Almanac of
Famous People

ISSN -1040-127X

Almanac of Famous People

A comprehensive reference guide to more
than 33,000 famous and infamous
newsmakers from Biblical times
to the present

SEVENTH EDITION

Volume 2
Biographies
S-Z
Indexes
Chronological by Year
Chronological by Date
Geographic
Occupation

Jennifer Mossman
Editor

GALE GROUP

Detroit
New York
San Francisco
London
Boston
Woodbridge, CT

Staff

Editor: Jennifer Mossman
Contributing Editor: Jerry Moore
Assistant Editor: Noah Schusterbauer

Manufacturing Manager: Dorothy Maki
Assistant Manager, Composition Purchasing and Electronic Prepress: Evi Seoud
Senior Buyer: Rita Wimberley

Design Manager: Kenn Zorn
Graphic Artist: Mike Logusz

Research Manager: Victoria B. Cariappa
Research Specialist: Barbara McNeil

Director, Technical Support Services: Theresa Rocklin
Programmer/Analyst: Natasha Mikheyeva
Oracle Applications Specialist: Lakshmi Narayana Sastry

Copyright ©2001
Gale Group, Inc.
27500 Drake Road
Farmington Hills, MI 48331-3535

ISBN 0-7876-4792-6 (two volume set)
ISBN 0-7876-4793-4 (volume one)
ISBN 0-7876-4794-2 (volume two)
ISSN 1040-127X

Gale Group Inc., an International Thomson Publishing Company.
Gale Group and Design is a trademark used herein under license.

Printed in the United States of America

Contents

Volume 1

Volume 2

Introduction

Almanac of Famous People is a biographical dictionary and an index to information about thousands of well-known individuals. It provides immediate, self-contained data on people who have made news, as well as citations to other widely available biographical sources that may be useful to the reader.

Almanac of Famous People includes both historic and contemporary figures in a wide range of occupations, from actor to zoologist. Fame is broadly defined to include renown resulting from "firsts," controversy or scandal, and awards, etc.

Highlights

Up-to-Date: Most of the 33,000 entries in the seventh edition have been updated with some kind of additional information, whether it be a death date, new sources, revised descriptor, or any combination of these things. This edition also contains approximately 3,000 new names, many of which have become well known in the years since the publication of the previous edition.

Easy-to-Use: Entries are arranged alphabetically by the person's best known name, with information listed in an easy-to-read format. Entries provide immediate concise information to users, while directing them to more detailed information through the listing of additional biographical reference sources.

Special Indexes: The second volume contains four indexes of interest to the researcher and trivia buff: a chronological index by year, a chronological index by date, a geographic index, and an occupation index. These indexes have been expanded and updated to reflect the new biographical material.

The Chronological Index by Year allows you to find all *Almanac of Famous People* entrants who were born in a designated year. Individuals born in a specific year are listed, followed by those who died in the same year.

The Chronological Index by Date contains all *Almanac of Famous People* listees who were born or died on a specific day. The year of birth or death appears before the name in chronological order.

The Geographic Index enables you to find everyone who was born or died in a specific location. The United States is subdivided by state and city; Canada, by province and city. Below each city are the names of those individuals listed in *Almanac of Famous People* who either were born or died in that location.

The Occupation Index lists all *Almanac of Famous People* entrants by the occupation(s) found in the main entry. This allows you to see everyone with a similar occupation grouped together. Listees with more than one occupation in their main entry listing can be found under each of those occupations.

Wide Audience: Information about famous people in this edition will appeal to a wide audience including students, educators, librarians, and researchers. Everyone from the casual reader to the trivia buff will enjoy these entries.

FORM AND CONTENT OF ENTRIES

[1] **Crawford, Joan**
[2] [Lucille Fay LeSueur]
[3] "Billie Cassin"
[4] American. [5] Actor
[6] Won Oscar for *Mildred Pierce*, 1945;
relationship with daughter subject of novel,
film *Mommie Dearest*, 1978, 1981.
[7] b. Mar 23, 1908 in San Antonio, Texas
[8] d. May 13, 1977 in New York, New York
[9] Source: *BiDD; IntWW 74, 75, 76, 77;*
InWom, SUP; LegTOT; MGM; MovMk;
OxCFilm; ThFT; TwYS; WhAm 7; WhoAm 74,
76, 78; WhoAmW 58, 61, 64, 66, 68, 70, 74, 75, 77;
WhoWest 74, 76; WhoWor 74; WorAl; WorAlBi

1. Person's name as most popularly known.
2. Pseudonym, real name, married name, or group affiliation in brackets.
3. Nickname in quotation marks.
4. Nationality (current or at time of death).
5. Occupation, career, or best known activity.
6. One-line descriptor.
7. Date and place of birth.
8. Date and place of death.
9. Alphabetically arranged codes for biographical reference sources which provide further information about the individual.

CODES AND LISTS OF TITLES INDEXED

Codes for the biographical reference sources indexed, along with complete bibliographic information on the titles of the volumes referred to by the codes, are given in the Key to Source Codes following the Introduction.

ACKNOWLEDGMENTS

The editors wish to thank Mr. Greg Smith of Graveline Tours, Hollywood, California, for his valuable assistance. We would also like to thank the many *Almanac of Famous People* users who sent in information about the people who appear in this edition.

AVAILABLE IN ELECTRONIC FORMATS

Diskette/Magnetic Tape. The *Almanac of Famous People* is available for licensing on diskette or magnetic tape in a fielded format. The database is available for internal data processing and nonpublishing purposes only. For more information, call 1-800-877-GALE.

Online. The *Almanac of Famous People* database is made available online as part of the Gale Biographies (GALBIO) database, accessible through LEXIS-NEXIS. For more information contact LEXIS-NEXIS, P.O. Box 933, Dayton, OH 45401-0933, phone: (937) 865-6800, toll-free: 800-543-6862.

SUGGESTIONS ARE WELCOME

The editors welcome comments or suggestions for future editions. Please address correspondence to: The Editor, *Almanac of Famous People*, Gale Group, Inc., 27500 Drake Road, Farmington Hills, MI 48331-3535; Fax 248-699-8062; or call 1-800-347-4253.

Key to Abbreviations

ABA	American Basketball Association	**CORE**	Committee (or Congress) on Racial Equality
ABC	American Broadcasting Company	**Corp.**	Corporation
ABL	American Basketball League	**Coty**	Fashion Critics Award
ACDA	Arms Control and Disarmament Agency	**CT**	Connecticut
ACLU	American Civil Liberties Union	**Ctr.**	Center
AFB	Air Force Base	**CUNY**	City University of New York
AFC	American Football Conference (of NFL)	**d.**	Died
AFL	American Federation of Labor, American Football League	**DC**	District of Columbia
		DE	Delaware
AFSCME	American Federation of State, County, and Municipal Employees	**Dec**	December
		Dem.	Democratic
AIDS	Acquired Immune Deficiency Syndrome	**Dept.**	Department
AIM	American Indian Movement	**Dist.**	District
AK	Alaska	**dj**	disc jockey
AL	Alabama, American League	**E**	East, Eastern
AMA	American Medical Association	**Edgar**	Edgar Allan Poe Mystery Writers Award
AP	Associated Press	**ERA**	Earned Run Average, Equal Rights Amendment
Apr	April		
AR	Arkansas	**ESP**	Extra Sensory Perception
ASCAP	American Society of Composers, Authors, and Publishers	**Exec.**	Executive
		FAA	Federal Aviation Administration
ASPCA	American Society for the Prevention of Cruelty to Animals	**FBI**	Federal Bureau of Investigation
		FCC	Federal Communications Commission
ASPCC	American Society for the Prevention of Cruelty to Children	**FDA**	Food and Drug Administration
		FDR	Franklin Delano Roosevelt
Assn.	Association	**Feb**	February
Asst.	Assistant	**FIBA**	International Amateur Basketball Federation
AT&T	American Telephone and Telegraph	**FL**	Florida
Aug	August	**fl.**	flourished
AWCTU	American Women's Christian Temperance Union	**Ft.**	Fort
		GA	Georgia
AZ	Arizona	**GE**	General Electric
b.	Born	**GM**	General Manager, General Motors
BAA	Basketball Association of America	**GOP**	Grand Old Party (Republican)
BBC	British Broadcasting Corporation	**Govt.**	Government
c.	Century, Circa	**Gr.**	Great
CA	California	**HBO**	Home Box Office
CAE	Central African Empire	**HEW**	Health, Education, and Welfare
Caldecott	Best Children's Illustrator Award	**HI**	Hawaii
Capt.	Captain	**hrs.**	Hours
CBO	Congressional Budget Office	**Hts.**	Heights
CBS	Columbia Broadcasting System	**HUD**	Housing and Urban Development
CEO	Chief Executive Officer	**Hugo**	Science Fiction Award
CFL	Canadian Football League	**IA**	Iowa
Chm.	Chairman	**IBM**	International Business Machines
CIA	Central Intelligence Agency	**ID**	Idaho
CIO	Congress of Industrial Organizations	**IL**	Illinois
CMA	Country Music Association	**ILA**	International Longshoremen's Association
CNN	Cable News Network	**ILGWU**	International Ladies Garment Workers Union
CO	Colorado		
Co.	Company, County	**ILWU**	International Longshoremen's and Warehousemen's Union
Com.	Committee		
Con.	Congressman, Congresswoman	**IN**	Indiana

Inc.	Incorporated		NFL	National Football League
INLA	Irish National Liberation Army		NH	New Hampshire
Int'l.	International		NHL	National Hockey League
IOC	International Olympic Committee		NJ	New Jersey
IRA	Irish Republic Army		NL	National League
IRS	Internal Revenue Service		NM	New Mexico
Is.	Island		Nov	November
ITT	International Telephone and Telegraph		NOW	National Organization for Women
IWW	Industrial Workers of the World		NPR	National Public Radio
Jan	January		NRA	National Recovery Administration
Jct.	Junction		NV	Nevada
Jr.	Junior		NY	New York
Jul	July		NYC	New York City
Jun	June		NY Met	New York Metropolitan Opera Company
KC	Kansas City		OAS	Organization of American States
KO	Knock-out		Obie	Off-Broadway Theater Award
KS	Kansas		Oct	October
KY	Kentucky		OH	Ohio
LA	Los Angeles, Louisiana		OK	Oklahoma
LC	Library of Congress		OMB	Office of Management and Budget
LPGA	Ladies Professional Golf Association		OR	Oregon
Lt.	Lieutenant		p.	Page
Ltd.	Limited		PA	Pennsylvania
MA	Massachusetts		Pac	Pacific
Mag	Magazine		PATCO	Professional Air Traffic Controllers
Mar	March			Organization
MCA	Music Corporation of America		PBA	Professional Bowlers Association
MCI	Microwave Communications Inc.		PBS	Public Broadcasting Service
MD	Maryland		PGA	Professional Golfers Association
ME	Maine		PLO	Palestine Liberation Organization
MGM	Metro-Goldwyn-Mayer		POW	Prisoner of War
Mgr.	Manager		PR	Puerto Rico
MI	Michigan		Pres.	President
min(s).	minute(s)		Prov.	Province
MIT	Massachusetts Institute of Technology		Pt.	Point, Port
ML	Major League(s)		Pte.	Pointe
MN	Minnesota		RBI	Runs Batted In
MO	Missouri		RCA	Radio Corporation of America
mo(s).	Month(s)		Rep.	Republican, Representative
MP	Member of Parliament, Military Police		Repub.	Republic
mph	miles per hour		Rev.	Reverend
MS	Mississippi		RI	Rhode Island
MT	Montana		RIF	Reading is Fundamental
Mt.	Mount, Mountain		Rpds.	Rapids
Mvmt.	Movement		S	South, Southern
MVP	Most Valuable Player		SALT	Strategic Arms Limitation Talks
N	North, Northern		SC	South Carolina
NAACP	National Association for the Advancement		SCLC	Southern Christian Leadership Conference
	of Colored People		SD	South Dakota
NASL	North American Soccer League		sec(s).	second(s)
NASA	National Aeronautics and Space		Sep	September
	Administration		SI	Sports Illustrated
NASCAR	National Association for Stock Car Auto		SLA	Symbionese Liberation Army
	Racing		SNCC	Student Nonviolent Coordinating
Nat.	National			Committee
NATO	North Atlantic Treaty Organization		Spingarn	NAACP Award
NBA	National Basketball Association		Sprgs.	Springs
NBC	National Broadcasting Company		Sq.	Square
NC	North Carolina		Sr.	Senior
NCAA	National Collegiate Athletic Association		St.	Saint, Sainte
ND	North Dakota		Sum.	Summit
NE	Nebraska		SUNY	State University of New York
Newbery	Best Children's Literature Award		TB	Tuberculosis
NFC	National Football Conference (of NFL)		TD	Touchdown

Terr.	Territory	**USSR**	Union of Soviet Socialist Republics
TM	Transcendental Meditation	**UT**	Utah
TN	Tennessee	**VA**	Virginia, Veteran's Administration
Tony	Antoinette Perry Broadway Award	**Vil.**	Village
tr.	Translated	**Vol(s).**	Volume, Volumes
TV	Television	**vp**	Vice President
TWA	Trans World Airlines	**VT**	Vermont
Twp.	Township	**W**	West, Western
TX	Texas	**WA**	Washington
U	University	**WASP**	White Anglo-Saxon Protestant
UAW	United Auto Workers	**WBA**	World Boxing Association
UFO	Unidentified Flying Object	**WBC**	World Boxing Council
UMW	United Mine Workers	**WHA**	World Hockey Association
UN	United Nations	**WCTU**	Women's Christian Temperance Union
UNESCO	United Nations Educational, Scientific, and	**WFL**	World Football League
	Cultural Organization	**WI**	Wisconsin
UNICEF	United Nations Children's Fund	**WPBA**	Women's Professional Bowlers Associationn
UPI	United Press International	**WV**	West Virginia
US	United States	**WW**	World War
USC	University of Southern California	**WY**	Wyoming
USCGA	United States Coast Guard Academy	**yds.**	Yards
USFL	United States Football League	**YMCA**	Young Men's Christian Association
USIA	United States Information Agency	**YWCA**	Young Women's Christian Association
USMC	United States Marine Corps	**yr(s).**	Year(s)

Source Codes

Code	Book Indexed
ABCCoAm	*The ABC-CLIO Companion to the 1960s Counterculture in America.* By Neil A. Hamilton. Santa Barbara, CA: ABC-CLIO, 1997.
ABCAmRe	*The ABC-CLIO Companion to American Reconstruction, 1862-1877.* By William L. Richter. Santa Barbara, CA: ABC-CLIO, 1996.
ABCDiRi	*The ABC-CLIO Companion to the Disability Rights Movement.* By Fred Pelka. Santa Barbara, CA: ABC-CLIO, 1997.
ABCMeAm	*The ABC-CLIO Companion to the Media in America.* By Daniel Webster Hollis, III. Santa Barbara, CA: ABC-CLIO, 1995.
ABCNaAm	*The ABC-CLIO Companion to the Native American Rights Movement.* By Mark Grossman. Santa Barbara, CA: ABC-CLIO, 1996.
ABCWHCa	*The ABC-CLIO World History Companion to Capitalism.* By Larry Allen. Santa Barbara, CA: ABC-CLIO, 1998.
AdMenW	*The Ad Men and Women.* A biographical dictionary of advertising. Edited by Edd Applegate. Westport, CT: Greenwood Press, 1994.
AfSS	*Africa South of the Sahara.* London: Europa Publications, 1978-1982.

        AfSS 78   Eighth edition, 1978-1979; 1978.
        AfSS 79   Ninth edition, 1979-1980; 1979.
        AfSS 80   10th edition, 1980-1981; 1980.
        AfSS 81   11th edition, 1981-1982; 1981.
        AfSS 82   12th edition, 1982-1983; 1982.

Biographies are located in the ''Who's Who in Africa South of the Sahara'' section.

Code	Book Indexed
AfrAmAl 8	*The African American Almanac.* Eighth edition. Edited by Jessie Carney Smith and Joseph Palmisano. Detroit: Gale Group, 2000. Formerly published as *The Negro Almanac.*

Use the Index to locate biographies.

AfrAmBi   *African American Biographies.* Profiles of ... current men and women. By Walter L. Hawkins. Jefferson, NC: McFarland & Co., 1992-1994.
                 AfrAmBi 1   First edition; 1992.
                 AfrAmBi 2   First edition supplement; 1994.

AfrAmG   *African American Generals and Flag Officers.* Biographies of over 120 blacks in the United States military. By Walter L. Hawkins. Jefferson, NC: McFarland & Co., 1993.

AfrAmPr   *African American History in the Press, 1851-1899.* From the coming of the Civil War to the rise of Jim Crow as reported and illustrated in selected newspapers of the time. Two volumes. Detroit: Gale Research, 1996.
            Use the Keyword Index to locate biographies.

AfrAmW   *African American Writers.* Edited by Valerie Smith, Lea Baechler, and A. Walton Litz. New York: Charles Scribner's Sons, 1991.

AfrA   *African Authors.* A Companion to Black African Writing. Volume I: 1300-1973. By Donald E. Herdeck. Washington, DC: Black Orpheus Press, 1973.

AfrWr   *African Writers.* Two volumes. Edited by C. Brian Cox. New York: Charles Scribner's Sons, 1997.

AfrAmAl 6   *The African-American Almanac.* Sixth edition. Detroit: Gale Research, 1994. Formerly published as *The Negro Almanac.*
            Use the Index to locate biographies.

AfrAmOr   *African-American Orators.* A bio-critical sourcebook. Edited by Richard W. Leeman. Westport, CT: Greenwood Press, 1996.

AfrAmSG   *African-American Sports Greats.* A biographical dictionary. Edited by David L. Porter. Westport, CT: Greenwood Press, 1995.

AfroAA   *Afro-American Artists.* A bio-bibliographical directory. Compiled and edited by Theresa Dickason Cederholm. Boston: Trustees of the Boston Public Library, 1973.

AgeMat   *The Age of Maturity, 1929-1941.* Concise Dictionary of American Literary Biography Series. Detroit: Gale Research, 1989.

ALA   *The ALA Yearbook.* A review of library events 1979. Volume 5, 1980. Chicago: American Library Association, 1980.
                 ALA 80   Biographies begin on page 73.
                 ALA 80N   Obituary section begins on page 227.

AllMGBl   *All Music Guide to the Blues.* The experts' guide to the best blues recordings. All Music Guide Series. San Francisco: Miller Freeman Books, 1996-1999.
                 AllMGBl 1   Edited by Michael Erlewine, Vladimir Bogdanov, Chris Woodstra, and Cub Koda; 1996.
                 AllMGBl 2   Second edition. Edited by Michael Erlewine et al; 1999.
                 AllMGBl 2A   Second edition. Edited by Michael Erlewine et al; 1999. "Blues in Jazz" section begins on page 528.

AllMGCo	*All Music Guide to Country.* The experts' guide to the best recordings in country music. Edited by Michael Erlewine, Vladimir Bogdanov, Chris Woodstra, and Stephen Thomas Erlewine. All Music Guide Series. San Francisco: Miller Freeman Books, 1997.
AllMGJa	*All Music Guide to Jazz.* The experts' guide to the best jazz recordings. Edited by Michael Erlewine. San Francisco, CA: Miller Freeman Books, 1996.
Alli	*Allibone's Critical Dictionary of English Literature.* British and American authors living and deceased from the earliest accounts to the latter half of the Nineteenth Century. Three volumes. By S. Austin Allibone. Philadelphia: J.B. Lippincott & Co., 1858-1871. Reprint. Detroit: Gale Research, 1965.
Alli SUP	*Allibone's Critical Dictionary of English Literature: A Supplement.* British and American authors. Two volumes. By John Foster Kirk. Philadelphia: J.B. Lippincott & Co., 1891. Reprint. Detroit: Gale Research, 1965.
AlmAP	*The Almanac of American Politics.* The senators, the representatives, the governors-- their records, states, and districts. By Michael Barone, Grant Ujifusa, and Douglas Matthews. New York: E.P. Dutton, 1977-1979.

AlmAP 78   1978 edition; 1977.
AlmAP 80   1980 edition; 1979.
Use the "Names Index" to locate biographies.

AlmAP 82	*The Almanac of American Politics.* The president, the senators, the representatives, the governors: their records and election results, their states and districts. 1982 edition. By Michael Barone and Grant Ujifusa. Washington, DC: Barone & Co., 1981.

Use the "Index of Persons" to locate biographies.

AlmAP	*The Almanac of American Politics.* The senators, the representatives, and the governors: their records and election results, their states and districts. By Michael Barone and Grant Ujifusa. Washington, DC: National Journal, 1983-1999.

AlmAP 84   1984 edition; 1983. Use the "Index of People" to locate biographies.
AlmAP 88   1988 edition; 1987. Use the "Index of People" to locate biographies.
AlmAP 92   1992 edition; 1991. Use the index to locate biographies.
AlmAP 96   1996 edition; 1995. Use the Index to locate biographies.
AlmAP 2000   2000 edition; 1999. Use the index to locate biographies.

AlmWMAP	*The Almanac of Women and Minorities in American Politics.* By Mart Martin. Boulder, CO: Westview Press, 1999.

Use the Index to locate biographies.

AmArch 70	*American Architects Directory.* Third edition. Edited by John F. Gane. New York: R.R. Bowker Co., 1970.
AmArt	*American Artists.* An illustrated survey of leading contemporary Americans. Edited by Les Krantz. New York: Facts on File Publications, 1985.

AmAu   *American Authors, 1600-1900.* A biographical dictionary of American literature.
                  Edited by Stanley J. Kunitz and Howard Haycraft. Wilson Authors Series. New
                  York: H.W. Wilson Co., 1938.

AmAu&B   *American Authors and Books.* 1640 to the present day. Third revised edition. By W.J.
                  Burke and Will D. Howe. Revised by Irving Weiss and Anne Weiss. New York:
                  Crown Publishers, 1972.

AmBench 79   *The American Bench.* Judges of the nation. Second edition. Edited by Mary Reincke
                  and Nancy Lichterman. Minneapolis: Reginald Bishop Forster & Associates,
                  1979.
                      Use the ''Name Index'' to locate biographies.

AmBench 97   *The American Bench.* Judges of the nation. Ninth edition, 1997/98. Edited by Ruth
                  A. Kennedy. Sacramento, CA: Forster-Long, 1997.
                      Use the alphabetical name index to locate entries.

AmBi   *American Biographies.* By Wheeler Preston. New York: Harper & Brothers
                  Publishers, 1940. Reprint. Detroit: Gale Research, 1974.

AmCath 80   *The American Catholic Who's Who.* Volume 23, 1980-1981. Edited by Joy
                  Anderson. Washington, DC: National Catholic News Service, 1979.

AmComp   *American Composers.* A biographical dictionary. By David Ewen. New York: G.P.
                  Putnam's Sons, 1982.

AmCulL   *American Cultural Leaders.* From colonial times to the present. By Justin Harmon et
                  al. Santa Barbara, CA: ABC-Clio, 1993.

AmDec   *American Decades.* Detroit: Gale Research, 1996.
                            AmDec 1900   1900-1909. Edited by Vincent Tompkins; 1996.
                            AmDec 1910   1910-1919. Edited by Vincent Tompkins; 1996.
                            AmDec 1920   1920-1929. Edited by Judith S. Baughman; 1996.
                            AmDec 1930   1930-1939. Edited by Victor Bondi; 1995.
                            AmDec 1940   1940-1949. Edited by Victor Bondi; 1995.
                            AmDec 1950   1950-1959. Edited by Richard Layman; 1994.
                            AmDec 1960   1960-1969. Edited by Richard Layman; 1995.
                            AmDec 1970   1970-1979. Edited by Victor Bondi; 1995.
                            AmDec 1980   1980-1989. Edited by Victor Bondi; 1996.
                  Biographies found in ''Headline Makers'' section of each chapter; use the
                  Index to locate.

AmEA 74   *American Economic Association, Directory of Members, 1974.* Edited by Rendigs
                  Fels. Published as Volume 64, Number 5 (October, 1974) of *The American
                  Economic Review.*

AmEnS   *The American Encyclopedia of Soccer.* Edited by Zandler Hollander. New York:
                  Everest House Publishers, 1980.

AmFD   *American Film Directors.* Edited by Stanley Hochman. A Library of Film Criticism.
                  New York: Frederick Ungar Publishing Co., 1974.

AmFkP	*American Folk Painters of Three Centuries.* Edited by Jean Lipman and Tom Armstrong. New York: Hudson Hills Press, 1980. Distributed by Simon & Schuster, New York. Published in association with the Whitney Museum of American Art. Use the Index to locate biographies.
AmGrD	*American Graphic Designers.* Thirty years of design imagery. By RitaSue Siegel. New York: McGraw-Hill Book Co., 1984. Use the Table of Contents to locate listings.
AmIndBi	*American Indian Biographies.* Edited by Harvey Markowitz and McCrea Adams. Magill's Choice. Pasadena, CA: Salem Press, 1999.
AmJust	*American Justice.* Two volumes. Edited by Joseph M. Bessette. Pasadena, CA: Salem Press, 1996.
AmLegL	*American Legislative Leaders, 1850-1910.* Edited by Charles F. Ritter and Jon L. Wakelyn. New York: Greenwood Press, 1989.

AmLY   *The American Literary Yearbook.* A biographical and bibliographical dictionary of living North American authors. Volume 1, 1919. Edited by Hamilton Traub. Henning, MN: Paul Traub, 1919. Reprint. Detroit: Gale Research, 1968.

AmLY	"Biographical and Bibliographical Dictionary of Living North American Authors" section begins on page 57.
AmLY XR	"Pen-names and Pseudonyms" section begins on page 49.

AmMWSc   *American Men & Women of Science.* A biographical directory of today's leaders in physical, biological and related sciences. New Providence, NJ: R.R. Bowker Co., 1971-1992.

AmMWSc 73P	12th edition, Physical & Biological Sciences. Seven volumes; 1971.
AmMWSc 73S	12th edition, Social & Behavioral Sciences. Two volumes; 1973.
AmMWSc 76P	13th edition, Physical & Biological Sciences. Seven volumes; 1976.
AmMWSc 78S	13th edition, Social & Behavioral Sciences. One volume; 1978.
AmMWSc 79	14th edition. Eight volumes; 1979.
AmMWSc 82	15th edition. Seven volumes; 1982.
AmMWSc 86	16th edition. Eight volumes; 1986.
AmMWSc 89	17th edition. Eight volumes; 1989.
AmMWSc 92	18th edition, 1992-1993. Eight volumes; 1992.

AmMWSc   *American Men & Women of Science™ [Bowker®].* A biographical directory of today's leaders in physical, biological and related sciences. Eight volumes. New Providence, NJ: R.R. Bowker Co., 1994-1998.

AmMWSc 95	19th edition; 1994.
AmMWSc 98	20th edition; 1998.

AmMilL   *American Military Leaders.* From colonial times to the present. Two volumes. By John C. Fredriksen. Santa Barbara, CA: ABC-CLIO Inc., 1999.

AmNatBi	*American National Biography.* 24 volumes. Edited by John A. Garraty and Mark C. Carnes. New York: Oxford University Press, 1999.
AmNatWr	*American Nature Writers.* Two volumes. Edited by John Elder. New York: Charles Scribner's Sons, 1996.
AmNov	*American Novelists of Today.* By Harry R. Warfel. New York: American Book Co., 1951. Reprint. Westport, Conn.: Greenwood Press, 1976.

AmNov X   "Index of Married Names and Pseudonyms" begins on page 477.

AmOrN	*American Orators before 1900.* Critical studies and sources. Edited by Bernard K. Duffy & Halford R. Ryan. New York: Greenwood Press, 1987.
AmOrTwC	*American Orators of the Twentieth Century.* Critical studies and sources. Edited by Bernard K. Duffy & Halford R. Ryan. New York: Greenwood Press, 1987.
AmPeW	*American Peace Writers, Editors, and Periodicals.* A dictionary. By Nancy L. Roberts. New York: Greenwood Press, 1991.
AmPB	*American Picturebooks from Noah's Ark to The Beast Within.* By Barbara Bader. New York: Macmillan Publishing Co.; London: Collier Macmillan Publishers, 1976.
AmPolLe	*American Political Leaders.* From colonial times to the present. By Steven G. O'Brien. Santa Barbara, CA: ABC-Clio, 1991.
AmPolW 80	*American Political Women.* Contemporary and historical profiles. By Esther Stineman. Littleton, CO: Libraries Unlimited, 1980.

AmPolW 80A   Appendix I: "Women of the Congress 1917-1980" begins on page 191.

AmPolW 80B   Appendix II: "Women Ambassadors of the United States Currently Serving" begins on page 198.

AmPolW 80C   Appendix III: "Women Chiefs of Mission 1933-1980" begins on page 199.

AmPolW 80D   Appendix IV: "Women Currently Serving as Federal Judges" begins on page 202.

AmPolW 80E   Appendix V: "Women Currently Serving in Government in Key Departmental, Agency, and White House Positions" begins on page 204.

AmPS	*American Popular Songs.* From the Revolutionary War to the present. Edited by David Ewen. New York: Random House, 1966.

AmPS A   The "All-Time Best-Selling Popular Recordings" section begins on page 485.

AmPS B   The "Some American Performers of the Past and Present" section begins on page 499.

AmRef&R	*American Reform and Reformers.* A biographical dictionary. Edited by Randall M. Miller and Paul A. Cimbala. Westport, CT: Greenwood Press, 1996.

AmRef   *American Reformers.* Edited by Alden Whitman. New York: H.W. Wilson Co., 1985.

AmRev   *The American Revolution, 1775-1783.* An encyclopedia. Two volumes. Edited by Richard L. Blanco. New York: Garland Publishing, 1993.

AmSetPR   *American Settlement Houses and Progressive Social Reform.* An encyclopedia of the American settlement movement. By Domenica M. Barbuto. Phoenix, AZ: Oryx Press, 1999.

AmSocL   *American Social Leaders.* By William McGuire and Leslie Wheeler. Santa Barbara, CA: ABC-Clio, 1993.

AmSong   *American Songwriters.* By David Ewen. New York: H.W. Wilson Co., 1987.

AmWom   *American Women.* A revised edition of *Woman of the Century,* 1,500 biographies with over 1,400 portraits; a comprehensive encyclopedia of the lives and achievements of American women during the nineteenth century. Two volumes. Edited by Frances E. Willard and Mary A. Livermore. New York: Mast, Crowell & Kirkpatrick, 1897. Reprint. Detroit: Gale Research, 1973.

AmWomD   *American Women Dramatists of the Twentieth Century.* A bibliography. By Brenda Coven. Metuchen, NJ: Scarecrow Press, 1982.

AmWomFW 97   *American Women Fiction Writers 1900-1960.* Volume 1. Edited by Harold Bloom. Women Writers of English and Their Works. Philadelphia: Chelsea House Publishers, 1997.

AmWomHi   *American Women Historians, 1700s-1990s.* A biographical dictionary. By Jennifer Scanlon and Shaaron Cosner. Westport, CT: Greenwood Press, 1996.

AmWomM   *American Women Managers and Administrators.* A selective biographical dictionary of twentieth-century leaders in business, education, and government. By Judith A. Leavitt. Westport, CT: Greenwood Press, 1985.

AmWomPl   *American Women Playwrights, 1900-1930.* A checklist. Compiled by Frances Diodato Bzowski. Bibliographies and Indexes in Women's Studies, no. 15. Westport, CT: Greenwood Press, 1992.

AmWomSc   *American Women in Science.* A biographical dictionary. By Martha J. Bailey. Denver: ABC-CLIO, 1994.

AmWomSc 1950   *American Women in Science, 1950 to the Present.* A biographical dictionary. By Martha J. Bailey. Santa Barbara, CA: ABC-Clio, 1998.

AmWomWr   *American Women Writers.* A critical reference guide from colonial times to the present. Four volumes. Edited by Lina Mainiero. New York: Frederick Ungar Publishing Co., 1979-1982.

AmWomWr 2   *American Women Writers.* A critical reference guide from colonial times to the present. Second edition. Four volumes. Edited by Taryn Benbow-Pfalzgraf. Detroit: St. James Press, 2000.

AmWomWr 92   *American Women Writers.* Diverse voices in prose since 1945. Edited by Eileen Barrett and Mary Cullinan. New York: St. Martin's Press, 1992.
Use the Table of Contents to locate biographies.

AmWomWr SUP   *American Women Writers.* A critical reference guide from colonial times to the present. Volume 5: Supplement. Edited by Carol Hurd Green and Mary Grimley Mason. New York: Continuum Publishing Co., 1994.

AmWr   *American Writers.* A collection of literary biographies. New York: Charles Scribner's Sons, 1974-1996.

     AmWr   Four volumes. Edited by Leonard Unger; 1974.
     AmWr RS1   Retrospective supplement 1. Edited by A. Walton Litz and Molly Weigel; 1998.
     AmWr S1   Supplement I. Two parts. Edited by Leonard Unger; 1979.
     AmWr S2   Supplement II. Two parts. Edited by A. Walton Litz; 1981.
     AmWr S3   Supplement III. Two parts. Edited by Lea Baechler and A. Walton Litz; 1991.
     AmWr S4   Supplement IV. Two parts. Edited by A. Walton Litz; 1996.

AmWrBE   *American Writers before 1800.* A biographical and critical dictionary. Three volumes. Edited by James A. Levernier and Douglas R. Wilmes. Westport, CT: Greenwood Press, 1983.

AncWr   *Ancient Writers: Greece and Rome.* Two volumes. Edited by T. James Luce. New York: Charles Scribner's Sons, 1982.

AnObit   *The Annual Obituary.* New York: St. Martin's Press, 1981-1983.

     AnObit 1980   *1980.*; 1981.
     AnObit 1981   *1981.*; 1982.
     AnObit 1982   *1982.*; 1983.
Use the "Alphabetical Index of Entrants" to locate biographies.

AnObit   *The Annual Obituary.* Detroit: St. James Press, 1984-1994.

     AnObit 1983   *1983.*; 1984.
     AnObit 1984   *1984.*; 1985.
     AnObit 1985   *1985.*; 1988.
     AnObit 1986   *1986.*; 1989.
     AnObit 1987   *1987.*; 1990.
     AnObit 1988   *1988.*; 1990.
     AnObit 1989   *1989.*; 1990.
     AnObit 1990   *1990.*; 1991.
     AnObit 1991   *1991.*; 1992.
     AnObit 1992   *1992.*; 1993.
     AnObit 1993   *1993.*; 1994.
Use the "Alphabetical Index of Entrants" to locate biographies.

AnCL   *Anthology of Children's Literature.* Fourth edition. Edited by Edna Johnson, Evelyn R. Sickels, and Frances Clarke Sayers. Boston: Houghton Mifflin Co., 1970.
Biographies begin on page 1217.

AnMV 1926	*Anthology of Magazine Verse for 1926 and Yearbook of American Poetry.* Edited by William Stanley Braithwaite. New York: G. Sully, 1926. Reprint. Granger Index Reprint Series. Freeport, N.Y.: Books for Libraries Press, 1972.

The "Biographical Dictionary of Poets in the United States" section begins on page 3 of part 4.

AntBDN *The Antique Buyer's Dictionary of Names.* By A.W. Coysh. Newton Abbot, England: David & Charles, 1970.

AntBDN A	"Art Nouveau" section begins on page 13.
AntBDN B	"Book Illustrations and Prints" section begins on page 23.
AntBDN C	"Bronzes" section begins on page 48.
AntBDN D	"Clocks and Barometers" section begins on page 59.
AntBDN E	"Fashion Plates" section begins on page 81.
AntBDN F	"Firearms" section begins on page 86.
AntBDN G	"Furniture" section begins on page 98.
AntBDN H	"Glass" section begins on page 123.
AntBDN I	"Maps, Charts, and Globes" section begins on page 137.
AntBDN J	"Miniatures" section begins on page 148.
AntBDN K	"Musical Instruments" section begins on page 170.
AntBDN L	"Netsuke" section begins on page 179.
AntBDN M	"Pottery and Porcelain" section begins on page 185.
AntBDN N	"Sheffield Plate" section begins on page 224.
AntBDN O	"Silhouettes or Profiles" section begins on page 231.
AntBDN P	"Silk Pictures, Portraits, and Bookmarks" section begins on page 243.
AntBDN Q	"Silver" section begins on page 250.

ApCAB *Appleton's Cyclopaedia of American Biography.* New York: D. Appleton & Co., 1888-1901.Reprint. Detroit: Gale Research, 1968.

ApCAB	Six volumes. Edited by James Grant Wilson and John Fiske; 1888.
ApCAB SUP	Volume VII, Supplement. Edited by James Grant Wilson; 1901.

ApCAB X *Appleton's Cyclopaedia of American Biography.* A supplement. Six volumes. Edited by L.E. Dearborn. New York: Press Association Compilers, 1918-1931. Originally published as *The Cyclopaedia of American Biography, Supplementary Edition.*

ArizL *Arizona in Literature.* A collection of the best writings of Arizona authors from early Spanish days to the present time. By Mary G. Boyer. Glendale, CA: Arthur H. Clark Co., 1935. Reprint. Ann Arbor, Mich.: Gryphon Books, 1971.
Use the Index to locate biographies.

ArtCS *The Art of the Comic Strip.* By Judith O'Sullivan. College Park, MD: University of Maryland, Department of Art, 1971.
Biographies begin on page 60.

ArtDirC *Art Directors in Cinema.* A worldwide biographical dictionary. By Michael L. Stephens. Jefferson, NC: McFarland & Co., 1998.

ArtLatA	*Art in Latin America.* The modern era, 1820-1980. By Dawn Ades. New Haven, CT: Yale University Press, 1989. Biographies begin on page 338.
ArtclWW 2	*Articles on Women Writers.* Volume 2, 1976-1984: A bibliography. By Narda Lacey Schwartz. Santa Barbara, CA: ABC-Clio, 1986.

ArtsAmW	*Artists of the American West.* A biographical dictionary. By Doris Ostrander Dawdy. Chicago: Sage Books/Swallow Press, 1974-1981.
	    ArtsAmW 1 Volume I; 1974.
	    ArtsAmW 2 Volume II; 1981.

ArtsAmW 3	*Artists of the American West.* A biographical dictionary. Volume III, *Artists Born before 1900.* By Doris Ostrander Dawdy. Athens, OH: Swallow Press/Ohio University Press, 1985.
ArtsCL	*Artists of a Certain Line.* A selection of illustrations for children's books. By John Ryder. London: The Bodley Head, 1960.
ArtsEM	*Artists of Early Michigan.* A biographical dictionary of artists native to or active in Michigan, 1701-1900. Compiled by Arthur Hopkin Gibson. Detroit: Wayne State University Press, 1975.
ArtsNiC	*Artists of the Nineteenth Century and Their Works.* A handbook containing two thousand and fifty biographical sketches. Revised edition. Two volumes. By Clara Erskine Clement and Laurence Hutton. Boston: J.R. Osgood & Co., 1885. Reprint. Two volumes in one. St. Louis: North Point, 1969.
ASCAP 66	*The ASCAP Biographical Dictionary.* Third edition. New York: American Society of Composers, Authors and Publishers, 1966.
ASCAP 80	*ASCAP Biographical Dictionary.* Fourth edition. Compiled for the American Society of Composers, Authors and Publishers by Jaques Cattell Press. New York: R.R. Bowker Co., 1980.
AsAmAlm	*The Asian American Almanac.* A reference work on Asians in the United States. Detroit: Gale Research, 1995. Use the Index to locate biographies.
AsAmLit	*Asian American Literature.* Reviews and criticism of works by American writers of Asian descent. Detroit: Gale Research, 1999.
AsAmWoW	*Asian-American Women Writers.* Edited by Harold Bloom. Women Writers of English and Their Works. Philadelphia: Chelsea House Publishers, 1997.
AsBiEn	*Asimov's Biographical Encyclopedia of Science and Technology.* The lives and achievements of 1,195 great scientists from ancient times to the present, chronologically arranged. New revised edition. By Isaac Asimov. New York: Avon, 1976. Use the ''Alphabetic List of Biographical Entries'' to locate biographies.

AsERC 80   *Association of Executive Recruiting Consultants, 1980 Directory.* New York: R.R. Bowker Co., 1980.

AstEnc   *The Astrology Encyclopedia.* By James R. Lewis. Detroit: Gale Research, 1994. Use the Index at the back of the book to locate entries.

AtlBL   *Atlantic Brief Lives.* A biographical companion to the arts. Edited by Louis Kronenberger. Boston: Little, Brown & Co., 1971.

AuLitCr   *Australian Literary Criticism: 1945-1988.* An annotated bibliography. By Robert L. Ross. Garland Reference Library of the Humanities, vol. 1075. New York: Garland Publishing, 1989.
                  Biographies are located in the "Major Writers" section, which begins on page 155.

AuWomWr   *Australian Women Writers.* A bibliographic guide. By Debra Adelaide. London: Pandora, 1988.

AuSpks   *The Author Speaks.* Selected "PW" interviews, 1967-1976. By *Publishers Weekly* editors and contributors. New York: R.R. Bowker Co., 1977.

Au&Arts   *Authors & Artists for Young Adults.* Detroit: Gale Research, 1989-1999.
                  Au&Arts 1   Volume 1; 1989.
                  Au&Arts 2   Volume 2; 1989.
                  Au&Arts 3   Volume 3; 1990.
                  Au&Arts 4   Volume 4; 1990.
                  Au&Arts 5   Volume 5; 1990.
                  Au&Arts 6   Volume 6; 1991.
                  Au&Arts 7   Volume 7; 1991.
                  Au&Arts 8   Volume 8; 1992.
                  Au&Arts 9   Volume 9; 1992.
                  Au&Arts 10   Volume 10; 1993.
                  Au&Arts 11   Volume 11; 1993.
                  Au&Arts 12   Volume 12; 1994.
                  Au&Arts 13   Volume 13; 1994.
                  Au&Arts 14   Volume 14; 1995.
                  Au&Arts 15   Volume 15; 1995.
                  Au&Arts 16   Volume 16; 1995.
                  Au&Arts 17   Volume 17; 1995.
                  Au&Arts 18   Volume 18; 1996.
                  Au&Arts 19   Volume 19; 1997.
                  Au&Arts 20   Volume 20; 1997.
                  Au&Arts 21   Volume 21; 1997.
                  Au&Arts 22   Volume 22; 1997.
                  Au&Arts 23   Volume 23; 1998.
                  Au&Arts 24   Volume 24; 1998.
                  Au&Arts 25   Volume 25; 1998.
                  Au&Arts 26   Volume 26; 1999.
                  Au&Arts 27   Volume 27; 1999.

Au&Arts   *Authors & Artists for Young Adults.* Detroit: Gale Group, 1999-2000.
                  Au&Arts 28   Volume 28; 1999.
                  Au&Arts 29   Volume 29; 1999.

Au&Arts 30	Volume 30; 1999.	
Au&Arts 31	Volume 31; 2000.	
Au&Arts 32	Volume 32; 2000.	

Au&Arts 33   *Authors and Artists for Young Adults.* Volume 33. Detroit: Gale Group, 2000.

AuBYP   *Authors of Books for Young People.* By Martha E. Ward et al. Metuchen, NJ: Scarecrow Press, 1971-1990.

AuBYP 2	Second edition; 1971.
AuBYP 2S	Supplement to the second edition; 1979.
AuBYP 2SA	Supplement to the second edition; 1979. Addendum to the Supplement begins on page 301.
AuBYP 3	Third edition; 1990.

Au&ICB   *Authors and Illustrators of Children's Books.* Writings on their lives and works. By Miriam Hoffman and Eva Samuels. New York: R.R. Bowker Co., 1972.

AuNews   *Authors in the News.* A compilation of news stories and feature articles from American newspapers and magazines covering writers and other members of the communications media. Edited by Barbara Nykoruk. Detroit: Gale Research, 1976.

AuNews 1	Volume 1.
AuNews 2	Volume 2.

Au&Wr 71   *The Author's and Writer's Who's Who.* Sixth edition. Darien, CT: Hafner Publishing Co., 1971.

AutoN 79   *Automotive News.* 1979 Market Data Book Issue, April 25, 1979.
The "Who's Who in the Auto Industry" section begins on page 130.

AZNatAW   *A to Z of Native American Women.* By Liz Sonneborn. Encyclopedia of Women. New York: Facts on File, 1998.

AZWoSci   *A to Z of Women in Science and Math.* By Lisa Yount. New York: Facts on File, 1999.

BakBD 78   *Baker's Biographical Dictionary of Musicians.* Sixth edition. Revised by Nicolas Slonimsky. New York: Schirmer Books; London: Collier Macmillan Publishers, 1978.

BakBD 84   *Baker's Biographical Dictionary of Musicians.* Seventh edition. Revised by Nicolas Slonimsky. New York: Macmillan, Schirmer Books, 1984.

BakBD 92   *Baker's Biographical Dictionary of Musicians.* Eighth edition. Revised by Nicolas Slonimsky. New York: Macmillan, 1992.

BakBDTw   *Baker's Biographical Dictionary of Twentieth-Century Classical Musicians.* By Nicolas Slonimsky. New York: Schirmer Books, 1997.

BakDcM   *Baker's Dictionary of Music.* By Nicolas Slonimsky. New York: Schirmer Books, 1997.

BakDcO   *Baker's Dictionary of Opera.* Edited by Laura Kuhn. New York: Schirmer Books, 2000.

Ballpl 90   *The Ballplayers.* Baseball's ultimate biographical reference. Edited by Mike Shatzkin. New York: William Morrow and Co., 1990.

BaseEn 88   *The Baseball Encyclopedia.* The Complete and Official Record of Major League Baseball. Edited by Joseph L. Reichler. New York: Macmillan, 1988.

BasBi   *Basketball Biographies.* 434 U.S. players, coaches and contributors to the game, 1891-1990. By Martin Taragano. Jefferson, NC: McFarland & Co., 1991.

BeaEPF   *Beacham's Encyclopedia of Popular Fiction.* Three volumes. Edited by Kirk H. Beetz, Ph.D. Biography Series. Osprey, FL: Beacham's Publishing Corp., 1996.

Benet 87   *Benet's Reader's Encyclopedia.* Third edition. New York: Harper & Row, 1987.

Benet 96   *Benet's Reader's Encyclopedia.* Fourth edition. Edited by Bruce Murphy. New York, NY: HarperCollins Publishers, 1996.

BenetAL 91   *Benet's Reader's Encyclopedia of American Literature.* First edition. Edited by George Perkins, Barbara Perkins, and Phillip Leininger. New York: HarperCollins Publishers, 1991.

BestMus   *The Best Musicals.* From *Show Boat* to *A Chorus Line.* Revised edition. By Arthur Jackson. New York: Crown Publishers, 1979.
                    Biographies are found in the ''Who's Who of Show and Film Music'' section beginning on page 135.

BestSel   *Bestsellers.* Books and authors in the news. Detroit: Gale Research, 1989-1991.
BestSel 89-1	89, Issue 1; 1989.
BestSel 89-2	89, Issue 2; 1989.
BestSel 89-3	89, Issue 3; 1989.
BestSel 89-4	89, Issue 4; 1990.
BestSel 90-1	90, Issue 1; 1990.
BestSel 90-2	90, Issue 2; 1990.
BestSel 90-3	90, Issue 3; 1991.
BestSel 90-4	90, Issue 4; 1991.

BibAL   *Bibliography of American Literature.* New Haven, CT: Yale University Press, 1955-1990.
BibAL	Volumes 1-7. Compiled by Jacob Blanck; 1955.
BibAL 8	Volume 8. Compiled by Jacob Blanck; edited and completed by Michael Winship; 1990.

BbD   *The Bibliophile Dictionary.* A biographical record of the great authors, with bibliographical notices of their principal works from the beginning of history. Originally published as Volumes 29 and 30 of *The Bibliophile Library of Literature, Art, and Rare Manuscripts.* Compiled and arranged by Nathan Haskell Dole, Forrest Morgan, and Caroline Ticknor. New York: International Bibliophile Society, 1904. Reprint. Detroit: Gale Research, 1966.

BbtC   *Bibliotheca Canadensis. Or, A manual of Canadian literature.* By Henry J. Morgan. Ottawa: G.E. Desbarats, 1867. Reprint. Detroit: Gale Research, 1968.

BgBands 74   *The Big Bands.* Revised edition. By George T. Simon. New York: Macmillan Publishing Co., Collier Books, 1974.
                    Use the Index to locate biographies.

BgBkCoM   *The Big Book of Country Music.* A Biographical Encyclopedia. By Richard Carlin. New York: Penguin Books, 1995.

BilGTRM   *The Billboard Guide to Tejano and Regional Mexican Music.* By Ramiro Burr. New York: Billboard Books, 1999.

BilIEnR   *The Billboard Illustrated Encyclopedia of Rock.* New York: Billboard Books, 1998.

BiGAW   *A Bio-Bibliography of German-American Writers, 1670-1970.* By Robert E. Ward. White Plains, NY: Kraus International Publications, 1985.

BiNAW   *A Biobibliography of Native American Writers, 1772-1924.* By Daniel F. Littlefield, Jr. and James W. Parins. Native American Bibliography Series, no. 2. Metuchen, NJ: Scarecrow Press, 1981.
                    BiNAW   Part I: ''A Bibliography of Native American Writers.''
                    BiNAW A   Part II: ''A Bibliography of Native American Writers Known Only by Pen Names'' begins on page 185.
                    BiNAW B   Part III: ''Biographical Notes'' begins on page 203.

BiNAW   *A Biobibliography of Native American Writers, 1772-1924: A Supplement.* By Daniel F. Littlefield, Jr. and James W. Parins. Native American Bibliography Series, no. 5. Metuchen, NJ: Scarecrow Press, 1985.
                    BiNAW Sup   Part I: ''A Bibliography of Native American Writers.''
                    BiNAW SupA Part II: ''A Bibliography of Native American Writers Known Only by Pen Names'' begins on page 159.
                    BiNAW SupB Part III: ''Biographical Notes'' begins on page 165.

Biodiv   *Biodiversity.* A reference handbook. By Anne Becher. Contemporary World Issues. Santa Barbara, CA: ABC-CLIO, 1998.
                    Biographical Sketches section begins on page 71.

BiB N   *Biographia Britannica Literaria: Anglo-Norman Period.* Biography of literary characters of Great Britain and Ireland, arranged in chronological order. By Thomas Wright. London: John W. Parker, 1846. Reprint. Detroit: Gale Research, 1968.
                    Use the Index to locate biographies.

BiB S   *Biographia Britannica Literaria: Anglo-Saxon Period.* Biography of literary characters of Great Britain and Ireland, arranged in chronological order. By Thomas Wright. London: John W. Parker, 1842. Reprint. Detroit: Gale Research, 1968.
                    Use the Index to locate biographies.

BiAUS   *Biographical Annals of the Civil Government of the United States.* During its first century; from original and official sources. By Charles Lanman. Washington, DC: James Anglim, 1876. Reprint. Detroit: Gale Research, 1976.
    BiAUS SUP   "Additional Facts" section begins on page 633.

BiCoLiE   *Biographical Companion to Literature in English.* By Antony Kamm. Lanham, MD: Scarecrow Press, 1997.

BiCAW   *The Biographical Cyclopaedia of American Women.* Two volumes. Detroit: Gale Research, 1974. Originally published in two volumes. Volume I: Compiled under the supervision of Mabel Ward Cameron, published by Halvord Publishing Co., 1924; Volume II: Compiled under the supervision of Erma Conkling Lee, published by Franklin W
    Use the Index in each volume to locate biographies.

BiDAfM   *Biographical Dictionary of Afro-American and African Musicians.* By Eileen Southern. Westport, CT: Greenwood Press, 1982.

BiDAmAr   *Biographical Dictionary of American Architects, Deceased.* By Henry F. Withey and Elsie Rathburn Withey. Los Angeles: New Age Publishing Co., 1956.

BiDAmBL 83   *Biographical Dictionary of American Business Leaders.* By John N. Ingham. Westport, CT: Greenwood Press, 1983.
    Use the Index to locate biographies.

BiDAmCa   *Biographical Dictionary of American and Canadian Naturalists and Environmentalists.* Edited by Keir B. Sterling, Richard P. Harmond, George A. Cevasco, and Lorne F. Hammond. Westport, CT: Greenwood Press, 1997.

BiDAmCu   *Biographical Dictionary of American Cult and Sect Leaders.* By J. Gordon Melton. Garland Reference Library of Social Science, vol. 212. New York: Garland Publishing, 1986.

BiDAmEd   *Biographical Dictionary of American Educators.* Three volumes. Edited by John F. Ohles. Westport, CT: Greenwood Press, 1978.

BiDAmJo   *Biographical Dictionary of American Journalism.* Edited by Joseph P. McKerns. New York: Greenwood Press, 1989.

BiDAmL   *Biographical Dictionary of American Labor.* Edited by Gary M. Fink. Westport, CT: Greenwood Press, 1984.
    Biographies begin on page 83.

BiDAmLL   *Biographical Dictionary of American Labor Leaders.* Edited by Gary M. Fink. Westport, CT: Greenwood Press, 1974.

BiDAmLf   *Biographical Dictionary of the American Left.* Edited by Bernard K. Johnpoll and Harvey Klehr. New York: Greenwood Press, 1986.

BiDAmM   *Biographical Dictionary of American Music.* By Charles Eugene Claghorn. West Nyack, NY: Parker Publishing Co., 1973.

BiDAmNC   *Biographical Dictionary of American Newspaper Columnists.* By Sam G. Riley. Westport, CT: Greenwood Press, 1995.

BiDAmS   *Biographical Dictionary of American Science.* The seventeenth through the nineteenth centuries. By Clark A. Elliott. Westport, CT: Greenwood Press, 1979.

BiDAmSp   *Biographical Dictionary of American Sports.* Edited by David L. Porter. Westport, CT: Greenwood Press, 1987-1992.
      BiDAmSp BB   *Baseball.*; 1987.
      BiDAmSp BK   *Basketball and Other Indoor Sports.*; 1989. Use the index to locate biographies.
      BiDAmSp FB   *Football.*; 1987.
      BiDAmSp OS   *Outdoor Sports.*; 1988. Use the Index to locate biographies.
      BiDAmSp Sup   1989-1992 supplement for baseball, football, basketball, and other sports; 1992. Use the Index to locate biographies.

BiDBrA   *A Biographical Dictionary of British Architects 1600-1840.* By Howard Colvin. New York: Facts on File, 1980.
      BiDBrA A   ''Appendix A'' begins on page 969.

BiDBrF   *   The Biographical Dictionary of British Feminists.* By Olive Banks. New York: New York University Press, 1985-1990.
      BiDBrF 1   Volume One: 1800-1930; 1985.
      BiDBrF 2   Volume Two: A supplement, 1900-1945; 1990.

BiDChrM   *Biographical Dictionary of Christian Missions.* Edited by Gerald H. Anderson. New York: Macmillan Reference USA, 1998.

BiDConf   *Biographical Dictionary of the Confederacy.* By Jon L. Wakelyn. Westport, CT: Greenwood Press, 1977.

BiDConC   *Biographical Dictionary of Contemporary Catholic American Writing.* Edited by Daniel J. Tynan. New York: Greenwood Press, 1989.

BiDD   *Biographical Dictionary of Dance.* By Barbara Naomi Cohen-Stratyner. New York: Macmillan Publishing Co., Schirmer Books; London: Collier Macmillan Publishers, 1982.

BiDEWW   *A Biographical Dictionary of English Women Writers, 1580-1720.* By Maureen Bell, George Parfitt, and Simon Shepherd. Boston: G.K. Hall & Co., 1990.

BiDExR   *Biographical Dictionary of the Extreme Right since 1890.* By Philip Rees. New York: Simon & Schuster, 1990.

BiDFedJ   *Biographical Dictionary of the Federal Judiciary.* Compiled by Harold Chase, Samuel Krislov, Keith O. Boyum, and Jerry N. Clark. Detroit: Gale Research, 1976.
      BiDFedJ A   Addendum begins on page 319.

BiDFilm   *A Biographical Dictionary of Film.* By David Thomson. New York: William Morrow & Co., 1976-1981.

                                 BiDFilm   First edition; 1976.

                                 BiDFilm 81   Second edition; 1981.

BiDFilm 94   *A Biographical Dictionary of Film.* By David Thomson. New York: Alfred A. Knopf, 1994.

BiDFrPL   *Biographical Dictionary of French Political Leaders since 1870.* Edited by David S. Bell, Douglas Johnson, and Peter Morris. New York: Simon & Schuster, 1990.

BiDHisA   *The Biographical Dictionary of Hispanic Americans.* By Nicholas E. Meyer. New York: Facts On File, 1997.

BiDHisL   *Biographical Dictionary of Hispanic Literature in the United States.* The literature of Puerto Ricans, Cuban Americans, and other Hispanic writers. Edited by Nicolas Kanellos. New York: Greenwood Press, 1989.

BiDInt   *Biographical Dictionary of Internationalists.* Edited by Warren F. Kuehl. Westport, CT: Greenwood Press, 1983.

BiDIrW   *A Biographical Dictionary of Irish Writers.* By Anne M. Brady and Brian Cleeve. New York: St. Martin's Press, 1985.

                                 BiDIrW   "Writers in English" section begins on page 1.

                                 BiDIrW A   Addendum begins on page 254.

                                 BiDIrW B   "Writers in Irish and Latin" section begins on page 255.

BiDJaL   *Biographical Dictionary of Japanese Literature.* By Sen'ichi Hisamatsu. Tokyo: Kodansha International, 1976. Distributed by Harper & Row, New York. Use the Index to locate biographies.

BiDJaz   *Biographical Dictionary of Jazz.* By Charles Eugene Claghorn. Englewood Cliffs, NJ: Prentice-Hall, 1982.

                                 BiDJaz A   "Index of Jazz and Various Small Groups" section begins on page 327.

BiDLAmC   *Biographical Dictionary of Latin American and Caribbean Political Leaders.* Edited by Robert J. Alexander. New York: Greenwood Press, 1988.

BiDLA   *A Biographical Dictionary of the Living Authors of Great Britain and Ireland.* Comprising literary memoirs and anecdotes of their lives; and a chronological register of their publications. London: Printed for Henry Colburn, Public Library, Hanover Square, 1816. Reprint. Detroit: Gale Research, 1966.

                                 BiDLA SUP   "Supplement of Additions and Corrections" begins on page 407.

BiDMarx   *Biographical Dictionary of Marxism.* Edited by Robert A. Gorman. Westport, CT: Greenwood Press, 1986.

BiDMoAE   *Biographical Dictionary of Modern American Educators.* By Frederik Ohles, Shirley M. Ohles, and John G. Ramsay. Westport, CT: Greenwood Press, 1997.

BiDMoER 1   *A Biographical Dictionary of Modern European Radicals and Socialists.* Volume
                    one: 1780-1815. Edited by David Nicholls and Peter Marsh. Sussex, England:
                    The Harvester Press; New York: St. Martin's Press, 1988.

BiDMoPL   *Biographical Dictionary of Modern Peace Leaders.* Edited by Harold Josephson.
                    Westport, CT: Greenwood Press, 1985.

BiDNeoM   *Biographical Dictionary of Neo-Marxism.* Edited by Robert A. Gorman. Westport,
                    CT: Greenwood Press, 1985.

BiDPara   *Biographical Dictionary of Parapsychology, 1964-1966.* Edited by Helene
                    Pleasants. New York: Garrett Publications, Helix Press, 1964.

BiDProW   *Biographical Dictionary of Professional Wrestling.* By Harris M. Lentz, III.
                    Jefferson, NC: McFarland & Co., 1997.

BiDcPsy   *Biographical Dictionary of Psychology.* Edited by Noel Sheehy, Antony J.
                    Chapman, and Wendy A. Conroy. London: Routledge, 1997.

BiDPsy   *Biographical Dictionary of Psychology.* By Leonard Zusne. Westport, CT:
                    Greenwood Press, 1984. A continuation of *Names in the History of Psychology:
                    A Biographical Sourcebook.*

BiDRP&D   *A Biographical Dictionary of Renaissance Poets and Dramatists, 1520-1650.* By
                    J.W. Saunders. Sussex, England: Harvester Press, 1983.

BiDScF   *A Biographical Dictionary of Science Fiction and Fantasy Artists.* By Robert
                    Weinberg. New York: Greenwood Press, 1988.

BiDSocW   *Biographical Dictionary of Social Welfare in America.* Edited by Walter I. Trattner.
                    New York: Greenwood Press, 1986.

BiDSA   *Biographical Dictionary of Southern Authors.* Compiled by Lucian Lamar Knight.
                    Atlanta: Martin & Hoyt Co., 1929. Reprint. Detroit: Gale Research, 1978.
                    Originally published as *Library of Southern Literature, Volume 15,
                    Biographical Dictionary of Authors.*

BiDSovU   *A Biographical Dictionary of the Soviet Union, 1917-1988.* By Jeanne Vronskaya
                    with Vladimir Chuguev. London: K.G. Saur, 1989.

BiD&SB   *Biographical Dictionary and Synopsis of Books Ancient and Modern.* Edited by
                    Charles Dudley Warner. Akron, OH: Werner Co., 1902. Reprint. Detroit: Gale
                    Research, 1965.

BiDTran   *Biographical Dictionary of Transcendentalism.* Edited by Wesley T. Mott.
                    Westport, CT: Greenwood Press, 1996.

BiDWomA   *A Biographical Dictionary of Women Artists in Europe and America since 1850.* By
                    Penny Dunford. Philadelphia: University of Pennsylvania Press, 1989.

BiDWWGF   *The Biographical Dictionary of World War II Generals and Flag Officers.* The U.S.
                    armed forces. By R. Manning Ancell. Westport, CT: Greenwood Press, 1996.

Use the Index to locate biographies.

BiDrACP 79   *Biographical Directory of the American College of Physicians.* 1979 edition. New York: R.R. Bowker Co., 1979.
Use the Index, which begins on page 1789, to locate biographies.

BiDrACR   *Biographical Directory of American Colonial and Revolutionary Governors, 1607-1789.* By John W. Raimo. Westport, CT: Microform Review, Meckler Books, 1980.
Use the Index to locate biographies.

BiDrAC   *Biographical Directory of the American Congress, 1774-1971.* The Continental Congress (September 5, 1774 to October 21, 1788) and the Congress of the United States (from the first through the ninety-first Congress March 4, 1789, to January 3, 1971, inclusive). Washington, DC: U.S. Government Printing Office, 1971.
Biographies begin on page 487.

BiDrAPH 79   *Biographical Directory of the American Public Health Association.* 1979 edition. New York: R.R. Bowker Co., 1979.

BiDrATG   *Biographical Directory of American Territorial Governors.* By Thomas A. McMullin and David Walker. Westport, CT: Meckler Publishing, 1984.
Use the Index to locate biographies.

BiDrAPA 77   *Biographical Directory: Fellows and Members of the American Psychiatric Association.* 1977 edition. New York: R.R. Bowker Co., 1977.

BiDrAPA 89   *Biographical Directory: Fellows and Members of the American Psychiatric Association.* 1989 edition. Washington, DC: American Psychiatric Association, 1989. Distributed by American Psychiatric Press, Washington, DC.

BiDrGov   *Biographical Directory of the Governors of the United States.* Westport, CT: Meckler, 1978-1989.
    BiDrGov 1789   *1789-1978.* Four volumes. Edited by Robert Sobel and John Raimo; 1978. Use the Index in each volume to locate biographies.
    BiDrGov 1978   *1978-1983.* Edited by John W. Raimo; 1985. Use the Index to locate biographies.
    BiDrGov 1983   *1983-1988.* By Marie Marmo Mullaney; 1989. Use the Index to locate biographies.

BiDrGov 1988   *Biographical Directory of the Governors of the United States. 1988-1994.* By Marie Marmo Mullaney. Westport, CT: Greenwood Press, 1994.
Use the Index to locate biographies.

BiDrLUS 70   *A Biographical Directory of Librarians in the United States and Canada.* Fifth edition. Edited by Lee Ash. Chicago: American Library Association, 1970.

BiDrUSC 89   *Biographical Directory of the United States Congress, 1774-1989.* The Continental Congress, September 5, 1774 to October 21, 1788 and the Congress of the United States from the first through the one hundredth Congresses, March 4,

1789, to January 3, 1989, inclusive. Bicentennial Edition. Washington, DC: U.S. Government Printing Office, 1989.
Biographies begin on page 507.

BiDrUSE   *Biographical Directory of the United States Executive Branch.* Edited by Robert Sobel. New York: Greenwood Press, 1971-1990.
    BiDrUSE 71   *1774-1971.*; 1971.
    BiDrUSE 89   *1774-1989.*; 1990.

BiESc   *A Biographical Encyclopedia of Scientists.* Two volumes. Edited by John Daintith, Sarah Mitchell, and Elizabeth Tootill. New York: Facts on File, 1981.

BiE&WWA   *The Biographical Encyclopaedia and Who's Who of the American Theatre.* Edited by Walter Rigdon. New York: James H. Heineman, 1966. Revised edition published as *Notable Names in the American Theatre.*
The "Biographical Who's Who" section begins on page 227.

BiHaHis   *A Biographical Handbook of Hispanics and United States Film.* By Gary D. Keller. Tempe, AZ: Bilingual Press, 1997.

BiHiMed   *A Biographical History of Medicine.* Excerpts and essays on the men and their work. By John H. Talbott. New York: Grune & Stratton, 1970.
Use the "Name Index," which begins on page 1193 to locate biographies.

BiInAmS   *Biographical Index to American Science.* The seventeenth century to 1920. Compiled by Clark A. Elliott. Bibliographies and Indexes in American History, no. 16. New York: Greenwood Press, 1990.

BioAmW   *Biographies of American Women.* An annotated bibliography. By Patricia E. Sweeney. Santa Barbara, CA: ABC-Clio, 1990.

BioIn   *Biography Index.* A cumulative index to biographical material in books and magazines. New York: H.W. Wilson Co., 1949-1998.
BioIn 1	Volume 1: January, 1946-July, 1949; 1949.
BioIn 2	Volume 2: August, 1949-August, 1952; 1953.
BioIn 3	Volume 3: September, 1952-August, 1955; 1956.
BioIn 4	Volume 4: September, 1955-August, 1958; 1960.
BioIn 5	Volume 5: September, 1958-August, 1961; 1962.
BioIn 6	Volume 6: September, 1961-August, 1964; 1965.
BioIn 7	Volume 7: September, 1964-August, 1967; 1968.
BioIn 8	Volume 8: September, 1967-August, 1970; 1971.
BioIn 9	Volume 9: September, 1970-August, 1973; 1974.
BioIn 10	Volume 10: September, 1973-August, 1976; 1977.
BioIn 11	Volume 11: September, 1976-August, 1979; 1980.
BioIn 12	Volume 12: September, 1979-August, 1982; 1983.
BioIn 13	Volume 13: September, 1982-August, 1984; 1984.
BioIn 14	Volume 14: September, 1984-August, 1986; 1986.
BioIn 15	Volume 15: September, 1986-August, 1988; 1988.
BioIn 16	Volume 16: September, 1988-August, 1990; 1990.
BioIn 17	Volume 17: September, 1990-August, 1992; 1992.
BioIn 18	Volume 18: September, 1992-August, 1993; 1993.
BioIn 19	Volume 19: September, 1993-August, 1994; 1994.
BioIn 20	Volume 20: September, 1994-August, 1995; 1995.
BioIn 21	Volume 21: September, 1995-August, 1996; 1996.

BioIn 22   Volume 22: September, 1996-August, 1997; 1997.
BioIn 23   Volume 23: September, 1997-August, 1998; 1998.

BioIn 24   *Biography Index.* A cumulative index to biographical material in books and magazines. Volume 24: September, 1998-August, 1999. New York: H. W. Wilson Co., 1999.

BioNews   *Biography News.* A compilation of news stories and feature articles from American news media covering personalities of national interest in all fields. Edited by Frank E. Bair. Detroit: Gale Research, 1974-1975.
                   BioNews 74   Volume 1, Numbers 1-12; 1974.
                   BioNews 75   Volume 2, Number 1, January-February; 1975.

BlkAmP   *Black American Playwrights, 1800 to the Present.* A bibliography. By Esther Spring Arata and Nicholas John Rotoli. Metuchen, NJ: Scarecrow Press, 1976. Updated by *More Black American Playwrights: A Bibliography.*

BlkAmWO   *Black American Women in Olympic Track and Field.* A complete illustrated reference. By Michael D. Davis. Jefferson, NC: McFarland & Co., 1992.

BlkAmW   *Black American Writers.* Bibliographical essays. Edited by M. Thomas Inge, Maurice Duke, and Jackson R. Bryer. New York: St. Martin's Press, 1978.
                   BlkAmW 1   Volume 1: The Beginnings through the Harlem Renaissance and Langston Hughes.
                   BlkAmW 2   Volume 2: Richard Wright, Ralph Ellison, James Baldwin, and Amiri Baraka.
                   Use the Index to locate biographies.

BlkAWP   *Black American Writers Past and Present.* A biographical and bibliographical dictionary. Two volumes. By Theressa Gunnels Rush, Carol Fairbanks Myers, and Esther Spring Arata. Metuchen, NJ: Scarecrow Press, 1975.

BlkAmsC   *Black Americans in Congress, 1870-1989.* By Bruce A. Ragsdale and Joel D. Treese. Washington, DC: U.S. Government Printing Office, 1990.

BlkAuIB 1999   *Black Authors and Illustrators of Books for Children and Young Adults.* A biographical dictionary. Third edition. By Barbara Thrash Murphy. Garland Reference Library of the Humanities, vol. 2157. New York: Garland Publishing, 1999. Earlier editions published as *Black Authors and Illustrators of Children's Books.*

BlkAuIl   *Black Authors and Illustrators of Children's Books.* By Barbara Rollock. New York: Garland Publishing, 1988-1992.
                   BlkAuIl   First edition. Garland Reference Library of the Humanities, vol. 660; 1988.
                   BlkAuIl 92   Second edition. Garland Reference Library of the Humanities, vol. 1316; 1992.

BlkCS   *The Black Composer Speaks.* Edited by David N. Baker, Lida M. Belt, and Herman C. Hudson. Metuchen, NJ: Scarecrow Press, 1978.

BlkCond   *Black Conductors.* By D. Antoinette Handy. Metuchen, NJ: Scarecrow Press, 1995. Use the Index to locate biographies.

BlkCO   *Black Congressional Reconstruction Orators and Their Orations, 1869-1879.* By
                   Annjennette Sophie McFarlin. Metuchen, NJ: Scarecrow Press, 1976.

BlkLC   *Black Literature Criticism.* Excerpts from criticism of the most significant works of
                   Black authors over the past 200 years. Three volumes. Detroit: Gale Research,
                   1992.

BlkLC SUP   *Black Literature Criticism Supplement.* Excerpts from criticism of the most
                   significant works of black authors over the past 200 years. Detroit: Gale
                   Research, 1999.

BlkMth   *Black Mathematicians and Their Works.* Edited by Virginia K. Newell, Joella H.
                   Gipson, L. Waldo Rich, and Beauregard Stubblefield. Ardmore, PA: Dorrance
                   & Co., 1980.
                   Biographies are located in the ''Biographical Index'' which begins on page
                   277.

BlkOlyM   *Black Olympian Medalists.* By James A. Page. Englewood, CO: Libraries Unlimited,
                   1991.

BlkWAm   *Black Women in America.* An historical encyclopedia. Two volumes. Edited by
                   Darlene Clark Hine. Brooklyn, NY: Carlson Publishing, 1993.

BlkWAB   *Black Women in American Bands and Orchestras.* By D. Antoinette Handy.
                   Metuchen, NJ: Scarecrow Press, 1981.
                   Use the ''Index to Profiles'' to locate biographies.

BlkWWr   *Black Women Writers (1950-1980).* A critical evaluation. Edited by Mari Evans.
                   Garden City, NY: Anchor Press/Doubleday, 1984.

BlkWr   *Black Writers.* A selection of sketches from *Contemporary Authors.* Detroit: Gale
                   Research, 1989-1994.
                   BlkWr 1   First edition; 1989.
                   BlkWr 2   Second edition; 1994.

BlkWr 3   *Black Writers.* A selection of sketches from *Contemporary Authors.* Third edition.
                   Detroit: Gale Group, 1999.

BlkWrNE   *Black Writers in New England.* A bibliography, with biographical notes, of books by
                   and about Afro-American writers associated with New England in the
                   Collection of Afro-American Literature. By Edward Clark. Boston: National
                   Park Service, 1985.
                   BlkWrNE A   Section II, ''Afro-American writers associated with New
                                      England not represented with books by or about them
                                      in the *Collection of Afro-American Literature,''* begins
                                      on page 70.

BlksAmF   *Blacks in American Films and Television.* An encyclopedia. By Donald Bogle.
                   Garland Reference Library of the Humanities, vol. 604. New York: Garland
                   Publishing, 1988.
                   Biographies are located in the ''Profiles'' section which begins on page
                   353.

BlksB&W	*Blacks in Black & White.* A source book on Black films. By Henry T. Sampson. Metuchen, NJ: Scarecrow Press, 1977.
	BlksB&W Biographies begin on page 192.
	BlksB&W C Appendix C, "Film Credits for Featured Players in Black-cast Films, 1915-1950," begins on page 311.
BlksBF	*Blacks in Blackface.* A source book on early Black musical shows. By Henry T. Sampson. Metuchen, NJ: Scarecrow Press, 1980. Biographies begin on page 330.
BlksCm	*Blacks in Communications.* Journalism, public relations, and advertising. By M.L. Stein. New York: Julian Messner, 1972.
BlkOpe	*Blacks in Opera.* An encyclopedia of people and companies, 1873-1993. By Eric Ledell Smith. Jefferson, NC: McFarland & Co., 1995.
BlksScM	*Blacks in Science and Medicine.* By Vivian Ovelton Sammons. New York: Hemisphere Publishing, 1990.
BlkwCE	*The Blackwell Companion to the Enlightenment.* By John W. Yolton, Roy Porter, Pat Rodgers, and Barbara Maria Stafford. Cambridge, MA: Basil Blackwell, 1991.
BlkwEAR	*The Blackwell Encyclopedia of the American Revolution.* Edited by Jack P. Greene and J.R. Pole. Cambridge, MA: Basil Blackwell, 1991. Biographies begin on page 695.
BlkwERR	*The Blackwell Encyclopedia of the Russian Revolution.* Edited by Harold Shukman. New York: Basil Blackwell, 1988. Biographies begin on page 297.
BlmGEL	*The Bloomsbury Guide to English Literature.* The new authority on English literature. Edited by Marion Wynne-Davies. New York: Prentice Hall General Reference, 1990. Originally published in hardcover as the *Prentice Hall Guide to English Literature.* Biographies begin on page 295.
BlmGWL	*The Bloomsbury Guide to Women's Literature.* Edited by Claire Buck. New York: Prentice Hall General Reference, 1992. Biographies begin on page 247.
BlueB 76	*The Blue Book.* Leaders of the English-speaking world. 1976 edition. London: St. James Press; New York: St. Martin's Press, 1976. Reprint. In two volumes by Gale Research, Detroit, 1979.
	BlueB 76N Obituary section begins on page 1837.
Blues	*The Blues.* From Robert Johnson to Robert Cray. By Tony Russell. New York: Schirmer Books, 1997.
	Blues "A-Z Blues Artists" section begins on page 86.
	Blues A "Blues Legends" section begins on page 36.
BluesWW	*Blues Who's Who.* A biographical dictionary of blues singers. By Sheldon Harris. New Rochelle, NY: Arlington House Publishers, 1979.

BkC   *The Book of Catholic Authors.* Informal self-portraits of famous modern Catholic writers. Edited by Walter Romig. Detroit: Walter Romig & Co., (n.d.).

BkC 1	First series; 1942.
BkC 2	Second series; 1943.
BkC 3	Third series; 1945.
BkC 4	Fourth series.
BkC 5	Fifth series.
BkC 6	Sixth series.

BkCL   *A Book of Children's Literature.* Third edition. Edited by Lillian Hollowell. New York: Holt, Rinehart & Winston, 1966.
Biographies begin on page 553.

BkIE   *Book Illustrators in Eighteenth-Century England.* By Hanns Hammelmann. Edited and completed by T.S.R. Boase. New Haven, CT: Yale University Press, 1975.

BkPepl   *The Book of People.* By Christopher P. Anderson. New York: Perigree Books, 1981.

BkP   *Books Are by People.* Interviews with 104 authors and illustrators of books for young children. By Lee Bennett Hopkins. New York: Citation Press, 1969.

BoxReg   *The Boxing Register.* International Boxing Hall of Fame official record book. By James B. Roberts and Alexander G. Skutt. Ithaca, NY: McBooks Press, 1997-1999.

BoxReg	First edition; 1997. Use the ''Inductees'' list, which begins on page 446, to locate biographies.
BoxReg 2	Second edition; 1999. Use the ''Inductees'' list, which begins on page 520, to locate biographies.

BriB   *Brilliant Bylines.* A biographical anthology of notable newspaperwomen in America. By Barbara Belford. New York: Columbia University Press, 1986.

BriBkM 80   *Britannica Book of Music.* Edited by Benjamin Hadley. Garden City, NY: Doubleday & Co., 1980.

BriEAA   *The Britannica Encyclopedia of American Art.* Chicago: Encyclopaedia Britannica Educational Corp., 1973. Distributed by Simon & Schuster, New York.

BritAS   *British and American Sporting Authors: Their Writings and Biographies.* By A. Henry Higginson. London: Hutchinson & Co., 1951.
Use the Index to locate biographies.

BritAu   *British Authors before 1800.* A biographical dictionary. Edited by Stanley J. Kunitz and Howard Haycraft. Wilson Authors Series. New York: H.W. Wilson Co., 1952.

BritAu 19   *British Authors of the Nineteenth Century.* Edited by Stanley J. Kunitz. Wilson Authors Series. New York: H.W. Wilson Co., 1936.

BritCA   *British Children's Authors.* Interviews at Home. By Cornelia Jones and Olivia R. Way. Chicago: American Library Association, 1976.

BritMNA	*The British Museum Encyclopedia of Native North America.* Edited by Rayna Green with Melanie Fernandez. Bloomington, IN: Indiana University Press, 1999.
BritPl	*British Playwrights, 1880-1956.* A research and production sourcebook. Edited by William W. Demastes and Katherine E. Kelly. Westport, CT: Greenwood Press, 1996.
BritWr	*British Writers.* New York: Charles Scribner's Sons, 1979-1999.

	BritWr 1	Volume I: William Langland to The English Bible; 1979. Use the "List of Subjects" to locate biographies.
	BritWr 2	Volume II: Thomas Middleton to George Farquhar; 1979. Use the "List of Subjects" to locate biographies.
	BritWr 3	Volume III: Daniel Defoe to The Gothic Novel; 1980. Use the "List of Subjects" to locate biographies.
	BritWr 4	Volume IV: William Wordsworth to Robert Browning; 1981. Use the "List of Subjects" to locate biographies.
	BritWr 5	Volume V: Elizabeth Gaskell to Francis Thompson; 1982. Use the "List of Subjects" to locate biographies.
	BritWr 6	Volume VI: Thomas Hardy to Wilfred Owen; 1983. Use the "List of Subjects" to locate biographies.
	BritWr 7	Volume VII: Sean O'Casey to Poets of World War II; 1984. Use the "List of Subjects" to locate biographies.
	BritWr S1	Supplement 1; 1987. Use the "List of Subjects" to locate biographies.
	BritWr S2	Supplement 2; 1992. Use the "List of Subjects" to locate biographies.
	BritWr S3	Supplement 3; 1996. Use the "List of Subjects" to locate biographies.
	BritWr S4	Supplement IV. Edited by George Stade and Carol Howard; 1997.
	BritWr S5	Supplement V. Edited by George Stade and Sarah Hannah Goldstein; 1999.

BroV	*Broadening Views, 1968-1988.* Concise Dictionary of American Literary Biography Series. Detroit: Gale Research, 1989.
BroadAu	*Broadside Authors and Artists.* An illustrated biographical directory. Compiled and edited by Leaonead Pack Bailey. Detroit: Broadside Press, 1974.
BuCMET	*Bud Collins' Modern Encyclopedia of Tennis.* Edited by Bud Collins and Zander Hollander. Detroit: Gale Research, 1994. Use the Index to locate biographies.
BusPN	*Business People in the News.* A compilation of news stories and feature articles from American newspapers and magazines covering people in industry, finance, and labor. Volume 1. Edited by Barbara Nykoruk. Detroit: Gale Research, 1976.

CabMA   *The Cabinetmakers of America.* Revised and corrected edition. By Ethel Hall Bjerkoe. Exton, PA: Schiffer, 1978. Originally published by Doubleday & Co., 1957.
                   Biographies begin on page 19.

Cald 1938   *Caldecott Medal Books: 1938-1957.* With the artist's acceptance papers & related material chiefly from the *Horn Book Magazine.* Edited by Bertha Mahony Miller and Elinor Whitney Field. Horn Book Papers, volume II. Boston: Horn Book, 1957.

CamBiEn   *The Cambridge Biographical Encyclopedia.* Second edition. Edited by David Crystal. Cambridge: Cambridge University Press, 1998.

CamDcSc   *The Cambridge Dictionary of Scientists.* By David Millar, Ian Millar, John Millar, and Margaret Millar. Cambridge: Cambridge University Press, 1996.

CamGEL   *The Cambridge Guide to English Literature.* Edited by Michael Stapleton. Cambridge: Cambridge University Press; Middlesex, England: Newnes Books, 1983.

CamGLE   *The Cambridge Guide to Literature in English.* Edited by Ian Ousby. Cambridge: Cambridge University Press; London: Hamlyn Publishing Group, 1988.

CamGWoT   *The Cambridge Guide to World Theatre.* Edited by Martin Banham. Cambridge: Cambridge University Press, 1988.

CamHAL   *The Cambridge Handbook of American Literature.* Edited by Jack Salzman. Cambridge: Cambridge University Press, 1986.

CaW   *Canada Writes!* The members' book of the Writers' Union of Canada. Edited by K.A. Hamilton. Toronto: Writers' Union of Canada, 1977.
                       CaW A   "Additional Members" section begins on page 387.

CaP   *Canada's Playwrights: A Biographical Guide.* Edited by Don Rubin and Alison Cranmer-Byng. Toronto: Canadian Theatre Review Publications, 1980.

CanNov   *Canadian Novelists, 1920-1945.* By Clara Thomas. Toronto: Longmans, Green & Co., 1946. Reprint. Folcroft, Penn.: Folcroft Library Editions, 1970.

CanParl 1998   *Canadian Parliamentary Guide. 1998-1999.* Detroit: Gale Group, 1999.
                   Use the Index to locate biographies.

CanWW 70   *Canadian Who's Who.* A biographical dictionary of notable living men and women. Volume 12, 1970-1972. Toronto: Who's Who Canadian Publications, 1972.

CanWW   *Canadian Who's Who.* Toronto: University of Toronto Press, 1979-1999.
                       CanWW 79   Volume 14. Edited by Kieran Simpson; 1979.
                       CanWW 80   Volume 15. Edited by Kieran Simpson; 1980.
                       CanWW 81   Volume 16. Edited by Kieran Simpson; 1981.
                       CanWW 83   Volume 18. Edited by Kieran Simpson; 1983.
                       CanWW 89   Volume 24. Edited by Kieran Simpson; 1989.
                       CanWW 96   Volume 31; 1996.

CanWW 97	Volume 32. Edited by Elizabeth Lumley; 1997.	
CanWW 98	Volume 33; 1998.	
CanWW 1999	Volume 34. Edited by Elizabeth Lumley; 1999.	

CanWr   *Canadian Writers*. A biographical dictionary. New edition, revised and enlarged. Edited by Guy Sylvestre, Brandon Conron, and Carl F. Klinck. Toronto: Ryerson Press, 1966.

CarWomW   *Caribbean Women Writers*. Edited by Harold Bloom. Women Writers of English and Their Works. Philadelphia: Chelsea House Publishers, 1997.

CaribW   *Caribbean Writers*. A bio-bibliographical-critical encyclopedia. Edited by Donald E. Herdeck. Washington: Three Continents Press, 1979.

CaribW 1	Volume I: *Anglophone Literature from the Caribbean,* begins on page 17.	
CaribW 1A	Volume I: *Supplementary List of Writers from Belize,* begins on page 230.	
CaribW 2	Volume II: *Francophone Literature from the Caribbean,* begins on page 283.	
CaribW 2A	Volume II: *Supplementary List of Writers from Haiti,* begins on page 531.	
CaribW 3	Volume III: *Literatures of the Netherlands Antilles and Surinam,* begins on page 561.	
CaribW 4	Volume IV: *Spanish Language Literature from the Caribbean,* begins on page 629.	

CarSB   *The Carolyn Sherwin Bailey Historical Collection of Children's Books*. A catalogue. Edited and compiled by Dorothy R. Davis. New Haven, CT: Southern Connecticut State College, 1966.

                Not in strict alphabetic sequence.

CasWL   *Cassell's Encyclopaedia of World Literature*. Two volumes. Edited by S.H. Steinberg. Revised and enlarged in three volumes by J. Buchanan-Brown. New York: William Morrow & Co., 1973.

                Biographies are found in Volumes 2 and 3 of the revised edition.

CathA   *Catholic Authors*. Contemporary biographical sketches. Edited by Matthew Hoehn. Newark, NJ: St. Mary's Abbey, 1948-1952.

CathA 1930	First volume: 1930-1947; 1948.	
CathA 1952	Second volume; 1952.	

CelCen   *Celebrities of the Century*. Being a dictionary of men and women of the nineteenth century. Two volumes. Edited by Lloyd C. Sanders. London: Cassell & Co., 1887. Reprint. Ann Arbor: Gryphon Books, 1971.

CelR   *Celebrity Register*. Third edition. Edited by Earl Blackwell. New York: Simon & Schuster, 1973.

CelR 90   *Celebrity Register, 1990*. Detroit: Gale Research, 1990.

Cen   *Censorship*. By Gail Blasser Riley. Library in a Book. New York, NY: Facts on File, 1998.

                Biographical Listing section begins on page 81.

CenC   *A Century of Ceramics in the United States, 1878-1978.* A study of its development. By Garth Clark. New York: E.P. Dutton, 1979.
              Biographies begin on page 269.

ChamBiD   *Chambers Biographical Dictionary.* Sixth edition. Edited by Melanie Parry. New York: Larousse Kingfisher Chambers, 1997.

Chambr   *Chambers's Cyclopaedia of English Literature.* A history critical and biographical of authors in the English tongue from the earliest times till the present day with specimens of their writings. Edited by David Patrick, revised by J. Liddell Geddie. Philadelphia: J.B. Lippincott, 1938. Reprint. Detroit: Gale Research, 1978.

Chambr 1	Volume I: 7th-17th Century.
Chambr 2	Volume II: 18th Century.
Chambr 3	Volume III: 19th-20th Century.

              Use the Index to locate biographies.

ChiLit   *Chicano Literature: A Reference Guide.* Edited by Julio A. Martinez and Francisco A. Lomeli. Westport, CT: Greenwood Press, 1985.

ChiLit A	"Appendix A" begins on page 441.

ChiSch   *Chicano Scholars and Writers.* A bio-bibliographical directory. Edited and compiled by Julio A. Martinez. Metuchen, NJ: Scarecrow Press, 1979.

ChhPo   *Childhood in Poetry.* A catalogue, with biographical and critical annotations, of the books of English and American poets comprising the Shaw Childhood in Poetry Collection in the Library of the Florida State University. By John Mackay Shaw. Detroit: Gale Research, 1967-1980.

ChhPo	First edition; 1967.
ChhPo S1	First Supplement; 1972.
ChhPo S2	Second Supplement; 1976.
ChhPo S3	Third Supplement; 1980.

ChlBIlD   *Children's Book Illustration and Design.* Edited by Julie Cummins. Library of Applied Design. New York: PBC International, 1992. Distributed by Rizzoli International Publications, New York.

ChlBkCr   *Children's Books and Their Creators.* Edited by Anita Silvey. Boston: Houghton Mifflin Co., 1995.

ChlFicS   *Children's Fiction Sourcebook.* A survey of children's books for 6-13 year olds. By Margaret Hobson, Jennifer Madden, and Ray Prytherch. Brookfield, VT: Ashgate Publishing Co., 1992.

ChlLR   *Children's Literature Review.* Excerpts from reviews, criticism, and commentary on books for children and young people. Detroit: Gale Research, 1976-1999.

ChlLR 1	Volume 1; 1976.
ChlLR 2	Volume 2; 1976.
ChlLR 3	Volume 3; 1978.
ChlLR 4	Volume 4; 1982.
ChlLR 5	Volume 5; 1983.
ChlLR 6	Volume 6; 1984.
ChlLR 7	Volume 7; 1984.

ChlLR 8	Volume 8; 1985.
ChlLR 9	Volume 9; 1985.
ChlLR 10	Volume 10; 1986.
ChlLR 11	Volume 11; 1986.
ChlLR 12	Volume 12; 1987.
ChlLR 13	Volume 13; 1987.
ChlLR 14	Volume 14; 1988.
ChlLR 15	Volume 15; 1988.
ChlLR 16	Volume 16; 1989.
ChlLR 17	Volume 17; 1989.
ChlLR 18	Volume 18; 1989.
ChlLR 19	Volume 19; 1990.
ChlLR 20	Volume 20; 1990.
ChlLR 21	Volume 21; 1990.
ChlLR 22	Volume 22; 1991.
ChlLR 23	Volume 23; 1991.
ChlLR 24	Volume 24; 1991.
ChlLR 25	Volume 25; 1991.
ChlLR 26	Volume 26; 1992.
ChlLR 27	Volume 27; 1992.
ChlLR 28	Volume 28; 1992.
ChlLR 29	Volume 29; 1993.
ChlLR 30	Volume 30; 1993.
ChlLR 31	Volume 31; 1994.
ChlLR 32	Volume 32; 1994.
ChlLR 33	Volume 33; 1994.
ChlLR 34	Volume 34; 1995.
ChlLR 35	Volume 35; 1995.
ChlLR 36	Volume 36; 1995.
ChlLR 37	Volume 37; 1996.
ChlLR 38	Volume 38; 1996.
ChlLR 39	Volume 39; 1996.
ChlLR 40	Volume 40; 1996.
ChlLR 41	Volume 41; 1997.
ChlLR 42	Volume 42; 1997.
ChlLR 43	Volume 43; 1997.
ChlLR 44	Volume 44; 1997.
ChlLR 45	Volume 45; 1997.
ChlLR 46	Volume 46; 1998.
ChlLR 47	Volume 47; 1998.
ChlLR 48	Volume 48; 1998.
ChlLR 49	Volume 49; 1998.
ChlLR 50	Volume 50; 1999.
ChlLR 51	Volume 51; 1999.
ChlLR 52	Volume 52; 1999.

ChlLR   *Children's Literature Review*. Excerpts from reviews, criticism, and commentary on books for children and young people. Detroit: Gale Group, 1999-2000.

ChlLR 53	Volume 53; 1999.
ChlLR 54	Volume 54; 1999.
ChlLR 55	Volume 55; 1999.
ChlLR 56	Volume 56; 1999.
ChlLR 57	Volume 57; 2000.
ChlLR 58	Volume 58; 2000.
ChlLR 59	Volume 59; 2000.

ChlLR 60	Volume 60; 2000.

ChrP   *The Children's Poets*. Analyses and appraisals of the greatest English and American poets for children. By Walter Barnes. Yonkers-on-Hudson, NY: World Book Co., 1924.

ChsFB   *The Child's First Books*. A critical study of pictures and texts. By Donnarae MacCann and Olga Richard. New York: H.W. Wilson Co., 1973.
       ChsFB A   "Author Biographies" begin on page 96.
       ChsFB I   "Illustrator Biographies" begin on page 47.

CivR 74   *Civil Rights: A Current Guide to the People, Organizations, and Events*. Second edition. By Joan Martin Burke. New York: R.R. Bowker Co., 1974.
       Biographies begin on page 21.

CivRSt   *The Civil Rights Struggle: Leaders in Profile*. By John D'Emilio. New York: Facts on File, 1979.

CivWDc   *The Civil War Dictionary*. By Mark Mayo Boatner, III. New York: David McKay Co., 1959.

ClMLC   *Classical and Medieval Literature Criticism*. Excerpts from criticism of the works of world authors from classical antiquity through the fourteenth century, from the first appraisals to current evaluations. Detroit: Gale Research, 1988-1999.

ClMLC 1	Volume 1; 1988.
ClMLC 2	Volume 2; 1988.
ClMLC 3	Volume 3; 1989.
ClMLC 4	Volume 4; 1990.
ClMLC 5	Volume 5; 1991.
ClMLC 6	Volume 6; 1991.
ClMLC 7	Volume 7; 1991.
ClMLC 8	Volume 8; 1992.
ClMLC 9	Volume 9; 1993.
ClMLC 10	Volume 10; 1993.
ClMLC 11	Volume 11; 1993.
ClMLC 12	Volume 12; 1994.
ClMLC 13	Volume 13; 1994.
ClMLC 14	Volume 14; 1995.
ClMLC 15	Volume 15; 1996.
ClMLC 16	Volume 16; 1996.
ClMLC 17	Volume 17; 1996.
ClMLC 18	Volume 18; 1996.
ClMLC 19	Volume 19; 1997.
ClMLC 20	Volume 20; 1997.
ClMLC 21	Volume 21; 1997.
ClMLC 22	Volume 22; 1997.
ClMLC 23	Volume 23; 1998.
ClMLC 24	Volume 24; 1998.
ClMLC 25	Volume 25; 1998.
ClMLC 26	Volume 26; 1998. Contains no biographies.
ClMLC 27	Volume 27; 1998.
ClMLC 28	Volume 28; 1999.
ClMLC 29	Volume 29; 1999.

ClMLC   *Classical and Medieval Literature Criticism.* Excerpts from criticism of the works of world authors from classical antiquity through the fourteenth century, from the first appraisals to current evaluations. Detroit: Gale Group, 1999-2000.

ClMLC 30	Volume 30; 1999.	
ClMLC 31	Volume 31; 1999.	
ClMLC 32	Volume 32; 1999.	
ClMLC 33	Volume 33; 1999.	
ClMLC 34	Volume 34; 2000.	
ClMLC 35	Volume 35; 2000.	
ClMLC 36	Volume 36; 2000.	
ClMLC 37	Volume 37; 2000.	

ClaDrA   *The Classified Directory of Artists' Signatures, Symbols, & Monograms.* Second edition, enlarged and revised. By H.H. Caplan. London: George Prior Publishers, 1982. Distributed by Gale Research, Detroit.

ColdWar   *The Cold War, 1945-1991.* Leaders and other important figures in the United States and Western Europe. Edited by Benjamin Frankel. Detroit: Gale Research, 1992.

ColdWar 1	Volume 1.
ColdWar 2	Volume 2.
ColdWar 3	Volume 3. Contains no biographies.

ColdWRG   *The Cold War Reference Guide.* A general history and annotated chronology, with selected biographies. By Richard Alan Schwartz. Jefferson, NC: McFarland & Co., 1997.

Biographies of U.S. Political Figures begin on page 137. Biographies of Superpower Leaders begin on page 248.

ColARen   *Colonization to the American Renaissance, 1640-1865.* Concise Dictionary of American Literary Biography Series. Detroit: Gale Research, 1988.

ClDMEL   *Columbia Dictionary of Modern European Literature.* New York: Columbia University Press, 1947-1980.

ClDMEL 47	First edition. Edited by Horatio Smith; 1947.
ClDMEL 80	Second edition. Edited by Jean-Albert Bede and William B. Edgerton; 1980.

ColCR   *Columbo's Canadian References.* By John Robert Columbo. New York: Oxford University Press, 1976.

CmdStar   *Comedy Stars at 78 RPM.* Biographies and discographies of 89 American and British recording artists, 1896-1946. By Ronald L. Smith. Jefferson, NC: McFarland & Co., 1998.

CmdGen 1991   *Commanding Generals and Chiefs of Staff, 1775-1991.* Portraits & biographical sketches of the United States Army's Senior Officers. Revised edition, 1775-1991. By William Gardner Bell. Washington, DC: Center of Military History, United States Army, 1992.

Use the Index to locate biographies.

CmCal   *A Companion to California.* By James D. Hart. New York: Oxford University Press, 1978.

CmFrR	*Companion to the French Revolution.* By John Paxton. New York: Facts on File Publications, 1988.
CmIrTM	*The Companion to Irish Traditional Music.* Edited by Fintan Vallely. New York: New York University Press, 1999.
CmMedTh	*A Companion to the Medieval Theatre.* Edited by Ronald W. Vince. New York: Greenwood Press, 1989.
CmMov	*A Companion to the Movies: From 1903 to the Present Day.* A guide to the leading players, directors, screenwriters, composers, cameramen and other artistes who have worked in the English-speaking cinema over the last 70 years. By Roy Pickard. New York: Hippocrene Books, 1972. Use the ''Who's Who Index'' to locate biographies.
CmOp	*A Companion to the Opera.* By Robin May. New York: Hippocrene Books, 1977. Use the ''Selective Index: I - People,'' beginning on page 349, to locate biographies.
CmScLit	*Companion to Scottish Literature.* By Trevor Royle. Detroit: Gale Research, 1983.
CmpBCM	*The Complete Book of Classical Music.* By David Ewen. Englewood Cliffs, NJ: Prentice-Hall, 1965. Use the index at the back of the book to locate biographies.
CmpEGui	*The Complete Encyclopedia of the Guitar.* The definitive guide to the world's most popular instrument. Edited by Terry Burrows. New York: Schirmer Books, 1998. *CmpEGui* ''A-Z of Guitarists'' section begins on page 126. *CmpEGui A* ''Legends of the Guitar'' section begins on page 94.
CmpEPM	*The Complete Encyclopedia of Popular Music and Jazz, 1900-1950.* Three volumes. By Roger D. Kinkle. New Rochelle, NY: Arlington House Publishers, 1974. Biographies are located in Volumes 2 and 3.
CmpGMD	*The Complete Guide to Modern Dance.* By Don McDonagh. Garden City, NY: Doubleday & Co., 1976. Use the Index at the back of the book to locate biographies.
CmpQue	*Completely Queer.* The gay and lesbian encyclopedia. By Steve Hogan and Lee Hudson. New York: Henry Holt & Co., 1998.
CompSN	*Composers since 1900.* A biographical and critical guide. Compiled and edited by David Ewen. New York: H.W. Wilson Co., 1969-1981. *CompSN* First edition; 1969. *CompSN SUP* *First Supplement.*; 1981.
CpmDNM	*Composium Directory of New Music.* Annual index of contemporary compositions. Sedro Woolley, WA: Crystal Musicworks, 1972-1983. *CpmDNM 72* 1972 edition; 1972. *CpmDNM 73* 1973 edition; 1973. *CpmDNM 74* 1974 edition; 1974.

CpmDNM 75	1975 edition; 1975.	
CpmDNM 76	1976 edition; 1976.	
CpmDNM 77	1977 edition; 1977.	
CpmDNM 78	1978 edition; 1978.	
CpmDNM 79	1979 edition; 1979.	
CpmDNM 80	1980 edition; 1980.	
CpmDNM 81	1981 edition; 1981.	
CpmDNM 82	1982/83 edition; 1983.	

CnDAL   *Concise Dictionary of American Literature.* Edited by Robert Fulton Richards. New York: Philosophical Library, 1955. Reprint. New York: Greenwood Press, 1969.

CnDBLB   *Concise Dictionary of British Literary Biography.* Detroit: Gale Research, 1992.

> *CnDBLB 1*   Volume 1: *Writers of the Middle Ages and Renaissance before 1660.*; 1992.
>
> *CnDBLB 2*   Volume 2: *Writers of the Restoration and Eighteenth Century, 1660-1789.*; 1992.
>
> *CnDBLB 3*   Volume 3: *Writers of the Romantic Period, 1789-1832.*; 1992.
>
> *CnDBLB 4*   Volume 4: *Victorian Writers, 1832-1890.*; 1991.
>
> *CnDBLB 5*   Volume 5: *Late Victorian and Edwardian Writers, 1890-1914.*; 1991.
>
> *CnDBLB 6*   Volume 6: *Modern Writers, 1914-1945.*; 1991.
>
> *CnDBLB 7*   Volume 7: *Writers After World War II, 1945-1960.*; 1991.
>
> *CnDBLB 8*   Volume 8: *Contemporary Writers, 1960 to the Present.*; 1992.

CnDWLB   *Concise Dictionary of World Literary Biography.* Detroit: Gale Group, 1999-2000.

> *CnDWLB 1*   Volume 1: *Ancient Greek and Roman Writers.*; 1999.
>
> *CnDWLB 2*   Volume 2: *German Writers.* Edited by James Hardin; 1999.
>
> *CnDWLB 3*   Volume 3: *African, Caribbean, and Latin-American Writers.*; 2000.

CnE&AP   *The Concise Encyclopedia of English and American Poets and Poetry.* Edited by Stephen Spender and Donald Hall. New York: Hawthorn Books, 1963.

CnMD   *The Concise Encyclopedia of Modern Drama.* By Siegfried Melchinger. Translated by George Wellwarth. Edited by Henry Popkin. New York: Horizon Press, 1964.

> *CnMD*   Biographies begin on page 159.
>
> *CnMD SUP*   ''Additional Entries'' section begins on page 287.

CnMWL   *The Concise Encyclopedia of Modern World Literature.* Second edition. Edited by Geoffrey Grigson. London: Hutchinson & Co., 1970.

CnThe   *A Concise Encyclopedia of the Theatre.* By Robin May. Reading, England: Osprey Publishing, 1974.

> Use the Index to locate biographies.

CnOxB   *Concise Oxford Dictionary of Ballet* By Horst Koegler. London: Oxford University Press, 1977.

CndCPOM   *Conductors and Composers of Popular Orchestral Music.* A biographical and discographical sourcebook. By Reuben Musiker and Naomi Musiker. Westport, CT: Greenwood Press, 1998.

CnfFoY   *Conflict in the Former Yugoslavia.* An encyclopedia. Edited by John B. Allcock, Marko Milivojevic, and John J. Horton. Roots of Modern Conflict. Denver: ABC-CLIO, 1998.

CngDr   *Congressional Directory.* Washington, DC: United States Government Printing Office, 1974-1999.

CngDr 74	93rd Congress, 2nd Session; 1974.
CngDr 77	95th Congress, 1st Session; 1977.
CngDr 78	*Supplement,* 95th Congress, 2nd Session; 1978.
CngDr 79	96th Congress, 1st Session; 1979.
CngDr 81	97th Congress; 1981.
CngDr 83	98th Congress, 1983-1984; 1983.
CngDr 85	99th Congress, 1985-1986; 1985.
CngDr 87	100th Congress, 1987-1988; 1987.
CngDr 89	101st Congress, 1989-1990; 1989.
CngDr 91	102d Congress, 1991-1992; 1991.
CngDr 93	103d Congress, 1993-1994; 1993.
CngDr 95	104th Congress, 1995-1996; 1995.
CngDr 99	106th Congress, 1999-2000; 1999.

Use the ''Name Index'' to locate biographies.

ConAAFP   *Contemporary African American Female Playwrights.* An annotated bibliography. Bibliographies and Indexes in Afro-American and African Studies, no. 37 Westport, CT: Greenwood Press, 1998.

ConAfAN   *Contemporary African American Novelists.* A bio-bibliographical critical sourcebook. Edited by Emmanuel S. Nelson. Westport, CT: Greenwood Press, 1999.

ConAmA   *Contemporary American Authors.* A critical survey and 219 bio-bibliographies. By Fred B. Millett. New York: Harcourt, Brace & World, 1940. Reprint. New York: AMS Press, 1970.

                                           Biographies begin on page 207.

ConAmBL   *Contemporary American Business Leaders.* A biographical dictionary. By John N. Ingham and Lynne B. Feldman. New York: Greenwood Press, 1990.

                                           Use the Index to locate biographies.

ConAmC   *Contemporary American Composers.* A biographical dictionary. Compiled by E. Ruth Anderson. Boston: G.K. Hall & Co., 1976-1982.

ConAmC 76	First edition; 1976.
ConAmC 76A	First edition; 1976. Addendum begins on page 495.
ConAmC 82	Second edition; 1982.

ConAmD   *Contemporary American Dramatists.* Edited by K.A. Berney. London: St. James Press, 1994.

ConAmL   *Contemporary American Literature.* Bibliographies and study outlines. By John Matthews Manly and Edith Rickert. Revised by Fred B. Millett. New York: Harcourt, 1929. Reprint. New York: Haskell House Publishers, 1974. Biographies begin on page 101.

ConAmTC   *Contemporary American Theater Critics.* A directory and anthology of their works. Compiled by M.E. Comtois and Lynn F. Miller. Metuchen, NJ: Scarecrow Press, 1977.

ConAmWS   *Contemporary American Women Sculptors.* By Virginia Watson-Jones. Phoenix, AZ: Oryx Press, 1986.

ConArch 80   *Contemporary Architects.* Edited by Muriel Emanuel. Contemporary Arts Series. New York: St. Martin's Press, 1980.
                    ConArch 80A   "Notes on Advisors and Contributors" section begins on page 927.

ConArch   *Contemporary Architects.* London: St. James Press, 1987-1994.
                    ConArch 87   Second edition. Edited by Ann Lee Morgan and Colin Naylor; 1987.
                    ConArch 94   Third edition. Edited by Muriel Emanuel; 1994.

ConArt   *Contemporary Artists.* Contemporary Arts Series. New York: St. Martin's Press, 1977-1983.
                    ConArt 77   First edition. Edited by Colin Naylor and Genesis P-Orridge; 1977.
                    ConArt 83   Second edition. Edited by Muriel Emanuel et al; 1983.

ConArt   *Contemporary Artists.* Contemporary Arts Series. Detroit: St. James Press, 1989-1996.
                    ConArt 89   Third edition. Edited by Colin Naylor; 1989.
                    ConArt 96   Fourth edition. Edited by Joann Cerrito; 1996.

ConAu   *Contemporary Authors.* A bio-bibliographical guide to current writers in fiction, general nonfiction, poetry, journalism, drama, motion pictures, television, and other fields. Detroit: Gale Research, 1967-1999.

ConAu 1R	Volumes 1-4, 1st revision; 1967.
ConAu 5R	Volumes 5-8, 1st revision; 1969.
ConAu 9R	Volumes 9-12, 1st revision; 1974.
ConAu 13R	Volumes 13-16, 1st revision; 1975.
ConAu 17R	Volumes 17-20, 1st revision; 1976.
ConAu 21R	Volumes 21-24, 1st revision; 1977.
ConAu 25R	Volumes 25-28, 1st revision; 1977.
ConAu 29R	Volumes 29-32, 1st revision; 1978.
ConAu 33R	Volumes 33-36, 1st revision; 1978.
ConAu 37R	Volumes 37-40, 1st revision; 1979.
ConAu 41R	Volumes 41-44, 1st revision; 1979.
ConAu 45	Volumes 45-48; 1974.
ConAu 49	Volumes 49-52; 1975.
ConAu 53	Volumes 53-56; 1975.
ConAu 57	Volumes 57-60; 1976.
ConAu 61	Volumes 61-64; 1976.
ConAu 65	Volumes 65-68; 1977.

ConAu 69	Volumes 69-72; 1978.
ConAu 73	Volumes 73-76; 1978.
ConAu 77	Volumes 77-80; 1979.
ConAu 81	Volumes 81-84; 1979.
ConAu 85	Volumes 85-88; 1980.
ConAu 89	Volumes 89-92; 1980.
ConAu 93	Volumes 93-96; 1980.
ConAu 97	Volumes 97-100; 1981.
ConAu 101	Volume 101; 1981.
ConAu 102	Volume 102; 1981.
ConAu 103	Volume 103; 1982.
ConAu 104	Volume 104; 1982.
ConAu 105	Volume 105; 1982.
ConAu 106	Volume 106; 1982.
ConAu 107	Volume 107; 1983.
ConAu 108	Volume 108; 1983.
ConAu 109	Volume 109; 1983.
ConAu 110	Volume 110; 1984.
ConAu 111	Volume 111; 1984.
ConAu 112	Volume 112; 1985.
ConAu 113	Volume 113; 1985.
ConAu 114	Volume 114; 1985.
ConAu 115	Volume 115; 1985.
ConAu 116	Volume 116; 1986.
ConAu 117	Volume 117; 1986.
ConAu 118	Volume 118; 1986.
ConAu 119	Volume 119; 1987.
ConAu 120	Volume 120; 1987.
ConAu 121	Volume 121; 1987.
ConAu 122	Volume 122; 1988.
ConAu 123	Volume 123; 1988.
ConAu 124	Volume 124; 1988.
ConAu 125	Volume 125; 1989.
ConAu 126	Volume 126; 1989.
ConAu 127	Volume 127; 1989.
ConAu 128	Volume 128; 1990.
ConAu 129	Volume 129; 1990.
ConAu 130	Volume 130; 1990.
ConAu 131	Volume 131; 1991.
ConAu 132	Volume 132; 1991.
ConAu 133	Volume 133; 1991.
ConAu 134	Volume 134; 1992.
ConAu 135	Volume 135; 1992.
ConAu 136	Volume 136; 1992.
ConAu 137	Volume 137; 1992.
ConAu 138	Volume 138; 1993.
ConAu 139	Volume 139; 1993.
ConAu 140	Volume 140; 1993.
ConAu 141	Volume 141; 1994.
ConAu 142	Volume 142; 1994.
ConAu 143	Volume 143; 1994.
ConAu 144	Volume 144; 1994.
ConAu 145	Volume 145; 1995.
ConAu 146	Volume 146; 1995.
ConAu 147	Volume 147; 1995.

ConAu 148	Volume 148; 1996.
ConAu 149	Volume 149; 1996.
ConAu 150	Volume 150; 1996.
ConAu 151	Volume 151; 1996.
ConAu 152	Volume 152; 1997.
ConAu 153	Volume 153; 1997.
ConAu 154	Volume 154; 1997.
ConAu 155	Volume 155; 1997.
ConAu 156	Volume 156; 1997.
ConAu 157	Volume 157; 1998.
ConAu 158	Volume 158; 1998.
ConAu 159	Volume 159; 1998.
ConAu 160	Volume 160; 1998.
ConAu 161	Volume 161; 1998.
ConAu 162	Volume 162; 1998.
ConAu 163	Volume 163; 1998.
ConAu 164	Volume 164; 1998.
ConAu 165	Volume 165; 1999.
ConAu 166	Volume 166; 1999.
ConAu 167	Volume 167; 1999.
ConAu 168	Volume 168; 1999.

ConAu   *Contemporary Authors.* A bio-bibliographical guide to current writers in fiction, general nonfiction, poetry, journalism, drama, motion pictures, television, and other fields. Detroit: Gale Group, 1999-2000.

ConAu 169	Volume 169; 1999.
ConAu 170	Volume 170; 1999.
ConAu 171	Volume 171; 1999.
ConAu 172	Volume 172; 1999.
ConAu 173	Volume 173; 1999.
ConAu 174	Volume 174; 1999.
ConAu 175	Volume 175; 1999.
ConAu 176	Volume 176; 1999.
ConAu 177	Volume 177; 1999.
ConAu 178	Volume 178; 2000.
ConAu 179	Volume 179; 2000.
ConAu 180	Volume 180; 2000.
ConAu 181	Volume 181; 2000.
ConAu 182	Volume 182; 2000.

ConAu   *Contemporary Authors, Autobiography Series.* Detroit: Gale Research, 1984-1999.

ConAu 1AS	Volume 1; 1984.
ConAu 2AS	Volume 2; 1985.
ConAu 3AS	Volume 3; 1986.
ConAu 4AS	Volume 4; 1986.
ConAu 5AS	Volume 5; 1987.
ConAu 6AS	Volume 6; 1988.
ConAu 7AS	Volume 7; 1988.
ConAu 8AS	Volume 8; 1989.
ConAu 9AS	Volume 9; 1989.
ConAu 10AS	Volume 10; 1989.
ConAu 11AS	Volume 11; 1990.
ConAu 12AS	Volume 12; 1990.
ConAu 13AS	Volume 13; 1991.
ConAu 14AS	Volume 14; 1991.

ConAu 15AS	Volume 15; 1992.	
ConAu 16AS	Volume 16; 1992.	
ConAu 17AS	Volume 17; 1993.	
ConAu 18AS	Volume 18; 1994.	
ConAu 19AS	Volume 19; 1994.	
ConAu 20AS	Volume 20; 1994.	
ConAu 21AS	Volume 21; 1995.	
ConAu 22AS	Volume 22; 1996.	
ConAu 23AS	Volume 23; 1996.	
ConAu 24AS	Volume 24; 1996.	
ConAu 25AS	Volume 25; 1997.	
ConAu 26AS	Volume 26; 1997.	
ConAu 27AS	Volume 27; 1997.	
ConAu 28AS	Volume 28; 1998.	
ConAu 29AS	Volume 29; 1998.	
ConAu 30AS	Volume 30; 1999.	

ConAu   *Contemporary Authors, Bibliographical Series*. Detroit: Gale Research, 1986-1989.

         ConAu 1BS   Volume 1: *American Novelists*. Edited by James J. Martine; 1986.

         ConAu 2BS   Volume 2: *American Poets*. Edited by Ronald Baughman; 1986.

         ConAu 3BS   Volume 3: *American Dramatists*. Edited by Matthew C. Roudane; 1989.

ConAu X   *Contemporary Authors, Index*. A bio-bibliographical guide to current writers in fiction, general nonfiction, poetry, journalism, drama, motion pictures, television, and other fields. Detroit: Gale Research, (n.d.).

     This code refers to Pseudonym Entries which appear only as Cross-References in the Cumulative Index.

ConAu   *Contemporary Authors, New Revision Series*. A bio-bibliographical guide to current writers in fiction, general nonfiction, poetry, journalism, drama, motion pictures, television, and other fields. Detroit: Gale Research, 1981-1999.

ConAu 1NR	Volume 1; 1981.	
ConAu 2NR	Volume 2; 1981.	
ConAu 3NR	Volume 3; 1981.	
ConAu 4NR	Volume 4; 1981.	
ConAu 5NR	Volume 5; 1982.	
ConAu 6NR	Volume 6; 1982.	
ConAu 7NR	Volume 7; 1982.	
ConAu 8NR	Volume 8; 1983.	
ConAu 9NR	Volume 9; 1983.	
ConAu 10NR	Volume 10; 1983.	
ConAu 11NR	Volume 11; 1984.	
ConAu 12NR	Volume 12; 1984.	
ConAu 13NR	Volume 13; 1984.	
ConAu 14NR	Volume 14; 1985.	
ConAu 15NR	Volume 15; 1985.	
ConAu 16NR	Volume 16; 1986.	
ConAu 17NR	Volume 17; 1986.	
ConAu 18NR	Volume 18; 1986.	
ConAu 19NR	Volume 19; 1987.	
ConAu 20NR	Volume 20; 1987.	
ConAu 21NR	Volume 21; 1987.	

ConAu 22NR	Volume 22; 1988.
ConAu 23NR	Volume 23; 1988.
ConAu 24NR	Volume 24; 1988.
ConAu 25NR	Volume 25; 1989.
ConAu 26NR	Volume 26; 1989.
ConAu 27NR	Volume 27; 1989.
ConAu 28NR	Volume 28; 1990.
ConAu 29NR	Volume 29; 1990.
ConAu 30NR	Volume 30; 1990.
ConAu 31NR	Volume 31; 1990.
ConAu 32NR	Volume 32; 1991.
ConAu 33NR	Volume 33; 1991.
ConAu 34NR	Volume 34; 1991.
ConAu 35NR	Volume 35; 1992.
ConAu 36NR	Volume 36; 1992.
ConAu 37NR	Volume 37; 1992.
ConAu 38NR	Volume 38; 1993.
ConAu 39NR	Volume 39; 1992.
ConAu 40NR	Volume 40; 1993.
ConAu 41NR	Volume 41; 1994.
ConAu 42NR	Volume 42; 1994.
ConAu 43NR	Volume 43; 1994.
ConAu 44NR	Volume 44; 1994.
ConAu 45NR	Volume 45; 1995.
ConAu 46NR	Volume 46; 1995.
ConAu 47NR	Volume 47; 1995.
ConAu 48NR	Volume 48; 1995.
ConAu 49NR	Volume 49; 1995.
ConAu 50NR	Volume 50; 1996.
ConAu 51NR	Volume 51; 1996.
ConAu 52NR	Volume 52; 1996.
ConAu 53NR	Volume 53; 1997.
ConAu 54NR	Volume 54; 1997.
ConAu 55NR	Volume 55; 1997.
ConAu 56NR	Volume 56; 1997.
ConAu 57NR	Volume 57; 1997.
ConAu 58NR	Volume 58; 1997.
ConAu 59NR	Volume 59; 1998.
ConAu 60NR	Volume 60; 1998.
ConAu 61NR	Volume 61; 1998.
ConAu 62NR	Volume 62; 1998.
ConAu 63NR	Volume 63; 1998.
ConAu 64NR	Volume 64; 1998.
ConAu 65NR	Volume 65; 1998.
ConAu 66NR	Volume 66; 1998.
ConAu 67NR	Volume 67; 1998.
ConAu 68NR	Volume 68; 1998.
ConAu 69NR	Volume 69; 1999.
ConAu 70NR	Volume 70; 1999.
ConAu 71NR	Volume 71; 1999.
ConAu 72NR	Volume 72; 1999.

ConAu   *Contemporary Authors, New Revision Series.* A bio-bibliographical guide to current writers in fiction, general nonfiction, poetry, journalism, drama, motion pictures, television, and other fields. Detroit: Gale Group, 1999-2000.

ConAu 73NR	Volume 73; 1999.
ConAu 74NR	Volume 74; 1999.
ConAu 75NR	Volume 75; 1999.
ConAu 76NR	Volume 76; 1999.
ConAu 77NR	Volume 77; 1999.
ConAu 78NR	Volume 78; 1999.
ConAu 79NR	Volume 79; 1999.
ConAu 80NR	Volume 80; 1999.
ConAu 81NR	Volume 81; 1999.
ConAu 82NR	Volume 82; 2000.
ConAu 83NR	Volume 83; 2000.
ConAu 84NR	Volume 84; 2000.
ConAu 85NR	Volume 85; 2000.
ConAu 86NR	Volume 86; 2000.

ConAu   *Contemporary Authors, Permanent Series.* A bio-bibliographical guide to current authors and their works. Detroit: Gale Research, 1975-1978.

ConAu P-1	Volume 1; 1975.
ConAu P-2	Volume 2; 1978.

ConBlAP 88   *Contemporary Black American Playwrights and Their Plays.* A biographical directory and dramatic index. By Bernard L. Peterson, Jr. New York: Greenwood Press, 1988.

ConBlB   *Contemporary Black Biography.* Profiles from the international black community. Detroit: Gale Research, 1992-1999.

ConBlB 1	Volume 1; 1992.
ConBlB 2	Volume 2; 1992.
ConBlB 3	Volume 3; 1993.
ConBlB 4	Volume 4; 1993.
ConBlB 5	Volume 5; 1994.
ConBlB 6	Volume 6; 1994.
ConBlB 7	Volume 7; 1994.
ConBlB 8	Volume 8; 1995.
ConBlB 9	Volume 9; 1995.
ConBlB 10	Volume 10; 1996.
ConBlB 11	Volume 11; 1996.
ConBlB 12	Volume 12; 1996.
ConBlB 13	Volume 13; 1997.
ConBlB 14	Volume 14; 1997.
ConBlB 15	Volume 15; 1997.
ConBlB 16	Volume 16; 1998.
ConBlB 17	Volume 17; 1998.
ConBlB 18	Volume 18; 1998.
ConBlB 19	Volume 19; 1999.
ConBlB 20	Volume 20; 1999.

ConBlB   *Contemporary Black Biography.* Profiles from the international black community. Detroit: Gale Group, 1999-2000.

ConBlB 21	Volume 21; 1999.
ConBlB 22	Volume 22; 1999.
ConBlB 23	Volume 23; 2000.

ConBrA 79   *Contemporary British Artists.* Edited by Charlotte Parry-Crooke. New York: St. Martin's Press, 1979.

Biographies are found in the "Directory" section.

ConBrDr	*Contemporary British Dramatists.* Edited by K.A. Berney. London: St. James Press, 1994.
ConCaAu 1	*Contemporary Canadian Authors.* A bio-bibliographic guide to current Canadian writers in fiction, general nonfiction, poetry, journalism, drama, motion pictures, television, and other fields. Volume 1. Toronto: Gale Canada, 1996.
ConCom 92	*Contemporary Composers.* Edited by Brian Morton and Pamela Collins. Chicago: St. James Press, 1992.
ConDes 84	*Contemporary Designers.* First edition. Edited by Ann Lee Morgan. Contemporary Arts Series. Detroit: Gale Research, 1984.
ConDes	*Contemporary Designers.* Contemporary Arts Series. Detroit: St. James Press, 1990-1997.

ConDes 90	Second edition. Edited by Colin Naylor; 1990.
ConDes 97	Third edition. Edited by Sara Pendergast; 1997.

ConDr   *Contemporary Dramatists.* London: St. James Press, 1999-1993.

ConDr 6	Sixth edition. Edited by Thomas Riggs; 1999.
ConDr 73	First edition. Edited by James Vinson; 1973.
ConDr 77	Second edition. Edited by James Vinson; 1977.
ConDr 77A	Second edition. Edited by James Vinson; 1977. "Screen Writers" section begins on page 893.
ConDr 77B	Second edition. Edited by James Vinson; 1977. "Radio Writers" section begins on page 903.
ConDr 77C	Second edition. Edited by James Vinson; 1977. "Television Writers" section begins on page 915.
ConDr 77D	Second edition. Edited by James Vinson; 1977. "Musical Librettists" section begins on page 925.
ConDr 77E	Second edition. Edited by James Vinson; 1977. "The Theatre of the Mixed Means" section begins on page 941.
ConDr 77F	Second edition. Edited by James Vinson; 1977. Appendix begins on page 969.
ConDr 82	Third edition. Edited by James Vinson; 1982.
ConDr 82A	Third edition. Edited by James Vinson; 1982. "Screen Writers" section begins on page 887.
ConDr 82(A	Third edition. Edited by James Vinson; 1982. "Screen Writers" section begins on page 887.
ConDr 82B	Third edition. Edited by James Vinson; 1982. "Radio Writers" section begins on page 899.
ConDr 82C	Third edition. Edited by James Vinson; 1982. "Television Writers" section begins on page 911.
ConDr 82D	Third edition. Edited by James Vinson; 1982. "Musical Librettists" section begins on page 921.
ConDr 82E	Third edition. Edited by James Vinson; 1982. Appendix begins on page 951.
ConDr 88	Fourth edition. Edited by D.L. Kirkpatrick; 1988.
ConDr 88A	Fourth edition. Edited by D.L. Kirkpatrick; 1988. "Screenwriters" section begins on page 591.

ConDr 88B	Fourth edition. Edited by D.L. Kirkpatrick; 1988. ''Radio Writers'' section begins on page 605.
ConDr 88C	Fourth edition. Edited by D.L. Kirkpatrick; 1988. ''Television Writers'' section begins on page 615.
ConDr 88D	Fourth edition. Edited by D.L. Kirkpatrick; 1988. ''Musical Librettists'' section begins on page 625.
ConDr 88E	Fourth edition. Edited by D.L. Kirkpatrick; 1988. Appendix begins on page 651.
ConDr 93	Fifth edition. Edited by K.A. Berney; 1993.

ConEn *Contemporary Entrepreneurs.* Profiles of entrepreneurs and the businesses they started. Edited by Craig E. Aronoff and John L. Ward. Detroit: Omnigraphics, 1992.

ConFash *Contemporary Fashion.* Edited by Richard Martin. Contemporary Arts Series. Detroit: St. James Press, 1995.

ConFLW 84 *Contemporary Foreign Language Writers.* Edited by James Vinson and Daniel Kirkpatrick. New York: St. Martin's Press, 1984.

ConGAN *Contemporary Gay American Novelists.* A bio-bibliographical critical sourcebook. Edited by Emmanuel S. Nelson. Westport, CT: Greenwood Press, 1993.

ConGrA *Contemporary Graphic Artists.* A biographical, bibliographical, and critical guide to current illustrators, animators, cartoonists, designers, and other graphic artists. Edited by Maurice Horn. Detroit: Gale Research, 1986-1988.

ConGrA 1	Volume 1; 1986.
ConGrA 2	Volume 2; 1987.
ConGrA 3	Volume 3; 1988.

ConHero *Contemporary Heroes and Heroines.* Detroit: Gale Research, 1990-1998.

ConHero 1	Book I; 1990. Use the Index to locate individuals found in group biographies.
ConHero 2	Book II; 1992.
ConHero 3	Book III; 1998.

ConICB *Contemporary Illustrators of Children's Books.* Compiled by Bertha E. Mahony and Elinor Whitney. Boston: Bookshop for Boys and Girls, 1930. Reprint. Detroit: Gale Research, 1978.

ConIsC *Contemporary Issues Criticism.* Excerpts from criticism of contemporary writings in sociology, economics, politics, psychology, anthropology, education, history, law, theology, and related fields. Detroit: Gale Research, 1982-1984.

ConIsC 1	Volume 1; 1982.
ConIsC 2	Volume 2; 1984.

ConJeAN *Contemporary Jewish-American Novelists.* A bio-critical sourcebook. Edited by Joel Shatzky and Michael Taub. Westport, CT: Greenwood Press, 1997.

ConLC *Contemporary Literary Criticism.* Excerpts from criticism of the works of today's novelists, poets, playwrights, short story writers, scriptwriters, and other creative writers. Detroit: Gale Research, 1973-1999.

ConLC 1	Volume 1; 1973.
ConLC 2	Volume 2; 1974.

ConLC 3	Volume 3; 1975.
ConLC 4	Volume 4; 1975.
ConLC 5	Volume 5; 1976.
ConLC 6	Volume 6; 1976.
ConLC 7	Volume 7; 1977.
ConLC 8	Volume 8; 1978.
ConLC 9	Volume 9; 1978.
ConLC 10	Volume 10; 1979.
ConLC 11	Volume 11; 1979.
ConLC 12	Volume 12; 1980.
ConLC 13	Volume 13; 1980.
ConLC 14	Volume 14; 1980.
ConLC 15	Volume 15; 1980.
ConLC 16	Volume 16; 1981.
ConLC 17	Volume 17; 1981.
ConLC 18	Volume 18; 1981.
ConLC 19	Volume 19; 1981.
ConLC 20	Volume 20; 1982.
ConLC 21	Volume 21; 1982.
ConLC 22	Volume 22; 1982.
ConLC 23	Volume 23; 1983.
ConLC 24	Volume 24; 1983.
ConLC 25	Volume 25; 1983.
ConLC 26	Volume 26; 1983.
ConLC 27	Volume 27; 1984.
ConLC 28	Volume 28; 1984.
ConLC 29	Volume 29; 1984.
ConLC 30	Volume 30; 1984.
ConLC 31	Volume 31; 1985.
ConLC 32	Volume 32; 1985.
ConLC 33	Volume 33; 1985.
ConLC 34	Volume 34: Yearbook 1984; 1985. Use the ''Cumulative Author Index'' to locate entries.
ConLC 35	Volume 35; 1985.
ConLC 36	Volume 36; 1986.
ConLC 37	Volume 37; 1986.
ConLC 38	Volume 38; 1986.
ConLC 39	Volume 39: Yearbook 1985; 1986. Use the ''Cumulative Author Index'' to locate entries.
ConLC 40	Volume 40; 1986.
ConLC 41	Volume 41; 1987.
ConLC 42	Volume 42; 1987.
ConLC 43	Volume 43; 1987.
ConLC 44	Volume 44: Yearbook 1986; 1987. Use the ''Cumulative Author Index'' to locate entries.
ConLC 45	Volume 45; 1987.
ConLC 46	Volume 46; 1988.
ConLC 47	Volume 47; 1988.
ConLC 48	Volume 48; 1988.
ConLC 49	Volume 49; 1988.
ConLC 50	Volume 50: Yearbook 1987; 1988. Use the ''Cumulative Author Index'' to locate entries.
ConLC 51	Volume 51; 1989.
ConLC 52	Volume 52; 1989.
ConLC 53	Volume 53; 1989.

ConLC 54	Volume 54; 1989.
ConLC 55	Volume 55: Yearbook 1988; 1989. Use the ''Cumulative Author Index'' to locate entries.
ConLC 56	Volume 56; 1989.
ConLC 57	Volume 57; 1990.
ConLC 58	Volume 58; 1990.
ConLC 59	Volume 59: Yearbook 1989; 1990. Use the ''Cumulative Author Index'' to locate entries.
ConLC 60	Volume 60; 1990.
ConLC 61	Volume 61; 1990.
ConLC 62	Volume 62; 1991.
ConLC 63	Volume 63; 1991.
ConLC 64	Volume 64; 1991.
ConLC 65	Volume 65: Yearbook 1990; 1991. Use the ''Cumulative Author Index'' to locate entries.
ConLC 66	Volume 66; 1991.
ConLC 67	Volume 67; 1992.
ConLC 68	Volume 68; 1992.
ConLC 69	Volume 69; 1992.
ConLC 70	Volume 70: Yearbook 1991; 1992. Use the ''Cumulative Author Index'' to locate entries.
ConLC 71	Volume 71; 1992.
ConLC 72	Volume 72; 1992.
ConLC 73	Volume 73; 1993.
ConLC 74	Volume 74; 1993.
ConLC 75	Volume 75; 1993.
ConLC 76	Volume 76: Yearbook 1992; 1993. Use the ''Cumulative Author Index'' to locate entries.
ConLC 77	Volume 77; 1993.
ConLC 78	Volume 78; 1994.
ConLC 79	Volume 79; 1994.
ConLC 80	Volume 80; 1994.
ConLC 81	Volume 81: Yearbook 1993; 1994. Use the ''Cumulative Author Index'' to locate entries.
ConLC 82	Volume 82; 1994.
ConLC 83	Volume 83; 1994.
ConLC 84	Volume 84; 1995.
ConLC 85	Volume 85; 1995.
ConLC 86	Volume 86: Yearbook 1994; 1995. Use the ''Cumulative Author Index'' to locate entries.
ConLC 87	Volume 87; 1995.
ConLC 88	Volume 88; 1995.
ConLC 89	Volume 89; 1996.
ConLC 90	Volume 90; 1996.
ConLC 91	Volume 91: Yearbook 1995; 1996. Use the ''Cumulative Author Index'' to locate entries.
ConLC 92	Volume 92; 1996.
ConLC 93	Volume 93; 1996.
ConLC 94	Volume 94; 1996.
ConLC 95	Volume 95; 1997.
ConLC 96	Volume 96; 1997.
ConLC 97	Volume 97; 1997.
ConLC 98	Volume 98; 1997.
ConLC 99	Volume 99: Yearbook 1996; 1997. Use the ''Cumulative Author Index'' to locate entries.

ConLC 100	Volume 100; 1997.
ConLC 101	Volume 101; 1997.
ConLC 102	Volume 102; 1998.
ConLC 103	Volume 103; 1998.
ConLC 104	Volume 104; 1998.
ConLC 105	Volume 105; 1998.
ConLC 106	Volume 106; 1998.
ConLC 107	Volume 107; 1998.
ConLC 108	Volume 108; 1998.
ConLC 109	Volume 109: Yearbook 1997; 1999. Use the "Cumulative Author Index" to locate entries.
ConLC 110	Volume 110; 1999.
ConLC 111	Volume 111; 1999.
ConLC 112	Volume 112; 1999.
ConLC 113	Volume 113; 1999.

ConLC   *Contemporary Literary Criticism.* Criticism of the works of today's novelists, poets, playwrights, short story writers, scriptwriters, and other creative writers. Detroit: Gale Group, 1999-2000.

ConLC 114	Volume 114; 1999.
ConLC 115	Volume 115; 1999.
ConLC 116	Volume 116; 1999.
ConLC 117	Volume 117; 1999.
ConLC 118	Volume 118; 1999.
ConLC 119	Volume 119: Yearbook 1998; 1999. Use the "Cumulative Author Index" to locate entries.
ConLC 120	Volume 120; 1999.
ConLC 121	Volume 121; 2000.
ConLC 122	Volume 122; 2000.
ConLC 123	Volume 123; 2000.
ConLC 124	Volume 124; 2000.
ConLC 125	Volume 125; 2000.
ConLC 126	Volume 126; 2000.

ConLCrt 77   *Contemporary Literary Critics.* First edition. By Elmer Borklund. London: St. James Press; New York: St. Martin's Press, 1977.

ConLCrt 82   *Contemporary Literary Critics.* Second edition. By Elmer Borklund. Detroit: Gale Research, 1982.

ConMuA   *Contemporary Music Almanac, 1980/81.* By Ronald Zalkind. New York: Macmillan Publishing Co., Schirmer Books, 1980.

ConMuA 80A	"Who's Who--Artists" section begins on page 157.
ConMuA 80B	"Music Business Professionals" section begins on page 351.

ConMus   *Contemporary Musicians.* Profiles of the people in music. Detroit: Gale Research, 1989-1999.

ConMus 1	Volume 1; 1989.
ConMus 2	Volume 2; 1990.
ConMus 3	Volume 3; 1990.
ConMus 4	Volume 4; 1991.
ConMus 5	Volume 5; 1991.
ConMus 6	Volume 6; 1992.
ConMus 7	Volume 7; 1992.

ConMus 8	Volume 8; 1993.
ConMus 9	Volume 9; 1993.
ConMus 10	Volume 10; 1994.
ConMus 11	Volume 11; 1994.
ConMus 12	Volume 12; 1994.
ConMus 13	Volume 13; 1995.
ConMus 14	Volume 14; 1995.
ConMus 15	Volume 15; 1996.
ConMus 16	Volume 16; 1996.
ConMus 17	Volume 17; 1997.
ConMus 18	Volume 18; 1997.
ConMus 19	Volume 19; 1997.
ConMus 20	Volume 20; 1998.
ConMus 21	Volume 21; 1998.
ConMus 22	Volume 22; 1998.
ConMus 23	Volume 23; 1999.

ConMus   *Contemporary Musicians.* Profiles of the people in music. Detroit: Gale Group, 1999-2000.

ConMus 24	Volume 24; 1999.
ConMus 25	Volume 25; 1999.
ConMus 26	Volume 26; 1999.
ConMus 27	Volume 27; 2000.

ConNews   *Contemporary Newsmakers.* A biographical guide to people in the news in business, education, technology, social issues, politics, law, economics, international affairs, religion, entertainment, labor, sports, design, psychology, medicine, astronautics, ecology, and other fields. Detroit: Gale Research, 1985-1988. Later editions published as *Newsmakers.*

ConNews 85-1	1985, Issue 1; 1985.
ConNews 85-2	1985, Issue 2; 1985.
ConNews 85-3	1985, Issue 3; 1986.
ConNews 85-4	1985, Issue 4; 1986.
ConNews 86-1	1986, Issue 1; 1986.
ConNews 86-2	1986, Issue 2; 1986.
ConNews 86-3	1986, Issue 3; 1987.
ConNews 86-4	1986, Issue 4; 1987.
ConNews 87-1	1987, Issue 1; 1987.
ConNews 87-2	1987, Issue 2; 1987.
ConNews 87-3	1987, Issue 3; 1988.
ConNews 87-4	1987, Issue 4; 1988.
ConNews 88-1	1988, Issue 1; 1988.

Use the "Cumulative Newsmaker Index" to locate entries in each quarterly edition.

ConNov   *Contemporary Novelists.* Detroit: St. James Press, 1972-1996.

ConNov 72	First edition. Edited by James Vinson; 1972.
ConNov 76	Second edition. Edited by James Vinson; 1976.
ConNov 82	Third edition. Edited by James Vinson; 1982.
ConNov 82A	Third edition. Edited by James Vinson; 1982. The Appendix is located at the back of this edition.
ConNov 86	Fourth edition. Edited by D.L. Kirkpatrick; 1986.
ConNov 86A	Fourth edition. Edited by D.L. Kirkpatrick; 1986. The Appendix is located at the back of this edition.
ConNov 91	Fifth edition. Edited by Lesley Henderson; 1991.

	ConNov 96	Sixth edition. Edited by Susan Windisch Brown; 1996.

ConPhot 82 — *Contemporary Photographers.* First edition. Edited by George Walsh, Colin Naylor, and Michael Held. Contemporary Arts Series. New York: St. Martin's Press, 1982.

ConPhot — *Contemporary Photographers.* Contemporary Arts Series. Detroit: St. James Press, 1988-1995.

	ConPhot 88	Second edition. Edited by Colin Naylor; 1988.
	ConPhot 95	Third edition. Edited by Martin Marix Evans; 1995.

ConPo — *Contemporary Poets.* Detroit: St. James Press, 1970-1996.

	ConPo 70	First edition. Edited by Rosalie Murphy; 1970.
	ConPo 75	Second edition. Edited by James Vinson; 1975.
	ConPo 80	Third edition. Edited by James Vinson; 1980.
	ConPo 80A	Third edition. Edited by James Vinson; 1980. The Appendix is located at the back of this edition.
	ConPo 85	Fourth edition. Edited by James Vinson and D.L. Kirkpatrick; 1985.
	ConPo 85A	Fourth edition. Edited by James Vinson and D.L. Kirkpatrick; 1985. The Appendix is located at the back of this edition.
	ConPo 91	Fifth edition. Edited by Tracy Chevalier; 1991.
	ConPo 96	Sixth edition. Edited by Thomas Riggs; 1996.

ConPopW — *Contemporary Popular Writers.* Edited by Dave Mote. Detroit: St. James Press, 1997.

ConSFA — *Contemporary Science Fiction Authors.* First edition. Compiled and edited by R. Reginald. New York: Arno Press, 1975. Previously published as *Stella Nova: The Contemporary Science Fiction Authors.* Los Angeles: Unicorn & Son, Publishers, 1970.

ConSFF — *Contemporary Science Fiction, Fantasy, and Horror Poetry.* A resource guide and biographical directory. By Scott E. Green. New York: Greenwood Press, 1989. Biographies are found in the "Biographical Directory of Poets" section which begins on page 85.

ConSoWr — *Contemporary Southern Writers.* Edited by Roger Matuz. Detroit: St. James Press, 1999.

ConSpAP — *Contemporary Spanish American Poets.* A bibliography of primary and secondary sources. Compiled by Jacobo Sefami. Bibliographies and Indexes in World Literature, no. 33. New York: Greenwood Press, 1992.

ConSSWr — *Contemporary Spanish-Speaking Writers and Illustrators for Children and Young Adults.* A biographical dictionary. Edited by Isabel Schon. Westport, CT: Greenwood Press, 1994.

ConTFT — *Contemporary Theatre, Film, and Television.* A biographical guide featuring performers, directors, writers, producers, designers, managers, choreographers, technicians, composers, executives, dancers, and critics in the United States, Canada, Great Britain and the world. Detroit: Gale Research, 1984-1999. Earlier editions published as *Who's Who in the Theatre.*

ConTFT 1	Volume 1; 1984.
ConTFT 2	Volume 2; 1986.
ConTFT 3	Volume 3; 1986.
ConTFT 4	Volume 4; 1987.
ConTFT 5	Volume 5; 1988.
ConTFT 6	Volume 6; 1989.
ConTFT 7	Volume 7; 1989.
ConTFT 8	Volume 8; 1990.
ConTFT 9	Volume 9; 1992.
ConTFT 10	Volume 10; 1993.
ConTFT 11	Volume 11; 1994.
ConTFT 12	Volume 12; 1994.
ConTFT 13	Volume 13; 1995.
ConTFT 14	Volume 14; 1996.
ConTFT 15	Volume 15; 1996.
ConTFT 16	Volume 16; 1997.
ConTFT 17	Volume 17; 1998.
ConTFT 18	Volume 18; 1998.
ConTFT 19	Volume 19; 1998.
ConTFT 20	Volume 20; 1999.
ConTFT 21	Volume 21; 1999.

ConTFT *Contemporary Theatre, Film, and Television.* A biographical guide featuring performers, directors, writers, producers, designers, managers, choreographers, technicians, composers, executives, dancers, and critics in the United States, Canada, Great Britain and the world. Detroit: Gale Group, 1999-2000.

ConTFT 22	Volume 22; 1999. Earlier editions published as *Who's Who in the Theatre.*
ConTFT 23	Volume 23; 1999.
ConTFT 24	Volume 24; 2000.
ConTFT 25	Volume 25; 2000.
ConTFT 26	Volume 26; 2000.
ConTFT 27	Volume 27; 2000.

ConTurW *Contemporary Turkish Writers.* A critical bio-bibliography of leading writers in the Turkish Republican Period up to 1980. By Louis Mitler. Uralic and Altaic Series, vol. 146. Bloomington, IN: Indiana University Research Institute for Inner Asian Studies, 1988.

ConWomA *Contemporary Women Artists.* Edited by Laurie Collier Hillstrom and Kevin Hillstrom. Detroit: St. James Press, 1999.

ConWomD *Contemporary Women Dramatists.* Edited by K.A. Berney. London: St. James Press, 1994.

ConWomP 98 *Contemporary Women Poets.* Edited by Pamela L. Shelton. Detroit: St. James Press, 1998.

ConWomW *Contemporary Women Writers of Spain.* By Janet Perez. Twayne's World Authors Series, no. 798, Spanish Literature. Boston: Twayne Publishers, 1988.
Use the Index to locate biographies.

ConWorW 93   *Contemporary World Writers.* Second edition. Edited by Tracy Chevalier. Contemporary Writers of the English Language Series. Detroit: St. James Press, 1993. First edition published as *Contemporary Foreign-Language Writers.*

ContDcW 89   *The Continuum Dictionary of Women's Biography.* Second edition. Edited by Jennifer S. Uglow. New York: Continuum Publishing, 1989. First edition published as *The International Dictionary of Women's Biography.*

Conv   *Conversations.* Conversations series. Detroit: Gale Research, 1977-1978.
         Conv 1   Volume 1: *Conversations with Writers.*; 1977.
         Conv 2   Volume 2: *Conversations with Jazz Musicians.*; 1977.
         Conv 3   Volume 3: *Conversations with Writers II.*; 1978.

CopCroC   *Cops, Crooks, and Criminologists.* An international biographical dictionary of law enforcement. By Alan Axelrod and Charles Phillips. New York: Facts on File, 1996.

CorpD   *Corpus Delicti of Mystery Fiction.* A guide to the body of the case. By Linda Herman and Beth Stiel. Metuchen, NJ: Scarecrow Press, 1974.
         Biographies begin on page 31.

CounME 74   *The Country Music Encyclopedia.* By Melvin Shestack. New York: Thomas Y. Crowell Co., 1974.
         CounME 74A   The "Discography" begins on page 325.

CreCan   *Creative Canada.* A biographical dictionary of twentieth-century creative and performing artists. Compiled by the Reference Division, McPherson Library, University of Victoria, British Columbia. Toronto: University of Toronto Press, 1971-1972.
         CreCan 1   Volume 1; 1971.
         CreCan 2   Volume 2; 1972.

CriJuSA   *Crime and the Justice System in America.* An encyclopedia. Edited by Frank Schmalleger with Gordon M. Armstrong. Westport, CT: Greenwood Press, 1997.

CrtSuDr   *Critical Survey of Drama.* Revised edition. Seven volumes. Edited by Frank N. Magill. Pasadena, CA: Salem Press, 1994.

CrtSuMy   *Critical Survey of Mystery and Detective Fiction.* Four volumes. Edited by Frank N. Magill. Pasadena, CA: Salem Press, 1988.

CrtT   *The Critical Temper.* A survey of modern criticism on English and American literature from the beginnings to the twentieth century. Edited by Martin Tucker. A Library of Literary Criticism. New York: Frederick Ungar Publishing Co., 1969-1979.
         CrtT 1   Volume I: From Old English to Shakespeare; 1969.
         CrtT 2   Volume II: From Milton to Romantic Literature; 1969.
         CrtT 3   Volume III: Victorian Literature and American Literature; 1969.
         CrtT 4   Volume IV: Supplement; 1979.

CroCAP   *Crowell's Handbook of Contemporary American Poetry.* By Karl Malkoff. New
                 York: Thomas Y. Crowell Co., 1973.
                 Biographies begin on page 43.

CroCD   *Crowell's Handbook of Contemporary Drama.* By Michael Anderson et al. New
                 York: Thomas Y. Crowell Co., 1971.

CroE&S   *Crowell's Handbook of Elizabethan & Stuart Literature.* By James E. Ruoff. New
                 York: Thomas Y. Crowell Co., 1975.

CubExWr   *Cuban Exile Writers.* A biobibliographic handbook. By Daniel C. Maratos and
                 Marnesba D. Hill. Metuchen, NJ: Scarecrow Press, 1986.
                 Biographies begin on page 19.

CulEncB   *The Cultural Encyclopedia of Baseball.* By Jonathan Fraser Light. Jefferson, NC:
                 McFarland & Co., 1997.

CurBio   *Current Biography Yearbook.* New York: H.W. Wilson Co., 1940-1998.

CurBio 40	*1940.;*	1940.
CurBio 41	*1941.;*	1941.
CurBio 42	*1942.;*	1942.
CurBio 43	*1943.;*	1943.
CurBio 44	*1944.;*	1944.
CurBio 45	*1945.;*	1945.
CurBio 46	*1946.;*	1946.
CurBio 47	*1947.;*	1947.
CurBio 48	*1948.;*	1948.
CurBio 49	*1949.;*	1949.
CurBio 50	*1950.;*	1950.
CurBio 51	*1951.;*	1951.
CurBio 52	*1952.;*	1952.
CurBio 53	*1953.;*	1953.
CurBio 54	*1954.;*	1954.
CurBio 55	*1955.;*	1955.
CurBio 56	*1956.;*	1956.
CurBio 57	*1957.;*	1957.
CurBio 58	*1958.;*	1958.
CurBio 59	*1959.;*	1959.
CurBio 60	*1960.;*	1960.
CurBio 61	*1961.;*	1961.
CurBio 62	*1962.;*	1962.
CurBio 63	*1963.;*	1963.
CurBio 64	*1964.;*	1964.
CurBio 65	*1965.;*	1965.
CurBio 66	*1966.;*	1966.
CurBio 67	*1967.;*	1967.
CurBio 68	*1968.;*	1968.
CurBio 69	*1969.;*	1969.
CurBio 70	*1970.;*	1970.
CurBio 71	*1971.;*	1971.
CurBio 71N	*1971.;*	1971. Obituary Section located in the back of the volume.
CurBio 72	*1972.;*	1972.

CurBio 72N	*1972.*; 1972. Obituary Section located in the back of the volume.
CurBio 73	*1973.*; 1973.
CurBio 73N	*1973.*; 1973. Obituary Section located in the back of the volume.
CurBio 74	*1974.*; 1974.
CurBio 74N	*1974.*; 1974. Obituary Section located in the back of the volume.
CurBio 75	*1975.*; 1975.
CurBio 75N	*1975.*; 1975. Obituary Section located in the back of the volume.
CurBio 76	*1976.*; 1976.
CurBio 76N	*1976.*; 1976. Obituary Section located in the back of the volume.
CurBio 77	*1977.*; 1977.
CurBio 77N	*1977.*; 1977. Obituary Section located in the back of the volume.
CurBio 78	*1978.*; 1978.
CurBio 78N	*1978.*; 1978. Obituary Section located in the back of the volume.
CurBio 79	*1979.*; 1979.
CurBio 79N	*1979.*; 1979. Obituary Section located in the back of the volume.
CurBio 80	*1980.*; 1980.
CurBio 80N	*1980.*; 1980. Obituary Section located in the back of the volume.
CurBio 81	*1981.*; 1981.
CurBio 81N	*1981.*; 1981. Obituary Section located in the back of the volume.
CurBio 82	*1982.*; 1982.
CurBio 82N	*1982.*; 1982. Obituary Section located in the back of the volume.
CurBio 83	*1983.*; 1983.
CurBio 83N	*1983.*; 1983. Obituary Section located in the back of the volume.
CurBio 84	*1984.*; 1985.
CurBio 84N	*1984.*; 1985. Obituary Section located in the back of the volume.
CurBio 85	*1985.*; 1985.
CurBio 85N	*1985.*; 1985. Obituary Section located in the back of the volume.
CurBio 86	*1986.*; 1987.
CurBio 86N	*1986.*; 1987. Obituary Section located in the back of the volume.
CurBio 87	*1987.*; 1988.
CurBio 87N	*1987.*; 1988. Obituary Section located in the back of the volume.
CurBio 88	*1988.*; 1989.
CurBio 88N	*1988.*; 1989. Obituary Section located in the back of the volume.
CurBio 89	*1989.*; 1990.
CurBio 89N	*1989.*; 1990. Obituary section located in the back of the volume.
CurBio 90	*1990.*; 1990.

CurBio 90N	*1990.*; 1990. Obituary section located in the back of the volume.	
CurBio 91	*1991.*; 1991.	
CurBio 91N	*1991.*; 1991. Obituary section located in the back of the volume.	
CurBio 92	*1992.*; 1992.	
CurBio 92N	*1992.*; 1992. Obituary section located in the back of the volume.	
CurBio 93	*1993.*; 1993.	
CurBio 93N	*1993.*; 1993. Obituary section located in the back of the volume.	
CurBio 94	*1994.*; 1994.	
CurBio 94N	*1994.*; 1994. Obituary section located in the back of the volume.	
CurBio 95	*1995.*; 1995.	
CurBio 95N	*1995.*; 1995. Obituary section located in the back of the volume.	
CurBio 96	*1996.*; 1996.	
CurBio 96N	*1996.*; 1996. Obituary section located in the back of the volume.	
CurBio 97	*1997.*; 1997.	
CurBio 97N	*1997.*; 1997. Obituary section located in the back of the volume.	
CurBio 98	*1998.*; 1998.	
CurBio 98N	*1998.*; 1998. Obituary section located in the back of the volume.	

CurBio 1999   *Current Biography Yearbook. 1999.* New York: H. W. Wilson Co., 1999.
  CurBio 1999   Obituary section located in the back of the volume

CyAG   *Cyclopedia of American Government.* Three volumes. Edited by Andrew C. McLaughlin and Albert Bushnell Hart. New York: D. Appleton & Co., 1914. Reprint. Gloucester, Mass.: Peter Smith, 1963.

CyAL   *Cyclopaedia of American Literature.* Embracing personal and critical notices of authors, and selections from their writings, from the earliest period to the present day; with portraits, autographs, and other illustrations. By Evert A. Duyckinck and George L. Duyckinck. Philadelphia: William Rutter & Co., 1875. Reprint. Detroit: Gale Research, 1965.
  CyAL   Two volumes. Use the Index in volume 2 to locate biographies.
  CyAL 1   Volume 1. Use the Index in Volume 2 to locate biographies.
  CyAL 2   Volume 2. Use the Index in Volume 2 to locate biographies.

CyEd   *A Cyclopedia of Education.* Five volumes. Edited by Paul Monroe. New York: Macmillan Co., 1911. Reprint. Detroit: Gale Research, 1968.

CyWA 58   *Cyclopedia of World Authors.* Edited by Frank N. Magill. New York: Harper & Row, Publishers, 1958. Also published as *Masterplots Cyclopedia of World Authors.*

CyWA 97   *Cyclopedia of World Authors.* Revised third edition. Five volumes. Edited by Frank N. Magill. Pasadena, CA: Salem Press, 1997.

CyWA 89	*Cyclopedia of World Authors II.* Four volumes. Edited by Frank N. Magill. Pasadena, CA: Salem Press, 1989.
DancEn 78	*The Dance Encyclopedia.* Revised and enlarged edition. Compiled and edited by Anatole Chujoy and P.W. Manchester. New York: Simon and Schuster, 1978.
DeafPAS	*Deaf Persons in the Arts and Sciences.* A biographical dictionary. By Harry G. Lang and Bonnie Meath-Lang. Westport, CT: Greenwood Press, 1995.
DetWom	*Detecting Women 2.* A reader's guide and checklist for mystery series written by women. By Willetta L. Heising. Dearborn, MI: Purple Moon Press, 1996.
DicTyr	*Dictators and Tyrants.* Absolute rulers and would-be rulers in world history. By Alan Axelrod and Charles Phillips. New York: Facts on File, 1995.
DcAfHiB 86	*Dictionary of African Historical Biography.* Second edition. By Mark R. Lipschutz and R. Kent Rasmussen. Berkeley, CA and Los Angeles: University of California Press, 1986.
	DcAfHiB 86S "Supplement of Post-1960 Political Leaders" begins on page 258.
DcAfAmP	*Dictionary of Afro-American Performers.* 78 RPM and cylinder recordings of opera, choral music, and songs, c. 1900-1949. By Patricia Turner. Garland Reference Library of the Humanities, vol. 590. New York: Garland Publishing, 1990.
DcAfL	*Dictionary of Afro-Latin American Civilization.* By Benjamin Nunez. Westport, CT: Greenwood Press, 1980.
DcAmAnt	*Dictionary of American Antiquarian Bookdealers.* By Donald C. Dickinson. Westport, CT: Greenwood Press, 1998.
DcAmArt	*Dictionary of American Art.* By Matthew Baigell. New York: Harper & Row, Publishers, 1979.
DcAmAu	*A Dictionary of American Authors.* Fifth edition, revised and enlarged. By Oscar Fay Adams. New York: Houghton Mifflin Co., 1904. Reprint. Detroit: Gale Research, 1969.
	Biographies are found in the "Dictionary of American Authors" section which begins on page 1 and in the "Supplement" which begins on page 441.
DcAmB	*Dictionary of American Biography.* New York: Charles Scribner's Sons, 1928-1995.

DcAmB	Volumes 1-20; 1928.
DcAmB S1	Supplement 1; 1944.
DcAmB S2	Supplement 2; 1958.
DcAmB S3	Supplement 3; 1973.
DcAmB S4	Supplement 4; 1974.
DcAmB S5	Supplement 5; 1977.
DcAmB S6	Supplement 6; 1980.
DcAmB S7	Supplement 7; 1981.
DcAmB S8	Supplement 8; 1988.
DcAmB S9	Supplement 9; 1994.

DcAmB S10   Supplement 10; 1995.

DcAmBC   *Dictionary of American Book Collectors.* By Donald C. Dickinson. New York: Greenwood Press, 1986.

DcAmChF   *Dictionary of American Children's Fiction.* Books of recognized merit. By Alethea K. Helbig and Agnes Regan Perkins. Westport, CT: Greenwood Press, 1986-1993.
         DcAmChF 1960 *1960-1984.*; 1986.
         DcAmChF 1985 *1985-1989.*; 1993.

DcAmC   *Dictionary of American Conservatism.* By Louis Filler. New York: Philosophical Library, 1987.

DcAmDH   *Dictionary of American Diplomatic History.* By John E. Findling. New York: Greenwood Press, 1980-1989.
         DcAmDH 80   First edition; 1980.
         DcAmDH 89   Second edition; 1989.

DcAmImH   *Dictionary of American Immigration History.* Edited by Francesco Cordasco. Metuchen, NJ: Scarecrow Press, 1990.

DcAmLiB   *Dictionary of American Library Biography.* Edited by Bohdan S. Wynar. Littleton, CO: Libraries Unlimited, 1978.

DcAmMeB   *Dictionary of American Medical Biography.* Lives of eminent physicians of the United States and Canada, from the earliest times. By Howard A. Kelly and Walter L. Burrage. New York: D. Appleton & Co., 1928. Reprint. Road Town, Tortola, British Virgin Islands: Longwood Press, 1979.

DcAmMeB 84   *Dictionary of American Medical Biography.* Two volumes. Edited by Martin Kaufman, Stuart Galishoff, and Todd L. Savitt. Westport, CT: Greenwood Press, 1984.

DcAmMiB   *Dictionary of American Military Biography.* Three volumes. Edited by Roger J. Spiller. Westport, CT: Greenwood Press, 1984.

DcAmNB   *Dictionary of American Negro Biography.* Edited by Rayford W. Logan and Michael R. Winston. New York: W.W. Norton & Co., 1982.

DcAmReB   *Dictionary of American Religious Biography.* By Henry Warner Bowden. Westport, CT: Greenwood Press, 1977-1993.
         DcAmReB 1   First edition; 1977.
         DcAmReB 2   Second edition; 1993.

DcAmSR   *A Dictionary of American Social Reform.* By Louis Filler. New York: Philosophical Library, 1963.

DcAmTB   *Dictionary of American Temperance Biography.* From Temperance Reform to Alcohol Research, the 1600s to the 1980s. By Mark Edward Lender. Westport, CT: Greenwood Press, 1984.

DcArch   *A Dictionary of Architecture.* By James Stevens Curl. Oxford: Oxford University Press, 1999.

DcArts   *Dictionary of the Arts.* New York: Facts on File, 1994.

DcBiA   *A Dictionary of Biographies of Authors Represented in the Authors Digest Series.* With a supplemental list of later titles and a supplementary biographical section. Edited by Rossiter Johnson. New York: Authors Press, 1927. Reprint. Detroit: Gale Research, 1974.
    ''Biographies of Authors'' begin on page 3 and ''Biographies of Authors Whose Works Are in Volume XVIII'' begin on page 437.

DcBiPP   *A Dictionary of Biography, Past and Present.* Containing the chief events in the lives of eminent persons of all ages and nations. Edited by Benjamin Vincent. Haydn Series. London: Ward, Lock, & Co., 1877. Reprint. Detroit: Gale Research, 1974.
    DcBiPP A   Addenda begin on page 638.

DcBrazL   *Dictionary of Brazilian Literature.* Edited by Irwin Stern. New York: Greenwood Press, 1988.

DcBrAmW   *A Dictionary of British and American Women Writers, 1660-1800.* Edited by Janet Todd. Totowa, NJ: Rowman & Allanheld, 1985.
    Biographies begin on page 27.

DcBrAr   *Dictionary of British Artists Working 1900-1950.* By Grant M. Waters. Eastbourne, England: Eastbourne Fine Art Publications, 1975-1976.
    DcBrAr 1   Volume I; 1975.
    DcBrAr 2   Volume II; 1976.

DcBrBI   *The Dictionary of British Book Illustrators and Caricaturists, 1800-1914.* By Simon Houfe. Woodbridge, England: Antique Collectors' Club, 1978.
    Biographies begin on page 215.

DcBrECP   *The Dictionary of British Eighteenth Century Painters in Oils and Crayons* By Ellis Waterhouse. Woodbridge, England: Antique Collectors' Club, 1981.

DcBrWA   *The Dictionary of British Watercolour Artists up to 1920.* By H.L. Mallalieu. Woodbridge, England: Antique Collectors' Club, 1976.

DcCanB   *Dictionary of Canadian Biography.* Toronto: University of Toronto Press, 1966-1998.
    DcCanB 1   *Volume I: 1000 to 1700.* Edited by George W. Brown; 1966.
    DcCanB 1A   *Volume I: 1000 to 1700.* Edited by George W. Brown; 1966. Appendix begins on page 675.
    DcCanB 2   *Volume II: 1701 to 1740.* Edited by David M. Hayne; 1969.
    DcCanB 3   *Volume III: 1741 to 1770.* Edited by Francess G. Halpenny; 1974.
    DcCanB 3A   *Volume III: 1741 to 1770.* Edited by Francess G. Halpenny; 1974. Appendix begins on page 675.

DcCanB 4	*Volume IV: 1771 to 1800.* Edited by Francess G. Halpenny; 1979.	
DcCanB 4A	*Volume IV: 1771 to 1800.* Edited by Francess G. Halpenny; 1979. Appendix begins on page 783.	
DcCanB 4S	*Volume IV: 1771 to 1800.* Edited by Francess G. Halpenny; 1979. Supplement begins on page 787.	
DcCanB 5	*Volume V: 1801 to 1820.* Edited by Francess G. Halpenny; 1983.	
DcCanB 5A	*Volume V: 1801 to 1820.* Edited by Francess G. Halpenny; 1983. Appendix begins on page 887.	
DcCanB 6	*Volume VI: 1821-1835.* Edited by Francess G. Halpenny; 1987.	
DcCanB 7	*Volume VII: 1836 to 1850.* Edited by Francess G. Halpenny; 1988.	
DcCanB 8	*Volume VIII: 1851-1860.* Edited by Francess G. Halpenny; 1985.	
DcCanB 8A	*Volume VIII: 1851-1860.* Edited by Francess G. Halpenny; 1985. Appendix begins on page 968.	
DcCanB 9	*Volume IX: 1861 to 1870.* Edited by Francess G. Halpenny; 1976.	
DcCanB 10	*Volume X: 1871 to 1880.* Edited by Marc La Terreur; 1972.	
DcCanB 11	*Volume XI: 1881 to 1890.* Edited by Henri Pilon; 1982.	
DcCanB 12	*Volume XII: 1891 to 1900.* Edited by Francess G. Halpenny; 1990.	
DcCanB 13	*Volume XIII: 1901 to 1910.* Edited by Ramsay Cook; 1994.	
DcCanB 14	*Volume XIV: 1911 to 1920.* Edited by Ramsay Cook; 1998.	

DcCathB   *Dictionary of Catholic Biography.* By John J. Delaney and James Edward Tobin. Garden City, NY: Doubleday & Co., 1961.

DcChlFi   *Dictionary of Children's Fiction from Australia, Canada, India, New Zealand, and Selected African Countries.* Books of recognized merit. By Alethea K. Helbig and Agnes Regan Perkins. Westport, CT: Greenwood Press, 1992.

DcCom 77   *The Dictionary of Composers.* Edited by Charles Osborne. London: Bodly Head, 1977.

DcCom&M 79   *The Dictionary of Composers and Their Music.* Every listener's companion. By Eric Gilder and June G. Port. New York: Ballantine Books, 1979.
  Entires are found in Part One.

DcCAA   *Dictionary of Contemporary American Artists.* By Paul Cummings. New York: St. Martin's Press, 1971-1994.

	DcCAA 71	Second edition; 1971.
	DcCAA 77	Third edition; 1977.
	DcCAA 88	Fifth edition; 1988.
	DcCAA 94	Sixth edition; 1994.

DcCAr 81   *Dictionary of Contemporary Artists.* Edited by V. Babington Smith. Oxford: Clio Press, 1981.

DcCLAA   *A Dictionary of Contemporary Latin American Authors.* Compiled by David William Foster. Tempe, AZ: Center for Latin American Studies, Arizona State University, 1975.

DcCM   *Dictionary of Contemporary Music.* Edited by John Vinton. New York: E.P. Dutton & Co., 1974.
         This book ignores prefixes in filing surnames.

DcCPCAm   *The Dictionary of Contemporary Politics of Central America and the Caribbean.* Edited by Phil Gunson and Greg Chamberlain. New York: Simon & Schuster, 1991.

DcCPSAm   *The Dictionary of Contemporary Politics of South America.* By Phil Gunson, Andrew Thompson, and Greg Chamberlain. New York: Macmillan Publishing Co., 1989.

DcCPSAf   *The Dictionary of Contemporary Politics of Southern Africa.* By Gwyneth Williams and Brian Hackland. New York: Macmillan Publishing Co., 1989.

DcD&D   *Dictionary of Design & Decoration.* A Studio Book. New York: Viking Press, 1973.

DcEcMov   *Dictionary of the Ecumenical Movement.* Edited by Nicholas Lossky et al. Geneva: WCC Publications; Grand Rapids, MI: William B. Eerdmans Publishing Co., 1991.

DcEnA   *A Dictionary of English Authors, Biographical and Bibliographical.* Being a compendious account of the lives and writings of upwards of 800 British and American writers from the year 1400 to the present time. New edition, revised with an appendix. By R. Farquharson Sharp. London: Kegan Paul, Trench, Trubner & Co., 1904. Reprint. Detroit: Gale Research, 1978.
         DcEnA A   Appendix begins on page 311.

DcEnL   *Dictionary of English Literature.* Being a comprehensive guide to English authors and their works. Second edition. By W. Davenport Adams. London: Cassell Petter & Galpin, (n.d.). Reprint. Detroit: Gale Research, 1966.

DcEuL   *A Dictionary of European Literature.* Designed as a companion to English studies. Second, revised edition. By Laurie Magnus. London: George Routledge & Sons; New York: E.P. Dutton & Co., 1927. Reprint. Detroit: Gale Research, 1974.
         The Appendix begins on page 595.

DcFM   *Dictionary of Film Makers.* By Georges Sadoul. Translated, edited, and updated by Peter Morris. Berkeley, CA and Los Angeles: University of California Press, 1972. Originally published as *Dictionnaire des Cineastes,* 1965.

DcHerTr   *Dictionary of Heresy Trials in American Christianity.* Edited by George H. Shriver. Westport, CT: Greenwood Press, 1997.

DcHiB   *Dictionary of Hispanic Biography.* Detroit: Gale Research, 1996.

DcInB   *Dictionary of Indian Biography.* By C.E. Buckland. London: Swan Sonnenschein &
                   Co., 1906. Reprint. Detroit: Gale Research, 1968.
                       DcInB A   Addenda begin on page 467.

DcInv   *Dictionary of Inventions & Discoveries.* Edited by E.F. Carter. Stevenage, England:
                   Robin Clark, 1978.

DcIrB 1   *A Dictionary of Irish Biography.* By Henry Boylan. New York: Barnes & Noble
                   Books, 1978.

DcIrB 2   *A Dictionary of Irish Biography.* Second edition. By Henry Boylan. New York: St.
                   Martin's Press, 1988.

DcIrB 3   *A Dictionary of Irish Biography.* Third edition. By Henry Boylan. Niwot, CO:
                   Roberts Rinehart Publishers, 1998.

DcIrL   *Dictionary of Irish Literature.* Edited by Robert Hogan. Westport, CT: Greenwood
                   Press, 1979-1996.
                       DcIrL   First edition; 1979.
                       DcIrL 96   Revised and expanded edition. Two volumes; 1996.

DcIrW   *Dictionary of Irish Writers.* By Brian Cleeve. Cork, Ireland: Mercier Press, 1967-
                   1971.
                       DcIrW 1   Volume 1: Fiction; 1967.
                       DcIrW 2   Volume 2: Non-fiction; 1969.
                       DcIrW 3   Volume 3: Writers in the Irish Language; 1971.

DcItL   *Dictionary of Italian Literature.* Edited by Peter Bondanella and Julia Conaway
                   Bondanella. Westport, CT: Greenwood Press, 1979-1996.
                       DcItL 1   First edition; 1979.
                       DcItL 2   Second edition; 1996.

DcLB   *Dictionary of Literary Biography.* Detroit: Gale Research, 1978-1994.
                       DcLB 1   Volume 1: *The American Renaissance in New England.*
                                   Edited by Joel Myerson; 1978.
                       DcLB 2   Volume 2: *American Novelists since World War II.*
                                   Edited by Jeffrey Helterman and Richard Layman;
                                   1978.
                       DcLB 3   Volume 3: *Antebellum Writers in New York and the*
                                   South. Edited by Joel Myerson; 1979.
                       DcLB 4   Volume 4: *American Writers in Paris, 1920-1939.* Edited
                                   by Karen Lane Rood; 1980.
                       DcLB 5   Volume 5: *American Poets since World War II.* Two
                                   parts. Edited by Donald J. Greiner; 1980.
                       DcLB 6   Volume 6: *American Novelists since World War II.*
                                   Second Series. Edited by James E. Kibler, Jr; 1980.
                       DcLB 7   Volume 7: *Twentieth-Century American Dramatists.*
                                   Two parts. Edited by John MacNicholas; 1981.
                       DcLB 8   Volume 8: *Twentieth-Century American Science-Fiction*
                                   Writers. Two parts. Edited by David Cowart and
                                   Thomas L. Wymer; 1981.
                       DcLB 9   Volume 9: *American Novelists, 1910-1945.* Three parts.
                                   Edited by James J. Martine; 1981.

DcLB 10	Volume 10: *Modern British Dramatists, 1900-1945.* Two parts. Edited by Stanley Weintraub; 1982.
DcLB 11	Volume 11: *American Humorists, 1800-1950.* Two parts. Edited by Stanley Trachtenberg; 1982.
DcLB 12	Volume 12: *American Realists and Naturalists.* Edited by Donald Pizer and Earl N. Harbert; 1982.
DcLB 13	Volume 13: *British Dramatists since World War II.* Two parts. Edited by Stanley Weintraub; 1982.
DcLB 14	Volume 14: *British Novelists since 1960.* Two parts. Edited by Jay L. Halio; 1983.
DcLB 15	Volume 15: *British Novelists, 1930-1959.* Two parts. Edited by Bernard Oldsey; 1983.
DcLB 16	Volume 16: *The Beats: Literary Bohemians in Postwar America.* Two parts. Edited by Ann Charters; 1983.
DcLB 17	Volume 17: *Twentieth-Century American Historians.* Edited by Clyde N. Wilson; 1983.
DcLB 18	Volume 18: *Victorian Novelists after 1885.* Edited by Ira B. Nadel and William E. Fredeman; 1983.
DcLB 19	Volume 19: *British Poets, 1880-1914.* Edited by Donald E. Stanford; 1983.
DcLB 20	Volume 20: *British Poets, 1914-1945.* Edited by Donald E. Stanford; 1983.
DcLB 21	Volume 21: *Victorian Novelists before 1885.* Edited by Ira B. Nadel and William E. Fredeman; 1983.
DcLB 22	Volume 22: *American Writers for Children, 1900-1960.* Edited by John Cech; 1983.
DcLB 23	Volume 23: *American Newspaper Journalists, 1873-1900.* Edited by Perry J. Ashley; 1983.
DcLB 24	Volume 24: *American Colonial Writers, 1606-1734.* Edited by Emory Elliott; 1984.
DcLB 25	Volume 25: *American Newspaper Journalists, 1901-1925.* Edited by Perry J. Ashley; 1984.
DcLB 26	Volume 26: *American Screenwriters.* Edited by Robert E. Morsberger, Stephen O. Lesser, and Randall Clark; 1984.
DcLB 27	Volume 27: *Poets of Great Britain and Ireland, 1945-1960.* Edited by Vincent B. Sherry, Jr; 1984.
DcLB 28	Volume 28: *Twentieth-Century American-Jewish Fiction Writers.* Edited by Daniel Walden; 1984.
DcLB 29	Volume 29: *American Newspaper Journalists, 1926-1950.* Edited by Perry J. Ashley; 1984.
DcLB 30	Volume 30: *American Historians, 1607-1865.* Edited by Clyde N. Wilson; 1984.
DcLB 31	Volume 31: *American Colonial Writers, 1735-1781.* Edited by Emory Elliott; 1984.
DcLB 31A	Volume 31: *American Colonial Writers, 1735-1781.* Edited by Emory Elliott; 1984. Appendix I: ''Eighteenth-Century Philosophical Background.'' Use the Table of Contents to locate entries.
DcLB 31B	Volume 31: *American Colonial Writers, 1735-1781.* Edited by Emory Elliott; 1984. Appendix II: ''Eighteenth-Century Aesthetic Theories.'' Use the Table of Contents to locate entries.
DcLB 32	Volume 32: *Victorian Poets before 1850.* Edited by William E. Fredeman and Ira B. Nadel; 1984.

DcLB 33	Volume 33: *Afro-American Fiction Writers after 1955*. Edited by Thadious M. Davis and Trudier Harris; 1984.
DcLB 34	Volume 34: *British Novelists, 1890-1929: Traditionalists*. Edited by Thomas F. Staley; 1985.
DcLB 35	Volume 35: *Victorian Poets after 1850*. Edited by William E. Fredeman and Ira B. Nadel; 1985.
DcLB 36	Volume 36: *British Novelists, 1890-1929: Modernists*. Edited by Thomas F. Staley; 1985.
DcLB 37	Volume 37: *American Writers of the Early Republic*. Edited by Emory Elliott; 1985.
DcLB 38	Volume 38: *Afro-American Writers after 1955: Dramatists and Prose Writers*. Edited by Thadious M. Davis and Trudier Harris; 1985.
DcLB 39	Volume 39: *British Novelists, 1660-1800*. Two parts. Edited by Martin C. Battestin; 1985.
DcLB 40	Volume 40: *Poets of Great Britain and Ireland since 1960*. Two parts. Edited by Vincent B. Sherry, Jr; 1985.
DcLB 41	Volume 41: *Afro-American Poets since 1955*. Edited by Trudier Harris and Thadious M. Davis; 1985.
DcLB 42	Volume 42: *American Writers for Children before 1900*. Edited by Glenn E. Estes; 1985.
DcLB 43	Volume 43: *American Newspaper Journalists, 1690-1872*. Edited by Perry J. Ashley; 1985.
DcLB 44	Volume 44: *American Screenwriters*. Second Series. Edited by Randall Clark; 1986.
DcLB 45	Volume 45: *American Poets, 1880-1945*. First Series. Edited by Peter Quartermain; 1986.
DcLB 46	Volume 46: *American Literary Publishing Houses, 1900-1980: Trade and Paperback*. Edited by Peter Dzwonkoski; 1986. Contains no biographies.
DcLB 47	Volume 47: *American Historians, 1866-1912*. Edited by Clyde N. Wilson; 1986.
DcLB 48	Volume 48: *American Poets, 1880-1945*. Second Series. Edited by Peter Quartermain; 1986.
DcLB 49	Volume 49: *American Literary Publishing Houses, 1638-1899*. Two parts. Edited by Peter Dzwonkoski; 1986. Contains no biographies.
DcLB 50	Volume 50: *Afro-American Writers before the Harlem Renaissance*. Edited by Trudier Harris; 1986.
DcLB 51	Volume 51: *Afro-American Writers from the Harlem Renaissance to 1940*. Edited by Trudier Harris; 1987.
DcLB 51A	Volume 51: *Afro-American Writers from the Harlem Renaissance to 1940*. Edited by Trudier Harris; 1987. Appendix. Use the Table of Contents to locate entries.
DcLB 52	Volume 52: *American Writers for Children since 1960: Fiction*. Edited by Glenn E. Estes; 1986.
DcLB 53	Volume 53: *Canadian Writers since 1960*. First Series. Edited by W.H. New; 1986.
DcLB 54	Volume 54: *American Poets, 1880-1945*. Third Series. Two parts. Edited by Peter Quartermain; 1987.
DcLB 55	Volume 55: *Victorian Prose Writers before 1867*. Edited by William B. Thesing; 1987.

DcLB 56	Volume 56: *German Fiction Writers, 1914-1945.* Edited by James Hardin; 1987.
DcLB 57	Volume 57: *Victorian Prose Writers after 1867.* Edited by William B. Thesing; 1987.
DcLB 58	Volume 58: *Jacobean and Caroline Dramatists.* Edited by Fredson Bowers; 1987.
DcLB 59	Volume 59: *American Literary Critics and Scholars, 1800-1850.* Edited by John W. Rathbun; 1987.
DcLB 60	Volume 60: *Canadian Writers since 1960.* Second Series. Edited by W.H. New; 1987.
DcLB 61	Volume 61: *American Writers for Children since 1960: Poets, Illustrators, and Nonfiction Authors.* Edited by Glenn E. Estes; 1987.
DcLB 62	Volume 62: *Elizabethan Dramatists.* Edited by Fredson Bowers; 1987.
DcLB 63	Volume 63: *Modern American Critics, 1920-1955.* Edited by Gregory S. Jay; 1988.
DcLB 64	Volume 64: *American Literary Critics and Scholars, 1850-1880.* Edited by John W. Rathbun and Monica M. Grecu; 1988.
DcLB 65	Volume 65: *French Novelists, 1900-1930.* Edited by Catharine Savage Brosman; 1988.
DcLB 66	Volume 66: *German Fiction Writers, 1885-1913.* Two parts. Edited by James Hardin; 1988.
DcLB 67	Volume 67: *Modern American Critics since 1955.* Edited by Gregory S. Jay; 1988.
DcLB 68	Volume 68: *Canadian Writers, 1920-1959.* First Series. Edited by W.H. New; 1988.
DcLB 69	Volume 69: *Contemporary German Fiction Writers.* First Series. Edited by Wolfgang D. Elfe; 1988.
DcLB 70	Volume 70: *British Mystery Writers, 1860-1919.* Edited by Bernard Benstock; 1988.
DcLB 71	Volume 71: *American Literary Critics and Scholars, 1880-1900.* Edited by John W. Rathbun and Monica M. Grecu; 1988.
DcLB 72	Volume 72: *French Novelists, 1930-1960.* Edited by Catharine Savage Brosman; 1988.
DcLB 73	Volume 73: *American Magazine Journalists, 1741-1850.* Edited by Sam G. Riley; 1988.
DcLB 74	Volume 74: *American Short-Story Writers before 1880.* Edited by Bobby Ellen Kimbel; 1988.
DcLB 75	Volume 75: *Contemporary German Fiction Writers.* Second Series. Edited by Wolfgang D. Elfe and James Hardin; 1988.
DcLB 76	Volume 76: *Afro-American Writers, 1940-1955.* Edited by Trudier Harris; 1988.
DcLB 77	Volume 77: *British Mystery Writers, 1920-1939.* Edited by Bernard Benstock and Thomas F. Staley; 1989.
DcLB 78	Volume 78: *American Short-Story Writers, 1880-1910.* Edited by Bobby Ellen Kimbel; 1989.
DcLB 79	Volume 79: *American Magazine Journalists, 1850-1900.* Edited by Sam G. Riley; 1989.
DcLB 80	Volume 80: *Restoration and Eighteenth-Century Dramatists.* First Series. Edited by Paula R. Backscheider; 1989.

DcLB 81	Volume 81: *Austrian Fiction Writers, 1875-1913*. Edited by James Hardin and Donald G. Daviau; 1989.
DcLB 82	Volume 82: *Chicano Writers*. First Series. Edited by Francisco A. Lomeli and Carl R. Shirley; 1989.
DcLB 83	Volume 83: *French Novelists since 1960*. Edited by Catharine Savage Brosman; 1989.
DcLB 84	Volume 84: *Restoration and Eighteenth-Century Dramatists*. Second Series. Edited by Paula R. Backscheider; 1989.
DcLB 85	Volume 85: *Austrian Fiction Writers after 1914*. Edited by James Hardin and Donald G. Daviau; 1989.
DcLB 86	Volume 86: *American Short-Story Writers, 1910-1945*. First Series. Edited by Bobby Ellen Kimbel; 1989.
DcLB 87	Volume 87: *British Mystery and Thriller Writers since 1940*. First Series. Edited by Bernard Benstock and Thomas F. Staley; 1989.
DcLB 88	Volume 88: *Canadian Writers, 1920-1959*. Second Series. Edited by W.H. New; 1989.
DcLB 89	Volume 89: *Restoration and Eighteenth-Century Dramatists*. Third Series. Edited by Paula R. Backscheider; 1989.
DcLB 90	Volume 90: *German Writers in the Age of Goethe, 1789-1832*. Edited by James Hardin and Christoph E. Schweitzer; 1989.
DcLB 91	Volume 91: *American Magazine Journalists 1900-1960*. First Series. Edited by Sam G. Riley; 1990.
DcLB 92	Volume 92: *Canadian Writers, 1890-1920*. Edited by W.H. New; 1990.
DcLB 93	Volume 93: *British Romantic Poets, 1789-1832*. First Series. Edited by John R. Greenfield; 1990.
DcLB 94	Volume 94: *German Writers in the Age of Goethe: Sturm und Drang to Classicism*. Edited by James Hardin and Christoph Schweitzer; 1990.
DcLB 95	Volume 95: *Eighteenth-Century British Poets*. First Series. Edited by John Sitter; 1990.
DcLB 96	Volume 96: *British Romantic Poets, 1789-1832*. Second Series. Edited by John R. Greenfield; 1990.
DcLB 97	Volume 97: *German Writers from the Enlightenment to Sturm und Drang, 1720-1764*. Edited by James Hardin and Christoph E. Schweitzer; 1990.
DcLB 98	Volume 98: *Modern British Essayists*. First Series. Edited by Robert Beum; 1990.
DcLB 99	Volume 99: *Canadian Writers before 1890*. Edited by W.H. New; 1990.
DcLB 100	Volume 100: *Modern British Essayists*. Second Series. Edited by Robert Beum; 1990.
DcLB 101	Volume 101: *British Prose Writers, 1660-1800*. First Series. Edited by Donald T. Siebert; 1991.
DcLB 102	Volume 102: *American Short-Story Writers, 1910-1945*. Second Series. Edited by Bobby Ellen Kimbel; 1991.
DcLB 103	Volume 103: *American Literary Biographers*. First Series. Edited by Steven Serafin; 1991.
DcLB 104	Volume 104: *British Prose Writers, 1660-1800*. Second Series. Edited by Donald T. Siebert; 1991.

DcLB 105	Volume 105: *American Poets since World War II*. Second Series. Edited by R.S. Gwynn; 1991.
DcLB 106	Volume 106: *British Literary Publishing Houses, 1820-1880*. Edited by Patricia J. Anderson and Jonathan Rose; 1991.
DcLB 107	Volume 107: *British Romantic Prose Writers, 1789-1832*. First Series. Edited by John R. Greenfield; 1991.
DcLB 108	Volume 108: *Twentieth-Century Spanish Poets*. First Series. Edited by Michael L. Perna; 1991.
DcLB 109	Volume 109: *Eighteenth-Century British Poets*. Second Series. Edited by John Sitter; 1991.
DcLB 110	Volume 110: *British Romantic Prose Writers, 1789-1832*. Second Series. Edited by John R. Greenfield; 1991.
DcLB 111	Volume 111: *American Literary Biographers*. Second Series. Edited by Steven Serafin; 1991.
DcLB 112	Volume 112: *British Literary Publishing Houses, 1881-1965*. Edited by Jonathan Rose and Patricia J. Anderson; 1991.
DcLB 113	Volume 113: *Modern Latin-American Fiction Writers*. First Series. Edited by William Luis; 1992.
DcLB 114	Volume 114: *Twentieth-Century Italian Poets*. First Series. Edited by Giovanna Wedel De Stasio, Glauco Cambon, and Antonio Illiano; 1992.
DcLB 115	Volume 115: *Medieval Philosophers*. Edited by Jeremiah Hackett; 1992.
DcLB 116	Volume 116: *British Romantic Novelists, 1789-1832*. Edited by Bradford K. Mudge; 1992.
DcLB 117	Volume 117: *Twentieth-Century Caribbean and Black African Writers*. First Series. Edited by Bernth Lindfors and Reinhard Sander; 1992.
DcLB 118	Volume 118: *Twentieth-Century German Dramatists, 1889-1918*. Edited by Wolfgang D. Elfe and James Hardin; 1992.
DcLB 119	Volume 119: *Nineteenth-Century French Fiction Writers: Romanticism and Realism, 1800-1860*. Edited by Catharine Savage Brosman; 1992.
DcLB 120	Volume 120: *American Poets since World War II*. Third Series. Edited by R.S. Gwynn; 1992.
DcLB 121	Volume 121: *Seventeenth-Century British Nondramatic Poets*. First Series. Edited by M. Thomas Hester; 1992.
DcLB 122	Volume 122: *Chicano Writers*. Second Series. Edited by Francisco A. Lomeli and Carl R. Shirley; 1992.
DcLB 123	Volume 123: *Nineteenth-Century French Fiction Writers: Naturalism and Beyond, 1860-1900*. Edited by Catharine Savage Brosman; 1992.
DcLB 124	Volume 124: *Twentieth-Century German Dramatists, 1919-1992*. Edited by Wolfgang D. Elfe and James Hardin; 1992.
DcLB 125	Volume 125: *Twentieth-Century Caribbean and Black African Writers*. Second Series. Edited by Bernth Lindfors and Reinhard Sander; 1993.
DcLB 126	Volume 126: *Seventeenth-Century British Nondramatic Poets*. Second Series. Edited by M. Thomas Hester; 1993.

DcLB 127	Volume 127: *American Newspaper Publishers, 1950-1990.* Edited by Perry J. Ashley; 1993.
DcLB 128	Volume 128: *Twentieth-Century Italian Poets.* Second Series. Edited by Giovanna Wedel De Stasio, Glauco Cambon, and Antonio Illiano; 1993.
DcLB 129	Volume 129: *Nineteenth-Century German Writers, 1841-1900.* Edited by James Hardin and Siegfried Mews; 1993.
DcLB 130	Volume 130: *American Short-Story Writers since World War II.* Edited by Patrick Meanor; 1993.
DcLB 131	Volume 131: *Seventeenth-Century British Nondramatic Poets.* Third Series. Edited by M. Thomas Hester; 1993.
DcLB 132	Volume 132: *Sixteenth-Century British Nondramatic Writers.* First Series. Edited by David A. Richardson; 1993.
DcLB 133	Volume 133: *Nineteenth-Century German Writers to 1840.* Edited by James Hardin and Siegfried Mews; 1993.
DcLB 134	Volume 134: *Twentieth-Century Spanish Poets.* Second Series. Edited by Jerry Phillips Winfield; 1994.
DcLB 135	Volume 135: *British Short-Fiction Writers, 1880-1914: The Realist Tradition.* Edited by William B. Thesing; 1994.
DcLB 136	Volume 136: *Sixteenth-Century British Nondramatic Writers.* Second Series. Edited by David A. Richardson; 1994.
DcLB 137	Volume 137: *American Magazine Journalists, 1900-1960.* Second Series. Edited by Sam G. Riley; 1994.
DcLB 138	Volume 138: *German Writers and Works of the High Middle Ages: 1170-1280.* Edited by James Hardin and Will Hasty; 1994.
DcLB 139	Volume 139: *British Short-Fiction Writers, 1945-1980.* Edited by Dean Baldwin; 1994.
DcLB 140	Volume 140: *American Book-Collectors and Bibliographers.* First Series. Edited by Joseph Rosenblum; 1994.
DcLB 141	Volume 141: *British Children's Writers, 1880-1914.* Edited by Laura M. Zaidman; 1994.
DcLB 142	Volume 142: *Eighteenth-Century British Literary Biographers.* Edited by Steven Serafin; 1994.
DcLB 143	Volume 143: *American Novelists Since World War II.* Third Series. Edited by James R. Giles and Wanda H. Giles; 1994.
DcLB 144	Volume 144: *Nineteenth-Century British Literary Biographers.* Edited by Steven Serafin; 1994.
DcLB 145	Volume 145: *Modern Latin-American Fiction Writers.* Second Series. Edited by William Luis and Ann Gonzalez; 1994.
DcLB 146	Volume 146: *Old and Middle English Literature.* Edited by Jeffrey Helterman and Jerome Mitchell; 1994.

DcLB	*Dictionary of Literary Biography.* Detroit: Gale Research, 1995-1999.
DcLB 147	Volume 147: *South Slavic Writers Before World War II.* Edited by Vasa D. Mihailovich; 1995.

DcLB 148	Volume 148: *German Writers and Works of the Early Middle Ages: 800-1170.* Edited by Will Hasty and James Hardin; 1995.
DcLB 149	Volume 149: *Late Nineteenth- and Early Twentieth-Century British Literary Biographers.* Edited by Steven Serafin; 1995.
DcLB 150	Volume 150: *Early Modern Russian Writers, Late Seventeenth and Eighteenth Centuries.* Edited by Marcus C. Levitt; 1995.
DcLB 151	Volume 151: *British Prose Writers of the Early Seventeenth Century.* Edited by Clayton D. Lein; 1995.
DcLB 152	Volume 152: *American Novelists Since World War II.* Fourth Series. Edited by James R. Giles and Wanda H. Giles; 1995.
DcLB 153	Volume 153: *Late-Victorian and Edwardian British Novelists.* First Series. Edited by George M. Johnson; 1995.
DcLB 154	Volume 154: *The British Literary Book Trade, 1700-1820.* Edited by James K. Bracken and Joel Silver; 1995.
DcLB 155	Volume 155: *Twentieth-Century British Literary Biographers.* Edited by Steven Serafin; 1995.
DcLB 156	Volume 156: *British Short-Fiction Writers, 1880-1914: The Romantic Tradition.* Edited by William F. Naufftus; 1996.
DcLB 157	Volume 157: *Twentieth-Century Caribbean and Black African Writers.* Third Series. Edited by Bernth Lindfors and Reinhard Sander; 1996.
DcLB 158	Volume 158: *British Reform Writers, 1789-1832.* Edited by Gary Kelly and Edd Applegate; 1996.
DcLB 159	Volume 159: *British Short-Fiction Writers, 1800-1880.* Edited by John R. Greenfield; 1996.
DcLB 160	Volume 160: *British Children's Writers, 1914-1960.* Edited by Donald R. Hettinga and Gary D. Schmidt; 1996.
DcLB 161	Volume 161: *British Children's Writers Since 1960.* First Series. Edited by Caroline C. Hunt; 1996.
DcLB 162	Volume 162: *British Short-Fiction Writers, 1915-1945.* Edited by John H. Rogers; 1996.
DcLB 163	Volume 163: *British Children's Writers, 1800-1880.* Edited by Meena Khorana; 1996.
DcLB 164	Volume 164: *German Baroque Writers, 1580-1660.* Edited by James Hardin; 1996.
DcLB 165	Volume 165: *American Poets Since World War II.* Fourth Series. Edited by Joseph Conte; 1996.
DcLB 166	Volume 166: *British Travel Writers, 1837-1875.* Edited by Barbara Brothers and Julia Gergits; 1996.
DcLB 167	Volume 167: *Sixteenth-Century British Nondramatic Writers.* Third Series. Edited by David A. Richardson; 1996.
DcLB 168	Volume 168: *German Baroque Writers, 1661-1730.* Edited by James Hardin; 1996.
DcLB 169	Volume 169: *American Poets Since World War II.* Fifth Series. Edited by Joseph Conte; 1996.

DcLB 170	Volume 170: *The British Literary Booktrade, 1475-1700.* Edited by James K. Bracken and Joel Silver; 1996.
DcLB 171	Volume 171: *Twentieth-Century American Sportswriters.* Edited by Richard Orodenker; 1996.
DcLB 172	Volume 172: *Sixteenth-Century British Nondramatic Writers.* Fourth Series. Edited by David A. Richardson; 1996.
DcLB 173	Volume 173: *American Novelists Since World War II.* Fifth Series. Edited by James R. Giles and Wanda H. Giles; 1997.
DcLB 174	Volume 174: *British Travel Writers, 1876-1909.* Edited by Barbara Brothers and Julia Gergits; 1997.
DcLB 175	Volume 175: *Native American Writers of the United States.* Edited by Kenneth M. Roemer; 1997.
DcLB 176	Volume 176: *Ancient Greek Authors.* Edited by Ward W. Briggs; 1997.
DcLB 177	Volume 177: *Italian Novelists Since World War II, 1945-1965.* Edited by Augustus Pallotta; 1997.
DcLB 178	Volume 178: *British Fantasy and Science-Fiction Writers Before World War I.* Edited by Darren Harris-Fain; 1997.
DcLB 179	Volume 179: *German Writers of the Renaissance and Reformation, 1280-1580.* Edited by James Hardin and Max Reinhart; 1997.
DcLB 180	Volume 180: *Japanese Fiction Writers, 1868-1945.* Edited by Van C. Gessel; 1997.
DcLB 181	Volume 181: *South Slavic Writers Since World War II.* Edited by Vasa D. Mihailovich; 1997.
DcLB 182	Volume 182: *Japanese Fiction Writers Since World War II.* Edited by Van C. Gessel; 1997.
DcLB 183	Volume 183: *American Travel Writers, 1776-1864.* Edited by James Schramer and Donald Ross; 1997.
DcLB 184	Volume 184: *Nineteenth-Century British Book-Collectors and Bibliographers.* Edited by William Baker and Kenneth Womack; 1997.
DcLB 185	Volume 185: *American Literary Journalists, 1945-1995.* First Series. Edited by Arthur J. Kaul; 1997.
DcLB 186	Volume 186: *Nineteenth-Century American Western Writers.* Edited by Robert L. Gale; 1997.
DcLB 187	Volume 187: *American Book Collectors and Bibliographers.* Second Series. Edited by Joseph Rosenblum; 1998.
DcLB 188	Volume 188: *American Book and Magazine Illustrators to 1920.* Edited by Steven E. Smith, Catherine A. Hastedt, and Donald H. Dyal; 1998.
DcLB 189	Volume 189: *American Travel Writers, 1850-1915.* Edited by Donald Ross and James J. Schramer; 1998.
DcLB 190	Volume 190: *British Reform Writers, 1832-1914.* Edited by Gary Kelly and Edd Applegate; 1998.
DcLB 191	Volume 191: *British Novelists Between the Wars.* Edited by George M. Johnson; 1998.
DcLB 192	Volume 192: *French Dramatists, 1789-1914.* Edited by Barbara T. Cooper; 1998.
DcLB 193	Volume 193: *American Poets Since World War II.* Sixth Series. Edited by Joseph Conte; 1998.

DcLB 194	Volume 194: *British Novelists Since 1960.* Second Series. Edited by Merritt Moseley; 1998.
DcLB 195	Volume 195: *British Travel Writers, 1910-1939.* Edited by Barbara Brothers and Julia M. Gergits; 1998.
DcLB 196	Volume 196: *Italian Novelists Since World War II, 1965-1995.* Edited by Augustus Pallotta; 1999.
DcLB 197	Volume 197: *Late-Victorian and Edwardian British Novelists.* Second Series. Edited by George M. Johnson; 1999.
DcLB 198	Volume 198: *Russian Literature in the Age of Pushkin and Gogol: Prose.* Edited by Christine A. Rydel; 1999.
DcLB 199	Volume 199: *Victorian Women Poets.* Edited by William B. Thesing; 1999.
DcLB 200	Volume 200: *American Women Prose Writers to 1820.* Edited by Carla Mulford, Angela Vietto, and Amy E. Winans; 1999.
DcLB 201	Volume 201: *Twentieth-Century British Book Collectors and Bibliographers.* First Series. Edited by William Baker and Kenneth Womack; 1999.
DcLB 202	Volume 202: *Nineteenth-Century American Fiction Writers.* Edited by Kent P. Ljungquist; 1999.

DcLB	*Dictionary of Literary Biography.* Detroit: Gale Group, 1999-2000.
DcLB 203	Volume 203: *Medieval Japanese Writers.* Edited by Steven D. Carter; 1999.
DcLB 204	Volume 204: *British Travel Writers, 1940-1997.* Edited by Barbara Brothers and Julia M. Gergits; 1999.
DcLB 205	Volume 205: *Russian Literature in the Age of Pushkin and Gogol: Poetry and Drama.* Edited by Christine A. Rydel; 1999.
DcLB 206	Volume 206: *Twentieth-Century American Western Writers.* First Series. Edited by Richard H. Cracroft; 1999.
DcLB 207	Volume 207: *British Novelists Since 1960.* Third Series. Edited by Merritt Moseley; 1999.
DcLB 208	Volume 208: *Literature of the French and Occitan Middle Ages: Eleventh to Fifteenth Centuries.* Edited by Deborah Sinnreich-Levi and Ian S. Laurie; 1999.
DcLB 209	Volume 209: *Chicano Writers.* Third Series. Edited by Francisco A. Lomeli and Carl R. Shirley; 1999.
DcLB 210	Volume 210: *Ernest Hemingway.* A Documentary Volume. Edited by Robert W. Trogdon; 1999.
DcLB 211	Volume 211: *Ancient Roman Writers.* Edited by Ward W. Briggs; 1999.
DcLB 212	Volume 212: *Twentieth-Century American Western Writers.* Second Series. Edited by Richard H. Cracroft; 1999.
DcLB 213	Volume 213: *Pre-Nineteenth-Century British Book Collectors and Bibliographers.* Edited by William Baker and Kenneth Womack; 1999.
DcLB 214	Volume 214: *Twentieth-Century Danish Writers.* Edited by Marianne Stecher-Hansen; 1999.
DcLB 215	Volume 215: *Twentieth-Century Eastern European Writers.* First Series. Edited by Steven Serafin; 1999.

DcLB 216	Volume 216: *British Poets of the Great War: Brooke, Rosenberg, Thomas.* A Documentary Volume. Edited by Patrick Quinn; 2000.
DcLB 217	Volume 217: *Nineteenth-Century French Poets.* Edited by Robert Beum; 2000.
DcLB 217A	Volume 217: *Nineteenth-Century French Poets.* Edited by Robert Beum; 2000. Other Poets section begins on page 299.
DcLB 218	Volume 218: *American Short-Story Writers Since World War II.* Second Series. Edited by Patrick Meanor and Gwen Crane; 2000.
DcLB 219	Volume 219: *F. Scott Fitzgerald's ''The Great Gatsby.''* A Documentary Volume. Edited by Matthew J. Bruccoli; 2000.
DcLB 220	Volume 220: *Twentieth-Century Eastern European Writers.*; 2000.
DcLB 221	Volume 221: *American Women Prose Writers, 1870-1920.* Edited by Sharon M. Harris; 2000.
DcLB 222	Volume 222: *H.L. Mencken.* A Documentary Volume. Edited by Richard J. Schrader; 2000.

DcLB *Dictionary of Literary Biography, Documentary Series.* An illustrated chronicle. Detroit: Gale Research, 1982-1999.

DcLB DS1	Volume 1. Edited by Margaret A. Van Antwerp; 1982.
DcLB DS2	Volume 2. Edited by Margaret A. Van Antwerp; 1982.
DcLB DS3	Volume 3. Edited by Mary Bruccoli; 1983.
DcLB DS4	Volume 4. Edited by Margaret A. Van Antwerp and Sally Johns; 1984.
DcLB DS5	Volume 5; 1987.
DcLB DS6	Volume 6. Edited by Matthew J. Bruccoli and Richard Layman; 1989.
DcLB DS7	Volume 7. Edited by Karen L. Rood; 1989.
DcLB DS8	Volume 8. Edited by Jeffrey Louis Decker; 1991.
DcLB DS9	Volume 9. Edited by Ronald Baughman; 1991.
DcLB DS10	Volume 10. Edited by Edward L. Bishop; 1992.
DcLB DS11	Volume 11. Edited by Jon Christian Suggs; 1993.
DcLB DS12	Volume 12. Edited by Mary Ann Wimsatt and Karen L. Rood; 1995.
DcLB DS13	Volume 13. Edited by John Delaney; 1995.
DcLB DS14	Volume 14. Edited by Caroline C. Hunt; 1996.
DcLB DS15	Volume 15. Edited by Matthew J. Bruccoli and Robert W. Trogdon; 1997.
DcLB DS16	Volume 16. Edited by John Delaney; 1997.
DcLB DS17	Volume 17. Edited by John Delaney; 1998.
DcLB DS18	Volume 18. Edited by Patrick Quinn; 1999.
DcLB DS19	Volume 19. Edited by Judith S. Baughman; 1999.

Use the Table of Contents to locate entries; multiple essays for the same name are often provided. Volumes 5 and 11 contain no biographies.

DcLB *Dictionary of Literary Biography, Yearbook.* Detroit: Gale Research, 1981-1998.

DcLB Y80A	*1980 Yearbook.* Edited by Karen L. Rood, Jean W. Ross, and Richard Ziegfeld; 1981. ''Updated Entries'' section begins on page 3.

DcLB Y80B	*1980 Yearbook.* Edited by Karen L. Rood, Jean W. Ross, and Richard Ziegfeld; 1981. ''New Entries'' section begins on page 127.
DcLB Y81A	*1981 Yearbook.* Edited by Karen L. Rood, Jean W. Ross, and Richard Ziegfeld; 1982. ''Updated Entries'' section begins on page 21.
DcLB Y81B	*1981 Yearbook.* Edited by Karen L. Rood, Jean W. Ross, and Richard Ziegfeld; 1982. ''New Entries'' section begins on page 139.
DcLB Y82A	*1982 Yearbook.* Edited by Richard Ziegfeld; 1983. ''Updated Entries'' section begins on page 121.
DcLB Y82B	*1982 Yearbook.* Edited by Richard Ziegfeld; 1983. ''New Entries'' section begins on page 203.
DcLB Y83A	*1983 Yearbook.* Edited by Mary Bruccoli and Jean W. Ross; 1984. ''Updated Entries'' section begins on page 155.
DcLB Y83B	*1983 Yearbook.* Edited by Mary Bruccoli and Jean W. Ross; 1984. ''New Entries'' section begins on page 175.
DcLB Y83N	*1983 Yearbook.* Edited by Mary Bruccoli and Jean W. Ross; 1984. Obituaries section begins on page 103.
DcLB Y84A	*1984 Yearbook.* Edited by Jean W. Ross; 1985. ''Updated Entry'' section begins on page 219.
DcLB Y84B	*1984 Yearbook.* Edited by Jean W. Ross; 1985. ''New Entries'' section begins on page 225.
DcLB Y84N	*1984 Yearbook.* Edited by Jean W. Ross; 1985. Obituaries section begins on page 163.
DcLB Y85A	*1985 Yearbook.* Edited by Jean W. Ross; 1986. ''Updated Entries'' section begins on page 279.
DcLB Y85B	*1985 Yearbook.* Edited by Jean W. Ross; 1986. ''New Entries'' section begins on page 319.
DcLB Y85N	*1985 Yearbook.* Edited by Jean W. Ross; 1986. Obituaries section begins on page 253.
DcLB Y86A	*1986 Yearbook.* Edited by J.M. Brook; 1987. ''Updated Entries'' section begins on page 247.
DcLB Y86B	*1986 Yearbook.* Edited by J.M. Brook; 1987. ''New Entries'' section begins on page 271.
DcLB Y86N	*1986 Yearbook.* Edited by J.M. Brook; 1987. Obituaries section begins on page 199.
DcLB Y87A	*1987 Yearbook.* Edited by J.M. Brook; 1988. ''Updated Entries'' section begins on page 241.
DcLB Y87B	*1987 Yearbook.* Edited by J.M. Brook; 1988. ''New Entries'' section begins on page 293.
DcLB Y87N	*1987 Yearbook.* Edited by J.M. Brook; 1988. Obituaries section begins on page 219.
DcLB Y88	*1988 Yearbook.* Edited by J.M. Brook; 1989. The Nobel Prize entry begins on page 3.
DcLB Y88N	*1988 Yearbook.* Edited by J.M. Brook; 1989. Obituaries section begins on page 199.
DcLB Y89	*1989 Yearbook.* Edited by J.M. Brook; 1990. The Nobel Prize entry begins on page 3.
DcLB Y89N	*1989 Yearbook.* Edited by J.M. Brook; 1990. Obituaries section begins on page 170.
DcLB Y90	*1990 Yearbook.* Edited by James W. Hipp; 1991. The Nobel Prize entry begins on page 3.

DcLB Y90N	*1990 Yearbook.* Edited by James W. Hipp; 1991. Obituaries section begins on page 206.
DcLB Y91	*1991 Yearbook.* Edited by James W. Hipp; 1992. Use the Table of Contents to locate entries.
DcLB Y91N	*1991 Yearbook.* Edited by James W. Hipp; 1992. Obituaries section begins on page 224.
DcLB Y92	*1992 Yearbook.* Edited by James W. Hipp; 1993. Use the Table of Contents to locate entries.
DcLB Y92N	*1992 Yearbook.* Edited by James W. Hipp; 1993. Obituaries section begins on page 286.
DcLB Y93	*1993 Yearbook.* Edited by James W. Hipp; 1994. Use the Table of Contents to locate entries.
DcLB Y93N	*1993 Yearbook.* Edited by James W. Hipp; 1994. Obituaries section begins on page 261.
DcLB Y94	*1994 Yearbook.* Edited by James W. Hipp; 1995. Use the Table of Contents to locate entries.
DcLB Y94N	*1994 Yearbook.* Edited by James W. Hipp; 1995. Obituaries section begins on page 236.
DcLB Y95	*1995 Yearbook.* Edited by James W. Hipp; 1996.
DcLB Y95N	*1995 Yearbook.* Edited by James W. Hipp; 1996. Obituaries section begins on page 306.
DcLB Y96	*1996 Yearbook.* Edited by Samuel L. Bruce; 1997.
DcLB Y96N	*1996 Yearbook.* Edited by Samuel L. Bruce; 1997. Obituaries section begins on page 298.
DcLB Y97	*1997 Yearbook.* Edited by Matthew Bruccoli and George Garrett; 1998. Use the Table of Contents to locate entries.
DcLB Y97N	*1997 Yearbook.* Edited by Matthew Bruccoli and George Garrett; 1998. Obituaries section begins on page 377.

DcLB   *Dictionary of Literary Biography, Yearbook.* 1998 Yearbook. Edited by Matthew J. Bruccoli and George Garrett. Detroit: Gale Group, 1999.

DcLB Y98	Use the Table of Contents to locate entries.
DcLB Y98N	Obituaries section begins on page 351.

DcLP   *Dictionary of Literary Pseudonyms.* A selection of popular modern writers in English. Fourth edition. By Frank Atkinson. Chicago: American Library Association; London: Library Association Publishing, 1987.

DcLP 87A	Part I: Alphabetical listing by authors' ''Real names'' begins on page 1.
DcLP 87B	Part II: Alphabetical listing by authors' ''Pseudonyms'' begins on page 140.

DcLEL   *A Dictionary of Literature in the English Language.* Compiled and edited by Robin Myers. Oxford: Pergamon Press, 1970-1978.

DcLEL	*From Chaucer to 1940.*; 1970.
DcLEL 1940	*From 1940 to 1970.*; 1978.

DcMexL   *Dictionary of Mexican Literature.* Edited by Eladio Cortes. Westport, CT: Greenwood Press, 1992.

DcMexR   *Dictionary of Mexican Rulers, 1325-1997.* By Juana Vazquez-Gomez. Westport, CT: Greenwood Press, 1997.
         Use the Index to locate biographies.

DcMidEa   *Dictionary of the Middle East.* By Dilip Hiro. New York: St. Martin's Press, 1996.

DcMPSA   *Dictionary of the Modern Politics of South-East Asia.* By Michael Leifer. London: Routledge, 1995.

DcNaB   *The Dictionary of National Biography.* London: Oxford University Press, 1953. Contains abstracts of the biographies found in *The Dictionary of National Biography, First Supplement* (Volume 22, New York: Macmillan Co.; London: Smith, Elder & Co., 1909).

      DcNaB   The Concise Dictionary. Part 1, From the beginnings to 1900; 1953.

      DcNaB 1912   *1912-1921.* Edited by H.W.C. Davis and J.R.H. Weaver; 1927.

      DcNaB 1922   *1922-1930.* Edited by J.R.H. Weaver; 1937.

      DcNaB 1931   *1931-1940.* Edited by L.G. Wickham Legg; 1949.

      DcNaB 1941   *1941-1950.* Edited by L.G. Wickham Legg and E.T. Williams; 1959.

      DcNaB 1951   *1951-1960.* Edited by E.T. Williams and Helen M. Palmer; 1971.

      DcNaB 1961   *1961-1970.* Edited by E.T. Williams and C.S. Nicholls; 1981.

      DcNaB 1971   *1971-1980.* Edited by Lord Blake and C.S. Nicholls; 1986.

      DcNaB 1981   *1981-1985.* Edited by Lord Blake and C.S. Nicholls; 1990.

      DcNaB 1986   *1986-1990.* Edited by C. S. Nicholls; 1996.

      DcNaB C   The Concise Dictionary. Part 1, From the beginnings to 1900; 1953. Corrigenda begins on page 1457.

      DcNaB MP   *Missing Persons.* Edited by C. S. Nicholls; 1993.

      DcNaB S1   The Concise Dictionary. Part 1, From the beginnings to 1900. First Supplement; 1953.

DcNaB S2   *The Dictionary of National Biography.* Second Supplement. Three volumes. Edited by Sir Sidney Lee. New York: Macmillan Co.; London: Smith, Elder & Co., 1912.

DcNAL   *Dictionary of Native American Literature.* Edited by Andrew Wiget. Garland Reference Library of the Humanities, vol. 1815. New York: Garland Publishing, 1994.

      Use the Index to locate biographies.

DcNiCA   *Dictionary of Ninteenth Century Antiques and Later Objets d'Art.* By George Savage. London: Barrie & Jenkins, 1978.

DcNAA   *A Dictionary of North American Authors Deceased before 1950.* Compiled by W. Stewart Wallace. Toronto: Ryerson Press, 1951. Reprint. Detroit: Gale Research, 1968.

DcNCBi   *Dictionary of North Carolina Biography.* Edited by William S. Powell. Chapel Hill, NC: University of North Carolina Press, 1979-1991.

      DcNCBi 1   Volume 1, A-C; 1979.

      DcNCBi 2   Volume 2, D-G; 1986.

      DcNCBi 3   Volume 3, H-K; 1988.

DcNCBi 4   Volume 4, L-O; 1991.

DcOrL   *Dictionary of Oriental Literatures.* New York: Basic Books, 1974.
                   DcOrL 1   Volume I: East Asia. Edited by Zbigniew Slupski.
                   DcOrL 2   Volume II: South and South-East Asia. Edited by Dusan
                                        Zbavitel.
                   DcOrL 3   Volume III: West Asia and North Africa. Edited by Jiri
                                        Becka.

DcPol   *A Dictionary of Politics.* Revised edition. Edited by Walter Laqueur. New York:
                   Macmillan Publishing Co., Free Press, 1974.

DcPseud   *Dictionary of Pseudonyms.* Third edition. By Adrian Room. Jefferson, NC:
                   McFarland & Co., 1998.

DcPup   *Dictionary of Puppetry.* By A.R. Philpott. Boston: Plays, 1969.

DcRusL   *Dictionary of Russian Literature.* By William E. Harkins. New York: Philosophical
                   Library, 1956. Reprint. Westport, CT: Greenwood Press, 1971.

DcRusLS   *Dictionary of Russian Literature since 1917.* By Wolfgang Kasack. New York:
                   Columbia University Press, 1988.

DcScanL   *Dictionary of Scandinavian Literature.* Edited by Virpi Zuck. New York:
                   Greenwood Press, 1990.

DcScB   *Dictionary of Scientific Biography.* New York: Charles Scribner's Sons, 1970-1990.
                   DcScB   Volumes I-XIV. Edited by Charles Coulston Gillispie;
                                        1970.
                   DcScB S1   Volume XV, Supplement I. Edited by Charles Coulston
                                        Gillispie; 1978.
                   DcScB S2   Volumes 17-18, Supplement II. Edited by Frederic L.
                                        Holmes; 1990.

DcSeaP   *Dictionary of Sea Painters.* By E.H.H. Archibald. Woodbridge, England: Antique
                   Collectors' Club, 1980.
                   Biographies begin on page 59.

DcSoc   *A Dictionary of Sociology.* Edited by G. Duncan Mitchell. Chicago: Aldine
                   Publishing Co., 1968.

DcSpL   *Dictionary of Spanish Literature.* By Maxim Newmark. New York: Philosophical
                   Library, 1956. Reprint. Totowa, N.J.: Littlefield, Adams & Co., 1970.

DcTxA   *Dictionary of Texas Artists, 1800-1945.* Compiled by Paula L. Grauer and Michael
                   R. Grauer. West Texas A&M University Series, Number Three. College
                   Station, TX: Texas A & M University Press, 1999.

DcTwBBL   *Dictionary of Twentieth Century British Business Leaders.* By David J. Jeremy and
                   Geoffrey Tweedale. London: Bowker-Saur, 1994.

DcTwCCu   *Dictionary of Twentieth Century Culture.* Detroit: Gale Research, 1994-1996.

DcTwCCu 1	Volume 1: *American Culture After World War II.* Edited by Karen L. Rood; 1994.	
DcTwCCu 2	Volume 2: *French Culture 1900-1975.* Edited by Catharine Savage Brosman; 1995.	
DcTwCCu 3	Volume 3: *Hispanic Culture of South America.* Edited by Peter Standish; 1995.	
DcTwCCu 4	Volume 4: *Hispanic Culture of Mexico, Central America, and the Caribbean.* Edited by Peter Standish; 1996.	
DcTwCCu 5	Volume 5: *African American Culture.* Edited by Sandra Adell; 1996.	

DcTwArt   *A Dictionary of Twentieth-Century Art.* By Ian Chilvers. Oxford: Oxford University Press, 1998.

DcTwCC   *A Dictionary of Twentieth-Century Composers, 1911-1971.* By Kenneth Thompson. New York: St. Martin's Press, 1973.
> ***DcTwCC A***   The Addenda begins on page 659.

DcTwCuL   *Dictionary of Twentieth-Century Cuban Literature.* Edited by Julio A. Martinez. New York: Greenwood Press, 1990.
> Use the Index to locate individuals found in group biographies.

DcTwDes   *Dictionary of Twentieth-Century Design.* By John Pile. New York: Facts on File, 1990.

DcTwHis   *Dictionary of Twentieth-Century History, 1914-1990.* By Peter Teed. Oxford: Oxford University Press, 1992.

DcVicP   *Dictionary of Victorian Painters.* By Christopher Wood. Suffolk, England: Baron Publishing, 1971.

DcVicP 2   *The Dictionary of Victorian Painters.* Second edition. By Christopher Wood. Woodbridge, England: Antique Collectors' Club, 1978.

DcWomA   *Dictionary of Women Artists.* An international dictionary of women artists born before 1900. By Chris Petteys. Boston: G.K. Hall & Co., 1985.

DirCG 82   *Directors: A Complete Guide.* Edited by Michael Singer. Beverly Hills: Lone Eagle Productions, Inc., 1982.

DrAF 76   *A Directory of American Fiction Writers.* Names and addresses of more than 800 contemporary fiction writers whose work has been published in the United States. 1976 edition. New York: Poets & Writers, 1976.
> Use the Index to locate listings.

DrAP 75   *A Directory of American Poets.* Names and addresses of more than 1,500 contemporary poets whose work has been published in the United States. 1975 edition. New York: Poets & Writers, 1974.
> Use the Index to locate listings.

DrAPF   *A Directory of American Poets and Fiction Writers.* Names and addresses of over 7,400 contemporary poets, fiction writers and performance writers. New York: Poets & Writers, 1980-1998.

DrAPF 80	1980-1981 edition; 1980. Use the Index to locate listings.
DrAPF 83	1983-1984 edition; 1983. Use the Index to locate listings.
DrAPF 85	1985-1986 edition; 1985. Use the Index to locate listings.
DrAPF 87	1987-1988 edition; 1987. Use the Index to locate listings.
DrAPF 89	1989-1990 edition; 1989. Use the Index to locate listings.
DrAPF 91	1991-1992 edition; 1990. Use the Index to locate listings.
DrAPF 93	1993-1994 edition; 1992. Use the Index to locate listings.
DrAPF 97	1997-1998 edition; 1997. Use the Index to locate listings.
DrAPF 1999	1999-2000 edition; 1998.

DrAS *Directory of American Scholars.* New York: R.R. Bowker Co., 1974-1982.

DrAS 74E	Sixth edition, Volume 2: English, Speech, & Drama; 1974.
DrAS 74F	Sixth edition, Volume 3: Foreign Languages, Linguistics, & Philology; 1974.
DrAS 74H	Sixth edition, Volume 1: History; 1974.
DrAS 74P	Sixth edition, Volume 4: Philosophy, Religion, & Law; 1974.
DrAS 78E	Seventh edition, Volume 2: English, Speech, & Drama; 1978.
DrAS 78F	Seventh edition, Volume 3: Foreign Languages, Linguistics, & Philology; 1978.
DrAS 78H	Seventh edition, Volume 1: History; 1978.
DrAS 78P	Seventh edition, Volume 4: Philosophy, Religion, & Law; 1978.
DrAS 82E	Eighth edition, Volume 2: English, Speech, & Drama; 1982.
DrAS 82F	Eighth edition, Volume 3: Foreign Languages, Linguistics, & Philology; 1982.
DrAS 82H	Eighth edition, Volume 1: History; 1982.
DrAS 82P	Eighth edition, Volume 4: Philosophy, Religion, & Law; 1982.

DrAS *Directory of American Scholars.* Detroit: Gale Group, 1999.

DrAS 99E	Ninth edition, Volume 2: English, Speech, & Drama.
DrAS 99F	Ninth edition, Volume 3: Foreign Languages, Linguistics, & Philology.
DrAS 99H	Ninth edition, Volume 1: History.
DrAS 99P	Ninth edition, Volume 4: Philosophy, Religion, & Law.

DrBlPA *Directory of Blacks in the Performing Arts.* By Edward Mapp. Metuchen, NJ: Scarecrow Press, 1978-1990.

DrBlPA	First edition; 1978.
DrBlPA 90	Second edition; 1990.

DrCnP 81 *Directory of Canadian Plays and Playwrights.* Edited by Jane Cunningham. Toronto: Playwrights Canada, 1981.

DrEEuF *Directory of Eastern European Film-Makers and Films, 1945-1991.* By Grzegorz Balski. Westport, CT: Greenwood Press, 1992.

DrIndFM *Directory of Indian Film-Makers and Films.* Compiled and edited by Sanjit Narwekar. Westport, CT: Greenwood Press, 1994.

DrInf	*The Directory of Infamy.* The best of the worst: an illustrated compendium of over 600 of the all-time great crooks. By Jonathon Green. London: Mills & Boon, 1980. Use the Index to locate biographies.
DrLC 69	*Directory of Library Consultants.* Edited by John N. Berry, III. New York: R.R. Bowker Co., 1969.
DrRegL 75	*Directory of Registered Lobbyists and Lobbyist Legislation.* Second edition. Chicago: Marquis Academic Media, 1975. Use the "Lobbyist Index," which begins on page 451, to locate listings.
Dis&D	*Disease and Destiny.* A bibliography of medical references to the famous. By Judson Bennett Gilbert. Additions and introduction by Gordon E. Mestler. London: Dawsons of Pall Mall, 1962.
DiAAPGL	*Distinguished African American Political and Governmental Leaders.* By James Haskins. Phoenix, AZ: Oryx Press, 1999.
DiAASTC	*Distinguished African American Scientists of the 20th Century.* By James H. Kessler, J. S. Kidd, Renee A. Kidd, and Katherine A. Morin. Phoenix, AZ: Oryx Press, 1996.
DivFut	*Divining the Future.* Prognostication from astrology to zoomancy. By Eva Shaw. New York: Facts on File, 1995.
Drake	*Drake's Dictionary of American Biography.* Including men of the time, containing nearly 10,000 notices of persons of both sexes, of native and foreign birth, who have been remarkable, or prominently connected with the arts, sciences, literature, politics, or history, of the American continent. By Francis S. Drake. Boston: James R. Osgood & Co., 1872. Reprint. Detroit: Gale Research, 1974. **Drake SUP** Supplement begins on page 1015.

DramC   *Drama Criticism.* Criticism of the most significant and widely studied dramatic works from all the world's literatures. Detroit: Gale Research, 1991-1999.

DramC 1	Volume 1; 1991.
DramC 2	Volume 2; 1992.
DramC 3	Volume 3; 1993.
DramC 4	Volume 4; 1994.
DramC 5	Volume 5; 1995.
DramC 6	Volume 6; 1996.
DramC 7	Volume 7; 1997.
DramC 8	Volume 8; 1998.
DramC 9	Volume 9; 1999.

DramC   *Drama Criticism.* Criticism of the most significant and widely studied dramatic works from all the world's literatures. Detroit: Gale Group, 1999-2000.

DramC 10	Volume 10; 1999.
DramC 11	Volume 11; 2000.

DrmM   *Dream Makers.* The uncommon men & women who write science fiction. Interviews by Charles Platt. New York: Berkley Books, 1980-1983.

DrmM 1	Volume 1; 1980.

DrmM 2	Volume II; 1983.

Use the Table of Contents to locate interviews.

Dun&B	*Dun & Bradstreet Reference Book of Corporate Managements.* Bethlehem, PA: Dun & Bradstreet, 1979-1999.

Dun&B 79	13th edition; 1979.
Dun&B 86	1986 edition; 1985.
Dun&B 88	1988 edition; 1988.
Dun&B 90	1990 edition; 1990.
Dun&B 98	1998 edition; 1998.
Dun&B 99	1999 edition; 1999.

Use the "Principal Officers and Directors Index" in the Cross-Reference volume to locate biographies. The "Principal Officers and Directors Index" often alphabetizes by titles of address, such as Dr., Mrs., and Baron. Names with prefixes, such as Mc, De, and De La, may sometimes be located in more than one place in the index.

DutArt	*Dutch Art.* An encyclopedia. Edited by Sheila D. Mulller. New York: Garland Publishing, 1997.

EarABI	*Early American Book Illustrators and Wood Engravers, 1670-1870.* A catalogue of a collection of American books illustrated for the most part with woodcuts and wood engravings in the Princeton University Library. By Sinclair Hamilton. Princeton, NJ: Princeton University Press, 1958-1968.

EarABI	Volume I: Main Catalogue; 1958.
EarABI SUP	Volume II: Supplement; 1968.

EarBlAP	*Early Black American Playwrights and Dramatic Writers.* A biographical directory and catalog of plays, films, and broadcasting scripts. By Bernard L. Peterson, Jr. New York: Greenwood Press, 1990.

Ebony	*The Ebony Success Library.* By the Editors of *Ebony.* Nashville, TN: Southwestern Co., 1973.

Ebony 1	Volume I: 1,000 Successful Blacks.
Ebony 3	Volume III: Career Guide.

EncAACR	*Encyclopedia of African-American Civil Rights.* From emancipation to the present. Edited by Charles D. Lowery and John F. Marszalek. Westport, CT: Greenwood Press, 1992.

EncAmaz 91	*The Encyclopedia of Amazons.* Women warriors from antiquity to the modern era. First edition. By Jessica Amanda Salmonson. New York: Paragon House, 1991.

EncAAc	*Encyclopedia of American Activism, 1960 to the Present.* By Margaret B. DiCanio. Santa Barbara, CA: ABC-Clio, 1998.

EncAAH	*Encyclopedia of American Agricultural History.* By Edward L. Schapsmeier and Frederick H. Schapsmeier. Westport, CT: Greenwood Press, 1975.

EncAAr 1	*Encyclopedia of American Architecture.* By William Dudley Hunt, Jr. New York: McGraw-Hill Book Co., 1980.

| *EncAAr 2* | *Encyclopedia of American Architecture.* Second edition. By Robert T. Packard. New York: McGraw-Hill, 1995. |

EncAB-A *Encyclopedia of American Biography.* New York and West Palm Beach, FL: The American Historical Society, 1934-1970.

EncAB-A 1	New Series. Volume 1; 1934.
EncAB-A 2	New Series. Volume 2; 1934.
EncAB-A 3	New Series. Volume 3; 1935.
EncAB-A 4	New Series. Volume 4; 1935.
EncAB-A 5	New Series. Volume 5; 1936.
EncAB-A 6	New Series. Volume 6; 1936.
EncAB-A 7	New Series. Volume 7; 1937.
EncAB-A 8	New Series. Volume 8; 1938.
EncAB-A 9	New Series. Volume 9; 1938.
EncAB-A 10	New Series. Volume 10; 1939.
EncAB-A 11	New Series. Volume 11; 1940.
EncAB-A 12	New Series. Volume 12; 1941.
EncAB-A 13	New Series. Volume 13; 1941.
EncAB-A 14	New Series. Volume 14; 1942.
EncAB-A 15	New Series. Volume 15; 1942.
EncAB-A 16	New Series. Volume 16; 1943.
EncAB-A 17	New Series. Volume 17; 1944.
EncAB-A 18	New Series. Volume 18; 1945.
EncAB-A 19	New Series. Volume 19; 1947.
EncAB-A 20	New Series. Volume 20; 1948.
EncAB-A 21	New Series. Volume 21; 1949.
EncAB-A 22	New Series. Volume 22; 1950.
EncAB-A 23	New Series. Volume 23; 1952.
EncAB-A 24	New Series. Volume 24; 1954.
EncAB-A 25	New Series. Volume 25; 1955.
EncAB-A 26	New Series. Volume 26; 1957.
EncAB-A 27	New Series. Volume 27; 1957.
EncAB-A 28	New Series. Volume 28; 1958.
EncAB-A 29	New Series. Volume 29; 1959.
EncAB-A 30	New Series. Volume 30; 1960.
EncAB-A 31	New Series. Volume 31; 1961.
EncAB-A 32	New Series. Volume 32; 1963.
EncAB-A 33	New Series. Volume 33; 1965.
EncAB-A 34	New Series. Volume 34; 1965.
EncAB-A 35	New Series. Volume 35; 1966.
EncAB-A 36	New Series. Volume 36; 1967.
EncAB-A 37	New Series. Volume 37; 1968.
EncAB-A 38	New Series. Volume 38; 1968.
EncAB-A 39	New Series. Volume 39; 1969.
EncAB-A 40	New Series. Volume 40; 1970.

Use the Index to locate biographies.

| *EncAB-H 1974* | *Encyclopedia of American Biography.* Edited by John A. Garraty. New York: Harper & Row Publishers, 1974. |

| *EncAB-H 1996* | *Encyclopedia of American Biography.* Edited by John A. Garraty and Jerome L. Sternstein. New York: HarperCollins, 1996. |

EncABHB	*Encyclopedia of American Business History and Biography.* New York: Facts on File, 1988-1994.

	EncABHB 1	*Railroads in the Age of Regulation, 1900-1980.* Edited by Keith L. Bryant, Jr; 1988.
	EncABHB 2	*Railroads in the Nineteenth Century.* Edited by Robert L. Frey; 1988.
	EncABHB 3	*Iron and Steel in the Nineteenth Century.* Edited by Paul F. Paskoff; 1989.
	EncABHB 4	*The Automobile Industry, 1896-1920.* Edited by George S. May; 1990. Use the index to locate biographies.
	EncABHB 5	*The Automobile Industry, 1920-1980.* Edited by George S. May; 1989. Use the index to locate biographies.
	EncABHB 6	*Banking and Finance to 1913.* Edited by Larry Schweikart; 1990.
	EncABHB 7	*Banking and Finance, 1913-1989.* Edited by Larry Schweikart; 1990.
	EncABHB 8	*The Airline Industry.* Edited by William M. Leary; 1992.
	EncABHB 9	*Iron and Steel in the Twentieth Century.* Edited by Bruce E. Seely; 1994.

EncACom	*The Encyclopedia of American Comics.* Edited by Ron Goulart. New York: Facts on File, 1990.
EncACr	*Encyclopedia of American Crime.* By Carl Sifakis. New York: Facts on File, Inc., 1982.
EncAFC	*Encyclopedia of American Film Comedy.* By Larry Langman. Garland Reference Library of the Humanities, vol. 744. New York: Garland Publishing, 1987.
EncAHmr	*Encyclopedia of American Humorists.* Edited by Steven H. Gale. New York: Garland Publishing, 1988.
EncAInd	*Encyclopedia of American Indian Wars, 1492-1890.* By Jerry Keenan. Santa Barbara, CA: ABC-CLIO, 1997.
EncAInt	*The Encyclopedia of American Intelligence and Espionage.* From the Revolutionary War to the present. By G.J.A. O'Toole. New York: Facts on File, 1988.
EncAJ	*The Encyclopedia of American Journalism.* By Donald Paneth. New York: Facts on File Publications, 1983.
EncAL	*Encyclopedia of the American Left.* Edited by Mari Jo Buhle, Paul Buhle, and Dan Georgakas. Garland Reference Library of the Social Sciences, vol. 502. New York: Garland Publishing, 1990. Cross-references appear before other entries with similar surnames.
EncALit	*Encyclopedia of American Literature.* Edited by Steven R. Serafin. New York: Continuum Publishing Co., 1999.
EncAPar	*Encyclopedia of American Parties, Campaigns, and Elections.* By William C. Binning, Larry E. Esterly, and Paul A. Sracic. Westport, CT: Greenwood Press, 1999.

EncAPoR   *Encyclopedia of American Political Reform.* By Richard A. Clucas. Santa Barbara, CA: ABC-CLIO, 1996.

EncARad   *The Encyclopedia of American Radio.* An A-Z guide to radio from Jack Benny to Howard Stern. By Ron Lackmann. New York: Facts on File, Inc., 2000.

EncARH   *The Encyclopedia of American Religious History.* Two volumes. By Edward L. Queen II, Stephen R. Prothero, and Gardiner H. Shattuck, Jr. New York: Facts on File, 1996.
                   Use the Index to locate biographies.

EncAR   *Encyclopedia of the American Revolution.* By Mark Mayo Boatner, III. New York: David McKay Co., 1966.

EncASM   *Encyclopedia of American Silver Manufacturers.* By Dorothy T. Rainwater. New York: Crown Publishers, 1975.

EncAWoR   *Encyclopedia of American Women and Religion.* By June Melby Benowitz. Santa Barbara, CA: ABC-Clio, 1998.

EncAnRW   *Encyclopedia of Animal Rights and Animal Welfare.* Edited by Marc Bekoff. Westport, CT: Greenwood Press, 1998.

EncApL   *Encyclopedia of Apocalyptic Literature.* By Valerie P. Zimbaro. Santa Barbara, CA: ABC-CLIO, 1996.

EncBrWW   *Encyclopedia of British Women Writers.* Edited by Paul Schlueter and June Schlueter. Garland Reference Library of the Humanities, vol. 818. New York: Garland Publishing, 1988.

EncCapP   *Encyclopedia of Capital Punishment.* By Mark Grossman. Santa Barbara, CA: ABC—CLIO, 1998.

EncChi   *Encyclopedia of China.* The essential reference to China, its history and culture. By Dorothy Perkins. New York: Facts on File, 1999.

EncClPh   *Encyclopedia of Classical Philosophy.* Edited by Donald J. Zeyl. Westport, CT: Greenwood Press, 1997.

EncCW   *Encyclopedia of the Cold War.* By Thomas S. Arms. New York: Facts on File, 1994.

EncCRAm   *The Encyclopedia of Colonial and Revolutionary America.* Edited by John Mack Faragher. New York: Facts on File, 1990.

EncCoWW   *Encyclopedia of Continental Women Writers.* Two volumes. Edited by Katharina M. Wilson. Garland Reference Library of the Humanities, vol. 698. New York: Garland Publishing, 1991.

EncDeaf   *The Encyclopedia of Deafness and Hearing Disorders.* By Carol Turkington and Allen E. Sussman. New York: Facts on File, 1992.

EncEarC   *Encyclopedia of Early Christianity.* Edited by Everett Ferguson. New York: Garland
                     Publishing, 1990-1997.
    EncEarC 90   Garland Reference Library of the Humanities, vol. 846;
                        1990.
    EncEarC 97   Second edition. Garland Reference Library of the
                        Humanities, vol. 1839; 1997.

EncEnl   *Encyclopedia of the Enlightenment.* By Peter Hanns Reill and Ellen Judy Wilson.
                     New York: Facts on File, 1996.

EncEnv   *The Encyclopedia of the Environment.* Edited by Ruth A. Eblen and William R.
                     Eblen. Boston: Houghton Mifflin Co., 1994.

EncE 75   *Encyclopedia of Espionage.* New edition. By Ronald Seth. London: New English
                     Library, 1975.

EncEth   *Encyclopedia of Ethics.* Two volumes. Edited by Lawrence C. Becker and Charlotte
                     B. Becker. New York: Garland Publishing, 1992.

EncEurC   *Encyclopedia of European Cinema.* Edited by Ginette Vincendeau. New York: Facts
                     on File, 1995.

EncFab   *Encyclopedia of Fable.* By Mary Ellen Snodgrass. ABC-CLIO Literary Companion.
                     Santa Barbara, CA: ABC-Clio, 1998.

EncFash   *The Encyclopaedia of Fashion.* By Georgina O'Hara. New York: Harry N. Abrams,
                     1986.

EncFiS   *The Encyclopedia of Figure Skating.* By John Malone. New York: Facts on File,
                     1998.

EncFCWM   *The Encyclopedia of Folk, Country & Western Music.* By Irwin Stambler and Grelun
                     Landon. New York: St. Martin's Press, 1969-1983.
    EncFCWM 69   First edition; 1969.
    EncFCWM 83   Second edition; 1983.

EncFoLi   *Encyclopedia of Folklore and Literature.* Edited by Mary Ellen Brown and Bruce A.
                     Rosenberg. Santa Barbara, CA: ABC-CLIO, 1998.

EncFrLi   *Encyclopedia of Frontier Literature.* By Mary Ellen Snodgrass. Santa Barbara, CA:
                     ABC-CLIO, 1997.

EncFWF   *Encyclopedia of Frontier and Western Fiction.* Edited by Jon Tuska and Vicki
                     Piekarski. New York: McGraw-Hill Book Co., 1983.

EncGRNM   *Encyclopedia of German Resistance to the Nazi Movement.* Edited by Wolfgang
                     Benz and Walter H. Pehle. New York, NY: Continuum Publishing, 1997.
                     The ''Biographical Sketches'' section begins on page 255.

EncGuW   *Encyclopedia of Guerilla Warfare.* By Ian F. W. Beckett. Santa Barbara, CA: ABC-
                     Clio, 1999.

EncHiCA	*An Encyclopedia of the History of Classical Archaeology.* Two volumes. Edited by Nancy Thomson de Grummond. Westport, CT: Greenwood Press, 1996.
EncHuEv	*Encyclopedia of Human Evolution and Prehistory.* Edited by Ian Tattersall, Eric Delson, and John Van Couvering. Garland Reference Library of the Humanities, vol. 768. New York: Garland Publishing, 1988.
EncJap	*Encyclopedia of Japan.* Japanese history and culture, from abacus to zori. By Dorothy Perkins. New York: Facts on File, 1991.
EncJzS	*Encyclopedia of Jazz in the Seventies.* By Leonard Feather and Ira Gitler. New York: Horizon Press, 1976.
EncJzS	*The Encyclopedia of Jazz in the Seventies.* By Leonard Feather and Ira Gitler. New York: Horizon Press, 1976.
EncLatA	*Encyclopedia of Latin America.* Edited by Helen Delpar. New York: McGraw-Hill Book Co., 1974.
EncLitE	*Encyclopedia of Literary Epics.* By Guida M. Jackson. Santa Barbara, CA: ABC-CLIO, 1996.
EncMcCE	*Encyclopedia of the McCarthy Era.* By William K. Klingaman. New York: Facts on File, 1996.
EncMA	*Encyclopedia of Modern Architecture.* Edited by Wolfgang Pehnt. New York: Harry N. Abrams, 1964. Biographies begin on page 28.
EncMot	*The Encyclopedia of Motorcycling.* By George Bishop. New York: G.P. Putnam's Sons, 1980.
EncMT	*Encyclopaedia of the Musical Theatre.* By Stanley Green. New York: Dodd, Mead & Co., 1976.
EncMys	*Encyclopedia of Mystery and Detection.* By Chris Steinbrunner and Otto Penzler. New York: McGraw-Hill Book Co., 1976.
EncNAB	*The Encyclopedia of Native American Biography.* Six hundred life stories of important people, from Powhatan to Wilma Mankiller. By Bruce E. Johansen and Donald A. Grinde, Jr. New York: Henry Holt and Co., 1997.
EncNAR	*The Encyclopedia of Native American Religions.* By Arlene Hirschfelder and Paulette Molin. New York: Facts on File, 1992.
EncNaHi	*An Encyclopedia of Naval History.* By Anthony Bruce and William Cogar. New York: Facts on File, 1998.
EncNoAI	*Encyclopedia of North American Indians.* Edited by Frederick E. Hoxie. Boston: Houghton Mifflin Co., 1996.

EncO&P   *Encyclopedia of Occultism & Parapsychology.* A compendium of information on the occult sciences, magic, demonology, superstitions, spiritism, mysticism, metaphysics, psychical science, and parapsychology, with biographical and bibliographical notes and comprehensive indexes. Edited by Leslie A. Shepard. Detroit: Gale Research, 1978-1991.

         EncO&P 1   First edition; 1978.
         EncO&P 1S1   First edition, *Occultism Update,* Issue Number 1; 1978.
         EncO&P 1S2   First edition, *Occultism Update,* Issue Number 2; 1980.
         EncO&P 1S3   First edition, *Occultism Update,* Issue Numbers 3-4; 1981.
         EncO&P 2   Second edition; 1984.
         EncO&P 2S1   Second edition, *Occultism Update.*; 1987.
         EncO&P 3   Third edition. Two volumes; 1991.

EncPaPR 91   *The Encyclopedia of Parapsychology and Psychical Research.* By Arthur S. Berger and Joyce Berger. New York: Paragon House, 1991.

EncPerG   *Encyclopedia of the Persian Gulf War.* By Richard A. Schwartz. Jefferson, NC: McFarland & Co., 1998.

EncPR&S 74   *Encyclopedia of Pop, Rock & Soul.* By Irwin Stambler. New York: St. Martin's Press, 1974.

EncPR&S 89   *The Encyclopedia of Pop, Rock & Soul.* Revised edition. By Irwin Stambler. New York: St. Martin's Press, 1989.

EncPopM 3   *The Encyclopedia of Popular Music.* Third edition. Eight volumes. Compiled and edited by Colin Larkin. London: MUZE, 1998. Distributed by Grove's Dictionaries, New York.

EncRelA   *Encyclopedia of Religion in American Politics.* Edited by Jeffrey D. Schultz, John G. West, Jr., and Iain Maclean. The American Political Landscape Series. Phoenix, AZ: Oryx Press, 1999.

EncRen   *Encyclopedia of the Renaissance.* Six volumes. New York: Charles Scribner's Sons, 1999.

EncRev   *The Encyclopedia of Revolutions and Revolutionaries.* From anarchism to Zhou Enlai. By Martin van Creveld. New York: Facts on File, 1996.

EncRhBD   *Encyclopedia of Rhythm & Blues and Doo-Wop Vocal Groups.* By Mitch Rosalsky. Lanham, MD: Scarecrow Press, 2000.

EncRk 88   *Encyclopedia of Rock.* By Phil Hardy and Dave Laing. New York: Schirmer Books, 1988.

EncRkSt   *Encyclopedia of Rock Stars.* By Dafydd Rees and Luke Crampton. New York: DK Publishing, 1996.

EncSPD   *The Encyclopedia of Schizophrenia and the Psychotic Disorders.* By Richard Noll. New York: Facts on File, 1992.

EncSF	*The Encyclopedia of Science Fiction.* An Illustrated A to Z. Edited by Peter Nicholls. London: Granada Publishing, 1979.
EncSF 93	*The Encyclopedia of Science Fiction.* Edited by John Clute and Peter Nicholls. New York: St. Martin's Press, 1993.
EncSoA	*Encyclopaedia of Southern Africa.* Sixth edition. Compiled and edited by Eric Rosenthal. London: Frederick Warne & Co., 1973.
EncSoB	*Encyclopedia of Southern Baptists.* Nashville, TN: Broadman Press, 1958-1971.
	EncSoB Two volumes; 1958.
	EncSoB SUP Volume III, Supplement; 1971.
EncSoH	*The Encyclopedia of Southern History.* Edited by David C. Roller and Robert W. Twyman. Baton Rouge, LA: Louisiana State University Press, 1979.
EncSoL	*Encyclopedia of Southern Literature.* By Mary Ellen Snodgrass. ABC-CLIO Literary Companion. Santa Barbara, CA: ABC-CLIO, 1997.
EncSUPP	*Encyclopedia of Strange and Unexplained Physical Phenomena.* By Jerome Clark. Detroit: Gale Research, 1993.
EncStYM	*Encyclopedia of Student and Youth Movements.* By David F. Burg. New York: Facts on File, 1998.
EncTelN	*Encyclopedia of Television News.* Edited by Michael D. Murray. Phoenix, AZ: Oryx Press, 1999.
EncTR	*Encyclopedia of the Third Reich.* By Louis L. Snyder. New York: McGraw-Hill Book Co., 1976.
EncTR 91	*The Encyclopedia of the Third Reich.* Two volumes. Edited by Christian Zentner and Friedemann Bedurftig. Translation edited by Amy Hackett. New York: Macmillan Publishing Co., 1991.
EncTwCJ	*Encyclopedia of Twentieth-Century Journalists.* By William H. Taft. Garland Reference Library of the Humanities, vol. 493. New York: Garland Publishing, 1986.
EncUnb	*The Encyclopedia of Unbelief.* Two volumes. Edited by Gordon Stein. Buffalo, NY: Prometheus Books, 1985.
EncUrb	*Encyclopedia of Urban Planning.* Edited by Arnold Whittick. New York: McGraw-Hill Book Co., 1974.
EncVaud	*Encyclopedia of Vaudeville.* By Anthony Slide. Westport, CT: Greenwood Press, 1994.
EncVieW	*Encyclopedia of the Vietnam War.* A political, social, and military history. Three volumes. Edited by Spencer C. Tucker. Santa Barbara, CA: ABC-CLIO, 1998.

Key to Source Codes

EncWar   *Encyclopedia of the War of 1812*. Edited by David S. Heidler and Jeanne T. Heidler. Santa Barbara, CA: ABC-CLIO, 1997.

EncWW   *The Encyclopedia of Witches and Witchcraft*. By Rosemary Ellen Guiley. New York: Facts on File, 1989.

EncWoAP   *Encyclopedia of Women in American Politics*. Edited by Jeffrey D. Schultz and Laura van Assendelft. The American Political Landscape Series. Phoenix, AZ: Oryx Press, 1999.

EncWomA   *An Encyclopedia of Women Artists of the American West*. By Phil Kovinick and Marian Yoshiki-Kovinick. Austin, TX: University of Texas Press, 1998.
                    EncWomA A   Artists II section begins on page 341.

EncWoAv   *Encyclopedia of Women in Aviation and Space*. By Rosanne Welch. Santa Barbara, CA: ABC-Clio, 1998.

EncWoSp   *Encyclopedia of Women and Sport in America*. Edited by Carole A. Oglesby, et al. Phoenix, AZ: Oryx Press, 1998.

EncWomS   *Encyclopedia of Women and Sports*. By Victoria Sherrow. Santa Barbara, CA: ABC-CLIO, 1996.

EncWomW   *Encyclopedia of Women and World Religion*. Two volumes. Edited by Serinity Young. New York: Macmillan Reference USA, 1999.

EncWHA   *The Encyclopedia of Women's History in America*. By Kathryn Cullen-DuPont. New York: Facts on File, 1996.

EncWB   *Encyclopedia of World Biography*. Detroit: Gale Research, 1998-1999.First edition published as *The McGraw-Hill Encyclopedia of World Biography* with six supplement volumes published as *Encyclopedia of World Biography: 20th Century Supplement*.
                    EncWB 98   Second edition. Seventeen volumes; 1998.
                    EncWB 99   Second edition supplement. Volume 18; 1999.

EncWB 2-19   *Encyclopedia of World Biography*. Second edition supplement. Volume 19. Detroit: Gale Group, 2000. First edition published as *The McGraw-Hill Encyclopedia of World Biography* with six supplement volumes published as *Encyclopedia of World Biography: 20th Century Supplement*.

EncWB   *Encyclopedia of World Biography: 20th Century Supplement*. Three volumes. Palatine, IL: Jack Heraty & Associates, 1987-1988. Earlier volumes published as *The McGraw-Hill Encyclopedia of World Biography*.

EncWL   *Encyclopedia of World Literature in the 20th Century*. New York: Frederick Ungar Publishing Co., 1981- 1967-1981.
                    EncWL 1   First edition. Three volumes and supplement. Edited by Wolfgang Bernard Fleischmann; 1967.
                    EncWL 2   Revised edition. Four volumes. Edited by Leonard S. Klein; 1981.

EncWL 2	Revised edition. Volume 4. Edited by Leonard S. Klein; 1981.
EncWL 2	Revised edition. Volume 2. Edited by Leonard S. Klein; 1981.
EncWL 2	Revised edition. Volume 3. Edited by Leonard S. Klein; 1981.
EncWL 2	Revised edition. Four volumes. Edited by Leonard S. Klein; 1981.
EncWL 2	Revised edition. Volume 1. Edited by Leonard S. Klein; 1981.

EncWL 2S　　*Encyclopedia of World Literature in the 20th Century.* Revised edition, supplement. Edited by Leonard S. Klein. New York: Continuum Publishing Co., 1993. Distributed by Gale Research, Detroit.

EncWL 3　　*Encyclopedia of World Literature in the 20th Century.* Third edition. Four volumes. Detroit: St. James Press, 1999.

EncWL SUP　　*Encyclopedia of World Literature in the 20th Century.* First edition, Supplement. Three volumes and supplement. Edited by Wolfgang Bernard Fleischmann. New York: Frederick Ungar Publishing Co., 1975. An enlarged and updated edition of the Herder *Lexikon der Weltliteratur im 20. Jahrhundert.*

EncWM　　*The Encyclopedia of World Methodism.* Two volumes. Edited by Nolan B. Harmon. Nashville, TN: United Methodist Publishing House, 1974.

EncWT　　*The Encyclopedia of World Theater.* Translated by Estella Schmid, edited by Martin Esslin. New York: Charles Scribner's Sons, 1977. Based on *Friedrichs Theaterlexikon,* by Karl Groning and Werner Kliess.

EncyDCo　　*An Encyclopedic Dictionary of Conflict and Conflict Resolution, 1945-1996.* By John E. Jessup. Westport, CT: Greenwood Press, 1998.

EncVatP　　*Encycolpedia of the Vatican and Papacy.* Edited by Frank J. Coppa. Westport, CT: Greenwood Press, 1999.

EngPo　　*English Poetry of the Second World War.* A Biobibliography. By Catherine W. Reilly. Boston: G.K. Hall & Co., 1986.
　　　　　　Biographies begin on page 21.

Ent　　*The Entertainers.* Edited by Clive Unger-Hamilton. New York: St. Martin's Press, 1980.
　　　　　　Use the "Index of Entries," beginning on page 306, to locate biographies.

Entr　　*Entrepreneurs.* The men and women behind famous brand names and how they made it. By Joseph J. Fucini and Suzy Fucini. Boston: G.K. Hall & Co., 1985.
　　　　　　Use the Index to locate biographies.

EnvEnDr　　*The Environment Encyclopedia and Directory.* London: Europa Publications, 1994.
　　　　　　"Who's Who in the Environment" section begins on page 329.

EnvEnc　　*Environmental Encyclopedia.* First edition. Detroit: Gale Research, 1994.

EnvJust   *Environmental Justice.* A reference handbook. By David E. Newton. Contemporary
                       World Issues. Santa Barbara, CA: ABC-CLIO, 1996.
                            Biographies begin on page 68.

EnvLit   *Environmental Literature.* An encyclopedia of works, authors, and themes. By
                       Patricia D. Netzley Santa Barbara, CA: ABC-Clio, 1999.

EuAu   *European Authors, 1000-1900.* A biographical dictionary of European literature.
                       Edited by Stanley J. Kunitz and Vineta Colby. Wilson Authors Series. New
                       York: H.W. Wilson Co., 1967.

EuWr   *European Writers.* New York: Charles Scribner's Sons, 1983-1990.
EuWr 1	Volume 1: *The Middle Ages and the Renaissance.* Edited by William T.H. Jackson and George Stade; 1983.
EuWr 2	Volume 2: *The Middle Ages and the Renaissance.* Edited by William T.H. Jackson and George Stade; 1983.
EuWr 3	Volume 3: *The Age of Reason and the Enlightenment.* Edited by George Stade; 1984.
EuWr 4	Volume 4: *The Age of Reason and the Enlightenment.* Edited by George Stade; 1984.
EuWr 5	Volume 5: *The Romantic Century.* Edited by Jacques Barzun and George Stade; 1985.
EuWr 6	Volume 6: *The Romantic Century.* Edited by Jacques Barzun and George Stade; 1985.
EuWr 7	Volume 7: *The Romantic Century.* Edited by Jacques Barzun and George Stade; 1985.
EuWr 8	Volume 8: *The Twentieth Century.* Edited by George Stade; 1989.
EuWr 9	Volume 9: *The Twentieth Century.* Edited by George Stade; 1989.
EuWr 10	Volume 10: *The Twentieth Century.* Edited by George Stade; 1990.
EuWr 11	Volume 11: *The Twentieth Century.* Edited by George Stade; 1990.
EuWr 12	Volume 12: *The Twentieth Century.* Edited by George Stade; 1990.
EuWr 13	Volume 13: *The Twentieth Century.* Edited by George Stade; 1990.

                       Use the "List of Subjects" to locate biographies.

EvEuW   *Everyman's Dictionary of European Writers.* By W.N. Hargreaves-Mawdsley.
                       London: J.M. Dent & Sons; New York: E.P. Dutton & Co., 1968.

EvLB   *Everyman's Dictionary of Literary Biography, English and American.* Compiled
                       after John W. Cousin by D.C. Browning. Revised edition. London: J.M. Dent &
                       Sons; New York: E.P. Dutton & Co., 1960.

ExpInc   *Experience, Inc.* Men and women who founded famous companies after the age of
                       40. By Joseph J. Fucini and Suzy Fucini. New York: Free Press, 1987.
                            Use the Index to locate biographies.

ExplAnT	*Explorers from Ancient Times to the Space Age.* Three volumes. Edited by John Logan Allen, E. Julius Dasch, and Barry M. Gough. New York: Macmillan Library Reference USA, 1999.
Expl 93	*Explorers and Discoverers of the World.* First edition. Edited by Daniel B. Baker. Detroit: Gale Research, 1993. Use the Table of Contents to locate biographies.
FacFEBW	*Facts on File Encyclopedia of Black Women in America.* Edited by Darlene Clark Hine. New York: Facts on File, 1997.

        FacFEBW DS   Dance, Sports, and Visual Arts. Use the Index to locate biographies.

        FacFEBW TA   Theater Arts and Entertainment. Biographies begin on page 49.

FacFETw	*The Facts on File Encyclopedia of the Twentieth Century.* Edited by John Drexel. New York: Facts on File, 1991.
FacPr	*Facts about the Presidents.* A compilation of biographical and historical information. By Joseph Nathan Kane. New York: H.W. Wilson Co., 1989-1993.

        FacPr 89   Fifth edition; 1989.

        FacPr 93   Sixth edition; 1993.

        Use the Index to locate biographies of the Presidents. Biographies of the First Ladies appear within the applicable President's biography.

FairDF	*Fairchild's Dictionary of Fashion.* By Charlotte Calasibetta. New York: Fairchild Publications, 1975.

        FairDF ENG   England section begins on page 548.

        FairDF FIN   Finland section begins on page 553.

        FairDF FRA   France section begins on page 554.

        FairDF IRE   Ireland section begins on page 577.

        FairDF ITA   Italy section begins on page 578.

        FairDF JAP   Japan section begins on page 583.

        FairDF SPA   Spain section begins on page 584.

        FairDF US   United States section begins on page 585.

FamA&A	*Famous Actors and Actresses on the American Stage.* Documents of American theater history. Two volumes. By William C. Young. New York: R.R. Bowker Co., 1975.
FamAIYP	*Famous Author-Illustrators for Young People.* By Norah Smaridge. New York: Dodd, Mead & Co., 1973.
FamAYP	*Famous Authors for Young People.* By Ramon P. Coffman and Nathan G. Goodman. New York: Dodd, Mead & Co., 1943.
FamMS	*Famous Modern Storytellers for Young People.* By Norah Smaridge. New York: Dodd, Mead & Co., 1969.
FamPYP	*Famous Poets for Young People.* By Laura Benet. New York: Dodd, Mead & Co., 1964.

FamSYP	*Famous Storytellers for Young People.* By Laura Benet. New York: Dodd, Mead & Co., 1968.
FanAl	*The Fantasy Almanac.* By Jeff Rovin. New York: E.P. Dutton, 1979.
FarE&A	*The Far East and Australasia.* A survey and directory of Asia and the Pacific. London: Europa Publications, 1978-1981.

	FarE&A 78	1978-1979 edition; 1978. Biographies are found in the ''Who's Who in the Far East and Australasia'' section.
	FarE&A 79	1979-1980 edition; 1979. Biographies are found in the ''Who's Who in the Far East and Australasia'' section.
	FarE&A 79A	1979-1980 edition; 1979. Wade-Giles/Pinyin spellings of Chinese names begin on page 1155.
	FarE&A 80	1980-1981 edition; 1980. Biographies are found in the ''Who's Who in the Far East and Australasia'' section.
	FarE&A 80A	1980-1981 edition; 1980. Wade-Giles/Pinyin spellings of Chinese names begin on page 1174.
	FarE&A 81	1981-1982 edition; 1981. Biographies are found in the ''Who's Who in the Far East and Australasia'' section.

FBI	*The FBI.* A comprehensive reference guide. Edited by Athan G. Theoharis with Tony G. Poveda, Susan Rosenfeld, and Richard Gid Powers. Phoenix, AZ: Oryx Press, 1999. Biographies section begins on page 309.
FemDram	*The Female Dramatist.* Profiles of women playwrights from the Middle Ages to contemporary times. By Elaine T. Partnow with Lesley Anne Hyatt. New York: Facts on File, 1998. ***FemDram A*** Supplemental Index begins on page 231.
FemPA	*The Female Poets of America.* With portraits, biographical notices, and specimens of their writings. Seventh edition, revised. By Thomas Buchanan Read. Philadelphia: E.H. Butler & Co., 1857. Reprint. Detroit: Gale Research, 1978.
FemiCLE	*The Feminist Companion to Literature in English.* Women writers from the Middle Ages to the present. By Virginia Blain, Patricia Clements, and Isobel Grundy. New Haven, CT: Yale University Press, 1990.
FemiWr	*Feminist Writers.* Edited by Pamela Kester-Shelton. Detroit: St. James Press, 1996.
FemmeNo	*Femme Noir.* Bad girls of film. By Karen Burroughs Hannsberry. Jefferson, NC: McFarland & Co., 1998.
FifBJA	*Fifth Book of Junior Authors & Illustrators.* Edited by Sally Holmes Holtze. New York: H.W. Wilson Co., 1983.
FifIDA	*Fifth International Directory of Anthropologists.* Current Anthropology Resource Series, edited by Sol Tax. Chicago: University of Chicago Press, 1975.
FifCWr	*Fifty Caribbean Writers.* A bio-bibliographical critical sourcebook. Edited by Daryl Cumber Dance. New York: Greenwood Press, 1986.

FifSWrA   *Fifty Southern Writers after 1900.* A bio-bibliographical sourcebook. Edited by Joseph M. Flora and Robert Bain. New York: Greenwood Press, 1987.

FifSWrB   *Fifty Southern Writers before 1900.* A bio-bibliographical sourcebook. Edited by Robert Bain and Joseph M. Flora. New York: Greenwood Press, 1987.

FifWWr   *Fifty Western Writers.* A bio-bibliographical sourcebook. Edited by Fred Erisman and Richard W. Etulain. Westport, CT: Greenwood Press, 1982.

FilmAG WE   *Film Actors Guide: Western Europe.* By James Robert Parish. Metuchen, NJ: Scarecrow Press, 1977.

FilmChD   *Film Choreographers and Dance Directors.* An illustrated biographical encyclopedia, with a history and filmographies, 1893 through 1995. By Larry Billman. Jefferson, NC: McFarland & Co., 1997.
                   Biographies of Choreographers and Dance Directors section begins on page 197.

FilmEn   *The Film Encyclopedia.* By Ephraim Katz. New York: Thomas Y. Crowell, 1979.

Film   *Filmarama.* Compiled by John Stewart. Metuchen, NJ: Scarecrow Press, 1975-1977.
                   Film 1   Volume I: *The Formidable Years, 1893-1919.*; 1975.
                   Film 2   Volume II: *The Flaming Years, 1920-1929.*; 1977.

FilmgC   *The Filmgoer's Companion.* Fourth edition. By Leslie Halliwell. New York: Hill & Wang, 1974. Later editions published as *Halliwell's Filmgoer's Companion.*

Focus   *Focus 101.* An illustrated biography of 101 poets of the 60's and 70's. By LaVerne Harrell Clark. Chico, CA: Heidelberg Graphics, 1979.

FolkA 87   *Folk Artists Biographical Index.* First edition. Edited by George H. Meyer. Detroit: Gale Research, 1987.

FootReg   *The Football Register.* St. Louis: The Sporting News, 1981-1985.
                   FootReg 81   1981 edition. Edited by Howard M. Balzar; 1981.
                   FootReg 85   1985 edition. Edited by Howard M. Balzar and Barry Siegel; 1985.

FootReg   *Football Register.* Edited by Howard M. Balzar and Barry Siegel. St. Louis: The Sporting News, 1986-1987.
                   FootReg 86   1986 edition; 1986.
                   FootReg 87   1987 edition; 1987.

ForWC 70   *Foremost Women in Communications.* A biographical reference work on accomplished women in broadcasting, publishing, advertising, public relations, and allied professions. New York: Foremost Americans Publishing Corp., 1970.

ForIl   *Forty Illustrators and How They Work.* By Ernest W. Watson. Cincinnati: Watson-Guptil Publications, 1946. Reprint. Freeport, New York: Books for Libraries Press, 1970.

ForYSC   *Forty Years of Screen Credits, 1929-1969.* Two volumes. Compiled by John T.
                  Weaver. Metuchen, NJ: Scarecrow Press, 1970.
                      Entries begin on page 57.

FourBJA   *Fourth Book of Junior Authors & Illustrators.* Edited by Doris De Montreville and
                  Elizabeth D. Crawford. New York: H.W. Wilson Co., 1978.

FreeExC   *Free Expression and Censorship in America.* An encyclopedia. By Herbert N.
                  Foerstel. Westport, CT: Greenwood Press, 1997.

FreeLaw 96   *Freedom's Lawmakers.* A directory of black officeholders during Reconstruction.
                  Revised edition. By Eric Foner. Baton Rouge, LA: Louisiana State University
                  Press, 1996.
                      FreeLaw 96A   Addenda to the revised edition on pages 239-243.

FrenWW   *French Women Writers.* A bio-bibliographical source book. Edited by Eva Martin
                  Sartori and Dorothy Wynne Zimmerman. New York: Greenwood Press, 1991.

FrSilen   *From Silents to Sound.* A biographical encyclopedia of performers who made the
                  transition to talking pictures. By Roy Liebman. Jefferson, NC: McFarland &
                  Co., 1998.

FrTalk   *From Talking Drums to the Internet.* An encyclopedia of communications
                  technology. By Robert Gardner and Dennis Shortelle. Santa Barbara, CA:
                  ABC-CLIO, 1997.

FrThres   *From the Threshold. (Desde el umbral.)* Contemporary Peruvian fiction in
                  translation. Bilingual edition. Edited by Luis Ramos-Garcia and Luis Fernando
                  Vidal. Austin, TX: Studia Hispanica Editors, 1987.
                      Biographies are found in the "Biographical Notes" section beginning on
                      page 310.

FronSpE   *Frontiers of Space Exploration.* By Roger D. Launis. Greenwood Press Guides to
                  Historic Events of the Twentieth Century. Westport, CT: Greenwood Press,
                  1998.
                      Biographies section begins on page 65.

FunnyW   *Funny Women.* American comediennes, 1860-1985. By Mary Unterbrink. Jefferson,
                  NC: McFarland & Co., 1987.
                      Use the Index to locate biographies.

Funs   *The Funsters.* By James Robert Parish and William T. Leonard. New Rochelle, NY:
                  Arlington House Publishers, 1979.

Future   *The Future.* A guide to information sources. Second edition. Edited by Edward S.
                  Cornish. Washington: World Future Society, 1979.
                      Biographies begin on page 125.

GaEncPs   *Gale Encyclopedia of Psychology.* Edited by Susan Gall. Detroit: Gale Research,
                  1996.

GangFlm   *Gangster Films.* A comprehensive, illustrated reference to people, films, and terms. By Michael L. Stephens. Jefferson, NC: McFarland & Co., 1996.

GayLesB   *Gay & Lesbian Biography.* Detroit: St. James Press, 1997.

GayLL   *Gay & Lesbian Literature.* Detroit: St. James Press, 1994-1998.
          GayLL 1   First edition; 1994.
          GayLL 2   Second edition; 1998.

GayN   *The Gay Nineties in America.* A cultural dictionary of the 1890s. By Robert L. Gale. Westport, CT: Greenwood Press, 1992.

GenMudB   *Generals in Muddy Boots.* A concise encyclopedia of combat commanders. By Dan Cragg. New York: Berkley Books, 1996.

Geog   *Geographers: Biobibliographical Studies.* London: Mansell Publishing, 1977-1986.
          Geog 1   Volume 1. Edited by T.W. Freeman, Marguerita Oughton, and Philippe Pinchemel; 1977.
          Geog 2   Volume 2. Edited by T.W. Freeman and Philippe Pinchemel; 1978.
          Geog 3   Volume 3. Edited by T.W. Freeman and Philippe Pinchemel; 1979.
          Geog 4   Volume 4. Edited by T.W. Freeman and Philippe Pinchemel; 1980.
          Geog 5   Volume 5. Edited by T.W. Freeman; 1981.
          Geog 6   Volume 6. Edited by T.W. Freeman; 1982.
          Geog 7   Volume 7. Edited by T.W. Freeman; 1983.
          Geog 8   Volume 8. Edited by T.W. Freeman; 1984.
          Geog 9   Volume 9. Edited by T.W. Freeman; 1985.
          Geog 10   Volume 10. Edited by T.W. Freeman; 1986.

GloEncH   *A Global Encyclopedia of Historical Writing.* Two volumes. Edited by D. R. Woolf. New York: Garland Publishing, 1998.

GolEC   *Golombek's Encyclopedia of Chess.* Edited by Harry Golombek. New York: Crown Publishers, 1977.

GoodHs   *The Good Housekeeping Woman's Almanac.* Edited by Barbara McDowell and Hana Umlauf. New York: Newspaper Enterprise Association, 1977.
          Use the Index to locate biographies.

GrAmP   *Great American Prints, 1900-1950.* 138 lithographs, etchings and woodcuts. By June Kraeft and Norman Kraeft. New York: Dover Publications, 1984.
          Biographies begin on page 139.

GrBIl   *The Great Bird Illustrators and Their Art, 1730-1930.* By Peyton Skipwith. New York: Hamlyn Publishing Group, 1979.

GrBr   *Great Britons.* Twentieth-century lives. By Harold Oxbury. Oxford: Oxford University Press, 1985.

GrComp	*Great Composers 1300-1900.* A biographical and critical guide. Compiled and edited by David Ewen. New York: H.W. Wilson Co., 1966.
GrEconB	*Great Economists before Keynes.* An introduction to the lives & works of one hundred great economists of the past. By Mark Blaug. Atlantic Highlands, NJ: Humanities Press International, 1986.
GrEconS	*Great Economists since Keynes.* An introduction to the lives & works of one hundred modern economists. By Mark Blaug. Totowa, NJ: Barnes & Noble Books, 1985.
GrFLW	*Great Foreign Language Writers.* Edited by James Vinson and Daniel Kirkpatrick. Great Writers Series. New York: St. Martin's Press, 1984.
GrLGrT	*Great Leaders, Great Tyrants?* Contemporary views of world rulers who made history. Edited by Arnold Blumberg. Westport, CT: Greenwood Press, 1995.
GrLiveH	*Great Lives from History.* Five volumes. Edited by Frank N. Magill. American Women Series. Pasadena, CA: Salem Press, 1995.
GrMetD	*The Great Metal Discography.* Edinburgh, Scotland: Canongate Books Ltd., 1998.
GrMovC	*Great Movie Comedians.* From Charlie Chaplin to Woody Allen. By Leonard Maltin. New York: Crown Publishers, 1978. Use the Table of Contents to locate biographies.
GrStDi	*The Great Stage Directors.* 100 distinguished careers of the theater. By Samuel L. Leiter. New York: Facts on File, 1994.
GrWomMW	*Great Women Mystery Writers.* Classic to contemporary. Edited by Kathleen Gregory Klein. Westport, CT: Greenwood Press, 1994.
GrWomW	*Great Women Writers.* The lives and works of 135 of the world's most important writers, from antiquity to the present. Edited by Frank N. Magill. New York: Henry Holt & Co., 1994.

GrWrEL	*Great Writers of the English Language.* Edited by James Vinson. New York: St. Martin's Press, 1979.
	    GrWrEL DR *Dramatists.*
	    GrWrEL N *Novelists and prose writers.*
	    GrWrEL P *Poets.*

Grk&L	*Greek and Latin Authors, 800 B.C.-A.D. 1000.* By Michael Grant. Wilson Authors Series. New York: H.W. Wilson Co., 1980.
GuAfrCi	*Guide to African Cinema.* By Sharon A. Russell. Reference Guides to the World's Cinema. Westport, CT: Greenwood Press, 1998.
GuBlues	*A Guide to the Blues.* History, who's who, research sources. By Austin Sonnier, Jr. Westport, CT: Greenwood Press, 1994. Biographies begin on page 93.

GuCinSp   *Guide to the Cinema of Spain.* By Marvin D'Lugo. Reference Guides to the World's Cinema. Westport, CT: Greenwood Press, 1997.
>   *GuCinSp A*   Directors, Producers, Cinematographers, and Critics section begins on page 115.
>   *GuCinSp B*   Actors and Actresses section begins on page 209.

GuFrLit   *Guide to French Literature.* By Anthony Levi. Detroit: St. James Press, 1992-1994.
>   *GuFrLit 1*   1789 to the present; 1992.
>   *GuFrLit 2*   Beginnings to 1789; 1994.

GuPsyc   *A Guide to Psychologists and Their Concepts.* By Vernon J. Nordby and Calvin S. Hall. San Francisco: W.H. Freeman & Co., 1974.

HalFC 80   *Halliwell's Filmgoer's Companion.* Seventh edition. By Leslie Halliwell. New York: Granada Publishing, 1980. Earlier editions published as *The Filmgoer's Companion.*

HalFC   *Halliwell's Filmgoer's Companion.* By Leslie Halliwell. New York: Charles Scribner's Sons, 1984-1988.Earlier editions published as *The Filmgoer's Companion.*
>   *HalFC 84*   Eighth edition; 1984.
>   *HalFC 88*   Ninth edition; 1988.

HanAmWH   *Handbook of American Women's History.* Edited by Angela Howard Zophy. Garland Reference Library of the Humanities, vol. 696. New York: Garland Publishing, 1990.

HanRL   *Handbook of Russian Literature.* Edited by Victor Terras. New Haven, CT: Yale University Press, 1985.

HarlReB   *Harlem Renaissance and Beyond.* Literary biographies of 100 black women writers, 1900-1945. By Lorraine Elena Roses and Ruth Elizabeth Randolph. Boston: G. K. Hall & Co., 1990.

HarEnCM 87   *The Harmony Illustrated Encyclopedia of Country Music.* By Fred Dellar, Allan Cackett, and Roy Thompson. New York: Harmony Books, 1987.
>   *HarEnCM 87A*   Appendix begins on page 197.

HarEnR 86   *Harmony Illustrated Encyclopedia of Rock.* Seventh edition. New York: Harmony Books, 1986.

HarEnMi   *The Harper Encyclopedia of Military Biography.* First edition. By Trevor N. Dupuy, Curt Johnson, and David L. Bongard. New York: HarperCollins Publishers, 1992.

HarEnUS   *Harper's Encyclopaedia of United States History: From 458 A.D. to 1915.* New edition entirely revised and enlarged. 10 volumes. By Benson John Lossing. New York: Harper & Brothers Publishers, 1915. Reprint. Detroit: Gale Research, 1974.

HealPre   *The Health of the Presidents.* The 41 United States presidents through 1993 from a physician's point of view. By John R. Bumgarner. Jefferson, NC: McFarland & Co., 1994.
    Use Table of Contents to locate biographies.

HerW   *Her Way.* A guide to biographies of women for young people. Chicago: American Library Association, 1976-1984.
        HerW   First edition. By Mary-Ellen Kulkin; 1976.
        HerW 84   Second edition. By Mary-Ellen Siegel; 1984.

HeroCon   *Heroes of Conscience.* A biographical dictionary. By Kathlyn Gay and Martin K. Gay. Santa Barbara, CA: ABC-CLIO, 1996.

HispLC   *Hispanic Literature Criticism.* Two volumes. Detroit: Gale Research, 1994.

HispLC SUP   *Hispanic Literature Criticism.* Supplement. Detroit: Gale Group, 1999.

HispWr   *Hispanic Writers.* A selection of sketches from *Contemporary Authors.* Detroit: Gale Research, 1991.

HispWr 2   *Hispanic Writers.* A selection of sketches from *Contemporary Authors.* Detroit: Gale Group, 1999.

HispAmA   *The Hispanic-American Almanac.* A reference work on Hispanics in the United States. By Nicolas Kanellos. Detroit: Gale Research, 1993.
    Use the Index to locate biographies.

HisWorL   *Historic World Leaders.* Five volumes. Edited by Anne Commire. Detroit: Gale Research, 1994.
    Use the "Biographies in *Historic World Leaders*" Index at the back of Volume 5 to locate biographies.

HisDcAR   *Historical Dictionary of American Radio.* Edited by Donald G. Godfrey and Frederic A. Leigh. Westport, CT: Greenwood Press, 1998.

HisDcAR   *Historical Dictionary of the American Revolution.* By Terry M. Mays. Historical Dictionaries of War, Revolution, and Civil Unrest, no. 7. Lanham, MD: Scarecrow Press, 1999.

HisDcBo   *Historical Dictionary of Bosnia and Herzegovina.* By Ante Cuvalo. European Historical Dictionaries, no. 25. Lanham, MD: Scarecrow Press, 1997.

HisDBrE   *Historical Dictionary of the British Empire.* Two volumes. Edited by James S. Olson and Robert Shadle. Westport, CT: Greenwood Press, 1996.

HisDCRM   *Historical Dictionary of the Civil Rights Movement.* By Ralph E. Luker. Historical Dictionaries of Religions, Philosophies, and Movements, No. 11. Lanham, MD: Scarecrow Press, 1997.

HisDcDP   *Historical Dictionary of Data Processing: Biographies.* By James W. Cortada. New York: Greenwood Press, 1987.

HisDcHu	*Historical Dictionary of Human Rights and Humanitarian Organizations.* By Robert F. Gorman and Edward S. Mihalkanin. Historical Dictionaries of International Organizations, no. 12. Lanham, MD: Scarecrow Press, 1997.
HisDcIr	*Historical Dictionary of Ireland.* By Colin Thomas and Avril Thomas. European Historical Dictionaries, no. 20. Lanham, MD: Scarecrow Press, 1997.
HisDcKW	*Historical Dictionary of the Korean War.* Edited by James I. Matray. New York: Greenwood Press, 1991.
HisDcPG	*Historical Dictionary of the Persian Gulf War 1990-1991.* By Clayton R. Newell. Historical Dictionaries of War, Revolution, and Civil Unrest, no. 9. Lanham, MD: Scarecrow Press, 1998.
HisDcPo	*Historical Dictionary of Poland, 1945-1996.* By Piotr Wrobel. Westport, CT: Greenwood Press, 1998. The entries in this source are arranged in the order of the Polish alphabet, whereas in *BGMI* the entries are arranged ignoring the diacritical markings. The user should consider this when looking up entries. See page ix of this source for a complete explanation.
HisDcSc	*Historical Dictionary of School Segregation and Desegregation.* The American experience. By Jeffrey A. Raffel. Westport, CT: Greenwood Press, 1998.
HisDcSE	*Historical Dictionary of the Spanish Empire, 1402-1975.* Edited by James S. Olson et al. New York: Greenwood Press, 1992.
HisDStE	*Historical Dictionary of Stuart England, 1603-1689.* Edited by Ronald H. Fritze and William B. Robison. Westport, CT: Greenwood Press, 1996.
HisDcTa	*Historical Dictionary of Taoism.* By Julian F. Pas. Historical Dictionaries of Religions, Philosophies, and Movements, no. 18. Lanham, MD: Scarecrow Press, 1998.
HisDcT	*Historical Dictionary of Terrorism.* By Sean Anderson and Stephen Sloan. Historical Dictionaries of Religions, Philosophies, and Movements, no. 4. Metuchen, NJ: Scarecrow Press, 1995.
HisDcWJ	*Historical Dictionary of War Journalism.* By Mitchel P. Roth. Westport, CT: Greenwood Press, 1997.
HisEAAC	*An Historical Encyclopedia of the Arab-Israeli Conflict.* Edited by Bernard Reich. Westport, CT: Greenwood Press, 1996.
HisEWW	*The Historical Encyclopedia of World War II.* Edited by Marcel Baudot et al. New York: Facts on File, 1980. Originally published as *Encyclopedie de la Guerre 1939-1945.* Paris: Editions Casterman, 1977.
HisPhAn	*History of Physical Anthropology.* An encyclopedia. Two volumes. Edited by Frank Spencer. New York: Garland Publishing, 1997.

HocEn   *The Hockey Encyclopedia.* The Complete Record of Professional Ice Hockey. By
               Stan Fischler and Shirley Walter Fischler. New York: Macmillan Publishing
               Co., 1983.

HocReg   *The Hockey Register.* Edited by Latty Wigge. St. Louis: The Sporting News, 1981-
               1987.
               HocReg 81   1981-82 edition; 1981.
               HocReg 85   1985-86 edition; 1985.
               HocReg 86   1986-87 edition; 1986.
               HocReg 87   1987-88 edition; 1987.

HolBB   *Hollywood Baby Boomers.* By James Robert Parish and Don Stanke. New York:
               Garland Publishing, 1992.

HolCA   *Hollywood Character Actors.* By James Robert Parish. Westport, CT: Arlington
               House Publishers, 1978.

HolP   *Hollywood Players.* New Rochelle, NY: Arlington House Publishers, 1976.
               HolP 30   *The Thirties.* By James Robert Parish and William T.
                                    Leonard.
               HolP 40   *The Forties.* By James Robert Parish and Lennard
                                    DeCarl.

HolStP   *Hollywood Stunt Performers.* A dictionary and filmography of over 600 men and
               women, 1922-1996. By Gene Scott Freese. Jefferson, NC: McFarland & Co.,
               1998.

HorFD   *Horror Film Directors, 1931-1990.* By Dennis Fischer. Jefferson, NC: McFarland &
               Co., 1991.
               Use the Table of Contents to locate entries.

HsB&A   *The House of Beadle and Adams and Its Dime and Nickel Novels.* The Story of a
               Vanished Literature. By Albert Johannsen. Norman, OK: University of
               Oklahoma Press, 1950-1962.
               HsB&A   Volumes I-II; 1950. Biographies are found in volume II.
               HsB&A SUP   Volume III, Supplement, Addenda, Corrigenda; 1962.

HumSex   *Human Sexuality.* An encyclopedia. Edited by Vern L. Bullough and Bonnie
               Bullough. Garland Reference Library of Social Science, vol. 685. New York:
               Garland Publishing, 1994.

ICPEnP   *ICP (International Center of Photography) Encyclopedia of Photography.* New
               York: Crown Publishers, 1984.
               ICPEnP A   ''Appendix 1'' begins on page 576.

IdentIs   *Identities and Issues in Literature.* Three volumes. Edited by David Peck. Pasadena,
               CA: Salem Press, 1997.

IlBBlP   *Illustrated Bio-Bibliography of Black Photographers, 1940-1988.* By Deborah
               Willis-Thomas. Garland Reference Library of the Humanities, vol. 760. New
               York: Garland Publishing, 1989.

IlBEAAW	*The Illustrated Biographical Encyclopedia of Artists of the American West.* By Peggy Samuels and Harold Samuels. Garden City, NY: Doubleday & Co., 1976.
IlDcG	*Illustrated Dictionary of Glass.* 2,442 entries, including definitions of wares, materials, processes, forms, and decorative styles, and entries on principal glass-makers, decorators, and designers, from antiquity to the present. By Harold Newman. London: Thames & Hudson, 1977.
IlEncBM 82	*Illustrated Encyclopedia of Black Music.* Edited by Ray Bonds. New York: Harmony Books, 1982.
IlEncCM	*The Illustrated Encyclopedia of Country Music.* By Fred Dellar, Roy Thompson, and Douglas B. Green. New York: Harmony Books, 1977.
IlEncJ	*The Illustrated Encyclopedia of Jazz.* By Brian Case and Stan Britt. New York: Harmony Books, 1978.
IlEncMy	*Illustrated Encyclopaedia of Mysticism and the Mystery Religions.* By John Ferguson. London: Thames & Hudson, 1976.
IlEncRk	*The Illustrated Encyclopedia of Rock.* Revised edition. Compiled by Nick Logan and Bob Woffinden. New York: Harmony Books, 1977.

IlWWBF	*The Illustrated Who's Who in British Films.* By Denis Gifford. London: Anchor Press, 1978.	
	IlWWBF A	The ''Biographical Bibliography'' section begins on page 317.

IlWWHD	*The Illustrated Who's Who of Hollywood Directors.* Volume 1: *The Sound Era.* By Michael Barson. New York: Farrar, Straus & Giroux, 1995.	
	IlWWHD 1	Biographies are located in the ''Directors'' section, beginning on page 1.
	IlWWHD 1A	Biographies are located in the ''Short Subjects'' section, beginning on page 479.

IlrAm 1880	*The Illustrator in America, 1880-1980.* A century of illustration. By Walt Reed and Roger Reed. New York: Madison Square Press, 1984. Distributed by Robert Silver Associates, New York. Use the Index to locate biographies.

IlrAm	*The Illustrator in America, 1900-1960's.* Compiled and edited by Walt Reed. New York: Reinhold Publishing Corp., 1966.	
	IlrAm A	''The Decade: 1900-1910'' begins on page 13.
	IlrAm B	''The Decade: 1910-1920'' begins on page 43.
	IlrAm C	''The Decade: 1920-1930'' begins on page 77.
	IlrAm D	''The Decade: 1930-1940'' begins on page 113.
	IlrAm E	''The Decade: 1940-1950'' begins on page 167.
	IlrAm F	''The Decade: 1950-1960'' begins on page 211.
	IlrAm G	''The Decade: 1960's'' begins on page 239.

IlsBYP   *Illustrators of Books for Young People.* Second edition. By Martha E. Ward and Dorothy A. Marquardt. Metuchen, NJ: Scarecrow Press, 1975.

IlsCB   *Illustrators of Children's Books.* Boston: Horn Book, 1947-1978.

	IlsCB 1744	*1744-1945.* Compiled by Bertha E. Mahony, Louise Payson Latimer, and Beulah Folmsbee; 1947. Biographies begin on page 267.
	IlsCB 1946	*1946-1956.* Compiled by Ruth Hill Viguers, Marcia Dalphin, and Bertha Mahony Miller; 1958. Biographies begin on page 62.
	IlsCB 1957	*1957-1966.* Compiled by Lee Kingman, Joanna Foster, and Ruth Giles Lontoft; 1968. Biographies begin on page 70.
	IlsCB 1967	*1967-1976.* Compiled by Lee Kingman, Grace Allen Hogarth, and Harriet Quimby; 1978. Biographies begin on page 93.

InB&W   *In Black and White.* A guide to magazine articles, newspaper articles, and books concerning Black individuals and groups. Edited by Mary Mace Spradling. Detroit: Gale Research, 1980-1985.

	InB&W 80	Third edition. Two volumes; 1980.
	InB&W 85	Third edition, Supplement; 1985.
	InB&W 85A	Third edition, Supplement; 1985. "Performing Groups" section begins on page 440.
	InB&W 85B	Third edition, Supplement; 1985. "Prominent Duos" section begins on page 451.

InSci   *Index to Scientists of the World from Ancient to Modern Times.* Biographies and portraits. By Norma Olin Ireland. Boston: F.W. Faxon Co., 1962.

InWom   *Index to Women of the World from Ancient to Modern Times.* Biographies and portraits. By Norma Olin Ireland. Westwood, MA: F.W. Faxon Co., 1970.

InWom SUP   *Index to Women of the World from Ancient to Modern Times: A Supplement.* By Norma Olin Ireland. Metuchen, NJ: Scarecrow Press, 1988.

IndAu 1816   *Indiana Authors and Their Books, 1816-1916.* Biographical sketches of authors who published during the first century of Indiana statehood with lists of their books. Compiled by R.E. Banta. Crawfordsville, IN: Wabash College, 1949.

IndAu 1917   *Indiana Authors and Their Books, 1917-1966.* A continuation of *Indiana Authors and Their Books, 1816-1916,* and containing additional names from the earlier period. Compiled by Donald E. Thompson. Crawfordsville, IN: Wabash College, 1974.

IndAu 1967   *Indiana Authors and Their Books, 1967-1980.* Biographical sketches of authors who published during the first century of Indiana statehood with lists of their books. Compiled by Donald E. Thompson. Crawfordsville, IN: Wabash College, 1981.

IndCTCL   *The Indiana Companion to Traditional Chinese Literature.* Edited and compiled by William H. Nienhauser, Jr. Bloomington, IN: Indiana University Press, 1986. Entries begin on page 195.

InnAst   *Innovations in Astronomy.* Innovations in Science Series. Santa Barbara, CA: ABC-CLIO Inc., 1999.
        The ''Biographical Sketches'' section begins on page 81.

InnESci   *Innovations in Earth Sciences.* Innovations in Science Series. Santa Barbara, CA: ABC-CLIO Inc., 1999.
        The ''Biographical Sketches'' section begins on page 57.

IntAu&W   *The International Authors and Writers Who's Who.* Cambridge: International Biographical Centre, 1976-1993.

IntAu&W 76	Seventh edition. Edited by Ernest Kay; 1976.
IntAu&W 76A	Seventh edition. Edited by Ernest Kay; 1976. Addendum begins on page 641.
IntAu&W 76X	Seventh edition. Edited by Ernest Kay; 1976. ''Pseudonyms of Included Authors'' section begins on page 645.
IntAu&W 77	Eighth edition. Edited by Adrian Gaster; 1977.
IntAu&W 77X	Eighth edition. Edited by Adrian Gaster; 1977. ''Pseudonyms of Included Authors'' section begins on page 1131.
IntAu&W 82	Ninth edition. Edited by Adrian Gaster; 1982.
IntAu&W 82X	Ninth edition. Edited by Adrian Gaster; 1982. ''Pseudonyms of Included Authors'' section begins on page 719.
IntAu&W 86	10th edition. Edited by Ernest Kay; 1986.
IntAu&W 86X	10th edition. Edited by Ernest Kay; 1986. ''Pseudonyms of Authors and Writers'' section begins on page 796.
IntAu&W 89	11th edition. Edited by Ernest Kay; 1989.
IntAu&W 91	12th edition. Edited by Ernest Kay; 1991.
IntAu&W 91X	12th edition. Edited by Ernest Kay; 1991. ''Pseudonyms of Authors'' section begins on page 940.
IntAu&W 93	13th edition, 1993-94. Edited by Ernest Kay; 1993.

IntDcAn   *International Dictionary of Anthropologists.* Edited by Christopher Winters. Garland Reference Library of the Social Sciences, vol. 638. New York: Garland Publishing, 1991.

IntDcAr   *International Dictionary of Architects and Architecture.* Volume 1: *Architects.* Edited by Randall J. Van Vynckt. Detroit: St. James Press, 1993.

IntDcAA 90   *International Dictionary of Art and Artists: Artists.* Edited by James Vinson. Chicago: St. James Press, 1990.

IntDcB   *International Dictionary of Ballet.* Two volumes. Edited by Martha Bremser. Detroit: St. James Press, 1993.

IntDcF   *The International Dictionary of Films and Filmmakers.* Detroit: St. James Press, 1984-1993.

IntDcF 1-2	First edition. Volume 2: *Directors/Filmmakers.* Edited by Christopher Lyon; 1984.
IntDcF 1-3	First edition. Volume 3: *Actors and Actresses.* Edited by James Vinson; 1986.

	IntDcF 1-4	First edition. Volume 4: *Writers and Production Artists.* Edited by James Vinson; 1987.
	IntDcF 2-2	Second edition. Volume 2: *Directors.* Edited by Nicholas Thomas; 1991.
	IntDcF 2-3	Second edition. Volume 3: *Actors and Actresses.* Edited by Nicholas Thomas; 1992.
	IntDcF 2-4	Second edition. Volume 4: *Writers and Production Artists.* Edited by Samantha Cook; 1993.

IntDcMo   *International Dictionary of Modern Dance.* Edited by Taryn Benbow-Pfalzgraf. Detroit: St. James Press, 1998.

IntDcOp   *International Dictionary of Opera.* Two volumes. Edited by C. Steven LaRue. Detroit: St. James Press, 1993.

IntDcT   *International Dictionary of Theatre.* Detroit: St. James Press, 1994-1996.

	IntDcT 2	Volume 2:*Playwrights.* Edited by Mark Hawkins-Dady; 1994.
	IntDcT 3	Volume 3: *Actors, Directors and Designers.* Edited by David Pickering; 1996.

IntDcWB   *The International Dictionary of Women's Biography.* Compiled and edited by Jennifer S. Uglow. New York: Continuum Publishing Co., 1982. Later edition published as *The Continuum Dictionary of Women's Biography.*

IntEnSS 79   *International Encyclopedia of the Social Sciences.* Volume 18: Biographical Supplement. Edited by David L. Sills. New York: Macmillan Publishing Co., 1979.

IntLitE   *International Literature in English.* Essays on the major writers. Edited by Robert L. Ross. New York: Garland Publishing, 1991.
Use the Index to locate biographies.

IntMed 80   *International Medical Who's Who.* A biographical guide in medical research. First edition. Two volumes. Harlow, United Kingdom: Longman Group, 1980.

IntMPA   *International Motion Picture Almanac.* New York: Quigley Publishing Co., 1975-1996.

	IntMPA 75	1975 edition; 1975.
	IntMPA 76	1976 edition; 1976.
	IntMPA 77	1977 edition; 1977.
	IntMPA 77	1977 edition; 1977.
	IntMPA 78	1978 edition; 1978.
	IntMPA 79	1979 edition; 1979.
	IntMPA 80	1980 edition; 1980.
	IntMPA 81	1981 edition; 1981.
	IntMPA 82	1982 edition; 1982.
	IntMPA 84	1984 edition; 1984.
	IntMPA 86	1986 edition; 1986.
	IntMPA 88	1988 edition; 1988.
	IntMPA 92	1992 edition; 1992.
	IntMPA 94	1994 edition; 1994.
	IntMPA 94N	1994 edition; 1994. Obituaries section is on page 386.
	IntMPA 96	1996 edition; 1996.

IntWW   *The International Who's Who.* London: Europa Publications, 1974-1999.

      IntWW 74   38th edition, 1974-1975; 1974.

      IntWW 75   39th edition, 1975-1976; 1975.

      IntWW 75N   39th edition, 1975-1976; 1975. The Obituary section is located at the front of the volume.

      IntWW 76   40th edition, 1976-1977; 1976.

      IntWW 76N   40th edition, 1976-1977; 1976. The Obituary section is located at the front of the volume.

      IntWW 77   41st edition, 1977-1978; 1977.

      IntWW 77N   41st edition, 1977-1978; 1977. The Obituary section is located at the front of the volume.

      IntWW 78   42nd edition, 1978-1979; 1978.

      IntWW 78N   42nd edition, 1978-1979; 1978. The Obituary section is located at the front of the volume.

      IntWW 79   43rd edition, 1979-1980; 1979.

      IntWW 79N   43rd edition, 1979-1980; 1979. The Obituary section is located at the front of the volume.

      IntWW 80   44th edition, 1980-1981; 1980.

      IntWW 81   45th edition, 1981-1982; 1981.

      IntWW 81N   45th edition, 1981-1982; 1981. The Obituary section is located at the front of the volume.

      IntWW 82   46th edition, 1982-1983; 1982.

      IntWW 82N   46th edition, 1982-1983; 1982. The Obituary section is located at the front of the volume.

      IntWW 83   47th edition, 1983-1984; 1983.

      IntWW 83N   47th edition, 1983-1984; 1983. The Obituary section is located at the front of the volume.

      IntWW 89   53rd edition, 1989-1990; 1989.

      IntWW 89N   53rd edition, 1989-1990; 1989. The Obituary section is located at the front of the volume.

      IntWW 91   55th edition, 1991-1992; 1991.

      IntWW 91N   55th edition, 1991-1992; 1991. The Obituary section is located at the front of the volume.

      IntWW 93   57th edition, 1993-1994; 1993.

      IntWW 93N   57th edition, 1993-1994; 1993. The obituary section is located at the front of the volume.

      IntWW 97   61st edition, 1997-1998; 1997.

      IntWW 97N   61st edition, 1997-1998; 1997. Obituary section is located at the front of the volume.

      IntWW 98   62nd edition, 1998-99; 1998.

      IntWW 98N   62nd edition, 1998-99; 1998. Obituary section is located at the front of the volume.

      IntWW 2000   63rd edition, 2000; 1999. 100 Entries from Previous Editions of *The International Who's Who* section begins on page vii.

      IntWW 2000   63rd edition, 2000; 1999.

      IntWW 2000   63rd edition, 2000; 1999. Obituary section is located at the front of the volume.

IntWWE   *International Who's Who in Energy and Nuclear Sciences.* Harlow, United Kingdom: Longman Group, 1983.

IntWWM	*International Who's Who in Music and Musicians' Directory.* Cambridge: International Who's Who in Music, 1977-1990.Distributed by Taylor and Francis International Publication Services, Bristol, Pa.

    IntWWM 77   Eighth edition; 1977.
    IntWWM 80   Ninth edition. Edited by Adrian Gaster; 1980.
    IntWWM 85   10th edition; 1984.
    IntWWM 90   12th edition, 1990-1991; 1990.

IntWWP   *International Who's Who in Poetry.* Edited by Ernest Kay. Cambridge: International Biographical Centre, 1977-1982.1982 edition is combined with *The International Authors and Writers Who's Who.*

    IntWWP 77   Fifth edition; 1977.
    IntWWP 77A   Fifth edition; 1977. Addendum begins on page 470.
    IntWWP 77X   Fifth edition; 1977. "Pseudonyms and Pen Names of Included Poets" section begins on page 702.
    IntWWP 82   Sixth edition; 1982. Biographies begin on page 759.
    IntWWP 82X   Sixth edition; 1982. "Pseudonyms of Included Poets" section begins on page 1035.

IntWWW 2   *International Who's Who of Women.* Second edition. London: Europa Publications, 1997.

IntYB   *The International Year Book and Statesmen's Who's Who.* West Sussex, England: Kelly's Directories, 1978-1981.

    IntYB 78   1978 edition; 1978.
    IntYB 79   1979 edition; 1979.
    IntYB 80   1980 edition; 1980.
    IntYB 81   1981 edition; 1981.
    Biographies are found in Part 3.

IntYB   *The International Yearbook and Statesmen's Who's Who.* 1982 edition. West Sussex, England: Thomas Skinner Directories, 1982.

    IntYB 82   Biographies are found in Part 3.
    IntYB 82A   "Late Information" section begins on page 749 of Part 3.

IntvTCA 2   *Interviews and Conversations with 20th-Century Authors Writing in English.* An index. Series II. By Stan A. Vrana. Metuchen, NJ: Scarecrow Press, 1986.

IntvLAW   *Interviews with Latin American Writers.* By Marie-Lise Gazarian Gautier. Elmwood Park, IL: Dalkey Archive Press, 1989.

IntvSpW   *Interviews with Spanish Writers.* By Marie-Lise Gazarian Gautier. Elmwood Park, IL: Dalkey Archive Press, 1991.

IntvWPC   *Interviews with Writers of the Post-Colonial World.* Edited by Feroza Jussawalla and Reed Way Dasenbrock. Jackson, MS: University Press of Mississippi, 1992. Use the Table of Contents to locate biographies.

IriPla   *Irish Playwrights, 1880-1995.* A research and production sourcebook. Edited by Bernice Schrank and William W. Demastes. Westport, CT: Greenwood Press, 1997.

ItaFilm   *Italian Film.* A who's who. By John Stewart. Jefferson, NC: McFarland & Co., 1994.

JapFilm   *The Japanese Filmography.* A complete reference to 209 filmmakers and the over
                   1250 films released in the United States, 1900 through 1994. By Stuart
                   Galbraith IV. Jefferson, NC: McFarland & Co., 1996.

JazzP   *Jazz Profiles.* The spirit of the nineties. By Reginald Carver and Lenny Bernstein.
                   New York: Billboard Books, 1998.
                       Use the Index to locate biographies.

JeHun   *The Jewish 100.* A ranking of the most influential Jews of all time. By Michael
                   Shapiro. New York: Carol Publishing Group, 1994.
                       Use the Index to locate biographies.

JeAmFiW   *Jewish American Fiction Writers.* An annotated bibliography. By Gloria L. Cronin,
                   Blaine H. Hall, and Connie Lamb. Garland Reference Library of the
                   Humanities, vol. 972. New York: Garland Publishing, 1991.

JeAmWW   *Jewish American Women Writers.* A bio-bibliographical and critical sourcebook.
                   Edited by Ann R. Shapiro. Westport, CT: Greenwood Press, 1994.

JeAmHC   *Jewish-American History and Culture.* An encyclopedia. Edited by Jack Fischel and
                   Sanford Pinkser. Garland Reference Library of the Social Sciences, vol. 429.
                   New York: Garland Publishing, 1992.

JoeFr   *Joe Franklin's Encyclopedia of Comedians.* Secaucus, NJ: Citadel Press, 1979.

JohnWSW   *John Willis' Screen World.* 1981, Volume 32. New York: Crown Publishers, Inc.,
                   1981.

JohnWTW 38   *John Willis' Theatre World.* 1981-82, Volume 38. New York: Crown Publishers,
                   Inc., 1983.

JouAdvM   *Journalistic Advocates and Muckrakers.* Three centuries of crusading writers. By
                   Edd Applegate. Jefferson, NC: McFarland & Co., 1997.

JrnUS   *Journalists of the United States.* Biographical sketches of print and broadcast news
                   shapers from the late 17th century to the present. By Robert B. Downs and Jane
                   B. Downs. Jefferson, NC: McFarland & Co., 1991.

JBA   *The Junior Book of Authors.* Edited by Stanley J. Kunitz and Howard Haycraft.
                   Wilson Authors Series. New York: H.W. Wilson Co., 1934-1951.
                       JBA 34   First edition; 1934.
                       JBA 51   Second edition, revised; 1951.

LadLa 86   *The Lady Laureates.* Women who have won the Nobel Prize. Second edition. By
                   Olga S. Opfell. Metuchen, NJ: Scarecrow Press, 1986.
                       Use the Index to locate biographies.

LarDcSc   *Larousse Dictionary of Scientists.* Edited by Hazel Muir. New York: Larousse, 1994.

LatAmCC   *Latin American Classical Composers.* A biographical dictionary. Compiled and edited by Miguel Ficher, Martha Furman Schleifer, and John M. Furman. Lanham, MD: Scarecrow Press, 1996.

LatAmLi   *Latin American Lives.* Selected Biographies from the five-volume *Encyclopedia of Latin American History and Culture.* Macmillan Compendium. New York: Macmillan Library Reference USA, 1996-1998.

LatAmWr   *Latin American Writers.* Three volumes. Edited by Carlos A. Sole and Maria Isabel Abreu. New York: Charles Scribner's Sons, 1989.
             Use the Index, which begins on page 1459 of Volume 3, to locate biographies.

Law&B   *Law & Business Directory of Corporate Counsel.* New York: Harcourt Brace Jovanovich, 1980-1984.
             Law&B 80   1980-1981 edition; 1980.
             Law&B 84   1984-1985 edition; 1984.
             Use the "Individual Name Index" to locate listings.

Law&B   *Law & Business Directory of Corporate Counsel.* Englewood Cliffs, NJ: Prentice Hall, 1989-1992.
             Law&B 89A   1989-1990 edition. Volume 1; 1989.
             Law&B 89B   1989-1990 edition. Volume 2; 1989.
             Law&B 92   1992-1993 edition; 1992.
             Use the "Individual Name Index" to locate biographies.

LNinSix   *Leaders from the 1960's.* A biographical sourcebook of American activism. Edited by David DeLeon. Westport, CT: Greenwood Press, 1994.
             Use the Index to locate biographies.

LAmCW   *Leaders of the American Civil War.* A biographical and historiographical dictionary. Edited by Charles F. Ritter and Jon L. Wakelyn. Westport, CT: Greenwood Press, 1998.

LEduc 74   *Leaders in Education.* Fifth edition. New York: R.R. Bowker Co., 1974.

LElec   *Leaders in Electronics.* New York: McGraw-Hill Book Co., 1979. Title page reads *McGraw-Hill's Leaders in Electronics.*

LeadWes   *Leading the West.* One hundred contemporary painters and sculptors. By Donald J. Hagerty. Flagstaff, AZ: Northland Publishing, 1997.
             Entries begin on page 191.

LegTOT   *Legends in Their Own Time.* New York: Prentice Hall General Reference, 1994.

LesBEnT   *Les Brown's Encyclopedia of Television.* By Les Brown. New York: New York Zoetrope, 1982. Earlier edition published as *The New York Times Encyclopedia of Television.*

LesBEnT 92 *Les Brown's Encyclopedia of Television.* Third edition. By Les Brown. Detroit: Gale Research, 1992.

LexLab   *The Lexicon of Labor.* More than 500 key terms, biographical sketches, and historical insights concerning labor in America. By R. Emmett Murray. New York: The New Press, 1998.

LibW   *Liberty's Women.* Edited by Robert McHenry. Springfield, MA: G. & C. Merriam Co., 1980.

LibrCom   *The Librarian's Companion.* A handbook of thousands of facts and figures on libraries/librarians, books/newspapers, publishers/booksellers. Second edition. By Vladimir F. Wertsman. Westport, CT: Greenwood Press, 1996.
Biographies begin on page 101.

LinLib   *The Lincoln Library of Language Arts.* Third edition. Two volumes. Columbus, OH: Frontier Press Co., 1978.

LinLib L	Biographies begin on page 345 of Volume 1 and are continued in Volume 2.
LinLib LP	''Pen Names'' section begins on page 331.

LinLib S   *The Lincoln Library of Social Studies.* Eighth edition. Three volumes. Columbus, OH: Frontier Press Co., 1978.
Biographies begin on page 865 of Volume 3.

LiExTwC   *Literary Exile in the Twentieth Century.* An analysis and biographical dictionary. Edited by Martin Tucker. New York: Greenwood Press, 1991.
Biographies begin on page 47.

LiHiK   *A Literary History of Kentucky.* By William S. Ward. Knoxville, TN: University of Tennessee Press, 1988.
Use the Index to locate biographies.

LiJour   *Literary Journalism.* A biographical dictionary of writers and editors. By Edd Applegate. Westport, CT: Greenwood Press, 1996.

LitC   *Literature Criticism from 1400 to 1800.* Critical discussion of the works of fifteenth-, sixteenth-, seventeenth-, and eighteenth-century novelists, poets, playwrights, philosophers, and other creative writers. Detroit: Gale Research, 1984-1999.

LitC 1	Volume 1; 1984.
LitC 2	Volume 2; 1985.
LitC 3	Volume 3; 1986.
LitC 4	Volume 4; 1986.
LitC 5	Volume 5; 1987.
LitC 6	Volume 6; 1987.
LitC 7	Volume 7; 1988.
LitC 8	Volume 8; 1988.
LitC 9	Volume 9; 1989.
LitC 10	Volume 10; 1989.
LitC 11	Volume 11; 1990.
LitC 12	Volume 12; 1990.
LitC 13	Volume 13; 1990.
LitC 14	Volume 14; 1991.
LitC 15	Volume 15; 1991.
LitC 16	Volume 16; 1991.
LitC 17	Volume 17; 1992.

LitC 18	Volume 18; 1992.
LitC 19	Volume 19; 1992.
LitC 20	Volume 20; 1993.
LitC 21	Volume 21; 1993.
LitC 22	Volume 22; 1993.
LitC 23	Volume 23; 1994.
LitC 24	Volume 24; 1994.
LitC 25	Volume 25; 1994.
LitC 26	Volume 26; 1995.
LitC 27	Volume 27; 1995.
LitC 28	Volume 28; 1995.
LitC 29	Volume 29; 1996.
LitC 30	Volume 30; 1996.
LitC 31	Volume 31; 1996.
LitC 32	Volume 32; 1996.
LitC 33	Volume 33; 1996.
LitC 34	Volume 34; 1997. Contains no biographies.
LitC 35	Volume 35; 1997.
LitC 36	Volume 36; 1997.
LitC 37	Volume 37; 1997.
LitC 38	Volume 38; 1998.
LitC 39	Volume 39; 1998.
LitC 40	Volume 40; 1998.
LitC 41	Volume 41; 1998.
LitC 42	Volume 42; 1998.
LitC 43	Volume 43; 1999.
LitC 44	Volume 44; 1999.
LitC 45	Volume 45; 1999.

LitC　　　　*Literature Criticism from 1400 to 1800.* Critical discussion of the works of fifteenth-, sixteenth-, seventeenth-, and eighteenth-century novelists, poets, playwrights, philosophers, and other creative writers. Detroit: Gale Group, 1999-2000.

LitC 46	Volume 46; 1999.
LitC 47	Volume 47; 1999. Contains no biographies.
LitC 48	Volume 48; 1999.
LitC 49	Volume 49; 1999.
LitC 50	Volume 50; 1999.
LitC 51	Volume 51; 2000. Contains no biographies.
LitC 52	Volume 52; 2000.
LitC 53	Volume 53; 2000.
LitC 54	Volume 54; 2000.

LiveLet　　　*Lives and Letters in American Parapsychology.* A biographical history, 1850-1987. By Arthur S. Berger. Jefferson, NC: McFarland & Co., 1988.
Use the Index to locate biographies.

LiveMA　　　*Lives of Mississippi Authors, 1817-1967.* Edited by James B. Lloyd. Jackson, MS: University Press of Mississippi, 1981.

LiveWoA　　　*Lives and Works in the Arts from the Renaissance to the 20th Century.* Nine volumes. Armonk, NY: Sharpe Reference, 1997.
Use index (volume nine) to locate entries.

LivgBAA　　　*Living Black American Authors.* A biographical directory. By Ann Allen Shockley and Sue P. Chandler. New York: R.R. Bowker Co., 1973.

LivgFWS	*The Living Female Writers of the South.* Edited by Mary T. Tardy. Philadelphia: Claxton, Remsen & Haffelfinger, 1872. Reprint. Detroit: Gale Research, 1978.
LngBDD	*Longman Biographical Directory of Decision-Makers in Russia and the Successor States.* Edited by Martin McCauley. Harlow, Essex, England: Longman Current Affairs, 1993. Distributed by Gale Research, Detroit.
LngCEL	*Longman Companion to English Literature.* Second edition. By Christopher Gillie. London: Longman Group, 1977. Also published as *A Companion to British Literature.* Detroit: Grand River Books, 1980.
LngCTC	*Longman Companion to Twentieth Century Literature.* By A.C. Ward. London: Longman Group, 1970.
LuthC 75	*Lutheran Cyclopedia.* Revised edition. Edited by Erwin L. Lueker. St. Louis: Concordia Publishing House, 1975.
MacBEP	*Macmillan Biographical Encyclopedia of Photographic Artists & Innovators.* By Turner Browne and Elaine Partnow. New York: Macmillan Publishing Co.; London: Collier Macmillan Publishers, 1983.
MacDCB 78	*The Macmillan Dictionary of Canadian Biography.* Fourth edition. Edited by W. Stewart Wallace. Revised, enlarged, and updated by W.A. McKay. Toronto: Macmillan of Canada, 1978.
MacDWB	*The Macmillan Dictionary of Women's Biography.* Edited by Jennifer S. Uglow. New York: Macmillan, 1982.
MacEA	*Macmillan Encyclopedia of Architects.* Four volumes. Edited by Adolf K. Placzek. New York: Macmillan Publishing Co., Free Press; London: Collier Macmillan Publishers, 1982. Use the "Index of Names," which begins on page 533 of Volume 4, to locate biographies.
MacEWoS	*Macmillan Encyclopedia of World Slavery.* Two volumes. Edited by Paul Finkelman and Joseph C. Miller. New York: Macmillan Reference USA, 1998.
MafEnc	*The Mafia Encyclopedia.* Second edition. By Carl Sifakis. New York: Facts On File, 1999.
MagIlD	*Magic Illustrated Dictionary.* By Geoffrey Lamb. London: Kaye & Ward, 1979.
MagSAmL	*Magill's Survey of American Literature.* Six volumes. Edited by Frank N. Magill. North Bellmore, NY: Marshall Cavendish, 1991.
MagSWL	*Magill's Survey of World Literature.* Six volumes. Edited by Frank N. Magill. North Bellmore, NY: Marshall Cavendish, 1993.
MajAI	*Major Authors and Illustrators for Children and Young Adults.* A selection of sketches from *Something about the Author.* Six volumes. Detroit: Gale Research, 1993.

MajAI SUP   *Major Authors and Illustrators for Children and Young Adults.* A selection of sketches from *Something about the Author.* Supplement. Detroit: Gale Group, 1998.

MajMD   *Major Modern Dramatists.* A Library of Literary Criticism. New York: Ungar Publishing Co., 1984-1986.

           MajMD 1   Volume I. Compiled and edited by Rita Stein and Friedhelm Rickert; 1984.

           MajMD 2   Volume II. Compiled and edited by Blandine M. Rickert, et al; 1986.

           Use the ''Dramatists Included'' list on page ix to locate biographies.

MajTwCW   *Major Twentieth-Century Writers.* A selection of sketches from *Contemporary Authors.* Detroit: Gale Research, 1991-1999.

           MajTwCW 1   First edition. Four volumes; 1991.

           MajTwCW 2   Second edition. Five volumes; 1999.

MakTCMA   *Makers of 20th Century Modern Architecture.* A bio-critical sourcebook. By Donald Leslie Johnson and Donald Langmead. Westport, CT: Greenwood Press, 1997.

MakMC   *Makers of Modern Culture.* Edited by Justin Wintle. New York: Facts on File, 1981.

MarqDCG 84   *Marquis Who's Who Directory of Computer Graphics.* First edition. Chicago: Marquis Who's Who, 1984.

McGCEnS   *McGraw-Hill Concise Encyclopedia of Science & Technology.* Fourth edition. Edited by Sybil P. Parker. New York: McGraw-Hill, 1997.

           Biographical Listing section begins on page 2218.

McGDA   *McGraw-Hill Dictionary of Art.* Five volumes. Edited by Bernard S. Myers. New York: McGraw-Hill Book Co., 1969.

McGEWB   *The McGraw-Hill Encyclopedia of World Biography.* New York: McGraw-Hill Book Co., 1973. Supplemental volumes published as *Encyclopedia of World Biography: 20th Century Supplement.*

McGEWD   *McGraw-Hill Encyclopedia of World Drama.* New York: McGraw-Hill Book Co., 1972-1984.

           McGEWD 72   First edition. Four volumes; 1972.

           McGEWD 84   Second edition. Five volumes; 1984.

McGMS 80   *McGraw-Hill Modern Scientists and Engineers.* Three volumes. New York: McGraw-Hill Book Co., 1980.

MedHR   *Medal of Honor Recipients, 1863-1978.* 96th Congress, 1st Session, Senate Committee Print No. 3. Prepared by the Committee on Veterans' Affairs, United States Senate. Washington, DC: U.S. Government Printing Office, 1979.

           Use the ''Medal of Honor Alphabetical Index,'' which begins on page 1023, to locate biographies.

MedHR 94   *Medal of Honor Recipients, 1863-1994.* Two volumes. Compiled by George Lang, Raymond L. Collins, and Gerard F. White. New York: Facts on File, 1995.

        Use the alphabetical Index, which begins on page 865, to locate biographies.

MedPD   *Media Personnel Directory.* An alphabetical guide to names, addresses, and telephone numbers of key editorial and business personnel at over 700 United States and international periodicals. Edited by Alan E. Abrams. Detroit: Gale Research Co., 1979.

MediEng   *Medieval England.* An Encyclopedia. Edited by Paul E. Szarmach, M. Teresa Tavormina, and Joel T. Rosenthal. Garland Encyclopedias of the Middle Ages, vol. 3. Garland Reference Library of the Humanities, vol. 907. New York: Garland Publishing, 1998.

MediFra   *Medieval France.* An encyclopedia. Edited by William W. Kibler and Grover A. Zinn. Garland Reference Library of the Humanities, vol. 932. New York: Garland Publishing, 1995.

MediWW   *Medieval Women Writers.* Edited by Katharina M. Wilson. Athens, GA: University of Georgia Press, 1984.
        Use the Table of Contents to locate biographies.

MemAm   *Memorable Americans, 1750-1950.* By Robert B. Downs, John T. Flanagan, and Harold W. Scott. Littleton, CO: Libraries Unlimited, 1983.

MnBBF   *The Men behind Boys' Fiction.* By W.O.G. Lofts and D.J. Adley. London: Howard Baker Publishers, 1970.

MnPM   *Men of Popular Music.* By David Ewen. Chicago: Ziff-Davis Publishing Co., 1944. Reprint. Freeport, N.Y.: Books for Libraries Press, 1972.

Meth   *The Methodists.* By James E. Kirby, Russell E. Richey, and Kenneth E. Rowe. Denominations in America, no. 8. Westport, CT: Greenwood Press, 1996.
        Biographies begin on page 257.

MetOEnc   *The Metropolitan Opera Encyclopedia.* A comprehensive guide to the world of opera. Edited by David Hamilton. New York: Simon and Schuster, 1987.

MexAmB   *Mexican American Biographies.* A historical dictionary, 1836-1987. By Matt S. Meier. New York: Greenwood Press, 1988.

MGM   *The MGM Stock Company.* The golden era. By James Robert Parish and Ronald L. Bowers. New Rochelle, NY: Arlington House, 1973.
        MGM A   "Capsule Biographies of MGM Executives" section begins on page 796.

MiSFD 9   *Michael Singer's Film Directors.* A complete guide. Ninth international edition. Edited by Michael Singer. Los Angeles: Lone Eagle Publishing Co., 1992.
        MiSFD 9N   The Obituary section begins on page 318.

MichAu 80   *Michigan Authors.* Second edition. By the Michigan Association for Media in Education. Ann Arbor, MI: Michigan Association for Media in Education, 1980.
        MichAu 80A   Addendum begins on page 339.

MidE	*The Middle East and North Africa.* London: Europa Publications, 1978-1982.

                MidE 78   25th edition, 1978-1979; 1978.
                MidE 79   26th edition, 1979-1980; 1979.
                MidE 80   27th edition, 1980-1981; 1980.
                MidE 81   28th edition, 1981-1982; 1981.
                MidE 82   29th edition, 1982-1983; 1982.
                Biographies are found in the "Who's Who in the Middle East and North Africa" section.

MilitOn   *The Military 100.* A ranking of the most influential military leaders of all time. By Michael Lee Lanning. Seacaucus, NJ: Citadel Press, 1996.
                Use the Index to locate biographies.

MinnWr   *Minnesota Writers.* A collection of autobiographical stories by Minnesota prose writers. Edited and annotated by Carmen Nelson Richards. Minneapolis: T.S. Denison & Co., 1961.
                Use the Table of Contents to locate biographies.

ModAL   *Modern American Literature.* A Library of Literary Criticism. New York: Frederick Ungar Publishing Co., 1969-1985.

                ModAL 4   Fourth edition. Volumes 1-3. Compiled and edited by Dorothy Nyren Curley, Maurice Kramer, and Elaine Fialka Kramer; 1969.
                ModAL 4S1   Volume 4, Supplement. Compiled and edited by Dorothy Nyren, Maurice Kramer, and Elaine Fialka Kramer; 1976.
                ModAL 4S2   Volume 5, Second Supplement. Compiled and edited by Paul Schlueter and June Schlueter; 1985.

ModAL 4S3   *Modern American Literature.* Volume 6, Third Supplement. Edited by Martin Tucker. A Library of Literary Criticism. New York: Continuum Publishing Co., 1997.

ModAL 5   *Modern American Literature.* Fifth edition. Three volumes. Detroit: St. James Press, 1999.

ModAWP   *Modern American Women Poets.* By Jean Gould. New York: Dodd, Mead & Co., 1984.
                Use the Table of Contents to locate biographies.

ModAWWr   *Modern American Women Writers.* Edited by Elaine Showalter, Lea Baechler, and A. Walton Litz. New York: Charles Scribner's Sons, 1991.

ModArCr   *Modern Arts Criticism.* A biographical and critical guide to painters, sculptors, photographers, and architects from the beginning of the modern era to the present. Detroit: Gale Research, 1991-1994.

                ModArCr 1   Volume 1; 1991.
                ModArCr 2   Volume 2; 1992.
                ModArCr 3   Volume 3; 1993.
                ModArCr 4   Volume 4; 1994.

ModBlW   *Modern Black Writers.* Compiled and edited by Michael Popkin. A Library of Literary Criticism. New York: Frederick Ungar Publishing Co., 1978.

ModBlW 2	*Modern Black Writers.* Second edition. Detroit: St. James Press, 2000.
ModBrL	*Modern British Literature.* Volumes 1-3. Compiled and edited by Ruth Z. Temple and Martin Tucker. A Library of Literary Criticism. New York: Frederick Ungar Publishing Co., 1966.
ModBrL 2	*Modern British Literature.* Second edition. Three volumes. Detroit: St. James Press, 2000.
ModBrL	*Modern British Literature.* A Library of Literary Criticism. New York: Frederick Ungar Publishing Co., 1975-1985.

          ModBrL S1   Volume 4, Supplement. Compiled and edited by Martin Tucker and Rita Stein; 1975.

          ModBrL S2   Volume 5, Second Supplement. Compiled and edited by Denis Lane and Rita Stein; 1985.

ModChi	*Modern China.* An encyclopedia of history, culture, and nationalism. Edited by Wang Ke-wen. New York: Garland Publishing, 1998.
ModCmwL	*Modern Commonwealth Literature.* Compiled and edited by John H. Ferres and Martin Tucker. A Library of Literary Criticism. New York: Frederick Ungar Publishing Co., 1977.
ModFrL	*Modern French Literature.* Two volumes. Compiled and edited by Debra Popkin and Michael Popkin. A Library of Literary Criticism. New York: Frederick Ungar Publishing Co., 1977.
ModGL	*Modern German Literature.* Two volumes. Compiled and edited by Agnes Korner Domandi. A Library of Literary Criticism. New York: Frederick Ungar Publishing Co., 1972.
ModIrL	*Modern Irish Literature.* Compiled and edited by Denis Lane and Carol McCrory Lane. A Library of Literary Criticism. New York: Ungar Publishing Co., 1988.
ModIrLi	*Modern Irish Lives.* Dictionary of 20th-century Irish biography. Edited by Louis McRedmond. New York: St. Martin's Press, 1996.
ModJap	*Modern Japan.* An encyclopedia of history, culture, and nationalism. Edited by James L. Huffman. New York: Garland Publishing, 1998.
ModLAL	*Modern Latin American Literature.* Two volumes. Compiled and edited by David William Foster and Virginia Ramos Foster. A Library of Literary Criticism. New York: Frederick Ungar Publishing Co., 1975.
ModRL	*Modern Romance Literatures.* Compiled and edited by Dorothy Nyren Curley and Arthur Curley. A Library of Literary Criticism. New York: Frederick Ungar Publishing Co., 1967.
ModSL	*Modern Slavic Literatures.* A Library of Literary Criticism. New York: Frederick Ungar Publishing Co., 1972-1976.

          ModSL 1   Volume 1: Russian Literature. Compiled and edited by Vasa D. Mihailovich; 1972.

ModSL 2   Volume 2: Bulgarian, Czechoslovak, Polish, Ukrainian and Yugoslav Literatures. Compiled and edited by Vasa D. Mihailovich et al; 1976.
Use the alphabetic listing of authors to locate biographies.

ModSpP   *Modern Spanish and Portuguese Literatures.* Compiled and edited by Marshall J. Schneider and Irwin Stern. A Library of Literary Criticism. New York: Continuum, 1988.

           ModSpP P   Biographies of Portuguese writers are located in the ''Portugal'' section, which begins on page 455.

           ModSpP S   Biographies of Spanish writers are located in the ''Spain'' section.

ModWoWr   *Modern Women Writers.* Four volumes. Compiled and edited by Lillian S. Robinson. New York, NY: Continuum Publishing Co., 1996.

ModWD   *Modern World Drama.* An encyclopedia. By Myron Matlaw. New York: E.P. Dutton & Co., 1972.

ModWr   *Modern Writers, 1900-1998.* Concise Dictionary of American Literary Biography. Detroit: Gale Research, 1999.

MorBAP   *More Black American Playwrights.* A bibliography. By Esther Spring Arata. Metuchen, NJ: Scarecrow Press, 1978. Updates *Black American Playwrights.*

MorBMP   *More Books by More People.* Interviews with sixty-five authors of books for children. By Lee Bennett Hopkins. New York: Citation Press, 1974.

MorJA   *More Junior Authors.* Edited by Muriel Fuller. Wilson Authors Series. New York: H.W. Wilson Co., 1963.

MorMA   *More Memorable Americans, 1750-1950.* By Robert B. Downs, John T. Flanagan, and Harold W. Scott. Littleton, CO: Libraries Unlimited, 1985.

MotPP   *Motion Picture Performers.* A bibliography of magazine and periodical articles, 1900-1969. Compiled by Mel Schuster. Metuchen, NJ: Scarecrow Press, 1971.

MouLC   *Moulton's Library of Literary Criticism.* English and American authors through the beginning of the twentieth century. Abridged, revised, and with additions by Martin Tucker. New York: Frederick Ungar Publishing Co., 1966.

           MouLC 1   Volume 1: The beginnings to the seventeenth century.
           MouLC 2   Volume 2: Neo-Classicism to the Romantic period.
           MouLC 3   Volume 3: The Romantic period to the Victorian age.
           MouLC 4   Volume 4: The mid-nineteenth century to Edwardianism.
Use the alphabetic listing at the front of the volume to locate biographies.

MovMk   *The Movie Makers.* By Sol Chaneles and Albert Wolsky. Secaucus, NJ: Derbibooks, 1974.
         The ''Directors'' section begins on page 506.

MugS   *Mug Shots.* Who's who in the new Earth. By Jay Acton, Alan Le Mond, and Parker Hodges. New York: World Publishing Co., 1972.

MurCaTw   *Murder Cases of the Twentieth Century.* Biographies and bibliographies of 280 convicted or accused killers. By David K. Frasier. Jefferson, NC: McFarland & Co., 1996.

MusmAFA   *Museum of American Folk Art Encyclopedia of Twentieth-Century American Folk Art and Artists.* By Chuck and Jan Rosenak. New York: Abbeville Press, 1990.

MusMk   *Music Makers.* By Clive Unger-Hamilton. New York: Harry N. Abrams, 1979.
                   Use the ''Alphabetical List of Entries'' at the front of the book to locate biographies.

Music   *Musicals.* By Michael Patrick Kennedy and John Muir. Glasgow, Scotland: HarperCollins Publishers, 1997. Distributed by Trafalgar Square, North Pomfret, VT.
                   Composer & Lyricist Biographies section begins on page 388.

MusSN   *Musicians since 1900.* Performers in concert and opera. Compiled and edited by David Ewen. New York: H.W. Wilson Co., 1978.

MysSW   *Mystery and Suspense Writers.* The literature of crime, detection, and espionage. Two volumes. Edited by Robin W. Winks. The Scribner Writers Series. New York: Charles Scribner's Sons, 1998.

NamesHP   *Names in the History of Psychology.* A biographical sourcebook. By Leonard Zusne. Washington, DC: Hemisphere Publishing Corp., 1975. Distributed by John Wiley & Sons, Halstead Press, New York. Continued by *Biographical Dictionary of Psychology.*
                   Use the ''Alphabetic List of Names,'' which begins on page ix, to locate biographies.

NatCAB   *The National Cyclopaedia of American Biography.* New York: James T. White & Co., 1891-1984.

NatCAB 1	Volume 1; 1891. Use the Index to locate biographies.
NatCAB 2	Volume 2; 1891. Use the Index to locate biographies.
NatCAB 3	Volume 3; 1891. Use the Index to locate biographies.
NatCAB 4	Volume 4; 1891. Use the Index to locate biographies.
NatCAB 5	Volume 5; 1891. Use the Index to locate biographies.
NatCAB 6	Volume 6; 1892. Use the Index to locate biographies.
NatCAB 7	Volume 7; 1892. Use the Index to locate biographies.
NatCAB 8	Volume 8; 1898. Use the Index to locate biographies.
NatCAB 9	Volume 9; 1899. Use the Index to locate biographies.
NatCAB 10	Volume 10; 1900. Use the Index to locate biographies.
NatCAB 11	Volume 11; 1901. Use the Index to locate biographies.
NatCAB 12	Volume 12; 1904. Use the Index to locate biographies.
NatCAB 13	Volume 13; 1906. Use the Index to locate biographies.
NatCAB 14	Volume 14; 1910. Use the Index to locate biographies.
NatCAB 15	Volume 15; 1914. Use the Index to locate biographies.
NatCAB 16	Volume 16; 1918. Use the Index to locate biographies.
NatCAB 17	Volume 17; 1921. Use the Index to locate biographies.
NatCAB 18	Volume 18; 1922. Use the Index to locate biographies.
NatCAB 19	Volume 19; 1926. Use the Index to locate biographies.
NatCAB 20	Volume 20; 1929. Use the Index to locate biographies.
NatCAB 21	Volume 21; 1931. Use the Index to locate biographies.

NatCAB 22	Volume 22; 1932. Use the Index to locate biographies.
NatCAB 23	Volume 23; 1933. Use the Index to locate biographies.
NatCAB 24	Volume 24; 1935. Use the Index to locate biographies.
NatCAB 25	Volume 25; 1936. Use the Index to locate biographies.
NatCAB 26	Volume 26; 1937. Use the Index to locate biographies.
NatCAB 27	Volume 27; 1939. Use the Index to locate biographies.
NatCAB 28	Volume 28; 1940. Use the Index to locate biographies.
NatCAB 29	Volume 29; 1941. Use the Index to locate biographies.
NatCAB 30	Volume 30; 1943. Use the Index to locate biographies.
NatCAB 31	Volume 31; 1944. Use the Index to locate biographies.
NatCAB 32	Volume 32; 1945. Use the Index to locate biographies.
NatCAB 33	Volume 33; 1947. Use the Index to locate biographies.
NatCAB 34	Volume 34; 1948. Use the Index to locate biographies.
NatCAB 35	Volume 35; 1949. Use the Index to locate biographies.
NatCAB 36	Volume 36; 1950. Use the Index to locate biographies.
NatCAB 37	Volume 37; 1951. Use the Index to locate biographies.
NatCAB 38	Volume 38; 1953. Use the Index to locate biographies.
NatCAB 39	Volume 39; 1954. Use the Index to locate biographies.
NatCAB 40	Volume 40; 1955. Use the Index to locate biographies.
NatCAB 41	Volume 41; 1956. Use the Index to locate biographies.
NatCAB 42	Volume 42; 1958. Use the Index to locate biographies.
NatCAB 43	Volume 43; 1961. Use the Index to locate biographies.
NatCAB 44	Volume 44; 1962. Use the Index to locate biographies.
NatCAB 45	Volume 45; 1962. Use the Index to locate biographies.
NatCAB 46	Volume 46; 1963. Use the Index to locate biographies.
NatCAB 47	Volume 47; 1965. Use the Index to locate biographies.
NatCAB 48	Volume 48; 1965. Use the Index to locate biographies.
NatCAB 49	Volume 49; 1966. Use the Index to locate biographies.
NatCAB 50	Volume 50; 1968. Use the Index to locate biographies.
NatCAB 51	Volume 51; 1969. Use the Index to locate biographies.
NatCAB 52	Volume 52; 1970. Use the Index to locate biographies.
NatCAB 53	Volume 53; 1972. Use the Index to locate biographies.
NatCAB 54	Volume 54; 1973. Use the Index to locate biographies.
NatCAB 55	Volume 55; 1974. Use the Index to locate biographies.
NatCAB 56	Volume 56; 1975. Use the Index to locate biographies.
NatCAB 57	Volume 57; 1977. Use the Index to locate biographies.
NatCAB 58	Volume 58; 1979. Use the Index to locate biographies.
NatCAB 59	Volume 59; 1980. Use the Index to locate biographies.
NatCAB 60	Volume 60; 1981. Use the Index to locate biographies.
NatCAB 61	Volume 61; 1982. Use the Index to locate biographies.
NatCAB 62	Volume 62; 1984. Use the Index to locate biographies.
NatCAB 63	Volume 63; 1984. Use the Index which begins on page 353 to locate biographies.
NatCAB 63N	Volume 63; 1984. Use the Index which begins on page 349 to locate biographies.

NatLAC   *National Leaders of American Conservation.* Edited by Richard H. Stroud. Washington, DC: Smithsonian Institution Press, 1985.

NatPD   *National Playwrights Directory.* Edited by Phyllis Johnson Kaye. Waterford, CT: The O'Neill Theater Center, 1977-1981.

NatPD 77	First edition; 1977.
NatPD 81	Second edition; 1981.

NatAL	*Native American Literatures.* An encyclopedia of works, characters, authors, and themes. By Kathy J. Whitson. Santa Barbara, CA: ABC-CLIO Inc., 1999.
NatNAFi	*Native North American Firsts.* Edited by Karen Gayton Swisher and AnCita Benally. Detroit: Gale Research, 1998. Use the General Index to locate biographies.
NatNAL	*Native North American Literature.* Biographical and critical information on native writers and orators from the United States and Canada from historical times to the present. Detroit: Gale Research, 1994. Use the Outline of Contents to locate biographies.
NegAl 76	*The Negro Almanac.* A reference work on the Afro American. Third edition. Edited by Harry A. Ploski and Warren Marr, II. New York: Bellwether Co., 1976. Later edition published as *The African-American Almanac.* Use the Index to locate biographies.
NegAl 83	*The Negro Almanac.* A reference work on the Afro-American. Fourth edition. Compiled and edited by Harry A. Ploski and James Williams. New York: John Wiley & Sons, 1983. Use the Index to locate biographies.

NegAl	*The Negro Almanac.* A reference work on the African American. Fifth edition. Detroit: Gale Research, 1989. Later edition published as *The African-American Almanac.*
	    NegAl 89 Use the Index to locate biographies.
	    NegAl 89A Unindexed biographies in ''The Black Voter and Elected Office Holder'' chapter are located on pages 386-468.

NewAgE 90	*New Age Encyclopedia.* A guide to the beliefs, concepts, terms, people, and organizations that make up the New Global Movement toward spritual development, health and healing, higher consciousness, and related subjects. First edition. Detroit: Gale Research, 1990.
NewAgMG	*The New Age Music Guide.* Profiles and recordings of 500 top New Age musicians. By Patti Jean Birosik. New York: Colliers Books, Macmillan Publishing Co., 1989.
NewAmDM	*The New American Dictionary of Music.* By Philip D. Morehead with Anne MacNeil. New York: Dutton, 1991.
NewCBEL	*The New Cambridge Bibliography of English Literature.* Five volumes. Edited by George Watson. Cambridge: Cambridge University Press, 1969-1977. Use the index in Volume 5 to locate entries.
NewC	*The New Century Handbook of English Literature.* Revised edition. Edited by Clarence L. Barnhart with the assistance of William D. Halsey. New York: Appleton-Century-Crofts, 1967.
NewCol 75	*The New Columbia Encyclopedia.* Edited by William H. Harris and Judith S. Levey. New York and London: Columbia University Press, 1975.

NewCBMT   *New Complete Book of the American Musical Theater.* By David Ewen. New York: Holt, Rinehart & Winston, 1970.
> Biographies are found in the ''Librettists, Lyricists and Composers'' section which begins on page 607.

NewCon   *The New Consciousness, 1941-1968.* Concise Dictionary of American Literary Biography Series. Detroit: Gale Research, 1987.

NewEAmW   *The New Encyclopedia of the American West.* Edited by Howard R. Lamar. New Haven, CT: Yale University Press, 1998.

NewEOp 71   *The New Encyclopedia of the Opera.* By David Ewen. New York: Hill & Wang, 1971.

NewEScF   *The New Encyclopedia of Science Fiction.* Edited by James Gunn. New York: Viking, 1988.

NewGrDA 86   *The New Grove Dictionary of American Music.* Four volumes. Edited by H. Wiley Hitchcock and Stanley Sadie. London: Macmillan Press, 1986.

NewGrDJ 88   *The New Grove Dictionary of Jazz.* Two volumes. Edited by Barry Kernfeld. London: Macmillan Press, 1988.

NewGrDJ 94   *The New Grove Dictionary of Jazz.* Edited by Barry Kernfeld. New York: St. Martin's Press, 1994.

NewGrDM 80   *The New Grove Dictionary of Music and Musicians.* 20 volumes. Edited by Stanley Sadie. London: Macmillan Publishers, 1980.

NewGrDO   *The New Grove Dictionary of Opera.* Four volumes. Edited by Stanley Sadie. London: Macmillan Press; New York: Grove's Dictionaries of Music, 1992.

NewOrJ   *New Orleans Jazz: A Family Album.* Revised edition. By Al Rose and Edmond Souchon. Baton Rouge, LA: Louisiana State University Press, 1978.
> *NewOrJ*   ''Who's Who in New Orleans Jazz'' begins on page 4.
> *NewOrJ SUP*   ''Who's Who in New Orleans Jazz Supplement'' begins on page 307.

NewOxM   *The New Oxford Companion to Music.* Two volumes. Edited by Denis Arnold. Oxford: Oxford University Press, 1983.

NewWmR   *New Women in Rock.* Edited by Liz Thompson. New York: Delilah Books, 1982.

NewYTBE   *The New York Times Biographical Edition.* A compilation of current biographical information of general interest. New York: Arno Press, 1970-1973.Continued by *The New York Times Biographical Service.*
> *NewYTBE 70*   Volume 1, Numbers 1-12; 1970.
> *NewYTBE 71*   Volume 2, Numbers 1-12; 1971.
> *NewYTBE 72*   Volume 3, Numbers 1-12; 1972.
> *NewYTBE 73*   Volume 4, Numbers 1-12; 1973.
> Use the annual Index to locate biographies.

NewYTBS   *The New York Times Biographical Service.* A compilation of current biographical
                   information of general interest. New York: Arno Press, 1974-1981.A
                   continuation of *The New York Times Biographical Edition.*
                       NewYTBS 74   Volume 5, Numbers 1-12; 1974.
                       NewYTBS 75   Volume 6, Numbers 1-12; 1975.
                       NewYTBS 76   Volume 7, Numbers 1-12; 1976.
                       NewYTBS 77   Volume 8, Numbers 1-12; 1977.
                       NewYTBS 78   Volume 9, Numbers 1-12; 1978.
                       NewYTBS 79   Volume 10, Numbers 1-12; 1979.
                       NewYTBS 80   Volume 11, Numbers 1-12; 1980.
                       NewYTBS 81   Volume 12, Numbers 1-12; 1981.
                       Use the annual Index to locate biographies.

NewYTBS   *The New York Times Biographical Service.* A compilation of current biographical
                   information of general interest. Sanford, NC: Microfilming Corp. of America,
                   1982-1983.
                       NewYTBS 82   Volume 13, Numbers 1-12; 1982.
                       NewYTBS 83   Volume 14, Numbers 1-12; 1983.
                       Use the annual Index to locate biographies.

NewYTBS   *The New York Times Biographical Service.* A compilation of current biographical
                   information of general interest. Ann Arbor, MI: University Microfilms
                   International, 1984-1993.
                       NewYTBS 84   Volume 15, Numbers 1-12; 1984.
                       NewYTBS 85   Volume 16, Numbers 1-12; 1985.
                       NewYTBS 86   Volume 17, Numbers 1-12; 1986.
                       NewYTBS 87   Volume 18, Numbers 1-12; 1987.
                       NewYTBS 88   Volume 19, Numbers 1-12; 1988.
                       NewYTBS 89   Volume 20, Numbers 1-12; 1989.
                       NewYTBS 90   Volume 21, Numbers 1-12; 1990.
                       NewYTBS 91   Volume 22, Numbers 1-12; 1991.
                       NewYTBS 92   Volume 23, Numbers 1-12; 1992.
                       NewYTBS 93   Volume 24, Numbers 1-12; 1993.
                       Use the annual Index to locate biographies.

NewYTBS   *The New York Times Biographical Service.* A compilation of current biographical
                   information of general interest. Ann Arbor, MI: UMI Co., 1994-1998.
                       NewYTBS 94   Volume 25, Numbers 1-12; 1994.
                       NewYTBS 95   Volume 26, Numbers 1-12; 1995.
                       NewYTBS 96   Volume 27, Numbers 1-12; 1996.
                       NewYTBS 97   Volume 28, Numbers 1-12; 1997.
                       NewYTBS 98   Volume 29, Numbers 1-12; 1998.
                       Use the annual Index to locate biographies.

NewYTBS 99   *The New York Times Biographical Service.* A compilation of current biographical
                   information of general interest. Volume 30, Numbers 1-12. Ann Arbor, MI:
                   Bell & Howell Information & Learning Co., 1999.
                       Use the annual index to locate biographies.

NewYTET   *The New York Times Encyclopedia of Television.* By Les Brown. New York: New
                   York Times Book Co., 1977. Later editions published as *Les Brown's
                   Encyclopedia of Television.*

NewbC   *Newbery and Caldecott Medal Books.* With acceptance papers, biographies and related material chiefly from the *Horn Book Magazine.* Edited by Lee Kingman. Boston: Horn Book, 1965-1975.

                     NewbC 1956   *1956-1965.*; 1965.
                     NewbC 1966   *1966-1975.*; 1975.

NewbC 1956   *Newbery and Caldecott Medal Books, 1956-1965.* With acceptance papers, biographies and related material chiefly from the *Horn Book Magazine.* Edited by Lee Kingman. Boston: Horn Book, 1965.

NewbC 1966   *Newbery and Caldecott Medal Books, 1966-1975.* With acceptance papers, biographies and related material chiefly from the *Horn Book Magazine.* Edited by Lee Kingman. Boston: Horn Book, 1975.

NewbMB   *Newbery Medal Books, 1922-1955.* With their authors' acceptance papers and
1922   related material chiefly from the *Horn Book Magazine.* Edited by Bertha Mahony Miller and Elinor Whitney Field. Horn Book Papers, vol. 1. Boston: Horn Book, 1955.

News   *Newsmakers.* The people behind today's headlines. Detroit: Gale Research, 1989-1998.Issues prior to 1988, Issue 2, were published as *Contemporary Newsmakers.*

News 88	1988 Cumulation; 1989.
News 89	1989 Cumulation; 1990.
News 90	1990 Cumulation; 1990.
News 91	1991 Cumulation; 1991.
News 92	1992 Cumulation; 1992.
News 93	1993 Cumulation; 1993.
News 94	1994 Cumulation; 1994.
News 95	1995 Cumulation; 1995.
News 96	1996 Cumulation; 1997.
News 97	1997 Cumulation; 1998.
News 98	1998 Cumulation; 1999.
News 88-2	1988, Issue 2; 1988.
News 88-3	1988, Issue 3; 1988.
News 89-1	1989, Issue 1; 1989.
News 89-2	1989, Issue 2; 1989.
News 89-3	1989, Issue 3; 1989.
News 90-1	1990, Issue 1; 1990.
News 90-2	1990, Issue 2; 1990.
News 90-3	1990, Issue 3; 1990.
News 91-1	1991, Issue 1; 1990.
News 91-2	1991, Issue 2; 1991.
News 91-3	1991, Issue 3; 1991.
News 92-1	1992, Issue 1; 1992.
News 92-2	1992, Issue 2; 1992.
News 92-3	1992, Issue 3; 1992.
News 93-1	1993, Issue 1; 1993.
News 93-2	1993, Issue 2; 1993.
News 93-3	1993, Issue 3; 1993.
News 94-1	1994, Issue 1; 1994.
News 94-2	1994, Issue 2; 1994.
News 94-3	1994, Issue 3; 1994.
News 95-1	1995, Issue 1; 1995.

News 95-2	1995, Issue 2; 1995.
News 95-3	1995, Issue 3; 1995.
News 96-1	1996, Issue 1; 1996.
News 96-2	1996, Issue 2; 1996.
News 96-3	1996, Issue 3; 1996.
News 97-1	1997, Issue 1; 1997.
News 97-2	1997, Issue 2; 1997.
News 97-3	1997, Issue 3; 1997.
News 98-1	1998, Issue 1; 1998.
News 98-2	1998, Issue 2; 1998.
News 98-3	1998, Issue 3; 1998.

Use the ''Cumulative Newsmaker Index'' to locate entries. Biographies in each quarterly issue can also be located in the annual cumulation.

News   *Newsmakers.* The people behind today's headlines. Detroit: Gale Group, 1999. Issues prior to 1988, Issue 2, were published as *Contemporary Newsmakers.*

News 99-1	1999, Issue 1; 1999. Use the ''Cumulative Newsmaker Index'' to locate entries. Biographies in each quarterly issue can also be located in the annual cumulation.
News 99-2	1999, Issue 2; 1999. Use the ''Cumulative Newsmaker Index'' to locate entries. Biographies in each quarterly issue can also be located in the annual cumulation.
News 1999	1999 Cumulation; 2000. Use the 'Cumulative Newsmaker Index' to locate entries. Biographies in each quarterly issue can also be located in the annual cumulation.
News 1999	1999, Issue 3; 1999. Use the 'Cumulative Newsmaker Index' to locate entries. Biographies in each quarterly issue can also be located in the annual cumulation.

NewYHSD   *The New-York Historical Society's Dictionary of Artists in America, 1564-1860.* By George C. Groce and David H. Wallace. New Haven, CT: Yale University Press, 1957.

NinCAWW   *Nineteenth-Century American Women Writers.* A bio-bibliographical critical sourcebook. Edited by Denise D. Knight. Westport, CT: Greenwood Press, 1997.

NinCLC   *Nineteenth-Century Literature Criticism.* Excerpts from criticism of various topics in nineteenth-century literature, including literary and critical movements, prominent themes and genres, anniversary celebrations, and surveys of national literatures. Detroit: Gale Research, 1981-1999.

NinCLC 1	Volume 1; 1981.
NinCLC 2	Volume 2; 1982.
NinCLC 3	Volume 3; 1983.
NinCLC 4	Volume 4; 1983.
NinCLC 5	Volume 5; 1984.
NinCLC 6	Volume 6; 1984.
NinCLC 7	Volume 7; 1984.
NinCLC 8	Volume 8; 1985.
NinCLC 9	Volume 9; 1985.
NinCLC 10	Volume 10; 1985.
NinCLC 11	Volume 11; 1986.
NinCLC 12	Volume 12; 1986.
NinCLC 13	Volume 13; 1986.

NinCLC 14	Volume 14; 1987.	
NinCLC 15	Volume 15; 1987.	
NinCLC 16	Volume 16; 1987.	
NinCLC 17	Volume 17; 1988.	
NinCLC 18	Volume 18; 1988.	
NinCLC 19	Volume 19; 1988.	
NinCLC 20	Volume 20; 1989. Contains no biographies.	
NinCLC 21	Volume 21; 1989.	
NinCLC 22	Volume 22; 1989.	
NinCLC 23	Volume 23; 1989.	
NinCLC 24	Volume 24; 1989. Contains no biographies.	
NinCLC 25	Volume 25; 1990.	
NinCLC 26	Volume 26; 1990.	
NinCLC 27	Volume 27; 1990.	
NinCLC 28	Volume 28; 1990. Contains no biographies.	
NinCLC 29	Volume 29; 1991.	
NinCLC 30	Volume 30; 1991.	
NinCLC 31	Volume 31; 1991.	
NinCLC 32	Volume 32; 1991. Contains no biographies.	
NinCLC 33	Volume 33; 1992.	
NinCLC 34	Volume 34; 1992.	
NinCLC 35	Volume 35; 1992.	
NinCLC 36	Volume 36; 1992. Contains no biographies.	
NinCLC 37	Volume 37; 1993.	
NinCLC 38	Volume 38; 1993.	
NinCLC 39	Volume 39; 1993.	
NinCLC 40	Volume 40; 1993. Contains no biographies.	
NinCLC 41	Volume 41; 1994.	
NinCLC 42	Volume 42; 1994.	
NinCLC 43	Volume 43; 1994.	
NinCLC 44	Volume 44; 1994. Contains no biographies.	
NinCLC 45	Volume 45; 1994.	
NinCLC 46	Volume 46; 1994.	
NinCLC 47	Volume 47; 1995.	
NinCLC 48	Volume 48; 1995. Contains no biographies.	
NinCLC 49	Volume 49; 1995.	
NinCLC 50	Volume 50; 1996.	
NinCLC 51	Volume 51; 1996.	
NinCLC 52	Volume 52; 1996. Contains no biographies.	
NinCLC 53	Volume 53; 1996.	
NinCLC 54	Volume 54; 1996.	
NinCLC 55	Volume 55; 1997.	
NinCLC 56	Volume 56; 1997. Contains no biographies.	
NinCLC 57	Volume 57; 1997.	
NinCLC 58	Volume 58; 1997.	
NinCLC 59	Volume 59; 1997.	
NinCLC 60	Volume 60; 1997.	
NinCLC 61	Volume 61; 1997.	
NinCLC 62	Volume 62; 1998.	
NinCLC 63	Volume 63; 1998.	
NinCLC 64	Volume 64; 1998. Contains no biographies.	
NinCLC 65	Volume 65; 1998.	
NinCLC 66	Volume 66; 1998.	
NinCLC 67	Volume 67; 1998.	
NinCLC 68	Volume 68; 1998. Contains no biographies.	

NinCLC 69	Volume 69; 1999.
NinCLC 70	Volume 70; 1999.
NinCLC 71	Volume 71; 1999.
NinCLC 72	Volume 72; 1999. Contains no biographies.

NinCLC   *Nineteenth-Century Literature Criticism.* Excerpts from criticism of the works of novelists, poets, playwrights, short story writers, philosophers, and other creative writers who died between 1800 and 1899, from the first published critical appraisals to current evaluations. Detroit: Gale Group, 1999.

NinCLC 73	Volume 73.
NinCLC 74	Volume 74.
NinCLC 75	Volume 75.
NinCLC 76	Volume 76. Contains no biographies.
NinCLC 77	Volume 77.
NinCLC 78	Volume 78.
NinCLC 79	Volume 79.
NinCLC 80	Volume 80.
NinCLC 81	Volume 81.
NinCLC 82	Volume 82.

NobelP   *Nobel Prize Winners.* New York: H.W. Wilson Co., 1987-1992.

NobelP	Edited by Tyler Wasson; 1987.
NobelP 91	Supplement 1987-1991. Edited by Paula McGuire; 1992.
NobelP 91N	Supplement 1987-1991. Edited by Paula McGuire; 1992. "Nobel Prize Winners Who Have Died since 1986" section appears on page 25.

NorAmWA   *North American Women Artists of the Twentieth Century.* A biographical dictionary. Edited by Jules Heller and Nancy G. Heller. Garland Reference Library of the Humanities, vol. 1219. New York: Garland Publishing, 1995.

NotAW   *Notable American Women, 1607-1950.* A biographical dictionary. Three volumes. Edited by Edward T. James. Cambridge: Harvard University Press, Belknap Press, 1971.

NotAW MOD   *Notable American Women, The Modern Period.* A biographical dictionary. Edited by Barbara Sicherman and Carol Hurd Green. Cambridge: Harvard University Press, Belknap Press, 1980.

NotAsAm   *Notable Asian Americans.* Detroit: Gale Research, 1995.

NotBlAM   *Notable Black American Men.* Edited by Jessie Carney Smith. Detroit: Gale Research, 1999.

NotBlAS   *Notable Black American Scientists.* Detroit: Gale Research, 1999.

NotBlAW   *Notable Black American Women.* Edited by Jessie Carney Smith. Detroit: Gale Research, 1992-1996.

NotBlAW 1	Book I; 1992.
NotBlAW 2	Book II; 1996.

NotHsAW   *Notable Hispanic American Women.* Detroit: Gale Research, 1993-1998.

NotHsAW 1	First edition; 1993.
NotHsAW 2	Book II; 1998.

NotLatA   *Notable Latino Americans.* A biographical dictionary. By Matt S. Meier. Westport, CT: Greenwood Press, 1997.

NotMat   *Notable Mathematicians.* From ancient times to the present. Detroit: Gale Research, 1998.

NotNAT   *Notable Names in the American Theatre.* Clifton, NJ: James T. White & Co., 1976. Earlier edition published as *The Biographical Encyclopaedia and Who's Who of the American Theatre.*

                                      NotNAT   "Notable Names in the American Theatre" section begins on page 489. This book often alphabetizes by titles of address, e.g.: Dr., Mrs., and Sir.

                                        NotNAT A   "Biographical Bibliography" section begins on page 309. This book often alphabetizes by titles of address, e.g.: Dr., Mrs., and Sir.

                                        NotNAT B   "Necrology" section begins on page 343. This book often alphabetizes by titles of address, e.g.: Dr., Mrs., and Sir.

NotNaAm   *Notable Native Americans.* Detroit: Gale Research, 1995.

NotPoe   *Notable Poets.* Three volumes. Magill's Choice. Pasadena, CA: Salem Press, 1998.

NotTwCP   *Notable Twentieth-Century Pianists.* A bio-critical sourcebook. Two volumes. By John Gillespie and Anna Gillespie. Westport, CT: Greenwood Press, 1995.

NotTwCS   *Notable Twentieth-Century Scientists.* Detroit: Gale Research, 1995-1998.
                                        NotTwCS 1   First edition. Four volumes; 1995.
                                        NotTwCS 1S   First edition, supplement; 1998.

NotWoAT   *Notable Women in the American Theatre.* A biographical dictionary. Edited by Alice M. Robinson, Vera Mowry Roberts, and Milly S. Barranger. New York: Greenwood Press, 1989.

NotWoLS   *Notable Women in the Life Sciences.* A biographical dictionary. Edited by Benjamin F. Shearer and Barbara S. Shearer. Westport, CT: Greenwood Press, 1996.

NotWoMa   *Notable Women in Mathematics.* A biographical dictionary. Edited by Charlene Morrow and Teri Perl. Westport, CT: Greenwood Press, 1998.

NotWoPS   *Notable Women in the Physical Sciences.* A biographical dictionary. Edited by Benjamin F. Shearer and Barbara S. Shearer. Westport, CT: Greenwood Press, 1997.

NotWoSc   *Notable Women Scientists.* Detroit: Gale Group, 1999.

Novels   *Novels and Novelists.* A guide to the world of fiction. Edited by Martin Seymour-Smith. New York: St. Martin's Press, 1980.
                Biographies are located in the "Novelists: An Alphabetical Guide" section, which begins on page 87.

ObitOF 79	*Obituaries on File.* Two volumes. Compiled by Felice Levy. New York: Facts on File, 1979.
ObitPA 96	*Obituaries in the Performing Arts, 1996.* Film, television, radio, theatre, dance, music, cartoons and pop culture. By Harris M. Lentz III. Jefferson, NC: McFarland & Co., 1997.
ObitT	*Obituaries from the Times.* Compiled by Frank C. Roberts. Reading, England: Newspaper Archive Developments, 1979-1978.

	ObitT 1951	*1951-1960.*; 1979.
	ObitT 1961	*1961-1970.*; 1975.
	ObitT 1971	*1971-1975.*; 1978.

ODwPR	*O'Dwyer's Directory of Public Relations Executives.* Edited by Jack O'Dwyer. New York: J.R. O'Dwyer Co., 1979-1990.

	ODwPR 79	1979 edition; 1979.
	ODwPR 91	1991 edition; 1990.

BaseReg	*Official Baseball Register.* Edited by Barry Siegel. St. Louis: The Sporting News, 1985-1988.

	BaseReg 85	1985 edition; 1985.
	BaseReg 86	1986 edition; 1986.
	BaseReg 87	1987 edition; 1987.
	BaseReg 88	1988 edition; 1988.

OfEnT	*Official Encyclopedia of Tennis.* United States Tennis Association. Revised and updated. Edited by Bill Shannon. New York: Harper & Row, 1979.
OfNBA	*Official NBA Register.* St. Louis: The Sporting News, 1981-1987.

	OfNBA 81	1981-1982 edition. Edited by Matt Winick; 1981.
	OfNBA 85	1985-1986 edition. Edited by Mike Douchant and Alex Sachare; 1985.
	OfNBA 86	1986-1987 edition. Edited by Mike Douchant and Alex Sachare; 1986.
	OfNBA 87	1987-1988 edition. Edited by Alex Sachare and Dave Sloan; 1987.

OfPGCP 86	*Official Price Guide to Collector Prints.* Seventh edition. By Ruth M. Pollard. Westminster, MD: House of Collectibles, 1986.
OhA&B	*Ohio Authors and Their Books.* Biographical data and selective bibliographies for Ohio authors, native and resident, 1796-1950. Edited by William Coyle. Cleveland: World Publishing Co., 1962.
OlFamFa	*Old Familiar Faces.* The great character actors and actresses of Hollywood's golden era. By Robert A. Juran. Sarasota, FL: Movie Memories Publishing, 1995.
OnHuMoP	*The One Hundred Most Popular Young Adult Authors.* Biographical sketches and bibliographies. By Bernard A. Drew. Englewood, CO: Libraries Unlimited, 1996.

OnHuYAF   *One Hundred Years of American Film.* Edited by Frank Beaver. New York: Macmillan Library Reference USA, 2000.

OnHuYeA   *One Hundred Years of American Women Writing, 1848-1948.* An annotated bio-bibliography. By Jane Missner Barstow. Magill Bibliographies. Pasadena, CA: Scarecrow Press, 1997.
         Use the table of contents to locate entries.

OnThGG   *One Thousand Great Guitarists.* By Hugh Gregory. San Francisco: Miller Freeman Books, 1994; London: Outline Press, 1994. Distributed by Publishers Group West, Emeryville, CA.

Opera   *Opera & Operetta.* By Michael White and Elaine Henderson. Glasgow, Scotland: HarperCollins Publishers, 1997. Distributed by Trafalgar Square, North Pomfret, VT.

OrJudAm   *Orthodox Judaism in America.* A biographical dictionary and sourcebook. By Moshe D. Sherman. Westport, CT: Greenwood Press, 1996.

OsStAZ   *The Oscar Stars from A-Z.* By Roy Pickard. London: Headline Book Publishing, 1996.

OutWomA   *Outstanding Women Athletes.* Who they are and how they influenced sports in America. Second edition. By Janet Woolum. Phoenix, AZ: Oryx Press, 1998.
         Biographies and Teams section begins on page 75.

OxCAfAL   *The Oxford Companion to African American Literature.* Edited by William L. Andrews, Frances Smith Foster, and Trudier Harris. New York: Oxford University Press, 1997.

OxCAmH   *The Oxford Companion to American History.* By Thomas H. Johnson. New York: Oxford University Press, 1966.

OxCAmL   *The Oxford Companion to American Literature.* By James D. Hart. New York: Oxford University Press, 1965-1995.
         OxCAmL 65   Fourth edition; 1965.
         OxCAmL 83   Fifth edition; 1983.
         OxCAmL 95   Sixth edition; 1995.

OxCAmT 84   *The Oxford Companion to American Theatre.* By Gerald Bordman. New York: Oxford University Press, 1984.

OxCArt   *The Oxford Companion to Art.* Edited by Harold Osborne. Oxford: Oxford University Press, Clarendon Press, 1970.

OxCAusL   *The Oxford Companion to Australian Literature.* By William H. Wilde, Joy Hooton, and Barry Andrews. Melbourne, Australia: Oxford University Press, 1985.

OxCBrHi   *The Oxford Companion to British History.* Edited by John Cannon. Oxford: Oxford University Press, 1997.

OxCCan   *The Oxford Companion to Canadian History and Literature.* Toronto: Oxford University Press, 1967-1973.
        OxCCan   By Norah Story; 1967.
        OxCCan SUP   Supplement. Edited by William Toye; 1973.

OxCCanL   *The Oxford Companion to Canadian Literature.* Toronto: Oxford University Press, 1983-1997.
        OxCCanL 1   Edited by William Toye; 1983.
        OxCCanL 2   Second edition. Edited by Eugene Benson and William Toye; 1997.

OxCCanT   *The Oxford Companion to Canadian Theatre.* Edited by Eugene Benson and L.W. Conolly. Toronto: Oxford University Press, 1989.

OxCChes 84   *The Oxford Companion to Chess.* By David Hooper and Kenneth Whyld. Oxford: Oxford University Press, 1984.

OxCChiL   *The Oxford Companion to Children's Literature.* By Humphrey Carpenter and Mari Prichard. Oxford: Oxford University Press, 1984.

OxCCAA   *The Oxford Companion to Christian Art and Architecture.* By Peter Murray and Linda Murray. New York: Oxford University Press, 1996.

OxCClC   *The Oxford Companion to Classical Civilization.* Edited by Simon Hornblower and Antony Spawforth. Oxford: Oxford University Press, 1998.

OxCClL   *The Oxford Companion to Classical Literature.* Oxford: Oxford University Press, 1937-1989.
        OxCClL   First edition. Edited by Sir Paul Harvey; 1937.
        OxCClL 89   Second edition. Edited by M.C. Howatson; 1989.

OxCDecA   *The Oxford Companion to the Decorative Arts.* Edited by Harold Osborne. Oxford: Oxford University Press, Clarendon Press, 1975.

OxCEng   *The Oxford Companion to English Literature.* Oxford: Oxford University Press, 1967-1995.
        OxCEng 67   Fourth edition. Compiled and edited by Sir Paul Harvey, revised by Dorothy Eagle; 1967.
        OxCEng 85   Fifth edition. Edited by Margaret Drabble; 1985.
        OxCEng 95   Revised fifth edition. Edited by Margaret Drabble; 1995.

OxCFaT   *The Oxford Companion to Fairy Tales.* Edited by Jack Zipes. New York: Oxford University Press, 2000.

OxCFilm   *The Oxford Companion to Film.* Edited by Liz-Anne Bawden. New York: Oxford University Press, 1976.

OxCFr   *The Oxford Companion to French Literature.* Compiled and edited by Sir Paul Harvey and J.E. Heseltine. Oxford: Oxford University Press, 1959. Reprinted with corrections, 1966.

OxCGer	*The Oxford Companion to German Literature.* Oxford: Oxford University Press, 1976-1997.

                      OxCGer 76   By Henry Garland and Mary Garland; 1976.
                      OxCGer 86   Second edition. By Mary Garland; 1986.
                      OxCGer 97   Third edition. By Mary Garland; 1997.

OxCIri   *The Oxford Companion to Irish Literature.* Edited by Robert Welch. Oxford: Oxford University Press, 1996.

OxCLaw   *The Oxford Companion to Law.* By David M. Walker. Oxford: Oxford University Press, Clarendon Press, 1980.

OxCLiW 86   *The Oxford Companion to the Literature of Wales.* Compiled and edited by Meic Stephens. Oxford: Oxford University Press, 1986.

OxCMed 86   *The Oxford Companion to Medicine.* Two volumes. Edited by John Walton, Paul B. Beeson, and Ronald Bodley Scott. Oxford: Oxford University Press, 1986.

OxCMus   *The Oxford Companion to Music.* 10th edition (corrected). By Percy A. Scholes. Edited by John Owen Ward. London: Oxford University Press, 1974.

OxCPhil   *The Oxford Companion to Philosophy.* Edited by Ted Honderich. Oxford: Oxford University Press, 1995.

OxCPMus   *The Oxford Companion to Popular Music.* By Peter Gammond. Oxford: Oxford University Press, 1991.

OxCShps   *The Oxford Companion to Ships and the Sea.* Edited by Peter Kemp. London: Oxford University Press, 1976.

OxCSpan   *The Oxford Companion to Spanish Literature.* Edited by Philip Ward. Oxford: Oxford University Press, Clarendon Press, 1978.

OxCSupC   *The Oxford Companion to the Supreme Court of the United States.* Edited by Kermit L. Hall. New York: Oxford University Press, 1992.

OxCThe   *The Oxford Companion to the Theatre.* Edited by Phyllis Hartnoll. Oxford: Oxford University Press, 1967-1983.

                      OxCThe 67   Third edition; 1967.
                      OxCThe 83   Fourth edition; 1983.

OxCTwCA   *The Oxford Companion to Twentieth-Century Art.* Edited by Harold Osborne. Oxford: Oxford University Press, 1981.

OxCTwCL   *The Oxford Companion to Twentieth-Century Literature in English.* Edited by Jenny Stringer. New York: Oxford University Press, 1996.

OxCTwCP   *The Oxford Companion to Twentieth-Century Poetry in English.* Edited by Ian Hamilton. Oxford: Oxford University Press, 1994.

OxCWoWr 95	*The Oxford Companion to Women's Writing in the United States.* Edited by Cathy N. Davidson and Linda Wagner-Martin. New York: Oxford University Press, 1995.
OxDcArt	*The Oxford Dictionary of Art.* Edited by Ian Chilvers and Harold Osborne. Oxford: Oxford University Press, 1988.
OxDcByz	*The Oxford Dictionary of Byzantium.* Three volumes. Edited by Alexander P. Kazhdan. New York: Oxford University Press, 1991.
OxDcJeR	*The Oxford Dictionary of the Jewish Religion.* Edited by R. J. Zwi Werblowsky and Geoffrey Wigoder. New York: Oxford University Press, 1997.
OxDcOp	*The Oxford Dictionary of Opera.* By John Warrack and Ewan West. Oxford: Oxford University Press, 1992.
OxDcP 86	*The Oxford Dictionary of Popes.* By J.N.D. Kelly. Oxford: Oxford University Press, 1986. Use the ''Alphabetical List of Popes and Antipopes'' which begins on page 1 to locate biographies.
PacWarE	*The Pacific War Encyclopedia.* Two volumes. By James F. Dunnigan and Albert A. Nofi. New York: Facts on File, 1998.
PenNWW	*Pen Names of Women Writers.* From 1600 to the present. A compendium of the literary identities of 2,650 women novelists, playwrights, poets, diarists, journalists and miscellaneous writers. By Alice Kahler Marshall. Camp Hill, PA: Alice Kahler Marshall, 1985.

PenNWW A   ''Alphabetical Listing by Author's Real Name'' begins on page 1.

PenNWW B   ''Alphabetical Listing by Author's Pen Name'' begins on page 95.

PenBWP	*The Penguin Book of Women Poets.* Edited by Carol Cosman, Joan Keefe, and Kathleen Weaver. New York: Viking Press, 1978.
PenC	*The Penguin Companion to World Literature.* New York: McGraw-Hill Book Co., 1971-1969.

PenC AM   *American Literature.* Edited by Malcolm Bradbury, Eric Mottram, and Jean Franco; 1971. Biographies are found in the ''U.S.A.'' and ''Latin America'' sections.

PenC CL   *Classical, Oriental and African Literature.* Edited by D.M. Lang and D.R. Dudley; 1969. Biographies are found in the ''Classical,'' ''Byzantine,'' ''Oriental,'' and ''African'' sections.

PenC ENG   *English Literature.* Edited by David Daiches; 1971.

PenC EUR   *European Literature.* Edited by Anthony Thorlby; 1969.

PenDiDA 89	*The Penguin Dictionary of Decorative Arts.* Revised edition. By John Fleming and Hugh Honour. London: Viking, 1989.

PenDiMP   *The Penguin Dictionary of Musical Performers.* A biographical guide to significant interpreters of classical music - singers, solo instrumentalists, conductors, orchestras and string quartets - ranging from the seventeenth century to the present day. By Arthur Jacobs. London: Viking, 1990.
          PenDiMP A   Biographies located in the "Index of Composers" begin on page 239.

PenEncH   *The Penguin Encyclopedia of Horror and the Supernatural.* Edited by Jack Sullivan. New York: Viking Penguin, 1986.

PenEncP   *The Penguin Encyclopedia of Popular Music.* Edited by Donald Clarke. New York: Viking, 1989.

PeoHis   *People in History.* An index to U.S. and Canadian biographies in history journals and dissertations. Two volumes. Edited by Susan K. Kinnell. Santa Barbara, CA: ABC-Clio, 1988.

PhDcTCA 77   *Phaidon Dictionary of Twentieth-Century Art.* Second edition. Oxford: Phaidon Press; New York: E.P. Dutton, 1977.

PhotEnc   *The Photography Encyclopedia.* By Gloria S. McDarrah, Fred W. McDarrah, and Timothy S. McDarrah. New York: Schirmer Books, 1999.

PiP   *The Pied Pipers.* Interviews with the influential creators of children's literature. By Justin Wintle and Emma Fisher. New York: Paddington Press, 1974.
          Use the Table of Contents to locate biographies.

PlP&P   *Plays, Players, and Playwrights.* An illustrated history of the theatre. By Marion Geisinger. Updated by Peggy Marks. New York: Hart Publishing Co., 1975.
          PlP&P   Use the Index, which begins on page 575, to locate biographies.
          PlP&P A   Use the Supplemental Index to the last chapter, which begins on page 797, to locate biographies.

PoeCrit   *Poetry Criticism.* Excerpts from criticism of the works of the most significant and widely studied poets of world literature. Detroit: Gale Research, 1991-1999.
          PoeCrit 1   Volume 1; 1991.
          PoeCrit 2   Volume 2; 1991.
          PoeCrit 3   Volume 3; 1991.
          PoeCrit 4   Volume 4; 1992.
          PoeCrit 5   Volume 5; 1992.
          PoeCrit 6   Volume 6; 1993.
          PoeCrit 7   Volume 7; 1994.
          PoeCrit 8   Volume 8; 1994.
          PoeCrit 9   Volume 9; 1994.
          PoeCrit 10   Volume 10; 1994.
          PoeCrit 11   Volume 11; 1995.
          PoeCrit 12   Volume 12; 1995.
          PoeCrit 13   Volume 13; 1995.
          PoeCrit 14   Volume 14; 1996.
          PoeCrit 15   Volume 15; 1997.
          PoeCrit 16   Volume 16; 1997.
          PoeCrit 17   Volume 17; 1997.

PoeCrit 18	Volume 18; 1997.
PoeCrit 19	Volume 19; 1997.
PoeCrit 20	Volume 20; 1998.
PoeCrit 21	Volume 21; 1998.
PoeCrit 22	Volume 22; 1999.
PoeCrit 23	Volume 23; 1999.

PoeCrit   *Poetry Criticism.* Excerpts from criticism of the works of the most significant and widely studied poets of world literature. Detroit: Gale Group, 1999-2000.

PoeCrit 24	Volume 24; 1999.
PoeCrit 25	Volume 25; 1999.
PoeCrit 26	Volume 26; 1999.
PoeCrit 27	Volume 27; 2000.
PoeCrit 28	Volume 28; 2000.

PoChrch   *The Poets of the Church.* A series of biographical sketches of hymn-writers with notes on their hymns. By Edwin F. Hatfield. New York: Anson D.F. Randolph & Co., 1884. Reprint. Detroit: Gale Research, 1978.

PoIre   *The Poets of Ireland.* A biographical and bibliographical dictionary of Irish writers of English verse. By D.J. O'Donoghue. Dublin, Ireland: Hodges Figgis & Co.; London: Henry Frowde, Oxford University Press, 1912. Reprint. Detroit: Gale Research, 1968.

      ''The Poets of Ireland'' begins on page 5. The Appendices begin on page 495.

PoLE   *The Poets Laureate of England.* Being a history of the office of poet laureate, biographical notices of its holders, and a collection of the satires, epigrams, and lampoons directed against them. By Walter Hamilton. London: Elliot Stock, 1879. Reprint. Detroit: Gale Research, 1968.

      Use the Index to locate biographies.

Po&Wr 77   *The Poets & Writers, Inc. 1977 Supplement.* A complete update to *A Directory of American Poets* (1975) and *A Directory of American Fiction Writers* (1976). New York: Poets & Writers, 1977.

      Use the Index to locate listings.

PolBiDi   *Polish Biographical Dictionary.* Profiles of nearly 900 Poles who have made lasting contributions to world civilization. By Stanley S. Sokol and Sharon F. Mrotek Kissane. Wauconda, IL: Bolchazy-Carducci Publishers, 1992.

PolCom   *Political Commentators in the United States in the 20th Century.* A bio-critical sourcebook. By Dan Nimmo and Chevelle Newsome. Westport, CT: Greenwood Press, 1997.

PolEnME   *Political Encyclopedia of the Middle East.* Edited by Avraham Sela. New York: Continuum Publishing Co., 1999.

PolLCME   *Political Leaders of the Contemporary Middle East and North Africa.* A biographical dictionary. Edited by Bernard Reich. New York: Greenwood Press, 1990.

PolLCWE   *Political Leaders of Contemporary Western Europe.* A biographical dictionary. Edited by David Wilsford. Westport, CT: Greenwood Press, 1995.

PolPar	*Political Parties and Elections in the United States.* An encyclopedia. Two volumes. Edited by L. Sandy Maisel. Garland Reference Library of Social Science, vol. 498. New York: Garland Publishing, 1991.

PolProf *Political Profiles.* New York: Facts on File, 1977-1978.

	PolProf E	*The Eisenhower Years.* Edited by Eleanora W. Schoenebaum; 1977.
	PolProf J	*The Johnson Years.* Edited by Nelson Lichtenstein; 1976.
	PolProf K	*The Kennedy Years.* Edited by Nelson Lichtenstein; 1976.
	PolProf NF	*The Nixon/Ford Years.* Edited by Eleanora W. Schoenebaum; 1979.
	PolProf T	*The Truman Years.* Edited by Eleanora W. Schoenebaum; 1978.

PolsAm 84	*Politics in America.* Members of Congress in Washington and at home. Edited by Alan Ehrenhalt. Washington: Congressional Quarterly, 1983. Use the Index to locate biographies.
PopAmC	*Popular American Composers.* From Revolutionary times to the present. A biographical and critical guide. Compiled and edited by David Ewen. New York: H.W. Wilson Co., 1962-1972.

	PopAmC	First edition; 1962.
	PopAmC SUP	First Supplement; 1972.
	PopAmC SUPN	First Supplement; 1972. The ''Necrology'' section appears on page vi.

PopDcHi	*A Popular Dictionary of Hinduism.* By Karel Werner. Richmond, Surrey, England: Curzon Press, 1994.
PopMus	*Popular Musicians.* Four volumes. Edited by Steve Hochman. Pasadena, CA: Salem Press, 1999.
PopNonf	*Popular Nonfiction Authors for Children.* A biographical and thematic guide. By Flora R. Wyatt, Margaret Coggins, and Jane Hunter Imber. Englewood, CO: Libraries Unlimited, 1998.
PorAmW	*Portraits of American Women.* From settlement to the present. By G.J. Barker-Benfield and Catherine Clinton. New York: St. Martin's Press, 1991. Use the Table of Contents to locate biographies.
PorSil	*Portraits in Silicon.* By Robert Slater. Cambridge: MIT Press, 1987. Use the Index to locate biographies.
PostFic	*Postmodern Fiction.* A bio-bibliographical guide. Edited by Larry McCaffery. Movements in the Arts, no. 2. New York: Greenwood Press, 1986. Biographies begin on page 247.
PresAR 1980	*Presidential Also-Rans and Running Mates, 1788-1980.* By Leslie H. Southwick. Jefferson, NC: McFarland & Co., 1984. Use the Index to locate biographies.

Key to Source Codes

PresAR 1996   *Presidential Also-Rans and Running Mates, 1788 through 1996.* Compiled by Leslie H. Southwick. Jefferson, NC: McFarland & Co., 1998.
Use the Index to locate biographies.

Pres 96   *The Presidents.* A reference history. Second edition. Edited by Henry F. Graff. New York: Charles Scribner's Sons, 1996.
Use the Table of Contents to locate biographies.

PrimTiR   *Prime-Time Religion.* An encyclopedia of religious broadcasting. By J. Gordon Melton, Philip Charles Lucas, and Jon R. Stone. Phoenix, AZ: Oryx Press, 1997.

PriCCJL 85   *The Princeton Companion to Classical Japanese Literature.* By Earl Miner, Hiroko Odagiri, and Robert E. Morrell. Princeton, NJ: Princeton University Press, 1985.
Biographies begin on page 141.

PrintW   *The Printworld Directory of Contemporary Prints & Prices.* Edited by Selma Smith. Bala Cynwyd, PA: Printworld, 1983-1985.
    PrintW 83   *1983/84,* second edition; 1983.
    PrintW 85   *1985/86,* third edition; 1985.
Not in strict alphabetical order.

ProFbHF   *The Pro Football Hall of Fame.* Players, coaches, team owners and league officials, 1963-1991. By Denis J. Harrington. Jefferson, NC: McFarland & Co., 1991.
Use the Index to locate entries.

Profile   *Profiles.* Authors and illustrators, children's literature in Canada. Edited by Irma McDonough. Ottawa: Canadian Library Association, 1975-1982.
    Profile 1   Revised edition; 1975.
    Profile 2   *Profiles 2.*; 1982.

ProfiWG 98   *Profiles of Worldwide Government Leaders.* 1998. Edited by Alan J. Day. Washington, DC: Keesing's Worldwide, L.L.C., 1998.
Use the Index to locate entries.

ProPowC   *Protest, Power, and Change.* An encyclopedia of nonviolent action from ACT-UP to women's suffrage. Edited by Roger S. Powers and William B. Vogele. New York: Garland Publishing, 1997.

PseudAu   *Pseudonyms of Authors.* Including anonyms and initialisms. By John Edward Haynes. New York: John Edward Haynes, 1882. Reprint. Detroit: Gale Research, 1969.
    PseudAu   Pseudonyms are given exactly as written by the author and are filed under the first letter of the pseudonym, including the articles ''a,'' ''an,'' and ''the.''
    PseudAu A   Addenda begins on page 104. Pseudonyms are given exactly as written by the author and are filed under the first letter of the pseudonym, including the articles ''a,'' ''an,'' and ''the.''

PseudN 82   *Pseudonyms and Nicknames Dictionary.* Second edition. Edited by Jennifer Mossman. Detroit: Gale Research Inc., 1982.

PueRA	*Puerto Rican Authors.* A biobibliographic handbook. By Marnesba D. Hill and Harold B. Schleifer. Translation of entries into Spanish by Daniel Maratos. Metuchen, NJ: Scarecrow Press, 1974.
PueRPas	*Puerto Rico Past and Present.* An encyclopedia. By Ronald Fernandez, Serafin Mendez Mendez, and Gail Cueto. Westport, CT: Greenwood Press, 1998.
PupTheA	*The Puppet Theatre in America.* A history, 1524-1948. By Paul McPharlin. With a supplement *Puppets in America since 1948.* By Marjorie Batchelder McPharlin. Boston: Plays, Inc., 1969.

> ***PupTheA*** — Biographies are found in Chapter XXI, ''A List of Puppeteers, 1524-1948,'' beginning on page 396.
> ***PupTheA SUP*** — Biographies are found in Chapter V of the Supplement ''Some Careers in Puppetry,'' beginning on page 606.

QDrFCA 92	*Quinlan's Illustrated Directory of Film Comedy Actors.* By David Quinlan. New York: Henry Holt and Co., 1992.
RadHan	*The Radicalism Handbook.* Radical activists, groups and movements of the twentieth century. By John Button. Santa Barbara, CA: ABC-CLIO, 1995. Use the Index to locate biographies.
RadStar	*Radio Stars.* An illustrated biographical dictionary of 953 performers, 1920 through 1960. By Thomas A. DeLong. Jefferson, NC: McFarland & Co., 1996.
RadMoSP	*Radio's Morning Show Personalities.* Early hour broadcasters and deejays from the 1920s to the 1990s. By Philip A. Lieberman. Jefferson, NC: McFarland & Co., 1996. Use the Index to locate biographies.
RanHWDS	*Random House Webster's Dictionary of Scientists.* New York: Random House, 1997.
RAdv 1	*The Reader's Adviser.* A layman's guide to literature. 12th edition. Volume 1: *The Best in American and British Fiction, Poetry, Essays, Literary Biography, Bibliography, and Reference..* Edited by Sarah L. Prakken. New York: R.R. Bowker Co., 1974. Use the ''Name Index'' to locate biographies.
RAdv 14	*The Reader's Adviser.* 14th edition. Six volumes. Edited by Marion Sader. New Providence, NJ: R.R. Bowker, 1994. Use the Name Index in Volume 6 to locate entries.
RAdv	*The Reader's Adviser.* A layman's guide to literature. New York: R.R. Bowker Co., 1986-1988.

> ***RAdv 13-1*** — 13th edition. Volume 1: *The Best in American and British Fiction, Poetry, Essays, Literary Biography, Bibliography, and Reference.* Edited by Fred Kaplan; 1986.
> ***RAdv 13-2*** — 13th edition. Volume 2: *The Best in American and British Drama and World Literature in English Translation.* Edited by Maurice Charney; 1986.

RAdv 13-3	13th edition. Volume 3: *The Best in General Reference Literature, the Social Sciences, History, and the Arts.* Edited by Paula T. Kaufman; 1986.
RAdv 13-4	13th edition. Volume 4: *The Best in the Literature of Philosophy and World Religions.* Edited by William L. Reese; 1988.
RAdv 13-5	13th edition. Volume 5: *The Best in the Literature of Science, Technology, and Medicine.* Edited by Paul T. Durbin; 1988.
	Use the ''Name Index'' to locate biographies.
RComAH	*The Reader's Companion to American History.* Edited by Eric Foner and John A. Garraty. Boston: Houghton Mifflin Co., 1991.
RComWL	*The Reader's Companion to World Literature.* Second edition. Revised and updated by Lillian Herlands Hornstein, Leon Edel, and Horst Frenz. New York: New American Library, 1973.
REn	*The Reader's Encyclopedia.* Second edition. By William Rose Benet. New York: Thomas Y. Crowell Co., 1965.
REnAL	*The Reader's Encyclopedia of American Literature.* By Max J. Herzberg. New York: Thomas Y. Crowell Co., 1962.
REnAW	*The Reader's Encyclopedia of the American West.* Edited by Howard R. Lamar. New York: Thomas Y. Crowell Co., 1977.
REnWD	*The Reader's Encyclopedia of World Drama.* Edited by John Gassner and Edward Quinn. New York: Thomas Y. Crowell Co., 1969.
RGAfL	*A Reader's Guide to African Literature.* Compiled and edited by Hans M. Zell and Helene Silver. New York: Africana Publishing Corp., 1971. Biographies begin on page 113.
RGFAP	*A Reader's Guide to Fifty American Poets.* By Peter Jones. London: Heinemann; Totowa, NJ: Barnes & Noble, 1980. Use the Index to locate biographies.
RGFBP	*A Reader's Guide to Fifty British Poets, 1300-1900.* By Michael Schmidt. London: Heinemann; Totowa, NJ: Barnes & Noble, 1980. Use the Index to locate biographies.
RGFMBP	*A Reader's Guide to Fifty Modern British Poets.* By Michael Schmidt. London: Heinemann; New York: Barnes & Noble, 1979. Use the Index to locate biographies.
RGFMEP	*Reader's Guide to Fifty Modern European Poets.* By John Pilling. London: Heinemann; Totowa, NJ: Barnes & Noble, 1982. Use the Index to locate biographies.
RGSF	*A Reader's Guide to Science Fiction.* By Baird Searles, Martin Last, Beth Meacham, and Michael Franklin. New York: Facts On File, 1979.

RGTwCSF   *Reader's Guide to Twentieth-Century Science Fiction.* Edited by Marilyn P. Fletcher. Chicago: American Library Association, 1989.

RGTwCWr   *A Reader's Guide to Twentieth-Century Writers.* Edited by Peter Parker. Oxford: Oxford University Press, 1996.

RealN   *Realism, Naturalism, and Local Color, 1865-1917.* Concise Dictionary of American Literary Biography Series. Detroit: Gale Research, 1988.

ReelWom   *Reel Women.* Pioneers of the cinema, 1896 to the present. By Ally Acker. New York: Continuum, 1991.
                     Use the Index to locate biographies.

RfGAmL   *Reference Guide to American Literature.* Detroit: St. James Press, 2000-1994.
                 RfGAmL 4   Fourth edition. Edited by Thomas Riggs; 2000.
                 RfGAmL 87   Second edition. Edited by D.L. Kirkpatrick; 1987.
                 RfGAmL 94   Third edition. Edited by Jim Kamp; 1994.

RfGEnL 91   *Reference Guide to English Literature.* Second edition. Three volumes. Edited by D.L. Kirkpatrick. Chicago: St. James Press, 1991.

RfGShF   *Reference Guide to Short Fiction.* Detroit: St. James Press, 1994-1999.
                 RfGShF 1   First edition. Edited by Noelle Watson; 1994.
                 RfGShF 2   Second edition. Edited by Thomas Riggs; 1999.

RfGWoL 95   *Reference Guide to World Literature.* Second edition. Two volumes. Edited by Lesley Henderson. Detroit: St. James Press, 1995.

RelLAm 1   *Religious Leaders of America.* A biographical guide to founders and leaders of religious bodies, churches, and spiritual groups in North America. By J. Gordon Melton. Detroit: Gale Research, 1991.

RelLAm 2   *Religious Leaders of America.* A biographical guide to founders and leaders of religious bodies, churches, and spiritual groups in North America. Second edition. By J. Gordon Melton. Detroit: Gale Group, 1999.

RkOn   *Rock On.* The illustrated encyclopedia of rock n' roll. By Norm N. Nite. New York: Thomas Y. Crowell Co., 1974-1978.
                 RkOn 74   Volume 1: *The Solid Gold Years*; 1974.
                 RkOn 74   Volume 1: *The Solid Gold Years*; 1974.
                 RkOn 78   Volume 2: *The Modern Years: 1964-Present*; 1978.
                 RkOn 78A   Volume 2: *The Modern Years: 1964-Present*; 1978.
                                     Appendix begins on page 543.

RkOn   *Rock On.* The illustrated encyclopedia of rock n' roll. By Norm N. Nite. New York: Harper & Row, 1982-1985.
                 RkOn 82   Volume 1: *The Solid Gold Years,* revised 1982; 1982.
                 RkOn 84   Volume 2: *The Years of Change, 1964-1978,* revised 1984; 1984.
                 RkOn 85   Volume 3: *The Video Revolution, 1978-Present.*; 1985.
                 RkOn 85A   Volume 3: *The Video Revolution, 1978-Present.*; 1985.
                                     The Appendix begins on page 413.

RkWho 96   *The Rock Who's Who.* Second edition. By Brock Helander. New York: Schirmer Books, 1996.

RkWW 82   *Rock Who's Who.* By Brock Helander. New York: Macmillan, Schirmer Books, 1982.

RkinSix   *The Rockin' '60s.* The people who made the music. By Brock Helander. New York: Schirmer Books, 1999.
　　　　　　　Use Index to locate biographies.

RolSEnR 83   *The Rolling Stone Encyclopedia of Rock & Roll.* Edited by Jon Pareles and Patricia Romanowski. New York: Rolling Stone Press/Summit Books, 1983.

RomantH   *Romantic Hearts.* Third edition. By Peggy J. Jaegly. Lanham, MD: Scarecrow Press, 1997.

SaTiSS   *Same Time, Same Station.* An a-z guide to radio from Jack Benny to Howard Stern. By Ron Lackmann. New York: Facts on File, 1996.

SchCGBL   *The Schomburg Center Guide to Black Literature.* From the eighteenth century to the present. Detroit: Gale Research, 1996.

ScF&FL   *Science Fiction and Fantasy Literature.* A checklist, 1700-1974. By R. Reginald. Detroit: Gale Research, 1979.
　　　　　ScF&FL 1　　　Volume 1.
　　　　　ScF&FL 1A　　Volume 1. Addendum begins on page 581.
　　　　　ScF&FL 2　　　Volume 2: *Contemporary Science Fiction Authors II.*

ScF&FL 92   *Science Fiction & Fantasy Literature, 1975-1991.* A bibliography of science fiction, fantasy, and horror fiction books and nonfiction monographs. By Robert Reginald. Detroit: Gale Research, 1992.

ScFSB   *The Science Fiction Source Book.* Edited by David Wingrove. New York: Van Nostrand Reinhold Co., 1984.
　　　　　Listings are located in the ''Science Fiction Writers: A Consumers' Guide'' section, which begins on page 87.

ScFEYrs   *Science Fiction: The Early Years.* A full description of more than 3,000 science-fiction stories from earliest times to the appearance of the genre magazines in 1930. By Everett F. Bleiler. Kent, OH: Kent State University Press, 1990.
　　　　　ScFEYrs A　　　First Addenda begins on page 843.
　　　　　ScFEYrs B　　　Second Addenda begins on page 851.

ScFWr   *Science Fiction Writers.* Critical studies of the major authors from the early nineteenth century to the present day. The Scribner Writers Series. New York: Charles Scribner's Sons, 1982-1999.
　　　　　ScFWr　　　　Edited by E.F. Bleiler; 1982.
　　　　　ScFWr 2　　　Second Edition. Edited by Richard Bleiler; 1999.

ScFnry   *The Science Fictionary.* An A-Z guide to the world of SF authors, films, and TV shows. Edited by Ed Naha. New York: Seaview Books, 1980.

Sc&ItsT 5	*Science and Its Times.* Understanding the social significance of scientific discovery. Volume Five: *1800-1899.* Detroit: Gale Group, 2000. Use the Index to locate biographies.
SciMath	*Scientists, Mathematicians, and Inventors.* Edited by Doris Simonis. Lives and Legacies: An Encyclopedia of People Who Changed the World. Phoenix, AZ: Oryx Press, 1999.
ScrEAmL	*The Scribner Encyclopedia of American Lives.* Edited by Kenneth T. Jackson. New York: Charles Scribner's Sons, 1998-1999.

	ScrEAmL 1	Volume One: 1981-1985; 1998.
	ScrEAmL 2	Volume Two: 1986-1990; 1999.

SelBAAf	*Selected Black American, African, and Caribbean Authors.* A bio-bibliography. Compiled by James A. Page and Jae Min Roh. Littleton, CO: Libraries Unlimited, 1985.
SelBAAu	*Selected Black American Authors.* An illustrated bio-bibliography. Compiled by James A. Page. Boston: G.K. Hall & Co., 1977.
SenS	*A Sense of Story.* Essays on contemporary writers for children. By John Rowe Townsend. London: Longman Group, 1971.
ShSCr	*Short Story Criticism.* Excerpts from criticism of the works of short fiction writers. Detroit: Gale Research, 1988-1999.

	ShSCr 1	Volume 1; 1988.
	ShSCr 2	Volume 2; 1989.
	ShSCr 3	Volume 3; 1989.
	ShSCr 4	Volume 4; 1990.
	ShSCr 5	Volume 5; 1990.
	ShSCr 6	Volume 6; 1990.
	ShSCr 7	Volume 7; 1991.
	ShSCr 8	Volume 8; 1991.
	ShSCr 9	Volume 9; 1992.
	ShSCr 10	Volume 10; 1992.
	ShSCr 11	Volume 11; 1992.
	ShSCr 12	Volume 12; 1993.
	ShSCr 13	Volume 13; 1993.
	ShSCr 14	Volume 14; 1994.
	ShSCr 15	Volume 15; 1994.
	ShSCr 16	Volume 16; 1994.
	ShSCr 17	Volume 17; 1995.
	ShSCr 18	Volume 18; 1995.
	ShSCr 19	Volume 19; 1995.
	ShSCr 20	Volume 20; 1995.
	ShSCr 21	Volume 21; 1996.
	ShSCr 22	Volume 22; 1996.
	ShSCr 23	Volume 23; 1996.
	ShSCr 24	Volume 24; 1997.
	ShSCr 25	Volume 25; 1997.
	ShSCr 26	Volume 26; 1997.
	ShSCr 27	Volume 27; 1998.
	ShSCr 28	Volume 28; 1998.

ShSCr 29	Volume 29; 1998.	
ShSCr 30	Volume 30; 1999.	
ShSCr 31	Volume 31; 1999.	

ShSCr   *Short Story Criticism.* Criticism of the works of short fiction writers. Detroit: Gale Group, 1999-2000.

ShSCr 32	Volume 32; 1999.
ShSCr 33	Volume 33; 1999.
ShSCr 34	Volume 34; 2000.
ShSCr 35	Volume 35; 2000.
ShSCr 36	Volume 36; 2000.

ShSWr   *Short Story Writers & Their Work.* A guide to the best. By Brad Hooper. Chicago: American Library Association, 1988.
Use the ''Author Index'' to locate biographies.

SigCnAF   *Significant Contemporary American Feminists.* A biographical sourcebook. Edited by Jennifer Scanlon. Westport, CT: Greenwood Press, 1999.

SilFlmP   *Silent Film Performers.* An annotated bibliography of published, unpublished, and archival sources for over 350 actors and actresses. By Roy Liebman. Jefferson, NC: McFarland & Co., 1996.

SingR   *Singing Roads.* A guide to Australian children's authors and illustrators. Edited by Hugh Anderson. Surry Hills, Australia: Wentworth Books, 1972-1970.

SingR 1	Part 1, Fourth edition; 1972.
SingR 2	Part 2; 1970.

SingPar   *Single Parents.* A reference handbook. By Karen L. Kinnear. Santa Barbara, CA: ABC-Clio, 1999.
Biographical Sketches section begins on page 95.

SixBJA   *Sixth Book of Junior Authors & Illustrators.* Edited by Sally Holmes Holtze. New York: H.W. Wilson Co., 1989.

SixAP   *Sixty American Poets, 1896-1944.* Revised edition. Selected, with preface and critical notes by Allen Tate. Washington, DC: Library of Congress, 1954. Reprint. Detroit: Gale Research, 1969.

SocPrL   *Social Protest Literature.* An encyclopedia of works, characters, authors, and themes. By Patricia D. Netzley. Santa Barbara, CA: ABC-CLIO Inc., 1999.

SmATA   *Something about the Author.* Facts and pictures about authors and illustrators of books for young people. Detroit: Gale Research, 1971-1999.

SmATA 1	Volume 1; 1971.
SmATA 2	Volume 2; 1971.
SmATA 3	Volume 3; 1972.
SmATA 4	Volume 4; 1973.
SmATA 5	Volume 5; 1973.
SmATA 6	Volume 6; 1974.
SmATA 7	Volume 7; 1975.
SmATA 8	Volume 8; 1976.
SmATA 9	Volume 9; 1976.
SmATA 10	Volume 10; 1976.

SmATA 11	Volume 11; 1977.
SmATA 12	Volume 12; 1977.
SmATA 13	Volume 13; 1978.
SmATA 14	Volume 14; 1978.
SmATA 15	Volume 15; 1979.
SmATA 16	Volume 16; 1979.
SmATA 17	Volume 17; 1979.
SmATA 18	Volume 18; 1980.
SmATA 19	Volume 19; 1980.
SmATA 20	Volume 20; 1980.
SmATA 20N	Volume 20, Obituary Notice; 1980.
SmATA 21	Volume 21; 1980.
SmATA 21N	Volume 21, Obituary Notice; 1980.
SmATA 22	Volume 22; 1981.
SmATA 22N	Volume 22, Obituary Notice; 1981.
SmATA 23	Volume 23; 1981.
SmATA 23N	Volume 23, Obituary Notice; 1981.
SmATA 24	Volume 24; 1981.
SmATA 24N	Volume 24, Obituary Notice; 1981.
SmATA 25	Volume 25; 1981.
SmATA 25N	Volume 25, Obituary Notice; 1981.
SmATA 26	Volume 26; 1982.
SmATA 26N	Volume 26, Obituary Notice; 1982.
SmATA 27	Volume 27; 1982.
SmATA 27N	Volume 27, Obituary Notice; 1982.
SmATA 28	Volume 28; 1982.
SmATA 28N	Volume 28, Obituary Notice; 1982.
SmATA 29	Volume 29; 1982.
SmATA 29N	Volume 29, Obituary Notice; 1982.
SmATA 30	Volume 30; 1983.
SmATA 30N	Volume 30, Obituary Notice; 1983.
SmATA 31	Volume 31; 1983.
SmATA 31N	Volume 31, Obituary Notice; 1983.
SmATA 32	Volume 32; 1983.
SmATA 32N	Volume 32, Obituary Notice; 1983.
SmATA 33	Volume 33; 1983.
SmATA 33N	Volume 33, Obituary Notice; 1983.
SmATA 34	Volume 34; 1984.
SmATA 34N	Volume 34, Obituary Notice; 1984.
SmATA 35	Volume 35; 1984.
SmATA 35N	Volume 35, Obituary Notice; 1984.
SmATA 36	Volume 36; 1984.
SmATA 36N	Volume 36, Obituary Notice; 1984.
SmATA 37	Volume 37; 1985.
SmATA 37N	Volume 37, Obituary Notice; 1985.
SmATA 38	Volume 38; 1985.
SmATA 38N	Volume 38, Obituary Notice; 1985.
SmATA 39	Volume 39; 1985.
SmATA 39N	Volume 39, Obituary Notice; 1985.
SmATA 40	Volume 40; 1985.
SmATA 40N	Volume 40, Obituary Notice; 1985.
SmATA 41	Volume 41; 1985.
SmATA 41N	Volume 41, Obituary Notice; 1985.
SmATA 42	Volume 42; 1986.
SmATA 42N	Volume 42, Obituary Notice; 1986.

SmATA 43	Volume 43; 1986.
SmATA 43N	Volume 43, Obituary Notice; 1986.
SmATA 44	Volume 44; 1986.
SmATA 44N	Volume 44, Obituary Notice; 1986.
SmATA 45	Volume 45; 1986.
SmATA 45N	Volume 45, Obituary Notice; 1986.
SmATA 46	Volume 46; 1987.
SmATA 46N	Volume 46, Obituary Notice; 1987.
SmATA 47	Volume 47; 1987.
SmATA 47N	Volume 47, Obituary Notice; 1987.
SmATA 48	Volume 48; 1987.
SmATA 48N	Volume 48, Obituary Notice; 1987.
SmATA 49	Volume 49; 1987.
SmATA 49N	Volume 49, Obituary Notice; 1987.
SmATA 50	Volume 50; 1988.
SmATA 50N	Volume 50, Obituary Notice; 1988.
SmATA 51	Volume 51; 1988.
SmATA 51N	Volume 51, Obituary Notice; 1988.
SmATA 52	Volume 52; 1988.
SmATA 52N	Volume 52, Obituary Notice; 1988.
SmATA 53	Volume 53; 1988.
SmATA 53N	Volume 53, Obituary Notice; 1988.
SmATA 54	Volume 54; 1989.
SmATA 54N	Volume 54, Obituary Notice; 1989.
SmATA 55	Volume 55; 1989.
SmATA 55N	Volume 55, Obituary Notice; 1989.
SmATA 56	Volume 56; 1989.
SmATA 56N	Volume 56, Obituary Notice; 1989.
SmATA 57	Volume 57; 1989.
SmATA 58	Volume 58; 1990.
SmATA 59	Volume 59; 1990.
SmATA 60	Volume 60; 1990.
SmATA 61	Volume 61; 1990.
SmATA 62	Volume 62; 1990.
SmATA 63	Volume 63; 1991.
SmATA 64	Volume 64; 1991.
SmATA 65	Volume 65; 1991.
SmATA 66	Volume 66; 1991.
SmATA 67	Volume 67; 1992.
SmATA 68	Volume 68; 1992.
SmATA 69	Volume 69; 1992.
SmATA 70	Volume 70; 1993.
SmATA 71	Volume 71; 1993.
SmATA 72	Volume 72; 1993.
SmATA 73	Volume 73; 1993.
SmATA 74	Volume 74; 1993.
SmATA 75	Volume 75; 1994.
SmATA 76	Volume 76; 1994.
SmATA 77	Volume 77; 1994.
SmATA 78	Volume 78; 1994.
SmATA 79	Volume 79; 1995.
SmATA 80	Volume 80; 1995.
SmATA 81	Volume 81; 1995.
SmATA 82	Volume 82; 1995.
SmATA 83	Volume 83; 1996.

SmATA 84	Volume 84; 1996.
SmATA 85	Volume 85; 1996.
SmATA 86	Volume 86; 1996.
SmATA 87	Volume 87; 1996.
SmATA 88	Volume 88; 1997.
SmATA 89	Volume 89; 1997.
SmATA 90	Volume 90; 1997.
SmATA 91	Volume 91; 1997.
SmATA 92	Volume 92; 1997.
SmATA 93	Volume 93; 1997.
SmATA 94	Volume 94; 1998.
SmATA 95	Volume 95; 1998.
SmATA 96	Volume 96; 1998.
SmATA 97	Volume 97; 1998.
SmATA 98	Volume 98; 1998.
SmATA 99	Volume 99; 1999.
SmATA 100	Volume 100; 1999.
SmATA 101	Volume 101; 1999.
SmATA 102	Volume 102; 1999.

SmATA   *Something about the Author.* Facts and pictures about authors and illustrators of books for young people. Detroit: Gale Group, 1999-2000.

SmATA 103	Volume 103; 1999.
SmATA 104	Volume 104; 1999.
SmATA 105	Volume 105; 1999.
SmATA 106	Volume 106; 1999.
SmATA 107	Volume 107; 1999.
SmATA 108	Volume 108; 2000.
SmATA 109	Volume 109; 2000.
SmATA 110	Volume 110; 2000.
SmATA 111	Volume 111; 2000.
SmATA 112	Volume 112; 2000.

SmATA   *Something about the Author, Autobiography Series.* Detroit: Gale Research, 1986-1998.

SmATA 1AS	Volume 1; 1986.
SmATA 2AS	Volume 2; 1986.
SmATA 3AS	Volume 3; 1987.
SmATA 4AS	Volume 4; 1987.
SmATA 5AS	Volume 5; 1988.
SmATA 6AS	Volume 6; 1988.
SmATA 7AS	Volume 7; 1989.
SmATA 8AS	Volume 8; 1989.
SmATA 9AS	Volume 9; 1990.
SmATA 10AS	Volume 10; 1990.
SmATA 11AS	Volume 11; 1991.
SmATA 12AS	Volume 12; 1991.
SmATA 13AS	Volume 13; 1992.
SmATA 14AS	Volume 14; 1992.
SmATA 15AS	Volume 15; 1993.
SmATA 16AS	Volume 16; 1993.
SmATA 17AS	Volume 17; 1994.
SmATA 18AS	Volume 18; 1994.
SmATA 19AS	Volume 19; 1995.
SmATA 20AS	Volume 20; 1995.

SmATA 21AS	Volume 21; 1996.
SmATA 22AS	Volume 22; 1996.
SmATA 23AS	Volume 23; 1997.
SmATA 24AS	Volume 24; 1997.
SmATA 25AS	Volume 25; 1998.
SmATA 26AS	Volume 26; 1998.

Songw   *Songwriters.* A biographical dictionary with discographies. By Nigel Harrison. Jefferson, NC: McFarland & Co., 1998.

SoulM   *Soul Music A-Z.* By Hugh Gregory. London: Blandford, 1991. Distributed by Sterling Publishing Co., New York.

SouSt   *A Sounding of Storytellers.* New and revised essays on contemporary writers for children. By John Rowe Townsend. New York: J.B. Lippincott, 1979.

SourALJ   *A Sourcebook of American Literary Journalism.* Representative writers in an emerging genre. Edited by Thomas B. Connery. New York: Greenwood Press, 1992.
      Use the Index to locate biographies.

SouBlCW   *Southern Black Creative Writers, 1829-1953.* Biobibliographies. Compiled by M. Marie Booth Foster. Bibliographies and Indexes in Afro-American and African Studies, no. 22. New York: Greenwood Press, 1988.

SouWr   *Southern Writers.* A biographical dictionary. Edited by Robert Bain, Joseph M. Flora, and Louis D. Rubin, Jr. Baton Rouge, LA: Louisiana State University Press, 1979.

SovUn   *The Soviet Union.* A biographical dictionary. Edited by Archie Brown. New York: Macmillan Publishing Co., 1990.
      SovUn A   Appendix 5: New Politburo Members begins on page 488.

SpAmA   *Spanish American Authors.* The twentieth century. By Angel Flores. New York: H.W. Wilson Co., 1992.

SpAmWar   *The Spanish American War.* A historical dictionary. By Brad K. Berner. Lanham, MD: Scarecrow Press, 1998.

SpAmWW   *Spanish American Women Writers.* A bio-bibliographical source book. Edited by Diane E. Marting. New York: Greenwood Press, 1990.

SpDramG   *Spanish Dramatists of the Golden Age.* A bio-bibliographical sourcebook. Edited by Mary Parker. Westport, CT: Greenwood Press, 1998.

Spies   *Spies.* A narrative encyclopedia of dirty deeds and double dealing from biblical times to today. By Jay Robert Nash. New York: M. Evans and Co., 1997.

SpreRhy   *Spreadin' Rhythm Around.* Black popular songwriters, 1880-1930. By David A. Jasen and Gene Jones. New York: Schirmer Books, 1998.
      Use the General Index to locate entries.

SpyCS	*Spy/Counterspy: Encyclopedia of Espionage.* By Vincent Buranelli and Nan Buranelli. New York: McGraw-Hill, 1982.
SpyFic	*Spy Fiction.* A connoisseur's guide. By Donald McCormick and Katy Fletcher. New York: Facts on File, 1990.
SJGBlA	*St. James Guide to Black Artists.* Edited by Thomas Riggs. Detroit: St. James Press, 1997.
SJGChWr 5	*St. James Guide to Children's Writers.* Fifth edition. Edited by Sara Pendergast and Tom Pendergast. Detroit: St. James Press, 1999. Earlier editions published as *Twentieth-Century Children's Writers.*

> ***SJGChWr 5A***   Appendix begins on page 1165.
> ***SJGChWr 5B***   "Foreign-Language Writers" section begins on page 1205.

SJGFanW	*St. James Guide to Fantasy Writers.* Edited by David Pringle. Detroit: St. James Press, 1996.

> Foreign-language authors section begins on page 649.

SJGHorW	*St. James Guide to Horror, Ghost, & Gothic Writers.* Edited by David Pringle. Detroit: St. James Press, 1998.
SJGNNAA	*St. James Guide to Native North American Artists.* Edited by Roger Matuz. Detroit: St. James Press, 1998.
SJGYouA 2	*St. James Guide to Young Adult Writers.* Second edition. Edited by Tom Pendergast and Sara Pendergast. Detroit: St. James Press, 1999. Earlier editions published as *Twentieth-Century Young Adult Writers.*
St&PR	*Standard & Poor's Register of Corporations, Directors and Executives.* New York: Standard & Poor's Corp., 1975-1998.

> ***St&PR 75***   1975 edition. Volume 2: *Directors and Executives.*; 1975.
> ***St&PR 84***   1984 edition. Volume 2: *Directors and Executives.*; 1984.
> ***St&PR 84N***   1984 edition. Volume 3; 1984. Obituary section begins on page 901.
> ***St&PR 87***   1987 edition. Volume 2: *Directors and Executives.*; 1987.
> ***St&PR 87N***   1987 edition. Volume 3; 1987. Obituary section begins on page 901.
> ***St&PR 91***   1991 edition. Volume 2: *Directors and Executives.*; 1991.
> ***St&PR 91N***   1991 edition. Volume 3; 1991. Obituary section begins on page 901.
> ***St&PR 93***   1993 edition. Volume 2: *Directors and Executives.*; 1993.
> ***St&PR 93N***   1993 edition. Volume 3; 1993. Obituary section begins on page 901.
> ***St&PR 96***   1996 edition. Volume 2: *Directors and Executives*; 1996.
> ***St&PR 96N***   1996 edition. Volume 3; 1996. Obituary section begins on page 901.

St&PR 97	1997 edition. Volume 2: *Directors and Executives*; 1997.
St&PR 97N	1997 edition. Volume 3; 1997. Obituary section begins on page 901.
St&PR 98	1998 edition. Volume 2: *Directors and Executives.*; 1998.
St&PR 98N	1998 edition. Volume 3; 1998. Obituary section begins on page 1001.

St&PR   *Standard & Poor's Register of Corporations, Directors and Executives.* Charlottesville, VA: Standard & Poor's, 1999.

St&PR 99	1999 edition. Volume 2: *Directors and Executives.*
St&PR 99N	1999 edition. Volume 3. Obituary section begins on page 1001.

St&PR   *Standard & Poor's Register of Corporations, Directors, and Executives.* 2000 edition. Charlottesville, VA: Standard & Poor's, 2000.

St&PR 2000	Volume 2: *Directors and Executives.*
St&PR 2000	Volume 3. Obituary section begins on page 1001.

StaCVF   *The Stanford Companion to Victorian Fiction.* By John Sutherland. Stanford, CA: Stanford University Press, 1989.

Str&VC   *Story and Verse for Children.* Third edition. By Miriam Blanton Huber. New York: Macmillan Co., 1965.
Biographies begin on page 793.

SupFW   *Supernatural Fiction Writers.* Fantasy and horror. Two volumes. Edited by E.F. Bleiler. New York: Charles Scribner's Sons, 1985.
Use the Index to locate biographies.

SupCtJu   *The Supreme Court Justices.* A biographical dictionary. Edited by Melvin I. Urofsky. Garland Reference Library of the Humanities, vol. 1851. New York: Garland Publishing, 1994.

Sw&Ld   *Sweet and Lowdown.* America's popular song writers. By Warren Craig. Metuchen, NJ: Scarecrow Press, 1978.

Sw&Ld A	Biographies appear in the "Before Tin Pan Alley" section, beginning on page 15.
Sw&Ld B	Biographies appear in the "Tin Pan Alley" section, beginning on page 23.
Sw&Ld C	Biographies appear in the "After Tin Pan Alley" section, beginning on page 91.

SweetSg   *Sweethearts of the Sage.* Biographies and filmographies of 258 actresses appearing in Western movies. By Buck Rainey. Jefferson, NC: McFarland & Co., 1992.

SweetSg A	"The Pathfinders" section begins on page 2.
SweetSg B	"The Trailblazers" section begins on page 98.
SweetSg C	"The Pioneers" section begins on page 240.
SweetSg D	"The Homesteaders" section begins on page 466.

TelevWe   *Television Western Players of the Fifties.* A biographical encyclopedia of all regular cast members in western series, 1949-1959. By Everett Aaker. Jefferson, NC: McFarland & Co., 1997.

TelT   *Tellers of Tales.* British authors of children's books from 1800 to 1964. Revised edition. By Roger Lancelyn Green. New York: Franklin Watts, 1964.

TexWr   *Texas Writers of Today.* By Florence Elberta Barns. Dallas: Tardy Publishing Co., 1935. Reprint. Ann Arbor, Mich.: Gryphon Books, 1971.

ThHDFas   *The Thames and Hudson Dictionary of Fashion and Fashion Designers.* By Georgina O'Hara Callan. New York: Thames and Hudson, 1998.

ThHEIm   *The Thames and Hudson Encyclopaedia of Impressionism.* By Bernard Denvir. New York: Thames and Hudson, 1990.

TheaDir   *Theatrical Directors.* A biographical dictionary. Edited by John W. Frick and Stephen M. Vallillo. Westport, CT: Greenwood Press, 1994.

ThFT   *They Had Faces Then.* Super stars, stars and starlets of the 1930's. By John Springer and Jack Hamilton. Secaucus, NJ: Citadel Press, 1974.

ThTwC 87   *Thinkers of the Twentieth Century.* Second edition. Edited by Roland Turner. Chicago: St. James Press, 1987.

ThrBJA   *Third Book of Junior Authors.* Edited by Doris De Montreville and Donna Hill. Wilson Authors Series. New York: H.W. Wilson Co., 1972.

ThrtnMM   *Thirteen Mistresses of Murder.* By Elaine Budd. New York: Ungar Publishing Co., 1986.
                    Use the Table of Contents to locate biographies.

Tw   *The Twenties, 1917-1929.* Concise Dictionary of American Literary Biography. Detroit: Gale Research, 1989.

TwCA   *Twentieth Century Authors.* A biographical dictionary of modern literature. Wilson Authors Series. New York: H.W. Wilson Co., 1942-1955.
        TwCA   Edited by Stanley J. Kunitz and Howard Haycraft; 1942.
        TwCA SUP   First Supplement. Edited by Stanley J. Kunitz; 1955.

TwCBDA   *The Twentieth Century Biographical Dictionary of Notable Americans.* Brief biographies of authors, administrators, clergymen, commanders, editors, engineers, jurists, merchants, officials, philanthropists, scientists, statesmen, and others who are making American history. 10 volumes. Edited by Rossiter Johnson. Boston: The Biographical Society, 1904. Reprint. Detroit: Gale Research, 1968.

TwCPaSc   *Twentieth Century Painters and Sculptors.* By Frances Spalding. Dictionary of British Art, vol. 6. Suffolk, England: Antique Collectors' Club, 1990.

TwCWr   *Twentieth Century Writing.* A reader's guide to contemporary literature. Edited by Kenneth Richardson. Levittown, NY: Transatlantic Arts, 1971.

TwCBrS   *Twentieth-Century Brass Soloists.* By Michael Meckna. Westport, CT: Greenwood Press, 1994.

TwCChW   *Twentieth-Century Children's Writers.* Edited by D.L. Kirkpatrick. Twentieth-Century Writers Series. New York: St. Martin's Press, 1978-1983.Later editions published as *St. James Guide to Children's Writers.*

TwCChW 1	First edition; 1978.
TwCChW 1A	First edition; 1978. Appendix begins on page 1391.
TwCChW 1B	First edition; 1978. "Children's Books in Translation" section begins on page 1481.
TwCChW 2	Second edition; 1983.
TwCChW 2A	Second edition; 1983. Appendix begins on page 859.
TwCChW 2B	Second edition; 1983. "Foreign-Language Writers" section begins on page 893.

TwCChW   *Twentieth-Century Children's Writers.* Detroit: St. James Press, 1989-1995.Later editions published as *St. James Guide to Children's Writers.*

TwCChW 3	Third edition. Edited by Tracy Chevalier; 1989.
TwCChW 3A	Third edition. Edited by Tracy Chevalier; 1989. Appendix begins on page 1083.
TwCChW 3B	Third edition. Edited by Tracy Chevalier; 1989. "Foreign-Language Writers" section begins on page 1119.
TwCChW 4	Fourth edition. Edited by Laura Standley Berger; 1995.
TwCChW 4A	Fourth edition. Edited by Laura Standley Berger; 1995. Appendix begins on page 1067.
TwCChW 4B	Fourth edition. Edited by Laura Standley Berger; 1995. "Foreign-Language Writers" section begins on page 1107.

TwCCr&M   *Twentieth-Century Crime and Mystery Writers.* Edited by John M. Reilly. Twentieth-Century Writers Series. New York: St. Martin's Press, 1980-1985.

TwCCr&M 80	First edition; 1980.
TwCCr&M 80A	First edition; 1980. "Nineteenth-Century Writers" section begins on page 1525.
TwCCr&M 80B	First edition; 1980. "Foreign-Language Writers" section begins on page 1537.
TwCCr&M 85	Second edition; 1985.
TwCCr&M 85A	Second edition; 1985. "Nineteenth-Century Writers" section begins on page 931.
TwCCr&M 85B	Second edition; 1985. "Foreign-Language Writers" section begins on page 939.

TwCCr&M 91   *Twentieth-Century Crime and Mystery Writers.* Third edition. Edited by Lesley Henderson. Twentieth-Century Writers Series. Chicago: St. James Press, 1991.

TwCCr&M 91A	"Nineteenth-Century Writers" section begins on page 1121.
TwCCr&M 91B	"Foreign-Language Writers" section begins on page 1129.

TwCLC   *Twentieth-Century Literary Criticism.* Excerpts from criticism of the works of novelists, poets, playwrights, short story writers, and other creative writers who lived between 1900 and 1960, from the first published critical appraisals to current evaluations. Detroit: Gale Research, 1978-1999.

TwCLC 1	Volume 1; 1978.
TwCLC 2	Volume 2; 1979.
TwCLC 3	Volume 3; 1980.

TwCLC 4	Volume 4; 1981.
TwCLC 5	Volume 5; 1981.
TwCLC 6	Volume 6; 1982.
TwCLC 7	Volume 7; 1982.
TwCLC 8	Volume 8; 1982.
TwCLC 9	Volume 9; 1983.
TwCLC 10	Volume 10; 1983.
TwCLC 11	Volume 11; 1983.
TwCLC 12	Volume 12; 1984.
TwCLC 13	Volume 13; 1984.
TwCLC 14	Volume 14; 1984.
TwCLC 15	Volume 15; 1985.
TwCLC 16	Volume 16; 1985.
TwCLC 17	Volume 17; 1985.
TwCLC 18	Volume 18; 1985.
TwCLC 19	Volume 19; 1986.
TwCLC 20	Volume 20; 1986.
TwCLC 21	Volume 21; 1986.
TwCLC 22	Volume 22; 1987.
TwCLC 23	Volume 23; 1987.
TwCLC 24	Volume 24; 1987.
TwCLC 25	Volume 25; 1988.
TwCLC 26	Volume 26; 1988. Contains no biographies.
TwCLC 27	Volume 27; 1988.
TwCLC 28	Volume 28; 1988.
TwCLC 29	Volume 29; 1988.
TwCLC 30	Volume 30; 1989. Contains no biographies.
TwCLC 31	Volume 31; 1989.
TwCLC 32	Volume 32; 1989.
TwCLC 33	Volume 33; 1989.
TwCLC 34	Volume 34; 1990. Contains no biographies.
TwCLC 35	Volume 35; 1990.
TwCLC 36	Volume 36; 1990.
TwCLC 37	Volume 37; 1991.
TwCLC 38	Volume 38; 1991. Contains no biographies.
TwCLC 39	Volume 39; 1991.
TwCLC 40	Volume 40; 1991.
TwCLC 41	Volume 41; 1991.
TwCLC 42	Volume 42; 1992. Contains no biographies.
TwCLC 43	Volume 43; 1992.
TwCLC 44	Volume 44; 1992.
TwCLC 45	Volume 45; 1992.
TwCLC 46	Volume 46; 1992. Contains no biographies.
TwCLC 47	Volume 47; 1993.
TwCLC 48	Volume 48; 1993.
TwCLC 49	Volume 49; 1993.
TwCLC 50	Volume 50; 1993. Contains no biographies.
TwCLC 51	Volume 51; 1994.
TwCLC 52	Volume 52; 1994.
TwCLC 53	Volume 53; 1994.
TwCLC 54	Volume 54; 1994. Contains no biographies.
TwCLC 55	Volume 55; 1995.
TwCLC 56	Volume 56; 1995.
TwCLC 57	Volume 57; 1995.
TwCLC 58	Volume 58; 1995. Contains no biographies.

TwCLC 59	Volume 59; 1995.
TwCLC 60	Volume 60; 1995.
TwCLC 61	Volume 61; 1996.
TwCLC 62	Volume 62; 1996. Contains no biographies.
TwCLC 63	Volume 63; 1996.
TwCLC 64	Volume 64; 1996.
TwCLC 65	Volume 65; 1997.
TwCLC 66	Volume 66; 1997. Contains no biographies.
TwCLC 67	Volume 67; 1997.
TwCLC 68	Volume 68; 1997.
TwCLC 69	Volume 69; 1997.
TwCLC 70	Volume 70; 1997. Contains no biographies.
TwCLC 71	Volume 71; 1997.
TwCLC 72	Volume 72; 1997.
TwCLC 73	Volume 73; 1998.
TwCLC 74	Volume 74; 1998. Contains no biographies.
TwCLC 75	Volume 75; 1998.
TwCLC 76	Volume 76; 1998.
TwCLC 77	Volume 77; 1998.
TwCLC 78	Volume 78; 1999. Contains no biographies.
TwCLC 79	Volume 79; 1999.
TwCLC 80	Volume 80; 1999.
TwCLC 81	Volume 81; 1999.

TwCLC   *Twentieth-Century Literary Criticism.* Criticism of the works of novelists, poets, playwrights, short story writers, and other creative writers who lived between 1900 and 1960, from the first published critical appraisals to current evaluations. Detroit: Gale Group, 1999-2000.

TwCLC 82	Volume 82; 1999. Contains no biographies.
TwCLC 83	Volume 83; 1999.
TwCLC 84	Volume 84; 1999.
TwCLC 85	Volume 85; 1999.
TwCLC 86	Volume 86; 2000. Contains no biographies.
TwCLC 87	Volume 87; 2000.
TwCLC 88	Volume 88; 2000.
TwCLC 89	Volume 89; 2000.
TwCLC 90	Volume 90; 2000. Contains no biographies.
TwCLC 91	Volume 91; 2000.
TwCLC 92	Volume 92; 2000.

TwCRGW   *Twentieth-Century Romance and Gothic Writers.* Edited by James Vinson. Detroit: Gale Research, 1982.

TwCRHW   *Twentieth-Century Romance and Historical Writers.* London: St. James Press, 1990-1994.

TwCRHW 90	Second edition. Edited by Lesley Henderson; 1990.
TwCRHW 94	Third edition. Edited by Aruna Vasudevan; 1994.

TwCSFW   *Twentieth-Century Science-Fiction Writers.* Twentieth-Century Writers Series. Chicago: St. James Press, 1981-1991.

TwCSFW 81	Edited by Curtis C. Smith; 1981.
TwCSFW 81A	Edited by Curtis C. Smith; 1981. ''Foreign-Language Writers'' section begins on page 613.
TwCSFW 81B	Edited by Curtis C. Smith; 1981. ''Major Fantasy Writers'' section begins on page 631.

TwCSFW 86	Second edition. Edited by Curtis C. Smith; 1986.
TwCSFW 86A	Second edition. Edited by Curtis C. Smith; 1986. ''Foreign-Language Writers'' section begins on page 837.
TwCSFW 86B	Second edition. Edited by Curtis C. Smith; 1986. ''Major Fantasy Writers'' section begins on page 863.
TwCSFW 91	Third edition. Edited by Noelle Watson and Paul E. Schellinger; 1991.
TwCSFW 91A	Third edition. Edited by Noelle Watson and Paul E. Schellinger; 1991. ''Foreign-Language Writers'' section begins on page 913.

TwCSAPR *Twentieth-Century Shapers of American Popular Religion.* Edited by Charles H. Lippy. New York: Greenwood Press, 1989.

TwCWW 82 *Twentieth-Century Western Writers.* First edition. Edited by James Vinson. Detroit: Gale Research, 1982.

TwCWW 91 *Twentieth-Century Western Writers.* Second edition. Edited by Geoff Sadler. Twentieth-Century Writers Series. Chicago: St. James Press, 1991.

TwCYAW 1 *Twentieth-Century Young Adult Writers.* First edition. Twentieth-Century Writers Series. Detroit: St. James Press, 1994.

TwYS *Twenty Years of Silents, 1908-1928.* Compiled by John T. Weaver. Metuchen, NJ: Scarecrow Press, 1971.

TwYS	''The Players'' section begins on page 27.
TwYS A	''Directors'' section begins on page 407.
TwYS B	''Producers'' section begins on page 502.

TwoTYeD *Two Thousand Years of Disbelief.* By James A. Haught. Amherst, NY: Prometheus Books, 1996.
     Use Index or Table of Contents to locate biographies.

USGovLe *U. S. Government Leaders.* Three volumes. Edited by Frank N. Magill. Pasadena, CA: Salem Press, 1997.

UFOEn-O *The UFO Encyclopedia.* The phenomenon from the beginning. Second edition. Two volumes. By Jerome Clark. Detroit: Omnigraphics, 1998.

UFOEn-P *The UFO Encyclopedia.* By Margaret Sachs. New York: G.P. Putnam's Sons, 1980.

UlDrSSP *The Ultimate Directory of the Silent Screen Performers.* A necrology of births and deaths and essays on 50 lost players. By Billy H. Doyle. Metuchen, NJ: Scarecrow Press, 1995.
     Biographies are found in the ''Lost Players'' section which begins on page 1.

USBiR 74 *United States. Department of State: The Biographic Register, July, 1974.* Washington, DC: United States Government Printing Office, 1974.

VarWW *Variety Who's Who in Show Business.* Edited by Mike Kaplan. New York: Garland Publishing, 1983-1985.

VarWW 83	1983 edition; 1983.	
VarWW 85	Revised edition, 1985; 1985.	

Vers   *The Versatiles.* A study of supporting character actors and actresses in the American motion picture, 1930-1955. By Alfred E. Twomey and Arthur F. McClure. South Brunswick, NJ: A.S. Barnes & Co.; London: Thomas Yoseloff, 1969.
        Vers A   "Biographical Section" begins on page 25.
        Vers B   "Non-Biographical Section" begins on page 249.

VicePre   *The Vice Presidents.* Biographies of the 45 men who have held the second highest office in the United States. By Carole Chandler Waldrup. Jefferson, NC: McFarland & Co., 1996.
        Use the Index to locate biographies.

VicBrit   *Victorian Britain.* An encyclopedia. Edited by Sally Mitchell. Garland Reference Library of Social Sciences, vol. 438. New York: Garland Publishing, 1988.

VioAm   *Violence in America: An Encyclopedia.* Three volumes. Edited by Ronald Gottesman. New York: Charles Scribner's Sons, 1999.

VixFlM   *Vixens, Floozies and Molls.* 28 Actresses of late 1920s and 1930s Hollywood. By Hans J. Wollstein. Jefferson, NC: McFarland & Co., 1999.

WarAmPC   *War and American Popular Culture.* A historical encyclopedia. Westport, CT: Greenwood Press, 1999.
        Use the Index to locate biographies.

Ward   *Ward's Who's Who among U.S. Motor Vehicle Manufacturers, 1977.* Detroit: Ward's Communications, 1977.
        Ward 77   "U.S. Big Four Biographical Section" begins on page 61.
        Ward 77A   "The Independent Truck, Off-Highway and Farm Vehicle Manufacturers" section begins on page 335.
        Ward 77B   "The Importers" section begins on page 355.
        Ward 77C   "United Auto Workers" section begins on page 371.
        Ward 77D   "Government Agencies" section begins on page 372.
        Ward 77E   "Auto Associations" section begins on page 376.
        Ward 77F   "The Automotive Press" section begins on page 387.
        Ward 77G   "Where Are They Now?" section begins on page 404.
        Ward 77H   "Automotive Suppliers' Section" begins on page 449.

WebAB   *Webster's American Biographies.* Edited by Charles Van Doren. Springfield, MA: G. & C. Merriam Co., 1974-1979.
        WebAB 74   1974 edition; 1974.
        WebAB 79   1979 edition; 1979.

WebAMB   *Webster's American Military Biographies.* Springfield, MA: G. & C. Merriam Co., 1978.

WebBD 83   *Webster's Biographical Dictionary.* 1983 edition. Springfield, MA: G. & C. Merriam Co., 1983.

WebE&AL	*Webster's New World Companion to English and American Literature.* Edited by Arthur Pollard. New York: World Publishing Co., 1973.

What	*Whatever Became of . . . ?* By Richard Lamparski. New York: Crown Publishers, 1967-1974. Also printed in a paperback edition by Ace Books.

What 1	Volume One; 1967.
What 2	Second Series; 1968.
What 3	Third Series; 1970.
What 4	Fourth Series; 1973.
What 5	Fifth Series; 1974.

WhDW	*Who Did What.* The lives and achievements of the 5,000 men and women -- leaders of nations, saints and sinners, artists and scientists -- who shaped our world. Edited by Gerald Howat. New York: Crown Publishers, 1974.

WhAm	*Who Was Who in America.* A companion biographical reference work to *Who's Who in America.* Chicago: A.N. Marquis Co., 1943-1963.

WhAm 1	Volume 1, 1897-1942; 1943.
WhAm 1C	Volume 1, 1897-1942; 1943. Corrigenda begins on page x.
WhAm 2	Volume 2, 1943-1950; 1963.
WhAm 2A	Volume 2, 1943-1950; 1963. Addendum begins on page 12.
WhAm 2C	Volume 2, 1943-1950; 1963. Corrigenda begins on page 5.

WhAm	*Who Was Who in America.* New Providence, NJ: Marquis Who's Who, 1966-1967.

WhAm 3	Volume 3, 1951-1960; 1966.
WhAm 3A	Volume 3, 1951-1960; 1966. Addendum begins on page 952.
WhAm 4	Volume 4, 1961-1968; 1968.
WhAm 4A	Volume 4, 1961-1968; 1968. Addendum begins on page 1049.
WhAm 5	Volume 5, 1969-1973; 1973.
WhAm 6	Volume 6, 1974-1976; 1976.
WhAm 7	Volume 7, 1977-1981; 1981.
WhAm 8	Volume 8, 1982-1985; 1985.
WhAm 9	Volume 9, 1985-1989; 1989.
WhAm 10	Volume 10, 1989-1993; 1993.
WhAm HS	Historical Volume, 1607-1896. Revised Edition; 1967.
WhAm HSA	Historical Volume, 1607-1896. Revised edition; 1967. Addendum begins on page 677.

WhAm	*Who Was Who in America*® *[Marquis*™*].* New Providence, NJ: Marquis Who's Who, 1996-1998.

WhAm 11	Volume 11, 1993-1996; 1996.
WhAm 12	Volume 12, 1996-1998; 1998.

WhAmArt 85	*Who Was Who in American Art.* Compiled from the original thirty-four volumes of *American Art Annual: Who's Who in Art, Biographies of American Artists Active from 1898-1947.* Edited by Peter Hastings Falk. Madison, CT: Sound View Press, 1985.

WhAmArt 85A	The "European Teachers of American Artists" section begins on page xxxiii.

WhAmP — *Who Was Who in American Politics.* A biographical dictionary of over 4,000 men and women who contributed to the United States political scene from colonial days up to and including the immediate past. By Dan and Inez Morris. New York: Hawthorn Books, 1974.

WhAmRev — *Who Was Who in the American Revolution.* New York: Facts on File, 1993.

WhBriIn — *Who Was Who in British India.* By John F. Riddick. Westport, CT: Greenwood Press, 1998.

WhCiWar — *Who Was Who in the Civil War.* By Stewart Sifakis. New York: Facts on File Publications, 1988.

WhE&EA — *Who Was Who among English and European Authors, 1931-1949.* Based on entries which first appeared in *The Author's and Writer's Who's Who and Reference Guide,* originally compiled by Edward Martell and L.G. Pine, and in *Who's Who among Living Authors of Older Nations,* originally compiled by Alberta Lawrence. Three volumes. Gale Composite Biographical Dictionary Series, Number 2. Detroit: Gale Research, 1978.

WhFla — *Who Was Who in Florida.* Written and compiled by Henry S. Marks. Huntsville, AL: Strode Publishers, 1973.

WhJnl — *Who Was Who in Journalism, 1925-1928.* A consolidation of all material appearing in the 1928 edition of *Who's Who in Journalism,* with unduplicated biographical entries from the 1925 edition of *Who's Who in Journalism,* originally compiled by M.N. Ask (1925 and 1928 editions) and S. Gershanek (1925 edition). Gale Composite Biographical Dictionary Series, Number 4. Detroit: Gale Research, 1978.
    WhJnl SUP — The "1925 Supplement" begins on page 639.

WhLit — *Who Was Who in Literature, 1906-1934.* Based on entries that first appeared in *Literary Yearbook* (1906-1913), *Literary Yearbook and Author's Who's Who* (1914-1917), *Literary Yearbook* (1920-1922), and *Who's Who in Literature* (1924-1934). Two volumes. Gale Composite Biographical Dictionary Series, Number 5. Detroit: Gale Research, 1979.

WhNaAH — *Who Was Who in Native American History.* Indians and non-Indians from early contacts through 1900. By Carl Waldman. New York: Facts on File, 1990.

WhNAA — *Who Was Who among North American Authors, 1921-1939.* Compiled from *Who's Who among North American Authors,* Volumes 1-7, 1921-1939. Two volumes. Gale Composite Biographical Dictionary Series, Number 1. Detroit: Gale Research, 1976.

WhScrn — *Who Was Who on Screen.* By Evelyn Mack Truitt. New York: R.R. Bowker Co., 1974-1977.
    WhScrn 74 — First edition; 1974.
    WhScrn 77 — Second edition; 1977.

WhScrn 77   *Who Was Who on Screen.* Second edition. By Evelyn Mack Truitt. New York: R.R. Bowker, 1977.

WhScrn 83   *Who Was Who on Screen.* Third edition. By Evelyn Mack Truitt. New York: R.R. Bowker Co., 1983.

WhThe   *Who Was Who in the Theatre: 1912-1976.* A biographical dictionary of actors, actresses, directors, playwrights, and producers of the English-speaking theatre. Compiled from *Who's Who in the Theatre,* Volumes 1-15 (1912-1972). Four volumes. Gale Composite Biographical Dictionary Series, Number 3. Detroit: Gale Research, 1978.

WhWE   *Who Was Who in World Exploration.* By Carl Waldman and Alan Wexler. New York: Facts on File, 1992.

WhWW-II   *Who Was Who in World War II.* Edited by John Keegan. London: Arms & Armour Press, 1978.

WhDun   *Whodunit?* Edited by H.R.F. Keating. New York: Van Nostrand Reinhold Co., 1982.

WhsNW 85   *Who's New Wave in Music.* An illustrated encyclopedia, 1976-1982 (the first wave). Edited by David Bianco. Ann Arbor, MI: Pierian Press, 1985.

WhsWeAm 98   *Who's Wealthy in America.* A prospecting list and directory of more than 110,000 affluent Americans. Two volumes. Detroit: The Taft Group, 1998.

Who   *Who's Who.* New York: St. Martin's Press, 1974-2000.

Who 74	126th Year of Issue, 1974-1975; 1974.
Who 82	134th Year of Issue, 1982-1983; 1982.
Who 82N	134th Year of Issue, 1982-1983; 1982. Obituary section.
Who 82R	134th Year of Issue, 1982-1983; 1982. The Royal Family section.
Who 82S	134th Year of Issue, 1982-1983; 1982. Supplement.
Who 83	135th Year of Issue, 1983-1984; 1983.
Who 83N	135th Year of Issue, 1983-1984; 1983. Obituary section.
Who 83R	135th Year of Issue, 1983-1984; 1983. The Royal Family section.
Who 83S	135th Year of Issue, 1983-1984; 1983. Supplement.
Who 85	137th Year of Issue, 1985-1986; 1985.
Who 85E	137th Year of Issue, 1985-1986; 1985. Errata section.
Who 85N	137th Year of Issue, 1985-1986; 1985. Obituary section.
Who 85R	137th Year of Issue, 1985-1986; 1985. The Royal Family section.
Who 85S	137th Year of Issue, 1985-1986; 1985. Supplement.
Who 88	140th Year of Issue, 1988; 1988.
Who 88N	140th Year of Issue, 1988; 1988. Obituary section.
Who 88R	140th Year of Issue, 1988; 1988. The Royal Family section.
Who 90	142nd Year of Issue, 1990; 1990.
Who 90N	142nd Year of Issue, 1990; 1990. Obituary section.
Who 90R	142nd Year of Issue, 1990; 1990. The Royal Family section.
Who 92	144th Year of Issue, 1992; 1992.

Who 92N	144th Year of Issue, 1992; 1992. Obituary section.	
Who 92R	144th Year of Issue, 1992; 1992. The Royal Family section.	
Who 94	146th Year of Issue, 1994; 1994.	
Who 94N	146th Year of Issue, 1994; 1994. Obituary section.	
Who 94R	146th Year of Issue, 1994; 1994. The Royal Family section.	
Who 98	150th Year of Issue, 1998; 1998.	
Who 98N	150th Year of Issue, 1998; 1998. Obituary section.	
Who 98R	150th Year of Issue, 1998; 1998. The Royal Family section.	
Who 99	151st Year of Issue, 1999; 1999.	
Who 99N	151st Year of Issue, 1999; 1999. Obituary section.	
Who 99R	151st Year of Issue, 1999; 1999. The Royal Family section.	
Who 2000	152nd Year of Issue, 2000; 2000. Obituary section.	
Who 2000	152nd Year of Issue, 2000; 2000. The Royal Family section.	
Who 2000	152nd Year of Issue, 2000; 2000.	

WhoAdv *Who's Who in Advertising.* Monroe, NY: Redfield Publishing Co., 1972-1980.

WhoAdv 72 Second edition. Edited by Robert S. Morgan; 1972. Biographies are found in ''U.S. Advertising Executives,'' beginning on page 1; ''Canadian Advertising Executives,'' beginning on page 585; and the Addendum beginning on page 637.

WhoAdv 80 Third edition. Edited by Catherine Quinn Serie; 1980.

WhoAdv 90 *Who's Who in Advertising.* First edition, 1990-1991. Wilmette, IL: Marquis Who's Who, 1989.

WhoAfr *Who's Who in Africa.* Leaders for the 1990s. By Alan Rake. Metuchen, NJ: Scarecrow Press, 1992.

Use the Index to locate biographies.

WhoAfA *Who's Who among African Americans.* Detroit: Gale Research, 1996-1998.Earlier editions published as *Who's Who among Black Americans.*

WhoAfA 9 Ninth edition, 1996/1997; 1996.
WhoAfA 10 Tenth edition, 1998/1999; 1997.
WhoAfA 10N Tenth edition, 1998/1999; 1997. Obituaries section.
WhoAfA 11 11th edition; 1998.

WhoAfA 12 *Who's Who among African Americans.* 12th edition. Detroit: Gale Group, 1999. Earlier editions published as *Who's Who among Black Americans.*

WhoAm *Who's Who in America.* New Providence, NJ: Marquis Who's Who, 1974-1993.

WhoAm 74 38th edition, 1974-1975; 1974.
WhoAm 76 39th edition, 1976-1977; 1976.
WhoAm 78 40th edition, 1978-1979; 1978.
WhoAm 80 41st edition, 1980-1981; 1980.
WhoAm 82 42nd edition, 1982-1983; 1982.
WhoAm 84 43rd edition, 1984-1985; 1984.
WhoAm 86 44th edition, 1986-1987; 1986.
WhoAm 88 45th edition, 1988-1989; 1988.

	WhoAm 90	46th edition, 1990-1991; 1990.
	WhoAm 92	47th edition, 1992-1993; 1992.
	WhoAm 94	48th edition, 1994; 1993.

WhoAm   *Who's Who in America® [Marquis™].* New Providence, NJ: Marquis Who's Who, 1994-1999.

	WhoAm 95	49th edition, 1995; 1994.
	WhoAm 96	50th edition, 1996; 1995.
	WhoAm 97	51st edition, 1997; 1996.
	WhoAm 98	52nd edition, 1998; 1997.
	WhoAm 99	53rd edition, 1999; 1998.
	WhoAm 2000	54th edition, 2000; 1999.

WhoAmA   *Who's Who in American Art.* New Providence, NJ: R.R. Bowker Co., 1973-1993.

	WhoAmA 73	11th edition; 1973.
	WhoAmA 76	12th edition; 1976.
	WhoAmA 76N	12th edition; 1976. The Necrology is located at the back of the volume.
	WhoAmA 78	13th edition; 1978.
	WhoAmA 78N	13th edition; 1978. The Necrology is located at the back of the volume.
	WhoAmA 80	14th edition; 1980.
	WhoAmA 80N	14th edition; 1980. The Necrology is located at the back of the volume.
	WhoAmA 82	15th edition; 1982.
	WhoAmA 82N	15th edition; 1982. The Necrology is located at the back of the volume.
	WhoAmA 84	16th edition; 1984.
	WhoAmA 84N	16th edition; 1984. The Necrology is located at the back of the volume.
	WhoAmA 86	17th edition; 1986.
	WhoAmA 86N	17th edition; 1986. The Necrology is located at the back of the volume.
	WhoAmA 89	18th edition, 1989-1990; 1989.
	WhoAmA 89N	18th edition, 1989-1990; 1989. The Necrology is located at the back of the volume.
	WhoAmA 91	19th edition, 1991-1992; 1990.
	WhoAmA 91N	19th edition, 1991-1992; 1990. The Necrology begins on page 1387.
	WhoAmA 93	20th edition, 1993-1994; 1993.
	WhoAmA 93N	20th edition, 1993-1994; 1993. The Necrology begins on page 1455.

WhoAmA 1999   *Who's Who in American Art® [Marquis™].* 23rd edition, 1999-2000 New Providence, NJ: Marquis Who's Who, 1999.

WhoAmJ 80   *Who's Who in American Jewry.* Incorporating *The Directory of American Jewish Institutions..* 1980 edition. Los Angeles: Standard Who's Who, 1980.

WhoAmL   *Who's Who in American Law.* New Providence, NJ: Marquis Who's Who, 1978-1994.

	WhoAmL 78	First edition; 1978.
	WhoAmL 79	Second edition; 1979.
	WhoAmL 83	Third edition; 1983.
	WhoAmL 85	Fourth edition, 1985-1986; 1985.

WhoAmL 87	Fifth edition, 1987-1988; 1987.
WhoAmL 90	Sixth edition, 1990-1991; 1989.
WhoAmL 92	Seventh edition, 1992-1993; 1991.
WhoAmL 94	Eighth edition, 1994-1995; 1994.

WhoAmL   *Who's Who in American Law® [Marquis™].* New Providence, NJ: Marquis Who's Who, 1996-1999.

WhoAmL 96	Ninth edition, 1996-1997; 1996.
WhoAmL 98	Tenth edition, 1998-1999; 1998.
WhoAmL 2000	11th edition, 2000-2001; 1999.

WhoAmM 83   *Who's Who in American Music: Classical.* First edition. New York: R.R. Bowker Co., 1983.

WhoAmP   *Who's Who in American Politics.* New Providence, NJ: R.R. Bowker, 1973-1993.

WhoAmP 73	Fourth edition, 1973-1974; 1973.
WhoAmP 75	Fifth edition, 1975-1976; 1975.
WhoAmP 77	Sixth edition, 1977-1978; 1977.
WhoAmP 79	Seventh edition, 1979-1980; 1979.
WhoAmP 81	Eighth edition, 1981-1982; 1981.
WhoAmP 83	Ninth edition, 1983-1984; 1983.
WhoAmP 85	10th edition, 1985-1986; 1985.
WhoAmP 87	11th edition, 1987-1988; 1987.
WhoAmP 89	12th edition, 1989-1990; 1989.
WhoAmP 91	13th edition, 1991-1992; 1991.
WhoAmP 93	14th edition, 1993-1994; 1993.

Use the Index to locate biographies.

WhoAmP 95   *Who's Who in American Politics™ [Bowker®].* 15th edition, 1995-1996. New Providence, NJ: R.R. Bowker, 1995.

Use the Index to locate biographies.

WhoAmP   *Who's Who in American Politics® [Marquis™].* New Providence, NJ: Marquis Who's Who, 1997-1999.

WhoAmP 97	16th edition, 1997-1998; 1997.
WhoAmP 1999	17th edition, 1999-2000; 1999.

Use the Index to locate biographies.

WhoAmW   *Who's Who of American Women.* New Providence, NJ: Marquis Who's Who, 1958-1993.

WhoAmW 58	First edition, 1958-1959; 1958.
WhoAmW 58A	First edition, 1958-1959; 1958. Addenda
WhoAmW 61	Second edition, 1961-1962; 1961.
WhoAmW 61A	Second edition, 1961-1962; 1961. Addenda
WhoAmW 64	Third edition, 1964-1965; 1963.
WhoAmW 64A	Third edition, 1964-1965; 1963. Addenda
WhoAmW 66	Fourth edition, 1966-1967; 1965.
WhoAmW 66A	Fourth edition, 1966-1967; 1965. Addenda
WhoAmW 68	Fifth edition, 1968-1969; 1967.
WhoAmW 68A	Fifth edition, 1968-1969; 1967. Addenda
WhoAmW 70	Sixth edition, 1970-1971; 1969.
WhoAmW 70A	Sixth edition, 1970-1971; 1969. Addenda
WhoAmW 72	Seventh edition, 1972-1973; 1971.
WhoAmW 74	Eighth edition, 1974-1975; 1973.

WhoAmW 74	Eighth edition, 1974-1975; 1973.
WhoAmW 75	Ninth edition, 1975-1976; 1975.
WhoAmW 77	10th edition, 1977-1978; 1978.
WhoAmW 79	11th edition, 1979-1980; 1979.
WhoAmW 81	12th edition, 1981-1982; 1981.
WhoAmW 83	13th edition, 1983-1984; 1983.
WhoAmW 85	14th edition, 1985-1986; 1984.
WhoAmW 87	15th edition, 1987-1988; 1986.
WhoAmW 89	16th edition, 1989-1990; 1988.
WhoAmW 91	17th edition, 1991-1992; 1991.
WhoAmW 93	18th edition, 1993-1994; 1993.

WhoAmW   *Who's Who of American Women® [Marquis™].* New Providence, NJ: Marquis Who's Who, 1995-1998.

WhoAmW 95	19th edition, 1995-1996; 1995.
WhoAmW 97	20th edition, 1997-1998; 1996.
WhoAmW 99	21st edition, 1999-2000; 1998.

WhoArab 81   *Who's Who in the Arab World.* Sixth edition, 1981-1982. Edited by Gabriel M. Bustros. Beirut, Lebanon: Publitec Publications, 1981.
    Biographies are located in Part III.

WhoArch   *Who's Who in Architecture from 1400 to the Present Day.* Edited by J.M. Richards. London: Weidenfeld & Nicolson, 1977.

WhoArt   *Who's Who in Art.* Biographies of leading men and women in the world of art today -- artists, designers, craftsmen, critics, writers, teachers and curators, with an appendix of signatures. Havant, England: Art Trade Press, 1980-1998.

WhoArt 80	19th edition; 1980.
WhoArt 80N	19th edition; 1980. The Obituary section is located at the back of the volume.
WhoArt 82	20th edition; 1982.
WhoArt 82N	20th edition; 1982. The Obituary section is located at the back of the volume.
WhoArt 84	21st edition; 1984.
WhoArt 84N	21st edition; 1984. The Obituary section is located at the back of the volume.
WhoArt 96	27th edition; 1996.
WhoArt 96N	27th edition; 1996. The Obituary section is located at the back of the volume.
WhoArt 98	28th edition; 1998.

WhoAsA 94   *Who's Who among Asian Americans.* 1994-1995 edition. Detroit: Gale Research, 1994.

WhoAsA 94N	The Obituaries section is located in the back of the volume.

WhoAsAP 91   *Who's Who in Asian and Australasian Politics.* First edition. London: Bowker-Saur, 1991.

WhoAtom 77   *Who's Who in Atoms.* Sixth edition. Edited by Ann Pernet. Guernsey, England: Francis Hodgson, 1977.

WhoBbl 73   *Who's Who in Basketball.* By Ronald L. Mendell. New Rochelle, NY: Arlington House, 1973.

WhoBlA   *Who's Who among Black Americans.* Northbrook, IL: Who's Who among Black Americans, 1976-1981.Later editions published as *Who's Who among African Americans.*
   WhoBlA 1   First edition, 1975-1976; 1976.
   WhoBlA 2   Second edition, 1977-1978; 1978.
   WhoBlA 3   Third edition, 1980-1981; 1981.

WhoBlA   *Who's Who among Black Americans.* Lake Forest, IL: Educational Communications, 1985-1988.Later editions published as *Who's Who among African Americans.*
   WhoBlA 4   Fourth edition, 1985; 1985.
   WhoBlA 5   Fifth edition, 1988; 1988.

WhoBlA   *Who's Who among Black Americans.* Detroit: Gale Research, 1990-1994.Later editions published as *Who's Who among African Americans.*
   WhoBlA 6   Sixth edition, 1990/1991; 1990.
   WhoBlA 6N Sixth edition, 1990/1991; 1990. The Obituary section is located in the back of the volume.
   WhoBlA 7   Seventh edition, 1992/1993; 1992.
   WhoBlA 7N Seventh edition, 1992/1993; 1992. The Obituary section is located in the back of the volume.
   WhoBlA 8   Eighth edition, 1994/1995; 1994.
   WhoBlA 8N Eighth edition, 1994/1995; 1994. The Obituary section is located in the back of the volume.

WhoBox 74   *Who's Who in Boxing.* By Bob Burrill. New Rochelle, NY: Arlington House, 1974.

WhoCan   *Who's Who in Canada.* An illustrated biographical record of men and women of the time in Canada. Toronto: International Press, 1973-1982.
   WhoCan 73 1973-1974 edition; 1973.
   WhoCan 75 1975-1976 edition; 1975.
   WhoCan 77 1977-1978 edition; 1977.
   WhoCan 80 1980-1981 edition; 1980.
   WhoCan 82 1982-1983 edition; 1982.
   Use the Index at the front of the volume to locate biographies.

WhoCan 84   *Who's Who in Canada.* An illustrated biographical record of Canada's leading men and women in business, government and academia. 1984-1985 edition. Agincourt, ON, Canada: Gage Publishing, Global Press, 1984.

WhoCanB 86   *Who's Who in Canadian Business.* Seventh edition, 1986-1987. Edited by Peggy M. Pasternak. Toronto: Trans-Canada Press, 1986.

WhoCanF 86   *Who's Who in Canadian Finance.* Eighth edition, 1986-1987. Edited by Peggy M. Pasternak. Toronto: Trans-Canada Press, 1986.

WhoCanL   *Who's Who in Canadian Literature.* By Gordon Ripley and Anne Mercer. Teeswater, ON, Canada: Reference Press, 1985-1992.
   WhoCanL 85 1985-1986 edition; 1985.
   WhoCanL 87 1987-1988 edition; 1987.
   WhoCanL 92 1992-1993 edition; 1992.

WhoChL	*The Who's Who of Children's Literature*. Compiled and edited by Brian Doyle. New York: Schocken Books, 1968. Biographies are found in "The Authors," beginning on page 1, and "The Illustrators," beginning on page 303.
WhoChr	*Who's Who in Christianity*. By Lavinia Cohn-Sherbok. New York: Routledge, 1998.
WhoColR	*Who's Who of the Colored Race*. A general biographical dictionary of men and women of African descent. Volume one. Edited by Frank Lincoln Mather. Chicago, 1915. Reprint. Detroit: Gale Research, 1976. ***WhoColR A*** Addenda begins on page xxvi.
WhoCom	*Who's Who in Comedy*. Comedians, comics, and clowns from vaudeville to today's stand-ups. By Ronald L. Smith. New York: Facts on File, 1992.
WhoCon 73	*Who's Who in Consulting*. A reference guide to professional personnel engaged in consultation for business, industry and government. Second edition. Edited by Paul Wasserman. Detroit: Gale Research, 1973.
WhoCtE 79	*Who's Who in Continuing Education*. Human resources in continuing library-information-media education, 1979. Compiled by CLENE (The Continuing Library Education Network and Exchange). New York and London: K.G. Saur, 1979.

WhoE   *Who's Who in the East*. New Providence, NJ: Marquis Who's Who, 1974-1992.

WhoE 74	14th edition, 1974-1975; 1974.
WhoE 75	15th edition, 1975-1976; 1975.
WhoE 77	16th edition, 1977-1978; 1977.
WhoE 79	17th edition, 1979-1980; 1979.
WhoE 81	18th edition, 1981-1982; 1981.
WhoE 83	19th edition, 1983-1984; 1983.
WhoE 85	20th edition, 1985-1986; 1984.
WhoE 85A	20th edition, 1985-1986; 1984. The Addendum is located at the back of the volume.
WhoE 86	21st edition, 1986-1987; 1986.
WhoE 89	22nd edition, 1989-1990; 1988.
WhoE 91	23rd edition, 1991-1992; 1990.
WhoE 93	24th edition, 1993-1994; 1992.

WhoE   *Who's Who in the East®* *[Marquis™]*. New Providence, NJ: Marquis Who's Who, 1994-1998.

WhoE 95	25th edition, 1995-1996; 1994.
WhoE 97	26th edition, 1996-1997; 1996.
WhoE 99	27th edition, 1999-2000; 1998.

WhoEc	*Who's Who in Economics*. A biographical dictionary of major economists, 1700-1986. Cambridge: MIT Press, 1983-1986.
	    WhoEc 81 First edition. Edited by Mark Blaug and Paul Sturges; 1983.
	    WhoEc 86 Second edition. Edited by Mark Blaug; 1986.

WhoEmL	*Who's Who of Emerging Leaders in America*. New Providence, NJ: Marquis Who's Who, 1987-1992.

WhoEmL 87	First edition, 1987-1988; 1987.
WhoEmL 89	Second edition, 1989-1990; 1988.
WhoEmL 91	Third edition, 1991-1992; 1991.
WhoEmL 93	Fourth edition, 1993-1994; 1992.

WhoEng   *Who's Who in Engineering.* Washington, DC: American Association of Engineering Societies, 1980-1988.

WhoEng 80	Fourth edition. Edited by Jean Gregory; 1980.
WhoEng 88	Seventh edition, 1988. Edited by Gordon Davis; 1988.
WhoEng 88A	Seventh edition, 1988. Edited by Gordon Davis; 1988. The ''Errata'' section follows page 852.

WhoEnt 92   *Who's Who in Entertainment.* Second edition, 1992-1993. Wilmette, IL: Marquis Who's Who, 1992.

WhoEnt 92A	Addendum follows page 700.

WhoEnt 98   *Who's Who in Entertainment® [Marquis™].* Third edition, 1998-1999. New Providence, NJ: Marquis Who's Who, 1997.

WhoEIO 82   *Who's Who in European Institutions and Organizations.* A biographical encyclopedia of the international red series containing some 4,000 biographies of the top administrators, chairmen, politicians and other leading personalities working with European institutions and organizations, and international institutions in Europe. First edition. Edited by Karl Strute and Theodor Doelken. Zurich, Switzerland: Who's Who, 1982.

WhoFash   *Who's Who in Fashion.* By Anne Stegemeyer. New York: Fairchild Publications, 1980-1988.

WhoFash	First edition; 1980.
WhoFash 88	Second edition; 1988.
WhoFash 88A	Second edition; 1988. ''Names to Know'' section begins on page 225.

WhoFI   *Who's Who in Finance and Industry.* New Providence, NJ: Marquis Who's Who, 1974-1993.

WhoFI 74	18th edition, 1974-1975; 1974.
WhoFI 75	19th edition, 1975-1976; 1975.
WhoFI 77	20th edition, 1977-1978; 1977.
WhoFI 79	21st edition, 1979-1980; 1979.
WhoFI 81	22nd edition, 1981-1982; 1981.
WhoFI 83	23rd edition, 1983-1984; 1983.
WhoFI 85	24th edition, 1985-1986; 1985.
WhoFI 87	25th edition, 1987-1988; 1987.
WhoFI 89	26th edition, 1989-1990; 1989.
WhoFI 92	27th edition, 1992-1993; 1991.
WhoFI 94	28th edition, 1994-1995; 1993.

WhoFI   *Who's Who in Finance and Industry® [Marquis™].* New Providence, NJ: Marquis Who's Who, 1995-1999.

WhoFI 96	29th edition, 1996-1997; 1995.
WhoFI 98	30th edition, 1998-1999; 1997.
WhoFI 00	31st edition, 2000-2001; 1999.

WhoFla   *Who's Who in Florida, 1973/74.* A composite of biographical sketches of outstanding men and women of the State of Florida. First edition. Lexington, KY: Names of Distinction, 1974.

WhoFtbl 74   *Who's Who in Football.* By Ronald L. Mendell and Timothy B. Phares. New Rochelle, NY: Arlington House, 1974.

WhoFr   *Who's Who in France.* Paris: Editions Jacques Lafitte, 1979-1986.
                           WhoFr 79   14th edition, 1979-1980; 1979.
                           WhoFr 79N   14th edition, 1979-1980; 1979. "Liste des Personnalites Decedees" begins on page cviii.
                           WhoFr 86   1986 edition; 1986.

WhoFrS 84   *Who's Who in Frontier Science and Technology.* First edition, 1984-1985. Chicago: Marquis Who's Who, 1984.

WhoGen 81   *Who's Who in Genealogy & Heraldry.* Volume 1. Edited by Mary Keysor Meyer and P. William Filby. Detroit: Gale Research, 1981.
                           WhoGen 81A   "Late Additions" section begins on page 231.

WhoGolf   *Who's Who in Golf.* By Len Elliott and Barbara Kelly. New Rochelle, NY: Arlington House Publishers, 1976.

WhoGov   *Who's Who in Government.* Chicago: Marquis Who's Who, 1972-1977.
                           WhoGov 72   First edition, 1972-1973; 1972.
                           WhoGov 75   Second edition, 1975-1976; 1975.
                           WhoGov 77   Third edition, 1977; 1977.

WhoGrA   *Who's Who in Graphic Art.* An illustrated book of reference to the world's leading graphic designers, illustrators, typographers and cartoonists. First edition. Edited by Walter Amstutz. Zurich, Switzerland: Amstutz & Herdeg Graphis Press, 1962.
                           WhoGrA 62   Use the "Index of Artists' Names," which begins on page 576, to locate biographies.

WhoGrA 82   *Who's Who in Graphic Art.* An illustrated world review of the leading contemporary graphic and typographic designers, illustrators and cartoonists. Volume Two. Edited and designed by Walter Amstutz. Dubendorf, Switzerland: De Clivo Press, 1982.
                     Use the "Index of Artists' Names," which begins on page 886, to locate biographies.

WhoHisp   *Who's Who among Hispanic Americans.* Detroit: Gale Research, 1991-1994.
                           WhoHisp 91   First edition, 1991-1992; 1991.
                           WhoHisp 91N   First edition, 1991-1992; 1991. The Obituaries section begins on page 423.
                           WhoHisp 92   Second edition, 1992-1993; 1992.
                           WhoHisp 92N   Second edition, 1992-1993; 1992. The Obituaries section begins on page 743.
                           WhoHisp 94   Third edition, 1994-1995; 1994.
                           WhoHisp 94N   Third edition, 1994-1995; 1994. The Obituaries section begins on page 887.

WhoHcky 73	*Who's Who in Hockey.* By Harry C. Kariher. New Rochelle, NY: Arlington House, 1973.
WhoHol 92	*Who's Who in Hollywood.* The largest cast of international film personalities ever assembled. Two volumes. By David Ragan. New York: Facts on File, 1992.
WhoHol	*Who's Who in Hollywood, 1900-1976.* By David Ragan. New Rochelle, NY: Arlington House, 1976.

	WhoHol A	The ''Living Players'' section begins on page 11.
	WhoHol B	The ''Late Players (1900-1974)'' section begins on page 539.
	WhoHol C	The ''Players Who Died in 1975 and 1976'' section begins on page 845.

WhoHr&F	*Who's Who in Horror and Fantasy Fiction.* By Mike Ashley. London: Elm Tree Books, 1977.
WhoHrs 80	*Who's Who of the Horrors and Other Fantasy Films.* The international personality encyclopedia of the fantastic film. First edition. By David J. Hogan San Diego: A.S. Barnes & Co.; London: Tantivy Press, 1980.
WhoIns	*Who's Who in Insurance.* Englewood, NJ: Underwriter Printing & Publishing Co., 1975-2000.

	WhoIns 75	1975 edition; 1975.
	WhoIns 76	1976 edition; 1976.
	WhoIns 76A	1976 edition; 1976. The Addenda appear at the back of the volume.
	WhoIns 77	1977 edition; 1977.
	WhoIns 77A	1977 edition; 1977. The Addenda appear at the back of the volume.
	WhoIns 78	1978 edition; 1978.
	WhoIns 78A	1978 edition; 1978. The Addenda appear at the back of the volume.
	WhoIns 79	1979 edition; 1979.
	WhoIns 79A	1979 edition; 1979. The Addenda appear at the back of the volume.
	WhoIns 80	1980 edition; 1980.
	WhoIns 80A	1980 edition; 1980. The Addenda appear at the back of the volume.
	WhoIns 81	1981 edition; 1981.
	WhoIns 81A	1981 edition; 1981. The Addenda appear at the back of the volume.
	WhoIns 82	1982 edition; 1982.
	WhoIns 82A	1982 edition; 1982. The Addenda appear at the back of the volume.
	WhoIns 84	1984 edition; 1984.
	WhoIns 84A	1984 edition; 1984. The Addenda appear at the back of the volume.
	WhoIns 86	1986 edition; 1986.
	WhoIns 86A	1986 edition; 1986. The Addenda appear at the back of the volume.
	WhoIns 88	1988 edition; 1988.
	WhoIns 90	1990 edition; 1990.

WhoIns 90A	1990 edition; 1990. The Addenda appear at the back of the volume.
WhoIns 92	1992 edition; 1992.
WhoIns 93	1993 edition; 1993.
WhoIns 94	1994 edition; 1994.
WhoIns 97	1997 edition; 1997.
WhoIns 98	1998 edition; 1998.
WhoIns 99	1999 edition; 1999.
WhoIns 2000	2000-2001 edition; 2000.

WhoIntA 2 *Who's Who in International Affairs.* Second edition. London: Europa Publications, 1997.

WhoIntG *Who's Who in International Golf.* Edited by David Emery. New York: Facts on File Publications, 1983.

WhoIntT *Who's Who in International Tennis.* Edited by David Emery. New York: Facts on File Publications, 1983.

WhoJazz 72 *Who's Who of Jazz: Storyville to Swing Street.* By John Chilton. Philadelphia: Chilton Book Co., 1972.

WhoLab 76 *Who's Who in Labor.* New York: Arno Press, 1976.

WhoLib 54 *Who's Who in Librarianship.* Edited by Thomas Landau. Cambridge: Bowes & Bowes, 1954.

WhoLib 72 *Who's Who in Librarianship and Information Science.* Second edition. Edited by T. Landau. London: Abelard-Schuman, 1972.

WhoLibI 82 *Who's Who in Library and Information Services.* Edited by Joel M. Lee. Chicago: American Library Association, 1982.

WhoLibS 55 *Who's Who in Library Service.* A biographical directory of professional librarians of the United States and Canada. Third edition. Edited by Dorothy Ethlyn Cole. New York: Grolier Society, 1955.

WhoLibS 66 *Who's Who in Library Service.* A biographical directory of professional librarians in the United States and Canada. Fourth edition. Edited by Lee Ash. Hamden, CT: Shoe String Press, 1966.

WhoLA *Who's Who among Living Authors of Older Nations.* Covering the literary activities of living authors and writers of all countries of the world except the United States of America, Canada, Mexico, Alaska, Hawaii, Newfoundland, the Philippine Islands, the West Indies, and Central America. Volume 1, 1931-1932. Edited by A. Lawrence. Los Angeles: Golden Syndicate Publishing Co., 1931. Reprint. Detroit: Gale Research, 1966.

WhoMedi 98 *Who's Who in the Media and Communications® [Marquis™].* 1st edition, 1998-1999. New Providence, NJ: Marquis Who's Who, 1997.

WhoMedH *Who's Who in Medicine and Healthcare® [Marquis™].* New Providence, NJ: Marquis Who's Who, 1997-1998.

WhoMedH 96	1st edition, 1996-1997; 1997.
WhoMedH 99	Second edition, 1999-2000; 1998.

WhoMW   *Who's Who in the Midwest.* New Providence, NJ: Marquis Who's Who, 1974-1994.

WhoMW 74	14th edition, 1974-1975; 1974.
WhoMW 76	15th edition, 1976-1977; 1976.
WhoMW 78	16th edition, 1978-1979; 1978.
WhoMW 80	17th edition, 1980-1981; 1980.
WhoMW 82	18th edition, 1982-1983; 1982.
WhoMW 84	19th edition, 1984-1985; 1984.
WhoMW 86	20th edition, 1986-1987; 1985.
WhoMW 88	21st edition, 1988-1989; 1987.
WhoMW 90	22nd edition, 1990-1991; 1989.
WhoMW 92	23rd edition, 1992-1993; 1992.
WhoMW 93	24th edition, 1994-1995; 1994.

WhoMW   *Who's Who in the Midwest® [Marquis™].* New Providence, NJ: Marquis Who's Who, 1996-1998.

WhoMW 96	25th edition, 1996-1997; 1996.
WhoMW 98	26th edition, 1998-1999; 1998.

WhoMilH 76   *Who's Who in Military History.* From 1453 to the present day. By John Keegan and Andrew Wheatcroft. New York: William Morrow & Co., 1976.

WhoMus 72   *Who's Who in Music and Musicians' International Directory.* Sixth edition. New York: Hafner Publishing Co., 1972. Later editions published as *International Who's Who in Music and Musicians' Directory.*

WhoNeCM   *Who's Who in New Country Music.* By Andrew Vaughan. New York: St. Martin's Press, 1989.

WhoNeCM A	Introduction begins on page 7.
WhoNeCM B	The "UK Country" section begins on page 115.
WhoNeCM C	The "Classic Country" section begins on page 119.

WhoNob   *Who's Who of Nobel Prize Winners.* Edited by Bernard S. Schlessinger and June H. Schlessinger. Phoenix, AZ: Oryx Press, 1986-1991.

WhoNob	First edtion; 1986. Use the "Name Index," which begins on page 195, to locate biographies.
WhoNob 90	Second edition; 1991.

WhoNob 95   *The Who's Who of Nobel Prize Winners.* Third edition. Edited by Bernard S. Schlessinger and June H. Schlessinger. Phoenix, AZ: Oryx Press, 1996. Use the "Name Index," which begins on page 229, to locate biographies.

WhoOcn 78   *Who's Who in Ocean and Freshwater Science.* First edition. Edited by Allen Varley. Essex, England: Longman Group, Francis Hodgson, 1978.

WhoOp 76   *Who's Who in Opera.* An international biographical directory of singers, conductors, directors, designers, and administrators. Also including profiles of 101 opera companies. Edited by Maria F. Rich. New York: Arno Press, 1976.

WhoPNW   *Who's Who among Pacific Northwest Authors.* Second edition. Edited by Frances Valentine Wright. Missoula, MT: Pacific Northwest Library Association, 1969.

Biographies are arranged alphabetically by state. Use the "Index of Authors" to locate listings.

WhoPRCh 81   *Who's Who in the People's Republic of China.* By Wolfgang Bartke. Armonk, NY: M.E. Sharpe, 1981.

         WhoPRCh 81A   Wade-Giles/Pinyin Conversion Table begins on page 719.

         WhoPRCh 81B   "Biographies of Important Deceased and Purged Cadres" section begins on page 573.

WhoPRCh   *Who's Who in the People's Republic of China.* By Wolfgang Bartke. Munich and New York: K.G. Saur, 1987-1991.

         WhoPRCh 87   Second edition; 1987.

         WhoPRCh 91   Third edition. Two volumes; 1991.

WhoPoA 96   *Who's Who in Polish America.* First edition, 1996-1997. New York: Bicentennial Publishing Corp., 1996. Distributed by Hippocrene Books, New York.

WhoPolA   *Who's Who in Polish America.* A biographical directory of Polish-American leaders and distinguished Poles resident in the Americas. Third edition. Edited by Francis Bolek. New York: Harbinger House, 1943. Reprint. The American Immigration Collection - Series II. New York: Arno Press and The New York Times, 1970.

WhoProB 73   *Who's Who in Professional Baseball.* By Gene Karst and Martin J. Jones, Jr. New Rochelle, NY: Arlington House, 1973.

WhoPubR   *Who's Who in Public Relations (International).* Edited by Adrian A. Paradis. Meriden, NH: PR Publishing Co., 1972-1976.

         WhoPubR 72   Fourth edition; 1972.

         WhoPubR 76   Fifth edition; 1976.

WhoPul   *Who's Who of Pulitzer Prize Winners.* By Elizabeth A. Brennan and Elizabeth C. Clarage. Phoenix, AZ: Oryx Press, 1999.

         Use the Index of Individual Winners to locate entries.

WhoReal 83   *Who's Who in Real Estate.* The directory of the real estate professions. Boston: Warren, Gorham & Lamont, 1983.

WhoRel   *Who's Who in Religion.* Wilmette, IL: Marquis Who's Who, 1975-1992.

         WhoRel 75   First edition, 1975-1976; 1975.

         WhoRel 77   Second edition, 1977; 1977.

         WhoRel 85   Third edition, 1985; 1985.

         WhoRel 92   Fourth edition, 1992-1993; 1992.

WhoRock 81   *Who's Who in Rock.* By Michael Bane. New York: Everest House, 1981.

WhoRocM 82   *Who's Who in Rock Music.* By William York. New York: Charles Scribner's Sons, 1982.

WhoRus   *Who's Who in Russia and the CIS Republics.* Edited by Vladimir Morozov. New York: Henry Holt & Co., 1995.

WhoSauA   *Who's Who in Saudi Arabia.* Jeddah, Saudi Arabia: Tihama; London: Europa
                 Publications, 1977-1978.
         WhoSauA 76   First edition, 1976-1977; 1977.
         WhoSauA 78   Second edition, 1978-1979; 1978.

WhoScEn 94   *Who's Who in Science and Engineering.* Second edition, 1994-1995. New
                 Providence, NJ: Marquis Who's Who, 1994.

WhoScEn   *Who's Who in Science and Engineering*® *[Marquis*™*].* New Providence, NJ:
                 Marquis Who's Who, 1996-1999.
         WhoScEn 96   Third edition, 1996-1997; 1996.
         WhoScEn 2000 Fifth edition, 2000-2001; 1999.

WhoScEu   *Who's Who in Science in Europe.* A biographical guide in science, technology,
                 agriculture, and medicine. Essex, England: Longman Group UK, 1991.
                 Distributed by Gale Research, Detroit.
         WhoScEu 91-1   Seventh edition. Volume 1: *United Kingdom.*
         WhoScEu 91-2   Seventh edition. Volume 2: *EC Countries A to F.*
         WhoScEu 91-3   Seventh edition. Volume 3: *EC Countries G to Z.*
         WhoScEu 91-4   Seventh edition. Volume 4: *Non-EC Countries.*
                 For volumes covering multiple countries, use the Table of Contents to
                 locate appropriate section. This book often alphabetizes by titles of address,
                 e.g., Dr., Mrs., and Sir.

WhoSciF   *Who's Who in Science Fiction.* By Brian Ash. London: Elm Tree Books, 1976.

WhoSecI 86   *Who's Who in the Securities Industry.* The Economist Securities Industry
                 Association Convention editions. Chicago: Economist Publishing Co., 1986.
         WhoSecI 86A   "The Executive Officers and the Principal Staff
                 Members of the Securities Industry Association"
                 section, begins on page 100.

WhoSocC 78   *Who's Who in the Socialist Countries.* A biographical encyclopedia of 10,000
                 leading personalities in 16 communist countries. First edition. Edited by Borys
                 Lewytzkyj and Juliusz Stroynowski. New York: K.G. Saur Publishing, 1978.
         WhoSocC 78A   The Appendix begins on page 713.

WhoSoCE 89   *Who's Who in the Socialist Countries of Europe.* A biographical encyclopedia of
                 more than 12,600 leading personalities in Albania, Bulgaria, Czechoslovakia,
                 German Democratic Republic, Hungary, Poland, Romania, Yugoslavia. Three
                 volumes. Edited by Juliusz Stroynowski. Munich, Germany: K.G. Saur, 1989.

WhoSSW   *Who's Who in the South and Southwest.* New Providence, NJ: Marquis Who's Who,
                 1973-1993.
         WhoSSW 73   13th edition, 1973-1974; 1973.
         WhoSSW 75   14th edition, 1975-1976; 1975.
         WhoSSW 76   15th edition, 1976-1977; 1976.
         WhoSSW 78   16th edition, 1978-1979; 1978.
         WhoSSW 80   17th edition, 1980-1981; 1980.
         WhoSSW 82   18th edition, 1982-1983; 1982.
         WhoSSW 84   19th edition, 1984-1985; 1984.
         WhoSSW 86   20th edition, 1986-1987; 1986.
         WhoSSW 88   21st edition, 1988-1989; 1988.

	WhoSSW 91	22nd edition, 1991-1992; 1990.
	WhoSSW 93	23rd edition, 1993-1994; 1993.

WhoSSW   *Who's Who in the South and Southwest® [Marquis™].* New Providence, NJ: Marquis Who's Who, 1995-1998.

	WhoSSW 95	24th edition, 1995-1996; 1995.
	WhoSSW 97	25th edition, 1997-98; 1997.
	WhoSSW 99	26th edition, 1999-2000; 1998.

WhoSpc   *Who's Who in Space.* The First 25 Years. By Michael Cassutt. Boston: G.K. Hall & Co., 1987.
Use the Index to locate biographies.

WhoSpc-   *Who's Who in Space.* The international space station edition. New York: Macmillan Library Reference USA, 1999.

	WhoSpc- A	By Michael Cassutt. The Astronaut biographies begin on page 41.
	WhoSpc- B	The Cosmonaut biographies begin on page 327.
	WhoSpc- C	The International Astronaut biographies begin on page 481.

WhoSpor   *A Who's Who of Sports Champions.* Their stories and records. By Ralph Hickok. New York, NY: Houghton Mifflin Co., 1995.

WhoSpyF   *Who's Who in Spy Fiction.* By Donald McCormick. London: Elm Tree Books, 1977.

WhoStg 1906   *Who's Who on the Stage.* The dramatic reference book and biographical dictionary of the theatre. Containing records of the careers of actors, actresses, managers and playwrights of the American stage. 1906 edition. Edited by Walter Browne and F.A. Austin. New York: Walter Browne & F.A. Austin, 1906.
Some entries are not in alphabetic sequence.

WhoStg 1908   *Who's Who on the Stage.* The dramatic reference book and biographical dictionary of the theatre. Containing careers of actors, actresses, managers and playwrights of the American stage. 1908 edition. Edited by Walter Browne and E. De Roy Koch. New York: B.W. Dodge & Co., 1908.
Some entries are not in alphabetic sequence.

WhoTech   *Who's Who in Technology.* Detroit: Gale Research, 1989-1995.

	WhoTech 89	Sixth edition. Two volumes; 1989.
	WhoTech 89N	Sixth edition. Two volumes; 1989. The "Obituaries" section begins on page 1819 of the *Biographies* volume.
	WhoTech 95	Seventh edition; 1995.
	WhoTech 95N	Seventh edition; 1995. The "Obituaries" section begins on page 1379.

WhoTech 82   *Who's Who in Technology Today.* Third edition. Four volumes. Edited by Jan W. Churchwell. Highland Park, IL: J. Dick & Co., 1982.
Use the "Index of Names," which begins on page 667 of Volume 4, to locate biographies.

WhoTech 84   *Who's Who in Technology Today.* Fourth edition. Five volumes. Edited by Barbara A. Tinucci. Lake Bluff, IL: Research Publications, J. Dick Publishing, 1984.

Use the "Index of Names," which begins on page 1125 of Volume 5, to locate biographies.

WhoTelC   *Who's Who in Television and Cable*. Edited by Steven H. Scheuer. New York: Facts on File, 1983.

WhoThe   *Who's Who in the Theatre*. A biographical record of the contemporary stage. London: Pitman Publishing; Detroit: Gale Research, 1972-1981.Continued as *Contemporary Theatre, Film, and Television*.
        WhoThe 72   15th edition. Compiled by John Parker; 1972.
        WhoThe 72   15th edition. Compiled by John Parker; 1972.
        WhoThe 77   16th edition. Edited by Ian Herbert; 1977.
        WhoThe 77   16th edition. Edited by Ian Herbert; 1977.
        WhoThe 81   17th edition. Edited by Ian Herbert; 1981.
        WhoThe 81N   17th edition. Edited by Ian Herbert; 1981. Obituary section begins on page 743.

WhoThe 77A   *Who's Who in the Theatre, 16th ed. Appendix*

WhoThSc 1996   *Who's Who in Theology and Science*. An international biographical and bibliographical guide to individuals and organizations interested in the interaction of theology and science. New York: Continuum Publishing Co., 1996.

WhoTr&F 73   *Who's Who in Track and Field*. By Reid M. Hanley. New Rochelle, NY: Arlington House, 1973.

WhoTran   *Who's Who in Translating and Interpreting*. Compiled by A. Flegon. London: Flegon Press, 1967.
        WhoTran AFR   Afrikaans section begins on page 5.
        WhoTran ALB   Albanian section begins on page 5.
        WhoTran ARB   Arabic section begins on page 5.
        WhoTran BEL   Belorussian section begins on page 9.
        WhoTran BUL   Bulgarian section begins on page 9.
        WhoTran CHI   Chinese section begins on page 11.
        WhoTran CZE   Czech section begins on page 12.
        WhoTran DAN   Danish section begins on page 16.
        WhoTran DUT   Dutch section begins on page 18.
        WhoTran ESP   Esperanto section begins on page 29.
        WhoTran EST   Estonian section begins on page 29.
        WhoTran FIN   Finnish section begins on page 30.
        WhoTran FLE   Flemish section begins on page 30.
        WhoTran FRE   French section begins on page 32.
        WhoTran GER   German section begins on page 70.
        WhoTran GRE   Greek section begins on page 110.
        WhoTran HEB   Hebrew section begins on page 112.
        WhoTran HIN   Hindi section begins on page 112.
        WhoTran HUN   Hungarian section begins on page 113.
        WhoTran ICE   Icelandic section begins on page 116.
        WhoTran IND   Indonesian section begins on page 116.
        WhoTran INT   Interlingua section begins on page 116.
        WhoTran IRI   Irish section begins on page 117.
        WhoTran ITA   Italian section begins on page 118.
        WhoTran JAP   Japanese section begins on page 130.

WhoTran LAT	Latvian section begins on page 132.
WhoTran LIT	Lithuanian section begins on page 133.
WhoTran MLT	Maltese section begins on page 134.
WhoTran MLY	Malay section begins on page 133.
WhoTran NOR	Norwegian section begins on page 136.
WhoTran POL	Polish section begins on page 137.
WhoTran POR	Portuguese section begins on page 143.
WhoTran RUM	Rumanian section begins on page 146.
WhoTran RUS	Russian section begins on page 148.
WhoTran SAN	Sanskrit section begins on page 162.
WhoTran SCA	Scandinavian section begins on page 162.
WhoTran SER	Serbo-Croat section begins on page 162.
WhoTran SPA	Spanish section begins on page 164.
WhoTran SWA	Swahili section begins on page 182.
WhoTran SWE	Swedish section begins on page 183.
WhoTran TUR	Turkish section begins on page 187.
WhoTran UKR	Ukranian section begins on page 188.

WhoTwCL   *Who's Who in Twentieth Century Literature.* By Martin Seymour-Smith. New York: Holt, Rinehart & Winston, 1976.

WhoUN 75   *Who's Who in the United Nations and Related Agencies.* New York: Arno Press, 1975.

WhoUN 92   *Who's Who in the United Nations and Related Agencies.* Second edition. Edited by Stanley R. Greenfield. Detroit: Omnigraphics, 1992.

WhoUSWr 88   *Who's Who in U.S. Writers, Editors & Poets.* A biographical directory. Second edition. Edited by Curt Johnson. Highland Park, IL: December Press, 1988.

WhoVenC 86   *Who's Who in Venture Capital.* Second edition. By A. David Silver. New York: John Wiley & Sons, 1986.
Biographies begin on page 101.

WhoWest   *Who's Who in the West.* New Providence, NJ: Marquis Who's Who, 1974-1993.

WhoWest 74	14th edition, 1974-1975; 1974.
WhoWest 76	15th edition, 1976-1977; 1976.
WhoWest 78	16th edition, 1978-1979; 1978.
WhoWest 80	17th edition, 1980-1981; 1980.
WhoWest 82	18th edition, 1982-1983; 1982.
WhoWest 84	19th edition, 1984-1985; 1983.
WhoWest 87	21st edition, 1987-1988; 1987.
WhoWest 89	22nd edition, 1989-1990; 1989.
WhoWest 92	23rd edition, 1992-1993; 1992.
WhoWest 94	24th edition, 1994-1995; 1993.

WhoWest   *Who's Who in the West® [Marquis™].* New Providence, NJ: Marquis Who's Who, 1999-1997.

WhoWest 96	25th edition, 1996-1997; 1995.
WhoWest 98	26th edition, 1998-1999; 1997.
WhoWest 00	27th edition, 2000-2001; 1999.

WhoWomW 91   *Who's Who of Women in World Politics.* First edition. New York: Bowker-Saur, 1991.

WhoWor	*Who's Who in the World.* New Providence, NJ: Marquis Who's Who, 1973-1992.

WhoWor 74	Second edition, 1974-1975; 1973.
WhoWor 76	Third edition, 1976-1977; 1976.
WhoWor 78	Fourth edition, 1978-1979; 1978.
WhoWor 80	Fifth edition, 1980-1981; 1980.
WhoWor 82	Sixth edition, 1982-1983; 1982.
WhoWor 84	Seventh edition, 1984-1985; 1984.
WhoWor 87	Eighth edition, 1987-1988; 1986.
WhoWor 89	Ninth edition, 1989-1990; 1988.
WhoWor 91	10th edition, 1991-1992; 1990.
WhoWor 93	11th edition, 1993-1994; 1992.

WhoWorJ 72 — *Who's Who in World Jewry.* A biographical dictionary of outstanding Jews. Edited by I.J. Carmin Karpman. New York: Pitman Publishing Corp., 1972.

WhoWorJ 78 — *Who's Who in World Jewry.* A biographical dictionary of outstanding Jews. Edited by I.J. Carmin Karpman. Tel-Aviv, Israel: Olive Books of Israel, 1978.

WhoWor — *Who's Who in the World® [Marquis™].* New Providence, NJ: Marquis Who's Who, 1994-1999.

WhoWor 95	12th edition, 1995-1996; 1994.
WhoWor 96	13th edition, 1996-1997; 1995.
WhoWor 97	14th edition, 1997; 1996.
WhoWor 98	15th edition, 1998; 1997.
WhoWor 99	16th edition, 1999; 1999.
WhoWor 2000	17th edition, 2000; 1999.

WhoWrEP — *Who's Who in Writers, Editors & Poets.* United States & Canada. Edited by Curt Johnson. Highland Park, IL: December Press, 1989-1995.

WhoWrEP 89	Third edition, 1989-1990; 1989.
WhoWrEP 92	Fourth edition, 1992-1993; 1992.
WhoWrEP 95	Fifth edition, 1995-1996; 1995.

WisWr — *Wisconsin Writers.* Sketches and studies. By William A. Titus. Chicago, 1930. Reprint. Detroit: Gale Research, 1974.
Use the Table of Contents to locate biographies.

Wiz — *Wizards and Sorcerers.* From Abracadabra to Zoroaster. By Tom Ogden. New York, NY: Facts on File, 1997.

WomWWA 14 — *Woman's Who's Who of America.* A biographical dictionary of contemporary women of the United States and Canada, 1914-1915. Edited by John William Leonard. New York: American Commonwealth Co., 1914. Reprint. Detroit: Gale Research, 1976.

WomWWA 14A	"Addenda and Corrections" and "Deaths during Printing" sections begin on page 29.

WomArch — *Women in Architecture.* A contemporary perspective. By Clare LLorenz. New York: Rizzoli International Publications, 1990.

WomArt — *Women Artists.* An historical, contemporary and feminist bibliography. By Donna G. Bachmann and Sherry Piland. Metuchen, NJ: Scarecrow Press, 1978.

	WomArt	Use the Table of Contents which begins on page 47 to locate biographies.
	WomArt A	The Addenda begins on page 322.

WomBeaG   *Women of the Beat Generation.* The writers, artists, and muses at the heart of a revolution. By Brenda Knight. Berkeley, CA: Conari Press, 1996.
Use the Index to locate biographies.

WomBioS   *Women in the Biological Sciences.* A bibliographic sourcebook. Edited by Louise S. Grinstein, Carol A. Biermann, and Rose K. Rose. Westport, CT: Greenwood Press, 1997.

WomChHR   *Women Champions of Human Rights.* Eleven U.S. leaders of the twentieth century. By Moira Davison Reynolds. Jefferson, NC: McFarland & Co., 1991.
Use the Index to locate biographies.

WomComm   *Women in Communication.* A biographical sourcebook. Edited by Nancy Signorielli. Westport, CT: Greenwood Press, 1996.

WomComp   *Women Composers.* Music through the ages. New York: G.K. Hall & Co., 1996-1999.

	WomComp 1	Volume 1: *Composers Born Before 1599.* Edited by Martha Furman Schleifer and Sylvia Glickman; 1996. Use the Index to locate entries.
	WomComp 2	Volume 2: *Composers Born 1600-1699.* Edited by Sylvia Glickman and Martha Furman Schleifer; 1996. Use the Index to locate entries.
	WomComp 3	Volume 3: *Composers Born 1700 to 1799, Keyboard Music.* Edited by Sylvia Glickman and Martha Furman Schleifer; 1998. Use the Index to locate entries.
	WomComp 4	Volume 4: *Composers Born 1700-1799, Vocal Music.* Edited by Sylvia Glickman and Martha Furman Schleifer; 1998. Use the Index to locate entries.
	WomComp 5	Volume 5: *Composers Born 1700-1799, Large and Small Instrumental Ensembles.* Edited by Sylvia Glickman and Martha Furman Schleifer; 1998. Use the Index to locate entries.
	WomComp 6	Volume 6: *Composers Born 1800-1899, Keyboard Music.* Edited by Sylvia Glickman and Martha Furman Schleifer; 1999. Use the Index to locate biographies.

WomCom   *Women Composers, Conductors and Musicians of the Twentieth Century.* Selected biographies. By Jane Weiner LePage. Metuchen, NJ: Scarecrow Press, 1980.

WomCon   *Women of Congress.* A twentieth-century odyssey. By Marcy Kaptur. Washington, DC: Congressional Quarterly, 1996.
Use the Index, beginning on page 252, to locate biographies.

WomEdUS   *Women Educators in the United States, 1820-1993.* A bio-bibliographical sourcebook. Edited by Maxine Schwartz Seller. Westport, CT: Greenwood Press, 1994.

WomFie   *Women in the Field.* America's pioneering women naturalists. By Marcia Myers Bonta. College Station, TX: Texas A & M University Press, 1991.

Key to Source Codes

Use the Index to locate biographies.

WomFilm	*Women Filmmakers & Their Films.* Edited by Amy L. Unterburger. Detroit: St. James Press, 1998.
WomHorF 1930	*Women in Horror Films, 1930s.* By Gregory William Mank. Jefferson, NC: McFarland & Co., 1999. Use the Index to locate biographies.
WomHorF 1940	*Women in Horror Films, 1940s.* By Gregory William Mank. Jefferson, NC: McFarland & Co., 1999. Use the Index to locate biographies.
WomIre	*Women of Ireland.* A biographic dictionary. By Kit O'Ceirin and Cyril O'Ceirin. Minneapolis: Irish Books and Media, 1996.
WomLaw	*Women in Law.* A bio-bibliographic sourcebook. Edited by Rebecca Mae Salokar and Mary L. Volcansek. Westport, CT: Greenwood Press, 1996.
WomMath	*Women of Mathematics.* A biobibliographic sourcebook. Edited by Louise S. Grinstein & Paul J. Campbell. New York: Greenwood Press, 1987.
WomMil	*Women and the Military.* An encyclopedia. By Victoria Sherrow. Santa Barbara, CA: ABC-CLIO, 1996.
WomNov	*Women Novelists, 1891-1920.* An index to biographical and autobiographical sources. By Doris Robinson. Garland Reference Library of the Humanities, vol. 491. New York: Garland Publishing, 1984.
WomPioE	*Women Pioneers for the Environment.* By Mary Joy Breton. Boston: Northeastern University Press, 1998. Use the Index to locate entries.
WomPlaD	*Women Playwrights of Diversity.* A bio-bibliographical sourcebook. By Jane T. Peterson and Suzanne Bennett. Westport, CT: Greenwood Press, 1997.
WomPEIS	*Women Playwrights in England, Ireland, and Scotland.* By David D. Mann and Susan Garland Mann. Bloomington, IN: Indiana University Press, 1996.
WomPsyc	*Women in Psychology.* A bio-bibliographic sourcebook. Edited by Agnes N. O'Connell and Nancy Felipe Russo. New York: Greenwood Press, 1990.
WomPO 76	*Women in Public Office.* A biographical directory and statistical analysis. Compiled by Center for the American Woman and Politics. New York: R.R. Bowker Co., 1976. Use the ''Name Index'' to locate listings.
WomPO 78	*Women in Public Office.* A biographical directory and statistical analysis. Second edition. Compiled by Center for the American Woman and Politics. Metuchen, NJ: Scarecrow Press, 1978. Use the ''Name Index'' to locate listings.

WomPubS 1800	*Women Public Speakers in the United States, 1800-1925.* A bio-critical sourcebook. Edited by Karlyn Kohrs Campbell. Westport, CT: Greenwood Press, 1993.
WomPubS 1925	*Women Public Speakers in the United States, 1925-1993.* A bio-critical sourcebook. Edited by Karlyn Kohrs Campbell. Westport, CT: Greenwood Press, 1994.
WomSc	*Women in Science.* Antiquity through the nineteenth century. By Marilyn Bailey Ogilvie. Cambridge: MIT Press, 1986. ***WomSc A*** The Appendix begins on page 181.
WomSoc	*Women in Sociology.* A bio-bibliographical sourcebook. Edited by Mary Jo Deegan. New York: Greenwood Press, 1991.
WomStre	*Women of Strength.* Biographies of 106 who have excelled in traditionally male fields, A.D. 61 to the present. By Louis Baldwin. Jefferson, NC: McFarland & Co., 1996. Use the Index to locate biographies.
WomThRe	*Women under the Third Reich.* A biographical dictionary. By Shaaron Cosner and Victoria Cosner. Westport, CT: Greenwood Press, 1998.
WomThWo	*Women in the Third World.* A reference handbook. By Karen L. Kinnear. Contemporary World Issues. Santa Barbara, CA: ABC-CLIO, 1997. Biographical Sketches section begins on page 75.

WomWMM	*Women Who Make Movies.* By Sharon Smith. Cinema Study Series. New York: Hopkinson & Blake, 1975.
	    WomWMM "Overview" section. Biographies can be located through the index beginning on page 299.
	    WomWMM A "The New Filmmakers" begin on page 145.
	    WomWMM B "Directory" begins on page 221.

WomWR	*Women Who Ruled.* By Guida M. Jackson. Santa Barbara, CA: ABC-Clio, 1990.
WomWrGe	*Women Writers of Germany, Austria, and Switzerland.* An annotated bio-bibliographical guide. Edited by Elke Frederiksen. Bibliographies and Indexes in Women's Studies, no. 8. New York: Greenwood Press, 1989.
WomWrGB	*Women Writers of Great Britain and Europe.* An encyclopedia. Edited by Katharina M. Wilson, Paul Schlueter, and June Schlueter. New York: Garland Publishing, 1997.
WomWrRR	*Women Writers of the Renaissance and Reformation.* Edited by Katharina M. Wilson. Athens, GA: University of Georgia Press, 1987. Use the Index to locate biographies.
WomWrS	*Women Writers of Spain.* An annotated bio-bibliographical guide. Edited by Carolyn L. Galerstein. Bibliographies and Indexes in Women's Studies, no. 2. New York: Greenwood Press, 1986.

WomWrSA   *Women Writers of Spanish America.* An annotated bio-bibliographical guide. Edited by Diane E. Marting. Bibliographies and Indexes in Women's Studies, no. 5. New York: Greenwood Press, 1987.

WomFir   *Women's Firsts.* Edited by Caroline Zilboorg. Detroit: Gale Research, 1997.
                  Use the Index to locate biographies.

WomIss   *Women's Issues.* Three volumes. Pasadena, CA: Salem Press, 1997.

WorAlBi   *The World Almanac Biographical Dictionary.* By the editors of *The World Almanac.* New York: World Almanac, 1990.

WorAl   *The World Almanac Book of Who.* Edited by Hana Umlauf Lane. New York: World Almanac Publications, 1980.
                  Use the ''Name Index,'' which begins on page 326, to locate biographies.

WorArt 1950 *World Artists, 1950-1980.* Edited by Claude Marks. New York: H.W. Wilson Co., 1984.

WorArt 1980 *World Artists, 1980-1990.* Edited by Claude Marks. New York: H.W. Wilson Co., 1991.

WorAu   *World Authors.* Wilson Authors Series. New York: H.W. Wilson Co., 1996-1995.
                  WorAu 1900   *1900-1950.* Four volumes. Edited by Martin Seymour-Smith and Andrew C. Kimmens; 1996.
                  WorAu 1950   *1950-1970.* Edited by John Wakeman; 1975.
                  WorAu 1970   *1970-1975.* Edited by John Wakeman; 1980.
                  WorAu 1975   *1975-1980.* Edited by Vineta Colby; 1985.
                  WorAu 1980   *1980-1985.* Edited by Vineta Colby; 1991.
                  WorAu 1985   1985-1990. Edited by Vineta Colby; 1995.

WorCh   *World of Chemistry.* Detroit: Gale Group, 2000.

WorDWW   *World Defence Who's Who.* Edited by Paul Martell and Grace P. Hayes. London: Macdonald & Jane's, 1974.

WorECar   *The World Encyclopedia of Cartoons.* Two volumes. Edited by Maurice Horn. Detroit: Gale Research, 1980. Published in association with Chelsea House Publishers, New York.
                  WorECar A   ''Notes on the Contributors'' section begins on page 631.

WorECom   *The World Encyclopedia of Comics.* Two volumes. Edited by Maurice Horn. New York: Chelsea House Publishers, 1976.
                  Biographies begin on page 65.

WorEFlm   *The World Encyclopedia of the Film.* Edited by John M. Smith and Tim Cawkwell. New York: A. & W. Visual Library, 1972.

WorESoc   *The World Encyclopedia of Soccer.* Detroit: Gale Research, 1994.
                  Biographies are located in the ''Who's Who in Soccer'' section which begins on page 49.

WorFshn   *World of Fashion.* People, places, resources. By Eleanor Lambert. New York: R.R. Bowker Co., 1976.
　　　Use the ''Name Index,'' which begins on page 351, to locate biographies.

WorFDir   *World Film Directors.* Edited by John Wakeman. New York: H.W. Wilson Co., 1987-1988.
　　　WorFDir 1　　Volume 1: 1890-1945; 1987.
　　　WorFDir 2　　Volume 2: 1945-1985; 1988.

WorInv   *World of Invention.* History's most significant inventions and the people behind them. Detroit: Gale Research, 1994.

WorLitC   *World Literature Criticism.* A selection of major authors from Gale's Literary Criticism Series. Detroit: Gale Research, 1992-1997.
　　　WorLitC　　　　Six volumes; 1992.
　　　WorLitC SUP　Supplement. Two volumes; 1997.

WorScD   *World of Scientific Discovery.* Scientific milestones and the people who made them possible. Detroit: Gale Research, 1994.

WorWaE   *World War II in Europe.* An encyclopedia. Two volumes. Edited by David T. Zabecki. Garland Reference Library of the Humanities, vol. 1254. Military History of the United States, vol. 6. New York: Garland Publishing, 1999.
　　　Biographies are found in section II, ''Leaders and Individuals,'' beginning on page 205.

WorWWEn   *World Who is Who and Does What in Environment & Conservation.* Edited by Nicholas Polunin. New York: St. Martin's Press, 1997.

WrChl   *Writers for Children.* Critical studies of major authors since the seventeenth century. Edited by Jane M. Bingham. New York: Charles Scribner's Sons, 1988.

WrCNE   *Writers of Colonial New England.* By Trentwell Mason White and Paul William Lehmann. Boston: Palmer Company, 1929. Reprint. Detroit: Gale Research, 1971.
　　　Use the Index to locate biographies.

WrDr   *The Writers Directory.* London: St. James Press; New York: St. Martin's Press, 1976-1979.
　　　WrDr 76　　Third edition, 1976-1978; 1976.
　　　WrDr 80　　Fourth edition, 1980-1982; 1979.

WrDr 82   *The Writers Directory.* Fifth edition, 1982-1984. Detroit: Gale Research, 1981.

WrDr   *The Writers Directory.* Detroit: St. James Press, 1983-2000.
　　　WrDr 84　　Sixth edition, 1984-1986; 1983.
　　　WrDr 86　　Seventh edition, 1986-1988; 1986.
　　　WrDr 88　　Eighth edition, 1988-1990; 1988.
　　　WrDr 90　　Ninth edition, 1990-1992; 1990.
　　　WrDr 92　　10th edition, 1992-1994; 1991.
　　　WrDr 94　　11th edition, 1994-1996; 1994.

WrDr 94N	11th edition, 1994-1996; 1994. The Obituaries section is located in the back of the volume.
WrDr 96	12th edition, 1996-1998; 1996.
WrDr 98	13th edition, 1998-2000; 1997.
WrDr 98N	13th edition, 1998-2000; 1997. The Obituaries section is located in the back of the volume.
WrDr 99	14th edition, 1999; 1999.
WrDr 2000	15th edition, 2000; 2000.

WrPh   *Writers and Philosophers.* A sourcebook of philosophical influences on literature. By Edmund J. Thomas and Eugene G. Miller. New York: Greenwood Press, 1990.

           WrPh P   ''Profiles of Philosophers'' section begins on page 215.

WrYoAd   *Writers for Young Adults.* Edited by Ted Hipple. New York: Charles Scribner's Sons, 1997-2000.

           WrYoAd   Three volumes; 1997.
           WrYoAd SUP1 Supplement One; 2000.

YABC   *Yesterday's Authors of Books for Children.* Facts and pictures about authors and illustrators of books for young people, from early times to 1960. Edited by Anne Commire. Detroit: Gale Research, 1977-1978.

           YABC 1   Volume 1; 1977.
           YABC 2   Volume 2; 1978.

YABC X   *Yesterday's Authors of Books for Children, Index.* Facts and pictures about authors and illustrators of books for young people, from early times to 1960. Detroit: Gale Research, 1977-1978.

        This code refers to pseudonym entries which appear only as cross-references in the cumulative index to *Yesterday's Authors of Books for Children.*

S

S(ymbionese) L(iberation) A(rmy)

[Angela Atwood; Donald David "Cinque Mtume" DeFreeze; Emily "Yolanda" Harris; William "Teko" Harris; Russell "Bo" Little; Nancy Ling Pery; Joseph "Osceola" Romero; Kathy Soliah; Steven Soliah; Patricia "Mizmoon" Soltysik; William "Cujo" Wolfe]
American. Revolutionaries
Kidnapped Patricia Hearst, February 1974.
Source: *GoodHs; NewYTBS 74*

Sa, Mem de

Portuguese. Jurist, Politician
Judge served as governor general of Brazil from 1558 to 1572, bringing peace and prosperity to Portuguese America.
b. 1504 in Coimbra, Portugal
d. Jan 12, 1572 in Salvador da Bahia, Brazil
Source: *EncWB 98; McGEWB*

Saadia ben Joseph al-Fayumi

Scholar
Considered the most important medieval Jewish scholar of literature and history, head of the prestigious Sura Academy in Babylonia.
b. 882, Egypt
d. 942, Babylon
Source: *EncWB 98; McGEWB; RAdv 13-4*

Saar, Alison

American. Artist
Sculptor known for her spiritual and political work that draws on both African American folk and European art; works shown in Biennial Exhibition, Whitney Museum of American Art, and other American museums; daughter of artist Betye Saar.
b. Feb 5, 1956 in Los Angeles, California
Source: *ConBlB 16; ConWomA; DcTwCCu 5; FacFEBW DS; NorAmWA; SJGBlA; WhoAm 97, 98, 99, 2000*

Saarinen, Aline Bernstein

American. Critic, Author
With *NY Times*, 1947-59; wrote *The Proud Possessors*, 1958; wife of Eero.
b. Mar 25, 1914 in New York, New York
d. Jul 13, 1972 in New York, New York
Source: *AmAu&B; AmNatBi; CurBio 56, 72; ForWC 70; NewYTBE 72; WhAm 5; WhoAmW 66, 68, 70, 72; WhoGov 72*

Saarinen, Eero

American. Architect
Often collaborated with father, Eliel; designed St. Louis' Jefferson Memorial Arch, 1947; husband of Aline.
b. Aug 20, 1910 in Kyrkslatt, Finland
d. Sep 1, 1961 in Ann Arbor, Michigan
Source: *AmCulL; AmDec 1940, 1950; AmNatBi; AtlBL; Benet 87; BioIn 2, 3, 4, 5, 6, 7, 8, 9, 10, 11, 12, 13, 14, 16, 19, 23; BriEAA; CamBiEn; CamDcAB; ChamBiD; ConArch 80, 87, 94; ConAu 113; ConDes 84; CurBio 49, 61; DcAmB S7; DcArch; DcArts; DcD&D; DcNiCA; DcTwDes; EncAAr 1, 2; EncMA; FacFETw; IntDcAr; LegTOT; LinLib S; MacEA; MakTCMA; McGDA; McGEWB; ModArCr 2; ObitT 1961; OxCAmH; OxCArt; PenDiDA 89; PIP&P; REn; WebAB 74, 79; WhAm 4; WhoAmA 78N, 80N, 82N, 84N, 86N, 89N, 91N, 93N; WhoArch; WorAl; WorAlBi*

Saarinen, Eliel

Flemish. Architect
Influenced modern architecture by rejecting edecticism with simple lines.
b. Aug 28, 1873 in Rantasalmi, Finland
d. Jul 1, 1950 in Bloomfield Hills, Michigan
Source: *AmNatBi; BioIn 1, 2, 3, 8, 10, 12, 13, 14, 16, 19, 21; BriEAA; ConArch 80, 87; CurBio 42, 50; DcArts; DcD&D; DcTwDes; EncAAr 1, 2; EncMA; FacFETw; IntDcAr; LegTOT; LinLib L, S; MacEA; McGDA; McGEWB; OxCAmH; OxCArt; PenDiDA 89; WebAB 74, 79; WhAm 3; WhAmArt 85; WhoArch*

Saatchi, Charles

English. Advertising Executive
Co-founder, director, Saatchi & Saatchi Co., an advertising agency, 1970-94.
b. Jun 9, 1943, England
Source: *BioIn 12, 13, 14, 15, 16; ConNews 87-3; DcTwArt; DcTwBBL; IntWW 91, 93, 97, 98, 2000; NewYTBS 80; Who 82, 83, 85, 88, 90, 92, 94, 98, 99, 2000; WhoAdv 90; WhoAm 88, 90, 92; WhoFI 89, 92, 96; WhoWor 89, 91, 93, 95, 96, 97, 98, 99, 2000*

Saatchi, Maurice

English. Advertising Executive
Cofounder (with brother Charles) of Saatchi & Saatchi, an advertising agency, 1970, chairman, 1985-94; cofounded New Saatchi Agency (with brother), 1995.
b. Jun 21, 1946 in Baghdad, Iraq
Source: *BioIn 12, 13, 14, 15, 16; CurBio 89; DcTwBBL; IntWW 91, 93; News 95; NewYTBS 80; Who 88, 90, 92, 94; WhoAdv 90; WhoAm 88, 90, 92, 94, 95, 96; WhoFI 89, 92, 94, 96; WhoWor 89, 91, 93, 95, 96, 97, 98, 99*

Saavdedra, Lamas Carlos

Argentine. Educator, Lawyer
Won Nobel Peace Prize, 1936, for espousal of antiwar pact submitted to League of Nations.
b. Nov 1, 1878 in Buenos Aires, Argentina
d. May 5, 1959 in Buenos Aires, Argentina
Source: *WhoNob*

Saavedra, Angel de

Spanish. Poet, Dramatist, Politician
Best known for his drama *Don Alvaro, or the Force of Destiny*, which signaled the advent of romanticism in Spain.
b. Mar 10, 1791 in Cordova, Spain
d. Jun 22, 1865 in Madrid, Spain
Source: *BiD&SB; DcBiPP; DcSpL; McGEWD 72, 84; NotNAT B; OxCThe 67; PenC EUR*

Sabatier, Paul
French. Chemist
Won Nobel Prize, 1912; studied organic
   processes, molecular structure.
b. Nov 5, 1854 in Carcassonne, France
d. Aug 14, 1941 in Toulouse, France
Source: AsBiEn; BiESc; BioIn 3, 6, 11,
   14, 15, 19, 20; CamBiEn; ChamBiD;
   ConAu 156; CurBio 41; DcScB; EncWB
   98; InSci; LarDcSc; McGCEnS;
   McGEWB; NobelP; NotTwCS 1;
   RanHWDS; WhoNob, 90, 95; WorAl;
   WorAlBi

Sabatini, Gabriela
Argentine. Tennis Player
As amateur, youngest player ever to win
   a round at US Open, 1984; won US
   Open, 1990; retired, 1996.
b. May 16, 1970 in Buenos Aires,
   Argentina
Source: BioIn 14, 15, 16; BuCMET;
   ChamBiD; ConNews 85-4; CurBio 92;
   DcHiB; IntWW 89, 91, 93, 97, 98, 2000;
   IntWWW 2; LegTOT; NewYTBS 92;
   WhoAm 92, 94, 95, 96, 97, 98, 99, 2000;
   WhoAmW 93, 95, 97, 99; WhoWor 93,
   95, 96

Sabatini, Rafael
Italian. Author, Dramatist
Wrote historical novels: Scaramouche,
   1921; Captain Blood, 1922.
b. Apr 29, 1875 in Jesi, Italy
d. Feb 13, 1950 in Aldenbogen,
   Switzerland
Source: BeaEPF; BioIn 2, 4, 11, 14, 22;
   CamBiEn; ChamBiD; ConAu 162;
   DcBiA; DcLEL; DcNaB MP; EvLB;
   FilmgC; HalFC 80, 84, 88; LegTOT;
   LngCTC; NewC; NotNAT B; REn;
   TwCA, SUP; TwCLC 47; TwCRGW;
   TwCRHW 90, 94; TwCWr; WhAm 2;
   WhE&EA; WhLit; WhoSpyF; WhThe;
   WorAu 1900

Sabato, Ernesto
Argentine. Author
Works examine human condition,
   survival of moral values; won Miguel
   de Cervantes Prize, 1985.
b. Jun 24, 1911 in Rojas, Argentina
Source: Benet 87, 96; BenetAL 91;
   BiCoLiE; BioIn 14, 16; CasWL;
   ChamBiD; CnDWLB 3; ConAu 32NR,
   97; ConLC 10, 23; CurBio 85; CyWA
   89, 97; DcArts; DcCLAA; DcHiB; DcLB
   145; DcTwCCu 3; EncLatA; EncWB 98;
   EncWL 1, 2, 2S, 3; HispLC; HispWr;
   IntAu&W 76, 77, 82, 86; IntvLAW;
   IntWW 74, 75, 76, 77, 78, 79, 80, 81, 82,
   83, 89, 91, 93, 97, 98, 2000; LatAmLi;
   LatAmWr; LegTOT; MajTwCW 1;
   McGEWB; ModLAL; OxCSpan; PenC
   AM; RAdv 14, 13-2; SpAmA; WhoWor
   74, 78, 80, 82, 87, 89, 91, 93, 95, 96;
   WorAu 1975

Sabbatai Zevi
Mystic, Religious Figure
Jewish mystic and pseudo-Messiah,
   founded the Sabbatean sect and

promised that 1666 would be the year
   of salvation.
b. 1626 in Smyrna, Turkey
d. 1676, Albania
Source: EncWB 98; JeHun; McGEWB

Saberhagen, Bret (William)
American. Baseball Player
Pitcher, KC, 1984-91; NY Mets 1992-95;
   Colorado, 1995; Boston, 1997—; fifth
   youngest in ML history to win 20
   games, 1985; youngest to win Cy
   Young Award, 1985; won Cy Young
   Award, 1989.
b. Apr 11, 1964 in Chicago Heights,
   Illinois
Source: Ballpl 90; BaseReg 86, 87;
   BioIn 14, 15; ConNews 86-1; NewYTBS
   85, 86, 91; WhoAm 90, 96, 97, 98, 99,
   2000; WhoMW 90; WorAlBi

Sabich, Spider
[Vladimir Sabich]
American. Skier
Two-time world champion skier
   accidentally killed by Claudine
   Longet.
b. 1943
d. Mar 21, 1976 in Aspen, Colorado
Source: BioIn 10, 11

Sabin, Albert Bruce
American. Biologist
Developed oral polio vaccine, 1954;
   superior in some ways to Salk vaccine.
b. Aug 26, 1906 in Bialystok, Russia
d. Mar 3, 1993 in Washington, District
   of Columbia
Source: AmMWSc 76P, 79, 82, 86, 89,
   92; AmNatBi; AsBiEn; BiESc; BioIn 4,
   5, 6, 7, 8, 10, 11, 12, 13; CamBiEn;
   CamDcAB; ChamBiD; ConAu 156;
   CurBio 58; EncWB, 98; FacFETw;
   InSci; IntWW 83, 91; LarDcSc;
   McGCEnS; McGMS 80; RanHWDS;
   WebAB 74, 79; Who 74, 85, 92; WhoAm
   80, 82, 84, 86, 88, 90, 92; WhoTech 89;
   WhoWor 89, 93; WorAl; WorAlBi;
   WorScD

Sabin, Florence Rena
American. Scientist
Known for her study of the lymphatic
   system and bloodcells.
b. Nov 9, 1871 in Central City, Colorado
d. Oct 3, 1953 in Denver, Colorado
Source: AmNatBi; AmWomSc; AZWoSci;
   BiDAmEd; BiHiMed; BioAmW; BioIn 1,
   2, 3, 4, 5, 8, 9, 10, 11, 12, 15, 16, 17,
   19, 20, 22, 23; CamDcAB; CamDcSc;
   ChamBiD; ConAu 156; ContDcW 89;
   CurBio 45, 53; DcAmB S5; DcAmMeB
   84; DcScB; EncWB 98; GoodHs; HerW
   84; InSci; IntDcWB; InWom, SUP;
   LibW; LinLib S; NatCAB 40; NotAW
   MOD; NotTwCS 1; NotWoLS; ObitOF
   79; OxCMed 86; PeoHis; RanHWDS;
   WhAm 3; WomBioS; WomFir; WomSc;
   WomWWA 14; WorScD

Sablon, Jean Georges
French. Singer, Composer
Has appeared in musicals, variety shows,
   and nightclubs worldwide; dubbed the
   "French Bing Crosby."
b. Mar 25, 1906 in Nogent-sur-Marne,
   France
d. Feb 24, 1994 in Cannes-la-Bocca,
   France
Source: BiE&WWA; BioIn 1; OxCPMus

Sabo, Chris(topher Andrew)
American. Baseball Player
Third baseman, Cincinnati Reds, 1988-
   94; Baltimore Orioles, 1994-95;
   Chicago White Sox, 1995—; NL
   rookie of year, 1988.
b. Jan 19, 1962 in Detroit, Michigan
Source: Ballpl 90; BaseReg 88; BioIn 16

Sabu
[Sabu Dastagir]
Indian. Actor
Best known for title role in Elephant
   Boy, 1937.
b. Mar 15, 1924, Mysore
d. Dec 2, 1963 in Chatsworth, California
Source: BioIn 6, 10, 15, 16; CmMov;
   DcArts; DcPseud; EncEurC; FilmEn;
   FilmgC; HalFC 80, 84, 88; HolP 40;
   IlWWBF; ItaFilm; LegTOT; MotPP;
   MovMk; NotNAT B; ObitT 1961;
   OxCFilm; WhoHol B; WhoHrs 80;
   WhScrn 74, 77, 83; WorEFlm

Sacagawea
[Mrs. Toussaint Charbonneau]
American. Native American Guide
Shoshone Indian who served as
   interpreter, guide on Lewis and Clark
   Expedition, 1804.
b. 1787?
d. Dec 2, 1812? in Fort Lisa, Nebraska
Source: DcAmB; LinLib S; OxCAmL 65,
   83, 95; REnAW; WebAB 74, 79; WhAm
   HS; WorAl; WorAlBi

Sacchini, Antonio
Italian. Composer
Operas include Oedipe a Colone, 1786;
   had short-lived fame.
b. Jun 14, 1730 in Florence, Italy
d. Oct 6, 1786 in Paris, France
Source: BakBD 78, 84, 92; BioIn 4;
   IntDcOp; MusMk; NewEOp 71;
   NewGrDM 80; NewOxM; OxCMus;
   OxDcOp

Sacco, Nicola
[Sacco and Vanzetti]
Italian. Political Activist
Tried, executed for murder during
   robbery; case became most notorious
   of century due to widespread charges
   of mistrial.
b. Apr 22, 1891 in Apulia, Italy
d. Aug 23, 1927 in Boston,
   Massachusetts
Source: AmBi; AmNatBi; BiDAmL; BioIn
   1, 2, 3, 4, 5, 6, 7, 8, 9, 10, 11, 12, 13,
   14, 15, 16, 17; ChamBiD; CopCroC;
   DcAmB; DcAmImH; EncCapP; LegTOT;

McGEWB; NewCol 75; WebAB 74, 79; WhAm 4; WhDW; WorAl; WorAlBi

Sacher, Paul
Swiss. Conductor
Founded Basel's Kammer Orchestra, 1926, introducing contemporary composers.
b. Apr 28, 1906 in Basel, Switzerland
d. May 26, 1999
Source: *BakBD 78, 84, 92; BakBDTw; BioIn 3, 4, 15; ChamBiD; DcArts; IntWW 74, 75, 76, 77, 78, 79, 80, 81, 82, 83, 89, 91, 93, 97, 98, 2000; IntWWM 77, 80, 85, 90; NewAmDM; NewGrDM 80; PenDiMP; WhoMus 72; WhoWor 74, 76, 78*

Sacher-Masoch, Leopold von
Austrian. Author
Word "masochism" derived from abnormality often depicted in his novels.
b. Jan 27, 1836? in Lemberg, Austria
d. Mar 9, 1895 in Lindheim, Germany
Source: *BbD; Benet 87, 96; BiD&SB; CamBiEn; ChamBiD; DcArts; Dis&D; EuAu; EvEuW; NinCLC 31; OxCGer 76; OxCMed 86; REn*

Sachs, Hans
German. Composer, Poet
Famed poet of the Meistersinger; wrote over 6000 works; main figure in Wagner's opera.
b. Nov 5, 1494 in Nuremberg, Germany
d. Jan 19, 1576 in Nuremberg, Germany
Source: *BakBD 78, 84, 92; BakDcM; BbD; Benet 87, 96; BiD&SB; BioIn 5, 7, 11, 23; CamBiEn; CasWL; ChamBiD; CmMedTh; CnDWLB 2; CnThe; CyWA 58, 97; DcArts; DcBiPP; DcEuL; DcLB 179; DcPup; EncWB 98; EncWT; Ent; EuAu; EvEuW; LinLib L; LuthC 75; McGEWB; McGEWD 72, 84; NewAmDM; NewC; NewCBEL; NewEOp 71; NewGrDM 80; NewOxM; NotNAT B; OxCEng 67, 95; OxCGer 76, 86, 97; OxCMus; OxCThe 67, 83; OxDcOp; PenC EUR; RAdv 14, 13-2; REn; REnWD; RfGWoL 95*

Sachs, Jeffrey D(avid)
American. Economist
Freelance economic adviser to foreign governments since 1985.
b. 1954 in Michigan
Source: *CamDcAB; CurBio 93; IntWW 97, 98, 2000; WhoEc 86*

Sachs, Nelly (Leonie)
German. Poet
Won Nobel Prize in literature, 1966, for poetry, dramas.
b. Dec 10, 1891 in Berlin, Germany
d. May 12, 1970 in Stockholm, Sweden
Source: *Benet 87, 96; BioIn 7, 8, 9, 10, 11, 20; BlmGWL; CamBiEn; CasWL; ChamBiD; ClDMEL 80; ConAu 25R, P-2; ConLC 14, 98; ContDcW 89; CurBio 67, 70; EncCoWW; EncWL 1, 2, 2S; FacFETw; GrWomW; IntDcWB; InWom; LadLa 86; LegTOT; LiExTwC; LinLib L,*

S; McGEWB; ModGL; ModWoWr; NewYTBE 70; NobelP; OxCGer 76, 86; PenBWP; PenC EUR; RAdv 14; RfGWoL 95; TwCWr; WhAm 5; WhoNob; WomFir; WomWrGe; WorAl; WorAlBi; WorAu 1950

Sachs, Samuel, II
American. Museum Director
Director, Detroit Institute of Arts, 1985—; co-author *Fakes and Forgeries.*
b. Nov 30, 1935 in New York, New York
Source: *WhoAm 76, 78, 80, 84, 86, 88, 90, 92, 94, 95, 96, 97, 98, 99; WhoAmA 73, 76, 78, 80, 82, 84, 86, 89, 91, 93, 1999; WhoMW 74, 76, 78, 86, 90, 92, 93, 96, 98*

Sachse, Leopold
German. Director
Stage director of Wagnerian operas, NY Met., 1935-43; Stage director of NY City Opera, 1945-51.
b. Jan 5, 1880 in Berlin, Germany
d. Apr 4, 1961 in Englewood Cliffs, New Jersey
Source: *BakBD 78, 84, 92; BakBDTw; BioIn 5; NewEOp 71*

Sack, Erna
"European Nightingale"
German. Opera Singer
Coloratura soprano, formerly contralto; American performances, 1930s, 1954.
b. 1903, Germany
d. Mar 2, 1972
Source: *BakBD 84; NewYTBE 72; WhoHol A; WhScrn 77, 83*

Sackheim, Maxwell Byron
American. Advertising Executive
Co-founded Book of the Month Club, 1926.
b. Sep 25, 1890 in Kovna, Russia
d. Dec 2, 1982 in Largo, Florida
Source: *BioIn 2, 8, 10; ConAu 108; WhAm 9*

Sackler, Howard Oliver
American. Dramatist
Won Pulitzer, 1969, for *The Great White Hope.*
b. Dec 19, 1929 in New York, New York
d. Oct 14, 1982 in Ibiza, Spain
Source: *AmNatBi; AnObit 1982; ChhPo S2; ConAu 61, 108; ConDr 73, 82; ConLC 14; McGEWD 84; NewYTBS 82; NotNAT; OxCAmL 83; OxCThe 83; PlP&P; WhAm 8; WhoAm 82; WrDr 76, 80*

Sacks, Oliver Wolf
American. Physician, Neurologist
Staff neurologist, Beth Abraham Hospital, New York, 1966—; author of *Awakenings,* 1973.
b. Jul 9, 1933 in London, England
Source: *CamBiEn; CamDcAB; ChamBiD; ConAu 76NR; IntWW 97, 98,*

2000; MajTwCW 2; Who 98, 99, 2000; WhoAm 98, 99, 2000; WrDr 98, 99, 2000

Sackville-West, Edward Charles
English. Author, Critic
Witty novels include *Piano Quintet,* 1925; *The Sun in Capricorn,* 1934; son of Victoria Mary.
b. Nov 13, 1901 in London, England
d. Jul 4, 1965 in Clogheen, Ireland
Source: *BioIn 3, 4; CathA 1952; ChhPo S2; DcLEL; DcNaB 1961; EvLB; LngCTC; ModBrL; NewC; NewCBEL; PenC ENG; REn; TwCA, SUP; TwCWr; WhE&EA*

Sackville-West, Vita
[Mrs. Harold Nicholson; Victoria Mary Sackville-West]
English. Poet, Author
Wrote *The Edwardians,* 1930, *Pepita,* 1937; mother of Nigel and Benjamin.
b. Mar 9, 1892 in Sevenoaks, England
d. Jun 2, 1962 in Cranbrook, England
Source: *ArtclWW 2; BioIn 3, 4, 5, 6, 7, 8, 10, 11, 12, 13; BlmGWL; CamBiEn; Chambr 3; ChhPo, S1, S2, S3; CmpQue; ConAu 93, 104; ContDcW 89; DcArts; DcLB 195; DcLEL; DcNaB 1961; EncBrWW; EncWL 1; EvLB; FacFETw; FemiCLE; GayLesB; GrBr; IntDcWB; InWom SUP; LngCTC; ModBrL; ModWoWr; NewC; NewCBEL; OxCEng 85, 95; PenC ENG; PenNWW B; RAdv 1, 14; REn; TwCA, SUP; TwCWr; WhoLA; WomFir; WomWrGB*

Sadat, Anwar el
Egyptian. Political Leader
Pres., 1970-81; awarded 1978 Nobel Peace Prize with Menachem Begin, for reaching Camp David peace agreement; slain in 1981.
b. Dec 25, 1918 in Mit Abul-Kum, Egypt
d. Oct 6, 1981 in Cairo, Egypt
Source: *BioIn 11; BioNews 75; BkPepl; ConAu 77NR, 101, 104; CurBio 71, 81; IntYB 79; NewCol 75; NewYTBE 70, 72; WhoNob; WhoWor 78*

Sadat, Jehan Raouf
Egyptian., Educator
Widow of Anwar Sadat; lecturer in Arabic literature at Cairo U; outspoken advocate of women's rights; wrote autobiography *A Woman of Egypt,* 1987.
b. Aug 1934? in Cairo, Egypt
Source: *BioIn 10, 11, 14, 15; CurBio 86; InWom SUP; NewYTBS 78, 87*

Saddler, Donald
American. Choreographer
Won Tonys for *Wonderful Town,* 1953; *No, No, Nanette,* 1971.
b. Jan 24, 1920 in Van Nuys, California
Source: *BiDD; BiE&WWA; BioIn 6, 9; CnOxB; ConTFT 2; DancEn 78; EncMT; NotNAT; VarWW 85; WhoAm 92; WhoEnt 92; WhoThe 77, 81*

Sade
[Helen Folasade Adu]
Nigerian. Singer
Debut album *Diamond Life,* 1984, sold
over six million copies; second albu m
Promise, 1985, was platinum.
b. Jan 16, 1959 in Ibadan, Nigeria
Source: *BakBD 92; BillEnR; BioIn 14,
15, 16; CelR 90; ConBlB 15; ConMus 2;
CurBio 86; DcPseud; DrBlPA 90;
EncPR&S 89; EncRk 88; LegTOT; News
93-2; PenEncP; Songw; SoulM; WhoAm
94, 95, 96, 97, 98; WhoEnt 98*

**Sade, Marquis (Donatien
Alphonse Francoise) de**
French. Author
Works first considered pornographic;
believed sexual, criminal acts to be
normal; term sadism derived from
name.
b. Jun 2, 1740 in Paris, France
d. Dec 2, 1814 in Charenton, France
Source: *AtlBL; CasWL; EuAu; EvEuW;
McGEWB; NewC; OxCEng 67; OxCFr;
PenC EUR; REn*

Sa'di
[Masharrif al-Din ibn Moslih al-Din;
Shaikh Muslih-al-Din Sadi]
Persian. Poet
One of the greatest figures in Persian
literature, he wrote the moralistic
classics *Bustan (The Orchard)* and
Gulistan (The Rose Garden).
b. c. 1200 in Shiraz, Persia
d. 1291 in Shiraz, Persia
Source: *EncWB 98*

Sadik, Nafis
Pakistani. Physician
Executive director, United Nations
Population Fund, 1987—; urges
equality between men and women in
order for population programs to be
successful.
b. Aug 18, 1929 in Jaunpur, India
Source: *CurBio 96; IntWW 89, 91, 93,
97, 98, 2000; IntWWW 2; WhoFI 00, 98;
WhoIntA 2; WhoWor 95, 96, 97, 98, 99,
2000*

Sadler, Barry
American. Singer
Wrote and sang popular Vietnam-era
song, "The Ballad of the Green
Berets," 1966.
b. 1941 in Leadville, Colorado
d. Nov 5, 1989 in Murfreesboro,
Kentucky
Source: *BioIn 7, 9, 15, 16; FacFETw;
NewYTBS 89; RkOn 74, 78; RolSEnR
83; WhoRock 81*

Sadr, Musa al-
[Imam Musa]
Iranian. Politician, Religious Leader
Shiite Moslem leader improved life for
ordinary Shiites in South Lebanon and
reduced the power of the Shiite elites.
b. 1928 in Qum, Iran
d. 1978

Source: *DcMidEa; EncWB, 98;
PolLCME*

**Saerchinger, Cesar Victor
Charles**
American. Author, Editor, Conductor
Editor, *Who's Who in Music and Musical
Gazetteer,* 1918; conductor, CBS radio
series, "The Story Behind the
Headlines," 1938-48.
b. Oct 23, 1889 in Aachen, Germany
d. Oct 10, 1971
Source: *AmAu&B; BakBD 84; BioIn 9;
ConAu 33R; CurBio 40; NewYTBE 71;
WhAm 5*

Safdie, Moshe
Israeli. Architect
Created master design in urban housing,
Habitat 67, for Montreal's Expo 67,
1967.
b. Jul 14, 1938 in Haifa, Palestine
Source: *BioIn 8, 9, 10, 11, 16, 22, 23;
BlueB 76; CanWW 70, 79, 80, 81, 83,
89, 96, 97, 98, 1999; ChamBiD;
ConArch 80, 87, 94; ConAu 69, 73NR;
CurBio 68; DcArch; IntAu&W 91, 93;
IntDcAr; IntWW 74, 75, 76, 77, 78, 79,
80, 81, 82, 83, 89, 91, 93, 97, 98, 2000;
WhoAm 74, 76, 78, 80, 82, 84, 86, 88,
90, 92, 94, 95, 96, 98, 99, 2000; WhoE
74; WhoScEn 2000; WhoWor 74, 76, 78,
84, 87, 89, 91, 93, 95; WrDr 80, 82, 84,
86, 88, 90, 92, 94, 96, 98, 99, 2000*

Safer, Morley
Canadian. Broadcast Journalist
Vietnam correspondent, 1964-71;
correspondent, "60 Minutes," 1970—
.
b. Nov 8, 1931 in Toronto, Ontario,
Canada
Source: *BioIn 11, 12, 13, 16; BlueB 76;
CelR 90; ConAu 93; ConCaAu 1;
ConTFT 12; CurBio 80; DcAmDH 80,
89; EncAJ; EncTelN; EncTwCJ;
HisDcWJ; IntMPA 84, 86, 88, 92, 94,
96; JrnUS; LegTOT; LesBEnT 92;
WhoAm 74, 76, 78, 80, 82, 84, 86, 88,
90, 92, 94, 95, 96, 97, 98, 99, 2000;
WhoE 91, 93; WhoEnt 98; WhoMedi 98;
WhoTelC; WorAl; WrDr 92, 94, 96, 98*

Safire, William L
American. Author, Journalist
Washington columnist, *NY Times,*
1973—; won Pulitzer, 1978.
b. Dec 17, 1929 in New York, New
York
Source: *BioIn 8, 9, 10, 11, 12, 13, 15,
16; CamDcAB; ConAu 17R, 31NR;
ConLC 10; CurBio 73; DcAmC;
EncTwCJ; IntAu&W 91; IntWW 91;
PolProf NF; WhoAm 86, 90; WhoAmP
91; WhoE 91; WhoGov 72; WhoPul;
WhoSSW 73; WhoUSWr 88; WhoWor
91; WorAlBi; WrDr 92*

Sagal, Katey
American. Actor
Plays Peg Bundy in TV series "Married
with Children," 1987—.
b. 1956

Source: *BioIn 15, 16; ConTFT 5;
LegTOT*

Sagan, Carl (Edward)
American. Astronomer, Biologist
Has popularized science through book
and TV series *Cosmos.*
b. Nov 9, 1934 in New York, New York
d. Dec 20, 1996 in Seattle, Washington
Source: *AmMWSc 73P, 76P, 79, 82, 86,
89, 92, 95; AsBiEn; Au&Arts 2; BiESc;
BioIn 6, 8, 10, 11, 12, 13, 14, 15, 16,
17, 20, 21; BlueB 76; CamBiEn;
CamDcAB; ChamBiD; ConAu 11NR,
25R, 36NR, 74NR, 155; ConHero 1;
ConIsC 2; ConLC 30; ConPopW;
CurBio 70; EncSF, 93; FacFETw;
IntAu&W 76, 89; IntWW 76, 77, 78, 79,
80, 81, 82, 83, 89, 91, 93; LarDcSc;
LegTOT; MajTwCW 1, 2; NewEScF;
NewYTBS 79, 85, 96; NotTwCS 1; RAdv
14, 13-5; RanHWDS; ScF&FL 92;
SmATA 58; UFOEn-P; WhAm 12;
WhoAm 74, 76, 78, 80, 82, 84, 86, 88,
90, 92, 94, 95, 96, 97; WhoE 74, 75, 77,
79, 81, 83, 85, 86, 89, 91, 93; WhoFrS
84; WhoScEn 94, 96; WhoTelC;
WhoUSWr 88; WhoWor 78, 80, 82, 84,
87, 89, 91, 93, 95; WhoWrEP 89, 92,
95; WorAl; WorAlBi; WorAu 1975;
WorScD; WrDr 76, 80, 82, 84, 86, 88,
90, 92, 94, 96*

Sagan, Francoise
[Francoise Quoirez]
French. Author
Wrote award-winning *Bonjour Tristesse,*
1945, filmed, 1958.
b. Jun 21, 1935 in Cajarc, France
Source: *Benet 87, 96; BiCoLiE; BioIn 3,
4, 5, 7, 8, 10, 11, 12, 13, 14, 16, 17, 23;
BlmGWL; CamBiEn; CasWL; ChamBiD;
ClDMEL 80; ConAu 6NR, 39NR, 49;
ConLC 3, 6, 9, 17, 36; ContDcW 89;
ConWorW 93; CurBio 60; CyWA 97;
DcArts; DcLB 83; DcPseud; DcTwCCu
2; EncCoWW; EncWL 1, 2, 2S, 3;
EvEuW; FacFETw; FemDram; FilmEn;
FilmgC; FrenWW; GuFrLit 1; HalFC
80, 84, 88; IntAu&W 76, 77, 89;
IntDcWB; IntWW 74, 75, 76, 77, 78, 79,
80, 81, 82, 83, 89, 91, 93, 97, 98, 2000;
IntWWW 2; InWom, SUP; ItaFilm;
LegTOT; LinLib L; LngCTC; MajTwCW
1; McGEWD 84; ModFrL; ModRL;
ModWoWr; Novels; PenC EUR;
PenNWW A, B; REn; TwCWr; WhDW;
Who 74, 82, 83, 85, 88, 90, 92, 94, 98,
99, 2000; WhoAmW 66, 68, 70, 72;
WhoFr 79; WhoTwCL; WhoWor 74, 82,
84, 87, 89, 91, 93, 95, 96; WorAl;
WorAlBi; WorAu 1950*

Sagansky, Jeff
American. TV Executive
Pres., entertainment programming, CBS,
1990-94; executive vp, Sony US,
1994-97, co-pres., 1997-98.
b. 1952 in Wellesley, Massachusetts
Source: *IntMPA 92; LesBEnT 92; News
93-2; WhoEnt 92*

Sage, Margaret Olivia
[Mrs. Russell Sage]
American. Philanthropist
Gave $10 million to found Russell Sage
Foundation, 1907, for improvement in
living conditions in US.
b. Sep 8, 1828 in Syracuse, New York
d. Nov 4, 1918 in New York, New York
Source: *AmBi; DcAmB; NotAW; WebAB
74; WhAm 1; WomWWA 14; WorAl;
WorAlBi*

Sage, Russell
American. Financier
Associated with Jay Gould in railroading,
stock market operations, 1850s-80s;
amassed fortune.
b. Aug 4, 1816 in Oneida County, New
York
d. Nov 4, 1906 in New York, New York
Source: *AmBi; AmNatBi; ApCAB;
BiAUS; BiDAmBL 83; BiDrAC;
BiDrUSC 89; BioIn 7, 21; CamDcAB;
DcAmB; HarEnUS; LinLib S; NatCAB
10; TwCBDA; WebAB 74, 79; WhAm 1;
WorAl; WorAlBi*

Sager, Carole Bayer
[Mrs. Robert Daly]
American. Singer, Songwriter
Won 1986 Grammy for "That's What
Friends Are For."
b. Mar 8, 1947 in New York, New York
Source: *BioIn 11, 14, 15; CelR 90;
ConAu 146; ConTFT 13; PenEncP;
RkOn 85; RolSEnR 83; WhoAm 80, 82,
84, 86, 88, 90, 92, 94, 95, 96, 97;
WhoAmW 95; WhoRocM 82*

Sager, Ruth
American. Geneticist
Discovered that genetic material was also
contained apart from the chromosomes
in the nucleus of the cell.
b. Feb 7, 1918
d. Mar 29, 1997 in Brookline,
Massachusetts
Source: *AmMWSc 73P, 76P, 79, 82, 86,
89, 92, 95; AmWomSc; BioIn 7, 8, 16,
20, 22, 23; ChamBiD; ConAu 158;
CurBio 97N; EncWB 98; InWom, SUP;
LibW; NotTwCS 1, 1S; WhAm 12;
WhoAm 82, 84, 90, 92, 94, 95, 96;
WhoAmW 68A, 79, 81, 83, 85, 89, 91,
93, 95; WhoFrS 84; WhoScEn 94, 96;
WomBioS*

Saget, Bob
[Robert Saget]
American. Actor, Comedian
Played Danny Tanner on TV comedy
"Full House," 1987-95; hosted TV
show "America's Funniest Home
Videos," 1990-97.
b. May 17, 1956 in Philadelphia,
Pennsylvania
Source: *BioIn 16; ConAu 173; ConTFT
7, 18; IntMPA 96; LegTOT; WhoEnt 92;
WhoHol 92*

Sahl, Mort (Lyon)
American. Comedian
Offbeat nightclub, TV political satirist;
known for ironic views of passing
scene; wrote autobiography,
Heartland, 1976.
b. May 11, 1927 in Montreal, Quebec,
Canada
Source: *BioIn 4, 5, 6, 7, 9, 10, 11, 13,
16; BioNews 74; CmCal; ConAu 113;
ConTFT 7; CurBio 60; Ent; FacFETw;
FilmgC; HalFC 84; IntWW 89, 91;
JoeFr; LegTOT; WhoAm 86, 90;
WhoCom; WhoEnt 92; WhoHol 92, A;
WorAl; WorAlBi*

Saibou, Ali
Nigerien. Political Leader
Appointed army chief of staff after the
1974 military coup led by Syni
Kountche, he was named president of
Niger 1987 and promised to continue
the process of democratization.
b. 1940 in Dingajibanda, Ouallam, Niger
Source: *BioIn 21; WhoAfr*

Saicho
Japanese. Clergy
Buddhist monk imported the Tendai sect
from China and founded a monastery
on Mt. Hiei; beliefs were based on the
Lotus Sutra, and the sect demanded
severe discipline.
b. 767 in Shiga, Omi, Japan
d. 822
Source: *EncJap; EncWB 98; McGEWB;
PriCCJL 85*

Said, Edward W
American. Political Activist, Educator
Prominent American spokesperson for
Palistinian Causes; wrote *Orientalism,*
1978.
b. Nov 1, 1935 in Jerusalem, Palestine
Source: *BioIn 15, 16; CamDcAB;
CamGLE; ConAu 21R, 74NR; ConLC
123; CurBio 89; CyWA 89; DcLB 67;
IntWW 91, 97, 98, 2000; LiExTwC;
MajTwCW 2; NewYTBS 80; Who 98, 99,
2000; WhoAm 90; WhoUSWr 88;
WhoWrEP 89; WorAu 1975; WrDr 92,
98, 99*

Said, Seyyid
Arab. Political Leader
Sultan of Oman transferred his capital
from Arabia to Zanzibar, where he
initiated clove production and greatly
expanded the East African slave trade.
b. 1790
d. Oct 19, 1856
Source: *EncWB 98; McGEWB*

Said bin Taimur
Ruler
Impoverished citizens of his oil-rich
country during reign as Sultan of
Muscat and Oman, 1932-70; deposed
by son, Quabus bin Said.
b. Aug 13, 1910 in London, England
d. Oct 19, 1972 in London, England
Source: *BioIn 4, 9, 10, 11, 17; CurBio
57, 78, 78N*

Saidenberg, Daniel
American. Musician, Conductor
Cellist; created Saidenberg Little
Symphony, 1940; led IL Symphony,
1930s.
b. Nov 12, 1906 in Winnipeg, Manitoba,
Canada
d. May 18, 1997 in New York, New
York
Source: *BioIn 2, 9, 22, 23; IntWWM 77,
80, 85; WhAm 12; WhoAm 74, 76, 78,
80, 82, 84, 86, 88, 90; WhoAmA 73, 76,
78, 80, 82, 84, 86, 89, 91, 93, 1999;
WhoEnt 92; WhoMus 72*

Said ibn Sultan
Arab. Ruler
Sayyid of Muscat, Oman, and Zanzibar,
1806-56; established Zanzibar as a
commerce capital.
b. 1791, Oman
d. Oct 19, 1856, At Sea

Saigo, Takamori
Japanese. Politician, Military Leader
Rebel and statesman led the Meiji
restoration, but he opposed rapid
Westernization and revolted against
the Meiji government in 1877.
b. Feb 7, 1827 in Kagoshima, Satsuma,
Japan
d. Sep 24, 1877
Source: *BioIn 1, 11, 19; EncWB 98;
HarEnMi; McGEWB*

Sain, Johnny
[John Franklin Sain]
American. Baseball Player, Baseball
Coach
Pitcher, 1942, 1946-55; had 139 career
wins; controversial pitching coach for
13 yrs.
b. Sep 15, 1918 in Havana, Arkansas
Source: *Ballpl 90; BioIn 1, 2, 3, 4, 6, 7,
8, 9, 10, 14, 15; WhoProB 73*

Saint, Assotto
American. Writer
Poetry collections include *Stations,* 1989;
also performed theatrical works.
b. Oct 2, 1957, Haiti
d. 1994
Source: *CmpQue; GayLesB; GayLL 2*

Saint, Eva Marie
American. Actor
Won Oscar, 1955, for *On the Waterfront,*
her first film; other films include *North
by Northwest,* 1959; *Grand Prix,* 1966.
b. Jul 4, 1924 in Newark, New Jersey
Source: *BiDFilm 94; BiE&WWA; BioIn
2, 3, 4, 10; BioNews 74; CamBiEn;
ConTFT 3, 5; CurBio 55; FilmEn;
FilmgC; ForYSC; GangFlm; HalFC 80,
84, 88; IntDcF 1-3, 2-3; IntMPA 77, 78,
79, 80, 81, 82, 84, 86, 88, 92, 94, 96;
InWom, SUP; LegTOT; MotPP; MovMk;
OsStAZ; WhoAm 74, 76, 78, 80, 82, 84,
86, 88, 90, 92, 94, 95, 96, 97, 98,
2000; WhoAmW 58, 61, 64, 66, 68, 70,
95, 97, 99; WhoEnt 92, 98; WhoHol 92,
A; WorAl; WorAlBi; WorEFlm*

Saint Clair, Arthur
American. Military Leader
First governor of Northwest Territory,
1787-1802; removed from office by
Jeffers on in 1802 for criticizing act
which made Ohio a state.
b. Mar 23, 1736 in Thurso, Scotland
d. Aug 31, 1818 in Ligonier,
Pennsylvania
Source: Alli; AmBi; ApCAB; BiAUS;
BiDrAC; BiDrUSE 71; DcAmB; Drake;
NewCol 75; OhA&B; OxCAmH; REnAL;
TwCBDA; WebAB 74; WebAMB; WhAm
HS; WorAl

St. Clair, Bob
American. Football Player
Tackle, San Francisco, 1953-63; Hall of
Fame, 1990.
b. Feb 18, 1931 in San Francisco,
California
Source: BioIn 17; WhoSpor

Saint Clair, James Draper
American. Lawyer
Chief Watergate counsel to Richard
Nixon, Jan-Aug 1974; argued against
impeachment before House Judiciary
Committee, Feb 1974.
b. Apr 14, 1920 in Akron, Ohio
Source: BioIn 10; NewYTBS 74; PolProf
NF; WhoAm 86, 90; WhoAmL 85, 92

Saint Cyr, Lillian
[Willis Marie VanSchaack]
American. Entertainer
Burlesque queen who made as much as
$7,500 per week at height of career.
b. Jun 3, 1917 in Minneapolis,
Minnesota
d. Jan 29, 1999 in Hollywood, California
Source: BioIn 10; DcPseud; InWom
SUP; WhoHol A

Saint Denis, Ruth
American. Dancer, Choreographer
Early modern dance exponent; noted for
eclectic style from Oriental
movements.
b. Jan 20, 1877 in Newark, New Jersey
d. Jun 21, 1968 in Los Angeles,
California
Source: BiDD; CurBio 49, 68; IntDcWB;
McGEWB; NotAW MOD; WebAB 79;
WhAm 5; WhoHol B; WhScrn 83

St. Denis, Ruth
American. Choreographer, Dancer
A founder of modern dance, known for
her mystical and Eastern-influenced
work.
b. Jan 20, 1877 in Newark, New Jersey
d. Jul 21, 1968 in Los Angeles,
California
Source: BiDD; BioAmW; CamDcAB;
ContDcW 89; DancEn 78; FilmChD;
IntDcWB; InWom SUP; NewGrDM 80;
NotNAT B; WebAB 74; WorAlBi

Sainte-Beuve, Charles Augustin
French. Critic
First professional literary critic; wrote
Port-Royal, 1840-59.
b. Dec 23, 1804 in Boulogne-sur-Mer,
France
d. Oct 13, 1869 in Paris, France
Source: AtlBL; BbD; Benet 87, 96;
BiD&SB; BioIn 1, 2, 3, 4, 5, 6, 7, 9, 10;
CamBiEn; CasWL; CelCen; ChamBiD;
CyWA 58, 97; DcArts; DcBiPP; DcEnL;
DcEuL; DcLB 217; Dis&D; EncWB 98;
EuAu; EvEuW; GloEncH; LinLib L, S;
McGEWB; NewC; NewCBEL; NinCLC
5; OxCEng 67, 85; OxCFr; OxCThe 67;
PenC EUR; RComWL; REn

**Sainte-Clair Deville, Henri
Etienne**
French. Chemist
Invented first cost-effective process for
making aluminum.
b. Mar 11, 1818 in Saint Thomas,
Danish West Indies
d. Jul 1, 1881 in Boulogne, France
Source: BioIn 3, 6

Sainte-Marie, Buffy
[Beverly Sainte-Marie]
American. Singer, Composer
Won Oscar for best song from An
Officer and a Gentleman, 1982; has
composed over 300 songs.
b. Feb 20, 1941 in Craven,
Saskatchewan, Canada
Source: AllMGCo; ASCAP 80; BiDAmM;
BillEnR; BioIn 14, 21, 22, 24;
ChamBiD; CivR 74; ConAu 107; ConLC
17; ConTFT 16; CurBio 69; EncFCWM
69, 83; EncRk 88; GoodHs; HarEnCM
87; IlEncCM; IlEncRk; InWom SUP;
LegTOT; NewAmDM; NewGrDA 86;
PenEncP; RkOn 74, 78; RolSEnR 83;
Songw; WhoAm 74, 76, 78, 80, 82;
WhoAmW 70, 72, 74, 75, 83; WhoRock
81; WhoRocM 82; WhoWor 74; WorAl;
WorAlBi

**Saint-Exupery, Antoine (Jean
Baptiste Marie Roger) de**
French. Author, Aviator
Wrote fable The Little Prince,
1943;autobiography Wind, Sand, and
Stars, 1939; opened transatlantic
airmail routes to S America, Africa.
b. Jun 29, 1900 in Lyons, France
d. Jul 31, 1944, France
Source: AtlBL; CasWL; ConAu 108;
CurBio 40, 45; MajAl; MajTwCW 2;
ModRL; OxCFr; PenC EUR; REn;
TwCA, SUP; TwCWr; WhoTwCL

Saint Gaudens, Augustus
American. Sculptor
Leading sculptor of late 19th c. known
for equestrian statue of General
Sherman in Central Park, NYC.
b. Mar 1, 1848 in Dublin, Ireland
d. Aug 3, 1907 in Cornish, New
Hampshire
Source: AmAu&B; AmBi; AmNatBi;
ApCAB; AtlBL; CamBiEn; CamDcAB;
ChamBiD; DcAmB; DcTwArt; EncAB-H

1974; EncWB 98; OxCAmL 65; REn;
REnAL; TwCBDA; WebAB 74; WhAm 1

Saint Georges, Jules
French. Author, Librettist
Wrote, alone or in collaboration, over 80
opera books for noted French
composers.
b. Nov 7, 1801 in Paris, France
d. Dec 23, 1875 in Paris, France
Source: NewEOp 71

Saint Jacques, Raymond
[Charles Arthur Johnson]
American. Actor
Films include Cotton Comes to Harlem,
1970; Glory, 1990.
b. Mar 1, 1930 in Hartford, Connecticut
d. Aug 27, 1990 in Los Angeles,
California
Source: BioIn 15; BlksAmF; ConTFT 9;
DrBlPA 90; FacFETw; FilmEn; FilmgC;
HalFC 88; IntMPA 86, 88; MovMk;
NewYTBE 73; NewYTBS 90; VarWW 85;
WhoAm 86, 90; WhoBlA 1, 7N; WhoHol
A

St. James, Lyn
[Evelyn Cornwall]
American. Auto Racer
First woman to be named rookie of the
year at the Indianapolis 500, 1992.
b. Mar 13, 1947 in Cleveland, Ohio
Source: BioIn 12, 16; EncWoSp; News
93-2; WhoAdv 90; WhoAm 94, 95, 96,
97, 98; WhoAmW 91, 93, 95, 97; WhoFI
89

Saint James, Susan
[Susan Jane Miller]
American. Actor
Appeared in TV series "The Name of
the Game," 1968-71; "McMillan and
Wife," 1971-76; "Kate and Allie,"
1984-89.
b. Aug 14, 1946 in Long Beach,
California
Source: BioIn 13, 14, 15; CelR 90;
ConTFT 2, 8, 18; DcPseud; FilmEn;
FilmgC; ForYSC; HalFC 80, 84, 88;
HolBB; IntMPA 77, 78, 79, 80, 81, 82,
84, 86, 88, 92, 94, 96; InWom SUP;
LegTOT; WhoAm 74, 76, 80, 82, 84, 86,
88, 90, 92; WhoAmW 72, 74, 75;
WhoEnt 92; WhoHol 92, A; WorAl;
WorAlBi

Saint James, Synthia
American. Artist, Entrepreneur
Self-taught artist known for brilliantly
colored paintings of figures and
scenes; illustrates book jackets,
children's books, and advertisements,
and licenses her designs for
reproduction of clothing and
decorative items.
b. Feb 11, 1949 in Los Angeles,
California
Source: AfrAmAl 8; ConBlB 12; SmATA
84; WhoAfA 11, 12; WhoAmW 97

Saint John, Betta
[Betty Streidler]
American. Actor
Ingenue in original Broadway cast of
  South Pacific, 1949; films include *The
  Law vs. Billy the Kid,* 1954.
b. Nov 26, 1929 in Hawthorne,
  California
Source: *FilmEn; FilmgC; HalFC 84, 88;
IntMPA 86, 88; WhoHol A*

Saint John, Howard
American. Actor
Films include *L'il Abner,* 1959; *Don't
  Drink the Water,* 1969.
b. Oct 9, 1905 in Chicago, Illinois
d. Mar 13, 1974 in New York, New
  York
Source: *BiE&WWA; FilmgC; MovMk;
WhoHol B; WhScrn 77*

Saint John, Jill
[Jill Oppenheim; Mrs. Robert Wagner]
American. Actor
Began acting at age 6; has appeared on
  radio, TV, film; appeared in film *Tony
  Rome,* 1967.
b. Aug 9, 1940 in Los Angeles,
  California
Source: *BioIn 13, 16; ConTFT 3;
EncAFC; FilmgC; HalFC 84, 88;
IntMPA 92; InWom SUP; MotPP;
MovMk; WhoAm 86, 90; WhoEnt 92;
WorAlBi*

Saint John, Robert
American. Journalist, Author
War correspondent with AP, WW II;
  books on Middle-Eastern affairs
  include *The Tongue of the Prophets,*
  1952.
b. Mar 9, 1902 in Chicago, Illinois
Source: *AmAu&B; ConAu 1R, 5NR;
CurBio 42; IntAu&W 91; WhoAm 84;
WhoWor 74; WrDr 86, 92*

Saint Johns, Adela Rogers
American. Author, Journalist
Noted for inside stories of Hollywood
  film community; wrote *The Tramp,*
  short story based on Hollywood
  experiences.
b. May 20, 1894 in Los Angeles,
  California
d. Aug 10, 1988 in Arroyo Grande,
  California
Source: *AmWomWr; AuNews 1; CelR;
ConAu 108; CurBio 76, 88; DcLB 29;
EncAJ; EncTwCJ; ForWC 70; GoodHs;
InWom SUP; LibW; WhoAm 74, 76, 78;
WhoAmW 64, 66, 68, 70, 72, 74, 75;
WorAl; WrDr 76, 80, 82, 84*

Saint-Just, Louis Antoine Leon de
French. Politician, Author
Radical political leader during the French
  Revolution and a member of the ruling
  Jacobin group in Paris during the
  Reign of Terror.
b. Aug 25, 1767 in Decize, France
d. Jul 28, 1794 in Paris, France
Source: *Benet 87, 96; BiDMoER 1;
BioIn 2, 5, 7, 13; Dis&D; EncEnl;*

*EncLitE; EncWB 98; McGEWB; OxCFr;
REn*

St. Laurent, Andre
"Ace"
Canadian. Hockey Player
Center, 1973-85; involved in
  controversial free agent compensation
  case with Dale McCourt, Rogie
  Vachon, 1979.
b. Feb 16, 1953 in Rouyn Noranda,
  Quebec, Canada
Source: *HocEn; HocReg 85*

St. Laurent, Louis Stephen
Canadian. Political Leader
Leader of the Liberal party of Canada
  served as prime minister of the
  country during a period of economic
  boom.
b. Feb 1, 1882 in Compton, Quebec,
  Canada
Source: *BioIn 1, 2, 3, 4, 6, 7, 8, 10, 13;
CamBiEn; ChamBiD; DcNaB 1971;
DcTwHis; FacFETw; LinLib L, S;
MacDCB 78; McGEWB; ObitT 1971;
OxCCan; WhAm 5*

Saint Laurent, Louis Stephen
Canadian. Political Leader
Prime Minister, Liberal Party, 1948-57.
b. Feb 1, 1882 in Compton, Quebec,
  Canada
d. Jul 24, 1973 in Quebec, Quebec,
  Canada
Source: *CanWW 70; CurBio 48, 73;
EncWB 98; NewYTBE 73; OxCCan;
WhAm 5; WhoWor 74*

Saint Laurent, Yves Mathieu
French. Fashion Designer
Responsible for "chic beatnik" and
  "little boy look" of 1960s.
b. Aug 1, 1936 in Oran, Algeria
Source: *BioIn 13, 16; BkPepl; CelR 90;
ConDes 90; CurBio 64; DcTwDes;
EncFash; Entr; FacFETw; IntWW 91;
NewYTBS 76, 83; Who 92; WhoFash 88;
WhoWor 84, 91; WorAlBi; WorFshn*

Saint-Pierre, Abbe de
[Charles Irenee Castel]
French. Political Scientist, Economist
Political and economic theorist was an
  early philosopher of the
  Enlightenment, known for his
  pamphleteering expressing intellectual
  upheaval and fascination with affairs
  of state.
b. 1658
d. 1743
Source: *EncWB 98*

Saint-Saens, (Charles) Camille
French. Musician, Composer
Best known for opera *Samson et Delila,*
  1877, several symphonies.
b. Oct 9, 1835 in Paris, France
d. Dec 16, 1921 in Algiers, Algeria
Source: *AtlBL; BakBD 78, 84, 92;
BakBDTw; BakDcM; Benet 87, 96; BioIn
1, 2, 3, 4, 5, 6, 7, 8, 9, 12, 13, 16, 20,*

*23; BriBkM 80; CamBiEn; CelCen;
ChamBiD; CmOp; CmpBCM; DancEn
78; DcArts; DcCom 77; DcCom&M 79;
DcPup; DcTwCCu 2; EncPaPR 91;
EncWB 98; GrComp; IntDcOp; LegTOT;
LinLib S; LuthC 75; McGEWB;
MetOEnc; MusMk; NewAmDM; NewEOp
71; NewGrDM 80; NewGrDO;
NewOxM; NotNAT B; OxCFr; OxCMus;
OxDcOp; PenDiMP A; REn; WhDW;
WorAl; WorAlBi*

**Saintsbury, George Edward
Bateman**
English. Author, Educator, Critic
Critical writings include *Elizabethan
  Literature,* 1906; *A Scrapbook,* 1922-
  24.
b. Oct 10, 1845 in Southampton,
  England
d. Jan 28, 1933 in Bath, England
Source: *Alli SUP; AtlBL; BbD; BiD&SB;
BioIn 1, 2, 5, 8, 11, 13; BlmGEL;
CamBiEn; ChamBiD; Chambr 3; ChhPo,
S2, S3; ConAu 160; DcEnA, A; DcLEL;
DcNaB 1931; EvLB; LngCEL; LngCTC;
ModBrL; NewC; NewCBEL; OxCEng 67,
85, 95; PenC ENG; RAdv 1; TwCA,
SUP; WhLit; WorAu 1900*

Saint-Simon, Duc de
[Louis de Rouvroy]
French. Author
Writer's *Memoirs* provide a major source
  of information on the court of the Sun
  King, Louis XIV.
b. Jan 16, 1675 in Paris, France
d. Mar 2, 1755 in Paris, France

**Saint-Simon, Claude-Henri de
Rouvroy**
French. Philosopher
Saint-Simonianism was system of social
  thought combining religious dogma
  with socialism.
b. Oct 17, 1760 in Paris, France
d. May 19, 1825 in Paris, France
Source: *ApCAB; BbD; BiD&SB;
CamBiEn; CasWL; ChamBiD; DcEuL;
EuAu; EvEuW; OxCEng 67, 95; OxCFr;
OxCPhil; REn*

Saint-Subber, Arnold
American. Producer
Productions include *The Little Foxes,*
  1967; *Gigi,* 1973.
b. Feb 18, 1918 in Washington, District
  of Columbia
Source: *BiE&WWA; BlueB 76;
CamGWoT; CelR; NotNAT; WhoAm 78;
WhoThe 72, 77, 81*

Saionji, Kimmochi
Japanese. Politician
Politically active during and after the
  Meiji restoration of 1868, he was the
  last elder statesman, or genro, of
  Japan.
b. Oct 23, 1849, Japan
d. Nov 24, 1940, Japan
Source: *BioIn 15; EncWB 98; McGEWB*

Saito, Yoshishige

Japanese. Artist

Rose to prominence with his surrealistic
series of Japanese demons, 1956; later
works moved to non-expressive mode.

b. May 4, 1904 in Tokyo, Japan

Source: *ConArt 77, 83, 89, 96; DcTwArt;
OxCTwCA; PhDcTCA 77; WhoWor 74;
WhWW-II*

Sajak, Pat

American. TV Personality

Host of game show "Wheel of
Fortune," 1981—, most successful
show ever syndicated.

b. Oct 26, 1947 in Chicago, Illinois

Source: *CelR 90; ConNews 85-4; CurBio
89; IntMPA 92; LegTOT; WhoAm 90,
92, 94, 95, 96, 97, 98, 99; WhoEnt 92,
98; WorAlBi*

Sakall, S. Z

[Eugene Gero Szakall]

"Cuddles"

Hungarian. Actor

Films include *Casablanca,* 1942; *Tea for
Two,* 1950.

b. Feb 2, 1883 in Budapest, Austria-
Hungary

d. Feb 12, 1955 in Los Angeles,
California

Source: *FilmgC; MotPP; MovMk; Vers
A; WhoHol B; WhScrn 74, 77*

Sakamoto, Ryuichi

Japanese. Composer, Musician

Composer and innovator in electronic
keyboard work; released first solo
album, *Thousand Knives,* in 1978;
formed the Yellow Magic Orchestra,
1978; wrote film score for *The Last
Emperor,* 1988, for which he won an
Oscar, a Grammy, a Golden Globe,
and the New York, Los Angeles, and
British Film Critics Association
awards for Best Original Score.

b. 1952, Japan

Source: *ConMus 18, 19*

Sakharov, Andrei Dmitrievich

Russian. Physicist

National hero for building hydrogen
bomb; led dissident movement in
Soviet Union; won Nobel Peace Prize,
1975; exiled to Gorky, 1980-87.

b. May 21, 1921 in Moscow, Union of
Soviet Socialist Republics

d. Dec 14, 1989 in Moscow, Union of
Soviet Socialist Republics

Source: *BiDSovU; BioIn 8, 9, 10, 11, 12,
13, 14, 15, 16, 17, 18, 19, 20, 23;
ColdWar 1; ConAu 105, 128, 130, 157;
CurBio 71, 90, 90N; EncWB; FacFETw;
IntWW 89; News 90-2; NewYTBE 73;
NewYTBS 75, 80, 86, 89; NobelP;
RanHWDS; Who 90; WhoNob, 90;
WhoWor 89; WorAlBi*

Saki

[Hector Hugh Munro]

Author

Satirist, short-story writer; works include
Chronicles of Clovis, 1911; killed in
WW I.

b. Dec 18, 1870 in Akyab, Burma

d. Nov 13, 1916 in Beaumont-Hamel,
France

Source: *Alli SUP; AtlBL; Benet 87, 96;
BiCoLiE; BioIn 1, 5, 9, 10, 12, 14, 15,
17, 18, 22; CamGEL; CamGLE; CasWL;
ChhPo; CnMWL; ConAu 104; CrtSuMy;
CyWA 58, 97; DcArts; DcLEL; DcNaB
1912; DcPseud; EncSF, 93; EvLB;
FacFETw; GrBr; GrWrEL N; LegTOT;
LngCTC; ModBrL, 2; NewC; NewCBEL;
NewEScF; Novels; OxCEng 67, 85, 95;
OxCTwCL; PenC ENG; PenEncH; RAdv
1, 13-1; REn; RfGEnL 91; RfGShF 1, 2;
RGTwCWr; ScFEYrs; ShSCr 12; ShSWr;
SJGHorW; SupFW; TwCA, SUP; TwCLC
3; TwCWr; WhDW; WhoTwCL;
WorAlBi; WorAu 1900; WorLitC*

Sakic, Joe

Canadian. Hockey Player

Center, Quebec, 1988-95; Colorado,
1995—; won Conn Smythe Trophy,
1996.

b. Jul 7, 1969 in Burnaby, British
Columbia, Canada

Source: *BioIn 22*

Sakiestewa, Ramona

American. Artist

Hopi weaver; creates designs based on
historic textiles.

b. 1949 in Albuquerque, New Mexico

Source: *AZNatAW; BioIn 21; NotNaAm*

Saks, Gene

American. Director

Won Tony for musical, *I Love My Wife,*
1977.

b. Nov 8, 1921 in New York, New York

Source: *BiE&WWA; BioIn 11;
CamDcAB; CamGWoT; ConTFT 2, 9,
21; EncAFC; FilmEn; FilmgC; HalFC
80, 84, 88; IntMPA 75, 76, 77, 78, 79,
80, 81, 82, 84, 86, 88, 92, 94, 96;
IntWW 91, 2000; ItaFilm; LegTOT;
MiSFD 9; NotNAT; TheaDir; WhoAm
74, 86, 90; WhoHol 92, A; WhoThe 72,
77, 81; WorAlBi*

Sala, George Augustus

English. Journalist

London *Daily Telegraph* correspondent,
covering American Civil War; wrote
travel books, novels.

b. Nov 24, 1828 in London, England

d. Dec 8, 1895 in Brighton, England

Source: *BbD; BenetAL 91; DcEnL;
EvLB; NinCLC 46; OxCAusL; OxCEng
85, 95; REnAL; ScFEYrs; StaCVF*

Saladin Yusuf ibn Ayyub

[Salah al-Din]

Moslem. Ruler

Sultan of Egypt, Syria, 1174; united
Muslim territories; considered great
Muslim hero.

b. 1138, Mesopotamia

d. 1193

Source: *NewC; NewCol 75; WebBD 83*

Salam, Abdus

Pakistani. Physicist

Shared 1979 Nobel Prize in physics with
Sheldon Glashow and Steven
Weinberg.

b. Jan 29, 1926 in Jhang, Pakistan

d. Nov 21, 1996 in Oxford, England

Source: *AmMWSc 86, 89, 92, 95; BiESc;
BioIn 12, 13, 14, 15, 16, 19, 20, 22, 23;
BlueB 76; CamBiEn; CamDcSc;
ChamBiD; ConAu 157; CurBio 88, 97N;
FacFETw; FarE&A 78, 79, 80, 81;
IntWW 74, 75, 76, 77, 78, 79, 80, 81, 82,
83, 89, 91, 93; IntWWE; LarDcSc;
McGCEnS; NewYTBS 96; NobelP;
NotTwCS 1, 1S; RAdv 14; WhAm 12;
Who 74, 82, 83, 85, 88, 90, 92, 94;
WhoAm 88, 90, 92, 94, 95; WhoAtom
77; WhoNob, 90, 95; WhoScEn 94, 96;
WhoScEu 91-3; WhoUN 75; WhoWor 74,
76, 78, 80, 82, 84, 87, 89, 91, 93, 95,
96, 97; WorAlBi; WorScD; WrDr 2000*

Salam, Saeb

Lebanese. Political Leader

Prime minister, 1952-53, 1960-61, 1970-
73.

b. Jan 17, 1905 in Beirut, Lebanon

d. Jan 23, 2000 in Beirut, Lebanon

Source: *BioIn 4; DcMidEa; IntWW 74,
75, 76, 77, 78, 79, 80, 81, 82, 83, 89,
91, 93; MidE 78, 79, 80, 81, 82;
WhoWor 74*

Salant, Richard S

American. Broadcasting Executive

President of CBS, 1961-79.

b. Apr 14, 1914 in New York, New
York

d. Feb 16, 1993 in Southport,
Connecticut

Source: *BioIn 16; CurBio 61; EncTwCJ;
IntMPA 86, 92; LesBEnT; WhoAm 86;
WorAlBi*

Salazar, Alberto

American. Track Athlete

Won NY City Marathon, 1980, 1981;
Boston Marathan, 1982.

b. Aug 7, 1958 in Havana, Cuba

Source: *BioIn 12, 13, 14, 16; CurBio 83;
NewYTBS 81; WhoAm 84, 86, 88, 92,
94, 95, 96, 97; WhoHisp 91, 92, 94*

Salazar, Antonio de Oliveira

Portuguese. Statesman

Premier, dictator of Portugal, 1932-68.

b. Apr 28, 1889, Portugal

d. Jul 27, 1970 in Lisbon, Portugal

Source: *BioIn 17, 21; ChamBiD; ConAu
113; CurBio 41, 52, 70; DcTwHis;
DicTyr; EncTR 91; FacFETw;
McGEWB; NewYTBE 70; PolLCWE;
WhDW; WorAlBi*

Sale, Charles Partlow
''Chic''
American. Actor
Films include *It's a Great Life,* 1936;
　You Only Live Once, 1937.
b. 1885 in Huron, South Dakota
d. Nov 7, 1936 in Los Angeles,
　California
Source: *BioIn 3; DcNAA; WhAm 1;*
WhScrn 74, 77

Sale, Richard Bernard
American. Author, Director, Screenwriter
Published more than 400 short stories;
　screenplays include *Mr. Belvidere*
　Goes to College, 1949; directed *The*
　Girl Next Door, 1953.
b. Dec 17, 1911 in New York, New
　York
d. Mar 4, 1993 in Los Angeles,
　California
Source: *BioIn 14; ConAu 9R, 61NR;*
EncAFC; HalFC 88; IntAu&W 91;
IntMPA 92; TwCCr&M 91; WrDr 92

Saleh, Ali Abdullah
Yemeni. Political Leader
President and commander in chief of the
　armed forces of The Yemen Arab
　Republic (North Yemen), he was
　elected the first president of unified
　Yemen in May 1990.
b. 1942 in Bayt al-Ahmar, Yemen
Source: *CamBiEn; ChamBiD; IntWW 79,*
80, 81, 82, 83, 89, 91, 93, 97, 98; MidE
78, 79, 80, 81, 82; WhoWor 80, 95

Salem, Mamdouh
Egyptian. Political Leader
Prime minister under Sadat, 1975-78;
　interior minister, 1971-75.
b. 1918 in Alexandria, Egypt
d. Feb 24, 1988 in London, England
Source: *BioIn 15; IntWW 74, 75, 83;*
NewYTBS 88

Salem, Peter
American. Patriot
Killed a British commander at the Battle
　of Bunker Hill, 1775.
b. 1750
d. 1816
Source: *BioIn 7, 8, 9, 10; DcAmNB;*
InB&W 80, 85

Salerno-Sonnenberg, Nadja
Italian. Violinist
Concert star, 1981—; youngest to win
　the Naumburg competition, 1981.
b. Jan 10, 1961 in Rome, Italy
Source: *BakBD 92; BakBDTw; BioIn 15,*
16; ConMus 3; CurBio 87; LegTOT;
News 88; NewYTBS 87; WhoAm 96, 97,
98, 99, 2000; WhoAmM 83; WhoAmW
93, 95, 97, 99; WhoEnt 92, 98

Sales, Soupy
[Milton Hines; Milton Supman]
American. TV Personality
Starred in ''Soupy Sales Show,'' 1953-
　66; known for pie-throwing act.

b. Jan 8, 1930 in Wake Forest, North
　Carolina
Source: *ASCAP 66, 80; BioIn 14, 16;*
CurBio 67; EncAFC; FilmgC; HalFC
88; LesBEnT 92; MotPP; WhoHol A;
WorAlBi

Salgado, Sebastiao
Brazilian. Photojournalist
Creator of photographic shows and
　books, including *Other Americas,*
　1984.
b. 1944 in Aimores, Brazil
Source: *ICPEnP A; LatAmLi; News 94,*
94-2; NewYTBS 91

Salhany, Lucie
[Lucille S Salhany]
American. Business Executive
Chm. Fox television, 1993-94; first
　woman to head a broadcast network;
　United ParamountNetwork, 1994—.
b. May 25, 1946 in Cleveland, Ohio
Source: *ConTFT 12; WomFir*

Salieri, Antonio
Italian. Conductor, Composer
Thirty five operas include *Tarare,* 1787;
　his envy of Mozart depicted in 1985
　Oscar-winning film, *Amadeus.*
b. Aug 18, 1750 in Legnano, Italy
d. May 7, 1825 in Vienna, Austria
Source: *BakBD 78, 84, 92; BakDcM;*
BioIn 4, 5, 6, 9, 12, 14, 18, 23; BriBkM
80; CamBiEn; ChamBiD; CmOp;
DcArts; DcBiPP; IntDcOp; MetOEnc;
MusMk; NewAmDM; NewEOp 71;
NewGrDM 80; NewGrDO; NewOxM;
NewYTBS 81; OxCMus; OxDcOp;
PenDiMP A

Salih, Ali Abdallah
Yemeni. Political Leader
Known as a consensus builder, he was
　elected president of the Yemeni Arab
　Republic (North Yemen) in 1978 and
　became the first president of the
　United Republic of Yemen in 1990.
b. 1942 in Bayt al-Ahmar, Yemen
Source: *BioIn 17; EncWB 98; WhoIntA*
2; WhoWor 96, 97, 98, 99, 2000

Salinas, Luis Omar
American. Poet
Poetry frequently uses surrealistic images
　and metaphors; published collection
　Crazy Gypsy, 1970.
b. Jun 27, 1937 in Robstown, Texas
Source: *BioIn 13, 16; ChiLit; ChiSch;*
ConAu 81NR, 131; ConLC 90; DcHiB;
DcLB 82; HispLC; HispWr, 2; IntWWP
77; MexAmB; WhoHisp 91, 92, 94

Salinas (y Serrano), Pedro
Spanish. Poet
Verse volumes include *Presagios,* 1923;
　La Voza Ti Debida, 1934.
b. Nov 27, 1891 in Madrid, Spain
d. Dec 4, 1951 in Boston, Massachusetts
Source: *Benet 87; BioIn 1, 2, 3, 4, 8, 10;*
CasWL; ClDMEL 47, 80; CnMWL;
ConAu 117; DcLB 134; DcSpL; EncWL

1, 2, 2S; EvEuW; LiExTwC; ModRL;
ModSpP S; OxCSpan; PenC EUR; RAdv
14, 13-2; REn; TwCA SUP; TwCLC 17;
TwCWr; WebBD 83; WhAm 3

Salinas de Gortari, Carlos
Mexican. Political Leader
Succeeded Miguel de la Madrid as pres.
　of Mexico, 1988-94.
b. Apr 3, 1948 in Mexico City, Mexico
Source: *BioIn 15, 16; DcCPCAm;*
DcHiB; DcMexR; EncWB 98; IntWW 89,
91, 93, 95, 98, 2000; LatAmLi; News 92;
NewYTBS 87, 88, 89; WhoAm 94, 95,
96; WhoIntA 2; WhoSSW 91, 93, 95;
WhoWor 91, 95, 96, 97, 98

Salinger, J(erome) D(avid)
American. Author
Best known for poignant human comedy,
　Catcher in the Rye, 1951, popular with
　teens at the time.
b. Jan 1, 1919 in New York, New York
Source: *AmAu&B; AmWr; Au&Arts 2;*
Au&Wr 71; Benet 87, 96; BenetAL 91;
BiCoLiE; BioIn 2, 4, 5, 6, 7, 8, 9, 10,
11, 12, 13, 14, 15, 16, 17, 19, 23;
CamBiEn; CamDcAB; CamGEL;
CamGLE; CamHAL; CasWL; CelR 90;
ChamBiD; ChLR 18; CnMWL; ConAu
5R, 39NR; ConLC 12, 56; ConNov 86,
91, 96; ConPopW; CyWA 89; DcArts;
DcLB 102; DcLEL 1940; DrAPF 87, 91;
EncAB-H 1974, 1996; EncALit;
FacFETw; IntAu&W 89, 91, 93; IntvTCA
2; IntWW 91, 93, 97, 98, 2000; MajAI;
MajTwCW 1, 2; MakMC; ModAL 4S1;
NewCon; OxCAmL 83, 95; OxCChiL;
OxCEng 85, 95; OxCTwCL; PenC AM;
RAdv 14, 13-1; REn; REnAL; RfGAmL
4, 87, 94; RfGShF 1, 2; RGTwCWr;
ShSCr 2; SJGYouA 2; SmATA 67;
TwCYAW 1; WebAB 74, 79; WhDW;
Who 74, 82, 83, 85, 88, 90, 92, 94, 98,
99, 2000; WhoAm 74, 76, 78, 80, 82, 84,
92, 94, 95, 96, 97, 98, 99, 2000;
WhoUSWr 88; WhoWor 74, 84, 95, 96,
97, 98, 99, 2000; WhoWrEP 89, 92, 95;
WorAlBi; WorAu 1900; WrDr 86, 90, 94,
96, 98, 99, 2000

Salinger, Pierre Emil George
American. Journalist, Politician
Press secretary to JFK; chief foreign
　correspondent for ABC News, 1979-
　87; senior editor, ABC News for
　Europe, 1988-90; senior editor, ABC
　News, 1988-93.
b. Jun 14, 1925 in San Francisco,
　California
Source: *BiDrAC; BiDrUSC 89; BioIn 14,*
15; ConAu 14NR, 17R; CurBio 61, 87;
EncTwCJ; IntAu&W 89; IntWW 91, 97,
98, 2000; LesBEnT 92; PolProf J, K;
Who 92, 98, 99, 2000; WhoAm 86, 90,
97, 98, 99, 2000; WhoTelC; WhoUSWr
88; WhoWrEP 89; WorAlBi; WrDr 86,
92, 98, 99, 2000

Salisbury, Harrison Evans
American. Journalist
Staff writer with *NY Times,* 1949-73;
　won Pulitzer, 1955; best-sellers

include *Black Nights, White Snow*,
1978.
b. Nov 14, 1908 in Minneapolis,
Minnesota
d. Jul 5, 1993 in Providence, Rhode
Island
Source: *AmAu&B; AmNatBi; Au&Wr 71;
BenetAL 91; BiDAmJo; BioIn 3, 4, 5, 6,
7, 10, 11, 12, 13, 14, 15, 16, 17, 19, 21;
CelR 90; ConAu 1R, 3NR, 15AS, 30NR;
ConLC 81; CurBio 55, 82; EncTwCJ;
EncWB, 98; HisDcWJ; IntAu&W 76, 77,
82, 89, 91, 93; IntWW 74, 75, 76, 77,
78, 79, 80, 81, 82, 83, 89, 91, 93;
MajTwCW 1; MinnWr; PolProf E, J;
REnAL; WhAm 11; Who 74, 82, 83, 85,
88, 90, 92; WhoAm 74, 76, 78, 80, 82,
84, 86, 88, 90, 92; WhoE 74; WhoPul;
WhoWor 74, 78; WorAl; WorAlBi;
WorAu 1950; WrDr 76, 86, 92*

Salisbury, Robert Arthur Talbot, 3rd Marquess

English. Statesman
Prime minister, 1885-1902, during
England's greatest power.
b. Feb 3, 1830 in Hatfield, England
d. Aug 22, 1903 in Hatfield, England
Source: *CelCen; DcInB; McGEWB;
WhDW*

Salk, Jonas E(dward)

American. Scientist, Physician
Developed anti-polio vaccine, one of the
greatest triumphs in medical history,
1953.
b. Oct 28, 1914 in New York, New York
d. Jun 23, 1995 in La Jolla, California
Source: *AmMWSc 76P, 79, 82, 86, 89,
92, 95; AmNatBi; AsBiEn; BiDrAPH 79;
BiESc; BioIn 3, 4, 5, 6, 7, 8, 9, 10, 11,
12, 13, 14, 15, 16; BioNews 75; BlueB
76; CamBiEn; CamDcAB; CelR 90;
ChamBiD; ConAu 49; ConHero 1;
CurBio 54, 95N; EncWB 98; FacFETw;
InSci; IntMed 80; IntWW 74, 75, 76, 77,
78, 79, 80, 81, 82, 83, 89, 91, 93; IntYB
78, 79, 80, 81, 82; JeAmHC; LarDcSc;
LngCTC; McGCEnS; McGEWB; McGMS
80; NewYTBS 90; OxCAmH; RanHWDS;
RComAH; WebAB 74, 79; WhAm 11;
WhDW; Who 74, 82, 83, 85, 88, 90, 92,
94; WhoAm 74, 76, 78, 80, 82, 84, 86,
88, 90, 92, 94, 95; WhoAmJ 80; WhoFrS
84; WhoScEn 94; WhoWest 76, 78, 80,
82, 84, 87, 89, 92, 94; WhoWor 74, 78,
80, 82, 84, 87, 89, 91, 93, 95; WhoWorJ
72, 78; WorAl; WorAlBi*

Salk, Lee

American. Psychologist, Author
Family columnist with *McCall's;* wrote
books on pediatric psychology;
*Familyhood: Nurturing the Values
That Matter*, 1992.
b. Dec 27, 1926 in New York, New
York
d. May 4, 1992 in New York, New York
Source: *AnObit 1992; AuNews 1; BioIn
10, 11, 12, 15, 17, 18, 19; ConAu 104,
137; CurBio 79, 92N; NewYTBS 92;
WhAm 10; WhoAm 80, 82, 84, 86, 88,
90; WhoWor 82*

Salle, David

American. Artist
Post-Modern painter known for his
disturbing meditations on modern
existence; he combined the human
figure with abstract forms in many of
his works.
b. 1952 in Norman, Oklahoma
Source: *AmArt; BioIn 12, 13; CamDcAB;
ConArt 89, 96; CurBio 86; DcCAA 88,
94; EncWB 98; IntWW 89, 91, 93, 97,
98, 2000; PrintW 83, 85; WhoAm 86, 88,
90, 92, 94, 95, 96; WhoAmA 82, 84, 86,
89, 91, 93, 1999; WhoE 85, 86; WorArt
1980*

Sallust

[Gaius Sallustius Crispus]
Roman. Politician, Historian
Statesman and innovative historian
rejected the more usual annalistic
historical style in order to treat
subjects of value and interest in a
narrative technique; wrote primarily of
the decline of the Roman Republic.
b. c. 86 in Amiternum
d. 35BC
Source: *AncWr; BbD; Benet 87, 96;
BiD&SB; BioIn 1, 3, 6, 7, 9, 24;
CamBiEn; CasWL; ChamBiD; CnDWLB
1; DcArts; DcLB 211; EncWB 98;
GloEncH; Grk&L; LegTOT; LinLib L, S;
LngCEL; McGEWB; NewC; OxCClC;
OxCCIL, 89; OxCEng 85, 95; PenC CL;
RAdv 14, 13-3; REn; RfGWoL 95;
WhDW*

Salmi, Albert

American. Actor
TV western actor; films include *Caddy
Shack*, 1980.
b. Mar 11, 1928 in New York, New
York
d. Apr 22, 1990 in Spokane, Washington
Source: *BiE&WWA; BioIn 16, 17;
ConTFT 5, 25; FilmEn; FilmgC;
ForYSC; HalFC 80, 84, 88; IntMPA 77,
80, 84, 86, 88; NewYTBS 90; NotNAT;
VarWW 85; WhoHol A*

Salome

Hebrew. Biblical Figure
Princess; granddaughter of Herod the
Great; asked for head of John the
Baptist in payment for dancing.
b. 14
d. 62
Source: *Dis&D; NewCol 75; WebBD 83*

Salomon, Alice

American. Educator
Founded first German school of social
work.
b. Apr 19, 1872 in Berlin, Germany
d. Aug 30, 1948 in New York, New
York
Source: *BioIn 1, 2; InWom SUP; ObitOF
79; WhE&EA; WhoLA*

Salomon, Charlotte

German. Artist
In the midst of World War II, Jewish
painter recorded her autobiography in

Life or Theater?, made up of more
than 1,300 paintings.
b. Apr 16, 1917 in Berlin, Germany
d. Oct 1943 in Auschwitz, Poland
Source: *BioIn 13, 20, 24; EncWB, 98;
WomThRe*

Salomon, Haym

American. Patriot
Aided finances of American Revolution;
made large loans to new govt., to
patriots.
b. 1740 in Leszno, Poland
d. Jan 6, 1785 in Philadelphia,
Pennsylvania
Source: *AmBi; AmNatBi; AmRev;
ApCAB; BiDAmBL 83; BioIn 1, 2, 3, 4,
5, 6, 7, 8, 9, 10, 11, 14, 15, 17, 22;
CamDcAB; DcAmB; DcAmSR; EncAInt;
HarEnUS; JeHun; NatCAB 11;
OxCAmH; PolBiDi; WebAB 74, 79;
WhAm HS; WhAmP; WhAmRev*

Salt

[Salt 'n Pepa; Cheryl James]
American. Rapper
Grammy. Best Rap Performance by a
Group or Duo, "None of Your
Business," 1994.
b. Mar 8, 1964 in New York, New York

Salt, Jennifer

American. Actor
Leading lady, 1960s-70s: *Midnight
Cowboy*, 1969; *Play It Again Sam*,
1972.
b. Sep 4, 1944 in Los Angeles,
California
Source: *ConTFT 7; FilmEn; HalFC 84,
88; WhoHol 92, A*

Salt, Waldo

American. Screenwriter
Won Oscars, 1969, 1978 for screenplays:
Midnight Cowboy; Coming Home.
b. Oct 18, 1914 in Chicago, Illinois
d. Mar 9, 1987 in Los Angeles,
California
Source: *AmNatBi; AnObit 1987; BioIn
15, 24; ConAu 77NR, 111, 121; ConTFT
6; DcLB 44; FilmEn; FilmgC; HalFC
80, 84, 88; IntDcF 1-4, 2-4; IntMPA 75,
76, 77, 78, 79, 80, 81, 82, 84, 86;
ScrEAmL 2; VarWW 85; WhAm 9;
WhoAm 84, 86*

Salten, Felix

[Siegmund Salzmann]
Hungarian. Children's Author
Wrote *Bambi*, 1926, translated, 1928, as
Bambi: A Life in the Woods.
b. Sep 6, 1869 in Budapest, Hungary
d. Oct 8, 1945 in Zurich, Switzerland
Source: *AuBYP 2; BioIn 1, 4, 5, 8, 13,
19, 20, 22; CamBiEn; ChamBiD;
ChlBkCr; ClDMEL 47; ConAu 108, 137;
CyWA 58, 97; DcPseud; LegTOT; LinLib
L; LngCTC; MajAl; OxCChiL; OxCGer
76, 86, 97; ScF&FL 1; SmATA 25;
TwCA, SUP; WhAm 2; WhE&EA;
WhoChL; WorAu 1900; WrChl*

Salter, Andrew
American. Psychologist
Developed techniques for autohypnosis; wrote *What Is Hypnosis?*, 1944.
b. May 9, 1914
d. Oct 7, 1996 in New York, New York
Source: *BioIn 22, 23; CurBio 97N; InSci*

Salt n Pepa
[Spinderella; Sandy "Pepa" Denton; Cheryl "Salt" James]
American. Rap Group
Popular female rap group; singles "Push It," 1987, "Let's Talk about Sex," 1992.
Source: *BioIn 20, 21; ConMus 6*

Saltonstall, Leverett
American. Politician
Rep. governor of MA, 1939-44; senator, 1945-66.
b. Sep 1, 1892 in Chestnut Hill, Massachusetts
d. Jun 17, 1979 in Dover, Massachusetts
Source: *AmNatBi; BiDrAC; BiDrGov 1789; BiDrUSC 89; BioIn 1, 3, 4, 7, 11, 12; BlueB 76; CamDcAB; CurBio 44, 56, 79, 79N; DcAmB S10; NewYTBS 79; PolProf E, J, K, T; WhAm 7; WhAmP; WhoAm 74, 76, 78; WhoAmL 78, 79; WhoAmP 73, 75, 77, 79*

Saltzman, Charles E(skridge)
American. Business Executive, Government Official
Assistant secretary of state for occupied areas, 1947-49; partner, Goldman, Sachs & Co., 1956-73.
b. Sep 19, 1903
d. Jun 16, 1994 in New York, New York
Source: *BiDWWGF; BioIn 1, 3; CurBio 94N; IntWW 74, 75, 76, 77, 78, 79, 80, 81, 82, 83, 89, 91, 93; WhAm 11; Who 74, 82, 83, 85, 88, 90, 92, 94; WhoAm 74, 76, 78, 80, 82, 84, 86, 88, 90, 92; WhoFI 74, 75, 77, 79*

Salvemini, Gaetano
Italian. Historian, Journalist
Scholar introduced economic and social analysis into Italian historiography; in his later years, he opposed the Fascist dictatorship.
b. Sep 8, 1873 in Molfetta, Italy
d. Sep 6, 1957 in Florence, Italy
Source: *BiDInt; BioIn 1, 4, 5, 11, 22; CIDMEL 47; EncWB 98; GloEncH; McGEWB; WhAm 3; WorAu 1900*

Sam and Dave
[Sam Moore; Dave Prater]
American. Music Group
Black singing duo known for pop, soul hits including "Soul Man," 1967.
Source: *BioIn 16; ConMuA 80A; ConMus 8; EncPR&S 89; EncRk 88; HarEnR 86; InB&W 80; NewYTBS 88; PenEncP; RkOn 78; RolSEnR 83; WhoHol 92; WhoRock 81; WhoRocM 82*

Samara, Noah (Azmi)
American. Entrepreneur
Founder and CEO of WorldSpace, Inc., a satellite broadcasting company dedicated to providing radio, fax, and cellular service to underserved, developing communities in Africa.
b. 1956 in Addis Ababa, Ethiopia
Source: *WhoAfA 9, 10, 11, 12; WhoBlA 7, 8*

Samaranch, Juan Antonio
[Juan Antonio Samaranch Torello]
Spanish. Olympic Official
Pres., International Olympic Committee, 1979—.
b. Jul 17, 1920 in Barcelona, Spain
Source: *BioIn 14, 15, 16; ChamBiD; ConNews 86-2; CurBio 94; IntWW 91; Who 82, 83, 85, 88, 90, 92, 94, 98, 99, 2000; WhoWor 84, 87, 89, 91, 93, 95, 96, 97, 98, 99, 2000*

Samaras, Lucas
American. Artist
Experimental artist, noted for his "assemblages," three dimensional still lifes: *The Room*, 1964.
b. Sep 14, 1936 in Kastoria, Greece
Source: *AmArt; BioIn 8, 9, 10, 14, 17; BriEAA; ChamBiD; ConArt 77, 83, 89, 96; ConPhot 82, 88, 95; CurBio 72; DcAmArt; DcCAA 71, 77, 88, 94; DcCAr 81; DcTwArt; ICPEnP A; MacBEP; OxCTwCA; OxDcArt; PhDcTCA 77; PrintW 83, 85; WhoAm 82, 84, 86, 88; WhoAmA 73, 76, 78, 80, 82, 84, 86, 89, 91, 93, 1999; WhoArt 80; WorArt 1980*

Samaroff, Olga
American. Pianist
Ranked among best pianists, early 1900s; wed to Leopold Stokowski, 1911-23.
b. Aug 8, 1882 in San Antonio, Texas
d. May 17, 1948 in New York, New York
Source: *AmNatBi; BakBD 78, 84, 92; BakBDTw; BiDAmEd; BioIn 15, 16, 20, 22, 23; BriBkM 80; CurBio 46, 48; DcAmB S4; DcPseud; FacFETw; InWom; LibW; MusSN; NewAmDM; NewGrDA 86; NewGrDM 80; NotAW; PeoHis; WhAm 2; WomFir*

Sammarco, Mario
Italian. Opera Singer
Baritone with European, American operas, from 1900; noted for *Tosca, Rigoletto* roles.
b. Dec 13, 1868 in Palermo, Sicily, Italy
d. Jan 24, 1930 in Milan, Italy
Source: *BakBD 78, 84; BioIn 10; CmOp; MetOEnc; NewEOp 71; NewGrDM 80; OxDcOp*

Sammartino, Peter
American. Educator
Founder, pres. Fairleigh Dickinson University, 1942-1967.
b. Aug 15, 1904 in New York, New York
d. Mar 29, 1992 in Rutherford, New Jersey

Source: *BiDAmEd; BioIn 3, 5, 14, 17, 18; ConAu 7NR, 57, 137; CurBio 92N; WhAm 10; WhoAm 74, 76, 78, 80, 82, 84, 86, 88, 90, 92; WhoGov 75; WhoWor 74*

Samms, Emma
[Emma Samuelson]
English. Actor
Succeeded Pamela Sue Martin in role of Fallon Carrington Colby in TV series "Dynasty," "The Colbys."
b. Aug 28, 1960 in London, England
Source: *BioIn 13, 14, 15; ConTFT 4; DcPseud; IntMPA 94, 96; LegTOT; WhoEnt 92; WhoHol 92; WorAlBi*

Samory Toure
African. Ruler
Created one of the most powerful and best-organized states in the western Sudan, and successfully opposed the French for 15 years.
b. 1830 in Milo Valley, Sudan
d. Jun 2, 1900, Gabon
Source: *EncWB 98*

Samoset
American. Native American Chief
Chief of the Abenaki; first chief to negotiate land transfer between native Americans and English settlers, 1625.
b. 1590?
d. 1653?
Source: *AmIndBi; ApCAB; CamDcAB; EncNAB; HarEnUS; NotNaAm; WebAB 74; WhNaAH*

Samper Pizano, Ernesto
Colombian. Political Leader
Pres., Colombia, 1994—.
b. Aug 3, 1950 in Bogota, Colombia
Source: *WhoIntA 2; WhoWor 95, 96, 97, 98, 99, 2000*

Sample, Bill
American. Police Officer
Founder, pres., Sunshine Foundation, 1977; grants wishes to terminally ill children.
b. Dec 2, 1935 in Philadelphia, Pennsylvania
Source: *BioIn 12, 15; ConNews 86-2*

Sample, Paul Starrett
American. Artist
Paintings of genre subjects in a simplified manner include *Janitor's Holiday*.
b. Sep 14, 1896 in Louisville, Kentucky
d. Feb 26, 1974 in Norwich, Vermont
Source: *AmNatBi; ArtsAmW 1; BioIn 1, 5, 6; IlBEAAW; McGDA; WhAm 6; WhAmArt 85; WhoAm 74; WhoAmA 73, 76, 78*

Samples, Junior
[Alvin Samples]
American. Comedian
Bib-overalled, 300 lb. star of TV's "Hee-Haw," 1969-83.

b. Apr 10, 1927? in Cumming, Georgia
d. Nov 13, 1983 in Cumming, Georgia
Source: *AllMGCo; BioIn 13; HarEnCM
87; NewYTBS 83*

Sampras, Pete(r)
American. Tennis Player
First American since 1984, youngest man
  ever to win US Open, 1990; ranked
  number one for 82 consecutive weeks
  until April 10, 1995; won Wimbledon
  six times: 1993-95, 1997-99;
  Australian Open, 1994, 1997; US
  Open, 1990, 1993, 1995-96.
b. Aug 12, 1971 in Washington, District
  of Columbia
Source: *BioIn 16; BuCMET; CurBio 94;
LegTOT; News 94, 94-1; NewYTBS 91;
Who 98, 99, 2000; WhoAm 92, 94, 95,
96, 97; WhoSpor; WhoWor 95, 96, 97*

Sampson, Charles
American. Rodeo Performer
First black world rodeo champion, 1982.
b. 1957?
Source: *BioIn 13; ConBlB 13*

Sampson, Deborah
[Robert Shirtliff]
American. Soldier
Spent three years in Continental Army
  disguised as a man.
b. Dec 17, 1760 in Massachusetts
d. 1827
Source: *AmBi; AmNatBi; AmRev;
ApCAB; BioAmW; BioIn 18, 20, 21;
CamDcAB; ContDcW 89; DcNAA;
Drake; EncAmaz 91; EncAR; EncAWoR;
EncCRAm; EncWHA; GoodHs;
HanAmWH; HarEnUS; HerW, 84;
HisDcAR; IntDcWB; InWom, SUP;
LibW; NatCAB 8; NotAW; NotBlAW 1;
OxCAmL 65, 83, 95; WebAMB;
WhAmRev; WomFir; WomMil*

Sampson, Edith Spurlock
American. Judge
First African-American woman to serve
  as circuit court judge, 1925 and as
  United Nations alternate delegate,
  1950.
b. Oct 13, 1901 in Pittsburgh,
  Pennsylvania
d. Oct 8, 1979 in Chicago, Illinois
Source: *AmNatBi; Ebony 1; InB&W 80,
85; InWom, SUP; NegAl 89A; NotBlAW
1; WhAm 7; WhoAm 74, 76; WhoAmW
66, 68, 70, 72, 74; WhoMW 74, 76*

Sampson, Ralph Lee
''The Stick''
American. Basketball Player
Seven-foot, four-inch center, played
  1983-92, mostly with Houston; NBA
  rookie of yr., 1984; with Akeem
  Olajuwon, formed team's famed
  ''Twin Towers'' combination.
b. Jul 7, 1960 in Harrisonburg, Virginia
Source: *BiDAmSp BK; BioIn 16;
NewYTBS 82, 83, 86; OfNBA 87;
WhoBlA 4, 5, 7*

Sampson, Will, Jr.
American. Actor
Acting debut as Chief Bromden in *One
  Flew Over the Cuckoo's Nest;* 1975.
b. 1943 in Okmulgee, Oklahoma
d. Jun 2, 1987 in Houston, Texas

Sampson, William T
American. Military Leader
Commanded North Atlantic squadron,
  Spanish-American War.
b. Feb 9, 1840 in Palmyra, New York
d. May 6, 1902 in Washington, District
  of Columbia
Source: *AmBi; ApCAB, SUP; NatCAB 9;
OxCAmH; TwCBDA; WebAMB; WhAm 1*

Samrin, Heng
Cambodian. Political Leader
Became pres. of Cambodia following
  Vietnam's invasion; held office 1979-
  93.
b. May 25, 1934 in Prey Veng Province
Source: *BioIn 11, 18; ColdWar 1, 2;
EncWB; IntWW 91; WhoWor 91*

Samson
Biblical Figure
Known for tremendous strength used
  against Philistines; secret betrayed by
  Delilah.
Source: *Benet 96; BiB N; BioIn 1, 2, 4,
6, 7, 8, 9, 10, 12, 17; CamBiEn;
ChamBiD; DcBiPP; DcCathB; DcNaB;
Dis&D; GrMetD; NewCol 75; OxCCAA;
OxDcJeR; WhoRocM 82*

Samsonov, Aleksandr Vasilievich
Russian. Military Leader
General; defeated by Germans at Battle
  of Tannenberg.
b. 1859
d. Aug 29, 1914 in Tannenberg, Prussia
Source: *HarEnMi; NewCol 75; WhoMilH
76*

Samstag, Nicholas
American. Advertising Executive, Author
Pres., Nicholas Samstag, Inc., 1933-39;
  wrote *The Uses of Ineptitude,* 1962.
b. Dec 25, 1903 in New York, New
  York
d. Mar 26, 1968
Source: *AuBYP 2, 3; BioIn 8; ConAu 5R,
25R*

Sam the Sham and the Pharaohs
[Butch Gibson; David Martin; Jerry
  Patterson; Domingo Samudio; Ray
  Stinnet]
American. Music Group
1960s rock-and-roll band best known for
  first hit, ''Wooly Bully,'' 1965.
Source: *Alli, SUP; BillEnR; BioIn 1, 15,
21; ChhPo S2; DcVicP 2; Drake;
DrAPF 89, 91, 93, 97; Dun&B 86, 88;
EncPR&S 74, 89; EncRk 88; InB&W 80;
MorBAP; NewYHSD; NewYTBS 95;
PenDiMP; PenEncP; RkOn 78, 84;
RolSEnR 83; St&PR 96, 97; WhoLibS
55; WhoRock 81; WhoRocM 82*

Samudragupta
Indian. Political Leader
Second emperor of the Gupta dynasty of
  India, reigned from 350 to 375; known
  as a benevolent imperial conqueror
  and a patron the arts and letters, he
  ushered in the Golden Age of India.
b. fl. 350

Samuel
Hebrew. Biblical Figure
Judge, great prophet who was influential
  in establishing Israeli monarchy.
b. fl. 11th cent. BC
Source: *CamBiEn; ChamBiD; DcCathB;
EncEarC 90; EncPaPR 91; NewC;
NewCol 75; OxDcJeR; WebBD 83; Who
92*

Samuel, Maurice
American. Journalist, Author
Writings on Jewish subjects include: *The
  Gentlemen and the Jew,* 1950.
b. Feb 8, 1895 in Macin, Romania
d. May 4, 1972 in New York, New York
Source: *AmAu&B; AmNatBi; AmNov;
BenetAL 91; BioIn 2, 4, 6, 9, 11, 22, 23;
ConAu 33R, 102; JeAmFiW; REnAL;
ScF&FL 1; TwCA SUP; WhAm 5;
WhoWorJ 72; WorAu 1900*

Samuels, Ernest
American. Educator, Author
Won Pulitzer for three-vol. biography on
  Henry Adams, 1965.
b. May 19, 1903 in Chicago, Illinois
d. Feb 12, 1996 in Evanston, Illinois
Source: *AmAu&B; DcLB 111; DrAS
74E, 78E, 82E; IntAu&W 82; OxCAmL
65, 83; WhAm 11; WhoAm 74, 76, 78,
80, 82, 84, 86, 88, 90, 92, 94, 95, 96;
WhoAmJ 80; WhoPul; WhoWorJ 72, 78;
WorAu 1950; WrDr 76, 80, 82, 84, 86,
92, 94, 96, 98N*

Samuelson, Joan
[Joan Benoit]
American. Track Athlete
Won Boston Marathon, 1983, posting
  fastest time ever for woman runner:
  2:22.42.
b. Mar 16, 1957 in Cape Elizabeth,
  Maine
Source: *ConNews 86-3; CurBio 96;
LegTOT; NewYTBS 83, 84; WhoAm 98;
WhoSpor; WomFir*

Samuelson, Paul Anthony
American. Economist
Won Nobel Prize, 1970; best known for
  writing textbook: *Economics: An
  Introductory Analysis,* 1948.
b. May 15, 1915 in Gary, Indiana
Source: *AmAu&B; AmMWSc 73S, 78S,
98; BioIn 5, 7, 9, 11, 12, 14, 15, 17, 19,
22, 23; BlueB 76; CamBiEn; CamDcAB;
ChamBiD; ConAu 5R; CurBio 65;
EncAB-H 1914, 1996; EncWB 98;
GrEconS; IndAu 1917; IntAu&W 91, 93;
IntWW 74, 75, 76, 77, 78, 79, 80, 81, 82,
83, 89, 91, 93, 97, 98, 2000; JeAmHC;
McGEWB; NewYTBE 70, 71; NewYTBS
86; NobelP; OxCTwCL; PolProf K, NF;*

*RAdv 14; ThTwC 87; WebAB 74, 79;
Who 92, 99, 2000; WhoAm 74, 76, 78,
80, 82, 84, 86, 88, 90, 92, 94, 95, 96,
97, 98, 99, 2000; WhoE 74, 77, 79, 81,
83, 85, 86, 89, 91, 93, 95, 97, 99;
WhoEc 81, 86; WhoFI 00, 79, 81, 83,
85, 89, 92, 94, 96, 98; WhoNob, 90, 95;
WhoScEn 96, 2000; WhoWor 74, 78, 80,
82, 84, 87, 89, 91, 93, 95, 96, 97, 98,
99, 2000; WorAl; WorAlBi; WrDr 76,
80, 82, 84, 86, 88, 90, 92, 94, 96, 98,
99, 2000*

Samuelsson, Bengt Ingemar
Swedish. Scientist
Shared 1982 Nobel Prize in medicine for
researching prostaglandins and their
role in lowering blood pressure.
b. May 21, 1934 in Halmstad, Sweden
Source: *AmMWSc 95, 98; BiESc; BioIn
13, 14, 15; CamBiEn; ChamBiD; ConAu
168; IntMed 80; IntWW 97, 98, 2000;
LarDcSc; McGCEnS; NewYTBS 82;
NobelP; RanHWDS; Who 85, 88, 90, 92,
94, 98, 99, 2000; WhoAm 88, 90, 92, 94,
95; WhoMedH 96, 99, 2000; WhoNob,
90, 95; WhoScEn 94, 96, 2000; WhoWor
78, 80, 82, 84, 87, 89, 91, 93, 95, 96,
97, 98, 99, 2000; WorAlBi*

Sananikone, Phoui
Laotian. Political Leader
Prime minister of Laos, 1950-51, 1959-
60; formed govt. in exile, 1978.
b. Sep 6, 1903, Laos
d. Dec 4, 1983 in Paris, France
Source: *BiDD; BioIn 8, 9, 10; CurBio
59, 84, 84N; FarE&A 78, 79, 80, 81;
IntWW 74, 75, 76, 77, 78, 79, 80, 81, 82,
83; WhoWor 74*

Sanapia
American. Physician
Last known Comanche eagle doctor.
b. 1895 in Fort Sill, Oklahoma
d. 1984 in Oklahoma
Source: *AZNatAW; BioIn 21; EncAWoR;
EncNAR; NotNaAm; RelLAm 1, 2*

Sanborn, David
American. Musician
Saxophonist; won Grammy for best
rhythm and blues instrumental
performance for *Voyeur,* 1981 and best
pop instrumental for *Close Up,* 1989.
b. Jul 30, 1945 in Tampa, Florida
Source: *AllMGJa; BillEnR; BioIn 13, 16;
ConMus 1; CurBio 92; EncJzS; LegTOT;
NewGrDJ 88; PenEncP; SoulM; WhoAm
94, 95, 96, 97, 98, 99, 2000*

Sanborn, Pitts
American. Critic, Author
Music editor, NYC papers, from 1905;
wrote *Metropolitan Book of the Opera,*
1937.
b. Oct 19, 1878 in Port Huron, Michigan
d. Mar 7, 1941 in New York, New York
Source: *BakBD 84; BiDAmM; CurBio
41; TwCA*

Sanchez, Salvador
"Chava"
Mexican. Boxer
WBC featherweight champ, 1980-82.
b. Feb 5, 1959 in Santiago de
Tianquistenco, Mexico
d. Aug 12, 1982 in Queretaro, Mexico
Source: *AnObit 1982; BoxReg, 2;
NewYTBS 82*

Sanchez, Sonia (Benita)
American. Author, Political Activist,
Educator
Award-winning poet and playwright
focuses on the relationships within
African American families and
communities, and urges black unity in
action against oppression; educator
advocates the inclusion of black
studies programs at colleges and
universities.
b. Sep 9, 1934 in Birmingham, Alabama
Source: *IntAu&W 89, 91, 93; WhoAfA 9,
10, 11, 12; WhoBlA 3, 4, 5, 6, 7, 8*

Sanchez de Lozada, Gonzalo
Bolivian. Political Leader
Multi-millionaire industrialist and leader
of the Nationalist Revolutionary
Movement (MNR), he was elected
president of Bolivia in 1993 and
worked to improve the economy and
increase investment in health and
education.
b. 1932

Sanchez-Vicario, Arantxa
Spanish. Tennis Player
Won French Open, 1989.
b. Dec 18, 1971 in Barcelona, Spain
Source: *CurBio 98; IntWW 93, 97, 98,
2000; IntWWW 2; WhoWor 2000*

Sanctorius
Italian. Physiologist, Physician
Physician is known for his application of
quantitative methods to the study of
human physiology and pathology, and
for his invention or perfection of
several medical instruments.
b. Mar 29, 1561 in Capo d'Istria, Italy
d. Feb 22, 1636 in Venice, Italy
Source: *CamBiEn; ChamBiD; DcScB;
EncWB 98; LarDcSc; McGCEnS;
McGEWB*

Sand, George
[Amandine Lucile Dupin Dudevant]
French. Author
Novels include *Lelia,* 1833; noted for her
unconventionality, liaison with Chopin.
b. Sep 1, 1804 in Paris, France
d. Jun 8, 1876 in Nohant, France
Source: *AtlBL; BbD; Benet 87, 96;
BiCoLiE; BiD&SB; BioIn 1, 2, 3, 4, 5, 6,
7, 8, 9, 10, 11, 12, 14, 15, 16, 17, 18,
19, 20, 22, 24; BlmGEL; BlmGWL;
CamBiEn; CasWL; CelCen; ChamBiD;
ContDcW 89; CyWA 58, 97; DcAmSR;
DcArts; DcBiA; DcEnL; DcEuL; DcLB
119, 192; DcPseud; DcPup; DcWomA;
EncWB 98; EuAu; EuWr 6; EvEuW;
FemiCLE; FemiWr; FrenWW; GoodHs;*

*GrFLW; GrWomW; GuFrLit 1; HerW
84; IntDcWB; InWom SUP; LegTOT;
LinLib L, S; McGEWB; NewCBEL;
NinCLC 2, 42, 57; NotNAT B; Novels;
OxCEng 67, 85, 95; OxCFr; PenC EUR;
PenNWW B; RAdv 14; RComWL; REn;
RfGWoL 95; ScF&FL 1; WhDW; WorAl;
WorAlBi; WorLitC*

Sand, Paul
[Pablo Sanchez]
American. Actor
TV series include "St. Elsewhere,"
1982-84; films: *The Main Event,* 1979.
b. Mar 5, 1941 in Los Angeles,
California
Source: *ConTFT 4; HalFC 88;
NewYTBE 71; NotNAT; VarWW 85;
WhoHol 92, A; WhoThe 81*

Sanda, Dominique
[Dominique Varaigne]
French. Actor
Top int'l star, 1970s; films include *The
Garden of Finzi-Continis,* 1971.
b. 1948 in Paris, France
Source: *BioIn 10, 17; FilmAG WE;
FilmEn; FilmgC; HalFC 80, 84, 88;
IntDcF 1-3, 2-3; ItaFilm; LegTOT;
MovMk; WhoHol 92, A*

Sandberg, Ryne (Dee)
American. Baseball Player
Infielder, Philadelphia, 1981; Chicago
Cubs, 1982-94; 1996—; known for
fielding; NL MVP, 1984.
b. Sep 18, 1959 in Spokane, Washington
Source: *Ballpl 90; BaseReg 86, 87;
BioIn 14, 15, 16; CurBio 94; LegTOT;
WhoAm 86, 88, 90, 92, 94; WhoMW 88,
90, 92, 93; WorAlBi*

Sandburg, Carl (August)
American. Poet, Author
Won three Pulitzers in Poetry, 1918,
1940, 1951.
b. Jan 6, 1878 in Galesburg, Illinois
d. Jul 22, 1967 in Flat Rock, North
Carolina
Source: *AmAu&B; AmCulL; AmDec
1910, 1930; AmWr; AnCL; ApCAB X;
ASCAP 66, 80; AtlBL; AuBYP 2, 3;
Benet 87, 96; BenetAL 91; BiDAmJo;
BiDAmM; BiDAmNC; BioIn 1, 2, 3, 4, 5,
6, 7, 8, 9, 10, 11, 12, 13, 14, 15, 16, 17,
18, 19, 20; CamDcAB; CamGEL;
CamGLE; CamHAL; CasWL; Chambr 3;
ChhPo, S1, S2, S3; ChlBkCr; CnDAL;
CnE&AP; CnMWL; ConAmA; ConAmL;
ConAu 5R, 25R, 35NR; ConLC 1, 4, 10,
15, 35; CurBio 40, 63; CyWA 58;
DcAmB S8; DcArts; DcLB 17, 54;
DcLEL; EncAAH; EncAB-H 1974, 1996;
EncAJ; EncAL; EncFCWM 69; EncWL
1, 2, 2S; EvLB; FacFETw; GrWrEL P;
HisDcWJ; LegTOT; LinLib L, S;
LngCTC; MagSAmL; MajAl; MajTwCW
1; MakMC; McGEWB; ModAL 4, 4S1,
4S2; MorMA; NewGrDA 86; ObitT
1961; OxCAmH; OxCAmL 65, 83, 95;
OxCEng 67, 85, 95; OxCTwCL;
OxCTwCP; PenC AM; PeoHis; PoeCrit
2; RAdv 1, 14, 13-1, 13-3; RealN; REn;*

REnAL; RfGAmL 87, 94; RGFAP; RGTwCWr; SixAP; SmATA 8; Str&VC; TwCA, SUP; TwCWr; WebAB 74, 79; WebE&AL; WhAm 4; WhDW; WhE&EA; WhoTwCL; WisWr; WorAl; WorAlBi; WorLitC; WrChl

Sandburg, Helga
American. Children's Author
Young adults novels include
  Gingerbread, 1964; daughter of Carl.
b. Nov 24, 1918 in Elmhurst, Illinois
Source: *AuBYP 2, 3; BioIn 8, 9, 11, 16; BlueB 76; ConAu 1R, 5NR; ConPo 70; ForWC 70; IntAu&W 82, 86, 91; IntWWP 77, 82; MichAu 80; SmATA 3, 10AS; ThRBJA; WhoAm 74, 76, 78, 80, 82, 84, 86, 88, 90, 92, 94, 95, 96, 97, 98, 99, 2000; WhoAmW 77; WhoEnt 98; WhoUSWr 88; WhoWrEP 89, 92, 95; WrDr 80, 82, 84, 86, 88, 90, 92, 94, 96, 98, 99, 2000*

Sande, Earl
American. Jockey
Winner of KY Derby, 1923, 1925, 1930; member of racing Hall of Fame.
b. 1898 in Groton, South Dakota
d. Aug 18, 1968 in Jacksonville, Florida
Source: *BioIn 3, 5, 6, 8, 10, 12, 22; CamDcAB; DcAmB S8; DcBiPP; LegTOT; WhScrn 83*

Sander, Jil
[Heidemarie Jiline Sander]
German. Fashion Designer
Established Jil Sander collection, 1973.
b. Nov 27, 1943 in Wesselburen, Germany
Source: *ConDes 97; ConFash; CurBio 97; News 95, 95-2; ThHDFas*

Sanderlin, George William
American. Children's Author
Historical books include *Benjamin Franklin: As Others Saw Him*, 1971.
b. Feb 5, 1915 in Baltimore, Maryland
Source: *BioIn 9; ConAu 13R; DrAS 74E, 78E, 82E; IntAu&W 89; SmATA 4; WhoUSWr 88; WhoWrEP 89; WrDr 86, 92*

Sanders, Barry
American. Football Player
Runningback, Detroit Lions 1989-98; won Heisman Trophy as junior at Oklahoma State, 1988.
b. Jul 16, 1968 in Wichita, Kansas
Source: *AfrAmSG; ConBlB 1; CurBio 93; News 92, 92-1; WhoAfA 9, 10, 11, 12; WhoAm 92, 94, 95, 96, 97, 98, 99, 2000; WhoBlA 7, 8; WhoMW 93, 96, 98*

Sanders, Bernard
American. Politician
In 1990, became the first independent, Socialist candidate elected to the US House of Representatives since 1920.
b. Sep 8, 1941 in New York, New York
Source: *AlmAP 92, 96, 2000; BioIn 16; CngDr 91, 93, 95; CurBio 91; EncAL; WhoAm 92, 94, 95, 96, 97, 98, 99, 2000;*

WhoAmP 85, 87, 89, 91, 93, 95, 97, 1999; WhoE 83, 85, 86, 91, 93, 95, 97, 99; WhoEmL 87

Sanders, Colonel
[Harland David Sanders]
American. Restaurateur
Established Kentucky Fried Chicken franchise, using a secret recipe, at age 66.
b. Sep 9, 1890 in Henryville, Indiana
d. Dec 16, 1980 in Louisville, Kentucky
Source: *AnObit 1980; BioIn 17; BusPN; ConAu 102; CurBio 73, 81; DcAmB S10; EncWB 2-19; NewYTBS 80; WhoAm 74; WhoSSW 73*

Sanders, Deion (Luwynn)
"Neion Deion"; "Prime Time"
American. Football Player, Baseball Player
Cornerback and punt returner, Atlanta, 1989-94, San Francisco, 1994-95, Dallas, 1995—; outfielder, NY Yankees, 1988-90; Atlanta Braves, 1991-94; Cincinnati Reds, 1994—.
b. Aug 9, 1967 in Fort Myers, Florida
Source: *AfrAmSG; BioIn 16; ConBlB 4; CurBio 95; News 92; WhoAfA 9, 10, 11, 12; WhoAm 92, 94, 95, 96, 97, 98, 99, 2000; WhoBlA 7, 8; WhoSSW 95, 97, 99*

Sanders, Dori(nda)
American. Writer
Author of *Clover*, 1990; *Her Own Place*, 1993.
b. c. 1935 in York, South Carolina
Source: *ConBlB 8; WhoAfA 9; WhoBlA 7, 8*

Sanders, Ed
[Black Hobart; James Edward Sanders]
American. Satirist
Anarchist, social critic; wrote best-selling non-fiction book *The Family: The Story of Charles Manson's Dune Buggy Attack Battalion*, 1971; organizer, lead singer, cult folk-rock group The Fugs, 1965-70.
b. Aug 17, 1939 in Kansas City, Missouri
Source: *AmAu&B; BioIn 10, 13, 17; ConAu 13NR, 13R; ConLC 53; ConPo 70, 75, 80, 85, 91; DcLB 16; DrAF 76; DrAP 75; DrAPF 80, 89; IntAu&W 91, 93; IntWWP 77; MugS; PenC AM; WrDr 76, 80, 82, 84, 86, 88, 90, 92*

Sanders, George
American. Actor
Won Oscar, 1950, for *All About Eve*; married to Zsa Zsa and Magda Gabor.
b. Jul 3, 1906 in Saint Petersburg, Russia
d. Apr 25, 1972 in Castelldefels, Spain
Source: *AmNatBi; BiDFilm, 81, 94; BioIn 2, 4, 5, 6, 8, 9, 10, 12, 18, 23; CurBio 43, 72, 72N; DcAmB S9; DcArts; Film 2; FilmEn; FilmgC; ForYSC; HalFC 80, 84, 88; IIWWBF, A; IntDcF 1-3, 2-3; ItaFilm; LegTOT; MotPP; MovMk; NewYTBE 72; NotNAT A; ObitT 1971; OsStAZ; OxCFilm; WhAm 5;*

WhoHol B; WhoHrs 80; WhScrn 77, 83; WorAl; WorAlBi; WorEFlm

Sanders, Joseph
[Joseph Richard Sanders, Jr.]
American. Designer
Designed exhibits *Moving Back Barriers: The Legacy of Carter G. Woodson*, Library of Congress, 1994; *Black Male: Representations of Masculinity in Contemprary Art*, 1994-95, Whitney Museum.
b. Oct 11, 1954 in Atchison, Kansas
Source: *ConBlB 11*

Sanders, Lawrence
American. Author
Best-selling novels include *The Anderson Tapes*, 1970, filmed 1971; *The First Deadly Sin*, 1973; *The Devil in the White House*, 1988.
b. 1920 in New York, New York
d. Feb 7, 1998 in Pompano Beach, Florida
Source: *AuSpks; BeaEPF; BestSel 89-4; BioIn 12, 14, 16, 17, 23, 24; ConAu 33NR, 62NR, 81, 165; ConLC 41; ConPopW; CrtSuMy; CurBio 89, 98N; EncSF, 93; IntAu&W 76, 77, 91, 93; LegTOT; MajTwCW 1; Novels; RAdv 14; ScF&FL 92; ScFSB; TwCCr&M 80, 85, 91; WhoAm 80, 82, 84, 86, 88, 90, 92, 94, 95, 96, 97, 98, 99; WhoEnt 98; WhoUSWr 88; WhoWrEP 89, 92, 95; WorAl; WorAlBi; WrDr 82, 84, 86, 88, 90, 92, 94, 96, 98, 99*

Sanders, Marlene
American. Broadcast Journalist
Correspondent, producer of CBS News documentaries since 1978.
b. Jan 10, 1931 in Cleveland, Ohio
Source: *BioIn 10, 11, 12, 14, 16; CamDcAB; ConAu 65; CurBio 81; EncTelN; EncTwCJ; ForWC 70; GoodHs; InWom SUP; LesBEnT, 92; Who 92; WhoAm 80, 82, 84, 86, 88, 90, 92, 94, 95, 96, 97, 98, 99, 2000; WhoAmW 79, 81, 83, 85, 87, 89, 91, 93, 95, 97, 99; WhoE 95; WhoEnt 92, 98; WhoTelC; WomFir; WomWMM*

Sanders, Marty
[Jay and the Americans]
American. Musician, Songwriter
Guitarist, songwriter with clean-cut vocal quintet of 1960s.
b. Feb 28, 1941
Source: *WhoRocM 82*

Sanders, Richard Kinard
American. Actor
Played Les Nessman on TV series "WKRP in Cincinnati," 1978-82.
b. Aug 23, 1940 in Harrisburg, Pennsylvania
Source: *ConAu 171; WhoAm 80, 82, 84, 86, 88, 90, 92, 94, 95, 96, 97, 98, 99, 2000; WhoEnt 92, 98*

Sanders, Summer
American. Swimmer
Won two gold medals in swimming
   events, 1992.
b. 1972
Source: *BioIn 21, 23; WhoAm 97, 98,
99, 2000; WhoAmW 93, 95, 97, 99;
WhoWor 95, 96*

Sanderson, Derek Michael
"Turk"
Canadian. Hockey Player
Colorful center, 1965-78, mostly with
   Boston; won Calder Trophy, 1966;
   wrote autobiography, *I've Got to Be
   Me,* 1970.
b. Jun 16, 1946 in Niagara Falls,
   Ontario, Canada
Source: *BioIn 9, 10, 11, 13; CurBio 75;
HocEn; NewYTBE 70, 72, 73; NewYTBS
74, 83; WhoAm 76, 78; WhoHcky 73*

Sanderson, Ivan Terence
[Terence Roberts]
American. Zoologist, Author
Importer of rare animals, 1950s; popular
   nature books include *Animal Treasure,*
   1937.
b. Jan 30, 1911 in Edinburgh, Scotland
d. Feb 19, 1973
Source: *AmAu&B; AmMWSc 73P;
AuBYP 2, 3; EncSF, 93; EncSUPP;
IlsCB 1744, 1946; LinLib L; NatCAB 57;
NewYTBE 73; REnAL; ScF&FL 1, 2;
SmATA 6; TwCA, SUP; UFOEn-O;
UFOEn-P*

Sanderson, Julia
[The Singing Sweethearts; Julia Sackett]
American. Singer, Actor
Often starred with husband, Frank
   Crumit, on stage, radio, 1900-40s;
   started Battle of Sexes Game Show,
   1939-43.
b. Aug 22, 1887 in Springfield,
   Massachusetts
d. Jan 27, 1975 in Springfield,
   Massachusetts
Source: *BiE&WWA; BioIn 3, 10;
CmpEPM; EncMT; Film 1; InWom;
NotNAT B; OxCAmT 84; OxCPMus;
RadStar; SaTiSS; WhAm 6; WhoStg
1908; WhScrn 77; WhThe*

Sanderson, Sybil
American. Opera Singer
Dramatic soprano; more successful in
   Paris than NY or London, 1880s-90s.
b. Dec 7, 1865 in Sacramento, California
d. May 15, 1903 in Paris, France
Source: *AmWom; BakBD 84; CmOp;
IntDcOp; InWom; NewEOp 71*

Sandiford, Lloyd Erskine
Barbadian. Political Leader, Educator
Known for his continuing commitment to
   education and dedication to a more
   unified Caribbean, the leader of the
   Democratic Labor Party (DLP) became
   prime minister of Barbados and
   Minister of Economic Affairs, Finance,
   Education, and Culture in 1987.

b. Mar 24, 1937 in Porters St. James,
   Barbados
Source: *IntWW 89, 91, 93, 97, 98, 2000;
Who 94, 98, 99, 2000; WhoWor 89, 91,
93, 95, 96*

Sandino, Augusto C(esar Calderon)
Nicaraguan. Political Leader
Leader of a guerrilla movement which
   successfully opposed United States
   Marine intervention in Nicaragua from
   1927 to 1933.
b. May 18, 1894 in Niquinohomo,
   Nicaragua
d. Feb 21, 1934 in Managua, Nicaragua

Sandler, Adam
American. Actor, Comedian
Appeared on "Saturday Night Live,"
   1991-95; films include *The Wedding
   Singer,* 1998.
b. Sep 9, 1966 in New York, New York
Source: *ConAu 176; CurBio 98;
LegTOT; News 99-2, 1999*

Sandler and Young
[Tony Sandler; Ralph Young]
American. Music Group
Popular singing duo, 1960s-70s,
   combining suave European Tony
   Sandler and comedic American Ralph
   Young.
Source: *CmpEPM*

Sando, Joe
American. Historian
Wrote works that chronicle the life,
   culture, and history of the Pueblo
   people; books include *The Pueblo
   Indians,* 1976.
b. Aug 1, 1923 in Jemez Pueblo, New
   Mexico
Source: *NotNaAm*

Sandow, Eugene
[Karl Frederick Mueller]
"The Mighty Monarch of Muscle"
German. Entertainer
Physical cultist; performed in London's
   music halls, 1800s.
b. Apr 10, 1867 in Konigsberg, Germany
d. Oct 14, 1925 in London, England
Source: *BiDD; BioIn 7, 12; ChamBiD;
EncVaud; Ent; Film 1; OxCAmT 84;
WhScrn 77, 83*

Sandoz, Mari
American. Author
Wrote *Old Jules,* 1935; books on Indians
   include *These Were the Sioux,* 1961.
b. May 11, 1900 in Sheridan County,
   Nebraska
d. Mar 10, 1966 in New York, New
   York
Source: *AmAu&B; AuBYP 2; CnDAL;
ConAu 1R; OxCAmL 65; REn; REnAL;
SmATA 5; ThrBJA; TwCA, SUP; WhAm
4; WhNAA*

Sandrich, Jay H
American. Director
Has directed TV sitcoms, including
   "Mary Tyler Moore Show," 1970-77;
   "Soap," 1977-79.
b. Feb 24, 1932 in Los Angeles,
   California
Source: *BioIn 15; ConTFT 4; IntMPA
88; LesBEnT; NewYTET; WhoAm 86, 88,
98, 99, 2000; WhoEnt 98; WhoTelC;
WhoWest 00, 98*

Sands, Bobby
[Robert Gerard Sands]
Irish. Hunger Striker, Revolutionary
IRA member, elected to Parliament while
   in prison; first of 10 hunger strikers to
   die demanding political prisoner rather
   than criminal status.
b. Mar 9, 1954 in Belfast, Northern
   Ireland
d. May 5, 1981 in Belfast, Northern
   Ireland
Source: *AnObit 1981; BioIn 12;
CamBiEn; ChamBiD; DcIrB 2, 3; DcIrL
96; ModIrLi; NewYTBS 81*

Sands, Diana Patricia
American. Actor
Best known for stage role in *A Raisin in
   the Sun,* 1960; won Obie, 1964.
b. Aug 22, 1934 in New York, New
   York
d. Sep 21, 1973 in New York, New
   York
Source: *BiE&WWA; DcAmB S9; HalFC
84; InWom SUP; MotPP; NewYTBE 73;
WhAm 6; WhoAmW 72, 74; WhoBlA 1;
WhoHol B; WhScrn 83; WomWMM*

Sands, Dorothy
American. Actor, Director
One of top performers in Grand Street
   Follies, 1920s.
b. Mar 5, 1893 in Cambridge,
   Massachusetts
d. Sep 11, 1980 in Croton-on-Hudson,
   New York
Source: *BiE&WWA; BioIn 12; ConAu
102; NotNAT; PIP&P; WhoAmW 58, 61;
WhoThe 72, 77, 81; WhScrn 83*

Sands, Tommy
[Thomas Adrian Sands]
American. Singer
Had hit song "Teenage Crush," 1957;
   film, TV star, 1950s-60s; first husband
   of Nancy Sinatra.
b. Aug 27, 1937 in Chicago, Illinois
Source: *ASCAP 66; BiDAmM; BioIn 4,
12; FilmEn; FilmgC; ForYSC; HalFC
80, 84, 88; IntMPA 75, 76, 77, 78, 79,
80, 81, 82, 84, 86, 88, 92, 94, 96;
LegTOT; MotPP; PenEncP; RkOn 74;
WhoHol A*

Sandwich, John Montagu
[4th Earl of Sandwich]
English. Politician
First Lord of Admiralty, 1771-82;
   selfishness led to ruin of British navy;
   much-hated man in 18th c. England;
   supposed inventor of sandwich.

b. Nov 3, 1718 in Wiltshire, England
d. Apr 30, 1792 in London, England
Source: *AmRev; BioIn 1, 2, 6, 17, 19; ChamBiD; EncAR; OxCBrHi; WhAmRev*

Sandy, Gary
American. Actor
Played Andy Travis on TV series "WKRP in Cincinnati," 1978-82.
b. Dec 25, 1946? in Dayton, Ohio
Source: *BioIn 11, 12; ConTFT 6; WhoAm 82*

Sandys, Edwin, Sir
English. Statesman
One of founders of VA; joint mgr. of colony, 1617.
b. Dec 9, 1561, England
d. Oct 1629
Source: *Alli; ApCAB; BioIn 1, 3, 6, 12, 24; DcBiPP; DcEnL; DcNaB; EncWB 98; HarEnUS; McGEWB; NewCBEL; NewCol 75; OxCAmH; WebBD 83*

Saneyev, Viktor
Russian. Track Athlete
Triple jumper; won gold medals, 1968, 1972 Olympics.
b. Oct 3, 1945, Union of Soviet Socialist Republics
Source: *BioIn 17; IntWW 81, 82, 83, 89, 91; LesBEnT; WhoTr&F 73*

Sanford, Isabel Gwendolyn
American. Actor
Best known for role of Louise Jefferson on TV series "The Jeffersons," 1974-85.
b. Aug 29, 1933? in New York, New York
Source: *BioIn 10, 13; ConTFT 2; IntMPA 88; WhoAm 86, 90; WhoAmW 91; WhoBlA 4, 5; WhoEnt 92; WhoTelC*

Sanford, Terry
American. Educator, Politician
Governor of NC, 1961-65; pres. of Duke U., 1969-85; senator from NC, 1987-93.
b. Aug 20, 1917 in Laurinburg, North Carolina
d. Apr 18, 1998 in Durham, North Carolina
Source: *AlmAP 88, 92; BiDrGov 1789; BiDrUSC 89; BioIn 6, 7, 8, 9, 10, 12, 14, 15, 23, 24; BlueB 76; CamDcAB; CngDr 87, 89, 91; ConAu 17R, 167; CurBio 61; IntWW 74, 75, 76, 77, 78, 79, 80, 81, 82, 83, 89, 91, 93, 97, 98; LEduc 74; NewYTBS 86, 98; PolPar; PolProf J, K, NF; WhAm 12; WhoAm 74, 76, 78, 80, 82, 84, 86, 88, 90, 92, 94, 95, 96, 97, 98; WhoAmL 90, 92, 94, 96; WhoAmP 73, 75, 77, 79, 81, 83, 85, 87, 89, 91, 93, 95, 97; WhoSSW 84, 86, 88, 91, 95, 97, 99; WhoUSWr 88; WhoWor 78, 84, 87, 89, 91; WhoWrEP 89, 92, 95*

Sang, Samantha
Australian. Singer
Soft rock singer; had hit single "Emotion," 1977, written by Barry and Robin Gibb.
b. Aug 5, 1953 in Melbourne, Australia
Source: *LegTOT; RkOn 78, 84; WhoRock 81*

Sangallo Family, The
[Antonio the Elder Sangallo; Antonio the Younger Sangallo; Giuliano Sangallo]
Italian. Artists
Large and important clan of Florentine artists, architects, and military engineers.
b. fl. 16
Source: *BioIn 12; MacEA; OxCArt*

Sangare, Oumou
Malian. Singer, Songwriter
One of Africa's biggest pop stars, singer/songwriter is known for her feminist music advocating gender equality; toured Europe and the United States, won European World Music Album of the Year for *Ko Sira,* 1993.
b. 1968 in Bamako, Mali
Source: *BioIn 24; ConBlB 18; ConMus 22; IntWWW 2*

Sanger, Frederick
English. Biologist
Won two Nobel Prizes in chemistry: in 1958 for studies on insulin, in 1980 for research on nucleic acids.
b. Aug 13, 1918 in Rendcomb, England
Source: *AmMWSc 89, 92, 95, 98; AsBiEn; BiESc; BioIn 5, 6, 8, 12, 14, 15, 16, 19, 20, 21; BlueB 76; CamBiEn; CamDcSc; ChamBiD; CurBio 81; EncWB 98; FacFETw; IntWW 74, 75, 76, 77, 78, 79, 80, 81, 82, 83, 89, 91, 93, 94, 98, 2000; LarDcSc; McGCEnS; McGEWB; McGMS 80; NewYTBS 80; NobelP; NotTwCS 1; RanHWDS; Who 74, 82, 83, 85, 88, 90, 92, 94, 98, 99, 2000; WhoAm 88, 90, 92, 94, 95, 99, 2000; WhoNob, 90, 95; WhoScEn 94, 96, 2000; WhoWor 74, 76, 78, 82, 84, 87, 89, 91, 93, 95, 96, 97, 98, 99, 2000; WorAlBi; WorScD*

Sanger, Margaret
[Margaret Higgins]
American. Nurse, Social Reformer
Founded National Birth Control League, 1914; wrote *Women, Morality, and Birth Control,* 1931.
b. Sep 14, 1883 in Corning, New York
d. Sep 6, 1966 in Tucson, Arizona
Source: *AmAu&B; BenetAL 91; BioIn 2, 3, 4, 7, 8, 9, 10, 11; ConAu 89; ContDcW 89; CurBio 44, 66; DcAmSR; EncAB-H 1974; FacFETw; HerW, 84; IntDcWB; LinLib L, S; LngCTC; LuthC 75; MemAm; ObitT 1961; OxCAmL 65, 83; OxCMed 86; TwoTYeD; WebAB 74; WhAm 4; WomFir; WorAlBi*

Sangster, Margaret Elizabeth
[Margaret Elizabeth Murson]
American. Social Reformer
Founded American Birth Control League, 1917; opened first clinic, 1921.
b. Feb 22, 1838 in New Rochelle, New York
d. Jun 4, 1912 in Glen Ridge, New Jersey
Source: *Alli SUP; AmAu; AmAu&B; AmBi; AmWom; ApCAB; BbD; BiD&SB; ChhPo S3; DcAmB; NotAW; REnAL; TwCBDA; WhAm 1; WomNov*

Sanguillen, Manny
[Manuel Dejesus Sanguillen]
Panamanian. Baseball Player
Catcher, 1967, 1969-80, mostly with Pittsburgh; had .296 lifetime batting average.
b. Mar 21, 1944 in Colon, Panama
Source: *Ballpl 90; BioIn 9, 10; InB&W 80; LegTOT; WhoBlA 2, 3, 4; WhoProB 73*

Sanguinetti, Julio Maria
Uruguayan. Political Leader
Leader of the Colorado Party, in 1984 he was elected the first civilian president of Uruguay after military rule; he worked to restore civil and political liberties and was elected a second time, in 1994.
b. Jan 6, 1936 in Montevideo, Uruguay
Source: *BiDLAmC; ChamBiD; DcCPSAm; IntWW 89, 91, 93, 97, 98, 2000; LatAmLi; NewYTBS 84; ProfiWG 98; WhoWor 87, 89, 91, 96, 97, 98, 99, 2000*

Sankara
Indian. Philosopher, Theologian
Founder of Advaita Vedanta School of thought, upon which modern Indian philosophy is based.
b. 700? in Kaladi, India
d. 750? in Kedarnath, India
Source: *CamBiEn; CasWL; ChamBiD; McGEWB*

Sankara, Thomas
Burkinabe. Political Leader
Marxist political and military leader attempted to eliminate poverty and power abuses in Upper Volta; became head of the country in a coup, 1983, changed country's name to Burkina Faso, and initiated major social reforms; assassinated, 1987.
b. Dec 21, 1949, Upper Volta
d. 1987 in Ouagadougou, Burkina Faso
Source: *ConBlB 17; RadHan*

San Martin, Jose de
Argentine. Revolutionary, Statesman
Fought in revolutions to liberate Argentina, Chile, Peru from Spain, 1812-22.
b. Feb 25, 1778 in Yapeyu, Argentina
d. Aug 17, 1850 in Boulogne-sur-Mer, France
Source: *ApCAB; Benet 87, 96; BenetAL 91; BiDLAmC; BioIn 1, 2, 3, 4, 5, 7, 8,*

9, 10, 11, 12, 15, 16, 17, 19, 20, 23;
CamBiEn; ChamBiD; Drake; EncLatA;
EncRev; EncWB 98; GenMudB;
HarEnMi; HisDcSE; HisWorL; LegTOT;
McGEWB; MilitOn; NewCol 75; REn;
WhDW; WhoMilH 76; WorAl; WorAlBi

Sanmicheli, Michele
Italian. Architect, Engineer
A military engineer, he introduced the
 Roman High Renaissance style of
 architecture to north Italy.
b. c. 1484 in Verona, Italy
d. 1559
Source: *BioIn 1; DcArch; DcBiPP;*
DcCathB; EncWB 98; IntDcAr; MacEA;
McGDA; McGEWB; WhoArch

Sann, Paul
American. Journalist
Executive editor, *NY Post*, 1949-77; non-
 fiction books include *The Lawless*
 Decade, 1957.
b. Mar 7, 1914 in New York, New York
Source: *AmAu&B; Au&Wr 71; BioIn 10;*
ConAu 5NR, 13R, 120; IntAu&W 86;
ScF&FL 92; WhAm 9; WhoAm 74, 76,
78, 80, 82, 84, 86; WhoE 74; WrDr 80,
82, 84, 86

Sansom, Odette Marie Celine
[Odette Marie Celine Churchill; Odette
 Marie Celine Hallowes]
British. Spy
British spy in France, 1942-43; captured,
 sent to concentration camp; freed,
 1945.
b. Apr 28, 1912 in Amiens, France
Source: *BioIn 2, 3, 4, 7; EncE 75;*
IntWW 74, 75, 76, 77, 78, 79, 80, 81, 82,
83, 89, 91, 93; InWom SUP; SpyCS;
Who 74, 82, 83, 85, 88, 90, 92, 94;
WhoWor 74, 76, 78; WhWW-II

Sansom, William
English. Author
Best known for sketches of London life:
 The Stories of William Sansom, 1963.
b. Jan 18, 1912 in London, England
d. Apr 20, 1976 in London, England
Source: *Au&Wr 71; Benet 87, 96; BioIn*
2, 4, 7, 10, 17, 20, 22; BlmGEL; BlueB
76; CamGLE; CnMWL; ConAu 5R,
42NR, 65; ConLC 2, 6; ConNov 72, 76;
CyWA 89, 97; DcLB 139; DcLEL 1940;
EncWL 1, 2, 2S, 3; GrWrEL N;
IntAu&W 76, 77; LngCTC; MajTwCW 1;
ModBrL, 2, S1; NewC; NewCBEL;
Novels; OxCEng 85, 95; PenC ENG;
RAdv 1; REn; RfGEnL 91; RfGShF 1, 2;
RGTwCWr; ScF&FL 1, 2; ShSCr 21;
TwCA SUP; TwCWr; WhAm 7; Who 74;
WhoHr&F; WhoWor 74; WorAu 1900;
WrDr 76

Sansovino, Andrea
[Andrea Andrea]
Italian. Artist
Renaissance sculptures include *Baptism*
 of Christ.
b. 1460 in Monte Sansavino, Italy
d. 1529

Source: *BioIn 9, 15, 18; LuthC 75;*
McGDA; NewCol 75; OxCArt; WhDW

Sansovino, Jacopo
[Jacopo Tatti]
Italian. Artist
Renaissance sculptures include *St. John*
 the Baptist.
b. 1486 in Florence, Italy
d. Nov 27, 1570 in Venice, Italy
Source: *BioIn 1, 2, 5, 10, 12, 14, 15, 17,*
18; CamBiEn; ChamBiD; DcArts;
DcCathB; DcPseud; EncWB 98;
IntDcAA 90; IntDcAr; MacEA;
McGEWB; NewCol 75; OxCArt;
OxDcArt; WhoArch

Sant, Alfred
Maltese. Political Leader
Reformed and modernized the Labor
 Party as its leader and was elected
 prime minister of Malta in 1996; he
 broke with past political traditions and
 withdrew his country's application for
 membership in the European Union.
b. Feb 28, 1948 in Sliema, Malta
Source: *IntWW 97, 98, 2000; ProfiWG*
98; Who 99, 2000; WhoFI 98; WhoWor
95, 96, 97, 98, 99

Santa Anna, Antonio Lopez de
"Perpetual Dictator"
Mexican. Political Leader
Pres. of Mexico intermittently, 1833-55;
 captured the Alamo in TX revolution,
 1836.
b. 1794 in Jalapa, Mexico
d. Jun 20, 1876 in Mexico City, Mexico
Source: *ApCAB; BiDLAmC; BioIn 15,*
16, 17, 18, 23, 24; DcHiB; DcMexR;
DicTyr; EncLatA; HarEnMi; HisWorL;
LatAmLi; NewEAmW; OxCAmH; REn;
REnAL; WhAm HS; WhoMilH 76;
WorAl; WorAlBi

Santa Cruz, Andres de
Bolivian. Political Leader, Military
 Leader
Supporter of a united Peru-Bolivia, he
 served as president of a short-lived
 confederation of the two.
b. Dec 5, 1792 in La Paz, Bolivia
d. 1865
Source: *BiDLAmC; DcHiB; EncWB 98;*
LatAmLi; McGEWB

Santamaria, Bartholomew
 Augustine
Australian. Political Activist, Social
 Reformer, Author
Roman Catholic publicist and organizer
 founded the Catholic Social Movement
 and opposed communism in Australia.
b. Aug 14, 1915 in Brunswick, Victoria,
 Australia
Source: *BioIn 7, 12, 24; CamBiEn;*
ChamBiD; EncWB 98; McGEWB

Santana
[Jose Areas; David Brown; Michael
 Carabello; Ndugu Chancler; Tom
 Coster; Armando Pereza; Gregg Rolie;
 Carlos Santana; Michael Shrieve; Greg
 Waler]
American. Music Group
Music is a mix of latin, jazz, rock; hits
 include "Evil Ways," 1970; "Hold
 On," 1982.
Source: *Alli; AllMGBl 2; AmMWSc 89;*
AntBDN D; ApCAB; BillEnR; BiNAW
Sup, SupB; BioIn 14; ConAu 129, X;
ConMuA 80A; DcBrECP; DcBrWA;
DcNaB; DrRegL 75; Dun&B 90;
EncASM; EncPR&S 89; EncRk 88;
EncRkSt; HarEnR 86; IlEncRk; InB&W
80; MacEA; NewAgMG; NewYHSD;
OxCPMus; PenEncP; RkOn 74, 78;
RkWho 96; RolSEnR 83; SmATA X; Who
94N; WhoAmW 66, 68; WhoRock 81;
WhoRocM 82; WhoScEu 91-1

Santana, Carlos
[Devadip Carlos Santana]
Mexican. Musician
Guitarist, founder of rock band Santana,
 1966; Grammy award, 1989.
b. Jul 20, 1947 in Autlan, Mexico
Source: *BakBD 84, 92; BiDHisA; BioIn*
11, 12, 13, 16, 17, 20, 22, 24; BkPepl;
CmpEGui; ConMus 1, 19; DcHiB;
EncPR&S 89; LegTOT; NewAmDM;
NewGrDA 86; NewGrDJ 88; OnThGG;
RkWW 82; WhoAm 80, 82, 84, 86, 88,
90, 92, 94, 95, 96, 97, 98, 99, 2000;
WhoEnt 92; WhoHisp 91, 92, 94;
WhoRocM 82

Santana, Pedro
Dominican. Political Leader, Military
 Leader
President of the Dominican Republic
 inflicted several decisive defeats on
 Haitian forces, met with internal
 conflict, and led his country to
 annexation by Spain.
b. 1801 in Hincha, Pedro, Dominican
 Republic
d. Jun 14, 1864 in Santo Domingo,
 Dominican Republic
Source: *ApCAB; BiDLAmC; BioIn 16;*
Drake; EncLatA; EncWB 98; HarEnUS;
LatAmLi; McGEWB

Santander, Francisco de Paula
Colombian. Revolutionary, Politician
Aided Bolivar in revolt against Spain;
 pres. of New Granada, 1832-36.
b. 1792
d. 1840
Source: *ApCAB; BioIn 16; CamBiEn;*
ChamBiD; DcHiB; Drake; LatAmLi

Santayana, George
Spanish. Philosopher, Author, Educator
Wrote philosophic *Realms of Being*,
 1927-40; novel *Last Puritan*, 1935;
 memoirs *Persons and Places*, 1944-53.
b. Dec 16, 1863 in Madrid, Spain
d. Sep 26, 1952 in Rome, Italy
Source: *AmAu&B; AmDec 1910;*
AmNatBi; AmWr; AtlBL; Benet 87, 96;

*BenetAL 91; BiD&SB; BiDHisA; BioIn
1, 2, 3, 4, 5, 6, 7, 8, 9, 11, 12, 13, 14,
15, 16, 18, 20, 22, 23; CamBiEn;
CamDcAB; CamGEL; CamGLE;
CamHAL; CasWL; ChamBiD; Chambr
3; ChhPo, S1, S2; CnDAL; ConAmA;
ConAmL; ConAu 115; CurBio 44, 52;
CyWA 58, 97; DcAmAu; DcAmB S5;
DcAmC; DcHiB; DcLB 54, 71, DS13;
DcLEL; DcPseud; DcTwArt; EncAB-H
1974, 1996; EncALit; EncEth; EncUnb;
EncWB 98; EncWL 1, 2, 2S, 3; EvLB;
FacFETw; GayLesB; GayN; GrWrEL N;
LegTOT; LiExTwC; LinLib L, S;
LngCTC; MakMC; McGEWB; ModAL 4,
4S1, 5; MorMA; NotLatA; Novels; ObitT
1951; OxCAmH; OxCAmL 65, 83, 95;
OxCArt; OxCEng 67, 85, 95; OxCPhil;
OxCTwCL; OxCTwCP; OxDcArt; PenC
AM; RAdv 14, 13-4; REn; REnAL;
RfGAmL 87; ThTwC 87; TwCA, SUP;
TwCBDA; TwCLC 40; TwCWr;
TwoTYeD; WebAB 74, 79; WebE&AL;
WhAm 3; WhE&EA; WhLit; WhoLA;
WhoTwCL; WorAl; WorAlBi; WorAu
1900; WrPh P*

Santee, Wes
American. Track Athlete
Known as America's greatest miler,
  1950s.
b. Mar 25, 1932 in Ashland, Kansas
Source: *BioIn 3, 4, 10, 21; WhoTr&F 73*

Santer, Jacques
Luxembourg. Political Leader
Leader of the centrist Christian Socialist
  Party (PCS), he was elected prime
  minister of Luxembourg in 1984 and
  served as the popular head of a
  coalition government.
b. May 18, 1937 in Wasserbillig,
  Luxembourg
Source: *BioIn 20; CamBiEn; ChamBiD;
IntWW 89, 91, 93, 97, 98, 2000; IntYB
78, 79, 80, 81, 82; Who 98, 99, 2000;
WhoEIO 82; WhoFI 00; WhoIntA 2;
WhoWor 95, 96, 97, 98, 99, 2000*

Santiago, Benito
American. Baseball Player
Catcher, San Diego, 1982-92; Florida,
  1992-94; Cincinnati, 1995;
  Philadelphia, 1996; Toronto, 1997-98;
  Chicago Cubs, 1999—; had 34-game
  hitting streak, 1987; NL rookie of the
  year, 1987.
b. Sep 3, 1965 in Ponce, Puerto Rico
Source: *Ballpl 90; BaseEn 88; BaseReg
87, 88; BioIn 15; LegTOT; WhoHisp 91,
92, 94*

Santillana, Inigo Lopez de
  Mendoza
Spanish. Poet
First to write sonnets in Spanish.
b. Aug 19, 1398 in Carrion, Spain
d. Mar 25, 1458 in Guadalajara, Spain
Source: *BbD; Benet 96; BiD&SB;
CasWL; ChamBiD; DcEuL; DcSpL;
EuAu; EvEuW; PenC EUR; REn*

Santmyer, Helen Hooven
American. Author
Wrote in obscurity for 60 yrs. before
  republication of fourth book *''.And
  Ladies of the Club,''* 1984, became
  best-seller.
b. Nov 25, 1895 in Xenia, Ohio
d. Feb 21, 1986 in Xenia, Ohio
Source: *AmAu&B; AnObit 1986;
BenetAL 91; BioIn 14, 15, 17, 21;
ConAu 1R, 15NR, 33NR, 118; ConLC
33; CurBio 85, 86, 86N; DcLB Y84B;
DrAPF 80; FacFETw; InWom SUP;
MajTwCW 1; NewYTBS 84; OhA&B;
TwCRHW 90, 94; WhoAmW 75; WorAu
1985; WrDr 76, 80, 82, 84*

Santo, Ron(ald Edward)
American. Baseball Player
Third baseman, 1960-74, mostly with
  Cubs; known for fielding; had lifetime
  .277 average.
b. Feb 25, 1940 in Seattle, Washington
Source: *Ballpl 90; BaseEn 88; BiDAmSp
BB; BioIn 7, 8, 9, 10, 15, 18, 19, 21;
WhoAm 74; WhoProB 73*

Santorum, Rick
American. Politician
Rep. senator from PA, 1995—.
b. May 10, 1958
Source: *AlmAP 92, 96, 2000; BioIn 20,
21, 22, 23, 24; CngDr 93; IntWW 97,
98, 2000; WhoAm 92, 94, 95, 96, 97, 98,
99, 2000; WhoE 93, 95, 97, 99*

Santos, Jose Eduardo dos
Angolan. Political Leader
Pres., Angola, 1979—.
b. Aug 28, 1942 in Luanda, Angola
Source: *BioIn 13, 15, 16, 17, 18, 19, 20,
21; ColdWar 1, 2; CurBio 94; DcAfHiB
86S; DcCPSAf; EncWB; FacFETw;
IntWW 91; WhoWor 91*

Santos-Dumont, Alberto
Brazilian. Balloonist
First to combine gasoline motor with
  propeller on a balloon, 1898; designed,
  flew box-kite type machine, 1906.
b. 1873 in Minas Gerais, Brazil
d. 1932, Brazil
Source: *BiDMoPL; BioIn 2, 3, 4, 6, 7, 8,
11, 12, 14, 19; CamBiEn; ChamBiD;
EncLatA; EncWB 98; InSci; LatAmLi;
LinLib S; McGEWB; REn; WhDW*

Saperstein, Abe
[Abraham Saperstein]
''Little Caesar''
American. Basketball Executive
Formed Harlem Globetrotters, 1927;
  clowning gradually became team
  trademark; Hall of Fame, 1970.
b. Jul 4, 1903 in London, England
d. Mar 15, 1966 in Chicago, Illinois
Source: *BioIn 1, 7, 21; LegTOT; ObitOF
79; WhoBbl 73; WhoSpor*

Sapir, Edward
American. Anthropologist, Author
Studied ethnology and linguistics of
  some Native Americans.
b. Jan 26, 1884 in Louenburg, Germany
d. Feb 4, 1939 in New Haven,
  Connecticut
Source: *AmNatBi; BenetAL 91; BiDPsy;
BioIn 1, 2, 4, 7, 12, 14, 16, 17, 22;
CamBiEn; CamDcAB; ChamBiD;
DcAmB S2; DcLB 92; DcNAA; EncWB
98; IntDcAn; MakMC; McGEWB;
NamesHP; NatCAB 33; NewEAmW;
OxCAmH; OxCCan; RAdv 14, 13-3;
REnAL; REnAW; ThTwC 87; WebAB 74,
79; WhAm 1; WhDW; WorAu 1900*

Sapir, Pinchas
Israeli. Government Official
Minister of commerce, finance, and other
  cabinet positions, 1955-74.
b. 1909 in Suwalki, Poland
d. Aug 12, 1975 in Beersheba, Israel
Source: *WhoWor 74; WhoWorJ 72*

Saporta, Vicki
American. Labor Union Official
First female organizer for the
  International Brotherhood of
  Teamsters, 1974-83; director of
  organizing for the union, 1983—,
  focusing on bringing in more clerical,
  service, and high-technology workers,
  including more women.
b. Sep 11, 1952
Source: *ConNews 87-3*

Sapp, Carolyn
American. Beauty Contest Winner
Miss America, 1992.

Sapphire
[Ramona Lofton]
American. Writer
Wrote book of poetry, *American Dreams*,
  1994; novel, *Push*, 1996.
b. c. 1951
Source: *News 96*

Sappho
''The Tenth Muse''
Greek. Poet
Lyric poet often compared to Homer;
  poems celebrate love of women.
b. 612BC, Greece
Source: *AtlBL; BbD; Benet 87, 96;
BiD&SB; BioIn 13, 14; CasWL; ClMLC
3; ContDcW 89; CyWA 58; EncAmaz
91; EncCoWW; FemiCLE; GayLesB;
GrFLW; GrWomW; IntDcWB; InWom
SUP; NewC; NewGrDM 80; OxCChiL;
OxCEng 85; PenC CL; RAdv 13-2;
RComWL; REn; RfGWoL 95*

Sapru, Tej Bahadur
Indian. Lawyer, Politician
Chairman of the Sapru Committee,
  charged with examining the communal
  question; contributed to the political
  and constitutional development of
  India.
b. 1875 in Aligarh, India

d. Jan 20, 1949, Italy
Source: *BioIn 1, 2, 8, 13; ChamBiD; EncWB 98; McGEWB*

Saragat, Giuseppe
Italian. Political Leader
One of founders of post-war Italian Republic; first socialist pres. of Italy, 1964-71.
b. Sep 19, 1898 in Turin, Italy
d. Jun 11, 1988 in Rome, Italy
Source: *AnObit 1988; BioIn 1, 4, 7, 16; CurBio 56, 65, 88, 88N; DcPol; FacFETw; IntWW 74, 75, 76, 77, 78, 79, 80, 81, 82, 83; IntYB 78, 79, 80; NewYTBS 88; WhAm 11; WhDW; Who 74, 82, 83, 85, 88; WhoGov 72; WhoWor 74, 91*

Sarah
Hebrew. Biblical Figure
Mother of Isaac, wife of Abraham; life was a continuous test of faith.
b. fl. 1900BC
Source: *BioIn 1; FolkA 87; InWom SUP*

Sarandon, Chris
American. Actor
Starred in *Dog Day Afternoon,* 1975; *Protocol,* 1984.
b. Jul 24, 1942 in Beckley, West Virginia
Source: *BioIn 15; ConTFT 4, 15, 27; HalFC 80, 84, 88; IntMPA 84, 86, 88, 92, 94, 96; LegTOT; NewYTBS 76; OsStAZ; WhoEnt 92; WhoHol 92, A; WhoThe 81*

Sarandon, Susan
[Susan Abigail Tomalin]
American. Actor
Films include *The Rocky Horror Picture Show,* 1975; *Atlantic City,* 1981; *Bull Durham,* 1988; and *Thelma and Louise,* 1991.
b. Oct 4, 1946 in New York, New York
Source: *BiDFilm 94; BioIn 13, 14, 15, 16; CamBiEn; CelR 90; ConNews 86-2; ConTFT 3, 10, 17; CurBio 89; DcPseud; EncWB 99; FilmEn; HalFC 80, 84, 88; HolBB; IntDcF 1-3, 2-3; IntMPA 80, 84, 86, 88, 92, 94, 96; InWom SUP; ItaFilm; LegTOT; News 95, 95-3; NewYTBS 83; OnHuYAF; OsStAZ; WhoAm 86, 90; WhoAmW 91; WhoEnt 92; WhoHol 92; WorAlBi*

Sarasate, Pablo de
[Martin Meliton S y Navascuez]
Spanish. Violinist, Composer
Celebrated virtuoso; had enormously successful worldwide tours, many noted works written for him.
b. Mar 10, 1844 in Pamplona, Spain
d. Sep 20, 1908 in Biarritz, France
Source: *BakBD 78, 84, 92; BakDcM; BioIn 1, 2, 4, 7, 8, 14; BriBkM 80; DcCom&M 79; GrComp; MusMk; NewAmDM; NewGrDM 80; NewOxM; OxCMus; PenDiMP*

Sarasin, Jean Francois
French. Author
Wrote witty, satirical verse, popular with Parisian society, 1640s.
b. 1614
d. Dec 5, 1654
Source: *OxCFr*

Sarazen, Gene
[Gene Saraceni; Eugene Sarazen]
American. Golfer
Turned pro, 1920; has seven major tournament wins including 1935 Masters; one of four players to win all major titles; invented the sand wedge, 1930s.
b. Feb 27, 1902 in Harrison, New York
d. May 13, 1999 in Naples, Florida
Source: *BiDAmSp OS; BioIn 2, 6, 9, 10, 13, 23, 24; CamDcAB; ChamBiD; DcPseud; LegTOT; News 1999; NewYTBE 72, 73; NewYTBS 82; WebAB 74, 79; WhoGolf; WorAl*

Sarbanes, Paul S(pyros)
American. Politician
Dem. senator from MD, 1977—.
b. Feb 3, 1933 in Salisbury, Maryland
Source: *AlmAP 80, 92; BiDrUSC 89; BioIn 10, 11; CngDr 83, 89; IntWW 77, 78, 79, 80, 81, 82, 83, 89, 91, 93, 97, 98, 2000; PolsAm 84; WhoAm 74, 76, 78, 80, 82, 84, 86, 88, 90, 92, 94, 95, 96, 97, 98, 99, 2000; WhoAmP 73, 77, 79, 81, 83, 85, 87, 89, 91, 93, 95, 97, 1999; WhoE 74, 75, 77, 79, 81, 83, 85, 86, 89, 91, 93, 95, 97, 99; WhoGov 72, 75, 77; WhoWor 80, 82, 84, 87, 89, 91*

Sarcey, Francisque
French. Journalist, Critic
Wrote influential eight-volume work on the theater, late 1800s.
b. Oct 8, 1827 in Dourban, France
d. May 15, 1899 in Paris, France
Source: *BbD; BiD&SB; BioIn 1; CamGWoT; ClDMEL 47; DcEuL; Dis&D; EncWT; NotNAT A, B; OxCFr; OxCThe 67*

Sardi, Vincent, Sr.
American. Restaurateur
Opened Sardi's restaurant in Manhattan's theatre district, 1921.
b. Dec 23, 1885 in Canelli, Italy
d. Nov 19, 1969 in New York, New York
Source: *BioIn 3, 4, 8, 9; CurBio 57, 70*

Sardi, Vincent, Jr.
American. Restaurateur
Owner, Sardi's restaurant, NY.
b. Jul 23, 1915 in New York, New York
Source: *BiE&WWA; BioIn 4, 12; CelR; WhoAm 76, 78, 80, 82, 84, 86*

Sardou, Victorien
French. Dramatist
Wrote over 70 popular plays including historical melodramas starring Sarah Bernhardt.
b. Sep 7, 1831 in Paris, France

d. Nov 8, 1908 in Paris, France
Source: *AtlBL; BbD; Benet 87, 96; BiD&SB; BioIn 1, 5, 7, 11, 24; CamBiEn; CamGWoT; CasWL; CelCen; ChamBiD; ClDMEL 47; CnThe; DcArts; DcBiPP A; DcEuL; DcLB 192; Dis&D; EncO&P 1, 2, 3; EncWT; Ent; EuAu; EvEuW; GuFrLit 1; IntDcT 2; LinLib L, S; LngCTC; McGEWD 72, 84; MetOEnc; ModWD; NewC; NewCBEL; NewEOp 71; NewGrDM 80; NewGrDO; NotNAT A, B; OxCAmT 84; OxCFr; OxCThe 67, 83; OxDcOp; PenC EUR; PIP&P; REn; REnWD; WhDW; WhLit; WhoStg 1908*

Sarduy, Severo
Cuban. Author
Author of novel *Cobra,* 1972.
b. Feb 25, 1937 in Camaguey, Cuba
d. Aug 1993
Source: *Benet 96; BenetAL 91; BioIn 18, 20; CaribW 4; ConAu 58NR, 81NR, 89, 142; ConLC 6, 81, 97; ConWorW 93; CubExWr; CyWA 97; DcCLAA; DcLB 113; DcTwCCu 4; DcTwCuL; EncWL 2, 2S, 3; HispWr, 2; IntvLAW; LatAmLi; LiExTwC; ModLAL; OxCSpan; RAdv 14; SpAmA*

Sarett, Lew R
American. Poet
Books of verse focus on Native American: *Slow Smoke,* 1925.
b. May 16, 1888 in Chicago, Illinois
d. Aug 17, 1954 in Gainesville, Florida
Source: *AmAu&B; AnMV 1926; ChhPo, S1, S2; CnDAL; ConAmA; ConAmL; OxCAmL 65; REn; REnAL; TwCA, SUP; WhAm 3; WhNAA; WorAu 1900*

Sarg, Tony
[Anthony Frederick Sarg]
American. Puppeteer, Children's Author
Created his famed marionettes, 1915; wrote, illustrated *Tony Sarg's Wonder Zoo,* 1927.
b. Apr 24, 1882, Guatemala
d. Mar 7, 1942 in Nantucket, Massachusetts
Source: *AmAu&B; ConICB; CurBio 42; DcAmB S3; IlrAm 1880, C; JBA 34, 51; OxCChiL; REnAL; WhAm 2; WorECar*

Sargeant, Winthrop
American. Critic, Author
Music critic for *New Yorker* mag., 1949-72.
b. Dec 10, 1903 in San Francisco, California
d. Aug 15, 1986 in Salisbury, Connecticut
Source: *AnObit 1986; BakBD 78, 84, 92; BakBDTw; BioIn 9, 15; BlueB 76; ConAu 29R, 75NR, 120; IntAu&W 77, 86; NewGrDA 86; NewYTBS 86; WhAm 9; WhoAm 74, 76, 78, 80, 82, 84, 86; WhoWor 74; WrDr 76, 80, 82, 84, 86*

Sargent, Alvin
American. Screenwriter
Wrote Oscar-winning screenplays for *Julia,* 1977; *Ordinary People,* 1980.

b. Apr 12, 1927 in Philadelphia,
  Pennsylvania
Source: ConAu 48NR, 111, 121; ConDr
88A; ConTFT 12; HalFC 88; IntMPA
92, 94, 96

Sargent, Ben
American. Cartoonist, Author
Won 1982 Pulitzer for editorial
  cartooning.
b. Nov 26, 1948 in Amarillo, Texas
Source: BioIn 15, 16, 23; ConAu 113,
114, 115, 116, 117, 118; ConGrA 2;
WhoAm 84, 86, 88, 90, 92, 94, 95;
WhoPul; WorECar

Sargent, Dick
American. Actor
Replaced Dick York as Darrin on TV
  series "Bewitched," 1969-72.
b. Apr 19, 1933 in Carmel, California
d. Jul 8, 1994 in Los Angeles, California
Source: BioIn 17, 20, 22; FilmgC;
HalFC 88; IntMPA 80, 81, 82, 84, 86,
88, 92; LegTOT; Who 92; WhoAm 74,
82; WhoHol 92, A

Sargent, George
English. Golfer
Touring pro, early 1900s; won US Open,
  1909; first to use movies for golf
  instruction, 1930.
b. 1880 in Dorking, England
d. Jun 18, 1962 in Atlanta, Georgia
Source: WhoGolf

Sargent, Herb
Writer
Won Emmys for "Lily," 1974;
  "Saturday Night Live," 1976, 1977.
Source: ConTFT 15; VarWW 85

Sargent, John Singer
American. Artist
Portrait painter who had many famous
  subjects; Madame X is in Metropolitan
  Museum of Art, NYC.
b. Jan 12, 1856 in Florence, Italy
d. Apr 15, 1925 in London, England
Source: AmBi; AmCulL; AmNatBi;
ApCAB, X; ArtsAmW 3; AtlBL; Benet 87,
96; BioIn 1, 2, 3, 4, 6, 7, 9, 10, 11, 12,
13, 14, 15, 16, 19, 20, 22, 23, 24;
BriEAA; CamBiEn; CamDcAB;
ChamBiD; ChhPo, S1; ClaDrA;
DcAmArt; DcAmB; DcArts; DcBrAr 1;
DcBrBI; DcBrWA; DcNaB 1922;
DcTwArt; DcVicP, 2; EncAB-H 1974,
1996; EncWB 98; FacFETw; GayN;
HarEnUS; IntDcAA 90; LegTOT; LinLib
S; LiveWoA; LngCTC; McGDA;
McGEWB; MorMA; NatCAB 11;
OxCAmH; OxCAmL 65; OxCArt;
OxCBrHi; OxDcArt; PeoHis; PhDcTCA
77; RComAH; REn; REnAL; ThHEIm;
TwCBDA; TwCPaSc; WebAB 74, 79;
WhAm 1; WhDW; WorAl; WorAlBi

Sargent, Malcolm, Sir
"Ambassador of Music"
English. Conductor
Led British orchestras, 1920s-60s; made
  frequent int'l tours; commemorative
  stamp issued in his honor, 1980.
b. Apr 29, 1895 in Stamford, England
d. Oct 3, 1967 in London, England
Source: BakBD 78, 84; BioIn 1, 2, 3, 4,
5, 7, 8, 11; BriBkM 80; CurBio 45, 68;
DcNaB 1961; FacFETw; MusSN;
NewAmDM; NewEOp 71; NewGrDM 80;
ObitT 1961; OxCMus; OxDcOp;
PenDiMP; WhScrn 77, 83

Sargon, II
Assyrian. King
Founder of the greatest line of Assyrian
  kings, reigned from 722-705 B.C;
  expanded the borders of the Assyrian
  empire, and built residence city
  Sargonsburg.
d. 705BC
Source: BioIn 11, 20; ChamBiD; EncWB
98; LegTOT; McGEWB

Sargon of Agade
Mesopotamian. King
First Semitic king of Mesopotamia and
  founder of the Akkadian dynasty;
  defeated the paramount ruler of the
  Sumerian city-states and other
  territories to become the first ruler in
  history to win and hold an empire;
  became legendary literary figure.
b. c. 2334BC in Saffron
d. 2279BC

Sarit Thanarat
Thai. Political Leader, Military Leader
Army officer led a coup to overthrow the
  government of Phibun Songkhram in
  1957, becoming prime minister;
  remembered for his effective economic
  development policies and promotion of
  education and social welfare.
b. Jun 16, 1908 in Bangkok, Thailand
d. Dec 8, 1963
Source: DcMPSA; DcPol; EncWB 98;
McGEWB

Sarkis, Elias
Lebanese. Political Leader
Pres. of Lebanon, 1976-82; also gained
  fame as head of Central Bank.
b. Jul 20, 1924 in Shibaniyah, Lebanon
d. Jun 27, 1985 in Paris, France
Source: AnObit 1985; BioIn 11, 12, 14,
15; ConNews 85-3; CurBio 79, 85, 85N;
DcMidEa; FacFETw; IntWW 78, 79, 80,
81, 82, 83; MidE 78, 79, 80, 81, 82;
NewYTBS 76, 85; PolEnME; WhoWor
78, 80, 82, 84

Sarmiento, Domingo Faustino
Argentine. Author, Political Leader,
  Educator, Journalist
Known as the "Teacher President" for
  his efforts to foster education in
  Argentina; he also wrote the classic
  Civilization and Barbarism; or, The
  Life of Juan Facundo Quiroga.
b. Feb 15, 1811 in San Juan, Argentina

d. Sep 11, 1888, Paraguay
Source: ApCAB; AtlBL; BbD; Benet 87,
96; BenetAL 91; BiD&SB; BiDLAmC;
BiDMoPL; BioIn 1, 2, 3, 4, 5, 6, 7, 8, 9,
11, 12, 15, 16, 17, 18, 19, 20, 21;
CasWL; ChamBiD; CyEd; DcHiB;
DcSpL; Drake; EncLatA; EncWB 98;
HispLC SUP; LatAmLi; LatAmWr;
McGEWB; OxCSpan; PenC AM; RAdv
14, 13-2; REn

Sarney, Jose
[Jose Ribamar Ferreira da Costa]
Brazilian. Political Leader
Brazil's first civilian pres. since 1964;
  assumed power, 1985.
b. Apr 30, 1930 in Sao Bento, Brazil
Source: BioIn 14, 15; CurBio 86;
DcCPSAm; IntWW 89, 91, 93, 97, 98,
2000; LatAmLi; NewYTBS 85; WhoWor
87

Sarnoff, David
American. Business Executive
Chairman, RCA; one of first to see that
  TV would replace radio in popularity.
b. Feb 27, 1891 in Minsk, Russia
d. Dec 12, 1971 in New York, New
  York
Source: AmDec 1920, 1950; AmNatBi;
BiDAmBL 83; BioIn 1, 2, 3, 4, 5, 6, 7, 8,
9, 10, 11, 12, 14, 15, 17, 19, 20, 23, 24;
CamBiEn; CamDcAB; ChamBiD; ConAu
113; CurBio 40, 51, 72, 72N; DcAmB
S9; EncAB-A 25; EncAB-H 1974, 1996;
EncAJ; EncTwCJ; EncWB, 98;
FacFETw; FrTalk; HisDcAR; InSci;
JeAmHC; JeHun; LinLib L, S;
McGEWB; NatCAB 56; NewYTBE 70,
71; ObitT 1971; PolProf E; SaTiSS;
WebAB 74, 79; WhAm 5; WhoWorJ 72;
WorAl; WorAlBi

Sarnoff, Robert W(illiam)
American. Business Executive
Chm., RCA, 1970-75.
b. Jul 2, 1918 in New York, New York
d. Feb 22, 1997 in New York, New
  York
Source: BioIn 2, 4, 8, 10, 11; BusPN;
CurBio 56, 97N; EncTwCJ; HisDcAR;
IntMPA 88; St&PR 84; Who 74; WhoAm
74; WorAl

Saro-Wiwa, Ken
Nigerian. Writer
Author of Sozaboy: A Novel in Rotten
  English.
b. Oct 10, 1941 in Bori, Nigeria
d. Nov 10, 1995 in Port Harcourt,
  Nigeria
Source: BlkWr 2; ChamBiD; ConLC
114; DcLB 157; HeroCon; ModBlW 2;
News 96, 96-2; OxCTwCL

Saroyan, William
American. Author, Dramatist
Won Pulitzer Prize, 1940, for The Time
  of Your Life.
b. Aug 31, 1908 in Fresno, California
d. May 18, 1981 in Fresno, California
Source: AmAu&B; AmNatBi; AmNov;
AnObit 1981; Au&Wr 71; Benet 87, 96;

BenetAL 91; BiCoLiE; BiE&WWA; BioIn
1, 2, 3, 4, 5, 6, 7, 8, 9, 10, 11, 12, 13,
14, 15, 17, 20, 22, 24; BlueB 76;
CamBiEn; CamDcAB; CamGLE;
CamGWoT; CamHAL; CasWL; CelR;
ChamBiD; CmCal; CnDAL; CnMD;
CnMWL; CnThe; ConAmA; ConAmD;
ConAu 5R, 30NR, 103; ConDr 73, 77,
93; ConLC 1, 8, 10, 11, 29, 56; ConNov
72, 76; CrtSuDr; CurBio 40, 72, 81,
81N; CyWA 58, 89, 97; DcArts; DcLB 7,
9, 86, Y81A; DcLEL; DrAF 76; DrAPF
80; EncALit; EncWB 98; EncWL 1, 2,
2S, 3; EncWT; Ent; EvLB; FacFETw;
FilmEn; FilmgC; GrWrEL DR, N;
HalFC 80, 84, 88; IdentIs; IntAu&W 76,
77; IntDcT 2; IntWW 74, 75, 77, 78, 79,
80, 81, 81N; LegTOT; LinLib L, S;
LngCTC; MagSAmL; MajTwCW 1, 2;
McGEWB; McGEWD 72, 84; ModAL 4,
4S1, 5; ModWD; ModWr; NewCBEL;
NewYTBS 75, 79, 81; NotNAT, A;
Novels; OxCAmL 65, 83, 95; OxCAmT
84; OxCThe 67, 83; OxCTwCL; PenC
AM; PlP&P; RAdv 1, 14, 13-2; REn;
REnAL; REnWD; RfGAmL 4, 87, 94;
RfGShF 1, 2; ScrEAmL 1; ShSCr 21;
SmATA 23, 24N; TwCA, SUP; TwCWr;
WebAB 74, 79; WebE&AL; WhAm 7;
WhE&EA; Who 74; WhoAm 74, 76, 78,
80; WhoPul; WhoThe 72, 77, 81;
WhoTwCL; WhoWor 74; WorAl;
WorAlBi; WorAu 1900; WorLitC; WrDr
76, 80, 82

Sarpi, Paolo
Italian. Politician, Historian
Prelate and statesman is considered one
of the greatest historians of early
modern Europe, and was a founder of
the modern historical method.
b. 1552 in Venice, Italy
d. 1623
Source: Benet 96; BioIn 7, 10, 13; DcItL
1, 2; DcScB; EncWB 98; GloEncH;
LinLib L; LuthC 75; McGEWB; PenC
EUR; REn

Sarraute, Nathalie
French. Author
Wrote novels Tropismes, 1939; Le
planetarium, 1959.
b. Jul 18, 1900 in Ivanovo-Voznessensk,
Russia
d. Oct 20, 1999 in Paris, France
Source: BeaEPF; Benet 96; BioIn 6, 7,
8, 9, 10, 11, 12, 13; CasWL; ConAu 9R,
23NR, 66NR; ConFLW 84; ConLC 1, 2,
8, 10, 31, 80; ConWorW 93; CyWA 89,
97; DcLB 83; DcTwCCu 2; EncCoWW;
EncWB; EncWL 2, 2S, 3; EuWr 12;
FacFETw; FrenWW; GrWomW; GuFrLit
1; IntAu&W 82, 86, 89, 91; IntDcT 2;
IntWW 80, 81, 82, 83, 89, 91, 93, 97, 98,
2000; IntWWW 2; InWom, SUP;
LiExTwC; LinLib L; MajTwCW 1, 2;
ModFrL; RfGWoL 95; Who 82, 83, 85,
88, 90, 92, 94, 98, 99, 2000; WhoEnt 98;
WhoFr 79; WhoWor 84, 87, 89, 91, 93,
95, 96, 97, 98, 99, 2000; WomWrGB

Sarrazin, Michael
[Jacques Michel Andre Sarrazin]
Canadian. Actor
Starred in The Reincarnation of Peter
Proud, 1975.
b. May 22, 1940 in Quebec, Quebec,
Canada
Source: ConTFT 5, 12, 21; FilmEn;
FilmgC; HalFC 80, 84, 88; IntMPA 77,
78, 79, 80, 81, 82, 84, 86, 88, 92, 94,
96; ItaFilm; LegTOT; NewYTBE 70;
WhoEnt 92; WhoHol 92, A; WorAl

Sarria, Jose
American. Entertainer
Pioneer in gay political theater; active in
AIDS fundraising.
Source: BioIn 24; GayLesB

Sarris, Andrew George
American. Author
Books on film include Politics and
Cinema, 1978.
b. Oct 31, 1928 in New York, New York
Source: AmAu&B; BioIn 13; OxCFilm;
WhoAm 76, 78, 80, 82, 84, 86, 88, 90,
92, 94, 95, 96, 97, 98, 99, 2000; WhoE
74, 75, 93; WhoEnt 92, 98; WhoMedi
98; WhoUSWr 88; WhoWor 78;
WhoWrEP 89, 92, 95

Sartain, John
American. Engraver
Pioneer mezzotint engraver; introduced
pictorial illustration to American
periodicals.
b. Oct 24, 1808 in London, England
d. Oct 25, 1897 in Philadelphia,
Pennsylvania
Source: Alli; AmAu&B; AmBi; AmNatBi;
ApCAB; ArtsNiC; BioIn 8; DcAmArt;
DcAmAu; DcAmB; DcNAA; Drake;
HarEnUS; McGDA; NatCAB 6;
NewYHSD; TwCBDA; WhAmArt 85;
WhAm HS

Sarti, Giuseppe
Italian. Composer, Conductor
Held musical posts in Denmark, Russia;
his 70 operas now forgotten.
b. Dec 1, 1729 in Faenza, Italy
d. Jul 28, 1802 in Berlin, Germany
Source: BakBD 78, 84, 92; BioIn 4;
BriBkM 80; DcBiPP; MusMk; NewEOp
71; NewGrDM 80; NewGrDO;
NewOxM; OxCMus; OxDcOp

Sarto, Andrea del
[Andrea Domenico d'Agnolodi
Francisco]
"Andrew the Faultless"
Italian. Artist
Noted for superbly colored religious
frescoes, easel painting: Madonna of
the Harpies, 1517.
b. Jul 16, 1486 in Florence, Italy
d. Sep 29, 1531 in Florence, Italy
Source: AtlBL; Benet 87, 96; BioIn 1, 2,
5, 7, 9; CambiEn; ChambiD; Dis&D;
LegTOT; McGDA; REn

Sarton, George
American. Historian
Founded the study of the history of
science in America; his major work
was Introduction to the History of
Science.
b. Aug 31, 1884 in Ghent, Belgium
d. Mar 22, 1956
Source: BioIn 3, 4, 5, 6, 12, 14, 22;
EncWB 98; GloEncH; LinLib L;
OxCAmH; RAdv 14

Sarton, May
[Eleanor Marie Sarton]
American. Author, Poet
Writings include verse vol. A Durable
Fire, 1972; novel As We Are Now,
1973.
b. May 3, 1912 in Wondelgem, Belgium
d. Jul 16, 1995 in York, Maine
Source: AmAu&B; AmNatBi;
AmWomWr; ArtclWW 2; Benet 87, 96;
BenetAL 91; BioAmW; BioIn 4, 5, 8, 10,
11, 12, 13, 14, 15, 16, 17, 18, 19, 20,
21, 22, 23, 24; BlmGWL; BlueB 76;
CamGLE; CamHAL; ConAu 1NR, 1R,
34NR; ConLC 4, 14, 49, 91; ConNov 72,
76, 82, 86, 91; ConPo 70, 75, 80, 85,
91; CurBio 82, 95N; CyWA 89, 97;
DcLB 48, Y81B; DrAF 76; DrAP 75;
DrAPF 80, 87, 91; DrAS 74E, 78E, 82E;
EncALit; EncWL 2, 3; FemiCLE;
GayLesB; GrWomW; IdentIs; IntAu&W
76, 77, 86, 91, 93; IntvTCA 2; IntWW
97, 98, 2000; IntWWP 77; InWom SUP;
LegTOT; MajTwCW 1; ModAL 4, 4S1,
4S2, 4S3, 5; ModWomWr; NewYTBS 83;
Novels; OxCAmL 65, 83; OxCWoWr 95;
PenC AM; RAdv 1; REnAL; ScF&FL 1;
SmATA 36; TwCA SUP; WhAm 12;
WhoAm 74, 76, 78, 80, 82, 90, 92;
WhoAmW 58, 64, 66, 68, 70, 72, 81, 83,
85, 87, 89, 91, 93, 95; WhoWor 74;
WorAu 1900; WrDr 76, 80, 82, 84, 86,
88, 90, 92, 94, 96, 98N

Sartre, Jean-Paul
French. Author, Dramatist
Major exponent of 20th-c. existentialism;
wrote Being and Nothingness, 1943;
refused Nobel Prize in literature, 1964.
b. Jun 21, 1905 in Paris, France
d. Apr 15, 1980 in Paris, France
Source: AnObit 1980; Au&Wr 71; Benet
87, 96; BiCoLiE; BiDFrPL; BiDNeoM;
BiDPsy; BiE&WWA; BioIn 22, 24;
BlmGEL; CambiEn; CamGWoT;
CasWL; CelR; ChambiD; ClDMEL 47,
80; CnMD; CnMWL; CnThe; ConAu 9R,
21NR, 97; ConLC 1, 4, 7, 9, 13, 18, 24,
52; CroCD; CurBio 71, 80N; CyWA 58,
89, 97; DcArts; DcLB 72; DcTwArt;
DcTwCCu 2; DramC 3; EncUnb;
EncWB 98; EncWL 1, 2, 2S, 3; EncWT;
Ent; EuWr 12; EvEuW; FacFETw;
FilmEn; FilmgC; GrFLW; GuFrLit 1;
HalFC 80, 84, 88; IntAu&W 76, 77;
IntWW 74, 75, 76, 77, 78, 79, 2000;
ItaFilm; LegTOT; LinLib L, S; LngCTC;
LuthC 75; MagSWL; MajMD 2;
MajTwCW 1, 2; MakMC; McGEWB;
McGEWD 72, 84; ModFrL; ModRL;
ModWD; NewYTBS 80; NobelP;
NotNAT, A; Novels; OxCEng 67, 85, 95;
OxCFr; OxCPhil; OxCThe 67; PenC

EUR; PlP&P; RadHan; RAdv 14, 13-2,
13-4; RComWL; REn; REnWD; ScF&FL
1, 2, 92; ShSCr 32; SocPrL; ThTwC 87;
TwCA SUP; TwCWr; TwoTYeD; WhAm
7; WhDW; Who 74; WhoChr; WhoFr
79; WhoNob; WhoThe 72, 77, 81;
WhoTwCL; WhoWor 74, 78; WhScrn 83;
WorAl; WorAlBi; WorAu 1900; WorLitC;
WrPh, P

Sasakawa, Ryoichi
Japanese. Industrialist, Philanthropist
Wealthy businessman amassed power
   through generous gifts to charitable
   organizarions; the UN has received
   more than $50 million from his
   foundation.
Source: BioIn 13, 15, 21; NewYTBS 74,
95

Sasser, James R(alph)
American. Politician
Dem. senator from TN, 1977-94; US
   ambassador to China, 1996—.
b. Sep 30, 1936 in Memphis, Tennessee
Source: AlmAP 82, 92; BiDrUSC 89;
CngDr 77, 79, 81, 83, 85, 87, 89;
CurBio 93; IntWW 81, 82, 83, 89, 91,
93, 97, 98, 2000; NewYTBS 90; WhoAm
78, 80, 82, 84, 86, 88, 90, 92, 94, 95,
97, 98, 99, 2000; WhoAmL 78; WhoAmP
77, 79, 81, 83, 85, 87, 89, 91, 93, 95,
97, 1999; WhoGov 77; WhoIntA 2;
WhoSSW 78, 80, 82, 86, 88, 91;
WhoWor 80, 82, 84, 87, 89, 91, 98, 99,
2000

Sassetta
[Stefano di Giovanni]
Italian. Artist
Noted painter of international Gothic
   style; drew panels on life of St.
   Francis, 1437-44.
b. 1395? in Siena, Italy
d. 1450 in Siena, Italy
Source: AtlBL; OxCArt

Sassoon, Siegfried
English. Poet, Soldier, Author
Prize-winning Memoirs of a Fox-Hunting
   Man, 1928, best known of semi-
   atobiographical trilogy.
b. Sep 8, 1886 in Brenchley, England
d. Sep 1, 1967 in Purton, England
Source: AtlBL; Benet 87, 96; BiCoLiE;
BioIn 12, 14, 15, 16, 17, 18, 21, 22, 24;
BlmGEL; BritAS; CamGEL; CamGLE;
CasWL; Chambr 3; CnE&AP; CnMWL;
ConAu 25R, 36NR, 104; ConLC 36;
CyWA 58, 97; DcArts; DcLB 20, 191,
DS18; EncWB 98; EncWL 2, 2S, 3;
EngPo; FacFETw; GrWrEL P; LinLib L;
LngCEL; LngCTC; MajTwCW 1;
ModBrL 2, S1, S2; NewC; ObitT 1961;
PenC ENG; PoeCrit 12; RAdv 14, 13-1;
REn; RfGEnL 91; TwCA SUP; WhAm 4;
WhDW; WhE&EA; WhoTwCL; WorAlBi

Sassoon, Vidal
English. Hairstylist
Founder, chm., Vidal Sassoon, Inc; wrote
   A Year of Beauty and Health, 1976.
b. Jan 17, 1928 in London, England

Source: AmDec 1960; BioIn 7, 8, 10, 12,
13; BioNews 74; BkPepl; CelR, 90;
ConAu 15NR, 65; CurBio 1999; Dun&B
86, 88; EncFash; IntWW 89, 91, 93, 97,
98, 2000; LegTOT; WhoAm 76, 78, 80,
82, 84, 86, 88, 90, 92, 96; WhoAmJ 80;
WhoFI 96; WhoWest 82, 84, 87, 89, 92,
94, 96; WhoWor 97; WorAl; WorFshn

Sassou-Nguesso, Denis
Congolese. Political Leader
Military officer was appointed President
   of the Republic of Congo 1979 and
   served until 1991; he approved a
   socialist constitution and instituted
   pro-Western foreign policy and liberal
   economic policy. He came to power
   again in 1997.
b. 1943 in Edou, Congo
Source: AfSS 81, 82; BioIn 15, 21;
ChamBiD; IntWW 89, 91, 93, 97, 98,
2000; ProfiWG 98; WhoAfr; WhoWor
82, 84, 87, 89, 93, 96, 99

Sasway, Benjamin H
American. Political Activist
First person indicted for violation of
   Selective Service Act since draft
   revival, 1980.
b. 1961? in Vista, California
Source: BioIn 13; NewYTBS 82

Satanta
American. Native American Chief
Principal war chief of the Kiowa; served
   prison sentences.
b. 1820 in Oklahoma
d. Sep 11, 1878 in Huntsville, Texas
Source: BioIn 21, 23; NotNaAm; PeoHis

Satcher, David
American. Government Official,
   Physician
Director, Centers for Disease Control and
   Prevention, 1994-98; Surgeon General,
   1998—.
b. Mar 2, 1941 in Anniston, Alabama
Source: AmMWSc 89, 92, 95, 98;
BiDrAPH 79; BioIn 19, 20, 22, 23, 24;
BlksScM; ConBlB 7; CurBio 97;
NotBlAM; NotTwCS 1; St&PR 84, 87,
91, 93, 96; WhoAfA 9, 10, 11, 12;
WhoAm 92, 95, 96, 97, 98, 99, 2000;
WhoAmP 1999; WhoBlA 2, 3, 4, 5, 6, 7,
8; WhoMedH 96, 99, 2000; WhoScEn
96, 2000; WhoSSW 84, 86; WhoWor 96,
98, 99, 2000

Sather, Glen Cameron
"Slats"
Canadian. Hockey Player, Hockey
   Coach, Hockey Executive
Left wing, 1966-77; coach, GM, pres.,
   Edmonton, 1977-89; won five Stanley
   Cups.
b. Sep 2, 1943 in High River, Alberta,
   Canada
Source: BioIn 14; HocEn; NewYTBE 71;
NewYTBS 85; WhoAm 84, 86, 90, 92,
94, 95, 96, 97, 98, 99, 2000; WhoHcky
73; WhoWest 87, 89, 92, 94, 96, 98

Satherly, Arthur Edward
"Uncle Art"
American. Music Executive
Record industry pioneer; helped launch
   careers of Gene Autry, Tex Ritter,
   Roy Rogers.
b. Oct 19, 1889 in Bristol, England
d. Feb 10, 1986 in Fountain Valley,
   California
Source: WhAm 9; WhoAm 76

Satie, Erik
French. Composer
Avant-garde works include Socrate,
   1918; influenced Debussy, Ravel, and
   Les Six group; wrote chiefly for piano.
b. May 17, 1866 in Honfleur, France
d. Jul 1, 1925 in Paris, France
Source: AtlBL; BakBD 78, 84; Benet 87;
BiDD; BioIn 1, 2, 3, 4, 5, 6, 7, 8, 9, 10,
11, 12, 16, 17, 18, 20, 21, 22; BriBkM
80; CmpBCM; CnOxB; CompSN, SUP;
ConMus 25; DancEn 78; DcCM; DcCom
77; DcCom&M 79; DcTwCC, A;
DcTwCCu 2; EncWB 98; FacFETw;
IntDcB; LegTOT; MakMC; McGEWB;
MusMk; NewAmDM; NewCol 75;
NewEOp 71; NewGrDM 80; NewOxM;
OxCFilm; OxCMus; OxDcOp; PenDiMP
A; RAdv 14; REn; WhDW; WhScrn 77,
83; WorAl; WorAlBi; WorEFlm

Sato, Eisaku
Japanese. Political Leader
Premier, 1964-72; developed Japan into
   major economic, industrial nation;
   shared 1974 Nobel Peace Prize for
   helping stabilize Pacific area.
b. Mar 27, 1901 in Tabuse, Japan
d. Jun 3, 1975 in Tokyo, Japan
Source: BioIn 6, 7, 8, 9, 10, 11, 15;
CurBio 65, 75, 75N; DcPol; EncWB 98;
EncyDco; FacFETw; IntWW 74, 75;
LegTOT; McGEWB; NewYTBS 74, 75;
NobelP; ObitT 1971; WhAm 6; WhoGov
72; WhoNob, 90, 95; WhoWor 74;
WorAlBi

Satriani, Joe
American. Musician
Lead guitarist for Mick Jagger's world
   tour, 1988; Hit album Surfing with the
   Alien.
b. 1957 in Carle Place, New York
Source: BioIn 16; ConMus 4; GrMetD;
News 89-3

Saubel, Katherine Siva
American. Historian
Helped found the Malki Museum, the
   first non-profit tribal museum on a
   Native American reservation in
   California; named Elder of the Year
   by the California State Indian
   Museum, 1987.
b. 1920
Source: BioIn 21; NotNaAm; WhoAmW
97

Saud (Ibn Abdul Aziz al Saud)
Saudi. Ruler
Ruled Saudi Arabia, 1953-64; deposed
   by brother, Faisal.

b. Jan 15, 1902, Kuwait
d. Feb 23, 1969 in Athens, Greece
Source: *BioIn 1, 3, 4, 5, 6, 7, 8, 9;*
CurBio 54, 69; NewCol 75

Saudek, Robert
American. TV Executive
Known for producing cultural
  programming, including "Omnibus";
  past president, NY's Museum of
  Broadcasting.
b. Apr 11, 1911 in Pittsburgh,
  Pennsylvania
d. Mar 13, 1997 in Baltimore, Maryland
Source: *BioIn 22, 24; BlueB 76;*
LesBEnT 92; St&PR 75; WhAm 12;
WhoEnt 92, 98; WhoWor 74, 76

Sauer, Carl Ortwin
American. Geographer, Anthropologist
Researcher was interested in historical
  fieldwork and other forms of
  geographical research, and concerned
  with the human imprint on the
  landscape.
b. Dec 24, 1889 in Warrenton, Missouri
d. Jul 18, 1975 in Warrenton, Missouri
Source: *AmMWSc 73S; AmNatBi;*
BiDAmCa; BioIn 1, 4, 10, 11, 13, 14,
15, 18, 23; CamBiEn; CamDcAB;
ChamBiD; ConAu 9NR, 57, 61; DcAmB
S9; EncWB 98; Geog 2; McGEWB;
OxCCan SUP; PeoHis; RAdv 14; WhAm
6

Sauer, George (Henry)
American. Football Coach
Head coach, Univ. of New Hampshire,
  1937-41; Univ. of Kansas, 1946-47,
  winner of two Bix Six titles.
b. Dec 11, 1910
d. Feb 5, 1994 in Waco, Texas
Source: *BiDAmSp Sup; BioIn 1; CurBio*
94N

Sauguet, Henri
French. Composer, Author
Neo-romantic was one of the most
  important composers, writers, and
  thinkers on French art and music of
  his time; his compositional style was
  characterized by clarity and simplicity.
b. May 18, 1901 in Bordeaux, France
d. 1989
Source: *BakBD 78, 84, 92; BakBDTw;*
BioIn 3, 8, 16, 17; CnOxB; CompSN,
SUP; DancEn 78; DcCM; EncWB, 98;
FacFETw; IntWW 89; NewAmDM;
NewEOp 71; NewGrDM 80; NewOxM;
OxCMus; OxDcOp; WhAm 10; WhoFr
79; WhoWor 74, 76

Saul
King
First king of Israel reigned from c. 1020
  to 1000 B.C., known as a generous,
  modest, and courageous leader.
b. fl. 1020
Source: *DicTyr; LegTOT*

Saunders, Allen
American. Cartoonist
Did comic strips Mary Worth, Steve
  Roper.
b. Mar 24, 1899 in Lebanon, Indiana
d. Jan 28, 1985 in Maumee, Ohio
Source: *BioIn 14; ConAu 69, 118;*
EncACom; NewYTBS 86; WhoAm 82;
WorECom

Saunders, Charles E, Sir
Canadian. Scientist
Developed early-maturing spring wheat
  grown in Western Canada: Marquis
  wheat, 1920s.
b. Feb 2, 1867 in London, Ontario,
  Canada
d. Jul 25, 1937 in Toronto, Ontario,
  Canada
Source: *Alli; McGEWB*

Saunders, Lori
American. Actor
Played Bobbi Jo on TV series "Petticoat
  Junction," 1965-70.
b. Oct 4, 1941 in Kansas City, Missouri
Source: *BioIn 24; WhoHol 92, A*

Saunders, Stuart T(homas)
American. Businessman
Headed PA Railroad, 1964; Penn Central
  Railroad, 1968-70.
b. Jul 16, 1909 in McDowell, Wyoming
d. Feb 7, 1987 in Richmond, Virginia
Source: *AmNatBi; BioIn 4, 6, 7, 8, 9, 11,*
12, 15; CurBio 66, 87, 87N; EncAB-A
35; EncABHB 1; IntWW 74, 75, 76, 77,
78, 79, 80, 81; NewYTBS 87; PolProf J,
NF; WhAm 9; WhoAm 74; WhoE 74

Saunders, William Laurence
American. Engineer, Inventor
Patented stone-cutting machines and
  drills.
b. Nov 1, 1856 in Columbus, Georgia
d. Jun 25, 1931 in Tenerife, Canary
  Islands, Spain
Source: *DcAmB; NatCAB 14, 26; WhAm*
1; WhNAA

Saura (Atares), Carlos
Spanish. Director, Screenwriter
Leading figure in Spanish cinema; films
  include *Cria,* 1976; *Carmen,* 1983.
b. Jan 4, 1932 in Huesca, Spain
Source: *BiDFilm 94; BioIn 11, 13, 16;*
ConAu 79NR, 114, 131; ConLC 20;
CurBio 78; EncEurC; FilmEn; HispWr;
IntDcF 1-2, 2-2; IntMPA 92, 94, 96;
IntWW 89, 91, 93; MiSFD 9; NewYTBE
71; WorEFlm; WorFDir 2

Saussure, Nicolas Thoedore de
Swiss. Chemist
Experiments in biochemistry of plants
  supplied groundwork for later
  development of phytochemistry.
b. Oct 14, 1767 in Geneva, Switzerland
d. Apr 18, 1845 in Geneva, Switzerland
Source: *BioIn 6; DcScB*

Sauter, Eddie
[Edward Ernest Sauter]
American. Jazz Musician, Songwriter
Trumpeter; arranged for Benny
  Goodman, Red Norvo, 1930s-40s; co-
  led Sauter-Finegan band, 1950s.
b. Dec 2, 1914 in New York, New York
d. Apr 21, 1981 in Nyack, New York
Source: *AmNatBi; AnObit 1981; ASCAP*
66, 80; BiDAmM; BioIn 12, 16;
CmpEPM; ConAmC 76A, 82; IlEncJ;
NewAmDM; NewGrDA 86; NewGrDJ
88, 94; NewYTBS 81; OxCPMus;
PenEncP; WhAm 7; WhoJazz 72

Sauve, Jeanne Mathilde Benoit
[Mrs. Maurice Sauve]
Canadian. Political Leader
First woman, 23rd governor-general
  (queen's representative) of Canada,
  1984-90.
b. Apr 26, 1922 in Prud'Homme,
  Saskatchewan, Canada
d. Jan 26, 1993 in Montreal, Quebec,
  Canada
Source: *AmCath 80; BioIn 13, 14, 15;*
CanWW 83, 89; ContDcW 89; CurBio
84; IntDcWB; IntWW 89; InWom SUP;
NewYTBS 83, 85; Who 92; WhoAm 86,
90; WhoAmW 91; WhoE 91; WhoWor 91

Sauveur, Albert
American. Scientist
A pioneer in the field of physical
  metallurgy.
b. Jun 21, 1863 in Louvain, Belgium
d. Jan 26, 1939 in Boston, Massachusetts
Source: *AmNatBi; BioIn 4, 12; DcAmB*
S2; DcNAA; DcScB; InSci; NatCAB 29;
WhAm 1; WhNAA

Savage, Augusta Christine
American. Sculptor
First black member National Assn. of
  Women Painters and Sculptors, 1934;
  noted for portrait sculpture.
b. Feb 29, 1892 in Green Cove Springs,
  Florida
d. Mar 26, 1962 in New York, New
  York
Source: *BiDWomA; BioIn 12, 20;*
ConWomA; DcWomA; EncWB 98;
InWom SUP; NotAW MOD; SJGBIA

Savage, Edward
American. Artist
Noted for portraits of George, Martha
  Washington.
b. Nov 26, 1761 in Princeton,
  Massachusetts
d. Jul 6, 1817 in Princeton,
  Massachusetts
Source: *AmBi; AmNatBi; ApCAB; BioIn*
1, 3, 5, 7, 10; BriEAA; CamDcAB;
DcAmArt; DcAmB; Drake; McGDA;
NewYHSD; WhAm HS

Savage, Fred
American. Actor
Played Kevin Arnold on "The Wonder
  Years," 1988-93.
b. Jul 9, 1976 in Chicago, Illinois

Source: *BioIn 16; ConTFT 8, 15, 27;*
IntMPA 92, 94, 96; LegTOT; News 90,
90-1; WhoHol 92

Savage, Henry Wilson
American. Impresario
Founded Boston Light Opera Co., 1895,
  presenting opera in English at
  moderate prices; also produced *Merry*
  Widow, 1907.
b. Mar 21, 1859 in Alton, New
  Hampshire
d. Nov 29, 1927 in Boston,
  Massachusetts
Source: *AmNatBi; BakBD 78, 84;*
BakBDTw; BiDAmM; DcAmB; EncMT;
NewEOp 71; NewGrDA 86; NotNAT B;
WhAm 1; WhThe

Savage, John
American. Journalist
Editorial writer for *States* (Washington,
  DC), 1857-61.
b. Dec 13, 1828 in Dublin, Ireland
d. Sep 9, 1888 in Laurelside,
  Pennsylvania
Source: *Alli; AmAu; AmAu&B; ApCAB;*
BbD; BiD&SB; ChhPo S1; CyAL 2;
DcAmAu; DcAmB; DcIrL 96; DcNAA;
DcNaB; Drake; HarEnUS; NatCAB 11;
PoIre; TwCBDA; WhAm HS

Savage, John
[John Youngs]
American. Actor
Films include *Salvador,* 1986; *The Onion*
  Field, 1979.
b. Aug 25, 1950? in Old Bethpage, New
  York
Source: *ConTFT 5; DcPseud; St&PR 87;*
VarWW 85; WhoEnt 92

Savage, Michael Joseph
New Zealander. Political Leader
Prime minister of New Zealand and a
  labor leader, known for his strong
  leadership during a time of depression.
b. Mar 23, 1872 in Victoria, Australia
d. Mar 27, 1940 in Wellington, New
  Zealand
Source: *BioIn 1; CamBiEn; DcTwHis;*
EncWB 98; FacFETw; McGEWB

Savage, Richard
English. Poet
Reputation gained from biography by
  Samuel Johnson, friendship with
  Alexander Pope.
b. 1697
d. Aug 1, 1743 in Bristol, England
Source: *Alli; BbD; Benet 87, 96; BioIn*
2, 3, 5, 9; BlmGEL; BritAu; CamBiEn;
CasWL; ChamBiD; Chambr 2; ChhPo,
S1; DcBiPP; DcEnA; DcEnL; DcEuL;
DcLB 95; EvLB; GrWrEL P; NewC;
NewCBEL; OxCEng 67, 85, 95; PenC
ENG; REn; RfGEnL 91; WebE&AL

Savage, Rick
[Def Leppard]
"Sav"
English. Musician
Bassist with heavy metal group formed
  1977.
b. Dec 2, 1960 in Sheffield, England

Savalas, Telly
[Aristoteles Savalas]
American. Actor
Played Kojak on TV police drama of
  same name, 1973-78; first shaved head
  for role of Pontius Pilate in *The*
  Greatest Story Ever Told, 1965.
b. Jan 21, 1923 in Garden City, New
  York
d. Jan 22, 1994 in Universal City,
  California
Source: *BioNews 74; BkPepl; ConTFT 2,*
7, 12; CurBio 76; FilmgC; HalFC 88;
IntMPA 92; IntWW 76, 77, 78, 79, 80,
81, 82, 89; MotPP; MovMk; NewYTBE
73; VarWW 85; WhoAm 86, 92; WhoEnt
92; WhoHol A; WorAlBi

Savant, Marilyn vos
American. Journalist
IQ of 228 is highest ever recorded;
  column, "Ask Marilyn," appears in
  Parade magazine.
b. Aug 11, 1946 in Saint Louis, Missouri
Source: *BioIn 15, 16; News 88-2*

Savard, Denis Joseph
Canadian. Hockey Player
Center, Chicago, 1980-90; Montreal,
  1990-93; Tampa Bay, 1993—.
b. Feb 4, 1961 in Pointe Gatineau,
  Quebec, Canada
Source: *HocEn; HocReg 87; WhoAm 96,*
97, 98, 99, 2000; WhoMW 90

Savard, Serge A
"The Senator"
Canadian. Hockey Player
Defenseman, 1966-83, mostly with
  Montreal; won Conn Smythe Trophy,
  1969, Masterton Trophy, 1979; Hall of
  Fame, 1986.
b. Jan 22, 1946 in Montreal, Quebec,
  Canada
Source: *BioIn 12; HocEn; WhoAm 84,*
86, 90; WhoE 91; WhoHcky 73

Savelli, Luca
Roman. Politician
Led middle class revolt against Pope
  Gregory IX, 1234.
d. 1266

Savery, Thomas
English. Inventor
Constructed the first steam engine.
b. 1650 in Shilstone, England
d. 1715 in London, England
Source: *AsBiEn; BiESc; BioIn 14;*
CamBiEn; ChamBiD; DcInv; DcNaB;
InSci; NewCBEL; OxCBrHi; RanHWDS;
WorInv

Savigny, Friedrich Karl von
German. Jurist
Most famous proponent of the historical
  school of jurisprudence, stressing
  historical rather than natural rights and
  historical facts rather than legal theory.
b. Jan 21, 1779 in Frankfurt am Main,
  Germany
d. Oct 25, 1861 in Berlin, Germany
Source: *BiD&SB; CamBiEn; CelCen;*
ChamBiD; DcBiPP; DcEuL; GloEncH;
McGEWB; OxCEng 67; OxCGer 76, 86,
97

Savimbi, Jonas Malheiro
Angolan. Political Leader
Founded National Union for the Total
  Independence of Angola, 1966.
b. Aug 3, 1934 in Munhango, Angola
Source: *BioIn 14, 15, 16; ChamBiD;*
ColdWar 1; ConBlB 2; ConNews 86-2;
CurBio 86; DcCPSAf; DcTwHis;
EncRev; EncWB; FacFETw; IntWW 91;
WhoAfr

Savitch, Jessica Beth
American. Broadcast Journalist
With NBC News, 1977-83; wrote
  autobiography, *Anchorwoman,* 1982.
b. Feb 2, 1948 in Kennett Square,
  Pennsylvania
d. Oct 23, 1983 in New Hope,
  Pennsylvania
Source: *BioIn 11; ConAu 108; CurBio*
83, 84; LesBEnT; NewYTBS 83; WhAm
8; WhoAm 82

Savitskaya, Svetlana Y
Russian. Cosmonaut
First woman to walk in space, Jul 25,
  1984.
b. 1947?
Source: *BiDSovU; BioIn 13, 14, 15;*
FacFETw; InWom SUP

Savitt, Jan
Russian. Bandleader
Led popular dance band, 1930s-40s.
b. Sep 4, 1913 in Saint Petersburg,
  Russia
d. Oct 4, 1948 in Sacramento, California
Source: *ASCAP 66, 80; CmpEPM;*
PenEncP

Savo, Jimmy
American. Actor, Comedian
Broadway performer who starred in
  several 1930s films.
b. 1896 in New York, New York
d. Sep 6, 1960 in Teni, Italy
Source: *BiDAmM; EncAFC; EncMT;*
JoeFr; NotNAT A, B; PlP&P; WhoCom;
WhoHol B; WhScrn 74, 77; WhThe

Savonarola, Girolamo
Italian. Religious Leader
Preached against corruptions in secular
  life; burned at stake for heresy, 1498.
b. Sep 21, 1452 in Ferrara, Italy
d. May 23, 1498 in Florence, Italy
Source: *BbD; Benet 87; BiD&SB; BioIn*
15, 16, 17, 20, 24; BlmGEL; CamBiEn;

CasWL; ChamBiD; DcCathB; DcItL 1, 2; Dis&D; EncCapP; EncRev; EncWB 98; EuAu; EvEuW; HisWorL; LegTOT; LinLib S; LuthC 75; McGEWB; NewC; OxCCAA; OxCEng 85, 95; PenC EUR; REn; WhDW; WhoChr; WorAl; WorAlBi

Savoy Brown

[Miller Anderson; Eric Dillon; James Leverton; Kim Simmonds; Stan Webb]
English. Music Group
Heavy rock group formed 1966; albums include *Rock & Roll Warriors, 1981.*
Source: *AllMGBl 2; ConMuA 80A; HarEnR 86; IlEncRk; OnThGG; PenEncP; RkOn 85A; RolSEnR 83; WhoRock 81; WhoRocM 82*

Sawchuk, Terry

[Terrance Gordon Sawchuk]
Canadian. Hockey Player
Goalie, 1949-70, mostly with Detroit; holds NHL record for career shutouts, 103; died of injuries received in fight with teammate; Hall of Fame, 1971.
b. Dec 28, 1929 in Winnipeg, Manitoba, Canada
d. May 31, 1970 in Mineola, New York
Source: *BioIn 10, 11; CamBiEn; ChamBiD; FacFETw; HocEn; LegTOT; NewYTBE 70; WhoHcky 73; WhoSpor*

Saw Maung

Burmese. Political Leader, Military Leader
Senior General of the tatmadaw (the Burmese armed forces) took power in a military coup in 1988; regime violently silenced dissidents, and refused to acknowledge the outcome of elections held in 1990.
b. 1928 in Mandalay, Burma
d. Jul 27, 1997
Source: *BioIn 23; EncWB 98; FacFETw; IntWW 97*

Sawyer, Amos

Liberian. Political Leader
Pres. interim government of Liberia, 1990.
b. Jun 15, 1945 in Greenville, Liberia
Source: *BioIn 16, 17, 21; ConBlB 2; WhoAfr*

Sawyer, Charles

American. Government Official
Ambassador to Belgium, 1944-45; secretary of Commerce, 1948-53.
b. Feb 10, 1887 in Cincinnati, Ohio
d. Apr 7, 1979 in Palm Beach, Florida
Source: *BiDrUSE 71, 89; BioIn 1, 2, 3, 10, 11, 12; ConAu 85, P-2; CurBio 79, 79N; NewYTBS 79; PolProf T; St&PR 75; WhAm 7; Who 74; WhoAm 74, 76; WhoAmP 73, 75, 77, 79*

Sawyer, Diane (K.)

[Mrs. Mike Nichols]
American. Broadcast Journalist
Former staff assistant to Nixon; first female correspondent on TV's "60 Minutes," 1984-89; co-anchor, "Prime

Time Live," 1989-98; co-anchor, "Day One," 1995; co-anchor, "Turning Point," 1994—; "20/20", 1998—.
b. Dec 22, 1945 in Glasgow, Kentucky
Source: *BioIn 12, 13, 16; CelR 90; ConAu 109, 115; ConTFT 10; CurBio 85; EncTwCJ; IntMPA 86, 88, 92, 94, 96; InWom SUP; JrnUS; LegTOT; LesBEnT 92; News 94; NewYTBS 81; WhoAm 86, 88, 90, 92, 94, 95, 96, 97; WhoAmW 87, 89, 91, 93, 95, 97; WhoE 91; WomStre; WorAlBi*

Sawyer, Eugene, Jr.

American. Politician
Alderman, elected acting mayor of Chicago replacing Harold Washington, 1987.
b. Sep 4, 1934 in Greensboro, Alabama
Source: *NewYTBS 87; WhoAm 88; WhoAmP 73, 75, 77, 79, 81, 83, 85, 87, 89, 91, 93, 95, 97, 1999*

Sawyer, Forrest

American. Broadcast Journalist
Covered Persian Gulf War for ABC; correspondent, Nightline, ABC, 1992—; anchor, World News Sunday, ABC; ABC News "Day One".
Source: *LesBEnT 92; WhoAm 88, 90, 92, 94, 95, 96, 97, 99, 2000; WhoE 95; WhoEnt 98; WhoMedi 98*

Sawyer, John E(dward)

American. Educator
Pres., Andrew W. Mellon Foundation, 1975-87; pres., Williams College, 1961-73.
b. May 5, 1917
d. Feb 7, 1995 in Woods Hole, Massachusetts
Source: *AmMWSc 73S, 78S; BioIn 5, 6, 7, 9; CurBio 95N; EncAInt; LEduc 74; WhAm 11; WhoAm 74, 76, 78, 80, 82, 84, 86, 88, 90, 92, 94, 95; WhoWor 76*

Sawyer, Ruth

American. Children's Author
Won Newbery Medal for autobiography *Roller Skates,* 1936.
b. Aug 5, 1880 in Boston, Massachusetts
d. Jun 3, 1970 in Hancock, Maine
Source: *AmAu&B; AmLY; AmNatBi; AmWomPl; AmWomWr; AnCL; AuBYP 2, 3; BioAmW; BioIn 2, 4, 6, 7, 8, 9, 11, 12, 14, 19, 22; BkCL; CarSB; ChhPo; ChlBkCr; ChlLR 36; ConAu 37NR, 73, 83NR; DcLB 22; HerW; InWom SUP; JBA 51; MajAI; NewbMB 1922; NotAW MOD; OxCChiL; SJGChWr 5; SmATA 17; TwCA, SUP; TwCCChW 1, 2, 3, 4; WhAm 5; WhE&EA; WhNAA; WhoAmW 58, 70, 72; WomNov; WrChl*

Sax, Adolphe (Antoine-Joseph)

Belgian. Inventor
Developed the saxophone, 1842, and other instruments used by military bands.
b. Nov 6, 1814 in Dinant, Belgium
d. Feb 4, 1894 in Paris, France

Source: *BakBD 78, 84, 92; BioIn 1, 2, 3, 5; BriBkM 80; MusMk; NewAmDM; NewGrDM 80; NewGrDO; NewOxM; WebBD 83; WhDW*

Sax, Charles Joseph

Belgian. Manufacturer
Made brass instruments at factory established in Brussels, 1815.
b. Feb 1, 1791 in Dinant, Belgium
d. Apr 26, 1865 in Paris, France
Source: *BakBD 84; WebBD 83*

Saxbe, William Bart

American. Diplomat
Rep. senator from OH, 1969-74; attorney general, 1973-74; ambassador to India, 1974-76.
b. Jun 25, 1916 in Mechanicsburg, Ohio
Source: *BiDrAC; BiDrUSC 89; CngDr 74; CurBio 74; IntWW 83, 89; NewYTBE 73; PolProf NF; WhoAm 76, 78, 82, 84, 86, 88, 90, 92, 94, 95, 96, 97, 98, 99, 2000; WhoAmP 85, 91; WhoGov 72*

Saxe, Maurice

French. Military Leader
One of greatest generals of his time for victories at Fontenoy, 1745, Racoux, 1746.
b. Oct 28, 1696 in Saxony, France
d. Nov 30, 1750 in Chambord, France
Source: *BioIn 2, 4, 6, 7, 16; ChamBiD; NewCol 75; OxCFr; OxCGer 76*

Saxon, Charles David

American. Cartoonist
Best known for humorous, satiric commentary on suburban upper class liftstyle in cartoons appearing on covers of *New Yorker* magazine since 1956.
b. Nov 13, 1920 in New York, New York
d. Dec 6, 1988 in Stamford, Connecticut
Source: *AmAu&B; ConAu 118, 127; WhAm 9; WhoAm 74, 76, 78; WhoAmA 73, 76, 78, 80, 82, 84, 86, 89, 91N, 93N; WhoE 74; WhoGrA 82*

Saxon, John

[Carmen Orrico]
American. Actor
Starred in TV series "The Bold Ones," 1969-72; film *The Cardinal,* 1963.
b. Aug 5, 1935 in New York, New York
Source: *BioIn 5; DcPseud; FilmEn; FilmgC; ForYSC; GangFlm; HalFC 80, 84, 88; IntMPA 75, 76, 77, 78, 79, 80, 81, 82, 84, 86, 88; ItaFilm; LegTOT; MotPP; MovMk; WhoHol A; WhoHrs 80; WorAl*

Say, Jean Baptiste

French. Economist, Educator
A founder of the classical school of economics, best known for his law of markets.
b. Jan 5, 1767 in Lyons, France
d. Nov 15, 1832
Source: *BiD&SB; BioIn 8, 14, 16; CamBiEn; CelCen; ChamBiD; CyEd;*

DcBiPP; EncWB 98; McGEWB; WhDW; WhoEc 81, 86

Sayao, Bidu
''The Brazilian Nightingale''
Brazilian. Opera Singer
Soprano prima donna with NY Met.,
  1937-52; noted for Manon role, jewel
  collection.
b. May 11, 1902 in Rio de Janeiro,
  Brazil
d. Mar 12, 1999 in Rockport, Maine
Source: *BakBD 78, 84, 92; BakBDTw;
BioIn 11, 13, 14, 15, 22; BriBkM 80;
CmOp; CurBio 42; IntDcOp; MetOEnc;
MusSN; NewAmDM; NewEOp 71;
NewGrDA 86; NewGrDM 80; OxDcOp;
PenDiMP*

Sayer, Leo
[Gerald Sayer]
English. Singer
Pop-rock hits include ''Have You Ever
  Been In Love,'' 1982.
b. May 21, 1948 in Shoreham, England
Source: *BillEnR; BioIn 11; BkPepl;
ConMuA 80A; DcPseud; EncRk 88;
EncRkSt; HarEnR 86; IlEncRk; LegTOT;
OxCPMus; PenEncP; RkOn 74, 78;
RolSEnR 83; Songw; WhoRock 81*

Sayers, Dorothy Leigh
English. Author
Dectective stories feature sleuth, Lord
  Peter Wimsey; first woman ever to
  receive degree from Oxford in
  medieval linguistics.
b. Jun 13, 1893 in Oxford, England
d. Dec 17, 1957 in Witham, England
Source: *ArtclWW 2; BiCoLiE; BioIn 2,
4, 8, 10, 11, 12, 13; CambiEn; CasWL;
ChamBiD; Chambr 3; CnMD; ConAu
60NR, 104, 119; CorpD; DcLEL; DcNaB
1951; EncMys; EncWL 1; EngPo; EvLB;
GrBr; GrWrEL N; InWom; LinLib S;
LngCTC; MajTwCW 2; ModBrL, S1;
ModWD; NewC; NewCBEL; NotNAT B;
OxCEng 67; OxCTwCL; PenC ENG;
PenNWW A; REn; TwCA, SUP; TwCWr;
WhAm 3; WhLit; WhoChr; WhThe;
WorAu 1900*

Sayers, Gale Eugene
American. Football Player
Four-time all pro running back, Chicago,
  1965-71; led NFL in rushing, 1966,
  1969; wrote *I Am Third*, 1970; Hall of
  Fame, 1977.
b. May 30, 1940 in Wichita, Kansas
Source: *BiDAmSp FB; ConAu 73;
InB&W 85; NewYTBE 70, 72; WhoAm
86, 88; WhoBlA 5; WhoFtbl 74*

Sayles, John
American. Filmmaker
Films include *Eight Men Out*, 1988;
  Passion Fish, 1992; *Lone Star*, 1996.
b. Sep 28, 1950 in Schenectady, New
  York
Source: *BiDFilm 94; BioIn 13, 14, 15,
16, 17, 19, 21, 22, 23; CelR 90; ConLC
7, 10, 14; ConTFT 1, 6, 13, 22; CurBio
84; EncSF 93; HalFC 88; IntDcF 1-4, 2-*

2; *IntMPA 84, 86, 88, 92, 94, 96;
LegTOT; LesBEnT; MiSFD 9; NewYTBS
83; Novels; WhoHol 92; WorAlBi;
WorFDir 2; WrDr 88, 90, 92, 94, 96, 98*

Sayles Belton, Sharon
American. Politician
Mayor of Minneapolis, 1994—.
b. c. 1952 in Saint Paul, Minnesota
Source: *ConBlB 9*

Sayre, Francis Bowes
American. Government Official, Educator
Law teacher and public official
  negotiated the treaties with European
  powers that ended extraterritoriality in
  Thailand.
b. Apr 30, 1885 in South Bethlehem,
  Pennsylvania
d. Mar 29, 1972 in Washington, District
  of Columbia
Source: *BioIn 1, 4, 8, 9; EncWB 98;
McGEWB; WhAm 5, 7; WhE&EA*

Sayyid Qutb
Egyptian. Author, Religious Leader,
  Educator
Islamic leader called for a revolution to
  establish an Islamic state and society;
  radical ideas influenced the Islamic
  resurgence of the late 20th century.
b. 1906 in Musha, Asyut, Egypt
d. Aug 25, 1966, Egypt
Source: *EncWB, 98*

Scaasi, Arnold
American. Fashion Designer
Made-to-order designer of First Lady
  Barbara Bush.
b. May 8, 1930 in Montreal, Quebec,
  Canada
Source: *BioIn 5, 11, 12, 13, 16; CelR
90; WhoAm 84*

Scaasi, Arnold
American. Fashion Designer
One of the last true custom designers in
  US; famous for his fur, feather-
  trimmed evening clothes.
b. May 8, 1931 in Montreal, Quebec,
  Canada
Source: *BioIn 13, 16; CelR 90;
ConFash; FairDF US; ThHDFas;
WhoFash 88; WorFshn*

Scaggs, Boz
[William Royce Scaggs]
American. Musician, Singer
Won Grammy for ''Lowdown,'' 1976;
  other hits include ''Miss Sun,'' 1980.
b. Jun 8, 1944 in Dallas, Texas
Source: *ASCAP 80; BillEnR; BioIn 16,
20, 24; ConMuA 80A; ConMus 12;
DcPseud; EncPR&S 89; EncRk 88;
EncRkSt; IlEncBM 82; IlEncRk;
LegTOT; NewAmDM; NewGrDA 86;
OnThGG; PenEncP; RkOn 74, 78;
RkWho 96; RolSEnR 83; Songw; SoulM;
WhoAm 78, 80, 82, 84, 86, 88, 90, 92,
94; WhoEnt 92, 98; WhoRock 81;
WorAlBi*

Scala, Gia
[Giovanna Sgoglio]
American. Actor
Leading lady, 1950s-60s: *The Guns of
  Navarone*, 1961; died of accidental
  drug, alcohol overdose.
b. Mar 3, 1934 in Liverpool, England
d. Apr 30, 1972 in Hollywood Hills,
  California
Source: *DcPseud; FilmEn; FilmgC;
HalFC 80, 84, 88; LegTOT; MotPP;
MovMk; NewYTBE 72; WhoHol B;
WhScrn 77, 83*

Scalchi, Sofia
Italian. Opera Singer
Noted mezzo-soprano; sang at NY Met.'s
  opening season, 1883; famed for high
  register.
b. Nov 29, 1850 in Turin, Italy
d. Aug 22, 1922 in Rome, Italy
Source: *BakBD 78, 84, 92; BioIn 1;
InWom; MetOEnc; NewEOp 71;
NewGrDM 80; NewGrDO*

Scalfaro, Oscar Luigi
Italian. Political Leader
Prominent Christian Democratic leader
  for over forty years, elected president
  of the Italian Republic in 1992.
b. Sep 9, 1918 in Novara, Italy
Source: *EncWB 98; IntWW 74, 75, 76,
89, 91, 93, 97, 98, 2000; ProfiWG 98;
WhoIntA 2; WhoWor 74, 84, 95, 96, 97,
98, 99, 2000*

Scali, John (Alfred)
American. Journalist, Diplomat
Senior correspondent, ABC News; US
  ambassador to UN, 1973-75.
b. Apr 27, 1918 in Canton, Ohio
d. Oct 9, 1995 in Washington, District of
  Columbia
Source: *BioIn 9, 10, 11, 12; CelR;
ConAu 65; CurBio 73, 96N; EncTwCJ;
IntAu&W 89, 91, 93; IntWW 74, 75, 76,
77, 78, 79, 80, 81, 82, 83, 89; LesBEnT
92; NewYTBE 71, 72; USBiR 74; WhAm
11; WhoAm 74, 76, 80, 82, 84, 86, 88,
90, 94, 95, 96; WhoAmP 73; WhoE 95;
WhoGov 75; WhoSSW 73; WhoUN 75;
WhoWor 74, 76, 78*

Scalia, Antonin
American. Supreme Court Justice
Appointed to court by Ronald Reagan,
  1986.
b. Mar 11, 1936 in Trenton, New Jersey
Source: *AmBench 97; AmPolLe; BioIn
14, 15, 17, 18, 22; CamDcAB; CngDr
83, 85, 87, 89, 91, 93, 95; ConAu 168;
CriJuSA; CurBio 86; EncCapP;
EncRelA; EncWB, 98; FacFETw; IntWW
89, 91, 93, 97, 98, 2000; LegTOT; News
88-2; NewYTBS 86; OxCSupC; SupCtJu;
Who 90, 94, 98, 99, 2000; WhoAm
74, 76, 78, 80, 82, 84, 86, 88, 90, 92,
94, 95, 96, 97, 98, 99, 2000; WhoAmL
78, 79, 83, 87, 90, 92, 94, 96, 98, 2000;
WhoAmP 87, 89, 91, 93, 95, 97, 1999;
WhoE 85, 86, 89, 91, 93; WhoGov 75,
77; WhoWor 89, 91, 93, 96; WorAlBi*

Scaliger, Joseph Justus
French. Scholar
Founded Julian period of scientific chronology.
b. Aug 4, 1540 in Agen, France
d. Jan 21, 1609 in Leyden, France
Source: *AsBiEn; BbD; BiD&SB; CamBiEn; ChamBiD; CyEd; DcBiPP; DcEuL; EncHiCA; EvEuW; InSci; LinLib L, S; LuthC 75; NewC; OxCEng 67, 85, 95; OxCFr; PenC EUR; WorAl; WorAlBi*

Scamozzi, Vincenzo
Italian. Architect
Influential designer of cathedrals, theaters, palaces; architectural theories helped usher in English Neoclassic era.
b. 1552 in Vicenza, Italy
d. 1616, Italy
Source: *CamGWoT; DcArch; DcBiPP; MacEA; McGDA; NotNAT B; OxCArt; OxCThe 67, 83; PlP&P; WhoArch*

Scanlon, Hugh Parr
English. Labor Union Official
Pres., Amalgamated Union of Engineering Workers, 1968-78.
b. Oct 26, 1913, Australia
Source: *BioIn 8, 9; IntWW 74, 75, 76, 77, 78, 93; Who 74*

Scarbury, Joey
American. Singer
Hit single "Believe It or Not," 1981, theme from TV show "Greatest American Hero."
b. Jun 7, 1955 in Ontario, California
Source: *RkOn 85*

Scargill, Arthur
English. Labor Union Official
Pres., Nat. Union of Mineworkers, 1981—; led Britain's longest, most violent post WW II strike, 1984-85.
b. Jan 11, 938 in Barnsley, England
Source: *BioIn 14, 15; CurBio 85; EncWB; FacFETw; IntWW 91; Who 92*

Scarlatti, Alessandro
Italian. Composer
Established Italian opera overture; wrote 200 masses, 115 operas, including *Il Tigrane,* 1715; father of Domenico.
b. May 2, 1660 in Palermo, Sicily, Italy
d. Nov 24, 1725 in Naples, Italy
Source: *AtlBL; BakBD 78, 84; BakDcM; Benet 87; BioIn 3, 4, 5, 7, 10, 12, 14; BriBkM 80; CmOp; CmpBCM; DcCom 77; DcCom&M 79; GrComp; IntDcOp; LegTOT; MetOEnc; MusMk; NewAmDM; NewCBEL; NewEOp 71; NewGrDM 80; NewOxM; OxCMus; OxDcOp; PenDiMP A; REn; WorAl; WorAlBi*

Scarlatti, Domenico Girolamo
Italian. Composer
Founded modern keyboard technique; first to use arpeggios in performances; wrote over 500 harpsichord sonatas.
b. Oct 26, 1685 in Naples, Italy

d. Jul 23, 1757 in Naples, Italy
Source: *AtlBL*

Scarne, John
American. Magician, Business Executive
Authority on games of chance; wrote *Scarne on Dice.*
b. Mar 4, 1903 in Steubenville, Ohio
d. Jul 7, 1985 in Englewood, New Jersey
Source: *BioIn 14, 24; ConAu 116, 159; MafEnc; ScrEAmL 1; WhoAm 76, 78, 80, 82, 84, 86, 88, 90, 92, 94, 95, 96, 97, 98, 99, 2000*

Scarpelli, Glenn
American. Actor
Played Alex in TV series "One Day at a Time," 1980-83.
b. Jul 6, 1968 in Staten Island, New York
Source: *VarWW 85*

Scarry, Richard (McClure)
American. Children's Author, Illustrator
Prolific writer of "best ever" picture books; won Edgar mystery award, 1976.
b. Jun 5, 1919 in Boston, Massachusetts
d. Apr 30, 1994 in Gstaad, Switzerland
Source: *AmNatBi; AuBYP 2, 3; BioIn 9, 10, 12, 14, 16, 19, 20; CamBiEn; CamDcAB; ChamBiD; ChlBkCr; ChlLR 3, 41; ConAu 17R, 18NR, 39NR, 83NR, 145; ConLC 86; DcLB 61; FamAIYP; IlsCB 1957; IntAu&W 77, 82, 86, 91, 93; MajAl, SUP; NewYTBS 94; OxCChiL; PiP; SJGChWr 5; SmATA 2, 35, 75, 90; ThrBJA; TwCChW 1, 2, 3, 4; WhAm 11; WhoAm 78, 80, 82, 84, 86, 88, 90, 92, 94; WrDr 76, 80, 82, 84, 86, 88, 90, 92, 94, 96*

Scavullo, Francesco
American. Photographer
Freelance photographer known for pictures of models, celebrities appearing in popular magazines.
b. Jan 16, 1929 in Staten Island, New York
Source: *BioIn 13, 14, 15, 17, 23; CelR 90; ConAu 43NR, 102; CurBio 85; EncFash; ICPEnP A; LegTOT; MacBEP; ThHDFas; WhoAdv 90; WhoAm 78, 80, 82, 84, 86, 88, 90, 92, 94, 95, 96, 97*

Schaap, Dick
[Richard J Schaap]
American. Journalist
Sportscaster with ABC News, 1980—; ESPN, 1990—; ESPN Radio, 1998—.
b. Sep 27, 1934 in New York, New York
Source: *AmAu&B; BioIn 15, 22; ConAu 5NR, 9R; LiJour; WhoE 74*

Schacht, Al(exander)
"Clown Prince of Baseball"
American. Baseball Player
Pitcher, Washington, 1919-21, with 14 ML wins; better known for entertaining fans before game.

b. Nov 11, 1892 in New York, New York
d. Jul 14, 1984 in Waterbury, Connecticut
Source: *Ballpl 90; BioIn 14; NewYTBS 84; WhoProB 73*

Schacht, Hjalmar Horace Greeley
German. Financier
Germany's "financial wizard"; saved country from inflation by issuing the Rentenmark, 1923; made Minister of Economics by Hitler; acquitted at Nuremberg trails.
b. Jan 22, 1877 in Tingleff, Germany
d. Jun 4, 1970 in Munich, Germany (West)
Source: *BiDExR; ConAu 113; CurBio 44, 70; EncWB 98; McGEWB; REn; WhWW-II*

Schadow, Gottfried
[Johann Gottfried Schadow]
German. Sculptor
Member of Neo-classic school; best known for monuments of Fredrick the Great, Blucher, Luther.
b. May 20, 1764 in Berlin, Germany
d. Jan 27, 1850 in Berlin, Germany
Source: *BioIn 2, 6, 11, 12; CelCen; DcBiPP; LuthC 75; McGDA; NewCol 75; OxCArt; OxDcArt; WorECar*

Schaefer, Germany
[Herman A Schaefer]
American. Baseball Player
Infielder, early 1900s; known for antics while stealing bases.
b. Feb 4, 1878 in Chicago, Illinois
d. May 16, 1919 in Saranac Lake, New York
Source: *BioIn 2, 3, 5; WhoProB 73*

Schaefer, Jack Warner
American. Author
Wrote dozens of Western novels including *Shane,* 1949, adapted to film, 1953, translated into 35 languages.
b. Nov 19, 1907 in Cleveland, Ohio
d. Jan 24, 1991 in Santa Fe, New Mexico
Source: *AmAu&B; Au&Wr 71; AuBYP 2, 3; BioIn 5, 8, 9, 11, 14; ConAu 15NR, 17R, 64NR, 133, P-1; DcAmChF 1960; EncFrLi; EncFWF; FifWWr; IntMPA 82, 86; NewEAmW; NewYTBS 91; OhA&B; REnAW; SJGChWr 5; SmATA 3, 66; ThrBJA; TwCChW 3; TwCWW 82, 91; WhoAm 74, 76, 78, 80, 82, 84, 86, 88, 90; WhoWest 74*

Schaefer, Rudolph Jay
American. Brewer
Chm., F & M Schaefer Brewing Co., 1950-69.
b. Jul 9, 1900 in Larchmont, New York
d. Sep 2, 1982 in New York, New York
Source: *NewYTBS 82; St&PR 75; WhoAm 74*

Schaefer, Thomas E
[The Hostages]
American. Hostage
One of 52 held by terrorists, Nov 1979-
Jan 1981.
b. 1931?
Source: *NewYTBS 81*

Schaefer, Vincent Joseph
American. Meteorologist
Performed experiments to investigate the
nature of precipitation.
b. Jul 4, 1906 in Schenectady, New York
d. Jul 25, 1993 in Schenectady, New
York
Source: *AmMWSc 73P, 76P, 79; AsBiEn;
BiESc; BioIn 1, 2, 5; CamBiEn;
CamDcAB; ChamBiD; ConAu 120;
CurBio 48; InSci; LarDcSc; McGMS 80;
WhoAm 74, 76, 78, 80, 82, 84; WhoTech
89*

Schaefer, William Donald
American. Politician
Dem. governor of MD, 1987—; mayor
of Baltimore, 1971-87.
b. Nov 2, 1921 in Baltimore, Maryland
Source: *AlmAP 88, 92; BiDrGov 1983,
1988; BioIn 12, 13, 16; CelR 90;
ConNews 88-1; CurBio 88; IntWW 89,
91, 93, 97, 98, 2000; WhoAm 78, 80, 82,
84, 86, 88, 90, 92, 94, 95; WhoAmP 73,
75, 77, 79, 81, 83, 85, 87, 89, 91, 93,
95, 97, 1999; WhoE 74, 75, 77, 79, 81,
83, 85, 86, 89, 91, 93, 95; WhoGov 75,
77; WhoWor 89, 91, 93, 95*

Schafer, Natalie
American. Actor
Veteran stage comedienne since 1944;
played Lovey on TV series
"Gilligan's Island," 1964-67.
b. Nov 5, 1902 in Rumson, New Jersey
d. Apr 10, 1991 in Beverly Hills,
California
Source: *FilmEn; HalFC 88; IntMPA 88;
NewYTBS 91; VarWW 85*

Schaff, Philip
American. Theologian
Noted church scholar; founder, first
president, American Society of Church
History, 1888.
b. Jan 1, 1819 in Chur, Switzerland
d. Oct 20, 1893 in New York, New York
Source: *Alli, SUP; AmAu; AmAu&B;
AmBi; AmNatBi; ApCAB; BbD;
BiD&SB; BioIn 1, 15, 17, 19, 23;
CamDcAB; ChamBiD; CyAL 2;
DcAmAu; DcAmB; DcAmReB 1, 2;
DcHerTr; DcLB DS13; DcNAA; Drake;
EncARH; EncRelA; EncWB 98;
HarEnUS; LuthC 75; McGEWB;
NatCAB 3; NewCol 75; OxCAmH;
PeoHis; RelLAm 1, 2; REnAL;
TwCBDA; WebAB 74, 79; WhAm HS*

Schaffner, Franklin James
American. Director
Won best director Oscar, 1970, for
Patton.
b. May 3, 1920 in Tokyo, Japan

d. Jul 2, 1989 in Santa Monica,
California
Source: *BioIn 16; ConTFT 7; FacFETw;
HalFC 88; IntMPA 88; IntWW 79, 80,
81, 82, 83, 89; LesBEnT 92; NewYTBS
89; PeoHis*

Schalk, Franz
Austrian. Conductor
Led Vienna State Opera, from 1918.
b. May 27, 1863 in Vienna, Austria
d. Sep 2, 1931 in Edlach, Austria
Source: *BakBD 78, 84, 92; BakBDTw;
CmOp; IntDcOp; MetOEnc; NewEOp
71; NewGrDM 80; NewGrDO; OxDcOp;
PenDiMP*

Schalk, Ray(mond William)
"Cracker"
American. Baseball Player
Catcher, 1912-29, mostly with Cubs;
known for fielding; Hall of Fame,
1955.
b. Aug 12, 1892 in Harvel, Illinois
d. May 19, 1970 in Chicago, Illinois
Source: *Ballpl 90; BiDAmSp BB; BioIn
7, 8, 14, 15; CamDcAB; DcAmB S8;
LegTOT; WhoProB 73*

Schally, Andrew Victor
American. Biochemist
Discovered pituitary hormone TRH,
1969, human ovulation hormone
LHRH, 1971; shared Nobel Prize,
1977.
b. Nov 30, 1926 in Wilno, Poland
Source: *AmMWSc 76P; WhoMedH 96,
99, 2000; WhoNob, 90, 95; WhoScEn 94,
96, 2000; WhoSSW 78, 80, 82, 84, 86,
88, 91, 93, 95, 97, 99; WhoTech 89;
WhoWor 78, 80, 82, 84, 87, 89, 91, 93,
95, 96, 97, 98, 99, 2000; WorAlBi;
WorScD*

Schaltzberg, Jerry Ned
American. Director
Films include *Panic in Needle Park*,
1972; *Honeysuckle Rose*, 1980.
b. Jun 26, 1927 in New York, New York
Source: *ConTFT 4; HalFC 84; WhoAm
86*

Schama, Simon
English. Historian, Educator
Wrote *Citizens: A Chronicle of the
French Revolution*, 1989, noted for its
unusual colorful narrative and stylistic
qualities.
b. Feb 13, 1945 in London, England
Source: *BestSel 89-4; ConAu 105;
CurBio 91; IntAu&W 91, 93; IntWW 91;
WhoAm 84, 94, 95, 96, 97, 98, 99, 2000;
WhoWor 93, 95; WrDr 90, 92*

Schanberg, Sydney Hillel
American. Journalist
Columnist, associate editor, *NY Times*,
1959-85; columnist, associate editor,
Newsday, 1986-99; APBNews.com,
1999—; won Pulitzer Prize, 1975.
b. Jan 17, 1934 in Clinton,
Massachusetts

Source: *BiDAmNC; BioIn 14, 15; ConAu
69; CurBio 90; IntAu&W 91; IntWW 89,
91, 93, 97, 98, 2000; WhoAm 76, 78, 80,
82, 84, 86, 88, 90, 92, 94, 95, 96, 97;
WhoAmJ 80; WhoE 77, 79, 81, 83, 85,
86, 89, 91, 95; WhoPul*

Schank, Roger C(arl)
American. Scientist
Creative computer scientist founded
Cognitive Science Society; Yale
professor and chairman of department
of Computer Science, from 1980;
founded Institute for the Learning
Sciences, 1989.
b. Mar 12, 1946 in New York, New
York
Source: *BioIn 13, 14, 15, 16; ConAu
132; News 89-2; WhoAm 84, 86, 88, 90,
92, 94, 95, 96, 97, 98, 99, 2000; WhoE
86; WhoFrS 84; WhoTech 89; WrDr 98,
99, 2000*

Schapiro, Meyer
[Meir Schapiro]
American. Historian, Educator
Art historian; faculty member of art
history dept. at Columbia U, 1928-
1973; professor emeritus, 1973-96.
b. Sep 23, 1904 in Siauliai, Lithuania
d. Mar 3, 1996 in New York, New York
Source: *AmAu&B; BioIn 7, 10, 11, 12,
14, 15, 17, 20, 21, 22, 23, 24;
CamDcAB; ChamBiD; ConAu 97, 151;
CurBio 84, 96N; DcTwArt; DrAS 74H,
78H; EncAL; FacFETw; IntAu&W 91;
NewYTBS 75, 96; ThTwC 87; WhAm 11;
Who 74, 82, 83, 85, 88, 90, 92, 94;
WhoAm 74, 76, 78, 82, 84, 86, 88, 90,
92, 94, 95, 96; WhoAmA 73, 76, 78, 80,
82, 84, 86, 89, 91, 93; WhoWorJ 72, 78;
WorAu 1975; WrDr 86, 88, 90, 92, 94,
96, 98N*

Schapiro, Miriam
American. Artist
A leader of the Feminist Art Movement
in the early 1970s, one of the first to
use the computer in creating art, and a
founder of the "Pattern and
Decoration Movement."
b. Nov 15, 1923 in Toronto, Ontario,
Canada
Source: *AmArt; BiDWomA; BioIn 5, 11,
12, 13, 15, 16, 23; CamDcAB; ConArt
77, 83, 89, 96; ConWomA; DcCAA 71,
77, 88, 94; DcCAr 81; DcTwArt; EncWB
98; IntWWW 2; InWom SUP;
NorAmWA; OxCTwCA; PrintW 83, 85;
WhoAm 82, 84, 86, 88, 90, 92, 94, 95,
96, 97, 98, 99, 2000; WhoAmA 73, 76,
78, 80, 82, 84, 86, 89, 91, 93, 1999;
WhoAmW 72, 74, 79, 81, 83, 97; WhoE
83*

**Scharnhorst, Gerhard Johann
David von**
Prussian. Military Leader
General rebuilt the Prussian army after
its collapse at Jena in 1806.
b. Nov 12, 1755 in Bordenau, Prussia
d. Jun 28, 1813 in Prague, Prussia

Source: *BioIn 24; CamBiEn; ChamBiD; HarEnMi; McGEWB; WhoMilH 76*

Scharping, Rudolf
German. Politician
Minister-president of Rhineland-
  Palatinate and chairman of the German
  Social Democratic Party, ran as its
  chancellor candidate in 1994.
b. Dec 2, 1947
Source: *EncWB 98; IntWW 97, 98, 2000; Who 98, 99, 2000; WhoWor 99, 2000*

Schary, Dore
American. Producer, Screenwriter
Early in career wrote several film scripts
  including *Boys Town*, 1938; later
  switched to producing.
b. Aug 31, 1905 in Newark, New Jersey
d. Jul 7, 1980 in New York, New York
Source: *AmAu&B; AmNatBi; AnObit 1980; BenetAL 91; BiDFilm, 81, 94; BiE&WWA; BioIn 1, 2, 3, 4, 5, 6, 9, 10, 12, 17, 20; BlueB 76; CamDcAB; ConAu 1NR, 1R, 101; ConDr 73, 77, 93; CurBio 48, 80, 80N; DcAmB S10; DcFM; EncMcCE; FacFETw; FilmEn; FilmgC; HalFC 80, 84, 88; IntDcF 1-4, 2-4; IntMPA 75, 76, 77, 78, 79, 80, 81, 82; LegTOT; LinLib L, S; MGM A; MiSFD 9N; ModWD; NatPD 77; NewYTBS 80; NotNAT; OxCFilm; REnAL; WhAm 7; WhoAm 74, 76, 78, 80; WhoAmJ 80; WhoE 74, 75, 77, 79, 81; WhoThe 72, 77, 81; WhoWor 74, 76, 78, 80; WhoWorJ 72, 78; WorAl; WorAlBi; WorAu 1950; WorEFlm; WrDr 76, 80*

Schaudinn, Fritz Richard
German. Zoologist
Discovered syphilis organism,
  Spirochaeta pallida, 1905.
b. Sep 19, 1871 in Roseningken, Prussia
d. Jun 22, 1906 in Hamburg, Germany
  (West)
Source: *AsBiEn; BiESc; BiHiMed; BioIn 9; CamBiEn; CamDcSc; ChamBiD; DcScB; InSci; LarDcSc; NewCol 75; OxCMed 86; RanHWDS; WebBD 83; WhDW*

Schauffler, Robert Haven
American. Poet, Essayist
Writings include *The Unknown Brahms*,
  1933; *The Days We Celebrate*, 1940.
b. Apr 8, 1879 in Brunn, Austria
d. Nov 24, 1964
Source: *AmAu&B; BakBD 78, 84; BenetAL 91; BioIn 4, 7, 22; ChhPo, S1, S2, S3; OhA&B; REn; REnAL; TwCA, SUP; WhAm 4; WhE&EA; WhNAA; WorAu 1900*

Schaufuss, Peter
Danish. Dancer
Principal dancer, NYC Ballet, 1974-77;
  Nat. Ballet of Canada, 1977-83;
  English Nat. Ballet, 1984-90.
b. Apr 26, 1949 in Copenhagen,
  Denmark
Source: *BiDD; BioIn 12, 13, 16; CamBiEn; ChamBiD; CnOxB; CurBio*

82; *FacFETw; IntDcB; IntWW 91; NewYTBS 75; Who 92; WhoAm 78, 80, 82, 90; WhoEnt 92; WhoWor 91*

Schawlow, Arthur L(eonard)
American. Physicist, Educator
With Nicolaas Bloembergen, shared 1981
  Nobel Prize in physics for studies of
  laser spectroscopy.
b. May 5, 1921 in Mount Vernon, New
  York
d. Apr 28, 1999 in Palo Alto, California
Source: *AmMWSc 76P, 79, 82, 86, 89, 92, 95, 98; BioIn 8, 11, 12, 13, 14, 15, 18, 20; BlueB 76; CamBiEn; CamDcAB; CamDcSc; ChamBiD; ConAu 157; IntWW 74, 75, 76, 77, 78, 79, 80, 81, 82, 83, 89, 91, 93, 97, 98, 2000; LarDcSc; McGCEnS; NobelP; RanHWDS; Who 83, 85, 88, 90, 92, 94, 98, 99; WhoAm 74, 76, 78, 80, 82, 84, 86, 88, 90, 92, 94, 95, 96, 97, 98, 99; WhoAtom 77; WhoEng 80, 88; WhoFrS 84; WhoNob, 90, 95; WhoScEn 94, 96; WhoTech 89; WhoWest 00, 74, 76, 78, 80, 82, 84, 87, 89, 92, 94, 96, 98; WhoWor 74, 76, 78, 82, 84, 87, 89, 91, 93, 95, 96, 97, 98, 99; WorAlBi*

Schayes, Dolph
[Adolph Schayes]
American. Basketball Player, Basketball
  Coach
Forward, 1949-64, mostly with Syracuse;
  led NBA in rebounding, 1951;
  coached five seasons; coach of year,
  1966; Hall of Fame, 1972.
b. May 19, 1928 in New York, New
  York
Source: *BasBi; BiDAmSp BK; BioIn 4, 5, 6, 8, 9, 10, 14, 22; LegTOT; OfNBA 87; PeoHis; WhoAm 74; WhoBbl 73; WhoE 74; WhoSpor*

Schechter, Solomon
American. Religious Leader, Scholar
President of the Jewish Theological
  Seminary of America, he laid the
  foundation for the development of
  Conservative Judaism in the United
  States.
b. Dec 1849 in Focsani, Romania
d. Nov 20, 1915
Source: *EncWB 98; McGEWB; NatCAB 13*

Scheel, Walter
German. Diplomat
Pres., Federal Republic of Germany,
  1974-79.
b. Jul 8, 1919 in Solingen, Germany
Source: *BioIn 8, 9, 10; CamBiEn; ChamBiD; CurBio 71; IntWW 74, 75, 76, 77, 78, 79, 80, 81, 82, 83, 89, 91, 93, 97, 98, 2000; IntYB 78, 79, 80, 81, 82; NewYTBS 74; Who 74, 82, 83, 85, 88, 90, 92, 94, 98, 99, 2000; WhoFI 96; WhoWor 74, 76, 78, 84, 87, 89, 91, 93, 95*

Scheele, Karl Wilhelm
Swedish. Chemist
Discovered oxygen, 1772, chlorine,
  1774; prior to Priestly's publications.
b. Dec 9, 1742 in Stralsund, Swedish
  Pomerania
d. May 26, 1786 in Koping, Sweden
Source: *AsBiEn; BiESc; BioIn 1, 3, 5, 6, 7, 9, 10, 12; EncWB 98; InSci; LinLib L, S; McGCEnS; McGEWB; RanHWDS; WhDW; WorAl; WorAlBi*

Scheer, Robert
American. Journalist
Anti-war activist, 1960s; wrote *How the United States Got Involved in Vietna m*, 1965; reporter, *LA Times*, 1976-
  1993.
b. Apr 14, 1936 in New York, New
  York
Source: *AmAu&B; BioIn 8, 11, 13; ConAu 106; PolProf J*

Scheff, Fritzi
''Little Devil of the Opera''
Austrian. Opera Singer
Soprano who sang over 30 roles; most
  noted for Broadway light opera, 1906-
  30s.
b. Aug 30, 1879 in Vienna, Austria
d. Apr 8, 1954 in New York, New York
Source: *BakBD 78, 84, 92; BakBDTw; BioIn 3; CmOp; CmpEPM; DcPseud; EncMT; EncVaud; Film 1; InWom, SUP; MetOEnc; NewEOp 71; NewGrDA 86; NewGrDM 80; NewGrDO; NotNAT B; OxCAmT 84; OxCPMus; WhoHol B; WhoStg 1906, 1908; WhScrn 74, 77, 83; WhThe*

Scheffer, Victor B(lanchard)
American. Conservationist, Zoologist
US government biologist, 1937-69;
  accepted idea that wildlife is a
  ''resource'' to be managed.
b. Nov 27, 1906 in Manhattan, Kansas
Source: *BioIn 10; CurBio 94; IntAu&W 93; WhoAm 74, 76; WrDr 94, 96*

Scheidemann, Philipp
German. Political Leader
Proclaimed start of Weimar Republic,
  1918; first chancellor, 1919.
b. Jun 26, 1865 in Kassel, Germany
d. Nov 29, 1939 in Copenhagen,
  Denmark
Source: *CamBiEn; ChamBiD; EncTR 91; FacFETw; NewCol 75; REn*

Scheider, Roy Richard
American. Actor
Starred in *Jaws I, II*, 1975, 1978; Oscar
  nominee: *All That Jazz*, 1979.
b. Nov 10, 1935 in Orange, New Jersey
Source: *BioIn 13; CelR 90; ConTFT 5; FilmgC; HalFC 84; IntMPA 86; NewYTBS 80; WhoAm 76, 78, 80, 82, 84, 86, 88, 90, 94; WhoEnt 92; WhoHol A; WorAl*

Schell, Johnathan Edward
American. Journalist
Staff writer,*New Yorker,* 1968-87; author of many books and articles on the Vietnam war.
b. Aug 21, 1943 in New York, New York
Source: *BioIn 12, 13; ConLC 35; CurBio 92; IntAu&W 91; WhoAm 88; WhoWrEP 89; WrDr 92*

Schell, Maria Margarethe
Austrian. Actor
Short American career debuted with *The Brothers Karamazov,* 1958; returned to European screen.
b. Jan 5, 1926 in Vienna, Austria
Source: *BioIn 14; ConTFT 6; CurBio 61; FilmEn; HalFC 84, 88; IntMPA 86, 92; InWom SUP; WorAlBi*

Schell, Maximilian
Austrian. Actor
Won Oscar, 1961, for *Judgment at Nuremberg;* brother of Maria Schell.
b. Dec 8, 1930 in Vienna, Austria
Source: *BiDFilm 94; BiE&WWA; BioIn 6, 7, 11, 14, 17; CelR; ConAu 116, 172; ConTFT 5, 18; CurBio 62; FilmAG WE; FilmEn; FilmgC; ForYSC; HalFC 80, 84, 88; IntDcF 1-3, 2-3; IntMPA 75, 76, 77, 78, 79, 80, 81, 82, 84, 86, 88, 92, 94, 96; IntWW 74, 75, 76, 77, 78, 79, 80, 81, 82, 83, 89, 91, 93, 97, 98, 2000; ItaFilm; LegTOT; MiSFD 9; MotPP; MovMk; OsStAZ; WhoAm 74, 76, 78, 80, 82, 84, 86, 88, 90, 92, 94, 95, 96, 97, 99, 2000; WhoEnt 92, 98; WhoHol 92, A; WhoWor 74, 78, 82, 84, 87, 89, 91, 93, 95, 96; WorAl; WorAlBi; WorEFlm*

Schell, Orville H, Jr.
American. Businessman
Chairman of NYC Ballet, 1975-87.
b. Jul 11, 1908 in New Rochelle, New York
d. Jun 17, 1987 in Danbury, Connecticut
Source: *NewYTBS 87; WhoAm 86*

Schell, Orville H(ickock), 3rd.
American. Journalist, Author
Books on China include *Modern China: The Story of a Revolution,* 1972.
b. May 20, 1940 in New York, New York
Source: *AuBYP 2S, 3; BioIn 11; ConAu 25R; IntAu&W 91; SmATA 10; WrDr 86, 92*

Schelling, Ernest Henry
"Uncle Ernest"
American. Pianist, Composer, Conductor
Led children's concerts, 1920s-30s; wrote fantasy *A Victory Ball,* 1923.
b. Jul 26, 1876 in Belvidere, New Jersey
d. Dec 8, 1939 in New York, New York
Source: *AmBi; AmNatBi; ASCAP 66; BakBD 84; BakBDTw; BiDAmM; CurBio 40; DcAmB S2; OxCMus; WhAm 1*

Schelling, Friedrich Wilhelm Joseph von
German. Philosopher
Spokesman of Romantic thought, ideals; father of existential tendencies in modern art.
b. Jan 27, 1775 in Wurttemberg, Germany
d. Aug 20, 1854 in Bad Ragaz, Switzerland
Source: *BbD; Benet 87, 96; BiD&SB; BiDPsy; BiDTran; BioIn 7, 11, 17, 23; BlkwCE; CamBiEn; CasWL; CelCen; ChamBiD; CyEd; DcBiPP; DcEuL; DcLB 90; Dis&D; EncEth; EuAu; EvEuW; InSci; LinLib L, S; LuthC 75; McGEWB; NamesHP; NewC; OxCEng 67, 85, 95; OxCGer 76, 86, 97; OxCPhil; PenC EUR; RAdv 13-4; REn; WhoChr*

Schembechler, Bo
[Glenn Edward Schembechler]
American. Football Coach, Baseball Executive
Assistant coach, Ohio State under Woody Hayes, 1958-62; head coach, U of M, 1969-89; president, Detroit Tigers, 1990—.
b. Apr 1, 1929 in Barberton, Ohio
Source: *BiDAmSp FB; BioIn 10, 11, 12, 16; ConAu 139; News 90, 90-3; NewYTBS 76; WhoAm 84, 86, 88, 90, 92, 94; WhoFtbl 74; WhoMW 92; WhoSpor*

Schenck, Joseph M
American. Film Executive, Producer
Chm., 20th Century-Fox, 1935-41; produced all of Buster Keaton's Silent films.
b. Dec 25, 1878 in Rybinsk, Russia
d. Oct 22, 1961 in Beverly Hills, California
Source: *FilmEn; FilmgC; OxCFilm; WhAm 4*

Schenck, Nicholas Michael
American. Film Executive
Pres., Loew's, Inc., 1927-55.
b. Nov 14, 1881 in Rybinsk, Russia
d. Mar 3, 1969 in Miami Beach, Florida
Source: *AmNatBi; BioIn 8; DcAmB S8; DcFM; FilmEn; FilmgC; OxCFilm; WhAm 5; WorEFlm*

Schenck, Robert Cumming
American. Politician
Whig-Rep. congressman from OH, 1843-51, 1863-71; minister to Brazil, 1851-53, to England, 1871-76.
b. Oct 4, 1809 in Franklin, Ohio
d. Mar 23, 1890 in Washington, District of Columbia
Source: *Alli SUP; AmBi; AmNatBi; ApCAB; BiAUS; BiDrAC; BiDrUSC 89; BioIn 7, 10, 12, 16; DcAmB; DcAmDH 80, 89; Drake; HarEnUS; NatCAB 3; OhA&B; TwCBDA; WhAm HS; WhAmP; WhCiWar*

Schenk, Ard
Dutch. Skater
Won three speed skating gold medals, 1972 Olympics.
b. Sep 19, 1944 in Anna Paulowna, Netherlands
Source: *BioIn 10*

Schenkel, Chris(topher Eugene)
American. Sportscaster
Broadcaster for more than 50 yrs. including 30 yrs. on ABC's Pro Bowling.
b. Aug 21, 1924 in Bippus, Indiana
Source: *BioIn 6, 9, 10; BioNews 74; LesBEnT, 92; WhoAm 86*

Schenkkan, Robert
American. Dramatist
Winner of Pulitzer Prize for drama, *The Kentucky Cycle,* 1992.
b. Mar 19, 1953 in Chapel Hill, North Carolina
Source: *ConAu 132; ConTFT 4; WhoPul*

Scherchen, Hermann
German. Conductor
Led European orchestras, from 1911; conducted premieres of many ultramodern works.
b. Jun 21, 1891 in Berlin, Germany
d. Jun 12, 1966 in Florence, Italy
Source: *BakBD 78, 84, 92; BakBDTw; BioIn 4, 5, 7, 11; BriBkM 80; CmOp; DcArts; FacFETw; MusSN; NewAmDM; NewEOp 71; NewGrDM 80; NewGrDO; OxDcOp; PenDiMP; WhAm 5*

Scherer, Ray(mond Lewis)
American. Broadcast Journalist, Business Executive
Former NBC News correspondent, now vp, RCA, 1975—.
b. Jun 7, 1919 in Fort Wayne, Indiana
d. Jul 1, 2000 in Washington, District of Columbia
Source: *ConAu 104; Dun&B 88; LElec; LesBEnT 92; St&PR 84, 87; WhoAm 74, 76, 78, 80, 82, 84, 86; WhoWor 74*

Scherman, Harry
American. Publisher, Author
Co-founded Book of the Month Club, 1926.
b. Feb 1, 1887 in Montreal, Quebec, Canada
d. Nov 12, 1969 in New York, New York
Source: *AmAu&B; AmNatBi; BioIn 1, 6, 7, 8, 9, 12; CurBio 43, 63, 70; DcAmB S8; EncTwCJ; NatCAB 58; WhAm 5; WhE&EA; WhoWorJ 72*

Scherman, Thomas Kielty
American. Conductor
Founded NYC's Little Orchestra Society, 1947-75; son of Harry.
b. Feb 12, 1917 in New York, New York
d. May 14, 1979 in New York, New York

Source: *BakBD 84; BakBDTw; BioIn 10; ConAu 106; CurBio 54, 79; NewYTBS 79; WhoWor 74*

Scherr, Max
American. Lawyer, Publisher
Founded the radical *Berkeley Barb*, 1965; editor until 1973.
b. 1916?
d. Oct 31, 1981 in Berkeley, California
Source: *AnObit 1982; BioIn 8, 12; ConAu 105*

Scheuer, Philip K(latz)
American. Critic, Editor
Film, drama critic, LA *Times*, 1927-67.
b. Mar 24, 1902 in Newark, New Jersey
d. Feb 18, 1985 in Hollywood, California
Source: *BiE&WWA; ConAu 115; IntMPA 75*

Schiaparelli
[Elsa Schiaparelli]
Italian. Fashion Designer
Known for exaggerated shoulders, nipped waistline, bizarre hats; introduced "shocking pink," 1939.
b. Sep 10, 1890 in Rome, Italy
d. Nov 14, 1973 in Paris, France
Source: *BioIn 1, 2, 3, 5, 9, 10; ConAu 113; ConFash; ContDcW 89; CurBio 40, 51, 74, 74N; EncFash; FairDF FRA; InWom SUP; LegTOT; LinLib S; NewYTBE 73; WhAm 6; Who 74; WhoFash 88; WhoWor 74; WomFir; WorAlBi; WorFshn*

Schiaparelli, Giovanni
Italian. Explorer, Scientist
Director, Milan Observatory, 1862-1900; discovered asteroid Hesperia, 1861.
b. Mar 14, 1835 in Savigliano, Italy
d. Jul 4, 1910 in Milan, Italy
Source: *AsBiEn; NewCol 75*

Schiavo, Mary (Fackler)
American. Political Activist, Government Official
Outraged at a lack of concern for safety at the Federal Aeronautics Agency (FAA), resigned from position as Inspector General of the United States Department of Transportation as a protest, 1996.
b. Sep 4, 1955 in Pioneer, Ohio
Source: *WhoAm 98, 99; WhoAmW 99*

Schick, Bela
American. Scientist, Physician
Developed Schick test for diphtheria, 1913; wrote *Child Care Today*, 1932.
b. Jul 16, 1877 in Bolgar, Austria-Hungary
d. Dec 6, 1967 in New York, New York
Source: *AmNatBi; BioIn 3, 4, 6, 8, 9, 22; CamDcAB; CurBio 44, 68; DcAmMeB 84; EncAB-A 40; InSci; JeAmHC; NatCAB 53; NotTwCS 1S; ObitT 1961; RanHWDS; WebAB 74, 79; WhAm 4*

Schick, Jacob
American. Inventor
Introduced electric razor, 1931.
b. Sep 16, 1877 in Des Moines, Iowa
d. Jul 3, 1937 in New York, New York
Source: *BioIn 11; Entr; NatCAB 30; WorAl; WorAlBi*

Schickel, Richard
American. Critic, Author
Time magazine movie critic, 1973—.
b. Feb 10, 1933 in Milwaukee, Wisconsin
Source: *AuNews 1; BioIn 10; ConAu 1NR, 1R, 34NR; ConTFT 10, 18; IntAu&W 91, 93; IntWW 89, 91, 93, 97, 98, 2000; WhoAm 74, 76, 78, 80, 82, 84, 86, 88, 92, 94, 95, 96, 97, 98, 99, 2000; WhoE 74; WhoEnt 92, 98; WhoUSWr 88; WhoWest 00; WhoWrEP 89, 92, 95; WorAu 1980; WrDr 76, 80, 82, 84, 86, 88, 90, 92*

Schickele, Peter
American. Composer, Musician
Created mythical, zany composer, PDQ Bach, who lampoons music classics; wrote score, lyrics for *Oh, Calcutta*.
b. Jul 17, 1935 in Ames, Iowa
Source: *ASCAP 66, 80; BakBD 78, 84, 92; BakBDTw; BakDcM; BioIn 8, 11, 12, 14; ConAmC 76, 76A, 82; ConAu 85; ConMus 5; CpmDNM 78, 79, 81, 82; CurBio 79; IntWWM 90; NewAmDM; NewGrDA 86; NewGrDM 80; NewGrDO; PenEncP; WhoAm 76, 78, 80, 82, 84, 86, 88, 90, 92, 94, 95, 96, 97, 98, 99, 2000; WhoAmM 83; WhoEnt 92, 98; WhoWor 74*

Schieffer, Bob
American. Broadcast Journalist
Anchor, correspondent, CBS News, since 1969.
b. Feb 25, 1937 in Austin, Texas
Source: *BioIn 15; ConAu 69; ConTFT 26; EncTelN; EncTwCJ; IntWW 91; JrnUS; LesBEnT, 92; WhoAm 86, 90; WhoAmP 1999; WhoTelC*

Schiele, Egon
Austrian. Artist
Expressionist painter; concentrated on the erotic portrayal of the human figure.
b. Jun 12, 1890 in Tulln, Austria
d. Oct 31, 1918 in Vienna, Austria
Source: *Benet 87, 96; BioIn 4, 5, 7, 9, 10, 11, 12, 14, 17, 23; CamBiEn; ChamBiD; DcArts; DcTwArt; EncWB, 98; FacFETw; IntDcAA 90; McGDA; ModArCr 4; OxCTwCA; OxDcArt; PhDcTCA 77*

Schiess, Betty Bone
American. Clergy
One of the "Philadelphia Eleven," a group of Episcopalian women ordained as priests in 1974; inducted into National Women's Hall of Fame, 1994.
b. Apr 2, 1923 in Cincinnati, Ohio
Source: *BioIn 10; EncWB 99; WhoAm 96, 97, 98, 99, 2000; WhoAmW 81, 83,*

85, 87, 89, 91, 93, 95, 97, 99; WhoE 97; WhoRel 77, 85, 92

Schiff, Dorothy
American. Publisher, Journalist
First woman publisher in US; bought controlling interest in *New York Post*, 1939; responsible for turning it into a tabloid with scandal, glamour, columnists; sold to Rupert Murdoch, 1976.
b. Mar 11, 1903 in New York, New York
d. Aug 30, 1989 in New York, New York
Source: *AmAu&B; AmNatBi; AnObit 1989; BiDAmBL 83; BiDAmNC; BioAmW; BioIn 4, 5, 7, 8, 10, 11, 16, 19, 22, 24; CelR; ConAu 114, 121, 129; CurBio 45, 65, 89, 89N; DcLB 127; EncAJ; EncTwCJ; ForWC 70; GoodHs; IntWW 74, 75, 76, 77, 78, 79, 80; InWom, SUP; LegTOT; LibW; NewYTBS 76, 89; ScrEAmL 2; WhoAm 74, 76; WhoAmW 58, 61, 64, 66, 68, 70, 72, 74, 75, 77; WhoE 74, 75, 77; WhoWor 74; WhoWorJ 72, 78; WorAl*

Schiff, Jacob Henry
American. Philanthropist
His banking syndicates played major role in railroad, industrial mergers, 1890s; created Semitic Museum at Harvard.
b. Jan 10, 1847 in Frankfurt am Main, Germany
d. Sep 25, 1920
Source: *AmBi; AmNatBi; AmSetPR; BiDAmBL 83; BioIn 5, 8, 9, 11, 12, 14, 15, 17, 19, 21, 22; CamDcAB; DcAmB; DcNAA; EncAB-H 1974, 1996; EncABHB 6; EncWB 98; HarEnUS; McGEWB; NatCAB 13; WhAm 1*

Schiffer, Claudia
German. Model
Model noted for her physical similarity to Brigitte Bardot.
b. Aug 24, 1971 in Dusseldorf, Germany
Source: *BioIn 16; IntWW 93, 97, 98, 2000; IntWWW 2*

Schifrin, Lalo Claudio
Argentine. Composer
Wrote for films, TV; four Grammys include score for TV's "Mission Impossible."
b. Jun 21, 1932 in Buenos Aires, Argentina
Source: *BakBD 84; BiDAmM; BioIn 8, 9; ConTFT 5; IntMPA 84, 92; NewAmDM; NewGrDA 86; NewGrDJ 88; NewGrDM 80; OxCPMus; PenEncP; RkOn 82; WhoAm 82, 88; WhoEnt 92; WorEFlm*

Schifter, Peter Mark
American. Conductor
Has been guest director of operas in Washington, DC; Seattle; Philadelphia; and other US cities.
b. 1950 in Westfield, New Jersey
d. Sep 10, 1993 in New York, New York

Source: *BioIn 12; WhoAmM 83*

Schikaneder, Emanuel
[Johann Jakob Schikaneder]
Austrian. Producer, Actor, Librettist
Collaborated with Mozart on *Die Zauberflote,* 1791.
b. Sep 1, 1748 in Straubing, Austria
d. Sep 21, 1812 in Vienna, Austria
Source: *BioIn 9; NewEOp 71; OxCMus*

Schildkraut, Joseph
American. Actor
Won Oscar, 1937, for *The Life of Emile Zola;* son of Rudolph.
b. Mar 22, 1896 in Vienna, Austria
d. Jan 21, 1964 in New York, New York
Source: *BiE&WWA; BioIn 10; CurBio 56, 64; DcAmB S7; EncAB-A 35; FamA&A; FilmgC; ForYSC; FrSilen; MotPP; MovMk; NotNAT A; TwYS; WhAm 4; WhoHol B; WhScrn 74, 77, 83; WhThe; WorAl; WorAlBi*

Schildkraut, Rudolph
American. Actor
Silent films include *Turkish Delight; The King of Kings,* 1927.
b. 1865 in Constantinople, Turkey
d. Jul 30, 1930 in Los Angeles, California
Source: *Film 1; FilmEn; NotNAT B; TwYS; WhoHol B; WhScrn 74, 77, 83*

Schillebeeckx, Edward (Cornelis Florentius Alfons)
Belgian. Theologian, Clergy
Priest was one of the most influential Roman Catholic thinkers of his day
b. Nov 12, 1914 in Antwerp, Belgium
Source: *CamBiEn; ChamBiD; WhoChr*

Schiller, Friedrich von
[Johann Christoph Friedrich von Schiller]
German. Author, Dramatist
Leading German playwright; wrote historical drama *Wilhelm Tell,* 1804.
b. Nov 10, 1759 in Marbach, Germany
d. May 9, 1805 in Weimar, Germany
Source: *AtlBL; BakBD 78, 84; BakDcM; BbD; Benet 87; BiD&SB; BioIn 1, 2, 3, 4, 5, 6, 7, 9, 10, 11, 13; BlkCE; CasWL; CelCen; ChhPo, S1, S2; CnThe; CyWA 58; DcArts; DcBiPP; DcEnL; DcEuL; EncWT; Ent; EuAu; EuWr 5; EvEuW; GrFLW; LegTOT; LinLib L, S; LuthC 75; McGEWB; McGEWD 72, 84; MetOEnc; NewC; NewCBEL; NewEOp 71; NotNAT A, B; OxCEng 67, 85, 95; OxCFr; OxCGer 76; OxCPhil; OxCThe 67, 83; OxDcOp; PenC EUR; RAdv 14, 13-2; RComWL; REn; REnWD; WorAlBi; WrPh*

Schiller, Karl (August Fritz)
German. Government Official
Directed reconstruction of Hamburg after WW II.
b. Apr 24, 1911
d. Dec 26, 1994 in Hamburg, Germany
Source: *BioIn 8, 9, 10, 20, 21; CurBio 71, 95N; IntWW 74, 75, 76, 77, 78, 79,*

80, 81, 82, 83, 89, 91, 93; *IntYB 78, 79, 80, 81, 82; Who 74, 82, 83, 85, 88, 90, 92, 94; WhoWor 74, 78, 80, 82*

Schilling, Peter
German. Singer
First single, "Major Tom (Coming Home)," was int'l hit, 1983.
b. Jan 28, 1956 in Stuttgart, Germany (West)
Source: *RkOn 85*

Schillinger, Joseph
American. Composer, Musician
Composers Gershwin, Levant and others used his musical system.
b. Sep 1, 1895 in Kharkov, Russia
d. Mar 23, 1943 in New York, New York
Source: *AmNatBi; BakBD 78, 84; BiDAmM; BioIn 1, 2, 11; CamDcAB; ConAmC 76, 82; CurBio 43; DcAmB S3; DcCM; EncAB-A 11; NewAmDM; NewGrDA 86; NewGrDM 80; OxCMus*

Schillings, Max von
German. Conductor, Composer
Wrote opera, *Mona Lisa,* 1915.
b. Apr 19, 1868 in Duren, Germany
d. Jul 23, 1933 in Berlin, Germany
Source: *BakBD 78, 84, 92; BakBDTw; MetOEnc; NewEOp 71; NewGrDM 80; NewGrDO; OxCGer 76, 86, 97; OxCMus; OxDcOp; PenDiMP A*

Schilt, Jan
American. Astronomer
Invented Schilt photometer, which measures distance of stars from Earth.
b. Feb 23, 1894 in Gouda, Netherlands
d. Jan 9, 1982 in Englewood, New Jersey
Source: *AmNatBi; AnObit 1982; BioIn 12, 13; NewYTBS 82; WhAm 8*

Schily, Otto
German. Politician
Lawyer, and one of the chief spokespersons for Germany's Greens Party, advocating peace and environmental protection; served in the Bundestag, the lower house of West Germany's parliament, 1983-86; involved in other environmental conservation efforts.
b. c. 1932 in Bochum, Germany
Source: *BioIn 16; ConNews 87-4; IntWW 89, 91, 93, 97, 98, 2000*

Schindler, Alexander Moshe
American. Religious Leader
Leader in nat. Jewish, Zionist organizations since early 1960s; pres., Union of American Hebrew Congregations, 1973—.
b. Oct 4, 1925 in Munich, Germany
Source: *BioIn 15; CurBio 87; IntWW 89, 91, 93, 97, 98, 2000; NewYTBE 73; WhoAm 76, 78, 80, 82, 84, 86, 88, 90, 92, 94, 95, 96, 97, 98, 99, 2000; WhoE 74, 75, 77, 86, 89, 91, 95, 97, 99;*

WhoRel 75, 77, 85, 92; WhoWor 78, 80, 82; WhoWorJ 72, 78

Schindler, Oskar
German. Business Executive
Employed more than one thousand Jews from Poland and Czechoslovakia in his factory during World War II, saving them from the Nazi death camps.
b. Apr 28, 1908 in Zwittau, Moravia, Austria-Hungary
d. Oct 9, 1974 in Frankfurt, Germany (West)
Source: *BioIn 10, 13, 16, 19, 20, 21, 23, 24; ConHero 3; EncGRNM; EncWB 99; HeroCon*

Schindler, Solomon
American. Clergy, Social Reformer
Rabbi and social theorist contributed to the reform movement in Judaism and to the religious socialism of his era.
b. Apr 24, 1842 in Neisse, Germany
d. May 5, 1915
Source: *Alli SUP; AmRef; BioIn 2, 3, 15; DcAmAu; DcAmB; DcNAA; EncWB 98; McGEWB; NatCAB 7; ScF&FL 1; ScFEYrs; WhAm 1*

Schine, G(erard) David
American. Businessman
Music, hotel exec., who produced *The French Connection,* 1971; directed special govt. investigations, 1952-53.
b. Sep 11, 1927 in Gloversville, New York
d. Jun 19, 1996 in Burbank, California
Source: *BioIn 3, 8, 10, 11; EncMcCE; PolProf E; St&PR 84, 91; WhAm 11; WhoAm 74, 76, 78, 80, 82, 84, 86, 88, 90, 92, 94, 95, 96; WhoWor 74*

Schinkel, Karl Friedrich
German. Architect, Painter, Designer
One of the most important and influential architects of his time, he worked in both the medieval and the classical traditions.
b. Mar 13, 1781 in Neuruppin, Germany
d. Oct 9, 1841 in Berlin, Germany
Source: *ArtsNiC; BioIn 2, 11, 12, 14, 15, 18, 19; CamBiEn; ChamBiD; DcArch; DcArts; DcBiPP; DcD&D; DcNiCA; EncMA; EncWB 98; EncWT; IntDcAr; LuthC 75; MacEA; McGEWB; MetOEnc; NewGrDM 80; NewGrDO; OxCArt; OxDcArt; OxDcOp; PenDiDA 89; WhDW; WhoArch*

Schioetz, Aksel
"The Voice of Denmark"
Danish. Singer, Educator
Broadcast daily patriotic songs defying Nazi occupation during WW II.
b. Sep 1, 1906 in Roskilde, Denmark
d. Apr 19, 1975 in Copenhagen, Denmark
Source: *ConAu 111; CurBio 49, 75; MusSN*

Schipa, Tito
Italian. Opera Singer
Tenor with NY Met., 1932-35, 1940;
noted for Rossini, Bellini roles.
b. Jan 2, 1889 in Lecce, Italy
d. Dec 16, 1965 in New York, New
York
Source: *BakBD 78, 84; BioIn 1, 4, 6, 7,
11, 12, 16, 18, 21; LegTOT; MusSN;
NewEOp 71; WhAm 4; WhoHol B;
WhScrn 74, 77, 83*

Schippers, Thomas
American. Conductor
Youngest ever to lead NY Met., 1955;
conducted record number of Met.
premieres; led Cincinnati Orchestra,
1970-77.
b. Mar 9, 1930 in Kalamazoo, Michigan
d. Dec 16, 1977 in New York, New
York
Source: *AmNatBi; BakBD 78, 84, 92;
BakBDTw; BiDAmM; BioIn 3, 4, 5, 6, 7,
8, 9, 10, 11, 21; BlueB 76; BriBkM 80;
CamDcAB; CelR; CmOp; CurBio 70, 78,
78N; DcAmB S10; IntDcOp; IntWW 74,
75, 76, 77; IntWWM 77, 80; MetOEnc;
MusSN; NewAmDM; NewEOp 71;
NewGrDA 86; NewGrDM 80;
NewGrDO; NewYTBS 77; OxDcOp;
PenDiMP; WhAm 7; WhoAm 74, 76, 78;
WhoMus 72; WhoMW 74, 76; WhoOp
76; WhoWor 74; WorAl; WorAlBi*

Schirmer, Gustave
German. Publisher, Musician
Founded Schirmer music publishing co.,
1866; published Wagner's works.
b. Sep 19, 1829 in Konigsee, Germany
d. Aug 6, 1893 in Eisenach, Germany
Source: *DcAmB; WebAB 74; WhAm HS*

Schirra, Wally
[Walter Marty Schirra, Jr]
American. Astronaut, Businessman
Pilot, Gemini 6, 1965; commander,
Apollo 7, 1968.
b. Mar 12, 1923 in Hackensack, New
Jersey
Source: *AmMWSc 73P; BioIn 6, 7, 8, 9,
10, 13, 16; CurBio 66; FacFETw;
IntWW 74, 75, 76, 77; LegTOT;
WebAMB; WhoAm 74, 76, 78, 80, 82,
84, 86, 88, 90, 92, 94, 95, 96, 97;
WhoFI 96; WhoScEn 94, 96; WhoSpc;
WhoTech 89; WhoWest 96; WhoWor 74,
78, 80, 82, 84, 87, 89, 91, 93, 95, 96,
97; WorAl; WorAlBi*

Schisgal, Murray Joseph
American. Dramatist
Avant-garde playwright with comic-sad
heroes: *Luv*, 1963, ran on Broadway
for 900 performances; screenplays
include *Tootsie*, 1982.
b. Nov 25, 1926 in New York, New
York
Source: *BiE&WWA; BioIn 15; CnMD
SUP; ConAu 86NR; ConDr 82, 88;
ConLC 6; ConTFT 5; CroCD; CurBio
68; DrAPF 87, 91; EncAHmr; IntAu&W
86; McGEWD 72; ModAL 4; ModWD;
NotNAT; WhoAm 86, 90, 97, 98, 99,*

2000; *WhoEnt 92, 98; WorAu 1950;
WrDr 86, 92*

Schlafly, Phyllis Stewart
American. Anti-Feminist, Author,
Politician
Outspoken ultra-conservative opponent of
ERA; wrote many books championing
conservatism, warning against
communism: *A Choice, Not an Echo*,
1964.
b. Aug 15, 1924 in Saint Louis, Missouri
Source: *AmSocL; AuNews 1; BiDAmNC;
BioIn 13, 14, 15; BioNews 74; ConAu
26NR; CurBio 78; DcAmC; DrAS 99H;
EncAWoR; EncWB; IntAu&W 89, 91,
93; InWom SUP; NewYTBS 80; PolProf
NF; WhoAm 76, 78, 80, 82, 84, 86, 88,
90, 92, 94, 95, 96, 97, 98, 99, 2000;
WhoAmP 73, 89, 91, 93, 95, 97, 1999;
WhoAmW 58, 61, 79, 81, 83, 85, 87, 89,
91, 93, 95, 97, 99; WhoEnt 92, 98;
WhoMW 84, 86, 88, 90, 92, 98;
WhoUSWr 88; WhoWor 99, 2000;
WhoWrEP 89, 92, 95*

Schlamme, Martha
Austrian. Singer, Actor
Known for singing folk songs in 12
languages; made Broadway debut,
1968, in *Fiddler on the Roof*.
b. 1930 in Vienna, Austria
d. Oct 6, 1985 in Jamestown, New York
Source: *BioIn 6, 7; CurBio 64, 86;
InWom; WhoAm 74*

Schlegel, Friedrich von
[Karl Wilhelm Friedrich von Schlegel]
German. Critic
Wrote history of literature; studies of
ancient Indian language; wrote novel
Lucinde, 1799.
b. Mar 10, 1772 in Hannover, Germany
d. Jan 12, 1829 in Dresden, Germany
Source: *AtlBL; BbD; BiD&SB; BiDTran;
BioIn 5, 7, 14, 16, 17, 23; BlkwCE;
CasWL; DcArts; DcBiPP; DcCathB;
DcEuL; EuAu; EuWr 5; LinLib L; LuthC
75; McGDA; McGEWB; NewC;
NewCBEL; OxCEng 67, 85, 95; OxCGer
76, 86; PenC EUR; REn; REnWD;
RfGWoL 95; WorAl; WorAlBi*

Schleicher, Kurt von
German. Political Leader
Chancellor of Germany, 1932-33;
succeeded by Hitler.
b. Apr 7, 1882 in Brandenburg, Germany
d. Jun 30, 1934 in Berlin, Germany
Source: *BioIn 5, 14; CamBiEn;
ChamBiD; DcTwHis; EncTR, 91;
NewCol 75; REn; WebBD 83*

Schleiden, Matthias Jakob
German. Botanist
Study of plant structure established that
plants are made up of cells; theorized
importance of nucleus in mitosis.
b. Apr 5, 1804 in Hamburg, Germany
d. Jun 23, 1881 in Frankfurt am Main,
Germany

Source: *AsBiEn; BiESc; BioIn 4, 12, 14;
ChamBiD; DcScB; LarDcSc; RanHWDS;
WorAlBi*

**Schleiermacher, Friedrich Ernst
Daniel**
German. Theologian, Philosopher
One of the founders of modern
Protestant theology.
b. Nov 21, 1768 in Breslau, Germany
d. Feb 12, 1834 in Berlin, Germany
Source: *Benet 87; BioIn 2, 7, 8, 9, 11,
12; CamBiEn; CelCen; ChamBiD;
DcBiPP; EncUnb; EncWB 98; LinLib L,
S; McGEWB*

Schlein, Miriam
[Miriam Weiss]
American. Children's Author
Writer since 1952: *Giraffe: The Silent
Giant*, 1976; *The Boy Who Became
Pharaoh*, 1979.
b. Jun 6, 1926 in New York, New York
Source: *AuBYP 2, 3; BioIn 5, 6, 7, 9;
ChlLR 41; ConAu 1R, 2NR, 52NR;
CurBio 59; IntAu&W 91; InWom;
MorJA; PenNWW A; SJGChWr 5;
SmATA 2, 87; TwCChW 3; WhoAmW 58,
61, 91; WrDr 92*

Schlemmer, Oskar
German. Artist, Designer
A painter, sculptor, and stage designer,
his works depict the human figure in
puppet-like, two-dimensional shapes
evoking the machine age.
b. 1888 in Stuttgart, Germany
d. Apr 1943 in Baden-Baden, Germany
Source: *Benet 87; BiDD; BioIn 2, 4, 9,
15, 17, 20; CamBiEn; CamGWoT;
ChamBiD; CnOxB; ConArt 77, 83;
DcArts; DcTwArt; DcTwDes; EncWB,
98; EncWT; Ent; FacFETw; IntDcAA
90; McGDA; OxCArt; OxCTwCA;
OxDcArt; PhDcTCA 77; TheaDir*

Schlesinger, Arthur M(eier), Jr.
American. Historian, Author
Special asst. to presidents Kennedy,
Johnson, 1961-64; wrote *A Thousand
Days*, 1965; *Robert Kennedy and His
Times*, 1978.
b. Oct 15, 1917 in Columbus, Ohio
Source: *AuNews 1; Benet 87, 96;
BenetAL 91; BioIn 1, 2, 3, 4, 5, 6, 7, 8,
10, 11, 12, 13, 14, 15; CamBiEn;
ChamBiD; ColdWar 2; ConAu 1NR, 1R,
28NR, 58NR; ConLC 84; CurBio 46, 79;
EncAB-H 1996; EncAInt; EncWB, 98;
IntAu&W 91; IntWW 89; MajTwCW 1,
2; NewYTBS 79; OhA&B; OxCAmL 65;
OxCTwCL; PenC AM; PolProf E, J, K,
T; RAdv 14, 13-3; REn; REnAL; SmATA
61; WebAB 79; Who 92, 98, 99, 2000;
WhoAm 86, 90, 97, 98, 99, 2000; WhoE
97; WhoEnt 98; WhoPul; WhoUSWr 88;
WhoWor 91, 97, 98, 99, 2000;
WhoWrEP 89; WorAlBi; WorAu 1900;
WrDr 92, 98, 99, 2000*

Schlesinger, Frank
American. Astronomer, Educator
Developed method for determining stellar
distances by photography.
b. May 11, 1871 in New York, New
York
d. Jul 10, 1943 in Old Lyme,
Connecticut
Source: *AmNatBi; BioIn 1, 20;
CamDcAB; CurBio 43; DcAmB S3;
DcScB; InSci; NatCAB 14, 32; WhAm 2;
WhNAA*

Schlesinger, James Rodney
American. Government Official
Secretary of Defense, 1973-75; Energy,
1977-79.
b. Feb 15, 1929 in New York, New
York
Source: *AmMWSc 73S; BioIn 9, 10, 11,
12, 14; CamDcAB; CngDr 74; ColdWar
2; CurBio 73; EncAInt; EncWB, 98;
IntWW 74, 75, 76, 77, 78, 79, 80, 81, 82,
83, 89, 91, 93, 97, 98; IntYB 78, 79, 80,
81, 82; NewYTBE 71, 72; NewYTBS 74,
76; Ward 77D; WhoAm 74, 76, 78, 80,
82, 84, 86, 88, 90, 92, 94, 95, 96, 97,
98, 99, 2000; WhoAmP 73, 75, 77, 79,
81, 83, 85, 87, 89, 91, 93, 95, 97, 1999;
WhoE 77, 79, 81, 83; WhoFI 79;
WhoGov 72, 75, 77; WhoSSW 73, 75,
76; WhoWor 74, 78, 80, 82, 84, 87, 89,
91, 93, 95, 96, 97, 98, 99, 2000;
WorAlBi*

Schlesinger, John Richard
English. Director
Won Oscar, 1969, for *Midnight Cowboy.*
b. Feb 16, 1926 in London, England
Source: *BiDFilm; BioIn 16; ChamBiD;
CurBio 70; DcFM; FilmgC; HalFC 88;
IntDcF 2-2; IntMPA 92; IntWW 74, 75,
76, 77, 78, 79, 80, 81, 82, 83, 89, 91,
93, 97, 98, 2000; MovMk; NewGrDO;
OxCFilm; Who 74, 82, 83, 85, 88, 90,
92, 94, 98, 99, 2000; WhoAm 78, 80, 82,
84, 86, 88, 90, 92, 94, 95, 96, 97, 98,
99, 2000; WhoEnt 92, 98; WhoThe 81;
WhoWor 74, 76, 78, 82, 84, 87, 89, 91,
93, 95, 96, 97, 98, 99, 2000; WorEFlm*

Schlessinger, David
American. Businessman
Founded Encore Books, discount
bookstore chain, 1973.
b. Mar 3, 1955 in Philadelphia,
Pennsylvania
Source: *ConNews 85-1*

Schlessinger, Laura
American. Author, Physiologist, Radio
Performer
Host of "The Dr. Laura Schlessinger
Show," 1990—; author of *Courage,
and Conscience,* 1996.
b. c. 1947 in New York, New York
Source: *ConAu 152; CurBio 97; News
96, 96-3; WrDr 99, 2000*

Schley, Winfield Scott
American. Naval Officer
Led battle of Santiago, Spanish-
American War, 1898; controversy

arose about credit of battle between
him and W T Sampson.
b. Oct 9, 1839 in Frederick County,
Maryland
d. Oct 2, 1909 in New York, New York
Source: *Alli SUP; AmBi; AmNatBi;
ApCAB, SUP, X; BiDSA; BioIn 1, 13;
CamDcAB; DcAmAu; DcAmB;
DcAmMiB; DcNAA; EncNaHi;
HarEnMi; HarEnUS; LinLib L, S;
NatCAB 4, 9; OxCShps; SpAmWar;
TwCBDA; WebAMB; WhAm 1*

Schlick, Friedrich Albert Moritz
German. Physicist, Philosopher
Founding spirit of the Vienna Circle, he
revived positivism as a leading force
in 20th-century thought.
b. Feb 28, 1882 in Berlin, Germany
d. Jun 22, 1936 in Vienna, Austria
Source: *EncWB 98; McGEWB; OxCPhil*

Schlicter, Art(hur E)
American. Football Player
Quarterback, Baltimore/Indianapolis,
1982, 1984-85; suspended for
gambling, 1983.
b. Apr 25, 1960 in Washington Court
House, Ohio
Source: *BioIn 15, 16; FootReg 85*

Schlieffen, Alfred, Graf von
German. Military Leader
WW I field marshal; developed
"swinging door" plan to crush French
resistance.
b. Feb 28, 1833 in Berlin, Germany
d. Jan 4, 1913 in Berlin, Germany
Source: *BioIn 24; CamBiEn; ChamBiD;
NewCol 75; WebBD 83; WhoMilH 76;
WorAl; WorAlBi*

Schliemann, Heinrich
German. Archaeologist
Excavated cities for remains of Homeric
age; known for discovery of ancient
Troy.
b. Jan 6, 1822 in Neubuckow, Germany
d. Dec 26, 1890 in Naples, Italy
Source: *Alli SUP; AmBi; BbD; Benet 87,
96; BiD&SB; BioIn 1, 2, 4, 5, 6, 7, 8, 9,
10, 11, 12, 13, 14, 16, 17, 19, 20, 21,
22, 24; CamBiEn; CelCen; ChamBiD;
CmCal; DcScB; EncHiCA; InSci;
LegTOT; McGDA; McGEWB; NewC;
OxCClL, 89; OxCGer 76, 86, 97; REn;
WhAm HS; WhDW; WorAl; WorAlBi*

Schlink, Frederick John
American. Consultant
Headed Consumers' Research until 1983;
wrote *Eat, Drink and Be Wary,* 1935.
b. Oct 26, 1891
d. Jan 15, 1995 in Phillpsburg, New
Jersey
Source: *AmAu&B; BioIn 8; ConAu 65,
147; CurBio 95N; InSci; WhE&EA;
WhNAA; WhoAm 74, 76, 78, 80*

Schlondorff, Volker
German. Director, Screenwriter
Directed, wrote screen adaptation of *The
Tin Drum,* 1980; won best foreign film
Oscar.
b. Mar 31, 1939 in Wiesbaden, Germany
Source: *BiDFilm, 81, 94; BioIn 12, 13,
14, 16; CurBio 83; EncEurC; FilmEn;
HalFC 84, 88; IntDcF 1-2, 2-2; IntMPA
81, 82, 84, 86, 88, 92, 94, 96; IntWW
89, 91, 93, 97, 98, 2000; MiSFD 9;
OxCFilm; WhoWor 84, 87, 89, 91, 93,
95, 96, 99; WorFDir 2*

Schlumberger, Jean
French. Jeweler
Had own salon at Tiffany's, 1956-87; set
well-known 128-carat Tiffany
diamond; prominent jewelry designer.
b. Jun 24, 1907 in Muhlhausen, Germany
d. Aug 29, 1987 in Paris, France
Source: *AnObit 1987; CelR; EncFash;
FacFETw; NewYTBS 87; St&PR 75;
ThHDFas; WhoFash 88; WorFshn*

Schlusnus, Heinrich
German. Opera Singer
Baritone with Berlin Opera, 1917-45;
noted as Lieder singer, had several US
tours.
b. Aug 6, 1888 in Braubach, Germany
d. Jun 19, 1952 in Frankfurt, Germany
(West)
Source: *BakBD 78, 84, 92; BakBDTw;
BioIn 2; CmOp; IntDcOp; MetOEnc;
NewEOp 71; NewGrDM 80; NewGrDO;
OxDcOp; PenDiMP*

Schluter, Andreas
German. Architect, Sculptor
Leading proponent of the baroque style
in northern Germany, known for the
powerful, dynamic, and dignified
works.
b. c. 1660, Germany
d. 1714 in St. Petersburg, Russia
Source: *EncWB 98; IntDcAr; McGDA;
McGEWB; OxCGer 97; OxDcArt;
WhoArch*

Schluter, Poul (Holmskov)
Danish. Political Leader
Conservative Party leader formed a
minority government and became
prime minister of Denmark for the
first time in 1982; he set out to
severely limit the welfare state.
b. 1929 in Tonder, South Jutland,
Denmark
Source: *CamBiEn; ChamBiD; IntWW 83,
89, 91, 93, 97, 98, 2000; WhoWor 84,
87, 89, 91, 93, 95*

Schmedes, Erik
Danish. Opera Singer
One of leading heroic tenors of his day;
with Vienna Opera, 1898-1924.
b. Aug 6, 1866 in Gjentofte, Denmark
d. Mar 23, 1931 in Vienna, Austria
Source: *BakBD 84; CmOp; NewEOp 71;
NewGrDM 80; NewGrDO; OxDcOp;
PenDiMP*

Schmeling, Max(imilian)
"The Black Uhlan"
German. Boxer
World heavyweight champ, 1930-32;
  KO'd Joe Louis, 1936; Hall of Fame,
  1970.
b. Sep 28, 1905 in Brandenburg,
  Germany
Source: *BioIn 1, 2, 5, 7, 8, 9, 10, 11, 14,
16, 19; BoxReg; EncTR, 91; FacFETw;
LegTOT; What 1; WhoBox 74; WhoHol
92, A; WorAl*

Schmemann, Alexander
Russian. Clergy, Theologian
Eastern Orthodox leader; promoted
  religious freedom in Soviet Union.
b. 1921 in Estonia, Union of Soviet
  Socialist Republics
d. Dec 13, 1983 in Crestwood, New
  York
Source: *AnObit 1983; BiDChrM; BioIn
13, 19; ConAu 111, 117; DcEcMov;
EncARH; NewYTBS 83; RelLAm 1, 2*

Schmid, Eduard
[Kasimir Edschmid]
German. Author
Wrote first German expressionist
  novellas.
b. Oct 5, 1890 in Darmstadt, Germany
d. Aug 31, 1966 in Vulpera, Switzerland
Source: *BioIn 1, 2, 7, 16; CasWL;
ClDMEL 47, 80; ConAu 113; DcLB 56;
EncWL 1; ModGL; OxCGer 76, 86;
PenC EUR*

Schmidt, Alfred
German. Hostage
Engineer in Lebanon seized by
  Strugglers for Freedom January 21,
  1987 and released September 7, 1987.
Source: *AmEA 74; WhoWor 80*

Schmidt, Benno C(harles), Jr.
American. University Administrator,
  Lawyer
Pres., Yale U, 1986-92; pres., CEO
  Edison Project, national private school
  system, 1992—.
b. Mar 20, 1942 in Washington, District
  of Columbia
Source: *CurBio 86; IntWW 91;
NewYTBS 85; Who 90, 92, 94, 98, 99,
2000; WhoAm 86, 88, 90, 92, 94, 95, 96;
WhoAmL 87, 90; WhoE 86, 89, 91;
WhoSSW 95, 97, 99; WhoWor 89, 91,
93, 95; WorAlBi; WrDr 92, 94, 96, 98,
99, 2000*

Schmidt, Helmut Heinrich Waldemar
German. Political Leader
Chancellor, W Germany, 1974-82; author
  of several books on political affairs.
b. Dec 23, 1918 in Hamburg, Germany
Source: *BioIn 16; CamBiEn; ChamBiD;
ColdWar 2; CurBio 74; FacFETw;
IntWW 76, 77, 91; IntYB 79; NewYTBS
74, 76, 77; Who 85, 92; WhoWor 84;
WorAlBi*

Schmidt, Joe
[Joseph Paul Schmidt]
American. Football Player, Football
  Coach
Ten-time all-pro middle linebacker,
  Detroit, 1953-65; head coach, Detroit,
  1967-72; Hall of Fame, 1973.
b. Jan 18, 1932 in Pittsburgh,
  Pennsylvania
Source: *BiDAmSp FB; BioIn 5, 6, 8, 17;
LegTOT; WhoFtbl 74*

Schmidt, Mike
[Michael Jack Schmidt]
American. Baseball Player
Infielder, Philadelphia, 1972-89; led NL
  in home runs eight times, RBIs four ti
  mes; NL MVP, 1980-81, 86.
b. Sep 27, 1949 in Dayton, Ohio
Source: *Ballpl 90; BaseEn 88; BaseReg
87, 88; BiDAmSp BB; BioIn 10, 11, 12,
13, 14, 15, 16, 17, 18, 20, 23; ConAu
126; CulEncB; FacFETw; LegTOT;
News 88-3; NewYTBS 74, 89; WhoAm
80, 82, 84, 86, 88, 90, 92, 94, 95, 96,
97; WhoE 86, 89, 95; WhoSpor; WorAl;
WorAlBi*

Schmidt, Milt(on Conrad)
Canadian. Hockey Player, Hockey
  Coach, Hockey Executive
Center, Boston, 1936-55; won Art Ross
  Trophy, 1940, Hart Trophy, 1951;
  coach, Boston, 1955-66, GM, 1967-73;
  Hall of Fame, 1961.
b. Mar 5, 1918 in Kitchener, Ontario,
  Canada
Source: *BioIn 9, 10; HocEn; WhoAm 76;
WhoE 74, 75; WhoHcky 73*

Schmidt, Tim(othy B)
[Poco; The Eagles]
American. Singer, Musician
Joined The Eagles, 1977, replacing
  Randy Meisner.
b. Oct 30, 1947 in Oakland, California
Source: *RkOn 85*

Schmidt-Isserstedt, Hans
German. Conductor
Led int'l orchestras, 1935-60s; had US
  debut, 1963.
b. May 5, 1900 in Berlin, Germany
d. May 28, 1973 in Hamburg, Germany
  (West)
Source: *BakBD 78, 84, 92; BakBDTw;
BioIn 9, 10; BriBkM 80; CmOp;
NewAmDM; NewEOp 71; NewGrDM 80;
NewGrDO; NewYTBE 73; OxDcOp;
PenDiMP; WhAm 6; WhoMus 72*

Schmidt-Rottluf, Karl
German. Artist
Helped form German Expressionist
  group, Die Brucke, 1905; drew vividly
  colored landscapes, nudes.
b. Dec 1, 1884 in Rottluff, Germany
d. Aug 9, 1976 in Wiesbaden, Germany
  (West)
Source: *ConArt 83; McGDA; OxCArt;
OxCGer 76; WhoWor 74*

Schmiechen, Richard Kurt
American. Producer
Won Academy Award for documentary
  The Times of Harvey Milk, 1984.
b. Jul 10, 1947 in Saint Louis, Missouri
d. Apr 7, 1993 in California

Schmitt, Bernadotte Everly
American. Author, Educator
Modern history authority; won Pulitzer,
  1931, for *The Coming of War*, 1914.
b. May 19, 1886 in Strasburg, Virginia
d. Mar 22, 1969 in Alexandria, Virginia
Source: *AmAu&B; BioIn 4, 5, 8, 10, 22;
ConAu 1R, 103; CurBio 42, 69; NatCAB
55; ObitOF 79; OhA&B; OxCAmL 65;
TwCA, SUP; WhE&EA; WhNAA;
WhoPul; WorAu 1900*

Schmitt, Gladys
American. Author, Editor
Wrote historical, biographical, biblical
  works with love as recurring theme.
b. May 31, 1909 in Pittsburgh,
  Pennsylvania
d. Oct 3, 1972 in Pittsburgh,
  Pennsylvania
Source: *AmAu&B; AmNov; AmWomWr;
Au&Wr 71; BenetAL 91; BioIn 1, 2, 3,
4, 9, 12, 22; ConAu 1R, 2NR, 37R;
CurBio 43, 72, 72N; OxCAmL 65, 83,
95; REnAL; TwCA SUP; WhAm 5;
WhoAmW 58, 64, 66, 68, 70, 72, 74;
WorAu 1900*

Schmitt, Harrison Hagan
American. Politician, Astronaut
Conservative Rep. senator from NM,
  1977-83; piloted lunar module, Apollo
  17, 1972.
b. Jul 3, 1935 in Santa Rita, New
  Mexico
Source: *AmMWSc 95, 98; BiDrUSC 89;
BioIn 10, 11, 12, 13, 14; CngDr 77, 79;
CurBio 74; FacFETw; IntWW 83, 91;
NewYTBE 72; NewYTBS 79; WhoAm 78,
80, 82, 84, 86, 88, 90, 92, 94, 95, 96,
97; WhoAmP 77, 79, 81, 83, 85, 87, 89,
91, 93, 95, 97, 1999; WhoEng 88;
WhoGov 72, 75, 77; WhoScEn 94, 96;
WhoSSW 73, 75, 76; WhoWest 78, 80,
82; WhoWor 80, 82; WorAlBi*

Schmoke, Kurt L(idell)
American. Politician
Mayor of Baltimore, 1987—.
b. Dec 1, 1949 in Baltimore, Maryland
Source: *BioIn 15, 16; CamDcAB;
ConBlB 1; CurBio 95; InB&W 85;
NegAl 89A; WhoAm 90; WhoAmP 89;
WhoBlA 7; WhoE 91*

Schmoller, Gustav Friedrich von
German. Economist
Broadened the study of economics by
  insisting that it be studied dynamically
  in the context of history and the social
  sciences.
b. Jun 24, 1838 in Wurttemberg-Baden,
  Germany
d. Jun 27, 1917 in Bad Harzburg, Prussia
Source: *McGEWB*

Schnabel, Artur
American. Pianist
Had US debut, 1921; interpreter of
   Beethoven, Bach.
b. Apr 17, 1882 in Lipnik, Austria
d. Aug 15, 1951 in Axenstein,
   Switzerland
Source: AmNatBi; BakBD 78, 84, 92;
BakBDTw; BakDcM; BioIn 1, 2, 3, 4, 6,
7, 9, 10, 11, 12, 16, 21; BriBkM 80;
CamBiEn; ChamBiD; CurBio 42, 51;
DcAmB S5; DcArts; FacFETw; LegTOT;
MusMk; MusSN; NewAmDM; NewGrDA
86; NewGrDM 80; NotTwCP; ObitT
1951; OxCMus; PenDiMP; REn; WhAm
3

Schnabel, Julian
American. Artist
Neo-expressionist whose paintings are
   encrusted with crockery, plaster; had
   one-man show, NYC, 1981.
b. Oct 26, 1951 in New York, New York
Source: AmArt; BioIn 12, 13, 14, 15;
ChamBiD; ConArt 83, 89, 96; ConAu
156; CurBio 83; DcCAA 88, 94; DcCAr
81; DcTwArt; IntWW 91, 93, 97, 98,
2000; LegTOT; News 97, 97-1;
NewYTBS 84; PrintW 85; WhoAm 84,
86, 88, 90, 92, 94, 95, 96; WhoAmA 86,
89, 91, 93, 1999; WhoE 85, 86; WhoWor
97; WorArt 1980

Schnabel, Karl Ulrich
Austrian. Musician
Performed duo-piano concerts with wife,
   Helen Fogel, 1939-74; son of Artur.
b. Aug 6, 1909 in Berlin, Germany
Source: BakBD 78, 84, 92; BakBDTw;
IntWWM 77, 80, 85, 90; NewGrDM 80;
PenDiMP; WhoAm 74, 76, 78, 80, 82,
84, 86, 88, 90, 92, 94, 95; WhoEnt 92,
98; WhoMus 72; WorAl; WorAlBi

Schneerson, Menachem M(endel)
American. Religious Leader
Spiritual leader of orthodox Lubavitch
   Sect, most powerful branch of
   Hasidism.
b. Apr 18, 1902 in Nikolayev, Russia
d. Jun 12, 1994 in New York, New York
Source: AmNatBi; BioIn 4, 13;
CamDcAB; CurBio 83, 94N; EncARH;
News 92, 94; OrJudAm; RelLAm 1, 2;
WhoAmJ 80; WhoRel 85; WhoWorJ 78

Schneider, Alan
[Abram Leopoldovich]
American. Director
Won Tony, 1962, for Who's Afraid of
   Virginia Woolf.
b. Dec 12, 1917 in Kharkov, Union of
   Soviet Socialist Republics
d. May 3, 1984 in London, England
Source: AnObit 1984; BiE&WWA; BioIn
8, 9, 13; BlueB 76; CamGWoT; CelR;
ConTFT 1; CurBio 69, 84, 84N; EncWT;
FacFETw; GrStDi; LesBEnT; NewYTBS
84; NewYTET; NotNAT; OxCAmT 84;
ScrEAmL 1; TheaDir; WhAm 8, 11;
WhoAm 82; WhoThe 72, 77, 81;
WhoWor 84, 87, 89, 91

Schneider, Alexander
American. Musician
First to present all of Bach's
   unaccompanied violin works in
   concert; often accompanied Casals.
b. Oct 21, 1908 in Vilna, Russia
d. Feb 4, 1993 in New York, New York
Source: AmNatBi; BakBD 78, 84;
BiDAmM; BioIn 2, 8, 9, 10, 11, 14, 15,
18, 19, 23; BriBkM 80; CamDcAB;
CurBio 76, 93N; IntWWM 90;
NewAmDM; NewGrDA 86; NewGrDM
80; NewYTBS 93; PenDiMP; WhAm 11;
WhoAm 74, 76, 78, 80, 82, 84, 86, 88,
90, 92; WhoWor 74

Schneider, Bert
American. Producer
Won Oscar, 1974, for documentary
   Hearts and Minds.
b. 1933?
Source: HalFC 88; NewYTBS 75;
WhoAm 76; WhoAmA 76

Schneider, Herman
American. Children's Author
Writes science books for juveniles with
   wife Nina: Let's Find Out about the
   Weather, 1956.
b. May 31, 1905 in Kreschov, Poland
Source: Au&Wr 71; AuBYP 2, 3; BioIn
6, 7, 10; ConAu 16NR, 29R; IntAu&W
76, 77, 82; MorJA; SmATA 7

Schneider, John
American. Actor, Singer
Played Bo Duke on TV series "The
   Dukes of Hazard."
b. Apr 8, 1954 in Mount Kisco, New
   York
Source: BgBkCoM; BioIn 12; ConTFT 5;
HarEnCM 87; IntMPA 92, 94, 96;
LegTOT; VarWW 85; WhoHol 92

Schneider, Maria
French. Actor
Starred with Marlon Brando in
   controversial film Last Tango in Paris,
   1972.
b. Mar 27, 1952 in Paris, France
Source: BioIn 9, 10, 17; FilmEn; HalFC
80, 84, 88; ItaFilm; LegTOT; MovMk;
NewYTBE 73; WhoHol 92, A

Schneider, Nina
[Mrs. Herman Schneider]
American. Children's Author
Writes juvenile books with husband; first
   adult novel The Woman Who Lived in
   a Prologue, 1980.
b. Jan 29, 1913 in Antwerp, Belgium
Source: Au&Wr 71; AuBYP 2, 3; BioIn
6, 7, 9; ConAu 15NR, 29R; DrAPF 80,
87, 91; MorJA; SmATA 2; WhoAmW 61,
64

Schneider, Rob
American. Comedian, Actor
Comic actor known for his portrayal of
   obnoxious characters, including "The
   Richmeister" on "Saturday Night

Live;" also appeared in various films
   and television shows.
b. Oct 31, 1965 in San Francisco,
   California
Source: BioIn 23; ConTFT 20; News 97

Schneider, Romy
[Rosemarie Albach-Retty]
Austrian. Actor
Starred in The Cardinal, 1963.
b. Sep 23, 1938 in Vienna, Austria
d. May 29, 1982 in Paris, France
Source: AnObit 1982; BiDFilm, 81, 94;
BioIn 4, 6, 7, 11, 12, 13, 17; ConTFT 2;
CurBio 65, 82, 82N; DcArts; DcPseud;
EncEurC; FilmAG WE; FilmEn; FilmgC;
ForYSC; HalFC 80, 84, 88; IntDcF 1-3,
2-3; IntMPA 75, 76, 77, 78, 79, 80, 81,
82; InWom, SUP; ItaFilm; LegTOT;
MotPP; MovMk; NewYTBS 82;
OxCFilm; WhoAm 74; WhoAmW 70, 72;
WhoHol A; WhoWor 74; WorAl;
WorEFlm

Schneiderman, Rose
American. Labor Union Organizer
Leader in labor organizing and in the
   improvement of working conditions
   for women, particularly through the
   National Women's Trade Union
   League (WTUL).
b. Apr 6, 1882, Poland
d. 1972
Source: AmNatBi; AmRef; AmSetPR;
BiDAmLL; BiDSocW; BioIn 12, 15, 18,
19, 21; ContDcW 89; DcAmB S9;
DcAmImH; EncWB; EncWoAP;
FacFETw; HanAmWH; HeroCon;
HisWorL; IntDcWB; InWom SUP;
NotAW MOD; PorAmW; WomFir

Schneirla, Theodore Christian
American. Animal Expert
Animal psychologist; studied the
   behavior patterns of army ants.
b. Jul 23, 1902 in Bay City, Michigan
d. Aug 20, 1968 in New York, New
   York
Source: BiDPsy; BioIn 4, 8; CurBio 55,
68; InSci; ObitOF 79; WhAm 5

Schnellenberger, Howard Leslie
American. Football Coach
Head coach, U of Miami, 1979-83; won
   nat. championship, 1983.
b. Mar 13, 1934 in Saint Meinrad,
   Indiana
Source: BioIn 13, 14; NewYTBS 85;
WhoAm 88; WhoSSW 84, 86, 88

Schnering, Otto
American. Candy Manufacturer
Made Baby Ruth candy bar, 1910s,
   named for Pres. Cleveland's daughter.
b. Oct 9, 1891 in Chicago, Illinois
d. Jan 19, 1953 in Cary, Illinois
Source: BioIn 2, 3, 4; Entr; NatCAB 41;
WhAm 3; WorAl

Schnittke, Alfred
Russian. Composer
Original experimental composer; works
    defy categorization.
b. Nov 24, 1934 in Engels, Union of
    Soviet Socialist Republics
d. Aug 3, 1998 in Hamburg, Germany
Source: BakBD 78, 84; BakDcM; BioIn
18, 19, 23, 24; CamBiEn; ChamBiD;
ConCom 92; CurBio 92, 98N; IntWW
89, 91, 93, 97, 98; IntWWM 90;
NewYTBS 98; PenDiMP A; Who 92, 94,
98

Schnitzler, Arthur
Austrian. Author, Dramatist
Plays are psychological observations,
    mostly with erotic themes: La Ronde,
    1900.
b. May 15, 1862 in Vienna, Austria
d. Oct 21, 1931 in Vienna, Austria
Source: AtlBL; Benet 87, 96; BioIn 1, 4,
6, 9, 10, 11, 13, 18, 22; CamBiEn;
CamGWoT; CasWL; ChamBiD; ClDMEL
47, 80; CnDWLB 2; CnMD; CnThe;
ConAu 104; CyWA 89, 97; DcArts;
DcLB 81, 118; Dis&D; EncWB 98;
EncWL 1, 2, 2S, 3; EncWT; Ent; EuWr
8; EvEuW; FacFETw; FilmgC; GrFLW;
HalFC 80, 84, 88; IntDcT 2; LinLib L,
S; LngCTC; MajMD 1; McGEWB;
McGEWD 72, 84; ModGL; ModWD;
NewCBEL; NotNAT A, B; Novels;
OxCGer 76, 86, 97; OxCThe 67, 83;
PenC EUR; RAdv 14, 13-2; REn;
REnWD; RfGShF 1, 2; RfGWoL 95;
ShSCr 15; TwCA, SUP; TwCLC 4;
WhDW; WhE&EA; WhoLA; WorAl;
WorAlBi; WorAu 1900

Schnorr, Ludwig von Carolsfeld
German. Opera Singer
Leading tenor with Dresden Opera,
    1860s; created role of Tristan in
    Wagner's opera, 1865.
b. Jul 2, 1836 in Munich, Germany
d. Jul 21, 1865 in Dresden, Germany
Source: BakBD 84; NewEOp 71;
NewGrDM 80

Schocken, Theodore
American. Publisher
Pres., Schocken Books, Inc., 1965-76.
b. Oct 8, 1914 in Zwickau, Germany
d. Mar 20, 1975 in White Plains, New
    York
Source: BioIn 10, 12; ConAu 104;
DcAmB S9; NatCAB 59; NewYTBS 75;
WhAm 6; WhoAm 74; WhoWor 74, 76;
WhoWorJ 72

Schoech, Othmar
Swiss. Composer, Conductor
Choral, orchestral leader, 1915-40s; song
    cycles include Elegie, 1923.
b. Sep 1, 1886 in Brunnen, Switzerland
d. Mar 8, 1957 in Zurich, Switzerland
Source: BakBD 84; BriBkM 80; NewEOp
71; NewGrDM 80; OxCMus

Schoellkopf, Caroline Rose Hunt
American. Businesswoman
Heiress to Hunt oil fortune; richest
    woman in US, 1987.
b. 1923? in Texas
Source: BioIn 12, 15; InWom SUP

Schoenbach, Sol Israel
American. Musician
Prize-winning bassoonist; with
    Philadelphia Orchestra, 1937-57.
b. Mar 15, 1915 in New York, New
    York
Source: NewGrDA 86; WhoAm 74, 76,
78, 80, 82, 84, 86, 88, 90; WhoAmJ 80;
WhoAmM 83; WhoEnt 92

Schoenberg, Arnold
American. Composer
Invented 12-tone musical system, 1921;
    wrote opera Moses und Aron, 1951,
    song cycle Pierrot Lunaire, 1912.
b. Sep 13, 1874 in Vienna, Austria
d. Jul 13, 1951 in Brentwood, California
Source: AmNatBi; ASCAP 66, 80; AtlBL;
BakBD 78, 84; Benet 87, 96; BioIn 14,
15, 16, 17, 19, 20, 22, 23, 24; BriBkM
80; CamBiEn; CmCal; CmOp; CnOxB;
CompSN, SUP; ConAmC 76, 82; ConAu
109; CurBio 42, 51; DcAmB S5; DcCM;
DcCom 77; DcCom&M 79; DcTwCC, A;
EncAB-H 1974, 1996; EncWB 98;
FacFETw; IntDcOp; JeHun; LegTOT;
LiveWoA; McGEWB; MetOEnc; MusMk;
NewAmDM; NewEOp 71; NewGrDA 86;
NewGrDM 80; NewOxM; Opera;
OxCAmH; OxCEng 85, 95; OxCGer 76;
OxCMus; OxDcOp; PenDiMP A; RAdv
14, 13-3; REn; ThTwC 87; TwCLC 75;
WebAB 74; WhAm 3; WhDW; WorAl;
WorAlBi

Schoenbrun, David
American. Journalist
War correspondent for CBS News, 1945-
    63; ABC News, 1963-79; author of
    seven best-selling books: Soldiers of
    the Night, 1980.
b. Mar 15, 1915 in New York, New
    York
d. May 23, 1988 in New York, New
    York
Source: AmAu&B; BioIn 5, 6; ConAu
3NR, 49, 125; CurBio 60, 88, 88N;
EncAJ; EncTelN; EncTwCJ; IntAu&W
91; LesBEnT; WhoAm 84; WhoWor 74;
WrDr 80, 82, 84, 86, 88, 90

Schoendienst, Red
[Albert Fred Schoendienst]
American. Baseball Player, Baseball
    Manager
Second baseman, 1945-63, mostly with
    St. Louis; known for fielding; had .289
    lifetime batting average; managed St.
    Louis to two pennants, one World
    Series win, 1960s.
b. Feb 2, 1923 in Germantown, Illinois
Source: Ballpl 90; BiDAmSp BB; BioIn
15, 19; CulEncB; CurBio 64; WhoAm
74, 76, 78, 90, 92, 94, 95, 96, 97;
WhoProB 73; WhoSpor

Schoenfeld, Gerald
American. Theater Owner
Chm., Shubert Organization, 1972—;
    owns 50 percent of Broadway's
    theaters.
b. 1924 in New York, New York
Source: BioIn 15; ConNews 86-2;
ConTFT 6; Dun&B 98; OxCAmT 84

Schoen-Rene, Anna
American. Teacher
Singing teacher at Juilliard School of
    Music whose students included Paul
    Robeson.
b. Jan 12, 1864 in Koblenz, Germany
d. Nov 13, 1942 in New York, New
    York
Source: BakBD 92; BakBDTw; CurBio
43; NewEOp 71

Schofield, John McAllister
American. Military Leader
Civil War general; commander of US
    Army, 1888-95, succeeding Sheridan.
b. Sep 29, 1831 in Gerry, New York
d. Mar 4, 1906 in Saint Augustine,
    Florida
Source: AmBi; AmNatBi; ApCAB;
BiAUS; BiDrUSE 71, 89; BiInAmS;
BioIn 1, 7, 9, 10; CamDcAB; ChamBiD;
CivWDc; CmdGen 1991; DcAmAu;
DcAmB; DcAmMiB; DcNAA; Drake;
HarEnMi; HarEnUS; MedHR 94;
NatCAB 4; SpAmWar; TwCBDA; WebAB
74, 79; WebAMB; WhAm 1; WhCiWar

Scholder, Fritz
American. Artist
Member of the Luiseno tribe; known for
    his paintings and lithographs; won
    New Mexico's Governor's Award in
    Visual Arts, 1983.
b. Oct 6, 1937 in Breckenridge,
    Minnesota
Source: AmArt; AmIndBi; BioIn 9, 10,
14, 15, 17, 21; CurBio 85; DcCAA 88,
94; EncNAB; IlBEAAW; NotNaAm;
PrintW 83, 85; SJGNNAA; WhoAm 76,
78, 80, 82, 84, 86, 88, 90, 92, 94, 95,
96, 97, 98, 99, 2000; WhoAmA 73, 76,
78, 80, 82, 84, 86, 89, 91, 93, 1999;
WhoWest 74, 76, 78, 84; WhoWor 78,
80, 82, 84, 87, 93; WorArt 1980

Scholem, Gershom Gerhard
Israeli. Educator, Author
Wrote, taught Jewish mysticism known
    as Kabbalah.
b. Dec 5, 1897 in Berlin, Germany
d. Feb 20, 1982 in Jerusalem, Israel
Source: AnObit 1982; BioIn 14, 15, 16,
17, 20; ConAu 39NR, 45, 106; IntWW
81, 82; McGEWB; MidE 80; OxDcJeR;
WhoWor 82; WhoWorJ 78; WorAu 1970

Scholes, Percy Alfred
English. Musicologist
Presented music appreciation in
    informative, interesting manner:
    Oxford Companion to Music, 1938.
b. Jul 1877 in Leeds, England
d. Aug 2, 1958 in Vevey, Switzerland

Source: *BakBD 84; BakBDTw; BioIn 22; CamBiEn; ChamBiD; LngCTC; OxCMus; TwCA SUP; WhoLA; WorAu 1900*

Scholl, William M
"Doctor Scholl"
American. Physician
Founder, pres., Scholl Manufacturing Co., 1908-68.
b. Jun 22, 1882 in LaPorte, Indiana
d. Mar 30, 1968 in Chicago, Illinois
Source: *IndAu 1917; WhAm 5*

Schollander, Don(ald Arthur)
American. Swimmer
Won two gold medals, 1964 Olympics.
b. Apr 30, 1946 in Charlotte, North Carolina
Source: *BiDAmSp BK; BioIn 7, 8, 9, 10; CmCal; CurBio 65*

Scholz, Jackson Volney
American. Track Athlete, Children's Author
Finished second in 1924 Olympic race which was adapted into 1981 film *Chariots of Fire;* wrote boys' sports books.
b. Mar 15, 1897 in Buchanan, Michigan
d. Oct 26, 1986 in Delray Beach, Florida
Source: *AmNatBi; AuBYP 2, 3; BiDAmSp OS; BioIn 6, 8, 13; ConAu 5R, 120; MorJA; NewYTBS 86*

Scholz, Tom
American. Singer, Musician
Founded hard-rock group Boston, 1975; hits include "Amanda," 1986; has also invented, made electronic equipment for musicians.
b. Mar 10, 1947 in Toledo, Ohio
Source: *BioIn 15, 16; BkPepl; ConNews 87-2; LegTOT; OnThGG; RkOn 84; RolSEnR 83; Songw; WhoEnt 98; WhoRocM 82*

Schomburg, Arthur Alfonso
[Arturo Alfonso Schomburg]
American. Historian
Private collection of African American books, prints, and artifacts became the basis for the 135th St. branch of the NY Public Library's Division of Negro Literature, History, and Prints; curator, 1932-38.
b. Jan 24, 1874 in San Juan, Puerto Rico
d. Jun 10, 1938 in New York, New York
Source: *AmNatBi; BioIn 1, 16, 19, 24; ConBlB 9; DcAmLiB; DcAmNB; DcTwCCu 5; NotBlAM; WhoColR*

Schonbein, Christian Friedrich
German. Chemist
Discovered ozone gas, 1840.
b. Oct 18, 1799 in Metzingen, Germany
d. Aug 29, 1868 in Sauersberg, Germany
Source: *AsBiEn; BiESc; BioIn 2; ChamBiD; DcBiPP; DcScB; InSci; LarDcSc; NewCol 75*

Schonberg, Harold C
American. Critic
With *NY Times,* 1960-80; won Pulitzer for distinguished criticism, 1971.
b. Nov 29, 1915 in New York, New York
Source: *AmAu&B; AuBYP 3; BakBD 84; BioIn 15, 16; ConAu 112; IntAu&W 91; IntWW 83, 91, 97, 98, 2000; IntWWM 90; NewGrDA 86; WhoAm 86, 90; WhoEnt 92; WrDr 92*

Schonfield, Hugh J
English. Author, Educator
Authority on Judaism; wrote controversial *The Passover Plot,* 1965.
b. May 17, 1901 in London, England
d. Jan 24, 1988 in London, England
Source: *Au&Wr 71; ConAu 9R, 124*

Schongauer, Martin
German. Artist, Engraver
First painter to practice engraving; historical, religious subjects include *Madonna of the Rose Bower,* 1473.
b. 1450 in Colmar, Germany
d. Feb 2, 1491 in Breisach, Germany
Source: *AtlBL; CamBiEn; ChamBiD; NewCol 75; WebBD 83*

Schonhuber, Franz Xaver
German. Politician
Leader of the Republicans, a right-wing political party, in West Germany in the 1980s.
b. Jan 19, 1923 in Trostberg an der Alz, Bavaria
Source: *EncWB 98*

Schoolcraft, Henry Rowe
American. Explorer, Naturalist
Native American culture expert; wrote *The Myth of Hiawatha,* 1856, which inspired Longfellow's poem.
b. Mar 28, 1793 in Albany County, New York
d. Dec 10, 1864 in Washington, District of Columbia
Source: *ABCNaAm; Alli; AmAu; AmAu&B; AmBi; AmNatBi; ApCAB; BbD; Benet 87, 96; BenetAL 91; BiAUS; BiDAmS; BiD&SB; BiInAmS; BioIn 1, 3, 4, 8, 9, 13, 16; CamBiEn; CamDcAB; CelCen; ChamBiD; CyAL 1; DcAmAu; DcAmB; DcBiPP; DcNAA; DcScB; Drake; EncAAH; EncAB-H 1974, 1996; EncALit; EncWB 98; HarEnUS; IlBEAAW; InSci; IntDcAn; LegTOT; LinLib L; McGEWB; MichAu 80; NatCAB 5; NewEAmW; NewYHSD; OxCAmH; OxCAmL 65, 83, 95; OxCCan; REn; REnAL; REnAW; TwCBDA; WebAB 74, 79; WhAm HS; WhNaAH; WhWE*

Schoonmaker, Frank Musselman
American. Author
Leading figure in US during Prohibition; wrote *The Complete Book of Wine,* 1934.
b. Aug 20, 1905 in Spearfish, South Dakota
d. Jan 11, 1976 in New York, New York

Source: *AmAu&B; BioIn 10; ConAu 61; NewYTBS 76; ObitOF 79*

Schoonmaker, Thelma
American. Filmmaker
Film editor of *Taxi Driver,* 1976; *The Age of Innocence,* 1993.
b. 1940 in Algiers, Algeria
Source: *BioIn 22, 23; CurBio 97; WomFilm*

Schopenhauer, Arthur
German. Philosopher, Author
Exponent of philosophical pessimism; major work: *The World as Will and Idea,* 1819.
b. Jan 22, 1788 in Danzig, Germany
d. Sep 20, 1860 in Frankfurt am Main, Germany
Source: *AtlBL; BakBD 78, 84, 92; BbD; Benet 87, 96; BiCoLiE; BiD&SB; BiDPsy; BioIn 1, 2, 3, 4, 5, 7, 8, 9, 10, 12, 13, 14, 16, 17, 20; CamBiEn; CasWL; CelCen; ChamBiD; CyEd; CyWA 58, 97; DcBiPP; DcEuL; DcLB 90; Dis&D; EncAnRW; EncEth; EncUnb; EncWB 98; EuAu; EuWr 5; EvEuW; IlEncMy; LegTOT; LinLib L, S; LngCEL; LuthC 75; McGEWB; NamesHP; NewC; NewCBEL; NewGrDM 80; NinCLC 51; OxCEng 67, 85, 95; OxCGer 76, 86, 97; OxCPhil; PenC EUR; RAdv 14, 13-4; RComWL; REn; TwoTYeD; WhDW; WhoChr; WorAl; WorAlBi; WrPh P*

Schopf, J(ames) William
American. Geologist, Educator, Chemist
Discovered oldest amino acids in 1967.
b. Sep 27, 1941 in Urbana, Illinois
Source: *AmMWSc 73P, 76P, 79, 82, 86, 89, 92, 95, 98; BioIn 11; CamDcAB; CurBio 95; WhoAm 78, 80, 82, 84, 86, 88, 96; WhoScEn 96, 2000; WhoWest 00, 74, 76, 98; WhoWor 97, 98*

Schorer, Mark
American. Author, Educator
Wrote encyclopedic biography, *Sinclair Lewis: An American Life,* 1961.
b. May 17, 1908 in Sauk City, Wisconsin
d. Aug 11, 1977 in Oakland, California
Source: *AmAu&B; AmNatBi; Au&Wr 71; Benet 87; BenetAL 91; BioIn 4, 11, 17, 22; BlueB 76; CnDAL; ConAu 5R, 7NR, 73; ConLC 9; ConLCrt 77, 82; ConNov 72, 76; DcAmB S10; DcLB 103; DrAF 76; DrAS 74E; IntAu&W 76, 77; IntWW 74, 75, 76, 77; LinLib L; Novels; OxCAmL 65, 83, 95; PenC AM; REn; REnAL; ScF&FL 1, 2; TwCA, SUP; WhoAm 74, 76; WhoWor 74; WorAu 1900; WrDr 76*

Schorr, Daniel Louis
American. Broadcast Journalist
Controversial CBS News correspondent, 1943-76; won three Emmys for Watergate coverage; suspended for disclosing confidential govt. information to *Village Voice* newspaper, 1976.

b. Aug 31, 1916 in New York, New York
Source: *BiDAmNC; BioIn 13, 14, 15; CamDcAB; ConAu 65; CurBio 59, 78; EncTwCJ; IntMPA 86, 92; JrnUS; LesBEnT, 92; NewYTBS 76; PolProf NF; WhoAm 74, 76, 78, 80, 82, 84, 86, 88, 90, 92, 94, 95, 96, 97, 98, 99, 2000; WhoAmJ 80; WhoE 95; WhoTelC; WhoWor 74; WorAl*

Schorr, Friedrich
Hungarian. Opera Singer
Baritone with NY Met., 1924-43; noted Wagnerian singer.
b. Sep 2, 1888 in Nagyvarad, Austria-Hungary
d. Aug 14, 1953 in Farmington, Connecticut
Source: *BakBD 78, 84, 92; BakBDTw; BiDAmM; BioIn 1, 2, 3, 4, 10, 11, 14; CmOp; CurBio 42, 54; IntDcOp; LegTOT; MetOEnc; MusSN; NatCAB 41; NewAmDM; NewEOp 71; NewGrDA 86; NewGrDM 80; NewGrDO; OxDcOp; PenDiMP*

Schott, Marge
[Margaret Schott]
American. Business Executive
Socialite; owner, Cincinnati Reds, 1985—; suspended from NL for one year following derogatory racial and ethnic remarks, 1992; suspended again in 1996 through the 1998 season.
b. Aug 18, 1928 in Cincinnati, Ohio
Source: *BioIn 14, 15, 16; ConNews 85-4; NewYTBS 85; WhoAm 88, 90, 92, 94, 95, 96, 97, 98, 99, 2000; WhoAmW 89, 91, 93, 95; WhoMW 88, 90, 92, 93, 96, 98*

Schottland, Charles I(rwin)
American. Government Official
Commissioner, US Social Security Administration, 1954-59.
b. Oct 29, 1906
d. Jun 27, 1995 in Tucson, Arizona
Source: *BioIn 4, 5, 21; BlueB 76; ConAu 13R, 149; CurBio 95N; WhAm 12; WhoAm 74, 76, 78, 80, 82, 84, 86, 88, 90, 92, 94, 95, 96; WhoAmJ 80; WhoWorJ 72, 78*

Schouten, William Cornelius
Dutch. Explorer
Navigator discovered a new route to the Pacific via Cape Horn in 1616.
b. c. 1580 in Hoorn, Netherlands
d. 1625 in Antongil Bay, Madagascar
Source: *EncWB 98; McGEWB*

Schrader, Paul Joseph
American. Director, Writer
Directed, wrote films *American Gigolo,* 1980; *Blue Collar,* 1978; *Hardcore,* 1979.
b. Jul 22, 1946 in Grand Rapids, Michigan
Source: *BioIn 10, 11, 13, 14, 15, 16; ChamBiD; ConAu 37R, 41NR; ConDr 82A, 88A; ConLC 26; ConTFT 4; CurBio 81; DcLB 44; HalFC 88; IntDcF*

2-2; *IntMPA 92; IntWW 91, 93, 97, 98, 2000; WhoAm 82, 88, 90, 92, 94, 95, 96, 97, 98; WhoEnt 92, 98; WhoWor 95; WorFDir 2*

Schram, Emil
American. Businessman
Pres. of NY Stock Exchange, 1941-51; pres. of United Service Organizations, 1953-57.
b. Nov 23, 1893 in Peru, Indiana
d. Sep 18, 1987 in Peru, Indiana
Source: *BioIn 1, 2, 3, 15; CurBio 41, 53, 87, 87N; NewYTBS 87; WhAm 9; Who 74, 82, 83, 85, 88; WhoAm 74*

Schramm, Tex(as Edward)
American. Football Executive
Dallas Cowboys, GM, 1960-1989; pres., 1966-1989; pres., World League of American Football, 1989-91.
b. Jun 2, 1920 in Los Angeles, California
Source: *BioIn 13, 16; WhoAm 86, 90; WhoFtbl 74; WhoSSW 73, 75, 86, 91*

Schranz, Karl
Austrian. Skier
World Cup Alpine champion, 1969, 1970.
b. Nov 18, 1938 in Saint Anton, Austria
Source: *BioIn 8, 9; CurBio 71; WhoWor 74*

Schreiber, Avery
[Burns and Schreiber]
American. Actor, Comedian
Starred with Jack Burns in "Burns and Schreiber Comedy Hour," 1973.
b. Apr 9, 1935 in Chicago, Illinois
Source: *ConTFT 7; EncAFC; LegTOT; WhoAm 74; WhoEnt 92; WhoHol 92, A*

Schreiber, Hermann Otto Ludwig
[Lujo Bassermann]
Austrian. Historian, Author
Books include *Vanished Cities,* 1957; *The Oldest Profession,* 1967.
b. May 4, 1920 in Wiener Neustadt, Austria
Source: *Au&Wr 71; ConAu 36NR; DcLP 87A; IntAu&W 86, 91; WrDr 76, 86, 88*

Schreker, Franz
German. Composer
Operas include *Der Ferne Klang,* 1912; *Christophorous,* cancelled by Nazis, 1933, first performed, 1978.
b. Mar 23, 1878, Monaco
d. Mar 21, 1934 in Berlin, Germany
Source: *BakBD 78, 84, 92; BakBDTw; BioIn 1, 3, 7, 8, 9, 12, 17, 18, 19, 23; CmOp; CompSN, SUP; DcCom 77; IntDcOp; MetOEnc; NewAmDM; NewEOp 71; NewGrDM 80; NewGrDO; OxCMus; OxDcOp*

Schreyer, Edward Richard
Canadian. Political Leader
Premier of Manitoba, 1969-77; governor-general, 1979-84, succeeded by Jeanne Sauve.

b. Dec 21, 1935 in Beausejour, Manitoba, Canada
Source: *AmCath 80; BioIn 11, 12, 13; BlueB 76; CanParl 1998; CanWW 80, 81, 83, 89, 96, 97, 98, 1999; CurBio 81; IntWW 74, 75, 76, 77, 78, 79, 80, 81, 82, 83, 89, 91, 93, 97, 98, 2000; IntYB 80, 81, 82; Who 82, 83, 85, 88, 90, 92, 94, 98, 99, 2000; WhoAm 74, 76, 78, 80, 82, 84; WhoCan 73, 75, 77, 80, 82, 84; WhoE 81, 83, 85; WhoMW 76, 78; WhoWor 74, 76, 78, 80, 82, 87*

Schrieffer, John Robert
American. Physicist, Educator
Shared 1972 Nobel Prize in physics for developing BCS (researchers' initials) theory of superconductivity.
b. May 31, 1931 in Oak Park, Illinois
Source: *AmMWSc 76P, 79, 82, 86, 89, 92, 95, 98; BioIn 9, 10, 15, 20; BlueB 76; CamBiEn; CamDcAB; CamDcSc; ChamBiD; IntWW 74, 75, 76, 77, 78, 79, 80, 81, 82, 83, 89, 91, 93, 97, 98, 2000; LarDcSc; McGCEnS; McGMS 80; NobelP; RanHWDS; WebAB 74, 79; Who 74, 82, 83, 85, 88, 90, 92, 94, 98, 99, 2000; WhoAm 74, 78, 80, 82, 84, 86, 88, 90, 92, 94, 95, 96, 97, 98, 99, 2000; WhoAtom 77; WhoE 74, 75, 77, 79, 81, 85; WhoFrS 84; WhoNob, 90, 95; WhoScEn 94, 96, 2000; WhoSSW 93, 95, 97, 99; WhoTech 89; WhoWest 82, 87, 89, 92; WhoWor 74, 80, 82, 84, 87, 89, 91, 93, 95, 96, 97, 98, 99, 2000; WorAl; WorAlBi; WorScD*

Schriner, Sweeney
[David Schriner]
Canadian. Hockey Player
Left wing, NY Americans, 1934-39, Toronto, 1939-46; won Calder Trophy, 1935, Art Ross Trophy, 1936, 1937; Hall of Fame, 1962.
b. Nov 30, 1911 in Calgary, Alberta, Canada
Source: *BioIn 17; HocEn; WhoHcky 73; WhoSpor*

Schroder, Gerhard
[Gerhard Schroeder]
German. Politician
Christian Democratic Union leader; foreign affairs minister, 1961-66, defense minister, 1966-69.
b. Sep 11, 1910 in Saarbrucken, Germany
d. Dec 31, 1989 in Sylt Island, Germany (West)
Source: *BioIn 5, 6, 7, 16, 17; CurBio 62, 90, 90N; IntWW 74, 75, 76, 77, 78, 79, 80, 81, 82, 83, 89; IntYB 78, 79, 80, 81, 82; NewYTBS 90; WhoWor 74, 76, 78*

Schroder, Rick
"Ricky"
American. Actor
Appeared in remake of *The Champ,* 1979; won Golden Globe award; starred in 1980s TV series "Silver Spoons;" on drama "NYPD Blue," 1998—.

b. Apr 13, 1970 in Staten Island, New
York
Source: BioIn 11, 12, 13, 14, 16;
ConTFT 2, 3, 17; HalFC 84, 88; IntMPA
84, 86, 88, 92; LegTOT; VarWW 85;
WhoAm 2000; WhoEnt 92

Schroder-Devrient, Wilhelmine
''The Queen of Tears''
German. Opera Singer
Famed soprano with Dresden Opera,
1822-47; first great singing actress.
b. Dec 6, 1804 in Hamburg, Germany
d. Jan 26, 1860 in Coburg, Germany
Source: BakBD 78, 84, 92; BioIn 7, 14,
15, 19, 24; BriBkM 80; CmOp;
IntDcOp; InWom, SUP; MetOEnc;
NewAmDM; NewEOp 71; NewGrDM 80;
NewGrDO; OxDcOp

Schroeder, Barbet
American. Director
Directed Reversal of Fortune, 1990; Kiss
of Death, 1995.
b. Apr 26, 1941 in Tehran, Iran
Source: BiDFilm 94; ConAu 143;
ConTFT 9; FilmEn; HalFC 84, 88;
IntMPA 88, 92, 94, 96; IntWW 91, 93,
97, 98, 2000; LegTOT; MiSFD 9; News
96, 96-1; WrDr 96, 98, 99, 2000

Schroeder, Jay Brian
American. Football Player
Minor league baseball player, 1980-83;
quarterback, Washington, 1985-88; LA
Raiders, 1989-93; Cincinnati, 1993;
Arizona, 1994.
b. Jun 28, 1961 in Milwaukee,
Wisconsin
Source: BioIn 14, 16; FootReg 86, 87

Schroeder, Patricia Scott
[Mrs. James White Schroeder]
American. Politician
Liberal Dem. congresswoman from CO,
1973-95.
b. Jul 30, 1940 in Portland, Oregon
Source: AlmAP 88; WhoWest 00, 74, 76,
78, 80, 82, 84, 87, 89, 92, 94, 96, 98;
WomPO 76

Schroeder, William J
American. Transplant Patient
Second human to receive artificial heart,
Nov 1984; survived longest, 620 days.
b. Feb 14, 1932 in Jasper, Indiana
d. Aug 6, 1986 in Louisville, Kentucky
Source: AmNatBi; ConNews 86-4;
NewYTBS 86

Schroedinger, Erwin
Austrian. Physicist
Shared 1933 Nobel Prize for quantum
mechanics concept; discovered new
productive forms of atomic theory.
b. Aug 12, 1887 in Vienna, Austria
d. Jan 4, 1961 in Alpbach, Austria
Source: AsBiEn; BiESc; ConAu 113;
DcScB; MakMC; McGEWB; WhAm 4;
WhDW; WhoNob; WorAl

Schuba, Beatrix
Austrian. Skater
Two-time world champion figure skater,
1971-72; won gold medal, 1972
Olympics.

Schubert, Franz Peter
Austrian. Composer
Created the German lieder; symphonies
include B Minor (The Unfinished,
1822) and C Major; wrote ''Ave
Maria.''
b. Jan 31, 1797 in Vienna, Austria
d. Nov 19, 1828 in Vienna, Austria
Source: AtlBL; BakBD 92; BakDcM;
BioIn 1, 2, 3, 4, 5, 6, 7, 8, 9, 10, 11, 12,
13; CamBiEn; CelCen; ChamBiD;
DcArts; DcBiPP; DcCathB; Dis&D;
EncWB 98; LinLib S; McGEWB; NewC;
NewEOp 71; NewGrDO; NotNAT B;
OxCEng 85, 95; OxCGer 76; OxCMus;
REn; WhDW; WorAl

Schuch, Ernst von
Austrian. Conductor
Led Dresden Court Opera for 40 yrs;
debuted 50 new operas, including Der
Rosenkavalier.
b. Nov 23, 1846 in Graz, Austria
d. May 10, 1914 in Dresden, Germany
Source: BakBD 78, 84, 92; CmOp;
IntDcOp; MetOEnc; NewEOp 71;
NewGrDM 80; OxDcOp; PenDiMP

Schul, Bob
American. Track Athlete
Middle-distance runner; first American to
win gold medal in 5,000-meters, 1964
Olympics.
b. Sep 28, 1937 in West Milton, Ohio
Source: WhoTr&F 73

Schulberg, Budd Wilson
American. Author, Journalist
Wrote What Makes Sammy Run? 1941;
prize-winning film scenario, On the
Waterfront, 1954.
b. Mar 27, 1914 in New York, New
York
Source: Benet 87; BenetAL 91; BioIn 14,
15, 16; ConAu 19NR; ConDr 73, 88A;
ConLC 48; ConNov 76, 91; ConTFT 6;
CurBio 41, 51; DcFM; DrAPF 87, 91;
FilmgC; HalFC 84, 88; IntMPA 77, 96;
IntvTCA 2; IntWW 74, 91; LngCTC;
ModAL 4; NewYTBE 72; NotNAT;
OxCAmL 65; OxCFilm; OxCTwCL;
PenC AM; REnAL; WhoAm 86, 90;
WhoUSWr 88; WhoWrEP 89; WorAlBi;
WrDr 92, 98, 99, 2000

Schulberg, Stuart
American. Producer
Exec. producer of news documentaries
for NBC; producer, ''Today Show,''
1968-76.
b. Nov 17, 1922 in Los Angeles,
California
d. Jun 28, 1979 in New York, New York
Source: BioIn 11, 12; ConAu 89;
NewYTBS 79; NewYTET

Schuler, Mike
[Michael Harold Schuler]
American. Basketball Coach
Coach, Portland, 1986-89; Clippers,
1990-92; NBA coach of year, 1987.
b. Sep 22, 1940 in Portsmouth, Ohio
Source: OfNBA 87; WhoAm 88, 90, 92;
WhoWest 87, 89, 92

Schuller, Gunther
American. Composer, Conductor
Noted horn player, 1940s-50s;
popularized ''cool jazz'' style;
instrumental in ragtime revival; wrote
operas, third-stream music.
b. Nov 22, 1925 in New York, New
York
Source: AllMGJa; AmComp; BakBD 78,
84; BakDcM; BiDAmM; BiDJaz; BioIn
6, 7, 8, 9, 10, 12, 14, 15; BlueB 76;
BriBkM 80; CamDcAB; CompSN, SUP;
ConAmC 76, 82; ConAu 28NR, 69,
73NR; ConCom 92; CpmDNM 77, 78,
80, 81, 82; CurBio 64; DcCM;
DcTwCCu 1; EncJzS; EncWB 98;
IntAu&W 91, 93; IntWW 74, 75, 76, 77,
78, 79, 80, 81, 82, 83, 89, 91, 93, 97,
98, 2000; IntWWM 77, 80, 90; LEduc
74; McGEWB; MetOEnc; MusMk;
NewAmDM; NewEOp 71; NewGrDA 86;
NewGrDJ 88; NewGrDM 80; NewOxM;
OxCMus; OxCPMus; PenDiMP, A;
PenEncP; WebAB 74, 79; WhoAm 74,
76, 78, 80, 82, 84, 86; WhoAmM 83;
WhoE 74, 77, 83; WhoWest 87; WhoWor
74; WrDr 76, 80, 82, 84, 86, 88, 90, 92,
94, 96, 98, 99, 2000

Schuller, Robert Harold
American. Evangelist, Author
Popular televangelist emphasizes
optimistic thinking; The Be Happy
Attitudes, 1985.
b. Sep 16, 1926 in Alton, Iowa
Source: BioIn 11, 12, 13, 14, 15, 16;
ConAu 9R, 14NR, 46NR; CurBio 79;
IntAu&W 77, 86, 91; RelLAm 1, 2;
WhoAm 76, 78, 80, 82, 84, 86, 88, 90,
95, 96, 97, 2000; WhoAmA 80; WhoRel
75, 77, 85, 92; WhoWest 80, 87, 89, 92,
94; WorAlBi; WrDr 76, 86, 92, 98

Schulman, Sarah (Miriam)
American. Writer
Wrote novel After Delores, 1988, winner
of the American Library Association
Gay/Lesbian Book Award.
b. Jul 28, 1958 in New York, New York
Source: BioIn 19, 20; ConAu 118;
GayLesB; GayLL 1

Schultes, Richard Evans
American. Educator, Scientist
Did botanical research in the Amazon
region, collecting 24,000 plant
specimens.
b. Jan 12, 1915 in Boston, Massachusetts
Source: AmMWSc 73P, 76P, 79, 82, 86,
89, 92, 95, 98; Biodiv; BioIn 12; ConAu
25NR, 50NR, 108; CurBio 95; EnvEnDr;
IntWW 89, 91, 93, 97, 98, 2000;
NotTwCS 1; WhoAm 74, 76, 78, 80, 82,
84, 86, 90, 92, 94, 95, 96, 97, 98; WhoE

95; WhoFrS 84; WhoRel 75, 77;
WhoScEn 94, 96, 2000; WorWWEn

Schultz, Dave
[David William Schultz]
''The Hammer''
Canadian. Hockey Player
Left wing, 1971-80, mostly with
Philadelphia; holds NHL record for
most penalties in season, 472 (1974-
75); second to Tiger Williams in
career penalties (2,294).
b. Oct 14, 1949 in Waldheim,
Saskatchewan, Canada
Source: BioIn 12, 13; HocEn; NewYTBS
74, 75

Schultz, Dutch
[Arthur Flegenheimer]
''The Dutchman''
American. Criminal
Major NYC bootlegger, racketeer of
Prohibition era; known for
ruthlessness; ordered rival ''Legs''
Diamond killed, 1931.
b. Aug 6, 1902 in New York, New York
d. Oct 24, 1935 in Newark, New Jersey
Source: AmNatBi; BioIn 1, 2, 6;
CopCroC; DcAmB S1; DrInf; FacFETw;
LegTOT; MafEnc; VioAm; WebAB 74,
79; WorAl; WorAlBi

Schultz, Harry D
American. Financier
Among books on stocks, investments:
Schultz's Bear Market Strategy, 1981.
b. Sep 11, 1923
Source: BioIn 13; ConAu 14NR, 21R

Schultz, Howard M.
American. Business Executive
Chairman and CEO, Starbucks Coffee
Co., 1987—.
b. 1953 in New York, New York
Source: CurBio 97

Schultz, Michael A.
American. Director
Directed Cooley High, 1975; The Last
Dragon, 1985.
b. Nov 10, 1938 in Milwaukee,
Wisconsin
Source: ConBlB 6; ConTFT 10; FilmEn;
WhoAfA 9, 10, 11, 12; WhoBlA 8;
WhoThe 72, 77, 81

Schultz, Richard D(ale)
American. Olympic Official
Executive director, United States
Olympic Committee, 1995—.
b. Sep 5, 1929 in Grinnell, Iowa
Source: CurBio 96; WhoAm 76, 78, 80,
82, 84, 86, 88, 90, 92, 94, 95, 96, 97,
98, 99, 2000; WhoFI 96; WhoMW 93,
96, 98; WhoWest 00, 98

Schultz, Theodore W(illiam)
American. Educator
Won Nobel Prize in economics, 1979.
b. Apr 30, 1902 in Arlington, South
Dakota

d. Feb 26, 1998 in Evanston, Illinois
Source: AmAu&B; AmMWSc 73S, 78S,
98; BiDMoAE; BioIn 4, 12, 15;
CamBiEn; CamDcAB; ChamBiD; ConAu
85, 165; GrEconS; IntAu&W 91; IntWW
91; LEduc 74; NewYTBS 79; WhAm 12;
Who 92; WhoAm 74, 76, 80, 82, 84, 86,
88, 90, 92, 94, 95, 96, 97, 98; WhoEc
86; WhoFI 83, 85, 89, 92, 94, 98;
WhoMW 80, 82, 84, 86, 88, 90, 92, 93,
96; WhoNob, 90, 95; WhoScEn 96;
WhoWor 74, 80, 82, 84, 87, 89, 91, 93,
95, 96, 97, 98; WorAlBi; WrDr 90

Schultze, Carl Emil
''Bunny''
American. Cartoonist
Drew ''Foxy Grandpa'' comic series,
1900-27.
b. May 25, 1866 in Lexington, Kentucky
d. Jan 18, 1939 in New York, New York
Source: AmAu&B; ChhPo; DcNAA;
WhAm 1; WhAmArt 85; WorECom

Schultze, Charles Louis
American. Economist
Chaired Jimmy Carter's Council of
Economic Advisers, 1977-81.
b. Dec 12, 1924 in Alexandria, Virginia
Source: AmEA 74; AmMWSc 92; BioIn
7, 8, 9, 11; ConAu 114; CurBio 70;
IntWW 74, 75, 76, 77, 78, 79, 80, 81, 82,
83, 89, 91, 93, 97, 98, 2000; IntYB 78,
79, 80, 81, 82; NewYTBS 76, 77;
PolProf J; WhoAm 74, 76, 78, 80, 84,
86, 88, 90, 92, 94, 95, 96, 97, 98, 99,
2000; WhoAmP 77, 79, 81; WhoE 77,
79, 81; WhoGov 77; WhoMedH 96, 99,
2000; WorAlBi

Schulz, Charles M(onroe)
American. Cartoonist
Created ''Peanuts'' comic strip, 1950;
won Emmy, 1966; strip ended 2000.
b. Nov 26, 1922 in Minneapolis,
Minnesota
d. Feb 12, 2000 in Santa Rosa,
California
Source: AmAu&B; AuBYP 2, 3;
BiDrAPA 89; BioIn 14, 15; BkPepl;
CamBiEn; CamDcAB; CelR 90;
ChamBiD; ConAu 6NR, 9R; ConLC 12;
CurBio 60; EncACom; EncTwCJ;
IntAu&W 91; IntWW 91, 97, 98, 2000;
LesBEnT 92; MinnWr; SmATA 10;
ThrBJA; WebAB 79; WhoAm 86, 90, 97,
98, 99, 2000; WhoAmA 84, 91, 1999;
WhoEnt 92, 98; WhoFI 00, 98; WhoWor
84, 89, 97, 98, 99, 2000; WorAlBi;
WrDr 86, 88, 92, 98, 99

Schumacher, E(rnst) F(riedrich)
English. Economist, Writer
Wrote Small Is Beautiful, 1973; A Guide
for the Perplexed, 1977; works fused
economic philosophy and Christian
and Buddhist theology.
b. Aug 16, 1911 in Bonn, Germany
d. Sep 4, 1977 in Romont, Switzerland
Source: BioIn 14; ConAu 34NR, 73, 81,
85NR; ConLC 80; DcNaB 1971;
EnvEnc; OxCTwCL

Schumacher, Joel
American. Writer
Films include St. Elmo's Fire, 1985.
b. 1942 in New York, New York
Source: HalFC 88; IntMPA 88; MiSFD
9; VarWW 85

Schumacher, Kurt
German. Politician
Leader, West German Social Democratic
Party, 1945-52.
b. Oct 13, 1895 in Kulm, Germany
d. Aug 21, 1952 in Bonn, Germany
Source: BioIn 1, 2, 3, 7, 18; ColdWar 1,
2; CurBio 52; DcTwHis; EncGRNM;
EncTR 91; EncWB, 98; ObitT 1951

Schuman, Patricia Glass
American. Publishing Executive
Pres., Neal-Schuman Publishers, 1976—;
pres., American Library Assn., 1990—
.
b. Mar 15, 1943 in New York, New
York
Source: ConAu 14NR, 33R; News 93-2;
WhoAm 98, 99, 2000; WhoAmW 83;
WhoAmW 91, 93, 95, 97, 99; WhoE 97,
99; WhoLibI 82

Schuman, Robert
French. Statesman, Economist
Founder, European Coal and Steel
Community.
b. Jun 29, 1886, Luxembourg
d. Sep 4, 1963 in Metz, France
Source: BiDInt; BioIn 1, 2, 3, 5, 6, 9,
17, 19; CamBiEn; ChamBiD; CurBio 48,
63; DcTwHis; EncCW; EncWB 98;
HisEWW; McGEWB; ObitT 1961; WhAm
4; WhDW; WorAl; WorAlBi

Schuman, William Howard
American. Composer
First to receive Pulitzer in music, 1943.
b. Aug 4, 1910 in New York, New York
d. Feb 15, 1992 in New York, New
York
Source: AmNatBi; BakBD 84; BakBDTw;
BiDAmM; BiDMoAE; BiE&WWA; BioIn
13, 14, 16; CamBiEn; CamDcAB;
ChamBiD; ConCom 92; CurBio 42, 62;
DancEn 78; DcCM; EncAB-H 1974;
FacFETw; IntWW 74, 91; MusMk;
NewAmDM; NewGrDA 86; NewOxM;
NewYTBS 85; OxCMus; PenDiMP A;
REnAL; WebAB 74; WhoAm 86, 90;
WhoMus 72; WhoWor 74, 91

**Schumann, Clara Josephine
Wieck**
German. Pianist
Brilliant performer; wife of Robert
Schumann, friend of Brahms.
b. Sep 13, 1819 in Leipzig, Germany
d. May 20, 1896 in Frankfurt am Main,
Germany
Source: BakBD 84; HerW; InWom, SUP

Schumann, Elisabeth
American. Opera Singer
Soprano with Vienna State Opera, 1919-
38; noted for Wagner, R Strauss roles.

b. Jun 13, 1885 in Merseburg, Germany
d. Apr 23, 1952 in New York, New
    York
Source: *BakBD 78, 84; BiDAmM; BioIn
4, 6, 10, 11, 12, 14, 15, 16, 18, 20;
BriBkM 80; CamBiEn; CmOp;
FacFETw; IntDcOp; MetOEnc; MusSN;
NewEOp 71; NewGrDM 80; ObitT 1951*

Schumann, Maurice
French. Politician
Foreign affairs minister, 1969-73.
b. Apr 10, 1911 in Paris, France
d. Feb 10, 1998 in Paris, France
Source: *BiDFrPL; BioIn 2, 7, 8, 9, 17,
23, 24; CurBio 70, 98N; HisEWW;
IntAu&W 76, 77, 82, 89; IntWW 74, 75,
76, 77, 78, 79, 80, 81, 82, 83, 89, 91,
93, 97; IntYB 78, 79, 80, 81, 82; WhAm
12; WhE&EA; Who 74, 82, 83, 85, 88,
90, 92, 94, 98; WhoEnt 98; WhoFr 79;
WhoWor 74, 78, 82, 84, 87, 89, 91, 93,
95, 96, 97, 98*

Schumann, Robert Alexander
German. Composer
Led Romantic movement; career as
    pianist ended due to hand injury.
b. Jun 8, 1810 in Zwickau, Germany
d. Jul 29, 1856 in Endenick, Germany
Source: *AtlBL; BakBD 84, 92; BakDcM;
BbD; BiD&SB; BioIn 1, 2, 3, 4, 5, 6, 7,
8, 9, 10, 11, 12, 13; CamBiEn; CelCen;
ChamBiD; DcArts; EncPaPR 91; EncWB
98; IntDcOp; LuthC 75; McGEWB;
NewGrDO; OxCGer 76; OxCMus; REn*

Schumann, Walter
American. Composer, Conductor
Won Emmy for theme to TV's
    "Dragnet," 1955.
b. Oct 8, 1913 in New York, New York
d. Aug 21, 1958 in Minneapolis,
    Minnesota
Source: *ASCAP 66, 80; BakBD 78, 84,
92; BakBDTw; BioIn 5; ConAmC 76, 82;
NotNAT B*

Schumann-Heink, Ernestine
    Rossler
American. Opera Singer
Brilliant contralto; famed for Wagnerian
    roles, German Lieder; noted radio
    performer.
b. Jun 15, 1861 in Lieben, Bohemia
d. Nov 16, 1936 in Hollywood,
    California
Source: *AmBi; BiDAmM; DcAmB S2;
InWom SUP; NotAW; REn; WebAB 74;
WhAm 1; WhScrn 77; WomWWA 14*

Schumer, Charles E(llis)
American. Politician
Dem. congressman from NY, 1981-99;
    Senator, 1999—.
b. Nov 23, 1950 in New York, New
    York
Source: *BiDrUSC 89; BioIn 13; CngDr
81, 83, 85, 87; CurBio 95; IntWW 2000;
NewYTBS 91; WhoAm 82, 84, 86, 88,
90, 92, 94, 95, 96, 97, 98, 99, 2000;
WhoE 83, 85, 86, 89, 91, 93, 95, 97, 99;
WhoGov 77*

Schumpeter, Joseph Alois
American. Economist
Wrote *Theory of Economic Development*,
    1911.
b. Feb 8, 1883 in Trest, Moravia
d. Jan 8, 1950 in Taconic, Connecticut
Source: *AmSocL; BioIn 2, 8, 10, 11, 12,
13, 14, 15, 16, 17, 18, 19, 20, 21, 22,
23; CamDcAB; ChamBiD; DcAmB S4;
EncAB-H 1974, 1996; EncWB 98;
McGEWB; NewCol 75; OxCAmH;
OxCTwCL; RAdv 14; REnAL; WebAB
74, 79; WhAm 2; WhoEc 81, 86*

Schurman, Jacob Gould
Canadian. Philosopher, Diplomat
Ambassador to China, 1921-25;
    Germany, 1925-30.
b. May 22, 1854 in Prince Edward
    Island, Canada
d. Aug 13, 1942
Source: *Alli SUP; AmAu&B; AmNatBi;
ApCAB; BbD; BiD&SB; BiDInt; BioIn 4,
5, 16, 22; CamDcAB; Chambr 3; CurBio
42; DcAmAu; DcAmB S3; DcAmDH 80,
89; DcNAA; HarEnUS; LinLib L;
NatCAB 4, 40; SpAmWar; TwCBDA;
WebAB 74, 79; WhAm 2*

Schurz, Carl
American. Politician
Reformist Rep. senator from MO, 1870-
    76; urged civil service revision.
b. Mar 2, 1829 in Cologne, Germany
d. May 14, 1906 in New York, New
    York
Source: *ABCNaAm; Alli, SUP; AmAu;
AmAu&B; AmBi; AmNatBi; AmPolLe;
AmRef; AmRef&R; ApCAB; BbD;
BenetAL 91; BiAUS; BiDAmJo; BiDrAC;
BiDrUSC 89; BiDrUSE 71, 89; BiDSA;
BioIn 1, 2, 3, 5, 6, 7, 8, 9, 10, 12, 15,
16, 17, 20, 21; CamBiEn; CamDcAB;
ChamBiD; CivWDc; CyAG; DcAmAu;
DcAmB; DcAmDH 80, 89; DcAmImH;
DcAmSR; DcLB 23; DcNAA; Drake;
EncAAH; EncAB-H 1974, 1996;
EncAInd; EncPaPR 91; EncSoH; EncWB
98; HarEnUS; JrnUS; LinLib L, S;
McGEWB; NatCAB 3; NatLAC;
NewEAmW; OxCAmH; OxCAmL 65, 83,
95; PolPar; REnAL; REnAW; TwCBDA;
USGovLe; WebAB 74, 79; WhAm 1;
WhAmP; WhCiWar; WhNaAH; WisWr;
WorAl; WorAlBi*

Schuschnigg, Kurt von
Austrian. Political Leader
Chancellor of Austria, 1934-38; taught in
    US for 20 yrs.
b. Dec 14, 1897 in Riva, Italy
d. Nov 18, 1977 in Innsbruck, Austria
Source: *BioIn 11, 14; CamBiEn; CathA
1952; ChamBiD; DcPol; DcTwHis;
EncTR; FacFETw; HisEWW; IntWW 74,
75, 76, 77; McGEWB; REn; WhDW;
Who 74; WhoWor 74*

Schussler Fiorenza, Elisabeth
Romanian. Scholar, Theologian
Feminist biblical scholar and theologian
    produced a model of Christianity in

which women shared the center and
    were restored to human subjectivity.
b. 1938, Romania
Source: *EncWB 98; FemiWr*

Schuster, Max Lincoln
American. Publisher
Founded Simon and Schuster, with
    Richard Simon, 1924.
b. Mar 2, 1897 in Kalusz, Austria
d. Dec 20, 1970 in New York, New
    York
Source: *AmAu&B; AmNatBi; BioIn 9;
ConAu 29R; CurBio 41, 71; DcAmB S8;
REnAL; WhAm 10; WhoWorJ 72, 78*

Schutz, Heinrich
German. Composer
Regarded as finest German composer
    before Bach; wrote first German opera,
    Daphne, 1627; composed over 500
    sacred works.
b. Oct 8, 1585 in Kostritz, Germany
d. Nov 6, 1672 in Dresden, Germany
Source: *AtlBL; BakBD 78, 84, 92;
BakDcM; Benet 87; BioIn 1, 4, 5, 7, 8,
12, 13, 15, 16, 17, 20; BriBkM 80;
CamBiEn; ChamBiD; DcArts; DcCom
77; DcCom&M 79; EncWB 98;
GrComp; LegTOT; LuthC 75; McGEWB;
MetOEnc; MusMk; MusSN; NewAmDM;
NewEOp 71; NewGrDM 80; NewGrDO;
NewOxM; OxCGer 76, 86, 97; OxCMus;
OxDcOp; PenDiMP A; REn; WhDW*

Schutzendorf, Gustav
German. Opera Singer
Best known of four brothers, all operatic
    baritones; with NY Met., 1922-35;
    wed to soprano Grete Stuckgold.
b. 1883 in Cologne, Germany
d. Apr 27, 1937 in Berlin, Germany
Source: *BakBD 78, 84, 92; MetOEnc;
NewEOp 71; NewGrDA 86; NewGrDM
80; OxDcOp*

Schuur, Diane
American. Singer
Two-time Grammy winner, best female
    jazz performance for *Timeless,* 1986
    and *Diane Schuur and the Count
    Basie Orchestra,* 1987.
b. Dec 10, 1953
Source: *AllMGJa; BioIn 16; ConMus 6;
WhoAmW 91; WhoEnt 92*

Schuyler, James Marcus
American. Poet
Won Pulitzer Prize for Poetry, 1981.
b. Nov 9, 1923 in Chicago, Illinois
d. Apr 12, 1991 in New York, New
    York
Source: *AmAu&B; Benet 87; BenetAL
91; BlueB 76; ConAu 101, 134; ConLC
5, 70; ConPo 70, 75, 91; CroCAP;
DcLEL 1940; DrAP 75; DrAPF 80, 91;
IntAu&W 86, 91, 93; IntWWP 77, 82;
NewYTBS 91; WhoAm 82, 84, 86, 88,
90; WhoUSWr 88; WhoWrEP 89, 92, 95;
WorAu 1975; WrDr 76, 90*

Schuyler, Philip John
American. Statesman
Member of Continental Congress, 1778-
81; one of NY's first two senators,
1780s-90s.
b. Nov 20, 1733 in Albany, New York
d. Nov 18, 1804 in Albany, New York
Source: *AmBi; AmNatBi; ApCAB;
BiAUS; BiDrAC; BiDrUSC 89; BioIn 6,
7, 8, 10, 16, 18; BlkwEAR; CamBiEn;
CamDcAB; ChamBiD; DcAmB; Drake;
EncAR; EncCRAm; EncWB 98;
GenMudB; HarEnMi; HisDcAR;
McGEWB; NatCAB 1; OxCAmH;
TwCBDA; WebAB 74, 79; WebAMB;
WebBD 83; WhAm HS; WhNaAH*

Schwab, Charles
American. Business Executive
Founder and president Charles Schwab &
Co., 1971—, largest discount
brokerage in US.
b. 1937 in Sacramento, California
Source: *BioIn 12, 13, 15; Dun&B 90;
News 89-3; NewYTBS 85; WhoAm 90;
WhoFI 92; WhoWest 92*

Schwab, Charles Michael
American. Industrialist
First pres. of US Steel, 1901-03; became
pres. of Bethlehem Steel, 1904,
making it huge independent steel
maker.
b. Feb 18, 1862 in Williamsburg,
Pennsylvania
d. Sep 18, 1939 in New York, New
York
Source: *AmBi; AmDec 1900; AmNatBi;
ApCAB X; BiDAmBL 83; BioIn 2, 3, 4,
7, 9, 10, 12; CamDcAB; DcAmB S2;
EncAB-H 1974, 1996; EncWB 98; LinLib
S; McGEWB; NatCAB 14; OxCAmH;
WebAB 74, 79; WhAm 1; WorAl*

Schwann, Theodor
German. Physiologist
Regarded as father of cytology; co-
founded cell theory; coined term
metabolism.
b. Dec 7, 1810 in Neuss, Prussia
d. Jan 11, 1882 in Liege, Belgium
Source: *AsBiEn; BiESc; BioIn 4, 8, 9,
12, 14; CamBiEn; CamDcSc; ChamBiD;
DcCathB; DcScB; EncWB 98; InSci;
LarDcSc; McGEWB; NewCol 75;
RanHWDS; WhDW; WorAl; WorAlBi*

Schwartz, Arthur
American. Songwriter
With Howard Dietz, wrote over 500
songs, including "Dancing in the
Dark," "That's Entertainment."
b. Nov 25, 1900 in New York, New
York
d. Sep 3, 1984 in Kintnersville,
Pennsylvania
Source: *AmNatBi, 80; LegTOT; Music;
NewAmDM; NewCBMT; NewGrDA 86;
NewGrDM 80; NewGrDO; NotNAT;
OxCAmT 84; OxCPMus; PenEncP;
PlP&P; PopAmC; SUP; ScrEAmL 1;
Songw; Sw&Ld C; WhAm 8; WhoAm 76;
WhoThe 77, 81; WorAl; WorAlBi*

Schwartz, David
American. Businessman
Founder and head of Rent-A-Wreck, an
agency renting low cost, late model
used vehicles, 1970—.
b. 1936
Source: *News 88-3; WhoAm 84*

Schwartz, Delmore (David)
American. Author, Editor, Critic
Edited *Partisan Review* mag., 1943-55.
b. Dec 8, 1913 in New York, New York
d. Jul 11, 1966 in New York, New York
Source: *AmAu&B; AmCulL; AmWr S2;
AtlBL; Benet 87, 96; BenetAL 91; BioIn
4, 5, 7, 8, 10, 11, 12, 13, 14, 15, 17, 18,
19; CamGLE; CamHAL; CasWL;
CnDAL; CnE&AP; CnMWL; ConAu
17R, 25R, 35NR, P-2; ConLC 2, 4, 10,
45, 87; ConLCrt 77, 82; ConPo 75, 80A;
CurBio 60, 66; CyWA 89; DcAmB S8;
DcArts; DcLB 28, 48; EncWL 1, 2, 2S;
FacFETw; GrWrEL P; JeAmFiW;
LegTOT; LinLib L; MajTwCW 1, 2;
ModAL 4, 4S1, 4S2; OxCAmL 65, 83,
95; OxCTwCP; PenC AM; PoeCrit 8;
RAdv 1, 14, 13-1; REn; REnAL;
RfGAmL 4, 87, 94; RGFAP; RGTwCWr;
SixAP; TwCA, SUP; TwCWr;
WebE&AL; WhAm 4; WhoTwCL; WorAl;
WorAlBi*

Schwartz, Felice N(ierenberg)
American. Social Reformer
Founder, pres., CEO, Catalyst, 1962-
1993.
b. Jan 16, 1925 in New York, New York
d. Feb 8, 1996 in New York, New York
Source: *AmWomM; CurBio 93; InWom
SUP; WhoAmW 58, 61, 64, 66, 70, 85,
91; WhoE 77*

Schwartz, Jean
American. Songwriter
Prolific Broadway composer, 1900-
1930s; wrote "Rock-a-Bye Your Baby
to a Dixie Melody," 1918;
"Chinatown My Chinatown," 1910.
b. Nov 4, 1878 in Budapest, Austria-
Hungary
d. Nov 30, 1956 in Sherman Oaks,
California
Source: *AmPS; AmSong; ASCAP 66, 80;
BiDAmM; BioIn 4, 5, 6, 15, 16;
CmpEPM; EncMT; NewCBMT;
NewGrDA 86; NotNAT B; OxCAmT 84;
OxCPMus; PopAmC; Songw; Sw&Ld C;
WhThe*

Schwartz, Maurice
American. Actor, Director, Producer
Films include *Bird of Paradise,* 1951;
Slaves of Babylon, 1953.
b. Jun 18, 1890 in Sedikov, Russia
d. May 10, 1960 in Tel Aviv, Israel
Source: *AmNatBi; BioIn 4, 5, 10, 20;
CamDcAB; CamGWoT; CurBio 56, 60;
FilmEn; NotNAT B; OxCAmT 84;
OxCThe 67; TheaDir; WhAm 4; WhoHol
B; WhScrn 74, 77; WhThe*

Schwartz, Melvin
American. Physicist
Shared Nobel Prize in physics, 1988, for
co-discovering neutrinos, subatomic
particles.
b. Nov 2, 1932 in New York, New York
Source: *AmMWSc 73P, 76P, 79, 82, 86,
89, 92, 95, 98; BioIn 16, 18, 20;
CamDcAB; ChamBiD; ConAu 168;
LarDcSc; LElec; McGCEnS; NobelP 91;
NotTwCS 1; RanHWDS; Who 90, 92, 94,
98, 99, 2000; WhoAm 74, 76, 78, 80, 82,
84, 86, 88, 90, 92, 94, 95, 96, 97, 98,
99, 2000; WhoE 95, 97, 99; WhoFrS 84;
WhoNob 90, 95; WhoScEn 94, 96, 2000;
WhoWor 91, 93, 95, 96, 97, 98, 99,
2000; WhoWorJ 72, 78; WorAlBi*

Schwartz, Stephen L(awrence)
American. Dramatist, Composer
Wrote music, lyrics for *Godspell,* 1971;
Butterflies Are Free, 1969.
b. Mar 6, 1948 in Roslyn, New York
Source: *ConAu 85; ConTFT 5; EncMT;
NotNAT; OxCPMus; SmATA 19; WhoAm
78, 80, 82, 84, 86, 88, 92, 94, 95, 96,
97, 98, 99, 2000; WhoEnt 92, 98;
WhoThe 81; WhoWor 2000*

Schwary, Ronald L
American. Producer
Films include *A Soldier's Story,* 1984;
won Oscar for *Ordinary People,* 1980.
b. May 23, 1944 in Oregon
Source: *VarWW 85; WhoAm 90; WhoEnt
92*

Schwarz, Gerard
American. Composer, Musician
Trumpet virtuoso who is one of most
sought-after conductors in US.
b. Aug 19, 1947 in Weehawken, New
Jersey
Source: *BakBD 84; BioIn 14, 15, 16;
BriBkM 80; CurBio 86; IntWW 89, 91,
93, 97, 98, 2000; IntWWM 90;
NewAmDM; NewGrDA 86; NewGrDM
80; NewYTBS 75, 86; PenDiMP; WhoAm
82, 96, 97, 98, 99, 2000; WhoAmM 83;
WhoEnt 98; WhoWest 00, 96, 98*

Schwarz-Bart, Andre
French. Author
His *Last of the Just* was a significant
post WWII Novel.
b. 1928 in Metz, France
Source: *Benet 87, 96; BioIn 5, 10;
ConAu 89; ConLC 2, 4, 24; CyWA 89,
97; IntAu&W 76, 77; REn; TwCWr; Who
74, 82, 83, 85, 88, 90, 92, 94, 98, 99,
2000; WhoWor 74; WorAu 1950*

Schwarzenegger, Arnold Alois
Austrian. Actor
Five times Mr. Universe, six times Mr.
Olympia; films include *Twins,* 1988;
Total Recall, 1990.
b. Jul 30, 1947 in Graz, Austria
Source: *BioIn 10, 13, 14, 15, 16; CelR
90; ConAu 21NR, 81; ConTFT 4;
CurBio 79, 91; HalFC 88; IntMPA 92;
IntWW 91, 93, 97, 98, 2000; News 91-1;
NewYTBS 76, 82; WhoAm 84, 86, 88,*

90, 92, 94, 95, 96, 97, 98, 99, 2000;
WhoEnt 92, 98; WorAlBi

Schwarzhaupt, Elisabeth
German. Politician
First woman cabinet member in West
Germany, health minister, 1961-66.
b. Jan 7, 1901 in Frankfurt am Main,
Germany
d. Oct 29, 1986 in Frankfurt, Germany
(West)
Source: BioIn 7, 8, 15; CurBio 67, 87,
87N; IntWW 74; InWom SUP; NewYTBS
86

Schwarzkopf, Elisabeth
German. Opera Singer
Soprano who performed in US, 1950s-
70s; renowned Mozart singer.
b. Dec 9, 1915 in Jarotschin, Poland
Source: BakBD 78, 84, 92; BakDcM;
BioIn 3, 4, 5, 6, 7, 8, 10, 11, 12, 13, 14,
15; BriBkM 80; ChamBiD; CmOp;
ContDcW 89; CurBio 55; DcArts;
FacFETw; IntDcOp; IntDcWB; IntWW
74, 75, 76, 77, 78, 79, 80, 81, 82, 83,
89, 91, 93; IntWWM 90; IntWWW 2;
InWom; LegTOT; MetOEnc; MusMk;
MusSN; NewAmDM; NewEOp 71;
NewGrDM 80; OxDcOp; PenDiMP;
Who 74, 82, 83, 85, 88, 90, 92, 94, 98,
99; WhoHol 92; WhoMus 72; WhoWor
80, 82, 93; WomThRe; WorAl; WorAlBi

Schwarzkopf, H. Norman
American. Military Leader
Retired army general; responsible for
military plan Operation Desert Shield/
Storm, January 16, 1991-February 28,
1991.
b. Aug 22, 1934 in Trenton, New Jersey
Source: CamBiEn; CurBio 91; EncPerG;
EncVieW; FacFETw; HisDcPG; IntWW
91, 97, 98, 2000; MilitOn; NewYTBS 91;
Who 98, 99, 2000; WhoAm 90; WhoWor
98, 99, 2000

Schwarzschild, Martin
American. Astronomer
Wrote Structure and Evolution of the
Stars, 1958; had a part in creating
Stratosphere-based astronomy.
b. May 21, 1912, Germany
d. Apr 10, 1997 in Langhorne,
Pennsylvania
Source: AmMWSc 73P, 76P, 79, 82, 86,
89, 92, 95; BioIn 5, 7, 8, 14, 22, 23, 24;
BlueB 76; CamDcAB; CurBio 97N;
IntWW 74, 75, 76, 77, 78, 79, 80, 81, 82,
83, 89, 91, 93, 97, 98; McGCEnS;
McGMS 80; NewYTBS 97; RanHWDS;
WhAm 12; WhoAm 74, 76, 78, 80, 82,
84, 86, 88, 90, 92, 94, 95, 96, 97, 98;
WhoE 95; WhoFrS 84; WhoScEn 94, 96;
WhoWor 74

Schwatka, Frederik
American. Explorer, Naturalist
Explored AK's Yukon River, 1883-84;
wrote Nimrod of the North, 1885.
b. Sep 29, 1849 in Galena, Illinois
d. Nov 2, 1892 in Portland, Oregon

Source: AmBi; ApCAB; DcAmB; NatCAB
1; TwCBDA; WhAm HS

Schweickart, Russell L
American. Astronaut
Lunar module pilot on Apollo 9, 1969.
b. Oct 25, 1935 in Neptune, New Jersey
Source: IntWW 74; WhoAm 86; WhoGov
72; WhoSSW 73; WhoWor 91

Schweiker, Richard Schultz
American. Government Official
Rep. senator from PA, 1969-81; secretary
of HHS, 1981-83.
b. Jun 1, 1926 in Norristown,
Pennsylvania
Source: BiDrAC; BiDrUSC 89; BiDrUSE
89; BioIn 8, 9, 10, 11, 12, 13, 14;
BioNews 74; CngDr 74, 77, 79; CurBio
77; IntWW 74, 75, 76, 77, 78, 79, 80,
81, 82, 83, 89, 91, 93, 97, 98, 2000;
NatCAB 63N; NewYTBS 76, 80; PolProf
NF; WhoAm 74, 76, 78, 80, 82, 84, 86,
88, 90, 92, 94, 95, 96, 97, 98, 99, 2000;
WhoAmP 73, 75, 77, 79, 81, 83, 85, 87,
89, 91, 93; WhoE 74, 75, 77, 79, 81;
WhoGov 72, 75, 77; WhoIns 86, 88, 90,
92, 93, 94; WhoWor 78, 80, 82; WorAl;
WorAlBi

Schweitzer, Albert
French. Missionary, Physician
Founded Lambarene Hospital, French
Equatorial Africa, 1913; won 1952
Nobel Peace Prize; known for
humanitarianism, "reverence of life"
philosohy.
b. Jan 14, 1875 in Kaysersberg, Germany
d. Sep 4, 1965 in Lambarene, Gabon
Source: BakBD 78, 84, 92; BakBDTw;
BakDcM; Benet 87, 96; BiDChrM;
BiDMoPL; BioIn 1, 2, 3, 4, 5, 6, 7, 8, 9,
10, 11, 12, 13, 14, 15, 16, 17, 18, 19,
20, 21, 22, 23, 24; BriBkM 80;
CamBiEn; ChamBiD; ConAu 93;
ConHero 2; CurBio 48, 65; CyWA 97;
DcAfHiB 86; DcTwHis; EncAnRW;
EncEth; EncWB 98; EnvEnc; FacFETw;
HeroCon; InSci; LegTOT; LinLib L, S;
LngCTC; LuthC 75; McGEWB; MusMk;
MusSN; NewAmDM; NewCol 75;
NewGrDM 80; NewYTBS 75; NobelP;
ObitT 1961; OxCGer 76, 86, 97;
OxCMed 86; OxCMus; PenDiMP;
RanHWDS; REn; ThTwC 87; TwCA
SUP; TwCWr; WebBD 83; WhAm 4;
WhDW; WhE&EA; WhoChr; WhoNob,
90, 95; WorAl; WorAlBi; WorAu 1900

Schweitzer, Pierre-Paul
French. Banker
Director of French treasury, 1953-60;
chairman, International Monetary
Fund, 1963-73; nephew of Albert
Schweitzer.
b. May 29, 1912
d. Jan 2, 1994 in Paris, France
Source: BioIn 19, 20; CurBio 94N;
IntWW 74, 75, 76, 77, 78, 79, 80, 81, 82,
83, 89, 91, 93; IntYB 78, 79, 80, 81, 82;
WhAm 11; Who 74, 82, 83, 85, 88, 90,
92, 94; WhoAm 74, 76, 78, 80, 82, 84,
86, 88, 90, 92; WhoFI 74, 75, 77, 79,

81, 83; WhoFr 79; WhoGov 72;
WhoSSW 73; WhoWor 74, 76, 78, 80,
82, 84, 87, 89

Schwenckfeld, Kasper von
Polish. Theologian, Nobleman
Broke with Luther over the doctrines he
formulated concerning the nature of
Christ and the Eucharist; spent much
of his life in exile as a religious
outlaw.
b. 1489 in Ossig, Silesia
d. 1561

Schweppe, Jacob
Swiss. Inventor
Pioneered method of carbonating still
water into soda water, 1792.
b. 1740
d. 1821
Source: Entr

Schwimmer, David
American. Actor
Plays Ross Geller on TV's "Friends,"
1994—.
b. Nov 12, 1966 in New York, New
York
Source: CamBiEn; ConTFT 15, 27; News
96, 96-2; WhoAm 98, 99, 2000; WhoEnt
98

Schwimmer, Rosika
Hungarian. Political Activist
Speechmaker and polemicist was a
feminist and international peace
activist during the First World War.
b. 1877 in Budapest, Hungary
d. 1948 in New York
Source: AmNatBi; AmPeW; AmRef;
BiDMoPL; BioIn 1, 10, 13, 15, 17, 19;
CamBiEn; ChamBiD; ContDcW 89;
DcAmB S4; DcAmSR; EncWB 98;
HisWorL; IntDcWB; InWom SUP; LibW;
NotAW; RadHan; WomFir

Schwinden, Ted
American. Politician
Dem. governor of Montana, 1981-89.
b. Aug 31, 1925 in Wolf Point, Montana
Source: AlmAP 82, 84, 88; BiDrGov
1978, 1983, 1988; BioIn 20; IntWW 81,
82, 83, 89, 91, 93; IntYB 82; PolsAm 84;
WhoAm 78, 80, 82, 84, 86, 88; WhoAmP
77, 79, 81, 83, 85, 87, 89, 91, 93, 95,
97, 1999; WhoWest 80, 82, 84, 87, 89,
92, 94, 96, 98; WhoWor 82, 87, 89, 91

Schwinger, Julian (Seymour)
American. Physicist, Educator
Shared 1965 Nobel Prize in physics for
developing theory of quantum
electrodynamics.
b. Feb 12, 1918 in New York, New
York
d. Jul 16, 1994 in Los Angeles,
California
Source: AmMWSc 73P, 76P, 79, 82, 86,
89, 92; AmNatBi; AsBiEn; BiESc; BioIn
1, 4, 7, 8, 12, 14, 15, 20, 21; BlueB 76;
CamBiEn; CamDcAB; CamDcSc; CurBio
67, 94N; IntWW 74, 75, 76, 77, 78, 79,

80, 81, 82, 83, 89, 91, 93; LarDcSc;
LegTOT; McGCEnS; McGMS 80;
NobelP; NotTwCS 1; RAdv 14;
RanHWDS; ThTwC 87; WebAB 79;
WhAm 11; Who 74, 82, 83, 85, 88, 90,
92, 94; WhoAm 74, 76, 78, 80, 82, 84,
86, 88, 90, 92, 94; WhoE 74; WhoFrS
84; WhoNob, 90, 95; WhoScEn 94;
WhoWest 78, 80, 82, 84, 87, 89, 92, 94;
WhoWor 74, 80, 82, 84, 87, 89, 91, 93;
WorAl; WorAlBi; WorScD; WrDr 86, 88,
90, 92, 94, 96

Schwinn, Edward R, Jr.
American. Business Executive
Pres., chief exec., Schwinn Bicycle Co.,
  1979—.
b. 1949?
Source: *BioIn 15; ConNews 85-4;*
Dun&B 90; WhoMW 82, 86

Schwinn, Ignaz
American. Manufacturer
Bicycle pioneer, whose design has been
  successful from outset of co., 1895.
b. 1860
d. 1948
Source: *Entr*

Schwitters, Kurt (Hermann Edward Karl Julius)
German. Artist, Poet
Dadaist painter, collagist, typographer,
  and writer created MERZ-art, two and
  three-dimensional collage-like works
  using text and discarded objects.
b. 1887 in Hannover, Germany
d. Jan 8, 1948 in Kendal, England
Source: *ConAu 158*

Schwob, Marcel
French. Journalist, Author
Wrote *The Book of Monelle*, 1929;
  Children's Crusade, 1898.
b. Aug 23, 1867 in Chaville, France
d. Feb 26, 1905 in Paris, France
Source: *BioIn 1, 7, 13, 15, 19; ClDMEL*
47, 80; ConAu 117; DcLB 123; EuAu;
GuFrLit 1; OxCFr; PenC EUR;
PenEncH; TwCLC 20

Scipio Africanus, Publius Cornelius
[Scipio the Elder]
Roman. Army Officer
Most famous Roman general before
  Julius Caesar, known for victory over
  Hannibal at Zama.
b. 234BC
d. 183BC in Liternum, Campania
Source: *DcBiPP; REn*

Scobee, Dick
[Francis Richard Scobee]
American. Astronaut
Spacecraft commander who died in
  explosion of space shuttle *Challenger*.
b. May 19, 1939 in Auburn, Virginia
d. Jan 28, 1986 in Cape Canaveral,
  Florida
Source: *BioIn 16; NewYTBS 86*

Scobie, Ronald Mackenzie
British. Army Officer
Commander of British Land Forces in
  Adriatic, WW II; commander-in-chief
  of Allied forces in Greece.
b. Jun 8, 1893
d. 1969
Source: *CurBio 45; WhWW-II*

Scofield, John
American. Musician
Jazz guitarist; albums include *Decoy*,
  1984 with Miles Davis.
b. Dec 26, 1951 in Dayton, Ohio
Source: *AllMGJa; BioIn 12, 13, 16;*
CmpEGui; ConMus 7; FacFETw;
NewGrDJ 88, 94; OnThGG; PenEncP;
WhoAm 94, 95, 96, 97, 98; WhoEnt 98

Scofield, Paul
[David Paul Scofield]
English. Actor
Won Oscar, 1966, for *A Man for All*
  Seasons.
b. Jan 21, 1922 in Hurstpierpoint,
  England
Source: *BiE&WWA; BioIn 2, 3, 4, 6, 7,*
8, 9, 10, 11, 14, 15, 16; BlueB 76;
CamGWoT; CnThe; ConTFT 4, 13;
CurBio 62; DcArts; EncMT; EncWT;
Ent; FilmEn; FilmgC; ForYSC; HalFC
80, 84, 88; IlWWBF; IntMPA 82, 84, 86,
88, 92, 94, 96; IntWW 74, 75, 76, 77,
78, 79, 80, 81, 82, 83, 89, 91, 93, 97,
98, 2000; ItaFilm; LegTOT; MotPP;
MovMk; NotNAT, A; OsStAZ; OxCAmT
84; OxCFilm; OxCThe 67, 83; PIP&P;
Who 74, 82, 83, 85, 88, 90, 92; WhoAm
94, 95, 96, 97, 98, 99, 2000; WhoEnt 98;
WhoHol 92, A; WhoThe 72, 77, 81;
WhoWor 74, 76, 78, 84, 87, 89, 91, 93,
95, 96, 97, 98, 99, 2000; WorAl;
WorAlBi

Scopas
Greek. Sculptor
First to depict violent emotions on
  marble faces; known for architectural
  works, statues.
b. fl. 6th cent. BC in Paros, Greece
Source: *CamBiEn; ChamBiD; DcBiPP;*
NewCol 75; OxCArt; OxCClL, 89;
OxDcArt; WebBD 83

Scopes, John Thomas
American. Teacher
Tried for teaching theory of evolution
  against state law, "monkey trial" of
  1925.
b. Aug 3, 1900 in Paducah, Kentucky
d. Oct 21, 1970 in Shreveport, Louisiana
Source: *AmNatBi; ChamBiD; DcAmB*
S8; LegTOT; NewYTBE 70; WorAl

Score, Herb(ert Jude)
American. Baseball Player, Sportscaster
Pitcher, 1955-62, mostly with Cleveland;
  AL rookie of year, 1955; never fully
  recovered when hit in eye by line
  drive, 1957.
b. Jun 7, 1933 in Rosedale, New York
Source: *Ballpl 90; BiDAmSp Sup; BioIn*
3, 4, 5, 6, 8, 11; WhoProB 73

Scorel, Jan van
Dutch. Artist
Portraitist, religious painter; most of
  great altarpieces have perished.
b. 1495
d. 1562
Source: *BioIn 4, 11; CamBiEn;*
ChamBiD; McGDA; NewCol 75;
OxCArt; OxDcArt

Scoresby, William
English. Explorer
Pioneered in study of the Arctic; charted
  Greenland's coasts, 1820s.
b. Oct 5, 1789 in Whitby, England
d. Mar 22, 1857 in Torquay, England
Source: *Alli; ApCAB; BioIn 4, 18, 24;*
BritAu 19; CamBiEn; CelCen;
ChamBiD; DcBiPP; DcNaB, C;
EncO&P 3; ExplAnT; Geog 4; LarDcSc;
NewCol 75; OxCShps; WhWE

Scorpions
[Francis Buchholz; Matthias Jabs; Klaus
  Meine; Herman Rarebell; Rudolph
  Schenker]
German. Music Group
Formed in 1971; first American tour,
  1979-80.
Source: *BillEnR; ConMus 12; EncRk 88;*
EncRkSt; GrMetD; IlEncRk; PenEncP;
RkOn 85; WhoRocM 82

Scorsese, Martin
American. Director, Screenwriter
Known for films *The Color of Money*,
  1986; *Taxi Driver*, 1976.
b. Nov 17, 1942 in New York, New
  York
Source: *AmCulL; AmDec 1980; BenetAL*
91; BiDFilm 81, 94; BioIn 10, 11, 12,
13, 14, 15, 16; CamBiEn; CamDcAB;
CelR 90; ChamBiD; ConAu 46NR,
85NR, 110, 114; ConLC 20, 89; ConTFT
1, 5, 12, 22; CurBio 79; DcArts;
DcTwCCu 1; FacFETw; FilmEn;
GangFlm; HalFC 84, 88; IlWWHD 1;
IntDcF 1-2, 2-2; IntMPA 86, 88, 92, 94,
96; IntWW 82, 83, 89, 91, 93, 97, 98,
2000; LegTOT; MiSFD 9; MovMk; News
89-1; NewYTBE 73; NewYTBS 76, 85;
OnHuYAF; Who 92, 94, 98, 99, 2000;
WhoAm 74, 76, 78, 80, 82, 84, 86, 88,
90, 92, 94, 95, 96, 97, 98, 99, 2000;
WhoEnt 92, 98; WhoHol 92, A; WhoWor
84, 87, 91, 93, 95, 96, 97, 98; WorAl;
WorAlBi; WorFDir 2

Scott, Adrian
[The Hollywood Ten]
American. Producer, Screenwriter
Blacklisted as Communist by film
  industry; sentenced to one yr. in
  prison.
b. Feb 6, 1912 in Arlington, New Jersey
d. 1973
Source: *FilmEn; FilmgC; GangFlm;*
HalFC 80, 84, 88; IntMPA 75, 76, 77,
78, 79, 80, 81, 82

Scott, Arleigh Winston, Sir
West Indian. Political Leader
Governor-general of Barbados, 1967-76.

b. Mar 27, 1900, Barbados
d. Aug 9, 1976 in Georgetown, Barbados
Source: *IntWW 74; Who 74; WhoGov 72; WhoWor 74, 76*

Scott, Austin
American. Educator
Pres. of Rutgers U, 1891-1906.
b. Aug 10, 1848 in Maumee, Ohio
d. Aug 16, 1922 in Granville Centre, Massachusetts
Source: *DcAmB; NatCAB 3; TwCBDA; WhAm 1*

Scott, Austin Wakeman
American. Author, Educator
Authority on trust law; wrote classic *Scott on Trusts*, 1939.
b. Aug 31, 1884 in New Brunswick, New Jersey
d. Apr 9, 1981 in Boston, Massachusetts
Source: *BioIn 24; ConAu 103; NewYTBS 74, 81; OxCLaw; ScrEAmL 1; WhAm 7*

Scott, Barbara Ann
Canadian. Skater
Two-time world champion figure skater; won gold medal, 1948 Olympics.
b. May 9, 1928 in Ottawa, Ontario, Canada
Source: *BioIn 1, 2, 3, 8, 10, 11, 16; CanWW 70; CurBio 48; InWom, SUP; WhoSpor*

Scott, Charles Prestwich
English. Editor
Editor, *Manchester Guardian*, 1872-1929, the forerunner of *The Guardian*.
b. Oct 26, 1846 in Bath, England
d. Jan 1, 1932 in Manchester, England
Source: *BioIn 1, 2, 5, 9, 14, 17; CamBiEn; ChamBiD; DcNaB 1931; GrBr; NewCBEL; WhDW*

Scott, Charles Wesly
[The Hostages]
American. Hostage
One of 52 held by terrorists, Nov 1979-Jan 1981.
b. 1933?
Source: *NewYTBS 81; WhoSSW 91*

Scott, Clarence
American. Businessman
Partner with brother, Edward, in million-dollar paper products business, begun 1879.
b. 1848 in Saratoga County, New York
d. 1912
Source: *Entr*

Scott, Cyril (Meir)
English. Composer, Author
Wrote opera *The Alchemist;* occult books include *The Initiate.*
b. Sep 27, 1879 in Oxton, England
d. 1970
Source: *BakBD 78, 84, 92; BakBDTw; BioIn 1, 3, 4, 8; BriBkM 80; CamBiEn; ChamBiD; CompSN, SUP; ConAu 111; DcNaB 1961; EncO&P 1S2, 1S3, 2, 3;*

MusMk; NewGrDM 80; NewGrDO; NewOxM; ObitT 1971; OxCMus; WhAm 6; WhE&EA; WhLit

Scott, David Randolph
American. Astronaut
On flights of Gemini 8, 1966; Apollo 9, 1969; Apollo 15, 1971.
b. Jun 6, 1932 in San Antonio, Texas
Source: *BioIn 9, 10; CurBio 71; IntWW 74; NewYTBE 71; WhoAm 86, 88; WhoSSW 73; WhoWor 80*

Scott, Dred
American. Slave
Sued for his freedom, 1846; lost in Supreme Court, 1857; "Dred Scott Case" because landmark decision upholding slavery.
b. 1795 in Southampton County, Virginia
d. Sep 17, 1858 in Saint Louis, Missouri
Source: *AfrAmAl 6, 8; AmBi; BenetAL 91; BioIn 1, 2, 6, 9, 10, 11, 12, 20; CamBiEn; CamDcAB; ChamBiD; DcAmB; DcAmNB; EncAB-H 1974, 1996; EncWB 98; InB&W 80, 85; LegTOT; McGEWB; NotBlAM; WhAm HS; WorAl*

Scott, Duncan Campbell
Canadian. Poet
Wrote extensively on N American Indian: *Collected Poems,* 1926.
b. Aug 2, 1862 in Ottawa, Ontario, Canada
d. Dec 19, 1947 in Ottawa, Ontario, Canada
Source: *Benet 87, 96; BenetAL 91; BiCoLiE; BiD&SB; BioIn 1, 4, 5, 10, 11, 17, 22; CamGEL; CamGLE; CanNov; CanWr; CasWL; Chambr 3; ChhPo, S1, S2, S3; ConAu 104, 153; ConCaAu 1; CreCan 2; DcLB 92; DcLEL; DcNAA; EvLB; GrWrEL P; LinLib L, S; LngCTC; MacDCB 78; OxCCan; OxCCanL 1, 2; OxCTwCL; PenC ENG; RAdv 14, 13-1; REn; REnAL; RfGEnL 91; TwCA, SUP; TwCLC 6; WebE&AL; WhE&EA; WhLit; WhNaAH*

Scott, Edward Irvin
American. Businessman
Partner with brother Clarence, in million-dollar paper products business, begun 1879.
b. 1846 in Saratoga County, New York
d. 1931
Source: *Entr*

Scott, Evelyn
[Elsie Dunn; Ernest Soiza]
American. Author
Novels include *Migrations,* 1927; *The Wave,* 1929.
b. Jan 17, 1893 in Clarksville, Tennessee
d. Aug 3, 1963
Source: *AmAu&B; AmNatBi; AmWomPl; AmWomWr; ArtclWW 2; BenetAL 91; BioAmW; BioIn 4, 9, 10, 12, 13, 14, 15, 16, 17, 22, 24; CnDAL; ConAmA; ConAmL; ConAu 64NR, 104, 112; ConLC 43; DcLB 9, 48; DcLEL; EncALit; FemiCLE; OxCAmL 65, 83, 95;*

OxCWoWr 95; PenNWW A; REnAL; SouWr; TwCA, SUP; TwCRHW 90, 94; WhE&EA; WhNAA; WorAu 1900

Scott, F(rancis) R(eginald)
"Frank Scott"
Canadian. Poet, Political Activist, Political Scientist
Writer and constitutional theorist advocated Canadian political, legal, and literary independence, human rights and fundamental freedoms in Canada, and Quebec nationalism.
b. 1899 in Quebec City, Quebec, Canada
d. 1985
Source: *Benet 96; BiCoLiE; BioIn 5, 14, 15, 16, 18; CanWr; CasWL; ConPo 70, 75; CreCan 1; DcArts; DcLEL, 1940; EncWB, 98; FacFETw; IntWWP 77, 82; OxCCan, SUP; OxCTwCL; OxCTwCP; PenC ENG; REn; REnAL; WebE&AL; WhE&EA; WhoCanL 85; WrDr 76*

Scott, Gene
[Jimmy Scott]
American. Evangelist
California preacher who shares his vision of a liberal, earthy God on late-night television; when Federal Communications Commission withdrew his license due to irregularities in management, he turned to closed circuit and satellite television and built his audience.
Source: *BioIn 15, 23; ConNews 86-1*

Scott, George C(ampbell)
American. Actor
First performer to refuse Oscar, 1970, for *Patton.*
b. Oct 18, 1927 in Wise, Virginia
d. Sep 22, 1999 in Westlake Village, California
Source: *BiDFilm; BiE&WWA; BioIn 6, 8, 9, 10, 11, 13, 14, 15; BkPepl; CamBiEn; CamDcAB; CamGWoT; CelR 90; ConTFT 7; DcArts; HalFC 84, 88; IntDcT 3; IntMPA 86, 92; IntWW 74, 75, 76, 77, 83, 91, 93, 97, 98, 2000; NewYTBS 82; NotNAT; OxCFilm; WhoAm 74, 76, 78, 80, 82, 84, 86, 88, 90, 92, 94, 95, 96, 97, 99, 2000; WhoEnt 92, 98; WhoThe 81; WhoWor 74, 78; WorAlBi*

Scott, George Charles, Jr.
"Boomer"
American. Baseball Player
First baseman, 1966-79, mostly with Boston; led AL in home runs, RBIs, 1975.
b. Mar 23, 1944 in Greenville, Mississippi
Source: *BaseEn 88; InB&W 85; WhoBlA 3*

Scott, George Gilbert, Sir
English. Architect
Led Gothic revival; restored Westminster Abbey; designed Albert Memorial, 1863-72.
b. Jul 13, 1811 in Gawcott, England
d. Mar 27, 1878 in London, England

Source: *Alli, SUP; ArtsNiC; BioIn 3, 5, 10, 11, 13, 14, 16, 23; CamBiEn; CelCen; ChamBiD; DcArch; DcBiPP; DcD&D; DcNaB; IntDcAr; MacEA; McGDA; NewCol 75; OxCArt; OxCBrHi; OxCCAA; VicBrit; WhBriIn; WhDW; WhoArch; WhoChr*

Scott, Gloria Dean Randle

American. University Administrator
Pres., Bennett College, 1987—; first
  African-American pres. of the Girl
  Scouts 1975-78.
b. Apr 14, 1938 in Houston, Texas
Source: *AfrAmBi 1; BlkWAm; InB&W 85; InWom SUP; NotBlAW 1; WhoAfA 9, 10, 11, 12; WhoAm 94, 95; WhoAmW 91; WhoBlA 4, 5, 6, 7, 8; WhoWor 96*

Scott, Gordon

[Gordon M Werschkul]
American. Actor
Was the 11th Tarzan in films, 1955-60.
b. Aug 3, 1927 in Portland, Oregon
Source: *DcPseud; FilmEn; FilmgC; ForYSC; HalFC 80, 84, 88; IntMPA 75, 76, 77, 78, 79, 80, 81, 82, 84, 86, 88, 92, 94, 96; ItaFilm; LegTOT; WhoHol 92, A; WhoHrs 80*

Scott, Hazel Dorothy

[Mrs. Adam Clayton Powell, Jr.]
American. Jazz Musician
Pianist, singer, popular in 1940s; sang
  "FDR Jones;" had own TV show.
b. Jun 11, 1920 in Port of Spain,
  Trinidad and Tobago
d. Oct 2, 1981 in New York, New York
Source: *AmNatBi; AmPS B; AnObit 1981; ASCAP 66; BiDAfM; BiDAmM; BioIn 6, 8, 10; CmpEPM; CurBio 43, 81; DrBlPA; InB&W 80; InWom; ScrEAmL 1; WhoAmW 58; WhoHol A*

Scott, Hugh (Doggett), Jr.

American. Politician
Rep. minority leader, 1969-77; senator
  from PA, 1959-77.
b. Nov 11, 1900 in Fredericksburg,
  Virginia
d. Jul 21, 1994 in Falls Church, Virginia
Source: *AmNatBi; BiDrAC; BiDrUSC 89; BioIn 1, 5, 6, 7, 8, 9, 10, 11, 12, 17, 20; BlueB 76; CelR; CurBio 94N; InB&W 85; IntWW 74, 75, 76, 77, 78, 79, 80, 81, 82, 83; NewYTBS 94; WhAm 11; WhoAm 74, 76, 78, 80, 82, 84, 86, 88, 90, 92, 94; WhoAmP 73, 75, 77, 79, 81, 83, 85, 87, 89, 91, 93; WhoWor 74; WorAl; WorAlBi*

Scott, Ken

[George Kenneth Scott]
American. Designer
First American to set up fashion house in
  Italy; known for scarves, colorful
  swimwear, 1950s-60s.
b. Nov 6, 1918 in Fort Wayne, Indiana
d. Feb 26, 1991 in Eze, France
Source: *BioIn 7, 8, 17; EncFash; NewYTBS 91; ThHDFas; WorFshn*

Scott, Lizabeth

[Emma Matzo]
American. Actor
Played tough, shiftless blondes in 1940s-
  50s films: *Bad for Each Other*, 1953.
b. Sep 29, 1922 in Scranton,
  Pennsylvania
Source: *BioIn 24; DcPseud; FemmeNo; FilmEn; FilmgC; HalFC 80, 84, 88; IntMPA 77, 82, 96; InWom SUP; LegTOT; MotPP; MovMk; What 3; WhoAm 80; WhoHol 92, A; WorEFlm*

Scott, Martha Ellen

American. Actor
Broadway, film character actress
  nominated for Oscar for *Our Town*,
  1940.
b. Sep 22, 1914 in Jamesport, Missouri
Source: *FilmgC; HalFC 88; HolP 40; InWom SUP; MovMk; NotNAT; WhoAm 74, 76, 82; WhoHol A; WhoThe 81; WorAlBi*

Scott, Mike

[Michael Warren Scott]
American. Baseball Player
Pitcher, 1980-92; threw no-hitter, 1986;
  won NL Cy Young Award, 1986.
b. Apr 26, 1955 in Santa Monica,
  California
Source: *Ballpl 90; BaseReg 86, 87; BioIn 15; NewYTBS 86; WhoAm 88, 90; WhoSpor; WorAlBi*

Scott, Norman

American. Opera Singer
Bass with NY Met., 1951-68.
b. Nov 30, 1928 in New York, New
  York
d. Sep 22, 1968 in New York, New
  York
Source: *BiDAmM; WhAm 5*

Scott, Paul Mark

English. Author
Wrote novels *The Raj Quartet*, 1976,
  adapted for TV, 1982.
b. Mar 25, 1920 in London, England
d. Mar 1, 1978 in London, England
Source: *Au&Wr 71; BioIn 10, 11, 12, 13; CamBiEn; ChamBiD; ConNov 72, 76, 82A; DcArts; DcLEL 1940; DcNaB 1971; GrBr; ObitOF 79; OxCEng 85, 95; OxCTwCL; TwCRHW 94; WhBriIn; WorAu 1950; WrDr 76*

Scott, Peter Markham, Sir

English. Author, Naturalist
Founded World Wildlife Fund, designed
  panda logo, 1961; advocated existence
  of Loch Ness Monster; son of Robert.
b. Sep 14, 1909, England
d. Aug 29, 1989 in Bristol, England
Source: *Au&Wr 71; BioIn 7, 8, 12, 14, 16, 22; BlueB 76; CamBiEn; ChamBiD; CurBio 89N; DcBrAr 1; DcNaB 1986; FacFETw; LngCTC; NewYTBS 89; OxCCan; RanHWDS; WhE&EA; Who 74, 82, 83, 85, 88, 90N; WhoArt 80, 82, 84; WhoOcn 78; WhoWor 74, 89*

Scott, Pippa

[Phillippa Scott]
American. Actor
Appeared in films *Auntie Mame*, 1958;
  Cold Turkey, 1970.
b. Nov 10, 1935 in Los Angeles,
  California
Source: *BiE&WWA; FilmgC; ForYSC; HalFC 80, 84, 88; MotPP; WhoHol A*

Scott, Randolph

American. Actor
Made name as a Western hero who was
  fast on the draw but short on words:
  Ride the High Country, 1962.
b. Jan 23, 1898 in Orange County,
  Virginia
d. Mar 2, 1987 in Los Angeles,
  California
Source: *AmNatBi; BiDFilm; BioIn 15, 16, 21, 22, 24; CmMov; ConNews 87-2; ConTFT 26; FilmgC; HalFC 88; IntMPA 82; LegTOT; MotPP; MovMk; NewYTBS 87; OxCFilm; WhoHol A; WorAlBi; WorEFlm*

Scott, Raymond

[Harry Warnow]
American. Songwriter, Bandleader
Led quintet, 1940s; with TV's "Your Hit
  Parade," 1950s; wrote "In an 18th
  Century Drawing Room."
b. Sep 10, 1909 in New York, New
  York
d. Feb 8, 1994 in North Hills, California
Source: *ASCAP 66, 80; BgBands 74; BiDAmM; BioIn 3, 6, 9, 12, 19, 20, 22; CmpEPM; CurBio 41, 94N; MnPM; NewGrDJ 88; OxCPMus; PenEncP; PopAmC; RadStar; WhoHol 92; WhoJazz 72*

Scott, Ridley

English. Director
Films include *Alien*, 1979; *Blade Runner*,
  1982; *Thelma and Louise* 1991.
b. 1939 in South Shields, England
Source: *BiDFilm 94; BioIn 13, 14, 15; ConTFT 5, 9; CurBio 91; DcArts; EncEurC; EncSF 93; HalFC 84, 88; IntDcF 2-2; IntMPA 92; IntWW 91; LegTOT; MiSFD 9; VarWW 85; WhoAm 92, 94, 95, 96, 97, 98, 2000; WhoEnt 92, 98*

Scott, Robert Falcon

English. Explorer
Led expedition to S Pole, 1912, only to
  find Roald Amundsen had already
  been there.
b. Jun 6, 1868 in London, England
d. Mar 27, 1912, South Pole
Source: *AnCL; AsBiEn; BioIn 1, 2, 3, 4, 5, 6, 7, 8, 9, 10, 11, 12, 13, 14, 15, 17, 18, 19, 20, 23, 24; CamBiEn; ChamBiD; CyWA 97; DcNaB 1912; EncNaHi; EncWB 98; Expl 93; ExplAnT; InSci; LinLib L, S; McGEWB; NewC; OxCBrHi; OxCEng 67, 85, 95; OxCShps; OxCTwCL; RAdv 14, 13-3; REn; WhDW; WhWE; WorAl*

Scott, Steve
American. Track Athlete
Second fastest miler in history.
b. 1956?
Source: BiDAmSp OS; BioIn 12, 13, 16;
NewYTBS 82

Scott, Thomas Alexander
American. Railroad Executive
Head of Union rail transportation, Civil
War; pres. of Pennsylvania Railroad,
1874-80.
b. Dec 28, 1823 in Fort Loudon,
Pennsylvania
d. May 21, 1881 in Darby, Pennsylvania
Source: AmBi; ApCAB; BiDAmBL 83;
CamDcAB; DcAmB; EncAB-H 1974,
1996; NewEAmW; NatCAB 13; NewEAmW;
OxCAmH; REnAW; TwCBDA; WhAm
HS; WhCiWar

Scott, Tony
American. Musician
Top jazz clarinetist, 1950s-60s; adapted
folk songs to jazz.
b. Jun 17, 1921 in Morristown, New
Jersey
Source: AllMGJa; BiDAmM; BiDJaz;
BioIn 5; CmpEPM; DcPseud; EncJzS;
NewGrDA 86; NewGrDJ 88, 94;
PenEncP; WhoAm 74; WhoE 74

Scott, Walter
"Death Valley Scotty"
American. Adventurer
Built $2 million Moorish castle in Death
Valley; tourist attraction today.
b. 1872
d. Jan 5, 1954 in Stovepipe Wells,
California
Source: BioIn 3, 7, 9, 10; CmCal;
DcAmB S5; WebAB 74

Scott, Walter, Sir
Scottish. Poet, Author, Historian
Father of historical novel; writings
include Ivanhoe, 1820.
b. Aug 15, 1771 in Edinburgh, Scotland
d. Sep 21, 1832 in Abbotsford, Scotland
Source: Alli; AnCL; AtlBL; Au&Arts 22;
BbD; Benet 87, 96; BiCoLiE; BiD&SB;
BiDLA, SUP; BioIn 1, 2, 3, 4, 5, 6, 7, 8,
9, 10, 11, 12, 13, 14, 15, 17, 18, 19, 20,
21, 22; BlmGEL; BritAu 19; BritWr 4;
CamBiEn; CamGEL; CamGLE; CarSB;
CasWL; CelCen; ChamBiD; Chambr 3;
ChhPo, S1, S2, S3; CmScLit; CnDBLB
3; CnE&AP; CrtT 2, 4; CyWA 58, 97;
DcArts; DcBiA; DcBiPP; DcEnA, A;
DcEnL; DcEuL; DcLB 93, 107, 116,
144, 159; DcLEL; DcNaB; DcPup;
Dis&D; EncFoLi; EncPaPR 91; EncWB
98; EvLB; FamAYP; GrWrEL N, P;
HalFC 80, 84, 88; HsB&A; LegTOT;
LinLib L, S; LngCEL; MagSWL;
McGEWB; MetOEnc; MnBBF; MouLC
3; NewC; NewCBEL; NewEOp 71;
NewGrDM 80; NewGrDO; NinCLC 15,
69; NotPoe; Novels; OxCBrHi;
OxCChiL; OxCEng 67, 85, 95; OxCMus;
OxCThe 83; OxDcOp; PenC ENG;
PenEncH; PoChrch; PoeCrit 13; RAdv
1, 14, 13-1; RComWL; REn; RfGEnL 91;

RfGShF 1, 2; ScF&FL 92; ShSCr 32;
SJGHorW; Str&VC; SupFW; WebE&AL;
WhDW; WhoChL; WhoHr&F; WorAl;
WorAlBi; WorLitC; YABC 2

Scott, Willard Herman, Jr.
American. TV Personality
Weatherman, "Today" show, 1980-95.
b. Mar 7, 1934 in Alexandria, Virginia
Source: BioIn 12, 13; ConAu 109;
NewYTBS 87; WhoAm 82, 84, 86, 88,
90, 92, 94, 95, 96, 97, 98, 2000; WhoE
95; WhoEnt 98; WhoTelC

Scott, Winfield
"Old Fuss and Feathers"
American. Army Officer
Led US in Mexican War, 1846-48; Whig
candidate for pres., 1852.
b. Jun 13, 1786 in Petersburg, Virginia
d. May 29, 1866 in West Point, New
York
Source: Alli; AmAu&B; AmBi; AmNatBi;
AmPolLe; ApCAB; BenetAL 91; BiAUS;
BiDSA; BioIn 1, 2, 3, 4, 6, 7, 8, 9, 10,
12, 20, 23, 24; CamBiEn; CamDcAB;
CelCen; ChamBiD; CivWDc; CmdGen
1991; CyAG; DcAmAu; DcAmB;
DcAmMiB; DcNAA; Drake; EncAB-H
1974, 1996; EncAPar; EncSoH;
EncWar; EncWB 98; GenMudB;
HarEnMi; HarEnUS; HisWorL; LegTOT;
LinLib S; McGEWB; MilitOn; NatCAB
3; NewEAmW; OxCAmH; PolPar;
PresAR 1980, 1996; REnAL; REnAW;
TwCBDA; WebAB 74, 79; WebAMB;
WhAm HS; WhCiWar; WhFla; WhNaAH;
WhoMilH 76; WorAl; WorAlBi

Scott, Zachary
American. Actor
Films include Bandido, 1956; It's Only
Money, 1962.
b. Feb 24, 1914 in Austin, Texas
d. Oct 3, 1965 in Austin, Texas
Source: BiE&WWA; BioIn 7, 10;
FilmEn; FilmgC; ForYSC; HalFC 80,
84, 88; HolP 40; MotPP; MovMk;
NotNAT B; WhoHol B; WhScrn 74, 77,
83; WorAl

Scotti, Antonio
Italian. Opera Singer
Famed dramatic baritone, NY Met.,
1900-33.
b. Jan 25, 1866 in Naples, Italy
d. Feb 26, 1936 in Naples, Italy
Source: BakBD 78, 84, 92; BakBDTw;
BiDAmM; BioIn 1, 3, 6, 11, 14; CmOp;
IntDcOp; LegTOT; MetOEnc; MusSN;
NewAmDM; NewEOp 71; NewGrDA 86;
NewGrDM 80; NewGrDO; OxDcOp;
PenDiMP; WhAm 1

Scotto, Renata
Italian. Opera Singer
Soprano who made NY Met. debut,
1965.
b. Feb 24, 1934 in Savona, Italy
Source: BakBD 78, 84; BioIn 14; CelR
90; CmOp; IntDcOp; IntWW 74, 75, 76,
77, 78, 79, 80, 81, 82, 83, 91; IntWWM
90; InWom SUP; MetOEnc; MusSN;

NewAmDM; NewEOp 71; NewGrDM 80;
NewGrDO; NewYTBE 72; PenDiMP;
WhoAm 86; WhoAmW 68, 70, 72, 74;
WhoE 74; WhoMus 72; WhoWor 74, 78;
WorAl; WorAlBi

Scottsboro Boys
[Olen Montgomery; Clarence Norris;
Haywood Patterson; Ozie Powell;
Willie Roberson; Charlie Weems;
Eugene Williams; Andy Wright; Roy
Wright]
American. Criminals
Young defendants charged with rape;
case dragged on for 20 years even
though one of rape charges was
recanted.
Source: InB&W 80; NewCol 75

Scourby, Alexander
American. Actor
Best known for resonant bass voice;
most memorable screen role in Giant,
1956.
b. Nov 13, 1913 in New York, New
York
d. Feb 22, 1985 in Boston,
Massachusetts
Source: BiE&WWA; BioIn 7, 8, 14, 24;
CurBio 65, 85, 85N; FilmEn; FilmgC;
ForYSC; GangFlm; HalFC 80, 84, 88;
ItaFilm; LegTOT; MotPP; MovMk;
NewYTBS 85; NotNAT; RadStar;
ScrEAmL 1; WhoE 74; WhoHol A;
WhoThe 72, 77, 81; WorAl; WorAlBi

Scowcroft, Brent
American. Presidential Aide
Head of National Security Council,
1975-77; 1989-93; member of Tower
commission investigating Iran-Contra
scandal, 1986-87.
b. Mar 19, 1925 in Ogden, Utah
Source: AmMWSc 73S; WhoWor 80;
WorDWW

Scranton, George Whitfield
American. Manufacturer
Founded Scranton, PA, 1840.
b. May 11, 1811 in Madison,
Connecticut
d. Mar 24, 1861 in Scranton,
Pennsylvania
Source: AmBi; AmNatBi; BiDrAC;
BiDrUSC 89; DcAmB; EncABHB 3;
NatCAB 9; WhAm HS; WhAmP; WorAl

Scranton, William Warren
American. Politician
Rep. governor of PA, 1963-66.
b. Jul 19, 1917 in Madison, Connecticut
Source: BiDrAC; BiDrGov 1789;
BiDrUSC 89; BioIn 6, 7, 10, 11, 12, 17;
BioNews 74; CurBio 64; IntWW 83, 89,
91, 93, 97, 98, 2000; IntYB 78, 79, 80,
81, 82; NewYTBE 70; NewYTBS 76;
PolProf J, K, NF; St&PR 75; WhoAm
74, 76, 78, 80, 82, 84; WhoAmP 73, 75,
77, 79, 81, 83, 85, 87, 89, 91, 93, 95,
97, 1999; WhoE 86; WhoFI 89; WhoGov
72, 75, 77; WhoWor 74, 78, 80, 82;
WorAl; WorAlBi

Scriabin, Alexander Nicholaevich

[Aleksandr Scryabin]
Russian. Composer, Musician
Best known for composition *Prometheus*.
b. Jan 6, 1872 in Moscow, Russia
d. Apr 27, 1915 in Moscow, Russia
Source: *AtlBL; BioIn 1, 3, 4, 6, 7, 8, 9, 10, 12; DcCM; REn*

Scribe, (Augustin) Eugene

French. Dramatist
Wrote an estimated three to four hundred works; wrote *Encore une nuit de la Garde Nationale*, 1815.
b. 1791 in Paris, France
d. 1861 in Paris, France
Source: *AtlBL; BakBD 78, 84, 92; BbD; Benet 87, 96; BiD&SB; BioIn 7, 10, 11, 14; BriBkM 80; CamBiEn; CasWL; CelCen; ChamBiD; CmOp; CnOxB; CnThe; DcArts; DcBiPP; DcEuL; Dis&D; DramC 5; EncWT; Ent; EuAu; EvEuW; GuFrLit 1; IntDcOp; IntDcT 2; LinLib L, S; McGEWD 72, 84; MetOEnc; NewCBEL; NewGrDM 80; NewGrDO; NinCLC 16; NotNAT A, B; OxCAmT 84; OxCFr; OxCThe 67, 83; OxDcOp; PenC EUR; REn; REnWD; RfGWoL 95*

Scribner, Charles

American. Publisher
Founded Baker and Scribner Publishers, 1846; changed to Charles Scribner's Sons, 1878.
b. Feb 21, 1821 in New York, New York
d. Aug 26, 1871 in Lucerne, Switzerland
Source: *AmAu&B; AmBi; AmNatBi; ApCAB; BioIn 1; CamBiEn; ChamBiD; DcAmB; LegTOT; NatCAB 6; TwCBDA; WhAm HS; WhDW; WorAl; WorAlBi*

Scribner, Charles, Jr.

American. Publisher
Chairman, Scribner Book Cos., 1978-86; president, Charles Scribner's Sons, 1952 -77, chairman, 1977-78; was Ernest Hemingway's personal editor.
b. Jul 13, 1921 in Quogue, New York
d. Nov 11, 1995 in New York, New York
Source: *AmAu&B; AmNatBi; BioIn 11, 14, 17, 19, 21, 22, 23; BlueB 76; CelR; ConAu 69, 150; DcLB Y95; IntAu&W 82; IntWW 74, 75, 76, 77, 78, 79, 80, 81, 82, 83, 89, 91, 93; LinLib L; PeoHis; SmATA 13, 87; St&PR 75, 84, 87; WhAm 11; WhoAm 74, 76, 78, 80, 82, 84, 86, 88, 90, 92, 94; WhoFI 74; WhoWor 74*

Scribner, Fred C(lark), Jr.

American. Government Official, Lawyer
Member, Republican National Committee, 1948-56; undersecretary of the Treasury, 1957-60; helped arrange Nixon-Kennedy debate, 1960.
b. Feb 14, 1908
d. Jan 5, 1994 in Portland, Maine
Source: *BioIn 4, 5; CurBio 94N; St&PR 75, 84, 87, 91, 93; WhAm 11; WhoAm 74, 76, 78, 80, 82, 84, 86, 88, 90, 92,*

94; WhoAmL 78, 79, 83, 87; WhoAmP 73, 75, 77, 79, 81, 83, 85, 87, 89, 91, 93; WhoFI 92, 94

Scripps, Edward Wyllis

American. Newspaper Publisher
Formed Scripps-McRae League of Newspapers which evolved into Scripps-Howard Newspapers; developed United Press International.
b. Jun 18, 1854 in Rushville, Illinois
d. Mar 12, 1926 in Monrovia, Liberia
Source: *AmAu&B; AmBi; BioIn 2, 3, 5, 7, 9, 10, 13, 14, 15, 16, 17, 20, 23; CamDcAB; ChamBiD; DcAmB; EncAB-H 1974, 1996; EncWB 98; FrTalk; McGEWB; NatCAB 28; OxCAmH; REnAL; WebAB 74, 79; WhAm 1*

Scripps, Robert Paine

American. Journalist
Editorial director of Scripps-Howard newspaper chain from 1917.
b. Oct 27, 1895 in San Diego, California
d. Mar 2, 1938
Source: *AmAu&B; AmBi; AmNatBi; BioIn 4, 13; DcAmB S2; LinLib L, S; NatCAB 62; WhAm 1, 1C*

Scruggs, Earl Eugene

[Flatt and Scruggs]
American. Musician, Songwriter
Won Grammy, 1969, for "Foggy Mountain Breakdown."
b. Jan 6, 1924 in Flint Hill, North Carolina
Source: *BakBD 84, 92; BiDAmM; BioIn 14, 15; ConMus 3; EncFCWM 69; EncRk 88; HarEnR 86; NewAmDM; NewGrDA 86; OxCPMus; WhoAm 76, 78, 80, 82, 84, 86, 88, 90, 92, 94, 95, 96, 97, 98, 99, 2000; WhoAmP 73; WhoEnt 92, 98; WhoGov 72; WhoWor 74, 78*

Scruggs, Jan

American. Veterans' Leader
Vietnam veteran; created concept of Vietnam Veterans Memorial, 1982, with wall of names of deceased soldiers.
Source: *BioIn 16; ConHero 1*

Scudery, Madeleine de

French. Author
Wrote huge novels, which epitomized sentimental romances of her day: *Almahide, or the Slave as Queen*, 1660-63.
b. Nov 15, 1607 in Le Havre, France
d. Jun 2, 1701 in Paris, France
Source: *BbD; Benet 87, 96; BiD&SB; BioIn 5, 7, 9, 11, 17; BlmGWL; CamBiEn; CasWL; ContDcW 89; CyWA 58, 97; DcEuL; EncCoWW; EvEuW; FemiCLE; FrenWW; IntDcWB; InWom, SUP; LegTOT; LitC 2; NewC; NewCBEL; OxCEng 67, 85, 95; OxCFr; PenC EUR; PenNWW A; REn; WhDW; WomWrGB*

Sculley, John

American. Business Executive
As president and CEO of Pepsi-Cola Co., 1977-83 used his marketing skills to create "the Pepsi generation;" Apple Computer, Inc., president and CEO, 1983-, chairman 1986-.
b. Apr 6, 1939 in New York, New York
Source: *BioIn 11, 13; ConAu 127; CurBio 88; Dun&B 79, 88, 90; IntWW 89, 91, 93, 97, 98; News 89; St&PR 84, 87, 91, 93, 96, 97, 98, 99, 2000; WhoAm 82, 84, 86, 88, 90, 92, 94, 95, 96; WhoFI 81, 87, 92, 94, 96; WhoTech 95; WhoWest 87, 89, 92, 94; WorAlBi*

Scullin, James Henry

Australian. Political Leader
First native-born Labour prime minister of Australia.
b. 1876 in Victoria, Australia
d. Jan 28, 1953
Source: *BioIn 3, 6, 8, 10; DcTwHis; EncWB 98; McGEWB*

Scully, Vin(cent Edward)

American. Sportscaster
With NBC Sports since 1982, covering among other things, baseball game of the week.
b. Nov 29, 1927 in New York, New York
Source: *BiDAmSp OS; BioIn 4, 6, 13; WhoAm 78, 80, 82, 84, 86, 88, 90, 92, 94, 95, 96, 97, 98, 99, 2000; WhoTelC; WhoWest 96*

Seaborg, Glenn T(heodore)

American. Chemist
Shared Nobel Prize, 1951, for identification of elements 94-102; chm., Atomic Energy Commission, 1961-71; element 106, seaborgium, was named in his honor.
b. Apr 19, 1912 in Ishpeming, Michigan
d. Feb 25, 1999 in Lafayette, California
Source: *AmMWSc 76P, 79, 82, 86, 89, 92, 95, 98; AsBiEn; BiESc; BioIn 1, 2, 3, 4, 5, 6, 7, 9, 10, 11, 12, 14, 15, 19, 20, 21; BlueB 76; CamBiEn; CamDcAB; CamDcSc; ConAu 2NR, 49; CurBio 48, 61; EncWB, 98; FacFETw; Future; InSci; IntAu&W 77, 93; IntWW 91, 97, 98; LinLib L, S; McGCEnS; McGMS 80; NobelP; OxCAmH; RAdv 14; RanHWDS; St&PR 87, 91; WebAB 74, 79; WhE&EA; Who 74, 82, 83, 85, 88, 90, 92, 94, 98, 99; WhoAm 74, 76, 78, 80, 82, 84, 86, 88, 90, 92, 94, 95, 96, 97, 98, 99; WhoAmP 73; WhoFrS 84; WhoNob, 90, 95; WhoScEn 94, 96; WhoWest 00, 78, 80, 82, 84, 87, 89, 92, 94, 98; WhoWor 74, 76, 78, 80, 82, 84, 87, 89, 91, 93, 95, 96, 97, 98, 99; WorAl; WorAlBi; WrDr 94, 96, 98, 99, 2000*

Seabury, Samuel

[A Westchester Farmer]
American. Theologian, Pamphleteer, Religious Leader
Loyalist during Revolution who was first American-born Episcopalian bishop.

b. Nov 30, 1729 in Groton, Connecticut
d. Feb 25, 1796 in New London,
Connecticut
Source: Alli; AmAu&B; AmBi; AmNatBi;
AmWrBE; ApCAB; BenetAL 91; BioIn 3,
5, 6, 9, 10, 11, 13, 14, 19; BlkwEAR;
CamBiEn; ChamBiD; CnDAL; CyAL 1;
DcAmAu; DcAmB; DcAmReB 1, 2;
DcLB 31; DcLEL; DcNAA; Drake;
EncAB-H 1974, 1996; EncALit;
EncARH; EncCRAm; EncWB 98;
HarEnUS; LuthC 75; McGEWB;
NatCAB 3; OxCAmH; OxCAmL 65, 83,
95; REnAL; TwCBDA; WebAB 74, 79;
WhAm HS

Seaga, Edward Phillip George
Jamaican. Political Leader
Prime minister of Jamaica, 1981-89.
b. May 28, 1930 in Boston,
Massachusetts
Source: BiDLAmC; BioIn 12, 13, 14, 16;
CurBio 81; IntWW 91; NewYTBS 80;
Who 92; WhoWor 87, 91

Seagal, Steven
American. Actor
Martial arts expert; movies include:
Above the Law, 1988; Under Siege,
1992.
b. Apr 10, 1951 in Lansing, Michigan
Source: FilmChD; IntMPA 92, 94;
IntWW 97, 98, 2000; WhoAm 94, 95, 96,
97, 98, 99; WhoEnt 98

Seagram, Joseph Edward Frowde
Canadian. Distiller
President of Joseph E Seagram & Sons
from 1937.
b. Aug 11, 1903 in Waterloo, Ontario,
Canada
d. Nov 28, 1979 in Waterloo, Ontario,
Canada
Source: CanWW 70, 79; IntYB 78, 79,
80; St&PR 75; WhAm 7; WhoAm 74;
WhoCan 73, 75, 77, 80; WhoE 74;
WhoFI 74; WhoMW 74; WhoWor 74

Seagrave, Gordon Stifler
American. Surgeon, Author
Founded hospitals in Burma, practiced
there for 40 yrs.
b. 1897 in Rangoon, Burma
d. Mar 28, 1965 in Namkham, Burma
Source: AmNatBi; BiDChrM; BioIn 1, 2,
3, 4, 5, 6, 7, 8; CurBio 43, 65; DcAmB
S7; InSci; OhA&B; WebAMB; WhAm 4

Seagren, Bob
[Robert Lloyd Seagren]
American. Track Athlete
Pole vaulter; first American to vault 18
feet, 1972; won gold medal, 1968
Olympics, silver medal, 1972
Olympics.
b. Oct 17, 1946 in Pomona, California
Source: BiDAmSp OS; BioIn 7, 8, 10;
CmCal; CurBio 74; WhoSpor; WhoTr&F
73

Seajay, Carol
American. Publisher
Co-founder of the feminist bookstore Old
Wives Tales, 1976, San Francisco;
publisher and editor, Feminist
Bookstore News, 1976—.
Source: BioIn 19; GayLesB

Seal
[Sealhenry Olumide Samuel]
English. Singer, Songwriter
Debut album, Seal, 1991; won three
Grammy Awards, 1996.
b. Feb 19, 1963 in Paddington, England
Source: BillEnR; ConAu 156; ConBlB
14; ConMus 14; CurBio 97; DcPseud;
Songw; WhoAm 2000

Seal, Elizabeth
Italian. Actor
Won Tony for Irma La Douce, 1961.
b. Aug 28, 1933 in Genoa, Italy
Source: BiE&WWA; ConTFT 5; EncMT;
HalFC 84, 88; NotNAT; VarWW 85;
WhoHol 92; WhoThe 72, 77, 81

Seale, Bobby G
American. Political Activist, Author
Co-founder, chairman, Black Panthers,
1966.
b. Oct 20, 1936 in Dallas, Texas
Source: BiDAmLf; BioIn 14, 15; BlkWr
1; BlkWrNE; ConBlB 3; Dun&B 90;
LivgBAA; MugS; NewYTBE 70; PolProf
J, NF; WhoBlA 4, 5

Seals, Dan Wayland
American. Singer, Songwriter
Member of pop duo England Dan and
John Ford Coley, 1969-80; solo career,
1983—; hits include "Bop," 1988.
b. Feb 8, 1948 in McCarney, Texas
Source: BioIn 14; ConMus 9; HarEnCM
87; WhoAm 94, 95, 96, 97, 98

Seals, Jim
[Seals and Crofts; James Seals]
American. Singer, Songwriter
Guitarist, vocalist with Seals and Crofts;
had hit album Diamond Girl, 1973.
b. Oct 17, 1942 in Sindey, Texas
Source: BkPepl; EncPR&S 89; WhoAm
82

Seals and Crofts
[Dash Crofts; Jim Seals]
American. Music Group
Hit rock duo, popular during 1970s;
songs show social concern.
Source: BkPepl; ConMus 3; EncPR&S
74, 89; EncRk 88; HarEnR 86; IlEncRk;
PenEncP; RkOn 74; WhoAm 78, 80, 82;
WhoRocM 82

Seaman, Owen, Sir
English. Editor
Editor of Punch, 1906-32.
b. Sep 18, 1861 in London, England
d. Feb 2, 1936 in London, England
Source: Alli SUP; BioIn 2, 11, 14, 22;
ChamBiD; Chambr 3; ChhPo, S1, S2,

S3; DcNaB 1931; EvLB; GrBr; LngCTC;
NewC; NewCBEL; NotNAT B; TwCA,
SUP; WhE&EA; WhLit; WhThe; WorAu
1900

Searchers, The
[Billy Adamson; Frank Allen; Bob
Jackson; John McNally; Mike Pender]
English. Music Group
Second to The Beatles in popularity,
1960s; hits include "Love Potion No.
9," 1964.
Source: BiDAmM; BillEnR; BioIn 12;
DrAPF 80, 83, 85, 87; EncRk 88;
EncRkSt; HarEnR 86; OxCPMus;
PenEncP; ProFbHF; RkOn 78, 84;
RolSEnR 83; WhoRock 81; WhoRocM 82

Searle, Ronald William Fordham
English. Artist
Children's writer, film illustrator; created
cartoon series, "St. Trinian's," 1941-
53.
b. Mar 3, 1920 in Cambridge, England
Source: Au&Wr 71; BioIn 14, 15;
CamBiEn; ChamBiD; ConAu 9R, 25NR;
FacFETw; IlsBYP; IlsCB 1946; IntWW
74, 91; NewC; OxCChiL; OxCTwCA;
SmATA 24, 42; TwCPaSc; Who 92, 98,
99, 2000; WhoAm 86, 88; WhoArt 84;
WhoGrA 62; WhoWor 74, 89; WrDr 76,
92, 98, 99, 2000

Sears, Eleonora Randolph
"Mother of Squash"
American. Athlete
Socialite, all-around sportswoman who
made breakthrough into all-male
sports; first woman squash champion,
1928.
b. Sep 28, 1881 in Boston,
Massachusetts
d. Mar 26, 1968 in Palm Beach, Florida
Source: AmNatBi; BiDAmSp OS; BioIn
12, 17, 21; CamDcAB; InWom SUP;
NotAW MOD

Sears, Heather
English. Actor
b. Sep 28, 1935 in London, England
Source: FilmEn, 78, 79, 80, 81, 82, 84,
86; MotPP; WhoHol 92, A; WhoThe 72,
77, 81

Sears, Isaac
"King Sears"
American. Patriot
Led anti-British demonstrations in New
York City before the American
Revolution.
b. Jul 1, 1730 in West Brewster,
Massachusetts
d. Oct 28, 1786 in Guangzhou, China
Source: AmNatBi; BioIn 12, 16;
BlkwEAR; DcAmB; EncAR; EncCRAm;
HisDcAR; NatCAB 1; WebAB 74, 79;
WhAm HS; WhAmRev

Sears, John Patrick

American. Lawyer
Deputy counsel to Nixon, 1969-70; managed Reagan's presidential campaign, 1975-76, 1979-80.
b. Jul 3, 1940 in Syracuse, New York
Source: *BioIn 8, 10, 11, 12; NewYTBS 76; WhoAm 74, 76, 78, 80, 82, 84, 86, 88, 90, 92, 94, 95, 96, 97, 98, 99, 2000; WhoAmL 78, 79; WhoAmP 79, 81, 83, 85, 87, 89, 91, 93, 95, 97, 1999; WhoSSW 73*

Sears, Richard Dudley

American. Tennis Player
First US nat. amateur tennis champ, 1881.
b. Oct 26, 1861 in Boston, Massachusetts
d. Apr 8, 1943 in Boston, Massachusetts
Source: *BiDAmSp OS; CamDcAB; DcAmB S3*

Sears, Richard Warren

American. Merchant
Issued first mail order catalog, 1887; Sears, Roebuck opened, 1893.
b. Dec 7, 1863 in Stewartville, Minnesota
d. Sep 28, 1914 in Waukesha, Wisconsin
Source: *AmBi; ApCAB X; BiDAmBL 83; BioIn 2, 6, 7, 10, 20, 24; CamBiEn; CamDcAB; DcAmB; EncAAH; WebAB 74, 79; WhAm 1; WhDW*

Sears, Robert Richardson

American. Psychologist, Educator
Psychology professor at several universities, specializing in child development; wrote *Patterns of Child Rearing*, 1957.
b. Aug 31, 1908 in Palo Alto, California
d. May 22, 1989 in Menlo Park, California
Source: *AmAu&B; AmMWSc 73S, 78S; AmNatBi; BiDcPsy; BiDMoAE; BioIn 2, 3, 10, 12, 16, 17, 24; ConAu 17R; CurBio 52, 89; InSci; NewYTBS 89; WhAm 10; WhoAm 74, 76, 78, 80, 82, 84, 86, 88*

Sears-Collins, Leah J.

American. Judge
First black woman to serve on the State Supreme Court of Georgia, 1992—.
b. Jun 13, 1955 in Heidelberg, Germany (West)
Source: *AfrAmBi 1; ConBlB 5; NotBlAW 2; WhoAmL 94, 96; WhoAmW 93, 95; WhoBlA 6; WhoSSW 93, 95*

Seaton, George

American. Screenwriter
Won Oscars for *Miracle on 34th Street*, 1947; *The Country Girl*, 1954.
b. Apr 17, 1911 in South Bend, Indiana
d. Jul 28, 1979 in Beverly Hills, California
Source: *AmNatBi; BiDFilm, 81, 94; BioIn 9, 11, 12, 15; ConAu 89, 105; DcFM; DcLB 44; DcPseud; EncAFC; FilmEn; FilmgC; HalFC 80, 84, 88; IlWWHD 1A; IndAu 1967; IntDcF 1-2; IntMPA 75, 76, 77, 78, 79; LegTOT;*

MiSFD 9N; MovMk; WhAm 7; WhoAm 74, 76, 78; WhoWor 74; WhScrn 83; WorEFlm

Seattle

American. Native American Chief
Chief of the Suquamish tribe; signed Port Elliott Treaty with the US government ceding native lands, 1855.
b. 1788?
d. Jun 7, 1866 in Washington
Source: *AmIndBi; CamDcAB; EncWB 98; NotNaAm; WhNaAH*

Seaver, Tom

[George Thomas Seaver]
"Tom Terrific"
American. Baseball Player
Pitcher, 1967-86, mostly with Mets; 17th in ML history to win 300 games, 1985; won NL Cy Young Award three times.
b. Nov 17, 1944 in Fresno, California
Source: *Ballpl 90; BaseReg 86, 87; BiDAmSp BB; BioIn 7, 8, 9, 10, 11, 12, 13, 14, 15, 16; BkPepl; CamBiEn; CelR; CmCal; CulEncB; CurBio 70; LegTOT; NewYTBE 70; NewYTBS 74, 77, 85; WhoAm 74, 76, 78, 80, 82, 84, 86, 88, 92, 94, 95, 96, 97, 98, 99, 2000; WhoE 95; WhoProB 73; WhoSpor*

Sebastian, John

[Lovin' Spoonful]
American. Singer
Co-founder, rock-folk group, Lovin' Spoonful, 1965.
b. Mar 17, 1944 in New York, New York
Source: *BakBD 84, 92; BillEnR; BioIn 13, 14; ConMuA 80A, 80B; EncRk 88; IlEncRk; LegTOT; NewGrDA 86; RkOn 78, 82; RolSEnR 83; Songw; WhoAm 74; WhoHol 92; WhoRock 81; WhoRocM 82; WorAlBi*

Sebastiani, Samuele

American. Vintner
Established prosperous trade selling bulk wine to bottlers in US, 1825.
b. 1874
d. 1944
Source: *Entr*

Sebelius, Keith George

American. Politician
Rep. congressman from KS, 1969-81.
b. Sep 10, 1916 in Alamena, Kansas
d. Sep 5, 1982 in Norton, Kansas
Source: *BiDrAC; WhoMW 74, 76, 78, 80, 82*

Seberg, Jean

American. Actor
Discovered by Otto Preminger; films include *Saint Joan*, 1957; *Lilith*, 1964.
b. Nov 13, 1938 in Marshalltown, Iowa
d. Aug 31, 1979 in Paris, France
Source: *BiDFilm, 78, 79; InWom SUP; ItaFilm; LegTOT; MotPP; MovMk; NewYTBS 80; OxCFilm; WhoAmW 74;*

WhoFr 79; WhoHol A; WhoWor 74; WhScrn 83; WorEFlm

Sebrell, W(illiam) H(enry), Jr.

American. Nutritionist
Medical director, Weight Watchers International, 1971-79; director, Weight Watchers Foundation, 1971-92.
b. Sep 11, 1901 in Portsmouth, Virginia
d. Sep 29, 1992 in Pompano Beach, Florida
Source: *AmMWSc 73P, 76P, 79; BiDrAPH 79; BioIn 2, 3, 18, 19; CurBio 92N; InSci; WhAm 10; WhoAm 74, 76, 78, 80, 82, 84, 86, 88, 90, 92; WhoWor 74*

Sebring, Jay

American. Hairstylist, Actor
Murdered, with Sharon Tate, by Charles Manson family.
b. Oct 10, 1933 in Alabama
d. Jul 8, 1969 in Los Angeles, California
Source: *BioIn 6; WhScrn 77, 83*

Secchi, Pietro Angelo

Italian. Astronomer
Jesuit priest known for work in spectroscopy; classified stars by their spectra, made solar-eclipse photo, 1860.
b. 1818 in Reggio Nell'Emilia, Italy
d. Feb 26, 1878 in Rome, Italy
Source: *AsBiEn; BiEsc; CamBiEn; DcAmB; DcCathB; DcScB; McGCEnS; NewCol 75; RanHWDS*

Secombe, Harry

Welsh. Actor, Comedian, Singer
With Spike Mulligan, Peter Sellers, originated, performed in BBC radio series, "The Goon Show," 1951-56.
b. Sep 8, 1921 in Swansea, Wales
Source: *BioIn 10, 13; BlueB 76; ConAu 57; EncMT; FilmgC; HalFC 80, 84, 88; IlWWBF; IntMPA 75, 76, 77, 78, 79, 80, 81, 82, 84, 86, 88, 92, 94, 96; Who 74, 82, 83, 85, 88, 90, 92; WhoHol 92, A; WhoMus 72; WhoThe 72, 77, 81; WrDr 76, 80, 82*

Secord, Laura Ingersoll

Canadian. Historical Figure
During War of 1812, warned British of surprise American attack at Beaver Dams, 1813.
b. 1775 in Massachusetts
d. Oct 17, 1868 in Chippewa, Ontario, Canada
Source: *BioIn 10; ColCR; EncWar; MacDCB 78; NewCol 75; OxCCan; WomFir*

Secunda, Arthur

[Holland Arthur Secunda]
American. Artist
Abstract paintings reflect California environment through use of vibrant colors.
b. Nov 12, 1927 in Jersey City, New Jersey

Source: *PrintW 83, 85; WhoAm 76, 78, 80, 82, 84, 86, 88, 90, 92, 94, 95, 96; WhoAmA 73, 76, 78, 80, 82, 84, 86, 89, 91, 1999*

Secunda, Sholom
Russian. Conductor
Wrote over 40 operettas for NYC Yiddish Theater; noted for "Bei Mir Bist Du Schon," 1933.
b. Aug 23, 1894 in Alexandria, Russia
d. Jun 13, 1974 in New York, New York
Source: *ASCAP 66, 80; BakBD 84, 92; BakBDTw; BioIn 2, 10, 12, 13; ConAmC 76, 82; ConAu 49; NatCAB 58; NewYTBS 74; WhAm 6; WhoAm 74; WhoMus 72; WhoWorJ 72*

Sedaka, Neil
American. Singer, Songwriter
Wrote songs "Breaking Up is Hard to Do," 1960; "Love Will Keep Us Together," 1975.
b. Mar 13, 1939 in New York, New York
Source: *AmSong; BilIEnR; BioIn 6, 10, 11, 12, 13, 14, 15, 16; BkPepl; ConAu 103; ConMuA 80A; ConMus 4; CurBio 78; EncPR&S 74, 89; EncRk 88; EncRkSt; HarEnR 86; IlEncRk; IntWW 97, 98, 2000; LegTOT; NewAmDM; NewGrDA 86; OxCPMus; PenEncP; RkOn 74, 78; RkWho 96; RolSEnR 83; Songw; WhoAm 78, 80, 82, 84, 86, 88, 90, 92, 94, 95, 96, 97, 98, 99, 2000; WhoEnt 92, 98; WhoHol 92; WhoRock 81; WhoRocM 82; WorAl; WorAlBi*

Seddon, Rhea
American. Astronaut
One of five women chosen for astronaut program, Jul, 1978.
b. 1947?
Source: *BioIn 11, 12; WhoSpc*

Seddon, Richard John
New Zealander. Political Leader
Liberal prime minister instituted liberal reforms and advocated imperial solidarity and expansion.
b. Jun 22, 1845 in St. Helens, Lancashire, England
d. Jun 10, 1906
Source: *BioIn 1, 4, 9, 14; CamBiEn; ChamBiD; DcNaB S2; EncWB 98; McGEWB*

Sedelmaier, Joe
[John Josef Sedelmaier]
American. Director, Filmmaker
Advertising director who created "Where's the Beef" commercial for Wendy's, 1984.
b. May 31, 1933 in Orrville, Ohio
Source: *BioIn 13, 14, 15; ConNews 85-3; WhoAdv 90; WhoAm 80, 82, 84, 86, 88, 90, 92, 94, 95, 96, 97; WhoEnt 92; WhoWor 80, 82, 84, 87*

Sedgman, Frank
[Francis Arthur Sedgman]
Australian. Tennis Player
First Australian to win US Nat. singles title, 1951, 1952; Wimbledon, 1952.
b. Oct 29, 1927 in Mont Albert, Australia
Source: *BioIn 2, 3, 12; BuCMET; CamBiEn; CurBio 51; Who 74, 82, 83, 85, 88, 90, 92, 94*

Sedgwick, Adam
English. Zoologist
Discovered an important zoological link between Annelida and Arthropoda.
b. Sep 28, 1854 in Norwich, England
d. Feb 27, 1913 in London, England
Source: *DcNaB 1912*

Sedgwick, Anne Douglas
American. Author
Wrote novels *Tante*, 1911; *Little French Girl*, 1924.
b. Mar 28, 1873 in Englewood, New Jersey
d. Jul 19, 1935
Source: *AmAu&B; AmBi; AmNatBi; AmWomWr; BenetAL 91; BioIn 1, 22; Chambr 3; CnDAL; ConAmA; ConAmL; DcAmB S1; DcLEL; DcNAA; EncALit; EvLB; FemiCLE; InWom, SUP; LibW; LngCTC; NotAW; OhA&B; OxCAmL 65, 83, 95; REnAL; ScF&FL 1; TwCA, SUP; WhAm 1; WhE&EA; WhLit; WomWWA 14; WorAu 1900*

Sedgwick, Catherine Maria
"Marie Edgeworth of America"
American. Author
Best-known historical novel: *Hope Leslie*, 1827.
b. Dec 28, 1789 in Stockbridge, Massachusetts
d. Jul 31, 1867 in West Roxbury, Massachusetts
Source: *Alli; AmWom; ApCAB; ArtclWW 2; BenetAL 91; CamDcAB; CarSB; ChhPo; DcAmB; DcEnL; DcLB 1; DcLEL; DcNAA; HarEnUS; NewCBEL; NotAW; OxCAmL 83; REnAL*

Sedgwick, John
American. Army Officer
Commanded Union troops at Antietam, Chancellorsville, etc; killed in Wilderness campaign.
b. Sep 13, 1813 in Cornwall Hollow, Connecticut
d. May 9, 1864 in Spotsylvania, Virginia
Source: *Alli; AmBi; AmNatBi; ApCAB; BioIn 1, 7, 12; CamDcAB; CivWDc; DcAmB; Drake; GenMudB; HarEnUS; NatCAB 4; NewCol 75; TwCBDA; WebAMB; WhAm HS; WhCiWar*

Sedney, Jules
Surinamese. Political Leader
Prime minister, Suriname, 1970-73; chm., Nat. Planning Council, 1980—.
b. Sep 28, 1922 in Paramaribo, Suriname
Source: *IntWW 74, 75, 76, 77, 78, 79, 80, 81, 82, 83, 89, 91, 93, 97, 98, 2000*

Sedran, Barney
[Heavenly Twins]
American. Basketball Player
Guard with several pro teams, 1912-26; Hall of Fame.
b. Jan 28, 1891 in New York, New York
d. Jan 14, 1969 in New York, New York
Source: *BioIn 9; ObitOF 79; WhoBbl 73; WhoSpor*

Seebeck, Thomas Johann
German. Physicist
Research in flow of electric current with a variety of conductors led to discovery of Seebeck effect.
b. Apr 9, 1770 in Tallinn, Estonia
d. Dec 10, 1831 in Berlin, Prussia
Source: *AsBiEn; BiESc; BioIn 12; CamBiEn; CamDcSc; ChamBiD; DcBiPP; DcInv; DcScB; InSci; LarDcSc; McGCEnS*

Seeckt, Hans von
German. Military Leader
As general and leader of the Reichswehr, strengthened German army by stressing efficiency and a Russo-German alliance.
b. Apr 22, 1866 in Schleswig, Prussia
d. Dec 27, 1936 in Berlin, Germany
Source: *BioIn 1, 2, 3, 5, 14; ChamBiD; DcTwHis; EncTR, 91; FacFETw; HarEnMi; ModChi; WhoMilH 76*

Seed, Jenny
South African. Author
Children's historical novels include *The Bushman's Dream*, 1974.
b. May 18, 1930 in Cape Town, South Africa
Source: *BioIn 11, 21; ConAu 21R, X; IntAu&W 86; SJGChWr 5; SmATA 8; TwCChW 1, 2, 3, 4; WhoEnt 98; WhoWor 95, 96, 97, 98, 99, 2000; WrDr 76, 82, 84, 86, 88, 90, 92, 94, 96, 98, 99, 2000*

Seefried, Irmgard Maria Theresia
German. Opera Singer
Soprano with Vienna State Opera, 1940s; made NY Met. debut, 1953.
b. Oct 9, 1919 in Kongetvied, Germany
d. Nov 24, 1988 in Vienna, Austria
Source: *BakBD 84; BriBkM 80; CurBio 56; IntWW 74; MusSN; NewGrDM 80; Who 74; WhoMus 72; WhoWor 74*

Seeger, Alan
American. Poet
Wrote "I Have a Rendevous with Death," 1916; killed in WW I.
b. Jun 22, 1888 in New York, New York
d. Jul 4, 1916 in Belloy en Senterre, France
Source: *AmAu&B; AmBi; AmNatBi; Benet 87, 96; BenetAL 91; BibAL; BioIn 6, 7, 10, 12, 13, 15, 22; CamDcAB; CamGEL; CamGLE; CamHAL; ChamBiD; Chambr 3; ChhPo, S3; CnDAL; DcAmB; DcAmC; DcLB 45; DcLEL; DcNAA; EncALit; EvLB; FacFETw; LinLib L, S; LngCTC; NatCAB 20; OxCAmL 65, 83, 95;*

OxCTwCL; OxCTwCP; REn; REnAL; TwCA; TwCWr; WebAMB; WhAm 4; WorAu 1900

Seeger, Pete(r)
[The Weavers]
American. Singer, Songwriter
Folksinger, guitarist, social activist; founded The Weavers, 1948; wrote modern folksong "If I Had a Hammer," 1958, popularized by Peter, Paul, and Mary, 1962.
b. May 3, 1919 in New York, New York
Source: *AmSocL; BakBD 78, 84, 92; BakBDTw; BakDcM; BgBkCoM; BioIn 6, 7, 8, 10, 11, 12, 13, 16; BioNews 74; BlueB 76; CamBiEn; CelR, 90; CmpEPM; ConAu 33NR, 69; ConHero 2; ConMuA 80A; ConMus 4; CurBio 63; DcArts; EncAAH; EncAL; EncFCWM 69, 83; EncMcCE; EncRk 88; EncWB; FacFETw; HarEnR 86; HeroCon; IlEncRk; LegTOT; LNinSix; MusMk; NewAmDM; NewGrDA 86; NewGrDM 80; OxCPMus; PenEncP; PolPar; RadHan; RolSEnR 83; SmATA 13; WebAB 74, 79; WhoAm 74, 76, 78, 80, 82, 84, 86, 88, 90, 92, 94, 95, 96, 97; WhoEnt 92; WhoHol 92, A; WhoRock 81; WhoRocM 82; WhoWor 74; WorAl; WorAlBi*

Seeley, Blossom
[Mrs. Benny Fields]
American. Actor
Vaudville performer with husband; their life filmed as *Somebody Loves Me.*
b. Jul 16, 1892 in San Pablo, California
d. Apr 17, 1974 in New York, New York
Source: *BiE&WWA; HalFC 80, 84, 88; LegTOT; NewYTBS 74; NotNAT B; OxCAmT 84; WhoHol B; WhScrn 77*

Seferiades, Giorgos Styljanou
Greek. Author, Diplomat
Won 1963 Nobel Prize in literature; best known for unique style of poetry.
b. Feb 22, 1900 in Izmir, Turkey
d. Sep 20, 1971 in Athens, Greece
Source: *ConAu 5NR, 5R; CurBio 64; WhoNob*

Seferis, George
[Giorgios Stylianou Seferiades]
Greek. Poet
Widely translated pioneer of symbolism in Greek literature; won Nobel Prize for Literature, 1963.
b. Mar 13, 1900 in Smyrna, Ottoman Empire
d. Sep 20, 1971 in Athens, Greece
Source: *Benet 87, 96; BiCoLiE; BioIn 1, 13, 15, 17; ChambBID; ClDMEL 80; CnMWL; ConAu 5NR, 5R, 33R, 36NR, X; ConLC 5, 11; CyWA 97; DcArts; DcPseud; EncWB 98; EncWL 1, 2, 2S, 3; EuWr 12; FacFETw; GrFLW; IntvTCA 2; LegTOT; LinLib L; MajTwCW 1; MakMC; McGEWB; NobelP; ObitOF 79; ObitT 1971; OxCEng 85, 95; PenC EUR; RAdv 14,*

13-2; RComWL; RfGWoL 95; RGFMEP; WhoNob; WhoTwCL; WorAu 1950

Sefton, William
[Heavenly Twins]
American. Track Athlete
With Earle Meadows, formed Heavenly Twins pole vaulting team; set world record, 1937.
b. Jan 21, 1915 in Los Angeles, California
Source: *WhoTr&F 73*

Segal, Erich Wolf
American. Author, Dramatist
Wrote *Love Story,* 1970; translated into 23 languages, filmed, 1970; *Oliver's Story,* 1977, filmed, 1978.
b. Jun 16, 1937 in New York, New York
Source: *AmAu&B; BioIn 8, 9, 10, 11, 12, 14, 15; BkPepl; ConAu 20NR, 36NR, 65NR; ConLC 3, 10; CurBio 71; DcLB Y86B; DrAS 82F; HalFC 84, 88; MajTwCW 1; NewYTBE 71; Who 85, 92; WhoAm 86, 88; WhoE 74; WhoHol A; WhoUSWr 88; WhoWor 84; WhoWorJ 72; WhoWrEP 89; WrDr 86, 92*

Segal, George
American. Sculptor
Known for life-size sculpture done in plaster.
b. Nov 26, 1924 in New York, New York
d. Jun 9, 2000 in South Brunswick, New Jersey
Source: *AmArt; AmCulL; Benet 87; BioIn 6, 7, 8, 9, 10, 11, 12, 13, 14, 16, 19; BriEAA; CamBiEn; CamDcAB; CelR; ChamBiD; ConArt 77, 83, 89, 96; CurBio 72; DcAmArt; DcCAA 71, 77, 88, 94; DcCAr 81; DcTwArt; EncWB 98; FacFETw; McGDA; OxCTwCA; OxDcArt; PhDcTCA 77; PrintW 83, 85; WebAB 74, 79; WhoAm 74, 76, 78, 80, 82, 84, 86, 88, 90, 92, 94, 95, 96, 97, 98, 99, 2000; WhoAmA 73, 76, 78, 80, 82, 84, 86, 89, 91, 93, 1999; WhoWor 74; WorAlBi; WorArt 1950*

Segal, George
American. Actor
Starred in *A Touch of Class,* 1973; *Carbon Copy,* 1981.
b. Feb 13, 1934 in New York, New York
Source: *BiDFilm, 81; BioIn 7, 9, 10, 11, 12, 14, 22; BkPepl; CamBiEn; ConTFT 3, 20; EncAFC; FilmEn; FilmgC; GangFlm; HalFC 80, 84, 88; IntMPA 75, 76, 77, 78, 79, 80, 81, 82, 84, 86, 88, 92, 94, 96; IntWW 77, 78, 79, 80, 81, 82, 83, 89, 91, 93, 97, 98, 2000; ItaFilm; LegTOT; MotPP; MovMk; OsStAZ; VarWW 85; WhoAm 86, 88, 90, 92, 94, 95, 96, 97, 99, 2000; WhoCom; WhoEnt 92; WhoHol 92, A; WorAl; WorAlBi*

Segal, Henry
American. Journalist
Editor, publisher of *American Israelite,* 1930-85, oldest English-Jewish newspaper in US.
b. 1901
d. Jul 18, 1985 in Cincinnati, Ohio
Source: *ConAu 116*

Segal, Lore Groszmann
American. Author
Children's fiction include *Lucinella,* 1976; *Tell Me a Trudy,* 1977.
b. Mar 8, 1928 in Vienna, Austria
Source: *AmAu&B; ConAu 5NR, 13R; DrAF 76; DrAPF 87, 91; IntAu&W 91; InWom SUP; LiExTwC; SmATA 4, 11AS, 66; WhoAm 86, 90; WhoAmW 87; WhoMW 84; WhoUSWr 88; WrDr 76, 86, 92*

Segal, Vivienne
American. Actor
Broadway star of operettas, musicals: *Desert Song,* 1926; *Pal Joey,* 1940.
b. Apr 19, 1897 in Philadelphia, Pennsylvania
d. Dec 29, 1992 in Los Angeles, California
Source: *BiDAmM; BiE&WWA; BioIn 6, 9, 16, 18; CmpEPM; EncMT; Film 2; FilmEn; ForYSC; HalFC 80, 84, 88; InWom SUP; MotPP; NotNAT; NotWoAT; OxCAmT 84; OxCPMus; ThFT; What 3; WhoHol 92, A; WhoThe 77A; WhThe*

Segantini, Giovanni
Artist
Portrayed allegorical scenes, peasants, alpine landscapes: *At The Watering Place.*
b. Jan 15, 1858 in Arco, Italy
d. Sep 28, 1899 in Samaden, Switzerland
Source: *BioIn 1, 13; ClaDrA; Dis&D; IntDcAA 90; McGDA; NewCol 75; OxCArt; OxDcArt; WebBD 83*

Segar, Elzie Crisler
American. Cartoonist
Created comic strip "Popeye," 1929.
b. Dec 8, 1894 in Chester, Illinois
d. Oct 13, 1938 in Santa Monica, California
Source: *AmNatBi; BioIn 17; CamBiEn; CamDcAB; ChambBID; DcNAA; WebAB 74, 79; WorECom*

Seger, Bob
[The Silver Bullet Band; Robert Clark Seger]
American. Singer, Musician
Triple platinum albums *Stranger in Town,* 1978; *Against the Wind,* 1980.
b. May 6, 1945 in Ann Arbor, Michigan
Source: *ASCAP 80; BillEnR; BioIn 11, 12, 13, 14, 16; ConLC 35; ConMuA 80A; ConMus 15; ConNews 87-1; EncPR&S 89; EncRk 88; EncRkSt; HarEnR 86; IlEncRk; LegTOT; NewAmDM; NewGrDA 86; PenEncP; RkOn 74, 78; RkWho 96; RolSEnR 83;*

Songw; WhoAm 86, 88, 90, 92, 94, 95;
WhoEnt 92, 98; WhoRock 81

Segni, Antonio
Italian. Political Leader
Premier of Italy, 1955-57, 1959-60;
  pres., 1962-64; founder of Christian
  Dem. Party.
b. Feb 2, 1891 in Sardinia, Italy
d. Dec 1, 1972 in Rome, Italy
Source: *BioIn 4, 5, 6, 9, 10; CurBio 55,*
73, 73N; LinLib S; NewYTBE 72; ObitT
1971; WhAm 5

Segovia, Andres
Spanish. Musician
Brought classical guitar into mainstream
  of musical world during 71-yr. career.
b. Feb 18, 1894 in Linares, Spain
d. Jun 2, 1987 in Madrid, Spain
Source: *BioIn 1, 2, 3, 4, 5, 6, 7, 10, 11;*
CambBiEn; CelR; ConAu 111; ConNews
87-3; CurBio 48, 64, 87; IntWW 74, 75,
76, 77, 78, 79, 80, 81, 82, 83; IntWWM
77; NewYTBS 86; WhAm 9; Who 74, 82,
83, 85; WhoAm 76, 78, 80, 82, 84, 86;
WhoAmM 83; WhoMus 72; WhoWor 74,
78, 87; WorAl; WorAlBi

Segrave, Henry O'Neal de Hane,
  Sir
English. Auto Racer, Boat Racer
Set several land and water speed records,
  1920s.
b. Sep 22, 1896 in Baltimore, Maryland
d. Jun 13, 1930 in Lake Windermere,
  England
Source: *BioIn 6, 7, 8; CambBiEn; DcNaB*
MP

Segre, Emilio Gino
American. Physicist
Shared Nobel Prize for physics, 1959.
b. Feb 1, 1905 in Tivoli, Italy
d. Apr 22, 1989 in Lafayette, California
Source: *AmMWSc 73P, 76P, 79, 82, 86,*
89, 92; AmNatBi; AsBiEn; BiESc; BioIn
14, 15, 16; BlueB 76; CambBiEn;
CamDcAB; CamDcSc; CmCal; ConAu
13NR, 128; CurBio 60, 89, 89N; InSci;
IntAu&W 91; IntWW 83, 89N;
McGCEnS; McGMS 80; NewYTBS 89;
NobelP; RanHWDS; ScrEAmL 2; WebAB
74, 79; WebBD 83; Who 85, 90N;
WhoAm 86, 88; WhoAmJ 80; WhoNob,
90, 95; WhoTech 89; WhoWest 87;
WhoWor 87, 89; WorAlBi; WorScD;
WrDr 86, 90

Segretti, Donald H
American. Lawyer
His "dirty trick" activities were the first
  uncovered by Woodward & Bernstein,
  1972; convicted of political espionage.
b. Sep 17, 1941 in San Marino,
  California
Source: *BioIn 9, 10, 11; NewYTBE 73;*
PolProf NF

Segura, Pancho
[Francisco Segura]
Ecuadorean. Tennis Player
First S. American to win nat.
  professional singles championship,
  1950, 1951.
b. Jun 20, 1921, Ecuador
Source: *BioIn 2, 3, 5, 10; BuCMET;*
CurBio 51; NewYTBE 71

Seiberling, Frank Augustus
American. Businessman
Founder, pres., Goodyear Tire & Rubber
  Co., 1898-1921.
b. Oct 6, 1859 in Western Star, Ohio
d. Aug 11, 1955 in Akron, Ohio
Source: *ApCAB X; BiDAmBL 83; BioIn*
7; DcAmB S5; WhAm 3

Seibert, Earl Walter
Canadian. Hockey Player
Defenseman, 1931-46, with three NHL
  teams; Hall of Fame, 1963; son of
  Oliver, also in Hall of Fame.
b. Dec 7, 1911 in Kitchener, Ontario,
  Canada
d. May 20, 1990 in Agawam,
  Massachusetts
Source: *BioIn 16; HocEn; WhoHcky 73*

Seibert, Florence B(arbara)
American. Biochemist, Inventor
Developed first test for tuberculosis
  infection, internationally adopted 1952.
b. Oct 6, 1897 in Easton, Pennsylvania
d. Aug 23, 1991 in Saint Petersburg,
  Florida
Source: *AmMWSc 73P, 76P, 79, 89, 92;*
AmWomSc; AZWoSci; BioIn 1, 2, 4, 6,
15; CurBio 91N; WhAm 10; WhoAm 74,
76; WhoAmW 58, 61, 64, 66, 68, 70, 72,
74; WomBioS

Seibert, Michael
[Blumberg and Seibert]
American. Skater
With Judy Blumberg, won bronze medal
  in ice dancing, 1983 world
  championships.
b. 1959? in Washington, Pennsylvania
Source: *BioIn 12, 13, 14; NewYTBS 83,*
84

Seibert, Oliver L
Canadian. Hockey Player
Played for amateur teams, early 1900s;
  Hall of Fame, 1961; father of Earl,
  also in Hall of Fame.
b. Mar 18, 1881 in Berlin, Ontario,
  Canada
d. May 15, 1944
Source: *WhoHcky 73*

Seidelman, Susan
American. Director, Producer
Directed film *Desperately Seeking Susan,*
  1984.
b. Dec 11, 1952 in Philadelphia,
  Pennsylvania
Source: *BioIn 14, 15, 16; ChamBiD;*
ConTFT 3, 12; CurBio 90; GrLiveH;
HalFC 88; IntMPA 92, 94, 96; IntWW

91, 93, 97, 98, 2000; IntWWW 2;
LegTOT; MiSFD 9; ReelWom; WhoAm
90, 92, 94, 95, 96, 97, 98; WhoAmW 91,
93, 95, 97, 99; WhoEnt 92, 98;
WomFilm; WomFir

Seidl, Anton
Hungarian. Conductor
Led NY Philharmonic, from 1891; noted
  Wagnerian.
b. May 7, 1850 in Budapest, Hungary
d. Mar 28, 1898 in New York, New
  York
Source: *AmNatBi; ApCAB SUP, X;*
BakBD 78, 84, 92; BiDAmM; BioIn 19;
BriBkM 80; CamDcAB; CmOp; DcAmB;
HarEnUS; IntDcOp; MetOEnc; NatCAB
8; NewAmDM; NewEOp 71; NewGrDA
86; NewGrDM 80; NewGrDO; OxCMus;
OxDcOp; PenDiMP; TwCBDA; WhAm
HS

Seifert, Elizabeth
American. Author
Wrote novels with a medical setting:
  Young Dr. Galahad, won Redbook
  Prize, 1938.
b. Jun 19, 1898 in Washington, Missouri
d. Jun 17, 1983 in Moberly, Missouri
Source: *AmWomWr; CurBio 51, 83N;*
IntAu&W 82X; InWom; WhoAmW 83;
WrDr 84

Seifert, Jaroslav
Czech. Poet
Won Nobel Prize for literature, 1984.
b. Sep 23, 1901 in Prague, Bohemia
d. Jan 10, 1986 in Prague,
  Czechoslovakia
Source: *AnObit 1986; Benet 87, 96;*
BioIn 14, 15, 17; CambBiEn; CasWL;
ChamBiD; ClDMEL 80; ConAu 127;
ConLC 34, 44, 93; DcArts; DcLB 215;
EncWL 2, 2S, 3; EvEuW; FacFETw;
IntWW 74, 75, 76, 77, 78, 79, 80, 81, 82,
83; IntWWP 77; LegTOT; MajTwCW 1,
2; ModSL 2; NewYTBS 86; NobelP;
PenC EUR; RAdv 14, 13-2; WhoNob, 90,
95; WhoSocC 78; WhoWor 74; WorAu
1975

Seiler, James, W
American. Broadcasting Executive
Founded American Research Bureau
  (later Arbitron), 1949; conducted first
  broadcast audience survey system.
b. 1917
d. Jan 2, 1983 in Silver Spring,
  Maryland
Source: *NewYTBS 82*

Seinfeld, Jerry
American. Comedian, Actor
Star of TV series "Seinfeld," 1989-98.
b. Apr 29, 1955 in New York, New
  York
Source: *BioIn 16; CurBio 92; IntWW*
2000; News 92; WhoAm 92, 94, 95, 96,
98, 99, 2000; WhoEnt 92, 98

Seiss, Joseph Augustus
American. Clergy
Founded General Council of Evangelical
    Lutheran Church in N America; wrote
    many books on religion.
b. Mar 18, 1823 in Frederick County,
    Maryland
d. Jun 20, 1904 in Philadelphia,
    Pennsylvania
Source: Alli, SUP; AmAu&B; AmNatBi;
    ApCAB; BiDSA; ChhPo; DcAmAu;
    DcAmB; DcNAA; Drake; LuthC 75;
    NatCAB 7; RelLAm 1, 2; TwCBDA;
    WhAm 1

Sejanus, Lucius Aelius
Roman.
Head administrator of Roman Empire
    under Tiberius.
d. Oct 18, 31
Source: BioIn 6, 8, 9; OxCClL, 89

Sejo
Korean. King
Ruthless but effective leader attempted to
    protect royal power in the face of
    aggression from Confucianist gentry-
    officials.
b. Nov 7, 1417
d. Sep 22, 1468, Republic of Korea
Source: EncWB 98; McGEWB

Sejong
Korean. King
King reigned from 1418 to 1450, a
    period considered to be the apex of
    the Yi dynasty; he made administrative
    reforms, protected the kingdom's
    borders, and was patron of the arts and
    inventor of the Korean alphabet.
b. May 7, 1397, Republic of Korea
d. Mar 30, 1450 in Seoul, Republic of
    Korea
Source: BioIn 13; DcOrL 1; EncWB 98;
    McGEWB

Selby, David
American. Actor
Starred in TV soap opera "Dark
    Shadows," 1966-71; played Richard
    Channing on TV drama "Falcon
    Crest," 1982-90.
b. Feb 5, 1941 in Morgantown, West
    Virginia
Source: ConTFT 5; IntMPA 84, 86, 88,
    92, 94, 96; WhoHol 92, A

Selby, Hubert, Jr.
American. Author
Wrote Last Exit to Brooklyn, 1964,
    subject of obscenity trial in England,
    banned in Italy.
b. Jul 23, 1928 in New York, New York
Source: AmAu&B; Benet 87, 96;
    BenetAL 91; BioIn 7, 8, 13, 17, 18;
    BlueB 76; CamDcAB; CamGLE;
    CamHAL; CasWL; ChamBiD; ConAu
    13R, 33NR, 85NR; ConLC 1, 2, 4, 8;
    ConNov 72, 76, 82, 86, 91, 96; DcArts;
    DcLB 2; DcLEL 1940; DrAF 76; DrAPF
    87; EncALit; IntAu&W 76, 77, 89;
    LegTOT; ModAL 4S1, 5; Novels;
    OxCAmL 83, 95; OxCTwCL; RGTwCWr;

ShSCr 20; WebE&AL; WhoAm 80, 82,
    84, 86, 88, 90, 92, 94, 95, 96, 97, 98,
    99, 2000; WhoEnt 92, 98; WorAu 1970;
    WrDr 76, 80, 82, 84, 86, 88, 90, 92, 94,
    96, 98, 99, 2000

Selden, George Baldwin
American. Inventor
Developed gasoline engine, 1879;
    patented, 1895.
b. Sep 14, 1846 in Clarkon, New York
d. Jan 17, 1922 in Rochester, New York
Source: AmNatBi; BioIn 9; DcAmB;
    InSci; LinLib S; NatCAB 20; WebAB 74,
    79; WhAm 4

Selden, John
English. Judge, Orientalist
Noted for collection of remarks over 20-
    yr. period: Table Talk, 1689.
b. Dec 10, 1584 in Salvington, England
d. Nov 30, 1654 in London, England
Source: Alli; Benet 87, 96; BiD&SB;
    BioIn 2, 3, 4, 9, 14, 15, 16; BritAu;
    CamBiEn; CamGEL; CamGLE; CasWL;
    ChamBiD; Chambr 1; CyEd; DcBiPP;
    DcEnA; DcEnL; DcEuL; DcLB 213;
    DcLEL; DcNaB; EvLB; GloEncH;
    HisDStE; NewC; NewCBEL; OxCBrHi;
    OxCEng 67, 85, 95; OxCLaw; OxCShps;
    PenC ENG; REn; WebE&AL; WhDW

Seldes, George (Henry)
American. Journalist
Foreign correspondent, Chicago Tribune,
    1919-28; advocate for freedom of the
    press; wrote Even the Gods Cannot
    Change History, 1976; Witness to a
    Century, 1987.
b. Nov 16, 1890 in Alliance, New Jersey
d. Jul 2, 1995 in Windsor, Vermont
Source: AmAu&B; Au&Wr 71; BenetAL
    91; BiDAmJo; BioIn 3, 4, 10, 14, 15, 16,
    17, 21; ConAu 2NR, 5R, 149; CurBio
    41, 95N; DcAmSR; EncAJ; IntAu&W 77,
    86, 91, 93; NewYTBS 95; OxCAmL 65,
    83; REnAL; TwCA, SUP; WhE&EA;
    WhJnl; WhNAA; WhoAm 74, 76, 78, 80,
    82, 84, 86, 88, 90, 92, 94, 95; WorAu
    1900; WrDr 76, 80, 82, 84, 86, 88, 90,
    92, 94, 96

Seldes, Gilbert Vivian
American. Critic, Author, Editor
CBS program director, 1937-45; wrote
    The Seven Lively Arts, 1924; novel
    The Wings of the Eagle, 1929; brother
    of George.
b. Jan 3, 1893 in Alliance, New Jersey
d. Sep 29, 1970 in New York, New
    York
Source: AmAu&B; AmNatBi; Au&Wr 71;
    BiDAmNC; BiE&WWA; BioIn 21, 22;
    CnDAL; ConAu 5R; NewYTBE 70;
    OxCAmL 83; OxCFilm; PenC AM;
    REnAL; TwCA SUP; WebAB 79; WhAm
    5; WorAu 1900

Seldes, Marian
American. Actor
Won 1967 Tony for A Delicate Balance.
b. Aug 23, 1928 in New York, New
    York

Source: BiE&WWA; BioIn 16; BlueB 76;
    CamGWoT; ConAu 19NR, 85; ConTFT
    2, 15, 27; ForYSC; NotNAT; NotWoAT;
    WhoAm 84, 86, 90; WhoE 74; WhoEnt
    92; WhoHol 92, A; WhoThe 72, 77, 81

Seldom Scene, The
[Mike Auldridge; T Michael Coleman;
    John Duffey; Ben Eldridge; Tom
    Gray; Phil Rosenthal; John Starling]
American. Music Group
Bluegrass band; name chosen because of
    infrequent concert appearnces; albums
    include Scenic Roots, 1990.
Source: AllMGCo; BgBkCoM; BioIn 14;
    ConMus 4; DcBrBI; DcVicP 2;
    EncFCWM 69; HarEnCM 87; MedHR;
    NewGrDA 86; NewYTBS 96; OnThGG;
    WhoRock 81; WhoRocM 82

Selena
[Selena Quintanilla Perez]
American. Singer
Grammy Award singer of Tejano songs.
b. Apr 16, 1971 in Lake Jackson, Texas
d. Mar 31, 1995 in Corpus Christi, Texas
Source: BilGTRM; BioIn 20, 21, 22, 23;
    ConMus 16; DcHiB; DcPseud; EncWB
    99; News 95; NotHsAW 2

Seles, Monica
Yugoslav. Tennis Player
Won Grand Slam, 1990; ranked number
    1 female tennis player by the
    Women's International Tennis
    Association, 1991. Stabbed during
    tennis match, 1994. Made comeback,
    1995.
b. Dec 2, 1973 in Novi Sad, Yugoslavia
Source: BioIn 15; BuCMET; CamBiEn;
    ChamBiD; CurBio 92; IntWW 91, 93,
    97, 98, 2000; IntWWW 2; LegTOT;
    News 91-3; NewYTBS 90; OutWomA;
    WhoAm 92, 94, 95, 96, 97, 98, 99, 2000;
    WhoAmW 95, 97, 99; WhoSpor;
    WhoWor 93, 95, 96, 97, 98, 99, 2000

Seleucus, I
Macedonian. King, Military Leader
King of Babylonia and Syria, and
    founder of the Seleucid empire and
    dynasty; general was also a companion
    of Alexander the Great.
b. c. 358BC, Macedonia
d. 281BC, Macedonia
Source: CamBiEn; DcBiPP; EncWB 98;
    McGEWB; OxCClC; WhDW

Selfridge, Harry Gordon
English. Businessman
Opened Selfridge and Co., Ltd., 1909.
b. Jan 11, 1858 in Ripon, Wisconsin
d. May 8, 1947 in London, England
Source: BioIn 1, 2, 4, 5, 12, 14;
    ChamBiD; DcNaB, 1941; DcTwBBL;
    GrBr; WebAB 74; WhAm 2; WhE&EA

Selfridge, Thomas Etholen
American. Soldier
First fatality of powered airplane travel;
    Selfridge AFB, MI named for him.

b. Feb 8, 1882 in San Francisco,
California
d. Sep 17, 1908 in Fort Meyer, Virginia
Source: *BioIn 6; InSci*

Selig, Bud
[Allan H. Selig]
American. Sports Executive
President and CEO, Milwaukee Brewers
baseball team, 1970—; interim
commissioner of Major League
Baseball, 1991—.
b. Jul 30, 1934 in Milwaukee, Wisconsin
Source: *CurBio 1999; News 95, 95-2;
WhoAm 74, 76, 78, 80, 82, 84, 86, 88,
90, 92, 94, 95, 96, 97; WhoMW 78, 80,
82, 84, 86, 88, 92, 93, 96*

**Seligman, Edwin Robert
Anderson**
American. Economist, Editor
Editor in chief of the *Encyclopaedia of
the Social Sciences* and editor of the
*Columbia University Studies in
History, Economics, and Public Law.*
b. Apr 25, 1861 in New York, New
York
d. 1939
Source: *AmBi; AmNatBi; ApCAB SUP,
X; BioIn 4, 15, 16; DcAmAu; DcAmB
S2; DcNAA; EncWB 98; GrEconB;
HarEnUS; McGEWB; NatCAB 10;
TwCBDA; WebAB 74, 79; WhAm 1;
WhNAA; WhoEc 81, 86*

Selim, III
Turkish. Political Leader
Twenty-eighth sultan of the Ottoman
Empire, instituted domestic reforms
and attempted to improve foreign
relations to slow the decay of the
weakening empire.
b. Dec 24, 1761
d. Jul 28, 1808
Source: *BioIn 4; CelCen; ChamBiD;
DcBiPP; EncWB 98; McGEWB*

Selim I
"Yavuz (The Grim)"
Ruler
Sultan, 1512-20; extended Ottoman
Empire to include Syria, the Hejaz,
and Egypt.
b. 1470 in Amasya, Ottoman Empire
d. Sep 22, 1520 in Corlu, Ottoman
Empire
Source: *EncWB 98; MilitOn*

Selke, Frank J, Sr.
Canadian. Hockey Executive
With Conn Smythe, helped build Toronto
Maple Leafs; became GM, Montreal,
1946-64, winning six Stanley Cups;
NHL trophy given to best defensive
forward named for him, 1978; Hall of
Fame, 1976.
b. May 7, 1893 in Kitchener, Ontario,
Canada
Source: *WhoHcky 73*

Selkirk, 5th Earl of
[Thomas Douglas]
Scottish. Colonizer
Colonist in Canada, devoted to
establishing new Scottish and Irish
communities in North America.
b. Jun 20, 1771 in Kirkcudbrightshire,
Scotland
d. Apr 8, 1820 in Pau, France
Source: *DcNaB; EncWB 98; OxCCan*

Selkirk, Alexander
Scottish. Adventurer
Lived alone on island, 1703-09; Daniel
Defoe based *Robinson Crusoe* on
account of his life.
b. 1676 in Largo, Scotland
d. 1721
Source: *Alli; ApCAB; Benet 87, 96;
BioIn 1, 4, 5, 8, 9, 12, 13; BlmGEL;
CamBiEn; ChamBiD; DcBiPP; DcEuL;
DcNaB; Drake; LngCEL; NewC;
NewCBEL; OxCEng 85, 95; OxCShps;
REn; WhWE*

Sellars, Peter
American. Director
Director, American National Theater, J F
Kennedy Center for Performing Arts.
b. 1958? in Pittsburgh, Pennsylvania
Source: *BioIn 13, 14, 15; CamBiEn;
CamDcAB; CamGWoT; ChamBiD;
CurBio 86; IntWW 91; IntWWM 90;
MetOEnc; NewGrDA 86; WhoAm 86;
WhoEnt 92*

Sellars, Wilfred
American. Philosopher
President of the American Philosophical
Association, he developed an
influential unified philosophical
system.
b. May 20, 1912 in Ann Arbor,
Michigan
d. 1989
Source: *EncWB 98*

Sellecca, Connie
[Mrs. John Tesh]
American. Actor
Played Christine Francis on TV series
"Hotel," 1983-88.
b. May 25, 1955 in New York, New
York
Source: *BioIn 11, 12, 15, 16; ConTFT 6,
13; DcPseud; IntMPA 92, 94, 96;
LegTOT; VarWW 85; WhoAm 92;
WorAlBi*

Selleck, Tom
[Thomas William Selleck]
"Clark Gable of the 80s"
American. Actor
Played Thomas Magnum on TV series
"Magnum PI," 1980-88; won Emmy,
1984; star of film *Three Men and a
Baby,* 1987.
b. Jan 29, 1945 in Detroit, Michigan
Source: *BioIn 12, 13, 14, 15, 16;
CamDcAB; CelR 90; ConTFT 1, 3, 12,
23; CurBio 83; HalFC 88; IntMPA 86,
88, 92, 94, 96; IntWW 89, 91, 93, 97,
98, 2000; LegTOT; VarWW 85; WhoAm*

86, 88, 90, 92, 94, 95, 96, 97, 99, 2000;
WhoEnt 92, 98; WhoHol 92, A;
WhoTelC; WorAlBi

Sellers, Peter
[Richard Henry Peter Sellers]
English. Actor
Played Inspector Jacques Clouseau in
The Pink Panther films, 1963-76.
b. Sep 8, 1925 in Portsmouth, England
d. Jul 24, 1980 in London, England
Source: *AmNatBi, 78, 79, 80; ItaFilm;
JoeFr; LegTOT; MotPP; MovMk;
OsStAZ; OxCFilm; QDrFCA 92; WhAm
7; Who 74; WhoCom; WhoHol A;
WhoWor 74, 78; WhScrn 83; WorAl;
WorAlBi; WorEFlm*

Sellinger, Frank
[Francis John Sellinger]
American. Brewer
Chief exec., Joseph Schlitz Brewing,
1980-82.
b. Jul 8, 1914 in Philadelphia,
Pennsylvania
Source: *Dun&B 90; St&PR 84; WhoAm
80, 82, 84; WhoFI 81; WhoMW 80, 82*

Sellinger, Joseph A
American. University Administrator
Pres., Loyola of Baltimore, 1964-1993;
transformed small commuter's college
into one of the nation's leading Jesuit
universities.
d. Apr 19, 1993 in Baltimore, Maryland

Selmon, Lee Roy
American. Football Player
Five-time all-pro defensive end, Tampa
Bay, 1976-85.
b. Oct 20, 1954 in Eufaula, Oklahoma
Source: *BiDAmSp FB; BioIn 13;
FootReg 85, 86; WhoAm 82, 84, 98, 99,
2000; WhoBlA 3, 4, 5, 6; WhoSpor*

Selvon, Samuel Dickson
[Sam Selvon]
Trinidadian. Author
Novels focus on Caribbean life: *Moses
Ascending,* 1975; *I Hear Thunder,*
1963.
b. May 20, 1923 in San Fernando,
Trinidad and Tobago
Source: *Benet 87; BenetAL 91; BioIn 13,
14; CamGLE; CasWL; ConAu 117, 128,
X; ConNov 86, 91; DcLB 125; FifCWr;
IntvWPC; LiExTwC; LngCTC;
MajTwCW 1; RAdv 13-2; RfGEnL 91;
SchCGBL; WebE&AL; Who 85, 92;
WorAu 1950; WrDr 86, 92, 98N*

Selye, Hans
[Hugo Bruno Selye]
Canadian. Scientist
Authority on stress who linked it to
disease, death; wrote *Stress without
Distress,* 1974.
b. Jan 26, 1907 in Vienna, Austria
d. Oct 16, 1982 in Montreal, Quebec,
Canada
Source: *AmMWSc 73P, 76P, 79, 82;
AnObit 1982; BiDPsy; BioIn 2, 3, 4, 5,*

6, 10, 11, 12, 13, 15; BlueB 76; CanWW
70, 79, 80, 81; ConAu 2NR, 5R, 85NR,
108; CurBio 51, 81, 83, 83N; FacFETw;
InSci; IntAu&W 76, 77; IntMed 80;
IntWW 74, 75, 76, 77, 78, 79, 80, 81,
82; NewYTBS 82; WhAm 8; WhoAm 74,
76, 78, 80, 82; WhoWor 74, 78; WrDr
76, 80, 82

Selzer, Richard (Alan)
American. Author
Wrote *Letters to a Young Doctor*, 1982;
   Raising the Dead, 1993; winner of the
   1982 Pushcart Prize for fiction.
b. Jun 24, 1928 in Troy, New York
Source: *BioIn 15, 16; ConAu 14NR, 65;
ConLC 74; CurBio 93; IntAu&W 86;
WhoAm 84, 86, 88, 90; WorAu 1985*

Selznick, David O(liver)
American. Producer
Won Oscar, 1939, for producing *Gone
   With the Wind*.
b. May 10, 1902 in Pittsburgh,
   Pennsylvania
d. Jun 22, 1965 in Hollywood, California
Source: *BiDFilm; BioIn 7, 8, 9, 10, 11,
12, 13; CamBiEn; CamDcAB; ChamBiD;
CurBio 41, 65; DcArts; DcFM; FilmgC;
NatCAB 54; OxCFilm; WebAB 74, 79;
WhAm 4; WorEFlm*

Selznick, Irene Mayer
American. Producer
Known for threatrical productions on
   London, NYC stages, 1940s-60s;
   former wife of David O Selznick.
b. Apr 2, 1907 in New York, New York
d. Oct 10, 1990 in New York, New York
Source: *BiE&WWA; BioIn 13, 16, 17,
24; ConAu 132; NewYTBS 90; NotNAT;
NotWoAT; ScrEAmL 2; WhAm 10;
WhoAm 84, 86, 88, 90*

Sembello, Michael
American. Singer, Musician
Guitarist for Stevie Wonder, 1973-79;
   had hit single "Maniac" from film
   Flashdance, 1983.
b. Apr 17, 1956? in Philadelphia,
   Pennsylvania
Source: *RkOn 85*

Sembene, Ousmane
Senegalese. Filmmaker
Made *La Noire de . . .*, (*Black Girl*)
   1965; *Camp de Thiaroye*, (*The Camp
   at Thiaroye*) 1987; several of his films
   have been banned in African nations.
b. Jan 1, 1923 in Ziguinchor, Senegal
Source: *AfrA; AfSS 78, 79, 80, 81, 82;
BiDFilm 94; BioIn 9, 11, 13, 14, 15, 16,
17, 18, 19, 20, 21; CasWL; ConBlB 13;
CurBio 94; CyWA 89, 97; DcAfHiB 86;
DrBlPA, 90; EncWB 98; EncWL 1, 2,
2S; GuAfrCi; InB&W 80; IntAu&W 76;
IntDcF 1-2, 2-2; MiSFD 9; ModBlW, 2;
ModFrL; PenC CL; RAdv 13-2; WorAu
1970; WorFDir 2*

Sembrich, Marcella
[Marcelline Kochanska]
Polish. Opera Singer
Soprano, great favorite of NY Met.,
   1898-1909; noted for Violetta role.
b. Feb 18, 1858 in Wisniewczyk, Poland
d. Jan 11, 1935 in New York, New York
Source: *BakBD 78, 84, 92; BiDAmM;
BioIn 1, 2, 3, 5, 7, 8, 10, 11, 13, 14, 22;
BriBkM 80; CmOp; DcAmB S1;
DcPseud; EncAB-A 5; IntDcOp; InWom
SUP; LibW; MetOEnc; MusSN; NatCAB
25; NewAmDM; NewEOp 71; NewGrDA
86; NewGrDM 80; NewGrDO; NotAW;
OxDcOp; PenDiMP; WhAm 1*

Semenenko, Serge
American. Financier, Business Executive
Consultant to ailing companies who led
   group that bought Warner Brothers;
   with First National Bank of Boston,
   1926-67.
b. Aug 23, 1903 in Odessa, Russia
d. Apr 24, 1980 in New York, New
   York
Source: *BioIn 6, 8, 12; IntYB 78;
NewYTBS 80; St&PR 75; WhAm 7;
WhoAm 74*

Semenov, Nikolai Nikolaevich
Russian. Chemist
First Soviet in homeland to win Nobel
   Prize, 1956, for research into
   mechanics of chemical reaction.
b. Apr 16, 1896 in Saratov, Russia
d. Sep 28, 1986 in Moscow, Union of
   Soviet Socialist Republics
Source: *BiESc; BioIn 14, 15; ConAu
157; EncWB 98; McGCEnS; McGEWB;
McGMS 80; NobelP; RanHWDS;
WhDW; Who 82, 83, 85, 88N; WhoAtom
77; WhoNob, 90, 95; WhoSocC 78;
WhoWor 74, 78, 80, 82; WorAl; WorAlBi*

Semmelweis, Ignaz Philipp
Hungarian. Physician
Discovered how pueperal fever is
   transmitted; helped greatly to reduce
   the death rate.
b. Jul 1, 1818 in Buda, Hungary
d. Aug 13, 1865 in Vienna, Austria
Source: *BiESc; BioIn 1, 2, 3, 4, 5, 6, 7,
9, 10, 12, 16; ChamBiD; DcCathB;
DcScB; EncWB 98; LarDcSc; McGEWB;
OxCMed 86; RanHWDS; WorAlBi;
WorScD*

Semmes, Raphael
American. Naval Officer
Confederate officer commanded the
   Sumter and Alabama in their daring
   raids on Northern shipping during the
   Civil War.
b. 1809 in Charles County, Maryland
d. 1877 in Mobile, Alabama
Source: *Alli, SUP; AmAu&B; AmBi;
AmNatBi; ApCAB; BenetAL 91;
BiDConf; BiDSA; BioIn 1, 3, 4, 5, 6, 7,
9, 20, 23, 24; CamBiEn; CamDcAB;
ChamBiD; CivWDc; DcAmAu; DcAmB;
DcAmMiB; DcCathB; DcLB 189;
DcNAA; EncNaHi; EncSoH; EncWB 98;
GenMudB; HarEnUS; LAmCW;*

McGEWB; NatCAB 4; OxCAmH;
OxCShps; REnAL; TwCBDA; WebAB 74,
79; WebAMB; WhAm HS; WhCiWar;
WorAl; WorAlBi*

Semple, Lorenzo, Jr.
Screenwriter
Films include *Never Say Never Again*,
   1983; TV movies include *Rearview
   Mirror*, 1986.
Source: *BioIn 13; ConAu 125, 129;
ConDr 88A; ConTFT 5; FilmgC; HalFC
80, 84, 88; IntDcF 1-4; IntMPA 84, 86,
88, 92, 94, 96; VarWW 85*

Semyonova, Marina
Russian. Dancer
Russia's first prima ballerina; best known
   for role of Nikya in *La Bayadere*.
b. Jun 12, 1908 in Saint Petersburg,
   Russia
Source: *BiDD; BioIn 14, 15, 17;
NewYTBS 87*

Senanayake, Don Stephen
Ceylonese. Political Leader
First prime minister of Ceylon, 1947-52;
   regarded as father of country.
b. Oct 20, 1884 in Botale, Ceylon
d. Mar 22, 1952 in Colombo, Ceylon
Source: *BioIn 2, 3, 5, 11; CamBiEn;
CurBio 50, 52; DcNaB 1951; DcTwHis;
NewCol 75; WhAm 3*

Senanayake, Dudley Shelton
Ceylonese. Statesman
Prime minister, 1952-53, 1960, 1965-70;
   son of Don Stephen.
b. Jun 19, 1911 in Colombo, Ceylon
d. Apr 12, 1973 in Colombo, Sri Lanka
Source: *BioIn 3, 5, 7, 9, 10; CurBio 52,
73N; NewCol 75; NewYTBE 73; WhAm
5; WhoGov 72*

Sendak, Maurice Bernard
American. Author, Illustrator
Won Caldecott for *Where the Wild
   Things Are*, 1963; first American to
   win H C Anderson's illustrator's
   award, 1970.
b. Jun 10, 1928 in New York, New York
Source: *AuBYP 3; BenetAL 91; BioIn 13,
16; CamBiEn; CamDcAB; CamGLE;
ChamBiD; ChlLR 17; ConAu 5R;
CurBio 68, 89; DcLB 61; FacFETw;
IlrAm 1880; IlsBYP; IlsCB 1946, 1957;
IntAu&W 91; IntWW 91, 97, 98, 2000;
MajTwCW 1, 2; MetOEnc; MorJA;
NewYTBE 70, 73; OxCChiL; PiP;
SJGChWr 5; SmATA 1; Str&VC; Who
92, 98, 99, 2000; WhoAm 86, 90, 97, 98,
99, 2000; WhoAmA 91, 1999; WhoEnt
92, 98; WhoUSWr 88; WhoWor 97, 98,
99, 2000; WhoWrEP 89; WorAlBi; WrDr
86, 92*

Sender, Ramon Jose
Spanish. Author
Numerous strong novels include
   Counterattack in Spain, 1937; award-
   winning *Mr. Witt among the Rebels*,
   1935.

b. Feb 3, 1902 in Alcolea de Cinca,
Spain
d. Jan 15, 1982 in San Diego, California
Source: *AmAu&B; AnObit 1982; Benet
87, 96; BioIn 12, 13; CasWL; ClDMEL
47, 80; ConAu 5R; DcSpL; EncWL 1;
EvEuW; IntAu&W 77; IntWW 80;
ModRL; REn; TwCA, SUP; TwCWr;
WhAm 8; Who 74, 82; WhoAm 74, 76*

Seneca, Lucius Annaeus, the Younger

Roman. Philosopher, Statesman,
Dramatist
Famed stoic; wrote eight tragedies;
committed suicide at Nero's command.
b. 4BC in Cordoba, Spain
d. 65AD in Rome, Italy
Source: *AtlBL; BbD; BiCoLiE; BiD&SB;
BioIn 1, 2, 5, 7, 8, 10, 11, 12, 14, 17;
CasWL; ClMLC 6; CnThe; CyEd; CyWA
58; DcArts; DcEnL; DcEuL; DcScB;
Dis&D; DramC 5; EncEth; EncWB 98;
EncWT; InSci; IntDcT 2; LinLib L, S;
LngCEL; LuthC 75; McGEWB;
McGEWD 72; NewC; NotNAT B;
OxCClL, 89; OxCEng 67, 85, 95;
OxCSpan; OxCThe 67, 83; PenC CL;
RComWL; REn; REnWD*

Senefelder, Aloys

German. Inventor
Invented lithography, 1796.
b. Nov 6, 1771 in Prague, Bohemia
d. Feb 26, 1834 in Munich, Germany
Source: *CamBiEn; ChamBiD; DcAmB;
DcBiPP; DcCathB; LinLib L, S; NewCol
75; OxCArt; OxDcArt; WebBD 83*

Senesh, Hannah

Hungarian. Social Reformer
Anti-Nazi activist; shot by Nazi firing
squad.
b. 1921 in Budapest, Hungary
d. Nov 7, 1944
Source: *BioIn 2, 4, 5, 7, 9, 10, 11, 13,
14, 15, 16, 17, 18, 19, 22, 24;
ChamBiD; ConAu 119; ContDcW 89;
EncAmaz 91; HerW, 84; IntDcWB;
InWom, SUP; WhWW-II*

Senesino

[Francesco Bernardi]
Italian. Opera Singer
Male mezzo-soprano; extremely popular
in London, 1720s-30s; took name from
hometown.
b. 1680 in Siena, Italy
d. 1750 in Siena, Italy
Source: *BakBD 84, 92; CmOp; DcPseud;
MetOEnc; NewAmDM; NewEOp 71;
NewGrDM 80; OxDcOp; PenDiMP*

Senfl, Ludwig

German. Composer
Master adopted the Franco-Flemish
imitative polyphony in his masses,
motets, and vernacular lieder.
b. c. 1486 in Basel, Switzerland
d. 1543
Source: *BakBD 78, 84, 92; EncWB 98;
LuthC 75; McGEWB; NewAmDM;
NewGrDM 80; NewOxM*

Senghor, Leopold Sedar

Senegalese. Political Leader, Poet
Pres. of Senegal, 1960-80; first book of
verse: *Chants d'Ombre*, 1945.
b. Oct 9, 1906 in Joal, Senegal
Source: *AfrA; AfrWr; AfSS 78, 79, 80,
81, 82; Benet 87, 96; BiCoLiE;
BiDFrPL; BioIn 5, 6, 7, 8, 9, 10, 11, 12,
13, 14, 17, 18, 20, 21, 23, 24; BlkLC;
BlkWr 1, 2; CamBiEn; CasWL;
ChamBiD; ClDMEL 80; ConAu 47NR,
74NR, 116, 117, 118, 119, 120, 121,
122, 123, 124, 125; ConBlB 12;
ConFLW 84; ConLC 54; ConWorW 93;
CurBio 62; DcAfHiB 86; DcArts;
DcTwCCu 2; DcTwHis; EncWB 98;
EncWL 1, 2, 2S, 3; FacFETw; GuFrLit
1; HisWorL; InB&W 80, 85; IntAu&W
77, 89, 91; IntWW 74, 75, 76, 77, 78,
79, 80, 81, 82, 83, 89, 91, 93, 97, 98,
2000; IntWWP 77, 82; IntYB 78, 79, 80,
81, 82; LegTOT; LiExTwC; LinLib L;
MajTwCW 1, 2; McGEWB; ModBlW, 2;
ModFrL; PenC CL; PoeCrit 25; RAdv
14, 13-2; RGAfL; SchCGBL; SelBAAf;
TwCWr; WhoGov 72; WhoTwCL;
WhoWor 74, 76, 78, 80, 82, 95; WorAl;
WorAlBi; WorAu 1950*

Sengstacke, John H(erman Henry)

American. Newspaper Publisher
President, editor of influential black
newspaper *Chicago Defender* and
affiliates since 1940; founded Negro
Newspaper Publishers' Assn., 1940.
b. Nov 25, 1912 in Savannah, Georgia
d. May 28, 1997 in Chicago, Illinois
Source: *AfrAmAl 6, 8; BioIn 2, 8; BlkWr
1; ConAu 101, 158; CurBio 49, 97N;
DcLB 127; EncTwCJ; InB&W 80, 85;
NegAl 83, 89; SelBAAf; SelBAAu; St&PR
84, 87, 91; WhAm 12; WhoAm 74, 76,
78, 80, 82, 84, 86, 88, 90, 92, 94, 95,
96, 97; WhoBlA 5, 7; WhoFI 75, 77, 92,
96, 98; WhoMedi 98; WhoMW 82, 88,
90, 92, 93, 96; WhoWor 95, 96, 97*

Senna, Ayrton

Brazilian. Auto Racer
Formula One World Champion, 1988,
1990, and 1991.
b. Mar 21, 1960 in Sao Paulo, Brazil
d. May 1, 1994 in Imola, Italy
Source: *BioIn 15, 16; CamBiEn;
ChamBiD; IntWW 91, 93; News 91, 94;
Who 94*

Sennacherib

Assyrian. Ruler
During reign destroyed Babylon, 689
BC, restored Nineveh; killed by son.
b. 705BC
d. 681BC
Source: *NewC; NewCol 75; WebBD 83;
WhDW*

Sennett, Mack

[Mikall Sinnott]
"King of Comedy"
American. Director, Producer
Created Keystone Kops; directed Charlie
Chaplin, Harold Lloyd.

b. Jan 17, 1884 in Richmond, Quebec,
Canada
d. Nov 5, 1960 in Woodland Hills,
California
Source: *Benet 87, 96; BenetAL 91; BioIn
2; BioNews 75; CmCal; CmMov; DcFM;
EncWB 98; Film 1; FilmEn; FilmgC;
McGEWB; MotPP; ObitT 1951;
OxCFilm; REn; REnAL; TwYS, B;
WebAB 74, 79; WhAm 4, HSA; WhScrn
83; WorAlBi; WorEFlm*

Seper, Franjo

Yugoslav. Religious Leader
Cardinal, Prefect, Sacred Congregation
Doctrine of Faith, 1968-81.
b. Oct 2, 1905 in Osijek, Yugoslavia
d. Dec 31, 1981 in Rome, Italy
Source: *AnObit 1981; BioIn 8, 11, 12;
IntWW 74, 75, 76, 77, 78, 79, 80, 81;
NewYTBS 81; WhoSocC 78; WhoWor 74,
76, 78, 80, 82*

Septimius Severus, Lucius

Roman. Emperor
His reign over the Roman Empire was
marked by the militarization of the
government, growing Oriental
influences in society, and the
development of civil law.
b. 146 in Leptis Magna, Africa
d. 211 in York, England

Sequoyah

[Sequoia; Sequoya; Sikwayi; Sogwal;
George Gist; George Guess]
American. Linguist, Scholar
Created Cherokee syllabary; taught
thousands to read, write; sequoia tree
named for him.
b. 1770? in Taskigi, Tennessee
d. 1843 in Tamaulipas, Mexico
Source: *ABCNaAm; AmBi; AmIndBi;
AmNatBi; ApCAB; BenetAL 91; BioIn 1,
2, 3, 4, 5, 7, 8, 9, 10, 17, 19, 21, 22, 23;
ChamBiD; DcAmB; DcAmSR; Drake;
EncAAH; EncNoAI; EncWB 98; FrTalk;
HarEnUS; McGEWB; NatCAB 5;
NatNAFi; NewCol 75; NewEAmW;
NotNaAm; OxCAmH; OxCAmL 65, 83,
95; PeoHis; REnAW; WebAB 74, 79;
WebBD 83; WhAm HS; WhDW;
WhNaAH; WorAl; WorAlBi*

Serafin, Tullio

Italian. Conductor
Led Milan's La Scala, Rome Opera Co.,
1909-50s; helped launch Maria Callas.
b. Dec 8, 1878 in Rottanova, Italy
d. Feb 2, 1968 in Rome, Italy
Source: *BakBD 84, 92; BakBDTw; BioIn
3, 4, 5, 6, 8, 11; BriBkM 80; CmOp;
IntDcOp; MetOEnc; MusSN;
NewAmDM; NewEOp 71; NewGrDA 86;
NewGrDM 80; NewGrDO; ObitT 1961;
OxDcOp; PenDiMP; WhAm 4A*

Seraphine, Danny

[Daniel Peter Seraphine]
American. Musician
Drummer with group since 1967; had
number one hit "Hard to Say I'm
Sorry," 1982.

b. Aug 28, 1948 in Chicago, Illinois
Source: *ASCAP 80; WhoAm 86, 90*

Serban, Andrei George
Romanian. Director
Associate director, Yale Repertory
   Theatre, 1977-78; directed opera
   Elektra, 1991.
b. Jun 21, 1943 in Bucharest, Romania
Source: *BioIn 11, 12, 13; CamGWoT;
   ConTFT 8; CurBio 78; IntWWM 90;
   MetOEnc; OxCThe 83; WhoAm 78, 80,
   82; WhoThe 81*

Seredy, Kate
Hungarian. Children's Author, Illustrator
Won 1938 Newbery Medal for *The
   White Stag.*
b. Nov 10, 1899 in Budapest, Austria-
   Hungary
d. Mar 7, 1975 in Middletown, New
   York
Source: *AnCL; Au&ICB; AuBYP 2;
   BioIn 13, 14, 19; BkCL; ChhPo;
   ChlBkCr; ChlLR 10; ConAu 5R, 57,
   83NR; CurBio 40, 75, 75N; DcLB 22;
   IlsCB 1744, 1946; JBA 51; LinLib L;
   MajAI; NewbMB 1922; OxCChiL;
   SJGChWr 5; SmATA 1, 24, 24N;
   Str&VC; TwCChW 1, 2, 3, 4*

Sereno, Paul C.
American. Paleontologist
Unearthed the most complete
   Herrerasaurus skeleton, 1988.
b. Oct 11, 1957 in Aurora, Illinois
Source: *CurBio 97*

Serkin, Peter A(dolf)
American. Pianist
Noted for chamber music, contemporary
   compositions, fresh interpretations of
   classic, romantic music; son of
   Rudolph.
b. Jul 24, 1947 in New York, New York
Source: *BakBD 84, 92; BakBDTw; BioIn
   14, 15, 16; CurBio 86; IntWW 89, 91,
   93, 97, 98, 2000; IntWWM 90;
   NewAmDM; NewGrDA 86; NewYTBE
   73; NewYTBS 80; NotTwCP; PenDiMP;
   WhoAm 84, 86, 90; WhoAmM 83; WhoE
   74; WhoEnt 92; WhoMus 72; WhoWor
   74*

Serkin, Rudolph
[Rudolf Serkin]
American. Pianist
Made US debut, 1933; specialized in
   Viennese classics.
b. Mar 28, 1903 in Eger, Bohemia
d. May 8, 1991 in Guilford, Vermont
Source: *AnObit 1991; BakBD 78, 84, 92;
   BiDAmM; BioIn 2, 3, 4, 5, 6, 9, 11, 15,
   16, 17, 18, 21; BlueB 76; BriBkM 80;
   CelR; CurBio 89, 91N; DcArts;
   DcTwCCu 1; FacFETw; IntWW 74, 75,
   76, 77, 78, 79, 80, 81, 82, 83, 89, 91,
   91N; IntWWM 77, 80, 90; LegTOT;
   MusMk; MusSN; NewAmDM; NewGrDA
   86; NewGrDM 80; News 92, 92-1;
   NewYTBS 91; NotTwCP; PenDiMP;
   REn; WhAm 10; Who 74, 82, 83, 85, 88,
   90, 92N; WhoAm 74, 76, 78, 80, 82, 84,*

86, 88, 90; WhoAmM 83; WhoE 74;
WhoGov 72, 75; WhoMus 72; WhoWor
74, 78, 80, 82, 84, 87, 89, 91; WorAl;
WorAlBi*

Serling, Rod
American. Author, Producer
Created, hosted TV series "Twilight
   Zone," 1959-65; "Night Gallery,"
   1970-73.
b. Dec 25, 1924 in Syracuse, New York
d. Jun 28, 1975 in Rochester, New York
Source: *AmAu&B; AmNatBi; Au&Arts
   14; AuNews 1; BenetAL 91; BioIn 4, 5,
   6, 7, 10, 14, 16, 19; CamBiEn; CelR;
   ChamBiD; ConAu 57, 65; ConDr 73;
   ConLC 30; ConTFT 14; CurBio 59,
   75N; DcLB 26; DcTwCCu 1; EncO&P
   1S2, 2, 3; EncSF, 93; FilmEn; FilmgC;
   HalFC 80, 84, 88; IntMPA 75, 76;
   LegTOT; LinLib L; NewEScF; NewYTBS
   75; NewYTET; REnAL; ScF&FL 1, 92;
   ScFSB; TwCSFW 81, 86, 91; WhAm 6;
   WhoAm 74; WhoHrs 80; WhoSciF;
   WhoWor 74; WhScrn 77, 83; WorAl;
   WorAlBi; WorEFlm*

Serpico, Frank
[Francisco Vincent Serpico]
American. Police Officer
Subject of film *Serpico,* 1973, which
   starred Al Pacino.
b. Apr 14, 1936 in New York, New
   York
Source: *BioIn 9, 13; CopCroC;
   NewYTBE 71*

Serra, Junipero
Spanish. Missionary
One of the most respected and best-
   known figures in California history,
   Franciscan founded the Spanish
   missions of the region.
b. 1713 in Majorca, Spain
d. Aug 1784 in California
Source: *AmNatBi; ApCAB SUP;
   BiDHisA; BioIn 1, 2, 3, 4, 5, 6, 7, 8, 9,
   11, 14, 15, 16, 17, 18, 19, 20, 21, 22,
   24; CamBiEn; CamDcAB; ChamBiD;
   CmCal; DcAmB; DcAmReB 1, 2;
   DcCathB; DcHiB; EncAB-H 1974, 1996;
   EncARH; EncCRAm; EncNAR; EncWB
   98; ExplAnT; HisDcSE; LatAmLi;
   LegTOT; LinLib S; LuthC 75; McGEWB;
   NewEAmW; NewGrDA 86; OxCAmH;
   OxCAmL 65; RComAH; REnAW; WebAB
   74, 79; WhAm HS; WhNaAH; WhWE;
   WorAl; WorAlBi*

Serra, Richard Anthony
American. Artist
Most innovative of minimalist sculptors.
b. Nov 2, 1939 in San Francisco,
   California
Source: *AmArt; BioIn 16; BriEAA;
   CamDcAB; ConArt 83, 89; CurBio 85;
   IntWW 91; NewYTBS 89; OxCTwCA;
   PrintW 85; WhoAm 84, 86, 90; WhoAmA
   84, 91*

Serraillier, Ian Lucien
English. Children's Author
Works depicting old English legends
   include *The Silver Sword,* 1960.
b. Sep 24, 1912 in London, England
d. Nov 28, 1994
Source: *Au&Wr 71; BioIn 15; ChlLR 2;
   ConAu 1NR, 1R, 83NR; EngPo;
   IntAu&W 91; MajAI SUP; OxCChiL;
   SJGYouA 2; SmATA 1, 3, 3AS; ThrBJA;
   TwCChW 2; WrDr 86, 92*

Serrano, Andres
American. Artist
Associated with debates on federal
   funding for artists and freedom of
   artistic expression due to work "Piss
   Christ," a photograph of a crucifix in
   urine.
b. Aug 15, 1950 in New York, New
   York
Source: *BioIn 17, 18, 23; ConPhot 95;
   WhoAm 97, 99, 2000; WhoAmA 89, 91,
   93, 1999*

Serrano Elias, Jorge Antonio
Guatemalan. Political Leader
The first active Protestant to be elected
   president of a Latin American nation,
   he served as president of Guatemala
   from 1991 to 1993.
b. 1945 in Guatemala City, Guatemala
Source: *EncWB 98; LatAmLi*

Serrault, Michel
French. Actor
Played the transvestite Zara in *La Cage
   aux Folles,* 1978.
b. 1928?
Source: *BioIn 12; ItaFilm; WhoFr 79*

Sert, Jose Luis
American. Architect
Dean, Harvard Graduate School of
   Design, 1953-69.
b. Jul 1, 1902 in Barcelona, Spain
d. Mar 15, 1983 in Barcelona, Spain
Source: *AmAu&B; AnObit 1983; BioIn
   10, 24; BlueB 76; CurBio 74, 83, 83N;
   EncMA; IntWW 74, 75, 76, 77, 78, 79,
   80, 81, 82; McGDA; NewYTBS 83;
   ScrEAmL 1; WhAm 8; WhoAm 74, 76,
   78, 82; WhoWor 74*

Serusier, Paul
[Louis Paul Henri Serusier]
French. Artist
Postimpressionist painter.
b. 1863? in Paris, France
d. Oct 6, 1927 in Morlaix, France
Source: *BioIn 4; ClaDrA; OxCTwCA;
   OxDcArt; PhDcTCA 77*

Servan-Schreiber, Jean-Jacques
French. Politician, Journalist
President, the Radical Party since 1977;
   founded news-magazine, *L'Express,*
   1953-69.
b. Feb 13, 1924 in Paris, France
Source: *BiDFrPL; BioIn 13, 14;
   CamBiEn; ConAu 102; EncWB, 98;
   IntAu&W 76, 77, 86, 89; IntWW 74, 75,*

76, 77, 78, 79, 80, 81, 82, 83, 89, 91, 93, 97, 98, 2000; LinLib L; Who 74, 82, 83, 85, 85E, 88, 90, 92, 94, 98, 99, 2000; WhoAm 94, 95, 96, 97; WhoFI 98; WhoFr 79; WhoWor 74, 76, 78, 80, 82, 84, 87, 89, 91, 93, 95, 96, 97

Servetus, Michael
Spanish. Physician, Theologian
Published *De Trinitatis Erroribus*, 1531, opposing doctrine of Trinity.
b. Sep 29, 1511 in Villanueva de Sixena, Spain
d. Oct 27, 1553 in Geneva, Switzerland
Source: *AsBiEn; BbD; BiD&SB; BiESc; BioIn 1, 2, 3, 4, 5, 7, 9, 12, 17, 23; CamBiEn; ChamBiD; DcScB; Dis&D; EncWB 98; InSci; LarDcSc; LuthC 75; McGCEnS; McGEWB; NewC; OxCEng 67, 85, 95; OxCMed 86; RanHWDS; WhoChr*

Service, John S(tewart)
American. Diplomat
Foreign service officer fired from State dept. over doubts of his loyalty, 1951; Supreme Court ruled his rights were violated.
b. Aug 8, 1909 in Chengdu, China
d. Feb 3, 1999 in Oakland, California
Source: *BioIn 2, 3, 7, 9, 11; CamDcAB; ConAu 113; EncCW; PolProf E, T*

Service, Robert William
"Canadian Kipling"
Canadian. Author, Poet
Wrote of northern frontier life: *Spell of the Yukon*, 1907; *Bar Room Ballads*, 1940.
b. Jan 16, 1874 in Preston, England
d. Sep 11, 1958 in Lancieux, France
Source: *BiCoLiE; BioIn 2, 3, 4, 5, 11, 12; CamBiEn; CanNov; CanWr; CasWL; ChamBiD; Chambr 3; ChhPo, S1, S2, S3; CnDAL; CnE&AP; ConAu 84NR; CreCan 1; DcAmB S6; DcArts; DcLEL; DcNaB 1951; EvLB; FacFETw; GrWrEL P; LinLib S; LngCTC; MacDCB 78; NewC; OxCAmL 65; OxCCan; OxCEng 85, 95; OxCTwCL; PenC ENG; REn; REnAL; TwCA, SUP; TwCWr; WebE&AL; WhAm 3; WhNAA; WhoLA; WorAl*

Sesshu, Toyo
Japanese. Artist
Zen priest, master of ink paintings; noted for landscape scrolls: *Four Seasons Landscape*, ca. 1470-90.
b. 1420
d. 1506
Source: *CamBiEn; ChamBiD; McGDA; McGEWB; NewCol 75; REn; WebBD 83*

Sessions, Jeff
American. Politician
Rep. senator, AL, 1997—.
b. Dec 24, 1946

Sessions, Roger Huntington
American. Composer
Most popular work was first major composition *The Black Masters*, 1923.
b. Dec 28, 1896 in New York, New York
d. Mar 16, 1985 in Princeton, New Jersey
Source: *AmAu&B; AmComp; AmNatBi; BakBDTw; BiDAmM; BioIn 1, 3, 4, 5, 6, 7, 8, 10, 11, 12, 13; CamDcAB; ConAmC 76, 82; ConAu 93; CurBio 75, 85; DcCM; EncWB 98; IntWW 74, 75, 76, 77, 78, 79, 80, 81, 82, 83; IntWWM 77; McGEWB; OxCAmL 65; REnAL; ScrEAmL 1; WebAB 74, 79; WhoAm 74, 76, 78, 80, 82, 84; WhoAmM 83; WhoE 85; WhoMus 72; WhoWor 74; WorAl*

Sessions, William Steele
American. Government Official
Director of FBI, 1987-93.
b. May 27, 1930 in Fort Smith, Arkansas
Source: *AmBench 79; BioIn 15, 16; CurBio 88; FBI; IntWW 91; NewYTBS 87; WhoAm 78, 86, 88, 90, 92, 94, 95, 96, 97, 98, 99, 2000; WhoAmL 79, 83, 85, 87, 90, 92, 94, 96, 98, 2000; WhoAmP 91; WhoGov 72, 75, 77; WhoSSW 82, 84, 86*

Seth, Vikram
Indian. Author
Published verse novel *The Golden Gate*, 1986; novel *A Suitable Boy*, 1993.
b. Jun 20, 1952 in Calcutta, India
Source: *AsAmAlm; BioIn 15, 18, 19, 20, 21; CamBiEn; CamGLE; ChamBiD; ConAu 50NR, 74NR, 121, 127; ConLC 43, 90; ConNov 96; ConPo 91, 96; DcLB 120; EncALit; EncWL 3; IntWW 93, 97, 98, 2000; MajTwCW 2; NotAsAm; OxCTwCL; OxCTwCP; RGTwCWr; WhoAm 94, 95, 96; WhoUSWr 88; WhoWrEP 89, 92, 95; WorAu 1985; WrDr 88, 90, 92, 94, 96, 98, 99, 2000*

Seton, Anya Chase
American. Author
Historical romances include *Dragonwyck*, 1944; daughter of Ernest Thompson.
b. 1916 in New York, New York
d. Nov 8, 1990 in Old Greenwich, Connecticut
Source: *AmAu&B; AmNov; Au&Wr 71; Benet 87; BenetAL 91; BioIn 14; ConAu 17R; CurBio 53; FacFWF; IntAu&W 89; InWom SUP; LngCTC; NewYTBS 90; OxCAmL 65; PenC AM; REn; REnAL; SmATA 3; TwCA SUP; TwCRHW 90; Who 85; WhoAm 86; WrDr 86*

Seton, Elizabeth Ann Bayley, Saint
[Mother Seton]
American. Religious Leader
Laid foundation of US parochial school system; founded Sisters of Charity, 1809; first American canonized, 1975.
b. Aug 28, 1774 in New York, New York
d. Jan 4, 1821 in Emmitsburg, Maryland

Source: *AmAu&B; AmBi; AmNatBi; AmSocL; ApCAB; AmNatBi; BiDAmEd; BioNews 75; BlmGWL; CamDcAB; DcAmAu; DcAmB; DcAmReB 1, 2; DcCathB; EncARH; EncAWoR; EncSoH; EncWB 98; GoodHs; InWom, SUP; LibW; McGEWB; NatCAB 2; NotAW; TwCBDA; WebAB 74, 79; WhAm HS; WomFir*

Seton, Ernest Thompson
American. Naturalist, Author
Noted animal fiction writer; instrumental in founding the Boy Scouts of America, 1910.
b. Aug 14, 1860 in South Shields, England
d. Oct 23, 1946 in Santa Fe, New Mexico
Source: *AmAu&B; AmLY; AmNatBi; AmNatWr; ApCAB X; ArtsAmW 1; Benet 87, 96; BenetAL 91; BiCoLiE; BioIn 1, 2, 3, 4, 5, 8, 10, 11, 12, 14, 15, 17, 22, 23; CamBiEn; CamDcAB; CamGEL; CamGLE; CanWr; ChamBiD; ChhPo, S1; ChlBkCr; ChlLR 59; ConAmL; ConAu 109; CreCan 2; DcAmB S4; DcArts; DcBrAr 1; DcBrBI; DcLB 92, DS13; DcNAA; DcPseud; DcVicP 2; EncSoH; EncWB, 98; EvLB; GayN; HarEnUS; IlBEAAW; IlsCB 1744; InSci; JBA 34; LinLib L, S; LngCTC; MacDCB 78; NatCAB 36; NatLAC; NewCBEL; OxCAmL 65, 83; OxCCan; OxCCanL 1, 2; OxCChiL; OxCTwCL; REn; REnAL; SmATA 18; TwCA, SUP; TwCChW 1, 2, 3; TwCLC 31; TwCWr; WhAm 2; WhAmArt 85; WhE&EA; WhLit; WhNAA; WhNaAH; WhoChL; WorAu 1900*

Seton-Watson, Hugh
[George Hugh Nicholas Seton-Watson]
English. Government Official
Authority on E European affairs; wrote *The Russian Empire*, 1967.
b. Feb 15, 1916 in London, England
d. Dec 19, 1984 in Washington, District of Columbia
Source: *AnObit 1984; Au&Wr 71; Benet 87; BioIn 10, 14; ConAu 114, 117; DcNaB 1981; NewYTBS 84; Who 74, 82, 83, 85; WorAu 1950*

Seurat, Georges Pierre
French. Artist
Devised pointillist style of painting, tiny dots of color.
b. Dec 2, 1859 in Paris, France
d. Mar 29, 1891 in Paris, France
Source: *AtlBL; BioIn 1, 2, 4, 5, 6, 7, 8, 9, 11, 12, 13, 14, 15, 16, 17, 18, 21; CamBiEn; ChamBiD; ClaDrA; EncWB 98; McGEWB; REn*

Seurat, Michel
French. Hostage
French researcher in Lebanon seized by Islamic Jihad May 22, 1985; reported dead March 5, 1986.

Seuss, Doctor
[Theodore Seuss Geisel]
American. Author, Illustrator
Wrote *How The Grinch Stole Christmas*,
1957; *The Cat in the Hat*, 1957; *Green
Eggs and Ham*, 1960.
b. Mar 2, 1904 in Springfield,
Massachusetts
d. Sep 24, 1991 in La Jolla, California
Source: *AmAu&B; ASCAP 66, 80;
AuBYP 3; Benet 87; BenetAL 91; BioIn
13, 14, 15, 16; CamBiEn; CamGLE;
CelR 90; ChlLR 1, 9; ConAu 13R, 32NR,
135, X; ConGrA 3; ConLC 70; DcPseud;
FacFETw; FamAIYP; IlsCB 1957;
MajTwCW 1; News 92; NewYTBS 86;
OxCChiL; REn; REnAL; SmATA 1, 67;
TwCA, SUP; WebAB 74; WhoAm 86, 88;
WhoWest 74; WhoWor 74; WrDr 86, 92*

Sevareid, Eric
[Arnold Eric Severeid]
American. Broadcast Journalist
Joined CBS as member of original news
team assembled, 1939.
b. Nov 26, 1912 in Velva, North Dakota
d. Jul 9, 1992 in Washington, District of
Columbia
Source: *AmAu&B; AmNatBi; AuNews 1;
BiDAmJo; BioIn 4, 5, 7, 8, 10, 11, 12,
16, 18, 19, 21, 23; CelR; ConAu 69;
ConTFT 12; CurBio 42, 66; DcAmDH
89; EncAJ; EncTelN; EncTwCJ;
FacFETw; HisDcWJ; IntMPA 75, 76, 77,
78, 79, 80, 81, 82, 84, 86, 88, 92;
IntWW 74, 75, 76, 77, 78, 79, 80, 83,
91; LegTOT; LesBEnT, 92; LinLib L, S;
News 93-1; NewYTBS 79, 92; NewYTET;
PeoHis; PolCom; RadStar; SaTiSS;
WhoAm 86, 90; WhoHol 92; WhoTelC;
WhoWor 74; WorAl; WorAlBi*

Severini, Gino
Italian. Artist
Futurist, cubist whose paintings include
*Dynamic Hieroglyph of the Bal
Tabarin*.
b. Apr 7, 1883 in Cortona, Italy
d. Feb 29, 1966 in Paris, France
Source: *BioIn 4, 6, 7, 10, 11, 13, 14, 17,
21; CamBiEn; ChamBiD; ClaDrA;
ConArt 77, 83; DcArts; DcTwArt;
EncWB 98; FacFETw; IntDcAA 90;
McGDA; McGEWB; NewCol 75;
OxCArt; OxCTwCA; OxDcArt;
PhDcTCA 77*

Severinsen, Doc
[Carl H Severinsen]
American. Musician, Bandleader
Joined "Tonight Show" orchestra, 1962;
music director 1967-92.
b. Jul 7, 1927 in Arlington, Oregon
Source: *AllMGJa; ASCAP 66, 80;
BakBD 84, 92; BakBDTw; BiDAmM;
BiDJaz; BioIn 8, 9, 10, 11, 12, 14, 16;
CmpEPM; ConMus 1; ConTFT 12;
EncJzS; EncJzS; NewAmDM; NewGrDA
86; NewGrDJ 88, 94; PenEncP; WhoAm
78, 80, 82, 84, 86, 88, 90, 92, 94, 95,
96, 97, 98, 99, 2000; WhoAmM 83;
WhoE 74; WhoEnt 92, 98; WhoMW 98;
WhoTelC; WhoWest 00, 94, 96, 98;
WhoWor 95; WorAl; WorAlBi*

Severn, William Irving
American. Author
Writes books of American history, magic
for children: *Magic with Coins and
Bills*, 1977; *Democracy's Messengers*,
1975.
b. May 11, 1914 in New York, New
York
Source: *AuBYP 3; ConAu 1NR, 1R,
16NR, 36NR; SmATA 1, 41*

Sevier, John
American. Politician
First governor of TN, 1796-1801, 1803-
09.
b. Sep 23, 1745 in New Market, Virginia
d. Sep 24, 1815 in Fort Decatur,
Alabama
Source: *AmAu&B; AmBi; AmNatBi;
AmRev; ApCAB; BiAUS; BiDrAC;
BiDrGov 1789; BiDrUSC 89; BioIn 1, 3,
4, 5, 6, 10, 16; CamDcAB; ChamBiD;
DcAmB; Drake; EncAAH; EncAR;
EncCRAm; EncSoH; EncWar; EncWB
98; HarEnUS; McGEWB; NatCAB 3;
NewEAmW; OxCAmH; REn; REnAW;
TwCBDA; WebAB 74, 79; WebAMB;
WhAm HS; WhAmP; WhAmRev;
WhNaAH*

Sevigne, Marie de Rabutin-
Chantal, Marquise de
French. Diarist
Prolific correspondent whose 1700 letters
to her daughter reflected the social
history of the reign of Louis XIV.
b. Feb 5, 1626 in Paris, France
d. Apr 17, 1696 in Grignan, France
Source: *Benet 87; BioIn 1, 4, 13, 14, 19;
BlmGWL; CasWL; DcArts; EncCoWW;
EuAu; FemiCLE; FrenWW; GuFrLit 2;
IntDcWB; InWom SUP; LitC 11;
OxCEng 85, 95; OxCFr; RAdv 13-2;
REn; WorAlBi*

Seville, David
[Ross S Bagdasarian]
American. Singer
Wrote "The Chipmunk Song," 1958; led
to animated TV series "The Alvin
Show," 1960.
b. Jan 27, 1919 in Fresno, California
d. Jan 16, 1972 in Beverly Hills,
California
Source: *ASCAP 80; BiDAmM; DcPseud;
EncPR&S 74; LegTOT; PenEncP; RkOn
74; Songw; WhoHol B; WhoRock 81;
WhScrn 77; WorAl*

Sevitzky, Fabien
Russian. Conductor
Led Indianapolis Symphony, 1937-55.
b. Sep 29, 1891 in Volotchok, Russia
d. Feb 2, 1967 in Athens, Greece
Source: *ASCAP 66; BakBD 78, 84, 92;
BakBDTw; CurBio 46, 67; NewGrDA
86; WhAm 4; WhoMus 72*

Sewall, Samuel
American. Judge
Sentenced 19 people to death at Salem
witchcraft trials, 1692; publicly
confessed his error, 1697.

b. Mar 28, 1652 in Bishopstoke, England
d. Jan 1, 1730 in Boston, Massachusetts
Source: *Alli; AmAu; AmAu&B; AmBi;
AmNatBi; AmWrBE; ApCAB; BbD;
Benet 87, 96; BenetAL 91; BiD&SB;
BioIn 1, 2, 3, 4, 7, 8, 10, 14, 15, 22, 24;
CamDcAB; CamGEL; CamGLE;
CamHAL; CasWL; ChamBiD; CnDAL;
DcAmAu; DcAmB; DcAmSR; DcLB 24;
DcLEL; DcNaB; Drake; EncAB-H 1974,
1996; EncALit; EncWB 98; HarEnUS;
LegTOT; LitC 38; MacEWoS; McGEWB;
NatCAB 5; OxCAmH; OxCAmL 65, 83,
95; OxCMus; PenC AM; REn; REnAL;
REnAW; RfGAmL 4, 87, 94; TwCBDA;
WebAB 74, 79; WebE&AL; WhAm HS;
WorAl; WorAlBi*

Seward, Anna
"The Swan of Lichfield"
English. Poet
Wrote poetic novel *Louisa*, 1782;
provided James Boswell gossip about
Samuel Johnson.
b. Dec 12, 1747 in Eyam, England
d. Mar 25, 1809 in Lichfield, England
Source: *Alli; ArtclWW 2; BiD&SB;
BlmGEL; BritAu; CamBiEn; CamGEL;
CamGLE; CasWL; ChamBiD; Chambr
2; ChhPo, S1; DcBiPP; DcBrAmW;
DcEnL; DcEuL; DcLEL; DcNaB, C;
EvLB; InWom, SUP; NewC; NewCol 75;
OxCEng 67, 85, 95; PenC ENG; REn*

Seward, William Henry
American. Government Official
Secretary of State, appointed by Lincoln,
1861-69; his purchase of Alaska from
Russia, 1867, was called "Seward's
Folly."
b. May 16, 1801 in Florida, New York
d. Oct 10, 1872 in Auburn, New York
Source: *Alli; AmAu&B; AmBi; AmNatBi;
AmPolLe; ApCAB; BbD; BenetAL 91;
BiAUS; BiD&SB; BiDrAC; BiDrGov
1789; BiDrUSC 89; BiDrUSE 71, 89;
BioIn 1, 3, 4, 5, 6, 7, 8, 9, 10, 11, 12,
14, 16, 17, 18, 19, 21, 22; CamBiEn;
CamDcAB; CelCen; ChamBiD; CivWDc;
CopCroC; CyAG; CyAL 2; DcAmAu;
DcAmB; DcAmDH 80, 89; DcAmSR;
DcBiPP; DcNAA; Drake; EncAAH;
EncAB-H 1974, 1996; EncWB 98;
HarEnUS; HisWorL; LAmCW; LegTOT;
LinLib L, S; McGEWB; MorMA;
NatCAB 2; OxCAmH; REn; REnAL;
TwCBDA; WebAB 74, 79; WhAm HS;
WhAmP; WhCiWar; WorAl*

Sewell, Anna
English. Author
Wrote *Black Beauty*, 1877.
b. Mar 30, 1820 in Yarmouth, England
d. Apr 25, 1878 in Norwich, England
Source: *ArtclWW 2; BioIn 1, 2, 4, 8, 9,
13, 16, 19, 22, 24; BlmGEL; BlmGWL;
BritAu 19; CamBiEn; CamGEL;
CamGLE; CarSB; CasWL; ChamBiD;
ChlBkCr; ChlLR 17; DcArts; DcLB 163;
DcLEL; DcNaB; EncAnRW; EncBrWW;
EvLB; FemiCLE; InWom; JBA 34;
LegTOT; MajAI; NewC; NewCBEL;
OxCChiL; OxCEng 67, 85, 95; REn;
SJGChWr 5A; SmATA 24, 100; StaCVF;*

TwCChW 1A, 2A, 3A, 4A; VicBrit;
WhoChL; WomWrGB; WrChl

Sewell, Joe
[Joseph Wheeler Sewell]
American. Baseball Player
Infielder, 1920-33, mostly with
  Cleveland; hold ML record for fewest
  strikeouts, with one every 64 at-bats;
  Hall of Fame, 1977.
b. Oct 9, 1898 in Titus, Alabama
d. Mar 6, 1990 in Mobile, Alabama
Source: *AmNatBi; Ballpl 90; BiDAmSp*
BB; BioIn 11, 14, 15, 16, 17; CulEncB;
FacFETw; LegTOT; NewYTBS 90

Sex Pistols, The
[Paul Cook; Steve Jones; Johnny Rotten;
Sid Vicious]
English. Music Group
Hit songs include "God Save the
  Queen," 1977; was banned from radio
  in England.
Source: *BillEnR; BioIn 11, 15, 17, 18;*
ChamBiD; ConMuA 80A; ConMus 5;
DcArts; DrAPF 85, 87, 89, 91, 93, 97;
EncPR&S 89; EncRk 88; EncRkSt;
HarEnR 86; IlEncRk; NewAmDM;
NewYTBS 79; OxCPMus; PenEncP;
RkWho 96; RolSEnR 83; St&PR 96, 97;
WhoHol 92; WhoRock 81; WhoRocM 82;
WhsNW 85

Sexton, Anne Harvey
American. Poet
Wrote "confessional" verse; won
  Pulitzer for *Live or Die,* 1967.
b. Nov 9, 1928 in Newton,
  Massachusetts
d. Oct 4, 1974 in Weston, Massachusetts
Source: *AmAu&B; CasWL; ChhPo S1;*
ConAu 1R, 3NR, 53; ConLC 2, 4, 6, 15;
ConPo 70, 75; CroCAP; ForWC 70;
GrWrEL P; MajTwCW 2; MakMC;
ModAL 4, 4S1; NewYTBS 74; PenBWP;
PenC AM; RAdv 1; SmATA 10;
WebE&AL; WhAm 6; WhoAm 74;
WhoAmW 68, 70, 72, 74, 75; WhoE 74;
WhoTwCL; WorAu 1950

Sexton, Leo
American. Track Athlete
Shot putter; won gold medal, 1932
  Olympics.
b. Aug 27, 1909 in Danvers,
  Massachusetts
d. Sep 6, 1968 in Perry, Oklahoma
Source: *BioIn 8; ObitOF 79; WhoTr&F*
73

Seymour, Anne Eckert
American. Actor
Performed in memorable radio series,
  "Bulldog Drummond," "Inner
  Sanctum," and "The Romance of
  Helen Trent," 1932-61.
b. Sep 11, 1909 in New York, New
  York
d. Dec 8, 1988 in Los Angeles,
  California
Source: *BiE&WWA; FilmgC; InWom*
SUP; MotPP; MovMk; NotNAT; WhoAm
82; WhoHol A

Seymour, Charles
American. Educator, Historian
President of Yale U, 1937-50; wrote
  Diplomatic Background of the War,
  1916.
b. Jan 1, 1884 in New Haven,
  Connecticut
d. Aug 11, 1963 in New Haven,
  Connecticut
Source: *AmAu&B; CurBio 41, 63;*
REnAL; WhAm 4; WhNAA

Seymour, Dan
American. Advertising Executive
Pres., chairman, J Walter Thompson Co.,
  1964-74.
b. Jun 28, 1914 in New York, New York
d. Jul 27, 1982 in New York, New York
Source: *BioIn 6, 7, 8, 13; NewYTBS 82;*
SaTiSS; St&PR 75; WhAm 8; WhoAdv
72; WhoAm 74, 76; WhoE 75; WhoFI
74, 75

Seymour, Dan
American. Actor
Character actor; appeared in films
  Casablanca, 1942; *Key Largo,* 1948.
b. Feb 22, 1915 in Chicago, Illinois
d. May 25, 1993 in Santa Monica,
  California
Source: *BioIn 4, 19; EncAFC; FilmEn;*
FilmgC; ForYSC; HalFC 80, 84, 88;
IntMPA 75, 76, 77, 78, 79, 80, 81, 82,
84, 86, 88, 92; MotPP; MovMk;
RadStar; Vers A; WhoHol A

Seymour, Horatio
American. Politician
Dem. presidential candidate, 1868; lost to
  Grant.
b. May 31, 1810 in Onondaga County,
  New York
d. Feb 12, 1886 in Utica, New York
Source: *AmBi; AmNatBi; AmPolLe;*
ApCAB; BiDrGov 1789; BioIn 5, 7, 8, 9,
24; CamDcAB; CivWDc; CyAG;
DcAmB; DcNAA; Drake; EncAPar;
EncWB 98; HarEnUS; McGEWB;
NatCAB 3; NewCol 75; PolPar; PresAR
1980, 1996; TwCBDA; WebAB 74, 79;
WhAm HS; WhCiWar

Seymour, Jane
English. Consort
Married Henry VIII, 1536; mother of
  Edward VI; died 12 days after son's
  birth.
b. 1509
d. Oct 24, 1537
Source: *Benet 87, 96; BioIn 18;*
CamBiEn; DcNaB; Dis&D; EncWB 99;
InWom SUP; NewCol 75; REn; WebBD
83

Seymour, Jane
[Joyce Penelope Wilhelmina
Frankenberg]
English. Actor
Starred in TV mini-series, "East of
  Eden," 1980; star of "Dr. Quinn,
  Medicine Woman," 1993-98.
b. Feb 15, 1951 in Hillingdon, England

Source: *BioIn 12, 16; CelR 90; ConTFT*
1, 6, 13, 22; DcPseud; HalFC 84, 88;
HolBB; IntMPA 84, 86, 88, 92, 94, 96;
IntWWW 2; LegTOT; News 94;
NewYTBS 80; WhoAm 80, 82, 84, 86,
88, 90, 92, 94, 95, 96, 97, 99, 2000;
WhoAmW 91, 93, 95, 97; WhoEnt 92;
WhoHol 92; WorAlBi

Seymour, Lynn
Canadian. Dancer
Popular dramatic ballerina with Royal
  Ballet, 1957-77; director, prima
  ballerina, Bayerische Staatsoper,
  Munich, 1978-79.
b. Mar 8, 1939 in Wainwright, Alberta,
  Canada
Source: *BiDD; BioIn 6, 11, 12, 13;*
CamBiEn; CanWW 70, 79, 80, 81, 83,
89; ChamBiD; CnOxB; CreCan 2;
CurBio 79; DancEn 78; DcArts;
DcPseud; IntDcB; IntWW 77, 78, 79, 80,
81, 82, 83, 89, 91, 93, 97, 98, 2000;
IntWWW 2; InWom SUP; Who 74, 82,
83, 85, 88, 90, 92, 94, 98, 99, 2000;
WhoAm 80, 82; WhoWor 74, 82, 87, 89,
91, 93, 95

Seyss-Inquart, Artur von
Austrian. Politician
German High Commissioner of The
  Netherlands, 1940-46; condemned,
  hanged by Int'l Military Tribunal for
  "ruthless terrorism."
b. Jul 2, 1892 in Stannern, Bohemia
d. Oct 16, 1946 in Nuremberg, Germany
Source: *BioIn 1, 14, 16, 18; ChamBiD;*
CurBio 41, 46; Dis&D; REn; WhDW;
WhWW-II

Sforza, Carlo
Italian. Author, Educator, Statesman
Foreign minister, 1920-22, 1947-51;
  writings display knowledge of int'l
  politics.
b. Sep 25, 1872 in Lucca, Italy
d. Sep 4, 1952 in Rome, Italy
Source: *BiDInt; BioIn 1, 2, 3; ClDMEL*
47; CurBio 42, 52; LinLib L, S; ObitOF
79; ObitT 1951; WhE&EA

Sforza, Ludovico
[Duke of Milan]
"Il Moro"
Italian. Nobleman
Ruled, 1481-99; defeated by Louis XII
  of France, 1499; imprisoned, 1500.
b. Jul 27, 1451 in Vigevano, Italy
d. May 27, 1508 in Loches, France
Source: *CamBiEn; NewCol 75; WebBD*
83

Shaaban Robert
Tanzanian. Author, Poet
Known for his poetry, fiction, and
  autobiography, he is considered the
  greatest author to have written in the
  Swahili language.
b. Jan 1, 1909 in Vibamba, Tanganyika
d. Jun 22, 1962
Source: *EncWB 98*

Shabaka
Ethiopian. King
Nubian king established the Twenty-fifth
Dynasty in Lower Egypt with his
reign from c. 712 to c. 696 B.C.,
becoming the first of the "Ethiopian"
(or black African) pharaohs.
b. fl. 712BC

Shabazz, Attallah
American. Actor, Director
Daughter of Malcolm X; formed theater
troupe, Nucleus, with Yolanda King,
daughter of Martin Luther King, Jr.
b. Nov 16, 1958 in Mount Vernon, New
York
Source: *BioIn 11, 12, 13, 16, 20;
ConBlB 6; InB&W 80, 85; NotBlAW 1*

Shabazz, Betty
American. Civil Rights Activist
Wife of Malcolm X.
b. May 28, 1936 in Detroit, Michigan
d. Jun 23, 1997 in New York, New York
Source: *ConBlB 7; ConHero 3; Ebony 1;
EncWB 98; InB&W 80; NegAl 76; News
97; NewYTBS 97; NotBlAW 2; WhoAfA
9, 10, 11; WhoBlA 1, 2, 8*

Shackelford, Ted
American. Actor
Played Gary Ewing on TV series "Knots
Landing," 1980-93.
b. Jun 23, 1946 in Oklahoma City,
Oklahoma
Source: *BioIn 13; ConTFT 8, 16, 26;
LegTOT; VarWW 85; WhoAm 82, 84, 86,
88, 90, 92; WhoEnt 92, 98; WhoHol 92;
WorAlBi*

Shackleton, Ernest Henry, Sir
Irish. Explorer
Wrote *The Heart of the Antarctic,* 1909,
which described expeditions.
b. Feb 15, 1874 in Kilkee, Ireland
d. Jan 5, 1922 in South Georgia,
Antarctica
Source: *BioIn 2, 3, 4, 5, 6, 7, 8, 10, 11,
12, 14, 17, 18, 20, 24; CamBiEn;
ChamBiD; ConAu 118; DcIrB 1, 2, 3;
DcNaB 1922; EncWB 98; ExplAnT;
FacFETw; GrBr; InSci; LinLib L, S;
LngCTC; McGEWB; ModIrLi; OxCBrHi;
OxCShps; REn; WhDW; WhWE; WorAl*

Shadrach
[Meshach and Abednego]
Hebrew. Biblical Figure
In Bible, one of three miraculously saved
from burning in a furnace.
Source: *BioIn 2, 4; NewCol 75*

Shadwell, Thomas
English. Dramatist, Poet
Wrote *Medal of John Bayes,* 1682;
succeeded Dryden as poet laureate,
1688-92.
b. 1642 in Bromhill, England
d. Nov 20, 1692 in London, England
Source: *Alli; AtlBL; BbD; Benet 87, 96;
BiCoLiE; BiD&SB; BioIn 3, 8, 12;
BlmGEL; BritAu; CamBiEn; CamGEL;*

*CamGLE; CamGWoT; CasWL;
ChamBiD; Chambr 1; CrtT 2; DcArts;
DcEnA; DcEnL; DcEuL; DcLEL;
DcNaB; EncWT; Ent; EvLB; GrWrEL
DR; LngCEL; NewC; NewCBEL;
NewC; NewCBEL; NewGrDM 80;
NotNAT B; OxCEng 67, 85, 95; OxClri;
OxCThe 67, 83; PenC ENG; PoLE;
REn; REnWD; WebE&AL; WhDW*

Shaffer, Anthony
English. Author
Won 1971 Tony for *Sleuth.*
b. May 15, 1926 in Liverpool, England
Source: *BioIn 10, 13, 14; ConAu 110,
116; ConDr 73, 77, 82, 88; ConLC 19;
ConTFT 6; CyWA 97; DcLB 13; DcLEL
1940; DcLP 87A; EncWT; HalFC 84,
88; IntvTCA 2; LegTOT; NewCBEL;
NotNAT; ScF&FL 92; TwCCr&M 85,
91; WhoThe 72, 77, 81; WrDr 76, 80,
82, 84, 86, 88, 90, 92*

Shaffer, Paul
Canadian. Musician, Composer
Best known as keyboardist, bandleader
on TV show "Late Night with David
Letterman," 1982-93, and "Late Show
With David Letterman," 1993—.
b. Nov 28, 1949 in Thunder Bay,
Ontario, Canada
Source: *BioIn 14, 15, 16; CanWW 96,
97, 98, 1999; ConMus 13; ConNews 87-
1; ConTFT 7, 15; LegTOT; WhoAm 92,
94, 95, 96, 97, 98; WhoEnt 92, 98;
WorAlBi*

Shaffer, Peter Levin
English. Dramatist
Wrote plays *Five Finger Exercise,* 1958;
Tony-winner *Equus,* 1975; *Amadeus,*
1981.
b. May 15, 1926 in Liverpool, England
Source: *Benet 87; BioIn 13, 14, 15;
BritWr S1; CamBiEn; CamGLE;
ChamBiD; ConAu 25NR, 74NR; ConDr
88; ConLC 18, 37; ConTFT 4; CurBio
67, 88; DcLP 87A; EncWB 98;
FacFETw; HalFC 84; IntAu&W 89;
IntvTCA 2; IntWW 91, 97, 98, 2000;
MajTwCW 2; McGEWD 84; ModBrL S2;
NewC; OxCAmT 84; OxCEng 85;
OxCTwCL; PenC ENG; RAdv 13-2;
REnWD; TwCCr&M 85; TwCWr; Who
92, 98, 99, 2000; WhoAm 90, 98, 99,
2000; WhoThe 81; WhoWor 87, 91, 98,
99, 2000; WrDr 86, 88, 98, 99, 2000*

Shafran, Daniel
Russian. Musician
Remarkable cellist, concertist; won first
prize in Moscow competition, 1937.
b. Feb 13, 1923 in Leningrad, Union of
Soviet Socialist Republics
Source: *BakBD 78, 84; BiDSovU; BioIn
5; PenDiMP*

Shafter, William Rufus
American. Military Leader
Led volunteer expeditionary force which
invaded Cuba, Spanish-American War,
1898.

b. Oct 16, 1835 in Kalamazoo County,
Michigan
d. Nov 12, 1906 in Bakersfield,
California
Source: *AmBi; AmNatBi; ApCAB SUP;
BioIn 1, 8, 16; CivWDc; DcAmB;
DcAmMiB; HarEnMi; HarEnUS; MedHR
94; NatCAB 9; SpAmWar; TwCBDA;
WebAB 74, 79; WebAMB; WhAm 1*

Shaftesbury, Anthony Ashley Cooper, Earl
English. Philosopher, Statesman
Collected writings appeared in
*Characteristics of Men, Manners,
Opinions, Times,* 1711.
b. Feb 26, 1671 in London, England
d. Feb 15, 1713 in Naples, Italy
Source: *BbD; BioIn 19; BritAu; CasWL;
ChamBiD; DcEnA; DcEnL; DcEuL;
DcLEL; EncEnl; EvLB; IlEncMy; NewC;
OxCEng 67, 95; PenC ENG; RAdv 14;
WebE&AL*

Shagan, Steve
[Stephen H Shagan]
American. Screenwriter
Oscar nominee for best screenplay: *Save
the Tiger,* 1973; *Voyage of the
Damned,* 1976.
b. Oct 25, 1927 in New York, New York
Source: *BioIn 12, 13; ConAu 6NR, 53;
ConTFT 5; HalFC 84, 88; IntMPA 86,
92, 94, 96; NewYTBS 79; ScF&FL 92;
VarWW 85; WhoAm 76, 78, 80, 82, 84,
86, 88, 90, 92, 94, 95, 96, 97, 98, 99,
2000; WhoEnt 98; WhoWor 82; WrDr
82, 84, 86, 88, 90, 92, 94, 96, 98, 99,
2000*

Shagari, Alhaji Shehu Usman Aliyu
Nigerian. Political Leader
Overthrown in bloodless coup, Dec 31,
1983, by military leader Mohammed
Buhari.
b. Apr 1925 in Shagari, Nigeria
Source: *AfSS 78, 79; BioIn 13, 14;
ChamBiD; CurBio 80; DcAfHiB 86;
InB&W 85; IntWW 75, 76, 77, 91;
NewYTBS 79; Who 92, 94, 98, 99, 2000;
WhoWor 74, 76*

Shah, Indries
Indian. Religious Leader
Author of books on the "secret
wisdom;" wrote *The Sufis,* 1964.
b. Jun 16, 1924
d. Nov 23, 1996 in London, England
Source: *BioIn 11*

Shaham, Gil
American. Violinist
Considered the finest violinist in his
generation; stood in for Itzhak Perlman
at the London Symphony Orchestra at
age 17, 1989.
b. 1971
Source: *BakBDTw; CurBio 97; WhoAm
98*

Shah Jahan
Indian. Ruler
Mughal emperor, 1628-58; directed
  building of the Taj Mahal.
b. Jan 5, 1592 in Lahore, India
d. Jan 22, 1666 in Agra, India

Shahn, Ben(jamin)
American. Artist
Noted for posters; used social, political
  themes in paintings: *Handball.*
b. Sep 12, 1898 in Kaunas, Lithuania
d. Mar 14, 1969 in New York, New
  York
Source: *AtlBL; Benet 87, 96; BioIn 1, 2,
  3, 4, 5, 6, 7, 8, 9, 10, 12, 13, 14, 17, 21;
  BriEAA; CambiEn; CamDcAB;
  ChambiD; ChhPo S1; ConArt 77, 83,
  89, 96; ConAu 89, 121; ConPhot 82, 88;
  CurBio 54, 69; DcAmArt; DcAmB S8;
  DcArts; DcCAA 71, 77, 88, 94; EncAB-
  H 1974, 1996; FacFETw; ICPEnP A;
  IlsCB 1957; IntDcAA 90; LegTOT;
  MacBEP; McGDA; McGEWB; ModArCr
  3; ObitT 1961; OxCAmL 65, 83, 95;
  OxCArt; OxCTwCA; OxDcArt;
  PhDcTCA 77; PrintW 83, 85; REn;
  SmATA 21N; WebAB 74, 79; WhAm 5;
  WhAmArt 85; WhoAmA 78N, 80N, 82N,
  84N, 86N, 89N, 91N, 93N; WhoGrA 62;
  WorAl; WorAlBi; WorArt 1950*

Shahpur, II
Persian. King
King of Persia whose 70-year reign
  marked the height of military power
  and territorial expansion in the
  Sassanian dynasty.
b. 310, Persia
d. 379, Persia
Source: *EncWB 98; McGEWB*

Shaka
African. Military Leader
Founder, chief of Zulu Empire, 1816;
  ruthless, highly trained army crushed
  neighboring tribes into submission or
  extermination; slain after his insanity
  led to murder of over 7,000 Zulus.
b. 1787
d. Sep 22, 1828
Source: *BioIn 4, 6, 7, 8, 9, 10, 12, 14,
  19, 20; ChambiD; DcAfHiB 86; DicTyr;
  EncWB 98; GenMudB; HarEnMi;
  McGEWB; MilitOn*

Shakespeare, William
[Bard of Avon]
English. Dramatist, Poet
Considered greatest dramatist ever; wrote
  154 sonnets, 37 plays.
b. Apr 23, 1564 in Stratford-upon-Avon,
  England
d. Apr 23, 1616 in Stratford-upon-Avon,
  England
Source: *Alli; AnCL; AtlBL; BbD; Benet
  87, 96; BiCoLiE; BiD&SB; BiDRP&D;
  BioIn 1, 2, 3, 4, 5, 6, 7, 8, 9, 10, 11, 12,
  13, 14, 15, 16, 17, 18, 19, 20, 21, 22,
  23, 24; BlmGEL; BritAu; BritWr 1;
  CamBiEn; CamGEL; CamGLE;
  CamGWoT; CarSB; CasWL; ChambiD;
  Chambr 1, 2, 3; ChhPo, S1, S2, S3;*

*CmpQue; CnDBLB 1; CnE&AP; CnThe;
  CroE&S; CrtSuDr; CrtT 1, 4; CyWA 58,
  97; DcArts; DcBiPP; DcEnA, A; DcEnL;
  DcEuL; DcLB 62, 172; DcLEL; DcNaB;
  DcPup; Dis&D; EncApL; EncFoLi;
  EncPaPR 91; EncWB 98; EncWT; Ent;
  EvLB; FamAYP; FilmgC; GloEncH;
  GrWrEL DR, P; HalFC 80, 84, 88;
  HisDStE; IntDcT 2; LegTOT; LinLib L;
  LiveWoA; LngCEL; LuthC 75; MagSWL;
  McGEWB; McGEWD 72, 84; MetOEnc;
  MouLC 1; NewC; NewCBEL; NewEOp
  71; NewGrDM 80; NewGrDO; NotNAT
  A, B; NotPoe; OxCAmT 84; OxCBrHi;
  OxCEng 67, 85, 95; OxCFilm; OxCFr;
  OxCGer 76; OxCThe 67, 83; OxDcOp;
  PenC ENG; PlP&P, A; RComWL; REn;
  REnWD; RfGEnL 91; TwoTYeD;
  WebE&AL; WhDW; WhoHrs 80; Wiz;
  WorAl; WorAlBi; WorLitC; WrYoAd*

Shakur, Assata
[JoAnne Deborah Byron]
American. Civil Rights Activist
Member of the Black Liberation Army,
  1970s; charged with several crimes;
  living in political asylum in Cuba.
b. Jul 16, 1947 in New York, New York
Source: *BioIn 20, 23, 24; ConBlB 6*

Shakur, Tupac
American. Rapper
Debut album *2Pacalypse Now,* 1992;
  died of gunshot wounds.
b. Jun 16, 1971 in New York, New York
d. Sep 13, 1996 in Las Vegas, Nevada
Source: *AfrAmAl 8; ConBlB 14; News
  97, 97-1; WhoAfA 9, 10N*

Shalala, Donna Edna
American. Political Scientist, University
  Administrator, Government Official
Secretary, Department of Health and
  Human Services, 1993—; chancellor
  of University of Wisconsin, Madison,
  1988-93; first woman in history to
  head a Big Ten university.
b. Feb 14, 1941 in Cleveland, Ohio
Source: *AmWomM; AmWomSc 1950;
  BioIn 12, 13, 15, 16; CamDcAB; CurBio
  91; EncWoAP; IntWW 91, 93, 97, 98,
  2000; IntWWW 2; InWom SUP; News
  92; NewYTBS 79, 87, 88; WhoAm 82,
  84, 86, 88, 90, 92, 94, 95, 96, 97, 98,
  99, 2000; WhoAmW 85, 87, 89, 91, 93,
  95, 97, 99; WhoE 83, 85, 86, 95;
  WhoMedH 96, 99, 2000; WhoMW 90,
  92, 93, 96, 98; WhoScEn 2000; WhoWor
  89, 91, 93, 95, 96, 97, 98, 99, 2000*

Shalamar
[Delisa Davis; Micki Free; Howard
  Hewett]
American. Music Group
Dance/pop group formed 1978; hits
  include "A Night to Remember,"
  1982.
Source: *BioIn 17; EncRk 88; EncRkSt;
  HarEnR 86; InB&W 85A; RkOn 85;
  RolSEnR 83; SoulM*

Shalamov, Varlam Tikhonovich
Russian. Poet, Author
Wrote about 17 yrs. in Gulag in *Kolyma
  Tales,* 1980.
b. Jun 18, 1907 in Vologda, Russia
d. Jan 17, 1982 in Moscow, Union of
  Soviet Socialist Republics
Source: *AnObit 1982; Benet 96; ConAu
  105; ConLC 18; NewYTBS 82; RfGShF
  2*

Shales, Tom
[Thomas William Shales]
American. Journalist
Syndicated columnist, *Washington Post,*
  1971—; wrote *American Film
  Heritage,* 1972; wone Pulitzer Prize,
  1988.
b. Nov 3, 1948 in Elgin, Illinois
Source: *BioIn 12, 15; ConAu 110, 112,
  X; ConTFT 15; LesBEnT 92; WhoAm 82,
  84, 86, 88, 90, 92, 94; WhoE 91, 93;
  WhoEnt 92*

**Shalikashvili, John (Malchase
  David)**
American. Military Leader
Drafted into U.S. Army, 1958;
  Chairman, Joint Chiefs of Staff, 1993-
  97.
b. Jun 27, 1936 in Warsaw, Poland
Source: *BioIn 18, 19, 20, 21; CurBio 95;
  EncWB 98; IntWW 93; News 94, 94-2;
  NewYTBS 93; Who 94, 98, 99, 2000*

Shalit, Gene
American. Critic, Journalist
With NBC since 1969; arts editor and
  critic, "Today," 1973—.
b. 1932 in New York, New York
Source: *BioIn 10; BkPepl; CelR 90;
  ConTFT 26; IntMPA 77, 78, 79, 80, 81,
  82, 84, 86, 88, 92, 94, 96; LegTOT;
  LesBEnT 92; NewYTET; WhoAm 84, 86;
  WhoTelC*

Shambaugh, Jessie Field
"Mother of 4-H"
American. Educator
Started nat. farm organization, 4-H,
  clubs, 1910.
b. Jun 26, 1881 in Shenandoah, Iowa
d. Jan 15, 1971 in Clarinda, Iowa
Source: *InWom SUP; NotAW MOD;
  PeoHis; WomFir*

Shamir, Yitzhak
[Yitzhak Yerzernitsky]
Israeli. Political Leader
Prime minister of Israel, 1983-84; 1986-
  92.
b. Nov 3, 1914 in Kuzinoy, Poland
Source: *BioIn 13, 14, 15, 16; CurBio 83,
  96; EncWB; FacFETw; HisDcPG;
  IntWW 91; MidE 82; NewYTBS 80, 83,
  88; PolLCME; WhoWor 87, 91*

Shammai
Sage
Jewish sage was a conservative scholar
  of the Oral Tradition, and rival of the
  liberal sage Hillel; founded the Bet

Shammai, the "House of Shammai," persistent opponent of Bet Hillel, the "House of Hillel."
b. 1st cent. BC
Source: *BioIn 5; CamBiEn; ChamBiD; EncWB 98; LuthC 75; McGEWB*

Sha Na Na
[Lenny Baker; John "Bowser" Bauman; Johnny Contrado; "Dennis" Frederick Greene; "Jocko" John; Dan McBride; "Chico" Dave Ryan; Tony Santini; Simon Scott; Donald York]
American. Music Group
Formed in 1969; albums include *Remember Then*, 1978.
Source: *BillEnR; EncPR&S 74, 89; EncRk 88; HarEnR 86; IlEncRk; NewYTBS 77, 82; NotNAT; PenEncP; RkOn 74, 78; RkWho 96; RolSEnR 83; WhoHol 92, A; WhoRock 81; WhoRocM 82*

Shandling, Garry
American. Comedian
Star of cable TV sitcom "It's Garry Shandling's Show," 1986-90; star of "The Larry Sanders Show," 1992—.
b. Nov 29, 1949 in Chicago, Illinois
Source: *BioIn 15, 16; ConTFT 9; CurBio 89; IntMPA 94, 96; LegTOT; News 95, 95-1; WhoAm 94, 95, 96, 97, 98; WhoCom; WhoEnt 98*

Shange, Ntozake
[Paulette Linda Williams]
American. Dramatist, Poet
Wrote play *For Colored Girls Who Have Considered Suicide/When the Rainbow is Enuf*, 1977, won Obie.
b. Oct 18, 1948 in Trenton, New Jersey
Source: *AfrAmAl 6, 8; AfrAmW; AmWomD; AmWomWr SUP; ArtclWW 2; Au&Arts 9; BenetAL 91; BioIn 11, 12, 13, 14, 15, 16; BlkLC; BlkWAm; BlkWr 1, 2; BlmGWL; CamGWoT; ConAfAN; ConAmD; ConAu 3BS, 27NR, 48NR, 74NR, 85; ConBlAP 88; ConBlB 8; ConDr 82, 88, 93; ConLC 8, 25, 38, 74, 126; ConPo 91, 96; ConTFT 5; ConWomD; ConWomP 98; CrtSuDr; CurBio 78, 79; CyWA 89, 97; DcLB 38; DcTwCCu 5; DramC 3; DrAPF 80, 91; DrBlPA, 90; EncALit; FacFEBW TA; FemDram; FemiCLE; FemiWr; GrWomW; IdentIs; InB&W 80, 85; IntDcT 2; IntWW 97, 98, 2000; InWom SUP; MagSAmL; MajTwCW 1, 2; ModAL 4S3, 5; ModBlW 2; ModWoWr; MorBAP; NatPD 81; NegAl 83, 89; NewYTBS 76; NotBlAW 1; NotWoAT; OxCAfAL; OxCAmL 95; OxCTwCL; OxCWoWr 95; RfGAmL 4; SchCGBL; SelBAAf; SelBAAu; SJGYouA 2; TwCYAW 1; WhoAfA 9, 10, 11, 12; WhoAm 80, 82, 84, 86, 88, 90, 92, 94, 95, 96, 97, 98; WhoAmW 83, 95; WhoBlA 3, 4, 5, 6, 7, 8; WhoThe 81; WhoUSWr 88; WhoWrEP 89, 92, 95; WomPlaD; WorAu 1975; WrDr 86, 92, 94, 96, 98, 99, 2000*

Shang Yang
Chinese. Philosopher, Politician
Statesman and political philosopher helped the Ch'in dynasty ascend to power; one of the founders of Chinese Legalism, he is credited with writing *Shang-Chun shu*, a collection of economic, legal, and political treatises.
b. c. 390BC in Wei, China
d. 338BC in Shang, China
Source: *EncChi; EncWB 98*

Shankar, Ravi
Indian. Musician, Composer
Plays the sitar; composed film score for *Ghandi*, 1982.
b. Apr 7, 1920 in Benares, India
Source: *ABCCoAm; AsAmAlm; ASCAP 80; AuBYP 3; BakBD 78, 84, 92; BakBDTw; BakDcM; BioIn 6, 7, 8, 9, 11, 13, 14; BriBkM 80; CamBiEn; CelR; ConMus 9; ConTFT 12; CurBio 68; DcArts; EncRk 88; FacFETw; FarE&A 78, 79, 80, 81; IntDcF 1-4, 2-4; IntWW 74, 75, 76, 77, 78, 79, 80, 81, 82, 83, 89, 91, 93, 97, 98, 2000; IntWWM 77, 80, 90; LegTOT; MusMk; NewAgMG; NewAmDM; NewGrDA 86; NewGrDM 80; PenDiMP; PenEncP; Who 90, 92; WhoEnt 98; WhoHol 92, A; WhoMus 72; WhoWor 74, 84, 87, 89, 91, 93, 95, 96; WorAl; WorEFlm*

Shankar, Uday
Indian. Dancer
Popularized Indian dance in West; created two ballets on Hindu themes.
b. 1901, India
d. Sep 26, 1977 in Calcutta, India
Source: *DcFM; IntWW 74; NewYTBS 77, 85; ObitOF 79*

Shankara
Indian. Philosopher
Reformer and Hindu philosopher founded the advaita, or nondual, school of vedanta philosophy based on the Upanishads, or esoteric teachings.
b. c. 788, India
d. 820
Source: *EncWB 98; HisWorL; McGEWB; WhDW*

Shanker, Albert
American. Teacher, Labor Union Official
Pres., NYC United Federation of Teachers, 1964-86.
b. Sep 14, 1928 in New York, New York
d. Feb 22, 1997 in New York, New York
Source: *AmDec 1980; BiDAmL; BiDAmLL; BiDMoAE; BioIn 8, 9, 10, 11, 12, 13, 14, 15; BlueB 76; CamDcAB; CurBio 69, 97N; EncWB 98; LEduc 74; NewYTBS 75, 97; PolProf J, NF; WhAm 12; WhoAm 76, 78, 80, 82, 84, 86, 88, 90, 92, 94, 95, 96, 97; WhoAmP 77, 79, 81, 83, 85, 87, 89, 91, 93, 95; WhoE 74, 75, 77, 79, 81, 91, 95; WhoLab 76; WhoWorJ 72, 78; WorAlBi*

Shanks, Michael
[Thomas William Shanks]
English. Economist, Government Official
Chm., National Consumer Council, 1977-84.
b. Apr 12, 1927 in London, England
d. Jan 13, 1984 in Sheffield, England
Source: *ConAu 8NR, 111; IntWW 74, 75, 76, 77, 78, 79, 80, 81, 82, 83; WhoWor 84*

Shanley, John Patrick
American. Dramatist
Wrote *Danny and the Deep Blue Sea: An Apache Dance*, 1984; wrote screenplay for film *Moonstruck*, 1987.
b. Oct 13, 1950 in New York, New York
Source: *ConAmD; ConAu 83NR, 128, 133; ConDr 93; ConLC 75; ConTFT 9; IntMPA 92, 94, 96; LegTOT; MiSFD 9; WhoAm 95, 96, 97; WrDr 94, 96, 98*

Shanley, Kathryn W.
American. Scholar
Served on many boards and committees including the American Indian Programm Steering Committee at Cornell Univ.
b. Dec 1, 1947 in Wolf Point, Montana
Source: *NotNaAm*

Shannon, Claude Elwood
American. Mathematician
The first to apply symbolic logic to the design of switching circuits, his work on the mathematics of communication is central to modern information theory.
b. Apr 30, 1916 in Gaylord, Michigan
Source: *AmMWSc 76P, 79, 82, 86, 89, 92, 95, 98; AsBiEn; BiESc; BioIn 4, 10, 14, 15, 17, 18, 20; CamBiEn; CamDcAB; CamDcSc; ChamBiD; ConAu 162; EncWB 98; HisDcDP; IntWW 74, 75, 76, 77, 78, 79, 80, 81, 82, 83, 89, 91, 93, 97, 98, 2000; LarDcSc; LElec; McGCEnS; McGEWB; McGMS 80; RanHWDS; WhoAm 74, 76, 78, 86, 88, 90, 92, 94, 95, 96, 97, 99, 2000; WhoWor 74, 78; WorAl*

Shannon, Del
[Charles Westover]
American. Singer, Songwriter
Early rock singer; wrote, recorded no. 1 hit "Runaway," 1961; popularity waned with Beatles-led British Invasion.
b. Dec 30, 1939 in Coopersville, Michigan
d. Feb 8, 1990 in Santa Clarita, California
Source: *AmPS A; AnObit 1990; BioIn 12, 16, 17; EncPR&S 89; EncRk 88; FacFETw; HarEnR 86; LegTOT; NewGrDA 86; NewYTBS 90; PenEncP; RkOn 74, 82; RolSEnR 83; WhoRock 81; WorAlBi*

Shannon, Fred Albert
American. Historian, Educator
Won 1929 Pulitzer for *Organization and Administration of the Union Army, 1861-65.*
b. Feb 12, 1893 in Sedalia, Missouri
d. Feb 14, 1963 in Urbana, Illinois
Source: *AmAu&B; AmNatBi; BioIn 4, 6; ConAu 111; DcAmB S7; EncAAH; OxCAmL 65; TwCA, SUP; WhAm 4; WhE&EA; WhNAA; WhoPul; WorAu 1900*

Shannon, James A(ugustine)
American. Physician
Director, National Institutes of Health, 1955-68; perfected usable form of quinacrine to combat malaira.
b. Aug 9, 1904
d. May 20, 1994 in Baltimore, Maryland
Source: *AmMWSc 76P, 79, 82, 86, 89, 92, 95; BioIn 7; BlueB 76; CurBio 94N; IntWW 74, 75, 76, 77, 78, 79, 80, 81, 82, 83, 89, 91, 93; WhoWor 74*

Shannon, William Vincent
American. Diplomat, Author
US ambassador to Ireland, 1977-81; wrote *Heir Apparent: Robert Kennedy and the Struggle for Power,* 1967.
b. Aug 24, 1927 in Worcester, Massachusetts
d. Sep 27, 1988 in Boston, Massachusetts
Source: *AmAu&B; AmCath 80; BiDAmNC; BioIn 11, 12, 13; ConAu 6NR, 9R; CurBio 79, 88; IntAu&W 76, 77, 89; IntWW 78, 79, 80, 81, 82, 83; IntYB 78, 79, 80, 81, 82; ScrEAmL 2; WhAm 9; WhoAm 74, 76, 78, 80, 82, 84, 86, 88; WhoAmP 85; WhoWor 78, 80, 82, 84*

Shante
[Lolita Gooden]
''Roxanne Shante''
American. Rapper
Controversial rap artist who recorded debut single ''Roxanne'e Revenge,'' 1985 and ''Have a Nice Day,'' 1987; released first album *Bad Sister,* 1990 and later *The Bitch is Back,* 1992.
b. 1970 in Long Island, New York
Source: *ConMus 10*

Shapey, Ralph
American. Composer, Conductor, Educator
Devoted to the cause of new music, he is known for powerful and complex compositions reflecting a personal vision.
b. Mar 12, 1921 in Philadelphia, Pennsylvania
Source: *AmComp; ASCAP 66, 80; BakBD 78, 84, 92; BakBDTw; BakDcM; BiDAmM; BioIn 12, 13; BlueB 76; BriBkM 80; ConAmC 76, 82; ConCom 92; CpmDNM 79, 80, 81, 82; DcCM; DcCom&M 79; EncWB, 98; IntWWM 85, 90; NewAmDM; NewGrDA 86; NewGrDM 80; WhoAm 74, 76, 78, 80, 82, 84, 86, 88, 94, 95, 96, 97, 98, 99,*

2000; *WhoAmJ 80; WhoAmM 83; WhoEnt 92, 98; WhoMW 74, 76; WhoWor 74; WhoWorJ 72, 78*

Shapira, Amitzur
Israeli. Olympic Athlete, Victim
One of 11 members of Israeli Olympic team kidnapped, killed by Arab terrorists during Summer Olympic Games.
b. 1932?
d. Sep 5, 1972 in Munich, Germany (West)
Source: *BioIn 9*

Shapiro, Arnold
American. Producer
Won Oscar for documentary *Scared Straight,* 1978.
b. Feb 1, 1941 in Los Angeles, California
Source: *LesBEnT 92; VarWW 85*

Shapiro, Harold Tafler
American. University Administrator, Educator
Pres., U of Michigan, 1979-87; Princeton, 1987—.
b. Jun 8, 1935 in Montreal, Quebec, Canada
Source: *BioIn 15; CanWW 89, 96, 97, 98, 1999; IntWW 91, 93, 97, 98, 2000; NewYTBS 87; WhoAm 80, 82, 84, 86, 88, 90, 92, 94, 95, 96, 97, 98, 99, 2000; WhoE 91, 93, 95, 97, 99; WhoMW 80, 82, 84, 86; WhoScEn 2000; WhoWor 80, 87, 89, 91, 93, 95, 96, 97, 98, 99, 2000; WrDr 98, 99, 2000*

Shapiro, Jane
American. Author
Wrote *After Moondog,* 1992.
Source: *ConLC 76*

Shapiro, Karl Jay
American. Poet, Critic
Poems of WW II, *V-Letters & Other Poems,* won Pulitzer Prize, 1945.
b. Nov 10, 1913 in Baltimore, Maryland
d. May 14, 2000 in New York, New York
Source: *AmAu&B; AmWr S2; AnCL; Benet 87; BioIn 22; CamBiEn; CamDcAB; CamGLE; CamHAL; CanWW 89; CasWL; ChamBiD; CnDAL; CnE&AP; ConAu 1NR, 6AS, 66NR, 132; ConLC 4, 15, 53; ConPo 85; DcLB 48; DrAPF 87; EncALit; IntAu&W 89; IntvTCA 2; IntWW 91, 97, 98, 2000; MajTwCW 2; ModAL 4S1, 4S2; OxCAmL 83; OxCTwCL; PenC AM; RAdv 13-1; RfGAmL 4, 87; TwCA SUP; WebAB 79; Who 92; WhoAm 86, 90, 98, 99, 2000; WhoE 91; WhoEnt 98; WhoWor 91; WrDr 86, 88, 98, 99, 2000*

Shapiro, Stanley
American. Screenwriter, Producer
Co-wrote screenplay for Oscar-winning film *Pillow Talk,* 1959.
b. Jul 16, 1925 in New York, New York

d. Jul 21, 1990 in Los Angeles, California
Source: *BioIn 6, 17; CmMov; ConAu 132; EncAFC; FilmEn; FilmgC; HalFC 80, 84, 88; ScF&FL 92; VarWW 85; WrDr 88, 90, 92, 94, 96*

Shaplen, Robert Modell
American. Journalist
Staff writer, *New Yorker* magazine, 1952-88; wrote *Bitter Victory,* 1986.
b. Mar 22, 1917 in Philadelphia, Pennsylvania
d. May 15, 1988 in New York, New York
Source: *AmAu&B; ConAu 9R; HisDcWJ; IntAu&W 77, 82; WhAm 9; WhoAm 74, 76, 78, 80, 82, 84, 86; WhoUSWr 88; WhoWor 74; WhoWrEP 89; WrDr 76, 80, 82, 84, 86, 88*

Shapley, Harlow T
American. Astronomer
Director of Harvard Observatory, 1921-52; known for studies of the Milky Way; wrote *Galaxies,* 1943; *Readings in the World of Science,* 1943.
b. Nov 2, 1885 in Nashville, Missouri
d. Oct 20, 1972 in Boulder, Colorado
Source: *AmAu&B; CurBio 41, 52, 72; DcScB; EncAB-H 1974; McGEWB; OxCAmH; REnAL; TwCA, SUP; WebAB 74; WhAm 5*

Shapp, Milton J(errold)
American. Politician
Dem. governor of PA, 1971-79.
b. Jun 25, 1912 in Cleveland, Ohio
d. Nov 24, 1994 in Wynnewood, Pennsylvania
Source: *BiDrGov 1789, 1978; BioIn 7, 9, 10, 11, 12, 17, 20, 21; BioNews 74; CurBio 73, 95N; IntWW 77, 78, 79, 80, 81, 82, 83; PolProf NF; WhoAm 74; WhoAmP 85, 91; WhoE 74; WhoGov 72*

Sharaff, Irene
American. Designer
Won four Oscars for costume designs including *West Side Story,* 1961; Tony for *The King and I,* 1952.
b. 1910 in Boston, Massachusetts
d. Aug 16, 1993 in New York, New York
Source: *AmNatBi; AnObit 1993; BiE&WWA; BioIn 16, 19; CamGWoT; ChamBiD; CnOxB; ConDes 84, 90, 97; DancEn 78; EncFash; FilmgC; HalFC 80, 84, 88; IntDcF 1-4, 2-4; IntMPA 84, 86, 88, 92; IntWW 83; NotNAT; NotWoAT; OxCAmT 84; ThHDFas; VarWW 85; WhoAm 84; WhoThe 77, 81; WomFilm*

Sharer, Donald A
[The Hostages]
American. Hostage
One of 52 held by terrorists, Nov 1979-Jan 1981.
b. 1941?
Source: *NewYTBS 81*

Sharett, Moshe
[Moshe Shertok]
Israeli. Government Official
Zionist leader; foreign minister, 1948-56;
premier, 1953-55.
b. Oct 3, 1894 in Kherson, Russia
d. Jul 7, 1965 in Jerusalem, Israel
Source: *BioIn 1, 2, 3, 4, 7, 8, 13, 22, 23;
ChamBiD; CurBio 48, 65; DcMidEa;
HisEAAC; ObitT 1961; WhAm 4*

Shariati, Ali
Iranian. Religious Leader
"Ideologue of the Iranian Revolution"
reinterpreted Islam in modern
sociological categories, preparing the
way for the Islamic revival that shook
Iran in 1979.
b. 1933 in Mazinan, Khurasan, Iran
d. 1977, England
Source: *BioIn 13; DcMidEa; EncRev;
EncWB, 98; PolEnME; RadHan*

Sharietmadari, Ayatollah Seyed
Iranian. Religious Leader
Islamic scholar who opposed Shah of
Iran, led nation's conservative forces
with Khomeini in exile.
b. 1902
Source: *BioIn 11*

Sharif, Nawaz
Pakistani. Political Leader
Prime minister of Pakistan, 1990-93,
1997—.
b. Dec 23, 1948 in Lahore, Pakistan
Source: *BioIn 19, 20, 24*

Sharif, Omar
[Michael Shalhoub]
Egyptian. Actor
Starred in *Dr. Zhivago*, 1965, *Funny
Girl*, 1968; bridge expert—daily
bridge lessons published in syndicated
newspapers.
b. Apr 10, 1932 in Alexandria, Egypt
Source: *BiDFilm, 81, 94; BioIn 8, 9, 10,
11, 13, 14, 16, 21; BkPepl; CamBiEn;
CelR; CmMov; ConTFT 5; CurBio 70;
DcArts; DcPseud; FilmEn; FilmgC;
HalFC 80, 84, 88; IntDcF 1-3, 2-3;
IntMPA 77, 78, 79, 80, 81, 82, 84, 86,
88, 92, 94, 96; IntWW 74, 75, 76, 77,
78, 79, 80, 81, 82, 83, 89, 91, 98;
ItaFilm; LegTOT; MidE 78, 79, 80, 81,
82; MotPP; MovMk; OsStAZ; OxCFilm;
WhoAm 80, 82, 84, 86, 88, 90, 92, 94,
95, 96, 97, 99, 2000; WhoEnt 92, 98;
WhoFr 79; WhoHol 92, A; WhoWor 74,
82, 84, 87, 89, 91, 2000; WorAl;
WorAlBi; WorEFlm*

Sharkey, Jack
[Joseph Paul Zukauskas]
"Big Skee"
American. Boxer
Popular, cocky world heavyweight
champ, 1932-33.
b. Oct 6, 1902 in Binghamton, New
York
Source: *BiDAmSp BK; BioIn 2, 5, 9, 10,
13, 20; BoxReg, 2; DcPseud; NewYTBS
83, 94; What 3; WhoBox 74*

Sharkey, Ray
American. Actor
Began acting on TV playing tough guys
who were emotionally vulnerable; best
known for his role of Sonny
Steelgrave on "Wiseguy."
b. Nov 14, 1952 in New York, New
York
d. Jun 11, 1993 in New York, New York
Source: *BioIn 12, 16; ConTFT 5; HalFC
84, 88; IntMPA 84, 86, 88, 92; LegTOT;
News 94; WhAm 11; WhoHol 92*

Sharman, Bill
[William Walton Sharman]
American. Basketball Player, Basketball
Coach
Guard, 1950-61, mostly with Boston; led
NBA in free throw percentage seven
yrs; coached seven yrs. in NBA,
mostly with LA; coach of year, 1972;
Hall of Fame, 1974.
b. May 25, 1926 in Abilene, Texas
Source: *Ballpl 90; BasBi; BiDAmSp BK;
CmCal; NewYTBE 72; OfNBA 87;
WhoAm 80, 82, 90; WhoBbl 73;
WhoSpor; WhoWest 80, 92*

Sharmat, Marjorie Weinman
American. Children's Author
Prolific writer of books for juveniles:
Rex, 1967, *Mooch the Messy*, 1976.
b. Nov 12, 1928 in Portland, Maine
Source: *AuBYP 2S, 3; BioIn 14, 19;
ChlBkCr; ConAu 12NR, 25R, 39NR,
84NR; FifBJA; FifWWr; IntAu&W 76,
77, 82, 86, 91, 93; MajAI; SJGChWr 5;
SmATA 4, 33, 74; TwCChW 1, 2, 3, 4;
WrDr 76, 80, 82, 84, 86, 88, 90, 92, 94,
96, 98, 99, 2000*

Sharon, Ariel
"Arik"
Israeli. Government Official
Defense minister forced to resign
because of role in Beirut massacre,
1982.
b. 1928 in Kafr Malal, Palestine
Source: *BioIn 9, 10, 11, 12, 13, 14, 15,
16; ChamBiD; ColdWar 1, 2; CurBio
81; DcMidEa; EncWB, 98; FacFETw;
HarEnMi; HisEAAC; IntWW 75, 76, 77,
78, 79, 80, 81, 82, 83, 89, 91, 93, 97,
98, 2000; MidE 78, 79, 80, 81, 82;
NewYTBS 81, 82, 90; PolEnME;
ProfiWG 98; WhoWor 82, 84, 87, 89, 91,
93, 97, 98, 99, 2000; WhoWorJ 78*

Sharon, Lois & Bram
[Sharon Hampson; Lois Lilienstein;
Bram Morrison]
Music Group
Popular children's singing group formed
in 1978.
Source: *ConMus 6*

Sharp, Granville
English. Philanthropist
Founded English Society for Abolition of
Slaves, 1787.
b. Nov 10, 1735 in Durham, England
d. Jul 6, 1813 in Fulham, England

Source: *BioIn 2, 6, 8, 9, 10; ChamBiD;
DcAfL; DcBiPP; DcNaB; HisDBrE;
MacEWoS; NewCBEL; NewCol 75;
OxCBrHi; WebBD 83*

Sharp, Margery
British. Author
b. 1905
Source: *Au&Wr 71; AuBYP 2, 3; BioIn
1, 2, 4, 8, 9, 13, 16, 17, 19, 22;
ChlBkCr; ChlLR 27; ConAu 18NR, 21R,
85NR, 134; ConNov 72, 76, 82, 86;
DcLB 161; DcLEL; EncBrWW; EvLB;
IntAu&W 76, 77, 89; IntWW 83, 91N;
LngCTC; MajAI; NewC; OxCChiL; RAdv
1; REn; ScF&FL 1, 2, 92; SJGChWr 5;
SmATA 1, 29, 67; ThrBJA; TwCA, SUP;
TwCChW 1, 2, 3, 4; WhLit; Who 85, 90,
92N; WhoWor 84, 91; WorAu 1900;
WrDr 76, 80, 82, 84, 86, 88, 90*

Sharp, William
[Fiona MacLeod]
Scottish. Poet, Author
Wrote literary biographies, novels under
own name; mystical verse prose under
feminine pseudonym.
b. Sep 12, 1855 in Paisley, Scotland
d. Dec 12, 1905 in Castello de Manlace,
Sicil, Italy
Source: *Alli SUP; AnCL; BbD; BiCoLiE;
BiD&SB; BioIn 12, 16, 21; BritAu 19;
CamGLE; CasWL; ChamBiD; Chambr
3; ChhPo, S1, S2, S3; CmScLit; ConAu
160; DcBiA; DcEnA, A; DcLB 156;
DcLEL; DcNaB S2; EvLB; GrWrEL N;
LngCTC; MnBBF; NewC; NewCBEL;
OxCEng 67, 85, 95; OxCIri; PenC ENG;
RfGEnL 91; ScF&FL 1; StaCVF;
SupFW; TwCLC 39; VicBrit*

Sharp, Zerna A
American. Teacher
Originated *Dick and Jane* reader series
for schools.
b. Aug 12, 1889 in Hillisburg, Indiana
d. Jun 17, 1981 in Frankfort, Indiana
Source: *AnObit 1981; BiDMoAE; BioIn
12, 13, 24; ConAu 104; NewYTBS 81;
SmATA 27N*

Sharpe, Sterling
American. Football Player
With Green Bay Packers, 1988-95; NFL
receiving leader, 1989, 1992, 1993.
b. Apr 6, 1965 in Chicago, Illinois
Source: *BioIn 20; News 94, 94-3;
WhoAm 95, 96, 97, 98, 99, 2000;
WhoSpor*

Sharpton, Al(fred), Jr.
American. Political Activist, Clergy
NY ordained minister involved in racial
crimes to promote justice; Tawana
Brawley case, 1987.
b. Oct 3, 1954 in New York, New York
Source: *AfrAmAl 6; BioIn 16; CurBio
95; LegTOT; News 91, 91-2; NewYTBS
91; RelLAm 2*

Shastri, Lal Badahur
Indian. Statesman
Prime minister of India, 1964-66.
b. Oct 2, 1904 in Mughalsarai, India
d. Jan 11, 1966 in Tashkent, Union of
Soviet Socialist Republics
Source: *BioIn 9; CurBio 64, 66; WhAm
2*

Shatner, William
American. Actor
Best known as James T Kirk on TV
series "Star Trek," 1966-69, films
based on series, 1979-89.
b. Mar 22, 1931 in Montreal, Quebec,
Canada
Source: *BiE&WWA; BioIn 10, 12, 13,
14, 15, 16, 17, 19, 20, 21, 22, 23, 24;
BioNews 74; CamBiEn; CamDcAB;
CanWW 83, 89, 96, 97, 98, 1999; CelR
90; ConAu 85NR, 146; ConCaAu 1;
ConTFT 1, 3, 17; CurBio 87; EncSF 93;
FilmEn; FilmgC; ForYSC; HalFC 80,
84, 88; IntMPA 84, 86, 88, 92, 94, 96;
IntWW 91, 93, 97, 98, 2000; ItaFilm;
LegTOT; LesBEnT 92; MiSFD 9;
MotPP; MovMk; NotNAT; OxCCanT;
ScF&FL 92; VarWW 85; WhoAm 74, 78,
80, 82, 84, 86, 88, 90, 92, 94, 95, 96,
97, 98, 99, 2000; WhoEnt 92, 98;
WhoHol 92, A; WhoHrs 80; WhoTelC;
WhoThe 77, 81; WorAl; WorAlBi*

Shattuck, Roger Whitney
American. Author, Educator
Wrote award-winner, *Marcel Proust,*
1974.
b. Aug 20, 1923 in New York, New
York
Source: *AmAu&B; Au&Wr 71; ConAu
5R, 71NR; DrAP 75; DrAPF 87, 91;
DrAS 82F; IntvTCA 2; SmATA 64;
WhoAm 86, 90, 97, 98, 99, 2000;
WhoEnt 98; WhoUSWr 88; WhoWrEP
89; WorAu 1950; WrDr 86, 92*

Shaughnessy, Clark Daniel
American. Football Coach
Head coach at several colleges and in
NFL, 1915-49; introduced modern T-
formation at Rose Bowl, 1941.
b. Mar 6, 1892 in Saint Cloud,
Minnesota
d. May 15, 1970 in Santa Monica,
California
Source: *AmNatBi; BiDAmSp FB; BioIn
4, 6, 8; DcAmB S8; NewYTBE 70;
WhAm 5; WhoFtbl 74*

Shaughnessy, Mickey
[Joseph C Shaughnessy]
American. Actor, Comedian
Often cast in tough guy roles; films
include *From Here to Eternity,* 1953;
Pocketful of Miracles, 1961.
b. 1920 in New York, New York
d. Jul 23, 1985 in Cape May Court
House, New Jersey
Source: *BioIn 14; EncAFC; FilmEn;
FilmgC; ForYSC; HalFC 80, 84, 88;
MovMk; NewYTBS 85; WhoHol A*

Shaver, Dorothy
American. Business Executive
Pres., Lord and Taylor specialty store
from 1945; promoted American
designers.
b. Jul 29, 1897 in Center Point, Arkansas
d. Jun 28, 1959 in Hudson, New York
Source: *AmWomM; BioIn 1, 2, 3, 4, 5, 7,
9, 11, 12, 17; ConAmBL; CurBio 46, 59;
EncAB-A 28; InWom, SUP; NatCAB 56;
NotAW MOD; WhAm 3; WhoAmW 58;
WorFshn*

Shaver, Helen
Canadian. Actor
Films include *The Amityville Horror,*
1979.
b. Feb 24, 1951 in Saint Thomas,
Ontario, Canada
Source: *BioIn 15; ConTFT 7, 14, 25;
IntMPA 92, 94, 96; VarWW 85; WhoHol
92*

Shavers, Ernie
American. Boxer
Heavyweight champion; 24 straight KOs,
1970s.
b. Aug 31, 1945 in Garland, Alabama
Source: *BioIn 11, 12, 13; NewYTBS 79;
WhoBox 74*

Shaw, Albert
American. Editor
Founded current events mag., *Review of
Reviews,* 1912-37.
b. Jul 23, 1857 in Shandon, Ohio
d. Jun 25, 1947 in New York, New York
Source: *Alli SUP; AmAu&B; AmNatBi;
ApCAB; BbD; BiDAmJo; BiD&SB; BioIn
1, 2, 10, 16, 17; DcAmAu; DcAmB S4;
DcAmSR; DcLB 91; DcNAA; HarEnUS;
LinLib L; NatCAB 9, 34; OhA&B;
OxCAmL 65; REnAL; TwCBDA; WhAm
2; WhNAA*

Shaw, Anna Howard
American. Social Reformer, Suffragist
Feminist leader and reformer was the
fourth president of the National
American Woman Suffrage
Association.
b. Feb 14, 1847 in Newcastle-upon-Tyne,
England
d. Jul 2, 1919 in Moylan, Pennsylvania
Source: *AmAu&B; AmBi; AmNatBi;
AmOrTwC; AmRef; AmWom;
AmWomWr; ApCAB X; BenetAL 91;
BioIn 1, 6, 10, 11, 15, 17, 19, 21, 24;
CamBiEn; CamDcAB; ChamBiD;
DcAmB; DcAmC; DcAmSR; DcAmTB;
DcNAA; EncAWoR; EncWB 98;
EncWHA; EncWM; EncWoAP;
FemiCLE; GrLiveH; HanAmWH; InSci;
InWom, SUP; LibW; McGEWB; Meth;
NatCAB 12; NotAW; OxCAmH; RelLAm
1, 2; REnAL; WhAm 1; WhAmP;
WomPubS 1800; WomWWA 14*

Shaw, Artie
[Arthur Arshowsky]
American. Musician
Clarinetist, prominent swing bandleader,
1930s-40s; had biggest hit with Cole
Po rter's "Begin the Beguine," 1938.
b. May 23, 1910 in New York, New
York
Source: *AllMGJa; ASCAP 66, 80;
BakBD 78, 84, 92; BakDcM; BiDAmM;
BiDJaz; BioIn 1, 2, 3, 6, 7, 8, 9, 12, 13,
14, 15, 16, 17, 20, 22; CamBiEn; CelR,
90; ChamBiD; CmpEPM; ConAu 144;
ConMus 8; CurBio 41; DcArts; DcLP
87B; DcPseud; FacFETw; HalFC 84,
88; IlEncJ; LegTOT; NewAmDM;
NewGrDA 86; NewGrDJ 88, 94;
NewGrDM 80; NewYTBE 73; NewYTBS
85; OxCPMus; PenEncP; PeoHis;
RadStar; What 2; WhoAm 74, 76, 78, 80,
82, 84, 86, 88, 90, 92, 94, 95, 96, 97,
98, 99, 2000; WhoE 74; WhoEnt 92, 98;
WhoHol 92, A; WhoJazz 72; WhoWor
74, 76; WorAl; WorAlBi; WrDr 96, 98,
99, 2000*

Shaw, Bernard
American. Broadcast Journalist
CNN's principal Washington anchor
1980—; one of three CNN
correspondents in Baghdad during the
Gulf War, 1991.
b. May 22, 1940 in Chicago, Illinois
Source: *AfrAmAl 6, 8; BioIn 11, 12, 16;
BlkWr 1; ConAu 109, 119; ConBlB 2;
CurBio 95; DcTwCCu 5; EncTelN;
NegAl 76; NotBlAM; PolCom; WhoAfA
9, 10, 11, 12; WhoAm 90, 92, 94, 95, 96,
97, 98, 99, 2000; WhoBlA 6, 7, 8; WhoE
93; WhoMedi 98; WhoWor 99, 2000*

Shaw, George Bernard
English. Dramatist, Critic
Greatest British dramatist since
Shakespeare; wrote *Pygmalion,* 1913;
won Nobel Prize, 1925.
b. Jul 26, 1856 in Dublin, Ireland
d. Nov 2, 1950 in Ayot Saint Lawrence,
England
Source: *Alli SUP; AtlBL; BakBD 78, 84,
92; BakBDTw; BakDcM; Benet 87, 96;
BiCoLiE; BiD&SB; BiDBrF 2; BiDIrW;
BioIn 1, 2, 3, 4, 5, 6, 7, 8, 9, 10, 11, 12,
13, 14, 15, 16, 17, 18, 19, 20, 23;
BlmGEL; BritPl; BritWr 6; CamBiEn;
CamGEL; CamGLE; CamGWoT;
CasWL; ChamBiD; Chambr 3; ChhPo,
S2, S3; CnMD; CnMWL; CnThe; ConAu
104, 128; CrtSuDr; CyWA 89, 97;
DcAmSR; DcArts; DcBiA; DcEnA A;
DcIrB 1, 2, 3; DcIrW 1, 2; DcLEL;
DcNaB 1941; DcPup; DcTwHis; Dis&D;
EncAnRW; EncFab; EncSF, 93;
EncUnb; EncWB 98; EncWL 1, 2, 2S, 3;
EncWT; Ent; EvLB; FacFETw; Film 2;
GrBr; GrStDi; GrWrEL DR; HalFC 84,
88; HisDcIr; IlWWBF A; IntDcT 2;
IntWW 2000; IriPla; LegTOT; LinLib L,
S; LngCEL; LuthC 75; MagSWL;
MajTwCW 1, 2; MakMC; McGEWB;
McGEWD 72, 84; ModBrL, 2, S1;
ModIrL; ModIrLi; NewC; NewCBEL;
NobelP; NotNAT A, B; Novels; OxCAmT
84; OxCBrHi; OxCEng 67, 85; OxCIri;
OxCMus; OxCThe 67, 83; OxCTwCL;*

PenC ENG; PlP&P; RAdv 14, 13-2;
RComWL; REn; RGTwCWr; ScF&FL 1;
ScFEYrs; ScFSB; SocPrL; StaCVF;
ThTwC 87; TwCA, SUP; TwCLC 3;
TwCWr; TwoTYeD; VicBrit; WebE&AL;
WhAm 3; WhDW; WhE&EA; WhLit;
WhoNob, 90, 95; WhoStg 1906, 1908;
WhoTwCL; WhScrn 77, 83; WorAl;
WorAlBi; WorAu 1900; WrPh

Shaw, Irwin
American. Author, Dramatist
Wrote *Rich Man, Poor Man*, 1970.
b. Feb 27, 1913 in New York, New
   York
d. May 16, 1984 in Davos, Switzerland
Source: AmAu&B; AmNatBi; AmNov;
AnObit 1984; Au&Wr 71; AuNews 1;
BeaEPF; Benet 87; BenetAL 91;
BiCoLiE; BiE&WWA; BioIn 1, 2, 4, 5, 6,
7, 8, 10, 12, 13, 14, 15, 16, 17, 20, 22,
24; BlueB 76; CelR; CnMD; CnThe;
ConAu 13R, 21NR, 112; ConDr 73, 77,
82; ConLC 7, 23, 34; ConNov 72, 76,
82; ConPopW; CurBio 84N; CyWA 89,
97; DcLB 6, 102, Y84N; DcTwCCu 1;
DrAF 76; EncALit; EncWL 1; EncWT;
Ent; FacFETw; FilmEn; IntAu&W 76,
77, 82; IntWW 74, 75, 76, 77, 78, 79,
80, 81, 82, 83; ItaFilm; JeAmFiW;
LinLib L; LngCTC; MajTwCW 1, 2;
McGEWD 72, 84; ModAL 4, 5; ModWD;
NewCon; NewYTBS 83, 84; NotNAT;
Novels; OxCAmL 65, 83, 95; OxCAmT
84; PenC AM; RAdv 1; REn; REnAL;
ShSWr; TwCA, SUP; TwCWr; WhAm 9;
Who 74, 82, 83; WhoAm 74, 76, 78, 80,
82, 84, 86, 88; WhoThe 72, 77, 81;
WhoTwCL; WhoWor 74, 78, 80, 82;
WorAl; WorAlBi; WorAu 1900;
WorEFlm; WrDr 76, 80, 82, 84

Shaw, Lemuel
American. Judge
Chief justice of the Supreme Judicial
   Court of Massachusetts, he was one of
   America's leading judges during the
   time the common law was being
   developed.
b. Jan 9, 1781 in Barnstable,
   Massachusetts
d. Mar 30, 1861
Source: Alli; AmBi; AmNatBi; ApCAB;
BiDTran; BioIn 3, 11, 23; CamDcAB;
DcAmB; Drake; EncAB-H 1974, 1996;
EncWB 98; HarEnUS; McGEWB;
NatCAB 5; OxCAmH; OxCLaw;
TwCBDA; WebAB 74, 79; WhAm HS

Shaw, Mary
American. Actor
One of first actresses to introduce
   American audiences to Ibsen, Shaw.
b. Jan 25, 1854 in Boston, Massachusetts
d. May 18, 1929 in New York, New
   York
Source: AmNatBi; AmWomPl; BioIn 16;
DcAmB; NotAW; NotNAT B; PeoHis;
PlP&P; WhAm 1; WhoStg 1906, 1908;
WhThe; WomWWA 14

Shaw, Richard Norman
English. Architect
Led revolution in domestic architecture;
   designed economical, smaller houses;
   important work, New Scotland Yard,
   1888-90.
b. Jul 5, 1831 in Edinburgh, Scotland
d. Jul 11, 1912 in Hampstead, England
Source: AntBDN G; BioIn 11, 13, 15,
16; CamBiEn; ChamBiD; DcArch;
DcBrAr 1; DcD&D; DcNaB 1912;
DcNiCA; EncMA; EncWB 98; IntDcAr;
McGDA; McGEWB; NewCol 75;
OxCArt; VicBrit; WhDW; WhoArch

Shaw, Robert
English. Actor, Dramatist, Author
Starred in *Jaws*, 1975; *The Deep*, 1977.
b. Aug 9, 1927 in Westhoughton,
   England
d. Aug 28, 1978 in Tourmakeady,
   Ireland
Source: AuNews 1; BiDFilm 81, 94;
BiDrAPA 77; BiE&WWA; BioIn 6, 7, 8,
9, 10, 11, 13, 14, 20, 21; BlueB 76;
CelR; ConAu 1R, 4NR, 81; ConDr 73,
77; ConLC 5; ConNov 72, 76; CroCD;
CurBio 78N; DcLB 13, 14; DcLEL 1940;
EncWT; FilmAG WE; FilmEn; FilmgC;
ForYSC; HalFC 80, 84, 88; IlWWBF;
IntAu&W 76, 77; IntDcF 1-3, 2-3;
ItaFilm; LegTOT; McGEWD 72;
MovMk; NotNAT; OsStAZ; PlP&P, A;
WhAm 7; Who 74; WhoAm 76, 78;
WhoHol A; WhoThe 72, 77; WhoWor 74;
WorAl; WorAlBi; WorAu 1950; WrDr 76

Shaw, Robert Gould
American. Military Leader
White commander of a black regiment,
   the 54th Massachusetts; his career and
   story of 54th featured in film *Glory*,
   1989.
b. Oct 10, 1837 in Boston, Massachusetts
d. Jul 18, 1863 in Charleston, South
   Carolina
Source: AmBi; AmNatBi; ApCAB; BioIn
4, 5, 7, 10, 12, 14, 15, 16, 17;
CamDcAB; Drake; EncAB-H 1974,
1996; GenMudB; NatCAB 8; NewCol
75; TwCBDA; WebAMB; WebBD 83;
WhAm HS; WhCiWar

Shaw, Robert Lawson
American. Conductor
Founder, director, Robert Shaw Chorale,
   1948-65; leader of Atlanta Symphony,
   1967-88; won many Grammys.
b. Apr 30, 1916 in Red Bluff, California
d. Jan 25, 1999 in New Haven,
   Connecticut
Source: BakBD 84, 92; BakBDTw;
BiDAmM; BioIn 1, 2, 4, 7, 8, 9, 11, 12;
CamDcAB; IntWWM 85; MusSN;
NewGrDA 86; NewYTBS 80; WebAB 74,
79; WhoAm 82, 84, 86, 88, 90, 92, 94,
95, 96, 97, 98, 99; WhoAmM 83;
WhoEnt 92, 98; WhoFI 87; WhoSSW 88,
95; WhoWor 95

Shaw, Wilbur
American. Auto Racer
Introduced crash helmet to US racing,
   1932; won Indy 500, 1937 in car made
   by him; won again, 1939, 1940.
b. Oct 31, 1902 in Shelbyville, Indiana
d. Oct 30, 1954 in Fort Wayne, Indiana
Source: AmNatBi; BioIn 3, 5, 7, 10, 11,
12; DcAmB S5; IndAu 1917; WhoSpor

Shawn, Dick
[Richard Schulefand]
American. Actor, Comedian
Appeared in films *It's a Mad Mad Mad
   Mad World*, 1963; *The Producers*,
   1968.
b. Dec 1, 1929 in Buffalo, New York
d. Apr 17, 1987 in La Jolla, California
Source: ConNews 87-3; ConTFT 5;
EncAFC; FilmEn; FilmgC; ForYSC;
HalFC 80; IntMPA 77, 80, 84, 86;
MotPP; MovMk; VarWW 85; WhoHol A;
WhoThe 77; WorAl; WorAlBi

Shawn, Ted
[Edwin Meyers Shawn]
American. Dancer
With wife Ruth St. Denis, organized
   Denishawn Dancers, 1915; established,
   directed Jacob's Pillow Dance
   Festival, 1932-49.
b. Oct 21, 1891 in Kansas City, Missouri
d. Jan 9, 1972 in Orlando, Florida
Source: AmAu&B; AmNatBi; BiDD;
BioIn 1, 2, 3, 4, 5, 6, 7, 8, 9, 10, 11, 12,
13, 17, 19, 21, 24; CamBiEn; ChamBiD;
CnOxB; ConAu 33R, X; CurBio 49, 72,
72N; DancEn 78; DcAmB S9; FilmChD;
IntDcMo; LegTOT; LinLib L; NewGrDM
80; NewYTBE 72; RAdv 14, 13-3;
REnAL; WebAB 74, 79; WhScrn 77

Shawn, Wallace
American. Actor, Dramatist
Known for collaboration, starring role in
   film *My Dinner with Andre*, 1981; son
   of *New Yorker* editor William Shawn.
b. Nov 12, 1943 in New York, New
   York
Source: BioIn 13, 14, 15; ConAmD;
ConAu 112; ConDr 77, 82, 88, 93;
ConLC 41; ConTFT 1, 6, 14, 25;
CrtSuDr; CurBio 86; CyWA 97;
IntAu&W 86; IntMPA 92, 94, 96; IntWW
2000; LegTOT; NatPD 77, 81; WhoAm
88, 90, 92, 94, 95, 96, 97, 98; WhoHol
92; WrDr 80, 82, 84, 86, 88, 90, 92, 94,
96

Shawn, William
American. Editor
Editor, *New Yorker* mag., 1952-87;
   second editor in mag.'s history;
   responsible for publishing excerpts of
   Catcher in the Rye, Silent Spring, and
   Hiroshima.
b. Aug 31, 1907 in Chicago, Illinois
d. Dec 8, 1992 in New York, New York
Source: AmAu&B; AmNatBi; AnObit
1992; BioIn 2, 9, 10, 12, 13, 14, 15;
BlueB 76; CamDcAB; CelR; ConAu
86NR, 108, 140; ConLC 76; DcLB 137;
DcPseud; EncTwCJ; EncWB 2-19;

IntWW 74, 75, 76, 77, 78, 79, 80, 81, 82, 83, 89, 91; LegTOT; LiJour; News 93-3; NewYTBS 92; WhAm 10; WhoAm 74, 76, 82, 84, 86, 88, 90, 92; WhoE 75, 85, 86; WhoWor 74; WorAlBi

Shays, Daniel
American. Soldier
Associated with 1786-87 rebellion, Springfield, MA.
b. 1747? in Hopkinton, Massachusetts
d. Sep 29, 1825 in Sparta, New York
Source: *AmBi; AmNatBi; AmRef; AmSocL; ApCAB; BioIn 1, 4, 7, 15, 19, 20; CamBiEn; CamDcAB; ChamBiD; DcAmB; DcAmMiB; Drake; EncAAH; EncAB-H 1974, 1996; EncAR; EncWB 98; HarEnUS; McGEWB; NatCAB 2; REn; TwCBDA; WebAB 74, 79; WebAMB; WhAm HS; WhAmRev; WhDW; WorAl; WorAlBi*

Shazar, Zalman
Israeli. Political Leader
Third pres. of Israel, 1963-73; leader of Zionist movement.
b. Nov 24, 1889 in Mir, Russia
d. Oct 5, 1974 in Jerusalem, Israel
Source: *ConAu 53, 101; CurBio 64, 74, 74N; IntWW 74; NewYTBS 74; WhAm 6; WhoGov 72; WhoWor 74*

Shcharansky, Anatoly Borisovich
Russian. Scientist
Jewish dissenter who served nine yrs. in Soviet prisons, 1977-86.
b. Jan 20, 1948 in Ukraine, Union of Soviet Socialist Republics
Source: *BioIn 14, 15, 16; ConNews 86-2; CurBio 87; EncWB, 98; FacFETw; IntWW 91; NewYTBS 78, 86; WorAlBi*

Shchedrin, Rodion Konstantinovich
Russian. Composer
Extremely popular works include Bizet's *Carmen* written as a ballet for ballerina wife, Maya Plisetskaya.
b. Dec 16, 1932 in Moscow, Union of Soviet Socialist Republics
Source: *BakBD 84, 92; BakBDTw; BiDSovU; BioIn 9; ChamBiD; CnOxB; CurBio 91N; DcCM; Dun&B 90; IntWW 80, 81, 82, 83, 89, 91, 93, 97, 98, 2000; NewGrDM 80; NewGrDO; NewYTBS 91; SovUn; WhoAm 90; WhoAmL 90; WhoE 91; WhoFI 89; WhoRus; WhoWor 82, 84, 87, 89, 91, 93, 95*

Shcherbo, Vitaly
Belarussian. Gymnast
Win six gold medals in the 1992 Olympics, more than any other gymnast in history.
b. Jan 13, 1972 in Kherson, Union of Soviet Socialist Republics
Source: *CurBio 96*

Shea, John
[Victor Shea, III]
American. Actor
Films include *Missing*, 1982; *Windy City*, 1984.
b. Apr 14, 1949? in North Conway, New Hampshire
Source: *BioIn 12; ConTFT 5, 13, 22; IntMPA 92, 94, 96; NewYTBS 79*

Shea, John A
American. Skater
Won two speed skating gold medals, 1932 Olympics.
Source: *DrRegL 75*

Shea, Lisa
American. Author
Wrote novel *Hula*, 1994.
b. Feb 13, 1953 in Washington, District of Columbia
Source: *ConAu 147; ConLC 86; WrDr 98, 99, 2000*

Shea, William Alfred
American. Lawyer
Credited with return of NL baseball to NYC, 1962; NY Mets' home stadium named for him.
b. Jun 21, 1907 in New York, New York
d. Oct 2, 1991 in New York, New York
Source: *BioIn 7, 17, 18, 19; CurBio 65; WhAm 10; WhoAm 86, 88, 90; WhoAmL 87, 90; WhoE 86, 89, 91; WhoFI 89; WhoMW 74; WhoRel 75*

Shean, Al
[Alfred Schoenberg]
American. Actor
Films include *52nd Street*, 1937; *People Are Funny*, 1946.
b. May 12, 1868 in Dornum, Germany
d. Aug 12, 1949 in New York, New York
Source: *AmNatBi; BioIn 2; DcPseud; EncMT; Ent; Film 2; FilmgC; ForYSC; HalFC 80, 84, 88; JoeFr; NotNAT B; WhoHol B; WhScrn 74, 77, 83; WhThe*

Shear, Murray Jacob
"Father of Chemotherapy"
American. Biochemist
Pioneer in development of chemotherapy treatment while at National Cancer Institute, 1939-69.
b. Nov 7, 1899 in New York, New York
d. Sep 27, 1983 in Bethesda, Maryland
Source: *NewYTBS 83; WhoAm 74; WhoWorJ 72*

Shearer, Douglas
American. Engineer
Pioneer in film sound recording; won 12 Oscars, 1951-63.
b. 1899
d. Jan 5, 1971 in Culver City, California
Source: *BioIn 9; FilmEn; FilmgC; HalFC 80, 84, 88; IntDcF 1-4, 2-4*

Shearer, Moira
Scottish. Dancer, Actor
Ballerina with Sadler's Wells, 1942-52; best known for leading film, *The Red Shoes*, 1948.
b. Jan 17, 1926 in Dunfermline, Scotland
Source: *BiDD; BioIn 1, 2, 3, 4, 5, 6, 8, 12, 15, 18, 20; CamBiEn; CnOxB; CurBio 50; DancEn 78; DcPseud; FilmEn; FilmgC; ForYSC; HalFC 80, 84, 88; IntDcB; IntWW 2000; IntWWW 2; InWom, SUP; LegTOT; MotPP; NewYTBS 88; Who 74, 82, 83, 85, 88, 90, 92, 94, 98, 99, 2000; WhoAmW 66, 68, 70, 72, 74, 75; WhoHol 92, A; WhoThe 77A; WhoWor 74; WhThe; WorAl; WorAlBi*

Shearer, Norma
"First Lady of the Screen"
American. Actor
Won 1930 Oscar for *The Divorcee*; married to Irving Thalberg, 1927.
b. Aug 10, 1900 in Montreal, Quebec, Canada
d. Jun 12, 1983 in Woodland Hills, California
Source: *AnObit 1983; BioIn 14, 16, 17, 24; CanWW 70; CmMov; DcPseud; Film 2; FilmEn; FilmgC; FrSilen; HalFC 80, 84, 88; IntDcF 1-3, 2-3; InWom, SUP; LegTOT; MGM; MotPP; MovMk; NewYTBS 83; OsStAZ; OxCFilm; ThFT; TwYS; WhoHol A; WorEFlm*

Sheares, Benjamin Henry
Singaporean. Political Leader
Pres., 1971-81; former gynecologist.
b. Aug 12, 1907, Singapore
d. May 12, 1981, Singapore
Source: *BioIn 10, 12, 13; FarE&A 78, 79, 80; IntWW 74, 75, 76, 77, 78, 79, 80, 81; IntYB 78, 79, 80, 81; NewYTBS 81; WhoWor 74, 76, 78, 80*

Shearing, George Albert
American. Musician
Popular blind pianist known for block chords; wrote jazz classic "Lullaby of Birdland."
b. Aug 13, 1919 in London, England
Source: *BakBD 78, 84, 92; BiDAmM; BiDJaz; BioIn 4, 5, 11, 12, 13, 16; CamDcAB; CelR 90; CmpEPM; CurBio 58; EncJzS; IntWW 98, 2000; MusMk; NewAmDM; NewGrDA 86; NewGrDJ 88, 94; OxCPMus; PenEncP; Who 98, 99, 2000; WhoAm 86, 90, 92, 94, 95, 96, 97, 98, 99, 2000; WhoEnt 92, 98; WhoHol A; WorAlBi*

Sheba
Ethiopian. Ruler
Biblical queen who made visit to Solomon to improve relations with Israel.
b. fl. 950BC, Ethiopia
Source: *WomWR*

Sheean, (James) Vincent
American. Journalist, Author
Covered world events from WW I to Korean War.

b. Dec 5, 1899 in Christian County,
Illinois
d. Mar 15, 1975 in Arolo, Italy
Source: *AmAu&B; AmNov; AuBYP 2S,
3; BenetAL 91; BioIn 1, 2, 3, 4, 5, 10,
14, 16, 20; CnDAL; ConAmA; ConAu
61; CurBio 41, 75, 75N; DcAmB S9;
EncAJ; HisDcWJ; IntAu&W 76, 77;
LiJour; LinLib L, S; NewYTBS 74;
OxCAmL 65, 83, 95; REn; REnAL;
ScF&FL 1, 2; TwCA, SUP; WhAm 6;
Who 74; WhoAm 74*

Sheed, Frank

[Francis Joseph Sheed]
Australian. Author, Publisher
Cofounded Roman Catholic publishing
house in London, Sheed & Ward,
1926; wrote *Society and Sanity*, 1953.
b. Mar 20, 1897 in Sydney, Australia
d. Nov 20, 1981 in Jersey City, New
Jersey
Source: *Au&Wr 71; BioIn 1, 9, 10, 12,
13, 14, 19; CathA 1930; ConAu 105,
129; CurBio 81, 82, 82N; FacFETw;
WhoAm 74*

Sheed, Wilfrid John Joseph

American. Author
Satirical novels, *A Middle-class
Education*, 1960; *The Hack*, 1963; son
of Frank.
b. Dec 27, 1930 in London, England
Source: *BenetAL 91; BiDConC; ConAu
30NR, 66NR; ConLC 2, 4, 10; ConNov
86, 91; CurBio 81; DcLB 6; DrAPF 91;
FacFETw; IntAu&W 91; IntWW 91, 97,
98, 2000; LiExTwC; MajTwCW 1, 2;
OxCAmL 83; WhoAm 84, 86, 90; WorAu
1950; WrDr 92, 98, 99, 2000*

Sheedy, Ally

[Alexandra Elizabeth Sheedy]
American. Actor
Films include *The Breakfast Club; St.
Elmos Fire*, 1985; member of
Hollywood's "brat pack.".
b. Jun 13, 1962 in New York, New York
Source: *BioIn 12, 13, 14, 15; ConAu 85,
173; ConTFT 2, 6, 8, 13, 22; HalFC 88;
IntMPA 86, 88, 92, 94, 96; InWom SUP;
LegTOT; News 89-1; NewYTBS 86;
SmATA 19, X; VarWW 85; WhoAm 92,
94, 95, 96, 97, 99, 2000; WhoAmW 91,
93; WhoEnt 92, 98; WhoHol 92;
WorAlBi*

Sheehan, Daniel P

American. Lawyer
Founder and chief counsel of the Christic
Institute, 1980-; legal team member
involved in "Pentagon Papers"
litigation.
b. 1945 in Warrensburg, New York
Source: *News 89-1*

Sheehan, Joseph Green

American. Psychologist, Educator,
Author
Authority on speech problems.
b. May 27, 1918 in Battle Creek,
Michigan

d. Nov 14, 1983 in Santa Monica,
California
Source: *AmMWSc 73S, 78S; ConAu 111;
WhAm 8; WhoAm 74, 76, 78, 80, 82*

Sheehan, Neil

American. Journalist, Author
Bureau chief for UPI during the Vietnam
War; book *A Bright Shining Lie*, won
Pulitzer Prize for nonfiction, 1988.
b. Oct 27, 1936 in Holyoke,
Massachusetts
Source: *BestSel 89-2; BioIn 11, 16;
ConAu 29R, 40NR; CurBio 89;
EncTwCJ; HisDcWJ; IntAu&W 91;
IntWW 93, 97, 98, 2000; LiJour;
NewYTBE 71; NewYTBS 90; OxCAmL
95; WhoAm 74, 76, 78, 80, 82, 84, 86,
88, 90, 92, 94, 95, 96, 97, 98, 99, 2000;
WhoE 93, 95, 97, 99; WhoPul;
WhoUSWr 88; WhoWrEP 89, 92, 95;
WrDr 90, 92, 94, 96, 98, 99, 2000*

Sheehy, Gail Henion

American. Journalist, Author
Wrote *Passages: Predictable Crises of
Adult Life*, 1976; *The Silent Passage:
Menopause*, 1992.
b. Nov 27, 1937 in Mamaroneck, New
York
Source: *AmWomSc 1950; BioIn 14, 15,
16; ConAu 1NR, 33NR, 49; CurBio 93;
ForWC 70; IntWWW 2; InWom SUP;
MajTwCW 1; WhoAm 78, 80, 82, 84, 86,
88, 90, 92, 94, 95, 96, 98, 99, 2000;
WhoAmW 81, 93, 95; WhoEnt 98;
WhoUSWr 88; WhoWrEP 89, 92, 95;
WorAl; WrDr 86, 92*

Sheekman, Arthur

American. Screenwriter
Collaborated on Marx Brothers' films;
helped found Screen Writers Guild,
1930s.
b. Feb 5, 1901 in Chicago, Illinois
d. Jan 12, 1978 in Santa Monica,
California
Source: *BioIn 11, 78*

Sheeler, Charles

American. Artist, Photographer
Abstractionist whose paintings include
Upper Deck; depicted factories,
machines.
b. Jul 16, 1883 in Philadelphia,
Pennsylvania
d. May 7, 1965 in Dobbs Ferry, New
York
Source: *AmCulL; AmNatBi; ArtsAmW 2;
Benet 87; BioIn 1, 2, 3, 4, 5, 6, 7, 8, 10,
11, 13, 14, 15, 16, 19, 20, 24; BriEAA;
CamBiEn; CamDcAB; ChamBiD;
ConPhot 82, 88; CurBio 50, 65;
DcAmArt; DcArts; DcCAA 71, 77, 88,
94; DcTwArt; DcTwDes; EncAB-H 1974,
1996; EncWB 98; FacFETw; GrAmP;
ICPEnP; LinLib S; MacBEP; McGDA;
McGEWB; WebAB 74, 79; WhAm 4;
WhAmArt 85; WhoAmA 78N, 80N, 82N,
84N, 86N, 89N, 91N, 93N; WorAlBi*

Sheen, Charlie

[Carlos Irwin Estevez]
American. Actor
Son of Martin Sheen; brother of Emilio
Estevez; in films *Ferris Bueller's Day
Off, Platoon*, 1986, *Major League*,
1988.
b. Sep 3, 1965 in Los Angeles,
California
Source: *BiDHisA; BiHaHis; BioIn 15,
16; CamBiEn; CelR 90; ConTFT 4, 10,
17; DcHiB; DcPseud; HalFC 88;
IntMPA 92, 94, 96; IntWW 91, 93, 97,
98, 2000; LegTOT; WhoAm 94, 95, 96,
97, 99, 2000; WhoHisp 92, 94; WhoHol
92; WorAlBi*

Sheen, Fulton John, Bishop

American. Religious Leader, Author
Well-known spokesman for Catholic
perspective, 1930s-70s; reached
millions through radio, TV series,
books: *Peace of Soul*, 1949.
b. May 8, 1895 in El Paso, Illinois
d. Dec 10, 1979 in New York, New
York
Source: *AmAu&B; AmCath 80;
AmNatBi; BiDChrM; BioIn 1, 2, 3, 4, 5,
7, 8, 9, 11, 12; CamBiEn; CamDcAB;
CathA 1930; ChamBiD; ConAu 5NR, 5R,
89; CurBio 41, 51; DcAmB S10;
DcAmReB 2; IntAu&W 77; IntWW 74,
75, 76, 77, 78, 79; LinLib S; RellAm 1,
2; REnAL; TwCA SUP; WebAB 74, 79;
WebBD 83; WhAm 7; Who 74; WhoAm
74, 76, 78; WhoE 74, 75; WhoHol A;
WhoRel 77; WhoWor 74, 78; WorAl;
WorAlBi; WorAu 1900; WrDr 76*

Sheen, Martin

[Ramon Estevez]
American. Actor
Films include *Apocalypse Now*, 1979;
Gandhi, 1982; father of Charlie,
Emilio Estevez.
b. Aug 3, 1940 in Dayton, Ohio
Source: *BiDFilm 94; BiDHisA; BiHaHis;
BioIn 11, 12, 13, 14, 16, 17, 18, 20, 22,
23; CamBiEn; CelR 90; ConTFT 2, 6,
13, 22; CurBio 77; DcHiB; DcPseud;
FilmEn; HalFC 80, 84, 88; HispAmA;
IntDcF 1-3, 2-3; IntMPA 75, 76, 77, 78,
79, 80, 81, 82, 84, 86, 88, 92, 94, 96;
IntWW 89, 91, 93, 98, 2000; LegTOT;
MiSFD 9; MovMk; NotLatA; NotNAT;
VarWW 85; WhoAm 78, 80, 82, 84, 86,
88, 90, 92, 94, 95, 96, 97, 99, 2000;
WhoEnt 92, 98; WhoHisp 91, 92, 94;
WhoHol 92, A; WhoThe 72, 77, 81;
WorAl; WorAlBi*

Sheffield, Gary (Antonian)

American. Baseball Player
Right fielder and formidable batter once
known for his hot temper, helped
Florida Marlins—a wild card team—
win their first World Series in 1997;
Sporting News Major League Player
of the Year, 1992.
b. Nov 18, 1968 in Tampa, Florida
Source: *WhoAfA 9, 10, 11, 12; WhoAm
94, 95, 96, 97, 98, 99, 2000; WhoBlA 7,
8; WhoSSW 95*

Shehu, Mehmet

"The Butcher"
Albanian. Politician
Prime Minister, 1954-81.
b. Jan 10, 1913 in Tirana, Albania
d. Dec 17, 1981 in Tirana, Albania
Source: *AnObit 1981; BioIn 4, 5, 12, 13;
CurBio 58, 82N; FacFETw; IntWW 74,
75, 76, 77, 78, 79, 80, 81; NewYTBS 81;
WhoSocC 78; WhoWor 78, 80*

Sheil, Bernard James, Archbishop

American. Religious Leader
Auxiliary bishop of Chicago, 1928-69;
founder, director, Catholic Youth
Organization, 1930-54.
b. Feb 18, 1888 in Chicago, Illinois
d. Sep 13, 1969 in Tucson, Arizona
Source: *BioIn 1, 2, 3, 4, 5, 7, 8; CurBio
68, 69; WhAm 5*

Sheila E

[Sheila Escovedo]
American. Singer, Musician
Has worked with Prince; had solo single
"The Glamorous Life," 1984.
b. Dec 12, 1959 in San Francisco,
California
Source: *BioIn 15; ConMus 3; DrBlPA
90; RkOn 85*

Sheinwold, Alfred

American. Bridge Player, Author
Has syndicated columns on bridge,
backgammon; author, *Five Weeks to
Winning Bridge*, 1959.
b. Jan 26, 1912 in London, England
d. Mar 8, 1997 in Sherman Oaks,
California
Source: *ConAu 61, 157; EncAInt;
WhoAm 86, 88*

Shekhar, Chandra

Indian. Political Leader
An idealist and self-styled socialist, he
formed the coalition Janata Party and
was appointed prime minister of India
in 1990.
b. Apr 1, 1927 in Ibrahimpatti, Uttar
Prades, India
Source: *NewYTBS 90; WhoWor 87, 89,
91, 93*

Shelby, Carroll (Hall)

American. Auto Racer, Business
Executive
Founder of Shelby-American, Inc., the
company that created the tube-frame
Cobra in 1962.
b. Jan 11, 1923 in Leesburg, Texas
Source: *BioIn 13, 14, 15, 16, 17, 19, 21;
ConAu 17R; CurBio 93*

Shelby, Richard C.

American. Politician
Rep. senator, AL, 1987—.
b. May 6, 1934 in Birmingham, Alabama
Source: *AlmAP 80, 82, 84, 88, 92, 96,
2000; BiDrUSC 89; CngDr 79, 81, 83,
85, 87, 89, 91, 93, 95; IntWW 91;
PolsAm 84; WhoAm 90; WhoAmP 91;
WhoSSW 91; WhoWor 91*

Sheldon, Alice Hastings Bradley

[Raccoona Sheldon; James Tiptree, Jr.]
American. Author
Science fiction novelist; works include
Starry Rift, 1986, *Brightness Falls
from the Air*, 1985.
b. Aug 24, 1915 in Chicago, Illinois
d. May 19, 1987 in McLean, Virginia
Source: *ConAu 34NR, 108, 122; ConLC
48, 50; DcLB 8; EncSF, 93; MajTwCW
1; NewEScF; Novels; PenNWW B;
RGTwCSF; ScF&FL 1, 92; ScFWr;
WrDr 86*

Sheldon, Charles M(onroe)

American. Social Reformer, Author
Pastor was an advocate of civil rights
and social services for African
Americans, but is best known for his
authorship of the best selling
inspirational novel *In His Steps*.
b. Feb 26, 1857 in Wellsville, New York
d. 1946
Source: *AmAu&B; AmNatBi; BiD&SB;
BioIn 1, 2, 4, 6, 10; ChhPo; DcAmAu;
DcAmB S4; DcAmReB 1, 2; DcLEL;
DcNAA; EncALit; EncARH; EncRelA;
EvLB; LngCTC; LuthC 75; NatCAB 34;
OxCAmL 65, 95; RelLAm 1, 2; REn;
REnAL; TwCA, SUP; TwCBDA; WhAm
2; WorAu 1900*

Sheldon, Sidney

American. Author
Wrote *The Other Side of Midnight*, 1973;
Rage of Angels, 1980; several
screenplays, TV series, plays.
b. Feb 11, 1917 in Chicago, Illinois
Source: *ASCAP 66, 80; AuNews 1;
BeaEPF; BestSel 89-1; BiE&WWA;
BioIn 10, 12, 16, 17, 20; BioNews 74;
CamDcAB; CelR 90; ConAu 29R, 33NR;
ConPopW; ConTFT 8, 16; CurBio 80;
FilmEn; FilmgC; HalFC 80, 84, 88;
IntAu&W 91, 93; IntMPA 82, 84, 86, 88,
92, 94, 96; IntWW 91, 93, 97, 98, 2000;
LegTOT; MajTwCW 1, 2; MiSFD 9;
Novels; RAdv 14; ScF&FL 92; WhoAm
78, 80, 82, 84, 86, 88, 90, 92, 94, 95,
96, 97, 98, 99, 2000; WhoEnt 92, 98;
WhoUSWr 88; WhoWrEP 89, 92, 95;
WorAl; WorAlBi; WrDr 80, 82, 84, 86,
88, 90, 92, 94, 96, 98, 99, 2000*

Sheldon, William Herbert

American. Physician, Psychologist
Correlated human somatypes with
physique, personality.
b. Nov 19, 1898 in Warwick, Rhode
Island
d. Sep 16, 1977 in Cambridge,
Massachusetts
Source: *AmNatBi; BiDPsy; BioIn 11;
ConAu 116; DcAmB S10; HisPhAn;
WhAm 7; WhoAm 74, 76, 78*

Shelepin, Aleksandr (Nikolaevich)

Russian. Government Official
First secretary, Young Communist
League, 1952-58; served in Politburo,
1964-75.
b. Aug 18, 1918
d. Oct 24, 1994

Source: *BiDSovU; BioIn 7, 8, 9, 10;
CurBio 71, 95N; SovUn; WhoSocC 78*

Shell, Art

American. Football Player, Football
Coach
Offensive tackle, Oakland, 1968-83; head
coach LA Raiders, 1989-94; first black
head coach in NFL history; Hall of
Fame 1989.
b. Nov 26, 1946 in Charleston, South
Carolina
Source: *AfrAmSG; BioIn 16, 20, 21;
ConBlB 1; NewYTBS 89; WhoAfA 9, 10,
11, 12; WhoAm 90; WhoBlA 7, 8;
WhoWest 92*

Shelley, Carole Augusta

English. Actor
Won Tony, 1979, for *The Elephant Man*;
Obie, 1982, for *Twelve Dreams*.
b. Aug 16, 1939 in London, England
Source: *ConTFT 4; NewYTBE 73;
NotNAT; VarWW 85; WhoAm 80, 82, 84,
86, 88, 90, 92, 94, 95, 96, 97; WhoAmW
81, 83, 87, 89, 91, 93, 95, 97; WhoEnt
92; WhoThe 81*

Shelley, Mary Wollstonecraft

[Mrs. Percy Bysshe Shelley]
English. Author
Wrote *Frankenstein*, 1818.
b. Aug 30, 1797 in London, England
d. Feb 1, 1851 in Bournemouth, England
Source: *Alli; ArtclWW 2; AtlBL; BbD;
Benet 87, 96; BiCoLiE; BiD&SB; BioIn
1, 2, 3, 4, 5, 7, 8, 9, 10, 11, 12, 13, 15,
16, 17, 18, 19, 20, 22, 23, 24; BlmGEL;
BlmGWL; BritAu 19; CamBiEn; CasWL;
ChamBiD; Chambr 3; CnDBLB 3; CrtT
4; CyWA 58, 97; DcArts; DcBiA;
DcBiPP; DcLB 110, 116, 159, 178;
DcNaB; EncApL; EncBrWW; EncSF, 93;
EncWB 98; FilmgC; GrWomW; HalFC
80, 84, 88; HerW; InWom; NewC;
NewEScF; NinCLC 59; OxCBrHi;
OxCEng 85, 95; PenC ENG; PenEncH;
RAdv 1, 14, 13-1; REn; ScF&FL 1, 92;
ScFWr 2; SmATA 29; WhDW; WhoHrs
80; WomWrGB; WorAl; WorAlBi*

Shelley, Percy Bysshe

English. Poet
Romantic lyricist known for *Prometheus
Unbound*, 1820.
b. Aug 4, 1792 in Field Place, England
d. Jul 8, 1822 in Viareggio, Italy
Source: *Alli; AtlBL; BbD; Benet 87, 96;
BiCoLiE; BiD&SB; BioIn 1, 2, 3, 4, 5, 6,
7, 8, 9, 10, 11, 12, 13, 14, 15, 16, 17,
18, 19, 20, 22, 24; BlmGEL; BritAu 19;
BritWr 4; CamBiEn; CamGEL;
CamGLE; CasWL; CelCen; ChamBiD;
Chambr 3; ChhPo, S1, S2, S3; CnDBLB
3; CnE&AP; CnThe; CrtSuDr; CrtT 2,
4; CyWA 58, 97; DcArts; DcBiPP;
DcEnA; DcEnL; DcEuL; DcLB 96, 110,
158; DcLEL; DcNaB, C; DcPup;
Dis&D; EncHiCA; EncPaPR 91;
EncUnb; EncWB 98; EncWT; EvLB;
GrWrEL P; IlEncMy; LegTOT; LinLib L,
S; LiveWoA; LngCEL; MagSWL;
McGEWB; McGEWD 72, 84; MouLC 2;*

NewC; NewCBEL; NinCLC 18; NotNAT B; NotPoe; OxCBrHi; OxCEng 67, 85, 95; OxCThe 67, 83; PenC ENG; PenEncH; PoeCrit 14; RadHan; RAdv 1, 14, 13-1; RComWL; REn; REnWD; RfGEnL 91; RGFBP; ScF&FL 1; TwoTYeD; WebE&AL; WhDW; WorAl; WorAlBi; WorLitC; WrPh

Shepard, Alan B(artlett), Jr.

American. Astronaut
First American to travel in space, 1961;
    commander of Apollo 14, 1971.
b. Nov 18, 1923 in East Derry, New
    Hampshire
d. Jul 21, 1998 in Monterey, California
Source: *AmMWSc 98; BioIn 5, 6, 7, 8, 9, 10, 12, 13, 16; CambiEn; CamDcAB; ChamBiD; ConHero 1; CurBio 61, 98N; EncNaHi; ExplAnT; FacFETw; InSci; IntWW 74, 91; RanHWDS; WebAMB; WhoAm 74, 76, 78, 80, 82, 84, 86, 88, 90, 92, 94, 95, 96, 97, 98; WhoFI 96, 98; WhoScEn 94, 96; WhoSpc; WhoSSW 73, 75, 76; WhoWor 74, 78, 80, 82, 84, 87, 89, 91, 93, 95, 96, 97, 98; WorAl; WorAlBi*

Shepard, Ernest Howard

English. Artist, Illustrator
Gained fame as illustrator of Milne's
    Pooh books.
b. Dec 10, 1879 in London, England
d. Mar 24, 1976 in Midhurst, England
Source: *Au&Wr 71; BioIn 1, 4, 5, 6, 8, 9, 10, 11, 12, 13; CambiEn; ChamBiD; ChhPo, S1, S2; ConAu 9R, 23NR, 65, 86NR; ConICB; DcBrAr 1, 2; DcBrBI; DcLB 160; DcNaB 1971; DcVicP 2; GrBr; IlsBYP; IlsCB 1744, 1946, 1957; MajAI; MorJA; NewYTBS 76; REn; SmATA 3, 24N, 33, 100; Who 74; WhoChL*

Shepard, Odell

American. Author
Co-founder, Thoreau Society of America;
    won Pulitzer for *Pedlar's Progress,
    the Life of Bronson Alcott*, 1938.
b. Jul 22, 1884 in Rock Falls, Illinois
d. Jul 19, 1967 in New London,
    Connecticut
Source: *AmAu&B; AmNatBi; BenetAL 91; BioIn 1, 4, 8, 22; ChhPo, S1; ConAu 3NR, 5R, 25R; OxCAmL 65, 83, 95; OxCCan; REnAL; TwCA, SUP; WhAm 4; WhoPul; WorAu 1900*

Shepard, Sam

[Samuel Shepard Rogers, III]
American. Dramatist, Actor
Won Pulitzer for *Buried Child*, 1979;
    won several Obies; wrote film *The
    Right Stuff*, 1983; appeared in some
    films.
b. Nov 5, 1943 in Fort Sheridan, Illinois
Source: *AmCulL; AmWr S3; Au&Arts 1; Benet 87, 96; BenetAL 91; BiCoLiE; BiDFilm 94; BioIn 10, 11, 12, 13, 14, 15, 16, 17, 18, 19, 20, 22, 23; CambiEn; CamDcAB; CamGLE; CamGWoT; CamHAL; CelR 90; ChamBiD; ConAmD; ConAu 3BS, 22NR, 69; ConDr*

73, 77, 82, 88, 93; ConLC 4, 6, 17, 34, 41, 44; CroCD; CrtSuDr; CurBio 79; CyWA 89, 97; DcArts; DcLB 7, 212; DcLEL 1940; DcPseud; DcTwCCu 1; DramC 5; EncALit; EncWB 98; EncWL 2, 2S, 3; EncWT; Ent; FacFETw; GrWrEL DR; HalFC 84, 88; IdentIs; IntAu&W 91, 93; IntDcF 2-4; IntDcT 2; IntMPA 84, 86, 88, 92, 94, 96; IntWW 89, 91, 93, 97, 98, 2000; LegTOT; LiExTwC; MagSAmL; MajTwCW 1; McGEWD 84; MiSFD 9; ModAL 4S1, 4S2, 4S3, 5; NatPD 77, 81; News 96; NewYTBS 80; NotNAT; OsStAZ; OxCAmL 83, 95; OxCAmT 84; OxCThe 83; OxCTwCL; RAdv 14, 13-2; RfGAmL 4, 87, 94; WhoAm 84, 86, 88, 90, 92, 94, 95, 96, 97, 98, 99; WhoEnt 92, 98; WhoHol 92; WhoPul; WhoThe 77, 81; WorAlBi; WorAu 1970; WrDr 76, 80, 82, 84, 86, 88, 90, 92, 94, 96, 98, 99, 2000

Shepherd, Cybill (Lynne)

American. Actor, Model
Played Maddie Hayes on TV series
    "Moonlighting," 1985-89; plays
    Cybill Sheridan on "Cybill," 1995—.
b. Feb 18, 1950 in Memphis, Tennessee
Source: *BioIn 16; ConAu 173; ConTFT 7; CurBio 87; HalFC 88; IntMPA 82, 92; InWom SUP; MovMk; WhoAm 86, 90; WhoEnt 92; WhoHol A; WomWMM; WorAlBi*

Shepherd, Jean Parker

American. Actor, Author
Writings include *The America of George
    Ade*, 1961; *The Ferrari in the
    Bedroom*, 1973.
b. Jul 26, 1929? in Chicago, Illinois
d. Oct 16, 1999 in Sanibel Island,
    Florida
Source: *AuNews 2; ConAu 77; WhoAm 74, 76*

Sheppard, Eugenia Benbow

American. Fashion Editor, Journalist
Wrote fashion column *Inside Fashion*.
b. 1910 in Columbus, Ohio
d. Nov 11, 1984 in New York, New
    York
Source: *AnObit 1984; BioIn 5, 6, 9; InWom, SUP; WhoAmW 61; WhoE 85A; WorFshn*

Sheppard, Jack

[John Sheppard]
English. Criminal
Thief, known for many escapes from
    prison; hanged; career is theme of
    several books, plays.
b. 1702 in Stepney, England
d. Nov 16, 1724 in London, England
Source: *BioIn 3, 4, 7, 8, 14; CambiEn; CamGEL; ChamBiD; DcNaB; DrInf; NewC; NewCol 75; OxCEng 85, 95; OxCLaw*

Sheppard, Sam(uel)

"Doctor Sam"
American. Physician
Accused of murdering wife, 1954.
b. Nov 5, 1923 in Fort Sheridan, Illinois

d. Apr 6, 1970 in Columbus, Ohio
Source: *BioIn 7, 8*

Sheppard, T. G

[Bill Browser]
American. Singer, Musician
Country singer, guitarist who sang
    "Make My Day," with Clint
    Eastwood, 1984.
b. Jul 20, 1944 in Jackson, Tennessee
Source: *BioIn 13, 14; HarEnCM 87; PenEncP; RkOn 85*

Shera, Jesse Hauk

American. Librarian, Educator
Leading authority on classification,
    documentation, history of US libraries.
b. Dec 8, 1903 in Oxford, Ohio
d. Mar 8, 1982 in Cleveland, Ohio
Source: *AmAu&B; AmNatBi; BiDAmEd; BioIn 2, 3, 6, 7, 8, 9, 12, 13, 15, 16, 17; BlueB 76; CamDcAB; ConAu 2NR, 5R, 106; CurBio 64, 82; LEduc 74; LibrCom; WhAm 8; WhoAm 74, 76, 78, 80, 82; WhoCon 73; WhoLibI 82*

Sheraton, Thomas

English. Designer, Furniture Designer
Advanced neoclassic designs; elegant
    style was delicate, simple, with
    emphasis on straight, vertical lines.
b. 1751 in Stockton, England
d. Oct 22, 1806 in London, England
Source: *Alli; AntBDN G; BioIn 2, 3, 4, 7, 16; BlmGEL; CambiEn; ChamBiD; DcArts; DcD&D; DcNaB; EncWB 98; LinLib L, S; LngCEL; McGDA; McGEWB; NewC; OxCBrHi; OxCDecA; OxCEng 67; PenDiDA 89; WorAl; WorAlBi*

Sheridan, Ann

[Clara Lou Sheridan]
"Oomph Girl"
American. Actor
Pin-up favorite, 1940s; films include *The
    Man Who Came to Dinner*, 1942.
b. Feb 21, 1915 in Denton, Texas
d. Jan 21, 1967 in Hollywood, California
Source: *BiDFilm, 81, 94; BioIn 1, 7, 8, 9, 14, 18, 23; DcPseud; EncAFC; Film 2; FilmEn; FilmgC; GangFlm; HalFC 80, 84, 88; IntDcF 1-3, 2-3; InWom, SUP; LegTOT; MotPP; MovMk; SweetSg D; ThFT; WhAm 4; WhoHol B; WhScrn 74, 77, 83; WorAl; WorAlBi; WorEFlm*

Sheridan, Clare Consuelo

English. Author, Artist
Sculpted bronze busts of many heads of
    state; wrote memoirs *To the Fair
    Winds*, 1957.
b. Sep 9, 1885 in London, England
d. May 31, 1970 in Sussex, England
Source: *BioIn 3, 4, 8, 11, 14, 22; CathA 1952; DcBrAr 1; DcNaB 1961; DcWomA; FemiCLE; GrBr; IntDcWB; WhLit*

Sheridan, Nicollette
American. Actor
Played Paige Mathison on TV series "Knot's Landing," 1988-93.
b. Nov 21, 1963 in Sussex, England
Source: *BioIn 14, 15; CelR 90; ConTFT 10; IntMPA 94, 96; LegTOT*

Sheridan, Philip Henry
American. Military Leader
Civil War Union general credited with forcing Lee's surrender by blocking retreat from Appomattox, 1865.
b. Mar 6, 1831 in Albany, New York
d. Aug 5, 1888 in Nonquitt, Massachusetts
Source: *Alli SUP; AmAu&B; AmBi; AmNatBi; ApCAB; BbD; BenetAL 91; BiD&SB; BioIn 1, 3, 4, 5, 6, 7, 8, 9, 11, 12, 14, 15, 16, 17, 18, 19, 20, 23, 24; CamBiEn; CamDcAB; CelCen; ChamBiD; CivWDc; CmdGen 1991; DcAmAu; DcAmB; DcAmMiB; DcCathB; DcIrB 1, 2, 3; DcNAA; Drake; EncAAH; EncAB-H 1974, 1996; EncAInd; EncWB 98; HarEnMi; HarEnUS; HisWorL; LAmCW; LinLib S; McGEWB; NatCAB 4; NewEAmW; OhA&B; OxCAmH; REn; REnAL; REnAW; TwCBDA; WebAB 74, 79; WebAMB; WhAm HS; WhCiWar; WhNaAH; WhoMilH 76; WorAl*

Sheridan, Richard Brinsley
Irish. Dramatist, Politician
Noted for three great comedies: *The Rivals*, 1775; *School for Scandal*, 1777; farce *The Critic*, 1779.
b. Oct 30, 1751 in Dublin, Ireland
d. Jul 7, 1816 in London, England
Source: *Alli; AtlBL; BbD; Benet 87, 96; BiCoLiE; BiD&SB; BiDIrW; BiDLA; BioIn 12, 24; BlkwCE; BlmGEL; BritAu; BritWr 3; CamGEL; CamGLE; CamGWoT; CasWL; ChamBiD; Chambr 2; ChhPo; CnDBLB 2; CnThe; CrtSuDr; CrtT 2; CyWA 58, 97; DcArts; DcEnA; DcEnL; DcEuL; DcInB; DcIrB 1, 2, 3; DcIrL, 96; DcIrW 1; DcLB 89; DcLEL; DcNaB; DramC 1; EncEnl; EncWB 98; EncWT; Ent; EvLB; GrWrEL DR; HisDcIr; LinLib L, S; McGEWB; McGEWD 72, 84; MouLC 2; NewC; NewCBEL; NewEOp 71; NewGrDO; NinCLC 5; NotNAT A, B; OxCAmT 84; OxCBrHi; OxCEng 67, 85, 95; OxCIri; OxCThe 67, 83; OxDcOp; PenC ENG; PIP&P; PoIre; RAdv 14, 13-2; REn; REnWD; RfGEnL 91; WebE&AL; WhDW; WorAlBi; WorLitC*

Sherman, Allan
American. Comedian
Known for satiric song, "Hello Muddah, Hello Faddah," 1963.
b. Nov 30, 1924 in Chicago, Illinois
d. Nov 20, 1973 in Los Angeles, California
Source: *ASCAP 66, 80; AuBYP 2, 3; BioIn 6, 7, 8, 9, 10, 19; ChhPo S1; ConAu 45, 101; CurBio 66, 74, 74N; DcAmB S9; DcPseud; JoeFr; LegTOT; RkOn 74; WhAm 6; WhoCom; WhoRock 81; WorAl*

Sherman, Bobby
American. Singer, Actor
1960s teen hero; first single, "Little Woman," 1969, went gold; starred in TV's "Here Come the Brides," 1968-70.
b. Jul 22, 1945 in Santa Monica, California
Source: *EncPR&S 74; PenEncP; RkOn 78, 84*

Sherman, Cindy
American. Artist
Performance art depicts feminist view of women's role in society.
b. Jan 19, 1954 in Glen Ridge, New Jersey
Source: *AmArt; BioIn 12, 13, 14, 15, 16; ConPhot 95; ConWomA; CurBio 90; EncWB 2-19; ICPEnP A; IntWW 91, 93, 97, 98, 2000; IntWWW 2; News 92, 92-3; NorAmWA; WhoAm 88, 90, 92, 94, 95, 96, 97, 98, 99, 2000; WhoAmA 86, 89, 91, 93, 1999; WhoAmW 85; WhoE 85, 86, 89; WorArt 1980*

Sherman, Frank Dempster
[Felix Carmen]
American. Poet, Educator, Architect
Wrote volumes of witty, light verse: *Lyrics of Joy*, 1904.
b. May 6, 1860 in Peekskill, New York
d. Sep 19, 1916
Source: *Alli SUP; AmAu; AmAu&B; BbD; BenetAL 91; BibAL; BiD&SB; BioIn 13; ChhPo, S1, S3; ChrP; CnDAL; DcAmAu; DcAmB; DcNAA; NatCAB 7; OxCAmL 65, 83, 95; REn; REnAL; ScF&FL 1; TwCBDA; WhAm 1, 4*

Sherman, George
American. Director
Director of low budget-westerns; first film *Wild Horse Rodeo*, 1937.
d. Mar 15, 1991 in Los Angeles, California
Source: *DcLP 87B; HalFC 88; IntMPA 75, 76, 78, 79, 81, 82, 84, 86; NewYTBS 91*

Sherman, Harry R
American. Producer
TV productions include "Eleanor and Franklin," 1976; "The Gathering," 1978; won three Emmys.
b. Sep 21, 1927 in Los Angeles, California
Source: *VarWW 85*

Sherman, James Schoolcraft
American. US Vice President
VP under William Howard Taft, 1909-12.
b. Oct 24, 1855 in Utica, New York
d. Oct 30, 1912 in Utica, New York
Source: *AmBi; AmPolLe; ApCAB X; BiDrAC; BiDrUSC 89; BiDrUSE 71, 89; BioIn 1, 4, 7, 8, 9, 10, 14, 22, 23; CamDcAB; DcAmB; HarEnUS; NatCAB 14; VicePre; WebAB 74, 79; WhAm 1; WhAmP*

Sherman, John
American. Politician
Senator was the most significant congressional figure in the development of American fiscal policy during the "gilded age."
b. May 10, 1823 in Lancaster, Ohio
d. Oct 22, 1900 in Washington, District of Columbia
Source: *ABCAmRe; Alli SUP; AmBi; AmNatBi; AmPolLe; ApCAB; BbD; BiAUS; BiD&SB; BiDrAC; BiDrUSC 89; BiDrUSE 71, 89; BioIn 4, 6, 7, 8, 9, 10, 12, 16, 22, 23; CamDcAB; ChamBiD; CyAG; DcAmAu; DcAmB; DcAmDH 80, 89; DcNAA; Drake; EncAAH; EncAB-H 1974, 1996; EncABHB 6; EncWB 98; HarEnUS; LinLib S; McGEWB; NatCAB 3; OhA&B; OxCAmH; PolPar; REnAL; SpAmWar; TwCBDA; WebAB 74, 79; WhAm 1; WhAmP; WhCiWar; WorAl; WorAlBi*

Sherman, Lowell
American. Actor, Director
Films include *Morning Glory*, 1933; *Born to Be Bad*, 1934.
b. Oct 11, 1885 in San Francisco, California
d. Dec 28, 1934 in Hollywood, California
Source: *BiDFilm, 81, 94; EncAFC; Film 1, 2; FilmEn; FilmgC; ForYSC; FrSilen; HalFC 80, 84, 88; MotPP; NotNAT B; SilFlmP; TwYS, A; WhoHol B; WhScrn 74, 77, 83; WhThe; WorEFlm*

Sherman, Richard Morton
American. Composer, Lyricist
Won Oscars for score of *Mary Poppins* and song "Chim, Chim, Cheree," 1964.
b. Jun 12, 1928 in New York, New York
Source: *ConAu 107; IntMPA 92; OxCPMus; WhoAm 74, 76, 78, 80, 82, 84, 86, 88*

Sherman, Roger
American. Continental Congressman
Influential member, first and second Continental Congress; signed Declaration of Independence, 1776; strict Puritan.
b. Apr 19, 1721 in Newton, Massachusetts
d. Jul 23, 1793 in New Haven, Connecticut
Source: *AmBi; AmNatBi; AmPolLe; ApCAB; BiAUS; BiDrAC; BiDrUSC 89; BioIn 3, 4, 7, 8, 9, 12, 13, 15, 16, 23; BlkwEAR; CamBiEn; CamDcAB; ChamBiD; CyAG; DcAmB; Drake; EncAB-H 1974, 1996; EncCRAm; EncWB 98; HarEnUS; HisWorL; McGEWB; NatCAB 2; OxCAmH; TwCBDA; USGovLe; WebAB 74, 79; WhAm HS; WhAmP; WhAmRev; WorAl; WorAlBi*

Sherman, Russell
American. Pianist
Pianist known for his personal and thoughtful interpretations of Romantic

and contemporary piano pieces; toured in the U.S. and abroad, is respected as a music teacher, and recorded on several labels.
b. 1930 in New York, New York
Source: *BakBD 92; BakBDTw; BioIn 16; BriBkM 80; ConNews 87-4; NewAmDM; NewGrDA 86*

Sherman, Vincent
[Abram Orovitz]
American. Director
TV shows include "The Waltons," 1972-81; "Baretta," 1975-78.
b. Jul 16, 1906 in Vienna, Georgia
Source: *BioIn 11, 12, 14, 21, 22; ConAu 159; DcPseud; FilmEn; FilmgC; ForYSC; GangFlm; HalFC 80, 84, 88; IlWWHD 1; IntMPA 75, 76, 77, 78, 79, 80, 81, 82, 84, 86, 88, 92, 94, 96; ItaFilm; MiSFD 9; VarWW 85; WhoHol 92, A; WomWMM; WorEFlm*

Sherman, William Tecumseh
American. Military Leader
Civil War Union general famous for march through Atlanta to the sea, 1864; said "War is Hell," 1880.
b. Feb 8, 1820 in Lancaster, Ohio
d. Feb 14, 1891 in New York, New York
Source: *Alli, SUP; AmAu&B; AmBi; AmNatBi; ApCAB; BbD; Benet 87, 96; BiAUS; BiD&SB; BiDrUSE 71, 89; BioIn 1, 2, 3, 4, 5, 6, 7, 8, 9, 10, 11, 12, 13; CamBiEn; CamDcAB; CelCen; ChamBiD; CivWDc; CmCal; CmdGen 1991; DcAmAu; DcAmB; DcAmMiB; DcBiPP; DcNAA; Drake; EncAB-H 1974, 1996; EncABHB 6; EncAInd; EncWB 98; GenMudB; HarEnMi; HarEnUS; HisWorL; LegTOT; LinLib S; McGEWB; MemAm; NatCAB 4; NewEAmW; OhA&B; OxCAmH; OxCAmL 95; RComAH; REn; REnAL; REnAW; TwCBDA; WebAB 74, 79; WebAMB; WhAm HS; WhCiWar; WhDW; WhNaAH; WhoMilH 76; WorAl; WorAlBi*

Sherriff, Robert Cedric
English. Author, Dramatist
Wrote *Journey's End*, 1929; translated, performed in every European language.
b. Jun 6, 1896 in Hampton-Wick, England
d. Nov 13, 1975 in Kingston-upon-Thames, England
Source: *Au&Wr 71; BiCoLiE; BiE&WWA; BioIn 2, 4, 5, 8, 10, 13, 14, 22, 23, 24; CamBiEn; ChamBiD; Chambr 3; CnMD; CnThe; ConAu 61; ConDr 73; CroCD; CyWA 58; DcLEL; DcNaB 1; EncWT; Ent; EvLB; GrBr; IntAu&W 76; IntWW 74, 75; LngCTC; McGEWD 72; ModBrL; ModWD; NewC; NewCBEL; NewYTBS 75; NotNAT A, B; OxCEng 67, 85; OxCThe 67; OxCTwCL; PenC ENG; REn; TwCA, SUP; TwCWr; WhE&EA; Who 74; WhoThe 72; WhoWor 74; WhThe; WorAu 1900*

Sherrill, Henry Knox
American. Theologian
Bishop of the Episcopal Church, 1946-58; pres., National Council of Churches, 1950-52.
b. Nov 6, 1890 in New York, New York
d. May 12, 1980 in Boxford, Massachusetts
Source: *AmNatBi; AnObit 1980; BiDInt; BioIn 1, 2, 5, 6, 12; BlueB 76; ConAu 97; CurBio 47, 80N; IntWW 74, 75, 76, 77, 78, 79, 80; RelLAm 1, 2; WhAm 7; Who 74; WhoAm 74, 76; WhoWor 74*

Sherrill, Robert Glenn
American. Author
Wrote controversial books on political issues, including, *The Last Kennedy: Edward M Kennedy*, 1976.
b. Dec 24, 1925 in Frogtown, Georgia
Source: *ConAu 15NR; WhoSSW 73, 75, 76, 82*

Sherrington, Charles Scott, Sir
English. Physician, Educator
Shared Nobel Prize in medicine, 1932, with Edgar Adrian.
b. Nov 27, 1857 in London, England
d. Mar 4, 1952 in Eastbourne, England
Source: *AsBiEn; BiDcPsy; BiDPsy; BiESc; BiHiMed; BioIn 2, 3, 4, 5, 6, 7, 9, 12, 14, 15, 20; CamBiEn; CamDcSc; ChamBiD; DcLEL; DcNaB 1951; DcScB; EncWB 98; EvLB; GrBr; LarDcSc; McGEWB; NamesHP; NewCBEL; NotTwCS 1; ObitOF 79; ObitT 1951; OxCMed 86; RanHWDS; WhoNob, 90, 95; WorAl; WorScD*

Sherrod, Clayton
American. Chef
Chef trained at Vestavia Country Club in Birmingham, AL, and the American Culinary Institute; founded successful catering company Chef Clayton's Food Systems, Inc., 1978; active in volunteer work.
b. 1944 in Birmingham, Alabama
Source: *ConBlB 17*

Sherrod, Robert (Lee)
American. Journalist, Editor
With the *New York Herald Tribune, Time, Saturday Evening Post;* wrote *History of the Marine Corps Aviation in World War II*, 1952.
b. Feb 8, 1909
d. Feb 13, 1994 in Washington, District of Columbia
Source: *AmAu&B; BioIn 3, 6, 17, 19, 20; ConAu 77; CurBio 94N; EncTwCJ; IntAu&W 76, 77, 89; IntWW 74, 75, 76, 77, 78, 79, 80, 81, 83, 89, 91, 93; WhAm 12; WhoAm 74, 76, 78, 80, 82, 84, 86, 88, 90, 92, 94; WhoE 79, 89; WhoSSW 73, 75, 76; WhoWor 78*

Sherwin, Henry Alden
American. Manufacturer
Developed formula for first premixed paint; joined Edward Williams to form paint co., 1873.
b. Sep 27, 1842 in Baltimore, Vermont

d. Jun 26, 1916 in Willoughby, Ohio
Source: *Entr; NatCAB 21; WhAm 1*

Sherwood, Frances
American. Author
Wrote *Vindication*, 1993, a fictional biography of the writer Mary Wollstonecraft.
b. Jun 4, 1940 in Washington, District of Columbia
Source: *BioIn 19; ConAu 146; ConLC 81; WrDr 98, 99, 2000*

Sherwood, Mary Martha
English. Children's Author
Wrote children's classic *History of the Fairchild Family*, 1818-47.
b. May 6, 1775 in Stamford, England
d. Sep 22, 1851 in Worcester, England
Source: *Alli; ArtclWW 2; BiD&SB; BioIn 1, 8, 10, 22; BritAu 19; CamGLE; CarSB; CasWL; ChamBiD; Chambr 3; DcBiPP; DcBrAmW; DcEnL; DcEuL; DcInB; DcLB 163; DcNaB; EvLB; FemiCLE; InWom; NewC; NewCBEL; OxCChiL; OxCEng 67, 85, 95; PenNWW A; ScF&FL 1; WhBriIn; WhoChL*

Sherwood, Robert Emmet
American. Dramatist, Author
Won Pulitzer for *Idiot's Delight*, 1936; *Abe Lincoln in Illinois*, 1938.
b. Apr 4, 1896 in New Rochelle, New York
d. Nov 14, 1955 in New York, New York
Source: *AmAu&B; AmNatBi; CamBiEn; CamDcAB; CasWL; ChamBiD; CnDAL; CnMD; ConAu 86NR; DcLEL; EncALit; EncWB 98; OxCAmL 65; OxCTwCL; PenC AM; RfGAmL 4; TwCA, SUP; WebAB 74; WorAu 1900*

Shestov, Lev
[Lev Isaakovich Schwarzmann]
Russian. Critic, Author
Jewish thinker and literary critic was an irrationalist and fideist; he concentrated on what he considered to be the inevitable struggle between religious faith and reason.
b. Jan 31, 1866 in Kiev, Ukraine
d. Nov 22, 1938 in Paris, France
Source: *BioIn 19; CasWL; ClDMEL 80; DcPseud; DcRusL; EncWB 98; RAdv 14, 13-4; REn; TwCLC 56*

Shevardnadze, Eduard Amvrosiyevich
Russian. Diplomat
Replaced Gromyko as minister of foreign affairs, 1985-90; resigned amid controversy.
b. Jan 25, 1928 in Mamati, Union of Soviet Socialist Republics
Source: *BiDSovU; BioIn 16; CamBiEn; ColdWar 1, 2; CurBio 86; FacFETw; IntWW 81, 82, 83, 89, 91, 93, 97, 98, 2000; Who 88, 90, 92, 94, 98, 99, 2000; WhoSocC 78; WhoWor 87, 89, 91, 93, 95, 96, 97, 98, 99, 2000; WorAlBi*

Shevchenko, Arkady N(ikolayevich)
Russian. Diplomat
Adviser to Andrei Gromyko, UN official, who defected to US, 1978; wrote *Breaking with Moscow*, 1985.
b. Oct 11, 1930 in Gorlovka, Union of Soviet Socialist Republics
d. Feb 28, 1998 in Bethesda, Maryland
Source: *BiDSovU; BioIn 11, 12; ConAu 129; CurBio 85, 98N; IntWW 76, 91; NewYTBS 78; WhoUN 75*

Shevchenko, Taras
Ukrainian. Poet
Allegorical poems include "Neofity," 1857; "Maruja," 1859.
b. Mar 9, 1814 in Morintsy, Russia
d. Mar 10, 1861 in Saint Petersburg, Russia
Source: *BbD; BiD&SB; BlkwERR; CasWL; DcArts; DcRusL; EuAu; HanRL; NinCLC 54; PenC EUR; RAdv 13-2*

Shields, Alexander
American. Fashion Designer
Menswear designer; introduced caftan for male beachwear, lounging, 1971.
Source: *Alli; WhoAm 82; WorFshn*

Shields, Brooke
[Mrs. Andre Agassi; Christa Brooke Camille Shields]
American. Actor, Model
Appeared on over 30 magazine covers, 1981; films include *The Blue Lagoon*, 1980, *Endless Love*, 1981; TV show "Suddenly Susan," 1997—.
b. May 31, 1965 in New York, New York
Source: *BioIn 11, 12, 13, 14, 15; BkPepl; CelR 90; ConTFT 3, 9; CurBio 82; FilmEn; HalFC 80, 84, 88; IntMPA 79, 80, 81, 82, 84, 86, 88, 92, 94, 96; InWom SUP; LegTOT; News 96, 96-3; WhoAm 88, 90; WhoEnt 92; WhoHol 92; WorAl; WorAlBi*

Shields, James
American. Politician
Governor, Oregon Territory, 1849; senator from IL, 1849-55, from MN, 1858-59.
b. May 10, 1810 in Altimore, Ireland
d. Jun 1, 1879 in Oregon
Source: *AmBi; ApCAB; BiAUS; BiDrAC; DcAmB; Drake; HarEnUS; NatCAB 8; TwCBDA; WhAm HS; WhAmP; WhCiWar*

Shields, Larry
American. Jazz Musician
Pioneered hot-style clarinet; star of Chicago's Original Dixieland Band, 1916.
b. May 17, 1893 in New Orleans, Louisiana
d. Nov 22, 1953 in Hollywood, California
Source: *AmNatBi; BiDAmM; BiDJaz; CmpEPM; NewGrDJ 88, 94; NewOrJ; WhoJazz 72*

Shields and Yarnell
[Robert Shields; Lorene Yarnell]
American. Entertainers
Mime duo; won first place Ted Mack amateur contest; on numerous TV specials.
Source: *DcEnL; DcNaB; VarWW 85; WhoAm 82, 84, 86, 88; WhoScEu 91-1*

Shihab, Fu'ad
Lebanese. Military Leader, Political Leader
Called the "Father of the Lebanese Army," he headed the military until his election as president of Lebanon in 1958; he helped develop a sense of national unity among Christian and Muslim Lebanese.
b. 1903 in Ghazir, Kisrwan, Lebanon
d. Apr 25, 1973
Source: *EncWB, 98*

Shih Ko-fa
Chinese. Military Leader
Scholar-soldier became a national hero with his gallant defense of Yangchow against Manchu troops.
d. 1644 in Yangchow, China
Source: *EncWB 98; HarEnMi*

Shih Le
Chinese. Political Leader
Man of humble social origins rose to rule almost all of North China, founding the Latter Chao empire; ruler was known to be astute and humane.
b. 274 in Shansi, China
d. 333, China
Source: *EncWB 98*

Shils, Edward Albert
American. Sociologist
Studied the sociology of culture, especially the role of ideology in culture and the role of intellectuals in the formation of ideology.
b. 1911
d. Jan 23, 1995 in Chicago, Illinois
Source: *BioIn 20, 21; EncWB 98*

Shilts, Randy (Martin)
American. Author, Journalist
Wrote *The Mayor of Castro Street: The Life and Times of Harvey Milk*, 1982; *And the Band Played On: Politics, People, and the AIDS Epidemic*, 1987.
b. Aug 8, 1951 in Davenport, Iowa
d. Feb 17, 1994 in Guerneville, California
Source: *AmNatBi; Au&Arts 19; BioIn 12; CmpQue; ConAu 45NR, 127, 144; ConLC 85, 86; CurBio 93, 94N; GayLesB; GayLL 1; LegTOT; News 94, 94-3; WhAm 11; WhoAm 94*

Shimkin, Leon
American. Publisher
Helped build Simon & Schuster into leading book publisher, eventually becoming owner; responsible for publishing Carnegie's *How to Win Friends and Influence People*, 1937.

b. Apr 7, 1907 in New York, New York
d. May 25, 1988 in New Rochelle, New York
Source: *AmAu&B; BioIn 2, 3, 7, 16, 24; CurBio 54, 88; NewYTBS 88; ScrEAmL 2; St&PR 84, 87; WhAm 9; WhoAm 74, 76, 78, 80, 82, 84; WhoFI 79, 81; WhoWorJ 72, 78*

Shimomura, Tsutomu
Japanese. Computer Scientist
Directed pursuit of noted computer hacker Kevin Mitnick, 1994-95.
b. 1965, Japan
Source: *ConAu 155; News 96, 96-1*

Shinburn, Mark
[Baron Shindell; Jimmy Valentine]
American. Criminal
Fenced stolen goods through Fredericka Mandelbaum, eventually retired to Monaco under alias.
b. 1842
d. 1916
Source: *BioIn 8*

Shinichiro Imaoka
Japanese. Theologian, Clergy, Educator
Revered religious figure greatly influenced the development of progressive and liberal religion.
b. Sep 16, 1881
d. Apr 11, 1988

Shinn, Everett
American. Artist
One of "the eight" versatile creator of mag., children's book illustrations; pastel scenes of Paris, NYC.
b. Nov 7, 1876 in Woodstown, New Jersey
d. May 1, 1953 in New York, New York
Source: *AmNatBi; BioIn 1, 3, 4, 5, 6, 10, 12, 14, 19, 20; BriEAA; CamDcAB; ChhPo, S2; CurBio 51, 53; DcAmArt; DcAmB S5; DcCAA 71, 77, 88, 94; DcTwArt; IlrAm 1880, A; IlsBYP; IlsCB 1744, 1946; McGDA; NatCAB 44; OxCTwCA; OxDcArt; PhDcTCA 77; SmATA 21; WhAm 3; WhAmArt 85; WhoAmA 78N, 80N, 82N, 84N, 86N, 89N, 91N, 93N*

Shinran
Japanese. Clergy
Buddhist monk was a disciple of Honen; founded True Pure Land sect rejecting monasticism, and was active in developing and transforming Amidist beliefs—that salvation is achieved by putting oneself completely at the mercy of the Buddha Amida.
b. 1173
d. 1262
Source: *BiDJaL; BioIn 4, 7, 8, 9; EncJap; EncWB 98; McGEWB; PriCCJL 85*

Shipley, Jenny
New Zealander. Political Leader
New Zealand's first female prime minister, the conservative politician

was occasionally criticized for her hard-line budget cuts effecting social services; former housewife joined National Party in 1975, became Minister of Social Welfare, 1990, and Prime Minister, 1997.
b. Feb 4, 1952 in Gore, New Zealand
Source: *BioIn 24; CamBiEn; IntWW 97, 98, 2000; News 98, 98-3; ProfiWG 98; WhoIntA 2; WhoWor 99, 2000*

Shipp, E. R.
American. Journalist
Sometimes controversial syndicated weekly columnist for *New York Daily News*, 1994—; won Pulitzer Prize for commentary, 1996.
b. 1955 in Conyers, Georgia
Source: *WhoAfA 9, 10, 11, 12; WhoBlA 5, 6, 7, 8; WhoPul*

Shippen, Edward
American. Jurist
A Tory during the Revolution, he later served as chief justice of the Supreme Court of Pennsylvania.
b. Feb 16, 1728
d. Apr 15, 1800 in Pennsylvania
Source: *DcAmB; EncWB 98; McGEWB*

Shippen, Katherine Binney
American. Children's Author
Historical children's books include *Passage to America*, 1950.
b. Apr 1, 1892 in Hoboken, New Jersey
d. Feb 20, 1980 in Suffern, New York
Source: *AnCL; AuBYP 2, 3; BioIn 2, 3, 6, 7, 9, 12, 13, 14; ConAu 5R, 86NR, 93; CurBio 54; IntAu&W 76; InWom; MorJA; SmATA 1, 23N; Str&VC*

Shippen, Margaret
"Peggy"
American. Spy
Loyalist, second wife of Benedict Arnold; collaborated in treasonable correspondence, fled to England.
b. 1760 in Philadelphia, Pennsylvania
d. 1804
Source: *AmBi; BioIn 2, 3, 8, 9, 10, 11; InB&W 80; InWom*

Shiras, George, Jr.
American. Supreme Court Justice
Served as associate justice, 1892-1903.
b. Jan 26, 1832 in Pittsburgh, Pennsylvania
d. Sep 2, 1924 in Pittsburgh, Pennsylvania
Source: *AmNatBi; ApCAB SUP; BiDFedJ; BioIn 2, 3, 5, 15; CamDcAB; DcAmB; HarEnUS; NatCAB 2; OxCSupC; SupCtJu; TwCBDA; WebAB 74, 79; WhAm 1*

Shire, David (Lee)
American. Composer
Won best song Oscar for *Norma Rae*, 1979; Grammy for *Saturday Night Fever*, 1978.
b. Jul 3, 1937 in Buffalo, New York

Source: *AmSong; ASCAP 66; BioIn 15; ConTFT 5; HalFC 80, 84, 88; IntMPA 80, 84, 86, 88, 92, 94, 96; VarWW 85; WhoAm 80, 82, 84, 86, 88, 90, 92, 94, 95, 96, 97, 98, 99, 2000; WhoEnt 92, 98; WhoWest 87, 89*

Shire, Talia Rose Coppola
[Mrs. Jack Schwartzman]
American. Actor
Played Adrian in *Rocky* films; sister of director Francis Ford Coppola.
b. Apr 25, 1946 in Jamaica, New York
Source: *BioIn 13; ConTFT 4; HalFC 88; InB&W 85; IntMPA 92; InWom SUP; NewYTBS 76, 82; WhoAm 86, 90; WhoEnt 92; WhoHol A; WorAlBi*

Shirelles, The
[Doris Kenner Jackson; Beverly Lee; Addie "Micki" Harris McFadden; Shirley Alston Owens]
American. Music Group
Their 1961 hit, "Dedicated to the One I Love," was the first million-selling singl e by an all-girl group.
Source: *AmPS A; BiDAmM; BillEnR; ConMus 11; EncPR&S 89; EncRk 88; EncRkSt; IlEncBM 82; InB&W 80, 85A; NewGrDA 86; PenEncP; RkOn 74; RkWho 96; RolSEnR 83; SoulM; WhoRock 81; WhoRocM 82*

Shirer, William L(awrence)
American. Author, Journalist
Blacklisted during McCarthy era for supporting Hollywood Ten; wrote best-sellers *Berlin Diary*, 1941, *The Rise and Fall of the Third Reich*, 1960.
b. Feb 23, 1904 in Chicago, Illinois
d. Dec 28, 1993 in Boston, Massachusetts
Source: *AmAu&B; AmNatBi; Au&Wr 71; AuBYP 2, 3; Benet 87, 96; BenetAL 91; BiDAmJo; BioIn 1, 2, 3, 4, 6, 7, 8, 11, 12, 13, 14, 15, 16; BlueB 76; CamBiEn; CamDcAB; ChamBID; ConAu 7NR, 9R, 55NR, 143; ConLC 81; CurBio 41, 62, 94N; DcLB 4; EncAJ; EncALit; EncTR; EncTwCJ; EncWB; FacFETw; HisDcWJ; IntAu&W 76, 77, 82, 86, 89, 91, 93; IntWW 74, 75, 76, 77, 78, 79, 80, 81, 82, 83, 89, 91, 93; JrnUS; LinLib L; MajTwCW 1, 2; NewYTBS 82, 86, 90; OxCAmL 65, 83; REn; REnAL; SmATA 45, 78; TwCA SUP; WebAB 74, 79; WhAm 11; WhE&EA; Who 74, 82, 83, 85, 88, 90, 92, 94; WhoAm 74, 76, 78, 80, 82, 84, 86, 88, 90, 92, 94; WhoUSWr 88; WhoWor 74, 78; WhoWrEP 89, 92; WorAl; WorAlBi; WorAu 1900; WrDr 76, 80, 82, 84, 86, 88, 90, 92, 94, 96*

Shirley, Anne
[Dawn O'Day; Dawn Evelyeen Paris]
American. Actor
Child star under name Dawn O'Day, 1922-34; received Oscar nomination for *Stella Dallas*, 1937.
b. Apr 17, 1918 in New York, New York

d. Apr 4, 1993 in Los Angeles, California
Source: *AnObit 1993; BioIn 10, 15, 19; DcPseud; EncAFC; Film 2; FilmEn; FilmgC; ForYSC; GangFlm; HalFC 80, 84, 88; InWom SUP; LegTOT; MotPP; MovMk; OsStAZ; ThFT; TwYS; WhoHol 92, A*

Shirley, George Irving
American. Opera Singer
Tenor; won Met. Opera audition, 1961.
b. Apr 18, 1934 in Indianapolis, Indiana
Source: *BakBD 84; BakBDTw; BioNews 75; DrBlPA 90; InB&W 85; IntWW 83, 91; MetOEnc; MusSN; NegAl 89; NewAmDM; NewGrDA 86; NewYTBE 72; WhoAm 86, 88; WhoAmM 83; WhoEnt 92*

Shirley, James
English. Dramatist
Wrote 40 plays, including tragedy *The Traitor*, 1631; comedy of manners, *Lady of Pleasure*, 1635.
b. Sep 18, 1596 in London, England
d. Oct 29, 1666 in London, England
Source: *Alli; AtlBL; Benet 87, 96; BiCoLiE; BiDRP&D; BioIn 1, 3, 4, 5, 8, 11, 12, 13, 16, 19, 22; BlmGEL; BritAu; CamBiEn; CamGEL; CamGLE; CamGWoT; CasWL; ChamBID; Chambr 1; ChhPo; CnE&AP; CnThe; CroE&S; CrtSuDr; CrtT 1; CyWA 58, 97; DcCathB; DcEnA; DcEnL; DcEuL; DcLB 58; DcLEL; DcNaB, C; EncWT; Ent; EvLB; GrWrEL DR; IntDcT 2; LngCEL; McGEWD 72, 84; MouLC 1; NewC; NewCBEL; NewGrDM 80; NewGrDO; NewOxM; NotNAT A, B; OxCEng 67, 85, 95; OxCIri; OxCMus; OxCThe 67, 83; PenC ENG; PlP&P; REn; REnWD; RfGEnL 91; WebE&AL*

Shirley, Ralph
[Rollo Ireton]
English. Publisher, Editor
Founded, edited *The Occult Review*, 1905-26.
b. Dec 30, 1865 in Oxford, England
d. Dec 29, 1946 in Oxford, England
Source: *ConAu 117; EncO&P 1, 2, 3; WhE&EA; WhLit*

Shirley, William
American. Colonial Figure
Governor of MA, 1740s-50s; headed British forces in America after Braddock's death.
b. Dec 2, 1694 in Preston, England
d. Mar 24, 1771 in Roxbury, Massachusetts
Source: *Alli; AmBi; AmNatBi; AmWrBE; BenetAL 91; BiDrACR; BioIn 4, 6, 9, 14; CamDcAB; DcAmB; DcAmMiB; DcNaB; Drake; EncAR; NatCAB 7; OxCAmH; REnAL; WebAB 74, 79; WhAm HS*

Shirley-Quirk, John Stanton
American. Opera Singer
Bass-baritone who sang multiple roles in
  Death in Venice, 1973; made NY Met.
  debut, 1974.
b. Aug 28, 1931 in Liverpool, England
Source: *BakBD 84, 92; BakBDTw;*
IntDcOp; IntWW 91; IntWWM 77, 90;
MetOEnc; NewAmDM; NewGrDM 80;
PenDiMP; Who 74, 82, 83, 85, 88, 90,
92, 94, 98, 99, 2000; WhoWor 74, 76, 78

Shirley-Smith, Hubert
English. Engineer
Expert designer, builder of int'l steel
  bridges.
b. Oct 13, 1901 in Hendon, England
d. Feb 10, 1981
Source: *ConAu 113; Who 74*

Shively, Charles
American. Educator
Professor of American Studies,
  University of Massachusetts; active in
  Boston's Gay Liberation Front,
  1970—.
b. Dec 8, 1937 in Stonelick Township,
  Ohio
Source: *DrAS 82H; GayLesB; WhoAmL*
85

Shklovsky, Iosif Samvilovitch
Russian. Astronomer, Educator
Researched extraterrestrial life; wrote
  Intelligent Life in the Universe, 1966.
b. Jul 1, 1916 in Glukhov, Russia
d. Mar 3, 1985 in Moscow, Union of
  Soviet Socialist Republics
Source: *ConAu 115; IntWW 83*

Shocked, Michelle
[Michelle Johnston]
American. Singer, Songwriter
Known for social commentary folk
  music; *The Texas Campfire Tapes;*
  Short, Sharp, Shocked; Captain Swing;
  Arkansas Traveller, 1992.
b. 1963
Source: *BioIn 16; ConMus 4; News 89;*
PenEncP; WhoAmW 97, 99

Shockley, William B(radford)
American. Scientist
Co-winner of 1956 Nobel Prize for
  inventing transistor, which
  revolutionized electronics; also known
  for theories on racial differences.
b. Feb 13, 1910 in London, England
d. Aug 12, 1989 in Palo Alto, California
Source: *AmMWSc 82, 92; AmNatBi;*
AsBiEn; BiEsc; BioIn 9, 10, 12; BlueB
76; CamBiEn; CamDcAB; CamDcSc;
ChamBiD; CmCal; ConAu 113, 129;
CurBio 89N; EncAB-H 1974, 1996;
FacFETw; HisDcDP; LarDcSc; LElec;
LinLib S; McGMS 80; NewYTBS 89;
NobelP; PolProf NF; PorSil; RanHWDS;
ScrEAmL 2; WebAB 74, 79; WhAm 10;
WhDW; Who 90N; WhoAm 74, 76, 78,
82, 84, 88; WhoFrS 84; WhoNob, 90,
95; WhoWest 87, 89; WhoWor 74, 76,
78, 80, 82, 84, 87, 89; WorAl; WorAlBi

Shoemaker, Vaughn Richard
American. Cartoonist
Political cartoons found in *Chicago Daily*
  News won Pulitzers, 1938, 1947.
b. Aug 11, 1902 in Chicago, Illinois
d. Aug 18, 1991 in Carol Stream, Illinois
Source: *AmAu&B; EncTwCJ; NewYTBS*
91; WhAmArt 85; WhoAm 86; WhoAmA
73, 91; WhoPul; WhoWor 74, 89

Shoemaker, Willie
[William Lee Shoemaker]
"The Shoe"
American. Jockey
Won over 8,500 races, including four
  Kentucky Derbys.
b. Aug 19, 1931 in Fabens, Texas
Source: *BiDAmSp OS; BioIn 2, 3, 5, 6,*
7, 8, 9, 10, 11, 12, 14, 15, 16, 17, 19;
CamBiEn; CelR; CmCal; ConAu 115;
CurBio 66; FacFETw; IntWW 89, 91,
93, 98, 2000; LegTOT; NewYTBE 70,
73; WebAB 74, 79; WhoAm 76, 78, 80,
82, 84, 86; WorAl; WorAlBi

Sholes, Christopher Latham
American. Journalist, Printer
Invented typewriter, 1868.
b. Feb 14, 1819 in Mooresburg,
  Pennsylvania
d. Feb 17, 1890 in Milwaukee,
  Wisconsin
Source: *AmBi; AmNatBi; ApCAB; BioIn*
3, 5, 7, 8, 11, 12, 13, 15, 21; CamBiEn;
CamDcAB; DcAmB; FrTalk; InSci;
JrnUS; LinLib S; NatCAB 3; OxCAmH;
WebAB 74, 79; WhAm HS; WorInv

**Sholokhov, Mikhail
Aleksandrovich**
Russian. Author
Novel *And Quiet Flows the Don,*
  depicted civil war as experienced by
  Cossack villagers; won Nobel Prize in
  literature, 1965.
b. May 24, 1905 in Kruzhilin, Russia
d. Feb 21, 1984 in Veshenskaya, Union
  of Soviet Socialist Republics
Source: *Benet 96; BiCoLiE; BioIn 1, 4,*
5, 6, 7, 9, 10, 11, 12, 22; CasWL;
ChamBiD; ClDMEL 47; CnMWL;
ConAu 101; CurBio 42, 60, 84; CyWA
58; DcRusL; EncWB 98; EncWL 1;
EvEuW; IntAu&W 76, 77; IntWW 74, 77,
78, 79, 80, 81, 82, 83; LngCTC;
MajTwCW 2; MakMC; McGEWB;
ModSL 1; PenC EUR; REn; TwCA,
SUP; TwCWr; Who 74, 82, 83;
WhoNob; WhoSocC 78; WhoTwCL;
WhoWor 82; WorAl

Shor, Toots
[Bernard Shor]
American. Restaurateur
Best known for NYC "watering spots"
  frequented by celebrities for over 35
  yrs.
b. May 6, 1905 in Philadelphia,
  Pennsylvania
d. Jan 24, 1977 in New York, New York
Source: *BusPN; LegTOT; WhAm 7;*
WhoAm 74, 76

Shore, Dinah
[Frances Rose Shore]
"Fannie"
American. Singer, Actor
Began singing, 1938; won ten Emmys
  for various TV shows; "Dinah Shore
  Chevy Show," 1956-63, where she
  sang the closing jingle, "See the
  U.S.A. in Your Chevrolet."
b. Mar 1, 1917 in Winchester, Tennessee
d. Feb 24, 1994 in Beverly Hills,
  California
Source: *AmNatBi; BakBD 84, 92;*
BioAmW; BioIn 1, 3, 4, 5, 6, 7, 9, 10,
11, 12, 16, 19, 20, 21, 22; BioNews 74;
BkPepl; CelR, 90; CmpEPM; ConTFT 3,
13; CurBio 42, 66, 94N; DcPseud;
EncWomS; FilmEn; FilmgC; ForYSC;
GoodHs; HalFC 80, 84, 88; IntMPA 84,
86, 88, 92, 94; InWom, SUP; LegTOT;
LesBEnT, 92; MotPP; NewAmDM;
NewGrDA 86; News 94, 94-3; NewYTBE
72; NewYTBS 81, 85, 94; OxCPMus;
PenEncP; RadStar; RkOn 74; SaTiSS;
WhoAm 86, 90; WhoEnt 92; WhoHol 92,
A; WorAlBi

Shore, Eddie
[Edward William Shore]
Canadian. Hockey Player
Defenseman, 1926-40, mostly with
  Boston; known for rough play; only
  defenseman to win Hart Trophy four
  times; Hall of Fame, 1945.
b. Nov 25, 1902 in Fort Qu'Appelle,
  Saskatchewan, Canada
d. Mar 16, 1985 in Springfield,
  Massachusetts
Source: *BioIn 2, 3, 5, 6, 8, 9, 10, 14, 24;*
HocEn; LegTOT; NewYTBS 85;
WhoHcky 73; WhoSpor; WorAl; WorAlBi

Shorr, Kehat
Israeli. Olympic Athlete, Victim
One of 11 members of Israeli Olympic
  team kidnapped, killed by Arab
  terrorists during Summer Olympic
  games.
b. 1919?, Romania
d. Sep 5, 1972 in Munich, Germany
  (West)

Shorrock, Glenn
[The Little River Band]
Australian. Singer
Formed Little River Band, 1975; began
  solo career, 1982, with album *Villain*
  of the Peace.
b. Jun 30, 1944 in Sydney, Australia
Source: *RkOn 85; Who 92*

Short, Bobby
[Robert Waltrip Short]
American. Pianist
Quintessential supper-club singer;
  celebrated 25th season at Cafe Carlyle,
  1992.
b. Sep 15, 1926 in Danville, Illinois
Source: *BakBD 84, 92; BakDcM;*
BiDAfM; BiDJaz; CelR, 90; ConAu 107;
CurBio 72; DcPseud; DrBlPA 90;
EncJzS; EncJzS; InB&W 85; NewGrDA
86; OxCPMus; PenEncP; WhoAm 82,

88; WhoBlA 1, 7; WhoEnt 92; WhoHol
92; WorAlBi

Short, James
Scottish. Astronomer, Manufacturer
Optician; invented the first accurate
  reflecting-telescope mirrors.
b. Jun 10, 1710 in Edinburgh, Scotland
d. Jun 14, 1768 in London, England
Source: Alli; DcBiPP; DcNaB; DcScB

Short, Martin
Canadian. Actor, Comedian
Regular cast member, "Saturday Night
  Live," 1984-85; created characters Ed
  Grimley, Nathan Thurm.
b. Mar 26, 1950 in Hamilton, Ontario,
  Canada
Source: BioIn 14, 15; ConNews 86-1;
ConTFT 5, 12, 23; CurBio 92; IntMPA
92, 94, 96; LegTOT; WhoAm 90, 2000;
WhoEnt 92; WhoHol 92

Short, Walter Campbell
American. Army Officer
Commanded armed forces at Pearl
  Harbor, Feb-Dec 1941; retired 1942;
  found directly responsible for failure
  of defenses.
b. Mar 30, 1880 in Fillmore, Illinois
d. Sep 3, 1949 in Dallas, Texas
Source: AmNatBi; BiDWWGF; BioIn 1,
2, 4, 24; CamDcAB; CurBio 46, 49;
DcAmB S4; DcAmMiB; HarEnMi;
NatCAB 40; ObitOF 79; WebAMB;
WhAm 2

Shorter, Frank C
American. Track Athlete
Long-distance runner; won gold medal in
  marathon, 1972 Olympics, silver
  medal, 1976 Olympics.
b. Oct 31, 1947 in Munich, Germany
  (West)
Source: BiDAmSp OS; BioIn 9, 13, 14;
CamDcAB; ChamBiD; ConAu 132;
NewYTBE 72, 73; NewYTBS 76; WhoAm
80, 82, 84, 86, 88; WhoTr&F 73;
WorAlBi

Shorter, Wayne
American. Composer, Musician
Saxophonist; co-leader of Weather
  Report 1970-85; formed own band
  1985; leading figure in post-modern
  jazz.
b. Aug 25, 1933 in Newark, New Jersey
Source: AllMGJa; BiDAfM; BiDJaz;
BioIn 13, 16; CamBiEn; ChamBiD;
ConMus 5; CurBio 96; DcTwCCu 5;
EncJzS; InB&W 80, 85; IntWW 89, 91,
93, 97, 98, 2000; LegTOT; NewAmDM;
NewGrDA 86; NewGrDJ 88, 94;
PenEncP; WhoAm 78, 80, 82, 84, 86, 88,
92, 94, 95, 96, 97; WhoEnt 92, 98;
WhoRocM 82

Shorthouse, Joseph Henry
English. Author, Manufacturer
Wrote historical, religious novel John
  Inglesant, 1881.
b. Sep 9, 1834 in Birmingham, England

d. Mar 4, 1903 in London, England
Source: BbD; BiCoLiE; BioIn 5, 9, 12,
13; BritAu 19; CamBiEn; CamGEL;
CamGLE; CasWL; CelCen; Chambr 3;
ConAu 121, 164; CyWA 58, 97; DcBiA;
DcEnA, A; DcEuL; DcLB 18; DcLEL;
DcNaB S2; EvLB; GrWrEL N; NewC;
NewCBEL; OxCEng 67, 85, 95; PenC
ENG; REn; RfGEnL 91; WebE&AL

Shortz, Will(iam Frederic)
American. Editor, Puzzle Maker
Editor in chief, Games magazine, 1989-
  93; puzzle editor, NY Times, 1993—.
b. Aug 26, 1952 in Crawfordsville,
  Indiana
Source: CurBio 96; IndAu 1967; WhoAm
94, 95, 96, 97

Shostakovich, Dmitri Dmitryevich
Russian. Composer
Best-known symphony, Fifth, celebrated
  20th anniversary of Russian
  Revolution, 1937.
b. Sep 25, 1906 in Saint Petersburg,
  Russia
d. Aug 9, 1975 in Moscow, Union of
  Soviet Socialist Republics
Source: BakBD 78; CurBio 41, 75;
DcCM; DcFM; NewEOp 71; NewYTBE
73; NewYTBS 75; OxCFilm; OxCMus;
WhAm 6; WorEFlm

Shostakovich, Maxim
Russian. Conductor
Son of Dmitri; led USSR State
  Orchestra, 1960s; noted for
  interpreting his father's works;
  defected to US, 1981.
b. May 10, 1938 in Leningrad, Union of
  Soviet Socialist Republics
d. Aug 9, 1975 in Moscow, Union of
  Soviet Socialist Republics
Source: BakBD 78, 84, 92; BakBDTw;
BiDSovU; BioIn 7, 8; IntWW 91;
IntWWM 90; NewAmDM; NewGrDM 80;
PenDiMP; WhoAm 90; WhoSSW 91;
WhoWor 82, 84, 87, 91

Shotoku Taishi
Japanese. Prince, Scholar
Known as the Prince of Holy Virtue, the
  Buddhist statesman and scholar
  prepared the Seventeen-article
  Constitution in 604, compiled the first
  history of Japan in 620, and
  contributed to the political-cultural
  development leading to the Taika
  Reform of 645-649.
b. 573, Japan
d. 621
Source: EncWB 98

Shotwell, James Thomson
American. Historian, Diplomat
Edited over 200 historical vols.:
  Economic and Social History of the
  World War, 1919-29.
b. Aug 6, 1874 in Strathroy, Ontario,
  Canada
d. Jul 15, 1965 in New York, New York
Source: AmAu&B; AmNatBi; AmPeW;
BiDInt; BioIn 4, 5, 6, 7, 10; CamDcAB;

CurBio 44, 65; DcAmB S7; MacDCB 78;
TwCA, SUP; WebBD 83; WhAm 4;
WhE&EA; WhLit; WhNAA

Show, Grant
American. Actor
Appears on TV's "Melrose Place."
b. Feb 27, 1962 in Detroit, Michigan
Source: ConTFT 15, 27

Shrady, Henry M
American. Sculptor
Executed equestrian statues of George
  Washington, R E Lee, General Grant,
  1901-02.
b. Oct 24, 1871 in New York, New York
d. Apr 12, 1922 in Elmsford, New York
Source: AmBi; DcAmB; NatCAB 13;
TwCBDA; WhAm 1; WhAmArt 85

Shrapnel, Henry
English. Army Officer
Invented shrapnel shells, c. 1804.
b. Jun 3, 1761 in Bradford-on-Avon,
  England
d. Mar 13, 1842 in Southampton,
  England
Source: CamBiEn; ChamBiD; DcBiPP;
DcNaB; HarEnMi; RanHWDS; WebBD
83

Shreve, Henry Miller
American. Pilot
Steamboat captain; assisted in the
  development of the lower Mississippi
  River system.
b. Oct 21, 1785 in Burlington County,
  New Jersey
d. Mar 6, 1851 in Saint Louis, Missouri
Source: AmBi; AmNatBi; ApCAB; BioIn
1, 3, 18; DcAmB; Drake; EncWB 98;
McGEWB; NatCAB 2; REnAW;
TwCBDA; WebAB 74, 79; WhAm HS;
WorAl; WorAlBi

Shreve, Susan Richards
American. Author
Won Edgar for juvenile mystery: Lucy
  Forever and Miss Rosetree, 1987.
b. May 2, 1939 in Toledo, Ohio
Source: AuBYP 3; BioIn 13, 15, 16;
ConAu 5AS, 5NR, 38NR, 49, 69NR;
ConLC 23; DcAmChF 1985; DrAPF 80,
91; IntWW 91, 93, 97, 98, 2000;
IntWWW 2; MajAI; ScF&FL 92; SixBJA;
SmATA 41, 46, 95; WhoAm 88, 90, 92,
94, 95, 96, 97, 98, 99, 2000; WhoAmW
87, 89, 91, 93, 95, 97, 99; WhoEnt 98;
WhoUSWr 88; WrDr 76, 80, 82, 84, 86,
92, 98, 99, 2000

Shrimpton, Jean Rosemary
"Shrimp"
English. Model
Popular model at same time as Twiggy,
  1960s.
b. Nov 6, 1942 in High Wycombe,
  England
Source: BioIn 7, 8, 13; InWom SUP;
WhoHol A

Shriner, Herb
American. TV Personality
Pioneer TV humorist, emcee; known for
  his Hoosier stories, 1950s.
b. May 29, 1918 in Toledo, Ohio
d. Apr 23, 1970 in Delray Beach, Florida
Source: *ASCAP 66; BiE&WWA; BioIn 1,
2, 3, 4, 8; JoeFr; LegTOT; LesBEnT;
NewYTBE 70; NewYTET; NotNAT B;
RadStar; WhAm 5; WhoHol B; WhScrn
74, 77, 83; WorAl; WorAlBi*

Shriver, Eunice Mary Kennedy
[Mrs. Robert Sargent Shriver]
American. Social Reformer
Sister of John F Kennedy; vp, Joseph P
  Kennedy Foundation, 1956—; founder
  of International Special Olympics.
b. Jul 10, 1920 in Brookline,
  Massachusetts
Source: *BioIn 13, 15; CelR 90; CurBio
96; InWom SUP; WhoAm 86, 90;
WhoAmW 77, 91*

Shriver, Maria (Owings)
[Mrs. Arnold Schwarzenegger]
American. Broadcast Journalist
Daughter of Sargent Shriver, Eunice
  Kennedy; co-anchor, CBS Morning
  News, 1985-86; "First Person with
  Maria Shriver," 1991—.
b. Nov 6, 1955 in Chicago, Illinois
Source: *BioIn 11, 16; ConNews 86-2;
ConTFT 12; CurBio 91; IntWWW 2;
LegTOT; LesBEnT 92; WhoAm 86, 88,
95, 96, 97, 99, 2000; WhoAmW 95, 97,
99; WhoEnt 92, 98; WhoMedi 98;
WomStre*

Shriver, Pam(ela Howard)
American. Tennis Player
Professional tennis player, 1979—;
  winner of 21 singles titles and 92
  doubles titles; gold medal in 1988
  Olympic games in doubles.
b. Jul 4, 1962 in Baltimore, Maryland
Source: *BiDAmSp OS; BioIn 11, 12, 13,
14, 15; BuCMET; EncWomS; LegTOT;
NewYTBS 82, 85; WhoAm 84, 86, 88,
90, 92, 94, 95, 96, 97, 98, 99; WhoAmW
93, 95, 97, 99; WhoE 95; WhoIntT;
WhoWor 96, 97, 98, 99*

Shriver, (Robert) Sargent
American. Lawyer, Government Official
Brother-in-law of John F Kennedy; first
  director of Peace Corps, 1961-66.
b. Nov 9, 1915 in Westminster,
  Maryland
Source: *AmCath 80; BioIn 5, 6, 7, 8, 9,
10, 11, 12, 14, 16; BlueB 76; CelR;
DcAmDH 80, 89; FacFETw; IntWW 74,
75, 76, 77, 78, 79, 80, 81, 82, 83, 89,
91, 93, 97, 2000; IntYB 78, 79, 80, 81,
82; LinLib S; NewYTBE 72; PresAR
1980; Who 74, 82, 83, 85, 88, 90, 92,
94, 98, 99, 2000; WhoAm 74, 76, 78, 80,
82, 84, 86, 88, 92, 94, 95, 96, 97, 98,
99, 2000; WhoAmP 73, 75, 77, 79, 81,
83, 85, 87, 89, 91, 93, 95, 97, 1999;
WhoE 95; WhoWor 74, 78, 80, 82*

Shrontz, Frank Anderson
American. Business Executive
President of Boeing, world's largest
  aircraft maker, since 1985.
b. Dec 14, 1931 in Boise, Idaho
Source: *BioIn 11, 15; Dun&B 90; IntWW
89, 91, 93, 97, 98, 2000; St&PR 84, 87,
91, 93, 96; WhoAm 76, 78, 80, 82, 84,
86, 88, 90, 92, 94, 95, 96, 97, 98, 99,
2000; WhoAmP 75, 77, 79; WhoFI 00,
87, 89, 92, 94, 96, 98; WhoGov 75, 77;
WhoWest 00, 80, 82, 87, 89, 92, 94, 96,
98; WhoWor 91, 93, 95, 96, 97, 98, 99,
2000*

Shubert, Jacob J
American. Manager, Producer
One of three brothers who built powerful
  Broadway theatrical empire; principal
  backer of Flo Ziegfeld.
b. Aug 15, 1880 in Shirvanta, Russia
d. Dec 26, 1963 in New York, New
  York
Source: *EncAB-H 1974; NotNAT A;
OxCThe 67; PlP&P; WhAm 4*

Shubert, Lee
American. Theater Owner, Producer
With brothers, major owner of legitimate
  theater empire, 1920-53; produced
  countless Broadway hits.
b. Mar 15, 1875 in Shirvanta, Russia
d. Dec 25, 1953 in New York, New
  York
Source: *BioIn 3, 8, 17, 18, 19;
CamGWoT; ChamBiD; CnThe; DcAmB
S5; EncWT; LegTOT; NotNAT A, B;
OxCThe 67; PlP&P; WebAB 74, 79;
WhAm 3; WhoStg 1908; WhThe; WorAl;
WorAlBi*

Shue, Andrew
American. Actor
Appears on TV's "Melrose Place."
b. Feb 20, 1967 in South Orange, New
  Jersey
Source: *ConTFT 16, 26; LegTOT*

Shue, Elizabeth
American. Actor
Starred in *Leaving Las Vegas,* 1995.
b. Jun 10, 1963 in Wilmington, Delaware

Shue, Gene
[Eugene William Shue]
American. Basketball Player, Basketball
  Coach
Guard, 1954-64; NBA coach 1966-89;
  with several teams; now with
  Washington, 1980—; coach of yr.,
  1969, 1982.
b. Dec 18, 1931 in Baltimore, Maryland
Source: *BasBi; BiDAmSp BK; OfNBA
87; WhoAm 84, 88, 92; WhoBbl 73;
WhoE 85; WhoWest 89*

Shukairy, Ahmed
Palestinian. Political Leader
Founder, first head of PLO, 1964-67.
b. 1908 in Acre, Palestine
d. Feb 26, 1980 in Amman, Jordan

Source: *AnObit 1980; HisEAAC;
NewYTBS 80*

Shukovsky, Joel
American. Writer
Co-created television comedy *Murphy
  Brown.*

Shukshin, Vasilii Makarovich
Russian. Actor, Author, Director
Short story writer identified with "New
  Slavophiles."
b. 1929, Union of Soviet Socialist
  Republics
d. Oct 2, 1974 in Moscow, Union of
  Soviet Socialist Republics
Source: *BiDSovU; BioIn 10, 11, 12, 16;
ObitOF 79; ObitT 1971*

Shula, Don(ald Francis)
American. Football Coach, Football
  Executive
Co-owner, head coach, Miami, 1970-95;
  won Super Bowl, 1972, 1973, 1974,
  1984, and 1985.
b. Jan 4, 1930 in Grand River, Ohio
Source: *BiDAmSp FB; BioIn 9, 10, 11,
12, 13, 14, 15; BioNews 74; CelR, 90;
ChamBiD; ConAu 106; CurBio 74;
FootReg 87; LegTOT; News 92, 92-2;
NewYTBE 73; NewYTBS 85; WhoAm 86,
88; WhoSSW 86, 91; WorAl; WorAlBi*

Shull, George Harrison
American. Botanist
Research on corn hybrids increased
  yields per acre 25-50%.
b. Apr 15, 1874 in Clark County, Ohio
d. Sep 28, 1954 in Princeton, New Jersey
Source: *AmNatBi; BioIn 1, 3, 4, 6, 12,
14; DcAmB S5; EncAAH; InSci; IntWW
83; WhAm 3; WhNAA; WhoAm 84*

Shulman, Irving
American. Author, Educator
Novels include *The Amboy Dukes,* 1947;
  biographies: *Harlow: An Intimate
  Biography,* 1964; adapted to film,
  1965.
b. May 21, 1913 in New York, New
  York
d. Mar 23, 1995 in Sherman Oaks,
  California
Source: *AmAu&B; AmNov; Au&Wr 71;
BioIn 2, 4, 11, 20, 21, 22; ConAu 1R,
6NR, 148; CurBio 56, 95N; SmATA 13;
WhAm 12; WhoAm 74, 76, 78, 80, 82,
84, 88, 90, 92; WhoE 74; WhoUSWr 88;
WhoWorJ 72, 78; WhoWrEP 89, 92, 95;
WrDr 76, 80, 82, 84, 86, 88, 90, 92, 94,
96*

Shulman, Max
American. Author, Dramatist
Humorous works include *Barefoot Boy
  with Cheek,* 1943; adapted to musical
  comedy, 1947; cowrote play *The
  Tender Trap,* 1954; creator, writer, TV
  series "The Many Loves of Dobie
  Gillis," 1959-63.
b. Mar 14, 1919 in Saint Paul, Minnesota

d. Aug 28, 1988 in Los Angeles,
California
Source: *AmAu&B; AmNov; BiE&WWA;
BioIn 2, 5, 6, 7, 13, 16, 24; ConAu 89,
126; CurBio 59, 88, 88N; DcLB 11;
DrAPF 80; IntMPA 75, 76, 77, 78, 79,
80, 81, 82, 84, 86, 88; LegTOT;
NewYTBS 88; NotNAT; ScrEAmL 2;
SmATA 59; St&PR 75; WhAm 9;
WhoAm 74, 76, 78, 80, 82, 84, 86, 88;
WhoE 74; WhoUSWr 88; WorAl*

Shulman, Morton
Canadian. Author, Physician
Wrote books on finance as a hobby: *How
to Invest Your Money & Profit from
Inflation,* 1979.
b. Apr 2, 1925 in Toronto, Ontario,
Canada
Source: *AmMWSc 73P, 92; AuNews 1;
BioIn 8, 10, 11, 12; CanWW 83, 89, 96;
ConAu 14NR, 21R; ConCaAu 1;
WhoMW 74*

Shultz, George Pratt
American. Government Official
Succeeded Alexander Haig as Reagan's
secretary of state, 1982-88.
b. Dec 13, 1920 in New York, New
York
Source: *AmMWSc 73S; AmPolLe;
BiDrUSE 71, 89; BioIn 8, 9, 10, 11, 12,
13, 14, 15, 16, 18, 19, 22, 23; CamBiEn;
CamDcAB; ChamBiD; CngDr 74, 83,
85, 87; ColdWar 2; ConAu 104; CurBio
69, 88; DcAmDH 89; EncWB, 98;
IntAu&W 89; IntWW 74, 75, 76, 77, 78,
79, 80, 81, 82, 83, 89, 91, 93, 97, 98,
2000; NewYTBE 70, 72, 73; NewYTBS
80, 82; PolProf NF; St&PR 84; Who 74,
82, 83, 85, 88, 90, 92, 94, 98, 99, 2000;
WhoAm 74, 76, 78, 80, 82, 84, 86, 88,
90, 92, 94, 95, 96, 97, 98, 99, 2000;
WhoAmP 73, 75, 77, 79, 85, 87, 89, 91,
93, 95, 97, 1999; WhoE 83, 85, 86, 89;
WhoFI 79, 92, 94; WhoGov 72;
WhoSSW 73, 75, 76; WhoWest 00, 92,
94, 96, 98; WhoWor 74, 82, 84, 87, 89,
91, 93, 95, 96, 97, 98, 99, 2000;
WorAlBi; WrDr 86, 92, 98, 99, 2000*

Shumlin, Herman Elliott
American. Producer, Director
Directed plays *Grand Hotel; The Deputy.*
b. Dec 6, 1898 in Atwood, Colorado
d. Jun 14, 1979 in New York, New York
Source: *BiE&WWA; BioIn 11; CurBio
41, 79; DcAmB S10; FilmgC; NewYTBS
79; NotNAT; WhAm 7; WhoAm 74, 76,
78; WhoThe 77; WorEFlm*

Shushkevich, Stanislav
Russian. Government Official
One of President Boris Yeltsin's key
partners during the establishment of
the Russian commonwealth.

Shuster, Frank
[Wayne and Shuster]
Canadian. Comedian
Had documentary-style TV show with
partner Johnny Wayne, "Wayne and

Schuster Take an Affectionate Look
at.,'' 1966.
b. Sep 5, 1916 in Toronto, Ontario,
Canada
Source: *BioIn 5, 11; CreCan 2*

Shuster, Joe
American. Cartoonist
Best known for "Superman" cartoons.
b. Jul 10, 1914 in Toronto, Ontario,
Canada
d. Jul 30, 1992 in Los Angeles,
California
Source: *BiDScF; BioIn 19; ConLC 21;
EncACom; JeHun; LegTOT; WorECom*

Shuster, Rosie
American. Writer
Multiple Emmy winner for NBC's
"Saturday Night Live," 1970s.
b. Jun 19, 1950 in Toronto, Ontario,
Canada
Source: *BioIn 12; ConTFT 4*

Shute, Denny
[Herman Densmore Shute]
American. Golfer
Turned pro, 1928; won British Open,
1933; last to win PGA two straight
yrs., 1936, 1937; Hall of Fame, 1957.
b. Oct 25, 1904 in Cleveland, Ohio
d. May 13, 1974 in Akron, Ohio
Source: *AmNatBi; LegTOT; NewYTBS
74; ObitOF 79; WhoGolf; WhoSpor*

Shute, Nevil
[Nevil Shute Norway]
English. Author, Aeronautical Engineer
Best known for novel of nuclear
holocaust, *On the Beach,* 1963.
b. Jan 17, 1899 in Ealing, Australia
d. Jan 12, 1960 in Melbourne, Australia
Source: *BeaEPF; Benet 87, 96;
BiCoLiE; BioIn 3, 4, 5, 7, 11, 14, 17,
22; CamBiEn; CamGLE; ChamBiD;
ConAu 93, 102; ConLC 30; CurBio 42,
60; DcArts; DcLEL; DcNaB 1951;
DcPseud; EncSF, 93; EvLB; FilmgC;
GrBr; HalFC 80, 84, 88; InSci;
LegTOT; LngCTC; ModBrL, 2; NewC;
NewCBEL; NewEScF; Novels; ObitT
1951; OxCAusL; OxCTwCL; PenC ENG;
RAdv 14, 13-1; REn; ScF&FL 1, 92;
ScFSB; TwCA, SUP; TwCCr&M 80;
TwCRHW 90, 94; TwCSFW 81, 86, 91;
TwCWr; WhAm 3, 4; WhE&EA;
WhoTwCL; WorAl; WorAu 1900*

Shutt, Steve
[Stephen John Shutt]
Canadian. Hockey Player
Left wing, 1972-85, mostly with
Montreal; set NHL record for most
goals in season by left wing, 60
(1976-77).
b. Jul 1, 1952 in Toronto, Ontario,
Canada
Source: *BioIn 11, 16; HocEn; HocReg
85; WhoAm 78, 80, 82, 84*

Shutta, Ethel
American. Actor
Sang in Ziegfeld Follies with Eddie
Cantor in *Whoopee.*
b. Dec 1, 1896 in New York, New York
d. Feb 5, 1976
Source: *BiDAmM; BioIn 9, 10; InWom
SUP; NewYTBE 70, 71; WhoHol C;
WhoThe 72; WhThe*

Shuttlesworth, Dorothy Edwards
American. Children's Author
Noted for natural history books.
b. 1907 in New York, New York
Source: *AuBYP 2, 3; BioIn 7, 9; ConAu
1R, 4NR; FifBJA; ForWC 70; SmATA 3*

Shuttlesworth, Fred Lee
American. Clergy, Civil Rights Leader
Aid to Martin Luther King, Jr; founder,
pres., AL Christian Movement for
Human Rights, 1956-69.
b. Mar 18, 1922 in Mugler, Alabama
Source: *AfrAmAl 8; BioIn 7, 11;
HisDCRM; InB&W 85; NegAl 89;
PolProf E, J, K; WhoBlA 4, 7*

Shyer, Charles
American. Screenwriter
Films include *Smokey and the Bandit,*
1977; *Private Benjamin,* 1980.
b. Oct 11, 1941 in Los Angeles,
California
Source: *BioIn 14; ConTFT 8; MiSFD 9;
VarWW 85*

Siad Barre, Mohamed
Somali. Political Leader
Pres., Somalia, 1969-91.
b. 1912? in Lugh, Somalia
d. Jan 2, 1995 in Lagos, Nigeria
Source: *BioIn 11, 13; ColdWar 1;
IntWW 91; WhoWor 91*

Sibelius, Jean
Finnish. Composer
Romantic composer who drew themes
from nature, folklore; known for seven
symphonies, 1899-1924.
b. Dec 8, 1865 in Tavastehus, Finland
d. Sep 20, 1957 in Jarvenpaa, Finland
Source: *AtlBL; BakBD 78, 84, 92;
BakBDTw; BakDcM; Benet 87, 96; BioIn
1, 2, 3, 4, 5, 6, 7, 8, 9, 10, 11, 12, 13,
14, 15, 16, 17, 19, 20, 23; BriBkM 80;
CnOxB; CompSN, SUP; DcCM; DcCom
77; DcCom&M 79; DcTwCC, A;
FacFETw; LegTOT; MakMC; MusMk;
NewAmDM; NewGrDM 80; NewOxM;
NotNAT B; ObitT 1951; OxCEng 85, 95;
OxCMus; OxDcOp; PenDiMP A; RAdv
14; REn; WhAm 3; WhDW; WorAl;
WorAlBi*

Siberry, Jane
Canadian. Singer, Songwriter
Albums include *No Borders Here,* 1984
and *Bound by the Beauty,* 1989.
b. 1950? in Toronto, Ontario, Canada
Source: *BioIn 16; ConMus 6*

Sibley, Hiram

American. Businessman
Pres., Western Union Telegraph Co.,
1856-69; built first transcontinental
line, 1861; established Sibley College
at Cornell U.
b. Feb 6, 1807 in North Adams,
Massachusetts
d. Jul 12, 1888 in Rochester, New York
Source: *AmBi; AmNatBi; ApCAB;
BiDAmBL 83; BioIn 4, 9, 15; DcAmB;
NatCAB 4; TwCBDA; WebAB 74, 79;
WebBD 83; WhAm HS*

Sickert, Walter Richard

English. Painter
Influenced by Degas, he was one of
England's greatest impressionist
painters and was known especially for
his cityscapes and music hall scenes.
b. 1860 in Munich, Germany
d. 1942 in Bath, England
Source: *AtlBL; BioIn 2, 3, 4, 5, 6, 7, 9,
10, 11, 12; CamBiEn; ChamBiD;
CnMWL; DcArts; DcBrAr 1; DcBrBI;
DcNaB 1941; DcTwArt; DcVicP, 2;
EncWB 98; GrBr; LngCTC; McGDA;
McGEWB; OxCArt; OxCBrHi;
OxCTwCA; OxDcArt; PhDcTCA 77;
ThHEIm; TwCPaSc*

Sickles, Daniel Edgar

American. Government Official, Soldier
Acquitted for shooting Philip Key, son of
Francis Scott; first time plea of
temporary insanity used, 1859;
credited with obtaining Central Park
for NYC.
b. Oct 20, 1825 in New York, New York
d. May 3, 1914 in New York, New York
Source: *AmBi; ApCAB; BiAUS; BiDrAC;
BioIn 3, 4, 6, 7, 8, 11, 12, 13;
CamDcAB; CivWDc; CopCroC; DcAmB;
Drake; NatCAB 12; TwCBDA; WebAB
74, 79; WebAMB; WhAm 1; WhAmP*

Sickmann, Rodney Virgil

[The Hostages]
"Rocky"
American. Hostage
One of 52 held by terrorists, Nov 1979-
Jan 1981.
b. 1958?
Source: *BioIn 12; NewYTBS 81*

Sidaris, Andy

American. Producer, Director
Won Emmys for "1968 Summer
Olympics," 1969; "XII Winter
Olympics," 1976.
b. Feb 20, 1932 in Chicago, Illinois
Source: *IntMPA 75, 76, 77, 78, 79, 80,
81, 82, 84, 86, 88, 92, 94, 96; VarWW
85*

Sidarouss, Stephanos, Cardinal

Egyptian. Religious Leader
Patriarch of Coptic Catholic Church,
1958-85; became cardinal, 1965.
b. Feb 22, 1904 in Cairo, Egypt
d. Aug 23, 1987 in Cairo, Egypt
Source: *BioIn 11, 15; IntWW 78; WhAm
11; WhoWor 76, 78, 80, 82, 84, 87*

Siddal, Elizabeth Eleanor

[Mrs. Dante Gabriel Rossetti]
"Lizzie"
English. Model, Artist
Body exhumed after death to recover
manuscript Rossetti had buried with
her.
b. 1834 in Sheffield, England
d. Feb 10, 1862
Source: *BioIn 9, 10, 11, 13; DcVicP, 2;
DcWomA; OxCArt; WomArt*

Siddons, Sarah Kemble

English. Actor
Best known for tragic roles, especially
Lady MacBeth, 1785-1812.
b. Jul 5, 1755 in Brecon, Wales
d. Jun 8, 1831 in London, England
Source: *CnThe; DcEuL; Ent; HerW, 84;
InWom, SUP; NewC; NewCol 75;
NotNAT A, B; OxCThe 67; PIP&P; REn*

Sidey, Hugh Swanson

American. Author, Journalist
Has written column, "The Presidency,"
for Time mag. since 1966.
b. Sep 3, 1927 in Greenfield, Iowa
Source: *BioIn 11, 15; ConAu 111, 124;
EncTwCJ; WhoAm 74, 76, 78, 80, 82,
84, 86, 88, 90, 92, 94, 95, 96, 97, 98,
99, 2000; WhoAmP 1999; WhoMedi 98;
WhoWor 74*

Sidgwick, Henry

English. Educator, Author
Best-known work: *Methods of Ethics,*
1874.
b. May 31, 1838 in Yorkshire, England
d. Aug 28, 1900 in Cambridge, England
Source: *Alli SUP; BbD; BiD&SB;
BiDBrF 1; BiDPara; BioIn 8, 9, 10, 16,
22; BritAu 19; CamBiEn; CamGEL;
CamGLE; CasWL; CelCen; ChamBiD;
Chambr 3; ConAu 120; DcEnA, A;
DcEuL; DcLEL; DcNaB S1; EncEth;
EncO&P 1, 2, 3; EncPaPR 91; EncWB
98; EvLB; GrEconB; LuthC 75;
McGEWB; NewC; NewCBEL; OxCEng
67, 85, 95; OxCPhil; PenC ENG; RAdv
14; WhoEc 81, 86*

Sidney, Algernon

English. Politician, Author
First to write "God helps those who help
themselves" in English in *Discourses
Government,* 1698; charged with
treason, executed for part in Ryehouse
Plot.
b. 1622 in Penshurst, England
d. Dec 7, 1683 in London, England
Source: *Alli; BiD&SB; BioIn 13, 14, 17,
21; CamBiEn; ChamBiD; DcBiPP;
DcEnA, A; DcEnL; DcNaB; EvLB;
NewC; NewCol 75; OxCBrHi; OxCEng
67, 85, 95; REn; WebBD 83*

Sidney, George

American. Director, Producer
Won Oscars for shorts *Quicker'n A
Wink,* 1940; *Of Pups and Puzzles,*
1941.
b. Oct 4, 1916 in New York, New York

Source: *BiDFilm; BioIn 15, 20; CmMov;
ConTFT 25; DcFM; EncAFC; FilmEn;
FilmgC; IlWWHD 1; IntDcF 1-2;
IntMPA 75, 76, 77, 78, 79, 80, 81, 82,
84, 86, 88, 92, 94, 96; MiSFD 9;
MovMk; WhoAm 74, 76, 78, 80, 82, 84;
WhoEnt 92; WorEFlm; WorFDir 1*

Sidney, Ivan

American. Native American Leader
Hopi tribal chairman beginning in 1983;
involved in a dispute with the Navajo
over 1.8 million acres of land in
northeastern Arizona, and although the
U.S. Congress ordered the land to be
divided, 1,000 Navajo residents
refused to relocate and the dispute
remained unresolved.
b. c. 1948 in Arizona
Source: *ConNews 87-2*

Sidney, Philip, Sir

English. Poet, Statesman, Soldier,
Courtier
Model of English chivalry; wrote
pastoral *Arcadia,* 1590.
b. Nov 30, 1554 in Kent, England
d. Oct 17, 1586 in Arnhem, Netherlands
Source: *Alli; AtlBL; BbD; Benet 87, 96;
BiCoLiE; BiD&SB; BiDRP&D; BioIn 1,
2, 3, 4, 5, 7, 8, 9, 10, 11, 12, 13, 14, 15,
16, 17, 18, 20, 21, 22, 24; BlmGEL;
BritAu; BritWr 1; CamBiEn; CamGEL;
CamGLE; CamGWoT; CasWL;
ChamBiD; Chambr 1; ChhPo, S2, S3;
CnDBLB 1; CnE&AP; CroE&S; CrtT 1,
4; CyWA 58, 97; DcArts; DcBiPP;
DcEnA; DcEnL; DcEuL; DcLB 167;
DcLEL; DcNaB; EncWB 98; EvLB;
GrWrEL N, P; LinLib L, S; LitC 19, 39;
LngCEL; LuthC 75; MagSWL;
McGEWB; MouLC 1; NewC; NewCBEL;
NotPoe; OxCBrHi; OxCEng 67, 85, 95;
PenC ENG; RAdv 1, 14, 13-1; REn;
RfGEnL 91; RGFBP; WebE&AL;
WhDW; WorAl; WorAlBi; WrPh*

Sidney, Sylvia

[Sophia Kosow]
American. Actor
Oscar nominee, 1973, for *Summer
Wishes, Winter Dreams.*
b. Aug 8, 1910 in New York, New York
d. Jul 1, 1999 in New York, New York
Source: *BiDFilm, 81, 94; BiE&WWA;
BioIn 9, 12, 21, 22; CelR; ConTFT 9;
CurBio 81; DcPseud; Film 2; FilmEn;
FilmgC; ForYSC; GangFlm; HalFC 80,
84, 88; IntDcF 1-3, 2-3; IntMPA 75, 76,
77, 78, 79, 80, 81, 82, 84, 86, 88, 92,
94, 96; InWom, SUP; LegTOT; MotPP;
MovMk; NotNAT; OsStAZ; OxCFilm;
ThFT; What 3; WhoAm 76, 78, 80, 82,
84, 86, 88, 90, 92, 94, 95, 96, 97, 98,
99; WhoEnt 92, 98; WhoHol 92, A;
WhoThe 72, 77, 81; WomWMM; WorAl;
WorAlBi; WorEFlm*

Siebert, Babe

[Albert Charles Siebert]
Canadian. Hockey Player
Left wing, 1925-39, with four NHL
teams; won Hart Trophy, 1937; Hall

of Fame, 1964; died from drowning at height of career.
b. Jan 14, 1904 in Plattsville, Ontario, Canada
d. Aug 25, 1939 in Saint Joseph, Ontario, Canada
Source: *HocEn; WhoHcky 73; WhoSpor*

Siebert, Muriel
"Rebel of Wall Street"
American. Business Executive
First female member of NY Stock Exchange, 1967; one of first to open discount brokerage.
b. 1932? in Cleveland, Ohio
Source: *BioIn 16; ConNews 87-2; CurBio 97; EncABHB 7; EncWB 99; InWom SUP; WhoAm 90; WhoAmW 91; WhoFI 89; WomFir*

Siegbahn, Kai Manne Boerje
Swedish. Physicist, Educator
Won 1981 Nobel Prize in physics for developing ESCA for chemical analysis; son of 1924 prize winner Manne.
b. Apr 20, 1918 in Lund, Sweden
Source: *AmMWSc 92; BioIn 13, 15; NobelP; Who 92; WhoAm 90; WhoNob, 90, 95; WhoWor 87, 91; WorAlBi*

Siegbahn, Karl Manne Georg
Swedish. Scientist
Won 1924 Nobel Prize in physics for discoveries in field of X-ray spectroscopy.
b. Dec 3, 1886 in Orebro, Sweden
d. Sep 26, 1978 in Stockholm, Sweden
Source: *AsBiEn; BiEsc; CamBiEn; ChamBiD; ConAu 161; DcScB S2; InSci; IntWW 74, 75, 76, 77, 78, 79N; LarDcSc; McGCEnS; McGMS 80; ObitOF 79; RanHWDS; WhAm 9; WhE&EA; Who 74; WhoNob, 90, 95; WhoWor 76; WorAl*

Siegel, Bernie S(hepard)
American. Surgeon
Promoter of self-healing; wrote *How to Live Between Office Visits,* 1993.
b. Oct 14, 1932 in New York, New York
Source: *ConAu 49NR; CurBio 93*

Siegel, Bugsy
[Benjamin Siegel]
American. Criminal
Helped organize Murder, Inc; began syndicate-controlled gambling in Las Vegas.
b. Feb 28, 1906 in New York, New York
d. Jun 20, 1947 in Beverly Hills, California
Source: *AmDec 1940; AmNatBi; BioIn 1, 2, 8, 11, 18, 24; DrInf; LegTOT*

Siegel, Don
American. Director
Won two Academy Awards for short films *Star in the Night,* and *Hitler Lives;* movies directed include *Dirty*

Harry, 1971 and *Escape from Alcatraz,* 1979.
b. Oct 16, 1912 in Chicago, Illinois
d. Apr 20, 1991 in Nipomo, California
Source: *AnObit 1991; BiDFilm 94; BioIn 12, 15, 17, 18, 19; ConTFT 6, 10; FilmEn; FilmgC; GangFlm; HalFC 80, 84, 88; IlWWHD 1; IntDcF 1-2, 2-2; IntMPA 75, 76, 77, 78, 79, 80, 81, 82, 84, 86, 88; LegTOT; MiSFD 9N; MovMk; NewYTBE 71, 72; NewYTBS 91; OxCFilm; PenEncH; WhAm 10; WhoAm 74, 76, 78, 80, 82, 84, 86, 88, 90; WhoHrs 80*

Siegel, Jerry
American. Cartoonist
Created comic book's most lucrative character, Superman, 1933; mistakenly sold rights for only $130 in 1938.
b. Oct 17, 1914 in Cleveland, Ohio
d. Jan 28, 1996 in Los Angeles, California
Source: *BioIn 10, 21, 22, 23; ChamBiD; ConAu X; EncACom; EncSF, 93; JeHun; LegTOT; ObitPA 96; WorECom*

Siegel, Larry
American. Writer
Won Emmys for "The Carol Burnett Show," 1971, 1973, 1978.
b. Oct 29, 1925 in New York, New York
Source: *VarWW 85*

Siegel, Morris J
American. Businessman
Chm., pres., Celestial Seasonings, biggest producer of herbal teas, 1971-84; sold to Kraft for $36 million.
b. Nov 21, 1949 in Salida, Colorado
Source: *BioIn 13; NewYTBS 83; WhoAm 80, 82, 84, 86, 88*

Siegel, Owen R
American. Manufacturer
Founded trophy-making co., RS Owens & Co., 1938; makes Oscars, Emmys, Clios, MTV Awards.
b. 1919 in Chicago, Illinois
Source: *BioIn 16; St&PR 84, 87, 98, 99, 2000*

Siegfried and Roy
[Siegfried Fischbacher; Roy Uwehudwigltorn]
American. Entertainers
Partners in illusion; have given over 10,000 performances in Las Vegas.
Source: *BioIn 17, 18, 19, 21*

Siegmeister, Elie
American. Composer, Conductor
Stage, orchestral works on native American themes include *Ozark Set,* 1943; founded, led American Ballad singers, 1939-44; wrote on music.
b. Jan 15, 1909 in New York, New York
d. Mar 10, 1991 in Manhasset, New York
Source: *AmAu&B; AmComp; ASCAP 66, 80; Au&Wr 71; AuBYP 2, 3; BakBD 78, 84, 92; BakBDTw; BiDAmM;*

BiE&WWA; BioIn 1, 2, 7, 8, 9, 11, 14, 16, 17; BlueB 76; BriBkM 80; CamDcAB; CompSN, SUP; ConAmC 76, 82; ConAu 1NR, 1R, 46NR, 133; CpmDNM 73, 79, 80; DcCM; EncAL; IntWWM 77, 80, 85, 90; LegTOT; MusMk; NewAmDM; NewGrDA 86; NewGrDM 80; NewGrDO; NewOxM; NewYTBS 91; NotNAT; OxCMus; WhAm 10; WhoAm 74, 76, 78, 80, 82, 84, 86, 88, 90; WhoAmJ 80; WhoAmM 83; WhoE 83, 85; WhoMus 72; WhoWorJ 72; WrDr 76, 80, 82, 84

Siemens, (Ernst) Werner von
German. Inventor, Industrialist
Developed electroplating process, 1841.
b. Dec 13, 1816 in Lenthe, Germany
d. Dec 6, 1892 in Berlin, Germany
Source: *BioIn 7, 12, 20; CamBiEn; CamDcSc; ChamBiD; DcScB; InSci; LarDcSc; McGCEnS; NewCol 75; RanHWDS; WhDW; WorAl; WorAlBi; WorInv*

Siemens, William, Sir
English. Inventor, Physicist, Engineer
Developed open-hearth steelmaking process, 1861; laid first cable between US and England, 1875.
b. Apr 4, 1823 in Lenthe, Germany
d. Nov 18, 1883 in London, England
Source: *AsBiEn; BioIn 16; DcNaB; McGCEnS; NewCol 75; WebBD 83; WorAl; WorAlBi*

Sienkiewicz, Henryk Adam Aleksander Pius
Polish. Author
Best known for historical novel *Quo Vadis,* 1895; won Nobel Prize for literature, 1905.
b. May 5, 1846 in Okrzejska, Poland
d. Nov 15, 1916 in Vevey, Switzerland
Source: *AtlBL; BbD; BiD&SB; CasWL; ClDMEL 47; CyWA 58; DcBiA; DcEuL; EncWL 1; EuAu; EvEuW; LngCTC; ModSL 2; PenC EUR; REn; RfGShF 2; WhoNob, 95*

Siepi, Cesare
Italian. Opera Singer
Bass with NY Met., 1950-74; noted for Don Giovanni, Verdi roles.
b. Feb 10, 1923 in Milan, Italy
Source: *BakBD 78, 84, 92; BakBDTw; BiE&WWA; BioIn 4, 5, 6, 7, 11; BriBkM 80; CelR; ChamBiD; CmOp; CurBio 55; FacFETw; IntDcOp; IntWWM 77, 80, 90; MetOEnc; MusSN; NewAmDM; NewEOp 71; NewGrDM 80; NewGrDO; NewYTBE 71; PenDiMP; WhoAm 74, 76, 78, 80, 82, 84, 86, 88, 90, 92, 94, 95, 96, 97, 98, 99, 2000; WhoEnt 92, 98; WhoHol 92, A; WhoMus 72; WhoOp 76; WhoWor 74*

Sierra (Garcia), Ruben Angel
Puerto Rican. Baseball Player
Outfielder, Texas, 1982-92; Oakland, 1992-95; NY Yankees, 1995—; led AL in rbis, 1989.

b. Oct 6, 1965 in Rio Piedras, Puerto
Rico
Source: *Ballpl 90; BaseEn 88; BaseReg
88; WhoAfA 9; WhoAm 90, 92, 94, 95;
WhoBlA 7, 8; WhoHisp 91, 92, 94;
WhoWest 92, 94; WorAlBi*

Sierra, Justo
Mexican. Writer, Educator, Historian,
Government Official
Mexico's leading liberal historians was,
as minister of education, responsible
for considerable educational reform
and expansion.
b. Jan 26, 1848 in Campeche, Yucatan,
Mexico
d. Sep 13, 1912 in Madrid, Spain
Source: *BioIn 1, 2; DcMexL; EncLatA;
EncWB 98; McGEWB; OxCSpan*

Sieyes, Emmanuel Joseph
French. Political Activist, Pamphleteer
Writings encouraged bourgeoisie during
French Revolution; participated in
political coup that brought Napoleon
to power.
b. May 3, 1748 in Frejus, France
d. Jun 20, 1836 in Paris, France
Source: *BiDMoER 1; BioIn 16, 23;
CamBiEn; CelCen; ChamBiD; CmFrR;
DcBiPP; EncEnl; EncRev; EncWB 98;
McGEWB; OxCFr; WhDW; WorAl;
WorAlBi*

Sifford, Charlie
[Charles Luther Sifford]
American. Golfer
First African-American to join
Professional Golfers' Assn. (PGA)
tour, 1960.
b. Jun 2, 1922 in Charlotte, North
Carolina
Source: *AfrAmAl 8; AfrAmSG; BioIn 8,
19, 21, 24; ConBlB 4; InB&W 85; NegAl
89; NotBlAM; WhoAfA 9, 10, 11, 12;
WhoBlA 7, 8*

Sifton, Clifford
Canadian. Politician
Federal cabinet member turned the
Canadian West into a premiere
agricultural area by organizing a
massive immigration into the region.
b. Mar 10, 1861 in Arva, Ontario,
Canada
d. Apr 17, 1929 in New York, New
York
Source: *ApCAB SUP; BioIn 1, 9; DcNaB
1922; EncWB 98; MacDCB 78; OxCCan*

Sigismund
Ruler
Ruled Holy Roman Empire, 1433-37;
German king, 1410-37; king of
Hungary, 1387-1437; son of Charles
IV.
b. Feb 15, 1368 in Nuremberg, Germany
d. Dec 19, 1437 in Znojmo, Bohemia
Source: *BioIn 8; CamBiEn; ChamBiD;
DcBiPP; DcCathB; Dis&D; EncWB 98;
LuthC 75; McGEWB; NewCol 75;
WebBD 83*

Sigmund, Barbara Boggs
American. Politician
Member of a family with a long history
of public service, she was the colorful
Democratic mayor of Princeton, NJ.
b. May 27, 1939 in New Orleans,
Louisiana
d. Oct 11, 1990 in Princeton, New Jersey
Source: *BioIn 13; News 91, 91-1;
NewYTBS 90; WhoAmP 81, 83, 85, 87,
89; WomPO 78*

Signac, Paul
French. Artist
Leading spokesman for the neo-
impressionist movement; painted
European coastal scenes.
b. Nov 11, 1863 in Paris, France
d. Aug 15, 1935 in Paris, France
Source: *AtlBL; BioIn 2, 3, 4, 5, 6, 8, 13,
14, 16; CamBiEn; ChamBiD; ClaDrA;
DcArts; DcTwArt; DcTwCCu 2;
McGDA; OxCArt; OxDcArt; PhDcTCA
77; REn; ThHEIm; WhDW*

Signorelli, Luca
Italian. Artist
Member of Umbrian school; best-known
frescoe: *Heaven and Hell*, 1499-1504.
b. 1441 in Cortona, Italy
d. Oct 16, 1523 in Cortona, Italy
Source: *AtlBL; BioIn 1, 5, 9, 16, 22;
CamBiEn; ChamBiD; DcCathB; IntDcAA
90; LuthC 75; McGDA; OxCArt;
OxCCAA; OxDcArt; REn*

**Signoret, Simone Henrietta
Charlotte**
[Simone Kaminker; Mrs. Yves Montand]
German. Actor
Won Oscar for *Room at the Top*, 1958.
b. Mar 25, 1921 in Wiesbaden, Germany
d. Sep 30, 1985 in Normandy, France
Source: *AnObit 1991; BiDAmM;
BiDFilm, 81, 94; BioIn 5, 9, 11, 13;
CelR, 90; ConMus 12; ConTFT 6, 10;
CurBio 60, 85, 88, 92N; DcArts;
DcTwCCu 2; EncEurC; FacFETw;
FilmAG WE; FilmEn; FilmgC; ForYSC;
HalFC 80, 84, 88; IntDcF 1-3, 2-3;
IntMPA 77, 80, 82, 84, 86, 88, 92;
IntWW 74, 75, 76, 77, 78, 79, 80, 81, 82,
83, 89, 91; ItaFilm; LegTOT; MotPP;
MovMk; News 92, 92-2; NewYTBS 91;
OxCFilm; OxCPMus; WhAm 10; Who
82; WhoAm 74, 82; WhoFr 79; WhoHol
92, A; WhoWor 74, 76, 78, 84, 87, 89,
91; WorAl; WorAlBi; WorEFlm*

Signorile, Michelangelo
American. Journalist
Known for denouncing closeted gays
who he felt most harmed the gay
community; wrote *Outing Yourself*,
1995.
b. 1960
Source: *GayLesB*

Sigourney, Lydia Howard
"The Mrs. Hemans of America"
American. Poet
Wrote over 60 volumes of sentimental,
sad verse: *Poems, Religious and
Elegiac*, 1841.
b. Sep 1, 1791 in Norwich, Connecticut
d. Jun 10, 1865 in Hartford, Connecticut
Source: *AmBi; AmWom; ApCAB; BioIn
3, 4, 7, 9, 11, 12, 13, 15, 19, 23;
CelCen; DcAmB; DcLB 1, 183; Drake;
FemiCLE; NatCAB 1; NotAW; TwCBDA;
WebAB 74; WhAm HS*

Sihanouk, Norodom
[Samdech Preah Norodom Sihanouk
(Varman)]
Cambodian. Ruler
Ruled Cambodia, 1941-55, 1960-70,
1975-76, 1993—; gained
independence from French rule, 1953.
b. Oct 31, 1922 in Pnom Penh,
Cambodia
Source: *CamBiEn; ChamBiD; ColdWar
2; ConAu 106, 129; CurBio 54, 93;
DcMPSA; DcTwHis; EncVieW; EncWB
98; EncyDCo; FacFETw; FarE&A 78,
79, 80, 81; IntWW 74, 75, 76, 77, 78,
79, 80, 81, 82, 83, 89, 91, 93;
McGEWB; NewYTBS 79, 93; WhoAsAP
91; WhoIntA 2; WhoWor 74, 82, 84, 87,
89, 91, 93, 95, 96, 98, 99, 2000;
WorAlBi*

Sikelianos, Angelos
Greek. Poet
Significant 20th c. Greek lyrical poet.
b. Mar 28, 1884 in Leucas Island,
Greece
d. Jun 19, 1951 in Athens, Greece
Source: *BioIn 1, 2, 10, 13; CasWL;
ClDMEL 80; EncWL 2, 2S, 3; GrFLW;
PenC EUR; RAdv 14; TwCLC 39;
WorAu 1950*

Sikking, James B
American. Actor
Played Lt. Howard Hunter on TV series
"Hill Street Blues," 1981-87.
b. Mar 5, 1934 in Los Angeles,
California
Source: *ConTFT 6, 25; IntMPA 92;
VarWW 85; WhoTelC*

Sikorsky, Igor Ivanovich
American. Aeronautical Engineer
Developed first successful helicopter,
1939.
b. May 25, 1889 in Kiev, Russia
d. Oct 26, 1972 in Easton, Connecticut
Source: *AmAu&B; AmMWSc 73P;
AmNatBi; CurBio 40, 56, 72; DcAmB
S9; FacFETw; McGMS 80; NewYTBE
72; WebAB 74; WhAm 5; WhDW; WorAl*

Silas, Paul Theron
American. Basketball Player, Basketball
Coach
Forward, 1964-80, with six NBA teams;
won three NBA championships; coach,
San Diego, 1980-83.
b. Jul 12, 1943 in Prescott, Arizona

Source: *BiDAmSp BK; OfNBA 81, 87;*
WhoAfA 9, 10, 11, 12; WhoBbl 73;
WhoBlA 4, 7, 8

Silber, John Robert
American. University Administrator
Pres. of Boston University, 1971-96;
   chancellor, Boston U, 1996—.
b. Aug 15, 1926 in San Antonio, Texas
Source: *BiDMoAE; BioIn 9, 10, 11, 12,*
13, 16; DrAS 82P, 99P; IntWW 91, 97,
98, 2000; News 90-1; NewYTBS 89;
WhoAm 90, 97, 98, 99, 2000; WhoE 91,
97, 99; WhoWor 84, 99; WrDr 92, 98,
99, 2000

Siles Zuazo, Hernan
Bolivian. Political Leader
Leader of revolution, 1952; pres., 1956-
   60, 1982-85.
b. Mar 19, 1914 in La Paz, Bolivia
d. Aug 6, 1996 in Montevideo, Uruguay
Source: *BioIn 5, 6, 13, 16, 22; CurBio*
58, 85, 96N; DcCPSAm; EncLatA;
EncWB 74; IntWW 74, 75, 76, 77, 78,
79, 80, 81, 82, 83, 89, 91, 93; LatAmLi;
NewYTBS 82; WhAm 12; WhoWor 74,
84, 87, 89, 91

Silhouette, Etienne de
French. Social Reformer
Controller of finance, 1759, scorned by
   nobility for savings reforms; name
   used for anything plain or cheap;
   ''silhouette'' applied to profile
   outlines, the poor man's miniature.
b. Jul 5, 1709
d. 1767
Source: *AntBDN O; Benet 87, 96;*
CambiEn; DcBiPP; REn; WebBD 83;
WorAl; WorAlBi

Silk, Dave
[David Silk]
American. Hockey Player
Center in NHL, 1980-86; member US
   Olympic gold medal-winning team,
   1980.
b. Jan 1, 1958 in Boston, Massachusetts
Source: *BioIn 13; HocEn; HocReg 86;*
NewYTBS 82

Silk, George
American. Photographer, Journalist
Staff photographer, *Life* magazine, 1943-
   72; best known for sports, war
   pictures.
b. Nov 17, 1916 in Levin, New Zealand
Source: *BioIn 4; ConPhot 82, 88;*
EncTwCJ; ICPEnP A; MacBEP; WhoAm
74, 76, 78, 80, 82, 84, 86, 88, 90, 92,
94, 95, 96, 97, 98, 99

Silkin, Jon
English. Poet
Books of verse include *The Lapidary*
   Poems, 1979.
b. Dec 2, 1930 in London, England
Source: *Au&Wr 71; BiCoLiE; BioIn 7,*
10, 12, 14, 16; CamGLE; ChhPo, S3;
CnE&AP; ConAu 5AS, 5R; ConLC 2, 6,
43; ConPo 70, 75, 80, 85, 91, 96; DcLB

27, 29; DcLEL 1940; EngPo; IntAu&W
77, 86, 89, 91, 93; IntvTCA 2; IntWW
76, 77, 78, 79, 80, 81, 82, 83, 89, 91,
93, 97; IntWWP 77; LinLib L; ModBrL,
2, S1, S2; NewC; OxCEng 85, 95;
OxCTwCL; OxCTwCP; RGFMBP;
RGTwCWr; WhAm 12; Who 74, 82, 83,
85, 88, 90, 92, 94, 98; WhoEnt 98;
WhoWor 82, 84, 87, 89, 91, 93, 95, 96,
97, 98; WorAu 1950; WrDr 76, 80, 82,
84, 86, 88, 90, 92, 94, 96, 98, 99, 2000

Silko, Leslie Marmon
American. Author
Writes novels with Native American
   themes; wrote *Ceremony*, 1977; *The*
   Almanac of the Dead, 1992.
b. Mar 5, 1948 in Albuquerque, New
   Mexico
Source: *AmIndBi; AmNatWr;*
AmWomWr, 92; AmWr S4; Au&Arts 14;
AZNatAW; Benet 96; BenetAL 91; BioIn
12, 13; BlmGWL; CamGLE; CamHAL;
ConAu 45NR, 65NR, 115, 122; ConLC
23, 74, 114; ConNov 86, 91, 96; ConPo
91, 96; ConPopW; ConWomP 98; CyWA
89, 97; DcLB 143, 175; DcNAL; DrAPF
80; EncALit; EncApL; EncFoLi;
EncNAB; EncWL 3; GrWomW; IdentIs;
InWom SUP; MagSAmL; MajTwCW 2;
ModAL 4S3, 5; ModWoWr; NatAL;
NatNAL; NewEAmW; NotNaAm;
OxCAmL 95; OxCTwCL; OxCWoWr 95;
RAdv 14; RfGAmL 4, 94; RfGShF 1, 2;
TwCWW 82, 91; WorAu 1985; WorLitC
SUP; WrDr 94, 96

Silkwood, Karen
American. Nuclear Technician
Exposed to radiation on job; active to
   improve safety; played by Meryl
   Streep in movie *Silkwood*, 1983.
b. Feb 19, 1946
d. Nov 13, 1974 in Oklahoma City,
   Oklahoma
Source: *BioIn 10, 11, 14, 16, 24;*
ConHero 1; EncWB 98; FacFETw;
LegTOT; NewYTBS 79

Sill, Edward Rowland
American. Poet, Educator
Best known for *The Hermitage and*
   Other Poems, 1868.
b. Apr 29, 1841 in Windsor, Connecticut
d. Feb 27, 1887 in Cleveland, Ohio
Source: *Alli, SUP; AmAu; AmAu&B;*
AmBi; AmNatBi; ApCAB; BenetAL 91;
BibAL; BiDAmEd; BiDAmM; BiD&SB;
BioIn 4, 13, 22; Chambr 3; ChhPo, S1,
S2; CmCal; CnDAL; CyEd; DcAmAu;
DcAmB; DcLEL; DcNAA; LinLib L;
NatCAB 7; OhA&B; OxCAmL 65, 83,
95; REn; REnAL; TwCBDA; WhAm HS

Sillanpaa, Frans E
Finnish. Author
Wrote novel *The Maid Silja*, 1931; won
   1939 Nobel Prize in literature.
b. Sep 16, 1888 in Hameenkyro, Finland
d. Jun 3, 1964 in Helsinki, Finland
Source: *CasWL; ConAu 93; CurBio 40,*
64; EncWL 1; EvEuW; Novels; PenC

EUR; REn; TwCA SUP; TwCWr; WhAm
4; WhoNob; WorAl

Silliman, Benjamin
American. Educator, Chemist, Geologist
Yale U professor; founded *American*
   Journal of Science, 1818.
b. Aug 8, 1779 in Trumbull, Connecticut
d. Nov 24, 1864 in New Haven,
   Connecticut
Source: *Alli; AmAu; AmBi; AmNatBi;*
ApCAB; AsBiEn; BbD; BbtC; BenetAL
91; BiDAmEd; BiDAmS; BiESc;
BiInAmS; BioIn 1, 2, 5, 7, 8, 9, 17, 23;
CamDcAB; ChamBiD; CyAL 1; CyEd;
DcAmAu; DcAmB; DcAmMeB, 84;
DcBiPP; DcLB 183; DcNAA; DcScB;
Drake; EncAB-H 1974, 1996; EncWB
98; HarEnUS; InSci; McGEWB; NatCAB
2; OxCAmH; OxCCan; PeoHis; REnAL;
TwCBDA; WebAB 74, 79; WhAm HS

Silliphant, Stirling Dale
American. Screenwriter, Producer
Won Oscar, Edgar for writing *In the*
   Heat of the Night, 1968.
b. Jan 16, 1918 in Detroit, Michigan
d. Apr 26, 1996 in Bangkok, Thailand
Source: *BioIn 14; CmMov; ConAu 14NR,*
42NR, 73, 152; ConTFT 3; DcLB 26;
HalFC 84, 88; IntMPA 86, 92; LesBEnT,
92; WhAm 11; WhoAm 76, 78, 80, 82,
84, 86, 88, 90, 92, 94, 95, 96; WhoEnt
92

Sillitoe, Alan
English. Author
Novels, short stories adapted to film:
   Saturday Night and Sunday Morning,
   1958.
b. Mar 4, 1928 in Nottingham, England
Source: *Au&Wr 71; AuNews 1; Benet*
87, 96; BiCoLiE; BioIn 6, 8, 9, 10, 13,
15, 16; BlmGEL; BlueB 76; BritWr S5;
CamBiEn; CamGLE; ChamBiD;
CnDBLB 8; ConAu 2AS, 8NR, 9R, 26NR,
55NR; ConLC 1, 3, 6, 10, 19, 57;
ConNov 72, 76, 82, 86, 91, 96; ConPo
70, 75, 80, 85, 91; CyWA 89, 97;
DcArts; DcLB 14, 139; DcLEL 1940;
EncSF, 93; EncWL 1, 2, 2S, 3;
FacFETw; GrWrEL N; HalFC 80, 84,
88; IntAu&W 76, 77, 91, 93; IntvTCA 2;
IntWW 74, 75, 76, 77, 78, 79, 80, 81, 82,
83, 89, 91, 93, 97, 98, 2000; IntWWP
77; LegTOT; LngCEL; LngCTC;
MajTwCW 1, 2; ModBrL, 2, S1, S2;
NewC; Novels; OxCEng 85, 95;
OxCTwCL; PenC ENG; RAdv 1, 14, 13-
1; REn; RfGEnL 91; RfGShF 1, 2;
RGTwCWr; ScF&FL 1, 2; ScFSB;
SmATA 61; TwCSFW 81; TwCWr;
WebE&AL; Who 74, 82, 83, 85, 88, 90,
92, 94, 98, 99, 2000; WhoEnt 98;
WhoTwCL; WhoWor 74, 76, 78, 80, 82,
84, 87, 89, 91, 93, 95, 96, 97, 98, 99,
2000; WorAl; WorAlBi; WorAu 1950;
WrDr 76, 80, 82, 84, 86, 88, 90, 92, 94,
96, 98, 99, 2000

Sillman, Leonard

American. Producer, Actor, Author
Wrote film *New Faces*, 1954; produced
    An Angel Comes to Brooklyn, 1945.
b. May 9, 1908 in Detroit, Michigan
d. Jan 23, 1982 in New York, New York
Source: *BiE&WWA; BioIn 5, 10, 12, 24;
ConAu 105; EncMT; NewYTBS 82;
NotNAT, A; WhoThe 72, 77, 81*

Sills, Beverly

[Mrs. Peter B Greenough; Belle
    Silverman]
"Bubbles"
American. Opera Singer
Coloratura soprano, made operatic debut,
    1947; director, NYC Opera, 1979-88;
    won two Emmys, Medal of Freedom,
    1980.
b. May 25, 1929 in New York, New
    York
Source: *BakBD 78, 84, 92; BakBDTw;
BakDcM; BiDAmM; BioIn 8, 9, 10, 11,
12, 13, 14, 15; BlueB 76; BriBkM 80;
CamDcAB; CelR, 90; ChamBiD; CmOp;
ConAu 89; ConHero 3; ConMus 5;
ContDcW 89; ConTFT 22; CurBio 69,
82; DcArts; DcPseud; DcTwCCu 1;
EncWB, 98; FacFETw; GoodHs;
GrLiveH; HerW 84; IntDcOp; IntDcWB;
IntWW 74, 75, 76, 77, 78, 79, 80, 81, 82,
83, 89, 91, 93, 97, 98, 2000; IntWWM
77, 80, 90; IntWWW 2; InWom SUP;
LegTOT; LibW; MetOEnc; MusMk;
MusSN; NewAmDM; NewEOp 71;
NewGrDA 86; NewGrDM 80;
NewGrDO; NewYTBE 71; NewYTBS 75,
76, 79, 87, 88; OxDcOp; PenDiMP;
RAdv 14; Who 74, 82, 83, 85, 88, 90,
92, 94, 98, 99, 2000; WhoAm 74, 76, 78,
80, 82, 84, 86, 88, 90, 92, 94, 95, 96,
99, 2000; WhoAmJ 80; WhoAmM 83;
WhoAmW 75, 77, 79, 81, 83, 85, 87, 89,
91, 93, 95, 97, 99; WhoE 74, 75, 77, 79,
81, 85, 86, 89, 91; WhoEnt 92, 98;
WhoGov 72, 75, 77; WhoOp 76;
WhoWor 74, 76, 78, 80, 82, 84, 87, 89,
91, 93, 95, 96; WhoWorJ 78; WomFir;
WorAl; WorAlBi*

Sills, Milton

American. Actor
Leading man in over 75 films, 1914-30.
b. Jan 10, 1882 in Chicago, Illinois
d. Sep 15, 1930 in Santa Barbara,
    California
Source: *AmNatBi; BioIn 9, 17; DcAmB;
DcNAA; Film 1, 2; FilmEn; FilmgC;
ForYSC; FrSilen; HalFC 80, 84, 88;
MovMk; NotNAT B; SilFlmP; TwYS;
WhAm 1; WhoHol B; WhScrn 74, 77, 83*

Silone, Ignazio

[Secondo Tranquilli]
Italian. Author
Founding member, Italian Communist
    Party, 1921; wrote *Bread and Wine*,
    1936.
b. May 1, 1900 in Pescina, Italy
d. Aug 22, 1978 in Geneva, Switzerland
Source: *Benet 87, 96; BiDMoPL; BioIn
1, 2, 3, 4, 5, 6, 7, 8, 10, 11, 12, 14, 15,
17; CamBiEn; CasWL; ClDMEL 47, 80;
CnMD; CnMWL; ConAu 34NR, 81, P-2;*

*ConLC 4; CyWA 58, 97; DcArts; DcItL
1, 2; DcPseud; EncWB 98; EncWL 1, 2,
2S, 3; EuWr 12; EvEuW; FacFETw;
GrFLW; IntAu&W 76; IntWW 74, 75,
76, 77, 78; LegTOT; LiExTwC; LinLib L,
S; LngCTC; MajTwCW 1; MakMC;
McGEWB; ModRL; NewYTBS 78;
Novels; OxCEng 85, 95; PenC EUR;
RAdv 14, 13-2; REn; RfGShF 2;
RfGWoL 95; TwCA, SUP; TwCWr; Who
74; WhoTwCL; WhoWor 74*

Silver, Abba Hillel

American. Religious Leader
Zionist leader, early advocate of the state
    of Israel.
b. Jan 28, 1893 in Sirvintos, Lithuania
d. Nov 28, 1963 in Cleveland, Ohio
Source: *AmAu&B; AmNatBi; BioIn 3, 6,
7, 8, 10, 16, 19; CamDcAB; ConAu 1R;
CurBio 41, 63, 64; DcAmB S7;
DcAmReB 2; EncAB-A 37; EncWB 98;
JeAmHC; McGEWB; NatCAB 50;
OhA&B; OxCAmH; RelLAm 1, 2; WhAm
4*

Silver, Franelle

Canadian. Writer
Won Emmy for "The Carol Burnett
    Show," 1978.
b. Sep 12, 1952 in Toronto, Ontario,
    Canada
Source: *VarWW 85; WhoEnt 92*

Silver, Horace Ward Martin Tavares

American. Jazz Musician
Outstanding pianist, accompanist; noted
    for "funky" style popular in late
    1950s.
b. Sep 28, 1928 in Norwalk, Connecticut
Source: *ASCAP 66; BakBD 84, 92;
BiDAfM; BiDAmM; BiDJaz; BioIn 13,
16; CamDcAB; CmpEPM; EncJzS;
IlEncJ; InB&W 80, 85; NewAmDM;
NewGrDA 86; NewGrDJ 88, 94;
NewGrDM 80; OxCPMus; PenEncP;
WhoAm 74, 76, 78, 80, 82, 84, 86, 88,
90, 92, 94, 95, 96, 97; WhoBlA 1, 2, 3,
4, 5, 6, 7; WhoE 74; WhoEnt 98; WorAl;
WorAlBi*

Silver, Ron

American. Actor
Won best actor Tony for *Speed-the-Plow*,
    1988; films include *Silkwood*, 1983.
b. Jul 2, 1946 in New York, New York
Source: *BioIn 15, 16, 17, 19; CelR 90;
ConTFT 1, 4, 11; DcPseud; IntMPA 86,
88, 92, 94, 96; LegTOT; WhoAm 90, 92,
94, 95, 96, 97, 99, 2000; WhoEnt 92, 98;
WhoHol 92*

Silvera, Frank

American. Actor
Character actor, 1952-70; appeared in
    TV series "High Chaparral," 1967-70.
b. Jul 24, 1914 in Kingston, Jamaica
d. Jun 11, 1970 in Pasadena, California
Source: *BiE&WWA; BiHaHis; BioIn 6,
8; BlkAWP; BlksAmF; DrBlPA, 90;
EarBlAP; FilmEn; FilmgC; ForYSC;
HalFC 80, 84, 88; MovMk; NewYTBE*

*70; NotNAT B; WhAm 5; WhoHol B;
WhScrn 74, 77, 83*

Silverberg, Robert

American. Author
Science fiction books include *Lord
    Valentine's Castle*, 1980.
b. Jan 15, 1935 in New York, New York
Source: *AmAu&B; Au&Arts 24; AuBYP
2, 3; BeaEPF; BenetAL 91; BioIn 12,
13, 15; ChlLR 59; ConAu 1NR, 1R, 3AS,
20NR, 36NR, 85NR; ConLC 7; ConNov
96; ConPopW; DcLB 8; DcLP 87A;
EncSF 93; IntAu&W 82, 91, 93; IntvTCA
2; LegTOT; MajAI; MajTwCW 1, 2;
NewEScF; OxCTwCL; RGTwCSF;
ScF&FL 1, 2, 92; ScFWr, 2; SmATA 13,
91, 104; ThrBJA; TwCSFW 81, 86, 91;
WhoAm 86, 90, 92, 94, 95, 96, 97, 98,
99, 2000; WhoEnt 98; WhoUSWr 88;
WhoWest 92, 94; WhoWrEP 89; WorAl;
WorAlBi; WrDr 84, 86, 88, 90, 92, 94,
96, 98, 99, 2000*

Silverheels, Jay

[Harold J. Smith]
American. Actor
Played Tonto in *Lone Ranger* movies
    and TV series, 1948-61.
b. May 26, 1919 in Six Nations Indian
    Reserva Ontario, Canada
d. Mar 5, 1980 in Woodland Hills,
    California
Source: *AmIndBi; AmNatBi; AnObit
1980; DcAmB S10; DcPseud; FilmEn;
FilmgC; HalFC 84, 88; LegTOT;
WhoHol A*

Silverman, Fred

American. TV Executive
Only man to run all three TV networks'
    entertainment divisions; CBS, 1963-
    75; ABC, 1975-78; NBC, 1978-81.
b. Sep 13, 1937 in New York, New
    York
Source: *BioIn 10, 11, 12, 13, 16;
ConTFT 7; CurBio 78; EncTwCJ;
IntMPA 76, 77, 78, 79, 80, 81, 82, 84,
86, 88, 92, 94, 96; IntWW 83, 89, 91,
93, 97, 98, 2000; LegTOT; LesBEnT, 92;
NewYTBS 78, 89; NewYTET; WhoAm 78,
80, 82, 84, 94, 95, 96, 97, 98; WhoE 79,
81; WhoEnt 92, 98; WhoFI 79, 81;
WhoTelC; WhoWor 82; WhsWeAm 98*

Silverman, Jonathan

American. Actor
Stage, screen, and television actor known
    for his wholesome, if mischievous,
    roles; creator and star of television
    comedy "The Single Guy," 1995—.
b. Aug 5, 1966 in Los Angeles,
    California
Source: *ConTFT 13, 25; IntMPA 94, 96;
News 97, 97-2; WhoAm 92, 94, 95, 96,
97, 99, 2000; WhoEnt 98; WhoHol 92*

Silverman, Sime

American. Publisher
Founder, editor of show business
    newspaper, *Variety*, 1905-33.
b. May 18, 1873 in Cortland, New York

d. Sep 22, 1933 in Los Angeles,
California
Source: *AmAu&B; CamDcAB; DcAmB;
EncAJ; EncVaud; LegTOT; NatCAB 24;
NotNAT A; OxCAmT 84; WebAB 74, 79;
WhAm 4, HSA*

Silvers, Phil
[Philip Silversmith]
American. Comedian
Won three Emmys for playing Sergeant
Bilko in TV series "The Phil Silvers"
Show, 1955-59; films include *A Funny
Thing Happened on the Way to the
Forum*, 1966.
b. May 11, 1911 in New York, New
York
d. Nov 1, 1985 in Los Angeles,
California
Source: *AmNatBi; AnObit 1985; ASCAP
66; BiE&WWA; CmMov; CmpEPM;
ConNews 85-4; CurBio 57, 86; EncMT;
Ent; FilmgC; ForYSC; Funs; IntMPA
81; LegTOT; MotPP; MovMk; NewYTBE
70; NotNAT, A; OxCAmT 84; QDrFCA
92; ScrEAmL 1; WhoAm 82; WhoHol A;
WhoThe 77, 81*

Silverstein, Alvin
[Dr. A]
American. Children's Author
Scientific, juvenile books include *Human
Anatomy & Physiology*, 1980.
b. Dec 30, 1933 in New York, New
York
Source: *AuBYP 2S, 3; BioIn 11; ChlLR
25; ConAu 2NR, 49; ConLC 17; FifBJA;
IntAu&W 76, 77, 82; MajAI; SmATA 8,
69; WhoE 91, 93*

Silverstein, Elliot
American. Director
Films include *Cat Ballou*, 1965; *A Man
Called Horse*, 1970.
b. Aug 3, 1927 in Boston, Massachusetts
Source: *BioIn 7; FilmEn; HalFC 84, 88;
IntMPA 86, 88, 92, 94, 96; MiSFD 9;
WorEFlm*

Silverstein, Shel(by)
American. Cartoonist, Author
Self-illustrated best-sellers include *Where
the Sidewalk Ends*, 1974; *A Light in
the Attic*, 1981.
b. Sep 25, 1932 in Chicago, Illinois
d. May 9, 1999 in Key West, Florida
Source: *BioIn 10, 11, 12, 13, 15, 16;
BlkWr 3; CamDcAB; ChlBkCr; ChlLR 5;
ConAu 47NR, 74NR, 81NR, 107, 179;
EncFCWM 83; FifBJA; HarEnCM 87;
IntAu&W 91, 93; LegTOT; MajAI;
MajTwCW 2; NewYTBS 81; PenEncP;
RAdv 14; SJGChWr 5; SmATA 27, 33,
92; TwCChW 2, 3, 4; WhoAm 74, 76,
78, 80, 82, 84, 86, 88, 90, 92, 94, 95,
96, 97, 98, 99; WhoUSWr 88; WhoWrEP
89, 92, 95; WrDr 86, 88, 90, 92, 94, 96,
98, 99, 2000*

Silverstone, Alicia
American. Actor
Filed for emancipation from her parents
at 15 so she could work in films as an

adult; appeared in several MTV
videos.
b. Oct 4, 1976 in San Francisco,
California
Source: *ConTFT 16, 27; IntWW 2000;
News 97; WhoAm 98, 99, 2000;
WhoAmW 99; WhoEnt 98*

Silvia
Swedish. Consort
Commoner who married King Carl
Gustaf of Sweden, 1976.
b. Dec 23, 1943 in Heidelberg, Germany
Source: *BioIn 10, 11; CamBiEn;
ChamBiD; NewYTBS 81; WhoWor 82,
87, 89, 91, 93, 95*

Sim, Alastair
English. Producer, Director
Films include *The Lavender Hill Mob*,
1951; starred in *A Christmas Carol*,
1951.
b. Oct 9, 1900 in Edinburgh, Scotland
d. Aug 19, 1976 in London, England
Source: *BioIn 11, 13, 16; CamBiEn;
ChamBiD; CmMov; EncEurC; FilmAG
WE; FilmEn; FilmgC; ForYSC; HalFC
80, 84, 88; IlWWBF; IntDcF 1-3, 2-3;
IntMPA 75, 76; MotPP; MovMk;
NewYTBS 76; OxCThe 83; QDrFCA 92;
WhAm 7; Who 74; WhoHol A; WhoThe
72, 77; WhoWor 74; WhScrn 83*

Simak, Clifford Donald
American. Author
Wrote highly acclaimed science fiction,
fantasy novels; won three Hugos; first
in Fandom Hall of Fame, 1973; Grand
Master, 1979.
b. Aug 3, 1904 in Millville, Wisconsin
d. Apr 25, 1988 in Minneapolis,
Minnesota
Source: *BioIn 6, 7, 10, 12; CamBiEn;
ChamBiD; ConAu 1NR, 1R; ConLC 1;
DcLB 8; DcLEL 1940; IntAu&W 77;
OxCTwCL; TwCSFW 86; WhoAm 84;
WorAu 1950; WrDr 86*

Simcoe, John Graves
English. Government Official
First lt. governor of Upper Canada,
1792-74; established capital at York
(now Toronto), 1793.
b. Feb 25, 1752 in Cotterstock, England
d. Oct 26, 1806 in Exeter, England
Source: *AmBi; AmRev; ApCAB; BioIn 8,
13; DcCanB 5; DcNaB; Drake; EncAR;
HarEnMi; HarEnUS; MacDCB 78;
NewC; NewCBEL; OxCCan; WebBD 83;
WhAmRev*

Simenon, Georges
[Georges Sim]
Belgian. Author
Wrote over 500 books; created Chief
Inspector Maigret, the Parisian
detective featured in over 80
mysteries.
b. Feb 13, 1903 in Liege, Belgium
d. Sep 4, 1989 in Lausanne, Switzerland
Source: *AnObit 1989; Au&Wr 71;
BeaEPF; Benet 87, 96; BiCoLiE; BioIn
2, 3, 4, 5, 7, 8, 9, 10, 12, 13, 14, 15, 16,*

*17, 18, 19, 20, 22, 23, 24; CasWL;
CIDMEL 80; CnMWL; ConAu 35NR, 85,
129; ConFLW 84; ConLC 1, 2, 3, 8, 18,
47; CorpD; CrtSuMy; CurBio 70, 89N;
CyWA 89, 97; DcArts; DcLB 72, Y89N;
DcTwCCu 2; EncEurC; EncMys; EncWB
98; EncWL 1, 2, 2S; EuWr 12; EvEuW;
FacFETw; FilmgC; GuFrLit 1; HalFC
80, 84, 88; IntAu&W 76, 77, 82, 86, 89,
91; IntWW 74, 75, 76, 77, 78, 79, 80,
81, 82, 83, 89; LegTOT; LinLib L;
LngCTC; MajTwCW 1; McGEWB;
ModFrL; ModRL; MysSW; NewYTBS 84,
89; Novels; OxCEng 67, 85, 95; OxCFr;
PenC EUR; RAdv 13-2; REn; REnAL;
TwCA, SUP; TwCCr&M 80B, 85B, 91,
91B; TwCWr; WhAm 10; WhDW;
WhE&EA; Who 74, 82, 83, 85, 88, 90N;
WhoFr 79; WhoTwCL; WhoWor 78, 82,
84, 87, 89; WorAlBi; WorAu 1900*

Simeon
[Symeon]
"The New Theologian"
Byzantine. Biblical Figure
Monk who preached mysticism; forced to
resign, 1009; wrote hymns, sermons.
b. 949?
d. 1022?
Source: *Alli; NewCol 75; WebBD 83*

Simeone, Harry
American. Composer
Arranger for Fred Waring; co-wrote
"The Little Drummer Boy," 1958.
b. May 9, 1911 in Newark, New Jersey
Source: *ASCAP 66, 80; ConAmC 76, 82;
RkOn 82*

Simeon Stylites, Saint
[Simeon the Elder]
Syrian. Religious Leader
First most famed stylite "Pillar
Dweller;" spent 35 yrs. on top of 50-
ft. high pillar.
b. 390?
d. 459?
Source: *BioIn 1, 2, 3, 4, 5, 6, 7, 8, 11,
12; DcBiPP; DcCathB; LuthC 75;
NewCol 75; WebBD 83; WhoChr*

Simic, Charles
American. Poet
Wrote award-winning verse, *Return to a
Place Lit by a Glass of Milk*, 1975.
b. May 9, 1938 in Belgrade, Yugoslavia
Source: *Benet 87, 96; BenetAL 91; BioIn
9, 10, 13, 14, 15, 17, 18, 21, 22, 24;
CamDcAB; ConAu 4AS, 12NR, 29R,
33NR, 52NR, 61NR; ConLC 6, 9, 22, 49,
68; ConPo 75, 80, 85, 91, 96; CyWA 97;
DcLB 105; DrAP 75; DrAPF 80, 91;
EncALit; Focus; IntvTCA 2; IntWW 91,
93, 97, 98, 2000; LegTOT; MajTwCW 2;
ModAL 5; OxCAmL 95; OxCTwCL;
OxCTwCP; RAdv 14, 13-1; RfGAmL 4;
WhoAm 78, 80, 82, 84, 86, 88, 90, 92,
94, 95, 96, 97, 98, 99, 2000; WhoE 91,
93, 95, 97, 99; WhoPul; WhoUSWr 88;
WhoWrEP 89, 92, 95; WhsWeAm 98;
WorAu 1970; WrDr 76, 80, 82, 84, 86,
88, 90, 92, 94, 96, 98, 99, 2000*

Simionato, Guilietta
Italian. Opera Singer
La Scala's leading contralto, 1939-59;
    with NY Met., 1959-65.
b. May 12, 1916 in Forli, Italy
Source: *BakBD 84; BioIn 11, 13, 14;
CurBio 60; IntWWM 90; InWom SUP;
MetOEnc; MusSN; NewAmDM; NewEOp
71; NewGrDM 80; PenDiMP; WhoEnt
92*

Simionescu, Mariana
Romanian. Tennis Player
Former wife of Bjorn Borg.
b. Nov 21, 1956 in Tirgu Neamt,
    Romania
Source: *BioIn 12, 13; WhoIntT*

Simitis, Costas
Greek. Political Leader
Known for his moderate style, the leader
    of the reformist wing of the
    Panhellenic Socialist Movement
    (PASOK) succeeded Andreas
    Papandreou as prime minister of
    Greece in 1996, then implemented a
    policy of reform.
b. Jan 26, 1936 in Athens, Greece

Simmel, Georg
German. Sociologist, Philosopher
Principal translated works include *The
    Sociology of Georg Simmel*, 1950.
b. Mar 1, 1858 in Berlin, Germany
d. Sep 26, 1918 in Strassburg, Germany
Source: *BioIn 4, 5, 7, 11, 12, 14, 22;
CamBiEn; ChamBiD; ConAu 157;
DcSoc; EncWB 98; GloEncH; MakMC;
McGEWB; NewCol 75; RAdv 14, 13-3;
ThTwC 87; TwCA SUP; TwCLC 64;
WorAu 1900*

Simmer, Charlie
[Charles Robert Simmer]
"Chaz"
Canadian. Hockey Player
Left wing, LA, 1977-84, Boston, 1984-
    87; first left wing in NHL history to
    score 100 pts. in two consecutive
    seasons (1979-81).
b. Mar 20, 1954 in Terrace Bay, Ontario,
    Canada
Source: *HocEn; HocReg 87*

Simmonds, Kennedy Alphonse
Kittsian. Political Leader
Leader of the People's Action Movement
    (PAM) became the premier of a
    coalition government in 1980, then
    was the first prime minister of St.
    Kitts-Nevis after independence in
    1983; he encouraged development
    through foreign investment.
b. Apr 12, 1936 in Basseterre, St. Kitts
    and Nevis
Source: *BiDLAmC; BioIn 16; CamBiEn;
ChamBiD; IntWW 89, 91, 93, 97, 98,
2000; Who 88, 90, 92, 94, 98, 99, 2000;
WhoWor 87, 89, 91, 93, 95, 96, 97, 98*

Simmons, Adele Smith
American. Philanthropist, Educator
Pres. of John D. and Catherine T.
    MacArthur Foundation, 1989—, the
    US's fourth largest private foundation.
b. Jun 21, 1941 in Lake Forest, Illinois
Source: *BioIn 11, 17; CurBio 91; IntWW
89, 91, 93, 97, 98; IntWWW 2; News 88;
WhoAm 80, 82, 86, 88, 90, 92, 94, 95,
96, 97; WhoAmW 87, 89, 91, 93, 95, 97;
WhoE 79, 81, 83, 86, 89; WhoEmL 87*

Simmons, Al(oysius Harry)
"Bucketfoot Al"
American. Baseball Player
Outfielder, 1924-41, 1943-44, mostly
    with Philadelphia; led AL in RBIs
    once, in batting twice; had .334
    lifetime batting average; Hall of Fame,
    1953.
b. May 22, 1903 in Milwaukee,
    Wisconsin
d. May 26, 1956 in Milwaukee,
    Wisconsin
Source: *BioIn 2, 3, 4, 5, 6, 7, 9, 10;
DcAmB S6; WhoPolA; WhoProB 73;
WhoSpor*

Simmons, Althea T. L
American. Lawyer, Civil Rights Leader
Worked her way through the ranks of the
    NAACP to become director of
    Washington office and chief lobbyist.
b. Apr 17, 1924 in Shreveport, Louisiana
d. Sep 13, 1990 in Washington, District
    of Columbia
Source: *BioIn 15; InB&W 80, 85;
NewYTBS 87, 90; NotBlAW 1; WhoBlA
2, 3, 4, 5, 7N*

Simmons, Calvin
"Maestro Kid"
American. Conductor
Led Oakland Symphony from 1979.
b. Apr 27, 1950 in San Francisco,
    California
d. Aug 21, 1982 in Connery Pond, New
    York
Source: *AnObit 1982; BakBD 84;
BiDAfM; BioIn 11, 12, 13, 21; BlkCond;
BlkOpe; DrBlPA 90; InB&W 80;
IntWWM 77, 80; NewAmDM; NewGrDA
86; NewYTBS 82; PenDiMP; WhoBlA 2,
3; WhoWest 80, 82*

Simmons, Franklin
American. Sculptor
Marble, bronze portraits, monuments
    include General Grant in the capitol
    rotunda, 1900.
b. Jan 11, 1839 in Webster, Maine
d. Dec 8, 1913 in Rome, Italy
Source: *AmBi; AmNatBi; ApCAB; BioIn
14; BriEAA; DcAmB; HarEnUS;
NatCAB 11; NewYHSD; TwCBDA;
WhAm 1; WhAmArt 85*

Simmons, Gene
[Kiss; Gene Klein]
American. Singer, Musician
Co-founded Kiss, 1972; dressed as fire-
    breathing, blood-spewing ghoul;
    invented Axe bass guitar, 1980.

b. Aug 25, 1949 in Haifa, Israel
Source: *BioIn 11, 12, 22, 24; ConTFT 8;
DcPseud; LegTOT; RkOn 85; WhoAm
82, 84, 86, 88, 90, 92, 94, 95, 96, 97,
98; WhoEnt 92; WhoHol 92; WhoRocM
82*

Simmons, Jean
English. Actor
Appeared in British, US films including
    Big Country, 1958; TV movies include
    "Thornbirds," 1983.
b. Jan 31, 1929 in London, England
Source: *BiDFilm, 81, 94; BioIn 1, 2, 3,
4, 5, 7, 10, 11, 16; BioNews 74;
CamBiEn; CelR, 90; CmMov; ConTFT
3, 4, 20; CurBio 52; DcArts; EncEurC;
FilmAG WE; FilmEn; FilmgC; ForYSC;
HalFC 80, 84, 88; IlWWBF; IntDcF 1-3,
2-3; IntMPA 75, 76, 77, 78, 79, 80, 81,
82, 84, 86, 88, 92, 94, 96; IntWW 82,
83, 89, 91, 93, 97, 98, 2000; IntWWW 2;
InWom, SUP; LegTOT; MotPP; MovMk;
OsStAZ; OxCFilm; Who 74, 82, 83, 85,
88, 90, 92, 94, 98, 99, 2000; WhoAm 74,
76, 78, 80, 82, 84, 86, 88, 90, 92, 94,
95, 96, 97, 99, 2000; WhoAmW 58, 68,
70, 72, 74, 83, 85, 87, 89, 91, 93, 95,
97, 99; WhoEnt 92, 98; WhoHol 92, A;
WorAl; WorAlBi; WorEFlm*

Simmons, Pat(rick)
[The Doobie Brothers]
American. Singer, Songwriter
Wrote Doobie hit "Black Water," 1974;
    began solo career, 1982.
b. Jan 23, 1950 in Aberdeen, Washington
Source: *OnThGG; RkOn 85; Songw*

Simmons, Richard
"The Clown Prince of Fitness"; "The
    Pied Piper of Pounds"
American. TV Personality, Author
Creator of diet program "Deal-a-Meal"
    and exercise video series "Sweatin' to
    the Oldies," author of *Never Say Diet*,
    1980.
b. Jul 12, 1948 in New Orleans,
    Louisiana
Source: *BioIn 12, 13; CelR 90; CurBio
82; LegTOT; NewYTBS 81; WhoTelC;
WorAlBi*

Simmons, Russell
American. Music Executive
Co-owner and founder Def Jam Records;
    head of Rush Artist Management,
    1985; produces rap artists Run-DMC
    and Public Enemy.
b. Oct 4, 1957 in New York, New York
Source: *AfrAmAl 8; BioIn 15, 16;
ConBlB 1; ConMus 7; CurBio 98;
Dun&B 88; NewYTBS 87; WhoAfA 12;
WhoAm 94, 95, 96, 97, 98, 99, 2000;
WhoEnt 98*

Simmons, Ruth J(ean)
American. Educator
President of Smith College, 1995—.
b. Jul 3, 1945 in Grapeland, Texas
Source: *CurBio 96*

Simmons, Zalmon G

American. Manufacturer
Invented inventor's patent for bedspring
as payment of debt, started bedding
products firm.
b. Sep 10, 1828 in Euphrates, New York
d. Feb 11, 1910 in Kenosha, Wisconsin
Source: *Entr; NatCAB 15*

Simms, Ginny

[Virginia E Simms]
American. Singer, Radio Performer
Popular vocalist, Kay Kyser's band,
1930s-40s; own radio, TV show, early
1950s.
b. May 25, 1916 in San Antonio, Texas
d. Apr 4, 1994 in Palm Springs,
California
Source: *CmpEPM; DcPseud; FilmgC;
HalFC 80, 84, 88; LegTOT; MotPP;
RadStar; WhoHol 92*

Simms, Hilda

American. Actor
Made Broadway debut in first play in US
with all-black cast, *Anna Lucasta*,
1944.
b. Apr 15, 1920 in Minneapolis,
Minnesota
d. Feb 6, 1994 in Buffalo, New York
Source: *BiE&WWA; BioIn 18, 19, 20,
22; CurBio 44, 94N; DcPseud; DrBlPA,
90; FacFEBW TA; InB&W 85; InWom;
NegAl 76, 83, 89; NotBlAW 1; NotNAT;
WhoHol 92, A; WhoThe 72, 77, 81*

Simms, Phil(ip)

American. Football Player
Quarterback, NY Giants, 1979-93; MVP,
Super Bowl, 1987; giants retire
number, 1 995.
b. Nov 3, 1955 in Lebanon, Kentucky
Source: *BioIn 12, 14, 15, 16, 17, 18, 20,
21; CelR 90; CurBio 94; FootReg 87;
NewYTBS 79, 81; WhoAm 90; WorAlBi*

Simms, William Gilmore

American. Author
Works include romantic novel *Master
Faber*, 1833; popular SC histories.
b. Apr 17, 1806 in Charleston, South
Carolina
d. Jun 11, 1870 in Charleston, South
Carolina
Source: *Alli; AmAu; AmAu&B; AmBi;
AmNatBi; ApCAB; BbD; Benet 87, 96;
BenetAL 91; BibAL; BiD&SB; BiDSA;
BioIn 1, 2, 3, 4, 5, 6, 8, 10, 11, 12, 13,
14, 15, 16, 18, 22; CamBiEn;
CamDcAB; CamGEL; CamGLE;
CamHAL; CasWL; ChambID; Chambr
3; ChhPo, S1, S2, S3; CnDAL; CyAL 2;
CyWA 58, 97; DcAmAu; DcAmB;
DcBiA; DcEnL; DcLB 3, 30, 59, 73;
DcLEL; DcNAA; Drake; EncALit;
EncFWF; EncSoH; EncSoL; EncWB 98;
EvLB; FifSWrB; GrWrEL N; HarEnUS;
HsB&A, SUP; InB&W 80; LinLib L, S;
McGEWB; NatCAB 6; NinCLC 3;
Novels; OxCAmH; OxCAmL 65, 83, 95;
OxCEng 67; PenC AM; PenEncH; RAdv
14; REn; REnAL; RfGAmL 4, 87, 94;*

*SouWr; TwCBDA; WebAB 74, 79;
WebE&AL; WhAm 3, HS; WhNaAH*

Simon, Carly

American. Singer, Songwriter
Hits include ''You're So Vain,'' 1972;
''Jesse,'' 1980; ''Coming Around
Again,'' 1987; Grammy award winner,
1971.
b. Jun 25, 1945 in New York, New York
Source: *AmSong; ASCAP 80; BiDAmM;
BillEnR; BioIn 9, 10, 11, 12, 13, 16;
BkPepl; CelR 90; ChambID; ConAu
105; ConLC 26; ConMuA 80A; ConMus
4, 22; CurBio 76; EncRk 88; EncRkSt;
FacFETw; GoodHs; HarEnR 86; HerW,
84; IlEncRk; IntWWW 2; InWom SUP;
LegTOT; NewAmDM; NewGrDA 86;
NewYTBS 74; PenEncP; RkOn 78;
RkWho 96; RolSEnR 83; Songw; WhoAm
86, 88, 90, 92, 94, 95, 96, 97, 98, 99,
2000; WhoAmW 89, 91, 93, 95, 97, 99;
WhoEnt 92, 98; WhoRock 81; WhoRocM
82; WorAl; WorAlBi*

Simon, Claude Eugene Henri

French. Author
Won Nobel Prize, 1985, for pioneering
work in new novel style of 1950s.
b. Oct 10, 1913 in Tananarive,
Madagascar
Source: *Benet 87; BioIn 14, 15;
CamBiEn; CasWL; ConAu 33NR, 89;
ConFLW 84; ConLC 4, 39; ConWorW
93; CurBio 92; CyWA 89; DcLB 83;
EncWL 1; EuWr 13; FacFETw; GuFrLit
1; IntAu&W 91; IntWW 74, 91;
MajTwCW 1; ModRL; NewYTBS 85;
PenC EUR; RAdv 13-2; REn; TwCWr;
Who 92; WhoNob, 90, 95; WhoTwCL;
WhoWor 74, 91, 93, 95, 96, 97, 98, 99,
2000; WorAlBi*

Simon, Herbert Alexander

American. Psychologist, Economist
Awarded 1978 Nobel Prize in
economics; developed a theory of
business decision-making.
b. Jun 15, 1916 in Milwaukee,
Wisconsin
Source: *AmMWSc 73S, 78S, 92;
BiDcPsy; BioIn 11, 12, 14, 15, 16, 17,
20, 21; BlueB 76; CamBiEn; CamDcAB;
ChambID; ConAu 9NR, 13R, 85NR;
EncWB, 98; GrEconS; HisDcDP; IntWW
91; NobelP; ThTwC 87; Who 83, 92, 98,
99, 2000; WhoAm 74, 76, 78, 80, 82, 84,
86, 90, 92, 94, 95, 96, 97, 98, 99, 2000;
WhoE 79, 81, 83, 85, 86, 91, 93, 95, 97,
99; WhoEc 86; WhoEng 88; WhoFI 00,
83, 85, 92, 94, 96, 98; WhoMW 92;
WhoNob, 90, 95; WhoScEn 96, 2000;
WhoTech 89; WhoWor 74, 80, 82, 84,
87, 91, 93, 95, 96, 97, 98, 99, 2000;
WrDr 86, 92, 98, 99, 2000*

Simon, Joe

American. Singer
Rhythm and blues, soul singer; hit single
''The Chokin' Kind,'' 1966.
b. Sep 2, 1943 in Simmesport, Louisiana

Source: *DrBlPA, 90; EncRk 88;
GuBlues; IlEncBM 82; RkOn 78; SoulM;
WhoRock 81*

Simon, John, Sir

English. Physician
His strong advocacy led to development
of public health system standards and
eventually to passage of Sanitary Act,
1866; Public Health Act, 1875.
b. Oct 10, 1816 in London, England
d. Jul 23, 1904 in London, England
Source: *Alli, SUP; BiHiMed; BioIn 1, 2,
7, 9; ChambID; DcBiPP; DcNaB, S2;
InSci; LarDcSc; OxCMed 86;
RanHWDS; WhDW*

Simon, John Ivan

American. Critic
Cultural critic for noted periodicals, from
1960; books on theater include *Movies
into Film*, 1971.
b. May 12, 1925 in Subotica, Yugoslavia
Source: *BiE&WWA; ConAmTC; NotNAT;
WhoAm 76, 78, 80, 82, 84, 90, 92, 94,
95, 96, 97, 98; WhoEnt 92, 98; WhoThe
77; WorAu 1950*

Simon, Jules Francois

French. Politician, Writer, Philosopher
Statesman led the moderate republican
faction during the early years of the
Third Republic.
b. Dec 27, 1814 in Lorient, France
d. Jun 8, 1896 in Paris, France
Source: *CyEd; EncWB 98; McGEWB*

Simon, Neil

[Marvin Neil Simon]
American. Dramatist
Most of his outstanding plays have been
adapted to film including *The Goodbye
Girl*, 1977; has won 4 Tonys; Pulitzer
Prize winner in drama for *Lost in
Yonkers*, 1991; wrote autobiography,
Rewrites 1996.
b. Jul 4, 1927 in New York, New York
Source: *AmAu&B; AmCulL; AmWr S4;
Au&Arts 32; AuNews 1; Benet 87;
BenetAL 91; BiE&WWA; BioIn 6, 7, 8,
9, 10, 11, 12, 13, 16; BlueB 76;
CamGLE; CamGWoT; CamHAL; CelR,
90; CnThe; ConAu 21R, 26NR; ConDr
73, 77, 82, 88; ConLC 6, 11, 31, 39, 70;
ConTFT 1, 6, 13; CroCD; CrtSuDr;
CurBio 68, 89; CyWA 89, 97; DcLB 7;
DcLEL 1940; DcTwCCu 1; EncAFC;
EncMT; EncWB 99; EncWT; Ent;
FacFETw; FilmEn; FilmgC; HalFC 80,
84, 88; IntAu&W 89, 91, 93; IntMPA 77,
80, 86, 88, 92, 94, 96; IntWW 74, 75,
76, 77, 78, 79, 80, 81, 82, 83, 89, 91,
93, 97, 98, 2000; ItaFilm; JeAmHC;
LegTOT; LesBEnT 92; LinLib L;
MagSAmL; MajTwCW 1; McGEWD 72,
84; ModAL 4, 5; ModWD; NatPD 81;
NewCBMT; NewYTBS 85, 91; NewYTET;
NotNAT; OxCAmT 84; OxCPMus;
OxCThe 83; PIP&P, A; RAdv 14;
WebAB 74, 79; Who 74, 82, 83, 85, 88,
90, 92, 94, 98, 99, 2000; WhoAm 74, 76,
78, 80, 82, 84, 86, 88, 90, 92, 94, 95,
96, 97, 98, 99, 2000; WhoAmJ 80; WhoE*

91, 93, 95, 97, 99; WhoEnt 92, 98;
WhoPul; WhoThe 72, 77, 81; WhoWor
74, 78, 93, 95, 96, 97, 98, 99, 2000;
WorAl; WorAlBi; WorAu 1950; WrDr
76, 82, 84, 86, 88, 90, 92, 94, 96, 98,
99, 2000

Simon, Norma Feldstein
American. Children's Author
Children are sources for writings: All
   Kinds of Families, 1976.
b. Dec 24, 1927 in New York, New
   York
Source: AuBYP 2, 3; ConAu 5R, 6NR,
21NR; SmATA 3, 68

Simon, Norton Winfred
American. Business Executive
Founded Norton Simon Inc., which
   included Hunt-Wesson Foods, Canada
   Dry Corp; art collection valued at $50
   million.
b. Feb 5, 1907 in Portland, Oregon
d. Jun 2, 1993 in Los Angeles, California
Source: AmNatBi; AnObit 1993; BioIn
12, 15; CamDcAB; ConAmBL; CurBio
68, 93N; NewYTBE 70; NewYTBS 74;
WhAm 11; WhoAm 78, 80, 82, 84, 86,
88; WhoAmA 84, 91; WhoWest 84, 87,
89

Simon, Paul
[Simon and Garfunkel]
American. Songwriter, Singer
Has successful solo career; won 1987
   Grammy for South African album
   Graceland; Emmy award winner,
   1977; Rock and Roll Hall of Fame,
   1990.
b. Oct 13, 1941 in Newark, New Jersey
Source: AmSong; BakBD 84, 92;
BakDcM; BillEnR; BioIn 12, 13, 14, 15;
BkPepl; CamBiEn; CelR, 90; ChamBiD;
ConAu 116; ConLC 17; ConMus 1, 16;
DcTwCCu 1; EncFCWM 83; EncPR&S
89; EncRk 88; EncRkSt; HalFC 88;
HarEnR 86; IlEncRk; IntMPA 92, 94,
96; NewAmDM; News 92, 92-2;
NewYTBE 72; OnThGG; OxCPMus;
PenEncP; RkWho 96; Songw; VarWW
85; WhoAm 86, 88, 90, 92, 94, 95, 96,
97; WhoEnt 92, 98; WhoRock 81;
WhoRocM 82; WhoWor 74; WorAl;
WorAlBi

Simon, Paul M(artin)
American. Politician
Dem. senator, IL, 1985-97; 1988
   presidential candidate.
b. Nov 29, 1928 in Eugene, Oregon
Source: AlmAP 92; BiDrUSC 89; BioIn
13, 14, 15, 16; CngDr 87, 89; ConAu
81; CurBio 88; EncWB; IntAu&W 89;
IntWW 91; PolsAm 84; WhoAm 86, 90;
WhoAmP 85, 91; WhoGov 77; WhoMW
92; WhoUSWr 88; WhoWor 87, 91;
WhoWrEP 89

Simon, Richard Leo
American. Publisher
With Max Schuster, founded Simon &
   Schuster Publishers, 1924.
b. Mar 6, 1899 in New York, New York

d. Jul 29, 1960 in Stamford, Connecticut
Source: AmAu&B; AmNatBi; BioIn 5, 6;
CamDcAB; CurBio 41, 60; DcAmB S6;
NatCAB 44; ObitOF 79; WhAm 4;
WorAl; WorAlBi

Simon, Saint
Biblical Figure
One of Twelve Disciples; preached in
   Egypt; feast day Oct 28.
Source: BioIn 2, 3, 4, 5, 6, 8, 9, 10, 11;
McGDA; NewCol 75

Simon, Simone
French. Actor
Movie idol in France, 1930s; US films
   include Seventh Heaven, 1937; The
   Cat People, 1942.
b. Apr 23, 1913 in Marseilles, France
Source: BiDFilm; FilmgC; HalFC 84;
HolP 30; IntMPA 76, 77; MotPP;
MovMk; OxCFilm; ThFT; WorEFlm

Simon, William E(dward)
American. Government Official
Secretary of Treasury, 1974-77.
b. Nov 27, 1927 in Paterson, New Jersey
d. Jun 3, 2000 in Santa Barbara,
   California
Source: BiDrUSE 89; BioIn 9, 10, 11,
12, 13, 14, 15, 16, 17, 19; BlueB 76;
CamDcAB; ConAmBL; ConAu 81;
CurBio 74; DcAmC; IntWW 74, 75, 76,
77, 78, 79, 80, 81, 82, 83, 89, 91, 93,
97, 98, 2000; LinLib S; NewYTBE 73;
NewYTBS 87; PolProf NF; Who 82, 85,
88, 90, 92, 94, 98, 99, 2000; WhoAm 74,
76, 78, 80, 82, 84, 86, 88, 90, 92, 95,
96, 97, 98; WhoAmP 75, 77, 79, 81, 83,
85, 87, 89, 91, 93, 95; WhoE 77; WhoFI
83; WhoGov 75, 77; WhoSSW 76;
WhoWor 76, 78; WorAl; WorAlBi

Simon and Garfunkel
[Arthur Garfunkel; Paul Simon]
American. Music Group
Sixth grade classmates who formed folk-
   rock duo; number one hits "Mrs.
   Robinson," 1967; "Bridge Over
   Troubled Waters," 1970.
Source: ABCCoAm; BillEnR; BioIn 17,
18, 19, 20; BlueB 76; ConMuA 80A;
ConMus 24; EncFCWM 69; EncPR&S
74, 89; EncRk 88; FacFETw; HarEnR
86; IntMPA 75, 76, 77, 78, 79, 80, 81;
IntWW 89, 91; NewAmDM; NewGrDA
86; NewYTBE 72; NewYTBS 82;
PenEncP; RkOn 74, 78; RkWho 96;
RolSEnR 83; WhoAm 74, 80, 82, 84, 86;
WhoRock 81; WhoRocM 82; WhoWor 74

Simone, Nina
[Eunice Wayman]
American. Singer
Jazz/soul singer, noted for club, festival
   performances; albums include Fodder
   On My Wings, 1984.
b. Feb 21, 1933 in Tryon, North Carolina
Source: AllMGJa; ASCAP 66, 80;
BakBD 84, 92; BakDcM; BiDAfM;
BiDAmM; BiDJaz; BillEnR; BioIn 6, 8,
9, 10, 12; BioNews 74; BlkWAm;
CamBiEn; CamDcAB; ChamBiD;

ConBlB 15; ContDcW 89; CurBio 68;
DcPseud; DcTwCCu 5; DrBlPA, 90;
EncJzS; EncJzS; EncRk 88; HarEnR 86;
IlEncBM 82; IlEncRk; InB&W 80, 85;
IntWW 89, 91, 93, 98, 2000; IntWWW 2;
InWom SUP; LegTOT; NegAl 89;
NewGrDA 86; NotBlAW 1; OxCPMus;
PenEncP; RolSEnR 83; SoulM; WhoAm
74, 76, 78, 80, 82; WhoAmW 70, 72, 74,
81; WhoBlA 1, 2, 3, 4, 7; WhoHol 92;
WhoRock 81; WorAl; WorAlBi

Simoneau, Leopold
Canadian. Opera Singer
Tenor; active during 1940s-70s; noted
   for Mozart roles.
b. May 3, 1918 in Quebec, Quebec,
   Canada
Source: BakBD 78, 84, 92; CanWW 70,
79, 80, 81, 83, 89, 96, 97, 98, 1999;
CreCan 1; IntDcOp; IntWWM 90;
MetOEnc; NewAmDM; NewGrDM 80;
OxDcOp; PenDiMP; WhoWor 74

Simonetta
Italian. Author, Fashion Designer
Rome's leading designer, 1950s;
   established first "haute boutique,"
   1965.
b. Apr 10, 1922 in Rome, Italy
Source: BioIn 4; ConFash; EncFash;
IntWW 74, 91; InWom; LegTOT;
ThHDFas; WorFshn

Simonov, Konstantin (Kirill)
Mikhailovich
Russian. Author, Poet
Writer was best known for his patriotic
   verse dealing with World War II, and
   for his prose descriptions of the
   courage of Soviet forces.
b. Nov 28, 1915 in St. Petersburg,
   Russia
d. 1979 in Moscow, Union of Soviet
   Socialist Republics
Source: Benet 96

Simons, Elwyn L(aVerne)
American. Scientist
Formulated a theory that all higher
   primates arose in Africa about forty
   million years ago in the form of
   squirrel-like tree-living animals.
b. Jul 14, 1930 in Lawrence, Kansas
Source: AmMWSc 76P, 79, 82, 86, 89,
92; ConAu 22NR, 105; CurBio 94;
IntAu&W 86; IntWW 89, 91, 93, 97, 98,
2000; WhoAm 74, 78, 80, 82, 84, 86, 88,
90, 92, 95, 99, 2000; WhoScEn 94,
96, 2000; WhoSSW 95, 97

Simons, Howard
American. Newspaper Editor
Managing editor, Washington Post, 1971-
   84; wrote Simm's List Book, 1977.
b. Jun 3, 1928 in Albany, New York
d. Jun 13, 1989 in Jacksonville Beach,
   Florida
Source: BioIn 14; ConAu 65, 128;
EncTwCJ; IntAu&W 89; NewYTBS 89;
WhoAm 86, 88; WhoSSW 82

Simple Minds
[Charlie Burchill; Mel Gaynor; John
Giblin; Jim Kerr; Mick Mac Neil]
Scottish. Music Group
Punk-dance style hits include "Alive and
Kicking," 1985.
Source: *BillEnR; ConMus 21; EncPR&S
89; EncRk 88; EncRkSt; HarEnR 86;
PenEncP; WhoRocM 82; WhsNW 85*

Simpson, Adele (Smithline)
American. Fashion Designer
Among highest paid designers in world,
1940s-50s; first to go "on tour" with
her collections.
b. Dec 8, 1903 in New York, New York
d. Aug 23, 1995 in Greenwich,
Connecticut
Source: *AmDec 1940; BioIn 9, 10, 11,
21; CelR; ConDes 90; CurBio 70, 95N;
FairDF US; InWom, SUP; LegTOT;
WhoAm 86, 90; WhoAmW 58, 64, 66,
68, 70, 72, 74, 91; WhoFash, 88;
WorFshn*

Simpson, Alan Kooi
American. Politician
Rep. senator from WY, 1979-97; co-
authored landmark Simpson-Mazzoli
immigration law, 1986.
b. Sep 2, 1931 in Cody, Wyoming
Source: *AlmAP 82, 92; BiDrUSC 89;
BioIn 13; CngDr 87, 89; CurBio 90;
IntWW 89, 91, 93, 97, 98, 2000;
NewYTBS 90; PolsAm 84; WhoAm 80,
82, 86, 88, 90, 92, 94, 95, 96, 97, 98,
99, 2000; WhoAmP 85, 91, 1999;
WhoGov 75, 77; WhoWest 00, 82, 89,
92, 94, 96, 98; WhoWor 80, 82, 84, 89,
91*

Simpson, Carole
[Carole Simpson Marshall]
American. Broadcast Journalist
Anchor, ABC's "World News
Saturday," 1988-93; anchor, ABC's
"World News Sunday," 1993—.
b. Dec 7, 1940 in Chicago, Illinois
Source: *AfrAmAl 6, 8; AfrAmBi 2; BioIn
18, 20; BlkWAm; ConBlB 6; ConTFT
26; CurBio 1999; DcTwCCu 5; Ebony 1;
EncTelN; InB&W 80; InWom SUP;
NotBlAW 1; WhoAfA 9, 10, 11, 12;
WhoAm 92, 94, 95; WhoBlA 1, 2, 3, 4,
5, 6, 7, 8*

Simpson, Cedric Keith
English. Physician, Author
Noted forensic scientist; wrote *Forty
Years of Murder* 1979.
b. Jul 20, 1907 in Brighton, England
d. Jul 21, 1985
Source: *Au&Wr 71; BioIn 12; ConAu
111, 117; CopCroC; IntWW 83;
RanHWDS; Who 74, 82, 83, 85*

Simpson, Donald C
American. Producer
Films include *Flash Dance*, 1983;
Beverly Hills Cop, 1984; *Top Gun*,
1986.
b. Oct 29, 1945 in Seattle, Washington

d. Jan 19, 1996 in Los Angeles,
California
Source: *ConTFT 5; IntMPA 86; VarWW
85*

Simpson, George Gaylord
American. Paleontologist
Curator of New York's American
Museum of Natural History, he
contributed to advances in
evolutionary theory and taxonomy.
b. Jun 16, 1902 in Chicago, Illinois
d. 1984
Source: *AmAu&B; AmMWSc 73P, 76P,
79, 82; AmNatBi; AnObit 1984; Au&Wr
71; BiDAmCa; BiESc; BioIn 1, 3, 4, 7,
11, 14, 15, 17, 20, 22, 23; BlueB 76;
CamBiEn; CamDcAB; ChamBiD; ConAu
16NR, 61NR, 114, P-1; CurBio 85N;
EncHuEv; EncWB, 98; FifIDA;
HisPhAn; IntWW 74, 75, 76, 77, 78, 79,
80, 81, 82, 83; LarDcSc; MajTwCW 1;
McGMS 80; NewYTBS 84; NotTwCS 1;
RanHWDS; TwCA SUP; WebAB 74, 79;
WhAm 9; WhoAm 74, 76, 78, 80, 82, 84;
WhoFrS 84; WhoWor 74, 78, 82, 84;
WorAu 1900*

Simpson, James Young, Sir
Scottish. Physician
One of founders of modern gynecology,
1840; first to use anesthesia in
childbirth.
b. Jun 7, 1811 in Bathgate, Scotland
d. May 6, 1870 in London, England
Source: *Alli, SUP; AsBiEn; BiESc;
BiHiMed; BioIn 1, 2, 3, 4, 6, 8, 9, 10,
14; CamBiEn; CelCen; ChamBiD;
ChhPo S1, S2; DcBiPP; DcNaB; InSci;
LarDcSc; LinLib S; OxCMed 86;
RanHWDS; WorAl; WorAlBi*

Simpson, Jim
American. Broadcaster
Play-by-play football commentator on
TV, 1962-79.
b. Dec 20, 1927 in Washington, District
of Columbia
Source: *BioIn 9, 21; LesBEnT, 92;
NewYTET; WhoTelC*

Simpson, Lorna
American. Artist
Known for conceptual photography.
b. Aug 13, 1960 in New York, New
York
Source: *AfrAmAl 6, 8; BioIn 21; ConBlB
4; ConWomA; DcTwCCu 5; IlBBlP;
SJGBlA; WhoAmW 91*

Simpson, Louis
[Louis Aston Marantz Simpson]
American. Author, Poet
Won 1964 Pulitzer for verse volume *At
the End of the Open Road.*
b. Mar 27, 1923 in Kingston, Jamaica
Source: *Benet 87; BenetAL 91; BiCoLiE;
BioIn 7, 8, 9, 10, 12, 13, 14, 15, 17, 20;
BlueB 76; CamGEL; CamGLE;
CamHAL; CaribW 1; ChhPo, S1, S3;
CnE&AP; ConAu 1NR, 1R, 4AS; ConLC
4, 7, 9, 32; ConPo 70, 75, 80, 85, 91,
96; CroCAP; CyWA 97; DcAfL; DcLB*

*5; DrAF 76; DrAP 75; DrAPF 80, 91;
FacFETw; GrWrEL P; IntAu&W 86, 89,
91, 93; IntWW 79, 80, 81, 82, 83, 89,
91, 93; IntWWP 77, 82; LegTOT; LinLib
L; MajTwCW 1; ModAL 4, 4S1, 5;
OxCAmL 65, 83, 95; OxCTwCP; PenC
AM; RAdv 1, 14, 13-1; REn; REnAL;
RfGAmL 87, 94; WebE&AL; WhoAm 74,
76, 78, 80, 82, 84, 86, 88, 90, 92, 94,
95, 96; WhoE 74; WhoPul; WhoTwCL;
WhoUSWr 88; WhoWor 74; WhoWrEP
89, 92, 95; WhsWeAm 98; WorAl;
WorAlBi; WorAu 1950; WrDr 76, 80, 82,
84, 86, 88, 90, 92, 94, 96*

Simpson, Mona Elizabeth
American. Author
Author's work includes *Anywhere but
Here,* 1986; *The Lost Father,* 1992.
b. Jun 14, 1957 in Green Bay, Wisconsin
Source: *BioIn 15, 16; ConAu 68NR, 122,
135; ConLC 44; CurBio 93; DrAPF 91;
OxCTwCL; WhoAm 2000; WrDr 92*

Simpson, Nicole Brown
[Mrs. O. J. Simpson]
American. Victim
Former wife of football star O. J.
Simpson and famous murder victim.
b. May 19, 1959, Germany
d. Jun 13, 1994 in Los Angeles,
California

Simpson, O(renthal) J(ames)
"Juice"
American. Football Player, Actor
Halfback, Buffalo, 1969-77, San
Francisco, 1978-79; set many NFL
rushing records including first to gain
2,000 yds. in season, 1973; Hall of
Fame, 1985; acquitted of the murder
of his former wife, Nicole Brown
Simpson, and her friend, Ronald
Goldman, 1995; found liable for those
deaths in a civil trial, 1997.
b. Jul 9, 1947 in San Francisco,
California
Source: *AfrAmBi 2; BiDAmSp FB; BioIn
8, 9, 10, 11, 12, 13, 14, 15, 16; BkPepl;
CamBiEn; CamDcAB; CelR 90;
ChamBiD; ConAu 50NR; ConTFT 7;
CriJuSA; CurBio 69; DrBlPA 90; HalFC
88; InB&W 85; IntMPA 86, 92;
LesBEnT, 92; NegAl 89; NewYTBE 70,
73; NewYTBS 75, 76; WhoAm 74, 86,
90; WhoBlA 2, 3, 4, 5, 6, 7; WhoFtbl
74; WhoHol A; WorAlBi*

Simpson, Scott
American. Golfer
Turned pro, 1977; won US Open, 1987.
b. Sep 17, 1955 in San Diego, California
Source: *BioIn 15, 16; ODwPR 91;
WhoIntG*

Simpson, Valerie
[Ashford and Simpson; Mrs. Nickolas
Ashford]
American. Singer
With husband, contributed original
material to soundtrack of *The Wiz;*
recorded two solo albums.

b. Aug 26, 1948 in New York, New
   York
Source: *BioIn 14, 15, 16; BioNews 74;*
BlkWAm; InB&W 85; NewGrDA 86;
NewYTBS 85; WhoBlA 4, 5, 7;
WhoRocM 82

**Simpson, Wallis (Bessie Wallis
   Warfield)**
[Duchess of Windsor]
American.
Two-time divorcee for whom Edward
   VIII abdicated his throne to marry,
   1936.
b. Jun 19, 1896 in Blue Ridge Summit,
   Pennsylvania
d. Apr 24, 1986 in Paris, France
Source: *AnObit 1986; BioIn 15; CelR;*
ConNews 86-3; CurBio 86N; FacFETw;
NewYTBS 86; WebAB 74; Who 82R,
83R, 85R; WhoAm 80, 82; WhoWor 76,
78, 80, 82

Simpson, William Hood
American. Army Officer
Commanded 9th Army in German
   invasion, WW II; four-star general,
   1954.
b. May 19, 1888 in Weatherford, Texas
d. Aug 15, 1980 in San Antonio, Texas
Source: *AmNatBi; AnObit 1980;*
BiDWWGF; BioIn 1, 3, 12; CurBio 45,
80; FacFETw; HarEnMi; NewYTBS 80;
WebAB 74; WebAMB

Sims, Billy Ray
American. Football Player
Halfback, won Heisman Trophy, 1978;
   in NFL with Detroit, 1980-86; career
   shortened by injuries.
b. Sep 18, 1955 in Saint Louis, Missouri
Source: *BiDAmSp FB; BioIn 11, 12, 14;*
FootReg 85, 86; InB&W 85; NewYTBS
78, 80; WhoBlA 4, 7

Sims, James Marion
American. Scientist, Physician, Engineer
Originator of operative gynecology;
   established Woman's Hospital of NY,
   1857.
b. Jan 25, 1813 in Lancaster County,
   Kentucky
d. Nov 13, 1883 in New York, New
   York
Source: *Alli, SUP; AmBi; ApCAB;*
BiDSA; BiHiMed; BioIn 1, 2, 3, 4, 5, 6,
7, 8, 9; CamDcAB; DcAmAu; DcAmB;
DcAmMeB; DcNAA; HarEnUS; InSci;
NatCAB 2; OxCAmH; OxCMed 86;
TwCBDA; WebAB 74, 79; WhAm HS

Sims, Naomi
American. Model, Business Executive
Haute couture model, 1967-73; founder
   and chm., Naomi Sims Beauty
   Products; author of several beauty
   books for black women.
b. Mar 30, 1948 in Oxford, Mississippi
Source: *BioIn 8, 9, 10, 12, 15; ConAu*
26NR, 69; InB&W 85; InWom SUP;
NegAl 89; NotBlAW 1; SelBAAf; WhoBlA
7

Sims, William Sowden
American. Military Leader
Wrote navigation textbook, 1880;
   adopted convoy system, WW I; co-
   wrote *The Victory at Sea*, won
   Pulitzer, 1920.
b. Oct 15, 1858 in Port Hope, Ontario,
   Canada
d. Sep 25, 1936 in Boston,
   Massachusetts
Source: *AmBi; AmNatBi; ApCAB X;*
BioIn 4, 6, 7, 8, 9, 23, 24; CamBiEn;
ChamBiD; DcAmB S2; DcAmMiB;
DcNAA; EncAB-H 1974, 1996; EncAInt;
EncNaHi; EncWB 98; HarEnMi; LinLib
S; McGEWB; NatCAB 27; OxCAmL 65;
OxCShps; SpAmWar; WebAB 74, 79;
WebAMB; WhAm 1; WhoPul; WorAl

Sims, Zoot
[John Haley Sims]
American. Jazz Musician
Saxophonist with Big Bands, 1940s; won
   Grammy, 1977.
b. Oct 29, 1925 in Inglewood, California
d. Mar 23, 1985 in New York, New
   York
Source: *AllMGJa; AmNatBi; AnObit*
1985; ASCAP 80; BakBD 84; CmpEPM;
EncJzS; FacFETw; IlEncJ; IntWWM 77;
LegTOT; NewAmDM; NewGrDA 86;
NewGrDJ 88, 94; NewYTBS 85;
OxCPMus; PenEncP; WhAm 8; WhoAm
74, 76, 78, 80, 82, 84

Sin, Jaime L(achica)
Philippine. Clergy
Archbishop of Manila, 1974—; elevated
   to Cardinal, 1976.
b. Aug 31, 1928 in New Washington,
   Philippines
Source: *BioIn 11, 12; CurBio 95;*
FarE&A 78, 79, 80, 81; IntWW 77, 78,
79, 80, 81, 82, 83; WhoRel 92; WhoWor
80, 82, 84, 87, 89, 91, 95, 96, 97, 98, 99

Sinan, Kodja Mimar
Turkish. Architect
Leading Ottoman architect known for his
   light but vast domes; his works
   include some of the most famous
   landmarks of the Turkish Empire.
b. Apr 15, 1489 in Kaisariya, Anatolia,
   Ottoman Empire
d. 1578
Source: *EncWB 98; McGEWB*

Sinatra, Barbara Marx Spencer
[Mrs. Frank Sinatra]
American.
Fourth, current wife of Frank Sinatra.
b. May 16, 1926 in Glendale, California
Source: *BioIn 10*

Sinatra, Christina
American.
Youngest daughter of Frank Sinatra.
b. Jun 20, 1948
Source: *BioIn 10*

Sinatra, Frank
[Francis Albert Sinatra]
"Ol' Blue Eyes"; "The Chairman of the
   Board"
American. Singer, Actor
Regarded as biggest entertainment
   attraction in 20th c; won Oscar, 1953,
   for *From Here to Eternity*.
b. Dec 12, 1915 in Hoboken, New Jersey
d. May 14, 1998 in Los Angeles,
   California
Source: *AllMGJa; AmCulL; AmDec*
1940; ASCAP 66, 80; BakBD 78, 84, 92;
BakDcM; BiDAmM; BiDFilm, 81, 94;
BiDJaz; BioIn 12, 13, 14, 15, 16, 17, 18,
19, 20, 21, 22, 23, 24; BkPepl;
CamBiEn; CelR 90; ChamBiD; CmCal;
CmMov; CmpEPM; ConMus 1, 23;
ConTFT 9; CurBio 43, 60, 98N; DcArts;
DcTwCCu 1; EncAB-H 1974; EncAFC;
EncJzS; EncPR&S 89; EncWB;
FacFETw; FilmEn; FilmgC; ForYSC;
GangFlm; HalFC 80, 84, 88; HarEnR
86; IntDcF 1-3, 2-3; IntMPA 75, 76, 77,
78, 79, 80, 81, 82, 84, 86, 88, 92, 94,
96; IntWW 74, 75, 76, 77, 78, 79, 80,
81, 82, 83, 89, 91, 93, 97; LegTOT;
LesBEnT 92; MafEnc; MGM; MiSFD 9;
MovMk; MusMk; NewAmDM; NewGrDA
86; NewGrDJ 88, 94; NewGrDM 80;
News 98; NewYTBS 90, 98; OsStAZ;
OxCFilm; OxCPMus; PenEncP;
RadStar; RAdv 14; RComAH; RkOn 74;
RolSEnR 83; WebAB 74; WhAm 12;
Who 82, 83, 85, 88, 90, 92, 94; WhoAm
74, 76, 78, 80, 82, 84, 86, 88, 90, 92,
94, 95, 96, 97, 98; WhoEnt 92, 98;
WhoHol 92; WhoMus 72; WhoRock 81;
WhoWor 78, 80, 82, 84, 87, 89, 91, 93,
95, 96, 97, 98; WorAl; WorAlBi;
WorEFlm

Sinatra, Frank, Jr.
American. Singer
Son of Frank; nightclub performer,
   cameo roles in TV, films.
b. Jan 10, 1944 in Jersey City, New
   Jersey
Source: *BioIn 6, 12; LegTOT; PenEncP;*
VarWW 85; WhoHol 92, A

Sinatra, Nancy
American. Singer
Recorded "Something Stupid," with
   father, 1969.
b. Jun 8, 1940 in Jersey City, New
   Jersey
Source: *BioIn 7, 8, 9, 10, 14; CelR;*
ConTFT 11; FilmgC; ForYSC; HalFC
80, 84, 88; InWom SUP; LegTOT;
PenEncP; RkOn 78; RolSEnR 83;
WhoAm 74; WhoHol 92, A; WhoRocM
82

Sinbad
[David Adkins]
American. Comedian, Actor
TV series "A Different World," 1988-
   91; "The Sinbad Show," 1993-94.
b. Nov 10, 1956 in Benton Harbor,
   Michigan
Source: *AfrAmAl 6, 8; BioIn 15; ConBlB*
1, 16; ConTFT 10, 17; CurBio 97; DcLP

87B; DcTwCCu 5; DrBlPA 90; IntMPA 96; WhoBlA 7; WhoEnt 92

Sinclair, Gordon

Canadian. Journalist, Radio Performer
Canadian editor who defended US in best-selling recorded editorial, "The Americans," 1973.
b. Jun 3, 1900 in Toronto, Ontario, Canada
d. May 17, 1984 in Toronto, Ontario, Canada
Source: *AuNews 1; BioIn 8, 10, 11, 13, 14; BioNews 74; CanWW 70, 79, 80, 81, 83; ConAu 102, 112; RkOn 78*

Sinclair, Harry Ford

American. Oilman
One of the key participants in the Teapot Dome scandal, 1922; founder of Sinclair Oil Corp.
b. Jul 6, 1876 in Wheeling, West Virginia
d. Nov 10, 1956 in Pasadena, California
Source: *AmNatBi; BiDAmBL 83; BioIn 1, 4; DcAmB S6; WebAB 74, 79; WhAm 3; WorAl; WorAlBi*

Sinclair, Iain

Welsh. Author
Wrote *Downriver; or, The Vessels of Wrath*, 1991; won the James Tait Black Memorial Book Prize, 1992.
b. Jun 11, 1943 in Cardiff, Wales
Source: *ConAu 81NR, 132; ConLC 76; ConPo 91, 96; OxCTwCL; ScF&FL 92; WrDr 92, 94, 96, 98, 99, 2000*

Sinclair, Jo

[Ruth Seid]
American. Author
Novelist, short story writer: *The Changelings*, 1955.
b. Jul 1, 1913 in New York, New York
d. Apr 4, 1995 in Jenkintown, Pennsylvania
Source: *AmAu&B; AmNov, X; AmWomWr; Au&Wr 71; BioAmW; BioIn 1, 2, 4, 14, 18, 20, 21, 22, 24; BlmGWL; ConAu 5R, 148, X; ConJeAN; ConNov 72, 76, 82, 86; CurBio 46, 95N; DcLB 28; DcLP 87B; DcPseud; IntAu&W 76, 77; InWom, SUP; JeAmWW; Novels; OhA&B; PenNWW B; TwCA SUP; WhoAm 74, 76, 78, 80, 82, 84, 86, 88, 90, 92, 94, 95, 96; WhoAmW 58, 61, 64, 66, 68, 70, 72, 74; WhoUSWr 88; WhoWorJ 72, 78; WhoWrEP 89, 92, 95; WorAu 1900; WrDr 76, 80, 82, 84, 86, 88*

Sinclair, Madge

[Madge Walters]
American. Actor
Three-time Emmy nominee for role on TV's "Trapper John, MD," 1980-86.
b. Apr 28, 1938 in Kingston, Jamaica
d. Dec 20, 1995 in Los Angeles, California
Source: *BioIn 14, 21, 22; BlksAmF; ConTFT 4, 15; DrBlPA 90; InB&W 85; IntMPA 92, 94, 96; WhoAfA 9, 10N; WhoEnt 92; WhoHol 92, A*

Sinclair, Mary

American. Political Activist
Former science writer and researcher, became an activist against nuclear power in 1967 when Consumer's Power proposed a nuclear power plant near her home in Midland, MI; lecturer on nuclear power and environmental issues.
b. Sep 23, 1918 in Chisholm, Minnesota
Source: *ConNews 85-2*

Sinclair, Upton Beall

[Clarke Fitch; Frederick Garrison; Arthur Stirling]
American. Author
Wrote *The Jungle*, 1906; 1943 Pulitzer winner *Dragon's Teeth*.
b. Sep 20, 1878 in Baltimore, Maryland
d. Nov 25, 1968 in Bound Brook, New Jersey
Source: *AmRef; AmSocL; BiDAmJo; CambBiEn; CamDcAB; CasWL; ChamBiD; ConLC 15; CurBio 62; DcAmB S8; EncAB-H 1996; EncALit; MajTwCW 2; ModAL 4; OxCAmL 65; OxCEng 67; OxCFilm; OxCTwCL; PenC AM; RAdv 1; REn; REnAL; SJGYouA 2; SmATA 9; TwCA, SUP; WebE&AL; WorAu 1900; WorEFlm*

Sinden, Donald (Alfred)

English. Actor
British films include *The Cruel Sea*, 1953; *That Lucky Touch*, 1975.
b. Oct 9, 1923 in Plymouth, England
Source: *BioIn 13, 19; CambBiEn; CamGWoT; CnThe; ConAu 132; ConTFT 7; DcArts; Ent; FilmAG WE; FilmEn; FilmgC; HalFC 80, 84, 88; IlWWBF; IntAu&W 89, 91; IntMPA 75, 76, 77, 78, 79, 80, 81, 82, 84, 86, 88, 92, 94, 96; IntWW 83, 89, 91, 93, 97, 98, 2000; OxCThe 83; VarWW 85; Who 74, 82, 83, 85, 88, 90, 92, 94, 98, 99, 2000; WhoEnt 92, 98; WhoHol 92, A; WhoThe 72, 77, 81; WhoWor 96; WrDr 94, 96, 98, 99, 2000*

Sinder, Dee

[Twisted Sister]
American. Singer
Flamboyant heavy metal singer and leader of band Twisted Sister, whose 1984 album *Stay Hungry* produced Top Ten hit "We're Not Gonna Take It;" band was singled out for criticism by the Parents' Music Resource Center (PMRC) in 1985, and the singer became a spokesman for rock musicians against the group.
b. Mar 1955 in New York, New York

Sinding, Christian

Norwegian. Composer
Wrote piano work, "Rustle of Spring;" operas, four symphonies.
b. Jan 11, 1856 in Kongsberg, Norway
d. Dec 3, 1941 in Oslo, Norway
Source: *BakBD 78, 84; BioIn 3, 8; ChamBiD; CompSN; CurBio 42; LinLib S; MusMk; NewAmDM; NewGrDM 80; NewOxM; OxCMus*

Singer, Burns James Hyman

American. Author
Best known for documentary novel, *Living Silver*, 1958.
b. Apr 29, 1928 in New York, New York
d. Sep 8, 1964 in Plymouth, England
Source: *ConAu 89, 102; ConPo 75; OxCTwCL; WorAu 1950*

Singer, Isaac Bashevis

[Isaac Warshofsky]
American. Author
Foremost living writer of Yiddish literature; won Nobel Prize, 1978; awarded American Academy and Institute of Arts and Letters gold medal, 1989.
b. Jul 14, 1904 in Radzymin, Poland
d. Jul 24, 1991 in Miami, Florida
Source: *AmAu&B; AmNatBi; AmWr; AnCL; AnObit 1991; Au&Arts 32; Au&Wr 71; AuBYP 2, 3; AuNews 1, 2; AuSpks; BeaEPF; Benet 87, 96; BenetAL 91; BiCoLiE; BioIn 6, 7, 8, 9, 10, 11, 12, 13, 14, 15, 16, 17, 18, 19, 20, 21, 22, 23, 24; BlueB 76; CamBiEn; CamDcAB; CasWL; CelR; ChamBiD; ChlBkCr; ChlLR 1; ConAu 1NR, 1R, 39NR, 134; ConLC 1, 3, 6, 9, 11, 15, 23, 38, 69, 70, 111; ConNov 72, 76, 82, 86; CurBio 69, 91N; CyWA 89, 97; DcArts; DcLB 6, 28, 52, Y91N; DcLP 87A; DcPseud; DcTwCCu 1; DrAF 76; EncAB-H 1996; EncALit; EncFoLi; EncWB 98; EncWL 1, 2, 2S, 3; FacFETw; GrWrEL N; IdentIs; IntAu&W 76, 77, 89, 91; IntvTCA 2; IntWW 74, 75, 76, 77, 78, 79, 80, 81, 82, 83, 89, 91; JeAmHC; LegTOT; LiExTwC; LinLib L, S; MagSWL; MajAI; MajTwCW 1, 2; McGEWB; ModAL 4S1, 4S2, 4S3, 5; MorBMP; NewCon; News 92, 92-1; NewYTBS 78, 91; NobelP; Novels; OxCAmL 83, 95; OxCChiL; OxCEng 85, 95; OxCTwCL; PenC AM; PenEncH; PeoHis; PolBiDi; RAdv 14, 13-2; RfGAmL 4, 87, 94; RfGShF 1, 2; RGTwCWr; ScF&FL 1, 2, 92; ShScr 3; ShSWr; SJGChWr 5; SJGHorW; SmATA 3, 27, 68; ThrBJA; TwCChW 1, 2, 3, 4; TwCWr; WebAB 74, 79; WebE&AL; WhAm 10; Who 82, 83, 85, 88, 90, 92N; WhoAm 74, 76, 78, 80, 82, 84, 86, 88, 90; WhoAmJ 80; WhoE 74, 79, 81, 83, 85, 86, 89, 91; WhoNob, 90, 95; WhoTwCL; WhoUSWr 88; WhoWor 74, 78, 80, 82, 84, 87, 89, 91; WhoWrEP 89; WorAl; WorAlBi; WorAu 1950; WorLitC; WrDr 76, 80, 82, 84, 86, 88, 90, 92, 94N; WrPh*

Singer, Isaac Merrit

American. Inventor
Manufactured first domestic sewing machine, 1851.
b. Oct 27, 1811 in Rensselaer, New York
d. Jul 23, 1875 in Torquay, England
Source: *AmBi; ApCAB; BioIn 5, 6, 7, 9, 11, 12; DcAmB; LegTOT; RanHWDS; TwCBDA; WebAB 74, 79; WhAm HS; WhDW*

Singer, Jane Sherrod
American. Author
Juvenile books include *Ernest Hemingway, Man of Courage*, 1963.
b. May 26, 1917 in Wichita Falls, Texas
Source: *BioIn 15; ConAu 17NR, 25R, 115; ForWC 70; SmATA 4, 42N; WhoAmW 61, 64, 66, 68, 70, 74, 75, 77; WhoWest 74, 76, 78*

Singer, Maxine (Frank)
American. Biochemist, Geneticist
Leading scientist in the field of human genetics, she advocated the responsible use of biochemical genetics research.
b. Feb 15, 1931 in New York, New York
Source: *AmMWSc 76P, 79, 82, 86, 89, 92, 95, 98; AmWomSc 1950; WhoAm 76, 78, 80, 82, 84, 86, 88, 90, 92, 94, 95, 96, 97, 98, 99, 2000; WhoAmW 66, 68, 70, 83, 85, 87, 89, 91, 93, 95, 97, 99; WhoFI 00, 96, 98; WhoFrS 84; WhoGov 72, 75, 77; WhoMedH 96, 99, 2000; WhoScEn 94, 96, 2000; WhoWor 91, 93, 95, 96, 97, 98, 99, 2000*

Singer, Peter
Austrian. Philosopher, Educator
Champion of animal rights; founder of the animal liberation movement; wrote *Animal Liberation: A New Ethic for Our Treatment of Animals*, 1975.
b. Jul 6, 1946 in Melbourne, Australia
Source: *ConAu 8NR, 57; CurBio 91; EnvEnc; IntWW 91; WrDr 84, 86, 88, 90, 92, 94, 96, 98, 99, 2000*

Singh, Giani Zail
Indian. Political Leader
Pres., India, 1982-87.
b. May 15, 1916 in Sandhwan, India
d. Dec 25, 1994 in Chandigarh, India
Source: *BioIn 13, 14, 15; CurBio 87, 95N; IntWW 83, 89, 91, 93; Who 88, 90, 92, 94; WhoWor 87*

Singh, (Sardar) Swaran
Indian. Government Official
Held various Indian cabinet positions, 1952-75.
b. Aug 19, 1907
d. Oct 30, 1994 in New Delhi, India
Source: *BioIn 7, 9, 20; CurBio 71, 95N; FarE&A 78, 79, 80, 81; IntWW 74, 75, 76, 77, 78, 79, 80, 81, 82, 83, 89, 91, 93; IntYB 78, 79, 80, 81, 82; Who 74, 82, 83, 85, 88, 90, 92, 94; WhoWor 74, 76, 78, 80*

Singh, V(ishwanath) P(ratap)
Indian. Political Leader
Prime Minister of India, 1989-1990; resigned after losing a parliamentary vote of confidence.
b. Jun 25, 1931 in Daiya, India
Source: *BioIn 15, 16; CamBiEn; ChamBiD; CurBio 90; EncWB 98; IntWW 89, 91, 93, 97, 98, 2000; NewYTBS 89, 90; Who 92, 94, 98, 99, 2000; WhoAsAP 91; WhoWor 91*

Singher, Martial
French. Opera Singer
Baritone with NY Met., 1943-60; noted for French operas.
b. Aug 14, 1904 in Oloron Saint Marie, France
d. Mar 10, 1990 in Santa Barbara, California
Source: *BakBD 78, 84; BioIn 1, 4, 5, 11, 15, 16; ConAu 131; CurBio 47, 90, 90N; IntWWM 90; MetOEnc; MusSN; NewAmDM; NewEOp 71; NewGrDA 86; NewGrDM 80; NewYTBS 90; PenDiMP; WhAm 10; WhoAm 74, 76, 78, 80, 82, 84, 86, 88; WhoAmM 83; WhoMus 72; WhoWest 74, 76, 78; WhoWor 74*

Singletary, Mike
[Michael Singletary]
American. Football Player
Four-time all-pro linebacker, Chicago, 1981-92; played major role in Super Bowl winning season, 1985-86.
b. Oct 9, 1958 in Houston, Texas
Source: *AfrAmSG; BiDAmSp FB; BioIn 14, 18, 19, 21; ConBlB 4; CurBio 93; FootReg 87; WhoAfA 9, 10; WhoAm 86, 88, 90, 92, 94, 95, 96, 97; WhoBlA 4, 5, 6, 7, 8; WhoMW 88, 90; WhoSpor; WorAlBi*

Singleton, John (Daniel)
American. Filmmaker
Writer and director of *Boyz N the Hood*, 1991; *Poetic Justice*, 1993; *Higher Learning*, 1995.
b. Jan 6, 1968 in Los Angeles, California
Source: *AfrAmAl 6; BlkWr 2; ConAu 138; ConBlB 2; ConTFT 12; IntMPA 94, 96; LegTOT; News 94, 94-3; NewYTBS 91; SchCGBL; WhoAm 95, 96, 97*

Singleton, Penny
[Dorothy McNulty]
American. Actor
Starred as "Blondie" in film series, 1938-50.
b. Sep 15, 1908 in Philadelphia, Pennsylvania
d. 1952
Source: *BioIn 10, 11; BioNews 74; BusPN; DcPseud; EncAFC; FilmEn; FilmgC; HalFC 80, 84, 88; HolP 30; IntMPA 77, 84, 86, 88, 92, 94, 96; InWom SUP; LegTOT; MotPP; MovMk; QDrFCA 92; RadStar; ThFT; WhoHol 92, A*

Singleton, Zutty
[Arthur James Singleton]
American. Musician
Drummer with leading jazz groups for over 50 yrs.
b. May 14, 1898 in Bunkie, Louisiana
d. Jul 14, 1975 in New York, New York
Source: *AmNatBi; BakBD 84, 92; BiDAfM; BiDAmM; BiDJaz; BioIn 7, 10, 16; CmpEPM; EncJzS; InB&W 80, 85; LegTOT; NewAmDM; NewGrDA 86; NewGrDJ 88, 94; NewGrDM 80; NewYTBS 75; OxCPMus; WhoHol C; WhoJazz 72; WhScrn 77, 83; WorAl; WorAlBi*

Singmaster, Elsie
American. Author
Her novels describe Pennsylvania Dutch country she lived in.
b. Aug 29, 1897 in Schuylkill, Pennsylvania
d. Sep 30, 1958 in Gettysburg, Pennsylvania
Source: *AmAu&B; ConAu 110; ObitOF 79; WhAm 3*

Sinise, Gary
American. Actor
Appeared in *Forrest Gump*, 1994; *Apollo 13*, 1995; founded the Steppenwolf Theatre Company, Chicago, 1974.
b. Mar 17, 1955 in Chicago, Illinois
Source: *ConTFT 16; CurBio 97; IntMPA 96; News 96, 96-1; OsStAZ; WhoAm 96, 97, 98, 99, 2000; WhoEnt 98*

Sinkford, Jeanne C(raig)
American. University Administrator, Dentist
Committed to social responsibility and community service, dentist, researcher, and educator rose to become dean emeritus of the Howard University College of Dentistry, 1991—, and director of Office of Women and Minority Affairs, American Association of Dental Schools, Washington, DC, 1991—.
b. Jan 30, 1933 in Washington, District of Columbia
Source: *NotBlAS; WhoAm 74, 76, 78, 80, 82, 84, 86, 90, 92, 94, 95, 96, 97, 98, 99, 2000; WhoAmW 79, 81, 83, 85, 89, 91, 93, 95, 97, 99; WhoE 95; WhoMedH 96, 99, 2000; WhoScEn 2000; WhoWor 76, 91, 93*

Sinkwich, Frank
"Fireball Frankie"
American. Football Player
All-America halfback, won Heisman Trophy, 1942; in NFL with Detroit, 1943-44; NFL MVP, 1944.
b. Oct 10, 1920 in McKees Rocks, Pennsylvania
d. Oct 22, 1990 in Athens, Georgia
Source: *BioIn 3, 8, 14, 17; NewYTBS 90; WhoFtbl 74; WhoSpor*

Sinner, George Albert
American. Politician
Dem. governor of ND, 1985-93.
b. May 29, 1928 in Fargo, North Dakota
Source: *AlmAP 88, 92; IntWW 89, 91, 93, 97, 98; St&PR 91; WhoAm 86, 88, 90, 92, 94, 95, 96, 97; WhoAmP 73, 85, 87, 91; WhoMW 88, 90, 92, 93, 96; WhoWor 87, 89, 91, 93, 95*

Sinopoli, Giuseppe
Italian. Conductor, Composer
Music director, London Philharmonia Orchestra, 1983-87; musical director, 1987—; known for his intense and individual interpretation of music.
b. Nov 2, 1946 in Venice, Italy
Source: *BakBD 84, 92; BakBDTw; BioIn 14, 15; ConNews 88-1; CurBio 91;*

IntDcOp; IntWW 89, 91, 93, 97, 98, 2000; IntWWM 90; MetOEnc; NewAmDM; NewGrDM 80; NewGrDO; PenDiMP; Who 94, 98, 99, 2000

Sinyavsky, Andrei D(onatovich)
[Abram Terts]
Russian. Author, Critic
Tried, convicted for slander to the Soviet State for literary work, *The Makepeace Experiment*, 1966; exiled to Paris, 1973.
b. Oct 8, 1925 in Moscow, Union of Soviet Socialist Republics
d. Feb 25, 1997 in Paris, France
Source: *Benet 87; BioIn 13, 15, 16, 21; ConAu 85; ConLC 8; CurBio 75, 97N; CyWA 89; DcRusLS; EncWL 2; FacFETw; HanRL; IntWW 91; LiExTwC; LinLib L; PenC EUR; RAdv 13-2; RfGShF 1; TwCWr; WhDW; WhoWor 91; WorAu 1950*

Siodmark, Curt
German. Producer, Director, Author
Science fiction books, films include *Donovan's Brain*, 1943.
b. Aug 10, 1902 in Dresden, Germany
Source: *ConAu 111, 113; ConDr 88A; DcLB 44; HalFC 88; IntMPA 92; NewEScF; ScFSB; TwCSFW 86, 91; WhoEnt 92; WhoSciF; WrDr 90*

Siouxie and the Banshees
[Budgie; John Klein; Martin McCarrick; Steven Severin; Siouxsie (Susan Dallion) Sioux]
English. Music Group
Punk rock band founded in 1976; the 1991 album *Superstition*, is their most cohesive work to date.
Source: *ConMus 8; EncRk 88; IlEncRk; PenEncP; WhoRocM 82; WhsNW 85*

Siple, Paul Allman
American. Explorer, Geographer
Originated wind-chill index.
b. Dec 18, 1908 in Montpelier, Ohio
d. Nov 25, 1968 in Arlington, Virginia
Source: *AmAu&B; AmNatBi; BioIn 4, 5, 6, 8; CurBio 57, 69; InSci; OhA&B; WhAm 5*

Siqueiros, David A
Mexican. Artist
Last of Mexican Renaissance giants; did boldly colored murals promoting proletarian revolution.
b. Dec 29, 1896 in Chihuahua, Mexico
d. Jan 6, 1974 in Cuernavaca, Mexico
Source: *CurBio 59, 74; NewCol 75; NewYTBS 74; WhAm 6; WhoAmA 73*

Sirhan, Sirhan Bishara
Jordanian. Assassin
Shot Robert Kennedy, Jun 5, 1968; serving life sentence in San Quentin Prison.
b. Mar 19, 1944? in Jerusalem, Palestine
Source: *BioIn 8, 9, 10, 11, 12, 13, 15; PolProf J; WorAlBi*

Sirica, John Joseph
American. Judge
Presided over Watergate trial, 1973-75.
b. Mar 19, 1904 in Waterbury, Connecticut
d. Aug 14, 1992 in Washington, District of Columbia
Source: *AmNatBi; BioIn 12, 13, 15; CamDcAB; CngDr 85, 87, 89; ConAu 110; CurBio 74; EncWB, 98; FacFETw; IntWW 77, 78, 79, 80, 81, 82, 83, 89, 91; News 93-2; NewYTBE 73; NewYTBS 92; WhoAm 86, 90; WhoAmL 83, 85; WhoSSW 73; WhoWor 84; WorAlBi*

Sirk, Douglas
[Dietlef Sierck]
Danish. Director
Films include *Magnificent Obsession*, 1954; *Imitation of Life*, 1959.
b. Apr 26, 1900 in Skagen, Denmark
d. Jan 14, 1987 in Lugano, Switzerland
Source: *AnObit 1987; BiDFilm, 81, 94; BioIn 10, 11, 12, 15, 16, 24; CmMov; DcArts; DcFM; DcPseud; FacFETw; FilmEn; FilmgC; HalFC 80, 84, 88; IlWWHD 1; IntDcF 1-2, 2-2; IntMPA 75, 76, 77, 78, 79, 80, 81, 82, 84, 86; ItaFilm; LegTOT; MakMC; MiSFD 9N; NewYTBS 87; OxCFilm; RAdv 14; WorEFlm; WorFDir 1*

Sironi, Mario
Italian. Artist
Founding member of the Novecento group: *House and Trees*, 1948.
b. May 12, 1885 in Tempio Pausania, Sardinia, Italy
d. Aug 13, 1961 in Milan, Italy
Source: *BioIn 4, 6, 17; ConArt 77, 83; DcTwArt; McGDA; ObitOF 79; OxCTwCA; PhDcTCA 77*

Sisco, Joseph John
American. Government Official
Asst. secretary of State, Near East and S Asian affairs, 1969-74; pres., American U, 1976-80.
b. Oct 31, 1919 in Chicago, Illinois
Source: *BioIn 10, 12; BlueB 76; CurBio 72; HisEAAC; IntWW 74, 75, 76, 77, 78, 79, 80, 81, 82, 83, 89, 91, 93, 97, 98, 2000; PolProf NF; USBiR 74; WhoAm 74, 76, 78, 80, 82, 84, 86, 88, 90, 92, 94, 95, 96, 97, 98, 99, 2000; WhoAmP 73, 75, 77, 79; WhoGov 72, 75; WhoSSW 73; WhoWor 78*

Siskel, Gene
[Eugene Karl Siskel]
American. Critic
Co-host of TV shows "Sneak Previews," 1978-82; "Siskel and Ebert," 1982-99.
b. Jan 26, 1946 in Chicago, Illinois
d. Feb 20, 1999 in Chicago, Illinois
Source: *BioIn 13; OnHuYAF; WhoAm 84, 86, 88, 90, 92, 94, 95, 96, 97, 98, 99; WhoEmL 87; WhoEnt 92, 98; WhoMW 88, 90, 92, 93*

Siskind, Aaron
American. Photographer
Abstract photographer best known for expressing moods/feelings through photography.
b. 1903 in New York, New York
Source: *AmArt; AnObit 1991; BioIn 10, 12, 13; BriEAA; CamDcAB; ConPhot 82, 88, 95; DcAmArt; DcArts; DcCAr 81; ICPEnP; MacBEP; NewYTBS 91; WhAm 10; WhAmArt 85; WhoAm 84, 88, 90*

Sisler, George Harold
"Gorgeous George"
American. Baseball Player
First baseman, 1915-22, 1924-30, mostly with St. Louis; holds ML record for hits in one season, 257, 1920; won AL batting title twice; Hall of Fame, 1939.
b. Mar 24, 1893 in Manchester, Ohio
d. Mar 26, 1973 in Richmond Heights, Missouri
Source: *AmNatBi; BiDAmSp BB; BioIn 2, 3, 4, 5, 6, 7, 8, 9, 10; CamDcAB; DcAmB S9; WhoProB 73*

Sisley, Alfred
French. Artist
Impressionist painter; *The Flood at Port Marly; Snow at Louveciennes*, both at Louvre.
b. Oct 30, 1839 in Paris, France
d. Jan 29, 1899 in Moret, France
Source: *AtlBL; Benet 87, 96; BioIn 2, 3, 4, 5, 6, 7, 9, 11, 12, 16, 18; CamBiEn; ChamBiD; ClaDrA; DcArts; DcNaB MP; IntDcAA 90; LegTOT; OxCArt; OxDcArt; REn; ThHEIm; WhDW; WorAl; WorAlBi*

Sismondi, Jean Charles Leonard Simonde de
Swiss. Economist, Historian
Political economist known for his histories of France and Italy emphasizing the development of constitutional government.
b. May 9, 1773, Switzerland
d. Jun 25, 1842
Source: *BioIn 18; GloEncH*

Sissle, Noble
American. Bandleader, Lyricist
Led Sizzling Syncopators, 1930s-60s; often collaborated with Eubie Blake; wrote "I'm Just Wild About Harry."
b. Jul 10, 1889 in Indianapolis, Indiana
d. Dec 17, 1975 in Tampa, Florida
Source: *AfrAmAl 6, 8; AllMGJa; AmNatBi; ASCAP 66, 80; BakDcM; BgBands 74; BiDAfM; BiDAmM; BiDJaz; BioIn 8, 9, 10, 11, 15; BlkAmP; BlkAWP; BlksB&W, C; BlksBF; CamGWoT; CmpEPM; ConAu 112; DrBlPA, 90; EncAACR; EncMT; EncVaud; MorBAP; NegAl 76, 83, 89; NewAmDM; NewGrDA 86; NewGrDJ 88; OxCPMus; Songw; SpreRhy; WhoJazz 72; WhScrn 77, 83*

Sissman, L(ouis) E(dward)
American. Poet, Essayist
Writings include "Dying: An Introduction," 1968; "Pursuit of Honor," 1971.
b. Jan 1, 1928 in Detroit, Michigan
d. Mar 10, 1976 in Boston, Massachusetts
Source: *BioIn 8, 10, 11, 12, 13; ConAu 13NR, 21R, 65; ConLC 9, 18; ConPo 75; DcLB 5; DcLEL 1940; DrAP 75; NatCAB 61; NewYTBS 76; OxCTwCP; WhAm 7; WhoAdv 72; WhoAm 74, 76; WhoE 74; WorAu 1950, 1975; WrDr 76*

Sisson, Charles Hubert
English. Poet
Satirical, politically critical works include "Anchises," 1976; "Exactions," 1980.
b. Apr 22, 1914 in Bristol, England
Source: *Au&Wr 71; BioIn 12, 14, 15; CamGLE; ConAu 1R, 3AS, 3NR, 84NR; ConLC 8; ConPo 70, 75, 91; DcLEL 27; EngPo; FacFETw; IntAu&W 77, 82, 86, 89, 91, 93; IntWW 77, 78, 79, 80, 81, 82, 83, 89, 91, 93, 97, 98, 2000; IntWWP 77, 82; MakMC; ModBrL S2; OxCEng 85; OxCTwCL; Who 74, 82, 83, 85, 88, 90, 92, 94, 98, 99, 2000; WhoTwCL; WhoWor 89; WrDr 76, 86, 92, 98, 99, 2000*

Sister Sledge
[Debbie Sledge; Joni Sledge; Kathy Sledge; Kim Sledge]
American. Music Group
Sister quartet known for hit "We Are Family," 1979, which became theme for world champ Pittsburgh Pirates, 1979.
Source: *BillEnR; DrBlPA 90; EncRk 88; InB&W 80, 85A; Law&B 92; RkOn 85; SoulM*

Sister Souljah
[Lisa Williamson]
American. Rapper
Released album, *360 Degrees of Power*, 1992; autobiography, *No Disrespect*, 1995.
b. 1964 in New York, New York
Source: *ConBlB 11*

Sisulu, Nontsikelelo Albertina
South African. Social Reformer, Political Activist
One of the most important women leaders of the anti-apartheid resistance in South Africa, she led the African National Congress Women's League and the Federation of South African Women in the 1950s.
b. 1918 in Transkei, South Africa
Source: *EncWB 98*

Sisulu, Walter Max Ulyate
South African. Social Reformer, Political Activist
General secretary of the African National Congress (ANC) of South Africa and a chief strategist and organizer of the Defiance Campaign in the 1950s, he

was a leader in the militant resistance to apartheid.
b. 1912 in Transkei, South Africa
Source: *ChamBiD; DcAfHiB 86; EncWB, 98; IntWW 91, 93, 97, 98, 2000; WhoAfr*

Sithole, Ndabaningi
Zimbabwean. Politician
Intellectual was a leader in the early nationalist movement in Zimbabwe (formerly Southern Rhodesia).
b. Jul 21, 1920 in Nyamanandhlovu, Zimbabwe
Source: *AfSS 78, 79, 80, 81, 82; BioIn 9, 10, 11, 21; ConAu 110; DcAfHiB 86; EncWB 98; EncyDCo; IntWW 74, 75, 76, 77, 78, 79, 80, 81, 82, 83, 89, 91, 93, 97, 98, 2000; McGEWB; NewYTBS 75, 79*

Sitter, Willem de
Dutch. Mathematician
His theoretical models regarding the nature of the universe were based on Einstein's theory of relativity.
b. May 6, 1872 in Sneek, Netherlands
d. Nov 20, 1934 in Leiden, Netherlands
Source: *AsBiEn; CamBiEn; CamDcSc; ChamBiD; DcScB; InSci; RanHWDS; WorScD*

Sitting Bull
American. Native American Chief
Organized Native American forces at Battle of Little Bighorn, 1876.
b. 1831 in Grand River, South Dakota
d. Dec 15, 1890 in Grand River, South Dakota
Source: *AmBi; AmIndBi; AmNatBi; ApCAB; BenetAL 91; BioIn 15, 16, 17, 19, 20, 22, 23, 24; CamDcAB; DcAmB; DcPseud; EncAB-H 1974; EncAInd; EncNoAI; FilmgC; GayN; HalFC 80, 84, 88; HarEnMi; LegTOT; NatNAL; NewEAmW; NotNaAm; RelLAm 1, 2; REnAW; VioAm; WebAB 74, 79; WebAMB; WhAm HS; WhDW; WhNaAH; WorAl; WorAlBi*

Sittler, Darryl Glen
Canadian. Hockey Player
Center, 1970-85, mostly with Toronto; set NHL record for most pts. in game, 10 (1976); Hall of Fame, 1989.
b. Sep 18, 1950 in Kitchener, Ontario, Canada
Source: *HocEn; HocReg 85; NewYTBS 76; WhoAm 78, 80, 82, 84; WhoHcky 73*

Sitwell, Edith, Dame
English. Poet
Wrote poetry volume *Street Songs*, 1943; biographical study *English Eccentrics*, 1933.
b. Sep 7, 1887 in Scarborough, England
d. Dec 9, 1964 in London, England
Source: *AnCL; ArtclWW 2; AtlBL; Benet 87, 96; BiCoLiE; BioIn 1, 2, 3, 4, 5, 6, 7, 8, 9, 10, 11, 12, 13, 14, 16, 17, 18, 20, 21, 22; BlmGEL; BlmGWL; BritWr 7; CamBiEn; CamGEL; CamGLE; CasWL; Chambr 3; ChhPo, S1, S2, S3; ClDMEL 47; CnDBLB 7; CnMWL;*

ConAu 9R, 35NR; ConLC 2, 9, 67; CyWA 97; DcArts; DcLB 20; DcLEL; EncBrWW; EncWB 98; EncWL 1, 2, 2S, 3; EngPo; EvLB; FacFETw; FemiCLE; GrWomW; GrWrEL P; InWom, SUP; LegTOT; LinLib L; LngCEL; LngCTC; MajTwCW 1; MakMC; McGEWB; ModBrL, 2, S1, S2; ModWoWr; NewC; NewCBEL; ObitT 1961; OxCEng 67; OxCMus; PenBWP; PenC ENG; PoeCrit 3; RAdv 1, 14, 13-1; REn; RfGEnL 91; RGFMBP; TwCA, SUP; TwCWr; WebE&AL; WhAm 4; WhDW; WhoTwCL; WorAl; WorAlBi; WorAu 1900*

Sitwell, Osbert, Sir
English. Author
Wrote novel *Before the Bombardment*, 1926; five-volume memoirs of his eccentric family, 1944-50.
b. Dec 6, 1892 in London, England
d. May 4, 1969 in Montagnana, Italy
Source: *Benet 87; BiCoLiE; BioIn 1, 2, 3, 4, 5, 6, 7, 8, 9, 10, 11, 12, 13, 14, 17, 22, 24; BlmGEL; CamBiEn; CamGEL; CamGLE; CasWL; Chambr 3; ConAu 25R, P-2; CurBio 65, 69; DcArts; DcLB 100, 195; DcLEL; DcNaB 1961; EncSF, 93; EncWL 1; EvLB; FacFETw; GrWrEL P; LinLib L, S; LngCEL; LngCTC; ModBrL, 2, S1; NewC; NewCBEL; Novels; ObitT 1961; OxCEng 67, 85; PenC ENG; RAdv 1, 13-1; REn; RfGEnL 91; ScF&FL 1, 2, 92; TwCA, SUP; TwCWr; WhAm 5; WhDW; WhE&EA; WhLit; WhoTwCL*

Sitwell, Sacheverell, Sir
English. Author, Critic
Known for art, music critiques: *German Baroque Art*, 1927; *Sacred and Profane Love*, 1940.
b. Nov 15, 1897 in Scarborough, England
d. Oct 1, 1988 in London, England
Source: *AnObit 1988; Au&Wr 71; Benet 87, 96; BiCoLiE; BioIn 2, 3, 4, 6, 8, 9, 10, 11, 12, 15, 16, 19, 22; BlmGEL; BlueB 76; CamBiEn; CamGEL; CamGLE; ChamBiD; Chambr 3; ChhPo, S2; CnE&AP; ConAu 21R, 86NR, 126; ConPo 70, 75, 80, 85; DcArts; DcLEL; DcNaB 1986; EncWL 1; EvLB; FacFETw; GrWrEL P; IntAu&W 76, 77, 82, 89, 91; IntWW 74, 75, 76, 77, 78, 79, 80, 81, 82, 83; IntWWP 77; LinLib L; LngCEL; LngCTC; ModBrL, 2, S1; NewC; NewCBEL; NewYTBS 88; OxCEng 67, 85, 95; OxCTwCL; OxCTwCP; PenC ENG; REn; RfGEnL 91; RGTwCWr; TwCA, SUP; TwCWr; WhDW; WhE&EA; Who 74, 82, 83, 85, 88; WhoTwCL; WhoWor 74, 76, 78; WorAu 1900; WrDr 76, 80, 82, 84, 86, 88*

Sivaji
[Sivaji Bhonsle]
Indian. King, Military Leader
Warrior ruled an independent Hindu nation in Maharashtra, and defended the Maratha people from the invading Mughals.

b. Apr 6, 1627 in Poona, Maharashtra,
India
d. Apr 3, 1680 in Rajgarh, India
Source: *BioIn 17; CamBiEn; EncWB 98;
WhoMilH 76*

Six, Robert Forman

American. Business Executive
Flamboyant founder of Continental
Airlines; introduced discount fares to
industry, 1962.
b. Jun 25, 1907 in Stockton, California
d. Oct 6, 1986 in Beverly Hills,
California
Source: *AmNatBi; BioIn 4, 5, 6, 7, 8, 9,
10, 11; BlueB 76; CamDcAB; CurBio
70, 86; IntWW 74, 75, 76, 77, 78, 79,
80, 81, 82, 83; IntYB 78, 79, 80, 81, 82;
NewYTBS 86; St&PR 75, 84; WhAm 9;
WhoAm 74, 76, 78, 80, 82, 84; WhoE
81, 83; WhoFI 74, 75, 77, 79, 81;
WhoWest 74, 76, 78, 82; WhoWor 74*

Sixtus, V

[Felice Peretti]
Italian. Religious Leader
Pope from 1585 to 1590, known for his
energy, intelligence, and
determination; reorganized the curial
system at the Vatican and changed the
face of Rome with new roads, palaces,
and aqueducts.
b. Dec 13, 1520 in Grottammare, Italy
d. Aug 27, 1590 in Rome, Italy
Source: *DcPseud; EncWB 98; LuthC 75;
McGEWB; OxDcP 86*

Siza, Alvaro (Joaquim Melo)

[Vieria]
Portuguese. Architect, Educator
Considered Portugal's greatest living
architect, his works are renowned for
their coherence, clarity, and
"simplism;" awarded the Pritzker
Prize, 1992.
b. Jun 25, 1933 in Matosinhos, Portugal

Sjoberg, Alf

Swedish. Director
Head director of Sweden's Royal
Dramatic Theater, 1930-40.
b. Jun 21, 1903 in Stockholm, Sweden
d. Apr 17, 1980 in Stockholm, Sweden
Source: *AnObit 1980; BiDFilm, 81, 94;
BioIn 12, 15, 20; CamGWoT; DcFM;
EncEurC; EncWT; FilmEn; FilmgC;
HalFC 80, 84, 88; IntDcF 1-2, 2-2;
IntDcT 3; IntWW 74, 75, 76, 77, 78;
MiSFD 9N; OxCFilm; OxCThe 83;
TheaDir; WhoWor 74, 76, 78; WhScrn
83; WorFDir 1*

Sjostrom, Victor

Swedish. Director
Pioneer of Swedish film industry.
b. Sep 20, 1879 in Silbodal, Sweden
d. Jan 3, 1960 in Stockholm, Sweden
Source: *BiDFilm, 81, 94; BioIn 15, 16;
CamBiEn; ChamBiD; DcFM; EncEurC;
Film 1; FilmEn; FilmgC; HalFC 80;
IntDcF 1-2, 2-2; MiSFD 9N; MovMk;
ObitT 1951; OxCFilm; WhoHol B;
WorEFlm; WorFDir 1*

Sjowall, Maj

Swedish. Author, Poet
With husband, Per Wahloo, wrote
detective novel series featuring Martin
Beck as protagonist, 1965-75.
b. Sep 25, 1935 in Malmo, Sweden
Source: *Benet 87; BioIn 9, 10, 24;
ConAu 65; ConLC 7; CrtSuMy; EncMys;
LegTOT; MyssW; NewYTBE 71; Novels;
TwCCr&M 85, 85B; WorAl; WorAlBi;
WorAu 1970*

Skaggs, M(arion) B

American. Merchant
Founder, head, Safeway Stores, Inc.,
1926-34; had 3,527 stores, 1931.
b. 1888
d. May 8, 1976 in Oakland, California
Source: *BioIn 10; NewYTBS 76; ObitOF
79*

Skaggs, Ricky

American. Musician, Singer
Won 1982 CMA awards for best male
vocalist and newcomer of year.
b. Jul 18, 1954 in Cordell, Kentucky
Source: *AllMGCo; BakBD 92;
BgBkCoM; BioIn 13, 14, 15, 16, 22, 24;
ConMus 5; EncRk 88; HarEnCM 87;
HarEnR 86; LegTOT; NewAmDM;
NewGrDA 86; OnThGG; PenEncP;
PrimTiR; WhoAm 90, 97, 98, 2000;
WhoEnt 92, 98; WhoNeCM*

Skate, Bill

[William Jack Skate]
Papua New Guinean. Political Leader
Following the Bougainville rebellion and
the resulting scandals, he replaced
Chan as prime minister of Papua New
Guinea in 1997.
b. Sep 26, 1953 in Ara'ara, Gulf, Papua
New Guinea

Skelly, Hal

American. Actor
Starred in seven films, 1929-33,
including *The Dance of Life*, 1929.
b. 1891 in Allegheny, Pennsylvania
d. Jun 16, 1934 in West Cornwall,
Connecticut
Source: *CmpEPM; Film 2; ForYSC;
HalFC 80, 84, 88; OxCAmT 84; WhoHol
B; WhScrn 74, 77, 83; WhThe*

Skelton, John

English. Poet
Poet laureate; tutor to Henry VIII;
irregular rhyme-scheme called
"skeltonic meter."
b. 1460?
d. Jun 21, 1529 in Westminster, England
Source: *Alli; AtlBL; Benet 87, 96;
BiCoLiE; BiD&SB; BioIn 1, 2, 3, 5, 7, 8,
9, 11, 12, 13, 17, 20, 24; BlmGEL;
BritAu; BritWr 1; CamBiEn; CamGEL;
CamGLE; CamGWoT; CasWL;
ChamBiD; Chambr 1; ChhPo, S1, S3;
CmMedTh; CnE&AP; CroE&S; CrtT 1,
4; CyWA 97; DcArts; DcCathB; DcEnL;
DcEuL; DcLEL; DcNaB; Dis&D;
EncWB 98; EvLB; GrWrEL P; LngCEL;
McGEWB; McGEWD 72, 84; MediEng;*

---

*MouLC 1; NewC; NewCBEL; OxCEng
67, 85, 95; OxCThe 67, 83; PenC ENG;
PoLE; RAdv 1, 14, 13-1; REn; RfGEnL
91; WebE&AL*

Skelton, Red

[Richard Skelton]
American. Comedian, Actor
Master of pantomime and slapstick
comedy; hosted comedy-variety TV
show, 1951-71.
b. Jul 18, 1913 in Vincennes, Indiana
d. Sep 17, 1997 in Rancho Mirage,
California
Source: *ASCAP 66, 80; AuBYP 2S, 3;
BioIn 2, 3, 4, 5, 6, 7, 10, 11, 12, 16, 23,
24; CamBiEn; CelR; CmMov; ConAu
104, 161; ConTFT 8, 18; CurBio 47,
97N; EncAFC; FilmEn; FilmgC; Funs;
HalFC 84, 88; IndAu 1967; IntMPA 84,
86, 88, 92, 94, 96; JoeFr; LegTOT;
LesBEnT, 92; MGM; MotPP; MovMk;
News 98, 98-1; NewYTBS 77, 97;
RadStar; SaTiSS; ScF&FL 1; WhAm 12;
WhoAm 76, 78, 80, 82, 88, 90, 92, 94,
95, 96, 97, 98; WhoCom; WhoEnt 92;
WhoHol A; WorAl; WorAlBi*

Skelton, Robin

English. Poet
Major books of poetry include *The
Hunting Dark*, 1971; *Timelight*, 1978.
b. Oct 12, 1925 in Easington, England
Source: *Au&Wr 71; AuNews 2; BioIn 10,
11, 14, 15, 16; CanWW 70, 79, 80, 81,
83, 89, 96, 97; CaW; ChhPo S1;
CnE&AP; ConAu 5AS, 5R, 28NR, 160;
ConCaAu 1; ConLC 13; ConPo 70, 75,
80, 85, 91, 96; DcLB 27, 53; DcLEL
1940; DrAP 75; DrAPF 80, 91; DrAS
74E, 78E, 82E; EngPo; IntAu&W 76, 77,
82, 89, 91, 93; IntWWP 77, 82;
OxCCanL 1, 2; OxCCan SUP;
OxCTwCP; ScF&FL 92; Who 74, 82, 83,
85, 88, 90, 92, 94; WhoAmA 78, 80, 82;
WhoCanL 85, 87, 92; WhoWest 74, 76;
WorAu 1950; WrDr 76, 80, 82, 84, 86,
88, 90, 92, 94, 96, 98, 99*

Skerritt, Tom

[Thomas Roy Skerritt]
American. Actor
Films include *Alien*, 1979; *The Dead
Zone*, 1983; in TV series "Picket
Fences," 1992-96.
b. Aug 25, 1933 in Detroit, Michigan
Source: *BioIn 21; ConTFT 6, 13, 25;
HalFC 84, 88; IntMPA 88, 92, 94, 96;
ItaFilm; LegTOT; VarWW 85; WhoAm
80, 82, 84, 94, 95, 96, 97, 98, 99, 2000;
WhoEnt 98; WhoHol 92, A; WorAlBi*

Skidmore, Louis

American. Architect
Partner in architectural firm that
constructed town of Oak Ridge, TN.
b. Apr 8, 1897 in Lawrenceburg, Indiana
d. Sep 27, 1962 in Winter Haven,
Florida
Source: *AmCulL; AmNatBi; BioIn 2, 4,
6, 8, 13; ConArch 80, 87, 94; CurBio
51, 62; DcAmB S7; DcD&D; DcTwDes;
EncAAr 1; EncMA; InSci; LegTOT;*

*MacEA; MakTCMA; McGDA; NatCAB
50; WhAm 4, 5; WorAl; WorAlBi*

Skinner, B(urrhus) F(rederic)
American. Psychologist, Author
Leading exponent of Behaviorism; father
of programmed instruction and
"Skinner" box.
b. Mar 20, 1904 in Susquehanna,
Pennsylvania
d. Aug 18, 1990 in Cambridge,
Massachusetts
Source: *AmAu&B; AmMWSc 73S, 78S;
AmSocL; Au&Wr 71; Benet 87, 96;
BenetAL 91; BiDAmEd; BioIn 1, 6, 7, 8,
9, 10, 11, 12, 13, 14, 17, 18, 19, 23;
CamBiEn; CamDcAB; ChamBiD; ConAu
9R, 18NR, 42NR, 132; EncAB-H 1974, 1996; EncSF;
EncWB 98; FacFETw; IntWW 74, 75,
76, 77, 78, 79, 80, 81, 82, 83, 89, 91N;
MajTwCW 1, 2; MakMC; McGEWB;
McGMS 80; News 91-1; NewYTBS 90;
RAdv 14, 13-3; RanHWDS; ScFSB;
ScrEAmL 2; ThTwC 87; WebAB 74, 79;
WhAm 10; Who 82, 83, 85, 88, 90;
WhoAm 74, 76, 78, 80, 82, 84, 86, 88,
90; WhoWor 74, 84; WorAlBi; WorAu
1970; WrDr 76, 80, 90*

Skinner, Cornelia Otis
American. Actor, Author
Daughter of Otis Skinner; appeared with
him in *Blood and Sand*, 1921.
b. May 30, 1901 in Chicago, Illinois
d. Jul 9, 1979 in New York, New York
Source: *AmAu&B; AmNatBi; AmWomD;
AmWomPl; AmWomWr; ArtclWW 2;
Au&Wr 71; Benet 87, 96; BenetAL 91;
BiE&WWA; BioIn 2, 3, 4, 5, 7, 9, 12,
13, 16, 22; CamGWoT; CelR; ChhPo;
ConAu 17R, 89; CurBio 42, 64, 79N;
DcAmB S10; DcLEL; EncWB 2-19;
EncWT; EvLB; FemiCLE; FilmgC;
ForYSC; HalFC 80, 84, 88; IntWW 74;
InWom, SUP; LegTOT; LinLib L;
LngCTC; NewYTBS 79; NotNAT, A;
NotWoAT; OxCAmL 65, 83, 95;
OxCAmT 84; PenC AM; REn; REnAL;
SmATA 2; TwCA SUP; TwCWr; Who
74; WhoAm 74; WhoHol A; WhoThe 72,
77; WhScrn 83; WorAl; WorAlBi;
WorAu 1900; WrDr 76*

Skinner, Halcyon
American. Inventor
Made power looms for weaving carpets,
1856.
b. Mar 6, 1824 in Mantua, Ohio
d. Nov 28, 1900 in Mantua, Ohio
Source: *DcAmB; NatCAB 5; WhAm HS*

Skinner, Otis
American. Actor
One of American theater's greatest
character actors; known for role in
Kismet, 1911-14.
b. Jun 28, 1858 in Cambridge,
Massachusetts
d. Jan 4, 1942 in New York, New York
Source: *AmAu&B; AmNatBi; BenetAL
91; BioIn 1, 2, 3, 4, 5, 9, 10, 13;
CamDcAB; CamGWoT; CurBio 42;*

*DcAmB S3; DcNAA; EncWT; FamA&A;
Film 1, 2; FilmgC; HalFC 80, 84, 88;
IntDcT 3; LinLib L, S; NatCAB 11, 32;
NotNAT A, B; OxCAmL 65; OxCAmT
84; OxCThe 67, 83; PlP&P; REn;
REnAL; TwYS; WebAB 74, 79; WhAm 1;
WhoHol B; WhScrn 74, 77; WhThe;
WorAl; WorAlBi*

Skinner, Sam
American. Government official
Attorney known for his ability to build
alliances, served as U.S. Secretary of
Transportation, 1989-91, and White
House Chief of Staff, 1991-92.
b. Jun 10, 1938 in Chicago, Illinois
Source: *News 92, 92-3*

Skinner, Samuel K(nox)
American. Government Official
US Secretary of Transportation 1988-92;
White House chief of staff, 1991-92.
b. Jun 10, 1938 in Chicago, Illinois
Source: *BiDrUSE 89; BioIn 16; CngDr
89, 91; CurBio 89; News 92; NewYTBS
91; Who 94, 98, 99, 2000; WhoAm 82,
90, 92, 94, 95, 96, 97; WhoAmL 78, 79,
83, 85, 87; WhoAmP 91, 93, 95, 97,
1999; WhoE 91, 93; WhoFI 92; WhoMW
96; WhoWor 91, 93*

Skipworth, Alison
American. Actor
Played dowagers, duchesses, 1930s; films
include *If I Had A Million*, 1932.
b. Jul 25, 1870? in London, England
d. Jul 5, 1952 in New York, New York
Source: *FilmgC; MovMk; ThFT; Vers B;
WhoHol B; WhoStg 1908; WhScrn 74,
83*

Skolnick, Mark H(enry)
American. Geneticist
Isolated two genes which cause breast
cancer, BRCA1 in 1994 and BRCA2
in 1996.
b. Jan 28, 1946 in Temple, Texas
Source: *AmMWSc 79, 82, 86, 89, 92, 95,
98; WhoAm 97*

Skolsky, Sidney
American. Journalist
Hollywood gossip columnist since 1933,
coined term "sneak preview."
b. May 5, 1905 in New York, New York
d. May 3, 1983 in Hollywood, California
Source: *BioIn 2, 78, 79, 80, 81, 82;
NewYTBS 83; ScrEAmL 1; WhAm 8;
WhoAm 74, 76, 78, 80, 82; WhoWorJ
72, 78*

Skouras, Spyros Panagiotes
American. Producer
Pres., 20th Century Fox, 1942-62;
launched cinemascope.
b. Mar 28, 1893 in Skourokhori, Greece
d. Aug 16, 1971 in Mamaroneck, New
York
Source: *AmNatBi; BioIn 5, 6, 8, 9;
CurBio 43, 71; DcAmB S9; DcFM;
FilmgC; NewYTBE 71; OxCFilm;
WebAB 74, 79; WhAm 5; WorEFlm*

Skowron, Bill
[William Joseph Skowron]
"Moose"
American. Baseball Player
First baseman, NY Yankees, 1954-62;
had lifetime .282 batting average.
b. Dec 18, 1930 in Chicago, Illinois
Source: *Ballpl 90; BaseEn 88; BiDAmSp
Sup; BioIn 6, 14, 15*

Skrowaczewski, Stanislaw
American. Composer, Conductor
Wrote symphony at age eight; led MN
Orchestra, 1960-79; Manchester,
England's Halle Orchestra, 1984-91;
musical advisor, St. Paul Chamber
Orchestra, 1986-87.
b. Oct 3, 1923 in Lwow, Poland
Source: *ASCAP 80; BakBD 78, 84, 92;
BakBDTw; BioIn 5, 7, 8, 9, 11; BlueB
76; BriBkM 80; CelR; ConAmC 82;
CurBio 64; IntWW 74, 75, 76, 77, 78,
79, 80, 81, 82, 83, 89, 91, 93, 97, 98,
2000; IntWWM 77, 80, 85, 90; MusSN;
NewAmDM; NewGrDA 86; NewGrDM
80; PenDiMP; WhoAm 74, 76, 78, 80,
82, 84, 86, 88, 90, 92, 94, 95, 96, 97,
98, 99, 2000; WhoAmM 83; WhoEnt 92,
98; WhoMus 72; WhoWM 74, 76, 78, 80,
82, 90; WhoOp 76; WhoPoA 96;
WhoSocC 78; WhoSoCE 89; WhoWor
74, 76, 78, 80, 82, 84, 87, 89, 91, 93,
95, 96, 97, 98, 99, 2000*

Skulnik, Menasha
Polish. Actor
Stage comedian, 1920-50, in Yiddish
theater.
b. May 15, 1898? in Warsaw, Poland
d. Jun 4, 1970 in New York, New York
Source: *BiE&WWA; NewYTBE 70;
WhAm 5; WhScrn 77*

Skurzynski, Gloria
American. Author
Juvenile books include *The Magic
Pumpkin*, 1971; *What Happened in
Hamelin*, 1979.
b. Jul 6, 1930 in Duquesne, Pennsylvania
Source: *ConAu 13NR, 30NR, 33R;
DcAmChF 1960, 1985; FifBJA;
PopNonf; SmATA 8, 9AS*

Slade, Bernard
[Bernard Slade Newbound]
Canadian. Dramatist
Stage plays include *Same Time Next
Year*, 1975; *Fatal Attraction*, 1984;
also wrote screenplays, TV scripts.
b. May 2, 1930 in Saint Catharines,
Ontario, Canada
Source: *BioIn 15; CanWW 89, 96, 97,
98, 1999; CaP; ConAu 9AS, 49NR, 81;
ConCaAu 1; ConDr 88, 93; ConLC 11,
46; ConTFT 1; CrtSuDr; DcLB 53;
IntAu&W 91, 93; LesBEnT, 92;
McGEWD 84; NatPD 81; NewYTBS 75;
OxCAmT 84; OxCCanT; WhoAm 84, 86,
88, 90, 92, 94, 95, 96, 97, 98, 99, 2000;
WhoEnt 92, 98; WhoWor 84; WrDr 88,
90, 92, 94, 96, 98, 99, 2000*

Slade, Jack
[Joseph A Slade]
American. Murderer
Ruthless gunman of the American West;
  known for his senseless cruelty;
  lynched by vigilantes.
b. 1824 in Carlyle, Illinois
d. Mar 10, 1864 in Virginia City,
  Montana
Source: *DrInf*

Slansky, Rudolf Salzmann
Czech. Politician
Founding member the Czechoslovak
  Communist Party and leader in the
  Communist takeover of
  Czechoslovakia in 1948; he was
  executed in the purges of "national
  Communists" ordered by Stalin.
b. Jul 31, 1901 in Nezvestice, Bohemia,
  Austria-Hungary
d. Dec 3, 1952 in Prague,
  Czechoslovakia
Source: *EncWB, 98*

Slash
[Guns N' Roses; Saul Hudson]
English. Musician
Debut album *Live? ! Like a Suicide,*
  1986.
b. 1965 in Stoke-on-Trent, England
Source: *DcPseud; LegTOT; OnThGG;*
WhoAm 94, 95, 96, 97, 98

Slater, Christian
[Christian Hawkins]
American. Actor
Appeared in *The Legend of Billie Jean,*
  1985; *Interview with the Vampire,*
  1994.
b. Aug 18, 1969 in New York, New
  York
Source: *CamBiEn; ConTFT 9, 16;*
DcPseud; IntMPA 92, 94, 96; IntWW 97,
98, 2000; LegTOT; News 94, 94-1;
WhoAm 94, 95, 96, 97, 99; WhoEnt 98;
WhoHol 92

Slater, Rodney E.
American. Government Official
Secretary of Transportation, 1997—.
b. Feb 23, 1955
Source: *AfrAmBi 2; ConBlB 15; IntWW*
97, 98, 2000; News 97; ProfiWG 98;
WhoAfA 9, 10, 11, 12; WhoAm 95, 96,
97, 98, 99, 2000; WhoAmP 97, 1999;
WhoBlA 5, 6, 7, 8; WhoFI 00, 96, 98;
WhoWor 98, 99, 2000

Slater, Samuel
American. Entrepreneur
In 1790, the manufacturer built the first
  successful cotton mill in the United
  States.
b. Jun 9, 1768 in Derbyshire, England
d. 1835
Source: *ABCWHCa; Alli; AmBi;*
AmNatBi; ApCAB; BiDAmBL 83;
BiInAmS; BioIn 3, 4, 6, 7, 8, 11, 14, 15,
16, 17, 20, 21; CamBiEn; CamDcAB;
ChamBiD; DcAmB; Drake; EncAB-H
1974, 1996; EncWB 98; HarEnUS;
InSci; LinLib S; McGEWB; NatCAB 4,

24; OxCAmH; PeoHis; RanHWDS;
TwCBDA; WebAB 74, 79; WhAm HS;
WorAl; WorAlBi; WorInv

Slatkin, Leonard
American. Conductor
Most promising American-born
  conductor since Leonard Bernstein;
  music director, St. Louis Symphony
  since 1979.
b. Sep 1, 1944 in Los Angeles,
  California
Source: *ASCAP 80; BakBD 78, 84;*
BakDcM; BioIn 14, 15, 16; CamDcAB;
CelR 90; CurBio 86; IntWW 91, 93, 97,
98, 2000; IntWWM 80, 90; LegTOT;
NewAmDM; NewGrDA 86; NewYTBS
84; PenDiMP; Who 98, 99, 2000;
WhoAm 84, 90; WhoEnt 92; WhoMW 82,
92

Slaughter, Enos Bradsher
"Country"
American. Baseball Player
Outfielder, 1938-42, 1946-59, mostly
  with St. Louis; led NL in RBIs, 1946;
  had lifetime .300 batting average.
b. Apr 27, 1916 in Roxboro, North
  Carolina
Source: *Ballpl 90; BiDAmSp BB; BioIn*
1, 2, 3, 4, 5, 7, 8, 10, 11, 15, 16;
WhoProB 73

Slaughter, Frank Gill
[C V Terry]
American. Author, Surgeon
Best known for medical novels: *That*
  None Should Die, 1941.
b. Feb 25, 1908 in Washington, District
  of Columbia
Source: *AmAu&B; AmNov; Au&Wr 71;*
AuNews 2; BenetAL 91; BioIn 1, 2, 3, 4,
5, 7, 10, 11, 14; ConAu 5NR, 5R, 85NR;
ConLC 29; CurBio 42; DcLP 87A;
InSci; IntAu&W 76, 77, 82, 86, 89, 91,
93; LngCTC; PenC AM; REnAL; TwCA
SUP; TwCRGW; TwCRHW 90; Who 74,
82, 83, 85, 88, 90, 92, 94, 98, 99, 2000;
WhoAm 86, 88, 90, 92, 94, 95, 96, 97,
98; WorAu 1900; WrDr 76, 86, 92, 98,
99

Slavenska, Mia
[Mia Corak]
Yugoslav. Dancer
Ballerina best known for role of
  "Blanche" in *Streetcar Named*
  Desire, 1952.
b. Feb 20, 1914 in Slavonski-Brod,
  Yugoslavia
Source: *BiDD; CnOxB; CurBio 54;*
DcPseud; IntDcB; WhoAm 82

Slavin, Mark
Israeli. Olympic Athlete, Victim
One of 11 members of Israeli Olympic
  team kidnapped and killed by Arab
  terrorists during Summer Olympic
  Games.
b. 1954?, Union of Soviet Socialist
  Republics
d. Sep 5, 1972 in Munich, Germany
  (West)

Source: *BioIn 9*

Slavitt, David R
[Henry Sutton]
American. Author
Wrote *Vital Signs,* 1975.
b. Mar 23, 1935 in White Plains, New
  York
Source: *BioIn 15, 16, 24; ConAu 3AS;*
ConLC 5, 14; ConNov 76; ConPo 85,
91; DcLP 87A; DrAP 75; DrAPF 91;
IntAu&W 91; IntWW 91; ScF&FL 1, 2,
92; WhoWrEP 89; WrDr 86, 92, 94

Slayton, Donald Kent
"Deke"
American. Astronaut
Flew on Apollo mission that docked with
  Russian Soyuz spaceship, 1975.
b. Mar 1, 1924 in Sparta, Wisconsin
d. Jun 13, 1993 in League City, Texas
Source: *AmMWSc 73P; AnObit 1993;*
BioIn 6, 9, 10, 11, 13, 16, 17, 19, 20,
22; ConAu 159; CurBio 76; FacFETw;
IntWW 83; NewYTBE 73; WebAMB;
WhAm 11; WhoAm 74, 76, 78, 80, 82,
84, 86, 88, 90, 92; WhoFI 87; WhoGov
72, 75, 77; WhoSpc; WhoSSW 73, 75,
76, 78, 93; WhoWor 74, 78, 80, 82, 84

Sledge, Debbie
[Sister Sledge]
American. Singer
Part of pop-rock group with three sisters,
  1970s-80s; best known hit: "We Are
  Family," 1979.
b. Jul 9, 1954 in Philadelphia,
  Pennsylvania
Source: *InB&W 85; InWom SUP*

Sledge, Joni
[Sister Sledge]
American. Singer
Late 1970s-early 1980s hits with three
  sisters include "We Are Family,"
  1979.
b. Sep 13, 1956 in Philadelphia,
  Pennsylvania
Source: *InB&W 85; InWom SUP*

Sledge, Kathy
[Sister Sledge]
American. Singer
Biggest hit with three sisters: "We Are
  Family," 1979.
b. Jan 6, 1959 in Philadelphia,
  Pennsylvania
Source: *InB&W 85; InWom SUP*

Sledge, Kim
[Sister Sledge]
American. Singer
Sang pop-rock tunes with three sisters,
  late 1970s-early 1980s.
b. Aug 21, 1957 in Philadelphia,
  Pennsylvania
Source: *InB&W 85; InWom SUP*

Sleet, Moneta, Jr.
American. Photojournalist
Staff photographer, *Ebony* and *Jet,*
1955—.
b. Feb 14, 1926 in Owensboro, Kentucky
d. Sep 30, 1996 in New York, New
York
Source: *AfrAmAl 6, 8; BioIn 19, 22, 23;*
ConBlB 5; NegAl 89; WhoE 74

Slenczynska, Ruth
American. Pianist
Acclaimed protege; stopped performing
at early age; wrote memoirs *Forbidden*
Childhood, 1957, recounts problems.
b. Jan 15, 1925 in Sacramento,
California
Source: *BakBD 78, 84, 92; BakBDTw;*
BiDAmM; BioIn 4, 5, 10; CmCal;
IntWWM 77, 80; InWom; NewGrDA 86;
WhoAm 76, 78; WhoAmW 58, 64, 66,
68, 70, 72, 74, 75, 77; WhoMus 72

Slesar, Henry
American. Writer
Head writer for "The Edge of Night,"
1968-83; "Capitol," 1984-87; won
Emmy, 1974.
b. Jun 12, 1927 in New York, New York
Source: *BioIn 14; ConAu 1NR, 1R,*
61NR; DcLP 87A; EncSF, 93; IntAu&W
91, 93; LegTOT; NewEScF; ScFSB;
TwCCr&M 80, 85, 91; TwCSFW 81, 86;
VarWW 85; WrDr 76, 80, 82, 84, 86, 88,
90, 92, 94, 96, 98, 99, 2000

Slezak, Erika
American. Actor
Won Emmys, 1984, 1986, for role of
Victoria Lord Buchanan in soap opera
"One Life to Live."
b. Aug 5, 1946 in Los Angeles,
California
Source: *BioIn 22; ConTFT 4; LegTOT;*
VarWW 85; WhoAm 90; WhoEnt 92

Slezak, Leo
Czech. Opera Singer
Tenor, noted for Lohengrin role; wrote
popular *What Time's the Next Swan;*
father of Walter.
b. Aug 18, 1875? in Schonberg, Moravia
d. Jun 1, 1946 in Egern, Germany
Source: *BakBD 84; BriBkM 80; CmOp;*
MusSN; WhAm 2; WhoHol B; WhScrn
74, 77, 83

Slezak, Walter
American. Actor
Won 1955 Tony for *Fanny,* best known
film role in *Lifeboat,* 1944.
b. May 3, 1902 in Vienna, Austria
d. Apr 21, 1983 in Flower Hill, New
York
Source: *AnObit 1983; BiDAmM;*
BiE&WWA; BioIn 3, 4, 5, 6, 13, 14;
CelR; CmMov; ConAu 109; CurBio 55,
83, 83N; EncAFC; EncMT; Film 2;
FilmEn; FilmgC; ForYSC; HalFC 80,
84, 88; IntMPA 75, 76, 77, 78, 79, 80,
81, 82; ItaFilm; MotPP; MovMk;
NewYTBS 83; NotNAT, A; OxCAmT 84;
OxDcOp; Vers A; WhAm 8; WhoAm 76;

WhoHol A; WhoThe 72, 77, 81; WhoWor
74; WorAl

Slick, Grace Wing
[Jefferson Airplane; Mrs. Skip Johnson;
Grace Barnett Wing]
American. Singer
Lead vocalist, Jefferson Starship, 1966-
78; rock hits include "White Rabbit,"
1967; pursued solo career.
b. Oct 20, 1939 in Chicago, Illinois
Source: *BakBD 84; BioIn 9, 10, 11;*
BkPepl; CamDcAB; CurBio 82;
IntDcWB; InWom SUP; RkOn 85;
WhoAm 74, 76, 78, 80, 82, 84, 86, 88,
90, 92, 94, 95, 96, 97; WhoAmW 70, 72,
74, 79, 81, 83, 85; WhoEnt 92;
WhoRocM 82; WorAlBi

Slidell, John
American. Politician, Diplomat
U.S. senator represented the Confederacy
in France during the American Civil
War.
b. 1793 in New York, New York
d. 1793, England
Source: *AmBi; AmNatBi; AmPolLe;*
ApCAB; BiAUS; BiDConf; BiDrAC;
BiDrUSC 89; BioIn 3, 5, 7, 9, 16;
CamDcAB; ChamBiD; CivWDc; CyAG;
DcAmB; DcAmDH 80, 89; DcBiPP;
Drake; EncAB-H 1974; EncSoH; EncWB
98; HarEnUS; McGEWB; NatCAB 2;
NewEAmW; OxCAmH; PolPar; REnAW;
TwCBDA; WebAB 74, 79; WhAm HS;
WhCiWar

Slim, William Joseph
English. Military Leader
Led Allied campaign to liberate Burma
from Japanese, WW II.
b. Aug 6, 1891 in Bristol, England
d. Dec 14, 1970 in London, England
Source: *BioIn 1, 2, 3, 15, 17, 24;*
ChamBiD; ConAu 107; CurBio 45, 71;
DcNaB 1961; DcTwHis; EncWB 99;
FacFETw; GenMudB; GrBr; HarEnMi;
HisEWW; WhAm 5; WhBriIn; WhoMilH
76; WhWW-II; WorAl; WorAlBi

Slipher, Vesto Melvin
American. Astronomer
First to provide evidence suggesting the
expanding universe theory.
b. Nov 11, 1875 in Mulberry, Indiana
d. Nov 8, 1969 in Flagstaff, Arizona
Source: *AmDec 1910; AmNatBi; AsBiEn;*
BiESc; BioIn 8, 9, 12, 14, 20; CamBiEn;
CamDcAB; ChamBiD; ChamBiD;
DcAmB S8; DcScB; InSci; LarDcSc;
RanHWDS; WebAB 74, 79; WhAm 5;
WorScD

Sliwa, Curtis
"The Rock"
American. Social Reformer
Founder, pres., Guardian Angels, 1979,
civilian patrol group launched to help
combat crime in NYC.
b. Mar 26, 1954 in New York, New
York

Source: *BioIn 12, 13, 14, 15, 16;*
CamDcAB; ConAu 111; CurBio 83;
NewYTBS 88

Sloan, Alfred Pritchard, Jr.
American. Industrialist
Founded Sloan-Kettering Institute for
Cancer Research, 1945.
b. May 23, 1875 in New Haven,
Connecticut
d. Feb 17, 1966 in New York, New
York
Source: *AmNatBi; ApCAB X; BiDAmBL*
83; BioIn 2, 3, 4, 5, 6, 7, 9, 10;
CamBiEn; CamDcAB; ChamBiD; CurBio
40, 66; DcAmB S8; EncAB-H 1996;
EncABHB 5; EncWB 98; FacFETw;
McGEWB; WhAm 4; WorAl

Sloan, Hugh W
American. Presidential Aide
Treasurer of Nixon's re-election
campaign, 1971.
b. Nov 1, 1940 in Princeton, New Jersey
Source: *BioIn 10; NewYTBE 73; PolProf*
NF; WhoAm 86, 90; WhoCanB 86

Sloan, John F
American. Artist
Member "The Eight" or "Ashcan"
school; drew somber genre scenes of
NY working people : *McSorley's Bar,*
1912.
b. Aug 2, 1871 in Lock Haven,
Pennsylvania
d. Sep 8, 1951 in Hanover, New
Hampshire
Source: *AtlBL; DcAmB S5; DcCAA 71;*
EncAB-H 1974; OxCAmL 65; REn;
REnAL; WebAB 74; WhAm 3

Sloan, Michael
American. Writer
Wrote for TV detective shows
"Columbo," 1971-77; "Harry-O,"
1974-76; "Switch," 1975-78.
b. Oct 14, 1946 in New York, New York
Source: *ConAu 130; ConTFT 5; ScF&FL*
92; VarWW 85; WhoEnt 92; WrDr 94

Sloan, Samuel
"Architect of Philadelphia"
American. Architect
Edited *The Architectural Review and*
American Builder's Journal, 1868-70,
first US periodical devoted to
architecture; internationally recognized
expert on designs for hospitals for the
insane.
b. 1815 in Chester County, Pennsylvania
d. Jul 19, 1884 in Raleigh, North
Carolina
Source: *Alli; ApCAB, X; BiDAmAr;*
BioIn 5, 14; BriEAA; CamDcAB;
DcAmAu; DcArch; DcNAA; Drake;
IntDcAr; MacEA; NewYHSD

Sloane, Dennis
American. Scientist
Wrote *Birth Defects and Drugs in*
Pregnancy, 1977, most comprehensive
report on subject.

b. Jan 9, 1930 in Pretoria, South Africa
d. May 10, 1982 in Lexington,
Massachusetts
Source: *BiDrACP 79; ConAu 106;
NewYTBS 82; WhoAm 80*

Sloane, Eric
[Everard Jean Hinrichs]
American. Artist
Known for portraying nostalgic aspects
of life in pre-industrial America.
b. Feb 27, 1910 in New York, New
York
d. Mar 6, 1985 in New York, New York
Source: *AmArt; AmAu&B; AnObit 1985;
ConAu 108, 115; CurBio 72, 85N;
IlBEAAW; IlsCB 1957; NewYTBS 85;
SmATA 42N, 52; WhAm 8; WhAmArt 85;
WhoAm 74, 76, 78; WhoAmA 73, 76, 78,
80, 82, 86N, 89N, 91N, 93N*

Sloane, Everett
American. Actor
Films include *The Patsy*, 1964;
Brushfire, 1962.
b. Oct 1, 1909 in New York, New York
d. Aug 6, 1965 in Brentwood, California
Source: *BiDFilm, 81, 94; BioIn 4, 7;
CurBio 57, 65; FilmEn; FilmgC; HalFC
80, 84, 88; HolCA; IntDcF 1-3, 2-3;
LegTOT; MotPP; MovMk; NotNAT B;
RadStar; SaTiSS; Vers A; WhoHol B;
WhScrn 74, 77, 83*

Sloane, Hans, Sir
English. Physician, Philanthropist
His collection of manuscripts, books,
specimens became the nucleus of
British Museum, 1759; physician to
George II.
b. Apr 16, 1660 in Killyleagh, Ireland
d. Jan 11, 1753 in London, England
Source: *Alli; ApCAB; BiDIrW; BiHiMed;
BioIn 2, 3, 5, 9, 10, 14, 17; BlkwCE;
CamBiEn; ChamBiD; DcBiPP; DcIrB 1,
2, 3; DcIrW 2; DcLEL; DcNaB; DcScB;
EncHiCA; HisDBrE; InSci; NewC;
NewCBEL; OxCEng 67, 85, 95; OxCMed
86; RanHWDS; REn; WhDW*

Sloane, John
Business Executive
Chm., W&J Sloane, 1933-55;
manufactured reproductions of antique
furniture.
b. Apr 20, 1883 in New York, New
York
d. Aug 3, 1971 in Bennington, Vermont
Source: *BioIn 9, 11; EncAB-A 30;
NatCAB 56; NewYTBE 71; WhAm 7*

Slobodkin, Louis
American. Sculptor, Author, Illustrator
Won Caldecott Medal for illustrating
James Thurber's *Many Moons*, 1943;
did sculptures for govt. buildings,
wrote *Sculpture: Principles and
Practice*, 1949.
b. Feb 19, 1903 in Albany, New York
d. May 8, 1975 in Miami Beach, Florida
Source: *AmAu&B; AuBYP 2, 3; BenetAL
91; BioIn 1, 2, 4, 5, 7, 8, 9, 10, 13, 14,
19; BkCL; BkP; Cald 1938; ChhPo;*

*ChlBkCr; ConAu 13R, 57, 83NR; CurBio
57, 75N; IlsBYP; IlsCB 1744, 1946,
1957; JBA 51; MajAI; NewYTBS 75;
OxCChiL; REnAL; ScF&FL 1, 2;
SJGChWr 5; SmATA 1, 26; TwCChW 1,
2, 3, 4; WhAm 6; WhAmArt 85; WhoAm
74; WhoAmA 73, 76N, 78N, 80N, 82N,
84N, 86N, 89N, 91N, 93N; WhoWorJ 72,
78*

Slobodkina, Esphyr
American. Children's Author, Illustrator
Self-illustrated books include *Long
Island Ducklings*, 1961.
b. Sep 22, 1909 in Siberia, Russia
Source: *AuBYP 2, 3; ChhPo; ConAu
1NR, 1R; ForWC 70; SmATA 1, 8AS;
ThrBJA; TwCChW 2, 3; WhoAmA 91;
WrDr 86, 92*

Slocum, Joshua
American. Author, Adventurer
Built ship *Spray;* sailed around the world
alone, 1895-98.
b. Feb 20, 1844 in Wilmont Township,
Nova Scotia, Canada
d. 1910?
Source: *AmAu&B; AmNatBi; BenetAL
91; BioIn 2, 3, 4, 5, 9, 11, 12, 18, 21,
24; CamBiEn; CamDcAB; ChamBiD;
DcAmAu; DcAmB; DcCanB 13; DcNAA;
LngCTC; NewYTBS 75; OxCAmL 65, 83,
95; OxCShps; OxCTwCL; PeoHis; RAdv
14, 13-3; REnAL; WhAm 4, HSA;
WhDW*

Slonimsky, Nicolas
American. Musicologist
Wrote *Music Since 1900*, 1971; revised
prestigious *Baker's Biographical
Dictionary*, 1958.
b. Apr 27, 1894 in Saint Petersburg,
Russia
d. Dec 25, 1995 in Los Angeles,
California
Source: *AmAu&B; AmNatBi; ASCAP 66,
80; BakBD 78, 84, 92; BakBDTw;
BakDcM; BiDAmM; BiDSovU; BioIn 1,
2, 3, 4, 5, 15, 16, 17, 21, 22; CamDcAB;
ConAmC 76, 82; ConAu 17R, 150;
CurBio 55, 91, 96N; DcCM; IntAu&W
82; IntWW 89, 91, 93; IntWWM 85, 90;
NewGrDA 86; NewGrDM 80; NewYTBS
95; OxCMus; PenDiMP; WhAm 11;
WhoAm 74, 76, 78, 80, 82, 84, 86, 88,
90, 92, 94, 95, 96; WhoAmM 83;
WhoEnt 92; WhoMus 72; WhoWest 96;
WhoWorJ 72; WrDr 76, 80, 82, 84*

Slotnick, Barry Ivan
American. Lawyer
Regarded as America's most successful
criminal defense attorney; clients have
included Bernhard Goetz, reputed
mobsters.
b. Jun 18, 1939
Source: *BioIn 14, 16; ConNews 87-4;
WhoAm 88, 90, 92; WhoAmL 90, 94;
WhoE 74, 75, 91; WhoFI 75*

Slotnick, Daniel Leonid
American. Scientist
Directed scientific team that developed
advance computer, Illiac IV.
b. Nov 12, 1931 in New York, New
York
d. Oct 25, 1985 in Baltimore, Maryland
Source: *AmMWSc 76P, 79, 82, 86, 89,
92; ConAu 117; WhAm 9; WhoAm 82,
84*

Slotta, Karl Heinrich
American. Biochemist
Discovered female hormone
progesterone, 1935; helped develop
birth control pill.
b. May 12, 1895 in Breslau, Germany
d. Jul 17, 1987 in Coral Gables, Florida
Source: *AmMWSc 76P, 79, 82, 86*

Slovik, Eddie
[Edward Donald Slovik]
American. Soldier
Only American executed during WW II
for desertion.
b. 1920 in Detroit, Michigan
d. Jan 31, 1945 in Sainte Marie Mines,
France
Source: *BioIn 3, 9, 10, 12, 15; BioNews
74; NewYTBS 87*

Slovo, Joe
South African. Political Leader, Lawyer
Founding member of South African
Communist Party, 1953; general
secretary, 1987.
b. 1926, Lithuania
d. Jan 6, 1995 in Johannesburg, South
Africa
Source: *BioIn 12; CamBiEn; ChamBiD;
ConAu 161; DcCPSAf; EncRev; IntWW
91, 93; News 89-2; NewYTBS 95;
RadHan; WhAm 11; WhoAfr; WhoWor
95*

Sluter, Claus
Dutch. Sculptor
Master of early Burgundian school, noted
for works at Dijon.
b. 1350?
d. 1406? in Dijon, France
Source: *CamBiEn; ChamBiD; EncWB
98; McGEWB; OxCArt; WebBD 83*

Sly and the Family Stone
[Gregg Errico; Lawence Graham, Jr;
Jerry Martini; Cynthia Robinson; Fred
Stone; Rose Stone; Sly Stone]
American. Music Group
Dance-rock hits include "Family
Affair," 1971.
Source: *AmPS B; BiDAmM; BioIn 15,
16; EncPR&S 74, 89; EncRk 88;
HarEnR 86; IlEncBM 82; IlEncRk;
InB&W 80, 85A; NewAmDM; NewGrDA
86; PenEncP; RkOn 74; SoulM; WhoHol
92; WhoRocM 82*

Slye, Maud
American. Pathologist
Doctor researched the inheritability of
cancer in mice.

b. Feb 8, 1879 in Minneapolis,
Minnesota
d. Sep 17, 1954 in Chicago, Illinois
Source: *BioAmW; BioIn 3, 11, 19, 20,
22, 23; EncWB 98; NotTwCS 1;
OxCMed 86; WhAm 3*

Smale, John Gray
American. Business Executive
Chm., Procter & Gamble, 1986-90;
director, General Motors Corp., 1992-
95; chm. of the board and chm.
executive committee, GM, 1996—.
b. Aug 1, 1927 in Listowel, Ontario,
Canada
Source: *BioIn 12, 15, 16, 18, 24;
CamDcAB; ConNews 87-3; Dun&B 90;
IntWW 91; St&PR 75, 84, 87, 91, 93, 96,
97, 98, 99, 2000; Who 98, 99, 2000;
WhoAm 76, 78, 80, 82, 84, 86, 88, 90,
94, 95, 96, 97, 98, 99, 2000; WhoFI 00,
75, 77, 79, 81, 85, 87, 89, 92, 94, 96,
98; WhoMW 74, 76, 78, 80, 82, 88, 90;
WhoWor 82, 84, 87, 89, 91, 95, 96, 97,
98, 99, 2000*

Small, Albion W(oodbury)
American. Sociologist
First U.S. professor of sociology; made
sociology a respected academic
discipline in America; wrote *An
Introduction to the Study of Society,*
1894.
b. May 11, 1854 in Buckfield, Maine
d. Mar 24, 1926 in Chicago, Illinois
Source: *Alli SUP; AmAu&B; AmBi;
AmLY; AmNatBi; BiDAmEd; BioIn 3, 5,
10, 11; CamDcAB; DcAmB; DcNAA;
DcSoc; EncARH; EncWB 98; McGEWB;
NatCAB 8, 25; TwCBDA; WhAm 1*

Smallens, Alexander
Russian. Conductor
Director, Radio City Music Hall, 1947-
50; original conductor, *Porgy and
Bess,* 1935.
b. Jan 1, 1889 in Saint Petersburg,
Russia
d. Nov 24, 1972 in Tucson, Arizona
Source: *BakBD 78, 84, 92; BakBDTw;
BiDAmM; BioIn 1, 2, 4, 8, 9, 10, 11;
CurBio 47, 73, 73N; DancEn 78;
MusSN; NewAmDM; NewEOp 71;
NewGrDA 86; NewGrDM 80; NewYTBE
72; OxDcOp; PenDiMP; WhAm 5*

Smalley, David Bruce
[The Raspberries]
American. Musician
Bassist, guitarist with power pop group,
1970-73.
b. Jul 10, 1949 in Oil City, Pennsylvania

Small Faces, The
[Kenny Jones; Ian MacLagan; Steve
Marriott; Rick Wills]
English. Music Group
Styled after rock group The Who; hits
include "Tin Soldier," 1967.
Source: *BillEnR; BioIn 21; EncRk 88;
EncRkSt; HarEnR 86; IlEncRk;
OxCPMus; PenEncP; RkOn 78, 84;*

*RkWho 96; RolSEnR 83; WhoRock 81;
WhoRocM 82*

Smalls, Charlie
American. Composer, Lyricist
Won Tonys for music, lyrics of *The Wiz,*
1975.
b. Oct 25, 1943 in New York, New York
d. Aug 27, 1987 in Bruges, Belgium
Source: *BioIn 12, 15; DrBlPA 90; WhAm
9; WhoAm 78, 80, 82, 84, 86; WhoBlA 4*

Smalls, Robert
American. Politician
Born a slave, he made a daring escape at
the beginning of the Civil War and
later served five terms in Congress as
the representative from South
Carolina.
b. Apr 5, 1839 in Beaufort, South
Carolina
d. Feb 22, 1916
Source: *ABCAmRe; AfrAmAl 6, 8;
AmNatBi; ApCAB; BiAUS; BiDrAC;
BiDrUSC 89; BioIn 4, 5, 6, 7, 8, 9, 10,
13, 17, 20; BlkAmsC; BlkCO;
CamDcAB; ChamBiD; DcAmB;
DcAmNB; DiAAPGL; EncAACR;
EncNaHi; EncSoH; EncWB 98; FreeLaw
96; InB&W 80, 85; McGEWB; NatCAB
12; NegAl 76, 83, 89A; NotBlAM;
TwCBDA; WebAB 74, 79; WebAMB;
WhAm 4, HSA; WhAmP*

Smallwood, Joey
[Joseph Roberts Smallwood]
Canadian. Political Leader
Led Newfoundland and Labrador into
Canadian Confederation; province's
first premier, 1949-79.
b. Dec 24, 1900 in Gambo,
Newfoundland, Canada
d. Dec 17, 1991 in Saint John's,
Newfoundland, Canada
Source: *AnObit 1991; BioIn 2, 3, 5, 9,
10, 11, 15; BlueB 76; CanWW 83, 89;
ConAu 105; CurBio 53; IntWW 83;
OxCCan; WhAm 10; WhoCan 73, 75, 77,
80; WhoE 74, 75*

Smaltz, Audrey
American. Fashion Show Coordinator
Fashion show coordinator founded The
Ground Crew, 1977, a company that
organizes the behind-the-scenes details
of fashion shows and provides dressers
and other assistants to the models;
clients include Vera Wang, Carolina
Herrerra, and Oscar de la Renta.
b. c. 1937 in New York, New York
Source: *ConBlB 12*

Smart, Christopher
English. Poet, Author
Noted for poem, "A Song to David,"
1763.
b. Apr 22, 1722 in Shipbourne, England
d. May 21, 1771 in Kings Bench,
England
Source: *Alli; AtlBL; Benet 87, 96;
BiCoLiE; BiD&SB; BioIn 1, 2, 3, 4, 5, 6,
7, 8, 10, 12, 13, 14, 15, 17, 18; BlkwCE;
BlmGEL; BritAu; CamGEL; CamGLE;*

*CasWL; ChamBiD; Chambr 2; ChhPo,
S1, S3; CnE&AP; CrtT 2; CyWA 97;
DcArts; DcBiPP; DcEnA; DcEnL; DcLB
109; DcLEL; DcNaB, C; Dis&D; EvLB;
LitC 3; LngCEL; MouLC 2; NewC;
OxCChiL; OxCEng 67, 85, 95; OxCLiW
86; PenC ENG; PoeCrit 13; RAdv 1, 14,
13-1; REn; RfGEnL 91; WebE&AL*

Smart, Jack Scott
American. Actor
Films include *Some Like It Hot,* 1939;
The Fat Man, 1951.
b. 1903
d. Jan 15, 1960 in Springfield, Illinois
Source: *WhoHol B; WhScrn 74, 77*

Smathers, George Armistead
American. Government Official
Dem. senator from FL, 1951-69.
b. Nov 14, 1913 in Atlantic City, New
Jersey
Source: *BiDrAC; BiDrUSC 89; BioIn 2,
3, 5, 6, 7, 9, 11; CurBio 54; IntWW 74;
PolProf E, J, K; WhoAm 74; WhoAmP
73, 75, 77, 79, 81, 83, 85, 87, 89, 91,
93, 95, 97, 1999*

Smeal, Eleanor Marie Cutri
American. Feminist
Pres. of NOW, 1977-82, 1985-87.
b. Jul 30, 1939 in Ashtabula, Ohio
Source: *BioIn 11, 12, 13; CamDcAB;
CurBio 80; EncWB; InWom SUP;
NewYTBS 77; WhoAm 84, 86, 90;
WhoAmP 91; WhoAmW 87, 91*

Smeaton, John
English. Engineer
Civil engineer transformed the handicraft
of engineering into a profession by
applying experimental science to
architectural and mechanical problems.
b. Jun 8, 1724 in Austhorpe, Yorkshire,
England
d. Oct 28, 1792 in Austhorpe, Yorkshire,
England
Source: *BioIn 2, 6, 7, 9, 10, 14;
CamBiEn; ChamBiD; DcArch; DcBiPP;
DcInv; DcNaB; DcScB; EncWB 98;
InSci; LarDcSc; MacEA; McGEWB;
OxCBrHi; OxCShps; RAdv 14;
RanHWDS; WorInv*

Smedley, Agnes
American. Author, Journalist
Wrote eye-witness reports on China for
magazines, newspapers, 1920s-40s;
books include *Chinese Destinies,* 1933.
b. 1894? in Missouri
d. May 6, 1950 in Oxford, England
Source: *AmAu&B; BioAmW; BioIn 2, 4,
10; CamDcAB; CurBio 44, 50; DcAmB
S4; EncAJ; HisDcWJ; InWom; LibW;
NotAW; TwCA, SUP; WhAm 3; WorAu
1900*

Smet, Pierre Jean de
Belgian. Missionary
Jesuit priest; mediated land talks between
the US government and native
American tribes.

b. Jan 30, 1801 in Dendermonde, Belgium
d. May 23, 1873 in Saint Louis, Missouri
Source: *AmAu&B; BenetAL 91; BioIn 1, 3, 4, 5, 6, 7, 9, 12, 15; DcNAA; EncNAB; MacDCB 78; NatCAB 2; OxCAmL 95; OxCCan; REnAL; WhAm HS*

Smetana, Bedrich
Czech. Musician, Conductor, Composer
Best known for opera *The Bartered Bride*, 1866.
b. Mar 2, 1824 in Litomischl, Bohemia
d. May 12, 1884 in Prague, Czechoslovakia
Source: *AtlBL; BakBD 78, 84, 92; BakDcM; Benet 87; BioIn 1, 2, 3, 4, 5, 6, 7, 8, 9, 11, 12, 14, 20, 21, 22, 23; BriBkM 80; CamBiEn; ChambID; CmOp; CmpBCM; DcArts; DcCom 77; DcCom&M 79; DcPup; Dis&D; EncDeaf; EncWB 98; GrComp; IntDcOp; LegTOT; McGEWB; MetOEnc; MusMk; NewamDM; NewEOp 71; NewGrDM 80; NewGrDO; NewOxM; Opera; OxCEng 85, 95; OxCMus; OxDcOp; PenDiMP A; RAdv 14; REn; WhDW; WorAl; WorAlBi*

Smibert, John
American. Painter
Portrait painter was a celebrated artist in the American Colonies.
b. 1688 in Edinburgh, Scotland
d. 1751
Source: *AmBi; AmNatBi; AtlBL; BioIn 1, 2, 4, 8, 11, 14, 21, 22; BriEAA; CamDcAB; DcAmArt; DcAmB; DcBrECP; EncCRAm; EncWB 98; FolkA 87; IntDcAA 90; McGDA; McGEWB; NewYHSD; OxCAmH; OxCAmL 65; OxCArt; OxDcArt; PeoHis; WebAB 74, 79; WhAm HS*

Smiley, Jane (Graves)
American. Author
Winner of Pulitzer Prize for *A Thousand Acres*, 1992.
b. Sep 26, 1949 in Los Angeles, California
Source: *BioIn 15, 16, 17, 18, 20, 21; ConAu 30NR, 50NR, 74NR, 104; ConLC 53, 76; ConNov 96; ConPopW; CurBio 90; GrWomW; IntWW 97, 98, 2000; IntWWW 2; MajTwCW 2; News 95; OxCWoWr 95; RAdv 14; WhoAm 90, 92, 94, 95, 96, 97, 98, 99, 2000; WhoAmW 93, 95, 97, 99; WhoMW 96, 98; WhoPul; WorAu 1985; WrDr 92, 94, 96, 98, 99, 2000*

Smiley, Tavis
American. Broadcaster, Author
Political commentator on radio and television, created 60-second syndicated radio commentary, "The Smiley Report," and host of Black Entertainment Television's "BET Tonight;" author of several political books, and named to *Time* magazine's List of 50 Future Leaders, 1994.
b. Sep 13, 1964 in Gulfport, Mississippi

Source: *AfrAmAl 8; ConBlB 20; WhoAfA 9, 10, 11, 12; WhoBlA 8*

Smirnoff, Yakov
[Yakov Pokhis]
American. Comedian
Known for TV beer commercial; comedy about native land.
b. Jan 24, 1951 in Odessa, Union of Soviet Socialist Republics
Source: *BioIn 13, 15, 16; ConNews 87-2; DcPseud; LegTOT; WhoCom; WhoEnt 92; WorAlBi*

Smith, A(rthur) J(ames) M(arshall)
Canadian. Poet, Critic
Leading figure in modern Canadian poetry: *Poems New and Collected*, 1967.
b. Nov 8, 1902 in Montreal, Quebec, Canada
d. Nov 21, 1980 in East Lansing, Michigan
Source: *AnObit 1980; Benet 87, 96; BiCoLiE; BioIn 1, 4, 5, 12, 13; CanWr; CasWL; ConAu 1R, 4NR, 102; ConCaAu 1; ConLC 15; ConPo 70, 75, 80; CreCan 2; DcLB 88; DcLEL, 1940; DrAP 75; DrAS 74E, 78E; IntWWP 77; LngCTC; ModCmwL; OxCCan; OxCCanL 1; OxCCan SUP; OxCTwCL; OxCTwCP; PenC ENG; REnAL; TwCA SUP; WebE&AL; WhAm 7; WhoAm 76, 78, 80; WorAu 1900; WrDr 76, 80, 82*

Smith, Adam
Scottish. Economist
Laid foundation for classical economics with *An Inquiry into the Nature and Causes of the Wealth of Nations*, 1776.
b. Jun 5, 1723 in Kirkcaldy, Scotland
d. Jul 17, 1790 in Edinburgh, Scotland
Source: *ABCWHCa; Alli; BbD; Benet 87, 96; BiCoLiE; BiD&SB; BiDPsy; BioIn 1, 2, 3, 4, 5, 6, 7, 8, 10, 11, 12, 13, 14, 15, 16, 17, 18, 19, 20, 21, 23; BlkwCE; BlkwEAR; BlmGEL; BritAu; CamBiEn; CamGEL; CamGLE; CasWL; ChambID; CmScLit; CyEd; CyWA 58, 97; DcAmC; DcBiPP; DcEnA; DcEnL; DcEuL; DcLB 104; DcLEL; DcNaB; Dis&D; EncEnl; EncEnv; EncEth; EncWB 98; EvLB; GrEconB; HisDBrE; LinLib L, S; LitC 36; LngCEL; LuthC 75; MacEWoS; McGEWB; NamesHP; NewC; OxCBrHi; OxCEng 67, 85, 95; OxCLaw; OxCPhil; PenC ENG; RAdv 14, 13-3; REn; WebE&AL; WhDW; WhoEc 81, 86; WorAl; WorAlBi*

Smith, Alex
Scottish. Golfer
Touring pro, early 1900s; won US Open, 1906, 1910; charter member, Hall of Fame, 1940.
b. 1872 in Carnoustie, Scotland
d. Apr 20, 1930 in Baltimore, Maryland
Source: *BiDAmSp OS; WhoGolf; WhoSpor*

Smith, Alexander
Scottish. Poet, Essayist
Labelled spasmodic poet; known for essays in *Dreamthorp*, 1863.
b. Dec 31, 1830? in Kilmarnock, Scotland
d. Jan 5, 1867 in Wardie, Scotland
Source: *Alli; BbD; BiCoLiE; BiD&SB; BioIn 2, 14, 15; BritAu 19; CamGEL; CamGLE; CasWL; ChamBiD; Chambr 3; ChhPo, S1, S2, S3; CmScLit; DcBiPP; DcEnA; DcEnL; DcEuL; DcLB 32; DcLEL; EvLB; NewC; OxCEng 67, 85, 95; PenC ENG; REn; StaCVF; WebE&AL*

Smith, Alexis
[Mrs. Craig Stevens]
American. Actor
Won 1971 Tony award for *Follies*.
b. Jun 8, 1921 in Penticton, British Columbia, Canada
d. Jun 9, 1993 in Los Angeles, California
Source: *AnObit 1993; BioIn 19, 20, 21; CelR; ConTFT 3, 12; FilmEn; FilmgC; ForYSC; HalFC 80, 84, 88; IntMPA 75, 76, 77, 78, 79, 80, 81, 82, 84, 86, 88, 92, 94; InWom SUP; LegTOT; MotPP; MovMk; NewYTBE 71; PlP&P, A; WhAm 11; WhoAm 74, 76, 78, 80, 82, 84, 86, 88, 90, 92; WhoAmW 81, 83; WhoHol 92, A; WhoThe 77, 81; WorAl; WorAlBi; WorEFlm*

Smith, Alfred
Canadian. Hockey Player
Amateur player with several teams, early 1900s; Hall of Fame, 1962.
b. Jun 3, 1873 in Ottawa, Ontario, Canada
d. Aug 21, 1953 in Ottawa, Ontario, Canada
Source: *WhoHcky 73*

Smith, Alfred Emanuel
American. Political Leader
Four-term Dem. governor of NY; first Catholic to run for pres., 1928.
b. Dec 30, 1873 in New York, New York
d. Oct 4, 1944 in New York, New York
Source: *AmAu&B; AmOrTwC; AmPolLe; AmSetPR; ApCAB X; BioIn 1, 2, 3, 4, 5, 6, 7, 8, 9, 10, 11, 13, 14, 16, 24; CamBiEn; CamDcAB; ChamBiD; CurBio 44; DcAmB S3; DcCathB; DcNAA; DcTwHis; EncAAH; EncAB-H 1974, 1996; HisDcAR; LinLib S; MorMA; NatCAB 32; OxCAmH; OxCAmL 65; REn; REnAL; WebAB 74, 79; WhAm 2; WhAmP*

Smith, Allison
American. Actor
Played Jennie Lowell on TV series "Kate & Allie," 1984-88.
b. Dec 9, 1969 in Bergen County, New Jersey
Source: *BioIn 14, 15; InWom SUP; WorAlBi*

Smith, Amanda W
American. Manufacturer
Baked pies; sold by son, commercialized
  into business bearing her name.
b. 1860
d. 1947
Source: *Entr*

Smith, Anna Deavere
American. Actor, Dramatist
Staged one-woman performance
  Twilight: Los Angeles 1992, 1993;
  won 1993 OBIE Award for Best New
  American Play.
b. Sep 18, 1950 in Baltimore, Maryland
Source: *ConAu 133; ConBlB 6; ConLC
86; ConTFT 2, 14, 25; CurBio 94;
FemDram; WhoAm 94, 95, 96, 97, 98,
99, 2000; WhoAmW 93, 95, 97, 99;
WrDr 94, 96, 98, 99, 2000*

Smith, Austin E(dward)
American. Physician
Wrote *The Drugs You Use,* 1948.
b. Nov 25, 1912
d. Oct 9, 1993 in Fort Myers, Florida
Source: *AmMWSc 73P; BioIn 2; CurBio
94N; InSci*

Smith, Barbara
American. Writer
Editor of *Home Girls: A Black Feminist
  Anthology,* 1983.
b. Nov 16, 1946 in Cleveland, Ohio
Source: *AfrAmAl 6, 8; BlkWr 2;
BlkWrNE; CmpQue; ConAu 142;
FemiWr; GayLesB; GayLL 1; SchCGBL;
SigCnAF; WhoAfA 9, 10, 11, 12;
WhoBlA 5, 6, 7, 8; WrDr 96*

Smith, Barbara
American. Restaurateur
Proprietor of B. Smith's, a restaurant in
  New York and Washington; wrote
  cookbook *B. Smith's Entertaining and
  Cooking for Friends,* 1995.
b. Aug 24, 1949 in Pittsburgh,
  Pennsylvania
Source: *ConBlB 11; CurBio 98*

Smith, Bessie
American. Singer, Songwriter
Blues singer, 1920s; discovered by Ma
  Rainey; first recording "Gulf Coast
  Blues," 1923.
b. Apr 15, 1894? in Chattanooga,
  Tennessee
d. Sep 26, 1937 in Clarksdale,
  Mississippi
Source: *AfrAmAl 6, 8; AllMGBl 1, 2;
AllMGJa; AmCulL; AmDec 1920;
AmNatBi; BakBD 78, 84, 92; BakDcM;
BiDAfM; BioAmW; BioIn 4, 5, 7, 8, 9,
10, 11, 12, 19, 20, 21, 22, 23, 24;
BlkWAm; BluesWW; ChamBiD;
CmpQue; ConBlB 3; ConMus 3; DcAmB
S2; DcAmNB; DcArts; DcTwCCu 5;
DrBlPA, 90; EncWB 98; GayLesB;
GoodHs; GrLiveH; GuBlues; HerW;
IlEncJ; InB&W 80; InWom SUP;
LegTOT; NegAl 76, 83, 89; NewAmDM;
NewGrDA 86; NewGrDJ 88, 94;
NewGrDM 80; NotAW; NotBlAW 1;*

*OxCAfAL; OxCPMus; PenEncP; WebAB
74; WhAm 4, HSA; WhoJazz 72; WhScrn
77, 83; WorAl; WorAlBi*

Smith, Betty
[Betty Wehner]
American. Author
Wrote best-seller *A Tree Grows in
  Brooklyn,* 1943; filmed, 1945; on
  Broadway, 1951.
b. Dec 15, 1904 in New York, New
  York
d. Jan 17, 1972 in Shelton, Connecticut
Source: *AmAu&B; AmNov; BeaEPF;
BenetAL 91; BioIn 1, 2, 3, 4, 5, 9, 10;
CnDAL; ConAu 5R; CurBio 43, 72, 72N;
CyWA 58; HalFC 84, 88; LegTOT;
LinLib L; LngCTC; NotWoAT; Novels;
OxCAmL 65, 83; PenC AM; REn;
REnAL; TwCA SUP; WhAm 5;
WhE&EA; WhoAmW 58, 61*

Smith, Billy
[William John Smith]
Canadian. Hockey Player
Goalie, NY Islanders, 1972-90; first
  goalie to score goal in NHL (1979);
  won Vezina Trophy, 1982, Jennings
  Trophy, 1983.
b. Dec 12, 1950 in Perth, Ontario,
  Canada
Source: *BioIn 13; HocEn; HocReg 87;
NewYTBS 83*

Smith, Bob
"Buffalo Bob"
American. Entertainer
Creator, star of children's TV show
  "Howdy Doody," 1947-60.
b. Nov 27, 1917 in Buffalo, New York
d. Jul 30, 1998 in Hendersonville, North
  Carolina
Source: *BioIn 15, 16; LegTOT; WhoAm
78; WorAl; WorAlBi*

Smith, Bruce (Bernard)
American. Football Player
Player with Buffalo, 1985—.
b. Jun 18, 1963 in Norfolk, Virginia
Source: *CurBio 95; WhoAfA 9, 10, 11,
12; WhoAm 92, 94, 95, 96, 97; WhoBlA
7, 8; WhoWor 95, 96*

Smith, Bruce P
"Boo"
American. Football Player
All-America halfback, won Heisman
  Trophy, 1941; in NFL with Green
  Bay, 1945-48, LA Rams, 1948.
b. Feb 8, 1920 in Faribault, Minnesota
d. Aug 28, 1967
Source: *BiDAmSp FB; BioIn 8, 11, 14;
WhoFtbl 74*

Smith, Bubba
[Charles Aaron Smith]
American. Football Player
Two-time all-pro defensive end-tackle,
  1967-76, mostly with Baltimore; made
  popular beer commercials.
b. Feb 28, 1945 in Orange, Texas

Source: *BiDAmSp FB; BioIn 9, 10, 11,
14, 15; ConTFT 7; LegTOT; WhoBlA 4,
5; WhoFtbl 74; WhoHol 92; WhoSpor*

Smith, C. Aubrey
English. Actor
Noted character actor in over 80 films,
  1920s-40s.
b. Jul 21, 1863 in London, England
d. Dec 20, 1948 in Beverly Hills,
  California
Source: *AmNatBi; Film 1; FilmgC;
MotPP; MovMk; PIP&P; Vers A;
WhoHol B; WhoStg 1908; WhScrn 74,
77*

Smith, Carleton Sprague
American. Musicologist
Expert on the Brazilian and Hispanic
  cultures; chief of the music division,
  New York Public Library, 1931-59.
b. Aug 8, 1905
d. Sep 19, 1994 in Washington,
  Connecticut
Source: *BakBD 78, 84, 92; BakBDTw;
BioIn 5, 17, 20; CurBio 94N; IntWWM
80; NewGrDA 86; NewGrDM 80*

Smith, Cathy Evelyn
Canadian. Singer
Convicted, sentenced to three yrs. in
  prison, for injecting fatal drug dose to
  John Belushi, 1986; paroled, 1988.
b. 1947?
Source: *BioIn 13*

Smith, Chard Powers
American. Author, Lecturer
Writings include verse *Along the Wind,*
  1925; novel *Ladies Day,* 1941.
b. Nov 1, 1894 in Watertown, New York
d. Oct 31, 1977
Source: *AmAu&B; AmNatBi; AmNov;
AnMV 1926; Au&Wr 71; BenetAL 91;
BioIn 2, 4, 11, 22; ChhPo S1; ConAu
5R, 73; OxCAmL 65, 83, 95; REnAL;
TwCA, SUP; WhAm 7; WhE&EA;
WhoAm 74, 76; WorAu 1900; WrDr 76*

Smith, Christopher Columbus
American. Manufacturer
Superior designs of his boats started
  venture of speedboat-building,
  marketing his Chris-Craft boats
  worldwide.
b. May 20, 1861 in Saint Clair, Michigan
d. Sep 9, 1939 in Mount Clemens,
  Michigan
Source: *BioIn 7; Entr; NatCAB 47*

Smith, Clarence
"Pinetop"
American. Jazz Musician
Pianist, vocalist; wrote "Pine Top's
  Boogie Woogie," 1928; accidentally
  murdered.
b. Jun 11, 1904 in Troy, Alabama
d. Mar 14, 1929 in Chicago, Illinois
Source: *BakBD 84, 92; BiDAfM;
BiDAmM; BiDJaz; BluesWW; GuBlues;
InB&W 80, 85; WhoJazz 72*

Smith, Claydes
[Kool and the Gang]
American. Musician
Lead guitarist with Kool and the Gang.
b. Sep 6, 1948 in Jersey City, New
   Jersey
Source: *OnThGG*

Smith, Courtney Craig
American. Educator
Pres. of Swarthmore College, 1953-69;
   proponent of academic freedom; died
   of he art attack during campus
   demonstration.
b. Dec 20, 1916 in Winterset, Iowa
d. Jan 16, 1969 in Swarthmore,
   Pennsylvania
Source: *CurBio 59, 69; DcAmB S8;*
WhAm 5

Smith, Cyrus Rowlett
American. Airline Executive
President, American Airlines, 1934-68.
b. Sep 9, 1899 in Minerva, Texas
d. Apr 4, 1990 in Annapolis, Maryland
Source: *AmNatBi; BiDAmBL 83;*
BiDrUSE 71, 89; BiDWWGF; BioIn 5, 8,
10, 16; CurBio 45, 90; FacFETw; InSci;
IntWW 83; NewYTBE 73; NewYTBS 90;
WhAm 10; WhoAm 74, 76, 78, 80, 82,
84, 86; WhoFI 74

Smith, David
American. Sculptor
Welded metal sculptures include *Zig.*
b. Mar 9, 1906 in Decatur, Indiana
d. May 23, 1965 in Albany, New York
Source: *AmNatBi; AtlBL; Benet 87, 96;*
BioIn 1, 2, 3, 4, 5, 6, 7, 8, 9, 10, 11, 12,
13, 14, 15, 19, 20, 22; BriEAA; CenC;
ConArt 77, 83, 89; ConAu 113;
DcAmArt; DcArts; DcCAA 71, 77, 88,
94; DcTwArt; DcTwCCu 1; EncAB-H
1974, 1996; EncWB 98; IntDcAA 90;
McGDA; McGEWB; OxCArt;
OxCTwCA; OxDcArt; PhDcTCA 77;
WebAB 74, 79; WhAm 4; WhAmArt 85;
WhDW; WhoAmA 78N, 80N, 82N, 84N,
86N, 89N, 91N, 93N; WorAlBi; WorArt
1950

Smith, Dean Edwards
American. Basketball Coach
Coach, U of NC, 1961—; won NCAA
   championship, 1982; Hall of Fame,
   1982.
b. Feb 28, 1931 in Emporia, Kansas
Source: *BiDAmSp BK; CurBio 94;*
WhoAm 78, 80, 82, 84, 86, 88, 90, 92,
94, 95, 96, 97, 98, 99, 2000; WhoSSW
86, 88, 91, 93, 95, 97, 99

Smith, Dennis
American. Author
Wrote *Report from Engine Co. 82,* 1972,
   about his experiences as a firefighter.
b. Sep 9, 1940 in New York, New York
Source: *BioIn 15; ConAu 10NR, 61;*
NewYTBE 72; WhoAm 82, 90; WhoE 79;
WrDr 80, 82, 84, 86

Smith, Dodie
[C L Anthony; Dorothy Gladys Smith]
English. Dramatist, Author
Wrote *The Hundred and One*
   Dalmations, 1956; filmed by Walt
   Disney, 1960.
b. May 3, 1896 in Whitefield, England
d. Nov 24, 1990
Source: *AnObit 1990; Au&Wr 71;*
BiE&WWA; BioIn 4, 9, 10, 11, 12, 13,
15, 17, 19, 21; BlmGWL; CamBiEn;
ChamBiD; Chambr 3; ConAu 37NR,
133; ConBrDr; ConDr 77, 82, 88, 93;
ConWomD; DcLB 10; DcLEL; DcLP
87A; FemDram; FemiCLE; IntAu&W 89,
91; IntWW 77, 78, 79, 80, 81, 82, 83,
89; InWom SUP; LegTOT; LngCTC;
MajAl; McGEWD 72, 84; NewC;
NotNAT; OxCChiL; OxCTwCL;
PenNWW A, B; PIP&P; REn;
RGTwCWr; ScF&FL 1, 92; SmATA 4,
65, 82; TwCChW 2, 3, 4; Who 82, 83,
85, 88, 90; WhoThe 77, 81; WorAu
1950; WrDr 76, 86

Smith, Donald Alexander
''Strathcona''
Canadian. Financier, Politician
A leader in syndicate that built Canadian
   Pacific Railway, 1880-85; pres., Bank
   of Montreal, 1887-1905.
b. Aug 6, 1820 in Morayshire, Scotland
d. Jan 21, 1914 in London, England
Source: *ApCAB; DcCanB 14; DcNaB*
1912; EncWB 98; McGEWB; OxCCan

Smith, Dora
American. Educator
Called ''The First Lady of the United
   States in the Teaching of English,''
   she researched, lectured, and wrote
   extensively about language arts and
   English curricula.
b. Feb 14, 1893 in Minneapolis,
   Minnesota
d. Jan 28, 1985
Source: *EncWB 98*

Smith, Edmund Kirby
[Edmund Kirby-Smith]
American. Military Leader
Last Confederate general to surrender in
   Civil War, May 1865; pres., U of
   Nashville, 1870-75.
b. May 16, 1824 in Saint Augustine,
   Florida
d. Mar 8, 1893 in Sewanee, Tennessee
Source: *AmBi; AmNatBi; ApCAB;*
BiDAmEd; BiDConf; BioIn 1, 3, 5, 9, 17,
18; CamDcAB; CivWDc; DcAmB;
DcAmMiB; Drake; EncSoH; HarEnMi;
HarEnUS; NatCAB 8; NewCol 75;
TwCBDA; WebAMB; WhAm HS;
WhCiWar; WhoMilH 76; WorAl;
WorAlBi

Smith, Ellison DuRant
''Cotton Ed''
American. Politician
Dem. senator from SC, 1909-44; critic of
   ''New Deal.''
b. Aug 1, 1864 in Lynchburg, South
   Carolina

d. Nov 17, 1944.in Lynchburg, South
   Carolina
Source: *AmNatBi; ApCAB X; BiDrUSC*
89; BioIn 1; CurBio 45; DcAmB S3;
EncSoH; FacFETw; WhAm 2

Smith, Emmitt
[Emmitt James Smith, III]
American. Football Player
Running back for the Dallas Cowboys,
   1990—; led NFL in rushing, 1991-93,
   1995.
b. May 15, 1969 in Pensacola, Florida
Source: *AfrAmSG; ConBlB 7; CurBio*
94; News 94, 94-1; WhoSpor

Smith, Ethel
[Ethel Goldsmith]
American. Organist
Film, radio performer, 1940s; helped
   popularize organ music.
b. Nov 22, 1910 in Pittsburgh,
   Pennsylvania
d. May 17, 1996 in Palm Beach, Florida
Source: *ASCAP 66, 80; BioIn 9;*
CmpEPM; InWom SUP; PenEncP; What
3; WhoHol A

Smith, Frances Scott Fitzgerald Lanahan
''Scottie''
American., Writer
Only child of F Scott, Zelda Fitzgerald;
   wrote for *Washington Post; New*
   Yorker.
b. 1922?
d. Jun 18, 1986 in Montgomery, Georgia

Smith, Francis Marion
American. Financier
Prospector; co-discovered Nevada borax
   deposits, 1872; monopolized borax
   market, using ''Twenty-Mule Team''
   trademark.
b. Feb 2, 1846 in Richmond, Wisconsin
d. Aug 27, 1931 in Oakland, California
Source: *AmNatBi; BiDAmBL 83; BioIn*
12; DcAmB; NatCAB 28; WebAB 74, 79;
WhAm 1

Smith, Frederick Wallace
American. Business Executive
Founded Federal Express, 1972; first
   corp. in history worth $1 billion in
   first decade of existence.
b. Aug 11, 1944 in Marks, Mississippi
Source: *CamDcAB; ConAmBL; ConNews*
85-4; St&PR 84, 87; WhoAm 82, 84, 86,
88, 90, 92, 94, 95, 96, 97, 98, 99, 2000;
WhoFI 00, 83, 85, 87, 89, 92, 94, 96,
98; WhoSSW 86, 88, 91, 93, 97, 99;
WhoWor 95, 96, 97, 98, 99, 2000

Smith, Geoff
English. Track Athlete
Won Boston Marathon, 1984, 1985.
b. 1954? in Liverpool, England
Source: *BioIn 13; NewYTBS 84*

Smith, Gerald Lyman Kenneth

American. Editor, Lecturer
Founded anti-Communist, anti-black,
  anti-Semitic group: Christian
  Nationalist Crusade.
b. Feb 27, 1898 in Pardeeville,
  Wisconsin
d. Apr 15, 1976 in Glendale, California
Source: *AmNatBi; AmSocL; BiDExR;
BioIn 1, 7, 8, 10, 11; ConAu 65; CurBio
43, 76; DcAmReB 2; RelLAm 1, 2*

Smith, Gerard C(oad)

American. Government Official
Head of US Arms Control and
  Disarmament Agency, 1969-73; led
  American delegation to SALT.
b. May 4, 1914
d. Jul 4, 1994 in Easton, Maryland
Source: *BioIn 8, 9, 12; CurBio 94N;
IntWW 74, 75, 76, 77, 78, 79, 80, 81, 82,
83, 89, 91, 93; PolProf NF; WhoAm 74,
76, 78; WhoAmP 73, 75, 77, 79, 81, 83,
85, 87, 89, 91, 93, 95; WhoGov 72*

Smith, Gerrit

American. Philanthropist
Aided temperance, abolition, women
  suffrage; helped John Brown.
b. Mar 6, 1797 in Utica, New York
d. Dec 28, 1874 in New York, New
  York
Source: *Alli; AmBi; AmNatBi; AmPeW;
AmRef; AmSocL; ApCAB; BbD; BiAUS;
BiD&SB; BiDMoPL; BiDrAC; BiDrUSC
89; BioIn 2, 8, 9, 12, 15, 19, 24;
CamBiEn; CamDcAB; ChamBiD;
DcAmAu; DcAmB; DcAmSR; DcAmTB;
DcNAA; Drake; EncRelA; EncWB 98;
HarEnUS; MacEWoS; McGEWB;
NatCAB 2; PolPar; TwCBDA; WebAB
74, 79; WhAm HS; WhCiWar*

Smith, Goldwin

English. Author
Wrote extensively on Canadian politics,
  urging separation from Britain, union
  with US: *Canada and the Canadian
  Question*, 1891.
b. Aug 13, 1823 in Reading, England
d. Jun 7, 1910 in Toronto, Ontario,
  Canada
Source: *Alli, SUP; ApCAB; BbD;
BiD&SB; BioIn 1, 2, 4, 12, 14, 17;
BritAu 19; CamGEL; CamGLE; CanWr;
CelCen; ChamBiD; Chambr 3; CyEd;
DcBiPP; DcCanB 13; DcEnA, A;
DcEnL; DcEuL; DcLB 99; DcLEL;
DcNAA; DcNaB S2; Drake; EvLB;
HarEnUS; HisDBrE; LinLib L, S;
LngCTC; MacDCB 78; NewC; OxCCan;
OxCCanL 1, 2; OxCEng 67, 85, 95;
REn; REnAL; WhAm 1; WhLit*

Smith, Gordon H.

American. Politician
Rep. senator, OR, 1997—.
b. May 25, 1952

Smith, H(arry) Allen

American. Author
Thirty-six books of humor include *Low
  Man on a Totem Pole*, 1941.

b. Dec 19, 1907? in McLeansboro,
  Illinois
d. Feb 24, 1976 in San Francisco,
  California
Source: *AmAu&B; AuNews 2; BiDrAC;
BioIn 1, 3, 4, 6, 8, 10, 11, 12, 13, 15,
22; CelR; ChhPo; ConAu 5NR, 5R, 65;
CurBio 42; DcAmB S10; EncSF, 93;
LngCTC; REn; REnAL; ScF&FL 2;
TwCA SUP; WhAm 6; WhE&EA;
WhoAm 74; WrDr 76*

Smith, Hamilton Othanel

American. Biologist, Physician
Won 1978 Nobel Prize in medicine for
  research on enzymes, molecular
  genetics.
b. Aug 23, 1931 in New York, New
  York
Source: *AmMWSc 76P, 79, 82, 86, 89,
92, 95, 98; BiEsc; BioIn 11, 12, 14, 15,
20; CamBiEn; CamDcSc; ChamBiD;
LarDcSc; McGCEnS; McGMS 80;
RanHWDS; Who 82, 83, 85, 88, 90, 92,
94, 98, 99, 2000; WhoAm 80, 82, 84, 86,
88, 90, 92, 94, 95, 96, 97, 99, 2000;
WhoE 79, 81, 83, 85, 86, 89, 91, 93, 95,
97; WhoFrS 84; WhoMedH 96, 99,
2000; WhoNob, 90, 95; WhoScEn 94, 96,
2000; WhoWor 80, 82, 84, 87, 89, 91,
93, 95, 96, 97*

Smith, Harold

American. Boxing Promoter
Chm., Muhammad Ali Professional
  Sports, Inc; sought by FBI for
  embezzlement, 1981.
b. 1944?
Source: *NewYTBS 81*

Smith, Hazel Brannon

American. Journalist
Won Pulitzer Prize, 1964; fought against
  racism; owned the Durant MS *News*,
  and Lexington MS *Advertiser*.
b. 1914?
d. May 14, 1994 in Cleveland, Tennessee
Source: *BiDAmNC; BioIn 19, 20; CurBio
73, 94N; DcLB 127; GoodHs; InWom
SUP; JrnUS; WhoPul; WomFir*

Smith, Hedrick Laurence

American. Journalist
Chief Washington correspondent for *NY
  Times*, 1979-85; won Pulitzers for
  cowriting *The Pentagon Papers*, 1972,
  for int'l reporting, 1974; wrote *The
  Power Game: How Washington
  Works*, 1988.
b. Jul 9, 1933 in Kilmacolm, Scotland
Source: *ConAu 11NR, 65; CurBio 91;
EncTwCJ; WhoAm 86, 90, 97, 98, 99,
2000; WhoPul; WorAlBi; WrDr 86, 92,
98, 99, 2000*

Smith, Holland McTeire

"Howlin' Mad"
American. Military Leader
Led Marine invasion of Iwo Jima, 1945;
  regarded as father of modern
  amphibious warfare; only third Marine
  in history to reach full general.
b. Apr 20, 1882 in Seale, Alabama

d. Jan 12, 1967 in San Diego, California
Source: *CurBio 45, 67; WhAm 4*

Smith, Hooley

[Reginald Joseph Smith]
Canadian. Hockey Player
Defenseman, 1924-41, with four NHL
  teams, Hall of Fame, 1972.
b. Jan 7, 1905 in Toronto, Ontario,
  Canada
d. Aug 24, 1963 in Montreal, Quebec,
  Canada
Source: *HocEn; WhoHcky 73*

Smith, Horace

[Smith and Wesson]
American. Manufacturer, Inventor
Produced the first revolvers, 1857.
b. Oct 28, 1808 in Cheshire,
  Massachusetts
d. Jan 15, 1893
Source: *AntBDN F; BioIn 18; DcAmB;
NatCAB 10; WhAm HS; WorInv*

Smith, Horton

"The Joplin Ghost"
American. Golfer
Turned pro, 1926; won 29 PGA
  tournaments, including first Masters,
  1934; pres. of PGA, 1952-54.
b. May 22, 1908 in Springfield, Missouri
d. Oct 15, 1963 in Detroit, Michigan
Source: *BiDAmSp OS; BioIn 6;
CamDcAB; DcAmB S7; LegTOT;
ObitOF 79; WhoGolf; WhoSpor*

Smith, Howard K(ingsbury)

American. Broadcast Journalist
Correspondent, CBS News, 1941-61;
  reporter, commentator, ABC News,
  1961-79.
b. May 12, 1914 in Ferriday, Louisiana
Source: *AmAu&B; BiDAmJo; BioIn 11,
16; BlueB 76; CamDcAB; ConAu 45,
71NR; CurBio 43, 76; EncTwCJ;
HisDcAR; HisDcWJ; IntAu&W 77, 82,
93; IntMPA 86, 92; IntWW 74, 75, 76,
77, 78, 83; JrnUS; LesBEnT; WhoAm
74, 76, 78, 80, 82; WhoSSW 73, 75, 76;
WhoTelC; WhoWor 74, 78; WorAlBi;
WrDr 76, 86, 90*

Smith, Howard Worth

American. Politician
Congressman, 1931-36; wrote Smith Act,
  1940, making illegal to be a
  Communist.
b. Feb 2, 1883 in Broad Run, Virginia
d. Oct 3, 1976 in Alexandria, Virginia
Source: *AmNatBi; BiDrAC; BiDrUSC
89; BioIn 3, 5, 6, 7, 11; CamDcAB;
DcAmB S10; NewYTBS 76; WhAm 7;
WhAmP; WhoAm 74, 76; WhoAmP 73,
75, 77, 79*

Smith, Iain Crichton

Scottish. Poet
Writes in English and Gaelic: *From
  Bourgeois Land*, 1969.
b. Jan 1, 1928 in Isle of Lewis, Scotland
d. Oct 15, 1998 in Taynuilt, Scotland

Source: *BiCoLiE; BioIn 15; CamGLE; CasWL; ChamBiD; ChhPo S2; CmScLit; ConAu 21R, 171; ConLC 64; ConNov 72, 76, 82, 86, 91, 96; ConPo 70, 75, 80, 85, 91, 96; DcLB 40, 139; DcLEL 1940; EngPo; IntAu&W 76, 77, 86, 89, 91, 93; IntWWP 77; OxCTwCL; OxCTwCP; PenC ENG; RfGShF 1, 2; RGTwCWr; WhoEnt 98; WhoTwCL; WhoWor 95, 96, 97, 98, 99; WorAu 1970; WrDr 84, 86, 88, 90, 92, 94, 96, 98, 99, 2000*

Smith, Ian Douglas
Rhodesian. Political Leader
Last prime minister of Rhodesia, 1964-79; declared country's independence, 1965.
b. Apr 8, 1919 in Seluwke, Rhodesia
Source: *BioIn 13, 21, 24; CamBiEn; ChamBiD; ColdWar 1; CurBio 66; DcAfHiB 86; EncWB 98; IntWW 83, 89, 97, 98, 2000; McGEWB; NewYTBS 76, 78; OxCBrHi; Who 85, 92, 98, 99, 2000*

Smith, Jack
[John Francis Smith, Jr.]
American. Auto Executive
President and CEO, General Motors, 1992-95; chairman, 1996—.
b. Apr 6, 1938 in Worcester, Massachusetts
Source: *IntWW 89, 91, 93; News 94, 94-3; WhoAm 86, 88, 90, 92, 94,'95, 96, 97; WhoFI 89, 92, 94, 96; WhoMW 93, 96; WhoWor 95, 96, 97*

Smith, Jaclyn
American. Actor
Starred in "Charlie's Angels," 1976-80; TV movie *Rage of Angels*, 1983; was married to actor Dennis Cole.
b. Oct 26, 1947 in Houston, Texas
Source: *BioIn 11, 12, 13, 16; BkPepl; CelR 90; ConTFT 2, 7, 14, 25; HolBB; IntMPA 84, 86, 88, 92, 94, 96; InWom SUP; LegTOT; WhoAm 86, 88, 90, 92, 94, 99, 2000; WhoEnt 92, 98; WhoHol 92; WhoTelC; WorAlBi*

Smith, Jada Pinkett
American. Actor
Television and film actor known for her portrayals of strong characters, including her debut film role in *Menace II Society*, 1993; married movie actor Will Smith, 1997.
b. Sep 18, 1971 in Baltimore, Maryland

Smith, James
American. Continental Congressman, Lawyer
Inconspicuous Pennsylvania delegate; signed Declaration of Independence.
b. 1713, Northern Ireland
d. Jul 11, 1806 in York, Pennsylvania
Source: *AmBi; ApCAB; BiAUS; BiDrAC; BiDrUSC 89; DcAmB; Drake; NatCAB 2; REnAL; WhAm HS; WhAmP; WhAmRev*

Smith, Jedediah Strong
American. Fur Trader, Explorer
Advocate of western expansion; explorations helped open up the West.
b. Jan 6, 1799? in Bainbridge, New York
d. May 27, 1831
Source: *AmAu&B; AmBi; AmNatBi; CamBiEn; ChamBiD; CmCal; DcAmB; EncAAH; EncWM; McGEWB; OxCAmH; OxCAmL 65; REnAW; WebAB 74, 79; WhAm HS; WhNaAH; WhWE; WorAl; WorAlBi*

Smith, Jeff
American. TV Personality, Chef, Author
Host of TV show "The Frugal Gourmet," 1973—, and author of 6 best-selling cookbooks.
b. Jan 22, 1939 in Seattle, Washington
Source: *BioIn 15; CurBio 91; News 91; NewYTBS 88; WrDr 92, 94, 96, 98, 99, 2000*

Smith, Jerome
[K C and the Sunshine Band]
American. Musician
Guitarist with the Sunshine Band since 1973.
b. Jun 18, 1953 in Miami, Florida
Source: *OnThGG*

Smith, Jerry
American. Football Player
All-pro tight end, Washington, 1965-78; first athlete to admit he had AIDS.
b. Jul 19, 1943 in Oakland, California
d. Oct 15, 1986 in Silver Spring, Maryland
Source: *ConNews 87-1*

Smith, Jessie Wilcox
American. Illustrator
Known for children's classics: *Little Women, Heidi.*
b. Sep 1863 in Philadelphia, Pennsylvania
d. May 3, 1935 in Philadelphia, Pennsylvania
Source: *AuBYP 2, 3; BioIn 2, 8, 11, 12, 13; DcWomA; IlrAm A; InWom SUP; JBA 34, 51; NatCAB 26; NotAW; OxCChiL; SmATA 21; WhAm 1*

Smith, Joe
[Smith and Dale; Joseph Seltzer]
American. Comedian
Part of vaudeville team, Smith and Dale, for 73 yrs.
b. Feb 17, 1884 in New York, New York
d. Feb 22, 1981 in Englewood, New Jersey
Source: *AnObit 1981; BioIn 8, 9, 10, 12; DcPseud; EncVaud; FacFETw; NewYTBS 81; QDrFCA 92; WhoHol A; WhScrn 83*

Smith, Joe
American. Jazz Musician
Trumpeter with Fletcher Henderson, McKinney's Cotton Pickers, 1920s.
b. Jun 28, 1902 in Ripley, Ohio

d. Dec 2, 1937 in New York, New York
Source: *AmNatBi; BakBD 84, 92; BiDAfM; BiDAmM; BiDJaz; CmpEPM; IlEncJ; InB&W 80, 85; LegTOT; NewGrDA 86; NewGrDJ 88, 94; PenEncP; WhoJazz 72; WorAl; WorAlBi*

Smith, John
English. Colonizer
Founder, leader of Jamestown, VA colony, 1607-09; explored, advocated colonization of New England.
b. Jan 1580? in Willoughby, England
d. Jun 21, 1631 in London, England
Source: *Alli; AmAu; AmAu&B; AmBi; AmNatBi; AmWrBE; ApCAB; Benet 87, 96; BenetAL 91; BiDAmCa; BiD&SB; BioIn 1, 2, 3, 4, 5, 6, 7, 8, 9, 10, 11, 12, 13, 14, 15, 16, 17, 18, 19, 20, 23, 24; CamBiEn; CamGEL; CasWL; ChamBiD; CnDAL; CyAL 1; DcAmAu; DcAmB; DcLB 24, 30; DcLEL; DcNaB; EncAInd; EncALit; EncCRAm; EncWB 98; EvLB; Expl 93; ExplAnT; FifSWrB; HisWorL; LinLib L, S; LitC 9; LuthC 75; McGEWB; NewC; OxCAmH; OxCAmL 65, 83, 95; OxCEng 67, 85, 95; PenC AM; PeoHis; RComAH; REn; REnAL; WebAB 74, 79; WebAMB; WebE&AL; WhAm HS; WhDW; WhNaAH; WhWE; WorAl; WorAlBi*

Smith, Joseph
American. Religious Leader
Founded Mormons, 1830; murdered by non-believers.
b. Dec 23, 1805 in Sharon, Vermont
d. Jun 27, 1844 in Carthage, Illinois
Source: *Alli; AmAu&B; AmBi; AmNatBi; AmRef&R; AmSocL; ApCAB; Benet 87, 96; BenetAL 91; BiDAmCu; BioIn 1, 3, 4, 5, 6, 8, 9, 10, 11, 12, 13, 14, 15, 16, 17, 18, 19, 20, 21, 22, 23, 24; CamBiEn; CamDcAB; CelCen; ChamBiD; CyAG; DcAmB; DcAmReB 1, 2; DcBiPP; DcNAA; Dis&D; Drake; EncAAH; EncAB-H 1974, 1996; EncARH; EncRelA; EncWB 98; HarEnUS; HisWorL; LegTOT; LinLib L, S; LuthC 75; McGEWB; MemAm; NatCAB 7, 16; NewEAmW; NinCLC 53; OhA&B; OxCAmH; OxCAmL 65, 83, 95; PeoHis; RAdv 14; RComAH; REn; REnAL; REnAW; TwCBDA; WebAB 74, 79; WhAm HS; WhDW; WhoChr; WorAl; WorAlBi*

Smith, Joseph Fielding
American. Religious Leader
10th pres., Mormon Church, pres., Council of Apostles.
b. Jul 19, 1876 in Salt Lake City, Utah
d. Jul 2, 1972 in Salt Lake City, Utah
Source: *AmAu&B; AmNatBi; BioIn 2, 5, 8, 9, 10, 18; ConAu 37R; DcAmB S9; RelLAm 1, 2; WhAm 5*

Smith, Joshua (Isaac)
American. Business Executive
President and CEO, MAXIMA Corp., 1978—.
b. Apr 8, 1941 in Garrard County, Kentucky

Source: *AfrAmBi 1; ConBlB 10; WhoAfA 9, 10, 11, 12; WhoBlA 4, 5, 6, 7, 8*

Smith, Juane Quick-to-See
American. Artist
Merged traditional Native American abstract art with contemporary styles; had several solo exhibitions of her work.
b. 1940 in Saint Ignatius, Montana
Source: *NotNaAm*

Smith, Kate
[Kathryn Elizabeth Smith]
American. Singer
Recorded over 2,000 songs, had 19 number one hits, best known for rendition of "God Bless America."
b. May 1, 1907 in Greenville, Virginia
d. Jun 17, 1986 in Raleigh, North Carolina
Source: *AmNatBi; AnObit 1986; BakBD 92; BakDcM; BioNews 74; ConAu 119; ConNews 86-3; CurBio 40, 65, 86; IntMPA 82; OxCPMus; PenEncP; RadStar; SaTiSS; ThFT; WebAB 74; WhAm 9; WhoAm 80, 82, 84*

Smith, Keely
American. Singer
Pop vocalist with husband, Louis Prima, 1950s-60s.
b. Mar 9, 1932 in Norfolk, Virginia
Source: *ASCAP 66; BiDAmM; BiDJaz; BioIn 13; CmpEPM; ForYSC; InWom, SUP; LegTOT; NewGrDJ 88; PenEncP; WhoAm 74; WhoHol 92, A; WorAl; WorAlBi*

Smith, Kenneth Danforth
American. Museum Director, Author
Director of Baseball Hall of Fame, Cooperstown, NY, 1963-79; baseball writer for *NY Mirror*, 1931-63.
b. Jan 8, 1902 in Danbury, Connecticut
d. Mar 1, 1991 in Tilantire Bridge, New York
Source: *ConAu 1NR; WhoAm 74, 76, 78*

Smith, Kent
American. Actor
Films include *Games,* 1967; *Taking Tiger Mountain,* 1983.
b. Mar 19, 1907 in New York, New York
d. Apr 23, 1985 in Los Angeles, California
Source: *AnObit 1985; BiE&WWA; BioIn 10, 14, 15; FilmEn; FilmgC; ForYSC; HalFC 80, 84, 88; HolP 40; IntMPA 77, 80, 82; MovMk; NewYTBS 85; NotNAT; VarWW 85; WhoHol A; WhoHrs 80; WhoThe 72, 77, 81*

Smith, Lee
American. Author
Fiction explores life in Appalachia; wrote *The Last Day the Dogbushes Bloomed,* 1968; *Black Mountain Breakdown,* 1981.
b. Mar 17, 1937 in New York, New York

Source: *ConAu 73, 114, 119; ConLC 25, 73*

Smith, Lee (Arthur)
American. Baseball Player
Relief pitcher, Chicago Cubs, 1980-87, Boston, 1988-90; St. Louis, 1990—; led NL in saves, 1983.
b. Dec 4, 1957 in Jamestown, Louisiana
Source: *Ballpl 90; BaseReg 87, 88; BiDAmSp Sup; WhoAfA 9, 10, 11, 12; WhoAm 92, 94, 95, 96, 97, 98, 99, 2000; WhoBlA 4, 5, 6, 7, 8; WhoE 95, 97; WhoWest 96*

Smith, Lillian
American. Author
Wrote popular novel *Strange Fruit,* 1944; banned in Boston.
b. Dec 12, 1897 in Jasper, Florida
d. Sep 28, 1966 in Atlanta, Georgia
Source: *AmAu&B; AmNov; AmWomWr; ArtclWW 2; Benet 87, 96; BenetAL 91; BioAmW; BlmGWL; CmpQue; CnDAL; ConAu 25R, P-2; DcAmSR; EncSoH; FacFETw; FemiCLE; FemiWr; LinLib L; LngCTC; NotAW MOD; ODwPR 79; OxCAmL 65, 83; REn; REnAL; TwCA SUP; WhAm 4; WhE&EA; WhoAmW 58, 64, 66*

Smith, Liz
[Mary Elizabeth Smith]
American. Journalist
Gossip column runs in *NY Daily News,* over 60 syndicated papers.
b. Feb 2, 1923 in Fort Worth, Texas
Source: *BiDAmNC; BioIn 15, 16; CelR 90; ConAu 65; ConTFT 9; CurBio 87; ForWC 70; HalFC 88; InWom SUP; JrnUS; LegTOT; WhoAm 86, 90, 96, 97, 98, 99, 2000; WhoAmW 85, 87, 95, 97, 99; WhoEnt 98; WhoWrEP 89; WorAlBi*

Smith, Loring
American. Actor
Films include *The Clown,* 1953; *Hurry Sundown,* 1967.
b. Nov 18, 1895 in Stratford, Connecticut
d. Jul 8, 1981
Source: *BiE&WWA; NotNAT; WhoHol A; WhoThe 72, 77A; WhScrn 83; WhThe*

Smith, Lowell Herbert
American. Aviator
Commanded first around the world flight, using two planes in 57 hops from Seattle, Apr-Sep 1924.
b. Oct 8, 1892 in Santa Barbara, California
d. Nov 4, 1945 in Tucson, Arizona
Source: *BioIn 3; NatCAB 37; ObitOF 79; WhAm 2*

Smith, Madeline Hamilton
Scottish. Murderer
Allegedly poisoned lover, who had blackmailed her with letters she'd written him, 1857.
b. 1835
d. Apr 12, 1928

Source: *BioIn 2, 5, 10, 11*

Smith, Maggie Natalie
English. Actor
Won Oscars for *The Prime of Miss Jean Brodie,* 1969; *California Suite,* 1978.
b. Dec 28, 1934 in Ilford, England
Source: *BiDFilm; BioIn 15, 16; ContDcW 89; ConTFT 4; CurBio 70; EncMT; FacFETw; FilmgC; HalFC 88; IntMPA 92; IntWW 74, 75, 76, 77, 78, 79, 80, 81, 82, 83, 89, 91, 93, 97, 98, 2000; IntWWW 2; InWom SUP; MotPP; MovMk; NewYTBE 70; NewYTBS 82, 90; OxCThe 83; PlP&P; Who 92; WhoAm 86, 90; WhoEnt 92; WhoThe 81; WhoWor 87, 91; WorAlBi*

Smith, Margaret
American. Educator, Author
Rehabilitation specialist for visually handicapped; wrote *If Blindness Strikes, Don't Strike Out,* 1984.
b. Feb 27, 1939 in Detroit, Michigan

Smith, Margaret (Madeline) Chase
American. Politician
Rep. senator from ME, 1948-72; served longer than any other woman.
b. Dec 14, 1897 in Skowhegan, Maine
d. May 29, 1995 in Skowhegan, Maine
Source: *AmPolLe; AmWomM; BiDRAC; BiDrUSC 89; BioAmW; BioIn 15, 16; ConAu 73, 148; ContDcW 89; CurBio 45, 62, 95N; EncWB; HerW 84; IntWW 83, 91; InWom SUP; NewYTBE 70, 72; NewYTBS 75; PolProf E, J, K, NF, T; WhoAm 74; WhoAmP 73, 91; WhoAmW 87; WorAlBi*

Smith, Martin Cruz
[Nick Carter; Jake Logan; Martin Quinn; Simon Quinn]
American. Author
Prolific writer of popular fiction, spy novels, westerns; wrote best-seller *Gorky Park,* 1981.
b. Nov 3, 1942 in Reading, Pennsylvania
Source: *BeaEPF; BenetAL 91; BestSel 89-4; BioIn 12, 14, 16; ConAu 6NR, 23NR, 43NR, 65NR, 85; ConLC 25; ConPopW; CrtSuMy; CurBio 90; CyWA 97; DcPseud; IntAu&W 91, 93; IntWW 91, 93, 97, 98, 2000; MajTwCW 2; NatNAL; NewYTBS 81; RfGAmL 4, 94; ScF&FL 1, 2, 92; SJGHorW; TwCCr&M 85, 91; WhoAm 92, 94, 95, 96, 97, 98, 99, 2000; WhoEnt 98; WorAlBi; WorAu 1975; WrDr 86, 88, 90, 92, 94, 96, 98, 99, 2000*

Smith, Mary Carter
American. Folklorist
Storyteller who helped preserve African American history and culture through various media.
b. Feb 10, 1919 in Birmingham, Alabama
Source: *BioIn 21, 22, 24; CurBio 96; WhoAfA 9, 10, 11, 12; WhoBlA 7, 8*

Smith, Mayo
[Edward Mayo Smith]
American. Baseball Manager
Appeared in 73 ML games as player; managed nine yrs. with three teams; won World Series with Detroit, 1968.
b. Jan 17, 1915 in New London, Missouri
d. Nov 24, 1977 in Boynton Beach, Florida
Source: *Ballpl 90; BaseEn 88; BioIn 11; NewYTBS 77; ObitOF 79*

Smith, Merriman
"Smitty"
American. Journalist
Chief Washington correspondent for UPI, 1941-70; won Pulitzer, 1964, for coverage of John F Kennedy assassination.
b. Feb 10, 1913 in Savannah, Georgia
d. Apr 13, 1970 in Alexandria, Virginia
Source: *AmAu&B; BiDAmJo; BioIn 8, 9, 11, 16, 19, 23, 24; ConAu 1R, 2NR, 29R; EncTwCJ; LegTOT; NatCAB 56; WhAm 5; WorAl; WorAlBi*

Smith, Michael John
American. Astronaut
Spacecraft pilot who died in explosion of space shuttle *Challenger.*
b. Apr 30, 1945 in Beaufort, North Carolina
d. Jan 28, 1986 in Cape Canaveral, Florida
Source: *NewYTBS 86*

Smith, Michael W
American. Singer
Album, *Somewhere Somehow* has Christian themes.
Source: *WhoAm 98, 99, 2000*

Smith, Oliver
American. Producer, Designer
Winner of eight Tonys for designs including *The Sound of Music,* 1960.
b. Feb 13, 1918 in Waupun, Wisconsin
d. Jan 23, 1994 in New York, New York
Source: *BiDD; BiE&WWA; BioIn 1, 2, 4, 6, 7, 9, 13, 15, 19, 20, 22; CamGWoT; CelR; CnOxB; ConDes 84, 90; CurBio 61, 94N; DancEn 78; EncWT; Ent; IntDcB; IntWW 83, 89, 91, 93; MetOEnc; NewYTBS 94; NotNAT; OxCAmT 84; PIP&P; WhAm 11; WhoAm 74, 76, 78, 80, 82, 84, 86, 88, 90, 92, 94; WhoE 74, 79, 81, 93; WhoEnt 92; WhoGov 72, 75, 77; WhoOp 76; WhoThe 72, 77, 81; WhoWor 74, 76*

Smith, Owen Guinn
American. Track Athlete
Pole vaulter; won gold medal, 1948 Olympics; set record that stood 25 yrs.
b. May 20, 1920 in McKinney, Texas
Source: *WhoTr&F 73*

Smith, Ozzie
[Osborne Earl Smith]
"Wizard of Oz"
American. Baseball Player
Shortstop with San Diego, 1977-82; St. Louis, 1982—; holds ML record for most assists by shortstop, 1980; seven-time NL All-Star; 2,000 career hit, 1992; NL record, 13 straight Gold Glove Awards.
b. Dec 26, 1954 in Mobile, Alabama
Source: *AfrAmSG; Ballpl 90; BaseReg 86, 87; BiDAmSp Sup; BioIn 11, 13, 16; CurBio 97; LegTOT; WhoAfA 9, 10, 11, 12; WhoAm 88, 90, 92, 94, 95, 96, 97, 98, 99, 2000; WhoBlA 4, 5, 6, 7, 8; WhoMW 90, 92, 93, 96, 98; WhoSpor; WorAlBi*

Smith, (Charles) Page
American. Historian
Writer of historical narratives including the 8 volume *People's History of the United States,* 1976-86.
b. Sep 6, 1917 in Baltimore, Maryland
d. Aug 28, 1995 in Santa Cruz, California
Source: *AmAu&B; BioIn 14; ConAu 1R, 2NR, 149; CurBio 90, 95N; DrAS 74H, 78H, 82H; IntAu&W 91, 93; WhoAm 74; WrDr 80, 82, 84, 86, 88, 90, 92, 94, 96*

Smith, Patti
American. Singer, Poet
Hit single "Because the Night," written with Bruce Springsteen, 1978.
b. Dec 30, 1946 in Chicago, Illinois
Source: *BillEnR; BioIn 16; ConAu 63NR, 93; ConLC 12; ConMuA 80A; CurBio 89; DcArts; DrAPF 89; EncPR&S 89; EncRk 88; EncRkSt; HarEnR 86; IlEncRk; IntWWW 2; InWom SUP; LegTOT; NewGrDA 86; NewWmR; PenEncP; RkOn 85; RkWho 96; RolSEnR 83; Songw; WhoEnt 92; WhoRock 81; WhoRocM 82; WorAl; WorAlBi*

Smith, Paul Joseph
American. Composer
Won Oscar, 1940, for work on Walt Disney classic *Pinocchio.*
b. Oct 30, 1906 in Calumet, Michigan
d. Jan 25, 1985 in Glendale, California
Source: *AmNatBi; ASCAP 80; BioIn 14*

Smith, Perry Edward
American. Murderer
Subject of Truman Capote's book, *In Cold Blood;* killed family of four with partner Richard Hickock, 1959; hanged after many appeals.
b. Oct 27, 1928? in Lansing, Kansas
d. Apr 14, 1965
Source: *BioIn 7; MurCaTw*

Smith, Pete
[Peter Schmidt]
American. Producer
Produced, narrated shorts for MGM, 1936-55; over 20 nominated for Oscars.
b. Sep 4, 1892 in New York, New York

d. Jan 12, 1979 in Los Angeles, California
Source: *BioIn 9, 78, 79; What 4; WhScrn 83*

Smith, Red
[Walter Wellesley Smith]
American. Journalist
Sportswriter whose column appeared in over 500 newspapers; won Pulitzer.
b. Sep 25, 1905 in Green Bay, Wisconsin
d. Jan 15, 1982 in Stamford, Connecticut
Source: *AmNatBi; AnObit 1982; BenetAL 91; BiDAmJo; BiDAmSp OS; BioIn 1, 2, 3, 4, 5, 6, 10, 11, 12, 13, 15, 16, 17, 22, 23, 24; CelR; ConAu 77; CulEncB; CurBio 59, 82, 82N; DcLB 29, 171; EncTwCJ; FacFETw; JrnUS; LegTOT; NewYTBS 82, 86; REnAL; WebAB 74, 79; WhAm 8; WhoAm 76, 78, 80, 82; WorAl; WorAu 1975*

Smith, Rex
American. Actor, Singer
Had hit single "You Take My Breath Away," 1981; starred in Broadway, film versions of *Pirates of Penzance,* 1980.
b. Sep 19, 1956? in Jacksonville, Florida
Source: *BioIn 12; ConTFT 7; LegTOT; RkOn 85; WhoHol 92; WhoSSW 91*

Smith, Robert C
American. Politician
Rep. senator, NH, 1990—.
b. Mar 30, 1941 in Trenton, New Jersey
Source: *AlmAP 88; BiDrUSC 89; BioIn 24; CngDr 89; NewYTBS 99; WhoAm 88; WhoAmP 87; WhoE 89*

Smith, Robert H
American. Social Reformer
Co-founder with William Griffith Wilson (Bill W) of Alcoholics Anonymous (AA).
b. Aug 8, 1879 in Saint Johnsbury, Vermont
d. Nov 16, 1950 in Akron, Ohio
Source: *WorAlBi*

Smith, Robert Lee
American. Inventor, TV Personality
Founder, Equal Relationships Institute, 1981—; host, TV series "You and Your Big Ideas," 1959-64.
b. Sep 18, 1928 in Saint Louis, Missouri
Source: *ConAu 111*

Smith, Robert Weston
"Wolfman Jack"
American. Radio Personality
Rock 'n' Roll jockey icon famous for his gravelly voice and wolf-man howls.
d. Jul 1, 1995 in Belvidere, North Carolina
Source: *BioIn 10, 21, 22; BioNews 74*

Smith, Robyn Caroline
[Mrs. Fred Astaire]
American. Jockey
First woman jockey to win major race.
b. Aug 14, 1944 in San Francisco,
California
Source: *BioIn* 9, 10, 11, 12; *CurBio* 76;
HerW 84; *InWom* SUP; *NewYTBE* 71;
NewYTBS 78; *WhoAm* 78, 80, 82

Smith, Roger
American. Actor
Films include *The First Time,* 1969;
husband, manager of Ann-Margret.
b. Dec 18, 1932 in South Gate,
California
Source: *BioIn* 16; *FilmgC; ForYSC;
HalFC* 80, 84, 88; *IntMPA* 75, 76, 77,
78, 79, 80, 81, 82, 84, 86, 88, 92, 94,
96; *ItaFilm; LegTOT; MotPP; MovMk;
WhoAm* 82; *WhoHol* 92, A; *WorAl*

Smith, Roger Bonham
American. Auto Executive
Chm., GM, 1981-90.
b. Jul 12, 1925 in Columbus, Ohio
Source: *AutoN* 79; *BioIn* 12, 13, 16;
ConAmBL; CurBio 84; *Dun&B* 79, 90;
EncABHB 5; *IntWW* 91; *NewYTBS* 85;
St&PR 84, 87, 91, 93; *Ward* 77; *Who*
82, 83, 85, 88, 90, 92, 94, 98, 99, 2000;
WhoAm 74, 76, 78, 80, 82, 84, 86, 88,
90, 92, 94, 95, 96; *WhoE* 85, 86, 89;
WhoFI 74, 81, 83, 85, 87, 89, 92;
WhoMW 84, 86, 88, 90, 92; *WhoWor* 84,
87, 89, 91

Smith, Roger Guenveur
American. Actor, Playwright, Director
Stage, television, and film actor known
for accepting challenging, provocative
roles such as Smiley in Spike Lee's
Do the Right Thing; also award-
winning playwright and director.
b. 1960 in Berkeley, California
Source: *ConBlB* 12

Smith, Ronnie
[K C and the Sunshine Band]
American. Musician
Trumpeter with Sunshine Band since
1973.
b. 1952 in Hialeah, Florida

Smith, Samantha
American. Student, Actor
Wrote letter to Soviet leader Andropov,
1982, visited USSR as his guest, 1983;
died in plane crash.
b. Jun 29, 1972 in Manchester, Maine
d. Aug 25, 1985 in Auburn, Maine
Source: *ConAu* 117; *ConNews* 85-3;
SmATA 45N

Smith, Sammi
American. Singer
Won best female country vocalist
Grammy, 1972, for "Help Me Make It
Through the Night."
b. Aug 5, 1943 in Orange, California
Source: *AllMGCo; BgBkCoM; BioIn* 14;
CounME 74, 74A; *EncFCWM* 83;

HarEnCM 87; *IlEncCM; PenEncP;
RkOn* 74, 78

Smith, Samuel Francis
American. Poet, Clergy
Wrote patriotic hymn, "America," 1831.
b. Oct 21, 1808 in Boston, Massachusetts
d. Nov 16, 1895 in Boston,
Massachusetts
Source: *Alli,* SUP; *AmAu; AmAu&B;
AmBi; AmNatBi; ApCAB; BiDAmM;
BiD&SB; BioIn* 1, 4, 13, 16; *ChhPo, S1;
CyAL* 2; *DcAmAu; DcAmB; DcLEL;
DcNAA; Drake; EvLB; HarEnUS; LinLib*
L; *LuthC* 75; *NatCAB* 6; *OxCAmL* 65,
83, 95; *PoChrch; REn; TwCBDA;
WebAB* 74, 79; *WebE&AL; WhAm* HS

Smith, Seba
[Major Jack Downing]
American. Journalist
Wrote America's first political satires on
Jacksonian democracy in newspapers,
magazines.
b. Sep 17, 1792 in Buckfield, Maine
d. Jul 28, 1868 in Patchogue, New York
Source: *Alli; AmAu; AmAu&B; AmBi;
AmNatBi; ApCAB; BbD; Benet* 87;
BenetAL 91; *BiD&SB; BioIn* 11, 12, 13,
15; *CamDcAB; ChhPo, S1; CnDAL;
CyAL* 2; *DcAmAu; DcAmB; DcEnL;
DcLB* 1, 11; *DcLEL; DcNAA; Drake;
EncAHmr; EncAJ; EncALit; NatCAB* 8;
OxCAmL 65, 83, 95; *REn; REnAL;
RfGAmL* 87, 94; *TwCBDA; WebAB* 74,
79; *WhAm* HS

Smith, (Robert) Sidney
American. Cartoonist
Started Andy Gump comic strip, 1917;
considered first to introduce continuity
to strips by continuing stories day
after day.
b. Feb 13, 1877 in Bloomington, Illinois
d. Oct 20, 1935 in Harvard, Illinois
Source: *AmAu&B; AmNatBi; DcAmB* S1;
DcNAA; EncACom; WhAm 1, 4;
WhAmArt 85; *WhAm* HSA; *WorECom*

Smith, Sophia
American. Philanthropist
Founded Smith College; opened, 1875.
b. Aug 27, 1796 in Hatfield,
Massachusetts
d. Jun 12, 1870 in Hadley, Massachusetts
Source: *AmAu&B; AmNatBi; ApCAB;
BioAmW; BioIn* 2, 10; *CamBiEn;
CamDcAB; ChamBiD; ContDcW* 89;
*DcAmB; IntDcWB; InWom; LibW;
MorMA; NatCAB* 7; *NotAW; OxCAmH;
TwCBDA; WhAm* HS; *WomFir*

Smith, Stan(ley Roger)
American. Tennis Player
Winner of over 25 US singles, doubles
titles.
b. Dec 14, 1946 in Pasadena, California
Source: *BiDAmSp* OS; *BioIn* 10, 12;
BuCMET; CelR; ConAu 85; *LegTOT;
NewYTBE* 70; *WhoAm* 76, 78, 80, 82,
84, 86, 88, 90, 92, 94, 95, 96, 97;
WhoIntT

Smith, Stevie
[Florence Margaret Smith]
English. Poet
Poems include "A Good Time Was Had
by All," 1937; "Novel on Yellow
Paper," 1936.
b. Sep 20, 1903 in Hull, England
d. Mar 7, 1971 in Ashburton, England
Source: *Au&Wr* 71; *CasWL; ConAu* P-2;
ConLC 25; *ConPo* 75; *DcLEL; LngCTC;
ModBrL* S1; *OxCEng* 85; *WorAu* 1950

Smith, Sydney
English. Clergy, Essayist
Co-founded *Edinburgh Review,* 1802;
wrote *Letters of Peter Plymley,* 1807,
defending Catholic emancipation.
b. Jun 6, 1771 in Woodford, England
d. Feb 22, 1845 in London, England
Source: *Alli; AtlBL; BbD; BenetAL* 91;
BiD&SB; BioIn 1, 3, 4, 5, 6, 7, 8, 9, 10,
11, 12, 13, 17; *BritAu* 19; *CamBiEn;
CamGEL; CamGLE; CasWL; CelCen;
ChamBiD; DcAmC; DcBiPP; DcEnA;
DcEnL; DcEuL; DcLB* 107; *DcLEL;
DcNaB; EvLB; LinLib* L, S; *NewC;
OxCAmL* 65, 83, 95; *OxCBrHi; OxCEng*
67, 85, 95; *PenC* ENG; *WebE&AL;
WhDW*

Smith, Theobald
American. Pathologist
Infectious disease specialist; did
important research on animals,
especially hogs, cattle.
b. Jul 31, 1859 in Albany, New York
d. Dec 10, 1934 in Princeton, New
Jersey
Source: *AmBi; AmNatBi; BiDSocW;
BiESc; BiHiMed; BioIn* 1, 2, 3, 5, 7, 9,
13; *CamBiEn; CamDcAB; CamDcSc;
ChamBiD; DcAmB* S1; *DcAmMeB* 84;
DcNAA; DcScB; EncAB-H 1974; *InSci;
LarDcSc; NatCAB* 35; *OxCMed* 86;
RanHWDS; WebAB 74, 79; *WhAm* 1

Smith, Thorne
American. Author
Humorous works include *Topper,* 1926;
became famous film series, TV show.
b. 1892? in Annapolis, Maryland
d. Jun 21, 1934 in Sarasota, Florida
Source: *AmAu&B; BeaEPF; Benet* 87;
BenetAL 91; *CnDAL; DcLEL; DcNAA;
EncAHmr; FilmgC; HalFC* 80, 84, 88;
LegTOT; LngCTC; OxCAmL 65, 83, 95;
REn; REnAL; TwCA

Smith, Tommie
American. Track Athlete
Sprinter; won gold medal in 200 meters,
1968 Olympics; on winner's stand
with John Carlos, protested treatment
of blacks in US by raising clenched
fists; expelled from games.
b. Jun 5, 1944 in Clarksville, Texas
Source: *AfrAmSG; BiDAmSp* OS; *BioIn*
7, 11; *BlkOlyM; CamBiEn; ChamBiD;
CmCal; InB&W* 80; *WhoAfA* 9, 10, 11,
12; *WhoBlA* 2, 3, 4, 5, 6, 7, 8;
WhoTr&F 73

Smith, Tommy
[Thomas J Smith]
Canadian. Hockey Player
Left wing, Quebec, 1919-20; Hall of
Fame, 1973.
b. Sep 27, 1885 in Ottawa, Ontario,
Canada
d. Aug 1, 1966
Source: *HocEn*

Smith, Tony
[Anthony Peter Smith]
American. Sculptor
Created huge minimalist sculptures:
Cigarette, 1961; *Throwback*, 1978.
b. 1912 in Orange, New Jersey
d. Dec 26, 1980 in New York, New
York
Source: *AmNatBi; AnObit 1980; BioIn 7,
8, 9, 12, 13; BriEAA; ConArt 77, 83, 89,
96; ConAu 105; DcAmArt; DcCAA 77,
88, 94; DcCAr 81; DcTwArt; McGDA;
NewYTBS 80; OxCTwCA; OxDcArt;
PhDcTCA 77; WhAm 7; WhoAm 74, 76,
78; WhoAmA 73, 76, 78, 80, 82, 84, 86,
89, 91N, 93N; WorArt 1950*

Smith, Tubby
[Orlando Smith]
American. Basketball Coach
Coached at several other universities,
then became the first African
American head basketball coach for
University of Kentucky Wildcats in
1997, and led the team to win the
National Collegiate Athletic
Association (NCAA) Championship
that year.
Source: *WhoAfA 9, 10, 11, 12*

Smith, W(illiam) Eugene
American. Photojournalist
Considered a master of modern
photojournalism, known for his
poignant images of war, social
injustice, and the mercury poisonings
in Minamata, Japan.
b. Dec 30, 1918 in Wichita, Kansas
d. Oct 15, 1978 in Tucson, Arizona
Source: *BiDAmJo; CamBiEn; ConAu
142; ConPhot 95; DcAmB S10*

Smith, Walter Bedell
"Beetle"
American. Army Officer
CIA director, 1950-53; ambassador to
USSR, 1946-49.
b. Oct 5, 1895 in Indianapolis, Indiana
d. Aug 9, 1961 in Washington, District
of Columbia
Source: *AmNatBi; BiDWWGF; BioIn 1,
2, 3, 6, 11, 16, 17, 18; CamDcAB;
ColdWar 1, 2; CurBio 44, 53, 61;
DcAmB S7; DcAmDH 80, 89;
DcAmMiB; DcCathB; EncCW; EncVieW;
HarEnMi; HisDcKW; HisEWW; IndAu
1917; PolProf E, T; REnAL; WebAB 74,
79; WebAMB; WhAm 4*

Smith, Will
[DJ Jazzy Jeff & The Fresh Prince]
"The Fresh Prince"
American. Actor, Rapper
Appeared on TV's "The Fresh Prince of
Bel Air," 1990-96; in *Independence
Day*, 1996.
b. Sep 25, 1968 in Philadelphia,
Pennsylvania
Source: *ConBlB 8, 18; ConMus 26;
ConTFT 23; CurBio 96; IntMPA 96;
IntWW 2000; LegTOT; News 97, 97-2;
WhoAfA 9, 10, 11, 12; WhoAm 98, 99,
2000; WhoEnt 98*

Smith, Willi Donnell
American. Fashion Designer
Began Willi Wear, Ltd, 1976; won 1983
Coty award for women's fashion.
b. Feb 29, 1948 in Philadelphia,
Pennsylvania
d. Apr 17, 1987 in New York, New
York
Source: *ConNews 87-3; InB&W 85;
WhAm 9; WhoAm 80, 82, 84, 86;
WhoBlA 4; WhoE 85, 86; WhoFash;
WorFshn*

Smith, William
English. Geologist
Founder of stratigraphical geology; wrote
Geological Map of England, 1815;
first recipient of geology's Wollaston
Medal, 1831.
b. Mar 23, 1769 in Churchill, England
d. Aug 28, 1839 in Northampton,
England
Source: *Alli; ApCAB; AsBiEn; BbtC;
BiESc; BioIn 2, 3, 7, 8, 12, 14; BritAu
19; CamBiEn; CamDcSc; ChamBiD;
DcBiPP; DcCanB 7; DcEnL; DcNAA;
DcNaB; DcScB; InSci; LarDcSc;
MacDCB 78; NewCol 75; OxCCan;
RanHWDS; WhDW*

Smith, William
[William Henry Joseph Berthol
Bonaparte Smith]
"Willie the Lion"
American. Jazz Musician, Songwriter
One of great "stride" pianists, active
from 1920s; subject of two short films,
1900s.
b. Nov 23, 1897 in Goshen, New York
d. Apr 18, 1973 in New York, New
York
Source: *ASCAP 66; BakBD 84;
CmpEPM; EncJzS; WhoJazz 72*

Smith, William French
American. Government Official
US attorney general under Ronald
Reagan, 1981-84.
b. Aug 26, 1917 in Wilton, New
Hampshire
d. Oct 29, 1990 in Los Angeles,
California
Source: *AnObit 1990; BiDrUSE 89;
BioIn 12, 13; CngDr 81, 83; CurBio 82,
91N; FacFETw; IntWW 81, 82, 83, 89,
91N; IntYB 82; LEduc 74; NewYTBS 80,
90; ScrEAmL 2; WhAm 10; Who 82, 83,
85, 88, 90, 92N; WhoAm 80, 82, 84, 86,*

88; *WhoAmL 78, 79, 83, 87; WhoAmP
73, 75, 77, 79, 81, 83, 85, 87, 89;
WhoBlA 6; WhoE 81, 83, 85; WhoGov
75, 77; WhoWest 74, 76, 78, 80;
WhoWor 80, 82, 84, 87, 89*

Smith, William Jay
American. Children's Author, Poet
Wrote *The Tin Can and Other Poems*,
1966; honored for poetry, translations.
b. Apr 22, 1918 in Winnfield, Louisiana
Source: *AuBYP 2S, 3; BenetAL 91; BioIn
6, 8, 9, 10, 11, 12, 17, 19; BkCL;
ChhPo, S1, S2, S3; ConAu 5R, 44NR;
ConLC 6; ConPo 70, 75, 80, 85, 91, 96;
ConSoWr; CurBio 74; DcLB 5; DcLEL
1940; DrAP 75; DrAPF 91; DrAS 74E,
78E; EncALit; FifBJA; IntAu&W 77;
IntWWP 77; MajAl; OxCAmL 83, 95;
OxCTwCP; PenC AM; SJGChWr 5;
SmATA 2, 22AS, 68; TwCChW 1, 2, 3,
4; WhoAm 74, 76, 78, 80, 82, 84, 86, 88,
90, 92, 94, 95, 96, 97, 98, 99, 2000;
WhoEnt 98; WhoUSWr 88; WhoWrEP
89, 92, 95; WorAu 1950; WrDr 76, 80,
82, 84, 86, 88, 90, 92, 94, 96, 98, 99,
2000*

Smith Brothers
[Andrew Smith; William Smith]
English. Manufacturers
First to market cough drops in prepacked
boxes, 1872.
Source: *Alli, SUP; AllMGCo; AntBDN
N; ArtsEM; BbtC; BiAUS; BiD&SB;
BiDBrA; BiDLA, SUP; BiDrAC;
BiDRP&D; BiDrUSC 89; BioIn 3, 9, 17,
18; BlmGEL; CabMA; CasWL; Chambr
1, 3; DcArch; DcBiPP; DcCanB 5;
DcNaB; DcNiCA; DcVicP, 2; Drake;
Entr; FolkA 87; IlDcG; IntMPA 82, 84,
86; LElec; MacDCB 78; MedHR; NegAl
83, 89; NewGrDM 80; NewYHSD;
NewYTBE 70; NewYTBS 93; OxCCanL
1; OxCShps; OxCThe 67, 83; PeoHis;
PoIre; ScF&FL 92; WhAm HS;
WhE&EA; WhoAmM 83; WhoHol 92, A;
WhoReal 83; WhoRocM 82; WhoScEu
91-1*

Smitherman, Geneva
American. Educator, Author
Linguist who specializes in black
language; author, *Black Language and
Culture*, 1975.
b. Dec 10, 1940 in Brownsville,
Tennessee
Source: *BlkAWP; BlkWrNE; ConAu 130;
DrAS 74E, 78F, 82F; InB&W 80, 85;
LEduc 74; WhoBlA 1, 2, 3, 4, 7; WrDr
94, 96, 98, 99*

Smithers, Jan
American. Actor
Played Bailey on TV series "WKRP in
Cincinnati," 1978-82.
b. Jul 3, 1949 in North Hollywood,
California
Source: *BioIn 15; ConTFT 7; LegTOT;
VarWW 85; WhoHol 92, A*

Smiths, The
[Mike Joyce; Johnny Marr; Steven
    Patrick Morrissey; Andy Rourke]
English. Music Group
Rock band formed in 1982 in
    Manchester, England; dissoved in
    1987.
Source: *BillEnR; BioIn 17; ConMus 3;
DcArts; EncRk 88; EncRkSt; PenEncP*

Smithson, Harriet Constance
Irish. Actor
Played Shakespearean roles to delighted
    Parisian audiences, 1827-28.
b. Mar 18, 1800 in Ennis, Ireland
d. Mar 3, 1854
Source: *BioIn 5, 10, 11, 13; CamGWoT;
CnThe; DcIrB 1, 2, 3; DcNaB; InWom;
OxCThe 67, 83*

Smithson, James (Louis Macie)
American. Scientist
Left estate money for founding of
    Smithsonian Institution, 1826.
b. 1765 in Paris, France
d. Jun 27, 1829 in Genoa, Italy
Source: *Alli; ApCAB; BiESc; BiInAmS;
BioIn 1, 6, 7, 10, 13; CamBiEn;
ChamBiD; DcNaB; DcScB; Drake;
EncAAH; InSci; LarDcSc; RanHWDS;
TwCBDA; WhAm HS; WorAl; WorAlBi*

Smithson, Robert (Irving)
American. Artist
Sculptor, essayist, and filmmaker is best
    known for his site-specific
    environmental earth works.
b. Jan 2, 1938 in Passaic, New Jersey
d. Jul 20, 1973 in Texas
Source: *AmNatBi; CamDcAB; ConArt 96*

Smits, Jimmy
American. Actor
Starred in TV dramas "LA Law," 1986-
    91; "NYPD Blue," 1994-98; won
    supporting actor Emmy, 1990.
b. Jul 9, 1955 in New York, New York
Source: *BiHaHis; BioIn 15; ConTFT 6,
15; DcHiB; HolBB; IntMPA 92, 94, 96;
LegTOT; WhoAm 95, 96, 97, 98, 99,
2000; WhoEnt 92, 98; WhoHisp 91, 92,
94; WhoHol 92; WorAlBi*

Smohalla
American. Religious Leader
Responsible for revitalizing the Washani
    religion of the Pacific Northwest.
b. 1815? in Washington
d. 1895
Source: *AmBi; AmIndBi; AmNatBi; BioIn
11, 21; DcAmB; EncNAR; EncNoAl;
EncWB 98; NotNaAm; RelLAm 1, 2;
WebAB 74, 79; WhAm 4, HSA; WhNaAH*

**Smokey Robinson and the
    Miracles**
[Pete Moore; Claudette Rogers Robinson;
    William "Smokey" Robinson; Bobby
    Rogers; Ronnie White]
American. Music Group
All-Detroit group, formed 1957; hit
    singles "I Second That Emotion,"
    1965; "The Tears of a Clown," 1970.
Source: *InB&W 85A; NewYTBS 95;
RolSEnR 83; WhoAmP 81; WhoRocM 82*

Smollett, Tobias George
"Smelfungus"
Scottish. Author, Physician, Translator
Novels include *Roderick Random,* 1748;
    Humphrey Clinker, 1770.
b. Mar 1721 in Dalquhurn, Scotland
d. Sep 17, 1771 in Monte Nero, Italy
Source: *Alli; AtlBL; BbD; Benet 96;
BiD&SB; BiHiMed; BioIn 1, 2, 3, 5, 7,
8, 9, 10, 11, 12, 14, 15, 17, 18; BlkwCE;
BlmGEL; BritAu; CamBiEn; CamGEL;
CasWL; ChamBiD; Chambr 2; ChhPo;
CrtT 2; CyWA 58; DcArts; DcBiA;
DcBiPP; DcEnA; DcEnL; DcEuL;
DcLEL; Dis&D; EncEnl; EncWB 98;
EvLB; LinLib S; LitC 46; LngCEL;
McGEWB; MouLC 2; NewC; NotNAT B;
OxCEng 67, 85, 95; OxCMed 86;
OxCShps; PenC ENG; RAdv 1, 14, 13-1;
REn; WebE&AL; WorAl*

Smoltz, John
American. Baseball Player
Pitcher, Atlanta Braves, 1988—; All
    Star, 1989, 1992-93; Cy Young award
    winner, 1996.
b. May 15, 1967 in Warren, Michigan
Source: *Ballpl 90; BioIn 22*

Smoot, George
[George Fitzgerald Smoot, III]
American. Physicist
Studied microwave radiation, the residual
    heat, of the big bang, resulting in a
    better understanding of the early days
    of the universe.
b. Feb 20, 1945 in Yukon, Florida
Source: *AmMWSc 76P, 79, 82, 86, 89,
92, 95; CurBio 94; WhoAm 92, 94, 95,
96, 97; WhoScEn 94, 96*

Smothers, Dick
[The Smothers Brothers; Richard
    Smothers]
American. Comedian, Singer
Starred with brother Tommy in 1960s
    TV series, in Broadway play *I Love
    My Wife,* 1978-79.
b. Nov 20, 1938 in New York, New
    York
Source: *BiDAmM; BioIn 7, 16; ConTFT
3; CurBio 68; HalFC 84; IntMPA 92;
NewYTBS 76; WhoAm 86, 90; WhoHol
A; WorAl; WorAlBi*

Smothers, Tommy
[The Smothers Brothers; Thomas Bolyn
    Smothers, III]
American. Comedian, Singer
b. Feb 2, 1937 in New York, New York

Source: *BioIn 16; ConTFT 3; CurBio
68; EncAFC; HalFC 88; IntMPA 92;
LegTOT; WhoAm 74, 90; WhoEnt 92;
WhoHol A; WorAlBi*

Smucker, Jerome
American. Manufacturer
In 1915 apple butter was main product in
    his preserves co; jellies, jams added
    later.
b. 1858
d. 1948
Source: *Entr*

Smuin, Michael
American. Choreographer
Won Tony for musical revival *Anything
    Goes,* 1988.
b. Oct 13, 1938 in Missoula, Montana
Source: *BiDD; BioIn 10, 11, 13, 16;
CnOxB; ConTFT 9; CurBio 84; EncWB
98; FilmChD; WhoAm 80, 82, 84, 92,
94, 95, 96, 97, 98, 99, 2000; WhoEnt
92A, 98; WhoWest 82*

Smuts, Jan Christian
South African. Soldier, Statesman
Commander of British forces in Africa
    during WW I; prime minister of S
    Africa, 1919-24, 1939-48.
b. May 24, 1870 in Cape Town, South
    Africa
d. Sep 11, 1950 in Irene, South Africa
Source: *Benet 87, 96; BioIn 2, 3, 4, 5, 6,
7, 8, 9, 10, 11, 12; ChamBiD; Chambr
3; CurBio 41, 50; DcNaB 1941;
DcTwHis; EncSoA; EncWB 98;
EncyDCo; GrBr; LngCTC; McGEWB;
NamesHP; OxCBrHi; OxCEng 67; REn;
WhAm 3*

Smyslov, Vasili Vasil'evich
Russian. Chess Player
Held world chess championships, 1957-
    58.
b. Mar 23, 1921 in Moscow, Union of
    Soviet Socialist Republics
Source: *BiDSovU; BioIn 8, 15;
ChamBiD; CurBio 67; OxCChes 84*

Smyth, Ethel, Dame
English. Composer
Composed *Mass in D Major,* 1893;
    memoir *Impressions That Remained,
    As Time Went On,* 1936.
b. 1858
d. May 1944
Source: *ArtclWW 2; BakBD 78, 84;
BakDcM; CmOp; CmpQue; ContDcW
89; DcCom&M 2; FemiCLE; GayLesB;
IntDcOp; IntDcWB; LngCTC; MetOEnc;
MusMk; NewAmDM; NewEOp 71;
NewGrDM 80; NewOxM; OxDcOp;
PenDiMP A; RadHan*

Smythe, Conn
[Constantine Falkland Kerry Smythe]
Canadian. Hockey Executive
One of original organizers of NY
    Rangers; first owner, Toronto Maple
    Leafs, 1926-61; built Maple Leaf
    Gardens, 1931; Conn Smythe Trophy,

NHL Smythe Division named for him;
Hall of Fame, 1958.
b. Feb 1, 1895 in Toronto, Ontario,
Canada
d. Nov 18, 1980 in Toronto, Ontario,
Canada
Source: *BioIn 1, 2, 10, 12; CanWW 70;
ColCR; DcPseud; NewYTBS 80; St&PR
75; WhoHcky 73*

Smythe, Reg(inald)

English. Cartoonist
Created ''Andy Capp,'' daily comic strip
for London's *Daily Mirror,* 1957.
b. Oct 7, 1917 in Hartlepool, England
d. Jun 13, 1998 in Hartlepool, England
Source: *AuNews 1; Who 92; WhoAm 86*

Snake, Reuben, Jr.

American. Native American Leader,
Religious Leader
Chairman of the American Indian
Movement, 1972-75; chairman of the
Winnebago Tribe, 1975-ca. 1987.
b. 1937 in Winnebago, Nebraska
d. 1993 in Nebraska
Source: *BioIn 21; EncNAB; NotNaAm*

Snead, Sam(uel Jackson)

''Slammin' Sammy''
American. Golfer
Turned pro, 1934; has over 100 career
wins, including PGA three times;
wrote several books on golf: *Golf
Begins at Forty,* 1978.
b. May 27, 1912 in Hot Springs, Virginia
Source: *BiDAmSp OS; BioIn 1, 2, 3, 5,
6, 9, 10, 11, 12, 13; CamBiEn;
CamDcAB; CelR; ConAu 114; CurBio
49; FacFETw; IntWW 81, 82, 83, 89, 91,
93, 97, 98, 2000; LegTOT; NewYTBE
72; NewYTBS 74, 75, 81, 82; WebAB 74,
79; WhoAm 76, 78, 80, 82, 84, 86, 88,
90, 92, 94, 95, 96, 97, 98; WhoGolf;
WorAl; WorAlBi*

Sneed, Paula A(nn)

American. Business Executive
Top marketing executive for Kraft
Foods, became head of marketing
services and senior vice-president of
the company, 1995; won M.B.A. of
the Year Award, Harvard Business
School Black Alumni Organization,
1987, and named one of *Black
Enterprise* magazine's ''21 Women of
Power and Influence,'' 1991.
b. Nov 10, 1947 in Everett,
Massachusetts
Source: *WhoAdv 90; WhoAmW 89, 91,
93; WhoFI 00*

Snegur, Mircea Ion

Moldovan. Political Leader
Former high-ranking Soviet Communist
Party official was elected president of
the Republic of Moldova in 1991;
considered a defender of Moldova's
interests, he has worked with Russia to
settle the conflict of the Trans-Dniestr
region.
b. 1940 in Trifaneshty, Moldova
Source: *LngBDD*

Sneider, Vernon John

American. Author
Wrote *Teahouse of the August Moon,*
1951; became play, film.
b. Oct 6, 1916 in Monroe, Michigan
d. May 1, 1981 in Monroe, Michigan
Source: *BioIn 4; ConAu 5R, 13NR, 103;
CurBio 56, 81; IntAu&W 77; NewYTBS
81*

Snell, George D(avis)

American. Scientist
Research on immune system greatly
enhanced organ transplants; shared
Nobel Prize, 1980.
b. Dec 19, 1903 in Bradford,
Massachusetts
d. Jun 6, 1996 in Bar Harbor, Maine
Source: *AmMWSc 73P, 76P, 79, 82, 86,
89, 92, 95; BiESc; BioIn 12, 14, 15, 20,
22; BlueB 76; CamBiEn; CamDcAB;
ChamBiD; ConAu 106, 152; CurBio 86,
96N; IntWW 74, 75, 76, 77, 78, 79, 80,
81, 82, 83, 89, 91, 93; LarDcSc;
McGCEnS; McGMS 80; NewYTBS 80;
NobelP; NotTwCS 1; WhAm 11; Who 82,
83, 85, 88, 90, 92, 94; WhoAm 74, 76,
78, 80, 82, 84, 86, 88, 90, 92, 94, 95,
96; WhoE 81, 83, 85, 86, 89, 91, 93, 95;
WhoFrS 84; WhoNob, 90, 95; WhoScEn
94, 96; WhoWor 78, 82, 84, 87, 89, 91,
93, 95, 96; WorAlBi*

Snell, Peter George

New Zealander. Track Athlete
Set five middle-distance records, 1962,
including the mile.
b. Dec 17, 1938 in Opunake, New
Zealand
Source: *CurBio 62; WhoTr&F 73*

Snelling, Richard

American. Politician
Rep. governor of VT, 1977-85; 1990-91.
b. Feb 18, 1927 in Allentown,
Pennsylvania
d. Mar 13, 1991
Source: *PolsAm 84; WhoAm 88;
WhoAmP 87; WhoE 85; WhoWor 84*

Snepp, Frank Warren, III

American. Government Official, Author
With CIA, 1968-76; in Saigon during S
Vietnam's fall, 1975; wrote *Decent
Interval,* 1977.
b. May 3, 1943? in Kinston, North
Carolina
Source: *BioIn 11, 13; ConAu 105*

Sneva, Tom

[Thomas Edsol Sneva]
American. Auto Racer
Won Indianapolis 500, 1983.
b. Jun 1, 1948 in Spokane, Washington
Source: *BiDAmSp OS; WhoAm 78, 80,
82, 84, 86, 88, 92, 94; WhoWest 94*

Snider, Dee

[Twisted Sister; Daniel Dee Snider]
American. Singer, Composer
Lead singer, Twisted Sister, 1976—;
composes most of group's original
songs.
b. Mar 15, 1955 in Massapequa, New
York
Source: *BioIn 15; ConNews 86-1; RkOn
85*

Snider, Duke

[Edwin Donald Snider]
''The Silver Fox''
American. Baseball Player
Outfielder, 1947-64, mostly with
Brooklyn/LA; led NL in home runs,
RBIs once; Hall of Fame, 1980.
b. Sep 19, 1926 in Los Angeles,
California
Source: *Ballpl 90; BiDAmSp BB; BioIn
3, 4, 5, 6, 7, 8, 9, 10, 14, 15, 16;
CmCal; CulEncB; CurBio 56; FacFETw;
LegTOT; WhoProB 73; WhoSpor*

Snider, Paul

Canadian. Murderer
Husband of Dorothy Stratten; killed wife,
himself in lover's quarrel.
b. 1951?
d. Aug 14, 1980 in Los Angeles,
California

Snipes, Wesley

American. Actor
Films include *Jungle Fever,* 1991; *White
Men Can't Jump,* 1992.
b. Jul 31, 1962 in Orlando, Florida
Source: *AfrAmAl 6, 8; ConBlB 3;
ConTFT 17; CurBio 93; DcTwCCu 5;
IntMPA 92, 94, 96; LegTOT; News 93-1;
WhoAfA 9, 10, 11, 12; WhoBlA 7, 8;
WhoHol 92*

Snively, William Daniel, Jr.

American. Physician, Author
Books on medicine include *Sea Within,*
1960.
b. Feb 9, 1911 in Rock Island, Illinois
Source: *AmMWSc 73P, 76P, 79;
BiDrACP 79; BioIn 8; IndAu 1967;
WhAm 12; WhoAm 74, 76, 78, 80, 82,
84, 86, 88, 90, 92; WhoWor 74, 82*

Snodgrass, W(illiam) D(eWitt)

[S S Gardens]
American. Poet
Won Pulitzer for *Heart's Needle,* 1959.
b. Jan 5, 1926 in Wilkinsburg,
Pennsylvania
Source: *BenetAL 91; BioIn 5, 6, 10, 11,
12, 16; BlueB 76; CamDcAB; CamGLE;
CamHAL; CasWL; ChhPo, S1; ClDMEL
47; ConAu 1R, 36NR; ConLC 18; ConPo
85, 91, 96; CroCAP; CurBio 60; DcLEL
1940; DcLP 87A; EncALit; IntAu&W 77,
82, 91; IntWW 74, 75, 76, 77, 78, 79,
80, 81, 82, 83, 89, 91, 93, 97, 98;
IntWWP 77, 82; MajTwCW 1; MichAu
80; ModAL 4S1, 4S2; OxCAmL 83, 95;
PenC AM; RAdv 14, 13-1; REn; REnAL;
RfGAmL 87, 94; WebE&AL; WhoAm 74,
76, 78, 80, 82, 90; WhoTwCL;*

WhoUSWr 88; WhoWrEP 89; WorAl;
WorAlBi; WorAu 1950; WrDr 86, 90, 94,
96

Snodgress, Carrie
American. Actor
1970 Oscar nominee for *Diary of a Mad*
Housewife.
b. Oct 27, 1946 in Chicago, Illinois
Source: *CelR; ConTFT 5; FilmEn;*
HalFC 80, 84, 88; IntMPA 82, 92;
InWom SUP; LegTOT; MovMk;
NewYTBE 70; OsStAZ; WhoHol A;
WorAl

Snoop Doggy Dogg
[Calvin Broadus]
American. Rapper
Debut album *Doggystyle,* 1993.
b. 1971? in Long Beach, California
Source: *BillEnR; DcPseud; EncRkSt*

Snorri, Sturluson
Icelandic. Historian
Best known for saga *Heimskringla,*
which tells history of Norway to 1177.
b. 1178
d. 1241
Source: *NewCol 75*

Snow, C(harles) P(ercy), Sir
English. Scientist, Author
His series of 11 novels, *Strangers and*
Brothers, depicts stresses of
contemporary British life.
b. Oct 15, 1905 in Leicester, England
d. Jul 1, 1980 in London, England
Source: *Au&Wr 71; AuSpks; Benet 96;*
BiCoLiE; BioIn 3, 4, 5, 12, 13, 14, 15,
17, 18; CasWL; ChamBiD; ConAu 5R,
101; ConLC 1, 4, 6, 9, 13; ConNov 72,
76; CurBio 54, 61, 80; DcArts; DcLEL;
DcNaB 1971; DcScB S2; EncMys;
EncSF 93; EncWB 98; EncWL 1, 2S, 3;
EvLB; GrBr; GrWrEL N; InSci;
IntAu&W 76, 77; LinLib L, S; LngCEL;
LngCTC; MajTwCW 2; McGEWB;
ModBrL, S1; NewC; NewCBEL; Novels;
OxCEng 67, 95; OxCTwCL; PenC ENG;
RAdv 1, 13-1, 13-5; REn; RGTwCWr;
ScF&FL 1, 2; TwCA SUP; TwCWr;
WebE&AL; WhE&EA; WhoTwCL;
WorAl; WrDr 76, 80

Snow, Carmel White
American. Fashion Editor
Edited *Harper's Bazaar,* 1932-57;
promoted Parisian designers.
b. Aug 21, 1887? in Dublin, Ireland
d. May 7, 1961 in New York, New York
Source: *CamDcAB; DcAmB S7; WhAm*
4; WorFshn

Snow, Clyde Collins
American. Scientist
Created the field of forensic
anthropology.
b. Jan 7, 1928 in Fort Worth, Texas
Source: *AmMWSc 73P, 76P, 79, 82, 86,*
89, 92, 95, 98; CurBio 97; FifIDA;
WhoScEn 94; WhoSSW 95

Snow, Don
Kenyan. Singer, Musician
Keyboardist, vocalist with Squeeze,
1982.
b. Jan 13, 1957, British East Africa
Source: *WhoRocM 82*

Snow, Dorothea Johnston
American. Children's Author
Wrote *Sequoyah: Young Cherokee*
Guide, 1960; *Tomahawk Claim,* 1968.
b. Apr 7, 1909 in McMinnville,
Tennessee
Source: *ConAu 1R, 3NR, 27NR; SmATA*
9

Snow, Edgar Parks
American. Journalist
Wrote of communism in China: *Red Star*
Over China, 1937; *The Other Side of*
the River, 1962.
b. Jul 19, 1905 in Kansas City, Missouri
d. Feb 15, 1972 in Eysins, Switzerland
Source: *AmAu&B; AmNatBi; Au&Wr 71;*
BenetAL 91; CamDcAB; ConAu 33R,
38NR, 81; CurBio 41, 72; JrnUS; REn;
REnAL; TwCA, SUP; WhAm 5; WorAu
1900

Snow, Hank
[Clarence Eugene Snow]
"The Singing Ranger"
American. Singer
Country music star, popular, 1950s;
wrote hit "I'm Movin' On."
b. May 9, 1914 in Brooklyn, Nova
Scotia, Canada
d. Dec 20, 1999 in Madison, Tennessee
Source: *AllMGCo; BakBD 84, 92;*
BgBkCoM; BiDAmM; BioIn 10, 12, 14,
15, 20, 22; CanWW 83, 89, 96, 97, 98,
1999; CmpEGui; CmpEPM; CounME
74, 74A; HarEnCM 69, 83; EncRk 88;
HarEnCM 87; IlEncCM; LegTOT;
NewAmDM; NewGrDA 86; OnThGG;
OxCPMus; PenEncP; Songw; WhoAm
76, 78, 80, 82, 84; WorAl; WorAlBi

Snow, Phoebe Laub
American. Singer
Albums include *Never Letting Go,* 1977;
Rock Away, 1980.
b. Jul 17, 1952 in New York, New York
Source: *BiDJaz; BioIn 10, 13, 16;*
ConMus 4; EncJzS; EncPR&S 89; EncRk
88; IlEncRk; InWom SUP; NewYTBS 76;
PenEncP; WhoAm 86; WhoRocM 82

Snowe, Olympia J(ean)
American. Politician
Rep. congresswoman from ME, 1979-95;
Senator, 1995—.
b. Feb 21, 1947 in Augusta, Maine
Source: *BiDrUSC 89; BioIn 12, 13;*
CurBio 95; EncWoAP; WhoAmP 75, 77,
79, 81, 83, 85, 87, 89, 91, 93, 95, 97,
1999; WhoE 79, 81, 83, 85, 86;
WhoWomW 91

Snyder, Gary Sherman
American. Poet
Won Pulitzer, 1975, for *Turtle Island.*

b. May 8, 1930 in San Francisco,
California
Source: *AmAu&B; CamBiEn; CamDcAB;*
CasWL; ConAu 17R, 60NR; ConLC 5;
ConPo 85; CroCAP; CurBio 78; DrAP
75; MajTwCW 2; ModAL 4S1; OxCAmL
83; OxCEng 85; OxCTwCL; PenC AM;
REn; REnAL; RfGAmL 4; WhoAm 86,
90, 98; WhoEnt 98; WhoUSWr 88;
WhoWrEP 89; WorAu 1950; WrDr 86,
98, 99, 2000

Snyder, Jimmy the Greek
[James Snyder; Demetrius George
Synodinos]
American. Journalist, Sportscaster
Former pro gambler; analyst for CBS
Sports, fired, 1988, for controversial
racial statements.
b. Sep 9, 1919 in Steubenville, Ohio
d. Apr 21, 1996 in Las Vegas, Nevada
Source: *BioIn 9, 10, 11, 12; NewYTBS*
88; WhoAm 76, 80, 82, 86; WhoTelC

Snyder, John Wesley
American. Banker, Government Official
Influential Truman adviser who was
secretary of Treasury, 1946-53; helped
design reconstruction programs after
WW II.
b. Jun 21, 1895 in Jonesboro, Arkansas
d. Oct 9, 1985 in Seabrook Is., South
Carolina
Source: *AmNatBi; BiDrUSE 71, 89;*
BioIn 3, 9, 10, 11; BlueB 76; CurBio 45,
86; IntWW 74, 75, 76, 77, 78, 79, 80,
81, 82, 83; IntYB 78, 79, 80, 81;
ScrEAmL 1; St&PR 75; WhAm 9; Who
74, 82, 83, 85; WhoAm 74, 76, 78, 80,
82, 84; WhoAmP 73, 75, 77, 79

Snyder, Mitch
American. Political Activist
Active with Community for Creative
Non-Violence since 1973, on behalf of
homeless people.
b. Aug 14, 1943 in New York, New
York
d. Jul 5, 1990 in Washington, District of
Columbia
Source: *AnObit 1990; BioIn 16;*
ConHero 1; HeroCon; News 91, 91-1;
NewYTBS 90; WhAm 10; WhoAm 88

Snyder, Richard Elliot
American. Publisher
Chairman of Simon & Schuster, 1975-
94; chairman and CEO, Golden Books
Family Entertainment, Inc., 1996—.
b. Apr 6, 1933 in New York, New York
Source: *BioIn 12; St&PR 84, 87, 91;*
WhoAm 76, 78, 80, 82, 84, 86, 88, 90,
92, 94, 98, 99, 2000; WhoE 74, 75, 77,
89, 91, 99; WhoEnt 98; WhoFI 79, 81,
87, 92, 94; WorAlBi

Snyder, Solomon H(albert)
American. Scientist
Identified, with Candace Pert, opiate
receptors in the brain, 1973.
b. Dec 26, 1938 in Washington, District
of Columbia

Source: *AmMWSc 73P, 76P, 79, 82, 86,
89, 92, 95; BiDrAPA 77, 89; BiESc;
BioIn 11, 13, 17; CamDcAB; CamDcSc;
ChamBiD; ConAu 14NR, 37R; CurBio
96; LarDcSc; RanHWDS; WhoAm 74,
76, 78, 80, 82, 84, 86, 88, 90, 92, 94,
95, 96, 97, 98, 99, 2000; WhoE 74;
WhoMedH 96, 99, 2000; WhoScEn 94,
96, 2000*

Snyder, Tom
American. Broadcast Journalist, TV
Personality
Best known as host of NBC latenight
interview show "Tomorrow," 1973-
81; host of "Late Late Show with
Tom Snyder," 1994-99.
b. May 12, 1936 in Milwaukee,
Wisconsin
Source: *BioIn 10, 11, 12, 13; BkPepl;
ConAu 109, 121; ConTFT 24; CurBio
80; EncAJ; EncTelN; EncTwCJ; IntMPA
77, 78, 79, 80, 81, 82, 84, 86, 88, 92,
94, 96; LegTOT; LesBEnT 92;
NewYTET; VarWW 85; WhoAm 78, 80,
82; WhoTelC*

Soames, Christopher
[Baron of Fletching; Arthur Christopher
John Soames]
English. Government Official
Governor of S Rhodesia, 1979-80;
presided over its transition into
independent Zimbabwe; son-in-law of
Winston Churchill.
b. Oct 12, 1920 in Penn, England
d. Sep 16, 1987 in London, England
Source: *BioIn 5, 10, 12, 15; BlueB 76;
CurBio 81, 87, 87N; IntWW 74, 75, 76,
77, 79; IntYB 78; NewYTBS 79, 87;
OxCLaw; Who 74, 85; WhoWor 74, 76,
78*

Soane, John, Sir
English. Architect, Art Collector
Best-known works include Bank of
England, 1788; Dulwich College
Picture Gallery, 1811.
b. Sep 10, 1753 in Whitchurch, England
d. Jan 20, 1837 in London, England
Source: *AtlBL; BiDBrA; BioIn 1, 2, 3, 4,
6, 9, 11, 13, 14, 15, 16, 17, 22;
CamBiEn; ChamBiD; DcArch; DcArts;
DcBiPP; DcD&D; DcNaB; EncHiCA;
EncMA; EncWB 98; IntDcAr; MacEA;
McGDA; McGEWB; NewCol 75;
OxCArt; OxCBrHi; OxCEng 85, 95;
WebBD 83; WhDW; WhoArch*

Soares, Mario Alberto Nobre Lopes
Portuguese. Political Leader
First civilian president of Portugal in 60
yrs., 1986-96.
b. Dec 7, 1924 in Lisbon, Portugal
Source: *ChamBiD; CurBio 75; IntWW
76, 77, 78, 79, 80, 81, 82, 83, 89, 91,
93, 97, 98, 2000; NewYTBS 76, 86; Who
92, 94, 98, 99, 2000; WhoIntA 2;
WhoWor 78, 80, 82, 84, 87, 89, 91, 93,
95, 96, 97, 98, 99, 2000; WorAlBi*

Sobchak, Anatoly Aleksandrovich
Russian. Politician
Mayor, St. Petersburg, Russia, 1991—.
b. 1937 in Chita, Union of Soviet
Socialist Republics
d. Feb 20, 2000 in Kaliningrad, Russia
Source: *CurBio 92; IntWW 91*

Sobell, Morton
American. Spy
Found guilty with Julius, Ethel
Rosenberg of conspiracy to sell
nuclear secrets, 1951.
b. Apr 11, 1917 in New York, New
York
Source: *BioIn 2, 3, 4, 5, 6, 7, 8, 11;
ConAu 53; EncCW; PolProf E, T; WrDr
76, 80, 82, 84*

Sobhuza II
"The Lion of Swaziland"
Swazi. Ruler
World's longest reigning monarch, 1921-
82; estimated to have had nearly 100
wives, 500 children.
b. Jul 22, 1899 in Mbabane, Swaziland
d. Aug 21, 1982 in Mbabane, Swaziland
Source: *AfSS 79; AnObit 1982; CurBio
82; EncyDCo; IntWW 78; NewCol 75;
NewYTBS 82; WhoGov 72; WhoWor 78*

Sobieski, Carol
American. Writer
TV shows include "Peyton Place,"
1964-69; films include *The Toy, Annie,*
19 82.
b. Mar 16, 1939 in Chicago, Illinois
Source: *BioIn 17; ConAu 124, 129, 132;
ConTFT 1, 9; NewYTBS 90; VarWW 85*

Sobieski, John, III
Polish. Ruler
King of Poland, 1674-96; later years
unsuccessful because of poor political
conditions.
b. Aug 17, 1624 in Lvov, Poland
d. Jun 17, 1696 in Wilanow, Poland
Source: *McGEWB; WebBD 83*

Sobol, Louis
American. Journalist, Author
Manhattan columnist for *NY Journal-
American,* King Features Syndicate.
b. Aug 10, 1896 in New Haven,
Connecticut
d. Jan 19, 1948
Source: *AmAu&B; BioIn 1, 8, 14; ConAu
118, P-2; IntMPA 75, 76, 77, 78, 79, 80,
81, 82, 84, 86; WhAm 2, 9; WhE&EA*

Sobrero, Ascanio
Italian. Chemist
Discovered nitroglycerine, 1847.
b. Oct 12, 1812 in Casale, Italy
d. May 26, 1888 in Turin, Italy
Source: *AsBiEn; BiESc; ChamBiD;
InSci; LarDcSc*

Sobukwe, Robert Mangaliso
South African. Political Activist
Militant opponent of white supremacy in
South Africa, he was a founder and
leader of the Pan-African Congress.
b. Dec 5, 1924 in Graaff-Reinet, South
Africa
d. 1978 in Kimberly, South Africa
Source: *BioIn 6, 7, 8, 10, 11, 16, 17, 18,
21, 23; CamBiEn; DcAfHiB 86; EncWB
98; FacFETw; WhoWor 74*

Soby, James Thrall
American. Critic, Author
Contended that modern art could only be
appreciated through knowledge of art
of the past.
b. Dec 14, 1906 in Hartford, Connecticut
d. Jan 29, 1979 in Norwalk, Connecticut
Source: *AmAu&B; BioIn 3, 4, 5, 6, 11,
22, 23; ConAu 103; DcTwArt; REnAL;
TwCA SUP; WhAm 7; WhoAm 74, 76,
78; WhoAmA 73, 76, 78, 80, 80N, 82N,
84N, 86N, 89N, 91N, 93N; WorAu 1900*

Socinus, Faustus
Theologian
His teachings led to the development of
Unitarianism.
b. Dec 5, 1539 in Siena, Italy
d. Mar 3, 1604 in Luclawice, Poland
Source: *BioIn 12; CamBiEn; ChamBiD*

Sockman, Ralph W
American. Religious Leader
Popular NYC pastor, 1916-61; broadcast
weekly sermons for 35 yrs.
b. Oct 1, 1889 in Mount Vernon, Ohio
d. Aug 29, 1970 in New York, New
York
Source: *AmAu&B; ConAu 5R, 89;
CurBio 70; NatCAB 55; OhA&B; WhAm
5; WhNAA*

Socrates
Greek. Philosopher
Viewed philosophy as necessary pursuit
of all intelligent men; teacher of Plato.
b. 470?BC in Athens, Greece
d. 399?BC in Athens, Greece
Source: *AsBiEn; AtlBL; BbD; Benet 96;
BiD&SB; BiDPsy; BioIn 1, 2, 3, 4, 5, 6,
7, 8, 9, 10, 11, 12, 13; BlmGEL;
CasWL; CyWA 58, 97; EncCapP;
EncEarC 97; EncEth; LegTOT; LngCEL;
LuthC 75; NamesHP; NewC; OxCEng
67; OxCPhil; PenC CL; PIP&P;
RComWL; REn; WhDW; WorAl;
WorAlBi; WrPh P*

Soddy, Frederick
English. Chemist
Won Nobel Prize, 1921, for work on the
origin of isotopes.
b. Sep 2, 1877 in Eastbourne, England
d. Sep 22, 1956 in Brighton, England
Source: *AsBiEn; BiESc; BioIn 3, 4, 5, 6,
12, 14, 15, 19, 20, 22; CamBiEn;
CamDcSc; ChamBiD; ConAu 167;
DcNaB 1951; DcScB; EncWB 98; GrBr;
InSci; LarDcSc; LinLib L, S; LngCTC;
McGCEnS; McGEWB; NobelP;
NotTwCS 1; ObitT 1951; RanHWDS;*

WhAm 3; WhDW; WhE&EA; WhoNob, 90, 95; WorAl; WorAlBi; WorScD

Soderbergh, Steven
American. Filmmaker
Wrote, edited, directed *Sex, Lies, and Videotape,* winner of several awards, 1989 Cannes Film Festival.
b. 1963 in Georgia
Source: *BiDFilm 94; BioIn 16; CelR 90; ConTFT 11; CurBio 98; IntMPA 96; IntWW 91, 93, 97, 98, 2000; LegTOT; MiSFD 9; NewYTBS 91; WhoAm 90; WhoEnt 92*

Soderblom, Nathan
Swedish. Theologian
Won Nobel Peace Prize, 1930, "for promotion of int'l understanding."
b. Jan 15, 1866 in Trono, Sweden
d. Jul 12, 1931 in Uppsala, Sweden
Source: *BiDInt; BioIn 1, 2, 6, 7, 8, 9, 11, 12, 15, 16; CamBiEn; ChamBiD; DcEcMov; EncWB 98; FacFETw; LuthC 75; McGEWB; NobelP; WhE&EA; WhoLA; WhoNob, 90, 95*

Soderman, Danuta
"Queen of Christian Broadcasting"
American. TV Personality
Co-host of Christian Broadcasting Company's "700 Club," 1985—.
Source: *BioIn 14; PrimTiR*

Sodero, Cesare
Italian. Conductor
Metropolitan Opera conductor who directed grand opera, symphony performances on radio.
b. Aug 2, 1886 in Naples, Italy
d. Dec 16, 1947 in New York, New York
Source: *ASCAP 66, 80; BakBD 78, 84, 92; BakBDTw; BiDAmM; BioIn 1, 3; ConAmC 76A, 82; CurBio 43, 48; MetOEnc; NatCAB 38; NewEOp 71; RadStar*

Soderstrom, Elisabeth Anna
Swedish. Opera Singer
Soprano, who is also versatile actress known for more than 50 operatic roles in ten languages.
b. May 7, 1927 in Stockholm, Sweden
Source: *CamBiEn; ChamBiD; CurBio 85; IntWW 74, 75, 76, 77, 78, 79, 80, 81, 82, 83, 89, 91, 93, 97, 98, 2000; IntWWM 77, 85; IntWWW 2; InWom SUP; NewAmDM; PenDiMP; WhoAmM 83; WhoMus 72; WhoOp 76*

Soeharto
Indonesian. Political Leader
Pres., Indonesia, 1967—.
b. Jun 8, 1921 in Java, Indonesia
Source: *BioIn 14, 15, 17, 18, 19, 22, 23, 24; CurBio 92; IntYB 78, 79, 80, 81, 82; Who 90, 92, 94; WhoAsAP 91; WhoWor 78, 80, 82, 84, 87, 89, 91, 93, 95, 96, 97, 98*

Soelle, Dorothee
German. Theologian, Political Activist, Feminist, Author
Leading liberation theologian reinterpreted the Christian message within the context of mysticism, feminism, and socialist pacifism.
b. Sep 1929 in Cologne, Germany
Source: *BioIn 19; ConAu 11NR, 69; EncWB, 98*

Soft Cell
[Marc Almond; Dave Ball]
English. Music Group
Formed 1979; hit single "Tainted Love," 1982, was on charts for 43 straight weeks.
Source: *BillEnR; EncRk 88; EncRkSt; HarEnR 86; RkOn 85; WhsNW 85*

Soft Machine
[Roy Babbington; Elton Dean; Hugh Hopper; Phil Howard; John Marshall; Mike Ratledge]
English. Music Group
Jazz sounding group; albums include *The Land of Cockayne,* 1981.
Source: *Alli, SUP; BiDJaz A; BioIn 9, 16, 17; CabMA; ConMuA 80A; DcVicP, 2; Dun&B 86, 88; EncRk 88; HarEnR 86; IlEncRk; MnBBF; NewCBEL; NewGrDJ 88, 94; NewYTBS 80; OxCChiL; PenEncP; PeoHis; PoIre; RolSEnR 83; Who 92, 94; WhoAm 90, 92, 94; WhoAmP 93, 95; WhoArt 80, 82, 84, 96; WhoE 97; WhoRock 81; WhoRocM 82; WhoSSW 88, 91, 93*

Soglo, Nicephore (Dieudonne)
Togolese. Political Leader
Led Benin from a totalitarian Marxist dictatorship to democracy; elected president of the country in 1991, becoming the first democratically elected civilian leader of a nation in the history of the entire African continent
b. 1935 in Lome, Togo
Source: *WhoWor 96, 97, 98, 99*

Soglow, Otto
American. Cartoonist
Created "Little King" comic strip, 1934.
b. Dec 23, 1900 in New York, New York
d. Apr 3, 1975 in New York, New York
Source: *AmAu&B; AmNatBi; BenetAL 91; BioIn 3, 10, 14; ChhPo, S3; ConAu 57, 93; CurBio 40, 75N; EncTwCJ; NatCAB 63; NewYTBS 75; REnAL; SmATA 39; WhAm 6; WhAmArt 85; WhoAm 74; WhoAmA 73, 76N, 78N, 80N, 82N, 84N, 86N, 89N, 91N, 93N; WorECom*

Sohappy, David, Sr.
American. Political Activist
Leading figure in battle for Northwest Coast Indian fishing rights.
b. Apr 25, 1925 in Yakima Indian Reservation,Washington
d. May 7, 1991 in Hood River, Washington

Source: *BioIn 21; EncNAB; NotNaAm*

Sokolsky, George E
American. Journalist, Author
Conservative columnist for Hearst Syndicate, 1944-62.
b. Sep 5, 1893 in Utica, New York
d. Dec 13, 1962 in Otis, Massachusetts
Source: *AmAu&B; ConAu 89; CurBio 41, 63; WhAm 4*

Solal, Martial
French. Pianist
Jazz pianist; has composed music for more than 30 films, among them *Breathless.*
b. Aug 23, 1927 in Algiers, Algeria
Source: *AllMGJa; BiDJaz; BioIn 6; CamBiEn; ConMus 4; EncJzS; NewGrDJ 88, 94; NewGrDM 80; PenEncP; WhoFr 79; WhoWor 74*

Solari, Andrea
[Andrea Del Gobbo]
Italian. Artist
A painter strongly influenced by Leonrdo da Vinci; student of the Milanese school.
d. 1524
Source: *OxDcArt*

Solarz, Stephen Joshua
American. Politician
Liberal Dem. congressman from NY, 1975-93
b. Sep 12, 1940 in New York, New York
Source: *AlmAP 88, 92; BiDrUSC 89; BioIn 12; CngDr 87; CurBio 86; NewYTBS 91; WhoAm 78, 80, 82, 84, 86, 88, 90, 92, 94, 95, 96; WhoAmJ 80; WhoAmP 87; WhoE 77, 79, 81, 85, 86, 89, 91, 93; WhoGov 75, 77*

Sol Ch'ong
Korean. Scholar
Known as one of the Ten Confucian Sages of Silla, scholar is credited with developing of a system for writing Korean.
b. c. 680
d. 750
Source: *EncWB 98*

Soleri, Paolo
American. Architect
Designed the planned community of Arcosanti, AZ, 1970; combines needs of architecture, ecology for 5,000 people.
b. Jun 21, 1919 in Turin, Italy
Source: *BioIn 8, 9, 10, 11, 12, 13, 14, 16; BriEAA; CelR; ChamBiD; ConArch 80, 87, 94; ConAu 106; CurBio 72; DcArch; IntDcAr; IntWW 82, 83, 89, 91, 93, 97, 98, 2000; MacEA; WhoAm 76, 82, 84, 86, 88, 90, 92, 94, 95, 96, 99, 2000; WhoAmA 73, 76, 78, 80, 82, 84, 86, 89, 91, 93, 1999; WhoWest 92, 94; WhoWor 84, 87, 89, 91, 93, 95; WrDr 82, 84, 86, 88, 90, 92, 94, 96, 98, 99, 2000*

Solis, Juan Diaz de
Portuguese. Explorer
Pilot major of Castile, he sailed under
   the Spanish flag to explore the
   Americas and discovered the Rio de la
   Plata.
b. c. 1470, Portugal
d. 1516, Uruguay
Source: *BioIn 18; EncLatA; Expl 93;
HisDcSE; McGEWB; WhDW*

Solomon
Hebrew. Ruler, Author
Ruled Israel; renowned for wisdom,
   wealth; during reign nation rose to its
   greatest; wrote *The Song of Solomon.*
b. 973?BC
d. 933?BC
Source: *DcOrL 3; Dis&D; NewC;
WebBD 83; WhDW*

Solomon
[Solomon Cutner]
English. Pianist
Child prodigy; concert repertoire focused
   on Mozart, Brahms, Shubert; retired,
   1956.
b. Aug 9, 1902 in London, England
d. Feb 22, 1988 in London, England
Source: *AnObit 1988; BakBD 78, 84, 92;
BakBDTw; BioIn 1, 2, 9, 21; BriBkM 80;
CamBiEn; ChamBiD; DcNaB 1986;
DcPseud; FacFETw; IntWWM 77, 80;
NewAmDM; NewGrDM 80; NewYTBS
88; NotTwCP; PenDiMP; Who 74, 82,
83, 85, 88*

Solomon, Hannah Greenebaum
American. Social Reformer
Founded National Council of Jewish
   Women, 1890.
b. Jan 14, 1858 in Chicago, Illinois
d. Dec 7, 1942 in Chicago, Illinois
Source: *AmNatBi; CamDcAB; EncAWoR;
HanAmWH; InWom SUP; LibW;
NatCAB 36; NotAW; WomFir;
WomWWA 14*

Solomon, Harold Charles
"Solly"
American. Tennis Player
Winner of Baltimore Grand Prix Tennis
   Tournament, 1979; German
   Championship, 1980.
b. Sep 17, 1952 in Washington, District
   of Columbia
Source: *OfEnT; WhoAm 78, 80, 82, 84;
WhoIntT*

Solomon, Izler
American. Conductor
Led Indianapolis Symphony, 1956-75.
b. Jan 11, 1910 in Saint Paul, Minnesota
Source: *BakBD 78, 84, 92; BakBDTw;
BiDAmM; BioIn 1, 2, 4, 11, 15; BlueB
76; MusSN; NewGrDA 86; NewYTBS
87; WhoAm 74, 76, 78, 80; WhoMus 72;
WhoMW 74, 76, 78, 80; WhoWorJ 72,
78*

Solomon, Neil
American. Physician, Journalist
Writes syndicated medical column, L.A.
   Times, 1974-.
b. Feb 27, 1932 in Pittsburgh,
   Pennsylvania
Source: *AmMWSc 73P, 76P, 79, 82, 86,
89, 92, 95, 98; ConAu 27NR; IntMed 80;
WhoAm 76, 78, 80, 82, 84, 86, 88;
WhoAmJ 80; WhoE 74, 75; WhoGov 77;
WhoMedH 96*

Solomon, Samuel Joseph
American. Airline Executive
Associated with various US airlines;
   chm., Aviation Historical Foundation.
b. Jul 11, 1899 in Washington, District
   of Columbia
d. Dec 8, 1977 in Bethesda, Maryland
Source: *BioIn 10, 12; IntYB 78; NatCAB
60; St&PR 75; WhAm 7; WhoAm 74, 76,
78*

Solon
Greek. Politician, Poet
Statesman and poet instituted major
   social reforms in the name of justice,
   developed an influential code of laws,
   and is regarded as the founder of
   Athenian democracy.
b. fl. 594

Solotaroff, Theodore
American. Author
Editor of *American Review* mag., 1972-
   77.
b. Oct 9, 1928 in Elizabeth, New Jersey
Source: *BioIn 13; ConAu 8NR, 9R;
DrAF 76; DrAPF 80, 91; WhoAm 90;
WhoWorJ 72; WhoWrEP 89*

Soloveitchik, Joseph Baer
American. Theologian, Philosopher
With an extensive knowledge of
   rabbinical tradition and of secular and
   non-Jewish thought, he illuminated the
   contemporary Jewish situation and the
   circumstances of modern man.
b. 1903 in Pruzhan, Poland
d. Apr 8, 1993 in Brookline,
   Massachusetts
Source: *BioIn 16; EncWB, 98*

Soloviev, Sergei Mikhailovich
Russian. Historian
Wrote *History of Russia,* 1851-79,
   describing story of Russian people,
   govt.
b. May 5, 1820 in Moscow, Russia
d. Oct 4, 1879
Source: *CasWL; NewCol 75; WebBD 83*

Soloviev, Vladimir Sergeevich
Russian. Philosopher
Religious thinker was an early leader of
   the ecumenical movement and of the
   modern reaction against extreme
   rationalism.
b. Jan 28, 1853, Russia
d. Aug 13, 1900 in Uzkoe, Russia
Source: *EncWB 98; McGEWB; WhoChr*

Solow, Robert Merton
American. Economist, Educator
MIT economics professor, 1958-95; W.
   Edwards Deming professor, NYU,
   1996—; won Nobel Prize in
   economics, 1987, for theories of
   economic growth of national income.
b. Aug 23, 1924 in New York, New
   York
Source: *BioIn 15, 16; CamBiEn;
CamDcAB; ChamBiD; IntWW 91, 97,
98, 2000; NewYTBS 87; Who 90, 92, 98,
99, 2000; WhoAm 86, 90, 97, 98, 99,
2000; WhoE 91, 97, 99; WhoFI 00, 83,
92, 98; WhoNob, 90, 95; WhoScEn
2000; WhoWor 91, 97, 98, 99, 2000;
WhoWorJ 78; WorAlBi; WrDr 98, 99*

Solti, Georg, Sir
English. Musician, Conductor
Winner of 22 Grammys, 1962-83; music
   director of Chicago Symphony 22
   years; artistic director of Salzburg
   Easter Festival, 1992.
b. Oct 21, 1912 in Budapest, Hungary
d. Sep 5, 1997 in Antibes, France
Source: *BakBD 78, 84, 92; BakBDTw;
BioIn 4, 5, 6, 8, 9, 10, 11, 12, 13, 14,
15, 18, 21, 22, 23, 24; BioNews 74;
BlueB 76; BriBkM 80; CamBiEn; CelR;
ChamBiD; CmOp; ConMus 13; CurBio
64, 97N; DcArts; FacFETw; IntDcOp;
IntWW 74, 75, 76, 77, 78, 79, 80, 81, 82,
83, 89, 91, 93, 97; IntWWM 77, 80, 85,
90; MetOEnc; MusMk; MusSN;
NewAmDM; NewEOp 71; NewGrDA 86;
NewGrDM 80; NewGrDO; News 98, 98-
1; NewYTBE 71, 72; NewYTBS 97;
OxDcOp; PenDiMP; VarWW 85; WhAm
12; Who 74, 82, 83, 85, 88, 92, 94;
WhoAm 74, 76, 78, 80, 82, 84, 86, 88,
90, 92, 94, 95, 96, 97, 98; WhoAmM 83;
WhoEnt 92; WhoFr 79; WhoMus 72;
WhoMW 74, 76, 78, 80, 82, 84, 86, 88,
90, 92, 93, 96; WhoOp 76; WhoWor 74,
76, 78, 80, 82, 84, 87, 89, 91, 93, 95;
WorAl; WorAlBi*

Soltysik, Patricia Michelle
[S(ymbionese) L(iberation) A(rmy)]
"Mizmoon"; "Zoya"
American. Revolutionary
Member of terrorist group that kidnapped
   Patricia Hearst, 1974.
b. May 17, 1950
d. May 24, 1974 in Los Angeles,
   California
Source: *BioIn 10; GoodHs*

Solzhenitsyn, Aleksandr (Isayevich)
Russian. Author
Exiled to Siberia, 1953; won Nobel Prize
   for literature, 1970; wrote *Gulag
   Archipelago,* 1973.
b. Dec 11, 1918 in Kislovodsk, Union of
   Soviet Socialist Republics
Source: *AuNews 1; IntYB 78, 79, 80, 81,
82; LiExTwC; MagSWL; MajTwCW 1, 2;
MakMC; ModSL 1; NewYTBE 72;
NewYTBS 74; NobelP; PenC EUR;
RadHan; RAdv 14, 13-2; RComWL;
REn; TwCWr; WhDW; Who 92; WhoAm
86, 90, 94, 95, 96, 97, 98, 99, 2000;*

WhoE 91, 95; WhoEnt 98; WhoNob 90; WhoTwCL; WhoWor 91, 95, 96, 97, 98, 99, 2000; WhoWrEP 89; WorAlBi; WorAu 1950; WorLitC; WrDr 98, 99, 2000

Sombart, Werner
German. Historian
Economic historian known for his work in both socialism and capitalism; he began as an admirer of Marxian socialism and ended as its bitter critic.
b. Jan 19, 1863 in Ermsleben, Germany
d. May 13, 1941 in Berlin, Germany
Source: *BioIn 8, 14, 16; EncWB 98; GrEconB; McGEWB; ThTwC 87; WhoEc 81, 86*

Some, Malidoma Patrice
Upper Voltan. Writer
Writer and speaker whose goal is to spread his knowledge of the spiritual life of his people to the whole world.
b. 1956 in Dano, Upper Volta
Source: *BioIn 20, 21, 24; ConAu 145; ConBlB 10; RelLAm 2; WrDr 98, 99, 2000*

Somers, Brett
American. Actor
Ex-wife of Jack Klugman.
b. Jul 11, 1927
Source: *LegTOT; WhoHol 92, A*

Somers, Suzanne
[Mrs. Alan Hamel; Suzanne Mahoney]
American. Actor
Star of TV's "Three's Company," 1977-81; also star of TV's "Step by Step," 1991 —.
b. Oct 16, 1946 in San Bruno, California
Source: *BioIn 11, 16; BkPepl; ConAu 139; ConTFT 3, 11; DcPseud; HalFC 84, 88; IntAu&W 91; IntMPA 81, 82, 84, 86, 88, 92, 94, 96; InWom SUP; LegTOT; TwCRHW 90; WhoAm 82; WhoAmW 97, 99; WhoEnt 92; WhoHol 92; WhoTelC; WorAl; WorAlBi; WrDr 92*

Somerset, Duke of
[Edward Seymour Hertford; Edward Seymour]
English. Politician
Lord protector advocated Protestantism and instituted the use of the English Prayer Book; he favored union with Scotland and economic change.
b. c. 1506
d. Jan 22, 1552, England

Somerville, Edith Anna OEnone
Irish. Author
In collaboration with her cousin, Violet Martin, she wrote the popular *Experiences of an Irish R. M.* stories and the novel *The Real Charlotte.*
b. May 2, 1858 in Corfu, Greece
d. Oct 8, 1949 in Castletownshend, Ireland
Source: *BioIn 14, 16, 17, 20, 22, 23, 24; BritAS; CamBiEn; CasWL; ChamBiD;*

Chambr 3; DcBrBI; DcIrB 1, 2, 3; DcLEL; DcNaB 1941; EncWB, 98; EvLB; GrWrEL N; HisDcIr; InWom SUP; ModIrLi; NewC; NewCBEL; OxCEng 67; PenC ENG; REn; RfGShF 1; RGTwCWr; TwCA, SUP; WomIre; WomNov; WorAu 1900

Somes, Michael (George)
English. Dancer
Leading male dancer with Royal Ballet, 1951-61; asst. director, 1963-70.
b. Sep 28, 1917 in Horsley, England
d. Nov 18, 1994 in London, England
Source: *BiDD; BioIn 3, 4, 5, 11, 20, 21; BlueB 76; CnOxB; CurBio 55, 95N; DancEn 78; IntDcB; NewYTBS 94; Who 74, 82, 83, 85, 88, 90, 92, 94; WhoHol 92, A; WhoThe 77A; WhoWor 74; WhThe; WorAl*

Sommer, Elke
[Elke Schletze]
American. Actor
Sexy blonde in films since 1959, including *A Shot in the Dark,* 1964; *The Prisoner of Zenda,* 1979.
b. Nov 5, 1941 in Berlin, Germany
Source: *BioIn 7, 10, 16; ConTFT 3, 21; FilmgC; ForYSC; HalFC 88; IntMPA 75, 76, 77, 78, 79, 80, 81, 82, 84, 86, 88; IntWW 91; InWom SUP; MotPP; MovMk; WhoAm 76, 78, 80, 82, 84, 86, 88, 90, 92; WhoAmW 74; WhoEnt 92; WhoHol A; WorAl; WorAlBi*

Sommer, Frederick
American. Photographer, Artist
Known for 1940s "assemblage" pictures: *Coyotes,* 1945; works have also included landscapes, geometric forms.
b. Sep 7, 1905 in Angri, Italy
d. Jan 23, 1999 in Prescott, Arizona
Source: *BioIn 17; BriEAA; ConPhot 82, 88, 95; DcCAr 81; ICPEnP; MacBEP; WhAmArt 85; WhoAm 82; WhoAmA 78, 80, 82, 84, 86, 89, 91, 93, 1999*

Sommers, Ben
American. Manufacturer
Pres., Capezio, makers of dance, theatrical shoes, 1940-85.
b. Dec 1, 1906 in New York, New York
d. Apr 30, 1985 in New York, New York
Source: *BiE&WWA; BioIn 14; NewYTBS 84; WhoAmJ 80; WhoE 74, 75, 77, 79, 81, 83, 85, 86*

Somogi, Judith
American. Conductor
Music director, conductor, Utica (NY) Symphony, 1977-88; first female to conduct an opera in US.
b. May 13, 1937 in New York, New York
d. Mar 23, 1988 in Long Island, New York
Source: *BakBD 84, 92; BakBDTw; BioIn 12; IntWWM 80; NewAmDM; NewGrDA 86; NewYTBS 80; WhoAm 84; WhoAmM 83*

Somoza, Anastasio
Nicaraguan. Political Leader
President, 1937-47, 1951-56; assassinated.
b. Feb 1, 1896 in San Marcos, Nicaragua
d. Sep 29, 1956 in Managua, Nicaragua
Source: *BioIn 1, 2, 3, 4, 7, 11, 12, 16, 17, 19; ColdWar 1; CurBio 42, 56; EncWB 98; LegTOT; McGEWB; WhAm 3; WorAl*

Somoza Debayle, Anastasio
Nicaraguan. Political Leader
Pres. of Nicaragua, 1967-72; 1974-79.
b. Dec 5, 1925 in Leon, Nicaragua
d. Sep 17, 1980 in Asuncion, Nicaragua
Source: *BiDLAmC; BioIn 8, 10, 11, 12; ColdWar 2; CurBio 78; DcCPCAm; DicTyr; EncLatA; EncWB, 98; EncyDCo; FacFETw; HisWorL; IntWW 74, 75, 76, 77, 78, 79, 80; IntYB 78, 79, 80; LatAmLi; LegTOT; NewYTBS 79, 80; WhoGov 72; WhoWor 74, 76, 78; WorAl; WorAlBi; WorDWW*

Sondergaard, Gale (Edith Holm)
[Mrs. Herbert Biberman]
American. Actor
Known for playing villainous women; won first supporting actress Oscar for *Anthony Adverse,* 1937; blacklisted with husband, late 1940s-50s.
b. Feb 15, 1899 in Litchfield, Minnesota
d. Aug 14, 1985 in Woodland Hills, California
Source: *AnObit 1985; BiE&WWA; BioIn 10, 11; BioNews 74; EncMcCE; FilmEn; FilmgC; HalFC 80, 84, 88; HolCA; IntMPA 82; InWom SUP; LegTOT; MotPP; MovMk; NotNAT; OlFamFa; ThFT; Vers A; WhoAm 82; WhoHol A; WhoHrs 80; WhoThe 77; WomFir*

Sondheim, Stephen (Joshua)
American. Composer, Lyricist
One of America's most acclaimed lyricists; wrote lyrics for *West Side Story,* 1957; *Gypsy,* 1959.
b. Mar 22, 1930 in New York, New York
Source: *AmCulL; AmDec 1970; AmPS; AmSong; ASCAP 66, 80; Au&Arts 11; BakBD 78, 84, 92; BakBDTw; Benet 87; BenetAL 91; BestMus; BiDAmM; BiE&WWA; BioIn 9, 10, 12, 13, 16; BkPepl; BlueB 76; BriBkM 80; CamBiEn; CamDcAB; CamGWoT; CamHAL; CelR, 90; ChamBiD; ConAmC 76, 82; ConAu 47NR, 67NR, 103; ConCom; ConLC 30, 39; ConMus 8; ConTFT 1, 11; CurBio 73; DcArts; DcTwCCu 1; EncMT; EncWB; EncWT; Ent; FacFETw; GayLesB; HalFC 80, 84, 88; IntMPA 88, 92, 94, 96; IntWW 76, 77, 78, 79, 80, 81, 82, 83, 89, 91, 93, 97, 98, 2000; IntWWM 77, 90; JeHun; LegTOT; NatPD 77; NewAmDM; NewCBMT; NewGrDA 86; NewGrDM 80; NewGrDO; NewOxM; News 94; NewYTBS 84; NotNAT, A; OxCAmL 95; OxCAmT 84; OxCPMus; OxCThe 83; OxDcOp; PenEncP; PlP&P, A; PopAmC SUP; RAdv 14; Who 82, 83, 85, 88, 90, 92, 94, 98, 99, 2000; WhoAm 74, 76, 78,*

80, 82, 84, 86, 88, 90, 92, 94, 95, 96, 97, 98, 99, 2000; WhoE 75, 77, 91, 93, 95; WhoEnt 92, 98; WhoThe 72, 77, 81; WhoWor 78, 80, 82, 84, 87, 89, 91, 93, 95; WorAl; WorAlBi; WrDr 82, 84, 86, 88, 90, 92, 94, 96, 98, 99, 2000

Song Sisters, The

[Ailing Song; Meiling Song; Qingling Song]
Chinese. Political Leaders
Sisters married men of political distinction, and each played a key role in modern Chinese history.
b. Dec 12, 1890 in Shanghai, China

Sonjo

Korean. King
Ruled Korea from 1567 to 1608, a time of serious economic and social discord, factional strife, and two destructive Japanese invasions.
b. Nov 26, 1552
d. Mar 16, 1608
Source: *EncWB 98; McGEWB*

Sonneck, Oscar George Theodore

American. Musicologist, Librarian
First chief, Music Division, Library of Congress, 1902-17; edited *Musicial Quarterly,* 1915-28; wrote on American music.
b. Oct 6, 1873 in Jersey City, New Jersey
d. Oct 30, 1928 in New York, New York
Source: *AmAu&B; AmNatBi; BakBD 78, 84; BakBDTw; BiDAmM; BiGAW; BioIn 1, 3, 17; ConAmC 76, 82; DcAmB; DcAmLiB; DcNAA; EncAAH; NatCAB 25; NewGrDM 80; OxCAmH; OxCMus; REnAL; WhAm 1*

Sonnenfeldt, Helmut

American. Government Official
Senior member of Nixon's National Security Council, 1969-74.
b. Sep 13, 1926 in Berlin, Germany
Source: *BioIn 10, 12; EncCW; IntWW 75, 76, 77, 78, 79, 80, 81, 82, 83, 89, 91, 93, 97, 98, 2000; NewYTBE 73; PolProf NF; USBiR 74; WhoAm 74, 76, 78, 80, 82, 84, 86, 88, 90, 92, 94, 95, 96, 97, 98, 99, 2000; WhoAmJ 80; WhoAmP 81, 83, 85, 87, 89, 91, 93, 95, 97, 1999; WhoE 91; WhoGov 72, 75, 77; WhoIntA 2*

Sonnier, Jo-El

American. Musician, Singer
Cajun music artist; recorded *Cajun Life,* 1984 for which he rececived a Grammy Award nomination; also released *Hello Happiness Again,* 1992, *Cajun Valentine,* and *The Scene in Cajun Music.*
b. 1946 in Rayne, Louisiana
Source: *AllMGCo; ASCAP 80; ConMus 10*

Sonny and Cher

[Cher; Sonny Bono]
American. Music Group
1960s pop hits include "I Got You Babe."
Source: *BioIn 9, 16, 17, 18, 20, 21; BioNews 74; EncPR&S 89; EncRk 88; HarEnR 86; IntMPA 75, 76, 77, 78, 79, 80, 81, 82; IntWW 89, 91, 93; LesBEnT, 92; NewGrDA 86; NewYTBS 84, 88, 95; PenEncP; RkOn 74; RolSEnR 83; WhoAmP 89, 91, 93; WhoHol A; WhoRocM 82*

Sons of the Pioneers

[Pat Brady; Roy Lanham; Rob Nolan; Lloyd Perryman; Rusty Richards; Roy Rogers; Tim Spencer; Dale Warren]
American. Music Group
One of first highly successful, durable Western singing groups, 1930s; hits include "Cool Water," 1948.
Source: *AllMGCo; AmPS B; ASCAP 66, 80; BgBkCoM; BiDAmM; BioIn 7, 15; BioNews 74; CmpEPM; ConMuA 80B; CounME 74, 74A; CurBio 48; EncFCWM 69, 83; HarEnCM 87; IlEncCM; MotPP; NewAmDM; NewGrDA 86; NewYTBE 72; ObitOF 79; OnThGG; OxCPMus; PenEncP; WhoHol 92, A; WhScrn 77, 83*

Sontag, Henriette

German. Opera Singer
Celebrated European soprano, 1820s-40s; noted for Rossini roles.
b. Jan 3, 1806 in Koblenz, Germany
d. Jun 17, 1854 in Mexico City, Mexico
Source: *ApCAB; BakBD 78, 84, 92; BioIn 7, 14, 15, 19; BriBkM 80; CmOp; ContDcW 89; DcPseud; IntDcOp; IntDcWB; InWom; MetOEnc; NewAmDM; NewEOp 71; NewGrDM 80; OxDcOp; PenDiMP*

Sontag, Susan

American. Author, Critic
One of most influential contemporary American critics, utilizing new sensibility to evaluate art; wrote novels *The Benefactor,* 1963; *Death Kit,* 1967.
b. Jan 16, 1933 in New York, New York
Source: *AmAu&B; AmWomWr; AmWr S3; ArtclWW 2; Benet 87, 96; BenetAL 91; BioIn 6, 7, 8, 9, 10, 11, 12, 13, 14, 15, 16, 17, 18, 19, 20, 21, 24; BlueB 76; CamBiEn; CamDcAB; CamGLE; CamHAL; CelR; ChamBiD; ConAu 17R, 25NR, 51NR, 74NR; ConJeAN; ConLC 1, 2, 10, 13, 31, 105; ConNov 72, 76, 82, 86, 91, 96; ConPopW; ContDcW 89; CurBio 69, 92; CyWA 89, 97; DcArts; DcLB 2, 67; DcLEL 1940; DrAF 76; DrAPF 80, 91; EncALit; EncWB, 98; EncWHA; EncWL 2, 2S, 3; FacFETw; FemiCLE; GayLesB; GrLiveH; HanAmWH; IdentIs; IntAu&W 76, 77; IntDcWB; IntWW 89, 91, 93, 97, 98, 2000; IntWWW 2; InWom SUP; JeAmFiW; JeAmWW; LegTOT; LibW; LiExTwC; LiJour; LinLib L; MajTwCW 1, 2; ModAL 4, 4S2, 4S3, 5; ModAWWr; ModWoWr; NewYTBS 78, 80; NotWoAT;*

Novels; OxCAmL 83, 95; OxCFilm; OxCTwCL; OxCWoWr 95; PenC AM; PolProf J; RAdv 1, 14, 13-1; RfGAmL 4, 94; ThTwC 87; TwCRHW 94; Who 85, 88, 90, 92, 94, 98, 99, 2000; WhoAm 86, 90, 96, 97, 98, 99, 2000; WhoAmW 87, 91, 97, 99; WhoTwCL; WomIss; WomWMM; WorAl; WorAlBi; WorAu 1950; WrDr 76, 80, 82, 84, 86, 88, 90, 92, 94, 96, 98, 99, 2000

Sonzogno, Edoardo

Italian. Publisher
Sole proprietor of newspaper, *Il Secolo,* 1861-1909; printed French, Italian operas, 1874-1909.
b. Apr 21, 1836 in Milan, Italy
d. Mar 14, 1920 in Milan, Italy
Source: *BakBD 78, 84, 92; MetOEnc; NewAmDM; NewEOp 71; NewGrDM 80; OxDcOp*

Soo, Jack

[Goro Suzuki]
American. Actor
Played Yemana on TV series "Barney Miller," 1975-79.
b. Oct 28, 1915 in Oakland, California
d. Jan 11, 1979 in Los Angeles, California
Source: *BioIn 11; MotPP; NewYTBS 79; WhoHol A; WhScrn 83*

Soong, T. V

[Sung Tsu-Wen]
Chinese. Statesman
Leading financier of Chinese Nationalist regime; brother of Madam Chiang-Kai-Shek; founded Bank of China, 1936.
b. Dec 4, 1894 in Shanghai, China
d. Apr 24, 1971 in San Francisco, California
Source: *CurBio 41, 71, 71N; NewYTBE 71; WhAm 5*

Sophocles

Greek. Poet, Dramatist
Wrote *Antigone, Oepidus Rex,* c. 429 BC.
b. 496?BC in Colonus, Greece
d. 406?BC in Athens, Greece
Source: *AncWr; AtlBL; BbD; Benet 87, 96; BiCoLiE; BiD&SB; BioIn 1, 2, 3, 5, 8, 10, 12; CamBiEn; CamGWoT; CasWL; ChamBiD; ChhPo S2; CIMLC 2; CnDWLB 1; CnThe; CyWA 58, 97; DcArts; DcEnL; DcLB 176; Dis&D; DramC 1; EncWB 98; EncWT; Ent; GrFLW; Grk&L; IntDcT 2; LegTOT; LuthC 75; MagSWL; McGEWB; McGEWD 72, 84; MetOEnc; NewC; NewEOp 71; NewGrDM 80; NewGrDO; NotNAT A, B; OxCClL, 89; OxCEng 67, 85, 95; OxCThe 67, 83; OxDcByz; PenC CL; PlP&P; RAdv 14, 13-2; RComWL; REn; REnWD; RfGWoL 95; WhDW; WorAl; WorAlBi; WorLitC SUP*

Sopwith, Thomas O. M, Sir

English. Aeronautical Engineer, Aviator
Founded Sopwith Aviation, 1912; designed Sopwith Pup, Sopwith

Camel, planes used extensively by
British in WW I.
b. Jan 18, 1888
d. Jan 27, 1989 in Winchester, England
Source: *AnObit 1989; BioIn 16;
FacFETw; IntWW 83, 89N; NewYTBS
89; Who 85, 88, 90N; WhoAm 88;
WhoWor 74*

Sor, Fernando
[Fernando Sors]
Spanish. Composer, Musician
Guitar virtuoso, popular in London,
Paris, 1820s; wrote guitar music.
b. Feb 13, 1778 in Barcelona, Spain
d. Jul 8, 1839 in Paris, France
Source: *BakBD 78, 84; BioIn 11;
CmpEGui; DcHiB; NewGrDM 80;
NewOxM; OxCMus; PenDiMP*

Sordello
[Sordel]
Italian. Troubador, Poet
Composer of about forty poems on love,
chivalry, and mortality.
b. c. 1189 in Goito, Italy
d. c. 1269
Source: *ClMLC 15; DcBiPP*

Sorel, Albert
French. Historian
Revered for his major work, *Europe and
the French Revolution,* which
profoundly influenced the
interpretation of the French
Revolution.
b. 1842, France
d. 1906
Source: *DcEuL; EncWB 98; GloEncH;
McGEWB; OxCEng 67; OxCFr; WhDW;
WhLit*

Sorel, Edward
[Edward Schwartz]
American. Artist
One of the founders of the Push Pin
Studios, 1953; drawings appear in
many American magazines including
The New Yorker and *Esquire.*
b. Mar 26, 1929 in New York, New
York
Source: *BioIn 8, 12, 15, 16, 17, 19, 20;
ConAu 9R, 33NR; ConGrA 1; CurBio
94; EncSF, 93; IlrAm 1880; IlsBYP;
IlsCB 1957; SmATA 37, 65; WhoAm 74,
76, 78, 80, 82, 84, 86, 88, 90, 92, 94,
95, 96, 97, 98, 99, 2000; WhoAmA 76,
78, 80, 82, 84, 86, 89, 91, 93, 1999;
WhoE 74; WhoGrA 82; WhoWor 74, 76;
WorECar*

Sorel, Georges
French. Philosopher
Political and social thinker inspired both
Communist and Fascist ideologists.
b. 1847 in Normandy, France
d. 1922
Source: *Benet 87, 96; BiDExR;
BiDFrPL; BiDNeoM; BioIn 1, 2, 8, 9,
10, 11, 12, 13, 14, 17; CamBiEn;
CasWL; ChamBiD; ClDMEL 47, 80;
ConAu 118; DcAmSR; DcTwCCu 2;
Dis&D; EncRev; EncWB 98; LngCTC;*

*McGEWB; OxCFr; OxCPhil; REn;
ThTwC 87; TwCLC 91; WhDW; WorAu
1950*

Soren, David
[Howard David Soren]
American. Archaeologist
Discovered lost Roman city of Kourion
(destroyed by earthquake in 364),
1984.
b. Oct 7, 1946 in Philadelphia,
Pennsylvania
Source: *AmMWSc 95, 98; ConNews 86-
3; DrAS 78H, 82H; WhoAm 90, 92, 94,
95, 96, 97, 98, 99, 2000; WhoEmL 87;
WhoScEn 94, 96, 2000; WhoWest 89, 92,
94, 96, 98*

Soren, Tabitha
American. Broadcast Journalist
MTV news correpondent.
b. Aug 19, 1967 in San Antonio, Texas
Source: *DcPseud; LegTOT*

Sorensen, Ted
[Theodore Chaikin Sorensen]
American. Government Official
Assistant, special counsel to JFK, 1953-
63; wrote *The Kennedy Legacy,* 1969.
b. May 8, 1928 in Lincoln, Nebraska
Source: *AmAu&B; ConAu 2NR, 45;
CurBio 61; IntWW 83, 91; PolProf K;
WhoAm 84, 86, 90, 97; WhoAmL 92;
WhoAmP 85, 91; WrDr 86, 92*

Sorensen, Virginia
[Mrs. Alec Waugh]
American. Children's Author
Won 1957 Newbery for *Miracles on
Maple Hill.*
b. Feb 17, 1912 in Provo, Utah
d. Dec 24, 1991
Source: *AmAu&B; AmNov; ArtclWW 2;
Au&Wr 71; AuBYP 2, 3; BenetAL 91;
BioIn 2, 4, 6, 7, 9, 10; ConAu 13R,
22NR, 139; CurBio 50; DcAmChF 1960;
DcLB 206; EncFWF; InWom; MajAl;
MorBMP; MorJA; NewbC 1956;
OxCAmL 83, 95; OxCChiL; SJGChWr 5;
SmATA 2, 15AS, 72; TwCA SUP;
TwCChW 1, 2, 3, 4; TwCWW 82, 91;
WhAm 10; WhoAm 74, 76, 78, 80, 82,
84, 86, 88, 90; WhoAmW 58, 72, 74;
WhoWor 74; WrDr 76, 80, 82, 84, 86,
88, 90, 92, 94N*

Sorge, Richard
German. Journalist, Spy
Soviet spy who organized spy ring in
Japan, 1935-44; caught and executed,
1944.
b. 1895 in Baku, Russia
d. 1944 in Tokyo, Japan
Source: *BiDSovU; BioIn 2, 3, 4, 7, 8, 11,
14, 17; EncCapP; EncTR, 91; HisEWW;
PacWarE; Spies; SpyCS; WhDW;
WhWW-II*

Soria, Dario
American. Business Executive
Pres., Cetra-Soria Records, 1950-53,
EMI, 1953-57; produced Met. Opera

Historic Broadcasting Recording
Series, 1975-80.
b. May 21, 1912 in Rome, Italy
d. Mar 28, 1980 in New York, New
York
Source: *BioIn 10, 11, 12; MetOEnc;
NewYTBS 80; WhAm 7; WhoAm 74, 76,
78, 80*

Sorin, Edward Frederick
American. Clergy, Educator
Roman Catholic priest; founder, first
pres., U of Notre Dame, 1844-65.
b. Feb 6, 1814 in Ahuille, France
d. Oct 31, 1893 in South Bend, Indiana
Source: *AmAu&B; AmNatBi; ApCAB;
BiDAmEd; CamDcAB; DcAmB;
TwCBDA; WebAB 74, 79; WhAm HS*

Sorokin, Pitirim A(lexandrovitch)
American. Sociologist, Educator
Social critic was a leading advocate of
the importance of values and broad
knowledge in an era dominated by
science and power.
b. Jan 21, 1889 in Turya, Russia
d. Feb 10, 1968 in Winchester,
Massachusetts
Source: *EncO&P 1, 2, 3; McGEWB;
WebAB 74, 79; WhAm 4A*

Soros, George
[Dzjchdzhe Shorash]
American. Financier
First American to earn $1 billion in one
year; started the Quantum Fund, 1969.
b. Aug 12, 1930 in Budapest, Hungary
Source: *BioIn 12; CamBiEn; CurBio 97;
IntWW 97, 98, 2000; Who 98, 99, 2000;
WhoAm 94, 95, 96, 97, 98, 99, 2000;
WhoE 99; WhoFI 92, 94; WhoIntA 2;
WhoWor 99, 2000*

Sorvino, Mira
American. Actor
Won Oscar, Best Supporting Actress,
Mighty Aphrodite, 1994.
b. 1969 in Tenafly, New Jersey
Source: *ConTFT 16*

Sorvino, Paul
American. Actor
Starred in *That Championship Season,* on
Broadway, 1972, film, 1982.
b. 1939 in New York, New York
Source: *BioIn 13, 14; ConTFT 4, 17;
EncAFC; FilmEn; HalFC 80, 84, 88;
IntMPA 80, 84, 86, 88, 92, 94, 96;
LegTOT; NewYTBE 72; NewYTBS 82;
PIP&P A; VarWW 85; WhoAm 86, 90,
95, 96, 97, 99, 2000; WhoEnt 92, 98;
WhoHol 92, A; WhoThe 77, 81; WorAl;
WorAlBi*

Sosa, Mercedes
Argentine. Singer
Songs reflect the pain of exile, fear of
political violence and struggle for
justice.
b. 1935 in Tucuman, Argentina
Source: *BioIn 16; ConMus 3; DcHiB;
NewYTBS 88*

Sosnik, Harry
American. Conductor
Led band, 1930s-40s; wrote TV scores,
    songs.
b. Jul 13, 1906 in Chicago, Illinois
Source: *ASCAP 66, 80; CmpEPM;
St&PR 75; WhoAm 74, 76, 78, 80, 82,
84, 86, 88; WhoEnt 92*

Soss, Wilma Porter
American. Business Executive
Founder, pres., Federation of Women
    Shareholders in American Business,
    1947-86.
b. Mar 13, 1900 in San Francisco,
    California
d. Oct 10, 1986 in New York, New York
Source: *AmNatBi; BioIn 15; CurBio 65,
87; NewYTBS 86; WhoAmW 87*

Sostratus
Greek. Architect
Built lighthouse for Ptolemy
    Philadelphus at Alexandria; model for
    similar structures of period.
b. fl. 3rd cent. BC
Source: *BioIn 14; DcBiPP; WebBD 83*

Sotatsu, Tawaraya
Japanese. Painter
One of the giants of Japanese art, his
    work is typically Japanese both subject
    matter and in its rather abstract,
    decorative design.
b. c. 1570
d. 1643
Source: *EncWB 98; McGEWB*

Sotheby, John
English. Auctioneer
Founded Covent Gardens Auction
    Rooms, 1744.
d. 1807
Source: *WebBD 83*

Sotheby, Samuel Leigh
English. Auctioneer
Entered family business, 1817; expert in
    Cataloguing; wrote on early printing.
b. Aug 31, 1805
d. Jun 19, 1861 in Buckfastleigh Abbey,
    England
Source: *Alli; BioIn 12; DcBiPP; DcNaB;
WebBD 83*

Sothern, Ann
[Harriet Lake]
American. Actor
Lighthearted heroine of *Maisie* film
    series, 1939-47; starred on TV in
    comedies "Private Secretary," 1954-
    57; "The Ann Sothern Show," 1958-
    61.
b. Jan 22, 1909 in Valley City, North
    Dakota
Source: *ASCAP 66; BioIn 16; CmpEPM;
ConTFT 8; CurBio 56; DcPseud;
EncAFC; EncMT; Film 2; FilmEn;
FilmgC; GangFlm; HalFC 80, 84, 88;
IntDcF 1-3; IntMPA 86, 92, 94, 96;
InWom SUP; LegTOT; MGM; MotPP;
MovMk; OsStAZ; OxCFilm; RadStar;*

*SaTiSS; ThFT; WhoAm 80, 82;
WhoCom; WhoHol A; WhoThe 77A;
WhThe; WorAlBi; WorEFlm*

Sothern, Edward Askew
English. Entertainer
Noted for role in *Our American Cousin,*
    from 1858; appeared night of Lincoln
    assassination.
b. Apr 1, 1826 in Liverpool, England
d. Jan 20, 1881 in London, England
Source: *Alli; AmBi; AmNatBi;
CamDcAB; DcAmB; DcNaB; EncWT;
FamA&A; NatCAB 5; NewC; NotNAT A;
OxCAmH; OxCAmL 65; OxCThe 67, 83;
REnAL; TwCBDA; WhAm HS*

Sothern, Edward Hugh
American. Entertainer
Founded Shakespearian Repertory Co.
    with wife, Julia Marlowe, 1900-16;
    son of Edward Askew.
b. Dec 6, 1859 in New Orleans,
    Louisiana
d. Oct 28, 1933 in New York, New York
Source: *AmAu&B; AmBi; AmNatBi;
ApCAB X; BioIn 1, 2, 3, 4, 5, 13;
ChhPo; DcAmB; DcNAA; FamA&A;
LinLib S; NatCAB 5; NotNAT A, B;
OxCAmH; OxCAmL 65; OxCThe 67, 83;
REn; REnAL; TwCBDA; WebAB 74, 79;
WhAm 1; WhoStg 1906, 1908; WhScrn
74, 77; WhThe*

Soto, Gary
American. Writer
Published poetry collections *The
    Elements of San Joaquin,* 1977; *Black
    Hair,* 1985; children's book *Pacific
    Crossing,* 1992; memoir *Living up the
    Street,* 1985.
b. Apr 12, 1952 in Fresno, California
Source: *Au&Arts 10; ChiLit; ChiSch;
ChlBkCr; ChlLR 38; ConAu 50NR,
74NR, 119, 125; ConLC 32, 80; ConPo
85, 91, 96; ConSSWr; DcHiB; DcLB 82;
DrAPF 80; EncALit; EncWL 3;
HispAmA; HispLC; HispWr, 2; IdentIs;
MajAI SUP; MajTwCW 2; MexAmB;
ModAL 4S3, 5; OnHuMoP; OxCAmL 95;
OxCTwCL; OxCTwCP; PoeCrit 28;
RfGAmL 4, 94; SJGYouA 2; SmATA 80;
TwCYAW 1; WhoAm 92; WhoHisp 91,
92, 94; WhoWest 87, 98; WorAu 1975;
WrDr 86, 88, 90, 92, 94, 96, 98, 99,
2000; WrYoAd*

Soto, Mario Melvin
Dominican. Baseball Player
Pitcher, Cincinnati, 1977—; led NL in
    complete games, 1983, 1984; three-
    time NL All-Star.
b. Jul 12, 1956 in Bani, Dominican
    Republic
Source: *Ballpl 90; BaseReg 86, 87;
BioIn 13; NewYTBS 84, 86*

Soufflot, Jacques Germain
French. Architect
Leader of the neoclassic movement that
    swept over Europe in the early 19th
    century, he was also inspired by
    Gothic designs.

b. Jul 22, 1713 in Irancy, Yonne, France
d. Aug 29, 1780 in Paris, France
Source: *BioIn 14; BlkwCE; CamBiEn;
DcArch; DcD&D; EncEnl; EncWB 98;
IntDcAr; McGEWB; OxCArt; WhDW*

Soul, David
American. Actor
Starred in TV shows "Here Come the
    Brides," "Starsky and Hutch."
b. Aug 28, 1946 in Chicago, Illinois
Source: *BioIn 13; ConTFT 3; HalFC 84;
IntMPA 88; WhoAm 80, 82; WhoHol A*

Soulages, Pierre
French. Painter
Artist was a major abstractionist of the
    School of Paris, known for his broad
    strokes of paint and subdued palette.
b. Dec 24, 1919 in Rodez, France
Source: *BioIn 4, 5, 10; ConArt 77, 83,
89, 96; DcTwArt; EncWB 98; IntWW 74,
75, 76, 77, 78, 79, 80, 81, 82, 83, 89,
91, 93, 97, 98, 2000; McGDA;
McGEWB; OxCTwCA; PhDcTCA 77;
PrintW 83, 85; WhoArt 80, 82, 84, 96,
98; WhoFr 79; WhoWor 74, 76, 78, 82,
84, 87, 89, 91, 93, 95, 96, 97, 98, 99,
2000; WorArt 1950*

Soule, Olan
American. Actor
Films include *The Apple Dumpling
    Gang,* 1975; *St. Ives,* 1976.
b. Feb 28, 1909 in La Harpe, Illinois
d. Feb 1, 1994 in Corona, California
Source: *BioIn 22; ConTFT 9, 13;
EncAFC; RadStar; VarWW 85; WhoHol
92, A*

Soule, Pierre
American. Politician, Lawyer, Diplomat
Active in Louisiana politics and pre-Civil
    War diplomacy, he was an advocate of
    American annexation of Cuba.
b. Aug 31, 1801 in Castillon-en-
    Couserans, France
d. Mar 26, 1870
Source: *AmNatBi; BiDConf; BiDrAC;
BiDrUSC 89; BioIn 2, 3, 4, 12, 16;
DcAmB; DcAmDH 80, 89; Drake;
EncSoH; EncWB 98; McGEWB; WebAB
74, 79; WhAm HS; WhAmP; WhCiWar*

Soundgarden
[Matt Cameron; Chris Cornell; Jason
    Everman; Hunter "Ben" Shepherd;
    Kim Thayil; Hiro Yamamoto]
American. Music Group
Heavy metal rock band; albums include
    Louder Than Love, 1989.
Source: *BillEnR; BioIn 20; ConMus 6;
EncRkSt; GrMetD*

Soupault, Philippe
French. Author
Wrote poem "The Magnetic Fields,"
    1919, with Andre Breton, considered
    the work that gave birth to the
    surrealist movement.
b. Aug 2, 1897 in Chaville, France
d. Mar 11, 1990 in Paris, France

Source: *AnObit 1990; Benet 87, 96; BioIn 1, 9, 10, 16, 17; CasWL; ClDMEL 47, 80; ConAu 116, 131, 147; ConLC 68; DcTwCCu 2; EncWL 1, 2, 2S, 3; FacFETw; GuFrLit 1; IntAu&W 77, 89, 91; IntWW 74, 75, 76, 77, 78, 79, 80, 81, 82, 83, 89; IntWWP 77; ModFrL; ModRL; ModWD; NewYTBS 90; OxCFr; REn; WhoFr 79; WhoWor 74; WorAu 1950*

Souphanouvong, Prince
Laotian. Political Leader
President of Laos, 1975-86.
b. 1912 in Luang Prabang, Laos
d. Jan 9, 1995, Laos
Source: *IntWW 83, 91; NewYTBE 70, 73; NewYTBS 74; WhoWor 84, 87, 91*

Sour, Robert B(andler)
American. Lyricist
Hit songs include ''Body and Soul,'' 1930.
b. Oct 31, 1905 in New York, New York
d. Mar 6, 1985 in New York, New York
Source: *BiDAmM; BioIn 14; ConAu 115; WhAm 8; WhoAm 74, 76, 78, 80*

Sousa, Henrique Teixeira de
Cape Verdean. Author
One of the most prolific and best-known novelists of Portuguese-speaking Africa.
b. Sep 1919 in Fogo, Cape Verde

Sousa, John Philip
American. Composer, Conductor
Wrote 140 marches, including ''Stars and Stripes Forever,'' 1897.
b. Nov 6, 1854 in Washington, District of Columbia
d. Mar 6, 1932 in Reading, Pennsylvania
Source: *AmAu&B; AmBi; AmCulL; AmNatBi; ApCAB SUP, X; ASCAP 66, 80; AtlBL; BakBD 78, 84, 92; BakBDTw; BakDcM; Benet 87, 96; BenetAL 91; BiDAmM; BioIn 1, 2, 3, 4, 5, 6, 7, 8, 9, 10, 13, 14, 15, 18, 19, 20, 22, 23, 24; BriBkM 80; CamBiEn; CamDcAB; ChamBiD; CmpEPM; ConMus 10; DcAmAu; DcAmB; DcArts; DcNAA; EncAB-H 1974, 1996; EncMT; EncWB 98; GayN; HalFC 80, 84, 88; LegTOT; LinLib L, S; LiveWoA; McGEWB; MemAm; MusMk; NatCAB 9, 33; NewAmDM; NewGrDA 86; NewGrDM 80; NewOxM; NotNAT B; OxCAmH; OxCAmL 65; OxCAmT 84; OxCMus; OxCPMus; OxDcOp; PenEncP; PopAmC; REn, REnAL; TwCBDA; WebAB 74, 79; WebAMB; WhAm 1; WhDW; WhoStg 1906, 1908; WhThe; WorAl; WorAlBi*

Sousa, Martim Afonso de
Portuguese. Colonizer
Founded the first permanent Portuguese settlement in South America; also served as viceroy of India.
b. c. 1500 in Vila Vicosa, Portugal
d. Jul 21, 1564 in Lisbon, Portugal
Source: *EncLatA; LatAmLi; McGEWB*

Soustelle, Jacques
French. Government Official, Anthropologist
Governor-general of Algeria, 1955-56; minister of information, 1958; has written extensively of anthropological expeditions to Mexico.
b. Feb 3, 1912 in Montpellier, France
d. Aug 7, 1990 in Neuilly-sur-Seine, France
Source: *AnObit 1990; BiDFrPL; BioIn 4, 5, 7, 9, 17; ConAu 132; CurBio 58, 90, 90N; DcPol; FacFETw; IntDcAn; IntWW 74, 75, 76, 77, 78, 79, 80, 81, 82, 83, 89, 91N; NewYTBS 90; Spies; Who 74, 82, 83, 85, 88, 90; WhoFr 79*

Soutar, William
Scottish. Poet
Prominent figure in the Scottish Renaissance movement; in later years wrote ''Whigmaleeries.''
b. Apr 28, 1898 in Perth, Scotland
d. Oct 15, 1943 in Perth, Scotland
Source: *BiCoLiE; BioIn 3, 12; CamBiEn; CamGEL; CamGLE; CasWL; ChamBiD; ChhPo, S1, S2, S3; CmScLit; DcLEL; EncWL 1; EngPo; EvLB; NewCBEL; OxCEng 85, 95; OxCTwCL; OxCTwCP; PenC ENG; RGTwCWr; TwCWr; WhE&EA; WhLit*

Souter, David Hackett
American. Supreme Court Justice
Conservative justice appointed to Supreme Court by George Bush, 1990, replacing retiring William Brennan.
b. Sep 17, 1939 in Melrose, Massachusetts
Source: *AmBench 97; CamDcAB; CngDr 91, 93, 95; CurBio 91; FacFETw; IntWW 91, 93, 97, 98, 2000; News 91-3; SupCtJu; Who 94, 98, 99, 2000; WhoAm 78, 80, 82, 84, 86, 88, 90, 92, 94, 95, 96, 97, 98, 99, 2000; WhoAmL 78, 85, 87, 90, 92, 94, 96, 98, 2000; WhoAmP 91, 1999; WhoE 79, 81, 83, 85, 86, 89, 91, 93, 95, 97, 99; WhoWor 96*

South, Joe
American. Musician, Singer, Songwriter
Won two Grammys, 1969, for ''Games People Play.''
b. Feb 28, 1942 in Atlanta, Georgia
Source: *BioIn 8; EncPR&S 89; HarEnR 86; IlEncRk; PenEncP; RkOn 74; RolSEnR 83; Songw; WhoRock 81*

Southall, Ivan Francis
Australian. Author
Novels for young adults deal with how children cope with various disasters: *Hills End*, 1962; *To the Wild Sky*, 1967.
b. Jun 8, 1921 in Canterbury, Australia
Source: *Au&Wr 71; AuBYP 2, 3; ChamBiD; ChlLR 2; ConAu 7NR, 9R; IntAu&W 91; IntWW 91; SenS; SJGYouA 2; SmATA 3, 68; ThrBJA; TwCChW 3; WhoAm 97, 98, 99, 2000; WhoWor 87, 91; WrDr 86, 92, 98, 99, 2000*

Southampton, Henry Wriothesley, Earl
English. Statesman
Active in London co. of VA, colonization of America, early 1600s; only benefactor acknowledged by Shakespeare.
b. Oct 6, 1573
d. Nov 10, 1624, Netherlands
Source: *ApCAB; Benet 87, 96; BioIn 7, 8, 11, 14; BlmGEL; ChamBiD; DcArts; DcBiPP; LngCEL; NewC; NewCBEL; OxCBrHi; REn*

Souther, J(ohn) D(avid)
[The Souther-Hillman-Furay Band]
American. Singer, Songwriter
Guitarist, vocalist with country-rock band, 1973-75.
b. Nov 2, 1945 in Detroit, Michigan
Source: *ConMuA 80A; RkOn 85; WhoRock 81*

Souther-Hillman-Furay Band, The
[Richie Furay; James Gordon; Paul Harris; Chris Hillman; Al Perkins; J(ohn) D(avid) Souther]
American. Music Group
Country-rock band formed 1973; first album was gold; disbanded, 1975, with members going on to solo careers.
Source: *Alli, SUP; AllMGCo; BiDLA; BiDSA; ChhPo S1, S3; ConMuA 80A; DcNaB; EngPo; IlEncRk; OnThGG; RkOn 78, 85; RolSEnR 83; WhoAmA 73, 76, 78; WhoHol 92; WhoNeCM A; WhoRock 81; WhoRocM 82*

Southern, Terry
American. Writer
Writes satirical novels, screenplays; known for satire on pornography, *Candy*, 1958, later published as *Lollipop*, 1962; films include *Easy Rider*, 1969.
b. May 1, 1924 in Alvarado, Texas
d. Oct 29, 1995 in New York, New York
Source: *AmAu&B; Au&Wr 71; BeaEPF; BioIn 6, 7, 8, 10; BlueB 76; CasWL; ConAu 1NR, 1R, 55NR, 150; ConDr 73, 77A; ConLC 7; ConNov 72, 76, 82, 86, 91, 96; ConTFT 15; DcLB 2; DrAF 76; DrAPF 91; HalFC 88; IntAu&W 76, 77, 91, 93; Novels; PenC AM; RGTwCWr; WhoAm 76, 78, 80, 82; WhoTwCL; WorAu 1950; WrDr 76, 80, 82, 84, 86, 88, 90, 92, 94, 96, 98N*

Southey, Robert
English. Poet, Author
One of ''Lake Poets;'' poet laureate, 1813-43.
b. Aug 12, 1774 in Bristol, England
d. Mar 21, 1843 in Keswick, England
Source: *Alli; AtlBL; BbD; Benet 87, 96; BiCoLiE; BiD&SB; BiDLA; BioIn 1, 2, 3, 5, 6, 7, 8, 9, 10, 11, 12, 13, 16, 17, 20, 23; BlmGEL; BritAu 19; BritWr 4; CamBiEn; CamGEL; CamGLE; CasWL; CelCen; ChamBiD; Chambr 3; ChhPo, S1, S2, S3; CnE&AP; CrtT 2, 4; CyWA*

58, 97; DcArts; DcBiPP; DcEnA, A;
DcEnL; DcEuL; DcLB 93, 107, 142;
DcLEL; DcNaB; Dis&D; EncLitE;
EncWB 99; EvLB; GrWrEL P; LegTOT;
LinLib L, S; LngCEL; MouLC 3; NewC;
NewCBEL; NinCLC 8; OxCBrHi;
OxCChiL; OxCEng 67, 85, 95; PenC
ENG; PoLE; RAdv 14; REn; RfGEnL
91; SmATA 54; WebE&AL; WhDW;
WhoChL

Southside Johnny and the Asbury Jukes

[Gene Bacia; Steve Becker; Al Berger;
Ricky Gazda; Kevin Kavanaugh;
"Southside" Johnny Lyon; Eddie
Manion; Carlo Novi; Tony Palligrosi;
Kenny Pentifallo; Richie Rosenberg;
Billy Rush]
American. Music Group
Rhythm and blues influenced rock band
formed 1974; albums featured Bruce
Springsteen songs.
Source: BillEnR; ConMuA 80A;
EncPR&S 89; EncRk 88; HarEnR 86;
IlEncRk; PenEncP; RkOn 78, 85;
RolSEnR 83; WhoRock 81; WhoRocM 82

Southworth, Emma Dorothy Eliza Nevitte

American. Author
Wrote novels of Southern life: The
Hidden Hand, 1859.
b. Dec 26, 1819 in Washington, District
of Columbia
d. Jun 30, 1899 in Georgetown, Virginia
Source: AmAu; AmBi; AmNatBi;
AmWom; AmWomWr; ApCAB; ArtclWW
2; BioIn 17; DcAmB; EncALit; InWom,
SUP; LibW; NatCAB 1; NewCol 75;
NinCLC 26; NotAW; PenNWW A; REn;
REnAL; SouWr; TwCBDA; WebAB 74,
79; WhAm 1

Soutine, Chaim

French. Artist
Expressionist, used heavy impasto; often
painted distorted portraits,
slaughterhouse scenes.
b. 1894 in Smilovich, Russia
d. Aug 9, 1943 in Paris, France
Source: AtlBL; BioIn 1, 2, 4, 6, 8, 10,
11, 12, 13, 14, 16, 18, 21; ConArt 83;
DcTwCCu 2; EncWB 98; MakMC;
McGDA; McGEWB; NewCol 75;
OxCArt; OxCTwCA; OxDcArt

Souvanna, Phouma

Laotian. Prince, Political Leader
Neutralist prime minister of Laos, 1951-
75.
b. Oct 7, 1901 in Luang Prabang, Laos
d. Jan 10, 1984 in Vientiane, Laos
Source: AnObit 1984; BioIn 5, 6, 7, 8, 9,
10; CurBio 62, 84; IntWW 74; NewYTBS
84; WhoGov 77; WhoWor 74

Souzay, Gerard

[Gerard Marcel Tisserand]
French. Opera Singer
Baritone, noted for Lieder, French art
songs; popular concertist, 1960s-80s.
b. Dec 8, 1920? in Angers, France

Source: BakBD 78, 84; BioIn 11; CurBio
66; IntWW 74, 75, 76, 77, 78, 79, 80,
81, 82, 83, 89, 91, 93; IntWWM 77, 80;
MusMk; MusSN; NewGrDM 80; Who
92; WhoFr 79; WhoMus 72; WhoOp 76;
WhoWor 74

Sovern, Michael I(ra)

American. University Administrator
Pres., Columbia U, 1980-93.
b. Dec 1, 1931 in New York, New York
Source: BioIn 8, 10, 12; BlueB 76;
CurBio 81; DrAS 74P, 78P, 82P; IntWW
89, 91, 93, 97, 98, 2000; NewYTBS 80;
WhoAm 74, 76, 78, 80, 82, 84, 86, 88,
90, 92, 94, 95, 96, 97, 98, 99, 2000;
WhoAmL 78, 79, 87, 90, 92, 94; WhoE
74, 83, 85, 86, 89, 91, 93; WhoFI 00,
98; WhoWor 84, 87, 89, 91, 93, 95, 96,
97, 98, 99, 2000

Sowell, Thomas

American. Economist, Author
Controversial conservative economist,
believes affirmative action and
minimum wages laws are detrimental
to black Americans; books include
Ethnic America, 1981; Preferential
Policies, 1990.
b. Jun 30, 1930 in Gastonia, North
Carolina
Source: AmEA 74; AmMWSc 73S, 78S;
BiDAmNC; BiDMoAE; BioIn 12, 13, 14,
15, 17, 24; BlkWr 1, 2; BlkWrNE A;
CamDcAB; ConAu 26NR, 41R, 61NR;
ConBlB 2; ConIsC 2; CurBio 81;
DcAmC; EncWB 2-19; InB&W 85;
NegAl 89; News 98, 98-3; SchCGBL;
SelBAAf; WhoAfA 9, 10, 11, 12; WhoAm
76, 82, 84, 86, 88, 90, 92, 94, 95, 96,
97; WhoBlA 1, 2, 3, 4, 6, 7, 8; WhoEc
81; WhoMedi 98; WrDr 92, 94, 96, 98

Sowerby, Leo

American. Organist, Composer
Wrote Pulitzer-winning poem, "Canticle
of the Sun," 1944.
b. May 1, 1895 in Grand Rapids,
Michigan
d. Jul 7, 1968 in Port Clinton, Ohio
Source: AmComp; ASCAP 66, 80;
BakBD 78, 84, 92; BakBDTw; BiDAmM;
BioIn 1, 3, 4, 8; BriBkM 80; CamBiEn;
ChamBiD; CompSN; ConAmC 76, 82;
DcCM; DcCom&M 79; MusMk;
NewAmDM; NewGrDA 86; NewGrDM
80; OxCAmL 65; OxCMus; REnAL;
WhAm 5; WhoPul

Soyer, David

American. Musician
Cellist; won five Grammys for Guarnieri
Quarter recordings, 1965-74.
b. Feb 24, 1923 in Philadelphia,
Pennsylvania
Source: BioIn 9, 11; IntWWM 77, 80;
NewYTBE 71; PenDiMP; WhoAm 76,
78, 80, 82, 84, 86, 88, 90, 92, 94, 95,
96, 97, 98, 99, 2000; WhoAmM 83;
WhoEnt 92, 98

Soyer, Isaac

American. Artist
With brothers, Moses, Raphael, leading
exponent of realism; paintings of
Depression Era working class:
Employment Agency, 1941.
b. Apr 20, 1907 in Tambov, Russia
d. Jul 8, 1981 in New York, New York
Source: BioIn 17; BriEAA; CamDcAB;
CurBio 41, 81, 81N; McGDA; WhAm 8;
WhAmArt 85; WhoAm 74, 76, 78; WhoE
74; WorArt 1950

Soyer, Moses

American. Artist
Twin brother of Raphael; social realism
genre painter; major works include
Girl at Sewing Machine, 1940.
b. Dec 25, 1899 in Tambov, Russia
d. Sep 2, 1974 in New York, New York
Source: BioIn 6, 7, 8, 10, 12, 14, 17;
BriEAA; CamDcAB; CelR; CurBio 41,
74, 74N; DcAmArt; DcAmB S9; DcCAA
71, 77, 88, 94; DcTwArt; McGDA;
NatCAB 58; NewYTBS 74; OxCTwCA;
OxDcArt; WhAm 6; WhAmArt 85;
WhoAm 74; WhoAmA 73, 76N, 78N,
80N, 82N, 84N, 86N, 89N, 91N, 93N;
WorArt 1950

Soyer, Raphael

American. Artist
Social realist; known for paintings
showing men, women during the
Depression.
b. Dec 25, 1899 in Tambov, Russia
d. Nov 4, 1987 in New York, New York
Source: AmArt; AmNatBi; AnObit 1987;
BiDSovU; BioIn 1, 2, 3, 6, 8, 9, 10, 11,
12, 13, 14, 15, 16, 17, 22, 24; BriEAA;
CamDcAB; CelR; ConAu 81, 124;
CurBio 41, 88, 88N; DcAmArt; DcCAA
71, 77, 88, 94; DcPseud; GrAmP;
McGDA; NewYTBE 72; NewYTBS 87;
OxDcArt; PhDcTCA 77; PrintW 83, 85;
ScrEAmL 2; WhAm 9; WhAmArt 85;
WhoAm 74, 76, 78, 80, 82, 84, 86;
WhoAmA 73, 76, 78, 80, 82, 84, 86;
WhoWorJ 72; WorArt 1950

Soyinka, Wole

[Akinwande Oluwole Soyinka]
Nigerian. Author
Works deal with life in Nigeria; first
African, first black to win Nobel Prize
for literature, 1986.
b. Jul 13, 1934 in Abeokuta, Nigeria
Source: AfrWr; AfSS 78, 79, 80, 81, 82;
Benet 87, 96; BiCoLiE; BioIn 8, 10, 12,
13; BlkLC; BlkWr 1, 2, 3; BlmGEL;
CamBiEn; CamGEL; CamGLE;
CamGWoT; CasWL; ChamBiD;
CnDWLB 3; CnThe; ConAu 13R, 27NR,
39NR, 82NR; ConBlB 4; ConDr 73, 77,
82, 88, 93; ConLC 3, 5, 14, 36, 44;
ConNov 96; ConPo 70, 75, 80, 85, 91,
96; ConTFT 6; CrtSuDr; CurBio 74;
CyWA 89, 97; DcArts; DcLB 125;
DramC 2; DrBlPA, 90; EncFoLi; EncWL
2, 2S, 3; EncWT; Ent; FacFETw;
GrWrEL DR; InB&W 80, 85; IntAu&W
76, 77; IntDcT 2; IntLitE; IntWW 74, 75,
76, 77, 78, 79, 80, 81, 82, 83, 89, 91,
93, 97, 98, 2000; IntWWP 77; LegTOT;

LiExTwC; LngCTC; MajTwCW 1, 2; MakMC; McGEWD 84; ModBlW, 2; ModCmwL; ModWD; NewYTBS 87; NobelP; Novels; OxCEng 85, 95; OxCThe 83; OxCTwCP; PenC CL, ENG; RadHan; RAdv 14, 13-2; REnWD; RfGEnL 91; RGAfL; SchCGBL; WebE&AL; Who 90, 92, 94, 98, 99, 2000; WhoNob 90, 95; WhoWor 74, 82, 84, 87, 89, 91, 93, 95, 96, 97, 98, 99, 2000; WorAlBi; WorAu 1950; WorLitC; WrDr 76, 80, 82, 84, 86, 88, 90, 92, 94, 96, 98, 99, 2000

Spaak, Paul-Henri
Belgian. Lawyer, Politician
Three-time premier of Belgium; among
 creators of NATO, secretary-general,
 1957-61.
b. Jan 25, 1899 in Schaerbeeck, Belgium
d. Jul 31, 1972 in Brussels, Belgium
Source: *BiDInt; BioIn 21; CamBiEn; ChamBiD; ConAu 37R; CurBio 45, 58, 72, 72N; DcTwHis; EncCW; EncWB 98; FacFETw; HisEWW; McGEWB; NewYTBE 72; ObitT 1971; PolLCWE; WhAm 5*

Spaatz, Carl Andrew
American. Army Officer
In charge of strategic bombing against
 Germany, Japan, WW II.
b. Jun 28, 1891 in Boyertown,
 Pennsylvania
d. Jul 14, 1974 in Washington, District
 of Columbia
Source: *AmNatBi; BioIn 10, 11, 12; ConAu 49; CurBio 42, 74; DcAmB S9; DcAmMiB; NatCAB 58; NewYTBS 74; WebAB 74; WhAm 6; Who 74*

Spacek, Sissy
[Mrs. Jack Fiske; Mary Elizabeth
 Spacek]
American. Actor
Won Oscar, 1980, for *Coal Miner's
 Daughter.*
b. Dec 25, 1949 in Quitman, Texas
Source: *BioIn 12, 13, 16; BkPepl; CelR 90; ConAu 77; CurBio 78; DcArts; DcPseud; FilmEn; HalFC 88; HolBB; IntDcF 1-3, 2-3; IntMPA 82, 88, 92, 94, 96; IntWW 83, 89, 91; IntWWW 2; LegTOT; NewYTBS 86; OsStAZ; WhoAm 86, 88, 90, 92, 94, 95, 96, 97, 98, 99, 2000; WhoAmW 81, 83, 85, 87, 89, 91, 93, 95, 97, 99; WhoEnt 98; WhoHol 92, A; WorAlBi*

Spacey, Kevin
American. Actor
Won Tony award, best featured actor
 (Drama), *Lost in Yonkers,* 1991;
 Oscar, best supporting actor, *The
 Usual Suspects,* 1995.
b. Jul 26, 1959 in South Orange, New
 Jersey
Source: *ConTFT 9, 17; CurBio 97; IntMPA 92, 94, 96; IntWW 98, 2000; LegTOT; News 96; OsStAZ; WhoAm 92, 94, 95, 96, 97, 98, 99, 2000; WhoEnt 92, 98; WhoHol 92*

Spader, James
American. Actor
Films include *sex, lies, and videotape,*
 1989; *White Palace,* 1990.
b. Feb 7, 1960 in Boston, Massachusetts
Source: *BioIn 15, 16; CamBiEn; CelR 90; ConTFT 9, 16; IntMPA 92, 94, 96; IntWW 97, 98, 2000; LegTOT; News 91, 91-2; WhoAm 92, 94, 95, 96, 97, 98, 99, 2000; WhoEnt 92, 98; WhoHol 92; WhoWor 95, 96, 97, 98, 99, 2000*

Spaeth, Sigmund Gottfried
"The Tune Detective"
American. Musicologist
Wrote syndicated column, books on
 music; helped popularize classical
 music.
b. Apr 10, 1885 in Philadelphia,
 Pennsylvania
d. Nov 12, 1965 in New York, New
 York
Source: *AmAu&B; ASCAP 66; BakBD 84; BiDAmM; ChhPo S1; CmpEPM; ConAu 5R; CurBio 42, 66; REnAL; TwCA, SUP; WhAm 4; WhNAA; WorAu 1900*

Spahn, Warren Edward
American. Baseball Player
Pitcher, Boston/Milwaukee Braves, 1942,
 1946-65; had 363 career wins, 63
 shutouts; Hall of Fame, 1973.
b. Apr 23, 1921 in Buffalo, New York
Source: *Ballpl 90; BiDAmSp BB; BioIn 4, 5, 6, 7, 8, 9, 10; CamBiEn; CamDcAB; CurBio 62; FacFETw; WebAB 74, 79; WhoAm 74; WhoProB 73; WorAlBi*

Spalding, Albert
American. Violinist
Int'l concertist, 1910-40s; wrote violin
 pieces; son of Albert Goodwill.
b. Aug 15, 1888 in Chicago, Illinois
d. May 26, 1953 in New York, New
 York
Source: *ASCAP 66, 80; BakBD 78, 84, 92; BakBDTw; BiDAmM; BioIn 1, 2, 3, 4, 5, 9, 10, 11, 14, 16; BriBkM 80; CamDcAB; ConAmC 76, 82; CurBio 44, 53; DcAmB S5; LinLib S; MusSN; NatCAB 42; NewAmDM; NewGrDA 86; RadStar; WebAB 74, 79; WhAm 3*

Spalding, Albert Goodwill
American. Baseball Player, Businessman
Pitcher, Chicago, 1876-78; won 47
 games, 1876; Hall of Fame, 1939;
 founded sporting goods firm, 1876.
b. Sep 2, 1850 in Byron, Illinois
d. Sep 9, 1915 in Point Loma, California
Source: *AmNatBi; BiDAmBL 83; BiDAmSp BB; BioIn 2, 3, 7, 11; CamDcAB; CulEncB; DcAmB; DcNAA; Entr; NatCAB 3; OxCAmH; WebAB 74, 79; WhAm 1; WhoProB 73*

Spallanzani, Lazzaro
Italian. Explorer, Scientist
Disproved theory of spontaneous
 generation.
b. Jan 12, 1729 in Scandiano, Italy

d. Feb 11, 1799 in Pavia, Italy
Source: *AsBiEn; BiESc; BiHiMed; BioIn 6, 9, 12, 14, 15; CamDcSc; DcCathB; DcScB; Dis&D; EncEnl; EncWB 98; InSci; McGEWB; NewCol 75; OxCMed 86; RanHWDS; WhDW; WorAl; WorAlBi; WorScD*

Spandau Ballet
[Tony Hadley; John Keeble; Gary Kemp;
 Martin Kemp; Steve Norman]
English. Music Group
Formed 1979; known for flamboyant,
 then classic dress; hit single "True,"
 1983.
Source: *Alli; BillEnR; BioIn 17; ConAu X; DrAPF 83, 85, 87, 89, 91, 93, 97; EncPR&S 89; EncRk 88; EncRkSt; HarEnR 86; PenEncP; RkOn 85; SmATA X; WhsNW 85*

Spanel, Abram N
American. Businessman, Inventor,
 Philanthropist
Founded International Latex (now
 Playtex) Corp., 1932; held over 2,000
 patents.
b. May 15, 1901 in Odessa, Russia
d. Mar 30, 1985 in Princeton, New
 Jersey
Source: *BioIn 14, 24; NewYTBS 85; WhoAm 82; WhoFI 74*

Spanier, Muggsy
[Francis Joseph Spanier]
American. Jazz Musician
Noted Dixieland cornetist; with Ted
 Lewis, 1929-36; led own band, early
 1940s; used plunger mute.
b. Nov 9, 1906 in Chicago, Illinois
d. Feb 12, 1967 in Sausalito, California
Source: *AllMGJa; BakBD 84, 92; BiDJaz; BioIn 7, 8; CmpEPM; EncJzS; IlEncJ; LegTOT; MusMk; NewAmDM; NewGrDA 86; NewGrDJ 88, 94; NewGrDM 80; ObitT 1961; OxCPMus; PenEncP; WhAm 4; WhoHol B; WhoJazz 72; WhScrn 74, 77; WorAl; WorAlBi*

Spann, Otis
American. Pianist
Blues music pianist and boogie-woogie
 piano master; played with Muddy
 Waters band, 1953-1969; released *Otis
 Spann Is the Blues,* 1960, which
 includes song "This Is the Blues,"
 and *Cryin' Time,* 1969; inducted into
 Blues Hall of Fame, 1980.
b. Mar 21, 1939 in Jackson, Mississippi
d. Apr 24, 1970 in Chicago, Illinois

Spano, Joe
American. Actor
Played Henry Goldblum on TV series
 "Hill Street Blues," 1981-87.
b. Jul 7, 1946 in San Francisco,
 California
Source: *ConTFT 5; VarWW 85; WhoAm 90; WhoEnt 92; WhoHol 92; WhoWest 89*

Spargo, John
American. Museum Director
Founder, director, curator, Bennington
Historical Museum, 1927-54.
b. Jan 31, 1876 in Stithians, England
d. Aug 17, 1966 in Bennington, Vermont
Source: *AmAu&B; AmLY; AmNatBi;
BiDAmLf; BioIn 1, 7, 9; CamDcAB;
ConAu 89; DcAmB S8; DcAmImH;
DcAmSR; EncAB-A 6, 39; EncAL;
LinLib L; NatCAB 52; OxCAmH;
REnAL; WhAm 4; WhLit; WhNAA*

Spark, Muriel Sarah
Scottish. Author
Satirist; best-known novel, *The Prime of
Miss Jean Brodie*, 1961, was adapted
to film, stage.
b. Feb 1, 1918 in Edinburgh, Scotland
Source: *BioIn 13, 16; CamBiEn;
ChamBiD; CmScLit; CnDBLB 7; ConAu
12NR, 36NR, 76NR; ConLC 18; ConNov
86, 91; ConPo 91; CyWA 89; DcLB 15;
EncBrWW; EncWB 98; FacFETw;
FemiCLE; HalFC 88; IntAu&W 91;
IntWW 83, 91; InWom SUP; LiExTwC;
MajTwCW 1, 2; ModBrL S1; NewC;
PenC ENG; RAdv 1; REn; RfGEnL 91;
SJGYouA 2; TwCWr; WebE&AL; Who
85, 92; WhoAm 86, 90, 99, 2000;
WhoWor 84, 91; WorAlBi; WorAu 1950;
WrDr 86, 92, 98, 99, 2000*

Sparkman, John Jackson
American. Government Official
Dem. senator from AL, 1947-79; Adlai
Stevenson's vice presidential running
mate, 1952.
b. Dec 20, 1899 in Morgan County,
Alabama
d. Nov 16, 1985 in Huntsville, Alabama
Source: *AmNatBi; BiDrAC; BiDrUSC
89; BioIn 2, 3, 5, 7, 9, 10, 11;
CamDcAB; CurBio 50, 86; EncSoH;
IntYB 83; IntYB 78, 79, 80; ScrEAmL
1; WhAm 9; Who 74; WhoAm 74;
WhoAmP 73; WhoGov 72, 75, 77;
WhoSSW 73*

Sparks, Jared
American. Editor, Historian
Pres. of Harvard, 1849-53; edited *North
American Review*, 1820s; wrote about
US history.
b. May 10, 1789 in Willington,
Connecticut
d. Mar 14, 1866
Source: *Alli; AmAu; AmAu&B; AmBi;
AmNatBi; ApCAB; Benet 87, 96;
BenetAL 91; BiDAmEd; BiD&SB; BioIn
3, 6, 9, 11, 14; CelCen; ChamBiD;
CyAL 1; DcAmAu; DcAmB; DcAmBC;
DcBiPP; DcLB 1, 30; DcNAA; Drake;
EncAB-H 1974, 1996; EncALit; EncWB
98; HarEnUS; LinLib L, S; LuthC 75;
McGEWB; NatCAB 5; OxCAmH;
OxCAmL 65, 83, 95; REn; REnAL;
TwCBDA; WebAB 74, 79; WhAm HS*

Sparks, Ned
[Edward A Sparkman]
American. Actor
Character actor, 1922-47; films include
Magic Town, 1947.
b. 1883 in Guelph, Ontario, Canada
d. Apr 2, 1957 in Apple Valley,
California
Source: *BioIn 4; DcPseud; EncAFC;
Film 1, 2; FilmEn; FilmgC; HalFC 80,
84, 88; LegTOT; MotPP; MovMk; TwYS;
Vers A; WhoHol B; WhScrn 74, 77, 83*

Spartacus
Thracian. Slave
Led slave revolt, Servile War, 73-71 BC;
finally beaten after winning several
battles against the Romans.
d. 71BC
Source: *Benet 87, 96; BioIn 1, 3, 5, 6, 7,
8, 9, 20, 24; CamBiEn; ChamBiD;
DcAmSR; EncRev; EncWB 98;
GenMudB; HarEnMi; LegTOT; LinLib S;
MacEWoS; McGEWB; OxCClL, 89;
REn; WebBD 83; WhDW; WorAl;
WorAlBi*

Spassky, Boris Vasilyevich
Russian. Chess Player, Journalist
World chess champion, 1969-72; lost
title to Bobby Fischer, 1972.
b. Jan 30, 1937 in Leningrad, Union of
Soviet Socialist Republics
Source: *BiDSovU; BioIn 15, 17, 18;
CamBiEn; CurBio 72; FacFETw;
IntAu&W 89; IntWW 74, 91; OxCChes
84; WhoWor 76, 78*

Spaulding, Charles Clinton
American. Insurance Executive
President, North Carolina Mutual Life
Insurance Co., 1923-52, building it
into the largest all-black business
enterprise in the world in 1952.
b. Aug 1, 1874 in Clarkton, North
Carolina
d. Aug 1, 1952 in Durham, North
Carolina
Source: *BiDAmBL 83; BioIn 1, 2, 3, 5,
6, 8, 9, 12, 20, 24; ConBlB 9; DcAmB
S5; DcAmNB; EncSoH; EncWB 98;
InB&W 80, 85; NatCAB 42; WhoColR*

Speaker, Tris(tram E)
"Spoke"; "The Grey Eagle"
American. Baseball Player
Outfielder, 1907-28, mostly with Boston,
Cleveland; holds ML record for
doubles in career, 793; Hall of Fame,
1937.
b. Apr 4, 1888 in Hubbard City, Texas
d. Dec 8, 1958 in Lake Whitney, Texas
Source: *Ballpl 90; BiDAmSp BB; BioIn
2, 3, 4, 5, 6, 7, 8, 9, 10, 13, 14, 15, 17;
CamBiEn; CamDcAB; FacFETw;
LegTOT; WhoProB 73; WhScrn 83;
WorAlBi*

Speakes, Larry Melvin
American. Government Official
Deputy press secretary under Reagan,
1981-87.

b. Sep 13, 1939 in Cleveland,
Mississippi
Source: *BioIn 15, 16; IntWW 91, 97, 98,
2000; WhoAm 84, 90, 97, 98, 99, 2000;
WhoAmP 91; WhoFI 92; WhoGov 75;
WrDr 98, 99, 2000*

Speaks, Oley
American. Songwriter
Hits include "On the Road to
Mandalay," 1907; "Sylvia," 1914.
b. Jun 28, 1874 in Canal Winchester,
Ohio
d. Aug 27, 1948 in New York, New
York
Source: *AmNatBi; ASCAP 66, 80;
BakBD 78, 84, 92; BakBDTw; BiDAmM;
CmpEPM; ConAmC 76, 82; DcAmB S4;
InWom SUP; NewAmDM; NewGrDA 86;
NotNAT B; OxCMus; OxCPMus;
PopAmC; WhAm 2*

Speare, Elizabeth George
American. Children's Author
Won Newbery Medals for *The Witch of
Blackbird Pond*, 1959; *The Bronze
Bow*, 1962.
b. Nov 21, 1908 in Melrose,
Massachusetts
d. Nov 15, 1994 in Tucson, Arizona
Source: *AmAu&B; AmWomWr; Au&Wr
71; AuBYP 2, 3; BioIn 14, 17, 19, 20,
21, 24; ChlBkCr; ChlLR 8; ConAu 1R,
147; CurBio 59, 95N; DcAmChF 1960;
ForWC 70; IntAu&W 77, 82; InWom;
MajAI, SUP; MorBMP; MorJA; NewbC
1956; OxCChiL; SJGYouA 2; SmATA 5,
62, 83; TwCChW 1, 2, 3; TwCYAW 1;
WhAm 11; WhoAm 74, 76, 78, 80, 82,
84, 86, 88, 90, 92, 94; WhoAmW 64, 66,
68, 70, 72, 74, 93; WrDr 76, 80, 82, 84,
86, 88, 90, 92, 94, 96*

Speck, Frank Gouldsmith
American. Anthropologist
Cultural anthropologist; pioneered studies
in ethnoscience and ethnomusicology;
known for work on Algonquin Indians.
b. Nov 8, 1881 in New York, New York
d. Feb 6, 1950 in Philadelphia,
Pennsylvania
Source: *AmAu&B; AmNatBi; BenetAL
91; BioIn 2, 13, 14; DcAmB S4;
OxCCan; REnAL; WhAm 2A; WhLit*

Speck, Richard Franklin
American. Murderer
Killed eight student nurses in Chicago,
July 13-14, 1966.
b. Dec 6, 1941 in Kirkwood, Illinois
d. Dec 5, 1991 in Joliet, Illinois
Source: *BioIn 7, 15; MurCaTw;
NewYTBS 91*

Specter, Arlen
American. Politician
Rep. senator from PA, 1981—.
b. Feb 12, 1930 in Wichita, Kansas
Source: *AlmAP 82, 84, 88, 92, 96, 2000;
BiDrUSC 89; BioIn 7, 12, 16; CngDr
81, 83, 85, 87, 89, 91, 93, 95; CurBio
88; IntWW 81, 82, 83, 89, 91, 93, 97,
98, 2000; IntYB 82; LegTOT; PolsAm*

84; WhoAm 84, 86, 88, 90, 92, 94, 95, 96, 97, 98, 99, 2000; WhoAmP 73, 75, 77, 79, 81, 83, 85, 87, 89, 91, 93, 95, 97, 1999; WhoAmW 70; WhoE 74, 75, 83, 85, 86, 89, 91, 93, 95, 97, 99; WhoWor 82, 87, 89, 91

Spector, Phil(lip Harvey)
American. Producer
Devised "wall of sound" technique of sound arrangement, 1962; highlights lead vocals; inducted into Rock-'n'-Roll Hall of Fame, 1989.
b. Dec 26, 1940 in New York, New York
Source: *BioIn 9, 12, 16; ConMus 4; CurBio 89; DcArts; EncPR&S 89; EncRk 88; IlEncBM 82; IlEncRk; LegTOT; MusMk; NewGrDA 86; News 89-1; OxCPMus; PenEncP; RkWW 82; RolSEnR 83; SoulM; WhoAm 78, 80, 82, 84, 86, 88, 90, 92, 94, 95, 96, 97; WhoEnt 92; WhoHol 92; WhoRock 81; WhoRocM 82; WhoWest 92, 94; WorAl; WorAlBi*

Spectorsky, Auguste Compte
American. Journalist
Associate publisher, *Playboy* mag., 1956-72; best known for witty book, *The Exurbanites*, 1955.
b. Aug 13, 1910 in Paris, France
d. Jan 17, 1972 in Saint Croix, Virgin Islands of the United States
Source: *AmAu&B; ConAu P-2; CurBio 60, 72; NewYTBE 72; REnAL; WhAm 5*

Spedding, Frank Harold
American. Chemist
Pioneered advances in cheaper production of rare-earth metals; was instrumental in developing methods of extracting pure uranium for use in nuclear chain reaction experiments.
b. Oct 22, 1902 in Hamilton, Ontario, Canada
d. Dec 15, 1984 in Ames, Iowa
Source: *AmMWSc 76P, 79, 82; AnObit 1984; AsBiEn; BioIn 1, 3, 8, 14, 15; BlueB 76; CamBiEn; ChamBiD; ConAu 162; IntWW 74, 75, 76, 77, 78, 79, 80, 81, 82, 83; LarDcSc; McGMS 80; NotTwCS 1; WhAm 8; WhoAm 74, 76; WhoTech 84; WhoWor 74*

Speer, Albert
German. Architect
Germany's official architect under Hitler; helped plan war economy with Goering.
b. Mar 19, 1905 in Mannheim, Germany
d. Sep 1, 1981 in London, England
Source: *AnObit 1981; BiDExR; BioIn 1, 2, 3, 8, 9, 10, 11, 12, 13, 14, 15, 16, 18, 21, 22, 24; CamBiEn; ChamBiD; ConArch 80; ConAu 40NR, 65, 104; CurBio 76, 81, 81N; DcArch; DcArts; DcTwHis; EncTR, 91; EncWB 2-19; FacFETw; HisEWW; HisWorL; LegTOT; MacEA; NewCol 75; NewYTBS 81; WhWW-II*

Speicher, Eugene Edward
American. Artist
Portraitist; best example of realistic painting, *Lilya*, 1930.
b. Apr 5, 1883 in Buffalo, New York
d. May 11, 1962 in Woodstock, New York
Source: *BioIn 1, 2, 4, 6; BriEAA; CamDcAB; CurBio 47, 62; DcCAA 71; McGDA; OxCAmH; WhAm 4*

Speidel, Hans
German. Military Leader
Part of abortive plot to assassinate Hitler, 1944; commanded Allied land forces in central Europe for NATO, 1957-63.
b. Oct 28, 1897 in Metzingen, Germany
d. Nov 28, 1984 in Bad Honnef, Germany (West)
Source: *BioIn 2, 3, 4, 11, 14, 17; CamBiEn; ChamBiD; ConAu 114, 133; CurBio 85, 85N; EncTR, 91; HarEnMi; IntWW 74, 75, 76, 77, 78, 79, 80, 81, 82, 83; IntYB 78, 79, 80, 81, 82; NewYTBS 84; Who 74, 82, 83, 85; WhWW-II*

Speight, Johnny
English. Writer
Created BBC series "Till Death Do Us Part," 1966-75; adapted in US as "All in the Family," 1971.
b. Jun 2, 1921? in London, England
Source: *BioIn 10; ConAu 117, 169; ConDr 73, 77, 82C; ConTFT 22; DcLEL 1940; IntAu&W 77, 91; Who 92; WrDr 76, 80, 82, 84, 86, 88, 90, 92, 94, 96, 99*

Speke, John Hanning
English. Explorer
Discovered Lake Victoria, 1858, confirmed as source of the Nile, 1862.
b. May 4, 1827 in Jordans, England
d. Sep 18, 1864 in Bath, England
Source: *Alli; BbD; BiD&SB; BioIn 4, 5, 6, 8, 9, 18, 20, 21, 22, 24; BritAu 19; CamBiEn; CamGEL; CamGLE; CelCen; ChamBiD; DcAfHiB 86; DcBiPP; DcLB 166; DcLEL; DcNaB; EncWB 98; EvLB; Expl 93; ExplAnT; HisDBrE; LinLib L, S; McGEWB; NewC; NewCBEL; OxCBrHi; OxCEng 67, 85, 95; WhWE*

Spelling, Aaron
American. Producer
Most successful TV producer; shows include "Charlie's Angels," "Dynasty," "Hotel," "Beverly Hills 90210."
b. Apr 22, 1923 in Dallas, Texas
Source: *BioIn 16; CamDcAB; CelR 90; ConTFT 3, 12, 23; CurBio 86; IntMPA 92; IntWW 2000; LesBEnT, 92; NewYTBS 91; St&PR 91; WhoAm 86, 90, 92, 94, 95, 96, 97, 98, 99, 2000; WhoEnt 92, 98; WhoHol A; WhoMedi 98; WhoTelC; WorAlBi*

Spelling, Tori
[Victoria Spelling]
American. Actor
Plays Donna Martin on TV series "Beverly Hills 90210;" daughter of Aaron Spelling.

b. May 16, 1973 in Los Angeles, California
Source: *ConTFT 26; LegTOT*

Spellman, Francis Joseph
American. Religious Leader
Appointed Archbishop of NY, 1939, cardinal, 1946 by Pope Pius XII.
b. May 4, 1889 in Whitman, Massachusetts
d. Dec 2, 1967 in New York, New York
Source: *AmAu&B; AmNatBi; BioIn 1, 2, 3, 4, 5, 6, 7, 8, 9, 11, 12; CamBiEn; CamDcAB; CathA 1930; ChhPo; ColdWar 2; ConAu 113; CurBio 40, 47, 68; DcAmB S8; DcAmReB 1, 2; EncAB-H 1974, 1996; EncARH; EncRelA; EncVieW; EncWB 98; LinLib S; McGEWB; WebAB 74, 79; WhAm 4; WhNAA; WorAl; WorAlBi*

Spemann, Hans
German. Educator, Biologist
Won Nobel Prize in medicine, 1935, for work on embryonic development.
b. Jun 27, 1869 in Stuttgart, Germany
d. Sep 12, 1941 in Freiburg, Germany
Source: *AsBiEn; BiESc; BioIn 3, 6, 12, 14, 15, 20; CamBiEn; ChamBiD; ConAu 162; DcScB; EncWB 98; InSci; LarDcSc; McGCEnS; McGEWB; NobelP; NotTwCS 1; RanHWDS; WhoNob, 90, 95; WorAl; WorAlBi*

Spence, Basil Urwin, Sir
English. Architect
Designed new Coventry Cathedral, 1951.
b. Aug 13, 1907 in Bombay, India
d. Nov 18, 1976 in Eye, England
Source: *Au&Wr 71; BioIn 3, 5, 9, 11, 14, 21; CamBiEn; ChamBiD; ConArch 87, 94; ConDes 84, 97; DcArch; DcBrAr 1; DcNaB 1971; GrBr; IntWW 74, 75, 76; OxCBrHi; WebBD 83; Who 74; WhoWor 74*

Spence, Lewis
[James Lewis Thomas Chalmers Spence]
Scottish. Editor, Poet, Folklorist
Wrote on occult, Mexican mythology: *The Occult Sciences in Atlantis*, 1943.
b. Nov 25, 1874 in Dundee, Scotland
d. Mar 3, 1955 in Edinburgh, Scotland
Source: *BioIn 3, 4, 22; ChhPo, S1, S3; CmScLit; ConAu 115; EncO&P 1, 2, 3; EvLB; ObitT 1951; OxCTwCP; PenC ENG; ScF&FL 1; TwCA SUP; WhLit; WhoLA; WorAu 1900*

Spencer, Herbert
English. Philosopher
Applied Darwin's doctrine of evolution to philosophy, ethics; wrote *Principles of Sociology*, 1876-96.
b. Apr 27, 1820 in Derby, England
d. Dec 8, 1903 in Brighton, England
Source: *Alli, SUP; AsBiEn; BbD; Benet 87, 96; BiCoLiE; BiD&SB; BiDPsy; BiESc; BioIn 1, 3, 4, 5, 6, 7, 8, 9, 10, 11, 13, 14, 15, 16, 19, 21, 23; BlmGEL; BritAu 19; CamBiEn; CamGEL; CamGLE; CasWL; CelCen; ChamBiD; Chambr 3; CyEd; DcAmC; DcAmSR;*

DcBiPP; DcEnA, A; DcEnL; DcLB 57;
DcLEL; DcNaB S2; DcScB; DcSoc;
Dis&D; EncEth; EncUnb; EncUrb;
EncWB 98; EvLB; InSci; IntDcAn;
LarDcSc; LinLib L, S; LngCEL; LuthC
75; McGEWB; ModJap; NamesHP;
NewC; NewCBEL; OxCBrHi; OxCEng
67, 85, 95; OxCLaw; OxCPhil; PenC
ENG; RAdv 14, 13-3, 13-4; REn;
VicBrit; WebE&AL; WhAm HS; WhDW;
WorAl; WorAlBi; WrPh P

Spencer, Percy Le Baron
American. Inventor
Invented the microwave oven, 1946.
b. Jul 9, 1894 in Howland, Maine
d. Sep 7, 1970 in Newton, Massachusetts
Source: NewYTBE 70; WhAm 5

Spencer, Stanley, Sir
English. Artist
Drew surrealistic religious paintings
  including Resurrection series, 1945-50.
b. Jun 30, 1891 in Cookham-on-Thames,
  England
d. Dec 14, 1959 in Taplow, England
Source: BioIn 1, 2, 3, 4, 5, 6, 7, 9, 11,
12, 14, 17, 22, 23; CamBiEn; ChambiD;
ConArt 77, 83; DcArts; DcBrAr 1;
DcNaB 1951; DcTwArt; FacFETw;
GrBr; IntDcAA 90; McGDA; NewCol
75; ObitT 1951; OxCArt; OxCCAA;
OxCTwCA; OxDcArt; PhDcTCA 77;
TwCPaSc; WhDW; WorArt 1950

Spencer, William
American. Author
Historical writings include Historical
  Dictionary of Morocco, 1980.
b. Jun 1, 1922 in Erie, Pennsylvania
Source: AuBYP 2, 3; BioIn 11; ConAu
8NR, 17R, 23NR; DrAS 74H, 78H;
Dun&B 90; IntAu&W 76, 77, 82, 86, 89,
91, 93; IntMed 80; SmATA 9; WhoFla;
WrDr 76, 80, 82, 84, 86, 88, 90, 92, 94,
96, 98, 99, 2000

Spencer Davis Group, The
[Spencer Davis; Muff Winwood; Stevie
  Winwood; Pete York]
English. Music Group
Hits include "Gimme Some Lovin',"
  1967.
Source: BillEnR; ConMuA 80A, 80B;
ConMus 19; EncPR&S 89; EncRk 88;
IlEncRk; RkOn 78; RolSEnR 83; WhoHol
92; WhoRock 81; WhoRocM 82; WhScrn
83

Spender, Stephen (Harold)
English. Author, Poet
Wrote autobiography World Within
  World, 1951; Collected Poems, 1954.
b. Feb 28, 1909 in London, England
d. Jul 16, 1995 in London, England
Source: Au&Wr 71; AuBYP 2S, 3; Benet
87, 96; BiCoLiE; BioIn 1, 2, 3, 4, 5, 8,
9, 10, 11, 12, 13, 14, 15, 16, 17, 18, 19,
20, 21; BlmGEL; BlueB 76; BritWr S2;
CamBiEn; CamGEL; CamGLE; CasWL;
Chambr 3; ChhPo, S2, S3; CnDBLB 7;
CnE&AP; CnMD; CnMWL; ConAu 9R,
31NR, 54NR, 149; ConLC 1, 2, 5, 10,

41, 91; ConLCrt 77, 82; ConPo 70, 75,
80, 85, 91, 96; CurBio 40, 77, 95N;
CyWA 58, 89; DcArts; DcLB 20;
DcLEL; EncWB, 98; EncWL 1, 2, 2S;
EngPo; EvLB; FacFETw; GayLL 1;
GrWrEL P; IntAu&W 76, 77, 91, 93;
IntWW 74, 75, 76, 77, 78, 79, 80, 81, 82,
83, 89, 91, 93; IntWWP 77; LegTOT;
LinLib L, S; LngCEL; LngCTC;
MajTwCW 1, 2; MakMC; ModBrL, S1,
S2; ModWD; NewC; NewCBEL;
NewYTBS 95; OxCEng 67, 85, 95;
OxCTwCL; OxCTwCP; PenC ENG;
RAdv 1, 14, 13-1; REn; RfGEnL 91;
RGTwCWr; TwCA, SUP; TwCWr;
WebE&AL; WhDW; WhE&EA; Who 74,
82, 83, 85, 88, 90, 92, 94; WhoAm 76;
WhoTwCL; WhoWor 74, 78, 80, 82, 91;
WorAl; WorAlBi; WorAu 1900; WrDr
76, 80, 82, 84, 86, 88, 90, 92, 94, 96,
98N

Spener, Philipp Jakob
German. Theologian
Regarded as the father of the movement
  called Pietism, he tried to infuse new
  spirit into the formal Lutheranism of
  the 17th century.
b. Jan 23, 1635 in Rappoltsweiler,
  Germany
d. Feb 5, 1705, Germany
Source: BiDChrM; BioIn 22; DcLB 164;
EncWB 98; McGEWB; OxCGer 76, 86,
97

Spengler, Oswald
German. Philosopher
Best known for Decline of the West,
  1918-22.
b. May 29, 1880 in Blankenburg,
  Germany
d. May 8, 1936 in Munich, Germany
Source: Benet 87, 96; BiDExR; BioIn 2,
4, 7, 9, 10, 12, 13, 14, 22; CamBiEn;
CasWL; ChambiD; ConAu 118;
EncGRNM; EncRev; EncTR, 91; EncWB
98; EvEuW; FacFETw; GloEncH;
LegTOT; LinLib L, S; LngCTC; LuthC
75; MakMC; McGEWB; OxCGer 76, 86,
97; RAdv 14, 13-3; REn; ThTwC 87;
TwCA, SUP; TwCLC 25; TwCWr;
WhDW; WorAl; WorAlBi; WrPh P

Spenkelink, John Arthur
American. Murderer
First person involuntarily executed in US
  since 1967.
b. 1949 in Buena Park, California
d. May 25, 1979 in Starke, Florida
Source: BioIn 11, 12

Spenser, Edmund
English. Poet
Developed Spenserian stanza used in
  allegorical epic The Faerie Queen,
  1596.
b. 1552? in London, England
d. Jan 13, 1599 in London, England
Source: Alli; AtlBL; BbD; Benet 87, 96;
BiCoLiE; BiD&SB; BiDRP&D; BioIn 1,
2, 3, 4, 5, 6, 7, 8, 9, 10, 11, 12, 14, 15,
18, 19, 20, 21, 22, 23, 24; BlmGEL;
BritAu; CamBiEn; CamGEL; CamGLE;

CasWL; ChambiD; Chambr 1; ChhPo,
S1, S2; CnDBLB 1; CnE&AP; CroE&S;
CrtT 1, 4; CyEd; CyWA 58, 97; DcArts;
DcEnA; DcEnL; DcEuL; DcIrL 96;
DcLB 167; DcLEL; DcNaB; EncApL;
EncWB 98; EvLB; GrWrEL P; LegTOT;
LinLib L, S; LitC 5, 39; LngCEL; LuthC
75; MagSWL; McGEWB; MouLC 1;
NewC; NewCBEL; NotPoe; OxCBrHi;
OxCEng 67, 85, 95; OxCIri; PenC ENG;
PoeCrit 8; PoLE; RAdv 1, 14, 13-1;
RComWL; REn; RfGEnL 91; RGFBP;
WebE&AL; WhDW; WorAl; WorAlBi;
WorLitC; WrPh

Speransky, Mikhail
Russian. Political Leader
Chief adviser to Czar Alexander, 1808-
  12, under Nicholas I was responsible
  for systemized Russian laws, 1833.
b. 1772
d. 1839
Source: ChambiD; NewCol 75

Sperling, Godfrey, Jr.
American. Journalist
Chief of Washington Bureau, Christian
  Science Monitor, 1973-83; senior
  Washington columnist, 1984—.
b. Sep 25, 1915 in Long Beach,
  California
Source: BiDAmNC; BioIn 9; WhoAm 74,
76, 78, 80, 82, 84, 86, 88, 90, 92, 94,
95, 96, 97, 98, 99, 2000; WhoSSW 73

Sperry, Armstrong W
American. Author, Illustrator, Children's
  Author
Most of writings based on his travel
  adventures throughout the world.
b. Nov 7, 1897 in New Haven,
  Connecticut
d. Apr 28, 1976 in Hanover, New
  Hampshire
Source: AnCL; CurBio 41; IlsCB 1744,
1946; JBA 34, 51; NewbMB 1922;
SmATA 1, 27; Str&VC

Sperry, Elmer Ambrose
American. Inventor
Invented gyrocompass and numerous
  electrical devices.
b. Oct 12, 1860 in Cortland, New York
d. Jun 10, 1930 in New York, New York
Source: AmBi; AmNatBi; ApCAB X;
AsBiEn; BiDAmBL 83; BiESc; BioIn 3,
4, 5, 6, 9, 12, 13, 19, 20, 21; CamBiEn;
CamDcAB; ChambiD; DcAmB; DcScB;
EncAB-H 1974, 1996; InSci; LinLib S;
NatCAB 15, 23; NewCol 75; OxCAmH;
OxCShps; RanHWDS; WebAB 74, 79;
WhAm 1; WhDW; WorAl

Sperry, Roger W(olcott)
American. Biologist
Won Nobel Prize, 1981, for contributions
  to understanding human brain.
b. Aug 20, 1913 in Hartford, Connecticut
d. Apr 17, 1994 in Pasadena, California
Source: AmMWSc 73S, 78S, 82, 86, 89,
92; BiDcPsy; BiESc; BioIn 12, 13, 14,
15, 19, 20, 21, 22; BlueB 76; CamBiEn;
CamDcAB; CamDcSc; ChambiD; ConAu

157; CurBio 86, 94N; IntWW 74, 75, 76, 77, 78, 79, 80, 81, 82, 83, 89, 91, 93; LarDcSc; McGCEnS; McGMS 80; NewYTBS 81; RanHWDS; WhAm 11; Who 83, 85, 88, 90, 92, 94; WhoAm 74, 76, 78, 80, 82, 84, 86, 88, 90, 92, 94; WhoFrS 84; WhoNob, 90, 95; WhoScEn 94; WhoUSWr 88; WhoWest 82, 84, 87, 89, 92, 94; WhoWor 74, 84, 87, 89, 91, 93; WhoWrEP 89, 92; WorAlBi

Sperti, George Speri
American. Scientist, Inventor
Holder of over 100 patents including Preparation H and Aspercreme.
b. Jan 17, 1900 in Covington, Kentucky
d. Apr 29, 1991 in Cincinnati, Ohio
Source: AmCath 80; AmMWSc 73P, 76P, 79, 82, 86, 89; AmNatBi; BioIn 2, 14, 17; CurBio 91N; InSci; IntWW 74, 75, 76, 77, 78, 79, 80, 81, 82, 83, 89, 91; InWom SUP; News 89-2; WhAm 10; WhoAm 74, 76, 78, 80, 86, 88; WhoEnt 92; WorInv

Spethmann, Dieter
German. Business Executive
Chairman of German steelmaker Thyssen since 1973.
b. 1926? in Essen, Germany
Source: BioIn 15; IntWW 77

Spewack, Bella Cohen
[Mrs. Samuel Spewack]
American. Dramatist, Journalist
With husband, wrote Broadway hits Boy Meets Girl, 1935, Kiss Me Kate, 1949.
b. Mar 25, 1899 in Bucharest, Romania
d. Apr 27, 1990 in New York, New York
Source: AmAu&B; AmWomD; AmWomPl; Au&Wr 71; BenetAL 91; BiDAmM; BiE&WWA; BioIn 4, 7, 9, 16; CnMD; ConAu 33R; ConDr 73, 82D; DcAmB S9; EncAFC; EncMT; FilmEn; IntMPA 88; InWom, SUP; McGEWD 72, 84; ModWD; NewCBMT; NewYTBS 76, 90; NotNAT, B; NotWoAT; OxCAmT 84; REn, REnAL; TwCA, SUP; WhAm 5, 10; WhJnl; WhoAm 74, 76; WhoThe 77; WhThe; WomWMM; WorAu 1900

Spewack, Samuel
Russian. Dramatist
With wife Bella, wrote Broadway hits Boy Meets Girl, 1935, Kiss Me Kate, 1949.
b. Sep 16, 1899 in Bachmut, Russia
d. Oct 14, 1971 in New York, New York
Source: AmAu&B; AmNatBi; Au&Wr 71; BenetAL 91; BiDAmM; BiE&WWA; BioIn 4, 7, 9, 16, 22; CnMD; ConAu 33R; DcAmB S9; EncAFC; FilmEn; McGEWD 72, 84; ModWD; NewCBMT; NewYTBE 71; NotNAT B; OxCAmT 84; REn, REnAL; TwCA, SUP; WhAm 5; WhJnl; WhThe; WorAu 1900

Spheeris, Penelope
American. Filmmaker
Founded music video production company, Rock n' Reel, 1974. Films The Decline of Western Civilization I-

II, 1980-88 depict punk and heavy-metal movements.
b. 1945
Source: ConTFT 11; IntMPA 88, 92, 94, 96; IntWWW 2; LegTOT; MiSFD 9; News 89-2; WhoAm 92, 94, 95, 96, 97, 98, 99, 2000; WhoAmW 95; WhoEnt 92, 98; WomFilm

Spicer, Jack
American. Poet
Wrote first book of poetry, After Lorca, 1957, in which he "communicates" with the Spanish poet Federico Garcia Lorca.
b. 1925 in Hollywood, California
d. 1965
Source: AmAu&B; BenetAL 91; BioIn 12, 13, 23, 24; ConAu 85; ConLC 8, 18, 72; ConPo 80A, 85A; CyWA 97; DcLB 5, 16, 193; EncALit; GayLL 1; OxCAmL 83, 95; OxCTwCL; OxCTwCP; PenC AM

Spiegel, Sam
[S P Eagle]
American. Producer
Won Oscars for On the Waterfront, 1954; The Bridge on the River Kwai, 1957; Lawrence of Arabia, 1962.
b. Nov 11, 1904 in Jaroslau, Austria
d. Dec 31, 1985, St. Martin
Source: BiDFilm, 81, 94; FilmgC; IntMPA 82; OxCFilm; WhoAm 78, 80, 82, 84; WhoAmA 73, 76, 78, 80, 82, 84; WhoAmJ 80; WhoWorJ 72, 78; WorEFlm

Spiegelman, Art
[Joe Cutrate; Al Flooglebuckle; Skeeter Grant]
American. Cartoonist, Writer
Published Maus: A Survivor's Tale I: My Father Bleeds History, 1986 and Maus: A Survivor's Tale II: And Here My Troubles Began, 1991; both about the experiences of a Jew in Nazi-occupied Poland; won Pulitzer Prize, 1992, for these books.
b. Feb 15, 1948 in Stockholm, Sweden
Source: Au&Arts 10; BioIn 10; ConAu 41NR, 55NR, 74NR, 125; ConGrA 3; ConJeAN; ConLC 76; CurBio 94; EncACom; MajTwCW 2; MugS; News 98, 98-3; SJGYouA 2; SmATA 109; TwCYAW 1; WhoAm 92, 94, 95, 96, 97, 98, 99, 2000; WhoE 95, 97, 99; WhoEnt 98; WhoPul

Spielberg, David
American. Actor
Noted for TV, stage, film work; won Obie for Sleep, 1971.
b. Mar 6, 1939 in Mercedes, Texas
Source: BioIn 11; ConTFT 1, 5; HalFC 84, 88; VarWW 85; WhoEnt 92; WhoHol 92

Spielberg, Steven
American. Director, Producer
Films include Jaws, 1975; ET, 1982; Schindler's List, 1993; Jurassic Park;

won 1999 best director Oscar for Saving Private Ryan.
b. Dec 18, 1947 in Cincinnati, Ohio
Source: AmDec 1980; JeHun; LegTOT; LesBEnT 92; MiSFD 9; NewEScF; News 93, 97; NewYTBS 82; OnHuYAF; ScF&FL 92; ScFSB; SmATA 32; Who 88, 90, 92, 94, 98, 99, 2000; WhoAm 80, 82, 84, 86, 88, 90, 92, 94, 95, 96, 97, 98; WhoEnt 92, 98; WhoFI 98; WorAlBi; WorFDir 2

Spielhagen, Friedrich von
German. Writer
Popular social novelist; wrote Problematische Naturen, 1861.
b. Feb 24, 1829 in Magdeburg, Prussia
d. Feb 25, 1911 in Berlin, Germany
Source: Benet 87; OxCGer 86

Spier, Peter Edward
American. Artist, Author
Self-illustrated children's books include Gobble, Growl, Grunt, 1971.
b. Jun 6, 1927 in Amsterdam, Netherlands
Source: AuBYP 2S, 2SA, 3; BioIn 16; BkP; ConAu 5R, 41NR; IlsBYP; IlsCB 1946, 1957; MajAI; SJGChWr 5; SmATA 4; ThrBJA; WhoAm 74, 76, 78, 80, 82, 84, 86, 88, 90, 94, 95, 96, 97, 98, 99, 2000; WhoAmA 76, 78, 80, 82, 84, 86, 89, 91, 93, 1999; WrDr 2000

Spigelgass, Leonard
American. Dramatist
Oscar nominee for best original story: Mystery Street, 1950.
b. Nov 26, 1908 in New York, New York
d. Feb 14, 1985 in Los Angeles, California
Source: BiE&WWA; BioIn 14; ConAu 103, 115; IntMPA 77, 80, 82; NotNAT; WhoAm 74, 76; WhoThe 72, 77

Spikes, Dolores
American. University Administrator
President of the University of Maryland-Eastern Shore (UMES), 1996—; committed to making college education accessible to more students, particularly through historically black land-grant universities.
b. Aug 24, 1936 in Baton Rouge, Louisiana
Source: ConBlB 18

Spillane, Mickey
[Frank Morrison Spillane]
American. Author
Known for Mike Hammer detective stories.
b. Mar 9, 1918 in New York, New York
Source: AmAu&B; BeaEPF; Benet 87, 96; BenetAL 91; BioIn 2, 3, 4, 5, 6, 9, 11, 12, 14, 15, 17, 21, 24; CamBiEn; CelR, 90; ChamBiD; ConAu 25R, 28NR, X; ConLC 3, 13; CorpD; CrtSuMy; CurBio 81; DcArts; DcTwCCu 1; EncMys; FacFETw; FilmgC; HalFC 80, 84, 88; IntAu&W 91; LegTOT; LinLib L; LngCTC; MajTwCW 1; MysSW; Novels;

OxCAmL 65, 83, 95; PenC AM; RAdv 14; REn; SmATA 66; SpyFic; TwCCr&M 80, 85, 91; TwCWr; VioAm; WebAB 74, 79; WhoAm 76, 78, 80, 82, 84, 86, 88, 90, 92, 94, 95, 96, 97, 98, 99, 2000; WhoHol 92, A; WhoWrEP 89; WorAl; WorAlBi; WrDr 76, 80, 82, 84, 86, 88, 90, 92, 94, 96, 98, 99, 2000

Spilsbury, Bernard Henry, Sir
English. Pathologist
Homicide expert; subject of *Scalpel of Scotland Yard,* 1952.
b. 1877 in Leamington, England
d. Dec 17, 1947 in London, England
Source: *BioIn 1, 2, 5, 7, 10, 14; CamBiEn; ChamBiD; CopCroC; DcNaB 1941; GrBr; InSci; LngCTC; ObitOF 79*

Spinal Tap
[Christopher (Nigel Tufnel) Guest; Michael (David St. Hubins) McKean; Harry (Derek Smalls) Shearer]
American. Music Group
Fictitious British heavy metal band made famous in the film *This Is Spinal Tap,* 1984; first appeared on television's "The TV Show," 1978.
Source: *BioIn 15, 18, 20; ConMus 8; ConTFT 3; EncRkSt; GrMetD; WhoAm 80, 82, 84, 86, 88, 90, 92, 94; WhoEnt 92*

Spingarn, Arthur Barnett
American. Lawyer, Civil Rights Leader
Pres., NAACP, 1940-65; honorary pres., 1966-71.
b. Mar 28, 1878 in New York, New York
d. Dec 1, 1971 in New York, New York
Source: *AmNatBi; BioIn 7, 9, 16; CurBio 65, 72; DcAmBC; DcAmB S9; EncAACR; NewYTBE 71; WhAm 5*

Spingarn, Joel Elias
American. Author, Educator
Founded NAACP, 1913, pres., 1930-31; originated Spingarn Medal, 1914.
b. May 17, 1875 in New York, New York
d. Jul 26, 1939 in New York, New York
Source: *AmAu&B; AmBi; AmLY; AmNatBi; AmRef; AmSocL; AnMV 1926; BioIn 3, 4, 9, 11, 15, 17, 19, 22; CamDcAB; ChamBiD; ChhPo; CnDAL; DcAmAu; DcAmB S2; DcLEL; DcNAA; EncAB-H 1974, 1996; LinLib L; NatCAB 17; OxCAmL 65; REn; REnAL; TwCA; WebAB 74, 79; WhAm 1; WhNAA; WorAl; WorAu 1900*

Spinks, Leon
American. Boxer
Won gold medal, 1976 Olympics; won world heavyweight title from Muhammad Ali, 1977.
b. Jul 11, 1953 in Saint Louis, Missouri
Source: *BiDAmSp BK; BioIn 11, 12, 16; BlkOlyM; LegTOT; NewYTBS 89*

Spinks, Michael
American. Boxer
Defeated Larry Holmes to become WBC heavyweight champ, 1985.
b. Jul 29, 1956 in Saint Louis, Missouri
Source: *BiDAmSp Sup; BioIn 12, 13, 16; BlkOlyM; BoxReg, 2; InB&W 80; LegTOT; WhoAfA 9, 10, 11, 12; WhoAm 86, 88, 90, 92, 94, 95, 96, 97, 98, 99, 2000; WhoBlA 5, 6, 7, 8*

Spinola, Antonio (Sebastiao Ribeiro) de
American. Military Leader, Political Leader
Pres., Portugal, 1974.
b. Apr 11, 1910
d. Aug 13, 1996 in Lisbon, Portugal
Source: *CurBio 96N; IntWW 74, 75, 76, 77, 78, 79, 80, 81, 82, 83, 89, 91, 93*

Spinoza, Baruch (Benedictus de)
Dutch. Philosopher
Exponent of rational pantheism; wrote *Ethics Demonstrated with Geometrical Order,* 1674.
b. Nov 24, 1632 in Amsterdam, Netherlands
d. Feb 20, 1677 in The Hague, Netherlands
Source: *BbD; Benet 87, 96; BiD&SB; BlkwCE; CasWL; DcEuL; Dis&D; EncUnb; EvEuW; IlEncMy; LegTOT; LinLib L, S; McGEWB; NewC; OxCEng 67; OxCLaw; OxCPhil; PenC EUR; RAdv 14, 13-4; RComWL; REn; TwoTYeD; WorAl; WorAlBi; WrPh P*

Spitalny, Phil
American. Bandleader
Conducted female orchestra, 1935-55.
b. Nov 7, 1890 in Odessa, Russia
d. Oct 11, 1970 in Miami, Florida
Source: *ASCAP 66, 80; BiDAmM; BioIn 9; CmpEPM; NewAmDM; NewGrDA 86; RadStar; SaTiSS; WhoHol B; WhScrn 74, 77, 83; WorAl*

Spitta, Philipp
[Julius August Philipp Spitta]
German. Author, Educator
Leading figure in late-19th c. musicology; wrote first comprehensive biography of Bach, 1873.
b. Dec 27, 1841 in Wechold, Germany
d. Apr 13, 1894 in Berlin, Germany
Source: *BakBD 78, 84; BriBkM 80; LuthC 75; NewGrDM 80; NewOxM; OxCMus*

Spitteler, Karl Friedrich Georg
[Felix Tandem]
Swiss. Poet
Best-known epic poem: *Olympischer Fruhling,* 1900-10; Nobelist, 1919.
b. Apr 24, 1845 in Liestal, Switzerland
d. Dec 28, 1924 in Lucerne, Switzerland
Source: *BioIn 15, 19; ChamBiD; ConAu 109; Dis&D; EvEuW; LinLib L; WhoNob*

Spitz, Mark Andrew
American. Swimmer
First athlete to win seven gold medals in single Olympic games, 1972; Sports Hall of Fame, 1991.
b. Feb 10, 1950 in Modesto, California
Source: *BiDAmSp BK; BioIn 16; BioNews 74; CamBiEn; ChamBiD; CurBio 72; FacFETw; NewYTBE 72, 73; WhoAm 74, 76; WorAlBi*

Spitzer, Andre
Israeli. Olympic Athlete, Victim
One of 11 members of Israeli Olympic team kidnapped and killed by Arab terrorists during Summer Olympic Games.
b. 1945?, Romania
d. Sep 5, 1972 in Munich, Germany (West)
Source: *BioIn 9*

Spitzer, Lyman, Jr.
American. Astronomer
Called the father of satellite astronomy.
b. Jun 26, 1914
d. Mar 31, 1997 in Princeton, New Jersey
Source: *AmMWSc 73P, 76P, 79, 82, 86, 89, 92, 95, 98; AsBiEn; BiESc; BioIn 5, 10, 14, 20, 22, 23; BlueB 76; CamBiEn; CamDcAB; ChamBiD; ConAu 116, 157; CurBio 97N; InSci; IntAu&W 77, 86, 89, 91, 93; IntWW 74, 75, 76, 77, 78, 79, 80, 81, 82, 83, 89, 91, 93; LarDcSc; McGMS 80; NotTwCS 1, 1S; RanHWDS; WhAm 12; Who 74, 82, 83, 85, 88, 90, 92, 94; WhoAm 74, 76, 78, 80, 82, 84, 86, 88, 90, 92, 94, 95, 96, 97, 98; WhoE 74, 75, 77; WhoFrS 84; WhoScEn 96; WhoTech 82, 84, 89, 95; WhoWor 74, 76, 78; WorAl; WorAlBi; WrDr 76, 80, 82, 84, 86, 88, 90, 92, 94, 96, 98N*

Spitzweg, Carl
German. Artist
Best known early Victorian painter in Germany.
b. Feb 5, 1808 in Munich, Germany
d. Sep 23, 1885 in Munich, Germany
Source: *BioIn 10, 11, 14, 20; ClaDrA; McGDA; OxCArt; OxCGer 76, 86, 97; WorECar*

Spivak, Charlie
American. Bandleader, Musician
Played lead trumpet with his popular band, 1940s-50s; disbanded with demise of big bands.
b. Feb 17, 1906 in New Haven, Connecticut
d. Mar 1, 1982 in Greenville, South Carolina
Source: *CmpEPM; NewYTBS 82; OxCPMus; PenEncP; WhoJazz 72*

Spivak, Lawrence E(dmund)
American. TV Personality, Producer
Co-founder, producer, panel member, *Meet the Press,* on radio, TV, 1945-1975.
b. Jun 11, 1900 in New York, New York

d. Mar 9, 1994 in Washington, District
   of Columbia
Source: *BioIn 4, 6, 9; CurBio 56, 94N;*
IntMPA 82, 92; WhAm 11; WhoAm 76,
78, 80, 82, 84, 86, 88, 90, 92; WhoAmJ
80; WhoEnt 92; WhoSSW 73; WhoWorJ
72; WorAlBi

Spivakov, Valdimir (Teodorovich)
Russian. Violinist
Founded the Moscow Virtuosi, a 26-
   member chamber orchestra, 1979.
b. Sep 12, 1944 in Ufa, Union of Soviet
   Socialist Republics
Source: *CurBio 96*

Spivakovsky, Tossy
Russian. Musician
Concert master of Berlin Philharmonic,
   pre-Nazism; violin soloist from 1941.
b. Feb 4, 1907 in Odessa, Russia
d. Jul 20, 1998 in Westport, Connecticut
Source: *BakBD 78, 84, 92; BakBDTw;*
BioIn 1, 2, 3, 4, 9; IntWW 74, 75, 76,
77, 78, 79, 80, 81, 82, 83, 89, 91, 93,
97, 98; IntWWM 85, 90; NewGrDA 86;
PenDiMP; WhoAmM 83; WhoWor 74;
WhoWorJ 72

Spock, Benjamin (McLane)
American. Physician, Author
Wrote *Common Sense Book of Baby*
Care, 1946; sold more than 40 million
   copies.
b. May 2, 1903 in New Haven,
   Connecticut
d. Mar 15, 1998 in San Diego, California
Source: *AmAu&B; AmMWSc 98;*
AmPeW; Au&Wr 71; AuNews 1;
BiDMoAE; BioIn 13, 16; BioNews 74;
CambBiEn; CamDcAB; CelR 90;
ChamBiD; ConAu 35NR, 65NR, 166;
ConHero 1; CurBio 56, 69, 98N;
EncAB-H 1974, 1996; FacFETw; IntWW
91, 97; MajTwCW 1, 2; NewYTBE 72;
PolProf NF; RanHWDS; RComAH;
REnAL; WebAB 79; WhAm 12; Who 90,
92, 98; WhoAm 86, 90, 97, 98; WhoAmP
91; WhoMedH 96; WhoWor 91, 97, 98;
WrDr 86, 92, 98, 99

Spode, Josiah
English. Artist
Potter; developed fine English porcelain
   called Spode ware, 1799.
b. Jul 16, 1754
d. 1827
Source: *ChamBiD; DcArts; LegTOT;*
NewCol 75; PenDiDA 89; WebBD 83;
WhDW

Spofford, Charles M(erville)
American. Lawyer
Pres. Metropolitan Opera Assn., 1946-50;
   initiator of Lincoln Center for the
   Performing Arts.
b. Nov 17, 1902 in Saint Louis, Missouri
d. Mar 23, 1991 in Hampton, New York
Source: *BiDWWGF; BiE&WWA; BioIn*
2, 9, 17; CurBio 91N; NewYTBS 91;
Who 74, 82, 83, 85, 88, 90, 92N;
WhoAmL 79; WhoE 74

Spohr, Louis Ludwig
German. Violinist, Composer, Conductor
Traveling violin virtuoso, opera
   conductor; known for chamber works.
b. Apr 5, 1784 in Brunswick, Germany
d. Oct 22, 1859 in Cassel, Germany
Source: *OxCMus*

Spokane Garry
American. Native American Chief
Chief of the Spokane; tribe signed treaty
   with US government ceding land,
   1887.
b. 1811? in Washington
d. Jan 12, 1892? in Washington
Source: *BioIn 21; EncNAB; NotNaAm;*
WhNaAH

Spong, John
American. Religious Leader
Controversial Episcopal bishop approves
   of women and homosexual clergy, and
   monogamous homosexual relationships
   affirmed by the church.
b. Jun 16, 1931 in Charlotte, North
   Carolina
Source: *BioIn 15; IntWW 91; News 91,*
91-3; WhoAm 90; WhoE 91; WhoRel 92

Spontini, Gasparo
Italian. Composer, Conductor
Wrote opera *La Vestale,* 1807; developed
   modern orchestral conducting.
b. Nov 14, 1774 in Majolati, Italy
d. Jan 24, 1851 in Majolati, Italy
Source: *BakBD 84; BakDcM; BioIn 1, 4,*
7, 8, 12, 23; BriBkM 80; CmOp; DcCom
77; DcCom&M 79; GrComp; MusMk;
NewEOp 71; NewOxM; OxCMus

Spooner, Bill
[The Tubes]
American. Musician
Guitarist with The Tubes since late
   1960s.
b. Apr 16, 1949 in Phoenix, Arizona

Spooner, John Coit
American. Politician
US Senator; wrote Spooner Act (1902),
   giving Pres. Theodore Roosevelt
   authority to build the Panama Canal.
b. Jan 6, 1843 in Lawrenceburg, Indiana
d. Jun 11, 1919 in New York, New York
Source: *AmBi; AmNatBi; ApCAB, X;*
BiDrAC; BiDrUSC 89; BioIn 5;
CamDcAB; DcAmB; EncAAH; EncAB-H
1974; HarEnUS; IndAu 1967; NatCAB
1, 14; TwCBDA; WebAB 74, 79; WhAm
1; WhAmP

Spooner, William Archibald
English. Educator
"Spoonerisms" are unconscious
   consonant transpositions.
b. Jul 22, 1844 in London, England
d. 1930
Source: *Benet 87, 96; BioIn 8, 11, 14;*
CambBiEn; ChamBiD; DcNaB 1922;
GrBr; LngCTC; REn

Spotswood, Alexander
English. Colonial Figure
Lt. governor, Colony of Virginia, 1710-
   22; improved tobacco production,
   Indian relationships.
b. 1676 in Tangiers, Morocco
d. Jun 7, 1740 in Annapolis, Maryland
Source: *AmBi; AmNatBi; AmWrBE;*
ApCAB; BenetAL 91; BiDrACR; BiDSA;
BioIn 8, 15; CamDcAB; DcAmB;
DcNaB, C; Drake; EncAB-H 1974, 1996;
EncCRAm; EncWB 98; McGEWB;
NatCAB 13; NewCol 75; OxCAmH;
OxCAmL 65, 83, 95; REnAL; TwCBDA;
WhAm HS; WhWE

Spotted Tail
[Sinte Gleska]
American. Native American Chief
Chief of the Sioux; proponent of
   nonviolent resolution with the white
   population; assassinated by fellow
   tribesman, Crow Dog.
b. 1823?
d. Aug 5, 1881
Source: *AmIndBi; AmNatBi; BioIn 5, 11;*
ChamBiD; EncNAB; EncNoAI; NotNaAm

Spottswood, Stephen Gill
American. Religious Leader
African Methodist Episcopal Zion
   bishop, who was chm., NAACP, 1961-
   74.
b. Jul 18, 1897 in Boston, Massachusetts
d. Dec 1, 1974 in Washington, District
   of Columbia
Source: *AfrAmAl 6, 8; AmNatBi; BioIn*
6, 10, 12; CurBio 62, 75, 75N; DcAmB
S9; Ebony 1; EncWM; InB&W 80;
NegAl 76, 83, 89; NewYTBS 74; WhAm
6; WhoAm 74; WhoBlA 1, 2, 3, 4;
WhoSSW 73; WhoWor 74

Sprague, Frank Julian
American. Engineer
Constructed first major electric trolley
   system in US in Richmond, VA, 1887.
b. Jul 25, 1857 in Milford, Connecticut
d. Oct 25, 1934 in New York, New York
Source: *AmBi; AmNatBi; ApCAB X;*
BioIn 1, 3, 7, 10; CambBiEn; CamDcAB;
ChamBiD; DcAmB S1; EncAB-H 1974,
1996; EncWB 98; InSci; McGEWB;
NatCAB 3, 24; WebAB 74, 79; WhAm 1

Sprague, R(obert) C(hapman)
American. Businessman
Founder of Sprague Electric Co., pioneer
   in electronic components of radio and
   TV receivers.
b. Aug 3, 1900 in New York, New York
d. Sep 27, 1991 in Williamstown,
   Massachusetts
Source: *AmMWSc 92; BioIn 2, 5, 17;*
CurBio 91N; Dun&B 88; IntYB 78, 79,
80, 81, 82; LElec; NewYTBS 91; St&PR
91; WhAm 10; WhoAm 74, 76, 78, 80,
86, 88, 90; WhoE 75, 77; WhoFI 74, 75,
77, 85

Spreckels, Claus
"Sugar King"
German. Manufacturer
Owner of largest sugar refinery on the
West Coast, 1883.
b. Jul 9, 1828 in Lamstedt, Germany
d. Jan 10, 1908 in San Francisco,
California
Source: *AmNatBi; BiDAmBL 83; BioIn
7; CmCal; DcAmB; WebAB 74, 79;
WhAm 1*

Springer, Axel Caesar
German. Publisher
Created Europe's largest newspaper
empire, including *Die Welt, Bild
Zeitung.*
b. May 2, 1912 in Hamburg, Germany
d. Sep 22, 1985 in Berlin, Germany
(West)
Source: *ConAu 117; CurBio 68, 85;
IntWW 74; WhoWor 74*

Springer, Jerry
American. Television Personality
Known as the "king of trash TV," host
of a talk show seen by 8 million
viewers daily; the show features real
people with shocking, usually off-color
stories confronting each other—and
often brawling—for the camera;
former mayor of Cincinnati, OH.
b. Feb 13, 1944 in London, England
Source: *ConTFT 22; News 98; WhoAm
2000*

Springer, Ya'acov
Israeli. Olympic Athlete, Victim
One of 11 members of Israeli Olympic
team kidnapped and killed by Arab
terrorists during Summer Olympic
Games.
b. 1920?
d. Sep 5, 1972 in Munich, Germany
(West)
Source: *BioIn 9*

Springfield, Dusty
[Mary Isabel Catherine O'Brien]
English. Singer
Popular vocalist; hits include "Wishin'
and Hopin','' 1964.
b. Apr 16, 1939 in Hampstead, England
d. Mar 2, 1999 in Henley-on-Thames,
England
Source: *BiDAmM; NewYTBS 99;
OxCPMus; PenEncP; RkOn 74, 78;
RolSEnR 83; WhoRock 81; WhoRocM
82; WorAl; WorAlBi*

Springfield, Rick
[Richard Springfield]
Australian. Actor, Musician, Singer
Former star of soap opera "General
Hospital" who had Grammy-winning
hit "Jessie's Girl," 1981.
b. Aug 23, 1949 in Sydney, Australia
Source: *BioIn 12, 13; ConMus 9;
ConTFT 19; DcPseud; EncPR&S 89;
EncRk 88; EncRkSt; IntMPA 88, 92, 94,
96; LegTOT; PenEncP; RkOn 78;
RolSEnR 83; Songw; WhoHol 92;
WhoTelC; WorAlBi*

Springsteen, Bruce
"The Boss"
American. Singer, Songwriter
Album *Born in the USA,* most popular
rock album of all time, 1985.
b. Sep 23, 1949 in Freehold, New Jersey
Source: *AmDec 1980; AmSong; ASCAP
80; BakBD 84, 92; BakDcM; BillEnR;
BioIn 10, 11, 12, 13, 16; CamBiEn;
CelR 90; ChamBiD; ConAu 111; ConLC
17; ConMuA 80A; ConMus 6, 25;
CurBio 78, 92; DcArts; DcTwCCu 1;
EncPR&S 89; EncRk 88; EncRkSt;
FacFETw; HarEnR 86; IlEncRk; IntWW
82, 83, 89, 91, 93, 97, 98, 2000;
LegTOT; NewAmDM; NewGrDA 86;
NewYTBS 85; OnThGG; OxCPMus;
PenEncP; RkOn 74, 78; RkWho 96;
RolSEnR 83; Songw; WhoAm 80, 82, 84,
86, 88, 90, 92, 94, 95, 96, 97, 98, 99,
2000; WhoEnt 92, 98; WhoRock 81;
WhoRocM 82; WhoWor 97, 98; WorAl;
WorAlBi*

Sprinkel, Beryl Wayne
American. Economist
Undersecretary of Treasury for monetary
affairs, Reagan administration, 1981-
85.
b. Nov 20, 1923 in Richmond, Missouri
Source: *CurBio 87; IntWW 91, 97, 98,
2000; NewYTBS 85; WhoAm 86, 90, 97,
98, 99, 2000; WhoAmP 89; WhoFI 92;
WrDr 92, 98, 99, 2000*

Sproul, Robert Gordon
American. Educator
Pres. of U of CA, 1930-58.
b. May 22, 1891 in San Francisco,
California
d. Sep 10, 1975 in Berkeley, California
Source: *AmNatBi; BiDAmEd; BioIn 1, 6,
7, 10, 11; CamDcAB; CmCal; CurBio
45, 75, 75N; DcAmB S9; EncAB-A 6;
LinLib S; WhAm 6; Who 74; WhoAm 74*

Spruance, Raymond Ames
American. Naval Officer, Statesman
Naval commander, US forces in Japanese
defeat at Midway, 1942.
b. Jul 3, 1886 in Baltimore, Maryland
d. Dec 13, 1969 in Pebble Beach,
California
Source: *AmNatBi; BiDWWGF; BioIn 16;
CamDcAB; CurBio 44, 70; DcAmB S8;
DcAmMiB; EncNaHi; FacFETw;
HarEnMi; NatCAB 55; OxCAmH;
OxCShps; WebAB 74, 79; WebAMB;
WhAm 5; WorAl*

Spry, Constance
English. Artist, Author
Internationally noted flower arranger;
wrote *Flower Decoration,* 1935.
b. Dec 5, 1886 in Derby, England
d. Jan 3, 1960 in Windsor, England
Source: *BioIn 5, 10, 14, 18; ChamBiD;
ContDcW 89; CurBio 60; DcNaB 1951;
GrBr; IntDcWB; InWom, SUP; ObitT
1951; WomFir*

Spurrier, Steve(n Orr)
American. Football Player
All-America quarterback, won Heisman
Trophy, 1966; in NFL, mostly with
San Francisco, 1967-76.
b. Apr 20, 1945 in Miami Beach, Florida
Source: *BiDAmSp FB; BioIn 7, 8, 21;
WhoFtbl 74; WhoSpor*

Spuzich, Sandra Ann
American. Golfer
Turned pro, 1962; won US Women's
Open, 1966.
b. Apr 3, 1937 in Indianapolis, Indiana
Source: *BioIn 7; WhoGolf*

Spy
[Leslie Ward]
English. Cartoonist
Contributed to *Vanity Fair* for 36 yrs;
recollections in *Forty Years of Spy,*
1915.
b. Nov 21, 1851 in London, England
d. May 15, 1922 in London, England
Source: *BioIn 8, 11, 12, 14, 16; ClaDrA;
DcBrAr 1; DcNaB 1922; DcPseud;
DcVicP, 2; GrBr; LinLib LP; LngCTC;
PseudAu; VicBrit; WorECar*

Spychalski, Marian
Polish. Architect, Politician
Organized Polish Worker's Party, 1942;
mayor of Warsaw, 1944-45; marshal
of Poland, 1963-80.
b. Dec 6, 1906 in Lodz, Poland
d. Jun 7, 1980 in Warsaw, Poland
Source: *AnObit 1980; BioIn 8; HisDcPo;
IntWW 74, 75, 76, 77, 78, 79, 80; IntYB
78, 79, 80; WhoSocC 78*

Spyri, Johanna Heuser
Swiss. Author
Best known for ever-popular *Heidi,*
1880; adapted to films, TV shows.
b. Jun 12, 1827 in Hirzel, Switzerland
d. Jul 7, 1901 in Zurich, Switzerland
Source: *AnCL; AuBYP 2; CarSB; JBA
34, 51; OxCChiL; OxCGer 76; SmATA
19; WhoChL*

Spyropoulos, Jannis
Greek. Artist
Painting style ranged from naturalistic to
abstract to non-objective abstract; later
paintings concentrate on surface,
texture.
b. Mar 12, 1912 in Pylos, Greece
Source: *BioIn 5, 6; IntWW 74, 75, 76,
77, 78, 79, 80, 81, 82, 83, 89, 91, 93;
OxCTwCA; WhoWor 74, 78*

Squanto
American. Native American Guide
Member of Wampanoag tribe; taught
Pilgrims wilderness survival.
b. 1585?
d. 1622 in Chatham Harbor,
Massachusetts
Source: *AmBi; DcAmB; WebAB 74;
WhAm HS*

Squeeze
[John Bentley; Paul Carrack; Chris
Difford; Julian Holland; Harry
Kakoulli; Gilson Lavis; Don Snow;
Glenn Tilbrook; Keith Wilkinson]
English. Music Group
Formed 1974 in London; had hit album
East Side Story, 1981.
Source: *Alli; BiDLA; BillEnR; BioIn 1;
ConMus 5; DcInB; DcNaB; EncPR&S
89; EncRk 88; EncRkSt; HarEnR 86;
IlEncRk; PenEncP; RkOn 85; RolSEnR
83; WhoRocM 82; WhsNW 85*

Squibb, Edward Robinson
American. Manufacturer
Founded E R Squibb pharmaceutical
firm, 1858.
b. Jul 4, 1819 in Wilmington, Delaware
d. Oct 25, 1900 in New York, New York
Source: *Alli SUP; AmNatBi; BiDAmS;
BiInAmS; BioIn 1, 4, 5, 6, 7; CamDcAB;
DcAmB; DcAmMeB 84; DcNAA; InSci;
NatCAB 19; WebAB 74, 79; WhAm HS*

Squier, Billy
American. Singer, Musician
Guitarist whose singles include
"Everybody Wants You," 1982; "Eye
On You," 1984.
b. May 12, 1950 in Wellesley,
Massachusetts
Source: *GrMetD; LegTOT; PenEncP;
RkOn 85; RolSEnR 83; WhoRocM 82*

Squire, Chris
English. Singer, Musician
Self-taught bassist who formed Yes,
1968; had solo album *Fish Out of the
Water,* 1975.
b. Mar 4, 1948 in London, England
Source: *WhoRocM 82*

Squires, James Radcliffe
American. Poet
Poetry was influenced by Greek
mythology; wrote *Cornar,* 1940.
b. May 23, 1917 in Salt Lake City, Utah
d. Feb 14, 1993
Source: *ConLC 51, 81; WhoAm 74, 76,
78, 80, 82, 84, 86, 88, 90, 92; WhoMW
74, 76; WhoUSWr 88*

Ssu-ma Ch'ien
Chinese. Historian
Called the "Grand Historian of China,"
completed a history of mankind begun
by his father; served as T'ai-shih, or
director of astrology, in the imperial
government.
b. 145BC
d. 90BC
Source: *EncWB 98*

Ssu-ma Hsiang-ju
Chinese. Poet
A leading poet of the Western Han
period, also served as a court official
and explored and colonized lands
southwest of the imperial territory.
b. c. 179BC, China
d. 117BC

Source: *Benet 96; EncWB 98*

Ssu-ma kuang
Chinese. Politician, Historian
Conservative statesman and academician
is known as one of the greatest
Chinese historians; author of *Tzu-chih
t'ung-chien* (*Comprehensive Mirror for
Aid in Government*).
b. Nov 17, 1019 in Kuang-shan, Hunan,
China
d. Oct 11, 1086
Source: *EncWB 98*

Stabile, Mariano
Italian. Opera Singer
Baritone; sang Falstaff more than 1,000
times; retired, 1960.
b. May 12, 1888 in Palermo, Sicily, Italy
d. Jan 11, 1968 in Milan, Italy
Source: *BakBD 78, 84, 92; BakBDTw;
BioIn 3, 8; CmOp; IntDcOp; MetOEnc;
NewEOp 71; NewGrDM 80; NewGrDO;
PenDiMP*

Stabler, Ken(neth Michael)
"Snake"
American. Football Player
Quarterback, 1970-84, mostly with
Oakland; known for passing; led NFL
in passing, 1973.
b. Dec 25, 1945 in Foley, Alabama
Source: *BioIn 16; CurBio 79; WhoAm
80, 82; WhoFtbl 74; WorAl; WorAlBi*

Stace, W(alter) T(erence)
Philosopher, Author
Combined naturalism and religion in his
theories; wrote prolifically in the field;
Mysticism and Philophy, 1960.
b. Nov 17, 1886 in London, England
d. Aug 2, 1967 in Laguna Beach,
California
Source: *AmAu&B; BioIn 3, 5, 6, 8, 10,
11; ConAu 1R, 2NR; NatCAB 55; WhAm
5, 7; WhLit*

Stacey, Thomas Charles Gerard
English. Author
Travel books include *A Malayan
Journey,* 1953; editor, *Chamber's
Encyclopedia Yearbook,* 1969-72.
b. Jan 11, 1930 in Bletchingley, England
Source: *Au&Wr 71; ConAu 9R, 21NR,
47NR; DcLEL 1940; IntAu&W 91;
WhoEnt 98; WhoWor 76, 95, 96, 97;
WrDr 86, 92*

Stack, Robert Langford
American. Actor
Starred in TV series "The
Untouchables," 1959-63.
b. Jan 13, 1919 in Los Angeles,
California
Source: *BiDFilm; FilmgC; HalFC 84;
MotPP; MovMk; WhoAm 74, 76, 78, 80,
82, 84, 86, 88, 90, 92, 94, 95, 96, 97,
98, 99, 2000; WhoEnt 92, 98; WorAl*

Stacton, David Derek
American. Author
Biographical-historical novels include
*Kaliyuga; or, A Quarrel with the
Gods,* 1965.
b. Apr 25, 1925 in Minden, Nevada
d. Jan 20, 1968 in Fredensborg, Sweden
Source: *AmAu&B; ConAu 5R, 6NR;
ObitOF 79; OxCAmL 83; WorAu 1950*

Stacy, Hollis
American. Golfer
Turned pro, 1974; won US Women's
Open, 1977, 1978, 1984.
b. Mar 16, 1954 in Savannah, Georgia
Source: *BiDAmSp Sup; BioIn 9, 11;
InWom SUP; WhoAm 86, 88, 2000;
WhoGolf; WhoIntG; WhoSpor*

Stacy, James
[Maurice W Elias]
American. Actor
Lost arm, leg in motorcycle accident;
starred in TV movie *Just a Little
Inconvenience,* 1977; once married to
Connie Stevens.
b. Dec 23, 1936 in Los Angeles,
California
Source: *BioIn 18, 22; ConTFT 6;
VarWW 85; WhoHol 92, A*

Stader, Maria
Swiss. Opera Singer
Lyric soprano; performances limited to
recordings, stage concerts.
b. Nov 5, 1911 in Budapest, Hungary
d. Apr 29, 1999 in Zurich, Switzerland
Source: *BakBD 84; BakBDTw; CurBio
58; WhoMus 72; WhoWor 74*

Stadler, Craig Robert
"The Walrus"
American. Golfer
Turned pro, 1975; won Masters, 1982;
leading money winner on tour, 1982.
b. Jun 2, 1953 in San Diego, California
Source: *NewYTBS 82; WhoAm 84, 86,
88, 90, 92, 94, 95, 96, 97, 98, 2000;
WhoIntG; WhoWest 94, 96*

Stael, Nicolas de
French. Artist
Painted mainly in watercolor; known for
Footballers series, 1952.
b. Jan 5, 1914 in Saint Petersburg,
Russia
d. Mar 22, 1955 in Antibes, France
Source: *AtlBL; BioIn 3, 4, 5, 6, 7, 11,
12, 16, 17; CamBiEn; ChamBiD;
DcTwArt; McGDA; McGEWB;
OxCTwCA; OxDcArt; WhDW*

**Stael-Holstein, Anne Louise
Germaine Necker, Baroness de**
French. Author, Socialite
Influenced French Romanticism;
Delphine, 1802, *Corinne,* 1807,
considered first modern, feminist,
romantic novels; critic of Napoleon,
consequently exiled from Paris many
times.
b. Apr 22, 1766 in Paris, France

d. Jul 14, 1817 in Paris, France
Source: *Benet 87; BioIn 14, 15; CasWL; CmFrR; FemiCLE; GuFrLit 1; IntDcWB; InWom SUP; McGEWB; OxCEng 85; OxCFr; OxCGer 86; REn; WorAlBi*

Stafford, Jean
American. Author
Collection of short stories, *Collected Stories,* won Pulitzer, 1970.
b. Jul 1, 1915 in Covina, California
d. Mar 26, 1979 in White Plains, New York
Source: *AmAu&B; AmNatBi; AmNov; AmWomWr, 92; ArtclWW 2; Benet 87, 96; BenetAL 91; BioAmW; BioIn 2, 3, 4, 7, 11, 12, 13, 14, 15, 16, 17, 18, 19, 20, 22, 23; BlmGWL; BlueB 76; CamBiEn; CamDcAB; CamGLE; CamHAL; ChamBiD; CnDAL; ConAu 1R, 3NR, 65NR, 85; ConLC 4, 7, 19, 68; ConNov 72, 76; CurBio 79N; CyWA 89, 97; DcAmB S10; DcLB 173; DcLEL 1940; DrAF 76; EncALit; EncWL 1; FacFETw; FemiCLE; GrWomW; GrWrEL N; IntAu&W 76, 77; InWom, SUP; LegTOT; LinLib L; MajTwCW 1, 2; ModAL 4, 4S3, 5; ModWoWr; Novels; OxCAmL 65, 83, 95; OxCTwCL; OxCWoWr 95; PenC AM; RAdv 1; REn; REnAL; RfGAmL 4, 87, 94; RfGShF 1, 2; ShSCr 26; ShSWr; SmATA 22N; TwCA SUP; TwCWW 82, 91; WhAm 7; WhoAm 74, 76, 78; WhoAmW 58, 64, 66, 68, 70, 72, 74; WhoE 74; WhoPul; WhoTwCL; WhoWor 74; WorAl; WorAlBi; WorAu 1900; WrDr 76, 80*

Stafford, Jim
[James Wayne Stafford]
American. Singer, Songwriter
Novelty songwriter; had hit singles "Spiders and Snakes," 1974; "My Girl Bill," 1974.
b. Jan 16, 1944 in Eloise, Florida
Source: *AllMGCo; BioIn 10, 14; EncFCWM 83; LegTOT; RkOn 74, 78*

Stafford, Jo
American. Singer
Popular performer, 1940s-50s; sang with Tommy Dorsey through mid-1944.
b. Nov 12, 1918 in Coalinga, California
Source: *BiDAmM; CmpEPM; InWom, SUP; LegTOT; RadStar; WhoAm 74, 90; WhoHol 92; WorAl; WorAlBi*

Stafford, Robert Theodore
American. Politician
Republican senator from VT, 1971-89.
b. Aug 8, 1913 in Rutland, Vermont
Source: *AlmAP 82; BiDrAC; BiDrUSC 89; BioIn 5, 9, 10, 12, 13, 16; CngDr 74, 77, 79, 81, 83, 85, 87; CurBio 60; NewYTBE 71; WhoAm 74, 76, 78, 80, 82, 84, 86, 88, 90, 92, 94, 95, 96, 97, 98, 99, 2000; WhoAmL 96; WhoAmP 85, 91; WhoE 74, 75, 77, 79, 81, 83, 85, 86, 89; WhoWor 80, 82, 87, 89*

Stafford, Thomas P(atten)
American. Astronaut, Businessman
Flew on Gemini VI, IX, and Apollo X flights.
b. Sep 17, 1930 in Weatherford, Oklahoma
Source: *AmMWSc 73P, 98; BioIn 7, 8, 9, 10, 11; CurBio 77; IntWW 74; Law&B 89A; NewYTBS 75; WhoAm 74, 76, 78, 80, 82, 84, 86, 88, 90, 92, 94, 95, 96, 97, 98; WhoScEn 94, 96; WhoSSW 73, 75, 95, 97; WhoWor 74, 78, 80, 82, 84, 87; WorAl; WorAlBi*

Stafford, William Edgar
American. Poet
Poems dealt with conflicts between natural, artificial worlds; won Nat. Book Award, 1962, for *Traveling through the Dark.*
b. Jan 17, 1914 in Hutchinson, Kansas
d. Aug 28, 1993 in Lake Oswego, Oregon
Source: *BenetAL 91; BioIn 15, 18, 19, 20; ConAu 5NR, 5R, 142; ConLC 4; ConPo 91; CroCAP; EncALit; ModAL 4S1; OxCAmL 65; PenC AM; RAdv 1; RfGAmL 4; WhoAm 84, 86, 90; WhoPNW; WhoUSWr 88; WhoWrEP 89; WorAu 1950; WrDr 92, 96*

Stagg, Amos Alonzo
American. Football Coach
Collegiate coach for 57 yrs., 1890-1946; introduced huddle and many innovative plays used today, including end around, double reverse.
b. Aug 16, 1862 in West Orange, New Jersey
d. Mar 17, 1965 in Stockton, California
Source: *AmNatBi; BasBi; BiDAmSp FB; BioIn 1, 2, 3, 4, 5, 6, 7, 8, 9, 10, 12, 20, 21; CamDcAB; CurBio 44, 65; DcAmB S7; FacFETw; LegTOT; NatCAB 11, 18; NewYTBS 81; OxCAmH; WebAB 74, 79; WhAm 4; WhNAA; WhoBbl 73; WhoFtbl 74; WhoSpor; WhScrn 83; WorAl; WorAlBi*

Staggers, Harley O(rrin)
American. Politician
Dem. WV Congressman, 1949-81.
b. Aug 3, 1907 in Keyser, Washington
d. Aug 20, 1991 in Cumberland, Maryland
Source: *AlmAP 78, 80, 88; BiDrAC; BiDrUSC 89; BioIn 9, 11, 12; CngDr 74, 77, 79; CurBio 71; NewYTBS 91; PolProf J, NF; PolsAm 84; WhAm 10; WhoAm 74, 76, 78, 80, 84, 86, 88; WhoAmP 73, 75, 77, 79, 81, 83, 85, 87, 89, 91; WhoE 74, 75, 77, 86; WhoGov 72, 75, 77; WhoSSW 78, 80, 82, 86, 88*

Stahl, Ben(jamin Albert)
American. Artist, Illustrator
Best known for illustrations in the *Saturday Evening Post,* 1933-63; won many awards.
b. Sep 7, 1910 in Chicago, Illinois
d. Oct 19, 1987 in Sarasota, Florida
Source: *BioIn 1, 2, 7, 8, 10, 11, 12, 15, 16; ConAu 29R, 123; IlrAm 1880, E;*

IlsBYP; IlsCB 1957; NewYTBS 87; ScF&FL 1, 2, 92; SmATA 5, 54N; WhAm 9; WhAmArt 85; WhoAm 74, 76, 78, 80, 82, 84, 86; WhoAmA 73, 76, 78, 80, 82, 84, 86; WhoSSW 73, 75, 76; WhoWor 80, 82

Stahl, Franklin William
American. Geneticist
Together with Mathew Meselsohn, 1958, demonstrated how DNA replicates itself.
b. Oct 8, 1929 in Boston, Massachusetts
Source: *AmMWSc 76P, 79, 82, 86, 89, 92, 95, 98; BioIn 14, 20, 23; LarDcSc; RanHWDS; WhoAm 99, 2000; WhoScEn 2000*

Stahl, Georg Ernst
German. Chemist
Founder of the phlogiston theory of combustion, he also developed a theory of medicine based upon vitalistic ideas.
b. Oct 21, 1660 in Anspach, Bavaria
d. May 14, 1734
Source: *AsBiEn; BiEsc; BioIn 1, 3, 5, 12, 14; BlkwCE; CamBiEn; CamDcSc; ChamBiD; DcBiPP; Dis&D; EncWB 98; InSci; LarDcSc; McGEWB; OxCMed 86; RanHWDS; WhDW; WorAl; WorAlBi*

Stahl, Lesley (Rene)
American. Broadcast Journalist
Longtime correspondent, CBS News; moderator, "Face the Nation," 1983-91; co-editor and correspondent "60 Minutes," 1991—; coined expression "The Peggy Principle."
b. Dec 16, 1941 in Lynn, Massachusetts
Source: *AuNews 2; BioIn 11, 14, 21; CelR 90; ConAu 107; ConTFT 12; CurBio 96; EncTwCJ; InWom SUP; LegTOT; LesBEnT 92; News 97-1; WhoAm 86, 90; WhoAmW 91; WhoE 91; WomStre; WorAlBi*

Stahl, Leslie
American. Journalist
Television journalist known for her tough reporting style, tempered by her charm; has been anchor of CBS-TV news programs, a White House correspondent, and moderator of "Face the Nation;" co-editor and correspondent for "60 Minutes," 1991—. Awards include an Emmy Award, the Matrix Award for broadcasting, and the Edward R. Murrow Award for Overall Excellence on Television.
b. Dec 16, 1941 in Swampscott, Massachusetts

Stahlberg, Kaarlo Juho
Finnish. Political Leader
Principle author of Finland's Constitution; independent Finland's first president, 1919-25.
b. Jan 28, 1865 in Suomusselmi, Finland
d. Sep 22, 1952 in Helsinki, Finland
Source: *BioIn 3, 8; CamBiEn; ChamBiD; OxCLaw*

Stakman, Elvin Charles
American. Agriculturist
Plant pathologist who pioneered
techniques to identify and fight food
crop diseases.
b. May 17, 1885 in Algoma, Wisconsin
d. Jan 22, 1979 in Saint Paul, Minnesota
Source: *AmMWSc 76P; AmNatBi; BioIn
1, 2, 3, 7, 8, 11, 12, 14; BlueB 76;
CurBio 49, 79N; InSci; IntWW 74, 75,
76, 77, 78, 79; NewYTBS 79; WhAm 7*

Stalin, Joseph
[Iosif Visarionovich Djugashvili]
Russian. Political Leader
Successor of Lenin who was dictator,
1929-53; attempted to establish
socialism by force, terror.
b. Dec 21, 1879 in Gori, Russia
d. Mar 5, 1953 in Moscow, Union of
Soviet Socialist Republics
Source: *Benet 87, 96; BioIn 13, 14, 15,
16, 17, 18, 19, 20, 21, 22, 23, 24;
CamBiEn; ChamBiD; ColdWar 1, 2;
ColdWRG; CurBio 42, 53; DcPseud;
DcRusL; EncMcCE; EncTR 91; EncWB
98; GrLGrT; HisDcKW; HisWorL;
LegTOT; LinLib L; MakMC; McGEWB;
ObitT 1951; OxCEng 85; RAdv 14, 13-3;
REn; TwCLC 92; WhAm 3, 4; WhDW;
WhoEc 81; WorAl; WorAlBi*

Stalin, Svetlana Alliluyeva
[Svetlana Peters]
Russian. Author
Daughter of Joseph Stalin who defected
to West, 1967; wrote memoirs *Twenty
Letters to a Friend,* 1967.
b. Feb 28, 1926 in Moscow, Union of
Soviet Socialist Republics
Source: *BioIn 15; CurBio 68; NewYTBE
73; WhoAm 74, 82, 84*

Staller, Ilona
"Cicciolina"
Italian. Actor, Politician
Actress in pornographic films; member
of Italian Parliament 1987—.
b. 1951 in Budapest, Hungary
Source: *IntWWW 2; News 88-3*

Stallings, George Augustus, Jr.
American. Religious Leader
Priest, founder of an independent
African-American Roman Catholic
church in Washington, DC, 1989—.
b. Mar 17, 1948 in New Bern, North
Carolina
Source: *AfrAmAl 6, 8; BioIn 16; News
90-1; RelLAm 1, 2; WhoAfA 9, 10, 11,
12; WhoBlA 4, 7, 8*

Stallings, Laurence
American. Dramatist, Screenwriter
Co-wrote play *What Price Glory?,* 1924.
b. Nov 25, 1894 in Macon, Georgia
d. Feb 28, 1968
Source: *AmAu&B; BenetAL 91;
BiE&WWA; BioIn 3, 4, 8, 10, 12, 15,
22; CnDAL; ConAmA; ConAmL; ConAu
89; CyWA 97; DcLB 7, 44; FilmEn;
FilmgC; HalFC 80, 84, 88; LegTOT;
McGEWD 72, 84; ModWD; NatCAB 55;*

*NotNAT B; Novels; OxCAmL 65, 83, 95;
PenC AM; PIP&P; REn; REnAL;
SouWr; TwCA, SUP; WhAm 4A; WhThe;
WorAl; WorAlBi; WorAu 1900*

Stallone, Sylvester (Enzio)
American. Actor, Director
Best known for *Rocky* film series, 1976-
90; *Rambo* films, 1984, 1985, 1988.
b. Jul 6, 1946 in New York, New York
Source: *BiDFilm 94; BioIn 11, 12, 13,
15, 16; BkPepl; CelR 90; ConAu 77;
ConTFT 1, 8; CurBio 77, 94; DcTwCCu
1; FilmEn; HalFC 80, 84, 88; HolBB;
IntDcF 1-3, 2-3; IntMPA 78, 79, 80, 81,
82, 84, 86, 88, 92, 94, 96; IntWW 89,
91, 93, 97, 98, 2000; LegTOT; MiSFD
9; News 94, 94-2; VarWW 85; WhoAm
78, 80, 82, 84, 86, 88, 90, 92, 94, 95,
96, 97, 98, 99, 2000; WhoEnt 92, 98;
WhoHol 92; WhoWor 97, 98, 99, 2000;
WorAl; WorAlBi*

Stallworth, John(ny Lee)
American. Football Player
Three-time all-pro wide receiver,
Pittsburgh, 1974-87; led NFL in
receiving, 1979; won four Super
Bowls.
b. Jul 15, 1952 in Tuscaloosa, Alabama
Source: *BiDAmSp FB; BioIn 16;
FootReg 87; WhoBlA 3, 4, 7*

Stambuliski, Aleksandr
[Alexandr Stamboliski]
Bulgarian. Political Leader
Leader of Peasant's Party; premier,
1920-23, until assassinated.
b. Mar 1, 1879 in Slavovitsa, Bulgaria
d. Jun 12, 1923 in Slavovitsa, Bulgaria
Source: *NewCol 75; WebBD 83*

Stammler, Rudolf
German. Judge
Renowned legal philosopher of the 20th
century; wrote *Lehre von dem
richtigen Rechte,* 1902.
b. Feb 19, 1856 in Alsfeld, Germany
d. Apr 25, 1938 in Wernigerode,
Germany

Stamos, John
American. Actor
Played Jesse on TV series "Full
House," 1987-95.
b. Aug 19, 1963 in Los Angeles,
California
Source: *BioIn 13, 14, 16; ConTFT 4, 13;
IntMPA 94, 96; LegTOT; WhoAm 95, 96,
97, 99, 2000; WhoHol 92*

Stamos, Theodoros
American. Painter
Abstract expressionist; painted in thin
washes of pigment.
b. Dec 31, 1922
d. Feb 2, 1997 in Yianina, Greece
Source: *BioIn 4, 5, 6, 11, 22, 23;
BriEAA; CamDcAB; ConArt 83, 89, 96;
CurBio 97N; DcAmArt; DcCAA 71, 77,
88, 94; DcCAr 81; McGDA; NewYTBS
97; OxCTwCA; PhDcTCA 77; PrintW*

*83, 85; WhAm 12; WhAmArt 85; WhoAm
82, 84, 86, 88, 90, 92, 94, 95, 96;
WhoAmA 73, 76, 78, 80, 82, 84, 86, 89,
91; WhoWor 74; WorArt 1950*

Stamp, Terence
English. Actor
Films include *Superman II,* 1980;
Monster Island, 1981.
b. Jul 22, 1940 in London, England
Source: *BioIn 14, 16, 20, 21; FilmEn;
FilmgC; HalFC 80, 84, 88; IIWWBF;
IntMPA 75, 76, 82, 92; IntWW 82, 91;
ItaFilm; MotPP; MovMk; OxCFilm;
WhoHol A; WorAl; WorEFlm; WrDr 92*

Stampfli, Jakob
Swiss. Political Leader
Pres. Swiss Confederation, 1856, 1859,
1862; helped fashion Swiss federal
bank and shaped its policies.
b. Feb 23, 1820 in Janzenhaus,
Switzerland
d. May 15, 1879 in Bern, Switzerland
Source: *IntWWM 90*

Stander, Lionel (Jay)
American. Actor
Played Max on TV series "Hart to
Hart," 1979-84.
b. Jan 11, 1909 in New York, New York
d. Nov 30, 1994
Source: *BiE&WWA; ConTFT 5;
EncAFC; FilmgC; HalFC 84, 88;
IntMPA 92; MotPP; MovMk; NewYTBE
71; NotNAT; Vers A; WhoAm 84;
WhoHol A*

Standing, Guy, Sir
Actor
Prominent on British, American stage;
appeared in Hollywood films, 1930s:
Death Takes a Holiday, 1934.
b. Sep 1, 1873 in London, England
d. Feb 24, 1937 in Los Angeles,
California
Source: *FilmEn; FilmgC; ForYSC;
HalFC 80, 84, 88; HolCA; MotPP;
NotNAT B; WhoHol B; WhoStg 1906,
1908; WhScrn 74, 77, 83; WhThe*

Standing Bear
American. Native American Leader
Leader of the Ponca tribe; led a band of
his tribesmen to resettle their former
lands in Nebraska, 1879.
b. 1829?
d. Sep 1908
Source: *AmIndBi; BioIn 4, 9, 11;
ConHero 3; NatNAFi; NotNaAm;
WhNaAH*

Standish, Miles
American. Colonial Figure
Military leader, Plymouth Colony, 1620-
25.
b. 1584 in Lancashire, England
d. Oct 3, 1656 in Duxbury,
Massachusetts
Source: *AmBi; Benet 87, 96; BenetAL
91; CamDcAB; DcAmMiB; Drake;
EncCRAm; HarEnUS; LegTOT; LinLib*

L, S; NatCAB 5; OxCAmH; OxCAmL 83;
REn; REnAL; WebAB 74, 79; WebAMB;
WhNaAH; WorAl; WorAlBi

Stanfield, Andy
[Andrew Stanfield]
American. Track Athlete
Sprinter; gold medalist in 200-meter,
400-meter relays, 1952 Olympics.
b. Dec 29, 1927 in Washington, District
of Columbia
Source: BlkOlyM; WhoSpor; WhoTr&F
73

Stanford, Charles Villiers, Sir
Irish. Composer, Conductor
b. Sep 30, 1852 in Fublin, Ireland
d. Mar 29, 1924 in London, England
Source: BakBD 78, 84, 92; BakBDTw;
BioIn 4, 5, 6, 11, 14, 16; BriBkM 80;
CamBiEn; CelCen; ChamBiD; CmOp;
DcArts; DcCom&M 79; DcIrB 1, 2, 3;
DcNaB 1922; GrBr; LuthC 75; ModIrLi;
MusMk; NewAmDM; NewEOp 71;
NewGrDM 80; NewGrDO; NewOxM;
OxCBrHi; OxCEng 85, 95; OxCMus;
OxDcOp; PenDiMP A; VicBrit

Stanford, John (Henry)
American. Educator
A retired Major General in the United
States Army known for his leadership
abilities, became the first African
American superintendent of the Seattle
school district, 1995, and instituted
sometimes controversial reforms.
b. Sep 14, 1938 in Darby, Pennsylvania
Source: AfrAmBi 1; AfrAmG; WhoAfA 9,
10, 11, 12; WhoBlA 7, 8

Stanford, Leland
[Amasa Leland Stanford]
American. Railroad Executive, Politician
Pres., Central Pacific, Southern Pacific
railroads, 1860s-90s; governor of CA,
1861-63; founded Stanford U, 1885, in
memory of son.
b. Mar 9, 1824 in Watervliet, New York
d. Jun 21, 1893 in Palo Alto, California
Source: AmBi; AmNatBi; AmSocL;
ApCAB; BiAUS; BiDAmBL 83; BiDrAC;
BiDrGov 1789; BiDrUSC 89; BioIn 2, 3,
6, 7, 8, 9, 10, 11, 12, 13, 15, 17, 19;
CmCal; DcAmB; Drake; EncAB-H 1974,
1996; EncABHB 2; EncWB 98; GayN;
HarEnUS; LegTOT; LinLib S;
McGEWB; MemAm; NatCAB 2;
NewEAmW; OxCAmH; REnAW;
TwCBDA; WebAB 74, 79; WhAm HS;
WhAmP; WhCiWar

Stanford, Sally
[Marcia Busby; Sally Gump]
American. Politician
Ran San Francisco's most celebrated
brothel, 1930s-40s; mayor of Sausalito,
CA, 1976-78.
b. May 5, 1903 in Baker City, Oregon
d. Feb 2, 1982 in Greenbrae, California
Source: AmNatBi; AnObit 1982; BioIn 2,
10, 11, 12, 14, 24; ConAu 105; InWom
SUP; NewYTBS 82; ScrEAmL 1;
WomPO 76

Stanford-Tuck, Robert Roland
English. Military Leader
WW II flying ace; decorated for fighting
in Battle of Britain.
b. Jul 1, 1916
d. May 5, 1987 in London, England
Source: Who 74, 82, 83, 85

Stang, Arnold
American. Comedian, Actor
Performer on radio beginning 1935;
known for film performance in The
Man With the Golden Arm, 1955.
b. Sep 28, 1925 in Chelsea,
Massachusetts
Source: ASCAP 66; BiE&WWA; ConTFT
2, 19; EncAFC; FilmEn; ForYSC;
IntMPA 86, 92; LegTOT; Vers A;
WhoEnt 92; WhoHol 92, A

Stangl, Franz Paul
Austrian. Government Official
Commanded Nazi concentration camps in
Poland, 1942-43, where 400,000 Jews
were killed under his supervision.
b. Mar 26, 1908? in Altmunster, Austria
d. Jun 28, 1971 in Dusseldorf, Germany
(West)
Source: BioIn 7, 8, 9, 10; NewYTBE 71;
WhWW-II

**Stanislavsky, Konstantin
Sergeyevich**
[Konstantin Sergeyevich Alexeyev]
Russian. Actor, Director
Co-founder, Moscow Art Theatre;
developed theory of actor identifying
with role, called Stanislavsky System.
b. Jan 17, 1863 in Moscow, Russia
d. Aug 7, 1938 in Moscow, Union of
Soviet Socialist Republics
Source: DcRusL; EncWT; IntWW 2000;
LngCTC; NewGrDM 80; NewGrDO;
OxCFilm; OxCThe 67; REn

Stankiewicz, Richard Peter
American. Artist
Pioneer in junk art; created sculptures
from scrap metal The Bride.
b. Oct 18, 1922 in Philadelphia,
Pennsylvania
d. Mar 27, 1983 in Worthington,
Massachusetts
Source: AmNatBi; BioIn 4, 5, 6, 7, 8;
BlueB 76; ConArt 77; CurBio 83;
DcAmArt; McGDA; WhoAm 74, 76, 78,
80, 82; WhoAmA 73, 76, 78, 80, 82;
WhoE 74, 83

Stanky, Eddie
[Edward Raymond Stanky]
"Muggsy"; "The Brat"
American. Baseball Player, Baseball
Manager
Infielder, 1943-53, known for brash play,
fielding; managed for eight yrs.
b. Sep 3, 1916 in Philadelphia,
Pennsylvania
d. Jun 6, 1999 in Fairhope, Alabama
Source: Ballpl 90; BaseEn 88; BiDAmSp
Sup; BioIn 1, 2, 3, 5, 7, 11, 12; CurBio
51; LegTOT; WhoProB 73

Stanley, Allan Herbert
Canadian. Hockey Player
Defenseman, 1948-69, with five NHL
teams; won four Stanley Cups with
Toronto; Hall of Fame, 1981.
b. Mar 1, 1926 in Timmins, Ontario,
Canada
Source: HocEn; WhoHcky 73

Stanley, Barney
[Russell Stanley]
Canadian. Hockey Player
Right wing in pro hockey 15 yrs,
through 1920s; Hall of Fame, 1962.
b. Jun 1, 1893 in Paisley, Ontario,
Canada
d. May 16, 1971
Source: WhoHcky 73

Stanley, Francis Edgar
American. Inventor, Auto Manufacturer
With twin brother, Freelan, built steam-
powered "Stanley Steamer," 1887;
founded Stanley Motor Co., 1902;
killed in auto accident.
b. Jun 1, 1849 in Kingfield, Maine
d. Jul 31, 1918 in Wenham,
Massachusetts
Source: AmNatBi; BioIn 5, 7, 21;
CamDcAB; ChamBiD; DcAmB; NatCAB
18; WebAB 74, 79; WhAm 4, HSA;
WorAl; WorInv

**Stanley, Frederick Arthur, Earl
of Derby**
[Lord Stanley of Preston]
English. Political Leader, Hockey
Pioneer
Governor-general of Canada, 1888-93;
donated Stanley Cup, presented to
amateur hockey teams, 1893-1912, to
pros ever since.
b. Jan 15, 1841 in London, England
d. Jun 14, 1908 in Kent, England
Source: ApCAB; CelCen; DcCanB 13;
DcNaB S2; WhoHcky 73

Stanley, Freelan O
American. Inventor, Auto Manufacturer
Built steam-powered "Stanley Steamer,"
1897, with twin brother, Francis; one
of their cars set world speed record,
1906.
b. Jun 1, 1849 in Kingfield, Maine
d. Oct 2, 1940 in Boston, Massachusetts
Source: BioIn 5, 7; CurBio 40;
EncABHB 4; InSci; WebAB 74, 79;
WhAm 1; WorAlBi

Stanley, Henry Morton, Sir
[Stanley and Livingstone; John
Rowlands]
English. Explorer, Journalist
Best known for finding David
Livingstone in Africa, 1871; fought on
both sides in US Civil War.
b. Jan 31, 1841 in Denbigh, Wales
d. May 10, 1904 in London, England
Source: ABCMeAm; Alli SUP; AmAu&B;
AmBi; AmNatBi; BbD; Benet 87, 96;
BiD&SB; BiDChrM; BioIn 1, 2, 3, 4, 5,
6, 7, 8, 9, 10, 11, 12; BritAu 19;
CamBiEn; CamDcAB; CamGEL;

*CamGLE; CarSB; ChamBiD; Chambr 3;
DcAfHiB 86; DcAmAu; DcAmB;
DcBrBI; DcEnA, A; DcNaB S2;
DcPseud; EncPaPR 91; EncWB 98;
EvLB; Expl 93; ExplAnT; HisDBrE;
HisDcWJ; LegTOT; LinLib L, S;
McGEWB; NatCAB 4; NewCBEL;
OxCAmH; OxCAmL 65, 83, 95;
OxCBrHi; OxCEng 67, 85, 95; OxCLiW
86; RAdv 14, 13-3; REn; REnAL;
VicBrit; WebAB 74, 79; WhAm 1;
WhCiWar; WhDW; WhoChr; WhWE;
WorAl*

Stanley, Kim
[Patricia Kimberly Reid]
American. Actor
Method actress; nominated for Oscar,
   1964, for *Seance on a Wet Afternoon*,
   1964.
b. Feb 11, 1925 in Tularosa, New
   Mexico
Source: *BiE&WWA; BioIn 1, 3, 4, 5, 6,
7, 12, 14, 16; CnThe; CurBio 55;
FilmEn; FilmgC; ForYSC; IntMPA 86,
88, 92, 94, 96; InWom, SUP; MotPP;
MovMk; NewYTBS 79; NotNAT;
NotWoAT; OsStAZ; OxCAmT 84;
WhoAm 74; WhoAmW 58, 66, 68, 70,
72, 74, 75, 91; WhoHol 92, A; WhoThe
72, 77; WorAl; WorAlBi*

Stanley, Mickey
[Mitchell Jack Stanley]
American. Baseball Player
Outfielder, Detroit, 1964-78, known for
   fielding; played errorless ball, 1968,
   1970; played shortstop, 1968 World
   Series.
b. Jul 20, 1942 in Grand Rapids,
   Michigan
Source: *Ballpl 90; BaseEn 88; WhoProB
73*

Stanley, Paul
[Kiss; Paul Eisen]
American. Singer, Musician
Guitarist who co-founded Kiss, 1972.
b. Jan 20, 1949 in New York, New York
Source: *WhoRocM 82*

Stanley, Ralph Edmond
American. Singer, Songwriter
One of the patriarchs of bluegrass; co-
   founder of Stanley Brothers and the
   Clinch Mountain Boys, 1946-66; now
   Ralph Stanley and the Clinch
   Mountain Boys.
b. Feb 25, 1927 in Stratton, Virginia
Source: *BiDAmM; BioIn 15; ConMus 5;
IlEncCM; NewAmDM; WhoAm 90;
WhoEnt 92*

Stanley, Wendell Meredith
American. Chemist
Won Nobel Prize, 1946, for work on
   viruses; isolated influenza virus,
   prepared vaccine against it.
b. Aug 16, 1904 in Ridgeville, Indiana
d. Apr 15, 1971 in Salamanca, Spain
Source: *AmMWSc 82; AmNatBi; AsBiEn;
BiEsc; BioIn 1, 3, 5, 6, 7, 8, 9, 10, 11,
15, 19, 20; CamBiEn; CamDcAB;*

*CamDcSc; ChamBiD; DcAmB S9;
DcAmMeB 84; DcScB S2; EncWB 98;
IndAu 1917; InSci; LarDcSc; McGCEnS;
McGEWB; McGMS 80; NatCAB 57;
NotTwCS 1; RanHWDS; WebAB 74, 79;
WhAm 5; WhDW; WhoNob, 90, 95;
WorAl; WorScD*

Stans, Maurice H(ubert)
American. Government Official
Secretary of Commerce, 1969-72, under
   Richard Nixon; involved in Vesco
   scandal.
b. Mar 22, 1908 in Shakopee, Minnesota
d. Apr 14, 1998 in Pasadena, California
Source: *BiDFilm; BiDrUSE 71, 89;
BioIn 4, 5, 6, 8, 9, 10, 12; ConAu 113,
167; CurBio 58, 98N; IntWW 74, 75, 76,
77, 78, 79, 80, 81, 82, 83, 91, 93, 97;
NewYTBE 70, 71, 73; WhAm 12;
WhoAm 74, 76, 78, 80, 82, 84, 86, 88,
90, 92, 94, 95, 96, 97, 98; WhoAmP 91;
WhoSSW 73; WorAl; WorAlBi*

Stansfield, Lisa
English. Singer
Pop/soul vocalist; formed group Blue
   Zone, 1986; first solo album *Affection*,
   1989.
b. Apr 11, 1966 in Rochdale, England
Source: *BillEnR; ConMus 9; EncRkSt;
LegTOT; Songw*

Stanton, Edwin McMasters
American. Statesman
Secretary of War, 1862-68; dismissal
   caused impeachment charges against
   Johnson, 1868.
b. Dec 19, 1814 in Steubenville, Ohio
d. Dec 24, 1869 in Washington, District
   of Columbia
Source: *ABCAmRe; Alli; AmBi;
AmNatBi; AmPolLe; ApCAB; BiAUS;
BiDrUSE 71, 89; BioIn 3, 5, 6, 7, 9, 10,
12, 15, 17; CamBiEn; CamDcAB;
ChamBiD; CivWDc; CyAG; DcAmB;
DcAmMiB; Drake; EncAB-H 1974,
1996; EncWB 98; HarEnUS; LinLib S;
McGEWB; NatCAB 2; OxCAmH;
TwCBDA; WebAB 74, 79; WhAm HS;
WhCiWar; WorAl*

Stanton, Elizabeth Cady
[Mrs. Henry Brewster Stanton]
American. Feminist, Social Reformer
Co-founded women's rights movement
   with Lucretia Mott; first pres.,
   National Woman Suffrage Assn.,
   1869-90.
b. Nov 12, 1815 in Johnstown, New
   York
d. Oct 26, 1902 in New York, New York
Source: *Alli SUP; AmAu; AmAu&B;
AmBi; AmJust; AmNatBi; AmOrN;
AmRef; AmRef&R; AmSocL; AmWom;
AmWomWr, 92; ApCAB; ArtclWW 2;
BbD; Benet 87, 96; BenetAL 91;
BiCAW; BiDAmJo; BiD&SB; BioAmW;
BioIn 14, 15, 16, 17, 18, 19, 20, 21, 22,
23, 24; BlmGWL; CamDcAB; CamHAL;
ChamBiD; ConAu 171; ContDcW 89;
CyWA 97; DcAmAu; DcAmB; DcAmReB
1, 2; DcAmSR; DcLB 79; DcNAA;*

*EncAB-H 1974, 1996; EncALit;
EncARH; EncAWoR; EncNAB; EncRelA;
EncRev; EncWB 98; EncWHA;
EncWoAP; FemiWr; GayN; GoodHs;
GrLiveH; HanAmWH; HarEnUS; HerW,
84; HisDcHu; HisWorL; IntDcWB;
InWom, SUP; LegTOT; LibW; LinLib L,
S; McGEWB; NatCAB 3; NotAW;
OnHuYeA; OxCAmH; OxCAmL 65, 83,
95; OxCWoWr 95; PolPar; PorAmW;
ProPowC; RadHan; RComAH; REn;
REnAL; TwCBDA; TwCLC 73;
TwoTYeD; WebAB 74, 79; WhAm 1;
WhAmP; WhoChr; WomFir; WomIss;
WorAl; WorAlBi*

Stanton, Frank Lebby
"Riley of the South"
American. Poet, Journalist
Wrote one of American journalism's first
   columns, "Just From GA" in *Atlanta
   Constitution*, beginning 1889;
   published poems *Up from GA*, 1902.
b. Feb 22, 1857 in Charleston, South
   Carolina
d. Jan 7, 1927 in Atlanta, Georgia
Source: *AmAu&B; AmNatBi; ASCAP 66,
80; BbD; BiDAmNC; BiDSA; ChhPo,
S1, S2; DcAmAu; DcAmB; DcNAA;
LinLib L, S; NatCAB 11; OxCAmL 65,
83, 95; REn; REnAL; WhAm 1*

Stanton, Frank Nicholas
American. TV Executive
Pres. of CBS, 1946-71; TV Academy
   Hall of Fame, 1986.
b. Mar 20, 1908 in Muskegon, Michigan
Source: *BiDAmJo; BiE&WWA; BioIn 15,
16; CamDcAB; CurBio 45, 65;
EncTwCJ; IntWW 83, 89, 97, 2000;
NewYTBE 71; WhoAm 86, 90; WhoTelC*

Stanton, Henry Brewster
American. Social Reformer
Active in anti-slavery activities,
   beginning 1834; married Elizabeth
   Cady, 1840.
b. Jun 27, 1805 in Griswold, Connecticut
d. Jan 7, 1887 in New York, New York
Source: *Alli, SUP; AmBi; ApCAB, X;
BiD&SB; DcAmAu; DcAmB; DcNAA;
HarEnUS; NatCAB 2; TwCBDA; WhAm
HS*

Stanton, Robert
American. Government Official
First African American director of the
   National Park Service; oversees 376
   sites across the country, including
   national parks, coastlines, national
   memorials, and historic sites, that draw
   265 million visitors annually.
b. Sep 22, 1940 in Fort Worth, Texas
Source: *ConBlB 20*

Stanwyck, Barbara
[Ruby Stevens]
American. Actor
Starred in over 80 films; received Oscar
   nominations for *Stella Dallas*, 1937,
   The Lady Eve, 1941, *Double
   Indemnity*, 1944, *Sorry, Wrong*

Number, 1948; won Emmys for ''The Big Valley'' and ''The Thorn Birds.''
b. Jul 16, 1907 in New York, New York
d. Jan 20, 1990 in Santa Monica, California
Source: *AmNatBi; AnObit 1990; BiDFilm, 81, 94; BiE&WWA; BioAmW; BioIn 1, 2, 3, 6, 9, 10, 11, 12, 13, 16; CamBiEn; CamDcAB; CelR, 90; ChamBiD; CmMov; ConTFT 3, 8; CurBio 47, 90, 90N; DcArts; DcPseud; EncAFC; FacFETw; FemmeNo; Film 2; FilmEn; FilmgC; ForYSC; GoodHs; HalFC 80, 84, 88; IntDcF 1-3, 2-3; IntMPA 77, 80, 84, 86, 88; IntWW 79, 80, 81, 82, 83, 89; InWom, SUP; LegTOT; MotPP; MovMk; NewYTBS 81, 90; OsStAZ; OxCFilm; ScrEAmL 2; SweetSg D; ThFT; WhAm 10; WhoAm 74, 76, 78, 80, 82, 84, 86, 88; WhoAmW 58, 61, 64, 66, 68, 70, 72, 87, 89; WhoHol A; WhoThe 77A; WhoWor 74, 89; WhThe; WorAl; WorAlBi; WorEFlm*

Stapledon, Olaf
[William Olaf Stapledon]
English. Educator, Author
Science fiction novels include *Death into Life,* 1946.
b. May 10, 1886 in Wallasey, England
d. Sep 6, 1950 in Cheshire, England
Source: *Benet 87; BioIn 2, 4, 7, 12, 13, 14, 17, 20, 21, 22; ConAu 111; CyWA 97; DcLB 15; EncSF; EvLB; LngCTC; NewCBEL; NewEScF; REn; RGSF; RGTwCSF; ScF&FL 1, 2, 92; ScFEYrs; ScFSB; ScFWr, 2; TwCA, SUP; TwCLC 22; TwCSFW 81, 86, 91; TwCWr; WhE&EA; WhLit; WhoSciF*

Staples, Brent
American. Journalist
Editorial writer, *New York Times,* 1983—; wrote *Parallel Time: Growing Up Black and White,* 1994.
b. 1951 in Chester, Pennsylvania
Source: *ConAu 153; ConBlB 8*

Staple Singers, The
[Cleotha Staple; Mavis Staple; Pervis Staple; Roebuck ''Pop'' Staple; Yvonne Staple]
American. Music Group
Family group formed, 1954; soul hits include ''Let's Do It Again,'' 1975.
Source: *AllMGBl 2; BiDAfM; BiDAmM; DcTwCCu 5; EncRk 88; EncRkSt; HarEnR 86; IlEncRk; InB&W 85A; NewGrDA 86; PenEncP; RkOn 78, 84; RkWho 96; SoulM; WhoRock 81*

Stapleton, Jean
[Jeanne Murray; Mrs. William Putch]
American. Actor
Played Edith Bunker on TV series ''All in the Family,'' 1971-79.
b. Jan 19, 1923 in New York, New York
Source: *BiE&WWA; BioIn 9, 10; BioNews 74; BkPepl; CamDcAB; CelR; ConTFT 1, 7, 25; CurBio 72; DcPseud; EncAFC; FilmEn; ForYSC; HalFC 80, 84, 88; IntMPA 77, 78, 79, 80, 81, 82, 84, 86, 88, 92; InWom SUP; LegTOT;*

NewYTBE 71, 72; NewYTBS 86; NotNAT; WhoAm 74, 86, 88, 90; WhoAmW 74, 75, 77, 87, 89; WhoCom; WhoHol 92, A; WhoTelC; WhoThe 77; WhoWest 74; WorAl; WorAlBi

Stapleton, Maureen
[Louis Maureen Stapleton]
American. Actor
Won Tony for *The Gingerbread Lady,* 1970; won Oscar for *Reds,* 1982.
b. Jun 21, 1925 in Troy, New York
Source: *BiE&WWA; BioIn 2, 3, 5, 6, 7, 9, 10, 12, 13, 14, 16, 18, 21, 22; BioNews 74; CamBiEn; CamGWoT; CelR, 90; ChamBiD; CnThe; ConTFT 4, 11; CurBio 59; EncAFC; Ent; FamA&A; FilmEn; FilmgC; ForYSC; HalFC 80, 84, 88; IntMPA 75, 76, 77, 78, 79, 80, 81, 82, 84, 86, 88, 92, 94, 96; IntWWW 2; InWom, SUP; ItaFilm; LegTOT; MotPP; MovMk; NewYTBE 71; NewYTBS 81; NotNAT; NotWoAT; OsStAZ; OxCAmT 84; OxCThe 83; WhoAm 74, 76, 78, 80, 82, 84, 86, 88, 90, 92, 94, 95, 96, 97, 98; WhoAmW 66, 68, 70, 72, 74, 75, 77, 81, 83, 85, 87, 89, 91, 93, 95, 97, 99; WhoEnt 92; WhoHol 92, A; WhoThe 72, 77, 81; WhoWor 74, 76; WorAl; WorAlBi*

Stapleton, Ruth Carter
American.
Baptist evangelist, spiritual healer; sister of Jimmy Carter.
b. Aug 7, 1929 in Archery, Georgia
d. Sep 26, 1983 in Fayetteville, North Carolina
Source: *AnObit 1983; BioIn 10; ConAu 81, 110; InWom SUP; NewYTBS 83*

Starch, Daniel
American. Advertising Executive, Psychologist
Marketing research expert; wrote *Principles of Advertising,* 1923.
b. Mar 8, 1883 in La Crosse, Wisconsin
d. Feb 8, 1979
Source: *AdMenW; AmAu&B; AmMWSc 73S, 78S; BioIn 4, 6, 10, 11, 12, 20; ConAu 37R, 85NR, 133; CurBio 63; NewYTBS 79; REnAL; WhAm 7; WhNAA; WhoAm 74, 76, 78*

Stargell, Willie
[Wilver Dornel Stargell]
''Pops''
American. Baseball Player
Outfielder, Pittsburgh, 1962-82; led NL in home runs twice, in RBIs once; Hall of Fame, 1988; coach, Ptiisgurgh, 1982-85; coach, Atlanta Braves, 1985-88.
b. Mar 4, 1941 in Earlsboro, Oklahoma
Source: *AfrAmSG; BiDAmSp BB; BioIn 9, 10, 11, 12, 13, 21; ConAu 118, 146; CurBio 80; InB&W 80; LegTOT; WhoAfA 79, 10, 11, 12; WhoAm 80, 82, 92, 94, 95, 96, 97, 98, 99, 2000; WhoBlA 2, 3, 4, 5, 6, 7, 8; WhoE 95; WhoProB 73; WhoSpor; WhoWor 96; WorAl; WorAlBi*

Starhawk
[Miriam Simos]
American. Psychotherapist, Religious Leader
Major contributor to the feminist spirituality movement, leading theorist and practitioner of Wicca (or witchcraft) in the United States.
b. Jun 17, 1951 in St. Paul, Minnesota
Source: *EncAWoR; EncWB 98; EncWW; FemiWr; NewAgE 90; RadHan; RelLAm 1, 2*

Stark, Harold Raynsford
American. Naval Officer
Chief of US naval operations, 1939-41; relieved of command after Pearl Harbor attack.
b. Nov 12, 1880 in Wilkes-Barre, Pennsylvania
d. Aug 20, 1972 in Washington, District of Columbia
Source: *BiDWWGF; BioIn 1, 10; CamBiEn; CamDcAB; ChamBiD; CurBio 72, 72N; DcAmB S9; DcAmMiB; EncNaHi; LinLib S; NewYTBE 72; ObitOF 79; OxCShps; WebAMB; WhAm 5; WhWW-II*

Stark, Johannes
German. Scientist
Discovered Doppler effect in canal rays; won 1919 Nobel Prize in physics.
b. Apr 15, 1874 in Schickenhof, Germany
d. Jun 21, 1957 in Traunstein, Germany (West)
Source: *AsBiEn; BiESc; BioIn 3, 4, 14, 15, 20; CamBiEn; CamDcSc; ChamBiD; DcScB; EncTR, 91; InSci; LarDcSc; McGCEnS; NobelP; NotTwCS 1; RanHWDS; WhoNob, 90, 95*

Stark, John
American. Army Officer
Revolutionary War officer; won battle of Bennington, VT, 1777.
b. Aug 28, 1728 in Londonderry, New Hampshire
d. May 8, 1822 in Manchester, New Hampshire
Source: *Alli; AmBi; AmNatBi; AmRev; ApCAB; BioIn 2, 3, 7, 9, 10, 16; CamDcAB; ChamBiD; DcAmB; Drake; EncAR; EncCRAm; GenMudB; HarEnUS; HisDcAR; LinLib S; NatCAB 1; OxCAmH; TwCBDA; WebAB 74, 79; WebAMB; WhAm HS; WhAmRev; WhoMilH 76; WorAl; WorAlBi*

Stark, Koo
[Kathleen Stark]
American. Actor
Involved in publicized romance with Britain's Prince Andrew, 1982.
b. 1957? in New York, New York
Source: *BioIn 13*

Stark, Ray
American. Filmmaker
Films produced include *Funny Girl,* 1968; *The Way We Were,* 1973; *Biloxi Blues,* 1987.

b. Oct 13, 1917?
Source: *CelR 90; ConTFT 6; HalFC 88; IntMPA 86; NewYTBS 80; WhoAm 84; WhoEnt 92; WhoWest 92*

Starker, Janos
Hungarian. Musician
Cello virtuoso; int'l reputation as first cellist with many symphonies.
b. Jul 5, 1924 in Budapest, Hungary
Source: *BakBD 78, 84, 92; BakBDTw; BakDcM; BioIn 4, 6, 9, 10, 11, 12, 13, 15, 22; BlueB 76; BriBkM 80; CurBio 63; FacFETw; IntWW 74, 75, 76, 77, 78, 79, 80, 81, 82, 83, 89, 91, 93, 97, 98, 2000; IntWWM 77, 80, 90; MusSN; NewAmDM; NewGrDA 86; NewGrDM 80; NewYTBE 72; NewYTBS 82; PenDiMP; Who 74, 82, 83, 85, 88, 90, 92, 94, 98, 99, 2000; WhoAm 74, 76, 78, 80, 82, 84, 86, 88, 90; WhoAmM 83; WhoEnt 92, 98; WhoMus 72*

Starkie, Walter Fitzwilliam
Irish. Author, Educator
Taught Romance languages, Trinity College, 1926-47; best known for stories of his life among the gypsies: *In Sara's Tents,* 1953.
b. Aug 9, 1894 in Killiney, Ireland
d. Nov 2, 1976 in Madrid, Spain
Source: *Au&Wr 71; BiDIrW; BioIn 1, 4, 6, 7, 11, 17, 22, 24; BlueB 76; CarSB; CathA 1930; ConAu 69, 77; CurBio 64, 77; DcIrB 2, 3; DcIrW 2; IntAu&W 77; IntWW 74, 75, 76; LngCTC; NewC; NewCBEL; NewGrDM 80; NewYTBS 76; TwCA, SUP; WhAm 7; WhE&EA; Who 74; WhoAm 74, 76; WhoMus 72; WorAu 1900*

Starkweather, Charles
American. Murderer
Killed 11 people, 1958; executed, 1959.
b. Nov 24, 1938 in Lincoln, Nebraska
d. Jun 24, 1959 in Lincoln, Nebraska
Source: *BioIn 10, 23; VioAm*

Starling, Ernest Henry
English. Physiologist
Collaborated with William Bayliss on digestive, kidney function studies; discovered secretin, 1912; wrote *Principles of Human Physiology,* 1912.
b. Apr 17, 1866 in London, England
d. May 2, 1927 in Kingston, Jamaica
Source: *AsBiEn; BiESc; BiHiMed; BioIn 2, 4, 8, 9, 14, 20; CamBiEn; CamDcSc; ChamBiD; DcNaB 1922; DcScB; InSci; LarDcSc; NewCol 75; OxCMed 86; RanHWDS; WhLit; WorAl; WorAlBi; WorScD*

Starr, Bart
[Bryan B Starr]
American. Football Player
Quarterback, Green Bay, 1956-71; set several NFL passing records; led league in passing three times; MVP, Super Bowl, 1967, 1968; Hall of Fame, 1977.
b. Jan 9, 1934 in Montgomery, Alabama

Source: *BioIn 7, 8, 9, 10, 11, 12, 13, 15, 17, 20, 23, 24; BioNews 75; CurBio 68; LegTOT; NewYTBS 81; WhoAm 82, 84, 86, 88, 92, 94, 95, 96; WhoFtbl 74; WhoSpor; WorAl; WorAlBi*

Starr, Belle
[Myra Belle Shirley]
American. Pioneer, Outlaw
Cattle rustler; harbored Jesse James, 1881.
b. Feb 5, 1848? in Carthage, Missouri
d. Feb 3, 1889 in Briartown, Oklahoma
Source: *AmAu&B; AmNatBi; BioIn 3, 5, 6, 7, 8, 9, 10, 11, 13, 14, 15, 16, 17, 24; ContDcW 89; DrInf; EncAmaz 91; GoodHs; HalFC 80, 84, 88; IntDcWB; LegTOT; LibW; NewEAmW; NotAW; REnAW; WhAm HS; WorAl; WorAlBi*

Starr, Kay
[Kathryn Stark]
American. Singer
Popular vocalist, 1940s-50s; combined blues, country, swing; hit single: "Wheel of Fortune," 1952.
b. Jul 21, 1924 in Doughtery, Oklahoma
Source: *BiDAmM; BioIn 2; CmpEPM; NewGrDJ 88; PenEncP; RkOn 74*

Starr, Kenneth
American. Lawyer
Attorney was named to the U.S. Court of Appeals, but stepped down in 1989 to become solicitor general, then appointed independent counsel in the Whitewater investigation; drew criticism for his obsessive investigation of President Bill Clinton's relationship with Monica Lewinsky, driving the scandal that led to the President's impeachment and eventual acquittal.
b. Jul 21, 1946 in Vernon, Texas
Source: *News 98, 98-3*

Starr, Ringo
[The Beatles; Richard Starkey]
English. Singer, Musician
Drummer with The Beatles; started solo career, 1970; starred in film *Caveman,* 1981; inducted into Rock and Roll Hall of Fame with The Beatles, 1988.
b. Jul 7, 1940 in Liverpool, England
Source: *BakBD 78, 84, 92; BakDcM; BillEnR; BioIn 6, 7, 8, 9, 10, 11, 12, 13, 16; BkPepl; BlueB 76; CamBiEn; CelR, 90; ConMuA 80A; ConMus 10, 24; ConTFT 7, 18; CurBio 65; DcPseud; EncPR&S 89; EncRk 88; EncRkSt; FilmEn; ForYSC; HarEnR 86; IlEncRk; IntMPA 92, 94, 96; IntWW 74, 75, 76, 77, 78, 79, 80, 81, 82, 83, 89, 91, 93, 98, 2000; ItaFilm; LegTOT; MiSFD 9; MotPP; NewAmDM; NewGrDM 80; OxCPMus; PenEncP; RkOn 78; RkWho 96; RolSEnR 83; WhoAm 78, 80, 82, 84, 86, 88, 90, 92, 94, 95, 96, 97, 98, 99, 2000; WhoEnt 92, 98; WhoHol 92, A; WhoRock 81; WhoRocM 82; WhoWor 74, 78, 80, 82, 84, 87, 89, 91, 93, 95, 96, 97, 98, 99, 2000; WorAl; WorAlBi*

Starrett, Vincent
[Charles Vincent Emerson Starrett]
American. Author, Critic
Books include *Bookman's Holiday,* 1942; *Private Life of Sherlock Holmes,* 1933.
b. Oct 26, 1886 in Toronto, Ontario, Canada
d. Jan 4, 1974 in Chicago, Illinois
Source: *AmAu&B; AuBYP 2, 3; BenetAL 91; BioIn 4, 7, 8, 10, 14, 22, 23; ChhPo, S2; ConAu 31NR, 45, 73; CrtSuMy; DcLB 187; DcLEL; EncMys; NewYTBS 74; REn; REnAL; ScF&FL 1, 92; TwCA, SUP; TwCCr&M 80, 85, 91; WhAm 6; WhLit; WhNAA; WorAu 1900*

Starship
[Don Baldwin; Craig Chaquico; Pete Sears; Grace Slick; Mickey Thomas]
American. Music Group
Made up of members of Jefferson Starship; hit album *Knee Deep in the Hoopla,* 1985.
Source: *ConMus 5; EncPR&S 89; EncRk 88; FacFETw; NewAmDM; PenEncP; WhoAmP 75; WhoRocM 82*

Starzl, Thomas Earl
American. Surgeon
Pioneer in organ transplantation; performed first human-liver transplant, 1963.
b. Mar 11, 1926 in Le Mars, Iowa
Source: *BioIn 11, 12; CamDcAB; CurBio 93; WhoAm 74, 76, 80, 82, 84, 88, 90, 92, 94, 95, 96, 97; WhoMedH 2000; WhoWest 74, 76, 78, 80; WrDr 98, 99, 2000*

Stassen, Harold Edward
American. Lawyer, Politician
Rep. Governor of MN, 1938-45; youngest governor in US history; best known for many attempts at presidential nomination.
b. Apr 13, 1907 in West Saint Paul, Minnesota
Source: *AmAu&B; BiDrGov 1789; BioIn 1, 2, 3, 4, 5, 6, 8, 10, 11; BlueB 76; CamBiEn; CamDcAB; ChamBiD; CurBio 40, 48; FacFETw; IntWW 83; IntYB 78, 79, 80, 81, 82; LinLib S; PolProf E, T; WebAB 74, 79; Who 74, 82, 83, 85, 88, 90, 92, 94, 98, 99, 2000; WhoAm 74, 76, 78, 80, 82; WhoAmL 83, 85; WhoAmP 73; WhoWor 78, 80, 82; WorAl; WorAlBi*

Stastny, Anton
Czech. Hockey Player
Left wing, Quebec, 1980—; defected with brothers Peter and Marian.
b. Aug 5, 1959 in Bratislava, Czechoslovakia
Source: *BioIn 12, 13; HocEn; HocReg 87; NewYTBS 81; WhoFI 92*

Stastny, Marian
Czech. Hockey Player
Right wing, Quebec, 1981-85, Toronto, 1985-87; defected with brothers Anton and Peter.

b. Jan 8, 1953 in Bratislava,
Czechoslovakia
Source: *BioIn 13; HocEn; HocReg 86;
NewYTBS 81*

Stastny, Peter
Czech. Hockey Player
Center, Quebec, 1980-1990, NJ, 1990—;
one of four players in NHL history to
break in with three consecutive 100-pt.
seasons; won Calder Trophy, 1981,
first non-North American player
honored.
b. Sep 18, 1956 in Bratislava,
Czechoslovakia
Source: *BioIn 12, 13; HocEn; HocReg
87; NewYTBS 81*

Statler, Ellsworth Milton
American. Hotel Executive
Started Statler chain of hotels, Buffalo,
NY, 1904.
b. Oct 26, 1863 in Somerset County,
Pennsylvania
d. Apr 16, 1928 in New York, New
York
Source: *AmNatBi; BioIn 2, 3, 7, 8, 10;
CamBiEn; ConMus 8; DcAmB; WebAB
74, 79; WhAm 1*

Statler Brothers
[Phillip Balsley; Lew C DeWitt; Don S
Reid; Harold W Reid]
American. Music Group
Durable country harmony group; hit
singles since early 1960s.
Source: *AllMGCo; BgBkCoM; BiDAmM;
ConMus 8; CounME 74, 74A;
EncFCWM 69, 83; HarEnCM 87;
IlEncCM; NewAmDM; NewGrDA 86;
PenEncP; RkOn 74, 78; WhoAmP 75,
77, 79, 81, 83, 85, 87; WhoHol 92;
WhoRock 81*

Status Quo
[Andy Bown; John Brown; Rick Parfitt;
Jeff Rich; Francis Rossi]
English. Music Group
Pop hits include *Dear John*, 1982; *The
Wanderer*, 1984.
Source: *AfrAmPr; Alli, SUP; BbtC;
BiAUS; BiDBrA; BiDLA; BiDrAC;
BiDrUSC 89; BillEnR; BioIn 11, 19;
CabMA; Chambr 2, 3; ChhPo, S1;
ConMuA 80A; CyAL 1; DcBiPP;
DcBrBl; DcBrWA; DcLP 87A; DcNaB,
C; EncRk 88; EncRkSt; FolkA 87;
GrMetD; IlEncRk; InB&W 80; Law&B
89A, 89B, 92; NewC; NewCBEL;
NewYHSD; OxCPMus; PenEncP;
PeoHis; PoIre; RkOn 78; RolSEnR 83;
St&PR 96, 97; WhAm HS; WhoAfA 9;
WhoAmP 85; WhoHol 92; WhoRock 81;
WhoRocM 82; WhScrn 77, 83*

Staub, Rusty
[Daniel Joseph Staub]
American. Baseball Player
Outfielder, 1963-85; led NL in pinch
hits, 1983, 1984; had .279 lifetime
batting average.
b. Apr 1, 1944 in New Orleans,
Louisiana

Source: *Ballpl 90; BaseReg 86;
BiDAmSp BB; BioIn 8, 9, 11, 12, 14, 15,
16; LegTOT; NewYTBE 72, 73;
NewYTBS 85; WhoAm 74, 76, 78;
WhoProB 73*

Staubach, Roger Thomas
American. Football Player
Quarterback, won Heisman Trophy,
1963; in NFL with Dallas, 1969-79;
MVP, Super Bowl, 1972; Hall of
Fame, 1985.
b. Feb 5, 1942 in Cincinnati, Ohio
Source: *BiDAmSp FB; BioIn 6, 9, 10,
11, 12, 15, 16; CamDcAB; ConAu 104;
CurBio 72; NewYTBE 71, 72; NewYTBS
84, 89; WhoAm 74, 76, 78, 80, 82, 84,
86, 88, 90, 92, 94, 95, 96; WhoFtbl 74;
WorAlBi*

Staudinger, Hermann
German. Chemist, Author
Won 1953 Nobel Prize for work in
synthetics.
b. Mar 23, 1881 in Worms, Germany
d. Sep 9, 1965 in Freiburg, Germany
(West)
Source: *AsBiEn; BiESc; BioIn 2, 3, 6, 7,
8, 14, 15, 19, 20; CamBiEn; CamDcSc;
ChamBiD; ConAu 113, 162; CurBio 65;
DcScB; InSci; LarDcSc; McGCEnS;
McGMS 80; NobelP; NotTwCS 1;
RanHWDS; WhAm 4; WhoNob, 90, 95*

**Stauffenberg, Claus (Schenk
Graf) Von**
[Klaus Graf Schenk von Stauffenberg]
German. Army Officer
Part of conspiracy against Hitler; failed
in assassination attempt, Jul 1944; shot
to death by firing squad.
b. Nov 15, 1907 in Upper Franconia,
Germany
d. Jul 20, 1944 in Rastenburg, Germany
Source: *BioIn 2, 8, 10; EncTR;
HisWorL; OxCGer 76; WhWW-II*

Staunton, Howard
English. Chess Player
Organizer of first world chess
tournament, 1851; wrote several books
on subject.
b. 1810 in Westmoreland, England
d. Jun 22, 1874 in London, England
Source: *Alli; BioIn 10, 11, 12, 14, 15;
CelCen; ChamBiD; DcBiPP; DcNaB;
GolEC; NewCBEL; OxCChes 84*

Staupers, Mabel K.
American. Civil Rights Activist
Executive secretary, National Association
of Colored Graduate Nurses, 1934-49;
president, 1940-50; helped pursuade
the American Nurses' Association to
remove all barriers to black
membership.
b. Feb 27, 1890, Barbados
d. Nov 29, 1989 in Washington, District
of Columbia
Source: *AfrAmAl 8; ConBlB 7*

Stautner, Ernie
[Ernest Stautner]
American. Football Player
Nine-time all-pro defensive tackle,
Pittsburgh, 1950-63; Hall of Fame,
1969.
b. Apr 2, 1925 in Calm, Bavaria
Source: *BiDAmSp FB; BioIn 10, 17;
LegTOT; WhoFtbl 74; WhoSpor*

Stavisky, Serge Alexandre
French. Criminal
Swindler; sold worthless bonds to French
working people.
b. Nov 10, 1886 in Slobodka, Russia
d. Jan 8, 1934 in Chamonix-Mont-Blanc,
France
Source: *BioIn 2, 4, 5, 10, 11, 14, 17;
CamBiEn; ChamBiD; REn*

Stavropoulos, George Peter
American. Fashion Designer
Best known for chiffon evening wear for
women; influenced by classical Greek
scu lpture; dressed such celebrities as
Elizabeth Taylor, Maria Callas.
b. Jan 22, 1920 in Tripolis, Greece
d. Dec 10, 1990 in New York, New
York
Source: *BioIn 14, 16; ConFash; CurBio
85, 91N; EncFash; FairDF US;
NewYTBS 90; WhAm 12; WhoAm 82;
WorFshn*

Stead, Christina (Ellen)
Australian. Author
Feminist novelist; best-known novel *The
Man Who Loved Children*, 1940.
b. Jul 17, 1902 in Sydney, Australia
d. Mar 31, 1983 in Sydney, Australia
Source: *AnObit 1983; ArtclWW 2;
Au&Wr 71; AuLitCr; AuWomWr; Benet
87, 96; BioIn 1, 4, 8, 9, 10, 11, 13, 14,
15, 16, 17, 18, 19, 20, 21; BlmGEL;
BlmGWL; CamBiEn; CamGLE; CasWL;
ChamBiD; ConAu 13R, 33NR, 40NR,
109; ConLC 2, 5, 8, 32, 80; ConNov 72,
76, 82; ContDcW 89; CyWA 89; DcArts;
DcLEL; EncBrWW; EncWL 2, 2S; EvLB;
FacFETw; FarE&A 78, 79, 80, 81;
FemiCLE; FemiWr; GrWomW; GrWrEL
N; IntAu&W 76, 77; IntDcWB; IntLitE;
IntWW 77, 78, 79, 80, 81, 82, 83N;
InWom, SUP; LegTOT; LngCTC;
MajTwCW 1, 2; ModCmwL; ModWoWr;
NewCBEL; NewYTBS 83; Novels;
OxCAusL; OxCEng 85, 95; OxCTwCL;
RAdv 1, 14, 13-1; RfGEnL 91; RfGShF
1, 2; RGTwCWr; ScF&FL 1, 2, 92;
TwCA, SUP; TwCWr; WhAm 8;
WhE&EA; Who 74, 82, 83; WhoTwCL;
WhoWor 74, 76; WorAl; WorAu 1900;
WrDr 76, 80, 82, 84*

Steber, Eleanor
American. Opera Singer
Soprano; NY Met., 1940-66; noted for
Mozart, Verdi, Puccini roles.
b. Jul 17, 1916 in Wheeling, West
Virginia
d. Oct 3, 1990 in Langhorne,
Pennsylvania

Source: *BakBD 78, 84; BiDAmM; BioIn 1, 2, 3, 4, 5, 9, 10, 11, 12, 13; BriBkM 80; CamDcAB; CmOp; CurBio 43, 91N; FacFETw; IntDcOp; IntWWM 90; InWom, SUP; MetOEnc; MusSN; NewAmDM; NewEOp 71; NewGrDA 86; NewGrDM 80; NewGrDO; NewYTBE 73; NewYTBS 90; PenDiMP; WhoAm 74, 76, 78, 80, 82, 84, 86, 90; WhoAmM 83; WhoAmW 58, 83, 87; WhoMus 72; WhoWor 74*

Stedman, Edmund Clarence
American. Author, Journalist
Edited *Victorian Poets*, 1875; 11-volume
  Library of American Literature, 1888-
  90.
b. Oct 8, 1833 in Hartford, Connecticut
d. Jan 18, 1908 in New York, New York
Source: *Alli, SUP; AmAu; AmAu&B; AmBi; AmNatBi; ApCAB, X; Benet 87; BenetAL 91; BibAL; BiD&SB; BioIn 3, 5, 13, 15, 16, 22; CamDcAB; ChamBiD; Chambr 3; ChhPo, S1, S2, S3; CivWDc; CnDAL; CyAL 2; DcAmAu; DcAmB; DcEnA A; DcEnL; DcLB 64; DcLEL; DcNAA; Drake; EvLB; GayN; HarEnUS; HisDcWJ; JrnUS; LinLib L; NatCAB 3; OxCAmL 65, 83, 95; OxCCan; REn; REnAL; TwCBDA; WhAm 1; WhCiWar; WhLit*

Steegmuller, Francis
American. Author
Best known for biographies; *Cocteau: A
  Biography* won Nat. Book Award,
  1971.
b. Jul 3, 1906 in New Haven,
  Connecticut
Source: *AmAu&B; Au&Wr 71; Benet 87, 96; BenetAL 91; BioIn 2, 4, 12, 17, 20, 22; ChhPo; ConAu 2NR, 49; ConNov 72, 79; DcLB 111; DcLP 87A; DrAPF 80, 91; IntAu&W 76, 77, 82, 86, 89, 91; NewYTBS 80; OxCAmL 83, 95; REnAL; TwCA SUP; WhAm 11; WhE&EA; Who 74, 82, 83, 85, 88, 90, 92, 94; WhoAm 74, 76, 78, 80, 82, 84, 86, 88, 90, 92, 94; WorAu 1900; WrDr 76, 80, 82, 84, 86, 88, 90, 92, 94, 96, 98, 99, 2000*

Steel, Anthony
English. Actor
Films include *The Monster Club*, 1981.
b. May 21, 1920 in London, England
Source: *FilmEn; FilmgC; ForYSC; HalFC 80, 84, 88; IIWWBF; IntMPA 75, 76, 77, 78, 79, 80, 81, 82, 84, 86, 88, 92; ItaFilm; WhoHol A*

Steel, Danielle Fernande
[Danielle Schuelein-Steel]
American. Author
Author of romantic bestsellers *The
  Promise*, 1979; *Full Circle*, 1984; *Fine
  Things*, 1987; *Jewels*, 1991.
b. Aug 14, 1947 in New York, New
  York
Source: *BioIn 16; CelR 90; ConAu 19NR, 36NR, 65NR, 81; CurBio 89; MajTwCW 2; SmATA 66; TwCRHW 90; WhoAm 86, 88, 90, 92, 94, 95, 96, 98, 99, 2000; WhoAmW 81, 83, 85, 89, 91,*

93, 95, 99; WhoEnt 98; WhoUSWr 88; WhoWor 95; WhoWrEP 89, 92, 95; WorAlBi; WrDr 92

Steel, David Martin Scott
Scottish. Politician
Member of Parliament and leader of the
  Liberal Party beginning in 1976.
b. Mar 31, 1938 in Kirkcaldy, Scotland
Source: *BioIn 11, 13; ChamBiD; EncWB, 98; IntAu&W 86, 89; IntWW 77, 78, 89, 91, 93, 97; IntYB 78, 79, 80, 81, 82; NewYTBS 76; Who 74, 83, 94; WhoWor 80, 82, 84; WrDr 94, 96, 98, 99, 2000*

Steel, Dawn
American. Producer, Film Executive
Films include *Fatal Attraction*, 1987;
  pres. of Columbia Pictures, 1987-90.
b. Aug 19, 1946 in New York, New
  York
d. Dec 20, 1997 in Los Angeles,
  California
Source: *BioIn 16; ChamBiD; ConAu 151, 163; ConTFT 5, 22; EncWB 99; IntMPA 86, 92, 94, 96; IntWW 89, 91, 93, 97; IntWWW 2; News 90, 98, 90-1, 98-2; NewYTBS 97; ReelWom; WhoAm 86, 88, 90; WhoAmW 89, 91; WhoEnt 92; WhoWest 89, 92; WomFir*

Steel, Flora Annie Webster
English. Author
Wrote on India: *On the Face of the
  Waters*, 1896.
b. Apr 2, 1847 in Harrow, England
d. Apr 12, 1929
Source: *BioIn 16, 21, 22; ConAu 116; InWom, SUP; LngCTC; TwCA*

Steele, Bob
[Robert North Bradbury, Jr.]
American. Actor
Cowboy star in over 150 films, 1927-71;
  appeared in TV comedy "F-Troop."
  1965-67.
b. Jan 23, 1906? in Pendleton, Oregon
d. Dec 21, 1988 in Burbank, California
Source: *BioIn 8, 16; Film 2; FilmEn; FilmgC; FrSilen; TwYS; Vers A; WhoHol A*

Steele, Claude Mason
American. Psychologist, Educator
Social psychologist researches alcohol
  addiction, negative self-image, and the
  effects of group stereotypes; developed
  theory of "stereotype vulnerability"
  involving the harmful effects of
  perceiving a negative stereotype about
  one's own group.
b. Jan 1, 1946 in Chicago, Illinois
Source: *ConBlB 13; NotBlAS; WhoAfA 9, 10, 11, 12; WhoBlA 3, 4, 5, 6, 7, 8; WhoScEn 94*

Steele, Richard, Sir
[Isaac Bickerstaff]
British. Author, Editor
Founded periodical papers *Tatler*, 1709,
  Spectator, 1711, *Guardian*, 1713;

wrote comedy *The Conscious Lover*,
  1712.
b. Mar 1672 in Dublin, Ireland
d. Sep 1, 1729 in Carmarthen, Wales
Source: *Alli; AtlBL; BbD; Benet 87, 96; BiCoLiE; BiD&SB; BiDIrW; BioIn 1, 2, 3, 4, 5, 6, 8, 9, 11, 12, 15, 17, 18, 21; BlkwCE; BlmGEL; BritAu; BritWr 3; CamBiEn; CamGEL; CamGLE; CamGWoT; CasWL; ChamBiD; Chambr 2; ChhPo; CnDBLB 2; CnThe; CrtSuDr; CrtT 2, 4; CyWA 58, 97; DcArts; DcEnA; DcEnL; DcEuL; DcIrB 1, 2, 3; DcIrL, 96; DcIrW 1, 2; DcLB 84, 101; DcLEL; DcNaB; Dis&D; EncEnl; EncWB 98; EncWT; Ent; EvLB; GrWrEL DR, N; IntDcT 2; LegTOT; LiJour; LinLib L, S; LitC 18; LngCEL; LuthC 75; McGEWB; McGEWD 72, 84; MouLC 2; NewC; NewCBEL; NotNAT A, B; OxCBrHi; OxCEng 67, 85, 95; OxCIri; OxCThe 67, 83; PenC ENG; PlP&P; PoIre; RAdv 1, 14, 13-1; REn; REnWD; RfGEnL 91; WebE&AL; WhDW; WorAl; WorAlBi*

Steele, Shelby
American. Author, Educator
Writing focuses on racial issues,
  specifically the notion that white
  society is inherently racist and all
  blacks are victimized by racism; book
  The Content of Our Character,
  nominated for National Book Award,
  1991.
b. Jan 1, 1946 in Chicago, Illinois
Source: *AfrAmAl 6, 8; AmDec 1980; ConAu 155; ConBlB 13; CurBio 93; CyWA 97; IdentIs; News 91, 91-2; NewYTBS 90; WhoAfA 9, 10, 11, 12; WhoAm 94, 95, 96, 97, 98, 99, 2000; WhoBlA 7, 8; WhoEnt 98; WrDr 92, 94, 96, 98*

Steele, Tommy
English. Actor
Films include *The Happiest Millionaire*,
  1967; *Finian's Rainbow*, 1968.
b. Dec 17, 1936 in London, England
Source: *BioIn 4, 5, 7, 8, 11, 13; BlueB 76; CamBiEn; ChamBiD; ConAu 129; ConTFT 3; DcPseud; EncMT; EncRk 88; EncRkSt; FilmAG WE; FilmEn; FilmgC; ForYSC; HalFC 80, 84, 88; IIWWBF, A; IntMPA 75, 76, 77, 78, 79, 80, 82, 84, 86, 88, 92, 94, 96; IntWW 79, 80, 81, 82, 83, 89, 91, 93, 97, 98, 2000; IntWWM 90; MotPP; OxCFilm; OxCPMus; PenEncP; RolSEnR 83; Who 74, 82, 83, 85, 88, 90, 92, 94, 98, 99, 2000; WhoHol 92, A; WhoRocM 82; WhoThe 72, 77, 81; WhoWor 76*

Steele, Willie
American. Track Athlete
Long jumper; won gold medal, 1948
  Olympics.
b. Jul 14, 1923 in Seeley, California
Source: *WhoTr&F 73*

Steeleye Span
[Kemp; Martin Carthy; Bob Johnson;
John Kirkpatrick; Peter Knight; Maddy
Prior]
British. Music Group
Pioneered electronic folk music; albums
include *Sails of Silver*, 1980.
Source: *Alli; SUP; AuBYP 2, 3; BiDLA;
BillEnR; BioIn 8, 17, 18; ConMuA 80A;
ConMus 19; EncPR&S 89; EncRk 88;
HarEnR 86; IlEncRk; NewYTBS 91;
PenEncP; PoIre; RolSEnR 83; WhoAm
84, 86; WhoAmP 83; WhoRock 81;
WhoRocM 82; WhoWest 87, 89*

Steelman, John Roy
American. Government Official
Held several govt. posts beginning 1934;
first to serve as asst. to US pres.,
under Truman, 1946-52.
b. Jun 23, 1900 in Thornton, Arkansas
d. Jul 14, 1999 in Naples, Florida
Source: *BioIn 1, 2, 3, 10, 11; CurBio 41,
52; PolProf T*

Steely Dan
[Jeff Baxter; Walter Becker; Denny Dias;
Donald Fagen; James Hodder; David
Palmer]
American. Music Group
Formed, 1972; lively, bluesy jazz hits
include FM, 1978; "Deacon Blues,"
1978.
Source: *Alli; BillEnR; BioIn 12; ChhPo,
S1; ConMuA 80A; ConMus 5; DcNaB;
DrAPF 85, 87, 89, 91, 93, 97; Dun&B
88, 90; EncPR&S 89; EncRk 88;
EncRkSt; HarEnR 86; IlEncRk;
NewAmDM; NewGrDA 86; OnThGG;
OxCCan; PenEncP; RkOn 74, 78;
RkWho 96; RolSEnR 83; WhoAm 80, 82,
84, 86, 94, 95, 96, 97; WhoEnt 92;
WhoHol 92; WhoRock 81; WhoRocM 82*

Steen, Alann
American. Hostage
Journalism professor in Lebanon seized
by Islamic Jihad January 24, 1987 and
held captive 1,774 days; released
December 3, 1991.
Source: *BioIn 19*

Steen, Jan
Dutch. Artist
Prolific painter of genre scenes depicting
taverns, middle-class life.
b. 1626 in Leiden, Netherlands
d. Feb 3, 1679 in Leiden, Netherlands
Source: *AtlBL; ChamBiD; ClaDrA;
DcArts; Dis&D; IntDcAA 90; LegTOT;
McGDA; OxCArt; WhDW*

Steen, Roger
[The Tubes]
American. Musician
Guitarist with The Tubes since late
1960s.
b. Nov 13, 1949 in Pipestone, Minnesota

Steenburgen, Mary
[Mrs. Ted Danson]
American. Actor
Won Oscar, 1981, for *Melvin and
Howard*; star of TV's "Ink," 1996-
97.
b. 1953 in Little Rock, Arkansas
Source: *BioIn 12, 13, 16; CelR 90;
ConTFT 7, 14, 25; HalFC 88; IntMPA
86, 88, 92, 94, 96; IntWW 97, 98, 2000;
IntWWW 2; JohnWSW; LegTOT;
OsStAZ; WhoAm 86, 88, 90, 92, 94, 95,
96, 97, 98, 99, 2000; WhoAmW 87, 89,
91, 93, 95, 97; WhoEnt 92; WhoHol 92;
WorAlBi*

Stefanik, Milan Rastislav
Czech. Astronomer, Military Leader
Army general who was one of
Czechoslovakia's founders in 1918.
b. Jul 21, 1880 in Kosariska, Austria-
Hungary
d. Apr 4, 1919 in Wenor,
Czechoslovakia
Source: *ChamBiD*

Stefansson, Vihjalmur
Canadian. Explorer
Led Canadian Arctic Expedition, 1913-
18; discovered new lands in Arctic
archipelago.
b. Nov 3, 1879 in Arnes, Manitoba,
Canada
d. Aug 26, 1962 in Hanover, New
Hampshire
Source: *CurBio 62; WebAB 74; WebBD
83; WorAl*

Steffani, Agostino
Italian. Composer
Noted operas include *SoloMe*, 1685.
b. Jul 25, 1654 in Castelfranco, Italy
d. Feb 12, 1728 in Frankfurt am Main,
Germany
Source: *BakBD 84, 92; BioIn 4; BriBkM
80; DcCathB; LuthC 75; MusMk;
NewAmDM; NewEOp 71; NewGrDM 80;
NewGrDO; NewOxM; OxCMus;
OxDcOp*

Steffens, Lincoln
[Joseph Lincoln Steffens]
American. Journalist, Social Reformer
Muckraking editor who exposed
government, business corruption.
b. Apr 6, 1866 in San Francisco,
California
d. Aug 9, 1936 in Carmel, California
Source: *AmAu&B; AmBi; AmDec 1900;
AmJust; AmNatBi; AmRef; AmSocL;
Benet 87; BenetAL 91; BiDAmJo;
BiDAmLf; BioIn 1, 2, 3, 4, 5, 6, 8, 9, 10,
11, 12, 13, 15, 16, 19, 22, 23;
CamDcAB; CmCal; ConAu 117; CyWA
89, 97; DcAmAu; DcAmB S2; DcAmSR;
DcLEL; DcNAA; EncAB-H 1974, 1996;
EncAJ; EncWB 98; FacFETw; GayN;
JouAdvM; JrnUS; LegTOT; LiJour;
LinLib L, S; LngCTC; McGEWB;
MemAm; ModAL 4, 5; NatCAB 14;
OxCAmH; OxCAmL 65, 83; PenC AM;
PeoHis; REn; REnAL; REnAW; TwCA,*

*SUP; TwCLC 20; WebAB 74, 79;
WebE&AL; WhAm 1; WorAl; WorAlBi*

Steger, Will
American. Pilot, Explorer
First person to fly solo around the world;
explored both the North & South
Poles.
b. 1945 in Minneapolis, Minnesota
Source: *BioIn 16; News 90*

Stegner, Wallace (Earle)
American. Author
Writings deal with American West; won
Pulitzer, 1972, for *Angle of Repose*.
b. Feb 18, 1909 in Lake Mills, Iowa
d. Apr 13, 1993 in Santa Fe, New
Mexico
Source: *AmAu&B; AmCulL; AmNatBi;
AmNov; AnObit 1993; Au&W 71;
AuNews 1; Benet 87, 96; BenetAL 91;
BestSel 90-3; BiDAmCa; BioIn 2, 3, 4,
9, 10, 11, 12, 13, 14, 15, 16, 17, 18, 19,
20, 21, 22, 23; BlueB 76; CamDcAB;
CmCal; CnDAL; ConAu 1NR, 1R, 9AS,
21NR, 46NR, 141; ConLC 9, 49, 81;
ConNov 72, 76, 82, 86, 91; CurBio 77,
93N; CyWA 89; DcLB 9, Y93N; DrAF
76; DrAPF 80, 91; DrAS 74E, 78E, 82E;
EncALit; EncFWF; FifWWr; IntAu&W
76, 77, 91, 93; LegTOT; LinLib L;
MajTwCW 1, 2; ModAL 4; NewYTBS 93;
Novels; OxCAmL 65, 83, 95; OxCCan;
OxCTwCL; PenC AM; RAdv 1, 14; REn;
REnAL; REnAW; RfGAmL 4, 94; TwCA,
SUP; TwCWW 82, 91; WhAm 11;
WhE&EA; WhNAA; WhoAm 74, 76, 78,
80, 82, 84, 86, 88, 90, 92; WhoUSWr
88; WhoWest 74, 76; WhoWrEP 89, 92;
WorAlBi; WorAu 1900; WrDr 76, 80, 82,
84, 86, 88, 90, 92, 94N*

Steichen, Edward Jean
American. Photographer, Artist
Brother-in-law of Carl Sandburg; pictures
ranged from impressionistic to straight
documentary.
b. Mar 27, 1879, Luxembourg
d. Mar 25, 1973 in West Redding,
Connecticut
Source: *BiDAmJo; BriEAA; CamBiEn;
ChamBiD; ConPhot 82; CurBio 73;
DcAmArt; DcAmB S9; DcTwDes;
EncAB-H 1974, 1996; HisDcWJ;
MacBEP; McGEWB; NatCAB 60;
NewYTBE 73; ObitOF 79; OxCAmL 65;
REn; REnAL; WebAB 74, 79; WhAm 5;
WorFshn*

Steig, William
American. Cartoonist, Illustrator,
Children's Author
Drawings featured in *The New Yorker*;
won 1970, 1977 Caldecotts; wrote *The
Amazing Bone*, 1977.
b. Nov 14, 1907 in New York, New
York
Source: *AmAu&B; AuBYP 2, 3; BenetAL
91; BioIn 8, 9, 10, 12, 13, 14, 15, 16,
17, 18, 19, 20, 23; CamDcAB; ChlBkCr;
ChlLR 15; ConAu 21NR, 77; CurBio 44;
DcAmChF 1960; DcLB 61; EncTwCJ;
IlsBYP; IlsCB 1967; MajAI; NewYTBE*

72; NewYTBS 97; OxCChiL; REnAL;
SJGChWr 5; SmATA 18, 70; ThrBJA;
TwCChW 1, 2, 3, 4; WhoAm 74, 76, 78,
80, 82, 84, 86, 88, 90, 92, 94, 95, 96,
97; WhoAmA 73, 76, 78, 80, 82, 84, 86,
89; WhoE 74; WhoGrA 82; WhoWor 74;
WhsWeAm 98; WorECar; WrDr 80, 82,
84, 86, 88, 90, 92, 94, 96, 98, 99, 2000

Steiger, Rod
American. Actor
Won Oscar, 1967, for In the Heat of the
  Night.
b. Apr 14, 1925 in Westhampton, New
  York
Source: BiDFilm, 81, 94; BiE&WWA;
BioIn 4, 5, 6, 7, 8, 10, 11, 12, 13, 14,
21, 23, 24; BkPepl; BlueB 76; CelR, 90;
CmMov; ConTFT 3, 10, 18; CurBio 65;
FilmEn; FilmgC; ForYSC; GangFlm;
HalFC 80, 84, 88; IntDcF 1-3, 2-3;
IntMPA 75, 76, 77, 78, 79, 80, 81, 82,
84, 86, 88, 92, 94, 96; IntWW 74, 75,
76, 77, 78, 79, 80, 81, 82, 83, 89, 91,
93, 97, 98, 2000; ItaFilm; LegTOT;
MotPP; MovMk; OsStAZ; OxCFilm;
WhoAm 74, 76, 78, 80, 82, 84, 86, 88,
90, 92, 94, 95, 96, 97, 99, 2000; WhoEnt
92, 98; WhoHol 92, A; WhoHrs 80;
WhoWor 74, 78; WorAl; WorAlBi;
WorEFlm

Stein, Aaron Marc
[George Bagby; Hampton Stone]
American. Author
Mystery story writer; won Grand Master
  Edgar Award, 1979.
b. Nov 15, 1906 in New York, New
  York
d. Aug 29, 1985 in New York, New
  York
Source: BioIn 14, 24; ConAu 6NR, 9R,
63NR, 117; EncMys; IntAu&W 77, 82;
Novels; ScrEAmL 1; TwCCr&M 80, 85,
91; WhAm 9; WhoAm 82, 84; WrDr 82,
84, 86

Stein, Clarence S
American. Architect, Urban Planner
Style emphasizes walls and minimal
  ornamentation; planned town of
  Greenbelt, MD.
b. Jun 19, 1882 in Rochester, New York
d. Feb 7, 1975 in New York, New York
Source: AmArch 70; BlueB 76; EncUrb;
IntWW 74, 75; WhAm 7; WhoAm 74, 76

Stein, Edith
German. Philosopher
Leading proponent of the
  phenomenological school of thought
  led by Edmund Husserl in the first
  half of the twentieth century; she
  attempted to reconcile phenomenology
  with her Catholic beliefs.
b. Oct 12, 1891 in Breslau, Germany
d. 1942 in Auschwitz, Poland
Source: BioIn 2, 4, 5, 6, 7, 8, 11, 12, 13,
15, 17, 19, 20, 21, 23, 24; BkC 5;
CamBiEn; ChamBiD; ContDcW 89;
DcCathB; EncCoWW; EncTR, 91;
EncWB 98; InWom, SUP; NewYTBS 98;
PolBiDi; WhoChr; WomFir; WomWrGB

Stein, Gertrude
American. Author
Center of American expatriates in 1920s
  Paris; named members the "Lost
  Generation."
b. Feb 3, 1874 in Allegheny,
  Pennsylvania
d. Jul 27, 1946 in Neuilly, France
Source: AmAu&B; AmCulL; AmNatBi;
AmWomD; AmWomPl; AmWomWr, 92;
AmWr; ArtclWW 2; AtlBL; Benet 87, 96;
BenetAL 91; BiCoLiE; BioAmW; BioIn
1, 2, 3, 4, 5, 6, 7, 8, 9, 10, 11, 12, 13,
14, 15, 17, 18, 19, 20, 21, 22, 23, 24;
BlmGWL; CamBiEn; CamDcAB;
CamGEL; CamGLE; CamHAL; CasWL;
ChamBiD; Chambr 3; ChhPo S1;
CmCal; CmpQue; CnDAL; CnE&AP;
CnMD; CnMWL; ConAmA; ConAmL;
ConAu 104, 132; ConJeAN; ContDcW
89; CyWA 89, 97; DcAmB S4; DcArts;
DcLB 4, 54, 86, DS15; DcLEL; DcNAA;
DcTwArt; EncAB-A 6; EncAB-H 1974,
1996; EncALit; EncWB 98; EncWHA;
EncWL 1, 2, 2S, 3; EncWT; EvLB;
FacFETw; FemDram; FemiCLE;
GayLesB; GayLL 1; GoodHs; GrLiveH;
GrWomW; GrWrEL N; HanAmWH;
HerW, 84; IdentIs; IntDcWB; InWom,
SUP; JeAmWW; JeHun; LegTOT; LibW;
LiExTwC; LinLib L, S; LngCTC;
MajTwCW 1, 2; MakMC; McGEWB;
MetOEnc; ModAL 4, 4S1, 4S2, 4S3, 5;
ModAWWr; ModWD; ModWoWr;
MorMA; NatCAB 38; NewEOp 71;
NewGrDA 86; NewGrDO; NotAW;
NotNAT A, B; NotWoAT; Novels;
OnHuYeA; OxCAmH; OxCAmL 65, 83,
95; OxCAmT 84; OxCChiL; OxCEng 67,
85, 95; OxCTwCL; OxCTwCP;
OxCWoWr 95; PenBWP; PenC AM;
PeoHis; PoeCrit 18; RAdv 1, 14, 13-1;
RComAH; RComWL; REn; REnAL;
RfGAmL 4, 87, 94; RfGShF 1, 2;
RGTwCWr; SixAP; Tw; TwCA, SUP;
TwCLC 1, 6, 28, 48; TwCWr; WebAB
74, 79; WebE&AL; WhAm 2; WhAmArt
85; WhDW; WhLit; WhNAA; WhoTwCL;
WomFir; WomIss; WomNov; WorAl;
WorAlBi; WorAu 1900; WorLitC

Stein, Heinrich Friedrich Karl vom und zum, Baron
Prussian. Politician
Statesman planned and initiated the
  Prussian recovery after the collapse of
  1806.
b. Oct 26, 1757 in Nassau, Prussia
d. Jun 29, 1831 in Kapfenberg, Austria
Source: EncWB 98

Stein, Herbert
American. Economist
Free-market advocate; member, Pres.
  Nixon's Council of Economic
  Advisers, 1969-72, chm., 1972-74;
  member, Pres. Reagan's Economic
  Policy Advisory Board, 1981.
b. Aug 27, 1916 in Detroit, Michigan
d. Sep 8, 1999 in Washington, District of
  Columbia
Source: AmAu&B; AmEA 74; AmMWSc
73S; BioIn 8, 9, 10, 12, 16, 17, 19, 20,
22; BlueB 76; ConAu 106; CurBio 73;
IntWW 74, 75, 76, 77, 78, 79, 80, 81, 82,

83, 89, 91, 93, 97, 98, 2000; NewYTBE
71; PolProf NF; St&PR 91; WhoAm 74,
76, 78, 80, 82, 84, 86, 88, 90, 92, 94,
95, 96, 97, 98, 99, 2000; WhoEc 81, 86;
WhoFI 83, 92; WhoGov 72, 75; WrDr
86, 88, 90, 92, 94, 96, 98, 99, 2000

Stein, Horst
German. Conductor
Led Hamburg State Opera, 1972-77,
  Hamburg Philharmonic, 1973-76.
b. May 28, 1928 in Elberfeld, Germany
Source: BakBD 78, 84; IntWWM 90;
NewEOp 71; NewGrDM 80; NewGrDO;
OxDcOp; PenDiMP; WhoMus 72;
WhoWor 74

Stein, James R
American. Writer
Won Emmys for "Lily," 1974; "The
  Carol Burnett Show," 1978.
b. Jan 9, 1950 in Chicago, Illinois
Source: St&PR 87; VarWW 85; WhoEnt
92

Stein, Joseph
American. Dramatist, Librettist
Won Tony for play Fiddler on the Roof,
  1965; wrote film version, 1972.
b. May 30, 1912 in New York, New
  York
Source: BiE&WWA; BioIn 15; CanWW
89; ConAu 13R, 31NR, 61NR; ConDr
77D, 82D; ConTFT 4; EncMT; IntMPA
77; LegTOT; NatPD 77; NewCBMT;
NotNAT; OxCAmT 84; VarWW 85;
WhoAm 80, 82, 84, 86, 90; WhoEnt 92;
WhoThe 72, 77, 81; WhoUSWr 88;
WhoWrEP 89, 92

Stein, Jules Caesar
American. Record Company Executive
Founder, pres., Music Corporation of
  America, 1924-46; chm., 1946-73;
  today MCA, Inc. is considered a major
  entertainment agency.
b. Apr 26, 1896 in South Bend, Indiana
d. Apr 29, 1981 in Los Angeles,
  California
Source: AmNatBi; BioIn 7, 8, 10, 13;
CurBio 81; IntMPA 79; NewYTBS 74;
WhAm 7; WhoAm 80; WhoFI 74;
WhoWest 76

Stein, Mark
[Vanilla Fudge]
American. Singer, Musician
Keyboardist, vocalist with group formed
  1966.
b. Mar 11, 1947 in Bayonne, New Jersey

Stein, William Howard
American. Chemist
Shared 1972 Nobel Prize in chemistry
  with Stanford Moore.
b. Jun 25, 1911 in New York, New York
d. Feb 2, 1980 in New York, New York
Source: AmMWSc 76P, 79; AmNatBi;
BiESc; BioIn 9, 10, 12; CamBiEn;
CamDcAB; ChamBiD; DcScB S2;
LarDcSc; McGCEnS; NotTwCS 1;
RanHWDS; WebAB 74, 79; WhAm 7;

Who 74; WhoAm 74, 76, 78, 80; WhoAmJ 80; WhoE 77, 79; WhoNob, 90, 95; WhoWor 74; WorAl

Steinbach, Terry Lee
American. Baseball Player
Catcher, Oakland, 1986—; MVP, 1988 All-Star Game.
b. Mar 2, 1962 in New Ulm, Minnesota
Source: *Ballpl 90; BaseEn 88; BaseReg 87, 88; WhoAm 97, 98, 99, 2000*

Steinbeck, John (Ernst)
American. Author
Won 1962 Nobel Prize; wrote *Of Mice and Men*, 1937; *The Grapes of Wrath*, 1939; *East of Eden*, 1952.
b. Feb 27, 1902 in Salinas, California
d. Dec 20, 1968 in New York, New York
Source: *AgeMat; AmAu&B; AmCulL; AmNov; AmWr; Au&Arts 12; AuBYP 2S, 3; Benet 87, 96; BenetAL 91; BiDAmJo; BiE&WWA; BioIn 1, 2, 3, 4, 5, 6, 7, 8, 9, 10, 11, 12, 13, 14, 15, 16, 17, 19, 20, 21; CamBiEn; CamDcAB; CamGEL; CamGLE; CamGWoT; CamHAL; CasWL; CmCal; CnDAL; CnMD; CnMWL; CnThe; ConAmA; ConAu 1NR, 1R, 25R, 35NR; ConLC 1, 5, 9, 13, 21, 34, 45, 59, 75; CurBio 40, 63; CyWA 58, 89; DcAmB S8; DcAmC; DcAmSR; DcArts; DcLB 7, 9, DS2; DcLEL; DcTwCCu 1; EncAAH; EncAB-H 1974, 1996; EncFWF; EncWB 98; EncWL 1, 2, 2S; EncWT; EvLB; FacFETw; FifWWr; FilmEn; FilmgC; GrWrEL N; HalFC 80, 84, 88; IntWW 2000; LegTOT; LinLib L, S; LngCTC; MagSAmL; MajTwCW 1, 2; MakMC; McGEWB; McGEWD 72, 84; ModAL 4, 4S2; ModWD; MorMA; NatCAB 61; NobelP; NotNAT B; Novels; ObitT 1961; OxCAmH; OxCAmL 65, 83, 95; OxCAmT 84; OxCEng 67, 85, 95; OxCFilm; OxCThe 67, 83; OxCTwCL; PenC AM; RAdv 1, 14, 13-1; RComAH; RComWL; REn; REnAL; REnAW; RfGAmL 4, 87, 94; RfGShF 1, 2; RGTwCWr; ScF&FL 1, 2, 92; ShSCr 11; ShSWr; SJGYouA 2; SmATA 9; TwCA, SUP; TwCRHW 90, 94; TwCWr; TwCYAW 82, 91; TwCYAW 1; WebAB 74, 79; WebE&AL; WhAm 5; WhDW; WhoNob, 90, 95; WhoTwCL; WhThe; WorAl; WorAlBi; WorAu 1900; WorLitC*

Steinberg, David
Canadian. Actor, Comedian
Off-beat comic; hosted David Frost, Dick Cavett shows on TV; directed film *Paternity*, 1981.
b. Aug 9, 1942 in Winnipeg, Manitoba, Canada
Source: *BioIn 9, 10, 12; CanWW 81, 83, 89, 96; ConTFT 7, 15, 27; IntMPA 88, 92, 94, 96; MiSFD 9; WhoAm 74, 76, 78, 80, 82, 84, 86, 88, 90, 92, 94, 96, 97, 98, 99, 2000; WhoCom; WhoEnt 92, 98; WhoHol A; WorAl*

Steinberg, Leigh
American. Agent, Lawyer
One of the top entertainment and sports agents in the U.S., known for his business acumen, his honesty, and his commitment to community service; successfully negotiated some of the most lucrative contracts in sports history.
b. Mar 27, 1949 in Los Angeles, California
Source: *ConNews 87-3*

Steinberg, Saul
American. Artist, Cartoonist
Known for cartoons, cover-art for *New Yorker*; works combine many styles including cubism, pointillism.
b. Jun 15, 1914 in Romanic-Sarat, Romania
d. May 12, 1999 in New York, New York
Source: *AmArt; AmAu&B; Benet 87; BenetAL 91; BioIn 1, 2, 3, 4, 5, 7, 8, 9, 11, 12, 13, 17; CamBiEn; CamDcAB; CelR; ChamBiD; ConArt 77, 83, 89, 96; ConAu 89; CurBio 57; DcAmArt; DcArts; DcCAA 71, 77, 88, 94; DcPseud; DcTwArt; EncAInt; IntWW 74, 75, 76, 77, 78, 79, 80, 81, 82, 83, 89, 91, 93, 97, 98, 2000; LegTOT; LinLib L; McGDA; OxCAmL 65, 83, 95; OxCTwCA; PhDcTCA 77; REn; SmATA 67; WebAB 74, 79; WhAmArt 85; WhoAm 74, 76, 78, 80, 82, 84, 86, 88, 90, 92, 94, 95, 96; WhoAmA 78, 80, 82, 84, 89, 91, 93; WhoGrA 62; WhoWor 74; WorArt 1950; WorECar*

Steinberg, William
[Hans Wilhelm Steinberg]
American. Conductor
Director, Pittsburgh Symphony, 1952-76; Boston Symphony, 1968-72.
b. Aug 1, 1899 in Cologne, Germany
d. May 16, 1978 in New York, New York
Source: *AmNatBi; BakBD 78, 84, 92; BakBDTw; BiDAmM; BioIn 4, 5, 6, 7, 8, 10, 11, 12; BlueB 76; BriBkM 80; CelR; CmOp; CurBio 40, 58, 78N; FacFETw; IntWW 74, 75, 76, 77, 78; IntWWM 77; LinLib S; MetOEnc; MusSN; NatCAB 60; NewAmDM; NewEOp 71; NewGrDA 86; NewGrDM 80; PenDiMP; WhAm 7; Who 74; WhoAm 74, 76, 78; WhoE 74, 75, 77; WhoWor 74*

Steinberger, Jack
American. Physicist
Shared Nobel Prize in physics, 1988, for codiscovering subatomic particles called neutrinos, with two other Americans.
b. May 25, 1921 in Bad Kissinger, Germany
Source: *AmMWSc 76P, 79, 82, 86, 89, 92, 95, 98; CamBiEn; CamDcAB; CamDcSc; ChamBiD; IntWW 74, 75, 76, 77, 78, 79, 80, 81, 82, 83, 89, 91, 93, 97, 98, 2000; LarDcSc; LegTOT; NobelP 91; NotTwCS 1; RanHWDS; Who 90, 92, 94, 98, 99, 2000; WhoAm 74, 76, 78, 88, 90, 92, 94, 95, 99, 2000; WhoNob 90,*

95; WhoScEn 94, 96, 2000; WhoWor 78, 91, 93, 95, 96, 97, 98, 99, 2000; WorAlBi

Steinbrenner, George Michael, III
American. Baseball Executive
Shipbuilding executive; controversial principal owner of NY Yankees, 1973-90; ordered by commissioner to give up managing partnership of Yankees for alleged association with gamblers.
b. Jul 4, 1930 in Rocky River, Ohio
Source: *BioIn 10, 11, 12, 16; BioNews 74; BusPN; CamDcAB; CamDcAB; CurBio 79; Dun&B 90; NewYTBE 73; St&PR 87, 91; WhoAm 76, 78, 80, 82, 84, 86, 88, 90, 92, 94, 95, 96, 97, 98, 99, 2000; WhoE 79, 81, 83, 85, 86, 89, 91, 93, 95, 97, 99; WhoFI 74, 75; WhoSSW 86, 88; WhoWor 98, 99, 2000*

Steinem, Gloria
American. Feminist, Journalist
Well-known activist for women's rights; co-founded *Ms.* mag., 1971; founded groups Coalition of Labor Union Women, Women USA; inducted into National Women's Hall of Fame, 1993.
b. Mar 25, 1934 in Toledo, Ohio
Source: *ABCCoAm; AmAu&B; AmDec 1970; AmSocL; AmWomWr SUP; BenetAL 91; BioIn 7, 8, 9, 10, 11, 12, 13, 16, 18; BioNews 74; BkPepl; BlmGWL; CamBiEn; CamDcAB; CelR 90; ChamBiD; ConAu 28NR, 51NR, 53; ConHero 1; ConLC 63; ContDcW 89; CurBio 72, 88; CyWA 97; DcTwCCu 1; EncAAc; EncAB-H 1996; EncTwCJ; EncWB, 98; EncWHA; EncWoAP; FacFETw; FemiCLE; FemiWr; ForWC 70; GoodHs; GrLiveH; HanAmWH; IntAu&W 89, 91, 93; IntDcWB; IntWW 89, 91, 93, 97, 98, 2000; IntWWW 2; InWom SUP; JouAdvM; LegTOT; LiJour; MajTwCW 1, 2; News 96; OxCAmL; OxCTwCL; OxCWoWr 95; PolPar; PolProf NF; RadHan; RComAH; SigCnAF; WhoAm 76, 78, 80, 82, 84, 86, 88, 90, 92, 94, 95, 96, 97, 98, 99, 2000; WhoAmW 74, 75, 77, 79, 81, 83, 85, 87, 89, 91, 93, 95, 97, 99; WhoEnt 98; WomFir; WomIss; WorAl; WorAlBi*

Steiner, Max
Austrian. Composer, Conductor
Wrote music for *Gone With the Wind*, 1939; Oscar-winning scores for *The Informer*, 1935; *Now, Voyager*, 1942.
b. May 10, 1888 in Vienna, Austria
d. Dec 28, 1971 in Hollywood, California
Source: *ASCAP 66, 80; BakBD 78, 84; BioIn 1, 6, 9, 10; CmMov; CmpEPM; CndCPOM; ConAmC 76, 82; CurBio 43, 72, 72N; DcFM; FacFETw; FilmEn; FilmgC; GangFlm; HalFC 80, 84, 88; IntDcF 1-4, 2-4; ItaFilm; LegTOT; NewAmDM; NewGrDA 86; NewGrDM 80; NotNAT B; OxCFilm; OxCPMus; PopAmC; Songw; WhAm 5; WhoHrs 80; WorAl; WorAlBi; WorEFlm*

Steiner, Rudolf

Austrian. Philosopher
Studied spirituality as independent of
   senses—"anthroposophy;" founded
   Anthroposophical Society, 1912.
b. Feb 27, 1861 in Kraljevic, Austria
d. Mar 30, 1925 in Durnach, Switzerland
Source: *BiDAmCu; BioIn 2, 4, 5, 9, 10,*
11, 12, 13, 14, 15, 17, 21, 23;
ChamBiD; ConAu 107; DcArch;
EncO&P 1, 2, 3; EncPaPR 91; LngCTC;
LuthC 75; MacEA; MakMC; NewAgE
90; OxCGer 76, 86, 97; RAdv 14;
RelLAm 1, 2; ThTwC 87; TwCLC 13;
WhoChr

Steinitz, Wilhelm

German. Chess Player
Editor of *International Chess Magazine,*
   1885-1891; won first official world
   championship, 1866.
b. May 17, 1836 in Prague, Bohemia
d. Aug 12, 1900 in New York, New
   York
Source: *BioIn 14, 15, 17, 18; CamDcAB;*
ChamBiD; GolEC; NewCol 75;
OxCChes 84

Steinman, David Barnard

American. Engineer, Designer
Known for designing world's great
   bridges, including George Washington
   Bridge, NY, 1938; Mackinac Bridge,
   MI, 1957.
b. Jun 11, 1886 in New York, New York
d. Aug 22, 1960 in New York, New
   York
Source: *AmAu&B; AmNatBi; BioIn 2, 4,*
5, 8, 20, 22; DcAmB S6; InSci; McGMS
80; WebAB 74, 79; WhAm 4; WhE&EA;
WhNAA

Steinmetz, Charles Proteus

[Karl August Rudolf Steinmetz]
American. Engineer
His more than 100 inventions turned
   electricity into useful household tool.
b. Apr 9, 1865 in Breslau, Prussia
d. Oct 26, 1923 in Schenectady, New
   York
Source: *AmBi; AmDec 1900; AmNatBi;*
AsBiEn; BioIn 2, 3, 4, 5, 6, 7, 8, 9, 11,
13, 18, 20, 21; CamBiEn; CamDcAB;
ChamBiD; DcAmAu; DcAmB; DcNAA;
DcPseud; DcScB; EncAB-H 1974, 1996;
EncWB 98; GayN; InSci; LarDcSc;
LinLib S; McGCEnS; McGEWB;
MemAm; NatCAB 13, 23; OxCAmH;
RanHWDS; WebAB 74, 79; WhAm 1;
WorAl; WorInv

Steinway, Henry Engelhard

[Henry Engelhard Steinweg]
German. Manufacturer
Founded Steinway and Sons piano
   manufacturers in NY, 1853.
b. Feb 15, 1797 in Wolfshagen, Germany
d. Nov 30, 1896 in New York, New
   York
Source: *AmBi; AmNatBi; ApCAB;*
BiDAmBL 83; BioIn 21; CamBiEn;
DcAmB; NatCAB 2; REn; WebAB 74;
WhAm HS; WorAl

Stella, Frank Philip

American. Artist
Leader of "Minimal Art" movement;
   paintings emphasize shape and color.
b. May 12, 1936 in Malden,
   Massachusetts
Source: *AmCulL; BioIn 12, 13; BriEAA;*
CamBiEn; CamDcAB; ChamBiD; ConArt
83; CurBio 71, 88; DcCAA 71; EncAB-H
1974, 1996; IntWW 83; MakMC;
McGEWB; OxCTwCA; WebAB 74, 79;
WhoAm 86, 90, 92, 94, 95, 96; WhoAmA
84

Stella, Joseph

American. Artist
Realist-turned-semiabstractionist painter:
   Battle of Lights, Coney Island, 1913;
   Brooklyn Bridge, 1919.
b. Jun 13, 1880 in Munra Lucano, Italy
d. Nov 5, 1946 in New York, New York
Source: *BioIn 1, 2, 4, 5, 6, 9, 11; ConArt*
83; CurBio 46; DcAmB S4; DcCAA 71;
McGDA; McGEWB; NatCAB 36;
OxCTwCA; REnAL; WhAm 2; WhAmArt
85

Stempel, Robert

American. Auto Executive
Succeeded Roger Smith as chm. of GM,
   1990-92; first engineer in GM history
   to hold position.
b. 1933 in New Jersey
Source: *AmMWSc 92; BioIn 11, 13, 15,*
16; Dun&B 90; IntWW 91, 2000; News
91, 91-3; St&PR 84; WhoAm 90; WhoFI
92; WhoMW 92; WhoWor 91

Stemrick, Greg(ory Earl, Sr.)

American. Football Player
Defensive back, 1975-83, mostly with
   Houston; suspended by NFL for drug
   involvement, 1983.
b. Oct 25, 1951 in Cincinnati, Ohio
Source: *FootReg 85*

Stendhal

[Marie Henri Beyle]
French. Author, Critic
Wrote *The Red and the Black,* 1831; *The*
   Charterhouse of Parma, 1839.
b. Jan 23, 1783 in Grenoble, France
d. Mar 23, 1842 in Paris, France
Source: *AtlBL; BakBD 78, 84, 92; Benet*
87, 96; BiCoLiE; BiD&SB; BioIn 1, 2, 3,
4, 5, 6, 7, 8, 9, 10, 11, 12, 13, 14, 15,
19, 20, 21, 22, 23, 24; CamBiEn;
CasWL; CelCen; ChamBiD; CyWA 58,
97; DcArts; DcBiA; DcBiPP; DcEuL;
DcLB 119; DcPseud; DcPup; Dis&D;
EncWB 98; EuAu; EuWr 5; EvEuW;
GrFLW; GuFrLit 1; LegTOT; LinLib L,
S; MagSWL; McGEWB; NewC;
NewCBEL; NewGrDM 80; NewGrDO;
NinCLC 23; Novels; OxCEng 67, 95;
OxCFr; OxDcOp; PenC EUR; PseudAu;
RAdv 14, 13-2; RComWL; REn; RfGWoL
95; ShSCr 27; WhDW; WorLitC

Stenerud, Jan

American. Football Player
Placekicker, 1967-85, mostly with
   Kansas City; set NFL record for most
   100-pt. seasons in career, seven.
b. Nov 26, 1943 in Fetsund, Norway
Source: *BioIn 9, 10, 13, 14; FootReg 85,*
86; NewYTBE 71; NewYTBS 83

Stengel, Casey

[Charles Dillon Stengel]
"The Old Professor"
American. Baseball Player, Baseball
   Manager
Outfielder, 1912-25; managed for 25 yrs.,
   including NY Yankees, 1949-60,
   where he won 10 pennants, seven
   World Series.
b. Jul 30, 1890 in Kansas City, Missouri
d. Sep 29, 1975 in Glendale, California
Source: *AmNatBi; BiDAmSp BB;*
CulEncB; CurBio 49, 75; DcAmB S9;
EncWB 2-19; NewYTBS 74, 75; WebAB
74; WhAm 6; WhoAm 74; WhoE 74;
WhoSpor; WhScrn 77, 83; WorAl;
WorAlBi

Stenmark, Ingemar

Swedish. Skier
World Cup Alpine champion, 1976-78;
   won gold medals in men's slalom,
   giant slalom, 1980 Olympics.
b. Mar 18, 1956 in Josesjo, Sweden
Source: *BioIn 11, 12, 13, 15; CamBiEn;*
ChamBiD; CurBio 82; FacFETw;
NewYTBS 82, 88; WorAl; WorAlBi

Stennis, John C(ornelius)

American. Politician
Dem. senator from MS, 1947-89.
b. Aug 3, 1901 in Kemper County,
   Mississippi
d. Apr 23, 1995 in Jackson, Mississippi
Source: *AmNatBi; BiDrAC; BiDrUSC*
89; BioIn 1, 3, 5, 6, 8, 9, 10, 11, 12;
BlueB 76; CngDr 74, 77, 79, 81, 83, 85,
87; CurBio 53, 95N; EncVieW; IntWW
74, 75, 76, 77, 78, 79, 80, 82, 83, 89,
91, 93; IntYB 78, 79, 80, 81, 82;
NewYTBS 85; PolProf E, J, K, NF, T;
WhAm 11; WhoAm 74, 76, 78, 80, 82,
84, 86, 88, 90, 92, 94, 95; WhoAmL 79;
WhoAmP 73, 75, 77, 79, 81, 83, 85, 87,
89, 91, 93; WhoGov 72, 75, 77;
WhoSSW 73, 75, 76, 78, 80, 82, 86, 88;
WhoWor 78, 80, 82, 84, 87, 89; WorAl;
WorAlBi

Steno, Nicolaus

Danish. Naturalist
Scientist established the law of
   superposition and the fundamental law
   of crystallography, the law of
   constancy of interfacial angles.
b. Jan 10, 1638 in Copenhagen, Denmark
d. Nov 26, 1686 in Schwerin, Germany
Source: *AsBiEn; BiESc; BioIn 2, 3, 4, 5,*
6, 7, 9, 12; CamBiEn; CamDcSc;
ChamBiD; DcCathB; DcScB; EncWB 98;
LarDcSc; McGEWB; RanHWDS

Stephanie, Princess
[Stephanie Marie Elisabeth Grimaldi]
Monacan. Princess
Daughter of Princess Grace, Prince
Rainier; career attempts include
swimsuit designer, model and singer.
b. Feb 1, 1965 in Monaco-Ville, Monaco
Source: *BioIn 7, 12, 13, 16; CurBio 86;
EncCoWW; IntWWW 2; LegTOT*

Stephanopoulos, George (Robert)
American. Government Official
Senior advisor to pres. Bill Clinton,
1993-96.
b. Feb 10, 1961 in Fall River,
Massachusetts
Source: *BioIn 13; CurBio 95; IntWW
2000; LegTOT; News 94, 94-3;
NewYTBS 92, 93; WhoAm 95, 96, 97,
98, 2000; WhoAmP 93, 95, 97, 1999*

Stephen
English. King
Ruled England from 1135 to 1154, but
claim to the throne was contested by
his cousin Matilda and his reign was
marked by civil war; Matilda's son
succeeded him as Henry II.
b. c. 1096
d. Oct 25, 1154
Source: *EncWB 98; McGEWB; MediEng;
OxCBrHi*

Stephen, I
Hungarian. King
Tribal leader of the Magyars was
baptized and crowned Christian king
of Hungary on Christmas Day, 1000;
successfully Christianized the country
in one generation and built the
foundation of a powerful European
nation.
b. c. 973, Hungary
d. 1038, Hungary
Source: *EncWB 98*

Stephen, Leslie, Sir
English. Author, Critic
First editor, *Dictionary of National
Biography,* 1882-91; wrote
biographies: *Thomas Hobbs,* 1904;
father of Virginia Woolf.
b. Nov 28, 1832 in London, England
d. Feb 22, 1904 in London, England
Source: *Alli, SUP; AtlBL; BbD; Benet
87, 96; BiD&SB; BioIn 1, 2, 3, 4, 5, 6,
7, 8, 9, 10, 11, 12, 13, 14, 16, 21, 23,
24; BlmGEL; BritAu 19; BritWr 5;
CamBiEn; CamGEL; CamGLE; CasWL;
CelCen; ChamBiD; Chambr 3; ChhPo
S1; ConAu 123; DcArts; DcEnA, A;
DcEnL; DcEuL; DcLB 57, 144, 190;
DcLEL; DcNaB S2; EncWB 98; EvLB;
LinLib L, S; LngCEL; LngCTC;
McGEWB; MouLC 4; NewC; NewCBEL;
OxCEng 67, 85, 95; PenC ENG; REn;
TwCLC 23; VicBrit; WebE&AL; WorAl;
WorAlBi*

Stephens, Alexander Hamilton
American. Politician
Elected vp of US Confederate States,
1862-65; imprisoned May-Oct 1865;

served in US Congress following Civil
War.
b. Feb 11, 1812 in Crawfordsville,
Georgia
d. Mar 4, 1883 in Atlanta, Georgia
Source: *Alli, SUP; AmAu&B; AmBi;
AmNatBi; ApCAB; BbD; BenetAL 91;
BiAUS; BiD&SB; BiDConf; BiDrAC;
BiDrGov 1789; BiDrUSC 89; BiDSA;
BioIn 1, 3, 4, 5, 6, 7, 9, 15, 16, 21;
CamBiEn; CamDcAB; ChamBiD;
CivWDc; CyAG; DcAmAu; DcAmB;
DcBiPP; DcNAA; Drake; EncAAH;
EncAB-H 1974, 1996; EncSoH; EncWB
98; HarEnUS; LAmCW; LinLib L, S;
McGEWB; NatCAB 3; OxCAmH;
REnAL; TwCBDA; WebAB 74, 79;
WhAm HS; WhAmP; WhCiWar; WorAl*

Stephens, Alice Barber
American. Artist
Noted magazine, book illustrator, 1875-
1904.
b. Jul 1, 1858 in Salem, New Jersey
d. Jul 13, 1932 in Rose Valley,
Pennsylvania
Source: *BioIn 15, 17, 24; ChhPo;
ConICB; DcAmB; DcLB 188; IlrAm
1880, A; InWom, SUP; LibW; NatCAB
13, 23; NorAmWA; NotAW; SmATA 66;
TwCBDA; WhAm 1; WhAmArt 85;
WomArt; WomWWA 14*

Stephens, Ann Sophia
American. Author, Editor
Wrote first dime novel *Malaeska; or the
Indian Wife of the White Hunter,*
1860.
b. May 30, 1810 in Seymour,
Connecticut
d. Aug 20, 1886 in Newport, Rhode
Island
Source: *BlmGWL; DcLB 73; EncALit;
FemiCLE; LibW; NinCAWW; NotAW;
OxCAmL 83, 95*

Stephens, Charlotte Andrews
American. Educator, Social Reformer
Lifelong educator was a teacher and
principal in the public schools of Little
Rock, AR, dedicated to the
improvement of life and education for
the African Americans of that city; a
school was named for her in 1909.
b. 1954 in Little Rock, Arkansas
d. 1951

Stephens, Helen
American. Track Athlete
Sprinter; won two gold medals, 1936
Olympics.
b. Feb 3, 1918 in Fulton, Missouri
d. Jan 17, 1994 in Saint Louis, Missouri
Source: *BiDAmSp OS; BioIn 3, 17, 19,
24; EncWB 2-19; WhoSpor; WhoTr&F
73*

Stephens, James
English. Author, Poet
Noted for prose fantasy *Crock of Gold,*
1912.
b. 1882 in Dublin, Ireland
d. Dec 26, 1950 in London, England

Source: *AnCL; AuBYP 2S, 3; Benet 87,
96; BiCoLiE; BiDIrW; BioIn 1, 2, 3, 4,
5, 6, 7, 10, 11, 12, 13, 14, 21, 22, 23;
CamGEL; CamGLE; CarSB; CasWL;
ChamBiD; Chambr 3; ChhPo, S1, S2,
S3; CnE&AP; ConAu 104; CyWA 58;
DcIrW 1; DcLB 19, 162; DcLEL;
EncWB 98; EncWL 1; EvLB; FacFETw;
GrWrEL P; LinLib L; LngCTC;
McGEWB; ModBrL, 2, S1; ModIrLi;
NewC; NewCBEL; OxCEng 67, 85, 95;
OxCTwCL; PenC ENG; PoIre; RAdv 1;
REn; ScF&FL 1, 92; Str&VC; SupFW;
TwCA, SUP; TwCLC 4; TwCWr; WhAm
3; WhDW*

Stephens, John Lloyd
American. Traveler, Author, Diplomat
Supervised construction of railway across
Isthmus of Panama; wrote of travels:
Incidents of Travel in Yucatan, 1843.
b. Nov 28, 1805 in Shrewsbury, New
Jersey
d. Oct 12, 1852 in New York, New York
Source: *Alli; AmAu&B; AmBi; ApCAB;
BbD; BenetAL 91; BiAUS; BiD&SB;
BioIn 1, 3, 6, 7, 8, 10; CamBiEn;
CamDcAB; ChamBiD; CyAL 2;
DcAmAu; DcAmB; DcAmDH 80, 89;
DcLB 183; DcNAA; Drake; EncLatA;
HarEnUS; InSci; IntDcAn; NatCAB 5;
OxCAmH; OxCAmL 65, 83, 95; REn;
REnAL; TwCBDA; WhAm HS; WhDW*

Stephens, Robert, Sir
English. Actor
Films include *Cleopatra,* 1963; *The
Shout,* 1978.
b. Jul 14, 1931 in Bristol, England
d. Nov 12, 1995 in London, England
Source: *BioIn 9, 21, 22, 23; BlueB 76;
CamGWoT; CnThe; ConTFT 6, 13, 15;
FilmAG WE; FilmEn; FilmgC; HalFC
80, 84, 88; IIWWBF; IntMPA 92, 94, 96;
IntWW 74, 75, 76, 77, 78, 79, 80, 81, 82,
83, 89, 91, 93; ItaFilm; NewYTBS 95;
VarWW 85; WhAm 11; Who 74, 82, 83,
85, 88, 90, 92, 94; WhoHol 92, A;
WhoThe 72, 77, 81; WhoWor 74, 84, 87,
91, 93, 95, 96*

Stephens, Uriah
American. Labor Union Official
Founder of the Knights of Labor, he
served as its leader for a decade.
b. Aug 3, 1821 in Cape May, New
Jersey
d. Feb 13, 1882
Source: *EncWB 98; LexLab*

Stephenson, George
English. Engineer, Inventor
Patented steam blast locomotive;
developed railway system.
b. Jun 9, 1781 in Wylam, England
d. Aug 12, 1848 in Chesterfield, England
Source: *AsBiEn; BiESc; BioIn 1, 2, 3, 4,
5, 6, 7, 8, 9, 10, 11, 12, 13, 14, 16, 17,
20; CamBiEn; CelCen; ChamBiD;
DcBiPP; DcInv; DcNaB; EncWB 98;
InSci; LinLib S; MacEA; McGDA;
McGEWB; NewCol 75; OxCBrHi;*

RanHWDS; SciMath; WebBD 83;
WhDW; WorAl; WorAlBi; WorInv

Stephenson, Henry
British. Actor
Character actor in over 100 films, 1917-
  49.
b. Apr 16, 1871, West Indies
d. Apr 24, 1956 in San Francisco,
  California
Source: *CmMov; DcPseud; EncAFC;*
Film 1, 2; FilmEn; FilmgC; HalFC 80,
84, 88; HolCA; MotPP; MovMk;
NotNAT B; Vers A; WhoHol B; WhScrn
74, 77, 83

Stephenson, Jan Lynn
American. Golfer
Turned pro, 1974; won US Women's
  Open, 1983; rookie of the year, 1974.
b. Dec 22, 1951 in Sydney, Australia
Source: *NewYTBS 76, 81, 82, 83;*
WhoAm 78, 84, 86, 88, 90, 92, 94, 95,
96, 97, 98, 99, 2000; WhoAmW 79, 89,
91, 93, 99; WhoGolf; WhoIntG

Stephenson, Skip
[Charles Frederick Stephenson]
American. TV Personality, Comedian
Co-host of TV series "Real People."
b. Apr 18, 1948? in Omaha, Nebraska
Source: *BioIn 12*

Stephenson, William
Spy
WW II spymaster; launched Anglo-
  American espionage program that
  helped defeat Nazis; subject of
  bestseller *A Man Called Intrepid.*
b. Jan 11, 1896 in Winnipeg, Manitoba,
  Canada
d. Jan 31, 1989 in Hamilton, Bermuda
Source: *AnObit 1989; BioIn 16;*
CamBiEn; FacFETw; NewYTBS 89; Who
85, 88, 90N

Stepinac, Alojzije
Yugoslav. Religious Leader
Roman Catholic archbishop of Zagreb,
  1937-53; cardinal, 1953-60;
  imprisoned by Communists, 1946-51.
b. May 8, 1898 in Krasic, Croatia
d. Feb 10, 1960 in Krasic, Yugoslavia
Source: *BioIn 1, 2, 3, 5, 6, 12, 15;*
CnfFoY; CurBio 53, 60; DcCathB;
EncWB, 98; LuthC 75

Steppenwolf
[George Biondo; Robert Cochran; Wayne
  Cook; Jerry Edmonton; John Kay]
American. Music Group
Songs include "Born to Be Wild,"
  1968.
Source: *Alli; BiDAmM; BillEnR;*
ConMuA 80A; ConMus 20; DcEnL;
DcNaB; DrAPF 80, 83, 85, 87, 89, 91,
93, 97; EncPR&S 74, 89; EncRk 88;
EncRkSt; FolkA 87; GrMetD; HarEnR
86; IlEncRk; InSci; MedHR; NewAmDM;
NewGrDA 86; PenEncP; PoLE; RkOn
78; RkWho 96; RolSEnR 83; WhDW;
WhoRock 81; WhoRocM 82; WorInv

Steptoe, Patrick Christopher
English. Physician
Gynecologist; with Robert Edwards,
  pioneered in vitro fertilization;
  responsible for first test-tube baby,
  Louise Brown, born, 1978.
b. Jun 9, 1913 in Oxford, England
d. Mar 21, 1988 in Canterbury, England
Source: *BioIn 11, 12; CamBiEn;*
ChamBiD; ConAu 163; CurBio 79, 88;
DcNaB 1986; FacFETw; LarDcSc;
NewYTBS 78, 88; RanHWDS; Who 82,
83, 85, 88; WhoWor 82, 84

Sterban, Richard
[The Oak Ridge Boys]
American. Singer
Bass vocalist with country-pop group.
b. Apr 24, 1943 in Camden, New Jersey
Source: *WhoAm 90*

Sterling, Bruce
American. Author
One of the founders of the cyberpunk
  movement; author of *The Hacker*
  Countdown: Law and Disorder on the
  Electronic Frontier, 1992.
b. Apr 14, 1954 in Brownsville, Texas
Source: *ConAu 44NR, 119; ConLC 72;*
EncSF 93; IntAu&W 89, 91, 93;
NewEScF; News 95; OxCTwCL;
ScF&FL 92; ScFWr 2; TwCSFW 86, 91;
WrDr 88, 90, 92, 94, 96, 98, 99, 2000

Sterling, Claire
Author
Author of *Time of the Assassins* and *The*
  Terror Network.
d. Jun 17, 1995 in Arezzo, Italy
Source: *BioIn 14, 21; InWom SUP;*
NewYTBS 81, 95

Sterling, Ford
[George Ford Stitch]
American. Actor
With Max Sennett's Keystone serials,
  1912-21.
b. Nov 3, 1880 in La Crosse, Wisconsin
d. Oct 13, 1939 in Los Angeles,
  California
Source: *Film 1; FilmEn; FilmgC;*
FrSilen; MovMk; QDrFCA 92; SilFlmP;
TwYS; WhoHol B; WhScrn 74, 77, 83

Sterling, George
American. Poet
Leader of bohemian art colony, Carmel,
  CA, 1908-15.
b. Dec 1, 1869 in Sag Harbor, New
  York
d. Nov 18, 1926 in San Francisco,
  California
Source: *AmAu&B; AmNatBi; AnMV*
1926; BenetAL 91; BibAL; BioIn 1, 2, 8,
12, 13, 15, 16, 22; CasWL; ChhPo, S1,
S2, S3; CmCal; ConAmL; ConAu 117,
165; DcAmB; DcLB 54; DcLEL;
DcNAA; OxCAmL 65, 83, 95; PenEncH;
REn; REnAL; TwCA, SUP; TwCLC 20;
WhAm 1; WhLit; WorAu 1900

Sterling, Jan
[Jan Sterling Andriance; Mrs. Paul
  Douglas]
American. Actor
Made Broadway debut, 1938; nominated
  for Oscar for *The High and the*
  Mighty, 1954.
b. Apr 3, 1923 in New York, New York
Source: *BiE&WWA; BioIn 2, 24;*
ConTFT 7; DcPseud; FemmeNo;
FilmEn; FilmgC; GangFlm; HalFC 80,
84, 88; IntMPA 75, 76, 77, 78, 79, 80,
81, 82, 84, 86, 88, 92, 94, 96; InWom,
SUP; LegTOT; MotPP; MovMk;
NotNAT; OsStAZ; WhoHol A; WhoThe
77, 81; WorAl; WorAlBi

Sterling, John Ewart Wallace
American. University Administrator
Pres., Stanford U, for two decades;
  received honorary knighthood from
  Elizabeth II, 1976.
b. Aug 6, 1906 in Linwood, Ontario,
  Canada
d. Jul 1, 1985 in Woodside, California
Source: *BiDAmEd; BioIn 1, 2, 3, 14, 24;*
CanWW 70, 79, 80, 81, 83; DrAS 74H,
78H, 82H; LEduc 74; WhAm 8, 11;
WhoAm 74, 76, 78, 80, 82, 84; WhoWest
84

Sterling, Robert
[William Sterling Hart]
American. Actor
Played George Kerby in TV's
  "Topper," 1953-56; appeared in some
  films.
b. Nov 13, 1917 in New Castle,
  Pennsylvania
Source: *BiE&WWA; BioIn 3; DcPseud;*
FilmEn; FilmgC; ForYSC; HalFC 80,
84, 88; IntMPA 75, 76, 77, 78, 79, 80,
81, 82, 84, 86, 88, 92, 94, 96; LegTOT;
MGM; MotPP; VarWW 85; WhoHol 92,
A

Stern, Arthur Cecil
American. Environmentalist
Pioneering expert in field of air
  pollution; co-author, *Fundamentals of*
  Air Pollution, 1984.
b. Mar 14, 1909 in Petersburg, Virginia
d. Apr 17, 1992 in Chapel Hill, North
  Carolina
Source: *BioIn 4, 8, 17, 18; InSci; WhAm*
10; WhoAm 74, 76, 78, 80, 86, 88, 90;
WhoCon 73; WhoEng 88; WhoTech 89

Stern, Bert
American. Photographer
Commercial photographer who ascribed
  to motto "less is more;" known for
  Smirnoff ads of martini glass in front
  of pyramids, 1955, portfolio of
  Marilyn Monroe silkscreen prints,
  1967.
b. Oct 3, 1929 in New York, New York
Source: *ConPhot 82, 88, 95; ICPEnP A;*
WhoAdv 90; WhoAm 74, 76

Stern, Bill
[William Stern]
American. Sportscaster
Sports announcer with NBC radio, TV, 1930s-50s; known for flamboyant anecdotes.
b. Jul 1, 1907 in Rochester, New York
d. Nov 19, 1971 in Rye, New York
Source: *BiDAmSp OS; BioIn 1, 5, 9; ConAu 89; CurBio 41, 72, 72N; DcAmB S9; EncAJ; IntMPA 75, 76, 77, 78, 79; NewYTBE 71; RadStar; SaTiSS; WhAm 5; WhoHol B; WhScrn 74, 77, 83*

Stern, Carl Leonard
American. Broadcast Journalist
NBC News legal affairs correspondent, 1967-93; director Office of Public Affairs, justice dept., 1993—.
b. Aug 7, 1937 in New York, New York
Source: *ConAu 97; EncTwCJ; WhoAm 80, 82, 84, 86, 88, 90, 92, 94, 95, 96, 97, 98, 99, 2000; WhoAmL 79, 83, 85, 94, 96, 98, 2000; WhoE 95; WhoMedi 98*

Stern, David Joel
American. Basketball Executive
Succeeded Larry O'Brien as commissioner of NBA, 1984—.
b. Sep 22, 1942 in New York, New York
Source: *BiDAmSp BK; WhoAm 86, 88, 90, 92, 94, 95, 96, 97, 98, 99, 2000; WhoE 86, 89, 91, 99*

Stern, Howard (Allan)
American. Radio Performer
Nationally syndicated, New York based radio host known for obnoxious behavior; movie *Private Parts*, 1997.
b. Jan 12, 1954 in New York, New York
Source: *BioIn 16; ConAu 146; ConTFT 12; CurBio 96; LegTOT; News 88-2, 93-3; WhoAm 94, 95, 96, 97, 98, 99, 2000; WhoE 95; WhoEnt 98; WhoMedi 98*

Stern, Isaac
American. Violinist
Made debut age 11; int'l concertist; made soundtrack for *Fiddler on the Roof*, 1971; French Legion of Honor, 1979.
b. Jul 21, 1920 in Kreminiecz, Union of Soviet Socialist Republics
Source: *AmMWSc 92; BakBD 78, 84, 92; BakBDTw; BakDcM; BiDAmM; BioIn 1, 2, 3, 4, 5, 7, 8, 9, 11, 12, 16; BlueB 76; BriBkM 80; CamBiEn; CamDcAB; CelR, 90; ChambID; CmCal; ConMus 7; ConTFT 15; CurBio 49, 89; DcTwCCu 1; EncWB 2-19; FacFETw; IntWW 74, 75, 76, 77, 78, 79, 80, 81, 82, 83, 89, 91, 93, 97, 98, 2000; IntWWM 77, 80, 90; LegTOT; MusMk; MusSN; NewAmDM; NewGrDA 86; NewGrDM 80; NewYTBE 70; PenDiMP; WebAB 74, 79; Who 74, 82, 83, 85, 88, 90, 92, 94, 98, 99, 2000; WhoAm 74, 76, 78, 80, 82, 84, 86, 88, 90, 92, 94, 95, 96, 97, 98, 99, 2000; WhoAmJ 80; WhoAmM 83; WhoE 74, 97, 99; WhoEnt 92, 98; WhoGov 72, 75, 77; WhoHol 92, A;*

WhoMus 72; WhoWor 74, 76, 78, 80, 82, 84, 87, 89, 91, 93, 95, 96, 97, 98, 99, 2000; WhoWorJ 72, 78; WorAl; WorAlBi

Stern, James
Irish. Author
Short story writer usually set in Ireland or Africa: *Something Wrong*, 1938.
b. Dec 26, 1904 in County Meath, Ireland
d. Nov 22, 1993 in Tisbury, England
Source: *BioIn 10, 19; ConAu 21R; ConNov 72, 76, 82, 86; IntAu&W 76, 77, 82, 86; WhoWor 76; WorAu 1950; WrDr 76, 80, 82, 84, 86, 88, 90, 92*

Stern, Leonard B
Writer, Producer
Won Emmys for scripts of "The Bilko Show," 1956; "Get Smart," 1967.
b. Dec 23, 1923 in New York, New York
Source: *BioIn 15, 16; ConAmBL; CurBio 91; LesBEnT 92; NewYTET; VarWW 85; WhoAm 88*

Stern, Leonard Norman
American. Business Executive
CEO, Hartz Group, Inc. (pet supplies), 1959—; owner of *The Village Voice*.
b. Mar 28, 1938 in New York, New York
Source: *BioIn 10, 11, 12; BusPN; Dun&B 90; WhoAm 74, 76, 78, 80, 82, 84, 86, 88, 90, 92, 95, 96, 97, 98, 99, 2000; WhoFI 00, 92*

Stern, Max
American. Business Executive
Founded, Hartz Mountain Corp., 1932.
b. 1898 in Fulda, Germany
d. May 20, 1982 in New York, New York
Source: *BioIn 5, 10, 11, 12, 13, 15; NewYTBS 82; WhAm 8*

Stern, Otto
American. Physicist, Educator
Won Nobel Prize in physics, 1943, for development of molecular beams, discovery of magnetic moment of the proton.
b. Feb 17, 1888 in Soran, Germany
d. Aug 17, 1969 in Berkeley, California
Source: *AmNatBi; AsBiEn; BiESc; BioIn 3, 5, 8, 9, 10, 13, 14, 15, 20; CamBiEn; CamDcAB; CamDcSc; ChamBiD; DcAmB S8; DcScB; EncWB 98; InSci; LarDcSc; LegTOT; LinLib S; McGCEnS; McGEWB; McGMS 80; NobelP; NotTwCS 1; ObitOF 79; RanHWDS; WebAB 74, 79; WebBD 83; WhAm 9; WhoNob, 90, 95; WorAl; WorAlBi*

Stern, Philip Van Doren
American. Author
Novelist, historian, widely acclaimed for Civil War era books.
b. Sep 10, 1900 in Wyalusing, Pennsylvania
d. Jul 31, 1984 in Sarasota, Florida

Source: *AmAu&B; AmNov; BenetAL 91; BioIn 22; ConAu 5R, 6NR, 86NR; NewYTBS 84; REnAL; ScF&FL 92; SmATA 13; WhE&EA; WhNAA; WhoAm 82, 84; WorAu 1900*

Stern, Richard Gustave
American. Author
Relatively obscure novelist since 1960; admired by other writers: *Packages*, 1980.
b. Feb 25, 1928 in New York, New York
Source: *AmAu&B; Au&Wr 71; BenetAL 91; BioIn 16; ConAu 1NR, 1R, 52NR; ConLC 4; ConNov 72, 76, 86, 91; CurBio 94; CyWA 89; DrAF 76; DrAPF 80; IntAu&W 91; PenC AM; WhoAdv 90; WhoAm 74, 76, 78, 80, 82, 84, 86, 88, 90, 92, 94, 95, 96, 97, 98, 99, 2000; WhoEnt 98; WhoUSWr 88; WhoWrEP 89, 92, 95; WorAu 1950; WrDr 76, 86, 92, 98, 99, 2000*

Stern, Sandor
Canadian. Writer, Director
Wrote screenplays *Fast Break; The Amityville Horror*.
b. Jul 13, 1936 in Timmins, Ontario, Canada
Source: *ConTFT 15; MiSFD 9; VarWW 85; WhoAm 99, 2000; WhoEnt 92, 98*

Stern, Stewart
American. Screenwriter
Films include *Rebel Without a Cause*, 1955; Oscar-winning *Rachel, Rachel*, 1966.
b. Mar 22, 1922 in New York, New York
Source: *BioIn 10, 14, 17; ConAu 113; ConDr 77, 77A; ConTFT 23; DcLB 26; FilmEn; IntMPA 75, 76, 77, 78, 79, 80, 81, 82, 84, 86, 88, 92, 94, 96; WorEFlm*

Sterne, Laurence
[Mister Yorick]
English. Author, Theologian
Wrote *Tristram Shandy*, 1760-67; *Sentimental Journey*, 1768.
b. Nov 24, 1713 in Clonmel, Ireland
d. Mar 18, 1768 in London, England
Source: *Alli; AtlBL; BbD; Benet 87, 96; BiCoLiE; BiD&SB; BiDIrW; BioIn 1, 2, 3, 4, 5, 6, 7, 8, 9, 10, 12, 13, 14, 15, 18, 20; BlkwCE; BlmGEL; BritAu; BritWr 3; CamBiEn; CamGEL; CamGLE; CasWL; ChamBiD; Chambr 2; ChhPo S3; CnDBLB 2; CrtT 2, 4; CyWA 58; DcArts; DcBiA; DcBiPP; DcEnA; DcEnL; DcEuL; DcIrB 1, 2, 3; DcIrL 96; DcIrW 1; DcLB 39; DcLEL; DcNaB; Dis&D; EncEnl; EncWB 98; EvLB; GrWrEL N; LegTOT; LinLib L, S; LitC 2, 48; LngCEL; MagSWL; McGEWB; MouLC 2; NewC; NewCBEL; Novels; OxCBrHi; OxCEng 67, 85, 95; OxCGer 76, 86, 97; OxCIri; PenC ENG; PoIre; RAdv 1, 14, 13-1; RComWL; REn; RfGEnL 91; WebE&AL; WhDW; WorAl; WorAlBi; WorLitC*

Sterne, Maurice
American. Artist
Modern classicist, painted 20 murals for
Dept. of Justice Bldg; works done on
Bali made island famous.
b. Jul 13, 1878 in Libau, Russia
d. Jul 23, 1957 in New York, New York
Source: *BioIn 1, 2, 4, 5, 7, 10, 22;
BriEAA; CamDcAB; CurBio 43, 57;
DcAmArt; DcAmB S6; DcCAA 71, 77,
88; IlBEAAW; McGDA; PhDcTCA 77;
WhAm 3; WhAmArt 85; WhoAmA 80N,
82N, 84N, 86N, 89N, 91N, 93N*

Sterrett, Cliff
American. Cartoonist
Creator of "Polly and her Pals" comic
strip, 1912-58.
b. Dec 12, 1883 in Fergus Falls,
Minnesota
d. Dec 28, 1964 in Ogunquit, Maine
Source: *BioIn 7; ConAu 155; WhAm 7;
WhAmArt 85; WhoAmA 89N, 91N, 93N;
WorECom*

Stetson, John Batterson
American. Manufacturer
Formed John B Stetson Co., 1885; made
wide-brimmed, high-crowned cowboy
hats.
b. May 5, 1830 in Orange, New Jersey
d. Feb 18, 1906 in De Land, Florida
Source: *AmBi; AmNatBi; BioIn 2, 6, 13,
18; CamDcAB; DcAmB; Entr; NatCAB
11; NewCol 75; TwCBDA; WebAB 74,
79; WhAm 1; WhFla*

Stettinius, Edward R, Jr.
American. Government Official
Lend-lease administrator, 1941-43;
secretary of State, 1944-45; first US
delegate to UN, 1945.
b. Oct 22, 1900 in Chicago, Illinois
d. Oct 31, 1949 in Greenwich,
Connecticut
Source: *CurBio 40, 49; DcAmB S4;
EncAB-H 1974; EncWB 98; McGEWB;
NatCAB 38; PolProf T; WhAm 1, 2*

**Steuben, Friedrich Wilhelm
Ludolf Gerhard Augustin,
Baron**
American. Soldier
American Revolutionary War general;
trained Continental Army;
Washington's advisor.
b. Sep 17, 1730 in Magdeburg, Prussia
d. Nov 28, 1794 in Remsen, New York
Source: *CamDcAB; DcNAA; McGEWB;
NewCol 75; OxCAmH; REnAL;
WebAMB*

Stevens, Albert William
American. Soldier, Balloonist
First photographer to capture Earth's
curving shape on camera in 1930; took
first photos of Earth during a solar
eclipse.
b. Mar 13, 1886 in Belfast, Maryland
d. Mar 26, 1949 in Redwood City,
California
Source: *BioIn 1, 2, 3; DcVicP 2; InSci;
NatCAB 37; ObitOF 79; WhAm 7*

Stevens, Andrew
American. Actor
Films include *The Fury*, 1978; played
Casey Denault on TV series "Dallas,"
1987-88; son of Stella.
b. Jun 10, 1955? in Memphis, Tennessee
Source: *BioIn 11; ConAu 175; ConTFT
3, 19; HalFC 80, 84, 88; IntMPA 82, 92,
94, 96; LegTOT; MiSFD 9; VarWW 85;
WhoAm 80, 82, 84, 86, 88, 90, 92, 94,
95, 96; WhoEnt 92; WhoHol 92;
WhoWor 80, 82*

Stevens, Cat
[Stephen Demetri Georgiou; Yosef
Islam]
English. Singer, Songwriter
Rock-folk singer; had hits "Moon
Shadow," 1971, "Morning Has
Broken," 1972; quit music business,
became Muslim, 1981.
b. Jul 21, 1948 in London, England
Source: *BiDAmM; BioIn 10, 12, 16;
BioNews 74; ConMuA 80A; ConMus 3;
EncPR&S 89; EncRk 88; HarEnR 86;
IlEncRk; NewAmDM; NewYTBE 71;
PenEncP; RkOn 78, 84; WhoAm 80, 82;
WhoRock 81; WhoRocM 82; WorAl;
WorAlBi*

Stevens, Connie
[Concetta Ingolia]
American. Actor, Singer
Starred in TV series "Hawaiian Eye,"
1959-63; "Wendy and Me," 1964-65,
with George Burns.
b. Aug 8, 1938 in New York, New York
Source: *BiDAmM; BioIn 6, 13, 16, 18;
ConTFT 3, 19; DcPseud; EncAFC;
FilmEn; FilmgC; ForYSC; HalFC 80,
84, 88; IntMPA 75, 76, 77, 78, 79, 80,
81, 82, 84, 86, 88, 92, 94, 96; InWom,
SUP; LegTOT; MotPP; RkOn 74;
WhoAm 86, 88, 90, 92, 94, 97, 98, 99,
2000; WhoEnt 92, 98; WhoHol 92, A;
WhoRock 81; WorAl; WorAlBi*

Stevens, Edmund William
American. Journalist
Pulitzer Prize for distinguished reporting
on international affairs; "This Is
Russia—Uncensored," 1950.
b. Jul 22, 1910 in Denver, Colorado
d. May 24, 1992 in Peredelkino, Russia
Source: *AmAu&B; BioIn 2; ConAu 109,
137; CurBio 92N; EncTwCJ; WhAm 10;
WhoAm 74, 76, 78, 80, 82, 84, 86, 88,
90; WhoPul; WhoWor 82, 91*

Stevens, Eileen
[Karen Stevens]
American. Social Reformer
Formed the Committee to Halt Useless
College Killings (CHUCK) after son
was killed in a hazing incident in
1978, to raise awareness and prevent
the dangerous binge drinking and
other activities involved in fraternity
initiations; named woman of the year
by *New York Daily News*, 1983, and
received the Clara Barton
Humanitarian Award from the Red
Cross.

b. Aug 31, 1939 in Long Island, New
York
Source: *ConNews 87-3*

Stevens, Emily A
American. Actor
Known for alluring woman roles: *The
Unchastened Woman*, 1915; died of
drug overdose; cousin of Minnie
Fiske.
b. Feb 27, 1882 in New York, New
York
d. Jan 2, 1928 in New York, New York
Source: *DcAmB; Film 1; WhoHol B;
WhScrn 74, 77, 83*

Stevens, George, Jr.
American. Producer
Won Emmys for "Salute to James
Cagney," 1975; "The Kennedy Center
Honors: A Celebration of the
Performing Arts," 1984.
b. Apr 3, 1932 in Los Angeles,
California
Source: *BioIn 7, 11; BlueB 76; CelR;
ConAu 118, 125; ConTFT 4; CurBio 65;
FilmEn; HalFC 84, 88; IntMPA 75, 76,
77, 78, 79, 80, 81, 82, 84, 86, 88, 92,
94, 96; LesBEnT 92; MiSFD 9; VarWW
85; WhoAm 74, 76, 78, 80, 82, 84, 86,
88, 90, 92, 94, 95, 96, 97, 98, 99, 2000;
WhoAmP 93, 95; WhoEnt 92, 98*

Stevens, George (Cooper)
American. Director
Won Oscars for *A Place in the Sun*,
1951; *Giant*, 1956.
b. Dec 18, 1904 in Oakland, California
d. Mar 8, 1975 in Lancaster, California
Source: *AmAu&B; BiDFilm, 81, 94;
BioIn 10, 12, 14, 15, 19; CelR; CmMov;
ConAu 116; CurBio 52, 75N; DcAmB
S9; DcArts; DcFM; EncAFC; FacFETw;
Film 1; FilmEn; FilmgC; HalFC 80, 84,
88; IlWWHD 1; IntDcF 1-2, 2-2;
IntMPA 75; IntWW 74; LegTOT; MiSFD
9N; MovMk; NewYTBS 75; OxCFilm;
WhAm 6; Who 74; WhoAm 74; WhoWor
74; WhScrn 77, 83; WorAl; WorAlBi;
WorEFlm; WorFDir 1*

Stevens, Inger
[Inger Stensland]
American. Actor
Starred in "The Farmer's Daughter,"
1963-66.
b. Oct 18, 1934 in Stockholm, Sweden
d. Apr 30, 1970 in Hollywood,
California
Source: *BiE&WWA; BioIn 6, 8, 16, 17;
DcPseud; FilmEn; FilmgC; ForYSC;
InWom; LegTOT; MotPP; MovMk;
NewYTBE 70; NotNAT B; WhAm 5;
WhScrn 74, 77*

Stevens, James (Richard)
English. Social Reformer
Founded Resurrection Home in Calcutta,
India, a sanctuary for children from
the slums of that city; the home
provides medical care, nutrition,
education and employment training to
thousands of children.

b. c. 1943

Stevens, Jeremy
Writer
Won Emmy for "The Electric
   Company," 1973; wrote for "What's
   Happening;" "Barbara Mandrell
   Show."
Source: *Alli; VarWW 85*

Stevens, John
American. Inventor, Shipbuilder
Built first oceangoing steamboat, 1808;
   first American steam locomotive,
   1825; established first US patent laws,
   1790.
b. 1749 in New York, New York
d. Mar 6, 1838 in Hoboken, New Jersey
Source: *AmBi; AmNatBi; ApCAB X;
BiDAmBL 83; BiInAmS; BioIn 1, 2, 3, 6,
9, 11, 14; BlkwEAR; ChamBiD; DcAmB;
Drake; EncWB 98; HarEnUS; InSci;
LinLib S; McGEWB; NatCAB 11;
OxCAmH; REn; WebAB 74, 79; WhAm
HS; WhAmRev; WhDW; WorInv*

Stevens, John Frank
American. Engineer
Civil engineer; aided in building of Great
   Northern Railway, 1890, Panama
   Canal, 1904-14.
b. Apr 25, 1853 in West Gardiner, Maine
d. Jun 2, 1943 in Southern Pines, North
   Carolina
Source: *AmNatBi; BioIn 8, 9; DcAmB
S3; NatCAB 32; WhAm 4*

Stevens, John Paul
American. Supreme Court Justice
Appointed 101st justice to Supreme
   Court, 1975—.
b. Apr 20, 1920 in Chicago, Illinois
Source: *AmBench 79, 97; BiDFedJ A;
BioIn 9, 10, 11, 12, 13; CamDcAB; CelR
90; CngDr 77, 79, 81, 83, 85, 87, 89,
91, 93, 95; ConAu 176; CriJuSA;
CurBio 76; DrAS 78P, 82P, 99P;
EncWB, 98; FacFETw; IntWW 76, 77,
78, 79, 80, 81, 82, 83, 89, 91, 93, 97,
98, 2000; LegTOT; LesBEnT; LinLib S;
NatCAB 63N; NewYTBS 75; OxCSupC;
PolProf NF; SupCtJu; WebAB 79; Who
82, 83, 85, 88, 90, 92, 94, 98, 99, 2000;
WhoAm 74, 76, 78, 80, 82, 84, 86, 88,
90, 92, 94, 95, 96, 97, 98, 99, 2000;
WhoAmL 78, 79, 83, 85, 87, 90, 92, 94,
96, 98, 2000; WhoAmP 85, 87, 89, 91,
93, 95, 97, 1999; WhoE 79, 81, 83, 85,
86, 89, 91, 93; WhoGov 75, 77; WhoMW
74; WhoWor 78, 80, 82, 84, 95, 96;
WorAl; WorAlBi*

Stevens, K. T
[Gloria Wood]
American. Actor
Films include *Bob, Carol, Ted, and
   Alice,* 1969; daughter of Sam Wood.
b. Jul 20, 1919 in Hollywood, California
Source: *ConTFT 2; FilmgC; HalFC 84,
88; IntMPA 86, 92; WhoHol A; WhoThe
77A*

Stevens, Leslie
American. Screenwriter
Co-wrote science fiction film *Buck
   Rogers in the 25th Century,* 1979.
b. Feb 3, 1924 in Washington, District of
   Columbia
d. Apr 24, 1998 in Los Angeles,
   California
Source: *BiE&WWA; BioIn 23, 24;
FilmEn; FilmgC; HalFC 80, 84, 88;
IntMPA 75, 76, 77, 78, 79, 80, 81, 82,
84, 86, 88, 92, 94, 96; LesBEnT 92;
MiSFD 9; NewYTBS 98; NewYTET;
NotNAT; VarWW 85; WorEFlm*

Stevens, Mark
American. Actor
Films include *Destination Tokyo,* 1944;
   Gun Fever, 1958.
b. Dec 13, 1922 in Cleveland, Ohio
Source: *BioIn 3; FilmEn; IntMPA 84,
86, 88, 92, 94, 96; MotPP; VarWW 85*

Stevens, Morton
American. Composer, Conductor
Won Emmys for themes to "You're
   Dead," 1970; "Hawaii 5-0," 1974.
b. Jan 30, 1929 in Newark, New Jersey
Source: *ASCAP 66, 80; BioIn 17;
NewYTBS 91; VarWW 85*

Stevens, Nettie Maria
American. Biologist, Geneticist
Among the first to discover that
   chromosomes determine sex.
b. Jul 7, 1861 in Cavendish, Vermont
d. May 4, 1912 in Baltimore, Maryland
Source: *AmNatBi; AmWomSc; AZWoSci;
BiInAmS; BioIn 11, 12, 15, 19, 20, 22,
23; CamDcSc; ChamBiD; DcNAA;
DcScB S2; EncWB 98; IntDcWB; InWom
SUP; LarDcSc; LibW; NotAW; NotTwCS
1; NotWoLS; RanHWDS; WomBioS;
WomFir; WomSc; WorScD*

Stevens, Onslow
[Onslow Ford Stevenson]
American. Actor
Appeared in films *This Side of Heaven,*
   1934; *The Couch,* 1962.
b. Mar 29, 1906 in Los Angeles,
   California
d. Jan 5, 1977 in Van Nuys, California
Source: *BiE&WWA; BioIn 11; FilmgC;
MovMk; NewYTBS 77; NotNAT; Vers A;
WhoHol A; WhoThe 72; WhThe*

Stevens, Ray
[Harold Ray Ragsdale]
American. Musician, Singer
Pianist, country-western singer, 1970s.
b. Jan 24, 1939 in Clarksdale, Georgia
Source: *AllMGCo; BgBkCoM; BioIn 14;
ConMus 7; EncFCWM 83; EncPR&S
74; EncRk 88; HarEnCM 87; IlEncCM;
IlEncRk; LegTOT; RkOn 82; WhoAm 76,
78, 80, 82; WhoRock 81*

Stevens, Rise
American. Opera Singer
Attractive mezzo-soprano; NY Met.,
   1938-61; films include *Going My Way,*
   1944.
b. Jun 11, 1913 in New York, New York
Source: *BakBD 78, 84, 92; BakBDTw;
BiDAmM; BioIn 1, 2, 3, 4, 5, 6, 7, 10,
11, 13, 15, 16, 18, 24; BriBkM 80;
CamDcAB; CmOp; CmpEPM; CurBio
41; DcPseud; FacFETw; FilmgC;
ForYSC; HalFC 80, 84, 88; IntDcOp;
IntWWM 90; InWom, SUP; LinLib S;
MetOEnc; MusSN; NewAmDM; NewEOp
71; NewGrDA 86; NewGrDM 80;
NewGrDO; OxDcOp; PenDiMP;
RadStar; What 4; WhoAm 82; WhoAmW
85; WhoHol 92, A; WorAl; WorAlBi*

Stevens, Robert Livingston
American. Inventor, Shipbuilder
Built over 20 ferries, steamboats;
   invented inverted T-rail for railroads,
   1830; son of John.
b. Oct 18, 1787 in Hoboken, New Jersey
d. Apr 20, 1856 in Hoboken, New Jersey
Source: *AmBi; AmNatBi; ApCAB;
BiDAmBL 83; BiInAmS; BioIn 11, 14;
CamBiEn; CamDcAB; ChamBiD;
DcAmB; Drake; HarEnUS; InSci;
NatCAB 11; OxCAmH; TwCBDA;
WebAB 74, 79; WhAm HS; WorInv*

Stevens, Robert Ten Broeck
American. Business Executive,
   Government Official
Pres., JP Stevens, 1929-45; secretary of
   Army, 1953-55, during close of
   Korean War testified at Army-
   McCarthy hearings.
b. Jul 31, 1899 in Fanwood, New Jersey
d. Jan 30, 1983 in Edison, New Jersey
Source: *ConAmBL; CurBio 53, 83;
EncMcCE; IntWW 80, 81; NewYTBS 83;
PolProf E; WhoAm 78; WhoWor 74*

Stevens, Roger L(acey)
American. Producer
Won Tonys for Broadway productions of
   A Man For All Seasons, 1962; *Death
   of a Salesman,* 1984; chm. of board,
   Kennedy Center, Washington, DC,
   1961-88.
b. Mar 12, 1910 in Detroit, Michigan
d. Feb 2, 1998 in Washington, District of
   Columbia
Source: *BioIn 3, 4, 5, 7, 11, 13; BlueB
76; CamGWoT; CurBio 55, 98N;
NewYTBE 71; NotNAT; VarWW 85;
WhAm 12; WhoAm 86, 90, 92, 94, 95,
96, 97, 98; WhoE 93; WhoEnt 92, 98;
WhoThe 81*

Stevens, S(tanley) S(mith)
American. Psychologist, Educator
Noted psychophysicist; founded
   Harvard's Psychoacoustic Laboratory,
   1940s.
b. Nov 4, 1906 in Ogden, Utah
d. Jan 18, 1973 in Vail, Colorado
Source: *AmMWSc 73P; AmNatBi;
BiDcPsy; BioIn 1, 9, 10, 11, 14;
CamBiEn; ChamBiD; ConAu 116;*

DcScB S2; GuPsyc; McGMS 80; ThTwC 87

Stevens, Shadoe
[Terry Ingstad]
American. TV Personality
Replaced Casey Kasem as host of "American Top 40."
b. Nov 3, 1947 in Jamestown, North Dakota
Source: *BioIn 16; CelR 90; ConTFT 18*

Stevens, Shane
American. Author
Novels deal with life in Harlem: *Go Down Dead*, 1967.
b. Oct 8, 1941 in New York, New York
Source: *ConAu 21R, 43NR; DrAF 76; DrAPF 80, 87; IntAu&W 76*

Stevens, Siaka Probyn
Sierra Leonean. Political Leader
First president, prime minister, of Sierra Leone, 1971-85.
b. Aug 24, 1905 in Moyamba, Sierra Leone
d. May 29, 1988 in Freetown, Sierra Leone
Source: *AfSS 78, 79, 80, 81, 82; BioIn 8, 15, 16, 18, 21; DcAfHiB 86; IntWW 74, 75, 76, 77, 78, 79, 80, 81, 82, 83; IntYB 79, 80, 81, 82; Who 85; WhoGov 72; WhoWor 74, 76, 78, 80, 82, 84*

Stevens, Stella
[Estelle Egglestone]
American. Actor
Best known for role of Appassionata von Climax in film *Lil' Abner*, 1959.
b. Oct 1, 1938 in Hot Coffee, Mississippi
Source: *BiDFilm, 81; BioIn 16, 21; ConTFT 7; FilmgC; HalFC 84, 88; IntMPA 77, 78, 79, 80, 81, 82, 84, 86, 88, 92; InWom SUP; MiSFD 9; MotPP; NewYTBE 73; WhoAm 74; WhoHol A; WorAlBi*

Stevens, Ted
[Theodore Fulton Stevens]
American. Politician
Rep. senator from AK, 1968—.
b. Nov 18, 1923 in Indianapolis, Indiana
Source: *AlmAP 78; WhoWest 76, 78, 80, 82, 84, 87, 89, 92, 94, 96; WhoWor 80, 82, 84, 87, 89, 91; WorAl; WorAlBi*

Stevens, Thaddeus
American. Abolitionist, Politician
Organized Rep. party in VT; fathered the 14th admendment; active during Reconstruction period.
b. Apr 4, 1792 in Danville, Vermont
d. Aug 11, 1868 in Washington, District of Columbia
Source: *ABCAmRe; AmBi; AmNatBi; AmPolLe; AmRef; ApCAB; BiAUS; BiDrAC; BiDrUSC 89; BioIn 1, 3, 4, 5, 7, 8, 9, 12, 13, 14, 15, 16, 20, 23; CamBiEn; CamDcAB; ChamBiD; CivWDc; CyAG; CyEd; DcAmB; DcAmSR; Drake; EncAACR; EncAAH; EncAB-H 1974, 1996; EncWB 98;*

HarEnUS; HisWorL; LAmCW; LegTOT; LinLib S; McGEWB; NatCAB 4, 7; OxCAmH; PeoHis; PolPar; RComAH; REn; REnAL; TwCBDA; USGovLe; WebAB 74, 79; WhAm HS; WhAmP; WhCiWar

Stevens, Wallace
American. Poet, Author
Won 1955 Pulitzer for *Collected Poems*; noted for verse theme: reality mixed with imagination.
b. Oct 2, 1879 in Reading, Pennsylvania
d. Aug 2, 1955 in Hartford, Connecticut
Source: *AgeMat; AmAu&B; AmCulL; AmNatBi; AmWr, RS1; AtlBL; Benet 87, 96; BenetAL 91; BiCoLiE; BioIn 1, 2, 3, 4, 5, 6, 7, 8, 9, 10, 11, 12, 13, 14, 15, 16, 17, 19, 22, 24; CamBiEn; CamDcAB; CamGLE; CamHAL; CasWL; ChamBiD; ChhPo S2; CnDAL; CnE&AP; CnMWL; ConAmA; ConAu 104, 124; CyWA 58, 97; DcAmB S5; DcArts; DcLB 54; DcLEL; DcTwCCu 1; EncAB-H 1974, 1996; EncALit; EncWB 98; EncWL 1, 2, 2S, 3; FacFETw; GrWrEL P; LegTOT; LinLib L, S; LngCTC; MagSAmL; MajTwCW 1, 2; MakMC; McGEWB; ModAL 4, 4S1, 4S2, 4S3, 5; MorMA; NewGrDA 86; NotPoe; OxCAmL 65, 83, 95; OxCEng 95; OxCTwCL; OxCTwCP; PenC AM; PoeCrit 6; RAdv 1, 14, 13-1; RComAH; REn; REnAL; RfGAmL 4, 87, 94; RGFAP; RGTwCWr; SixAP; TwCA, SUP; TwCLC 3, 12, 45; TwCWr; WebAB 74, 79; WebE&AL; WhAm 3; WhDW; WhoPul; WhoTwCL; WorAl; WorAlBi; WorAu 1900; WorLitC; WrPh*

Stevenson, Adlai Ewing
American. US Vice President
Served under Grover Cleveland, 1893-97.
b. Oct 23, 1835 in Christian County, Kentucky
d. Jun 14, 1914 in Chicago, Illinois
Source: *AmBi; AmNatBi; AmPolLe; ApCAB SUP; BiDrAC; BiDrUSC 89; BiDrUSE 71, 89; BiDSA; BioIn 1, 4, 7, 8, 9, 10, 17, 22, 23; CamDcAB; DcAmB; DcNAA; EncAAH; HarEnUS; NatCAB 2; TwCBDA; VicePre; WebAB 74, 79; WhAm 1; WhAmP; WorAl*

Stevenson, Adlai Ewing, II
American. Diplomat, Politician
UN ambassador, 1961-65; lost to Eisenhower in presidential races, 1952, 1956.
b. Feb 5, 1900 in Los Angeles, California
d. Jul 14, 1965 in London, England
Source: *AmAu&B; AmDec 1950; AmNatBi; AmOrTwC; AmPolLe; BiDInt; BioIn 1, 2, 3, 4, 5, 6, 7, 8, 9, 10, 11, 12, 13; CamBiEn; CamDcAB; ChamBiD; ColdWar 2; ConAu P-1; CurBio 49, 61, 65; DcAmB S7; DcAmDH 80, 89; DcPol; DcTwHis; EncAAH; EncAB-A 36; EncAB-H 1974, 1996; EncWB 98; FacFETw; LinLib S; McGEWB; NatCAB 53; OxCAmH; OxCAmL 65; PresAR 1980; REn; REnAL; WebAB 74, 79;*

WhAm 4; WhAmP; WhDW; WhScrn 77; WorAl

Stevenson, Adlai Ewing, III
American. Politician, Lawyer
Dem. senator from IL, 1970-81.
b. Oct 10, 1930 in Chicago, Illinois
Source: *BiDrAC; BiDrUSC 89; BioIn 3, 7, 8, 9, 10, 11, 13; CurBio 74; IntWW 83, 91; LElec; WhoAm 74, 76, 78, 80, 82, 84, 86, 88, 90, 92, 94, 95, 96, 97, 2000; WhoAmL 85, 90, 92, 94, 96, 2000; WhoAmP 73, 75, 77, 79, 81, 83, 85, 87, 89, 91, 93, 95, 97, 1999; WhoGov 72, 75, 77; WhoMW 74, 76, 78, 80, 82; WhoWor 80, 82, 84, 2000; WorAl; WorAlBi*

Stevenson, Bryan (Allen)
American. Lawyer
Founder and director, Equal Justice Initiative of Alabama, 1995—; works to fight inequities in the justice system.
b. Nov 14, 1959 in Milton, Delaware
Source: *BioIn 21; CurBio 96; WhoAm 96, 97, 98, 99, 2000; WhoAmL 92, 94*

Stevenson, Coke Robert
American. Politician
Prominent in TX politics, 1920s-40s; governor of TX, 1943-47.
b. Mar 20, 1888 in Mason County, Texas
d. Jun 28, 1975 in San Angelo, Texas
Source: *BioIn 1, 10, 11; WhAm 6*

Stevenson, Janet
American. Author
Many of her writings deal with women in unexpected roles: *Woman Aboard*, 1969.
b. Feb 4, 1913 in Chicago, Illinois
Source: *AuBYP 2S, 3; BioIn 11; ConAu 13R, 29NR; ForWC 70; SmATA 8; WhoAmW 61, 66, 68, 70*

Stevenson, McLean
American. Actor
Played Henry Blake on "M*A*S*H," 1972-75.
b. Nov 14, 1929 in Bloomington, Illinois
d. Feb 15, 1996 in Tarzana, California
Source: *BioIn 10, 12, 17, 21, 22, 23; BioNews 74; ConTFT 6, 16; CurBio 80, 96N; LegTOT; News 96, 96-3; ObitPA 96; WhoAm 80; WhoCom; WhoHol 92, A; WhoTelC*

Stevenson, Parker
American. Actor
Starred in TV series "Hardy Boys Mysteries," 1978-79.
b. Jun 4, 1951? in Philadelphia, Pennsylvania
Source: *BioIn 12, 13; IntMPA 86, 92*

Stevenson, Robert
American. Director
Films include Disney classics *Mary Poppins*, 1964; *The Love Bug*, 1968.
b. Mar 31, 1905 in London, England

d. Apr 30, 1986 in Santa Barbara,
California
Source: *AnObit 1986; BioIn 14, 15;
ConAu 120; FilmEn; FilmgC; HalFC 80,
84, 88; IlWWBF; IlWWHD 1; IntAu&W
77; IntDcF 2-2; IntMPA 75, 76, 77, 78,
79, 80, 81, 82, 84, 86; MiSFD 9N;
MovMk; NewYTBS 86; WhAm 9; Who
74, 82, 83, 85; WhoAm 78, 80, 82;
WhoHrs 80; WhoWest 80; WorEFlm;
WorFDir 1*

Stevenson, Robert Louis (Balfour)
Scottish. Author, Poet, Essayist
Wrote *Treasure Island; A Child's
Garden of Verses; Dr. Jekyll and Mr.
Hyde.*
b. Nov 13, 1850 in Edinburgh, Scotland
d. Dec 3, 1894 in Vailima, Samoa
Source: *Alli SUP; AnCL; ApCAB SUP;
AtlBL; AuBYP 2, 3; BbD; Benet 87, 96;
BenetAL 91; BiD&SB; BioIn 1, 2, 3, 4,
5, 6, 7, 8, 9, 10, 11, 12, 13, 14, 15, 16,
17, 18, 19, 20, 21; BlmGEL; BritAu 19;
BritWr 5; CamBiEn; CamGEL;
CamGLE; CarSB; CasWL; CelCen;
ChamBiD; Chambr 3; ChhPo, S1, S2,
S3; ChlBkCr; ChlLR 10, 11; ChrP;
CmCal; CmScLit; CnDBLB 5; CrtSuMy;
CrtT 3; CyWA 58; DcArts; DcBiA;
DcBrBl; DcEnA, A; DcEuL; DcLB 18,
57, 141, 156, 174, DS13; DcLEL;
DcNaB, C; DcPup; Dis&D; EncMys;
EncPaPR 91; EncSF, 93; EvLB;
FamAYP; FilmgC; GrWrEL N; HalFC
80, 84, 88; JBA 34; LegTOT; LinLib L,
S; LngCEL; MagSWL; MajAl;
McGEWB; MnBBF; MouLC 4; NewC;
NewCBEL; NewEScF; NinCLC 5, 14;
Novels; OxCAmL 65, 83, 95; OxCAusL;
OxCChiL; OxCEng 67, 85, 95; OxCMus;
PenC ENG; PenEncH; PeoHis; RAdv 1,
14, 13-1; REn; REnAL; RfGEnL 91;
RfGShF 1; ScF&FL 1, 92; ScFSB;
ShSCr 11; ShSWr; SJGHorW; SJGYouA
2; SmATA 100; StaCVF; Str&VC;
SupFW; TwCChW 1A, 2A, 3A, 4A;
TwCYAW 1; VicBrit; WebE&AL;
WhDW; WhoChL; WhoHr&F; WhoHrs
80; WorAl; WorAlBi; WorLitC; WrChl;
YABC 2*

Stevenson, Teofilo
Cuban. Boxer
Amateur heavyweight boxer; second man
to win three successive Olympic
boxing gold medals, 1972-1980.
b. Mar 23, 1952 in Delicias, Cuba
Source: *BioIn 15, 22; BlkOlyM;
ChamBiD; InB&W 80; NewYTBS 82*

Stevin, Simon
[Simon Stevinus]
Dutch. Mathematician, Engineer
Introduced decimal fractions into
common use; developed hydrostatics;
wrote *La Thiende*, 1585.
b. 1548 in Bruges, Belgium
d. 1620 in The Hague, Netherlands
Source: *AsBiEn; BiEsc; BioIn 1, 8, 14,
15, 16; CamBiEn; CamDcSc; CasWL;
ChamBiD; DcBiPP; DcCathB; DcInv;
DcScB; InSci; LarDcSc; NewCol 75;*

*NotMat; WhDW; WorAl; WorAlBi;
WorInv; WorScD*

Steward, Emanuel
American. Boxing Trainer
Trainer of Thomas Hearns, Milton
McCrory.
b. Jul 7, 1944 in Bluefield, West Virginia
Source: *BioIn 12, 23; BoxReg, 2;
ConBlB 18; WhoAfA 9, 10, 11, 12;
WhoBlA 4, 5, 6, 7, 8*

Steward, Julian Haynes
American. Anthropologist
Founded cultural ecology theory.
b. Jan 31, 1902 in Washington, District
of Columbia
d. Feb 6, 1972 in Urbana, Illinois
Source: *AmNatBi; BioIn 9, 10;
CamBiEn; CamDcAB; ChamBiD; ConAu
33R; FacFETw; IntEnSS 79; WhAm 5*

Stewart, Al
Scottish. Singer
Hit singles include "Year of the Cat,"
1977; "Time Passages," 1978.
b. Sep 5, 1945 in Glasgow, Scotland
Source: *ASCAP 80; BillEnR; BioIn 11;
ConMuA 80A; EncRkSt; HarEnR 86;
IlEncRk; LegTOT; PenEncP; RkOn 74,
78; RolSEnR 83; Songw; WhoAm 80, 82;
WhoRock 81*

Stewart, Alexander Peter
American. Military Leader
General active during Civil War in
western, Atlanta campaigns;
commanded Army of Tennessee.
b. Oct 2, 1821 in Rogersville, Tennessee
d. Aug 30, 1908 in Biloxi, Mississippi
Source: *AmBi; AmNatBi; ApCAB;
BiDConf; BioIn 1, 3, 5, 17; CivWDc;
DcAmB; NatCAB 4; TwCBDA;
WebAMB; WhAm 1; WhCiWar*

Stewart, Alexander Turney
American. Merchant, Philanthropist
Started NYC dry-goods store, 1823;
developed into world's largest retail
store, 1862; founded Garden City,
1869.
b. Oct 12, 1803 in Lisburn, Northern
Ireland
d. Apr 10, 1876 in New York, New
York
Source: *AmBi; AmNatBi; ApCAB;
BiAUS; BiDAmBL 83; BioIn 1, 4, 6, 7,
10, 15, 18; ChamBiD; DcAmB; Dis&D;
Drake; EncAB-H 1974; EncWB 98;
HarEnUS; McGEWB; NatCAB 7;
OxCAmH; TwCBDA; WebAB 74, 79;
WhAm HS*

Stewart, Alison
American. Broadcaster
Television journalist writes, produces,
and delivers stories for the news
department at cable channel Music
Television (MTV), and hosts
"Unfiltered," a news program; stories
generally focus on racial, feminist, and
political issues.

b. c. 1966 in Glen Ridge, New Jersey
Source: *ConBlB 13*

Stewart, Anita
American. Actor
Starred for Vitagraph, 1911-17; with
Louis B. Mayer, 1918-28; retired with
advent of talkies.
b. Feb 17, 1896 in New York, New
York
d. May 4, 1961 in Beverly Hills,
California
Source: *Film 1; FilmgC; TwYS; WhoHol
B; WhScrn 74, 77*

Stewart, Black Jack
[John Sherratt Stewart]
Canadian. Hockey Player
Defenseman, 1938-52, mostly with
Detroit; Hall of Fame, 1964.
b. May 6, 1917 in Pilot Mound,
Manitoba, Canada
Source: *HocEn; WhoHcky 73*

Stewart, Dave
[David Keith Stewart]
American. Baseball Player
Pitcher since 1981, with Oakland, 1986-
92; Toronto, 1993—; has won at least
20 games, 1987-90; MVP, 1989 World
Series; with Fernando Valenzuela,
pitched no-hitter on same day, 1990;
first pitchers to accomplish since 1898.
b. Feb 19, 1957 in Oakland, California
Source: *Ballpl 90; BaseEn 88; BaseReg
88; BioIn 16; News 91, 91-1; NewYTBS
89; WhoAfA 9; WhoBlA 4, 5, 6, 7, 8;
WhoWest 92; WorAlBi*

Stewart, David
[The Eurythmics]
English. Musician
Guitarist with Eurythmics; singles
include "Would I Lie to You?" 1985.
b. Sep 19, 1952 in Sunderland, England

Stewart, Donald Ogden
American. Author, Actor
Hollywood scenarist, humorist; wrote
Parody Outline of History, 1921.
Hollywood scenarist, humorist; wrote
Parody Outline of History, 1921.
b. Nov 30, 1894 in Columbus, Ohio
d. Aug 2, 1980 in London, England
Source: *AmAu&B; AmNatBi; AnObit
1980; BenetAL 91; BiE&WWA; BioIn 4,
10, 12, 13, 14, 15, 17, 22; CarSB;
ConAu 43NR, 81, 101; Conv 1; CurBio
41, 80N; DcAmB S10; DcLB 4, 11, 26;
DcLEL; EncAFC; EncALit; FilmEn;
FilmgC; HalFC 80, 84, 88; IntDcF 1-4,
2-4; LegTOT; NotNAT; OhA&B;
OxCAmL 65, 83, 95; PenC AM; REnAL;
TwCA, SUP; WhAm 7, 10; WhJnl;
WhNAA; WhoAm 74; WhoThe 77A;
WhScrn 83; WhThe; WorAu 1900;
WorEFlm*

Stewart, Dugald
Scottish. Philosopher
A proponent of Reid's commonsense
philosophy, he was concerned with

formulating a philosophy of mind through the use of the inductive method of Sir Francis Bacon.
b. Nov 22, 1735 in Edinburgh, Scotland
d. Jun 11, 1828
Source: *OxCPhil*

Stewart, Ellen
American. Producer
Opened boutique, La Mama, NYC, 1962; produced, directed plays by int'l, avant-garde playwrights.
b. Oct 7, 1931 in New Orleans, Louisiana
Source: *BioIn 10, 13; CamDcAB; CelR; ConTFT 5; CurBio 73; NotNAT; PIP&P; WhoThe 77, 81; WhThe*

Stewart, George Rippey
American. Author, Educator
Versatile writer, known for novels *Storm*, 1941; *Earth Abides*, 1951.
b. May 31, 1895 in Sewickley, Pennsylvania
d. Aug 22, 1980 in San Francisco, California
Source: *AmAu&B; AmNatBi; AmNov; Au&Wr 71; BioIn 1, 2, 4, 9, 12, 13, 22; CnDAL; ConAu 1R, 3NR, 101; CurBio 42, 80; EncSF; FifWWr; IntAu&W 77; OxCAmL 65; REnAL; ScF&FL 1, 2; SmATA 3, 23N; TwCA SUP; TwCSFW 81; WhAm 7; WhE&EA; WhNAA; WhoAm 74; WorAu 1900; WrDr 76, 80, 82*

Stewart, J(ohn) I(nnes) M(ackintosh)
[Michael Innes]
Scottish. Author
Wrote detective stories concerning sleuth Inspector Appleby: *The Spider Strikes*, 1939.
b. Sep 30, 1906 in Edinburgh, Scotland
d. Nov 12, 1994
Source: *Au&Wr 71; Benet 96; BiCoLiE; BioIn 14, 15, 16, 17, 20; CamBiEn; ChamBiD; ConAu 47NR, 85, 147; ConLC 7, 14, 32, 86; ConNov 72, 76; CrtSuMy; DcLEL; EncMys; EvLB; LegTOT; LngCTC; MajTwCW 2; NewC; NewCBEL; Novels; OxCAusL; OxCEng 95; OxCTwCL; PenC ENG; REn; RGTwCWr; TwCA, SUP; TwCCr&M 80, 85, 91; TwCWr; Who 74, 82, 83, 85, 88, 90, 92, 94; WhoSpyF; WorAl; WorAlBi; WorAu 1900; WrDr 76, 94, 96*

Stewart, Jackie
[John Young Stewart]
Scottish. Auto Racer
World Grand Prix champ, 1969, 1971, 1973; auto racing commentator, ABC.
b. Jun 11, 1939 in Dunbartonshire, Scotland
Source: *BioIn 8, 9, 10, 11, 12, 16; CamBiEn; ChamBiD; FacFETw; IntWW 76, 77, 78, 79, 80, 81, 82, 83, 89, 91, 93; LegTOT; Who 74, 82, 83, 85, 88, 90, 92, 94; WorAl; WorAlBi*

Stewart, James (Maitland)
[Jimmy Stewart]
American. Actor
Hollywood great; best known for *Mr. Smith Goes to Washington*, 1939, *It's a Wonderful Life*, 1946.
b. May 20, 1908 in Indiana, Pennsylvania
d. Jul 2, 1997 in Beverly Hills, California
Source: *AmCulL; BiDFilm, 81, 94; BiE&WWA; BioIn 1, 2, 3, 4, 5, 6, 7, 8, 9, 10, 11, 12, 13; BkPepl; BlueB 76; CamBiEn; CamDcAB; CelR, 90; ChamBiD; CmCal; CmMov; ConTFT 4; CurBio 97N; DcArts; EncAFC; FacFETw; FilmEn; FilmgC; ForYSC; GangFlm; HalFC 80, 84, 88; IntDcF 1-3, 2-3; IntMPA 77, 84, 86, 88, 92, 94, 96; IntWW 74, 75, 76, 77, 78, 79, 80, 81, 82, 83, 89, 91, 93, 97; LegTOT; MGM; MotPP; MovMk; NewYTBS 90; OxCFilm; PIP&P; VarWW 85; WhAm 12; Who 74, 82, 83, 85, 88, 90, 92, 94; WhoAm 74, 76, 78, 80, 82, 84, 86, 88, 90, 92, 94, 95, 96, 97; WhoEnt 92; WhoHol 92, A; WhoHrs 80; WhoThe 77, 81; WhoWor 74, 78, 84, 89, 91, 93, 95, 96, 97; WorAl; WorAlBi; WorEFlm*

Stewart, John
American. Singer, Songwriter
Best known for writing song "Daydream Believer," 1967, which was number one hit for The Monkees, 1967; member of Kingston Trio, 1961-67.
b. Sep 5, 1939 in San Diego, California
Source: *AllMGCo; BioIn 14; ConMuA 80A; EncFCWM 83; HarEnCM 87; HarEnR 86; IlEncCM; IlEncRk; IntWWM 80; PenEncP; RkOn 85; RolSEnR 83; Songw; WhoAdv 90; WhoAm 74, 76; WhoEnt 92; WhoRock 81*

Stewart, Jon
[Jon Stuart Liebowitz]
American. TV Personality, Actor, Comedian
Host of "The Jon Stewart Show."
b. 1963 in Lawrence, New Jersey

Stewart, Luisa Harris
American. Basketball Player
Led Delta State to three national championships in the 1970s; one of first two women inducted into Basketball Hall of Fame, 1992.
b. Feb 10, 1955 in Minter City, Mississippi

Stewart, Maria W. Miller
American. Political Activist, Writer, Educator
Thought to be the first American woman to give a public lecture, spoke out in the 1830s for the abolition of slavery, black economic progress and self-determination, and women's rights; also an essayist and teacher.
b. 1803 in Hartford, Connecticut
d. Dec 1879

Source: *AmWomWr; ConBlB 19; EncWHA; InB&W 80, 85; InWom, SUP; NotAW*

Stewart, Martha
American. Author
Author of gourmet food and lifestyle books; was lifestyle contributor to NBC's "Today;" created own line of paints.
b. 1941? in Nutley, New Jersey
Source: *AmDec 1980; BioIn 12, 16; CurBio 93; EncWB 2-19; GrLiveH; News 92-1*

Stewart, Mary (Florence Elinor)
English. Author
Wrote trilogy about Merlin, King Arthur: *The Last Enchantment*, 1979.
b. Sep 17, 1916 in Sunderland, England
Source: *ArtclWW 2; Au&Wr 71; Benet 87, 96; BioIn 5, 8, 9, 10, 11, 12, 14, 16; BlmGWL; ChlBkCr; ConAu 1NR, 1R, 59NR; ConLC 7, 35; ConPopW; CrtSuMy; DcLEL 1940; EncBrWW; EncMys; FemiCLE; IntAu&W 76, 77, 82, 89, 91, 93; InWom SUP; LngCEL; LngCTC; NewYTBS 79; Novels; OxCChiL; OxCTwCL; ScF&FL 1, 2, 92; SJGFanW; SJGYouA 2; SmATA 12; TwCCr&M 80, 85, 91; TwCRGW; TwCRHW 90, 94; TwCWr; TwCYAW 1; Who 74, 82, 83, 85, 88, 90, 92, 94, 98, 2000; WhoAm 74, 76, 78, 80, 82, 84, 86, 88, 90, 92, 94, 95, 96, 97, 98, 99, 2000; WhoAmW 70, 72, 74, 75, 77; WhoUSWr 88; WhoWor 74, 76; WhoWrEP 89, 92, 95; WorAlBi; WorAu 1950; WrDr 76, 80, 82, 84, 86, 88, 90, 92, 94, 96, 98, 99, 2000*

Stewart, Michael
[Michael Rubin]
American. Dramatist
Won Tonys for *Bye, Bye Birdie*, 1961; *Hello Dolly!* 1964.
b. Aug 1, 1929 in New York, New York
d. Sep 20, 1987 in New York, New York
Source: *BiE&WWA; BioIn 12, 15; ConTFT 1, 5; EncMT; NewCBMT; NotNAT; OxCAmT 84; VarWW 85; WhAm 9; WhoAm 82, 84, 86; WhoThe 77, 81*

Stewart, Nels(on Robert)
"Old Poison"
Canadian. Hockey Player
Center, 1925-40, mostly with Montreal Maroons; won Hart Trophy, 1926, 1930, Art Ross Trophy, 1926; first to score 300 goals; Hall of Fame, 1962.
b. Dec 29, 1902 in Montreal, Quebec, Canada
d. Aug 21, 1957 in Toronto, Ontario, Canada
Source: *BioIn 2, 4; HocEn; ObitOF 79; WhoHcky 73*

Stewart, Patrick
English. Actor
Played Captain Jean-Luc Picard on "Star Trek: The Next Generation," 1987-94;

won and was nominated for several
Lawrence Olivier Awards.
b. Jul 13, 1940 in Mirfield, England
Source: *BioIn 18, 19, 20, 21, 22, 23, 24;
CamBiEn; ConTFT 7, 14, 25; CurBio
94; IntMPA 94, 96; News 96, 96-1;
WhoAm 94, 95, 96, 97, 98, 99, 2000;
WhoEnt 98; WhoHol 92, A; WhoThe 72,
77, 81*

Stewart, Paul
American. Actor
Made acting debut in Orson Welles'
Citizen Kane, 1941; typically cast in
gangster roles.
b. Mar 13, 1908 in New York, New
York
d. Feb 17, 1986 in Los Angeles,
California
Source: *AnObit 1986; BioIn 14; ConTFT
21; DcPseud; FilmEn; FilmgC; ForYSC;
GangFlm; HalFC 80, 84, 88; HolCA;
IntMPA 84, 86; MovMk; RadStar; Vers
A; WhoAm 74, 76, 78, 80, 82, 84;
WhoHol A*

Stewart, Paul Wilbur
American. Curator
Curator dedicated to documenting the
role of African Americans in building
of the American West, founded the
Black American West Museum and
Heritage Center, a collection of over
35,000 items, in 1971.
b. Dec 18, 1925 in Clinton, Iowa
Source: *ConBlB 12; WhoAfA 9, 10, 11,
12; WhoBlA 2, 3, 4, 6, 7, 8*

Stewart, Potter
American. Supreme Court Justice
Conservative Eisenhower Rep; justice,
1958-81; youngest to resign.
b. Jan 13, 1915 in Jackson, Michigan
d. Dec 7, 1985 in Hanover, New
Hampshire
Source: *AmBench 79; AmNatBi; AnObit
1985; BiDFedJ; BioIn 5, 6, 7, 8, 9, 10,
11, 12, 13, 14, 15, 17, 24; BlueB 76;
CamDcAB; CelR; CngDr 74, 77, 79, 81,
83, 85, 87; ConNews 86-1; CurBio 59,
86, 86N; DrAS 74P, 78P, 82P; EncRelA;
EncWB, 98; FacFETw; IntWW 74, 75,
76, 77, 78, 79, 80, 81, 82, 83; IntYB 78,
79, 80, 81, 82; LegTOT; LinLib S;
NewYTBS 85; OxCSupC; PolProf E, J,
K, NF; ScrEAmL 1; SupCtJu; WebAB
74, 79; Who 74, 82, 83, 85; WhoAm 74,
76, 78, 80, 82, 84; WhoAmL 78, 79, 83,
85; WhoAmP 73, 75, 77, 79, 81, 83, 85;
WhoE 79, 81, 83, 85; WhoGov 72, 75,
77; WhoSSW 73, 75, 76; WhoWor 74,
78, 80, 82, 84; WorAl; WorAlBi*

Stewart, Rod(erick David)
English. Singer
Singer with Jeff Beck Group, 1968-69;
Faces, 1969-75; solo performer,
1975—.
b. Jan 10, 1945 in North London,
England
Source: *ASCAP 80; BioIn 9, 10, 11, 12,
13, 16; BkPepl; CamBiEn; CelR 90;
ConMuA 80A; ConMus 2; CurBio 79;*

*EncPR&S 74, 89; EncRk 88; EncRkSt;
HarEnR 86; IlEncRk; IntWW 89, 91, 93;
LegTOT; NewAmDM; OxCPMus;
PenEncP; RkOn 74, 78; RolSEnR 83;
WhoAm 78, 80, 82, 84, 86, 88, 90, 92,
94, 95, 96, 97, 98, 99; WhoEnt 92A, 98;
WhoMW 90; WhoRock 81; WhoRocM
82; WhoWor 95, 96, 97, 98, 99, 2000;
WorAl; WorAlBi*

Stewart, Slam
[Leroy Stewart]
American. Jazz Musician, Composer
Innovative bassist with Art Tatum,
Benny Goodman; recorded "Flat Foot
Floogie" with Slim Gaillard, 1938.
b. Sep 21, 1914 in Englewood, New
Jersey
d. Dec 10, 1987 in Binghamton, New
York
Source: *AllMGJa; AmNatBi; AnObit
1987; BiDAmM; BiDJaz; BioIn 15, 16,
24; CmpEPM; DrBlPA 90; EncJzS;
InB&W 80, 85; NewGrDA 86; NewGrDJ
88, 94; NewYTBS 87; PenEncP; WhoAm
82, 84, 86; WhoJazz 72*

Stewart, Thomas
[Thomas James Stewart, Jr.]
American. Opera Singer
Baritone with various operas including
the NY Met, 1960—; Wagnerian
soloist.
b. Aug 19, 1928 in San Saba, Texas
Source: *BakBD 78, 84; BiDAmM; BioIn
11, 13; CmOp; CurBio 74; IntWW 78,
79, 80, 81, 82, 83, 89, 91, 93, 97, 98,
2000; IntWWM 80; MetOEnc; MusSN;
NewAmDM; NewEOp 71; NewGrDA 86;
NewGrDM 80; OxDcOp; WhoAm 78, 80,
82, 84, 86, 88, 90, 92, 94, 95, 96, 97;
WhoAmM 83; WhoEnt 92; WhoOp 76;
WhoWor 78, 80, 82, 84*

Stewart, Wynn
American. Singer, Songwriter
Formed country-western band, The
Tourists, 1960s; hit single "Something
Pretty," 1968.
b. Jun 7, 1934 in Morrisville, Missouri
d. Jul 17, 1985 in Hendersonville,
Tennessee
Source: *AllMGCo; BgBkCoM; BiDAmM;
BioIn 14; ConAu 116, 154; CounME 74,
74A; EncFCWM 69, 83; HarEnCM 87;
IlEncCM; PenEncP*

Stibitz, George R.
American. Inventor, Mathematician
Inventor of first electric calculator.
d. Jan 13, 1995 in Hanover, New
Hampshire
Source: *NewYTBS 95*

Stich, Michael
Tennis Player
Won Grand Slam, 1991.
Source: *BioIn 17, 23; NewYTBS 91*

Stich-Randall, Teresa
American. Opera Singer
Soprano; NY Met debut, 1961; sang
Aida at age 15.
b. Dec 24, 1927 in West Hartford,
Connecticut
Source: *BakBD 84, 92; BakBDTw;
CmOp; IntDcOp; IntWWM 80, 90;
MetOEnc; NewAmDM; NewEOp 71;
NewGrDA 86; NewGrDM 80;
NewGrDO; OxDcOp; PenDiMP; WhoAm
74; WhoMus 72*

Stickley, Gustav
[Gustav Stoeckel]
American. Journalist, Furniture Designer
Editor, publisher, *The Craftsman
Magazine,* 1901; founded furniture
works hops; created Mission style
furniture.
b. Mar 9, 1858 in Osceola, Wisconsin
d. Apr 21, 1942 in New York, New
York
Source: *AmCulL; AmNatBi; AmRef;
BioIn 3, 7, 11, 13, 15, 16, 19, 20;
CamBiEn; CamDcAB; ChamBiD;
NatCAB 14; WhAm 4*

Stickney, Dorothy
American. Actor, Centenarian
Co-starred in Broadway's *Life With
Father* with husband Howard Lindsay,
1939-43.
b. Jun 21, 1896 in Dickinson, North
Dakota
d. Jun 1, 1998 in New York, New York
Source: *BiE&WWA; BioIn 24; CurBio
42, 98N; ForYSC; InWom, SUP; MotPP;
NotNAT; WhoHol 92, A; WhoThe 72, 77,
81*

Stieb, Dave
[David Andrew Stieb]
American. Baseball Player
Pitcher, Toronto, 1979-92; led AL in
ERA, 1985; five-time AL All-Star;
pitched no-hitter, 1990.
b. Jul 22, 1957 in Santa Ana, California
Source: *Ballpl 90; BaseReg 86, 87;
BiDAmSp Sup; BioIn 13; WhoAm 84, 86,
88, 90, 92; WhoE 89*

Stiedry, Fritz
Austrian. Conductor
Principal Wagner conductor, NY Met.,
1946-58.
b. Oct 11, 1883 in Vienna, Austria
d. Aug 9, 1968 in Zurich, Switzerland
Source: *BakBD 78, 84, 92; BakBDTw;
BiDAmM; BiDSovU; BioIn 2, 4, 8, 11;
CmOp; MetOEnc; MusSN; NewEOp 71;
NewGrDA 86; NewGrDM 80;
NewGrDO; PenDiMP*

Stiegel, Henry William
American. Manufacturer
Iron, glass maker; founder Flint Glass
Co., 1772; glassware now collector's
items.
b. May 13, 1729 in Cologne, Germany
d. Jan 10, 1785 in Charming Forge,
Pennsylvania

Source: *AmBi; AmNatBi; AntBDN H; BioIn 1, 3, 8, 17; BriEAA; DcAmB; EncCRAm; EncWB 98; IlDcG; McGEWB; NewCol 75; OxCAmH; OxCDecA; PenDiDA 89; WebAB 74, 79; WhAm HS*

Stieglitz, Alfred

"Father of Modern Photography"
American. Photographer, Editor
Work characterized by technical innovations taking pictures at night or in rain; influenced by artists Matisse, Picasso.
b. Jan 1, 1864 in Hoboken, New Jersey
d. Jul 13, 1946 in New York, New York
Source: *AmAu&B; AmCulL; AmNatBi; AtlBL; Benet 87, 96; BiDAmJo; BioIn 1, 2, 4, 5, 6, 7, 8, 9, 10, 11, 12, 13, 14, 15, 16, 17, 18, 19, 20, 21, 22; BriEAA; CamBiEn; CamDcAB; ChambiD; ConPhot 82, 88; CurBio 46; DcAmArt; DcAmB S4; DcArts; DcTwArt; DcTwDes; EncAB-H 1974, 1996; EncAJ; EncWB 98; FacFETw; GayN; ICPEnP; JeAmHC; LegTOT; MacBEP; McGDA; McGEWB; ObitOF 79; OxCAmH; OxCAmL 65; OxCTwCA; OxDcArt; REn; REnAL; WebAB 74, 79; WhAm 2; WhAmArt 85; WhNAA; WorAl; WorAlBi*

Stiers, David Ogden

American. Actor
Played Major Winchester on "M*A*S*H," 1977-83.
b. Oct 31, 1942 in Peoria, Illinois
Source: *BioIn 11, 12, 13; ConTFT 6; HalFC 88; IntMPA 92, 94, 96; LegTOT; VarWW 85; WhoAm 80, 82, 84, 86, 88, 90, 92, 94, 95, 96, 97, 99; WhoEnt 92, 98; WhoHol 92; WhoWest 82*

Stiffel, Theodopholous

American. Businessman
Started TA Stiffel Co., 1932, artfully fashioned, high-priced lamps.
b. 1899 in Memphis, Tennessee
d. 1971
Source: *Entr*

Stigler, George Joseph

American. Economist
Intellectual anchor of Chicago school of economics movement; won Nobel Prize in economics, 1982; wrote *The Economist as Preacher*, 1982.
b. Jun 17, 1911 in Renton, Washington
d. Dec 1, 1991 in Chicago, Illinois
Source: *AmAu&B; AmMWSc 73S, 78S; BioIn 13, 14, 15, 16, 17, 18, 19, 20; BlueB 76; CamBiEn; CamDcAB; ChambiD; ConAu 41R; CurBio 83; GrEconS; IntWW 74, 75, 76, 77, 78, 79, 80, 81, 82, 83, 89, 91; NewYTBS 82; NobelP; RAdv 14; WhAm 10; Who 85, 88, 90, 92; WhoAm 74, 76, 78, 80, 82, 84, 86, 88, 90; WhoEc 81, 86; WhoFI 83, 85, 89, 92; WhoMW 84, 86, 88, 90; WhoNob, 90, 95; WhoWor 82, 84, 87, 89, 91; WorAlBi; WrDir 76, 84, 92*

Stignani, Ebe

Italian. Opera Singer
Mezzo-soprano; with Milan's La Scala, 1926-56; known for Italian roles.
b. Jul 10, 1907 in Naples, Italy
d. Oct 5, 1974 in Imola, Italy
Source: *BakBD 84; BioIn 1, 2, 3, 4, 9, 10, 11, 14, 17; BriBkM 80; CurBio 49, 91N; InWom; MusSN; NewEOp 71; NewGrDM 80; WhAm 6*

Stigwood, Robert Colin

Australian. Producer
Won Tony for *Evita*, 1980.
b. Apr 16, 1934 in Adelaide, Australia
Source: *ConAu 102; ConTFT 5; CurBio 79; HalFC 84, 88; IntMPA 86, 92; IntWW 83, 89, 91, 93, 97, 98, 2000; VarWW 85; WhoAm 86, 88, 90, 92, 94, 95, 96, 97, 98, 99, 2000; WhoE 93; WhoEnt 92, 98; WhoWor 84, 87*

Stilicho, Flavius

Roman. Military Leader
General of Vandal origin maintained the territorial integrity of the Western Roman Empire during the reign of the emperor Honorius.
d. Aug 22, 408
Source: *CamBiEn; DcBiPP; EncWB 98; McGEWB*

Still, Andrew Taylor

American. Physician
Founder of osteopathy; believed all disease derived from dislocation of vertebrae.
b. Aug 6, 1828 in Jonesville, Virginia
d. Dec 12, 1917 in Kirksville, Missouri
Source: *AmBi; AmNatBi; BioIn 2, 4, 9; DcAmB; DcAmMeB 84; DcNAA; LinLib L, S; NatCAB 14, 26; NewAgE 90; NewCol 75; WebAB 74, 79; WhAm 1*

Still, Clyfford

American. Artist
Pioneer in use of mural sized canvas.
b. Oct 30, 1904 in Grandin, North Dakota
d. Jun 23, 1980 in Baltimore, Maryland
Source: *AmNatBi; AnObit 1980; BioIn 1, 3, 5, 6, 8, 9, 10, 12, 14, 15, 19, 20, 21; BriEAA; CamBiEn; CamDcAB; CelR; ChambiD; ConArt 77, 83, 89, 96; CurBio 71, 80N; DcAmArt; DcAmB S10; DcArts; DcCAA 71, 77, 88, 94; DcCAr 81; DcTwArt; EncWB, 98; McGDA; NewCol 75; NewYTBS 80; OxCTwCA; OxDcArt; PhDcTCA 77; REn; WhAm 4, 7, 8; WhAmArt 85; WhoAm 74, 76, 78, 80; WhoAmA 73, 76, 78, 80, 82N, 84N, 86N, 89N, 91N, 93N; WhoE 74; WhoWor 74; WorArt 1950*

Still, William

American. Abolitionist, Business Executive, Author
An important strategist for the Underground Railroad, he wrote an account of the hundreds of slaves he aided.
b. Oct 7, 1821 in Shamong, New Jersey
d. 1902

Source: *Alli SUP; AmAu&B; AmNatBi; AmRef; AmSocL; ApCAB; BiD&SB; BioIn 5, 6, 8, 9, 15, 19, 20, 23; BlkAWP; DcAmAu; DcAmB; DcAmNB; DcAmSR; DcNAA; EncWB 98; HarEnUS; InB&W 80; McGEWB; NatCAB 2; NegAl 76, 83; NotBlAM; OxCAfAL; SchCGBL; SelBAAf; SelBAAu; WhAm 1*

Still, William Grant

"Dean of Afro-American Composers"
American. Composer, Conductor
First black to lead major US orchestra, LA Philharmonic, 1936; wrote "Afro-American Symphony," 1931.
b. May 11, 1895 in Woodville, Mississippi
d. Dec 3, 1978 in Los Angeles, California
Source: *AfrAmAl 6, 8; AmComp; AmNatBi; ASCAP 66, 80; BakBD 78, 84, 92; BakBDTw; BakDcM; BiDAfM; BiDAmM; BioIn 1, 2, 3, 4, 6, 8, 9, 10, 11, 12, 13; BlkOpe; BriBkM 80; CamBiEn; CamDcAB; ChambiD; CmCal; CompSN, SUP; ConAmC 76, 82; CurBio 41, 79, 79N; DcAfAmP; DcAmB S10; DcCM; DcTwCCu 5; DrBlPA, 90; Ebony 1; EncAACR; EncWB 98; FacFETw; InB&W 80, 85; McGEWB; MetOEnc; NegAl 76, 83, 89; NewAmDM; NewCol 75; NewEAmW; NewEOp 71; NewGrDA 86; NewGrDM 80; NewGrDO; NewOxM; NewYTBS 78; NotBlAM; ObitOF 79; OxCMus; OxDcOp; REnAL; SelBAAu; WebAB 74, 79; WhoAm 74, 76; WhoBlA 1, 2; WhoMus 72*

Stiller, Ben

American. Actor, Director
Appeared in *Empire of the Sun*, 1987 and *Reality Bites*, 1994.
b. Nov 30, 1965 in New York, New York
Source: *ConTFT 12, 23; CurBio 1999; IntMPA 96; News 99-1, 1999*

Stiller, Jerry

[Stiller and Meara]
American. Comedian, Actor
Formed successful comedy team with wife Anne Meara; in film *Those Lips, Those Eyes*; played Frank Costanza on "Seinfeld," 1993-98.
b. Jun 8, 1926? in New York, New York
Source: *BioNews 75; CelR 90; LegTOT; VarWW 85; WhoAm 86, 88; WhoHol A*

Stiller, Mauritz

Swedish. Director
Pioneer of Swedish cinema; discovered Greta Garbo.
b. Jul 17, 1883 in Helsinki, Finland
d. Nov 8, 1928 in Stockholm, Sweden
Source: *BiDFilm, 81, 94; BioIn 9, 10, 12, 15; CamBiEn; ChambiD; DcFM; EncEurC; FilmEn; FilmgC; HalFC 80, 84, 88; IntDcF 1-2, 2-2; MiSFD 9N; MovMk; OxCFilm; TwYS, A; WhScrn 77, 83; WorEFlm; WorFDir 1*

Stillman, Irwin Maxwell
American. Physician
Wrote *The Doctor's Quick Weight-Loss Diet*, 1966.
b. Sep 11, 1895 in New York, New York
d. Aug 27, 1975 in Bal Harbour, Florida
Source: *BioIn 10, 12; BioNews 74; ConAu 49, 61; NatCAB 59; NewYTBS 75*

Stillman, James
American. Banker
Pres. of NY's National City Bank (now Citibank) made it one of the more powerful institutions in US.
b. Jun 9, 1850 in Brownsville, Texas
d. Mar 15, 1918 in New York, New York
Source: *AmNatBi; BiDAmBL 83; BioIn 3, 10, 21; DcAmB; EncABHB 6; NatCAB 15; WhAm 1*

Stills, Stephen
[Buffalo Springfield; Crosby, Stills, Nash, and Young]
American. Musician, Singer, Songwriter
Vocalist, guitarist, Buffalo Springfield band, 1966-68; Crosby, Stills, Nash, 1968-69, 1977, 1982; Crosby, Stills, Nash, & Young, 1969-71; solo career, 1971—; solo hits include "Love the One You're With," 1971.
b. Jan 3, 1945 in Dallas, Texas
Source: *ASCAP 80; BillEnR; BioIn 13; ConMuA 80A; ConMus 5; EncPR&S 74, 89; EncRk 88; HarEnR 86; IlEncRk; LegTOT; OnThGG; PenEncP; Songw; WhoAm 94, 95, 96, 97, 99, 2000; WhoEnt 98; WhoRocM 82; WorAl; WorAlBi*

Stilwell, Joseph Warren
"Vinegar Joe"
American. Army Officer
Commander of the 6th Army; chief-of-staff to Chiang Kai-Shek; disagreement over role of Chinese forces led to his loss of command by FDR, 1944.
b. Mar 19, 1883 in Palatka, Florida
d. Oct 12, 1946 in San Francisco, California
Source: *AmNatBi; BiDWWGF; BioIn 1, 5, 9, 10, 11, 13, 17, 18, 23, 24; CamBiEn; CamDcAB; ChamBiD; CurBio 42, 46; DcAmB S4; DcAmMiB; DcTwHis; EncAB-H 1974, 1996; EncChi; EncWB 98; HarEnMi; McGEWB; ModChi; NatCAB 33; REnAL; WebAB 74, 79; WebAMB; WhAm 2; WhoMilH 76; WhWW-II; WorAl*

Stilwell, Richard Dale
American. Opera Singer
Lyric baritone who joined NYC Opera, 1970; known for role of Pelleas in *Pelleas et Melisande.*
b. May 6, 1942 in Saint Louis, Missouri
Source: *BakBD 92; BakBDTw; BioIn 10, 11; ColdWar 2; CurBio 86; IntWW 89, 91, 93, 97, 98, 2000; NewAmDM; PenDiMP; WhoAm 74, 76, 78, 80, 82,*

84, 86, 88, 90, 92, 94, 95, 96, 97, 98, 99, 2000; WhoOp 76

Stimson, Henry Lewis
[Harry Stimson]
American. Government Official
Secretary of War, 1940-45; led expansion, operation of US Army, WW II; advised use of atomic bomb on Japan.
b. Sep 21, 1867 in New York, New York
d. Oct 20, 1950 in Huntington, New York
Source: *AmNatBi; AmPolLe; BiDInt; BiDrUSE 71, 89; BioIn 1, 2, 3, 4, 5, 6, 7, 8, 9, 10, 11, 13, 15, 16, 17, 18; CamBiEn; CamDcAB; ChamBiD; ColdWar 2; CurBio 40, 50; DcAmB S4; DcAmDH 80, 89; DcAmMiB; DcPol; DcTwHis; EncAB-H 1974; EncTR 91; EncWB 98; FacFETw; HarEnUS; HisEWW; HisWorL; LinLib S; McGEWB; NatCAB 37; OxCAmH; REnAL; WebAB 74, 79; WhAm 3; WorAl*

Stine, R. L.
American. Author
Teen horror fiction writer known for *Goosebumps* series.
b. Oct 8, 1943 in Columbus, Ohio
Source: *BioIn 20, 21, 23, 24; ChlLR 37; ConAu 22NR; CurBio 1999; OnHuMoP; WhoWrEP 89; WrYoAd SUP1*

Sting
[The Police; Gordon Matthew Sumner]
English. Musician, Singer, Songwriter
Self-taught musician, force behind success of *The Police*, 1976-83; solo performer, 1985—.
b. Oct 2, 1951 in Newcastle-upon-Tyne, England
Source: *BakBD 92; BillEnR; BioIn 16; CamBiEn; CelR 90; ConAu 167; ConMus 2, 19; ConTFT 2, 7, 18; CurBio 85; DcArts; DcPseud; EncPR&S 89; EncRkSt; EnvEnDr; HalFC 88; IntMPA 88, 92, 94, 96; IntWW 89, 91, 93; ItaFilm; LegTOT; NewAmDM; News 91; NewYTBS 84; Songw; WhoAm 84, 86, 88, 90, 92, 94, 95, 96, 97, 98, 99, 2000; WhoEnt 92, 98; WhoHol 92; WhoRocM 82; WhoWor 93, 95, 96, 97, 98, 99, 2000; WorAlBi*

Stingley, Darryl
American. Football Player
Wide receiver, New England, 1973-78; paralyzed by Jack Tatum tackle during preseason game, 1978.
b. Sep 18, 1951 in Chicago, Illinois
Source: *BioIn 11, 12, 13, 18; BlkWrNE A; InB&W 85; NewYTBS 78, 82; WhoBlA 3, 4, 5*

Stipe, Michael
[R.E.M; John Michael Stipe]
American. Singer, Songwriter
Grammy, Best Pop Vocal—Group, "Losing My Religion," 1991.
b. Jan 4, 1960 in Decatur, Georgia

Source: *CurBio 97; IntWW 2000; LegTOT; WhoAm 94, 95, 96, 97, 98, 99, 2000; WhoEnt 98*

Stirling, Lord
[William Alexander]
American. Military Leader
Continental army general; defended the NYC area in various battles, Mar 1776-Jan 1780.
b. 1726 in New York, New York
d. Sep 15, 1783 in New York, New York
Source: *AmBi; AmRev; ApCAB; BiInAmS; BioIn 8, 12, 15; DcAmB; DcNaB; Drake; EncAR; EncCRAm; HarEnMi; HarEnUS; NatCAB 1; TwCBDA; WebAB 74; WebAMB; WhAm HS; WhAmP; WhAmRev*

Stirling, James
Scottish. Architect
Major designs include Queen's College-Oxford, 1967-71; Fogg Museum, Harvard U., 1979.
b. Apr 22, 1926 in Glasgow, Scotland
d. Jun 25, 1992 in London, England
Source: *AnObit 1992; ChamBiD; ConArch 80; DcArts; DcD&D; EncWB, 98; IntDcAr; IntWW 75, 76, 77, 78, 79, 80, 81, 82, 83, 89, 91; MacEA; MakTCMA; NewYTBS 92; WhAm 10; Who 92; WhoArch; WhoArt 96; WhoWor 78, 82, 84, 87, 89, 91*

Stirner, Max
[Johann Kaspar Schmidt]
German. Philosopher
Writings lent ideological inspiration to anarchists; wrote *Der Einzige und Sein Eigentum*, 1845.
b. Oct 25, 1806 in Bayreuth, Bavaria
d. Jun 26, 1856 in Berlin, Germany
Source: *BioIn 9, 10, 11, 19; DcLB 129; DcPseud; Dis&D; EncWB 98; McGEWB; OxCGer 76, 86, 97; OxCPhil; REn*

Stitt, Sonny
[Edward Stitt]
American. Jazz Musician
Saxophonist with Dizzy Gillespie, 1940s; led own combo, 1950s-60s.
b. Feb 2, 1924 in Boston, Massachusetts
d. Jul 22, 1982 in Washington, District of Columbia
Source: *AllMGBl 2A; AllMGJa; AmNatBi; AnObit 1982; BakBD 84, 92; BiDAfM; BiDAmM; BiDJaz; BioIn 13, 16; CmpEPM; DrBlPA, 90; EncJzS; IlEncJ; InB&W 80, 85; LegTOT; NewAmDM; NewGrDA 86; NewGrDJ 88, 94; NewYTBS 82; PenEncP; WhoAm 82; WorAl; WorAlBi*

Stock, Frederick A
American. Conductor
Led Chicago Symphony for 48 yrs.
b. Nov 11, 1872 in Dulich, Germany
d. Oct 20, 1942 in Chicago, Illinois
Source: *BakBD 78, 84; BiDAmM; BriBkM 80; CurBio 42; DcAmB S3;*

MusSN; NewGrDM 80; OxCMus; WhAm 2

Stockdale, James
American. Army Officer
Vietnam War POW; Ross Perot's vice-presidential candidate, 1992.
b. Dec 23, 1923 in Abington, Illinois
Source: *BioIn 11, 12, 13, 18, 20, 21, 22, 24; WhoAm 90; WhoAmP 1999*

Stocker, Wally
[The Babys]
English. Singer, Musician
Guitarist, vocalist with power pop group, 1976-81.
b. Mar 17, 1954 in London, England

Stockhausen, Karlheinz
German. Composer
Avant-garde works emphasize time-space music, electronic devices, audience participation; *Sirius* dedicated to space pioneers, 1976.
b. Aug 28, 1928 in Modrath, Germany
Source: *BakBD 78, 84, 92; BakBDTw; BakDcM; BioIn 6, 7, 8, 9, 10, 12, 13, 14, 15, 20, 21, 23, 24; BriBkM 80; CamBiEn; ChamBiD; CnOxB; CompSN; SUP; ConCom 92; CurBio 71; DcArts; DcCM; DcCom 77; DcCom&M 79; EncWB 98; FacFETw; IntDcOp; IntWW 74, 75, 76, 77, 78, 79, 80, 81, 82, 83, 89, 91, 93, 97, 98, 2000; IntWWM 77, 80, 90; MakMC; McGEWB; MetOEnc; MusMk; NewAmDM; NewGrDM 80; NewGrDO; NewOxM; NewYTBE 71; OxCMus; OxDcOp; PenDiMP A; RAdv 14; WhDW; Who 74, 82, 83, 85, 88, 90, 92, 94, 98, 99, 2000; WhoEnt 98; WhoMus 72; WhoWor 74, 78, 82, 84, 87, 89, 91, 93, 95, 96, 97, 98, 99, 2000*

Stockman, David Allen
American. Government Official
Directed OMB, 1981-85; wrote *Triumph of Politics*, 1986.
b. Nov 10, 1946 in Fort Hood, Texas
Source: *AlmAP 80; CngDr 78; CurBio 81; IntWW 81, 82, 83, 89, 91, 93, 97, 98, 2000; IntYB 82; NewYTBS 80, 85; WhoAm 78, 80, 82, 84, 86, 92, 94, 95, 96, 97, 98, 99, 2000; WhoAmP 85, 91, 95, 97, 1999; WhoFI 83, 85, 89, 92, 94; WhoGov 77; WhoMW 78, 80; WrDr 98*

Stockton, Dave
[David Knapp Stockton]
American. Golfer
Turned pro, 1964; won PGA, 1970, 1976.
b. Nov 2, 1941 in San Bernardino, California
Source: *BioIn 19, 21; NewYTBE 71; NewYTBS 74; WhoAm 78, 80, 82, 84, 86, 88, 90, 92, 94, 95, 96, 97; WhoGolf; WhoIntG; WhoWest 94, 96*

Stockton, Dick
American. Tennis Player
US Open mixed champion, 1975; World mixed champion, 1975-77; WCT World champion, 1977.
b. Feb 18, 1951 in New York, New York
Source: *BioIn 10, 11; WhoIntT*

Stockton, Frank
[Francis Richard Stockton]
American. Author
Known for puzzling short story *The Lady or the Tiger*, 1884.
b. Apr 5, 1834 in Philadelphia, Pennsylvania
d. Apr 20, 1902 in Washington, District of Columbia
Source: *Alli SUP; AmBi; ApCAB, X; BiD&SB; BioIn 14, 15, 19; Chambr 3; CnDAL; ConAu 108, 137; DcAmAu; DcAmB; DcBiA; DcEnA A; DcNAA; EncMys; FamSYP; JBA 34; LinLib L; LngCTC; MajAl; NatCAB 1; NewYHSD; OxCAmL 65; OxCEng 67; RAdv 1; REn; REnAL; ScFEYrs; SmATA 44; TwCBDA; WebAB 74, 79; WhAm 1; WhAmArt 85*

Stockton, John (Houston)
American. Basketball Player
With Utah Jazz, 1984—; member, US Olympic Basketball Team, 1992.
b. Mar 26, 1962 in Spokane, Washington
Source: *BasBi; CurBio 95; LegTOT; WhoAm 92, 94, 95, 96, 97, 98, 99, 2000; WhoWest 00, 98; WhoWor 99, 2000; WorAlBi*

Stockton, Richard
American. Continental Congressman, Lawyer
Signed Declaration of Independence, 1776; promoted Princeton College; grandfather of Robert Field.
b. Oct 1, 1730 in Princeton, New Jersey
d. Feb 28, 1781 in Princeton, New Jersey
Source: *AmBi; AmNatBi; AmPolLe; ApCAB; BiAUS; BiDrAC; BiDrUSC 89; BioIn 1, 3, 4, 7, 8, 9, 10, 11, 18, 23; CamDcAB; DcAmB; Drake; EncAR; EncCRAm; HarEnUS; HisDcAR; NatCAB 12; TwCBDA; WhAm HS; WhAmP; WhAmRev*

Stockton, Robert Field
American. Naval Officer
Captured Santa Barbara, Los Angeles in Mexican War; declared CA a territory of US; Stockton, CA named for him.
b. Aug 20, 1795 in Princeton, New Jersey
d. Oct 7, 1866 in Princeton, New Jersey
Source: *AmBi; AmNatBi; ApCAB; BiAUS; BiDrAC; BiDrUSC 89; BioIn 1, 2, 4, 16; CamDcAB; CmCal; DcAmB; DcAmDH 80, 89; DcAmMiB; Drake; EncNaHi; EncWB 98; HarEnMi; HarEnUS; McGEWB; NatCAB 4; NewEAmW; OxCAmH; REnAW; TwCBDA; WebAB 74, 79; WebAMB; WhAm HS; WhAmP*

Stockwell, Dean
American. Actor
Child star of 1940s; films include *Blue Velvet*, 1986, *Married to the Mob*, 1988; stars as TVs first holographic character in "Quantum Leap," 1988-93.
b. Mar 5, 1936 in Hollywood, California
Source: *BiDFilm 94; BioIn 1, 2, 9, 16; ConTFT 5, 12, 23; CurBio 91; FilmEn; FilmgC; ForYSC; HalFC 84, 88; IntMPA 77, 84, 86, 92; LegTOT; MGM; MotPP; MovMk; OsStAZ; VarWW 85; WhoAm 90, 92, 94, 95, 96, 97, 99, 2000; WhoEnt 92A, 98; WhoHol 92, A; WhoWor 95, 96, 97, 98; WorAl*

Stockwell, Guy
American. Actor
Films include *Please Don't Eat the Daisies*, 1960; *Airport 1975*, 1974.
b. Nov 16, 1938 in North Hollywood, California
Source: *FilmgC; ForYSC; HalFC 88; WhoHol A*

Stoddard, Alexandra
American. Interior Decorator
Wrote *Style for Living*, 1974; host of "Homes Across America" on the Home and Garden cable network, 1994—.
b. Nov 6, 1941 in Weston, Massachusetts
Source: *CurBio 96; WhoAm 98, 99, 2000; WhoWor 91*

Stoddard, Brandon
American. Broadcasting Executive
Pres. of ABC's Entertainment, 1985-89; pres. ABC Productions, 1989—.
b. Mar 31, 1937 in Bridgeport, Connecticut
Source: *BioIn 11, 12, 13, 14, 15, 16; CurBio 89; IntMPA 92, 94, 96; LesBEnT 92; WhoAm 80, 82, 84, 86, 88, 90, 92, 94, 95, 96, 97; WhoEnt 92; WhoFI 85*

Stoddard, Richard Henry
"Nestor of American Literature"
American. Poet
Literary editor, *NY Mail and Express*, 1880-1903.
b. Jul 12, 1825 in Hingham, Massachusetts
d. May 12, 1903
Source: *Alli, SUP; AmAu; AmAu&B; AmBi; AmNatBi; ApCAB; BbD; BenetAL 91; BibAL 8; BiD&SB; BioIn 4, 9, 12, 16, 22; ChamBiD; Chambr 3; ChhPo, S1; CnDAL; ConAu 114; CyAL 2; DcAmAu; DcAmB; DcEnA A; DcEnL; DcLB 3, 64, DS13; DcLEL; DcNAA; Drake; EncALit; EvLB; HarEnUS; LinLib L; NatCAB 3; OxCAmL 65, 83, 95; REn; REnAL; TwCBDA; WhAm 1*

Stoddard, Solomon
American. Clergy
Colonial Congregational minister was the dominant civil and religious figure in western Massachusetts for nearly 60 years.
b. Sep 1643 in Boston, Massachusetts

d. Feb 11, 1728
Source: *Alli; AmAu; AmNatBi; AmWrBE; ApCAB; BenetAL 91; BioIn 5, 9, 12, 14, 15, 17, 19; CamDcAB; CamGLE; CamHAL; ChamBiD; DcAmAu; DcAmB; DcAmReB 1, 2; DcLB 24; DcNAA; Drake; EncALit; EncARH; EncWB 98; LuthC 75; McGEWB; NatCAB 7; OxCAmH; OxCAmL 65, 83, 95; REnAL; WebAB 74, 79; WhAm HS; WrCNE*

Stoessel, Albert
American. Conductor, Composer, Violinist
Associated with NY Oratorio Society, Juilliard School; wrote *Technic of the Baton*, 1920.
b. Oct 11, 1894 in Saint Louis, Missouri
d. May 12, 1943 in New York, New York
Source: *ASCAP 66, 80; BakBD 78, 84; ConAmC 76, 82; CurBio 43; DcAmB S3; NewAmDM; NewGrDA 86; NewGrDM 80; OxCMus; WhAm 2*

Stoffels, Hendrikje
Dutch. Mistress, Model
Housekeeper, mistress of Rembrandt, 1645-63.
b. 1622
d. 1663
Source: *BioIn 9*

Stofflet, Ty(rone Earl)
American. Softball Player
Known as fastest softball pitcher in the world, at speeds exceeding 100 mph.
b. Jul 29, 1941 in Coplay, Pennsylvania
Source: *BioIn 12, 16; ConNews 87-1; NewYTBS 85*

Stokely, Alfred Jehu
American. Business Executive
With Stokely-Van Camp, Inc. since 1938; chm., CEO, 1978-81.
b. Mar 26, 1916 in Newport, Tennessee
Source: *BioIn 9; St&PR 75, 84, 87, 91; WhoAm 74, 76, 78, 80, 82; WhoFI 74, 75, 77, 79, 81; WhoWor 74*

Stokely, Anna
American. Business Executive
With sons established canning business, 1898; has become major nat. food packer.
b. 1852
d. 1916
Source: *Entr*

Stokely, James
American. Businessman
With mother, brother, established food packing business, 1898.
b. 1875
d. 1922
Source: *Entr*

Stokely, John
American. Businessman
With brother, mother established cannery which grew in six years to major industry.
b. 1876
d. 1919
Source: *Entr*

Stoker, Bram
Irish. Author
Published best-selling horror story *Dracula*, 1897.
b. Nov 8, 1847 in Dublin, Ireland
d. Apr 20, 1912 in London, England
Source: *Alli SUP; Au&Arts 23; BeaEPF; Benet 87, 96; BiCoLiE; BioIn 5, 6, 8, 10, 11, 12, 13, 14, 15, 16, 17, 18, 20, 21, 22, 23, 24; BritWr S3; CamBiEn; CamGLE; ChamBiD; CnDBLB 5; ConAu 150; CyWA 58, 97; DcArts; DcIrL, 96; DcLB 36, 70, 178; DcLEL; EncFoLi; EncMys; EncO&P 1, 2, 3; EncSF; EncWB 98; EvLB; FilmgC; GrWrEL N; HalFC 80, 84, 88; LegTOT; LngCTC; NewEScF; NotNAT B; Novels; OxCEng 85, 95; OxCIri; PenC ENG; PenEncH; RAdv 14; REn; RfGEnL 91; ScF&FL 1, 92; SJGHorW; StaCVF; SupFW; TwCA, SUP; TwCCr&M 80; TwCLC 8; VicBrit; WhDW; WhLit; WhoChL; WhoHr&F; WhoHrs 80; WorAl; WorAlBi; WorAu 1900; WorLitC*

Stokes, Carl B(urton)
American. Politician
Mayor, Cleveland, 1967-71; one of the first big city black mayors in America.
b. Jun 21, 1927 in Cleveland, Ohio
d. Apr 4, 1996 in Cleveland, Ohio
Source: *BioIn 7, 8, 9, 10, 11, 12; BlueB 76; CamDcAB; ConAu 69, 152; CurBio 68, 96N; DiAAPGL; Ebony 1; InB&W 80, 85; PolProf J, NF; WhAm 11; WhoAfA 9, 10N; WhoAm 74, 76, 78, 80, 82, 84, 86, 88, 90, 92, 94, 95, 96; WhoAmP 73, 75, 77, 79, 81, 83, 85, 87, 89, 91, 93, 95; WhoBlA 1, 2, 3, 4, 5, 6, 7, 8; WhoWor 74*

Stokes, Donald Gresham Stokes, Baron
English. Auto Executive
Pres. British Leyland, 1975-79; Dutton-Forshaw Motor Group Ltd., 1980-90.
b. Mar 22, 1914 in London, England
Source: *BioIn 10; BlueB 76; IntWW 74, 75, 76, 77, 78, 79, 80, 81; IntYB 80, 81; Who 74; WhoAm 84, 86, 90; WhoWor 74*

Stokes, Doris
English. Psychic, Author
Internationally known psychic medium; wrote *Voices in My Ear: The Autobiography of a Medium*, 1980.
b. 1919 in Grantham, England
Source: *BioIn 16; ConAu 115, 122; EncO&P 1S3, 2, 3*

Stokes, George Gabriel, Sir
English. Physicist, Mathematician
Developed law of viscosity, which has to do with a solid globe's motion in

fluid; created theorem of vector analysis called Stokes's theorem.
b. Aug 13, 1819 in Skreen, Ireland
d. Feb 1, 1903 in Cambridge, England
Source: *Alli, SUP; AsBiEn; BiESc; BioIn 8, 12, 14, 16, 17; BritAu 19; CamBiEn; CamDcSc; CelCen; ChamBiD; DcBiPP; DcInv; DcIrB 1, 2, 3; DcNaB S2; DcScB; InSci; LarDcSc; McGCEnS; NotMat; NotTwCS 1S; RanHWDS*

Stokes, Louis
American. Politician
Dem. congressman representing Ohio, 1969—.
b. Feb 23, 1925 in Cleveland, Ohio
Source: *AfrAmAl 6, 8; AfrAmBi 1; AlmAP 78, 80, 82, 84, 88, 92, 96; BiDrAC; BiDrUSC 89; BioIn 9, 12, 13, 14, 16; BlkAmsC; BlueB 76; CamDcAB; CivR 74; CngDr 74, 77, 79, 81, 83, 85, 87, 89, 91, 93, 95; ConBlB 3; DiAAPGL; DrAS 99P; Ebony 1; PolsAm 84; WhoAfA 9, 10, 11, 12; WhoAm 74, 76, 78, 80, 82, 84, 86, 88, 90, 92, 94, 95, 96, 97, 98, 99, 2000; WhoAmL 78, 79; WhoAmP 73, 75, 77, 79, 81, 83, 85, 87, 89, 91, 93, 95, 97, 1999; WhoBlA 1, 2, 3, 4, 5, 6, 7, 8; WhoGov 72, 75, 77; WhoMW 74, 76, 78, 80, 82, 84, 86, 88, 90, 92, 93, 96, 98; WhoWor 74*

Stokes, William
Irish. Physician
Most renowned modern doctor in Europe; leader in Dublin School of anatomical diagnosis.
b. Oct 1, 1804 in Dublin, Ireland
d. Jan 10, 1878 in Howth, Ireland
Source: *Alli, SUP; BiHiMed; BioIn 5, 9, 14; CelCen; DcBiPP; DcIrB 1, 2, 3; DcNaB; HisDcIr; InSci; OxCMed 86; RanHWDS; WhDW*

Stokowski, Leopold (Anton Stanislaw Boleslawawicz)
American. Conductor, Musician
Led Philadelphia Orchestra, 1914-36; formed American Symphony Orchestra, 1962; film *Fantasia*, 1940, helped popularize the classics.
b. Apr 18, 1882 in London, England
d. Sep 13, 1977 in Nether Wallop, England
Source: *ASCAP 66; BakBD 78, 84; BiDAmM; BioIn 15, 16, 17, 19, 21; BioNews 74; BlueB 76; BriBkM 80; CelR; ChhPo S2; ConAmC 76, 82; CurBio 41, 53, 77, 77N; DcArts; FacFETw; FilmEn; FilmgC; HalFC 80, 84, 88; IntWW 76, 77; IntWWM 77; LegTOT; MetOEnc; MusMk; MusSN; NewAmDM; NewEOp 71; NewGrDA 86; NewGrDM 80; NewYTBE 70; NewYTBS 77; OxCAmH; PenDiMP; PolBiDi; RadStar; REn; WebAB 74, 79; WhAm 7; Who 74; WhoAm 74, 78; WhoE 74; WhoHol A; WhoMus 72; WhoWor 74; WhScrn 83; WorAl; WorAlBi*

Stoll, George E
American. Composer
Film scores include *For Me and My Gal,*
1942; won Oscar for *Anchors Aweigh,*
1945.
b. May 7, 1905 in Minneapolis,
Minnesota
d. Jan 18, 1985 in Monterey, California
Source: *CmpEPM; FilmEn; FilmgC;*
VarWW 85

Stoltz, Rosine
[Victorine Noel]
French. Opera Singer
Paris Opera mezzo-soprano, 1830s-40s;
noted for adventuresome life.
b. Feb 13, 1815 in Paris, France
d. Jul 28, 1903 in Paris, France
Source: *BakBD 78, 84, 92; BioIn 3, 11;*
DcPseud; InWom; MetOEnc; NewEOp
71; NewGrDM 80; NewGrDO; OxDcOp;
PenDiMP

Stoltzman, Richard Leslie
American. Musician
Clarinet virtuoso, known for combining
traditional, contemporary material
from classical, jazz sources.
b. Jul 12, 1942 in Omaha, Nebraska
Source: *BakBD 92; BakBDTw; CurBio*
86; IntWWM 77, 80, 90; WhoAm 80, 82,
84, 86, 88, 90, 92, 94, 95, 96, 97, 98,
99, 2000; WhoAmM 83; WhoEnt 92, 98

Stolypin, Piotr Arkadevich
Russian. Political Leader
Premier, minister of Interior for Czar
Nicholas II, 1906-11.
b. Apr 14, 1862 in Baden, Russia
d. Sep 14, 1911 in Kiev, Russia
Source: *BioIn 10; EncWB 98; McGEWB;*
NewCol 75

Stolz, Robert
German. Composer
Wrote 2,000 songs, 50 operettas, music
for films; won Oscars, 1941, 1944.
b. Aug 25, 1886 in Graz, Austria
d. Jun 27, 1975 in Berlin, Germany
(West)
Source: *BiE&WWA; CurBio 43, 75, 75N;*
WhoMus 72; WhoWor 74; WhThe

Stolz, Teresa
[Teresina Stolzova]
Bohemian. Opera Singer
Soprano; first Italian Aida, 1872; often
sang Verdi roles.
b. Jun 2, 1834 in Elbe Kosteletz,
Bohemia
d. Aug 23, 1902 in Milan, Italy
Source: *BakBD 78, 84, 92; BioIn 15;*
CmOp; IntDcOp; InWom; MetOEnc;
NewEOp 71; NewGrDM 80; NewGrDO;
OxDcOp; PenDiMP

Stommel, Henry Melson
American. Oceanographer, Meteorologist
Ocean current research led to
development of means for determining
absolute velocity of mean ocean

currents from observations of the
density alone.
b. Sep 27, 1920 in Wilmington,
Delaware
Source: *AmMWSc 73P, 76P, 79, 82, 86,*
89, 92; BioIn 14; CamBiEn; CamDcAB;
ConAu 155; IntWW 74; McGMS 80;
WhAm 10; WhoAm 90; WhoFrS 84;
WhoWor 74

Stompanato, Johnny
American. Criminal
Killed by Lana Turner's daughter after
argument; death judged justifiable
homicide.
b. 1926
d. Apr 4, 1958 in Hollywood, California
Source: *EncACr*

Stone, Chuck
[Charles Sumner Stone]
American. Journalist
Special asst. to US congressman, Adam
Clayton Powell, 1965-67; syndicated
columnist, *Philadelphia Daily News,*
1973-91.
b. Jul 21, 1924 in Saint Louis, Missouri
Source: *AfrAmAl 8; BiDAmNC; BioIn*
12; BlkAWP; BlkWr 2; BlkWrNE; ConAu
77; ConBlB 9; DcTwCCu 5; InB&W 80,
85; LivgBAA; WhoAfA 9, 10, 11, 12;
WhoBlA 6, 7, 8; WhoE 74

Stone, Dick
[Richard Bernard Stone]
American. Politician
Senator from FL, 1975-81; ambassador
to Central America, 1980-84.
b. Sep 22, 1928 in New York, New
York
Source: *BiDrUSC 89; CngDr 77, 79;*
NewYTBS 80, 83; Who 74; WhoAm 78,
80; WhoAmJ 80; WhoAmP 73, 75, 77,
79, 81, 83, 85, 87, 89, 91, 93, 95;
WhoGov 72, 75, 77; WhoSSW 78, 80;
WhoWor 80, 82

Stone, Dorothy
American. Actor, Dancer
Daughter of Fred Stone; dance partner
with husband, Charles Collins, in *The*
Gay Divorcee, 1933, 1941; *The Red*
Mill, 1945.
b. Jun 3, 1905 in New York, New York
d. Sep 24, 1974 in Montecito, California
Source: *BiDD; BiE&WWA; NotNAT B;*
WhoHol B; WhoMus 72; WhScrn 77, 83;
WhThe

Stone, Doug
[Doug Brooks]
American. Singer, Songwriter
Country music singer; released debut
album *Doug Stone,* 1990, which
became platinum record; also recorded
I Thought It Was You, 1992 and *From*
the Heart, 1992.
b. Jun 19, 1956 in Atlanta, Georgia
Source: *AllMGCo; BgBkCoM; ConMus*
10; LegTOT

Stone, Edward C, Jr.
American. Physicist, Educator
Project Scientist for Voyager Project,
1972—; Director, Jet Propulsion
Laboratory, 1991—.
b. Jan 23, 1936 in Knoxville, Iowa
Source: *AmMWSc 73P, 92; BioIn 11, 12,*
16; CurBio 90; WhoAm 90; WhoTech
89; WhoWest 92

Stone, Edward Durell
American. Architect
Designed JFK Center, Washington, DC;
New York Cultural Center; US
Embassy in New Delhi.
b. Mar 9, 1902 in Fayetteville, Arkansas
d. Aug 6, 1978 in New York, New York
Source: *AmArch 70; AmNatBi;*
BiE&WWA; BioIn 4, 5, 6, 7, 9, 11, 14;
BlueB 76; BriEAA; CamBiEn;
CamDcAB; CelR; ChamBiD; ConArch
80, 87, 94; DcAmB S10; DcTwDes;
EncAAr 1, 2; EncAB-A 33; EncMA;
FacFETw; IntDcAr; IntWW 74, 75, 76,
77, 78; MacEA; NewYTBS 78; WebAB
74, 79; WhAm 7; WhoAm 74, 76, 78;
WhoAmA 80N, 82N, 84N, 86N, 89N,
91N, 93N; WhoFI 74; WhoWor 74;
WorAl; WorAlBi

Stone, Ezra (Chaim)
American. Director, Producer
Best known as Henry Aldrich on radio
show "The Aldrich Family;" director
of numerous movies, plays, TV shows.
b. Dec 2, 1917 in New Bedford,
Massachusetts
d. Mar 3, 1994 in Perth Amboy, New
Jersey
Source: *AmAu&B; BiE&WWA; BioIn 19,*
21; BlueB 76; ConTFT 1, 13; IntMPA
82, 92, 94; LesBEnT 92; NotNAT;
WhAm 11; WhoAm 74, 76, 78, 80, 82,
84, 86, 88, 90, 92, 94; WhoE 89;
WhoEnt 92; WhoHol 92, A

Stone, Fred Andrew
American. Actor
Scarecrow in original Broadway version
of *The Wizard of Oz,* 1903.
b. Aug 19, 1873 in Valmont, Colorado
d. Mar 6, 1959 in North Hollywood,
California
Source: *BioIn 3, 5; EncMT; Film 1, 2;*
FilmEn; NotNAT A, B; PIP&P; TwYS;
Vers A; WhAm 3; WhoHol B; WhScrn
74, 77; WhThe

Stone, George Robert
American. Baseball Player
Outfielder, 1903, 1905-10, mostly with
St. Louis; led AL in batting, 1906; had
.301 lifetime batting average.
b. Sep 7, 1877 in Lost Nation, Iowa
d. Jan 3, 1945 in Clinton, Iowa
Source: *BioIn 4; WhoProB 73*

Stone, Grace Zaring
American. Author
Wrote *The Heaven and Earth of Dona*
Elena, 1929.
b. Jan 9, 1891 in New York, New York

d. Sep 29, 1991 in Stonington,
Connecticut
Source: *AnObit 1991; BioIn 17, 18;
ConAu 135, P-2; ConLC 70; WorAu
1900*

Stone, Harlan Fiske
American. Supreme Court Justice
Associate justice, 1925-41; chief justice,
1941-46.
b. Oct 11, 1872 in Chesterfield, New
Hampshire
d. Apr 22, 1946 in Washington, District
of Columbia
Source: *AmDec 1920; AmJust; AmNatBi;
AmPolLe; ApCAB X; BiDFedJ; BiDrUSE
71, 89; BioIn 1, 2, 3, 4, 5, 7, 8, 9, 10,
11, 15; CamBiEn; CamDcAB; ChamBiD;
CopCroC; CurBio 41, 46; DcAmB S4;
EncAB-H 1974, 1996; EncRelA; EncWB
98; FacFETw; LegTOT; McGEWB;
NatCAB 34; OxCAmH; OxCLaw;
OxCSupC; PolProf T; RComAH;
SupCtJu; WebAB 74, 79; WhAm 2;
WorAl; WorAlBi*

Stone, Harold J
American. Actor
Starred in TV series "The Goldbergs,"
1952; "My World and Welcome to
It," 1969-72; "Bridget Loves
Bernie," 1972-73.
b. 1911
Source: *FilmgC; HalFC 88; WhoHol A*

Stone, I(sidor) F(einstein)
"Godfather of New Left Journalism"
American. Journalist, Author,
Pamphleteer
Edited newsletter *I F Stone's Bi-Weekly,*
1953-71; wrote *Underground to
Palestine,* 1946; *The Trial of Socrates,*
1988.
b. Dec 24, 1907 in Philadelphia,
Pennsylvania
d. Jun 18, 1989 in Boston, Massachusetts
Source: *ABCMeAm; AmPeW; AmSocL;
BiDAmJo; BioIn 8, 9, 10, 11, 12, 13, 14,
15, 16, 17, 18, 19, 20, 23; CamBiEn;
CelR; ChamBiD; ConAu 40NR, 61;
CurBio 72; EncAB-H 1996; EncAJ;
EncTwCJ; EncWB; JrnUS; NewYTBS 78;
PolProf E, J, K; ScrEAmL 2; WebAB 74,
79; WhE&EA; WhoAm 74, 76, 78, 80,
82, 84, 86, 88; WhoWor 74; WorAl;
WorAu 1970; WrDr 80*

Stone, Irving
American. Author
Noted for biographical novels: *Lust for
Life; The Agony and the Ecstasy; The
Origin.*
b. Jul 14, 1903 in San Francisco,
California
d. Aug 26, 1989 in Los Angeles,
California
Source: *AmAu&B; AmNatBi; AmNov;
AnObit 1989; Au&Wr 71; AuNews 1;
BeaEPF; Benet 87, 96; BenetAL 91;
BioIn 2, 4, 5, 6, 7, 8, 9, 10, 12, 14, 15,
16, 17, 22, 24; BlueB 76; CamBiEn;
CamDcAB; CelR; ChamBiD; CmCal;
ConAu 1NR, 1R, 3AS, 23NR, 129;*

*ConLC 7; ConNov 72, 76, 82, 86;
ConPopW; CurBio 67, 89, 89N; CyWA
89, 97; DcPseud; DrAS 74E, 78E, 82E;
EncALit; FacFETw; HalFC 84, 88;
IntAu&W 76, 77, 89, 91; IntWW 74, 75,
76, 77, 78, 79, 80, 81, 82, 83, 89;
LegTOT; LinLib L; LngCTC; MajTwCW
1, 2; News 90, 90-2; NewYTBS 80, 89;
Novels; OxCAmL 83, 95; PenC AM;
RAdv 14; REn; RENAL; ScrEAmL 2;
SmATA 3, 64; TwCA, SUP; TwCRHW
90, 94; TwCWr; WhAm 10; WhE&EA;
WhNAA; WhoAm 74, 76, 78, 80, 82, 84,
86, 88; WhoAmJ 80; WhoWor 74, 78;
WhoWorJ 72, 78; WorAl; WorAlBi;
WorAu 1900; WrDr 76, 80, 82, 84, 86,
88, 90*

Stone, John Richard Nicholas, Sir
English. Economist, Educator
Won 1984 Nobel Prize in economics.
b. Aug 30, 1913 in London, England
Source: *CamBiEn; ChamBiD; IntWW 89;
NewYTBS 84; Who 74, 85, 92; WhoEc
81, 86; WhoNob, 90, 95*

Stone, Lewis
American. Actor
Was Judge Hardy in Andy Hardy film
series.
b. Nov 15, 1879 in Worcester,
Massachusetts
d. Sep 11, 1953 in Los Angeles,
California
Source: *BioIn 3, 7, 17, 21; EncAFC;
Film 1, 2; FilmEn; FilmgC; ForYSC;
HalFC 80, 84, 88; HolCA; IntDcF 1-3;
LegTOT; MGM; MotPP; MovMk;
NotNAT B; OlFamFa; OsStAZ; TwYS;
Vers B; WhAm 3; WhoHol B; WhoHrs
80; WhScrn 74, 77; WorAl*

Stone, Louis
American. Businessman, Publisher
Founder, *Louis Stone Monthly Investment
Letter,* 1953-85.
b. 1910 in New York, New York
d. Mar 16, 1985 in New York, New
York
Source: *ConAu 115*

Stone, Lucy
American. Feminist, Suffragist, Editor
Founded *Woman's Journal,* 1870; voice
of Woman's Suffrage Assn. for 50 yrs.
b. Aug 13, 1818 in West Brookfield,
Massachusetts
d. Oct 18, 1893 in Dorchester,
Massachusetts
Source: *AmAu&B; AmBi; AmNatBi;
AmOrN; AmRef; AmSocL; AmWom;
ApCAB; Benet 87, 96; BenetAL 91;
BiDAmJo; BiD&SB; BioAmW; BioIn 3,
4, 6, 8, 9, 10, 11, 12, 13, 14, 15, 16, 18,
19, 21, 23; CamBiEn; CamDcAB;
ChamBiD; ContDcW 89; DcAmB;
DcAmSR; DcLB 79; Drake; EncWB 98;
EncWHA; EncWoAP; FemiCLE;
GoodHs; GrLiveH; HanAmWH;
HarEnUS; HerW, 84; HisWorL;
IntDcWB; InWom, SUP; LegTOT; LibW;
McGEWB; NatCAB 2, 29; NotAW;
OxCAmH; OxCAmL 65, 83, 95; PolPar;*

*REn; TwCBDA; WebAB 74, 79; WhAm
HS; WhAmP; WhCiWar; WomFir;
WomIss; WorAl; WorAlBi*

Stone, Marvin Lawrence
American. Editor
Editor-in-chief, *US News & World
Report,* mag., 1976-85.
b. Feb 26, 1924 in Burlington, Vermont
d. May 1, 2000 in Falls Church, Virginia
Source: *ConAu 69; WhoAm 74, 76, 78,
80, 82, 84, 86, 88, 90, 92, 94, 95, 96,
97, 98, 99, 2000; WhoE 85, 86, 89;
WhoSSW 76, 95, 97, 99; WhoWorJ 72*

Stone, Matt
American. Filmmaker
Creator, with partner Trey Parker, of
"South Park," the wildly popular
animated series featuring the crude and
cruel children of South Park, CO, for
cable channel Comedy Central; feature
film *South Park: Bigger, Longer &
Uncut* released in 1999.
b. 1971 in Houston, Texas
Source: *ConTFT 21*

Stone, Melville Elijah
American. Newspaper Publisher
Founded Chicago's first penny
newspaper, *Daily News,* 1875; general
manager, AP in IL and later in NY,
1893-1921.
b. Aug 22, 1848 in Hudson, Illinois
d. Feb 15, 1929 in New York, New
York
Source: *AmAu&B; AmBi; AmNatBi;
ApCAB, X; BiDAmJo; BioIn 7, 9;
CamDcAB; ChhPo S1; DcAmB; DcNAA;
EncAB-H 1974, 1996; JrnUS; LinLib L,
S; NatCAB 1, 21; RENAL; WebAB 74,
79; WhAm 1*

Stone, Michael Patrick William
American. Government Official
Secretary of the Army, 1989-93; presided
over Army's response to the Iraqi
invasion of Kuwait in 1990.
d. May 18, 1995 in San Francisco,
California

Stone, Milburn
American. Actor
Played Doc Adams on "Gunsmoke,"
1955-75; won Emmy, 1968.
b. Jul 5, 1904 in Burton, Kansas
d. Jun 12, 1980 in La Jolla, California
Source: *AnObit 1980; BioIn 4, 5, 12;
EncAFC; FilmEn; FilmgC; ForYSC;
HalFC 80, 84, 88; HolCA; LegTOT;
MotPP; TelevWe; WhoHol A; WhoHrs
80; WhScrn 83*

Stone, Oliver
American. Screenwriter, Director
Won best picture, best director Oscars
for *Platoon,* 1986; best director Oscar
for *Born on the Fourth of July,* 1990;
also made *JFK,* 1991.
b. Sep 15, 1946 in New York, New
York

Source: *Au&Arts 15; BiDFilm 94; BioIn 12, 16; CamBiEn; CamDcAB; CelR 90; ChambiD; ConAu 110; ConLC 73; ConTFT 1, 6, 13, 25; CurBio 87; DcTwCCu 1; EncWB 98; GangFlm; HalFC 88; IntDcF 2-2; IntMPA 86, 88, 92, 94, 96; IntWW 89, 91, 93, 97, 98, 2000; LegTOT; MiSFD 9; News 90; NewYTBS 81, 84; OnHuYAF; WhoAm 82, 84, 86, 88, 90, 92, 94, 2000; WhoEnt 92; WhoHol 92; WhoWor 80; WorAlBi*

Stone, Paula
American. Producer
Starred with family as *The Stepping Stones* in vaudeville.
b. Jan 20, 1916 in New York, New York
Source: *BiE&WWA; BioIn 3; ForYSC; NotNAT; WhoHol A; WhoThe 77A; WhThe*

Stone, Peter H
American. Screenwriter
Won Oscar for *Father Goose*, 1964; won Tonys for *1776*, 1969; *Woman of the Year*, 1980; *Titanic*, 1997.
b. Feb 27, 1930 in Los Angeles, California
Source: *ConAu 7NR; ConDr 82D; ConTFT'6, 23; HalFC 84, 88; IntAu&W 91; IntMPA 86; NotNAT; SmATA 65; VarWW 85; WhoAm 86, 90; WhoE 89; WhoEnt 92*

Stone, Robert Anthony
American. Author
Wrote *A Hall of Mirrors*, 1967; *Children of Light*, 1986.
b. Aug 21, 1937 in New York, New York
Source: *AmAu&B; BioIn 13; CamDcAB; ConAu 66NR, 85; ConLC 23; ConNov 86; CurBio 86; EncWB 98; OxCAmL 83; OxCTwCL; WhoAm 86, 90, 97, 98, 99, 2000; WhoUSWr 88; WhoWrEP 89; WrDr 98, 99, 2000*

Stone, Sharon
American. Actor
Films include *Basic Instinct*, 1992; *Casino*, 1995.
b. Mar 10, 1958 in Meadville, Pennsylvania
Source: *ChambiD; ConTFT 7, 14; CurBio 96; IntMPA 94, 96; IntWW 97, 98, 2000; IntWWW 2; LegTOT; News 93; OsStAZ; WhoAm 94, 95, 96, 97, 98, 99; WhoAmW 93, 95, 97, 99; WhoEnt 98*

Stone, Sidney
American. TV Personality
Commercial announcer for Milton Berle's TV series, 1948-51; coined phrase, "Tell ya what I'm gonna do!"
b. 1903?
d. Feb 12, 1986 in New York, New York
Source: *LesBEnT*

Stone, Sly
[Sly and the Family Stone; Sylvester Stewart]
American. Singer, Musician
Led rock/blues group, 1970s; hits include "If You Want Me to Stay," 1973.
b. Mar 15, 1944 in Dallas, Texas
Source: *BiDAmM; BioIn 10, 12, 16, 24; ConMus 8; DcPseud; DrBlPA, 90; InB&W 80, 85; NewAmDM; NewGrDA 86; Songw; WhoBlA 3; WhoRocM 82; WorAl; WorAlBi*

Stone, Thomas
American. Lawyer, Continental Congressman
Signed Declaration of Independence, 1776; moderate patriot; rarely spoke in Congress.
b. 1743 in Charles County, Maryland
d. Oct 5, 1787 in Alexandria, Virginia
Source: *AmBi; ApCAB; BiAUS; BiDrAC; BiDrUSC 89; BioIn 7, 8, 9, 23; DcAmB; Drake; EncAR; EncCRAm; HarEnUS; HisDcAR; NatCAB 8; TwCBDA; WhAm HS; WhAmP; WhAmRev*

Stone, Toni
[Marcenia Lyle Stone]
American. Baseball Player
As second base player for the Negro American League's Indianapolis Clowns, she was the first woman to play as a regular on a big-league professional baseball team; inducted into the Baseball Hall of Fame, 1991.
b. 1921 in St. Paul, Minnesota
d. Nov 10, 1996
Source: *ConBlB 15; WhoSpor*

Stone, W. Clement
American. Businessman, Philanthropist
Founder, CEO, chm. of board, worldwide Combined Insurance Co. of America, 1939-81; exponent of Positive Mental Attitude; editor, publisher, *Success: The Magazine of Achievers*.
b. May 4, 1902 in Chicago, Illinois
Source: *Au&Wr 71; CurBio 72; Dun&B 90, 98; St&PR 91; WhoAm 86, 90; WhoAmP 85, 89, 97, 1999; WhoIns 92, 98, 99; WhoMW 90*

Stoneham, Horace
American. Baseball Executive
Principal owner, pres., NY/San Francisco Giants, 1936-76; known for moving team to San Francisco following 1957 season.
b. Jul 10, 1903 in Jersey City, New Jersey
d. Jan 7, 1990 in Scottsdale, Arizona
Source: *AnObit 1990; BiDAmSp BB; BioIn 7, 15, 16, 24; FacFETw; NewYTBS 90*

Stoneman, George
American. Military Leader, Politician
Union general; commanded troops that brought on Battle of Williamsburg, 1862; part of Atlanta campaign, 1864; Dem. governor of CA, 1883-87.

b. Aug 8, 1822 in Busti, New York
d. Sep 5, 1894 in Buffalo, New York
Source: *AmBi; AmNatBi; ApCAB; BiDrGov 1789; BioIn 1, 7, 11; CivWDc; CmCal; DcAmB; Drake; HarEnUS; NatCAB 4; TwCBDA; WebAMB; WhAm HS; WhCiWar*

Stones, Dwight
American. Track Athlete
High jumper; won bronze medal, 1972, 1976 Olympics; set world record 10 times.
b. Dec 6, 1953 in Los Angeles, California
Source: *BioIn 10, 11, 12, 14, 21; NewYTBS 75, 79, 84; WhoTr&F 73; WorAl; WorAlBi*

Stonesifer, Patty
American. Computer Executive
Vice president, consumer division, Microsoft Corp, 1994-96.
b. 1956 in Indiana
Source: *News 97, 97-1*

Stoney, George Johnstone
English. Physicist
Coined the word "electron."
b. Feb 15, 1826 in Oakley Park, Ireland
d. Jul 5, 1911 in London, England
Source: *AsBiEn; BiESc; BioIn 14; CamBiEn; CamDcSc; ChambiD; DcNaB S2; DcScB; InSci; LarDcSc*

Stoodard, George Dinsmore
American. University Administrator
President, U of IL, 1946-53; wrote *The Meaning of Intelligence*, 1943.
b. Oct 8, 1897 in Carbondale, Pennsylvania
d. Dec 28, 1981 in New York, New York
Source: *AmAu&B; AmMWSc 73S; BiDAmEd; ConAu 106; CurBio 46, 82; WhoAm 80, 82; WhoWor 80*

Stookey, Paul
[Peter, Paul, and Mary; Noel Paul Stockey]
American. Singer, Songwriter
Member, folk-singing group, Peter, Paul and Mary, 1961-1971; 1978—; wrote, recorded The "Wedding Song (There Is Love,)" 1971.
b. Dec 30, 1937 in Baltimore, Maryland
Source: *ASCAP 66; BioIn 12, 14, 21, 24; EncFCWM 69; LegTOT; WhoAm 84, 86, 90; WhoEnt 92; WorAlBi*

Stoopnagle, Lemuel Q, Colonel
[Stoopnagle and Budd; F Chase Taylor]
American. Actor
Part of radio team, 1930-37, famous for nonsense words, silly inventions.
b. Oct 4, 1897 in Buffalo, New York
d. May 29, 1950 in Boston, Massachusetts
Source: *CurBio 47, 50; JoeFr; WhScrn 77*

Stopes, Marie Charlotte Carmichael

English. Scientist

Cofounded first birth control clinic in Britain, 1921; candid books on marriage were forerunners of today's books on sex: *Married Love*, 1918.

b. Oct 15, 1880 in Edinburgh, Scotland

d. Oct 2, 1958 in Dorking, England

Source: *BiDBrF 1; BioIn 14, 16, 17, 20; CamBiEn; ChamBiD; ChhPo S2; ConAu 115; DcNaB 1951; GrBr; HumSex; InWom SUP; LngCTC; NewCol 75; OxCEng 85, 95; OxCMed 86; RanHWDS; WebBD 83; WhoLA; WomFir; WomNov*

Stoppard, Tom

[Tomas Straussler]

English. Author

Award-winning dramatist: *Rosencrantz and Guildenstern Are Dead*, 1967; *The Real Thing*, 1984; *Arcadia*, 1995.

b. Jul 3, 1937 in Zlin, Czechoslovakia

Source: *Au&Wr 71; Benet 87, 96; BiCoLiE; BioIn 8, 9, 10, 11, 12, 13; BlmGEL; BlueB 76; BritWr S1; CamBiEn; CamGEL; CamGLE; CamGWoT; CelR 90; ChamBiD; CnDBLB 8; CnThe; ConAu 39NR, 67NR, 81; ConBrDr; ConDr 73, 77, 82, 88, 93; ConLC 1, 3, 4, 5, 8, 15, 29, 34, 63, 91; ConTFT 1, 4, 12; CroCD; CrtSuDr; CurBio 74; CyWA 89, 97; DcArts; DcLB 13, Y85A; DcLEL 1940; DcPseud; DramC 6; EncWB; EncWL 1, 2, 2S, 3; EncWT; Ent; FacFETw; GrWrEL DR; HalFC 88; IntAu&W 76, 89, 91, 93; IntDcT 2; IntMPA 92, 94, 96; IntWW 74, 75, 76, 77, 78, 79, 80, 81, 82, 83, 89, 91, 93, 97, 98, 2000; LegTOT; MagSWL; MajMD 1; MajTwCW 1, 2; MakMC; McGEWD 72, 84; MiSFD 9; ModBrL 2, S1, S2; ModWD; News 95; NewYTBE 72; NewYTBS 74, 84; NotNAT; OxCAmT 84; OxCEng 85, 95; OxCThe 83; OxCTwCL; PIP&P A; RAdv 14, 13-2; RfGEnL 91; RGTwCWr; WebE&AL; Who 74, 82, 83, 85, 88, 90, 92, 94, 98, 99, 2000; WhoAm 80, 82, 84, 86, 88, 90, 92, 94, 95, 96, 97, 98, 99, 2000; WhoEnt 92, 98; WhoThe 72, 77, 81; WhoTwCL; WhoWor 82, 84, 87, 89, 91, 93, 95, 96, 97, 98, 99, 2000; WorAl; WorAlBi; WorAu 1970; WorLitC; WrDr 76, 80, 82, 84, 86, 88, 90, 92, 94, 96, 98, 99, 2000*

Storch, Larry

American. Actor, Comedian

Starred on TV series "F Troop," 1965-67.

b. Jan 8, 1923 in New York, New York

Source: *BiE&WWA; BioIn 3; ConTFT 4; ForYSC; HalFC 80, 84, 88; IntMPA 96; LegTOT; MotPP; NotNAT; WhoCom; WhoHol 92, A*

Storey, David Malcolm

English. Author, Dramatist

Wrote *This Sporting Life*, 1960, filmed, 1963.

b. Jul 13, 1933 in Wakefield, England

Source: *CamBiEn; ChamBiD; CnThe; ConAu 81; ConDr 73, 77; ConNov 76;*

CurBio 73; DcLEL 1940; EncWT; IntAu&W 91; IntMPA 81; IntWW 91, 97, 98, 2000; McGEWD 84; ModBrL S1; NotNAT; OxCEng 85; TwCWr; Who 92, 98, 99, 2000; WhoThe 81; WhoWor 91; WrDr 98, 99, 2000

Storm, Gale

[Josephine Cottle]

American. Actor

Starred in "My Little Margie," 1952-55; "The Gale Storm Show," 1956-62.

b. Apr 5, 1922 in Bloomington, Texas

Source: *BiDAmM; BioIn 3, 4, 10, 12, 18; DcPseud; FilmEn; FilmgC; ForYSC; HalFC 80, 84, 88; HolP 40; IntMPA 75, 76, 77, 78, 79, 80, 81, 82, 84, 86, 88, 92, 94, 96; InWom, SUP; LegTOT; MotPP; MovMk; PenEncP; RadStar; RkOn 74; SweetSg D; WhoAmW 58; WhoHol 92, A; WhoRock 81; WorAl; WorAlBi*

Storm, (Hans) Theodor (Woldsen)

German. Author, Poet

Outstanding lyric poet of German literature and a recognized master of the novella.

b. Sep 14, 1817 in Husum, Germany

d. Jul 4, 1888 in Hademarschen, Germany

Source: *CamBiEn; RfGShF 1, 2; RfGWoL 95*

Stormer, Fredrik (Carl Mulertz)

Norwegian. Physicist, Mathematician

Created mathematical theory of auroral phenomena.

b. Sep 3, 1874 in Skien, Norway

d. Aug 13, 1957 in Oslo, Norway

Source: *BioIn 2, 4, 5, 20; CamBiEn; ChamBiD; DcScB; InSci; NotTwCS 1*

Storr, (Charles) Anthony

English. Psychiatrist

Wrote *Human Aggression*, 1968; *The Art of Psychotherapy*, 1979.

b. May 18, 1920 in Bentley, England

Source: *ConAu 17NR, 41NR, 97; CurBio 94; IntAu&W 89, 91, 93; IntWW 91, 93, 97, 2000; Who 74, 82, 83, 85, 88, 90, 92, 94, 98, 99, 2000; WhoWor 95, 96, 97; WorAu 1985; WrDr 86, 88, 90, 92, 94, 96, 98, 99, 2000*

Story, Joseph

American. Supreme Court Justice

Associate justice, 1811-45; pioneer in organizing, directing teaching at Harvard Law School; wrote *Equity Jurisprudence*, 1836.

b. Sep 18, 1779 in Marblehead, Massachusetts

d. Sep 10, 1845 in Cambridge, Massachusetts

Source: *Alli; AmAu; AmAu&B; AmBi; AmJust; AmNatBi; AmPolLe; ApCAB; BenetAL 91; BiAUS; BiDAmEd; BiD&SB; BiDFedJ; BiDrAC; BiDrUSC 89; BioIn 1, 2, 3, 5, 6, 8, 9, 11, 14, 15, 23; CamBiEn; CamDcAB; ChamBiD; CyAG; CyAL 2; DcAmAu; DcAmB; DcAmC; DcBiPP; DcEnL; DcNAA;*

Drake; EncAB-H 1974, 1996; EncRelA; EncWB 98; HarEnUS; LinLib L, S; McGEWB; NatCAB 2; OxCAmH; OxCAmL 65, 83, 95; OxCLaw; OxCSupC; REnAL; SupCtJu; TwCBDA; WebAB 74, 79; WhAm HS; WhAmP; WorAl; WorAlBi

Story, Liz

American. Pianist, Composer

First solo album *Solid Colors* released in 1983.

b. Oct 28, 1956 in San Diego, California

Source: *BakBD 92; BakBDTw; BioIn 16; ConMus 2; NewAgMG*

Story, William Wetmore

American. Sculptor, Author, Lawyer

Best known as neoclassic sculptor; wrote books on Italy: *Vallombrosa*, 1881.

b. Feb 12, 1819 in Salem, Massachusetts

d. Oct 7, 1895 in Vallombrosa, Italy

Source: *Alli, SUP; AmAu; AmAu&B; AmBi; AmNatBi; ApCAB; BbD; BenetAL 91; BibAL 8; BiD&SB; BiDTran; BioIn 4, 5, 7, 8, 9, 10, 11, 22, 23; BriEAA; CamDcAB; CasWL; ChamBiD; Chambr 3; ChhPo, S1; CyAL 2; DcAmArt; DcAmAu; DcAmB; DcBiPP; DcEnL; DcLB 1; DcLEL; DcNAA; Drake; EvLB; HarEnUS; McGDA; NatCAB 5; NewYHSD; OxCAmH; OxCAmL 65, 83, 95; REnAL; TwCBDA; WhAmArt 85; WhAm HS*

Stoss, Veit

German. Sculptor

Master wood carver, active in Krakow, Nuremberg.

b. 1445 in Nuremberg, Germany

d. 1533 in Nuremberg, Germany

Source: *EncWB 98; McGEWB; NewCol 75*

Stottlemyre, Mel(vin Leon)

American. Baseball Player

Pitcher, NY Yankees, 1964-74; had three 20-game winning seasons, 164 career wins.

b. Nov 13, 1941 in Hazelton, Missouri

Source: *Ballpl 90; BaseEn 88; BiDAmSp Sup; BioIn 14, 18; WhoAm 74; WhoProB 73*

Stotz, Charles Morse

American. Architect, Author

Pioneer in architectural restoration; wrote on PA architecture.

b. Aug 1, 1898 in Pittsburgh, Pennsylvania

d. Mar 5, 1985 in Fort Myers, Florida

Source: *AmArch 70; ConAu 115; WhoAm 74, 76*

Stouffer, Samuel A.

American. Sociologist, Statistician

Leader in applying rigorous survey research techniques and statistical methodology to sociological investigations.

b. Jun 6, 1900 in Sac City, Iowa

d. Aug 24, 1960

Source: *EncWB 98; RAdv 13-3*

Stouffer, Vernon B
American. Businessman, Restaurateur
Operated chain of restaurants, formed
corp., 1929; introduced frozen dishes,
1954.
b. Aug 22, 1901 in Cleveland, Ohio
d. Jul 26, 1974 in Lakewood, Ohio
Source: *Entr; ObitOF 79; WhAm 6;
WhoAm 74*

Stout, Juanita Kidd
American. Judge
First African-American woman elected
judge in the US; Municipal Court of
Philadelphia, 1959.
b. Mar 7, 1919 in Wewoka, Oklahoma
d. Aug 21, 1998 in Philadelphia,
Pennsylvania
Source: *AmBench 79; BioIn 6, 7, 16, 24;
BlkWAm; Ebony 1; InWom; NegAl 89;
NotBlAW 1; WhoAfA 9, 10, 11, 12;
WhoAm 76, 78, 96, 97, 98, 99; WhoAmL
79, 83; WhoAmP 91; WhoAmW 61, 64,
66, 68, 72, 74, 75, 85, 87, 89, 91, 93,
95, 97, 99; WhoBlA 1, 2, 3, 4, 5, 6, 7, 8;
WhoE 74, 75, 91; WomPO 78*

Stout, Rex Todhunter
American. Author
Founded Vanguard Press, 1926; created
detective Nero Wolfe, 1934.
b. Dec 1, 1886 in Noblesville, Indiana
d. Oct 27, 1975 in Danbury, Connecticut
Source: *AmAu&B; AuNews 2; CamBiEn;
CamDcAB; CasWL; ChamBiD; ConAu
61, 71NR; ConLC 3; ConNov 76;
CorpD; CurBio 46; EncALit; EncMys;
EvLB; IndAu 1917; LngCTC; OxCTwCL;
PenC AM; REn; RfGAmL 4; TwCA SUP;
WhAm 6; WhoAm 74, 76; WorAu 1900*

Stout, William Bushnell
American. Engineer, Inventor
Built first commercial monoplane, 1919;
gasoline driven passenger rail car,
1933.
b. Mar 16, 1880 in Quincy, Illinois
d. Mar 20, 1956
Source: *BioIn 2, 3, 4, 9, 19; CurBio 57;
FacFETw; InSci; WhAm 3*

Stoutenburg, Adrien Pearl
[Lace Kendall]
American. Children's Author
Books include *Fee, Fi, Fo, Fum:
Friendly & Funny Giants*, 1969; *A Cat
Is*, 1971.
b. Dec 1, 1916 in Dafur, Minnesota
Source: *AmAu&B; Au&Wr 71; AuBYP 2,
3; ConAu 5R, 176; ConPo 75; DrAP 75;
MinnWr; PenNWW A, B; SmATA 3;
ThrBJA; WhoAm 82; WhoWest 74; WrDr
86*

Stovall, Luther McKinley
"Lou Stovall"
American. Printmaker
Artist transformed silkscreen printmaking
from a commercial craft to a true art
form.

b. Jan 1, 1937 in Athens, Georgia
Source: *EncWB 98; WhoAmA 73, 76, 78,
80, 82, 84, 86, 89, 91, 93, 1999*

Stove, Betty
Dutch. Tennis Player
One of best doubles players; currently
coaches Hana Mandlikova.
b. Jun 24, 1945 in Rotterdam,
Netherlands
Source: *BuCMET; InWom SUP; OfEnT;
WhoIntT*

Stover, Russell
American. Candy Manufacturer
Perfected Eskimo Pie, 1921; pres.,
Russell Stover Candies, 1925-43.
b. May 6, 1888 in Alton, Kansas
d. May 11, 1954 in Miami Beach,
Florida
Source: *BioIn 3, 4, 6; Entr; NatCAB 43*

Stow, (Julian) Randolph
Australian. Author
Novels on Australia include *Tourmaline*,
1963.
b. Nov 28, 1935 in Geraldton, Australia
Source: *AuLitCr; Benet 87, 96; BioIn 6,
9, 10, 17; BlueB 76; CamGLE; CasWL;
ChamBiD; ConAu 13R, 33NR; ConLC
23, 48; ConNov 72, 76, 82, 86, 91, 96;
ConPo 70, 75, 80, 85; CyWA 89;
DcChlFi; DcLEL 1940; EncSF 93;
GrWrEL N; IntAu&W 76, 77, 82, 89, 91,
93; IntLitE; IntWWP 77; LiExTwC;
MajTwCW 1; ModCmwL; NewC;
OxCAusL; OxCTwCP; PenC ENG; RAdv
14, 13-1; RfGEnL 91; RGTwCWr;
ScF&FL 1, 2, 92; ScFSB; TwCWr;
WebE&AL; Who 74, 82, 83, 85, 90, 92,
94, 98, 99, 2000; WorAu 1950; WrDr
76, 80, 82, 84, 86, 88, 90, 92, 94, 96,
98, 99, 2000*

**Stowe, Harriet (Elizabeth)
Beecher**
American. Author
Wrote *Uncle Tom's Cabin*, 1852.
b. Jun 14, 1811 in Litchfield,
Connecticut
d. Jul 1, 1896 in Hartford, Connecticut
Source: *Alli, SUP; AmAu; AmAu&B;
AmBi; AmRef; AmSocL; AmWomWr;
AtlBL; BbD; BiD&SB; CamBiEn;
CamDcAB; CarSB; CasWL; ChamBiD;
Chambr 3; CyWA 58; DcAmB;
DcAmReB 1, 2; EncAAH; EncAB-H
1974, 1996; EncALit; EncWB 98;
HarEnUS; InWom, SUP; LibW; LinLib
S; MajAI; McGEWB; NatCAB 1;
NotAW; OxCAmL 95; OxCEng 85, 95;
PenC AM; RAdv 1; REn; RfGAmL 4, 94;
TwCBDA; WebAB 74, 79; WhAm HS;
WhAmP*

Stowe, Leland
American. Journalist
Foreign correspondent, *NY Herald
Tribune*, 1926-39; won Pulitzer, 1930;
war correspondent, *Chicago Daily
News*, 1939-43.
b. Nov 10, 1899 in Southbury,
Connecticut

d. Jan 16, 1994 in Ann Arbor, Michigan
Source: *AmAu&B; BiDAmJo; BioIn 1, 3,
4, 16, 17, 19, 20, 22; BlueB 76; ConAu
53NR, 77, 143; CurBio 40, 94N; DcLB
29; EncAJ; EncTwCJ; HisDcWJ;
IntAu&W 77, 89, 91; IntWW 74, 75, 76,
77, 78, 79, 80, 81, 82, 83, 89, 91, 93;
JrnUS; LinLib L; NewYTBS 94; REnAL;
SmATA 60, 78; TwCA SUP; WhoAm 74,
76, 78, 80, 82, 84, 86, 88, 90, 92, 94,
95, 96, 97; WhoPul; WhoWor 74;
WorAu 1900*

Stowe, Madeleine
American. Actor
Appeared in *The Last of the Mohicans*.
b. Aug 18, 1958 in Los Angeles,
California
Source: *ConTFT 12, 24; IntMPA 94, 96;
IntWW 97, 98, 2000; IntWWW 2;
LegTOT; NotHsAW 2; WhoAm 95, 96,
97, 98, 99, 2000; WhoAmW 95, 97;
WhoHisp 94; WhoHol 92*

Strabo
Greek. Geographer, Historian
Wrote *Historical Sketches; Geographical
Sketches* describing earth as a globe.
b. 63?BC in Amasia, Pontus
d. 22AD
Source: *AsBiEn; BbD; BiD&SB; BiESc;
BioIn 18, 20, 23, 24; DcScB;
Grk&L; InSci; OxCEng 67, 85, 95;
OxDcByz; PenC CL; RanHWDS; REn;
WhWE; WorAl; WorAlBi*

Stracciari, Riccardo
Italian. Opera Singer
Baritone who sang *Figaro* over 90 times.
b. Jun 26, 1875 in Casalecchio, Italy
d. Oct 10, 1955 in Rome, Italy
Source: *BakBD 84, 92; BakBDTw; BioIn
4, 10, 12; CmOp; IntDcOp; MetOEnc;
NewEOp 71; NewGrDM 80; NewGrDO;
OxDcOp*

Strachan, John
Canadian. Educator, Clergy
Leading member of the ruling oligarchy
in Upper Canada, he was the first
Anglican bishop of Toronto and
founder of the University of Toronto.
b. Apr 12, 1778 in Aberdeen, Scotland
d. Nov 1, 1867 in Toronto, Ontario,
Canada
Source: *Alli; ApCAB; BbtC; BioIn 1, 5,
8, 9, 11, 12; ChamBiD; CyEd; DcBiPP;
DcCanB 9; DcNaB; Drake; EncWar;
EncWB 98; MacDCB 78; McGEWB;
OxCCan*

Strachey, (Giles) Lytton
English. Biographer, Historian
Revolutionized art of biography with
humanized criticism; most famous
work: *Queen Victoria*, 1921.
b. Mar 1, 1880 in London, England
d. Jan 21, 1932 in Hungerford, England
Source: *AtlBL; Benet 87, 96; BiCoLiE;
BiDMoPL; BioIn 1, 2, 3, 4, 5, 8, 9, 10,
12, 13, 14, 15, 19, 20, 21; BlmGEL;
BritWr S2; CamBiEn; CamGEL;
CamGLE; CasWL; ChamBiD; Chambr*

3; CnMWL; ConAu 110, 178; CyWA 58;
DcArts; DcLB 149, DS10; DcLEL;
DcNaB 1931; EncWB 98; EncWL 1, 2,
2S; EvLB; FacFETw; GayLesB; GayLL
2; GrBr; LegTOT; LinLib L, S; LngCEL;
LngCTC; MajTwCW 2; MakMC;
ModBrL; NewC; NewCBEL; OxCEng 67,
85, 95; OxCTwCL; PenC ENG; RAdv
13-3; REn; TwCA, SUP; TwCLC 12;
TwCWr; WebE&AL; WhDW; WhE&EA;
WhLit; WhoLA; WhoTwCL; WorAl;
WorAlBi; WorAu 1900

Stradella, Alessandro
Italian. Composer
Adventuresome life subject of 19th-c.
    operas, books; wrote opera *Il
    Corispeo.*
b. Oct 1, 1642 in Naples, Italy
d. Feb 28, 1682 in Genoa, Italy
Source: *BakBD 84; BioIn 3, 4;
CamBiEn; ChamBiD; CmOp; MusMk;
NewEOp 71; OxCMus*

Stradivari, Antonio
[Antonius Stradivarius]
Italian. Violin Maker
Workmanship perfected violin; earliest
    known, 1666.
b. 1644 in Cremona, Italy
d. Dec 17, 1737 in Cremona, Italy
Source: *BakBD 78, 84, 92; BakDcM;
BioIn 1, 2, 3, 6, 10, 15; BriBkM 80;
CamBiEn; ChamBiD; DcArts; DcCathB;
Dis&D; EncWB 98; LegTOT; LinLib S;
MusMk; NewAmDM; NewCol 75;
NewGrDM 80; NewOxM; OxCMus;
WebBD 83*

Strafford, 1st Earl of
[Thomas Wentworth]
English. Politician
Lord deputy of Ireland from 1632 to
    1640, he instituted the King's rule and
    the King's peace through the hated
    policy of "Thorough;" he later
    became Charles I's chief adviser.
b. Apr 13, 1593, England
d. May 12, 1641 in London, England
Source: *Benet 87, 96; BioIn 15;
CamBiEn; EncWB 98*

Straight, Beatrice Whitney
American. Actor
Won Tony, 1953, for performance in *The
    Crucible;* Oscar, 1976, for *Network.*
b. Aug 2, 1918 in Long Island, New
    York
Source: *BiE&WWA; ConTFT 7; ForWC
70; HalFC 88; IntMPA 92; InWom SUP;
NotNAT; VarWW 85; WhoAm 78, 80, 82,
84, 86, 88, 90, 92, 94, 95, 96; WhoAmW
85; WhoE 89, 91, 93, 95; WhoEnt 92;
WhoHol A; WhoThe 81; WhoWor 91;
WorAlBi*

Strait, George
American. Singer
Country singer; CMA entertainer of year,
    1989, 1990; album *Does Fort Worth
    Ever Cross Your Mind* was CMA
    album of year, 1985.
b. May 10, 1952 in Pearsall, Texas

Source: *AllMGCo; BgBkCoM; CelR 90;
ConMus 5; HarEnCM 87; LegTOT;
News 98, 98-3; PenEncP; WhoAm 88,
90, 92, 94, 95, 96, 97, 98, 99, 2000;
WhoEnt 92, 98; WhoNeCM*

Strakosch, Maurice
Czech. Impresario
Presented first season of Italian Opera,
    NYC, 1850s.
b. Jan 15, 1825 in Butschowitz, Moravia
d. Oct 9, 1887 in Paris, France
Source: *AmNatBi; ApCAB; BakBD 78,
84, 92; MetOEnc; NewEOp 71;
NewGrDA 86; NewGrDO; WhAm HS*

Strand, Mark
American. Poet
Publications include *Reasons for Moving,*
    1968; won Edgar Award for *The Story
    of Our Lives,* 1974; published
    collection of poems *The Continuous
    Life,* 1990; won 1999 Pulitzer Prize
    for Poetry for *Blizzard of One.*
b. Apr 11, 1934 in Summerside, Prince
    Edward Island, Canada
Source: *AmAu&B; AmWr S4; Benet 87,
96; BenetAL 91; BioIn 9, 10, 11, 12, 13,
15, 17, 20, 24; CamDcAB; ChamBiD;
ChhPo S2; ConAu 21R, 40NR, 65NR;
ConLC 6, 8, 18, 41, 71; ConPo 70, 75,
80, 85, 91, 96; CroCAP; CyWA 97;
DcLB 5; DcLEL 1940; DrAP 75; DrAPF
80, 91; DrAS 82E; EncALit; EncWB 98;
EncWL 2S, 3; Focus; IntAu&W 86;
IntWWP 77; LegTOT; LinLib L; ModAL
4S2, 5; ODwPR 91; OxCAmL 83, 95;
OxCTwCL; OxCTwCP; RAdv 1, 14, 13-
1; RfGAmL 4; SmATA 41; WhoAm 76,
78, 80, 82, 84, 86, 88, 90, 92, 94, 95,
96, 97, 2000; WhoE 74; WhoUSWr 88;
WhoWest 94; WhoWrEP 89, 92, 95;
WorAu 1970; WrDr 76, 80, 82, 84, 86,
88, 90, 92, 94, 96, 98, 99, 2000*

Strand, Paul
American. Photographer, Filmmaker
First to use "candid camera" trick;
    produced film documentaries.
b. Oct 16, 1890 in New York, New York
d. Mar 31, 1976 in Yvelines, France
Source: *AmNatBi; Benet 87, 96; BioIn 6,
7, 8, 9, 10, 11, 12, 13, 16, 17, 18, 20,
24; BriEAA; CamBiEn; CamDcAB;
ChamBiD; ConAu 65; ConPhot 82, 88;
CurBio 65, 76N; DcAmArt; DcAmB S10;
DcArts; DcFM; DcTwDes; EncAJ;
EncWB 2-19; FacFETw; FilmEn;
ICPEnP; LegTOT; MacBEP; NewYTBS
76; OxCFilm; WebAB 74, 79; WhAm 7;
WhAmArt 85; WhoAm 74, 76; WhoWor
74; WorEFlm*

Strang, Ruth May
American. Educator
Professor at Columbia University and the
    University of Arizona, known for her
    achievements in the fields of student
    guidance, reading and communication,
    child study, mental health, and
    development and adjustment.
b. Apr 3, 1895 in Chatham, New Jersey
d. Jan 1971

Source: *AmNatBi; BiDAmEd; BioIn 12;
ConAu 2NR; EncWB 98; InWom SUP;
NotAW MOD*

Strange, Curtis
American. Golfer
Turned pro, 1976; leading money winner
    on tour, 1985; won US Open, 1988,
    1989.
b. Jan 30, 1955 in Norfolk, Virginia
Source: *BioIn 16; IntWW 91; LegTOT;
News 88; NewYTBS 90; WhoAm 90;
WhoE 86; WhoEmL 87; WhoFI 87;
WhoIntG; WhoWor 89; WorAlBi*

Strasberg, Lee
[Israel Strassberg]
American. Actor, Acting Teacher
Directed Actor's Studio, 1950-82; taught
    Stanislavsky acting method, also
    known as "method acting."
b. Nov 17, 1901 in Budzanow, Austria
d. Feb 17, 1982 in New York, New
    York
Source: *AmNatBi; AnObit 1982; BiDFilm
94; BiE&WWA; BioIn 5, 6, 10, 11, 12,
13, 14, 20, 24; BlueB 76; CamBiEn;
CamDcAB; CamGWoT; CelR; ChamBiD;
CnThe; ConAu 13R, 29NR, 106; CurBio
60, 82, 82N; DcPseud; EncWB, 98;
EncWT; Ent; FacFETw; FilmEn;
FilmgC; HalFC 80, 84; IntDcT 3;
IntMPA 81, 82; IntWW 74, 75, 76, 77,
78, 79, 80, 81; LegTOT; NewYTBS 75,
82; NotNAT; OsStAZ; OxCAmT 84;
OxCThe 83; PIP&P; ScrEAmL 1;
TheaDir; WhAm 8; WhoAm 74, 76, 78,
80; WhoE 77, 79, 81; WhoHol A;
WhoThe 72, 77, 81; WhoWor 74; WorAl;
WorAlBi*

Strasberg, Susan Elizabeth
American. Actor, Author
Created lead role on stage in *Diary of
    Anne Frank,* 1955.
b. May 22, 1938 in New York, New
    York
d. Jan 21, 1999 in New York, New York
Source: *BiE&WWA; ConAu 120, 174;
CurBio 58; FilmgC; HalFC 88; IntMPA
92; InWom, SUP; MotPP; MovMk;
NewYTBS 80; NotNAT; WhoAm 86, 90;
WhoEnt 92; WhoHol A; WorAlBi*

Strasburger, Eduard Adolf
German. Biologist
Plant cytologist who explained nuclear
    division in plants.
b. Feb 1, 1844 in Warsaw, Poland
d. May 18, 1912 in Bonn, Germany
Source: *AsBiEn; BiESc; BioIn 2;
CamBiEn; CamDcSc; ChamBiD; DcScB;
LarDcSc; RanHWDS*

Strasfogel, Ignace
Polish. Conductor
Associate conductor, Metropolitan Opera
    Assn., 1951-1974.
b. Jul 17, 1909 in Warsaw, Poland
d. Feb 6, 1994 in New York, New York
Source: *BioIn 10, 19; BlueB 76; WhAm
11; WhoAm 74, 76, 78, 80, 82, 84, 86,
88, 90, 92, 94; WhoEnt 92; WhoMus 72;*

WhoOp 76; WhoWor 74, 76; WhoWorJ 72, 78

Strasser, Valentine (E. M.)
Sierra Leonean. Political Leader
Military officer became president of Sierra Leone after protesting soldiers ousted Joseph Momoh in a 1992 coup; he ruled the troubled nation from exile.
b. Sep 15, 1966 in Allen Town, Sierra Leone
Source: *WhoWor 96, 97*

Strassman, Marcia
American. Actor
Played Julie Kotter in TV series "Welcome Back, Kotter," 1975-79.
b. Apr 28, 1948 in New York, New York
Source: *BioIn 11, 13; ConTFT 7, 18; LegTOT; VarWW 85; WhoHol 92*

Strassmann, Fritz
German. Chemist
Opened field of atomic energy when he found neutron-induced nuclear fissure in uranium.
b. Feb 22, 1902 in Boppard, Germany
d. Apr 22, 1980 in Mainz, Germany
Source: *BiESc; BioIn 12, 20; McGMS 80; NotTwCS 1; WhoWor 74, 76, 78*

Stratas, Teresa
[Anastasia Strataki]
Canadian. Opera Singer
Soprano; NY Met., since late 1950s; won three Grammys, one Tony.
b. May 26, 1939 in Toronto, Ontario, Canada
Source: *BakBD 84; BioIn 16; CanWW 89; CreCan 2; FacFETw; IntWW 91; IntWWM 90; NewAmDM; NewYTBS 90; PenDiMP; WhoAm 74, 76, 78, 80, 86, 90; WhoAmW 66, 68, 70, 72, 74, 75; WhoHol 92; WhoMus 72; WhoWor 84, 91*

Stratemeyer, Edward L
American. Children's Author
Syndicate produced *The Rover Boys, Hardy Boys, Bobbsey Twins, Nancy Drew,* etc.
b. Oct 4, 1862 in Elizabeth, New Jersey
d. May 10, 1930 in Newark, New Jersey
Source: *AmAu&B; BiD&SB; CamBiEn; CamDcAB; CarSB; ConAu P-2; DcAmAu; EncMys; HsB&A; OxCAmL 65; REn; REnAL; SmATA 1, 100; TwCBDA; WebAB 74; WhAm 1*

Stratemeyer, George E, General
American. Army Officer
US Air Force general, commanding general China-Burma-India, WW II; Far East Air Forces, 1949-52.
b. Nov 24, 1890 in Cincinnati, Ohio
d. Aug 9, 1969 in Winter Park, Florida
Source: *CurBio 51, 69; WhAm 5*

Stratten, Dorothy
[Dorothy Hoogstratten; Mrs. Paul Snider]
Canadian. Actor, Model
Former Playboy centerfold shot to death by estranged husband; life story subject of film *Star 80,* 1983.
b. Feb 28, 1960 in Vancouver, British Columbia, Canada
d. Aug 14, 1980 in Los Angeles, California
Source: *BioIn 12, 16, 17; DcPseud*

Stratton, Julius A(dams)
American. Scientist
President, MIT, 1959-66; expert on radar for US Secretary of War during World War II.
b. May 18, 1901
d. Jun 22, 1994 in Boston, Massachusetts
Source: *AmMWSc 76P, 79, 82, 86, 89, 92; BioIn 1, 4, 5, 6, 7, 20, 21; BlueB 76; CurBio 94N; LElec; WhAm 11; Who 74, 82, 83, 85, 88, 90, 92, 94; WhoAm 74, 76, 78, 80, 84, 86, 88, 90, 92, 94; WhoE 83, 85, 86, 89; WhoWor 74*

Stratton, Monty Franklin Pierce
"Gander"
American. Baseball Player
Pitcher, White Sox, 1934-38; lost leg in hunting accident, 1938; life story filmed, 1949, starring Jimmy Stewart.
b. May 21, 1912 in Celeste, Texas
d. Sep 29, 1982 in Greenville, Texas
Source: *NewYTBS 82; WhoProB 73*

Stratton, Samuel S(tuddiford)
American. Politician
Fifteen term US representative from NY.
b. Sep 27, 1916 in Yonkers, New York
d. Sep 13, 1990 in Gaithersburg, Maryland
Source: *AlmAP 78, 80, 82, 84, 88; BiDrAC; BiDrUSC 89; BioIn 7; CngDr 74, 77, 79, 81, 83, 85, 87; CurBio 91N; NewYTBS 90; PolsAm 84; WhAm 10; WhoAm 74, 76, 78, 80, 82, 84, 86, 88, 90; WhoAmP 73, 75, 77, 79, 81, 83, 85, 87, 89; WhoE 74, 75, 77, 79, 81, 83, 85, 86, 89; WhoGov 72, 75, 77*

Straub, Peter
American. Author
Horror novelist's titles include *Ghost Story,* 1979 and *The Talisman,* 1984, co-written with Stephen King and the fastest-selling book in publishing history.
b. Mar 2, 1943 in Milwaukee, Wisconsin
Source: *BeaEPF; BestSel 89-1; BioIn 12, 13, 14, 15, 16; ConAu 28NR, 85; ConLC 28, 107; CurBio 89; DcLB Y84B; IntAu&W 91; IntvTCA 2; LegTOT; MajTwCW 1; OxCTwCL; PenEncH; RAdv 14; ScF&FL 92; ScFSB; WhoAm 90; WhoEnt 92; WhoWrEP 89; WrDr 80, 82, 84, 86, 88, 90, 92*

Straus, Isidor
American. Merchant, Philanthropist
Purchased R H Macy & Co., 1896; developed Abraham & Straus, 1892; lost in Titanic disaster.

b. Feb 6, 1845 in Otterberg, Germany
d. Apr 15, 1912 in At Sea
Source: *AmBi; AmNatBi; ApCAB X; BiDAmBL 83; BiDrAC; BiDrUSC 89; BioIn 4, 5, 23; CamDcAB; DcAmB; EncWB 98; JeAmHC; McGEWB; NatCAB 10; OxCAmH; WebAB 74, 79; WhAm 1; WorAl; WorAlBi*

Straus, Jack Isidor
American. Merchant
Pres., chief exec., Macy's, beginning 1940, who oversaw company's expansion to 93 stores in 14 states.
b. Jan 13, 1900 in New York, New York
d. Sep 19, 1985 in New York, New York
Source: *BiDAmBL 83; BioIn 2, 3, 6, 7, 8, 9, 14; BlueB 76; CurBio 52, 85N; IntWW 74; IntYB 78, 79, 80, 81, 82; NewYTBS 85; St&PR 75, 84; WhAm 9; WhoAm 74, 76, 80, 82, 84; WhoFI 74; WhoWorJ 72, 78; WorAl; WorAlBi*

Straus, Nathan
American. Merchant, Philanthropist
With brother Isidor became owner of R H Macy & Co., 1896; leader in campaign for pasteurized milk in NY, 1892.
b. Jan 31, 1848 in Otterberg, Bavaria
d. Jan 11, 1931 in New York, New York
Source: *AmBi; ApCAB X; BiDAmBL 83; BioIn 1, 2, 4, 8, 9, 14, 17; CamDcAB; DcAmB; DcAmMeB 84; DcNAA; JeAmHC; LinLib S; NatCAB 10, 22; OxCAmH; WebAB 74, 79; WhAm 1; WorAl; WorAlBi*

Straus, Oscar Solomon
American. Lawyer, Diplomat
First ambassador to Turkey; secretary of Commerce, Labor under Theodore Roosevelt, 1906-09; wrote *The Hague Tribunal,* 1904.
b. Dec 23, 1850 in Otterberg, Germany
d. May 3, 1926 in New York, New York
Source: *Alli SUP; AmAu&B; AmBi; AmNatBi; AmPeW; ApCAB, SUP; BiDAmBL 83; BiD&SB; BiDInt; BiDrUSE 71, 89; BiDSA; BioIn 1, 2, 4, 5, 8, 9, 10, 14, 16; CamDcAB; CyAG; DcAmAu; DcAmB; DcNAA; HarEnUS; JeAmHC; NatCAB 10, 14, 40; REnAL; TwCBDA; WebAB 74, 79; WhAm 1*

Straus, Oskar
Austrian. Composer
Wrote 50 operettas including *Chocolate Soldier,* 1909; filmed, 1941.
b. Apr 6, 1870 in Vienna, Austria
d. Jan 11, 1954 in Bad Ischl, Austria
Source: *BakBD 78; BioIn 3, 4; ChamBiD; CmpEPM; CurBio 44, 54; NotNAT B; ObitOF 79; OxCMus; REn; WhAm 3; WhThe*

Straus, Roger W(illiams), Jr.
American. Publisher
Founder, pres., Farrar, Straus & Co., 1945.
b. Jan 3, 1917 in New York, New York

Source: *AmMWSc 73P; BiDAmBL 83; BioIn 12, 16; CelR 90; CurBio 80; IntWW 91; NewYTBS 80; WhE&EA; WhoAm 86, 90; WorAlBi*

Strauss, David Friedrich
German. Theologian
Described Gospels as ''historical myth;'' his *Leben Jesu*, 1835, was turning point in study of historical Jesus.
b. Jan 27, 1808 in Stuttgart, Germany
d. Feb 28, 1874 in Ludwigsburg, Germany
Source: *Benet 87, 96; BiD&SB; BiDTran; BioIn 7, 10, 13, 14, 20, 23; CamBiEn; CelCen; ChamBiD; DcBiPP; DcEuL; DcLB 133; EncUnb; EncWB 98; LuthC 75; McGEWB; NewCBEL; NewCol 75; OxCEng 85, 95; OxCGer 76, 86, 97; REn; WhoChr*

Strauss, Franz Josef
German. Politician
West German Defense Minister, 1956-62; Finance Minister, 1966-69; pres. of Bavaria, 1978-80.
b. Sep 6, 1915 in Munich, Germany
d. Oct 3, 1988 in Munich, Germany
Source: *AnObit 1988; BioIn 4, 5, 6, 7, 8, 9, 10, 11, 12, 13, 15, 16, 18, 21; CamBiEn; ChamBiD; ColdWar 1, 2; CurBio 57, 87, 88, 88N; DcTwHis; EncCW; EncWB, 98; FacFETw; IntWW 74, 75, 76, 77, 78, 79, 80, 81, 82, 83; IntYB 78, 79, 80, 81, 82; NewYTBS 88; WhAm 11; Who 74, 82, 83, 85, 88; WhoWor 74, 84, 87, 89*

Strauss, Johann, Sr.
''The Father of the Waltz''
Austrian. Composer, Conductor
Published 152 waltzes; led orchestra at Viennese dance halls.
b. Mar 14, 1804 in Vienna, Austria
d. Sep 25, 1849 in Vienna, Austria
Source: *BakBD 78, 84; BioIn 1, 4, 5, 7, 9, 11, 12, 16, 20, 23; BriBkM 80; CamBiEn; ChamBiD; DcCom 77; LegTOT; NewAmDM; NewCol 75; NewGrDM 80; NotNAT B; OxCMus; OxCPMus; OxDcOp; WebBD 83*

Strauss, Johann, Jr.
''The Waltz King''
Austrian. Composer, Conductor, Violinist
Wrote 16 operettas, 400 waltzes, including *The Blue Danube*, 1864.
b. Oct 25, 1825 in Vienna, Austria
d. Jun 3, 1899 in Vienna, Austria
Source: *AtlBL; BakBD 78, 84; Benet 87, 96; BiDD; BioIn 1, 2, 3, 4, 5, 6, 7, 9, 10, 11, 12, 16, 20, 23; BriBkM 80; CamBiEn; CelCen; ChamBiD; CmOp; CmpBCM; CnOxB; DancEn 78; DcCom 77; DcCom&M 79; EncWB 98; GrComp; LinLib S; McGEWB; MetOEnc; MusMk; NewAmDM; NewEOp 71; NewGrDM 80; NotNAT B; Opera; Opera; OxCAmT 84; OxCGer 76, 86, 97; OxCMus; OxCPMus; OxDcOp; PenDiMP A; REn; WhDW; WorAl; WorAlBi*

Strauss, Joseph Baermann
American. Engineer
Best known as chief engineer for Golden Gate Bridge, 1937.
b. Jan 9, 1870 in Cincinnati, Ohio
d. May 16, 1938 in Los Angeles, California
Source: *AmBi; AmNatBi; BioIn 2, 4, 7, 15; DcAmB S2; InSci; LinLib S; NatCAB 27; OhA&B; WhAm 1*

Strauss, Leo
German. Philosopher
Controversial Socratic political philosopher aroused bitter opposition from the academic and intellectual establishment.
b. Sep 20, 1899 in Kirchhain, Hesse, Germany
d. 1973
Source: *AmAu&B; AmNatBi; Au&Wr 71; BioIn 10, 11, 12, 13; CamDcAB; ConAu 45, 101; DcAmC; EncWB 98; IntEnSS 79; PeoHis; ThTwC 87; WhAm 6; WhoWorJ 72*

Strauss, Levi
American. Manufacturer
Settled in San Francisco, 1850, to make denim pants for miners.
b. 1829?
d. 1902
Source: *AmNatBi; BioIn 4, 11, 14, 16, 17, 18, 20, 23; CamBiEn; ChamBiD; EncAB-H 1996; Entr; JeHun; LegTOT; WebAB 74, 79; WorAl; WorAlBi*

Strauss, Lewis Lichtenstein
American. Author, Government Official
Chm., Atomic Energy Commission, 1953-58; helped shape US thermonuclear policy; wrote *Men & Decisions*, 1962.
b. Jan 31, 1896 in Charleston, West Virginia
d. Jan 21, 1974 in Brandy Station, Virginia
Source: *AmNatBi; BiDrUSE 71, 89; BioIn 1, 3, 4, 5, 6, 10, 11; BioNews 74; CamDcAB; ConAu 45; CurBio 47, 74; LinLib S; PolProf E, T; WhAm 6; Who 74; WhoWor 74*

Strauss, Peter
American. Actor
Won Emmy, 1979, for *The Jericho Mile*; starred in *Rich Man, Poor Man*, 1976.
b. Feb 20, 1947 in Croton-on-Hudson, New York
Source: *ConTFT 5, 25; IntMPA 77, 78, 79, 80, 81, 82, 84, 86, 88, 92, 94, 96; ItaFilm; WhoAm 78, 80, 82, 84, 86, 88, 90, 92, 94, 95, 96, 97, 98, 99, 2000; WhoEnt 92; WhoHol 92, A; WorAl; WorAlBi*

Strauss, Richard Georg
German. Conductor, Composer
Wrote operas *Salome*, 1905; *Rosenkavalier*, 1911; one of last German romantics.
b. Jun 11, 1864 in Munich, Germany

d. Sep 8, 1949 in Garmisch, Germany (West)
Source: *AtlBL; BakBD 84; BakBDTw; BakDcM; CurBio 44, 49; DcCM; NewYTBS 91; OxCGer 76; REn; WhAm 2; WhoAm 90; WhoAmL 90; WhoAmP 91*

Strauss, Robert
American. Actor
In films, 1942-61; appeared in *Stalag 17*, 1953; *The Seven Year Itch*, 1955.
b. Nov 8, 1913 in New York, New York
d. Feb 20, 1974 in New York, New York
Source: *BiE&WWA; BioIn 10; BioNews 75; EncAFC; FilmEn; FilmgC; ForYSC; HalFC 80, 84, 88; HolCA; IntMPA 75; MovMk; NewYTBS 75; NotNAT B; OsStAZ; Vers A; WhoHol C; WhScrn 77, 83*

Strauss, Robert Schwarz
American. Presidential Aide, Lawyer
Chm., Dem. Nat. Committee, 1972-77; worked to reelect Carter, 1979-81; US Ambassador to Russia, 1991-93.
b. Oct 19, 1918 in Lockhart, Texas
Source: *BioIn 10, 11, 12; CurBio 74, 92; EncWB, 98; IntWW 89, 91, 93, 97, 98, 2000; NewYTBS 76, 80, 91; PolProf NF; WhoAm 78, 80, 82, 84, 86, 88, 90, 92, 94, 95, 96; WhoAmL 87, 90; WhoAmP 85; WhoGov 77; WhoSSW 95; WhoWor 93, 95; WorAl*

Strauss, Theodore
Writer
TV shows include ''Born of Fire;'' won Emmy for ''They've Killed President Lincoln,'' 1971.
Source: *VarWW 85*

Stravinsky, Igor Fedorovich
American. Composer
Noted for ballets *The Firebird*, 1910, *Rite of Spring*, 1913; greatly influenced modern music.
b. Jun 17, 1882 in Oranienbaum, Russia
d. Apr 6, 1971 in New York, New York
Source: *AmAu&B; AmCulL; AmCL; ASCAP 66; BakBD 84; BiDAmM; ConAu 29R, 107; CurBio 40, 53, 71; DcCM; EncAB-H 1974; EncWB 98; FacFETw; MakMC; McGEWB; MusSN; NewGrDM 80; REn; WebAB 74, 79; WhAm 5, 7*

Stravinsky, Vera de Bossett
Russian. Artist
Second wife of Igor Stravinsky, married, 1940.
b. Dec 25, 1888 in Saint Petersburg, Russia
d. Sep 17, 1982 in New York, New York
Source: *AnObit 1982; NewYTBE 71; NewYTBS 82*

Straw, Syd
American. Singer, Songwriter
Performed backup singer for musician Pat Benatar in late 1970s; released

debut album, *Surprise,* 1989; later
recorded *War and Peace,* 1996 and
contributed song "People of Earth" to
Party of Five television soundtrack,
1996.
b. c. 1958 in Vermont
Source: *ConMus 18*

Strawberry, Darryl (Eugene)
American. Baseball Player
Outfielder, NY Mets, 1983-90; LA,
1991-93; San Francisco, 1994; NY
Yankees, 1995—; NL rookie of year,
1983; led NL in home runs, 1988.
b. Mar 12, 1962 in Los Angeles,
California
Source: *Ballpl 90; BaseReg 86, 87;
BioIn 16; CurBio 84; NewYTBS 82, 83,
84; WhoAm 90; WhoBlA 7; WhoWest
92; WorAlBi*

Strawbs
[Rod Coombes; Dave Cousins; Chas
Cronk; Dave Lambert]
British. Music Group
Music mixes folk/bluegrass; songs
include "Part of the Union," 1973.
Source: *BillEnR; ConMuA 80A; EncRk
88; HarEnR 86; IlEncRk; ObitOF 79;
PenEncP; RolSEnR 83; WhoRock 81;
WhoRocM 82*

Strawser, Neil Edward
American. Broadcast Journalist
CBS News correspondent since 1952.
b. Aug 16, 1927 in Rittman, Ohio
Source: *WhoAm 76, 78, 80, 82, 84, 86*

Stray Cats
[Jim "Slim Jim Phantom" McDonnell;
Lee Rocker; Brian Setzer]
American. Music Group
Rock group formed, 1979; albums
include *Built for Speed,* 1982.
Source: *BioIn 15; ConMus 11; EncRk
88; EncRkSt; HarEnR 86; IlEncRk;
PenEncP; RkOn 85; RolSEnR 83;
WhsNW 85*

Strayhorn, Billy
[William Strayhorn]
American. Jazz Musician
Pianist, arranger, Duke Ellington's band,
1938-67; wrote "Take the A' Train,"
1941.
b. Nov 29, 1915 in Dayton, Ohio
d. May 31, 1967 in New York, New
York
Source: *AfrAmAl 6; AllMGJa; AmNatBi;
ASCAP 66, 80; BakBD 78, 84, 92;
BakDcM; BiDAfM; BiDAmM; BiDJaz;
BioIn 7, 8, 22; CamBiEn; CmpEPM;
ConAmC 76, 82; ConMus 13; DrBlPA,
90; EncJzS; EncJzS; IlEncJ; LegTOT;
NewAmDM; NewGrDA 86; NewGrDJ
88, 94; NewGrDM 80; OxCPMus;
PenEncP; Songw; WhoJazz 72*

Streep, Meryl
[Mary Louise Streep]
American. Actor
Won Oscar for *Sophie's Choice,* 1983;
Emmy, 1978, for *Holocaust.*
b. Jun 22, 1949 in Summit, New Jersey
Source: *AmDec 1980; BiDFilm 94; BioIn
11, 12, 13, 16; CamGWoT; CelR 90;
ChamBiD; ContDcW 89; ConTFT 8, 16;
CurBio 80, 97; DcArts; DcTwCCu 1;
GrLiveH; HalFC 84, 88; HolBB; IntDcF
1-3, 2-3; IntMPA 82, 84, 86, 88, 92, 94,
96; IntWW 83, 89, 91, 93, 98, 2000;
IntWWW 2; InWom SUP; LegTOT; News
90, 90-2; NewYTBS 76, 79, 91;
OnHuYAF; OsStAZ; Who 90, 92;
WhoAm 86, 90, 92, 94, 95, 96, 97, 98,
99, 2000; WhoAmW 87, 89, 91, 93, 95,
97, 99; WhoEnt 92, 98; WhoHol 92;
WhoThe 81; WhoWor 89, 91, 93, 95, 96,
97, 98, 99, 2000; WorAlBi*

Street, George Edmund
English. Architect
A champion of Gothic revival; designed
over 250 buildings including London's
Royal Courts of Justice, 1874-81.
b. Jun 20, 1824 in Woodford, England
d. Dec 18, 1881 in London, England
Source: *Alli, SUP; ArtsNiC; BioIn 5, 14,
16; CamBiEn; CelCen; ChamBiD;
DcArch; DcArts; DcBiPP; DcD&D;
DcNaB; IntDcAr; MacEA; McGDA;
NewCBEL; NewCol 75; OxCArt;
OxCCAA; VicBrit; WhoArch*

Streeter, Edward
American. Author
Wrote *Father of the Bride,* 1949;
Chairman of the Bored, 1961.
b. Aug 1, 1891 in New York, New York
d. Mar 31, 1976 in New York, New
York
Source: *AmAu&B; AmNatBi; Au&Wr 71;
BioIn 1, 5, 7, 10, 13, 15; ConAu 1R,
2NR, 65; DcLB 11; EncAHmr; EncALit;
OxCAmL 65, 83, 95; REnAL; WhAm 7;
WhNAA; WhoAm 74, 76; WorAu 1950*

Streeter, Ruth
American. Military Leader
Commanded Marine Corps. Women's
Reserve during WWII.
b. Oct 2, 1895 in Brookline,
Massachusetts
d. Sep 30, 1990 in Morristown, New
Jersey
Source: *BioIn 1; CurBio 91N; InWom
SUP; NewYTBS 90; WebAMB*

Streeton, Arthur Ernest
Australian. Painter
Leading landscape artist of the
Heidelberg school, the Australian
version of impressionism.
b. Apr 8, 1867 in Mount Duneed,
Victoria, Australia
d. Sep 1, 1943 in Olinda, Victoria,
Australia
Source: *CamBiEn; ChamBiD; EncWB
98; McGEWB*

Strehler, Giorgio
Italian. Director
Responsible for bringing Italian theatre
to international attention via his
Piccolo Teatro di Milano, founded
1947; an advocate of theatre as a force
in contemporary society.
b. Aug 14, 1921 in Trieste, Italy
d. Dec 25, 1997 in Lugano, Switzerland
Source: *BakBDTw; BioIn 11, 15, 17, 20,
23, 24; CamBiEn; CamGWoT; CmOp;
CurBio 91, 98N; DcItL 2; EncWT; Ent;
GrStDi; IntDcOp; IntDcT 3; IntWW 93,
97; MetOEnc; NewGrDM 80;
NewGrDO; OxCThe 83; OxDcOp;
TheaDir; WhoOp 76; WhoWor 97, 2000*

Streibert, Theodore Cuyler
American. Government Official
First director, US Information Agency,
1953-57.
b. Aug 29, 1899 in Albany, New York
d. Jan 18, 1987 in Syosset, New York
Source: *BioIn 3, 4, 11; CurBio 55, 87;
PolProf E; WhAm 9; WhoAm 74, 76, 78;
WhoWor 74*

Streich, Rita
German. Opera Singer
Soprano; Vienna debut, 1953; noted for
Mozart, Strauss roles.
b. Dec 18, 1920 in Barnaul, Union of
Soviet Socialist Republics
Source: *BakBD 84, 92; BakBDTw; BioIn
4, 14; CmOp; IntDcOp; IntWW 74;
MetOEnc; NewAmDM; NewGrDM 80;
NewGrDO; OxDcOp; PenDiMP;
WhoMus 72; WhoOp 76; WhoWor 74*

Streicher, Julius
German. Journalist, Politician
Edited anti-Semitic *The Stormer,* 1923-
45; executed after Nuremberg trial.
b. Feb 12, 1885 in Fleinhausen, Germany
d. Oct 16, 1946 in Nuremberg, Germany
Source: *BiDExR; BioIn 1, 12, 14, 16, 18,
24; CamBiEn; ChamBiD; CurBio 46;
DcTwHis; Dis&D; EncTR, 91; HisEWW;
REn; WhDW; WhWW-II*

Streisand, Barbra (Joan)
[Mrs. James Brolin; Barbara Streisand]
American. Singer, Actor, Director
Won Oscar, 1968, for *Funny Girl;*
albums include *The Lodgers,* 1985;
received special Grammy Legend
Award for lifetime achievement, 1992;
directed and starred in *The Mirror Has
Two Faces,* 1996; Emmy award
winner, 1964, for TV special, "My
Name is Barbra."
b. Apr 24, 1942 in New York, New
York
Source: *AmDec 1960; ASCAP 80;
BakBD 84, 92; BiDAmM; BiDFilm, 81,
94; BiE&WWA; BioAmW; BioIn 6, 7, 8,
9, 10, 11, 12, 13, 16; BkPepl; BlueB 76;
CelR, 90; CmMov; ConAu 144; ConMuA
80A; ConMus 2; ContDcW 89; ConTFT
1, 7; CurBio 64, 92; DcArts; DcTwCCu
1; EncAFC; EncMT; EncPR&S 89;
FacFETw; FilmEn; FilmgC; ForWC 70;
ForYSC; GoodHs; GrLiveH; HalFC 80,*

84, 88; IntDcF 1-3, 2-3; IntDcWB; IntMPA 75, 76, 77, 78, 79, 80, 81, 82, 84, 86, 88, 92, 94, 96; IntWW 74, 75, 76, 77, 78, 79, 80, 81, 82, 83, 89, 91, 93, 97, 98, 2000; IntWWW 2; InWom, SUP; LegTOT; LibW; MiSFD 9; MotPP; MovMk; NewAmDM; NewGrDA 86; News 92, 92-2; NotNAT, A; OxCFilm; OxCPMus; PenEncP; PIP&P; ReelWom; RkOn 78; WebAB 74, 79; Who 94, 98, 99, 2000; WhoAm 74, 76, 78, 80, 82, 84, 86, 88, 90, 92, 94, 95, 96, 97, 98, 99, 2000; WhoAmJ 80; WhoAmW 66, 68, 70, 72, 74, 75, 79, 81, 83, 85, 87, 89, 91, 93, 95, 97, 99; WhoE 74; WhoEnt 92, 98; WhoHol 92, A; WhoRock 81; WhoThe 72, 77, 81; WhoWor 74, 78, 89, 98, 99, 2000; WomFir; WomWMM; WorAl; WorAlBi

Streithorst, Tom
American. Broadcast Journalist
Covered Middle East, Latin America for NBC News from early 1960s.
b. 1932
d. Feb 19, 1981 in Palo Alto, California
Source: *ConAu 103; WhAm 7*

Strenger, Hermann Josef
German. Business Executive
Chairman of Bayer, prominent German chemical firm, since 1984.
b. Sep 26, 1928? in Cologne, Germany
Source: *BioIn 15; IntWW 82, 83, 89, 91, 97, 98, 2000; WhoFI 00, 96, 98; WhoWor 95, 96, 97, 98, 99, 2000*

Strepponi, Giuseppina
Italian. Opera Singer
Famed soprano, late 1830s; wife of Verdi.
b. Sep 18, 1815 in Lodi, Italy
d. Nov 15, 1897 in Busseto, Italy
Source: *BakBD 78, 84, 92; CmOp; IntDcOp; InWom; MetOEnc; NewAmDM; NewEOp 71; NewGrDM 80; NewGrDO; OxDcOp; PenDiMP*

Stresemann, Gustav
German. Statesman
Chancellor, then foreign minister, who helped negotiate Locarno Pact, 1925; shared 1926 Nobel Peace Prize with Aristide Briand.
b. May 10, 1878 in Berlin, Germany
d. Oct 3, 1929 in Berlin, Germany
Source: *BiDInt; BioIn 3, 4, 6, 9, 10, 11, 15, 16; CamBiEn; ChamBiD; DcTwHis; Dis&D; EncTR, 91; EncWB 98; HisWorL; McGEWB; NewCol 75; NobelP; OxCGer 76, 86, 97; REn; WhDW; WorAl; WorAlBi*

Stribling, Thomas Sigismund
American. Author
Trilogy depicting life in the South includes 1933 Pulitzer-winning novel, *The Store.*
b. Mar 4, 1881 in Clinton, Tennessee
d. Jul 8, 1965 in Florence, Alabama
Source: *AmAu&B; BioIn 7, 8, 10, 12, 13, 14, 15; CasWL; CnDAL; ConAmA; DcAmB S7; DcLEL; EncAAH; EncALit;*

EncMys; EncSoH; EncWL 1; LngCTC; OxCAmL 65; PenC AM; REn; RfGAmL 4; TwCA; WhAm 4; WhE&EA; WhNAA; WorAu 1900

Stribling, Young
[William Lawrence Stribling]
"Georgia Peach"
American. Boxer
Had 126 KOs out of 286 fights; defeated by Schmeling for heavyweight crown, 1931.
b. Dec 26, 1904 in Bainbridge, Georgia
d. Oct 2, 1933 in Macon, Georgia
Source: *BioIn 8; BoxReg, 2; WhoBox 74*

Strindberg, August
[Johan August Strindberg]
Swedish. Dramatist, Author
Developed realism, symbolism in work: *Miss Julie; The Ghost Sonata.*
b. Jan 22, 1849 in Stockholm, Sweden
d. May 14, 1912 in Stockholm, Sweden
Source: *AtlBL; Benet 87; BiD&SB; BioIn 1, 2, 3, 4, 5, 6, 7, 8, 9, 10, 11, 12, 13, 14, 15, 16, 17, 18, 19, 22; BlmGEL; CamGWoT; CasWL; CIDMEL 47, 80; CnMD; CnThe; ConAu 104, 135; CyWA 58, 97; DcArts; DcEuL; DcScanL; Dis&D; EncWB 98; EncWL 1, 2, 2S, 3; EncWT; Ent; EuAu; EuWr 7; EvEuW; FacFETw; GrFLW; IntDcT 2; LegTOT; LinLib L, S; LngCEL; LngCTC; MagSWL; MajMD 2; McGEWB; McGEWD 72, 84; ModWD; NewC; NewCBEL; NewEOp 71; NewYTBS 74; NotNAT A, B; OxCAmT 84; OxCEng 67, 85; OxCGer 76, 86, 97; OxCThe 67, 83; PenC EUR; PhDcTCA 77; PIP&P A; RAdv 14, 13-2; RComWL; REn; REnWD; RfGWoL 95; TwCA, SUP; TwCLC 1, 8, 21, 47; WhDW; WhLit; WhoTwCL; WorAl; WorAlBi; WorLitC; WrPh*

Stringer, C. Vivian
American. Basketball Coach
Women's basketball coach for University of Iowa, 1983-95, and Rutgers University, 1995—; led both teams to National Collegiate Athletic Association (NCAA) Final Four appearances, and was named National Coach of the Year three times; highest-paid women's coach in the United States.
b. 1948 in Edenborn, Pennsylvania
Source: *BioIn 21; BlkWAm; ConBlB 13; WhoAfA 9, 10, 11; WhoBlA 5, 6, 7, 8*

Stringfield, Sherry
American. Actor
Played Dr. Susan Lewis on TV's "ER," 1994-96.
b. Jun 24, 1967 in Colorado Springs, Colorado
Source: *BioIn 24; ConTFT 26*

Stritch, Elaine
American. Actor, Singer
Film, stage performer; appeared in film *September,* 1987.
b. Feb 2, 1928 in Detroit, Michigan

Source: *BiE&WWA; BioIn 16; CelR, 90; ConTFT 7; CurBio 88; EncMT; FilmgC; HalFC 88; IntMPA 92; IntWW 91; InWom SUP; MotPP; NewYTBE 70; NotNAT; OxCAmT 84; WhoAm 76, 90; WhoEnt 92; WhoHol A; WhoThe 77; WorAlBi*

Strode, Hudson
American. Author, Educator, Lecturer
Biographies include *Jefferson Davis; Confederate President,* 1959.
b. Oct 31, 1893 in Cairo, Illinois
d. Sep 22, 1976 in Tuscaloosa, Alabama
Source: *AmAu&B; BioIn 2, 4, 10; ConAu 13R, 69; REnAL; TwCA, SUP; WhNAA; WhoAm 74*

Strode, Woody
[Woodrow Wilson Woolwine Strode]
American. Actor
In films since 1941: *The Cotton Club,* 1984.
b. Jul 25, 1914 in Los Angeles, California
d. Dec 31, 1994 in Glendora, California
Source: *BioIn 13, 20, 21, 22; BlksAmF; CelR; CmMov; ConTFT 18; DrBlPA, 90; FilmEn; FilmgC; HalFC 84, 88; IntMPA 88, 92, 94; ItaFilm; NewYTBE 71; WhoHol 92, A*

Stroessner, Alfredo
Paraguayan. Political Leader
President of Paraguay, longest ruling political leader in Latin America, 1954-89; ousted in military coup.
b. Nov 3, 1912 in Encarnacion, Paraguay
Source: *BiDLAmC; BioIn 5, 8, 9, 11, 12, 13, 16; CamBiEn; ChamBiD; CurBio 58, 81; DcCPSAm; DcHiB; DcPol; DcTwHis; DicTyr; EncLatA; EncWB 98; EncyDCo; FacFETw; IntWW 74, 75, 76, 77, 78, 79, 80, 81, 82, 83, 89, 91, 93, 97, 98, 2000; LatAmLi; McGEWB; WhoWor 82, 87, 89, 91; WorDWW*

Stroh, Bernard
American. Brewer
Established brewery, 1850; introduced Bohemian-style beer.
b. 1822
d. 1882
Source: *BusPN; Entr*

Stroh, Peter W
American. Brewer
Chairman and CEO Stroh Brewery, 1982-97.
b. Dec 18, 1927 in Detroit, Michigan
Source: *BioIn 15; ConNews 85-2; Dun&B 98; St&PR 98, 99, 2000; WhoAm 88; WhoFI 87; WhoMW 92*

Stromberg, Hunt
American. Producer
Produced Nelson Eddy-Jeanette MacDonald films, *The Thin Man* series for MGM, 1930s.
b. Jul 12, 1894 in Louisville, Kentucky
d. Aug 23, 1968 in Los Angeles, California

Source: *FilmEn; FilmgC; HalFC 80, 84, 88; IntDcF 1-4, 2-4; WhAm 5*

Stromgren, Bengt Georg Daniel
Danish. Physicist, Astronomer
Pioneered studies of gas clouds in space.
b. Jan 21, 1908 in Goteborg, Sweden
d. Jul 4, 1987 in Copenhagen, Denmark
Source: *BiESc; BioIn 2, 14, 15, 16; FacFETw; IntWW 74, 75, 76, 77, 78, 79, 80; McGCEnS; McGMS 80; NewYTBS 87; RanHWDS; WhAm 9; WhoAm 74, 76; WhoWor 74, 78*

Strong, Anna Louise
American. Journalist
Advocated communism in her newsletter, *Letter from China.*
b. Nov 24, 1885 in Friend, Nebraska
d. Mar 29, 1970 in Beijing, China
Source: *AmAu&B; AmNatBi; AmWomWr; BioIn 1, 2, 3, 4, 8, 9, 11, 13, 14, 15, 19, 22; CamDcAB; ConAu 29R; CurBio 49, 70; DcAmB S8; EncAJ; FemiCLE; InWom, SUP; JrnUS; LibW; NewYTBE 70; NotAW MOD; ObitT 1961; OhA&B; TwCA, SUP; WhAm 5; WhNAA; WomWWA 14; WorAu 1900*

Strong, Austin
American. Author
Wrote play *Seventh Heaven,* 1920, which was filmed, 1937.
b. Jan 18, 1881 in San Francisco, California
d. Sep 17, 1952 in Nantucket, Massachusetts
Source: *AmAu&B; AmNatBi; BenetAL 91; BioIn 1, 3; LngCTC; ModWD; NotNAT B; OxCAmL 65, 83; REnAL; WhAm 3; WhLit; WhNAA; WhThe*

Strong, James Matthew
Irish. Politician
Member, N Ireland Parliament, killed with father, by IRA terrorists.
b. Jun 21, 1932
d. Jan 21, 1981 in Armagh, Northern Ireland
Source: *AnObit 1981; BioIn 12*

Strong, Josiah
American. Clergy, Social Reformer
Developed Christian Socialism and was a leading religious and social figure in the United States around the turn of the twentieth century.
b. Jan 19, 1847 in Naperville, Illinois
d. Apr 28, 1916 in New York, New York
Source: *Alli SUP; AmAu&B; AmNatBi; ApCAB; BenetAL 91; BiDChrM; BioIn 16, 17, 19; CamDcAB; DcAmAu; DcAmB; DcAmDH 80, 89; DcAmReB 1, 2; DcAmSR; DcNAA; EncAB-H 1974, 1996; EncARH; EncWB 98; HarEnUS; NatCAB 9; OhA&B; OxCAmH; OxCAmL 65, 83, 95; PeoHis; RelLAm 1, 2; WebAB 74, 79; WhAm 1*

Strong, Ken(neth E)
American. Football Player
Halfback-kicker, 1929-39, 1944, 1947, mostly with NY Giants; led NFL in field goals, 1944; Hall of Fame, 1967.
b. Aug 6, 1906 in West Haven, Connecticut
d. Oct 5, 1979 in New York, New York
Source: *Ballpl 90; BioIn 12, 17; LegTOT; NewYTBS 79; WhoFtbl 74; WhoSpor*

Strong, Maurice Frederick
Canadian. Environmentalist
Known for his environmetal activism; secretary-general, UN Conference on Environment and Development, 1990-92 (better known as the Earth Summit).
b. Apr 29, 1929 in Oak Lake, Manitoba, Canada
Source: *BioIn 9, 10, 11, 13, 15, 16; BlueB 76; CanWW 83, 89; CurBio 73; IntWW 91; News 93-1; NewYTBE 71; Who 92, 99, 2000; WhoAm 74, 76, 78, 80, 82, 84, 86, 94, 95; WhoCanB 86; WhoCanF 86; WhoFI 81, 83, 94; WhoIntA 2; WhoScEn 96; WhoUN 75, 92; WhoWest 84; WhoWor 98*

Strong, Philip Duffield
American. Author
Wrote *State Fair,* 1932; made into film several times.
b. Jan 27, 1899 in Keosauqua, Iowa
d. Apr 26, 1957 in Washington, Connecticut
Source: *AmAu&B; AuBYP 2S; ConAmA*

Stronge, Norman, Sir
[Charles Norman Lockhart Stronge]
Irish. Politician
Speaker of House of Commons, N Ireland, 1945-69; killed in terrorist attack on his home.
b. Jul 23, 1894 in Bryansford, Northern Ireland
d. Jan 21, 1981 in Armagh, Northern Ireland
Source: *AnObit 1981; BioIn 12; IntWW 74, 75, 76, 77, 78, 79, 80; Who 74; WhoWor 74, 76, 78*

Stroud, Robert Franklin
"Birdman of Alcatraz"
American. Ornithologist, Criminal
60 yrs. in prison for murder portrayed in film starring Burt Lancaster, *Birdman of Alcatraz,* 1961.
b. 1890 in Seattle, Washington
d. Nov 21, 1963 in Springfield, Missouri
Source: *BioIn 4, 6; WebAB 74*

Strougal, Lubomir
Czech. Political Leader
Prime minister of Czechoslovakia, 1970-88.
b. Oct 19, 1924 in Veseli nad Luznici, Czechoslovakia
Source: *BioIn 8, 9; IntWW 74, 75, 76, 77, 78, 79, 80, 81, 82, 83, 89, 91, 93; IntYB 81, 82; WhoGov 72; WhoSocC 78;*

WhoSoCE 89; WhoWor 74, 76, 78, 80, 82, 84, 87, 89, 91

Stroup, Thomas Bradley
American. Educator, Author
Wrote *Religious Rite and Ceremony in Milton's Poetry,* 1968.
b. Dec 21, 1903 in Fletcher, North Carolina
Source: *DrAS 74E, 78E, 82E*

Strouse, Charles
American. Composer
Won Tonys for *Bye Bye Birdie,* 1959; *Applause,* 1970; *Annie,* 1977.
b. Jun 7, 1928 in New York, New York
Source: *AmPS; AmSong; ASCAP 66, 80; BakBD 84; BakDcM; BiDAmM; BiE&WWA; BioIn 9, 10, 12; CelR 90; ConAmC 82; ConTFT 1, 11; EncMT; Music; NewAmDM; NewCBMT; NewGrDA 86; NewGrDM 80; NotNAT; OxCAmT 84; OxCPMus; PopAmC SUP; WhoAm 74, 76, 78, 80, 82, 84, 86, 88, 90; WhoThe 72, 77, 81; WorAl; WorAlBi*

Strouse, Norman H(ulbert)
American. Advertising Executive
Became pres. of J Walter Thompson in 1955.
b. Nov 4, 1906 in Olympia, Washington
d. Jan 19, 1993 in Saint Helena, California
Source: *BioIn 5, 6, 7, 8; ChhPo S1; CurBio 60, 93N; St&PR 75*

Strout, Richard Lee
American. Journalist
Known for political analyses in *Christian Science Monitor* and weekly column "TRB From Washington" in *New Republic.*
b. Mar 14, 1898 in Cohoes, New York
d. Aug 19, 1990 in Washington, District of Columbia
Source: *AmAu&B; BiDAmJo; BiDAmNC; BioIn 8, 10, 11, 12, 13, 16, 17, 24; ConAu 69, 132; CurBio 80, 90, 90N; NewYTBS 90; ScrEAmL 2; WhAm 10; WhoAm 74, 76, 78, 80, 82, 84, 86; WhoPul*

Strudwick, Shepperd
American. Actor
Career began in 1928; over 200 roles in plays, movies, TV.
b. Sep 22, 1907 in Hillsboro, North Carolina
d. Jan 15, 1983 in New York, New York
Source: *BiE&WWA; BioIn 13; FilmEn; FilmgC; ForYSC; HalFC 80; IntMPA 75, 76, 77, 78, 79, 80, 81, 82, 84; LegTOT; MovMk; NewYTBS 83; NotNAT; WhAm 8; WhoAm 74, 76, 82; WhoHol A; WhoThe 72, 77, 81*

Strug, Kerri
American. Gymnast
Member of the 1996 U.S. Olympic gymnastic team; even though she had just sprained her ankle on the same move, completed a performance on the

vault and helped win the gold medal, simultaneously becoming known for her determination and strength.
b. Nov 19, 1977 in Tucson, Arizona
Source: *BioIn 22, 23, 24; ConAu 169; News 97, 97-3; SmATA 108; WhoAm 99; WhoAmW 97, 99; WhoWor 97, 98, 99, 2000*

Struss, Karl
American. Filmmaker
Won first Oscar given for cinematography, 1927.
b. Nov 30, 1886 in New York, New York
d. Dec 16, 1981 in Santa Monica, California
Source: *AnObit 1981; BioIn 12, 19, 22; CmMov; FilmEn; FilmgC; ICPEnP; IntDcF 1-4, 2-4; MacBEP; NewYTBS 81; WhoHrs 80; WorEFlm*

Struther, Jan
[Joyce Maxtone Graham]
English. Author
Best known for *Mrs. Miniver*, 1940.
b. Jun 6, 1901 in London, England
d. Jul 20, 1953 in New York, New York
Source: *BioIn 1, 3, 4, 16, 22; CamBiEn; ChamBiD; ChhPo, S1, S2; CurBio 41, 53; DcPseud; EncAB-A 24; EncBrWW; EngPo; FemiCLE; InWom; LngCTC; NewC; REn; TwCA, SUP; WhAm 3; WorAu 1900*

Struthers, Sally Anne
American. Actor
Played Gloria on "All in the Family," 1971-78; won two Emmys.
b. Jul 28, 1948 in Portland, Oregon
Source: *BkPepl; ConTFT 2, 7; CurBio 74; HalFC 84, 88; IntMPA 92; InWom SUP; NewYTBE 72; WhoAm 78, 80, 82, 84, 86, 88, 90; WhoHol A; WhoTelC; WorAl; WorAlBi*

Strutt, Joseph
English. Author
Wrote *Manners, Customs, Habits of People of England,* 1774-76.
b. Oct 27, 1749 in Chelmsford, England
d. Oct 16, 1802 in London, England
Source: *Alli; BioIn 3, 11; BkIE; BritAu; CamGLE; DcBiPP; DcBrECP; DcBrWA; DcEnL; DcLEL; DcNaB; DcPup; NewC; NewCBEL; OxCEng 67, 85, 95; REn*

Struve, Friedrich Georg Wilhelm von
Russian. Astronomer, Scientist
Geodesist and astronomer known for observing binary stars and for measuring the meridional arc from the north coast of Norway to Ismail on the Danube.
b. Apr 15, 1793 in Altona, Germany
d. Nov 23, 1864, Russia
Source: *AsBiEn; BioIn 14, 16; DcBiPP; DcScB; McGCEnS; McGEWB; RanHWDS; WorAl*

Struve, Otto
American. Astronomer, Educator
Director, Yerkes and McDonald Observatories, 1932-47.
b. Aug 12, 1897 in Kharkov, Russia
d. Apr 6, 1963 in Berkeley, California
Source: *AmNatBi; AsBiEn; BiDSovU; BiESc; BioIn 2, 3, 4, 5, 6, 7; CamBiEn; ChamBiD; DcAmB S7; DcScB; InSci; LarDcSc; McGMS 80; WebAB 74, 79; WebBD 83; WhAm 4*

Stryper
[Oz Fox; Timothy Gaines; Richard Martinez; Michael Sweet; Robert Sweet]
American. Music Group
Christian rock band that tosses miniature Bibles into the audience during concerts.
Source: *Alli; BiDrAPA 89; BioIn 16, 17; ConMus 2; GrMetD; WhoHisp 91, 92, 94*

Stuart, Bruce
Canadian. Hockey Player
Amateur player for several teams, early 1900s; Hall of Fame, 1961.
b. 1882 in Ottawa, Ontario, Canada
d. Oct 28, 1961 in Ottawa, Ontario, Canada
Source: *WhoHcky 73*

Stuart, Charles Edward Louis Philip
"Bonnie Prince Charlie"
English.
Grandson of James II who unsuccessfully tried to seize Hanoverian throne, 1745.
b. Dec 31, 1720 in Rome, Italy
d. Jan 31, 1788 in Rome, Italy
Source: *Alli; McGEWB; NewC; REn; WhoMilH 76*

Stuart, Gilbert Charles
American. Artist
Noted for three portraits of George Washington, 1795-96.
b. Dec 3, 1755 in North Kingstown, Rhode Island
d. Jul 9, 1828 in Boston, Massachusetts
Source: *AmBi; AmCulL; ApCAB; AtlBL; BriEAA; CamBiEn; CamDcAB; ChamBiD; DcAmB; DcArts; DcBiPP; Drake; EncAB-H 1974; HarEnUS; IlBEAAW; McGEWB; NatCAB 5; NewYHSD; OxCAmL 65; REn; REnAL; TwCBDA; WebAB 74, 79; WhAm HS; WorAl*

Stuart, Hod
[Horace Hodgson Stuart]
Canadian. Hockey Player
Defenseman, 1898-1907, with several amateur teams; Hall of Fame, 1945; drowned.
b. 1880 in Ottawa, Ontario, Canada
d. Jun 23, 1907 in Belleville, Ontario, Canada
Source: *WhoHcky 73*

Stuart, James
English. Architect, Artist
Published *The Antiquities of Athens,* 1762, which had first illustrations of Greek architecture; work spurred the classic revival period.
b. 1713
d. 1788
Source: *Alli; BiDBrA; BlkwCE; DcArch; DcArts; DcBiPP; DcBrECP; DcNaB; EncHiCA; IntDcAr; MacEA; McGDA; NewCBEL; NewCol 75; OxCArt; PenDiDA 89; WhoArch*

Stuart, Jeb
[James Ewell Brown Stuart]
American. Army Officer
Commanded all Confederate cavalry, 1862-64.
b. Feb 6, 1833 in Patrick County, Virginia
d. May 12, 1864 in Richmond, Virginia
Source: *AmBi; ApCAB; BiDConf; BioIn 1, 3, 4, 5, 6, 7, 8, 9, 12, 15, 18, 19, 20, 21, 23, 24; CamBiEn; CivWDc; DcAmB; DcAmMiB; EncAB-H 1974, 1996; EncSoH; GenMudB; HarEnMi; HarEnUS; HisWorL; McGEWB; NatCAB 4; OxCAmH; TwCBDA; WebAB 74, 79; WebAMB; WhAm HS; WhCiWar; WhoMilH 76*

Stuart, Jesse Hilton
American. Author, Poet
Prolific regional writer named poet laureate of KY, 1954; best-known work: *Man with a Bull-Tongue Plow,* 1934.
b. Aug 8, 1907 in W-Hollow, Kentucky
d. Feb 17, 1984 in Ironton, Ohio
Source: *AmAu&B; AmNov; Au&Wr 71; AuBYP 3; ConAu 5R; ConLC 14; ConNov 72, 76; CurBio 84; CyWA 58; OxCAmL 65; RAdv 1; REn; SixAP; SmATA 2; TwCA SUP; TwCWr; WhAm 8; WhoAm 82*

Stuart, Kenneth James
American. Illustrator, Art Director
Art editor *Saturday Evening Post,* 1943-62; art director, Reader's Digest Assn., 1962-77.
b. Sep 21, 1905 in Milwaukee, Wisconsin
d. Feb 27, 1993 in Norwalk, Connecticut
Source: *BioIn 18; WhAmArt 85; WhoAm 74, 76, 78, 80, 82, 84, 86, 88, 90, 92, 94, 95, 96; WhoAmA 91, 93; WhoE 85, 86, 89; WhoWor 80*

Stuart, Lyle
American. Publisher
Pres. of Lyle Stuart, Inc., 1954-89; wrote *The Secret Life of Walter Winchell,* 1953.
b. Aug 11, 1922 in New York, New York
Source: *BioIn 6, 8, 9, 11; CelR; ConAu 81; DcAmSR; IntWW 91, 93, 97, 98, 2000; WhoAm 78, 80, 82, 84, 86, 88, 90, 92, 94, 95, 96, 97, 98, 99, 2000; WhoEnt 98; WhsWeAm 98*

Stuart, Marty
[John Marty Stuart]
American. Singer, Songwriter, Musician
Country and bluegrass singer, guitarist
  and mandolinist; debut album, *Ridge
  Runner*, 1982; won 1993 Grammy for
  "The Whiskey Ain't Workin'".
b. Sep 30, 1958 in Philadelphia,
  Mississippi
Source: *AllMGCo; BgBkCoM; ConMus
9; LegTOT; WhoAm 94, 95, 96, 97, 98,
99, 2000; WhoEnt 98; WhoNeCM*

Stuart, Mel
American. Director
Won Emmys for "The Roots of
  Madness," 1967; "Making of the
  President," 1970.
b. Sep 2, 1928 in New York, New York
Source: *FilmgC; HalFC 88; LesBEnT
92; MiSFD 9; NewYTET; VarWW 85;
WhoAm 80, 82*

Stuart, Ruth McEnery
American. Author
Wrote Southern life tales in dialect: *In
  Simpkinsville*, 1897.
b. May 21, 1849 in Marksville,
  Louisiana
d. May 6, 1917 in White Plains, New
  York
Source: *AmNatBi; DcLB 202;
NinCAWW; NotAW; REn*

Stubbs, George
English. Artist
Animal painter, noted for drawings of
  horses.
b. Aug 24, 1724 in Liverpool, England
d. Jul 10, 1806 in London, England
Source: *Alli; AtlBL; Benet 87; BioIn 1,
2, 3, 4, 5, 6, 7, 9, 10, 11, 13, 14, 15;
BlkwCE; BritAS; CamBiEn; ChamBiD;
DcArts; DcBiPP; DcBrECP; DcBrWA;
DcNaB; EncEnl; IntDcAA 90; LegTOT;
LiveWoA; McGDA; NewCol 75; OxCArt;
OxCBrHi; OxDcArt; WhDW; WorAl;
WorAlBi*

Stubbs, Levi
[The Four Tops]
American. Singer
Original member of group.
b. Jun 6, 1936 in Detroit, Michigan
Source: *BioIn 15; WhoBlA 7; WhoRocM
82*

Stuckey, Williamson Sylvester
American. Businessman
Opened first candy shop, 1938; became
  nat. restaurant chain, with stores off
  US highways, after WW II.
b. 1909
d. Jan 7, 1977 in Eastman, Georgia
Source: *BioIn 8, 11; NewYTBS 77*

Studds, Gerry E(astman)
American. Politician
Dem. congressman from MA, 1973-83,
  1983-96; censured by House, Jul 1983,
  for homosexual affair with page.
b. May 12, 1937 in Mineola, New York

Source: *AlmAP 92; BiDrUSC 89;
CmpQue; CngDr 87, 89; GayLesB;
LesBEnT; WhoAm 74, 76, 78, 80, 82, 84,
86, 88, 90, 92, 94, 95, 96, 97, 98, 99,
2000; WhoAmP 73, 75, 77, 79, 81, 83,
85, 87, 89, 91, 93, 95, 97, 1999; WhoE
77, 79, 81, 83, 85, 86, 89, 91, 93, 95,
97, 99; WhoGov 75, 77*

Studebaker, Clement
American. Manufacturer
Formed wagon co., 1852; experimented
  with autos, 1897; major product, 1902.
b. Mar 12, 1831 in Pinetown,
  Pennsylvania
d. Nov 27, 1901 in South Bend, Indiana
Source: *AmNatBi; BiDAmBL 83;
CamBiEn; CamDcAB; DcAmB; EncWM;
NatCAB 11; WebAB 74, 79; WhAm 1;
WorAl; WorAlBi*

Studebaker, John Mohler
American. Auto Manufacturer
Joined brother's firm, 1858, pres. from
  1901.
b. Oct 10, 1833 in Gettysburg,
  Pennsylvania
d. Mar 16, 1917
Source: *AmNatBi; BioIn 1; NatCAB 11;
WhAm 1*

Studer, Cheryl
American. Opera Singer
Internationally known versatile soprano.
b. Oct 24, 1955 in Midland, Michigan
Source: *BakBD 92; BakBDTw; BakDcM;
CurBio 92; IntWW 97, 98, 2000;
IntWWM 90; IntWWW 2; NewGrDO;
NewYTBS 91; OxDcOp; WhoAm 92;
WhoEnt 92, 98*

Studi, Wes
[Wesley Studie]
American. Actor
Appeared in films *Dances With Wolves,
  The Last of the Mohicans*, and
  Geronimo.
b. c. 1944 in Nofire Hollow, Oklahoma
Source: *ConTFT 16; EncWB 98; News
94, 94-3*

Stuhldreher, Harry A
[Four Horsemen of Notre Dame]
American. Football Player
All-America quarterback under Knute
  Rockne at Notre Dame, 1922-24.
b. Oct 14, 1901 in Massillon, Ohio
d. Jan 22, 1965 in Pittsburgh,
  Pennsylvania
Source: *DcAmB S7; OhA&B; WhoFtbl
74; WhScrn 83*

Stulberg, Louis
American. Labor Union Official
Pres. of International Ladies Garment
  Workers Union, 1966-75.
b. Apr 14, 1901, Poland
d. Dec 14, 1977 in New York, New
  York
Source: *BiDAmL; BiDAmLL; BioIn 5,
11; NewYTBS 77; WhAm 7; WhoAm 74,
76; WhoLab 76; WhoWorJ 72, 78*

Stumpf, Richard J
American. Engineer
Co-inventor, Sensurround; won two
  Oscars for sound engineering, 1974,
  1981.
b. Oct 15, 1926 in Glendale, California
Source: *VarWW 85*

Sturgeon, Theodore Hamilton
[Edward Hamilton Waldo]
American. Author
Books include *My People Is the Enemy*,
  1964.
b. Feb 26, 1918 in Staten Island, New
  York
d. May 8, 1985 in Eugene, Oregon
Source: *AmAu&B; BioIn 7, 10, 12;
ConAu 81; LinLib L; MajTwCW 2;
OxCTwCL; PenC AM; REnAL;
SJGHorW; WhoAm 74, 76, 78, 80, 82,
84; WorAl; WorAu 1950*

Sturgeon, William
English. Physicist
Developed the electromagnet.
b. May 22, 1783 in Whittington, England
d. Dec 4, 1850 in Prestwich, England
Source: *Alli; AsBiEn; BiESc; BioIn 2, 3,
14; CamBiEn; CamDcSc; CelCen;
ChamBiD; DcBiPP; DcInv; DcNaB;
DcScB; InSci; LarDcSc; McGCEnS;
RanHWDS; WhDW*

Sturges, Preston
[Edmond P Biden]
American. Director, Screenwriter
Wrote, directed Oscar-winning *The Great
  McGinty*, 1940.
b. Aug 29, 1898 in Chicago, Illinois
d. Aug 6, 1959 in New York, New York
Source: *AmFD; AmNatBi; BenetAL 91;
BiDFilm, 81, 94; BioIn 1, 4, 5, 7, 8, 9,
10, 12, 13; CamBiEn; CamDcAB;
ChamBiD; CmMov; ConAu 114, 149;
CurBio 41, 59; DcAmB S6; DcArts;
DcFM; DcLB 26; DcPseud; EncAFC;
EncWB 2-19; FacFETw; FilmEn;
FilmgC; HalFC 80, 84, 88; IIWWHD 1;
IntDcF 1-2, 2-2; LegTOT; MiSFD 9N;
ModWD; MovMk; NatCAB 61; ObitT
1951; OxCFilm; REnAL; TwCLC 48;
WhAm 3; WhThe; WorEFlm; WorFDir 1*

Sturm, Charles Francois
[Jacques Charles Francois Sturm]
French. Mathematician
Sturm's theorem, concerning the theory
  of equations, was named in honor of
  his work.
b. Sep 29, 1803 in Geneva, Switzerland
d. Dec 18, 1855 in Paris, France
Source: *DcBiPP; DcScB; InSci; LarDcSc*

Sturt, Charles
English. Explorer, Government Official
Led three major expeditions into the
  interior of eastern Australia.
b. Apr 28, 1795, India
d. Jun 16, 1869 in Cheltenham, England
Source: *BioIn 2, 3, 6, 8, 10, 18, 24;
CamBiEn; DcNaB; EncWB 98; Expl 93;
ExplAnT; McGEWB; NewCBEL;
OxCAusL; WhDW; WhWE*

Sturtevant, Alfred Henry
American. Geneticist
Responsible for mapping specific genes
of chromosomes in fruit flies.
b. Nov 21, 1891 in Jacksonville, Illinois
d. Apr 5, 1970 in Pasadena, California
Source: *AmDec 1910; AmNatBi; BiESc;
BioIn 6, 8, 9, 20; CamBiEn; CamDcAB;
CamDcSc; ChamBiD; ConAu 158;
DcScB; LarDcSc; McGMS 80;
RanHWDS; WhAm 5; WorScD*

Sturtzel, Howard Allison
[Paul Annixter]
American. Children's Author
Wrote nature novels with wife: *Windigo*,
1963.
b. Jun 25, 1894 in Minneapolis,
Minnesota
Source: *BioIn 6, 9; ConAu 1R, 6NR,
70NR; DcLP 87A; SmATA 1*

Sturtzel, Jane Levington
American. Children's Author
With husband, wrote nature novels: *The
Year of the She-Grizzly*, 1978.
b. Jun 22, 1903 in Detroit, Michigan
Source: *AuBYP 3; BioIn 9; ConAu 1R,
6NR; DcLP 87A; PenNWW A; SmATA 1*

Stuyvesant, Peter
[Petrus Stuyvesant]
Dutch. Colonial Figure
One-legged governor of New
Amsterdam, now NY, 1647-64.
b. 1610 in Scherpenzeel, Netherlands
d. Feb 1672 in New York, New York
Source: *AmBi; AmNatBi; DcAmB;
EncAB-H 1974; EncAInd; EncCRAm;
EncWB 98; HisWorL; LegTOT;
McGEWB; RComAH; REn; REnAL;
WebAB 74, 79; WhAm HS; WhNaAH;
WorAl*

Stydahar, Joe
[Joseph Leo Stydahar]
''Jumbo Joe''
American. Football Player
Four-time all-pro defensive tackle,
Chicago, 1936-42, 1945-46; Hall of
Fame, 1967.
b. Mar 17, 1912 in Kaylor, Pennsylvania
d. Mar 23, 1977 in Beckley, West
Virginia
Source: *BioIn 6, 8, 11, 17; LegTOT;
NewYTBS 77; WhoFtbl 74*

Styles, Re
[The Tubes]
American. Singer
Dancer, singer with The Tubes since late
1960s.
b. Mar 3, 1950

Styne, Jule
[Julius Kerwin Stein]
American. Songwriter
Won best song Oscar for ''Three Coins
in the Fountain,'' 1954; other songs
included in films ''I'll Walk Alone,''
1945; ''Funny Girl,'' 1968.
b. Dec 31, 1905 in London, England

d. Sep 20, 1994 in New York, New
York
Source: *AmNatBi; AmPS; AmSong;
ASCAP 66, 80; BakBD 78, 84, 92;
BakDcM; BestMus; BiDAmM;
BiE&WWA; BioIn 1, 5, 6, 9, 10, 11, 12,
13, 14, 15, 16, 20, 21, 22; CamBiEn;
CamDcAB; CelR, 90; CmpEPM;
ConAmC 76, 82; ConMus 21; ConTFT
4, 13; CurBio 83, 94N; DcPseud;
EncMT; FacFETw; FilmEn; FilmgC;
HalFC 80, 84, 88; IntMPA 77, 80, 92,
94; IntWW 89, 91, 93; LegTOT; Music;
NewAmDM; NewCBMT; NewGrDA 86;
NewGrDM 80; NewGrDO; News 95, 95-
1; NewYTBS 87, 94; NotNAT; OxCAmT
84; OxCPMus; PopAmC, SUP; Songw;
Sw&Ld C; WhAm 11; WhoAm 74, 76,
78, 80, 82, 84, 86, 88, 90, 92, 94;
WhoThe 72, 77, 81; WhoWor 74; WorAl;
WorAlBi*

Styron, William Clark, Jr.
American. Author
Won Pulitzer for *The Confessions of Nat
Turner*, 1968; wrote novel *Sophie's
Choice*, 1979, filmed, 1982.
b. Jun 11, 1925 in Newport News,
Virginia
Source: *Benet 87; BenetAL 91; BioIn 15,
16; BroV; CamGLE; CamHAL; CasWL;
CelR 90; ConAu 5NR, 5R, 33NR; ConLC
15, 60; ConNov 86, 91; CurBio 86;
CyWA 89; DrAPF 91; EncWB;
FacFETw; FifSWrA; IntAu&W 91;
IntvTCA 2; IntWW 91; MajTwCW 1;
ModAL 4S1, 4S2; OxCAmL 65; PenC
AM; PeoHis; RAdv 1, 13-1; REn;
REnAL; RfGAmL 87; TwCRHW 90;
TwCWr; WhoAm 86, 90; WhoE 91;
WhoUSWr 88; WhoWor 87, 91;
WhoWrEP 89; WorAlBi; WrDr 86, 92;
WrPh*

Styx
[John Curulewski; Dennis DeYoung;
Chuck Panozzo; John Panozzo;
Tommy Shaw; James Young]
American. Music Group
Hard pop group formed 1963, popular
among young teens; hit single
''Babe,'' 1979.
Source: *Alli; AntBDN Q; ASCAP 80;
BillEnR; ConMuA 80A; DcCanB 1;
DcNaB; EncPR&S 89; EncRk 88;
EncRkSt; Film 1; GrMetD; InB&W 80;
NewGrDA 86; NewYTBS 96; OxCCan;
PenEncP; RkOn 78, 85, 85A; RolSEnR
83; WhoHol 92; WhoRock 81; WhoRocM
82*

Suarez, Francisco
Spanish. Philosopher, Theologian
Laid the foundation for a theory of
international law and developed an
eclectic metaphysical theory.
b. Jan 5, 1548 in Granada, Spain
d. Sep 25, 1617 in Lisbon, Portugal
Source: *BioIn 2; CamBiEn; CasWL;
DcBiPP; DcCathB; EncEth; EncWB 98;
HisDcSE; InSci; LuthC 75; McGEWB;
OxCLaw; OxCPhil; OxCSpan; RAdv 14,
13-4*

Suarez, Xavier Louis
Cuban. Politician, Lawyer
Mayor, Miami, FL, 1985-93, 1997—;
first Cuban-American mayor in Miami.
b. May 21, 1949 in Las Villas, Cuba
Source: *ConNews 86-2; NewYTBS 85;
WhoAm 86, 88, 90, 92, 94, 95, 96, 97,
98; WhoAmL 94, 96, 98; WhoAmP 87,
89, 91, 93, 95, 97, 1999; WhoHisp 92;
WhoSSW 88, 91, 93, 95*

Suarez Gonzales, Adolfo
Spanish. Political Leader
Prime minister, 1976-81.
b. Sep 25, 1932 in Cebreros, Spain
Source: *CurBio 77; WhoWor 84, 91;
WorAl; WorAlBi*

Suazo Cordova, Roberto
Honduran. Politician, Physician
Became president of Honduras in 1982
after military rulers agreed to restore
civilian government; he promoted the
democratic process and moderate
economic reform, and cooperated with
U.S. military build-up in the country.
b. Mar 17, 1927 in La Paz, Honduras
Source: *BioIn 13; DcCPCAm; EncWB,
98; LatAmLi; WhoWor 84*

Subic, Joseph, Jr.
[The Hostages]
American. Hostage
One of 52 held by terrorists, Nov 1979-
Jan 1981.
b. 1957?
Source: *NewYTBS 81*

Sublette, William L
American. Explorer, Naturalist
Established firm to transport people
across Rocky Mts., 1823-30.
b. 1799 in Lincoln County, Kentucky
d. Jul 23, 1845 in Pittsburgh,
Pennsylvania
Source: *DcAmB; WhAm HS*

Suchocka, Hanna
Polish. Politician
Prime minister, Poland, 1992-93.
b. Apr 3, 1946 in Pleszew, Poland
Source: *CurBio 94; HisDcPo; IntWW 93,
97, 98, 2000; IntWWW 2; NewYTBS 93;
ProfiWG 98; WhoWor 93, 95, 99, 2000*

Suckling, John
English. Poet, Dramatist
One of the Cavalier poets, sophisticated
courtiers loyal to Charles I.
b. Feb 1609
d. 1642
Source: *Alli; Benet 87, 96; BiCoLiE;
BiD&SB; BiDRP&D; BioIn 2, 3, 5, 12,
15, 16, 17, 19, 21, 24; BlmGEL; BritAu;
BritWr 2; CamBiEn; CamGEL;
CamGLE; CasWL; ChamBiD; Chambr
1; ChhPo; CnE&AP; CnThe; CroE&S;
CrtT 1, 4; CyWA 97; DcArts; DcBiPP;
DcEnA; DcEnL; DcEuL; DcLB 58, 126;
DcLEL; DcNaB, C; EncWB 98; EvLB;
GrWrEL P; LngCEL; McGEWB; MouLC
1; NewC; NewCBEL; OxCEng 67, 85,*

95; OxCThe 67; PenC ENG; REn;
REnWD; RfGEnL 91; WebE&AL

Suckow, Ruth
American. Author
Books describe small-town Iowa: *The*
   Folks, 1934.
b. Aug 6, 1892 in Hawarden, Iowa
d. Jan 23, 1960 in Claremont, California
Source: *AmAu&B; AmNatBi; AmNov;*
AmWomPl; AmWomWr; ArtclWW 2;
BenetAL 91; BioAmW; BioIn 2, 4, 5, 7,
8, 12, 17, 22; ChhPo; CnDAL; ConAmA;
ConAmL; ConAu 113; CyWA 97; DcLB
9, 102; DcLEL; EncALit; EncFWF;
FemiCLE; FifWWr; GrWrEL N; InWom,
SUP; LngCTC; ModWoWr; NotAW
MOD; OxCAmL 65, 83, 95; PeoHis;
REn; REnAL; RfGAmL 4, 87, 94; ShSCr
18; TwCA, SUP; TwCWW 91; WhoAmW
58; WorAu 1900

Sucre, Antonio J. de
Venezuelan. Revolutionary
Pres. of Bolivia, 1825-28.
b. 1795 in Cumana, Venezuela
d. Jun 4, 1830 in Pasto, Colombia
Source: *ApCAB; Drake; REn*

Sudarkasa, Niara
[Gloria Albertha Marshall]
American. University Administrator
First woman pres. of historically black
   Lincoln U, PA 1987—.
b. Aug 14, 1938 in Fort Lauderdale,
   Florida
Source: *AmWomSc 1950; BioIn 16;*
BlkWAm; ConBlB 4; IntWWW 2;
NotBlAS; NotBlAW 1; WhoAfA 9, 10, 11,
12; WhoAm 88, 90, 94; WhoAmW 91,
93, 97; WhoBlA 4, 5, 6, 7, 8; WhoWor
96

Sudermann, Hermann
German. Dramatist
Works concerned ideas of honor,
   reputation: *Honor,* 1893; *St. John's*
   Fire, 1900.
b. Sep 30, 1857 in Matziken, Prussia
d. Nov 21, 1928 in Berlin, Germany
Source: *BbD; Benet 87, 96; BiD&SB;*
BioIn 1, 5, 18, 22; CamGWoT; CasWL;
ChamBiD; ClDMEL 47, 80; CnMD;
ConAu 107; CyWA 58, 97; DcLB 118;
Dis&D; EncWB 98; EncWT; Ent;
EvEuW; IntDcT 2; LinLib L, S; LngCTC;
McGEWB; McGEWD 72, 84; ModWD;
NewC; NewCBEL; NotNAT B; OxCEng
67; OxCGer 76, 86, 97; OxCThe 67, 83;
PenC EUR; REn; TwCA, SUP; TwCLC
15; WhDW; WorAu 1900

Sue, Eugene Joseph Marie
French. Author, Physician
Wrote romances *The Wandering Jew,*
   1845; *Mysteries of Paris,* 1842.
b. Jan 20, 1804 in Paris, France
d. Aug 3, 1857 in Annecy, France
Source: *BbD; BiD&SB; CasWL; CyWA*
58; DcBiA; DcEuL; EncMys; EuAu;
EvEuW; NewC; OxCEng 67; OxCFr;
OxCThe 67; PenC EUR; REn

Suenens, Leon Joseph, Cardinal
American. Religious Leader
Primate, Belgium, 1961-79.
b. Jul 6, 1904
d. May 6, 1996 in Brussels, Belgium
Source: *BioIn 6, 7, 8, 9, 10, 11, 12, 13,*
20; ConAu 61, 152; CurBio 96N;
WhoWor 74, 76, 78, 80, 82

Suesse, Dana Nadine
''Girl Gershwin''
American. Composer, Musician
Child prodigy pianist; composed
   orchestral pieces as well as pop tunes:
   ''You Oughta Be in Pictures,'' 1934.
b. Dec 3, 1911 in Shreveport, Louisiana
d. Oct 16, 1987 in New York, New York
Source: *BakBD 84; CmpEPM; ConAmC*
82; CurBio 40, 88; InWom, SUP

Suetonius
Roman. Biographer
Wrote lives of Roman literary figures,
   biographies of first 11 emperors.
b. 69?
d. 140?
Source: *AncWr; AtlBL; BiCoLiE;*
BiD&SB; CasWL; ChamBiD; CyWA 97;
DcArts; DcLB 211; NewC; OxCEng 67;
RAdv 14, 13-2, 13-3; REn; RfGWoL 95;
WorAl; WorAlBi

Suggs, Louise
American. Golfer
Turned pro, 1948; has 50 LPGA wins
   including US Women's Open, 1949,
   1952; Hall of Fame, 1961.
b. Sep 7, 1923 in Lithia Springs, Georgia
Source: *BiDAmSp OS; BioIn 1, 6;*
CurBio 62; EncWomS; EncWoSp;
InWom, SUP; LegTOT; WhoGolf;
WhoSpor

Sugiura, Kanematsu
American. Scientist
Pioneer in development of chemotherapy
   for cancer treatment, 1912.
b. Jun 5, 1892 in Tsushima-Shi, Japan
d. Oct 21, 1979 in White Plains, New
   York
Source: *AmMWSc 79; DcAmB S10;*
NewYTBS 79

Suharto
Indonesian. Political Leader
Pres., Indonesia, 1968-98.
b. Jun 8, 1921 in Kemusa, Dutch East
   Indies
Source: *BioIn 10, 14, 23; CamBiEn;*
CurBio 67; EncWB 98; EncyDCo;
FacFETw; FarE&A 79; IntWW 80, 81,
82, 83, 91; IntYB 78; NewYTBS 91; Who
92; WhoWor 87, 91, 98; WorAlBi

Suhl, Yuri
American. Author
Wrote on Holocaust for children, adults:
   On the Other Side of the Gate, 1975.
b. Jul 30, 1908 in Podhajce, Poland
d. Nov 8, 1986 in New York, New York
Source: *AuBYP 2S, 3; BioIn 11, 15, 16,*
19; ChlLR 2; ConAu 2NR, 45, 121;

IntAu&W 76; SmATA 1AS, 8, 50N;
WhoWorJ 72, 78

Sui, Anna
American. Fashion Designer
Launched own fashion line, c. 1980.
b. c. 1955 in Dearborn Heights,
   Michigan
Source: *AsAmAlm; ConFash; CurBio 93;*
IntWWW 2; News 95, 95-1; NotAsAm;
ThHDFas; WhoAm 94, 95, 96, 2000;
WhoAmW 95, 97, 99; WhoAsA 94;
WhoWor 97

Sui, Yang Chien
Chinese. Political Leader
First of Sui emperors; reunited China,
   killed, succeeded by son.
b. 541
d. 604
Source: *McGEWB; NewCol 75*

Suiko
Japanese. Empress
First empress regnant of Japan ruled for
   35 years and enthusiastically promoted
   Buddhism, during the reign both the
   12 grades in court ranking and the
   Seventeen-article Constitution were
   proclaimed.
b. 554, Japan
d. 628
Source: *EncJap; EncWB 98*

Suits, C(hauncey) G(uy)
American. Physicist, Inventor
Developed method of measuring
   temperature of arcs, determined
   practical applications like radio
   circuits, beacons, and submarine
   signals.
b. Mar 12, 1905 in Oshkosh, Wisconsin
d. Aug 14, 1991 in Pilot Knob, New
   York
Source: *AmMWSc 73P, 76P, 79, 82, 86,*
89, 92; BioIn 1, 2, 4, 7, 17, 20; BlueB
76; CurBio 91N; InSci; IntWW 74, 75,
76, 77, 78, 79, 80, 81, 82, 83, 89, 91;
McGMS 80; NewYTBS 91; WhAm 10;
WhoAm 74, 76, 78, 86, 88, 90; WhoEng
88; WhoWor 74

Sui Wen-ti
[Yang Chien]
Chinese. Emperor
Founder of the Sui dynasty, conquered
   the South of China to unify the state
   after 300 years of internal political
   conflict.
b. 541, China
d. 604, China
Source: *EncWB 98; WorAlBi*

Suk, Josef
Bohemian. Violinist, Composer
Wrote symphony *Asrael,* 1907; son-in-
   law of Dvorak.
b. Jan 4, 1874 in Krecovic, Bohemia
d. May 29, 1935 in Beneschau,
   Czechoslovakia
Source: *BakBD 78, 84, 92; BakBDTw;*
BakBDTw; BioIn 3, 4, 8, 14; DcCom&M

79; NewAmDM; NewCol 75; NewGrDM 80; NewOxM; OxCMus

Sukarno, Achmed
Indonesian. Political Leader
First pres. of Indonesia, 1945-67, headed authoritarian government with strong ties to Communist China.
b. Jun 1, 1901 in Surabaya, Dutch East Indies
d. Jun 21, 1970 in Jakarta, Indonesia
Source: *ConAu 113; CurBio 47, 70; DcPol; EncyDCo; McGEWB; NewYTBE 70; WhAm 5; WhWW-II*

Sukenik, Eliazer Lipa
Israeli. Archaeologist
Expert on Biblical manuscripts.
b. 1889
d. Feb 28, 1953 in Jerusalem, Israel
Source: *BioIn 3; ObitOF 79*

Sukhomlinov, Vladimir Aleksandrovich
Russian. Military Leader
General most responsible for prematurely involving Russia in World War I.
b. Aug 16, 1848, Russia
d. Feb 2, 1926 in Berlin, Germany
Source: *BiDSovU; BioIn 17*

Sukman, Harry
American. Composer, Conductor, Pianist
Won Oscar for score of *Song Without End,* 1960.
b. Dec 2, 1912 in Chicago, Illinois
d. Dec 2, 1984
Source: *ASCAP 66, 80; BioIn 14; VarWW 85*

Suleiman I
[Suleiman the Magnificent]
Turkish. Ruler
Ottoman sultan, 1520-66; empire reached height of power under him.
b. Apr 27, 1496 in Trebizona, Turkey
d. Sep 5, 1566 in Szigetvar, Hungary
Source: *McGEWB; NewCol 75; REn; WebBD 83; WhDW; WhoMilH 76*

Sulla, Lucius C
Roman. Army Officer, Political Leader
Used army to seize control of state, 82 BC; revived Roman office of dictator; his was notorious for cruelty.
b. 138BC
d. 78BC in Campania, Campania
Source: *LinLib S; McGEWB; NewCol 75; REn*

Sullavan, Margaret
American. Actor
First wife of Henry Fonda; won Drama Critics award for *The Voice of the Turtle,* 1943.
b. May 16, 1896 in Norfolk, Virginia
d. Jan 1, 1960 in New Haven, Connecticut
Source: *BiDFilm; BioAmW; CmMov; CurBio 44, 60; FilmgC; MotPP;*

MovMk; OxCFilm; OxCThe 67; ThFT; WhAm 3; WhScrn 77

Sullivan, A(loysius) M(ichael)
American. Editor
Edited *Dun's Review,* 1954-61.
b. Aug 9, 1896 in Harrison, New Jersey
d. Jun 10, 1980 in Montclair, New Jersey
Source: *AmCath 80; AnCL; BioIn 1, 3, 12; BkC 3; CathA 1930; ChhPo, S1, S2; ConAu 97, P-2; CurBio 53, 80; Po&Wr 77; REnAL; WhAm 7; WhE&EA*

Sullivan, Andrew
American. Editor, Writer
Editor, *New Republic,* 1991—.
b. c. 1964, England
Source: *News 96, 96-1*

Sullivan, Anne
[Mrs. John A. Macy]
American. Teacher
Perkins Institute teacher of Helen Keller, 1887; companion until death, 1936.
b. Apr 14, 1866 in Feeding Hills, Massachusetts
d. Oct 20, 1936 in Forest Hills, New York
Source: *AmBi; BioIn 14, 18, 20, 21, 23, 24; CamBiEn; CamDcAB; InWom, SUP; LegTOT; NotAW; WebAB 74*

Sullivan, Arthur Seymour, Sir
[Gilbert and Sullivan]
English. Composer, Author
With W S Gilbert produced 14 comic operas; wrote "Onward Christian Soldiers," 1871.
b. May 14, 1842 in London, England
d. Nov 22, 1900 in London, England
Source: *Alli; AtlBL; AuBYP 2S; BakBD 78, 84; BakDcM; BioIn 1, 2, 3, 4, 5, 6, 7, 8, 9, 10, 11, 12, 13; BriBkM 80; CamBiEn; CelCen; ChamBiD; CmOp; DcCom 77; DcCom&M 79; DcNaB S1; Dis&D; EncWB 98; FilmgC; GrComp; LinLib L, S; McGEWB; MusMk; NewC; NewGrDM 80; NotNAT A, B; OxCMus; REn; REnWD*

Sullivan, Barry
[Patrick Barry]
American. Actor
Leading man in films since 1940s:
Another Time, Another Place, 1958; *Harlow,* 1965.
b. Aug 12, 1912 in New York, New York
d. Jun 6, 1994 in Sherman Oaks, California
Source: *BiE&WWA; BioIn 4, 18, 19, 20, 22; DcPseud; FilmEn; FilmgC; ForYSC; GangFlm; HalFC 80, 84, 88; IntMPA 75, 76, 78, 79, 80, 81, 82, 84, 86, 88, 92, 94; ItaFilm; LegTOT; MotPP; MovMk; NotNAT; VarWW 85; WhoAm 82, 84; WhoHol 92, A; WorAl*

Sullivan, C(harles) Gardner
American. Screenwriter, Filmmaker
Wrote scenarios of early Western films.
b. Sep 18, 1886? in Stillwater, Minnesota

d. Sep 5, 1965 in Hollywood, California
Source: *ConAu 113; DcLB 26; OxCFilm*

Sullivan, Daniel P
American. Government Official
FBI agent who helped track down John Dillinger and Barker-Karpis gang.
b. 1912 in Washington, District of Columbia
d. Jul 4, 1982 in Miami, Florida
Source: *NewYTBS 82*

Sullivan, Danny
American. Auto Racer
Won Indianapolis 500, 1985.
b. Mar 9, 1950 in Louisville, Kentucky
Source: *BioIn 15; CelR 90; NewYTBS 85; WhoAm 94, 95, 96, 97, 98*

Sullivan, Ed(ward Vincent)
American. TV Personality
"Toast of the Town" variety show evolved into "The Ed Sullivan Show," 1948-71.
b. Sep 28, 1902 in New York, New York
d. Oct 13, 1974 in New York, New York
Source: *AmDec 1950; BiDAmJo; BiDAmNC; BiDD; BioIn 2, 3, 4, 5, 6, 7, 8, 10, 12, 16, 17, 19; CamBiEn; CamDcAB; CelR; ChamBiD; ConAu 89; CurBio 52, 74, 74N; EncAJ; EncTwCJ; FacFETw; IntMPA 75; IntWW 74; LegTOT; LinLib L, S; NewYTBS 74; NewYTET; PlP&P; SaTiSS; WebAB 74, 79; WhAm 6; WhoAm 74; WhoHol B; WhoWor 74; WhScrn 77, 83; WorAl; WorAlBi*

Sullivan, Francis Loftus
English. Actor
Character actor, often in villainous roles:
Oliver Twist, 1948; *The Prodigal,* 1955.
b. Jan 6, 1903 in London, England
d. Nov 19, 1956 in New York, New York
Source: *BioIn 3, 4; FilmAG WE; FilmEn; FilmgC; ForYSC; HalFC 80; IlWWBF; MotPP; NotNAT B; PlP&P; Vers A; WhAm 3; WhoHol B; WhScrn 74, 77, 83; WhThe*

Sullivan, Frank
American. Journalist
Best known for cliche phrases; wrote Christmas poems for *The New Yorker,* 1932-74.
b. Sep 22, 1892 in Saratoga, New York
d. Feb 19, 1976 in Saratoga, New York
Source: *AmAu&B; AmNatBi; Benet 87, 96; BenetAL 91; BiDAmNC; BioIn 3, 4, 7, 9, 10, 13, 14, 15, 22; ChhPo S1; ConAu 65, P-2; EncALit; JrnUS; LegTOT; LngCTC; NewYTBS 76; OxCAmL 83, 95; REn; REnAL; TwCA, SUP; WhAm 6; WhoAm 74, 76; WorAu 1900*

Sullivan, Harry Stack
American. Psychiatrist
Based his approach to mental illness
  primarily upon interpersonal theory.
b. Feb 21, 1892 in Norwich, New York
d. Jan 14, 1949 in Paris, France
Source: *AmDec 1940; AmNatBi;*
BiDcPsy; BiDPsy; BioIn 1, 2, 9, 10, 11,
12, 13, 14, 18, 22, 23; CamDcAB;
ChamBiD; DcAmB S4; DcAmMeB 84;
DcNAA; EncAB-H 1974, 1996; EncSPD;
EncWB 98; GuPsyc; InSci; McGEWB;
NamesHP; RAdv 14; REnAL; ThTwC 87;
WebAB 74, 79; WhAm 4, HSA; WorAu
1900

Sullivan, Haywood Cooper
American. Baseball Executive
Catcher, Boston Red Sox, 1952, 1955-
  60; Kansas City, 1961-63; appeared in
  312 ML games in seven yrs., mostly
  as catcher; co-owner Boston Red Sox,
  1985-94.
b. Dec 15, 1930 in Donaldsonville,
  Georgia
Source: *BaseEn 88; WhoAm 84, 86, 88,*
90, 92, 94, 95; WhoE 83, 85, 86, 91, 95

Sullivan, John
American. Politician
President (before title of governor) of
  NH, 1786, 1787, 1789; member of
  first, second Continental Congresses,
  1774, 1775.
b. Feb 17, 1740 in Somersworth, New
  Hampshire
d. Jan 23, 1795 in Durham, North
  Carolina
Source: *Alli; AmBi; AmRev; ApCAB;*
BenetAL 91; BiAUS; BiDFedJ; BiDrAC;
BiDrACR; BiDrUSC 89; BioIn 4, 6, 7, 8,
10, 11; BlkwEAR; CamBiEn; CamDcAB;
ChamBiD; DcAmB; DcAmMiB; Drake;
EncAR; EncCRAm; HarEnMi; HarEnUS;
HisDcAR; NatCAB 1; NewCBEL;
OxCAmH; REnAL; TwCBDA; WebAB
74, 79; WebAMB; WhAm HS; WhAmP;
WhAmRev; WhNaAH; WhoMilH 76

Sullivan, John L(awrence)
"Boston Strong Boy"
American. Boxer
Last bare-knuckle heavyweight champ,
  1882-92; Hall of Fame, 1954.
b. Oct 15, 1858 in Boston, Massachusetts
d. Feb 2, 1918 in Abingdon,
  Massachusetts
Source: *AmBi; BiDAmSp BK; BioIn 1, 2,*
3, 4, 5, 6, 9, 10, 11, 12; CamBiEn;
CamDcAB; DcAmB; DcAmTB; DcNAA;
EncWB 98; McGEWB; OxCAmH;
REnAL; WebAB 74, 79; WhAm 4, HS,
HSA; WhoBox 74

Sullivan, Kathleen
American. Broadcast Journalist
Anchors "ABC World News This
  Morning."
b. May 17, 1954? in Pasadena, California
Source: *BioIn 15, 16; CelR 90; InWom*
SUP; LegTOT; WhoAm 90; WhoRel 92

Sullivan, Kathryn D
American. Astronaut
First woman to walk in space, with
  shuttle *Challenger,* Oct 1984.
b. 1951? in New Jersey
Source: *AmMWSc 98; AmWomSc 1950;*
BioIn 11; IntWWW 2; NewYTBS 84;
WhoAmW 91; WhoSpc

Sullivan, Leon H
American. Civil Rights Leader, Clergy
Pioneer of protest economic boycotts for
  stores failing to employ blacks; created
  job-training agency Opportunities
  Industrialization Centers of America,
  Inc.
b. Oct 16, 1922 in Charleston, West
  Virginia
Source: *AfrAmAl 8; BioIn 8, 9, 10, 11,*
12, 13; ConBlB 3; CurBio 69; NegAl 89;
NotBlAM; WhoAm 90; WhoBlA 7;
WhoRel 92

Sullivan, Louis Henri
American. Architect
Pioneer in modern functional architecture
  who abandoned Victorian Gothic
  ornamentation for simple, uncluttered
  lines.
b. Sep 3, 1856 in Boston, Massachusetts
d. Apr 14, 1924 in Chicago, Illinois
Source: *AmAu&B; AmBi; AmNatBi;*
AtlBL; BiDAmAr; BriEAA; CamDcAB;
DcAmB; DcNAA; EncAAr 1, 2; EncAB-H
1974, 1996; EncWB 98; McGDA;
McGEWB; MemAm; OxCAmH; OxCAmL
65; REn; REnAL; WebAB 74, 79; WhAm
1; WhDW; WhoArch

Sullivan, Louis W(ade)
American. Government Official
US Secretary of Health and Human
  Services 1989-93.
b. Nov 3, 1933 in Atlanta, Georgia
Source: *AfrAmAl 6; AfrAmBi 1;*
AmMWSc 73P, 76P, 79, 82, 86, 89, 92,
95, 98; BiDrUSE 89; BioIn 16;
BlksScM; CngDr 89, 91; CurBio 89;
DiAAPGL; DiAASTC; InB&W 85;
IntWW 89, 91, 93, 97, 98, 2000;
NotBlAS; WhoAfA 9, 10, 11, 12; WhoAm
78, 82, 84, 86, 88, 90, 92, 94, 95, 96,
97, 98; WhoAmP 89, 91, 93, 95;
WhoBlA 3, 4, 5, 6, 7, 8; WhoE 91, 93;
WhoFrS 84; WhoMedH 96, 99, 2000;
WhoScEn 94; WhoSSW 95, 97, 99;
WhoWor 91, 93, 95

Sullivan, Mark
American. Author
Wrote six-vol. history, *Our Times: The*
  United States, 1900-1925, 1926-36.
b. Sep 10, 1874 in Avondale,
  Pennsylvania
d. Aug 13, 1952 in Avondale,
  Pennsylvania
Source: *AmAu&B; AmNatBi; Benet 87;*
BenetAL 91; BiDAmNC; BioIn 3, 4, 5, 9,
14, 22; CamDcAB; CathA 1952; DcAmB
S5; DcAmSR; EncAJ; JouAdvM;
MorMA; NatCAB 42; OxCAmH;
OxCAmL 65, 83, 95; REn; REnAL;

TwCA, SUP; WhAm 3; WhLit; WhNAA;
WorAu 1900

Sullivan, Maxine
American. Singer, Musician
Famous for 1937 rendition of "Loch
  Lomond."
b. May 13, 1911 in Pittsburgh,
  Pennsylvania
d. Apr 7, 1987 in New York, New York
Source: *AllMGJa; AmNatBi; AnObit*
1987; BiDAfM; BiDAmM; BiDJaz; BioIn
10, 14, 15, 17, 22; BlkWAm; CmpEPM;
DcPseud; DrBlPA, 90; EncJzS; IlEncJ;
InB&W 80, 85; InWom SUP; NegAl 83,
89; NewAmDM; NewGrDA 86;
NewGrDJ 88, 94; NewYTBS 87;
NotBlAW 2; OxCPMus; PenEncP;
WhoJazz 72

Sullivan, Mike
[Michael J Sullivan]
American. Politician
Dem. governor of Wyoming, 1987-93.
b. Sep 23, 1939 in Omaha, Nebraska
Source: *AlmAP 88, 92; BiDrGov 1983,*
1988; BioIn 16; IntWW 89, 91, 93;
WhoAm 88, 90; WhoAmP 87, 89, 91, 93,
95; WhoWest 87, 89, 92; WhoWor 89,
91

Sullivan, Pat(rick J)
American. Football Player
All-America quarterback, won Heisman
  Trophy, 1971; in NFL with Atlanta,
  1972-75.
b. Jan 18, 1950 in Birmingham,
  Michigan
Source: *BiDAmSp FB; BioIn 14;*
NewYTBE 71; WhoFtbl 74

Sullivan, Susan
American. Actor
Played Maggie Gioberti Channing on TV
  series "Falcon Crest," 1981-89.
b. Nov 18, 1944 in New York, New
  York
Source: *BioIn 15; ConTFT 2, 18;*
LegTOT; VarWW 85

Sullivan, Tom
American. Singer, Actor, Composer
Blind performer who wrote *If You Could*
  See What I Hear, 1976; made into
  movie, 1982.
b. Mar 27, 1947 in Boston,
  Massachusetts
Source: *BioIn 10, 11, 12, 17; ConTFT 2,*
19; VarWW 85; WhoEnt 92, 98

Sullivan, Walter
[Walter Seager Sullivan, Jr.]
American. Journalist
Science editor of *NY Times* 1964-87;
  wrote *We Are Not Alone,* 1964.
b. Jan 12, 1918 in New York, New York
d. Mar 19, 1996 in Riverside,
  Connecticut
Source: *AmAu&B; AmMWSc 92; ConAu*
2NR, 151; CurBio 80; EncTwCJ;
IntAu&W 91; IntWW 83, 91; JrnUS;
NewYTBS 96; WhAm 11; WhoAm 82, 90;

WhoWrEP 89; WrDr 80, 82, 84, 86, 88, 90, 92

Sullivan, William Hallisey, Jr.
American. Football Executive
Owner, pres., New England Patriots, 1975-88; pres., AFL, 1963-65.
b. Sep 13, 1915 in Lowell, Massachusetts
d. Feb 23, 1998 in Atlantis, Florida
Source: *BioIn 23; NewYTBS 86; WhoAm 74, 76, 78, 80, 82, 84, 86, 88, 90, 92, 94, 95, 96, 97; WhoE 74, 79, 81, 83, 85, 86, 93; WhoFtbl 74*

Sullivan, William Healy
American. Diplomat
US ambassador to Iran, 1977-79, to Philippines, 1973-77.
b. Oct 12, 1922 in Cranston, Rhode Island
Source: *BioIn 9, 11, 12, 14; CurBio 79; EncVieW; IntWW 74, 75, 76, 77, 78, 79, 80, 81, 82, 83, 89; MidE 78, 79, 80, 81, 82; NewYTBS 79; PolProf J, K; USBiR 74; WhoAm 76, 78; WhoAmP 77, 79; WhoGov 72, 75, 77; WhoWor 74, 76, 78*

Sully, Maximilien de Bethune, Duc
French. Statesman
Wrote *Royal Economics*, 1638.
b. 1560, France
d. 1641, France
Source: *BiD&SB; CamBiEn; ChamBiD; OxCFr; REn*

Sully, Thomas
American. Artist
Painted over 2,000 portraits, 500 historical scenes.
b. Jun 8, 1783 in Horncastle, England
d. Nov 5, 1872 in Philadelphia, Pennsylvania
Source: *Alli SUP; AmBi; AmNatBi; ApCAB; ArtsNiC; Benet 87, 96; BioIn 1, 2, 4, 7, 9, 10, 11, 12, 13, 14, 22; BriEAA; CamBiEn; CamDcAB; ChamBiD; ChhPo; DcAmArt; DcAmAu; DcAmB; Drake; EncAB-H 1974, 1996; HarEnUS; LegTOT; LinLib S; McGDA; NatCAB 5; NewYHSD; OxCAmH; OxCAmL 65; OxCArt; OxDcArt; REn; TwCBDA; WebAB 74, 79; WhAm HS; WorAl; WorAlBi*

Sully Prudhomme
[Rene-Francois-Armand Prudhomme]
French. Poet
Won first Nobel Prize for literature, 1901.
b. Mar 16, 1839 in Paris, France
d. Sep 7, 1907 in Paris, France
Source: *AtlBL; Benet 87, 96; BiD&SB; CamBiEn; CasWL; ChamBiD; ClDMEL 47, 80; EuAu; LinLib L, S; OxCFr; PenC EUR; REn; TwCLC 31; WorAl; WorAlBi*

Sulzberger, Arthur Hays
American. Journalist
Board chm. of *NY Times* from 1957, publisher from 1935.
b. Sep 12, 1891 in New York, New York
d. Dec 11, 1968 in New York, New York
Source: *AmAu&B; AmNatBi; BioIn 1, 2, 3, 7, 8, 12, 16, 19, 24; ConAu 89; CurBio 43, 69; DcAmB S8; DcLB 127; EncAJ; JrnUS; LinLib L, S; ObitT 1961; REnAL; WebAB 74, 79; WhAm 5*

Sulzberger, Arthur O(chs)
"Punch"
American. Newspaper Executive
Pres., publisher of *NY Times* 1963-92; CEO *NY Times*, 1963-97.
b. Feb 5, 1926 in New York, New York
Source: *BioIn 7, 8, 10, 11, 13, 15, 16, 17, 18, 19, 23, 24; BlueB 76; CelR, 90; CurBio 66; DcLB 127; Dun&B 79, 88, 90, 98; EncAJ; EncWB, 98; IntWW 74, 75, 76, 77, 78, 79, 80, 81, 82, 83, 89, 91, 93, 97, 98, 2000; NewYTBS 87; PolProf K; St&PR 93, 96, 97, 98, 99, 2000; Who 74, 82, 83, 85, 88, 90, 92, 94, 98, 99, 2000; WhoAm 74, 76, 78, 80, 82, 84, 86, 88, 90, 92, 94, 95, 96, 97, 98, 99, 2000; WhoE 74, 75, 77, 79, 81, 83, 85, 86, 89, 91, 93, 95, 97, 99; WhoFI 00, 74, 75, 77, 79, 81, 83, 85, 87, 89, 92, 94, 96, 98; WhoMedi 98; WhoWor 74, 78, 87; WorAlBi*

Sulzberger, Arthur O(chs), Jr.
American. Newspaper Executive
Publisher, *NY Times*, 1992—; CEO, 1997—.
b. Sep 22, 1951 in Mount Kisco, New York
Source: *NewYTBS 87; WhoAm 92, 94, 95, 96, 97, 98, 99, 2000; WhoE 89, 91, 93, 95, 97, 99; WhoMedi 98; WhoWor 96*

Sulzberger, C(yrus) L(eo)
American. Author
Books include *Such a Peace: The Roots and Ashes of Yalta*, 1982.
b. Oct 27, 1912 in New York, New York
d. Sep 20, 1993 in Paris, France
Source: *Au&Wr 71; BiDAmNC; BioIn 3, 4, 7, 8, 9, 10, 11, 19; ConAu 23NR, 53; CurBio 44; HisDcWJ; IntAu&W 76; IntWW 74, 75, 76, 77, 78, 79, 80, 81, 82, 83, 89, 91, 93; REnAL; WhAm 11; WhoAm 74, 76, 78, 80, 82, 84, 86, 90, 92, 94; WhoPul; WhoWor 74, 89; WrDr 92*

Sulzer, Salomon
"Father of Modern Synagogue Music"
Austrian. Composer
Most renowned cantor of 19th century.
b. Mar 30, 1804 in Hohenems, Austria
d. Jan 17, 1890 in Vienna, Austria
Source: *BakBD 78, 84, 92; BioIn 2; NewGrDM 80; OxDcJeR*

Sumac, Yma
Peruvian. Singer
Flamboyant concertist, billed as Inca princess; voice ranged five octaves.
b. Sep 10, 1928 in Ichocan, Peru
Source: *BakBD 84; CurBio 55; DcPseud; ForYSC; HalFC 80, 84, 88; PenEncP; WhoAmW 58, 61, 68, 72, 74; WhoHol A; WhoMus 72*

Summer, Donna
[LaDonna Andrea Gaines]
American. Singer
Disco hits include "Hot Stuff," 1979; "Last Dance," 1978; "Dinner With Gershwin," 1987; Grammy award winner, 1984.
b. Dec 31, 1948 in Boston, Massachusetts
Source: *AfrAmAl 8; ASCAP 80; BiDAfM; BillEnR; BioIn 11, 12, 13; BkPepl; CamBiEn; CelR 90; ConMuA 80A; ConMus 12; CurBio 79; DcPseud; DrBlPA 90; EncPR&S 89; EncRk 88; EncRkSt; HerW; IlEncBM 82; IntWW 89, 91, 93, 97, 98, 2000; IntWWW 2; InWom SUP; LegTOT; NewGrDA 86; OxCPMus; PenEncP; RkOn 74; RkWho 96; RolSEnR 83; SoulM; WhoAm 80, 82, 84, 86, 88, 90, 92, 99, 2000; WhoAmW 87, 89, 91, 99; WhoBlA 4; WhoEnt 92; WhoHol 92; WhoRock 81; WorAlBi*

Summerall, Pat
[George Summerall]
"Gary Cooper of Sportscasters"
American. Sportscaster
Announcer for CBS Sports, 1962-94; covered 11 Super Bowls; Sportscaster of Year, 1977; announcer for Fox Sports, 1994—.
b. 1931? in Lake City, Florida
Source: *LegTOT; LesBEnT; WhoAm 86, 92, 94, 95, 96, 97, 98, 99, 2000; WhoFtbl 74; WhoWest 96*

Summerfield, Arthur Ellsworth
American. Government Official
Postmaster General under Eisenhower, 1953-61.
b. Mar 17, 1899 in Pinconning, Michigan
d. Apr 26, 1972 in West Palm Beach, Florida
Source: *BiDrUSE 71, 89; BioIn 2, 3, 4, 5, 9, 10, 11, 17; CurBio 52, 72; DcAmB S9; IntYB 78; LinLib S; NewYTBE 72; PolProf E; WhAm 5; Who 74*

Summers, Andy
[The Police; Andrew James Somers; Andrew James Summers]
English. Musician, Songwriter
Guitarist with The Police; scored movie *Down and Out in Beverly Hills*, 1986; now solo.
b. Dec 31, 1942 in Poulton-Fylde, England
Source: *BioIn 12, 13, 16; CmpEGui; ConMus 3; LegTOT; OnThGG; WhoAm 94, 95, 96, 97, 98, 99, 2000; WhoRocM 82*

Summers, Anne Fairhurst
Editor, Writer
Editor-in-chief of Ms. magazine, 1987-
    89; author of *Damned Whores and
    God's Police*, 1975.
b. Mar 12, 1945 in Deniliquin, Australia
Source: *AmWomWr; BioIn 16; CamBiEn;
News 90-2; OxCAusL; WhoAm 94;
WhoAmW 91, 93; WhoE 91, 93, 95*

Summersby, Kay
[Kathleen McCarthy-Morrogh]
English. Secretary
Wartime companion romantically linked
    to Eisenhower.
b. 1908 in County Cork, Ireland
d. Jan 20, 1975 in Southampton, England
Source: *AmNatBi; BioIn 1, 7, 10, 11, 17;
BioNews 74*

**Summerskill, Edith Clara,
    Baroness**
English. Physician
Member, House of Commons, 1938-61;
    chm., Labour Party, 1954-55.
b. Apr 19, 1901 in London, England
d. Feb 4, 1980 in London, England
Source: *BioIn 7, 8, 12;
ChamBiD; CurBio 43, 63, 80N; DcNaB
1971; InSci; IntWW 77; InWom, SUP;
NewYTBS 80; WhoWor 74; WomFir*

Summerville, Slim
[George J Summerville]
American. Comedian
One of original Keystone Cops, known
    for "hick" roles; films include *All
    Quiet on the Western Front*, 1930.
b. Jul 10, 1896 in Albuquerque, New
    Mexico
d. Jan 6, 1946 in Laguna Beach,
    California
Source: *CurBio 46; Film 1; FilmgC;
HalFC 84; MotPP; MovMk; NotNAT B;
TwYS; WhScrn 77, 83*

Sumner, Charles
American. Politician, Orator
Senator from MA, 1851-74; abolitionist;
    injured by Southern colleague for
    ardent attacks against slavery, 1856.
b. Jan 6, 1811 in Boston, Massachusetts
d. Mar 11, 1874 in Washington, District
    of Columbia
Source: *ABCAmRe; Alli, SUP; AmAu;
AmAu&B; AmBi; AmNatBi; AmOrN;
AmPeW; AmPolLe; AmRef; ApCAB;
BbD; Benet 87, 96; BenetAL 91; BiAUS;
BiD&SB; BiDMoPL; BiDrAC; BiDrUSC
89; BiDTran; BioIn 2, 3, 4, 5, 6, 7, 8, 9,
11, 12, 13, 15, 16, 17, 20, 21, 22, 23;
CamBiEn; CamDcAB; CelCen;
ChamBiD; CivWDc; CyAG; CyAL 2;
DcAmAu; DcAmB; DcAmDH 80, 89;
DcAmSR; DcBiPP; Dis&D; Drake;
EncAACR; EncAAH; EncAB-H 1974,
1996; EncWB 98; HarEnUS; LAmCW;
LegTOT; LinLib L, S; McGEWB;
NatCAB 3; OxCAmH; OxCAmL 65, 83,
95; PolPar; RComAH; REn; REnAL;
TwCBDA; USGovLe; WebAB 74, 79;
WhAm HS; WhAmP; WhCiWar; WorAl;
WorAlBi*

Sumner, Edwin V
American. Army Officer
Commander, Department of the West,
    1858-61.
b. Jan 30, 1797 in Boston, Massachusetts
d. Mar 21, 1863 in Syracuse, New York
Source: *AmBi; ApCAB; DcAmB; Drake;
TwCBDA; WebAMB; WhAm HS*

Sumner, James Batcheller
American. Chemist
Shared Nobel Prize, 1946, for
    crystallization of enzymes.
b. Nov 19, 1887 in Canton,
    Massachusetts
d. Aug 19, 1955 in Buffalo, New York
Source: *AmNatBi; AsBiEn; BiESc; BioIn
1, 3, 4, 6, 15, 19, 20; CamBiEn;
CamDcAB; ChamBiD; DcAmB S5;
DcScB; InSci; LarDcSc; McGCEnS;
McGMS 80; NatCAB 46; RanHWDS;
WebAB 74, 79; WhAm 3; WhoNob, 90,
95; WorAl; WorScD*

Sumner, Jessie
American. Politician
Rep. congresswoman from IL, 1939-47;
    opposed to Pres. Roosevelt's New
    Deal programs.
b. 1899?
d. Aug 10, 1994 in Watseka, Illinois

Sumner, William Graham
American. Educator, Economist,
    Sociologist
Laissez-faire economist whose best-
    known work was *Folkways*, 1907.
b. Oct 30, 1840 in Paterson, New Jersey
d. Apr 12, 1910 in Englewood, New
    Jersey
Source: *Alli SUP; AmAu; AmAu&B;
AmBi; AmNatBi; AmSocL; ApCAB;
BenetAL 91; BiDAmEd; BiD&SB; BioIn
1, 2, 3, 10, 11, 14, 19; CamDcAB;
CyWA 97; DcAmAu; DcAmB; DcAmC;
DcAmSR; DcSoc; EncAB-H 1974, 1996;
EncABHB 6; EncWB 98; GayN;
HarEnUS; LinLib L, S; McGEWB;
MorMA; NatCAB 11, 25; OxCAmH;
OxCAmL 65, 83, 95; REn; REnAL;
WebAB 74, 79; WhAm 1; WorAl*

Sumners, Rosalyn
American. Skater
World champion figure skater, 1983.
b. Apr 20, 1964 in Palo Alto, California
Source: *BioIn 13*

Sumter, Thomas
American. Army Officer
Brigadier general in Revolution; Dem.
    senator from SC, 1802-10; Fort
    Sumter, SC named for him.
b. Aug 14, 1734 in Hanover County,
    Virginia
d. Jun 1, 1832 in Stateburg, Virginia
Source: *AmBi; AmNatBi; AmRev;
ApCAB; BiAUS; BiDrAC; BiDrUSC 89;
BioIn 5, 16; BlkwEAR; CamBiEn;
CamDcAB; ChamBiD; DcAmB; Drake;
EncAR; EncCRAm; EncGuW; EncSoH;
HarEnMi; HarEnUS; NatCAB 1;
TwCBDA; WebAB 74, 79; WebAMB;*

*WhAm HS; WhAmP; WhAmRev;
WhoMilH 76*

Sunay, Cevdet
Turkish. Political Leader
Pres. of Turkey, 1966-73.
b. Feb 10, 1900 in Trabzon, Turkey
d. May 22, 1982 in Istanbul, Turkey
Source: *AnObit 1982; BioIn 7, 8, 11, 12,
13; CurBio 69, 82N; DcPol; IntWW 75,
76, 77, 78, 79, 80, 81, 82; IntYB 78, 79,
81; MidE 78, 79, 80, 81; PolEnME;
WhoGov 72; WhoWor 74, 78*

Sundance Kid, The
[Harry Longabaugh]
American. Outlaw
Celebrated bankrobber, trainrobber,
    1901-09; portrayed by Robert Redford
    in popular 1969 film.
d. 1909?
Source: *BioIn 10, 13; LegTOT;
NewEAmW; PeoHis; REnAW*

Sunday, Billy ·
[William Ashley Sunday]
"Parson"; "The Evangelist"
American. Baseball Player, Evangelist
Outfielder, 1883-90, known for fielding,
    base stealing; as popular evangelist,
    fought against Sunday baseball.
b. Nov 18, 1862 in Ames, Iowa
d. Nov 6, 1935 in Chicago, Illinois
Source: *AmBi; AmNatBi; AmSocL; Ballpl
90; BioIn 15, 17, 18, 19, 23; ConAu
120; DcAmB S1; DcAmReB 1, 2;
DcAmTB; DcNAA; EncAAH; EncARH;
GayN; HisWorL; LngCTC; LuthC 75;
McGEWB; PrimTiR; RelLAm 1, 2;
TwCSAPR; WebAB 74, 79; WhAm 1;
WhoProB 73; WorAl*

Sundberg, Jim
[James Howard Sundberg]
American. Baseball Player
Catcher, TX, 1974-83, 1988-89;
    Milwaukee, 1984; KC, 1985-86;
    Chicago Cubs, 1987-88; led AL
    catchers in fielding seven times;
    awarded golden glove, 1980.
b. May 18, 1951 in Galesburg, Illinois
Source: *BaseReg 86, 87*

Sunderland, Thomas E(lbert)
American. Businessman, Lawyer
Antitrust law and international
    negotiations expert; progressive pres.
    of United Fruit Co.
b. Apr 28, 1907 in Ann Arbor, Michigan
d. Mar 1, 1991 in Scottsdale, Arizona
Source: *BioIn 5, 6, 17; BlueB 76;
CurBio 91N; IntWW 74, 75, 76, 77, 78,
79, 80, 81, 82, 83, 89, 91; NewYTBS 91;
WhAm 10; WhoAm 74, 76, 78, 80, 82,
84, 86, 88, 90; WhoAmL 78, 79, 83, 85,
87, 90; WhoWor 74, 76, 78, 80*

Sundiata Keita
Malian. Ruler
National hero of the Malinke-speaking
    people defeated the Susu army to
    found the West African empire of

Mali, regarded as a brilliant magician-king.
b. c. 1210 in Kangaba
d. 1260, Mali
Source: *McGEWB*

Sundlun, Bruce George
American. Politician
Dem. governor, RI, 1990—.
b. Jan 19, 1920 in Providence, Rhode Island
Source: *AlmAP 92; BioIn 11, 12; Dun&B 88; IntWW 91, 93, 97, 98, 2000; St&PR 75, 84, 87, 91; WhoAm 74, 76, 78, 80, 82, 84, 86, 88, 90, 92; WhoAmP 91; WhoE 79, 81, 93; WhoWor 76, 82*

Sung Chiao-jen
Chinese. Political Activist
Founded Kuomintang Nationalist Party; assassinated while boarding a train; death helped start second revolution of 1913.
b. Apr 5, 1882 in Taoyuan, China
d. Mar 22, 1913 in Shanghai, China
Source: *BioIn 9*

Sung T'ai-tsu
Chinese. Emperor
Founder of the great Sung dynasty, ruled during a period of economic transition and cultural development.
b. 927, China
d. 976
Source: *EncWB 98*

Sun Ra
[Herman "Sonny" Blount]
American. Bandleader, Composer, Musician
Leader of the Sun Ra Arkestra; influenced modern jazz for more than four decades.
b. May 22, 1914 in Birmingham, Alabama
d. May 30, 1993 in Birmingham, Alabama
Source: *AllMGJa; AmNatBi; AnObit 1993; BakBD 92; BakBDTw; BakDcM; BioIn 11, 12, 13, 16; ConMus 5, 27; DcPseud; DcTwCCu 5; DrBlPA 90; EncJzS; FacFETw; InB&W 85; NewAmDM; NewGrDA 86; NewGrDJ 88, 94; News 94, 94-1; OxCPMus; PenEncP; WhoAm 90*

Sunshine, Linda
American. Author
Author *Plain Jane Works Out*, 1983, spoof of *Jane Fonda's Workout Book*.
b. 1948?
Source: *ConAu 154; WrDr 99, 2000*

Sununu, John Henry
American. Presidential Aide, Politician
Chief of staff under George Bush, 1989-91; Rep. governor of NH, 1983-89.
b. Jul 2, 1939 in Havana, Cuba
Source: *AlmAP 88; AmMWSc 73P, 79, 82, 86, 89, 92, 95, 98; BioIn 13; CamDcAB; WhoAm 86; WhoAmP 85,*

87; *WhoE 83, 85, 86; WhoGov 75, 77; WhoWor 87*

Sun Yat-Sen
[Sun Wen]
"Father of Modern China"
Chinese. Political Leader
Led revolution that overthrew Manchu dynasty, 1911; principal founder of Chinese Nationalist Party, 1912; pres., South China Republic, 1921.
b. Nov 12, 1866, Macao
d. Mar 12, 1925 in Beijing, China
Source: *Benet 96; BioIn 18, 20; ChamBiD; EncChi; EncRev; EncWB 98; HisWorL; LegTOT; McGEWB; ModChi; NewCol 75; OxCEng 67; RadHan; REn; WhDW; WorAl; WorAlBi*

Sun Yat-Sen, Chingling Soong, Madame
[Ching-ling Sung Sun]
Chinese. Political Leader
Widow of Sun Yat-sen; deputy chairman of People's Republic of China; ardent communist.
b. Jan 27, 1893 in Shanghai, China
d. May 29, 1981 in Beijing, China
Source: *BioIn 1, 4, 5, 9, 10; CurBio 44, 81; NewYTBS 81*

Supertramp
[Bob C Benberg; Richard Davies; John Anthony Helliwell; Rodger Hodgson; Dougie Thompson]
English. Music Group
Albums include *.Famous Last Words*, 1982.
Source: *Alli; BilIEnR; ConMuA 80A; ConMus 25; DcNaB, C; DrRegL 75; EncRk 88; EncRkSt; EngPo; HarEnR 86; IlEncRk; NewCBEL; PenEncP; RkOn 85; RolSEnR 83; WhoAmP 75, 77, 79, 81, 83; WhoRock 81; WhoRocM 82*

Supervia, Conchita
Spanish. Opera Singer
Mezzo-soprano; London debut, 1930; noted for Rossini roles, controversial Carmen.
b. Dec 8, 1899 in Barcelona, Spain
d. Mar 30, 1936 in London, England
Source: *BakBD 84; BioIn 3, 5, 7, 10; InWom; NewEOp 71*

Suppe, Franz von
Austrian. Composer
Influenced development of German and Austrian light opera; prolific until middle of 20th century.
b. Apr 18, 1819 in Spalato, Austria
d. May 21, 1895 in Vienna, Austria
Source: *BakBD 84; BioIn 4, 7, 12; CamBiEn; ChamBiD; DcPseud; MetOEnc; NewAmDM; NewOxM; OxCPMus*

Supremes, The
[Florence Ballard; Cindy Birdsong; Diana Ross; Jean Terrell; Mary Wilson]
American. Music Group
Detroit trio, formed 1962; hits include "Baby Love," 1964; Hall of Fame, 1988.
Source: *Alli, SUP; BilIEnR; BioIn 9, 14, 15, 16, 17, 18, 19, 20; BlkWAm; ConAu X; DcLP 87B; DcWomA; EncPR&S 74; EncRk 88; EncRkSt; EngPo; HarEnR 86; IlEncBM 82; InB&W 80, 85, 85A; IntMPA 75, 76, 78, 79, 81, 82; InWom, SUP; NegAl 76, 83, 89; NewGrDA 86; NewYTBE 72; NewYTBS 76; ObitOF 79; PenEncP; PenNWW A; ScF&FL 92; SmATA X; SoulM; TwCRHW 90, 94; WhoAm 74, 76, 78, 80, 82, 84, 86; WhoAmW 70, 72, 74, 75, 77, 79, 81, 83, 85, 87; WhoBlA 1, 2, 3; WhoHol 92; WhoRocM 82; WhoWest 74, 76; WhoWor 84, 87; WomPO 78; WrDr 84, 86, 88, 90, 92, 96*

Surratt, John Harrison
American. Criminal
Friend of John Wilkes Booth, tried as conspirator in assassination of A Lincoln.
b. 1844 in Prince George's County, Maryland
d. Apr 21, 1916
Source: *BioIn 7, 17; DcNAA; HarEnUS; WhAm HS; WhCiWar*

Surratt, Mary Eugenia Jenkins
American. Criminal
Boardinghouse operator; hanged as conspirator in Lincoln's assassination.
b. May 1820 in Waterloo, Maryland
d. Jul 7, 1865 in Washington, District of Columbia
Source: *BioIn 1, 3; LibW; NatCAB 4; NotAW; WebAB 74, 79*

Surtees, John
British. Auto Racer
Motorcycle, car racing champ, 1950s-60s.
b. Feb 11, 1934
Source: *BioIn 7, 8, 10, 11, 12; CamBiEn; ChamBiD; EncMot; IntWW 81, 82, 83, 89, 91, 93, 97, 98, 2000; Who 74, 82, 83, 85, 88, 90, 92, 94, 98, 99, 2000*

Surtees, Robert Smith
English. Author
Humorous character, sporting grocer John Jorrocks appeared in *Jorrocks's Jaunts and Jollities*, 1838.
b. May 17, 1805 in Newcastle-upon-Tyne, England
d. Mar 16, 1864 in Brighton, England
Source: *AtlBL; BioIn 14; BlmGEL; BritAS; BritAu 19; Chambr 3; CyWA 58; DcEuL; DcLEL; DcNaB, C; EvLB; LngCEL; NewC; NinCLC 14; OxCEng 67, 85, 95; PenC ENG; REn; StaCVF; WebE&AL*

Survivor
[Dave Bickler; Marc Droubay; Stephan Ellis; Dennis Keith Johnson; Jim Peternik; R Gary Smith; Frankie Sullivan]
American. Music Group
Had number one hit "Eye of the Tiger," theme song from *Rocky III*, 1982.
Source: *BioIn 13; EncRkSt; GrMetD; PenEncP; RkOn 85; WhoRocM 82*

Susann, Jacqueline
American. Author, Actor
Wrote sex-filled novels *Valley of the Dolls*, 1966; *Once Is Not Enough*, 1973.
b. Aug 20, 1921 in Philadelphia, Pennsylvania
d. Sep 21, 1974 in New York, New York
Source: *AmAu&B; ArtclWW 2; AuNews 1; AuSpks; BioAmW; BioIn 10, 11, 13, 15, 17, 21, 23; BlmGWL; ConAu 53, 65; ConLC 3; CurBio 72, 74, 74N; DcAmB S9; ForWC 70; HalFC 80, 84, 88; InWom SUP; LegTOT; LibW; MajTwCW 1, 2; NewYTBE 73; NewYTBS 74; WhAm 6; WhoAm 74; WhoHol B; WhScrn 77, 83; WorAl*

Su Shih
[Su Tung-p'o]
Chinese. Poet
Considered to be the greatest poet of the Sung dynasty.
b. 1036 in Mei-shan, China
d. 1101
Source: *BioIn 18; ClMLC 15*

Suslov, Mikhail Andreevich
Russian. Politician
Worked under Stalin, Khrushchev, Brezhnev; senior member of Politburo, 1952-82.
b. Nov 21, 1902 in Shakhovskol, Russia
d. Jan 26, 1982 in Moscow, Union of Soviet Socialist Republics
Source: *AnObit 1982; BiDSovU; BioIn 4, 5, 6, 7, 8, 9, 12, 13, 16, 18; ColdWar 1; CurBio 57, 82; IntWW 74, 78; IntYB 78, 79; NewYTBS 82; SovUn; WhoSocC 78; WhoWor 74*

Suso, Heinrich
[Heinrich Seuse]
"Sweet Suso"
German. Mystic
Popular Dominican preacher; thought to have written first German prose autobiography, early 1360s.
b. Mar 21, 1295? in Uberlingen, Germany
d. Jan 25, 1366 in Ulm, Germany
Source: *CasWL; DcBiPP; DcEuL; EvEuW; LuthC 75; NewCol 75; OxCGer 76*

Susskind, David Howard
American. Producer
Well-known TV talk show host; producer of films, plays, TV shows; won Emmys, 1970s.
b. Dec 19, 1920 in Brookline, Massachusetts
d. Feb 22, 1987 in New York, New York
Source: *BiE&WWA; BioIn 11; BkPepl; ConNews 87-2; ConTFT 5; CurBio 60, 87; FilmgC; IntMPA 82; IntWW 74, 75, 76, 77, 78, 79, 80, 81, 82, 83; NotNAT; ScrEAmL 2; WhAm 9; WhoAm 74, 76, 78, 80, 82, 84, 86; WhoE 74; WhoWor 74, 78; WorAl*

Susskind, Walter
British. Conductor
Led St. Louis Symphony, 1968-75.
b. May 1, 1913 in Prague, Bohemia
d. Mar 25, 1980 in Berkeley, California
Source: *AnObit 1980; BakBD 78, 84; BioIn 2, 10, 12; BlueB 76; CanWW 70; CreCan 2; IntWW 74, 75, 76, 77, 78, 79; IntWWM 77; MusMk; NewAmDM; NewGrDA 86; NewGrDM 80; PenDiMP; WhAm 7; Who 74; WhoAm 74, 76, 78, 80; WhoMus 72; WhoMW 74, 80; WhoWor 74, 76, 78, 80*

Sutcliffe, Rick
[Richard Lee Sutcliffe]
American. Baseball Player
Pitcher, LA Dodgers, 1976-81; Cleveland Indians, 1982-84; Chicago Cubs, 1984—; won NL rookie of year, 1979, Cy Young Award, 1984.
b. Jun 21, 1956 in Independence, Missouri
Source: *Ballpl 90; BaseReg 86, 87; WhoMW 90; WhoSpor*

Suter, Gary
American. Hockey Player
Defenseman, Calgary, 1985—; won Calder Trophy, 1986.
b. Jun 24, 1964 in Madison, Wisconsin
Source: *BioIn 21; HocReg 87*

Sutermeister, Heinrich
Swiss. Composer
Works include *Madam Bovary*, 1967; radio, TV operas.
b. Aug 12, 1910 in Feuerthalen, Switzerland
Source: *BakBD 78, 84, 92; BakBDTw; BioIn 8; CmOp; CompSN, SUP; CpmDNM 80; DcCM; IntWW 74, 75, 76, 77, 78, 79, 80, 81, 82, 83, 89, 91, 93; IntWWM 77, 80, 85, 90; NewEOp 71; NewGrDM 80; NewGrDO; OxDcOp; PenDiMP A; WhoMus 72*

Sutherland, Donald
Canadian. Actor
Played Hawkeye in film version of *M*A*S*H*, 1970; other films include *Ordinary People*, 1980.
b. Jul 17, 1934 in Saint John, New Brunswick, Canada
Source: *BiDFilm, 94; BioIn 13, 14, 16, 17, 24; BkPepl; CamBiEn; CanWW 81, 83, 89, 1999; CelR, 90; ConTFT 6, 13, 25; CurBio 81; DcArts; FilmEn; FilmgC; IntDcF 1-3, 2-3; IntMPA 82, 84, 86, 88; LegTOT; MovMk; NewYTBE 70; OxCCanT; VarWW 85; WhoAm 76, 78, 80, 82, 84, 86; WhoHol 92, A; WomWMM; WorAl; WorAlBi*

Sutherland, Earl Wilbur, Jr.
American. Scientist, Physician, Engineer
Won Nobel Prize in medicine, 1971, for his career research on hormones.
b. Nov 19, 1915 in Burlingame, Kansas
d. Mar 9, 1974 in Miami, Florida
Source: *AmMWSc 73P; BioIn 14, 15, 20; CamDcAB; ChambID; ConAu 49, 163; DcAmB S9; DcAmMeB 84; LarDcSc; McGCEnS; McGMS 80; NewYTBE 71; NewYTBS 74; OxCMed 86; RanHWDS; WebAB 74, 79; WhAm 6; Who 74; WhoAm 74; WhoNob, 90, 95; WhoSSW 73, 75; WhoWor 74; WorAl*

Sutherland, Graham Vivian
English. Artist
Commissioned to paint a portrait of Winston Churchill, 1954; so disliked, Churchill's family destroyed it.
b. Aug 24, 1903 in London, England
d. Feb 17, 1980 in Hampstead, England
Source: *AnObit 1980; BioIn 22; CamBiEn; ChambID; CurBio 55, 80; DcBrAr 1; IntWW 74, 75, 76, 77, 78, 79; Who 74; WhoWor 74*

Sutherland, Joan, Dame
Australian. Opera Singer
Leading coloratura soprano, 1960s-70s; won Grammy for best classical vocalist, 1981.
b. Nov 7, 1929 in Sydney, Australia
Source: *BakBD 84; CelR; CurBio 60; IntWW 83; InWom; NewEOp 71; NewYTBE 70; NewYTBS 82; Who 85; WhoAm 86; WhoAmM 83*

Sutherland, Keifer
Canadian. Actor
Films include *Stand By Me*, 1986, *Bright Lights, Big City*, 1988, *Flatliners*, 1990; son of Donald.
b. Dec 21, 1966 in London, England
Source: *BioIn 13; CelR 90; ConTFT 5*

Sutherland, Thomas M
American. Hostage
Dean, American University of Beirut seized by Islamic Jihad June 19, 1985 and held captive for 2,353 days; released November 18, 1991.
Source: *BioIn 10*

Sutter, Bruce
[Howard Bruce Sutter]
American. Baseball Player
Relief pitcher, 1976-89; set NL records for saves in season, in career; won NL Cy Young Award, 1979.
b. Jan 8, 1953 in Lancaster, Pennsylvania
Source: *Ballpl 90; BaseReg 86, 87; BioIn 12, 13; WhoAm 82, 84, 86, 88; WhoSpor; WhoSSW 86, 88*

Sutter, John Augustus
[Johann August Suter]
American. Pioneer
Discovery of gold on his land started
   1848 CA gold rush.
b. Feb 15, 1803 in Kandern, Germany
d. Jun 18, 1880 in Washington, District
   of Columbia
Source: *AmAu&B; AmBi; ApCAB;*
BenetAL 91; BioIn 1, 2, 3, 4, 6, 7, 8, 9,
12, 20, 24; CamBiEn; CamDcAB;
ChamBiD; CmCal; DcAmB; EncAAH;
EncWB 98; HarEnUS; McGEWB;
NatCAB 4; NewEAmW; OxCAmH;
OxCAmL 65, 83, 95; PeoHis; REnAW;
WebAB 74, 79; WhAm HS; WhNaAH;
WorAl; WorAlBi

Suttner, Bertha Felicie Sophie Kinsky von
Austrian. Editor, Writer
First woman to win Nobel Peace Prize,
   1905; wrote *Lay Down Your Arms,*
   1889.
b. Jun 9, 1843 in Prague, Czechoslovakia
d. Jun 21, 1914 in Vienna, Austria
Source: *CasWL; EuAu; EvEuW; HerW;*
LuthC 75; OxCGer 76; ScF&FL 1;
WhLit; WhoNob

Sutton, Carol
American. Editor
First woman to head news operation of
   major US daily newspaper, 1974.
b. Jun 29, 1933 in Saint Louis, Missouri
d. Feb 19, 1985 in Louisville, Kentucky
Source: *BioIn 10, 14, 24; ConAu 115;*
InWom SUP; WhoAmW 75, 77; WomFir

Sutton, Don(ald Howard)
American. Baseball Player
Pitcher, 1966-88; tied NL record for
   most one-hit games in career, five;
   19th ML pitcher to win 300 games,
   1986; Hall of Fame, 1998.
b. Apr 2, 1945 in Clio, Alabama
Source: *Ballpl 90; BaseReg 86, 87;*
BiDAmSp BB; BioIn 11, 12, 13;
LegTOT; WhoAm 78, 80, 82, 84, 86, 88,
92; WhoWest 87; WorAl; WorAlBi

Sutton, Hal Evan
American. Golfer
Touring pro, 1980s; won PGA, 1983;
   leading money winner on tour, 1983.
b. Apr 28, 1958 in Shreveport, Louisiana
Source: *WhoAm 84, 86, 88, 2000;*
WhoWor 2000

Sutton, Horace (Ashley)
American. Author
Travel books include *Travelers: The*
American Tourist from Stagecoach to
Space Shuttle, 1980; editor-in-chief of
Citicorp Publishing Co. 1984-87.
b. May 17, 1919 in New York, New
   York
d. Oct 26, 1991 in New York, New York
Source: *BioIn 3, 5, 17; CelR; ConAu*
10NR, 13R, 135; WhAm 10; WhoAm 74,
76, 78, 80, 82, 84, 86, 88, 90; WhoWor
74

Sutton, John
English. Actor
In films since 1937, usually playing
   hero's rival: *Of Human Bondage,*
   1964.
b. Oct 22, 1908 in Rawalpindi, India
d. 1963
Source: *FilmEn; FilmgC; ForYSC;*
HalFC 80, 84, 88; IntMPA 75, 76, 78,
79, 80, 81, 82; MotPP; MovMk; WhoHol
A, B; WhScrn 74, 77, 83

Sutton, Margaret Beebe
Children's Author
Best known for Judy Bolton series.
b. Jan 22, 1903
Source: *AuBYP 2, 3; ConAu 1R; ForWC*
70; SmATA 1

Sutton, Walter Stanborough
American. Geneticist
Proved that chromosones contain the
   building blocks of inheritance.
b. 1877 in Utica, New York
d. Nov 10, 1916 in Kansas City, Kansas
Source: *BiInAmS; BioIn 20; CamDcAB;*
DcScB; NotTwCS 1; WorScD

Sutton, Willie
[William Francis Sutton, Jr]
''The Actor''
American. Criminal
Stole $2 million in 35 years of bank
   robbing; disguises earned him
   nickname.
b. Jun 30, 1901 in New York, New York
d. Nov 2, 1980 in Spring Hill, Florida
Source: *AmNatBi; BioIn 2, 3, 8, 9, 10,*
11, 12, 23; DcAmB S10; DrInf;
FacFETw; LegTOT

Suu Kyi, Aung San
Burmese. Political Activist
Political dissident, under house arrest in
   Rangoon, 1989-95; won Nobel Peace
   Prize, 1991.
b. 1945? in Rangoon, Burma
Source: *BioIn 16; ConHero 2; News 92,*
96, 92-2, 96-2

Suvorov, Aleksandr V
Russian. Military Leader
Commanded Austro-Russian forces
   against French in French
   Revolutionary Wars, 1798-99; never
   beaten in battle.
b. Nov 25, 1729 in Moscow, Russia
d. May 17, 1800 in Saint Petersburg,
   Russia
Source: *McGEWB; NewCol 75*

Suzman, Helen
South African. Politician
Member of South African Parliament,
   1953-89; noted for her battle against
   apartheid.
b. Jul 11, 1917 in Germiston, South
   Africa
Source: *BioIn 7, 8, 9, 10, 11, 15, 16;*
CamBiEn; ChamBiD; ConAu 145;
ContDcW 89; CurBio 68; DcCPSAf;
EncSoA; EncWB, 98; IntDcWB; IntWW

*91, 93, 97, 98, 2000; IntWWW 2; News
89-3; NewYTBE 70; RadHan; Who 74,
82, 83, 85, 88, 90, 92, 94, 98, 99, 2000;
WomFir; WomLaw; WrDr 98, 99, 2000*

Suzman, Janet
South African. Actor
Active in British theater since 1962;
   Oscar nominee for *Nicholas and*
   Alexandra, 1971.
b. Feb 9, 1939 in Johannesburg, South
   Africa
Source: *BioIn 10, 11, 12; CamBiEn;*
*CamGWoT; ChamBiD; CnThe; ConTFT
1, 4; CurBio 76; Ent; FilmAG WE;
FilmgC; HalFC 80, 84, 88; IntDcT 3;
IntMPA 84, 86, 88, 92, 94, 96; IntWW
76, 78, 79, 80, 81, 82, 83, 89, 91, 93,
97, 98, 2000; IntWWW 2; InWom SUP;
ItaFilm; OsStAZ; OxCThe 83; Who 82,
83, 85, 88, 90, 92, 94, 98, 99, 2000;
WhoEnt 92, 98; WhoHol 92, A; WhoThe
72, 77, 81; WhoWor 74*

Suzuki, Daisetz Teitaro
Japanese. Author, Educator, Philosopher
Introduced Zen Buddhism to Western
   world.
b. Oct 18, 1870 in Kanazawa, Japan
d. Jul 12, 1966 in Tokyo, Japan
Source: *BiDAmCu; BioIn 4, 5, 15, 17,
19, 22; ConAu 111, 121; CurBio 58, 66;
DcAmReB 1, 2; EncARH; EncWB, 98;
IlEncMy; MajTwCW 1, 2; NewCol 75;
RelLAm 1, 2; WhE&EA*

Suzuki, David T(akayoshi)
Canadian. Broadcast Journalist,
   Environmentalist
Host of CBC's ''The Nature of Things
   with David Suzuki,'' 1979—.
b. Mar 24, 1936 in Vancouver, British
   Columbia, Canada
Source: *AmMWSc 73P, 76P, 79, 82, 86,
89, 92, 95, 98; CurBio 95; WhoAm 78,
86, 88; WhoWest 00, 98*

Suzuki, Pat
[Chiyoko Suzuki]
American. Singer, Actor
Starred in *Flower Drum Song,* 1958.
b. Sep 23, 1931 in Cressy, California
Source: *CurBio 60; InWom; WhoAm 74;
WhoAmW 66, 68, 70, 72; WhoHol 92, A;
WhoWor 74*

Suzuki, Shin'ichi
Japanese. Violinist, Educator
Innovative music teacher, developed a
   method of teaching very young
   children to play by ear, before learning
   to read music: the method is based on
   the idea that native languages are
   learned within a nurturing
   environment, by listening and
   imitating; method is taught by
   instructors around the world.
b. Oct 17, 1898 in Nagoya, Japan
d. Jan 26, 1998 in Matsumoto, Japan
Source: *BakBD 84, 92; BakBDTw;
BakDcM; BioIn 10, 11, 13, 14, 18, 23,
24; CamBiEn; NewAmDM; NewGrDM
80; News 98, 98-3; NewYTBS 98;*

PenDiMP; WhAm 12; WhoWor 74, 78, 84, 95, 97

Suzuki, Zenko
Japanese. Political Leader
Prime minister, 1980-82.
b. Jan 11, 1911? in Yamada, Japan
Source: *BioIn 12, 13; CamBiEn; ChamBiD; CurBio 81; FarE&A 78, 79, 80, 81; IntWW 77, 78, 79, 80, 81, 82, 83, 89, 91, 93, 97, 98; NewYTBS 80, 81; WhoWor 80, 82, 84, 87, 89, 91, 93*

Suzy
[Aileen Elder]
American. Journalist
Gossip column syndicated to more than 100 newspapers.
b. Jun 10, in El Paso, Texas
Source: *BioIn 6, 7, 10, 15, 16; CelR, 90; FairDF FRA; InWom, SUP; PenNWW B; WhoAm 78, 80, 82, 84, 86*

Svanholm, Set
Swedish. Opera Singer, Director
Tenor, formerly baritone, noted for Wagner roles; NY Met., 1946-56; director, Swedish Royal Opera, 1956-63.
b. Sep 2, 1904 in Vasteras, Sweden
d. Oct 4, 1964 in Saltsjoe-Duvnaes, Sweden
Source: *BakBD 78, 84; BioIn 3, 4, 7, 11, 16; CmOp; CurBio 56, 64; IntDcOp; MetOEnc; MusSN; NewEOp 71; NewGrDM 80; ObitT 1961; OxDcOp; PenDiMP; WhAm 4*

Svedberg, Theodor H. E
Swedish. Chemist
Won 1926 Nobel Prize for developing the ultracentrifuge; work later used for studying polymers.
b. Aug 30, 1884 in Flerang, Sweden
d. Feb 25, 1971 in Orebro, Sweden
Source: *AsBiEn; BiESc; DcScB; NewYTBE 71; WhAm 5; WhoNob; WorAl*

Sverdrup, H(arald) U(lrik)
Norwegian. Meteorologist, Oceanographer
His research explained equatorial countercurrents; assisted in the creation of methods to predict surf and breakers.
b. Nov 15, 1888 in Sogndal, Norway
d. Aug 21, 1957 in Oslo, Norway
Source: *AmNatBi; BioIn 2, 4; ChamBiD; DcScB; LarDcSc; McGMS 80; ObitOF 79; WhAm 3*

Sverdrup, Otto
Norwegian. Explorer
Famous for expedition to N Pole, 1898-1902, aboard the *Fram.*
b. Jan 1, 1855 in Helgeland, Norway
d. Nov 26, 1930 in Oslo, Norway
Source: *ChamBiD; MacDCB 78; NewCol 75; OxCCan*

Svetlanov, Evgeni Fyodorovich
Russian. Composer, Conductor
Led State Orchestra of USSR, 1965-79.
b. Sep 6, 1928 in Moscow, Union of Soviet Socialist Republics
Source: *BakBD 84; IntWW 74, 75, 83; WhoWor 74*

Svetlova, Marina
American. Dancer, Choreographer
Prima ballerina with Met. Opera, 1943-50.
b. May 3, 1922 in Paris, France
Source: *BiDD; BioIn 5; CnOxB; DancEn 78; IntWWM 77; IntWWW 2; WhoAm 74, 76, 78, 80, 82, 84, 86, 88, 90, 92, 94, 95, 96, 97, 98, 99, 2000; WhoAmW 61, 64, 66, 68, 70, 72, 74, 77, 79, 81, 83, 85, 87, 89, 91, 93, 95, 97; WhoEnt 92, 98; WhoWor 74, 76*

Svevo, Italo
[E. Samigli; Aron Hector Schmitz]
Italian. Author
One of the first Italian novelists to consequentially apply psychoanalytical discoveries to literature.
b. Dec 19, 1861 in Trieste, Italy
d. Sep 13, 1928 in Motta di Livenza, Italy
Source: *Benet 87, 96; BiCoLiE; BioIn 17, 22; CamBiEn; CasWL; ChamBiD; ClDMEL 47, 80; CnMWL; CyWA 89, 97; DcArts; DcItL 1, 2; DcPseud; Dis&D; EncWB 98; EncWL 1, 2, 3; EuWr 8; EvEuW; FacFETw; GrFLW; LngCTC; MakMC; McGEWB; McGEWD 84; ModRL; Novels; OxCEng 67, 85, 95; PenC EUR; RAdv 14; REn; RfGWoL 95; ShSCr 25; TwCA, SUP; TwCLC 2, 35; TwCWr; WhoTwCL; WorAu 1900*

Svoboda, Ludvik
Czech. Political Leader
Pres. of Czechoslovakia, 1968-75.
b. Nov 25, 1895 in Horznatin, Moravia
d. Sep 20, 1979 in Prague, Czechoslovakia
Source: *BioIn 8, 12; CamBiEn; ChamBiD; EncCW; FacFETw; IntWW 74, 75, 76, 77, 78, 79; IntYB 78, 79; NewYTBS 79; WhoGov 72; WhoSocC 78; WhoWor 74; WorDWW*

Swados, Elizabeth A
[Liz Swados]
American. Author, Composer, Director
Composer, director for *Nightclub Cantata,* 1977.
b. Feb 5, 1951 in Buffalo, New York
Source: *ConAu 97; ConLC 12; ConTFT 1; CurBio 79; IntWWW 2; NewYTBS 77, 78; WhoAm 86, 98; WhoThe 81*

Swados, Harvey
American. Author
Works concerned disillusionment of American life; *Standing Fast,* 1970.
b. Oct 28, 1920 in Buffalo, New York
d. Dec 11, 1972 in Holyoke, Massachusetts
Source: *AmAu&B; AmNatBi; AuBYP 2S, 3; BenetAL 91; BioIn 5, 6, 9, 10; ConAu*

5R, 6NR, 37R; ConLC 5; ConNov 72; DcLB 2; DcLEL 1940; EncAL; EncALit; IntAu&W 76; JeAmFiW; JouAdvM; LiJour; LinLib L; ModAL 4, 5; NewYTBE 72; Novels; OxCAmL 65, 83, 95; PenC AM; REnAL; WhAm 5; WorAu 1950

Swaggart, Jimmy Lee
American. Evangelist
TV preacher who claims to have 200 million followers; strong right-wing views; involved in sex scandal, banned from pulpit, 1988.
b. Mar 15, 1935 in Ferriday, Louisiana
Source: *BioIn 13; ConNews 87-3; CurBio 87; RelLAm 1, 2; WhoAm 95, 96, 97, 98, 99, 2000; WhoRel 92*

Swaminathan, M(onkombu) S(ambisivan)
Indian. Geneticist
Leader in "Green Revolution" introducing high-yield rice, wheat crops; promoted improved farming tehcniques.
b. Aug 7, 1925 in Kumbakonam, India
Source: *IntWW 91; Who 74; WhoWor 91*

Swammerdam, Jan
Dutch. Scientist
Natural scientist was skilled in the art of microdissection and was a founder of comparative anatomy and entomology.
b. Feb 12, 1637 in Amsterdam, Netherlands
d. Feb 17, 1680
Source: *AsBiEn; BiESc; BiHiMed; BioIn 4, 9, 12, 14; CamBiEn; CamDcSc; ChamBiD; DcBiPP; DcInv; DcScB; EncWB 98; InSci; LarDcSc; McGEWB; OxCMed 86; RanHWDS; WhDW; WorScD*

Swan, Joseph Wilson, Sir
English. Physicist, Chemist
Inventor of dry photographic plate; created electric light bulb that became prototype for Edison's later invention.
b. Oct 31, 1828 in Sunderland, England
d. May 27, 1914 in Warlingham, England
Source: *AsBiEn; BiESc; BioIn 1, 8, 12, 20; CamBiEn; ChamBiD; DcNaB 1912; ICPEnP; InSci; LarDcSc; MacBEP; OxCBrHi; WhDW; WorAl; WorAlBi*

Swanberg, William Andrew
American. Author
Pulitzer-winning biographer whose books include *Citizen Hearst,* 1961; *Luce and His Empire,* 1972.
b. Nov 23, 1907 in Saint Paul, Minnesota
d. Sep 17, 1992 in Southbury, Connecticut
Source: *Au&Wr 71; BioIn 10; ConAu 5R, 8NR; ConLC 76; DcLEL 1940; MinnWr; WhAm 10; WhoAm 74, 76, 78, 80, 82, 84, 86, 88, 90, 92; WorAu 1950; WrDr 76, 80, 86*

Swann, Donald (Ibrahim)
Welsh. Composer, Lyricist, Entertainer
Starred with Michael Flanders in two-
    man show *At the Drop of a Hat*,
    1950s.
b. Sep 30, 1923 in Llanelly, Wales
d. Mar 23, 1994 in London, England
Source: *Au&Wr 71; BiE&WWA; BioIn 5,
7, 8, 9, 19, 20; BlueB 76; ConAu 16NR,
21R, 41NR, 144; CurBio 70, 94N;
IntAu&W 77, 82; IntWW 74, 75, 76, 77,
78, 79, 80, 81, 82, 83, 89, 91, 93;
IntWWM 77, 80, 85, 90; JoeFr;
NewYTBS 94; NotNAT; OxCPMus;
OxCThe 67; WhAm 11; Who 74, 82, 83,
85, 88, 90, 92, 94; WhoMus 72; WhoThe
72, 77, 81; WhoWor 74, 76, 78, 89;
WrDr 76, 80, 82, 84, 86, 88, 90, 92, 94,
96*

Swann, Lynn Curtis
American. Football Player
Wide receiver, Pittsburgh, 1974-82; led
    NFL in receiving TDs, 1975.
b. Mar 7, 1952 in Alcoa, Tennessee
Source: *BiDAmSp FB; BioIn 11;
NewYTBS 77, 78, 79; WhoAfA 9, 10, 11,
12; WhoAm 78, 80, 82, 84, 86, 88, 90,
92, 94, 95, 96, 97, 98, 99, 2000;
WhoBlA 2, 3, 4, 6, 7, 8; WhoFtbl 74*

Swann, Michael Meredith, Sir
English. Educator
Chancellor of U of York since 1980.
b. Mar 1, 1920 in Shortlands, England
Source: *BioIn 3, 9; BlueB 76; DcNaB
1986; IntWW 74, 76, 77, 78, 79, 80;
WhAm 10; Who 74; WhoWor 74, 76, 78,
82, 84, 87*

Swanson, Carl A
American. Businessman
Food processing firm in 1920s was
    nucleus of first frozen dinner
    production, 1953.
b. May 1, 1876 in Karlskrona, Sweden
d. Oct 9, 1949 in Chicago, Illinois
Source: *Entr; NatCAB 40*

Swanson, Gloria May Josephine
[Josephine Swenson]
American. Actor
Starred in *Sunset Boulevard*, 1950.
b. Mar 27, 1897 in Chicago, Illinois
d. Apr 4, 1983 in New York, New York
Source: *AnObit 1983; BiDFilm;
BiE&WWA; CurBio 83; Film 1; FilmgC;
IntMPA 82; MovMk; NewYTBS 83;
OxCFilm; ThFT; WhAm 8; Who 82;
WhoAm 82; WhoHol A; WhoThe 81*

Swart, Charles Robberts
South African. Political Leader
First South African state president, 1961-
    67; last governor general, 1960-61.
b. Dec 5, 1894, Orange Free State
d. Jul 16, 1982 in Bloemfontein, South
    Africa
Source: *AfSS 78, 79, 80, 81, 82; AnObit
1982; BioIn 5, 13; CurBio 60; EncSoA;
IntWW 74, 75, 76, 77, 78, 79, 80, 81, 82,
83; IntYB 78, 79, 80, 81; NewYTBS 82;*

*WhAm 8; WhE&EA; Who 74, 82;
WhoWor 74*

Swarthout, Gladys
American. Opera Singer
NY Met. mezzo-soprano, 1929-45;
    renowned as Carmen; made five films.
b. Dec 25, 1904 in Deepwater, Missouri
d. Jul 6, 1969 in La Ragnaia, Italy
Source: *AmNatBi; BakBD 84; BiDAmM;
BioIn 1, 3, 4, 8, 9, 11, 14; CamDcAB;
CmOp; CurBio 44, 69; FilmEn; FilmgC;
ForYSC; HalFC 80, 84, 88; InWom,
SUP; LegTOT; LinLib S; MusSN;
NewEOp 71; NewGrDM 80; ObitT 1961;
RadStar; ThFT; WhAm 5; What 2;
WhoAmW 58, 61, 64, 66, 68, 70;
WhoHol B; WhoMus 72; WhScrn 74, 77,
83*

Swarthout, Glendon (Fred)
American. Author
Books include *Where the Boys Are*,
    1960; *Skeletons*, 1979.
b. Apr 8, 1918 in Pinckney, Michigan
d. Sep 23, 1992 in Scottsdale, Arizona
Source: *AnObit 1992; AuBYP 2, 3;
BenetAL 91; BioIn 4, 11, 13; ConAu
1NR, 1R, 47NR, 139; ConLC 35, 76;
ConNov 72, 76, 82, 86, 91; DcAmChF
1960; DcLEL 1940; DrAPF 80;
EncFWF; FourBJA; IntAu&W 76, 77,
86, 91, 93; MagSAmL; MichAu 80;
Novels; SJGYouA 2; SmATA 26;
TwCWW 82, 91; TwCYAW 1; WhAm 10;
WhoAm 80, 82, 86, 88, 90; WhoUSWr
88; WhoWest 74, 76, 78; WhoWrEP 89,
92, 95; WrDr 76, 80, 82, 84, 86, 88, 90,
92, 94N*

Swayne, Noah Haynes
American. Supreme Court Justice
Appointed by Abraham Lincoln; served,
    1862-81.
b. Dec 7, 1804 in Frederick County,
    Virginia
d. Jun 8, 1884 in New York, New York
Source: *AmNatBi; ApCAB; BiAUS;
BiDFedJ; BioIn 2, 5, 15; CamDcAB;
DcAmB; Drake; HarEnUS; NatCAB 4;
OxCSupC; SupCtJu; TwCBDA; WebAB
74, 79; WhAm HS; WhCiWar*

Swayze, John Cameron, Sr.
American. Journalist
Did commercials for Timex watches;
    radio, TV news commentator, NBC,
    1947-56.
b. Apr 4, 1906 in Wichita, Kansas
d. Aug 15, 1995 in Sarasota, Florida
Source: *BioIn 3, 13, 21, 22; CamDcAB;
ConAu 102, 149; EncAJ; EncTelN;
EncTwCJ; IntMPA 75, 76, 78, 79, 80,
81, 82, 84, 86, 88, 92, 94; LegTOT;
LesBEnT; News 96, 96-1; NewYTET;
SaTiSS; WhAm 11; WhoAm 74, 76, 78,
80, 82, 84, 86, 88, 90, 92, 94, 95; WhoE
74; WhoEnt 92; WhoWor 78, 82, 84, 87,
89; WorAl; WorAlBi*

Swayze, Patrick
American. Actor
In films *Dirty Dancing*, 1987, *Ghost*,
    1990.
b. Aug 18, 1952 in Houston, Texas
Source: *ConTFT 4, 16, 27; CurBio 91;
FilmChD; HolBB; IntMPA 94, 96;
LegTOT; VarWW 85; WhoHol 92*

Swearingen, John Eldred
American. Business Executive
Chm., CEO of Continental Illinois Corp.,
    1984-87; CEO of Standard Oil of
    Indiana, 1960-83.
b. Sep 7, 1918 in Columbia, South
    Carolina
Source: *AmMWSc 73P, 79, 82, 86, 89,
92, 95, 98; BioIn 6, 11, 12, 13; CurBio
79; IntWW 74, 75, 76, 77, 78, 79, 80,
81, 82, 83, 89, 91, 93; NewYTBS 84;
WhoAm 74, 76, 78, 80, 82, 84, 86, 88,
90, 92; WhoFI 74, 75, 77, 79, 81, 83,
87, 89; WhoMW 74, 76, 78, 80, 82, 86,
88, 92; WhoWor 74, 76, 78, 80, 82, 84,
87, 89*

Sweat, Keith
American. Singer
Successful singer was a pioneer of
    "New Jack Swing" music, a fusion
    style of rhythm and blues, soul, and
    hip-hop; album *Make It Last Forever*
    went double platinum; named No. 1
    New Male Artist, Black Radio
    Exclusive, 1988.
b. c. 1961 in New York, New York
Source: *ConBlB 19*

Swedenborg, Emanuel
Swedish. Scientist, Mystic
Religious works rejected traditional
    doctrines of original sin, eternal
    damnation.
b. Jan 29, 1688 in Stockholm, Sweden
d. Mar 29, 1772
Source: *BbD; Benet 87, 96; BenetAL 91;
BiD&SB; BiDPsy; BiHiMed; BioIn 1, 3,
4, 5, 6, 7, 8, 9, 10, 14, 15, 16, 18, 19,
20, 22; BlmGEL; CamBiEn; CasWL;
ChamBiD; CyWA 58, 97; DcEuL;
DcPseud; DcScanL; DcScB; Dis&D;
EncEnl; EncO&P 1, 2, 3; EncPaPR 91;
EncSF, 93; EncWB 98; EuAu; EvEuW;
IlEncMy; LarDcSc; LinLib L, S;
LngCEL; LuthC 75; McGEWB;
NamesHP; NewC; NewCBEL; OxCEng
67, 85, 95; RAdv 14; RComWL; REn;
WhoChr; WorAl; WorAlBi; WrPh P*

Sweelinck, Jan Pieterszoon
Dutch. Composer, Organist
Famed organ teacher; wrote choral,
    church music.
b. 1562 in Amsterdam, Netherlands
d. Oct 16, 1621 in Amsterdam,
    Netherlands
Source: *AtlBL; BakBD 78, 84, 92;
BakDcM; BioIn 1, 4, 7, 12; CamBiEn;
ChamBiD; DcCathB; EncWB 98; LuthC
75; McGEWB; MusSN; NewAmDM;
NewGrDM 80; NewOxM; OxCMus;
WhDW*

Sweeney, John J(oseph)

American. Labor Union Official
President, AFL-CIO, 1995—.
b. May 5, 1934 in New York, New York
Source: *CurBio 96; IntWW 97, 98, 2000;
NewYTBS 76; WhoAm 98, 99, 2000;
WhoE 99; WhoFI 00*

Sweet, Blanche

[Sarah Blanche Sweet]
American. Actor
Starred in first feature length film made
    in US: *Judith of Bethulia,* 1913.
b. Jun 18, 1896 in Chicago, Illinois
d. Sep 6, 1986 in New York, New York
Source: *AmNatBi; AnObit 1986;
BiE&WWA; BioIn 9, 10, 11, 15, 18;
Film 1, 2; FilmgC; ForYSC; IntDcF 1-3,
2-3; MotPP; MovMk; NewYTBS 86;
NotNAT; OxCFilm; SweetSg A; TwYS;
WhoHol A*

Sweet, John Howard

Canadian. Publisher
Publisher of *US News and World Report,*
    1951-78; board chm., 1973-83.
b. Mar 21, 1907 in Emerson, Manitoba,
    Canada
d. Aug 14, 1988 in Bethesda, Maryland
Source: *BioIn 16; BlueB 76; CanWW 70,
79, 80, 81, 83; EncTwCJ; IntYB 78, 79;
WhAm 9; WhoAm 74, 76, 78, 80, 82, 84,
86, 88; WhoE 77, 79, 81, 83, 85, 86;
WhoFI 74; WhoSSW 73; WhoWor 74*

Sweet, Matthew

American. Singer, Songwriter, Musician
Rock and roll singer/guitarist; began solo
    career 1986; albums include
    Girlfriend, 1991.
b. Oct 6, 1964 in Lincoln, Nebraska
Source: *BillEnR; ConMus 9*

Sweet, Rachel

American. Singer
Hit album *Fool Around;* single "Baby."
b. 1966 in Akron, Ohio
Source: *BioIn 12; NewWmR*

Sweet Honey in the Rock

[Ysaye Maria Barnwell; Nitanju Bolade;
    Evelyn Harris; Aisha Kahlil; Bernice
    Johnson Reagon]
American. Music Group
Politically active gospel singers; album
    *B'lieve I'll Rin On. See, What the
    Ends Gonna Be,* 1978.
Source: *BlkWAm; ConMus 1, 26; InB&W
85A; PenEncP; PeoHis; WomPO 76, 78*

Swenson, Inga

American. Actor
Played Gretchen Kraus on TV series
    "Benson," 1979-85.
b. Dec 29, 1932 in Omaha, Nebraska
Source: *BiE&WWA; EncMT; FilmgC;
HalFC 80, 84, 88; InWom SUP;
LegTOT; NotNAT; WhoAm 74; WhoHol
A; WhoTelC; WhoThe 77, 81*

Swenson, May

American. Poet
Wrote *New and Selected Things Taking
    Place,* 1978.
b. May 28, 1919 in Logan, Utah
Source: *AmAu&B; AnCL; AnObit 1989;
ArtclWW 2; AuBYP 2S, 3; Benet 87, 96;
BenetAL 91; BioIn 8, 9, 10, 12, 14, 15,
16, 17, 19, 20, 23; ChhPo S1, S2;
ConAu 5R, 36NR, 61NR, 130; ConLC 4,
14, 61, 106; ConPo 70, 75, 80, 85;
CroCAP; CyWA 97; DcLEL 1940; DrAP
75; EncALit; FemiCLE; Focus; IntWWP
77, 82; InWom SUP; MajTwCW 1, 2;
ModAL 4S2; ModWoWr; OxCTwCL;
OxCTwCP; OxCWoWr 95; PoeCrit 14;
RAdv 1, 14; SmATA 15; WhoAm 74, 76,
78, 80, 82, 84, 86, 88; WhoAmW 81, 85,
87, 89; WhoUSWr 88; WhoWor 74;
WhoWrEP 89; WorAu 1950; WrDr 76,
80, 82, 84, 86, 88, 90*

Swenson, Rick

American. Athlete
Five-time winner of the Alaskan Iditarod
    Trail sled dog race.

Swerling, Jo

American. Screenwriter, Dramatist
Co-author of play *Guys and Dolls,* 1951;
    won Tony.
b. May 18, 1897 in Bardichov, Russia
Source: *BiE&WWA; BioIn 15; DcLB 44;
FilmEn; FilmgC; HalFC 84; IntDcF 1-4,
2-4; IntMPA 75, 76, 78, 79, 80, 81, 82,
84, 86, 88, 92, 94, 96; NotNAT; VarWW
85; WorEFlm*

Swift, Elizabeth Ann

[The Hostages]
American. Hostage
One of 52 held by terrorists, Nov 1979-
    Jan 1981.
b. Dec 3, 1940 in Washington, District
    of Columbia
Source: *BioIn 12; NewYTBS 81; USBiR
74; WhoGov 72; WhoSSW 99*

Swift, Graham (Colin)

English. Author
Wrote novels *The Sweet-Shop Owner,*
    1980; *Ever After,* 1992.
b. Aug 16, 1949 in London, England
Source: *BioIn 14, 17; CamGLE; ConAu
46NR, 71NR, 117, 122; ConLC 41, 88;
ConNov 86, 91, 96; CyWA 89; IntAu&W
91, 93; IntWW 91, 93, 97, 98, 2000;
MajTwCW 2; RGTwCWr; Who 94, 98,
99, 2000; WorAu 1980; WrDr 86, 88,
90, 92, 94, 96*

Swift, Gustavus Franklin

American. Manufacturer
Developed refrigerated railroad cars.
b. Jun 24, 1839 in Sandwich,
    Massachusetts
d. Mar 29, 1903 in Chicago, Illinois
Source: *AmBi; AmNatBi; ApCAB X;
BiDAmBL 83; BioIn 3, 6, 7, 15;
CamBiEn; CamDcAB; DcAmB; EncAAH;
EncAB-H 1974, 1996; NatCAB 14;
OxCAmH; WebAB 74, 79; WhAm 1;
WorAl*

Swift, Jonathan

[Isaac Bickerstaff]
English. Satirist, Author, Clergy
Wrote *Gulliver's Travels,* 1726.
b. Nov 30, 1667 in Dublin, Ireland
d. Oct 19, 1745 in Dublin, Ireland
Source: *Alli; AtlBL; BbD; Benet 87, 96;
BiCoLiE; BiD&SB; BiDIrW; BioIn 1, 2,
3, 4, 5, 6, 7, 8, 9, 10, 11, 12, 13, 14, 15,
16, 17, 18, 20, 21, 22; BlkwCE;
BlmGEL; BritAu; BritWr 3; CamBiEn;
CamGEL; CamGLE; CarSB; CasWL;
ChamBiD; Chambr 2; ChhPo, S1, S3;
ChlLR 53; CnDBLB 2; CnE&AP; CrtT
2, 4; CyWA 58, 97; DcArts; DcBiA;
DcBiPP; DcEnA, A; DcEnL; DcEuL;
DcIrB 1, 2, 3; DcIrL, 96; DcIrW 1, 2;
DcLB 95, 101; DcLEL; DcNaB; DcPup;
Dis&D; EncEnl; EncSF, 93; EncWB 98;
EvLB; GrWrEL N, P; HalFC 80, 84, 88;
HisDcIr; HsB&A; JouAdvM; LegTOT;
LinLib L, S; LitC 1; LiveWoA; LngCEL;
LuthC 75; MagSWL; McGEWB; MouLC
2; NewC; NewCBEL; NewEScF; Novels;
OxCBrHi; OxCEng 67, 85, 95; OxCIri;
OxCMus; PenC ENG; PoeCrit 9; PoIre;
RadHan; RAdv 1, 14; RComWL; REn;
RfGEnL 91; RGFBP; ScF&FL 1;
ScFEYrs; ScFSB; SmATA 19; SocPrL;
WebE&AL; WhDW; WhoChL; WhoChr;
WorAl; WorAlBi; WorLitC; WrChl;
WrPh*

Swift, Kay

American. Musician, Songwriter
Pianist-arranger; songs include "Forever
    and a Day."
b. Apr 19, 1897 in New York, New
    York
d. Jan 28, 1993 in Southington,
    Connecticut
Source: *AnObit 1993; ASCAP 66; BioIn
18, 19; CmpEPM; ConAmC 76; EncMT;
InWom SUP; NewGrDA 86; NewYTBS
93*

Swigert, Ernest Goodnough

American. Manufacturer
Founder, pres., Hyster Co., 1929-71,
    manufacturer of lift trucks, cranes.
b. Aug 4, 1892 in Portland, Oregon
d. Nov 30, 1986 in Portland, Oregon
Source: *BioIn 4, 15; CurBio 57, 87;
WhAm 9*

Swigert, Jack

[John Leonard Swigert, Jr]
American. Astronaut, Politician
Commanded *Apollo 13;* elected to
    Congress from CO, 1982; died before
    sworn in.
b. Aug 30, 1931 in Denver, Colorado
d. Dec 27, 1982 in Washington, District
    of Columbia
Source: *AmMWSc 73P, 79; AnObit 1982;
BioIn 21, 23; IntWW 74, 75, 76, 77;
NewYTBS 82; WhAm 8; WhoAm 76, 78,
80, 82; WhoAmP 75, 77, 79; WhoGov
72, 75; WhoSSW 73, 75, 76; WhoWest
82, 84; WhoWor 78; WorDWW*

Swimmer, Ross
American. Native American Chief, Government Official, Business Executive
Principal chief of the Cherokee, 1975-85; head of the Bureau of Indian Affairs, 1985-89; president, Cherokee Nation Industries, Inc., 1992—.
b. Oct 26, 1943 in Oklahoma City, Oklahoma
Source: *NotNaAm*

Swinburne, Algernon Charles
English. Poet, Dramatist, Critic
Wrote *Atalanta in Calydon*, 1865; *Poems and Ballads*, 1866.
b. Apr 5, 1837 in London, England
d. Apr 10, 1909 in London, England
Source: *AtlBL; BbD; Benet 87, 96; BiCoLiE; BiD&SB; BioIn 1, 2, 3, 5, 6, 7, 8, 9, 10, 11, 12, 13, 14, 16, 17, 18, 19, 20, 23, 24; BlmGEL; BritAu 19; BritWr 5; CamBiEn; CamGEL; CamGLE; CarSB; CasWL; CelCen; ChamBiD; Chambr 3; ChhPo, S1, S2, S3; CnDBLB 4; CnE&AP; ConAu 105, 140; CrtSuDr; CrtT 3, 4; CyWA 58, 97; DcArts; DcBiPP; DcEnA, A; DcEnL; DcEuL; DcLEL; DcNaB S2; Dis&D; EncUnb; EncWB 98; EvLB; GrWrEL P; LinLib S; LngCEL; MagSWL; McGEWB; MouLC 4; NewC; NewCBEL; NotNAT B; OxCEng 67, 85, 95; PenC ENG; PoeCrit 24; RAdv 1; RComWL; REn; RfGEnL 91; RGFBP; TwoTYeD; VicBrit; WebE&AL; WhDW; WhLit; WorAl; WorAlBi*

Swinburne, Laurence
American. Children's Author
Books include *RFK: The Last Knight*, 1969; *Detli*, 1970.
b. Jul 2, 1924 in New York, New York
Source: *BioIn 11; ConAu 15NR, 61; SmATA 9*

Swing, Raymond Gram
American. Broadcast Journalist
Best known for radio commentaries in 1930s; liberal views attacked by House Committee on Un-American Activities.
b. Mar 25, 1887 in Cortland, New York
d. Dec 22, 1968 in Washington, District of Columbia
Source: *AmAu&B; BiDAmJo; ConAmC 76, 82; ConAu 89; CurBio 40, 69; DcAmDH 80, 89; EncAJ; LegTOT; LngCTC; OhA&B; OxCAmH; RadStar; TwCA SUP; WhAm 5; WorAl*

Swinnerton, Frank Arthur
[Simon Pure]
English. Author, Critic
Wrote popular tale *Nocturne*, 1917; critique *Georgian Literary Scene*, 1935.
b. Aug 12, 1884 in Wood Green, England
d. Nov 6, 1982 in Cranleigh, England
Source: *AnObit 1982; BioIn 5, 6, 11, 13; Chambr 3; ChhPo S3; ConAu 108; ConNov 72, 76; CyWA 58; DcLEL; DcNaB 1981; EvLB; IntWW 74, 75, 76,*

77, 78, 79, 80, 81, 82; *LngCTC; ModBrL; NewC; NewCBEL; NewYTBS 76, 82; PenC ENG; RAdv 1; REn; TwCA, SUP; TwCWr; WhAm 8; WhE&EA; Who 74, 82, 83; WhoLA; WhoWor 74, 76, 78, 80; WorAu 1900; WrDr 76, 80*

Swinnerton, James Guilford
American. Cartoonist
Created early comic strips "Little Jimmy," "The Canyon Kiddies."
b. Nov 13, 1875 in Eureka, California
d. Sep 5, 1974 in Palm Springs, California
Source: *AmNatBi; ArtsAmW 1; BioIn 6, 9, 10; ConAu 93; IlBEAAW; NewYTBS 74; WhAm 6; WhoAmA 84N; WorECom*

Swinton, Ernest Dunlop, Sir
English. Army Officer
Instrumental in development of tank, WW I.
b. Oct 21, 1868 in Bangalore, Mysore
d. Jan 15, 1951 in Oxford, England
Source: *BioIn 2, 3, 9; CamBiEn; ChamBiD; DcNaB 1951; InSci; WhDW; WhLit*

Swit, Loretta
[Mrs. Dennis Holahan]
American. Actor
Played Margaret Houlihan in TV series "M*A*S*H," 1972-83; won Emmy award for best supporting actress in a comedy series 1979-81.
b. Nov 4, 1939 in Passaic, New Jersey
Source: *BioNews 74; ConTFT 19; HalFC 84; IntMPA 86, 94, 96; WhoAm 84, 86, 95, 96, 97, 98, 99, 2000; WhoAmW 85, 87, 95; WhoEnt 98; WhoHol A*

Switzer, Barry
American. Football Coach
Head coach, U of Oklahoma, 1973-89; won three national championships; head coach, Dallas, 1994-98; won Super Bowl, 1996.
b. Oct 5, 1937 in Crossett, Arkansas
Source: *BiDAmSp FB; BioIn 13; ConAu 143; NewYTBS 86; WhoAm 80, 82, 84, 86, 88, 95, 96, 97, 98; WhoFtbl 74; WhoSpor; WhoSSW 78, 80, 82, 84, 95; WrDr 96*

Switzer, Carl
[Our Gang]
"Alfalfa"
American. Actor
In *Our Gang* film series, 1935-42; specialty was off-key singing; shot in brawl.
b. Aug 7, 1927 in Paris, Illinois
d. Jan 21, 1959 in Sepulveda, California
Source: *BioIn 5, 9; FilmEn; FilmgC; MotPP; NotNAT B; WhoHol B; WhScrn 74, 77, 83*

Switzer, Katherine Virginia
American. Track Athlete
First woman to officially run in Boston Marathon, 1967.
b. Jan 5, 1947 in Amberg, Germany
Source: *BioIn 12; NewYTBS 76, 82; WhoAmW 77, 85, 87*

Switzer, Mary E.
American. Government Official, Social Reformer
Dedicated to the cause of rehabilitation, she helped establish the World Health Organization and was an administrator with the Office of Vocational Rehabilitation and the Social and Rehabilitation Service at the Department of Health, Education and Welfare.
b. Feb 16, 1900 in Newton Upper Falls, Massachusetts
d. Oct 16, 1971 in Washington, District of Columbia
Source: *CurBio 71N; EncWB, 98*

Swoopes, Sheryl
American. Basketball Player
Member of gold-medal winning US Women's Olympic Basketball Team, 1996.
b. Mar 25, 1971 in Brownfield, Texas
Source: *BioIn 22, 23, 24; ConBlB 12; CurBio 96; EncWoSp; News 98, 98-2; WhoAfA 10; WhoAm 99, 2000; WhoAmW 99*

Swope, Gerard
American. Industrialist
Pres., General Electric, 1922-39, 1942-44.
b. Dec 1, 1872 in Saint Louis, Missouri
d. Nov 20, 1957 in New York, New York
Source: *AmNatBi; BiDAmBL 83; BioIn 1, 4, 5, 6, 11; CamDcAB; CurBio 41, 58; DcAmB S6; EncAB-A 2; EncWB, 98; InSci; NatCAB 45; ObitOF 79; OxCAmH; WebAB 74, 79; WhAm 3*

Swope, Herbert Bayard
American. Journalist, Editor
Won Pulitzer for WW I coverage; executive editor of *NY World*, 1920-29.
b. Jan 5, 1882 in Saint Louis, Missouri
d. Jun 20, 1958 in Sands Point, New York
Source: *AmNatBi; BiDAmJo; BioIn 1, 4, 5, 6, 7, 13, 14, 16; CamDcAB; CurBio 44, 58; DcAmB S6; EncAJ; HisDcWJ; JrnUS; NatCAB 45; REn; REnAL; WebAB 74, 79; WhAm 3; WhoPul; WorAl; WorAlBi*

Syberberg, Hans Jurgen
German. Director, Screenwriter
Films include seven-hr. *Our Hitler: A Film from Germany*, 1977.
b. 1935 in Pomerania, Prussia
Source: *BioIn 10, 11, 12, 13, 14, 16, 17, 19; ConAu 93; CurBio 83; EncEurC; IntWW 97, 98, 2000; WorFDir 2*

Sydenham, Baron
[Charles Edward Poulett Thomson]
English. Politician
Governor general of British North
America, attempted to implement the
reforms recommended in the Durham
Report.
b. Sep 13, 1799
d. Sep 19, 1841 in Kingston, Ontario,
Canada

Sydenham, Thomas
''The English Hippocrates''
English. Scientist, Engineer, Physician
Introduced use of quinine; invented
liquid laudanum.
b. Sep 10, 1624
d. Dec 29, 1689 in London, England
Source: *Alli; BiESc; BiHiMed; BioIn 5,
7, 9, 17; CamBiEn; CamDcSc;
ChamBiD; DcBiPP; DcNaB; DcScB;
EncWB 98; InSci; LarDcSc; McGCEnS;
McGEWB; NewCBEL; OxCMed 86;
RanHWDS; WhDW; WorScD*

Syed Ahmed Khan
Indian. Religious Leader, Educator,
Government Official
Helped establish the Moslem foundation
for adapting to the intellectual and
political changes accompanying
Western rule in southern Asia.
b. Oct 17, 1817
d. Mar 27, 1898
Source: *EncWB 98; McGEWB*

Sykes, George
''Tardy George''
American. Military Leader
Commanded Union's Fifth Corps at
Gettysburg, 1863.
b. Oct 9, 1822 in Dover, Delaware
d. Feb 8, 1880 in Brownsville, Texas
Source: *AmBi; AmNatBi; ApCAB; BioIn
7; CivWDc; DcAmB; HarEnUS; NatCAB
4; TwCBDA; WhAm HS; WhCiWar*

Sykes, Mark, Sir
English. Statesman
Expert on Mideast policy who helped
promote Balfour Declaration, 1917.
b. Mar 16, 1879 in London, England
d. Feb 16, 1919 in Paris, France
Source: *BioIn 2, 10; DcNaB 1912;
HisDBrE*

Sykes, Roosevelt
[Dobby Bragg]
American. Musician
Considered the father of modern blues
piano, the pianist and singer performed
with bands such as the Honeydrippers
and as a solo act beginning in the
1920s.
b. Jan 31, 1906 in Elmar, Arkansas
d. Jul 17, 1984 in New Orleans,
Louisiana
Source: *AllMGBl 1, 2; AmNatBi; AnObit
1983; BiDAfM; BioIn 13; Blues;
BluesWW; ConAu 110; ConBlB 20;
ConMus 20; GuBlues; InB&W 85;
NewGrDA 86; PenEncP; WhAm 8*

Sylbert, Paul
Designer, Director
Won Oscar, 1978, for *Heaven Can Wait.*
b. 1928
Source: *BioIn 13; ConTFT 9; VarWW
85; WhoAm 96, 97, 98, 99, 2000;
WhoEnt 98*

Sylbert, Richard
American. Art Director
Films include *Breathless; The Cotton
Club;* won Oscar for *Who's Afraid of
Virginia Woolf,* 1966.
b. Apr 16, 1928 in New York, New
York
Source: *ArtDirC; BioIn 12, 13; ConDes
90, 97; ConTFT 9; FilmgC; HalFC 84,
88; IntDcF 1-4, 2-4; VarWW 85;
WhoAm 96, 97, 98, 99, 2000*

Sylvers, The
[Charmaine Sylver; Edmund Sylver;
Foster Sylver; James Sylver; Joseph
Sylver; Leon Sylver; Olympia-Ann
Sylver]
American. Music Group
Family group of singers, began
recording, 1972; soul hits include
''Boogie Fever,'' 1976; ''Hot Line,''
1977.
Source: *BioIn 11; InB&W 80; RkOn 84*

Sylvester, James Joseph
English. Mathematician
Co-founder of algebraic invariants theory
with Arthur Cayley.
b. Sep 3, 1814 in London, England
d. Mar 15, 1897 in London, England
Source: *Alli SUP; AmBi; AmNatBi;
ApCAB; BiDAmS; BiESc; BiInAmS;
BioIn 15, 22, 24; CamBiEn; CamDcSc;
ChamBiD; DcAmB; DcBiPP; DcNaB;
DcScB; InSci; LarDcSc; NotMat;
OxCAmH; PeoHis; RanHWDS; WhAm
HS; WhDW*

Sylvis, William (H.)
American. Labor Union Official
Pioneered many trade union methods and
inspired the first attempt to form a
united trade union movement.
b. Jan 26, 1828 in Armagh, Pennsylvania
d. 1869
Source: *AmNatBi; AmRef; BiDAmL;
BioIn 2, 4, 6, 7, 8, 9, 10, 15; CamDcAB;
DcAmB; LexLab; McGEWB; WebAB 74,
79; WhAm HS*

Symington, J. Fife, III
American. Politician
Rep. governor, AZ, 1991-97; indicted on
23 counts of attempted extortion and
wire and bankruptcy fraud in 1996.
b. Aug 12, 1945 in New York, New
York
Source: *AlmAP 92; WhoAm 98;
WhoWest 92, 98*

Symington, Stuart
[William Stuart Symington]
American. Politician
Democratic senator from MO, 1952-77;
known champion of the military; first
US Air Force secretary, 1947-50.
b. Jun 26, 1901 in Amherst,
Massachusetts
d. Dec 14, 1988 in New Canaan,
Connecticut
Source: *AmNatBi; AnObit 1988;
BiDrAC; BiDrUSC 89; BioIn 1, 2, 3, 4,
5, 6, 9, 10, 11, 12, 16, 24; BlueB 76;
CamBiEn; CamDcAB; CelR; CngDr 74;
CurBio 45, 56, 89, 89N; EncCW;
EncMcCE; FacFETw; InSci; IntWW 74,
75, 76, 77, 78, 79, 80, 81; IntYB 78, 79;
LinLib S; NewYTBS 88, 89; PolPar;
PolProf E, J, K, NF, T; WhAm 9; Who
74, 82, 83, 85, 88; WhoAm 74, 76, 84,
86, 88; WhoAmP 73, 75, 77, 79, 89;
WhoGov 72, 75, 77; WhoMW 74, 76;
WhoWor 74; WorAl; WorAlBi*

Symms, Steven Douglas
American. Politician
Rep. senator from ID, 1980—.
b. Apr 23, 1938 in Nampa, Idaho
Source: *AlmAP 88; BiDrUSC 89; CngDr
87; IntWW 81, 82, 83, 89, 91, 93;
WhoAm 74, 76, 78, 80, 82, 84, 86, 88,
90; WhoAmP 87; WhoWest 74, 76, 78,
80, 82, 84, 87, 89; WhoWor 82, 87, 91*

Symonds, John Addington
English. Historian, Poet, Translator
Noted for seven-volume *History of
Italian Renaissance,* 1875-86;
translation of Cellini autobiography,
1888.
b. Oct 5, 1840 in Bristol, England
d. Apr 19, 1893 in Rome, Italy
Source: *Alli, SUP; AtlBL; BbD; Benet
87, 96; BiD&SB; BioIn 7, 8, 9, 10, 14,
16, 20, 21; BritAu 19; CamBiEn;
CamGEL; CamGLE; CasWL; CelCen;
ChamBiD; ChhPo, S1, S2, S3; CmpQue;
DcEnA; DcEuL; DcLB 144; DcLEL;
Dis&D; EvLB; GayLesB; GloEncH;
LinLib L, S; MouLC 4; NewC;
NewCBEL; NinCLC 34; OxCEng 67, 85,
95; PenC ENG; REn; VicBrit*

Symons, Arthur William
Welsh. Critic, Poet
Wrote verse volume *Silhouettes,* 1892;
critique *Symbolist Movement in
Literature,* 1899.
b. Feb 28, 1865 in Milford Haven, Wales
d. Jan 22, 1945 in Wittersham, England
Source: *Alli SUP; AtlBL; BiD&SB;
CamBiEn; CasWL; ChamBiD; Chambr
3; CnE&AP; DcNaB 1941; EvLB;
LngCTC; ModBrL; NewC; OxCEng 67,
85, 95; OxCTwCP; PenC ENG; REn;
TwCA, SUP; TwCWr; WebE&AL;
WorAu 1900*

Symons, George James
English. Meteorologist
Worked to make meteorology more
accurate and standardized in its
measurements.

b. Aug 6, 1838 in London, England
d. Mar 10, 1900 in London, England
Source: *BioIn 4; CamBiEn; ChamBiD;
DcNaB S1; InSci; LarDcSc*

Symons, Julian (Gustave)
English. Author
Mystery writer; won 1961 Edgar for
Progress of a Crime.
b. May 30, 1912 in London, England
d. Nov 19, 1994
Source: *Benet 87, 96; BioIn 4, 9, 13, 14,
15, 17, 19, 20, 21; BlueB 76; ChamBiD;
ConAu 3AS, 3NR, 33NR, 49, 59NR, 147;
ConLC 2, 14, 32, 86; ConNov 82, 86,
91; ConPo 80, 85, 91; CrtSuMy; DcLB
87, 155, Y92; DcLEL 1940; EncMys;
EngPo; IntAu&W 76, 77, 89, 91, 93;
IntWW 91, 93; LngCTC; MajTwCW 1;
ModBrL; NewCBEL; NewYTBS 94;
Novels; OxCTwCL; OxCTwCP;
RGTwCWr; ScF&FL 92; TwCA SUP;
TwCCr&M 80, 85, 91; WhAm 11;
WhE&EA; Who 74, 82, 83, 85, 88, 90,
92, 94; WhoAm 82, 84, 86, 88, 90, 92,
94, 95; WhoSpyF; WorAl; WorAlBi;
WrDr 76, 80, 82, 84, 86, 88, 90, 92, 94,
96*

Syms, Sylvia
American. Singer
Popular Cabaret singer.
b. Dec 2, 1917 in New York, New York
d. May 10, 1992 in New York, New
York
Source: *BioIn 17, 18, 22; DcPseud;
NewYTBS 92*

Syms, Sylvia
English. Actor
Leading lady in films: *The World of
Suzie Wong,* 1960; *The Victim,* 1961.
b. Dec 3, 1934 in London, England
Source: *BioIn 19; ConTFT 3, 13;
FilmAG WE; FilmEn; FilmgC; HalFC
80, 84, 88; IlWWBF; IntMPA 75, 76, 78,
79, 80, 81, 82, 84, 88, 92, 94, 96;
IntWW 98, 2000; IntWWW 2; ItaFilm;
MotPP; WhoHol 92, A*

Synge, John Millington
Irish. Author, Dramatist
Wrote about peasants of W Ireland; *The
Playboy of the Western World,* 1907.
b. Apr 16, 1871 in Dublin, Ireland
d. Mar 24, 1909 in Dublin, Ireland
Source: *AtlBL; Benet 87, 96; BiCoLiE;
BiDIrW; BioIn 1, 3, 4, 5, 6, 7, 8, 9, 10,
11, 12, 13, 14, 17, 18, 23; BlmGEL;
CamBiEn; CamGEL; CamGWoT;
CasWL; Chambr 3; ChhPo S1; CnDBLB
5; CnMD; CnMWL; CnThe; CrtSuDr;
CyWA 58, 97; DcEuL; DcIrB 1, 2, 3;
DcIrL; DcIrW 1; DcLEL; DcNaB S2;
Dis&D; DramC 2; EncFoLi; EncWL 1,
2, 2S, 3; EncWT; Ent; EvLB; FacFETw;
HisDcIr; IriPla; LinLib L, S; LngCEL;
LngCTC; MagSWL; McGEWD 72, 84;
ModBrL, 2, S1, S2; ModIrL; ModIrLi;
ModWD; NewC; NewEOp 71;
NewGrDO; NotNAT B; OxCEng 67, 85;
OxCThe 67, 83; OxCTwCL; PenC ENG;
PlP&P; PoIre; RAdv 14; RComWL;*

*REn; REnWD; TwCA; TwCLC 37;
TwCWr; WebE&AL; WhDW; WhoTwCL;
WorAl; WorAlBi*

Synge, Richard Laurence Millington
English. Chemist
Shared Nobel Prize, 1952, for invention
of partition chromatography.
b. Oct 28, 1914 in Liverpool, England
Source: *AmMWSc 98; AsBiEn; BiESc;
BioIn 3, 6; BlueB 76; CamBiEn;
ChamBiD; IntWW 74, 75, 76, 77, 78, 79,
80, 81, 82, 83, 89, 91, 93; LarDcSc;
McGCEnS; McGMS 80; RanHWDS;
Who 74, 82, 83, 85, 88, 90, 92, 94;
WhoNob, 90, 95; WhoScEn 94, 96;
WhoWor 74, 76, 78, 82, 84, 87, 89, 91,
93, 95, 96, 97; WorAl*

Szabo, Violette Bushell
English. Spy
Special Operations Executive agent, WW
II; captured while on mission,
executed in concentration camp; life
was subject of film *Carve Her Name
With Pride,* 1958.
b. 1918
d. Jan 26, 1945, Germany
Source: *BioIn 7, 8; WhWW-II*

Szabolcsi, Bence
Hungarian. Musicologist, Educator
Authority on Hungarian composer, Bela
Bartok.
b. Aug 2, 1899 in Budapest, Austria-
Hungary
d. Jan 21, 1973 in Budapest, Hungary
Source: *BakBD 78, 84, 92; BakBDTw;
ConAu 116; NewGrDM 80; WhoMus 72;
WhoWor 74; WhoWorJ 72, 78*

Szasz, Thomas Stephen
American. Psychiatrist, Educator
Books on mental illness include *Insanity:
The Idea and Its Consequences,* 1986.
b. Apr 15, 1920 in Budapest, Hungary
Source: *AmAu&B; AmMWSc 73S, 76P,
79, 82, 86, 89, 92, 95, 98; BiDrAPA 77;
BioIn 9, 10, 12, 13, 15; CamBiEn;
CamDcAB; ChamBiD; ConAu 9NR, 17R;
CurBio 75; IntAu&W 77, 82, 86, 89, 91,
93; IntWW 76, 77, 78, 79, 80, 81, 82,
83, 89, 91, 93, 97, 98, 2000; MakMC;
NewYTBE 71; WhoAm 74, 76, 78, 80,
82, 84, 86, 88, 90, 92, 94, 95, 96, 97,
98, 99, 2000; WhoE 91, 95; WhoMedH
96; WhoScEn 94, 96, 2000; WhoWor 74;
WorAu 1975; WrDr 76, 80, 82, 84, 86,
88, 90, 92, 94, 96, 98, 99, 2000*

Szell, George
American. Conductor
Led Cleveland Symphony, from 1946,
molding it into one of nation's finest.
b. Jun 7, 1897 in Budapest, Austria-
Hungary
d. Jul 30, 1970 in Cleveland, Ohio
Source: *AmNatBi; BakBD 78, 84, 92;
BakBDTw; BakDcM; BiDAmM; BioIn 1,
2, 3, 4, 6, 9, 11, 13, 18; BriBkM
80; CamBiEn; CamDcAB; ChamBiD;
CurBio 45, 70; DcAmB S8; FacFETw;*

*IntDcOp; LegTOT; LinLib S; MetOEnc;
MusSN; NatCAB 61; NewAmDM;
NewGrDA 86; NewGrDM 80;
NewGrDO; NewYTBE 70; ObitT 1961;
OxCAmH; OxDcOp; PenDiMP; WebAB
74, 79; WorAl; WorAlBi*

Szenkar, Eugen
Brazilian. Conductor
Directed Dusseldorf Symphony, 1950s;
Brazilian Symphony, 1940s.
b. Apr 9, 1891 in Budapest, Austria-
Hungary
d. Mar 28, 1977 in Duesseldorf,
Germany
Source: *BakBD 78, 84, 92; BakBDTw;
NewEOp 71*

Szent-Gyorgyi, Albert (von Nagyrapolt)
American. Biochemist
Won Nobel Prize, 1937, for discovery of
Vitamin C; first Hungarian to win
Nobel.
b. Sep 16, 1893 in Budapest, Austria-
Hungary
d. Oct 22, 1986 in Woods Hole,
Massachusetts
Source: *AmMWSc 73P, 76P, 79, 82, 86;
AsBiEn; BioIn 2, 3, 4, 10, 11, 14, 15, 16,
20; BlueB 76; CamBiEn; ChamBiD;
ConAu 120; ConNews 87-2; CurBio 55,
87, 87N; FacFETw; IntWW 74, 75, 76,
77, 78, 79, 80, 81, 82, 83; LarDcSc;
LinLib S; McGCEnS; McGEWB;
McGMS 80; NewYTBS 86; NobelP;
NotTwCS 1; RanHWDS; WebAB 74, 79;
WhAm 9; Who 74, 82, 83, 85; WhoAm
74, 76, 78, 80, 84, 86; WhoE 77, 79, 81,
83, 85, 86; WhoNob, 90, 95; WhoWor
74, 76, 78, 82, 84, 87; WorAl; WorAlBi;
WorScD*

Szeryng, Henryk
Mexican. Violinist
Int'l concertist since 1933; recorded
nearly 250 works, mostly in Romantic
style.
b. Sep 22, 1921? in Zelazowa Wola,
Poland
d. Mar 3, 1988 in Kassel, Germany
(West)
Source: *BakBD 84; BioIn 6, 8; CurBio
68, 86; IntWW 74, 75, 76, 77; MusSN;
NewGrDM 80; NewYTBS 83; Who 74;
WhoAm 86; WhoAmM 83; WhoFr 79;
WhoSSW 73, 75; WhoWor 74*

Szewinska, Irena Kirszenstein
Polish. Track Athlete
Sprinter; won gold medal in 200 meters,
1968 Olympics.
b. May 24, 1946 in Leningrad, Union of
Soviet Socialist Republics
Source: *WhoTr&F 73*

Szigeti, Joseph
American. Violinist
Great concert performer; pioneered in
performing Bartok, contemporary
composers.
b. Sep 2, 1892 in Budapest, Hungary
d. Feb 20, 1973 in Lucerne, Switzerland

Source: *BakBD 78, 84, 92; BakBDTw;
BakDcM; BioIn 1, 2, 3, 4, 5, 7, 9, 10,
11, 12, 13, 14, 18; BriBkM 80; ConAu
P-1; CurBio 40, 58, 73, 73N; FacFETw;
MusMk; MusSN; NewAmDM; NewGrDM
80; NewYTBE 73; ObitT 1971;
PenDiMP; WhAm 5; WhoMus 72;
WhScrn 83*

Szilard, Leo
American. Scientist
With Enrico Fermi, achieved first nuclear
  chain reaction, 1942.
b. Feb 11, 1898 in Budapest, Austria-
  Hungary
d. May 30, 1964 in La Jolla, California
Source: *AmNatBi; AmPeW; AsBiEn;
BiDMoPL; BiESc; BioIn 1, 5, 6, 7, 8, 9,
10, 11, 12, 13; CamBiEn; CamDcAB;
CamDcSc; ChamBiD; ConAu 113, 158;
CurBio 47, 64; DcAmB S7; DcScB;
EncSF, 93; EncWB, 98; FacFETw;
InSci; JeHun; LarDcSc; McGEWB;
McGMS 80; NotTwCS 1; ObitT 1961;
OxCAmH; PeoHis; PolProf T;
RanHWDS; ScF&FL 1; ScFSB;
TwCSFW 81, 86, 91; WebAB 74, 79;
WhAm 4; WhoSciF; WorAl; WorAlBi;
WorInv*

Szmuness, Wolf
Polish. Scientist
Epidemiologist, best known for hepatitis-
  B vaccine.
b. Mar 12, 1919 in Warsaw, Poland
d. Jun 6, 1982 in Flushing, New York
Source: *AnObit 1982; BioIn 12, 13;
NewYTBS 82*

Szoka, Edmund Casimir, Cardinal
American. Religious Leader
Archbishop of Detroit, 1981-90; chief
  financial officer at the Vatican, 1990—
  .
b. Sep 14, 1927 in Grand Rapids,
  Michigan
Source: *AmCath 80; BioIn 13; IntWW
89, 91, 93, 97, 98, 2000; RelLAm 1, 2;
WhoAm 76, 78, 80, 82, 84, 86, 88, 90,
95, 96, 97, 98, 99, 2000; WhoMW 82,
84, 88, 90; WhoRel 85, 92; WhoWor 91,
95, 96, 98, 99*

Szold, Henrietta
American. Social Reformer
Founder, pres., Hadassah, US women's
  Zionist group, 1912-26; practiced
  nursing in Holy Land.
b. Dec 21, 1860 in Baltimore, Maryland
d. Feb 13, 1945 in Jerusalem, Palestine
Source: *AmNatBi; BioAmW; BioIn 1, 2,
3, 4, 5, 6, 7, 8, 9, 10, 11, 12, 13, 14, 15,
16, 17, 19, 21, 22, 23, 24; CamDcAB;
ChamBiD; ContDcW 89; CurBio 40, 45;
DcAmB S3; DcAmImH; DcAmReB 1, 2;
EncARH; EncAWoR; EncWB 98;
EncWHA; EncWomW; FacFETw;
GoodHs; GrLiveH; HerW; IntDcWB;
InWom, SUP; JeAmHC; JeHun; LibW;
McGEWB; NotAW; RelLAm 1, 2; WhAm
2; WomFir; WomWWA 14; WorAl;
WorAlBi*

Szyk, Arthur
Polish. Artist
Miniaturist, manuscript illuminator; noted
  for fine book illustration.
b. Jun 3, 1894 in Lodz, Poland
d. Sep 13, 1951 in New Canaan,
  Connecticut
Source: *BioIn 1, 2, 3, 5, 16; ChhPo;
CurBio 46, 51; DcAmB S5; IlsBYP;
IlsCB 1946; PolBiDi; WhAm 3;
WhAmArt 85; WhoAmA 84, 89N, 91N,
93N; WorECar*

Szymanowski, Karol Maciej
Russian. Composer
Works include opera *Krol Roger*, 1926.
b. Oct 6, 1882 in Timoshovka, Russia
d. Mar 29, 1937 in Lausanne,
  Switzerland
Source: *BakBD 84; BakBDTw; DcCM*

T

T, Mr.
[Lawrence Tero; Lawrence Tureaud]
American. Actor
Former celebrity bodyguard; star of TV's
"A-Team."
b. May 21, 1952 in Chicago, Illinois
Source: *BioIn 13; BlksAmF; ConTFT 5;
DcPseud; InB&W 85; VarWW 85;
WhoAfA 9, 10, 11, 12; WhoBlA 4, 5, 6,
7, 8; WhoHol 92; WorAlBi*

T. Rex
[Marc Bolan; Steven Currie; Mickey
Finn; Jack Green; Bill Legend; Steven
Peregrine Took]
English. Music Group
Rock group formed 1967; up and down
career eventually landed hit song
"Bang A Gong (Get it On)," 1972.
Source: *BiDrAPA 89; BillIEnR; BioIn 13;
ConMus 11; EncPR&S 89; EncRk 88;
EncRkSt; ForYSC; IntMPA 94; LinLib
LP; RkOn 78; RolSEnR 83; WhoHol 92;
WhoRock 81; WhoRocM 82*

Tabai, Ieremia Tienang
Kiribatian. Political Leader
Optimistic yet serious, he was elected the
first president of Kiribati in 1978;
popular leader promoted the interests
of his nation in international
negotiations, and worked to preserve
the traditional Kiribati lifestyle and
culture.
b. Dec 16, 1950, Kiribati
Source: *WhoWor 95*

Tabari, Muhammad ibn Jarir al-
Persian. Scholar, Historian, Author
Moslem religious scholar wrote a
monumental commentary on the
Koran; his annals are the most
important source for the early history
of Islam.
b. 839 in Amol, Tabaristan, Persia
d. Feb 15, 923
Source: *EncWB 98; McGEWB; PenC CL*

Tabb, John Banister
American. Poet
Wrote religious verse *The Rosary in
Rhyme,* 1904.
b. Mar 22, 1845 in Amelia County,
Virginia
d. Nov 19, 1909
Source: *AmAu; AmAu&B; AmBi;
AmNatBi; BenetAL 91; BibAL 8;
BiD&SB; BiDSA; BioIn 22; Chambr 3;
ChhPo, S1; CnDAL; DcAmAu; DcAmB;
DcLEL; DcNAA; EvLB; LinLib L;
NatCAB 13; OxCAmL 65, 83; REnAL;
SouWr; TwCBDA; WhAm 1*

Tabbert, William
American. Actor, Singer
Broadway shows include *South Pacific;
Seven Lively Arts; Fanny.*
b. Oct 5, 1921 in Chicago, Illinois
d. Oct 20, 1974 in Dallas, Texas
Source: *BiE&WWA; BioIn 10; CmpEPM;
EncMT; NewYTBS 74; NotNAT B;
ObitOF 79; WhThe*

Tabei, Junko
Japanese. Mountaineer
First woman to climb to summit of Mt.
Everest, 1975.
b. 1940 in Tokyo, Japan
Source: *GoodHs; InWom SUP; WorAl;
WorAlBi*

Taber, Gladys Bagg
American. Journalist, Author
Wrote popular "Stillmeadow" books;
columnist, *Ladies Home Journal,*
1938-49.
b. Apr 12, 1899 in Colorado Springs,
Colorado
d. Mar 11, 1980 in Hyannis,
Massachusetts
Source: *AmAu&B; AmNov; Au&Wr 71;
BioIn 15; ConAu 4NR, 5R, 97; CurBio
52, 80; ForWC 70; WhoAm 74*

Tabor, Elizabeth Bonduel
McCourt Doe
[Mrs. Horace Tabor]
"Baby Doe"; "Silver Queen"
American. Pioneer
Douglas Moore's opera, *The Ballad of
Baby Doe,* 1955, based on marriage to
Horace Tabor.
b. 1854 in Oshkosh, Wisconsin
d. Mar 7, 1935 in Leadville, Colorado
Source: *NewCol 75*

Tabor, Horace Austin Warner
"Hod"; "Silver Dollar"
American. Government Official
Wealth gained from silver mine; first
mayor of Leadville, CO, 1878; went
broke when US adopted gold standard.
b. Nov 26, 1830 in Holland, Vermont
d. Apr 10, 1899 in Denver, Colorado
Source: *AmBi; AmNatBi; ApCAB;
BiDAmBL 83; BiDrAC; BiDrUSC 89;
BioIn 4, 10; CamDcAB; DcAmB; EncWB
98; McGEWB; NatCAB 11; NewEAmW;
REnAW; TwCBDA; WhAm HS; WhAmP*

Tabori, Kristoffer
American. Actor
Son of actress Viveca Lindfors; starred
in TV series "Chicago Story," 1982.
b. Aug 4, 1952 in Los Angeles,
California
Source: *ConTFT 17; NotNAT; WhoHol
92, A*

Tabouis, Genevieve
French. Journalist
Noted European political analyst; foreign
news editor of *L'Oeuvre,* 1932-40.
b. Feb 23, 1892
d. Sep 22, 1985 in Paris, France
Source: *ConAu 117; CurBio 40, 85;
WhE&EA; Who 82, 83, 85; WhoFr 79*

Tacitus, Cornelius
[Gaius Tacitus; Publius Tacitus]
Roman. Historian, Orator
Writings on Roman history include
Annals, Dialogue on Oratory.
b. 55
d. 117

Source: *Alli; AtlBL; BbD; Benet 87, 96; BiCoLiE; BiD&SB; BioIn 1, 4, 5, 7, 8, 9, 10, 11, 12; BlmGEL; CasWL; CyWA 58; DcEnL; LngCEL; LuthC 75; NewC; OxCEng 67, 85, 95; OxCGer 76; PenC CL; RComWL; REn; WhDW*

Taddei, Giuseppe
Italian. Opera Singer
Dramatic baritone, noted for Verdi, buffo roles.
b. Jun 26, 1916 in Genoa, Italy
Source: *BakBD 84, 92; BakBDTw; BioIn 14, 16; CmOp; IntWWM 90; MetOEnc; NewAmDM; NewEOp 71; NewGrDM 80; NewGrDO; OxDcOp; PenDiMP; WhoMus 72; WhoOp 76*

Taeuber, Conrad F.
American. Sociologist
Together with wife Irene Barnes-Taeuber, contributed to founding of demography as a field; directed US Federal census, 1960, 1970.
b. Jun 15, 1906 in Hosmer, South Dakota
d. Sep 11, 1999 in Nashua, New Hampshire
Source: *ConAu 28NR, 45; IntEnSS 79; IntYB 78, 79, 80, 81, 82; RAdv 14; WhoAm 74, 76, 78, 80, 82, 84, 86, 88, 90, 92, 94, 95, 96, 97; WhoE 77; WhoSSW 73, 75, 76; WhoTech 89*

Taeuber-Arp, Sophie
Swiss. Artist
Sculptor; active in Dada movement; wed to Jean Arp; best work done, 1935-38.
b. Jan 19, 1889 in Davos, Switzerland
d. Jan 13, 1943 in Zurich, Switzerland
Source: *ChamBiD; ConArt 77, 83; ConWomA; DcTwArt; DcWomA; EncWB, 98; InWom SUP; McGDA; OxCTwCA; OxDcArt; PhDrTCA 77; WomArt*

Taewon'gun, Hungson
Korean. Political Leader
One of the most powerful figures at the end of the Yi dynasty, he was the imperial regent and the father of king Kojong.
b. 1820
d. Feb 1898
Source: *EncWB 98; McGEWB*

Taft, Charles Phelps
American. Lawyer, Religious Leader
One of the founders, World Council of Churches; son of Pres. William Howard Taft.
b. Sep 20, 1897
d. Jun 24, 1983 in Cincinnati, Ohio
Source: *AmAu&B; AmNatBi; Au&Wr 71; BioIn 1, 3, 7, 9, 13; BlueB 76; ConAu 105; CurBio 45, 83; IntWW 74, 75, 76, 77, 78, 79, 80, 81, 82, 83; NewYTBS 83; OhA&B; REnAL; WhAm 8; Who 74, 82, 83; WhoAm 74, 76, 78, 80, 82; WhoAmP 83*

Taft, Helen Herron
American. First Lady
Persuaded mayor of Tokyo to donate 3,000 cherry trees to nation's capital; wife of US pres. William Howard Taft.
b. Jun 2, 1861 in Cincinnati, Ohio
d. May 22, 1943 in Washington, District of Columbia
Source: *AmNatBi; BioIn 16, 17, 19, 22; DcNAA; EncWoAP; FacPr 89; GoodHs; InWom, SUP; NatCAB 14; NotAW; OhA&B; WomWWA 14*

Taft, Henry Waters, II
American. Business Executive
Former pres. Outward Bound, U.S.A; pres. and treasurer Brystal-Myers Co., 1962-73; grand nephew of pres. William Howard Taft.
b. Jul 5, 1926 in New York, New York
d. Mar 18, 1991 in Camden, Maine
Source: *BioIn 17; NewYTBS 91; WhoAm 74, 76, 78, 80, 82, 84, 86; WhoE 74; WhoFI 74*

Taft, Lorado
American. Sculptor
Best-known works include *Solitude of the Soul*, Chicago; Ferguson Fountain of the Great Lakes, Chicago.
b. Apr 29, 1860 in Elmwood, Illinois
d. Oct 30, 1936 in Chicago, Illinois
Source: *AmBi; AmLY; AmNatBi; ApCAB SUP; BioIn 1, 4, 8, 11; DcAmAu; DcAmB S2; DcNAA; DcTwArt; EncAB-A 2; EncWB 98; GayN; HarEnUS; LinLib L, S; McGDA; OxCAmH; OxCAmL 65; REnAL; TwCBDA; WebAB 74; WhAm 1, 4A; WhNAA*

Taft, Robert A(lphonso)
"Mr. Republican"
American. Politician
Rep. senator from OH, 1939-53; son of William Howard; sponsored Taft-Hartley Labor Relations Act, 1947.
b. Sep 8, 1889 in Cincinnati, Ohio
d. Jul 31, 1953 in New York, New York
Source: *AmDec 1950; AmNatBi; AmPolLe; BiDrAC; BiDrUSC 89; BioIn 1, 2, 3, 4, 5, 6, 7, 8, 9, 10, 11, 13; CamBiEn; ColdWar 2; CurBio 40, 48, 53; DcAmB S5; EncAAH; EncAB-H 1974, 1996; EncWB, 98; FacFETw; LinLib S; NatCAB 47; OhA&B; PolProf E, T; REn; REnAL; WebAB 74, 79; WhAm 3; WhAmP; WhoAmW 58; WorAl*

Taft, Robert A(lphonso), Jr.
American. Politician
Rep. senator from OH, 1971-76; grandson of Pres. Taft; son of Sen. Taft.
b. Feb 26, 1917 in Cincinnati, Ohio
d. Dec 6, 1993 in Cincinnati, Ohio
Source: *BiDrAC; BioIn 3, 4, 5, 6, 7, 8, 9, 10, 11, 12; CngDr 74; CurBio 67; IntWW 83; NewYTBE 70; PolProf NF; WhoAm 86*

Taft, William (Howard)
American. US President
Rep., 27th pres., 1909-13; created labor dept., 1911; Supreme Court justice, 1921-30.
b. Sep 15, 1857 in Cincinnati, Ohio
d. Mar 8, 1930 in Washington, District of Columbia
Source: *AmBi; AmDec 1900; AmJust; AmLY; AmNatBi; AmPeW; AmPolLe; ApCAB SUP, X; Ballpl 90; Benet 87, 96; BenetAL 91; BiDFedJ; BiDInt; BiDrAC; BiDrUSE 71, 89; BioIn 1, 2, 3, 4, 5, 6, 7, 8, 9, 10, 11, 12, 13; CamBiEn; CamDcAB; ChambiD; CyAG; DcAmB; DcAmC; DcAmSR; DcNAA; Dis&D; EncAAH; EncAB-H 1974, 1996; EncApar; EncSoH; EncWB 98; FacFETw; FacPr 89, 93; HarEnUS; HealPre; HisWorL; LegTOT; LinLib L, S; McGEWB; NatCAB 14, 23; OhA&B; OxCAmH; OxCAmL 65, 83; OxCLaw; OxCSupC; PolPar; Pres 96; PresAR 1996; RComAH; REn; REnAL; SupCtJu; TwCBDA; USGovLe; WebAB 74, 79; WhAm 1; WhAmP; WhDW; WorAl; WorAlBi*

Taggard, Genevieve
American. Poet, Editor
Founder, editor of *Measure*, 1920-26; wrote *Slow Music*, 1946.
b. Nov 28, 1894 in Waitsburg, Washington
d. Nov 8, 1948 in New York, New York
Source: *AmAu&B; AmNatBi; BenetAL 91; BioIn 1, 4, 15, 22; ChhPo, S1, S2, S3; CmCal; CnDAL; ConAmA; ConAu 166; DcAmB S4; DcNAA; EncALit; FemiCLE; InWom, SUP; LibW; ModWoW; NewCol 75; NotAW; OxCAmL 65, 83, 95; OxCTwCP; REn; REnAL; SixAP; TwCA, SUP; WhAm 2; WhE&EA; WorAu 1900*

Tagliabue, Carlo
Italian. Opera Singer
Internationally known baritone; noted for Verdi, Wagner roles.
b. Jan 13, 1898 in Como, Italy
d. Apr 5, 1978 in Monza, Italy
Source: *BakBD 84, 92; BakBDTw; BioIn 11; CmOp; MetOEnc; NewAmDM; NewEOp 71; NewGrDM 80; NewGrDO; WhScrn 83*

Tagliabue, Paul John
American. Football Executive, Lawyer
Commissioner of NFL, 1989—.
b. Nov 24, 1940 in Jersey City, New Jersey
Source: *BioIn 16; CurBio 92; News 90-2; NewYTBS 89; WhoAm 90, 92, 94, 95, 96, 97, 98, 99, 2000; WhoAmL 90, 92; WhoE 91, 93, 99*

Tagliavini, Ferrucio
Italian. Opera Singer
Leading Italian lyric tenor during WW II; with NY Met., 1946-54.
b. Aug 14, 1913 in Reggio Emilia, Italy
d. Jan 28, 1995 in Reggio Emilia, Italy

Source: *BakBD 84; CurBio 47; ItaFilm; MussN; NewYTBS 95*

Taglioni, Maria
Italian. Dancer
Member of dancing family; known for ballet *La Sylphide.*
b. Apr 23, 1804 in Stockholm, Sweden
d. Apr 24, 1884 in Marseilles, France
Source: *CelCen; ChamBiD; DancEn 78; InWom; NewC; NewCol 75; OxCFr; WebBD 83; WhDW*

Tagore, Rabindranath, Sir
[Ravindranath Thakur]
Indian. Poet
Won Nobel Prize for literature, 1913; known for mysticism, religious feeling.
b. May 6, 1861 in Calcutta, India
d. Aug 7, 1941 in Calcutta, India
Source: *Benet 87, 96; BiCoLiE; BiDMoPL; BioIn 1, 2, 4, 5, 6, 7, 8, 9, 10, 11, 12, 13, 14, 15, 16, 17, 20, 21, 22, 23, 24; CamBiEn; CamGEL; CasWL; ChamBiD; Chambr 3; ChhPo, S1, S2; CnMD; CnThe; ConAu 120; CurBio 41; DcAmSR; DcArts; DcLEL; DcNaB 1941; DcOrL 2; DcTwArt; DcTwHis; EncWL 1, 2, 2S, 3; EncWT; Ent; EvLB; FacFETw; GrWrEL P; HisWorL; IlEncMy; IntDcT 2; LegTOT; LinLib L, S; LngCTC; MajTwCW 1, 2; MakMC; McGEWB; McGEWD 84; ModCmwL; ModWD; NewC; NewGrDM 80; NobelP; NotNAT B; Novels; OxCEng 67, 85, 95; OxCPhil; OxCThe 67, 83; OxCTwCL; PenC CL, ENG; PoeCrit 8; RAdv 14; REn; REnWD; RfGEnL 91; RfGShF 1, 2; RfGWoL 95; TwCA, SUP; TwCLC 53; TwCWr; WebE&AL; WhDW; WhLit; WhoNob, 90, 95; WhoTwCL; WorAl; WorAlBi; WorAu 1900*

Taha Hussein
Egyptian. Educator, Author
Outstanding Islamic scholar, author of over 40 books; blinded in childhood; wrote *An Egyptian Childhood,* 1932; *The Tree of Misfortune,* 1944.
b. Nov 14, 1889 in Maghagha, Egypt
d. Oct 28, 1973 in Cairo, Egypt
Source: *ConAu 45; CurBio 53, 73; NewYTBE 73; WhAm 6; WhoWor 74*

Taharqa
Egyptian. Ruler
Nubian pharaoh of Egypt was the last ruler of the so-called Ethiopian Dynasty, reigned until he was driven from Lower Egypt by the Assyrians.
d. 662BC
Source: *EncWB 98; McGEWB*

Tahse, Martin
American. Producer
Exec. producer of ABC's "Afternoon Specials;" won Emmys, 1980, 1981.
b. Apr 24, 1930 in Cincinnati, Ohio
Source: *BiE&WWA; VarWW 85; WhoAm 74, 76, 78; WhoWor 74*

Tailleferre, Germaine
[Les Six]
French. Composer
Only woman composer in group of post-WW I composers.
b. Apr 19, 1892 in Pau-Saint Maur, France
d. Nov 7, 1983 in Paris, France
Source: *AnObit 1983; BakBD 78, 84; BakDcM; BioIn 3, 4, 13, 15, 17, 19; BriBkM 80; CamBiEn; ChamBiD; ContDcW 89; IntDcWB; IntWWM 80; InWom; NewAmDM; NewGrDM 80; NewOxM; NewYTBS 82, 83; OxCMus; PenDiMP A; WhoFr 79; WomComp 6; WomFir*

Taine, Hippolyte Adolphe
French. Philosopher
Attempted scientific study of human nature, history; wrote *History of English Literature,* 1864.
b. Apr 21, 1828 in Vouziers, France
d. Mar 9, 1893 in Paris, France
Source: *AtlBL; BbD; BiD&SB; BiDPsy; BioIn 1, 2, 3, 5, 7, 9, 10; CamBiEn; CasWL; CelCen; ChamBiD; ClDMEL 47; CyWA 58, 97; DcArts; DcBiPP; DcEnL; DcEuL; Dis&D; EncWB 98; EuAu; EvEuW; GloEncH; LinLib L, S; McGEWB; NamesHP; NewC; NewCBEL; NinCLC 15; OxCEng 67; OxCFr; PenC EUR; REn; WhDW; WorAl; WorAlBi*

Tairov, Aleksandr Yakovlevich
[Aleksandr Kornblit]
Russian. Producer, Director
Founded Moscow's Kamerny (Chamber) Theatre 1914; producer-director 1914-49; known for avant garde staging style.
b. Jun 24, 1885 in Romny, Russia
d. Sep 25, 1950 in Moscow, Union of Soviet Socialist Republics
Source: *BiDSovU; BioIn 3, 14; CamGWoT; FacFETw; NotNAT B; OxCThe 83; SovUn*

Taishoff, Sol Joseph
American. Editor, Publisher
Co-founded *Broadcasting* magazine.
b. Oct 8, 1904 in Minsk, Russia
d. Aug 15, 1982 in Washington, District of Columbia
Source: *BiDAmJo; BioIn 12, 13, 16; ConAu 73; EncTwCJ; NewYTBS 82; NewYTET; St&PR 75; WhAm 8; WhoAm 74, 76, 78, 80, 82; WhoFI 74, 75, 77, 79, 81; WhoSSW 73; WhoWor 74, 76, 78, 80; WhoWorJ 72*

Tait, Arthur Fitzwilliam
English. Artist
Self-taught painter for Currier & Ives; specialized in animal subjects: *The Life of a Hunter.*
b. Aug 5, 1819 in Liverpool, England
d. Apr 28, 1905 in Yonkers, New York
Source: *ApCAB; BioIn 3, 7, 9, 10, 14, 15; BriEAA; CamDcAB; DcAmArt; DcAmB; EarABI; IlBEAAW; NewEAmW; NewYHSD; TwCBDA; WhAm 1; WhAmArt 85*

Tait, Peter Guthrie
Scottish. Physicist, Mathematician
Co-developer of quaternions, a form of advanced algebra.
b. Apr 28, 1831 in Dalkeith, Scotland
d. Jul 4, 1901 in Edinburgh, Scotland
Source: *Alli, SUP; BioIn 4; BritAu 19; CamBiEn; CelCen; ChamBiD; DcNaB, S2; DcScB; InSci; LarDcSc*

Tai-Tsung
Chinese. Ruler
Second emperor of Sung Dynasty, 960-1249; consolidated power, developed civil-service examination system.
b. 939, China
d. 997, China

T'ai-tsung, T'ang
Chinese. Emperor
Established the Tang dynasty in imperial China; he conquered much of Asia and initiated a cultural and economic flowering.
b. 600 in Ta-hsing-ch'eng, China
d. 649 in Chang'an, China
Source: *EncWB 98*

Taj Mahal
[Henry Saint Clair Fredericks Williams]
American. Singer, Songwriter, Composer
Blues performer; composed scores for films *Sounder, Sounder II,* and *Brothers.*
b. May 17, 1942 in New York, New York
Source: *BiDJaz A; Blues; CmpEGui; ConMus 6; EncFCWM 83; InB&W 80, 85; NewGrDA 86; OnThGG*

Tajo, Italo
b. Apr 25, 1915 in Pinerolo, Italy
d. Mar 29, 1993 in Cincinnati, Ohio
Source: *BakBD 84, 92; BakBDTw; BioIn 1, 3, 4, 11, 13, 14, 18; CmOp; IntDcOp; IntWWM 77, 80, 90; MetOEnc; NewAmDM; NewEOp 71; NewGrDA 86; NewGrDM 80; NewGrDO; NewYTBS 93; OxDcOp; PenDiMP; WhAm 11; WhoAm 78, 80, 82, 84, 86, 88; WhoAmM 83; WhoEnt 92; WhoOp 76*

Takada, Kenzo
Japanese. Fashion Designer
Ready-to-wear designs sold around the world; specializes in clothing, shoes, accessories.
b. Feb 28, 1940, Japan
Source: *WhoFash; WorFshn*

Takahama Kyoshi
Japanese. Poet
Contributed much to modern Japanese haiku; wrote *Susumu beki haiku no michi,* 1918.
b. Feb 22, 1874 in Matsuyama, Japan
d. Apr 8, 1959 in Kamakura, Japan

Takahashi, Korekiyo
Japanese. Politician
Economically liberal finance minister
resisted military spending and was
assassinated in the attempted military
coup of 1936.
b. Jul 24, 1854 in Tokyo, Japan
d. Feb 26, 1936
Source: *BioIn 14; EncWB 98; McGEWB*

Takamine, Jokichi
Japanese. Biochemist
First person to isolate a pure hormone
(adrenalin or epinephrine) in its natural
state.
b. Nov 3, 1854 in Takaoka, Japan
d. Jul 22, 1922 in New York, New York
Source: *AmNatBi; AsAmAlm; AsBiEn;
BiDAmS; BiESc; BioIn 3, 4, 11, 20;
CamBiEn; CamDcAB; CamDcSc;
DcAmB; DcAmMeB 84; NatCAB 40;
NotAsAm; SciMath; WhAm 1*

Take 6
[Alvin "Vinnie" Chea; Cedric Dent;
Mark Kibble; Claude V. McKnight,
III; David Thomas; Mervyn Warren]
American. Music Group
Gospel/jazz group; Grammy Awards:
best jazz vocal group for "Spread
Love," 1989 and best soul gospel
album *Take 6*, 1989.
Source: *Alli; BioIn 16, 17; ConMus 6;
DcTwCCu 5; DrRegL 75; NewCBEL;
WhoAmP 85; WhoHol 92, A; WhoRocM
82*

Takehara Han
Japanese. Dancer
Became Japan's best known Jiutamai
dancer of the 20th c.
b. Feb 4, 1903 in Tokushima, Japan

Takei, George
American. Actor
Played Sulu on TV's "Star Trek," 1966-
69, also in film series.
b. Apr 20, 1937 in Los Angeles,
California
Source: *ConTFT 5, 14; EncSF 93;
IntMPA 86, 92, 94, 96; VarWW 85*

Takei, Kei
Japanese. Choreographer, Dancer
Founder of the Moving Earth dance
company, 1969; choreography blurs
traditional distinction between dance
and drama.
b. Dec 30, 1946 in Tokyo, Japan
Source: *BiDD; News 90, 90-2; WhoEnt
92*

Takemitsu, Toru
Japanese. Composer
Co-founded an experimental laboratory
in Tokyo, 1951, to examine oriental
music and avant-garde western
techniques.
b. Oct 8, 1930 in Tokyo, Japan
d. Feb 20, 1996 in Tokyo, Japan
Source: *BakBD 78, 84, 92; BakBDTw;
BakDcM; BioIn 8, 11, 17, 21, 22, 23;*

*BriBkM 80; ChamBiD; CompSN SUP;
ConCom 92; ConMus 6; DcCM; IntDcF
1-4, 2-4; IntWWM 77, 80, 90; JapFilm;
NewAmDM; NewGrDM 80; NewOxM;
NewYTBS 96; ObitPA 96; PenDiMP A;
WhoWor 78, 80, 82*

Takeshita, Noboru
Japanese. Political Leader
Succeeded Yasuhiro Nakasone as prime
minister, 1987.
b. Feb 26, 1924 in Shimane, Japan
d. Jun 19, 2000 in Tokyo, Japan
Source: *CamBiEn; ChamBiD; CurBio
88; FacFETw; FarE&A 80, 81; IntWW
80, 81, 82, 83, 89, 91, 93, 97, 98, 2000;
NewYTBS 87; WhoAsAP 91; WhoWor
87, 89, 91, 93*

Takhtadzhian, Armen Leonovich
Russian. Botanist
Expert on plant classification; author of
*Flowering Plants: Classification and
Phylogeny*, 1993.
b. May 28, 1910 in Shusha, Russia
Source: *WhoSocC 78*

Taktakishvili, Otar Vasilevich
Russian. Composer
Music shows Caucasus influence; has
written piano concertos, symphonic
poems.
b. Jul 27, 1924 in Tiflis, Union of Soviet
Socialist Republics
Source: *BakBD 84; BioIn 9*

Tal, Josef
Israeli. Composer, Pianist, Educator
Teacher and musician in the mainstream
of contemporary European music, he
was influenced by Middle Eastern
music.
b. 1910 in Pinne, Poland
Source: *BakBD 84, 92; BakBDTw;
BakDcM; BioIn 10, 23; DcCM; EncWB,
98; IntWW 74, 75, 76, 77, 78, 79, 80,
81, 82, 83; IntWWM 77, 80, 85, 90;
MidE 78, 79, 80, 81, 82; NewAmDM;
NewGrDM 80; NewGrDO; OxDcOp;
PenDiMP A; WhoEnt 98; WhoWor 82,
84, 91, 93, 95, 96, 97, 98, 99, 2000;
WhoWorJ 72*

Tal, Mikhail Nekhemyevich
Russian. Chess Player
International Grandmaster, 1957, world
champion, 1960-61.
b. 1936 in Riga, Union of Soviet
Socialist Republics
d. Jun 28, 1992 in Moscow, Union of
Soviet Socialist Republics
Source: *BioIn 11; GolEC; OxCChes 84*

Talbert, Mary Morris Burnett
American. Educator, Civil Rights
Activist, Lecturer
Teacher and principal was an active
feminist and civil rights advocate.
b. Sep 18, 1866 in Oberlin, Ohio
d. Oct 15, 1923
Source: *BlkWAm; EncWB, 98*

Talbot, John Michael
American. Musician, Singer
Member of country-rock band Mason
Proffit, 1969-1973; became a
Franciscan monk, late 1970s;
developed a classical, contemplative
musical style.
b. May 8, 1954 in Oklahoma City,
Oklahoma
Source: *BioIn 14, 15; ConMus 6;
NewAgMG; WhoMW 98*

Talbot, Lyle
[Lyle Henderson]
American. Actor
Character actor in over 100 films since
1932; in TV series "The Bob
Cummings Show," 1955-59.
b. Feb 8, 1902 in Pittsburgh,
Pennsylvania
d. Mar 3, 1996 in San Francisco,
California
Source: *BiE&WWA; BioIn 23; ConTFT
7, 16; EncAFC; FilmEn; FilmgC; HalFC
84; HolCA; IntMPA 94, 96; MovMk;
NotNAT; ObitPA 96; Vers B; WhDW;
WhoAm 74; WhoHol A*

Talbot, Nita
American. Comedian
Appeared in film *The Day of the Locust*,
1975.
b. Aug 8, 1930 in New York, New York
Source: *ConTFT 8; DcPseud; EncAFC;
FilmgC; ForWC 70; ForYSC; HalFC 80,
84, 88; InWom SUP; WhoHol 92, A;
WorAl*

Talbot, William Henry Fox
"Father of Photography"
English. Photographer, Inventor
Developed several photographic
processes, including method for taking
instant pictures, 1851.
b. Feb 11, 1800 in Lacock Abbey,
England
d. Sep 17, 1877 in Lacock Abbey,
England
Source: *Alli; AsBiEn; BioIn 2, 4, 7, 8, 9,
10, 11, 12, 13, 16, 18, 19, 20; CamBiEn;
CamDcSc; CelCen; ChamBiD; DcBiPP,
A; DcBrWA; DcInv; DcScB; EncAJ;
ICPEnP; InSci; LarDcSc; MacBEP;
McGCEnS; NewCol 75; OxCBrHi;
OxCDecA; RanHWDS; VicBrit; WhDW;
WorInv*

Talese, Gay
American. Author, Journalist
Wrote *Honor Thy Father*, 1971; *Thy
Neighbor's Wife*, 1980.
b. Feb 7, 1932 in Ocean City, New
Jersey
Source: *BioIn 9, 10, 12; CamBiEn;
ChamBiD; ConAu 9NR, 58NR; ConLC
37; CurBio 72; DcLB 185; EncAJ;
EncTwCJ; IntAu&W 86; LegTOT;
LiJour; LinLib L; MajTwCW 1, 2;
NewYTBS 80; WhoAm 74, 76, 78, 80,
82, 84, 86, 88, 90, 92, 94, 95, 96, 97,
98, 99, 2000; WhoE 74; WhoEnt 98;
WhoUSWr 88; WhoWor 74, 76, 93;
WhoWrEP 89, 92, 95; WorAu 1975;*

WrDr 86, 88, 90, 92, 94, 96, 98, 99, 2000

Talking Heads, The
[David Byrne; Chris Frantz; Jerry Harrison; Martina Weymouth]
American. Music Group
New wave group begun, 1977; combine traditional rock styles with Afro-'American music; had hit single ''Burning Down the House,'' 1983.
Source: *BakDcM; BillEnR; BioIn 14, 15, 16, 17, 20; ConMuA 80A; ConMus 1; DcArts; EncPR&S 89; EncRk 88; EncRkSt; HarEnR 86; NewAmDM; NewYTBS 85, 86; OxCPMus; PenEncP; RkOn 85; RkWho 96; RolSEnR 83; WhoRock 81; WhoRocM 82; WhsNW 85*

Tallchief, Maria
American. Dancer
Prima ballerina who appeared in film *Million Dollar Mermaid*, 1952.
b. Jan 24, 1925 in Fairfax, Oklahoma
Source: *AmIndBi; AZNatAW; BiDD; BioAmW; BioIn 2, 3, 4, 5, 6, 7, 9, 10, 12, 13; BlueB 76; CamBiEn; CamDcAB; ChamBiD; CnOxB; ConHero 3; CurBio 51; DancEn 78; EncWB 98; FacFETw; GoodHs; GrLiveH; HanAmWH; HerW; IntDcB; IntWW 97, 98, 2000; IntWWW 2; InWom, SUP; LegTOT; LibW; LinLib S; NatNAFi; NotNaAm; WebAB 74, 79; WhoAm 74, 76, 78, 80, 82, 84, 86, 88, 90, 92, 94, 95, 96, 97, 98, 99, 2000; WhoAmW 58, 61, 64, 66, 68, 70, 72, 74, 81, 83, 85, 87, 89, 91, 93, 95; WhoEnt 92, 98; WhoHol 92, A; WhoMus 72; WhoMW 80, 82, 84, 86, 88, 92; WhoThe 77A; WhoWor 74, 76, 78, 80, 82, 84; WhThe*

Tallchief, Marjorie
American. Dancer
Ballerina; first American to achieve position of premiere danseuse etoile with Paris Opera.
b. Oct 19, 1927 in Fairfax, Oklahoma
Source: *BiDD; BioIn 3, 4, 5, 9, 10, 11, 13; CnOxB; DancEn 78; IntWW 74, 75, 76, 77, 78, 79, 80, 81, 82, 83, 89, 91, 93, 97, 98, 2000; IntWWW 2; InWom, SUP; WhoHol 92*

Tallent, Garry Wayne
[E Street Band]
American. Musician
Bassist who joined Bruce Springsteen's band, 1971.
b. Oct 27, 1949 in Detroit, Michigan
Source: *WhoRocM 82*

Talley, Gary
[The Box Tops]
American. Musician
Bass guitarist with Memphis-based group, 1966-70.
b. Aug 17, 1947
Source: *WhoRocM 82*

Talleyrand-Perigord, Charles Maurice de
French. Statesman
Minister of Foreign Affairs, 1797-99; opposed Louisiana Purchase, 1803.
b. Feb 13, 1754 in Paris, France
d. May 17, 1838 in Paris, France
Source: *BbD; Benet 87, 96; BiD&SB; BioIn 12, 19, 20, 21; CamBiEn; CelCen; ChambBiD; CmFrR; DcBiPP; Dis&D; HarEnUS; LinLib L, S; LuthC 75; OxCFr; REn; WhAm HS; WhDW; WorAl; WorAlBi*

Tallis, Thomas
[Thomas Tallys]
''Father of English Cathedral Music''
English. Organist, Composer
Among first to set English words to music for Anglican liturgy; organist of the chapel royal.
b. 1515? in Greenwich, England
d. Nov 23, 1585 in Greenwich, England
Source: *Alli; AtlBL; BakBD 84; DcBiPP; DcCathB; DcNaB; LuthC 75; NewCol 75; OxCMus; WhDW*

Tallmadge, Thomas Eddy
American. Architect
Designed numerous churches; wrote *Architecture in America*, 1927.
b. Apr 24, 1876 in Washington, District of Columbia
d. Jan 1, 1940
Source: *AmNatBi; BiDAmAr; DcNAA; MacEA; WhAm 1; WhAmArt 85; WhNAA*

TallMountain, Mary
American. Poet
Published poetry collections *There Is No Word for Goodbye*, 1981; *A Quick Brush of Wings*, 1991.
b. 1918 in Nulato, Alaska
d. Sep 2, 1994
Source: *AZNatAW; BioIn 21, 24; ConAu 146, 161; ConLC 86; DcLB 193; NatAL; NatNAL; NotNaAm; WrDr 98, 99*

Talma, Francois Joseph
French. Actor
Greatest tragic actor of his time; introduced realistic scenery, costuming.
b. Jan 15, 1763 in Paris, France
d. Oct 19, 1826 in Paris, France
Source: *BbD; BioIn 2, 3, 4, 5, 7; CamGWoT; CelCen; ChamBiD; CnThe; DcBiPP; Dis&D; EncWT; NewCol 75; NotNAT A, B; OxCFr; OxCThe 67; WebBD 83*

Talmadge, Constance
American. Comedian
Silent film star, 1914-29; retired when talking pictures began.
b. Apr 19, 1900 in New York, New York
d. Nov 23, 1973 in Los Angeles, California
Source: *BioAmW; BioIn 7, 10, 15; DcAmB S9; EncAFC; Film 1, 2; FilmEn; FilmgC; InWom, SUP; MotPP; MovMk; NewYTBE 73; ObitT 1971; OxCFilm;*

TwYS; WhAm 6; What 1; WhoAmW 72; WhoHol B; WhScrn 77; WorEFlm

Talmadge, Eugene
American. Politician
Dem. governor of GA, 1933-37, 1940-43.
b. Sep 23, 1884 in Forsyth, Georgia
d. Dec 21, 1946 in Atlanta, Georgia
Source: *AmNatBi; AmOrTwC; BioIn 1, 3, 4, 9, 10; CamBiEn; CamDcAB; CurBio 41, 47; DcAmB S4; EncAB-A 1; EncSoH; NatCAB 38; PolPar; WhAm 2*

Talmadge, Herman Eugene
American. Politician
Dem. governor of GA, 1948-55; US senator, 1957-81; son of Eugene.
b. Aug 9, 1913 in Telfair County, Georgia
Source: *AlmAP 80; BiDrAC; BiDrUSC 89; BioIn 1, 2, 3, 4, 5, 8, 9, 10, 11, 12; BlueB 76; CamDcAB; CngDr 74, 77, 79; CurBio 47; EncAAH; IntWW 74, 75, 76, 77, 78, 79, 80, 81, 82, 83; NewYTBS 79; WhoAm 74, 76, 78, 80, 82, 84; WhoAmP 73, 75, 77, 79; WhoWor 78, 80; WorAl*

Talmadge, Norma
American. Actor
Played suffering heroine in films, 1910-30.
b. May 26, 1897 in Jersey City, New Jersey
d. Dec 24, 1957 in Las Vegas, Nevada
Source: *BiDFilm, 81, 94; BioAmW; BioIn 4, 5, 6, 7, 9, 12, 18, 22; DcAmB S6; EncAFC; Film 1; FilmEn; FilmgC; ForYSC; HalFC 84; IntDcF 1-3, 2-3; InWom; MotPP; MovMk; NatCAB 48; NotNAT B; OxCFilm; ThFT; TwYS; WhAm 3; WhScrn 83; WorAl; WorEFlm*

Talmadge, Thomas de Witt
American. Clergy, Author
Chaplain for Union Army during Civil War; sermons printed weekly in various papers for 30 yrs; wrote *The Earth Girdled*, 1895.
b. Jan 7, 1832 in Bound Brook, New Jersey
d. Apr 12, 1902 in Washington, District of Columbia
Source: *AmAu&B; NewCol 75; WhAm 1*

Talman, William
American. Actor
Played D.A. Burger on TV show ''Perry Mason,'' 1957-66.
b. Feb 4, 1915 in Detroit, Michigan
d. Aug 30, 1968 in Encino, California
Source: *FilmgC; ForYSC; HalFC 80, 84, 88; MotPP; WhoHol B; WhScrn 77, 83*

Talon, Jean
French. Government Official
As intendant of New France, he was responsible for implementing the French policy of colonial development in Canada.
b. Jan 8, 1626 in Champagne, France
d. Nov 24, 1694 in Paris, France

Source: *DcCanB 1; EncWB 98;*
McGEWB

Talvela, Martti Olavi
Finnish. Opera Singer
Bass, noted for portrayal of bass roles by
Wagner and Mussorgsky.
b. Feb 4, 1935 in Hiitola, Finland
d. Jul 22, 1989 in Juva, Finland
Source: *BakBD 84; BakBDTw; CurBio*
83, 89; IntWW 74, 75, 76, 77, 78, 79,
80, 81, 82, 89; MusSN; NewYTBS 74;
WhoAm 84, 86, 88; WhoOp 76; WhoWor
84, 87, 89

Tamagno, Francesco
Italian. Opera Singer
Probably greatest tenor di forza of all
time; created role of Othello, 1887.
b. Dec 28, 1850 in Turin, Italy
d. Aug 31, 1905 in Varese, Italy
Source: *BakBD 78, 84, 92; BriBkM 80;*
CmOp; IntDcOp; MetOEnc; NewAmDM;
NewEOp 71; NewGrDM 80; NewGrDO;
OxDcOp; PenDiMP

Tamayo, Rufino
Mexican. Artist
Fused ancient Mexican with modern
French art; painted nationalistic murals
in Mexico City, 1950s.
b. Aug 26, 1899 in Oaxaca, Mexico
d. Jun 24, 1991 in Mexico City, Mexico
Source: *AnObit 1991; ArtLatA; BioIn 1,*
2, 3, 4, 5, 6, 8, 9, 10, 11, 12, 13, 14, 15,
17, 18; CamBiEn; ChamBiD; ConArt 83,
89, 96; CurBio 53; DcArts; DcHiB;
DcTwArt; DcTwCCu 4; EncLatA;
IntDcAA 90; LatAmLi; McGDA; NewCol
75; News 92, 92-1; NewYTBS 91;
OxCArt; OxCTwCA; OxDcArt;
PhDcTCA 77; PrintW 83, 85; REn;
WhoAm 74, 76, 78, 80, 82; WhoAmA 73,
76, 78, 80, 82, 84, 86, 89, 91, 93N;
WhoSSW 73, 75; WhoWor 74; WorArt
1950

Tamayo y Baus, Manuel
Spanish. Dramatist
Internationally known for play, *Un*
drama nuevo, 1867.
b. Sep 15, 1829 in Madrid, Spain
d. Jun 20, 1898 in Madrid, Spain
Source: *BioIn 1, 3, 7, 10; CamGWoT;*
CasWL; ClDMEL 47; DcEuL; DcSpL;
EuAu; EvEuW; LinLib L; McGEWD 72,
84; NinCLC 1; NotNAT B; OxCSpan;
OxCThe 67, 83; PenC EUR

Tamberlik, Enrico
Italian. Singer
Internationally renowned tenor of the
19th c. known for powerful, resonant
high notes.
b. Mar 16, 1820 in Rome, Italy
d. Mar 13, 1889 in Paris, France
Source: *BakBD 78, 84, 92; BioIn 4, 7,*
14; BriBkM 80; CmOp; DcBiPP;
MetOEnc; NewAmDM; NewGrDM 80;
NewGrDO; OxDcOp; PenDiMP

Tamblyn, Russ
American. Actor
Oscar nominee for *Peyton Place,* 1957;
dancing star of *Seven Brides for Seven*
Brothers, 1954; *West Side Story,* 1961.
b. Dec 30, 1935 in Los Angeles,
California
Source: *BiDD; CmMov; ConTFT 9;*
FilmgC; ForYSC; HalFC 84; IntMPA
84, 88, 92, 94, 96; MotPP; MovMk;
WhoHol A

Tambo, Oliver
South African. Political Activist
Pres. of South Africa's outlawed African
National Congress, 1949—; formally
ap pointed pres., 1977-89.
b. Oct 27, 1917 in Transkei, South
Africa
d. Apr 24, 1993 in Johannesburg, South
Africa
Source: *AfSS 78, 79, 80, 81, 82; BioIn*
13; CamBiEn; ChamBiD; CurBio 87,
93N; EncRev; FacFETw; IntWW 74, 75,
76, 77, 78, 79, 80, 81, 82, 83, 89, 91;
LegTOT; News 91, 91-3; RadHan;
WhoWor 74

Tamburini, Antonio
Italian. Opera Singer
Celebrated baritone, idol of London,
Paris, 1830s-40s; created many roles.
b. Mar 28, 1800 in Faenza, Italy
d. Nov 9, 1876 in Nice, France
Source: *BakBD 78, 84, 92; BioIn 7, 14;*
BriBkM 80; CelCen; CmOp; DcBiPP;
MetOEnc; NewAmDM; NewEOp 71;
NewGrDM 80; NewGrDO; OxDcOp;
PenDiMP

Tamerlane
[Timur]
''The Prince of Destruction''
Mongolian. Conqueror
Descendant of Genghis Khan; invaded
Russia, Asia Minor.
b. 1336 in Kesh, Persia
d. 1405
Source: *Benet 87, 96; BioIn 1, 2, 3, 4, 5,*
6, 7, 8, 10, 11, 12, 15, 17, 20; DcBiPP;
DicTyr; EncChi; EncWB 98; GenMudB;
HarEnMi; HisWorL; LegTOT; LinLib S;
McGEWB; MilitOn; NewCol 75;
OxCChes 84; OxDcByz; WebBD 83;
WhDW

Tamiris, Helen
American. Choreographer, Dancer
Choreographed Broadway musical *Annie*
Get Your Gun, 1948.
b. Apr 24, 1902? in New York, New
York
d. Aug 25, 1966 in New York, New
York
Source: *AmNatBi; BiDD; InWom SUP;*
NotAW MOD; NotNAT B; NotWoAT;
WhAm 4

Tamiroff, Akim
American. Actor
Character actor who played villain roles,
1933-70; Oscar nominee for *For*
Whom the Bell Tolls.

b. Oct 29, 1901 in Baku, Russia
d. Sep 17, 1972 in Palm Springs,
California
Source: *BiDFilm; BiE&WWA; FilmgC;*
MotPP; MovMk; NewYTBE 72; NotNAT
B; OxCFilm; Vers A; WhAm 5; WhoHol
B; WhScrn 77; WorEFlm

Tamm, Igor Evgenevich
Russian. Physicist, Educator
Shared Nobel Prize in physics, 1958,
with I M Frank.
b. Jul 8, 1895 in Vladivostok, Russia
d. Apr 12, 1971 in Moscow, Union of
Soviet Socialist Republics
Source: *AmMWSc 82; BiDSovU; BiESc;*
McGMS 80; ObitOF 79; ObitT 1971;
WhoNob, 90, 95; WhoSocC 78; WorAl

Tammann, Gustav Heinrich
Johann Apollon
Russian. Chemist
One of the founders of metallurgy;
pioneered research of metals and
alloys and their internal structure and
physical properties.
b. Jun 9, 1861 in Jamburg, Russia
d. Dec 17, 1938 in Gottingen, Germany
Source: *BioIn 2; DcScB*

Tan, Amy
American. Author
Wrote *The Joy Luck Club,* 1989, *The*
Kitchen God's Wife, 1991, and *The*
Hundred Secret Senses, 1995.
b. Feb 19, 1952 in Oakland, California
Source: *AmWomWr 92, SUP; AsAmAlm;*
AsAmLit; AsAmWoW; Au&Arts 9;
BeaEPF; BestSel 89-3; BlmGWL; ConAu
136; ConLC 59, 120; CurBio 92; CyWA
97; DcLB 173; EncAL; EncChi; EncWB
98; GrLiveH; IdentIs; IntAu&W 91;
IntWWW 2; LegTOT; ModAL 5;
ModWoWr; ModWr; News 98, 98-3;
NotAsAm; OxCAmL 95; OxCTwCL;
OxCWoWr 95; SJGYouA 2; SmATA 75;
TwCYAW 1; WorAu 1985; WrDr 94, 96,
98, 99, 2000

Tanaka, Kakuei
Japanese. Political Leader
Prime minister, 1972-74; convicted of
bribery, 1983.
b. May 4, 1918 in Kariwa, Japan
d. Dec 16, 1993 in Tokyo, Japan
Source: *AnObit 1993; BioIn 12, 13;*
CamBiEn; ChamBiD; CurBio 72, 94N;
EncWB, 98; EncyDCo; FacFETw;
FarE&A 78, 79, 80, 81; IntWW 74, 75,
76, 77, 78, 79, 80, 81, 82, 83, 91, 93;
IntYB 78, 79; NewCol 75; NewYTBE 72;
NewYTBS 76, 93; WhoWor 74; WorAl;
WorAlBi

Tanaka, Tomoyuki
Japanese. Filmmaker
Film producer made more than 200 films
over six decades; best known as the
creator of Godzilla, the dinosaur-like
creature awakened by U.S. atomic
testing that terrorized Japanese cities
and gained a cult following.
b. Apr 26, 1910 in Osaka, Japan

d. Apr 2, 1997 in Tokyo, Japan
Source: *BioIn 22, 23, 24; JapFilm; News 97, 97-3*

Tanana, Frank Daryl
American. Baseball Player
Pitcher, 1973—; seventh in ML history to record 2,000 strikeouts.
b. Jul 3, 1953 in Detroit, Michigan
Source: *BaseReg 86, 87; BiDAmSp Sup; BioIn 11*

Tandy, James Napper
Irish. Revolutionary
Founder, Society of United Irishmen, 1791; hero of ballad "The Wearing of the Green."
b. 1740 in Dublin, Ireland
d. Apr 24, 1803 in Bordeaux, France
Source: *DcIrB 1, 3; DcNaB; NewCol 75*

Tandy, Jessica
[Mrs. Hume Cronyn]
American. Actor
Three-time Tony winner; performances include *A Streetcar Named Desire,* 1948; oldest to win Oscar, 1990, for *Driving Miss Daisy.*
b. Jun 7, 1909 in London, England
d. Sep 11, 1994 in Easton, Connecticut
Source: *AmNatBi; BiDFilm 94; BiE&WWA; BioIn 1, 2, 4, 5, 7, 10, 11, 12, 13; CamBiEn; CamDcAB; CamGWoT; CelR, 90; CnThe; ConTFT 1, 7, 13; CurBio 56, 84, 94N; FacFETw; FilmEn; FilmgC; ForYSC; GrLiveH; HalFC 80, 84, 88; IntDcT 3; IntMPA 75, 76, 78, 79, 80, 81, 82, 84, 88, 92, 94; IntWW 91, 93; InWom, SUP; LegTOT; MotPP; MovMk; News 90, 95, 95-1; NewYTBS 74, 81, 82; NotNAT; NotWoAT; OxCAmL 83; OxCAmT 84; OxCThe 83; PlP&P; WhAm 11; Who 74, 82, 83, 85, 88, 90, 92, 94; WhoAm 74, 76, 78, 80, 82, 84, 86, 88, 90, 92, 94; WhoAmW 58, 61, 64, 66, 68, 70, 72, 74, 79, 81, 83, 85, 87, 89, 91, 93; WhoE 91, 93; WhoEnt 92; WhoHol 92, A; WhoThe 72, 77, 81; WhoWor 74, 76; WorAl; WorAlBi*

Tanen, Ned Stone
Producer
Films include *The Breakfast Club,* 1985; *St. Elmo's Fire,* 1985.
b. 1931 in Los Angeles, California
Source: *BioIn 13, 14, 16; Dun&B 79; VarWW 85; WhoAm 80, 82, 84, 86, 88, 90, 95, 96, 97; WhoWest 89*

Taney, Roger Brooke
American. Supreme Court Justice
Appointed, 1836; ruled against Scott in Dred Scott case, 1857, arguing that blacks needed to remain slaves as long as they were in US.
b. Mar 17, 1777 in Calvert County, Maryland
d. Oct 12, 1864 in Washington, District of Columbia
Source: *Alli; AmBi; AmJust; AmNatBi; AmPoLe; ApCAB; BiAUS; BiDFedJ; BiDrUSE 71, 89; BiDSA; BioIn 2, 3, 4,*

5, 6, 7, 8, 9, 10, 11, 12, 14, 15, 18, 19, 20, 23; CamBiEn; CamDcAB; ChamBiD; ChhPo; CyAG; DcAmB; DcCathB; Drake; EncAB-H 1974, 1996; EncRelA; EncSoH; EncWar; EncWB 98; HarEnUS; LinLib L, S; McGEWB; MorMA; NatCAB 1; OxCAmH; OxCLaw; OxCSupC; REn; REnAL; SupCtJu; TwCBDA; WebAB 74, 79; WhAm HS; WhCiWar; WhDW; WorAl

Taneyev, Sergey Ivanovich
Russian. Composer, Pianist
Chief composer of counterpoint in 19th c. Russia; composed operatic trilogy *Oresteia,* 1895.
b. Nov 25, 1856 in Vladimir, Russia
d. Jun 19, 1915 in Moscow, Russia
Source: *BakBD 84; BioIn 1; BriBkM 80; CamBiEn; MetOEnc; NewAmDM; NewGrDM 80; NewGrDO; NewOxM*

Tange, Kenzo
Japanese. Architect, Educator
Combines modern designs with Japanese traditions for urban buildings, cultural centers, sports facilities, and govt. headquarters.
b. Sep 4, 1913 in Osaka, Japan
Source: *BioIn 5, 6, 7, 9, 11, 12, 13; CamBiEn; ChamBiD; ConArch 80, 87, 94; CurBio 87; DcArch; DcArts; DcD&D; EncMA; EncWB, 98; FarE&A 78, 79, 80, 81; IntDcAr; IntWW 74, 75, 76, 77, 78, 79, 80, 81, 82, 83, 89, 91, 93, 97, 98, 2000; MacEA; MakMC; MakTCMA; McGDA; McGEWB; NewCol 75; WhoAm 74, 76, 82; WhoArch; WhoScEn 96; WhoWor 74, 76, 78, 89, 91*

T'ang Hsuan-tsung
Chinese. Emperor
Able ruler was the seventh emperor of the T'ang dynasty; he abdicated after the massive rebellion of An Lu-shan broke out in 755.
b. 685
d. 762

Tanguay, Eva
"I Don't Care Girl"
Canadian. Actor
Vaudeville, musical, comedy darling; starred in *Sambo Girl.*
b. Aug 1, 1878 in Marbleton, Quebec, Canada
d. Jan 11, 1947 in Los Angeles, California
Source: *AmNatBi; AmPS B; BiDD; BioIn 1, 5, 16, 17; CamDcAB; CmdStar; CmpEPM; DcAmB S4; EncVaud; Ent; Film 1; InWom, SUP; LibW; NewAmDM; NewGrDA 86; NotAW; NotNAT B; NotWoAT; OxCAmT 84; OxCPMus; WhoCom; WhoHol B; WhoStg 1908; WhScrn 77, 83; WhThe*

Tanguy, Yves
American. Artist
Surrealist painter whose permanent collections are in museums throughout US, Paris.

b. Jan 5, 1900 in Paris, France
d. Jan 15, 1955 in Woodbury, Connecticut
Source: *BioIn 1, 3, 4, 14, 22; BriEAA; CamBiEn; CamDcAB; ChamBiD; ConArt 77, 83; DcArts; DcCAA 71, 77, 88, 94; DcTwArt; DcTwCCu 2; EncWB 98; FacFETw; IntDcAA 90; LegTOT; McGDA; McGEWB; NewCol 75; OxCArt; OxCTwCA; OxDcArt; PhDcTCA 77; REn; WhAm 3; WhoAmA 78N, 80N, 82N, 86N, 89N, 91N, 93N; WorArt 1950*

Tanizaki Jun'ichiro
Japanese. Author
Works alternately marked by both eroticism and an adherence to traditional standards of beauty.
b. Jul 24, 1886 in Tokyo, Japan
d. Jul 30, 1965 in Yugawara, Japan
Source: *Benet 87; BiCoLiE; BioIn 7, 10, 12, 13; CasWL; ChamBiD; ConAu 25R, 93; ConLC 8, 14, 28; DcLB 180; EncWL 2, 3; GrFLW; McGEWB; ModJap; ObitOF 79; RfGShF 2*

Tannen, Deborah Frances
American. Linguist, Author
Author of *You Just Don't Understand: Women and Men in Conversation,* 1990.
b. Jun 7, 1945 in New York, New York
Source: *CurBio 94; WhoAm 94, 95, 96, 97, 98, 99, 2000; WhoAmW 95, 97, 99; WhoEnt 98*

Tannenbaum, Frank
American. Educator, Historian
Expert on Mexico, Latin America; wrote *Peace By Revolution,* 1933.
b. Mar 1893, Austria
d. Jun 1, 1969 in New York, New York
Source: *AmAu&B; BioIn 2, 8, 16; CamBiEn; CamDcAB; ConAu 9R; IntEnSS 79; LatAmLi; MacEWoS; NewCol 75; RAdv 14; WhNAA*

Tanner, Alain
Swiss. Filmmaker
Films include *Charles Dead or Alive,* and *The Women from Rose Hill.*
b. Dec 6, 1929 in Geneva, Switzerland
Source: *BiDFilm 94; BioIn 13, 16; ConTFT 8; CurBio 90; EncEurC; FilmEn; HalFC 88; IntDcF 1-2, 2-2; IntWW 91; MiSFD 9; WhoWor 89, 95; WorFDir 2*

Tanner, Henry Ossawa
American. Artist
Most renowned of all black artists; member National Academy of Art and Design.
b. Jun 21, 1859 in Pittsburgh, Pennsylvania
d. May 25, 1937 in Etaples, France
Source: *AfrAmAl 6, 8; AfroAA; AmBi; AmNatBi; ApCAB X; BioIn 1, 3, 4, 6, 7, 8, 9, 11, 17, 19, 21, 22, 23; BriEAA; CamDcAB; ConBlB 1; DcAmArt; DcAmB S2; DcAmNB; EncAB-H 1974, 1996; EncWB 98; GayN; InB&W 80, 85;*

McGDA; McGEWB; ModArCr 4;
NatCAB 3; NegAl 76, 83, 89; NotBlAM;
SJGBlA; WebAB 74, 79; WhAm 1;
WhoAmA 80N, 82N, 86N, 89N, 91N,
93N; WhoColR

Tanner, Marion
American. Philanthropist, Socialite
Real life model for Auntie Mame,
   immortalized in novel by nephew
   Patrick Dennis.
b. Mar 6, 1891 in Buffalo, New York
d. Oct 30, 1985 in New York, New York
Source: BioIn 14; NewYTBS 85

Tanner, Roscoe
[Leonard Roscoe Tanner, III]
"Cannonball Kid"
American. Tennis Player
Serve timed at 155 mph; lost to Borg in
   five-set Wimbledon final, 1979.
b. Oct 15, 1951 in Lookout Mountain,
   Tennessee
Source: BioIn 10, 12, 14; LegTOT;
NewYTBS 84; WhoAm 80, 82; WhoIntT

Tanner, Valno Alfred
Finnish. Statesman
Headed Social Democratic Party, 1950s-
   60s; opposed Soviet expansion.
b. Mar 12, 1881 in Helsinki, Finland
d. Apr 19, 1966 in Helsinki, Finland
Source: BioIn 1, 4, 5, 7, 8; CurBio 60,
66; ObitOF 79

Tanny, Vic
[Victor A Iannidinardo]
American. Businessman
Owner, first chain of stylish gyms, health
   clubs, 1939.
b. 1912
d. Jun 11, 1985 in Tampa, Florida
Source: BioIn 5; ConNews 85-3;
NewYTBS 85

Tao-an
Chinese. Religious Leader
The most important figure in early
   Chinese Buddhism, monk led disciples
   to rely on the best translations of
   Buddhist texts from India, and to
   interpret them critically.
b. 312 in Hopei Province, China
d. 385 in Ch'ang-an, China
Source: EncWB 98; McGEWB

Tao-chi
Chinese. Artist
One of first Individualist painters well
   known in China, the West; landscapes
   have often been forged.
b. 1630 in Wuzhou, China
d. 1717?
Source: BioIn 3; McGDA; OxCArt

T'ao Ch'ien
Chinese. Poet
Principal lyrical poet of the five-word
   shih style was extremely influential to
   younger poets.

b. 365 in Ch'ai-sang, Kiangsi Provin,
   China
d. 427
Source: EncWB 98; RAdv 14

Tao-hsuan
Chinese. Religious Leader
Buddhist monk, scholar, and mystic
   founded Lu-tsung, the Disciplinary
   school of Chinese Buddhism.
b. 596, China
d. 667, China
Source: EncWB 98; McGEWB

Taoka Kazuo
"Kuma"
Japanese. Criminal
Leader of Yamaguchi-gumi criminal
   organization which dealt in exortion,
   gambling, labor racketeering,
   loansharking, prostitution, show
   business, smuggling.
b. Mar 28, 1912 in Sanshomura, Japan
d. Jul 30, 1981 in Amagasaki, Japan
Source: BioIn 11

Tapahonso, Luci
American. Poet
Poetry collections include One More
   Shiprock Night, 1981; Saanii
   Dahataal, The Women Are Singing,
   1993.
b. 1953 in Shiprock, New Mexico
Source: AmIndBi; AZNatAW; BioIn 14,
21, 22; ConAu 72NR, 145; DcLB 175;
NatAL; NatNAL; NotNaAm; WrDr 98,
99, 2000

Tappan, Eva March
American. Children's Author, Educator
Wrote educational books: American Hero
   Stories, 1906.
b. Dec 26, 1854 in Blackstone,
   Massachusetts
d. Jan 29, 1930 in Worcester,
   Massachusetts
Source: AmAu&B; AmLY; BiDAmEd;
BiD&SB; BioIn 15, 22; CarSB; ChhPo,
S1; DcAmAu; DcAmB; DcNAA; InWom
SUP; JBA 34; NatCAB 22; NotAW;
REnAL; TwCA; TwCBDA; WhAm 1;
WhNAA; WomNov; WomWWA 14;
WorAu 1900

Tappan, William J
American. Manufacturer
Founded stove co., 1881, which later
   diversified into microwave ovens.
b. 1860
d. 1937
Source: Entr

Tappan Brothers
[Arthur Tappan; Lewis Tappan]
American. Religious Figures, Social
   Reformers
Religious reformers and abolitionists
   helped found the Antislavery Society
   and the American Missionary
   Association in the mid-1800s.
Source: EncWB 98; MacEWoS

Taqi Khan Amir-e Kabir, Mirza
Iranian. Political Leader
Greatest prime minister of the Qajar
   dynasty, served from 1848 to 1851.
b. c. 1806
d. 1852 in Kashan, Iran
Source: EncWB 98; McGEWB

Tarantino, Quentin
American. Director, Writer, Actor
Oscar, Best Original Screenplay, Pulp
   Fiction, 1994.
b. Mar 27, 1963 in Knoxville, Tennessee
Source: ChamBiD; ConLC 125; ConTFT
13, 23; CurBio 95; IntMPA 96; IntWW
97, 98, 2000; LegTOT; News 95, 95-1;
NewYTBS 92; WhoAm 95, 96, 97, 98,
99, 2000; WhoEnt 98; WhoWor 96, 97,
98

Tarasova, Alla Konstantinovna
Russian. Actor
Award winning actress with the Moscow
   Art Theatre; played Anna in Anna
   Karenina, 1937.
b. Jan 25, 1898 in Kiev, Russia
d. Apr 5, 1973 in Moscow, Union of
   Soviet Socialist Republics
Source: BiDSovU; EncWT; SovUn;
WhoWor 74; WhScrn 77; WhThe

Tarbell, Ida Minerva
American. Author, Editor
Leader of "muckracking" movement in
   journalism; wrote Life of Abraham
   Lincoln, 1900.
b. Nov 5, 1857 in Erie County,
   Pennsylvania
d. Jan 6, 1944 in Bethel, Connecticut
Source: AmAu&B; AmRef; AmSocL;
AmWomHi; AmWomWr; ApCAB X;
ArtclWW 2; BiDAmJo; BiD&SB; BioIn
1, 2, 3, 4, 5, 6, 8, 9, 10, 11, 13;
CamBiEn; CamDcAB; ChamBiD;
CnDAL; ConAu 181; CurBio 44;
DcAmAu; DcAmB S3; DcLEL; DcNAA;
EncAB-H 1974, 1996; EncTwCJ; EncWB
98; GoodHs; HarEnUS; HerW; InWom,
SUP; LibW; LinLib S; McGEWB;
NatCAB 14; NotAW; OxCAmH;
OxCAmL 65, 83; REn; REnAL; TwCA,
SUP; WebAB 74, 79; WhAm 2; WhLit;
WhNAA; WomComm; WomNov;
WomWWA 14; WorAl; WorAu 1900

Tarde, Gabriel
[Jean Gabriel de Tarde]
French. Sociologist, Criminologist
Introduced theory of social interaction
   placing emphasis on individuals
   instead of group.
b. Mar 12, 1843 in Sarlat, France
d. May 13, 1904 in Paris, France
Source: BiDPsy; BioIn 1, 6; ClDMEL
47; CopCroC; DcSoc; EncSF 93;
NamesHP; OxCFr; OxCLaw; REn;
ScF&FL 1; ScFEYrs

Targ, William
American. Publisher
Senior editor, Putnam's Sons, 1974—;
   writes on book collecting.
b. Mar 4, 1907 in Chicago, Illinois

d. Jul 22, 1999 in New York, New York
Source: *AmAu&B; BioIn 10; ChhPo, S3;
ConAu 61; St&PR 75; WhoAm 74, 76,
78, 80, 82, 84, 86, 88, 90, 92, 95;
WhoWor 82, 84, 87, 89; WhoWorJ 72,
78*

Tarkanian, Jerry
American. Basketball Coach
Coach, UNLV, 1973-1992; Fresno State,
1995—.
b. Aug 8, 1930 in Euclid, Ohio
Source: *BiDAmSp BK; BioIn 9, 11, 13,
14, 15, 16, 17, 18, 19, 21, 22, 23;
LegTOT; News 90; NewYTBS 83;
WhoAm 86, 88, 92, 94; WhoBbl 73;
WhoSpor; WhoSSW 95*

Tarkenton, Fran(cis Asbury)
American. Football Player, TV
Personality
Scrambling quarterback, 1961-79; mostly
with Minnesota; Hall of Fame, 1986;
co-host TV series, "That's
Incredible," 1980-84.
b. Feb 3, 1940 in Richmond, Virginia
Source: *BiDAmSp FB; BioIn 6, 7, 8, 9,
10, 11, 12, 13, 15, 17, 21; CamBiEn;
CamDcAB; CelR; ChamBiD; ConAu
103; CurBio 69; FacFETw; LegTOT;
NewYTBE 70, 71, 72; WhoAm 74, 76,
78, 80, 82, 84, 86, 88, 92, 94, 95, 96;
WhoFtbl 74; WorAl; WorAlBi*

Tarkington, Booth
[Newton Booth Tarkington]
American. Author, Dramatist
Won Pulitzers for *The Magnificent
Ambersons,* 1919; *Alice Adams,* 1922.
b. Jul 29, 1869 in Indianapolis, Indiana
d. May 16, 1946 in Indianapolis, Indiana
Source: *AmAu&B; AmCulL; AmNatBi;
ApCAB X; AtlBL; BbD; BeaEPF; Benet
87; BenetAL 91; BiD&SB; BioIn 1, 2, 3,
4, 5, 6, 8, 10, 11, 12, 13, 14, 16, 17, 19,
22; CamGLE; CamGWoT; CamHAL;
CarSB; CasWL; Chambr 3; ChhPo S2;
ChlBkCr; CnDAL; ConAmA; ConAmL;
ConAu 110; CurBio 46; CyWA 58, 97;
DcAmAu; DcAmB S4; DcAmC; DcArts;
DcBiA; DcLB 102; DcLEL; DcNAA;
EncAAH; EncAB-A 15; EvLB; FacFETw;
FilmgC; GayN; GrWrEL N; HalFC 80,
84, 88; IndAu 1816; JBA 34; LegTOT;
LinLib L, S; LngCTC; McGEWB;
McGEWD 72, 84; MnBBF; ModAL 4, 5;
ModWD; MorMA; NatCAB 4, 42;
NotNAT B; Novels; OxCAmL 65, 83;
OxCAmT 84; OxCEng 67, 85; OxCThe
67, 83; PenC AM; PIP&P; REn; REnAL;
RfGAmL 87; SmATA 17; TwCA, SUP;
TwCBDA; TwCChW 3; TwCWr; WebAB
74, 79; WebE&AL; WhAm 2; WhAmArt
85; WhE&EA; WhLit; WhNAA;
WhoChL; WhoPul; WorAl; WorAlBi;
WorAu 1900*

Tarkovsky, Andrei (Arsenyich)
Russian. Director
Made films *My Name is Ivan,* 1963;
Andrei Rublev, 1966.
b. Apr 4, 1932 in Sarvrashye, Union of
Soviet Socialist Republics

d. Dec 29, 1986 in Paris, France
Source: *AnObit 1986; BiDFilm, 81, 94;
ConAu 127; ConLC 75; DcArts; EncSF
93; FilmEn; HalFC 80, 84, 88; IntDcF
1-2, 2-2; MiSFD 9N; NewYTBS 86;
OxCFilm; WorFDir 2*

Tarleton, Banastre, Sir
English. Army Officer
Led British Troops in American
Revolution; with Cornwallis at
surrender; noted for cruelty.
b. Aug 21, 1754 in Liverpool, England
d. Jan 25, 1833 in Shropshire, England
Source: *Alli; AmBi; AmRev; ApCAB;
BiDLA; BiDSA; BioIn 4, 7, 10;
BlkwEAR; CamBiEn; ChamBiD; DcNaB;
Drake; EncAR; EncCRAm; EncGuW;
EncWB 98; GenMudB; HarEnMi;
HarEnUS; HisDcAR; McGEWB;
NewCBEL; WhAmRev*

Tarlton, Richard
English. Comedian
Queen Elizabeth I's favorite clown;
probably model for Yorick in
Shakespeare's *Hamlet.*
d. Sep 3, 1588 in London, England
Source: *Alli; BiDRP&D; BioIn 2, 3;
BlmGEL; CamBiEn; CamGLE;
CamGWoT; LngCEL; NewC; NewCBEL;
OxCEng 85, 95; OxCMus; REn*

Tarnower, Herman
American. Physician, Author
Wrote *The Complete Scarsdale Medical
Diet,* 1979; murdered by longtime
companion, Jean Harris.
b. Mar 18, 1910 in New York, New
York
d. Mar 10, 1980 in Purchase, New York
Source: *AmNatBi; BiDrACP 79; BioIn
12, 13; ConAu 89, 97; LegTOT;
NewYTBS 80*

Tarsis, Valery Yakovlevich
Swiss. Author
Dissident deprived of Soviet citizenship
during lecture of Britain, 1966.
b. Sep 23, 1906 in Kiev, Russia
d. Mar 3, 1983 in Bern, Switzerland
Source: *ConAu 109; DcRusLS; HanRL;
NewYTBS 83; TwCWr; WhoAm 78;
WorAu 1950*

Tarski, Alfred
American. Mathematician
Major contributor to algebra,
mathematical logic, measure theory,
metamathematics, set theory; wrote
number of books including *Ordinal
Algebras,* 1956.
b. Jan 14, 1902 in Warsaw, Poland
d. Oct 26, 1983 in Berkeley, California
Source: *AmAu&B; AmMWSc 73P;
AnObit 1983; BiEsc; BioIn 15; BlueB
76; CamBiEn; ChamBiD; ConAu 111;
DcScB S2; EncWB 98; IntWW 74, 75,
76, 77, 78, 79, 80, 81, 82, 83; LarDcSc;
McGEWB; OxCPhil; ScrEAmL 1;
ThTwC 87; WhAm 8; WhoAm 74, 76;
WhoWor 74, 76, 78*

Tartaglia, Niccolo (Fontana)
Italian. Mathematician
Pioneered work on ballistics and falling
bodies, and was the first to apply
mathematics to the solution of artillery
problems.
b. 1500 in Brescia, Italy
d. Dec 13, 1557 in Venice, Italy

Tartikoff, Brandon
American. TV Executive
Pres., NBC Entertainment, 1980-90,
credited with successes "The Cosby
Show," "Cheers;" Chairman, NBC
Entertainment, 1989-91; Chairman,
Paramount Pictures, 1991-92;
Chairman, New World Entertainment,
Ltd., 1994-97.
b. Jan 13, 1949 in Long Island, New
York
d. Aug 27, 1997 in Los Angeles,
California
Source: *ConAu 166; ConNews 85-2;
ConTFT 5, 10, 17, 18; CurBio 87, 97N;
IntMPA 84, 86, 88, 92, 94, 96; LegTOT;
LesBEnT; News 98, 98-1; WhAm 12;
WhoAm 86, 88, 90, 92, 94, 95, 96, 97,
98; WhoEnt 92; WhoFI 94, 96;
WhoMedi 98; WhoTelC; WhoWest 89,
92, 94*

Tartini, Giuseppe
Italian. Composer, Violinist
Wrote 50 violin sonatas; developed
"Tartini harmonic" for finer
intonation.
b. Apr 8, 1692 in Istria, Italy
d. Feb 26, 1770 in Padua, Italy
Source: *BakBD 78, 84, 92; BakDcM;
BioIn 1, 2, 3, 4, 6, 7, 8, 12, 14; BriBkM
80; CamBiEn; ChamBiD; CmpBCM;
DcArts; DcBiPP; DcCathB; DcCom 77;
EncWB 98; GrComp; McGEWB;
MusMk; NewAmDM; NewCol 75;
NewGrDM 80; NewOxM; OxCMus;
REn; WebBD 83; WhDW*

Tartt, Donna (Louise)
American. Author
Wrote *The Secret History,* 1992.
b. 1964? in Greenwood, Mississippi
Source: *ConAu 142; ConLC 76; LegTOT*

Tashman, Lilyan
American. Actor
Elegant leading lady of silents and early
talkies, 1921-34, in *No, No Nanette.*
b. Oct 23, 1899 in New York, New York
d. Mar 21, 1934 in New York, New
York
Source: *BioIn 10; EncAFC; Film 2;
FilmEn; FilmgC; FrSilen; HalFC 80, 84,
88; InWom SUP; LegTOT; MovMk;
NotNAT B; SilFlmP; ThFT; TwYS;
VixFIM; WhoHol B; WhScrn 74, 77;
WhThe; WorAl*

Tasman, Abel Janszoon
Dutch. Explorer
Discovered Tasmania and New Zealand,
1642.
b. 1603
d. 1659

Source: *BioIn 5, 11, 12, 18, 19, 20, 24; CambiEn; ChambiD; EncWB 98; Expl 93; ExplAnT; LegTOT; McGEWB; NewC; NewCol 75; OxCAusL; OxCShps; REn; WebBD 83; WhDW; WhWE*

Tassell, Gustave
American. Designer
With the death of Norman Norell, 1972, carried on the designer's classic, luxurious line.
b. Feb 4, 1926 in Philadelphia, Pennsylvania
Source: *ConFash; EncFash; FairDF US; ThHDFas; WhoAm 74, 76, 78; WhoFash 88; WorFshn*

Tasso, Torquato
Italian. Author
Best-known epic *Jerusalem Delivered*, 1575; re-wrote because of criticism, 1587.
b. Mar 11, 1544 in Sorrento, Italy
d. Apr 25, 1595 in Rome, Italy
Source: *AtlBL; BbD; Benet 87, 96; BiCoLiE; BiD&SB; BioIn 1, 2, 5, 7, 8, 13, 14, 20, 24; BlmGEL; CambiEn; CamGWoT; CasWL; ChambiD; CnThe; CroE&S; CyWA 58, 97; DcArts; DcBiPP; DcCathB; DcEuL; DcItL 1, 2; Dis&D; EncLitE; EncWB 98; EncWT; Ent; EuAu; EuWr 2; EvEuW; GrFLW; IntDcT 2; LinLib L, S; LitC 5; LngCEL; McGEWB; McGEWD 72, 84; NewC; NewCBEL; NewEOp 71; NewGrDM 80; NewGrDO; NotNAT B; OxCEng 67, 85, 95; OxCThe 67, 83; OxDcOp; PenC EUR; PlP&P; RAdv 14; RComWL; REn; REnWD; RfGWoL 95; WhDW; WorAl; WorAlBi*

Tata, J(ehangir) R(atanji) D(adbhoy)
Indian. Industrialist
Grandson of Jamshedji Nusserwanji Tata; became chairman of Tata Sons, 1938.
b. Jul 29, 1904
d. Nov 29, 1993, Switzerland
Source: *BioIn 5, 8; CurBio 94N; IntYB 78, 79, 80, 81, 82*

Tata, Jamshedji Nusserwanji
Indian. Industrialist, Philanthropist
Major architect of India's industrial development; gave generously to fund several research institutions.
b. Mar 3, 1839 in Navsari, India
d. May 19, 1904 in Nauheim, Germany
Source: *BioIn 1, 6, 7; DcNaB S2*

Tate, Allen (John Orley)
American. Poet, Critic
Poems include *The Golden Mean and Other Poems*, 1923; novels include *The Fathers*, 1938.
b. Nov 19, 1899 in Winchester, Kentucky
d. Feb 9, 1979 in Nashville, Tennessee
Source: *AmAu&B; AmWr; Au&Wr 71; Benet 87; BenetAL 91; BiDConC; BioIn 3, 4, 5, 7, 8, 9, 10, 11, 12, 13, 14, 15, 16, 17, 18, 19, 21; BlueB 76; CamGEL; CamGLE; CamHAL; CasWL; CathA*

1952; *ChhPo, S2, S3; CnDAL; CnE&AP; ConAmA; ConAu 5R, 32NR, 85; ConLC 2, 4, 6, 9, 11, 14, 24; ConLCrt 77, 82; ConNov 72, 76; ConPo 70, 75; ConSpo 79N; DrAF 76; DrAP 75; DrAS 74E, 78E, 82E; EncWL 1, 2, 2S; FacFETw; FifSWrA; GrWrEL P; IntAu&W 76, 77; IntWW 74, 75, 76, 77, 78; IntWWP 77; LegTOT; LiHiK; LinLib L; LngCTC; MajTwCW 1; McGEWB; ModAL 4, 4S1, 4S2; NewYTBS 79; OxCAmL 65, 83; OxCEng 85; OxCTwCP; PenC AM; PeoHis; RAdv 1, 14; REn; REnAL; RfGAmL 87; RGFAP; SixAP; SouWr; TwCA, SUP; TwCWr; WebAB 74, 79; WebE&AL; WhAm 7; WhE&EA; WhoAm 74, 76, 78; WhoSSW 73, 75, 76; WhoTwCL; WhoWor 74, 76, 78; WorAl; WorAlBi; WrDr 76, 80*

Tate, Eleanora E(laine)
American. Author, Journalist
Author of novels focusing on African American girls, credited with shattering racial stereotypes and promoting the value of community; her best known works are the novels in the *South Carolina Trilogy*.
b. Apr 16, 1948 in Canton, Missouri
Source: *BlkAuII, 92; BlkWr 2, 3; ConAu 43NR, 81NR; MajAI SUP; SJGChWr 5; SmATA 94; TwCYAW 1; WhoAfA 9, 10, 11, 12; WhoBlA 6, 7, 8*

Tate, Henry, Sir
English. Art Collector, Manufacturer
Sugar magnate; founded Britain's renowned Tate Gallery, 1897.
b. 1819
d. 1899
Source: *BioIn 6, 8; CambiEn; ChambiD; DcNaB S1; REn*

Tate, James
American. Poet
Winner of Pulitzer Prize for poetry, *Selected Poems*, 1992.
b. Dec 8, 1943 in Kansas City, Missouri
Source: *BenetAL 91; BioIn 9, 12, 22; CambiEn; ConAu 21R, 29NR; ConLC 25; ConPo 80, 85, 91; CyWA 97; DcLB 169; EncALit; EncWL 3; OxCAmL 83; OxCTwCL; OxCTwCP; RAdv 14; RfGAmL 4; WhoAm 74, 76, 78, 82, 84; WhoPul; WhoUSWr 88; WhoWrEP 89, 92, 95; WorAu 1970; WrDr 80, 82, 84, 86, 88, 90, 92*

Tate, Larenz
American. Actor
Actor in films and television, first drew attention with performance in *Menace II Society*, 1993; also appeared in TV drama series "South Central" and as the lead in the film *Love Jones*.
b. Sep 8, 1975 in Chicago, Illinois
Source: *ConBlB 15; ConTFT 22*

Tate, Nahum
English. Poet
Poet laureate, 1692-1715, best known for "Panacea, a poem on Tea," 1700.
b. Sep 12, 1652 in Dublin, Ireland

d. Aug 12, 1715 in London, England
Source: *Alli; AnCL; Benet 87, 96; BiCoLiE; BiDIrW; BioIn 3, 9, 12; BlmGEL; BritAu; CambiEn; CamGLE; CamGWoT; CasWL; ChambiD; Chambr 2; ChhPo; DcArts; DcBiPP; DcEnA; DcEnL; DcEuL; DcIrB 1, 2, 3; DcIrL, 96; DcIrW 1; DcLEL; DcNaB; EvLB; GrWrEL DR; IntDcT 2; LuthC 75; NewC; NewCBEL; NewGrDM 80; NewGrDO; NotNAT B; OxCEng 67, 85, 95; OxCIri; OxCMus; OxCThe 67, 83; PenC ENG; PlP&P; PoChrch; PoIre; PoLE; REn; RfGEnL 91*

Tate, Sharon
[Mrs. Roman Polanski]
American. Actor
Murdered by Charles Manson family.
b. Jan 24, 1943 in Dallas, Texas
d. Aug 9, 1969 in Bel Air, California
Source: *BioIn 7, 8, 11, 13; FilmgC; ForYSC; HalFC 80, 84, 88; ItaFilm; LegTOT; MotPP; WhoHol B; WhoHrs 80; WhScrn 74, 77, 83*

Tati, Jacques
[Jacques Tatischeff]
French. Comedian, Director
Won Oscar, 1958, for *Mon Oncle*; inspired by Charlie Chaplin and Buster Keaton.
b. Oct 9, 1908 in Le Pecq, France
d. Nov 5, 1982 in Paris, France
Source: *AnObit 1982; BiDFilm, 81, 94; BioIn 3, 5, 6, 9, 11, 12; CambiEn; ChambiD; ConAu 108; CurBio 61, 83N; DcArts; DcFM; DcPseud; DcTwCCu 2; EncEurC; Ent; FacFETw; FilmAG WE; FilmEn; FilmgC; HalFC 80, 84, 88; IntDcF 1-2, 2-2; IntWW 74, 75, 76, 77, 78, 79, 80, 81, 82, 83N; ItaFilm; JoeFr; LegTOT; MiSFD 9N; MotPP; MovMk; NewYTBS 82; OxCFilm; QDrFCA 92; Who 74, 82, 83, 83N; WhoCom; WhoHol A; WhoWor 74, 82; WorEFlm; WorFDir 2*

Tatlin, Vladimir Yevgrapovich
Ukrainian. Artist, Sculptor
Led Constructivism movement in Moscow; known for monument to the Third International, 1920.
b. Dec 28, 1885 in Kharkov, Ukraine
d. May 31, 1953 in Moscow, Union of Soviet Socialist Republics
Source: *BioIn 13, 14, 15, 16; ConArt 83; DcTwDes; FacFETw; IntDcAA 90; OxCArt; OxDcArt; PenDiDA 89; WhoArch*

Tatum, Art(hur)
American. Jazz Musician
All-time great jazz pianist, noted for original technique, improvisation; led trio, 1943-55; recorded "Sweet Lorraine."
b. Oct 13, 1910 in Toledo, Ohio
d. Nov 4, 1956 in Los Angeles, California
Source: *AmCulL; BakBD 84, 92; BakDcM; BiDAfM; BiDAmM; BiDJaz; BioIn 4, 5, 10, 11, 12, 13, 14, 15, 16,*

17, 19, 20; CambiEn; ChamBiD;
CmpEPM; DcAmB S6; DcArts; DrBlPA,
90; EncJzS; IlEncJ; InB&W 80;
LegTOT; NegAl 76, 83, 89; NewAmDM;
NewGrDM 80; WebAB 74, 79; WhAm 4;
WhoJazz 72; WhScrn 77, 83; WorAl;
WorAlBi

Tatum, Donn B
American. Business Executive
Chm., Walt Disney Co., 1971-80; major
figure in the development of Walt
Disney World and Tokyo Disneyland.
b. Jan 9, 1913 in Los Angeles, California
d. May 31, 1993 in Pacific Palisades,
California
Source: BioIn 9; IntMPA 92; WhoAm
90; WhoEnt 92; WhoFI 89

Tatum, Edward Lawrie
American. Biochemist, Geneticist,
Educator, Author
Won 1958 Nobel Prize for work in
genetics.
b. Dec 14, 1909 in Boulder, Colorado
d. Nov 5, 1975 in New York, New York
Source: AmNatBi; AsBiEn; BiESc; BioIn
3, 4, 5, 6, 7, 10, 11, 12, 13, 14, 15, 20;
BlueB 76; CamBiEn; CamDcAB;
ChamBiD; ConAu 113; CurBio 59;
DcAmB S9; DcAmMeB 84; LarDcSc;
McGCEnS; McGMS 80; NotTwCS 1;
OxCMed 86; RanHWDS; WebAB 74, 79;
WhAm 6; WhoAm 74, 76; WhoNob, 90,
95; WorAl; WorScD

Tatum, Jack
[John David Tatum]
"The Assassin"
American. Football Player
Three-time all-pro defensive back, 1971-
80, mostly with Oakland; known for
aggressiveness; wrote They Call Me
Assassin, 1979.
b. Nov 18, 1948 in Cherryville, North
Carolina
Source: BiDAmSp FB; BioIn 10, 12;
ConAu 104; NewYTBS 80; WhoAm 78,
80; WhoBlA 2, 3, 4, 6; WhoFtbl 74

Taube, Henry
American. Educator
Won Nobel Prize in chemistry, 1983.
b. Nov 30, 1915 in Neudorf,
Saskatchewan, Canada
Source: AmMWSc 73P, 76P, 79, 82, 86,
89, 92, 95, 98; BiESc; BioIn 3, 5, 7, 8,
9, 13; BlueB 76; CamBiEn; CamDcAB;
CanWW 98, 1999; ChamBiD; IntWW 74,
75, 76, 77, 78, 79, 80, 81, 82, 83, 89,
91, 93, 97, 98, 2000; LarDcSc;
McGCEnS; McGMS 80; NobelP;
NotTwCS 1; RanHWDS; Who 85, 88, 90,
92, 94, 98, 99, 2000; WhoAm 74, 76, 78,
80, 82, 84, 86, 88, 90, 92, 94, 95, 96,
97, 98, 99, 2000; WhoFrS 84; WhoNob,
90, 95; WhoScEn 94, 96, 2000; WhoWest
00, 87, 89, 92, 94, 96, 98; WhoWor 74,
84, 87, 89, 91, 93, 95, 96, 97, 98, 99,
2000; WorAlBi

Tauber, Richard
British. Opera Singer, Actor
Tenor, noted for Mozart, Lehar operetta
roles; films include Blossom Time,
1932.
b. May 16, 1892 in Linz, Austria
d. Jan 8, 1948 in London, England
Source: BakBD 78, 84; BioIn 1, 2, 3, 4,
5, 7, 9, 11, 12, 14, 17, 18; BriBkM 80;
CamBiEn; ChamBiD; CmOp; EncMT;
FacFETw; FilmgC; ForYSC; HalFC 80,
84, 88; IlWWBF, A; MusMk; MusSN;
NewCol 75; NewEOp 71; NewOxM;
OxCFilm; OxCPMus; OxDcOp; WhAm
2; WhoHol B; WhScrn 74, 77, 83

Taubes, Frederic
American. Artist
Exhibits at one-man shows, museums
throughout US, Europe, Palestine;
books on art include The Technique of
Oil Painting, 1941.
b. Apr 15, 1900 in Lvov, Poland
d. Jun 21, 1981 in Nyack, New York
Source: BioIn 1, 2, 3, 10; ConAu 9NR,
17R, 104; CurBio 43; DcCAA 71, 77,
88, 94; McGDA; WhAmArt 85; WhoAmA
73, 76, 78, 80, 82N, 86N, 89N, 91N, 93N

Taubman, A(dolph) Alfred
American. Businessman
Founder and chm. Taubman Co., 1950—
, a major developer of successful
shopping malls nationwide.
b. Jan 31, 1925 in Pontiac, Michigan
Source: BioIn 13, 14, 15; CurBio 93;
Dun&B 90; IntWW 91; NewYTBS 83;
WhoAm 90; WhoE 89; WhoFI 92;
WhoMW 92

Taubman, (Hyman) Howard
American. Journalist, Author, Critic
Drama critic, NY Times, 1960-72.
b. Jul 4, 1907 in New York, New York
d. Jan 8, 1996 in Sarasota, Florida
Source: AmAu&B; BakBD 78, 84, 92;
BiDAmM; BiE&WWA; BioIn 5, 20, 21;
BlueB 76; CurBio 59, 96N; IntAu&W 76,
77; IntWW 74, 75, 76, 77, 78, 79, 80,
81, 82, 83, 89, 91, 93; NewGrDA 86;
NewGrDM 80; NewYTBS 96; NotNAT;
WhoAm 74, 76; WhoThe 72, 77A;
WhThe

Taulbert, Clifton Lemoure
American. Author, Business Executive
Author of much-acclaimed memoir Once
Upon a Time When We Were Colored,
about his own childhood during the
Jim Crow era in the Deep South;
successful marketing consultant and
CEO of a manufacturing company.
b. Feb 19, 1945 in Glen Allen,
Mississippi
Source: BlkWr 2; ConAu 143; ConBlB
19; WhoAfA 9, 10, 11, 12; WhoBlA 7, 8;
WrDr 96, 98, 99, 2000

Taupin, Bernie
English. Lyricist
Wrote lyrics for Elton John's gold
records; inducted into Songwriters Hall
of Fame, 1992.

b. May 22, 1950 in Sleaford, England
Source: BioIn 11, 12; ConMus 22;
EncPR&S 74; EncRk 88; IlEncRk;
LegTOT; Songw; WhoRocM 82

Taurog, Norman
American. Director
Won Oscar for Skippy, 1931.
b. Feb 23, 1899 in Chicago, Illinois
d. Apr 7, 1981 in Rancho Mirage,
California
Source: AnObit 1981; BioIn 12, 15;
CmMov; DcFM; EncAFC; Film 1;
FilmEn; FilmgC; HalFC 80, 84, 88;
IlWWHD 1; IntDcF 1-2; IntMPA 75, 76,
78, 79, 80, 81; LegTOT; MiSFD 9N;
MovMk; NewYTBS 81; TwYS, A; WhAm
7; WhoAm 74, 76, 78, 80; WhScrn 83;
WorEFlm; WorFDir 1

Tausig, Karl
Polish. Pianist, Composer
Internationally renowned concert pianist
known for excellent dexterity and
tone; student of Liszt.
b. Nov 4, 1841 in Warsaw, Poland
d. Jul 17, 1871 in Leipzig, Germany
Source: BakBD 84; BioIn 2, 7, 16;
NewAmDM; OxCMus; PenDiMP

Taussig, Frank William
American. Economist
Major contributor to trade theory; wrote
text Princples of Economics, 1911.
b. Dec 28, 1859 in Saint Louis, Missouri
d. Nov 11, 1940 in Saint Louis, Missouri
Source: Alli SUP; AmAu&B; AmLY;
AmNatBi; BiDAmEd; BioIn 2, 3, 4, 14;
CurBio 40; DcAmAu; DcAmB S2;
DcNAA; HarEnUS; NatCAB 8, 30;
ObitOF 79; OxCAmH; REnAL; WhAm 1;
WhNAA; WhoEc 81, 86

Taussig, Helen Brooke
American. Physician
Developed surgical procedure for treating
"blue babies;" warned US of
Thalidomide peril.
b. May 24, 1898 in Cambridge,
Massachusetts
d. May 20, 1986 in Kennett Square,
Pennsylvania
Source: AmMWSc 76P, 79, 82;
AmNatBi; AmWomSc; BiDrACP 79;
BioIn 1, 2, 3, 5, 7, 8, 9, 11, 13, 14, 15,
16, 18, 20, 22, 23, 24; CamBiEn;
ChamBiD; ConAu 163; ContDcW 89;
CurBio 46, 86; EncWB 98; GoodHs;
InSci; IntDcWB; InWom, SUP; LarDcSc;
LibW; McGMS 80; NewYTBS 86;
NotTwCS 1; NotWoLS; RanHWDS;
ScrEAmL 2; WhAm 9; WhoAm 74, 76,
78; WhoAmW 58, 61, 64, 66, 68, 70, 72,
74, 79, 83, 85; WhoWor 74; WomBioS;
WomFir; WorScD

Tavernier, Bertrand
French. Director
Films center around basic human
experiences: 'Round Midnight, 1986;
Let Joy Reign Supreme, 1975.
b. Apr 25, 1941 in Lyons, France

Source: *BiDFilm 94; BioIn 13; ChamBiD; ConAu 123; ConTFT 7; CurBio 88; EncEurC; FilmEn; HalFC 80, 84, 88; IntDcF 1-2, 2-2; IntMPA 79, 80, 81, 82, 84, 86, 88, 92, 94, 96; LegTOT; MiSFD 9; NewYTBS 85; WhoFr 86; WhoWor 87; WorFDir 2*

Tawley, Howard
Canadian. Politician
New Democratic Party premier of Manitoba, 1981—.
b. Nov 21, 1934 in Brampton, Ontario, Canada

Tawney, Richard Henry
English. Historian, Author
Best known for his comparative study *Religion and the Rise of Capitalism*, 1926.
b. Nov 30, 1880 in Calcutta, India
d. Jan 16, 1962 in London, England
Source: *BioIn 2, 4, 5, 6, 10, 12, 14; CambiEn; CasWL; ChamBiD; ConAu 93; DcLEL; DcNaB 1961; DcSoc; DcTwHis; EncWB 98; GloEncH; GrBr; LngCTC; MakMC; McGEWB; NewC; NewCBEL; OxCEng 85; OxCTwCL; PenC AM, ENG; REn; TwCA, SUP; WhE&EA; WhLit; WhoEc 81, 86*

Tax, Sol
American. Anthropologist
Studies of native American tribes led to pioneering use of transactional analysis.
b. Oct 30, 1907 in Chicago, Illinois
d. Jan 4, 1995 in Chicago, Illinois
Source: *AmAu&B; AmMWSc 73S, 76P; BioIn 17, 20, 21; BlueB 76; CamDcAB; ConAu 5R; EncNAB; FifIDA; IntDcAn; IntEnSS 79; IntWW 74, 75, 76, 77, 78, 79, 80, 81, 82, 83, 89, 91, 93; WhAm 12; WhoAm 74, 76, 78, 80, 82, 84, 88, 90; WhoGov 72, 75; WhoWor 74; WhoWorJ 72, 78*

Taya, Maaouya Ould Sid'Ahmed
Mauritian. Political Leader
Military leader deposed President Haidalla in a bloodless coup in 1983, becoming president of the Islamic Republic of Mauritania; his leadership is characterized by human rights violations, press censorship, ethnic unrest, and setbacks in the democratization process.
b. 1943 in Atar, Mauritania

Tayback, Vic
[Victor Tabback]
American. Actor
Played Mel on TV series "Alice," 1976-85.
b. Jan 6, 1929 in New York, New York
d. May 25, 1990 in Glendale, California
Source: *BioIn 11, 16, 17; DcPseud; HalFC 88; LegTOT; WhoAm 80, 82, 84; WhoHol A; WhoTelC*

Taylor, A(lan) J(ohn) P(ercivale)
English. Author, Historian
Britain's most popular historian; wrote at least 30 books; his 60-year career convinced him that events are often shaped by accident.
b. Mar 25, 1906 in Birkdale, England
d. Sep 7, 1990 in Barnet, England
Source: *Au&Wr 71; Benet 87, 96; BioIn 4, 7, 10, 11, 13, 15, 17, 18, 19, 20; BlueB 76; CamBiEn; ChamBiD; ConAu 5R; CurBio 83, 90; DcNaB 1986; EncTR; GloEncH; IntAu&W 76, 77, 91; IntWW 74, 75, 76, 77, 78, 79, 80, 81, 82, 83, 89; LngCTC; MajTwCW 1, 2; NewC; NewCBEL; NewYTBS 90; OxCCan SUP; OxCEng 85, 95; OxCTwCL; RAdv 14; REn; WhAm 10; WhDW; WhE&EA; Who 74, 82, 83, 85, 88, 90; WhoWor 74, 76, 78, 84, 87, 89; WorAu 1950; WrDr 76, 80, 82, 84, 86, 90*

Taylor, Ann
English. Children's Author, Poet
With sister Jane, wrote *Original Poems for Infant Minds*, 1804.
b. Jun 30, 1782 in London, England
d. Dec 20, 1866
Source: *Alli; BioIn 8, 14, 15, 16, 22; BlmGEL; BlmGWL; BritAu 19; CarSB; ChhPo, S1, S2, S3; ChrP; DcBiPP; DcEnL; DcEuL; DcLB 163; DcNaB; EncBrWW; EvLB; InWom, SUP; NewC; NewCBEL; OxCChiL; OxCEng 67; PenNWW A; SmATA 35, 41; Str&VC; WhoChL*

Taylor, Arthur Robert
American. TV Executive
President, CBS, Inc., 1972-76.
b. Jul 6, 1935 in Elizabeth, New Jersey
Source: *BioIn 9, 10, 11; BlueB 76; IntWW 74, 75, 76, 77, 78, 79, 80, 81, 82, 83, 89, 91, 93, 97, 98, 2000; NewYTBE 72; Who 83, 85, 88, 90, 92, 94, 98, 99, 2000; WhoAm 74, 76, 78, 80, 82, 84, 86, 88, 90, 92, 94, 95, 96, 97, 98, 99, 2000; WhoE 89; WhoFI 74, 77, 79, 81, 83; WhoWor 87, 89*

Taylor, Bayard
[James Bayard Taylor]
American. Traveler, Author
Wrote *Travels in Arabia*, 1872; *Egypt and Iceland*, 1874.
b. Jan 11, 1825 in Kennett Square, Pennsylvania
d. Dec 19, 1878 in Berlin, Germany
Source: *Alli, SUP; AmAu; AmAu&B; AmBi; AmNatBi; ApCAB; ArtsAmW 1; BbD; Benet 87; BenetAL 91; BibAL 8; BiD&SB; BiGAW; BioIn 1, 2, 3, 9, 10, 15, 16, 22, 23, 24; CamDcAB; CamGEL; CamGLE; CamHAL; CasWL; CelCen; Chambr 3; ChhPo, S1, S3; CmCal; CnDAL; CyAL 2; DcAmAu; DcAmB; DcAmDH 80, 89; DcBiA; DcBiPP; DcEnA A; DcEnL; DcLB 3, 189; DcLEL; DcNAA; Drake; EncAHmr; EncALit; EvLB; FolkA 87; GrWrEL P; HarEnUS; IlBEAAW; JrnUS; LinLib L, S; NatCAB 3; NewEAmW; NewYHSD; OxCAmH; OxCAmL 65, 83; OxCEng 67; PenC AM; PeoHis; REn; REnAL;*

REnAW; RfGAmL 4, 87, 94; TwCBDA; WebAB 74, 79; WhAm HS

Taylor, Billy
[William Edward Taylor]
American. Jazz Musician
Noted jazz pianist, since 1937; had weekly TV show, 1960s; member, Jazz Hall of Fame, 1979.
b. Jul 24, 1921 in Greenville, North Carolina
Source: *AfrAmAl 6; AllMGJa; ASCAP 80; BakBD 84, 92; BiDJaz; BioIn 13, 14, 16, 17; BlkCond; CmpEPM; ConMus 13; DcTwCCu 5; DrBlPA, 90; Ebony 1; EncJzS; FacFETw; InB&W 80, 85; IntWWM 77; LegTOT; NewAmDM; NewGrDA 86; NewGrDJ 88, 94; NewYTBE 71; OxCPMus; PenEncP; WhoAfA 9; WhoAm 74, 76, 78, 80, 82, 84, 86, 88, 96, 97; WhoBlA 2, 3, 4, 6, 7, 8; WhoJazz 72; WorAl; WorAlBi*

Taylor, Brook
English. Mathematician
Best known for the Taylor series, expressing the value of a function in the neighborhood of a point in terms of the derivatives at the point.
b. Aug 1685
d. 1731
Source: *Alli; BiESc; BioIn 14; CamBiEn; ChamBiD; DcBiPP; DcNaB; DcScB; EncEnl; EncWB 98; InSci; LarDcSc; McGCEnS; McGEWB; NewGrDM 80; NotMat*

Taylor, Cecil Percival
American. Musician
Jazz pianist, who combines classical, contemporary music; innovator in harmony rhythm.
b. Mar 15, 1933 in Long Island, New York
Source: *BakBD 92; BakBDTw; BiDAfM; BiDJaz; CamBiEn; CamDcAB; ChamBiD; ConMus 9; CurBio 86; EncJzS; InB&W 80, 85; WhoAm 80, 82, 84, 86, 88, 90, 92, 94, 95, 96, 97, 98, 99*

Taylor, Charles
Liberian. Political Leader
Elected president of Liberia, 1997, in a landslide victory; had been one of the forces behind the country's bloody and economically disastrous seven-year civil war.
b. Jan 28, 1948 in Arthington, Liberia
Source: *ConBlB 20; CurBio 92; WhoAfr*

Taylor, Charles Alonzo
"The Master of Melodrama"
American. Producer, Dramatist
Suspense plays include *The Child Wife*, 1901.
b. Jan 20, 1864 in Greenfield, Massachusetts
d. Mar 20, 1942 in Glendale, California
Source: *AmNatBi; CurBio 42; DcAmB S3*

Taylor, Charles McArthur
Liberian. Military Leader
Self-proclaimed president of Liberia.
b. 1948?, Liberia
Source: *BioIn 16; CurBio 92*

Taylor, Charley
American. Football Player
Halfback, receiver, 1965-77, mostly with
Washington; Hall of Fame, 1984.
b. Sep 28, 1942 in Dallas, Texas
Source: *BioIn 9; LegTOT; WhoBlA 4*

Taylor, Cyclone
[Fred Taylor]
Canadian. Hockey Player
Forward-defenseman, 1906-21; Hall of
Fame, 1945.
b. Jun 23, 1883 in Tara, Ontario, Canada
d. Jun 10, 1979
Source: *BioIn 8, 11; WhoHcky 73*

Taylor, Dave
[David Andrew Taylor]
Canadian. Hockey Player
Right wing, LA, 1977—; with Marcel
Dionne, Charlie Simmer, formed high-
scoring Royal Line, early 1980s.
b. Dec 4, 1955 in Levack, Ontario,
Canada
Source: *HocEn; HocReg 87*

Taylor, (Joseph) Deems
American. Composer, Critic
Editor, *Musical America*, 1927-29;
commentator, narrator on radio, 1933-
66.
b. Dec 22, 1885 in New York, New
York
d. Jul 3, 1966 in New York, New York
Source: *AmAu&B; AmComp; ApCAB X;
ASCAP 66, 80; BakBD 78, 84, 92;
BakBDTw; BiDAmM; BioIn 1, 3, 4, 5, 6,
7, 8, 11; CamDcAB; ChhPo, S2;
CompSN; ConAmC 76, 82; ConAu 89;
CurBio 40, 66; DcAmB S8; DcCM;
DcCom&M 79; FilmgC; LegTOT; LinLib
L, S; MetOEnc; NewAmDM; NewCol 75;
NewEOp 71; NewGrDA 86; NewGrDM
80; NewGrDO; NotNAT B; OxCAmH;
OxCAmL 65; OxCAmT 84; OxCMus;
OxDcOp; RadStar; REnAL; TwCA, SUP;
WebAB 74, 79; WhAm 4; WhJnl;
WhScrn 77, 83; WhThe*

Taylor, Edward
American. Poet
Only two of his works were published in
his lifetime, re-discovered, 1939:
"God's Determinations Touching His
Elect," 1685.
b. 1642 in Coventry, England
d. Jun 24, 1729 in Westfield,
Massachusetts
Source: *Alli; AmAu&B; AmBi; AmNatBi;
AmWr; AmWrBE; ApCAB; AtlBL; Benet
87, 96; BenetAL 91; BioIn 5, 6, 7, 9, 10,
12, 14, 17; CasWL; ChhPo, S1; CnDAL;
CnE&AP; CrtT 3; CyWA 58; DcAmB
S1; DcLEL; EncALit; EncWB 98;
GrWrEL P; LinLib L; LitC 11;
McGEWB; OxCAmL 65; OxCEng 67;
PenC AM; RAdv 1, 14; REn; REnAL;*

*RfGAmL 4, 87, 94; RGFAP; WebE&AL;
WhAm HS*

Taylor, Elizabeth Rosemond
English. Actor
Won Oscars for *Butterfield 8*, 1960;
Who's Afraid of Virginia Woolf? 1966.
b. Feb 27, 1932 in London, England
Source: *BiDFilm; IntWWW 2; MovMk;
OxCFilm; Who 94, 98, 99, 2000;
WhoAm 86, 95, 96, 97, 98, 99, 2000;
WhoAmW 87, 95, 97, 99; WhoEnt 98;
WhoWor 87, 95, 96, 97, 98, 99, 2000;
WorAl; WorEFlm*

Taylor, Estelle
[Estelle Boylan]
American. Actor
Married Jack Dempsey, 1925-31; films
include *The Ten Commandments*,
1956.
b. May 20, 1899 in Wilmington,
Delaware
d. Apr 15, 1958 in Hollywood,
California
Source: *BioIn 4; DcPseud; Film 2;
FilmEn; FilmgC; ForYSC; FrSilen;
HalFC 80, 84, 88; InWom, SUP;
LegTOT; MotPP; NotNAT B; SilFlmP;
ThFT; TwYS; WhoHol B; WhScrn 74,
77, 83; WorAl*

Taylor, Frederick Winslow
American. Engineer, Inventor
Conducted first time-and-motion studies
to improve efficiency, 1881.
b. Mar 20, 1856 in Germantown,
Pennsylvania
d. Mar 21, 1915 in Philadelphia,
Pennsylvania
Source: *AmBi; AmDec 1900; AmNatBi;
AsBiEn; BiDAmBL 83; BiDAmSp OS;
BilnAmS; BioIn 2, 4, 5, 7, 8, 9, 10, 11,
12, 13, 17, 20, 21, 22, 23; CamBiEn;
CamDcAB; ChamBiD; DcAmB; DcNAA;
DcScB; EncAB-H 1974, 1996; EncABHB
4; MemAm; NatCAB 14, 23; NewCol 75;
NotTwCS 1; OxCAmH; PeoHis; TwCLC
76; WebAB 74, 79; WhAm 1; WorAl*

Taylor, George
American. Colonial Figure, Continental
Congressman
Ironmaster; served less than a year in
Congress; signed Declaration of
Independence, 1776.
b. 1716, Northern Ireland
d. Feb 22, 1781 in Easton, Pennsylvania
Source: *AmBi; ApCAB; BiAUS; BiDrAC;
BiDrUSC 89; BioIn 7, 8, 9, 23; DcAmB;
DcIrB 1, 2, 3; Drake; EncAR;
EncCRAm; HarEnUS; HisDcAR;
NatCAB 5; NewCol 75; TwCBDA;
WhAm HS; WhAmP; WhAmRev*

Taylor, Graham
American. Clergy, Sociologist
Founder, warden, Chicago Commons
Social Settlement, 1894-1938.
b. May 2, 1851 in Schenectady, New
York
d. Sep 26, 1938

Source: *AmLY; AmNatBi; AmSetPR;
BiDSocW; BioIn 3, 4, 7; CamDcAB;
DcAmB S2; DcNAA; NatCAB 29;
OxCAmH; OxCAmL 65, 83, 95; WhAm
1; WorAl; WorAlBi*

Taylor, Henry Junior
American. Journalist, Diplomat
Non-fiction works include *Men and
Power*, 1946.
b. Sep 2, 1902 in Chicago, Illinois
d. Feb 26, 1984 in New York, New
York
Source: *AmAu&B; BiDAmNC; BioIn 1;
ConAu 112, P-2; IntWW 74; St&PR 75;
WhAm 8; WhoAm 74, 76, 78, 80, 82*

Taylor, J(ohn) H(enry)
[Great Triumvirate]
English. Golfer
With James Braid, Harry Vardon,
dominated game, late 19th, early 20th
c; won British Open five times.
b. Mar 19, 1871 in North Devon,
England
d. Feb 10, 1963 in Devonshire, England
Source: *BioIn 6, 13, 14; CamBiEn;
ChamBiD; DcNaB 1941, 1961; GrBr;
ObitT 1961; WhoGolf*

Taylor, J. T
[Kool and the Gang; James Taylor]
American. Singer
Vocalist with Kool and the Gang since
1978.
b. Aug 16, 1953 in South Carolina

Taylor, James Vernon
"Sweet Baby James"
American. Singer, Songwriter
Has nine gold albums, four platinum
albums, three gold singles for his folk-
rock songs.
b. Mar 12, 1948 in Boston,
Massachusetts
Source: *BakBD 92; BkPepl; CamDcAB;
HarEnR 86; RkOn 74; WhoAm 74, 76,
78, 80, 82, 84, 86, 88, 90, 92, 94, 95,
96, 97, 98, 99, 2000; WhoEnt 92, 98;
WhoWest 74*

Taylor, Jane
English. Poet
Wrote *Twinkle, Twinkle Little Star*; sister
of Ann.
b. Sep 26, 1783 in Holborn, England
d. Apr 12, 1824 in Ongar, England
Source: *Alli; ArtclWW 2; BioIn 2, 6, 8,
13, 15, 16, 22; BlmGEL; BlmGWL;
CarSB; ChhPo, S1, S3; Drake; DcBiPP;
DcEnL; DcEuL; DcNaB; EncBrWW;
EvLB; FemiCLE; InWom, SUP;
NewCBEL; OxCChiL; OxCEng 67, 85,
95; PenNWW A; PoChrch; SmATA 35,
36, 41; Str&VC; WhoChL*

Taylor, Jeremy
Irish. Religious Leader
Anglican minister; wrote *Holy Living,
Holy Dying*, 1650-51.
b. Aug 1613 in Cambridge, England

d. Aug 13, 1667 in Lisburn, Northern
Ireland
Source: *Alli; BbD; Benet 87, 96;
BiCoLiE; BiD&SB; BioIn 1, 2, 3, 5, 8, 9,
10, 12, 21; BlmGEL; BritAu; CamBiEn;
CamGEL; CamGLE; CasWL; ChambiD;
Chambr 1; ChhPo, S1; CrtT 1; CyEd;
DcBiPP; DcEnA; DcEnL; DcEuL; DcLB
151; DcLEL; DcNaB, C; EvLB;
IlEncMy; LinLib L, S; LngCEL; LuthC
75; MouLC 1; NewC; NewCBEL;
OxCBrHi; OxCEng 67, 85, 95; PenC
ENG; REn; WebE&AL; WhoChr*

Taylor, Jim
[James Taylor]
American. Football Player
Fullback, 1958-67, mostly with Green
Bay; had greatest success paired with
Paul Hornung in backfield; Hall of
Fame, 1976.
b. Sep 20, 1935 in Baton Rouge,
Louisiana
Source: *BioIn 6, 7, 8, 15, 17; LegTOT;
WhoFtbl 74; WhoSpor*

Taylor, John
American. Politician
Political theorist was a spokesman for
southern planter society after the
Revolutionary War.
b. 12, 1753 in Virginia
d. Aug 21, 1824 in Virginia
Source: *Alli; AmAu; AmAu&B; AmBi;
AmNatBi; AmWrBE; BenetAL 91;
BiDrUSC 89; BiDSA; BioIn 1, 3, 5, 8,
19; CamDcAB; DcAmAu; DcAmB;
DcNAA; EncAAH; EncAB-H 1974, 1996;
EncCRAm; EncSoH; EncWar; EncWB
98; McGEWB; OxCAmH; OxCAmL 65,
83, 95; PenC AM; REnAL; SouWr;
WebAB 74, 79; WhAm HS*

Taylor, John
English. Lawyer, Politician, Broadcaster
Barrister active in Tory politics, was
made Lord (Baron) of Warwick,
County Warwickshire, in 1996, and
became the first black man in the
British House of Lords, as well as its
youngest member; also producer and
presenter, British Broadcasting
Corporation (BBC), Radio and
Television.
b. Sep 21, 1952 in Birmingham, England
Source: *ConBlB 16; InB&W 85;
TwCPaSc*

Taylor, John Russell
English. Critic
Film critic, London *Times*, 1962-73;
books include *Hollywood 1940s*, 1985.
b. Jun 19, 1935 in Dover, England
Source: *Au&Wr 71; ConAu 5R, 37NR;
ConTFT 5; DcLEL 1940; IntAu&W 77,
89, 91, 93; IntMPA 92, 94, 96; IntWW
77, 78, 79, 80, 81, 82, 83, 89, 91, 93,
97, 98, 2000; Who 74, 82, 85, 88, 90,
92, 94, 98, 99, 2000; WhoArt 96, 98;
WhoFI 98; WhoThe 72, 77, 81; WhoWest
76, 78; WhoWor 84, 87, 89, 91, 93, 95,
96, 97, 98; WrDr 76, 80, 82, 84, 86, 88,
90, 92, 94, 96, 98, 99, 2000*

Taylor, June
[June Taylor Dancers]
American. Choreographer, Dancer
Best known for TV work; signature
routine done for "Jackie Gleason
Show," 1952-59, 1962-70 was the
overhead shot of a circular formation.
b. 1918 in Chicago, Illinois
Source: *BiDD; BiE&WWA; CnOxB;
NotNAT*

Taylor, Kenneth Douglas
Canadian. Diplomat
Ambassador to Iran, 1977-80; helped six
Americans escape from Iran during
hostage crisis, 1980.
b. Oct 5, 1934 in Calgary, Alberta,
Canada
Source: *CanWW 81, 83, 89, 96, 97, 98,
1999; WhoAm 82, 84, 86, 88*

Taylor, Kent
[Louis Weiss]
American. Actor
Hero in B-pictures: *Tangier, Tombstone;*
began film career, 1931; played
Blackie in TV series "Boston
Blackie," 1951-53.
b. May 11, 1907 in Nashua, Iowa
d. Apr 13, 1987 in Los Angeles,
California
Source: *BioIn 15, 17; DcPseud; FilmEn;
FilmgC; ForYSC; HalFC 80, 84, 88;
IntMPA 75, 76, 78, 79, 80, 81, 82, 84,
86; MovMk; VarWW 85; WhoHol A;
WhoHrs 80; WorAl*

Taylor, KoKo
[Cora Walton]
American. Singer, Songwriter
Blues singer; recorded million-selling
single "Wang Dang Doodle," 1964;
won Grammy Award for best blues
recording for *Blues Explosion*, 1984;
recipient of annual W.C. Handy
Award, 1983-1992.
b. 1935 in Memphis, Tennessee
Source: *AfrAmAl 8; AllMGBl 1, 2; BioIn
19, 23, 24; BlkWAm; Blues; BluesWW;
ConMus 10; DcPseud; DcTwCCu 5;
PenEncP; RolSEnR 83*

Taylor, Kristin Clark
American. Business Executive
Director of White House media relations,
1989-90; vice-president of external
affairs, Student Loan Marketing
Association, 1994—.
b. Mar 26, 1959 in Detroit, Michigan
Source: *ConBlB 8; WhoAm 90, 94, 95,
96, 97, 98, 99; WhoAmW 91, 93, 99;
WhoEmL 93; WhoWor 99*

Taylor, Laurette
[Laurette Cooney]
American. Actor
Star of plays *Peg o' My Heart*, 1912;
Glass Menagerie, 1945.
b. Apr 1, 1887? in New York, New
York
d. Dec 7, 1946 in New York, New York
Source: *CurBio 45, 47; DcAmB S4;
FamA&A; FilmgC; NotAW; ObitOF 79;*

*OxCAmL 65; OxCThe 67, 83; PIP&P;
TwYS; WhAm 2; WhoHol B; WhScrn 74,
77*

Taylor, Lawrence Julius
American. Football Player
Linebacker, NY Giants, 1981-93; MVP,
1987.
b. Feb 4, 1959 in Williamsburg, Virginia
Source: *BioIn 13; ConNews 87-3;
FootReg 87; WhoAfA 9, 10, 11, 12;
WhoBlA 4, 6, 7, 8*

Taylor, Livingston
American. Singer
Brother of James Taylor; hit single "I
Will Be in Love with You," 1978.
b. Nov 21, 1950 in Boston,
Massachusetts
Source: *RkOn 85; RolSEnR 83*

Taylor, Lucy Beaman Hobbs
American. Dentist, Social Reformer
First woman to receive degree in
dentistry, 1866.
b. Mar 14, 1833 in Franklin County,
New York
d. Oct 3, 1910 in Lawrence, Kansas
Source: *AmNatBi; GoodHs; InWom SUP;
LibW; NotAW*

Taylor, Margaret (Smith)
American. First Lady
Devoted wife of pres. Zachary Taylor
who was without social ambition;
daughter acted as White House
hostess.
b. Sep 21, 1788 in Calvert County,
Maryland
d. Aug 18, 1852 in Pascagoula,
Kentucky
Source: *AmWom; ApCAB; BioIn 16, 17;
FacPr 89; GoodHs; NatCAB 4; NotAW;
TwCBDA*

Taylor, Maxwell Davenport
American. Military Leader
Chm., US Joint Chiefs of Staff, 1962-64;
played a major role in determining
American military, diplomatic strategy
from WW II to Vietnam War.
b. Aug 26, 1901 in Keytesville, Missouri
d. Apr 19, 1987 in Washington, District
of Columbia
Source: *AmNatBi; BiDWWGF; BioIn 1,
3, 4, 5, 6, 7, 8, 9, 11, 12; BlueB 76;
CamBiEn; CmdGen 1991; ColdWar 2;
ConNews 87-3; CurBio 46, 61, 87;
DcAmDH 80, 89; DcAmMiB; EncVieW;
FacFETw; HarEnMi; IntWW 74, 75, 76,
77, 78, 79, 80, 81, 82, 83; ScrEAmL 2;
WebAMB; WhAm 9; Who 74, 82, 83, 85;
WhoAm 74, 76, 78, 80, 82, 84; WhoWor
74, 78; WorAl*

Taylor, Meshach
American. Actor
Played Anthony on TV series
"Designing Women," 1986-93; plays
Shel on TV series "Dave's World,"
1993—.
b. Apr 11, in Boston, Massachusetts

Source: *BioIn 16, 18, 19; ConTFT 8, 18; IntMPA 92, 94, 96; WhoAfA 9, 10, 11, 12; WhoAm 92, 94, 95, 96, 97; WhoBlA 7, 8; WhoEnt 92, 98*

Taylor, Mick
[The Rolling Stones]
English. Musician
Guitarist; replaced Brian Jones, 1969-74.
b. Jan 17, 1948 in Hertfordshire, England
Source: *BioIn 8, 11; CmpEGui; LegTOT; OnThGG; WhoRocM 82*

Taylor, Paul
American. Choreographer
Award-winning productions include *Musette*, 1983; formed own co., NYC, 1952—.
b. Jul 29, 1930 in Allegheny, New York
Source: *BiDD; BioIn 5, 6, 7, 8, 10, 11, 12, 13, 14, 15, 17, 18, 19, 21, 24; BlueB 76; CamDcAB; CelR 90; CmpGMD; CnOxB; ConTFT 12; CurBio 64; DancEn 78; DcArts; DcTwCCu 1; FacFETw; IntDcB; IntDcMo; LegTOT; News 92, 92-3; NewYTBS 81, 87; RAdv 14; WhoAm 74, 76, 78, 80, 82, 84, 86, 88, 92, 94, 95, 96, 97, 98, 99, 2000; WhoE 74, 99; WhoEnt 98; WhoWor 74, 76, 78, 80, 82, 84, 87, 89, 91, 93, 95; WorAlBi*

Taylor, Peter (Hillsman)
American. Author
Master storyteller; won PEN/Faulkner best fiction award, 1985.
b. Jan 8, 1917 in Trenton, New Jersey
d. Nov 2, 1994 in Charlottesville, Virginia
Source: *AmAu&B; AmNatBi; Benet 96; BenetAL 91; BiCoLiE; BioIn 3, 4, 8, 9, 13, 14, 15, 17, 20, 21, 22, 23; BlueB 76; CamBiEn; CamDcAB; CamGLE; CamHAL; ChamBiD; ConAu 9NR, 50NR, 147; ConLC 1, 4, 18, 37, 44, 50, 71; ConNov 82, 86, 91; CurBio 84, 87, 95N; CyWA 89; DcLB Y94N; DcLEL 1940; EncALit; FifSWrA; LegTOT; MajTwCW 1, 2; ModAL 4, 4S2; NewYTBS 94; Novels; OhA&B; OxCAmL 83, 95; PenC AM; REnAL; RfGShF 1, 2; RGTwCWr; ShSCr 10; ShSWr; SouWr; TwCA SUP; WhoAm 74, 76, 78, 80, 84; WhoPul; WhoUSWr 88; WhoWrEP 89, 92, 95; WorAlBi; WrDr 82*

Taylor, Phoebe Atwood
[Alice Tilton]
American. Author
Crime novels include *The Cape Cod Mystery*, 1931; *Punch with Care*, 1946.
b. May 18, 1910 in Boston, Massachusetts
d. Jan 9, 1976 in Boston, Massachusetts
Source: *ConAu 61; EncMys; TwCA, SUP; TwCCr&M 80*

Taylor, Regina
American. Actor
Won Golden Globe, 1993, for best actress, "I'll Fly Away," 1991-93.
b. c. 1959 in Dallas, Texas

Source: *ConBlB 9*

Taylor, Richard Edward
Canadian. Physicist
Shared Nobel Prize in physics, 1990, for breakthrough discoveries about the structure of matter; first to observe traces of quarks, subatomic particles forming the basis of 99% of earth's matter.
b. Nov 2, 1929 in Medicine Hat, Alberta, Canada
Source: *AmMWSc 79, 82, 86, 89, 92, 95, 98; BioIn 17, 18, 20; ChamBiD; IntWW 91, 93, 97, 98, 2000; LarDcSc; McGCEnS; Who 92, 94, 98, 99, 2000; WhoAm 86, 88, 90, 92, 94, 95, 96, 97, 98, 99, 2000; WhoScEn 94, 96, 2000; WhoWest 00, 74, 76, 87, 89, 92, 94, 96, 98; WhoWor 95, 96, 97, 98, 99, 2000*

Taylor, Robert
[Arlington Spangler Brugh]
"The Man with the Perfect Profile"
American. Actor
Romantic star with MGM for 25 years.
b. Aug 5, 1911 in Filley, Nebraska
d. Jun 8, 1969 in Santa Monica, California
Source: *AmNatBi; BiDFilm, 81, 94; BioIn 2, 3, 5, 6, 8, 9, 10, 14, 17; CmMov; CurBio 52, 69; DcAmB S8; DcPseud; EncMcCE; FacFETw; FilmEn; FilmgC; ForYSC; GangFlm; HalFC 80, 84, 88; IntDcF 1-3, 2-3; LegTOT; MGM; MotPP; MovMk; OxCFilm; WhoHol B; WhScrn 74, 77, 83; WorAl; WorAlBi; WorEFlm*

Taylor, Rod(ney)
Australian. Actor
Best known as resourceful hero in Hitchcock's *The Birds*, 1963.
b. Jan 11, 1930 in Sydney, Australia
Source: *CelR; ConTFT 6; FilmgC; HalFC 84; IntMPA 92, 94, 96; MotPP; MovMk; WhoAm 74, 76, 78, 80, 82, 84, 86, 88, 90, 92; WhoEnt 92A; WhoHol A; WorAl*

Taylor, Ronnie
English. Filmmaker
Won Oscar for cinematography of *Gandhi*, 1982.
Source: *HalFC 84, 88; VarWW 85; WhoRocM 82*

Taylor, Samuel (Albert)
American. Dramatist
Plays include *Sabrina Fair*, 1953; *No Strings*, 1962.
b. Jun 13, 1912 in Chicago, Illinois
d. May 26, 2000 in Blue Hill, Maine
Source: *AmAu&B; BiE&WWA; ConAu 25R; ConDr 73, 77D; McGEWD 72, 84; NotNAT; OxCAmT 84; WhoAm 74, 76, 78, 80, 82, 84, 86, 88, 90, 92, 94, 95, 96, 97; WhoEnt 92; WhoThe 72, 77, 81; WhoWor 80; WrDr 76, 80, 82, 84, 86, 88, 90, 92, 94, 96*

Taylor, Susan L.
American. Editor, Journalist
Editor of black women's magazine, *Essence*, 1981-99; publications director, 2000—.
b. Jan 23, 1946 in New York, New York
Source: *AfrAmAl 8; BioIn 18, 20, 21, 22, 23, 24; ConBlB 10; CurBio 97; InB&W 85; News 98, 98-2; NotBlAW 1; WhoAfA 9, 10, 11, 12; WhoAm 84, 98, 99, 2000; WhoBlA 8*

Taylor, Susie Baker King
American.
Author of *Reminiscences of My Life in Camp*, 1902 about her life as a slave and Civil War nurse.
b. Aug 5, 1848 in Isle of Wight, Georgia
d. Oct 12, 1912 in Boston, Massachusetts
Source: *BlksScM; BlkWAm; BlkWrNE; FemiCLE; HerW 84; InB&W 85; InWom SUP; NotBlAW 1*

Taylor, Sydney Brenner
American. Children's Author
Wrote *All-of-a-Kind Family* series.
b. Oct 31, 1904? in New York, New York
d. Feb 12, 1978 in New York, New York
Source: *AuBYP 2; BkCL; ConAu 4NR, 5R, 77; MorBMP; MorJA; SmATA 1; WrDr 76*

Taylor, Walter
American. Vintner
Established winery, 1880, in NY's Finger Lake district.
b. 1858
d. 1934
Source: *Entr*

Taylor, William Desmond
[William Cunningham Dean Tanner]
American. Director
Pres., Screen Actors Guild; homicide victim whose death was a scandal when affairs with popular leading ladies discovered.
b. Apr 26, 1877 in Carlow, Ireland
d. Feb 2, 1922 in Hollywood, California
Source: *BioIn 15, 16, 17; EncAFC; FilmEn; LegTOT; MiSFD 9N; TwYS, A; WhoHol B; WhScrn 74, 77, 83*

Taylor, Zachary
"Old Rough and Ready"
American. US President
12th pres., 1849-50; hero of US-Mexican War, 1846-48.
b. Nov 24, 1784 in Orange County, Virginia
d. Jul 9, 1850 in Washington, District of Columbia
Source: *AmAu&B; AmBi; AmNatBi; AmPolLe; ApCAB; BenetAL 91; BiAUS; BiDrAC; BiDrUSE 71, 89; BiDSA; BioIn 1, 2, 3, 4, 5, 6, 7, 8, 9, 10, 11, 12, 13, 14, 15, 16, 17, 18, 19, 20, 22, 23, 24; CamBiEn; CamDcAB; CelCen; ChamBiD; CyAG; DcAmB; DcAmMiB; DcBiPP; DcNaB; Drake; EncAAH; EncAB-H 1974, 1996; EncAPar;*

EncSoH; EncWar; EncWB 98; FacPr 89, 93; GenMudB; HarEnMi; HarEnUS; HealPre; HisWorL; LegTOT; LinLib L, S; McGEWB; NatCAB 4; NewEAmW; OxCAmH; OxCAmL 65, 83; PolPar; Pres 96; RComAH; REnAL; REnAW; TwCBDA; USGovLe; WebAB 74, 79; WebAMB; WhAm HS; WhAmP; WhDW; WhFla; WhNaAH; WhoMilH 76; WorAl; WorAlBi

Tchaikovsky, Peter Ilyich
[Petr Ilich Chaikovshy]
Russian. Composer
Known for classical ballet scores *Swan Lake*, 1877; *Nutcracker Suite*, 1892; *Sleeping Beauty*, 1889.
b. May 7, 1840 in Votiwsk, Russia
d. Nov 6, 1893 in Saint Petersburg, Russia
Source: *AtlBL; BakBD 84; CmOp; EncWB 98; GayLesB; LegTOT; LiveWoA; McGEWB; MetOEnc; MusMk; NewC; NewEOp 71; OxCEng 67, 85; REn; WorAl; WorAlBi*

Tchelitchew, Pavel
American. Artist, Designer
Stage designer; abstract painter, portraitist, noted for multiple imagery.
b. Sep 21, 1898, Russia
d. Jul 31, 1957 in Rome, Italy
Source: *AmNatBi; Bioln 11, 21, 22; BriEAA; CamDcAB; CamGWoT; ChhPo; ConArt 77, 83; CurBio 43, 57; DcAmB S6; DcCAA 71, 77, 88, 94; DcTwArt; IntDcB; McGDA; NewCol 75; OxCTwCA; OxDcArt; PhDcTCA 77*

Tcherepnin, Alexander Nikolayevich
American. Pianist, Composer
Experimented with nine-note scale, rhythmic polyphony; wrote opera, *Farmer and the Nymph*, 1952.
b. Jan 20, 1899 in Saint Petersburg, Russia
d. Sep 29, 1977 in Paris, France
Source: *BakBD 84; DcCM; IntWW 74; WebBD 83; WhAm 7; WhoAm 74; WhoMus 72; WhoWor 74*

Tcherepnin, Nicholas
[Nicolai Tcherepnin]
Russian. Composer, Conductor
Wrote ballets, symphonies; led Diaghilev Ballet, 1909-14; father of Alexander.
b. May 14, 1873 in Saint Petersburg, Russia
d. Jun 26, 1945 in Paris, France
Source: *BakBD 84; BiDD; CnOxB; NewEOp 71; NewOxM; OxCMus; WebBD 83*

Tcherkassky, Marianna Alexsavena
American. Dancer
Principal dancer, American Ballet Theatre since 1976, known for purity of style.
b. Oct 28, 1952 in Glen Cove, New York

Source: *CurBio 85; IntWWW 2; WhoAm 78, 80, 82, 84, 86, 88, 92, 94, 95, 96, 97; WhoAmW 83, 85, 89, 91, 93, 95; WhoWor 95, 96, 97, 98*

Tchernichowski, Saul Gutmanovich
Israeli. Poet
Poems, sonnets reflect fervent Jewish nationalism.
b. Aug 20, 1875 in Crimea, Ukraine
d. Oct 14, 1943 in Jerusalem, Palestine
Source: *CasWL; ConAu 116; PenC CL; WorAu 1950*

Teacher, Brian
American. Tennis Player
Won Australian Open, 1980.
b. Dec 23, 1954 in San Diego, California
Source: *WhoIntT*

Teagarden, Charles
''Little T''
American. Jazz Musician
Trumpeter with Big Bands, late 1920s-63; brother of Jack.
b. Jul 19, 1913 in Vernon, Texas
d. Dec 10, 1984 in Las Vegas, Nevada
Source: *AnObit 1984; BiDAmM; BiDJaz; CmpEPM; EncJzS; IlEncJ*

Teagarden, Jack
[Weldon John Teagarden]
''Big T''
American. Jazz Musician, Bandleader
Great jazz trombonist, vocalist; led own band, 1939-46; in film *Birth of the Blues*, 1941.
b. Aug 20, 1905 in Vernon, Texas
d. Jan 15, 1964 in New Orleans, Louisiana
Source: *AllMGJa; AmNatBi; BakBD 92; BgBands 74; Bioln 4, 5, 6, 7, 9, 12, 13, 20, 22; CamBiEn; CmpEPM; ConMus 10; FacFETw; IlEncJ; LegTOT; NewAmDM; NewGrDA 86; NewGrDJ 88, 94; NewGrDM 80; OxCAmH; OxCPMus; PenEncP; WhAm 4; WhoHol B; WhoJazz 72; WhScrn 74, 77; WorAlBi*

Teague, Olin E
American. Politician
Dem. senator from TX, 1946-79; identified with veterans affairs.
b. Apr 6, 1910 in Woodward, Oklahoma
d. Jan 23, 1981 in Bethesda, Maryland
Source: *AlmAP 78; AnObit 1981, 1984; BiDrAC; CurBio 52, 81, 81N; NewYTBS 81; WhAm 7*

Teague, Walter Dorwin
''Dean of Industrial Design''
American. Designer
Known for industrial designs for Kodak, Ford Motor Co., US Steel.
b. Dec 18, 1883 in Decatur, Indiana
d. Dec 5, 1960 in Flemington, New Jersey
Source: *AmAu&B; Bioln 5, 6, 8; CamBiEn; CamDcAB; ChamBiD; ChhPo S1; ConDes 84; CurBio 42, 61; DcArch; DcArts; DcD&D; DcTwDes; EncAB-A*

32; *FacFETw; IndAu 1917; McGDA; NatCAB 50; ObitOF 79; PenDiDA 89; WhAm 4; WhAmArt 85*

Teale, Edwin Way
American. Naturalist, Author
Wrote over 25 books; won Pulitzer for *Wandering Through Winter*, 1966.
b. Jun 2, 1899 in Joliet, Illinois
d. Oct 18, 1980 in Norwich, Connecticut
Source: *AmAu&B; AmNatBi; AmNatWr; AnObit 1980; Au&Wr 71; AuBYP 2, 3; BenetAL 91; BiDAmCa; Bioln 1, 2, 3, 4, 5, 6, 7, 8, 9, 10, 12, 13, 15, 22, 23; CamDcAB; ConAu 1R, 2NR, 102; CurBio 61, 81, 81N; InSci; LinLib L, S; NewYTBS 80; OxCAmL 83, 95; REnAL; SmATA 7, 25N; Str&VC; ThrBJA; TwCA SUP; WhAm 7; WhNAA; WhoAm 74, 76, 78, 80; WhoPul; WhoWor 74; WorAu 1900; WrDr 76, 80, 82, 84*

Teannaki, Teatao
Political Leader
Legislator and former vice president was elected president of Kiribati in 1991.
b. 1939 in Nonouti, Kiribati

Tears for Fears
[Roland Orzabal; Curt Smith]
English. Music Group
Bath, England duo; had number one hit ''Everybody Wants to Rule the World,'' 1985.
Source: *BillEnR; ConMus 6; EncRk 88; EncRkSt; HarEnR 86; PenEncP; RkOn 85*

Teasdale, Sara
American. Author, Poet
Writings include *Rivers to the Sea*, 1915; *Stars Tonight*, 1930.
b. Aug 8, 1884 in Saint Louis, Missouri
d. Jan 28, 1933 in New York, New York
Source: *AmAu&B; AmNatBi; AmWomPl; AnCL; AnMV 1926; ApCAB X; ArtclWW 2; Benet 87, 96; BenetAL 91; BiDAmM; BiDSA; BioAmW; Bioln 4, 5, 8, 11, 12, 14, 15, 16, 22; BkCL; BlmGWL; CamBiEn; CamDcAB; CasWL; ChamBiD; ChhPo, S1, S2, S3; CnDAL; ConAmA; ConAmL; ConAu 104, 163; DcAmB; DcLEL; DcNAA; EncALit; EvLB; FacFETw; FemiCLE; GayLL 1; GrLiveH; GrWrEL P; InWom, SUP; LegTOT; LibW; LinLib L; LngCTC; ModWoWr; NatCAB 39; NotAW; OnHuYeA; OxCAmL 65, 83, 95; OxCTwCP; OxCWoWr 95; PeoHis; RAdv 1; REn; REnAL; RfGAmL 4, 87, 94; SixAP; SmATA 32; Str&VC; TwCA, SUP; TwCWr; WebAB 74, 79; WhAm 1, 7; WhNAA; WhoPul; WomWWA 14; WorAl; WorAlBi; WorAu 1900*

Tebaldi, Renata
Italian. Opera Singer
Outstanding postwar soprano; noted for Verdi, Puccini roles.
b. Feb 1, 1922 in Pesaro, Italy
Source: *BakBD 78, 84, 92; BakBDTw; BakDcM; Bioln 2, 3, 4, 5, 6, 7, 9, 10, 11, 14, 15, 18, 21, 22; BriBkM 80;*

CamBiEn; ChamBiD; CmOp; CurBio 55; DcArts; FacFETw; IntDcOp; IntWW 74, 75, 76, 77, 78, 79, 80, 81, 82, 83, 89, 91, 93, 97, 98, 2000; IntWWM 77, 80; IntWWW 2; InWom, SUP; LegTOT; MetOEnc; MusMk; MusSN; NewAmDM; NewEOp 71; NewGrDA 86; NewGrDM 80; NewGrDO; NewYTBE 73; OxDcOp; PenDiMP; Who 74, 82, 83, 85, 88, 90, 92, 94, 98, 99, 2000; WhoAm 74, 76, 78, 80, 82, 86, 88, 90, 92, 94, 95, 96, 97; WhoAmM 83; WhoAmW 66, 68, 70, 72, 74, 75, 83; WhoHol 92, A; WhoMus 72; WhoOp 76; WhoWor 74; WorAl; WorAlBi

Tebbel, John William
American. Author, Educator
Writings include *Your Body: How to Keep It Healthy,* 1950; *A Voice in the Streets,* 1954.
b. Nov 16, 1912 in Boyne City, Michigan
Source: *BioIn 3; ConAu 85; CurBio 53; DrAS 74E, 78E, 82E; WhoAm 86*

Tebbetts, Birdie
[George Robert Tebbetts]
American. Baseball Player, Baseball Manager
Catcher, 1936-42, 1946-52, mostly with Detroit; managed for 11 yrs.
b. Nov 10, 1912 in Burlington, Vermont
d. Mar 24, 1999 in Bradenton, Florida
Source: *Ballpl 90; BioIn 16, 21; WhoProB 73*

Tebbit, Norman Beresford
English. Political Leader
Conservative member of Parliament, 1970-92; chm., Conservative Party, 1985-87.
b. Mar 29, 1931 in London, England
Source: *ChamBiD; CurBio 87; IntWW 82, 83, 89, 91, 93; IntYB 78, 79, 80, 81, 82; NewYTBS 86; WhoWor 87, 89*

Tebelak, John Michael
American. Dramatist, Director
Wrote, directed rock musical *Godspell.*
b. 1949
d. Apr 2, 1985 in New York, New York
Source: *ConAu 115*

Technotronic
[MC Eric; Thomas (Jo Bogaert) DeQuincey; Manuela Barbara (Ya Kid K) Kamosi]
American. Music Group
Studio house band with rap and vocals; debut album *Pump Up the Jam: The Album,* 1989 went gold.
Source: *ConMus 5; OxCMus*

Tecumseh
American. Native American Chief
Shawnee Indian chief, tried to unite tribes to resist westward expansion of whites.
b. Mar 1768 in Oldtown, Ohio
d. Oct 5, 1813 in Thamesville, Ontario, Canada

Source: *AmBi; AmIndBi; AmNatBi; ApCAB; Benet 87, 96; BenetAL 91; BioIn 1, 2, 4, 5, 6, 7, 8, 9, 10, 11, 12, 14, 15, 16, 17, 18, 19, 20, 23, 24; CamBiEn; CamDcAB; ChamBiD; DcAmB; DcAmMiB; DcCanB 5; EncAAH; EncAB-H 1974, 1996; EncAInd; EncNAB; EncNoAI; EncWar; EncWB 98; GenMudB; HarEnMi; HarEnUS; HisWorL; MacDCB 78; McGEWB; MorMA; NatCAB 11; NatNAL; NewEAmW; NotNaAm; OxCAmH; OxCAmL 65, 83, 95; OxCCan; RComAH; REn; REnAL; REnAW; WebAB 74, 79; WebAMB; WhAm HS; WhNaAH; WhoMilH 76; WorAl; WorAlBi*

Tedder, Arthur William Tedder, Baron
English. Military Leader, Author, University Administrator
Marshall of Royal Air Force; responsible for Allied Air Forces in Mediterranean, 1943.
b. Jul 11, 1890 in Stirling, Scotland
d. Jun 3, 1967 in Surrey, England
Source: *BioIn 1, 3, 7, 8, 11, 14; CurBio 43, 67; HisEWW; ObitOF 79; ObitT 1961; WhAm 4; WhWW-II; WorAl*

Teena Marie
[Mary Christine Brockert]
"Lady T"
American. Singer
Often works with Rick James; hits include "I Need Your Lovin';" "It Must be Magic."
b. 1957 in Santa Monica, California
Source: *DcPseud; EncPR&S 89; IlEncBM 82; RkOn 85*

Teggart, Frederick J.
American. Historian, Librarian, Sociologist, Educator
An advocate of the fruitful interchange between history and sociology, he initiated sociology at the University of California.
b. 1870 in Belfast, Ireland
d. 1946
Source: *EncWB 98*

Teicher, Louis
[Ferrante and Teicher]
American. Pianist, Composer
Part of the Ferrante and Teicher piano team, 1947—.
b. Aug 24, 1924 in Wilkes-Barre, Pennsylvania
Source: *ASCAP 66, 80; BioIn 6, 7; LegTOT; WhoAm 74, 76, 78, 80, 82, 84, 86, 88; WhoAmJ 80*

Teichmann, Howard Miles
American. Dramatist, Biographer
Best-known play: *The Solid Gold Cadillac,* 1953; biographies include those of Henry Fonda, Alexander Woollcott.
b. Jan 22, 1916 in Chicago, Illinois
d. Jul 7, 1987 in New York, New York

Source: *AmNatBi; BiE&WWA; ConAu 69; ConTFT 1; McGEWD 72; NatPD 77; NewYTBS 87; NotNAT; WhAm 9; WhoAm 80, 82, 84, 86; WhoE 79, 83, 85, 86*

Teilhard de Chardin, Pierre
French. Clergy, Philosopher, Paleontologist
Attempted to reconcile evolution with Catholic doctrine; helped discover Peking Man, 1929; wrote *Phenomenon of Man,* published 1955.
b. May 1, 1881 in Auvergne, France
d. Apr 10, 1955 in New York, New York
Source: *Benet 87, 96; BioIn 3, 4, 5, 6, 7, 8, 9, 10, 11, 12, 13; CamBiEn; CasWL; ChamBiD; ClDMEL 80; ConAu 105; CyWA 97; DcCathB; DcScB; DcTwCCu 2; EncHuEv; EncUnb; FacFETw; Geog 7; GuFrLit 1; HisPhAn; InSci; LarDcSc; LegTOT; LinLib L, S; LngCTC; LuthC 75; MakMC; McGEWB; NewCol 75; OxCEng 85, 95; RAdv 14; ThTwC 87; WhAm 4, HSA; WhoChr; WorAl; WorAlBi; WorAu 1950; WrPh P*

Teisserenc de Bort, Leon-Philippe
French. Meteorologist
Discoverer of the stratosphere.
b. Nov 5, 1855 in Paris, France
d. Jan 2, 1913 in Cannes, France
Source: *ChamBiD; McGCEnS*

Tekakwitha, Kateri, Saint
[Catherine Tegakovita]
"Lily of the Mohawks"
American. Religious Figure
First Native American to be canonized by the Roman Catholic Church.
b. 1656 in Ossernenon, New York
d. Apr 17, 1680 in Caughnawaga, Quebec, Canada
Source: *AmIndBi; AmNatBi; AZNatAW; BioAmW; BioIn 2, 3, 4, 5, 6, 7, 11, 18, 19, 21, 22; DcAmReB 1; DcCanB 1; EncARH; EncAWoR; EncNAR; EncNoAI; InWom, SUP; LibW; MacDCB 78; NatNAFi; NotAW; NotNaAm; WebAB 74, 79; WhNaAH*

Te Kanawa, Kiri, Dame
New Zealander. Opera Singer
Soprano; performed at wedding of Prince Charles, Lady Diana Spencer, 1981.
b. Mar 6, 1944 in Gisborne, New Zealand
Source: *BakBD 84, 92; BakBDTw; BakDcM; BriBkM 80; CamBiEn; CelR 90; CmOp; ConMus 2; ContDcW 89; CurBio 78; DcArts; EncWB, 98; FarE&A 81; IntWW 81, 82, 83, 89, 91, 93, 97, 98, 2000; IntWWM 90; IntWWW 2; ItaFilm; MetOEnc; NewAmDM; NewGrDM 80; NewGrDO; NewYTBS 82; OxDcOp; PenDiMP; Who 82, 83, 85, 88, 90, 92; WhoAm 86, 88, 90, 92, 94, 95, 96, 97, 98, 99, 2000; WhoAmW 87; WhoEnt 98; WhoWor 84, 87, 89, 91, 93, 95, 96, 97, 98, 99, 2000; WorAlBi*

Tekere, Edgar Zivanai
Zimbabwean. Government Official
Secretary general who was arrested for
murder during guerrilla attacks in
Zimbabwe, 1980.
b. Apr 1, 1937, Rhodesia
Source: *BioIn 12; NewYTBS 80*

Tekulve, Kent(on Charles)
American. Baseball Player
Relief pitcher, 1975-89; pitched in more
games as reliever than anyone in ML
history, 1,050.
b. Mar 5, 1947 in Cincinnati, Ohio
Source: *Ballpl 90; BaseReg 86, 87;
BiDAmSp Sup; BioIn 12, 13; LegTOT;
NewYTBS 79; WhoAm 82, 84*

Telemann, Georg Philipp
German. Composer
Wrote over 600 overtures, 50 operas,
including *Sokrates*, 1721.
b. Mar 14, 1681 in Magdeburg, Germany
d. Jun 25, 1767 in Hamburg, Germany
Source: *AtlBL; BakBD 78, 84, 92;
BakDcM; BioIn 1, 4, 7, 10, 12, 20, 23;
BriBkM 80; CamBiEn; ChamBiD;
CmOp; CmpBCM; DcArts; DcCom 77;
DcCom&M 79; EncEnl; EncWB 98;
GrComp; IntDcOp; LuthC 75;
McGEWB; MetOEnc; MusMk;
NewAmDM; NewCol 75; NewGrDM 80;
NewGrDO; NewOxM; OxCMus;
OxDcOp; WorAl; WorAlBi*

Telesio, Bernardino
Italian. Philosopher
Leader in the Renaissance movement
against medieval Aristotelianism.
b. 1509 in Cosenza, Italy
d. 1588 in Cosenza, Italy
Source: *CasWL; DcBiPP; DcCathB;
DcScB; Dis&D; EncWB 98; McGEWB;
REn*

Telkes, Maria (de)
American. Chemist
Pioneer in application of solar energy to
water distillation and home heating,
1970s.
b. Dec 12, 1900, Austria-Hungary
d. Dec 2, 1995 in Budapest, Hungary
Source: *AmMWSc 73P, 76P, 79, 82, 86,
89, 92, 95; BioIn 2, 4, 15, 20; CurBio
96N; ForWC 70; InSci; NotTwCS 1;
WhoAm 74, 76, 78, 80, 82; WhoAmW
58, 64, 66, 68, 70, 72, 79, 81; WhoFrS
84; WhoWor 74, 78*

Tell, William
[Wilhelm Tell]
Swiss. Legendary Figure
In legend, shot an apple from son's head
with arrow.
b. 1282
Source: *NewCol 75; OxCGer 76*

Teller, Edward
"Father of the Hydrogen Bomb"
American. Physicist, Educator, Author
Worked on the Manhattan Project
developing atomic bomb, 1940s.

b. Jan 15, 1908 in Budapest, Austria-
Hungary
Source: *AmAu&B; AmDec 1940;
AmMWSc 73P, 73S, 76P, 79, 82, 86, 89,
92, 95, 98; AsBiEn; BiESc; BioIn 3, 4,
5, 6, 8, 11, 12, 13, 14, 15, 16, 17, 18,
20, 24; BlueB 76; CamBiEn; CamDcAB;
CamDcSc; CelR; ChamBiD; CmCal;
ColdWar 1, 2; ConAu 33NR, 65NR, P-1;
CurBio 54, 83; EncAB-H 1974, 1996;
EncWB, 98; FacFETw; InSci; IntWW 74,
75, 76, 77, 78, 79, 80, 81, 82, 83, 89,
91, 93, 97, 98, 2000; IntWWE; IntYB 78,
79; LarDcSc; LegTOT; LinLib L, S;
MajTwCW 1; McGCEnS; McGMS 80;
NotTwCS 1; OxCAmH; PolProf E, K, T;
RAdv 14; RanHWDS; WebAB 74, 79;
WhDW; Who 74, 82, 83, 85, 88, 90, 92,
94, 98, 99, 2000; WhoAm 74, 76, 78, 80,
82, 84, 86, 88, 90, 92, 94, 95, 96, 97,
98, 99, 2000; WhoFrS 84; WhoScEn 94,
96, 2000; WhoTech 82, 84, 89, 95;
WhoWest 82, 84; WhoWor 74, 78, 80,
82, 84; WhoWorJ 72, 78; WorAl;
WorAlBi; WorInv*

Telva, Marion
American. Opera Singer
Contralto, NY Met., 1920-33.
b. Sep 26, 1897 in Saint Louis, Missouri
d. Oct 23, 1962 in Norwalk, Connecticut
Source: *BakBD 84; BiDAmM; BioIn 6;
InWom, SUP; MetOEnc; NewEOp 71;
WhAm 4*

Temin, Howard Martin
American. Scientist, Educator
Shared 1975 Nobel Prize in medicine for
work with tumor viruses, cells.
b. Dec 10, 1934 in Philadelphia,
Pennsylvania
Source: *AmMWSc 73P, 76P, 79, 82, 86,
89, 92; BiESc; BioIn 10, 14, 15, 19, 20,
21, 22; CamBiEn; CamDcAB; ChamBiD;
FacFETw; LarDcSc; McGCEnS;
RanHWDS; WhAm 11; WhoAm 74, 76,
78, 80, 82, 84, 86, 88, 90, 92, 94;
WhoFrS 84; WhoMW 78, 80, 82, 84, 86,
88, 90, 92, 93; WhoNob, 90, 95;
WhoScEn 94; WhoWor 78, 80, 82, 84,
87, 89, 91, 93; WorAl; WorScD*

Tempest, Marie
English. Actor
Appeared in stage comedies, 1899-1942,
including *Marriage of Kitty*.
b. Jul 15, 1864 in London, England
d. Oct 15, 1942 in London, England
Source: *BioIn 3, 5, 10, 14; CnThe;
ContDcW 89; CurBio 42; DcNaB 1941;
DcPseud; EncMT; EncWT; Ent;
FamA&A; Film 1; FilmgC; GrBr;
HalFC 80, 84, 88; IntDcWB; LegTOT;
OxCAmT 84; OxCPMus; OxCThe 67,
83; PIP&P; REn; WhAm 2; WhoHol B;
WhoStg 1906, 1908; WhScrn 77, 83;
WhThe; WorAl*

Temple, William
English. Clergy
Religious and civic leader achieved
world status in the ecumenical

movement as archbishop of
Canterbury.
b. 1881 in Exeter, England
d. 1944
Source: *BiDChrM; BioIn 1, 4, 5, 6, 7, 9,
14; CamBiEn; ChamBiD; ConAu 120;
DcEcMov; DcLEL; DcNaB 1941;
DcTwHis; EncWB, 98; FacFETw; GrBr;
LuthC 75; NewCBEL; OxCBrHi;
PrimTiR; ThTwC 87; WhoChr*

Templeton, Alec
American. Pianist
Famed blind entertainer, noted for piano
parodies, novelty vocals, 1930s-40s;
own radio show, 1940.
b. Jul 4, 1910 in Cardiff, Wales
d. Mar 28, 1963 in Greenwich,
Connecticut
Source: *AmNatBi; ASCAP 66, 80;
BakBD 84; BiDAmM; BioIn 1, 5, 6, 11;
CmpEPM; ConAmC 76; CurBio 40, 63;
NewGrDA 86; NotNAT B; RadStar;
WhAm 4; WhoHol B*

Templeton, Fay
American. Actor
Appearances on stage, vaudeville
included *Fiddle-Dee-Dee*.
b. Dec 25, 1865 in Little Rock, Arkansas
d. Oct 3, 1939 in San Francisco,
California
Source: *BioIn 3; CamGWoT; CmpEPM;
EncMT; InWom, SUP; LibW; NewGrDA
86; NotAW; NotNAT B; OxCAmH;
OxCAmT 84; OxCPMus; WhAm 1;
WhoHol B; WhoStg 1906, 1908; WhScrn
74, 77; WhThe*

Templeton, Garry Lewis
"Jump Steady"; "Tempy"
American. Baseball Player
Shortstop, Padres, 1976—; led NL in
hits, 1979.
b. Mar 24, 1956 in Lockney, Texas
Source: *BaseReg 86, 87; BiDAmSp Sup;
InB&W 80; WhoAfA 9, 10, 11, 12;
WhoBlA 5, 6, 7, 8*

Temptations, The
[Dennis Edwards; Melvin Franklin;
Eddie Kendricks; David Ruffin; Otis
Williams; Paul Williams]
American. Music Group
Group formed in 1964; hits include "My
Girl;" "Just My Imagination."
Source: *AmBench 79; BakDcM;
BiDAmM; BillEnR; BioIn 12, 17, 18;
ConMuA 80A; ConMus 3; DcTwCCu 5;
EncPR&S 74, 89; EncRk 88; EncRkSt;
HarEnR 86; IlEncRk; InB&W 80, 85,
85A; IntMPA 75, 76, 77, 78, 79, 80, 81,
82, 84, 86, 88, 92; NewAmDM;
NewGrDA 86; NewYTBS 92, 95;
OxCPMus; PenEncP; RkOn 84; RkWho
96; SoulM; WhAmArt 85; WhoHol 92, A;
WhoRock 81; WhoRocM 82; WorAl;
WorAlBi*

Tenace, Gene
[Fury Gene Tenace]
American. Baseball Player
Catcher-first baseman, 1969-83, mostly
with Oakland; holds ML record for
hitting home run in first two at-bats,
1972 World Series; fifth ML player to
hit four home runs in World Series,
1972.
b. Oct 10, 1946 in Russellton,
Pennsylvania
Source: *Ballpl 90; BaseEn 88; BioIn 9,
10, 11; NewYTBE 73; WhoProB 73*

Ten Boom, Corrie
Dutch. Author
Wrote of experiences in concentration
camp: *The Hiding Place*, 1971; movie
starred Julie Harris, 1975.
b. Apr 15, 1892 in Amsterdam,
Netherlands
d. Apr 15, 1983 in Placentia, California
Source: *BioIn 10, 11, 12, 13; ChamBiD;
ConAu 109, 111; ConHero 2; EncAWoR;
FacFETw; HeroCon; RelLAm 1, 2;
WomFir; WomThRe*

Ten CC
[Paul Burgess; Lol Creme; Kevin
Godley; Graham Gouldman; Eric
Stewart]
English. Music Group
Formed in 1972; albums include
Windows in the Jungle, 1983.
Source: *BillEnR; BioIn 11; ConMuA
80A; EncRk 88; HarEnR 86; IlEncRk;
MiSFD 9; OxCPMus; PenEncP; RkOn
78; RkWho 96; RolSEnR 83; WhoRock
81; WhoRocM 82*

Tenggren, Gustaf Adolf
American. Illustrator
Books include *Canterbury Tales*, 1961;
*King Arthur and the Knights of the
Round Table*, 1962.
b. Nov 3, 1896, Sweden
d. Apr 6, 1970 in West Southport, Maine
Source: *BioIn 8; IlsBYP; IlsCB 1744,
1946; MorJA; SmATA 18; WhAm 6;
WhAmArt 85*

Teniers, David, the Younger
Flemish. Artist
Paintings express tone, atmosphere: *The
Dance in Front of the Castle*, 1645.
b. Dec 14, 1610 in Antwerp, Belgium
d. Apr 25, 1690 in Brussels, Belgium
Source: *AtlBL; BioIn 2, 11, 12;
CamBiEn; ClaDrA; DcBiPP; DcCathB;
IntDcAA 90; McGDA; OxCArt; OxCEng
85, 95; OxDcArt*

Tennant, Veronica
Canadian. Dancer
Principal dancer with National Ballet
Canada, 1965-89.
b. Jan 15, 1946 in London, England
Source: *BiDD; BioIn 14, 16; CanWW
79, 80, 81, 83; CnOxB; CreCan 1;
SmATA 36; WhoAm 84*

Tennenbaum, Silvia
American. Author, Lecturer
Wrote *Rachel, the Rabbi's Wife*, 1978;
articles, book reviews for *Midstream;
Newsday* mags.
b. Mar 10, 1928, Germany
Source: *ConAu 21NR, 77*

Tennent, Gilbert
American. Clergy, Evangelist
Presbyterian clergyman and evangelist
was active in the Great Awakening
revival movement in New England and
the Middle colonies.
b. Feb 5, 1703 in County Armagh,
Ireland
d. Jul 23, 1764 in Philadelphia,
Pennsylvania
Source: *Alli; AmAu; AmNatBi; AmWrBE;
ApCAB; BioIn 1, 3, 9, 15, 18, 19, 20;
CamDcAB; DcAmAu; DcAmB;
DcAmReB 1, 2; DcNAA; Drake;
EncARH; EncCRAm; EncWB 98; LuthC
75; McGEWB; NatCAB 8; OxCAmH;
TwCBDA; WebAB 74, 79; WhAm HS*

Tenniel, John, Sir
English. Illustrator, Artist
Best known for illustrations in *Alice's
Adventures in Wonderland.*
b. Feb 28, 1820 in London, England
d. Feb 25, 1914 in London, England
Source: *Alli; AntBDN B; ArtsNiC; Benet
87, 96; BioIn 1, 2, 3, 8, 9, 11, 12, 13,
16, 17, 19; CamBiEn; CamGLE;
CelCen; ChamBiD; ChhPo, S1, S2;
ChlBkCr; ChlLR 18; ClaDrA; ConAu
111; DcArts; DcBiPP; DcBrWA;
DcBrWA; DcNaB 1912; DcPup; DcVicP,
2; IlsBYP; JBA 34, 51; LegTOT; LinLib
L; LngCTC; MajAl; McGDA; NewC;
NewCBEL; OxCArt; OxCChiL; OxCEng
85, 95; OxDcArt; REn; SmATA 27, 74;
StaCVF; Str&VC; VicBrit; WhDW;
WhLit; WhoChL; WorECar*

Tennille, Toni
[The Captain and Tennille; Mrs. Daryl
Dragon]
American. Singer
Had 1975 hit "Love Will Keep Us
Together," written by Neil Sedaka.
b. May 8, 1943 in Montgomery,
Alabama
Source: *BioIn 11, 12, 13, 21, 24;
BkPepl; LegTOT; WhoAmW 81, 83;
WorAl; WorAlBi*

Tennstedt, Klaus
German. Conductor
Musical director, conductor of London
Philharmonic Orchestra, 1983-87;
conductor laureate, 1987-98.
b. Jun 6, 1926 in Merseburg, Germany
d. Jan 11, 1998 in Kiel, Germany
Source: *BakBD 78, 84, 92; BakBDTw;
BioIn 11, 12, 13, 23, 24; CurBio 83,
98N; DcArts; IntWW 82, 83, 89, 91, 93,
97; IntWWM 90; MetOEnc; NewAmDM;
NewGrDA 86; NewGrDM 80;
NewGrDO; NewYTBS 77, 98; PenDiMP;
WhAm 12; Who 85, 88, 90, 92, 94, 98;
WhoAm 80, 82, 84, 86, 88, 90, 92, 94,*

*95, 96, 97, 98; WhoEnt 92; WhoWor 84,
87, 89, 91, 93,, 95*

Tennyson, Alfred, Lord
English. Poet
Poet laureate, 1850-92; wrote *Idylls of
the King*, 1885; "Charge of the Light
Brigade," 1854.
b. Aug 6, 1809 in Somersby, England
d. Oct 6, 1892 in Haslemere, England
Source: *Alli, SUP; AnCL; AtlBL; AuBYP
2, 3; BbD; Benet 87, 96; BiCoLiE;
BiD&SB; BioIn 12, 13, 16, 17, 18, 19,
20; BlmGEL; BritAu; BritWr 4;
CamGEL; CamGWoT; CasWL; CelCen;
ChamBiD; Chambr 3; ChhPo, S1, S2,
S3; CnDBLB 4; CnE&AP; CnThe;
CrtSuDr; CrtT 3, 4; CyWA 58, 97;
DcArts; DcBiPP; DcEnA, A; DcEnL;
DcEuL; DcLEL; DcNaB; DcPup;
Dis&D; EncLitE; EncPaPR 91; EncWB
98; EvLB; GrWrEL P; IlEncMy;
LegTOT; LngCEL; LuthC 75; MagSWL;
McGEWB; McGEWD 72, 84; MouLC 4;
NewC; NewCBEL; NewEOp 71; NinCLC
30, 65; NotNAT B; NotPoe; OxCBrHi;
OxCEng 67, 85, 95; OxCMus; OxCThe
67, 83; PenC ENG; PenEncH; PoLE;
RAdv 1, 14; RComWL; REn; REnWD;
RfGEnL 91; Str&VC; VicBrit;
WebE&AL; WhDW; WorAl; WorAlBi;
WorLitC*

Ten Thousand Maniacs
[Jerry Augustyniak; Robert Buck; Dennis
Drew; Steve Gustafson; Natalie
Merchant]
American. Music Group
Rock group; hit singles include *Like the
Weather*, 1987 and *Trouble Me*, 1989.
Source: *Alli; BillEnR; BioIn 15, 16, 21;
ConMus 3; EncRkSt; OnThGG*

Ten Years After
[Chick Churchill; Alvin Lee; Rick Lee;
Leo Lyons]
British. Music Group
Major blues band, 1967-75; albums
include *Goin' Home*, 1975.
Source: *AllMGBI 2; BillEnR; BioIn 11;
ConMuA 80A; EncPR&S 89; EncRk 88;
EncRkSt; GrMetD; HarEnR 86; IlEncRk;
PenEncP; RolSEnR 83; WhoRock 81;
WhoRocM 82*

Tenzing Norgay
[Namgyal Wangdi]
Mountaineer
With Sir Edmund Hillary, first to reach
summit of Mt. Everest, 1953.
b. May 15, 1914 in Solo Khumbu, Nepal
d. May 9, 1986 in Darjeeling, India
Source: *BioIn 3, 4, 5, 7, 8, 9, 10, 11, 14,
15, 16, 17, 19, 24; CamBiEn; ChamBiD;
CurBio 54; DcPseud; FarE&A 78, 79,
80, 81; IntWW 76, 77, 78, 79, 81, 82,
83; NewYTBS 86; Who 82, 83, 85*

Ter-Arutunian, Rouben
Russian. Designer
Best known for innovative stage designs
for ballet, Broadway including

Redhead, 1959; works in both realism, abstractionism.
b. Jul 24, 1920 in Tiflis, Union of Soviet Socialist Republics
d. Oct 17, 1992 in New York, New York
Source: *AnObit 1992; BiDD; BiE&WWA; BioIn 6, 7, 8, 19; CamGWoT; CnOxB; ConDes 84, 90, 97; ConTFT 7; CurBio 63, 93N; DancEn 78; EncWT; NewEOp 71; NewYTBS 92; NotNAT; WhoAm 74, 76, 78, 80, 82; WhoE 74; WhoOp 76; WhoThe 72, 77, 81; WhoWor 74*

Ter Borch, Gerard
Dutch. Artist
Noted for small portraits, genre painting, including *Guitar Lesson.*
b. 1617 in Zwolle, Netherlands
d. Dec 8, 1681 in Deventer, Netherlands
Source: *McGDA; McGEWB; NewCol 75; OxCArt*

Terbrugghen, Hendrick
Dutch. Artist
Genre works, influenced by Caravaggio, include *The Flute Player,* 1621.
b. 1588
d. 1629
Source: *BioIn 5, 19; DcArts; DutArt; IntDcAA 90; McGDA; NewCol 75; OxCArt; OxDcArt; WhDW*

Terence
[Publius Terentius Afer]
Roman. Dramatist, Poet
Comedies modeled on Greek originals; more subtle, refined than Plautus's.
b. 185?BC
d. 159BC
Source: *AtlBL; BbD; Benet 87, 96; BiCoLiE; BiD&SB; CasWL; ClMLC 14; CnThe; CyWA 58; DcEnL; LngCEL; LuthC 75; McGEWD 84; NewC; OxCEng 67; OxCThe 67; PenC CL; PlP&P; RComWL; REn; REnWD*

Teresa, Mother
[Agnes Gonxha Bojaxhiu]
"Saint of the Gutters"
Albanian. Missionary
Catholic nun widely respected for int'l humanitarian efforts for poor; founded Missionaries of Charity, 1950, Superior General, 1950-97; awarded Nobel Peace Prize, 1979.
b. Aug 27, 1910 in Skopje, Yugoslavia
d. Sep 5, 1997 in Calcutta, India
Source: *BiDChrM; BioIn 16, 17, 18, 19, 20, 22, 23, 24; CurBio 73, 97N; DcPseud; EncWB 98; FacFETw; FarE&A 81; IntDcWB; IntWW 89, 91, 93, 97, 2000; IntWWW 2; InWom SUP; News 93-1; NewYTBS 79, 97; RelLAm 2; WhAm 12; Who 92, 94; WhoChr; WhoNob, 90; WhoRel 92; WhoWor 87, 91, 93, 95, 96, 97, 98; WomThWo; WorAlBi*

Tereshkova-Nikolaeva, Valentina
Russian. Cosmonaut
First woman in space; orbited earth 48 times, 1963.

b. Mar 6, 1937 in Maslennikovo, Union of Soviet Socialist Republics
Source: *IntWW 74; WhoWor 74*

TerHorst, Jerald Franklin
American. Journalist
White House press secretary under Ford, who resigned after 30 days because of Ford's pardon of Richard Nixon, 1974.
b. Jul 11, 1922 in Grand Rapids, Michigan
Source: *AuNews 1; BiDAmNC; BioIn 10, 12; BioNews 74; ConAu 107; CurBio 75; EncTwCJ; NewYTBS 74; PolProf NF; WhoAm 74, 76, 78, 80, 82, 84, 86, 88, 90, 92, 94, 95, 96, 97, 98, 99, 2000; WhoSSW 95*

Terhune, Albert Payson
American. Journalist, Author
Popular canine stories include *Lad, a Dog,* 1928.
b. Dec 21, 1872 in Newark, New Jersey
d. Feb 18, 1942 in Pompton Lakes, New Jersey
Source: *AmAu&B; AmLY; AmNatBi; AuBYP 2, 3; BenetAL 91; BiD&SB; BioIn 2, 5, 7, 8, 9, 11, 12, 19, 22; CamDcAB; ChhPo; ChlBkCr; CnDAL; ConAu 111, 136; CurBio 42; DcAmAu; DcAmB S3; DcLB 9; DcNAA; EvLB; JBA 34; LinLib L; MajAl; NatCAB 34; OxCAmL 65, 83, 95; OxCChiL; REnAL; SJGchWr 5; SmATA 15; TwCA, SUP; TwCBDA; TwCChW 3, 4; WebAB 74, 79; WhAm 2; WhLit; WhNAA; WorAl; WorAlBi; WorAu 1900*

Terhune, Mary Virginia
American. Author
Wrote romantic novels, household quotes; mother of Albert Payson.
b. Dec 31, 1831 in Dennisville, Virginia
d. Jun 3, 1922 in New York, New York
Source: *Alli SUP; AmAu; AmAu&B; AmBi; AmWom; ApCAB; BbD; BiD&SB; BiDSA; CarSB; Drake; NotAW; OxCAmL 83; REnAL; TwCBDA; WhAm 1*

Terkel, Studs (Louis)
American. Author, Journalist
Books based on tape-recorded interviews include Pulitzer winner *The Good War,* 1985.
b. May 16, 1912 in New York, New York
Source: *AmAu&B; AuNews 1; BenetAL 91; BioIn 7, 10, 11, 12, 13, 14, 16, 17, 18, 19, 21; CelR 90; ConAu 57; ConLC 38; CurBio 74; EncAJ; FacFETw; IntAu&W 89; IntWW 83, 89, 91, 93, 97, 98, 2000; LegTOT; LiJour; LinLib L; OxCAmL 83, 95; WhoAm 74, 76, 78, 80, 82, 84, 86, 88, 90, 92, 94, 95, 96, 97; WhoHol 92; WhoMW 74, 76, 80, 82, 84, 86, 88, 92, 93, 96; WhoUSWr 88; WhoWor 95, 96, 97; WhoWrEP 89, 92, 95; WorAl; WorAlBi; WrDr 76, 86, 94, 96, 98, 99, 2000*

Terman, Lewis Madison
American. Psychologist
Publisher of the Stanford-Binet intelligence test.
b. Jan 15, 1877 in Johnson County, Indiana
d. Dec 21, 1956 in Palo Alto, California
Source: *AmDec 1910; AmNatBi; BiDAmEd; BiDcPsy; BiDPsy; BioIn 4, 5, 9, 10, 12, 14, 16, 18, 23, 24; CamBiEn; CamDcAB; ChamBiD; DcAmB S6; DcAmImH; EncWB, 98; IndAu 1917; InSci; NamesHP; ObitOF 79; OxCAmH; REnAL; WebAB 74, 79; WhAm 3; WhE&EA; WhNAA*

Ternina, Milka
Croatian. Opera Singer
Outstanding Wagnerian soprano; sang first NY, London *Tosca,* 1901.
b. Dec 19, 1863 in Belgisc
d. May 18, 1941 in Zagreb, Yugoslavia
Source: *BakBD 78, 84, 92; BakBDTw; BioIn 1, 11; CmOp; InWom; MetOEnc; MusSN; NewEOp 71; NewGrDM 80; NewGrDO; OxDcOp; PenDiMP*

Ter-Petrosyan, Levon
Armenian. Political Leader
An advocate for the liberation Nagorno Karabakh, he was elected president following Armenia's declaration of independence in 1991 and reelected in 1996.
b. Jan 9, 1945 in Aleppo, Syria
Source: *WhoWor 96, 97, 98*

Terra, Daniel J(ames)
American. Art Collector, Diplomat
Founded Terra Museum of American Art, Chicago, 1980; ambassador at large for cultural affairs, 1981-89.
b. Jun 9, 1911 in Philadelphia, Pennsylvania
d. Jun 28, 1996 in Washington, District of Columbia
Source: *BioIn 12, 13; CurBio 87, 96N; St&PR 87; WhAm 11; WhoAm 76, 78, 80, 82, 84, 86, 90, 92, 94, 95, 96; WhoAmA 84; WhoAmP 81, 83, 85, 87, 89, 91, 93, 95; WhoFI 74, 75, 77, 79, 81, 83, 85; WhoMW 74, 76, 78, 80, 82, 86; WhoWor 76, 78, 82, 84*

Terra, Gabriel
Uruguayan. Political Leader
President by election overthrew his government by a coup d'etat in 1933, then ruled the authoritarian government until 1938.
b. 1873 in Montevideo, Uruguay
d. 1942 in Montevideo, Uruguay
Source: *BiDLAmC; BioIn 3, 16; DcCPSAm; EncLatA; EncWB 98; LatAmLi; McGEWB*

Terrell, Mary Church
American. Social Reformer
Worked to improve women's rights, equality for black people; first pres., Nat. Association of Colored Women, 1896-1904.
b. Sep 23, 1863 in Memphis, Tennessee

d. Jul 24, 1954 in Annapolis, Maryland
Source: *BiDSocW; BioIn 17, 18, 19, 20, 21, 23; BlkWrNE; CamDcAB; ConBlB 9; CurBio 42, 54; DcAmB S5; DcAmNB; EncAACR; EncSoH; EncWoAP; HanAmWH; InWom; LegTOT; NegAl 76, 83, 89; NotBlAW 1; OxCAfAL; PeoHis; SelBAAf; WhAm 3; WomEdUS; WomFir; WorAl; WorAlBi*

Terrell, Tammi
American. Singer
Best known for duets with Marvin Gaye: "Your Precious Love," 1967; "Ain't Nothing Like the Real Thing," 1968.
b. Apr 29, 1945 in Philadelphia, Pennsylvania
d. Mar 16, 1970 in Philadelphia, Pennsylvania
Source: *DcPseud; RolSEnR 83*

Terris, Norma
American. Actor
Played Magnolia Hawks in *Showboat*, 1927, 1932.
b. Nov 13, 1904 in Columbus, Kansas
d. Nov 15, 1989 in Lyme, Connecticut
Source: *AnObit 1989; DcPseud; EncMT; Film 2; WhoHol A; WhoThe 77A; WhThe*

Terris, Susan
American. Children's Author
Writings include *The Upstairs Witch and the Downstairs Witch*, 1970; *Ammanda, the Panda, and the Redhead*, 1975.
b. May 6, 1937 in Saint Louis, Missouri
Source: *AuBYP 2S; BioIn 9; ConAu 12NR, 29R; FifBJA; IntAu&W 76, 77, 82, 89, 91, 93; SmATA 3, 77; WhoAmW 75; WhoWrEP 89, 92, 95; WrDr 76, 80, 82, 84, 86, 88, 90, 92, 94, 96, 98, 99, 2000*

Terry, Alfred Howe
American. Military Leader, Lawyer
Major-general who led campaign against Sioux involving Custer massacre at Little Big Horn, 1876.
b. Nov 10, 1827 in Hartford, Connecticut
d. Dec 16, 1890 in New Haven, Connecticut
Source: *AmBi; AmNatBi; ApCAB; BioIn 7, 17, 23; CamDcAB; CivWDc; DcAmB; DcAmMiB; Drake; EncAInd; HarEnUS; NatCAB 4; NewCol 75; NewEAmW; REnAW; TwCBDA; WebAB 74, 79; WebAMB; WebBD 83; WhAm HS; WhCiWar; WhNaAH*

Terry, Bill
[William Harold Terry]
"Memphis Bill"
American. Baseball Player, Baseball Manager
First baseman, NY Giants, 1923-36; last player to bat .400 in NL, 1930; Hall of Fame, 1954.
b. Oct 30, 1898 in Atlanta, Georgia
d. Jan 9, 1989 in Jacksonville, Florida
Source: *AmNatBi; AnObit 1989; BiDAmSp BB; BioIn 2, 4, 5, 7, 8, 9, 14,*
15, 16, 20, 24; *NewYTBS 89; WhoProB 73; WhoSpor*

Terry, Ellen Alicia, Dame
English. Actor
Acting partner with Henry Irving, 1878-1902; carried on famed correspondence with George Bernard Shaw.
b. Feb 27, 1848 in Coventry, England
d. Jul 21, 1928 in Kent, England
Source: *FamA&A; Film 1; HerW; IntDcWB; LngCTC; NewC; OxCThe 67; PlP&P; REn; WhAm 1; WhDW; WhoStg 1906, 1908; WhScrn 77; WorAl*

Terry, Luther Leonidas
American. Physician
Surgeon general, whose study revealed smoking hazardous to health, 1964.
b. Sep 15, 1911 in Red Level, Alabama
d. Mar 29, 1985 in Philadelphia, Pennsylvania
Source: *AmMWSc 73P, 76P, 79, 82; BiDrACP 79; BioIn 5, 6, 11; ConAu P-2; CurBio 61; FacFETw; InSci; IntWW 74, 75, 76, 77, 78, 79, 80, 81, 82, 83; ScrEAmL 1; SmATA 11; St&PR 84; WhAm 8; WhoAm 74, 76, 78, 80, 82, 84; WhoE 85; WhoWor 82*

Terry, Megan
[Megan Duffy]
American. Dramatist
Plays include Obie winner, *The Tommy Allen Show*, 1970.
b. Jul 22, 1932 in Seattle, Washington
Source: *AmWomD; AmWomWr; ArtclWW 2; BenetAL 91; BioIn 10, 12, 15, 16; CamGWoT; ConAmD; ConAu 3BS, 43NR, 77; ConDr 73, 77, 82, 88, 93; ConLC 19; ConTFT 5; ConWomD; CroCD; CrtSuDr; CyWA 97; DcPseud; DrAP 75; DrAPF 80; EncWT; FemDram; FemiCLE; GayLL 2; GrLiveH; IntAu&W 89, 91, 93; IntDcT 2; InWom SUP; McGEWD 84; ModWoWr; NatPD 81; NotNAT; NotWoAT; OxCThe 83; OxCTwCL; OxCWoWr 95; PlP&P; RAdv 14; WhoAm 76, 78, 80, 82, 84, 86, 88, 90, 92, 94, 95, 96, 97, 98, 99; WhoAmW 95, 97, 99; WhoEnt 92; WhoThe 77, 81; WhoWor 80; WhsWeAm 98; WorAu 1970; WrDr 76, 80, 82, 84, 86, 88, 90, 92, 94, 96, 98, 99, 2000*

Terry, Paul H
American. Cartoonist, Producer
Best known for animation of Mighty Mouse.
b. Feb 19, 1887 in San Mateo, California
d. Oct 25, 1971 in New York, New York
Source: *BioIn 9; DcFM; FilmgC; WorECom*

Terry, Randall A.
American. Social Reformer
Controversial leader of anti-abortion group Operation Rescue, 1984—.
b. Apr 25, 1959 in Rochester, New York
Source: *BioIn 16; CurBio 94; EncRelA; News 91; St&PR 87*

Terry, Sonny
[Saunders Terrell]
American. Singer, Musician
Harmonica player and blues singer; partner to guitarist Brownie McGhee.
b. Oct 24, 1911 in Greensboro, Georgia
d. Mar 11, 1986 in Mineola, New York
Source: *AllMGBI 2; AmNatBi; AnObit 1986; BakBD 92; BiDAfM; BiDAmM; BiDJaz; BluesWW; CamDcAB; CmpEPM; DcPseud; DrBlPA, 90; EncFCWM 69; EncJzS; EncRk 88; GuBlues; IlEncJ; InB&W 80; NewAmDM; NewGrDA 86; NewYTBS 86; OxCPMus; PenEncP; WhAm 9; WhoRock 81*

Terry, Walter
American. Critic, Author
Dance critic, 1936-82; wrote 22 books.
b. May 14, 1913 in New York, New York
d. Oct 4, 1982 in New York, New York
Source: *AmAu&B; AmNatBi; AnObit 1982; AuBYP 2, 3; BioIn 8, 13, 24; CnOxB; ConAu 10NR, 21R, 107; DancEn 78; FacFETw; NewYTBS 82; ScrEAmL 1; SmATA 14; WhAm 8; WhoAm 74, 76, 78, 80, 82*

Terry-Thomas
[Thomas Terry Hoar-Stevens]
English. Actor, Comedian
Character actor known for gap-toothed smile; films include *I'm All Right, Jack*, 1960, *Those Magnificent Men in Their Flying Machines*, 1965.
b. Jul 14, 1911 in London, England
d. Jan 8, 1990 in Godalming, England
Source: *AnObit 1990; BioIn 4, 5, 6, 7, 11, 13, 16, 17; CamBiEn; ChamBiD; ConTFT 10; CurBio 61, 90, 90N; DcArts; DcNaB 1986; DcPseud; EncEurC; FacFETw; FilmEn; FilmgC; ForYSC; HalFC 80, 84, 88; IlWWBF; IntDcF 2-3; IntMPA 75, 76, 78, 79, 80, 81, 82; IntWW 82, 83, 89; ItaFilm; LegTOT; MotPP; MovMk; NewYTBS 90; QDrFCA 92; Who 74, 82, 83, 85, 88, 90; WhoCom; WhoHol A; WhoHrs 80; WhoWor 74, 76; WorAl; WorAlBi*

Tertullian, Quintus Septimus Florens
Roman. Writer
Known as one of fathers of church; writings attack official attitude toward Christianity.
b. 160?
d. 230?
Source: *BbD; BiD&SB; BioIn 1, 2, 3, 5, 6, 7, 9; CasWL; DcCathB; Grk&L; LinLib L, S; McGEWB; NewC; OxCEng 67; PenC CL; WhDW*

Terzi, Zehdi Labib
Palestinian. Diplomat
Representative of the Palestine Liberation Organization (PLO) to the United Nations (1975—), and advocate of a separate Palestinian state and armed resistance to Israel; successful in building modest support for his cause.

b. Feb 20, 1924 in Jerusalem, Palestine
Source: *BioIn 12; ConNews 85-3;*
NewYTBS 79

Teschemacher, Frank
American. Jazz Musician
Hot clarinetist, active, 1920s-30s.
b. Mar 14, 1906 in Kansas City,
Missouri
d. Feb 29, 1932 in Chicago, Illinois
Source: *AllMGJa; BiDAmM; BiDJaz;*
BioIn 16; CmpEPM; IlEncJ; NewAmDM;
NewGrDA 86; NewGrDJ 88, 94;
NewGrDM 80; OxCPMus; PenEncP;
WhAm 4, HSA; WhoJazz 72

Teschner, Richard
Austrian. Puppeteer
Improved on existing Javanese rod
puppets; helped popularize ro puppets
in Europe and the US.
b. Mar 22, 1879 in Carlsbad, Bohemia
d. Jul 4, 1948 in Vienna, Austria
Source: *BioIn 2; DcPup; Ent*

Tesh, John
American. TV Personality, Musician
Co-host, syndicated entertainment news
program "Entertainment Tonight,"
1986-96; producer of recording artists,
under name John Tesh Project, 1994—
.
b. Jul 9, 1953 in Garden City, New York
Source: *BioIn 16; ConMus 20; ConTFT*
11; WhoAm 95, 96, 97, 98, 99, 2000;
WhoEnt 98; WhoWest 00, 96, 98

Teshigahara, Hiroshi
Japanese. Director
Films include *The Pitfall; Woman in the*
Dunes.
b. Jan 28, 1927 in Tokyo, Japan
Source: *BiDFilm, 81; BioIn 10; DcFM;*
FilmEn; IntDcF 1-2; JapFilm; MiSFD 9;
OxCFilm; WorEFlm

Tesich, Steve
[Stoyan Tesich]
American. Screenwriter
Best known for *Breaking Away,* 1979;
The World According to Garp, 1982.
b. Sep 29, 1942 in Titovo Utice,
Yugoslavia
d. Jul 1, 1996 in Sydney, Nova Scotia,
Canada
Source: *BioIn 14, 17, 21, 22, 23; ConAu*
105, 152; ConDr 82; ConLC 40;
ConTFT 5, 18; CrtSuDr; CurBio 91,
96N; HalFC 84; IntMPA 86, 92, 94, 96;
NewYTBS 80, 82, 96; ObitPA 96;
VarWW 85; WhAm 11; WhoAm 82, 84,
86, 88, 90, 92, 94, 95, 96; WhoEnt 92;
WorAu 1985; WrDr 84, 86, 88, 90, 92,
94, 96, 98N

Tesla, Nikola
American. Engineer, Inventor
Pioneer in electric power, marketed first
electric appliance, three blade fan,
1889.
b. Jul 10, 1856 in Smiljan, Austria-
Hungary

d. Jan 7, 1943 in New York, New York
Source: *AmNatBi; ApCAB SUP; AsBiEn;*
BiESc; BioIn 12, 13, 14, 15, 16, 18, 20,
21, 22, 23, 24; CamBiEn; CamDcAB;
CamDcSc; ChamBiD; ChhPo S3; ConAu
157; CurBio 43; DcAmB S3; DcNAA;
DcScB; EncO&P 2S1, 3; EncWB 98;
GayN; InSci; LarDcSc; LegTOT;
McGEWB; NewCol 75; NotTwCS 1;
ObitOF 79; OxCAmH; RanHWDS;
SciMath; TwCLC 88; WebAB 74, 79;
WhAm 2; WhDW; WorAl; WorAlBi;
WorInv

Testaverde, Vinny
"Miami Nice"
American. Football Player
Quarterback, won Heisman Trophy,
1986; signed with Tampa Bay as
America's richest draft pick, 1987;
with Tampa Bay, 1987-92; Cleveland,
1993-1995; Baltimore, 1996-97; NY
Jets, 1998—.
b. Nov 13, 1963 in New York, New
York
Source: *ConNews 87-2; LegTOT;*
WhoSpor

Tetrazzini, Luisa
Italian. Opera Singer
Soprano who debuted in NYC, 1908; 33
operas include *Rigoletto, Lakme.*
b. Jun 29, 1874 in Florence, Italy
d. Apr 28, 1940 in Milan, Italy
Source: *BioIn 1; CurBio 40; InWom;*
LinLib S; WhAm 1

Tevis, Walter
American. Author
Wrote novel *The Hustler,* 1959, which
became 1961 film, sequel *The Color of*
Money, 1984.
b. Feb 28, 1928 in San Francisco,
California
d. Aug 9, 1984 in New York, New York
Source: *BioIn 13; ConAu 113; ConLC*
42; DrAPF 80; LiHiK; NewEScF;
NewYTBS 83, 84; ScF&FL 92; ScFSB;
TwCSFW 81, 86, 91; WorAu 1975;
WrDr 84

Tewfik Pasha
Egyptian. Ruler
Khedive of Egypt ruled during the
British occupation of 1882 and the
establishment of British overrule.
b. 1852, Egypt
d. 1892, Egypt
Source: *EncWB 98; McGEWB*

Tewodros II
"Kassa"
Ethiopian. Ruler
Ethiopia's emperor 1855-68; known as
first modern leader of Ethiopia;
reunited Ethiopia's kingdoms.
b. 1818
d. Apr 13, 1868 in Magdela, Ethiopia
Source: *DcAfHiB 86; McGEWB*

Tex, Joe
[Joseph Arrington, Jr.]
American. Singer
Had 1964 hit "Hold On to What You've
Got."
b. Aug 8, 1933 in Rogers, Texas
d. Aug 13, 1982 in Navasota, Texas
Source: *BillEnR; BioIn 13; DcPseud;*
EncPR&S 89; EncRk 88; GuBlues;
InB&W 80; LegTOT; NewGrDA 86;
OxCPMus; PenEncP; RkOn 78; RolSEnR
83; Songw; SoulM; WhoBlA 2; WhoRock
81

Tex and Jinx
[Jinx Falkenburg; Tex McCrary]
American. Radio Performers
Husband and wife team; produced own
radio, TV shows, 1940s-50s.
Source: *BioIn 1, 2, 3, 12, 17; CurBio 53*

Texas Tornadoes, The
[Freddie (Baldemar Huerta) Fender;
Flaco (Leonardo Jiminez) Jiminez;
Augie Meyers; Doug Sahm]
American. Music Group
Country/rock group; solo performers
before joining together in 1989;
Grammy award for best Mexican-
American performance, 1991.
Source: *ConMus 8; WhoRocM 82*

Tey, Josephine
[Elizabeth Mackintosh]
Scottish. Author
Mystery novels include *Brat Farrar,*
1949; *To Love and Be Wise,* 1950.
b. 1897 in Inverness, Scotland
d. Feb 13, 1952
Source: *CamGLE; ChamBiD; Chambr 3;*
DcLEL; DcPseud; EncMys; EvLB;
InWom SUP; LegTOT; LngCTC; NewC;
OxCTwCL; PenC ENG; REn; TwCA
SUP; TwCCr&M 80, 85, 91; TwCLC 14;
TwCWr

Teyte, Maggie, Dame
[Margaret Tate]
English. Opera Singer
Lead singer in opera, 1907-19; London
stage musicals include *A Little Dutch*
Girl, 1920.
b. Apr 17, 1888 in Wolverhampton,
England
d. May 27, 1976 in London, England
Source: *BakBD 78, 84, 92; BakBDTw;*
BioIn 10, 11, 12, 14; BriBkM 80;
CamBiEn; CmOp; ConAu 65; ContDcW
89; CurBio 45, 76, 76N; DcArts;
DcPseud; EncMT; FacFETw; IntDcOp;
IntDcWB; InWom SUP; MetOEnc;
MusSN; NewAmDM; NewEOp 71;
NewGrDA 86; NewGrDM 80;
NewGrDO; NewYTBS 76; OxCBrHi;
OxDcOp; PenDiMP; Who 74

Thackeray, William Makepeace
[Jeames; Mister Brown; George Savage
Fitzboodle; Michael Angelo Titmarsh;
Theophile Wagstaff; Charles James
Yellowplush]
British. Author
Wrote satirical novel *Vanity Fair,* 1848.

b. Jul 18, 1811 in Calcutta, India
d. Dec 24, 1863 in London, England
Source: *Alli; AtlBL; BbD; Benet 87, 96; BiCoLiE; BiD&SB; BioIn 1, 2, 3, 4, 5, 6, 7, 8, 9, 10, 11, 12, 13, 14, 15, 16, 18, 21, 22, 23; BlmGEL; BritAu 19; BritWr 5; CamBiEn; CamGEL; CamGLE; CarSB; CasWL; CelCen; ChambiD; Chambr 3; ChhPo, S1, S2, S3; CnDBLB 4; CrtT 3, 4; CyWA 58, 97; DcArts; DcBiA; DcBiPP; DcBrBI; DcBrWA; DcEnA, A; DcEnL; DcEuL; DcInB; DcIrL 96; DcLB 159, 163; DcLEL; DcPup; Dis&D; EncCapP; EncO&P 3; EncWB 98; EvLB; FamSYP; GrWrEL N; HsB&A; LegTOT; LinLib L, S; LngCEL; MagSWL; McGEWB; MouLC 3; NewC; NewCBEL; NinCLC 5, 14, 22, 43; Novels; OxCAmL 65, 83, 95; OxCBrHi; OxCEng 67, 85, 95; OxCIri; PenC ENG; PseudAu; RAdv 1, 14; RComWL; REn; RfGEnL 91; ScF&FL 1A, 92; SmATA 23; StaCVF; VicBrit; WebE&AL; WhDW; WhoChL; WorAl; WorAlBi; WorLitC*

Thalberg, Irving Grant
"The Boy Wonder"
American. Producer
Head of MGM production under Louis Mayer, 1923-36.
b. May 30, 1899 in New York, New York
d. Sep 14, 1936 in Santa Monica, California
Source: *AmCulL; BiDFilm; BioIn 16, 17, 19; CamDcAB; ChambiD; CmCal; ConAu 41R; DcAmB S2; DcArts; DcFM; FilmgC; NatCAB 27; OxCFilm; WebAB 74, 79; WhAm 4, HSA; WorAl; WorEFlm*

Thales
Greek. Philosopher
First to search for rational explanation of natural phenomenon replacing superstition with science.
b. 600BC in Miletus, Asia Minor
d. 540BC
Source: *AsBiEn; BiD&SB; BiESc; CasWL; DcInv; Grk&L; NewC; PenC CL; REn; WorAl*

Thalheimer, Richard
American. Businessman
Founder and pres. The Sharper Image, 1977—.
b. 1948 in Little Rock, Arkansas
Source: *BioIn 13; ConNews 85-2; News 88; St&PR 91*

Thalmann, Ernst
German. Political Leader
Communist leader responsible for creating Kommunistische Partei Deutschlands into second most powerful Communist Party; executed at Buchenwald concentration camp.
b. Apr 16, 1886 in Hamburg, Germany
d. Aug 18, 1944 in Buchenwald, Germany
Source: *EncGRNM; EncTR 91*

Thang, Ton Duc
Vietnamese. Government Official
Pres., Vietnam, 1969-80.
b. Aug 20, 1888 in Long Xuyen Province, Vietnam
d. Mar 30, 1980 in Hanoi, Vietnam
Source: *AnObit 1980; BioIn 8, 9; IntWW 74; WhoWor 74, 76, 78*

Thani, Shiekh Khalifa Ben Hamad al
Qatari. Ruler
Amir of Qatar, 1972—; expanded economic, social reform; stopped most of royal family's extravagance, privileges.
b. 1932 in Rayyan, Qatar
Source: *WhoWor 74*

Than Shwe
Burmese. Political Leader
Rose to prominence after the 1988 military coup d'etat that put the State Law and Order Restoration Council (SLORC) into power, and was named prime minister of Myanmar in 1992.
Source: *IntWW 93, 97, 98, 2000; WhoWor 95*

Thant, U
Burmese. Statesman
Secretary-general, UN, 1962-72; focused on problems of Third World.
b. Jan 22, 1909 in Pantanaw, Burma
d. Nov 25, 1974 in New York, New York
Source: *BioIn 12, 18; CamBiEn; ChambiD; ColdWar 1; ConAu 108; CurBio 62, 75N; EncCW; EncWB 98; IntWW 74; LegTOT; LinLib S; McGEWB; NewYTBS 74; ObitT 1971; OxCLaw; WhAm 6; WhDW; Who 74; WhoAm 74; WhoWor 74; WorAl; WorAlBi*

Thao, Tran Duc
Vietnamese. Philosopher
Existentialist thinker with ties to Sartre.
b. 1917 in Hanoi, Vietnam
d. Apr 24, 1993 in Paris, France

Thapa, Surya Bahadur
Nepalese. Political Leader
Advocate of a more democratic system and founder of the Rashtriya Prajatantra Party (RPP), he served as prime minister of Nepal several times, the first in 1967 and the latest in 1997.
b. Mar 21, 1928 in Muga, Nepal
Source: *FarE&A 78, 79, 80, 81; IntWW 74, 75, 76, 77, 78, 79, 80, 81, 82, 83, 89, 91, 93, 97, 98, 2000; ProfiWG 98; WhoWor 74, 80, 82*

Tharaud, Jean
French. Author
With brother Jerome, wrote many magazine articles and books; *Notre cher Peguy*, 1926.
b. May 9, 1877 in Saint-Junien, France
d. Apr 9, 1952 in Paris, France

Source: *BioIn 1, 2, 3, 4, 22; ObitOF 79; ObitT 1951; WorAu 1900*

Tharaud, Jerome
French. Author
With brother Jean, wrote many magazine articles and books; *Dingley*, 1902.
b. May 18, 1874 in Saint-Junien, France
d. Jan 28, 1953 in Varengeville-sur-Mer, France
Source: *BioIn 1, 3, 4, 22; ObitOF 79; ObitT 1951; TwCA; WorAu 1900*

Tharoor, Shashi
Indian. Author
Author of *The Great Indian Novel*, 1991, a retelling of India's history.
b. 1956 in London, England
Source: *BioIn 19, 20, 21; ConAu 141; ConLC 70; ConNov 96; IntAu&W 91; NotAsAm; WhoAm 2000; WhoE 99; WorAu 1985; WrDr 96, 98, 99, 2000*

Tharp, Louise Hall
American. Author
Biographies include *The Peabody Sisters of Salem*, 1950; *Mrs. Jack*, 1965.
b. Jun 19, 1898 in Oneonta, New York
Source: *AmAu&B; Au&Wr 71; AuBYP 2, 3; ChhPo; ConAu 1R, 33NR; CurBio 55; ForWC 70; MorJA; RAdv 1; SmATA 3; WhoAm 74; WorAu 1950*

Tharp, Marie
American. Cartographer, Geologist
Known for her maps showing the structure and evolution of ocean floors.
b. Jul 30, 1920 in Ypsilanti, Michigan
Source: *AmWomSc 1950; BioIn 20; EncWB 98; NotTwCS 1*

Tharp, Twyla
American. Choreographer, Dancer
Choreographer, Paul Taylor Dance Co., 1963-65; founder Twyla Tharp Dance Founda tion, 1965-87; artistic associate and resident choreographer American Ballet Th eatre, 1987-91.
b. Jul 1, 1941 in Portland, Indiana
Source: *BiDD; BioIn 10; CamDcAB; CelR 90; ChambiD; ConTFT 12; CurBio 75; DcArts; DcTwCCu 1; EncWB 98; FacFETw; FilmChD; GoodHs; GrLiveH; IntDcB; IntDcMo; IntWW 89, 91, 93, 97, 98, 2000; IntWWW 2; InWom SUP; LegTOT; LibW; NewGrDA 86; News 92; NewYTBS 76; NotWoAT; RAdv 14; Who 98, 99, 2000; WhoAm 78, 80, 82, 84, 86, 88, 92, 94, 95, 96, 97, 98, 99, 2000; WhoAmW 79, 81, 83, 85, 87, 89, 91, 93, 95, 97, 99; WhoE 79, 81, 83, 85, 86, 89, 91, 93, 95, 97, 99; WhoEnt 92, 99; WomFir; WorAl; WorAlBi*

Thatcher, Margaret (Hilda Roberts)
"Iron Lady"
British. Political Leader
Britian's first female prime minister, 1979-91.
b. Oct 13, 1925 in Grantham, England

Source: *ColdWar 1, 2; ConHero 1; ContDcW 89; CurBio 75, 89; DcAmC; EncCW; EncWB; HisDBrE; HisWorL; IntDcWB; IntWW 74; InWom SUP; LegTOT; NewYTBS 75, 79, 83, 95; PolLCWE; Who 82, 83, 85, 88, 90, 92; WhoAmW 74; WhoWor 87; WomStre; WomWR; WorAlBi*

Thaw, Harry Kendall
American. Murderer
Killed architect Stanford White in Madison Square Garden, 1906; ruled insane.
b. Feb 1, 1871 in Pittsburgh, Pennsylvania
d. Feb 22, 1947 in Miami Beach, Florida
Source: *AmNatBi; BioIn 1, 5, 6, 8, 9, 11, 24; DcAmB S4; EncACr; WorAl*

Thaxter, Celia
American. Poet
Verse volumes include *Driftwood,* 1879.
b. Jun 29, 1835 in Portsmouth, New Hampshire
d. Aug 26, 1894 in Appledore, New Hampshire
Source: *AmNatWr; BenetAL 91; BioIn 1, 2, 6, 13; ChrP; FemiCLE; NotAW; OxCAmL 83; REn*

Thaxter, Phyllis
American. Actor
Mother of Skye Aubrey; films include *Sea of Grass,* 1947.
b. Nov 20, 1920 in Portland, Maine
Source: *BiE&WWA; FilmgC; HalFC 84; MGM; MovMk; NotNAT; WhoHol A; WhoThe 77, 81*

Thayer, Abbott Handerson
American. Artist
Painted landscapes, portraits, 1879-91; turned later to figure paintings.
b. Aug 12, 1849 in Boston, Massachusetts
d. May 29, 1921 in Monadnock, New Hampshire
Source: *AmBi; AmNatBi; ApCAB; BioIn 2, 4, 9, 11, 13; BriEAA; DcAmB; DcTwArt; McGDA; PeoHis; WhAm 1*

Thayer, Eli
American. Politician, Social Reformer
Agitator and promoter turned his progressive ideals into money-making ventures, including the New England Emigrant Aid Company's drive to make Kansas a free state.
b. Jun 11, 1819 in Mendon, Massachusetts
d. Apr 1899
Source: *AmBi; AmNatBi; ApCAB; BiAUS; BiDrAC; BiDrUSC 89; BioIn 6; DcAmAu; DcAmB; DcAmSR; DcNAA; EncWB 98; HarEnUS; McGEWB; NatCAB 11; OxCAmH; TwCBDA; WhAm HS; WhAmP; WhCiWar*

Thayer, Ernest L
American. Author
Wrote *Casey at the Bat,* 1888.

b. Aug 14, 1863 in Lawrence, Massachusetts
d. Aug 21, 1940 in Santa Barbara, California
Source: *AuBYP 2; BioIn 6; EvLB*

Thayer, Mary Van Rensselaer
[Molly Thayer]
American. Journalist, Author
Wrote two biographies of Jacqueline Kennedy.
b. 1903? in Southampton, New York
d. Dec 12, 1983 in Washington, District of Columbia
Source: *ConAu 111*

Thayer, Sylvanus, General
"Father of the Military Academy"
American. Educator, Military Leader
Superintendent, West Point, 1817-33; instituted reforms, established efficient organization.
b. Jun 9, 1785 in Braintree, Massachusetts
d. Sep 7, 1872 in Braintree, Massachusetts
Source: *Alli; AmBi; AmNatBi; ApCAB; BiDAmEd; BioIn 4, 5, 8, 11, 13, 23; CamDcAB; CivWDc; CyEd; DcAmAu; DcAmB; DcAmMiB; DcNAA; Drake; EncWB 98; HarEnUS; McGEWB; NatCAB 7; OxCAmH; TwCBDA; WebAB 74, 79; WebAMB; WhAm HS; WhCiWar*

Thayer, Tiffany Ellsworth
American. Screenwriter, Actor
Appeared in films, 1920-25; wrote *Devil on Horseback,* 1936; *Chicago Deadline,* 1949.
b. Mar 1, 1902 in Freeport, Illinois
d. Aug 23, 1959 in Nantucket, Massachusetts
Source: *AmAu&B; TwCA, SUP; WhAm 3; WhE&EA; WorAu 1900*

Thebom, Blanche
American. Opera Singer
Mezzo-soprano; starred with NY Met., 1940-67.
b. Sep 19, 1919 in Monessen, Pennsylvania
Source: *BakBD 84; BiDAmM; BioIn 2, 3, 4, 5, 10; BioNews 74; CurBio 48; IntWWM 77, 80; InWom, SUP; NewEOp 71; WhoAm 74, 76; WhoAmW 58, 64, 66, 68, 70, 72, 74, 75; WhoWor 74*

Thedosius I
Roman. Ruler
Ruled Holy Roman Empire before division of East, West, 379-395; proclaimed son, Honorius, emperor of the West, 395.
b. Jan 11, 346? in Cauca, Spain
d. Jan 17, 395 in Milan, Spain
Source: *BioIn 1, 6, 9; LinLib S; McGEWB; NewCol 75; WebBD 83*

Theiler, Max
American. Scientist, Physician, Engineer
Research on yellow fever led to developing vaccine; won Nobel Prize in medicine, 1951.
b. Jan 30, 1899 in Pretoria, South Africa
d. Aug 11, 1972 in New Haven, Connecticut
Source: *AmNatBi; AsBiEn; BiESc; BioIn 2, 3, 4, 5, 6, 9, 10, 14, 15, 20; CamBiEn; CamDcAB; CamDcSc; ChamBiD; ConAu 164; CurBio 52, 72, 72N; DcAmMeB 84; EncSoA; EncWB 98; InSci; LarDcSc; McGCEnS; McGEWB; McGMS 80; NewYTBE 72; NobelP; NotTwCS 1; OxCMed 86; RanHWDS; WhAm 5; WhoNob, 90, 95*

Theismann, Joe
[Joseph Robert Theismann]
American. Football Player, Sportscaster
Two-time all-pro quarterback, 1971-85, mostly with Washington; suffered career-en ding broken leg during game; anallyst, CBS NFL broadcasts, 1987-88; analyst, ESPN NFL broadcasts, 1988—.
b. Sep 9, 1949 in New Brunswick, New Jersey
Source: *BiDAmSp FB; BioIn 12, 13; ConAu 171; FootReg 86; NewYTBS 82, 84; WhoAm 80, 82, 84, 86, 88, 94, 95, 96, 97; WhoE 85; WhoFtbl 74; WhoSSW 95; WhoWor 80*

Themistocles
Greek. Military Leader
Athenian commander who developed naval strength; led victory against Persians at Salamis, 480 BC.
b. 524?BC
d. 460?BC
Source: *BioIn 20, 21, 24; DcBiPP; GenMudB; LegTOT; McGEWB; NewCol 75; OxCClC; OxCClL 89; REn; WhDW; WorAl; WorAlBi*

Theocritus
Greek. Poet
Originator of pastoral poetry; sensitivity to nature imitated by later poets.
b. 310BC in Syracuse, Sicily, Italy
d. 250BC
Source: *BbD; BiCoLiE; BiD&SB; CamBiEn; CasWL; ChamBiD; ChhPo; CyWA 58; DcArts; DcBiPP; DcEnL; EncWB 98; Grk&L; LegTOT; McGEWB; NewC; OxCEng 67; PenC CL; RAdv 14; RComWL; REn; WhDW; WorAlBi*

Theodora
Roman. Consort
Married Justinian I, 523; became joint ruler of Byzantine empire, 527.
b. 508
d. 548
Source: *Benet 87, 96; DcBiPP; Dis&D; InWom, SUP; NewCol 75; PlP&P; REn; WebBD 83; WomFir*

Theodoracopulos, Taki
Greek. Journalist
Columnist for the English magazine
Spectator.
b. Aug 11, 1937 in Athens, Greece
Source: *BioIn 12; CelR 90; ConAu 129*

Theodorakis, Mikis
Greek. Composer
Revitalized modern Greek music; wrote
score for *Zorba the Greek*, 1964.
b. Jul 29, 1925 in Chios, Greece
Source: *BakBD 78, 84, 92; BakBDTw;
BakDcM; BioIn 8, 9, 10, 12, 16, 18;
CamBiEn; ChamBiD; CurBio 73;
EncEurC; FilmEn; IntDcF 1-4, 2-4;
IntMPA 88, 92, 94, 96; IntWW 74, 75,
76, 77, 78, 79, 80, 81, 82, 83, 89, 91,
93, 97, 98, 2000; IntWWM 80; ItaFilm;
MusMk; NewGrDM 80; OxCFilm;
OxCPMus; WhoFr 79; WhoWor 74, 78,
80, 82, 84, 87, 89, 91, 93, 95; WorEFlm*

Theodorescu, Ion N
Romanian. Poet, Translator
Romania's poet laureate; wrote verse
volume *Cuvinte Potrivite*, 1927.
b. May 20, 1880 in Bucharest, Romania
d. Jul 14, 1967 in Bucharest, Romania
Source: *ClDMEL 80; ConAu 116;
WorAu 1970*

Theodoric the Great
Italian. King, Military Leader
King of the Ostrogoths conquered Italy,
becoming the second barbarian king of
Italy after the fall of the Roman
Empire.
b. c. 453 in Pannonia
d. 526
Source: *EncWB 98; McGEWB*

Theodosius
Roman. Emperor
Sometimes called "The Great," he
subdued the Goths through diplomacy
and unified the empire, and was a
champion of Christian orthodoxy.
b. c. 346
d. Jan 17, 395
Source: *BioIn 1, 6, 9; CamBiEn;
DcBiPP; DcCathB; EncEarC 90, 97;
EncWB 98; LuthC 75; McGEWB;
WhoChr*

Theorell, (Axel) Hugh Teodor
Swedish. Biochemist
Won 1955 Nobel Prize for medicine;
pioneered enzyme research.
b. Jul 6, 1903 in Linkoping, Sweden
d. Aug 15, 1982 in Stockholm, Sweden
Source: *AnObit 1982; AsBiEn; CurBio
56, 82N; IntWW 81; NewYTBS 82; Who
83N; WhoNob; WhoWor 78*

Theresa, Saint
Spanish. Religious Figure, Author
Noted for mystic visions; reformed
Carmelite order.
b. Mar 28, 1515 in Avila, Spain
d. Oct 4, 1582 in Alva, Spain

Source: *DcBiPP; DcEuL; EncWB 98;
InWom; LinLib L; McGEWB; NewC;
NewCol 75; OxCEng 67, 85, 95; REn*

Theresa, St.
[Teresa de Cepeda y Ahumada]
Spanish. Clergy
Carmelite nun reformed her order to
conform with the primitive, and more
rigorous, rule; she is known as one of
the world's most outstanding mystical
writers.
b. Mar 28, 1515 in Avila, Spain
d. Oct 15, 1582 in Avila, Spain
Source: *DcBiPP; EncWB 98; InWom;
LinLib L; McGEWB; NewC; OxCEng 67,
85, 95; REn*

Therese of Lisieux, Saint
"The Little Flower"
French. Religious Figure
Carmelite nun called the "greatest saint
of modern times"; patron of aviators,
foreign ministers.
b. Jan 2, 1873 in Alencon, France
d. Sep 30, 1897 in Lisieux, France
Source: *BiDChrM; ChamBiD; DcCathB;
Dis&D; EncWomW; LuthC 75; NewCol
75*

Theriault, Yves
Canadian. Author
Prolific writer for radio and TV; books
include *Agaguk*, 1958; *N'Tsuk*.
b. Nov 28, 1916 in Quebec, Quebec,
Canada
d. Oct 20, 1983 in Montreal, Quebec,
Canada
Source: *BenetAL 91; BioIn 10; CanWr;
CanWW 70, 79, 80, 81, 83; CasWL;
ConAu 102; ConLC 79; CreCan 1;
DcLB 88; OxCCan; OxCCanT; REnAL*

Theroux, Paul Edward
American. Author
Wrote prize-winning novel *Picture
Palace*, 1978; best-selling travel yarn
Kingdom By the Sea, 1983.
b. Apr 10, 1941 in Medford,
Massachusetts
Source: *Au&Wr 71; CamBiEn;
CamDcAB; ChamBiD; ConAu 74NR;
ConLC 28; ConNov 86; ConPo 70;
IntWW 97, 98, 2000; MajTwCW 2;
NewYTBS 76, 78; OxCAmL 83;
OxCTwCL; SJGHorW; SmATA 44; Who
98, 99, 2000; WhoAm 86, 98, 99, 2000;
WhoEnt 98; WhoWor 98, 99, 2000;
WrDr 86*

Thespis
Greek. Actor, Dramatist, Poet
Invented tragedy in Greek tradition;
originated actor's role; actors called
thespians in his honor.
b. fl. 6th cent. BC in Attica, Greece
Source: *Benet 87, 96; BlmGEL;
CamBiEn; CamGWoT; CasWL;
ChamBiD; DcArts; DcBiPP; EncWT;
Ent; Grk&L; LegTOT; LinLib L, S;
NewC; NewCol 75; NotNAT B; OxCCIL,
89; OxCThe 67, 83; PenC CL; REn;
WorAl; WorAlBi*

They Might Be Giants
[John Flansburgh; John Linnell]
American. Music Group
Pop-rock duo; wildly inventive videos
caught the attention of MTV viewers.
Source: *AntBDN G; BilIEnR; BioIn 16;
ConMus 7; CurBio 1999; DcBrWA;
DcVicP 2*

Thibault, Conrad
American. Singer
Baritone; active in radio, 1930s.
b. Nov 13, 1908 in Northbridge,
Massachusetts
d. Aug 1, 1987 in New York, New York
Source: *BiDAmM; CmpEPM; WhoAm
74, 76, 78, 80, 82, 84, 86*

Thibaut, IV
French. King, Nobleman, Poet
Count of Champagne and Brie and, as
Thibaut I, king of Navarre; courtly
poet was considered the greatest
trouvere, or troubadour.
b. May 30, 1201 in Troyes, Champagne,
France
d. Jul 7, 1253 in Pamplona, Navarre,
France
Source: *BakBD 78, 84, 92; CasWL;
DcEuL; EncWB 98; LuthC 75;
McGEWB; MusMk; NewGrDM 80;
NewOxM; OxCFr; PenC EUR*

Thicke, Alan
Canadian. Actor
Star of TV series "Growing Pains,"
1985-92.
b. Mar 1, 1947 in Kirkland Lake,
Ontario, Canada
Source: *ConTFT 6, 25; CurBio 87;
IntMPA 96; LegTOT; WhoHol 92;
WorAlBi*

Thiebaud, (Morton) Wayne
American. Artist
Realist painter best known for use of
light, structure.
b. Nov 15, 1920 in Mesa, Arizona
Source: *AmArt; BioIn 10, 11, 12, 15, 17,
19, 20, 21; CmCal; ConArt 77, 83, 89,
96; ConAu 45; CurBio 87; DcAmArt;
DcCAA 71, 77, 88, 94; DcCAr 81;
IntWW 89, 91; News 91, 91-1;
OxCTwCA; PhDcTCA 77; PrintW 83,
85; WhoAm 74, 76, 78, 80, 82, 84, 86,
88, 92, 96; WhoAmA 73, 76, 78, 80, 82,
84, 86, 89, 91, 93, 1999; WhoWor 74,
76; WorArt 1950*

Thierry, Augustin
[Jacques-Nicolas-Augustin Thierry]
French. Historian
Best known for Romantic interpretations
of Middle Ages.
b. 1795 in Blois, France
d. 1856
Source: *BioIn 11; DcEuL; Dis&D;
GloEnch; OxCFr; WebBD 83*

Thiers, Adolphe
[Louis-Adolphe Thiers]
French. Statesman
Held public office, 1832-73; premier,
1836, 1840; first pres. of Third
Republic, 1871-73, resigned.
b. Apr 15, 1797 in Marseilles, France
d. Sep 3, 1877 in Saint-Germain-en-
Laye, France
Source: *BiDFrPL; BioIn 8, 9, 10, 11, 17,
23; GloEncH; OxCFr; WebBD 83*

Thigpen, Bobby
[Robert Thomas Thigpen]
American. Baseball Player
Relief pitcher, Chicago White Sox,
1986—; set ML record for saves in a
season, 57, 1990, breaking Dave
Righetti's mark.
b. Jul 17, 1963 in Tallahassee, Florida
Source: *Ballpl 90; LegTOT; WhoAm 92,
94*

Thigpen Lynne
American. Actor
Stage, screen, and television actor known
for her wide range of work; starred in
the long-running PBS-TV children's
program "Where in the World Is
Carmen Sandiego?" and won a Tony
Award for her performance in Wendy
Wasserstein's *An American Daughter.*
b. c. 1948 in Joliet, Illinois

Thill, Georges
French. Opera Singer
Leading tenor, Paris Opera, 1925 to end
of WW II.
b. Dec 14, 1897 in Paris, France
d. Oct 17, 1984 in Draguignan, France
Source: *AnObit 1984; BakBD 84, 92;
BakBDTw; BioIn 4, 10, 14, 24; CmOp;
IntDcOp; MetOEnc; NewEOp 71;
NewGrDM 80; NewGrDO; NewYTBS 84;
OxDcOp; PenDiMP*

Thin Lizzy
[Eric Bell; Brian Downey; Scott Gorham;
Phil Lynott; Garry Moore; Brian
Robertson; Midge Ure; Darren
Wharton; Snowy White]
Irish. Music Group
Hard-nosed rock band, known for
successful album *Jailbreak,* 1976.
Source: *BillEnR; ConMuA 80A; ConMus
13; CurBio 48, 54; EncPR&S 89; EncRk
88; EncRkSt; GrMetD; HarEnR 86;
IlEncRk; LesBEnT, 92; ModIrLi;
OnThGG; PenEncP; RkOn 78; RolSEnR
83; WhoRock 81; WhoRocM 82*

Thinnes, Roy
American. Actor
On TV in "Long, Hot Summer," 1965-
66; "Invaders," 1966-68; "Falcon
Crest," 1983.
b. Apr 6, 1936 in Chicago, Illinois
Source: *ConTFT 6; FilmgC; IntMPA 84;
WhoAm 82, 84; WhoHol A*

Third World
[Bunny "Rugs" Clarke; Michael "Ibo"
Cooper; Stephen "Cat" Coore;
Richard Daley; Orvin "Carrot"
Jarrett; Willie Stewart]
Jamaican. Music Group
Reggae band formed 1973; hits include
"Sense of Purpose," 1985.
Source: *BioNews 74; ConMus 13;
EncPR&S 89; InB&W 85A; RkOn 85*

Thirty-Eight Special
[Don Barnes; Steve Brookins; Jeff
Carlisi; Jack Grondin; Larry Junstron;
Donnie Van Zandt]
American. Music Group
Formed 1979; albums include *Tour de
Force,* 1984.
Source: *EncPR&S 89; GrMetD; HarEnR
86; PenEncP; RkOn 85; RolSEnR 83;
WhoRock 81; WhoRocM 82*

Thoma, Hans
German. Artist
Influenced by Courbet; early landscapes
depict native Black Forest.
b. Oct 2, 1839 in Bernau, Germany
d. Nov 7, 1924 in Karlsruhe, Germany
Source: *CloDrA; DcTwArt; Dis&D;
LuthC 75; McGDA; NewCol 75;
OxCArt; OxDcArt; WebBD 83*

Thomas, Saint
[Teoma]
"Doubting Thomas"
Biblical Figure
One of 12 Apostles; his life is outlined
in John's Gospel; remembered for
doubting the Resurrection.
d. 53
Source: *Alli; Benet 87, 96; BiB N; BioIn
1, 2, 3, 4, 5, 6, 7, 8, 9, 10, 11, 14, 15;
CamBiEn; ChamBiD; ChamBiD; ChhPo;
DcBrECP; DcCathB; DcNaB; DcVicP 2;
DcWomA; InWom SUP; McGDA; NewC;
REn; WebBD 83; WhoChr*

Thomas, Alma (Woodsy)
American. Painter, Educator
Painter drew inspiration from nature and
created colorful, abstract works; art
teacher and founder and vice president
of Barnett-Aden Gallery in
Washington, DC; had her first major
exhibitions—at the Whitney Museum
in New York and the Corcoran
Gallery in Washington, DC—in 1972,
when she was 80 years old.
b. Sep 22, 1891 in Columbus, Georgia
d. Feb 24, 1978 in Washington, District
of Columbia

**Thomas, (Charles Louis)
Ambroise**
French. Composer
Wrote operas *Mignon,* 1866; *Hamlet,*
1868.
b. Aug 5, 1811 in Metz, France
d. Feb 12, 1896 in Paris, France
Source: *BakBD 78, 84, 92; BioIn 3, 4, 7,
12; BriBkM 80; CamBiEn; CelCen;
ChamBiD; CmOp; CmpBCM; DcCathB;
DcCom 77; DcCom&M 79; Dis&D;*

*GrComp; IntDcOp; LinLib S; MetOEnc;
MusMk; NewAmDM; NewCol 75;
NewEOp 71; NewGrDM 80; NewGrDO;
NewOxM; NotNAT B; OxCEng 85, 95;
OxCMus; OxDcOp; PenDiMP A*

Thomas, B(illy) J(oe)
American. Singer
Hits include "Raindrops Keep Fallin' On
My Head," 1970; "Somebody Done
Somebody Wrong Song," 1974.
b. Aug 7, 1942 in Houston, Texas
Source: *EncFCWM 83; EncPR&S 74;
WhoAm 84, 86, 88, 90, 92, 94; WhoEnt
92, 98*

Thomas, Betty
[Betty Thomas Nienhauser]
American. Actor
Played Lucy Bates on TV series "Hill
Street Blues," 1981-87.
b. Jul 27, 1948 in Saint Louis, Missouri
Source: *BioIn 13; ConTFT 7, 15, 27;
IntMPA 92, 94, 96; VarWW 85;
WhoTelC*

Thomas, Bill
American. Costume Designer
Won Oscar for costume designs in
Spartacus, 1960.
b. Oct 13, 1921 in Chicago, Illinois
d. May 30, 2000 in Beverly Hills,
California
Source: *IntMPA 75, 76, 77, 78, 79, 80,
81, 82, 84, 86, 88; VarWW 85*

Thomas, Billy
[Our Gang]
"Buckwheat"
American. Actor
Played Buckwheat in "Our Gang"
comedies, 1934-44.
b. Mar 12, 1931 in Los Angeles,
California
d. Oct 10, 1980 in Los Angeles,
California
Source: *NewYTBS 80; WhScrn 83*

Thomas, Brandon
English. Actor, Dramatist
Wrote *Charley's Aunt,* 1892.
b. Dec 25, 1856 in Liverpool, England
d. Jun 19, 1914 in London, England
Source: *BioIn 4, 5; CamGWoT;
LngCTC; McGEWD 72, 84; ModWD;
NotNAT A, B; OxCThe 83; WhLit;
WhThe*

Thomas, Caitlin Macnamara
[Mrs. Dylan Thomas]
Welsh. Author
Married Dylan Thomas, 1937; wrote of
life together in *Leftover Life to Kill,*
1957.
b. Dec 8, 1913 in London, England
Source: *BioIn 4*

Thomas, Charles Allen
American. Business Executive
Pres., Monsanto Chemical Co., 1951-60;
chairman, 1960-65.

b. Feb 15, 1900 in Scott County,
  Kentucky
d. Mar 30, 1982 in Albany, Georgia
Source: *AmMWSc 73P, 76P, 79, 82;
AnObit 1982; BioIn 1, 2, 3, 4, 5, 12, 13;
CurBio 50, 82N; FacFETw; InSci;
IntWW 74; IntYB 78, 79, 80, 81, 82;
NewYTBS 82; St&PR 75; WhAm 8;
WhoAm 74, 76, 78, 80, 82; WhoWor 74,
76, 78, 80*

Thomas, Clarence
American. Supreme Court Justice
Member of US Supreme Court, 1991—;
  controversy surrounding nomination
  involved accusations of sexual
  harassment by former EEOC colleague
  Anita Hill.
b. Jun 23, 1948 in Savannah, Georgia
Source: *AfrAmAl 6, 8; AfrAmBi 1;
AmBench 97; BioIn 13, 14, 15, 18;
BlkWr 3; CamBiEn; CamDcAB; CngDr
91, 93, 95; ConAu 166; ConBlB 2;
CriJuSA; CurBio 92; DiAAPGL; DrAS
99P; EncAPoR; EncRelA; EncWB 98;
InB&W 85; LegTOT; News 92, 92-2;
NewYTBS 91; NotBlAM; OxCSupC;
SupCtJu; Who 98, 99, 2000; WhoAfA 9,
10, 11, 12; WhoAm 82, 84, 86, 88, 92,
94, 95, 96, 97, 98, 99, 2000; WhoAmL
92, 94, 96, 98, 2000; WhoAmP 89, 91,
93, 95, 97, 1999; WhoBlA 4, 5, 6, 7, 8;
WhoE 93; WhoEmL 89; WhoFI 87, 89,
92, 94; WhoWor 96*

Thomas, Craig
American. Politician
Rep. senator from WY, 1995—.
b. Feb 17, 1933
Source: *AlmAP 92, 96, 2000; BioIn 20,
21, 22, 24; CngDr 91, 93, 95; IntWW
97, 98, 2000; WhoAm 90, 92, 94, 95, 96,
97, 98, 99, 2000; WhoAmP 91, 93, 95,
97, 1999; WhoWest 00, 92, 94, 96, 98*

Thomas, Craig D
[David Grant]
Welsh. Author
Best-selling novel *Firefox*, 1977, adapted
  to successful film, 1982.
b. Nov 24, 1942 in Cardiff, Wales
Source: *ConAu 108, 112; Novels; WrDr
86, 94*

Thomas, D(onald) M(ichael)
English. Author
Wrote best-seller *The White House*,
  1981.
b. Jan 27, 1935 in Carnkie, England
Source: *BiCoLiE; BioIn 12; CamBiEn;
ConAu 45NR, 61, 74NR, 75NR; ConNov
96; ConPo 70, 75, 96; DcLEL 1940;
EncSF 93; IntAu&W 77, 82, 89, 91, 93;
IntWW 89, 91, 93, 97, 98, 2000;
MajTwCW 2; OxCEng 95; OxCTwCL;
OxCTwCP; RGTwCWr; SJGHorW; Who
85, 88, 90, 92, 94, 98, 99, 2000;
WhoWor 87; WrDr 76, 80, 94, 96, 98,
99, 2000*

Thomas, Danny
[Amos Jacobs]
American. Actor, Comedian, Producer
Starred in "Make Room for Daddy,"
  1953-64, later called "Danny Thomas
  Show"; father of Marlo.
b. Jan 6, 1914 in Deerfield, Michigan
d. Feb 6, 1991 in Los Angeles,
  California
Source: *BiDAmM; BioIn 3, 4, 5, 6, 8, 9,
10, 11, 13, 14, 15; BioNews 74; CelR,
90; CmpEPM; ConTFT 3; CurBio 59,
91N; EncAFC; FilmEn; FilmgC;
ForYSC; HalFC 80, 84, 88; IntMPA 75,
76, 77, 80, 84, 86, 88; JoeFr; LegTOT;
MotPP; News 91, 91-3; NewYTET;
WhAm 10; WhoAm 74, 76, 78, 80, 82,
84, 86, 88, 90; WhoHol A; WorAl;
WorAlBi*

Thomas, Dave
[Rex David Thomas]
American. Business Executive,
  Restaurateur
Founder of Wendy's International, 1969;
  known for his folksy TV commercials.
b. Jul 2, 1932 in Atlantic City, New
  Jersey
Source: *ConHero 3; ConNews 86-2;
CurBio 95; EncWB 99; LegTOT; News
93-2; St&PR 87; WhoAm 84, 86; WhoFI
83*

Thomas, Dave
[McKenzie Brothers; Doug McKenzie]
Canadian. Comedian, Screenwriter
As Doug McKenzie, had hit album with
  Rick Moranis *Great White North*,
  1981.
b. May 20, 1949 in Saint Catharines,
  Ontario, Canada
Source: *BioIn 12, 13; ConAu 115, 152;
ConTFT 6, 13; IntMPA 96; News 93-2*

Thomas, Debi
American. Skater
First black figure skater to win world
  championship, 1986; won bronze
  medal, 1988 Olympics.
b. Mar 25, 1967 in Poughkeepsie, New
  York
Source: *AfrAmAl 8; AfrAmBi 1;
BlkOlyM; CelR 90; ConNews 87-2;
EncWomS; FacFEBW DS; IntWWW 2;
LegTOT; NewYTBS 85; NotBlAW 2;
WhoAfA 9, 10, 11, 12; WhoAm 94, 95,
96, 97, 98, 99, 2000; WhoAmW 89, 91;
WhoBlA 5, 6, 7, 8; WhoSpor*

Thomas, Dennis
[Kool and the Gang]
"Dee Tee"
American. Musician
Plays flute, saxophone with Kool and the
  Gang.
b. Feb 9, 1951 in Jersey City, New
  Jersey

Thomas, Dylan Marlais
Welsh. Author
Wrote *A Child's Christmas in Wales;
  Under Milk Wood*, 1954.
b. Oct 27, 1914 in Swansea, Wales

d. Nov 9, 1953 in New York, New York
Source: *AtlBL; BlmGEL; CamBiEn;
CasWL; ChamBiD; ConAu 65NR; ConPo
75; DcArts; DcLEL; DcNaB 1951;
EncWB 98; EncWL 1; EvLB; GrBr;
LinLib S; LngCEL; LngCTC; MakMC;
McGEWB; McGEWD 72; ModBrL, S1;
ModWD; NewC; OxCEng 67, 85, 95;
OxCTwCL; PenC ENG; RfGShF 1, 2;
TwCA; TwCWr; WhAm 4, HSA;
WhE&EA*

Thomas, E. Donall
American. Physician
Won Nobel Prize in medicine, 1990, for
  work in transplanting human organs
  and bone marrow.
b. Mar 15, 1920 in Mart, Texas
Source: *AmMWSc 92; Who 92; WhoAm
90; WhoNob 90; WhoWest 92*

Thomas, Edith Matilda
American. Poet, Editor
Wrote *The Inverted Torch*, 1890.
b. Aug 12, 1854 in Chatham, Ohio
d. Sep 13, 1925 in New York, New
  York
Source: *Alli SUP; AmAu; AmAu&B;
AmBi; AmWom; AmWomPl; ApCAB, X;
BbD; BenetAL 91; BiD&SB; BlmGWL;
ChhPo, S1, S2, S3; DcAmAu; DcAmB;
DcNAA; InWom, SUP; LibW; NatCAB 9;
NotAW; OhA&B; OxCAmL 65, 83, 95;
REn; REnAL; TwCBDA; WhAm 1;
WomWWA 14*

Thomas, Edward
English. Poet, Author
Writings focus on nature, melancholy;
  wrote travel books, biographies before
  meeting Robert Frost and switching to
  poetry.
b. Mar 3, 1878 in London, England
d. Apr 9, 1917 in Arras, France
Source: *AnCL; AtlBL; Benet 87; BioIn 3,
4, 5, 6, 8, 9, 10, 11, 12, 13, 14, 15, 16,
17, 21, 22, 23, 24; BritWr S3; CamGEL;
CamGLE; ChhPo, S1, S2, S3; CnE&AP;
CnMWL; ConAu 106; DcLB 19, 98, 156,
216; DcLEL; DcNaB 1922, 1, 2S, 3;
FacFETw; GrWrEL P; LngCTC;
ModBrL, 2, S1, S2; NewC; NewCBEL;
OxCEng 67, 85; OxCLiW 86;
OxCTwCP; PenC ENG; RAdv 14; REn;
RfGEnL 91; RGFMBP; TwCA, SUP;
TwCLC 10; TwCWr; WebE&AL; WhDW;
WhoTwCL; WorAu 1900*

Thomas, Elizabeth Marshall
American. Writer
Wrote books based on her study of
  animal behavior, *The Hidden Life of
  Dogs*, 1993; *The Tribe of the Tiger*,
  1994.
b. Sep 13, 1931 in Boston,
  Massachusetts
Source: *Au&Wr 71; BioIn 15, 19, 21,
22; ConAu 17R; CurBio 96; IntAu&W
82, 93; ScF&FL 92; WhoAm 98, 99,
2000; WhoAmW 99*

Thomas, Elmer
American. Politician
Dem. senator from OK, 1927-51.
b. Sep 8, 1876 in Greencastle, Indiana
d. Sep 19, 1965
Source: *AmNatBi; BioIn 1, 2, 7, 11; CurBio 49, 65; DcAmB S7; WhAm 4*

Thomas, Frank
[Frank Edward Thomas, Jr.]
''The Big Hurt''
American. Baseball Player
First baseman, designated hitter, Chicago White Sox, 1990—; AL MVP, 1993-94; AL batting champion, 1997.
b. May 27, 1968 in Columbus, Georgia
Source: *AfrAmSG; ConBlB 12; CurBio 94; News 94, 94-3; WhoAfA 9; WhoAm 92, 94, 95, 96, 97; WhoBlA 8; WhoMW 93, 96*

Thomas, Franklin Augustine
American. Lawyer
Pres. of Ford Foundation, 1979-96.
b. May 27, 1934 in New York, New York
Source: *BioIn 11, 12, 13; CurBio 81; Ebony 1; InB&W 80, 85; NewYTBS 79; Who 83, 85, 88, 90, 92, 94, 98, 99, 2000; WhoAm 76, 78, 80, 82, 84, 86, 88, 90, 92, 94, 95, 96, 97, 98, 99, 2000; WhoBlA 5; WhoE 95, 97, 99; WhoFrS 84*

Thomas, George Henry
''The Rock of Chickamauga''
American. Military Leader
Distinguished Civil War general; accepted surrender of Atlanta, 1864.
b. Jul 31, 1816 in Southampton County, Virginia
d. Mar 28, 1870 in San Francisco, California
Source: *AmBi; AmNatBi; ApCAB; BioIn 1, 3, 6, 7, 8, 9, 10, 13, 15, 17, 23; CamBiEn; CamDcAB; ChamBiD; CivWDc; DcAmB; DcAmMiB; DcBiPP; Drake; EncAB-H 1974, 1996; EncSoH; EncWB 98; HarEnMi; HarEnUS; LAmCW; LinLib S; McGEWB; NatCAB 4; OxCAmH; PeoHis; TwCBDA; WebAB 74, 79; WebAMB; WhAm HS; WhCiWar; WhoMilH 76; WorAl*

Thomas, Gerald
English. Producer, Director
Noted for *Carry On* comedy film series, 1957-70s.
b. Dec 20, 1920 in Hull, England
Source: *BioIn 19; ConTFT 5; FilmEn; FilmgC; HalFC 80, 84, 88; IIWWBF; IntMPA 75, 76, 77, 78, 79, 80, 81, 82, 84, 86, 88, 92, 94; MiSFD 9*

Thomas, Gwyn
Welsh. Author
Wrote *Where Did I Put My Pity?; The Love Man; The Keep.*
b. Jul 6, 1913 in Porth, Wales
d. Apr 13, 1981 in Cardiff, Wales
Source: *AnObit 1981; ArtclWW 2; Au&Wr 71; BioIn 8, 10, 11, 12, 13, 19; CasWL; ConAu 9NR, 65, 103; ConDr*

73, 77, 93; ConNov 76; CroCD; DcLB 15; DcLEL 1940; DcNaB 1981; EncWT; IntAu&W 76, 77; LngCTC; OxCLiW 86; TwCWr; Who 74; WhoThe 72, 77, 81; WorAu 1950; WrDr 76, 80, 82

Thomas, Helen A.
[Mrs. Douglas B. Cornell]
American. Journalist
UPI White House bureau chief, 1974—.
b. Aug 4, 1920 in Winchester, Kentucky
Source: *BioIn 12; BioNews 75; ConAu 101; CurBio 93; IntWWW 2; WhoAm 74, 76, 78, 80, 82, 84, 86, 88, 90, 92, 94, 95, 96, 97, 98, 99, 2000; WhoAmP 1999; WhoAmW 66, 68, 70, 72, 74, 81, 85, 89, 91, 93, 95, 97, 99; WhoE 95; WhoWor 74; WomFir*

Thomas, Henry
American. Actor
Played Elliott, ET's ''friend,'' in film *ET*, 1981.
b. Sep 8, 1972 in San Antonio, Texas
Source: *BioIn 13; ConTFT 6; LegTOT; VarWW 85*

Thomas, Isaiah
American. Publisher
Founded American Antiquarian Society, 1812.
b. Jan 30, 1750 in Boston, Massachusetts
d. Apr 4, 1831 in Worcester, Massachusetts
Source: *Alli; AmAu; AmAu&B; AmBi; ApCAB; BiD&SB; BioIn 15, 16, 17, 23; CyAL 1; DcAmB; DcLB 43, 73, 187; Drake; EarABI; JrnUS; OxCAmL 65; OxCChiL; REnAL; TwCBDA; WebAB 74; WhAm HS*

Thomas, Isiah
[Isiah Lord Thomas, III]
''Pocket Magic''
American. Basketball Player, Basketball Executive
Guard, Detroit, 1981-94; holds NBA record for most assists in season, 1985; MVP, All-Star Game, 1984, 1986; MVP, championship series, 1990; vice president, Toronto Raptors, 1994—.
b. Apr 30, 1961 in Chicago, Illinois
Source: *AfrAmBi 1; AfrAmSG; BasBi; BiDAmSp BK; BioIn 12; CelR 90; ConBlB 7; CurBio 89; News 89-2; NewYTBS 81; OfNBA 87; WhoAfA 9; WhoAm 86, 88, 90, 92, 94, 95, 96, 97; WhoBlA 5, 6, 7, 8; WhoE 97; WhoMW 88, 90, 92, 93, 96*

Thomas, Jess
American. Opera Singer
Tenor, noted for Wagner roles; NY Met. debut, 1963.
b. Apr 8, 1927 in Hot Springs, South Dakota
d. Oct 11, 1993 in San Francisco, California
Source: *AnObit 1993; BakBD 84; BiDAmM; BioIn 6, 7, 9, 11, 13, 16, 19, 20; CmOp; CurBio 64, 94N; IntWWM 77, 80, 90; MetOEnc; MussN; NewEOp*

71; NewGrDA 86; NewGrDM 80; NewYTBE 71; NewYTBS 93; OxDcOp; PenDiMP; WhAm 11; WhoAm 74, 76, 78, 80, 82, 84, 86, 88, 90, 92, 94; WhoAmM 83; WhoE 74; WhoEnt 92, 98; WhoOp 76; WhoWor 74, 78, 82, 87, 89

Thomas, John Charles
American. Opera Singer
Baritone; radio, film star; popular concert performer, 1940s-50s; NY Met., 1933-45.
b. Sep 6, 1891 in Meyersdale, Pennsylvania
d. Dec 13, 1960 in Apple Valley, California
Source: *AmNatBi; BakBD 78, 84, 92; BakBDTw; BioIn 1, 2, 4, 5; CamDcAB; CurBio 43, 61; DcAmB S6; MetOEnc; MussN; NewEOp 71; NewGrDA 86; NewGrDO; OxCAmT 84; PenDiMP; RadStar; WhAm 4; WhoHol B; WhScrn 74, 77*

Thomas, Jonathan Taylor
[Jonathan Weiss]
American. Actor
Plays Randy Taylor on TV's ''Home Improvement,'' 1991—.
b. Sep 8, 1981 in Bethlehem, Pennsylvania
Source: *ConTFT 16, 27*

Thomas, Joyce Carol
American. Author
Wrote 1982 award-winning young adult novel *Marked By Fire.*
b. May 25, 1938 in Ponca City, Oklahoma
Source: *Au&Arts 12; BioIn 13; BlkAuIl, 92; BlkWr 1, 2, 3; ChlLR 19; ConAfAN; ConAu 48NR, 113, 116; ConBlAP 88; ConLC 35; DcLB 33; DrAPF 80; FemDram A; FemiCLE; MajAl; MajTwCW 1, 2; MorBAP; OnHuMoP; OxCAfAL; OxCWoWr 95; ScF&FL 92; SchCGBL; SJGYouA 2; SmATA 7AS, 40, 78; TwCYAW 1; WhoAfA 9, 10, 11, 12; WhoAm 88, 97; WhoAmW 87, 89; WhoBlA 1, 2, 3, 4, 5, 6, 7, 8; WhoUSWr 88; WhoWor 96, 97; WhoWrEP 89, 92, 95; WrYoAd*

Thomas, Kurt
American. Gymnast
First US male to win gold medal in world gymnastic competition, 1978.
b. Mar 29, 1956 in Terre Haute, Indiana
Source: *BiDAmSp BK; BioIn 11, 12; ConAu 114, 154; LegTOT; WhoHol 92; WhoSpor; WorAl*

Thomas, Lewis
American. Physician, Author
Wrote *The Lives of a Cell: Notes of a Biology Watcher,* 1974; *The Medusa and the Snail,* 1979.
b. Nov 25, 1913 in Flushing, New York
d. Dec 3, 1993 in New York, New York
Source: *AmDec 1970; AmMWSc 73P, 76P, 79, 82, 86, 89, 92; AmNatBi; AmNatWr; AnObit 1993; Benet 96; BioIn 10, 12, 13, 14, 16, 17, 19, 20, 21, 22;*

CamDcAB; ConAu 38NR, 60NR, 85,
143; ConLC 35; CurBio 75, 94N; CyWA
89, 97; DcNaB; IntMed 80; IntWW 77,
78, 79, 80, 81, 82, 83, 89, 91, 93; LEduc
74; MajTwCW 1, 2; NewYTBS 79, 93;
RAdv 14, 13-1, 13-5; RanHWDS; WhAm
11; WhoAm 74, 76, 78, 80, 82, 84, 86,
88, 90, 92, 94; WhoE 74; WhoFrS 84;
WhoWor 78, 80, 82, 84, 87, 89, 91;
WorAlBi; WorAu 1975; WrDr 82, 84, 86,
88, 90, 92, 94, 96

Thomas, Lowell Jackson
American. Author, Radio Performer
Wrote With Lawrence in Arabia, 1924;
  hosted "High-Adventure," 1957-59.
b. Apr 6, 1892 in Woodington, Ohio
d. Aug 29, 1981 in Pawling, New York
Source: AmAu&B; AmSocL; Au&Wr 71;
AuBYP 2, 3; AuNews 1, 2; BiDAmJo;
CamDcAB; ConAu 3NR, 45, 104;
CurBio 40, 81; HisDcAR; HisDcWJ;
IntMPA 79; JBA 34; NewYTBS 78;
OhA&B; OxCCan; REnAL; ScrEAmL 1;
TwCA, SUP; WebAB 74, 79; WhE&EA;
WhNAA; Who 74; WhoAm 80; WhoHol
A; WorAl; WorAu 1900; WrDr 80

Thomas, Lowell Jackson, Jr.
American. Author, Producer
Writings include The Silent War in Tibet,
  1959; Famous First Flights That
  Changed History, 1968.
b. Oct 6, 1923 in London, England
Source: AmAu&B; AuBYP 2, 3; ConAu
85; IntMPA 82; SmATA 15; WhoAm 84,
86; WhoAmP 85; WhoHol A; WhoWest
74

Thomas, Marlo
[Mrs. Phil Donahue; Margaret Thomas]
American. Actor
Starred in "That Girl," 1966-71; won
  Emmys for "Free to Be. You and
  Me," 1977; "Nobody's Child," 1986.
b. Nov 21, 1938 in Detroit, Michigan
Source: BioIn 8, 9, 10, 11; BkPepl;
CelR, 90; ConAu 165; ConTFT 10, 17;
HalFC 84; IntMPA 77, 78, 79, 80, 81,
82, 84, 86, 88, 92, 94, 96; LegTOT;
NewYTBE 73; VarWW 85; WhoAm 86;
WhoAmW 85; WhoHol 92, A

Thomas, Martha Carey
American. Educator, Feminist
Pres., Bryn Mawr College, 1894-1922.
b. Jan 2, 1857 in Baltimore, Maryland
d. Dec 2, 1935 in Philadelphia,
  Pennsylvania
Source: AmAu&B; AmBi; AmRef;
AmWomM; BiDAmEd; BioIn 1, 10, 11,
12, 14, 15, 19, 20; CamBiEn;
CamDcAB; ChamBiD; CmpQue;
ContDcW 89; DcAmAu; DcAmB S1;
DcNAA; EncAB-H 1996; EncWoAP;
FemiWr; GayLesB; GoodHs; GrLiveH;
IntDcWB; InWom, SUP; LibW;
McGEWB; NotAW; TwCBDA; WebAB
74, 79; WomEdUS; WomFir; WomWWA
14; WorAl; WorAlBi

Thomas, Michel
American. Linguist
Unorthodox language teacher encourages
  students to relax and listen to
  recordings of celebrity novices
  learning the new language, instead of
  the more traditional tapes of fluent
  speakers; founder of Michel Thomas
  Language Center, 1982, and dialect
  coach for film actors.
b. c. 1911 in Bordeaux, France
Source: ConNews 87-4

Thomas, Norman Mattoon
"Conscience of America"
American. Author, Political Leader
Writings include The Conscientious
  Objector in America, 1923; What's the
  Matter with New York?, 1932.
b. Nov 20, 1884 in Marion, Ohio
d. Dec 19, 1968 in Huntington, New
  York
Source: AmNatBi; Benet 96; CamBiEn;
CamDcAB; ChamBiD; ConAu 101;
CurBio 44, 62, 69; EncAB-H 1974,
1996; EncWB 98; OhA&B; OxCAmL 65;
PenC AM; REn; REnAL; WebAB 74;
WhAm 5

Thomas, Philip Michael
American. Actor
Played Ricardo Tubbs on TV series
  "Miami Vice," 1984-89.
b. May 26, 1949 in Los Angeles,
  California
Source: BlksAmF; ConTFT 6; IntMPA
88, 92, 94, 96; LegTOT; WhoAfA 9, 10,
11, 12; WhoBlA 4, 5, 6, 7, 8; WhoHol
92, A

Thomas, Pinklon
American. Boxer
WBC heavyweight champion, 1984; lost
  title to Trevor Berbick, 1986.
b. 1957? in Pontiac, Michigan
Source: BioIn 12; NewYTBS 82, 85

Thomas, Piri
American. Author
Wrote autobiographies Down These
  Mean Streets, 1967; Seven Long
  Times, 1974.
b. Sep 30, 1928 in New York, New
  York
Source: AmAu&B; BiDHisA; BiDHisL;
BioIn 7, 8, 9, 10, 13, 16, 17, 20, 23, 24;
CaribW 4; ConAu 73; ConLC 17;
DcHiB; DrAF 76; DrAP 75; DrAPF 80;
EncALit; HispAmA; HispLC SUP;
HispWr; IntAu&W 77; MorBAP;
NotLatA; OxCAfAL; WhoE 74; WhoHisp
92, 94; WrDr 76

Thomas, Richard Earl
American. Actor
Played John Boy in "The Waltons,"
  1972-77; published two books of
  poetry.
b. Jun 13, 1951 in New York, New York
Source: ConAu 107; CurBio 75; FilmgC;
HalFC 84; IntMPA 86; WhoAm 84, 86

Thomas, Robert B
American. Publisher
Founded, edited Old Farmer's Almanac,
  1792-1844.
b. Apr 24, 1766 in Grafton,
  Massachusetts
d. May 19, 1846 in West Bolyston,
  Massachusetts
Source: Alli; AmAu&B; AmBi; CasWL;
DcAmAu; DcAmB; REnAL; WhAm HS

Thomas, Ronald Stuart
Welsh. Poet
Poems express bleak view of man: The
  Stones of the Field, 1946.
b. Mar 29, 1913 in Cardiff, Wales
Source: BiCoLiE; BioIn 6, 10, 12, 14,
15, 17, 18; CamBiEn; CasWL;
ChamBiD; ChhPo, S1, S2; CnE&AP;
ConAu 89; ConLC 6, 13; ConPo 70, 75;
DcLEL 1940; EncWL 3; IntAu&W 89,
91, 93; IntWW 79, 80, 81, 82, 83, 89,
91, 93, 97, 98, 2000; LngCTC; ModBrL,
S1; NewC; NewCBEL; NewYTBS 83;
OxCLiW 86; OxCTwCL; PenC ENG;
TwCWr; WebE&AL; Who 85, 88, 90, 92,
94, 98, 99, 2000; WhoTwCL; WorAu
1950; WrDr 76, 98, 99, 2000

Thomas, Ross (Elmore)
"Oliver Bleeck"
American. Writer
Author of political thrillers such as
  Chinaman's Chance, 1978.
b. Feb 19, 1926 in Oklahoma City,
  Oklahoma
d. Dec 18, 1995 in Santa Monica,
  California
Source: Au&Wr 71; BioIn 14, 15, 21;
ConAu 22NR, 33R, 63NR, 150; ConLC
39; CrtSuMy; EncMys; Novels;
OxCTwCL; SpyFic; TwCCr&M 80, 85,
91; WhAm 11; WhoAm 74, 76, 78, 80,
82, 84, 86, 88, 90, 92, 94, 95, 96;
WhoSSW 73; WrDr 76, 80, 82, 84, 86,
88, 90, 92, 94, 96

Thomas, Rufus
American. Singer, Songwriter
Rhythm and blues singer and songwriter
  was a successful recording artist and
  disc jockey, probably best known for
  his novelty songs like "Walking the
  Dog" and "Do the Funky Chicken."
b. Mar 26, 1917 in Cayce, Mississippi
Source: AllMGBl 2; ASCAP 80;
BiDAmM; BioIn 12; BluesWW; ConBlB
20; DcTwCCu 5; EncPR&S 89; EncRk
88; NewGrDA 86; PenEncP; RolSEnR
83; SoulM; WhoRock 81

Thomas, Samuel Bath
American. Manufacturer, Businessman
Introduced English muffins to US, 1880.
b. 1855
d. 1919
Source: Entr

Thomas, Seth
American. Manufacturer
Founded Seth Thomas Clock Co., 1853.
b. Aug 19, 1785 in Wolcott, Connecticut
d. Jan 29, 1859 in Plymouth, Connecticut

Source: *AmBi; AmNatBi; ApCAB X;*
BiDAmBL 83; BioIn 2, 6; CamBiEn;
CamDcAB; DcAmB; DcNiCA; Entr;
LegTOT; NatCAB 3; RanHWDS; WebAB
74, 79; WhAm HS

Thomas, Sidney Gilchrist
English. Inventor, Scientist
Discovered method to allow phosphoric
ores to be used, Bessemer converter,
1875.
b. Apr 16, 1850 in London, England
d. Feb 1, 1885 in Paris, France
Source: *BiESc; BioIn 2, 7; ChamBiD;*
DcNaB; DcScB; InSci; LarDcSc;
OxCLiW 86; RanHWDS; WorInv

Thomas, Theodore
German. Conductor
Director, Cincinnati College of Music,
1878-98; violinist with symphonies.
b. Oct 11, 1835 in Essen, Germany
d. Jan 4, 1905 in Chicago, Illinois
Source: *AmBi; AmNatBi; ApCAB;*
BakBD 78, 84; BakDcM; BioIn 1, 2, 3,
7, 8, 9; BriBkM 80; DcAmB; DcNAA;
EncWB 98; HarEnUS; LinLib S;
McGEWB; MetOEnc; NatCAB 2;
NewAmDM; NewEOp 71; NewGrDA 86;
NewGrDM 80; OxCAmH; OxCAmL 65;
OxCMus; PenDiMP; REn; TwCBDA;
WebAB 74, 79; WhAm 1; WhDW

Thomas, Thurman Lee
American. Football Player
NFL running back, Buffalo Bills, 1988—
; AP MVP, 1991.
b. May 16, 1966 in Houston, Texas
Source: *News 93-1; WhoAfA 11, 12;*
WhoBlA 7

Thomas, Tony
Writer
Co-created *Blossom, Nurses,* and
Herman's Head.
Source: *BioIn 16, 23; ConTFT 13;*
NewYTBS 97; SelBAAf; WhoAm 99,
2000; WhoEnt 98; WhoHol A

Thomas, Vivien
American. Scientist
With no formal medical training, helped
develop intricate surgical techniques;
surgical research technician, Vanderbilt
Univ. Medical School, 1930-41;
research assoc., Johns Hopkins Univ.
School of Medicine, 1941-70.
b. 1910 in Nashville, Tennessee
d. 1985
Source: *AfrAmAl 8; ConBlB 9*

Thomas, W(illiam) I(saac)
American. Sociologist, Educator
Sociology professor; author of *Sex and
Society,* 1907.
b. Aug 13, 1863 in Russell County,
Virginia
d. Dec 5, 1947 in Berkeley, California
Source: *AmNatBi; BioIn 1, 6, 10, 11, 14;*
CamDcAB; DcAmB S4; DcNAA; DcSoc;
EncWB 98; McGEWB; NatCAB 44;
RAdv 14, 13-3; ThTwC 87; WhAm 2

Thomas a Kempis
[Thomas Hamerken]
German. Theologian, Author
Wrote influential *The Imitation of Christ,*
c. 1427.
b. 1380? in Kempen, Germany
d. Jul 25, 1471 in Agnietenberg,
Netherlands
Source: *AtlBL; Benet 87, 96; BiCoLiE;*
BiD&SB; BioIn 1, 2, 5, 6, 7, 20;
CasWL; CyWA 58; DcCathB; DcEnL;
DcEuL; DcPseud; DcSpL; EuAu; LitC
11; McGEWB; NewC; OxCEng 67, 85,
95; OxCGer 76; PenC EUR; PseudAu;
RComWL; REn; WhDW; WhoChr;
WorAl

Thomas Aquinas, Saint
[Tommaso d'Aquino]
"Angelic Doctor"; "Doctor of the
School"
Italian. Theologian, Philosopher
Synthesis of theology, philosophy known
as Thomism; wrote *Summa
Theologica.*
b. 1225 in Roccasecca, Italy
d. Mar 7, 1274 in Fossannova, Italy
Source: *BbD; BiD&SB; BiDChrM; BioIn*
1, 2, 3, 4, 5, 6, 7, 8, 9, 10, 11, 12, 13,
14, 15, 17, 18, 20, 23; CasWL; CyWA
58; DcCathB; DcEuL; EncEth; EuAu;
EvEuW; IlEncMy; McGDA; NewC;
OxCCAA; OxCEng 67; OxCFr; PenC
EUR; RAdv 13-4; RComWL; REn;
WebBD 83; WhoChr

Thomasius
[Christian Thomasius]
German. Philosopher, Jurist, Educator
One of the most respected and influential
university teachers of his day, he
helped popularize the Enlightenment in
Germany.
b. Jan 1, 1655 in Leipzig, Germany
d. Sep 23, 1728 in Halle, Germany
Source: *EncWB 98*

Thomason, Harry
American. Writer
Co-created television comedies
Designing Women and *Evening Shade.*
Source: *BioIn 12, 17, 18, 22, 24;*
WhoAm 92, 2000

Thomason, John William, Jr.
American. Military Leader
WW I colonel; wrote, illustrated from
military experiences: *Fix Bayonets,*
1926.
b. Feb 28, 1893 in Huntsville, Texas
d. Mar 12, 1944 in San Diego, California
Source: *AmAu&B; ArtsAmW 1; BioIn 1,*
4, 6, 8, 13; CurBio 44; DcNAA;
EncFWF; IlBEAAW; NatCAB 33;
REnAL; TexWr; TwCA, SUP; TwCWW
82; WhAm 2; WhAmArt 85; WorAu 1900

Thomaz, Americo
[Americo Deus Rodrigues Tomas]
Portuguese. Political Leader
Elected pres., 1958; twice again, under
suspicious circumstances, until ousted
in 1974.

b. Nov 19, 1894 in Lisbon, Portugal
d. Sep 18, 1987 in Cascais, Portugal
Source: *CurBio 58, 87; DcPol;*
FacFETw; IntWW 74; WhoWor 74

Thomopoulos, Anthony Denis
American. TV Executive
Pres., ABC Broadcast Group, 1983-85;
pres., ABC, 1978-83; chm. and CEO,
United Artists Pictures, 1986—.
b. Feb 7, 1938 in Mount Vernon, New
York
Source: *BioIn 11; IntMPA 86; LesBEnT;*
VarWW 85; WhoAm 86; WhoFI 83;
WhoTelC

Thompson, Bradbury James
American. Designer
On faculty of Yale School of Art and
Architecture, 1956—; designed Time-
Life *Library of Art* series, 1965;
designer of over 100 US postage
stamps, 1958-92.
b. Mar 25, 1911 in Topeka, Kansas
d. Nov 1, 1995
Source: *WhoAm 84, 86; WhoAmA 84;*
WhoGrA 62; WhoWor 87

Thompson, Daley
[Francis Daley Thompson]
English. Track Athlete
Second person to win two gold medals
in decathlon, 1980, 1984 Olympics.
b. Jul 30, 1958 in London, England
Source: *BioIn 11, 12, 13; CamBiEn;*
CurBio 86; DcPseud; FacFETw; IntWW
89, 91; NewYTBS 79, 84

Thompson, David
English. Explorer, Geographer
First white man to explore Columbia
River from source to mouth, 1811;
maps helped outline US-Canadian
boundary, 1816-26.
b. Apr 30, 1770 in London, England
d. Feb 10, 1857 in Montreal, Quebec,
Canada
Source: *AmBi; AmNatBi; ApCAB; BbtC;*
BenetAL 91; BiDAmCa; BioIn 1, 4, 5, 7,
8, 9, 12, 14, 17, 18, 20, 22, 23, 24;
CamBiEn; ChamBiD; DcAmB; DcCanB
8; DcLB 99; DcLEL; EncWB 98; Expl
93; ExplAnT; HarEnUS; IntDcAn;
MacDCB 78; McGEWB; NewCBEL;
NewEAmW; OxCAmH; OxCAmL 65;
OxCCan; REnAL; REnAW; WebAB 74,
79; WhAm HS; WhDW; WhNaAH;
WhWE; WorAl; WorAlBi

Thompson, David O'Neil
American. Basketball Player
Guard, Denver, 1976-82; Seattle, 1982-
84; MVP, NBA All-Star game, 1979.
b. Jul 13, 1954 in Shelby, North Carolina
Source: *BiDAmSp BK; NewYTBS 82;*
WhoAm 84; WhoBbl 73; WhoBlA 4

Thompson, Dorothy
American. Journalist
Columnist for *NY Herald Tribune
Syndicate,* 1936-41; writer, *Ladies
Home Journal,* mag, 1937-61.

b. Jul 9, 1894 in Lancaster, New York
d. Jan 31, 1961 in Lisbon, Portugal
Source: *AmAu&B; AmSocL; AmWomWr; Benet 87, 96; BenetAL 91; BioAmW; BioIn 1, 2, 4, 5, 6, 7, 8, 9, 10, 11; CamDcAB; ChamBiD; ConAu 89, 179; ContDcW 89; CurBio 40, 61; EncAB-H 1974, 1996; EncAJ; EncTR; EncTwCJ; EncWB, 98; EvLB; FacFETw; GoodHs; HisDcAR; IntDcWB; InWom; LegTOT; LibW; LinLib L, S; ObitT 1961; OxCAmH; OxCAmL 65, 83, 95; RadStar; REn; REnAL; TwCA, SUP; WebAB 74, 79; WhAm 4; WhE&EA; WhoAmW 58, 61; WomFir; WomPO 76; WomStre; WorAl; WorAlBi*

Thompson, Edward Herbert
American. Archaeologist, Explorer, Author
Studied Mayan sites in Mexico; wrote *People of the Serpent,* 1932.
b. Sep 28, 1856 in Worcester, Massachusetts
d. May 11, 1935 in Plainfield, New Jersey
Source: *BioIn 4, 6, 8; CamDcAB; DcAmB S1*

Thompson, Emma
English. Actor
Appeared in *Henry V,* 1989; won Oscar, Best Actress, *Howard's End,* 1993; Oscar, Best Adapted Screenplay, *Sense and Sensibility,* 1995.
b. Apr 15, 1959 in London, England
Source: *BiDFilm 94; BiNAW Sup, SupB; CamBiEn; ChamBiD; ConAu 154; ConTFT 11; CurBio 95; DcArts; IntMPA 92, 94, 96; IntWW 91, 93, 97, 98, 2000; IntWWW 2; LegTOT; News 93-2; OsStAZ; Who 94, 98, 99, 2000; WhoAm 94, 95, 96, 97, 99, 2000; WhoAmW 97; WhoEnt 98; WhoWor 95, 96, 97, 98, 99, 2000*

Thompson, Ernest
[Richard Ernest Thompson]
American. Author
Wrote play *On Golden Pond,* 1978; won 1982 Oscar for screen adaptation.
b. Nov 6, 1950 in Bellows Falls, Vermont
Source: *ConAu 115; MiSFD 9; VarWW 85*

Thompson, Francis Joseph
English. Poet, Essayist
First volume *Poems,* 1893, contained best known poem "The Hound of Heaven."
b. Dec 18, 1859 in Preston, England
d. Nov 13, 1907 in London, England
Source: *AtlBL; BiD&SB; CasWL; CnE&AP; ConAu 104; CrtT 3; DcEuL; DcLEL; EncWL 1; EvLB; LngCTC; MouLC 4; NewC; OxCEng 67; PenC ENG; RAdv 1; REn; WebE&AL*

Thompson, Frank, Jr.
American. Politician
Dem. congressman from NJ, 1955-69, 1971-81.

b. Jul 26, 1918 in Trenton, New Jersey
d. Jul 22, 1989 in Baltimore, Maryland
Source: *AlmAP 78, 80; BiDrAC; BiDrUSC 89; BioIn 5, 8, 10, 11, 12, 16; CngDr 74, 77, 79; CurBio 59, 89N; NewYTBS 76, 80, 89; PolProf E, J, K; WhoAm 74, 76, 78, 80; WhoAmP 73, 75, 77, 79, 81, 83; WhoE 74, 75, 77, 79; WhoGov 72, 75, 77*

Thompson, Fred
American. Politician
Rep. senator from TN, 1994—.
b. Aug 19, 1942
Source: *AlmAP 96; CngDr 95; CurBio 1999; News 98, 98-2; WhoAm 97, 98, 99, 2000; WhoAmP 1999; WhoSSW 97, 99*

Thompson, George Selden
[George Selden]
American. Children's Author
Best known for *The Cricket in Times Square,* which won Newbery Medal, 1961, and was adapted to film, 1973.
b. May 14, 1929 in Hartford, Connecticut
d. Dec 5, 1989 in New York, New York
Source: *AuBYP 2, 3; BioIn 8, 9, 10, 14, 15, 16, 17, 19; ChlBkCr; ChlLR 8; ConAu 5R, 21NR, 37NR, 130; DcAmChF 1960; DcLB 52; FourBJA; IntAu&W 91; MajAl; OxCChiL; ScF&FL 1, 2, 92; SJGFanW; SmATA 4, 63, 73, X; TwCChW 1, 2, 3, 4; WrDr 80, 82, 84, 86, 88, 90*

Thompson, Hank
American. Singer, Musician, Bandleader
Led country music-swing band, Brazos Valley Boys, 1950s-70s; had 100 hit-chart records by 1966.
b. Sep 3, 1925 in Waco, Texas
Source: *AllMGCo; ASCAP 66; Ballpl 90; BgBkCoM; BioIn 14, 15, 20; CounME 74, 74A; EncFCWM 69, 83; HarEnCM 87; IlEncCM; NewAmDM; NewGrDA 86; PenEncP*

Thompson, Hunter S(tockton)
[Sebastian Owl]
American. Journalist, Editor
Wrote *Hell's Angels: A Strange and Terrible Saga,* 1966; nat. affairs editor, *Rolling Stone* mag, 1969-74.
b. Jul 18, 1939 in Louisville, Kentucky
Source: *AmSocL; BioIn 12, 13; CamBiEn; ChamBiD; ConAu 17R, 46NR, 74NR, 77NR; ConLC 17, 40; ConPopW; CurBio 81; EncWB 98; IntAu&W 76, 77, 82; MajTwCW 2; News 92; NewYTBS 79; OxCTwCL; WhoAm 76, 78, 80, 82, 84, 86, 88, 90, 92; WhoE 74; WhoUSWr 88; WhoWest 89; WhoWrEP 89, 92, 95; WrDr 94, 96, 98, 99, 2000*

Thompson, J(ames) Walter
American. Advertising Executive
Founded one of major advertising firms, 1878; specialized in mag. marketing.
b. Oct 28, 1847 in Pittsfield, Massachusetts
d. Oct 16, 1928 in New York, New York

Source: *AdMenW; ApCAB X; BiDAmBL 83; BioIn 6, 7, 20; CamDcAB; NatCAB 15, 21; WebAB 74, 79; WebBD 83*

Thompson, James Robert
American. Politician
Republican governor of IL, 1977-90, succeeded by Jim Edgar.
b. May 8, 1936 in Chicago, Illinois
Source: *AlmAP 88; AmMWSc 95, 98; BiDrGov 1789; BioIn 10, 11; CurBio 79; IntYB 79, 80, 81, 82; WhoAm 78, 80, 82, 84, 86, 88, 90, 92, 94, 95, 96, 97, 98, 99, 2000; WhoAmL 79, 96, 98, 2000; WhoGov 75, 77; WhoMW 78, 80, 82, 84, 86, 88, 90, 92; WhoScEn 94; WhoWor 82, 87, 89, 91; WorAl*

Thompson, John
American. Basketball Coach
Coach at Georgetown University, 1972—; coached US Olympic men's basketball team, 1988.
b. Sep 2, 1941 in Washington, District of Columbia
Source: *AfrAmAl 8; AfrAmSG; BasBi; BiDAmSp BK; BioIn 12; CelR 90; CurBio 89; News 88-3; WhoAm 84, 86, 88, 90, 92, 94, 95, 96, 97, 98, 99, 2000; WhoBbl 73; WhoE 89; WhoSpor; WorAlBi*

Thompson, John S(parrow) D(avid), Sir
Canadian. Judge, Politician
Conservative prime minister, 1892-94; died while visiting Queen Victoria.
b. Nov 10, 1844 in Halifax, Nova Scotia, Canada
d. Dec 2, 1894 in Windsor Castle, England
Source: *ApCAB; BioIn 1, 4, 7, 8; DcCathB; DcNaB; MacDCB 78; OxCCan; PeoHis*

Thompson, John Taliaferro
American. Inventor
US military officer; invented firearms, machinery, airplane devices; "Tommy Gun" named for him, 1920.
b. Dec 31, 1860 in Newport, Kentucky
d. Jun 21, 1940
Source: *ApCAB X; ChamBiD; CurBio 40; NatCAB 16, 29; WebAMB; WhAm 1*

Thompson, Karen
American. Social Reformer
Was involved in a case for guardianship of her companion, Sharon Kowalski, which Kowalski's parents opposed; was granted guardianship, 1991.
Source: *BioIn 15, 17; CmpQue; GayLesB*

Thompson, Kay
American. Author, Singer
Noted for singing career with Williams Brothers, 1947-53; invented popular character in book, *Eloise,* 1955.
b. Nov 9, 1912 in Saint Louis, Missouri
d. Jul 2, 1998 in New York, New York

Source: *AmAu&B; ASCAP 66, 80; BioIn 22; CamDcAB; CmpEPM; ConAu 85, 169; CurBio 59; FourBJA; InWom; MotPP; SmATA 16; WhoAm 74; WhoHol A*

Thompson, Llewellyn E, Jr.
American. Diplomat
US ambassador to the Soviet Union, 1957-62; 1967-69.
b. Aug 24, 1904 in Las Animas, Colorado
d. Feb 6, 1972 in Washington, District of Columbia
Source: *BioIn 4, 5, 6, 7, 8, 9, 11, 16, 23; CamDcAB; ColdWar 2; DcAmDH 89; NewYTBE 72; PolProf J*

Thompson, Marshall
[James Marshall Thompson]
American. Actor
Played in TV show "Daktari," 1966-69.
b. Nov 27, 1926 in Peoria, Illinois
d. May 25, 1992 in Royal Oak, Michigan
Source: *FilmgC; ForYSC; HalFC 84; IntMPA 84, 86, 88, 92; MGM; MotPP; MovMk; WhoHol A; WhoHrs 80*

Thompson, Mary
American. Centenarian
One of the oldest Americans, dying at age 120; daughter of slaves.
b. Mar 27, 1876?
d. Aug 3, 1996 in Orlando, Florida
Source: *BioIn 22; NewYTBS 96*

Thompson, Mickey
American. Auto Racer
First American to exceed 400 mph on land, 1960, but not officially recognized for record because of car's mechanical problems; shot to death with wife.
b. 1928
d. Mar 23, 1988 in Bradbury, California
Source: *BioIn 6, 8, 9, 11, 12, 13; FacFETw*

Thompson, Moose
[Wilbur Thompson]
American. Track Athlete
Shot putter; won gold medal, 1948 Olympics.
b. Apr 6, 1921 in Frankfort, South Dakota
Source: *WhoTr&F 73*

Thompson, Oscar
American. Critic, Author
Editor, *Musical America,* 1936-43.
b. Aug 10, 1887 in Crawfordsville, Indiana
d. Jul 2, 1945 in New York, New York
Source: *AmAu&B; AmNatBi; BakBD 78, 84, 92; BakBDTw; BiDAmM; CamDcAB; CurBio 45; DcAmB S3; DcNAA; IndAu 1917; NewGrDA 86; NewGrDM 80; OxCAmH; WhAm 2; WhNAA*

Thompson, Paul W(illiams)
American. Publishing Executive
With *Reader's Digest,* 1957-71, retiring as vp.
b. Dec 19, 1906
d. Feb 9, 1996 in Daytona Beach, Florida
Source: *BiDWWGF; BioIn 21, 22; CurBio 96N; InSci; WhoAm 74, 76, 78*

Thompson, Randall
American. Composer, Teacher
Wrote *Second Symphony,* 1932; choral piece, *Festival of Freedom,* 1942.
b. Apr 12, 1899 in New York, New York
d. Jul 9, 1984 in Boston, Massachusetts
Source: *AmComp; AmMWSc 73P; AmNatBi; AnObit 1984; ASCAP 66, 80; BakBD 78, 84, 92; BakBDTw; BakDcM; BiDAmM; BioIn 1, 4, 8, 14, 17, 24; BriBkM 80; CamBiEn; CamDcAB; CompSN, SUP; ConAmC 76, 82; ConAu 113; CpmDNM 82; IntWWM 77, 80; LegTOT; MusMk; NewAmDM; NewGrDA 86; NewGrDM 80; NewGrDO; NewYTBS 84; OxCMus; WhAm 8; WhoAm 74, 76, 78, 80, 82, 84; WhoE 75; WhoWor 74*

Thompson, Richard
English. Singer, Musician
Founding member of Fairport Convention 1967-1972; albums include *Shoot Out the Lights,* 1982 and *Amnesia,* 1988.
b. Apr 3, 1949 in London, England
Source: *BillEnR; BioIn 13; ChamBiD; CmpEGui; ConMus 7; DcArts; EncRk 88; EncRkSt; OnThGG; PenEncP; RolSEnR 83; Songw*

Thompson, Ruth Plumly
"Royal Historian of Oz"
American. Historian, Author
Wrote 19 "Oz" books after Baum's death, including *The Enchanted Island of Oz,* 1976.
b. Jul 27, 1891 in Philadelphia, Pennsylvania
d. Apr 6, 1976
Source: *ConAu 113, 134; DcLB 22; SmATA 66*

Thompson, Sada Carolyn
American. Actor
Played Kate Lawrence in "Family," 1976-79; won Tony for *Twigs,* 1971.
b. Sep 27, 1929 in Des Moines, Iowa
Source: *BiE&WWA; BioNews 75; ConTFT 4; CurBio 73; HalFC 84; InWom SUP; NewYTBE 71; NotNAT; PIP&P A; WhoAm 74, 76, 78, 80, 82, 84, 86, 88, 92, 99, 2000; WhoAmW 81, 83; WhoEnt 92, 98; WhoHol A; WhoThe 81; WorAl*

Thompson, Sam(uel Luther)
American. Baseball Player
Outfielder, 1885-98, 1906; led NL in batting, 1887; had lifetime .331 batting average; Hall of Fame, 1974.
b. Mar 5, 1860 in Danville, Indiana

d. Nov 7, 1922 in Detroit, Michigan
Source: *AmNatBi; Ballpl 90; BioIn 14, 15; WhoProB 73*

Thompson, Starley
American. Scientist
Climatologist and creator of computer model that allows him to make extremely long-term weather predictions, used in exploring the possible results of a nuclear war or the "Greenhouse Effect."
b. Jan 16, 1954 in Victoria, Texas
Source: *ConNews 87-3*

Thompson, Tazewell (Alfred)
American. Director
Director the works of up and coming African American playwrights as well as classics of world theater, dedicated to bringing more minorities into American theater; won the Helen Hayes Award, 1987, for *Abyssinia.*
b. May 27, 1954 in New York, New York
Source: *WhoAm 95; WhoEnt 92*

Thompson, Thomas
American. Journalist
At age 23 became youngest city editor with a major daily newspaper, *Houston Press,* 1957; wrote nonfiction best-sellers.
b. Oct 3, 1933 in Fort Worth, Texas
d. Oct 29, 1982 in Los Angeles, California
Source: *BioIn 13; ConAu 14NR, 65, 108; LiJour; NewYTBS 82; WrDr 80*

Thompson, Tiny
[Cecil Thompson]
Canadian. Hockey Player
Goalie, 1928-40, mostly with Boston; won Vezina Trophy four times; Hall of Fame, 1959.
b. May 31, 1905 in Sandon, British Columbia, Canada
d. Feb 9, 1981 in Calgary, Alberta, Canada
Source: *HocEn; WhoHcky 73; WhoSpor*

Thompson, Tommy George
American. Politician
Rep. governor of Wisconsin, 1987—.
b. Nov 19, 1941 in Elroy, Wisconsin
Source: *AlmAP 88; CurBio 95; IntWW 89, 91, 93, 97, 98, 2000; WhoAm 88, 90, 92, 94, 95, 96, 97, 98, 99, 2000; WhoAmL 79; WhoAmP 73, 75, 77, 79, 81, 83, 85, 87, 89, 91, 93, 95, 97, 1999; WhoMW 74, 76, 78, 80, 88, 90, 92, 93, 96, 98; WhoWor 89, 91*

Thompson, Vivian Laubach
American. Children's Author
Best known for book on the experience of moving: *Sad Day, Glad Day,* 1962.
b. Jan 7, 1911 in Jersey City, New Jersey
Source: *AuBYP 2, 3; BioIn 8, 9; ConAu 1NR, 1R; ForWC 70; SmATA 3; WrDr 76, 86*

Thompson, William Tappan

American. Humorist, Writer
Founder and editor of *Savannah Morning News*, 1850-82; wrote *Major Jones's Courtship*, 1843.
b. Aug 31, 1812 in Ravenna, Ohio
d. Mar 24, 1882 in Savannah, Georgia
Source: *AmAu; AmAu&B; AmBi; AmNatBi; ApCAB; BenetAL 91; BibAL 8; BiDSA; BioIn 3, 8, 12, 13, 15; CnDAL; DcAmAu; DcAmB; DcLB 3, 11; DcLEL; DcNAA; EncAHmr; EncALit; FifSWrB; NatCAB 9; OhA&B; OxCAmL 65, 83, 95; PeoHis; REnAL; SouWr; TwCBDA; WhAm HS*

Thompson Twins

[Tom Bailey; Alannan Currie; Joe Leway]
English. Music Group
Chesterfield, England group; hit singles include "Hold Me Now," 1984; "King for Just One Day," 1986.
Source: *BillEnR; EncPR&S 89; EncRk 88; EncRkSt; HarEnR 86; PenEncP; RkOn 85; WhsNW 85*

Thomson, Bobby

[Robert Brown Thomson]
"Nick the Greek"
American. Baseball Player
Outfielder, 1946-60; best known for home run that won pennant for NY Giants—"the shot heard round the world"—1951.
b. Oct 25, 1923 in Glasgow, Scotland
Source: *Ballpl 90; BiDAmSp Sup; BioIn 3, 4, 10, 11, 15, 16, 17; LegTOT; WhoProB 73*

Thomson, Charles Wyville, Sir

Scottish. Naturalist
Pioneered in deep-sea study; wrote oceanographic classic *Depths of the Sea*, 1873.
b. Mar 5, 1830 in Bonsyde, Scotland
d. Mar 10, 1882 in Bonsyde, Scotland
Source: *Alli SUP; AsBiEn; BiESc; BioIn 2, 6; BritAu 19; CamBiEn; CamDcSc; CelCen; ChamBiD; DcBiPP; DcNaB; DcScB; InSci; NewCol 75; WhDW; WhWE*

Thomson, Earl

Canadian. Track Athlete
Hurdler; won gold medal in 110-meter hurdles, 1920 Olympics.
b. Feb 15, 1895 in Prince Albert, Saskatchewan, Canada
d. Apr 19, 1971 in Annapolis, Maryland
Source: *BioIn 10; WhoTr&F 73*

Thomson, Elihu

American. Inventor, Scientist
Invented electric welding; obtained over 700 patents.
b. Mar 29, 1853 in Manchester, England
d. Mar 13, 1937 in Swampscott, Massachusetts
Source: *AmBi; AmNatBi; ApCAB; BiESc; BioIn 3, 4, 5, 11, 17, 21; CamBiEn; CamDcAB; ChamBiD; DcAmB S2; DcScB; HarEnUS; InSci; LarDcSc;*

LinLib S; NatCAB 10, 27; OxCAmH; RanHWDS; TwCBDA; WebAB 74, 79; WhAm 1; WhDW; WorInv

Thomson, George Paget, Sir

English. Physicist
Shared Nobel Prize in physics, 1937, with Clinton J Davisson.
b. May 3, 1892 in Cambridge, England
d. Sep 10, 1975 in Cambridge, England
Source: *AsBiEn; BiESc; BioIn 1, 2, 3, 5, 10, 11, 14, 15, 20; BlueB 76; CamBiEn; CamDcSc; ChamBiD; ConAu 4NR, 5R, 61; CurBio 47, 75, 75N; DcNaB 1971; DcScB S2; EncWB 98; InSci; IntWW 74, 75; LarDcSc; LngCTC; McGCEnS; McGEWB; McGMS 80; NotTwCS 1; ObitOF 79; RanHWDS; WhAm 6; WhE&EA; Who 74; WhoLA; WhoNob, 90, 95; WhoWor 74, 76; WorAl*

Thomson, Gordon

Canadian. Actor
Played Adam Carrington on TV drama "Dynasty," 1982-89.
b. Mar 2, 1951 in Ottawa, Ontario, Canada
Source: *BioIn 13; ConTFT 8*

Thomson, James

Scottish. Poet
Best known collection *The Seasons*, 1730, emphasized blank verse, nature as a theme within itself.
b. Sep 11, 1700 in Ednam, Scotland
d. Aug 27, 1748 in Richmond, England
Source: *Alli; AtlBL; BbD; Benet 87, 96; BiCoLiE; BiD&SB; BioIn 1, 2, 3, 4, 5, 6, 7, 9, 10, 12, 16, 17; BlkwCE; BlmGEL; BritAu; BritWr S3; CamBiEn; CamGEL; CamGLE; CasWL; ChamBiD; ChhPo, S1, S3; CmScLit; CnE&AP; CrtT 2, 4; CyWA 97; DcArts; DcBiPP; DcEnA; DcEnL; DcEuL; DcLB 95; DcLEL; DcNaB; EncWB 98; EvLB; GrWrEL P; LinLib L; LitC 16, 29, 40; LngCEL; McGEWB; MouLC 2; NewC; NewCBEL; NotNAT B; OxCEng 67, 85, 95; OxCMus; OxCThe 67; PenC ENG; RAdv 1, 14, 13-1; REn; RfGEnL 91; RGFBP; WebE&AL; WhDW*

Thomson, James

[B V; Bysshe Vanolis]
Scottish. Poet, Essayist
Best known for "The City of Dreadful Night," 1874, which expressed his despair of current political affairs.
b. Nov 23, 1834, Scotland
d. Jun 3, 1882 in London, England
Source: *Alli SUP; AtlBL; BbD; Benet 87, 96; BiCoLiE; BiD&SB; BioIn 2, 9, 11, 14; BlmGEL; BritAu 19; CamBiEn; CamGEL; CamGLE; CasWL; CelCen; ChamBiD; ChhPo, S1, S2; CmScLit; CnE&AP; DcArts; DcEnA; DcEuL; DcLB 35; DcLEL; DcNaB; DcPseud; EvLB; GrWrEL P; LngCEL; MouLC 4; NewC; NewCBEL; NinCLC 18; OxCEng 67, 85, 95; PenC ENG; REn; RfGEnL 91; WebE&AL*

Thomson, Joseph John, Sir

English. Scientist
Won 1906 Nobel Prize in physics for experiments in conduction of electricity through gases.
b. Dec 18, 1856 in Manchester, England
d. Aug 30, 1940 in Cambridge, England
Source: *AsBiEn; BiESc; BioIn 1, 2, 3, 4, 5, 7, 9, 11, 12, 13, 14, 15, 17, 20, 23; CamBiEn; CamDcSc; ChamBiD; CurBio 40; DcInv; DcNaB 1931; DcScB; EncWB 98; FacFETw; GrBr; InSci; LinLib L, S; McGCEnS; McGEWB; RAdv 14; RanHWDS; WhDW; WhE&EA; WhoLA; WhoNob, 90, 95; WorAl; WorScD*

Thomson, Ken(neth Roy)

[Lord Thomson of Fleet]
Canadian. Business Executive
Owner Thomson Newspapers, Toronto, 1953—; chairman, International Thomson Organization, Ltd; son of Roy.
b. Sep 1, 1923 in Toronto, Ontario, Canada
Source: *St&PR 84, 87, 91, 93, 96, 97, 98, 99, 2000; WhoAm 74, 76, 78, 80, 82, 84, 86, 88; WhoE 85, 89; WhoFI 83, 85, 87; WhoWor 74, 87*

Thomson, Peter William

Australian. Golfer
International golfer, 1950-65; won British Open five times.
b. Aug 23, 1929 in Melbourne, Australia
Source: *BioIn 8, 9, 13; FarE&A 81; IntWW 83, 89, 91, 93, 97, 98, 2000; WhoGolf*

Thomson, Roy Herbert

[Lord Thompson of Fleet]
English. Newspaper Publisher, Business Executive
Founded media empire, Thomson Organization Ltd; today has publishing, travel, oil.
b. Jun 5, 1894 in Toronto, Ontario, Canada
d. Aug 4, 1976 in London, England
Source: *BioIn 3, 5, 6, 7, 8, 10, 11, 17, 20; CanWW 70; ConAu 69; CurBio 60, 76; DcNaB 1971; DcTwBBL; FacFETw; IntWW 74; WhAm 7; Who 74; WorAl*

Thomson, Tom

Canadian. Artist
Short painting career ended when found mysteriously drowned; his Canadian landscapes directly influenced the Group of Seven.
b. Aug 4, 1877 in Claremont, Ontario, Canada
d. Jul 8, 1917 in Canoe Lake, Ontario, Canada
Source: *ArtsAmW 3; BioIn 1, 2, 4, 8, 9, 10, 11, 13, 18; CamBiEn; CreCan 1; DcTwArt; EncWB 98; IlBEAAW; McGDA; McGEWB; OxCArt; OxDcArt; PhDcTCA 77*

Thomson, Vernon Wallace
American. Politician
Rep. congressman from WI, 1960-75;
member of Federal Election
Commission, 1975-79.
b. Nov 5, 1905 in Richland Center,
Wisconsin
d. Apr 2, 1988 in Washington, District of
Columbia
Source: *BiDrAC; BiDrGov 1789;
BiDrUSC 89; BioIn 4, 5, 15, 16; CngDr
74; CurBio 58, 88; WhAm 9; WhoAm
74, 76, 78, 80; WhoAmP 73, 75, 77, 79,
81, 83, 85, 87; WhoGov 72, 75; WhoMW
74, 76*

Thomson, Virgil Garnett
American. Composer, Musician, Critic
Wrote 100 musical portraits; opera *Four
Saints in Three Acts,* 1934; won Oscar
for score of *Louisiana Story,* 1948.
b. Nov 25, 1896 in Kansas City,
Missouri
d. Sep 30, 1989 in New York, New
York
Source: *AmComp; ASCAP 66; BakBD
84; BakBDTw; Benet 96; BiDAmM;
BiE&WWA; CamDcAB; CurBio 40, 66;
DcCM; EncAAH; EncAB-H 1974, 1996;
IntWW 83; McGEWB; NewYTBE 71;
NotNAT; REn; REnAL; TwCA; WebAB
74, 79; WhoAm 86; WhoAmM 83;
WhoMus 72; WorAu 1900*

Thon, William
American. Artist
Leans toward cubism; paintings are of
architectural subjects.
b. Aug 8, 1906 in New York, New York
Source: *BioIn 1, 3, 4, 6, 7; McGDA;
WhAmArt 85; WhoAm 74, 76, 78, 80, 82,
84, 86, 88, 90, 92, 94, 95, 96, 97, 98,
99, 2000; WhoAmA 73, 76, 78, 80, 82,
84, 86, 89, 91, 93*

Thorarensen, Jakob
Icelandic. Poet
Wrote poetry that championed the
worker; *Snaljos,* 1914.
b. May 18, 1886 in Hunavatnssysla,
Iceland
d. 1972, Iceland
Source: *BioIn 2; WhE&EA*

Thorborg, Kerstin
Swedish. Opera Singer
Sometimes considered greatest
Wagnerian Mezzo-soprano of all time;
NY Met., 1936-50.
b. May 19, 1896 in Hedemora, Sweden
d. Apr 12, 1970 in Falun, Sweden
Source: *BakBD 78, 84, 92; BakBDTw;
BioIn 6, 8, 9, 11; CurBio 40, 70;
IntDcOp; MetOEnc; MusSN; NewEOp
71; NewGrDA 86; NewGrDM 80;
NewGrDO; NewYTBE 70; OxDcOp;
PenDiMP*

Thoreau, Henry David
American. Author
Wrote essay *Civil Disobedience,* 1849;
novel *Walden,* 1854.

b. Jul 12, 1817 in Concord,
Massachusetts
d. May 6, 1862 in Concord,
Massachusetts
Source: *ABCCoAm; Alli; AmAu;
AmAu&B; AmBi; AmCulL; AmNatBi;
AmNatWr; AmRef; AmSocL; AmWr;
AnCL; ApCAB; AtlBL; BbD; BbtC;
Benet 87, 96; BenetAL 91; BibAL 8;
BiCoLiE; BiDAmCa; BiD&SB;
BiDMoPL; BiDTran; BioIn 1, 2, 3, 4, 5,
6, 7, 8, 9, 10, 11, 12, 13, 14, 15, 16, 17,
18, 19, 20, 21, 22, 23, 24; CamBiEn;
CamDcAB; CamGEL; CamGLE;
CamHAL; CasWL; CelCen; ChamBiD;
Chambr 3; ChhPo; CnDAL; CnE&AP;
ColARen; CrtT 3, 4; CyAL 2; CyWA 58,
97; DcAmAu; DcAmB; DcArts; DcEnA;
DcLB 1, 183; DcLEL; DcNAA; Dis&D;
Drake; EncAAH; EncAB-H 1974, 1996;
EncALit; EncARH; EncEnv; EncEth;
EncRelA; EncWB 98; EnvEnc; EvLB;
GrWrEL N; HarEnUS; IlEncMy; InSci;
LegTOT; LinLib L, S; LiveWoA;
MagSAmL; McGEWB; MemAm; MouLC
3; NatCAB 2; NewEAmW; NewGrDA 86;
NinCLC 7, 21, 61; OxCAmH; OxCAmL
65, 83, 95; OxCCan; OxCEng 67, 85,
95; OxCPhil; PenC AM; PeoHis;
ProPowC; RadHan; RAdv 1, 14, 13-1;
RComAH; RComWL; REn; REnAL;
REnAW; RfGAmL 4, 87, 94; RGFAP;
TwCBDA; TwoTYeD; WebAB 74, 79;
WebE&AL; WhAm HS; WorAl; WorAlBi;
WorLitC; WrPh*

Thorek, Max
American. Surgeon
Founded International College of
Surgeons, 1935; developed successful
gall bladder surgery technique.
b. Mar 10, 1880, Austria-Hungary
d. Jan 25, 1960 in Chicago, Illinois
Source: *AmNatBi; BioIn 2, 5, 7; CurBio
51, 60; DcAmB, S6; NatCAB 48; WhAm
3; WhAmArt 85*

Thorez, Maurice
French. Politician
Leader of French Communist party,
secretary general, 1930-64, first pres.,
1964.
b. Apr 28, 1900 in Noyelles Godault,
France
d. Jul 11, 1964
Source: *BiDFrPL; BioIn 1, 2, 3, 4, 6, 7,
9, 17; ChamBiD; ConAu 113; CurBio
46, 64; DcPol; DcTwCCu 2; DcTwHis;
EncWB, 98; ObitOF 79; ObitT 1961;
WhAm 4*

Thorn, Gaston
Luxembourg. Politician
Pres., European Commission, exec.
section of European Economic
Community, 1981-84; prime minister
of Luxembourg, 1974-79.
b. Sep 3, 1928, Luxembourg
Source: *EncWB, 98; IntWW 74, 75, 76,
77, 78, 79, 80, 81, 82, 83, 89, 91, 93,
97, 98, 2000; IntYB 82; NewYTBS 75;
Who 82, 83, 85; WhoEIO 82; WhoIntA
2; WhoWor 74, 76, 78*

Thornburgh, Dick
[Richard Lewis Thornburgh]
American. Politician
Rep. governor of PA, 1979-87;
succeeded Edwin Meese as US
attorney general, 1988-91.
b. Jul 16, 1932 in Pittsburgh,
Pennsylvania
Source: *AlmAP 88; BiDrGov 1978,
1983; BiDrUSE 89; BioIn 11; IntWW 89,
91, 93, 97, 98, 2000; NewYTBS 75, 78,
90; Who 92, 94; WhoAm 76, 78, 80, 82,
86, 88, 90, 92, 94, 95, 96, 97, 98, 99;
WhoAmL 78, 79, 83, 90, 92, 94, 96, 98;
WhoAmP 79, 85, 97, 1999; WhoE 74,
75, 77, 79, 81, 83, 85, 86, 89, 91, 93;
WhoGov 72, 75, 77; WhoWor 82, 87, 89,
91*

Thorndike, Edward L(ee)
American. Psychologist
Animal behavior studies created
groundwork for connectionism theory.
b. Aug 31, 1874 in Williamsburg,
Massachusetts
d. Aug 9, 1949 in Montrose, New York
Source: *AmAu&B; AmDec 1900; AmLY;
AmNatBi; AmSocL; ApCAB X;
BiDAmEd; BiDcPsy; BiDPsy; BioIn 2, 3,
4, 8, 12, 14, 15; CamBiEn; CamDcAB;
ChamBiD; ConAu 121; CurBio 49;
DcAmAu; DcAmB S4; DcAmImH;
DcNAA; EncAB-H 1974, 1996; EncWB
98; InSci; LinLib L, S; LuthC 75;
McGEWB; NamesHP; NatCAB 15, 51;
ObitOF 79; OxCAmH; RAdv 14; REnAL;
WebAB 74, 79; WhAm 2; WhE&EA;
WhNAA*

Thorndike, Lynn
American. Historian
Wrote eight-vol. *History of Magic and
Experimental Science,* 1923-58.
b. Jul 24, 1882 in Lynn, Massachusetts
d. Dec 28, 1965 in New York, New
York
Source: *AmAu&B; AmNatBi; BioIn 4, 5,
7, 8, 22; CamDcAB; ConAu 111;
DcAmB S7; NatCAB 51; OhA&B;
REnAL; TwCA SUP; WhAm 4;
WhE&EA; WhNAA*

Thorndike, Sybil, Dame
[Agnes Sybil Thorndike]
English. Actor
Best known for her lead role in *Saint
Joan,* 1923.
b. Oct 24, 1882 in Gainsborough,
England
d. Jun 9, 1976 in Chelsea, England
Source: *BiE&WWA; BioIn 2, 3, 4, 9, 10,
11, 14; BlueB 76; CamGWoT; CnThe;
ContDcW 89; CurBio 53, 76N; DcArts;
DcNaB 1971; EncWT; Ent; Film 2;
FilmEn; FilmgC; GrBr; HalFC 80, 84,
88; IlWWBF, A; IntDcWB; IntWW 74,
75, 76; InWom, SUP; LegTOT; MotPP;
MovMk; NewC; NewYTBS 76; NotNAT
A, B; OxCThe 67, 83; PlP&P; REn;
WhAm 7; WhDW; Who 74; WhoAmW
74; WhoHol A; WhoThe 72, 77, 81N;
WhoWor 74; WhScrn 83; WorAl;
WorAlBi*

Thorne, Jim
American. Author, Adventurer
First non-Mexican to make successful
dive off Acapulco cliff, 1965.
b. 1922 in Milwaukee, Wisconsin
Source: *ConAu 1NR, 1R*

Thornell, Jack Randolph
American. Photographer
With AP, 1964—; won Pulitzer, 1967.
b. Aug 29, 1939 in Vicksburg,
Mississippi
Source: *WhoAm 74, 76, 78, 80, 82, 84,
86, 88, 90, 92, 94, 95, 96, 97, 98, 99,
2000; WhoPul; WhoSSW 73*

Thorneycroft, (George Edward) Peter
English. Politician
Member of Parliament, 1948-66;
chairman, Conservative Party, 1975-
81.
b. Jul 26, 1909
d. Jun 4, 1994 in London, England
Source: *BioIn 3, 4, 20; CurBio 94N;
IntWW 93; WhAm 11; WhoWor 74, 76,
78, 84, 87, 89, 91, 93*

Thornhill, Claude
American. Songwriter, Bandleader
Led major dance band, 1940s; noted for
novelty arrangements.
b. Aug 10, 1908 in Terre Haute, Indiana
d. Jul 1, 1965 in Caldwell, New Jersey
Source: *ASCAP 66, 80; BakBD 84;
BiDAmM; BioIn 7, 9, 12; CmpEPM;
WhoHol B; WhoJazz 72; WhScrn 74, 77,
83*

Thornton, Billy Bob
American. Actor, Filmmaker
Actor on television and in films; wrote,
directed, and starred in the critically
acclaimed film *Sling Blade,* 1996, for
which he received Best Actor and Best
Screenplay Academy Award
nominations; signed three-film deal
with Miramax Pictures, 1997.
b. c. 1956 in Arkansas
Source: *News 97*

Thornton, Charles Bates
"Tex"
American. Businessman
Helped establish Litton Industries, served
as chm., CEO, 1953-81; headed
"Whiz Kids" team at Ford Motor
Co., 1946-48.
b. Jul 22, 1913 in Haskell, Texas
d. Nov 24, 1981 in Holmby Hills,
California
Source: *AnObit 1981; BiDAmBL 83;
BioIn 6, 8, 9, 12, 13, 23; CamDcAB;
CelR; CurBio 70, 82; Dun&B 79; IntWW
74, 75, 76, 77, 78, 79, 80, 81; LElec;
NewYTBS 81; WhAm 8; WhoAm 74, 76,
78, 80, 84; WhoFI 74, 75, 79, 81;
WhoWest 74, 76, 78, 80, 82; WhoWor 74*

Thornton, Matthew
American. Continental Congressman,
Physician
Congressman from NH; signed
Declaration of Independence, 1776.
b. 1714?, Ireland
d. Jun 24, 1803 in Newburyport,
Massachusetts
Source: *Alli; AmBi; AmNatBi; ApCAB;
BiAUS; BiDrAC; BiDrACR; BiDrUSC
89; BioIn 7, 8, 9, 23; DcAmB;
DcAmMeB, 84; DcIrB 1, 2, 3; Drake;
EncAR; EncCRAm; HarEnUS; NatCAB
11; TwCBDA; WhAm HS; WhAmP;
WhAmRev*

Thornton, Willie Mae
"Big Mama"
American. Singer
Known for renditions of "Have Mercy
Baby"; "Hound Dog"; "Ball and
Chain."
b. Dec 11, 1926 in Montgomery,
Alabama
d. Jul 25, 1984 in Los Angeles,
California
Source: *AmNatBi; AnObit 1984;
BiDAfM; BioIn 19, 23; BluesWW;
ConAu 113; EncRk 88; GuBlues;
HanAmWH; InB&W 80, 85; NewYTBS
84; NotBlAW 2; PenEncP; RkOn 74*

Thorp, Willard Long
American. Economist
Helped draft the Marshall Plan for the
economic recovery of Europe after
WW II.
b. May 24, 1899 in Oswego, New York
d. May 10, 1992 in Pelham,
Massachusetts
Source: *AmMWSc 73S; BioIn 1, 2, 11,
16, 17, 18, 19; BlueB 76; ConAu 1R,
28NR, 85NR, 130, 137; IntWW 74, 75,
76, 77, 78, 79, 80, 81, 82, 83, 89, 91;
NewYTBS 90; WhAm 10; WhoAm 74, 76,
78; WhoE 91; WhoWor 74; WrDr 76*

Thorpe, Grace F.
American. Political Activist
Daughter of Olympian Jim Thorpe; made
efforts to reinstate her father's medals
and to establish a museum in his
honor; former lobbyist for the National
Congress of American Indians.
b. 1921
Source: *BioIn 21, 22; NotNaAm*

Thorpe, Jeremy
[John Jeremy Thorpe]
English. Political Leader
Liberal MP, 1959-79; held balance of
power in govt., mid-1970s.
b. Apr 29, 1929 in London, England
Source: *BioIn 7, 8, 10, 11, 12, 17; BlueB
76; CurBio 74; DcPol; FacFETw;
IntWW 74, 75, 76, 77, 78, 79, 80, 81, 82,
83, 89, 91, 98; IntYB 78, 79, 80, 81, 82;
NewYTBS 74, 78; Who 74, 82, 83, 85,
88, 90, 92; WhoWor 74, 76, 78, 80, 82*

Thorpe, Jim
[James Francis Thorpe]
American. Track Athlete
Called "greatest athlete ever"; only
person ever to win gold medals in
decathalon, pentathlon, 1912
Olympics; played pro baseball,
football; first pres. of NFL, 1920-21;
Burt Lancaster starred in film of life,
1951.
b. May 28, 1888 in Shawnee, Oklahoma
d. Mar 28, 1953 in Los Angeles,
California
Source: *AmDec 1910; AmIndBi;
AmNatBi; BiDAmSp FB; BiNAW SupB;
BioIn 2, 3, 4, 5, 6, 7, 8, 9, 10, 11, 12,
13, 14, 15, 16, 17, 18, 19, 20, 21, 22,
23, 24; CamBiEn; ConHero 2; CurBio
50, 53; DcAmB S5; DcPseud; EncAB-H
1974, 1996; EncNAB; EncWB, 98;
FacFETw; HalFC 80, 84, 88; LegTOT;
NatNAFi; OxCAmH; RComAH; WebAB
74, 79; WhAm 4, HSA; WhoFtbl 74;
WhoHol B; WhoProB 73; WhoSpor;
WhoTr&F 73; WhScrn 74, 77; WorAl*

Thorpe, Thomas Bangs
American. Humorist
Created tall-tale "The Big Bear of
Arkansas."
b. Mar 1, 1815 in Westfield,
Massachusetts
d. Sep 20, 1878 in New York, New
York
Source: *Alli; AmAu; AmAu&B; ApCAB;
BibAL 8; BiDSA; BioIn 4, 6, 8, 12, 13,
15; CnDAL; CyAL 2; DcAmAu; DcAmB;
DcEnL; DcLB 3, 11; DcLEL; DcNAA;
Drake; EncAAH; EncAHmr; EncALit;
FifSWrB; GrWrEL N; HarEnUS;
HisDcWJ; NatCAB 6; NewEAmW;
NewYHSD; OxCAmL 65, 83; PeoHis;
RAdv 14; REnAL; REnAW; RfGAmL 4,
87, 94; SouWr; TwCBDA; WebAB 74,
79; WebE&AL; WhAm HS*

Thorvaldsen, Albert Bertel
[Bertel Thorwaldsen]
Danish. Sculptor
Statues of various figures include Venus,
Psyche, Jason.
b. 1770 in Copenhagen, Denmark
d. 1844
Source: *DcArts; DcNiCA; NewCol 75;
OxCArt; WebBD 83*

Thou, Jacques Auguste de
French. Historian, Statesman
Wrote *Historia sui Temporis*, 1604-08.
b. Oct 8, 1553
d. May 7, 1617
Source: *DcBiPP; DcCathB; DcEuL;
NewCBEL; NewCol 75; OxCFr; REn;
WebBD 83*

Threadgill, Henry
American. Jazz Musician, Composer
Jazz saxophinist and composer; albums
include *Easily Slip into Another
World,* 1987.
b. Feb 14, 1944 in Chicago, Illinois
Source: *AllMGJa; BiDJaz; BioIn 15;
ConMus 9; NewGrDJ 88; PenEncP*

Three Dog Night
[Michael Allsup; James Greenspoon; Daniel Hutton; Skip Konte; Charles Negron; Joseph Schermine; Floyd Sneed; Cory Wells]
Australian. Music Group
Rock band formed, 1968; hits include "Joy to the World," 1971.
Source: *BiDAmM; BilIEnR; ConMuA 80A; ConMus 5; EncPR&S 74, 89; EncRk 88; EncRkSt; HarEnR 86; IlEncRk; NewAmDM; PenEncP; RkOn 78, 84; RkWho 96; RolSEnR 83; WhoRock 81; WhoRocM 82*

Three Stooges, The
[Joe Besser; Joe DeRita; Larry Fine; Curly Howard; Moe Howard; Shemp Howard]
American. Comedy Team
Performed in vaudeville, 1923; made 200 short films, 1934-58.
Source: *AmNatBi; BioIn 10, 11; CamBiEn; EncAFC; FacFETw; FilmEn; ForYSC; Funs; GrMovC; HalFC 84, 88; IntDcF 1-3, 2-3; IntMPA 94N; JoeFr; MotPP; NewYTBS 75, 88; ObitOF 79; What 4; WhoCom; WhoHol 92, B; WhoHrs 80*

Threlkeld, Richard D
American. Broadcast Journalist
Correspondent CBS News, 1966-82; chief correspondent ABC News, 1982-89.
b. Nov 30, 1937 in Cedar Rapids, Iowa
Source: *ConAu 65; WhoAm 84, 86; WhoAmP 87, 89, 91, 93, 95, 97, 1999; WhoTelC*

Throckmorton, Cleon
American. Designer
Pioneer in stage, set design; began career while working on Eugene O'Neill's plays, 1920s.
b. Oct 8, 1897 in Atlantic City, New Jersey
d. Oct 23, 1965
Source: *BiE&WWA; BioIn 7; CamGWoT; CurBio 43, 65; LegTOT; NotNAT B; OxCAmT 84; PIP&P; WhAm 4; WhAmArt 85; WhThe*

Throneberry, Marv(in Eugene)
"Marvelous Marv"
American. Baseball Player
First baseman, 1955, 1958-63; best known for time with NY Mets, where he became symbol of team's inept play in early yrs.
b. Sep 12, 1933 in Collierville, Tennessee
Source: *Ballpl 90; BaseEn 88; BioIn 20; LegTOT; WhoProB 73*

Thucydides
Greek. Historian
Wrote *History of the Peloponnesian War,* called first modern history.
b. c. 460BC in Athens, Greece
d. c. 399BC in Athens, Greece
Source: *AncWr; AtlBL; BbD; Benet 87, 96; BiCoLiE; BiD&SB; CamBiEn;*

CasWL; ChamBiD; ClMLC 17; CyWA 58; DcBiPP; DcEnL; Dis&D; EncWB 98; GloEncH; GrFLW; Grk&L; McGEWB; NewC; OxCClC; OxCClL, 89; OxCEng 67, 85, 95; OxDcByz; PenC CL; RAdv 14; RComWL; REn; RfGWoL 95; WhDW

Thuilier, Raymond
French. Chef
Known for his classic French cuisine with distinct sauces and multiple courses.
b. Jan 11, 1897 in Chambery, France
d. Jun 20, 1993 in Carita, France
Source: *AnObit 1993; BioIn 19; WhoFr 79*

Thuku, Harry
Kenyan. Politician
Pioneer in the development of modern African nationalism in Kenya.
b. 1895 in Kambui, Kenya
d. 1970
Source: *BioIn 9; EncWB 98; McGEWB*

Thulin, Ingrid
Swedish. Actor
Films include *Wild Strawberries; The Damned; Cries and Whispers.*
b. Jan 27, 1929 in Solleftea, Sweden
Source: *BiDFilm, 81, 94; BioIn 6, 11, 17; CelR; ConTFT 9; EncEurC; EncWT; FilmEn; FilmgC; ForYSC; HalFC 80, 84, 88; IntDcF 1-3, 2-3; IntMPA 75, 76, 77, 78, 79, 80, 81, 82, 84, 86, 88, 92, 94, 96; IntWW 74, 75, 76, 77, 78, 79, 80, 81, 82, 83, 89, 91, 93, 97, 98, 2000; IntWWW 2; InWom SUP; ItaFilm; LegTOT; MotPP; MovMk; OxCFilm; WhoEnt 92, 98; WhoHol 92, A; WhoWor 74, 76, 78, 84, 87, 89, 91, 95, 96, 97, 98, 99, 2000; WomWMM; WorAl; WorAlBi; WorEFlm*

Thum, Marcella
American. Children's Author
Won Edgar for first book, *Mystery at Crane's Landing,* 1964; other books include *Margarite,* 1987.
Source: *AuBYP 2S, 3; BioIn 9, 13; ConAu 6NR, 9R, 21NR, 49NR; DcAmChF 1960; IntAu&W 77, 86, 89, 91, 93; SmATA 3, 28; TwCRHW 90, 94; WrDr 76, 80, 82, 84, 86, 88, 90, 92*

Thurber, Charles
American. Inventor
Patented, 1843, hand printing machine that preceded typewriter.
b. Jan 2, 1803 in East Brookfield, Massachusetts
d. Nov 7, 1886 in Nashua, New Hampshire
Source: *BioIn 12; DcAmB; WhAm HS*

Thurber, James Grover
American. Author
Major contributor to *New Yorker* mag., 1927-52; known for whimsical writings, cartoons; best-known short story: "The Secret Life of Walter

Mitty"; book: *The Thurber Carnival,* 1945.
b. Dec 8, 1894 in Columbus, Ohio
d. Nov 2, 1961 in New York, New York
Source: *AmAu&B; AnCL; AtlBL; AuBYP 2; Benet 96; BiDAmNC; BkCL; CamBiEn; CamDcAB; CasWL; ChamBiD; CnDAL; CnMWL; ConAmA; ConAu 73; ConLC 5, 11; CurBio 40, 62; EncAB-H 1996; MajTwCW 2; OxCAmL 65; OxCTwCL; PenC AM; RfGAmL 4; RfGShF 2; RGTwCWr; SJGChWr 5; SJGFanW; TwCA; WorAu 1900*

Thurman, Howard
American. Educator
Baptist minister since 1925; taught theology, dean of chapel, Howard U., 1932-44; first full-time black professor, Boston U., School of Theology, 1953-65.
b. Nov 18, 1900 in Daytona Beach, Florida
d. Apr 10, 1981 in San Francisco, California
Source: *AnObit 1981; BioIn 19; BlkAWP; BlkWr 1; BlueB 76; CmCal; ConAu 25NR, 97, 103; ConBlB 3; CurBio 55, 81, 81N; DcAmReB 2; Ebony 1; LinLib L, S; LivgBAA; NegAl 83, 89; NewYTBS 81; NotBlAM; RelLAm 1, 2; SchCGBL; SelBAAf; SelBAAu; WhAm 7; WhoAm 74, 76, 78; WhoBlA 1, 2; WhoRel 77*

Thurman, Uma
[Mrs. Ethan Hawke]
American. Actor
Appeared in *Dangerous Liaisons,* 1988; *Henry and June,* 1990; *Pulp Fiction,* 1994.
b. Apr 29, 1970 in Boston, Massachusetts
Source: *ConTFT 10; CurBio 96; IntMPA 92, 94, 96; IntWW 97, 98, 2000; IntWWW 2; LegTOT; News 94, 94-2; OsStAZ; WhoHol 92*

Thurman, Wallace (Henry)
[Patrick Casey; Ethel Belle Mandrake]
American. Author, Journalist
A novelist, playwright, critic, and editor active during the Harlem Renaissance of the 1920s, published literary journals the *Messenger* and *Fire!!*; became cynical and vehemently critical of the artistic movement.
b. Aug 16, 1902 in Salt Lake City, Utah
d. Dec 21, 1934 in New York, New York
Source: *BlkWr 3; ConAu 81NR; DcLB 51; EncALit; GayLL 2*

Thurmond, Nate
[Nathaniel Thurmond]
American. Basketball Player
Center, 1963-77, mostly with San Francisco-Golden State; known for rebounding; Hall of Fame, 1984.
b. Jul 25, 1941 in Akron, Ohio
Source: *BasBi; BiDAmSp BK; InB&W 80; NewYTBS 76; OfNBA 87; WhoAfA 9,*

10, 11, 12; *WhoAm 78; WhoBbl 73;*
WhoBlA 1, 2, 3, 4, 5, 6, 7, 8; WhoSpor

Thurmond, Strom
[James Strom Thurmond]
American. Politician
Dem., then Rep. senator from SC,
    1955—; led segregationists, 1940s-
    50s; conducted longest Senate
    filibuster, 24 hrs., 1957.
b. Dec 5, 1902 in Edgefield, South
    Carolina
Source: *AlmAP 82, 84, 88, 92, 96, 2000;*
AmPolLe; BiDrAC; BiDrGov 1789;
BiDrUSC 89; BioIn 1, 4, 5, 6, 7, 8, 9,
10, 11, 13, 18, 20, 21, 22, 23, 24; BlueB
76; CelR, 90; CivRSt; CngDr 74, 77, 79,
81, 83, 85, 87, 89, 91, 93, 95; ConAu
89; CurBio 92; EncAAH; EncSoH;
EncWB; IntWW 74, 75, 76, 77, 78, 79,
80, 81, 82, 83, 89, 91, 93, 97, 98, 2000;
IntYB 78, 79, 80, 81, 82; LegTOT;
PolPar; PolProf E, J, K, NF; PolsAm
84; PresAR 1996; WebAB 74, 79;
WhoAm 74, 76, 78, 80, 82, 84, 86, 88,
90, 92, 94, 95, 96, 97, 98, 99, 2000;
WhoAmP 73, 75, 77, 79, 81, 83, 85, 87,
89, 91, 93, 95, 97, 1999; WhoGov 72,
75, 77; WhoSSW 73, 75, 76, 78, 80, 82,
84, 86, 88, 91, 93, 95, 97, 99; WhoWor
74, 78, 80, 82, 84, 87, 89, 91; WorAl;
WorAlBi

Thurow, Lester C
American. Economist, Educator
Most influential economist of his
    generation; wrote *Zero-Sum Society,*
    1980.
b. May 7, 1938 in Livingston, Montana
Source: *AmEA 74; BioIn 9, 10, 12, 15;*
ConAu 81; CurBio 90; WhoAm 88;
WhoEc 86; WhoFI 85; WrDr 92

Thurston, Howard
American. Magician
Practiced magic since childhood; toured
    US, 1907-08.
b. Jul 20, 1869 in Columbus, Ohio
d. Apr 13, 1936 in Miami, Florida
Source: *AmNatBi; BioIn 4, 5, 7, 16;*
CamDcAB; ChhPo; DcAmB S2; DcNAA;
MagIlD; NatCAB 10; OhA&B; OxCAmT
84; WhAm 1; WhJnl

Thurstone, Louis Leon
American. Psychologist
The most renowned psychometrician of
    his time, he pioneered mental
    measurement and testing through
    quantitative methods.
b. May 29, 1887 in Chicago, Illinois
d. Sep 29, 1955 in Chapel Hill, North
    Carolina
Source: *AmNatBi; BiDAmEd; BiDcPsy;*
BiDPsy; BioIn 1, 2, 4, 6; CamBiEn;
ChamBiD; DcAmB S5; EncWB 98;
InSci; McGEWB; NamesHP; WhAm 3;
WhNAA

Thutmose, III
Egyptian. King
Ruler stabilized his empire by
    reestablishing Egyptian rule in Syria
    and Palestine.
b. 1504BC
d. 1450BC
Source: *BioIn 20; ChamBiD; DicTyr;*
EncWB 98; GenMudB; McGEWB

Thyssen, Fritz
German. Industrialist
Early Nazi supporter; broke with party,
    fled to Switzerland, WW II.
b. Nov 9, 1873
d. Feb 8, 1951, Argentina
Source: *BioIn 1, 2, 3, 14; CurBio 40, 51;*
EncTR, 91; WorAl; WorAlBi

Thyssen-Bornemisza de Kaszan,
    Hans Heinrich, Baron
Netherlands. Art Collector
Art collection considered finest in the
    world, second only to the Queen of
    England.
b. Apr 13, 1921 in The Hague,
    Netherlands
Source: *BioIn 12; CurBio 89; IntWW 91;*
Who 92

Tiant, Luis Clemente
Cuban. Baseball Player
Pitcher, 1964-82, mostly with Boston;
    led AL in ERA twice.
b. Nov 23, 1940 in Havana, Cuba
Source: *BioIn 9, 10, 11; InB&W 80, 85;*
WhoAm 78, 80, 82; WhoBlA 2, 3;
WhoProB 73; WorAl

Tibbets, Paul Warfield
American. Pilot
Piloted the *Enola Gay,* plane that
    dropped atomic bomb on Hiroshima,
    Aug 6, 1945.
b. 1915
Source: *BioIn 10, 11, 12; St&PR 84, 87;*
WhWW-II

Tibbett, Lawrence Mervil
American. Opera Singer, Actor
Popular leading baritone, NY Met.,
    1923-50; starred in film *New Moon*
    with Grace Moore, 1931.
b. Nov 16, 1896 in Bakersfield,
    California
d. Jul 15, 1960 in New York, New York
Source: *BakBD 84; ChamBiD; CurBio*
45, 60; DcAmB S6; FilmgC; LinLib S;
WhAm 4; WhoHol B; WhScrn 74, 77

Tiberius Julius Caesar Augustus
[Tiberius Claudius Nero]
Roman. Ruler
Second Roman Emperor, AD 14-37.
b. Nov 16, 42BC in Rome, Italy
d. Mar 16, 37AD in Campania, Italy
Source: *EncWB 98; GenMudB;*
McGEWB; NewCol 75; REn

Tiburzi, Bonnie
American. Pilot
First woman hired by a major airline,
    American Airlines 727 fleet, 1973.
b. 1948?
Source: *BioIn 9, 12, 17; ConAu 136;*
SmATA 65; WomFir; WrDr 94

Tichatschek, Joseph
German. Opera Singer
Principal tenor, Dresden Opera, 1837-70;
    admired by Wagner.
b. Jul 11, 1807 in Weckseldorf, Germany
d. Jan 18, 1886 in Dresden, Germany
Source: *BakBD 84, 92; BioIn 14, 16;*
NewEOp 71; OxDcOp

Tickner, Charlie
[Charles Tickner]
American. Skater
Four-time US champion figure skater,
    1977-80; world champion, 1978.
b. Nov 13, 1953 in Oakland, California
Source: *BiDAmSp BK; BioIn 11, 12;*
LegTOT; WhoSpor; WorAl

Ticknor, George
American. Historian
Wrote *History of Spanish Literature,*
    1849; founded Boston Public Library,
    1852.
b. Aug 1, 1791 in Boston, Massachusetts
d. Jan 26, 1871 in Boston, Massachusetts
Source: *Alli, SUP; AmAu; AmAu&B;*
AmBi; AmNatBi; ApCAB; BbD; Benet
87; BenetAL 91; BiDAmEd; BiD&SB;
BiDTran; BioIn 1, 2, 3, 5, 7, 11, 12, 16,
20, 23; CasWL; ChamBiD; Chambr 3;
ChhPo S1; CyAL 1; DcAmAu; DcAmB;
DcAmBC; DcAmLiB; DcBiPP; DcEnL;
DcLB 1, 59, 140; DcNAA; DcSpL;
Drake; EncALit; EvLB; HarEnUS;
LegTOT; NatCAB 6; NewYHSD;
OxCAmH; OxCAmL 65, 83, 95; OxCEng
67; OxCSpan; PeoHis; REn; REnAL;
TwCBDA; WebAB 74, 79; WhAm HS

Tidyman, Ernest
American. Author, Screenwriter
Wrote novel, screenplay *Shaft,* won best
    screenplay Oscar for *The French*
    Connection, 1971.
b. Jan 1, 1928 in Cleveland, Ohio
d. Jul 14, 1984 in London, England
Source: *AnObit 1984; BioIn 8, 9, 12;*
ConAu 29NR, 73, 113; EncSF, 93;
GangFlm; HalFC 84, 88; ScF&FL 92;
TwCCr&M 80, 85, 91; WhAm 8; WhoAm
76, 78, 80, 82; WrDr 82, 84

Tieck, (Johann) Ludwig
German. Author
Novelist is considered the most versatile
    and productive writer of the German
    Romantic Movement.
b. May 5, 1773 in Berlin, Germany
d. Apr 28, 1853 in Berlin, Germany
Source: *BiD&SB; BioIn 3, 4, 5, 7, 8, 9,*
11; CamBiEn; CelCen; ChamBiD;
DcArts; DcEuL; EuAu; McGEWD 72,
84; NewGrDO; RfGWoL 95; WhoHr&F

Tiede, Tom Robert
American. Journalist
Expert on war; correspondent for
  Newspaper Enterprise Assn., 1964-92.
b. Feb 24, 1937 in Huron, South Dakota
Source: AmAu&B; BiDAmNC; WhoAm
  74, 76, 78, 80, 82, 84, 86, 88, 90, 92,
  96, 97, 98, 99, 2000; WhoE 74, 99;
  WhoFI 98; WhoSSW 95; WhoWor 91,
  93, 95, 96, 97, 98, 2000

Tiegs, Cheryl
American. Actor, Model
Highest paid model of 1970s; wrote The
  Way to Natural Beauty, 1980.
b. Sep 25, 1947 in Alhambra, California
Source: BioIn 11, 12, 13; BkPepl; CelR
  90; CurBio 82; InWom SUP; LegTOT;
  NewYTBS 78; WhoAm 84, 86; WhoAmW
  85, 87

Tiepolo, Giambattista
[Giovanni Battista Tiepol]
Italian. Artist
Works include frescoes, portraits, palace
  facades.
b. Mar 5, 1696 in Venice, Italy
d. Mar 27, 1770 in Madrid, Spain
Source: AtlBL; LiveWoA; McGEWB;
  OxCArt; REn; WebBD 83

Tiepolo, Giovanni Domenico
Italian. Artist
Paintings include decorations of royal
  palace at Wurzburg.
b. 1727
d. 1804
Source: BioIn 1, 3, 5, 9, 13, 22, 24;
  ClaDrA; McGDA; WebBD 83

Tieri, Frank
"Funzi"; "Funzola"; "The Old Man"
Italian. Criminal
First man ever convicted of heading an .
  organized-crime family, 1980; died
  before serving 10 yr. sentence.
b. 1904 in Castel Gandolfo, Italy
d. Mar 29, 1981 in New York, New
  York
Source: BioIn 11, 12; MafEnc; NewYTBS
  81

Tierney, Gene
American. Actor
Played title role in Laura, 1944; wrote
  Self-Portrait, 1979.
b. Nov 11, 1920 in New York, New
  York
d. Nov 6, 1991 in Houston, Texas
Source: AnObit 1991; BiDFilm, 81, 94;
  BioIn 5, 8, 9, 10, 11, 17, 18, 23, 24;
  CmMov; ConAu 116; ConTFT 11;
  FemmeNo; FilmEn; FilmgC; ForYSC;
  GangFlm; HalFC 80, 84, 88; IntDcF 1-
  3, 2-3; IntMPA 75, 76, 77, 78, 79, 80,
  81, 82, 84, 86, 88, 92; InWom, SUP;
  LegTOT; MotPP; MovMk; NewYTBS 91;
  OsStAZ; WhAm 10; What 5; WhoHol 92,
  A; WorAl; WorAlBi; WorEFlm

Tietjen, Heinz
German. Conductor, Producer
Director, Bayreuth Festival, 1931-44;
  noted Wagnerian producer.
b. Jun 24, 1881 in Tangiers, Morocco
d. Nov 1, 1967 in Bayreuth, Germany
  (West)
Source: BakBD 84, 92; BakBDTw;
  CmOp; NewEOp 71; NewGrDO;
  OxDcOp

Tietjens, Eunice
American. Poet, Author
Wrote poems Profiles on China, 1917;
  novel Jake, 1921.
b. Jul 29, 1884 in Chicago, Illinois
d. Sep 6, 1944 in Chicago, Illinois
Source: AmAu&B; AmNatBi; BenetAL
  91; BioAmW; BioIn 4; ChhPo, S1, S2,
  S3; ConAmL; CurBio 44; DcLB 54;
  DcLEL; DcNAA; FemiCLE; InWom,
  SUP; JBA 34; NotAW; OxCAmL 65, 83,
  95; OxCTwCP; REn; REnAL; TwCA,
  SUP; WhAm 2; WhNAA

Tiffany
[Tiffany Renee Darwish]
American. Singer
Million-selling album, 1987; included
  "Could've Been," "I Think We're
  Alone Now."
b. Oct 2, 1971 in Norwalk, California
Source: DcPseud; EncRkSt; LegTOT

Tiffany, Charles Lewis
American. Jeweler
Founded exclusive jewelry store, Tiffany
  & Co., 1837; manufactured silverware,
  jewelry, art pieces.
b. Feb 15, 1812 in Killingly, Connecticut
d. Feb 18, 1902 in Irvington-on-Hudson,
  New York
Source: AmBi; AmNatBi; BioIn 7, 13,
  15; CamBiEn; ChamBiD; DcAmB; Entr;
  LinLib S; NatCAB 2; TwCBDA; WebAB
  74, 79; WhAm 1, 2; WorAl

Tiffany, Louis Comfort
American. Artist, Designer
VP, director, Tiffany and Co. who
  discovered formula for making
  decorative glass, "Tiffany Favrile
  glass"; known for Tiffany lamps.
b. Feb 18, 1848 in New York, New
  York
d. Jan 17, 1933 in New York, New York
Source: AmBi; AmCulL; AmDec 1900;
  AmNatBi; AntBDN A; ApCAB; ArtsAmW
  3; Benet 87, 96; BioIn 1, 2, 3, 4, 5, 6, 7,
  8, 9, 10, 11, 12, 13, 15, 16, 17, 18, 19,
  22, 24; BriEAA; CamBiEn; CamDcAB;
  CenC; ChamBiD; DcAmB; DcArts;
  DcD&D; DcNiCA; DcTwArt; DcTwDes;
  EncAB-H 1974, 1996; EncWB 98; GayN;
  IlDcG; LinLib S; McGDA; McGEWB;
  NatCAB 7, 36; OxCDecA; OxDcArt;
  PenDiDA 89; PeoHis; PhDcTCA 77;
  REn; TwCBDA; WebAB 74, 79; WebBD
  83; WhAm 1; WorAl; WorAlBi

Tiffeau, Jacques Emile
French. Fashion Designer
Winner of two Coty Awards who
  designed coats, sportswear for
  Originala since 1976.
b. Oct 11, 1927 in Chenevelles, France
Source: WhAm 9; WhoAm 74, 76, 78, 80,
  82; WorFshn

Tiffin, Pamela Kimberley
American. Model, Actor
Films include The Pleasure Seekers,
  1964; Harper, 1966.
b. Oct 13, 1942 in Oklahoma City,
  Oklahoma
Source: FilmgC; ForWC 70; HalFC 84;
  IntMPA 86; MotPP; WhoAm 74, 76, 78;
  WhoAmW 74; WhoHol A

Tiglath-pileser, III
Assyrian. King
Reigned as king of Assyria from 745 to
  727 B.C; known as an outstanding
  administrator and warrior, he restored
  the empire to its former position of
  power.
d. 731BC, Babylon
Source: BioIn 9; McGEWB

Tikaram, Tanita
American. Singer, Songwriter
Folk-rock performer; debut album
  Ancient Heart, 1988.
b. 1970, Germany (West)
Source: BioIn 16; ConMus 9

Tikhomirov, Vasily Dmitrievich
Russian. Dancer
Premier danseur Bolshoi Ballet 1893;
  Bolshoi teacher and director; helped
  maintain Bolshoi's classic techniques.
b. Mar 30, 1876 in Moscow, Russia
d. Jun 20, 1956 in Moscow, Union of
  Soviet Socialist Republics
Source: BiDSovU; BioIn 4, 14;
  FacFETw

Tilberis, Elizabeth
American. Editor
Editor-in-chief, Harper's Bazaar, 1992-
  99.
b. Sep 7, 1947 in Bath, England
d. Apr 21, 1999 in New York, New
  York
Source: News 94, 94-3; Who 92

Tilbrook, Glenn
English. Singer, Musician
Guitarist, vocalist; collaborated with
  Chris Difford on over 600 songs.
b. Aug 31, 1957 in London, England
Source: LegTOT; OnThGG; WhoRocM
  82

Tilden, Bill
[William Tatem, Jr. Tilden]
"Big Bill"
American. Tennis Player
US tennis champion, 1920-25, 1929;
  only man to win US championship six
  consecutive yrs.

b. Feb 10, 1893 in Philadelphia,
Pennsylvania
d. Jun 5, 1953 in Hollywood, California
Source: *AmNatBi; BioIn 17, 21, 23;*
BuCMET; CamBiEn; ChamBiD;
CmpQue; DcAmB S5; FacFETw;
LegTOT; NotNAT B; RComAH; WebAB
74; WhAm 4; WhoHol B; WhoSpor;
WhScrn 74, 77, 83

Tilden, Samuel Jones
American. Politician, Lawyer
Dem. governor, NY, 1875-76; ran for
pres. against Rutherford B Hayes.
b. Feb 9, 1814 in New Lebanon, New
York
d. Aug 4, 1886 in Yonkers, New York
Source: *Alli SUP; AmAu&B; AmBi;*
AmNatBi; AmPolLe; ApCAB; BiAUS;
BiDrGov 1789; BioIn 2, 5, 7, 8, 9, 10;
CamBiEn; CamDcAB; CelCen;
ChamBiD; CyAG; DcAmAu; DcAmB;
DcNAA; Drake; EncAAH; EncAB-H
1974, 1996; EncWB 98; HarEnUS;
LinLib S; McGEWB; NatCAB 3;
OxCAmH; REn; REnAL; TwCBDA;
WebAB 74, 79; WhAm HS; WhAmP;
WhCiWar; WorAl

Till, Emmett (Louis)
American. Victim
Lynched for allegedly whistling at a
white woman; event was a catalyst for
protests asking Congress for an anti-
lynching bill.
b. Jul 25, 1941 in Chicago, Illinois
d. Aug 28, 1955 in Tallahatchie County,
Mississippi
Source: *AmNatBi; BioIn 10, 11; ConBlB*
7; EncAACR; HisDCRM; InB&W 80

Tiller, Rogers
[Terence Rogers Tiller]
English. Poet, Writer
Major poetry works include *The Inward*
Animal, 1943; *Unarm, Eros* 1947.
b. Sep 19, 1916 in Truro, England
Source: *ConAu 101; ConPo 70, 75, 85;*
DcLEL 1940; IntWWP 77; ModBrL;
TwCWr; WrDr 76, 86

Tilley, Samuel Leonard, Sir
Canadian. Politician
Created the National Policy trade
protection program.
b. May 8, 1818 in Gagetown, New
Brunswick, Canada
d. Jun 25, 1896 in Saint John, New
Brunswick, Canada
Source: *ApCAB; DcCanB 12; DcNaB;*
Drake; EncWB 98; MacDCB 78;
McGEWB; OxCCan

Tillich, Paul Johannes
American. Theologian
Wrote *The Shaking of the Foundation,*
1948; *Theology of Culture,* 1959.
b. Aug 20, 1886 in Starzeddal, Germany
d. Oct 22, 1965 in Chicago, Illinois
Source: *AmAu&B; Benet 96; BioIn 3, 4,*
5, 6, 7, 8, 9, 10, 11, 12; BioNews 74;
CamBiEn; CamDcAB; ChamBiD; ConAu
5R; CurBio 54, 65; DcAmReB 1, 2;

EncAB-A 37; EncAB-H 1974, 1996;
EncARH; EncWB 98; LngCTC;
MajTwCW 2; McGEWB; OxCAmL 65;
OxCGer 76; RAdv 14, 13-4; REn;
REnAL; TwCA SUP; WebAB 74, 79;
WhAm 4; WhoChr; WorAu 1900

Tillis, Mel(vin)
American. Singer, Songwriter
Has written over 450 songs; CMA
entertainer of year, 1976.
b. Aug 8, 1932 in Pahokee, Florida
Source: *BakBD 84, 92; BgBkCoM;*
BiDAmM; BioIn 12, 13; BkPepl;
ConMus 7; CounME 74, 74A;
EncFCWM 69, 83; HarEnCM 87;
IllEncCM; LegTOT; PenEncP; WhoAm
78, 80, 82, 84, 86, 88, 92, 94, 95, 96,
97, 98, 99, 2000; WhoEnt 92, 98

Tillis, Pam
American. Singer, Songwriter
Album *Put Yourself in My Place,* 1991
includes hits *Don't Tell Me What to*
Do and *I've Already Fallen.*
b. Jul 24, 1957 in Plant City, Florida
Source: *AllMGCo; BgBkCoM; BioIn 13,*
24; ConMus 8, 25; LegTOT; WhoAm 94,
95, 96, 97, 98, 99, 2000

Tillman, Benjamin Ryan
American. Politician
Known as "Pitchfork Ben," demagogue
conducted political campaigns on
behalf of poor whites in the post-
Reconstruction era.
b. Aug 11, 1847 in Edgefield Country,
South Carolina
d. Apr 3, 1918 in Washington, District of
Columbia
Source: *AmBi; AmNatBi; AmPolLe;*
ApCAB SUP; BiDrAC; BiDrGov 1789;
BiDrUSC 89; BiDSA; BioIn 2, 5, 7, 12,
14; CamDcAB; CyAG; DcAmB;
EncAAH; EncAB-H 1974; EncSoH;
EncWB 98; HarEnUS; McGEWB;
NatCAB 1, 12, 60; OxCAmH; TwCBDA;
WebAB 74, 79; WhAm 1; WhAmP

Tillman, George, Jr.
American. Screenwriter, Director
Writer and director of popular 1997 film
Soul Food, about a family coming
together despite difficulties to share
Sunday dinner; won Midwestern
Student Academy Award and Black
Filmmakers Hall of Fame Award for
short film *Paula,* 1990.
b. c. 1968 in Milwaukee, Wisconsin
Source: *ConBlB 20*

Tillstrom, Burr
American. Puppeteer
Creator, puppeteer, "Kukla, Fran, &
Ollie" puppet show, on TV, 1947-57.
b. Oct 13, 1917 in Chicago, Illinois
d. Dec 6, 1985 in Palm Springs,
California
Source: *AmNatBi; ASCAP 66, 80; BioIn*
2, 3, 10, 14, 15, 24; CamDcAB; CelR;
ConNews 86-1; CurBio 51, 86, 86N;
FacFETw; IntMPA 75, 76, 77, 78, 79,
80, 81, 82, 84, 86; LegTOT; PupTheA,

SUP; ScrEAmL 1; WebAB 74, 79; WhAm
9; WhoAm 74, 76, 78, 80, 82, 84;
WorAl; WorAlBi

Tilly, Jennifer
American. Actor
Film actor sometimes compared to
cartoon character Betty Boop and
noted for her distinctive voice;
frequently cast as a "bimbo," even
while trying to break from the genre—
received an Academy Award
nomination for Best Supporting
Actress for just such a role in Woody
Allen's *Bullets Over Broadway,* 1994.
b. 1958 in Harbor City, California
Source: *IntMPA 96; LegTOT; News 97,*
97-2

Tilson Thomas, Michael
American. Conductor
Principal guest conductor, LA
Philharmonic, 1981-85; principal
conductor of the London Symphony
Orchestra 1988-95; conductor, San
Francisco Symphony, 1995—; winner
of two Grammy awards.
b. Dec 21, 1944 in Hollywood,
California
Source: *BakBD 84; BiDAmM; BioIn 21,*
22, 24; ConMus 24; CurBio 71, 96;
IntWW 91, 93, 97, 98, 2000; IntWWM
77, 80; MusSN; NewGrDM 80;
NewYTBE 71; Who 90, 92, 94, 98, 99,
2000; WhoAm 86, 95, 96, 97, 98, 99,
2000; WhoAmM 83; WhoEnt 98;
WhoMus 72; WhoWest 00, 96, 98;
WhoWor 84, 96, 97, 98, 99, 2000

Tilton, Charlene
American. Actor
Played Lucy Ewing Cooper on TV
drama "Dallas", 1978-85, 1988—.
b. Dec 1, 1958? in San Diego, California
Source: *BioIn 12, 20; ConTFT 8; InWom*
SUP; LegTOT; WhoHol 92; WhoTelC

Timbuk 3
[Barbara Kooyman MacDonald; Pat
McDonald]
American. Music Group
Pop/rock duo; made *Cutting Edge,* MTV
showcase, 1985.
Source: *ConMus 3*

Timerman, Jacobo
Argentine. Author, Journalist
Wrote *Prisoner Without a Name, Cell*
Without a Number, 1981, detailing
events during capture in Argentina,
1977-79.
b. Jan 6, 1923 in Bar, Union of Soviet
Socialist Republics
d. Nov 11, 1999 in Buenos Aires,
Argentina
Source: *BioIn 11, 12, 13, 14, 17; ConAu*
32NR, 109, 120; CurBio 81; DcHiB;
EncWB; HeroCon; HispWr;
LatAmLi; LegTOT; NewYTBS 79;
WhoWor 89

Timken, Henry
American. Inventor, Manufacturer
Patented Timken spring, 1877.
b. Aug 16, 1831 in Bremen, Germany
d. Mar 16, 1909 in San Diego, California
Source: *BioIn 21; CamDcAB; DcAmB; WhAm 4, HSA*

Timmerman, George Bell, Jr.
American. Politician
Governor, SC, 1955-59; made efforts to oppose racial desegregation.
b. Aug 12, 1912
d. Nov 29, 1994 in Columbia, South Carolina
Source: *AmBench 79; BiDrGov 1789; BioIn 4, 5, 11, 20, 21; CurBio 95N; PolProf E; WhAm 11; WhoAm 74, 76, 78, 80, 82, 84, 86, 88, 90, 92; WhoAmL 78, 79, 83, 90; WhoGov 75, 77; WhoWor 82, 84, 87, 89, 93*

Timmermans, Felix
Flemish. Author
Prolific novelist and short story writer; wrote *Pallieter*, 1916.
b. Jul 5, 1886 in Lier, Belgium
d. Jan 24, 1947 in Lier, Belgium
Source: *Benet 87, 96; BioIn 1, 3, 22; CasWL; CathA 1952; CIDMEL 47, 80; DcCathB; EncWL 1, 2, 2S, 3; EvEuW; ScF&FL 1; TwCWr; WorAu 1900*

Timoshenko, Semen Konstantinovich
Russian. Army Officer
WW II hero helped defeat German troops on Soviet western front.
b. Feb 19, 1895 in Urmanka, Russia
d. Mar 31, 1970 in Moscow, Union of Soviet Socialist Republics
Source: *BiDSovU; BioIn 1, 4, 6, 8, 9; CurBio 70; HarEnMi; LinLib S; ObitOF 79; ObitT 1961; SovUn; WhoMilH 76; WorAl*

Timrod, Henry
"Laureate of the Confederacy"
American. Poet
Wrote war verse inspirational to Southern cause.
b. Dec 8, 1828 in Charleston, South Carolina
d. Oct 6, 1867 in Columbia, South Carolina
Source: *Alli; AmAu; AmAu&B; AmBi; Benet 87, 96; BenetAL 91; BibAL 8; BiD&SB; BiDSA; BioIn 1, 2, 3, 7, 8, 9, 12, 22; CamGEL; CamGLE; CamHAL; CasWL; Chambr 3; ChhPo, S1, S2; CnDAL; CyAL 1; DcAmAu; DcAmB; DcLB 3; DcLEL; DcNAA; EncALit; EvLB; FifSWrB; GrWrEL P; HisDcWJ; LinLib L, S; NinCLC 25; OxCAmL 65, 83, 95; PenC AM; RAdv 14, 13-1; REn; REnAL; RfGAmL 4, 87, 94; SouWr; TwCBDA; WebAB 74, 79; WhAm HS; WhCiWar*

Tinbergen, Jan
Dutch. Economist
Shared 1969 Nobel Prize for work in econometrics, math economics.

b. Apr 12, 1903 in The Hague, Netherlands
d. Jun 9, 1994
Source: *AmEA 74; BioIn 8, 9, 13, 14, 15, 17, 20, 21, 23; CamBiEn; ChamBiD; ConAu 2NR, 5R, 145; EncWB 98; Future; GrEconS; IntEnSS 79; IntWW 74, 75, 76, 77, 78, 79, 80, 81, 82, 83, 89, 91, 93; IntYB 78, 79, 80, 81, 82; McGEWB; NobelP; ThTwC 87; WhAm 11; Who 74, 82, 83, 85, 88, 90, 92, 94; WhoAm 74, 76, 90, 92, 94; WhoEc 81, 86; WhoFI 92, 94; WhoNob, 90, 95; WhoUN 75; WhoWor 74, 76, 78, 80, 82, 84, 87, 89, 91, 93*

Tinbergen, Nikolaas
Dutch. Scientist
Shared 1973 Nobel Prize for animal behavior studies; noted for researching gulls; one of the founders of ethology.
b. Apr 15, 1907 in The Hague, Netherlands
d. Dec 21, 1988 in London, England
Source: *AmMWSc 89, 92; AnObit 1988; Au&Wr 71; BiDcPsy; BiESc; BioIn 10, 11, 12; BlueB 76; CamBiEn; CamDcSc; ChamBiD; CurBio 75, 89; DcNaB 1986; EncWB 98; FacFETw; IntAu&W 77; IntDcAn; IntEnSS 79; IntWW 74, 75, 76, 77, 78, 79, 80, 81, 82, 83; LarDcSc; MakMC; McGCEnS; McGMS 80; NewYTBS 88; NotTwCS 1; RAdv 14, 13-3, 13-5; RanHWDS; WhAm 9; Who 74, 82, 83, 85, 88; WhoAm 74, 76, 88; WhoNob, 90, 95; WhoWor 74, 76, 78, 80, 82, 84, 87, 89; WorAl; WorAlBi; WrDr 88*

Tindemans, Leo(nard)
Belgian. Political Leader
Active in politics since 1960s; prime minister of Belgium, 1974-78; minister of Foreign Relations, 1981-89.
b. Apr 16, 1922 in Zwijndrecht, Belgium
Source: *BioIn 11, 21; CurBio 78; IntWW 74, 75, 76, 77, 78, 79, 80, 81, 82, 83, 89, 91, 93; IntYB 78, 79, 80, 81, 82; PolLCWE; Who 82, 83, 85, 88, 90, 92, 94; WhoWor 76, 78, 84, 87, 89, 91*

Ting, Samuel Chao Chung
American. Scientist
Shared 1976 Nobel Prize in physics; co-discovered subatomic particle J/psi.
b. Jan 27, 1936 in Ann Arbor, Michigan
Source: *AmMWSc 86; BiESc; BioIn 11, 12; CamBiEn; CamDcAB; CamDcSc; ChamBiD; IntWW 77, 78, 79, 80, 81, 82, 83, 89, 91, 93, 97, 98, 2000; LarDcSc; McGMS 80; NewYTBS 76; RanHWDS; Who 82, 83, 85, 88, 90, 92, 94, 98, 99, 2000; WhoAm 76, 78, 80, 82, 84, 86, 88, 90, 92, 94, 95, 96, '97, 98, 99, 2000; WhoE 77, 79, 81, 83, 85, 86, 89, 91, 93, 95, 97, 99; WhoNob, 90, 95; WhoScEn 94, 96, 2000; WhoWor 78, 80, 82, 84, 87, 89, 91, 93, 95, 96, 97, 98, 99, 2000; WorAl; WorScD*

Tinguely, Jean
Swiss. Sculptor
Began using motion in sculpture, 1940s; advanced to complex machine art: *Homage to NY*, 1960.
b. May 22, 1925 in Fribourg, Switzerland
d. Aug 30, 1991 in Bern, Switzerland
Source: *AnObit 1991; BioIn 5, 6, 7, 8, 10, 11, 13, 17, 18, 22; CamBiEn; ChamBiD; ConArt 77, 83, 89, 96; CurBio 66, 91N; DcCAr 81; DcTwArt; DcTwCCu 2; EncWB, 98; McGDA; ModArCr 4; NewCol 75; NewYTBS 91; OxCTwCA; OxDcArt; PhDcTCA 77; WhoAm 74; WhoWor 74; WorArt 1950*

Tinker, Grant Almerin
American. TV Executive, Producer
Pres., MTM Enterprises, 1970-81; chm, CEO, NBC, 1981-86; former husband of Mary Tyler Moore.
b. Jan 11, 1926 in Stamford, Connecticut
Source: *ConTFT 5; CurBio 82; IntMPA 86; LesBEnT; NewYTBS 86; NewYTET; St&PR 84, 87; WhoAm 86; WhoE 83; WhoFI 83; WhoTelC*

Tinker, Joe
[Joseph Bert Tinker]
American. Baseball Player
Shortstop, 1902-16, mostly with Cubs; part of double play combination of Tinker to Evers to Chance; Hall of Fame, 1946.
b. Jul 27, 1880 in Muscotah, Kansas
d. Jul 27, 1948 in Orlando, Florida
Source: *Ballpl 90; BiDAmSp BB; BioIn 1, 3, 7, 10, 14, 15; CulEncB; LegTOT; WhoProB 73*

Tinney, Cal(vin Lawrence)
American. Radio Performer
Homespun philosopher with Texas accent; known for radio show, early 1940s.
b. Feb 2, 1908 in Pontotoc County, Oklahoma
Source: *CurBio 43; JoeFr; RadStar*

Tintoretto
[Jacopo Robusti]
Italian. Artist
Paintings known for unusual body movement, light, spacing.
b. Sep 29, 1518 in Venice, Italy
d. May 31, 1594 in Venice, Italy
Source: *AtlBL; Benet 87, 96; BioIn 1, 23; CamBiEn; ChamBiD; DcArts; DcCathB; DcPseud; Dis&D; EncWB 98; IntDcAA 90; LegTOT; LinLib S; LuthC 75; McGDA; McGEWB; NewC; NewCol 75; OxDcArt; REn; WebBD 83; WorAl; WorAlBi*

Tiny Tim
[Herbert Buckingham Khaury]
American. Entertainer
Falsetto singer, best known for song "Tiptoe through the Tulips."
b. Apr 12, 1922 in New York, New York

d. Nov 30, 1996 in Minneapolis, Minnesota
Source: *BioIn 8, 9, 10, 11, 14, 21; BioNews 75; DcPseud; LegTOT; ObitPA 96; WhoAm 74; WhoHol A*

Tiomkin, Dimitri
American. Composer, Pianist
Wrote music for over 100 films; four Oscar-winning scores include *High Noon*, 1952.
b. May 10, 1899 in Saint Petersburg, Russia
d. Nov 11, 1979 in London, England
Source: *AmPS; BakBD 84; BiDAmM; BioIn 1, 3, 5, 6, 8, 9, 12, 15; BlueB 76; CmMov; CmpEPM; ConAu 93; DcArts; DcFM; FacFETw; FilmEn; FilmgC; IntDcF 1-4, 2-4; IntMPA 77; IntWW 74, 75, 76, 77, 78, 79; IntWWM 77; MusMk; OxCFilm; PopAmC, SUP; Songw; WebAB 74, 79; WhAm 7; WhoAm 74, 76, 78; WhoHrs 80; WhoWor 74, 78; WorEFlm*

Tippett, Michael Kemp, Sir
English. Composer
Works include oratorio *A Child of Our Time*, 1941; opera *The Knot Garden*, 1970.
b. Jan 2, 1905 in London, England
d. Jan 8, 1998 in London, England
Source: *BakBD 84, 92; BakBDTw; BakDcM; BioIn 1, 4, 6, 7, 8, 10, 11, 12, 13; BioNews 74; CamBiEn; ChamBiD; ConAu 109, 164; CurBio 74, 98N; DcArts; DcCM; EncWB 98; IntWW 74, 75, 76, 77, 78, 79, 80, 81, 82, 83, 89, 91, 93, 97; IntWWM 77; McGEWB; MusSN; NewGrDO; NewOxM; OxCEng 85; OxCMus; WhAm 12; WhDW; Who 94, 98; WhoMus 72; WhoWor 74, 76, 78, 82, 84, 87, 89, 91, 93, 95, 96, 97, 98*

Tippu Tib
[Muhammed Bin Hamid]
Arab. Businessman
Trader; monopolized elephant hunting, built roads and plantations in the upper Congo area.
b. 1837
d. Jun 14, 1905, Zanzibar

Tipu Sultan
Indian. Ruler
Moslem ruler of Mysore was the most powerful of all the native princes of India, and was the chief rival of British aggression in South India.
b. 1750 in Devanhalli, India
d. 1799
Source: *EncWB 98; McGEWB*

Tiradentes
[Joaquim da Silva Xavier]
Brazilian. Patriot, Rebel Leader
National hero of Brazil led the Minas Gerais conspiracy to achieve Brazilian independence in 1789; executed by the Portuguese.
b. Nov 12, 1748 in Pombal, Minas Gerais, Brazil
d. Apr 21, 1792 in Rio de Janeiro, Brazil

Source: *ChamBiD; DcPseud; EncWB 98; McGEWB*

Tirpitz, Alfred von
German. Naval Officer
Cruiser squadron commander, East Asia, 1896-97; secretary of State in Imperial Navy, 1897-1916.
b. Mar 19, 1849 in Kustrin, Prussia
d. Mar 6, 1930 in Ebenhausen, Germany
Source: *BioIn 6, 7, 17; DcTwHis; EncNaHi; FacFETw; HarEnMi; LinLib S; NewCol 75; OxCGer 76, 86, 97; OxCShps; REn; WebBD 83; WhDW; WorAl; WorAlBi*

Tirso de Molina
[Fray Gabriel Tellez]
Spanish. Author
Dramatist is regarded as one of the three greatest dramatists of Spain's Golden Age of literature, and is credited with originating the Don Juan theme.
b. 1584 in Madrid, Spain
d. 1648
Source: *EncWB 98; Ent; McGEWB; RAdv 14, 13-2; WhDW*

Tisch, Laurence Alan
American. Business Executive
Known for rescuing failing companies like CBS, 1986.
b. Mar 15, 1923 in New York, New York
Source: *BioIn 5, 8, 10, 12, 13; CamDcAB; ConAmBL; ConTFT 5; CurBio 87; IntWW 89, 91, 93; News 88-2; WhoAm 74, 76, 78, 80, 82, 84, 86, 88, 90, 92, 94, 95, 96, 97, 98, 99, 2000; WhoE 74, 83, 85, 86, 89, 91, 93, 95, 97, 99; WhoEnt 92, 98; WhoFI 00, 74, 75, 77, 79, 81, 83, 85, 87, 89, 92, 94, 96, 98; WhoWor 87, 89, 91, 93, 95, 96*

Tisdale, Wayman Lawrence
American. Basketball Player
Forward, Indiana, 1985; member, US Olympic team, 1984.
b. Jun 9, 1964 in Tulsa, Oklahoma
Source: *BiDAmSp BK; NewYTBS 84; OfNBA 87; WhoAfA 9, 10; WhoBlA 7, 8*

Tiselius, Arne Wilhelm Kaurin
Swedish. Chemist
Won Nobel Prize, 1948, for research on serum protein.
b. Aug 10, 1902 in Stockholm, Sweden
d. Oct 29, 1971 in Stockholm, Sweden
Source: *AsBiEn; BiEsc; BioIn 14, 15, 19, 20; CamBiEn; CamDcSc; ChamBiD; DcScB; EncWB 98; InSci; LarDcSc; McGCEnS; McGEWB; McGMS 80; ObitOF 79; RanHWDS; WhAm 5; WhoNob, 90, 95; WorScD*

Tissot, James Joseph Jacques
French. Artist
Painter known for portrayal of people in late Victorian society.
b. Oct 15, 1836 in Nantes, France
d. Aug 8, 1902 in Buillon Abbey, France

Source: *BioIn 8, 9, 10, 11, 12, 14, 15, 16; CamBiEn; ChamBiD; ClaDrA; DcVicP 2; EncO&P 2, 3; McGDA; OxCArt; OxDcArt; ThHEIm*

Tisza, Kalman
Hungarian. Politician
Prime minister, 1875-90; wide-ranging reforms strengthened, modernized Hungary.
b. Dec 16, 1830 in Geszt, Hungary
d. Mar 23, 1902 in Budapest, Austria-Hungary
Source: *WhDW*

Titchener, Edward Bradford
American. Psychologist
Leader of the structural school of psychology and head of the department of psychology at Cornell University.
b. Jan 11, 1867 in Chichester, England
d. Aug 3, 1927 in Ithaca, New York
Source: *AmAu&B; AmBi; AmNatBi; BiDAmEd; BiDcPsy; BiDPsy; BioIn 7, 9, 13, 14, 17, 23; CamDcAB; ChamBiD; DcAmAu; DcAmB; DcNAA; EncWB 98; InSci; LinLib L, S; LuthC 75; McGEWB; NamesHP; NatCAB 22; REnAL; ThTwC 87; WebAB 74, 79; WhAm 1; WhLit*

Titian
[Tiziano Vecellio]
Italian. Artist
Works include *Assumption of the Virgin*, 1518; *La Bella*, 1537; master colorist.
b. 1477 in Pieve di Cadore, Italy
d. Aug 27, 1576 in Venice, Italy
Source: *AtlBL; Benet 87, 96; BioIn 1, 2, 3, 4, 5, 6, 7, 8, 9, 10, 11, 12, 13; ClaDrA; DcBiPP; DcCathB; Dis&D; LinLib S; LuthC 75; McGDA; McGEWB; NewC; NewCol 75; OxCArt; REn; WebBD 83; WhoChr*

Tito
[Josip Broz Tito]
Yugoslav. Political Leader
Established Yugoslavia as communist state after WW II; pres., 1953-80.
b. May 25, 1892 in Kumrovec, Yugoslavia
d. May 4, 1980 in Ljubljana, Yugoslavia
Source: *AnObit 1980; BiDMarx; BioIn 1, 2, 3, 4, 5, 6, 7, 8, 9, 10, 11, 12, 13, 14, 15, 16, 17, 18, 19, 20, 21; CamBiEn; ChamBiD; ColdWar 1, 2; ConAu 97; CurBio 43, 55, 80N; DcAmSR; DcPol; DcPseud; DicTyr; EncCW; EncRev; EncyDCo; FacFETw; GenMudB; GrLGrT; HisEWW; IntWW 74, 75, 76, 77, 78, 79; IntYB 78, 79, 80; LegTOT; LinLib S; McGEWB; MilitOn; NewCol 75; NewYTBS 80; WhDW; Who 74; WhoGov 72; WhoMilH 76; WhoWor 74, 76, 78; WhWW-II; WorAl; WorAlBi*

Tito, Teburoro
Political Leader
After years as the opposition leader in the legislature, the head of the Christian Democratic Unity Party

(CDUP) was elected the third president of Kiribati in 1994.
b. Aug 25, 1953 in Tabiteaua North, Kiribati
Source: *IntWW 97, 98, 2000; WhoIntA 2; WhoWor 96, 97, 98, 99, 2000*

Titov, Gherman Stepanovich
Russian. Cosmonaut
Pilot of first space flight of more than 24 hrs., 1961.
b. Sep 11, 1935 in Verkhneye, Union of Soviet Socialist Republics
Source: *BioIn 6, 7, 15, 17; CurBio 62; IntWW 83; WhoWor 74*

Tittle, Y(elberton) A(braham)
American. Football Player
Three-time all-pro quarterback, 1948-64, enjoying greatest success with NY Giants; led NFL in passing, 1963; Hall of Fame, 1971.
b. Oct 24, 1926 in Marshall, Texas
Source: *BiDAmSp FB; BioIn 4, 6, 7, 8, 9, 10, 11, 15, 17; CurBio 64; NewYTBE 70; WhoFtbl 74*

Titulescu, Nicolae
Romanian. Politician, Diplomat
Outstanding diplomat played a major role in the League of Nations.
b. Mar 4, 1882 in Craiova, Romania
d. Mar 17, 1941 in Cannes, France
Source: *BiDInt; BioIn 14; EncWB 98; McGEWB*

Titus
Roman. Ruler
Ruled, AD 79-81; empire was peaceful during reign; aided Pompeii after volcano, Rome after fires.
b. Dec 30, 40 in Rome, Italy
d. Sep 13, 81 in Rome, Italy
Source: *BioIn 2, 4, 5, 10, 14, 17; REn; WhDW*

Tizard, Henry Thomas, Sir
English. Scientist
Developed Watson-Watts radio beam aircraft detector—radar.
b. Aug 23, 1885 in Gillingham, England
d. Oct 9, 1959 in Oxford, England
Source: *BiESc; BioIn 1, 2, 3, 5, 6, 7, 8, 14, 20, 24; ChamBiD; ConAu 161; CurBio 59; DcNaB 1951; GrBr; HisEWW; InSci; LarDcSc; WhWW-II*

Tjader, Cal(len Radcliffe, Jr.)
American. Jazz Musician
Vibist; with Brubeck octet, 1949-51, George Shearing, 1950s; won 1981 Grammy.
b. Jul 16, 1925 in Saint Louis, Missouri
d. May 5, 1982, Philippines
Source: *AllMGJa; BioIn 12, 13, 16; CmpEPM; EncJzS; FacFETw; LegTOT; NewAmDM; NewGrDA 86; NewGrDJ 88; NewYTBS 82; PenEncP; WhoAm 74*

TLC
[Lisa "Left Eye" Lopes; Rozonda "Chilli" Thomas; Tionne "T-Boz" Watkins]
American. Music Group
Released albums *Oooooooohhh. . .On the TLC Tip*, 1992; *Crazysexycool*, 1994.
Source: *BillEnR; ConMus 15; EncRkSt; News 96, 96-1*

Toba Sojo
Japanese. Painter, Clergy
Buddhist painter-priest is credited with producing the Choju Giga (or Animal Caricature) scrolls, regarded as the finest examples of Japanese narrative scroll painting.
b. 1053
d. 1140
Source: *EncWB 98*

Tobey, Mark
American. Artist
Painter known for calligraphy in white on a dark background; influenced by Chinese calligraphers.
b. Dec 11, 1890 in Centerville, Wisconsin
d. Apr 24, 1976 in Basel, Switzerland
Source: *ArtsAmW 3; BioIn 1, 2, 3, 4, 5, 6, 7, 9, 10, 11, 13, 14, 18; BriEAA; CamBiEn; CamDcAB; CelR; ConArt 77, 83, 89, 96; ConAu 65; CurBio 57, 76N; DcAmArt; DcAmB S10; DcCAA 71, 77, 88, 94; DcTwArt; EncWB, 98; IntDcAA 90; IntWW 74, 75, 76; McGDA; ObitOF 79; OxCArt; OxCTwCA; OxDcArt; PeoHis; PhDcTCA 77; PrintW 83, 85; REn; WebAB 74, 79; WhAm 7; WhAmArt 85; WhDW; WhoAm 74, 76; WhoAmA 73, 76, 78N, 80N, 82N, 84N, 86N, 89N, 91N, 93N; WhoWor 74; WorArt 1950*

Tobias, Andrew Previn
American. Writer
Columnist, *Playboy* mag., 1983-87; *Time*, 1989—; contributor *Worth Magazine*; noted for books on money management.
b. Apr 20, 1947 in New York, New York
Source: *BioIn 9; ConAu 14NR, 37R; WhoAm 84, 86, 88, 90, 92, 94, 95, 96, 97, 98, 99, 2000; WhoUSWr 88; WhoWrEP 89, 92, 95; WrDr 86*

Tobias, Channing Heggie
American. Social Reformer
Minister active in NAACP, 1940s-50s.
b. Feb 1, 1882 in Augusta, Georgia
d. Nov 5, 1961 in New York, New York
Source: *AmNatBi; BioIn 2, 3, 4, 6, 12; CurBio 45, 62; DcAmB S7; DcAmNB; InB&W 80; WhAm 4*

Tobias, George
American. Actor
Character actor as the hero's sidekick, 1939-70; films include *Ninotchka; Silk Stockings*.
b. Jul 14, 1901 in New York, New York
d. Feb 27, 1980 in Hollywood, California

Source: *BiE&WWA; BioIn 12; EncAFC; FilmEn; FilmgC; ForYSC; HalFC 80, 84, 88; HolCA; IntMPA 78, 79, 80; LegTOT; MotPP; MovMk; NewYTBS 80; NotNAT; Vers A; WhoHol A; WhoThe 81N; WhScrn 83; WorAl*

Tobin, Daniel Joseph
American. Labor Union Official
Pres., Teamsters, 1907-52.
b. Apr 1875 in County Clare, Ireland
d. Nov 14, 1955
Source: *AmNatBi; BiDAmL; BiDAmLL; BioIn 1, 3, 4, 5, 11; DcAmB S5; DcCathB; NatCAB 42; WhAm 3; WorAl*

Tobin, James
American. Economist
Follower of John Maynard Keynes who believed in government intervention in economics; won Nobel Prize, 1981.
b. Mar 5, 1918 in Champaign, Illinois
Source: *AmEA 74; AmMWSc 73S, 78S, 98; BioIn 4, 5, 7, 9, 11, 12, 13, 14, 15; BlueB 76; CamBiEn; CamDcAB; ChamBiD; ConAu 5NR, 53; CurBio 84; GrEconS; IntAu&W 77; IntWW 74, 75, 76, 77, 78, 79, 80, 81, 82, 83, 89, 91, 93, 97, 98, 2000; NewYTBS 81, 85; NobelP; PolProf K; Who 83, 85, 88, 90, 92, 94, 98, 99, 2000; WhoAm 74, 76, 78, 80, 82, 84, 86, 88, 90, 92, 94, 95, 96, 97, 98, 99, 2000; WhoE 85, 86, 89, 91, 93, 95, 97, 99; WhoEc 81, 86; WhoFI 00, 87, 89, 92, 94, 96, 98; WhoNob, 90, 95; WhoScEn 96, 2000; WhoWor 82, 84, 87, 89, 91, 93, 95, 96, 97, 98, 99, 2000; WorAlBi; WrDr 76, 80, 82, 84, 86, 88, 90, 92, 94, 96, 98, 99, 2000*

Tobin, Richard L(ardner)
American. Journalist
With *NY Herald Tribune*, 1932-56; wrote *Invasion Journal*, 1944.
b. Aug 9, 1910
d. Sep 10, 1995 in Southbury, Connecticut
Source: *AmAu&B; BioIn 1, 5; ConAu 1NR, 1R, 149; CurBio 95N; St&PR 75; WhoAm 74, 76, 78; WhoMW 86, 88*

Toch, Ernst
American. Composer, Musician
Seven symphonies include 1956 Pulitzer-winning *Third Symphony;* wrote piano pieces, film scores.
b. Dec 7, 1887 in Vienna, Austria
d. Oct 1, 1964 in Los Angeles, California
Source: *AmComp; ASCAP 66, 80; BakBD 78, 84, 92; BakBDTw; BakDcM; BioIn 1, 2, 3, 7, 8, 12, 22; BriBkM 80; CamDcAB; CompSN, SUP; ConAmC 76, 82; DcCM; HalFC 84, 88; IntWWM 77, 80; LegTOT; NewAmDM; NewEOp 71; NewGrDA 86; NewGrDM 80; NewGrDO; NewOxM; OxCAmH; OxCMus; PenDiMP A; WhAm 4; WhoPul*

Tocqueville, Alexis, Comte de
French. Author
Noted for classic, two-volume:
  Democracy in America, 1835.
b. Jul 29, 1805 in Vernevil, France
d. Apr 16, 1859 in Cannes, France
Source: *AmBi; ApCAB; AtlBL; BbD;
BiD&SB; CasWL; CnDAL; CyAG;
DcEuL; Drake; EuAu; GuFrLit 1;
NewC; NewCBEL; NewCol 75;
OxCAmH; OxCAmL 65, 83, 95; OxCEng
67; OxCFr; PenC AM; REn; REnAL;
WhDW*

Todd, Alexander (Robertus), Sir
English. Chemist
Won Nobel Prize for work in
  biochemistry, 1957.
b. Oct 2, 1907 in Glasgow, Scotland
d. Jan 10, 1997 in Cambridge, England
Source: *AmMWSc 95; AsBiEn; BiESc;
ConAu 146, 156; CurBio 58, 97N; InSci;
IntWW 93; LarDcSc; LinLib S;
NewYTBS 97; NobelP; NotTwCS 1;
RanHWDS; WhAm 12; WhoAm 76, 90,
92, 94, 95; WhoNob, 90, 95; WhoScEn
94; WhoWor 74, 76, 78, 80, 82, 87, 89,
91, 93, 95, 96, 97; WorScD*

Todd, Ann
English. Actor
Films include *The Paradine Case,* 1947;
  The Seventh Veil, 1946.
b. Jan 24, 1909 in Hartford, England
d. May 6, 1993 in London, England
Source: *BiE&WWA; BioIn 1, 12, 18, 19;
ConAu 129; EncEurC; FilmAG WE;
FilmEn; FilmgC; HalFC 80, 84, 88;
IlWWBF; IntMPA 86, 88, 92; ItaFilm;
LegTOT; MotPP; MovMk; OxCFilm;
Who 85; WhoHol 92, A; WhoThe 81*

Todd, Garfield
Zimbabwean. Political Leader, Educator,
  Rancher
Southern Rhodesian prime minister took
  up the cause of independence and
  freedom for blacks; he was seen as an
  enlightened white African hero by
  Westerners and as a traitor by white
  Rhodesians.
b. Jul 13, 1908 in Invercargill, New
  Zealand
Source: *AfSS 78, 79, 80, 81, 82; BioIn
11; DcPol; EncWB 99; IntWW 76, 77,
78, 79, 80, 81, 82, 83, 89, 98; IntYB 78,
79, 80, 81, 82; WhDW*

Todd, Mabel Loomis
American. Author
First editor of poems, letters of Emily
  Dickinson, 1890-95.
b. Nov 10, 1856 in Cambridge,
  Massachusetts
d. Oct 14, 1932 in Hog Island, Maine
Source: *AmAu&B; AmWomWr; BenetAL
91; BiD&SB; BioIn 14, 15, 17, 22, 23;
ChhPo; CnDAL; DcAmAu; DcAmB;
DcNAA; InWom, SUP; LibW; NatCAB
28, 41; NotAW; OxCAmL 65, 83, 95;
REnAL; TwCA, SUP; WhNAA; WorAu
1900*

Todd, Mike
[Avron Hirsch Goldbogen; Michael
  Todd]
American. Producer
Produced 1956 Oscar-winning *Around
  the World in 80 Days;* wed to
  Elizabeth Taylor; killed in plane crash.
b. Jun 22, 1909 in Minneapolis,
  Minnesota
d. Mar 22, 1958 in Grants, New Mexico
Source: *CamBiEn; ChamBiD; CurBio
55, 58; DcAmB S6; DcFM; EncMT;
FilmgC; LegTOT; NatCAB 62; ObitOF
79; OxCFilm; WhAm 3; WorAl; WorAlBi*

Todd, Richard
[Richard Andrew Palethorpe-Todd]
Irish. Actor
Oscar nominee for *The Hasty Heart,*
  1949.
b. Jun 11, 1919 in Dublin, Ireland
Source: *BioIn 4, 11, 13, 19; CmMov;
ConTFT 3, 20; CurBio 55; FilmAG WE;
FilmEn; FilmgC; ForYSC; HalFC 80,
84, 88; IlWWBF; IntMPA 75, 76, 77, 78,
79, 80, 81, 82, 84, 86, 88, 92, 94, 96;
ItaFilm; LegTOT; MotPP; MovMk;
NewYTBS 78, 84; OsStAZ; Who 74, 82,
83, 85, 88, 90, 92, 94, 98, 99, 2000;
WhoAm 74, 76; WhoHol 92, A; WhoThe
77, 81; WhoWor 74; WorAl*

Todd, Richard
American. Football Player
Quarterback, 1976-85, mostly with NY
  Jets; set NFL record for completed
  passes in game: 42, 1980.
b. Nov 19, 1953 in Birmingham,
  Alabama
Source: *BioIn 11, 12, 13; CurBio 82;
FootReg 86, 87; NewYTBS 84; WhoAm
84*

Todd, Sweeney
"Demon Barber of Fleet Street"
English. Murderer
Life was subject of Broadway musical
  Sweeney Todd; supposedly slashed hi
  s victims' throats, used bodies in meat
  pies.
Source: *ChamBiD*

Todd, Thelma
American. Actor
Made over 60 films, 1926-36, last
  released post-humously.
b. Jul 29, 1905 in Lawrence,
  Massachusetts
d. Dec 18, 1935 in Santa Monica,
  California
Source: *BiDD; BioIn 11; EncAFC; Film
2; FilmEn; FilmgC; ForYSC; FrSilen;
Funs; HalFC 80, 84, 88; InWom SUP;
JoeFr; LegTOT; MotPP; MovMk;
NotNAT B; QDrFCA 92; ThFT; TwYS;
WhoCom; WhoHol B; WhoHrs 80;
WhScrn 74, 77, 83; WorAl*

Todman, Bill
[William Seldon Todman]
American. Producer
With Mark Goodson, created TV game
  shows "What's My Line"; "Match
  Game."
b. Jul 31, 1916 in New York, New York
d. Jul 29, 1979 in New York, New York
Source: *ConAu 89; IntMPA 77; LegTOT;
NatCAB 62; NewYTBS 79; WhAm 7, 8;
WhoAm 82; WhoTelC*

Toffenetti, Dario Louis
Italian. Restaurateur
Owner, operator, Toffenetti restuarants,
  Hotel, 1950s-62.
b. Jan 20, 1889 in Valdi Sole, Austria
d. Jan 16, 1962 in New York, New York
Source: *BioIn 1, 6, 9; NatCAB 53;
ObitOF 79; WhAm 4*

Toffler, Alvin
American. Author
Wrote *Future Shock,* 1970; *The Third
  Wave,* 1980.
b. Oct 4, 1928 in New York, New York
Source: *AmAu&B; BioIn 10, 12, 13;
ConAu 13R, 15NR, 46NR, 67NR; ConIsC
1; ConPopW; CurBio 75; DcLEL 1940;
EncSF, 93; Future; IdentIs; IntAu&W
89, 91, 93; LegTOT; MajTwCW 1, 2;
NewYTBS 80; WhoAm 74, 76, 78, 80,
82, 84, 86, 88, 92, 94, 95, 96; WhoE 75;
WhoUSWr 88; WhoWrEP 89, 92, 95;
WrDr 76, 80, 82, 84, 86, 88, 90, 92, 94,
96, 98, 99, 2000*

Togliatti, Palmiro
[Ercole Ercoli]
Italian. Political Leader
A founder, head of Italian Communist
  Party, 1921-44; exiled under Mussolini
  for 18 yrs.
b. Mar 26, 1893 in Genoa, Italy
d. Aug 21, 1964 in Yalta, Union of
  Soviet Socialist Republics
Source: *BioIn 1, 2, 3, 4, 7, 9, 21;
ChamBiD; ConAu 113, 133; CurBio 47,
64; DcTwHis; EncCW; EncRev; EncWB,
98; EncyDCo; ObitT 1961; PolLCWE;
WhAm 4; WhDW; WorAl; WorAlBi*

Togo, Heihachiro
Japanese. Naval Officer
Considered Japan's greatest naval hero;
  led Japanese fleet in Russo-Japanese
  War, 1904-05.
b. Dec 22, 1848 in Kagoshima, Japan
d. May 30, 1934 in Tokyo, Japan
Source: *BioIn 5, 8, 24; GenMudB;
HarEnMi; MilitOn; NewCol 75; WebBD
83; WorAlBi*

Tojo, Hideki
[Eiki Tojo]
Japanese. Army Officer, Political Leader
Prime minister, 1941; directed Japanese
  military operations, WW II; hanged
  for war crimes.
b. Dec 30, 1884 in Tokyo, Japan
d. Dec 23, 1948 in Tokyo, Japan
Source: *BioIn 1, 2, 3, 7, 8, 9, 10, 12, 13,
15, 18, 20, 24; CurBio 41, 49; DcPol;*

EncCapP; EncWB 98; FacFETw; HarEnMi; HisEWW; LegTOT; LinLib S; McGEWB; NewCol 75; PacWarE; REn; WhoMilH 76; WhWW-II; WorAl

Tokatyan, Armand
Bulgarian. Opera Singer
Tenor; with NY Met., 1922-46.
b. Feb 12, 1899 in Plovdiv, Bulgaria
d. Jun 12, 1960 in Pasadena, California
Source: *BakBD 84; NewEOp 71*

Toklas, Alice B(abette)
American. Secretary
Close companion of Gertrude Stein from
1907; her famed *Autobiography,* was
actually written by Stein, 1933.
b. Apr 30, 1877 in San Francisco,
California
d. Mar 7, 1967 in Paris, France
Source: *AmAu&B; AmWomWr; BioIn 1,
6, 8, 9, 10, 11, 12, 13; CmCal; CnDAL;
ConAu 25R, 81; DcAmB S8; GayLesB;
GayLL 1; InWom SUP; LngCTC; NotAW
MOD; ObitOF 79; OxCAmL 65, 95; REn*

Tokutomi Soho
[Tokutomi Ichiro]
Japanese. Publisher
Exerted influence in Japan through the
publication of Japan's first general
periodical and the respected
newspaper, *Kokumn Shimbum.*
b. Mar 13, 1863 in Tsumori, Japan
d. Nov 3, 1957 in Atami, Japan
Source: *BioIn 12; GloEncH; ModJap*

Tokyo Rose
[Iva Toguri d'Aquino]
American. Traitor
WW II propaganda commentator for
Radio Tokyo; imprisoned, then
received presidential pardon, 1977.
b. Jul 4, 1916 in Los Angeles, California
Source: *FacFETw; GoodHs; HisDcAR;
LegTOT; NewYTBS 76; What 3; WhWW-
II; WorAl; WorAlBi*

Toland, Gregg
American. Filmmaker
Photography talents in chiaroscuro and
deep-focus photography are showcased
in movies such as *Citizen Kane,* 1941.
b. May 29, 1904 in Charleston, Illinois
d. Sep 28, 1948 in Hollywood, California
Source: *BiDFilm 94; BioIn 1, 13;
CamDcAB; CurBio 48; DcArts; DcFM;
FilmEn; FilmgC; GangFlm; HalFC 80,
84, 88; IntDcF 1-4, 2-4; ObitOF 79;
OxCFilm; WorEFlm*

Toland, John
British. Scholar, Author
Controversial deist worked as a linguist,
translator, political and religious
polemicist, and diplomat.
b. Nov 30, 1670 in Londonderry, Ireland
d. Mar 11, 1722 in London, England
Source: *Alli; BiD&SB; BioIn 2, 3, 14,
17, 22; BlkwCE; BritAu; CamBiEn;
CamGEL; CamGLE; Chambr 2; DcEnL;
DcIrB 1, 2, 3; DcNaB; EncEnl; EncUnb;*

*EncWB 98; EvLB; LuthC 75; McGEWB;
NewCBEL; OxCEng 85, 95; OxCIri;
OxCPhil; PenC ENG; PoIre; WhoChr*

Toland, John Willard
American. Journalist, Author, Historian
Historical works include 1970 Pulitzer
winner *The Rising Sun.*
b. Jun 29, 1912 in La Crosse, Wisconsin
Source: *AmAu&B; Au&Wr 71; ConAu
1R, 6NR; MajTwCW 2; SmATA 38;
WhoAm 86, 97, 98, 99, 2000; WhoE 99;
WhoEnt 98; WhoWor 87, 97, 98, 99,
2000; WorAu 1950; WrDr 86, 98, 99,
2000*

Tolbert, William Richard, Jr.
Liberian. Political Leader
Pres. of Liberia, 1971-80.
b. May 13, 1913 in Bensonville, Liberia
d. Apr 12, 1980 in Monrovia, Liberia
Source: *AfSS 78, 79; BioIn 9, 10, 12;
CurBio 74, 80; DcAfHiB 86S; InB&W
80, 85; IntWW 74, 75, 76, 77, 78, 79;
NewYTBE 72; WhoAm 74, 76; WhoGov
72; WhoWor 74, 76, 78*

Toledano, Ralph de
American. Journalist, Author
Syndicated columnist, King Features,
1960-71; publications include *RFK:
The Man Who Would Be President,*
1967; *J Edgar Hoover: The Man &
His Times,* 1973.
b. Aug 17, 1916 in Tangiers, Morocco
Source: *AmAu&B; AuNews 1;
BiDAmNC; BioIn 22; ConAu 9R, 31NR;
CurBio 62; DcAmC; IntAu&W 76, 86;
LinLib L; WhoAm 74, 76, 78, 80, 82, 84,
86, 88, 90, 92, 94, 95, 96, 97, 98, 99,
2000; WhoUSWr 88; WhoWrEP 89, 92,
95; WrDr 76, 80, 82, 84, 86, 88, 90, 92,
94, 96, 98, 99, 2000*

Toledano, Vicente Lombardo
Mexican. Politician, Educator, Labor
Union Official, Journalist
Marxist intellectual led the national and
international labor movements and was
the founder and head of Mexico's
Popular party.
b. Jul 16, 1894 in Tezlutlan, Puebla,
Mexico
d. Nov 16, 1968 in Mexico City, Mexico
Source: *BioIn 16; EncWB 98; McGEWB*

Toledo, Fernando Alvarez de
[Duke of Alva]
Spanish. Army Officer
Through use of cautious tactics rose to
chief of Spanish Army, 1541;
governor-general of Netherlands,
1567-73.
b. Jul 10, 1515 in Oropesa, Spain
d. Apr 21, 1582 in Thomar, Spain
Source: *ApCAB*

Toledo, Francisco de
Spanish. Government Official
Fifth Spanish viceroy of Peru was
considered one of the most talented

and energetic administrators of the
Spanish Empire in America.
b. 1515 in Oropesa, New Castile, Spain
d. 1584
Source: *DcCathB; EncLatA; EncWB 98;
McGEWB*

Toler, Sidney
American. Actor
Replaced Warner Oland in Charlie Chan
film series, 1938-47.
b. Apr 28, 1874 in Warrensburg,
Missouri
d. Feb 12, 1947 in Beverly Hills,
California
Source: *BioIn 1; DcNAA; EncAFC; Film
2; FilmEn; FilmgC; ForYSC; GangFlm;
HalFC 80, 84, 88; HolCA; LegTOT;
MotPP; MovMk; NotNAT B; ObitOF 79;
WhoHol B; WhoHrs 80; WhScrn 74, 77,
83; WhThe; WorAl*

Tolkien, J(ohn) R(onald) R(euel)
English. Author
Wrote *The Hobbit,* 1938; *The Lord of the
Rings,* 1954-56.
b. Jan 3, 1892 in Bloemfontein, South
Africa
d. Sep 2, 1973 in Bournemouth, England
Source: *AnCL; Au&Arts 10; Au&Wr 71;
AuBYP 2; AuNews 1; Benet 96;
BiCoLiE; BioIn 4, 6, 7, 8, 9, 10, 11, 12,
13, 14, 16, 17, 18, 19, 20, 23; CamBiEn;
CasWL; CelR; ChamBiD; ChhPo, S1,
S2, S3; ChlLR 56; CnMWL; ConAu 45,
117; ConLC 1, 2, 3; ConNov 72, 76;
ConPopW; DcArts; DcLEL; DcNaB
1971; EncSF 93; EncWL 1, 2S, 3; GrBr;
LngCTC; MajAI; MajTwCW 2; MakMC;
ModBrL, S1; MorJA; NewC; NewCBEL;
OxCEng 67, 95; OxCTwCL; PenC ENG;
RAdv 1; REn; RGTwCWr; SJGChWr 5;
SJGFanW; SJGYouA 2; SmATA 2, 100;
TwCChW 1, 4; TwCWr; TwCYAW 1;
WebE&AL; WhAm 6; WhDW; WhoChL;
WhoTwCL; WhoWor 74; Wiz; WorAu
1950*

Toller, Ernst
German. Poet, Dramatist
Pacifist who organized Students' League
for Peace during WW I.
b. Dec 1, 1893 in Samotschin, Germany
d. May 22, 1939 in New York, New
York
Source: *Benet 87, 96; BiDMoPL;
BiGAW; BioIn 1, 4, 7, 9, 17, 19, 22;
CamGWoT; CasWL; ClDMEL 47, 80;
CnMD; CnMWL; CnThe; ConAu 107;
DcLB 124; EncGRNM; EncStYM;
EncTR, 91; EncWB 98; EncWL 1, 2, 2S,
3; EncWT; Ent; EvEuW; FacFETw;
IntDcT 2; LiExTwC; LinLib L; LngCTC;
McGEWB; McGEWD 72, 84; ModGL;
ModWD; NotNAT B; OxCEng 67, 85,
95; OxCGer 76, 86; OxCThe 67, 83;
PenC EUR; PlP&P; RAdv 14, 13-2;
REn; REnWD; RfGWoL 95; TwCA, SUP;
TwCLC 10; WhAm 4, HSA; WhDW;
WhE&EA; WhoTwCL; WhThe; WorAu
1900*

Tolliver, William (Mack)
American. Artist
Created many paintings of the deep
South including *High Cotton*, 1985;
Ceremony in Red, 1986.
b. Dec 1951 in Vicksburg, Mississippi
Source: *ConBlB 9; WhoSSW 88, 91*

Tolman, Edward Chace
American. Psychologist
Behaviorist; advanced theory of
behaviorial unit as purposive and not
merely conditioned reflex.
b. Apr 14, 1886 in West Newton,
Massachusetts
d. Nov 19, 1959 in Berkeley, California
Source: *AmNatBi; BiDcPsy; BiDPsy;
BioIn 5, 6, 14, 15, 23; CamBiEn;
CamDcAB; ChamBiD; DcAmB, S6;
EncWB 98; McGEWB; NamesHP;
ThTwC 87; WhAm 4*

Tolman, Richard C(hace)
American. Chemist, Physicist
Experiments led to discovery of electron
as charged particle in electrical flow in
metals; determined mass of electron.
b. Mar 4, 1881 in West Newton,
Massachusetts
d. Sep 5, 1948 in Pasadena, California
Source: *AmNatBi; BioIn 1, 2, 3; DcAmB
S4; DcNAA; DcScB; InSci; WhAm 2;
WhNAA*

Tolson, Clyde Anderson
American. Government Official
Joined FBI, 1928; named associate
director, 1947.
b. May 22, 1900 in Laredo, Missouri
d. Apr 14, 1975 in Washington, District
of Columbia
Source: *AmNatBi; BioIn 3, 9, 10, 11;
WhAm 6; WhoAm 74; WhoGov 72;
WhoSSW 73*

Tolstoy, Alexey Nikolaevich
Russian. Author
Historical novel, *Peter the Great*, 1929-
34, called a masterpiece of Soviet
literature.
b. Jan 10, 1883 in Nikolaevski-
Samarskom, Russia
d. Feb 22, 1945 in Moscow, Union of
Soviet Socialist Republics
Source: *ConAu 107; EncWL 2, 2S, 3;
McGEWD 84; RAdv 13-2; WhDW*

Tolstoy, Leo Nikolayevich
Russian. Author
Wrote *War and Peace*, 1865-69; *Anna
Karenina*, 1875-77.
b. Sep 9, 1828 in Yasnaya Polyana,
Russia
d. Nov 20, 1910 in Astapovo, Russia
Source: *AtlBL; CamBiEn; ChamBiD;
ClDMEL 47; CnMD; CyWA 58; DcEuL;
EncAnRW; EncWT; EuAu; FilmgC;
LngCTC; McGEWD 72; ModWD;
NewGrDM 80; NotNAT B; OxCChes 84;
OxCChiL; OxCEng 67; OxCThe 67;
PIP&P; RComWL; REn; REnWD; WorAl*

Tomasi di Lampedusa, Guiseppe
Italian. Author
Novelist; wrote of decline of Sicilian
upper class in 1860s: *The Leopard*,
published posthumously, 1960.
b. Dec 23, 1896 in Palermo, Sicily, Italy
d. Jul 26, 1957 in Rome, Italy
Source: *CasWL; ConAu 111; EvEuW;
OxCEng 67*

Tomasson, Helgi
Icelandic. Dancer, Choreographer
"Premier danseur" with NY City Ballet,
1970-85; artistic director, San
Francisco ballet, 1985—.
b. Oct 8, 1942 in Reykjavik, Iceland
Source: *BiDD; BioIn 7, 8, 11, 12, 13;
CnOxB; CurBio 82; IntDcB; WhoAm 78,
80, 82, 84, 86, 88, 90, 92, 94, 95, 96,
97, 98, 99, 2000; WhoE 79, 81, 83;
WhoEnt 92, 98; WhoWest 00, 87, 89, 92,
94, 98; WhoWor 95*

Tomba, Alberto
"Tomba la Bomba"
Italian. Skier
Won gold medals in slalom, giant
slalom, 1988, 1992 Olympics.
b. Dec 19, 1966 in San Lazzaro di
Savenna, Italy
Source: *ChamBiD; CurBio 93; LegTOT;
News 92, 92-3; WhoWor 95, 96*

Tombalbaye, Nagarta Francois
Chadian. Political Leader
Pres. of Chad since 1960; killed in
military coup.
b. Jun 15, 1918 in Badaya, Chad
d. Apr 13, 1975 in Fort Lamy, Chad
Source: *WhAm 6; WhoWor 74*

Tombaugh, Clyde W(illiam)
American. Astronomer
Discovered planet, Pluto, 1930.
b. Feb 4, 1906 in Streator, Illinois
d. Jan 17, 1997 in Las Cruces, New
Mexico
Source: *AmMWSc 86; AsBiEn; BiESc;
BioIn 4, 6, 10, 12; CamBiEn;
CamDcAB; CamDcSc; ChamBiD;
FacFETw; InnAst; InSci; IntWW 74, 75,
76, 77, 78, 79, 80, 81, 82, 83, 89, 91,
93; LarDcSc; RanHWDS; WhAm 12;
WhDW; WhoAm 74, 76, 88, 90, 92, 94,
95, 96, 97; WhoScEn 94, 96; WhoWest
74, 76, 78; WhoWor 74*

Tomei, Marisa
American. Actor
Won Oscar, best supporting actress, *My
Cousin Vinny*, 1993.
b. Dec 4, 1964 in New York, New York
Source: *ConTFT 12, 23; IntMPA 94, 96;
LegTOT; News 95, 95-2; OsStAZ;
WhoAm 94, 95, 96, 97, 98, 99;
WhoAmW 95, 97, 99*

Tomes, Margot
American. Illustrator
Award winning artist/illustrator of more
than 40 books.
b. Aug 10, 1917 in Yonkers, New York

d. Jun 25, 1991 in New York, New York
Source: *BioIn 8, 13, 14, 16, 17, 18, 19;
ChlBkCr; FifBJA; NewYTBS 91; SmATA
27, 36; WhoAmA 91*

Tomlin, Bradley Walker
American. Artist
Abstract painter; body of work consists
mainly of poetic Cubist still lifes.
b. Aug 19, 1899 in Syracuse, New York
d. May 11, 1953 in New York, New
York
Source: *AmNatBi; BioIn 3, 4, 10, 14;
BriEAA; CamDcAB; ConArt 77, 83;
DcAmArt; DcAmB S5; DcCAA 71, 77,
88, 94; DcTwArt; EncAB-A 7; McGDA;
OxCTwCA; OxDcArt; PhDcTCA 77;
WhAm 3; WhAmArt 85; WhoAmA 78N,
80N, 82N, 84N, 86N, 89N, 91N, 93N;
WorArt 1950*

Tomlin, Lily
[Mary Jane Tomlin; Mary Jane
Tomlinson]
American. Comedian
Starred in *Nine to Five*, 1980; won Tony
for *The Search for Signs of Intelligent
Life in the Universe*, 1986.
b. Sep 1, 1939 in Detroit, Michigan
Source: *ASCAP 80; BioIn 9, 10, 11, 12;
BkPepl; CamDcAB; CelR; ConLC 17;
ConTFT 2, 6, 13, 24; CurBio 73;
EncAFC; GoodHs; GrLiveH; HalFC 80,
84, 88; IntMPA 84, 86, 88, 92, 94, 96;
IntWWW 2; JoeFr; LegTOT; NewYTBE
73; NewYTBS 76, 85; OsStAZ; QDrFCA
92; WhoAm 74, 76, 78, 80, 82, 84, 86,
88, 90, 92, 94, 95, 96, 99, 2000;
WhoAmW 79, 81, 83, 85, 89, 91, 93, 95,
97, 99; WhoCom; WhoEnt 92, 98;
WhoHol 92, A; WorAl; WorAlBi*

Tomlin, Pinky
American. Songwriter
Co-wrote popular hit, "The Object of
My Affection," 1934; used in film
Times Square Lady, 1935.
b. Sep 9, 1908 in Eros, Arkansas
d. Dec 15, 1987 in Los Angeles,
California
Source: *ASCAP 66, 80; BioIn 12, 15;
CmpEPM; WhoHol A*

Tomlinson, Henry Major
English. Author
Noted for travel tale *The Sea and the
Jungle*, 1912; novel *All Our
Yesterdays*, 1930.
b. Jun 21, 1873 in London, England
d. Feb 5, 1958 in London, England
Source: *BioIn 1, 2, 3, 4, 5, 6, 9, 13, 14,
17; CamBiEn; ChamBiD; ConAu 161;
CyWA 58; DcLB 36; DcLEL; DcNaB
1951; EvLB; InSci; LngCTC; ModBrL;
NewC; NewCBEL; OxCEng 67;
OxCShps; OxCTwCL; PenC ENG; REn;
REnAL; TwCA, SUP; TwCWr; WhDW;
WorAu 1900*

Tomlinson, Jill
English. Children's Author
Animal tales include *Penguin's Progress*,
1975.

b. Dec 27, 1931 in Twickenham,
England
d. 1976, England
Source: *Au&Wr 71; BioIn 9, 13; ConAu
P-2; IntAu&W 76; SmATA 3, 24, 24N;
WrDr 76, 80, 82, 84, 86*

Tomonaga Shinichiro
Japanese. Physicist
Shared 1965 Nobel Prize; researched
quantum electrodynamics.
b. Mar 31, 1906 in Tokyo, Japan
d. Jul 8, 1979 in Tokyo, Japan
Source: *WhoNob*

Tom Petty and the Heartbreakers
[Ron Blair; Mike Campbell; Stan Lynch;
Tom Petty; Benmont Tench]
American. Music Group
Rock group formed by Tom Petty, 1975;
album *Damn the Torpedoes*, 1979,
sold over 2.5 million copies.
Source: *BioIn 11, 12, 17, 20, 21;
ConMus 26; EncPR&S 89; EncRk 88;
HarEnR 86; IlEncRk; PenEncP; RkOn
85; RolSEnR 83; WhoHol 92; WhoRocM
82*

Tompkins, Daniel D
American. US Vice President
Vp under James Monroe, 1817-25.
b. Jun 21, 1774 in Scarsdale, New York
d. Jun 11, 1825 in Staten Island, New
York
Source: *AmNatBi; BiAUS; BiDrGov
1789; BioIn 22, 23; CamDcAB; EncWar;
HarEnUS; NatCAB 6; WebAB 79*

Tompkins, Sally Louisa
American. Philanthropist
Operated Civil War hospital in own
home; commissioned captain in
Confederate calvary, only woman to
be so honored.
b. Nov 9, 1833 in Mathews County,
Virginia
d. Jul 25, 1916 in Richmond, Virginia
Source: *AmNatBi; BiDConf; BioIn 5, 16,
21; DcAmB; EncSoH; InWom SUP;
LibW; NotAW; WebAB 74, 79;
WebAMB; WhCiWar; WomFir; WomMil*

Tompkins, Susie
American. Fashion Designer, Business
Executive
Founder, owner of Esprit Clothing, noted
for mail order catalogue, trendy,
colorful outfits.
b. 1943
Source: *ConNews 87-2*

Toms, Carl
English. Designer
Won Tony for stage designs in *Sherlock
Holmes*, 1974; first head of design,
associate director with National
Theater beginning in 1970.
b. May 29, 1927, England
d. Aug 4, 1999 in Hertfordshire, England
Source: *ConDes 84, 90, 97; ConTFT 6,
13; IntWWM 77, 80; NotNAT; VarWW*

85; Who 82, 83, 85, 88, 90, 92, 94, 98,
99; WhoOp 76; WhoThe 72, 77, 81*

Tomseth, Victor Lloyd
[The Hostages]
American. Hostage
One of 52 held by terrorists, Nov 1979-
Jan 1981.
b. Apr 14, 1941 in Springfield, Oregon
Source: *BioIn 12; NewYTBS 81; USBiR
74*

Tom Thumb, General
[Charles Sherwood Stratton]
American. Circus Performer
Midget, whose height never exceeded 33
inches; hired by PT Barnum, 1842.
b. Jan 4, 1838 in Bridgeport, Connecticut
d. Jul 15, 1883 in Middleboro,
Massachusetts
Source: *AmBi; AmNatBi; ApCAB; BioIn
1, 2, 3, 4, 5, 6, 8, 11, 12, 22; DcAmB;
Drake; NatCAB 10; NewCol 75; NotNAT
A; OxCAmH; WhAm HS*

Tone, Franchot
[Stanislas Pascal Franchot Tone]
American. Actor
Typecast in playboy roles at MGM,
1930s; Oscar nominee for *Mutiny on
the Bounty*, 1935.
b. Feb 27, 1905 in Niagara Falls, New
York
d. Sep 18, 1968 in New York, New
York
Source: *BiDFilm 94; BiE&WWA; BioIn
8, 9, 14; CmMov; CurBio 68; DcAmB
S8; EncAFC; FilmEn; FilmgC; ForYSC;
HalFC 80, 84, 88; ItaFilm; LegTOT;
MGM; MotPP; MovMk; NotNAT B;
ObitOF 79; OsStAZ; OxCAmT 84;
OxCFilm; PIP&P; WhAm 5; WhoHol A;
WhScrn 74, 77, 83; WorAl; WorAlBi;
WorEFlm*

Tone, Theobald Wolfe
Irish. Revolutionary
One of the founders of United Irishmen,
1791.
b. 1763
d. 1798
Source: *Alli; BiCoLiE; BiDIrW; BioIn
13, 16, 17, 18, 24; CamBiEn; CasWL;
ChambiD; Chambr 2; CmFrR; DcBiPP;
DcIrB 1, 2, 3; DcIrW 2; DcNaB;
HisDcIr; NewCol 75; OxCIri; PoIre;
REn; WebBD 83; WhDW*

Tonegawa, Susumu
Japanese. Scientist
Won Nobel Prize in medicine, 1987, for
discovering how body makes
antibodies to fight disease.
b. Sep 5, 1939 in Nagoya, Japan
Source: *AmMWSc 86, 89, 92, 95, 98;
BioIn 15, 18, 20; ChambiD; IntWW 89,
91, 93, 97, 98, 2000; LarDcSc;
McGCEnS; NobelP 91; NotTwCS 1;
RanHWDS; Who 90, 92, 94, 98, 99,
2000; WhoAm 84, 86, 88, 90, 92, 94, 95,
96, 97, 98, 99, 2000; WhoAsA 94; WhoE
91, 95, 97, 99; WhoMedH 96, 99, 2000;
WhoNob 90, 95; WhoScEn 94, 96, 2000;*

*WhoWor 89, 91, 93, 95, 96, 97, 98, 99,
2000; WorAlBi*

Tone-Loc
[Anthony Terrell Smith]
American. Rapper
Rap singer; had multi-platinum hit single
"Wild Thing," 1988; won several
Grammys, 1990.
b. Mar 3, 1966 in Los Angeles,
California

Tonge, Israel
English. Revolutionary
With Titus Oakes, invented Popish Plot,
1678, plan to assassinate Charles II,
replace with brother James.
b. 1621
d. 1680
Source: *BioIn 2; DcNaB*

Tonnies, Ferdinand
German. Sociologist
Pioneered sociology as a rigorous
scientific discipline based on original
studies in the history of ideas,
epistemology, political science,
economics, and social anthropology.
b. Jul 26, 1855 in Eiderstedt, Germany
d. Apr 9, 1936
Source: *BioIn 9; DcSoc; EncWB 98;
McGEWB; RAdv 14, 13-3*

Toole, John Kennedy
American. Author
Wrote posthumously published best-seller
The Confederacy of Dunces, 1980,
which won Pulitzer.
b. 1937 in New Orleans, Louisiana
d. Mar 26, 1969 in Biloxi, Mississippi
Source: *AmNatBi; BeaEPF; BenetAL 91;
BiDConC; BioIn 12, 13, 15, 17, 19;
CamBiEn; CamGLE; CamHAL; ConAu
104; ConLC 19, 64; CyWA 89, 97;
DcLB Y81B; EncAHmr; MajTwCW 2;
OxCAmL 83, 95; OxCTwCL; RGTwCWr;
WhoPul; WorAlBi; WorAu 1975*

Toombs, Robert Augustus
American. Statesman
Dem. con. from GA, 1845-53; left to
become secretary of State of
Confederacy.
b. Jul 2, 1810 in Wilkes County, Georgia
d. Dec 15, 1885 in Washington, Georgia
Source: *AmBi; AmNatBi; ApCAB;
BiAUS; BiDConf; BiDrAC; BioIn 5, 7,
16; CamDcAB; CivWDc; CyAG;
DcAmB; DcAmDH 80, 89; Drake;
EncSoH; EncWB 98; McGEWB; NatCAB
4; NewCol 75; TwCBDA; WebAB 74,
79; WebBD 83; WhAm HS; WhAmP;
WhCiWar*

Toomer, Jean
[Nathan Pinchback Toomer]
American. Author, Poet
A Harlem Renaissance writer; wrote
Cane, 1923.
b. Dec 26, 1894 in Washington, District
of Columbia

d. Mar 30, 1967 in Doylestown,
Pennsylvania
Source: *AfrAmAl 6, 8; AfrAmW;
AmAu&B; AmNatBi; AmWr S3; BioIn 2,
8, 9, 10, 12, 14, 15, 17, 19, 20, 23, 24;
BlkAmP; BlkAmW 1; BlkAWP; BlkLC;
BlkWr 1; BlkWrNE; BroadAu; CamGLE;
CamHAL; ChamBiD; ConAu 85; ConBlB
6; ConLC 1, 4, 13, 22; CyWA 89, 97;
DcAmNB; DcLB 45, 51; DcTwCCu 5;
EarBlAP; EncAACR; EncALit; EncSoH;
EncWL 2, 2S, 3; FifSWrA; GrWrEL N;
InWom SUP; LegTOT; LinLib L;
MajTwCW 1, 2; ModAL 4S1, 5;
ModBlW, 2; MorBAP; NegAl 76, 83, 89;
OxCAfAL; OxCAmL 65, 83, 95;
OxCTwCL; OxCTwCP; PenC AM;
PoeCrit 7; RAdv 14; REnAL; RfGAmL 4,
87, 94; RfGShF 1, 2; SchCGBL;
SelBAAf; SelBAAu; ShScr 1; SocPrL;
SouBlCW; SouWr; Tw; WebE&AL;
WorAu 1950; WorLitC SUP*

Toomer, Ronald V
American. Designer, Business Executive
Designed more than 80 roller coasters
worldwide.
b. 1930 in Pasadena, California
Source: *BioIn 16; News 90-1*

Toomey, Bill
[William Toomey]
American. Track Athlete
Won gold medal in decathlon, 1968
Olympics.
b. Jan 10, 1939 in Philadelphia,
Pennsylvania
Source: *CmCal; WhoSpor; WhoTr&F 73*

Toomey, Mary Rand
[Mrs. Bill Toomey]
American. Track Athlete
As member of British team, won gold
medal in long jump, silver in
pentathlon, bronze in 400 meter relay,
1960 Olympics.
b. Feb 10, 1940
Source: *WhoTr&F 73*

Toomey, Regis
American. Actor
Character actor in over 150 films,
1929—, TV shows "Burke's Law,"
1963-65.
b. Aug 13, 1898 in Pittsburgh,
Pennsylvania
d. Oct 12, 1991 in Woodland Hills,
California
Source: *AnObit 1991; BioIn 17, 18; Film
2; FilmgC; HalFC 84; IntMPA 82, 84,
86, 92; MotPP; MovMk; NewYTBS 91;
Vers A; WhoHol A; WorAl*

Toon, Malcolm
American. Diplomat
Has served as US ambassador to
Czechoslovakia, Yugoslavia, Israel,
USSR.
b. Jul 4, 1916 in Troy, New York
Source: *BioIn 8, 11, 16; BlueB 76;
CurBio 78; DcAmDH 80, 89; IntWW 74,
75, 76, 77, 78, 79, 80, 81, 82, 83, 89,
91, 93, 97, 98, 2000; IntYB 78, 79, 80,*

*81, 82; USBiR 74; WhoAm 74, 76, 78,
80, 82, 84, 86, 88, 90, 92, 94, 95, 96,
97, 98, 99, 2000; WhoAmP 73, 75, 77,
79, 81, 83, 85, 87, 89, 91, 93, 95, 97,
1999; WhoGov 72, 75, 77; WhoWor 74,
76, 78, 82*

Toone, Bill
American. Ornithologist
Avian biologist, serves as director of
condor (a kind of vulture) breeding
program at San Diego Wild Animal
Park, working to rescue the California
condor from the brink of extinction.
b. c. 1956 in California
Source: *ConNews 87-2*

Toots and the Maytals
[Raleigh Gordon; Frederick "Toots"
Hibbert; Nathaniel "Jerry" Mat]
Jamaican. Music Group
Reggae band, 1962-83; hit albums
include *Reggae Greats*, 1985.
Source: *ConMuA 80A; HarEnR 86;
IlEncRk; RolSEnR 83*

Toplady, Augustus Montague
English. Clergy
Wrote "Rock of Ages," 1776.
b. Nov 4, 1740 in Farnham, England
d. Aug 11, 1778 in London, England
Source: *Alli; BbD; BiD&SB; BioIn 3;
BritAu; CasWL; ChamBiD; Chambr 2;
ChhPo; DcBiPP; DcEnL; DcLEL;
DcNaB; EncWM; EvLB; LuthC 75;
NewC; NewCBEL; OxCEng 67, 85, 95;
OxCMus; PoChrch*

Topol, Chaim
Israeli. Actor
Oscar nominee for Tevye in *Fiddler on
the Roof*, 1971.
b. Sep 9, 1935 in Tel Aviv, Palestine
Source: *BioIn 8, 9, 13; FilmgC; IntWW
77, 78, 79, 80, 81, 82, 83, 89, 91, 93,
97, 98, 2000; NewYTBE 71; OxCThe 83;
WhoHol A; WhoWor 82, 84, 87, 89, 91,
93, 95, 96, 97, 98, 99, 2000; WhoWorJ
78*

Topolski, Feliks
English. Artist
Official war artist, 1940-45; mural in
Buckingham Palace: *The Coronation
of Elizabeth II*.
b. Aug 14, 1907 in Warsaw, Poland
d. Aug 24, 1989 in London, England
Source: *AnObit 1989; BioIn 1, 4, 5, 7,
11, 14, 16; BlueB 76; CamBiEn;
ChamBiD; ConAu 112; DcBrAr 1;
DcNaB 1986; DcTwArt; IlsBYP; IlsCB
1946; IntWW 74, 75, 76, 77, 78, 79, 80,
81, 82, 83, 89; NewYTBS 89; OxCArt;
OxCTwCA; OxDcArt; PhDcTCA 77;
PolBiDi; TwCPaSc; WhAm 10; Who 74,
82, 83, 85, 88; WhoArt 80, 82, 84;
WhoGrA 62, 82; WhoSoCE 89; WhoWor
74, 82; WorArt 1950*

Topping, Dan(iel Reid)
American. Baseball Executive
Owner, NY Yankees, 1945-66.

b. Jun 11, 1912 in Greenwich,
Connecticut
d. May 18, 1974 in Miami, Florida
Source: *BiDAmSp BB; BioIn 10, 15;
NewYTBS 74; WhAm 6*

Torborg, Jeff(rey Allen)
American. Baseball Manager
ML catcher, 1964-73; manager,
Cleveland, 1977-79, Chicago White
Sox, 1989—; AL manager of year,
1990.
b. Nov 26, 1941 in Westfield, New
Jersey
Source: *Ballpl 90; BaseEn 88; WhoAm
74, 76, 78, 90, 92; WhoMW 90*

Toren, Marta
Swedish. Actor
Films include *Casbah, Sword in the
Sand.*
b. May 21, 1926 in Stockholm, Sweden
d. Feb 19, 1957 in Stockholm, Sweden
Source: *BioIn 1, 4; FilmEn; FilmgC;
HalFC 80, 84, 88; ItaFilm; MotPP;
NotNAT B; ObitOF 79; WhoHol B;
WhScrn 74, 77, 83*

Tork, Peter
[The Monkees]
American. Singer, Musician
Bass guitarist, vocalist with The
Monkees on popular TV series, 1966-
68.
b. Feb 13, 1944 in Washington, District
of Columbia
Source: *LegTOT*

Torme, Mel(vin Howard)
"The Velvet Fog"
American. Singer, Songwriter
Versatile film, TV entertainer from
1940s; wrote "The Christmas Song";
won 1983 Grammy.
b. Sep 13, 1925 in Chicago, Illinois
d. Jun 5, 1999 in Los Angeles, California
Source: *AllMGJa; ASCAP 66, 80;
BakBD 84, 92; BakDcM; BiDAmM;
BiDJaz; BioIn 6, 11, 12, 13, 15, 16, 17,
20; CamDcAB; CelR, 90; ChamBiD;
CmpEPM; ConAu 118, 143, 181;
ConMus 4; CurBio 83; EncJzS; FilmgC;
ForYSC; IlEncJ; IntMPA 84, 86, 88, 92,
94, 96; LegTOT; NewAmDM; NewGrDA
86; NewGrDJ 88, 94; OxCPMus;
PenEncP; RadStar; RkOn 74; WhoAm
74, 76, 78, 80, 82, 84, 86, 88, 90;
WhoHol 92, A; WorAl; WorAlBi; WrDr
96, 98, 2000*

Torn, Rip
[Elmore Torn, Jr.]
American. Actor
Films from 1956 include *Sweet Bird of
Youth; Heartland;* married Geraldine
Page, 1961.
b. Feb 6, 1931 in Temple, Texas
Source: *BiE&WWA; BioIn 8, 9, 11, 12,
20, 21, 22; ConTFT 4, 16; CurBio 77;
DcPseud; FilmEn; FilmgC; ForYSC;
HalFC 80, 84, 88; IntDcF 1-3; IntMPA
75, 76, 77, 78, 79, 80, 81, 82, 84, 86,
88, 92, 94, 96; LegTOT; MiSFD 9;*

MovMk; NotNAT; OsStAZ; WhoAm 78,
80, 82, 84, 86, 88, 90, 92, 94, 95, 96,
97, 99, 2000; WhoEnt 92, 98; WhoHol
92, A; WhoThe 72, 77, 81; WorAl;
WorAlBi

Torquemada, Tomas de

Spanish. Religious Figure
Monk, Inquisitor-General, who organized
   the Spanish Inquisition, 1483; in
   charge of removing Jews, Muslims
   from Spain.
b. 1420, Spain
d. 1498
Source: BioIn 2, 4, 7, 20; BlmGEL;
CamBiEn; ChamBiD; DcBiPP;
DcCathB; DicTyr; LngCEL; LuthC 75;
NewC; OxCEng 85, 95; OxCSpan;
WhDW; WhoChr; WorAl; WorAlBi

Torrance, Jack

"Baby Elephant"; "Baby Jack"
American. Track Athlete
Shot putter; held world record, 1934-59.
b. Jun 20, 1913 in Weathersby,
   Mississippi
d. Nov 10, 1969 in Baton Rouge,
   Louisiana
Source: BioIn 8; WhoTr&F 73

Torre, Joe

[Joseph Paul Torre]
American. Baseball Player, Baseball
   Manager
Catcher-infielder, Milwaukee/Atlanta
   Braves, 1960-69; St. Louis, 1969-74;
   NY Mets, 1974-77; led NL in batting,
   RBIs, won MVP, 1971; manager, NY
   Mets, 1977-82; Atlanta, 1982-84; St.
   Louis, 1990-94; NY Yankees, 1996—.
b. Jul 18, 1940 in New York, New York
Source: Ballpl 90; BiDAmSp BB; BioIn
7, 8, 9, 11, 15, 22, 23; CurBio 72, 97;
LegTOT; News 97, 97-1; NewYTBE 71;
NewYTBS 74, 77; WhoAm 74, 76, 78,
80, 82, 84, 92, 94, 95; WhoE 79, 81, 97;
WhoMW 92, 93; WhoProB 73; WorAl;
WorAlBi

Torrence, Dean

[Jan and Dean]
American. Singer
Formed singing duo with junior high
   school friend, Jan Berry, 1958; has
   designed album covers.
b. Mar 10, 1941 in Los Angeles,
   California

Torrence, Ernest

American. Actor, Opera Singer
Films, 1921-33, include Covered Wagon;
   King of Kings.
b. Jun 16, 1878 in Edinburgh, Scotland
d. May 15, 1933 in New York, New
   York
Source: BioIn 17; Film 2; FilmEn;
FilmgC; ForYSC; FrSilen; HalFC 80,
84, 88; HolCA; MotPP; MovMk;
NotNAT B; SilFlmP; TwYS; WhoHol B;
WhScrn 74, 77, 83; WhThe

Torrence, Gwen(dolyn Lenna)

American. Track Athlete
Won two gold medals, 200-meter and
   4x100-meter relay, 1992 Olympics;
   won gold in 4x100-meter relay, 1996
   Olympics.
b. Jun 12, 1965 in Atlanta, Georgia
Source: CurBio 96; EncWomS; WhoAmW
97; WhoWor 97

Torrence, Jackie

American. Folklorist
Began telling stories to three and four-
   year olds; became known as "The
   Story Lady."
b. Feb 12, 1944 in Chicago, Illinois
Source: BioIn 18, 20; EncWB 2-19;
NotBlAW 1; WhoBlA 7

Torrence, Ridgely

[Frederic Ridgely Torrence]
American. Poet, Dramatist
His Plays for a Negro Theater, 1917,
   sparked interest in blacks as a source
   of literary material; won many awards
   for poetry, admired by A E
   Houseman, other poets.
b. Feb 27, 1875 in Xenia, Ohio
d. Dec 25, 1950 in New York, New
   York
Source: AmAu&B; BenetAL 91; BioIn 2,
3, 4, 8, 9, 15, 22; CnDAL; ConAmL;
DcAmAu; EvLB; ModAL 4, 5; OhA&B;
OxCAmL 65, 83; OxCTwCP; REnAL;
TwCA, SUP; WhAm 3; WhNAA

Torre-Nilsson, Leopoldo

Argentine. Director
Art cinema director; The House of the
   Angel, 1957, brought world attention
   to him, Argentinian films.
b. May 5, 1924 in Buenos Aires,
   Argentina
d. Sep 8, 1978 in Buenos Aires,
   Argentina
Source: DcFM; FilmEn; FilmgC; HalFC
84; IntWW 74, 79N; OxCFilm; WorEFlm

Torresola, Griselio

Puerto Rican. Attempted Assassin
Tried to shoot way into Blair House to
   kill Harry Truman; killed in attempt.
d. Nov 1, 1950 in Washington, District
   of Columbia
Source: BioIn 8, 9, 10

Torrey, Bill

[William Arthur Torrey]
Canadian. Hockey Executive
NY Islanders, 1972-93; Florida Panthers
   1993—; built team that won four
   consecutive Stanley Cups, 1979-83.
b. Jun 23, 1934 in Montreal, Quebec,
   Canada
Source: BioIn 12, 13; NewYTBS 80, 81;
WhoAm 74, 76, 78, 80, 82, 84, 86, 88,
92, 95; WhoE 79, 81, 85, 86, 89, 91

Torricelli, Evangelista

Italian. Scientist
Developed barometer, invented its
   earliest form, 1643; also improved
   telescope.
b. Oct 15, 1608 in Piancaldoli, Italy
d. Oct 25, 1647 in Florence, Italy
Source: AsBiEn; BiESc; BioIn 5, 9, 12,
14; CamBiEn; CamDcSc; ChamBiD;
DcBiPP; DcCathB; DcInv; DcScB;
Dis&D; EncWB 98; InSci; LarDcSc;
LinLib S; McGCEnS; McGEWB; NewC;
NewCol 75; RanHWDS; SciMath;
WebBD 83; WhDW; WorAl; WorAlBi;
WorInv; WorScD

Torricelli, Robert G.

American. Politician
Dem. senator, NJ, 1997—.
b. Aug 26, 1951
Source: AlmAP 84, 88, 92, 96, 2000;
BioIn 21, 22, 23, 24; CngDr 83, 85, 87,
89, 91, 93, 95; IntWW 97, 98, 2000;
PolsAm 84; WhoAm 84, 86, 88, 90, 92,
94, 95, 96, 97, 98, 99, 2000; WhoAmP
75, 77, 79, 81, 83, 85, 87, 89, 91, 93,
95, 97, 1999; WhoE 83, 85, 86, 89, 91,
93, 95, 97, 99

Torrijos Herrera, Omar

Panamanian. Political Leader
Engineered 1968 coup, instituted reforms
   as Chief of Government, 1972-78;
   main architect of Panama Canal
   treaties with US, 1979; against
   opposition granted asylum to Shah of
   Iran, 1979; killed in plane crash.
b. Feb 13, 1929 in Santiago de Veraguas,
   Panama
d. Jul 31, 1981, Panama
Source: BiDLAmC; BioIn 9, 10, 11, 12,
14, 16, 17; BioNews 74; ChamBiD;
CurBio 73, 81, 81N; DcCPCAm;
EncyDCo; IntWW 74, 75, 76, 77, 78, 79,
80, 81; IntYB 78, 79, 80, 81; LatAmLi;
NewYTBE 73; NewYTBS 77, 81;
WhoWor 78, 80; WorAl

Torrio, Johnny

[John Torrio]
American. Criminal
Prohibition-era crime boss involved in
   Chicago brothel chain, bootlegging
   and casinos; cohort of Al Capone;
   served various prison sentences, but
   retired wealthy.
b. Feb 1882 in Orsara, Italy
d. Apr 16, 1957 in New York, New
   York
Source: BioIn 9, 16; CopCroC

Torroja (y Miret), Eduardo

Spanish. Architect, Engineer
Pioneered concrete-shell structure design;
   founded Technical Institute of
   Construction and Cement, 1951-61.
b. Aug 27, 1899 in Madrid, Spain
d. Jun 15, 1961 in Madrid, Spain
Source: ConArch 80, 87; DcArch;
DcD&D; EncMA; McGDA; WhoArch

Tors, Ivan
Hungarian. Producer, Director
Produced TV shows "Sea Hunt," 1957-61; "Flipper," 1964-68.
b. Jun 12, 1916 in Budapest, Austria-Hungary
d. Jun 4, 1983 in Mato Grosso, Brazil
Source: *BioIn 7, 8, 12, 13; CelR; ConAu 103, 110; CurBio 69, 83N; FilmEn; FilmgC; HalFC 80, 84, 88; IntMPA 75, 76, 77, 78, 79, 80, 81, 82; LesBEnT; NewYTBS 83; NewYTET; WhAm 8; WhoAm 74, 76, 78, 80, 82; WhoHol A; WhoHrs 80*

Tortelier, Paul
French. Musician, Composer
Noted cellist; wrote cello concertos.
b. Mar 21, 1914
d. Dec 18, 1990 in Villarceaux, France
Source: *AnObit 1990; BakBD 78, 84, 92; BakBDTw; BioIn 11, 14, 16, 17; CamBiEn; ChamBiD; IntWW 74, 75, 76, 77, 78, 79, 80, 81, 82, 83, 89; IntWWM 77, 80, 90; MusMk; NewAmDM; NewGrDM 80; NewYTBS 90; PenDiMP; WhAm 10; Who 74, 82, 83, 85, 88, 90; WhoMus 72; WhoWor 74, 76, 78, 89*

Torvill, Jayne
[Torvill and Dean]
English. Skater
With Christopher Dean, won gold medal in ice dancing, 1984 Olympics.
b. 1958? in Nottingham, England
Source: *BioIn 13*

Toscanini, Arturo
Italian. Conductor
Considered finest maestro of his time; director, La Scala, from 1898; NBC Symphony, 1937-54; directed from memory.
b. Mar 25, 1867 in Parma, Italy
d. Jan 16, 1957 in New York, New York
Source: *AmCulL; AmNatBi; BakBD 78, 84, 92; BakBDTw; BakDcM; BiDAmM; BioIn 1, 2, 3, 4, 5, 6, 7, 8, 10, 11, 12, 13, 14, 15, 16, 17, 19, 20, 23; BriBkM 80; CamBiEn; CamDcAB; ChamBiD; CmOp; ConMus 14; CurBio 42, 54, 57; DcAmB S6; DcArts; DcCathB; EncWB 98; FacFETw; IntDcOp; LegTOT; LinLib S; McGEWB; MetOEnc; MusMk; MusSN; NewAmDM; NewEOp 71; NewGrDA 86; NewGrDM 80; NewGrDO; ObitT 1951; OxCAmH; OxCMus; OxDcOp; PenDiMP; RadStar; REn; WebAB 74, 79; WhAm 3; WhDW; WhScrn 77, 83; WorAl; WorAlBi*

Tosh, Peter
[Bob Marley and the Wailers; Winston Hubert MacIntosh MacIntosh]
Jamaican. Singer
Original Wailer; one of the founding fathers of Jamaica's vibrant music of revolution—reggae.
b. Oct 9, 1944 in Westmoreland, Jamaica
d. Sep 11, 1987 in Kingston, Jamaica
Source: *AnObit 1987; BillEnR; BioIn 12, 15, 16; ConBlB 9; ConMuA 80A; ConMus 3; DcPseud; DcTwCCu 5;*

DrBlPA 90; EncPR&S 89; EncRk 88; HarEnR 86; InB&W 80, 85; LegTOT; News 88-2; NewYTBS 87; OnThGG; RkOn 85; RolSEnR 83; WhoRock 81

Tosovsky, Josef
Czech. Banker, Political Leader
As governor of the Czech National Bank, he was one of the key figures in the newly privatized Czech economy; named Prime Minister of the Czech Republic in 1997.
b. Sep 28, 1950 in Nachod, Czechoslovakia
Source: *EncWB 99; IntWW 91, 93, 97, 98, 2000; ProfiWG 98; WhoFI 96; WhoWor 95, 96, 97, 98, 99, 2000*

Tosti, Francesco Paolo
Italian. Composer
Singing teacher to Britain's royal family; wrote "Goodbye Forever and Forever."
b. Apr 7, 1846 in Ortona, Italy
d. Dec 6, 1916 in Rome, Italy
Source: *BakBD 78, 84; BioIn 7, 12; ChamBiD; GrComp; NewGrDM 80; OxCMus; WebBD 83*

Totenberg, Nina
American. Journalist
Legal affairs correspondent National Public Radio, 1975—; interviewed Anita Hill about her claim of sexual harassment against then-nominee to the Supreme Court Clarence Thomas, 1991; reporter, "Inside Washington," 1992—; reporter "Nightline", 1993—
.
b. Jan 14, 1944 in New York, New York
Source: *CurBio 96; News 92, 92-2; WhoAm 94, 95, 96, 97, 98, 99, 2000; WhoAmW 97, 99; WhoE 93, 95; WhoMedi 98; WomStre*

Totheroh, Dan
American. Dramatist
Plays include *Wild Birds*, 1922.
b. Jul 22, 1894 in Oakland, California
d. 1976
Source: *AmAu&B; AmNatBi; CnDAL; CnMD; ConAmA; ModWD; OxCAmL 65; PenC AM; REnAL; WhoThe 77A; WhThe*

Toto
[Bobby Kimball; Steve Lukather; David Paich; Jeff Porcaro; Mike Porcaro; Steve Porcaro]
American. Music Group
Formed late 1970s; hits include "Rosanna," 1982; "Africa," 1983.
Source: *BillEnR; ConMuA 80A; DcPseud; EncAFC; EncPR&S 89; EncRk 88; EncRkSt; Film 1; FilmAG WE; HarEnR 86; ItaFilm; MotPP; NewGrDA 86; ObitOF 79; PenEncP; RkOn 85; RolSEnR 83; WhoHol 92; WhoRock 81; WhoRocM 82*

Totter, Audrey
American. Actor
Played in TV show "Medical Center," 1972-76; appeared on stage, film.
b. Dec 20, 1918 in Joliet, Illinois
Source: *BioIn 16, 18, 24; FemmeNo; FilmEn; FilmgC; ForYSC; GangFlm; HalFC 80, 84, 88; IntMPA 84, 86, 94, 96; LegTOT; MGM; MotPP; MovMk; WhoHol 92, A*

Tough, Dave
American. Jazz Musician
A top drummer, 1940s; with Spivak, Goodman, Woody Herman, others.
b. Apr 26, 1908 in Oak Park, Illinois
d. Dec 6, 1948 in Newark, New Jersey
Source: *BiDAmM; BiDJaz; CmpEPM; IlEncJ; WhoJazz 72*

Touhy, Roger
"The Terrible"
American. Criminal
Chicago crime boss involved in bootlegging, gambling; imprisoned 1934-59 for a kidnapping, later found to be a hoax; killed by gunmen shortly after release.
b. 1898 in Chicago, Illinois
d. Dec 17, 1959 in Chicago, Illinois
Source: *BioIn 5, 24; DrInf; MafEnc*

Toulmin, Stephen Edelston
English. Philosopher
Influential ethical philosopher of the latter half of the 20th century.
b. 1922 in London, England
Source: *Au&Wr 71; BioIn 3; ConAu 5NR, 9R, 20NR; EncWB, 98; Who 74, 82, 83, 85, 88, 90, 92, 94, 98, 99, 2000; WhoAm 74, 76, 78, 80, 82, 88, 90, 92, 94, 95, 96, 97, 98, 99, 2000; WhoGov 72, 75; WhoWor 74; WrDr 94, 96, 98*

Toulouse-Lautrec (Monfa), (Henri Marie Raymond de)
French. Artist
Postimpressionist painter known for physical deformity; drawings of Paris cabarets.
b. Nov 24, 1864 in Albi, France
d. Sep 9, 1901 in Malrome, France
Source: *AntBDN A; AtlBL; CamBiEn; ChamBiD; Dis&D; NewCol 75; OxCFr; REn; WorAl*

Toumanova, Tamara
Russian. Dancer
Prima ballerina from age 12; starred in film *Days of Glory*, 1944.
b. Mar 2, 1919 in Siberia, Russia
d. May 29, 1996 in Santa Monica, California
Source: *BiDD; BioIn 21, 22, 23; CnOxB; ContDcW 89; DancEn 78; FilmgC; HalFC 84; IntDcB; IntDcWB; NewYTBS 96; ObitPA 96; WhoHol A; WhoThe 77A*

Touraine, Alain (Louis)
French. Sociologist
Studied social movements while they were in the process of formation; best

known as the originator of the phrase
"post-industrial society."
b. Aug 3, 1925 in Hermanville, France
Source: *WhoWor 97*

Toure, Ahmed Sekou
Guinean. Political Leader
Leader of Guinea since its independence,
1958-84; black Africa's longest
surviving head of state.
b. Jan 9, 1922 in Faranah, Guinea
d. Mar 26, 1984 in Cleveland, Ohio
Source: *AfSS 78, 79, 80, 81, 82; AnObit
1984; BiDMarx; BioIn 14, 18, 20, 21;
ChamBiD; CurBio 59; DcAfHiB 86;
DcTwHis; EncyDCo; InB&W 80, 85;
IntWW 74, 75, 76, 77, 78, 79, 80, 83;
IntYB 79, 80, 81, 82; NewCol 75;
NewYTBS 84; WhoGov 72; WhoWor 78,
80, 82*

Toure, Ali Farka
Malian. Singer, Musician
Malian guitarist who played with
American blues legend John Lee
Hooker in France in the 1970s;
collaborated with Ry Cooder to
produce *Talking Timbuktu*, 1994,
which received *Down Beat* Critics
Poll's "Beyond Album of the Year"
Award; also released *The Source* in
1992.
b. 1942 in Niafenke, Mali
Source: *ConMus 18*

Toure, Amadou Toumani
Malian. Army Officer, Government
Official
Led military rebellion to oust dictator
Moussa Traore, 1991; served as
interim president, leading the country
to democratic elections in 1992;
became a diplomat promoting peace in
central Africa.
b. c. 1948 in Mpoti, Mali
Source: *ConBlB 18*

Toure, Sekou
Guinean. Political Leader
Radical socialist served as president of
the Republic of Guinea after
independence; he opposed the De
Gaulle referendum in 1958,
contributing to the destruction of the
old French West African Federation.
b. 1922 in Faranah, Guinea
d. Mar 26, 1984 in Cleveland, Ohio
Source: *BioIn 5, 6, 7, 8, 9, 13; ConBlB
6; CurBio 84N; DcPol; DicTyr; EncWB
98; IntWW 81, 82; IntYB 78; McGEWB;
WhoGov 72; WhoWor 74, 76, 82*

Tourel, Jennie
American. Opera Singer
Mezzo-soprano, noted for Carmen; NY
Met., 1944-57.
b. Jun 18, 1910 in Montreal, Quebec,
Canada
d. Nov 23, 1973 in New York, New
York
Source: *BakBD 84; BiDAmM; BioIn 1,
2, 3, 4, 6, 9, 10, 11; BioNews 74;
CamDcAB; CmOp; CurBio 47, 74, 74N;*

*InWom, SUP; NewEOp 71; NewYTBE
73; WhAm 6; WhoAmW 58, 61, 64;
WhoHol B; WhoWor 74; WhoWorJ 72;
WhScrn 77, 83*

Tourgee, Albion Winegar
American. Jurist, Author, Civil Rights
Activist
Known for his attempts to extend justice
to blacks and his denunciations of Ku
Klux Klan terrorism, he was also a
novelist and a pioneer in social
criticism.
b. May 2, 1838 in Williamsfield, Ohio
d. May 21, 1905 in Bordeaux, France
Source: *Alli SUP; AmAu; AmAu&B;
AmBi; AmNatBi; AmRef; AmSocL;
ApCAB; BbD; BibAL 8; BiD&SB; BioIn
1, 3, 6, 7, 8, 12, 15, 19; CamDcAB;
CasWL; ChhPo; CnDAL; CyWA 97;
DcAmAu; DcAmB; DcBiA; DcLEL;
DcNAA; EncALit; EncSoH; EncWB 98;
GrWrEL N; HarEnUS; LinLib L;
McGEWB; NatCAB 7; OhA&B;
OxCAmL 65, 95; PenC AM; REn;
REnAL; RfGAmL 4, 94; TwCBDA;
WebE&AL; WhAm 1*

Tournefort, Joseph Pitton de
"The Father of Botany"
French. Scientist
Founded system of classifying plants,
discarded, mid-18th c.
b. Jun 3, 1656 in Aix-en-Provence,
France
d. Nov 28, 1708 in Paris, France
Source: *BioIn 4; CamBiEn; ChamBiD;
DcBiPP; DcCathB; DcScB; InSci;
LarDcSc; RanHWDS*

Tourneur, Cyril
English. Dramatist
The Revenger's Tragedy, 1607; *The
Atheist's Tragedy*, 1611, are
considered most important of his
dramas.
b. 1575
d. Feb 28, 1626 in Kinsdale, Ireland
Source: *Alli; AtlBL; Benet 87, 96;
BiCoLiE; BiD&SB; BiDRP&D; BioIn 1,
3, 5, 7, 12, 16; BlmGEL; BritAu; BritWr
2; CamBiEn; CamGEL; CamGLE;
CamGWoT; CasWL; ChamBiD; Chambr
1; CnE&AP; CnThe; CroE&S; CrtSuDr;
CrtT 1, 4; CyWA 58, 97; DcArts;
DcEnL; DcLEL; DcNaB; EncWT; Ent;
EvLB; GrWrEL DR; IntDcT 2; LngCEL;
McGEWD 72, 84; MouLC 1; NewC;
NewCBEL; NotNAT B; OxCEng 67, 85,
95; OxCThe 67, 83; PenC ENG; RAdv
14, 13-2; REn; REnWD; RfGEnL 91;
WebE&AL*

Tournier, Michel
French. Author
Novel *Le Roides Aulnes*, 1970, awarded
Prix Goncourt, France's highest
literary award.
b. Dec 19, 1924 in Paris, France
Source: *Benet 96; BioIn 10, 13, 16;
ConAu 3NR, 36NR, 49; ConFLW 84;
ConLC 6, 23, 36, 95; CurBio 90; CyWA
89, 97; DcLB 83; DcTwCCu 2; EncWL*

*1, 2, 2S, 3; GuFrLit 1; IntAu&W 76, 77,
82, 91; IntWW 74, 75, 76, 77, 78, 79,
80, 81, 82, 83, 89, 91, 93, 97, 98, 2000;
MajTwCW 1; ModFrL; PostFic; RAdv
14, 13-2; SmATA 23; TwCChW 2B;
WhoEnt 98; WhoFr 79; WhoWor 84, 87,
89, 91, 93, 95, 96, 97, 98, 99, 2000;
WorAu 1975*

Toussaint l'Ouverture, Pierre Dominique
Haitian. Slave, Political Leader
Self-educated slave who played dominant
role in Negro Rebellion, 1791,
bringing law, order to Haiti by 1801.
b. May 20, 1743 in Cape Francois, Haiti
d. Apr 7, 1803 in Fort-de-Joux, France
Source: *Drake; LinLib S; NewCol 75;
REn; WhAm HS*

Tovey, Donald Francis, Sir
English. Musicologist, Composer, Author
Wrote opera *The Bride of Dionysus*,
1935.
b. Jul 17, 1875 in Eton, England
d. Jul 10, 1940 in Edinburgh, Scotland
Source: *BakBD 78, 84; BakBDTw; BioIn
2, 3, 4, 6, 9, 10, 12, 21, 22; BriBkM 80;
CamBiEn; CurBio 40; DcNaB, 1931;
EvLB; LngCTC; MusMk; NewCBEL;
NewGrDM 80; REn; TwCA SUP;
WhDW; WorAu 1900*

Tower, Joan Peabody
American. Composer
Works include *Percussion Quartet*, 1963;
Hexachords for Flute, 1972.
b. Sep 6, 1938 in New Rochelle, New
York
Source: *BakBD 84, 92; BakBDTw; BioIn
13; ConAmC 82; IntWWW 2; WhoAm
88, 90, 92, 94, 95; WhoAmW 74, 75, 77,
85, 87, 89, 91, 93; WhoEnt 92*

Tower, John Goodwin
American. Politician
Conservative Rep. senator from TX,
1961-85; nomination to be Bush's
secretary of defense rejected by
Senate, 1989.
b. Sep 29, 1925 in Houston, Texas
d. Apr 5, 1991 in Brunswick, Georgia
Source: *BiDrAC; BiDrUSC 89; BioIn 5,
6, 8, 9, 10, 11, 12, 13; BlueB 76;
CamDcAB; CngDr 74, 77, 79, 81, 83;
ConAu 106; CurBio 68; IntWW 83, 89;
IntYB 82; NewYTBS 80, 83; WhAm 10;
WhoAm 74, 76, 78, 80, 82, 84, 86, 88,
90; WhoAmP 73, 75, 77, 79, 81, 83, 85,
87, 89; WhoGov 72, 75, 77; WhoSSW
73, 75, 76, 78, 80, 82; WhoWor 78, 80,
82; WorAl; WorAlBi*

Towers, John Henry
American. Naval Officer
One of the first officers of Navy in
aviation service; Asst. director, Naval
Aviation, WW I.
b. Jan 30, 1885 in Rome, Georgia
d. Apr 1, 1955 in Washington, District of
Columbia
Source: *AmNatBi; BiDWWGF; BioIn 1,
3, 4, 16, 17; CamDcAB; DcAmB S5;*

EncNaHi; NatCAB 41; ObitT 1951; WebAMB; WebBD 83; WhAm 3

Towle, Katherine Amelia
American. Military Leader, Educator
First director of Women's Marines; in
regular Marine Corps, 1948-53.
b. Apr 30, 1898 in Towle, California
d. Mar 1, 1986 in Pacific Grove,
California
Source: BioIn 1, 2; CurBio 86; InWom,
SUP; LibW; WebAMB; WhAm 9;
WhoAmW 58, 61, 64, 66

Towne, Charles Hanson
American. Poet, Editor
Wrote Pretty Girls Get There, 1940;
Gentlemen Behave, 1941.
b. Feb 2, 1877 in Louisville, Kentucky
d. Feb 28, 1949 in New York, New
York
Source: AmAu&B; ASCAP 66, 80;
BenetAL 91; BioIn 1, 4, 5, 22; ChhPo,
S1, S2; DcAmB S4; DcNAA; NotNAT B;
OxCCan; REnAL; TwCA, SUP; WhAm
2; WhScrn 83; WorAu 1900

Towne, Robert (Burton)
[P. H. Vazak; Edward Wain]
American. Writer, Filmmaker
Won Oscar for Chinatown, 1974.
b. 1936 in San Pedro, California
Source: BioIn 10, 12, 13, 15, 16, 17, 21;
ConAu 108; ConDr 82A; ConLC 87;
ConTFT 8; CurBio 89; DcLB 44; HalFC
84, 88; IntMPA 84, 86, 92, 94, 96;
LegTOT; MiSFD 9; VarWW 85; WhoAm
84, 86, 94, 95, 96, 97

Townes, Charles Hard
American. Physicist
Shared Nobel Prize, 1964, for work in
quantum electronics; one of builders of
first successful maser, 1954.
b. Jul 28, 1915 in Greenville, South
Carolina
Source: AmMWSc 76P, 79, 82, 86, 89,
92, 95, 98; AsBiEn; BiESc; BioIn 6, 7,
8, 9, 11, 12; BlueB 76; CamBiEn;
CamDcSc; ChamBiD; EncWB 98;
FacFETw; IntWW 74, 75, 76, 77, 78, 79,
80, 81, 82, 83, 89, 91, 93, 97, 98, 2000;
LarDcSc; LElec; McGCEnS; McGMS
80; RanHWDS; WebAB 74, 79; Who 74,
82, 83, 85, 88, 90, 92, 94, 98, 99, 2000;
WhoAm 74, 76, 78, 80, 82, 84, 86, 88,
90, 92, 94, 95, 96, 97, 98, 99, 2000;
WhoFrS 84; WhoNob, 90, 95; WhoScEn
94, 96, 2000; WhoWest 00, 74, 76, 78,
80, 82, 84, 87, 89, 92, 94, 96, 98;
WhoWor 74, 80, 82, 84, 87, 89, 91, 93,
95, 96, 97, 98, 99, 2000

Towns, Edolphus
American. Politician
Representative of a predominantly
African American and Hispanic
section of Brooklyn, New York, in the
United States Congress, 1982—; chair
of the Congressional Black Caucus,
1991—.
b. Jul 21, 1934 in Chadbourn, North
Carolina

Source: AfrAmBi 2; AlmAP 84, 88, 92,
96, 2000; BiDrUSC 89; BioIn 13, 17;
BlkAmsC; CngDr 83, 85, 87, 89, 91, 93,
95; ConBlB 19; DiAAPGL; PolsAm 84;
WhoAfA 9, 10, 11, 12; WhoAm 84, 86,
88, 90, 92, 94, 95, 96, 97, 98, 99, 2000;
WhoAmP 83, 85, 87, 89, 91, 93, 95, 97,
1999; WhoBlA 4, 5, 6, 7, 8; WhoE 85,
86, 89, 91, 93, 95, 97, 99

Towns, Forrest
American. Track Athlete
Hurdler; won gold medal, 110 meter
hurdles, 1936 Olympics; first to run
hurdles under 14 seconds.
b. Feb 6, 1914 in Fitzgerald, Georgia
d. Apr 9, 1991 in Athens, Georgia
Source: WhoTr&F 73

Townsend, Francis Everett
American. Social Reformer, Physician
Pres., Townsend National Weekly, Inc.,
United Publishing Co., pres.,
Townsend Foundation.
b. Jan 13, 1867 in Livingston City,
Illinois
d. Sep 1, 1960 in Los Angeles,
California
Source: AmDec 1930; AmNatBi; AmRef;
AmSocL; BioIn 1, 5, 7, 13, 15, 19;
CamDcAB; ChamBiD; DcAmB S6;
DcTwHis; FacFETw; OxCAmH; WebAB
74, 79; WhAm 4; WorAl

Townsend, George Alfred
"Gath"
American. Author
Wrote Campaigns of a Non-Combatant,
1865; The Entailed Hat, 1884.
b. Jan 30, 1841 in Georgetown,
Delaware
d. Apr 15, 1914 in New York, New
York
Source: Alli, SUP; AmAu; AmAu&B;
AmBi; ApCAB; BbD; BenetAL 91;
BiD&SB; BioIn 1, 3, 22; ChhPo S1;
CivWDc; DcAmAu; DcAmB; DcNAA;
HarEnUS; HisDcWJ; JrnUS; NatCAB 1;
OxCAmL 65, 83, 95; REnAL; TwCBDA;
WhAm 1; WhCiWar

Townsend, John Sealy Edward, Sir
Irish. Physicist
Pioneer in electrical conduction of gases;
first person to measure the unit
electrical charge (e).
b. Jun 7, 1868 in Galway, Ireland
d. Feb 16, 1957 in Oxford, England
Source: BiESc; BioIn 1, 4, 8, 14;
CamBiEn; ChamBiD; DcNaB 1951;
DcScB; InSci; LarDcSc; McGCEnS;
RanHWDS; WhLit

Townsend, Lynn Alfred
American. Auto Executive
Pres., Chrysler Corp., 1961-66; board
chm., 1967-75.
b. May 12, 1919 in Flint, Michigan
Source: BioIn 6, 7, 8, 10, 11; BlueB 76;
BusPN; CamDcAB; CurBio 66;
EncABHB 5; IntWW 81; IntYB 78, 79,
80, 81, 82; PolProf J; St&PR 75;

WhoAm 74, 76, 78, 80; WhoFI 74, 75;
WhoMW 74, 76; WhoWor 74

Townsend, Peter Wooldridge
English. Author
Books on history, travel include Earth,
My Friend, 1959; Duel of Eagles,
1961.
b. Nov 22, 1914 in Rangoon, Myanmar
d. Jun 19, 1995 in Paris, France
Source: Au&Wr 71; Who 85; WrDr 86

Townsend, Robert
American. Filmmaker, Actor
Co-wrote, directed, produced, and
appeared in Hollywood Shuffle, 1987,
and The Five Heartbeats, 1991.
b. Feb 6, 1957 in Chicago, Illinois
Source: AfrAmAl 8; Au&Arts 24; BioIn
14, 15, 16; ConAu 162; ConBlB 4, 23;
ConTFT 3, 13; CurBio 94; DrBlPA 90;
IntMPA 88, 92, 94, 96; LegTOT; MiSFD
9; WhoAfA 9, 10, 11, 12; WhoAm 94,
95, 96, 97, 98, 99, 2000; WhoBlA 7, 8;
WhoEnt 92, 98

Townsend, Willard Saxby
American. Labor Union Official
Pres., United Transport Service
Employees of America, 1940-57.
b. Dec 4, 1895 in Cincinnati, Ohio
d. Feb 3, 1957 in Chicago, Illinois
Source: AmNatBi; BiDAmL; BiDAmLL;
BioIn 1, 4; CurBio 48; DcAmB S6;
InB&W 80, 85; WhAm 3; WorAl

Townsend, William Cameron
American. Missionary
Founded Wycliffe Bible Translators, Inc.,
1935, nonprofit group that translated
New Testament into over 130
languages.
b. 1896
d. Apr 23, 1982 in Lancaster, South
Carolina
Source: AmNatBi; BiDChrM; BioIn 10,
12, 13, 15, 19, 22; ConAu 106;
DcAmReB 2

Townsend, William H(enry)
American. Lawyer, Author
Expert on Pres. Lincoln; held one of
largest collections of Lincoln
memorabilia in US; wrote Lincoln the
Litigant.
b. May 31, 1890 in Glensboro, Kentucky
d. Jul 25, 1964 in Lexington, Kentucky
Source: AmAu&B; BioIn 6, 7, 8; ConAu
111; EncAB-A 6; EncAB-H 1974;
NatCAB 51; WhAm 4

Townshend, Peter Dennis Blandford
[The Who]
English. Musician
Called one of rock music's most
intelligent, inventive songwriters;
wrote opera Tommy.
b. May 19, 1945 in London, England
Source: ConAu 107; CurBio 83; HarEnR
86; IntWW 89, 91, 93, 97, 98, 2000;

IntWWM 90; Who 98, 99, 2000; WhoAm 80

Toye, Clive Roy
English. Soccer Executive
Chm. of the now defunct NASL;
    president, Toronto Blizzard, 1979—;
    has written books about soccer for
    children.
b. Nov 23, 1932 in Plymouth, England
Source: *SmATA 30; WhoAm 84, 86;
WhoE 77, 79, 81, 83, 85, 86*

Toye, Francis
English. Author, Journalist
Music critic for London newspapers;
    wrote *Guiseppi Verdi: His Life and
    Work,* 1931.
b. Jan 27, 1883 in Winchester, England
d. Oct 31, 1964 in Florence, Italy
Source: *BakBD 78, 84; BioIn 1, 4, 7;
NewGrDM 80; OxCMus*

Toynbee, Arnold Joseph
English. Historian
Writings include *Nationality and War,*
    1915; *Hellenism,* 1959; *Mankind and
    Mother Earth,* 1976.
b. Apr 14, 1889 in London, England
d. Oct 22, 1975 in York, England
Source: *Au&Wr 71; AuNews 2; BioIn 1,
2, 3, 4, 5, 6, 7, 8, 10, 11, 12, 13, 14, 15,
16, 20, 22; CamBiEn; CasWL;
ChamBiD; ConAu 5R, 61; CurBio 47;
CyWA 58; DcLEL; DcNaB 1971; EncWB
98; EvLB; GloEncH; GrBr; IntWW 74,
75; LinLib S; LngCTC; MakMC;
McGEWB; NewC; NewCBEL; OxCEng
67, 85, 95; OxCTwCL; REn; TwCA,
SUP; TwCWr; WebE&AL; WhAm 6;
WhDW; WhE&EA; WhLit; Who 74;
WhoAm 74; WhoLA; WhoWor 74;
WorAu 1900*

Toynbee, Philip
[Theodore Philip Toynbee]
English. Author, Critic, Journalist
Wrote *Tea with Mrs. Goodman,* 1947;
    The Garden to the Sea, 1953.
b. Jun 25, 1916 in Oxford, England
d. Jun 15, 1981 in Saint Briavels,
    England
Source: *AnObit 1981; Au&Wr 71; BioIn
4, 12; BlueB 76; ConAu 1R, 4NR, 104;
ConNov 72, 76; ConPo 70, 75, 80;
DcLEL; DcNaB 1981; EvLB; IntAu&W
76, 77; IntWWP 77; LngCTC; ModBrL,
2; NewCBEL; Novels; PenC ENG; REn;
TwCA SUP; TwCWr; WhE&EA; Who
74; WhoTwCL; WorAu 1900; WrDr 76,
80, 82*

Toyoda, Eiji
Japanese. Auto Executive
With Toyota Motor Co. since 1937;
    chm., 1982—.
b. Sep 12, 1913 in Kinjo, Japan
Source: *ConNews 85-2; EncWB 98;
FarE&A 78, 79, 80, 81; IntWW 74, 75,
76, 77, 78, 79, 80, 81; WhoAm 74, 76,
78, 80, 82, 84, 86, 88, 92, 94, 95, 96;
WhoWor 74, 78, 80, 82, 84, 87, 89, 91,
93, 95, 97*

Toyoda, Shoichiro
"The Crown Prince"
Japanese. Auto Executive
President, Toyota Motor Corporation,
    1982-92; chm., 1992-99; hon. chm.,
    1999—.
b. Feb 27, 1925, Japan
Source: *IntWW 93, 97, 98, 2000; WhoAm
99, 2000; WhoFI 00, 96, 98; WhoWor
74, 76, 89, 91, 93, 95, 96, 97, 98, 99,
2000*

Toyotomi Hideyoshi
Japanese. Military Leader, Dictator
Warrior commander successfully
    completed the military unification of
    Japan, became its central ruler, and
    twice invaded Korea.
b. 1536
d. 1598
Source: *DicTyr; EncJap; EncWB 98*

Tozzer, Alfred Marston
American. Anthropologist, Archaeologist
Expert on Mayan Indians attempted to
    decipher their hieroglyphics; wrote
    many scholarly works on the subject.
b. Jul 4, 1877 in Lynn, Massachusetts
d. Oct 5, 1954 in Cambridge,
    Massachusetts
Source: *BioIn 3, 4; CamDcAB; InSci;
IntDcAn; WhAm 3; WhLit; WhNAA*

Tozzi, Giorgio
American. Opera Singer, Actor
Bass-baritone; NY Met. debut, 1955;
    starred in Broadway's *Most Happy
    Fella,* 1979-80.
b. Jan 8, 1923 in Chicago, Illinois
Source: *BakBD 78, 84, 92; BakBDTw;
BioIn 4, 5, 6, 8, 11; CelR; CmOp;
CurBio 61; IntDcOp; IntWWM 90;
MetOEnc; MusSN; NewAmDM; NewEOp
71; NewGrDA 86; NewGrDM 80;
NewGrDO; PenDiMP; WhoAm 74, 76,
78, 80, 82, 84, 86, 88; WhoAmM 83;
WhoMus 72; WhoOp 76; WhoWor 74*

Trabert, Tony
[Marion Anthony Trabert]
American. Tennis Player
Won US Open championship singles
    title, 1953, 1955; doubles, 1954;
    Wimbledon championship, 1955.
b. Sep 16, 1930 in Cincinnati, Ohio
Source: *BiDAmSp OS; BioIn 3, 4, 10,
12; BuCMET; CurBio 54; LegTOT;
WhoHol A; WhoSpor; WhoTelC*

Tracy, Arthur
[Abba Tracowtsky]
"The Street Singer"
American. Singer
Appeared with accordion on radio shows,
    films, 1930s-50s: film *The Big
    Broadcast,* 1932.
b. Jun 25, 1903 in Kamenetz-Podolsk,
    Moldova
d. Oct 5, 1997 in New York, New York
Source: *BioIn 7, 10; EncVaud; FilmgC;
ForYSC; HalFC 80, 84, 88; SaTiSS;
WhoHol 92, A*

Tracy, Edward A
American. Hostage
Writer in Lebanon seized by
    Revolutionary Justice Organization Oct
    21, 1986 and held captive 1,755 days;
    released Aug 11, 1991.

Tracy, Lee
American. Actor
Oscar nominee for *The Best Man,* 1964.
b. Apr 4, 1898 in Atlanta, Georgia
d. Oct 18, 1968 in Santa Monica,
    California
Source: *BiE&WWA; BioIn 5, 8, 11, 18,
21; CamGWoT; EncAFC; Film 2;
FilmEn; FilmgC; ForYSC; HalFC 80,
84, 88; HolP 30; LegTOT; MotPP;
MovMk; NotNAT B; OlFamFa; OsStAZ;
OxCAmT 84; WhAm 5; WhoHol B;
WhScrn 74, 77, 83; WhThe; WorAl;
WorAlBi*

Tracy, Spencer Bonaventure
American. Actor
Leading man considered one of world's
    greatest actors; won Oscars for
    Captains Courageous, 1937; *Boy's
    Town,* 1938; co-starred with Katharine
    Hepburn in nine films.
b. Apr 5, 1900 in Milwaukee, Wisconsin
d. Jun 10, 1967 in Beverly Hills,
    California
Source: *BiDFilm; BiE&WWA; CmMov;
CurBio 43, 67; DcAmB S8; EncWB, 98;
FilmEn; FilmgC; MotPP; MovMk;
OxCFilm; PIP&P; WebAB 79; WhAm 4;
WhScrn 83; WorEFlm*

Traetta, Tommaso
Italian. Composer
Operas include *Il Farnace,* 1751; works
    now neglected.
b. Mar 30, 1727 in Bitonto, Italy
d. Apr 6, 1779 in Venice, Italy
Source: *BakBD 78, 84, 92; BlkwCE;
DcBiPP; MusMk; NewAmDM; NewEOp
71; NewGrDM 80; NewOxM; OxCMus;
OxDcOp*

Traffic
[Jim Capaldi; Dave Mason; Stevie
    Winwood; Chris Wood]
English. Music Group
Rock band formed 1967; known for hit
    albums: *Traffic,* 1968.
Source: *BillEnR; ConMuA 80A; ConMus
19; EncPR&S 74, 89; EncRk 88;
EncRkSt; HarEnR 86; IlEncRk;
OxCPMus; PenEncP; RkOn 78; RkWho
96; RolSEnR 83; WhoRock 81;
WhoRocM 82*

Trafficante, Santo, Jr.
American. Criminal
Mafia don; testified before Congress that
    he was part of a 1960 assassination
    plot against Fidel Castro.
b. Nov 14, 1915? in Tampa, Florida
d. Mar 17, 1987 in Houston, Texas
Source: *BioIn 11*

Trafton, George
American. Football Player
Center, Chicago, 1920-33; Hall of Fame,
1964.
b. Dec 6, 1896 in Chicago, Illinois
d. Sep 5, 1971
Source: *AmNatBi; BiDAmSp FB; BioIn
8, 17; LegTOT; WhoFtbl 74; WhoSpor*

Trafzer, Clifford Earl
American. Historian
Writings include *The Kit Carson
Campaign,* 1982; *Yakima, Palouse,
Cayuse, Umatilla, Walla Walla, and
Wanapum Indians: An Historical
Bibliography,* 1992.
b. Mar 1, 1949 in Mansfield, Ohio
Source: *ConAu 26NR, 109; DrAS 78H,
82H, 99H; NotNaAm*

Traglia, Luigi, Cardinal
Italian. Religious Leader
Dean of Roman Catholic Sacred College
of Cardinals, 1974-77.
b. Apr 3, 1896 in Albano Laziale, Italy
d. Nov 22, 1977 in Rome, Italy
Source: *BioIn 5, 11; IntWW 74; WhoWor
74*

Traikov, Georgi
Bulgarian. Politician
Chief of state, 1964-72; first deputy
prime minister, 1949-64.
b. 1898, Bulgaria
d. Jan 14, 1975
Source: *IntWW 74; NewCol 75; WhoGov
72; WhoSocC 78; WhoWor 74*

Traill, Catharine Parr
Canadian. Naturalist, Author
Best known for her accurate accounts of
pioneer conditions in Upper Canada,
she also wrote books for children and
studies of Canadian flowers and plants.
b. 1802 in London, England
d. 1899 in Lakefield, Canada
Source: *BbtC; BiCoLiE; CamGLE;
CanWr; DcLB 99; EncWB 98; FemiCLE;
NinCLC 31; OxCCan; OxCCanL 1, 2;
OxCChiL*

Train, Arthur Cheney
American. Lawyer, Author
Wrote *Mr. Tutt* stories.
b. Sep 6, 1875 in Boston, Massachusetts
d. Dec 22, 1945 in New York, New
York
Source: *BioIn 22; CamDcAB; ConAu
159; DcAmB S3; REnAL; TwCA; WhAm
2; WorAu 1900*

Train, Russell Errol
American. Government Official
EPA administrator, 1973-77; pres.,
World Wildlife Fund, 1978-85.
b. Jun 4, 1920 in Washington, District of
Columbia
Source: *BioIn 8, 9, 10, 12; BlueB 76;
CurBio 70; IntWW 74, 75, 76, 77, 78,
79, 80, 81, 82, 83, 89, 91, 93, 97;
NatLAC; NewYTBE 70; NewYTBS 84;
PolProf NF; WhoAm 74, 76, 78, 82, 84,*

*86, 88, 92, 94, 95, 96, 97, 99, 2000;
WhoAmP 73, 75, 77, 79; WhoGov 72,
75, 77; WhoSSW 73; WhoWor 84, 93*

Trajan
[Marcus Ulpius Trajanus]
Roman. Ruler
Ruled, 98-117; known for building
bridges, roads, Trajan's Forum,
Trajan's Column.
b. Sep 18, 53? in Italica, Spain
d. Aug 8, 117 in Selinus, Cilicia
Source: *BioIn 5, 7, 8, 9, 14, 17, 20, 23,
24; CamBiEn; ChamBiD; DicTyr;
EncEarC 90, 97; EncWB 98; GrLGrT;
HarEnMi; HisWorL; LegTOT; LinLib S;
McGEWB; NewC; NewCol 75; OxCClC;
OxCClL 89; REn; WebBD 83; WhDW;
WorAl; WorAlBi*

Trammell, Alan Stuart
American. Baseball Player
Shortstop, Detroit, 1977-96; MVP, 1984
World Series.
b. Feb 21, 1958 in Garden Grove,
California
Source: *BaseReg 86, 87; BiDAmSp Sup;
WhoAm 86, 88, 92; WhoMW 88, 90*

Trampler, Walter
American. Musician
Viola virtuoso; known for performances
with Budapest String Quartet.
b. Aug 25, 1915 in Munich, Germany
d. Sep 27, 1997 in Port Joli, Nova
Scotia, Canada
Source: *BakBD 78, 84, 92; BakBDTw;
BakDcM; BioIn 9, 11, 23, 24; BriBkM
80; CamDcAB; CurBio 71, 98N;
IntWWM 77, 80; MusSN; NewAmDM;
NewGrDA 86; NewGrDM 80; NewYTBS
77, 97; PenDiMP; WhoAm 74, 76;
WhoAmM 83; WhoE 74, 75; WhoMus
72; WhoWor 74*

Traore, Moussa
Malian. Political Leader
President, Republic of Mali, 1968-91;
ousted, Mar 26, 1991.
b. Sep 25, 1936 in Kayes, Mali
Source: *AfSS 78, 79, 80, 81, 82; BioIn
21; DcAfHiB 86S; EncRev; IntWW 74,
75, 76, 77, 78, 79, 80, 81, 82, 83, 89,
91, 93, 97, 98, 2000; WhoGov 72;
WhoWor 74, 76, 78, 80, 82, 84, 87, 89,
91*

Traphagen, Ethel Leigh
American. Fashion Designer
Founded first school of fashion design in
US, 1923.
b. Oct 10, 1882 in New York, New York
d. Apr 29, 1963 in New York, New
York
Source: *CurBio 48, 63; NatCAB 54*

Trapp, Maria Augusta von
American. Singer, Author
Fled Nazi-occupied Austria, formed
Trapp Family Singers, 1930s; life
story was inspiration for play *The
Sound of Music,* 1959.

b. Jan 26, 1905 in Vienna, Austria
d. Mar 28, 1987 in Morrisville, Vermont
Source: *AmAu&B; BioIn 12, 13; ConAu
81; ConNews 87-3; CurBio 68, 87;
InWom SUP; NewYTBS 87; SmATA 16;
WhAm 12; WhoAm 74, 76, 78, 80, 82,
84, 86; WhoE 74; WorAl*

Trask, Diana
Australian. Singer, Actor
Folk singer with Grand Ole Opry, 1960s-
70s.
b. Jun 23, 1940
Source: *AllMGCo; BioIn 5, 14; CounME
74, 74A; EncFCWM 83; HarEnCM 87;
IlEncCM*

Traub, Marvin Stuart
American. Business Executive
Chm., Bloomingdales dept. store chain,
1978-92.
b. Apr 14, 1925 in New York, New
York
Source: *ConNews 87-3; St&PR 87;
WhoAm 76, 78, 80, 82, 84, 86, 88, 90,
95; WhoFI 89, 92*

Traube, Shepard
American. Producer, Director
Founder, Society of Stage Directors and
Choreographers; directed *Angel Street,*
1940s.
b. Feb 27, 1907 in Malden,
Massachusetts
d. Jul 23, 1983 in New York, New York
Source: *BiE&WWA; BioIn 13; ConAu
111; NotNAT; WhAm 8; WhoAm 78, 80,
82; WhoThe 72, 77, 81*

Traubel, Helen
American. Opera Singer
Leading NY Met. Wagnerian soprano,
1939-53; forced to resign due to
nightclub appearances.
b. Jun 20, 1899 in Saint Louis, Missouri
d. Jul 28, 1972 in Santa Monica,
California
Source: *BakBD 78, 84; BiDAmM; BioIn
12, 15, 19, 20; BriBkM 80; CamBiEn;
CamDcAB; ChamBiD; CmOp; CurBio
40, 52, 72; DcAmB S9; FilmgC; HalFC
80, 84, 88; IntDcOp; InWom; LinLib S;
MetOEnc; MusSN; NewAmDM; NewEOp
71; NewGrDA 86; NewGrDM 80;
NewYTBE 72; OxDcOp; PenDiMP;
WhAm 5; WhScrn 77; WorAl; WorAlBi*

Trauner, Alexander
French. Art Director
Set designer; won Oscar for *The
Apartment,* 1960.
b. Aug 3, 1906 in Budapest, Hungary
Source: *ArtDirC; FilmEn; FilmgC;
HalFC 80, 84, 88; OxCFilm; VarWW
85; WorEFlm*

Travanti, Daniel J(ohn)
American. Actor
Won two Emmys for role of Frank
Furillo on TV series "Hill Street
Blues," 1981-87.
b. Mar 7, 1940 in Kenosha, Wisconsin

Source: *VarWW 85; WhoAm 86, 95, 96, 97, 98, 99, 2000; WhoTelC*

Traven, B.
[Ret Marut; Berick Traven Torsvan]
Mexican. Author
Wrote *Treasure of the Sierra Madre*, 1935; filmed, 1948.
b. Feb 23, 1882? in Schwiebus, Germany
d. Mar 27, 1969 in Mexico City, Mexico
Source: *AmAu&B; CamBiEn; CasWL; CnMWL; ConAu P-2; ConLC 11; DcPseud; EncWL 1, 3; HalFC 80; OxCAmL 83; OxCEng 85; OxCGer 76; PenC AM, EUR; REnAL; RfGAmL 4; TwCA SUP; WebE&AL; WhAm 5; WorAu 1900*

Travers, Ben
English. Dramatist
Known for series of farces, 1920s-30s: *Rookery Nook*, 1926.
b. Nov 12, 1886 in London, England
d. Dec 18, 1980 in London, England
Source: *AnObit 1980; Au&Wr 71; BiE&WWA; BioIn 4, 10, 11, 12, 13, 14; BlmGEL; CamGLE; CamGWoT; ConAu 102, 133; ConDr 73, 77, 93; CroCD; DcLB 10; EncWT; Ent; FilmgC; GrWrEL DR; HalFC 80, 84, 88; IntAu&W 76, 77; LngCTC; McGEWD 72, 84; NewCBEL; NewYTBS 80; NotNAT, A; OxCEng 85, 95; OxCThe 83; OxCTwCL; RfGEnL 91; WhDW; WhE&EA; Who 74; WhoThe 72, 77, 81; WrDr 76, 80, 82*

Travers, Bill
English. Actor, Producer, Director
Films include *Born Free*, 1966; *Ring of Bright Water*, 1969.
b. Jan 3, 1922 in Newcastle-upon-Tyne, England
Source: *BioIn 19, 20, 22; DcPseud; FilmEn; FilmgC; HalFC 80, 84, 88; IlWWBF; IntMPA 77, 80, 88, 92, 94; MovMk; VarWW 85; WhoHol 92, A*

Travers, Jerry
[Jerome Dunstan Travers]
American. Golfer
One of five amateurs to win US Open, 1915; charter member, Hall of Fame, 1940.
b. May 19, 1887 in New York, New York
d. Mar 29, 1951 in East Hartford, Connecticut
Source: *BiDAmSp OS; BioIn 2; DcAmB S5; ObitOF 79; WhoGolf; WhoSpor*

Travers, Mary
[Peter, Paul, and Mary]
American. Singer
Member of folk music trio, popular in 1960s; hits include number-one single "Leavin' on a Jet Plane," 1969.
b. Nov 7, 1937 in Louisville, Kentucky
Source: *ASCAP 66; BioIn 12, 14, 21, 24; EncFCWM 69; WhoAm 74; WhoRock 81; WhoRocM 82; WhoWor 74*

Travers, P(amela) L(yndon)
Australian. Author
Wrote *Mary Poppins*, 1934; filmed by Walt Disney, 1964.
b. Aug 9, 1906 in Queensland, Australia
d. Apr 23, 1996 in London, England
Source: *AnCL; ArtclWW 2; AuBYP 2; AuWomWr; Benet 96; BioIn 1, 2, 3, 4, 6, 7, 8, 9, 10, 11, 13; CamBiEn; ChlLR 2; ConAu 33R; CurBio 96; JBA 51; LngCTC; MorBMP; NewC; NewCBEL; RAdv 14; REn; ScF&FL 1; SJGChWr 5; SmATA 4, 100; TwCA; SUP; TwCChW 1, 2, 4; WhoChL; WrDr 86, 94, 96*

Travis, Dempsey Jerome
American. Real Estate Executive, Mortgage Banker
Founded, heads many businesses including Travis Realty Co., 1949—; wrote *Autobiography of Black Politics*, 1987.
b. Feb 25, 1920 in Chicago, Illinois
Source: *BioIn 9, 10, 13; ConAu 15NR, 85; InB&W 85; WhoAm 74, 76, 78, 80, 82, 84, 86, 88, 90, 92, 94, 95, 96, 97, 98, 99, 2000; WhoBlA 4, 5; WhoFI 74, 75, 77, 79, 81, 85; WhoMW 74, 76, 78, 80, 82, 84; WhoWor 74, 76*

Travis, Merle Robert
American. Musician, Singer
Country Music Hall of Fame, 1977; compositions include "16 Tons," "Old Mountain Dew"; created "Travis-style" guitar playing.
b. Nov 29, 1917 in Rosewood, Kentucky
d. Oct 20, 1983 in Park Hill, Oklahoma
Source: *BakBD 84; BiDAmM; CounME 74, 74A; EncFCWM 83; IlEncCM; NewYTBS 83; VarWW 85; WhAm 8; WhoAm 76, 80, 82*

Travis, Randy
[Randy Traywick]
American. Singer
Country singer; had number one single "Forever and Ever, Amen," 1987; Grammy award winner, 1987; has won numerous other awards.
b. May 4, 1959 in Monroe, North Carolina
Source: *AllMGCo; BakBD 92; CelR 90; ConMus 9; CurBio 89; DcPseud; EncRkSt; LegTOT; News 88; PenEncP; Songw; WhoAm 88; WhoHol 92; WorAlBi*

Travis, William Barret
American. Military Leader
Hero of Texas Revolution; commanded The Alamo, where all were slain by Santa Anna.
b. Aug 9, 1809 in Red Banks, South Carolina
d. Mar 6, 1836 in San Antonio, Texas
Source: *AmBi; AmNatBi; BioIn 1, 3, 4, 5, 6, 7, 8, 10, 11, 16; CamDcAB; ChamBiD; DcAmB; Drake; EncAAH; EncSoH; EncWB 98; HarEnMi; McGEWB; NewEAmW; WebAB 74, 79; WebAMB; WhAm HS; WorAlBi*

Travolta, John
American. Actor
Starred in TV's "Welcome Back Kotter," 1975-79; films: *Saturday Night Fever*, 1977; *Grease*, 1978; *Look Who's Talking*, 1989; *Pulp Fiction*, 1994; *Get Shorty*, 1995.
b. Feb 18, 1954 in Englewood, New Jersey
Source: *BiDD; BiDFilm 81, 94; BioIn 11, 12, 13; BkPepl; CamBiEn; CelR 90; ChamBiD; ConAu 169; ConTFT 2, 13, 22; CurBio 78, 96; FilmEn; HalFC 80, 84, 88; HarEnR 86; HolBB; IntDcF 1-3, 2-3; IntMPA 84, 86, 88, 92, 94, 96; IntWW 81, 82, 83, 89, 91, 93, 97, 98, 2000; LegTOT; News 95, 95-2; NewYTBS 83; OsStAZ; RkOn 78; WhoAm 78, 80, 82, 84, 86, 88, 90, 92, 94, 95, 96, 97, 98, 99, 2000; WhoEnt 92; 98; WhoHol 92; WhoRock 81; WorAl; WorAlBi*

Traynor, John
[Jay and the Americans; Jay Traynor]
American. Singer
Lead singer, original "Jay" of Jay and the Americans, 1961-62.
Source: *BiDAmM; ConMuA 80A; EncPR&S 89; EncRk 88; NewAmDM; PenEncP; RkOn 74; RolSEnR 83; WhoRock 81; WhoRocM 82*

Traynor, Pie
[Harold Joseph Traynor]
American. Baseball Player
Infielder, Pittsburgh, 1920-37; had 100 or more RBIs seven times, .320 lifetime batting average; Hall of Fame, 1948.
b. Nov 11, 1899 in Framingham, Massachusetts
d. Mar 16, 1972 in Pittsburgh, Pennsylvania
Source: *AmNatBi; Ballpl 90; BiDAmSp BB; BioIn 2, 3, 4, 6, 7, 8, 9, 10, 13, 14, 15; CulEncB; DcAmB S9; FacFETw; LegTOT; NewYTBE 72; ObitOF 79; WhoProB 73; WhoSpor*

Treacher, Arthur
[Arthur Veary]
American. Actor
Played butler in films, 1930s-40s; sidekick on Merv Griffin's TV show.
b. Jul 2, 1894 in Brighton, England
d. Dec 14, 1975 in Manhasset, New York
Source: *AmNatBi; BiE&WWA; BioIn 8, 10; CelR; DcPseud; EncAFC; Film 2; FilmEn; FilmgC; ForYSC; HalFC 80, 84, 88; HolCA; IntMPA 75; LegTOT; MotPP; MovMk; NewYTBS 75; NotNAT B; Vers B; WhoHol C; WhScrn 77, 83; WorAl; WorAlBi*

Treas, Terri
American. Actor
Films include *All That Jazz*, 1979; *The Best Little Whorehouse in Texas*, 1982.
b. Jul 19, 1959 in Kansas City, Kansas
Source: *VarWW 85*

Treat, Lawrence
[Lawrence Arthur Goldstone]
American. Author
Mystery novels include *Venus Unarmed,*
    1961; *Murder in the Mind,* 1967.
b. Dec 21, 1903 in New York, New
    York
d. Jan 7, 1998 in Martha's Vineyard,
    Massachusetts
Source: *BioIn 12, 16, 23; ConAu 49,
    64NR, 164; CrtSuMy; DcPseud;
    IntAu&W 89, 91, 93; SmATA 59;
    TwCCr&M 80, 85, 91; WhAm 12;
    WhoAm 82, 84, 86, 88, 90, 92, 94, 95,
    96, 97, 98; WhoEnt 98; WhoUSWr 88;
    WhoWrEP 89, 92, 95; WrDr 82, 84, 86,
    88, 90, 92, 94, 96, 98, 99*

Trebek, Alex
American. TV Personality
Host of syndicated TV game show
    "Jeopardy!," 1984—.
b. Jul 22, 1940 in Sudbury, Ontario,
    Canada
Source: *LegTOT; VarWW 85; WhoAm
    90, 92, 94, 95, 96, 97, 98, 99, 2000;
    WhoEnt 92, 98; WhoTelC; WhoWest 96*

Tree, Herbert Beerbohm
English. Actor, Manager
Began acting, 1878; managed the
    Haymarket Theatre, 1887-97; produced
    18 Shakespeare plays.
b. Dec 17, 1853 in Kensington, England
d. Jul 2, 1917 in London, England
Source: *BioIn 2, 3, 4, 5, 6, 9, 10, 12;
    BlmGEL; CamGWoT; CnThe; DcNaB
    1912; FamA&A; Film 1; NewC; NotNAT
    A, B; OxCAmT 84; OxCThe 67; PlP&P;
    VicBrit; WhAm 1; WhDW; WhLit;
    WhoHol B; WhScrn 77; WhThe; WorAl*

Tree, Marietta Endicott Peabody
American. Government Official
US rep. to Human Rights Committee,
    UN, 1961-64; served on staff of UN
    Secretariat until 1967.
b. Apr 12, 1917 in Lawrence,
    Massachusetts
d. Aug 15, 1991 in New York, New
    York
Source: *CurBio 61; WhoAm 86;
    WhoAmW 79*

Treece, Henry
English. Author, Poet, Dramatist
Versatile writer whose novels include
    Red Queen, White Queen, 1958;
    Oedipus, 1964.
b. Dec 22, 1911 in Staffordshire,
    England
d. Jun 10, 1966 in Barton-on-Humber,
    England
Source: *AuBYP 2, 3; BiCoLiE; BioIn 19,
    22; CamBiEn; CamGLE; ChlBkCr;
    ConAu 1R, 6NR, 25R; DcLB 160;
    DcLEL; EvLB; LngCEL; LngCTC;
    ModBrL; MorJA; NewC; NewCBEL;
    OxCChiL; OxCTwCL; PenC ENG; REn;
    ScF&FL 1, 2; SmATA 2; TwCA SUP;
    TwCChW 1, 2, 3; TwCRHW 90, 94;
    TwCWr; TwCYAW 1; WhoChL; WorAu
    1900*

Trefflich, Henry Herbert Frederick
"Monkey King of America"
American. Animal Dealer
Sold over 1.5 million monkeys, many of
    which were used for research and lab
    experiments; supplied Cheetah for
    Tarzan films.
b. Jan 9, 1908 in Hamburg, Germany
d. Jul 7, 1978 in Bound Brook, New
    Jersey
Source: *BioIn 3, 11; ConAu 77, P-2;
    CurBio 53, 78; WhAm 7; WhoAm 74, 76,
    80*

Tregaskis, Richard William
American. Author
Wrote best-selling *Guadalcanal Diary,*
    1943.
b. Nov 28, 1916 in Elizabeth, New
    Jersey
d. Aug 15, 1973 in Honolulu, Hawaii
Source: *AmAu&B; Au&Wr 71; AuBYP 2,
    3; BioIn 7, 9, 10, 12, 13; ConAu 1R,
    2NR, 45; CurBio 73; NatCAB 59;
    NewYTBE 73; SmATA 3, 26; WebAMB;
    WhAm 6; WhoAm 74*

Treitel, Jonathan
English. Writer
Author of *The Red Cabbage Cafe,* 1991,
    a novel of post-Revolution Russia.
b. 1959, England
Source: *ConLC 70*

Treitschke, Heinrich Gotthard von
German. Historian
Member of Prussian school of history,
    19th-c. Germany; supported idea of
    united Germany under Prussian
    leadership.
b. Sep 15, 1834 in Dresden, Germany
d. Apr 28, 1896 in Berlin, Germany
Source: *BiD&SB; BioIn 1, 4, 7, 9;
    CasWL; DcEuL; EuAu; McGEWB;
    OxCGer 76; REn*

Trelawny, Edward John
English. Adventurer
Wrote *Recollections of the Last Days of
    Shelley and Byron,* 1858.
b. Nov 13, 1792 in London, England
d. Aug 13, 1881 in Sompting, England
Source: *Alli; Benet 87, 96; BiD&SB;
    BioIn 17, 18, 21; BritAu 19; CamBiEn;
    CasWL; CelCen; ChamBiD; DcAmAu;
    DcEnA; DcLB 110, 116, 144; DcLEL;
    DcNaB; EvLB; NewC; NewCBEL;
    OxCEng 67, 85, 95; PenC ENG; REn*

Tremayne, Les
American. Actor
Long-time radio actor in "The First
    Nighter," 1933-43; "The Thin Man,"
    1945-50; had character roles in US
    films from 1951: *The Fortune Cookie,*
    1966.
b. Apr 16, 1913 in London, England
Source: *FilmgC; ForYSC; HalFC 84, 88;
    IntMPA 75, 76, 77, 78, 79, 80, 81, 82,
    84, 86, 88, 92, 94, 96; RadStar; SaTiSS;*

*WhoAm 74, 76, 78, 80, 82; WhoHol 92,
    A; WhoWor 80, 82*

Tremblay, Michel
Canadian. Dramatist
Plays include *Les Belles-Soeurs,* 1968.
b. Jun 25, 1942 in Montreal, Quebec,
    Canada
Source: *Benet 96; BioIn 11, 15, 16, 17,
    24; CamBiEn; CamGWoT; CanWW 96,
    97, 98, 1999; CaP; ClDMEL 80; ConAu
    116, 128; ConCaAu 1; ConLC 29, 102;
    ConWorW 93; DcLB 60; EncWL 2S, 3;
    GayLL 1; IntDcT 2; IntWW 91, 93, 97,
    98, 2000; MajTwCW 1, 2; McGEWD 84;
    OxCCanL 1, 2; OxCCan SUP;
    OxCCanT; OxCThe 83; WhoCanL 85,
    87, 92; WhoWor 95; WorAu 1970*

Trenary, Jill
American. Skater
Three-time US figure skating champion;
    world champion, 1990.
b. 1969 in Minneapolis, Minnesota
Source: *EncFiS*

Trench, Richard Chenevix
Irish. Poet, Scholar
Noted philologist who popularized study
    of language: *Study of Words.*
b. Sep 5, 1807 in Dublin, Ireland
d. Mar 28, 1886 in London, England
Source: *Alli, SUP; BbD; Benet 87, 96;
    BiD&SB; BiDIrW; BioIn 5, 12, 19;
    BritAu 19; CamBiEn; CamGEL;
    CamGLE; CelCen; ChamBiD; Chambr
    3; ChhPo, S1, S2; DcBiPP; DcEnL;
    DcEuL; DcIrB 1, 2, 3; DcIrL 96;
    DcLEL; DcNaB, C; EvLB; LuthC 75;
    NewC; NewCBEL; OxCEng 67, 85, 95;
    OxCIri; PoIre; REn*

Trenchard, Hugh Montague, First Viscount
"Father of the RAF"
English. Military Leader
Marshall of Royal Air Force from 1927.
b. Feb 3, 1873 in Taunton, England
d. Feb 10, 1956 in London, England
Source: *CopCroC; DcNaB 1951;
    DcTwHis; GrBr; HarEnMi; HisEWW;
    WhAm 3; WhE&EA; WhoMilH 76;
    WorAl; WorAlBi*

Trendelenburg, Friedrich Adolf
German. Educator, Philosopher
Professor; wrote a number of scholarly
    books supporting the philosophy of
    Plato and Aristotle, against that of
    Kant and Hegel.
b. Nov 30, 1802 in Eutin, Germany
d. Jan 24, 1872 in Berlin, Germany
Source: *BiD&SB; CelCen; CyEd;
    OxCLaw*

Trendle, George Washington
American. Producer
Creator of "The Lone Ranger," "The
    Green Hornet," "Sergeant Preston of
    the Yukon" radio series, 1930s-40s.
b. Jul 4, 1884 in Norwalk, Ohio

d. May 11, 1972 in Grosse Pointe, Michigan
Source: *BioIn 9; EncMys; HisDcAR; NewYTBE 72; WhAm 5*

Trenet, Charles
French. Singer, Songwriter
Writer of pop classic *Beyond the Sea.*
b. May 18, 1913 in Perpignan, France
Source: *BioIn 1, 6, 15, 16, 22; CurBio 89; DcTwCCu 2; NewYTBS 87; OxCPMus; PenEncP; Songw; WhoFr 79; WhoHol 92*

Treptow, Martin A
American. Soldier
Ronald Reagan made reference to him in Inaugural speech, 1981.
b. 1894 in Bloomer, Wisconsin
d. Jul 28, 1918 in Chateau Thierry, France
Source: *BioIn 12*

Tretiak, Vladislav
Russian. Hockey Player
Goalie, Soviet national team, 1970s; wrote *The Hockey I Love,* translated, 1977; Hall of Fame, 1989.
b. Apr 25, 1952, Union of Soviet Socialist Republics
Source: *BioIn 10, 11, 13*

Treurnicht, Andries Petrus
South African. Politician
Leader of South African Conservative Party; advocate of separate national areas based on race.
b. Feb 19, 1921 in Piketberg, South Africa
Source: *AfSS 78, 79, 80, 81, 82; BioIn 12; CamBiEn; ChamBiD; DcCPSAf; IntWW 74, 75, 76, 77, 78, 79, 80, 81, 82, 83, 89, 91; IntYB 81, 82; News 92; NewYTBS 82; WhAm 11; WhoWor 89, 91, 93*

Trevelyan, George Macaulay
English. Historian, Author
Known for dramatic histories of England, including *England under Queen Anne,* 1930-34.
b. Feb 16, 1876 in Stratford-upon-Avon, England
d. Jul 21, 1962 in Cambridge, England
Source: *ArizL; BioIn 1, 2, 3, 4, 5, 6, 7, 10, 11, 13, 14, 18, 19, 22, 23; BlueB 76; CamBiEn; CamGEL; CasWL; ChamBiD; Chambr 3; ChhPo S2; ConAu 89; CyWA 97; DcLEL; DcNaB 1961; EncWB 98; EvLB; GloEncH; GrBr; LinLib L; LngCTC; McGEWB; ModBrL; NewC; NewCBEL; OxCEng 67; OxCTwCL; PenC ENG; RAdv 14, 13-3; REn; TwCA, SUP; WebE&AL; WhAm 4; WhE&EA; WhLit; WhoLA; WorAl; WorAlBi; WorAu 1900*

Trevino, Elizabeth Borton de
American. Children's Author
Won Newbery Medal for *I, Juan de Pareja,* 1966.
b. Sep 2, 1904 in Bakersfield, California

Source: *AuBYP 2; BioIn 14, 19; ConAu 9NR, 17R; DcAmChF 1960; NewbC 1966; ScF&FL 1, 2; SmATA 1, 5AS, 29; ThrBJA; WhoAm 74, 76, 78, 80, 82; WhoAmW 70, 72, 74; WhoSSW 73, 75, 76*

Trevino, Lee Buck
American. Golfer
Turned pro, 1960; first to win US, British, Canadian opens in same yr., 1971; struck by lightning on golf course, 1975, which changed his swing; wrote autobiography *They Call Me Super Mex,* 1983.
b. Dec 1, 1939 in Dallas, Texas
Source: *BiDAmSp OS; CamDcAB; ChamBiD; ConAu 113; CurBio 71; FacFETw; IntWW 81, 82, 83, 89, 91, 93, 97, 98, 2000; WebAB 74, 79; WhoAm 74, 76, 78, 80, 82, 84, 86, 88, 90, 92, 94, 95, 96, 97, 98, 99, 2000; WhoGolf; WhoIntG; WhoSSW 73, 75, 76, 78, 80, 82; WhoWor 74, 98, 99, 2000*

Trevithick, Richard
English. Inventor
Built first passenger steam train, 1801.
b. Apr 13, 1771 in Illogan, England
d. Apr 22, 1833 in Dartford, England
Source: *AsBiEn; BioIn 1, 2, 3, 4, 5, 6, 7, 9, 12, 14; CamBiEn; ChamBiD; DcBiPP; DcInv; DcNaB; InSci; NewCol 75; OxCBrHi; OxCLiW 86; RanHWDS; WebBD 83; WhDW; WorAl; WorAlBi; WorInv*

Trevor, Claire
American. Actor
Won Oscar for *Key Largo,* 1948.
b. Mar 8, 1909 in New York, New York
d. Apr 8, 2000 in Newport Beach, California
Source: *BiDFilm, 81, 94; BioIn 9, 18, 24; CmMov; ConTFT 9; DcPseud; FemmeNo; FilmEn; FilmgC; ForYSC; GangFlm; HalFC 80, 84, 88; IntDcF 2-3; IntMPA 84, 86, 88; InWom SUP; LegTOT; MotPP; MovMk; OsStAZ; OxCFilm; ThFT; VarWW 85; WhoAm 74; WhoHol 92, A; WhoThe 77A; WhThe; WomWMM; WorAl; WorAlBi; WorEFlm*

Trevor, William
[William Trevor Cox]
Irish. Author, Dramatist
Works deal with domestic, private relationships in English, Irish counties, towns; wrote *The Children of Dynmouth,* 1976; *Two Lives: Reading Turgenev; My House in Umbria,* 1991.
b. May 24, 1928 in Mitchelstown, Ireland
Source: *Benet 87, 96; BiDIrW; BioIn 10, 13, 14, 17, 18, 19, 20, 23; BlueB 76; BritWr S4; CamBiEn; CamGLE; ChamBiD; ConAu 4NR, 9NR, 9R, 37NR, 55NR, X; ConBrDr; ConDr 73, 77, 82, 88, 93; ConLC 7, 9, 14, 25, 71, 116; ConNov 72, 76, 82, 86, 91, 96; CurBio 84; CyWA 89, 97; DcIrL, 96; DcIrW 1; DcLB 14, 139; DcLEL 1940; DcPseud;*

EncWB, 98; EncWL 2S, 3; FacFETw; IntAu&W 76, 77, 82, 86, 89, 91, 93; IntWW 81, 82, 83, 89, 91, 93, 97, 98, 2000; MajTwCW 1; ModBrL 2, S1, S2; ModIrL; ModIrLi; NewC; Novels; OxCEng 85, 95; OxCIri; OxCTwCL; RfGEnL 91; RfGShF 1, 2; ScF&FL 92; ShSCr 21; ShSWr; TwCWr; Who 74, 82, 83, 85, 88, 90, 92, 94, 98, 99, 2000; WhoWor 74, 76, 84, 87, 89, 91, 93, 95; WorAu 1950; WrDr 76, 80, 82, 84, 86, 88, 90, 92, 94, 96, 98, 99, 2000

Trevor-Roper, Hugh Redwald
[Baron Dacre of Glanton]
English. Historian
Books covering period from Roman Empire to Nazi Germany include *The Crisis of the Seventeenth Century,* 1967; *The Last Days of Hitler,* 1947.
b. Jan 15, 1914 in Glanton, England
Source: *CamBiEn; ChamBiD; ConAu 101; CurBio 83; GloEncH; GloEncH; IntWW 83; LngCTC; OxCTwCL; REn; TwCA SUP; Who 85; WhoWor 97, 98, 99, 2000; WorAu 1900; WrDr 86, 98, 99, 2000*

Treybig, James G
American. Computer Executive
Pres. and CEO Tandem Computers, 1974—.
b. 1940 in Clarendon, Texas
Source: *BioIn 13, 15; Dun&B 90; News 88-3; WhoFI 89; WhoWest 92*

Tribble, Isreal, Jr.
[Israel Tribble, Jr.]
American. Educator
President and CEO, Florida Education Fund, 1985—.
b. Sep 4, 1940 in Philadelphia, Pennsylvania
Source: *BioIn 20; ConBlB 8; WhoAfA 9; WhoBlA 2, 7, 8*

Tribe, Laurence Henry
American. Lawyer, Educator
Authority on Constitutional law; clients include Sun Myung Moon, Hare Krishnas.
b. Oct 10, 1941 in Shanghai, China
Source: *CamDcAB; CurBio 88; DrAS 74P, 78P, 82P, 99P; IntWW 89, 91, 93, 97, 98, 2000; WhoAm 82, 84, 86, 88, 90, 92, 94, 95, 96; WhoAmL 83, 85, 90, 92, 94; WhoE 91, 93, 95; WhoEmL 87; WrDr 98, 99, 2000*

Tribe Called Quest, A
[Ali (Ali Shaheed Muhammed); Jonathan (Q-Tip) Davis; (Phife) Malik Taylor]
American. Rap Group
Have won accolades for their use of complex musical structures and the fresh collage of sonic information they have produced.
Source: *BioIn 8; ConMus 8; McGEWB; NewYTBE 73*

Trible, Paul Seward, Jr.
American. Politician
Rep. senator from VA, 1983-89.
b. Dec 29, 1946 in Baltimore, Maryland
Source: *AlmAP 88; BiDrUSC 89; BioIn 13; CngDr 77, 79, 81, 87; IntWW 83, 89, 91, 93; WhoAm 78, 80, 82, 84, 86, 88, 90, 96, 97, 98, 99, 2000; WhoAmP 77, 79, 81, 83, 85, 87, 89, 91, 93, 95, 97, 1999; WhoEmL 87; WhoFI 00, 96, 98; WhoGov 77; WhoSSW 78, 80, 82, 84, 86, 88; WhoWor 84, 87, 89*

Tricky
[Adrian Thaws]
English. Producer, Composer, Singer, Songwriter
Invented the genre known as "trip-hop;" member of group Massive Attack, 1990-1995; released solo debut album, *Maxinquaye,* 1995 and later *Tricky Presents Grass Roots,* 1996; also recorded *Nearly God,* 1996.
b. c. 1967 in Bristol, England
Source: *ConMus 18*

Trifa, Valerian
American. Religious Leader
Orthodox archbishop ordered out of U.S. for hiding pro-Nazi activities while a student leader in pre-WW II Romania.
b. Jun 28, 1914 in Campeni, Romania
d. Jan 28, 1987 in Cascais, Portugal
Source: *AnObit 1987; BlueB 76; NewYTBS 87; RelLAm 1, 2; WhoAm 82, 84; WhoRel 85*

Trifonov, Yuri Valentinovich
Russian. Author
Major contributor to 20th-c. Russian literature; tales of Stalinist era include *The House on the Embankment,* 1983.
b. Aug 28, 1925 in Moscow, Union of Soviet Socialist Republics
d. Mar 21, 1981 in Moscow, Union of Soviet Socialist Republics
Source: *AnObit 1981; ClDMEL 80; ConAu 103; EncWL 2; FacFETw; IntWW 80; WhoSocC 78; WorAu 1975*

Trigere, Pauline
American. Fashion Designer
Leading designer of ladies' ready-to wear clothes; known for cutting, designing directly from bolts of cloth; won Coty Award, 1949, 1951, 1959.
b. Nov 4, 1912 in Paris, France
Source: *AmDec 1940; BioIn 2, 5, 10, 11; BioNews 74; CelR, 90; ConDes 84, 90, 97; ConFash; CurBio 60; EncFash; FairDF US; GoodHs; InWom, SUP; LegTOT; LibW; ThHDFas; WhoAm 74, 76, 78, 80, 82, 84, 86, 88, 92, 94, 95, 96, 97, 98, 99, 2000; WhoAmW 58, 61, 64, 66, 68, 70, 72, 74, 81, 83, 91, 93, 95, 97, 99; WhoFash 88; WorFshn*

Trihey, Harry
[Henry Judah Trihey]
Canadian. Hockey Player
Center, Montreal Shamrocks, 1897-1901; Hall of Fame, 1950.

b. Dec 25, 1877 in Montreal, Quebec, Canada
d. Dec 9, 1942 in Montreal, Quebec, Canada
Source: *WhoHcky 73*

Trillin, Calvin Marshall
American. Author
Books include *Uncivil Liberties,* 1982; *If You Can't Say Something Nice,* 1987; *American Stories,* 1991.
b. Dec 5, 1935 in Kansas City, Missouri
Source: *AuNews 1; CamDcAB; ConAu 67NR, 85; MajTwCW 2; OxCAmL 83; WhoAm 86, 97, 98; WhoEnt 98*

Trilling, Diana (Rubin)
American. Author, Critic
Wife of Lionel; wrote *Mrs. Harris: The Death of the Scarsdale Diet Doctor,* 1981.
b. Jul 21, 1905 in New York, New York
d. Oct 23, 1996 in New York, New York
Source: *AmWomM; AmWomWr; ArtclWW 2; Au&Wr 71; BenetAL 91; BioIn 3, 11, 12, 13; ConAu 5R, 10NR, 46NR, 154; CurBio 79; ForWC 70; IntAu&W 86, 89; InWom SUP; MajTwCW 1, 2; NewYTBS 96; OxCAmL 83, 95; REnAL; WhoAm 80, 82, 84, 86, 88, 90, 92, 94, 95, 96, 97; WhoWorJ 72, 78; WorAu 1975; WrDr 86, 88, 90, 92, 94, 96*

Trilling, Lionel
American. Author, Critic
Volumes of essays include *The Opposing Self,* 1955; *The Middle of the Journey,* 1947.
b. Jul 4, 1905 in New York, New York
d. Nov 5, 1975 in New York, New York
Source: *AmAu&B; AmNatBi; AmNov; AmWr S3; Benet 87, 96; BenetAL 91; BiCoLiE; BioIn 1, 2, 3, 4, 10, 11, 12, 13, 14, 15, 16, 17, 19, 20, 22, 24; BlueB 76; CamBiEn; CamDcAB; CamGLE; CamHAL; CasWL; CelR; ChamBiD; CnDAL; ConAu 9R, 10NR, 61; ConJeAN; ConLC 9, 11, 24; ConLCrt 77, 82; ConNov 72, 76; CyWA 89, 97; DcAmB S9; DcAmC; DcArts; DcLB 28, 63; DcLEL; DrAS 74E; EncALit; EncWL 1, 2, 2S, 3; FacFETw; GrWrEL N; IntAu&W 76; IntWW 74, 75; JeAmFiW; JeAmHC; LegTOT; LinLib L; LngCTC; MajTwCW 1, 2; MakMC; ModAL 4, 4S2, 5; NewYTBE 71; NewYTBS 75, 76; Novels; ObitT 1971; OxCAmL 65, 83, 95; OxCEng 85, 95; OxCTwCL; PenC AM; PeoHis; RAdv 1, 14, 13-1; REn; REnAL; RfGAmL 4, 87, 94; RGTwCWr; ThTwC 87; TwCA SUP; TwCWr; WebAB 74, 79; WhAm 6, 7; Who 74; WhoAm 74, 76; WhoE 74, 75; WhoTwCL; WhoWor 74; WhoWorJ 72, 78; WorAl; WorAlBi; WorAu 1900*

Trimble, (William) David
Irish. Politician
Member of the British parliament was a key figure in the historic Northern Ireland peace agreement of 1998, for

which he was awarded the Nobel Peace Prize.
b. Oct 15, 1944 in Belfast, Northern Ireland
Source: *ModIrLi; Who 92, 94, 98, 99, 2000*

Trintignant, Jean-Louis Xavier
French. Actor
Films include *And God Created Woman,* 1957; *A Man and a Woman,* 1966.
b. Dec 11, 1930 in Polenc, France
Source: *BiDFilm; BioNews 74; CurBio 88; FilmgC; IntMPA 84; IntWW 83, 97, 2000; MotPP; MovMk; OxCFilm; VarWW 85; WhoHol A; WhoWor 74; WorAl; WorEFlm*

Tripp, Paul
American. Children's Author, Actor, Producer
Created, produced TV shows for children; wrote script, lyrics for film *The Christmas That Almost Wasn't,* 1966; also starred in film.
b. Feb 20, 1916 in New York, New York
Source: *ASCAP 66, 80; ConAu 21R; ConTFT 2; SmATA 8; WhoAm 84, 86, 88, 90, 92; WhoE 74, 75, 77, 81, 83, 85, 86, 89; WhoEnt 92; WhoHol A*

Trippe, Juan Terry
American. Airline Executive
Founded Pan Am, 1928; had first transatlantic passenger service, 1939.
b. Jun 27, 1899 in Sea Bright, New Jersey
d. Apr 3, 1981 in New York, New York
Source: *AmNatBi; BiDAmBL 83; BioIn 1, 2, 3, 4, 7, 8, 12, 13, 15, 16; CamBiEn; CamDcAB; ChamBiD; CurBio 42, 55, 81; EncWB 98; FacFETw; InSci; OxCAmH; ScrEAmL 1; St&PR 75; WhAm 7; Who 74; WhoE 74; WhoFI 74, 75, 77; WorAl*

Trippi, Charlie
[Charles L Trippi]
"Scintillating Sicilian"; "Triple-Threat Trippi"
American. Football Player
Running back, Chicago Cards, 1947-55; Hall of Fame, 1968.
b. Dec 14, 1922 in Pittston, Pennsylvania
Source: *BioIn 1, 8; LegTOT; WhoFtbl 74*

Tripplehorn, Jean
American. Actor
Appeared in *Basic Instinct.*
b. 1963 in Tulsa, Oklahoma

Trist, Nicholas Philip
American. Lawyer, Diplomat
Best known for negotiating the Treaty of Guadalupe Hidalgo, ending the war with Mexico in 1848.
b. Jun 2, 1800 in Charlottesville, Virginia
d. Feb 11, 1874 in Alexandria, Virginia
Source: *AmBi; AmNatBi; ApCAB; BioIn 3, 9, 12, 16, 17; CamDcAB; DcAmB;*

DcAmDH 80, 89; Drake; EncAB-H 1974; EncSoH; EncWB 98; HarEnUS; McGEWB; NatCAB 7; OxCAmH; WebAB 74, 79; WhAm HS

Tristano, Leonard Joseph
"Lennie"
American. Jazz Musician
Blind avant-garde pianist, active, late 1940s; noted for jazz improvisations.
b. Mar 19, 1919 in Chicago, Illinois
d. Nov 18, 1978 in Jamaica, New York
Source: *BakBD 84; BiDAmM; BioIn 5, 8, 11, 12, 15, 16; CamDcAB; CmpEPM; DcAmB S10; EncJzS; NewGrDM 80; WhoE 74*

Tritt, Travis
American. Singer, Songwriter, Musician
Country music singer; debut album *Country Club*, 1990 went gold; Grammy, vocal collaboration with Mary Stuart, for "The Whisky Ain't Workin,'" 1992.
b. Feb 9, 1963 in Marietta, Georgia
Source: *AllMGCo; BgBkCoM; ConMus 7; LegTOT; WhoAm 94, 95, 96, 97, 98, 99, 2000; WhoEnt 98*

Triumph
[Rick Emmet; Mike Levine; Gil Moore]
Canadian. Music Group
Albums include *Best Of*, 1985.
Source: *BioIn 19; EncPR&S 89; GrMetD; HarEnR 86; RkOn 85; WhoRocM 82*

Trnka, Jiri
Czech. Filmmaker, Illustrator
Award-winning puppet film producer: *The Animals and the Brigands*, 1946; *Favorite Tales from Grimm and Andersen*, 1959.
b. Feb 24, 1912 in Pilsen, Bohemia
d. Dec 30, 1969 in Prague, Czechoslovakia
Source: *BioIn 14, 15, 19; ConAu 111; DcFM; EncEurC; FilmEn; HalFC 84; IlsCB 1957; IntDcF 1-2, 2-4; MajAl; OxCFilm; SmATA 32, 43; ThrBJA; WhoGrA 62; WorECar; WorEFlm*

Troell, Jan
Swedish. Director
Films include *The Emigrants*, 1971; *The New Land*, 1973; *Flight of the Eagle*, 1978; often edits, photographs works.
b. Jul 23, 1931 in Limhamn, Sweden
Source: *ConTFT 8; EncEurC; FilmEn; HalFC 80, 84, 88; IntDcF 1-2; IntMPA 75, 76, 77, 78, 79, 80, 81, 82, 84, 86, 88, 92, 94, 96; MiSFD 9; MovMk; WorEFlm; WorFDir 2*

Troeltsch, Ernst
German. Theologian, Historian, Sociologist
Intellectual utilized the objective methods of modern scholarship and contributed to the sociology of religion and the problems of historicism.
b. 1865 in Augsburg, Germany

d. 1923
Source: *BiDChrM; BioIn 8, 11, 14, 18, 19; EncWB 98; GloEncH; McGEWB; ThTwC 87; WhoChr*

Troger, Paul
Austrian. Painter
Known for his frescoes, the artist's highly dramatic style and use of light colors was tremendously influential.
b. Oct 30, 1698 in Welsberg, Austria
d. 1762
Source: *EncWB 98; McGDA; McGEWB*

Troggs, The
[Ronnie Bond; Chris Britton; Tony Murray; Reg Presley]
British. Music Group
Cabaret, club performers since 1966; albums include *Love is All Around*, 1967.
Source: *BillEnR; BioIn 12; ConMuA 80A; EncRk 88; EncRkSt; HarEnR 86; RkOn 78, 84; RolSEnR 83; WhoRock 81; WhoRocM 82*

Trohan, Walter
American. Journalist
With *Chicago Tribune*, 1929-71, as Washington correspondent, executive director; wrote *Political Animals*, 1975.
b. Jul 4, 1903 in Mount Carmel, Pennsylvania
Source: *BioIn 1, 10; ConAu 81; EncTwCJ; WhoAm 74, 76, 78, 80, 82, 84, 86, 88, 90, 92, 94, 95; WhoWor 80, 82, 84, 87, 89, 91, 93, 95*

Trollope, Anthony
English. Author
Wrote 50 novels including *Barsetshire Chronicles*, 1850s-60s.
b. Apr 24, 1815 in London, England
d. Dec 6, 1882 in London, England
Source: *Alli, SUP; AtlBL; BbD; Benet 87, 96; BenetAL 91; BiCoLiE; BiD&SB; BioIn 1, 2, 3, 4, 5, 6, 7, 8, 9, 10, 11, 12, 13, 14, 15, 16, 17, 18, 19, 22, 23; BlmGEL; BritAS; BritAu 19; BritWr 5; CamBiEn; CamGEL; CamGLE; CasWL; CelCen; ChamBiD; Chambr 3; ChhPo S2; CnDBLB 4; CrtT 3, 4; CyWA 58, 97; DcArts; DcBiA; DcBiPP; DcEnA; DcEnL; DcEuL; DcIrL 96; DcLB 21, 57, 159; DcLEL; DcNaB; Dis&D; EncSF, 93; EncWB 98; EvLB; GrWrEL N; HsB&A; LegTOT; LinLib L, S; LngCEL; MagSWL; McGEWB; MouLC 4; NewC; NewCBEL; NinCLC 6, 33; Novels; OxCAusL; OxCBrHi; OxCEng 67, 85, 95; PenC ENG; RAdv 1, 14, 13-1; REn; REnAL; RfGEnL 91; RfGShF 1, 2; ScF&FL 1; ScFEYrs; ScFSB; ShSCr 28; SmATA 22; StaCVF; VicBrit; WebE&AL; WhDW; WorAl; WorAlBi; WorLitC; WrPh*

Trollope, Frances
English. Author
Wrote controversial, much resented *Domestic Manners of the Americans*, 1832; mother of Anthony.

b. Mar 10, 1780 in Bristol, England
d. Oct 6, 1863 in Florence, Italy
Source: *Alli; ArtclWW 2; BbD; Benet 87, 96; BenetAL 91; BiD&SB; BioIn 1, 2, 3, 4, 5, 6, 8, 9, 10, 11, 12, 13; BlmGEL; BritAu 19; CamGEL; CamGLE; CasWL; ChamBiD; Chambr 3; ContDcW 89; DcAmImH; DcEnA; DcEnL; DcLEL; DcNaB; EvLB; FemiCLE; LegTOT; NewC; NewCBEL; NinCLC 30; OhA&B; OxCAmH; OxCAmL 65, 83, 95; OxCEng 67, 85, 95; PenC ENG; REn; REnAL*

Tromp, Solco Walle
Dutch. Geologist, Author
Wrote *Neo-Materialism; Physical Physics*.
b. Mar 9, 1909 in Batavia, Dutch East Indies
d. Mar 17, 1983, Netherlands
Source: *BiDPara; ConAu 116; EncO&P 2*

Trotman, Alexander J.
American. Auto Executive
Chairman and CEO of Ford Motor Co., 1993—.
b. Jul 22, 1933 in Middlesex, England
Source: *AutoN 79; Dun&B 86, 88, 90, 98; WhoAm 90, 96, 97, 98, 99, 2000; WhoE 99; WhoFI 00, 87, 94, 96, 98; WhoMW 96, 98; WhoWor 96, 97, 98, 99, 2000*

Trotsky, Leon
[Lev Davidovitch Bronstein]
Russian. Political Leader, Author
Organized 1917 revolution; banished, 1929, after power struggle with Stalin.
b. Nov 8, 1879 in Elisavetgrad, Russia
d. Aug 21, 1940 in Mexico City, Mexico
Source: *Benet 87, 96; BiDMarx; BiDSovU; BioIn 1, 2, 3, 4, 5, 6, 7, 8, 9, 10, 11, 12, 13, 14, 15, 16, 17, 18, 19, 20, 21, 22, 23; CamBiEn; CasWL; ChamBiD; ColdWar 1, 2; ConAu 118, 167; CurBio 40; DcAmC; DcAmSR; DcPseud; DcRusL; DcTwHis; EncRev; EncWB 98; Film 1; GloEncH; HarEnMi; HisEWW; HisWorL; JeHun; LegTOT; LinLib L, S; LngCTC; MakMC; McGEWB; OxCPhil; RadHan; RAdv 14, 13-3; REn; ThTwC 87; TwCLC 22; WhoHol B; WhScrn 77, 83; WorAl; WorAlBi*

Trotta, Margarethe Von
German. Filmmaker
Work focuses on concerns and relationships of women; films include *Rosa Luxemburg*, 1986; *Love and Fear*, 1988.
b. Feb 21, 1942 in Berlin, Germany
Source: *BioIn 14, 16; ConAu 126; ContDcW 89; CurBio 88; EncEurC; HalFC 84; IntDcF 2-2; ReelWom; WorFDir 2*

Trotta, Maurice S
American. Educator, Author
Labor arbitrator, wrote books on industrial labor relations.

b. Aug 15, 1907 in New York, New
York
d. Jul 11, 1976 in Newton, New Jersey
Source: *AmMWSc 73S; ConAu 111;
WhoLab 76*

Trotter, John Scott
American. Musician, Songwriter
Pianist, arranger for Bing Crosby radio
shows, 1930s-40s; won Oscar for
scoring *Pennies From Heaven,* 1961.
b. Jun 14, 1908 in Charlotte, North
Carolina
d. Oct 29, 1975 in Los Angeles,
California
Source: *ASCAP 66, 80; BioIn 4, 10;
CmpEPM; NewYTBS 75; ObitOF 79;
RadStar; WhoHol C; WhScrn 77, 83*

Trotter, Mildred
American. Anatomist, Anthropologist
Formulated a method for using bone
length to estimate the height of the
body from which it came; her studies
contributed to a wide range of
disciplines, including medicine,
forensics, engineering, and aeronautics.
b. Feb 3, 1899 in Beaver, Pennsylvania
d. Aug 23, 1991
Source: *AmMWSc 79, 82, 86, 89; BioIn
18, 20; CamDcAB; EncWB 98; FifIDA;
HisPhAn; McGMS 80; NotTwCS 1;
WhAm 11; WhoAm 74, 76, 80, 82, 84,
86, 88; WhoAmW 58, 70, 72*

Trotter, Monroe
[William Monroe Trotter]
American. Civil Rights Activist, Editor
Co-founder and editor, *The Guardian,* a
Boston newspaper, 1901-34.
b. Apr 7, 1872 in Chillicothe, Ohio
d. Apr 7, 1934 in Boston, Massachusetts
Source: *AfrAmAl 6; AmDec 1900;
BiDAmJo; BioIn 1, 5, 8, 9, 16, 21;
BlkWrNE; ConBlB 9; DcAmNB;
DcTwCCu 5; EncAB-H 1974, 1996;
EncAJ; EncWB; InB&W 80, 85; NegAl
76, 83, 89; NotBlAM; SelBAAf;
SelBAAu; WhoColR*

Trottier, Bryan John
"Trots"
American. Hockey Player
Center, NY Islanders, 1975-90;
Pittsburgh, 1990-93; won Art Ross,
Hart trophies, 1979; 15th player in
NHL history to score 500 goals
(1990).
b. Jul 17, 1956 in Val Marie,
Saskatchewan, Canada
Source: *CurBio 85; HocEn; HocReg 87;
NewYTBS 75, 78; WhoAm 80, 82, 84,
86, 88, 90, 92, 94, 95, 96, 97, 98; WhoE
95*

Troup, Bobby
[Robert William Troup]
American. Actor, Songwriter, Singer
Former bandleader who played Dr. Joe
Early in TV series "Emergency,"
1972-77; wrote "Daddy," 1941;
"Route 66," 1946.

b. Oct 18, 1918 in Harrisburg,
Pennsylvania
d. Feb 7, 1999 in Los Angeles,
California
Source: *AllMGJa; ASCAP 66, 80; BioIn
10; CmpEPM; ForYSC; PenEncP;
Songw; WhoEnt 92; WhoHol 92, A*

Trout, Dizzy
[Paul Howard Trout]
American. Baseball Player
Pitcher, 1939-52, 1957, mostly with
Detroit; led AL in wins, 1943.
b. Jun 29, 1915 in Sandcut, Indiana
d. Feb 28, 1972 in Chicago, Illinois
Source: *Ballpl 90; BiDAmSp Sup; BioIn
2, 3, 9; NewYTBE 72; ObitOF 79*

Trout, Robert
"Iron Man of Radio"
American. Broadcast Journalist
Coined term "fireside chats" for FDR's
radio broadcasts, which he announced;
known for ad-libbing, stamina.
b. Oct 15, 1908 in Wake County, North
Carolina
Source: *BiDAmJo; BioIn 1, 7; CelR;
CurBio 65; EncAJ; EncTeIN; EncTwCJ;
HisDcAR; LesBEnT; NewYTET; RadStar;
SaTiSS; WhoAm 74, 76*

Troutt, Kenny A.
American. Entrepreneur
Founder and CEO of Excel
Communications, one of the fastest-
growing providers of
telecommunications services in the
United States with sales of $507
million in 1995.
b. Jan 8, 1948 in Mt. Vernon, Illinois
Source: *Dun&B 98; News 98, 98-1*

Trovoada, Miguel
Sao Tomean. Political Leader
Founder of the Acao Democratica
Independente (ADI) party, he was
elected president of Sao Tome and
Principe in 1991 and reelected in
1996; his priority was turning around
the country's failing economy.
b. Dec 27, 1936, Sao Tome and Principe
Source: *ProfiWG 98; WhoWor 96, 97,
98, 99, 2000*

Trowbridge, John Townsend
American. Journalist, Author
Best known for juvenile antislavery
novels, *Cudjo's Cave,* 1864; *Jack
Hazard Series,* 1871-74; narrative
poem, "Darius Green and His Flying
Machine," 1903.
b. Sep 18, 1827 in Ogdensburg, New
York
d. Feb 12, 1916 in Arlington,
Massachusetts
Source: *Alli, SUP; AmAu; AmAu&B;
AmBi; AmNatBi; ApCAB; BbD; BenetAL
91; BibAL 8; BiD&SB; BioIn 1, 2, 5;
CarSB; ChhPo, S1; CyAL 2; CyWA 58,
97; DcAmAu; DcAmB; DcBiA; DcEnL;
DcLB 202; DcLEL; DcNAA; Drake;
HarEnUS; LinLib L, S; NatCAB 3;*

*OxCAmL 65; REnAL; TwCBDA; WhAm
1*

Trower, Robin
[Procol Harum]
English. Musician
Albums include *Beyond the Mist,* 1985.
b. Mar 9, 1945 in London, England
Source: *AllMGBl 2; ConMuA 80A;
EncPR&S 74, 89; EncRk 88; GrMetD;
HarEnR 86; IlEncRk; LegTOT;
PenEncP; RolSEnR 83; WhoRock 81;
WhoRocM 82*

Troy, Hannah
American. Fashion Designer
Creator of the petite size for women;
introduced Italian styles to the US.
b. Feb 10, 1905 in New York, New
York
d. Jun 22, 1993 in Miami Beach, Florida
Source: *WhoAmW 58, 61, 64, 66*

Troyanos, Tatiana
American. Opera Singer
Mezzo-soprano; starred in *Ariodante,*
opening of Kennedy Center, 1971.
b. Sep 12, 1938 in New York, New
York
d. Aug 21, 1993 in New York, New
York
Source: *AnObit 1993; BakBD 84, 92;
BakBDTw; BioIn 12, 13, 19, 20; CelR
90; CmOp; CurBio 79, 93N; IntDcOp;
IntWWM 90; InWom SUP; LegTOT;
MetOEnc; NewAmDM; NewGrDA 86;
NewGrDM 80; NewGrDO; NewYTBS 76,
93; OxDcOp; PenDiMP; WhAm 11;
WhoAm 78, 80, 82, 84, 86, 88, 92, 94;
WhoAmM 83; WhoAmW 81, 83, 85;
WhoMus 72; WhoOp 76*

Troyat, Henri
[Lev Tarassoff]
French. Author
Well-known French author, wrote a
series of biographical novels on
Russian literary figures.
b. Nov 1, 1911 in Moscow, Russia
Source: *Benet 87, 96; BiDSovU; BioIn
17, 18; CasWL; ClDMEL 80; ConAu
2NR, 33NR, 45, 67NR; ConLC 23;
CurBio 92; DcPseud; DcTwCCu 2;
EncWL 1; GuFrLit 1; IntAu&W 76, 77,
82, 89; IntWW 74, 75, 76, 77, 78, 79,
80, 81, 82, 83, 89, 91, 93, 97, 98, 2000;
LinLib L; MajTwCW 1; PenC EUR;
REn; TwCWr; Who 74, 82, 83, 85, 88,
90, 92, 94, 98, 99, 2000; WhoAm 74, 76,
78, 80, 82; WhoFr 79; WhoWor 74, 76,
78, 87; WorAu 1950*

Troyon, Constant
French. Artist
Member, Barbizon School; noted for
landscapes and animal scenes,
particularly cows.
b. Aug 18, 1810 in Sevres, France
d. Feb 21, 1865 in Paris, France
Source: *ArtsNiC; BioIn 1, 4, 5, 8;
CamBiEn; ClaDrA; McGDA; McGEWD
72; NewCol 75; OxDcArt*

Trudeau, Arthur G(ilbert)
American. Military Leader
Chief Army Research & Development
  Command, 1958-62; won Silver Star
  for gallantry at Porkchop Hill.
b. Jul 5, 1902 in Middlebury, Vermont
d. Jun 5, 1991 in Chevy Chase,
  Maryland
Source: *BiDWWGF; BioIn 3, 4, 5, 11,
17; CurBio 91N; EncAInt; InSci;
NewYTBS 91; PolProf K; WhAm 10;
WhoAm 74, 76*

Trudeau, Edward Livingston
American. Physician
First to establish sanitarium, laboratories
  for pulmonary tuberculosis study in
  US, 1884, at Saranac Lake, NY.
b. Oct 5, 1848 in New York, New York
d. Nov 15, 1915
Source: *AmAu&B; AmBi; AmNatBi;
BiInAmS; BioIn 1, 2, 3, 4, 5, 8, 9;
CamDcAB; DcAmB; DcAmMeB, 84;
DcNAA; NatCAB 13; OxCMed 86;
WhAm 1*

Trudeau, Garry
[Garretson Beckman Trudeau]
American. Cartoonist
Created comic strip "Doonesbury"; won
  Pulitzer, 1975.
b. 1948 in New York, New York
Source: *AmDec 1970; Au&Arts 10;
AuNews 2; CelR 90; ChamBiD; ConAu
81; ConLC 12; ConTFT 7; CurBio 75;
EncACom; EncAJ; EncTwCJ; FacFETw;
LegTOT; News 91, 91-2; WhoAm 84, 86,
95, 96, 97, 98; WhoAmA 84; WhoE 95;
WorAlBi; WorECom; WrDr 86, 88, 90,
92*

Trudeau, Margaret Joan Sinclair
Canadian. Author, Socialite
Ex-wife of Pierre Trudeau; wrote *Beyond
  Reason,* 1979.
b. Sep 10, 1948 in Vancouver, British
  Columbia, Canada
Source: *BioNews 74; BkPepl; ConAu 93;
InWom SUP*

Trudeau, Pierre Elliott
Canadian. Political Leader
Colorful Liberal prime minister, 1969-79,
  1980-84.
b. Oct 18, 1919 in Montreal, Quebec,
  Canada
Source: *BioIn 8, 9, 10, 11, 12, 13; BlueB
76; CamBiEn; CanParl 1998; CanWW
70, 79, 80, 81, 83, 89, 96, 97, 98, 1999;
ChamBiD; ConAu 3NR, 45; CurBio 68;
DcTwHis; EncWB, 98; FacFETw;
IntWW 74, 75, 76, 77, 78, 79, 80, 81, 82,
83, 89, 91, 93, 97, 98, 2000; IntYB 78,
79, 80, 81, 82; LinLib L, S; NewYTBS
80, 84; OxCCan SUP; Who 74, 82, 83,
85, 88, 90, 92, 94, 98, 99, 2000; WhoAm
74, 76, 78, 80, 82, 84, 86, 88, 90, 92,
94, 95, 96, 97, 98, 99, 2000; WhoAmL
94; WhoCan 73, 75, 77, 80, 82; WhoE
74, 75, 77, 79, 81, 83, 85, 86, 89, 91,
93; WhoFI 98; WhoWor 74, 76, 78, 80,
82, 84, 87, 89, 91, 93, 95, 96, 97, 98,
99, 2000; WorAl; WorAlBi*

Trudell, John
American. Actor, Musician, Political
  Activist
Joined group that occupied Alcatraz
  Island, 1969; took part in the Trail of
  Broken Treaties, 1972.
b. 1947 in Niobrara, Nebraska
Source: *AmIndBi; BioIn 21; EncNAB;
NotNaAm*

Trueblood, D(avid) Elton
American. Theologian
Philosophy professor; wrote *The Essence
  of Spiritual Religion,* 1936.
b. Dec 12, 1900
d. Dec 20, 1994 in Lansdale,
  Pennsylvania
Source: *AmAu&B; BioIn 2, 3, 6, 7, 10,
12; CamBiEn; ChamBiD; ConAu 41R;
CurBio 95N; DrAS 74P, 78P, 82P;
IndAu 1967; WhAm 12; WhE&EA;
WhoAm 74, 76, 78, 82, 84, 86, 88, 90,
92, 94; WhoRel 77*

Truex, Ernest
American. Actor
Films include *It's a Wonderful World,*
  1939; *Fluffy,* 1965.
b. Sep 19, 1890? in Kansas City,
  Missouri
d. Jun 27, 1973 in Fallbrook, California
Source: *BiE&WWA; BioIn 9, 10; CurBio
41, 73, 73N; EncAFC; EncMT; Film 1,
2; FilmEn; FilmgC; HalFC 80, 84, 88;
MotPP; MovMk; NatCAB 62; ObitOF
79; TwYS; Vers A; WhoHol B; WhScrn
77; WhThe; WorAl*

Truffaut, Francois
French. Director
New Wave director who was admired for
  depictions of children, obsessed men,
  and women driven by strong passions;
  won Oscar, 1973.
b. Feb 6, 1932 in Paris, France
d. Oct 21, 1984 in Neuilly-sur-Seine,
  France
Source: *AnObit 1984; Benet 87, 96;
BiDFilm, 81, 94; BioIn 6, 7, 8, 9, 10, 11,
12, 13, 14, 15, 16, 17, 18, 20, 24;
CamBiEn; CelR; ChamBiD; ConAu
34NR, 81, 113; ConLC 20, 101; ConTFT
2; CurBio 69, 85N; DcArts; DcFM;
DcTwCCu 2; EncEurC; EncWB 98;
FacFETw; FilmEn; FilmgC; HalFC 80,
84, 88; IntDcF 1-2, 2-2; IntMPA 75, 76,
77, 78, 79, 80, 81, 82, 84; IntWW 74,
75, 76, 77, 78, 79, 80, 81, 82, 83;
ItaFilm; LegTOT; MakMC; McGEWB;
MiSFD 9N; MovMk; NewYTBS 84;
OxCFilm; RAdv 14, 13-3; WhAm 8, 11;
Who 74, 82, 83; WhoAm 74, 76, 78, 80,
82, 84; WhoFr 79; WhoHol A; WhoHrs
80; WhoWor 74, 76, 78, 80, 82, 84, 95,
96; WorAl; WorAlBi; WorEFlm;
WorFDir 2*

Truitt, Anne
American. Artist, Sculptor
Produced paintings and sculptures over
  the last five decades; helped create
  American abstract art.
b. Mar 16, 1921 in Baltimore, Maryland

Source: *BiDWomA; BioIn 13, 15, 19, 20,
21, 23; BriEAA; ConAmWS; ConArt 77,
83, 89, 96; ConWomA; DcCAA 77, 88,
94; InWom SUP; News 93-1; NorAmWA;
WhoAm 90; WhoAmA 73, 76, 78, 80, 82,
84, 86, 89, 91; WrDr 88, 90, 92, 94, 96,
98*

Trujillo (Molina), Rafael Leonidas
Dominican. Politician
Dictator of Dominican Republic, 1931-
  61; assassinated.
b. Oct 24, 1891 in San Cristoban,
  Dominican Republic
d. May 30, 1961 in Ciudad Trujillo,
  Dominican Republic
Source: *BiDLAmC; BioIn 1, 2, 3, 4, 5, 6,
7, 8, 9, 10, 12, 16, 17, 18, 23; CamBiEn;
CamBiEn; ColdWar 1, 2; CurBio 41, 61;
DcHiB; DicTyr; EncLatA; EncWB 98;
LatAmLi; McGEWB; ObitT 1961; WhAm
4; WorAl*

Truly, Richard H
American. Astronaut, Government
  Official
Commander, Columbia Flight 2, NASA,
  1981; commander, Columbia Flight 2,
  Challenger Flight 3, 1983; dir, Space
  Shuttle program, 1986-89;
  administrator, NSASA, 1989-92.
b. Nov 12, 1937 in Fayette, Mississippi
Source: *AmMWSc 98; WhoAm 98, 99,
2000; WhoScEn 2000; WhoSSW 73;
WhoWest 00; WhoWor 74; WorDWW*

Truman, Bess
[Elizabeth Virginia Wallace Truman]
"The Boss"
American. First Lady
Publicity shy, gracious, unassuming
  White House hostess, married Harry
  Truman, 1919.
b. Feb 13, 1885 in Independence,
  Missouri
d. Oct 18, 1982 in Kansas City, Missouri
Source: *AmNatBi; AnObit 1982; BioIn 1,
2, 3, 5, 6, 7, 8, 9, 10, 11, 12, 13; CurBio
47, 83; LegTOT; NewYTBE 72;
NewYTBS 82; WhoAm 74, 76, 78, 80;
WhoAmW 72, 74*

Truman, Harry S
"Give 'em Hell, Harry"
American. US President
Dem., 33rd pres., 1945-53; made
  decision to drop atomic bomb on
  Japan, 1945.
b. May 8, 1884 in Lamar, Missouri
d. Dec 26, 1972 in Kansas City,
  Missouri
Source: *AmNatBi; Au&Wr 71; BiDrAC;
BiDrUSE 71; BioIn 22, 23, 24;
CamBiEn; CamDcAB; ChamBiD;
ColdWar 2; ColdWRG; ConAu 106;
CurBio 42, 45, 73; DcAmSR; EncAB-H
1974; EncAPar; EncVieW; EncWB 98;
EncyDCo; HisDcAR; HisDcSc;
HisEWW; ObitT 1971; OxCAmH;
OxCAmL 65; PacWarE; Pres 96; REn;
USGovLe; WhAm 5; WhDW; WhoGov
72; WorAl*

Truman, Margaret

[Mary Margaret Truman]
American. Author
Daughter of Harry Truman; wrote *Letters from Father*, 1981; author of many Washington, DC-based mystery novels; wife of Clifton Daniel.
b. Feb 17, 1924 in Independence, Missouri
Source: *BestSel 90-1; BiDAmM; BioIn 1, 2, 3, 4, 5, 6, 7, 8, 9, 10, 12, 15, 17, 21; BioNews 74; CelR, 90; ConAu 29NR, 105; CurBio 50, 87; GrWomMW; InWom, SUP; MajTwCW 1; NewYTBS 80; WhoAm 74, 76, 78, 80, 82, 84, 86, 88, 90, 92, 94, 95, 96, 97, 98, 99, 2000; WhoAmW 91, 93, 95, 97, 99; WrDr 86, 88, 90, 92, 94, 96, 98, 99, 2000*

Trumbauer, Frank(ie)

American. Songwriter, Bandleader
C-melody saxist; with Paul Whiteman, 1927-36; recorded classics with Beiderbecke.
b. May 30, 1901 in Carbondale, Illinois
d. Jun 11, 1956 in Kansas City, Missouri
Source: *AmNatBi; ASCAP 66, 80; BgBands 74; BiDAmM; BiDJaz; BioIn 4, 7, 20; CmpEPM; NewAmDM; NewGrDA 86; NewGrDJ 88, 94; OxCPMus; PenEncP; WhAm 4; WhoJazz 72*

Trumbauer, Horace

American. Architect
Built French Renaissance-style mansions, mostly in NYC, Philadelphia
b. Dec 28, 1869 in Philadelphia, Pennsylvania
d. Sep 18, 1938 in Philadelphia, Pennsylvania
Source: *BiDAmAr; BioIn 4; BriEAA; DcAmB S2; MacEA; NatCAB 28; WhAm 4, HSA*

Trumbo, Dalton

[The Hollywood Ten]
American. Screenwriter, Author
Wrote novel *Johnny Got His Gun*, 1939; screenplays *Thirty Seconds Over Tokyo*, 1945; *Exodus*, 1960.
b. Dec 9, 1905 in Montrose, Colorado
d. Sep 10, 1976 in Los Angeles, California
Source: *AmAu&B; AmNatBi; AuSpks; Benet 87, 96; BenetAL 91; BioIn 2, 4, 5, 9, 11, 14, 16, 17, 19, 22; CmCal; ConAu 10NR, 21R, 69; ConDr 73, 77A; ConLC 19; ConNov 72, 76; CurBio 41, 76N; DcFM; DcLB 26; EncALit; EncMcCE; FilmEn; FilmgC; HalFC 80, 84, 88; IntAu&W 76, 77; IntDcF 1-4, 2-4; IntMPA 75, 76; ItaFilm; LegTOT; LiExTwC; Novels; ObitOF 79; OxCAmL 95; OxCFilm; PolProf T; REnAL; RGTwCWr; ScF&FL 1, 2; SJGYouA 2; TwCA, SUP; TwCYAW 1; WhAm 7; WhE&EA; WhoAm 74, 76, 78; WhoWor 76; WorAu 1900; WorFEFlm; WrDr 76*

Trumbull, John

American. Poet, Judge
Most popular of Hartford Wits; wrote mock epic *M'Fingal*, 1782, satirizing stupidity of British.
b. Apr 24, 1750 in Watertown, Connecticut
d. May 11, 1831 in Detroit, Michigan
Source: *Alli; AmAu; AmAu&B; AmBi; AmNatBi; AmWrBE; ApCAB; Benet 87, 96; BenetAL 91; BiAUS; BibAL 8; BiD&SB; BioIn 2, 3, 9, 10, 12, 14, 15; CamBiEn; CamDcAB; CamGEL; CamGLE; CamHAL; CasWL; ChhPo, S1; CnDAL; CyAL 1; DcAmAu; DcAmB; DcEnL; DcLB 31; DcLEL; DcNAA; Drake; EncAHmr; EncALit; EncCRAm; EvLB; GrWrEL P; HarEnUS; NatCAB 7; NinCLC 30; OxCAmL 65, 83, 95; PenC AM; REn; REnAL; RfGAmL 4, 87, 94; TwCBDA; WebAB 74, 79; WebE&AL; WhAm HS; WhAmRev*

Trumbull, John

American. Artist
Did historical scenes, portraits of eminent Americans.
b. Jun 6, 1756 in Lebanon, Connecticut
d. Nov 10, 1843 in New York, New York
Source: *Alli; AmAu&B; AmBi; AmNatBi; AmRev; AntBDN J; ApCAB; BiAUS; BioIn 1, 2, 3, 4, 5, 6, 7, 8, 9, 10, 11, 13, 14, 15, 22, 23; BriEAA; CamBiEn; CamDcAB; ChamBiD; DcAmArt; DcAmB; DcArts; DcBiPP; DcBrECP; DcLB 183; DcNAA; Drake; EncAB-H 1974, 1996; EncAR; EncCRAm; EncWB 98; HarEnUS; IntDcAA 90; LegTOT; LinLib S; McGDA; McGEWB; MorMA; NatCAB 3; NewYHSD; OxCAmH; OxCAmL 65; OxDcArt; TwCBDA; WebAB 74, 79; WhAm HS; WhAmRev; WorAl; WorAlBi*

Trumbull, Jonathan

"Brother Jonathan"
American. Politician, Judge
Governor of CT, 1769-84; friend, counselor to George Washington.
b. Oct 12, 1710 in Lebanon, Connecticut
d. Aug 17, 1785 in Lebanon, Connecticut
Source: *Alli; AmBi; AmNatBi; AmRev; ApCAB; BiAUS; BiDAmBL 83; BiDrACR; BioIn 1, 3, 4, 6, 8, 10; CamDcAB; ChamBiD; CyAL 1; DcAmB; DcAmSR; Drake; EncAR; EncCRAm; HarEnUS; HisDcAR; NatCAB 10; OxCAmH; OxCAmL 65, 83, 95; REn; TwCBDA; WebAB 74, 79; WhAm HS; WhDW; WorAl; WorAlBi*

Trumbull, Lyman

American. Politician
Influential senator from Illinois during the Civil War and Reconstruction.
b. Oct 12, 1813 in Colchester, Connecticut
d. Jun 25, 1896 in Chicago, Illinois
Source: *ABCAMRe; AmBi; AmNatBi; AmPolLe; ApCAB; BiAUS; BiDrAC; BiDrUSC 89; BioIn 7, 9, 12; CamDcAB; DcAmB; DcAmSR; Drake; EncWB 98; HarEnUS; McGEWB; NatCAB 12;*

OxCAmH; PolPar; TwCBDA; WhAm HS; WhAmP; WhCiWar

Trumka, Richard Louis

American. Labor Union Official, Lawyer
National pres., UMW, 1981-82; sec. treasurer, AFL-CIO, 1995—.
b. Jul 24, 1949 in Waynesburg, Pennsylvania
Source: *CurBio 86; IntWW 89, 91, 93, 97, 98, 2000; NewYTBS 82; WhoAm 84, 86, 88, 92, 95, 96, 97, 98, 99, 2000; WhoE 89; WhoFI 00, 87, 89, 92, 96, 98*

Trump, Donald John

American. Business Executive
Pres., billion-dollar Trump Organization, one of Manhattan's most grandiose builders.
b. 1946 in New York, New York
Source: *CamBiEn; CamDcAB; ConAmBL; CurBio 84; EncWB 98; IntWW 89, 91, 93, 97, 98, 2000; NewYTBS 84; WhoAm 84, 86, 88, 90, 92, 94, 95, 96, 97, 98, 99, 2000; WhoE 91, 93, 95, 97, 99; WhoFI 00, 87, 89, 92, 94, 96, 98; WhoSSW 88, 91*

Trump, Ivana Winkelmayr

American. Businesswoman
Former wife of NY billionaire Donald Trump; wrote tell-all *For Love Alone*, 1992.
b. Feb 20, 1949 in Zlin, Czech Republic
Source: *BioIn 14, 15, 16; CelR 90*

Truth, Sojourner

[Isabella VanWagener]
American. Abolitionist, Feminist
Freed slave who advocated emancipation, women's rights; noted orator.
b. 1797 in Ulster County, New York
d. Nov 26, 1883 in Battle Creek, Michigan
Source: *AfrAmAl 6, 8; AfrAmOr; AmBi; AmOrN; AmRef; AmSocL; AmWomWr 92; BenetAL 91; BioAmW; BioIn 1, 3, 4, 5, 6, 7, 8, 9, 10, 11, 13; BlksScM; BlmGWL; CamBiEn; CamDcAB; ChamBiD; ContDcW 89; DcAmNB; DcAmReB 1, 2; DcPseud; EncAB-H 1974, 1996; EncARH; EncAWoR; EncRelA; EncWB 98; EncWHA; FemiCLE; FemiWr; GoodHs; GrLiveH; HerW, 84; HisWorL; InB&W 80, 85; IntDcWB; InWom, SUP; LegTOT; LibW; MacEWoS; McGEWB; NegAl 76, 83, 89; NewCol 75; NotAW; NotBlAW 1; OxCAfAL; OxCAmL 95; ProPowC; RadHan; RComAH; WebAB 74, 79; WhAmP; WomPubS 1800; WorAl; WorAlBi*

Tryon, Thomas

American. Author, Actor
Writes supernatural fiction: *The Other*, 1971; *Harvest Home*, 1973 ; *By the Rivers of Babylon*, 1992.
b. Jan 14, 1926 in Hartford, Connecticut
d. Sep 4, 1991 in Los Angeles, California
Source: *AnObit 1991; AuNews 1; AuSpks; BeaEPF; BioIn 10, 11; BioNews*

75; BkPepl; CamDcAB; CelR; ConAu
29R, 32NR, 77NR, 135; ConLC 3, 11;
ConPopW; ConTFT 5, 10; Conv 1;
CurBio 77, 91N; IntAu&W 76, 77, 91,
93; IntMPA 82; LegTOT; MajTwCW 1;
NewYTBS 91; Novels; PenEncH;
ScF&FL 1, 2, 92; SJGHorW; WhAm 10;
WhoAm 74, 76, 78, 80, 82, 84, 86, 88,
90; WorAl; WrDr 76, 80, 82, 84, 86, 88

Tryon, William
English. Politician, Government Official
Governor of both North Carolina and
  New York colonies, he led a loyalist
  force during the American Revolution.
b. 1729 in Surrey, England
d. Jan 27, 1788 in London, England
Source: AmBi; AmNatBi; AmRev;
BiDrACR; BioIn 1, 4, 5, 12, 17;
CamDcAB; DcAmB; EncAAH; EncAR;
EncCRAm; EncSoH; EncWB 98;
HarEnMi; HisDcAR; McGEWB; WhAm
HS; WhAmRev

Ts'ai, Lun
Chinese. Inventor
Made paper from bamboo pulp, circa
  105.
b. 50? in Guiyang, China
d. 118?
Source: AsBiEn; WebBD 83

Ts'ai Yuan-p'ei
Chinese. Educator
Leading liberal educator, known
  primarily for his synthesis of Chinese
  and Western ideas.
b. 1867 in Chekiang Province, China
d. Mar 3, 1940 in Hong Kong, China
Source: EncWB 98

Tsang, Daniel C.
American. Librarian
Co-founded Alliance Working for Asian
  Rights and Empowerment (AWARE),
  1993; research topics include the
  lesbian/gay Asian press.
b. Oct 27, 1949, Hong Kong
Source: GayLesB

Tsankov, Aleksandur
Bulgarian. Political Leader
Became prime minister of Bulgaria after
  a 1923 military coup; served until
  1926, a period of civil unrest.
b. 1879 in Oriakhova, Bulgaria
d. Jul 17, 1959 in Belgrano, Argentina
Source: BiDExR; ObitOF 79

Ts'ao Ts'ao
Chinese. Military Leader, Politician
Most popular hero of Chinese folklore
  was a brilliant general and statesman
  who rescued North China from chaos
  when the Han dynasty disintegrated.
b. 155
d. Mar 15, 220
Source: DicTyr; EncWB 98; HarEnMi

Tsatsos, Constantinos
Greek. Political Leader
First elected pres. of the republic of
  Greece, 1975-80.
b. Jul 1, 1899 in Athens, Greece
d. Oct 8, 1987 in Athens, Greece
Source: IntWW 83; WhoWor 87

Tschernichowsky, Saul
Russian. Poet, Translator, Physician
One of the fathers of modern Hebrew
  poetry, his work is closely tied to
  nature.
b. 1875 in Mikilovka, Russia
d. 1943
Source: EncWB 98; McGEWB

Tschirky, Oscar
"Oscar of the Waldorf"
American. Hotel Executive
Maitre d'hotel, Waldorf-Astoria, NYC,
  1931-43; executive, 1943-50;
  originated Waldorf salad.
b. Sep 28, 1866 in Locle, Switzerland
d. Nov 6, 1950 in New Paltz, New York
Source: BioIn 1, 2; CurBio 47, 50;
LegTOT; WhAm 3; WorAl; WorAlBi

Tsedenbal, Yumzahgin
Mongolian. Politician
Chm. of Presidium of People's Great
  Hural (head of state), 1974-84.
b. Sep 17, 1916
d. Apr 20, in Moscow, Russia
Source: BioIn 9; IntWW 83; WhoWor 84

Tsegaye, Gabre-Medhin
Ethiopian. Poet, Dramatist
Plays deal with Ethiopian life and
  history; author of more than 20 plays;
  most famous English verse play, Oda
  Oak Oracle, 1965.
b. Aug 17, 1935 in Ambo, Ethiopia
Source: AfrA; BioIn 10; CamGWoT;
ConAu X; ConDr 82, 88

Tseng Kuo-fan
Chinese. Government Official, Military
  Leader, Scholar
Considered to be a model Confucian
  official, the statesman and general
  suppressed the Taiping Rebellion.
b. Nov 26, 1811 in Hsiang-hsiang,
  Hunan, China
d. Mar 12, 1872 in Nanking, China
Source: EncWB 98

Tshabalala, Headman
South African. Singer
Member of Ladysmith Black Mambazo.
d. Dec 10, 1991 in Pinetown, South
  Africa
Source: BioIn 17; NewYTBS 91

Tshombe, Moise
Congolese. Political Leader
Prominent in secession of Katanga
  Province from Congo, 1960; president
  of Katanga, 1960-63; premier of
  Congo, 1963-65.
b. Nov 10, 1919 in Musumba, Congo

d. Jun 29, 1969 in Algiers, Algeria
Source: BioIn 5, 6, 18, 21; ColdWar 1;
CurBio 61, 69; DcPol; FacFETw; LinLib
S; McGEWB; NewCol 75; ObitOF 79;
ObitT 1961; WhDW; WorAl

**Tsiolkovsky, Konstantin
Eduardovich**
Russian. Scientist
Formulated mathematical fundamentals
  of modern astronautics; advocated
  space travel via rocket propulsion,
  1883; presented plans for multistage
  rocket, 1929.
b. Sep 17, 1857 in Izhevskoye, Union of
  Soviet Socialist Republics
d. Sep 19, 1935 in Kaluga, Union of
  Soviet Socialist Republics
Source: AsBiEn; BiESc; BioIn 10;
CamBiEn; ChamBiD; ConAu 119, 164;
DcScB; DeafPAS; EncSF 93; EncWB 98;
LarDcSc; McGEWB; NewCol 75;
RanHWDS; ScFEYrs; TwCSFW 86A;
WorAl

Tsiranana, Philibert
African. Political Leader
Pres. of Madagascar, 1959-72; first of
  the republic; declared independence in
  1960.
b. Oct 18, 1912 in Anahidrano,
  Madagascar
d. Apr 16, 1978 in Tananarive,
  Madagascar
Source: BioIn 21; ChamBiD; IntWW 74,
75, 76, 77; NewCol 75; NewYTBS 78;
ObitOF 79; WhoGov 72; WhoWor 74

Tsongas, Paul E(fthemios)
American. Politician, Lawyer
Dem. senator from MA, 1979-85;
  presidential candidate, 1992.
b. Feb 14, 1941 in Lowell,
  Massachusetts
d. Jan 18, 1997 in Boston, Massachusetts
Source: AlmAP 78, 80, 82, 84; BiDrUSC
89; BioIn 10, 11, 12, 13; CngDr 79;
ConAu 108, 156; CurBio 81, 97N;
IntWW 81, 82, 83, 89, 91, 93; NewYTBS
85, 92; PolsAm 84; WhAm 12; WhoAm
78, 80, 82, 84, 86, 88, 90, 92, 94, 95,
96, 97; WhoAmP 75, 77, 79, 81, 83, 85,
87, 89, 91, 93, 95; WhoE 79, 81, 83, 85;
WhoWor 80, 82

Tso Tsung-t'ang
Chinese. Military Leader, Government
  Official
General and statesman was a leading
  military figure and proponent of "self-
  strengthening," or adopting Western
  military tactics to protect traditional
  Chinese culture.
b. Nov 10, 1812 in Hsiangyin, Hunan,
  China
d. Sep 5, 1885 in Foochow, China
Source: EncWB 98; HarEnMi

Tsou Yen
Chinese. Philosopher
Developed the Five Element theory—
  identifying the five agents as fire,
  water, wood, metal, and earth—that

became integral to Chinese philosophy and science.
b. fl. 4th cent. BC
Source: *EncWB 98*

Tsui, Kitty
American. Writer
Books include *The Words of a Woman Who Breathes Fire*, 1983; *Breathless*, 1995.
b. 1952, Hong Kong
Source: *BioIn 19; CmpQue; DrAPF 80; GayLesB; GayLL 2*

Tsvetayeva, Marina Ivanovna
Russian. Poet
Modernist poet influenced by Pasternak, folk music.
b. Sep 26, 1892? in Moscow, Russia
d. Aug 31, 1941 in Yelabuga, Union of Soviet Socialist Republics
Source: *BioIn 14; CasWL; ClDMEL 47, 80; DcRusL; DcRusLS; EvEuW; IntDcWB; ModSL 1; PenBWP; PenC EUR; WorAu 1950*

Tu, Fu
Chinese. Poet
Verse shows hatred of war, love of nature.
b. 712 in Gongxian, China
d. 777 in Tanzhou, China
Source: *Benet 87; BioIn 2, 3, 4, 8, 9, 14; CasWL; DcOrL 1; GrFLW; IndCTCL; LinLib L; McGEWB; PenC CL; REn; WhDW; WorAl*

Tubb, Ernest
''The Texas Trubadour''
American. Singer, Musician, Songwriter
Country music legend who wrote over 150 songs including hit ''Walking the Floor over You,'' 1941.
b. Feb 9, 1914 in Crisp, Texas
d. Sep 6, 1984 in Nashville, Tennessee
Source: *AmNatBi; AnObit 1984; BakBD 84; BakDcM; BgBkCoM; BioIn 14, 15, 22, 24; CamDcAB; CmpEPM; ConAu 114; ConMus 4; CounME 74, 74A; CurBio 83, 84N; EncFCWM 69, 83; HarEnCM 87; IlEncCM; LegTOT; NewAmDM; NewGrDA 86; NewGrDM 80; NewYTBS 84; OxCPMus; PenEncP; RadStar; Songw; WhoAm 80*

Tubes, The
[Rich Anderson; Michael Cotten; Prairie Prince; Bill Spooner; Roger Steen; Re Styles; Fee Waybill; Vince Welnick]
American. Music Group
Begun late 1960s, combining rock, theater, satire; appeared in film *Xanadu*, 1980.
Source: *BilIEnR; ConMuA 80A; EncRk 88; EncRkSt; HarEnR 86; IlEncRk; RkOn 85; RkWho 96; RolSEnR 83; WhDW; WhoRock 81; WhoRocM 82; WorAl*

Tubman, Harriet Ross
''Moses of Her People''
American. Abolitionist
Leader of Underground Railroad; helped over 300 slaves escape.
b. 1826 in Dorchester, Maryland
d. Mar 10, 1913 in Auburn, New York
Source: *AfrAmAl 8; AmBi; ApCAB; BioAmW; DcAmB; EncAB-H 1974; GoodHs; HerW; InB&W 80; InWom; NewCol 75; NotAW; NotBlAW 1; REnAL; WebAB 74; WhAm HSA; WhAmP; WorAl*

Tubman, William Vacanarat Shadrach
Liberian. Political Leader
President of Liberia, 1944-71.
b. Nov 29, 1895 in Harper, Liberia
d. Jul 23, 1971 in London, England
Source: *BioIn 1, 3, 4, 5, 6, 7, 8, 9, 10, 11, 18, 20, 21, 23; CurBio 55, 71; DcAfHiB 86; DcTwHis; EncWB 98; EncWM; InB&W 80, 85; McGEWB; NewCol 75; WhAm 5; WhoGov 72*

Tuchman, Barbara Wertheim
American. Author, Historian
Wrote about people at war or at brink of war; won Pulitzers for *The Guns of August*, 1962, *Stillwell and the American Experience in China, 1911-45*, 1971.
b. Jan 30, 1912 in New York, New York
d. Feb 6, 1989 in Greenwich, Connecticut
Source: *AmAu&B; AmNatBi; AmWomWr; Au&Wr 71; Benet 87; BenetAL 91; BioIn 13, 16; BlueB 76; ChamBiD; ConAu 1R, 3NR, 24NR, 127; CurBio 63, 89, 89N; EncWB; GloEncH; IntAu&W 91; IntWW 83, 89N; InWom; SUP; LibW; MajTwCW 1, 2; NewYTBS 78, 89; OxCAmL 65; RAdv 13-3; RfGAmL 4; ScrEAmL 2; WhAm 9; WhoAm 74, 76, 78, 80, 82, 84, 86, 88; WhoAmJ 80; WhoAmW 58, 61, 64, 66, 68, 70, 72, 74, 75, 77, 81, 83, 85, 87, 89; WhoE 74; WhoUSWr 88; WhoWor 74, 78, 80, 82, 87, 89; WomFir; WorAu 1950; WrDr 76, 86, 88*

Tuck, Lily
American. Author
Wrote *Interviewing Matisse, or, The Women Who Died Standing Up*, 1991.
b. 1938, France
Source: *ConAu 139; ConLC 70; WrDr 96, 98, 99, 2000*

Tucker, C(ynthia) DeLores (Nottage)
American. Civil Rights Activist, Organization Executive
Rose to national prominence in African American civil rights circles through her tireless activism and political fundraising; she founded or led several activist organizations.
b. Oct 4, 1927 in Philadelphia, Pennsylvania
Source: *InB&W 85; WhoAm 76, 78, 80, 82, 84, 86, 88, 90, 96, 97, 98, 99, 2000;*

WhoE 74, 75, 79, 81, 83, 85, 86, 89; WhoGov 75, 77; WhoWor 2000

Tucker, Chris
American. Comedian, Actor
Stand-up comedian known for his high-pitched, fast-paced delivery; actor in films such as *House Party III*, 1994, and *Friday*, 1995.
b. c. 1973 in Atlanta, Georgia
Source: *ConBlB 13, 23; News 99-1, 1999; WhoAm 2000; WhoWor 2000*

Tucker, Cynthia (Anne)
American. Journalist
Syndicated political columnist reaches 40 markets across the United States; became first African American woman to edit the editorial page of a major daily newspaper, the *Atlanta Constitution*, 1991; commentator on ''Jim Lehrer's NewsHour'' and ''CNN and Company.''
b. Mar 13, 1955 in Monroeville, Alabama
Source: *BiDAmNC; WhoAfA 9, 10, 11, 12; WhoAm 94, 95, 96, 97, 98, 99, 2000; WhoBlA 8*

Tucker, Forrest Meredith
American. Actor
Crusty character actor best known as Sgt. O'Rourke on TV series ''F Troop,'' 1965-67.
b. Feb 12, 1919 in Plainfield, Indiana
d. Oct 25, 1986 in Woodland Hills, California
Source: *BiE&WWA; BioNews 74; ConNews 87-1; ConTFT 3, 4; FilmgC; IntMPA 82; MotPP; MovMk; WhAm 9; WhoAm 74, 76, 80, 82, 84, 86; WhoHol A*

Tucker, George
American. Historian
Most important historian from the South in the era preceding the Civil War.
b. Aug 20, 1775 in St. George's, Bermuda
d. Apr 10, 1861 in Charlottesville, Virginia
Source: *Alli; AmAu; AmAu&B; AmNatBi; ApCAB; BenetAL 91; BiAUS; BiDAmEd; BiD&SB; BiDrAC; BiDrUSC 89; BioIn 1, 3, 5, 6, 7, 8, 12, 14; ChhPo S1; CnDAL; DcAmAu; DcAmB; DcLB 3, 30; DcLEL; DcNAA; Drake; EncABHB 6; EncALit; EncSoH; EncWB 98; EvLB; FifSWrB; HarEnUS; McGEWB; NatCAB 7; NewEScF; OxCAmL 65, 83, 95; REnAL; ScF&FL 92; ScFEYrs; SouWr; TwCBDA; WhAm HS; WhAmP; WhoEc 81, 86*

Tucker, Lorenzo
''The Black Valentino''
American. Actor
One of the first major black screen actors; starred in many all-black movies, 1920s-40s.
b. Jun 27, 1907 in Philadelphia, Pennsylvania

d. Aug 19, 1986 in Los Angeles,
California
Source: *AmNatBi; BioIn 15, 16;
BlksAmF; BlksB&W, C; DrBlPA, 90;
InB&W 80; WhoBlA 3, 4*

Tucker, Mary Bradham
American. Model
The first Pepsi girl, seen on calendars,
early 1900s.
b. 1903
d. May 26, 1984 in Edenton, North
Carolina
Source: *BioIn 13*

Tucker, Orrin
American. Bandleader
Led dance bands, 1930s-40s; recorded
"Oh, Johnny, Oh" with Bonnie
Baker, 1939.
b. Feb 17, 1911 in Saint Louis, Missouri
Source: *ASCAP 66, 80; BgBands 74;
BiDAmM; CmpEPM; PenEncP; SaTiSS;
WhoHol 92*

Tucker, Preston Thomas
American. Auto Manufacturer
Developed rear engine car, 1940s.
b. Sep 21, 1903 in Capac, Michigan
d. Jan 7, 1956 in Ypsilanti, Michigan
Source: *AmNatBi; BioIn 2, 4, 5, 9, 10,
11, 13; BusPN; EncABHB 5; FacFETw;
ObitOF 79; WhAm 3*

Tucker, Richard
[Reuben Tickel]
American. Opera Singer, Actor
Considered best operatic tenor, 1940s-
50s.
b. Aug 28, 1913 in New York, New
York
d. Jan 8, 1975 in Kalamazoo, Michigan
Source: *AmNatBi; BakBD 78, 84, 92;
BakDcM; BioIn 2, 3, 4, 5, 6,
7, 8, 9, 10, 11, 13, 21; CamDcAB; CelR;
CurBio 56, 75, 75N; DcAmB S9;
DcPseud; FacFETw; IntDcOp; IntWW
74; MetOEnc; MusSN; NewAmDM;
NewEOp 71; NewGrDA 86; NewGrDM
80; NewGrDO; NewYTBE 73; OxDcOp;
PenDiMP; WhAm 6; WhoAm 74;
WhoWor 74; WhScrn 77*

Tucker, Rosina
American. Labor Union Official, Civil
Rights Activist, Educator
Union organizer and civil rights activist
worked with the Brotherhood of
Sleeping Car Porters to fight racism
and improve life for African American
workers; founder and secretary-
treasurer of the International Ladies'
Auxiliary, 1937, to further support the
union.
b. Nov 4, 1881 in Washington, District
of Columbia
d. Mar 3, 1987
Source: *ConBlB 14; NotBlAW 2*

Tucker, Sophie
[Sophia Kalish]
American. Singer
Vaudeville performer billed as "last of
the red-hot Mamas."
b. Jan 13, 1884, Russia
d. Feb 9, 1966 in New York, New York
Source: *AmAu&B; AmNatBi; BakBD 92;
BakDcM; BiDAmM; BiE&WWA;
BioAmW; BioIn 2, 3, 7, 11, 12, 13, 16;
CamBiEn; CamDcAB; CamGWoT;
ChamBiD; CmdStar; CmpEPM; ConMus
12; ContDcW 89; CurBio 45, 66;
DcPseud; EncMT; Film 2; FilmgC;
ForYSC; FunnyW; GoodHs; GrLiveH;
HalFC 80, 84, 88; IntDcWB; InWom;
JoeFr; LegTOT; LibW; NewGrDA 86;
NotAW MOD; NotNAT A; ObitT 1961;
OxCAmH; OxCAmT 84; OxCPMus;
PenEncP; ThFT; WebAB 74, 79; WhAm
4; WhoAmW 61, 64; WhoCom; WhoHol
B; WhScrn 74, 77, 83; WhThe; WorAl;
WorAlBi*

Tucker, Sterling
American. Civil Rights Leader
Executive director, Washington, DC
Urban League, 1956-78; books include
Black Reflections on White Power,
1969; *For Blacks Only*, 1970.
b. Dec 21, 1923 in Akron, Ohio
Source: *CivR 74; InB&W 80; LivgBAA;
SelBAAf; WhoAm 78, 80, 82, 84, 86, 88;
WhoAmP 73, 75, 77, 79; WhoGov 72, 75*

Tucker, Tanya (Denise)
American. Singer
First hit at age 14; millionaire by 16; hit
song "Delta Dawn," 1973.
b. Oct 10, 1958 in Seminole, Texas
Source: *BgBkCoM; BioIn 10, 11, 12, 14,
16, 20; BioNews 75; CelR 90; ConMus
3; CounME 74, 74A; EncFCWM 83;
EncRk 88; HarEnCM 87; IlEncCM;
LegTOT; RkOn 78, 85; RolSEnR 83;
WhoAm 80, 82, 84, 86, 88, 90, 92, 94,
95, 96, 97, 98, 99, 2000; WhoAmW 81,
83, 85, 95, 97, 99; WhoEnt 92; WhoHol
92, A; WhoNeCM; WhoRock 81;
WhoWest 82; WorAlBi*

Tucker, Tommy
"Little Tommy Tucker"
American. Bandleader
Led hotel-style dance bands, 1930s-50s;
best known song was "I Don't Want
to Set the World on Fire."
b. May 18, 1908 in Souris, North Dakota
d. Jul 10, 1989 in Sarasota, Florida
Source: *ASCAP 66, 80; BgBands 74;
BiDAmM; CmpEPM; LegTOT; WhoAm
74; WhoMus 72; WhoRocM 82*

Tuckwell, Barry Emmanuel
Australian. Musician
Virtuoso horn player; edited horn
literature.
b. Mar 5, 1931 in Melbourne, Australia
Source: *BakBD 84, 92; BakBDTw; BioIn
16; CamBiEn; ChamBiD; CurBio 79;
IntWW 81, 82, 83, 89, 91, 93, 97, 98,
2000; NewAmDM; NewGrDM 80;
NewYTBS 78; PenDiMP; TwCBrS; Who*

*82, 83, 85, 88, 90, 92, 94, 98, 99, 2000;
WhoAm 80, 82, 84, 86, 88, 90, 92, 94,
95, 96, 97, 98, 99, 2000; WhoAmM 83;
WhoMus 72; WhoWor 76, 82, 84*

Tudjman, Franjo
Croatian. Political Leader
Pres. of Croatia, 1990-99.
b. May 14, 1922 in Veliko-Tgrovisce,
Croatia
d. Dec 10, 1999 in Zagreb, Croatia
Source: *ChamBiD; CnfFoY; CurBio 97;
EncWB 98; IntWW 93, 97, 98, 2000;
News 96, 96-2; ProfiWG 98; WhoIntA 2;
WhoSoCE 89; WhoWor 95, 96, 97, 98,
99, 2000*

Tudor, Antony
[William Cook]
English. Choreographer
Best known for revolutionary use of
psychological themes in ballet.
b. Apr 4, 1908? in London, England
d. Apr 20, 1987 in New York, New
York
Source: *AmNatBi; AnObit 1987; BiDD;
BiE&WWA; BioIn 11, 13; CamBiEn;
ChamBiD; CnOxB; ConNews 87-4;
CurBio 45, 87; DcPseud; DcTwCCu 1;
IntDcB; LegTOT; NewGrDA 86;
NewOxM; NewYTBS 87; ScrEAmL 2;
WhAm 9; WhoAm 74, 76, 80, 82, 84, 86;
WorAl*

Tudor, John Thomas
American. Baseball Player
Pitcher, 1979-91; led NL in shutouts,
1985.
b. Feb 2, 1954 in Schenectady, New
York
Source: *Ballpl 90; BaseReg 86, 87;
BioIn 14*

Tuffin, Sally
English. Fashion Designer
Fashions designed for youth; firm of
Foale & Tuffin, Ltd. was major
fashion influence during the Youth
Rebellion, 1965.
Source: *EncFash; WorFshn*

Tufts, Sonny
[Bowen Charles Tufts, III]
American. Actor
Began film career, 1943; appeared in *No
Escape*, 1953.
b. Jul 16, 1911 in Boston, Massachusetts
d. Jun 5, 1970 in Santa Monica,
California
Source: *BioIn 8, 10; DcPseud; EncAFC;
FilmEn; FilmgC; HalFC 80, 84, 88;
HolP 40; LegTOT; MotPP; MovMk;
NewYTBE 70; ObitOF 79; What 2;
WhoHol B; WhoHrs 80; WhScrn 74, 77*

Tugwell, Rexford Guy
American. Author, Political Scientist
Adviser to FDR during Depression;
appointed gov. of Puerto Rico, 1941.
b. Jul 10, 1891 in Sinclairville, New
York

d. Jul 21, 1979 in Santa Barbara,
California
Source: *AmAu&B; AmMWSc 73S;
AmNatBi; AmPolLe; BioIn 1, 6, 7, 8, 10,
11, 12; BlueB 76; CamDcAB; ConAu 85,
89; CurBio 41, 79; DcAmB S10;
EncAAH; EncAB-H 1974, 1996; EncWB,
98; IntAu&W 76; IntWW 74, 75, 76, 77,
78, 79; LatAmLi; NewYTBE 70;
NewYTBS 79; OxCAmH; PolProf T;
REnAL; WebAB 74, 79; WhAm 7;
WhoAm 74, 76, 78; WhoEc 86; WhoWest
74, 76, 78; WhoWor 74, 78; WrDr 76,
80*

**Tukhachevski, Mikhail
Nikolayevich**
Russian. Military Leader
Commanded Russian offensive in Russo-
Polish War, 1919-20; led
modernization of Red Army, 1935;
charged with treason by Stalin,
executed.
b. Feb 16, 1893 in Slednevo, Russia
d. Jun 11, 1937 in Moscow, Union of
Soviet Socialist Republics
Source: *NewCol 75; WebBD 83;
WhoMilH 76*

Tulane, Paul
American. Merchant, Philanthropist
New Orleans clothier; donated fortune to
U of Louisiana; name changed to
Tulane U, 1884.
b. May 10, 1801 in Princeton, New
Jersey
d. Mar 27, 1887 in Princeton, New
Jersey
Source: *AmBi; ApCAB; BioIn 3; DcAmB;
HarEnUS; NatCAB 9; TwCBDA; WhAm
HS*

Tully, Alice
American. Singer, Philanthropist
Former operatic soprano; donated Alice
Tully Hall, chamber music recital hall
in Lincoln Center for Performing Arts,
NYC.
b. Oct 11, 1902 in Corning, New York
d. Dec 10, 1993 in New York, New
York
Source: *AnObit 1993; BakBD 84, 92;
BakBDTw; BioIn 13, 14, 15, 16, 17, 19,
20, 21; CelR 90; CurBio 84, 94N;
InWom, SUP; NewAmDM; NewGrDA
86; NewYTBS 77, 82, 93*

Tully, Grace George
American. Secretary
Personal secretary to FDR, 1928-45;
wrote memoirs, *F.D.R.: My Boss,*
1949.
b. Aug 9, 1900 in Bayonne, New Jersey
d. Jun 15, 1984 in Washington, District
of Columbia
Source: *AmNatBi; BioIn 2, 12, 14, 24;
ConAu 113; NewYTBS 80, 84; WhoGov
72*

Tully, Tom
American. Actor
Oscar nominee for *The Caine Mutiny,*
1954.

b. Aug 21, 1902 in Durango, California
d. Apr 27, 1982 in Newport Beach,
California
Source: *FilmgC; ForYSC; IntMPA 82;
MotPP; MovMk; Vers A; WhoHol A*

Tune, Tommy
[Thomas James Tune]
American. Director, Choreographer
Won Tonys for *A Day in Hollywood/A
Night in the Ukraine,* 1980; *Nine,*
1982; only person to win 9 Tonys in 4
different categories.
b. Feb 28, 1939 in Wichita Falls, Texas
Source: *BiDD; BioIn 13, 14; CamDcAB;
CelR 90; CnOxB; ConTFT 1, 7, 14;
CurBio 83; FilmChD; GrStDi; IntMPA
86, 88, 92, 94, 96; IntWW 89, 91, 93,
98, 2000; LegTOT; News 94, 94-2;
NewYTBS 80; OxCAmT 84; TheaDir;
WhoAm 80, 82, 84, 86, 88, 90, 92, 94,
95, 96, 97, 98, 99, 2000; WhoE 91, 93;
WhoEnt 92, 98; WhoHol 92, A; WhoThe
81; WhoWor 98, 99, 2000; WorAl;
WorAlBi*

Tung Chee-hwa
Chinese. Political Leader
Chief Executive, Hong Kong, 1997—.
b. May 29, 1937 in Shanghai, China
Source: *ChamBiD; IntWW 97, 98, 2000;
ProfiWG 98; Who 99; WhoIntA 2*

Tung Ch'i-ch'ang
Chinese. Artist, Historian
Calligrapher, painter, and art historian
founded the Sung-chiang school of
literati painting
b. 1555 in Shanghai, China
d. 1636
Source: *EncWB 98*

Tung Chung-shu
Chinese. Author
Man of letters known for formulating the
system of thought that came to be
called Confucianism.
b. c. 179BC, China
d. 104BC, China

Tunis, Edwin Burdett
American. Children's Author
Self-illustrated works include *Frontier
Living,* 1961.
b. Dec 8, 1897 in New York
d. Aug 7, 1973
Source: *AuBYP 2; ConAu 5R, 45; IlsCB
1946, 1957; MorJA; SmATA 1; WhoAmA
73*

Tunnard, Christopher
American. Architect
Urban planning authority; known for
idea of "linear" or "super" city on
Atlantic sea board; won National Book
Award, 1963, for *Man-Made America:
Chaos or Control.*
b. Jul 7, 1910 in Victoria, British
Columbia, Canada
d. Feb 14, 1979 in New Haven,
Connecticut

Source: *AmAu&B; BioIn 5, 11, 12;
ConAu 5R, 6NR, 85; CurBio 59, 79N;
NewYTBS 79; WhAm 7; WhoAm 74, 76,
78; WhoWor 74*

Tunnell, Em(len)
American. Football Player, Football
Coach
Defensive back, 1948-61, mostly with
NY Giants; first black full-time coach
in NFL as assistant coach with Giants,
1963-73; first black man in Hall of
Fame, 1967.
b. Mar 29, 1925 in Bryn Mawr,
Pennsylvania
d. Jul 22, 1975 in Pleasantville, New
York
Source: *AfrAmSG; AmNatBi; BiDAmSp
FB; BioIn 6, 10, 17, 21; InB&W 80;
LegTOT; NewYTBS 75; ObitOF 79;
WhoFtbl 74; WhoSpor*

Tunney, Gene
[James Joseph Tunney]
American. Boxer, Businessman
Beat Jack Dempsey in famous "long
count fight," 1922, to become
heavyweight champ; retired unbeaten.
b. May 25, 1898 in New York, New
York
d. Nov 7, 1978 in Greenwich,
Connecticut
Source: *AmAu&B; BiDAmSp BK; BioIn
1, 2, 3, 4, 5, 6, 7, 8, 9, 10, 11, 12, 14,
17, 21, 22; CelR; ConAu 111; CurBio
40, 79N; FacFETw; Film 2; IntWW 74;
LegTOT; NewYTBS 78; OxCAmH;
REnAL; WebAB 74, 79; WhoAm 74;
WhoBox 74; WhScrn 83; WorAl;
WorAlBi*

Tunney, John Varick
American. Politician
Dem. senator from CA, 1971-77; son of
boxer Gene.
b. Jun 26, 1934 in New York, New York
Source: *BiDrAC; BiDrUSC 89; BioIn 7,
8, 9, 10, 11; BlueB 76; CngDr 74;
ConAu 61; CurBio 71; IntWW 83, 91;
NewYTBE 71; WhoAm 74, 76, 78, 80,
82, 84, 86, 88, 92, 94, 95, 96, 97, 99;
WhoAmP 73, 75, 77, 79, 81, 83, 85, 87,
89, 91, 93, 95, 97, 1999; WhoGov 75,
77; WhoWest 74, 76*

Tupac Amaru
[Jose Gabriel Condorcanqui]
Peruvian. Nobleman
Inca, who lead Indian rebellion in
Americas, 1780, resulting in minor
reforms in Peru.
b. 1742 in Tinta, Peru
d. 1781
Source: *ApCAB; EncLatA; HisDcSE;
McGEWB; NewCol 75*

Tupolev, Andrei Nikolaevich
Russian. Engineer, Army Officer
Aeronautical engineer and military man
was the leading designer of large and
heavy aircraft in the former U.S.S.R.
b. Nov 10, 1888 in Pustomazovo, Russia
d. 1972

Source: *BiDSovU; BioIn 2, 3, 4, 5, 9, 10, 11; EncWB 98; McGEWB; WhAm 5*

Tupou, IV
Political Leader
The king of Tonga since 1967, he heads
a constitutional monarchy faced with
severe socio-economic problems and
the pains of modernization.
b. Jul 4, 1918
Source: *BioIn 8*

Tupper, Charles
Canadian. Political Leader
One of the Canadian fathers of
confederation, he served as a cabinet
minister, high commissioner to the
United Kingdom, and prime minister
of Canada.
b. Jul 2, 1821 in Amherst, Nova Scotia,
Canada
d. Oct 30, 1915, England
Source: *ApCAB; BbtC; CelCen; DcCanB
14; DcNaB 1912; EncWB 98; LinLib S;
MacDCB 78; McGEWB; OxCCan;
OxCMed 86*

Tupper, Earl Silas
American. Inventor
Former DuPont chemist who founded
Tupperware Home Parties, Inc., 1945.
b. Jul 28, 1907 in Berlin, New
Hampshire
d. Oct 3, 1983 in San Jose, California
Source: *AmNatBi; Entr; NewYTBS 83;
ScrEAmL 1*

Tura, Cosme
[Cosimo Tura]
Italian. Artist
Founder, master of Ferrarese school of
painting; works include allegorical
frescoes, Pieta, 1472.
b. 1430 in Ferrara, Italy
d. 1495 in Ferrara, Italy
Source: *AtlBL; CamBiEn; DcCathB;
IntDcAA 90; McGEWB; NewCol 75;
OxCArt; OxDcArt; WebBD 83*

Turbay Ayala, Julio Cesar
Colombian. Political Leader
Pres., 1978-82; permanent representative
UN, 1967; ambassador to US, 1974-
76.
b. Jun 18, 1916 in Bogota, Colombia
Source: *BioIn 11, 12; CurBio 79;
DcCPSAm; IntWW 74, 79, 80, 81, 82,
83, 89, 91, 93, 97, 98, 2000; IntYB 79,
80, 81, 82; LatAmLi; NewYTBS 78;
WhoWor 74, 80, 82*

Turcotte, Ron
Canadian. Jockey
Leading jockey, 1960s-70s; rode
Secretariat to Triple Crown, 1973.
b. Jul 22, 1941 in Drummond, New
Brunswick, Canada
Source: *BioIn 10, 11, 12, 13, 16; CurBio
74*

Tureck, Rosalyn
American. Pianist
Specialized in Bach; founded Int'l Bach
Society, 1966.
b. Dec 14, 1914 in Chicago, Illinois
Source: *BakBD 78, 84, 92; BakBDTw;
BioIn 1, 2, 4, 5, 8, 11, 12, 14, 21; BlueB
76; BriBkM 80; CamDcAB; CurBio 59;
IntAu&W 82, 89; IntWW 74, 75, 76, 77,
78, 80, 81, 82, 83, 89, 91, 93, 97, 98,
2000; IntWWM 77, 80, 90; IntWWW 2;
InWom; MusSN; NewAmDM; NewGrDA
86; NewGrDM 80; NotTwCP; PenDiMP;
Who 74, 82, 83, 85, 88, 90, 92, 94, 98,
99, 2000; WhoAm 74, 76, 78, 80, 82, 84,
86, 88, 90, 92, 94, 95, 96, 97, 98, 99,
2000; WhoAmW 66, 68, 70, 74, 79, 81,
83, 85, 87, 89, 91, 93, 95, 97, 99;
WhoEnt 92, 98; WhoMus 72; WhoWor
74; WhoWorJ 72, 78; WomCom; WrDr
76, 80, 82, 84, 86, 88, 90, 92, 94, 96*

**Turenne, Henri de La Tour
Auvergne, Viscount**
French. Military Leader
Fought in Thirty Years War; emphasized
mobility, surprise in military
operations.
b. Sep 11, 1611 in Sedan, France
d. Jul 27, 1675 in Sasbach, Germany
Source: *LinLib S; NewCol 75; OxCFr;
REn; WhDW; WorAl*

Turgenev, Ivan Sergeevich
Russian. Author
First major 19th-c. Russian novelist
known abroad; wrote his masterpiece,
Fathers and Sons, 1862; a popular
comedy, *A Month in the Country*,
1850.
b. Nov 9, 1818 in Orel, Russia
d. Sep 3, 1883 in Bougival, France
Source: *AtlBL; BbD; BiD&SB; BioIn 12,
13, 14, 15, 16, 20, 24; BlmGEL;
CamGWoT; CasWL; ClDMEL 47;
CnThe; CyWA 58; DcBiA; DcEuL;
DcRusL; EuAu; HanRL; LinLib L;
McGEWB; McGEWD 84; OxCEng 85,
95; OxCThe 83; PenC EUR; RComWL;
RfGShF 1, 2; RfGWoL 95*

**Turgot, A(nne) R(obert)
J(acques), Baron de l'Aulne**
French. Economist
Controller general under Louis XVI
unsuccessfully attempted to reform the
Old Regime.
b. 1721
d. 1781
Source: *EncWB 98*

Turing, Alan (Mathison)
English. Mathematician
Was instrumental in the design of an
automatic computing engine while
with England's National Physical
Laboratory, 1946-48.
b. Jun 23, 1912 in London, England
d. Jun 1954
Source: *BiESc; BioIn 3, 4, 5, 8, 11, 12,
13, 14, 15, 17, 18, 20, 21, 24; CamBiEn;
CamDcSc; ChamBiD; CmpQue; DcNaB
1951; DcScB; EncWB, 98; FacFETw;*

*GayLesB; GrBr; HisDcDP; InSci;
LarDcSc; LegTOT; MakMC; McGCEnS;
NotTwCS 1; OxCPhil; PorSil; RAdv 14;
RanHWDS*

Turischeva, Ludmila
[Mrs. Valeri Borzov]
Russian. Gymnast
Won gold medals, 1968, 1972, 1976
Olympics.
b. Oct 7, 1952 in Grozny, Union of
Soviet Socialist Republics
Source: *BiDSovU; BioIn 11; ContDcW
89; InWom SUP; WorAl*

Turkle, Brinton Cassaday
American. Children's Author
Self-illustrated juvenile books include
The Adventures of Obadiah, 1972;
Rachel & Obadiah, 1978.
b. Aug 15, 1915 in Alliance, Ohio
Source: *BioIn 8, 9, 10, 12, 14, 20; BkP;
ChhPo S2; FamAIYP; IlsBYP; IlsCB
1957; SmATA 2; ThrBJA; TwCChW 3;
WrDr 86, 92*

Turkus, Burton B
"Mr. Arsenic"
American. Lawyer
Cracked organized crime syndicate,
Murder, Inc., 1940s.
b. 1902? in New York, New York
d. Nov 22, 1982 in New York, New
York
Source: *AnObit 1982; BioIn 2, 13;
ConAu 108; NewYTBS 82; WhoAmL 79;
WhoLab 76*

Turlington, Christy
American. Model
Her face was used on mannequins at the
Metropolitan Museum of Art's
costume galleries.
b. Jan 2, 1969 in Walnut Creek,
California
Source: *IntWW 97, 98, 2000; IntWWW
2; NotHsAW 2; WhoAm 95, 96, 97;
WhoAmW 95, 99; WhoEnt 98; WhoWor
97, 98, 99, 2000*

Turnbull, Agnes Sligh
American. Author
Wrote of rural PA in 14 novels including
Rolling Years, 1936.
b. Oct 14, 1888 in New Alexandria,
Pennsylvania
d. Jan 31, 1982 in Livingston, New
Jersey
Source: *AmAu&B; AmNov; AmWomWr;
AnObit 1982; Au&Wr 71; AuBYP 2, 3;
BenetAL 91; BioIn 22; ConAu 1R, 2NR,
86NR, 105; InWom, SUP; NewYTBS 82;
REnAL; TwCA, SUP; WhE&EA;
WhNAA; WhoAm 74, 76, 78, 80, 82;
WhoAmW 58, 61, 64, 66, 68, 70, 72, 74;
WorAu 1900*

Turnbull, Collin M(acmillan)
English. Anthropologist
Best known for studies on Pygmy
groups: *The Forest People*, 1961; *The
Mountain People*, 1971.

b. Nov 25, 1924 in Harrow, England
d. Jul 28, 1994 in Kilmarnock, Virginia
Source: *AmMWSc 73S; BioIn 11, 14;
ConAu 3NR; CurBio 80; WhoAm 86, 88;
WorAu 1970; WrDr 92*

Turnbull, Walter (J.)
American. Musician, Educator
A singer himself, became founder and
director of the Choir Academy and the
highly respected Boys Choir of
Harlem, 1968; group has recorded
albums, appeared on film soundtracks,
and toured the world.
b. Jul 19, 1944 in Greenville, Mississippi
Source: *WhoAfA 9, 10, 11, 12; WhoBlA
8*

Turnbull, Wendy
"Rabbit"
Australian. Tennis Player
Won mixed doubles with John Lloyd:
1982 French Open, 1983 Wimbledon.
b. Nov 26, 1952 in Brisbane, Australia
Source: *BioIn 14, 16; NewYTBS 84;
WhoIntT*

Turner, Donald F(rank)
American. Lawyer
Specialist in antitrust law; wrote *Antitrust
Policy,* 1959; *Antitrust Law,* 1980.
b. Mar 19, 1921
d. Jul 19, 1994 in Derwood, Maryland
Source: *BioIn 7, 8, 11, 20; BlueB 76;
CurBio 94N; DrAS 74P, 78P; PolProf J;
WhAm 11; WhoAm 74, 76, 78, 80, 82,
84, 86, 88, 90, 92, 94, 95; WhoAmL 83,
85, 90, 92; WhoE 74*

Turner, Eva, Dame
English. Opera Singer
Dramatic soprano; 35-year career earned
her the unofficial title of England's
greatest soprano; won renown in title
role in Puccini's "Turandot."
b. Mar 10, 1892 in Oldham, England
d. Jun 16, 1990 in London, England
Source: *AnObit 1990; BakBD 92;
BakBDTw; BioIn 2, 3, 5, 14, 15, 17, 21;
CamBiEn; ChamBiD; CmOp; DcArts;
DcNaB 1986; FacFETw; IntDcOp;
IntWWM 90; InWom; MetOEnc;
NewEOp 71; NewGrDM 80; NewGrDO;
NewYTBS 90; OxDcOp; PenDiMP; Who
83, 85, 88, 90; WhoMus 72*

Turner, Frederick Jackson
American. Historian
Originated frontier theory emphasizing
significance of receding frontier in
American social, economic
development.
b. Nov 14, 1861 in Portage, Wisconsin
d. Mar 14, 1932 in Pasadena, California
Source: *AmAu&B; AmBi; AmNatBi;
AmSocL; Benet 87, 96; BenetAL 91;
BioIn 1, 3, 5, 7, 8, 9, 10, 11, 12, 13, 14,
15, 19, 20, 22, 23; CamBiEn;
CamDcAB; CamGEL; CamGLE;
CamHAL; CasWL; ChamBiD; ConAu
113; CyWA 97; DcAmB; DcLB 17, 186;
DcNAA; EncAAH; EncAB-H 1974, 1996;
EncWB 98; EvLB; FacFETw; GayN;*

*GloEncH; HarEnUS; MakMC;
McGEWB; MemAm; NatCAB 13;
NewEAmW; OxCAmH; OxCAmL 65, 83,
95; PenC AM; PeoHis; RAdv 14, 13-3;
RComAH; REn; REnAL; REnAW;
ThTwC 87; TwCA, SUP; WebAB 74;
WebE&AL; WhAm 1; WisWr; WorAu
1900*

Turner, Henry McNeal
American. Religious Leader
Commissioned chaplain by Lincoln, first
black commissioned, 1863; forced out,
1865.
b. Feb 1, 1834 in Abbeville, South
Carolina
d. May 8, 1915 in Windsor, Ontario,
Canada
Source: *AfrAmAl 6, 8; AmNatBi;
BiDChrM; BiDSA; BioIn 6, 8, 9, 10, 11,
17, 18, 19, 22; DcAmAu; DcAmB;
DcAmNB; DcAmReB 1, 2; EncAACR;
EncAB-H 1974, 1996; EncSoH; EncWB
98; EncWM; McGEWB; NotBlAM;
RelLAm 1, 2; TwCBDA; WhAm 1;
WhoColR; WorAlBi*

Turner, Ike
[Ike and Tina Turner]
American. Singer, Songwriter
Wrote, sang hit songs "A Fool in Love
(Tell Me What's Wrong)," 1960;
"Goodbye, So Long," 1971.
b. Nov 5, 1931 in Clarksdale, Mississippi
Source: *AllMGBl 1, 2; BakBD 84, 92;
BiDAfM; BioIn 15; Blues; ConMus 24;
DcTwCCu 1; DrBlPA 90; EncPR&S 89;
EncRk 88; LegTOT; NewAmDM;
OnThGG; OxCPMus; PenEncP; SoulM;
WhoHol 92, A; WhoRock 81; WorAlBi*

Turner, Janine
[Janine Gauntt]
American. Actor
Plays Maggie O'Connell on the Emmy
winning TV show, "Northern
Exposure."
b. Dec 1962 in Lincoln, Nebraska
Source: *IntMPA 94, 96; LegTOT; News
93-2*

Turner, Jesse
American. Hostage
Computer science instructor in Lebanon
seized by Islamic Jihad January 24,
1987 and held captive 1,731 days;
released October 21, 1991.
Source: *BioIn 13, 17*

Turner, Joe
"Big Joe"
American. Jazz Musician
Blues vocalist; rock pioneer; recorded
classic "Shake, Rattle, and Roll,"
1954.
b. May 18, 1911 in Kansas City,
Missouri
d. Nov 24, 1985 in Hollywood,
California
Source: *BiDJaz; BioIn 11, 12, 14, 15,
16, 17, 24; Blues; DrBlPA 90; EncPR&S
74, 89; EncRk 88; NewGrDA 86;*

*NewGrDJ 88, 94; RkOn 74, 78;
RolSEnR 83; WhoJazz 72; WhoRocM 82*

Turner, John Napier
Canadian. Political Leader
Liberal Party leader who succeeded
Pierre Trudeau as prime minister,
1984; defeated by Conservative Brian
Mulroney, Sep 1984.
b. Jun 7, 1929 in Richmond, England
Source: *AmCath 80; BlueB 76;
CamBiEn; CanParl 1998; ChamBiD;
CurBio 84; FacFETw; IntWW 74, 75,
76, 77, 78, 79, 80, 81, 82, 83, 89, 91,
93, 97, 98, 2000; NewYTBS 84; Who 82,
83, 85, 88, 90, 92, 94, 98, 99, 2000;
WhoAm 74, 76, 78, 80, 82, 84, 88, 94,
95, 96, 97, 98, 99, 2000; WhoCan 73,
75, 77, 80, 82, 84; WhoE 74, 75, 77, 85;
WhoWor 74, 76, 78, 84, 89, 93, 95, 96,
97, 98, 99, 2000*

Turner, Joseph Mallord William
English. Artist
Foremost English Romantic painter;
noted for impressionistic oils,
watercolors of seascapes.
b. Apr 23, 1775 in London, England
d. Dec 19, 1851 in London, England
Source: *Alli; ArtsNiC; AtlBL; Benet 87,
96; BioIn 1, 2, 3, 4, 5, 6, 7, 8, 9, 10, 11,
12, 13, 14, 15, 16, 23; CamBiEn;
CelCen; ChamBiD; ChhPo, S1, S3;
ClaDrA; DcArts; DcBiPP; DcBrBI;
DcBrECP; DcBrWA; DcNaB; DcSeaP;
DcVicP, 2; EncEnv; EncWB 98; LinLib
S; McGDA; McGEWB; NewC;
NewCBEL; OxCArt; OxCBrHi;
OxCShps; OxDcArt; RAdv 14, 13-3;
REn; VicBrit; WhDW*

Turner, Kathleen
[Mary Kathleen Turner]
American. Actor
Star of feature films *Romancing the
Stone,* 1984; *Jewel of the Nile,* 1985.
b. Jun 19, 1954 in Springfield, Missouri
Source: *BiDFilm 94; BioIn 14, 15, 16;
CamBiEn; CelR 90; ChamBiD; ConNews
85-3; ConTFT 5, 12, 24; CurBio 86;
EncAFC; HalFC 88; HolBB; IntDcF 1-3,
2-3; IntMPA 86, 88, 92, 94, 96; IntWW
89, 91, 93, 97, 98, 2000; IntWWW 2;
ItaFilm; LegTOT; NewYTBS 86; OsStAZ;
VarWW 85; WhoAm 86, 88, 90, 92, 94,
95, 96, 97, 99, 2000; WhoAmW 89, 91,
93, 95, 97, 99; WhoEnt 92, 98; WhoHol
92*

Turner, Lana
[Julia Jean Mildred Frances Turner]
"The Sweater Girl"
American. Actor
Allegedly discovered while drinking a
soda at Top Hat Malt Shop; films
include *Imitation of Life,* 1959.
b. Feb 8, 1920 in Wallace, Idaho
d. Jun 29, 1995 in Los Angeles,
California
Source: *AmNatBi; BiDFilm, 94;
BioAmW; BioIn 1, 2, 4, 6, 8, 9, 10, 11,
12, 13, 14, 15, 16, 18, 21, 22, 23, 24;
BlueB 76; CelR, 90; ChamBiD; CmMov;*

CurBio 43, 95N; DcArts; DcPseud; EncWB 2-19; FilmEn; FilmgC; ForYSC; GoodHs; HalFC 80, 84, 88; IntDcF 1-3, 2-3; IntMPA 84, 86, 88, 92; InWom, SUP; LegTOT; MGM; MotPP; MovMk; NewYTBE 71; NewYTBS 95; OsStAZ; OxCFilm; ThFT; VarWW 85; WhoAm 74, 76, 78, 80, 82, 84, 86, 88, 92, 94; WhoEnt 92; WhoHol A; WorAl; WorAlBi; WorEFlm

Turner, Morrie
American. Cartoonist, Author
Broke cartoon strip color barrier with syndicated comic *Wee Pals*, 1970s; books include *All God's Chillun Got Soul*, 1980.
b. Dec 11, 1923 in Oakland, California
Source: *BioIn 15; ConAu 15NR, 29R, X; Ebony 1; EncACom; WhoAm 80; WorECom*

Turner, Nat
American. Slave
Led only effective slave rebellion in US history, 1831.
b. Oct 2, 1800 in Southampton County, Virginia
d. Nov 11, 1831 in Jerusalem, Virginia
Source: *AfrAmAl 6, 8; AmBi; AmNatBi; ApCAB; BenetAL 91; BioIn 1, 3, 4, 6, 7, 8, 9, 10, 11, 16, 17, 18, 19, 20, 21, 23, 24; CamBiEn; CamDcAB; ChamBiD; DcAmB; DcAmNB; DcAmSR; EncAAH; EncAB-H 1974, 1996; EncARH; EncRelA; EncSoH; HarEnUS; HisWorL; LegTOT; LinLib S; MacEWoS; NatCAB 13; NegAl 76, 83, 89; NewCol 75; NotBlAM; OxCAfAL; OxCAmL 83; WebAB 74, 79; WhAm HS; WhCiWar; WorAl; WorAlBi*

Turner, Roscoe Wilson
American. Aviator
Stunt flier, air racer; held cross-country speed records, nat. air races, 1933-38; awarded Distinguished Flying Cross, 1952.
b. Sep 29, 1895 in Corinth, Mississippi
d. Jun 23, 1970 in Indianapolis, Indiana
Source: *NewYTBE 70; WhAm 5; WhoSSW 82; WhScrn 83*

Turner, Stansfield
American. Government Official
Retired Naval admiral; directed CIA, 1977-81.
b. Dec 1, 1923 in Chicago, Illinois
Source: *BioIn 11, 12, 13, 14; ConAu 118, 124; CurBio 78; EncAInt; EncNaHi; IntAu&W 89; IntWW 77, 78, 79, 80, 81, 82, 83, 89, 91, 93, 97, 98, 2000; IntYB 78, 79, 80, 81, 82; NewYTBS 77; WhoAm 74, 76, 78, 80, 82, 84, 86, 88, 90, 92, 94, 95, 96, 97, 98, 99, 2000; WhoAmP 77, 79, 81, 83, 85, 87, 89, 91, 93, 95, 97, 1999; WhoE 79, 81; WhoFI 89, 92; WhoGov 72, 77; WhoSSW 88; WorAl; WorAlBi*

Turner, Ted
[Robert Edward Turner, III]
''The Mouth of the South''
American. Impresario, Businessman
Winner of America's Cup, 1977; owner of Atlanta Braves, Hawks; developed first all-news cable network, Cable News Network (CNN).
b. Nov 19, 1938 in Cincinnati, Ohio
Source: *AmDec 1970; Ballpl 90; BiDAmSp OS; BiDProW; BioIn 13, 14, 15, 16, 17, 18, 19, 20, 21, 22, 23, 24; CamBiEn; CelR 90; ChamBiD; ConAmBL; ConAu 120, X; ConHero 3; ConTFT 5, 25; CurBio 79, 98; DcTwCCu 1; EncAB-H 1996; EncTeIN; EncTwCJ; EncWB, 98; FacFETw; IntMPA 86, 88, 92, 94, 96; IntWW 91, 93, 98, 2000; LegTOT; LesBEnT, 92; News 89-1; NewYTBE 72; St&PR 93, 96, 97; WhoAm 80, 82, 84, 86, 88, 90, 92, 94, 95, 96, 97, 98, 99, 2000; WhoEnt 92, 98; WhoFI 00, 83, 85, 87, 89, 94, 96, 98; WhoMedi 98; WhoSpor; WhoSSW 86, 88, 91, 95, 97, 99; WhoWor 96, 97, 98, 99, 2000; WorAl; WorAlBi*

Turner, Thomas Wyatt
American. Civil Rights Leader, Educator
Charter member, NAACP; founded Federation of Colored Catholics, 1915; active in black voter registration, 1920s.
b. Apr 16, 1877 in Hughesville, Maryland
d. Apr 21, 1978 in Washington, District of Columbia
Source: *AmNatBi; BiDMoAE; BioIn 13, 19, 21, 24; BlksScM; CamDcAB; FacFETw; InB&W 80; NatCAB 61; NewYTBS 78; NotBlAS; ObitOF 79; WhoColR*

Turner, Tina
[Ike and Tina Turner; Anna Mae Bullock]
American. Singer
Won Grammys for ''Proud Mary,'' 1972; ''What's Love Got to Do With It?,'' 1984.
b. Nov 26, 1939 in Nutbush, Tennessee
Source: *AfrAmAl 6, 8; BakBD 84, 92; BakDcM; BiDAfM; BillEnR; BioIn 8, 9, 13, 14, 15, 16; BlkWAm; CamBiEn; CelR 90; ConAu 147; ConMus 1; CurBio 84; DcTwCCu 5; DrBIPA, 90; EncPR&S 89; EncRk 88; EncRkSt; EncWB 98; GrLiveH; HarEnR 86; InB&W 80, 85; IntMPA 88, 92, 94, 96; IntWW 91, 98, 2000; InWom SUP; NegAl 89; NewAmDM; NewGrDA 86; NotBlAW 1; OxCPMus; PenEncP; RkOn 85; SoulM; WhoAm 84, 86, 88, 90, 92, 94, 95, 96, 97, 98, 99, 2000; WhoAmW 89, 91; WhoBlA 7; WhoEnt 92, 98; WhoHol 92, A; WhoRock 81; WhoRocM 82; WorAl; WorAlBi*

Turnesa, Jim
[James Turnesa]
American. Golfer
Turned pro, 1931; won PGA, 1952.
b. Dec 9, 1914 in Elmsford, New York
d. Aug 27, 1971 in Elmsford, New York

Source: *BioIn 9; NewYTBE 71; ObitOF 79; WhoGolf*

Turow, Scott
American. Author
Lawyer-turned-best-selling author; wrote *The Burden of Proof*, 1990; *Presumed Innocent* filmed, 1990, starring Harrison Ford.
b. Apr 12, 1949 in Chicago, Illinois
Source: *BeaEPF; BestSel 90-3; BioIn 11, 15, 16; ConAu 40NR, 65NR, 73; ConPopW; CurBio 91; LegTOT; MajTwCW 2; OxCTwCL; TwCCr&M 91; WhoAm 88, 90; WhoMW 92; WorAu 1985; WrDr 92*

Turpin, Ben
American. Comedian
Known for crossed eyes, somersaults; appeared in film *Swing High*, 1930s.
b. Sep 17, 1869 in New Orleans, Louisiana
d. Jul 1, 1940 in Santa Barbara, California
Source: *BioIn 2, 4, 11, 17; CurBio 40; DcAmB S2; Film 1; FilmgC; FrSilen; Funs; LegTOT; MotPP; MovMk; SilFlmP; TwYS; WhAm 4, HSA; WhScrn 74, 77, 83; WorAl; WorAlBi; WorEFlm*

Turpin, Dick
[Richard Turpin]
English. Criminal
Horse thief hanged at York; subject of W H Ainsworth's novel, *Rockwood*, 1834.
b. 1706 in Essex, England
d. Apr 10, 1739 in York, England
Source: *Benet 87, 96; BioIn 1, 4, 6, 8, 10; BlmGEL; CamBiEn; CamGEL; DcArts; DcNaB; DrInf; FilmgC; HalFC 84, 88; LngCEL; NewC; NewCol 75; OxCBrHi; REn; WhDW*

Turtle Island String Quartet
[Darol Anger; David Balakrishnan; Jeremy Cohen; Mark Summer]
American. Music Group
Acoustic string quartet; albums include *Skylife*, 1990.
Source: *ConMus 9; DrAS 82H; NewAgMG*

Turtles, The
[Howard Kaylan; Don Murray; Al Nichol; Jim Pons; Chuck Portz; John Seiter; Jim Tucker]
American. Music Group
Underrated cult band during Beatles era; hits include ''Happy Together,'' 1967.
Source: *BiDAmM; BillEnR; ConMuA 80A; CurBio 59; EncPR&S 89; EncRk 88; EncRkSt; HarEnR 86; IlEncRk; InB&W 80; PenEncP; RkOn 78, 84; RkWho 96; RolSEnR 83; WhoHol 92; WhoRock 81; WhoRocM 82*

Turturro, John

American. Actor
Films include *Do the Right Thing,* 1989; *Quiz Show,* 1994; *Unstrung Heroes,* 1995.
b. Feb 28, 1957 in New York, New York
Source: *BiDFilm 94; BioIn 14, 15, 17, 18, 19, 20, 22, 23; CamBiEn; ConTFT 9, 16; CurBio 96; IntMPA 92, 94, 96; IntWW 93, 97, 98, 2000; LegTOT; MiSFD 9; WhoAm 92, 94, 95, 96, 97, 98, 99, 2000; WhoEnt 92, 98; WhoHol 92; WhoWest 98; WhoWor 95, 96, 97, 98, 99, 2000*

Tushingham, Rita

English. Actor
Had award-winning performance in *A Taste of Honey,* 1961.
b. Mar 14, 1942 in Liverpool, England
Source: *BioIn 7, 11; BlueB 76; ConTFT 7; CurBio 65; FilmEn; FilmgC; HalFC 84, 88; IlWWBF; IntMPA 75, 76, 77, 78, 79, 80, 81, 82, 84, 86, 92, 94, 96; IntWWW 2; InWom, SUP; MotPP; MovMk; OxCFilm; Who 74, 82, 83, 85, 88, 90, 92, 94, 98, 99, 2000; WhoAmW 70, 72, 74; WhoHol A; WhoThe 72, 77, 81; WhoWor 74, 76; WorAl; WorAlBi; WorEFlm*

Tussaud, Marie Gresholtz, Madame

Swiss. Wax Modeler
Created Madame Tussaud museum of waxwork figures in London.
b. Dec 7, 1760 in Bern, Switzerland
d. Apr 15, 1850 in London, England
Source: *InWom; NewCol 75; WebBD 83*

Tutankhamen

[Tut-Ankh—Amen]
"King Tut"
Egyptian. Ruler
Boy ruler of 18th Dynasty; tomb, with magnificent contents, found 1922, in Valley of Kings.
b. 1358BC
d. 1340BC
Source: *DcBiPP; NewCol 75; WebBD 83*

Tuthill, Harry J

American. Cartoonist
Created wryly cynical syndicated comic strip, "The Bungle Family," 1925-45.
b. 1886 in Chicago, Illinois
d. Jan 25, 1957 in Saint Louis, Missouri
Source: *WorECom*

Tuttle, Lurene

American. Actor
TV shows include "Life With Father," 1953-55; Julia, 1968-71.
b. Aug 20, 1906 in Pleasant Lake, Indiana
d. May 28, 1986 in Encino, California
Source: *ForWC 70; LegTOT; Vers A; WhoHol A*

Tuttle, Merlin Devere

American. Animal Expert
World-renowned authority on bats.
b. Aug 26, 1941 in Honolulu, Hawaii
Source: *AmMWSc 76P, 79, 82, 86, 89, 92, 95, 98; BioIn 15, 16; CamDcAB; CurBio 92*

Tutu, Desmond (Mpilo)

South African. Religious Leader
First black Anglican bishop of Johannesburg, S Africa; won Nobel Peace Prize, 1984.
b. Oct 7, 1931 in Klerksdrop, South Africa
Source: *AfSS 81, 82; BioIn 12, 13, 14, 15, 16; BlkLC; BlkWr 1, 3; CamBiEn; ChamBiD; ConAu 67NR, 81NR, 125; ConBlB 6; ConHero 1; ConLC 80; CurBio 85; DcCPSAf; DcEcMov; DcTwHis; EncWB; FacFETw; HeroCon; IntWW 81, 82, 83, 89, 91, 93, 97, 98, 2000; LegTOT; NewYTBS 84; NobelP; RadHan; SchCGBL; Who 82, 83, 88, 92, 98, 99, 2000; WhoAfr; WhoIntA 2; WhoNob, 90, 95; WhoRel 92; WhoWor 87, 89, 91, 93, 95, 96, 97, 98, 99, 2000; WrDr 98, 99, 2000*

Tutuola, Amos

Nigerian. Author
Novels with Yoruba folklore as background include *The Feather Woman of the Jungle,* 1962; *The Wild Herbalist of the Remote Town,* 1980.
b. Jun 20, 1920 in Abeokuta, Nigeria
d. Jun 8, 1997 in Ibadan, Nigeria
Source: *AfrA; AfrWr; AfSS 78, 79, 80, 81, 82; Au&Wr 71; Benet 87, 96; BiCoLiE; BioIn 3, 6, 7, 10, 13, 14; BlkLC; BlkWr 1, 2, 3; CamBiEn; CamGEL; CamGLE; CasWL; ChamBiD; CnDWLB 3; CnMWL; ConAu 9R, 27NR, 66NR, 159; ConLC 5, 14, 29; ConNov 72, 76, 82, 86, 91, 96; CyWA 89, 97; DcAfHiB 86; DcLB 125; DcLEL 1940; EncFoLi; EncWB 98; GrWrEL N; IntAu&W 76, 77, 82; IntvTCA 2; IntWW 74, 75, 76, 77, 78, 79, 80, 81, 82, 83, 89, 91, 93, 97; LegTOT; LinLib L; LngCTC; MajTwCW 1, 2; McGEWB; ModBlW, 2; ModCmwL; NewYTBS 97; Novels; OxCTwCL; PenC CL, ENG; RAdv 14, 13-2; RfGEnL 91; RGAfL; RGTwCWr; ScF&FL 1, 2; SchCGBL; SelBAAf; TwCWr; WebE&AL; WhDW; WhoHr&F; WhoWor 84, 87, 89, 91, 93, 95, 96; WorAu 1950; WrDr 76, 80, 82, 84, 86, 88, 90, 92, 94, 96, 98N*

Tutwiler, Margaret (DeBardeleben)

American. Government Official
Appointed assistant secretary of state for public affairs and State Department spokesperson, 1989; criticized for her lack of knowledge of foreign affairs, but also praised and respected for her dedication and candor.
b. Dec 28, 1950 in Birmingham, Alabama
Source: *IntWWW 2; WhoAm 84, 86, 90, 92, 94, 95, 96; WhoAmP 81, 83, 85, 87,*

89, 91, 93, 95, 97, 1999; WhoAmW 89, 91, 93, 95; WhoEmL 87

Tuve, Merle Antony

American. Physicist
Scientific discoveries led to development of radar and nuclear energy.
b. Jun 27, 1901 in Canton, South Dakota
d. May 20, 1982 in Bethesda, Maryland
Source: *AmMWSc 76P, 79, 82; AmNatBi; BiESc; BioIn 5, 6, 12, 13; BlueB 76; CamDcSc; ConAu 106; DcScB S2; IntWW 74, 75, 76, 77, 78, 79, 80, 81, 82, 83N; McGMS 80; WhAm 8; WhoAm 74, 76, 78, 80; WhoGov 72; WhoWor 74*

Twachtman, John Henry

American. Artist
Impressionist landscape painter; known for scenes of Yellowstone, Niagara: "Snowbound," 1902.
b. Aug 4, 1853 in Cincinnati, Ohio
d. Aug 8, 1902 in Gloucester, Massachusetts
Source: *AmBi; AmNatBi; ApCAB; ArtsAmW 3; BioIn 1, 12, 19, 20, 22; BriEAA; CamDcAB; DcAmArt; DcAmB; EncWB 98; IlBEAAW; McGDA; McGEWB; NatCAB 13; NewCol 75; OxCAmH; WebBD 83; WhAmArt 85*

Twain, Mark

[Samuel Langhorne Clemens]
"The People's Author"
American. Author, Journalist
Wrote *Tom Sawyer,* 1876; *Huckleberry Finn,* 1885.
b. Nov 30, 1835 in Florida, Missouri
d. Apr 21, 1910 in Redding, Connecticut
Source: *Alli, SUP; AmAu; AmAu&B; AmBi; AmCulL; AmNatBi; AmOrN; AmRef; AmWr; AnCL; ApCAB; ArizL; AtlBL; Au&Arts 20; AuBYP 2, 3; BbD; BeaEPF; Benet 87, 96; BenetAL 91; BiCoLiE; BiDAmJo; BiD&SB; BiDPara; BiDSA; BioIn 1, 2, 3, 4, 5, 6, 7, 8, 9, 10, 11, 12, 13, 14, 15, 16, 17, 18, 19, 20, 21, 22, 23, 24; CamBiEn; CamGEL; CamGLE; CamHAL; CarSB; CasWL; CelCen; ChamBiD; Chambr 3; ChhPo, S1; ChlBkCr; ChlLR 58, 60; CnDAL; ConAu 104, 135; CrtSuMy; CrtT 3, 4; CyAL 2; CyWA 58, 89, 97; DcAmAu; DcAmB; DcAmC; DcArts; DcBiPP; DcEnA, A; DcEnL; DcLB 11, 12, 23, 64, 74; DcLEL; DcNAA; DcPseud; Dis&D; Drake; EncAAH; EncAB-H 1974, 1996; EncAHmr; EncApL; EncFoLi; EncFrLi; EncFWF; EncMys; EncO&P 1, 2, 3; EncPaPR 91; EncSF, 93; EncSoH; EncSoL; EncUnb; EncWB 98; EncWL 1; EvLB; FamAYP; FifSWrB; FilmgC; GayN; GrWrEL N; HalFC 80, 84, 88; HarEnUS; JBA 34; JrnUS; LegTOT; LiJour; LinLib L, S; LiveWoA; LngCTC; MagSAmL; MajAl; McGEWB; MemAm; ModAL 4, 4S1, 5; NatCAB 6; NewEAmW; NewEScF; NewGrDA 86; NotNAT B; Novels; OnHuMoP; OxCAmH; OxCAmL 65, 83, 95; OxCAusL; OxCChiL; OxCEng 67, 85, 95; PenC AM; RAdv 1, 14, 13-1; RComAH; RComWL; RealN; REn;*

REnAL; REnAW; RfGAmL 4, 87, 94;
RfGShF 1, 2; ScF&FL 1, 92; ScFEYrs;
ScFSB; ShSCr 6, 26, 34; ShSWr;
SJGChWr 5A; SJGFanW; SJGYouA 2;
SouWr; SupFW; TwCA; TwCBDA;
TwCChW 1A, 2A, 3A, 4A; TwCLC 6, 12,
19, 36, 48; TwCSFW 81, 86, 91;
TwCYAW 1; TwoTYeD; WebAB 74, 79;
WebE&AL; WhAm 1; WhCiWar; WhDW;
WhLit; WhoChL; WhoTwCL; WorAl;
WorAlBi; WorLitC; WrChl; WrYoAd;
YABC 2

Twain, Shania
[Eileen Twain]
Canadian. Singer, Songwriter
Won Grammy, Best Country Album, The
Woman in Me, 1995; entertainer of the
year, CMA Awards, 1999.
b. 1965 in Windsor, Ontario, Canada
Source: AllMGCo; CanWW 96, 98;
ConMus 17; News 96, 96-3

Tway, Bob
[Robert Tway]
American. Golfer
Touring pro, 1980s; won PGA, 1986.
b. May 4, 1958 in Oklahoma City,
Oklahoma
Source: BioIn 15; NewYTBS 87

Tweed, Boss
[William Marcy Tweed]
American. Politician
Tammany Hall boss; stole millions from
city treasury; exposed by Nast
cartoons, 1870.
b. Apr 3, 1823 in New York, New York
d. Apr 12, 1878 in New York, New
York
Source: AmBi; AmPolLe; ApCAB; Benet
87, 96; BiAUS; BiDrAC; BiDrUSC 89;
BioIn 5, 6, 7, 10, 11, 16, 17, 21;
CabMA; CyAG; DcAmB; EncAB-H 1974,
1996; HarEnUS; LegTOT; McGEWB;
NatCAB 3; OxCAmH; REn; WebAB 74,
79; WhAm HS; WhAmP; WorAl;
WorAlBi

Tweedale, Violet Chambers
British. Author
Wrote over 30 works dealing with
occult: Ghosts I Have Seen, 1919.
b. 1862
d. Dec 10, 1936
Source: ConAu 116; EncO&P 1

Twelvetrees, Helen
[Helen Jurgens]
American. Actor
1930s films include Millie, Bedtime
Story.
b. Dec 25, 1908 in New York, New
York
d. Feb 14, 1958 in Pennsylvania
Source: BioIn 4, 5, 11; Film 2; FilmgC;
ForYSC; HalFC 80, 84, 88; HolP 30;
MotPP; MovMk; NotNAT B; ObitOF 79;
ThFT; WhoHol B; WhoHrs 80; WhScrn
74, 77, 83

Twiggy
[Leslie Hornby]
English. Model
Ultra-thin model, 1966-76; sang and
danced in critically acclaimed musical
My One and Only, with Tommy Tune,
1983.
b. Sep 19, 1949 in London, England
Source: ABCCoAm; AmDec 1960;
CamBiEn; CelR, 90; ChamBiD; ConAu
103; ConTFT 3; CurBio 68; EncFash;
FilmgC; GoodHs; HalFC 84, 88;
IntMPA 75, 76, 77, 78, 79, 80, 81, 82,
84, 86, 88, 92, 94, 96; IntWW 91;
InWom, SUP; LegTOT; NewYTBS 83;
ThHDFas; Who 85, 88, 90, 92, 94;
WhoAm 84, 86, 92, 94; WhoEnt 92;
WhoHol 92, A; WorAl

Twining, Nathan F(arragut)
American. Air Force Officer
Became general, 1950; chm., Joint
Chiefs of Staff, 1957-60; instrumental
in formulating Indochina policy.
b. Oct 11, 1897 in Monroe, Wisconsin
d. Mar 29, 1982 in Lackland Air Force
Base, Texas
Source: AmNatBi; AnObit 1982;
BiDWWGF; BioIn 1, 2, 3, 4, 5, 11, 12,
13, 24; BlueB 76; CamBiEn; CurBio 53,
82; EncVieW; HarEnMi; IntWW 74, 75,
76, 77, 78, 79, 80, 81, 82N; NewYTBS
82; PolProf E; ScrEAmL 1; WebAMB;
WhAm 8; Who 74, 83N; WhoAm 74, 76,
78; WhoWor 74; WhWW-II; WorAl;
WorAlBi

Twining, Thomas
English. Merchant
Known for specialty teas; popularized tea
in England by opening first tea house,
1717.
b. 1675
d. 1741
Source: Entr

Twisted Sister
[Jay Jay French; Mark "the Animal"
Mendoza; Eddie "Fingers" Ojeda; A J
Pero; Dee Snider]
American. Music Group
Heavy metal group formed 1976, known
for wild attire, hard rock sound; first
single "We're Not Gonna Take It,"
1984.
Source: BillEnR; BioIn 15; EncPR&S
89; GrMetD; PenEncP; RkOn 85

Twitchell, Paul
Cultist, Author
Founder, cult sect Eck, 1968.
b. 1908?
d. 1971
Source: ConAu 111, 132; EncO&P 1S3,
2, 3; ScF&FL 1A, 2, 92

Twitty, Conway
[Harold Lloyd Jenkins]
"The High Priest of Country Music"
American. Singer, Songwriter
Began as rock-n-roll singer, later turned
to country music: "Lonely Boy

Blue," 1960; inducted into Country
Music Hall of Fame, 1999.
b. Sep 1, 1933 in Friars Point,
Mississippi
d. Jun 5, 1993 in Springfield, Missouri
Source: AllMGCo; BakBD 84, 92;
BgBkCoM; BioIn 14, 15, 16, 18, 19, 20,
21; BioNews 75; CelR 90; ConMus 6;
CounME 74, 74A; DcPseud; EncFCWM
83; EncRk 88; ForYSC; HarEnCM 87;
HarEnR 88; IllEncM; LegTOT;
NewAmDM; NewGrDA 86; News 94, 94-
1; OxCPMus; PenEncP; RolSEnR 83;
WhoAm 78, 80, 82, 84, 86, 88; WhoEnt
92; WhoHol 92, A; WhoRock 81;
WhoRocM 82; WorAl; WorAlBi

Twombly, Cy
[Edward Parker Twombly, Jr.]
American. Artist
Paintings, drawings reflect his love for
antiquity: Discoveries on Commodus,
1963; elected to the American
Academy and Institute of Arts and
Letters, 1987.
b. Apr 25, 1929 in Lexington, Virginia
Source: AmArt; BioIn 8, 11, 12, 14, 15,
16, 17, 20, 21; ConArt 77, 83, 89, 96;
CurBio 88; DcAmArt; DcCAA 71, 77,
88; DcTwArt; IntWW 91, 93, 97, 98,
2000; OxCTwCA; OxDcArt; PhDcTCA
77; PrintW 85; WhoAm 82, 84, 86, 88,
94, 96; WhoAmA 84, 91; WorArt 1980

Tworkov, Jack
American. Artist
Leader of NY school of Abstract
Expressionism.
b. Aug 15, 1900 in Biala, Poland
d. Sep 4, 1982 in Provincetown,
Massachusetts
Source: AmNatBi; AnObit 1982; BioIn 3,
5, 6, 7, 10, 13, 14, 16; BriEAA;
CamBiEn; CamDcAB; ConArt 77, 83,
89, 96; ConAu 107; CurBio 82, 82N;
DcAmArt; DcCAA 71, 77, 88, 94; DcCAr
81; DcTwArt; NewYTBS 82; OxCTwCA;
OxDcArt; PhDcTCA 77; PrintW 83, 85;
SmATA 31N, 47; WhAm 8; WhAmArt 85;
WhoAm 74, 76, 78, 80, 82; WhoAmA 73,
76, 78, 80, 82, 84N, 86N, 89N, 91N,
93N; WhoAmJ 80; WhoWor 74;
WhoWorJ 72, 78; WorArt 1950

Twyman, Jack
[John Kennedy Twyman]
American. Basketball Player
Forward, 1955-66, mostly with
Cincinnati; led NBA in field goal
percentage, 1958; Hall of Fame, 1982.
b. May 11, 1934 in Pittsburgh,
Pennsylvania
Source: BasBi; BiDAmSp BK; BioIn 6;
Dun&B 86, 88, 90, 98; OfNBA 87;
WhoAm 86, 90, 94, 95, 96, 97; WhoBbl
73; WhoFI 87, 89, 94, 96; WhoMW 88,
90; WhoSpor

Tydings, Millard Evelyn
American. Politician
Dem. senator from MD, 1927-51; headed
McCarthy investigation which cleared
State Dept., 1950.

b. Apr 6, 1890 in Havre de Grace, Maryland
d. Feb 9, 1961 in Havre de Grace, Maryland
Source: *AmNatBi; BiDrAC; BiDrUSC 89; BioIn 2, 5, 6, 11; CurBio 45, 61; DcAmB S7; EncAB-A 32; EncSoH; NewCol 75; WhAm 4; WhAmP; WorAl*

Tyler, Anne
American. Author
Called chronicler of modern American family: *Morgan's Passing,* 1980; *Dinner at the Homesick Restaurant,* 1982; won Pulitzer Prize for fiction for *Breathing Lessons,* 1989.
b. Oct 25, 1941 in Minneapolis, Minnesota
Source: *AmWomWr; AmWr S4; ArtclWW 2; Au&Arts 18; BeaEPF; Benet 96; BenetAL 91; BestSel 89-1; BiCoLiE; BioIn 10, 11, 12, 13, 14, 15, 16, 17, 18, 19, 20, 21, 22; BlmGWL; CamBiEn; CamDcAB; ChamBiD; ConAu 9R, 11NR, 33NR, 53NR; ConLC 7, 11, 18, 28, 44, 59, 103; ConNov 72, 76, 82, 86, 91, 96; ConPopW; ConSoWr; CurBio 81; CyWA 89, 97; DcLB 6, 143, Y82A; DcLEL 1940; DcTwCCu 1; DrAF 76; DrAPF 80, 83, 87, 91; EncALit; EncWB 98; EncWL 2S, 3; FemiCLE; FifSWrA; GrWomW; IntAu&W 76, 77, 91, 93; IntvTCA 2; IntWW 91, 93, 97, 98, 2000; IntWWW 2; InWom SUP; LegTOT; MagSAmL; MajTwCW 1, 2; ModAL 4S2, 4S3, 5; ModAWWr; ModWoWr; ModWr; News 95; NewYTBS 77; OxCAmL 83, 95; OxCTwCL; OxCWoWr 95; RAdv 14; RfGAmL 4, 94; RGTwCWr; SJGYouA 2; SmATA 7, 90; TwCYAW 1; Who 94, 98, 99, 2000; WhoAm 76, 78, 80, 82, 84, 86, 88, 90, 92, 94, 95, 96, 97, 98, 99, 2000; WhoAmW 68, 70, 72, 74, 75, 79, 81, 83, 85, 87, 89, 91, 93, 95, 97, 99; WhoE 74, 75, 77, 95, 97, 99; WhoEmL 87; WhoEnt 98; WhoPul; WhoUSWr 88; WhoWor 95, 96, 97, 98, 99, 2000; WhoWrEP 89, 92, 95; WorAlBi; WorAu 1970; WrDr 76, 80, 82, 84, 86, 88, 90, 92, 94, 96, 98, 99, 2000*

Tyler, Bonnie
[Gaynor Hopkins]
Welsh. Singer
Raspy-voiced singer who had number one hit "Total Eclipse of the Heart," 1983.
b. Jun 8, 1953 in Swansea, Wales
Source: *BioIn 13, 14; EncFCWM 83; EncRkSt; LegTOT; PenEncP; RkOn 85; WhoRock 81; WhoRocM 82*

Tyler, John
American. US President
Took office after Harrison's death, 1841-45, making him first vice president to take such action.
b. Mar 29, 1790 in Charles City, Virginia
d. Jan 18, 1862 in Richmond, Virginia
Source: *Alli; AmAu&B; AmBi; AmNatBi; AmPolLe; ApCAB; BenetAL 91; BiAUS; BiDConf; BiDrAC; BiDrGov 1789; BiDrUSC 89; BiDrUSE 71, 89; BioIn 1,*

2, 3, 4, 5, 6, 7, 8, 9, 10, 11, 12, 13, 14, 15, 16, 17, 18, 19, 20, 22, 23, 24; CamBiEn; CamDcAB; CelCen; ChamBiD; CyAG; DcAmB; DcBiPP; Drake; EncAAH; EncAB-H 1974, 1996; EncAPar; EncSoH; EncWB 98; FacPr 89, 93; HarEnUS; HealPre; LegTOT; LinLib L, S; McGEWB; NatCAB 6; OxCAmH; OxCAmL 65, 83; OxCSupC; PolPar; Pres 96; PresAR 1980, 1996; RComAH; REn; REnAL; TwCBDA; USGovLe; VicePre; WebAB 74, 79; WhAm HS; WhAmP; WhCiWar; WhDW; WorAl; WorAlBi

Tyler, Julia Gardiner
American. First Lady
Became John Tyler's second wife in secret ceremony, 1844.
b. May 4, 1820 in Gardiner's Island, New York
d. Jul 10, 1889 in Richmond, Virginia
Source: *AmNatBi; AmWom; ApCAB; BioIn 16, 17, 22; EncWoAP; FacPr 89; GoodHs; InWom, SUP; NatCAB 6; NotAW*

Tyler, Letitia Christian
American. First Lady
First president's wife to die in White House; wife of John Tyler.
b. Nov 12, 1790 in New Kent County, Virginia
d. Sep 10, 1842 in Washington, District of Columbia
Source: *Alli; AmAu&B; AmBi; AmPolLe; ApCAB; BenetAL 91; BiAUS; BiDConf; BiDrAC; BiDrGov 1789; BiDrUSC 89; BiDrUSE 71, 89; BioIn 1, 2, 3, 4, 5, 6, 7, 8, 9, 10, 11, 12, 13, 14, 15, 16, 17, 18, 19, 20; CelCen; CyAG; DcAmB; DcBiPP; Drake; EncAAH; EncAB-H 1974, 1996; EncSoH; EncWoAP; FacPr 89, 93; GoodHs; HarEnUS; HealPre; InWom, SUP; LegTOT; LinLib L, S; McGEWB; NatCAB 6; NotAW; OxCAmH; OxCAmL 65, 83; OxCSupC; PolPar; PresAR 1980; RComAH; REn; REnAL; TwCBDA; VicePre; WebAB 74, 79; WhAm HS; WhAmP; WhCiWar; WhDW; WorAl; WorAlBi*

Tyler, Liv
American. Actor
Appeared in *Silent Fall,* 1994.
b. Jul 1, 1977 in New York, New York
Source: *ConTFT 16; IntWW 2000; LegTOT; WhoAm 2000*

Tyler, Moses Coit
American. Historian
Literary historian was a pioneer in the development of American intellectual history.
b. Aug 2, 1835 in Griswold, Connecticut
d. Dec 28, 1900
Source: *Alli SUP; AmAu; AmAu&B; AmBi; ApCAB; BbD; Benet 87, 96; BenetAL 91; BiDAmEd; BiD&SB; BioIn 3, 8, 14, 15, 16; Chambr 3; DcAmAu; DcAmB; DcLB 47, 64; DcNAA; Drake; EncWB 98; HarEnUS; LinLib L; McGEWB; NatCAB 4; OxCAmH;*

OxCAmL 65, 83; PenC AM; REn; REnAL; TwCBDA; WebAB 74, 79; WhAm 1

Tyler, Parker
American. Poet, Critic
Wrote *The Young and Evil,* 1933; *Chaplin,* 1948; *Classics of the Foreign Film,* 1962.
b. Mar 6, 1907 in New Orleans, Louisiana
d. Jul 24, 1974 in New York, New York
Source: *AmAu&B; BenetAL 91; BioIn 4, 10, 14, 22; ConAu 5NR, 5R, 49; GayLL 1; OxCFilm; REnAL; TwCA SUP; WorAu 1900*

Tyler, Ralph W(infred)
American. Educator, Scholar
Regarded as the father of behavioral objectives, he contributed to curriculum theory and development and educational assessment and evaluation.
b. Apr 22, 1902 in Chicago, Illinois
d. 1994
Source: *BiDAmEd; BioIn 4, 8, 11, 13, 14, 16, 17, 19, 20, 21; BlueB 76; ConAu 109, 144*

Tyler, Richard
Australian. Fashion Designer
Started Richard Tyler collection with wife Lisa Trafficante, late 1980s, opened Los Angeles showroom, Tyler Trafficante, 1988.
b. Sep 22, 1950 in Sunshine, Australia
Source: *CurBio 97; WhoAm 97, 98, 99, 2000; WhoWor 97, 98, 99, 2000*

Tyler, Royall
American. Dramatist, Author, Jurist
Playwright and novelist wrote the first successful American play. He also served as justice of the Supreme Court of Vermont.
b. 1757 in Boston, Massachusetts
d. 1826 in Brattleboro, Vermont
Source: *Alli; AmAu; AmAu&B; AmBi; AmNatBi; AmWrBE; ApCAB; BbD; Benet 87, 96; BenetAL 91; BiAUS; BibAL 8; BiD&SB; BioIn 7, 10, 11, 12, 13, 14, 16; CamDcAB; CamGEL; CamGLE; CamHAL; CasWL; ChhPo; CnDAL; CnThe; CrtSuDr; CyAL 1; DcAmAu; DcAmB; DcLB 37; DcLEL; DcNAA; Drake; EncALit; EncCRAm; EncWB 98; EncWT; EvLB; GrWrEL DR; McGEWB; McGEWD 72, 84; NatCAB 7; NinCLC 3; NotNAT B; OxCAmL 65, 83, 95; OxCAmT 84; OxCThe 67, 83; PenC AM; PlP&P; RAdv 14; REn; REnAL; REnWD; RfGAmL 4, 87, 94; TwCBDA; WebAB 74, 79; WebE&AL; WhAm HS; WhAmRev*

Tyler, Steven
[Aerosmith; Steven Tallarico]
American. Musician, Singer
Vocalist with heavy-metal band since 1970; hit album *Toys in the Attic,* 1975, went platinum.
b. Mar 26, 1948 in Yonkers, New York

Source: *BioIn 22, 24; BkPepl; CurBio 96; DcPseud; LegTOT; WhoAm 95, 96, 97, 98, 99, 2000; WhoRocM 82*

Tyler, Wat
English. Revolutionary
Lead Peasant's Revolt, 1381, against Richard II; was killed after demands were met; Richard II revoked agreement.
d. 1381 in Smithfield, England
Source: *BioIn 7; BlmGEL; CamBiEn; ChambiD; DcAmSR; DcBiPP; DcNaB; EncCapP; EncRev; LinLib S; LngCEL; NewCol 75; OxCBrHi; OxCEng 85, 95; WhDW*

Tylor, Edward Bennett, Sir
English. Anthropologist
Founder of modern anthropology; developed theory of animism in *Primitive Culture*, 1871.
b. Oct 2, 1832 in London, England
d. Jan 2, 1917 in Wellington, England
Source: *DcBiPP; DcEnA; NamesHP; WhDW*

Tynan, Kenneth Peacock
English. Critic, Author
Reviewer for *London Observer*, 1954-58, 1960-63; wrote musical *Oh! Calcutta*, 1969.
b. Apr 2, 1927 in Birmingham, England
d. Jul 26, 1980 in Santa Monica, California
Source: *Benet 87, 96; BiE&WWA; BlueB 76; ChambiD; ConAu 13R, 63NR, 101; CroCD; CurBio 63, 80; DcArts; DcLEL 1940; DcNaB 1971; IntAu&W 76, 77; IntWW 74, 77, 78, 79, 80; LngCTC; MajTwCW 2; ModBrL; NewC; NotNAT; OxCEng 85, 95; OxCThe 83; OxCTwCL; PenC ENG; Who 74; WhoThe 77; WhoWor 74, 78, 80; WorAu 1950; WrDr 76*

Tyndale, William
[William Hutchins; William Tindale]
English. Translator
Translated New Testament into English, 1525; basis for King James version.
b. 1484? in Gloucester, England
d. Oct 6, 1536 in Antwerp, Belgium
Source: *Alli; BritAu; CasWL; Chambr 1; CroE&S; DcBiPP; DcEnA; DcEnL; DcEuL; DcLEL; EvLB; LngCEL; NewC; NewCol 75; OxCEng 67; PenC ENG; REn; WebBD 83; WebE&AL*

Tyndall, John
English. Physicist, Author
Helped popularize science; his experiments showed why the sky is the color blue; wrote *On Radiation*, 1865.
b. Aug 2, 1820 in Leighlin Bridge, Ireland
d. Dec 4, 1893 in Hindhead, England
Source: *Alli, SUP; AsBiEn; BakBD 78, 84; BbD; BiD&SB; BiDIrW; BiDTran; BiESc; BiHiMed; BioIn 1, 2, 6, 8, 9, 10, 12, 14, 23; BritAu 19; CamBiEn; CamDcSc; CamGLE; CelCen; ChambiD;*

Chambr 3; CyEd; DcBiPP; DcEnA; DcEnL; DcIrB 1, 2, 3; DcIrW 2; DcNaB; DcScB; EncWB 98; EvLB; InSci; LarDcSc; LinLib L, S; LuthC 75; McGCEnS; McGEWB; NewCBEL; OxCBrHi; OxCEng 67, 85, 95; RanHWDS; WorAl; WorAlBi; WorScD

Tyne, George
American. Actor, Director
Directed TV shows: "Sanford and Son," 1972-77; "The Ghost and Mrs. Muir," 1968-70.
b. Aug 6, 1917 in Philadelphia, Pennsylvania
Source: *VarWW 85; WhoAm 80, 82; WhoHol 92*

Tyner, McCoy Alfred
[Sulaimon Saud]
American. Pianist, Composer
Jazz recording artist; member of John Coltrane Quartet 1960-65.
b. Dec 11, 1938 in Philadelphia, Pennsylvania
Source: *BakBD 84; BiDJaz; BioIn 12, 13, 16; ConMus 7; NewAmDM; NewGrDA 86; NewGrDJ 88; PenEncP; WhoBlA 7*

Tyner, Rob
[MC5; Robert Derminer]
American. Singer
Lead singer for rock group MC5; the band was formed in the mid-1960s and was considered one of the inspirations for the punk rock movement, with its revolutionary politics and anarchic musical tendencies; hit song was "Kick Out the Jams."
b. c. 1945
d. Sep 17, 1991 in Royal Oak, Michigan
Source: *News 92, 92-2*

Typhoid Mary
[Mary Mallon]
American. Cook
Immune to typhoid fever, but carried virus during NY epidemics, 1904, 1914.
b. 1870
d. Nov 11, 1938 in New York, New York
Source: *BioIn 5; ChambiD; GoodHs; InWom SUP; LegTOT; LibW; WebAB 74, 79; WorAl; WorAlBi*

Tyrrell, George
Irish. Clergy
Jesuit priest best known for his contributions to the Catholic "Modernist" movement, which sought to revise traditional views of revelation and church teaching to stress their historical dimensions.
b. Feb 6, 1861 in Dublin, Ireland
d. Jul 15, 1909 in Storrington, England
Source: *BioIn 6, 8, 9, 12, 13, 17, 22; DcNaB S2; EncWB 98; LuthC 75; NewC; NewCBEL; OxCEng 67, 85, 95; PoIre; TwCA; WhoChr; WorAu 1900*

Tyrrell, James, Sir
English. Courtier
Sir Thomas More claimed he was responsible for murders of Edward V, brother Richard.
d. May 6, 1502 in London, England
Source: *BioIn 3, 11; DcNaB; NewC*

Tyrrell, Joseph Burr
Canadian. Geologist
Pioneered in Canadian metal mining, mineral findings; discovered Kirkland Lake gold deposits, 1900s.
b. Nov 1, 1858 in Weston, Ontario, Canada
d. Aug 26, 1957 in Toronto, Ontario, Canada
Source: *BiDAmCa; BioIn 1, 2, 4, 5, 11, 12, 23; DcScB; InSci; LarDcSc; MacDCB 78; OxCCan; RAdv 14; WhLit; WhNAA*

Tyrrell, Susan
American. Actor
Oscar nominee for *Fat City*, 1972.
b. 1946 in San Francisco, California
Source: *ConTFT 6; FilmEn; HalFC 80, 84, 88; IntMPA 75, 76, 77, 78, 79, 80, 81, 82, 84, 86, 88, 92, 94, 96; ItaFilm; NewYTBE 72; OsStAZ; WhoHol 92, A*

Tyson, Cicely
[Mrs. Miles Davis]
American. Actor
Won Emmy, 1973, for "The Autobiography of Miss Jane Pitman"; star of film, *Sounder*, 1972.
b. Dec 19, 1939 in New York, New York
Source: *AfrAmAl 8; BioIn 9, 10, 11, 12, 13, 14, 15, 16; BlksAmF; BlkWAm; CelR 90; CurBio 75; DrBlPA, 90; FacFEBW TA; GoodHs; GrLiveH; HalFC 84, 88; InB&W 85; IntMPA 86, 92; InWom SUP; MovMk; NegAl 89; NewYTBE 72; NotBlAW 1; NotNAT; NotWoAT; WhoAm 86, 90; WhoAmW 85, 87, 91; WhoBlA 4, 7; WhoEnt 92; WhoHol A; WhoThe 81; WorAlBi*

Tyson, Don
American. Business Executive
President, Tyson Foods, 1956-67, chairman and CEO, 1967-95.
b. Apr 21, 1930 in Olathe, Kansas
Source: *Dun&B 86, 88, 90, 98; News 95, 95-3; St&PR 75, 84, 87, 91, 93; WhoFI 74*

Tyson, Ian
[Ian and Sylvia]
Canadian. Singer, Songwriter
Former rodeo performer; played blues, folk material; formed duo, 1959.
b. Sep 25, 1933 in Victoria, British Columbia, Canada
Source: *AllMGCo; BiDAmM; BioIn 8, 10, 14, 16, 20, 21, 22, 24; DcCAr 81; Songw; TwCPaSc; WhoRocM 82*

Tyson, Laura D'Andrea
American. Economist, Government Official
Chm., President's Council of Economic Advisors, 1993-95; chair, National Economics Council, 1995—.
b. Jun 28, 1947 in Bayonne, New Jersey
Source: *AmEA 74; AmMWSc 78S, 98; AmWomSc 1950; BioIn 18, 19, 20, 21, 22, 23; CurBio 96; EncWoAP; News 94, 94-1; NewYTBS 93; WhoAm 95, 96, 97, 2000; WhoAmW 95, 97, 99; WhoE 95; WhoFI 00, 96, 98; WhoScEn 96; WhoWor 96, 97, 98, 99, 2000*

Tyson, Mike
American. Boxer
Youngest heavyweight champion ever, defeating defending WBC champ, Trevor Berbick, Nov 1986; lost championship to "Buster" Douglas, Feb 1990; sentenced to 6-year prison term for the rape of Desiree Washington, 1992.
b. Jun 1, 1966 in New York, New York
Source: *AfrAmSG; AmDec 1980; BioIn 16; CamBiEn; CelR 90; ChamBiD; ConNews 86-4; CurBio 88; IntWW 91; LegTOT; NegAl 89; NewYTBS 86, 91; WhoAfA 9, 10, 11, 12; WhoAm 90; WhoBlA 7, 8; WhoSpor; WhoWor 89; WorAlBi*

Tyson, Neil de Grasse
American. Astrophysicist, Author
Eminent astrophysicist and author of magazine columns and books, known

for his ability to explain complex scientific concepts to the general public; director of Hayden Planetarium in New York City, 1996—.
b. Oct 5, 1958 in New York, New York
Source: *ConBlB 15; NotBlAS*

Tyson, Sylvia Fricker
[Ian and Sylvia; Mrs. Ian Tyson]
Canadian. Singer, Songwriter
With husband formed folksinging country duo; hits include "You Were on My Mind," 1964.
b. Sep 19, 1940 in Chatham, Ontario, Canada
Source: *ASCAP 80; WhoRocM 82*

Tyus, Wyomia
American. Track Athlete
Sprinter; first woman to win gold medal in 100 meters twice, 1964, 1968 Olympics.
b. Aug 29, 1945 in Griffin, Georgia
Source: *AfrAmBi 1; BiDAmSp OS; BioIn 10, 11, 15, 16, 17, 19, 21, 22, 24; BlkAmWO; BlkOlyM; ChamBiD; EncWoSp; FacFEBW DS; InB&W 80, 85; InWom SUP; NotBlAW 2; OutWomA; WhoAfA 9, 10, 11, 12; WhoBlA 2, 3, 4, 5, 6, 7, 8; WhoSpor; WhoTr&F 73; WorAl; WorAlBi*

Tyzack, Margaret Maud
English. Actor
Noted for work on London stage; plays include *Mornings at Seven*, 1984; a lso on TV, films.
b. Sep 9, 1931
Source: *FilmgC; HalFC 84, 88; IntWWW 2; Who 82, 83, 85, 88, 90, 92, 94, 98, 99, 2000; WhoHol A; WhoThe 72, 81*

Tzara, Tristan
Romanian. Author, Poet
Leader of Dada movement in French literature; edited *Dada* magazine, 1916-20.
b. Apr 4, 1896 in Moinesti, Romania
d. Dec 24, 1963 in Paris, France
Source: *Benet 87, 96; BiDMoPL; BioIn 4, 6, 8, 9, 10, 11, 12, 17; CasWL; ChamBiD; ClDMEL 80; ConAu 153; ConLC 47; DcPseud; DcTwCCu 2; EncWL 1, 2, 2S, 3; EvEuW; FacFETw; LiExTwC; MajTwCW 2; MakMC; ModFrL; ModWD; OxCFr; PenC EUR; PoeCrit 27; REn; TwCWr; WhE&EA; WhoTwCL; WorAlBi; WorAu 1950*

Tz'u Hsi
Chinese. Ruler
Empress Dowager 1861-1908, who resisted foreign encroachment, modernization; last great Manchu leader.
b. Nov 29, 1835 in Beijing, China
d. Nov 14, 1908 in Beijing, China
Source: *EncWB 98; McGEWB; NewCol 75; WhDW*

U

U2
[Adam Clayton; David Howell "The Edge" Evans; Paul "Bono Vox" Hewson; Larry Mullen, Jr.]
Irish. Music Group
Rock band; albums include *War*, 1983; Grammy winner *The Joshua Tree*,2 1987.
Source: *BillEnR; CelR 90; ConMus 2, 12; DcArts; EncPR&S 89; EncRk 88; EncRkSt; HarEnR 86; ModIrLi; NewAmDM; OxCPMus; PenEncP; RkOn 85; RkWho 96; RolSEnR 83; WhsNW 85*

UB 40
[James Brown; Ali Campbell; Robin Campbell; Earl Falconer; Norman Hassan; Brian Travers; Michael Virture; Terence "Astro" Wilson]
English. Music Group
Reggae group formed 1978; named for number of British unemployment benefits card.
Source: *Alli, SUP; BbtC; BiDLA; BioIn 15, 16, 17, 18, 20; BlkAmP; BlkAmWO; BlkAWP; CabMA; ChhPo; ConAu 151; ConMuA 80A; ConMus 4; DcBrBI; DcNAA; DrAPF 80, 83, 85, 87, 89, 91, 93, 97; DrRegL 75; Dun&B 88, 90; EncPR&S 89; EncRk 88; FolkA 87; HarEnR 86; InB&W 80; Law&B 84; LesBEnT 92; MedHR; NewYTBS 84, 92; PenEncP; RkOn 85; SmATA 85; Who 83S; WhoAfA 9; WhoAmA 80, 82, 84, 86, 89, 91, 93; WhoAmP 85; WhoBlA 3, 4; WhoRocM 82; WhoScEu 91-1; WhsNW 85*

Ubell, Earl
American. Broadcast Journalist
Health editor *Parade* mag., 1983—; director TV news, NBC News, 1972-76.
b. Jun 21, 1926 in New York, New York
Source: *BioIn 5, 9; ConAu 37R; SmATA 4; St&PR 96, 97, 98, 99, 2000; WhoAm 74, 76, 78, 80, 82, 84, 86, 88, 90, 92, 94, 95, 96, 97, 98, 99, 2000; WhoUSWr 88; WhoWrEP 89, 92, 95*

Ubico y Castaneda, Jorge
Guatemalan. Political Leader, Military Leader
Controversial president of Guatemala from 1931 to 1944, achieved many accomplishments through a harsh and repressive dictatorship.
b. Nov 10, 1878 in Guatemala City, Guatemala
d. Jun 14, 1946 in New Orleans, Louisiana
Source: *BiDLAmC; DcCPCAm; EncWB, 98; LatAmLi*

Uccello, Paolo
[Paolo di Dono]
Italian. Artist
Developed foreshortening, linear perspective: *Rout of San Romano*, 1450s.
b. 1396 in Florence, Italy
d. Dec 10, 1475 in Florence, Italy
Source: *AtlBL; BioIn 14, 19; ChamBiD; DcBiPP; DcCathB; REn; WhDW*

Uchida, Mitsuko
Japanese. Pianist
Japanese Suntory Music Award for outstanding contribution to interntional music in Japan, 1987.
b. Dec 20, 1948 in Tokyo, Japan
Source: *BakBD 92; BakBDTw; BakDcM; BioIn 16; CurBio 91; IntWW 89, 91, 93, 97, 98, 2000; IntWWM 90; IntWWW 2; News 89-3; NewYTBS 88; NotTwCP; PenDiMP; Who 98, 99, 2000; WhoWor 99, 2000*

Udall, Morris K(ing)
American. Politician
Sought Dem. presidential nomination, 1976; keynote speaker, Dem. Nat. Convention, 1980; congressman from AZ, 1961-91.
b. Jun 15, 1922 in Saint Johns, Arizona
d. Dec 12, 1998 in Washington, District of Columbia
Source: *AlmAP 88, 92; BiDrAC; BiDrUSC 89; BioIn 8, 9, 10, 11, 12, 13, 16; BioNews 74; BlueB 76; CngDr 85, 87, 89; ConAu 45, 172; CurBio 69; IntWW 91; NewYTBS 80; PolsAm 84;*

REnAW; WhoAm 74, 76, 78, 80, 82, 84, 86, 88, 90, 92, 94, 95, 96; WhoAmL 79; WhoAmP 73, 75, 77, 79, 81, 83, 85, 87, 89, 91, 93, 95, 97; WhoE 95; WhoGov 72, 75, 77; WhoWest 74, 76, 78, 80, 82, 84, 87, 89, 92, 94; WorAl; WorAlBi

Udall, Nicholas
English. Dramatist
Wrote *Ralph Roister Doister*, first complete English comedy, c. 1553.
b. 1505 in Hampshire, England
d. Dec 1556 in London, England
Source: *Alli; BbD; BiD&SB; BiDRP&D; BioIn 3, 4, 5, 7, 11, 12, 16; BlmGEL; BritAu; CamGEL; CamGLE; CamGWoT; CasWL; CmMedTh; CnThe; CroE&S; CrtSuDr; CyWA 58, 97; DcArts; DcEnA; DcEnL; DcEuL; DcLEL; DcNaB; EncWT; Ent; EvLB; GrWrEL DR; LngCEL; McGEWD 72, 84; NewC; NewCBEL; NotNAT B; OxCBrHi; OxCEng 67, 85; OxCThe 67, 83; PenC ENG; REn; WebE&AL*

Udall, Stewart Lee
American. Government Official
Secretary of Interior, 1961-69; brother of Morris.
b. Jan 31, 1920 in Saint Johns, Arizona
Source: *AmAu&B; BiDrAC; BiDrUSC 89; BiDrUSE 71, 89; BioIn 5, 6, 7, 8, 9, 10, 11, 12; CamBiEn; CamDcAB; ConAu 69; CurBio 61; EncAAH; IntWW 74, 75, 76, 77, 78, 79, 80, 81, 82, 83, 89, 91, 93, 97, 98, 2000; LinLib L, S; NewYTBS 93; REnAW; WhoAm 74, 76, 78, 80, 82, 84, 86, 88; WhoWor 78; WorAl; WorAlBi*

Udet, Ernst
German. Aviator
Stunt flier who shot down 62 planes during WW I; killed while experimenting with "new weapon."
b. Apr 26, 1896 in Frankfurt am Main, Germany
d. Nov 17, 1941
Source: *BioIn 5, 8, 11, 12, 14, 16; CamBiEn; ChamBiD; EncTR, 91; HisEWW; InSci; ObitOF 79; WhoMilH 76; WhWW-II*

Udry, Janice May
American. Children's Author
Writings include *Danny's Pig*, 1960; *The Sunflower Garden*, 1969.
b. Jun 14, 1928 in Jacksonville, Illinois
Source: *AuBYP 2, 3; BkP; ConAu 5R; SmATA 4; ThrBJA; WrDr 92*

Ueberroth, Peter Victor
American. Businessman, Baseball Executive
Pres., LA Olympic Organizing Committee, 1979-84; succeeded Bowie Kuhn as baseball commissioner, 1984-89, succeeded by A Bartlett Giamatti.
b. Sep 2, 1937 in Evansville, Illinois
Source: *Ballpl 90; BiDAmSp OS; BioIn 13, 14, 15, 16; CamDcAB; CurBio 85; EncWB, 98; IntWW 91; NewYTBS 84; St&PR 75; WhoAm 86, 88, 92, 98; WorAlBi*

Uecker, Bob
[Robert George Uecker]
American. Baseball Player, Actor
Catcher, 1962-67, known for beer commercials, starring role in TV series "Mr. Belvedere," 1984-90.
b. Jan 26, 1935 in Milwaukee, Wisconsin
Source: *Ballpl 90; BioIn 13; LegTOT; WhoAm 86, 88, 90, 92, 94, 95, 96, 97, 99, 2000; WhoEnt 92; WhoHol 92; WhoProB 73; WorAlBi*

Ufer, Walter
American. Artist
Painter known for his Indian portraits and southwestern landscapes.
b. Jul 22, 1876 in Louisville, Kentucky
d. Aug 2, 1936 in Santa Fe, New Mexico
Source: *ArtsAmW 1; BioIn 1, 9, 11, 14; IlBEAAW; WhAm 1; WhAmArt 85*

UFO
[Neil Carter; Paul Chapman; Phil Mogg; Andy Parker; Michael Schenker; Pete Way]
British. Music Group
Formed 1971; hard-rock band whose hits include *The Wild, the Willing, and the Innocent*, 1982.
Source: *BiDProW; BillEnR; ConMuA 80A; EncRk 88; GrMetD; HarEnR 86; IlEncRk; PenEncP; RolSEnR 83; WhAmArt 85; WhoRock 81; WhoRocM 82*

Uggams, Leslie (Marian Crayne)
American. Singer, Actor
Won Tony for *Hallelujah Baby*, 1968; played Kizzy in TV epic, "Roots," 1977.
b. May 25, 1943 in New York, New York
Source: *AfrAmAl 6; BiDAfM; BiDAmM; BioIn 6, 7, 8, 11, 14; BlksAmF; CelR, 90; ConTFT 6; CurBio 67; DcTwCCu 5; DrBlPA, 90; EncMT; FilmgC; HalFC 84, 88; InB&W 85; IntMPA 75, 76, 77, 78, 79, 80, 81, 82, 84, 86, 88, 92, 94, 96; InWom, SUP; LegTOT; NegAl 76, 83, 89; NewAmDM; NewYTBS 86;*

NotBlAW 2; NotNAT; WhoAfA 9; WhoAm 74, 76, 78, 80, 82, 84, 86, 88, 90, 92, 94, 95; WhoAmW 68, 70, 74, 75, 81, 83, 95, 97; WhoBlA 1, 2, 3, 4, 5, 6, 7, 8; WhoEnt 92; WhoHol 92, A; WorAl; WorAlBi

Uhde, Hermann
German. Opera Singer
Noted bass-baritone, noted for Wagnerian roles; died on stage.
b. Jul 20, 1914 in Bremen, Germany
d. Oct 10, 1965 in Copenhagen, Denmark
Source: *BakBD 84, 92; BakBDTw; BioIn 7; CmOp; MetOEnc; NewEOp 71; NewGrDM 80; NewGrDO; OxDcOp; PenDiMP; WhAm 4*

Uhlenbeck, Karen (Keskulla)
American. Mathematician, Educator
Her research has contributed to theoretical physics and the study of instantons, and she was awarded a MacArthur Fellowship for her work in geometry and partial differential equations.
b. Aug 24, 1942 in Cleveland, Ohio
Source: *AmWomSc 1950; ConAu 160; WhoAm 86, 88, 90, 92, 94, 95, 96, 97, 98, 99, 2000; WhoAmW 89, 91, 93, 95, 97, 99; WhoScEn 94, 96, 2000; WhoSSW 95; WrDr 2000*

Uhlman, Wes(ley Carl)
American. Politician, Lawyer
Mayor of Seattle, 1970-78.
b. Mar 13, 1935 in Cashmere, Washington
Source: *WhoAm 84; WhoAmP 73, 75, 77, 79, 81, 83, 85, 87, 89, 91, 93, 95, 97, 1999; WhoGov 77; WhoWest 74, 80*

Uhnak, Dorothy
American. Author
Crime novels include *The Ledger*, 1970.
b. 1933 in New York, New York
Source: *AmWomWr; ArtclWW 2; AuNews 1; BioIn 13, 14; ConAu 29NR, 63NR, 81; EncMys; FemiCLE; GrWomMW; IntAu&W 91, 93; InWom SUP; NewYTBE 71; NewYTBS 81; Novels; ThrtnMM; TwCCr&M 80, 85, 91; WrDr 76, 82, 84, 86, 88, 90, 92, 94, 96, 98, 99, 2000*

Uhry, Alfred
American. Dramatist
Won 1988 Pulitzer for first play, *Driving Miss Daisy*.
b. 1937?
Source: *BioIn 16; ConAu 127, 133; ConLC 55; OxCAmL 95; WhoAm 90; WhoEnt 92; WhoWor 91; WrDr 92*

Ukrainka, Lesia
[Larisa Kvitka-Kosach]
Russian. Poet
Wrote collection of poems *On the Wings of Song*, 1892; play *Cassandra*, 1908.
b. 1871 in Ukraine, Russia
d. 1913

Source: *NewCol 75*

Ulanova, Galina
Russian. Dancer
Retired from Russian ballet to teach; appeared on film, 1950s.
b. Jan 10, 1910 in Saint Petersburg, Russia
d. Mar 21, 1998 in Moscow, Russia
Source: *BiDD; BiDSovU; BioIn 3, 4, 5, 6, 10, 14, 17, 23, 24; CnOxB; ContDcW 89; CurBio 58; DancEn 78; DcArts; EncWB 98; FacFETw; IntDcB; IntDcWB; IntWW 83, 91; InWom SUP; NewGrDM 80; NewYTBS 98; RAdv 14; WhDW; Who 85, 92; WhoAmW 66, 68, 70, 72; WhoHol A; WhoWor 74; WorAlBi*

Ulbricht, Walter
German. Political Leader
Member, People's Chamber, 1949-73; chm., Council of State of German Democratic Republic, 1960-73.
b. Jun 30, 1893 in Leipzig, Germany
d. Aug 1, 1973 in Berlin, German Democratic Republic
Source: *BioIn 6, 7, 8, 9, 10, 14, 18, 20; ChamBiD; ColdWar 1, 2; ConAu 113; CurBio 52, 73, 73N; DcTwHis; DicTyr; EncCW; EncGRNM; EncRev; EncTR 91; EncWB 98; EncyDCo; FacFETw; HisEWW; HisWorL; McGEWB; NewYTBE 73; ObitT 1971; OxCGer 76, 86, 97; WhAm 5; WhDW; WhoGov 72; WorAl; WorAlBi*

Ulfilas
Translator, Scholar
Arian bishop of the Visigoths (or West Goths), developed a Gothic alphabet based on the Greek and Roman alphabets and translated part of the Bible into Gothic.
b. c. 311
d. 382
Source: *BbD; BiD&SB; BioIn 4, 5, 10, 22; CamBiEn; CasWL; ChamBiD; DcCathB; EncEarC 90, 97; EncWB 98; LinLib L, S; McGEWB; NewC; OxCEng 67, 85, 95; OxCGer 76; OxDcByz*

Ulibarri, Sabine (Reyes)
American. Writer
Published collection of poetry *Al cielo se sube a pie*, 1961; also published several collections of short stories.
b. Sep 21, 1919 in Santa Fe, New Mexico
Source: *ChiLit; ConAu 81NR, 105; ConLC 83; DrAS 74F, 78F, 82F; HispAmA; HispWr 2; RfGShF 2*

Ullman, Al(bert Conrad)
American. Politician
Dem. congressman from OR, 1956-81.
b. Mar 9, 1914 in Great Falls, Montana
d. Oct 11, 1986 in Bethesda, Maryland
Source: *AlmAP 78, 80; BiDrAC; BiDrUSC 89; BioIn 10, 15; BioNews 75; BlueB 76; CngDr 74, 77, 79; CurBio 75, 87, 87N; IntWW 78, 79, 80, 81, 82, 83; NewYTBS 74; WhAm 9; WhoAm 74, 76,*

78, 80, 82, 84, 86; WhoAmP 73, 75, 77, 79, 81, 83, 85; WhoGov 72, 75, 77; WhoWest 74; WorAl

Ullman, James Ramsey
American. Author
Wrote books about mountaineering: *Kingdom of Everest*, 1947.
b. Nov 24, 1907 in New York, New York
d. Jun 20, 1971 in Boston, Massachusetts
Source: *AmAu&B; Au&Wr 71; AuBYP 2, 3; BenetAL 91; BioIn 1, 2, 4, 7, 9, 10, 11, 14, 22; ConAu 1R, 3NR, 29R; CurBio 45, 71; FourBJA; LngCTC; NatCAB 56; NewYTBE 71; REn; REnAL; ScF&FL 1, 2; SmATA 7; TwCA SUP; WhAm 5; WhNAA; WorAu 1900*

Ullman, Norm(an Victor Alexander)
Canadian. Hockey Player
Center, 1955-77, mostly with Detroit, Toronto; scored 490 goals in NHL; Hall of Fame, 1982.
b. Dec 26, 1935 in Provost, Alberta, Canada
Source: *HocEn; WhoAm 74, 76; WhoHcky 73*

Ullman, Tracey
English. Actor
First American hit "They Don't Know," 1984; star of TV show "The Tracey Ullman Show," 1986-90; films include *I Love You to Death*, 1990.
b. Dec 30, 1959 in Slough, England
Source: *BioIn 14, 15, 16; CamBiEn; CelR 90; ChamBiD; ConTFT 4, 9; CurBio 88; EncRk 88; IntMPA 92, 94, 96; IntWW 93, 97, 98, 2000; IntWWW 2; LegTOT; NewYTBS 89; PenEncP; RkOn 85; WhoAm 90, 92, 94, 95, 96, 97, 98, 99, 2000; WhoAmW 91, 93, 95, 97, 99; WhoCom; WhoEnt 92, 98; WhoHol 92; WhoWor 91*

Ullmann, Liv (Johanne)
[Mrs. Donald Saunders]
Norwegian. Actor
Star of Ingmar Bergman films; goodwill ambassador, UNICEF, 1980—.
b. Dec 16, 1938 in Tokyo, Japan
Source: *BiDFilm; BioIn 13, 14, 16; BioNews 74; CelR 90; ConAu 102; ContDcW 89; ConTFT 3; CurBio 73; EncEurC; HalFC 84, 88; IntDcWB; IntMPA 84, 86, 92; IntWW 76, 77, 78, 79, 80, 81, 82, 83, 89, 91, 93, 97, 98, 2000; IntWWW 2; InWom SUP; LegTOT; MovMk; NewYTBE 72; NewYTBS 82; Who 82, 83, 85, 88, 90, 92, 94, 98, 99, 2000; WhoAm 84, 86, 88, 90, 92, 94, 95, 96, 97; WhoEnt 92; WhoHol 92, A; WhoWor 87, 89, 91, 93, 95, 96; WorAlBi*

Ullstein, Hermann
German. Publisher
Partner, Ullstein Publisher, which was taken over by Nazis.
b. 1875

d. Nov 23, 1943 in New York, New York
Source: *ConAu 116; CurBio 44; ObitOF 79*

Ulmanis, Guntis
Latvian. Political Leader
Great-nephew of Karlis Ulmanis, the last president of independent Latvia, he was elected resident of Latvia in 1993 as a Farmers' Union candidate and reelected in 1996; his government faces difficult citizenship issues and economic declines.
b. Sep 13, 1939 in Riga, Latvia
Source: *IntWW 97, 98, 2000; ProfiWG 98; WhoIntA 2; WhoWor 95, 96, 97, 98, 99, 2000*

Ulmer, James
"Blood"
American. Musician
Sound based on blues, hard rock, avant-garde jazz; albums include *Free Lancing*, 1982.
b. Feb 2, 1942 in Saint Matthews, South Carolina
Source: *BiDJaL; BiDJaz; BioIn 12, 15; InB&W 85; NewAmDM; NewGrDA 86; NewGrDJ 88, 94; PenEncP; RolSEnR 83*

Ulpian, Domitius
Roman. Jurist
One of the most distinguished Roman legal scholars, he was a praetorian prefect and chief adviser to the emperor Alexander Severus.
d. 228
Source: *EncWB 98; McGEWB*

Ulreich, Nura Woodson
American. Illustrator
Wrote, illustrated children's book *The Kitten Who Listened*, 1950.
b. Dec 1899 in Kansas City, Missouri
d. 1950
Source: *IlsBYP; IlsCB 1744, 1946; InWom; PenNWW A*

Ulric, Lenore
American. Actor
Played in *Tiger Rose; Camille; Intrigue*.
b. Jul 21, 1894 in New Ulm, Minnesota
d. Dec 30, 1970 in Orangeburg, New York
Source: *BiE&WWA; FamA&A; Film 1; FilmgC; InWom; MotPP; MovMk; NewYTBE 70; ObitOF 79; ThFT; TwYS; WhScrn 74, 77*

Ulrichs, Karl Heinrich
German. Writer
Played an early role in the fight for gay rights in Germany; came out with his own scientific theories defending his sexuality, 1862.
b. Aug 28, 1825, Germany
d. Jul 14, 1895
Source: *BioIn 20; CmpQue; GayLesB; HumSex*

Ulufa'alu, Bart
[Bartholomew Ulufa'alu]
Solomon Islander. Political Leader
The organizer of the first labor unions in the Protectorate and an agitator for independence, he replaced Solomon Mamaloni as prime minister of the Solomon Islands in 1997.
b. 1950 in Alite'e Village, Laulasi, Solomon Islands

Ulvaeus, Bjorn
Swedish. Singer, Musician
With group since 1973; hits include "Dancing Queen," 1977; "Take a Chance on Me," 1978.
b. Apr 25, 1945 in Stockholm, Sweden
Source: *RolSEnR 83*

Umberto II
[Umberto Nicola Giovanni Maria of Savoy]
Italian. Ruler
Italy's last king; reigned May 9-Jun 2, 1946; monarchy abolished by Mussolini.
b. Sep 15, 1904 in Racconigi, Italy
d. Mar 18, 1983 in Geneva, Switzerland
Source: *CamBiEn; ChamBiD; CurBio 43, 83N; NewYTBS 83*

Umeki, Miyoshi
Japanese. Singer, Actor
Films include *Flower Drum Song*, 1961; won Oscar for *Sayonara*, 1957.
b. Apr 3, 1929 in Holdaido, Japan
Source: *BioIn 5, 6, 9; FilmEn; FilmgC; ForYSC; HalFC 84, 88; InWom SUP; LegTOT; MotPP; MovMk; OsStAZ; VarWW 85; WhoHol 92, A; WorAl*

Unamuno (y Jugo), Miguel de
Spanish. Philosopher, Author
Major work *The Tragic Sense of Life in Men and Nations*, 1913.
b. Sep 29, 1864 in Bilbao, Spain
d. Dec 31, 1936 in Salamanca, Spain
Source: *AtlBL; WrPh*

Unanue, Jose Hipolito
Peruvian. Educator, Scientist, Journalist
Leading physician and thinker of the transition period from the colonial to the independence era.
b. Aug 13, 1755 in Arica, Peru
d. Jul 15, 1833
Source: *DcScB; EncWB 98; McGEWB*

Underhill, Evelyn
English. Author
Through her lectures and works furthered the development and acceptance of mystical theology.
b. Dec 6, 1875 in Wolverhampton, England
d. Jun 15, 1941 in London, England
Source: *ArtclWW 2; BioIn 1, 2, 5, 10, 11, 12, 16, 17, 19, 22, 23; CamBiEn; ChamBiD; Chambr 3; ContDcW 89; DcLEL; DcNaB 1941; DivFut; EncBrWW; EncWomW; EvLB; FemiCLE; IntDcWB; InWom; LngCTC; LuthC 75;*

NewC; NewCBEL; OxCCanL 1; OxCEng 85, 95; REn; ScF&FL 1; TwCA, SUP; TwCWr; WhE&EA; WhLit; WhoChr; WomNov; WorAu 1900

Underhill, John

American. Military Leader, Judge
Magistrate was a leader in the early
Indian Wars in New England and in
New York.
b. c. 1597
d. Sep 21, 1672
Source: *Alli; AmBi; AmNatBi; AmWrBE; ApCAB; BenetAL 91; CamDcAB; DcAmB; Drake; EncAInd; EncWB 98; McGEWB; NatCAB 1; NewCBEL; OxCAmL 65, 83, 95; REnAL; WebAB 74, 79; WebAMB; WhAm HS; WhNaAH*

Underwood, Blair

American. Actor
Appeared on TV's "L.A. Law," 1987-
94; won NAACP Image Award, 1994.
b. Aug 25, 1964 in Tacoma, Washington
Source: *AfrAmBi 2; ConBlB 7; DrBlPA 90; IntMPA 94, 96; LegTOT; WhoAfA 9, 10, 11, 12; WhoAm 99, 2000; WhoBlA 7, 8; WhoEnt 98; WhoHol 92*

Underwood, John Thomas

American. Manufacturer
Introduced Underwood typewriter, 1897.
b. Apr 12, 1857 in London, England
d. Jul 2, 1937 in Wianno, Massachusetts
Source: *BiDAmBL 83; BioIn 4; DcAmB S2; NatCAB 29; WhAm 4, HSA*

Underwood, Oscar Wilder

American. Government Official
Dem. senator from AL, 1914-27.
b. May 6, 1862 in Louisville, Kentucky
d. Jan 25, 1929 in Fairfax County,
Virginia
Source: *AmBi; AmNatBi; AmPolLe; ApCAB SUP, X; BiDrAC; BiDrUSC 89; BioIn 4, 8, 12, 15; CamBiEn; CamDcAB; DcAmB; DcNAA; EncAAH; EncAB-H 1974; EncSoH; FacFETw; NatCAB 12, 21; TwCBDA; WebAB 74, 79; WhAm 1; WhAmP*

Undset, Sigrid

Norwegian. Author
Won Nobel Prize in literature, 1928;
wrote three-vol. historical novel,
Kristin Lavransatter, 1922.
b. May 20, 1882 in Kalundborg,
Denmark
d. Jun 10, 1949 in Lillehammer, Norway
Source: *AtlBL; AuBYP 2, 3; Benet 87, 96; BioIn 1, 2, 3, 4, 5, 7, 8, 9, 10, 11, 12, 14, 15, 17, 20, 22; BlmGWL; CamBiEn; CasWL; CathA 1930; ChamBiD; ClDMEL 47, 80; ConAu 104, 129; ContDcW 89; CurBio 40, 49; CyWA 58, 97; DcArts; DcCathB; DcScanL; EncCoWW; EncWB 98; EncWL 1, 2, 2S, 3; EuWr 9; EvEuW; FacFETw; FemiWr; GoodHs; GrFLW; GrWomW; InWom, SUP; LadLa 86; LegTOT; LiExTwC; LinLib L, S; LngCTC; MajTwCW 1, 2; McGEWB; ModWoWr; NobelP; Novels; OxCEng*

67; PenC EUR; RAdv 14, 13-2; REn; RfGWoL 95; TwCA, SUP; TwCLC 3; TwCWr; WhAm 2; WhoNob, 90, 95; WomFir; WomWrGB; WorAl; WorAlBi; WorAu 1900; WorLitC

Ungaretti, Giuseppe

Italian. Poet
Themes of personal sorrow, grief are
based on self: *Il Dolore*, 1946.
b. Feb 10, 1887 in Alexandria, Egypt
d. Jun 1, 1970 in Milan, Italy
Source: *CasWL; ClDMEL 47; CnMWL; ConAu P-2; ConLC 7, 15; EncWL 1; EvEuW; ModRL; NewYTBE 70; PenC EUR; REn; TwCWr; WhoTwCL; WorAu 1950*

Ungaro, Emanuel Matteotti

French. Fashion Designer
Avant-garde designs are noted for print
patterns, flowers, abstracts.
b. Feb 13, 1933 in Aix-en-Provence,
France
Source: *BioIn 9, 14, 15, 16; ConDes 90; CurBio 80; DcTwDes; EncFash; IntWW 91, 93, 97, 98, 2000; WhoAm 96, 98, 99, 2000; WhoFash 88; WhoWor 91, 93, 95, 96, 98, 99, 2000; WorFshn*

Unger, Caroline

Austrian. Opera Singer
Contralto known for turning Beethoven
around to see audience applause after
first performance of ninth symphony,
1824.
b. Oct 28, 1803 in Vienna, Austria
d. Mar 23, 1877 in Florence, Italy
Source: *BakBD 78, 84, 92; CmOp; InWom; MetOEnc; NewEOp 71; NewGrDM 80; OxDcOp*

Unger, Garry Douglas

"Iron Man"
Canadian. Hockey Player
Center, 1967-83; held NHL record for
consecutive games played (914, from
1968-79) until broken by Doug Jarvis,
1986.
b. Dec 7, 1947 in Edmonton, Alberta,
Canada
Source: *HocEn; WhoAm 74, 76, 78, 80, 82, 84; WhoHcky 73*

Unger, Irwin

American. Educator, Historian
Won Pulitzer for history, 1965; writings
include *The Vulnerable Years: The
United States, 1896-1917*.
b. May 2, 1927 in New York, New York
Source: *ConAu 7NR, 9R; DrAS 74H, 78H, 82H, 99H; EncAAH; OxCAmL 65; WhoAm 74, 76, 78, 80, 82, 84, 86, 88, 90, 92, 94, 95, 96, 97, 98, 99, 2000; WhoPul*

Ungerer, Tomi

[Jean Thomas Ungerer]
French. Children's Author, Illustrator
Writings include *Moon Man*, 1967; *The
Joy of Frogs*, 1985.
b. Nov 28, 1931 in Strasbourg, France

Source: *AmAu&B; Au&Wr 71; AuBYP 2, 3; BioIn 5, 7, 8, 9, 10, 11, 12, 13, 14, 16, 19, 24; BkP; ChhPo; ChlBkCr; ChlLR 3; ConAu 41R, X; FamAIYP; IlsCB 1957; IntAu&W 77; LinLib L; OxCChiL; SJGChWr 5; SmATA 5; ThrBJA; TwCChW 1, 2, 3, 4; Who 90, 92, 94, 98, 99; WhoAm 86, 88; WhoGrA 62, 82; WhoUSWr 88; WhoWrEP 89*

Unitas, Johnny

[John Constantine Unitas]
American. Football Player
Quarterback, 1956-73, mostly with
Baltimore; holds many NFL passing
records, including most 300-yd.
passing games, 27; MVP, three times;
Hall of Fame, 1979.
b. May 7, 1933 in Pittsburgh,
Pennsylvania
Source: *BiDAmSp FB; BioIn 13, 16, 17, 20; BioNews 74; CamBiEn; CurBio 62; FacFETw; LegTOT; NewYTBE 71; NewYTBS 74; WebAB 79; WhoAm 74, 76, 78, 80, 82, 84, 86, 88, 90, 92; WhoFtbl 74; WhoSpor; WorAlBi*

Unkelbach, Kurt

American. Children's Author
Books on cats, dogs include *Uncle
Charlie's Poodle*, 1975; wrote *Straw
Hat*, 1937, which was produced on
Broadway.
b. Nov 21, 1913 in New Britain,
Connecticut
Source: *ApCAB SUP; AuBYP 2S, 3; BioIn 9; ConAu 8NR, 21R; SmATA 4; WhoE 74*

Unruh, Howard B

American. Murderer
Killed 13 people in 12 minutes in
Camden, NJ, Jun 9, 1949.
b. 1921? in Camden, New Jersey
Source: *BioIn 2; DrInf*

Unruh, Jesse Marvin

American. Politician
Influential CA assemblyman who aided
John, Robert Kennedy presidential
campaigns.
b. Sep 30, 1922 in Newton, Kansas
d. Aug 4, 1987 in Marina del Rey,
California
Source: *BioIn 5, 6, 7, 8, 9, 11; CamDcAB; CurBio 69, 87; PolProf J, K; ScrEAmL 2; WhAm 9; WhoAm 74, 76, 78, 80, 82, 84, 86; WhoGov 75; WhoWest 74, 84, 87*

Unseld, Wes(tley Sissel)

American. Basketball Player
Center, 1968-81, mostly with
Washington; led NBA in rebounding,
1975; NBA MVP, 1969; Hall of
Fame, 1988.
b. Mar 14, 1946 in Louisville, Kentucky
Source: *BasBi; BiDAmSp BK; BioIn 16; InB&W 85; LegTOT; OfNBA 87; WhoAfA 9; WhoAm 90, 92, 94, 95, 96, 97, 98, 2000; WhoBbl 73; WhoBlA 2, 3, 4, 5, 6, 7, 8; WhoE 89, 91, 95, 97, 99; WorAl; WorAlBi*

Unser, Al, Sr.

American. Auto Racer
One of three drivers to win Indianapolis
500 four times.
b. May 29, 1939 in Albuquerque, New
Mexico
Source: *BiDAmSp OS; BioIn 9, 11, 12,
13, 14, 21; CamBiEn; CamDcAB; CelR;
ChamBiD; LegTOT; WhoAm 74, 76, 78,
80, 82, 84, 86, 88, 92, 94, 95, 96, 97,
98, 99, 2000; WhoWest 00, 94, 96, 98;
WorAl; WorAlBi*

Unser, Al, Jr.

"Little Al"
American. Auto Racer
Raced with father for first time, 1983
Indianapolis 500; won Indianapolis
500 by .043 second, closest finish in
race's history.
b. Apr 19, 1962
Source: *BioIn 13, 14, 15, 16; LegTOT;
NewYTBS 83, 85*

Unser, Bobby

[Robert William Unser]
American. Auto Racer
Won Indianapolis 500, 1968, 1975, 1981.
b. Feb 20, 1934 in Albuquerque, New
Mexico
Source: *BiDAmSp OS; BioIn 9, 10, 11,
12, 13; ConAu 97; LegTOT; NewYTBS
74; WhoAm 74, 76, 78, 80, 82, 84, 86,
88, 90, 92, 94, 95, 96, 97; WhoSpor;
WhoWest 94; WorAl; WorAlBi*

Unsworth, Barry (Foster)

English. Author
Won Booker Prize for Fiction for *Sacred
Hunger*, 1992.
b. Aug 10, 1930 in Wingate, England
Source: *BioIn 21; ChamBiD; ConAu
25R, 30NR; ConLC 76; IntWW 93;
WrDr 76, 80, 82, 84, 86, 88, 90, 92*

Unsworth, Geoffrey

English. Filmmaker
Cameraman, who won Oscar for
cinematography, 1972, for *Cabaret*.
b. 1914 in London, England
d. 1978
Source: *ConTFT 25; EncEurC; FilmEn;
FilmgC; HalFC 80, 84, 88; IntDcF 1-4,
2-4; ItaFilm; WorEFlm*

Untermeyer, Jean Starr

American. Author
Wrote *Growing Pains*, 1918; translated
Hermann Broch's *The Death of Virgil*,
1945.
b. Mar 13, 1886 in Zanesville, Ohio
d. Jul 27, 1970 in New York, New York
Source: *AmAu&B; AmNatBi;
AmWomWr; AnMV 1926; Au&Wr 71;
BenetAL 91; ChhPo, S2, S3; CnDAL;
ConAmL; ConAu 29R; ForWC 70;
InWom, SUP; NewYTBE 70; OhA&B;
OxCAmL 65, 83, 95; REnAL; TwCA
SUP; WhAm 5, 7; WhNAA; WhoAmW
58, 61, 64, 66, 68, 70, 72; WhoWorJ 72,
78*

Untermeyer, Louis

American. Author, Editor
Best known for anthologies used by
colleges.
b. Oct 1, 1885 in New York, New York
d. Dec 18, 1977 in Newtown,
Connecticut
Source: *AmAu&B; AmLY; AmNatBi;
AnCL; AnMV 1926; ApCAB X; Au&Wr
71; AuBYP 2, 3; Benet 87, 96; BenetAL
91; BioIn 1, 4, 5, 6, 7, 8, 9, 11, 13, 14,
15, 22; BlueB 76; CelR; Chambr 3;
ChhPo, S1, S2, S3; CnDAL; ConAmA;
ConAmL; ConAu 5R, 31NR, 73; ConPo
70, 75; CurBio 67, 78N; DcAmB S10;
DcLEL; EvLB; FacFETw; IntAu&W 76,
77; IntWW 74, 75, 76, 77; IntWWP 77,
82; LegTOT; LinLib L, S; LngCTC;
NewYTBS 77; OxCAmL 65, 83, 95;
OxCTwCP; REn; REnAL; ScF&FL 1, 2;
SmATA 2, 26N, 37; TwCA, SUP;
TwCWr; WhAm 7; WhNAA; Who 74;
WhoAm 74, 76; WhoWorJ 72; WorAl;
WorAlBi; WorAu 1900; WrDr 76*

Unwin, Stanley, Sir

English. Publisher, Author
Founder, George Allen & Unwin Ltd.,
book publishers, 1914.
b. Dec 19, 1884 in London, England
d. Oct 13, 1968 in London, England
Source: *BioIn 1, 2, 5, 8, 14, 18;
CamBiEn; ChamBiD; ConAu 5R; CurBio
49, 68; DcNaB 1961; GrBr; LinLib L;
LngCTC; ObitT 1961; WhAm 5;
WhE&EA; WhLit*

Upchurch, John Jorden

American. Labor Union Official
Founded Ancient Order of United
Workmen, 1868; forerunner of
fraternal societies.
b. Mar 26, 1820 in Franklin County,
North Carolina
d. Jan 18, 1887 in Steelville, Missouri
Source: *ApCAB; DcAmB; DcNAA;
HarEnUS; WhAm HS*

Updike, Daniel Berkeley

American. Printer, Publisher
Known for improving typography in US;
founded The Merrymount Press,
Boston, 1893.
b. Feb 24, 1860 in Providence, Rhode
Island
d. Dec 28, 1941 in Boston,
Massachusetts
Source: *AmNatBi; BenetAL 91; BioIn 1,
4, 10, 12; CamDcAB; CurBio 42;
DcAmBC; DcAmB S3; DcNAA; LinLib
L; OxCAmL 65, 83, 95; OxCDecA;
REnAL; WhAm 2; WhAmArt 85*

Updike, John (Hoyer)

American. Author
Won Pulitzer, 1981, for *Rabbit Is Rich*;
National Book Critics Circle Award,
Pultizer Prize, for *Rabbit at Rest*,
1990.
b. Mar 18, 1932 in Shillington,
Pennsylvania
Source: *AmAu&B; AmCulL; AmWr;
AnCL; Au&Wr 71; AuBYP 2, 3; Benet

87, 96; BenetAL 91; BioIn 5, 6, 7, 8, 9,
10, 11, 12, 13, 14, 15, 16; BlueB 76;
BroV; CamBiEn; CamDcAB; CamGEL;
CamGLE; CamHAL; CasWL; CelR, 90;
ChamBiD; ChhPo; ConAu 1BS, 1NR,
1R, 4NR, 33NR, 51NR; ConLC 1, 2, 3,
5, 7, 9, 13, 15, 23, 34, 43, 45, 70;
ConNov 72, 76, 82, 86, 91, 96; ConPo
70, 75, 80, 85, 91, 96; ConPopW;
CurBio 84; CyWA 89; DcArts; DcLB 2,
5, 143, DS3, Y80A, Y82A; DcLEL 1940;
DcTwCCu 1; DrAF 76; DrAPF 80, 91;
EncAB-H 1974, 1996; EncALit; EncSF
93; EncWL 1, 2, 2S; FacFETw; FolkA
87; GrWrEL N; IntAu&W 76, 77, 89, 91,
93; IntvTCA 2; IntWW 74, 75, 76, 77,
78, 79, 80, 81, 82, 83, 89, 91, 93, 97,
98, 2000; IntWWP 77; LegTOT; LinLib
L, S; MagSAmL; MajTwCW 1, 2;
MakMC; ModAL 4, 4S1, 4S2; NewYTBS
89; Novels; OxCAmL 65, 83, 95;
OxCEng 85, 95; OxCTwCL; PenC AM;
RAdv 1, 14, 13-1; REn; REnAL;
RfGAmL 4, 87, 94; RfGShF 1, 2;
RGTwCWr; ScF&FL 1, 2, 92; ShSCr 13,
27; ShSWr; SJGHorW; TwCWr; WebAB
74, 79; WebE&AL; Who 74, 82, 83, 85,
88, 90, 92, 94, 98, 99, 2000; WhoAm 74,
76, 78, 80, 82, 84, 86, 88, 90, 92, 94,
95, 96, 97, 98, 99, 2000; WhoE 85, 86,
91, 93, 95, 97, 99; WhoEnt 98; WhoPul;
WhoTwCL; WhoUSWr 88; WhoWor 74,
78, 80, 82, 84, 87, 91, 93, 95, 96, 97,
98, 99, 2000; WhoWrEP 89, 92, 95;
WorAl; WorAlBi; WorAu 1950; WorLitC;
WrDr 76, 80, 82, 84, 86, 88, 90, 92, 94,
96, 98, 99, 2000; WrPh*

Upjohn, Lawrence Northcote

American. Manufacturer
Pres., Upjohn Pharmaceuticals, 1930-44.
b. 1873
d. Jun 2, 1967 in Kalamazoo, Michigan
Source: *BioIn 7, 9; EncAB-A 39;
NatCAB 53; ObitOF 79*

Upjohn, Richard

American. Architect
Designs include Trinity Church, NYC.
b. Jan 22, 1802 in Shaftesbury, England
d. Aug 17, 1878 in Garrison, New York
Source: *Alli; AmBi; AmCulL; AmNatBi;
ApCAB; BiDAmAr; BioIn 1, 8, 9, 15, 19;
BriEAA; CamBiEn; CamDcAB; DcAmB;
DcArch; DcD&D; EncAAr 1, 2; EncWB
98; HarEnUS; IntDcAr; LegTOT;
MacEA; McGDA; McGEWB; NatCAB 2;
NewYHSD; OxCAmH; OxCAmL 65;
TwCBDA; WebAB 74, 79; WhAm HS;
WhFla; WhoArch; WorAl; WorAlBi*

Uppman, Theodor

American. Opera Singer
Baritone, created title role in Britten's
Billy Budd, 1951.
b. Jan 12, 1920 in San Jose, California
Source: *BakBD 84, 92; BakBDTw; BioIn
4, 6, 9, 13; CmOp; IntWWM 77, 80, 90;
MetOEnc; NewAmDM; NewEOp 71;
NewGrDA 86; NewGrDM 80;
NewGrDO; PenDiMP; WhoAm 74, 76,
78, 80, 82, 84, 86, 88, 90, 92, 94, 95,
96, 97, 98, 99, 2000; WhoAmM 83;
WhoEnt 92, 98; WhoOp 76; WhoWor 74*

Upshaw, Dawn
American. Singer
Lyric soprano has performed with most
outstanding orchestras and chamber
groups in the US and Europe.
b. Jul 17, 1960 in Nashville, Tennessee
Source: *BakBD 92; BakBDTw; BakDcM;
BioIn 16; ConMus 9; CurBio 90;
IntWWW 2; NewGrDO; News 91, 91-2;
Who 2000; WhoAm 92, 94, 95, 96, 97,
98, 99, 2000; WhoAmW 93*

Upshaw, Gene
[Eugene Upshaw]
American. Football Player, Football
Executive
Guard, Los Angeles Raiders, 1967-82;
exec. director, NFL Players Assn.,
1980—; Hall of Fame, 1987.
b. Aug 15, 1945 in Robstown, Texas
Source: *AfrAmAl 8; AfrAmBi 2;
AfrAmSG; BiDAmSp FB; BioIn 12, 13,
14, 15; ConBlB 18; ConNews 88-1;
InB&W 80; LegTOT; WhoAfA 9, 10, 11,
12; WhoAm 86, 88, 90, 94, 95, 96, 97,
98, 99, 2000; WhoBlA 2, 3, 4, 5, 6, 7, 8;
WhoFtbl 74; WhoSpor; WhoWor 96;
WorAlBi*

Upshaw, William David
American. Author, Politician
Dem. congressman from GA, 1919-27.
b. Oct 15, 1866 in Newnan, Georgia
d. Nov 21, 1952
Source: *BiDrAC; BiDrUSC 89; BiDSA;
BioIn 3, 4; DcAmB S5; DcAmTB;
NatCAB 41; RelLAm 2; WhAm 3;
WhAmP*

Upson, Ralph Hazlett
American. Aeronautical Engineer
Chief engineer, aeronautical dept.,
Goodyear Tire & Rubber Co., 1914-
20; produced many US balloons,
airships, WW I.
b. Jun 21, 1888 in New York, New York
d. Aug 13, 1968
Source: *BioIn 8, 10; NatCAB 54; WhAm
5*

Upton, Florence Kate
English. Illustrator
Created "Golliwogg" series for children,
popular, 1890s-1910.
b. Feb 22, 1873 in Flushing, New York
d. Oct 17, 1922 in London, England
Source: *BioIn 8, 14, 18, 20; DcBrAr 2;
DcWomA*

Upton, Francis Robbins
American. Mathematician, Physicist
As asst. to Edison, helped with various
inventions that led to the modern use
of electricity.
b. 1852 in Peabody, Massachusetts
d. Mar 10, 1921 in Orange, New Jersey

Urban, VI
[Bartolomeo Prignano]
Italian. Religious Leader
Pope from 1378 to 1389, angered several
cardinals and ignited the Great

Schism, when rival popes in Rome
and Avignon both claimed papal
authority.
b. 1318 in Naples, Italy
d. Oct 15, 1389
Source: *BioIn 5, 7; DcBiPP; DcCathB;
DcPseud; EncVatP; EncWB 98; LuthC
75; McGEWB; OxDcP 86; WhoChr*

Urban, Joseph Maria
Austrian. Designer, Architect
Designed the Tsar's Bridge, Leningrad,
USSR; best known for interior, set
designs of theaters, opera houses.
b. May 26, 1872 in Vienna, Austria
d. Jul 10, 1933 in New York, New York
Source: *AmBi; DcAmB; MacEA;
OxCAmH; OxCThe 67; WebAB 74, 79;
WhAm 1*

Urban, Matt
American. Soldier
Most decorated soldier in U.S. military
history, he received 29 medals and
awards for bravery, including the
Congressional Medal of Honor, for his
20 months of service in Europe during
World War II.
b. Aug 25, 1919 in Buffalo, New York
d. Mar 4, 1995 in Holland, Michigan
Source: *BioIn 12; EncWB 2-19*

Urban II
[Odo of Lagery]
French. Religious Leader
French pope, 1088-99; launched First
Crusade, 1095.
b. 1035? in Chatillon-sur-Marne, France
d. Oct 29, 1099
Source: *ChamBiD; DcCathB; DcPseud;
McGEWB; NewCol 75; WebBD 83;
WorAl*

Ure, Mary
Scottish. Actor
Married John Osborne, Robert Shaw;
films include *Sons and Lovers,* 1960.
b. Feb 18, 1933 in Glasgow, Scotland
d. Apr 3, 1975 in London, England
Source: *BiE&WWA; BioIn 9, 10;
EncWT; FilmAG WE; FilmEn; FilmgC;
ForYSC; HalFC 80, 84, 88; IntMPA 75;
LegTOT; MotPP; MovMk; NewYTBE 72;
NewYTBS 75; NotNAT B; ObitOF 79;
ObitT 1971; OsStAZ; OxCThe 83;
PIP&P; WhAm 6; Who 74; WhoAmW
68, 70, 72, 74; WhoHol C; WhoWor 74;
WhScrn 77, 83; WhThe*

U'Ren, William Simon
American. Statesman
Best known for bringing about direct
election of senators, the direct
presidential primary.
b. Jan 10, 1859 in Lancaster, Wisconsin
d. Mar 8, 1949 in Portland, Oregon
Source: *AmNatBi; AmRef; BioIn 1, 8,
15; CamDcAB; DcAmB S4; WebAB 74,
79; WhAm 4*

Urey, Harold Clayton
American. Chemist
Work with separation of isotopes aided
in making first atomic bomb; won
Nobel Prize, 1934.
b. Apr 29, 1893 in Walkerton, Indiana
d. Jan 6, 1981 in La Jolla, California
Source: *AllMGCo; AmAu&B; AmMWSc
76P, 79; AmNatBi; AnObit 1981;
AsBiEn; BiESc; BioIn 1, 3, 5, 6, 9, 10,
11, 12, 13, 14, 15, 19, 20, 24; CamBiEn;
CamDcAB; CamDcSc; ChamBiD; ConAu
102, 157; CurBio 41, 60, 81; DcScB S2;
EncAB-H 1974; EncWB 98; IndAu 1917;
InnESci; InSci; IntWW 74, 75, 76, 77,
78, 79, 80, 81; LarDcSc; LinLib S;
McGCEnS; McGEWB; McGMS 80;
NewYTBS 81; OxCAmH; ScrEAmL 1;
WebAB 74, 79; WhAm 7; WhDW; Who
74, 82; WhoAm 74, 76, 78, 80;
WhoAtom 77; WhoNob, 90, 95; WhoWest
78, 80, 82; WhoWor 74; WorAl; WorScD*

Uriah Heep
[Mick Box; David Byron; Ken Hensley;
Al Napier; Paul Newton]
English. Music Group
Rock group whose albums include
Demons And Wizards, 1972; not liked
by critics.
Source: *BillEnR; ConMuA 80A; ConMus
19; EncPR&S 74, 89; EncRk 88;
GrMetD; HarEnR 86; IlEncRk;
PenEncP; RkOn 78; RolSEnR 83;
WhoRock 81; WhoRocM 82*

Urich, Robert
American. Actor
Actor has appeared on numerous TV
series, including "S.W.A.T.," 1975-76
and "Spenser for Hire," 1985-88.
b. Dec 19, 1947 in Toronto, Ohio
Source: *BioIn 15, 16, 22, 24; ConNews
88-1; ConTFT 3; HalFC 88; IntMPA 86,
88, 92; LesBEnT 92; VarWW 85;
WhoAm 86, 90, 94, 95, 96, 97, 99, 2000;
WhoEnt 92, 98; WorAlBi*

Uris, Harold David
American. Philanthropist
With brother, Percy, financed many of
NYC's skyscrapers.
b. May 26, 1905 in New York, New
York
d. Mar 28, 1982 in Palm Beach, Florida
Source: *NewYTBS 82; St&PR 75;
WhoAm 74, 76*

Uris, Leon Marcus
American. Author
Wrote *Exodus,* 1958; *Trinity,* 1976.
b. Aug 3, 1924 in Baltimore, Maryland
Source: *AmAu&B; Au&Wr 71; AuNews
1, 2; CamBiEn; CamDcAB; ChamBiD;
ConAu 1NR, 1R; ConLC 7, 32; ConNov
86; CurBio 59; EncALit; IntWW 83, 97,
98, 2000; MajTwCW 2; REn; REnAL;
WebAB 79; WhoAm 86, 98, 99, 2000;
WrDr 86, 98, 99, 2000*

Urquhart, Brian Edward
English. Diplomat
Served as chief aide to UN secretaries-general, 1945-85; wrote biography
Hammarskjold, 1972.
b. Feb 28, 1919 in Bridport, England
Source: *BioIn 13, 14, 15, 16; BlueB 76;
ConAu 26NR, 105; CurBio 86; IntWW
83, 91; NewYTBS 82; Who 74, 82, 83,
85, 92, 94, 98, 99, 2000; WhoE 83, 85,
86, 89; WhoUN 75; WhoWor 80, 82, 84,
89; WrDr 76, 80, 82, 84, 86, 88, 90, 92,
94, 96, 98, 99, 2000*

Urquhart, Jane
Canadian. Author
Novels set in the Victorian Era include
The Whirlpool, 1986.
b. Jun 21, 1949 in Geraldton, Ontario,
Canada
Source: *BioIn 23; BlmGWL; CanWW 89,
96, 97, 98, 1999; ConAu 32NR, 68NR,
113; ConCaAu 1; ConLC 90; IntAu&W
93; IntWWW 2; OxCCanL 2; ScF&FL
92; WhoCanL 85, 87, 92*

Urquiza, Justo Jose
Argentine. Political Leader, Military
Leader
Dictator, general, and statesman was an
ardent federalist and fought against the
dominance of the province of Buenos
Aires over the interior provinces.
b. Oct 18, 1801 in Arroyo de la China,
Entre, Argentina
d. Apr 1870
Source: *EncWB 98; McGEWB*

Urrutia Lleo, Manuel
Cuban. Judge, Political Leader
Pres. of Cuba, 1959; dismissed by Castro
six months later.
b. Dec 8, 1901 in Yaguajay, Cuba
d. Jul 5, 1981 in New York, New York
Source: *AnObit 1981; BioIn 5, 12;
ConAu 104; CurBio 59, 81, 81N;
LatAmLi; NewYTBS 81*

Ursuleac, Viorica
Romanian. Opera Singer
Considered the ideal soprano by R
Strauss; noted also for Mozart,
Wagner roles.
b. Mar 26, 1899 in Czernowitz, Romania
Source: *BakBD 78, 84; BioIn 14, 15;
CmOp; InWom; MetOEnc; NewEOp 71;
PenDiMP*

Urtain, Jose Manuel Ibar
Spanish. Boxer
European heavyweight champ, 1970.
b. May 14, 1943, Spain
Source: *BioIn 8; WhoBox 74*

Uspenskii, Petr Dem'yanovich
[P D Uspensky]
Russian. Author
Writings include *Tertium Organum*,
1920; *A New Model of the Universe*,
1931.
b. 1878 in Moscow, Russia
d. 1947 in Virginia Water, England

Source: *BioIn 1; LngCTC; TwCA SUP*

Ussachevsky, Vladimir Alexis
Composer
Works using electronic sound include
The Creation, 1961; a founder,
Princeton Electronic Music Center,
1959.
b. Nov 3, 1911 in Hailar, China
d. Jan 4, 1990 in New York, New York
Source: *AmComp; BakBD 84; BakBDTw;
BakDcM; BioIn 15, 16; ConAmC 82;
DcCM; NewAmDM; NewGrDA 86;
NewYTBS 90; WhoAm 86, 88; WhoAmM
83*

Ussher, James
Irish. Religious Leader
Archbishop of Armagh, 1625; upheld
doctrine of divine right of kings.
b. Jan 4, 1581 in Dublin, Ireland
d. Mar 21, 1656 in Reigate, England
Source: *Alli; BbD; Benet 87, 96;
BiD&SB; BiDIrW; BioIn 1, 3, 5, 8, 12;
BritAu; CamBiEn; CamGLE; ChamBiD;
Chambr 1; DcBiPP; DcEnA; DcEnL;
DcIrB 1, 2, 3; DcIrW 2; DcLB 213;
DcNaB; EvLB; HisDcIr; LinLib L, S;
LuthC 75; NewC; NewCBEL; OxCBrHi;
OxCEng 67, 85, 95; OxCIri; REn;
WhoChr*

Ustinov, Dmitri Fedorovich
Russian. Government Official
Politburo member, minister of defense,
1976-84.
b. Oct 30, 1908 in Samara, Russia
d. Dec 20, 1984 in Moscow, Union of
Soviet Socialist Republics
Source: *ColdWar 1; IntWW 74, 75, 76,
81, 82, 83; IntYB 81, 82; NewYTBS 76,
84; WhoWor 74, 80, 82*

Ustinov, Peter Alexander
English. Actor
All-around entertainer in films, stage,
TV; Oscar nominee for *Quo Vadis*,
1951.
b. Apr 16, 1921 in London, England
Source: *Benet 87; BiE&WWA; BioIn 13,
14, 15, 16; CamBiEn; CelR 90;
ChamBiD; ConAu 13R, 25NR, 51NR;
ConDr 82, 88; ConTFT 8; FacFETw;
HalFC 88; IntAu&W 91; IntMPA 92;
IntvTCA 2; IntWW 91, 97, 98, 2000;
MajTwCW 2; MovMk; NewYTBS 84;
NotNAT; OxCFilm; OxCThe 67; PIP&P;
TwCWr; Who 85, 92, 98, 99, 2000;
WhoAm 86, 90, 97, 98, 99, 2000;
WhoEnt 92, 98; WhoHol A; WhoThe 81;
WhoWor 87, 91, 97, 98, 99, 2000;
WorAlBi; WorEFlm; WrDr 86, 92, 98,
99, 2000*

Ut, Huynh Cong
Vietnamese. Photojournalist
Won 1973 Pulitzer for photograph of
children running, crying from their
napalmed village near Saigon.
b. Mar 29, 1951 in Saigon, Vietnam
Source: *AsAmAlm; MacBEP; NotAsAm;
WhoAm 74, 76; WhoPul*

Utamaro, Kitagawa
Japanese. Artist
Best known Japanese master of color
print; paintings center around beautiful
women's occupations, amusements.
b. 1753
d. 1806
Source: *BioIn 2; CamBiEn; DcArts;
EncWB 98; McGDA; McGEWB; NewCol
75; OxCArt*

Uthman don Fodio
African. Educator, Theologian
Moslem teacher, theologian, and spiritual
leader was one of the leading
reformers of Islam in Hausaland in
Northern Nigeria; founder of an
Islamic empire in West Africa.
b. 1755 in Hausa, Gobir
d. 1816
Source: *EncWB 98; McGEWB*

Utley, Freda
American. Journalist, Author
Wrote *Will the Middle East Go West?*,
1957.
b. Jan 23, 1898 in London, England
d. Jan 21, 1978 in Washington, District
of Columbia
Source: *AmAu&B; BioIn 1, 2, 5, 8, 11;
BlueB 76; ConAu 77, 81; CurBio 58, 78,
78N; DcAmB S10; EncAJ; EncMcCE;
FacFETw; InWom, SUP; NewYTBS 78;
WhAm 7; WhoAm 74, 76; WhoAmW 58,
64, 66, 68, 70, 72; WhoSSW 73*

Utley, (Clifton) Garrick
American. Journalist
Foreign correspondent for NBC, 1963-
64; British correspondent, 1973-79.
b. Nov 19, 1939 in Chicago, Illinois
Source: *ConAu 69; IntAu&W 89;
LegTOT; LesBEnT 92; Who 82, 83, 85,
88, 90, 92, 94, 98, 99, 2000; WhoAm 76,
78, 80, 82, 84, 86, 88, 90, 92, 94; WhoE
91; WhoSSW 73, 75*

Utley, Mike
American. Football Player
Offensive lineman for Detroit Lions until
a paralyzing spinal column injury
occurred during a game, 1991.
b. Dec 20, 1965 in Seattle, Washington

Utrillo, Maurice
French. Artist
Style based on modified form of Cubism;
known for Parisian street scenes,
houses.
b. Dec 25, 1883 in Paris, France
d. Nov 5, 1955 in Dax, France
Source: *AtlBL; Benet 87, 96; BioIn 1, 2,
3, 4, 5, 7, 8, 9, 10, 12, 13, 16, 17;
CamBiEn; ChamBiD; ClaDrA; CurBio
53, 56; DcArts; DcPseud; DcTwArt;
DcTwCCu 2; LegTOT; McGDA; ObitT
1951; OxCArt; OxCFr; OxCTwCA;
OxDcArt; PhDcTCA 77; REn; WhDW*

Uttley, Alice Jane Taylor
[Alison Uttley]
English. Children's Author
Books based on farm life, animals
include *Little Grey Rabbit's
Christmas,* 1939.
b. Dec 17, 1884 in Derbyshire, England
d. May 7, 1976 in High Wycombe,
England
Source: *Au&Wr 71; AuBYP 2, 3; BioIn
3, 8, 10, 12, 14, 16; BlmGWL; CamGLE;*
*ChhPo; ConAu 7NR, 53, 65, X; DcLB
160; DcLEL; FemiCLE; LngCTC;
OxCChiL; OxCEng 85, 95; PenNWW B;
ScF&FL 1; SmATA 3, 26, X; TwCChW
1, 2, 3, 4; WhoChL; WrDr 76*

Utzon, Jorn
Danish. Architect
Best known for designing Opera House,
Sydney, Australia, 1956; built, 1960-
73.
b. Apr 9, 1918 in Copenhagen, Denmark
Source: *BioIn 7, 10, 11, 12, 14, 23;
CamBiEn; ChamBiD; ConArch 80, 87,
94; DcArch; DcD&D; DcTwDes;
EncMA; IntDcAr; IntWW 74, 75, 76, 77,
78, 79, 80, 81, 82, 83, 89, 91, 93, 97,
98, 2000; MacEA; MakTCMA; WhDW;
WhoArch; WhoScEn 96*

V

Vaaler, Johan
Norwegian. Inventor, Educator
Patented the paper clip, 1899.

Vaccaro, Brenda
American. Actor
Husky-voiced entertainer on TV, film,
    stage; nominated for three Tonys, won
    Emmy for "The Shape of Things,"
    1974.
b. Nov 18, 1939 in New York, New
    York
Source: *BiE&WWA; BioIn 8; CelR;
ConTFT 2, 7, 15; EncAFC; FilmEn;
FilmgC; HalFC 80, 84, 88; IntMPA 76,
77, 78, 79, 80, 81, 82, 84, 86, 88, 92,
94, 96; InWom SUP; LegTOT; NotNAT;
OsStAZ; WhoAm 74, 76, 78, 80, 82, 84,
86, 88, 90, 92, 94, 99, 2000; WhoAmW
74, 83; WhoEnt 92, 98; WhoHol 92, A;
WhoThe 72, 77, 81; WorAl*

Vachon, Rogie
[Rogatien Rosaire Vachon]
Canadian. Hockey Player
Goalie, 1966-82, with four NHL teams;
    won Vezina Trophy, 1968; involved in
    controversial free agent compensation
    case with Dale McCourt, 1978-79.
b. Sep 8, 1945 in Palmarolle, Quebec,
    Canada
Source: *BioIn 11, 23; HocEn; WhoAm
78, 80, 82, 90, 92, 94, 95, 96, 97;
WhoHcky 73; WhoWest 87, 89, 92, 94,
96*

Vadim, Roger
[Roger Vadim Plemiannikov]
French. Director
Wrote book about former wives: *Bardot,
    Deneuve, Fonda,* 1983.
b. Jan 26, 1928 in Paris, France
d. Feb 12, 2000 in Paris, France
Source: *BiDFilm, 81, 94; BioIn 4, 5, 10,
11, 13, 14, 15, 16; CamBiEn; ConAu
143; ConTFT 5; CurBio 84; DcFM;
DcPseud; DcTwCCu 2; EncEurC;
FilmEn; FilmgC; HalFC 84, 88; IntDcF
1-2, 2-2; IntMPA 84, 86, 88, 92, 94, 96;
IntWW 74, 75, 76, 77, 78, 79, 80, 81, 82,
83, 89, 91, 98; ItaFilm; MiSFD 9;
MovMk; NewYTBE 70; OxCFilm;*

*WhoEnt 92; WhoFr 79; WhoHol 92, A;
WhoWor 74, 84, 87, 91; WorAl;
WorEFlm; WorFDir 2*

Vagelos, P. Roy
[Pindaros Vagelos]
American. Businessman
Enjoys highest credibility in
    pharmaceutical industry as president
    and CEO of Merck & Co., 1985-.
b. Aug 10, 1929 in Westfield, New
    Jersey
Source: *AmMWSc 92, 98; BioIn 7, 14,
15; Dun&B 90; IntWW 91; News 89;
St&PR 91, 98, 99, 2000; WhoAm 90;
WhoE 91; WhoFI 92*

Vai, Steve
American. Musician, Songwriter
Guitarist; performed and recorded with
    Frank Zappa, David Lee Roth and
    Whitesnake.
b. 1961 in New York, New York
Source: *ConMus 5*

Vaid, Urvashi
American. Writer
Public Information Director and
    Executive Director for the National
    Gay and Lesbian Task Force, 1986-92;
    wrote book *Virtual Equality,* 1995.
b. 1958, India
Source: *BioIn 20, 22; ConAu 156;
GayLesB; GayLL 2; NotAsAm; WrDr 99,
2000*

Vail, Alfred Lewis
American. Manufacturer, Inventor
Manufactured telegraph, 1838; received
    test message between Washington, DC
    and Baltimore, "What hath God
    wrought!" 1844.
b. Sep 25, 1807 in Morristown, New
    Jersey
d. Jan 18, 1859 in Morristown, New
    Jersey
Source: *AmBi; ApCAB; DcAmB; NatCAB
4; RanHWDS; TwCBDA; WebAB 74, 79;
WhAm HS*

Vail, Theodore Newton
American. Businessman
Pres., American Telegraph & Telephone
    Co., 1907-20.
b. Jul 16, 1845 in Carroll County, Ohio
d. Apr 16, 1920 in Baltimore, Maryland
Source: *AmBi; AmNatBi; ApCAB X;
BiDAmBL 83; BioIn 6, 7, 10;
CamDcAB; DcAmB; DcNAA; EncAB-H
1974, 1996; HarEnUS; InSci; NatCAB
28; OhA&B; OxCAmH; WebAB 74, 79;
WhAm 1; WorAl*

Vaive, Rick Claude
Canadian. Hockey Player
Right wing, 1978-93, mostly with
    Toronto, currently with Chicago; had
    three 50-goal seasons.
b. May 14, 1959 in Ottawa, Ontario,
    Canada
Source: *HocEn; HocReg 87*

Vajpayee, Atal Behari
Indian. Political Leader
Prime minister of India representing the
    Bharatiya Janata Party (Indian
    People's Party), 1998—; sparked
    worldwide controversy when his
    country detonated three nuclear
    devices in tests held in 1998.
b. Dec 25, 1926 in Gwalior, Madahya
    Pradesh, India
Source: *EncWB 2-19; News 98*

Valachi, Joe
[Joseph M. Valachi]
American. Criminal
Hit man, turned informer to Justice
    Dept., 1963.
b. Sep 22, 1904 in New York, New
    York
d. Apr 3, 1971 in El Paso, Texas
Source: *BioIn 8, 9; NewYTBE 71;
ObitOF 79*

Valadon, Suzanne
French. Artist
Mother of Utrillo; influenced in painting
    by Gauguin, Degas; figures usually
    from working class.
b. Sep 23, 1869 in Bessines, France

d. Apr 7, 1938 in Paris, France
Source: *CamBiEn; ChamBiD; IntDcWB; McGDA; OxCArt; OxCTwCA*

Valdengo, Giuseppe
Italian. Opera Singer
Baritone with NY Met., 1947-60.
b. May 24, 1920 in Turin, Italy
Source: *BakBD 84; BioIn 13; IntWWM 90; MetOEnc; PenDiMP; WhoWor 74*

Valdes-Leal, Juan de
Spanish. Artist
Paintings include *The Two Cadavers*; series on life of St. Jerome.
b. 1622
d. 1690
Source: *NewCol 75; WebBD 83*

Valdez, Luis (Miguel)
American. Director, Writer
Founder, El Teatro Campesino, 1965—, most influential Chicano theater in US; won Obie, 1969; Emmy, 1973.
b. Jun 26, 1940 in Delano, California
Source: *BenetAL 91; BioIn 12, 14, 15, 16; CamGWoT; ChiLit; ChiSch; ConAmD; ConAu 32NR, 81NR, 101; ConDr 82, 88, 93; ConLC 84; ConTFT 5; CrtSuDr; CyWA 89, 97; DcHiB; DcLB 122; EncALit; EncFoLi; HispAmA; HispLC; HispWr; MiSFD 9; TheaDir; VarWW 85; WhoHisp 92; WhoThe 81; WhoWest 89; WrDr 84, 86, 88, 90, 92, 94, 96, 98, 99, 2000*

Valdivia, Pedro de
Spanish. Conqueror, Soldier
Conquistador fought in Europe and in the civil wars of Peru, and initiated the conquest of Chile.
b. c. 1502 in La Serena, Estremadura, Spain
d. 1553
Source: *HisDcSE; McGEWB*

Vale, Jerry
[Gerano Louis Vitaliamo]
American. Singer
Hit singles include "Innamorata," 1956; "Dommage, Dommage," 1966.
b. Jul 8, 1932 in New York, New York
Source: *AmPS A, B; PenEncP; RkOn 74, 82*

Valens, Ritchie
[Richard Valenzuela]
American. Singer
Had number one single "La Bamba," 1958; life story filmed, 1987.
b. May 13, 1941 in Pacoima, California
d. Feb 3, 1959 in Clear Lake, Iowa
Source: *BiDHisA; BiHaHis; BillEnR; BioIn 15, 20, 22; DcHiB; DcPseud; EncPR&S 74; EncRk 88; EncRkSt; HarEnR 86; LegTOT; PenEncP; RkOn 74; RolSEnR 83; WhoRock 81*

Valente, Benita
American. Opera Singer
Lyric soprano with NY Met. since 1973.

Source: *BakBD 84; BioIn 12, 13, 14, 15, 16, 19; CurBio 88; IntWWM 85, 90; MetOEnc; NewAmDM; NewGrDA 86; NewYTBE 73; NewYTBS 75, 85; WhoAm 78, 80, 82, 84, 86, 88, 90; WhoAmM 83; WhoAmW 97; WhoOp 76*

Valenti, Jack Joseph
American. Film Executive, Government Official
Assistant to LBJ, 1963-66; pres., Motion Picture Assn., 1966—.
b. Sep 5, 1921 in Houston, Texas
Source: *BioIn 6, 7, 8, 10, 11, 13, 16; BlueB 76; BusPN; CamDcAB; CelR 90; ConAu 73; CurBio 68; EncWB 98; FilmgC; HalFC 84, 88; IntMPA 86, 92; IntWW 83, 91; LesBEnT, 92; NewYTBS 82, 91; WhoAm 74, 76, 78, 80, 82, 84, 86, 88, 90, 92, 94, 95, 96, 97, 98, 99, 2000; WhoE 85, 86; WhoEnt 92, 98; WhoGov 72, 75; WhoMedi 98; WhoSSW 73; WhoTelC; WhoWor 74, 78, 80, 82, 84, 87; WorAl*

Valentina
[Nicholaena Sanina Schlee]
American. Fashion Designer
Known for soft, flowing, bias-cut clothing, 1930s-40s.
b. May 1, 1904 in Kiev, Russia
d. Sep 14, 1989 in New York, New York
Source: *AmDec 1930; BioIn 1, 2, 3, 6, 16, 21; ConFash; CurBio 89N; EncFash; FairDF US; InWom, SUP; WorFshn*

Valentine, Dean
American. Broadcasting Executive
One of the most powerful executives in television comedy; pres., Disney Television.
Source: *BioIn 24; WhoAm 99, 2000*

Valentine, Karen
American. Actor
TV shows include "Room 222," 1969-74; "Karen," 1975.
b. May 25, 1947 in Santa Rosa, California
Source: *BioIn 10, 13; ConTFT 3, 20; HalFC 84, 88; IntMPA 84, 86, 88, 92, 94, 96; LegTOT; WhoAmW 87; WhoEmL 87; WhoHol 92*

Valentine, Scott
American. Actor
Played Nick in TV series "Family Ties," 1985-87.
b. Jun 3, 1958 in Saratoga Springs, New York
Source: *BioIn 15; ConTFT 5; WhoHol 92*

Valentino
[Valentino Garavani]
Italian. Fashion Designer
Opened ready-to-wear boutique in Milan, 1969; designs known for elegance, simple lines, styles.
b. May 11, 1932 in Milan, Italy

Source: *BioIn 7, 10, 12, 14, 16; CelR, 90; ConDes 84, 90, 97; ConFash; CurBio 73; DcArts; DcPseud; EncFash; IntWW 91, 93, 98, 2000; LegTOT; ThHDFas; WhoAm 76, 78, 96, 97; WhoFash, 88; WhoWor 82, 84, 87, 89, 91, 93, 95, 96, 97, 98; WorFshn*

Valentino, Rudolph
[Rodolfo d'Antonguella]
American. Actor
Starred in *The Sheik*, 1921; *Blood and Sand*, 1922.
b. May 6, 1895 in Castellaneta, Italy
d. Aug 23, 1926 in New York, New York
Source: *AmBi; AmCulL; AmNatBi; BiDD; BiDFilm, 81, 94; BioIn 1, 2, 3, 5, 6, 7, 8, 9, 10, 11, 12, 14, 15, 16, 17, 18, 19, 20; CamBiEn; ChamBiD; CmCal; CmMov; ConTFT 22; DcArts; DcNAA; DcPseud; FacFETw; Film 1, 2; FilmEn; FilmgC; HalFC 80, 84, 88; IntDcF 1-3, 2-3; LegTOT; MotPP; MovMk; NotNAT B; OxCFilm; SilFlmP; TwYS; WebAB 74, 79; WhAm 1; WhDW; WhoHol B; WhScrn 74, 77, 83; WomWMM; WorAl; WorAlBi; WorEFlm*

Valenzuela, Fernando
[Fernando Anguamea]
"El Toro"
Mexican. Baseball Player
Pitcher, LA Dodgers, 1980-91; CA Angels, 1991-92; won NL rookie of year, Cy Young Award, 1981; first Mexican to win 20 games in NL, 1986; with Dave Stewart, pitched no-hitter on same day, 1990, first with same-day no-hitters since 1898.
b. Nov 1, 1960 in Navajoa, Mexico
Source: *Ballpl 90; BaseReg 85, 86, 87; BiDHisA; BioIn 12, 13, 14, 15, 16; CurBio 82; HispAmA; LegTOT; NewYTBS 81, 86; WhoAm 84, 86, 88, 90, 92; WhoHisp 91, 92, 94; WhoSpor; WhoWest 87, 89; WorAlBi*

Valera y Alcala Galiano, Juan
Spanish. Author, Critic, Diplomat
Best remembered for his novel *Pepita Jimenez*, published in 1874.
b. 1824 in Cabra, Cordova, Spain
d. 1905
Source: *Benet 87, 96; BioIn 1, 5, 7, 10; CasWL; ConAu 106; CyWA 58; EncWB 98; EuAu; EvEuW; LinLib L; McGEWB; OxCSpan; REn*

Valerian
[Publius Licinius Valerianus]
Roman. Emperor
Emperor was known for his ruthless persecution of Christians, and his attempts to repel the invasions of barbarians and Persians on Roman territory.
b. c. 200
d. 260
Source: *EncEarC 90, 97; EncWB 98; McGEWB*

Valeriani, Richard Gerard
American. Broadcast Journalist
With NBC News since, 1961; Pentagon correspondent since, 1982.
b. Aug 29, 1932 in Camden, New Jersey
Source: *ConAu 12NR, 65; EncTwCJ; WhoAm 74, 76, 78, 80, 82, 84, 86, 88, 90, 92, 94, 95, 96, 97, 98, 99, 2000; WhoE 95; WhoSSW 73; WhoTelC*

Valerio, James Robert
American. Artist
Realist painter; won many awards.
b. Dec 2, 1938 in Chicago, Illinois
Source: *BioIn 13; DcCAA 88; PrintW 85; WhoAm 84, 86, 88; WhoAmA 78, 80, 82, 84, 86, 89, 91, 93, 1999; WhoE 83, 85, 86*

Valery, Paul Ambroise
French. Poet, Critic
Wrote *The Graveyard by the Sea*.
b. Oct 30, 1871 in Sete, France
d. Jul 20, 1945 in Paris, France
Source: *AtlBL; BiCoLiE; CasWL; ChhPo S2; ClDMEL 47, 80; CnMD; CnMWL; CurBio 45; Dis&D; EncWB 98; EncWL 1; EvEuW; LngCTC; McGEWB; ModRL; NewC; OxCEng 67; OxCFr; PenC EUR; REn; TwCA, SUP; TwCWr; WhAm 4; WhDW; WhoLA; WhoTwCL*

Valla, Lorenzo
Italian. Critic, Scholar
Humanist's textual criticism initiated the reappraisal of Europe's historical and religious scholarship during the Renaissance.
b. c. 1407 in Rome, Italy
d. 1457
Source: *BbD; BiD&SB; BioIn 14; CamBiEn; CasWL; DcEuL; DcItL 1, 2; EncWB 98; EuAu; GloEncH; McGEWB; OxCLaw; OxCPhil; PenC EUR; RAdv 14, 13-4; REn*

Vallandigham, Clement Laird
American. Politician
Leading Peace Democrat during the Civil War, he sought to end the conflict and reunite the Union but became a symbol of treasonous activity.
b. Jul 29, 1820 in New Lisbon, Ohio
d. Jun 17, 1871 in Hamilton, Ohio
Source: *AmBi; AmNatBi; AmPolLe; ApCAB; BiDrAC; BiDrUSC 89; BioIn 4, 6, 7, 9; CamDcAB; CivWDc; DcAmB; DcNAA; EncAB-H 1974, 1996; EncWB 98; HarEnUS; McGEWB; NatCAB 3; OhA&B; OxCAmH; TwCBDA; WebAB 74, 79; WhAm HS; WhAmP; WhCiWar; WorAl*

Vallee, Rudy
[Hubert Prior Vallee]
"The Vagabond Lover"
American. Actor, Singer
Saxophonist, vaudeville performer; known for using megaphone, theme song "My Time Is Your Time."
b. Jul 28, 1901 in Island Pond, Vermont
d. Jul 3, 1986 in Hollywood, California

Source: *AmCulL; AmNatBi; AmPS; AnObit 1986; ASCAP 66, 80; BakBD 92; BakDcM; BgBands 74; BiE&WWA; BioIn 1, 2, 6, 9, 10, 11, 12, 15, 16, 19, 22, 24; CmpEPM; ConAu 2NR, 119, X; CurBio 63, 86, 86N; DcArts; DcPseud; EncAFC; EncMT; EncVaud; FacFETw; Film 2; FilmEn; FilmgC; ForYSC; HalFC 80, 84, 88; IntMPA 75, 76, 77, 78, 79, 80, 81, 82, 84, 86; LegTOT; MotPP; MovMk; NewAmDM; NewGrDA 86; NewGrDM 80; NewYTBS 86; OxCPMus; PenEncP; RadStar; WebAB 74, 79; WhoHol A; WorAl; WorAlBi*

Valle Inclan, Ramon Maria del
[Ramon (Jose Simon) del Valle y Pena]
Spanish. Author, Dramatist, Poet
Member of the Generation of '98 wrote plays, novels, and poetry; he was influenced by foreign literary trends, particularly the modernist movement.
b. c. 1866 in Puebla de Caraminal, Spain
d. 1936, Spain
Source: *CasWL; ClDMEL 47, 80; CnMD SUP; CnMWL; ConAu 80NR, 153; DcArts; DcSpL; EncWB 98; EncWL 1; EncWT; Ent; EvEuW; HispWr 2; IntDcT 2; McGEWB; McGEWD 72, 84; ModRL; ModWD; OxCSpan; OxCThe 67, 83; PenC EUR; REn; RfGWoL 95; TwCA, SUP; TwCWr; WhDW; WhoTwCL*

Vallejo, Cesar Abraham
Peruvian. Poet
Regarded as one of Peru's best 20th-century poets, his work is characterized by regional themes and characters.
b. Mar 16, 1892 in Santiago de Chuco, Peru
d. 1938
Source: *BioIn 14, 16, 18; ChamBiD; ConAu 153; EncWB 98; LiExTwC; McGEWB; OxCSpan; RfGWoL 95*

Valleria, Alwina
[Alwina Schoening]
American. Opera Singer
Soprano, noted for Wagnerian roles; with NY Met., 1883.
b. Oct 12, 1848 in Baltimore, Maryland
d. Feb 17, 1925 in Nice, France
Source: *BakBD 78, 84, 92; BiDAmM; BioIn 13; DcPseud; InWom SUP; MetOEnc; NewEOp 71; NewGrDA 86; NewGrDM 80; NewGrDO*

Valletti, Cesare
Italian. Opera Singer
Tenor with NY Met., 1952-62; admired for Mozart, Rossini roles.
b. Dec 18, 1922 in Rome, Italy
d. May 20, 2000 in Genoa, Italy
Source: *BakBD 84, 92; BakBDTw; IntDcOp; IntWWM 90; MetOEnc; NewEOp 71; NewGrDM 80; NewGrDO; WhoMus 72*

Valli, Alida
[Alida Maria Altenburger]
Italian. Actor
Films include *Third Man; Paradise Case*.
b. May 31, 1921 in Pola, Italy
Source: *BiDFilm, 81, 94; BioIn 11; DcPseud; EncEurC; FilmAG WE; FilmEn; FilmgC; ForYSC; HalFC 80, 84, 88; IntDcF 1-3, 2-3; IntMPA 75, 76, 77, 78, 79, 80, 81, 82, 84, 86, 88, 92, 94, 96; InWom SUP; ItaFilm; LegTOT; MotPP; MovMk; OxCFilm; WhoHol 92, A; WorEFlm*

Valli, Frankie
[The Four Seasons; Francis Castelluccio]
American. Singer
Hits include "Sherry"; "Big Girls Don't Cry"; "My Eyes Adored You."
b. May 3, 1937 in Newark, New Jersey
Source: *BillEnR; BioIn 15, 23; BkPepl; ConMus 10; DcPseud; IlEncRk; LegTOT; NewAmDM; NewGrDA 86; RkOn 74, 78; WhoAm 78, 80, 82, 84, 86, 88, 92, 94; WhoEnt 92, 98; WorAl; WorAlBi*

Vallone, Raf(faele)
Italian. Actor
Leading man in Italian films; films include *Obsession*, 1976; *The Godfather: Part III*, 1991.
b. Feb 17, 1918 in Tropea, Italy
Source: *ConTFT 1; FilmgC; HalFC 84, 88; IntMPA 84, 86, 92; MovMk; WhoHol A; WorEFlm*

Valtman, Edmund Siegfried
American. Cartoonist
Won 1962 Pulitzer for political, anti-Castro cartoon.
b. May 31, 1914 in Tallinn, Russia
Source: *WhoAm 74, 76; WhoAmA 84, 91; WhoE 91; WhoPul; WorECar*

Valvano, Jim
[James Thomas Valvano]
American. Basketball Coach, Sportscaster
Coach, NC State U, 1980-1990; won NCAA championship, 1983; college basketball analyst.
b. Mar 10, 1946 in New York, New York
d. Apr 28, 1993 in Durham, North Carolina
Source: *BioIn 13, 15, 16; NewYTBS 80, 83, 89; WhAm 11; WhoAm 84, 86, 88, 90, 92; WhoEmL 87; WhoSSW 86*

Van Allen, James Alfred
American. Physicist
Specialist in earth's radiation belts; won many awards.
b. Sep 7, 1914 in Mount Pleasant, Iowa
Source: *AmMWSc 73P, 76P, 79, 82, 86, 89, 92, 95, 98; AsBiEn; BiESc; BioIn 5, 6, 8, 11, 12, 14, 16, 17, 20, 24; BlueB 76; CamBiEn; CamDcAB; ChamBiD; ConAu 162; CurBio 59; FacFETw; InnAst; IntWW 74, 75, 76, 77, 78, 79, 80, 81, 82, 83, 89, 91, 93, 97, 98, 2000; LarDcSc; LegTOT; McGCEnS; McGMS*

80; OxCAmH; RanHWDS; WebAB 74,
79; Who 74, 82, 83, 85, 88, 90, 92, 94,
98, 99, 2000; WhoAm 74, 76, 78, 80, 82,
84, 86, 88, 90, 92, 94, 95, 96, 98, 99,
2000; WhoFrS 84; WhoScEn 94, 96,
2000; WhoWor 74; WorAl

VanAllsburg, Chris

American. Children's Author, Illustrator
Won Caldecotts for *Jumanji*, 1981; *The
Polar Express*, 1985.
b. Jun 18, 1949 in Grand Rapids,
Michigan
Source: *AuBYP 3; BioIn 14, 15, 16;
ChlLR 5, 13; ConAu 113, 117; CurBio
96; DcLB 61; FifBJA; NewYTBS 89;
TwCChW 3; WhoAm 86, 90*

VanAlstyne, Egbert Anson

American. Songwriter, Musician
Wrote over 700 songs, including "In the
Shade of the Old Apple Tree."
b. Mar 5, 1882 in Chicago, Illinois
d. Jul 9, 1951 in Chicago, Illinois
Source: *AmPS; ASCAP 66, 80;
BiDAmM; BioIn 2, 3, 4, 6, 10;
CmpEPM; NotNAT; REnAL; Songw*

Van Andel, Jay

American. Business Executive
Co-founder, chairman of Amway Corp.,
1970—.
b. Jun 3, 1924 in Grand Rapids,
Michigan
Source: *BioIn 9, 10, 11, 12, 13, 17, 24;
ConAmBL; ConAu 181; Dun&B 86, 88,
90; St&PR 75, 84, 87, 91; WhoAm 74,
76, 78, 80, 82, 84, 86, 88, 90, 92, 94,
95, 96, 97, 98, 99, 2000; WhoFI 00, 74,
75, 85, 87, 89, 92, 94, 96, 98; WhoMW
76, 78, 84, 86, 90, 92, 93; WhoWor 74*

Van Ark, Joan

American. Actor
Played Val Ewing on TV series "Knots
Landing," 1979-92.
b. Jun 16, 1946 in New York, New York
Source: *BioIn 6, 12, 15, 16; CelR 90;
ConTFT 7; IntMPA 92; WhoAm 86, 90;
WhoAmW 87, 91; WhoEnt 92; WhoHol
A; WorAlBi*

Vanbiesbrouck, John

American. Hockey Player
Goalie, NY Rangers, 1983-93; FL
Panthers, 1993—; won Vezina
Trophy, 1986.
b. Sep 4, 1963 in Detroit, Michigan
Source: *BioIn 14, 21, 23; HocReg 87;
NewYTBS 85; WhoAm 92, 94, 95, 96,
97, 98, 99, 2000; WhoSSW 95, 97*

Van Brocklin, Norm (an Mack)

"The Dutchman"
American. Football Player, Football
Coach
Quarterback, 1949-60, mostly with LA
Rams; holds NFL record for yds.
passing, 554, in single game, 1951;
MVP, 1960; Hall of Fame, 1971.
b. Mar 15, 1926 in Parade, South Dakota
d. May 2, 1983 in Monroe, Georgia

Source: *AnObit 1983; CmCal; ConAu
109; LegTOT; NewYTBS 83; WhoAm 74;
WhoFtbl 74; WorAl; WorAlBi*

Vanbrugh, John, Sir

English. Dramatist, Architect
Designed Castle Howard, Yorkshire;
Blenheim Palace, Woodstock; plays
include *The Provoked Wife*, 1697.
b. Jan 24, 1664 in London, England
d. Mar 16, 1726 in London, England
Source: *Alli; AtlBL; BbD; Benet 87, 96;
BiCoLiE; BiD&SB; BiDBrA; BioIn 1, 2,
3, 5, 6, 7, 8, 10, 12, 13, 14, 16, 17, 18;
BlkwCE; BlmGEL; BritAu; BritWr 2;
CamBiEn; CamGEL; CamGLE;
CamGWoT; CasWL; ChamBiD; Chambr
2; ChhPo S1; CnThe; CrtSuDr; CrtT 2;
CyWA 58, 97; DcArch; DcArts;
DcD&D; DcEnA; DcEnL; DcEuL; DcLB
80; DcLEL; DcNaB; EncWB 98; EncWT;
Ent; EvLB; GrWrEL DR; IntDcAr;
IntDcT 2; LitC 21; LngCEL; MacEA;
McGDA; McGEWB; McGEWD 72, 84;
MouLC 2; NewC; NewCBEL; NewCol
75; NewGrDO; NotNAT A, B; OxCArt;
OxCBrHi; OxCEng 67, 85, 95; OxCThe
67, 83; PenC ENG; PlP&P; RAdv 14,
13-2; REn; REnWD; RfGEnL 91;
WebE&AL; WhDW; WhoArch*

Van Buren, Abigail

[Pauline Esther Friedman; Mrs. Morton
Phillips]
"Dear Abby"; "Popo"
American. Journalist
Wrote *Dear Abby on Marriage*, 1962;
twin sister of Ann Landers.
b. Jul 4, 1918 in Sioux City, Iowa
Source: *AmAu&B; BioAmW; BioIn 14,
15, 16, 24; CamDcAB; CelR, 90;
ChamBiD; ConAu 1R, X; CurBio 60;
DcLP 87B; DcPseud; EncAJ; EncTwCJ;
ForWC 70; LegTOT; LibW; PenNWW B; WebAB 74,
79; WhoAm 74, 76, 78, 80, 82, 84, 86,
88, 90, 92, 94, 95, 96, 97, 98, 99, 2000;
WhoAmJ 80; WhoAmW 66, 68, 70, 72,
74, 75, 77, 79, 81, 83, 85, 95, 97, 99;
WorAl; WorAlBi*

Van Buren, Hannah (Hoes)

American.
Died 18 yrs. before husband Martin Van
Buren became pres.
b. Mar 8, 1783 in Kinderhook, New
York
d. Feb 5, 1819 in Albany, New York
Source: *AmNatBi; ApCAB; BioIn 16, 17;
FacPr 89; GoodHs; InWom, SUP;
NotAW*

Van Buren, Martin

American. US President
Eighth pres., Dem., 1837-41; opposed
annexation of Texas, established
independent treasury system.
b. Dec 5, 1782 in Kinderhook, New
York
d. Jul 24, 1862 in Kinderhook, New
York
Source: *Alli; AmAu&B; AmBi; AmNatBi;
AmPolLe; ApCAB; BbD; Benet 87, 96;*

BenetAL 91; BiAUS; BiD&SB; BiDrAC;
BiDrGov 1789; BiDrUSC 89; BiDrUSE
71, 89; BioIn 1, 2, 3, 4, 5, 6, 7, 8, 9, 10,
11, 12, 13, 14, 15, 16, 17, 18, 19, 20,
22, 23, 24; CamBiEn; CamDcAB;
CelCen; ChamBiD; CyAG; DcAmAu;
DcAmB; DcAmDH 80, 89; DcAmSR;
DcNAA; Drake; EncAAH; EncAB-H
1974, 1996; EncAPar; EncWar; EncWB
98; FacPr 89, 93; HealPre; LegTOT;
LinLib L, S; McGEWB; NatCAB 6;
OxCAmH; OxCAmL 65, 83; PolPar;
Pres 96; PresAR 1980, 1996; RComAH;
REn; REnAL; TwCBDA; USGovLe;
VicePre; WebAB 74, 79; WhAm HS;
WhAmP; WhCiWar; WhDW; WorAl;
WorAlBi

Van Buren, Steve W

American. Football Player
Four-time all-pro halfback, Philadelphia,
1944-51; led NFL in rushing four
times; Hall of Fame, 1965.
b. Dec 28, 1920 in La Ceiba, Honduras
Source: *BiDAmSp FB; BioIn 1, 2, 6, 7,
8, 9, 10; WhoFtbl 74*

Van Camp, Gilbert C

American. Business Executive
Pres., Van Camp Packing Co, 1882-98.
b. Dec 25, 1817 in Brookline, Indiana
d. Apr 4, 1900 in Indianapolis, Indiana
Source: *NatCAB 28*

Vance, Courtney B.

American. Actor
Theater, film, and television actor, his
many performances include the
Broadway production of *Fences*, 1987,
and the film *The Preacher's Wife*,
1996.
b. Mar 12, 1960 in Detroit, Michigan
Source: *BioIn 22; ConBlB 15; ConTFT
16; DrBlPA 90; IntMPA 96; WhoAfA 11,
12*

Vance, Cyrus Roberts

American. Lawyer, Government Official
Secretary of State, 1977-80.
b. Mar 27, 1917 in Clarksburg, West
Virginia
Source: *AmPolLe; BiDrUSE 89; BioIn 6,
8, 10, 11, 12, 13, 14, 16; BlueB 76;
CamBiEn; CamDcAB; ChamBiD; CngDr
77, 79; ColdWar 2; ConAu 121; CurBio
62; DcAmDH 80, 89; EncVieW; EncWB;
IntWW 74, 75, 76, 77, 78, 79, 80, 81, 82,
83, 89, 91, 93, 97, 98, 2000; IntYB 78,
79, 80, 81, 82; NewYTBS 76; Who 88,
92, 94, 98, 99, 2000; WhoAm 74, 76, 78,
80, 82, 84, 86, 88, 90, 92, 94, 95, 96,
97, 98, 99, 2000; WhoAmL 78, 79, 87,
90, 92; WhoAmP 73, 75, 77, 79, 81, 83,
85, 87, 89, 91, 93, 95, 97, 1999; WhoE
74, 77, 79, 81, 83, 85, 86, 89, 91, 93,
95, 97, 99; WhoFI 89; WhoGov 72, 77;
WhoIntA 2; WhoWor 78, 80, 82, 84;
WorAlBi*

Vance, Dazzy

[Clarence Arthur Vance]
American. Baseball Player
Pitcher, 1915, 1918, 1922-35, mostly
  with Brooklyn; led NL in strikeouts
  seven straight yrs; Hall of Fame, 1955.
b. Mar 4, 1891 in Orient, Iowa
d. Feb 16, 1961 in Homosassa Springs,
  Florida
Source: *AmNatBi; Ballpl 90; BioIn 5, 6,
7, 8, 14, 15; CulEncB; LegTOT;
WhoProB 73; WhoSpor*

Vance, Kenny

[Jay and the Americans]
American. Singer
Part of clean-cut vocal quintet of 1960s;
  solo debut, 1975.
b. Dec 9, 1943
Source: *WhoRocM 82*

Vance, Louis Joseph

American. Author
Wrote *The Lone Wolf,* 1914; *The
Trembling Flame,* 1931.
b. Sep 19, 1879 in Washington, District
  of Columbia
d. Dec 16, 1933 in New York, New
  York
Source: *AmAu&B; AmBi; BioIn 14, 22;
ConAu 112; DcAmB S1; DcNAA;
EncMys; LngCTC; ScF&FL 1; TwCA;
TwCCr&M 80, 85, 91; WhAm 1; WhLit;
WhNAA; WorAu 1900*

Vance, Vivian

American. Actor
Best known as Ethel Mertz in "I Love
  Lucy," 1951-59; also starred in "The
  Lucy Show," 1962-65.
b. Jul 26, 1912 in Cherryvale, Kansas
d. Aug 17, 1979 in Belvedere, California
Source: *AmNatBi; BioIn 4, 7, 8, 10, 11,
12; DcAmB S10; FilmgC; ForYSC;
IntMPA 77; InWom, SUP; MotPP;
WhoAm 74; WhoCom; WhoHol A;
WorAl*

Vance, Zebulon Baird

American. Politician
U.S. senator and congressman served as
  the Civil War governor of North
  Carolina; he was known for his
  concern for the common Southerner
  and his lack of cooperation with
  Confederate authorities.
b. May 13, 1830 in Buncombe County,
  North Carolina
d. Apr 14, 1894
Source: *AmBi; AmNatBi; ApCAB;
BiAUS; BiDConf; BiDrAC; BiDrUSC 89;
BiDSA; BioIn 1, 3, 5, 6, 7, 8, 9;
CamDcAB; ChhPo; CivWDc; DcAmB;
Drake; EncSoH; EncWB 98; HarEnUS;
McGEWB; NatCAB 2, 4; TwCBDA;
WebAB 74, 79; WhAm HS; WhAmP;
WhCiWar*

Van Cleef, Lee

American. Actor
Western/action films include *High Noon,*
  1952; *The Good, the Bad, and the
  Ugly,* 1967.

b. Jan 9, 1925 in Somerville, New Jersey
d. Dec 16, 1989 in Oxnard, California
Source: *AnObit 1989; BioIn 16, 17, 24;
CmMov; ConTFT 8; FilmEn; FilmgC;
ForYSC; GangFlm; HalFC 80, 84, 88;
IntDcF 1-3, 2-3; IntMPA 75, 76, 77, 78,
79, 80, 81, 82, 84, 86, 88; ItaFilm;
LegTOT; MotPP; MovMk; NewYTBS 89;
OxCFilm; WhAm 10; WhoAm 78, 80, 82,
84, 86, 88; WhoHol A; WhoHrs 80;
WorAl; WorAlBi*

Van Cortlandt, Oloff Stevenszen

Dutch. Politician
Deputy mayor of NYC, 1667; Van
  Cortlandt Park, NYC, named after
  him.
b. 1600 in Wijk, Netherlands
d. Apr 5, 1684 in New York, New York
Source: *ApCAB; BiDAmBL 83; DcAmB;
WhAm HS*

Van Cortlandt, Stephanus

American. Politician
Merchant who was first American-born
  mayor of NYC, 1677.
b. May 7, 1643 in New York, New York
d. Nov 25, 1700 in New York, New
  York
Source: *AmBi; AmNatBi; ApCAB;
BiDAmBL 83; DcAmB; EncCRAm;
NatCAB 5; TwCBDA; WebAB 74, 79;
WhAm HS*

Vancouver, George

English. Explorer
Wrote *A Voyage of Discovery to the
North Pacific Ocean and Round the
World,* 1798.
b. Jun 22, 1757 in King's Lynn, England
d. May 10, 1798 in Petersham, England
Source: *Alli; AmNatBi; ApCAB; BbD;
BbtC; BenetAL 91; BiD&SB; BioIn 3, 4,
5, 9, 11, 12, 18, 20, 24; BritAu;
CamBiEn; ChamBiD; DcCanB 4;
DcNaB, C; Drake; Expl 93; ExplAnT;
MacDCB 78; NewC; OxCAmL 65;
OxCCan; OxCEng 67; REn; WhAm HS;
WhWE; WorAl; WorAlBi*

Van Damme, Jean-Claude

[Jean-Claude Van Varenberg]
"Muscles from Brussels"
Belgian. Bodybuilder, Actor
Martial-arts films include *Bloodsport;
Universal Soldier,* 1992.
b. Oct 18, 1960 in Brussels, Belgium
Source: *CurBio 1999; FilmChD; IntMPA
92, 94; WhoHol 92*

Vandegrift, Alexander Archer

American. Army Officer
Entered Marines, 1909; became general,
  1945; received Medal of Honor.
b. Mar 13, 1887 in Charlottesville,
  Virginia
d. May 8, 1973 in Bethesda, Maryland
Source: *AmNatBi; BiDWWGF; BioIn 1,
2, 6, 7, 9, 10; CamDcAB; CurBio 43, 73,
73N; DcAmB S9; DcAmMiB; HarEnMi;
MedHR, 94; WebAB 74, 79; WebAMB;
WhAm 6; WorAl*

Vandenberg, Arthur Hendrick

American. Politician
Rep. senator from MI, 1928-51.
b. Mar 22, 1884 in Grand Rapids,
  Michigan
d. Apr 18, 1951 in Grand Rapids,
  Michigan
Source: *AmAu&B; AmNatBi; AmPeW;
AmPolLe; ApCAB X; BiDInt; BiDrAC;
BiDrUSC 89; BioIn 1, 2, 3, 5, 6, 9, 10,
11; CamBiEn; CamDcAB; ChamBiD;
ColdWar 2; ConAu 120; CurBio 51;
DcAmB S5; DcAmDH 80, 89; DcTwHis;
EncAB-H 1974, 1996; FacFETw; LinLib
L, S; OxCAmH; WebAB 74, 79; WhAm
3; WhAmP; WhLit; WhWW-II; WorAl*

Vandenberg, Arthur Hendrick, Jr.

American. Government Official,
  Presidential Aide
Exec. asst. to General Dwight D
  Eisenhower, 1952; director, Govt.
  Affairs Foundation, Inc., 1953-68.
b. Jun 30, 1907 in Grand Rapids,
  Michigan
d. Jan 18, 1968 in Grand Rapids,
  Michigan
Source: *BioIn 3, 10, 11; WhAm 4A*

Vandenberg, Hoyt Sanford

American. Army Officer
Chief of Staff, US Air Force, 1948-53;
  head of air mission to Russia, 1943-
  44.
b. Jan 24, 1899 in Milwaukee, Wisconsin
d. Apr 2, 1954 in Washington, District of
  Columbia
Source: *AmNatBi; BiDWWGF; BioIn 1,
2, 3, 4, 11, 12, 16; CurBio 45, 54;
DcAmB S5; DcAmMiB; EncAInt;
WebAMB; WhAm 3*

Van Depoele, Charles Joseph

American. Inventor, Scientist
Held over 250 patents, including the
  electric railway, 1883.
b. Apr 27, 1846 in Lichtervelde, Belgium
d. Mar 18, 1892 in Lynn, Massachusetts
Source: *BiInAmS; DcAmB; NatCAB 13;
TwCBDA; WebAB 74, 79; WhAm HS*

Vanderbilt, Alfred G(wynne)

English. Horse Racing Official
Chm. of NY Racing Association, 1971-
  75.
b. Sep 22, 1912 in London, England
d. Nov 12, 1999 in Mill Neck, New
  York
Source: *BioIn 1; NewYTBS 75; WhoAm
76*

Vanderbilt, Amy

American. Journalist, Author
Etiquette expert who wrote syndicated
  newspaper column, regularly revised
  Complete Book of Etiquette, 1952.
b. Jul 22, 1908 in Staten Island, New
  York
d. Dec 27, 1974 in New York, New
  York
Source: *AmAu&B; AmNatBi;
AmWomWr; Au&Wr 71; BiDAmNC;*

BioIn 3, 5, 6, 7, 9, 10; CamDcAB; CelR; ConAu 1R, 3NR, 53; CurBio 54, 75, 75N; DcAmB S9; EncAJ; EncTwCJ; InWom, SUP; LegTOT; LinLib L; NewYTBS 74; ObitOF 79; WhAm 6; WhoAm 74; WhoAmW 58, 61, 64, 66, 68, 70; WhoE 74; WorAl; WorAlBi

Vanderbilt, Cornelius
American. Financier
Fortune made in shipping business, stock market, estimated at $100 million; Vanderbilt U., Nashville, named after him.
b. May 27, 1794 in Staten Island, New York
d. Jan 4, 1877 in New York, New York
Source: *AmBi; AmNatBi; ApCAB; BiDAmBL 83; BioIn 1, 3, 5, 6, 7, 9, 11, 13, 14, 15, 16, 17, 21, 22; CamBiEn; CamDcAB; CelCen; ChamBiD; DcAmB; DcAmDH 80, 89; Drake; EncAB-H 1974, 1996; EncABHB 2; EncWB 98; HarEnUS; LegTOT; LinLib S; McGEWB; MemAm; NatCAB 6; OxCAmH; RComAH; REn; REnAL; TwCBDA; WebAB 74, 79; WhAm HS; WhCiWar; WhDW; WorAl; WorAlBi*

Vanderbilt, Cornelius
American. Financier, Philanthropist
Eldest son of William H, grandson of Cornelius Vanderbilt.
b. Nov 27, 1843 in Staten Island, New York
d. Sep 12, 1899 in New York, New York
Source: *AmBi; ApCAB, SUP; BiDAmBL 83; BioIn 2, 3, 7, 12, 16; CamDcAB; DcAmB; EncABHB 2; HarEnUS; NatCAB 6, 34; TwCBDA; WebAB 74, 79; WhAm 1*

Vanderbilt, Cornelius, Jr.
American. Journalist, Filmmaker
Founder, pres., Vanderbilt Newspapers, Inc., 1923; wrote *Park Avenue,* 1930; *Farewell to Fifth Avenue,* 1935.
b. Apr 30, 1898 in New York, New York
d. Jul 7, 1974 in Miami Beach, Florida
Source: *AmAu&B; Au&Wr 71; AuNews 1; BioIn 5, 10, 16; BlueB 76; ConAu 49, P-1; DcAmB S9; LinLib L; WhAm 6; WhNAA; Who 74; WhoAm 74*

Vanderbilt, Gloria Morgan
[Gloria Cooper]
American. Designer
Best known for Gloria Vanderbilt jeans that influenced ''designer jeans'' craze, 1980s; appeared on stage, film; writes poetry, designs fabrics.
b. Feb 20, 1924 in New York, New York
Source: *BiDAmBL 83; BiE&WWA; BioAmW; BioIn 4, 5, 8, 9, 10, 11, 12, 13, 14, 15, 16; BioNews 74; CelR 90; ConAu 22NR, 89; CurBio 72; Entr; ForWC 70; IntWWW 2; InWom SUP; NewYTBS 79, 85, 87; NotNAT; WhoAm 76, 78, 80, 82, 84, 86, 88; WhoAmW 83, 85, 87, 89, 91, 93, 95; WomFir*

Vanderbilt, Harold Stirling
American. Businessman
Invented card game contract bridge, 1925.
b. Jul 6, 1884 in Oakdale, New York
d. Jul 4, 1970 in Newport, Rhode Island
Source: *BioIn 7, 8, 9, 21; CamBiEn; CamDcAB; NewYTBE 70; ObitOF 79; OxCShps; WebAB 74, 79; WhAm 5, 7*

Vanderbilt, William Henry
American. Financier, Railroad Executive
Succeeded father Cornelius as pres., NY Central Railroad, 1877.
b. May 8, 1821 in New Brunswick, New Jersey
d. Dec 8, 1885 in New York, New York
Source: *AmBi; AmNatBi; ApCAB; BiDAmBL 83; BiDrGov 1789; BioIn 3, 5, 7; CamDcAB; DcAmB; EncAB-H 1974, 1996; HarEnUS; NatCAB 6, 30; NewYTBS 81; TwCBDA; WebAB 74, 79; WhAm HS; WorAl*

Vanderbilt, William Henry
American. Politician, Philanthropist
Rep. governor of RI, 1939-40; founded non-profit South Forty Corp to help rehabilitate prisoners.
b. Nov 24, 1902 in New York, New York
d. Apr 14, 1981 in South Williamston, Massachusetts
Source: *NewYTBS 81; St&PR 75; WhoAm 74*

Vanderbilt, William Kissam
American. Businessman
Pres., P.& L.E. Railroad; director NY Central Railroad; founder, pres., The New Theater.
b. Dec 12, 1849 in New York, New York
d. Jul 22, 1920 in Paris, France
Source: *AmNatBi; ApCAB SUP; BiDAmBL 83; BioIn 16; CurBio 44; DcAmB; NatCAB 6, 30; WebAB 74, 79; WhAm 1; WorAl*

Vandercook, John Womack
American. Author, Broadcast Journalist
Writings include *Tom-Tom,* 1926; *Murder in New Guinea,* 1959.
b. Apr 22, 1902 in London, England
d. Jan 6, 1963 in Delhi, New York
Source: *AmAu&B; BioIn 1, 6; CurBio 42, 63; EncMys; NotNAT B; REnAL; WhAm 4; WhE&EA; WhNAA*

Van der Klugt, Cor
Dutch. Business Executive
President of Philips, Dutch electronics firm, since 1986.
b. 1924?, Netherlands

Vanderlyn, John
American. Artist
First nude exhibited in US caused scandal, 1815; portraits of famous people include Andrew Jackson, James Monroe.
b. Oct 15, 1775 in Kingston, New York

d. Sep 23, 1852 in Kingston, New York
Source: *AmBi; ApCAB; BiAUS; DcAmB; Drake; OxCAmL 65; TwCBDA; WebAB 74; WhAm HS*

Vander Meer, Johnny
[John Samuel Vander Meer]
''Double No-Hit''; ''The Dutch Master''
American. Baseball Player
Pitcher, 1937-51; only pitcher to throw consecutive no-hitters, 1938.
b. Nov 2, 1914 in Prospect Park, New Jersey
d. Oct 6, 1997 in Tampa, Florida
Source: *Ballpl 90; BiDAmSp Sup; BioIn 2, 6, 9, 11, 23; FacFETw; LegTOT; WhoProB 73; WorAl*

Van der Meer, Simon
Dutch. Physicist
Shared Nobel Prize in physics with Carlo Rubbia, 1984; studied subatomic particles, links to basic forces of nature.
b. Nov 24, 1925 in The Hague, Netherlands
Source: *AmMWSc 89, 92, 95, 98; BioIn 13, 14, 15; CamBiEn; ChamBiD; IntWW 89, 91, 93, 97, 98, 2000; LarDcSc; LegTOT; McGCEnS; NobelP; NotTwCS 1; RanHWDS; Who 88, 90, 92, 94, 98, 99, 2000; WhoAm 99, 2000; WhoNob, 90, 95; WhoScEn 94, 96, 2000; WhoWor 87, 89, 91, 93, 95, 96, 97, 98, 99, 2000; WorAlBi*

Van Der Post, Laurens (Jan), Sir
South African. Author
Wrote *In a Province,* 1934; *The Heart of the Hunter,* 1961.
b. Dec 13, 1906 in Philioppis, South Africa
d. Dec 15, 1996 in London, England
Source: *Au&Wr 71; Benet 87, 96; BioIn 4, 8, 9, 10, 13, 15, 16; BlueB 76; CamBiEn; CamGEL; CamGLE; CasWL; ChamBiD; ConAu 5R, 35NR, 155; ConLC 5; ConNov 72, 76, 82, 86, 91, 96; DcArts; DcLEL; EncSoA; GrWrEL N; IntAu&W 76, 77, 82, 89, 91, 93; IntWW 74, 75, 76, 77, 78, 79, 80, 81, 82, 83, 89, 91, 93; LiExTwC; LinLib L; LngCTC; ModCmwL; NewYTBS 96; Novels; OxCEng 85, 95; OxCTwCL; PenC ENG; RAdv 14, 13-3; REn; RfGEnL 91; RGTwCWr; TwCWr; Who 74, 82, 83, 85, 85N, 88, 90, 92, 94; WhoAm 74, 76, 78; WhoWor 74, 76, 78; WorAu 1950; WrDr 76, 80, 82, 84, 86, 88, 90, 92, 94, 96, 98N*

Vandervelde, Emile
Belgian. Statesman
Belgian minister of justice, 1919, foreign affairs, 1925; first pres., International Socialist Bureau.
b. Jan 25, 1866 in Ixelles, Belgium
d. Dec 27, 1938 in Brussels, Belgium
Source: *BiDInt; NewCol 75; WebBD 83*

Vander Zalm, William
[Wilhelmus Nicholass Theodoros Maria Vander Zalm]
Canadian. Political Leader
Social Credit premier of British Columbia, 1986-91.
b. May 29, 1934 in Noordwykerhout, Netherlands
Source: *BioIn 15, 16; CanWW 83, 89; ConNews 87-3; IntWW 91; Who 92; WhoAm 90; WhoWest 92*

VanDerZee, James
American. Photographer
Known for photographs of Harlem, begun in 1915.
b. Jun 29, 1886 in Lenox, Massachusetts
d. May 15, 1983 in Washington, District of Columbia
Source: *BioIn 9, 10, 12; ConAu 104, 109; ConPhot 82; InB&W 80; NegAl 83; NewYTBE 71; NewYTBS 83; PeoHis; WhAm 7; WhAmArt 85; WhoAm 74, 76, 78*

Van Devanter, Willis
American. Supreme Court Justice
Served on US Supreme Court, 1910-37.
b. Apr 17, 1859 in Marion, Indiana
d. Feb 8, 1941 in Washington, District of Columbia
Source: *AmNatBi; BiDFedJ; BioIn 1, 2, 5, 8, 11, 15; CamDcAB; CurBio 41; DcAmB S3; NatCAB 12; NewEAmW; OxCSupC; REnAW; SupCtJu; WebAB 74, 79; WhAm 1*

van de Velde, Henry
Belgian. Painter, Designer, Architect, Writer
Influential in developing a new architectural expression in Europe during the early 20th century.
b. Apr 3, 1863 in Antwerp, Belgium
d. Oct 27, 1957 in Zurich, Switzerland
Source: *BioIn 14, 15, 20; ConArch 80; DcD&D; EncMA; EncWB 98; IntDcAr; MacEA; PenDiDA 89*

Van Devere, Trish
[Patricia Dressel; Mrs. George C Scott]
American. Actor
Co-starred with husband in several films: *Where's Poppa?*, 1970, *Day of the Dolphin*, 1973.
b. Mar 9, 1945 in Englewood Cliffs, New Jersey
Source: *BioIn 9, 11; ConTFT 3; FilmEn; HalFC 88; IntMPA 84, 86, 88, 92, 94, 96; InWom SUP; WhoAm 88*

Vandeweghe, Kiki
[Ernest Maurice Vandeweghe]
American. Basketball Player
Forward, Denver, 1980-84, Portland, 1984-89; NY Knicks, 1989-92; LA Clippers, 1992-93; led NBA in three-point field goal percentage, 1987.
b. Aug 1, 1958 in Wiesbaden, Germany (West)
Source: *BasBi; BioIn 15; OfNBA 87*

Van Diemen, Anthony Meuza
Dutch. Government Official, Merchant
Governor general of the Dutch East Indies, he helped develop Batavia and the Indies and expand Dutch influence in East Asia.
b. 1593 in Culemborg, Netherlands
d. May 19, 1645 in West Java, Indonesia

Van Dine, S. S
[Willard Huntington Wright]
American. Author, Critic
Wrote popular Philo Vance detective stories including *Canary Murder Case*, 1927.
b. Oct 15, 1888 in Charlottesville, Virginia
d. Apr 11, 1939 in New York, New York
Source: *AmAu&B; BenetAL 91; BioIn 4, 6, 14, 18, 24; CnDAL; ConAu 115; DcAmB S2; DcNAA; EncMys; EvLB; FilmgC; LngCTC; OxCAmL 65, 83, 95; OxCTwCL; PenC AM; REnAL; TwCA; SUP; TwCWr; WhAm 1; WhLit; WhNAA*

Van Doren, Carl Clinton
American. Critic, Biographer
Won Pulitzer for biography of *Benjamin Franklin*, 1938; brother of Mark.
b. Sep 10, 1885 in Hope, Illinois
d. Jul 18, 1950 in Torrington, Connecticut
Source: *CamBiEn; CamDcAB; ChamBiD; CnDAL; ConAmA; ConAmL; ConAu 111, 168; DcAmB S4; DcLEL; EvLB; LngCTC; NatCAB 39; OxCAmL 83; REn; REnAL; TwCA; TwCWr; WebAB 79; WhAm 3; WorAu 1900*

Van Doren, Charles Lincoln
American. Editor
VP, *Encyclopedia Britannica*, 1973-82.
b. Feb 12, 1926 in New York, New York
Source: *BioIn 4, 5, 6, 10, 11, 20, 22, 24; ConAu 4NR, 5R; DrAS 74E, 78E, 82E; IntAu&W 89; PolProf E; WhoAm 84, 86, 90; WhoFI 83; WhoUSWr 88; WhoWrEP 89*

Van Doren, Dorothy Graffe
American. Author
Writings include *Strangers*, 1926; *The Country Wife*, 1950; *Men, Women and Cats*, 1962.
b. May 2, 1896 in San Francisco, California
d. Feb 21, 1993 in Sharon, Connecticut
Source: *AmAu&B; AmNov; BioIn 18; ConAu 1R, 141; ForWC 70; InWom; REnAL; WhAm 10; WhE&EA; WhLit; WhoAm 74, 76, 78; WhoAmW 58, 61, 64, 66, 68, 70, 72, 74*

Van Doren, Mamie
[Joan Lucille Olander]
American. Actor
Films include *Untamed Youth; Ain't Misbehavin'*.
b. Feb 6, 1933 in Rowena, South Dakota
Source: *BioIn 3, 14, 15; DcPseud; FilmgC; ForYSC; HalFC 80, 84, 88;*

IntMPA 75, 76, 77, 78, 79, 80, 81, 82, 84, 86, 88, 92, 94, 96; InWom, SUP; ItaFilm; LegTOT; MotPP; MovMk; WhoHol A; WhoHrs 80; WorAl; WorAlBi

Van Doren, Mark
American. Poet, Critic, Author
Won Pulitzer for poetry, 1939; writings include *That Shining Place*, 1969.
b. Jun 13, 1894 in Hope, Illinois
d. Dec 10, 1972 in Torrington, Connecticut
Source: *AmAu&B; AmNatBi; Au&Wr 71; Benet 87, 96; BenetAL 91; BiDAmEd; BiE&WWA; BioIn 1, 3, 4, 5, 7, 8, 9, 10, 12, 15, 17, 22; CamDcAB; CasWL; ChhPo, S1, S2, S3; CnDAL; CnE&AP; ConAmA; ConAu 1R, 3NR, 37R; ConLC 6, 10; ConNov 72; ConPo 70; CurBio 40, 73, 73N; DcArts; DcLB 45; DcLEL; EncALit; EvLB; GrWrEL P; LinLib L; LngCTC; MajTwCW 1, 2; ModAL 4, 4S1, 5; NewYTBE 72; Novels; OxCAmL 65, 83; OxCTwCP; PenC AM; RAdv 1; REn; REnAL; RfGAmL 87; ScF&FL 1, 2; SixAP; TwCA, SUP; TwCWr; WebAB 74, 79; WhAm 5; WhNAA; WhoPul; WorAl; WorAlBi; WorAu 1900*

Vandross, Luther
American. Singer, Musician
With *Power of Love*, 1991, has created 8 consecutive platinum records.
b. Apr 20, 1951 in New York, New York
Source: *AfrAmAl 6, 8; BillEnR; BioIn 12, 13, 14, 15, 16; ConBlB 13; ConMus 2, 24; CurBio 91; DrBlPA 90; EncPR&S 89; EncRk 88; EncRkSt; InB&W 85; IntWW 91; LegTOT; NewYTBS 91; PenEncP; RkOn 85; Songw; SoulM; WhoEnt 92*

Van Druten, John William
American. Dramatist
Plays include *I Remember Mama*, 1944, from Kathryn Forbes' book; *Anatomy of Murder*, 1957, from Robert Traver's book.
b. Jun 1, 1901 in London, England
d. Dec 19, 1957 in Indio, California
Source: *AmNatBi; ConAu 161; CurBio 44, 58; McGEWD 72; ModAL 4; ModBrL; ModWD; NewC; OxCAmL 65; OxCThe 67; PenC AM; PlP&P; REn; REnAL; RfGAmL 4; TwCA, SUP; TwCWr; WhAm 3; WorAu 1900*

Van Dusen, Henry Pitney
American. Clergy, Educator
Helped found World Council of Churches, 1948.
b. Dec 11, 1897 in Philadelphia, Pennsylvania
d. Feb 13, 1975 in Belle Meade, New Jersey
Source: *AmAu&B; BiDAmEd; BioIn 2, 3, 6, 7, 10, 11, 18, 19; ConAu 1R, 3NR, 57; CurBio 50, 75; DcAmReB 1, 2; DrAS 74P; RelLAm 1, 2; WhAm 6; WhNAA; WhoAm 74*

Van Duyn, Mona
American. Poet
US poet laureate, 1992-93; won Pulitzer
    Prize for poetry, *Near Changes*, 1991.
b. May 9, 1921 in Waterloo, Iowa
Source: *AmAu&B; AmWomWr SUP;*
ArtclWW 2; Benet 96; BenetAL 91;
BioIn 12, 16; ConAu 7NR, 9R; ConLC 3,
7, 63, 116; ConPo 70, 75, 80, 85, 91;
ConWomP 98; CurBio 98; CyWA 97;
DcLB 5; DrAP 75; DrAPF 80, 91;
EncALit; EncWB 98; EncWHA;
FemiCLE; GrWomW; IntWW 93, 97, 98,
2000; InWom SUP; ModAL 5; News 93-
2; OxCAmL 95; OxCTwCL; OxCTwCP;
OxCWoWr 95; RAdv 14; WhoAm 90;
WhoAmW 91; WhoPul; WhoWrEP 89;
WorAu 1970; WrDr 76, 80, 82, 84, 86,
88, 90, 92, 94, 96

Van Dyck, Anthony, Sir
Flemish. Artist
Court painter to Charles I of England;
    set style for English portraiture which
    lasted a century.
b. Mar 22, 1599 in Antwerp, Belgium
d. Dec 9, 1641 in London, England
Source: *AtlBL; Benet 96; BioIn 14;*
CamBiEn; ChambiD; EncWB 98;
IntDcAA 90; LegTOT; LiveWoA;
McGDA; McGEWB; NewC; NewCol 75;
OxCArt; OxCBrHi; OxCEng 95; REn;
WebBD 83; WorAlBi

Van Dyke, Dick
American. Actor, Comedian
Won three Emmys for TV series "The
    Dick Van Dyke Show," 1961-66.
b. Dec 13, 1925 in West Plains, Missouri
Source: *BioIn 6, 7, 9, 10, 11, 16, 18, 22,*
24; CamBiEn; CamDcAB; CelR, 90;
ChamBiD; ConAu 112, 166; ConTFT 3,
13, 24; CurBio 63; EncAFC; FilmEn;
FilmgC; ForYSC; Funs; HalFC 80, 84,
88; IntMPA 75, 76, 77, 78, 79, 80, 81,
82, 84, 86, 88, 92, 94, 96; JoeFr;
LegTOT; LesBEnT 92; MotPP; MovMk;
OxCPMus; QDrFCA 92; WhoAm 74, 76,
78, 80, 82, 84, 86, 88, 90, 92, 94, 95,
96, 97, 99, 2000; WhoCom; WhoEnt 92,
98; WhoHol 92, A; WhoTelC; WhoWest
74; WhoWor 74, 76; WorAl; WorAlBi;
WorEFlm

Vandyke, Henry Jackson, Jr.
American. Clergy, Poet, Educator
Wrote *The White Bees, and Other*
    Poems, 1909; *Chosen Poems*, 1927.
b. Nov 10, 1852 in Germantown,
    Pennsylvania
d. Apr 10, 1933 in Princeton, New
    Jersey
Source: *Alli SUP; AmAu&B; AmBi;*
ApCAB; BbD; BiD&SB; Chambr 3;
ChhPo, S1, S2; ConAmL; DcAmAu;
DcAmB; DcNAA; EvLB; JBA 34;
LngCTC; REnAL; Str&VC; TwCA, SUP;
WhAm 1; WhNAA

Van Dyke, Jerry
American. Actor
Brother of Dick Van Dyke; starred in
    TV series "My Mother the Car,"
    1965-66; "Coach," 1989-97.
b. Jul 27, 1931 in Danville, Illinois
Source: *BioIn 16; ConTFT 12, 23;*
ForYSC; IntMPA 96; MotPP; VarWW
85; WhoCom; WhoEnt 92; WhoHol 92,
A; WorAl

Van Dyke, W(oodbridge) S(trong)
"One Shot Woody"; "Woody"
American. Director, Producer
Nickname earned from reputation as
    casual director; resulted in spontaneous
    performances from actors.
b. Mar 21, 1887 in San Diego, California
d. Feb 5, 1943 in Brentwood, California
Source: *BiDFilm; CmMov; DcFM; Film*
1; FilmgC; MovMk; ObitOF 79;
OxCFilm; TwYS; WhScrn 77; WorEFlm

Van Dyken, Amy
American. Swimmer
First American woman to win four gold
    medals in any event during a single
    Olympic Game, 1996.
b. Feb 1, 1973 in Engelwood, Colorado
Source: *BioIn 23, 24; EncWomS;*
EncWoSp; News 97, 97-1; WhoAm 98,
99, 2000; WhoAmW 97, 99; WhoWor 97,
98, 99, 2000

Vane, Henry
English. Politician
Served as governor of the Massachusetts
    Bay Colony and led the Long
    Parliament and the English
    Commonwealth.
b. 1613
d. 1662
Source: *Alli; AmBi; AmNatBi; BiDrACR;*
BioIn 2, 3, 6, 8, 9, 10, 14; CamBiEn;
ChamBiD; DcAmB; DcNaB; EncWB 98;
LuthC 75; McGEWB; OxCAmH;
OxCBrHi; REn; WhAm HS

Vane, John Robert, Sir
English. Scientist
Shared Nobel Prize in medicine, 1982,
    for discoveries relating to
    prostaglandins.
b. Mar 29, 1927 in Tardebigg, England
Source: *AmMWSc 89, 92, 95, 98; BiESc;*
BioIn 13, 14, 15; BlueB 76; CamBiEn;
ChamBiD; ConAu 160; CurBio 86;
IntMed 80; IntWW 83, 89, 91, 93, 97,
98, 2000; LarDcSc; McGCEnS;
NewYTBS 82; NobelP; RanHWDS; Who
74, 82, 83, 85, 88, 92, 94, 98, 99, 2000;
WhoAm 88, 90, 92, 94, 95, 99, 2000;
WhoMedH 96, 99, 2000; WhoNob, 90,
95; WhoScEn 94, 96, 2000; WhoWor 78,
80, 82, 84, 87, 89, 91, 93, 95, 96, 97,
98, 99, 2000; WorAlBi; WrDr 2000

Van Eekelen, Willem Frederik
Dutch. Politician
Minister of defense of the Netherlands
    became secretary-general of the
    Western European Union in 1989.
b. 1931 in Utrecht, Netherlands

Source: *EncWB 98; IntWW 89, 91, 93,*
97, 98, 2000; WhoWor 89, 95, 96, 97,
98, 99, 2000

Van Eyck, Hubert
Flemish. Artist
Co-founder, with brother Jan, of Flemish
    School; only extant piece, Lamb
    altarpiece, Ghent.
b. 1370
d. 1426
Source: *AtlBL; LegTOT; LinLib S;*
McGDA; McGEWB; NewC; REn

Van Eyck, Jan
Flemish. Artist
Noted for descriptive realism, intensive
    color; perfected, but did not discover
    oil technique.
b. 1371 in Maeseyck, Netherlands
d. 1440
Source: *ClaDrA; McGDA; McGEWB;*
NewC; REn

Van Fleet, James Alward
American. Army Officer
Served in Mexican Border campaign,
    1916-17; deputy chief of staff
    European Command, Germany, 1947-
    48.
b. Mar 19, 1892 in Coytesville, New
    Jersey
d. Sep 23, 1992 in Polk City, Florida
Source: *BiDWWGF; BioIn 1, 2, 3, 4, 9,*
18, 19, 24; CamDcAB; CurBio 48;
DcAmMiB; HarEnMi; WebAMB; WhoAm
74, 76, 78, 80, 82, 84; WhoWor 74, 76

Van Fleet, Jo
[Mrs. William Bales]
American. Actor
Won Oscar for her first film *East of*
    Eden, 1955; Tony for *Trip to*
    Bountiful, 1954.
b. Dec 30, 1919 in Oakland, California
d. Jun 10, 1996 in New York, New York
Source: *BiE&WWA; ConTFT 5; FilmEn;*
FilmgC; ForYSC; HalFC 80, 84, 88;
HolCA; IntMPA 86, 92, 94, 96; InWom
SUP; ItaFilm; LegTOT; MotPP; MovMk;
NotNAT; ObitPA 96; OsStAZ; VarWW
85; Vers A; WhoAm 82; WhoEnt 92;
WhoHol 92, A; WhoThe 81; WorAl

Vangelis
[Evangelos Papathanassiou]
Greek. Composer
Won Oscar for score of *Chariots of Fire*,
    1982.
b. Mar 29, 1943 in Volos, Greece
Source: *BioIn 13; ConMus 21; ConTFT*
21; DcPseud; EncEurC; EncRk 88;
EncRkSt; HalFC 88; HarEnR 86;
IlEncRk; IntMPA 92, 94, 96; IntWW 91;
ItaFilm; LegTOT; NewAgMG; RkOn 85;
RolSEnR 83; WhoRocM 82

Van Gogh, Vincent Willem
Dutch. Artist
Works in brilliant colors, swirling brush
    strokes became popular 50 years after
    death, include *Sunflowers*.

b. Mar 30, 1853 in Groot Zundert,
Netherlands
d. Jul 29, 1890 in Auvers, France
Source: *AtlBL; McGDA; NewCol 75;
OxCFr; REn*

Van Halen

[Michael Anthony; Sammy Hagar; David
Lee Roth; Alex Van Halen; Eddie
(Edward) Van Halen]
American. Music Group
California-based, heavy metal rock band;
first number-one hit was "Jump,"
1984.
Source: *BillEnR; BioIn 14, 15, 16, 17,
21; BlkOlyM; CelR 90; ConMuA 80A;
ConMus 8, 25; EncPR&S 89; EncRk 88;
EncRkSt; GrMetD; HarEnR 86;
PenEncP; RkOn 85; RkWho 96;
RolSEnR 83; WhoRock 81; WhoRocM 82*

Van Halen, Alex

[Van Halen]
American. Musician
Drummer, brother of Eddie Van Halen;
inducted into Hollywood Rock Walk,
1991.
b. May 8, 1955 in Nijmegen,
Netherlands
Source: *EncPR&S 89; LegTOT*

Van Halen, Eddie

[Van Halen; Edward Van Halen]
Dutch. Musician, Singer
One of world's top guitarists with band
Van Halen since 1974.
b. Jan 26, 1957 in Nijmegen,
Netherlands
Source: *BioIn 12, 14, 15; CmpEGui;
ConNews 85-2; EncPR&S 89; LegTOT;
OnThGG; WhoAm 86, 88, 90, 92, 94, 95,
96, 97, 98, 99, 2000; WhoEnt 92, 98;
WhoRocM 82; WorAlBi*

Van Hamel, Martine

Canadian. Dancer
Principal dancer, American Ballet
Theatre, 1973—; won dance awards.
b. Nov 16, 1945 in Brussels, Belgium
Source: *BiDD; BioIn 8, 10, 11, 12, 13,
14; CreCan 2; CurBio 79; IntDcB;
IntWW 2000; InWom SUP; WhoAm 78,
80, 82, 84, 86, 88; WhoAmW 83, 85, 89,
91; WhoE 85, 86, 89; WhoEnt 98*

Van Heusen, Jimmy

[Edward Chester Babcock; James Van
Heusen]
American. Songwriter
"Architect of melody," known for
collaborations with Sammy Kahn; with
Kahn, won Oscars for "All the Way,"
1957, "High Hopes," 1959, "Call Me
Irresponsible," 1963.
b. Jan 26, 1913 in Syracuse, New York
d. Feb 7, 1990 in Rancho Mirage,
California
Source: *AmNatBi; AmSong; AnObit
1990; ASCAP 66, 80; BakBD 92;
BestMus; BiE&WWA; BioIn 4, 9, 14, 15,
16, 17, 24; CelR; CmpEPM; ConTFT
11; CurBio 70, 86, 90, 90N; FacFETw;
FilmgC; HalFC 84, 88; IntMPA 86, 88;*

*LegTOT; NewAmDM; NewGrDA 86;
NewGrDM 80; NewYTBS 90; NotNAT;
OxCPMus; PopAmC, SUP; Songw;
WhAm 10; WhoThe 81; WorAl; WorAlBi*

Van Heusen, John

American. Designer
Designed first semisoft shirt collar, 1919.
b. Apr 14, 1869 in Albany, New York
d. Dec 18, 1931 in Scarsdale, New York
Source: *Entr; NatCAB 24*

Van Horne, Harriet

American. Critic, Journalist
Columnist whose writings focused on
quality of radio, TV; reviewed many
of the early TV shows.
b. May 17, 1920 in Syracuse, New York
d. Jan 15, 1998 in New York, New York
Source: *BiDAmNC; BioIn 3, 5, 11, 23,
24; CelR; ConAu 113, 164; CurBio 54,
98N; EncTwCJ; InWom, SUP; NewYTBS
98; WhoAm 80, 84; WhoAmW 58, 61,
64, 66, 68, 72, 74, 83*

Van Horne, William Cornelius, Sir

American. Railroad Executive
Pres., C.,M.&St.P. Railroad, 1888-99.
b. Feb 3, 1843 in Will County, Illinois
d. Sep 11, 1915 in Montreal, Quebec,
Canada
Source: *ApCAB; BiDAmBL 83; DcAmB;
DcNaB 1912; HarEnUS; OxCCan;
WhAm 1*

Vanik, Charles Albert

American. Politician
Dem. congressman from OH, 1954-79.
b. Apr 7, 1913 in Cleveland, Ohio
Source: *AlmAP 80; BiDrAC; BiDrUSC
89; BioIn 11, 12; CngDr 79; PolProf J,
NF; WhoAm 80; WhoAmP 85, 91;
WhoGov 77*

Vanilla Fudge

[Carmine Appice; Tim Bogert; Vincent
Martell; Mark Stein]
American. Music Group
One of first heavy-rock bands, formed
1966; known for psychedelic light
shows.
Source: *BiDAmM; BillEnR; ConMuA
80A; EncPR&S 74; EncRk 88; EncRkSt;
GrMetD; IlEncRk; PenEncP; RkOn 78;
RolSEnR 83; WhoRock 81; WhoRocM 82*

Vanilla Ice

[Robert Van Winkle]
American. Rapper
White solo rap star; received American
Music Award, 1991.
b. Oct 31, 1967 in Miami, Florida
Source: *ConMus 6; News 91, 91-3*

Van Itallie, Jean-Claude

American. Dramatist
Won Obie for *The Serpent*, 1969; other
plays include *The Traveler*, 1986.
b. May 23, 1936 in Brussels, Belgium

Source: *BioIn 15; CamGWoT; ConAmD;
ConAu 1NR, 2AS, 45, 48NR; ConDr 73,
77, 82, 88, 93; ConLC 3; ConTFT 3;
CroCD; CyWA 97; DcLB 7; Ent;
IntAu&W 82; IntDcT 2; IntWWP 77, 82;
McGEWD 72, 84; ModWD; NatPD 77;
NotNAT; OxCThe 83; PIP&P; RAdv 13-
2; WhoAm 74, 76, 78, 84, 86, 88, 90, 92,
94, 95, 96, 97, 98, 99, 2000; WhoEnt 92,
98; WhoThe 72, 77, 81; WhoUSWr 88;
WhoWor 74, 76; WhoWrEP 89, 92, 95;
WorAu 1970; WrDr 76, 80, 82, 84, 86,
88, 90, 92, 94, 96, 98, 99, 2000*

Vanity

[Denise Mathews]
American. Singer, Actor
Recorded album *Nasty Girl* with Vanity
6; solo *Wild Animal*, 1985; in film *The
Last Dragon*, 1985.
b. Jan 3, 1961 in Niagara Falls, New
York
Source: *BioIn 14, 15, 16; DrBlPA 90;
IntAu&W 86*

VanKamp, Merete

[Merete Kamp]
Danish. Actor
Played Daisy in TV movie "Princess
Daisy," 1983.
b. Nov 17, 1961 in Kolding, Denmark
Source: *BioIn 13; ConTFT 4*

Van Lew, Elizabeth

American. Spy
VA unionist; federal agent during Civil
War.
b. Oct 17, 1818 in Richmond, Virginia
d. Sep 25, 1900 in Richmond, Virginia
Source: *BioIn 3, 6, 9, 11, 19, 22, 24;
GoodHs; HerW, 84; InWom; NotAW;
WebAMB; WomMil*

Van Leyden, Lucas

[Lucas Hugensz]
Dutch. Artist
Noted for copperplate engravings;
considered founder of Dutch genre
painting.
b. 1494 in Leiden, Netherlands
d. 1533 in Leiden, Netherlands
Source: *AtlBL; DutArt; McGDA; NewCol
75; OxCArt*

Van Loon, Hendrik Willem

American. Historian, Author
Wrote six best-sellers including *The
Story of Mankind*, 1921.
b. Jan 14, 1882 in Rotterdam,
Netherlands
d. Mar 10, 1944 in New York, New
York
Source: *AmAu&B; AmNatBi; AnCL;
AuBYP 2, 3; Benet 87; BenetAL 91;
BioIn 1, 2, 3, 4, 7, 8, 9, 12, 14, 22;
CamBiEn; ChamBiD; ChhPo S2;
ChlBkCr; ConAmA; ConAmL; ConAu
117; CurBio 44; DcAmB S3; DcLEL;
DcNAA; JBA 34; LinLib L, S; LngCTC;
NatCAB 33; NewbMB 1922; OxCAmL
65, 83, 95; REn; REnAL; ScF&FL 1;
SmATA 18; TwCA, SUP; WhAm 2;*

WhAmArt 85; WhNAA; WorAu 1900; WrChl

Vannelli, Gino
Canadian. Singer, Songwriter
One of first pop artists to perform
   without guitars or bass "Wheels of
   Life," 1979; "Living Inside Myself."
b. Jun 16, 1952 in Montreal, Quebec,
   Canada
Source: *ASCAP 80; BioIn 11, 12;
LegTOT; RkOn 85*

Van Niel, Cornelius B(ernardus)
American. Biologist, Educator
Microbiologist who was first to explain
   photosynthesis.
b. Nov 4, 1897 in Haarlem, Netherlands
d. Mar 10, 1985 in Carmel, California
Source: *AmMWSc 82; ConAu 115;
FacFETw; McGMS 80; WhAm 8;
WhoAm 76*

Van Nostrand, David
American. Publisher
Publishing co. was largest US outlet for
   scientific, military, technical works.
b. Dec 5, 1811 in New York, New York
d. Jun 14, 1886
Source: *AmAu&B; ApCAB; DcAmB*

Vanocur, Sander
American. Broadcast Journalist
With ABC News since 1977; chief
   diplomatic correspondent since 1981.
b. Jan 8, 1928 in Cleveland, Ohio
Source: *BiDAmNC; BioIn 6, 9; ConAu
109, 120; ConTFT 12, 23; CurBio 63;
EncTelN; EncTwCJ; IntMPA 84, 86, 92,
94, 96; LegTOT; LesBEnT, 92; WhoAm
74, 76, 78, 80, 82, 84, 86; WhoHol A;
WhoSSW 73*

Van Paassen, Pierre
[Pieter Antonie Laurusse Van Paassen]
Canadian. Journalist, Author, Clergy
Religious writings include *Days of Our
   Years,* 1939; *To Number Our Days,*
   1964.
b. Feb 7, 1895 in Goreum, Netherlands
d. Jan 8, 1968 in New York, New York
Source: *AmAu&B; BenetAL 91; BioIn 1,
4, 7, 8, 11, 22; CurBio 42, 68; EncAJ;
REnAL; TwCA, SUP; WhAm 4A; WorAu
1900*

Van Patten, Dick Vincent
American. Actor
Appeared in "I Remember Mama,"
   1949-57; played Tom Bradford on
   "Eight Is Enough," 1977-81.
b. Dec 9, 1928 in Kew Gardens, New
   York
Source: *BiE&WWA; BioIn 12; EncAFC;
HalFC 84, 88; IntMPA 86, 92; NotNAT;
WhoAm 78, 80, 82, 84, 86, 88, 92, 94,
95, 96, 97; WhoEnt 92, 98; WhoHol A;
WhoThe 77; WorAl; WorAlBi*

Van Patten, Joyce
American. Actor
Began career as child actress in radio,
   stage; TV shows include "Danny
   Kaye Show."
b. Mar 9, 1934 in New York, New York
Source: *BiE&WWA; ConTFT 4;
EncAFC; FilmEn; FilmgC; HalFC 80,
84, 88; IntMPA 88, 92; LegTOT;
NotNAT; WhoEnt 92; WhoHol 92, A;
WhoThe 72, 77, 81*

Van Patten, Vince(nt)
American. Actor, Tennis Player
Supporting actor, 1970s; films include
   Wild Horses; son of Dick Van Patten.
b. Oct 17, 1957 in New York, New York
Source: *BioIn 14, 21; ItaFilm; NewYTBS
84; WhoHol 92, A; WhoIntT*

Van Peebles, Mario
American. Actor
Films included *The Cotton Club,* 1984;
   Heartbreak Ridge, 1987; *New Jack
   City,* 1991.
b. Jan 15, 1957 in Mexico City, Mexico
Source: *BioIn 15, 16; ConBlB 2;
ConTFT 6, 13, 22; CurBio 93;
DcTwCCu 5; DrBlPA 90; InB&W 85;
IntMPA 92, 94, 96; IntWW 97, 98, 2000;
LegTOT; NewYTBS 91; WhoAm 99,
2000; WhoBlA 7; WhoEnt 98; WhoHol
92*

Van Peebles, Melvin
American. Actor, Dramatist, Composer
Wrote, directed play *Ain't Supposed to
   Die a Natural Death,* 1971.
b. Aug 21, 1932 in Chicago, Illinois
Source: *AfrAmAl 8; ASCAP 80; BiDAfM;
BioIn 8, 9, 10, 12, 13, 15, 16, 17, 19,
20, 21, 23; BlkAmP; BlkAWP; BlksAmF;
BlkWr 1, 2, 3; CelR; ConAu 27NR,
67NR, 82NR, 85; ConBlAP 88; ConBlB
7; ConDr 77D, 82D, 88D; ConLC 2, 20;
ConTFT 7, 18; DcTwCCu 5; DrBlPA,
90; Ebony 1; EncAFC; FilmEn; FilmgC;
HalFC 80, 84, 88; InB&W 80, 85;
IntDcF 1-2; IntMPA 77, 80, 86, 92, 94,
96; LegTOT; LinLib L; LivgBAA;
MiSFD 9; MorBAP; NegAl 76;
NewYTBE 72; NotBlAM; NotNAT;
PIP&P A; SchCGBL; SelBAAf; SelBAAu;
WhoAfA 9, 10, 11, 12; WhoBlA 1, 2, 3,
4, 5, 6, 7, 8; WhoHol 92, A; WhoThe 77,
81*

Van Rensselaer, Kiliaen
Dutch. Merchant, Colonizer
Director of the Dutch West India
   Company and first patroon of
   Rensselaerswyck Manor in the colony
   of New Netherland.
b. c. 1580 in Amsterdam, Netherlands
d. 1643 in Amsterdam, Netherlands
Source: *EncCRAm; EncWB 98;
McGEWB*

Van Rensselaer, Stephen
American. Army Officer, Politician
Congressman from NY, 1822-29; first
   pres., NY Board of Agriculture, 1820.
b. Nov 1, 1764 in New York, New York

d. Jan 26, 1839 in Albany, New York
Source: *AmBi; AmNatBi; ApCAB;
BiAUS; BiDrAC; BiDrUSC 89; BiInAmS;
BioIn 19; CamDcAB; CyEd; DcAmB;
DcAmMiB; Drake; EncAAH; EncAR;
EncWar; HarEnMi; NatCAB 2;
OxCAmH; WebAB 74, 79; WebAMB;
WhAm HS; WhAmP*

Van Rooy, Anton
Dutch. Opera Singer
Bass-baritone; Wagnerian star, banned
   from Bayreuth, 1903.
b. Jan 1, 1870 in Rotterdam, Netherlands
d. Nov 28, 1932 in Munich, Germany
Source: *BakBD 78, 84; MetOEnc;
NewEOp 71; NewGrDA 86; NewGrDM
80; PenDiMP*

Van Sant, Gus
American. Filmmaker
Films directed include *Drugstore
   Cowboy,* 1989; *My Own Private
   Idaho.*
b. 1952 in Louisville, Kentucky
Source: *Au&Arts 17; ConAu 152;
ConTFT 26; CurBio 92; IntMPA 94, 96;
IntWW 2000; LegTOT; News 92, 92-2;
NewYTBS 91; WhoAm 95, 96, 97, 98,
99, 2000*

Van Shelton, Ricky
American. Singer, Songwriter
Country singer; debut album *Wild-Eyed
   Dream,* 1987 went gold.
b. Jan 12, 1952 in Grit, Virginia
Source: *BioIn 16; ConMus 5; WhoAm
90, 92, 94, 95; WhoEnt 92*

Van Slyke, Andy
[Andrew James Van Slyke]
American. Baseball Player
Centerfielder, St. Louis Cardinals 1979-
   87; currently with the Philadelphia
   Phillies.
b. Dec 21, 1960 in Utica, New York
Source: *Ballpl 90; BioIn 16, 21; News
92; WhoAm 92, 94, 95, 96, 97; WhoE
95; WhoSpor; WhoWor 96*

Van Slyke, Helen Lenore Vogt
American. Author
Wrote best-sellers *A Necessary Woman,*
   1979; *No Love Lost,* 1979.
b. Jul 9, 1919 in Washington, District of
   Columbia
d. Jul 3, 1979 in New York, New York
Source: *AmNatBi; ConAu 89; InWom
SUP; WhoAdv 72; WrDr 76*

Van't Hoff, Jacobus Henricus
Dutch. Chemist
First to win Nobel Prize, 1901;
   researched stereochemistry.
b. Aug 30, 1852 in Rotterdam,
   Netherlands
d. Mar 1, 1911 in Berlin, Germany
Source: *AsBiEn; BiESc; BioIn 14, 15,
19; DcScB; Dis&D; InSci; LarDcSc;
McGEWB; RanHWDS; WhoNob, 90, 95;
WorAl; WorScD*

Van Vechten, Carl

American. Author, Critic
Wrote *Parties*, 1930; *Pavlova*, 1947.
b. Jun 17, 1880 in Cedar Rapids, Iowa
d. Dec 21, 1964 in New York, New
    York
Source: *AmAu&B; AmNatBi; AmWr S2;
BakBD 78, 84, 92; BakBDTw; Benet 87,
96; BenetAL 91; BiDAmM; BioIn 2, 3, 4,
5, 6, 7, 8, 12, 15, 16, 20, 22; CmpQue;
CnDAL; ConAmA; ConAmL; ConAu 89;
ConLC 33; ConPhot 82, 88; CyWA 58,
97; DancEn 78; DcAmB S7; DcLB 4, 9,
51A; DcLEL; EncALit; EncWB 99;
GayLesB; GrWrEL N; ICPEnP A;
LegTOT; LngCTC; MacBEP; NewGrDA
86; NotNAT B; OxCAmL 65, 83, 95;
OxCTwCL; PenC AM; REn; REnAL;
RfGAmL 87, 94; RGTwCWr; TwCA,
SUP; WebE&AL; WhAm 4; WorAu 1900*

Van Vleck, John Hasbrouck

American. Physicist
Shared Nobel Prize in physics, 1977,
    with Anderson, Mott; studied
    electronic structures.
b. Mar 13, 1899 in Middletown,
    Connecticut
d. Nov 28, 1980 in Cambridge,
    Massachusetts
Source: *AmNatBi; AnObit 1980; BioIn
12, 13, 14, 15, 19, 20; CamBiEn;
CamDcAB; CamDcSc; ChamBiD; ConAu
102; DcAmB S10; DcScB S2; IntWW 74;
LarDcSc; NewYTBS 80; RanHWDS;
WhAm 7; Who 74; WhoAm 74; WhoNob,
90, 95; WhoWor 74; WorScD*

Van Vooren, Monique

American. Actor, Author
Appeared in movie *Damn Yankees*, 1958;
    wrote novel *Night Sanctuary*, 1981.
b. Mar 17, 1933 in Brussels, Belgium
Source: *BiE&WWA; ConAu 107;
ForYSC; InWom; MotPP; WhoAm 74,
76; WhoAmW 70, 72; WhoHol 92, A;
WhoHrs 80*

Van Wachem, Lodewijk
Christiaan

Dutch. Business Executive
President of Royal Dutch Petroleum Co.
    since 1982.
b. Jul 31, 1931 in Pangkalan Brandan,
    Dutch East Indies
Source: *BioIn 15; Dun&B 90; IntWW 78,
79, 80, 81, 82, 83, 89, 91, 93, 97, 98,
2000; St&PR 91; Who 82, 83, 85, 88,
90, 92, 94, 98, 99, 2000; WhoAm 88, 90,
92, 94, 95, 96, 97, 98, 99, 2000; WhoFI
00, 89, 92, 94, 96, 98; WhoSSW 88, 91,
93; WhoWor 89, 93, 95, 96, 97, 98, 99,
2000*

Van Westerborg, Edward

American. Publisher
Founded *Facts on File*, 1941; headed
    publications until 1975.
b. 1900?, Netherlands
d. May 7, 1988 in Walnut Creek,
    California

Van Zandt, Marie

American. Opera Singer
Coloratura soprano; Paris Opera-
    Comique, 1880s.
b. Oct 8, 1861 in New York, New York
d. Dec 31, 1919 in Cannes, France
Source: *AmWom; ApCAB; BakBD 78,
84; BioIn 22; InWom; NewEOp 71;
NewGrDM 80; PenDiMP*

Vanzant, Iyanla (Rhonda)

American. Author, Lecturer, Clergy,
    Lawyer
Known for her powerful speaking and
    writing abilities, minister and former
    lawyer is dedicated to teaching women
    of color to improve life for themselves
    and their communities; best-selling
    books include *Acts of Faith*, 1993, and
    Faith in the Valley, 1996.
b. Sep 13, 1953 in New York, New
    York

Van Zant, Ronnie

[Lynyrd Skynard; Ronald Van Zant]
American. Musician, Singer
Founding member of one of best rock
    bands in history, 1973-77; group
    ended when he and others were killed
    in plane crash.
b. Jan 15, 1949 in Jacksonville, Florida
d. Oct 20, 1977 in Gillsburg, Mississippi
Source: *BioIn 11, 24; LegTOT;
WhoRocM 82*

Vanzetti, Bartolomeo

[Sacco and Vanzetti]
Italian. Political Activist
Tried, executed for murder during
    robbery; case became most notorious
    of century due to widespread charges
    of mistrial.
b. Jun 11, 1888 in Villafalletto, Italy
d. Aug 23, 1927 in Boston,
    Massachusetts
Source: *AmBi; BiDAmL; BioIn 2, 3, 4, 5,
6, 7, 8, 9, 10, 11, 12, 13, 14, 15, 16, 17,
20; CopCroC; DcAmB; DcAmSR;
LegTOT; REn; WebAB 74, 79; WhAm 4;
WhDW; WorAl; WorAlBi*

Varda, Agnes

French. Screenwriter, Director
Directed *Elsa*, 1966; *Lions Love*, 1969.
b. May 30, 1928 in Brussels, Belgium
Source: *BiDFilm, 81, 94; BioIn 7, 9, 12,
13, 15, 16; ChamBiD; ConAu 116, 122;
ConLC 16; ContDcW 89; ConTFT 8;
CurBio 70; DcFM; DcTwCCu 2;
EncEurC; FilmEn; FilmgC; HalFC 80,
84, 88; IntAu&W 76, 77, 82; IntDcF 1-2,
2-2; IntDcWB; IntMPA 79, 80, 81, 82,
84, 86, 88; IntWW 74, 75, 76, 77, 78,
79, 80, 81, 82, 83, 89, 91, 93, 97, 98,
2000; IntWWW 2; InWom SUP; ItaFilm;
MiSFD 9; OxCFilm; ReelWom;
WhoAmW 70, 72; WhoFr 79; WhoHol A;
WhoWor 74, 76, 78, 84, 91; WomFilm;
WomWMM; WorEFlm; WorFDir 2*

Vardon, Harry

"Great Triumvirate"
English. Golfer
With James Braid, JH Taylor, dominated
    game, late 19th, early 20th c; only
    player to win British Open six times.
b. May 9, 1870 in Isle of Jersey,
    England
d. Mar 20, 1937 in London, England
Source: *BioIn 9, 13; CamBiEn;
ChamBiD; WhoGolf*

Vare, Glenna Collett

American. Golfer
Dominated women's golf, 1922-35; won
    49 amateur titles; Vare Trophy, given
    to women golfers, named for her;
    charter member, Hall of Fame.
b. Jun 20, 1903 in New Haven,
    Connecticut
d. Feb 3, 1989 in Gulfstream, Florida
Source: *BiDAmSp OS; BioIn 11, 16, 17,
24; FacFETw; GoodHs; InWom SUP;
NewYTBS 89; OutWomA; ScrEAmL 2;
WhoGolf; WorAl; WorAlBi*

Varese, Edgar

American. Composer, Author
Founded, directed International
    Composers Guild, 1921-27; developed
    electronic music, 1917.
b. Dec 22, 1883 in Paris, France
d. Nov 6, 1965 in New York, New York
Source: *AtlBL; BakBD 78, 84; BriBkM
80; DcAmB S7; DcCM; DcTwCC;
FacFETw; NewGrDM 80; OxCMus;
WebAB 74; WhAm 4*

Varesi, Felice

French. Opera Singer
Baritone, noted for Verdi roles.
b. 1813 in Calais, France
d. Mar 13, 1889 in Milan, Italy
Source: *BakBD 84, 92; CmOp;
MetOEnc; NewEOp 71; NewGrDM 80;
NewGrDO; OxDcOp*

Vargas, Alberto

[Joaquin Alberto Vargas y Chavez]
American. Artist
Created pinups for *Esquire*; *Playboy*
    magazines.
b. Feb 9, 1895 in Arequipa, Peru
d. Dec 30, 1983 in Los Angeles,
    California
Source: *BioIn 11; NewYTBS 83*

Vargas, Getulio Dornelles

Brazilian. Lawyer, Political Leader
Pres. of Brazil, 1930-45.
b. Apr 19, 1883 in Sao Borja, Brazil
d. Aug 24, 1954 in Rio de Janeiro,
    Brazil
Source: *BiDLAmC; CamBiEn; CurBio
40, 51, 54; DcPol; EncWB 98; LatAmLi;
McGEWB; WhAm 3; WhDW; WhWW-II*

Vargas Llosa, Mario

Peruvian. Author
Work includes *The Real Life of
    Alejandro Mayta*, 1986.
b. Mar 28, 1936 in Arequipa, Peru

Source: *BeaEPF; Benet 87; BenetAL 91; BiCoLiE; BioIn 7, 10, 11, 12, 14, 15, 16, 17, 18, 19, 20, 21, 22, 23; CasWL; CnDWLB 3; ConAu 18NR, 32NR, 73; ConFLW 84; ConLC 3, 6, 9, 10, 15, 31, 42, 85; CurBio 76; CyWA 89, 97; DcArts; DcCLAA; DcCPSAm; DcHiB; DcLB 145; DcTwCCu 3; EncLatA; EncWB 98; EncWL 1, 2, 2S, 3; FacFETw; HispLC; HispWr; IntAu&W 89; IntvLAW; IntWW 74, 75, 76, 77, 78, 79, 80, 81, 82, 83, 89, 91, 93, 97, 98, 2000; LatAmLi; LatAmWr; LegTOT; LiExTwC; MagSWL; MajTwCW 1; ModLAL; NewYTBS 89, 90; Novels; OxCSpan; PenC AM; PostFic; RAdv 14, 13-2; SpAmA; TwCWr; Who 98, 99, 2000; WhoAm 86, 88; WhoTwCL; WhoWor 74, 78, 80, 82, 84, 87, 91, 93, 95; WorAu 1970*

Varipapa, Andy
American. Bowler
Won national bowling championships in 1940s.
b. 1894
d. Aug 25, 1984 in Huntington, New York
Source: *BioIn 1, 10; NewYTBS 84; WhoSpor*

Varley, F(rederick) H(orseman)
[Group of Seven]
Canadian. Artist
Landscape, portrait painter; original member of group influential in Canadian painting, 1920s; famous for *Stormy Weather, Georgian Bay,* 1920.
b. Jan 2, 1881 in Sheffield, England
d. Sep 8, 1969 in Toronto, Ontario, Canada
Source: *BioIn 11; CreCan 1; IlBEAAW; McGDA; WhoAmA 78N*

Varmus, Harold E(lliot)
American. Government Official, Scientist
With J. Michael Bishop won the 1989 Nobel Prize for Physiology or medicine for their work on the origins of cancer; director, National Institutes of Health, 1993-99; pres. and chief executive, Sloan-Kettering Cancer Center, 2000—.
b. Dec 18, 1939 in Oceanside, New York
Source: *AmMWSc 82, 86, 89, 92, 95, 98; CamDcAB; ChamBiD; CurBio 96; IntWW 91; LarDcSc; RanHWDS; Who 92; WhoAm 90; WhoNob 90; WhoWest 92; WhoWor 91; WorAlBi*

Varnay, Astrid
Swedish. Opera Singer
Dramatic soprano; made NY Met., debut, 1941, substituting for Lotte Lehmann without rehearsal.
b. Apr 25, 1918 in Stockholm, Sweden
Source: *BakBD 78, 84; BiDamM; BioIn 2, 3, 4, 6, 10, 11, 23, 24; BriBkM 80; CamDcAB; CmOp; CurBio 51; IntWWM 80, 90; InWom, SUP; MetOEnc; MusSN; NewAmDM; NewEOp 71; NewGrDA 86; NewGrDM 80; NewYTBS 74; OxDcOp; PenDiMP; WhoMus 72*

Varnedoe, (John) Kirk (Train)
American. Art Historian
Director of the Dept. of Painting and Sculpture at the Museum of Modern Art, 1989—.
b. Jan 18, 1946 in Savannah, Georgia
Source: *BioIn 15, 16, 17; CamDcAB; CurBio 91; NewYTBS 90; WhoAm 90, 92, 94, 95, 96, 97, 98, 99, 2000; WhoAmA 76, 78, 80, 82, 84, 86, 89, 91, 93, 1999; WhoE 95*

Varney, Jim
American. Actor
Plays TV commercial character Ernest P Worrell; star of film *Ernest Goes to Camp,* 1987.
b. Jun 15, 1949 in Lexington, Kentucky
d. Feb 10, 2000 in White House, Tennessee
Source: *ConNews 85-4; ConTFT 11; IntMPA 92, 94, 96; WhoHol 92*

Varnhagen, Francisco Adolfo de
Brazilian. Historian
Best known for his colonial history of Brazil, *Historia geral do Brasil.*
b. 1816
d. 1878
Source: *BioIn 8; EncWB 98; GloEncH; LatAmLi; McGEWB*

Varro, Marcus Terentius
Roman. Scholar, Author
Prolific writer is considered the greatest Roman scholar; it is estimated that he wrote 74 separate works in 620 volumes covering all aspects of contemporary learning.
b. 116BC in Reate
d. 27BC
Source: *BiD&SB; BioIn 5; CamBiEn; CasWL; ChamBiD; DcScB; EncWB 98; Grk&L; InSci; LibrCom; McGEWB; NewGrDM 80; OxCClL, 89; OxCThe 83; PenC CL; REn; WhDW*

Varsi, Diane
American. Actor
Won Oscar for her first film *Peyton Place,* 1957.
b. Feb 23, 1938 in San Francisco, California
d. Nov 19, 1992 in Los Angeles, California
Source: *AnObit 1992; BioIn 18, 19; FilmgC; ForYSC; HalFC 80, 84, 88; IntMPA 84, 86, 88, 92; InWom SUP; LegTOT; MotPP; MovMk; NewYTBE 72; WhoAm 74; WhoHol 92, A; WorAl*

Varthema, Ludovico di
Italian. Adventurer
Traveled widely in the East and was the first European to visit several sites.
b. c. 1470 in Bologna, Italy
d. 1517 in Rome, Italy
Source: *EncWB 98; McGEWB; WhWE*

Varviso, Silvio
Swiss. Conductor
Director, Stockholm Royal Opera, 1965-72; Paris Opera, since 1981.
b. Feb 26, 1924 in Zurich, Switzerland
Source: *BakBD 78, 84, 92; BakBDTw; IntWWM 90; MetOEnc; NewAmDM; NewEOp 71; NewGrDM 80; NewGrDO; PenDiMP; WhoOp 76; WhoWor 74*

Vasarely, Victor
French. Artist
Considered originator of post-war Op Art; geometric works include *Orion MC,* 1963.
b. Apr 9, 1908 in Pecs, Austria-Hungary
d. Mar 15, 1997 in Paris, France
Source: *BioIn 8, 9, 10, 22, 23; ClaDrA; ConArt 77, 83, 89; CurBio 71, 97N; DcArts; DcCAr 81; DcTwArt; DcTwCCu 2; EncWB, 98; IntDcAA 90; IntWW 74, 75, 76, 77, 78, 79, 80, 81, 82, 83, 89, 91, 93; McGDA; OxCTwCA; OxDcArt; PhDcTCA 77; PrintW 83, 85; WhAm 12; WhoAm 74, 76, 78, 80, 82, 84, 86, 88, 95; WhoArt 80, 82, 84; WhoFI 85; WhoFr 79; WhoWor 82, 84, 87, 89; WorArt 1950*

Vasari, Giorgio
Italian. Architect, Artist, Author
Published *Lives of Most Eminent Painters and Sculptors,* 1550, first work of art history.
b. Jul 30, 1511 in Arezzo, Italy
d. Jun 27, 1574 in Florence, Italy
Source: *AtlBL; Benet 87, 96; BiD&SB; BioIn 14, 18, 21; CamBiEn; CamGWoT; CasWL; ChamBiD; ClaDrA; DcArch; DcArts; DcCathB; DcEuL; DcItL 1, 2; EncHiCA; EncWB 98; EncWT; EuAu; GloEncH; IntDcAA 90; IntDcAr; LegTOT; LinLib L, S; MacEA; McGDA; McGEWB; NewC; NewCBEL; OxCArt; OxCCAA; OxCEng 67, 85, 95; OxDcArt; PenC EUR; REn; WhDW; WhoArch; WorAl; WorAlBi*

Vasconcelos (Calderon), Jose
Mexican. Philosopher, Sociologist, Historian
Best known for his four-volume autobiography documenting his experiences around the time of the Mexican Revolution.
b. Feb 27, 1882 in Oaxaca, Mexico
d. Jun 30, 1959 in Mexico City, Mexico

Vashti
Persian. Ruler
Dethroned, maybe beheaded, for refusing to flaunt her beauty for group of princes at her husband's, the king's, request.
b. fl. 519BC
Source: *BioIn 9; EncAmaz 91; NewCol 75*

Vasily III
[Vasily Ivanovich]
Russian. Ruler
Grand prince of Moscow 1505-1533; consolidated several independent

principalities into Muscovite state;
father of Ivan the Terrible.
b. 1479
d. Dec 3, 1533 in Moscow, Russia

Vassallo, Jesse
American. Swimmer
World's best individual medley
   swimmer, 1978-82.
b. 1961
Source: *BioIn 11, 13; NewYTBS 84*

Vassar, Matthew
English. Brewer, Merchant
Founded Vassar College, 1865.
b. Apr 29, 1792 in East Tuddingham,
   England
d. Jun 23, 1868 in Poughkeepsie, New
   York
Source: *AmBi; AmNatBi; ApCAB; BioIn
10, 15; CyAL 2; DcAmB; HarEnUS;
LinLib L, S; NatCAB 5; NewCol 75;
OxCAmH; TwCBDA; WebAB 74, 79;
WebBD 83; WhAm HS*

Vassilenko, Sergei
Russian. Composer
Wrote operas *Christopher Columbus,*
1933; *Buran,* 1939; works inspired by
Russian folk songs, the East.
b. Mar 30, 1872 in Moscow, Russia
d. Mar 11, 1956 in Moscow, Union of
   Soviet Socialist Republics
Source: *BakBD 78, 84; NewEOp 71*

Vassiliou, George (Vassos)
Cypriot. Political Leader
Marketing executive was elected
   president of Republic of Cyprus as an
   independent candidate in 1988; he
   favored a free market approach and
   entrepreneurism.
b. May 20, 1931 in Famagusta, Cyprus
Source: *IntWW 89, 91, 93, 97, 98, 2000;
Who 98, 99, 2000; WhoWor 82, 84, 87,
89, 91, 93, 95, 96, 97, 98, 99, 2000*

Vauban, Sebastien LePrestre de
French. Engineer, Military Leader
Foremost military engineer under Louis
   the XIV, contributed to France's
   domination of Western Europe.
b. May 15, 1633 in Saint-Leger-de-
   Foucherest, France
d. Mar 30, 1707 in Paris, France
Source: *BbD; BiD&SB; DcScB; EncWB
99; MacEA; OxCFr; WhoArch; WhoEc
81; WhoMilH 76; WorAl*

Vaudreuil-Cavagnal, Marquis de
[Pierre Francois de Rigaud]
Canadian. Politician
Governor of Louisiana and governor
   general of New France, he surrendered
   Canada to the British in 1760.
b. Nov 22, 1698 in Quebec, Canada
d. 1778, France

Vaughan, Arky
[Joseph Floyd Vaughan]
American. Baseball Player
Shortstop, 1932-43, 1947-48, mostly with
   Pittsburgh; led NL in batting, 1935;
   had lifetime .318 batting average.
b. Mar 9, 1912 in Clifty, Arkansas
d. Aug 30, 1952 in Eagleville, California
Source: *AmNatBi; Ballpl 90; BiDAmSp
BB; BioIn 14, 15; CulEncB; LegTOT;
WhoProB 73; WhoSpor*

Vaughan, Bill
[William Edward Vaughan]
American. Journalist, Author
Wrote nationally syndicated column
   "Starbeams."
b. Oct 8, 1915 in Saint Louis, Missouri
d. Feb 26, 1977 in Kansas City, Kansas
Source: *BiDAmNC; BioIn 6, 11; ConAu
5R, 69; WhAm 7; WhoAm 74, 76;
WhoMW 74, 76*

Vaughan, Harry Hawkins
American. Army Officer
Military aide to Harry S Truman during
   vice presidential, presidential years,
   1944-53.
b. Nov 26, 1893 in Glasgow, Missouri
d. May 20, 1981 in Fort Belvoir,
   Virginia
Source: *AmNatBi; BioIn 1, 2, 8, 11, 12;
CurBio 49, 81; PolProf T*

Vaughan, Henry
Welsh. Poet
Best known for *The Retreat; The World.*
b. Apr 17, 1622 in Llansantfraed, Wales
d. Apr 23, 1695 in Newton, England
Source: *Alli; AtlBL; BbD; Benet 87, 96;
BiCoLiE; BiD&SB; BiDRP&D; BioIn 1,
2, 3, 5, 6, 7, 10, 12, 19, 21, 24;
BlmGEL; BritAu; BritWr 2; CamBiEn;
CamGEL; CasWL; ChamBiD; ChhPo,
S2; CnE&AP; CroE&S; CrtT 1; CyWA
97; DcArts; DcEnA; DcEnL; DcEuL;
DcLEL; DcNaB; EvLB; GrWrEL P;
IlEncMy; LinLib S; LngCEL; MouLC 1;
NewC; NewCBEL; OxCBrHi; OxCEng
67; PenC ENG; RAdv 1, 14, 13-1; REn;
WebE&AL; WhoChr*

Vaughan, Sarah Lois
American. Singer
Jazz vocalist, pianist; career took off
   after winning contest at Apollo
   Theater, NYC, 1940s.
b. Mar 27, 1924 in Newark, New Jersey
d. Apr 3, 1990 in Hidden Hills,
   California
Source: *AfrAmAl 8; BakBD 84; BiDJaz;
BioIn 13, 14, 15, 16; BioNews 74;
CamBiEn; CamDcAB; CelR 90;
ChamBiD; CmpEPM; ConMus 2;
ContDcW 89; CurBio 57, 80, 90, 90N;
DrBlPA 90; EncJzS; EncWB 98;
FacFETw; IntWW 83, 89; InWom SUP;
NegAl 89; NewAmDM; NewGrDA 86;
NewGrDJ 88; News 90; NewYTBS 90;
NotBlAW 1; OxCPMus; PenEncP;
ScrEAmL 2; WhoAm 86, 88; WhoAmW
85, 87; WhoBlA 4, 6, 7N; WhoWor 84,
89; WorAlBi*

Vaughan, Stevie Ray
American. Musician
Guitarist; Grammy for "In Step," 1990;
   died in helicopter crash.
b. Oct 3, 1954 in Dallas, Texas
d. Aug 27, 1990 in East Troy, Wisconsin
Source: *AllMGBl 1, 2; AmNatBi; AnObit
1990; BioIn 13, 16; Blues; CamDcAB;
CmpEGui; EncPR&S 89; EncRkSt;
FacFETw; News 91-1; NewYTBS 90;
OnThGG; PenEncP; ScrEAmL 2*

Vaughan Williams, Ralph
English. Composer
Works include chorals, songs,
   symphonies including "London,"
   1914; "Pastoral," 1922.
b. Oct 12, 1872 in Ampney, England
d. Aug 26, 1958 in London, England
Source: *AtlBL; BakBD 78, 84, 92;
BakBDTw; BakDcM; Benet 87, 96; BioIn
1, 2, 3, 4, 5, 6, 7, 8, 9, 10, 11, 12, 14,
15, 16, 20, 23, 24; BriBkM 80;
CamBiEn; ChamBiD; CmOp; CompSN;
SUP; ConAu 115; CurBio 53, 58;
DcArts; DcCM; DcCom 77; DcCom&M
79; DcNaB 1951; DcTwCC, A; EncWB
98; FacFETw; GrBr; IntDcOp; LegTOT;
LinLib S; MakMC; McGEWB; MetOEnc;
MusMk; NewAmDM; NewEOp 71;
NewGrDM 80; NewGrDO; NewOxM;
ObitT 1951; OxCBrHi; OxCEng 85, 95;
OxCFilm; OxCMus; OxDcOp; PenDiMP
A; RAdv 14; REn; WhAm 3; WhDW;
WhE&EA; WhoChr*

Vaughn, Mo
[Maurice Samuel Vaughn]
American. Baseball Player
First baseman for the Boston Red Sox,
   1991—; named the American
   League's Most Valuable Player in
   1995 for his consistently excellent
   hitting, base stealing, team leadership,
   and community service.
b. Dec 15, 1967 in Norwalk, Connecticut
Source: *BioIn 22, 23, 24; ConBlB 16;
News 99-2, 1999; WhoAfA 9, 10, 11, 12;
WhoBlA 8*

Vaughn, Robert
American. Actor
Played Napoleon Solo in TV series "The
   Man from UNCLE," 1964-67.
b. Nov 22, 1932 in New York, New
   York
Source: *BioIn 7, 8, 10, 11, 17; BioNews
74; BlueB 76; ConAu 61; ConTFT 3, 5,
18; CurBio 67; FilmEn; FilmgC;
ForYSC; HalFC 80, 84, 88; IntMPA 75,
76, 77, 78, 79, 80, 81, 82, 84, 86, 88,
92, 94, 96; ItaFilm; LegTOT; MotPP;
MovMk; OsStAZ; WhoAm 74, 76, 78, 80,
82, 84, 86, 88, 90, 92, 94, 95, 96, 97;
WhoHol 92, A; WhoHrs 80; WhoTelC;
WorAlBi; WorEFlm*

Vaux, Calvert
American. Architect
Park landscapes include Central Park,
   NYC; South Park, Chicago.
b. Dec 20, 1824 in London, England

d. Nov 19, 1895 in New York, New
York
Source: *Alli; AmBi; AmNatBi; ApCAB;
BiDAmAr; BioIn 2, 3, 9, 13, 23;
CambiEn; CamDcAB; DcAmAu;
DcAmB; DcArch; DcNAA; HarEnUS;
IntDcAr; MacEA; NatCAB 9; OxCAmH;
TwCBDA; WhAm HS; WhoArch*

Vavilov, Nikolai Ivanovich

Russian. Botanist, Geneticist
Scientist is best known for his theory on
the origin of cultivated plants and his
law of the homologous series of
inherited variation.
b. Nov 25, 1887 in Moscow, Russia
d. Jan 26, 1943 in Magadan, Russia
Source: *BiDSovU; BioIn 1, 3, 5, 7, 8, 10,
11, 12, 14, 15, 16, 18; ChamBiD;
EncWB 98; LarDcSc; McGEWB; WhDW*

Vazquez, Horacio

Dominican. Political Leader
Twice president of the Dominican
Republic, he officiated over the most
democratic era in the history of the
country.
b. 1860
d. 1936
Source: *EncWB 98*

Veblen, Thorstein Bunde

American. Economist
Divided society into economic classes;
wrote *The Theory of the Leisure Class*,
1899.
b. Jul 30, 1857 in Valders, Wisconsin
d. Aug 3, 1929 in Palo Alto, California
Source: *AmAu&B; AmBi; AmNatBi;
CambiEn; CamDcAB; ChamBiD; ConAu
165; DcAmB; DcAmSR; DcLEL; EncAB-
H 1974, 1996; EncWB 98; EvLB; LinLib
S; LngCTC; ModAL 4; OxCAmH;
OxCAmL 65, 83; OxCTwCL; PenC AM;
REn; REnAL; WhoTwCL; WorAl; WorAu
1900*

Vedder, Eddie

[Pearl Jam; Eddie Mueller]
American. Singer, Songwriter
Debut album *Ten*, 1991.
b. Dec 23, 1964 in Chicago, Illinois

Vedder, Elihu

American. Artist
Painted five decorative panels, mosaic
Minerva in the Congressional Library
in Washington, DC.
b. Feb 26, 1836 in New York, New
York
d. Jan 29, 1923 in Rome, Italy
Source: *AmAu&B; AmBi; AmLY;
AmNatBi; ApCAB, X; ArtsNiC; BenetAL
91; BioIn 5, 7, 9, 12, 15, 22; BriEAA;
CambiEn; CamDcAB; ChamBiD; ChhPo
S1; DcAmArt; DcAmB; DcNAA; Drake;
EarABI, SUP; HarEnUS; IlrAm 1880;
LinLib S; McGDA; NatCAB 6;
NewYHSD; OxCAmL 65, 83, 95;
PeoHis; REnAL; TwCBDA; WhAm 1;
WhAmArt 85*

Vee, Bobby

[Robert Velline]
American. Singer
Teen idol singer similar to Frankie
Avalon, Fabian; songs include "Take
Good Care of My Baby," 1961.
b. Apr 30, 1943 in Fargo, North Dakota
Source: *AmPS A; BiDAmM; BillEnR;
BioIn 12; DcPseud; EncPR&S 89;
EncRk 88; EncRkSt; HarEnR 86;
LegTOT; PenEncP; RkOn 74, 82;
RolSEnR 83; WhoHol 92, A; WhoRock
81*

Veeck, Bill

[William Louis Veeck]
"P T Barnum of Baseball"
American. Baseball Executive
Owner of three ML baseball teams;
introduced gimmicks such as
exploding scoreboards, ethnic nights to
game.
b. Feb 9, 1914 in Chicago, Illinois
d. Jan 2, 1986 in Chicago, Illinois
Source: *AmNatBi; AnObit 1986; Ballpl
90; BiDAmSp BB; BioIn 11, 13;
BioNews 74; CambiEn; ConAu 118;
ConNews 86-1; CulEncB; CurBio 48, 86,
86N; FacFETw; LegTOT; NewYTBS 82,
86; WebAB 74, 79; WhAm 9; WhoAm
76, 78, 80, 82, 84; WhoMW 78, 80;
WhoProB 73*

Vega, Suzanne

American. Singer, Songwriter
Blends jazz, rock and roll, and
minimalism; had hit single "Luka,"
1987.
b. Jul 11, 1959 in Santa Monica,
California
Source: *BillEnR; BioIn 14, 15; ConMus
3; ConNews 88-1; CurBio 94; EncRkSt;
LegTOT; NewGrDA 86; PenEncP;
Songw; WhoAm 94; WhoAmW 95*

Veidt, Conrad

British. Actor
Played in German films, 1917-34,
including *Diary of a Lost Girl*.
b. Jan 22, 1893 in Berlin, Germany
d. Apr 3, 1943 in Hollywood, California
Source: *BiDFilm, 81, 94; BioIn 9, 15,
20; CurBio 43; DcArts; EncEurC; Film
1, 2; FilmAG WE; FilmEn; FilmgC;
ForYSC; FrSilen; HalFC 80, 84, 88;
IlWWBF; IntDcF 1-3, 2-3; ItaFilm;
LegTOT; MotPP; MovMk; NotNAT B;
OxCFilm; PenEncH; TwYS; WhoHol B;
WhoHrs 80; WhScrn 74, 77, 83; WorAl;
WorEFlm*

Veil, Simone Annie Jacob

French. Political Leader
Pres., European Parliament, 1979-82;
chm., legal affairs committee, 1982,
1984-89.
b. Jul 13, 1927 in Nice, France
Source: *BiDFrPL; BioIn 16; ContDcW
89; CurBio 80; IntWW 83, 91; IntYB 82;
InWom SUP; NewYTBS 74; Who 83, 92;
WhoWor 87, 91*

Velarde, Pablita

American. Artist
Her art chronicles the lives of the Pueblo
people; she revived traditional forms
of making art; won the Palmes
Academiques from the French
government, 1954.
b. Sep 19, 1918 in Santa Clara, New
Mexico
Source: *AZNatAW; BioIn 7, 9, 10, 11,
19, 20, 21; HerW, 84; InWom SUP;
NatNAFi; NotNaAm; SJGNNAA;
WhoAmA 73, 76, 78, 80, 82*

Velasco, Luis de

Spanish. Government Official
The second viceroy of New Spain, he
consolidated Spanish control and
implemented legislation ending Indian
slavery.
b. 1511 in Carrion de los Condes, Spain
d. Jul 31, 1564
Source: *DcMexR; HisDcSE; LatAmLi;
McGEWB*

Velasco Alvarado, Juan

Peruvian. Political Leader
Pres. of Peru after 1958 coup; ousted in
1975 coup.
b. Jun 16, 1910 in Piura, Peru
d. Dec 24, 1977 in Lima, Peru
Source: *BiDLAmC; BioIn 8, 9, 10, 11,
13; CurBio 70, 78, 78N; DcCPSAm;
EncLatA; EncWB, 98; EncyDCo; IntWW
74, 75, 76, 77, 78; LatAmLi; NewCol 75;
NewYTBS 77; WhoGov 72; WhoWor 74,
76; WorDWW*

Velasco Ibarra, Jose Maria

Ecuadorean. Political Leader
Served as pres. of Ecuador five times
between 1934-72; ousted by military
off and on.
b. Mar 19, 1893 in Quito, Ecuador
d. Mar 30, 1979 in Quito, Ecuador
Source: *BiDLAmC; BioIn 1, 5, 6, 8, 9,
11, 12, 16, 21; CurBio 52, 79, 79N;
DcCPSAm; DcHiB; DictTyr; EncLatA;
EncWB 98; EncyDCo; FacFETw; IntWW
74, 75, 76, 77, 78; LatAmLi; McGEWB;
NewCol 75; NewYTBS 79; WhoGov 72;
WhoWor 74*

Velazquez, Diego Rodriguez de Silva

Spanish. Artist
Greatest Spanish Baroque painter; superb
colorist, noted for portraits, genre
scenes.
b. Jun 6, 1599 in Seville, Spain
d. Aug 6, 1660 in Madrid, Spain
Source: *AtlBL; CambiEn; EncHiCA;
McGDA; McGEWB; NewC; NewCol 75;
OxCArt; RAdv 14; REn*

Velazquez, Nydia Margarita

American. Politician
In 1992, the Democrat became the first
Puerto Rican woman to be elected to
the U.S. House of Representatives.
b. Mar 23, 1953 in Yabucoa, Puerto Rico
Source: *BiDHisA; DcHiB; EncWB 98;
NotHsAW 1; WhoHisp 94*

Velazquez de Cuellar, Diego
Spanish. Conqueror, Soldier, Government
Official
Conquistador founded Cuba and was
indirectly responsible for the conquest
of Aztec Mexico and Mayan Yucatan.
b. c. 1465 in Cuellar, Spain
d. 1523
Source: *CamBiEn; ChamBiD*

Velde, Willem van de
Dutch. Artist
Known for paintings of naval battles;
member of family of famous 17th
century painters, draftsmen.
b. 1633 in Leiden, Netherlands
d. 1707 in London, England
Source: *BioIn 23; CamBiEn; ChamBiD;
McGDA; NewCol 75; WebBD 83;
WhDW*

Velez, Clemente Soto
Puerto Rican. Social Reformer, Poet
Campaigned to prevent Puerto Rico from
becoming the 51st state.
d. Apr 16, 1993 in San Juan, Puerto
Rico
Source: *BiDHisL; BioIn 16*

Velez, Eddie
[Edwin Velez]
American. Actor
Best known for episodic TV; films
include *Extremities*, 1986.
b. Jun 4, 1958 in New York, New York
Source: *BiHaHis; ConTFT 5; WhoHol
92*

Velez, Lupe
[Maria Guadalupe Velez de Villalobos]
Mexican. Actor
Starred in *Mexican Spitfire* film series,
1940s; married Johnny Weissmuller,
1933-38.
b. Jul 18, 1910 in San Luis Potosi,
Mexico
d. Dec 14, 1944 in Beverly Hills,
California
Source: *BioIn 7, 10; CurBio 45; FilmEn;
FilmgC; InWom; MotPP; MovMk;
NotNAT B; ThFT; TwYS; WhoHol B;
WhScrn 74, 77*

Velluti, Giovanni Battista
Italian. Opera Singer
Male soprano, considered last great
castrato; shocked, fascinated
Londoners, 1820s.
b. Jan 28, 1780 in Monterone, Italy
d. Jan 22, 1861 in Sambruson, Italy
Source: *CmOp; NewEOp 71; NewGrDO;
OxCMus; OxDcOp*

Velvet Underground, The
[John Cale; Sterling Morrison; Lou Reed;
Marueen Tucker]
American. Music Group
Formed, 1965; never sold many records
but influenced David Bowie, the Cars,
the Sex Pistols, and others.
Source: *ABCCoAm; BakDcM; BiDAmM;
BilEnR; BioIn 12, 14, 15, 16, 17, 21;*

*ConAu X; ConMuA 80A; ConMus 7;
DcArts; EncPR&S 74, 89; EncRk 88;
EncRkSt; HarEnR 86; IlEncRk;
NewAmDM; NewGrDA 86; NewYTBS
95; OxCPMus; PenEncP; RkWho 96;
RolSEnR 83; WhoRock 81; WhoRocM 82*

Vendler, Helen Hennessy
American. Educator, Critic
Harvard English professor; poetry
criticism appears in *New Yorker; New
Yorker Review of Books.*
b. Apr 30, 1933 in Boston,
Massachusetts
Source: *AmWomWr; BioIn 14, 15;
CamBiEn; CamDcAB; ConAu 25NR,
41R, 72NR; CurBio 86; DrAS 82E;
IntAu&W 77, 91; IntWW 97, 98, 2000;
IntWWW 2; MajTwCW 1, 2; WhoAm 86,
90, 97, 98, 99, 2000; WhoAmW 85, 87,
91, 97, 99; WhoUSWr 88; WhoWrEP 89;
WorAu 1975; WrDr 86, 92, 98, 99, 2000*

Venetiaan, Renaldo
Surinamese. Political Leader, Educator
Member of the Creole Surinamese
National party (NPS), he was elected
president of Suriname in 1991; he
helped end the guerrilla insurgency
and is committed to stripping the
military of its political role in the
country.

Veneziano, Domenico
Italian. Painter
Early Renaissance artist was known for
his subtle observation of the reaction
of colors to conditions of natural light.
b. c. 1410 in Venice, Italy
d. 1461
Source: *EncWB 98*

Venizelos, Eleutherios Kyriakos
Greek. Statesman
Premier of Greece, 1910; leader of
opposition to Tsaldares govt., 1933-35;
condemned to death but received
amnesty from King George II.
b. Aug 23, 1864 in Mournies, Crete
d. Mar 18, 1936 in Paris, France
Source: *CamBiEn; McGEWB; WebBD
83; WhDW*

Venkataraman, Ramaswamy
Indian. Political Leader
President of India, 1987-92.
b. Dec 4, 1910 in Rajamadam, India
Source: *BioIn 15, 16, 19, 21; IntWW 83,
89, 91, 93, 97, 98, 2000; NewYTBS 87;
Who 83, 85, 88, 90, 92, 94, 98, 99,
2000; WhoAsAP 91; WhoWor 82, 84, 87,
91, 93, 95*

Venter, J. Craig
American. Scientist
With the Institute for Genomic Research,
Gaithersburg, MD, 1992—; pres. and
ch ief scientific officer, Celera
Genomics; received King Faisal
International Pri ze for Science
(Biology); his company was first to
sequence the human genome, 2 000.

b. Oct 14, 1946 in Salt Lake City, Utah
Source: *AmMWSc 82, 86, 89, 92, 95, 98;
CurBio 95; WhoFrS 84*

Ventura, Charlie
American. Jazz Musician
Noted tenor saxist; with Gene Krupa,
1940s.
b. Dec 2, 1916 in Philadelphia,
Pennsylvania
d. Jan 17, 1992 in Pleasantville, New
Jersey
Source: *AllMGJa; AmNatBi; AnObit
1992; BgBands 74; BiDJaz; BioIn 17,
19; CmpEPM; EncJzS; EncJzS;
NewAmDM; NewGrDJ 88, 94; PenEncP;
WhoJazz 72*

Ventures, The
[Bob Bogle; Johnny Durrill; Nokie
Edwards; Howie Johnston; Jerry
McGee; Mel Taylor; Don Wilson]
American. Music Group
Instrumental rock group, formed 1960;
hits include "Walk, Don't Run,"
1960; "Hawaii Five-O," 1969.
Source: *AmPS A; BillEnR; ConMus 19;
CurBio 44; DrRegL 75; EncPR&S 74,
89; EncRk 88; EncRkSt; HarEnR 86;
NewAmDM; NewGrDA 86; NewYTBS
82, 88, 96; ObitOF 79; PenEncP; RkOn
74; RolSEnR 83; WhoHol 92, A;
WhoRock 81; WhoRocM 82*

Venturi, Ken(neth)
American. Sportscaster, Golfer
Won US Open, 1964; golf commentator
for CBS since 1968.
b. May 15, 1931 in San Francisco,
California
Source: *BioIn 4, 5, 7, 9, 10, 11; CmCal;
CurBio 66; WhoGolf; WhoTelC*

Venturi, Robert
American. Architect
Winner, Pritzker Architecture Prize,
1991; best-known works are the
Salisbury Wing of the British National
Gallery and the Seattle Art Museum.
b. Jun 25, 1925 in Philadelphia,
Pennsylvania
Source: *AmArch 70; AmCulL; AmDec
1960, 1970; BioIn 9, 10, 11, 12, 13;
BlueB 76; BriEAA; CamBiEn;
CamDcAB; CelR; ChamBiD; ConArch
80; ConAu 61; CurBio 75; DcArts;
DcTwCCu 1; DcTwDes; EncAAr 2;
EncAB-H 1996; EncWB, 98; IntDcAr;
IntWW 76, 77, 78, 79, 80, 81, 82, 83, 89,
91, 93, 97, 98, 2000; MacEA;
MakTCMA; NatCAB 63N; News 94;
PenDiDA 89; Who 88, 90, 92, 94, 98,
99, 2000; WhoAm 74, 76, 78, 80, 82, 84,
86, 88, 90, 92, 94, 95, 96, 97, 98, 99,
2000; WhoAmA 78, 80, 82, 84, 86, 89,
91, 93, 1999; WhoE 74, 77, 85A, 86, 89,
93, 95, 97, 99; WhoWor 74; WrDr 76,
80, 82, 84, 86, 88, 90, 92, 94, 96*

Venuta, Benay
[Venuta Rose Crooke]
American. Actor, Singer
Played on stage since 1928 in *Anything Goes; Annie Get Your Gun.*
b. Jan 27, 1911 in San Francisco, California
Source: *BiE&WWA; BioIn 21, 22; CmpEPM; DcPseud; NewYTBS 95; NotNAT; WhoHol A; WhoThe 72, 77, 81*

Vera
[Vera Neumann]
American. Designer
Founded Vera Co., 1945.
b. Jul 24, 1910 in Stamford, Connecticut
d. Jun 15, 1993 in North Tarrytown, New York
Source: *DcLP 87B; FairDF US; WorFshn*

Vera, Billy
[Billy Vera & the Beaters]
American. Singer
Had number one single "At This Moment," 1986.
b. May 28, 1945 in Riverside, California
Source: *BioIn 15*

Vera-Ellen
[Vera-Ellen Rohe]
American. Dancer, Actor
Films include *White Christmas,* 1954; *Web of Violence,* 1959.
b. Feb 16, 1926 in Cincinnati, Ohio
d. Aug 30, 1981 in Los Angeles, California
Source: *AmNatBi; AnObit 1981; BioIn 5, 11, 12, 13, 22, 23; CmMov; CmpEPM; CurBio 59, 81, 81N; FilmEn; FilmgC; HalFC 80; InWom, SUP; MotPP; MovMk; WhoHol A; WhScrn 83; WorEFlm*

Vercingetorix
French. Military Leader, Chieftain
Revered as France's first national hero, Celtic leader battled valiantly but unsuccessfully to keep the Roman army from overrunning the territory of Gaul.
b. c. 75BC, Gaul
d. 46BC, Roman Empire
Source: *EncWB 2-19*

Verdi, Giuseppe Fortunino Francesco
Italian. Composer
Composed 27 operas, including *Rigoletto; La Traviata; Aida.*
b. Oct 10, 1813 in Le Roncole, Italy
d. Jan 27, 1901 in Milan, Italy
Source: *AtlBL; BakDcM; CamBiEn; ChamBiD; EncWB 98; NewC; NewCol 75; REn; WebBD 83*

Verdi-Fletcher, Mary (Regina)
American. Dancer
President and founder, Cleveland Ballet Dancing Wheels, the first dance company in the US that included people in wheelchairs, 1980—.

b. Jun 4, 1955 in Bratenahl, Ohio
Source: *WhoEnt 98*

Verdon, Gwen
[Gwyneth Evelyn Verdon]
American. Dancer, Actor
Won Tonys for *Can Can,* 1953; *Damn Yankees,* 1956; *New Girl in Town,* 1958; *Red Head,* 1959.
b. Jan 13, 1925 in Culver City, California
Source: *BiDD; BiE&WWA; BioIn 3, 4, 5, 6, 8, 12, 16, 18; CamGWoT; CelR, 90; ConTFT 3, 20; CurBio 60; DancEn 78; EncAFC; EncMT; FilmChD; FilmEn; GrLiveH; HalFC 80, 84, 88; IntMPA 88, 92, 94, 96; InWom, SUP; LegTOT; MotPP; NewAmDM; NewGrDA 86; NewYTBS 81; NotNAT; NotWoAT; OxCAmT 84; OxCPMus; WhoAm 74, 76, 78, 80, 82, 86, 88, 90, 92, 94, 95, 96, 97, 98, 99, 2000; WhoAmW 83, 85; WhoEnt 92, 98; WhoHol 92, A; WhoThe 77, 81; WorAl; WorAlBi*

Verdugo, Elena
American. Actor
Played Millie Bronson in "Meet Millie," 1952-56; Nurse Consuelo Lopez in "Marcus Welby, MD," 1969-76.
b. Apr 20, 1926 in Hollywood, California
Source: *FilmEn; FilmgC; ForYSC; HalFC 80, 84, 88; LegTOT; MovMk; WhoHol A*

Verdy, Violette
[Nelly Guillerm]
French. Dancer, Director
Toured US, Europe, 1957-58; artistic director Boston Ballet, 1980-84; teaches NYC Ballet, 1984—.
b. Dec 1, 1933 in Pont-L'Abbe, France
Source: *BioIn 11, 12, 13, 14; CamBiEn; ChamBiD; CnOxB; CurBio 80; DancEn 78; DcPseud; IntDcB; IntWWW 2; InWom SUP; WhoAm 74, 76, 78, 80, 82, 84, 86, 88; WhoAmW 70, 72, 74, 75, 83, 85; WhoE 83, 85; WhoFr 79; WhoWor 74*

Vereen, Ben(jamin Augustus)
American. Entertainer
Won Tony for *Pippin',* 1972; played Chicken George in TV miniseries "Roots ," 1977.
b. Oct 10, 1946 in Miami, Florida
Source: *BakBD 84, 92; BiDAfM; BiDD; BioIn 9, 10, 11, 12, 16; CelR, 90; ConBlB 4; ConTFT 2, 8; CurBio 78; DcBiPP; DcTwCCu 5; DrBlPA, 90; EncMT; HalFC 80, 84, 88; InB&W 80, 85; IntMPA 84, 86, 88, 92, 94, 96; LegTOT; NegAl 89; NewYTBE 72; NotNAT; WhoAm 76, 78, 80, 82, 84, 86, 88, 90, 92, 94, 95, 96, 97; WhoBlA 7; WhoEnt 92; WhoHol 92, A; WhoThe 77, 81; WorAl; WorAlBi*

Vereshchagin, Vasily Vasilyevich
Russian. Artist
Best known subjects are of the military, Turkish, Oriental life including *Blessing the Dead.*
b. Oct 26, 1842 in Cherepovets, Russia
d. 1904 in Lushun, China
Source: *BioIn 9; NewCol 75; WebBD 83*

Verga, Giovanni
Italian. Author
Novels, short stories of Sicilian life include *Mastro Don Gesnaldo,* 1889; *Cavalleria Rusticana,* 1880.
b. Aug 31, 1840 in Catania, Sicily, Italy
d. Jan 27, 1922 in Catania, Sicily, Italy
Source: *AtlBL; BbD; Benet 87, 96; BiCoLiE; BiD&SB; BioIn 1, 3, 4, 5, 6, 8, 9, 11, 12, 14, 22; CamBiEn; CamGWoT; CasWL; ChamBiD; ClDMEL 47, 80; CnThe; ConAu 104, 123; CyWA 58, 97; DcBiA; DcEuL; DcItL 1, 2; EncWL 1, 2, 2S, 3; EncWT; EuWr 7; EvEuW; GrFLW; LinLib L; LngCTC; McGEWD 72, 84; ModRL; ModWD; NewGrDO; Novels; OxCEng 67, 85, 95; OxCThe 67, 83; PenC EUR; RAdv 14, 13-2; RComWL; REn; REnWD; RfGShF 1, 2; RfGWoL 95; ShSCr 21; TwCA SUP; TwCLC 3; WhDW; WhoTwCL; WhThe; WorAl; WorAlBi; WorAu 1900*

Vergil
[Virgil; Publius Vergilius Maro]
Roman. Poet
Unfinished epic poem *Aeneid* was about the founding of Rome.
b. Oct 15, 70BC in Mantua, Gaul
d. Sep 21, 19BC in Brundisium, Italy
Source: *AncWr; AtlBL; BbD; Benet 87, 96; BiDLA; BioIn 1, 2, 4, 5, 6, 7, 9, 10, 12, 13; BlmGEL; CasWL; ClMLC 9; CyWA 97; DcArts; DcBiA; DcEnL; DcEuL; Dis&D; EncLitE; GrFLW; Grk&L; LegTOT; LinLib L; LngCEL; MagSWL; McGEWB; MetOEnc; NewC; NewCBEL; NewEOp 71; NewGrDM 80; NewGrDO; NotPoe; OxCClL, 89; OxCEng 67, 85, 95; OxDcByz; PenC CL; PoeCrit 12; RAdv 14, 13-2; RComWL; REn; RfGWoL 95; WhDW; WorAl; WorAlBi; WorLitC SUP*

Verissimo, Erico Lopes
Brazilian. Author
Novels set in Brazil, full of character, broad in scope include *Crossroads,* 1935.
b. Dec 17, 1905 in Rio Grande do Sul, Brazil
d. Nov 28, 1975 in Porto Alegre, Brazil
Source: *CasWL; ConAu 174; EncWL 1; HispWr 2; IntAu&W 76, 77; IntWW 74, 75; PenC AM; REn; TwCWr; WhoWor 74; WorAu 1950*

Verity, C(alvin) William, Jr.
American. Government Official
Succeeded Malcolm Baldrige as secretary of Commerce, 1987-89.
b. Jan 26, 1917 in Middletown, Ohio
Source: *BiDrUSE 89; BioIn 7, 10, 12, 15, 16; BlueB 76; CurBio 88; Dun&B*

79; *IntWW 74, 75, 76, 77, 78, 79, 80, 81, 82, 83, 89, 91, 93; NewYTBS 87; St&PR 75, 84, 87; WhoAm 74, 76, 78, 80, 82, 84, 88; WhoE 89; WhoFI 74, 75, 77, 81, 89; WhoMW 82; WhoWor 74, 89*

Verlaine, Paul (Marie)
French. Poet
Lyrics are known for musical tone, gracefulness: *Sagesse*, 1881.
b. Mar 30, 1844 in Metz, France
d. Jan 8, 1896 in Paris, France
Source: *AtlBL; BbD; Benet 87, 96; BiD&SB; BioIn 20; CamBiEn; CasWL; ClDMEL 47, 80; CyWA 58; DcArts; DcEuL; Dis&D; EncWB 98; EuAu; EuWr 7; EvEuW; GayLesB; GrFLW; GuFrLit 1; LegTOT; LinLib L, S; MagSWL; ModRL; NewC; NewCBEL; NewGrDM 80; NinCLC 2, 51; OxCEng 67, 85, 95; OxCFr; OxCMus; PenC EUR; PoeCrit 2; RAdv 14, 13-2; RComWL; REn; RGFMEP; WhDW; WorAl; WorAlBi*

Vermeer, Jan
[Jan van Delft; Jan van der Meer]
Dutch. Artist
Painted Dutch interiors, genre subjects; interested in light, color: *The Lacemaker*.
b. Oct 30, 1632 in Delft, Netherlands
d. Dec 15, 1675 in Delft, Netherlands
Source: *AtlBL; Benet 87, 96; BioIn 14, 15, 16, 17, 19; CamBiEn; ChamBiD; DcArts; EncWB 98; IntDcAA 90; LegTOT; LiveWoA; McGDA; McGEWB; NewC; NewCol 75; OxCArt; OxDcArt; REn; WebBD 83; WhDW; WorAl; WorAlBi*

Vermeij, Geerat J(acobus)
American. Biologist
Blind scientist who studies mollusks; demonstrated the importance of predation as a force in evolution.
b. Sep 28, 1946 in Groningen, Netherlands
Source: *AmMWSc 76P, 79, 82, 86, 89, 92, 95, 98; BioIn 9, 11; CurBio 95; WhoAm 99, 2000; WhoScEn 96, 2000*

Vermeil, Dick
[Richard Albert Vermeil]
American. Football Coach, Sportscaster
Coach, Philadelphia Eagles, 1976-82; analyst for CBS Sports and ABC Sports, 1983-97; coach, St. Louis Rams, 1997—.
b. Oct 30, 1936 in Calistoga, California
Source: *BioIn 12, 13, 23; NewYTBS 81; WhoAm 82; WhoTelC*

Verne, Jules
"The Founder of Science Fiction"
French. Author
Wrote *Twenty Thousand Leagues Under the Sea*, 1870; *Around the World in Eighty Days*, 1873; both adapted to film, 1954, 1956.
b. Feb 8, 1828 in Nantes, France
d. Mar 24, 1905 in Amiens, France

Source: *AtlBL; Au&Arts 16; AuBYP 2; BbD; Benet 87, 96; BiCoLiE; BiD&SB; BioIn 1, 2, 3, 4, 5, 6, 7, 8, 9, 10, 11, 12, 13, 14, 17, 18, 19, 21, 22, 23; CamBiEn; CarSB; CasWL; CelCen; ChamBiD; ChlBkCr; ClDMEL 80; ConAu 110, 131; CyWA 58, 97; DcArts; DcBiA; DcBiPP; DcCathB; DcEnL; DcEuL; DcLB 123; DcPup; Dis&D; DivFut; EncSF; EncWB 98; EuAu; EvEuW; FilmgC; GuFrLit 1; HalFC 80, 84, 88; JBA 34, 51; LegTOT; LinLib L, S; LngCEL; LngCTC; MagSWL; McGEWB; MnBBF; NewC; NewCBEL; NewEScF; Novels; OxCChiL; OxCEng 67, 85, 95; OxCFr; OxCShps; PenC EUR; REn; RGSF; ScF&FL 1, 92; ScFEYrs; ScFSB; ScFWr, 2; SmATA 21; SocPrL; TwCLC 6, 52; TwCSFW 81A, 86A, 91A; WhDW; WhoChL; WhoHrs 80; WhoSciF; WorAl; WorAlBi; WrChl*

Vernier, Pierre
French. Mathematician
Developed vernier scale for measuring linear or angular magnitudes.
b. Aug 19, 1580 in Ornans, France
d. Sep 14, 1637 in Ornans, France
Source: *BiESc; CamBiEn; DcBiPP; DcCathB; DcScB; InSci; McGCEnS; RanHWDS; WebBD 83*

Vernon, Edward, Sir
"Old Grog"
English. Naval Officer
First to issue rum mixed with water, later called grog, 1740.
b. 1684
d. 1757
Source: *Alli; ApCAB; BioIn 3; CamBiEn; ChamBiD; DcBiPP; DcNaB; Drake; EncAR; EncNaHi; HarEnUS; HisDBrE; NewCol 75; OxCBrHi; OxCShps; WebBD 83*

Vernon, Jackie
American. Comedian
Known for off-beat, satirical humor; played nightclubs, TV, films; trademark saying, "You had to be there."
b. 1928 in New York, New York
d. Nov 10, 1987 in Los Angeles, California
Source: *WhoCom; WhoHol A*

Vernon, John
[Adolphus Vernon Agopsowicz]
Canadian. Actor
Films include *Dirty Harry; Topaz; National Lampoon's Animal House.*
b. Feb 24, 1932 in Regina, Saskatchewan, Canada
Source: *ColCR; ConTFT 7, 15; DcPseud; DrAPF 91; FilmEn; FilmgC; HalFC 88; IntMPA 84, 92, 94, 96; ItaFilm; WhoHol 92, A*

Vernon, Lillian
American. Business Executive
Started a mail order business from her home, 1951; issued first catalog, 1956; company became the Lillian Vernon Corporation, 1965.

b. 1927 in Leipzig, Germany
Source: *CurBio 96; NewYTBS 97; WhoAm 92, 94, 95, 96, 97, 98, 99, 2000; WhoAmW 93, 95, 99; WhoE 97, 99; WhoFI 94*

Vernon, Mickey
[James Barton Vernon]
American. Baseball Player
First baseman, 1939-43, 1946-60, mostly with Washington; won AL batting title, 1946, 1953; set several AL fielding records.
b. Apr 22, 1918 in Marcus Hook, Pennsylvania
Source: *Ballpl 90; BaseEn 88; BiDAmSp BB; BioIn 3, 4, 11, 15, 18; WhoProB 73*

Vernon, Mike
[Michael Vernon]
Canadian. Hockey Player
Goaltender, Calgary, 1982-94; Detroit, 1994—; won Conn Smythe Trophy, 1997.
b. Feb 24, 1963 in Calgary, Alberta, Canada
Source: *BioIn 23, 24; WhoAm 98, 99, 2000*

Veronese, Paolo
[Paolo Caliari]
"Painter of Pageants"
Italian. Artist
Noted for decorative, many-figured frescoes, altarpieces: *Marriage of Cana.*
b. 1528 in Verona, Italy
d. Apr 9, 1588 in Venice, Italy
Source: *AtlBL; Benet 87, 96; BioIn 1, 2, 4, 5, 6, 9, 15, 16; CamBiEn; ClaDrA; DcArts; DcCathB; DcPseud; EncWB 98; IntDcAA 90; LegTOT; McGDA; McGEWB; OxDcArt; REn; WhDW; WorAl; WorAlBi*

Veronis, John James
American. Publisher
Co-founder, *Psychology Today* mag; pres., Communications/Research/ Machines, Inc., 1967-71; founder, pres., *Book Digest* mag., NYC, 1973-79.
b. Mar 6, 1928 in New Brunswick, New Jersey
Source: *EncTwCJ; WhoAm 76, 78, 86, 88; WhoE 74, 75, 77; WhoFI 74, 75*

Verrazano, Giovanni da
Italian. Navigator, Explorer
Discovered mouth of Hudson River, 1524.
b. 1485? in Val di Greve, Italy
d. Nov 1528 in Puerto del Pico, Spain
Source: *AmBi; ApCAB; Benet 87, 96; BenetAL 91; BioIn 1, 2, 8, 9, 11, 15, 16, 18, 19, 20, 24; CnDAL; EncCRAm; EncWB 98; ExplAnT; McGEWB; OxCCan; REn; REnAL; WhAm HS; WhDW; WhNaAH; WhWE; WorAl; WorAlBi*

Verrett, Shirley Carter
American. Opera Singer
Mezzo-soprano; made NY Met. debut,
1968; 1955 Marion Anderson winner.
b. May 31, 1933 in New Orleans,
Louisiana
Source: *BakBD 84; BioIn 13, 16;*
BioNews 75; CelR 90; DrBlPA 90;
InB&W 85; IntWW 83, 91; IntWWM 90;
InWom SUP; MetOEnc; MusSN; NegAl
89; NewAmDM; NewGrDA 86;
NewYTBS 74; PenDiMP; WhoAm 86, 90;
WhoAmM 83; WhoAmW 85, 87; WhoBlA
4, 7; WhoEnt 92; WhoWor 84, 91

Verrill, Alpheus Hyatt
American. Explorer, Author, Inventor
Developed autochrome natural color
photo process; wrote over 100 books.
b. Jul 23, 1871 in New Haven,
Connecticut
d. Nov 14, 1954 in Chiefland, Florida
Source: *AmAu&B; AmNatBi; BioIn 3;*
DcAmB S5; ObitOF 79; REnAL; WhAm
3; WhNAA

Verrocchio, Andrea del
[Andrea di Michele di Francesco Cioni]
Italian. Artist
Sculptures include bronze of David;
paintings include *Baptism of Christ.*
b. 1435 in Florence, Italy
d. Oct 7, 1488 in Venice, Italy
Source: *AtlBL; BioIn 1, 5, 8, 11, 15, 18;*
CamBiEn; ChamBiD; DcArts; DcCathB;
DcPseud; EncWB 98; IntDcAA 90;
LegTOT; McGDA; McGEWB; NewCol
75; OxCArt; OxDcArt; REn; WebBD 83

Versace, Gianni
Italian. Fashion Designer
Known for bondage inspired designs and
his use of metal-mesh materials.
b. Dec 2, 1946 in Reggio di Calabria,
Italy
d. Jul 15, 1997 in Miami Beach, Florida
Source: *BioIn 15, 16, 17, 18, 19, 20, 21,*
22, 23, 24; CamBiEn; ConDes 84, 90,
97; ConFash; ConNews 88-1; CurBio
93, 97N; DcArts; EncFash; EncWB 2-
19; IntWW 89, 91, 93, 97; LegTOT;
News 98, 98-2; ThHDFas; WhAm 12;
WhoAm 84, 86, 88, 92, 94, 95, 96, 97;
WhoFash 88; WhoWor 84, 87, 89, 91,
93, 95, 97

Versalles, Zoilo Casanova
''Zorro''
Cuban. Baseball Player
Shortstop, Washington Senators 1959-60,
Minnesota Twins 1961-67, Los
Angeles Dodgers 1968, Cleveland
Indians 1969, Washington Senators
1969, Atlanta Braves 1971. American
League MVP, 1965.
b. Dec 18, 1939 in Vedado, Cuba
d. Jun 9, 1995 in Bloomington,
Minnesota
Source: *Ballpl 90; BaseEn 88; BioIn 7,*
8, 11

Vertes, Marcel
Hungarian. Artist
Designed scenery, costumes for ballets:
Bluebeard; Helen of Troy; exhibits in
museums around the world.
b. Aug 10, 1895 in Ujpest, Austria-
Hungary
d. Oct 31, 1961 in Paris, France
Source: *BioIn 1, 2, 3, 4, 5, 6; ClaDrA;*
CurBio 61, 62; DancEn 78; EncFash;
McGDA; NotNAT B; ThHDFas; WhAm
4; WhAmArt 85; WhoAmA 80N, 82N,
84N, 86N, 89N, 91N, 93N; WhoArt 80,
82, 84; WhoGrA 62

Veruschka
[Countess Vera VonLehndorff]
German. Model, Actor
Films include *Blow Up,* 1966.
b. 1943
Source: *BioIn 10, 11, 14, 15; InWom*
SUP; WhoHol A

Verwoerd, Hendrik F
South African. Political Leader
Prime minister, 1958-66; assassinated.
b. Sep 8, 1901 in Amsterdam,
Netherlands
d. Sep 6, 1966 in Cape Town, South
Africa
Source: *BioIn 5, 6, 7, 8; CurBio 59, 67;*
WhAm 4

Very, Jones
American. Author
Wrote religious verse, 1837; wrote
sonnets, 1839; published book *Essays*
and Poems, 1839.
b. Aug 28, 1813 in Salem, Massachusetts
d. May 8, 1880 in Salem, Massachusetts
Source: *Alli, SUP; AmAu; AmAu&B;*
AmBi; AmNatBi; ApCAB; AtlBL; Benet
87, 96; BenetAL 91; BiBAL 8; BiDAmM;
BiD&SB; BiDTran; BioIn 6, 8, 11, 12,
22, 23; CamBiEn; CamDcAB; CamGEL;
CamGLE; CamHAL; CasWL; ChamBiD;
Chambr 3; ChhPo, S1; CnDAL; CyAL 2;
DcAmAu; DcAmB; DcLB 1; DcLEL;
DcNAA; Drake; EncALit; EvLB;
GrWrEL P; MouLC 3; NatCAB 6;
NinCLC 9; OxCAmL 65, 83, 95; PenC
AM; RAdv 14, 13-1; REn; REnAL;
RfGAmL 4, 87, 94; WebAB 74, 79;
WebE&AL; WhAm HS

Vesalius, Andreas
Belgian. Scientist
Anatomist who was the first to dissect
the human body.
b. Dec 31, 1514 in Brussels, Belgium
d. Oct 15, 1564 in Zante, Greece
Source: *AsBiEn; BiD&SB; BiDPsy;*
BiEsc; BiHiMed; BioIn 1, 2, 3, 4, 5, 6,
7, 8, 9, 11, 12, 13, 14, 15, 16, 18, 19,
20; CamBiEn; CamDcSc; ChamBiD;
DcBiPP; DcCathB; DcScB; EncWB 98;
HisPhAn; InSci; LarDcSc; LinLib L, S;
McGCEnS; McGEWB; OxCMed 86;
RAdv 14; RanHWDS; REn; SciMath;
WorAl; WorAlBi; WorScD

Vesco, Robert Lee
American. Financier
Indicted for using illegal funds to gain
control of US companies, 1970s;
contributed large sum to re-elect
Nixon used to finance Watergate
break-in, 1972; fled to Costa Rica to
avoid charges.
b. Dec 4, 1935 in Detroit, Michigan
Source: *BioIn 10, 11, 12, 13; BioNews*
74; BusPN; LatAmLi; PolProf NF;
WhoE 74

Vesey, Denmark
American. Carpenter, Slave, Abolitionist
Brilliant freedom fighter planned an
abortive slave insurrection.
b. 1767, Africa
d. Jun 23, 1822 in Charleston, South
Carolina
Source: *AfrAmAl 6, 8; AmBi; AmNatBi;*
ApCAB; BioIn 1, 5, 6, 8, 9, 10, 12, 17,
20, 23; CamDcAB; ChamBiD; DcAmB;
DcAmNB; DcAmSR; EncAAH; EncAB-H
1974, 1996; EncARH; EncRelA;
EncSoH; EncWB 98; HarEnUS; InB&W
80, 85; LegTOT; McGEWB; NegAl 76,
83, 89; NotBlAM; WebAB 74, 79; WhAm
HS; WhCiWar

Vespasian
[Titus Flavius Sabinus Vespasianus]
Roman. Ruler
During reign, suppressed revolt of
Batavians; began erection of
Colosseum, AD 69-79.
b. Nov 17, 8 in Reate, Italy
d. Jun 24, 79 in Reate, Italy
Source: *PenC CL; REn*

Vespucci, Amerigo
[Americus Vespucius]
Italian. Navigator
America was named for him; discovered
mouth of Rio de la Plata.
b. Mar 9, 1451 in Florence, Italy
d. Feb 22, 1512 in Seville, Spain
Source: *BbD; Benet 87, 96; BiD&SB;*
BioIn 1, 3, 4, 5, 7, 8, 9, 12, 14, 16, 17,
18, 19, 20, 24; ChamBiD; DcBiPP;
DcCathB; Dis&D; Drake; Expl 93;
ExplAnT; HisDcSE; LinLib S; NatCAB
3; NewC; OxCAmH; OxCAmL 65;
OxCShps; RAdv 14, 13-3; REn; REnAL;
TwCBDA; WebAB 74; WhAm HS;
WhWE

Vessels, Billy
''Curly''
American. Football Player
Halfback, won Heisman Trophy, 1952;
had brief NFL career with Baltimore,
1956.
b. Mar 22, 1931 in Cleveland, Ohio
Source: *BiDAmSp FB; BioIn 14;*
WhoFtbl 74

Vessey, John William, Jr.
American. Military Leader
First man to rise through ranks from
private to four-star general to chairman
of Joint Chiefs of Staff, 1979-85;
succeeded by William Crowe.

b. Jun 29, 1922 in Minneapolis,
Minnesota
Source: *BioIn 13, 14, 15; IntWW 83, 91;
NewYTBS 82, 84; WhoAm 82, 84, 86,
88, 90, 97, 98, 99, 2000; WhoMW 90,
92; WhoWor 87*

Vestris, Lucia Elizabeth, Madame
English. Opera Singer, Actor
Star of London stage, 1820-54; noted for
"breeches parts, burlesques."
b. Jan 3, 1797 in London, England
d. Aug 8, 1856 in London, England
Source: *BioIn 8, 10; CelCen; ChamBiD;
DcBiPP; IntDcT 3; InWom; NewGrDM
80; NewGrDO; OxCThe 67; OxDcOp;
PenDiMP*

Vezina, Georges
"The Chicoutimi Cucumber"
Hockey Player
Goalie, Montreal, 1917-25, considered
best of his time; died of TB; Hall of
Fame, 1945; Vezina Trophy, awarded
to goalies, named in his honor.
b. Jan 1887 in Chicoutimi, Quebec,
Canada
d. Mar 26, 1925
Source: *BioIn 2; HocEn; WhoHcky 73;
WhoSpor*

Vianney, Jean (Marie) Baptiste
French. Clergy
Known for his personal holiness and his
ability to help the troubled, he served
as the cure (parish priest) of Ars; he
was canonized in 1925.
b. May 8, 1786 in Lyons, France
d. Aug 4, 1859 in Ars, France

Viardot-Garcia, Pauline
French. Opera Singer, Composer
Mezzo-soprano, noted for range,
technique; friend of Turgenev.
b. Jul 18, 1821 in Paris, France
d. May 18, 1910 in Paris, France
Source: *BakBD 78, 84; BioIn 1, 4, 5, 7,
8, 10, 11; CmOp; InWom; NewAmDM;
NewCol 75; NewEOp 71; PenDiMP*

Vicente, Gil
Portuguese. Poet, Dramatist
Known for his poetry and plays in both
Portuguese and Spanish, he was an
outstanding figure of the Iberian
Renaissance.
b. c. 1465
d. 1536
Source: *BiCoLiE; BioIn 23; CmMedTh;
CnThe; EncWB 98; EncWT; Ent;
GrFLW; IntDcT 2; McGEWB;
NewGrDM 80; OxCSpan; OxCThe 67,
83; RAdv 14, 13-2; REnWD; RfGWoL 95*

Vicious, Sid
[The Sex Pistols; John Simon Ritchie]
English. Singer
Bass player, vocalist with punk rock
group, 1977-78; arrested for murder,
1978; died of drug overdose.
b. May 10, 1957 in London, England
d. Feb 2, 1979 in New York, New York

Source: *BioIn 11, 22, 23; DcPseud;
LegTOT; NewYTBS 79; WhoRocM 82*

Vickers, Edward
English. Manufacturer
Co-founded Vickers' Sons & Co., 1867,
for steel manufacturing.
b. 1804
d. 1897
Source: *WebBD 83*

Vickers, Jon
Canadian. Opera Singer
Among finest postwar heroic tenors;
made recordings, operatic films; had
NY Met. debut, 1960.
b. Oct 29, 1926 in Prince Albert,
Saskatchewan, Canada
Source: *BakBD 78, 84; BioIn 5, 6, 7, 8,
10, 11, 15, 16, 17, 19, 21; BlueB 76;
BriBkM 80; CanWW 70, 79, 80, 81, 83,
89, 96, 97, 98, 1999; CmOp; CreCan 1;
CurBio 61; FacFETw; IntDcOp; IntWW
74, 75, 76, 77, 78, 79, 80, 81, 82, 83,
89, 91, 93; IntWWM 77, 80, 90;
LegTOT; MetOEnc; MusSN; NewAmDM;
NewEOp 71; NewGrDM 80; OxDcOp;
PenDiMP; Who 74, 82, 83, 85, 88, 90,
92, 94, 98, 2000; WhoAm 74, 76, 78, 80,
82, 84, 86, 88; WhoAmM 83; WhoOp
76; WhoWor 74; WorAl; WorAlBi*

Vickers, Martha
[Martha MacVicar]
American. Actor
Married Mickey Rooney, 1949-51; films
include *The Big Sleep*, 1946.
b. May 28, 1925 in Ann Arbor,
Michigan
d. Nov 2, 1971 in Van Nuys, California
Source: *BioIn 10; DcPseud; FilmEn;
FilmgC; ForYSC; HalFC 80, 84, 88;
HolP 40; LegTOT; ObitOF 79; WhoHol
B; WhScrn 74, 77, 83*

Vickrey, Robert (Remsen)
American. Artist
Paintings are of detailed, eerie tempera:
The Labyrinth, 1951.
b. Aug 20, 1926 in New York, New
York
Source: *AmArt; BioIn 3, 4, 7, 12;
DcCAA 88; McGDA; PrintW 85; WhoAm
74, 76, 78, 80, 82, 84, 86, 88, 90, 92,
94, 95, 96; WhoAmA 73, 76, 78, 80, 82,
84, 86, 89, 91, 93, 1999; WhoWor 84,
87, 89*

Vickrey, William
American. Economist
Won Nobel Prize in economics, 1996.
b. Jun 21, 1914, Canada
d. Oct 11, 1996 in New York
Source: *AmEA 74; CamBiEn; ConAu
41R; WhoEc 81, 86*

Vico, Giovanni Battista
Italian. Philosopher
Writings dealt with laws of evolution in
society.
b. Jun 23, 1668 in Naples, Italy
d. Jan 23, 1744 in Naples, Italy

Source: *BioIn 3, 7, 8, 10, 13, 14, 15, 17,
19, 20; CyEd; DcBiPP; DcEuL; EuAu;
EuWr 3; LngCTC; LuthC 75; NewCol
75; OxCLaw; REn; WhoChr*

Victor, Paul-Emile
French. Explorer
Founded French Polar Expeditions, 1947;
explored polar regions from 1934 to
1987.
b. Jun 28, 1907 in Geneva, Switzerland
d. Mar 8, 1995 in Bora Bora, French
Polynesia
Source: *BioIn 20; IntWW 74, 75, 76, 77,
78, 79, 80, 81, 82, 83, 89, 91, 93;
NewYTBS 95; WhoFr 79; WhoWor 78*

Victor, Sally Josephs
American. Designer
Opened hat shop, 1934-68; won Coty,
1956.
b. Feb 23, 1905 in Scranton,
Pennsylvania
d. May 14, 1977 in New York, New
York
Source: *BioIn 12; CurBio 54, 77N;
FairDF US; InWom; NatCAB 59;
NewYTBS 77; WorFshn*

Victor Amadeus, II
Italian. King
Known as an enlightened despot, he was
the Duke of Savoy, king of Sicily, and
king of Sardinia; achieved freedom
from foreign domination for his
domains, and brought them justice and
prosperity.
b. May 14, 1666
d. Oct 31, 1732
Source: *BioIn 13; DcBiPP; EncWB 98;
McGEWB; WhoMilH 76*

Victor Emmanuel II
Italian. Ruler
First king of Italy, 1861-78, who freed
Italy from Austrian domination.
b. Mar 14, 1820 in Turin, Italy
d. Jan 9, 1878 in Rome, Italy
Source: *CamBiEn; CelCen; ChamBiD;
Dis&D; EncWB 98; LinLib S; NewCol
75*

Victor Emmanuel III
Italian. Ruler
King of Italy, 1900-46; relinquished
power to son, 1944; abdicated, 1946.
b. Nov 11, 1869 in Naples, Italy
d. Dec 28, 1947 in Alexandria, Egypt
Source: *BioIn 24; CamBiEn; ChamBiD;
EncWB 98; NewCol 75; WebBD 83*

Victoria, Queen
[Alexandrina Victoria]
English. Ruler
Had longest reign in British history,
1837-1901; featured growing
industrialization, middle class
prosperity.
b. May 24, 1819 in London, England
d. Jan 22, 1901 in Isle of Wight,
England

Source: *Alli, SUP; BbD; Benet 87, 96; BiD&SB; BioIn 1, 2, 3, 4, 5, 6, 7, 8, 9, 10, 11, 12, 13, 14, 15, 16, 17, 18, 19, 20, 21, 22, 23, 24; BlmGWL; CamBiEn; ChambBiD; ChhPo; ContDcW 89; DcBiPP; DcBrWA; DcEnL; DcLB 55; DcLEL; DcNaB; DcWomA; Dis&D; EncBrWW; EncFash; EncO&P 3; EncPaPR 91; EncWB 98; EvLB; FemiCLE; GoodHs; HalFC 84, 88; HerW, 84; HisDBrE; HisWorL; IntDcWB; InWom, SUP; LegTOT; LinLib L, S; LngCEL; McGEWB; NewC; OxCBrHi; OxCEng 67, 85, 95; REn; ThHDFas; VicBrit; WhCiWar; WhDW; WomFir; WomWR; WorAl; WorAlBi*

Victoria, Tomas Luis de
Spanish. Composer
Most renowned Spanish Renaissance polyphonist, known for his mystical fervor and the nobility of his musical concepts.
b. c. 1548 in Avila, Spain
d. 1611
Source: *AtlBL; BakBD 84, 92; BakDcM; Benet 87, 96; BioIn 4, 7, 10, 14, 20; BriBkM 80; CamBiEn; ChamBiD; CmpBCM; EncWB 98; GrComp; McGEWB; MusMk; NewAmDM; NewGrDM 80; NewOxM; REn*

Victoria Ingrid Alice Desiree
Swedish. Princess
First child of King Carl Gustaf XVI of Sweden; will succeed father to throne.
b. Jul 4, 1977 in Stockholm, Sweden

Victorio
American. Native American Leader
Led small bands of Native Americans in resistance to US and Mexican troops.
b. 1820?
d. Oct 15, 1880
Source: *NotNaAm*

Vidal, Gore
[Eugene Luther Gore Vidal, Jr.]
American. Author, Dramatist
Wrote *Lincoln: A Novel*, 1984; *Empire*, 1987; won National Book Award for *United States: Essays, 1952-92*, 1993.
b. Oct 3, 1925 in West Point, New York
Source: *AmAu&B; AmCulL; AmNov; AmWr S4; AuNews 1; AuSpks; BeaEPF; Benet 87, 96; BenetAL 91; BestSel 90-2; BiCoLiE; BiE&WWA; BioIn 2, 3, 4, 5, 6, 7, 8, 9, 10, 11, 12, 13, 14, 15, 16, 17, 18, 19, 20, 21, 22, 23; BioNews 74; BkPepl; BlueB 76; CamGEL; CamGLE; CamHAL; CasWL; CelR, 90; CmpQue; CnMD; ConAmD; ConAu 5R, 13NR, 45NR, 65NR; ConDr 73, 77, 82, 88, 93; ConGAN; ConLC 2, 4, 6, 8, 10, 22, 33, 72; ConNov 72, 76, 82, 86, 91, 96; ConPopW; ConTFT 3, 20; CroCD; CurBio 83; CyWA 89, 97; DcArts; DcLB 6, 152; DcLEL 1940; DcLP 87A; DrAF 76; DrAPF 80, 87, 91; EncALit; EncMys; EncSF; EncWL 1, 2, 2S, 3; EncWT; FacFETw; FilmEn; GayLesB; GrWrEL N; IdentIs; IntAu&W 76, 77, 89, 91, 93; IntvTCA 2; IntWW 74, 75,*

76, 77, 78, 79, 80, 81, 82, 83, 89, 91, 93, 97, 98, 2000; *ItaFilm; JouAdvM; LegTOT; LiExTwC; LiJour; LinLib L; LngCTC; LNinSix; MagSAmL; MajTwCW 1, 2; MakMC; McGEWD 72, 84; ModAL 4S2, 4S3, 5; ModWD; ModWr; NatPD 81; NewEScF; News 96, 96-2; NotNAT, A; Novels; OxCAmL 65, 83, 95; OxCAmT 84; OxCTwCL; PenC AM; RAdv 1, 14, 13-1; REn; REnAL; RfGAmL 87; ScF&FL 1, 2, 92; ScFSB; TwCA SUP; TwCCr&M 91; TwCRHW 90, 94; TwCSFW 81, 86; TwCWr; WebAB 74, 79; WebE&AL; Who 74, 82, 83, 85, 88, 90, 92, 94, 98, 99, 2000; WhoAm 74, 76, 78, 80, 82, 84, 86, 88, 90, 92, 94, 95, 96, 97, 98, 99, 2000; WhoSpyF; WhoThe 72, 77, 81; WhoTwCL; WhoUSWr 88; WhoWor 74, 84; WhoWrEP 89, 92, 95; WorAl; WorAlBi; WorAu 1900; WorEFlm; WrDr 76, 80, 82, 84, 86, 88, 90, 92, 94, 96, 98, 99, 2000*

Vidal de la Blache, Paul
French. Geographer
Founded the modern French school of geography through his writings on human and regional geography; his *Atlas* was first published in 1894.
b. Jan 22, 1845 in Pezenas, Herault, France
d. May 5, 1918 in Tamaris-sur-Mer, France

Videla, Jorge Rafael
Argentine. Political Leader
Pres. of Argentina, 1976-81; led coup that ousted Pres. Peron.
b. Aug 2, 1925 in Mercedes, Argentina
Source: *BiDLAmC; BioIn 10, 11, 12, 16; CurBio 78; DcCPSAm; EncWB, 98; IntWW 76, 77, 78, 79, 80, 81, 82, 83, 89, 91, 93, 97, 98, 2000; IntYB 78, 79, 80, 81, 82; LatAmLi; NewYTBS 75; WhoWor 78, 80*

Videnov, Zhan (Vassilev)
Bulgarian. Political Leader
Leader of the Bulgarian Socialist Party (BSP), associated with the former Communist Party, he was elected prime minister in 1995 and promised to improve the economy and increase social benefits.
b. 1959 in Plovdiv, Bulgaria
Source: *WhoWor 96, 97, 98, 99*

Vidor, Florence
[Florence Cobb]
American. Actor
Successful on silent films; career ended with talkies.
b. Jul 23, 1895 in Houston, Texas
d. Nov 3, 1977 in Pacific Palisades, California
Source: *BioIn 9, 11; DcAmB S10; DcPseud; EncAFC; Film 1, 2; FilmEn; FilmgC; FrSilen; HalFC 80, 84, 88; MotPP; MovMk; NewYTBS 77; ObitOF 79; SilFlmP; TwYS; WhoHol A; WhScrn 83*

Vidor, King Wallis
American. Director
Directed *Hallelujah*, 1929; first Hollywood movie with all black cast.
b. Feb 8, 1894 in Galveston, Texas
d. Nov 1, 1982 in Paso Robles, California
Source: *AnObit 1982; BiDFilm; BioIn 3, 4, 8, 9, 10, 11, 12, 13; BkPepl; CamBiEn; CamDcAB; ChamBiD; CmMov; CurBio 57, 83; Film 1; FilmgC; IntMPA 82; IntWW 83N; MovMk; NewYTBE 72; NewYTBS 82; OxCFilm; ScrEAmL 1; TwYS; Who 82; WhoAm 82*

Vidov, Oleg
Russian. Actor, Director
Handsome star of 37 Russian, Scandinavian, and Eastern European films, but when he questioned the tight Soviet political control over film production, he was denied work; defected to the United States, 1985.
b. Jun 11, 1940 in Moscow, Union of Soviet Socialist Republics
Source: *ConNews 87-4*

Vieira, Antonio
Portuguese. Clergy, Missionary
Foremost orator in the Portuguese Empire in the 17th century, he defended Jewish, Native, and black Americans from exploitation and persecution.
b. Feb 6, 1608 in Lisbon, Portugal
d. Aug 18, 1697 in Salvador, Brazil
Source: *ApCAB; Benet 87, 96; BiDChrM; BioIn 1, 2, 4, 7, 9, 24; CamBiEn; CasWL; DcBiPP; DcBrazL; DcCathB; EncLatA; EncWB 98; InB&W 80; LatAmLi; MacEWoS; McGEWB; PenC EUR; REn; WhDW*

Vieira, Joao (Bernardo)
Guinean. Political Leader
Became president of Guinea-Bissau in a 1980 coup, and faced building the economy of one of the world's poorest nations; helped lead the successful rebellion against the Portuguese colonists that resulted in the country's independence in 1974.
b. Apr 27, 1939 in Bissau, Guinea-Bissau
Source: *AfSS 78, 79, 80, 81, 82; BioIn 21; CamBiEn; ChamBiD; IntWW 78, 79, 80, 81, 82, 83, 89, 91, 93, 97, 98, 2000; ProfiWG 98; WhoAfr; WhoWor 80, 82, 87, 89, 91, 93, 95, 96, 97, 98, 99*

Vieira Da Silva, Maria Helena
French. Artist
Abstract painter, inspired by the seasons, landscapes, urban streets, games and the horror of WW II.
b. Jun 13, 1908 in Lisbon, Portugal
d. Mar 6, 1992 in Paris, France
Source: *BiDWomA; BioIn 17, 18; ConArt 89; CurBio 92N; WhoArt 84*

Viereck, George Sylvester
American. Author, Editor
Edited *American Editor*, 1914-27; imprisoned during WW II for pro-German propaganda.
b. Dec 31, 1884 in Munich, Germany
d. Mar 18, 1962 in Holyoke, Massachusetts
Source: *AmAu&B; AmLY; AmNatBi; BenetAL 91; BioIn 4, 6, 9, 11, 15, 22; CamDcAB; CasWL; ChhPo; ConAu 116; CurBio 40, 62; DcAmB S7; DcLB 54; EncAJ; LinLib L; OxCAmL 65, 83, 95; REnAL; ScF&FL 1, 92; SJGFanW; TwCA SUP; WhAm 4; WhJnl; WhLit; WhNAA; WorAu 1900*

Viereck, Peter Robert Edwin
American. Poet, Educator
Won 1949 Pulitzer for verse vol., *Terror and Decorum.*
b. Aug 5, 1916 in New York, New York
Source: *AmAu&B; BenetAL 91; BioIn 22; CnDAL; CnE&AP; ConAu 1NR, 1R; ConPo 85, 91; CurBio 43; DrAPF 87, 91; DrAS 82E; IntAu&W 91; IntvTCA 2; IntWW 83, 91; ModAL 4; OxCAmL 65; PenC AM; REn; REnAL; TwCWr; WhoAm 86, 90; WhoUSWr 88; WhoWrEP 89; WorAu 1900; WrDr 86, 92, 98, 99, 2000*

Viertel, Peter
American. Author
Writings include *The Canyon*, 1940; *White Hunter, Black Heart*, 1953.
b. Nov 16, 1920 in Dresden, Germany
Source: *AmAu&B; AmNov; BioIn 2, 7, 12; ConAu 13R, 52NR; DcLEL 1940*

Vieuxtemps, Henri Francois Joseph
Belgian. Musician, Composer
Violinist who was professor, Brussels Conservatory of Music, 1871-81.
b. Feb 20, 1820 in Verviers, Belgium
d. Jun 6, 1881 in Mustapha, Algeria
Source: *NewCol 75; OxCMus*

Vig, Butch
American. Producer, Musician
Formed band Spooner with Duke Erikson, 1979; founded Smart Studios with Steve Marker, late 1970s; formed band Fire Town with Steve Marker and released debut album, *The Good Life*, in 1989; produced Nirvana's album *Nevermind*, 1991; formed group Garbage and released self-titled debut album, 1995.
b. 1956 in Viroqua, Wisconsin
Source: *ConMus 17*

Vigee-Lebrun, Marie-Louise-Elisabeth
French. Artist
Best known for her portraits, including over 25 of Marie-Antoinette.
b. Apr 16, 1755 in Paris, France
d. Mar 30, 1842 in Paris, France
Source: *CamBiEn; NewCol 75; WebBD 83*

Vigeland, Gustav
[Adolf Gustav Vigeland]
Norwegian. Sculptor
His famous work, Fountain Square (located in Oslo's Frogner Park), consists of sculptures of all the periods in the human life cycle.
b. Apr 11, 1869 in Mandal, Norway
d. Mar 12, 1943 in Oslo, Norway
Source: *BioIn 1, 2, 5, 9; DcArts; DcTwArt; McGDA; OxCArt; OxCTwCA; OxDcArt; PhDcTCA 77*

Vignola, Giacomo da
[Giacomo Barocchio; Giacomo Barozzi]
Italian. Architect
Succeeded Michelangelo as chief architect of St. Peter's, 1564; wrote on architectural theory.
b. Oct 1, 1507 in Vignola, Italy
d. Jul 7, 1573 in Rome, Italy
Source: *AtlBL; EncWB 98; LuthC 75; McGEWB; NewCol 75; WebBD 83; WhDW*

Vigny, Alfred Victor, Comte de
French. Author, Poet, Dramatist
Early exponent of French romanticism; wrote historical novel *Cliq-Mars*, 1826; verse *Les Destinees*, 1864.
b. Mar 27, 1797 in Loches, France
d. Sep 17, 1863 in Paris, France
Source: *AtlBL; BbD; BiD&SB; BioIn 1, 2, 3, 4, 5, 6, 7, 8, 9, 11; CamBiEn; CasWL; ChamBiD; CnThe; CyWA 58; DcBiA; DcEuL; Dis&D; EuAu; EvEuW; McGEWB; McGEWD 72; NewC; OxCEng 67; OxCFr; PenC EUR; RComWL; REn; REnWD; WorAl; WorAlBi*

Vigo, Jean
French. Director
Experimental films banned as "anti-French" because they attacked the establishment.
b. Apr 26, 1905 in Paris, France
d. Oct 5, 1934 in Paris, France
Source: *BiDFilm, 81, 94; BioIn 9, 12, 15, 24; ChamBiD; DcArts; DcFM; DcPseud; DcTwCCu 2; EncEurC; FilmEn; FilmgC; HalFC 80, 84, 88; IntDcF 1-2, 2-2; MiSFD 9N; MovMk; OxCFilm; WorEFlm; WorFDir 1*

Vigoda, Abe
American. Actor
Played Detective Fish on "Barney Miller," 1975-77.
b. Feb 24, 1921 in New York, New York
Source: *BioIn 10, 16, 22; ConTFT 3, 20; EncAFC; HalFC 84, 88; IntMPA 96; LegTOT; WhoAm 78, 80, 82, 84, 86, 88, 92, 94, 99, 2000; WhoCom; WhoEnt 92A, 98; WhoHol A; WorAlBi*

Viguerie, Richard A(rt)
"Godfather of the New Right"
American. Publisher
Founder of the *Conservative Digest*, 1975.
b. Sep 23, 1933 in Golden Acres, Texas

Source: *BioIn 12, 13, 15; CurBio 83; DcAmC; IntWW 89, 91, 93, 97, 98; St&PR 84; WhoAdv 90; WhoAm 80, 82, 86, 88*

Vila, Bob
[Robert Joseph Vila]
American. TV Personality
Host of PBS's "This Old House," 1979-89, "Home Again With Bob Vila," 1990—.
b. Jun 20, 1946 in Miami, Florida
Source: *DcHiB; LegTOT; WhoAm 88, 90, 92, 94, 95, 96, 97; WhoEnt 92; WhoHisp 91, 92, 94*

Vila, George Raymond
American. Business Executive
Best known for contributions to rubber industry; chm., US Rubber Co., 1965-75, now called Uniroyal.
b. Mar 12, 1909 in Philadelphia, Pennsylvania
d. Jul 8, 1987 in New York, New York
Source: *BioIn 6, 7; BlueB 76; CurBio 63, 87; IntWW 74, 75, 76, 77, 78, 79, 80, 81; IntYB 78, 79, 80, 81, 82; NewYTBS 87; WhoAm 74, 76, 78, 80, 82, 84, 86, 88; WhoFI 74, 75; WhoWor 74*

Vilas, Guillermo
"Young Bull of the Pampas"
Argentine. Tennis Player
Won US Open, 1977; Italian, 1980.
b. Aug 17, 1952 in Mar del Plata, Argentina
Source: *BioIn 10, 11, 12, 13, 14, 16; BuCMET; CurBio 78; LegTOT; NewYTBS 77, 84; WhoIntT; WhoWor 78; WorAl*

Villa, Luz Corral de
[Mrs. Francisco "Pancho" Villa]
"Dona Lucha"
Mexican.
Known for her successful efforts to gain official recognition of her husband's revolutionary contributions to Mexico.
b. 1892 in Chihuahua, Mexico
d. Jul 6, 1981 in Chihuahua, Mexico
Source: *AnObit 1981; NewYTBS 81*

Villa, Pancho
[Doroteo Arango; Francisco Villa]
Mexican. Revolutionary
Notorious as bandit before fighting in revolution; viewed jointly as criminal, hero.
b. Jun 5, 1878 in Rio Grande, Mexico
d. Jul 20, 1923 in Parral, Mexico
Source: *AmNatBi; BioIn 14, 15, 16, 17, 19, 20, 22, 23, 24; CamBiEn; DcHiB; EncRev; EncWB 98; FacFETw; HisWorL; LegTOT; McGEWB; NewC; OxCAmH; REn; WhAm 4, HSA; WhDW; WorAl; WorAlBi*

Villa, Pancho
[Francisco Guilledo Villa]
Philippine. Boxer
World flyweight champ, 1923; Hall of
Fame, 1961.
b. Aug 1, 1901 in Iloilo, Philippines
d. Jul 14, 1925 in Oakland, California
Source: *BoxReg, 2; WhoBox 74*

Village People, The
[Alex Briley; David Hodo; Glenn M
Hughes; Randy Jones; Jeff Olson;
Felipe Rose; Ray Simpson; Victor
Willis]
American. Music Group
Formed late 1970s; known for
outrageous macho stage costumes; hit
single "YMCA," 1979.
Source: *BillEnR; BioIn 10, 11; ConMuA
80A; ConMus 7; EncRk 88; EncRkSt;
InB&W 85A; MorBAP; NewYTBS 76,
77; RkOn 85; RolSEnR 83; TwCPaSc;
WhoAm 92, 94; WhoHol 92; WhoRock
81*

Villa-Lobos, Heitor
Brazilian. Composer
Wrote over 1,400 works including
Bachianas Brasileiras, 1930-44,
featuring national folk music.
b. Mar 5, 1887 in Rio de Janeiro, Brazil
d. Nov 17, 1959 in Rio de Janeiro,
Brazil
Source: *AtlBL; BakBD 78, 84, 92;
BakBDTw; BakDcM; BriBkM 80;
CamBiEn; ChamBiD; CompSN, SUP;
CurBio 45, 60; DcArts; DcBrazL;
DcCM; DcCom 77; DcCom&M 79;
EncLatA; EncWB 98; FacFETw; HalFC
88; IntDcOp; LatAmCC; LatAmLi;
LegTOT; MacGEWB; MusMk;
NewAmDM; NewGrDM 80; NewGrDO;
NewOxM; ObitT 1951; OxCMus;
OxDcOp; PenDiMP A; REn; WhAm 3;
WhDW; WorAl; WorAlBi*

Villani, Giovanni
Italian. Historian, Merchant
Chronicled the history of Florence from
its origins to the age of Dante.
b. c. 1270 in Florence, Italy
d. 1348 in Florence, Italy
Source: *EncWB 98; McGEWB*

Villanueva, Carlos Raul
Venezuelan. Architect
Responsible for the development of
modern Venezuelan architecture.
b. May 30, 1900 in Croydon, England
d. Aug 16, 1975 in Caracas, Venezuela
Source: *BioIn 11; ConArch 80, 87, 94;
DcArch; DcD&D; DcHiB; DcTwCCu 3;
EncLatA; EncMA; IntDcAr; IntWW 74,
75, 76; MacEA; McGDA; OxCArt;
WhoArch; WhoWor 74*

Villard, Helen Francis Garrison
American. Social Reformer
Worked to further the women's
movement, advancement of black
people.
b. Dec 16, 1844 in Boston,
Massachusetts

d. Jul 5, 1928 in Dobbs Ferry, New
York
Source: *DcAmB; DcNAA*

Villard, Henry
[Ferdinand H G Hilgard]
American. Journalist, Businessman
Helped found Edison General Electric
Co., 1890s; most important railroad
promoter in US, 1879-83.
b. Apr 10, 1835 in Speyer, Bavaria
d. Nov 12, 1900 in Dobbs Ferry, New
York
Source: *AmAu&B; AmBi; AmNatBi;
ApCAB; BenetAL 91; BiDAmBL 83;
BiDAmJo; BioIn 1, 3, 11, 16, 17;
CamDcAB; CivWDc; DcAmB; DcLB 23;
DcNAA; DcPseud; EncAB-H 1974, 1996;
EncABHB 2; EncAJ; HarEnUS;
HisDcWJ; JrnUS; NatCAB 3;
NewEAmW; OhA&B; OxCAmH;
OxCAmL 65, 83, 95; REnAL; REnAW;
TwCBDA; WebAB 74, 79; WhAm HS;
WhCiWar; WorAl; WorAlBi*

Villard, Oswald (Garrison)
American. Journalist
Involved in founding NAACP; capital
correspondent for *Evening Post,*
Washington, DC, 1915.
b. Mar 13, 1872 in Wiesbaden, Germany
d. Oct 1, 1949 in New York, New York
Source: *AmAu&B; AmDec 1910;
AmNatBi; AmPeW; AmRef; AmSocL;
BenetAL 91; BiDAmJo; BioIn 2, 4, 5, 6,
7, 10, 14, 15, 16, 17, 19, 22; CamDcAB;
ConAu 113, 162; CurBio 40, 49; DcAmB
S4; DcAmSR; DcLB 25, 91; DcNAA;
EncAACR; EncAB-H 1974, 1996; EncAJ;
EncWB 98; JrnUS; LegTOT; McGEWB;
OxCAmH; OxCAmL 65, 83, 95; REn;
REnAL; TwCA, SUP; WebAB 74, 79;
WhAm 2; WhNAA; WorAl; WorAlBi;
WorAu 1900*

Villechaize, Herve Jean Pierre
French. Actor
Played Tattoo on TV series "Fantasy
Island," 1978-83.
b. Apr 23, 1943 in Paris, France
d. Sep 4, 1993 in Los Angeles,
California
Source: *BioIn 13; ConTFT 5; HalFC 84,
88; IntMPA 84, 86, 92; News 94; WhAm
11; WhoAm 80, 82, 84, 86, 88; WhoEnt
92; WhoHol A; WhoTelC; WhoWest 82*

Villehardouin, Geffroi de
French. Historian, Soldier
First French chronicler to write in the
vernacular and whose writings deserve
literary recognition, his topic was the
Fourth Crusade.
b. c. 1150 in Villehardouin, Champagne,
France
d. 1213
Source: *EncWB 98; McGEWB*

Villella, Edward Joseph
American. Dancer, Choreographer
Member, NY City Ballet, 1957—;
soloist, 1958-60; principle soloist,
1960-83; artistic director, OK Ballet,

1983-86; founding artistic director,
Miami City Ballet, 1985—.
b. Oct 1, 1936 in New York, New York
Source: *BiDD; BioIn 13; BioNews 74;
CelR 90; ChamBiD; CurBio 65;
FacFETw; IntWW 83, 91; NewYTBS 80;
St&PR 87; WhoAm 74, 76, 78, 80, 82,
84, 86, 88, 90, 92, 94, 95, 96, 97, 98,
99, 2000; WhoE 85, 86; WhoEnt 92, 98;
WhoGov 72, 75; WhoHol A; WhoSSW
86, 91, 93, 95, 97, 99; WhoWor 74, 78,
80, 82, 84, 87, 89, 91, 93, 95, 96, 97,
98, 99, 2000; WorAlBi*

Villeneuve, Gilles
"Air Canada"
Canadian. Auto Racer
Won six Grand Prix races.
b. Jan 18, 1950 in Berthierville, Quebec,
Canada
d. May 8, 1982 in Zolder, Belgium
Source: *AnObit 1982; WhoWor 82*

Villeneuve, Jacques
Canadian. Auto Racer
Won Indianapolis 500, 1995.
b. Apr 9, 1971 in Saint-Jean-sur-
Richelieu, Quebec, Canada
Source: *CamBiEn; CanWW 97, 98,
1999; IntWW 98, 2000; News 97, 97-1;
WhoWor 99, 2000*

Villers, George
[Duke of Buckingham]
English. Nobleman, Dramatist
Prominent writer of the restoration;
satirized Dryden in play *The
Rehearsal,* 1671.
b. Jan 30, 1628 in London, England
d. Apr 16, 1687 in Yorkshire, England
Source: *AtlBL; DcEnL; DcLEL; EvLB;
McGEWB; NewCol 75; OxCEng 67;
OxCThe 67; REn*

Villiers, Alan John
Australian., Author
Writings include *Whaling in the Frozen
South,* 1925; *The Bounty Ships of
France,* 1972.
b. Sep 23, 1903 in Melbourne, Australia
d. Mar 3, 1982 in Oxford, England
Source: *AuBYP 3; BioIn 1, 4, 7, 10, 11,
13, 22, 24; BlueB 76; ConAu 1NR;
IntAu&W 76, 77; IntWW 74, 75, 76, 77,
78, 79, 80, 81, 82N; OxCAusL;
OxCShps; SmATA 10; WhE&EA; Who
74, 82, 83N; WhoAm 74; WhoWor 74,
76, 78; WorAu 1900; WrDr 82*

Villiger, Kaspar
Swiss. Political Leader, Business
Executive
Pro-business member of the moderate
Radical Democratic Party (FDP), he
served as president of Switzerland's
coalition government in the early
1990s.
b. Feb 5, 1941 in Lucern, Switzerland
Source: *IntWW 97, 98, 2000; WhoFI 00;
WhoIntA 2; WhoWor 93, 95, 96, 97, 98,
99, 2000*

Villon, Francois
[Francois Des Loges; Francois de
  Montcorbier]
French. Poet
Wrote *Grand Testament,* 1461; became
  Rogue-hero of 19th c.
b. 1431? in Paris, France
d. 1463 in Paris, France
Source: *AtlBL; BbD; Benet 87, 96;
BiCoLiE; BiD&SB; BioIn 1, 2, 4, 5, 6, 7,
8, 9, 13, 17; CamBiEn; CasWL;
ChamBiD; ChhPo, S2, S3; CyWA 58, 97;
DcArts; DcBiPP; DcEuL; DcLB 208;
DcPseud; Dis&D; EncWB 98; EuAu;
EuWr 2; EvEuW; HalFC 84, 88;
LegTOT; LinLib L; McGEWB; MediFra;
NewC; NewCol 75; NewEOp 71;
OxCEng 67, 85, 95; OxCFr; PenC EUR;
PoeCrit 13; RAdv 14, 13-2; RComWL;
REn; WorAl; WorAlBi*

Vinay, Ramon
Chilean. Opera Singer
Tenor, baritone with NY Met., 1946-61;
  famed for role, recording of *Otello.*
b. Aug 31, 1912 in Chillan, Chile
Source: *BakBD 84, 92; BakBDTw; BioIn
7, 21, 23; IntDcOp; IntWWM 90;
MetOEnc; NewEOp 71; NewGrDM 80;
NewGrDO; NewYTBS 96; ObitPA 96;
OxDcOp; PenDiMP*

Vincennes, Francois Marie Bissot
[Sieur DeVincennes]
Canadian. Explorer
Established fort on Wabash River, 1731.
b. 1700 in Montreal, Quebec, Canada
d. Mar 25, 1736
Source: *AmBi; DcAmB*

Vincent, Fay
[Francis Thomas Vincent, Jr.]
American. Baseball Executive
Succeeded A. Bartlett Giamatti as
  baseball commissioner, 1989-92.
b. May 29, 1938 in Waterbury,
  Connecticut
Source: *Ballpl 90; BioIn 15, 16; CurBio
91; Dun&B 88; IntMPA 88; IntWW 93;
News 90, 90-2; NewYTBS 90; WhoAm
80, 82, 84, 86, 90, 92, 94; WhoE 83, 85,
86, 91, 93; WhoFI 87; WhoSSW 88;
WhoWor 84*

Vincent, Gene
[Vincent Eugene Craddock]
American. Singer
Known for wild habits on/off stage;
  recorded "Pistol Packin' Mama,"
  1960.
b. Feb 11, 1935 in Norfolk, Virginia
d. Oct 12, 1971 in Hollywood, California
Source: *AllMGCo, 83*

Vincent, Jan-Michael
American. Actor
Films include *Buster and Billie; White
Line Fever.*
b. Jul 15, 1944 in Ventura, California
Source: *BioIn 13; ConTFT 5; FilmEn;
HalFC 80, 84, 88; IntMPA 80, 84, 86,
88, 92; LegTOT; WhoEnt 92; WhoHol A;
WorAl; WorAlBi*

Vincent, John Heyl
American. Educator, Religious Leader
Methodist minister helped establish the
  Chautauqua lectures, an important
  means of adult education in 19th-
  century America.
b. Feb 23, 1832 in Tuscaloosa, Alabama
d. May 9, 1920
Source: *Alli SUP; AmBi; AmNatBi;
ApCAB, X; BbD; BiDAmEd; BiD&SB;
BiDSA; BioIn 1, 12, 14; DcAmAu;
DcAmB; DcNAA; EncAAH; EncWB 98;
EncWM; HarEnUS; LuthC 75;
McGEWB; Meth; NatCAB 9, 24;
PeoHis; RelLAm 1, 2; TwCBDA; WebAB
74, 79; WhAm 1; WorAl; WorAlBi*

Vincent, Marjorie Judith
American. Beauty Contest Winner
Miss America, 1991; first black woman
  to be crowned by reigning black
  queen.
b. Nov 21, 1964 in Chicago, Illinois
Source: *ConBlB 2; WhoAfA 9, 10, 11,
12; WhoBlA 7, 8*

Vincent de Paul, Saint
French. Religious Leader
Founded charities, Vincentians, Sisters of
  Charity, circa 1625; helped revive
  French Catholicism.
b. Apr 24, 1581 in Pouy, France
d. Sep 27, 1660 in Paris, France
Source: *DcCathB; LinLib S; McGEWB;
NewCol 75; OxCFr*

Vines, Ellsworth
[Henry Ellsworth Vines, Jr.]
American. Tennis Player, Author
Youngest player to win US amateur
  championship, 1931; writings include
  How to Play Tennis, 1938.
b. Sep 28, 1911 in Pasadena, California
Source: *BiDAmSp OS; BioIn 1, 6, 7, 12,
14, 17, 19; BuCMET; CmCal; ConAu
109; NewYTBS 94; WhoGolf; WhoSpor*

Vinogradoff, Paul Gavrilovitch
Russian. Educator, Historian
Wrote and edited many works of
  political and legal history.
b. Dec 1, 1854 in Kostroma, Russia
d. Dec 19, 1925 in Oxford, England
Source: *DcNaB 1922; EncWB 98;
GloEnch; McGEWB; OxCLaw*

Vinson, Carl
American. Politician
Dem. congressman from GA, 1914-65.
b. Nov 18, 1883 in Milledgeville,
  Georgia
d. Jun 1, 1981 in Milledgeville, Georgia
Source: *AmNatBi; AnObit 1981;
BiDrAC; BiDrUSC 89; BioIn 1, 2, 4, 5,
6, 7, 11, 12, 23, 24; CamBiEn;
CamDcAB; CurBio 42, 81, 81N;
EncCW; FacFETw; NewYTBS 81;
PolProf E, J, K, T; ScrEAmL 1; WhAm
7; WhAmP*

Vinson, Cleanhead
[Eddie Vinson]
American. Jazz Musician, Singer
Saxophonist, vocalist; sang with Cootie
  Williams, 1940s; own band, 1960s.
b. Dec 18, 1917 in Houston, Texas
d. Jul 2, 1988 in Los Angeles, California
Source: *AllMGJa; AnObit 1988; BakBD
92; BiDAfM; BiDJaz; BioIn 13;
BluesWW; CmpEPM; EncJzS; GuBlues;
InB&W 80, 85; NewGrDJ 88, 94;
NewYTBS 88; PenEncP; WhoJazz 72*

Vinson, Frederick Moore
American. Supreme Court Justice
Served on US Supreme Court, 1946-53;
  advocate of civil rights, liberal
  construction of the Constitution.
b. Jan 22, 1890 in Louisa, Kentucky
d. Sep 8, 1953 in Washington, District of
  Columbia
Source: *AmPolLe; BiDrAC; BiDrUSC
89; BiDrUSE 71, 89; BioIn 1, 2, 3, 4, 5,
10, 11, 15, 23; CamDcAB; ChamBiD;
EncSoH; HisDcSc; LinLib S; OxCSupC;
SupCtJu; WebAB 74, 79; WhAmP;
WorAl*

Vinson, Helen
American. Actor
Supporting roles in films during 1930s-
  40s include *The Thin Man Goes
  Home,* 1945.
b. Sep 17, 1907 in Beaumont, Texas
Source: *BioIn 21; DcPseud; FilmEn;
FilmgC; ForYSC; GangFlm; HalFC 80,
84, 88; HolCA; InWom SUP; MovMk;
OlFamFa; ThFT; VixFlM; WhoHol 92,
A; WhoThe 77; WhThe*

Vinton, Bobby
[Stanley Robert Vinton]
"The Polish Prince"
American. Singer
Hits include "Blue Velvet"; had sold
  over 25 million records by 1974.
b. Apr 16, 1935 in Canonsburg,
  Pennsylvania
Source: *ASCAP 66; BiDAmM; BioNews
74; ConAu 120; CurBio 77; EncPR&S
89; EncRk 88; EncRkSt; LegTOT;
PenEncP; WhoAm 86; WhoEnt 92;
WhoHol 92, A; WhoRock 81; WhoRocM
82; WorAl; WorAlBi*

Vinton, Will
American., Filmmaker
Uses claymation to create TV
  commercial characters.
b. Nov 17, 1938 in McMinnville, Oregon
Source: *BioIn 12, 13, 15; WhoAdv 90;
WhoEnt 92*

Viola, Frank John, Jr.
American. Baseball Player
Pitcher, Minnesota Twins, 1982-89; NY
  Mets, 1989-91; Boston Red Sox,
  1992-94; Toronto Blue Jays, 1994—.
b. Apr 19, 1960 in East Meadow, New
  York
Source: *Ballpl 90; BaseEn 88; BaseReg
87, 88; BioIn 14, 15, 16; NewYTBS 87;*

WhoAm 90, 92, 94, 95, 96, 97; WhoE 95; WorAlBi

Violet, Arlene
American. Lawyer
First elected female attorney general in the United States (for state of Rhode Island); took on high-profile challenges, such as the retrial of socialite Claus von Bulow, who was eventually acquitted of charges that he killed his wife; former nun is known for her dedication and zeal in her duties.
b. Aug 19, 1943 in Providence, Rhode Island
Source: *ConNews 85-3; WhoAm 86; WhoAmL 85; WhoAmP 85, 87, 89, 91, 93, 95, 97, 1999; WhoAmW 87; WhoE 86*

Viollet le Duc, Eugene Emmanuel
French. Architect
Supporter of Gothic revival in France; noted for restorations of churches, town halls.
b. Jan 27, 1814 in Paris, France
d. Sep 17, 1879 in Lausanne, Switzerland
Source: *CamBiEn; ChamBiD; DcArch; EncHiCA; EncWB 98; McGEWB; NewCol 75*

Vionnet, Madeleine
French. Fashion Designer
Invented revolutionary bias cut for Women's Fashion, 1930s.
b. Jun 22, 1877 in Chilleurs-aux-Bois, France
d. Mar 2, 1975 in Paris, France
Source: *BioIn 5, 10; ConDes 90; ContDcW 89; DcTwDes; EncFash; IntDcWB; InWom SUP; NewYTBS 75; WhoFash 88; WomFir; WorFshn*

Viorst, Judith (Stahl)
American. Author, Poet
Writings include *The Village Square*, 1965; *People and Other Aggravations*, 1971.
b. Feb 2, 1931 in Newark, New Jersey
Source: *ArtclWW 2; AuBYP 3; BenetAL 91; BestSel 90-1; BioIn 15, 16; ChlBkCr; ConAu 2NR, 26NR, 49; ConPopW; DcLB 52; EncALit; IntAu&W 86; InWom SUP; LegTOT; MajAl; SmATA 7, 70; TwCChW 2, 3, 4; WhoAm 82, 84, 86, 88, 90, 92, 94, 95, 96, 97, 98, 99, 2000; WhoAmW 95, 97, 99; WhoEnt 98; WhoSSW 73; WhoUSWr 88; WhoWrEP 89, 92, 95; WrDr 88, 92, 94, 96*

Viotti, Giovanni Battista
"The Father of the Modern Technique"
Italian. Musician, Composer
Foremost violinist of his time; played for royalty, directed the Paris Opera.
b. May 23, 1753 in Vercelli, Italy
d. Mar 3, 1824 in London, England
Source: *BakBD 84; BioIn 1, 2, 3, 4, 7, 8, 14, 22; CelCen; ChamBiD; DcBiPP; DcCathB; OxCMus; WebBD 83*

Virchow, Rudolf
German. Pathologist, Political Leader
Founded cellular pathology.
b. Oct 31, 1821 in Schivelbein, Prussia
d. Sep 5, 1905 in Berlin, Germany
Source: *AsBiEn; BbD; BiD&SB; BiDMoPL; BiHiMed; CelCen; ChamBiD; HisPhAn; InSci; LarDcSc; OxCGer 76, 86, 97; WebBD 83*

Viren, Lasse
Finnish. Track Athlete
Distance runner; won two gold medals, 1972 Olympics; won gold medals, 1972, 1976 Olympics for the 5,000- and 10,000- metre races.
b. Jul 22, 1949
Source: *BioIn 12, 22, 24; IntWW 81, 82, 83, 89, 91, 93, 97, 98, 2000; WhoTr&F 73*

Virtanen, Artturi Llmari
Finnish. Chemist
Won Nobel Prize, 1945, for work on preservation of fodder crops.
b. Jan 15, 1895 in Helsinki, Finland
d. Nov 11, 1973 in Helsinki, Finland
Source: *BiESc; McGMS 80; WhoNob*

Viscardi, Henry, Jr.
American. Businessman
Founder, trustee of Abilities Inc., NY, since 1942; pres., chm., Human Resources Center, since 1955.
b. May 10, 1912 in New York, New York
Source: *ABCDiRi; BioIn 2, 3, 7, 9, 15; ConAu 5NR, 5R; CurBio 54, 66; NewYTBE 72; WhoAm 74, 76, 78, 80; WhoE 74*

Visconti, Gian Galeazzo, Duke of Milan
Italian. Nobleman
Conquered most of northern Italy while attempting to control the entire Italian peninsula.

Visconti, Luchino
Italian. Director
Films' recurrent theme was moral disintegration of a family including *The Damned*, 1961.
b. Nov 2, 1906 in Milan, Italy
d. Mar 17, 1976 in Rome, Italy
Source: *BakBD 84; Benet 87, 96; BiDFilm, 81, 94; BioIn 5, 6, 7, 8, 9, 10, 11, 12, 13, 14, 15, 18, 20, 23; CamBiEn; CamGWoT; CelR; ChamBiD; CmOp; CnThe; ConAu 39NR, 65, 81; ConLC 16; CurBio 65, 76N; DcArts; DcBiPP; DcFM; EncEurC; EncWT; Ent; FacFETw; FilmEn; FilmgC; HalFC 80, 84, 88; IntDcF 1-2, 2-2; IntDcOp; IntDcT 3; IntMPA 75, 76; IntWW 74, 75; ItaFilm; LegTOT; MakMC; MetOEnc; MiSFD 9N; MovMk; NewEOp 71; NewGrDM 80; NewYTBS 76; OxCFilm; OxCThe 67, 83; OxDcOp; RAdv 14, 13-3; TheaDir; WhAm 6; Who 74; WhoOp 76; WhoWor 74; WhScrn 83; WorAl; WorAlBi; WorEFlm; WorFDir 1*

Vishnevskaya, Galina (Pavlovna)
Russian. Opera Singer
First Russian diva to sing with Metropolitan Opera, 1961, in title role of *Aida*.
b. Oct 25, 1926 in Leningrad, Union of Soviet Socialist Republics
Source: *BakBD 78, 84, 92; BakBDTw; BiDSovU; BioIn 14, 15, 21; BriBkM 80; CmOp; CurBio 66; FacFETw; IntDcOp; IntWW 74, 75, 76, 77, 78, 79, 80, 81, 82, 83, 89, 91, 93, 97, 98, 2000; IntWWM 77, 80, 85, 90; IntWWW 2; InWom, SUP; MetOEnc; MusSN; NewAmDM; NewEOp 71; NewGrDM 80; NewGrDO; OxDcOp; PenDiMP; SovUn; Who 74, 82, 83, 85, 88, 90, 92, 94; WhoAm 80, 82, 84, 86, 88, 90, 92, 94, 95, 96, 97; WhoAmM 83; WhoOp 76*

Vishnevsky, Alexandr Alekandrovich
Russian. Surgeon
Director, Institute of Surgery, 1948-75; noted for working with local anesthesia and open-heart surgery, late 1960s.
b. May 24, 1906 in Kazan, Russia
d. Nov 19, 1975, Union of Soviet Socialist Republics
Source: *IntWW 74; NewYTBS 75; WhoWor 74*

Vishniac, Roman
American. Photographer
Best known for photographs documenting doomed Jews in Nazi Germany.
b. Aug 19, 1897 in Saint Petersburg, Russia
d. Jan 22, 1990 in New York, New York
Source: *AnObit 1990; BioIn 4, 5, 7, 8, 10, 13, 16; ConPhot 82, 88, 95; CurBio 67, 90, 90N; FacFETw; ICPEnP; InSci; MacBEP; NewYTBS 90; WhAm 10; WhoAm 86, 88*

Visscher, William Lightfoot
American. Poet
Wrote over 1,000 poems which were published in newspapers.
b. Nov 25, 1842 in Owingsville, Kentucky
d. Feb 10, 1924 in Chicago, Illinois
Source: *AmAu&B; AmLY; DcAmB; DcNAA; JrnUS; WhAm 1*

Visser T. Hooft, Willem Adolf
Dutch. Religious Leader
Founding general-secretary, World Council of Churches, 1948-66.
b. Sep 20, 1900 in Haarlem, Netherlands
d. Jul 4, 1985 in Geneva, Switzerland
Source: *BiDChrM; CamBiEn; ChamBiD; ConAu 116; CurBio 49, 85; EncWB 98*

Vitale, Dick
[Richard Vitale]
American. Basketball Coach, Sportscaster
Coach, Detroit Pistons, 1978-79; flamboyant basketball commentator for ABC, ESPN.
b. Jun 9, 1939 in Garfield, New Jersey

Source: *BioIn 15, 16; News 88, 94; NewYTBS 79*

Vitale, Milly
Italian. Actor
Films since 1950s include *The Juggler*, 1953; *War and Peace*, 1956.
b. Jul 16, 1938 in Rome, Italy
Source: *FilmgC; ForYSC; HalFC 84, 88; IntMPA 75, 76, 77, 78, 79, 80, 81, 82, 84, 86, 88; WhoHol A*

Vitellius, Aulus
Roman. Ruler
Roman emperor, 69, after death of Otho; defeated, killed by Primus.
b. 15
d. 69
Source: *BioIn 14, 20, 22; CamBiEn; ChamBiD; DcBiPP; NewCol 75; OxCClL; REn; WebBD 83*

Vitoria, Francisco de
Spanish. Theologian
First great theorist of modern international law, he developed a justification for Spain's conquests in the New World.
b. c. 1483
d. Aug 12, 1546 in Salamanca, Spain
Source: *BiDChrM; CasWL; EncWB 98; McGEWB; OxCLaw*

Vitruvius
[Marcus Vitruvius Pollio]
Roman. Architect
Wrote only source of classical Greek, Roman architecture *De Architectura*, c.27-23 BC.
b. 70BC
d. 16BC
Source: *AsBiEn; AtlBL; PlP&P; REn*

Vitry, Philippe de
French. Poet, Composer, Clergy
Considered an outstanding poet of his day, the bishop's treatise *Ars nova* became the rallying cry for all "modern" composers after about 1320.
b. 1291 in Paris, France
d. 1360
Source: *BakBD 78, 84, 92; BakDcM; BriBkM 80; DcLB 208; EncWB 98; McGEWB; MusMk; NewAmDM; NewGrDM 80; NewOxM; OxCMus*

Vitti, Monica
[Maria Louisa Ceciarelli]
Italian. Actor
Appeared mostly on stage in classical roles; first leading role in film: *L'Avventura*.
b. Nov 3, 1931 in Rome, Italy
Source: *BiDFilm; BioIn 11, 17; ContDcW 89; DcPseud; EncEurC; FilmAG WE; FilmEn; FilmgC; HalFC 84, 88; IntDcF 1-3, 2-3; IntDcWB; IntMPA 86, 92; IntWW 79, 80, 81, 82, 83, 89, 91, 93, 98, 2000; IntWWW 2; InWom SUP; ItaFilm; MotPP; MovMk; OxCFilm; WhoHol 92, A; WorEFlm*

Vittorini, Elio
Italian. Author
Known for his autobiographical novels, he anticipated the Italian neorealist movement.
b. Jul 23, 1908 in Siracusa, Italy
d. Feb 14, 1966 in Milan, Italy
Source: *Benet 87, 96; BiCoLiE; BioIn 2, 4, 7, 8, 22; CamBiEn; CasWL; ChamBiD; ClDMEL 80; CnMWL; ConAu 25R, 133; ConLC 6, 9, 14; CyWA 89, 97; DcItL 1, 2; EncWB 98; EncWL 1, 2, 3; EuWr 12; EvEuW; GrFLW; McGEWB; ModRL; Novels; PenC EUR; RAdv 14, 13-2; REn; RfGWoL 95; TwCA SUP; TwCWr; WhoTwCL; WorAu 1900*

Vivaldi, Antonio (Lucio)
"The Red Priest"
Italian. Musician, Composer
Violinist, famous for over 100 concertos including *The Four Seasons*.
b. Mar 4, 1678 in Venice, Italy
d. Jul 27, 1741 in Vienna, Austria
Source: *AtlBL; BakDcM; CamBiEn; ChamBiD; NewCol 75; REn; WebBD 83*

Vivekananda
Indian. Religious Leader
Hindu missionary and spiritual leader founded the Vedanta Society to introduce Indian philosophical and religious beliefs to the West, and the Ramakrishna mission to bring about reforms in India.
b. 1863 in Calcutta, India
d. 1902
Source: *BiDAmCu; BioIn 3, 5, 6, 7, 8, 11, 12, 20; CasWL; ChamBiD; DcAmReB 1, 2; DcInB; DcPseud; EncO&P 2, 3; EncWB 98; McGEWB; NewAgE 90; PopDcHi; RAdv 14; RelLAm 1, 2; TwCLC 88*

Vizenor, Gerald
American. Author
Poetry collections include *Seventeen Chirps*, 1964; short stories collected in *Wordarrows*, 1978.
b. Oct 22, 1934 in Minneapolis, Minnesota
Source: *BenetAL 91; CamDcAB; CamGLE; CamHAL; ConAu 22AS; ConLC 103; CyWA 97; DcLB 175; DcNAL; EncNAB; IdentIs; IntWWP 77; NatAL; NatNAL; NotNaAm; OxCAmL 95; OxCTwCL; TwCWW 91; WrDr 92*

Vladimir, I
"Vladimir the Great"
Russian. Prince
Grand prince of Kievan Russia from c. 980 to 1015, solidified the first Russian state through conquest and conversion to Christianity.
b. c. 956
d. 1015
Source: *BioIn 5, 14, 20; CamBiEn; DcCathB; LuthC 75; WhDW; WhoChr*

Vlaminck, Maurice de
French. Artist
Painted in broad strokes, straight from paint tube to canvas; began with Fauvism ended with sinister realism.
b. Apr 4, 1876 in Paris, France
d. Oct 11, 1958 in Paris, France
Source: *AtlBL; Benet 87, 96; BioIn 1, 3, 4, 5, 6, 7, 8, 17; CamBiEn; ChamBiD; ClaDrA; ConArt 83; DcArts; DcTwArt; DcTwCCu 2; IntDcAA 90; LegTOT; McGDA; McGEWB; NewCol 75; ObitT 1951; OxCArt; OxCTwCA; OxDcArt; PhDcTCA 77; REn*

Vlasic, Joseph
American. Business Executive
Created Vlasic Pickle Co., 1959; successful ad campaign made Vlasic synonymous with pickles.
b. 1904?, Yugoslavia
d. Jul 10, 1986 in Phoenix, Arizona
Source: *BioIn 15; Entr*

Vlieger, Simon Jacobsz de
Dutch. Artist
Best known for *Rescue*, 1630; *Seascape with a Boat*.
b. 1600 in Rotterdam, Netherlands
d. 1653 in Weesp, Netherlands
Source: *BioIn 5, 19, 23; McGDA; OxCArt; OxCShps*

Voegelin, Eric (Herman Wilhelm)
American. Political Scientist, Philosopher, Historian
Regarded as the most subtle rethinker of Augustine's *City of God*, and as the leading Christian philosopher of history of the 20th century.
b. Jan 3, 1901 in Cologne, Germany
d. Jan 19, 1985
Source: *CamDcAB*

Voelker, John Donaldson
[Robert Traver]
American. Judge, Author
Wrote *Anatomy of a Murder*, 1957; made into film, 1959.
b. Jun 29, 1903 in Ishpeming, Michigan
d. Mar 18, 1991 in Ishpeming, Michigan
Source: *AmAu&B; BioIn 4, 5, 10, 17, 18; BlueB 76; ConAu 1R, 134, X; ConNov 72, 76; DcLP 87A; IntAu&W 76, 77; MichAu 80; NewYTBS 91; WhAm 10; WhoAm 74, 76, 78; WhoAmA 91; WorAu 1950; WrDr 76, 80, 82, 84, 86, 88, 90, 92, 94N*

Voelker, Paul Frederick
American. Educator, Author
Pres., Battle Creek College, 1925-33; wrote *Function of Ideals in Social Education*, 1921.
b. Sep 30, 1875 in Evart, Michigan
Source: *WhAm 5; WhNAA*

Vogel, Hans-Jochen
German. Politician
Leader, Social Dem. party, 1982-91; minister of justice, 1974-81.
b. Feb 3, 1926 in Gottingen, Germany

Source: *BioIn 10, 13, 14; CamBiEn;
ChamBiD; CurBio 84; EncWB, 98;
IntWW 83, 89, 91, 93, 97, 98, 2000;
IntYB 79, 80, 81, 82; Who 85, 88, 90,
92, 94, 98, 99, 2000; WhoWor 84, 87,
89, 91, 93, 95; WrDr 92*

Vogel, Julius
English. Political Leader, Journalist
New Zealand journalist, financier,
 politician, and prime minister led the
 country to economic recovery after the
 post-gold rush depression.
b. Feb 24, 1835 in London, England
d. Mar 12, 1899 in East Molesey,
 England
Source: *Alli SUP; BioIn 1, 9; CamBiEn;
ChamBiD; DcLEL; DcNaB S1; EncSF
93; EncWB 98; McGEWB; ScF&FL 1;
ScFEYrs; StaCVF*

Vogel, Paula (Anne)
American. Dramatist
Wrote play *The Baltimore Waltz,* 1989;
 won Obie Award, 1992; won Pulitzer
 for *How I Learned to Drive,* 1998.
b. Nov 16, 1951 in Washington, District
 of Columbia
Source: *ConAmD; ConAu 108; ConDr
93; ConLC 76; ConWomD; RfGAmL 4;
WhoAm 2000; WhoAmW 99; WhoEnt 92,
98*

Vogelstein, Bert
American. Biologist
Cancer researcher who studies the
 genetics of cancer; helped to identify
 the genes called ''tumor-supressors.''
b. Jun 2, 1949
Source: *CurBio 96*

Vogelweide, Walther von der
German. Poet, Composer, Singer
Known for his genuine feeling and
 meticulous skill in metrics and rhyme
 patterns, he was the greatest producer
 of minnesongs and Spruche—gnomic
 or didactic songs—of the Middle
 Ages.
b. c. 1170 in Bolzano, Austria
d. 1229
Source: *BakBD 92; EncWB 98; WhDW*

Vogl, Heinrich
German. Opera Singer
Leading Wagnerian tenor at Bayreuth,
 1876-97.
b. Jan 15, 1845 in Aue, Germany
d. Apr 21, 1900 in Munich, Germany
Source: *BakBD 78, 84, 92; CmOp;
MetOEnc; NewEOp 71; NewGrDM 80;
NewGrDO; OxDcOp; PenDiMP*

Vogues, The
[Charles Blasko; William Burkette; Hugh
 Geyer; Don Miller]
American. Music Group
Formed, 1960; hits include ''Turn
 Around Look At Me,'' 1968.
Source: *DrRegL 75; EncPR&S 74; RkOn
78; WhoRock 81; WhoRocM 82*

Vohor, (Rialuth) Serge
Vanuatuan. Political Leader
Member of the Union of Moderate
 Parties (UMP), which rejects the
 influence of foreigners, he was elected
 the fourth prime minister of Vanuatu
 in 1995, resigned after only two
 months, and regained the office in
 1996.
b. Apr 24, 1955 in Espiritu Santo,
 Vanuatu

Voight, Jon
American. Actor
Won Oscar, 1979, for *Coming Home.*
b. Dec 29, 1938 in Yonkers, New York
Source: *BiDFilm 94; BioIn 8, 10, 11, 12,
13, 14, 15, 23, 24; BioNews 74; BkPepl;
CelR, 90; ConAu 179; ConTFT 2, 7, 17;
CurBio 74; DcArts; FilmEn; FilmgC;
ForYSC; HalFC 80, 84, 88; IntDcF 2-3;
IntMPA 75, 76, 77, 78, 79, 80, 81, 82,
84, 86, 88, 92, 94, 96; IntWW 79, 80,
81, 82, 83, 89, 91, 93, 97, 98, 2000;
ItaFilm; LegTOT; MovMk; NewYTBS 79;
OsStAZ; OxCFilm; WhoAm 74, 76, 78,
80, 82, 84, 86, 88, 90, 92, 94, 95, 96,
97, 99, 2000; WhoEnt 92, 98; WhoHol
92, A; WhoThe 77, 81; WhoWor 95, 96,
97, 98, 99, 2000; WorAl; WorAlBi*

Voinovich, George V(ictor)
American. Politician
Mayor of Cleveland, 1979-90; Rep.
 governor, OH, 1991-99; Rep. Senator
 from OH, 1999—.
b. Jul 15, 1936 in Cleveland, Ohio
Source: *AlmAP 92; St&PR 75; WhoAm
84, 86, 88; WhoAmP 73, 85, 91;
WhoMW 82, 92*

Voit, Willard Darby
American. Business Executive
Chm. of W J Voit Rubber Corp., 1960-
 70.
b. Nov 8, 1910 in Seattle, Washington
d. Feb 1980 in Newport Beach,
 California
Source: *St&PR 75; WhoAm 74, 76, 78*

Volcker, Paul Adolph
American. Government Official, Banker
Chm., Federal Reserve Board, 1979-87;
 known for reducing double-digit
 inflation.
b. Sep 5, 1927 in Cape May, New Jersey
Source: *AmPolLe; BioIn 6, 9, 10, 12, 13,
14, 15, 16; ChamBiD; ConAu 114, 129;
CurBio 73; EncABHB 7; EncWB; IntWW
83, 91; NewYTBS 75, 79, 88; PolProf
NF; Who 85, 92; WhoAm 86, 88;
WhoAmP 85, 91; WhoE 86; WhoFI 85,
92; WhoWor 82, 84, 87, 91; WorAlBi*

Volkov, Leon
American. Journalist
Defected to US from USSR, 1945;
 Soviet affairs specialist with *Newsweek*
 mag. for 20 yrs.
b. Jan 22, 1920
d. Jan 22, 1974 in Bethesda, Maryland
Source: *ConAu 45; NewYTBS 74*

Volkov, Vladislav Nikolayevich
Russian. Cosmonaut
Flight engineer, *Soyuz 7,* 1969; died in
 space due to faulty depressurization.
b. Nov 23, 1935 in Moscow, Union of
 Soviet Socialist Republics
d. Jun 30, 1971
Source: *NewYTBE 71; WhAm 5*

Vollbracht, Michaele J
American. Fashion Designer, Artist
Asst. to Geoffrey Beene, 1968-70;
 partner, chm., Michaele Vollbracht,
 NYC; won Coty, 1980.
b. Nov 17, 1947 in Quincy, Illinois
Source: *BioIn 11; WhoAm 82, 84*

Vollenweider, Andreas
Swiss. Musician
Cult harpist who combines jazz, classical
 styles; has million-selling albums
 Behind the Gardens, 1981; *Caverna
 Magica,* 1982.
b. 1953 in Zurich, Switzerland
Source: *BakBD 92; BakBDTw; BioIn 14,
15; ConNews 85-2; CurBio 87; LegTOT;
NewAgMG*

Vollmann, William T.
American. Author
Often compared to Wolfe and Pynchon;
 wrote *An Afghanistan Picture Show,*
 1992.
b. 1959 in Santa Monica, California
Source: *ConAu 67NR, 134; ConLC 89;
ConPopW; EncALit; EncSF 93;
MajTwCW 2; WrDr 94, 96, 98, 99*

Vollmer, Lula
American. Dramatist
Plays include *The Shame Woman,* 1923;
 Sentinels, 1931.
b. 1898 in Keyser, North Carolina
d. May 2, 1955
Source: *AmAu&B; AmWomD;
AmWomPl; BioIn 1, 3, 4, 16, 22; CnMD;
FemDram A; InWom SUP; ModWD;
NotNAT B; OxCAmL 65; TwCA, SUP;
WhAm 3; WhNAA; WhThe; WorAu 1900*

Volner, Jill Wine
American. Lawyer
Asst. special prosecutor during Watergate
 trial, 1973-75.
b. May 5, 1943 in Chicago, Illinois
Source: *BioNews 74; CamDcAB;
GoodHs; InWom SUP; NewYTBE 73;
WhoAm 74, 76, 78, 80; WhoAmL 78, 79;
WhoAmP 77, 79, 81, 83; WhoAmW 77,
79, 81, 83; WhoGov 75*

**Volney, (Constantin) Francois
 Chasseboeuf, Comte de**
French. Author
Best known for essay on the philosophy
 of history: *Les Ruines, ou Meditation
 sur les Revolutions des Empires,* 1791.
b. Feb 3, 1757 in Craon, France
d. Apr 25, 1820 in Paris, France
Source: *ApCAB; BbD; BbtC; BiD&SB;
DcEuL; EncEnl; EuAu; OxCFr*

Volpe, John A(nthony)
American. Diplomat
US secretary of transportation, 1969-73;
ambassador to Italy, 1973-77; Rep.
governor of MA, 1960s.
b. Dec 8, 1908 in Wakefield,
Massachusetts
d. Nov 11, 1994 in Nahunt,
Massachusetts
Source: *AmCath 80; BiDrAC; BiDrGov
1789; BiDrUSE 71, 89; BioIn 6, 8, 10,
11, 12, 15; BlueB 76; CurBio 62, 95N;
IntWW 74, 75, 76, 77, 78, 79, 80, 81, 82,
83, 89; PolProf K, NF; USBiR 74;
WhoAm 74, 76; WhoAmP 73, 75, 77, 79;
WhoEng 88; WhoFI 74; WhoGov 72, 75,
77; WhoSSW 73; WhoWor 74, 76*

Volpi, Alfredo
Brazilian. Artist
Abstract paintings marked by intricate
geometric forms in bright colors.
b. 1895 in Lucca, Italy
d. May 30, 1988 in Sao Paulo, Brazil
Source: *McGDA; OxCTwCA*

Volstead, Andrew J
American. Politician
Ten-term congressman who personified
Prohibition with passage of Volstead
Act, 1919.
b. Oct 31, 1860 in Kenyon, Minnesota
d. Jan 20, 1947 in Granite Falls,
Minnesota
Source: *BiDrAC; CamBiEn; DcAmB S4;
LinLib S; ObitOF 79; WhAm 2; WhAmP;
WorAl*

**Volta, Alessandro Giuseppe
Antonio Anastasio**
Italian. Physicist
The volt, a unit of electrical
measurement, is named for him.
b. Feb 18, 1745 in Como, Italy
d. May 7, 1827 in Como, Italy
Source: *AsBiEn; CamBiEn; DcScB;
EncEnl; NewCol 75; RanHWDS; WebBD
83*

Voltaire
[Francois-Marie Arouet]
French. Author, Philosopher
Wrote *Candide*, 1759.
b. Nov 21, 1694 in Paris, France
d. May 30, 1778 in Paris, France
Source: *AsBiEn; AtlBL; BbD; Benet 87;
BiCoLiE; BiD&SB; BiDPsy; BioIn 14,
15, 17, 18, 20; BlkwCE; BlmGEL;
CamBiEn; CamGWoT; CasWL;
ChamBiD; CnThe; CrtSuMy; CyWA 58,
97; DcArts; DcBiA; DcEnL; DcEuL;
DcPseud; DcPup; Dis&D; EncEth;
EncLitE; EncSF, 93; EncWB 98;
EncWT; Ent; EuAu; EuWr 4; EvEuW;
GloEncH; GrFLW; GuFrLit 2; IntDcT 2;
LegTOT; LitC 14; LngCEL; LuthC 75;
MagSWL; McGEWB; McGEWD 72, 84;
MetOEnc; NamesHP; NewC; NewEOp
71; NewEScF; NewGrDO; Novels;
OxCCan; OxCEng 67, 85, 95; OxCFr;
OxCGer 76; OxCMus; OxCThe 67, 83;
OxDcOp; PenC EUR; RAdv 14, 13-2;
RComWL; REn; REnWD; RfGShF 2;*

*RfGWoL 95; ScF&FL 1, 92; ScFEYrs;
ScFSB; ShSCr 12; WhoChr; WorAlBi;
WorLitC; WrPh P*

Von Bekesy, Georg
American. Scientist
Won 1961 Nobel Prize in medicine for
research on hearing.
b. Jun 3, 1899 in Budapest, Austria-
Hungary
d. Jun 13, 1972 in Honolulu, Hawaii
Source: *BiESc; BioIn 6, 9, 10, 11, 14,
15, 20; CurBio 62, 72; DcAmMeB 84;
SciMath; WhAm 5; WhoNob, 90, 95*

VonBraun, Wernher
American. Scientist
Led development of V-2 missiles for
Germany during WW II; directed
rocket research in US.
b. Mar 23, 1912 in Wirsitz, Germany
d. Jun 1977 in Alexandria, Virginia
Source: *AmAu&B; AmMWSc 73P, 76P;
AuBYP 2; BlueB 76; CelR; ConAu 5R,
9NR, 69; CurBio 52; InSci; IntWW 74;
McGEWB; NewYTBE 70; WebAB 74, 79;
WhAm 7; Who 74; WhoAm 74, 76;
WhoSSW 73; WhoWor 74; WrDr 76*

Von Bulow, Claus
[Claus Borberg]
British. Businessman
Convicted, 1982, of injecting wife with
insulin, resulting in irreversible coma.
b. Aug 11, 1926 in Copenhagen,
Denmark
Source: *AmDec 1980; BioIn 12, 13, 14,
15, 16; DcPseud; FacFETw; LegTOT*

Von Bulow, Sunny
[Martha Sharp Crawford Von Bulow;
Mrs. Claus Von Bulow]
American. Socialite, Victim
Husband convicted, 1982, of trying to
murder her with insulin injection.
b. Sep 1, 1932 in Manassas, Virginia
Source: *BioIn 12, 13, 14, 15, 16;
LegTOT*

VonDaeniken, Erich
Swiss. Author
Wrote *Chariots of the Gods?* 1968;
Unsolved Mysteries of the Past, 1969.
b. Apr 14, 1935 in Zofingen, Switzerland
Source: *AuNews 1; BioNews 75; ConAu
17NR*

Vondel, Joost van den
Dutch. Poet, Dramatist
Considered the greatest of all Dutch
writers, he was the national poet as the
Netherlands was emerging as a
national state.
b. Nov 17, 1587 in Cologne, Germany
d. Feb 5, 1679 in Amsterdam,
Netherlands
Source: *CamBiEn; CamGWoT;
ChamBiD; EncWB 98; RAdv 14;
RfGWoL 95; WhDW*

VonDoderer, Heimito
Austrian. Author
Best known for novel *Die
Strudelhofstiege*, 1951.
b. Sep 5, 1896
d. Dec 23, 1966 in Vienna, Austria
Source: *CasWL; ConAu 25R; EncWL 1;
EvEuW; LinLib L; ModGL; OxCGer 76;
PenC EUR; REn; TwCWr; WhoTwCL;
WorAu 1950*

Von Eckardt, Wolf
German. Critic, Author
Design critic, *Time* mag., 1981-85;
writings include *Back to the Drawing
Board! Planning Livable Cities*, 1979.
b. Mar 6, 1918 in Berlin, Germany
d. Aug 27, 1995 in Jaffrey, New
Hampshire
Source: *ConAu 5R, 149; IntAu&W 89,
91, 93; WhAm 12; WhoAm 74, 76, 78,
80, 82, 84, 86, 88, 90, 92, 94, 95, 96*

Von Euler, Ulf
Swedish. Biochemist
Co-winner of 1970 Nobel Prize for work
on nerve hormones.
b. Feb 7, 1905 in Stockholm, Sweden
d. Mar 1983 in Stockholm, Sweden
Source: *AmMWSc 82; AnObit 1983;
BiESc; IntWW 83; Who 83; WhoAm 82;
WhoNob; WhoWor 82*

VonFurstenberg, Betsy
[Elizabeth Caroline Maria Agatha
Felicitas Therese Furstenberg-
Hedringen]
German. Actor
Stage performances include *Wonderful
Town*, 1959, 1967.
b. Aug 16, 1932 in Westphalia, Germany
Source: *BiE&WWA; ConTFT 5; InWom
SUP; MotPP; NotNAT; WhoAm 86, 90;
WhoEnt 92; WhoHol A; WhoThe 81;
WorAl*

VonHoffman, Nicholas
American. Journalist
Writings include *Mississippi Notebook*,
1964; *Two, Three, Many More*, 1969.
b. Oct 16, 1929 in New York, New York
Source: *AmAu&B; CelR 90; ConAu
34NR, 81; EncTwCJ; WhoAm 86, 90;
WhoE 91; WhoSSW 73; WrDr 92*

von Hugel, Friedrich, Baron
Italian. Philosopher
Wrote extensively on the philosophy of
religion, particularly relating to the
importance of the truth claims of
modern science to believing
Christians.
b. May 5, 1852 in Florence, Italy
d. Jan 27, 1925 in London, England
Source: *BioIn 14; DcNaB 1922; OxCEng
67, 85, 95; ThTwC 87; WhoChr*

Von Karman, Theodore
American. Aeronautical Engineer
Helped found, chm. of advisory group
for aeronautical research, development
for NATO, 1951-63.

b. May 11, 1881 in Budapest, Austria-Hungary
d. May 7, 1963 in Aachen, Germany (West)
Source: *BioIn 1, 2, 3, 4, 5, 6, 7, 8, 10, 12, 13, 14, 18, 20; EncWB 98; LinLib L, S; McGCEnS; McGMS 80; NotTwCS 1; OxCAmH; PeoHis; WebAB 74; WhAm 4*

Von Klitzing, Klaus
German. Physicist
Won 1985 Nobel Prize in physics for discovering the quantized Hall effect of electrical conductivity.
b. Jun 28, 1943 in Schroda, Germany
Source: *AmMWSc 89, 92, 95, 98; BioIn 13, 14, 15, 20; CamBiEn; ChamBiD; IntWW 89, 91, 93, 97, 98, 2000; LarDcSc; NewYTBS 85; NobelP; NotTwCS 1; RanHWDS; Who 88, 90, 92, 94, 98, 99, 2000; WhoNob, 90; WhoScEu 91-3; WhoWor 87*

von Lipsey, Roderick K.
American. Pilot, Government Official
Aide-de-camp to Chairman of Joint Chiefs of Staff John Colin Powell, 1991-93; US Marine Corps pilot, 1980-91.
b. Jan 13, 1959 in Philadelphia, Pennsylvania
Source: *AfrAmAl 8; ConBlB 11*

von Mehren, Robert Brandt
American. Lawyer
Activist and expert on international law, he helped create the legal structure of the International Atomic Energy Agency.
b. Aug 10, 1922 in Albert Lea, Minnesota
Source: *EncWB, 98; WhoAm 90, 92, 94, 95, 96, 97, 98, 99, 2000; WhoAmL 78, 79, 83, 85, 92; WhoE 75, 77, 79, 81, 83, 95, 97, 99*

von Mises, Ludwig (Edler)
Austrian. Economist, Philosopher
Leading 20th century exponent of the Austrian school, he was a conservative in matters of economic and social policy.
b. Sep 29, 1881 in Lemburg, Austria-Hungary
d. 1973 in Geneva, Switzerland

Vonnegut, Kurt, Jr.
American. Author, Journalist
Wrote *Slaughterhouse Five*, 1969; *Breakfast of Champions*, 1973; *Hocus Pocus*, 1990, his 13th novel.
b. Nov 11, 1922 in Indianapolis, Indiana
Source: *ABCCoAm; AmAu&B; AmCulL; AmDec 1960; AmWr S2; Au&Arts 6; Au&Wr 71; AuNews 1; AuSpks; BeaEPF; Benet 87, 96; BenetAL 91; BestSel 90-4; BiCoLiE; BioIn 2, 8, 9, 10, 11, 12, 13, 14, 15, 16, 17, 19, 21, 22, 23, 24; BlueB 76; BroV; CamBiEn; CamDcAB; CamGEL; CamGLE; CamHAL; CasWL; CelR; ChamBiD; ConAu 1NR, 1R, 25NR, 49NR, 75NR; ConDr 77, 82, 93; ConLC 1, 2, 3, 4, 5, 8, 12, 22, 40, 60, 111; ConNov 72, 76,*

82, 86, 91, 96; ConPopW; ConSFA; ConTFT 6; CurBio 70, 91; CyWA 89, 97; DcArts; DcLB 2, 8, 152, DS3, Y80A; DcLEL 1940; DcTwCCu 1; DrAF 76; DrAPF 80, 91; DrmM 1; EncAB-H 1974, 1996; EncALit; EncApL; EncSF, 93; EncWB 98; EncWL 1, 2, 2S, 3; FacFETw; GrWrEL N; IdentIs; IndAu 1917; IntAu&W 76, 77, 89, 91, 93; IntvTCA 2; IntWW 74, 75, 76, 77, 78, 79, 80, 81, 82, 83, 89, 91, 93, 97, 98, 2000; LegTOT; LinLib L, S; MagSAmL; MajTwCW 1, 2; MakMC; ModAL 4S1, 4S2, 4S3, 5; MugS; NatPD 77, 81; NewEScF; News 98; Novels; OxCAmL 83, 95; OxCEng 85, 95; OxCTwCL; PenC AM; PostFic; RAdv 1, 14, 13-1; RfGAmL 4, 87, 94; RGTwCSF; RGTwCWr; ScF&FL 1, 2, 92; ScFSB; ScFWr, 2; ShSCr 8; SJGYouA 2; SocPrL; SpyFic; TwCSFW 81, 86, 91; TwCYAW 1; TwoTYeD; WebAB 74, 79; WebE&AL; Who 83, 85, 88, 90, 92, 94, 98, 99, 2000; WhoAm 74, 76, 78, 80, 82, 84, 86, 88, 90, 92, 94, 95, 96, 97, 98, 99, 2000; WhoE 91, 93, 95, 97, 99; WhoEnt 92, 98; WhoHol 92; WhoHrs 80; WhoSciF; WhoSpyF; WhoTwCL; WhoUSWr 88; WhoWor 74, 76, 78, 80, 82, 84, 87, 89, 91, 93, 95, 96, 97, 98, 99, 2000; WhoWrEP 89, 92, 95; WorAl; WorAlBi; WorAu 1950; WorLitC; WrDr 76, 80, 82, 84, 86, 88, 90, 92, 94, 96, 98, 99, 2000

Vonnegut, Mark
American. Author
Wrote *The Eden Express*, 1975; son of Kurt.
b. May 11, 1947 in Chicago, Illinois
Source: *AuNews 2; BioIn 11, 12; ConAu 65*

Von Neumann, John
American. Mathematician
Helped develop atomic, hydrogen bombs.
b. Dec 3, 1903 in Budapest, Austria-Hungary
d. Feb 8, 1957 in Washington, District of Columbia
Source: *AmDec 1930; BiDPsy; BiESc; BioIn 3, 4, 5, 6, 7, 8, 11, 12, 13, 14, 15, 16, 17, 18, 19, 20, 21, 23, 24; CamBiEn; CamDcAB; ChamBiD; ConAu 117; CurBio 55, 57; DcAmB S6; EncAB-H 1974, 1996; EncWB 98; FacFETw; HisDcDP; InSci; JeHun; LarDcSc; MakMC; McGCEnS; McGEWB; McGMS 80; NatCAB 46; NotMat; NotTwCS 1; OxCAmH; PorSil; RAdv 14, 13-3; RanHWDS; RComAH; SciMath; ThTwC 87; WebAB 74; WhAm 3*

Vonnoh, Robert William
American. Artist
Paintings exhibited at Metropolitan Museum, NYC, include *President Wilson's Family, La Mere Adele*.
b. Sep 17, 1858 in Hartford, Connecticut
d. Dec 28, 1933 in Lyme, Connecticut
Source: *AmBi; AmNatBi; ApCAB, X; BioIn 15, 19; BriEAA; CamDcAB; DcAmArt; DcAmB; NatCAB 7; TwCBDA; WhAm 1; WhAmArt 85*

von Praunheim, Rosa
[Holger Mischwitki]
German. Filmmaker
Films include *Army of Lovers*, 1979; *Dolly, Lotte and Maria*, 1988.
b. 1942 in Riga, Latvia
Source: *CmpQue; GayLesB; MiSFD 9*

von Rad, Gerhard
German. Theologian
Developed the "tradition history" approach to the Old Testament that dominated Bible study through the end of the 20th century.
b. Oct 21, 1901 in Nurnberg, Germany
d. Oct 31, 1971

VonSchmidt, Harold
American. Illustrator
Known for drawings of Western subjects in mags., private sales.
b. May 19, 1893 in Alameda, California
d. Jun 3, 1982 in Westport, Connecticut
Source: *ArtsAmW 1; BioIn 1, 2, 7, 9, 10, 12, 13; IlBEAAW; IlrAm 1880; NewYTBS 82; WhAm 8; WhAmArt 85*

VonStade, Frederica
[Mrs. Peter Elkus]
"Flicka"
American. Opera Singer
Mezzo-soprano; had NY Met. debut in 1970; noted for Wagner, Rossini roles.
b. Jun 1, 1945 in Somerville, New Jersey
Source: *BioIn 16; CelR 90; FacFETw; IntWW 91; IntWWM 90; InWom SUP; NewAmDM; NewGrDA 86; NewYTBS 83; PenDiMP; WhoAm 86, 88, 90; WhoAmW 83, 89*

VonSternberg, Josef
Austrian. Director
Films include *The Blue Angel*, 1931, which starred Marlene Dietrich, whom he discovered.
b. May 29, 1894 in Vienna, Austria
d. Dec 22, 1969 in Hollywood, California
Source: *BiDFilm; DcFM; FilmEn; FilmgC; MovMk; ObitOF 79; OxCFilm; TwYS; WhScrn 74, 77; WorEFlm*

VonStroheim, Erich
[Erich Oswald Stroheim]
German. Actor, Director
As actor, called "the man you love to hate"; directed many silent films including *Greed*, 1928.
b. Sep 22, 1885 in Vienna, Austria
d. May 12, 1957 in Paris, France
Source: *BiDFilm; DcFM; Film 1; FilmgC; MotPP; MovMk; ObitOF 79; OxCFilm; REn; TwYS; WebAB 74, 79; WhAm 3; WhoHol A; WhScrn 74, 83; WorAl; WorEFlm*

VonSydow, Max Carl Adolf
Swedish. Actor
Sensitive, versatile, powerful screen actor: *Hannah and Her Sisters*, 1985, *Pelle the Conqueror*, 1988.
b. Apr 10, 1929 in Lund, Sweden

Source: *BiDFilm; BioIn 16; CelR 90;
ConTFT 5; CurBio 67; FilmgC; HalFC
84, 88; IntMPA 84, 86, 92; IntWW 74;
MotPP; MovMk; OxCFilm; WhoAm 76,
78, 80, 82, 84, 86, 90; WhoEnt 92;
WhoHol A; WhoWor 74, 76, 78, 91;
WorAl; WorAlBi; WorEFlm*

Von Tilzer, Albert
[Albert Gumm]
American. Composer
Best known for song "Take Me Out to
the Ball Game."
b. Mar 29, 1878 in Indianapolis, Indiana
d. Oct 1, 1956 in Los Angeles,
California
Source: *AmPS; AmSong; ASCAP 66, 80;
BiDAmM; BioIn 4, 6, 14, 15, 16;
CmpEPM; DcPseud; NewGrDA 86;
NotNAT B; OxCPMus; PopAmC; Songw;
Sw&Ld C*

VonTilzer, Harry
[Harry Gumm]
American. Publisher, Songwriter
Published two thousand songs including
"Wait Till the Sun Shines, Nellie";
"In the Sweet Bye-and-Bye."
b. Jul 8, 1872 in Detroit, Michigan
d. Jan 10, 1946 in New York, New York
Source: *ASCAP 66; CurBio 46; DcAmB
S4; REnAL*

Von Wangenheim, Chris
German. Photographer
Fashion photographer whose admirable
love of women produced "daring,
provocative, brilliantly inventive
photos."
b. Feb 21, 1942 in Breslau, Germany
d. Mar 9, 1981, St. Martin
Source: *ConAu 103; MacBEP; NewYTBS
81*

Von Zell, Harry
American. Actor
Known for mellow voice; featured on
"George Burns and Gracie Allen
Show," 1956-58; appeared in 30
movies.
b. Jul 11, 1906 in Indianapolis, Indiana
d. Nov 21, 1981 in Woodland Hills,
California
Source: *BioIn 12, 13; CurBio 44, 82,
82N; ForYSC; LegTOT; RadStar;
SaTiSS; WhoHol A; WhScrn 83; WorAl*

Voorhees, Donald
American. Conductor
Directed popular weekly radio concerts,
Bell Telephone Hour, 1940s.
b. Jul 26, 1903 in Allentown,
Pennsylvania
d. Jan 10, 1989 in Cape May Court
House, New Jersey
Source: *BakBD 92; BakBDTw; BioIn 2,
4, 16; CurBio 50, 89, 89N; FacFETw;
NewYTBS 89; RadStar; WhAm 9;
WhoAm 74*

Voroshilov, Kliment Efremovich
Russian. Soldier, Politician
In command on the Leningrad front at
outbreak of war with Germany, 1941;
succeeded Stalin as chm. of Presidium,
1953-57.
b. Feb 4, 1881 in Verkhneye, Russia
d. Dec 2, 1969 in Moscow, Union of
Soviet Socialist Republics
Source: *BiDSovU; BioIn 13, 16, 18;
ColdWar 1, 2; CurBio 40, 70;
FacFETw; WebBD 83; WhoMilH 76*

Vorster, Balthazar Johannes
[John Vorster]
South African. Lawyer, Politician
Prime minister, 1966-78; Pres., 1978-79;
introduced "banning" (internal exile).
b. Dec 13, 1915 in Jamestown, South
Africa
d. Sep 10, 1983 in Cape Town, South
Africa
Source: *AfSS 78, 79, 80, 81, 82; AnObit
1983; BioIn 7, 8, 9, 10, 11, 12, 13, 21;
CurBio 67, 83N; DcAfHiB 86S; DcPol;
DcTwHis; EncSoA; EncWB 98;
EncyDCo; HisWorL; IntWW 74, 75, 76,
77, 78, 79, 80, 81, 82, 83; IntYB 78, 79,
80, 81, 82; McGEWB; NewYTBS 76, 83;
WhAm 8; WhDW; Who 74, 82, 83;
WhoGov 72; WhoWor 74, 76, 78;
WorAl; WorAlBi*

Vos, Cornelis de
Flemish. Artist
Best known for straightforward portraits
including one of his family, 1621.
b. 1584
d. 1651
Source: *NewCol 75; OxCArt; OxDcArt*

Vos, Martin de
Flemish. Artist
Student of Frans Floris; after Floris'
death he became leading Italianate
artist in Antwerp.
b. 1532
d. Dec 4, 1603
Source: *EncHiCA; McGDA; NewCol 75;
OxCArt*

Voskovec, George
Czech. Actor, Director, Dramatist
On Broadway *Cabaret,* 1969; in film
Twelve Angry Men, 1957.
b. Jun 19, 1905 in Sazova,
Czechoslovakia
d. Jul 1, 1981 in Pearblossom, California
Source: *AnObit 1981; BiE&WWA; BioIn
6, 11, 12; ConAu 104; FilmgC; ForYSC;
HalFC 80, 84, 88; MotPP; NewYTBS
81; NotNAT; OxCThe 67; WhoHol A;
WhoThe 72, 77, 81; WhScrn 83*

Votipka, Thelma
American. Opera Singer
Debut in *Marriage of Figaro,* 1927;
soprano with Metropolitan Opera,
1935-63.
b. Dec 20, 1898 in Cleveland, Ohio
d. Oct 24, 1972
Source: *InWom; NewYTBE 72; WhAm 5*

Vouet, Simon
French. Artist
Best-known paintings: *The Presentation,*
1641; *Allegory of Peace,* 1648.
b. Jan 9, 1590 in Paris, France
d. Jun 30, 1649 in Paris, France
Source: *BioIn 6, 11, 13, 19; CamBiEn;
ChamBiD; ClaDrA; DcBiPP; IntDcAA
90; McGDA; NewCol 75; OxCArt;
OxDcArt*

Vought, Chance Milton
American. Aeronautical Engineer
Taught to fly by the Wright brothers,
1910; designed planes Vought VE-7,
1919; Vought UO-1, 1922-25.
b. Feb 26, 1890 in New York, New
York
d. Jul 25, 1930 in Long Island, New
York
Source: *CamBiEn; CamDcAB; DcAmB;
WebAB 74, 79; WhAm 4, HSA*

Vo Van Kiet
Vietnamese. Political Leader
Prime minister, Vietnam, 1991—.
b. 1922 in Cuu Long, Vietnam
Source: *DcMPSA; EncVieW; FarE&A
78, 79, 80, 81; IntWW 78, 79, 80, 81,
82, 83, 89, 91, 93, 97, 98, 2000;
WhoIntA 2; WhoWor 93, 95, 96, 97, 98*

Vranitzky, Franz
Austrian. Government Official
Federal Chancellor of Austria 1986-97.
b. Oct 4, 1937 in Vienna, Austria
Source: *BioIn 16; CamBiEn; ChamBiD;
CurBio 89; IntWW 89, 91, 93, 97, 98,
2000; PolLCWE; WhoIntA 2; WhoWor
82, 87, 89, 91, 93, 95, 96, 97, 98, 99,
2000*

Vrba, Elisabeth S.
South African. Paleontologist
Was the first person to hypothesize that
climate played a major role in the
extinction of species and evolution.
b. 1942
Source: *CurBio 97*

Vreeland, Diana (Dalziel)
American. Fashion Editor
Fashion editor, *Harper's Bazaar,* 1937-
62, editor-in-chief, *Vogue,* 1962-71;
created spectacular fashion exhibits at
Metropolitan Museum of Art 1971-89.
b. 1903 in Paris, France
d. Aug 22, 1989 in New York, New
York
Source: *AmNatBi; AnObit 1989; BioIn 6,
7, 11, 12, 13, 14, 16; BlueB 76; CelR;
ConAu 111, 129; ContDcW 89; CurBio
78, 89, 89N; EncTwCJ; FacFETw;
ForWC 70; GrLiveH; IntDcWB; InWom,
SUP; LegTOT; LibW; News 90, 90-1;
NewYTBS 84, 89; WhoAm 86, 88;
WhoAmW 89; WhoFash, 88; WorAlBi;
WorFshn*

Vronsky, Vitya
[Vronsky and Babin; Victoria Vronsky]
American. Pianist
Performed two-piano concerts with
husband, Victor, since 1937.
b. Aug 22, 1909 in Evpatoria, Russia
Source: *BakBD 78, 84, 92; BakBDTw;
BioIn 3, 4, 6, 11; InWom; NewGrDA 86;
NewGrDM 80; PenDiMP; WhoAm 74;
WhoAmM 83; WhoAmW 58, 64*

Vuckovich, Pete(r Dennis)
American. Baseball Player
Pitcher, 1975-83; led AL in wins, 1981;
won AL Cy Young Award, 1982.
b. Oct 27, 1952 in Johnstown,
Pennsylvania
Source: *Ballpl 90; BaseEn 88; BioIn 13;
LegTOT; NewYTBS 83*

Vuillard, (Jean) Edouard
French. Artist
Painted commonplace subjects, domestic
interiors: *Woman Sweeping,* 1892.
b. Nov 11, 1868 in Cuiseaux, France

d. Jun 21, 1940 in La Baule, France
Source: *AtlBL; BioIn 3, 4, 6, 8, 9, 11,
15, 16; CamBiEn; ChamBiD; ClaDrA;
DcTwCCu 2; EncWB 98; IntDcAA 90;
LegTOT; McGDA; McGEWB; OxCArt;
OxCTwCA; OxDcArt; PhDcTCA 77;
WhDW; WorAl; WorAlBi*

Vynnychenko, Volodymyr
Ukrainian. Author
Known for realistic, unexpected conflicts;
writings include *Nova Zapovid,* 1950.
b. Jul 27, 1880 in Kherson, Russia
d. Mar 6, 1951 in Paris, France
Source: *BlkwERR; ClDMEL 80; EncRev;
EncWL 2, 2S, 3; LiExTwC; ModSL 2;
PenC EUR*

Vyshinsky, Andrei Yanuarievich
Russian. Judge, Diplomat
Foreign minister, Soviet Union, 1949-53.
b. Dec 10, 1883 in Odessa, Union of
Soviet Socialist Republics
d. Nov 22, 1954 in New York, New
York

Source: *BiDSovU; CurBio 55; EncWB;
FacFETw; WhAm 3*

Vysotsky, Vladimir Semyonovich
Russian. Actor, Singer, Songwriter
Best known as ballad singer whose songs
were mildly critical of Soviet officials.
b. Jan 25, 1938 in Moscow, Union of
Soviet Socialist Republics
d. Jul 25, 1980 in Moscow, Union of
Soviet Socialist Republics
Source: *AnObit 1980; CamGWoT;
DcRusLS; HanRL; NewYTBE 70;
NewYTBS 80*

Vyvyan, Jennifer Brigit
English. Opera Singer
London's Covent Garden soprano,
1950s-60s; noted for Handel, Britten
roles.
b. Mar 13, 1925 in Broadstairs, England
d. Apr 5, 1974 in London, England
Source: *BakBD 84; BakBDTw; Who 74;
WhoMus 72*

W

Waals, Johannes Diderik van der
Dutch. Scientist
Won 1910 Nobel Prize in physics;
known for theory of binary solutions,
thermodynamic theory of capillarity.
b. Nov 23, 1837 in Leiden, Netherlands
d. Mar 9, 1923 in Amsterdam,
Netherlands
Source: *AsBiEn; BiESc; BioIn 20, 22;
CamDcSc; ChamBiD; DcScB; WhDW;
WhoNob; WorScD*

Wachner, Linda
American. Business Executive
Owner and pres. Warnaco, Inc., an
apparel conglomerate, 1986-; chm.,
CEO, authentic fitness Corp., 1991—.
b. Feb 3, 1946 in New York, New York
Source: *AmWomM; BioIn 15; ConAmBL;
CurBio 98; Dun&B 90; News 97, 88-3,
97-2; WhoAm 90; WhoAmW 91; WhoE
91; WhoFI 92; WhoWest 92*

Wachter, Ed(ward)
American. Basketball Player
Center, 1896-1924; first pro player to be
sold to another team, 1902; Hall of
Fame.
b. Jun 30, 1883 in Troy, New York
d. Mar 12, 1966 in Troy, New York
Source: *BioIn 9; WhoBbl 73*

Waddell, Rube
[George Edward Waddell]
American. Baseball Player
Pitcher, 1897, 1899-1901; led AL in
strikeouts once, NL six consecutive
yrs; Hall of Fame, 1946.
b. Oct 13, 1876 in Bradford,
Pennsylvania
d. Apr 1, 1914 in San Antonio, Texas
Source: *AmNatBi; Ballpl 90; BiDAmSp
BB; BioIn 2, 3, 4, 5, 6, 7, 8, 9, 10, 14,
15, 16; CulEncB; LegTOT; WhoProB
73; WhoSpor*

Waddell, Tom
[Thomas Flubacher; Thomas Waddell]
American. Physician, Olympic Athlete
Olympic decathlon athlete, 1968;
founded Gay Games, 1982.

b. 1937 in Paterson, New Jersey
d. Jul 11, 1987 in San Francisco,
California
Source: *BioIn 15, 20, 22; CmpQue;
GayLesB; News 88-2; NewYTBS 87*

Waddles, Charleszetta, Mother
American.
Founder, Mother Waddles Perpetual Help
Mission, Detroit, 1956—; provides
help for the needy.
b. Oct 7, 1912 in Saint Louis, Missouri
Source: *AfrAmAl 8; BioIn 8, 9; ConBlB
10; Ebony 1; InB&W 85; NegAl 76, 89;
NotBlAW 1; WhoBlA 5, 7*

Wade, Benjamin Franklin
American. Politician
Senator from OH, 1851-69; opposed
Lincoln's reconstruction policy;
awaited Johnson's impeachment, as
head of senate, he would succeed him.
b. Oct 27, 1800 in Springfield,
Massachusetts
d. Mar 2, 1878 in Jefferson, Ohio
Source: *AmBi; AmNatBi; AmPolLe;
ApCAB; BiAUS; BiDrAC; BiDrUSC 89;
BioIn 1, 3, 6, 7; CamDcAB; ChamBiD;
CivWDc; DcAmB; Drake; EncAB-H
1974, 1996; EncWB 98; HarEnUS;
McGEWB; NatCAB 2; OxCAmH;
TwCBDA; WebAB 74, 79; WhAm HS;
WhAmP; WhCiWar*

Wade, Virginia
"Ginny Fizz"; "Our Ginny"
English. Tennis Player
Women's singles champion, Wimbledon,
1977.
b. Jul 10, 1945 in Bournemouth, England
Source: *BioIn 10, 11, 12, 13, 14;
BuCMET; ConAu 132; CurBio 76;
IntWW 81, 82, 83, 91, 98; InWom SUP;
LegTOT; NewYTBS 83; Who 88, 90, 92;
WhoIntT; WhoWor 78, 80, 82, 84, 87,
89, 91, 93, 95, 96; WorAl*

Wadkins, Lanny
American. Golfer
Turned pro, 1971; won PGA, 1977.
b. Dec 5, 1949 in Richmond, Virginia

Source: *BioIn 9, 11, 13; LegTOT; Who
98, 99, 2000; WhoAm 74, 76, 92, 94, 95,
96, 97, 98, 99, 2000; WhoGolf;
WhoIntG; WhoWor 95, 96*

Wadsworth, James Jeremiah
[Jerry Wadsworth]
American. Government Official
Helped negotiate partial ban on nuclear
weapons as head of US delegation to
UN, 1960.
b. Jun 12, 1905 in Groveland, New York
d. Mar 13, 1984 in Rochester, New York
Source: *AmNatBi; BioIn 3, 4, 5, 8, 11,
12, 13, 14; BlueB 76; ConAu 112, P-2;
CurBio 56, 84; IntWW 74, 75, 76;
NewYTBS 84; WhoAm 74*

Wadsworth, James Samuel
American. Military Leader
Brigadier general of volunteers from
1861; played key role in Union victory
at Gettysburg, 1863.
b. Oct 30, 1807 in Geneseco, New York
d. May 8, 1864 in Fredericksburg,
Virginia
Source: *AmBi; AmNatBi; ApCAB; BioIn
7; CivWDc; DcAmB; Drake; HarEnUS;
NatCAB 5; TwCBDA; WhCiWar*

Waggoner, Lyle
American. Actor
TV shows include "Wonder Woman,"
1977-79; "Carol Burnett Show,"
1967-74.
b. Apr 13, 1935 in Kansas City, Kansas
Source: *ConTFT 7; IntMPA 75, 76, 77,
78, 79, 80, 81, 82, 84, 86, 88, 92, 94,
96; LegTOT; WhoAm 82; WhoHol 92;
WorAl*

Wagnalls, Adam Willis
American. Publisher
With Isaac Funk founded publishing
house, Funk & Wagnalls, 1890.
b. Sep 24, 1843 in Lithopolis, Ohio
d. Sep 3, 1924 in Northport, New York
Source: *AmAu&B; NatCAB 23; WhAm 1*

Wagner, Barbara
Canadian. Skater
Figure skater; with partner Bob Paul,
  won gold medal, pairs skating, 1960
  Olympics.
b. May 5, 1938 in Toronto, Ontario,
  Canada
Source: *BioIn 10*

Wagner, Cosima Liszt
[Mrs. Richard Wagner]
Hungarian.
Daughter of Franz Liszt; married
  Wagner, 1870; created Bayreuth
  Festival.
b. Dec 25, 1837 in Bellagio, Austria
d. Apr 1, 1930 in Bayreuth, Germany
Source: *BakBD 84; IntDcWB; NewCol
75; NewEOp 71; WebBD 83*

Wagner, Honus
[John Peter Wagner]
"The Flying Dutchman"
American. Baseball Player
Infielder, 1897-1917, mostly with
  Pittsburgh; led NL in batting eight
  times; had lifetime .329 batting
  average; one of five original Hall of
  Fame inductees, 1936.
b. Feb 24, 1874 in Mansfield,
  Pennsylvania
d. Dec 6, 1955 in Carnegie, Pennsylvania
Source: *AmDec 1900; AmNatBi; Ballpl
90; BiDAmSp BB; BioIn 1, 2, 3, 4, 5, 6,
7, 8, 9, 10, 13, 14, 15, 17, 20, 21, 22,
24; CamBiEn; CulEncB; DcAmB S5;
FacFETw; LegTOT; WebAB 74, 79;
WhoProB 73; WhoSpor; WorAl; WorAlBi*

Wagner, Jack Peter
American. Actor, Singer
Plays Frisco Jones on daytime drama
  "General Hospital"; hit single "All I
  Need," 1984.
b. Oct 3, 1959 in Washington, Missouri

Wagner, Jane
American. Writer, Director
Won three Emmys for Lily Tomlin
  specials; wrote film *The Incredible
  Shrinking Woman*, 1980.
b. Feb 2, 1935 in Morristown, Tennessee
Source: *AuBYP 2S, 3; BioIn 14; ConAu
42NR, 109; ConTFT 6; IntMPA 88, 92,
94, 96; InWom SUP; LegTOT; LesBEnT;
MiSFD 9; SmATA 33; VarWW 85*

Wagner, Lindsay J
American. Actor
Emmy-winning star of TV series
  "Bionic Woman," 1976-78; TV films
  include *This Child Is Mine*, 1985.
b. Jun 22, 1949 in Los Angeles,
  California
Source: *BioIn 13, 15; CelR 90; ConTFT
3; HalFC 84, 88; IntMPA 92; InWom
SUP; LesBEnT 92; NewAgE 90; WhoAm
86, 90, 98, 99, 2000; WhoEnt 92;
WhoHol A; WorAlBi*

Wagner, Otto
Austrian. Architect, Educator
A founder of modern European
  architecture, he advocated a break
  from historicist architecture.
b. Jul 13, 1841 in Vienna, Austria
d. Apr 11, 1918 in Vienna, Austria
Source: *BioIn 9, 12, 13; CamBiEn;
ChamBiD; DcArch; DcArts; DcD&D;
DcTwDes; EncMA; EncUrb; EncWB, 98;
IntDcAr; MacEA; McGDA; OxCArt;
WhoArch*

Wagner, Richard
[Wilhelm Richard Wagner]
German. Composer, Librettist, Poet
Opera themes derived from medieval
  legends; wrote *Lohengrin, Tristan, Die
  Meistersinger*; founded Bayreuth
  Festival, 1876.
b. May 22, 1813 in Leipzig, Germany
d. Feb 13, 1883 in Venice, Italy
Source: *AtlBL; BakBD 78, 84; BbD;
Benet 87, 96; BiD&SB; BioIn 1, 2, 3, 4,
5, 6, 7, 8, 9, 10, 11, 12, 13, 14, 15, 16,
17, 18, 19, 20, 22, 23, 24; BriBkM 80;
CamGWoT; CasWL; CelCen; ClDMEL
47, 80; CmOp; CmpBCM; CnOxB;
DancEn 78; DcArts; DcBiPP; DcCom
77; DcCom&M 79; DcEuL; DcLB 129;
Dis&D; EncRev; EncTR, 91; EncWB 98;
EuAu; EuWr 6; EvEuW; GrComp;
IntDcOp; LegTOT; LinLib L; LiveWoA;
LuthC 75; McGEWB; MetOEnc; MusMk;
NewAmDM; NewC; NewCBEL; NewCol
75; NewEOp 71; NewGrDM 80;
NewOxM; NinCLC 9; NotNAT B; Opera;
OxCEng 67, 85, 95; OxCFr; OxCGer 76,
86, 97; OxCMus; OxCThe 67; OxDcOp;
PenC EUR; PenDiMP A; RAdv 14, 13-3;
REn; REnWD; WebBD 83; WhDW;
WorAl; WorAlBi*

Wagner, Robert F(erdinand)
American. Politician
Dem. senator from NY, 1926-49; helped
  draft several New Deal measures.
b. Jun 8, 1877 in Hesse-Nasseau,
  Germany
d. May 4, 1953 in New York, New York
Source: *AmPolLe; AmSetPR; BiDrAC;
BiDrUSC 89; BioIn 1, 2, 3, 7, 8, 11;
CamDcAB; ChamBiD; CurBio 41, 53;
DcAmB S5; DcAmSR; DcCathB; EncAB-
H 1974, 1996; EncWB 98; LinLib S;
McGEWB; NatCAB 48; NewYTBE 72;
PolProf T; WebAB 74, 79; WhAm 3;
WhAmP; WorAl*

Wagner, Robert Ferdinand, Jr.
American. Lawyer, Politician
NYC's 102nd mayor, 1954-65; U.S.
  ambassador to Spain, 1968; envoy to
  the Vatican, 1978-81.
b. Apr 20, 1910 in New York, New
  York
d. Feb 12, 1991
Source: *AmNatBi; BiE&WWA; BioIn 3,
4, 5, 6, 7, 8, 9, 10, 11, 17, 18; CurBio
54; EncWB, 98; IntWW 74; LinLib S;
NewCol 75; NewYTBS 91; PolProf E;
WhoAm 86, 90; WhoAmL 79, 90;
WhoAmP 85; WhoE 89; WorAl; WorAlBi*

Wagner, Robert John, Jr.
"R J"
American. Actor
Star of TV series, 1960s-80s: "It Takes
  a Thief;" "Switch;" "Hart to Hart;"
  in films since 1951: *Prince Valiant*,
  1954; widower of Natalie Wood.
b. Feb 10, 1930 in Detroit, Michigan
Source: *BioIn 4, 5, 9, 10, 11; BkPepl;
CamBiEn; ChamBiD; FilmgC; MovMk;
WhoAm 86; WhoHol A; WhoTelC;
WorAl; WorEFlm*

Wagner, Robin
American. Designer
Won Tony for set design of *On the 20th
  Century*, 1978; other plays include
  42nd Street, Dream Girls.
b. Aug 31, 1933 in San Francisco,
  California
Source: *BiE&WWA; BioIn 21;
CamGWoT; ConDes 84, 90; ConTFT 3,
11; MetOEnc; NotNAT; VarWW 85;
WhoAm 88, 90; WhoEnt 92; WhoThe 72,
77, 81*

Wagner, Roger Frances
American. Musician
Founded chorale group which toured
  extensively in US, Canada, Latin
  America, 1946-65.
b. Jan 16, 1914 in Le Puy, France
d. Sep 17, 1992, France
Source: *ASCAP 66; BakBD 84; WhoAm
86; WhoWest 87, 92*

Wagner, Siegfried (Helferich)
German. Composer, Conductor
Son of Richard Wagner; conducted
  father's works at Bayreuth Festival.
b. Jan 6, 1869 in Stiebschen, Switzerland
d. Aug 4, 1930 in Bayreuth, Germany
Source: *BakBD 78, 84; BioIn 8, 10, 19;
MetOEnc; NewCol 75; NewEOp 71;
NewGrDM 80; OxCMus; OxDcOp;
PenDiMP*

Wagner, Wieland Adolf Gottfried
German. Director, Producer
Scenic director of Bayreuth Festival from
  1951; grandson of Richard Wagner,
  son of Siegfried.
b. Jan 5, 1917 in Bayreuth, Germany
d. Oct 16, 1966 in Munich, Germany
  (West)
Source: *BakBD 84; BakBDTw; BioIn 7,
8, 9, 13; ConDes 84; EncWT; IntDcOp;
ObitT 1961; WhAm 4*

Wagner, Wolfgang
German. Producer
Director of Bayreuth Festival since 1966;
  grandson of Richard Wagner, son of
  Siegfried.
b. Aug 30, 1919 in Bayreuth, Germany
Source: *BakBD 84; BioIn 11; IntAu&W
82; IntDcOp; IntWW 83, 89, 91, 93, 97,
98, 2000; IntWWM 90; MetOEnc;
NewEOp 71; NewGrDM 80; OxDcOp;
WhoEnt 92, 98; WhoMus 72; WhoOp 76;
WhoWor 74, 76, 78, 84*

Wagner-Jaurregg, Julius, von
Austrian. Scientist
Won 1927 Nobel Prize in medicine for discovery of therapeutic value of malaria inoculation in treatment of syphilitic paralysis.
b. Mar 7, 1857 in Wels, Austria
d. Sep 27, 1940 in Vienna, Austria
Source: *BiESc; CurBio 40; DcScB; WhoNob*

Wagner-Regeny, Rudolf
Romanian. Composer
Operas include *Johanna Balk,* 1941; director of the State Conservatory in East Berlin, 1950.
b. Aug 28, 1903 in Regen, Romania
d. Sep 18, 1969 in Berlin, German Democratic Republic
Source: *BakBD 78, 84, 92; BakBDTw; BioIn 8; CmOp; DcCM; NewEOp 71; NewGrDM 80; NewGrDO; NewOxM; OxCMus; OxDcOp*

Wagoner, Porter
American. Singer
With Grand Ole Opry, 1957—; won three CMA awards with Dolly Parton.
b. Aug 12, 1927 in West Plains, Missouri
Source: *BakBD 84, 92; BioIn 14; EncFCWM 83; HarEnCM 87; LegTOT; NewAmDM; NewGrDA 86; PenEncP; WhoAm 74, 76, 78, 80, 82, 84, 86, 88, 90, 92, 94, 95, 96, 97, 98; WhoEnt 92, 98; WhoHol 92; WorAl; WorAlBi*

Wahl, Ken
American. Actor
Played undercover cop Vinnie Terranova on TV series, "Wiseguy," 1987-90.
b. Feb 14, 1957 in Chicago, Illinois
Source: *BioIn 12; CelR 90; ConTFT 7; HalFC 88; IntMPA 84, 86, 88, 92; WhoHol 92*

Wahlberg, Donnie
[New Kids on the Block]
American. Singer
Lead vocals of the group.
b. Aug 17, 1969 in Massachusetts
Source: *BioIn 17, 22*

Wahlberg, Mark
"Marky Mark"
American. Actor, Rapper
Albums include *You Gotta Believe;* brother of singer Donnie Wahlberg; starred in film *Boogie Nights,* 1997.
b. 1971? in Boston, Massachusetts
Source: *ConTFT 21; LegTOT; News 93-3; WhoAm 2000*

Wahloo, Per
Swedish. Journalist, Author
With wife, Maj Sjowall, wrote police procedure mysteries.
b. Aug 5, 1926 in Gothenburg, Sweden
d. Jun 22, 1975 in Malmo, Sweden
Source: *BioIn 9, 10, 24; ConAu 57, 61, 73NR; ConLC 7; DetWom; EncMys; EncSF, 93; InWom SUP; LegTOT;*

LinLib L; NewYTBE 71; ScF&FL 92; ScFSB; TwCCr&M 80B, 85B, 91B; WorAl; WorAlBi

Waihee, John David, III
American. Politician
Dem. governor of Hawaii, 1986-94.
b. May 19, 1946 in Honokaa, Hawaii
Source: *AlmAP 88, 92; IntWW 89, 91, 93, 97, 98, 2000; PolsAm 84; WhoAm 84, 86, 88, 90, 92, 94, 95; WhoAmP 85, 87; WhoAsA 94; WhoWest 84, 87, 89, 92, 94; WhoWor 89, 91, 93, 95*

Wain, Bea
American. Singer
Famous for renditions of "My Reverie," "Deep Purple," 1938; popular in 1930s-40s.
b. Apr 30, 1917 in New York, New York
Source: *CmpEPM; IntMPA 79; InWom SUP; RadStar*

Wain, John Barrington
English. Author, Critic
Wrote novel, *Hurry on Down,* 1953; critical appraisal, *Living World of Shakespeare,* 1964.
b. Mar 14, 1925 in Stoke-on-Trent, England
d. May 24, 1994 in Oxford, England
Source: *Au&Wr 71; Benet 87; BioIn 13; CamBiEn; CamGLE; CasWL; ChamBiD; CnDBLB 8; ConAu 4AS, 5R, 23NR, 145; ConLC 11, 15, 46; ConNov 86, 91; ConPo 85, 91; CyWA 89; EncWL 1; EngPo; IntAu&W 91; IntWW 83, 91; LngCTC; MajTwCW 1, 2; ModBrL, S2; OxCEng 85, 95; OxCTwCL; PenC ENG; REn; Who 92; WhoTwCL; WhoWor 91; WorAu 1950; WrDr 86, 92, 96*

Wainwright, James
American. Actor
TV shows include "Jigsaw," 1972-73; "Daniel Boone," 1968.
b. Mar 5, 1938 in Danville, Illinois
Source: *HalFC 84, 88; WhoAm 78, 80, 82; WhoFI 87; WhoHol 92, A*

Wainwright, Jonathan Mayhew
American. Army Officer
Led US forces at Bataan, Corregidor, WW II; awarded Congressional Medal of Honor.
b. Aug 23, 1883 in Walla Walla, Washington
d. Sep 2, 1953 in San Antonio, Texas
Source: *AmNatBi; BiDWWGF; BioIn 1, 3, 6, 7, 9, 10, 12, 17, 24; CamBiEn; CamDcAB; ChamBiD; CurBio 42, 53; DcAmB S5; EncWB 98; HarEnMi; McGEWB; MedHR 94; NatCAB 44; WebAMB; WhAm 3; WhWW-II; WorAl*

Wainwright, Loudon, III
American. Musician, Singer
Acoustic guitarist; albums include *Fame and Wealth,* 1983.
b. Sep 5, 1947 in Chapel Hill, North Carolina

Source: *ASCAP 80; BioIn 9, 10, 11, 14, 15, 16; ConMuA 80A; EncRk 88; HarEnR 86; IlEncRk; NewYTBS 74, 88; PenEncP; RkOn 82; RolSEnR 83; WhoRocM 82*

Waissman, Kenneth
American. Producer
Won Tony for *Torch Song Trilogy,* 1983.
b. Jan 24, 1940 in Baltimore, Maryland
Source: *ConTFT 5; NewYTBS 74; NotNAT; VarWW 85; WhoThe 81*

Waite, John
[The Babys]
English. Singer, Songwriter
Had hit single, "Missing You," 1984.
b. Jul 4, 1955 in Lancaster, England
Source: *BillEnR; LegTOT; RkOn 85; WhoRocM 82*

Waite, Morrison Remick
American. Supreme Court Justice
Appointed by U S Grant; served on bench, 1874-88.
b. Nov 29, 1816 in Lyme, Connecticut
d. Mar 23, 1888 in Washington, District of Columbia
Source: *AmBi; AmJust; AmNatBi; AmPolLe; ApCAB; BiAUS; BiDFedJ; BioIn 2, 3, 5, 6, 9, 11, 15; CamDcAB; ChamBiD; DcAmB; EncAB-H 1974, 1996; EncWB 98; HarEnUS; McGEWB; NatCAB 1, 26; OxCAmH; OxCLaw; OxCSupC; SupCtJu; TwCBDA; WebAB 74, 79; WhAm HS*

Waite, Ralph
American. Actor
Played John Walton in TV series "The Waltons," 1972-80.
b. Jun 22, 1928 in White Plains, New York
Source: *BioIn 13; ConTFT 1, 8, 16; HalFC 80, 84, 88; IntMPA 86, 92; LegTOT; MiSFD 9; WhoAm 86, 90; WhoEnt 92; WhoHol 92, A; WorAlBi*

Waite, Ric
Filmmaker
Cinematographer who won Emmy for *Captains and Kings,* 1977; theatrical films include *Brewster's Millions,* 1985.
Source: *IntMPA 86, 88, 92, 94; VarWW 85; WhoEnt 92*

Waite, Terry
[Terence Hardy Watte]
"Anglican Henry Kissinger"
English. Clergy, Diplomat
Special Anglican Church envoy to Mideast who helped negotiate release of hostages in Lebanon, 1986-87; kidnapped, held hostage himself, 1987-1991.
b. May 31, 1939 in Styal, England
Source: *BioIn 14, 15; CamBiEn; ChamBiD; ConHero 2; CurBio 86; EncWB 98; FacFETw; HeroCon; IntWW 91; LegTOT; NewYTBS 85; Who 85, 92*

Waits, Tom

American. Musician, Singer, Songwriter
Beatnik revivalist; was opening act for
    Frank Zappa, 1970s; Grammy award
    for *Bone Machine*, 1993.
b. Dec 7, 1949 in Pomona, California
Source: *BakBD 92; BakDcM; BillEnR;
    BioIn 14, 15, 16, 17, 19, 23, 24;
    CamBiEn; ChamBiD; ConMuA 80A;
    ConMus 1, 12, 27; ConTFT 6, 13;
    CurBio 97; DcArts; EncFCWM 83;
    EncPR&S 89; EncRk 88; EncRkSt;
    HarEnR 86; IlEncRk; IntMPA 92, 94,
    96; LegTOT; NewGrDA 86; NewGrDJ
    88, 94; PenEncP; RkWho 96; RolSEnR
    83; Songw; WhoAm 90; WhoEnt 92;
    WhoHol 92; WhoRock 81; WhoRocM 82;
    WorAlBi*

Waitt, Tedd

[Theodore W. Waitt]
American. Computer Executive,
    Entrepreneur
Dropped out of college in 1987 and
    borrowed money to start up computer
    marketing business, which became
    Gateway 2000; by 1997, the company
    was the second-largest direct marketer
    of personal computers and brought in
    more than $5 billion in sales annually.
b. c. 1963 in Sioux City, Iowa

Waitz, Grete

Norwegian. Track Athlete
Won NY Marathon seven times.
b. Oct 1, 1953 in Oslo, Norway
Source: *BioIn 12, 13, 14, 15, 17, 20, 22,
    24; CamBiEn; ContDcW 89; CurBio 81;
    EncWoSp; InWom SUP; NewYTBS 79,
    84*

Wajda, Andrzej

Polish. Director
Films include *Man of Marble, 1977;
    Man of Iron, 1981,* about Solidarity
    labor movement.
b. Mar 6, 1926 in Suwalki, Poland
Source: *Benet 87, 96; BiDFilm, 81;
    BioIn 10, 11, 12, 13, 14, 16, 18, 20;
    CamBiEn; ChamBiD; ConAu 102;
    ConLC 16; ConTFT 2, 8, 16; CurBio 82;
    DcArts; DcFM; DrEEuF; FilmEn;
    FilmgC; GrStDi; HalFC 80, 84, 88;
    HisDcPo; IntDcF 2-2; IntMPA 81, 92,
    96; IntWW 74, 75, 76, 77, 78, 79, 80,
    81, 82, 83, 89, 91, 93, 97, 98, 2000;
    ItaFilm; LegTOT; MiSFD 9; MovMk;
    NewYTBS 81, 89; OxCFilm; PolBiDi;
    TheaDir; WhDW; Who 92, 94, 98, 99,
    2000; WhoSocC 78; WhoSoCE 89;
    WhoWor 74, 76, 78, 84, 89, 91, 93, 95,
    96, 97, 98; WorEFlm; WorFDir 2*

Wakefield, Dan

American. Author
First novel, *Island in the City,* 1959, was
    an insight into the world of Spanish
    Harlem.
b. May 21, 1932 in Indianapolis, Indiana
Source: *AmAu&B; AuSpks; BioIn 10, 11,
    15, 16; BlueB 76; ConAu 7AS, 21R;
    ConLC 7; ConNov 86, 91, 96; DcLEL
    1940; DrAF 76; DrAPF 80, 91; IndAu*

*1917; LiJour; WhoAm 74, 76, 78, 80,
82, 84, 86, 88, 90, 92, 94, 95, 96, 97,
98, 99, 2000; WhoEnt 92, 98; WhoFI
85; WhoUSWr 88; WhoWrEP 89, 92, 95;
WorAu 1985; WrDr 80, 82, 84, 86, 88,
90, 92, 94, 96, 98, 99, 2000*

Wakefield, Dick

[Richard Cummings Wakefield]
American. Baseball Player
Baseball's first bonus baby; signed
    $52,000 contract with Detroit, 1940;
    had .293 career batting average.
b. May 6, 1921 in Chicago, Illinois
d. Aug 26, 1985 in Detroit, Michigan
Source: *Ballpl 90; BioIn 2, 11, 14;
    WhoProB 73*

Wakefield, Edward Gibbon

English. Social Reformer, Author
Colonial reformer, promoter, and
    advocate of systematic colonization.
b. Mar 20, 1796
d. May 16, 1862 in Wellington, New
    Zealand
Source: *Alli; BbtC; BioIn 2, 5, 6, 8, 9,
    10, 16; BritAu 19; CamBiEn; CelCen;
    ChamBiD; DcBiPP; DcCanB 9; DcNaB;
    EncWB 98; GrEconB; HisDBrE;
    MacDCB 78; McGEWB; OxCAusL;
    OxCBrHi; OxCCan; WhoEc 81, 86*

Wakefield, Ruth G

American. Manufacturer
Created tollhouse chocolate chip cookie.
b. 1905?
d. 1977 in Plymouth, Massachusetts
Source: *BioIn 11*

Wakely, Jimmy

American. Actor, Singer, Songwriter
Starred in movie westerns, 1940s; had
    CBS radio show, 1952-57.
b. Feb 16, 1914 in Mineola, Arkansas
d. Sep 23, 1982 in Los Angeles,
    California
Source: *AllMGCo; AmNatBi; ASCAP 66,
    80; BgBkCoM; BiDAmM; BioIn 8, 11,
    18; CmpEPM; CounME 74, 74A;
    EncFCWM 69; ForYSC; HarEnCM 87;
    IlEncCM; IntMPA 75, 76, 77, 78, 79, 80,
    81, 82, 84, 86, 88; OxCPMus; PenEncP;
    WhoHol A*

Wakeman, Frederic

American. Author
Wrote best-seller *The Hucksters,* 1946.
b. Dec 26, 1909 in Scranton, Kansas
Source: *AmAu&B; AmNov; BioIn 1, 2, 4,
    22; CurBio 46; LngCTC; REn; REnAL;
    TwCA SUP; TwCWr; WhoSSW 73;
    WorAu 1900*

Wakeman, Rick

English. Musician
Wrote film scores for *The Burning,* 1981;
    Journey to the Center of the Earth,
    1974.
b. May 18, 1949 in London, England
Source: *BillEnR; BioIn 10, 11; ConMuA
    80A; ConMus 27; EncPR&S 89; EncRk
    88; HarEnR 86; IlEncRk; LegTOT;*

*OxCPMus; WhoAm 82, 90, 92, 94, 95,
96, 97, 98; WhoEnt 92; WhoRock 81;
WhoRocM 82*

Wakoski, Diane

American. Poet
Linked with confessional school;
    collections include *Cap of Darkness,*
    1980.
b. Aug 3, 1937 in Whittier, California
Source: *AmWomWr; ArtclWW 2;
    BenetAL 91; BioIn 10, 11, 12, 14, 15;
    CamDcAB; CamGLE; CamHAL; ConAu
    1AS, 9NR, 13R, 60NR; ConLC 2, 4, 7, 9,
    11, 40; ConPo 70, 75, 80, 85, 91, 96;
    ConWomP 98; CroCAP; CyWA 97;
    DcLB 5; DcLEL 1940; DrAP 75; DrAPF
    80, 91; EncALit; FemiCLE; Focus;
    IntAu&W 86, 89, 91; IntvTCA 2; IntWW
    98, 2000; IntWWP 77; InWom SUP;
    MajTwCW 2; ModAL 4S1, 5;
    ModWoWr; OxCAmL 83, 95; OxCTwCL;
    OxCTwCP; OxCWoWr 95; PenC AM;
    RAdv 1, 13-1; WhoAm 80, 82, 84, 86,
    88, 90, 92, 94, 95, 96, 97, 98, 99, 2000;
    WhoEnt 98; WhoUSWr 88; WhoWrEP
    89, 92, 95; WorAu 1970; WrDr 76, 80,
    82, 84, 86, 88, 90, 92, 94, 96, 98, 99,
    2000*

Waksman, Selman Abraham

American. Scientist, Physician, Engineer
Main discoverer of streptomycin, 1943;
    coined term ''antibiotic''; won Nobel
    in medicine, 1952.
b. Jul 22, 1888 in Priluki, Ukraine
d. Aug 16, 1973 in Hyannis,
    Massachusetts
Source: *AmNatBi; AsBiEn; BiDAmCa;
    BiESc; BioIn 1, 2, 3, 4, 5, 6, 8, 10, 11,
    14, 15, 20, 22; CamBiEn; CamDcAB;
    CamDcSc; ChamBiD; CurBio 46, 73;
    DcAmB S9; DcAmMeB 84; DcScB S2;
    EncAAH; EncWB 98; FacFETw; InSci;
    LarDcSc; McGCEnS; McGEWB;
    McGMS 80; NewCol 75; NewYTBE 73;
    OxCMed 86; PeoHis; RanHWDS;
    WebAB 74, 79; WhAm 6; WhoAm 74;
    WhoNob, 90, 95; WhoWor 74; WorAl;
    WorScD*

Walbrook, Anton

[Adolf Anton Wilhelm Wohlbruck]
British. Actor
Films include *The Red Shoes,* 1948;
    Gaslight, 1940.
b. Nov 19, 1900 in Vienna, Austria
d. Aug 9, 1967 in Munich, Germany
    (West)
Source: *BiDFilm, 81, 94; BioIn 14;
    DcPseud; EncWT; Film 2; FilmEn;
    FilmgC; ForYSC; HalFC 80, 84, 88;
    IlWWBF; ItaFilm; MotPP; MovMk;
    NotNAT B; ObitT 1961; OxCFilm;
    WhoHol B; WhScrn 74, 77, 83; WhThe;
    WorEFlm*

Walburn, Raymond

American. Actor
Character actor in over 80 films, 1929-
    55, including *Broadway Bill,* 1934.
b. Sep 9, 1887 in Plymouth, Indiana
d. Jul 26, 1969 in New York, New York

Source: BiE&WWA; BioIn 8, 21;
EncAFC; Film 2; FilmEn; FilmgC;
ForYSC; HalFC 80, 84, 88; HolCA;
MotPP; MovMk; NotNAT B; OlFamFa;
Vers A; WhoHol B; WhScrn 74, 77, 83

Walcott, Derek (Alton)
West Indian. Poet
Winner of Nobel Prize in Literature,
    1992; work includes In a Green Night,
    1962; Another Life, 1973; Omeros,
    1990.
b. Jan 23, 1930 in Castries, St. Lucia
Source: Benet 87; BenetAL 91; BioIn 9,
10, 11, 12, 13, 14, 15, 16; BlkAmP;
BlkLC; BlkWr 1, 2; BlkWrNE; BlmGEL;
CamGEL; CamGLE; CamGWoT;
CaribW 1; CasWL; ChamBiD; ConAu
26NR, 47NR, 75NR, 80NR, 89; ConBlB
5; ConBrDr; ConDr 73, 77, 82, 88, 93;
ConLC 2, 4, 9, 14, 25, 42, 67, 76;
ConPo 70, 75, 80, 85, 91, 96; ConTFT
6, 13; CrtSuDr; CurBio 84; CyWA 89;
DcAfL; DcArts; DcLB 117, Y81B, Y92;
DcLEL 1940; DcTwCCu 5; DrAP 75;
DrAPF 80, 91; DrBlPA, 90; EncLitE;
IntLitE; IntWW 91; IntWWP 77;
LegTOT; LiExTwC; LngCTC; MagSWL;
MajTwCW 1, 2; ModBlW; ModCmwL;
MorBAP; NewYTBS 79, 82, 92; OxCEng
85, 95; OxCTwCL; OxCTwCP; PenC
ENG; PIP&P A; RAdv 14, 13-2; RfGEnL
91; RGTwCWr; SchCGBL; SelBAAf;
WebE&AL; WhDW; Who 98, 99, 2000;
WhoAm 92, 94, 95, 96, 97, 98, 99, 2000;
WhoE 95; WhoNob 95; WhoWor 82, 84,
89, 91, 93, 95, 96, 97, 98, 99, 2000;
WorAu 1950; WrDr 82, 84, 86, 88, 90,
92, 94, 96, 98, 99, 2000

Walcott, Joe
[Arnold Raymond Cream]
''Jersey Joe''
American. Boxer
Heavyweight champion, 1951-52; lost
    title to Marciano; Hall of Famer.
b. Jan 31, 1914 in Merchantville, New
    Jersey
d. Feb 25, 1994 in Camden, New Jersey
Source: BiDAmSp BK; BioIn 1, 2, 3, 5,
6, 7, 8, 9, 10, 11; CurBio 49, 94N;
InB&W 80; What 1; WhoAfA 9; WhoBlA
7; WhoBox 74; WorAl; WorAlBi

Walcott, Mary Morris Vaux
''Audubon of American Wild Flowers''
American. Artist, Naturalist
Illustrated five-volume North American
    Wild Flowers, 1925.
b. Jul 31, 1860 in Philadelphia,
    Pennsylvania
d. Aug 22, 1940 in Saint Andrew's, New
    Brunswick, Canada
Source: AmWomSc; InWom SUP; LibW;
NotAW; WomFir

Wald, George
American. Biologist
Shared Nobel Prize in medicine, 1967,
    for researching vision.

b. Nov 18, 1906 in New York, New
    York
d. Apr 12, 1997 in Cambridge,
    Massachusetts
Source: AmMWSc 73P, 76P, 79, 86, 89,
92, 95; AsBiEn; BiESc; BioIn 5, 7, 8,
11, 14, 15, 20, 22, 23; BlueB 76;
CamBiEn; CamDcAB; ChamBiD; ConAu
159; CurBio 68, 97N; EncWB, 98;
IntWW 74, 75, 76, 77, 78, 79, 80, 81, 82,
83, 89, 91, 93, 97; LarDcSc; McGCEnS;
McGMS 80; NobelP; NotTwCS 1, 1S;
RanHWDS; WebAB 74, 79; WhAm 12;
Who 74, 82, 83, 85, 88, 90, 92, 94;
WhoAm 74, 76, 78, 80, 82, 84, 86, 88,
90, 92, 94, 95, 96, 97; WhoE 74, 77, 79,
81, 85, 86, 89, 91, 95, 97; WhoFrS 84;
WhoMedH 96; WhoNob, 90, 95;
WhoScEn 94, 96; WhoWor 74, 80, 82,
84, 87, 89, 91, 93, 95, 96, 97; WhoWorJ
72, 78; WhsWeAm 98; WorAl; WorAlBi;
WorScD

Wald, Jerry
[Jerome Irving Wald]
American. Producer
Films include Flamingo Road, 1949;
    Mildred Pierce, 1945; Peyton Place,
    1957.
b. Sep 16, 1911 in New York, New
    York
d. Jul 13, 1962 in Beverly Hills,
    California
Source: BiDFilm, 94; BioIn 1, 2, 3, 4, 5,
6, 9; CurBio 62; FilmEn; FilmgC;
GangFlm; HalFC 80, 84, 88; IntDcF 1-
4, 2-4; LegTOT; ObitOF 79; WhAm 4;
WorAl; WorEFlm

Wald, Lillian D
American. Social Worker
Founded Henry Street Settlement, NYC;
    founded first public health nursing
    service, 1902.
b. Mar 10, 1867 in Cincinnati, Ohio
d. Sep 1, 1940 in Westport, Connecticut
Source: AmAu&B; AmNatBi; AmSetPR;
CamBiEn; CamDcAB; CmpQue; CurBio
40; DcAmB S2; EncAB-A 2; EncAB-H
1974; HerW; NotAW; OhA&B; WebAB
74; WhAm 1; WhNAA; WomWWA 14

Walden, Robert
American. Actor
Played Joe Rossi on TV series ''Lou
    Grant.''
b. Sep 25, 1943 in New York, New
    York
Source: DcPseud; WhoAm 80, 82, 84,
86, 88, 90, 92, 94; WhoHol 92, A

Waldheim, Kurt
Austrian. Statesman
Elected pres. of Austria, 1986, in spite of
    Nazi allegations; secretary-general of
    UN, 1972-81.
b. Dec 21, 1918 in Woerdern, Austria
Source: BioIn 9, 10, 11, 12, 13, 14, 15,
16; CamBiEn; CelR; ChamBiD; ConAu
89; CurBio 72, 84, 87; DcPol;
DcTwHis; EncCW; EncWB, 98;
EncyDCo; FacFETw; IntWW 74, 75, 76,
77, 78, 79, 80, 81, 82, 83, 89, 91, 93,

97, 98, 2000; IntYB 78, 79, 80, 81, 82;
LegTOT; LinLib S; NewYTBE 71;
NewYTBS 81, 88; OxCLaw; WhDW;
Who 74, 82, 83, 85, 88, 90, 92, 94, 98,
99, 2000; WhoAm 74, 76, 78, 80, 82, 86;
WhoE 74, 75, 77; WhoGov 72; WhoIntA
2; WhoUN 75; WhoWor 74, 76, 78, 80,
82, 84, 87, 89, 91, 93, 95; WorAlBi

Waldman, Max
American. Photographer
Known for black and white theater and
    classical dance subjects, 1947-81.
b. Jun 2, 1920 in New York, New York
d. Mar 1, 1981 in New York, New York
Source: AnObit 1981; ConAu 103, 105;
MacBEP; NewYTBS 81

Waldo, Peter
French. Religious Leader
Was An advocate of voluntary poverty
    and religious simplicity; his followers
    were considered heretics by the
    Church.
d. 1218
Source: EncWB 98; McGEWB; WhDW

Waldock, Humphrey Meredith,
Sir
[Claud Humphrey Meredith Waldock]
British. Statesman
An expert in international law; sat on
    International Court of Justice, 1973-81.
b. Aug 13, 1904 in Colombo, Ceylon
d. Aug 15, 1981 in The Hague,
    Netherlands
Source: AnObit 1981; ConAu 108;
IntWW 78, 82N; OxCLaw; Who 82N;
WhoUN 75; WhoWor 80

Waldron, Charles D
American. Actor
Specialized in playing stern fathers; films
    include The Nurse's Secret, 1941; The
    Gay Sisters, 1942.
b. Dec 23, 1875 in Waterford, New York
d. Mar 4, 1946 in Hollywood, California
Source: Film 1; NotNAT B; ObitOF 79;
WhoHol B; WhScrn 74, 77; WhThe

Waldron, Hicks Benjamin
American. Cosmetics Executive,
    Consultant
President, chairman, Avon Products,
    1983-89; currently chairman,
    Boardroom Consultants Inc.
b. Oct 31, 1923 in Amsterdam, New
    York
Source: BioIn 13, 14, 15, 16; ConNews
87-3; CurBio 88; Dun&B 88; InB&W
85; NewYTBS 83, 85; St&PR 84, 87, 91;
WhoAm 76, 78, 80, 82, 84, 86, 88, 90;
WhoE 83, 85, 86, 89; WhoFI 77, 79, 81,
85, 87, 89, 92; WhoWor 84

Waldseemuller, Martin
German. Geographer, Cartographer
The first to suggest that the New World
    should be called America; he
    published an influential world map in
    1507.
b. c. 1470 in Radolfzell, Germany

d. 1518
Source: *ApCAB; CamBiEn; DcCathB; DcScB; Drake; EncWB 98; HarEnUS; LinLib S; McGEWB; REn; WhAm HS; WhDW; WhWE*

Wales, Salem Howe
American. Journalist
Editor, *Scientific American*, 1848-71.
b. Oct 4, 1825 in Wales, Massachusetts
d. 1902
Source: *ApCAB; NatCAB 3; WhAm 1*

Walesa, Lech
Polish. Political Leader, Labor Union Official
Organized Solidarity, only independent trade union in Communist world, 1980; won Nobel Peace Prize, 1983; pres., Poland, 1990-95.
b. Sep 29, 1943 in Popowo, Poland
Source: *BioIn 12; LegTOT; News 91, 91-2; NewYTBS 81, 83, 88, 89; NobelP; PolBiDi; ProPowC; RadHan; Who 85, 88, 90, 92, 94, 98, 99, 2000; WhoFI 98; WhoHol 92; WhoIntA 2; WhoNob, 90, 95; WhoSoCE 89; WhoWor 82, 84, 87, 89, 91, 93, 95, 96, 97, 98, 99, 2000; WorAlBi*

Waley, Arthur David
English. Author
Scholar, translator of Oriental literature.
b. Aug 19, 1889 in London, England
d. Jun 27, 1966
Source: *CasWL; ChhPo, S1, S2; CnE&AP; CnMWL; ConAu 85; DcLEL; DcNaB 1961; EncJap; EvLB; GrBr; LngCTC; MakMC; NewC; NewCBEL; OxCEng 67, 85, 95; OxCTwCL; OxCTwCP; PenC ENG; REn; TwCA, SUP; TwCWr; WhDW*

Walford, Roy L(ee, Jr.)
American. Physician, Author
Researcher on aging; wrote *Maximum Life Span*, 1983.
b. Jun 29, 1924 in San Diego, California
Source: *AmMWSc 73P, 92; BioIn 13; ConAu 111*

Walgreen, Charles Rudolph
American. Merchant
Founded Walgreen drugstore chain, 1916.
b. Oct 9, 1873 in Knox County, Illinois
d. Dec 11, 1939 in Chicago, Illinois
Source: *AmNatBi; BiDAmBL 83; BioIn 4, 13; CamDcAB; DcAmB S2; LegTOT; NatCAB 29; WebAB 74, 79; WhAm 1*

Walgreen, Charles Rudolph, Jr.
American. Businessman
Pres. of Walgreen's, 1939-63; converted stores to self-service after WW II.
b. Mar 4, 1906 in Chicago, Illinois
Source: *BioIn 1, 10; IntWW 74; WhoAm 74, 76, 78; WhoFI 74*

Walgreen, Charles Rudolph, III
American. Business Executive
Chairman and CEO of Walgreen Company, drugstore chain, 1971-99.
b. Nov 11, 1935 in Chicago, Illinois
Source: *BiDAmBL 83; BioIn 13, 15, 16; ConNews 87-4; Dun&B 90; St&PR 87, 91; WhoAm 74, 76, 78, 80, 82, 84, 86, 88, 90, 92, 94, 95, 96, 97, 98; WhoFI 74, 75, 77, 79, 87, 89, 92, 94, 96, 98; WhoMW 82, 84, 86, 88, 90, 92, 93, 96; WhoWor 95, 96*

Walinsky, Adam
American. Lawyer
Chm. of NY State Commission of Investigation, 1978-81.
b. Jan 10, 1937 in New York, New York
Source: *BioIn 7, 9, 10; WhoAmL 85, 87, 96; WhoFI 81, 83; WhoWor 91, 93*

Walken, Christopher
American. Actor
Won Oscar for best supporting actor, 1978, for *The Deer Hunter*.
b. Mar 31, 1943 in New York, New York
Source: *BiDFilm 94; BioIn 11, 12, 15; CamBiEn; ConTFT 3, 12, 20; CurBio 90; FilmEn; HalFC 80, 84, 88; IntMPA 80, 81, 82, 84, 86, 88, 92, 94, 96; IntWW 91, 93, 97, 98, 2000; LegTOT; NewYTBS 78; NotNAT; OsStAZ; WhoAm 80, 82, 84, 86, 88, 90, 92, 94, 95, 96, 97, 99, 2000; WhoEnt 92, 98; WhoHol 92, A; WhoThe 77, 81; WorAlBi*

Walker, A. Maceo, Sr.
American. Insurance Executive
Pres., CEO, Universal Life Insurance Co., 1952-83, 1985-90; co-founder, pres., Tri-State Bank of Memphis.
b. Jun 7, 1909 in Indianola, Mississippi
Source: *DcWomA; Dun&B 90; WhoBlA 4, 5, 7; WhoIns 92*

Walker, Adam
English. Inventor, Teacher, Author
Taught math at age 15; traveling lecturer on natural philosophy; invented a machine for raising water level.
b. 1766 in Kendal, England
d. 1821
Source: *Alli; BiDLA*

Walker, Albertina
American. Singer
Formed gospel group Caravans, 1952, disbanded, 1967; a force in traditional gosepl music.
b. 1929 in Chicago, Illinois
Source: *AfrAmAl 8; ConBlB 10; ConTFT 12; WhoAfA 9, 10, 11, 12; WhoBlA 3, 6, 7, 8*

Walker, A'lelia
American. Art Patron, Socialite
Daughter of Madam C. J. Walker, founder of a hair-care products empire; a lavish entertainer during the Harlem Renaissance, a devoted patron of the arts, and founder of ''The Dark Tower,'' a lavish salon for writers and artists.
b. Jun 6, 1885 in Vicksburg, Mississippi
d. Aug 16, 1931 in Long Branch, New York
Source: *BioIn 18; BlkWAm; ConBlB 14; DcTwCCu 5; InB&W 80, 85; NotBlAW 1*

Walker, Alice
American. Author
Won Pulitzer for novel *The Color Purple*, 1982; filmed, 1985.
b. Feb 9, 1944 in Eatonton, Georgia
Source: *AfrAmAl 6, 8; AfrAmW; AmWomWr, 92; AmWr S3; ArtclWW 2; Au&Arts 3, 33; AuSpks; BeaEPF; Benet 87, 96; BenetAL 91; BestSel 89-4; BiCoLiE; BioIn 11, 13, 14, 15, 16, 17, 18, 19, 20, 21, 22, 23, 24; BlkAull, 92; BlkAWP; BlkLC; BlkWAm; BlkWr 1; BlkWrNE; BlkWWr; BlmGWL; BroadAu; BroV; CamGLE; CamHAL; CelR 90; ConAfAN; ConAu 9NR, 27NR, 37R; ConBlB 1; ConHero 1; ConLC 5, 6, 9, 19, 27, 46, 58, 103; ConNov 86, 91; ConSoWr; ContDcW 89; CurBio 84; CyWA 89, 97; DcArts; DcLB 6, 33, 143; DcTwCCu 1, 5; DcVicP 2; DrAF 76; DrAP 75; DrAPF 80, 91; EncAACR; EncFoLi; EncSF 93; EncSoL; EncWB; EncWL 2S, 3; FacFETw; FemiCLE; GrLiveH; GrWomW; HanAmWH; IdentIs; InB&W 80, 85; IntAu&W 82, 91; IntDcWB; IntWW 91; InWom SUP; JouAdvM; LegTOT; LivgBAA; MagSAmL; MajTwCW 1; ModAL 4S2, 4S3, 5; ModAWWr; ModBlW, 2; ModWoWr; NegAl 83, 89; News 99-1, 1999; NewYTBS 83; NotBlAW 1; OxCAfAL; OxCAmL 83; OxCWoWr 95; PeoHis; PostFic; RadHan; RAdv 14; RfGAmL 87; ScF&FL 92; SchCGBL; ShSCr 5; SigCnAF; SmATA 31; SocPrL; WhoAm 74, 76, 78, 90; WhoAmW 74, 91; WhoBlA 1, 2, 3, 4, 5, 7; WhoPul; WhoUSWr 88; WhoWrEP 89; WomFir; WomIss; WorAlBi; WorAu 1975; WorLitC SUP; WrDr 86, 88, 90, 92, 94, 96, 99, 2000*

Walker, C. J., Madame
[Sarah Breedlove]
American. Businesswoman
President and owner, Madame C. J. Walker Manufacturing Co., 1906-19, a producer and distributor of a line of hair and beauty preparations for black women.
b. Dec 23, 1867 in Delta, Louisiana
d. May 25, 1919 in Irvington-on-Hudson, New York
Source: *AfrAmAl 6, 8; BioIn 16, 17, 18, 19, 20, 23, 24; DcAmNB; EncWB 98; NotBlAW 1; RComAH*

Walker, Cedric Ricky
American. Circus Owner
Former music promoter and theater producer is the founder and chairman UniverSoul Big Top Circus, a nationally-touring African American circus.
b. c. 1953 in Baltimore, Maryland

Walker, Chet

[Chester Walker]
American. Basketball Player
Forward, 1962-75, mostly with
  Philadelphia, Chicago; led NBA in
  free throw percentage, 1971.
b. Feb 22, 1940 in Benton Harbor,
  Michigan
Source: BasBi; BiDAmSp BK; BioIn 6,
  15, 21; OfNBA 87; WhoAfA 9; WhoAm
  74; WhoBbl 73; WhoBlA 7, 8

Walker, Clint

American. Actor
Star of TV series "Cheyenne," 1955-63.
b. May 30, 1927 in Hartford, Illinois
Source: BioIn 4, 22; FilmEn; FilmgC;
  ForYSC; HalFC 80, 84, 88; IntMPA 75,
  76, 77, 78, 79, 80, 81, 82, 84, 86, 88,
  92, 94, 96; LegTOT; MotPP; TelevWe;
  WhoHol 92, A; WorAl

Walker, Cyril

English. Golfer
Touring pro, 1920s; won US Open,
  1924.
b. 1892 in Manchester, England
d. Aug 5, 1948 in Hackensack, New
  Jersey
Source: BioIn 1; WhoGolf

Walker, Daniel

American. Politician
Dem. governor of IL, 1973-77; convicted
  of fraud, perjury, 1987.
b. Aug 6, 1922 in San Diego, California
Source: BiDrGov 1789; BioIn 9, 10, 11,
  20; BlueB 76; CurBio 76; IntWW 74, 75,
  76, 77, 78, 79, 80, 81, 82, 83, 89;
  PolPar; WhoAm 74, 76, 78; WhoAmL
  79; WhoGov 75, 77; WhoMW 74, 76, 78,
  80

Walker, Danton MacIntyre

American. Journalist
Broadway columnist, NY Daily News;
  wrote Danton's Inferno, 1955.
b. Jul 26, 1899 in Marietta, Georgia
d. Aug 8, 1960 in Hyannis,
  Massachusetts
Source: AmAu&B; BiDAmNC; BioIn 3,
  5; ConAu 93; REnAL; WhAm 4

Walker, David

American. Abolitionist, Author
Wrote Walker's Appeal, a pamphlet
  urging slaves to resort to violence
  when necessary to win their freedom.
b. Sep 28, 1785 in Wilmington, North
  Carolina
d. Jun 28, 1830 in Boston, Massachusetts
Source: AfrAmAl 8; BenetAL 91; BioIn
  6, 8, 11, 12, 20, 23; BlkAmW 1;
  BlkAWP; BlkWrNE; CamDcAB;
  ChamBiD; DcAmB; DcAmNB; DcNAA;
  EncSoH; EncWB 98; InB&W 80, 85;
  MacEWoS; McGEWB; NatCAB 14;
  NegAl 76, 83, 89; OxCAfAL; OxCAmL
  83, 95; RComAH; SchCGBL; SelBAAf;
  SelBAAu; WebAB 74, 79; WhAm HS

Walker, David Harry

Canadian. Author
Wrote Geordie, 1950; The Pillar, 1952.
b. Feb 9, 1911, Scotland
d. Mar 5, 1992
Source: BenetAL 91; BioIn 6, 10, 11;
  CanWr; CanWW 70, 79, 80, 81, 83, 89;
  CasWL; ConAu 1NR, 1R; ConLC 14, 76;
  ConNov 72, 76; DcLEL 1940; LngCTC;
  OxCCan, SUP; OxCChiL; REnAL;
  SJGChWr 5; SmATA 8; Who 74, 82, 83,
  85, 88, 90, 92; WhoAm 76, 78, 80, 82,
  84, 86, 88, 90; WhoCan 73, 75, 77, 80,
  82, 84; WhoCanL 92; WhoWor 80;
  WorAu 1950; WrDr 76

Walker, Dixie

[Fred Walker]
"The Peepul's Cherce"
American. Baseball Player
Outfielder, 1931, 1933-49, mostly with
  Brooklyn; led NL in batting, RBIs;
  had .306 lifetime batting average.
b. Sep 24, 1910 in Villa Rica, Georgia
d. May 17, 1982 in Birmingham,
  Alabama
Source: Ballpl 90; BiDAmSp BB; BioIn
  1, 2, 3, 8, 15, 24; FacFETw; LegTOT;
  NewYTBS 82; WhoProB 73

Walker, Doak

[Ewell Doak Walker, Jr.]
"Doaker"
American. Football Player
Halfback, won Heisman Trophy, 1948;
  in NFL with Detroit, 1950-56; led
  league in scoring twice; Hall of Fame,
  1986.
b. Jan 1, 1927 in Dallas, Texas
d. Sep 27, 1998 in Steamboat Springs,
  Colorado
Source: BiDAmSp FB; BioIn 1, 2, 3, 5,
  8, 9, 10, 14, 16, 17, 23; LegTOT; St&PR
  75, 84, 87, 91; WhoFtbl 74; WhoSpor

Walker, Edyth

American. Opera Singer
Mezzo-soprano, noted for Wagner roles;
  among first Americans accepted in
  European opera houses.
b. Mar 27, 1867 in Hopewell, New York
d. Feb 19, 1950 in New York, New
  York
Source: AmNatBi; BakBD 78, 84, 92;
  BakBDTw; CmOp; InWom SUP;
  MetOEnc; NewEOp 71; NewGrDA 86;
  NewGrDM 80; NewGrDO; NotAW;
  PenDiMP

Walker, Emery, Sir

English. Type Designer, Printer
Influenced William Morris to start
  Kelmscott Press, 1891; cofounded
  Doves Press, 1900.
b. Apr 2, 1851 in London, England
d. Jul 22, 1933 in London, England
Source: BioIn 2, 10, 16; DcNaB 1931;
  NewCol 75

Walker, Eric A(rthur)

American. Educator
Pres., PA State U, 1956-70.
b. Apr 29, 1910

d. Feb 17, 1995 in State College,
  Pennsylvania
Source: BioIn 4, 5, 9; BlueB 76; CurBio
  95N; WhAm 11; WhoAm 74, 76, 78, 80,
  82, 84, 86, 88, 90, 92, 94, 95, 96; WhoE
  74; WhoFI 74; WhoFrS 84; WhoGov 72,
  75, 77

Walker, Harold Blake

American. Clergy, Author, Journalist
Presbyterian minister; wrote Prayers to
  Live By, 1966.
b. May 7, 1904 in Denver, Colorado
Source: BlueB 76; ConAu 17R; WhoAm
  74, 76, 78, 80, 82, 84, 86, 88, 90, 92,
  94, 95, 96, 97, 98, 99, 2000; WhoMW
  92; WhoRel 92

Walker, Henry Oliver

American. Artist
Figural, mural painter; did congressional
  library scenes.
b. May 14, 1843 in Boston,
  Massachusetts
d. Jan 14, 1929 in Belmont,
  Massachusetts
Source: AmBi; DcAmB; NatCAB 9, 13,
  22; TwCBDA; WhAm 1

Walker, Herschel

American. Football Player
Running back, won Heisman Trophy,
  1982; in NFL with Dallas, 1986-89,
  Minnesota, 1989-92, Philadelphia,
  1992-95, New York Giants, 1995—.
b. Mar 3, 1962 in Wrightsville, Georgia
Source: AfrAmSG; BiDAmSp FB; BioIn
  12, 13, 14, 15, 16; ConBlB 1; CurBio
  85; FootReg 87; InB&W 85; LegTOT;
  NewYTBS 81, 82, 83, 84, 85, 86, 88;
  WhoAfA 9, 10, 11, 12; WhoAm 92, 94,
  95, 96, 97, 98; WhoBlA 4, 5, 6, 7, 8;
  WhoE 95; WhoWor 96; WorAlBi

Walker, Hiram

American. Distiller
Opened Hiram Walker and Sons,
  Canada; town of Walkerville, ON,
  named for him.
b. Jul 4, 1816 in East Boston,
  Massachusetts
d. Jan 12, 1899 in Detroit, Michigan
Source: DcCanB 12; MacDCB 78

Walker, Jack

[John Philip Walker]
Canadian. Hockey Player
Left wing. Detroit, 1926-28; Hall of
  Fame, 1960.
b. Nov 28, 1888 in Silver Mountain,
  Ontario, Canada
d. Feb 16, 1950
Source: HocEn; WhoHcky 73

Walker, Jimmie

[James Carter Walker]
American. Actor, Comedian
Played J J on TV series "Good Times,"
  1974-78; known for phrase "Dy-no-
  mite."
b. Jun 25, 1948 in New York, New York

Source: *BioIn 10, 13, 14, 15; BlksAmF;*
ConTFT 7; DrBlPA 90; EncAFC;
InB&W 80, 85; VarWW 85; WhoBlA 3,
4, 7; WhoHol A

Walker, Jimmy
[James John Walker]
American. Politician, Songwriter
Colorful mayor of NYC, 1925-32;
   investigation of widespread corruption
   led to resignation.
b. Jun 19, 1881 in New York, New York
d. Nov 18, 1946 in New York, New
   York
Source: *ASCAP 66, 80; BiDAmM; BioIn*
1, 2, 3, 4, 5, 6, 10; ChamBiD; CopCroC;
DcAmB S4; DcCathB; NatCAB 34;
ObitOF 79; OxCAmH; REn; REnAL;
WebAB 74, 79; WhAm 2; WorAl

Walker, John
American. Curator
Founding chief curator, National Gallery
   of Art, 1939-56; director, 1956-69.
b. Dec 24, 1906
d. Oct 15, 1995 in Sussex, England
Source: *BioIn 4, 5, 8, 9, 10, 11, 21, 22;*
BlueB 76; ConAu 5R, 6NR; CurBio 96N;
IntWW 74, 75, 76, 77, 78, 79, 80, 81, 82,
83, 89, 91, 93; NewYTBS 95; WhAmArt
85; Who 74, 82, 83, 85, 88, 90, 92, 94;
WhoAm 74, 76; WhoGov 72; WhoWor
74; WrDr 80, 82, 84, 86, 88, 90

Walker, Joseph
American. Photographer, Inventor
Developed first zoom lens, 1922;
   patented panoramic camera; received
   special Oscar, 1982.
b. 1892
d. Aug 1, 1985 in Las Vegas, Nevada
Source: *BioIn 14, 15; CamDcAB; ConAu*
117; FacFETw; FilmEn; FilmgC;
GangFlm; HalFC 80, 84, 88; IntMPA
77, 80, 81

Walker, Joseph Reddeford
American. Explorer, Naturalist
First white man to lead party across
   Sierra Nevadas; Walker Lake Pass
   named for him.
b. Dec 13, 1798 in Virginia
d. Oct 27, 1876 in Ignacio Valley,
   California
Source: *ApCAB; BioIn 2, 7, 13, 15, 18,*
24; CmCal; DcAmB; EncWB 98; Expl
93; ExplAnT; HarEnUS; NatCAB 5;
NewEAmW; REnAW; WebAB 74, 79;
WhAm HS; WhNaAH; WhWE

Walker, Junior
[Jr. Walker and the All-Stars; Autry
DeWalt, Jr.]
American. Musician, Singer
Saxophonist; hits include "Shotgun,"
   1965; "How Sweet It Is," 1966.
b. Jun 14, 1942 in Blythesville, Arkansas
d. Nov 23, 1995 in Battle Creek,
   Michigan
Source: *BioIn 22; EncRk 88; HarEnR*
86; LegTOT; NewGrDA 86; News 96,
96-2; NewYTBS 95; PenEncP; RkOn 84;
RolSEnR 83; WorAl

Walker, Kara
American. Artist
Controversial and critically acclaimed
   artist known for her political,
   sometimes shocking silhouette
   depictions of ante-Bellum blacks and
   whites interacting; work debuted at the
   Drawing Center in New York City and
   was shown in the Whitney Museum
   Biennial, 1997.
b. 1969 in Stockton, California
Source: *ConBlB 16; News 99-2, 1999;*
WhoAm 2000; WhoAmA 1999

Walker, LeRoy Tashreau
American. Educator, University
   Administrator
In 1992, he became the first African
   American elected to serve as president
   and chief executive officer of the
   United States Olympic Committee.
b. Jun 14, 1918 in Atlanta, Georgia
Source: *BioIn 13; EncWB 98; WhoAfA 9,*
10, 11, 12; WhoAm 78, 80, 82, 86, 88,
90, 92, 96, 97, 98, 99; WhoBlA 2, 3, 5,
6, 7, 8; WhoSSW 82, 84, 86, 88;
WhoWor 84, 93

Walker, Maggie Lena
American.
First US woman bank pres., 1903-32, St.
   Luke's Penny Thrift Savings Bank,
   now called the Consolidated Bank and
   Trust Co.
b. Jul 15, 1867 in Richmond, Virginia
d. Dec 15, 1934 in Richmond, Virginia
Source: *AfrAmAl 6, 8; AmWomM;*
BiDAmBL 83; BioIn 6, 8, 10, 16, 20, 21,
22, 23, 24; BlkWAm; ConBlB 17;
DcAmNB; EncWB, 98; GrLiveH; InB&W
85; InWom, SUP; LibW; NegAl 76, 83,
89; NotAW; NotBlAW 1; PeoHis;
WhoBlA 7

Walker, Margaret (Abigail)
[Margaret Walker Alexander]
American. Author, Poet, Educator
Powerful and prolific writer best known
   for her collection of poetry about
   racial affirmation, *For My People*
   (1942), and her Civil War novel
   Jubilee (1963).
b. Jul 7, 1915 in Birmingham, Alabama
Source: *AfrAmAl 6; ArtclWW 2; BenetAL*
91; BlkWAm; BlkWr 1, 2, 3; BroadAu;
ConAu 26NR, 54NR, 73, 76NR, 172;
ConNov 96; ConPo 96; InB&W 85;
InWom, SUP; MajTwCW 2; OxCAmL
95; OxCTwCL; RfGAmL 4, 94; SelBAAf;
SouBlCW; TwCRHW 94; WhoAfA 9, 10,
11, 12; WhoBlA 7, 8; WrDr 94, 96, 98,
99, 2000

Walker, Mary Edwards
American. Physician
First woman physician in US, 1855; only
   woman to receive Medal of Honor,
   1865.
b. Nov 26, 1832 in Oswego, New York
d. Feb 21, 1919 in Oswego, New York
Source: *AmBi; AmRef; AmWom;*
BioAmW; BioIn 2, 5, 6, 8, 11, 12, 15,
21, 22, 23, 24; CamDcAB; ChamBiD;

CivWDc; ConHero 3; ContDcW 89;
DcAmB; DcAmMeB 84; DcAmSR;
DcBiPP; DcNAA; EncWoAP;
HanAmWH; HerW; InSci; IntDcWB;
InWom, SUP; LibW; MedHR, 94;
MorMA; NatCAB 13; NotAW; NotWoLS;
OhA&B; WebAMB; WhAm 1; WomFir;
WomMil; WorAl

Walker, Mickey
[Edward Patrick Walker]
"Toy Bulldog"
American. Boxer, Artist
World welterweight champion, 1922-26;
   middleweight champion, 1926-31.
b. Jul 13, 1901 in Elizabeth, New Jersey
d. Apr 28, 1981 in Freehold, New Jersey
Source: *AmNatBi; AnObit 1981;*
BiDAmSp BK; BioIn 3, 4, 5, 6, 8, 10, 12,
24; BoxReg, 2; ConAu 108; LegTOT;
NewYTBS 81; WhoBox 74; WhoSpor;
WorAl

Walker, Mort
[Mortimer Walker Addison]
American. Cartoonist
Created *Beetle Bailey,* 1950; *Hi and*
Lois, 1954.
b. Sep 3, 1923 in El Dorado, Kansas
Source: *BioIn 11, 14, 15, 16; ConAu*
3NR, 25NR, 49; ConGrA 2; EncACom;
EncTwCJ; LegTOT; LinLib L; SmATA 8;
WhoAm 74, 76, 78, 80, 82, 84, 86, 88,
90, 92, 94, 95, 96, 97, 98, 99, 2000;
WhoAmA 73, 76, 78, 80, 82, 84, 86, 89,
91, 93, 1999; WhoE 74; WhoWor 74

Walker, Nancy
[Anna Myrtle Swoyer]
American. Actor
TV shows include "McMillan and
   Wife," 1971-76, "Rhoda," 1974-76.
b. May 10, 1921 in Philadelphia,
   Pennsylvania
d. Mar 25, 1992 in Studio City,
   California
Source: *BiE&WWA; BioNews 74;*
ConTFT 3; CurBio 65; EncMT; HalFC
80, 84, 88; IntMPA 92; InWom SUP;
LegTOT; LesBEnT, 92; MotPP; MovMk;
News 92; NewYTBE 73; NewYTBS 76;
NotNAT; OxCAmT 84; OxCPMus;
WhoAm 74, 78, 80, 82, 86, 88;
WhoCom; WhoEnt 92; WhoHol A;
WhoThe 77, 81; WorAl; WorAlBi

Walker, Ralph Thomas
American. Architect
Leading proponent, designer of Art Deco
   skyscrapers, 1920s.
b. Nov 28, 1889 in Waterbury,
   Connecticut
d. Jan 17, 1973
Source: *AmArch 70; AmNatBi; BioIn 4,*
5, 9, 10, 13; CamDcAB; CurBio 57, 73;
DcArch; MacEA; WhAm 5; WhoE 74

Walker, Robert
American. Actor
Starred in Hitchcock's *Strangers on a*
Train, 1951.
b. Oct 13, 1918 in Salt Lake City, Utah

d. Aug 28, 1951 in Santa Monica,
California
Source: *BiDFilm, 81, 94; EncAFC;
FilmEn; FilmgC; IntDcF 1-3, 2-3;
MovMk; NotNAT B; OxCFilm; WhScrn
74, 77; WorEFlm*

Walker, Robert James
American. Government Official
Secretary of Treasury under James Polk,
1845-49; helped create dept. of
Interior, 1849.
b. Jul 23, 1801 in Northumberland,
Pennsylvania
d. Nov 11, 1869 in Washington, District
of Columbia
Source: *Alli; BiAUS; BiDrAC; BiDrUSE
71, 89; BiDSA; BioIn 9; Drake;
HarEnUS; WhAm HS; WhAmP*

**Walker, Sarah Breedlove
McWilliams**
[Madame C. J. Walker]
American. Business Executive,
Philanthropist
Made fortune from beauty products
designed for black women's hair,
1905.
b. Dec 23, 1867 in Delta, Louisiana
d. May 25, 1919 in New York, New
York
Source: *InB&W 80; NotAW; WhoColR*

Walker, Stanley
American. Journalist
Wrote *City Editor,* 1934; city editor of
NY Herald Tribune, 1928-35.
b. Oct 21, 1898 in Lampasas, Texas
d. Nov 25, 1962 in Lampasas, Texas
Source: *AmAu&B; AmNatBi; BioIn 1, 6;
ConAu 93; CurBio 44, 63; EncAJ;
EncTwCJ; REnAL; TexWr; WhAm 4*

Walker, Stuart Armstrong
American. Producer, Director
Founded experimental mobile
Portmanteau Theatre, 1915.
b. Mar 4, 1880 in Augusta, Kentucky
d. Mar 13, 1941 in Beverly Hills,
California
Source: *DcAmB S3; NatCAB 38; WhAm
1*

Walker, T-Bone
[Aaron Thibeaux Walker]
"Daddy of the Blues"
American. Singer, Musician, Songwriter
Blues guitarist who popularized the use
of the electric guitar.
b. May 28, 1910 in Linden, Texas
d. Mar 16, 1975 in Los Angeles,
California
Source: *AllMGBl 1, 2; AmNatBi;
BiDAfM; BiDAmM; BillEnR; BioIn 15;
BluesWW; CamBiEn; CmpEGui;
ConMus 5; DcArts; DcTwCCu 5;
EncJzS; EncRk 88; IlEncJ; LegTOT;
NewAmDM; NewGrDA 86; NewGrDM
80; OnThGG; OxCPMus; PenEncP;
RolSEnR 83; Songw; WhoJazz 72;
WhoRock 81; WhoRocM 82*

Walker, T. J.
[Thomas Walker]
American. Fashion Designer
Co-founded, with Carl Jones, Cross
Colours, 1990.
b. c. 1961 in Toomsuba, Mississippi

Walker, Wesley Darcel
American. Football Player
Wide receiver, NY Jets, 1977-88; led
NFL in receiving, 1978.
b. May 26, 1955 in San Bernardino,
California
Source: *BioIn 14; FootReg 87; NewYTBS
78; WhoAfA 9, 10, 11, 12; WhoBlA 4, 7,
8*

Walker, William
American. Adventurer
Overthrew Nicaraguan govt., pres., 1856;
captured, executed in Honduras.
b. May 8, 1824 in Nashville, Tennessee
d. Sep 12, 1860 in Trujillo, Honduras
Source: *Alli SUP; AmAu&B; AmBi;
AmNatBi; ApCAB; BenetAL 91;
BiD&SB; BiDLAmC; BiDSA; BioIn 1, 2,
3, 4, 6, 8, 9, 11, 12, 16, 24; CamBiEn;
CamDcAB; ChambID; CmCal; DcAmAu;
DcAmB; DcAmDH 80, 89; DcAmSR;
DcBiPP; DcNAA; Drake; EncCapP;
EncLatA; EncRev; EncSoH; EncWB 98;
HarEnUS; HisWorL; LatAmLi; LinLib S;
McGEWB; NatCAB 11; OxCAmH;
PeoHis; REnAL; WebAB 74, 79; WhAm
HS; WhCiWar*

Walker, Zena
English. Actor
Won Tony for *A Day in the Death of
Joe Egg,* 1968.
b. Mar 7, 1934 in Birmingham, England
Source: *ConTFT 5; HalFC 84, 88;
VarWW 85; WhoHol 92; WhoThe 72, 77,
81*

Wall, Art(hur Jonathan), Jr.
American. Golfer
Turned pro, 1949; had 19 PGA wins
including Masters, 1959; leading
money winner, 1959.
b. Nov 25, 1923 in Honesdale,
Pennsylvania
Source: *BioIn 2, 5, 10, 21; CurBio 59;
WhoGolf*

Wallace, Alfred Russell
English. Engineer, Scientist, Physician
Proposed theory of evolution
simultaneously, but independently, of
Charles Darwin, 1858.
b. Jan 8, 1823 in Usk, England
d. Nov 7, 1913 in Broadstone, England
Source: *Alli SUP; BbD; BiD&SB;
BiDPara; BritAu 19; Chambr 3; DcEnA
A; DcEnL; DcEuL; DcLEL; EvLB; Expl
93; McGEWB; NewC; OxCEng 85; REn;
WebBD 83*

Wallace, Amy
American. Author
Wrote, with father *The People's Almanac
Presents the Book of Lists,* 1977.

b. Jul 3, 1955 in Los Angeles, California
Source: *ArtclWW 2; BiDrAPA 89; BioIn
11, 12, 15; ConAu 27NR, 81; WhAmArt
85; WhoWest 92*

Wallace, Bobby
[Roderick John Wallace]
"Rhody"
American. Baseball Player
Shortstop, 1894-1918, mostly with St.
Louis Browns; known for fielding;
first AL shortstop elected to Hall of
Fame, 1953.
b. Nov 4, 1874 in Pittsburgh,
Pennsylvania
d. Nov 3, 1960 in Torrance, California
Source: *WhoProB 73*

Wallace, Chris(topher)
American. Broadcast Journalist
White House correspondent, NBC News,
1982-1989; Prime Time Live 1989—;
son of Mike Wallace.
b. Oct 12, 1947 in Chicago, Illinois
Source: *BioIn 12, 14; Dun&B 90;
WhoAm 84, 86, 88, 90, 92, 94, 95, 96,
97, 98, 99, 2000; WhoE 95; WhoMedi
98; WhoTelC; WhoWor 96*

Wallace, Cornelia Folsom
American.
Second wife of AL governor, George
Wallace, 1971-78.
b. Jan 28, 1939 in Elba, Alabama
Source: *BioIn 10, 11, 12*

Wallace, DeWitt
[William Roy DeWitt Wallace]
American. Publisher
With wife, Lila, founded *Reader's
Digest,* 1922.
b. Nov 12, 1889 in Saint Paul,
Minnesota
d. Mar 30, 1981 in Mount Kisco, New
York
Source: *AmAu&B; AmNatBi; AnObit
1981; BiDAmJo; BioIn 1, 2, 3, 4, 5, 6, 8,
12, 15, 16, 17, 19, 20, 23, 24; BlueB 76;
CamBiEn; ChambID; ConAu 103;
CurBio 44, 56, 81, 81N; DcLB 137;
EncAB-H 1974, 1996; EncAJ; EncTwCJ;
EncWB, 98; IntWW 74, 75, 76, 77, 78,
79, 80; LegTOT; LinLib L, S; NewYTBS
81; RComAH; St&PR 75; WebAB 74,
79; WhAm 7; WhDW; WhoAm 74, 76,
78, 80; WhoWor 74; WorAl; WorAlBi*

Wallace, Ed(ward Tatum)
American. Journalist
Human interest stories were featured in
NY Daily News.
b. Aug 9, 1906
d. Oct 10, 1976 in New York, New York
Source: *BioIn 11; ConAu 69; NewYTBS
76*

Wallace, Edgar
[Richard Horatio Edgar Wallace]
English. Author
Wrote popular thrillers including *The
Terror,* 1930.
b. Dec 1875 in Greenwich, England

d. Feb 10, 1932 in Hollywood, California
Source: *Benet 87, 96; BiCoLiE; BioIn 2, 7, 8, 10, 14, 22, 24; CamGWoT; CasWL; ConAu 115; CrtSuMy; DcArts; DcLB 70; DcLEL; DcNaB 1931; DcPseud; EncMys; EncSF, 93; EncSoA; EvLB; FilmgC; GrBr; GrWrEL N; HalFC 84, 88; HisDcWJ; ItaFilm; LngCTC; MnBBF; ModBrL, 2; MysSW; NewC; NewCBEL; Novels; OxCEng 67, 85; OxCThe 67; PenC ENG; RAdv 14; REn; RfGEnL 91; ScF&FL 1, 92; ScFEYrs; ScFSB; TwCA, SUP; TwCCr&M 80, 85, 91; TwCLC 57; TwCSFW 81, 86, 91; TwCWr; WhoSpyF; WhoTwCL; WorAl; WorAlBi; WorAu 1900*

Wallace, George C(orley)
American. Politician
Four-term Dem. governor of AL, 1960s-80s; paralyzed in assassination attempt, 1972; gained renown as strong segregationist, but moderated views, becoming symbol of "New South."
b. Aug 25, 1919 in Clio, Alabama
d. Sep 13, 1998 in Montgomery, Alabama
Source: *AmOrTwC; AmPolLe; BiDrGov 1789, 1978, 1983; BioIn 5, 6, 7, 8, 9, 10, 11, 12, 13, 14, 15, 16, 17, 19, 20, 21, 22, 23, 24; BlueB 76; CamBiEn; CamDcAB; ChamBiD; CivRSt; ConAu 114, 170; CurBio 63, 98N; DcAmC; DcTwHis; EncAAH; EncAB-H 1974, 1996; EncAPar; EncSoH; EncVieW; EncWB 98; FacFETw; HisDCRM; HisDcSc; IntWW 74, 75, 76, 77, 78, 79, 80, 81, 82, 83, 89, 91, 93, 97, 98; LinLib S; McGEWB; NewYTBE 72; NewYTBS 74, 86; PolProf J, K, NF; PolsAm 84; PresAR 1980; RComAH; WebAB 74, 79; WhDW; WhoAm 74, 76, 78, 80, 82, 84, 86, 88, 90, 92, 94, 95, 98, 99; WhoAmL 79; WhoAmP 73, 75, 77, 79, 81, 83, 85, 87, 89, 91, 93, 95, 97; WhoGov 72, 75, 77; WhoSSW 73, 75, 76, 78, 84, 86, 88, 91, 95, 97; WhoWor 74, 78, 84, 87; WorAl; WorAlBi*

Wallace, Henry
American. Publicist, Editor
Agricultural publicist edited of the newspaper *Wallaces' Farmer* from 1895 to 1916.
b. Mar 19, 1836 in West Newton, Pennsylvania
d. Feb 22, 1916
Source: *AmAu; AmAu&B; AmBi; AmNatBi; BioIn 1, 9; ChamBiD; DcAmB; DcNAA; EncAAH; EncWB 98; McGEWB; OxCAmH; RAdv 14; REnAL; WhAm 1, 1C*

Wallace, Henry Agard
American. US Vice President
VP under FDR, 1941-45; Progressive Party presidential candidate, 1948.
b. Oct 7, 1888 in Adair County, Iowa
d. Nov 18, 1965 in Danbury, Connecticut
Source: *AmAu&B; AmNatBi; AmOrTwC; AmPeW; AmPolLe; BiDInt; BiDrAC; BiDrUSC 89; BiDrUSE 71, 89; BioIn 1, 2, 4, 5, 6, 7, 8, 9, 10, 11, 12, 14, 15, 16,*

17, 18, 19, 20, 22, 23, 24; *CamBiEn; CamDcAB; ChamBiD; ColdWar 2; ConAu 89; CurBio 40, 47, 66; DcAmB S7; DcTwHis; EncAAH; EncAB-A 1, 23; EncAB-H 1974, 1996; EncWB 98; LinLib S; McGEWB; MorMA; NatCAB 53; NewEAmW; ObitT 1961; OxCAmH; REnAL; REnAW; VicePre; WebAB 74, 79; WhAm 4; WhAmP; WhNAA; WorAl*

Wallace, Horace Binney
American. Author, Critic, Poet
Wrote verse "Hand That Rocks the Cradle."
b. Feb 26, 1817 in Philadelphia, Pennsylvania
d. Dec 16, 1852 in Paris, France
Source: *Alli; AmAu&B; AmBi; ApCAB; BiD&SB; CyAL 2; DcAmAu; DcAmB; DcNAA; Drake; NatCAB 6; OxCAmL 65, 83, 95; WhAm HS*

Wallace, Irving
[Irving Wallechinsky]
American. Author
One of best-read and best-selling 20th-century American authors; wrote *The Chapman Report*, 1960, filmed starring Jane Fonda, Shelley Winters, 1962.
b. Mar 19, 1916 in Chicago, Illinois
d. Jun 29, 1990 in Los Angeles, California
Source: *AmAu&B; AmNatBi; AnObit 1990; Au&Wr 71; AuNews 1; AuSpks; BeaEPF; BioIn 6, 8, 9, 10, 11, 12, 13, 14, 15, 16, 17, 24; BioNews 74; BkPepl; BlueB 76; CelR, 90; ConAu 1AS, 1NR, 1R, 27NR, 132; ConLC 7, 13; ConPopW; CurBio 79, 90, 90N; DcArts; DcLEL 1940; DcPseud; FacFETw; FilmEn; HalFC 84, 88; IntAu&W 76, 89, 91; IntMPA 75, 76, 77, 78, 79, 80, 81, 82, 84, 86, 88; LegTOT; MajTwCW 1, 2; News 91, 91-1; NewYTBS 90; Novels; RAdv 14; ScF&FL 92; ScrEAmL 2; TwCWr; WhAm 10; Who 74, 82, 83, 85, 88, 90; WhoAm 74, 76, 78, 80, 82, 84, 86, 88; WhoUSWr 88; WhoWrEP 89; WorAl; WorAlBi; WrDr 76, 80, 82, 84, 86, 88, 90*

Wallace, Lew(is)
American. Author, Soldier
Wrote best-sellers *Ben Hur*, 1880; *Prince of India*, 1893.
b. Apr 10, 1827 in Brookville, Indiana
d. Feb 15, 1905 in Crawfordsville, Indiana
Source: *Alli SUP; AmAu; AmAu&B; AmBi; ApCAB, X; ArtsAmW 1; BbD; Benet 87, 96; BenetAL 91; BibAL 8; BiD&SB; BiDrATG; BioIn 1, 2, 3, 5, 6, 7, 12, 14, 16; CamBiEn; CamDcAB; CamGEL; CamGLE; CamHAL; CarSB; CasWL; ChamBiD; Chambr 3; ChhPo, S3; CivWDc; CnDAL; ConAu 120, 176; CyWA 58, 97; DcAmAu; DcAmB; DcAmDH 80, 89; DcAmMiB; DcBiA; DcEnA A; DcLEL; DcNAA; EncAB-H 1974, 1996; EncWB 98; EvLB; GayN; GrWrEL N; HalFC 84, 88; HarEnUS; IlBEAAW; JBA 3; LegTOT; LinLib L, S; McGEWB; NatCAB 4; NewYHSD; NotNAT B; Novels; OxCAmL 65, 83, 95;*

PenC AM; RAdv 1, 14, 13-1; REn; REnAL; RfGAmL 4, 87, 94; TwCBDA; WebAB 74, 79; WebAMB; WhAm 1; WhAmArt 85; WhCiWar; WorAl

Wallace, Lila Bell Acheson
American. Publisher, Editor
Organizer, YWCA, 1921-22; co-founder, editor *Reader's Digest*, 1921-65.
b. Dec 25, 1889 in Virden, Manitoba, Canada
d. May 8, 1984 in Mount Kisco, New York
Source: *AmAu&B; AmNatBi; AnObit 1984; BlueB 76; CamDcAB; CanWW 83; ConAu 105, 112; CurBio 56; ForWC 70; InWom, SUP; WebAB 74, 79; WhoAm 74; WhoAmW 81; WhoE 74; WhoWor 74*

Wallace, Lurleen Burns
[Mrs. George Wallace]
American. Politician
Succeeded husband to become first woman governor of AL, 1967.
b. Sep 19, 1926 in Tuscaloosa, Alabama
d. May 7, 1968 in Montgomery, Alabama
Source: *AmNatBi; AmPolW 80; BiDrGov 1789; CurBio 67, 68; DcAmB S8; EncWoAP; InWom, SUP; LegTOT; WhAm 5; WhoAmW 68*

Wallace, Michele Faith
American. Educator, Author
Feminist scholar has taught at several universities, including the City University of New York, and is a columnist for the *Village Voice;* sparked controversy for criticizing the Civil Rights and Black Power movements in her 1978 book *Black Macho and the Myth of the Superwoman.*
b. Jan 4, 1952 in New York, New York
Source: *ConAu 58NR, 108; ConBlB 13; WhoAmW 79, 81, 83, 85, 87; WhoEmL 87*

Wallace, Mike
[Myron Leon Wallace]
American. Broadcast Journalist
CBS correspondent, 1963-76; co-editor, "60 Minutes," 1968—; inducted into Television Academy Hall of Fame 1991.
b. May 9, 1918 in Brookline, Massachusetts
Source: *BioIn 4, 6, 8, 11, 12, 13, 14, 17, 18, 19, 20, 21, 22, 23, 24; BkPepl; BlueB 76; CelR, 90; ConAu 65; ConTFT 10, 17; CurBio 57, 77; EncAJ; EncTelN; EncTwCJ; IntMPA 75, 76, 77, 78, 79, 80, 81, 82, 84, 86, 88, 92, 94, 96; JrnUS; LegTOT; LesBEnT; NewYTET; PolCom; WhoAm 74, 76, 78, 80, 82, 84, 86, 88, 90, 92, 94, 95, 96, 97, 98, 99, 2000; WhoAmJ 80; WhoE 74, 91, 93, 95, 97, 99; WhoEnt 98; WhoMedi 98; WhoWorJ 72, 78; WorAl; WorAlBi*

Wallace, Phyllis A(nn)
American. Economist, Educator
Professor of economics, Massachusetts
Institute of Technology, 1975-86;
member, Minimum Wage Study
Commission, 1978-82.
b. c. 1920 in Baltimore, Maryland
d. Jan 10, 1993
Source: *NotBlAW 1*

Wallace, Richard, Sir
English. Art Collector, Philanthropist
His inherited 19th-c. art collection was
bequeathed to British nation, 1897.
b. Jun 21, 1818 in London, England
d. Jul 20, 1890 in Paris, France
Source: *BioIn 2, 12; CamBiEn;
ChamBiD; DcArts; DcBiPP; DcBrWA;
DcNaB; OxCArt*

Wallace, Sippie
[Beulah Thomas]
''Texas Nightingale''
American. Singer
Major 1920s blues singer; received
Grammy nomination for *Sippie,* 1983.
b. Nov 1, 1898 in Houston, Texas
d. Nov 1, 1986 in Detroit, Michigan
Source: *AllMGBl 1, 2; AmNatBi; AnObit
1986; BiDAfM; BiDJaz; BioIn 9, 12, 13,
15, 16, 17, 18, 19, 20, 23, 24; BlkWAm;
Blues; ConBlB 1; ConMus 6; InWom
SUP; NewGrDJ 88, 94; NewYTBS 86;
NotBlAW 1; PenEncP; ScrEAmL 2;
WhoJazz 72*

Wallace, William
Scottish. Military Leader
Champion of Scottish nationalism led the
Rising of 1297, an attempt to reverse
the loss of Scottish independence to
England.
b. c. 1270
d. 1305 in London, England
Source: *BlmGEL; CamBiEn; CmScLit;
DcBiPP; DcCathB; EncWB 98;
GenMudB; HarEnMi; LinLib S;
LngCEL; McGEWB*

**Wallace-Johnson, Isaac
Theophilus Akunna**
African. Politician, Journalist, Labor
Union Official
West African trade union organizer,
nationalist political leader, and
journalist was a pan-Africanist.
b. 1895 in Wilberforce, Sierra Leone
d. May 10, 1965, Ghana
Source: *EncWB 98; McGEWB*

Wallach, Eli
American. Actor
Films include *Baby Doll,* 1956; *The
Misfits,* 1961.
b. Dec 7, 1915 in New York, New York
Source: *BiE&WWA; BioIn 3, 5, 6, 8, 14,
17, 20; CamGWoT; CelR, 90; CnThe;
ConTFT 1, 7, 18; FilmEn; FilmgC;
ForYSC; GangFlm; HalFC 80, 84, 88;
IntDcF 1-3, 2-3; IntMPA 77, 78, 79, 80,
81, 82, 84, 86, 88, 92, 94, 96; IntWW
76, 77, 78, 79, 80, 81, 82, 83, 89, 91,
93, 97, 98, 2000; ItaFilm; LegTOT;*

*MotPP; MovMk; NotNAT; OxCAmT 84;
OxCFilm; PIP&P; WhoAm 74, 76, 78,
80, 82, 84, 86, 88, 90, 92, 94, 95, 96,
97, 98, 99, 2000; WhoAmJ 80; WhoEnt
92, 98; WhoHol 92, A; WhoThe 72, 77,
81; WhoWor 74, 78, 80, 82, 84;
WhoWorJ 72, 78; WorAl; WorAlBi;
WorEFlm*

Wallach, Otto
German. Chemist
Won 1910 Nobel Prize for pioneering
field of alicyclic compounds, organic
chemistry.
b. Mar 27, 1847 in Konigsberg, Prussia
d. Feb 26, 1931 in Gottingen, Germany
Source: *AsBiEn; BiESc; BioIn 1, 3, 5, 6,
15, 19, 20; ChamBiD; DcScB; InSci;
LarDcSc; McGCEnS; NobelP; NotTwCS
1; RanHWDS; WhoNob, 90, 95; WorAl;
WorAlBi*

Wallack, James William
American. Actor, Manager
Operated Wallack's Theater in NY,
1852-64.
b. Aug 24, 1795 in London, England
d. Dec 25, 1864 in New York, New
York
Source: *AmBi; AmNatBi; ApCAB; BioIn
2; CamGWoT; DcAmB; DcNaB; Drake;
EncWT; FamA&A; HarEnUS; NatCAB
4; OxCThe 67; TwCBDA; WebAB 74,
79; WhAm HS*

Wallant, Edward Lewis
American. Author
Wrote *The Pawnbroker,* 1961, filmed
1965.
b. Oct 19, 1926 in New Haven,
Connecticut
d. Dec 5, 1962 in Norwalk, Connecticut
Source: *AmAu&B; BenetAL 91; BioIn 6,
9, 10, 12, 14, 17, 21, 24; ConAu 1R,
22NR; ConJeAN; ConLC 5, 10; ConNov
76; CyWA 97; DcLB 2, 28, 143; DcLEL
1940; EncALit; EncWL 1, 2, 2S, 3;
GrWrEL N; JeAmFiW; MajTwCW 1, 2;
ModAL 4, 5; Novels; OxCAmL 65, 83,
95; OxCTwCL; PenC AM; RfGAmL 4,
87, 94; WebE&AL; WhoTwCL; WorAu
1950*

Wallas, Graham
British. Sociologist, Political Scientist
Anti-rationalist; was a proponent of a
psychological approach to the study of
politics.
b. 1858
d. 1932
Source: *BioIn 2, 9, 12, 14, 16, 22;
ChamBiD; DcNaB 1931; EncWB 98;
EvLB; GrBr; LngCTC; McGEWB;
NamesHP; NewCBEL; ThTwC 87;
TwCA, SUP; TwCLC 91; WorAu 1900*

Wallechinsky, David
American. Author
Co-author: *The People's Almanac,* 1975;
The Book of Lists, 1977; son of Irving
Wallace.
b. Feb 5, 1948 in Los Angeles,
California

Source: *BioIn 15; ConAu 27NR, 55NR,
61*

Wallenberg, Marcus
Swedish. Banker
Business empire controlled one-third of
all Swedish industry.
b. Oct 5, 1899 in Stockholm, Sweden
d. Sep 13, 1982 in Stockholm, Sweden
Source: *AnObit 1982; BioIn 11, 12, 13,
14; ChamBiD; IntWW 74, 75, 76, 77, 78,
79, 80, 81, 82, 83N; IntYB 78, 79, 80,
81, 82; NewYTBS 82; WhAm 8; WhoFI
74; WhoWor 74, 76, 78, 80, 82*

Wallenberg, Raoul Gustav
Swedish. Diplomat
Saved nearly 100,000 Budapest Jews in
WW II.
b. Aug 4, 1912 in Stockholm, Sweden
d. Jul 17, 1947 in Moscow, Union of
Soviet Socialist Republics
Source: *BioIn 4; HisEWW; NewYTBS 80*

Wallenda, Karl
American. Circus Performer
Patriarch of famed high-wire troupe;
killed in 100-foot fall.
b. Jan 21, 1905 in Magdeburg, Germany
d. Mar 22, 1978 in San Juan, Puerto
Rico
Source: *BioIn 9, 10, 11, 12; DcAmB
S10; LegTOT; NewYTBS 78*

**Wallenstein, Albrecht Wenzel
Eusebius von**
Bohemian. Military Leader
Soldier of fortune was one of the richest
and most powerful men in Europe, and
one of the major figures in the Thirty
Years War.
b. Sep 24, 1583 in Hermanitz, Bohemia
d. Feb 25, 1634 in Eger, Bohemia
Source: *BioIn 18, 20, 24; ChamBiD;
EncWB 98*

Wallenstein, Alfred Franz
American. Musician, Conductor
Cellist; one of first native American
symphonic conductors to gain national
status; directed LA Philharmonic,
1943-56.
b. Oct 7, 1898 in Chicago, Illinois
d. Feb 8, 1983 in New York, New York
Source: *AnObit 1983; BakBD 78;
BiDAmM; BioIn 1, 2, 3, 4, 11, 13;
CurBio 40, 52, 83; NewYTBS 83;
ScrEAmL 1; WhAm 8; WhoAm 74, 76,
78, 80, 82; WorAl*

Waller, Edmund
English. Poet
Served in Parliament under Charles II;
lyrics were set to music by Henry
Lawes.
b. Mar 3, 1606 in Coleshill, England
d. Oct 21, 1687 in Beaconsfield, England
Source: *Alli; AtlBL; BbD; Benet 87, 96;
BiCoLiE; BiD&SB; BiDRP&D; BioIn 2,
3, 5, 9, 12, 19, 24; BlmGEL; BritAu;
BritWr 2; CamBiEn; CamGEL;
CamGLE; CasWL; ChamBiD; Chambr*

1; *ChhPo, S1; CnE&AP; CroE&S;*
CyWA 97; DcArts; DcEnA; DcEnL;
DcLB 126; DcLEL; DcNaB; EvLB;
GrWrEL P; LngCEL; MouLC 1; NewC;
NewCBEL; OxCBrHi; OxCEng 67, 85,
95; PenC ENG; REn; RfGEnL 91;
WebE&AL; WhDW

Waller, Fats

[Thomas Wright Waller]
American. Jazz Musician, Songwriter
Stride pianist, famed entertainer, singer;
wrote "Ain't Misbehavin',"
"Honeysuckle Rose."
b. May 21, 1904 in New York, New
York
d. Dec 15, 1943 in Kansas City,
Missouri
Source: *AllMGJa; AmNatBi; AmSong;*
ASCAP 66; BakBD 78, 84, 92; BakDcM;
BiDAfM; BiDJaz; BioIn 14, 15, 16, 22;
CamBiEn; ChamBiD; CmpEPM;
ConMus 7; CurBio 42, 44; DcAmB S3;
DcAmNB; DcArts; DcPseud; DcTwCCu
5; DrBlPA, 90; FilmgC; HalFC 80, 84,
88; IlEncJ; InB&W 80, 85; LegTOT;
NewAmDM; NewGrDA 86; NewGrDJ
88, 94; NewGrDM 80; NewOxM;
NotBlAM; NotNAT 0; OxCPMus;
PenEncP; PopAmC; RAdv 14; Songw;
SpreRhy; WhAm 4; WhoHol B; WhoJazz
72; WhScrn 77; WorAl; WorAlBi

Waller, Fred(erick)

American. Inventor
Invented Cinerama, 1952; invented,
patented first water ski.
b. Mar 10, 1886 in New York, New
York
d. May 18, 1954 in Huntington, New
York
Source: *BioIn 3; CurBio 53, 54; DcFM;*
FilmEn; FilmgC; HalFC 80, 84, 88

Waller, Gordon

[Peter and Gordon]
Scottish. Singer, Musician
Part of Peter and Gordon duo, 1961-68;
biggest hit "World without Love,"
1964, written by Paul McCartney.
b. Jun 4, 1945 in Braemar, Scotland

Waller, Robert James

American. Author, Educator
Author of *The Bridges of Madison
County*, 1991.
b. Aug 1, 1939 in Rockford, Iowa
Source: *BeaEPF; BioIn 18, 19, 20, 21,
23; ConAu 65NR, 147; ConPopW;
CurBio 94; IntWW 98, 2000; WhoAm 95,
96, 97, 98, 99, 2000; WrDr 98, 99, 2000*

Waller, William, Sir

"William the Conqueror"
English. Army Officer, Statesman
Fought in Thirty Years War, 1620-22;
served in Parliament as member of
Presbyterian party.
b. 1597 in Knole, England
d. Sep 19, 1668 in London, England
Source: *Alli; BioIn 9, 16, 23; ChamBiD;
DcBiPP; DcEnL; DcNaB; HarEnMi;
NewC; WhoMilH 76*

Wallerstein, Jusith S.

American. Psychologist
Studied the effects of divorce on adults
and children, proving that many of
those affected were feeling poorer one
year after the event; wrote *How
Children and Parents Cope with
Divorce*, 1990.
b. Dec 27, 1921 in New York, New
York
Source: *CurBio 96*

Wallerstein, Lothar

Czech. Director
Conducted at La Scala, Milan, 1929;
producer at NY Met., 1941.
b. Nov 6, 1882 in Prague, Bohemia
d. Nov 13, 1949 in New Orleans,
Louisiana
Source: *BakBD 78, 84, 92; BakBDTw;
BioIn 2; CmOp; IntDcOp; NewEOp 71;
NewGrDA 86; ObitOF 79; OxDcOp;
PenDiMP*

Walley, Deborah

American. Actor
Played in TV show "Mothers-in-law,"
1967-69; starred in film *Gidget Goes
Hawaiian*, 1961.
b. Aug 13, 1943 in Bridgeport,
Connecticut
Source: *BioIn 16; ForWC 70; ForYSC;
MotPP; WhoHol A*

Wallington, Jimmy

[James S Wallington]
American. Actor
Radio announcer on "The Eddie Cantor
Show," "The Burns and Allen
Show."
b. Sep 15, 1907 in Rochester, New York
d. Dec 22, 1972 in Fairfax, Virginia
Source: *BioIn 9; NewYTBE 72; ObitOF
79; RadStar; WhoHol B; WhScrn 77, 83*

Wallis, Barnes Neville, Sir

English. Engineer, Inventor
Designed "Grand Slam," "Tall Boy
bombs," WW II."
b. Sep 26, 1887 in Ripley, England
d. Oct 30, 1979 in Leatherhead, England
Source: *BiESc; BioIn 4, 9, 12, 13, 14;
CamBiEn; ChamBiD; DcNaB 1971;
FacFETw; GrBr; IntWW 78; LarDcSc;
NewYTBS 79; RanHWDS; WhDW; Who
74; WhWW-II*

Wallis, Hal Brent

American. Producer
Produced over 400 films, including
Casablanca, 1942; *The Maltese
Falcon*, 1941; 32 of his films won
Oscars.
b. Sep 14, 1899 in Chicago, Illinois
d. Oct 5, 1986 in Rancho Mirage,
California
Source: *BiDFilm; BlueB 76; ConNews
87-1; ConTFT 4; FilmgC; HalFC 84;
IntMPA 86; OxCFilm; VarWW 85;
WebAB 74, 79; WhAm 9; WhoAm 86;
WhoWor 82; WorAl; WorEFlm*

Wallis, Samuel

English. Navigator
Around the world voyage, 1766-68;
discovered Easter Island, Tahiti.
b. Apr 23, 1728 in Fentonwoon
d. Jan 21, 1795 in London
Source: *ApCAB; BioIn 18, 20, 24;
CamBiEn; ChamBiD; DcNaB; Expl 93;
ExplAnT; OxCShps; WebBD 83; WhWE*

Wallis, Shani

English. Actor
Films include *Terror in the Wax
Museum*, 1973.
b. Apr 16, 1933 in London, England
Source: *FilmgC; HalFC 84, 88; WhoHol
A; WhoThe 72, 77A; WhThe*

Wallmann, Margherita

Austrian. Producer
Productions in opera, film, TV, stage
known internationally.
b. Jun 22, 1904 in Vienna, Austria
d. May 2, 1992 in Monte Carlo, Monaco
Source: *CmOp; IntDcOp; MetOEnc;
NewEOp 71; WhoMus 72*

Wallop, Douglass

[John Douglass, III Wallop]
American. Author
Wrote *The Year the Yankees Lost the
Pennant*, 1954, basis for hit musical
Damn Yankees, 1955.
b. Mar 8, 1920 in Washington, District
of Columbia
d. Apr 1, 1985 in Georgetown, Maryland
Source: *AmAu&B; BiE&WWA; BioIn 14;
ConAu 13NR, 73, 115; CurBio 85, 85N;
DrAPF 80, 83; NotNAT; ScF&FL 1, 92;
WhoAm 76*

Wallop, Malcolm

American. Politician
Rep. senator from WY, 1976-94.
b. Feb 27, 1933 in New York, New
York
Source: *AlmAP 78, 80, 82, 84, 88, 92;
BiDrUSC 89; BioIn 13; CngDr 77, 79,
81, 83, 85, 87, 89, 91, 93; IntWW 89,
91, 93, 97, 98, 2000; NewYTBS 82;
PolsAm 84; WhoAm 78, 80, 84, 86, 88,
90, 92, 94, 95; WhoAmP 73, 75, 77, 79,
81, 83, 85, 87, 89, 91, 93, 95, 97, 1999;
WhoGov 77; WhoWest 78, 80, 82, 84,
87, 89, 92, 94; WhoWor 80, 84, 87,
89, 91*

Walls, Everson Collins

American. Football Player
Four-time all-pro cornerback, Dallas,
1981-89; NY Giants 1989-92;
Cleveland, 1992—.
b. Dec 28, 1959 in Dallas, Texas
Source: *BioIn 14; FootReg 87; WhoBlA
4, 7*

Walmsley, Jon

American. Actor
Played Jason Walton on TV series "The
Waltons," 1972-79.
b. Feb 6, 1956 in Lancashire, England
Source: *BioIn 11, 12; WhoHol 92, A*

Waln, Nora

American. Journalist
Wrote *House of Exile,* 1933.
b. Jun 4, 1895 in Grampian,
  Pennsylvania
d. Sep 27, 1964 in Madrid, Spain
Source: *AmAu&B; BioIn 4, 7, 22; ConAu
89; CurBio 40, 64; InWom; LngCTC;
REnAL; TwCA, SUP; WhAm 4;
WhE&EA; WorAu 1900*

Walpole, Horace

[Fourth Earl of Oxford]
English. Author
His work *The Castle of Otranto,* 1765,
  began fad for Gothic novels; brilliant
  prolific letter writer.
b. Sep 24, 1717 in London, England
d. Mar 2, 1797 in London, England
Source: *Alli; AtlBL; BbD; Benet 87, 96;
BiCoLiE; BiD&SB; BioIn 1, 2, 3, 4, 5, 6,
7, 8, 9, 10, 11, 12, 13, 15, 17, 21, 24;
BlkwCE; BlmGEL; BritAu; CamGEL;
CamGLE; CasWL; ChamBiD; Chambr
2; ChhPo, S2; CrtT 2, 4; CyWA 58, 97;
DcArch; DcArts; DcBiA; DcBiPP;
DcEnA; DcEnL; DcEuL; DcLB 39, 104,
213; DcLEL; DcNaB; Dis&D; EncAR;
EncEnl; EvLB; GrWrEL N; LegTOT;
LinLib L, S; LitC 2, 49; LngCEL;
MacEA; MouLC 2; NewC; NewCBEL;
OxCArt; OxCBrHi; OxCEng 67, 85, 95;
OxDcArt; PenC ENG; PenEncH; RAdv
1, 14, 13-1; REn; RfGEnL 91; ScF&FL
1; SJGHorW; SupFW; WebE&AL;
WhDW; WhoHr&F; WorAl; WorAlBi*

Walpole, Hugh Seymour, Sir

English. Author
Novels include *The Dark Forest,* 1916.
b. Mar 13, 1884 in Auckland, New
  Zealand
d. Jun 1, 1941 in Brackenburg, England
Source: *CamBiEn; CasWL; ChamBiD;
Chambr 3; ChhPo S2; ConAu 165;
CyWA 58; DcBiA; DcLEL; DcNaB 1941;
Dis&D; EvLB; FilmgC; GrBr; GrWrEL
N; HalFC 80; LinLib L, S; LngCTC;
MajTwCW 2; MnBBF; ModBrL; NewC;
NewCBEL; NotNAT B; OxCEng 67, 85,
95; OxCTwCL; PenC ENG; REn;
ScF&FL 1; SJGHorW; TwCA, SUP;
TwCRHW 94; TwCWr; WebE&AL;
WhLit; WhoChL; WhoHol B; WhoHr&F;
WhoLA; WhoTwCL; WhScrn 74, 77;
WhThe; WorEFlm*

Walpole, Robert

[First Earl of Oxford]
English. Statesman
Secretary of war, 1708-1710; treasurer of
  the navy, 1710-1711; father of Horace
  Walpole.
b. Aug 26, 1676 in Houghton, England
d. Mar 18, 1745 in Houghton, England
Source: *Alli; Benet 87, 96; BioIn 14, 15,
17, 21, 24; BlmGEL; CamBiEn;
ChamBiD; DcBiPP; DcNaB; EncEnl;
EncWB 98; HisDBrE; HisWorL;
LegTOT; LinLib S; LngCEL; McGEWB;
NewC; NewCBEL; OxCBrHi; OxCEng
85, 95; OxCMus; REn; WhDW; WorAl;
WorAlBi*

Walras, Marie Esprit Leon

French. Economist
Influenced modern economic theory by
  his discovery of the general
  equilibrium theory, a single model
  designed to include theories of
  exchange, production, capital, and
  money.
b. 1834 in Evreux, Normandy, France
d. 1910
Source: *BioIn 14, 18; EncWB 98;
McGEWB; WhoEc 81, 86*

Walsh, Bill

[William Ernest Walsh]
American. Football Coach
Head coach, San Francisco, 1979-88;
  won Super Bowl, 1982, 1985, 1989.
b. Nov 30, 1931 in Los Angeles,
  California
Source: *BiDAmSp FB; BioIn 12, 13, 14,
16, 18, 19, 20, 22, 24; ConNews 87-4;
CurBio 89; FootReg 87; LesBEnT 92;
NewYTBS 82; WhoAm 86; WhoSpor;
WorAlBi*

Walsh, Chad

American. Author, Clergy
Wrote numerous books including *Faith
  and Behavior,* 1954, *God at Large,*
  1971.
b. May 10, 1914 in South Boston,
  Virginia
d. Jan 17, 1991 in Shelburne, Vermont
Source: *AmAu&B; Au&Wr 71; BioIn 2,
4, 6, 10, 17; ConAu 1R, 6NR, 133;
ConPo 70, 75, 80, 85, 91; CurBio 91N;
DrAP 75; DrAPF 80, 91; DrAS 74E,
78E, 82E, 99E; IntWWP 77; NewYTBS
91; ScF&FL 1, 2, 92; WhoAm 74, 76,
78; WorAu 1950; WrDr 76, 80, 82, 84,
86, 88, 90, 92, 94N*

Walsh, Ed(ward Augustine)

''Big Ed''
American. Baseball Player
Pitcher, 1904-17, mostly with White
  Sox; won 40 games, 1908; holds ML
  record for lowest career ERA; Hall of
  Fame, 1946.
b. May 14, 1881 in Plains, Pennsylvania
d. May 26, 1959 in Pompano Beach,
  Florida
Source: *AmNatBi; Ballpl 90; BiDAmSp
BB; BioIn 14, 15; CamDcAB; DcAmB
S6; LegTOT; WhoProB 73*

Walsh, James Edward

American. Religious Leader
Roman Catholic bishop who spent more
  than 40 yrs. as missionary to China,
  12 yrs. in Shanghai prison.
b. Apr 30, 1891? in Cumberland,
  Maryland
d. Jul 29, 1981 in Ossining, New York
Source: *AmCath 80; AnObit 1981;
BiDChrM; BioIn 1, 5, 6, 9, 11, 12;
CathA 1930; ConAu 104; NewYTBS 81;
WhAm 8; WhoAm 74, 76, 78, 80*

Walsh, Joe

[The Eagles; The James Gang; Joseph
  Fidler Walsh]
American. Musician, Singer
Joined James Gang, 1971; Eagles, 1976-
  82; solo albums include *The
  Confessor,* 1985.
b. Nov 20, 1947 in Wichita, Kansas
Source: *ASCAP 80; BillEnR; BioIn 11,
13; ConMus 5; EncRk 88; EncRkSt;
GrMetD; HarEnR 86; LegTOT;
OnThGG; PenEncP; RkOn 74; RolSEnR
83; Songw; WhoAm 76, 80, 82, 84, 86,
88, 92, 94, 95, 96; WhoEnt 92A*

Walsh, Lawrence E

American. Government Official, Lawyer
Special prosecutor of the Iran-Contra
  affair.
b. Jan 8, 1912 in Port Maitland, Nova
  Scotia, Canada
Source: *BioIn 4, 15; CurBio 91; IntWW
91; NewYTBE 71; NewYTBS 75, 86, 87;
WhoAm 90; WhoAmL 90; WhoWor 91*

Walsh, Michael Patrick

American. University Administrator
Pres., Boston College, 1958-68; Fordham
  U, 1969-72.
b. Feb 28, 1912 in Boston,
  Massachusetts
d. Apr 23, 1982 in Boston,
  Massachusetts
Source: *AmCath 80; AmMWSc 76P, 79;
BioIn 12, 13; LEduc 74; NewYTBS 82;
WhAm 8; WhoE 74*

Walsh, Raoul

American. Actor, Director
Directed Hollywood's first outdoor
  talking movie, *In Old Arizona,* 1929.
b. Mar 11, 1887 in New York, New
  York
d. Dec 31, 1980 in Los Angeles,
  California
Source: *AmNatBi; AnObit 1980;
BiDFilm, 81, 94; BiHaHis; BioIn 12, 15,
16; CmMov; ConAu 102; DcAmB S10;
DcArts; DcFM; EncAFC; FacFETw;
Film 1; FilmEn; FilmgC; GangFlm;
HalFC 80, 84, 88; IlWWHD 1; IntDcF
1-2, 2-2; IntMPA 77; ItaFilm; LegTOT;
MiSFD 9N; MovMk; NewYTBS 81;
OxCFilm; TwYS; WhoHol A; WhScrn
83; WorEFlm; WorFDir 1; WrDr 76, 80*

Walsh, Stella

[Stanislawa Walasiewicz]
Polish. Track Athlete
Sprinter; won gold medal in 100-meter
  run, 1932 Olympics.
b. Apr 3, 1911 in Wierzchownia, Poland
d. Dec 4, 1980 in Cleveland, Ohio
Source: *AmNatBi; AnObit 1980;
BiDAmSp OS; BioIn 11, 12; DcPseud;
EncWB 2-19; EncWomS; GoodHs;
InWom SUP; LegTOT; NewYTBS 80;
PolBiDi; WhoSpor; WhoTr&F 73; WorAl*

Walsh, Thomas James
American. Lawyer, Politician
Dem. senator from MT, 1913-33;
uncovered Teapot Dome Scandal,
1923.
b. Jun 12, 1859 in Two Rivers,
Wisconsin
d. Mar 2, 1933 in Wilson, North
Carolina
Source: *AmBi; AmNatBi; AmPeW;
ApCAB X; BiDInt; BiDrAC; BiDrUSC
89; BioIn 4, 7; DcAmB; EncAAH;
EncAB-H 1974; EncWB 98; McGEWB;
NatCAB 15, 24; WebAB 74, 79; WhAm
1; WhAmP*

Walsh, William B(ertalan)
American. Physician
CEO and medical director, People-to-
People Health Foundation, parent
organization of Project HOPE, 1958-
92.
b. Apr 26, 1920
d. Dec 27, 1996 in Bethesda, Maryland
Source: *BioIn 6; ConAu 155; CurBio
97N; WhAm 12; WhoAm 74, 76, 78, 80,
82, 84, 86, 88, 90, 92; WhoWor 76, 78,
80*

Walsingham, Francis, Sir
English. Statesman
Entered service of Elizabeth I, 1563;
established spy system that revealed
plot of Mary Stuart, led to her
execution.
b. 1530? in Footscray, England
d. Apr 6, 1590 in London, England
Source: *Alli; Benet 87, 96; BioIn 3, 4, 7,
8, 9, 10, 11; CamBiEn; ChamBiD;
DcBiPP; DcNaB; REn; SpyCS*

Walston, Ray
American. Actor, Director
Won Tony for *Damn Yankees,* 1955;
starred in TV series "My Favorite
Martian," 1963-66.
b. Nov 22, 1918 in New Orleans,
Louisiana
Source: *BiE&WWA; BioIn 18, 21, 24;
ConTFT 3, 10, 17; EncAFC; FilmEn;
FilmgC; ForYSC; HalFC 84, 88;
IntMPA 75, 76, 77, 78, 79, 80, 81, 82,
84, 86, 88, 92, 94, 96; MovMk; NotNAT;
WhoAm 86, 88, 90; WhoEnt 92; WhoHol
A; WhoThe 81; WhoWor 89; WorAlBi*

Waltari, Mika
Finnish. Critic, Author, Editor
Popular historical novels include *The
Egyptian,* 1945.
b. Sep 19, 1908 in Helsinki, Finland
d. Aug 26, 1979 in Helsinki, Finland
Source: *Au&Wr 71; BioIn 22; CasWL;
ConAu 9R, 89; CurBio 50, 79N; DcLEL
1940; EncEurC; EncWL 1; IntAu&W 76,
77; IntWW 74, 75, 76, 77, 78, 79; LinLib
L; PenC EUR; REn; ScF&FL 1, 92;
TwCA SUP; WhE&EA; Who 74;
WhoWor 74, 76*

Walter, Bruno
[Bruno Schlesinger]
American. Conductor, Pianist
An authority on the interpretation of the
works of Mahler, Mozart.
b. Sep 15, 1876 in Berlin, Germany
d. Feb 17, 1962 in Beverly Hills,
California
Source: *AmNatBi; BakBD 78, 84, 92;
BakBDTw; BakDcM; BiDAmM; BioIn 1,
2, 3, 4, 5, 6, 7, 8, 9, 10, 11, 12, 18;
BriBkM 80; CamBiEn; CamDcAB;
ChamBiD; CmCal; CmOp; ConAmC 76,
82; CurBio 42, 62; DcAmB S7;
DcPseud; EncAB-A 33; EncTR, 91;
FacFETw; IntDcOp; LegTOT; LinLib S;
MetOEnc; MusMk; MusSN; NatCAB 52;
NewAmDM; NewEOp 71; NewGrDA 86;
NewGrDM 80; NewGrDO; NotNAT B;
ObitT 1961; OxCAmH; OxCMus;
OxDcOp; PenDiMP; REn; WebAB 74,
79; WhAm 4; WorAl; WorAlBi*

Walter, Cyril
[Cy Walter]
American. Pianist, Songwriter
Played in sophisticated style on radio,
TV, nightclubs, 1940s-50s.
b. Sep 16, 1925 in Minneapolis,
Minnesota
d. Aug 18, 1968 in New York, New
York
Source: *ASCAP 66, 80; BiDAmM;
CmpEPM*

Walter, Eugene
American. Dramatist, Screenwriter
Wrote plays *Trail of the Lonesome Pine,*
1911; *Easiest Way,* 1909.
b. Nov 27, 1874 in Cleveland, Ohio
d. Sep 26, 1941 in Hollywood, California
Source: *AmAu&B; AmNatBi; BenetAL
91; CamGWoT; CnDAL; CurBio 41;
DcAmB S3; DcNAA; LinLib L;
McGEWD 72, 84; ModWD; NotNAT B;
OhA&B; OxCAmL 65, 83, 95; OxCAmT
84; OxCThe 67, 83; REn; REnAL;
WhAm 1; WhThe*

Walter, Jessica
[Mrs. Ron Leibman]
American. Actor
Won Emmy for "Amy Prentiss," 1974-
75; films include *Play Misty For Me,*
1971.
b. Jan 31, 1944 in New York, New York
Source: *BioIn 14; ConTFT 1, 7, 18;
FilmgC; HalFC 80, 84, 88; IntMPA 77,
86, 92, 94, 96; WhoAm 86, 88, 90, 92,
99; WhoEnt 92, 98; WhoHol A; WorAlBi*

Walter, Johann
German. Composer
As musical adviser to Luther he
constructed a new liturgy and
composed tunes for many Lutheran
hymns; he also pioneered the
"dramatic" musical setting of the
Passion in German.
b. 1496 in Kahla, Thuringia, Germany
d. 1570 in Torgau, Germany

Source: *BakBD 78, 84; EncWB 98;
McGEWB; NewGrDM 80; NewOxM;
OxCGer 76, 86, 97*

Walter, John, I
English. Newspaper Publisher
Founded *Daily Universal Register,* 1785,
which was renamed London *Times,*
1788.
b. 1739 in London
d. Nov 16, 1812 in Teddington
Source: *Alli; CamBiEn; ChamBiD;
DcBiPP; DcEnL; DcEuL; DcNaB;
NewCBEL; REn; WebBD 83; WhDW*

Walter, Marie Therese
French. Model
Mistress of Pablo Picasso.
b. 1909?
d. 1977 in Antibes, France
Source: *BioIn 10, 11, 13*

Walter, Thomas Ustick
American. Architect
Built legislative wings, cast iron dome
on Capitol, Washington, DC.
b. Sep 4, 1804 in Philadelphia,
Pennsylvania
d. Oct 30, 1887 in Philadelphia,
Pennsylvania
Source: *Alli; AmBi; AmNatBi; ApCAB;
BiAUS; BiDAmAr; BioIn 1, 3, 14, 16;
BriEAA; DcAmB; DcArch; DcNAA;
Drake; EncAAr 1, 2; HarEnUS; LinLib
S; McGDA; NatCAB 9; NewYHSD;
OxCAmH; OxCAmL 65; WhAm HS;
WhoArch*

Walters, Barbara
American. Broadcast Journalist
First woman to co-anchor the "Today"
show, 1963-76; with ABC News since
1976; known for one-on-one
interviews, correspondent, "20/20,"
1981-84, co-host, 1984—.
b. Sep 25, 1931 in Boston,
Massachusetts
Source: *AuNews 2; BioIn 8, 9, 10, 11,
12, 13, 14, 15, 16, 17, 18, 19, 20, 21,
22, 23, 24; BioNews 74; BkPepl; BlueB
76; CamDcAB; CelR, 90; ConAu 65;
ContDcW 89; ConTFT 6, 13, 25; CurBio
71; EncAJ; EncTwCJ; EncWB, 98;
FacFETw; ForWC 70; GoodHs;
GrLiveH; HerW 84; IntDcWB; IntMPA
77, 78, 79, 80, 81, 82, 84, 86, 88, 92,
94, 96; IntWW 77, 78, 79, 80, 81, 82,
83, 89, 91, 93, 97, 98, 2000; IntWWW 2;
InWom SUP; JrnUS; LegTOT; LesBEnT,
92; LibW; News 98, 98-3; NewYTBE 72;
NewYTBS 76; NewYTET; WhoAm 74, 76,
78, 80, 82, 84, 86, 88, 90, 92, 94, 95,
96, 97, 98, 99, 2000; WhoAmW 70, 72,
74, 75, 77, 79, 81, 83, 85, 87, 89, 91,
93, 95, 97, 99; WhoE 99; WhoEnt 92,
98; WhoFI 00, 98; WhoMedi 98;
WhoWor 78, 80, 82, 84, 87, 89, 91, 93,
95, 96, 97, 98, 99, 2000; WomComm;
WomFir; WomStre; WorAl*

Walters, Bucky
[William Henry Walters]
American. Baseball Player
Pitcher, 1931-48, 1950; led NL in wins
three times, in ERA twice; NL MVP,
1939.
b. Apr 19, 1910 in Philadelphia,
Pennsylvania
d. Apr 18, 1991 in Abington,
Pennsylvania
Source: *Ballpl 90; BiDAmSp BB; BioIn
2, 10, 15; NewYTBS 91; WhoProB 73*

Walters, Charles
American. Director
Directed musicals *Easter Parade*, 1948;
Unsinkable Molly Brown, 1964.
b. Nov 17, 1903? in Pasadena, California
d. Aug 13, 1982 in Malibu, California
Source: *AnObit 1983; BiDFilm; CmMov;
DcFM; EncMT; FilmgC; IntMPA 82;
MovMk; WhoAm 82; WorEFlm*

Walters, David
American. Politician
Dem. governor, OK, 1991—.
b. Nov 20, 1951 in Elk City, Oklahoma
Source: *AlmAP 92; BiDrGov 1988;
WhoAm 92, 94, 95; WhoAmP 91, 93, 95,
97, 1999; WhoSSW 93*

Walters, Henry
American. Businessman
With father, developed the Atlantic Coast
Line Railroad; established Walters Art
Gallery in Boston.
b. Sep 26, 1848 in Baltimore, Maryland
d. Nov 30, 1931 in Baltimore, Maryland
Source: *BiDAmBL 83; BioIn 3, 7, 16, 20,
21; DcAmB; DcAmBC; DcLB 140;
EncABHB 1; EncHiCA; NatCAB 37;
WhAm 1; WhAmArt 85*

Walters, Julie
English. Actor
Received Oscar nomination for role of
Rita in film *Educating Rita*, 1984.
b. Feb 22, 1950 in Birmingham, England
Source: *CamBiEn; ChamBiD; ConTFT 7,
15, 26; HalFC 88; IntMPA 92, 94, 96;
IntWW 91, 93, 97, 98, 2000; OsStAZ;
VarWW 85; Who 88, 90, 92, 94, 98, 99,
2000*

Walters, Lou
American. Business Executive
Operated NYC's famous Latin Quarter
nightclub; father of Barbara Walters.
b. 1897
d. 1977 in Miami, Florida
Source: *NewYTBS 77; ObitOF 79*

Walters, Peter Ingram, Sir
English. Business Executive
Chairman of British Petroleum, 1981-90.
b. Mar 11, 1931 in Birmingham, England
Source: *IntWW 89, 91, 97, 98, 2000;
Who 85, 88, 92, 98, 99, 2000; WhoAm
88; WhoE 89; WhoFI 89; WhoWor 87,
91, 98, 99, 2000*

Walters, Vernon Anthony
American. Diplomat
US ambassador to UN, replacing Jeanne
Kirkpatrick, 1985.
b. Jan 3, 1917 in New York, New York
Source: *BioIn 10, 11, 12, 13, 14, 15, 16;
ConAu 122; CurBio 88; DcAmDH 89;
IntWW 74, 75, 76, 77, 78, 79, 80, 81, 82,
83, 89, 91, 93, 97, 98, 2000; NewYTBS
82, 85; WhoAm 74, 76, 84, 86, 88, 90,
92, 94, 95, 96; WhoAmP 87, 91;
WhoGov 75; WhoWor 87, 89, 91;
WorDWW*

Walthall, Henry B
American. Actor
First actor to wear motion picture
makeup, 1914; starred in film *Birth of
a Nation*, 1914.
b. Mar 16, 1878 in Shelby City,
Alabama
d. Jun 17, 1936 in Monrovia, California
Source: *DcAmB S2; Film 1; FilmgC;
MotPP; MovMk; OxCFilm; TwYS; Vers
B; WhScrn 74, 77*

Walton, Bill
[William Theodore Walton]
American. Basketball Player
Center, Portland 1974-79; Los Angeles,
1979-85; Boston 1985-87; led NBA in
rebounding, 1977; NBA MVP, 1978;
sportscaster NBC Sports, 1993—.
b. Nov 5, 1952 in La Mesa, California
Source: *BasBi; BiDAmSp BK; BioIn 9,
10, 11, 12, 13, 14, 19, 20, 23; BioNews
74; CmCal; CurBio 77; LegTOT;
NewYTBS 74, 75, 79, 80, 82; OfNBA 87;
WhoAm 78, 80, 82, 84, 86, 88, 92, 94,
95, 96, 97, 98, 99, 2000; WhoBbl 73;
WhoSpor; WorAl; WorAlBi*

Walton, Ernest Thomas Sinton
Irish. Physicist, Educator
Shared Nobel Prize in physics, 1951, for
work on transmutation of atomic
nuclei.
b. Oct 6, 1903 in Dungorvan, Ireland
d. Jun 25, 1995 in Belfast, Northern
Ireland
Source: *AsBiEn; BiESc; BioIn 1, 2, 3,
14, 15; BlueB 76; CamBiEn; ChamBiD;
CurBio 95N; InSci; IntWW 74, 75, 76,
77, 78, 79, 80, 81, 82, 83, 89, 91, 93;
LarDcSc; McGCEnS; McGMS 80;
ModIrLi; NobelP; RanHWDS; WhAm 11;
Who 74, 82, 83, 85, 88, 90, 92, 94;
WhoNob, 90, 95; WhoScEn 94; WhoWor
74, 76, 78, 82, 84, 87, 89, 91, 93, 95;
WorAl; WorAlBi; WorScD*

Walton, George
American. Lawyer, Continental
Congressman
Signed Declaration of Independence,
1776; active patriot; governor of GA,
1789; US senator.
b. 1741 in Farmville, Virginia
d. Feb 2, 1804 in College Hill, Georgia
Source: *AmBi; ApCAB; BiAUS; BiDrGov
1789; BiDSA; BioIn 1, 7, 8, 9, 23;
DcAmB; Drake; EncAR; HarEnUS;
HisDcAR; WhAm HS; WhAmRev*

Walton, Izaak
English. Biographer, Author
Wrote *Compleat Angler*, 1676,
biographies of John Donne and
George Herbert.
b. Aug 9, 1593 in Staffordshire, England
d. Dec 15, 1683 in Winchester, England
Source: *Alli; AtlBL; BbD; Benet 87, 96;
BiD&SB; BiDRP&D; BioIn 1, 2, 3, 4, 5,
7, 12, 13, 16, 17, 18, 19, 20, 21; BritAu;
BritWr 2; CamBiEn; CamGEL;
CamGLE; CarSB; ChamBiD; Chambr 1;
CnDBLB 1; CroE&S; CyWA 58, 97;
DcArts; DcEnA; DcEnL; DcEuL; DcLB
151, 213; DcLEL; DcNaB, C; DcScB;
EncWB 98; EvLB; GrWrEL N; LegTOT;
LinLib L, S; LngCEL; McGEWB; NewC;
NewCBEL; OxCBrHi; OxCEng 67, 85,
95; OxCMus; PenC ENG; REn; RfGEnL
91; WebE&AL; WorAl; WorAlBi*

Walton, Jerome O'Terrell
American. Baseball Player
Outfielder, Chicago Cubs, 1989—; NL
rookie of year, 1989.
b. Jul 8, 1965 in Newnan, Georgia
Source: *Ballpl 90; WhoAfA 9, 10;
WhoBlA 8*

Walton, Joe
[Joseph Frank Walton]
American. Football Coach
Head coach, NY Jets, 1983-89.
b. Dec 15, 1935 in Beaver Falls,
Pennsylvania
Source: *BioIn 13, 16; FootReg 87;
NewYTBS 83; WhoAm 84, 86, 88; WhoE
85, 86, 89*

Walton, Sam Moore
American. Business Executive
Chm., CEO Wal-Mart; richest man in
US, 1991; worth 4.4 billion.
b. Mar 29, 1918 in Kingfisher, Oklahoma
d. Apr 5, 1992 in Little Rock, Arkansas
Source: *BioIn 13, 14, 15, 16; ConAmBL;
ConNews 86-2; CurBio 92; Dun&B 90;
EncWB 98; IntWW 91; News 93-1;
WhoAm 86, 90; WhoFI 92; WhoSSW 91;
WhoWor 91*

Walton, Tony
English. Designer
Won Tony for set design of *Pippin*,
1973; Oscar for art direction of *All
That Jazz*, 1979.
b. Oct 24, 1934 in Walton-on-Thames,
England
Source: *BiE&WWA; BioIn 12, 13, 14;
ConDes 97; ConTFT 4, 12; HalFC 84,
88; NotNAT; VarWW 85; WhoAm 92;
WhoEnt 92; WhoThe 72, 77, 81*

Walton, William Turner, Sir
English. Composer
Composed "Orb and Sceptre"
(Coronation March), 1953, for
coronation of Elizabeth II.
b. Mar 29, 1902 in Oldham, England
d. Mar 8, 1983 in Ischia, Italy
Source: *BakBD 92; BakBDTw; BioIn 1,
2, 3, 4, 5, 6, 8, 10, 12, 13; CamBiEn;
ChamBiD; CurBio 40, 83, 83N; DcArts;*

DcNaB 1981; EncWB 98; FilmgC; IntWW 75, 76, 77, 78, 79, 80, 81, 82; McGEWB; NewGrDO; OxCEng 85, 95; OxCFilm; OxCMus; REn; WhAm 8; WhDW; Who 74, 82; WhoAm 74, 76, 78, 80, 82; WhoMus 72; WhoWor 74, 76, 78

Waltrip, Darrell Lee

American. Auto Racer
Stock car driver; won Daytona 500, 1989; won Winston Cup three times.
b. Feb 5, 1947 in Owensboro, Kentucky
Source: *BiDAmSp OS; BioIn 11, 13, 14; CelR 90; CrtSuMy; HalFC 88; IntAu&W 91; IntvTCA 2; IntWW 91; MajTwCW 1; NewYTBS 86; TwCCr&M 91; WhoAm 80, 82, 84, 86, 88, 90, 92, 94, 95, 96, 97, 98, 99, 2000; WorAlBi; WrDr 92*

Walworth, William, Sir

English. Politician
Lord mayor, London, 1374-1381; money lender to Richard II; defended London Bridge against the Kentish peasants, 1381.
d. 1385
Source: *BioIn 6; DcBiPP; DcCathB; DcNaB, C; WebBD 83*

Walz, Ken

American. Producer
Has produced music videos for Cyndi Lauper, Huey Lewis, Billy Joel; won Billboard, MTV Awards, 1984.
b. Apr 29, 1942 in Holland, Michigan
Source: *BioIn 15; ConTFT 4; WhoAdv 90; WhoEnt 92*

Wambaugh, Joseph Aloysius, Jr.

American. Author
With LA police, 1960-74; wrote police novels *The New Centurions,* 1971; *The Blue Knight,* 1972; *The Choir Boys,* 1975.
b. Jan 22, 1937 in Pittsburgh, Pennsylvania
Source: *AuNews 1; AuSpks; BioIn 10, 11, 12; ConAu 65NR; ConLC 18; CurBio 80; HalFC 84; MajTwCW 2; NewYTBE 73; Novels; TwCCr&M 85; WhoAm 74, 84; WorAl; WrDr 86*

Wambsganss, Bill

[William Adolph Wambsganss]
American. Baseball Player
Second baseman, 1914-26, mostly with Cleveland; best known for only unassisted triple play in World Series history, 1920.
b. Mar 19, 1894 in Garfield Heights, Ohio
d. Dec 8, 1985 in Lakewood, Ohio
Source: *Ballpl 90; BioIn 7, 14; WhoProB 73*

Wanamaker, John

American. Merchant
Started Wanamakers Store in NYC, 1896; US postmaster-general, 1889-93.
b. Jul 11, 1838 in Philadelphia, Pennsylvania

d. Dec 12, 1922 in Philadelphia, Pennsylvania
Source: *AmBi; AmNatBi; ApCAB; BiDAmBL 83; BiDrUSE 71, 89; BioIn 1, 2, 3, 6, 7, 8, 9, 10, 12, 18, 20; CamDcAB; ChhPo S2; DcAmB; DcNAA; EncAB-H 1974, 1996; HarEnUS; LinLib S; OxCAmH; PeoHis; REnAL; TwCBDA; WebAB 74, 79; WhAm 1; WorAl; WorAlBi*

Wanamaker, Lewis Rodman

American. Merchant
Owner, director of Wanamaker dept. stores, 1922-28; began public concerts in stores; son of John.
b. 1863 in Philadelphia, Pennsylvania
d. Mar 9, 1928 in Atlantic City, New Jersey
Source: *BiDAmBL 83; DcAmB; NatCAB 21; WhAmArt 85*

Wanamaker, Sam

American. Actor, Director
On Hollywood black list, 1950s, for leftist political associations.
b. Jun 14, 1919 in Chicago, Illinois
Source: *BiE&WWA; BioIn 1, 15, 19, 22, 23; BlueB 76; CamBiEn; CamDcAB; ChamBiD; CnThe; ConTFT 3, 12; FilmEn; FilmgC; ForYSC; HalFC 80, 84, 88; IIWWBF; IntMPA 75, 76, 77, 78, 79, 80, 81, 82, 84, 86, 88, 92, 94; IntWW 74, 75, 76, 77, 78, 79, 80, 81, 82, 83, 89, 91, 93; ItaFilm; LegTOT; LesBEnT; MiSFD 9; MotPP; MovMk; NewYTET; NotNAT; OxCThe 83; RadStar; WhAm 11; Who 74, 82, 83, 85, 88, 90, 92, 94; WhoAm 80, 82, 84, 86, 88, 90, 92, 94; WhoEnt 92; WhoHol 92, A; WhoThe 72, 77, 81; WhoWor 74, 78; WorAlBi*

Waner, Lloyd James

"Little Poison"
American. Baseball Player
Outfielder, 1927-42, 1944-45, mostly with Pittsburgh; had .316 lifetime batting average; Hall of Fame, 1967.
b. Mar 16, 1906 in Harrah, Oklahoma
d. Jul 22, 1982 in Oklahoma City, Oklahoma
Source: *BiDAmSp BB; BioIn 10, 11, 13; ScrEAmL 1; WhoProB 73*

Waner, Paul Glee

"Big Poison"
American. Baseball Player
Outfielder, 1926-45, mostly with Pittsburgh with brother Lloyd; won NL batting title three times; NL MVP, 1927; Hall of Fame, 1952.
b. Apr 16, 1903 in Harrah, Oklahoma
d. Aug 29, 1965 in Sarasota, Florida
Source: *AmNatBi; BiDAmSp BB; BioIn 2, 3, 7, 9, 10; CamDcAB; DcAmB S7; WhoProB 73*

Wang, An

American. Business Executive, Engineer
Pioneering giant in computer industry; founded Wang Labs, 1951; developed

desktop calculator, 1964; earned more than 40 patents.
b. Feb 7, 1920 in Shanghai, China
d. Mar 24, 1990 in Boston, Massachusetts
Source: *AmMWSc 73P, 79, 82, 86, 89, 92; AmNatBi; AnObit 1990; AsAmAlm; BioIn 12, 13, 15; CamBiEn; CamDcAB; ChamBiD; ConAmBL; ConAu 132; ConNews 86-1; CurBio 87, 90, 90N; Dun&B 79, 86, 88, 90; EncWB, 98; Entr; FacFETw; HisDcDP; LElec; News 90, 90-3; NewYTBS 90; NotAsAm; NotTwCS 1; RanHWDS; ScrEAmL 2; St&PR 75, 84, 87; WhAm 10; WhoAm 74, 76, 78, 80, 82, 84, 86, 88; WhoE 83, 85, 86, 89; WhoFI 83, 85, 87, 89; WhoTech 84, 89; WhoWor 84; WorInv*

Wang, Vera

American. Fashion Designer
Designer of wedding gowns, evening gowns, and figure skating costumes, known for her minimalism and her use of sheer materials; celebrity fans include Holly Hunter and Sharon Stone, and Nancy Kerrigan wore costumes she designed in the 1994 Olympics.
b. Jun 27, 1949 in New York, New York
Source: *News 98; NotAsAm; WhoAmW 99*

Wang An-shih

Chinese. Political Reformer, Poet, Scholar
Most famous reformer in Chinese history, developed a sweeping program of agricultural, economic, educational, and administrative reforms.
b. Dec 18, 1021 in Kiangsi, China
d. May 21, 1086 in Nanking, China
Source: *EncWB 98; RAdv 14*

Wang Chang

[Darren Costin; Nick Feldman; Jack Hues]
English. Music Group
Jazz/rock group formed 1981; name is Chinese for "perfect pitch."
Source: *RkOn 85*

Wang Ching-wei

Chinese. Revolutionary
Follower of Sun Yat-sen; president and prime minister of the Nationalist government before World War II, then leader of the Japanese puppet regime at Nanking during the war.
b. 1883 in Canton, China
d. 1944
Source: *EncWB 98; FacFETw*

Wangchuk, Jigme Singye

Bhutanese. Political Leader
King of Bhutan since 1972, he is committed to continuing reforms to help modernize the country's political institutions and develop a constitutional monarchy.
b. Nov 11, 1955

Source: *FarE&A 78, 79, 80, 81; IntWW 76, 77, 78, 79, 80, 81, 82, 83, 89, 91, 93; WhoWor 78, 80, 82, 84, 87*

Wang Ch'ung

Chinese. Philosopher
Thinker was critical of the validity of contemporary belief, and applied standards of ordered systematic inquiry to the natural world
b. 27, China
d. 100
Source: *EncWB 98; HisDcTa*

Wanger, Walter

[Walter Feuchtwanger]
American. Producer
Regarded his films as foremost medium of communication, instrument to promote int'l understanding: *Stagecoach,* 1939.
b. Jul 11, 1894 in San Francisco, California
d. Nov 18, 1968 in New York, New York
Source: *AmNatBi; BiDFilm, 81, 94; BioIn 1, 8, 9, 21; CamBiEn; CmMov; CurBio 47, 69; DcAmB S8; DcFM; DcPseud; FilmEn; FilmgC; GangFlm; HalFC 80, 84, 88; IntDcF 1-4, 2-4; LegTOT; OxCFilm; WorAl; WorAlBi; WorEFlm*

Wang Fu-chih

Chinese. Philosopher
Proto-nationalist philosopher developed a evolutionary theory of history; provides an intellectual link between imperial and revolutionary China.
b. Oct 7, 1619 in Hunan, China
d. 1692
Source: *EncWB 98*

Wang Hung-Wen

[Wang Hongwen]
Chinese. Political Leader
Sentenced to life imprisonment for being member of "gang of four," 1981.
b. 1937, China
Source: *NewYTBE 73; NewYTBS 76*

Wang Kon

Korean. Military Leader, King
Member of the powerful maritime clan at Songdo, served as general under Kungye of Later Koguryo, then became king and founder of the Koryo dynasty.
b. 877
d. 943
Source: *EncWB 98*

Wang Mang

Chinese. Emperor
Statesman of the Former Han dynasty, took the throne as emperor in 9 A.D. and founded the Hsin dynasty.
b. 45BC
d. Oct 6, 23AD, China
Source: *EncWB 98*

Wang Ming

[Chen Shaoyu]
Chinese. Political Leader
Major rival of Mao Tse-Tung within the Chinese Communist Party, led the "Internationalist" group that required compliance with the Comintern line in opposition to Mao's nationalism.
b. 1904 in Anwei, China
d. Mar 27, 1974 in Moscow, Union of Soviet Socialist Republics
Source: *BioIn 17; EncRev; EncWB 98; ModChi*

Wang Pi

Chinese. Philosopher
Known as one of the most brilliant Chinese philosophers, he reinterpreted the Tao-te ching and the I ching, and developed an influential new Confucian metaphysics.
b. 226
d. 249
Source: *EncWB 98; HisDcTa*

Wang Shih-chieh

Chinese. Diplomat
Close adviser of Nationalist China's Chiang Kai-shek.
b. Mar 10, 1891 in Hupeh
d. Apr 1981? in Taipei, Taiwan
Source: *BioIn 1; CurBio 45, 81*

Wang T'ao

Chinese. Author, Political Activist
Reformer advocated the adoption of Western learning and nationalist ideals, advanced economic and political modernization, and pioneered modern Chinese journalism.
b. Nov 10, 1828 in Kiangsu Province, China
d. 1897 in Shanghai, China
Source: *EncWB 98; ModChi*

Wang Wei

Chinese. Poet, Artist
Considered to be the founder of the Southern school of landscape painting, and one of the greatest poets of the T'ang dynasty, called the golden age of Chinese poetry.
b. 699 in P'u-chou, China
d. 759
Source: *Benet 96; CamBiEn; ChamBiD; EncChi; EncWB 98; PoeCrit 18*

Wang Yang-ming

Chinese. Philosopher, Government Official
Scholar-official led a revolt against the Neo-Confucian rationalism of Chu Hsi, and founded the influential Yang-ming school of Neo-Confucian idealism.
b. 1472 in Hangchow, China
d. 1529
Source: *CamBiEn; EncChi; EncEth; EncWB 98; OxCPhil*

Wank, Roland A

American. Architect
Renowned designer of towns, public buildings; architect, Tennessee Valley Authority, 1933-44.
b. Oct 2, 1898 in Budapest, Austria-Hungary
d. Apr 22, 1970 in New Rochelle, New York
Source: *CurBio 43, 70; NewYTBE 70; WhAm 5*

Wanke, Daouda Malam

Nigerien. Political Leader
Head of the Presidential Guard unit responsible for the assassination of Ibrahim Bare Mainassara during the 1999 military coup d'etat, he became head of state of Niger.
b. 1954 in Yelou, Gaya, Niger

Wankel, Felix

German. Engineer, Inventor
Developed first viable rotary internal combustion engine, 1934-56.
b. Aug 13, 1902 in Lahr, Germany
d. Oct 9, 1988 in Lindau, Germany (West)
Source: *AnObit 1988; BioIn 12, 16, 20; CamBiEn; CamDcSc; ChamBiD; DcTwDes; FacFETw; IntWW 74, 75, 76, 77, 78, 79, 80, 81, 82, 83; NewYTBE 72; NewYTBS 88; NotTwCS 1; RanHWDS; WhDW*

Wanzer, Bobby

American. Basketball Player
Guard, Rochester Royals, 1948-57; five-time All-Star; Hall of Fame, 1987.
b. Jun 4, 1921 in New York, New York
Source: *BiDAmSp BK; WhoBbl 73; WhoSpor*

Wapner, Joseph A

American. TV Personality
Arbitrated cases as presiding judge on syndicated TV series "The People's Court," 1981-92; California Superior Court judge, 1961-79.
b. Nov 15, 1919 in Los Angeles, California
Source: *BioIn 13, 14, 15, 16; ConNews 87-1; CurBio 89; WhoAm 90; WhoEnt 98*

War

[Harold Brown; Ron Hammaon; Lonnie Jordan; Charles Miller; Lee Ostar; Luther Rabb; Pat Rizzo; Howard Scott; Tweed Smith]
American. Music Group
Pop hits includes *Me and Baby Brother,* 1974; *Low Rider,* 1975.
Source: *Alli; BiDAfM; BillEnR; BioIn 1, 13, 17; ConMuA 80A; ConMus 14; CurBio 61; EncPR&S 89; EncRk 88; EncRkSt; Film 1; IlEncRk; InB&W 80, 85A; InSci; IntMPA 82, 84, 86, 88; NewGrDA 86; NewYHSD; NewYTBS 76; PenEncP; RkOn 78; RkWho 96; RolESEnR 83; SoulM; TwYS A; WhAmArt 85; What 2; WhFla; WhoHol 92; WhoRock 81; WhoRocM 82*

Warburg, Felix Moritz

American. Philanthropist, Banker
Member of Kuhn, Loeb & Co., NYC,
1896-1937; known for philanthropies.
b. Jan 14, 1871 in Hamburg, Germany
d. Oct 20, 1937 in New York, New York
Source: *AmBi; ApCAB X; BakBD 78, 84;
BioIn 1, 4, 11; DcAmB S2; NatCAB 30;
NewGrDA 86; WebBD 83; WhAm 1;
WorAl*

Warburg, Frederick Marcus

American. Banker
Son of Felix Moritz Warburg; partner in
Kuhn, Loeb & Co., 1931-73.
b. Oct 14, 1897 in New York, New York
d. Jul 10, 1973 in Winchester, Virginia
Source: *BioIn 10, 11; NatCAB 57;
NewYTBE 73; WhAm 6; WhoWorJ 72*

Warburg, James Paul

American. Businessman, Philanthropist,
Author
Book subjects include US political,
economic affairs; member of FDR's
"Brain Trust."
b. Aug 18, 1896 in Hamburg, Germany
d. Jun 3, 1969 in Greenwich,
Connecticut
Source: *AmAu&B; AmNatBi; AmPeW;
ASCAP 66; BiDInt; BioIn 1, 4, 6, 8, 9,
11, 19, 22; ConAu P-2; CurBio 48, 69;
DcAmB S8; NatCAB 56; REnAL; TwCA
SUP; WhAm 5; WhE&EA; WhoWorJ 72,
78; WorAl; WorAu 1900*

Warburg, Otto Heinrich

German. Scientist
Won Nobel Prize in medicine, 1931, for
discovery of nature and mode of
action of the respiratory enzyme.
b. Oct 8, 1883 in Freiburg, Germany
d. Apr 1, 1970 in Berlin, Germany
(West)
Source: *AsBiEn; BiESc; BioIn 3, 5, 9,
12; CamBiEn; CamDcSc; ChamBiD;
ConAu 158; DcScB; InSci; LarDcSc;
McGCEnS; McGMS 80; ObitT 1961;
OxCMed 86; RanHWDS; WhAm 5, 7;
WhoNob, 90, 95; WorAl; WorAlBi;
WorScD*

Warburg, Paul Moritz

American. Banker
Spokesman for the large bankers of
America, he favored a highly
centralized banking system that,
greatly modified, became the Federal
Reserve System.
b. 1868 in Hamburg, Germany
d. 1932
Source: *AmBi; ApCAB X; BiDAmBL 83;
BioIn 5, 8; DcAmB; DcNAA; EncAB-A
9; EncAB-H 1974, 1996; EncWB 98;
McGEWB; NatCAB 26; WhAm 1*

Ward, Artemus

[Charles Farrar Browne]
American. Journalist, Lecturer
Best known as "moral" lecturer
throughout country; humorous
comments influenced Mark Twain.
b. Apr 26, 1834 in Waterford, Maine

d. Mar 6, 1867 in Southampton, England
Source: *Alli, SUP; AmAu; AmAu&B;
AmBi; ApCAB; BbD; Benet 87, 96;
BenetAL 91; BibAL; BiDAmJo; BiD&SB;
BioIn 1, 2, 3, 5, 6, 7, 9, 10, 11, 12, 13,
16; CamGEL; CamGLE; CamHAL;
CasWL; CelCen; Chambr 3; ChhPo;
CnDAL; DcAmAu; DcAmB; DcArts;
DcCathB; DcEnA A; DcEnL; DcLB 11;
DcLEL; DcNAA; DcPseud; Dis&D;
Drake; EncAAH; EncAJ; EncWB 98;
EvLB; GrWrEL N; HarEnUS; LegTOT;
LinLib L, S; McGEWB; NatCAB 1;
NinCLC 37; Novels; OhA&B; OxCAmL
65, 83, 95; OxCEng 67, 85, 95; PenC
AM; PeoHis; REn; REnAL; RfGAmL 4,
87, 94; TwCBDA; WebAB 74, 79;
WebE&AL; WhAm HS; WhCiWar;
WhDW*

Ward, Barbara Mary

English. Author, Economist
Wrote on political, economic affairs:
India and the West, 1961.
b. May 23, 1914 in York, England
d. May 31, 1981 in Lodsworth, England
Source: *CamBiEn; CathA 1930; ConAu
103; CurBio 50, 77, 81; DcNaB 1981;
IntAu&W 77; IntWW 78; InWom, SUP;
TwCA SUP; WhE&EA; WhoAm 78;
WhoAmW 75; WhoEc 86; WhoWor 78;
WrDr 80*

Ward, Benjamin

American. Government Official
First black NYC police commissioner,
1984-89.
b. Aug 10, 1926 in New York, New
York
Source: *BioIn 13, 16; CopCroC; CurBio
88; NewYTBS 75, 83; WhoAfA 9, 10, 11,
12; WhoAm 86, 88, 90; WhoBlA 1, 2, 3,
4, 5, 6, 7, 8; WhoE 89, 91*

Ward, Burt

[Bert John Gervais, Jr.]
American. Actor
Played Robin on TV series "Batman,"
1966-68.
b. Jul 6, 1946 in Los Angeles, California
Source: *BioIn 13, 16; HalFC 88;
IntMPA 84, 86, 88, 92; WhoHol A*

Ward, David S

American. Screenwriter
Wrote films *The Sting,* 1973; *The Sting
II,* 1983; won Oscar, 1973.
b. Oct 24, 1945 in Providence, Rhode
Island
Source: *IntMPA 92; VarWW 85; WhoAm
90; WhoEnt 92*

Ward, Deighton Harcourt Lisle, Sir

West Indian. Political Leader
Governor-General of Barbados, 1976-84.
b. May 16, 1909, Barbados
d. Jan 9, 1984, Barbados
Source: *IntYB 82; Who 83, 85N;
WhoWor 78, 80*

Ward, Douglas Turner

American. Director, Dramatist, Actor
Artistic director, co-founder, Negro
Ensemble Co., 1967; won Obie for
distinguished performance in *River
Niger,* 1973.
b. May 5, 1930 in Burnside, Louisiana
Source: *BioIn 9, 10, 11, 12, 14, 20;
BlkWr 1; CamDcAB; CamGWoT;
ConAmD; ConAu 27NR, 81; ConBlAP
88; ConDr 73, 77, 82, 88, 93; ConLC
19; ConTFT 4; CurBio 76; DcLB 7, 38;
DcTwCCu 5; DrBlPA, 90; Ent; InB&W
80; IntvTCA 2; LivgBAA; McGEWD 84;
MorBAP; NotBlAM; NotNAT; OxCAfAL;
PlP&P A; SchCGBL; SelBAAf; TheaDir;
WhoAfA 9, 10, 11, 12; WhoAm 74, 76,
78, 80, 82, 84, 86, 88; WhoBlA 1, 2, 3,
5, 6, 7, 8; WhoThe 72, 77, 81; WorAu
1970; WrDr 76, 80, 82, 84, 86, 88, 90,
92, 94*

Ward, Fannie

American. Actor
Films include *The Cheat,* 1915; *Betty to
the Rescue,* 1917.
b. Nov 23, 1872 in Saint Louis, Missouri
d. Jan 27, 1952 in New York, New York
Source: *BioIn 2, 3, 9, 15; DcPseud;
EncAFC; Film 1, 2; HalFC 80; InWom;
MotPP; NotNAT B; ObitT 1951; OxCThe
67, 83; TwYS; WhAm 3; WhoHol B;
WhScrn 74, 77, 83; WhThe*

Ward, J(ohn) Q(uincy) A(dams)

American. Sculptor
Famous for portrait busts, equestrian
monuments.
b. Jun 29, 1830
d. 1910
Source: *AmBi; AmNatBi; ApCAB; BioIn
1, 5, 7, 9, 14; BriEAA; CamDcAB;
DcAmArt; DcAmB; DcBiPP; Drake;
GayN; HarEnUS; IlBEAAW; McGDA;
NatCAB 2; NewYHSD; OxCAmH;
OxCAmL 65; OxCArt; OxDcArt; PeoHis;
TwCBDA; WebAB 74, 79; WebBD 83;
WhAm 1; WhAmArt 85*

Ward, Jay

American. Cartoonist
Created cartoon characters Rocky the
Flying Squirrel and Bullwinkle Moose
with partner Bill Scott, 1959.
b. Sep 21, 1920 in San Francisco,
California
d. Oct 12, 1989 in Los Angeles,
California
Source: *AnObit 1989; BioIn 16; ConTFT
8; LesBEnT 92; NewYTBS 89; SmATA
63; WhoSSW 84; WhoWest 74, 76*

Ward, Lester Frank

American. Sociologist
Wrote *The Geological Distribution of
Fossil Plants,* 1888; professor of
sociology, Brown U., 1906-13.
b. Jun 18, 1841 in Joliet, Illinois
d. Apr 18, 1913 in Washington, District
of Columbia
Source: *Alli SUP; AmAu; AmBi;
AmNatBi; AmRef; ApCAB; BiDAmEd;
BiDAmS; BiInAmS; BioIn 1, 2, 3, 4, 11,*

14, 15, 21; *CamDcAB; DcAmAu;*
DcAmB; DcNAA; DcSoc; EncAB-H
1974, 1996; EncWB 98; GayN;
McGEWB; NatCAB 13; OxCAmH;
OxCAmL 65, 83, 95; REnAL; TwCBDA;
WebAB 74, 79; WhAm 1, 4A, HSA

Ward, Lynd
American. Artist
Noted for woodcut illustrations; won
   1952 Caldecott for *The Biggest Bear.*
b. Jun 26, 1905 in Chicago, Illinois
d. Jun 28, 1985 in Reston, Virginia
Source: *BiDScF; ChlBkCr; ConAu 116;*
ConGrA 1; DcLB 22; FourBJA;
IlrAm 1880, E; LinLib L; McGDA; PenEncH;
ScF&FL 1, 2, 92; SmATA 36, 42N;
WhAmArt 85; WhoAm 84; WhoAmA 73,
76, 78, 80, 82, 84, 86N, 89N, 91N;
WrDr 84

Ward, Mary Jane
American. Author
Wrote novel *The Snake Pit,* 1946.
b. Aug 27, 1905 in Fairmount, Indiana
Source: *AmAu&B; AmNov; AmWomWr;*
BenetAL 91; BioIn 1, 2, 4, 22; CurBio
46; InWom, SUP; LngCTC; REnAL;
TwCA SUP; WhNAA; WhoAmW 58, 66,
68; WorAu 1900

Ward, Monte
[John Montgomery Ward]
American. Baseball Player
Pitcher-infielder, 1878-94; won 158
   games as pitcher; converted to
   shortstop after arm injury; Hall of
   Fame, 1964.
b. Mar 3, 1860 in Bellefonte,
   Pennsylvania
d. Mar 4, 1925 in Augusta, Georgia
Source: *Ballpl 90; BiDAmSp BB; BioIn*
3, 7, 14, 15, 16, 17; WhoProB 73;
WhoSpor

Ward, Montgomery
[Aaron Montgomery Ward]
American. Merchant
Founded Montgomery Ward & Co., first
   mail-order house, 1872.
b. Feb 17, 1843 in Chatham, New Jersey
d. Dec 7, 1913 in Highland Park, Illinois
Source: *BiDAmBL 83; BioIn 3, 4, 15;*
DcAmB; EncAAH; LegTOT; LinLib S;
McGEWB; WebAB 74, 79; WebBD 83;
WhAm 4, HSA; WorAlBi

Ward, Nancy
American. Native American Leader
"Beloved Woman" among the Cherokee
   people; against land cession; roles
   included peace neggotiator and
   General Council voting member.
b. 1738? in Chota, Georgia
d. 1824 in Chota, Georgia
Source: *ABCNaAm; AmIndBi; AmNatBi;*
AZNatAW; BioIn 14, 18, 21; EncAmaz
91; EncCRAm; EncNAB; HerW, 84;
InWom SUP; LibW; NotAW; NotNaAm;
PorAmW; WhNaAH; WommMil

Ward, Paul W
American. Journalist
Won 1948 Pulitzer for articles on USSR.
b. Oct 9, 1905 in Lorain, Ohio
d. Nov 24, 1976 in Chevy Chase,
   Maryland
Source: *BiDInt; BioIn 11, 12, 15; ConAu*
69; NatCAB 59; WhAm 7; WhoAm 74,
76

Ward, Phillip R
[The Hostages]
American. Hostage
One of 52 held by terrorists, Nov 1979 -
   Jan 1981.
b. Mar 22, 1940
Source: *NewYTBS 81; USBiR 74*

Ward, Rachel
[Mrs. Bryan Brown]
English. Actor, Model
Starred in TV mini-series "The Thorn
   Birds," 1983; film *Against All Odds,*
   1984.
b. 1957 in London, England
Source: *BioIn 12, 13, 16; ConTFT 6;*
HalFC 84, 88; IntMPA 86, 88, 92, 94,
96; IntWWW 2; ItaFilm; LegTOT;
NewYTBS 82; VarWW 85; WhoAmW 87,
89, 91, 93

Ward, Robert Eugene
American. Composer, Conductor
Won Pulitzer in music for opera *The
   Crucible,* 1962.
b. Sep 13, 1917 in Cleveland, Ohio
Source: *BakBD 84; BakBDTw; BioIn 13,*
14, 15; DcCM; DcLP 87B; IntWWM 90;
MetOEnc; NewAmDM; NewGrDA 86;
WhoAm 86, 90; WhoPul; WhoSSW 73;
WhoWor 84

Ward, Simon
English. Actor
Portrayed Winston Churchill in film
   Young Winston, 1971.
b. Oct 19, 1941 in London, England
Source: *ConTFT 5, 16; FilmgC; HalFC*
80, 84, 88; IntMPA 75, 76, 77, 78, 79,
80, 81, 82, 84, 86, 88, 92, 94, 96;
IntWW 82, 83, 89, 91, 93, 97, 98, 2000;
ItaFilm; Who 88; WhoHol 92, A;
WhoHrs 80; WhoThe 72, 77, 81;
WhoWor 84, 93, 95; WorAl

Warden, Jack
American. Actor
Oscar nominee for *Shampoo,* 1975;
   Heaven Can Wait, 1978; starred in
   mid-1980s TV show "Crazy Like a
   Fox."
b. Sep 18, 1920 in Newark, New Jersey
Source: *BiE&WWA; BioIn 12, 14;*
ConTFT 1, 8, 16; EncAFC; FilmEn;
FilmgC; ForYSC; HalFC 80, 84, 88;
HolCA; IntDcF 1-3; IntMPA 84, 86, 88,
92, 94, 96; LegTOT; MotPP; MovMk;
NotNAT; OsStAZ; WhoAm 78, 80, 82,
84, 86, 88, 90, 92, 94, 95, 96, 97, 99,
2000; WhoEnt 92; WhoHol 92, A;
WorAl; WorAlBi

Ware, Andre
American. Football Player
Quarterback, U. of Houston; first black
   in this position to win Heisman
   Trophy, 1989; Detroit Lions, 1990-93;
   Minnesota Vikings, 1994—.
b. Jul 31, 1968 in Dickinson, Texas
Source: *BioIn 21; WhoSpor*

Warfield, David
American. Actor
Starred in Belasco plays including *Return
   of Peter Grimm,* 1911.
b. Nov 28, 1866 in San Francisco,
   California
d. Jun 27, 1951 in New York, New York
Source: *AmNatBi; ApCAB X; BioIn 1, 2,*
3, 4, 10; CamDcAB; CamGWoT;
CmCal; DcAmB S5; DcPseud; EncWT;
FamA&A; NatCAB 14, 38; NotNAT B;
ObitOF 79; OxCAmH; OxCAmL 65;
OxCAmT 84; OxCThe 67, 83; PIP&P;
REn; REnAL; WhAm 3; WhoStg 1906,
1908; WhThe

Warfield, Marsha
American. Actor, Comedian
Played bailiff Roz Russell on TV series
   "Night Court," 1986-91.
b. Mar 5, 1955 in Chicago, Illinois
Source: *BioIn 12, 13, 15, 16, 17;*
ConBlB 2; ConTFT 7; DrBlPA 90;
FacFEBW TA; FunnyW; InB&W 85;
LegTOT; WhoAfA 9, 10, 11, 12; WhoBlA
7, 8; WhoHol 92

Warfield, Paul Dryden
American. Football Player
End, 1964-77, with Cleveland, Miami;
   Hall of Fame, 1983.
b. Nov 28, 1942 in Warren, Ohio
Source: *BiDAmSp FB; NegAl 89;*
NewYTBE 72; WhoAm 74, 78; WhoBlA
4, 7; WhoFtbl 74

Warfield, William Caesar
American. Singer
Best known for roles in *Showboat,* 1951;
   Porgy & Bess, 1952; husband of
   Leontyne Price.
b. Jan 22, 1920 in West Helena,
   Arkansas
Source: *BakBD 84, 92; BakBDTw;*
BiDAfM; BiE&WWA; BioIn 14;
CamDcAB; DcAfAmP; InB&W 80, 85;
NewGrDA 86; NotNAT; WhoAm 74, 76,
78, 80, 82, 84, 86, 88, 90, 92, 94, 95,
96, 97, 98, 99, 2000; WhoAmM 83;
WhoBlA 1, 3, 5; WhoEnt 92, 98;
WhoHol A; WhoWor 74, 76; WorAl

Warham, William
English. Religious Leader
Archbishop of Canterbury, 1504-15;
   signed Henry VIII's petition to pope
   for divorce from Katherine of Aragon,
   1527.
b. 1450, England
d. Aug 22, 1532, England
Source: *BioIn 3, 11; ChambID; DcBiPP;*
DcCathB; DcNaB, C; NewCol 75;
OxCBrHi; WebBD 83

Warhol, Andy
[Andrew Warhola, Jr.]
American. Artist, Author
Leader of pop artists since early 1960s; known for paintings of soup cans, celebrities; published *Interview* mag., made several films.
b. Aug 6, 1927 in McKeesport, Pennsylvania
d. Feb 22, 1987 in New York, New York
Source: *AmAu&B; CamBiEn; CelR; ConArt 83; ConAu 89, 121; ConNews 87-2; ConPhot 82; CurBio 68, 86, 87; DcPseud; EncAB-H 1974; EncWB 98; FacFETw; FilmEn; FilmgC; GayLesB; ItaFilm; MiSFD 9N; OxCArt; OxCFilm; WebAB 79; WhoAmA 76, 78, 86; WhoAmA 84; WhoWor 78, 87*

Wariner, Steve
American. Musician, Singer, Songwriter
Country guitarist and vocalist; released first top-ten hit "Your Memory," 1980; released debut album *Steve Wariner*, 1982; recorded first gold record, *I Am Ready*, 1991; won Grammy Award for best country vocal collaboration for single "Restless," 1992; inducted as member of the Grand Ole Opry, 1996.
b. Dec 25, 1954 in Noblesville, Indiana
Source: *AllMGCo; BgBkCoM; ConMus 18; HarEnCM 87; LegTOT; PenEncP; WhoNeCM*

Waring, Fred Malcolm
"The Man Who Taught America to Sing"
American. Bandleader, Inventor
Music conductor of The Pennsylvanians, 1923-84; invented the Waring blender.
b. Jun 9, 1900 in Tyrone, Pennsylvania
d. Jul 29, 1984 in State College, Pennsylvania
Source: *AnObit 1984; ASCAP 66; BakBD 84; BioNews 74; CmpEPM; CurBio 40, 84; IntMPA 84; NewYTBS 80, 84; WhoAm 84; WhoHol A; WorAl*

Warmerdam, Dutch
[Cornelius Warmerdam]
American. Track Athlete
Pole vaulter; first to vault 15 feet, 1940; held world record, 1940-57.
b. Jun 22, 1915 in Long Beach, California
Source: *BiDAmSp OS; BioIn 3, 5, 6, 8, 9, 10; BioNews 74; WhoSpor; WhoTr&F 73*

Warne, William E(lmo)
American. Government Official
Irrigation expert; director, CA Dept. of Water Resources, 1961-67.
b. Sep 2, 1905
d. Mar 9, 1996 in Menlo Park, California
Source: *AmMWSc 73S, 78S; BioIn 3, 21, 22; ConAu 41R, 151; CurBio 96N; IndAu 1917; WhAm 11; WhoAm 74, 76, 78, 80, 82, 84, 88, 90, 92, 94, 95, 96; WhoFI 94; WhoScEn 94, 96; WhoWest 74, 76, 78, 80, 82, 84, 87, 89,*

92, 94, 96; *WhoWor 76, 78, 80, 82, 84, 87, 89, 91, 93, 95*

Warneke, Lon(nie)
"The Arkansas Humming Bird"
American. Baseball Player, Baseball Umpire
Pitcher, 1930-43, 1945; had 193 career wins, 31 shutouts, one no-hitter; NL umpire, 1949-55.
b. Mar 28, 1909 in Mount Ida, Arkansas
d. Jun 23, 1976 in Hot Springs, Arkansas
Source: *Ballpl 90; BiDAmSp BB; BioIn 3, 10, 15; LegTOT; NewYTBS 76; ObitOF 79; WhoProB 73*

Warner, Albert
[Warner Brothers]
American. Film Executive
Co-founded Warner Brothers Pictures, Inc., 1923.
b. Jul 23, 1884 in Kraznashiltz, Poland
d. Nov 26, 1967 in Miami Beach, Florida
Source: *AmNatBi; BiDAmBL 83; BioIn 19; DcFM; NatCAB 54; ObitT 1961; WebAB 74, 79; WhAm 4A; WorAl; WorAlBi*

Warner, Charles Dudley
American. Editor, Author
Best known for collaborating with Mark Twain on *The Gilded Age*, 1873; said, "Everybody talks about the weather but nobody does anything about it."
b. Sep 12, 1829 in Plainfield, Massachusetts
d. Oct 20, 1900 in Hartford, Connecticut
Source: *Alli SUP; AmAu; AmAu&B; AmBi; AmNatBi; ApCAB; BbD; Benet 87, 96; BenetAL 91; BibAL 8; BiDAmJo; BiD&SB; BioIn 9, 12, 16, 17; CamDcAB; CamGLE; CamHAL; CasWL; CelCen; ChamBiD; Chambr 3; ChhPo, S2; CnDAL; CyAL 2; DcAmAu; DcAmB; DcBiA; DcEnA A; DcEnL; DcLB 64; DcLEL; DcNAA; EncALit; GrWrEL N; HarEnUS; LinLib L, S; NatCAB 2; OxCAmL 65, 83, 95; OxCCan; PenC AM; PeoHis; REn; REnAL; RfGAmL 4, 87, 94; TwCBDA; WebAB 74, 79; WhAm 1*

Warner, Curt
American. Football Player
Running back, Seattle, 1983-89; LA Rams 1989-90.
b. Mar 18, 1961 in Wyoming, West Virginia
Source: *BiDAmSp FB; BioIn 13; FootReg 87; NewYTBS 82; WhoAfA 9, 10; WhoBlA 5, 7, 8*

Warner, David
English. Actor
Starred in *Morgan*, 1965; *Time After Time*, 1979; *Time Bandits*, 1980.
b. Jul 29, 1941 in Manchester, England
Source: *CanWW 96, 97, 98, 1999; CnThe; ConTFT 5, 20; Dun&B 90; FilmAG WE; FilmEn; FilmgC; ForYSC; HalFC 80, 84, 88; IlWWBF; IntMPA 78, 79, 80, 81, 82, 84, 86, 88, 92, 94, 96;*

IntWW 82, 83, 89, 91, 93, 97, 98, 2000; NewYTBE 71; OxCFilm; WhoHol 92, A; WhoHrs 80; WhoThe 72, 77, 81; WhoWor 84, 87, 89, 91, 93, 95, 96

Warner, Denis Ashton
Australian. Author, Journalist
Contributor to leading Australian, US newspapers; specialist on Far Eastern affairs.
b. Dec 12, 1917 in Hobart, Australia
Source: *ConAu 3NR, 5R; IntAu&W 77, 89; IntWW 89, 91, 93, 97, 98, 2000; WhoWor 74, 76, 78*

Warner, Emily Howell
American. Pilot
First woman pilot for major US passenger airline (Frontier).
b. 1940 in Denver, Colorado
Source: *BioIn 13*

Warner, Harry Morris
[Warner Brothers]
American. Film Executive
Co-founder, pres., Warner Brothers Pictures, Inc., 1923-56.
b. Dec 12, 1881 in Kraznashiltz, Poland
d. Jul 25, 1958 in Hollywood, California
Source: *AmNatBi; BiDAmBL 83; BioIn 5; CurBio 45, 58; DcAmB S6; DcFM; ObitOF 79; WebAB 74; WhAm 3*

Warner, Jack, Jr.
American. Film Executive
Organized Jack M Warner Productions, Inc., 1949.
b. Mar 27, 1916 in San Francisco, California
d. Apr 1, 1995 in Los Angeles, California
Source: *BioIn 20, 21, 22; IntMPA 75, 76, 77, 78, 79, 80, 81, 82, 84, 86, 88, 92, 94; WhoAm 74, 76, 78, 80, 82, 84, 86, 88, 90, 92, 94, 95, 96, 97; WhoEnt 92; WhoWor 78*

Warner, Jack Leonard
[Warner Brothers; Jack Eichelbaum]
American. Film Executive
With brothers, introduced first successful sound film, *The Jazz Singer*, 1927; produced award-winning *My Fair Lady*, 1964.
b. Aug 2, 1892 in London, Ontario, Canada
d. Sep 9, 1978 in Los Angeles, California
Source: *AmNatBi; BiDAmBL 83; BioIn 9, 10, 11; ChamBiD; ConAu 108; CurBio 45, 78; DcAmB S10; DcFM; FilmgC; IntMPA 77; IntWW 74; WebAB 74; WhAm 7; Who 74; WhoAm 80; WhoHol A; WorAl*

Warner, John William
American. Politician
Rep. senator from VA, 1979—; husband of Elizabeth Taylor, 1976-82.
b. Feb 18, 1927 in Washington, District of Columbia

Source: *AlmAP 88, 92; BiDrUSC 89;*
BioIn 8, 11, 12, 13, 16; CngDr 79, 81,
83, 85, 87, 89; IntWW 91; IntYB 81, 82;
WhoAm 74, 76, 78, 80, 82, 84, 86, 88,
90, 92, 94, 95, 96, 97, 98, 99, 2000;
WhoAmL 90; WhoAmP 73, 75, 77, 79,
81, 83, 85, 87, 89, 91, 93, 95, 97, 1999;
WhoSSW 80, 82, 84, 86, 88, 91, 93, 95,
97, 99; WhoWor 78, 80, 82, 84, 87, 89,
91; WorAl; WorAlBi

Warner, Malcolm-Jamal
American. Actor
Played Theo Huxtable on "The Cosby
   Show," 1984-92.
b. Aug 18, 1970 in Jersey City, New
   Jersey
Source: *BioIn 14, 15, 16; ConBlB 22;*
ConTFT 5, 10; DrBlPA 90; IntMPA 92,
94, 96; WhoAfA 9, 10, 11, 12; WhoAm
92; WhoBlA 7; WhoEnt 92

Warner, Pop
[Glenn Scobey Warner]
American. Football Coach
Collegiate coach, 1895-1938; one of
   game's great innovators, introducing
   numbering of players, headgear.
b. Apr 5, 1871 in Springville, New York
d. Sep 7, 1954 in Palo Alto, California
Source: *AmNatBi; BiDAmSp FB; BioIn*
3, 4, 6, 7, 8, 9, 10, 12, 21; CmCal;
DcAmB S5; LegTOT; OxCAmH; WebAB
74, 79; WhAm 3; WhoFtbl 74; WhoSpor

Warner, Rawleigh, Jr.
American. Oilman
Chm. of Mobil Corp., 1976-85.
b. Feb 13, 1921 in Chicago, Illinois
Source: *AmMWSc 92; BioIn 10, 12, 14;*
BlueB 76; Dun&B 79, 86, 88; IntWW 74,
75, 76, 77, 78, 79, 80, 81, 82, 83, 89,
91, 93, 97, 98; St&PR 75, 84, 87, 91;
WhoAm 74, 76, 78, 80, 82, 84, 86, 88,
90, 92, 94, 95, 96, 97, 98, 99, 2000;
WhoE 74, 77, 79, 81, 83, 85; WhoFI 74,
75, 77, 79, 81, 83, 85; WhoWor 74, 76,
78, 80, 82, 84, 87, 89

Warner, Roger Sherman, Jr.
American. Engineer
Developed atomic, hydrogen bombs,
   amphibious equipment for US troops.
b. Jun 12, 1907 in Boston, Massachusetts
d. Aug 3, 1976 in Washington, District
   of Columbia
Source: *BioIn 6; ObitOF 79; WhAm 7*

Warner, Sam(uel Louis)
[Warner Brothers]
American. Film Executive
Opened studios in CA with brothers,
   1918.
b. Aug 10, 1887 in Baltimore, Maryland
d. Oct 5, 1927 in Los Angeles,
   California
Source: *BioIn 1; NatCAB 21; WebAB 74*

Warner, Susan Bogert
[Elizabeth Wetherell]
American. Author
Wrote sentimental juvenile novels: *Wide,*
   Wide World, 1851; *Queechy,* 1852.
b. Jul 11, 1819 in New York, New York
d. Mar 17, 1885 in Highland Falls, New
   York
Source: *Alli, SUP; AmAu; AmAu&B;*
AmBi; AmNatBi; AmWomWr; ApCAB;
ArtclWW 2; BbD; BenetAL 91; BibAL 8;
BiD&SB; BioIn 1, 4, 8, 12, 15;
BlmGWL; CamDcAB; CarSB; ChamBiD;
Chambr 3; ChhPo, S1, S2; CyAL 2;
DcAmAu; DcAmB; DcBiA; DcEnL;
DcLB 42; DcLEL; DcNAA; EvLB;
FemiCLE; InWom, SUP; LibW; NatCAB
5; NotAW; OxCAmL 65, 83, 95;
OxCChiL; PenNWW A, B; REnAL;
SJGChWr 5A; TwCBDA; TwCChW 4A;
WhAm HS; WhoChL

Warner, Sylvia Townsend
English. Author, Poet, Biographer
Best known for short stories in *New*
   Yorker mag; wrote biography of Jane
   Austen.
b. Dec 6, 1893 in Harrow, England
d. May 1, 1978 in Maiden Newton,
   England
Source: *ArtclWW 2; WhoTwCL; WhoWor*
74, 76; WomWrGB; WorAu 1900; WrDr
76

Warnes, Jennifer
American. Singer
Sang Oscar-winning song "Up Where
   We Belong," 1983, with Joe Cocker.
b. 1947? in Orange County, California
Source: *BioIn 14, 15; ConMus 3;*
EncFCWM 83; EncRkSt; LegTOT; RkOn
84; WhoRocM 82

Warnke, Paul Culliton
American. Lawyer, Government Official
Director, ACDA, 1977-78; chief US
   negotiator for SALT, 1977-78.
b. Jan 31, 1920 in Webster,
   Massachusetts
Source: *BioIn 8, 10, 11; ColdWar 2;*
CurBio 77; DcAmDH 80, 89; IntWW 77,
78, 79, 80, 81, 82, 83, 89, 91, 93, 97,
98, 2000; NewYTBE 72; NewYTBS 77;
PolProf J; WhoAm 74, 76, 78, 80, 82,
84, 86, 88, 90, 92, 94, 95, 96, 97, 98,
99, 2000; WhoAmL 83, 92, 96; WhoAmP
77, 79, 81, 83, 85, 87, 89, 91, 93, 95,
97, 1999; WhoE 86, 91, 95; WhoGov 77;
WorAl; WorAlBi

Warnock, (Helen) Mary (Wilson)
British. Philosopher
Leader in the philosophical community
   of the 20th century, she wrote on
   ethics, imagination, and Sartre.
b. Apr 14, 1924 in Winchester, England
Source: *EncWB 98*

Warren, Austin
American. Critic, Author
Texts include *The Theory of Literature,*
   1949.

b. Jul 4, 1899 in Waltham,
   Massachusetts
d. Aug 20, 1986 in Providence, Rhode
   Island
Source: *AmAu&B; AmNatBi; BenetAL*
91; BioIn 4, 15, 21, 22; ConAu 17R,
120; ConLCrt 77, 82; REnAL; TwCA
SUP; WhAm 9; WhoAm 74, 76, 78, 86;
WorAu 1900; WrDr 80, 82, 84, 86

Warren, Earl
American. Supreme Court Justice
Chief Justice, 1953-69; wrote many
   landmark liberal decisions; headed
   investigation of John F Kennedy
   assassination.
b. Mar 19, 1891 in Los Angeles,
   California
d. Jul 9, 1974 in Washington, District of
   Columbia
Source: *AmDec 1950; AmJust; AmNatBi;*
AmPolLe; AmRef; BiDFedJ; BiDInt;
BiDrGov 1789; BioIn 1, 2, 3, 4, 5, 6, 7,
8, 9, 10, 11, 12, 13, 14, 15, 16, 18, 20,
21, 23, 24; BioNews 74; CamDcAB;
CelR; ChambiD; CmCal; CngDr 74;
ConAu 49, 123; CopCroC; CriJuSA;
CurBio 44, 54, 74, 74N; DcAmB S9;
DcAmC; DcPol; DcTwHis; EncAB-H
1974, 1996; EncAPoR; EncMcCE;
EncWB 98; FacFETw; FreeExC;
HisDcSc; LegTOT; LinLib L, S;
McGEWB; NewYTBS 74; ObitT 1971;
OxCAmH; OxCLaw; OxCSupC; PolPar;
PolProf E, J, K, T; PresAR 1980, 1996;
RComAH; REn; SupCtJu; WebAB 74,
79; WhAm 6; WhDW; Who 74; WhoAm
74; WhoAmP 73; WhoGov 72; WhoWor
74; WorAl; WorAlBi

Warren, Gerald Lee
American. Presidential Aide, Editor
Asst. press secretary to Nixon, 1969-74;
   Ford, 1974-75; editor, *San Diego*
   Union, 1975-92; editor, *San Diego*
   Union-Tribune 1992-95.
b. Aug 17, 1930 in Hastings, Nebraska
Source: *WhoAm 74, 76, 78, 80, 84, 92,*
94, 95, 96, 97; WhoGov 72, 75;
WhoSSW 73; WhoWest 82, 84, 87, 89,
94, 96, 98

Warren, Harry
[Salvatore Guaragna]
American. Songwriter
Wrote hundreds of popular songs for
   plays, films; won Oscars for hits
   "Lullaby of Broadway," 1935;
   "You'll Never Know," 1940; "On
   the Atchison, Topeka and the Santa
   Fe," 1946.
b. Dec 24, 1893 in New York, New
   York
d. Sep 22, 1981 in Los Angeles,
   California
Source: *AmCulL; AmNatBi; AmPS;*
AmSong; AnObit 1981; ASCAP 66, 80;
BakBD 78, 84, 92; BestMus; BiDAmM;
BiE&WWA; BioIn 2, 4, 6, 9, 10, 11, 12,
14, 15, 16, 19, 24; CmpEPM; ConAmC
76, 82; ConAu 105; CurBio 43, 81, 81N;
DcPseud; FacFETw; FilmEn; HalFC 84,
88; IntMPA 75, 76, 77, 78, 79, 80, 81,
82; LegTOT; NewAmDM; NewGrDA 86;

NewGrDM 80; NotNAT; OxCFilm;
OxCPMus; PenEncP; PopAmC, SUP;
ScrEAml 1; Songw; WhAm 9; WhoAm
74, 76; WhScrn 83

Warren, Joseph
American. Military Leader
Revolutionary general known for sending
  Paul Revere, William Dawes on their
  famous ride.
b. Jun 11, 1741 in Roxbury,
  Massachusetts
d. Jun 17, 1775 in Charlestown,
  Massachusetts
Source: *Alli; AmBi; AmNatBi; AmRev;*
AmWrBE; ApCAB; BiHiMed; BioIn 6, 8,
9, 19; BlkwEAR; CamDcAB; CyAL 1;
DcAmB; DcAmMeB, 84; Drake; EncAR;
EncCRAm; HarEnUS; HisDcAR;
NatCAB 1; OxCAmH; TwCBDA; WebAB
74, 79; WebAMB; WhAm HS;
WhAmRev; WhoHol A; WorAl; WorAlBi

Warren, Leonard
American. Opera Singer
Leading baritone from 1940s; noted for
  Rigoletto role; died on stage at NY
  Met.
b. Apr 21, 1911 in New York, New
  York
d. Mar 4, 1960 in New York, New York
Source: *AmNatBi; BakBD 78, 84, 92;*
BakBDTw; BiDAmM; BioIn 1, 2, 3, 4, 5,
7, 10, 11; BriBkM 80; CamDcAB;
CmOp; CurBio 53, 60; DcAmB S6;
DcPseud; IntDcOp; LegTOT; MetOEnc;
MusSN; NatCAB 47; NewAmDM;
NewEOp 71; NewGrDA 86; NewGrDM
80; NewGrDO; OxDcOp; PenDiMP;
RadStar; WhAm 3; WhScrn 77, 83;
WorAl; WorAlBi

Warren, Lesley Ann
American. Actor, Dancer
Made TV debut in musical
  "Cinderella," 1964.
b. Aug 16, 1946 in New York, New
  York
Source: *BioIn 14, 16; ConTFT 1, 2, 6,*
13; ForYSC; HalFC 84, 88; IntMPA 86,
88, 92, 96; LegTOT; VarWW 85;
WhoAm 88, 90; WhoEnt 92; WhoHol 92,
A; WorAlBi

Warren, Mercy Otis
American. Dramatist, Historian
Wrote political satires attacking
  Loyalists, history of Revolution, 1805.
b. Sep 14, 1728 in Barnstable,
  Massachusetts
d. Oct 19, 1814
Source: *Alli; AmAu; AmAu&B; AmBi;*
AmNatBi; AmWomHi; AmWomWr;
AmWrBE; ApCAB; ArtclWW 2; Benet
96; BenetAL 91; BiD&SB; BioAmW;
BioIn 14, 15, 16, 18, 20, 21, 23, 24;
BlkwEAR; BlmGWL; CamBiEn;
CamDcAB; CamGLE; CamGWoT;
CamHAL; ChamBiD; ChhPo; CnDAL;
CyAL 1; DcAmAu; DcAmB; DcBrAmW;
DcLB 31, 200; DcNAA; Drake; EncAB-
H 1974, 1996; EncALit; EncCRAm;
EncWB 98; EncWHA; FemDram;

GloEncH; GoodHs; GrLiveH; GrWrEL
DR; InWom, SUP; LibW; McGEWB;
NatCAB 7; NinCLC 13; NotAW; NotNAT
B; NotWoAT; OxCAmH; OxCAmL 65,
83, 95; OxCAmT 84; OxCWoWr 95;
PenNWW A; PeoHis; PorAmW; REn;
REnAL; WebAB 74, 79; WhAm HS;
WhAmP; WhAmRev; WorAl; WorAlBi

Warren, Michael
American. Actor
Played Bobby Hill on TV series "Hill
  Street Blues," 1981-87; former All-
  American basketball player.
b. Mar 5, 1946 in South Bend, Indiana
Source: *BioIn 13; ConAu 174; ConTFT*
7, 18; DrBlPA 90; WhoAfA 9, 10, 11,
12; WhoAm 86, 88, 90, 92; WhoBlA 5,
6, 7, 8; WhoHol 92; WhoTelC

Warren, Robert Penn
American. Author, Poet, Critic
Three-time Pulitzer Prize winner, best
  known for *All the King's Men*, 1946;
  first US poet laureate, 1986-87.
b. Apr 24, 1905 in Guthrie, Kentucky
d. Sep 15, 1989 in Stratton, Vermont
Source: *AmAu&B; AmNatBi; AmNov;*
AmWr; AnObit 1989; Au&Wr 71;
AuNews 1; BeaEPF; Benet 87, 96;
BenetAL 91; BiCoLiE; BioIn 2, 3, 4, 5,
6, 7, 8, 9, 10, 11, 12, 13, 14, 15, 16, 17,
19, 20, 21, 22, 23, 24; BlueB 76; BroV;
CamBiEn; CamDcAB; CamGEL;
CamGLE; CamHAL; CasWL; ChamBiD;
ChhPo S3; CnDAL; CnE&AP; CnMD;
ConAmA; ConAu 10NR, 13R, 47NR,
129; ConLC 1, 4, 6, 8, 10, 13, 18, 39,
53, 59; ConLCrt 77, 82; ConNov 72, 76,
82, 86; ConPo 70, 75, 80, 85; Conv 1;
CurBio 70, 89, 89N; CyWA 58, 89, 97;
DcArts; DcLB 2, 48, 152, Y80A, Y89N;
DcLEL; DcTwCCu 1; DrAF 76; DrAP
75; DrAPF 80, 89; EncALit; EncSoH;
EncWB 98; EncWL 1, 2, 2S, 3; EvLB;
FacFETw; FifSWrA; FilmgC; GrWrEL
N, P; HalFC 80, 84, 88; IntAu&W 76,
77, 82, 86, 89; IntvTCA 2; IntWW 74,
75, 76, 77, 78, 79, 80, 81, 82, 83, 89;
IntWWP 77, 82; LegTOT; LiHiK; LinLib
L, S; LngCTC; MagSAmL; MajTwCW 1,
2; McGEWB; ModAL 4, 4S1, 4S2, 5;
ModWD; News 90, 90-1; NewYTBS 89;
NotPoe; Novels; OxCAmL 65, 83, 95;
OxCEng 85, 95; OxCTwCL; OxCTwCP;
PenC AM; PeoHis; RAdv 1, 14, 13-1;
RComWL; REn; REnAL; RfGAmL 4, 87,
94; RfGShF 1, 2; RGFAP; RGTwCWr;
ScrEAmL 2; ShScr 4; SixAP; SmATA 46,
63; SouWr; TwCA, SUP; TwCRHW 90,
94; WebAB 74, 79; WebE&AL; WhAm
10; WhDW; WhE&EA; WhNAA; Who
74, 82, 83, 85, 88, 90N; WhoAm 74, 76,
78, 80, 82, 84, 86, 88; WhoPul;
WhoTwCL; WhoUSWr 88; WhoWor 74,
80, 82, 84, 87, 89; WhoWrEP 89;
WorAl; WorAlBi; WorAu 1900; WorLitC;
WrDr 76, 80, 82, 84, 86, 88, 90; WrPh

Warrick, Ruth
American. Actor
In film *Citizen Kane*, 1941; longtime role
  on TV daytime drama "All My
  Children."

b. Jun 29, 1915 in Saint Louis, Missouri
Source: *BiE&WWA; BioIn 16; ConTFT*
3; FilmEn; FilmgC; ForYSC; HalFC 80,
84, 88; IntMPA 77, 80, 84, 88, 92;
InWom SUP; LegTOT; MovMk; NotNAT;
RadStar; VarWW 85; WhoAm 90;
WhoEnt 92; WhoHol 92, A; WhoThe 77

Warrington, Lewis
American. Naval Officer
US secretary of navy ad interim, 1844;
  town in VA named in his honor.
b. Nov 3, 1782 in Williamsburg, Virginia
d. Oct 12, 1851 in Washington, District
  of Columbia
Source: *AmNatBi; ApCAB; BioIn 2;*
DcAmB; Drake; EncWar; HarEnUS;
NatCAB 6; TwCBDA; WebAMB; WhAm
HS

Warton, Joseph
English. Author, Poet, Critic
Literary critic known for esssays on
  Pope, 1756, 1782.
b. Apr 1722 in Dunsfold, England
d. Feb 23, 1800 in Wickham, England
Source: *Alli; BbD; BiD&SB; BioIn 3, 8,*
10, 17; BlmGEL; BritAu; CamGEL;
CamGLE; CasWL; ChamBiD; Chambr
2; ChhPo; CnE&AP; DcArts; DcBiPP;
DcEnL; DcEuL; DcLB 104, 109;
DcLEL; DcNaB; EvLB; GrWrEL P;
NewC; NewCBEL; OxCEng 67, 85, 95;
PenC ENG; RfGEnL 91; WebE&AL

Warton, Thomas
English. Author
Poet-laureate, 1785-90; wrote *Triumph of*
  Iris, 1749; brother of Joseph.
b. Jan 9, 1728 in Basingstoke, England
d. May 21, 1790 in Oxford, England
Source: *Alli; BbD; Benet 87, 96;*
BiCoLiE; BiD&SB; BioIn 2, 3, 10, 12,
17; BlkwCE; BlmGEL; BritAu;
CamBiEn; CamGEL; CamGLE; CasWL;
ChamBiD; ChhPo, S1; CnE&AP;
DcBiPP; DcEnA; DcEnL; DcEuL; DcLB
104, 109; DcLEL; DcNaB, C; EvLB;
GrWrEL P; LitC 15; MouLC 2; NewC;
NewCBEL; OxCEng 67, 85, 95; PenC
ENG; PoLE; REn; RfGEnL 91;
WebE&AL

Warwick, Dionne
[Marie Dionne Warwick]
American. Singer
Three-time Grammy winner; hits include
  "Alfie," 1967; "That's What Friends
  are For," 1985.
b. Dec 12, 1940 in East Orange, New
  Jersey
Source: *BakBD 84; BiDAfM; BillEnR;*
BioIn 8, 10, 12, 13, 15, 16; BlkWAm;
CelR 90; ChamBiD; ConBlB 18;
ConMus 2; CurBio 69; DcPseud;
DcTwCCu 5; DrBlPA, 90; EncPR&S 89;
EncRkSt; IlEncBM 82; InB&W 80, 85;
IntWW 91; InWom SUP; LegTOT;
NewAmDM; NotBlAW 1; OxCPMus;
PenEncP; RkOn 74; RkWho 96; SoulM;
WhoAfA 9, 10, 11, 12; WhoAm 86, 88,
95, 96, 97, 98; WhoAmW 70, 72, 77, 91,

95, 97, 99; WhoBlA 1, 7, 8; WhoEnt 92, 98; WhoRock 81; WorAlBi

Warwick, Robert
[Robert Taylor Bien]
American. Actor
Matinee idol of Broadway, films, 1914-
   59; in film *Adventures of Robin Hood*,
   1938.
b. Oct 9, 1876 in Sacramento, California
d. Jun 4, 1964 in Los Angeles, California
Source: *FilmgC; MotPP; MovMk;
   NotNAT B; WhScrn 77; WhThe*

**Warwick and of Salisbury, Earl
of**
[Richard Neville]
English. Nobleman
Known as the "Kingmaker," he was the
   most powerful English noble of his
   time and the principal baronial figure
   in the Wars of the Roses.
b. Nov 22, 1428, England
d. Apr 14, 1471, England
Source: *EncWB 98*

Was (Not Was)
[Sweet Pea Atkinson; Harry Bowens;
   Donald (Don Was) Fagenson; David
   (David Was) Weis]
American. Music Group
Rhythm-and-blues group formed in early
   1980s; albums include *What Up,
   Dog?*, 1988 and *Are You OK?*, 1990.
Source: *ConMus 6; EncRk 88; PenEncP;
   WhsNW 85*

Washakie
American. Native American Chief
Chief of Eastern Shoshone tribe; ally of
   white settlers; signed treaty
   establishing a Shoshone reservation in
   Wyoming, 1868.
b. 1804? in Montana
d. 1900 in Flathead Village, Montana
Source: *AmIndBi; BioIn 1, 3, 5, 7, 11;
   CamDcAB; DcAmB; EncNoAI; EncWB
   98; NewEAmW; NotNaAm; OxCAmH;
   REnAW; WebAB 74, 79; WhAm HS;
   WhNaAH*

Washam, Wisner McCamey
American. Writer
Head writer for soap opera "All My
   Children," 1971—.
b. Sep 8, 1931 in Mooresville, North
   Carolina
Source: *VarWW 85*

Washburn, Charles
American. Journalist, Dramatist
Best known as theatrical press agent;
   clients included Al Jolson, John
   Barrymore.
b. 1890 in Chicago, Illinois
d. 1972 in Jersey City, New Jersey
Source: *ConAu 104; NewYTBE 72*

Washington, Booker T(aliafero)
American. Educator, Author
Leading black of his time; founded
   Tuskegee Institute, 1881, turned it into
   foremost college for blacks; wrote
   autobiographical *Up From Slavery*,
   1901.
b. Apr 5, 1856 in Franklin County,
   Virginia
d. Nov 14, 1915 in Tuskegee, Alabama
Source: *AmAu&B; AmBi; ApCAB;
   BiD&SB; BiDSA; BlkAWP; CasWL;
   Chambr 3; CyAG; DcAmB; DcLEL;
   OxCAmH; PenC AM; REnAL; WebAB
   79; WhAm 1; WorAl*

Washington, Buck
[Buck and Bubbles; Ford Lee
   Washington]
American. Jazz Musician, Comedian
Part of comedy team with John Sublett,
   1919-53.
b. Oct 16, 1903 in Louisville, Kentucky
d. Jan 31, 1955 in New York, New York
Source: *BiDJaz; DrBlPA, 90; NewGrDJ
   88, 94; WhoJazz 72*

Washington, Denzel, Jr.
American. Actor
Played Dr. Phillip Chandler on TV series
   "St. Elsewhere," 1982-84; *Glory*,
   1990; *Malcolm X*, 1992.
b. Dec 28, 1954 in Mount Vernon, New
   York
Source: *AfrAmAl 6, 8; AfrAmBi 2;
   BiDFilm 94; BioIn 14, 15, 16, 18;
   CamBiEn; ChamBiD; ConBlB 1, 16;
   ConTFT 9, 17; CurBio 92; DcTwCCu 5;
   DrBlPA, 90; InB&W 85; IntMPA 92, 94,
   96; IntWW 91, 93, 97, 98, 2000;
   LegTOT; News 93-2; NotBlAM; OsStAZ;
   VarWW 85; WhoAfA 9, 10, 11, 12;
   WhoAm 90, 94, 95, 96, 97, 98, 99, 2000;
   WhoBlA 7, 8; WhoEnt 92, 98; WhoHol
   92*

Washington, Dinah
[Ruth Jones]
"Queen of the Blues"
American. Singer
Adapted blues style to pop songs; with
   Lionel Hampton's band, 1943-49.
b. Aug 29, 1924 in Tuscaloosa, Alabama
d. Dec 14, 1963 in Detroit, Michigan
Source: *AfrAmAl 6, 8; AllMGBl 1, 2;
   AllMGJa; AmNatBi; BakBD 84, 92;
   BakDcM; BiDAfM; BiDAmM; BiDJaz;
   BioAmW; BioIn 6, 12, 13, 15, 16, 18, 19,
   20; BlkWAm; Blues; BluesWW;
   CamBiEn; CamDcAB; ChamBiD;
   CmpEPM; ConBlB 22; ConMus 5;
   DcAmB S7; DcPseud; DcTwCCu 5;
   DrBlPA, 90; EncPR&S 89; EncRk 88;
   IlEncBM 82; IlEncJ; InB&W 80, 85;
   InWom, SUP; LegTOT; NegAl 89;
   NewAmDM; NewGrDA 86; NewGrDJ
   88, 94; NotBlAW 1; NotNAT B; ObitOF
   79; OxCPMus; PenEncP; RkOn 74;
   RolSEnR 83; WhoHol B; WhoRock 81;
   WhScrn 77, 83; WorAl; WorAlBi*

Washington, Fredi
[Fredericka Carolyn Washington]
American. Actor
Stage productions included *Porgy and
   Bess*, 1943 and *Cry the Beloved
   Country*, 1952.
b. Dec 23, 1903 in Savannah, Georgia
d. Jun 28, 1994 in Stamford, Connecticut
Source: *AfrAmAl 8; BioIn 18, 20, 22;
   BlksAmF; BlkWAm; ConBlB 10;
   DcTwCCu 5; DrBlPA, 90; FacFEBW
   TA; InB&W 85; InWom SUP; NewYTBS
   94; NotBlAW 1; ThFT; WhoHol 92*

Washington, George
American. US President
First president, 1789-97; commander-in-
   chief, Continental Forces, 1775-83;
   warned against foreign alliances.
b. Feb 22, 1732 in Westmoreland,
   Virginia
d. Dec 14, 1799 in Mount Vernon,
   Virginia
Source: *Alli; AmAu&B; AmBi; AmNatBi;
   AmOrN; AmPolLe; AmRev; AmWrBE;
   ApCAB; BbD; Benet 87, 96; BenetAL
   91; BiAUS; BiD&SB; BiDrAC; BiDrUSC
   89; BiDrUSE 71, 89; BiDSA; BioIn 1, 2,
   3, 4, 5, 6, 7, 8, 9, 10, 11, 12, 13, 14, 15,
   16, 17, 18, 19, 20, 21, 22, 23, 24;
   BlkwCE; BlkwEAR; BlmGEL; CamBiEn;
   CamDcAB; ChamBiD; Chambr 3;
   CmdGen 1991; CyAG; CyAL 1;
   DcAmAu; DcAmB; DcAmC; DcAmMiB;
   DcBiPP; DcLB 31; DcLEL; DcNAA;
   Dis&D; Drake; EncAAH; EncAB-H
   1974, 1996; EncAInt; EncAPar; EncAR;
   EncCRAm; EncRelA; EncRev; EncSoH;
   EncWB 98; FacPr 89, 93; GenMudB;
   HalFC 80, 84, 88; HarEnMi; HarEnUS;
   HealPre; HisDBrE; HisDcAR; HisWorL;
   LegTOT; LinLib L; LitC 25; LngCEL;
   MacEWoS; McGEWB; MemAm; MilitOn;
   NewCBEL; NewEAmW; OxCAmH;
   OxCAmL 65, 83, 95; OxCBrHi;
   OxCCan; OxCSupC; PeoHis; PolPar;
   Pres 96; RAdv 13-3; RComAH; REn;
   REnAL; REnAW; Spies; TwCBDA;
   USGovLe; WebAB 74, 79; WebAMB;
   WhAm HS; WhAmP; WhAmRev; WhDW;
   WhNaAH; WhoMilH 76; WorAl;
   WorAlBi*

Washington, Grover, Jr.
American. Musician
Jazz saxophonist; Grammy Award, 1981,
   for "best jazz fusion performance,
   vocal or instrumental" for album
   Winelight.
b. Dec 12, 1943 in Buffalo, New York
d. Dec 17, 1999 in New York, New
   York
Source: *AllMGBl 2A; AllMGJa; ASCAP
   80; BiDAfM; BiDJaz; BioIn 13; ConBlB
   17; ConMus 5; DrBlPA, 90; EncJzS;
   EncPR&S 89; IlEncBM 82; InB&W 80,
   85; LegTOT; NewGrDJ 88, 94; News
   89-1; PenEncP; RkOn 85; RolSEnR 83;
   SoulM; WhoAfA 9, 10, 11, 12; WhoAm
   80, 82, 84, 86, 88, 90, 92, 94, 95, 96,
   97, 98, 99, 2000; WhoBlA 7, 8; WhoEnt
   92, 98; WhoRock 81*

Washington, Harold

American. Politician
First black Dem. mayor of Chicago,
1983-87; suffered massive heart attack
in office.
b. Apr 15, 1922 in Chicago, Illinois
d. Nov 25, 1987 in Chicago, Illinois
Source: *AfrAmAl 6, 8; AfrAmBi 1;*
AlmAP 82; AmNatBi; AnObit 1987;
BiDrUSC 89; BioIn 12, 13; BlkAmsC;
CamDcAB; CngDr 81, 83; ConBlB 6;
ConNews 88-1; CurBio 84, 88, 88N;
DiAAPGL; Ebony 1; InB&W 80; NegAl
76, 83; NewYTBS 83, 87; NotBlAM;
PolPar; ScrEAmL 2; WhAm 9; WhoAm
76, 84, 86; WhoAmP 73, 75, 77, 79, 81,
83, 85, 87; WhoBlA 1, 2, 3, 4, 5, 6N;
WhoMW 82, 84, 86, 88

Washington, Laura S.

American. Journalist, Publisher
Frequent contributor the *Chicago Tribune*
and to Chicago radio and television
programs, influential editor and
publisher of the *Chicago Reporter,* a
Chicago monthly dealing mainly with
race and economic issues.
b. c. 1956 in Chicago, Illinois
Source: *ConBlB 18*

Washington, Lawrence

American.
Half-brother of George Washington;
George inherited Mount Vernon from
him.
b. 1718
d. Jul 1752
Source: *BioIn 11, 18; HarEnUS; PeoHis*

Washington, MaliVai

American. Tennis Player
Winner, U.S. Men's Clay Court
Championships, 1992.
b. Jun 20, 1969 in Glen Cove, New
York
Source: *ConBlB 8; WhoAfA 9, 10, 11,*
12; WhoAm 94, 95, 96, 97, 98, 99, 2000;
WhoE 95

Washington, Martha (Dandridge Custis)

American. First Lady
Widow who married George
Washington, Jan 6, 1759.
b. Jun 2, 1732 in New Kent County,
Virginia
d. May 22, 1802 in Mount Vernon,
Virginia
Source: *Alli; AmAu&B; AmBi; AmOrN;*
AmPolLe; AmRev; AmWom; AmWrBE;
ApCAB; BbD; Benet 87, 96; BenetAL
91; BiAUS; BiD&SB; BiDrAC; BiDrUSC
89; BiDrUSE 71, 89; BiDSA; BioIn 1, 2,
3, 4, 5, 6, 7, 8, 9, 10, 11, 12, 13, 14, 15,
16, 17, 18, 19, 20, 21; BlkwCE;
BlkwEAR; BlmGEL; Chambr 3; CmdGen
1991; CyAG; CyAL 1; DcAmAu;
DcAmB; DcAmC; DcAmMiB; DcBiPP;
DcLB 31; DcLEL; DcNAA; Dis&D;
Drake; EncAAH; EncAB-H 1974, 1996;
EncAInt; EncAR; EncCRAm; EncRev;
EncSoH; FacPr 89, 93; GenMudB;
GoodHs; HalFC 80, 84, 88; HarEnMi;

HarEnUS; HealPre; HerW; HisDBrE;
HisWorL; LegTOT; LinLib L; LitC 25;
LngCEL; McGEWB; MemAm; NatCAB
1; NewCBEL; NewCol 75; NotAW;
OxCAmH; OxCAmL 65, 83, 95;
OxCCan; OxCSupC; PeoHis; PolPar;
RAdv 13-3; RComAH; REn; REnAL;
REnAW; TwCBDA; WebAB 74, 79;
WebAMB; WhAm HS; WhAmP;
WhAmRev; WhDW; WhNaAH; WhoMilH
76; WorAl; WorAlBi

Washington, Patrice Clarke

American. Airline Pilot
Pilot was named captain for United
Parcel Service in 1994, becoming the
first black commercial airline captain
in the United States; believed to be the
first African American female pilot
with a commercial airline.
b. Sep 11, 1961 in Nassau, Bahamas
Source: *ConBlB 12*

Washington, Thomas L.

American. Organization Official
President, National Rifle Association,
1994-95.
d. Dec 5, 1995 in Dearborn, Michigan
Source: *BioIn 21; NewYTBS 95*

Washington, Val J.

American. Politician, Business Executive
Pre-Civil Rights era director of
minorities for the Republican National
Committee and advisor to President
Dwight D. Eisenhower, assisted in the
appointments of several African
Americans to government positions;
resigned when John F. Kennedy took
office in 1961.
b. Sep 18, 1903 in Columbus, Indiana
d. 1995 in Washington, District of
Columbia

Washington, Walter Edward

American. Politician, Lawyer
Mayor of Washington, DC, 1975-79.
b. Apr 15, 1915 in Dawson, Georgia
Source: *AfrAmBi 1; BioIn 8, 9, 10, 11;*
BioNews 74; BlueB 76; CurBio 68;
DiAAPGL; InB&W 80; IntWW 82, 91;
WhoAm 86, 88, 90, 92; WhoBlA 3, 7;
WhoE 89, 91; WhoGov 72, 75, 77;
WhoWor 82, 87

Washkansky, Louis

"Washy"
South African. Businessman, Transplant
Patient
Received first heart transplant, Dec 3,
1967, performed by Dr. Christiaan
Barnard.
b. 1913, Lithuania
d. Dec 21, 1967 in Cape Town, South
Africa
Source: *BioIn 8*

Wasmosy, Juan Carlos

Paraguayan. Political Leader
Elected president of Paraguay in 1993, in
the country's first truly democratic
elections.

b. 1939
Source: *EncWB 98*

Wasow, Omar

American. Entrepreneur
Founder and president of Diaspora inc.,
an online venture firm; creator of New
York Online (NYO), a popular
Internet community where subscribers
discuss city politics and culture.
b. Dec 22, 1970 in Nairobi, Kenya
Source: *BioIn 24; ConBlB 15*

Wasserburg, Gerald Joseph

American. Scientist
Known for calculating age of moon
rocks; oldest 4.6 billion yrs.
b. Mar 25, 1927 in New Brunswick,
New Jersey
Source: *AmMWSc 76P, 79, 82, 86, 89,*
92, 95, 98; BioIn 12, 13, 14, 15; BlueB
76; CurBio 86; IntWW 74, 75, 76, 77,
78, 79, 80, 81, 82, 83, 89, 91, 93, 97,
98, 2000; McGMS 80; WhoAm 74, 76,
78, 80, 82, 84, 88, 90, 92, 94, 95, 96,
97, 98, 99, 2000; WhoScEn 94, 96,
2000; WhoWest 94, 96

Wasserman, Dale

American. Dramatist
Won best musical Tony for *Man of La*
Mancha, 1965.
b. Nov 2, 1917 in Rhinelander,
Wisconsin
Source: *AmAu&B; BiE&WWA; BlueB*
76; ConAu 49; ConDr 73, 77D, 88D;
ConTFT 5; EncMT; IntMPA 75, 76, 77,
78, 79, 80, 81, 82, 84, 86, 88, 92, 94,
96; LesBEnT 92; NatPD 81; NewYTET;
NotNAT; WhoAm 74, 76, 78, 80, 82, 84,
86, 88, 90, 92, 94, 95, 96, 97, 98;
WhoEnt 92, 98; WrDr 76, 80, 82, 84, 86,
88, 90, 92, 94, 96, 98, 99, 2000

Wasserman, Lew(is Robert)

American. Film Executive
Chief exec., MCA, Inc., 1946-90; won
special Oscar, 1973.
b. Mar 15, 1913 in Cleveland, Ohio
Source: *BiDAmBL 83; BioIn 10, 11, 14,*
16; CelR, 90; CurBio 91; Dun&B 90;
IntMPA 77, 80, 84, 92, 94, 96; IntWW
91; NewYTBS 85; St&PR 91; WhoAm
86, 88; WhoEnt 92; WhoFI 92; WhoWest
92

Wasserman, Lew R

American. Business Executive
Pres. of MCA (Music Corporation of
America) 1946-1990, when it was
purchased by the Matsushita Corp. of
Japan.
b. Mar 15, 1913 in Cleveland, Ohio
Source: *BioIn 14, 16, 22, 23, 24; CurBio*
91; Dun&B 90, 98; IntMPA 92; IntWW
91, 97, 98, 2000; NewYTBS 74, 83, 85;
St&PR 91, 98, 99, 2000; WhoAm 88, 98,
99, 2000; WhoEnt 98; WhoFI 00, 92,
98; WhoMedi 98; WhoWest 00, 92, 98

Wassermann, August von
German. Physician
Known for discovering method of
  detecting syphilis in blood, 1906.
b. Feb 21, 1866 in Bamberg, Bavaria
d. Mar 15, 1925 in Berlin, Germany
Source: *AsBiEn; BioIn 5, 20; CamDcSc;
IntMed 80; McGCEnS; NewCol 75;
WebBD 83; WhDW*

Wassermann, Jakob
German. Author
Novelist best known for strange
  characters, startling plots: *Doctor
  Keerkhoven*, 1931.
b. Mar 10, 1873 in Furth, Bavaria
d. Jan 1, 1934 in Altaussee, Austria
Source: *Benet 87, 96; BioIn 1, 3, 5, 16,
22; CasWL; ClDMEL 47, 80; ConAu
104; CyWA 58, 97; DcLB 66; Dis&D;
EncWB 98; EncWL 1, 2, 2S, 3; EvEuW;
McGEWB; ModGL; Novels; OxCGer 76,
86, 97; PenC EUR; REn; TwCA, SUP;
TwCLC 6; WhE&EA; WhoLA*

Wasserstein, Wendy
American. Dramatist
Playwright's work details changes in
  modern womens' lives; *The Heidi
  Chronicles*, 1989.
b. Oct 18, 1950 in New York, New York
Source: *AmWomD; AmWomWr SUP;
Benet 96; BioIn 12, 13, 14, 15, 16;
BlmGWL; CamGWoT; CelR 90;
ConAmD; ConAu 3BS, 53NR, 75NR,
121, 129; ConDr 88, 93; ConLC 32, 59,
90; ConTFT 1, 8, 21; ConWomD;
CrtSuDr; CurBio 89; CyWA 97;
DcTwCCu 1; DramC 4; EncALit; EncWL
3; FemDram; FemiCLE; FemiWr;
GrWomW; IdentIs; IntAu&W 91; IntWW
93, 97, 98, 2000; IntWWW 2; InWom
SUP; JeAmWW; LegTOT; MajTwCW 2;
ModAL 5; NatPD 81; News 91, 91-3;
NewYTBS 81, 92; NotWoAT; OxCAmL
95; OxCTwCL; OxCWoWr 95; RAdv 14;
SmATA 94; WhoAm 90, 92, 94, 95, 96,
97, 98, 99, 2000; WhoAmW 85, 87, 91,
93, 95, 97, 99; WhoE 91, 93, 95, 97, 99;
WhoEmL 87; WhoEnt 92, 98; WhoPul;
WhoWor 95; WorAu 1980*

Wasson, R(obert) Gordon
American. Journalist, Scientist
Mushroom expert; wrote *The Wondrous
  Mushroom*, 1980.
b. Sep 22, 1898 in Great Falls, Montana
d. Dec 23, 1986 in New York, New
  York
Source: *AmAu&B; AmMWSc 76P, 79,
82, 86; BioIn 15, 16; ConAu 116, 153;
EncO&P 1, 2, 3; NewYTBS 86; WhAm
9; WhJnl*

Waterfield, Bob
[Robert Stanton Waterfield]
"Rifle"
American. Football Player
Quarterback, Cleveland-LA Rams, 1945-
  52; led NFL in passing twice; helped
  perfect long TD pass—"bomb;" Hall
  of Fame, 1965.
b. Jul 26, 1920 in Elmira, New York

d. Mar 26, 1983 in Burbank, California
Source: *AmNatBi; BioIn 3, 8, 9, 10, 13,
17, 21, 24; CmCal; LegTOT; NewYTBS
83; WhoFtbl 74; WhoSpor*

Waterhouse, Benjamin
American. Physician
First American doctor to use Jenner's
  smallpox vaccine in general practice,
  1800.
b. Mar 4, 1754 in Newport, Rhode Island
d. Oct 2, 1846 in Cambridge,
  Massachusetts
Source: *Alli; AmNatBi; ApCAB;
BiDAmS; BiHiMed; BiInAmS; BioIn 2, 3,
4, 6, 9; CamDcAB; CyAL 1; DcAmAu;
DcAmB; DcAmMeB, 84; DcNAA; Drake;
EncAAH; EncAB-H 1974, 1996; EncWB
98; InSci; McGEWB; NatCAB 9;
NewCol 75; OxCAmH; OxCMed 86;
TwCBDA; WebAB 74, 79; WhAm HS*

Waterhouse, Ellis Kirkham, Sir
American. Museum Director, Art
  Historian
Prominent art historian; wrote *Painting
  in Britain*, 1953.
b. Feb 16, 1905 in Epsom, England
d. Sep 7, 1985 in Oxford, England
Source: *BioIn 9; BlueB 76; ConAu 65,
117; DcNaB 1981; IntWW 74, 75, 76,
77, 78, 79, 80, 81, 82, 83; Who 74*

Waterhouse, Keith Spencer
English. Author
Best-seller, *Billy Liar*, 1959; successful
  play, 1960; film, 1963 and a musical,
  1974.
b. Feb 6, 1929 in Hunslet, England
Source: *BioIn 10, 13; CamBiEn;
CamGLE; ChamBiD; ConAu 5R, 67NR;
ConDr 88; ConLC 47; ConNov 91;
ConTFT 5; CroCD; DcLB 15; DcLP
87A; HalFC 88; IntAu&W 91; IntMPA
92; IntWW 97, 98, 2000; MajTwCW 2;
OxCThe 83; OxCTwCL; Who 92, 98, 99,
2000; WrDr 92, 98, 99, 2000*

Waterman, Lewis Edson
American. Inventor
Introduced the first practical fountain
  pen; operated own co., 1883-1901.
b. Nov 20, 1837 in Decatur, New York
d. May 1, 1901 in New York, New York
Source: *AmBi; BioIn 11; DcAmB;
NatCAB 1; WebAB 74, 79; WebBD 83;
WhAm HS; WhDW*

Waters, Ethel
American. Singer, Actor
Starred in plays *Cabin in the Sky*, 1940;
  The Member of the Wedding, 1950;
  Oscar nominee for *Pinky*, 1949; active
  in Billy Graham's crusades from
  1950s.
b. Oct 31, 1896 in Chester, Pennsylvania
d. Sep 1, 1977 in Chatsworth, California
Source: *AfrAmAl 8; AllMGBl 1, 2;
AllMGJa; AmNatBi; BakBD 78, 84, 92;
BiDAfM; BiDJaz; BiE&WWA; BioIn 11,
12, 13, 16, 17, 18, 19, 20; BlksAmF;
BlkWAm; BluesWW; CamGWoT;
ChamBiD; CmpQue; ConAu 73, 81;*

*CurBio 41, 51, 77, 77N; DcAmB S10;
DcTwCCu 5; DrBlPA, 90; EncMT;
FacFEBW TA; FamA&A; FilmEn;
FilmgC; GuBlues; HalFC 84, 88;
IntMPA 77; LegTOT; LibW; MotPP;
NewAmDM; NewGrDA 86; NewGrDJ
88, 94; NewGrDM 80; NewYTBS 77;
NotBlAW 1; NotNAT; OsStAZ;
OxCAfAL; OxCPMus; PIP&P; WebAB
79; WhoAm 76; WhoHol A; WhoRel 77;
WhoThe 77; WhScrn 83; WorAl*

Waters, Frank (Joseph)
American. Author
Author of more than two dozen books
  about the Native American culture and
  the American west.
b. 1902 in Colorado
d. Jun 3, 1995 in Taos, New Mexico
Source: *AmAu&B; AmNov; BioIn 2, 9,
10, 12, 13, 14, 15, 16, 21; CnDAL;
ConAu 3NR, 5R, 13AS, 18NR, 63NR,
149; ConLC 88; CyWA 89; DcLB Y86B;
DrAF 76; DrAPF 80; EncFWF; FifWWr;
IntAu&W 76, 77, 82; OxCAmL 95;
REnAW; RfGAmL 4, 94; TwCWW 82,
91; WhNAA; WhoAm 74, 76, 78;
WhoWest 74, 76; WrDr 84, 86, 88, 90,
92, 94, 96, 98N*

Waters, John
American. Filmmaker
Off-beat outrageous films include *Pink
  Flamingos*, 1972; transvestite Divine
  featured in many films.
b. Apr 22, 1946 in Baltimore, Maryland
Source: *Au&Arts 16; BioIn 16, 17, 19,
20, 22, 23, 24; CmpQue; ConAu 126,
130; ConTFT 5, 10, 26; CurBio 90;
DcLP 87A; GayLesB; IntMPA 92, 94,
96; LegTOT; MiSFD 9; News 88-3;
WhoAm 92, 94, 95, 96, 97, 98, 2000;
WhoE 93, 95, 97, 99; WhoEnt 92, 98;
WrDr 94*

Waters, Maxine
American. Politician
US Dem. rep from CA, 1991—;
  founder, Black Women's Forum.
b. Aug 15, 1938 in Saint Louis, Missouri
Source: *AfrAmAl 6, 8; AlmAP 92, 96,
2000; BioIn 13, 14, 16; BlkWAm; CngDr
91, 93, 95; ConBlB 3; CurBio 92;
DiAAPGL; EncWB 98; EncWoAP;
InB&W 85; LegTOT; News 98; NotBlAW
2; WhoAm 92, 94, 95, 96, 97, 98, 99,
2000; WhoAmP 91, 1999; WhoAmW 87,
89, 91, 93, 95, 97, 99; WhoBlA 7;
WhoWest 00, 87, 89, 92, 94, 96, 98;
WomPO 78; WomStre*

Waters, Muddy
[McKinley Morganfield]
American. Singer, Musician
Won five Grammys; hits include "I'm a
  Man"; "I've Got My Mojo
  Working."
b. Apr 4, 1915 in Rolling Fork,
  Mississippi
d. Apr 30, 1983 in Downers Grove,
  Illinois
Source: *AfrAmAl 6, 8; AllMGBl 1, 2;
AmNatBi; AnObit 1983; BakBD 84, 92;*

*BakDcM; BiDAfM; BiDAmM; BiDJaz;
BioIn 8, 9, 11, 12, 13, 14, 15, 16, 17,
19, 20, 24; BluesWW; CamBiEn;
CamDcAB; ChamBiD; CmpEGui A;
ConMuA 80A; ConMus 4, 24; CurBio
81, 83N; DcPseud; DrBlPA, 90;
EncFCWM 69, 83; EncJzS; EncPR&S
89; EncRk 88; EncRkSt; EncWB 98;
GuBlues; HarEnR 86; IlEncJ; IlEncRk;
InB&W 80, 85; LegTOT; NewGrDM 80;
NewYTBS 83; OnThGG; OxCPMus;
PenEncP; PeoHis; RkOn 74; RkWho 96;
RolSEnR 83; ScrEAmL 1; Songw; WhAm
8; WhoAm 76, 78, 80, 82; WhoBlA 2, 3;
WhoRock 81; WhoRocM 82*

Waterston, Sam(uel Atkinson)
American. Actor
Film, TV, stage performer since 1963;
   Oscar nominee for *The Killing Fields,*
   1984.
b. Nov 15, 1940 in Cambridge,
   Massachusetts
Source: *BioIn 12, 14; CamGWoT;
ConTFT 3, 10; CurBio 85; FilmEn;
HalFC 80, 84, 88; IntMPA 77, 80, 81,
82, 84, 86, 88, 92, 94, 96; LegTOT;
NotNAT; PIP&P A; VarWW 85; WhoAm
80, 84, 86, 88, 92, 94, 95, 96, 97, 98,
99, 2000; WhoEnt 92, 98; WhoHol 92,
A; WhoThe 81; WorAlBi*

Watie, Stand
American. Military Leader, Native
   American Leader
Signed the Treaty of New Echota, 1835,
   which relocated the Cherokee to
   Oklahoma; Confederate Brigadier
   General.
b. 1806 in Georgia
d. Sep 9, 1871 in Oklahoma
Source: *AmAu&B; AmBi; AmIndBi;
AmNatBi; BiDConf; BioIn 5, 11, 21;
CamDcAB; CivWDc; DcAmB;
DcAmMiB; EncNAB; EncNoAI; EncSoH;
NatNAFi; NewEAmW; NotNaAm;
PeoHis; REnAW; WebAMB; WhAm HS;
WhCiWar; WhNaAH*

Watkins, Arthur V(ivian)
American. Politician, Lawyer
Dem. senator from UT, 1947-59; led
   committee considering charges against
   Joe McCarthy, 1954.
b. Dec 18, 1886 in Midway, Utah
d. Sep 1, 1973 in Orem, Utah
Source: *ABCNaAm; AmNatBi; BiDrAC;
BiDrUSC 89; BioIn 2, 3, 5, 7, 10, 11;
ConAu 111; CurBio 50, 73N; DcAmB
S9; NewYTBE 73; PolProf E; WhAm 6,
7; WhAmP*

Watkins, James (David)
American. Government Official
Secretary of Energy, 1988-93.
b. Mar 7, 1927 in Alhambra, California
Source: *AmMWSc 98; BiDrUSE 89;
BioIn 13, 16; CngDr 89; CurBio 89;
IntWW 83, 89, 91, 93; NewYTBS 92, 91;
WhoAm 78, 82, 84, 86, 88, 90, 92, 95,
98, 99, 2000; WhoAmP 91; WhoE 91,
93; WhoFI 92; WhoScEn 94, 2000;
WhoWor 91, 93*

Watkins, Levi, Jr.
American. Surgeon
Introduced a procedure that has saved
   the lives of patients suffering from
   arrhythmia known as the Automatic
   Implantable Defibrillator (AID), 1980.
b. Jun 13, 1945 in Parsons, Kansas
Source: *AfrAmAl 8; BioIn 12, 20;
BlksScM; ConBlB 9; NotTwCS 1*

Watkins, Perry
American. Army Officer, Entertainer
Openly homosexual U.S. Army sergeant
   first class, drafted by the Army in
   1968, discharged 15 years later for
   being gay; the officer fought the
   dismissal to the U.S. Supreme Court,
   and was ultimately reinstated.
b. Aug 20, 1948 in Joplin, Missouri
d. Mar 13, 1996 in Tacoma, Washington
Source: *ConBlB 12*

Watkins, Shirley R.
American. Government Official
Dedicated to nutrition education,
   nominated by President Bill Clinton to
   head the US Department of
   Agriculture's Food, Nutrition and
   Consumer Services Agency in 1997,
   becoming the first African American
   to hold that position; the agency
   administers such programs as the Food
   Stamp Program and the School Lunch
   Program.
b. Jan 7, 1938 in Hope, Arkansas
Source: *ConBlB 17; WhoAfA 9, 10, 11,
12*

Watley, Jody
American. Singer
Won Grammy for best new artist, 1988;
   hits include "Looking for a New
   Love," 1987; granddaughter of Jackie
   Wilson.
b. Jan 30, 1961 in Chicago, Illinois
Source: *BioIn 15, 16; ConMus 9;
WhoBlA 7*

Watson, Bryan Joseph
"Bugsy"; "Superpest"
Canadian. Hockey Player
Defenseman, 1963-79, with seven NHL
   teams; best known for shadowing
   Bobby Hull, late 1960s; had career
   2,212 penalty minutes.
b. Nov 14, 1942 in Bancroft, Ontario,
   Canada
Source: *HocEn; WhoHcky 73*

Watson, Charles
"Tex"
American. Cultist
Member of Manson cult.
b. Dec 2, 1945 in Coppeville, Texas
Source: *BioIn 8, 10, 11*

Watson, Doc
[Arthel Lane Watson]
American. Musician
Country music entertainer, considered
   finest interpreter of guitar flat-picking

in world; with son, Merle, won two
   Grammys, 1970s.
b. Mar 2, 1923 in Deep Gap, North
   Carolina
Source: *AllMGCo; BgBkCoM; BioIn 14,
15, 16; ChamBiD; ConMus 2; CounME
74, 74A; EncFCWM 69, 83; HarEnCM
87; IlEncCM; LegTOT; NewAmDM;
NewGrDA 86; OnThGG; PenEncP;
WhoAm 76, 78, 80, 82, 84, 86, 88, 90,
92, 94, 95, 96, 97, 98, 99; WhoEnt 92,
98*

Watson, Elizabeth
American. Police Chief
Chief of Police, Houston, TX, 1990-92.
b. Aug 25, 1949 in Philadelphia,
   Pennsylvania
Source: *News 91, 91-2*

Watson, Elkanah
American. Merchant, Banker
Noted for his efforts in organizing
   agricultural societies and fairs.
b. Jan 22, 1758 in Plymouth,
   Massachusetts
d. 1842
Source: *Alli; AmNatBi; ApCAB; BioIn 1,
3, 11; CamDcAB; CyAL 1; DcAmAu;
DcAmB; DcNAA; Drake; EncAAH;
EncWB 98; HarEnUS; McGEWB;
NatCAB 5; NewCBEL; PeoHis; WebAB
74, 79; WhAm HS*

Watson, Jack Hearn, Jr.
American. Lawyer, Government Official
Appointed chief of the White House
   staff, assistant to the pres., by Carter,
   1980.
b. Oct 24, 1938 in El Paso, Texas
Source: *BioIn 10, 11, 12; CurBio 80;
NewYTBS 76, 80; WhoAm 88; WhoE 79,
81*

Watson, James Dewey
American. Biochemist
Shared 1962 Nobel Prize in medicine for
   DNA studies.
b. Apr 6, 1928 in Chicago, Illinois
Source: *AmAu&B; LarDcSc; MakMC;
McGCEnS; McGEWB; McGMS 80;
NewYTBS 80; NobelP; RAdv 14, 13-5;
RanHWDS; ThTwC 87; WebAB 74, 79;
Who 74, 82, 83, 85, 88, 90, 92, 94, 98,
99, 2000; WhoAm 74, 76, 78, 80, 82, 84,
86, 88, 90, 92, 94, 95, 96, 97, 98, 99,
2000; WhoE 81, 83, 85, 86, 89, 91, 95,
97, 99; WhoFrS 84; WhoMedH 96, 99,
2000; WhoNob, 90, 95; WhoScEn 94, 96,
2000; WhoTech 89; WhoWor 74, 76, 78,
80, 82, 84, 87, 89, 91, 93, 95, 96, 97,
98, 99, 2000; WorAl; WorScD; WrDr 88,
98, 99, 2000*

Watson, John
Irish. Auto Racer
Formula One racer, racing in Grand Prix
   around world.
b. May 4, 1946 in Belfast, Northern
   Ireland
Source: *BioIn 11, 13, 14; ModIrLi;
WhoWor 82*

Watson, John Broadus
American. Psychologist
Founded behaviorist psychology, 1913;
　denied role of heredity in personality
　development.
b. Jan 9, 1878 in Greenville, South
　Carolina
d. Sep 25, 1958 in New York, New
　York
Source: *AmNatBi; ApCAB X; AsBiEn;
BiDAmEd; BiDcPsy; BiDPsy; BioIn 5, 7,
12, 14, 15, 16, 18; CamBiEn;
CamDcAB; ChamBiD; CurBio 42, 58;
DcAmB S6; EncAB-A 30; EncAB-H
1974, 1996; EncWB 98; FacFETw;
GaEncPs; InSci; LinLib L, S; LuthC 75;
MakMC; McGCEnS; McGEWB;
NamesHP; NatCAB 48; OxCAmH;
OxCPhil; PeoHis; REnAL; WebAB 74,
79; WhAm 3; WorAl*

Watson, Johnny "Guitar"
American. Musician
An accomplished vocalist and blues
　guitarist with several funk-infused hit
　albums during the 1970s, including
　Ain't That a Bitch and *A Real Mother
　for Ya;* played as a sideman for avant-
　garde musician Frank Zappa, and
　during the 1990s music was revived
　by rap and hip-hop musicians.
b. Feb 3, 1935 in Houston, Texas
d. May 17, 1996 in Yokohama, Japan
Source: *BioIn 12; OnThGG; WhoAfA
10N*

Watson, Mark Skinner
American. Journalist
Won 1945 Pulitzer for distinguished
　reporting of international events, WW
　II.
b. Jun 24, 1887 in Plattsburg, New York
d. Mar 25, 1966 in Baltimore, Maryland
Source: *BioIn 1, 2, 7, 15, 23; ConAu 89;
CurBio 46, 66; WhAm 4; WhoPul*

Watson, Moose
[Harry E Watson]
Canadian. Hockey Player
Played amateur hockey, 1920s; Hall of
　Fame, 1962.
b. Jul 14, 1898 in Saint John's,
　Newfoundland, Canada
d. Sep 11, 1957 in Toronto, Ontario,
　Canada
Source: *WhoHcky 73*

Watson, Thomas Edward
American. Politician
Populist; congressman, 1891-93; senator
　from GA, 1921-27; wrote *Life of
　Thomas Jefferson,* 1900.
b. Sep 5, 1856 in Thomson, Georgia
d. Sep 26, 1922 in Washington, District
　of Columbia
Source: *AmAu&B; AmBi; AmNatBi;
AmPolLe; AmRef; BiDRAC; BiDrUSC
89; BiDSA; BioIn 1, 4, 10, 15, 21, 24;
CamDcAB; ChamBiD; CyAG; DcAmAu;
DcAmB; DcAmSR; DcNAA; EncAAH;
EncAB-H 1974, 1996; EncSoH; EncWB
98; HarEnUS; McGEWB; NatCAB 3;
TwCBDA; WebAB 74, 79; WhAm 1*

Watson, Thomas J(ohn), Sr.
American. Business Executive
With IBM, 1914-56, chairman, chief
　exec., 1949-56; brought company into
　computer era.
b. Feb 17, 1874 in Campbell, New York
d. Jun 19, 1956 in New York, New York
Source: *AmNatBi; BiDAmBL 83; BiDInt;
BioIn 1, 2, 3, 4, 5, 6, 7, 8, 9, 10;
CamDcAB; CurBio 40, 50, 56; DcAmB
S6; EncAB-A 27; EncAB-H 1974, 1996;
HisDcDP; McGEWB; NatCAB 47;
PorSil; WebAB 74, 79; WhAm 3; WorAl*

Watson, Thomas J(ohn), Jr.
American. Business Executive
Chairman, IBM, 1961-71; oversaw
　growth of company into new fields;
　ambassador to USSR, 1979-81.
b. Jan 8, 1914 in Dayton, Ohio
d. Dec 31, 1993 in Greenwich,
　Connecticut
Source: *AmNatBi; BiDAmBL 83; BioIn
2, 3, 4, 5, 7, 9, 10, 11, 12, 13, 15;
CamDcAB; ChamBiD; ConAu 138, 143;
CurBio 56, 94N; DcAmDH 89;
HisDcDP; IntWW 83, 91; IntYB 78, 79,
82; NewYTBS 90; PolProf E, K; St&PR
75; WhoAm 84, 90; WhoAmP 85; WhoFI
74; WhoWor 84; WorAl; WorAlBi*

Watson, Tom
[Thomas Sturges Watson]
American. Golfer
Turned pro, 1971; won British Open five
　times; Masters twice, US Open once.
b. Sep 4, 1949 in Kansas City, Missouri
Source: *BiDAmSp OS; BioIn 12, 13, 15,
20, 21; CamBiEn; CelR 90; ChamBiD;
CurBio 79; FacFETw; IntWW 81, 82,
83, 89, 91, 93; LegTOT; NewYTBS 79,
80, 82; WhoAm 78, 80, 82, 84, 86, 88,
90, 92, 94, 95, 96, 97; WhoGolf;
WhoIntG; WhoSpor; WhoWor 95, 96,
97; WorAl; WorAlBi*

Watson-Watt, Robert Alexander, Sir
Scottish. Scientist, Engineer
Developed the radiolocator (radar), secret
　weapon of Battle of Britain.
b. Apr 13, 1892 in Brechin, Scotland
d. Dec 5, 1973 in Inverness, Scotland
Source: *AsBiEn; Au&Wr 71; BioIn 1, 2,
3, 4, 5, 6, 7, 9, 10, 12, 14, 20;
CamBiEn; CamDcSc; ChamBiD; ConAu
45, P-1; CurBio 45, 74; DcNaB 1971;
DcScB S2; EncWB 98; GrBr; InSci;
LarDcSc; McGEWB; NewYTBE 73;
ObitOF 79; ObitT 1971; RanHWDS;
WhAm 6; WhDW; Who 74; WorAl*

Watt, Douglas Benjamin
American. Composer, Author
Drama critic for *NY Daily News,* 1937-
　70; contributor, *New Yorker* mag;
　wrote *After All These Years.*
b. Jan 20, 1914 in New York, New York
Source: *ASCAP 66; NotNAT; OxCAmT
84; WhoAm 86, 90; WhoE 74, 86*

Watt, George Willard
American. Chemist
Worked with Manhattan Project, U of
　Chicago, 1943-45; with Exxon Nuclear
　Co., 1970-80.
b. Jan 8, 1911 in Bellaire, Ohio
d. Mar 29, 1980 in Austin, Texas
Source: *AmMWSc 76P, 79; AmNatBi;
BioIn 10, 12; NewYTBS 80; WhAm 7;
WhoAm 74, 76, 78, 80*

Watt, James
Scottish. Engineer, Inventor
Defined unit of power (horsepower)
　1783; the watt was named for him.
b. Jan 19, 1736 in Greenock, Scotland
d. Aug 19, 1819 in Heathfield, England
Source: *Alli; AsBiEn; BiDLA; BiESc;
BioIn 1, 2, 3, 4, 5, 6, 7, 8, 9, 10, 11, 12,
13, 14, 17, 20; BlkwCE; BlmGEL;
CamBiEn; CamDcSc; CelCen;
ChamBiD; DcBiPP; DcInv; DcNaB;
DcScB; Dis&D; EncEnl; EncWB 98;
InSci; LarDcSc; LegTOT; LngCEL;
MacEA; McGCEnS; McGEWB; NewC;
NewCol 75; OxCBrHi; RanHWDS;
SciMath; WebBD 83; WhDW; WorAl;
WorAlBi; WorInv*

Watt, James Gaius
American. Government Official
Outspoken secretary of Interior, 1981-83;
　known for controversial environmental
　policies.
b. Jan 31, 1938 in Lusk, Wyoming
Source: *BiDrUSE 89; BioIn 12, 13, 14;
CurBio 82; DcAmC; EnvEnc; IntWW 81,
82, 83, 89, 91, 93, 97, 98, 2000; IntYB
82; NatCAB 63N; NewYTBS 80; WhoAm
76, 78, 80, 82, 84, 86, 88, 90, 92, 94,
95, 96, 97; WhoAmP 73, 75, 77, 79, 83,
85, 87, 89, 91, 93, 95, 97, 1999; WhoE
81, 83; WhoGov 72, 75, 77; WhoWor 82*

Watt, Richard Martin
American. Author
Wrote *Dare Call It Treason,* 1963; *The
　Kings Depart,* 1969.
b. Nov 10, 1930 in Berwyn, Illinois
Source: *ConAu 5R; St&PR 87, 91; WhoE
75, 77, 79*

Watteau, Jean Antoine
French. Artist
Rococo painter; noted for pastel coloring,
　courtly fantasies: *Embarkation of
　Cythera,* 1717.
b. Oct 10, 1684 in Valenciennes, France
d. Jul 18, 1721 in Nogent-sur-Marne,
　France
Source: *AtlBL; BioIn 1, 2, 3, 4, 6, 8, 9,
11, 12, 13, 14, 15, 19; CamBiEn;
ChamBiD; ClaDrA; DcBiPP; DcCathB;
Dis&D; EncEnl; LiveWoA; McGDA;
McGEWB; OxCArt; OxCFr; REn;
WhDW; WorAl*

Wattenberg, Ben J
American. Author
Demographer; book *The Good News Is
　the Bad News Is Wrong,* 1984, says
　quality of life in all segments of US
　society is improving.

b. Aug 26, 1933 in New York, New
York
Source: *BioIn 14; ConAu 33NR, 57;
CurBio 85; WhoAm 86, 90; WhoE 89;
WhoEnt 98; WhoMedi 98; WhoUSWr 88;
WhoWrEP 89; WrDr 86, 92, 98*

Watterson, Bill
[William B. Watterson, II]
American. Cartoonist
Drew syndicated comic strip "Calvin
and Hobbes," 1985-95.
b. 1958?
Source: *Au&Arts 9; BioIn 15, 16, 18;
ConAu 134; EncACom; LegTOT; News
90, 90-3; SmATA 66; WhoAm 90, 92, 94,
95, 96, 97; WrDr 94, 96, 98*

Watterson, Henry
"Marse Henry"
American. Newspaper Editor
Editor, *Courier-Journal*, 1868-1918,
Louisville; won Pulitzer, 1917.
b. Feb 16, 1840 in Washington, District
of Columbia
d. Dec 22, 1921 in Jacksonville, Florida
Source: *Alli SUP; AmAu&B; AmBi;
AmNatBi; ApCAB, X; BbD; BenetAL 91;
BiDAmJo; BiD&SB; BiDConf; BiDRAC;
BiDrUSC 89; BiDSA; BioIn 2, 3, 4, 5, 9,
10, 14, 16, 23; CamDcAB; DcAmAu;
DcAmB; DcLB 25; DcNAA; EncAAH;
EncAJ; EncSoH; HarEnUS; JrnUS;
LinLib L, S; MorMA; NatCAB 1;
OxCAmH; OxCAmL 65, 83, 95; REnAL;
SouWr; TwCBDA; WebAB 74, 79;
WhAm 1; WhAmP; WhCiWar*

Wattleton, Faye
[Alice Fay Wattleton]
American. Business Executive, Feminist
Pres., Planned Parenthood Federation of
America, 1978-92.
b. Aug 7, 1943 in Saint Louis, Missouri
Source: *AfrAmAl 8; AmWomM; BioIn 11,
12, 15, 16; BlksScM; BlkWAm;
CamDcAB; ConBlB 9; ConNews 85-3;
CurBio 90; EncWB 99; IntWWW 2;
LegTOT; News 89-1; NewYTBS 89;
NotBlAW 1; WhoAfA 10, 11, 12; WhoAm
90, 96, 97, 99, 2000; WhoAmW 91, 95,
97, 99; WhoBlA 6, 7, 8*

Watts, Alan Wilson
American. Philosopher
Proponent of Eastern philosophy,
Western culture; wrote *The Spirit of
Zen*, 1936.
b. Jan 6, 1915 in Chislehurst, England
d. Nov 16, 1973 in Mill Valley,
California
Source: *AmAu&B; AmNatBi; BiDAmCu;
BioIn 5, 6, 7, 9, 10, 11, 12, 15, 17, 19;
CamDcAB; ConAu 41R, 45; CurBio 62,
74; DcAmB S9; DcAmReB 2; EncARH;
EncWB, 98; NewYTBE 73; RAdv 14;
RelLAm 1, 2; WebAB 74; WhAm 6;
WhoAm 74; WhoWor 74; WomWMM;
WorAl; WorAu 1950*

Watts, Andre
American. Musician
Internationally famous pianist; played at
Nixon's inaugural concert, 1969.
b. Jun 20, 1946 in Nuremberg
Source: *AfrAmAl 6, 8; BakBD 78, 84,
92; BakBDTw; BakDcM; BiDAfM;
BiDAmM; BioIn 6, 8, 9, 10, 11, 12, 13,
14, 15, 16, 21; BioNews 75; BriBkM 80;
CamBiEn; CamDcAB; CelR, 90; CurBio
68; DcTwCCu 1; DrBlPA, 90; Ebony 1;
InB&W 80, 85; IntWWM 77, 80, 90;
LegTOT; MusSN; NegAl 89; NewAmDM;
NewGrDA 86; NewGrDM 80; NewYTBE
71; NewYTBS 88; NotBlAM; NotTwCP;
PenDiMP; WhoAfA 9, 10, 11, 12;
WhoAm 76, 78, 80, 82, 84, 86, 92, 94,
95, 96, 97, 98; WhoAmM 83; WhoBlA 1,
2, 3, 4, 5, 6, 7, 8; WhoE 74; WhoEnt 92,
98; WhoWor 74, 78, 80, 82, 84; WorAl;
WorAlBi*

Watts, Charlie
[The Rolling Stones; Charles Robert
Watts]
English. Singer, Musician
Drummer, original member of Rolling
Stones, 1964—.
b. Jun 2, 1941 in Islington, England
Source: *AllMGJa; BioIn 13, 15; IntWW
98, 2000; LegTOT; WhoAm 80, 82, 84,
86, 88; WhoAmP 89; WhoEnt 98;
WhoRocM 82; WhoWor 98*

Watts, George Frederic
English. Artist, Sculptor
Best known for 19th-c. British
portraiture, busts.
b. 1817 in London, England
d. 1904 in London, England
Source: *BioIn 11; DcNaB S2; DcVicP;
McGDA; OxDcArt; VicBrit; WhDW*

Watts, Heather
[Linda Heather Watts]
American. Dancer
Member NYC Ballet, 1970-78; soloist,
1978-79; principle ballerina, 1979-95.
b. Sep 27, 1953 in Los Angeles,
California
Source: *BiDD; BioIn 13, 14; CurBio 83;
IntDcB; IntWWW 2; InWom SUP;
WhoAm 80, 82, 84, 86, 88, 90, 92, 94,
95, 96, 97; WhoAmW 81, 89, 91, 93, 95*

Watts, Isaac
English. Theologian
Best known for hymns: "O God Our
Help in Ages Past"; children's songs:
"How Doth the Little Busy Bee."
b. Jul 17, 1674 in Southampton, England
d. Nov 25, 1748 in Stoke Poges, England
Source: *Alli; AnCL; BbD; Benet 87, 96;
BiCoLiE; BiD&SB; BioIn 1, 2, 3, 4, 6, 7,
8, 10, 16, 17; BlkwCE; BlmGEL; BritAu;
CamBiEn; CamGEL; CamGLE; CarSB;
CasWL; ChamBiD; ChhPo, S1, S2, S3;
CnE&AP; DcBiPP; DcEnA; DcEnL;
DcEuL; DcLB 95; DcLEL; DcNaB;
EncWM; EvLB; LegTOT; LinLib L, S;
LngCEL; LuthC 75; NewC; NewCBEL;
OxCChiL; OxCEng 67, 85, 95; OxCMus;*

*PenC ENG; PoChrch; REn; SmATA 52;
Str&VC; WebE&AL; WhoChr*

Watts, J(ulius) C(aesar), (Jr.)
American. Politician, Clergy, Football
Player
In 1994, the former football star became
the first African American Republican
from a Southern state to win a seat in
Congress since Reconstruction.
b. Nov 18, 1957 in Eufaula, Oklahoma
Source: *EncWB 99*

Watts, Pete
[Mott (the Hoople)]
"Overend"
English. Musician
Bassist with hard-rock group, 1969-74.
b. May 13, 1947 in Birmingham,
England

Watts, Richard, Jr.
American. Critic
Career spanned 40 yrs. for the *NY
Herald Tribune, Post.*
b. Jan 12, 1898 in Parkersburg, West
Virginia
d. Jan 2, 1981 in New York, New York
Source: *AmAu&B; BiE&WWA; BioIn 12;
CamGWoT; ConAmTC; ConAu 102;
IntAu&W 82; NewYTBS 81; NotNAT;
OxCAmT 84; OxCThe 67; WhoE 74;
WhoThe 72, 77*

Watts, Rolonda
American. TV Personality
Host of "Rolonda," a talk show, 1994—
.
b. Jul 12, 1959 in Winston-Salem, North
Carolina
Source: *ConBlB 9*

Watts-Dunton, Theodore
[Walter Theodore Watts-Dunton]
English. Critic, Poet
Benefactor, companion of Swinburne;
wrote *Aylwin*, 1898.
b. Oct 12, 1832 in Saint Ives, England
d. Jun 7, 1914 in London, England
Source: *BiD&SB; BioIn 2, 3, 6, 9, 10;
BritAu 19; CamGEL; CamGLE; Chambr
3; ChhPo, S1, S2, S3; DcEnA, A;
DcEuL; DcLEL; DcNaB 1912; DcPseud;
EvLB; LngCTC; MouLC 4; NewC;
NewCBEL; NewCol 75; OxCEng 67, 85;
PenC ENG; REn; ScF&FL 1; StaCVF*

Waugh, Alec
[Alexander Raban Waugh]
English. Author
Wrote best-seller *Island in the Sun*,
1955; brother of Evelyn Waugh.
b. Jul 8, 1898 in London, England
d. Sep 3, 1981 in Tampa, Florida
Source: *AnObit 1981; Au&Wr 71; BioIn
4, 5, 6, 7, 8, 10, 11, 12, 24; BlueB 76;
CamBiEn; CamGLE; ChamBiD; ConAu
17R, 22NR, 104, X; ConNov 76, 82;
DcLB 191; DcLEL; DcNaB 1981; EvLB;
FacFETw; IntAu&W 76, 77; IntWW 74,
75, 76, 77, 78, 79, 80, 81; LegTOT;
LngCTC; MnBBF; ModBrL, 2; NewC;*

NewCBEL; NewYTBS 81; Novels;
OxCEng 85, 95; OxCTwCL; PenC ENG;
RAdv 1; REn; RGTwCWr; TwCA, SUP;
TwCWr; WhAm 8; WhE&EA; WhLit;
Who 74; WhoWor 74, 76, 78, 80, 82;
WorAl; WorAlBi; WorAu 1900; WrDr
76, 80, 82

Waugh, Auberon
English. Critic, Author
Writes novels; contributes articles, book
reviews for several newspapers; son of
Evelyn Waugh.
b. Nov 17, 1939 in Dulverton, England
Source: *Au&Wr 71; Benet 87; BioIn 6,*
9, 11, 13, 14, 16; BlueB 76; ConAu
6NR, 22NR, 45; ConLC 7; ConNov 72,
76, 82; CurBio 90; DcLB 14, 194;
DcLEL 1940; DcLP 87A; FacFETw;
IntAu&W 77, 91; IntvTCA 2; IntWW 83,
91; LegTOT; Who 85, 92; WhoWor 91;
WorAu 1975; WrDr 76, 80, 82, 84, 86,
88, 90, 92

Waugh, Evelyn Arthur St. John
English. Author, Satirist
Wrote *Decline and Fall*, 1928;
Brideshead Revisited, 1945.
b. Oct 28, 1903 in London, England
d. Apr 10, 1966 in Taunton, England
Source: *AtlBL; CasWL; CathA 1930;*
ChamBiD; CnMWL; ConAu 85; ConLC
1, 3; CyWA 58; DcArts; DcLEL; DcNaB
1961; EncWB 98; EncWL 1; EvLB;
FacFETw; GayLL 1; GrBr; HisDcWJ;
MakMC; McGEWB; ModBrL S1;
NewYTBE 73; OxCEng 85, 95;
OxCTwCL; PenC ENG; RfGShF 1, 2;
TwCA SUP; WhAm 4; WorAl

Waugh, Frederick Judd
American. Artist
Principally painted marine scenes;
designed church of St. Mary's of the
Harbor, Provincetown, MA.
b. Sep 13, 1861 in Bordentown, New
Jersey
d. Sep 11, 1940 in Provincetown,
Massachusetts
Source: *BioIn 1, 2, 4, 7, 8; BriEAA;*
CamDcAB; CurBio 40; DcAmB S2;
DcSeaP; WhAm 1

Wauneka, Annie Dodge
American. Native American Leader,
Social Reformer
Won Medal of Freedom, 1963, for
efforts to improve health services
among Navajos.
b. Apr 10, 1910 in Sawmill, Arizona
d. Nov 10, 1997 in Flagstaff, Arizona
Source: *AmIndBi; AZNatAW; BioIn 21,*
23; ConHero 3; EncWB 99; GrLiveH;
HerW, 84; InWom SUP; NotNaAm

Wavell, Archibald Percival
Wavell, Earl
English. Military Leader
Commander in chief for Middle East,
1938-41; Viceroy of India, 1943-47.
b. May 5, 1883 in Colchester, England
d. May 24, 1950 in London, England

Source: *BioIn 1, 2, 5, 6, 7, 8, 10, 11, 13,*
14; CamBiEn; ChamBiD; CurBio 41, 50;
DcLEL; WhAm 3

Waxman, Al
Actor
Played Lt. Samuels in TV series
"Cagney and Lacey," 1982-88.
b. Mar 2, 1934 in Toronto, Ontario,
Canada
Source: *BioIn 15; ConTFT 3*

Waxman, Franz
German. Conductor, Composer
Only composer to receive consecutive
Academy Awards for musical scores
of *Sunset Boulevard*, 1950; *A Place in
the Sun*, 1951.
b. Dec 24, 1906 in Koenigsbutte,
Germany
d. Feb 24, 1967 in Los Angeles,
California
Source: *AmNatBi; ASCAP 66, 80;*
BakBD 78, 84, 92; BakBDTw; BakDcM;
BioIn 1, 2, 3, 7, 18; CamDcAB; CmMov;
CmpEPM; CndCPOM; ConAmC 76, 82;
DcAmB S8; DcPseud; FilmEn; FilmgC;
GangFlm; HalFC 80, 84, 88; IntDcF 1-
4, 2-4; LegTOT; NewAmDM; NewGrDA
86; NewGrDM 80; OxCPMus; WhAm 4;
WorEFlm

Waxman, Henry Arnold
American. Politician
US Dem. rep. from CA, 1975—.
b. Sep 12, 1939 in Los Angeles,
California
Source: *AlmAP 92; BiDrUSC 89; BioIn*
13, 15, 16; CngDr 89; CurBio 92;
PolsAm 84; WhoAm 78, 80, 82, 84, 86,
88, 90, 92, 94, 95, 96, 97, 98, 99, 2000;
WhoAmJ 80; WhoAmP 73, 75, 77, 79,
81, 83, 85, 87, 89, 91, 93, 95, 97, 1999;
WhoE 95; WhoWest 00, 87, 89, 92, 94,
96, 98

Wayans, Damon
American. Actor, Comedian
Appeared on TV's "In Living Color,"
1990-92.
b. 1961 in New York, New York
Source: *ConBlB 8; ConTFT 10; WhoAfA*
9, 10, 11, 12; WhoAm 94, 95, 96, 97, 99,
2000; WhoEnt 98

Wayans, Keenen Ivory
American. Comedian, Filmmaker
Writer, director, and star of *I'm Gonna
Get You Sucka!*, 1988; TV series "In
Living Color," 1990-92; won Emmy
Award, 1990.
b. Jun 8, 1958 in New York, New York
Source: *BioIn 16; BlkWr 2; ConAu*
82NR, 140; ConBlB 18; ConTFT 10, 17;
CurBio 95; DcTwCCu 5; IntMPA 92, 94,
96; LegTOT; MiSFD 9; News 91, 91-1;
SchCGBL; WhoAm 94, 95, 96, 97, 99,
2000; WhoBlA 7; WhoEnt 92, 98;
WhoHol 92

Waybill, Fee
[The Tubes; John Waldo]
American. Singer
Lead singer for The Tubes since late
1960s.
b. Sep 17, 1950 in Omaha, Nebraska
Source: *LegTOT*

Wayland, Francis
American. Clergy, Educator
Pres. of Brown U., 1827-55.
b. Mar 11, 1796 in New York, New
York
d. Sep 30, 1865 in Providence, Rhode
Island
Source: *Alli; AmAu&B; AmBi; AmNatBi;*
AmPeW; ApCAB; BbD; BiDAmEd;
BiD&SB; BiDMoPL; BioIn 6, 16, 19;
CamDcAB; CyAL 1; CyEd; DcAmAu;
DcAmB; DcAmReB 1, 2; DcAmSR;
DcAmTB; DcNAA; Drake; EncRelA;
EncWB 98; HarEnUS; McGEWB;
NatCAB 1, 8; TwCBDA; WebAB 74, 79;
WhAm HS

Waymack, W(illiam) W(esley)
American. Editor
Editor of *Des Moines Register, Tribune*;
won Pulitzer for editorial writing,
1938.
b. Oct 18, 1888 in Savanna, Illinois
d. Nov 5, 1960 in Des Moines, Iowa
Source: *BioIn 1, 5, 6; ConAu 93; CurBio*
47, 61; DcAmB S6; WhAm 4; WhoPul

Wayman, Dorothy
[Theodate Geoffrey]
American. Author
Wrote on Quaker history, 1960s.
b. Jan 7, 1893 in San Bernardino,
California
d. Oct 27, 1975 in Olean, New York
Source: *AmAu&B; BioIn 1, 3, 10, 11;*
CathA 1952; ConAu 61; PenNWW B;
WhAm 6; WhNAA; WhoAm 74

Wayne, Anthony
"Mad Anthony"
American. Soldier
American Revolutionary General; helped
open the Northwest Territory to
settlement, 1794.
b. Jan 1, 1745 in Waynesboro,
Pennsylvania
d. Dec 15, 1796 in Erie, Pennsylvania
Source: *Alli; AmBi; AmNatBi; AmRev;*
ApCAB; BiAUS; BiDrAC; BiDrUSC 89;
BioIn 1, 3, 5, 6, 7, 8, 9, 10, 14, 16, 24;
BlkwEAR; CamBiEn; CamDcAB;
ChamBiD; CmdGen 1991; DcAmB;
DcAmMiB; Drake; EncAAH; EncAB-H
1974, 1996; EncAInd; EncAR;
EncCRAm; EncWB 98; GenMudB;
HarEnMi; HarEnUS; HisDcAR;
HisWorL; LinLib S; McGEWB; MorMA;
NatCAB 1; NewEAmW; OxCAmH; REn;
REnAL; REnAW; TwCBDA; WebAB 74,
79; WebAMB; WhAm HS; WhAmP;
WhAmRev; WhNaAH; WorAl; WorAlBi

Wayne, Bernie
American. Composer
Composed the beauty contest theme
  song, "There She Is, Miss America."
d. Apr 18, 1993 in Marina del Rey,
  California
Source: *BioIn 18, 19; NewYTBS 93*

Wayne, David
[Wayne David McKeeken; Wayne James
  McMeekan]
American. Actor
Films include *Three Faces of Eve,* 1957;
  Front Page, 1931.
b. Jan 30, 1914 in Traverse City,
  Michigan
d. Feb 9, 1995 in Santa Monica,
  California
Source: *BiDFilm; BiE&WWA; BioIn 4,
20, 21, 22; CmpEPM; ConAu 28NR;
ConTFT 7, 14; CurBio 56, 95N;
DcPseud; EncAFC; EncMT; FilmEn;
FilmgC; ForYSC; HalFC 80, 84, 88;
IntMPA 88, 92, 94, 96; LegTOT; MotPP;
MovMk; News 95, 95-3; NewYTBS 95;
NotNAT; OxCAmT 84; PIP&P; VarWW
85; WhoHol 92, A; WhoThe 72, 77, 81;
WorAl; WorAlBi; WorEFlm*

Wayne, John
[Marion Robert Morrison]
"Duke"
American. Actor, Director
Biggest box office attraction in
  Hollywood history; starred in over 200
  westerns; won Oscar, 1968, for *True
  Grit.*
b. May 26, 1907 in Winterset, Iowa
d. Jun 11, 1979 in Los Angeles,
  California
Source: *AmNatBi, 78, 79; IntWW 74, 75,
76, 77, 78, 79N; ItaFilm; LegTOT;
MiSFD 9N; MotPP; MovMk;
NewEAmW; NewYTBE 72; NewYTBS 79;
OnHuYAF; OsStAZ; OxCFilm;
RComAH; WebAB 74, 79; WhAm 7;
WhoAm 74, 76, 78; WhoHol A; WhoHrs
80; WhoWor 78; WhScrn 83; WorAl;
WorAlBi; WorEFlm*

Wayne, Johnny
[Wayne and Shuster]
Canadian. Comedian
Had documentary-style TV show with
  Frank Shuster, Wayne and Shuster
  Take an Affectionate Look at., 1966;
  got first break in US on Ed Sullivan's
  show, 1950s.
b. May 28, 1918 in Toronto, Ontario,
  Canada
d. Jul 18, 1990 in Toronto, Ontario,
  Canada
Source: *AnObit 1990; BioIn 5; CreCan
2; DcPseud; NewYTBS 90*

Wayne, Patrick
American. Actor
Son of John Wayne, appeared with father
  in several films: *McClintock!,* 1963;
  leading man in own right, 1970s.
b. Jul 15, 1939 in Los Angeles,
  California

Source: *BioIn 10, 11, 15; ConTFT 3, 20;
FilmEn; FilmgC; HalFC 80, 84, 88;
IntMPA 78, 79, 80, 81, 82, 84, 86, 88,
92, 94, 96; ItaFilm; NewYTBE 71;
WhoHol 92, A; WhoHrs 80*

Wayne, Paula
American. Actor
Career in theater, TV, films; dubbed
  voices for over 50 foreign films.
b. Nov 3, 1937 in Hobart, Oklahoma
Source: *BiE&WWA; NotNAT; WhoAm 74*

Wayne and Shuster
[Frank Shuster; Johnny Wayne]
Canadian. Comedy Team
Ed Sullivan first gave them US exposure,
  1950s; popular on Canadian radio, TV,
  1940s-60s.
Source: *BioIn 17; LesBEnT; NewYTET*

Weatherford, Teddy
American. Jazz Musician
Pianist, leading exponent of "Chicago-
  style" jazz, 1920s.
b. Oct 11, 1903 in Bluefield, West
  Virginia
d. Apr 25, 1945 in Calcutta, India
Source: *BakBD 84, 92; BiDAfM;
BiDAmM; BiDJaz; InB&W 85; LegTOT;
NewGrDJ 88, 94; OxCPMus; PenEncP;
WhoJazz 72; WorAl; WorAlBi*

Weather Report
[Alejandro Acuna; Alphonso Johnson;
  Jaco Pastorius; Wayne Shorter;
  Chester Thompson; Norada Walden;
  Josef Zawainul]
American. Music Group
Instrumental hit "Birdland," 1978.
Source: *AllMGJa; BiDJaz A; BillEnR;
BioIn 12, 14, 15, 16, 21; ConMuA 80A;
ConMus 19; EncJzS; EncRk 88;
FacFETw; HarEnR 86; IlEncBM 82;
IlEncJ; IlEncRk; LElec; NewAmDM;
NewGrDA 86; NewGrDJ 88, 94;
NewYTBS 87; OxCPMus; PenEncP;
RolSEnR 83; WhoRock 81; WhoRocM 82*

Weathers, Carl
American. Actor
Played Apollo Creed in *Rocky,* 1976;
  starred in TV's "Street Justice,"
  1991-92.
b. Jan 14, 1948 in New Orleans,
  Louisiana
Source: *ConBlB 10; DrBlPA 90; IntMPA
92, 94, 96; WhoHol 92*

Weathers, Felicia
American. Opera Singer
Soprano with Hamburg State Opera,
  1966-70; made NY Met. debut, 1965.
b. Aug 13, 1937 in Saint Louis, Missouri
Source: *BakBD 84, 92; BakBDTw;
BiDAfM; BioIn 7, 8, 16; BlkOpe; CmOp;
InB&W 85; IntWWM 90; NewEOp 71;
PenDiMP; WhoAm 74, 76, 78; WhoAmW
68, 70, 72, 74; WhoWor 74*

Weatherwax, Rudd B
American. Animal Trainer
Most famous pupils were seven male
  collies who played Lassie in films,
  TV.
b. 1908?
d. Feb 25, 1985 in Mission Hills,
  California

Weaver, Dennis
American. Actor
Starred in TV series "Gunsmoke,"
  1955-64; "McCloud," 1970-77;
  "Buck James," 1985-87.
b. Jun 4, 1925 in Joplin, Missouri
Source: *BioIn 9, 10, 11, 12, 15; ConTFT
3; CurBio 77; FilmgC; HalFC 84, 88;
IntMPA 75, 76, 77, 78, 79, 80, 81, 82,
84, 86, 88, 92, 94, 96; MotPP; MovMk;
NewAgE 92; VarWW 85; WhoAm 86, 90;
WhoEnt 92; WhoHol 92, A; WorAlBi*

Weaver, Doodles
[Winstead Sheffield Glendening Dixon
  Weaver]
American. Actor
Played hayseed comedic roles in over 60
  films, 1930s-40s; appeared with Spike
  Jones band as Professor Feedelbaum,
  1948-51.
b. May 11, 1914 in Los Angeles,
  California
d. Jan 15, 1983 in Burbank, California
Source: *BioIn 10, 13; EncAFC; ForYSC;
JoeFr; NewYTBS 83; What 4; WhoHol A*

Weaver, Earl Sidney
American. Baseball Manager
Manager, Baltimore, 1968-82, 1985-86;
  won four pennants, one World Series;
  admitted to Baseball Hall of Fame,
  1996.
b. Aug 14, 1930 in Saint Louis, Missouri
Source: *Ballpl 90; BiDAmSp BB; BioIn
10, 12, 13, 14, 15, 16; CamDcAB;
ConAu 116; CurBio 83; WhoAm 74, 76,
78, 80, 82, 84, 86; WhoE 81; WhoProB
73; WorAl; WorAlBi*

Weaver, Fritz William
American. Actor
Won Tony for *Child's Play,* 1970.
b. Jan 19, 1926 in Pittsburgh,
  Pennsylvania
Source: *BiE&WWA; CamGWoT;
ConTFT 8; CurBio 67; FilmgC; HalFC
88; IntMPA 84, 92; NotNAT; OxCAmT
84; WhoAm 74, 76, 78, 80, 82, 84, 86,
88, 92, 94, 95, 96, 97; WhoEnt 92, 98;
WhoHol A; WhoThe 81; WorAl; WorAlBi*

Weaver, James Baird
American. Politician
Unsuccessful presidential candidate,
  1880, 1892.
b. Jun 12, 1833 in Dayton, Ohio
d. Feb 6, 1913 in Des Moines, Iowa
Source: *AmBi; AmNatBi; AmPolLe;
ApCAB; BiDrAC; BiDrUSC 89; BioIn 8,
24; CamBiEn; CamDcAB; CivWDc;
DcAmB; DcNAA; EncAAH; EncAB-H
1974, 1996; EncWB 98; McGEWB;
NatCAB 11, 16; NewCol 75; NewEAmW;*

OhA&B; OxCAmH; REnAL; REnAW; TwCBDA; WebAB 74, 79; WhAm 1; WhAmP

Weaver, Mike
[Michael Dwayne Weaver]
American. Boxer
Won 1980 WBA heavyweight title.
b. Jun 4, 1952 in Gatesville, Texas
Source: *BioIn 13, 15; InB&W 85; IntWW 91; NewYTBS 79; WhoAm 82*

Weaver, Pat
[Sylvester L(aflin) Weaver, Jr.]
American. TV Executive
An executive with the National Broadcasting Company (NBC), he was responsible for some of the most innovative and entertaining programming on both radio and television.
b. Dec 21, 1908 in Los Angeles, California
Source: *EncTelN; EncWB 2-19; WrDr 98, 99*

Weaver, Robert C(lifton)
American. Government Official
First secretary of HUD, 1966-69; first black US cabinet member.
b. Dec 29, 1907 in Washington, District of Columbia
d. Jul 17, 1997 in New York, New York
Source: *AmMWSc 73S; AmPolLe; BiDrUSE 71, 89; BioIn 5, 6, 7, 8, 9, 10, 11, 15, 20, 23; BlkWrNE A; BlueB 76; CamDcAB; ConAu 9R, 159; CurBio 61, 97N; DiAAPGL; EncAB-H 1974, 1996; EncSoH; FacFETw; InB&W 80, 85; IntWW 83, 91; IntYB 82; OxCAmH; PeoHis; PolProf J, K; SelBAAf; SelBAAu; WebAB 74, 79; WhAm 12; WhoAm 74, 76, 78, 80, 82, 86, 88, 90, 92, 94; WhoAmP 73, 75, 77, 79, 81, 83, 85, 87, 89, 91, 93, 95, 97; WhoBlA 4, 7; WhoE 74; WorAlBi*

Weaver, Sigourney
[Susan Weaver]
American. Actor
Starred in *Alien*, 1979; *Ghostbusters*, 1984; *Working Girl*, 1988.
b. Oct 8, 1949 in New York, New York
Source: *BiDFilm 94; BioIn 14, 15, 16; CamBiEn; CelR 90; ChamBiD; ConTFT 3, 10, 17; CurBio 89; DcPseud; EncAFC; HalFC 84, 88; HolBB; IntDcF 2-3; IntMPA 86, 88, 92, 94, 96; IntWW 89, 91, 93, 97, 98, 2000; IntWWW 2; JohnWSW; LegTOT; News 88-3; NewYTBS 86; OsStAZ; VarWW 85; WhoAm 88, 90, 92, 94, 95, 96, 97, 98, 99, 2000; WhoAmW 89, 91, 93, 95, 97, 99; WhoEnt 92, 98; WhoHol 92; WhoHrs 80; WorAlBi*

Weaver, Thomas
American. Anthropologist, Author
Professor of anthropology, U of AZ, 1975—; writings include *Mexican Migration*, 1976.
b. May 1, 1929 in Grenville, New Mexico

Source: *AmMWSc 73S, 76P; ConAu 13NR, 61; FifIDA; WhoAm 80, 82, 84; WhoUSWr 88; WhoWest 74, 76, 78, 80, 82; WhoWrEP 89, 92, 95*

Weaver, William
American. Translator, Journalist
Award-winning translator of Italian prose.
b. Jul 24, 1923 in Washington, District of Columbia
Source: *Au&Wr 71; BioIn 14, 16, 18; CamDcAB; ConAu 112, 116; WhoAm 74, 76; WhoWor 74*

Weavers, The
[Erik Darling; Lee Hays; Fred Hellerman; Bernie Krause; Pete Seeger]
American. Music Group
Popular folk group, 1948-63; hits include "On Top of Old Smoky," 1951; "Good Night Irene," 1950; pioneered in making folk music commercially successful.
Source: *AmPS A, B; BiDAmM; BioIn 12, 14, 15, 16, 17, 18, 19, 20, 21; BioNews 74; ConMus 8; CurBio 63; EncFCWM 69, 83; EncRk 88; FacFETw; NewAmDM; NewGrDA 86; NewYTBS 80, 81; OxCPMus; PenEncP; PeoHis; RkOn 74, 78; RolSEnR 83; WhoHol 92*

Webb, Beatrice Potter
[Mrs. Sidney James Webb]
English. Sociologist
Collaborated with husband on many books: *The Truth about Soviet Russia*, 1942.
b. Jan 22, 1858 in Gloucester, England
d. Apr 30, 1943 in Liphook, England
Source: *BioIn 14, 15, 16, 17, 18, 19, 21, 22, 24; BlmGWL; CurBio 43; DcAmSR; DcLEL; EncBrWW; EncWB 98; EvLB; InWom SUP; LngCTC; McGEWB; NewC; OxCEng 67, 95; PenNWW A; TwCA SUP; VicBrit; WomFir; WomWrGB; WorAu 1900*

Webb, Chick
[William Webb]
American. Jazz Musician
Drummer, bandleader, 1920s-30s; noted for "Stompin' at the Savoy"; introduced Ella Fitzgerald.
b. Feb 10, 1902 in Baltimore, Maryland
d. Jun 16, 1939 in Baltimore, Maryland
Source: *BgBands 74; BiDAmM; BiDJaz; BioIn 6, 9, 10, 12; CmpEPM; IlEncJ; NewGrDM 80; WhoJazz 72*

Webb, Clifton
[Webb Parmelee Hollenbeck]
American. Actor
Oscar nominee for *Laura*, 1944; *Razor's Edge*, 1946.
b. Nov 19, 1891 in Indianapolis, Indiana
d. Oct 13, 1966 in Beverly Hills, California
Source: *AmNatBi; BiDD; BiDFilm, 94; BiE&WWA; CmpEPM; CurBio 43, 66; EncAFC; EncMT; FacFETw; FilmEn; FilmgC; Funs; HalFC 84; IntDcF 1-3,*

2-3; LegTOT; MotPP; MovMk; OsStAZ; OxCPMus; WhAm 4; WhScrn 77; WorAl; WorEFlm

Webb, Jack Randolph
[John Farr; Tex Grady]
American. Director, Author
Played Sgt. Joe Friday on Emmy-winning TV series "Dragnet," 1952-59, 1967-70; also produced "Adam 12," 1968-75.
b. Apr 2, 1920 in Santa Monica, California
d. Dec 23, 1982 in Los Angeles, California
Source: *AnObit 1982; ConAu 108; ConTFT 1; CurBio 55, 83N; FilmgC; HalFC 84; IntMPA 82; LesBEnT; MotPP; NewYTBS 82; OxCFilm; WhAm 8; WhoAm 82; WhoHol A; WhoWest 74; WorEFlm*

Webb, James Edwin
American. Government Official
NASA administrator, 1961-68.
b. Oct 7, 1906 in Granville City, North Carolina
d. Mar 27, 1992 in Washington, District of Columbia
Source: *AmMWSc 73S, 78S; AmNatBi; BioIn 1, 2, 3, 5, 6, 7, 8, 11; BlueB 76; CamBiEn; FacFETw; IntWW 74, 75, 76, 77, 78, 79, 80, 81, 82, 83; WhAm 10; WhoAm 74, 76, 78, 80, 82; WhoSSW 73; WrDr 90*

Webb, James H(enry), Jr.
American. Government Official
Secretary of Navy, 1987-88; novels on Vietnam War include *Fields of Fire*, 1978; *A Sense of Honor*, 1981.
b. Feb 9, 1946 in Saint Joseph, Missouri
Source: *BioIn 15, 16; ConAu 81; ConLC 22; CurBio 87; IntWW 91; NewYTBS 83, 87; WhoAm 88; WhoAmP 91; WhoWor 89*

Webb, Jim
American. Composer
Wrote songs "Up, Up, and Away," 1967; "MacArthur Park," 1968; "Galveston," 1969.
b. Aug 15, 1946 in Elk City, Oklahoma
Source: *BioIn 8, 13, 14; CelR, 90; EncPR&S 89; EncRk 88; NewAmDM; OxCPMus; PenEncP*

Webb, Sidney James
[Baron Passfield]
English. Political Leader
Among founders of Fabian Society, 1885; wrote many books with wife, Beatrice.
b. Jul 13, 1859 in London, England
d. Oct 13, 1947 in Liphook, England
Source: *BbD; BiD&SB; CamBiEn; ChamBiD; ConAu 163; DcAmSR; DcLEL; DcNaB 1941; DcTwHis; EncWB 98; EvLB; GrBr; LngCTC; MakMC; McGEWB; NewC; NewCBEL; OxCEng 67; TwCA, SUP; VicBrit; WebBD 83; WhE&EA; WhoEc 81, 86; WorAl; WorAlBi*

Webb, Spud
[Anthony Jerome Webb]
American. Basketball Player
Guard, Atlanta, 1985-91; Sacramento, 1991—; one of shortest players in NBA; sl am-dunk winner, 1986.
b. Jul 13, 1963 in Dallas, Texas
Source: *BasBi; BioIn 13, 14, 15, 16; NewYTBS 86; OfNBA 87; WhoAfA 9, 10, 11, 12; WhoBlA 7*

Webb, Veronica
American. Model, Actor
Films include *Jungle Fever*, 1991 and *Malcolm X*, 1993; spokesperson for Revlon.
b. Dec 25, 1965 in Detroit, Michigan
Source: *ConAu 169; ConBlB 10; WhoAm 95, 96, 97, 98; WhoAmW 95, 99; WhoWor 97, 98, 99, 2000*

Webb, Walter Prescott
American. Author
Writings include *More Water for Texas*, 1954.
b. Apr 3, 1888 in Panola County, Texas
d. Mar 8, 1963 in Austin, Texas
Source: *AmAu&B; AmNatBi; BenetAL 91; BioIn 3, 4, 5, 6, 7, 8, 9, 10, 11, 13, 14, 16, 22; ConAu 113; CyWA 97; DcAmB S7; DcLB 17; EncAB-A 36; NatCAB 51; NewEAmW; OxCAmL 65, 83, 95; RAdv 14; REnAL; REnAW; TexWr; WhAm 4; WhE&EA*

Webb, Wellington
American. Politician
Mayor Denver, CO, 1991—.
b. Feb 17, 1941 in Chicago, Illinois
Source: *AfrAmAl 8; BioIn 11, 14; ConBlB 3; WhoAmP 91; WhoBlA 7; WhoWest 92*

Webb, William Seward
American. Railroad Executive
Pres. of Mohawk and Malone railroad.
b. Jan 31, 1851 in New York, New York
d. Oct 29, 1926
Source: *ApCAB SUP; DcAmAu; DcNAA; NatCAB 1; TwCBDA; WhAm 1*

Webber, Chris
[Mayce Edward Christopher Webber]
American. Basketball Player
Drafted by Orlando, 1993; forward, Golden State, 1993-94; Washington, 1994-98; Sacramento, 1998—.
b. Mar 1, 1973 in Detroit, Michigan
Source: *ConBlB 15; News 94, 94-1; WhoAfA 9, 10, 11, 12; WhoAm 97, 98, 2000; WhoBlA 8; WhoWest 00*

Weber, Carl
Director
Has directed for stage, TV, all over the world; won Obie Award, 1973, for *Kaspar*.
b. Aug 7, 1925 in Dortmund, Germany
Source: *ConTFT 3, 21*

Weber, Carl Maria von
German. Composer
Founder, German Romantic school; wrote operas *Der Freischutz*, 1821; *Oberon*, 1826.
b. Nov 18, 1786 in Eutin, Denmark
d. Jun 5, 1826 in London, England
Source: *AtlBL; BakBD 84; BioIn 14, 16, 23; BriBkM 80; CmOp; CmpBCM; CnOxB; DancEn 78; DcCom 77; DcCom&M 79; DcPup; GrComp; MetOEnc; MusMk; NewAmDM; NewCol 75; NewEOp 71; NewGrDM 80; NewOxM; Opera; OxCEng 67, 85, 95; OxCGer 76; OxDcOp; PenDiMP A; WebBD 83; WorAl; WorAlBi*

Weber, Dick
[Richard Anthony Weber]
American. Bowler
Only pro bowler to win PBA titles in four decades; PBA Hall of Fame; father of Pete Weber.
b. Dec 23, 1929 in Indianapolis, Indiana
Source: *BiDAmSp BK; BioIn 8, 9, 10, 14, 15; CurBio 70; NewYTBS 85; WhoSpor; WhoWor 74*

Weber, Ernst
American. Engineer
Research in microwave technology helped in the production of microwave communications equipment.
b. Sep 6, 1901 in Vienna, Austria
d. Feb 15, 1996 in Columbus, South Carolina
Source: *AmMWSc 73P, 79, 82, 86, 89, 92, 95; BioIn 3, 4, 5, 8, 21, 23; BlueB 76; IntWW 74, 75, 76, 77, 78, 79, 80, 81, 82, 83, 89; LElec; McGMS 80; NotTwCS 1S; WhAm 11; WhoAm 74, 76, 88, 90, 92, 94, 95, 96; WhoEng 80, 88*

Weber, Joseph M
[Weber and Fields]
American. Comedian
Formed comedy team with Lewis Fields, 1895-1904; reunited to play in *Roly Poly*, 1912.
b. Aug 11, 1867 in New York, New York
d. May 10, 1942 in Los Angeles, California
Source: *BiDAmM; CurBio 42; DcAmB S3; FamA&A; OxCThe 67; REnAL; WhAm 2; WhoStg 1908*

Weber, Lois
American. Actor, Director, Screenwriter
First woman film director, early 1900s.
b. Jun 13, 1881 in Allegheny, California
d. Nov 13, 1939 in Los Angeles, California
Source: *GrLiveH; IntDcWB; InWom SUP; LibW; NotAW; WhAm 1; WomFir*

Weber, Max
German. Sociologist, Author
Rejected Marx's economic determinism, concentrating on religious roots of modern institutions.
b. Apr 21, 1864 in Erfurt, Prussia
d. Jun 14, 1920 in Munich, Germany

Source: *Benet 87, 96; BiDPsy; BioIn 1, 2, 4, 5, 7, 8, 9, 10, 11, 12, 13, 14, 15, 16, 17, 18, 22, 23; CamBiEn; CasWL; ChamBiD; ConAu 109; CyWA 89, 97; DcSoc; EncEth; EncRelA; EncWB 98; EncWomW; FacFETw; GloEncH; GrEconB; IlEncMy; LegTOT; LuthC 75; MakMC; McGEWB; NamesHP; NewCol 75; NewGrDM 80; OxCGer 76, 86, 97; OxCLaw; RAdv 14, 13-3; REn; ThTwC 87; TwCA SUP; TwCLC 69; WhDW; WhoEc 81, 86; WorAl; WorAlBi*

Weber, Max
American. Artist, Author
Social themes depicted in *Chinese Restaurant*.
b. Apr 18, 1881 in Bialystok, Russia
d. Oct 4, 1961 in Great Neck, New York
Source: *AmAu&B; AmNatBi; AtlBL; Benet 87, 96; BioIn 1, 2, 4, 5, 6, 9, 10, 11, 12, 14, 17; BriEAA; CamBiEn; CamDcAB; ChamBiD; ConArt 83; DcAmArt; DcAmB S7; DcArts; DcCAA 71, 77, 88, 94; DcTwArt; EncWB 98; McGDA; McGEWB; OxCAmH; OxCArt; OxCTwCA; OxDcArt; PhDcTCA 77; REn; REnAL; WebAB 74, 79; WhAm 4; WhAmArt 85; WhoAmA 78N, 80N, 82N, 84N, 86N, 89N, 91N, 93N; WorArt 1950*

Weber, Pete(r)
American. Bowler
Son of Dick; pro bowler, 1979—; one of tour's money leaders; PBA Hall of Fame, 1998.
b. Aug 21, 1962 in Saint Louis, Missouri
Source: *BioIn 14, 15, 16; ConNews 86-3; NewYTBS 85; St&PR 91; WhoSpor*

Weber, Robert Maxwell
American. Cartoonist
With *New Yorker* mag. since 1962; contributor of cartoons to US newspapers.
b. Apr 22, 1924 in Los Angeles, California
Source: *WhoAm 82, 84, 86, 88, 90, 92, 94, 95, 96, 97, 98, 99, 2000*

Weber, Wilhelm Eduard
German. Physicist
Devised an electromagnetic telegraph.
b. Oct 24, 1804 in Wittenberg, Germany
d. Jun 23, 1891 in Gottingen, Germany
Source: *AsBiEn; BiESc; BioIn 8, 12, 14; CamBiEn; ChamBiD; DcScB; InSci; LarDcSc; LinLib S; McGCEnS; NewCol 75; RanHWDS; WebBD 83*

Weber and Fields
[Lew Fields; Joseph Weber]
American. Comedy Team
Began theatrical co., 1885; managed Broadway Music Hall, 1895-1904; shows include *Roly Poly*, 1912.
Source: *CamGWoT; CurBio 41; EncAFC; EncVaud; FacFETw; ObitOF 79; OxCPMus; OxCThe 67, 83; REn; WebBD 83; WhoHol 92; WhoTech 82*

Webern, Anton Friedrich Ernst von
Austrian. Composer
Pupil of Schoenberg; works banned by Nazis, 1933, as "cultural Bolshevism."
b. Dec 3, 1883 in Vienna, Austria
d. Sep 15, 1945 in Mittersill, Austria
Source: AtlBL; CamBiEn; CompSN SUP; DcCM; MakMC; NewCol 75; WhAm 4; WhDW; WorAl

Webster, Ben(jamin)
English. Actor
Movies include Mrs. Miniver, 1942; Lassie Come Home, 1943; father of Margaret Webster.
b. Jun 2, 1864 in London, England
d. Feb 26, 1947 in Hollywood, California
Source: BioIn 1, 5, 10; DcNaB 1941; Film 1, 2; HalFC 80, 84, 88; IIWWBF; NotNAT A, B; ObitOF 79; OxCThe 67; WhoHol B; WhScrn 74, 77, 83; WhThe

Webster, Daniel
American. Orator, Statesman
Senator from MA, 1820s-50s; noted for brilliant constitutional speeches; secretary of state, 1850-52.
b. Jan 18, 1782 in Salisbury, New Hampshire
d. Oct 24, 1852 in Marshfield, Massachusetts
Source: Alli; AmAu; AmAu&B; AmBi; AmNatBi; AmOrN; AmPolLe; ApCAB; BbD; Benet 87, 96; BenetAL 91; BiAUS; BiD&SB; BiDrAC; BiDrUSC 89; BiDrUSE 71, 89; BiDTran; BioIn 1, 2, 3, 4, 5, 7, 8, 9, 10, 11, 12, 13, 14, 15, 16, 17, 20, 22, 23, 24; CamBiEn; CamDCAB; CelCen; ChamBiD; Chambr 3; ChhPo, S1; CyAG; CyAL 1; DcAmAu; DcAmB; DcAmC; DcAmDH 80, 89; DcAmSR; DcBiPP; DcLEL; DcNAA; Dis&D; Drake; EncAAH; EncAB-H 1974, 1996; EncWar; EncWB 98; EvLB; HarEnUS; HisWorL; LegTOT; LinLib L, S; McGEWB; MemAm; NatCAB 3; OxCAmH; OxCAmL 65, 83; OxCEng 85, 95; OxCSupC; PenC AM; PolPar; PresAR 1980, 1996; RAdv 13-3; RComAH; REn; REnAL; TwCBDA; USGovLe; WebAB 74, 79; WhAm HS; WhAmP; WhCiWar; WorAl; WorAlBi

Webster, H(arold) T(ucker)
American. Cartoonist
Newspaper cartoonist known for "The Timid Soul," its character Caspar Milquetoast.
b. Sep 21, 1885 in Parkersburg, West Virginia
d. Sep 22, 1952 in Stamford, Connecticut
Source: AmAu&B; BioIn 1, 2, 3, 5; CurBio 45, 52; DcAmB S5; ObitOF 79; REnAL; WhAm 3; WhAmArt 85; WorECom

Webster, Jean
American. Author
Wrote Daddy Long-Legs, 1912.
b. Jul 24, 1876 in Fredonia, New York
d. Jun 11, 1916 in New York, New York

Source: AmAu&B; AmNatBi; AmWomPl; AmWomWr; BenetAL 91; BioIn 8, 12, 14, 22; BlmGWL; CarSB; ChhPo, S3; ChlBkCr; CnDAL; DcAmB; DcNAA; EvLB; InWom SUP; JBA 34; LibW; LngCTC; NotAW; NotNAT B; OxCAmL 65, 83, 95; REn; REnAL; SJGChWr 5; TwCA; TwCChW 2, 3, 4; TwCRGW; TwCRHW 90, 94; TwCWr; WhAm 1; WhoChL; WomWWA 14

Webster, John
English. Dramatist
Wrote The White Devil, 1612; The Duchess of Malfi, 1613.
b. 1580? in London, England
d. 1634?
Source: AtlBL; Benet 87, 96; BiCoLiE; BiD&SB; BioIn 2, 3, 4, 5, 7, 8, 9, 11, 12, 16, 18, 19; BritAu; BritWr 2; CamBiEn; CamGEL; CamGLE; CamGWoT; CasWL; ChamBiD; ChhPo; CnDBLB 1; CnE&AP; CnThe; CroE&S; CrtT 1, 4; CyWA 58; DcArts; DcEnA; DcEnL; DcEuL; DcLEL; DcNaB; DramC 2; EncWB 98; EncWT; Ent; EvLB; GrWrEL DR; LinLib L, S; LitC 33; LngCEL; McGEWB; McGEWD 72, 84; MouLC 1; NewC; NewCBEL; NotNAT A, B; OxCEng 67; OxCThe 67, 83; PenC ENG; PlP&P; RAdv 14, 13-2; REn; REnWD; WebE&AL; WhDW; WorLitC

Webster, Margaret
American. Actor, Director
Revived Shakespeare on Broadway stage, 1930s-40s; daughter of May Whitty.
b. Mar 15, 1905 in New York, New York
d. Nov 13, 1972 in London, England
Source: AmAu&B; AmNatBi; BiE&WWA; BioIn 1, 2, 8, 9, 10, 12, 16, 17, 19, 20, 24; CamGWoT; ChamBiD; CnThe; ConAu 37R; CurBio 40, 50, 73, 73N; DcAmB S9; GrStDi; InWom, SUP; MetOEnc; NewYTBE 72; NotAW MOD; NotNAT A, B; NotWoAT; ObitT 1971; OxCAmT 84; OxCThe 67, 83; REn; TheaDir; WhAm 5; WhoAmW 58, 64, 66, 68, 70, 72, 74; WhoThe 72, 77; WhScrn 77, 83

Webster, Mike
[Michael Lewis Webster]
American. Football Player
Eight-time all-pro center, Pittsburgh, 1974-88; KC Chiefs, 1989-90; won four Super Bowls.
b. Mar 18, 1952 in Tomahawk, Wisconsin
Source: BiDAmSp FB; BioIn 12, 14, 15; FootReg 87; NewYTBS 80, 85

Webster, Noah
American. Lexicographer, Author
Compiled American Dictionary of the English Language, 1828; his work helped standardize American pronunciation.
b. Oct 16, 1758 in West Hartford, Connecticut

d. May 28, 1843 in New Haven, Connecticut
Source: ABCMeAm; Alli; AmAu; AmAu&B; AmBi; AmNatBi; AmRef; AmSocL; AmWrBE; ApCAB; BbD; Benet 87, 96; BenetAL 91; BiDAmEd; BiDAmJo; BiD&SB; BiInAmS; BioIn 1, 2, 3, 4, 5, 6, 7, 8, 9, 10, 11, 12, 13, 14, 15, 16, 17, 19, 20, 24; BlkwCE; BlkwEAR; CamBiEn; CamDcAB; CasWL; CelCen; ChamBiD; ChhPo S3; CnDAL; CyAL 1; CyEd; DcAmAu; DcAmB; DcAmMeB, 84; DcBiPP; DcEnL; DcInv; DcLB 1, 37, 42, 43, 73; DcLEL; DcNAA; Dis&D; Drake; EncAB-H 1974, 1996; EncCRAm; EncWB 98; EvLB; FrTalk; HarEnUS; JrnUS; LegTOT; LinLib L, S; McGEWB; MemAm; MouLC 3; NatCAB 2; NinCLC 30; OxCAmH; OxCAmL 65, 83, 95; OxCEng 67, 85, 95; PenC AM; REn; REnAL; TwCBDA; WebAB 74, 79; WebE&AL; WhAm HS; WhDW; WorAl; WorAlBi

Webster, Paul Francois
American. Lyricist
Wrote over 500 songs including Oscar-winning "Shadow of Your Smile," 1965.
b. Dec 20, 1907 in New York, New York
d. Mar 22, 1984 in Beverly Hills, California
Source: AmPS; BiE&WWA; ConAu 112; VarWW 85; WhoAm 82

Webster, William Hedgcock
American. Government Official
FBI director, 1978-87; director, CIA, 1987-91.
b. Mar 6, 1924 in Saint Louis, Missouri
Source: BiDFedJ A; BioIn 11, 12, 14, 15, 16; CamDcAB; EncAInt; IntWW 78, 79, 80, 81, 82, 83, 89, 91, 93, 97, 98, 2000; NewYTBS 78, 87, 88; WhoAm 74, 76, 78, 80, 82, 84, 86, 88, 90, 92, 94, 95, 96, 97, 98, 99, 2000; WhoAmL 79, 83, 85, 87; WhoAmP 91; WhoE 95; WhoGov 77; WhoMW 74, 76; WorAlBi

Wechsberg, Joseph
American. Author, Journalist
Wrote for The New Yorker, 1938-75.
b. Aug 29, 1907 in Ostrava, Czechoslovakia
d. Apr 10, 1983 in Vienna, Austria
Source: AmAu&B; Au&Wr 71; BenetAL 91; BiGAW; BioIn 1, 3, 4, 9, 10, 12, 13; BlueB 76; ConAu 34NR, 105, 109; CurBio 55, 83N; EncAJ; EncTwCJ; NewYTBS 83; OxCAmL 65, 83, 95; REnAL; WhAm 8; WhE&EA; WhoAm 74, 76, 78, 80, 82; WhoMus 72; WhoWor 74, 76; WrDr 80, 82, 84

Wechsler, David
American. Psychologist
Wrote popular intelligence test.
b. Jan 12, 1896 in Lespedi, Romania
d. May 2, 1981 in New York, New York
Source: AmMWSc 73S; AmNatBi; BiDcPsy; BiDMoAE; BiDPsy; BioIn 12,

13, 15, 24; CamBiEn; CamDcAB;
ConAu 103; IntEnSS 79; RAdv 14;
ScrEAmL 1; WhAm 7; WhoAm 74, 76;
WhoWorJ 72

Wechsler, James Arthur
American. Author, Journalist
Columnist, editor, *New York Post.*
b. Oct 31, 1915 in New York, New York
d. Sep 11, 1983 in New York, New
    York
Source: *AmAu&B; AnObit 1983;
BiDAmNC; BioIn 1, 3, 6, 9, 11, 13;
ConAu 101; IntWW 74; NewYTBS 83;
ScrEAmL 1; WhAm 8; WhoAm 82;
WhoE 74; WhoWor 74; WhoWorJ 72*

Weddell, James
English. Explorer
Made voyage to S Pole, 1822-24; sea
    named after him.
b. Aug 24, 1787 in Ostend, Austria
d. Sep 9, 1834 in London, England
Source: *Alli; BioIn 14; CamBiEn;
ChamBiD; DcNaB; NewCol 75;
OxCShps; WhDW; WhWE; WorAl;
WorAlBi*

Wedekind, Frank
German. Dramatist
Expressionist, social critic; plays on
    sexual issues include *Pandora's Box,*
    1918; play's character, Lulu, subject of
    Alban Berg's opera, *Lulu,* 1934.
b. Jul 24, 1864 in Hannover, Hannover
d. Mar 9, 1918 in Munich, Germany
Source: *AtlBL; Benet 87, 96; BioIn 1, 2,
5, 7, 8, 10, 15, 18, 22; CamBiEn;
CamGWoT; CasWL; ChamBiD; ClDMEL
47, 80; CnDWLB 2; CnMD; CnThe;
ConAu 104; CyWA 58; DcArts; EncWB
98; EncWL 1, 2, 2S, 3; EncWT; Ent;
EuWr 8; EvEuW; GrFLW; LinLib L, S;
LngCTC; MajMD 1; McGEWB;
McGEWD 72, 84; ModGL; ModWD;
NewEOp 71; NotNAT A, B; OxCGer 76,
86, 97; OxCThe 67, 83; PenC EUR;
RAdv 14, 13-2; REn; REnWD; TwCA,
SUP; TwCLC 7; TwCWr; WhDW;
WhoTwCL*

Wedemeyer, Albert Coady
American. Military Leader
Army general, military planner;
    originated WW II "Victory Program,"
    which eventually led to invasion of
    Normandy, June 1944.
b. Jul 9, 1897 in Omaha, Nebraska
d. Dec 17, 1989 in Fort Belvoir, Virginia
Source: *BiDWWGF; BioIn 1, 2, 3, 5, 9,
11, 13, 14, 16; CamDcAB; ConAu 130;
CurBio 45, 90, 90N; DcAmMiB;
FacFETw; NewYTBS 89; PeoHis;
PolProf T; ScrEAmL 2; WebAMB;
WhAm 10; WhoAm 76, 78, 80, 82, 84,
86, 88; WhoWor 74, 76, 78; WhWW-II*

Wedgwood, C(icely) V(eronica)
English. Historian
Speicalist in 17th century British history;
    wrote *The Thirty Years War,* 1938.
b. Jul 20, 1910
d. Mar 9, 1997 in London, England

Source: *Benet 87; BioIn 4, 16, 17, 23;
CamBiEn; CamGEL; CamGLE;
ChambiD; ConAu 21NR, 67NR, 105,
157; CurBio 97N; DcLEL; EncWB, 98;
GloEncH; IntAu&W 76, 77, 91, 93;
IntWW 74, 75, 78, 83, 89; IntWWW 2;
LngCTC; MajTwCW 1; ModBrL;
NewCBEL; OxCTwCL; REn; WhE&EA;
Who 74, 82, 83, 85, 88, 90, 92; WhoAm
74; WhoAmW 68, 70, 72; WhoWor 74,
76, 78; WrDr 76, 80, 82, 84, 86, 88, 90,
92, 94, 96, 98N*

Wedgwood, Josiah
English. Artist
Founded firm, 1759; invented translucent,
    unglazed semiporcelain called jasper
    ware.
b. Jul 12, 1730 in Burslem, England
d. Jan 3, 1795 in Etruria, England
Source: *Alli; AntBDN M; BioIn 1, 2, 3,
4, 5, 6, 7, 9, 10, 11, 12, 14, 15, 20, 21,
22, 24; BlmGEL; CamBiEn; ChamBiD;
DcArts; DcBiPP; DcD&D; DcInv;
DcNaB; DcScB; Dis&D; EncEnl;
EncHiCA; EncWB 98; EncWM; Entr;
LegTOT; LinLib S; McGDA; McGEWB;
NewC; NewCol 75; OxCBrHi;
OxCDecA; OxCEng 85, 95; OxDcArt;
PenDiDA 89; RanHWDS; WhDW;
WorAl; WorAlBi*

Wedgwood, Thomas
English. Photographer
Credited with inventing several
    photographic processes; never able to
    make an image permanent; son of
    Josiah.
b. May 14, 1771 in Stoke-on-Trent,
    England
d. Jul 11, 1805
Source: *BioIn 4, 10; BlmGEL;
CamDcSc; DcBiPP; DcNaB; ICPEnP;
MacBEP*

Weed, Steven Andrew
American. Educator
Fiance of Patty Hearst at time of
    abduction by SLA; wrote *My Search
    for Patty Hearst,* 1976.
b. 1947
Source: *BioIn 10*

Weed, Thurlow
American. Journalist, Politician
Influential newspaper owner, head of NY
    state Whig party; helped elect Rep.
    presidential candidates, 1840s-50s.
b. Nov 15, 1797 in Cairo, New York
d. Nov 22, 1882 in New York, New
    York
Source: *ABCMeAm; Alli, SUP;
AmAu&B; AmBi; AmNatBi; ApCAB;
BbD; BenetAL 91; BiDAmJo; BiD&SB;
BioIn 1, 8, 9, 14, 16, 17; CyAG;
DcAmAu; DcAmB; DcNAA; Drake;
EncAB-H 1974, 1996; EncAJ; EncWB
98; HarEnUS; JrnUS; LinLib L;
McGEWB; NatCAB 3; OxCAmH;
PolPar; REnAL; TwCBDA; WebAB 74,
79; WhAm HS; WhCiWar*

Weede, Robert
American. Singer
Baritone with NY Met., San Francisco
    Opera; starred in Broadway's *Most
    Happy Fella,* 1956; Tony nominee for
    Cry for Us All, 1970.
b. Feb 22, 1903 in Baltimore, Maryland
d. Jul 10, 1972 in Walnut Creek,
    California
Source: *BakBDTw; BiDAmM;
BiE&WWA; BioIn 1, 4, 9; CurBio 57,
72, 72N; DcAmB S9; EncMT; MetOEnc;
NewGrDA 86; NewGrDO; NewYTBE 72;
NotNAT B*

Weeks, Sinclair
American. Government Official
Secretary of Commerce, 1953-58, under
    Eisenhower.
b. Jun 15, 1893 in West Newton,
    Massachusetts
d. Jan 27, 1972 in Concord,
    Massachusetts
Source: *AmNatBi; BiDrAC; BiDrUSC
89; BiDrUSE 71, 89; BioIn 3, 4, 5, 9,
10, 11; CurBio 53, 72, 72N; DcAmB S9;
LinLib S; NewYTBE 72; ObitOF 79;
PolProf E; WhAm 5; WhAmP*

Weems, Mason Locke
American. Clergy, Author
Episcopal minister was also a book
    salesman and popular writer; he is best
    known for his fictionalized biographies
    of the American founding fathers.
b. Oct 1, 1759 in Anne Arundel County,
    Maryland
d. May 23, 1825 in Beaufort, South
    Carolina
Source: *Alli; AmAu; AmAu&B; AmNatBi;
AmWrBE; Benet 87, 96; BenetAL 91;
BiD&SB; BiDSA; BioIn 3, 4, 5, 6, 10,
12, 13, 14, 15, 16; CamBiEn;
CamDcAB; ChamBiD; CyAL 1;
DcAmAu; DcAmB; DcArts; DcLB 30, 37,
42; DcNAA; EncALit; EncAR; EncSoH;
EncWB 98; McGEWB; MemAm;
OxCAmH; OxCAmL 65, 83, 95; PenC
AM; REn; REnAL; WebAB 74, 79;
WebE&AL; WhAm HS*

Weems, Ted
[Wilfred Theodore Weems]
American. Bandleader
Led popular dance style band, late
    1920s-40s; wrote "The Martins and
    the Coys," 1930s.
b. 1900 in Pitcairn, Pennsylvania
d. May 6, 1963 in Tulsa, Oklahoma
Source: *ASCAP 66; BioIn 6, 9; WhoHol
B; WhScrn 74, 77*

Wegener, Alfred Lothar
German. Geologist, Explorer
Expert on Greenland who was one of
    first to propose continental drift
    theory, 1910.
b. Nov 1, 1880 in Berlin, Germany
d. Nov 1930, Greenland
Source: *AsBiEn; BiESc; BioIn 10, 12,
14, 15, 20, 23, 24; CamBiEn; ChamBiD;
DcScB; EncWB 98; ExplAnT; FacFETw;
InnESci; InSci; LarDcSc; McGCEnS;*

McGEWB; RanHWDS; SciMath; WhDW;
WhWE

Wegman, William George
American. Artist
Known for work in photography of dogs
detailing the dog's innate dignity
contrasted with human consumerism.
b. Feb 12, 1942 in Holyoke,
Massachusetts
Source: *AmArt; BioIn 13, 16; ConArt 89;*
ConPhot 88; CurBio 92; ICPEnP A;
News 91-1; PrintW 85; WhoAm 90;
WhoAmA 91; WhoArt 80

Wehrwein, Austin Carl
American. Journalist
With *Minneapolis Star*, 1966-82; won
1953 Pulitzer for int'l. reporting.
b. Jan 12, 1916 in Austin, Texas
Source: *ConAu 77; EncTwCJ; WhoAm*
74, 76, 78, 80, 82, 84, 86, 88, 90, 98,
99, 2000; WhoMW 93, 96, 98; WhoPul

Weicker, Lowell Palmer, Jr.
American. Politician
Independent governor of CT, 1991—;
Republican US senator, 1971-89.
b. May 16, 1931 in Paris, France
Source: *AlmAP 92; BiDrAC; BiDrUSC*
89; BioIn 9, 10, 11, 13, 15; BlueB 76;
CngDr 87; CurBio 74, 93; IntWW 74,
75, 76, 77, 78, 79, 80, 81, 82, 83, 89,
91, 93, 97, 98, 2000; News 93-1;
NewYTBS 90, 91; PolsAm 84; WhoAm
74, 76, 78, 80, 82, 84, 86, 88, 92, 94,
95; WhoAmP 73, 75, 77, 79, 81, 83, 85,
87, 89, 91, 93, 95, 97, 1999; WhoE 74,
89, 91, 93, 95; WhoGov 72, 75, 77;
WhoWor 80, 82, 84, 87, 89, 93, 95;
WorAl; WorAlBi

Weidenbaum, Murray Lew
American. Government Official,
Economist
Chm., Council of Economic Advisers,
1981-82; director, Center for Study of
American Business, 1975-81, 1982-95.
b. Feb 10, 1927 in New York, New
York
Source: *AmEA 74; AmMWSc 73S, 78S;*
BioIn 9, 12, 13; BlueB 76; ConAu 37R;
CurBio 82; IntWW 81, 82, 83, 89, 91,
93, 97, 98, 2000; NewYTBS 81; Who 82,
83, 85, 88, 90, 92, 94, 98, 99, 2000;
WhoAm 74, 76, 78, 80, 82, 84, 86, 88,
90, 92, 94, 95, 96, 97, 98, 99, 2000;
WhoAmP 73, 75, 77, 79, 81, 83, 85, 87,
89, 91, 93, 95, 97, 1999; WhoFI 83, 85,
87, 89, 94, 96; WhoGov 72; WhoMW
92; WrDr 86, 92

Weidenreich, Franz
German. Anatomist, Anthropologist
Known for his outstanding contributions
in the areas of hematology and human
evolution.
b. Jun 7, 1873 in Edenkoben, Germany
d. Jul 11, 1948
Source: *BioIn 1, 2, 13, 20; CamBiEn;*
CamDcAB; ChamBiD; ConAu 164;
DcAmB S4; DcNAA; EncHuEv; EncWB

98; HisPhAn; IntDcAn; LarDcSc;
McGEWB; NotTwCS 1

Weidman, Charles Edward, Jr.
American. Dancer
Best known for enhancing the
participation of men in dance.
b. Jul 22, 1901 in Lincoln, Nebraska
d. Jul 15, 1975 in New York, New York
Source: *AmNatBi; BiE&WWA;*
CamBiEn; CamDcAB; CamDcAB;
CurBio 42; WhAm 6; WhoAm 74

Weidman, Jerome
American. Author
Won Pulitzer for play, *Fiorello,* 1960.
b. Apr 4, 1913 in New York, New York
d. Oct 6, 1998 in New York, New York
Source: *AmAu&B; AmNov; Au&Wr 71;*
AuNews 2; AuSpks; Benet 87, 96;
BenetAL 91; BiE&WWA; BioIn 2, 3, 4,
5, 6, 7, 8, 10, 11, 14, 15, 22, 24; BlueB
76; CnDAL; ConAmD; ConAu 1NR, 1R,
171; ConDr 73, 77, 88D, 93; ConJeAN;
ConLC 7; ConNov 72, 76, 82, 86, 91;
ConTFT 6, 24; CurBio 42, 1999; DcLB
28; DcLEL; DrAF 76; DrAPF 80, 87,
91; EncALit; EncMT; IntAu&W 76, 77,
82; JeAmFiW; LegTOT; LngCTC;
NewCBMT; NewYTBS 98; NotNAT;
Novels; OxCAmL 65, 83, 95; PenC AM;
REn; REnAL; RGTwCWr; TwCA, SUP;
WhE&EA; WhNAA; WhoAm 74, 76, 78,
80, 82, 84, 86, 88, 90, 92, 94, 95, 96,
97, 98; WhoAmJ 80; WhoEnt 98;
WhoPul; WhoThe 72, 77, 81; WhoTwCL;
WhoUSWr 88; WhoWorJ 72, 78;
WhoWrEP 89, 92, 95; WorAu 1900;
WrDr 76, 80, 82, 84, 86, 88, 90, 92, 94,
96, 98, 99

Wei Hsiao-Wen-ti
Chinese. Emperor
Sixth emperor of the Northern Wei
dynasty, he represented the zenith of
the dynasty's power and probably laid
the foundation for its subsequent
decline.
b. Oct 13, 467 in P'ing-ch'eng, China
d. Apr 26, 499 in Hupei, China

Weil, Andrew (Thomas)
American. Physician
Studied effects of smoking marijuana on
patients, proving that the "high"
experienced comes from within rather
than the drug; wrote *Spontaneous*
Healing, 1995.
b. Jun 8, 1942 in Philadelphia,
Pennsylvania
Source: *AmMWSc 79, 82, 86, 89, 92, 95,*
98; BiDrAPA 89; BioIn 9, 10, 12;
ConAu 20NR, 43NR, 73; CurBio 96;
NewAgE 90; WhoAm 98, 99, 2000;
WhoEmL 89; WhoWest 87

Weil, Joseph R
"Yellow Kid"
American. Criminal
Made over $8 million as a con man;
known for innovative swindles.
b. Jun 30, 1875? in Chicago, Illinois
d. Feb 26, 1976 in Chicago, Illinois

Source: *BioIn 1, 4, 5, 10; EncACr;*
NewYTBS 76

Weil, Simone
French. Philosopher
Mystic; activist in French Resistance,
WW II; wrote *Gravity and Grace,*
published 1952.
b. Feb 3, 1909 in Paris, France
d. Aug 24, 1943 in Ashford, England
Source: *Benet 87, 2S, 3; EncWomW;*
EuWr 12; EvEuW; FacFETw; FrenWW;
GuFrLit 1; IlEncMy; InWom SUP;
LegTOT; LiExTwC; LngCTC; LuthC 75;
MakMC; ModFrL; ModRL; ModWoWr;
OxCEng 85, 95; OxCFr; OxCPhil; PenC
EUR; RAdv 14, 13-2; REn; ThTwC 87;
TwCA SUP; TwCLC 23; TwCWr;
WhoChr; WhoTwCL; WomWrGB;
WorAl; WorAlBi

Weiland, Cooney
[Ralph Weiland]
Canadian. Hockey Player
Center, 1928-39, mostly with Boston;
won Art Ross Trophy, 1930; Hall of
Fame, 1971.
b. Nov 5, 1904 in Seaforth, Ontario,
Canada
d. Jul 4, 1985 in Boston, Massachusetts
Source: *BioIn 14; HocEn; WhoHcky 73;*
WhoSpor

Weill, Claudia
American. Director
Films include *It's My Turn,* 1980;
Girlfriends, 1977.
b. 1947 in New York, New York
Source: *BioIn 10, 11, 12; ConTFT 1;*
FilmEn; HalFC 84, 88; IntMPA 92, 94,
96; InWom SUP; MiSFD 9; NewYTBS
78; ReelWom; WhoAm 82, 84, 86, 88;
WomFilm; WomWMM A

Weill, Kurt
American. Composer
Best known work *Threepenny Opera,*
1928; also wrote *One Touch of Venus,*
and "September Song."
b. Mar 2, 1900 in Dessau, Germany
d. Apr 3, 1950 in New York, New York
Source: *AmComp; AmNatBi; AmPS;*
AmSong; ASCAP 66, 80; AtlBL; BakBD
78, 84; Benet 87, 96; BenetAL 91;
BestMus; BiDAmM; BioIn 1, 2, 3, 4, 5,
6, 8, 9, 10, 11, 12, 13, 14, 15, 16, 18,
19, 20, 21, 22, 23; BriBkM 80;
CamBiEn; CamDcAB; CamHAL;
ChamBiD; CmOp; CmpEPM;
CndCPOM; CompSN, SUP; ConAmC 76,
82; ConMus 12; CurBio 41, 50; DancEn
78; DcAmB S4; DcCM; DcCom 77;
EncMT; EncTR, 91; EncWB 98; EncWT;
FacFETw; FilmgC; HalFC 80, 84, 88;
IntDcOp; LegTOT; MakMC; McGEWB;
MetOEnc; MorBAP; Music; MusMk;
NewAmDM; NewCBMT; NewEOp 71;
NewGrDA 86; NewGrDM 80; NewOxM;
NewYTBS 87; NotNAT B; Opera;
OxCAmT 84; OxCEng 85, 95; OxCFilm;
OxCGer 76, 86, 97; OxCMus;
OxCPMus; OxDcOp; PenDiMP A;
PenEncP; PlP&P; PopAmC, SUP; REn;

Songw; WebAB 74, 79; WhAm 3; WhDW; WhThe; WorAl; WorAlBi; WorEFlm

Weill, Sanford I.
American. Business Executive
CEO of Shearson/Lehman Bros. Inc. 1960-1984; CEO of Primerica Corp. 1989—; chairman and CEO of Travelers Group, 1996-98; co-CEO, Citigroup, 1998—.
b. Mar 16, 1933 in New York, New York
Source: *BioIn 13, 14, 15, 16; CurBio 1999; Dun&B 90, 98; IntWW 91, 97, 98, 2000; NewYTBS 98; St&PR 84, 87, 98, 99, 2000; WhoAm 84, 90, 98, 99, 2000; WhoE 83, 91, 99; WhoFI 00, 83, 92, 98; WhoWor 87, 98, 99, 2000*

Wein, George Theodore
American. Musician, Producer
Founded Newport Jazz Festival, 1954; produces jazz festivals throughout country.
b. Oct 3, 1925 in Boston, Massachusetts
Source: *BiDAmM; BiDJaz; BioIn 13, 14; CamDcAB; CmpEM; CurBio 85; NewGrDJ 88; WhoAm 84, 86, 88; WhoEnt 92, 98*

Weinberg, Chester
American. Fashion Designer
Director of design/production, Calvin Klein Jeans, 1983-85; won Coty, 1970.
b. Sep 23, 1930 in New York, New York
d. Apr 24, 1985 in New York, New York
Source: *BioIn 14; FairDF US; NewYTBS 85; WhAm 9; WhoAm 78, 80, 82, 84; WhoE 74; WhoFash 88; WorFshn*

Weinberg, Max M
[E Street Band]
"Mighty One"
American. Musician
Drummer with Bruce Springsteen's band since 1974.
b. Apr 13, 1951 in South Orange, New Jersey
Source: *BioIn 15; WhoRocM 82*

Weinberg, Moshe
Israeli. Olympic Athlete, Victim
One of 11 members of Israeli Olympic team kidnapped and killed by Arab terrorists during Summer Olympic Games.
b. 1940?
d. Sep 5, 1972 in Munich, Germany (West)
Source: *BioIn 9*

Weinberg, Steven
American. Physicist
Shared 1979 Nobel Prize in physics with Sheldon Glashow, Abdus Salam.
b. May 3, 1933 in New York, New York
Source: *AmMWSc 73P, 76P, 79, 82, 86, 89, 92, 95, 98; BiEsc; BioIn 12, 15; BlueB 76; CamBiEn; CamDcAB;*

CamDcSc; ChamBiD; ConAu 5NR, 36NR, 53; DrAS 99P; EncWB 98; FacFETw; IntWW 74, 75, 76, 77, 78, 79, 80, 81, 82, 83, 89, 91, 93, 97, 98, 2000; LarDcSc; McGCEnS; McGMS 80; NobelP; NotTwCS 1; RAdv 14, 13-5; RanHWDS; Who 82, 83, 85, 88, 90, 92, 94, 98, 99, 2000; WhoAm 74, 76, 78, 80, 82, 84, 86, 88, 90, 92, 94, 95, 96, 97, 98, 99, 2000; WhoE 81, 85, 86; WhoFrS 84; WhoNob, 90, 95; WhoScEn 94, 96, 2000; WhoSSW 84, 86, 88, 91, 93, 95, 97, 99; WhoTech 82, 84, 89, 95; WhoWor 80, 82, 84, 87, 89, 91, 93, 95, 96, 97, 98, 99, 2000; WorAlBi; WorScD; WrDr 90, 92, 94, 96, 98, 99, 2000

Weinberger, Caspar Willard
"Cap the Knife"
American. Government Official
Secretary of HEW, 1973-75; Secretary of Defense, 1981-87; chm., *Forbes* magazine, 1989—.
b. Aug 18, 1917 in San Francisco, California
Source: *AmPolLe; BiDrUSE 89; BioIn 8, 9, 10, 12, 13, 14, 15, 16; BlueB 76; CamBiEn; CamDcAB; ChamBiD; CngDr 74, 81, 83, 85, 87; ColdWar 2; ConAu 133; CurBio 73; EncWB; IntWW 79, 80, 81, 82, 83, 89, 91, 93, 98, 2000; NatCAB 63N; NewYTBE 72; NewYTBS 80, 89; Who 82, 83, 85, 88, 90, 92, 94, 98, 99, 2000; WhoAm 74, 76, 78, 80, 82, 84, 86, 88, 90, 92, 94, 95, 96, 97, 98, 99, 2000; WhoAmL 79; WhoAmP 73, 75, 77, 79, 81, 83, 85, 87, 89, 91, 93, 95, 97, 1999; WhoE 81, 83, 85, 86, 89, 91, 93, 95, 97, 99; WhoEnt 98; WhoFI 00, 74, 92, 94, 96, 98; WhoGov 72, 75, 77; WhoIntA 2; WhoSSW 75; WhoWor 82, 84, 87, 89, 91, 93, 95, 96, 97, 98, 99, 2000; WorAlBi; WrDr 98, 99, 2000*

Weinberger, Edwin B
Writer
Won Emmys for "Mary Tyler Moore Show"; "Taxi."
Source: *VarWW 85*

Weinberger, Jaromir
American. Composer
Wrote immensely popular Bohemian-style opera, *Schwanda the Bagpiper*, 1927.
b. Jan 8, 1896 in Prague, Bohemia
d. Aug 6, 1967 in Saint Petersburg, Florida
Source: *AmComp; ASCAP 66, 80; BakBD 78, 84, 92; BakBDTw; BiDAmM; BioIn 1, 2, 4, 8, 16; BriBkM 80; CamBiEn; ChamBiD; CmOp; CompSN; ConAmC 76, 82; DcCom&M 79; IntDcOp; IntWWM 77, 80; MetOEnc; NewEOp 71; NewGrDA 86; NewGrDM 80; NewGrDO; NewOxM; OxCMus; OxDcOp; PenDiMP A*

Weingarten, Violet Brown
American. Journalist, Author
Novels include *Half a Marriage*, 1976; films include *Debbie*, 1964.

b. Feb 23, 1915 in San Francisco, California
d. Jul 17, 1976 in New York, New York
Source: *ConAu 7NR, 9R, 65; ForWC 70; IntAu&W 77; NewYTBS 76; SmATA 3, 27N*

Weingartner, Felix
[Paul Felix Weingartner]
Austrian. Conductor, Composer
Succeeded Gustav Mahler as director of Vienna State Opera, 1908-11, 1930s; wrote operas, seven symphonies.
b. Jun 2, 1863 in Zara, Austria
d. May 7, 1942 in Winterthur, Switzerland
Source: *BakBD 78, 84; BioIn 2, 4, 6, 8, 11, 19; BriBkM 80; CmOp; CurBio 42; FacFETw; IntDcOp; MetOEnc; MusMk; MusSN; NewAmDM; NewEOp 71; NewGrDM 80; NewOxM; OxCMus; OxDcOp; PenDiMP; WhE&EA; WhoLA*

Weinman, Adolph A
American. Sculptor
Designed 1916 dime, half dollar.
b. Dec 11, 1870 in Karlsruhe, Germany
d. Aug 8, 1952 in Port Chester, New York
Source: *NatCAB 62; WhAm 3; WhAmArt 85; WhoAmA 84N*

Weinmesiter, Arnie
[Arnold Weinmesiter]
American. Football Player
Tackle, 1948-53, mostly with NY Giants; Hall of Fame, 1984.
b. Mar 23, 1923 in Rhein, Saskatchewan, Canada
d. Jun 28, 2000 in Seattle, Washington
Source: *BiDAmSp FB; BioIn 2, 3; WhoFtbl 74*

Weinstein, Bob
American. Film Executive
Co-founder and co-chairman, Miramax Films, 1978—.
b. Oct 18, 1954 in New York, New York
Source: *CurBio 97*

Weinstein, Harvey
American. Film Executive
Co-founder and co-chairman, Miramax Films, 1978—.
b. Mar 19, 1952 in New York, New York
Source: *ConTFT 21; CurBio 97*

Weintal, Edward
American. Journalist
Award-winning diplomatic correspondent *Newsweek*, 1944-69; special consultant, USIA, 1967-73.
b. Mar 21, 1901 in Warsaw, Poland
d. Jan 24, 1973 in Washington, District of Columbia
Source: *BioIn 9; ConAu 41R; NewYTBE 73; WhAm 5*

Weintraub, Jerry
American. Producer, Agent
Talent agent, clients include Frank
  Sinatra, Neil Diamond, John Denver.
b. Sep 26, 1937 in New York, New
  York
Source: *BioIn 11, 12, 15; ConNews 86-
  1; ConTFT 7, 14; IntMPA 84, 86, 88,
  92, 94, 96; WhoAm 84, 86, 95, 96, 97,
  98; WhoEnt 92A, 98*

Weir, Benjamin T
American. Hostage
Minister in Lebanon seized by Islamic
  Jihad May 6, 1984 and released
  September 14, 1985.
Source: *BioIn 14, 15, 16*

Weir, Bob
[The Grateful Dead; Robert Hall Weir]
American. Singer, Musician
Recorded solo album *Bombs Away,*
  1978.
b. Oct 16, 1949 in San Francisco,
  California
Source: *RkOn 85*

Weir, John F(erguson)
American. Artist
Industrial scenes include *Forging the
  Shaft;* son of Robert.
b. Aug 28, 1841 in West Point, New
  York
d. Apr 8, 1926 in Providence, Rhode
  Island
Source: *AmBi; AmNatBi; ApCAB;
  ArtsNiC; BioIn 4, 12, 23; BriEAA;
  DcAmArt; DcAmAu; DcAmB; DcNAA;
  EarABI SUP; HarEnUS; NatCAB 6;
  OxCAmH; TwCBDA; WhAm 1;
  WhAmArt 85*

Weir, Julian Alden
American. Artist
Semi-Impressionist works include *The
  Green Bodice;* son of Robert.
b. Aug 30, 1852 in West Point, New
  York
d. Dec 8, 1919 in New York, New York
Source: *AmBi; AmNatBi; ApCAB; BioIn
  5, 9, 20, 21, 22; BriEAA; CamDcAB;
  DcAmArt; DcAmB; LinLib S; NatCAB
  11, 22; OxCAmH; OxCAmL 65;
  TwCBDA; WhAm 1; WhAmArt 85*

Weir, Peter
Australian. Director
Compared with Alfred Hitchcock for
  ability to combine everyday life with
  unspeakable terror: *The Year of Living
  Dangerously,* 1983.
b. Aug 8, 1944 in Sydney, Australia
Source: *BiDFilm 94; BioIn 14, 15, 16,
  24; ConAu 113, 123; ConLC 20;
  ConTFT 1, 6, 13; CurBio 84; FacFETw;
  HalFC 84, 88; IntDcF 1-2, 2-2; IntMPA
  84, 86, 88, 92, 94, 96; IntWW 91;
  LegTOT; MiSFD 9; Who 92; WhoEnt
  92; WhoWor 91; WorFDir 2*

Weir, Robert W
American. Artist, Educator
Noted for *Embarkation of the Pilgrims,*
  in Capitol rotunda, 1836-40.
b. Jun 18, 1803 in New Rochelle, New
  York
d. May 1, 1889 in New York, New York
Source: *Alli; AmBi; ApCAB; ArtsNiC;
  BiAUS; DcAmArt; DcAmB; Drake;
  EarABI, SUP; TwCBDA; WhAm HS*

Weisgall, Hugo (David)
Czech. Composer, Conductor
Operas include *Night,* 1932; *The Tenor,*
  1950; ballets include *Quest,* 1938.
b. Oct 13, 1912 in Ivanice,
  Czechoslovakia
d. Mar 11, 1997 in Manhasset, New
  York
Source: *AmComp; ASCAP 66, 80;
  BakBD 78, 84, 92; BakBDTw; BiDAmM;
  BioIn 7, 8, 9, 18; BriBkM 80;
  CamDcAB; CompSN, SUP; ConAmC 76,
  82; CpmDNM 79, 81, 82; DcCM;
  IntWWM 77, 80, 90; MetOEnc;
  NewAmDM; NewEOp 71; NewGrDA 86;
  NewGrDM 80; NewGrDO; NewYTBS 76;
  OxDcOp; WhAm 12; WhoAm 74, 76, 78,
  80, 82, 84, 86, 88, 90, 92, 94, 95, 96,
  97, 98; WhoAmM 83; WhoEnt 98;
  WhoMus 72; WhoWor 74, 76; WhoWorJ
  72*

Weiskopf, Bob
American. Writer, Producer
Won Emmys for "Red Skelton Show,"
  1971; "All in the Family," 1978.
b. Mar 13, 1914 in Chicago, Illinois
Source: *ConAu 118, 123, X; ConTFT 2;
  VarWW 85*

Weiskopf, Tom
[Thomas Daniel Weiskopf]
American. Golfer
Turned pro, 1964; won British Open,
  1973; has won $2.5 million on PGA
  tour. Won U.S. Senior Open, 1995.
b. Nov 9, 1942 in Massillon, Ohio
Source: *BiDAmSp OS; BioIn 10, 12, 13;
  BioNews 74; CurBio 73; NewYTBE 73;
  NewYTBS 81; WhoAm 74, 76, 78, 80,
  82, 84, 86; WhoGolf; WhoIntG*

Weismann, August Friedrich Leopold
German. Biologist
Originator of germ-plasm theory of
  heredity; wrote *The Germ Plasm,*
  1892.
b. Jan 17, 1834 in Frankfurt am Main,
  Germany
d. Nov 6, 1914 in Freiburg, Germany
Source: *AsBiEn; BbD; BiESc; CamBiEn;
  ChamBiD; DcScB; LarDcSc; McGEWB;
  NewCol 75; RanHWDS*

Weiss, George Martin
American. Baseball Executive
With NY Yankees in several capacities,
  1932-62, helping to build team in
  dynasty yrs; first pres., NY Mets,
  1962-67; Hall of Fame, 1971.

b. Jun 23, 1894 in New Haven,
  Connecticut
d. Aug 13, 1972 in Greenwich,
  Connecticut
Source: *DcAmB S9; NatCAB 57; WhAm
  5; WhoProB 73*

Weiss, Peter Ulrich
German. Dramatist
Wrote *Marat/Sade;* won Tony, 1966.
b. Nov 8, 1916 in Nowawes, Germany
d. May 10, 1982 in Stockholm, Sweden
Source: *CamBiEn; CasWL; ChamBiD;
  ConAu 3NR, 106; CurBio 68; NotNAT;
  OxCFilm; OxCGer 76; PenC EUR;
  PlP&P, A; REnWD; TwCWr; Who 82;
  WhoThe 81; WhoWor 74; WorAu 1950;
  WorEFlm*

Weiss, Ted
[Theodore S Weiss]
American. Politician
Dem. congressman from NY, 1976-87;
  advocated end to arms race.
b. Sep 17, 1927 in Budapest, Hungary
d. Sep 14, 1992 in New York, New
  York
Source: *AlmAP 88, 92; AnObit 1992;
  BiDrUSC 89; BiGAW; BioIn 14, 18, 19;
  CngDr 77, 79, 81, 83, 85, 87, 89, 91;
  CurBio 85, 92N; DrAPF 91; NewYTBS
  92; PolsAm 84; WhoAm 78, 80, 82, 84,
  86, 90; WhoAmJ 80; WhoAmP 77, 79,
  81, 83, 85, 87, 89, 91; WhoE 79, 85, 91*

Weiss, Theodore (Russell)
American. Poet, Editor
Poem verses include *A Slow Fuse,* 1984;
  editor, publisher, *Quarterly Review
  Literature,* 1943—.
b. Dec 16, 1916 in Reading,
  Pennsylvania
Source: *AmAu&B; BenetAL 91; BioIn
  10, 12, 15; BlueB 76; ConAu 2AS, 9R,
  46NR; ConLC 3, 8, 14; ConPo 70, 75,
  80, 85, 91, 96; CroCAP; DcLB 5;
  DcLEL 1940; DrAP 75; DrAPF 80;
  DrAS 74E, 78E, 82E; EncALit; IntAu&W
  77, 82, 86; IntWWP 77, 82; LinLib L;
  OxCTwCL; OxCTwCP; PenC AM;
  WhoAm 74, 76, 78, 80, 82, 84, 86, 88,
  90, 94, 95, 96, 97, 98, 99, 2000;
  WhoAmJ 80; WhoE 74; WhoEnt 98;
  WhoUSWr 88; WhoWorJ 72; WhoWrEP
  89, 92, 95; WorAu 1950; WrDr 76, 80,
  82, 84, 86, 88, 90, 92, 94, 96, 98, 99,
  2000*

Weiss, Walt(er William, Jr.)
American. Baseball Player
Shortstop, Oakland, 1987—; AL rookie
  of year, 1988.
b. Nov 28, 1963 in Tuxedo, New York
Source: *Ballpl 90; BaseReg 88; BioIn 16*

Weissenberg, Alexis Sigismund
American. Pianist
Gives over 85 int'l concerts yearly; has
  made several records.
b. Jul 26, 1929 in Sofia, Bulgaria
Source: *BakBD 84; BiDAmM; BioIn 8,
  11, 12, 13, 14; BriBkM 80; CurBio 78;
  IntWW 91; IntWWM 90; MusSN;*

NewAmDM; NewGrDA 86; NewGrDM 80; NewYTBE 71; NotTwCP; PenDiMP; WhoAm 86, 88; WhoSoCE 89; WhoWor 91

Weissmuller, Johnny
[Peter John Weissmuller]
American. Actor, Swimmer
Played Tarzan in 19 movies, 1934-48; won five gold medals in 1924, 1928 Olympics.
b. Jun 2, 1904 in Windber, Pennsylvania
d. Jan 20, 1984 in Acapulco, Mexico
Source: *AmNatBi; AnObit 1984; BiDAmSp BK; BiDFilm 94; BioIn 3, 6, 7, 8, 9, 10, 12, 13, 14, 16, 17, 22, 23, 24; CamBiEn; CmCal; ConAu 111; FacFETw; Film 2; FilmEn; FilmgC; ForYSC; HalFC 80, 84, 88; IntDcF 1-3, 2-3; IntMPA 75, 76, 77, 78, 79, 80, 81, 82; LegTOT; MGM; MotPP; MovMk; NewYTBE 72; NewYTBS 84; OxCFilm; WebAB 74, 79; What 1; WhoHol A; WhoSpor; WorAl; WorAlBi; WorEFlm*

Weitz, Bruce Peter
American. Actor
Played Mick Belker on TV series "Hill Street Blues," 1981-87; won Emmy award, 1984.
b. May 27, 1943 in Norwalk, Connecticut
Source: *BioIn 13, 15; ConNews 85-4; ConTFT 7; VarWW 85; WhoAm 88, 90; WhoEnt 92; WhoTelC*

Weitz, John
American. Fashion Designer
Founded own fashion house, 1954; won Coty, 1974.
b. May 25, 1923 in Berlin, Germany
Source: *BioIn 8, 12; CelR, 90; ConAu 29R; ConDes 84, 90, 97; ConFash; CurBio 79; FairDF US; NewYTBE 72; WhoAm 76, 78, 80, 82, 84, 86, 88, 90, 92, 94, 95, 96, 97, 98, 99, 2000; WhoAmJ 80; WhoFash 88; WhoWor 78, 82, 84, 87, 89, 91, 95; WorFshn*

Wei Yuan
Chinese. Historian, Geographer
One of the first Chinese to study the history and geography of the West, he compiled his research in the *Illustrated Gazetteer of the Countries Overseas.*
b. Apr 23, 1794 in Shaoyang, Hunan, China
d. 1856 in Hangchow, China
Source: *EncWB 98; GloEncH; ModChi*

Weizman, Ezer
Israeli. Politician
Minister of communications, 1984-88; science, 1988-92; elected Pres., 1993.
b. Jun 15, 1924 in Tel Aviv, Palestine
Source: *BioIn 8, 9, 11, 12; ConAu 111; CurBio 79; EncWB, 98; HisEAAC; IntAu&W 86; IntWW 74, 75, 76, 77, 78, 79, 80, 81, 82, 83, 89, 91, 93, 97, 98, 2000; IntYB 79, 80, 81, 82; MidE 78, 79, 80, 81, 82; NewYTBS 78; ProfiWG 98; Who 94, 98, 99, 2000; WhoIntA 2;*

WhoWor 80, 82, 95, 96, 97, 98, 99, 2000; WhoWorJ 78

Weizmann, Chaim
Israeli. Political Leader, Religious Leader
Provisional pres. of Israel, 1948-49; first elected pres., 1949-52; first pres., World Zionist Organization, 1923.
b. Nov 27, 1874 in Grodno, Russia
d. Nov 9, 1952 in Rehovot, Israel
Source: *AsBiEn; BioIn 1, 2, 3, 4, 5, 6, 7, 8, 9, 10, 11, 12, 13, 14, 15, 16, 17, 18, 20, 22, 23, 24; CurBio 42, 48, 52; DcNaB 1951; DcPol; DcScB; EncTR 91; EncWB 98; EncyDCo; FacFETw; GrBr; HisDBrE; HisEAAC; HisWorL; InSci; JeHun; LarDcSc; LegTOT; LinLib L, S; McGEWB; NewYTBS 86; ObitT 1951; PolLCME; WhAm 3, 4; WhWW-II; WorAl; WorAlBi*

Weizsacker, Richard Freiherr von
German. Political Leader
Succeeded Karl Carstens as sixth pres. of W Germany, 1984.
b. Apr 15, 1920 in Stuttgart, Germany
Source: *BioIn 14; CurBio 85; IntWW 91; NewYTBS 84; WhoWor 91*

Wek, Alek
Sudanese. Model
Called "the hottest face in fashion" by *Newsweek* magazine, model known for her very dark skin, very short hair, and distinctive smile, appeared on November 1997 cover of *Elle.*
b. c. 1977, Sudan
Source: *ConBlB 18*

Welch, Bob
[Fleetwood Mac]
American. Musician
Guitarist with Fleetwood Mac, 1971-75; had solo single "Sentimental Lady," 1977.
b. Jul 31, 1946 in Los Angeles, California
Source: *ConAu X; ConMuA 80A; LegTOT; NewYTBS 80; RkOn 78; WhoRock 81; WhoRocM 82*

Welch, Bob
[Robert Lynn Welch]
American. Baseball Player
Pitcher, LA, 1979-87, Oakland, 1988—; his 27 wins in 1990 was most in AL in 22 years; won AL Cy Young Award, 1990.
b. Nov 3, 1956 in Detroit, Michigan
Source: *Ballpl 90; BaseEn 88; BaseReg 88; BioIn 12, 13, 14, 15, 16, 17, 21; ConAu 112; Dun&B 88; News 91, 91-3; WhoAm 94; WhoSpor; WhoWest 94*

Welch, Herbert
American. Religious Leader
Chm. of Methodist Committee for Overseas Relief, 1940-48; pres., Ohio Wesleyan U, 1905-16.
b. Nov 7, 1862 in New York, New York
d. Apr 4, 1969 in New York, New York

Source: *BioIn 1, 6, 8, 9; ConAu P-1; EncWM; NatCAB 14; OhA&B; WhAm 5; WhE&EA*

Welch, James
American. Author
Themes of novels include Native American acculturation; novels include *Winter in the Blood,* 1975.
b. 1940
Source: *AmIndBi; BenetAL 91; BiNAW, B; BioIn 10, 12, 17, 21, 22; CamDcAB; CamGLE; CamHAL; ConAu 42NR, 66NR, 85; ConLC 6, 14, 52; ConNov 91, 96; ConPo 75, 80, 85, 91, 96; ConPopW; CyWA 97; DcLB 175; DcNAL; DrAP 75; DrAPF 80; EncALit; EncFWF; EncNAB; IdentIs; NatAL; NatNAL; NewEAmW; NotNaAm; OxCAmL 95; OxCTwCL; RfGAmL 4, 94; SocPrL; TwCWW 82, 91; WorAu 1980; WrDr 76, 80, 82, 84, 86, 88, 90, 92, 94, 96*

Welch, John Francis, Jr.
American. Business Executive
Chm., CEO of General Electric Co., 1981—.
b. Nov 19, 1935 in Peabody, Massachusetts
Source: *AmMWSc 79, 92; BioIn 12, 13, 14, 15, 16; CurBio 88; Dun&B 90; IntWW 89, 91, 93, 97, 98, 2000; St&PR 84, 87, 91, 93, 96, 97, 98, 99, 2000; WhoAm 78, 80, 82, 84, 86, 88, 90, 92, 94, 95, 96, 97, 98, 99, 2000; WhoE 83, 85, 86, 89, 91, 93, 95, 97, 99; WhoFI 00, 81, 83, 85, 87, 89, 92, 94, 96, 98; WhoMedi 98; WhoWor 84, 87, 89, 91, 95, 96, 97, 98, 99, 2000*

Welch, Joseph Nye
American. Lawyer, Actor
Counsel for US Army during McCarthy hearings, 1954; known for civil trials.
b. Oct 22, 1890 in Primghar, Iowa
d. Oct 6, 1960 in Hyannis, Massachusetts
Source: *AmNatBi; BioIn 3, 5, 6, 11; CamDcAB; CurBio 54, 60; DcAmB S6; EncMcCE; WebAB 74, 79; WebBD 83; WhAm 4; WhScrn 74, 77*

Welch, Ken
American. Writer, Composer, Songwriter
With wife, Mitzie, won Emmys for music for TV specials including "Linda in Wonderland," 1981.
b. Feb 4, 1926 in Kansas City, Missouri
Source: *VarWW 85*

Welch, Larry Dean
American. Military Leader
Vice Chief of Staff of Air Force, 1981-85; commander-in-chief, SAC (Strategic Air Command), 1985-86; chief of staff, USAF, 1986—.
b. Jun 9, 1934 in Guymon, Oklahoma
Source: *BioIn 15; NewYTBS 86; St&PR 91; WhoAm 84, 86, 90; WhoMW 88*

Welch, Mickey
[Michael Francis Welch]
''Smiling Mickey''
American. Baseball Player
Pitcher, 1880-92, mostly with NY
　Giants; had 311 career wins; thought
　to be first to throw screwball; Hall of
　Fame, 1973.
b. Jul 4, 1859 in New York, New York
d. Jul 30, 1941 in Nashua, New
　Hampshire
Source: *AmNatBi; Ballpl 90; BiDAmSp
BB; BioIn 14, 15; CulEncB; WhoProB
73; WhoSpor*

Welch, Mitzie
[Marilyn Cottle]
American. Writer, Composer, Songwriter
With husband, Ken, won several Emmys
　including ''Carol Burnett Show,''
　1976.
b. Jul 25, in McDonald, Pennsylvania
Source: *VarWW 85*

Welch, Raquel
[Raquel Tejada]
American. Actor, Model
Film star known for figure, sexiness: *One
　Million Years, BC*, 1967; starred on
　Broadway in *Woman of the Year*,
　1982.
b. Sep 5, 1940 in Chicago, Illinois
Source: *BiDHisA; BiHaHis; BioIn 8, 9,
10, 11, 12, 13, 14, 16, 18, 20, 22, 23;
BioNews 74; BkPepl; CamBiEn; CelR,
90; ChamBiD; ConTFT 3, 19; CurBio
71; DcArts; DcHiB; DcPseud; FilmEn;
FilmgC; HalFC 80, 84, 88; HispAmA;
IntDcF 1-3, 2-3; IntMPA 82, 92, 94, 96;
IntWW 82, 83, 89, 91, 93, 97, 98, 2000;
IntWWW 2; InWom SUP; ItaFilm;
LegTOT; MotPP; MovMk; NewYTBE 72;
NotHsAW 1; NotLatA; VarWW 85;
WhoAm 84, 86, 88, 92, 94, 95, 96, 97,
99, 2000; WhoAmW 85, 95, 97, 99;
WhoEnt 92, 92A, 98; WhoHisp 91, 92,
94; WhoHol 92, A; WhoHrs 80;
WorAlBi; WorEFlm*

Welch, Robert Henry Winborne, Jr.
American. Political Activist
Founder of ultraconservative, anti-
　communist John Birch Society, 1958.
b. Dec 1, 1899 in Chowan County, North
　Carolina
d. Jan 6, 1985 in Winchester,
　Massachusetts
Source: *BiDExR; BioIn 5, 6, 7, 10, 11;
CurBio 76; PolProf J; St&PR 75;
WebAB 74, 79; WhoAm 80, 82; WhoWor
74*

Welch, Thomas B
American. Dentist, Businessman
Prohibitionist, who developed
　unfermented wine, Welch's Grape
　Juice, 1872.
b. 1825
d. 1903
Source: *Entr*

Welch, William Henry
American. Pathologist, Bacteriologist
First professor of pathology at Johns
　Hopkins Hospital & Medical School,
　1889; helped establish Rockefeller
　Institute, NY.
b. Apr 8, 1850 in Norfolk, Connecticut
d. Apr 30, 1934 in Baltimore, Maryland
Source: *AmAu&B; AmBi; AmDec 1910;
AmNatBi; ApCAB SUP; BiDAmEd;
BiESc; BiHiMed; BioIn 1, 2, 3, 5, 7, 8,
9, 10, 11, 13, 15, 19; CamDcAB;
DcAmAu; DcAmB; DcAmMeB 84;
DcNAA; DcScB; EncAB-H 1974, 1996;
EncWB 98; InSci; LarDcSc; McGEWB;
NatCAB 10, 26; OxCAmH; OxCMed 86;
RanHWDS; REnAL; WebAB 74, 79;
WhAm 1*

Welchman, Gordon
American. Mathematician
Solved Nazis' decoding machine; wrote
　*Hut Six Story: Breaking the Enigma
　Code*, 1982.
b. 1906, England
d. Oct 8, 1985 in Newburyport,
　Massachusetts
Source: *AnObit 1985; ConAu 117;
DcNaB 1981*

Weld, Theodore Dwight
American. Abolitionist, Clergy, Editor
Preacher was one of the most influential
　leaders in the early days of the
　antislavery movement.
b. Nov 23, 1803 in Hampton,
　Connecticut
d. Feb 3, 1895 in Massachusetts
Source: *AmBi; AmNatBi; AmRef;
AmSocL; ApCAB; Benet 87, 96; BenetAL
91; BioIn 2, 12, 15, 19; CamDcAB;
ChamBiD; DcAmAu; DcAmB; DcAmReB
1, 2; DcAmSR; DcNAA; EncAAH;
EncAB-H 1974, 1996; EncARH;
EncRelA; EncStYM; EncWB 98;
HarEnUS; McGEWB; NatCAB 2;
OhA&B; OxCAmH; OxCAmL 65, 83, 95;
REn; REnAL; WebAB 74, 79; WhAm HS;
WhCiWar*

Weld, Tuesday
[Susan Ker Weld]
American. Actor
Starred in *Return to Peyton Place*, 1961;
　Looking for Mr. Goodbar, 1977.
b. Aug 27, 1943 in New York, New
　York
Source: *BiDFilm, 81, 94; BioIn 5, 6, 9,
10, 11, 14, 15, 16, 22; CelR; ConTFT 3,
18; CurBio 74; DcPseud; EncAFC;
FilmEn; FilmgC; ForYSC; HalFC 80,
84, 88; IntDcF 1-3, 2-3; IntMPA 75, 76,
77, 78, 79, 80, 81, 82, 84, 86, 88, 92,
94, 96; IntWW 91; InWom, SUP;
LegTOT; MotPP; MovMk; NewYTBE 71;
OsStAZ; WhoAm 86, 90; WhoAmW 74,
91; WhoEnt 92; WhoHol 92, A; WorAl;
WorAlBi; WorEFlm*

Weld, William F(loyd)
American. Politician
Rep. governor, MA, 1990-97.
b. Jul 31, 1945 in Smithtown, New York

Source: *BioIn 14, 15, 16; CurBio 93;
IntWW 91, 93, 97, 98, 2000; NewYTBS
88, 90, 91, 92; WhoAm 80, 82, 84, 86,
88, 92, 94, 95, 96, 97, 98; WhoAmL 83,
85, 87, 90, 92, 94, 96; WhoAmP 91;
WhoE 93, 95, 97; WhoWor 93, 95, 96,
97, 98*

Weldon, Fay
English. Author
Novels focus on issues in women's lives;
　The Life and Loves of a She-Devil,
　1983; *Leader of the Band*, 1988.
b. Sep 22, 1931 in Alvechurch, England
Source: *BiCoLiE; BioIn 9, 13, 14, 16;
BlmGEL; BlmGWL; BritWr S4;
ChamBiD; CnDBLB 8; ConAu 63NR;
ConLC 59, 122; ConNov 86, 91, 96;
ConPopW; ContDcW 89; CurBio 90;
CyWA 89, 97; DcArts; DcLB 14, 194;
EncBrWW; EncSF 93; FemiCLE;
FemiWr; IntAu&W 86, 89, 91, 93;
IntWW 83, 89, 91, 93, 97, 98, 2000;
IntWWW 2; InWom SUP; LegTOT;
MajTwCW 1, 2; RfGEnL 91; RfGShF 2;
RGTwCWr; ScF&FL 92; SJGHorW;
Who 85, 88, 90, 92, 94, 98, 99, 2000;
WhoWor 97, 98, 99, 2000; WrDr 92, 94,
96, 98, 99, 2000*

Weldon, Joan
American. Actor
Films include *So This Is Love*, 1953;
　Home Before Dark, 1958.
b. Aug 5, 1933 in San Francisco,
　California
Source: *ForYSC; IntMPA 75, 76, 77, 78,
79, 80, 81, 82, 84, 86, 88; WhoHol 92,
A; WhoHrs 80*

Weldon, John
[Brinsley MacNamara]
Irish. Actor, Dramatist
Plays include *Margaret Gillan*, 1935.
b. Sep 6, 1890? in Hiskenstown, Ireland
d. Feb 4, 1963 in Dublin, Ireland
Source: *BiDIrW; BioIn 13; CasWL;
CnMD; ConAu 115; DcIrB 2; DcIrL, 96;
DcLB 10; IriPla; LngCTC; McGEWD
72, 84; ModIrL; ModWD; OxCIri;
OxCThe 83; RfGEnL 91; WhE&EA*

Welensky, Roy
Rhodesian. Political Leader
Dominant white supremacist in British
　south-central Africa, served as prime
　minister of the Federation of Rhodesia
　and Nyasaland from 1956 to 1963.
b. Jan 20, 1907 in Salisbury, Rhodesia
d. Dec 5, 1991
Source: *AfSS 78, 79, 80, 81, 82; AnObit
1991; BioIn 5, 6, 7, 17, 18, 20, 21;
CamBiEn; ChamBiD; CurBio 92N;
DcAfHiB 86; DcPol; DcTwHis; EncWB
98; FacFETw; HisDBrE; IntWW 74, 75,
76, 77, 78, 79, 80, 81, 82, 83, 89, 91;
IntYB 78, 79, 80, 81, 82; McGEWB;
NewYTBS 91; Who 74, 82, 83, 85, 88,
90, 92; WhoWor 74, 76, 78*

Welitsch, Ljuba
Austrian. Opera Singer
Soprano, noted for Salome role; with NY
Met., 1949-52.
b. Jul 10, 1913 in Borissova, Bulgaria
d. Sep 1, 1996 in Vienna, Austria
Source: *BakBD 78, 84, 92; BakBDTw;*
BioIn 1, 2, 3, 4, 7, 9, 11, 13, 14, 15, 22,
23; CmOp; CurBio 49, 96N; DcPseud;
IntDcOp; IntWWM 80, 90; InWom, SUP;
MetOEnc; MusSN; NewAmDM;
NewGrDM 80; NewGrDO; NewYTBE
72; NewYTBS 96; ObitPA 96; OxDcOp;
PenDiMP; WhoMus 72

Welk, Lawrence
''The King of Champagne Music''
American. Bandleader
Started band, 1927; host of TV's ''The
Lawrence Welk Show,'' 1955-71,
longest-running show in TV history.
b. Mar 11, 1903 in Strasburg, North
Dakota
d. May 17, 1992 in Santa Monica,
California
Source: *AmNatBi; AnObit 1992; ASCAP*
66, 80; BakBD 78, 84, 92; BakDcM;
BgBands 74; BiDAmM; BiDJaz; BioIn 4,
7, 8, 9, 10, 11, 12, 13, 17, 18, 19, 24;
BioNews 74; CamDcAB; CelR, 90;
CmpEPM; ConAu 105, 134; ConMuA
80B; ConMus 13; ConTFT 12; CurBio
57, 92N; DcTwCCu 1; FacFETw;
IntMPA 77, 80, 84, 86, 88, 92; LegTOT;
NewAmDM; NewGrDA 86; NewYTBS
92; OxCPMus; PenEncP; RadStar; RkOn
74; WebAB 74, 79; WhoAm 74, 76, 78,
80, 82; WhoMus 72; WorAl; WorAlBi;
WrDr 80, 82, 84, 86, 88, 90

Welland, Colin
English. Screenwriter
Wrote Oscar-winning film *Chariots of
Fire*, 1981.
b. Jul 4, 1934, England
Source: *ConDr 77C, 88C; ConTFT 7;*
DcPseud; FilmgC; HalFC 80, 84, 88;
IntAu&W 89, 91, 93; IntWW 89, 91, 93,
98, 2000; VarWW 85; Who 82, 83, 85,
88, 90, 92, 94, 98, 99, 2000

Wellcome, Henry Solomon, Sir
American. Manufacturer
Founded pharmaceutical firm, 1880;
pioneered the field in US, England;
established museums, foundations.
b. Aug 21, 1853 in Wisconsin
d. Jul 25, 1936 in London, England
Source: *BioIn 2, 3, 9, 13; DcNaB 1931;*
DcTwBBL; OxCMed 86

Wellek, Rene
American. Author, Educator
Writings include *Confrontations*, 1965;
Chekhov: New Perspectives, 1984.
b. Aug 22, 1903 in Vienna, Austria
d. Nov 10, 1995 in Hamden, Connecticut
Source: *AmAu&B; AmNatBi; Au&Wr 71;*
BioIn 4, 10, 16; BlueB 76; CamDcAB;
ConAu 5R, 7AS, 8NR, 150; ConLC 28;
ConLCrt 77, 82; DcLB 63; DrAS 74F,
82F; EncALit; EncWL 1, 2, 2S, 3;
IntAu&W 76, 82, 86; IntvTCA 2; IntWW

75, 76, 77, 78, 79, 80, 81, 82, 83, 89,
91, 93; LiExTwC; NewYTBS 74; WhoAm
74, 76, 78, 80, 82, 84, 86, 88; WhoWor
74, 76, 78; WorAu 1950; WrDr 76, 80,
82, 84, 86, 88, 90, 92, 94, 96, 98N

Weller, Michael
American. Dramatist, Screenwriter
Wrote films *Hair*, 1979; *Ragtime*, 1981.
b. Sep 27, 1942 in New York, New
York
Source: *BioIn 10, 12, 16; CamGWoT;*
ConAmD; ConAu 85; ConDr 73, 77, 82,
88, 93; ConLC 10, 53; ConTFT 2;
CurBio 89; McGEWD 84; NatPD 81;
OxCAmT 84; VarWW 85; WhoAm 90,
92, 94, 95, 96, 97, 98; WhoEnt 92, 98;
WhoThe 81; WrDr 76, 80, 82, 84, 86,
88, 90, 92, 94, 96, 98, 99, 2000

Weller, Thomas Huckle
American. Physician
Shared Nobel Prize in medicine, 1954,
with Frederick C Robbins.
b. Jun 15, 1915 in Ann Arbor, Michigan
Source: *AmMWSc 76P, 79, 82, 86, 89,*
92, 95, 98; AsBiEn; BiESc; BioIn 3, 4,
15, 20; BlueB 76; CamBiEn; ChamBiD;
IntWW 74, 75, 76, 77, 78, 79, 80, 81, 82,
83, 89, 91, 93, 97, 98, 2000; LarDcSc;
McGCEnS; McGMS 80; NobelP;
RanHWDS; WebAB 74, 79; WebBD 83;
Who 74, 82, 83, 85, 88, 90, 92, 94, 98,
99, 2000; WhoAm 74, 76, 78, 80, 82, 84,
86, 88, 90, 92, 94, 95, 96, 97, 98, 99,
2000; WhoE 77, 79, 81, 83, 85, 86, 89,
91, 93, 95, 97, 99; WhoMedH 96, 99,
2000; WhoNob, 90, 95; WhoScEn 94, 96,
2000; WhoWor 74, 82, 84, 87, 89, 91,
93, 95, 96, 97, 98, 99, 2000; WorAl;
WorAlBi

Welles, Gideon
American. Politician
Secretary of Navy, 1861-69; credited
with building Union Navy, blockading
Confederacy; his *Diary of Gideon
Welles* was published in 1911.
b. Jul 1, 1802 in Glastonbury,
Connecticut
d. Feb 11, 1878 in Hartford, Connecticut
Source: *Alli SUP; AmAu&B; AmBi;*
AmNatBi; ApCAB; BiAUS; BiDrUSE 71,
89; BioIn 4, 5, 7, 10; CamBiEn;
CamDcAB; CivWDc; DcAmAu; DcAmB;
DcAmMiB; DcNAA; Drake; EncAB-H
1974, 1996; EncNaHi; EncWB 98;
HarEnUS; McGEWB; NatCAB 2;
NewCol 75; OxCAmH; OxCShps; REn;
REnAL; TwCBDA; WebAB 74, 79;
WebBD 83; WhAm HS; WhCiWar

Welles, Orson
[George Orson Welles]
American. Actor, Director, Producer,
Writer
Considered major film genius; gained
reputation with 1938 radio adaptation
of *War of the Worlds*; starred in
Citizen Kane, 1940.
b. May 6, 1915 in Kenosha, Wisconsin
d. Oct 10, 1985 in Los Angeles,
California

Source: *AmAu&B; AmCulL; AmDec*
1940; AmFD; AmNatBi; Benet 87;
BenetAL 91; BiDFilm, 81, 94;
BiE&WWA; BioIn 1, 2, 3, 4, 5, 6, 7, 8,
9, 10, 11, 12, 13, 14, 15, 16, 17, 18, 19,
20, 21, 22, 23, 24; BkPepl; BlueB 76;
CamGWoT; CelR; CmCal; CmMov;
CnThe; ConAu 93, 117; ConDr 73, 77A;
ConLC 20, 80; ConTFT 3; CurBio 65,
85N; DcAmSR; DcFM; EncAB-H 1974,
1996; EncMT; EncWB, 98; EncWT; Ent;
FacFETw; FamA&A; FilmEn; FilmgC;
FrTalk; GrStDi; HalFC 80, 84, 88;
IlWWHD 1; IntAu&W 76, 77; IntMPA
77, 82, 84, 86; IntWW 74, 75, 76, 77,
78, 79, 80, 81, 82, 83; ItaFilm; LegTOT;
LinLib L, S; MakMC; MiSFD 9N;
MotPP; MovMk; NewYTBE 72;
NewYTBS 85; NotNAT, A; OnHuYAF;
OsStAZ; OxCAmH; OxCAmT 84;
OxCFilm; OxCThe 67, 83; PIP&P;
RadStar; RAdv 13-3; RComAH; REn;
REnAL; SaTiSS; ScF&FL 1, 92;
ScrEAmL 1; VarWW 85; WebAB 74, 79;
WhAm 9; WhDW; WhE&EA; Who 74,
82, 83, 85; WhoAm 74, 76, 78, 80, 82,
84; WhoHol A; WhoHrs 80; WhoThe 72,
77A; WhoWor 74; WhThe; WorAl;
WorAlBi; WorEFlm; WorFDir 1; WrDr
80, 82, 84

Welles, Sumner
American. Diplomat, Author
Roosevelt's assistant secretary and
undersecretary of state, 1933-43;
helped form ''good neighbor'' policy
with Latin America.
b. Oct 14, 1892 in New York, New York
d. Sep 24, 1961 in Bernardsville, New
Jersey
Source: *AmAu&B; AmNatBi; AmPeW;*
BiDInt; BioIn 1, 2, 4, 6, 16, 22; CurBio
40, 61; DcAmB S7; EncAB-H 1974;
EncLatA; EncTR 91; EncWB 98;
LegTOT; McGEWB; ObitT 1961;
REnAL; TwCA SUP; WhAm 4;
WhE&EA; WorAl; WorAlBi; WorAu
1900

Wellesley, Dorothy Violet
[Duchess of Wellington]
English. Poet
Wrote collection of poems, *Early Light*,
1956.
b. Jul 30, 1889 in White Waltham,
England
d. Jul 11, 1956 in Withyham, England
Source: *Chambr 3; DcLEL; DcNaB*
1951; ModBrL; OxCEng 85; OxCTwCL;
REn

Wellesley, Richard Colley, 1st
Marquess Wellesley
English. Government Official
Vigorous expansionist served as governor
general of India.
b. Jun 20, 1760 in Dangan Castle,
Ireland
d. Sep 26, 1842 in Brompton, England
Source: *Alli; BiDLA; BioIn 12; CelCen;*
DcInB; DcNaB; EncWB 98; HisDBrE;
McGEWB; PoIre

Wellesz, Egon

Austrian. Composer, Musicologist
Expert on Byzantine music; wrote many
operas.
b. Oct 21, 1885 in Vienna, Austria
d. Nov 9, 1974 in Oxford, England
Source: *BakBD 78, 84; BriBkM 80;*
CmOp; ConAu 53; DcCM; IntWW 74;
NewAmDM; NewEOp 71; NewGrDM 80;
NewOxM; NewYTBS 74; ObitT 1971;
OxCMus; OxDcOp; WhAm 6; Who 74

Wellington, Arthur Wellesley, Duke

English. Army Officer, Statesman
Commander, Peninsular War, 1808-14,
fighting Napoleon; prime minister,
1828-30.
b. May 1, 1769 in Dublin, Ireland
d. Sep 14, 1852 in Kent, England
Source: *Alli; Benet 87, 96; BioIn 1, 2, 3,*
4, 5, 6, 7, 8, 9, 10, 11, 12, 13, 14, 16,
18, 19, 20, 21, 22, 23, 24; BlmGEL;
CamBiEn; CelCen; ChamBiD; DcBiPP;
DcInB; HarEnMi; LinLib S; LngCEL;
McGEWB; NewC; OxCBrHi; OxCEng
85, 95; REn; WhDW; WhoMilH 76;
WorAl; WorAlBi

Wellman, Paul Iselin

American. Journalist, Author
Novels include *Bowl of Brass,* 1944;
Magnificent Destiny, 1962.
b. Oct 14, 1898 in Enid, Oklahoma
d. Sep 17, 1966 in Los Angeles,
California
Source: *AmAu&B; AmNov; Au&Wr 71;*
AuBYP 2, 3; BioIn 1, 2, 4, 7, 8, 9, 22;
ConAu 1R, 16NR, 64NR; CurBio 49;
REn; REnAL; REnAW; SmATA 3; TwCA
SUP; TwCWW 82; WhAm 4; WorAu
1900

Wellman, Walter

American. Journalist
Founded *Cincinnati Post,* 1879; known
for travels, record-breaking stunts.
b. Nov 3, 1858 in Mentor, Ohio
d. Jan 31, 1934 in New York, New York
Source: *AmBi; AmNatBi; ApCAB X;*
BioIn 5, 8, 22; CamDcAB; DcAmB;
DcNAA; EncAB-A 3; InSci; JrnUS;
OhA&B; TwCBDA; WebAB 74, 79;
WhAm 1

Wellman, William Augustus

"Wild Bill"
American. Director
Films known for "documentary realism"
include *Wings,* 1927; *The High and*
the Mighty, 1954.
b. Feb 29, 1896 in Brookline,
Massachusetts
d. Dec 9, 1975 in Los Angeles,
California
Source: *AmNatBi; BiDFilm; BioIn 2, 9,*
10, 11, 12, 13, 15, 16, 17, 18; CmMov;
ConAu 61; CurBio 50, 76; DcAmB S9;
DcFM; Film 1; FilmEn; FilmgC;
IntMPA 75; MovMk; ObitOF 79; ObitT
1971; OxCFilm; TwYS; WhAm 6;
WhoAm 74, 76; WhoWor 74; WorAl

Wells, Carolyn

American. Author
Wrote over 170 mysteries, nonsense
tales, children's books.
b. Jun 18, 1869 in Rahway, New Jersey
d. Mar 26, 1942 in New York, New
York
Source: *AmAu&B; AmLY; AmNatBi;*
AmWomPl; AmWomWr; BenetAL 91;
BiD&SB; BioIn 13, 14, 15, 21, 22;
CarSB; ChhPo, S1, S2; ConAu 113;
CurBio 42; DcAmAu; DcLB 11; DcNAA;
DetWom; EncAHmr; EncMys; EvLB;
InWom; NatCAB 13; PenNWW A; REn;
REnAL; TwCA; TwCCr&M 80, 85, 91;
TwCWr; WhAm 2; WhNAA; WorAu 1900

Wells, Edward

American. Engineer
Former Boeing Co. chief engineer; held
20 patents for plane parts designs.
b. Aug 26, 1910 in Boise, Idaho
d. Jul 1, 1986 in Bellevue, Washington
Source: *AmMWSc 82; St&PR 84;*
WhoAm 84; WhoFrS 84

Wells, George

Screenwriter
Won Oscar for *Designing Woman,* 1957.
b. 1909
Source: *EncAFC; FilmEn; FilmgC;*
HalFC 80, 84, 88; VarWW 85; WorEFlm

Wells, H(erbert) G(eorge)

English. Author
Wrote *The Time Machine,* 1895; *The*
Invisible Man, 1897; *The War of the*
Worlds, 1898.
b. Sep 21, 1866 in Bromley, England
d. Aug 13, 1946 in London, England
Source: *Benet 96; BiCoLiE; BiDInt;*
BioIn 1, 2, 3, 4, 5, 6, 7, 8, 9, 10, 11, 12,
13, 14, 15, 16, 17, 18, 19, 23; CamBiEn;
CasWL; ChambiD; Chambr 3; CurBio
46; DcAmSR; DcArts; DcBiA; DcEnA A;
DcLEL; DcNaB 1941; EncSF 93;
EncUnb; EncWB 98; EncWL 1, 2S, 3;
EvLB; GloEnch; GrBr; IntWW 2000;
LinLib S; LngCEL; LngCTC; MajTwCW
2; MakMC; McGEWB; MnBBF;
NewCBEL; NotNAT B; OxCEng 67, 95;
OxCTwCL; PenC ENG; PIP&P; RAdv 1;
RComWL; REn; RfGShF 1, 2;
RGTwCWr; SJGHorW; SJGYouA 2;
TwCA, SUP; TwCWr; TwCYAW 1;
VicBrit; WebE&AL; WhAm 2; WhDW;
WhE&EA; WhoHol B; WhoLA;
WhoTwCL; WhScrn 74, 77; WorAu 1900

Wells, Henry

American. Businessman
With William Fargo, organized express
service, Wells, Fargo, & Co. during
California gold rush, 1852.
b. Dec 12, 1805 in Thetford, Vermont
d. Dec 10, 1878 in Glasgow, Scotland
Source: *AmBi; CamBiEn; DcAmB; EncAAH;*
BioIn 4; CamBiEn; DcAmB; EncAAH;
EncABHB 6; NatCAB 39; NewEAmW;
REnAW; TwCBDA; WebAB 74, 79;
WhAm HS

Wells, Horace

American. Dentist
Pioneered in anesthesia for dentistry,
1840s.
b. Jan 21, 1815 in Hartford, Vermont
d. Jan 24, 1848 in New York, New York
Source: *Alli; AmBi; AmNatBi; ApCAB;*
BiESc; BiInAmS; BioIn 1, 2, 3, 4, 6, 7,
14; CamDcAB; DcAmB; DcAmMeB, 84;
DcNAA; Drake; EncWB 98; HarEnUS;
InSci; LinLib S; McGEWB; NatCAB 6;
OxCAmH; OxCMed 86; RanHWDS;
TwCBDA; WebAB 74, 79; WhAm HS

Wells, James Lesesne

American. Artist
Artwork was influenced by African art;
art instructor and professor, Howard
University, 1929-68.
b. Nov 2, 1902 in Atlanta, Georgia
d. 1993
Source: *AfrAmAl 8; AfroAA; AnObit*
1993; ConBlB 10; DcTwCCu 5; InB&W
80, 85; SJGBlA; WhAmArt 85; WhoAfA
9; WhoAm 78; WhoAmA 73, 76, 78, 80;
WhoBlA 1, 2, 3, 4, 6, 7, 8

Wells, Junior

[Amos Blackmore]
American. Musician
Blues harmonica player; played with the
Muddy Waters band, 1952-53; toured
and recorded with Buddy Guy;
recorded songs "Little by Little,"
"Messin' With the Kid," and "Let
Me Love You Baby;" released albums
It's My Life, 1966, *Junior Wells's*
Southside Blues Jam, 1970 and
Everybody's Gettin' Some, 1995.
b. Dec 9, 1934 in West Memphis,
Arkansas
d. Jan 15, 1998 in Chicago, Illinois
Source: *AllMGBl 1, 2; BioIn 17, 23, 24;*
Blues; ConMus 17; NewAmDM;
NewGrDA 86; NewYTBS 98; PenEncP;
RolSEnR 83; WhoAfA 11; WhoRock 81

Wells, Kitty

[Muriel Deason Wright]
American. Singer
Award-winning Grand Ole Opry star
since 1950s; Country Music Hall of
Fame, 1976.
b. Aug 30, 1919 in Nashville, Tennessee
Source: *BakBD 84, 92; BgBkCoM;*
BiDAmM; BioIn 14, 15, 17, 19, 22, 23;
CamDcAB; ChamBiD; ConMuA 80A;
ConMus 6; CounME 74, 74A; DcPseud;
EncFCWM 69, 83; IlEncJ; InWom SUP;
NewAmDM; NewGrDA 86; PenEncP;
WhoAm 76, 78, 80, 82, 84, 86, 88, 94,
95, 96, 97, 98

Wells, Linton

American. Journalist
War correspondent, staff writer for
newspapers, mags., 1911-76.
b. Apr 1, 1893 in Louisville, Kentucky
d. Jan 31, 1976 in Washington, District
of Columbia
Source: *AmAu&B; BioIn 10, 12; ConAu*
61, 97; NatCAB 59; WhAm 6, 7;
WhE&EA; WhNAA; WhoAm 74, 76

Wells, Mary

American. Singer
Sang "Bye, Bye, Baby," 1961; "Two
　Lovers," 1962; "My Guy," 1964.
b. May 13, 1943 in Detroit, Michigan
d. Jul 26, 1992 in Los Angeles,
　California
Source: *AfrAmAl 6, 8; AfrAmBi 2;*
AnObit 1992; BiDEWW; BillEnR; BioIn
15, 18, 19; DcWomA; DrBlPA 90;
EncPR&S 74, 89; EncRk 88; FemiCLE;
InB&W 85; LegTOT; NewAmDM;
NewGrDA 86; News 93-1; NewYTBS 92;
PenEncP; RkOn 74, 78; RolSEnR 83;
SoulM; WhoRock 81

Wells, Sharlene

American. Beauty Contest Winner
Won Miss America pageant in 1985; a
　wholesome Mormon from Utah, she
　stood in contrast to 1984's Miss
　America, Vanessa Williams, who was
　forced to resign her crown after
　Penthouse magazine published nude
　photos of her.
b. c. 1965
Source: *ConNews 85-1*

Wells-Barnett, Ida Bell

American. Journalist
Regular writer for the black press
　throughout the country; civil rights
　activist honored by the US Postal
　Service with a stamp in 1990.
b. Jul 16, 1862 in Holly Springs,
　Mississippi
d. Mar 25, 1931 in Chicago, Illinois
Source: *AfrAmOr; AmNatBi; AmRef;*
AmSocL; BiDSocW; BioIn 13, 15;
BlkWAm; BriB; CamDcAB; ContDcW
89; EncAB-H 1974; EncSoH; EncWHA;
HarlReB; HerW 84; InWom SUP;
JrnUS; LibW; NotAW; PenNWW A;
WomFir

Wellstone, Paul David

American. Politician
Dem. Senator from MN, 1991—.
b. Jul 21, 1944 in Washington, District
　of Columbia
Source: *AlmAP 92; BioIn 13; ConAu*
107; CurBio 93; NewYTBS 91; WhoAmP
91, 93, 95, 97, 1999; WhoMW 92

Welnick, Vince(nt)

[The Tubes]
American. Musician
Keyboardist with The Tubes since late
　1960s.
b. Feb 21, 1951 in Phoenix, Arizona
Source: *WhoRocM 82*

Welsbach, Carl Auer von, Baron

Austrian. Chemist, Inventor
Discovered earth elements neodymium
　and praseodymium, 1885; lutetium,
　1908.
b. Sep 1, 1858
d. Aug 4, 1929
Source: *DcInv; NewCol 75; WebBD 83;*
WhDW

Welsh, Matthew E(mpson)

American. Politician
Dem. governor of IN, 1961-65.
b. Sep 15, 1912
d. May 28, 1995 in Indianapolis, Indiana
Source: *BiDrGov 1789; BioIn 6, 7, 9;*
BlueB 76; CurBio 95N; IntWW 74, 75,
76, 77, 78, 79, 80, 81; WhAm 11;
WhoAm 74, 76, 78, 80, 82, 84, 86, 88,
90, 92, 94; WhoAmL 83; WhoAmP 73,
75, 77, 79, 81, 83, 85, 87, 89, 91, 93;
WhoWor 78, 82

Welsing, Frances Cress

American. Psychiatrist
Wrote *The Cress Theory of Color-*
　Confrontation and Racism (White
　Supremacy), 1970, proposing that the
　origin of racism is rooted in skin
　pigment.
b. Mar 18, 1935 in Chicago, Illinois
Source: *BioIn 19; BlksScM; BlkWr 2;*
ConAu 142; ConBlB 5; Ebony 1; InB&W
80; NegAl 76; NotBlAW 2; SchCGBL;
WhoAfA 9, 10, 11, 12; WhoBlA 2, 3, 4,
6, 7, 8; WrDr 96, 98, 99, 2000

Welty, Eudora

American. Author
Won Pulitzer for *The Optimist's*
　Daughter, 1972; won National Book
　Award, 1991, for distinguished
　contribution to American letters.
b. Apr 13, 1909 in Jackson, Mississippi
Source: *AmAu&B; AmNov; AmWomWr,*
92; AmWr, RS1; ArtclWW 2; BeaEPF;
Benet 87, 96; BenetAL 91; BiCoLiE;
BioAmW; BioIn 1, 2, 3, 4, 5, 6, 7, 8, 9,
10, 11, 12, 13, 14, 15, 16, 17, 18, 19,
20, 21, 22, 23, 24; BlmGWL; BlueB 76;
CamBiEn; CamDcAB; CamGLE;
CamHAL; CasWL; CelR; ChambiD;
ChhPo; CnDAL; ConAu 1BS, 9R, 32NR,
65NR; ConLC 1, 2, 5, 14, 22, 33, 105;
ConNov 72, 76, 82, 86, 91; ConSoWr;
ContDcW 89; CurBio 42, 75; CyWA 58,
89, 97; DcArts; DcLB 102, 143, DS12,
Y87A; DcLEL 1940; DcTwCCu 1; DrAF
76; DrAPF 80, 91; EncAB-H 1996;
EncFoLi; EncSoH; EncSoL; EncWB 98;
EncWHA; EncWL 1, 2, 2S, 3; FacFETw;
FemiCLE; FifSWrA; GrWomW; GrWrEL
N; ICPEnP A; IdentIs; IntAu&W 76, 77,
89, 91; IntDcWB; IntvTCA 2; IntWW 74,
75, 76, 77, 78, 79, 80, 81, 82, 83, 89,
91, 93, 97, 98, 2000; IntWWW 2;
InWom, SUP; LegTOT; LibW; LinLib L,
S; LiveMA; LngCTC; MacBEP;
MagSAmL; MajTwCW 1, 2; ModAL 4,
4S1, 4S2, 4S3, 5; ModAWWr;
ModWoWr; NewCon; Novels; OxCAmL
65, 83, 95; OxCTwCL; OxCWoWr 95;
PenC AM; PenEncH; RAdv 1, 14, 13-1;
REn, REnAL; RfGAmL 87; ShSCr 1, 27;
ShSWr; SouWr; TwCA SUP; WebAB 74,
79; WebE&AL; WhDW; Who 85, 92;
WhoAm 86, 90; WhoAmW 87, 91;
WhoPul; WhoTwCL; WhoUSWr 88;
WhoWor 87, 91; WhoWrEP 89; WorAl;
WorAlBi; WorLitC; WrDr 76, 80, 82, 84,
86, 88, 90, 92, 94, 96, 98, 99, 2000

Wenceslaus

Bohemian. Emperor
Holy Roman emperor from 1376 to 1400
　and, as Wénceslaus IV, king of
　Bohemia from 1378 to 1419; faced
　internal political rivalry and the
　religious problem of the Great Schism.
b. 1361, Bohemia
d. Aug 19, 1419
Source: *DcCathB; Dis&D; EncWB 98;*
LuthC 75; McGEWB

Wendell Oliver, Scott, Sr.

American. Auto Racer
One of very few African American stock
　car racers, competed in 506 Winston
　Cup Grand Nationals between 1961
　and 1973; won National Association
　for Stock Car Auto Racing (NASCAR)
　championship in 1963; inducted into
　the National Black Athletic Hall of
　Fame, 1977.
b. Aug 29, 1921 in Danville, Virginia
d. Dec 24, 1990

Wenders, Wim

[Wilhelm Wenders]
German. Director
Films include *Hammett; American*
　Friend.
b. Aug 14, 1945 in Dusseldorf, Germany
Source: *BiDFilm 81, 94; BioIn 10, 11,*
12, 13, 14, 15, 16; CamBiEn; ChamBiD;
ConAu 93; ConTFT 5, 14, 24; CurBio
84; EncEurC; FilmEn; HalFC 84, 88;
IntDcF 1-2, 2-2; IntMPA 79, 80, 81, 82,
84, 86, 88, 92, 94, 96; IntWW 89, 91,
93, 97, 98, 2000; LegTOT; MiSFD 9;
WhoAm 95, 96, 97, 98; WhoWor 87, 93,
95, 96, 97, 98, 99, 2000; WorFDir 2

Wendt, George (Robert)

American. Actor
Played Norm Peterson on TV series
　"Cheers," 1982-93.
b. Oct 17, 1948 in Chicago, Illinois
Source: *BioIn 14; ConTFT 7; IntMPA*
92, 94, 96; WhoAm 99, 2000; WhoEnt
98

Weng, Will

American. Puzzle Maker
Editor, *NY Times* crossword puzzle,
　1968-78.
b. 1907? in Terre Haute, Indiana
d. May 2, 1993 in New York, New York
Source: *BioIn 10, 11, 16, 18, 19*

Wengenroth, Stow

American. Lithographer
Called "greatest black-and-white artist in
　America."
b. Jul 25, 1906 in New York, New York
d. Jan 22, 1978 in Gloucester,
　Massachusetts
Source: *BioIn 8, 10, 11, 12; CamDcAB;*
ConAu 104; DcAmArt; GrAmP; McGDA;
NatCAB 60; WhAm 7; WhAmArt 85;
WhoAm 74, 76, 78; WhoAmA 73, 76,
78N, 80N, 82N, 84N, 86, 86N, 89, 89N,
91N, 93N

Wen-hsiang

Chinese. Government Official

Manchu statesman was a leader of the Self-strengthening movement, advocating Westernization and friendly relations with foreigners with the goal of preserving traditional Chinese culture.

b. Oct 18, 1818 in Mukden, China
d. 1876
Source: *EncWB 98; McGEWB*

Wenner, Jann

American. Journalist, Publisher

Founder, publisher *Rolling Stone* mag, 1967—; also owns *Us* mag.

b. Jan 7, 1946 in New York, New York
Source: *AmDec 1960; BioIn 9, 10, 11, 14, 15; ConAu 101; CurBio 80; EncTwCJ; LegTOT; LiJour; MugS; NewGrDA 86; News 93-1; NewYTBS 87; RkWho 96; WhoAm 86, 90; WhoE 86; WhoEnt 92; WhoUSWr 88; WhoWrEP 89*

Wenner-Gren, Axel (Lenard)

Swedish. Industrialist

Founder, chm., Electrolux Co., 1921; manufactured vacuums, refrigerators.

b. Jun 5, 1881 in Uddevalla, Sweden
d. Nov 24, 1961 in Stockholm, Sweden
Source: *BioIn 1, 2, 3, 4, 6; CurBio 42, 62*

Wenrich, Percy

American. Songwriter

Wrote songs "Moonlight Bay," "Put on Your Old Gray Bonnet."

b. Jan 23, 1887 in Joplin, Missouri
d. Mar 17, 1952 in New York, New York
Source: *AmPS; ASCAP 66, 80; BiDAmM; BioIn 4, 6, 9; CmpEPM; NewAmDM; NewGrDA 86; NewGrDM 80; NotNAT B; PopAmC*

Wen T'ien-hsiang

Chinese. Government Official

Statesman in the late Sung dynasty, became the Chinese model of the ideal loyal minister.

b. Jun 6, 1236 in Chi-an, Kiangsi, China
d. Jan 1283
Source: *EncWB 98*

Wentworth, William Charles

Australian. Politician, Writer

Statesman championed the cause of the emancipists (ex-convicts and their offspring) against the elite English exclusives in Australia.

b. 1790
d. Mar 20, 1872 in Dorset, England
Source: *BioIn 24; CamBiEn; EncWB 98; ExplAnT; HisDBrE; McGEWB*

Wenzel, Hanni

Liechtenstein. Skier

Won gold medals, women's slalom, giant slalom, 1980 Olympics.

b. 1957
Source: *BioIn 12*

Werblin, Sonny

[David Abraham Werblin]
American. Businessman

Signed Joe Namath to New York Jets 1965; Pres., CEO, Madison Square Garden Corp., 1977-84; chm., MSG Corp., 1984-92; pres., MCA-TV, 1951-65; created $340 million Meadowlands Sports Complex in New Jersey.

b. Mar 17, 1910 in New York, New York
d. Nov 21, 1991 in New York, New York
Source: *BiDAmSp OS; BioIn 6, 7, 11, 12, 17, 18; CurBio 79; NewYTBS 79, 91; WhoAm 74*

Werfel, Franz

Austrian. Author

Noted expressionist; wrote *The Song of Bernadette,* 1942; filmed, 1943.

b. Sep 10, 1890 in Prague, Bohemia
d. Aug 26, 1945 in Beverly Hills, California
Source: *Benet 87, 96; BiDAmM; BiGAW; CamBiEn; CamGWoT; CasWL; ChamBiD; ClDMEL 47, 80; CmCal; CnMD; CnThe; ConAu 104; CurBio 40, 45; CyWA 58, 97; DcArts; DcLB 81, 124; DcNAA; EncGRNM; EncSF, 93; EncTR, 91; EncWB 98; EncWL 1, 2, 2S, 3; Ent; EvEuW; FacFETw; LegTOT; LiExTwC; LinLib L, S; LngCTC; LuthC 75; McGEWB; McGEWD 72, 84; ModGL; ModWD; NewEOp 71; NewGrDM 80; NewGrDO; NotNAT B; Novels; OxCGer 76, 86, 97; OxCThe 67, 83; PenC EUR; PIP&P; RAdv 14, 13-2; REn; REnWD; RfGWoL 95; ScF&FL 1; ScFSB; TwCA, SUP; TwCLC 8; TwCSFW 81A, 86A; TwCWr; WhAm 2; WorAu 1900*

Werner, Abraham Gottlob

German. Naturalist

Leading proponent of the Neptunian theory of the earth, he wrote the first modern textbook of descriptive mineralogy.

b. Sep 25, 1749 in Upper Lusatia, Prussia
d. Jun 30, 1817 in Dresden, Germany
Source: *CamDcSc; ChamBiD; DcScB; EncEnl; EncWB 98; InSci; LarDcSc; McGEWB; RanHWDS*

Werner, Alfred

French. Chemist

Won 1913 Nobel Prize for linking atoms in molecules; noted for inorganic research.

b. Dec 12, 1866 in Mulhouse, France
d. Nov 15, 1919 in Zurich, Switzerland
Source: *AsBiEn; BiESc; BioIn 3, 6, 7, 14, 15, 16, 19, 20; CamDcSc; ChamBiD; DcScB; InSci; LarDcSc; LinLib S; McGCEnS; NobelP; NotTwCS 1; RanHWDS; WhDW; WhoNob, 90, 95; WorScD*

Werner, Helmut (Eberhard)

German. Business Executive

Known as a brilliant and innovative manager, he was chief executive officer and chairperson of the board of Mercedes-Benz from 1993 to 1997.

b. Sep 2, 1936 in Cologne, Germany

Werner, Oskar

[Oskar Josef Bschliessmayer]
Austrian. Actor

Starred in *Jules et Jim,* 1961; *Ship of Fools,* 1965; *Fahrenheit 451,* 1966.

b. Nov 13, 1922 in Vienna, Austria
d. Oct 23, 1984 in Marburg, Germany (West)
Source: *AnObit 1984; BiDFilm, 81, 94; BioIn 7, 8, 9, 14; CelR; CurBio 66, 85N; DcPseud; EncEurC; EncWT; FilmAG WE; FilmEn; FilmgC; ForYSC; HalFC 80, 84, 88; IntDcF 1-3, 2-3; IntMPA 75, 76, 77, 78, 79, 80, 81, 82, 84; LegTOT; MotPP; MovMk; NewYTBS 84; OsStAZ; OxCFilm; WhoAm 74, 76, 78, 80, 82; WhoHol A; WorAl; WorAlBi; WorEFlm*

Werner, Pierre

Luxembourg. Lawyer, Politician

Prime minister of Luxembourg, 1959-84.

b. Dec 29, 1913 in Saint-Andre, France
Source: *IntWW 74, 75, 76, 77, 78, 79, 80, 81, 82, 83, 89, 91, 93, 97, 98, 2000; IntYB 78, 79, 80, 81, 82; WhoEIO 82; WhoGov 72; WhoWor 74, 76, 78, 80, 82, 84*

Werner, Tom

American. Producer

Developed *The Cosby Show* and *Roseanne.*

b. Apr 12, 1950
Source: *ConTFT 12, 25; LegTOT; NewYTBS 90; WhoEnt 92*

Werth, Alexander

English. Journalist, Author

WW II newspaper correspondent in USSR; wrote *Russia at War: 1941-45,* 1964.

b. Feb 4, 1901, Russia
d. Mar 5, 1969 in Paris, France
Source: *BioIn 8, 9; ConAu 25R, P-1; CurBio 43, 69; WhAm 5*

Wertham, Fredric

German. Author

Influential in suggesting violence in films, TV is dangerous to youth; with NYC Dept. of Hospitals, 1932-81.

b. 1895 in Munich, Germany
d. Nov 18, 1981 in Kempton, Pennsylvania
Source: *AmAu&B; Au&Wr 71; BiDrAPA 77; BioIn 1, 2, 4, 12, 13; BlueB 76; ConAu 5R, 105; CurBio 49, 82, 82N; EncACom; InSci; IntAu&W 76, 77, 82; ScF&FL 1, 2, 92; TwCA SUP; WhAm 8; WhoAm 74, 76, 78; WhoWor 74; WorAu 1900*

Wertheimer, Linda (Cozby)
American. Broadcast Journalist
With NPR since 1971; host of "All Things Considered," 1989—.
b. Mar 19, 1943 in Carlsbad, New Mexico
Source: *CurBio 95*

Wertheimer, Max
American. Psychologist
Co-founder, Gestalt movement, 1912.
b. Apr 15, 1880 in Prague, Bohemia
d. Oct 12, 1943 in New Rochelle, New York
Source: *AmNatBi; BiDcPsy; BiDPsy; BioIn 1, 7, 14, 17, 23; CamBiEn; CamDcAB; ChamBiD; ConAu 123; DcAmB S3; EncWB 98; FacFETw; GuPsyc; InSci; McGEWB; NamesHP*

Wertmuller, Lina von Eigg
[Arcangela Felice Assunta Wertmuller von Elgg]
Italian. Director
In popular films: *Seven Beauties,* 1976; *Seduction of Mimi,* 1974.
b. Aug 14, 1928 in Rome, Italy
Source: *Benet 87; BioIn 14; ConAu 97; ConLC 16; ContDcW 89; ConTFT 6; CurBio 76; FilmEn; HalFC 84, 88; IntDcWB; IntMPA 84, 86, 92; MovMk; NewYTBS 75; WomWMM; WorAl*

Wescott, Glenway
American. Author
Novels include *The Grandmothers,* 1927; *The Pilgrim Hawk,* 1940.
b. Apr 11, 1901 in Kewaskum, Wisconsin
d. Feb 22, 1987 in Rosemont, New Jersey
Source: *AmAu&B; AmNatBi; AmNov; AnObit 1987; Benet 87; BenetAL 91; BioIn 2, 4, 5, 7, 8, 9, 12, 13, 15, 16, 17, 22, 24; BlueB 76; CamDcAB; CamGLE; CamHAL; CasWL; ChhPo S3; CnDAL; ConAmA; ConAmL; ConAu 13R, 23NR, 70NR, 121; ConLC 13; ConNov 72, 76, 82, 86; CyWA 58, 97; DcLB 4, 9, 102; DcLEL; GrWrEL N; LngCTC; ModAL 4, 5; NewYTBS 87; Novels; OxCAmL 65, 83, 95; OxCTwCL; PenC AM; RAdv 1; REn; REnAL; RfGAmL 4, 87, 94; ScrEAmL 2; ShSCr 35; TwCA, SUP; TwCWr; WhAm 9; WhoAm 74, 76, 78, 86; WisWr; WorAu 1900; WrDr 76, 80, 82, 84, 86*

Wesendonck, Mathilde Luckemeyer
German. Poet
Friend of Richard Wagner; he set five of her poems to music as "The Wesendonck Songs."
b. Dec 23, 1828 in Elberfeld, Austria
d. Aug 31, 1902 in Traunblick, Austria
Source: *BakBD 78; OxCGer 76*

Wesker, Arnold
English. Dramatist
Plays include *Their Very Own Golden City,* 1966; *The Merchant,* 1977.
b. May 24, 1932 in London, England

Source: *Au&Wr 71; Benet 87, 96; BiCoLiE; BiE&WWA; BioIn 6, 7, 8, 9, 10, 11, 12, 13, 14, 17, 18, 22; BlmGEL; BlueB 76; CamBiEn; CamGEL; CamGLE; CamGWoT; CasWL; ChamBiD; CnDBLB 8; CnMD; CnThe; ConAu 1NR, 1R, 7AS, 33NR; ConBrDr; ConDr 73, 77, 82, 88, 93; ConLC 3, 5, 42; ConTFT 7, 14; CroCD; CrtSuDr; CurBio 62; CyWA 89, 97; DcArts; DcLB 13; DcLEL 1940; EncWL 1, 2, 2S, 3; EncWT; Ent; GrWrEL DR; IntAu&W 76, 77, 82, 86, 89, 91, 93; IntDcT 2; IntvTCA 2; IntWW 74, 75, 76, 77, 78, 79, 80, 81, 82, 83, 89, 91, 93, 97, 98, 2000; LinLib L; LngCEL; LngCTC; MajMD 1; MajTwCW 1; MakMC; McGEWD 72, 84; ModBrL, 2, S1, S2; ModWD; NewC; NotNAT, A; OxCEng 85, 95; OxCThe 67, 83; OxCTwCL; PenC ENG; PlP&P; RAdv 14, 13-2; REnWD; RfGEnL 91; RGTwCWr; TwCWr; WebE&AL; Who 74, 82, 83, 85, 88, 90, 92, 94, 98, 99, 2000; WhoEnt 98; WhoThe 72, 77, 81; WhoTwCL; WhoWor 74, 76, 78, 84, 87, 89, 91, 93, 95, 96, 97, 98, 99, 2000; WorAu 1950; WrDr 76, 80, 82, 84, 86, 88, 90, 92, 94, 96, 98, 99, 2000*

Wesley, Charles
English. Clergy, Composer
Preacher started Methodism with his brother and composed thousands of hymns to express its religious ideals.
b. Dec 18, 1707 in Epworth, Lincolnshire, England
d. Mar 29, 1788 in London, England
Source: *BakBD 92; Benet 87, 96; BiDAmM; BiDChrM; BioIn 1, 2, 3, 4, 5, 6, 7, 8, 9, 11, 12, 15, 16, 17, 21; BlmGEL; CamBiEn; CamGEL; CamGLE; ChamBiD; DcLB 95; DcNaB; EncSoH; EncWB 98; EncWM; GrWrEL P; LegTOT; LinLib L, S; LngCEL; LuthC 75; McGEWB; NewCBEL; OxCBrHi; OxCEng 85, 95; OxCMus; RfGEnL 91; WhoChr*

Wesley, Charles Harris
American. Historian, Educator
Leading figure in modern study of black history; wrote several books, including *Negro Labor in the United States, 1850-1925,* 1927.
b. Dec 2, 1891 in Louisville, Kentucky
d. Aug 16, 1987 in Washington, District of Columbia
Source: *AmNatBi; BiDAmEd; BioIn 2, 3, 5, 6, 7, 9, 15, 23, 24; ConAu 101; CurBio 44, 87; EncSoH; InB&W 80; LivgBAA; OhA&B; SelBAAf; WhAm 9; WhoAm 74, 76, 78; WhoBlA 4*

Wesley, Dorothy Porter
American. Librarian, Author
Librarian and curator of the Moorland-Spingarn Research Center at Howard University, building the collection of African American history into one of largest and most comprehensive in the world; received the Charles Frankel Award, National Endowment for the Humanities, 1994.

b. May 25, 1905 in Warrenton, Virginia
d. Dec 17, 1995 in Fort Lauderdale, Florida
Source: *BioIn 23; ConBlB 19*

Wesley, John
English. Religious Leader
Founded Methodism at Oxford U, 1729; name derived from methodical devotion to study, religion.
b. Jun 28, 1703 in Lincoln, England
d. Mar 3, 1791 in London, England
Source: *Alli; ApCAB; AtlBL; BakBD 78, 84, 92; BbD; Benet 87, 96; BiCoLiE; BiDAmM; BiD&SB; BiDChrM; BioIn 1, 2, 3, 4, 5, 6, 7, 8, 9, 10, 11, 12, 13, 14, 16, 17, 19, 20, 21, 23, 24; BlkwCE; BlmGEL; BritAu; CamBiEn; CamGEL; CamGLE; CasWL; ChamBiD; Chambr 2; ChhPo, S1; CyEd; DcAfL; DcBiPP; DcEnA; DcEnL; DcEuL; DcLB 104; DcLEL; DcNaB; Dis&D; Drake; EncAAH; EncEnl; EncSoH; EncWB 98; EncWM; EvLB; HarEnUS; HisWorL; IlEncMy; LegTOT; LinLib L, S; LngCEL; LuthC 75; McGEWB; NatCAB 5; NewC; NewCBEL; NewCol 75; NewGrDM 80; OxCBrHi; OxCEng 67, 85, 95; OxCMus; PenC ENG; PoChrch; RAdv 14, 13-4; RComWL; REn; WebE&AL; WhDW; WhoChr; WorAl; WorAlBi*

Wesley, Valerie Wilson
American. Author, Journalist
Mystery writer whose novels focus on a working class African American heroine in Newark, NJ; also author of children's books and contributor to *Essence* magazine.
b. c. 1940
Source: *ConBlB 18*

Wesselmann, Tom
American. Artist
Best known for series of *The Great American Nude* paintings in different set-ups, media.
b. Feb 23, 1931 in Cincinnati, Ohio
Source: *AmArt; BioIn 12, 13, 14, 15; BlueB 76; BriEAA; CamBiEn; ChamBiD; ConArt 77, 83, 89, 96; ConAu 108; DcAmArt; DcCAA 71, 77, 88, 94; DcCAr 81; DcTwArt; IntWW 74, 75, 76, 77, 78, 79, 80, 81, 82, 83, 89, 91, 93, 97, 98, 2000; OxCTwCA; OxDcArt; PhDcTCA 77; PrintW 83, 85; WhoAm 74, 76, 78, 80, 82, 84, 86, 98; WhoAmA 73, 76, 78, 80, 82, 84, 86, 89, 91, 93, 1999; WhoE 83, 85, 86; WhoWor 74; WorArt 1950*

Wesson, Daniel Baird
[Smith and Wesson]
American. Manufacturer
With Horace Smith, developed repeating action pistol, 1854; open cylinder revolver, 1857.
b. May 25, 1825 in Worcester, Massachusetts
d. 1906

Source: *BioIn 2, 18; CamBiEn; CamDcAB; ChamBiD; DcAmB; NatCAB 10; WhAm 1; WorInv*

Wesson, David
American. Chemist
Discovered refining process for cottonseed oil, 1899, marketed under trade name, Wesson Oil.
b. Jan 14, 1861 in New York, New York
d. May 22, 1934 in Montclair, New Jersey
Source: *EncAB-A 4; Entr; NatCAB 27; WhAm 1*

West, Adam
[William West Anderson]
American. Actor
Played Bruce Wayne/Batman on TV series "Batman," 1966-68.
b. Sep 19, 1938 in Walla Walla, Washington
Source: *BioIn 15, 16; ConTFT 8; FilmgC; HalFC 88; IntMPA 92; WhoHol A*

West, Benjamin
American. Artist
Realistic, historic paintings include *Death of General Wolfe.*
b. Oct 10, 1738 in Springfield, Pennsylvania
d. Mar 11, 1820 in London, England
Source: *Alli; AmBi; AmCulL; AmNatBi; ApCAB; AtlBL; Benet 87, 96; BiDLA; BioIn 1, 2, 3, 4, 5, 6, 7, 8, 9, 10, 11, 12, 13, 14, 19, 22; BkIE; BriEAA; CamBiEn; CamDcAB; CelCen; ChamBiD; ClaDrA; DcAmArt; DcAmB; DcArts; DcBiPP; DcBrECP; DcBrWA; DcNaB; Drake; EncAB-H 1974, 1996; EncCRAm; EnchiCA; EncWB 98; FolkA 87; HarEnUS; IlBEAAW; IntDcAA 90; LegTOT; LinLib S; LiveWoA; McGDA; McGEWB; NatCAB 5; NewYHSD; OxCAmH; OxCAmL 65; OxCArt; OxCBrHi; OxDcArt; REn; TwCBDA; WebAB 74, 79; WhAm HS; WhDW; WorAlBi*

West, Cornel
American. Educator, Author
Professor, Union Theological Seminary, 1977-84, 1987-88; Yale University, 1984-87, Princeton University, 1988-94; Harvard University, 1994—.
b. Jun 2, 1953 in Tulsa, Oklahoma
Source: *AfrAmAl 8; BlkLC SUP; CamDcAB; ConBlB 5; CurBio 93; CyWA 97; DcTwCCu 5; DrAS 99F; EncWB 98; News 94, 94-2; NewYTBS 91; NotBlAM; OxCAfAL; WhoAfA 9, 10, 11, 12; WhoAm 95, 96; WhoBlA 8*

West, Dorothy
American. Author, Editor
Wrote *Living it Easy,* 1948; *The Richer, the Poorer: Stories, Sketches and Reminiscences,* 1995; founded *Challenge* magazine, 1934.
b. Jun 2, 1907 in Boston, Massachusetts
d. Aug 16, 1998 in Boston, Massachusetts

Source: *AfrAmAl 8; BioIn 23, 24; BlkWAm; BlkWr 2; ConAfAN; ConAu 143, 169; ConBlB 12; ConLC 119; CurBio 98N; DcLB 76; DcTwCCu 5; HarlReB; News 96, 96-1; NewYTBS 98; NotBlAW 1; OxCAfAL; OxCWoWr 95; SchCGBL; WhoAfA 9, 10, 11, 12; WhoBlA 7, 8*

West, Dottie
[Dorothy Marie Marsh; Mrs. Alan Winters]
American. Singer
First woman to win country music Grammy for "Here Comes My Baby," 1964; won Clio for co-writing "Country Sunshine" for commercials, 1973, the first awarded to a country artist.
b. Oct 11, 1932 in McMinnville, Tennessee
d. Sep 4, 1991 in Nashville, Tennessee
Source: *AllMGCo; AnObit 1991; BakBD 84, 92; BgBkCoM; BioIn 12, 13, 14, 15, 17, 18, 19, 21; ConMus 8; CounME 74, 74A; EncFCWM 69, 83; HarEnCM 87; IlEncCM; LegTOT; News 92, 92-2; NewYTBS 91; OxCPMus; PenEncP; RkOn 85; WhoAm 86, 88; WhoAmW 87, 89; WhoHol 92*

West, James Edward
American. Social Worker
First leader of US Boy Scouts, 1911.
b. May 16, 1876 in Washington, District of Columbia
d. May 15, 1948 in New Rochelle, New York
Source: *AmAu&B; AmNatBi; BioIn 1, 2, 3, 7; DcAmB S4; NatCAB 34; WhAm 2*

West, Jerry
[Jerome Alan West]
"Mr. Clutch"
American. Basketball Player
Ten-time all-star guard, LA, 1960-74; led NBA in scoring, 1970, in assists, 1972; Hall of Fame, 1979.
b. May 28, 1938 in Cabin Creek, West Virginia
Source: *BasBi; BiDAmSp BK; BioIn 5, 6, 8, 9, 10, 11, 12, 20, 21; CelR; CmCal; ConAu X; FacFETw; LegTOT; NewYTBS 74; OfNBA 87; WhoAm 74, 78, 80, 86, 90; WhoBbl 73; WhoSpor; WhoWest 92; WorAl; WorAlBi*

West, Jessamyn
American. Author
Wrote stories based on Quaker ancestors; first collection *The Friendly Persuasion,* 1945.
b. Jul 18, 1902 in Indiana
d. Feb 25, 1984 in Napa, California
Source: *AmNatBi; AmWomWr; AnObit 1984; BenetAL 91; BioIn 11, 12, 13, 24; CmCal; ConAu 9R, 27NR, 112; ConLC 7, 17; ConNov 76, 82; CurBio 77, 84N; CyWA 89, 97; DcLB 6, Y84N; EncALit; EncFWF; FemiCLE; InWom SUP; LegTOT; LibW; MajTwCW 1; NewYTBS 84; REnAL; ScF&FL 92; SmATA 37N; TwCA SUP; TwCRHW 90; TwCWW 91;*

WhAm 8; WhoAm 76, 78, 80, 82; WhoAmW 79, 81, 83; WrDr 84

West, Mae
American. Actor
Known for sex appeal, frankness, films with W C Fields, including *My Little Chickadee,* 1940.
b. Aug 17, 1893 in New York, New York
d. Nov 22, 1980 in Hollywood, California
Source: *AmAu&B; AmNatBi; AmWomWr; BioAmW; CamBiEn; CamDcAB; CamGWoT; ChamBiD; CmdStar; ConAu 89, 102, 107; CurBio 67, 81, 81N; DcAmB S10; EncWB 2-19; EncWT; Ent; FunnyW; GrLiveH; JoeFr; ModWD; MotPP; MovMk; NewYTBE 70; NewYTBS 80; NotNAT, A; OxCAmH; OxCFilm; ReelWom; REnAL; ThFT; WebAB 74; WhDW; WhoAm 74; WhoCom; WhoHol A; WhoThe 77; WhoWor 74; WomWMM; WorEFlm*

West, Morris L(anglo)
Australian. Author
Wrote *The Shoes of the Fisherman,* 1963; filmed, 1968.
b. Apr 26, 1916 in St. Kilda, Australia
d. Oct 9, 1999 in Sydney, Australia
Source: *Au&Wr 71; Benet 87; BioIn 13; CamBiEn; ChamBiD; ConAu 5R, 24NR, 64NR; ConLC 6, 33; ConNov 86, 91; CurBio 66; DcLP 87A; HalFC 84, 88; IntAu&W 91; IntWW 83, 91, 97, 2000; MajTwCW 1, 2; ModBrL; OxCAusL; REn; SpyFic; TwCSAPR; TwCWr; Who 85, 92, 98, 99, 2000; WhoAm 90, 98, 99, 2000; WhoEnt 98; WhoWor 87, 91, 98, 99, 2000; WhoWrEP 89; WorAlBi; WorAu 1950; WrDr 86, 92, 98, 99, 2000*

West, Nathanael
[Nathan Wallenstein Weinstein]
American. Author
Wrote *Miss Lonelyhearts,* 1933; *The Day of the Locust,* 1939.
b. Oct 17, 1903 in New York, New York
d. Dec 22, 1940 in El Centro, California
Source: *AgeMat; AmAu&B; AmNatBi; AmWr; AtlBL; BeaEPF; BioIn 14, 15, 17, 22; CamBiEn; CamDcAB; CamGEL; CamGLE; CamHAL; CasWL; ChamBiD; CmCal; CnMWL; ConAu 104, 125; CurBio 41; CyWA 58, 97; DcLB 4, 9, 28; DcLEL; DcNAA; DcPseud; EncALit; EncApL; EncWB 98; EncWL 1, 2, 2S, 3; FacFETw; FilmgC; IdentIs; LegTOT; LngCTC; MagSAmL; MajTwCW 1, 2; McGEWB; ModAL 4, 4S1, 4S2, 4S3, 5; OxCAmL 65, 83, 95; OxCTwCL; PenC AM; RAdv 1; REn; REnAL; RfGAmL 4, 87, 94; RGTwCWr; ScF&FL 1; ShScr 16; TwCA, SUP; TwCLC 1, 14, 44; TwCWr; WebAB 74, 79; WebE&AL; WhAm 4; WhDW; WhoTwCL; WorAl; WorAlBi; WrPh*

West, Rebecca, Dame
[Cecily Isobel Fairfield Andrews]
Irish. Author, Journalist
Wrote *The Fountain Overflows*, 1957;
nonfiction *The Meaning of Treason*,
1949.
b. Dec 25, 1892 in County Kerry, Ireland
d. Mar 15, 1983 in London, England
Source: *AnObit 1983; ArtcIWW 2;
Au&Wr 71; BeaEPF; Benet 87, 96;
BiCoLiE; BiDBrF 2; BioIn 1, 2, 3, 4, 5,
6, 7, 8, 9, 10, 11, 12, 13, 14, 15, 16, 17,
18, 21, 22, 24; BlmGWL; BlueB 76;
BritWr S3; CamBiEn; CamGEL;
CamGLE; CasWL; ChamBiD; Chambr
3; ConAu 5R, 19NR, 109; ConLC 7, 9,
31; ConNov 72, 76, 82; ContDcW 89;
CurBio 68, 83N; CyWA 58, 89, 97;
DcArts; DcLB 36, Y83N; DcLEL;
DcNaB 1981; DcPseud; EncBrWW;
EncWL 1, 2, 2S, 3; EvLB; FacFETw;
FemiCLE; FemiWr; GrWrEL N;
IntAu&W 76, 77; IntDcWB; IntWW 74,
75, 76, 77, 78, 79, 80, 81, 82; InWom,
SUP; LegTOT; LinLib L, S; LngCTC;
MajTwCW 1, 2; ModBrL, 2, S1, S2;
ModWoWr; NewC; NewCBEL; NewYTBS
82, 83; Novels; OxCEng 67, 85, 95;
PenC ENG; PenNWW B; RadHan; RAdv
1, 14, 13-1; REn; RfGEnL 91;
RGTwCWr; ScF&FL 1, 2, 92; TwCA,
SUP; TwCWr; WhAm 8; WhE&EA; Who
74, 82, 83; WhoAmW 66, 68, 70, 72, 74,
75; WhoLA; WhoTwCL; WhoWor 74;
WomFir; WomWrGB; WorAl; WorAlBi;
WorAu 1900; WrDr 76, 80, 82, 84*

West, Riff
[Molly Hatchet]
American. Musician
Bass player with heavy metal band since
1982.
b. Apr 3, 1950 in Orlando, Florida

West, Togo D., Jr.
American. Government Official
Secretary of the Army, 1993—.
b. Jun 21, 1942
Source: *ConBlB 16*

Westall, Robert Atkinson
English. Children's Author
Author of over 30 children's books; won
the Carnegie Medal for *The Machine-
Gunners*, 1975 and *Scarecrows*, 1980.
b. Oct 7, 1929 in Tynemouth, England
d. Apr 15, 1993 in Cheshire, England
Source: *BioIn 13, 15; ChlLR 13; ConAu
18NR, 68NR; ConLC 81; DcVicP 2;
FifBJA; IntAu&W 91; MajAl SUP;
OxCChiL; SJGYouA 2; SmATA 2AS;
TwCChW 3; Who 92; WrDr 92*

Westbrook, Peter (J.)
American. Fencer, Business Executive
Champion fencer, one of the few African
Americans to excel in the sport; won
National Collegiate Athletic
Association fencing championships
and was considered the nation's best
college sabrist, 1973, and bronze
medal winner at the 1984 Olympic
Games; founded the Peter Westbrook

Foundation, a fencing clinic for inner-
city children, 1991.
b. Apr 16, 1952 in St. Louis, Missouri
Source: *BlkOlyM; ConAu 164*

Westerman, Floyd
American. Entertainer, Songwriter
Albums include *Custer Died for Your
Sins* and *The Land is Your Mother*;
played Ten Bears in *Dances with
Wolves,*.
b. 1936 in Sissenton-Wahpeton
ReservaSouth Dakota
Source: *BioIn 21; NotNaAm*

Westermann, H(orace) C(lifford)
American. Sculptor
Works of metal, wood take on a comic
strip flare; known for surrealist
displacement.
b. Dec 11, 1922 in Los Angeles,
California
d. Nov 3, 1981 in Danbury, Connecticut
Source: *AnObit 1981; BioIn 8, 11, 12,
13, 14, 17; BriEAA; ConArt 77, 83;
DcAmArt; DcCAA 71; DcCAr 81;
OxCTwCA; PhDcTCA 77; WhAm 8;
WhoAm 74, 76, 78, 80, 86, 88, 90, 92,
94, 95, 96, 97; WhoAmA 73, 76, 78, 80,
82N, 84N, 86N, 89N, 91N, 93N; WhoE
83, 85, 86; WhoWor 74*

Westermarck, Edward Alexander
Finnish. Anthropologist, Philosopher
Defender of conservative morality; traced
origin of marriage to apes.
b. Nov 20, 1862 in Helsingfors, Finland
d. Sep 3, 1939 in Lapinlahti, Finland
Source: *CamBiEn; DcSoc; LinLib S;
REn; WhDW; WhE&EA; WhLit*

Westheimer, Irvin Ferdinand
American. Businessman
Credited with the idea for Big Brothers,
1903; started Big Brothers
organization, Cincinnati, 1912.
b. Sep 19, 1879 in Newark, New Jersey
d. Dec 29, 1980 in Cincinnati, Ohio
Source: *AnObit 1980; BlueB 76;
NewYTBS 81; WhAm 7; WhoAm 74, 76,
78; WhoFI 74, 75*

Westheimer, Ruth
[Karola Ruth Siegel]
''Dr. Ruth''
American. Psychiatrist
Hosts radio, TV shows on sexual
relationships.
b. 1929 in Frankfurt am Main, Germany
Source: *BioIn 12, 13, 14, 15, 16; CelR
90; CurBio 87; InWom SUP; NewYTBS
85, 87; WhoAmW 91; WhoTelC; WrDr
92*

Westinghouse, George
American. Inventor, Manufacturer
Invented air brake and automatic railroad
signals; held over 400 patents.
b. Oct 6, 1846 in Central Bridge, New
York
d. Mar 12, 1914 in New York, New
York

Source: *AmBi; AmNatBi; ApCAB X;
AsBiEn; BiDAmBL 83; BiESc; BiInAmS;
BioIn 1, 3, 4, 5, 6, 7, 8, 9, 11, 12, 13,
14, 16, 18, 21, 23; CamBiEn;
CamDcAB; ChamBiD; DcAmB; DcInv;
DcTwBBL; EncAB-H 1974, 1996;
EncABHB 2; EncWB 98; Entr; GayN;
InSci; LarDcSc; LegTOT; LinLib S;
McGEWB; MemAm; NatCAB 11, 15;
OxCAmH; RanHWDS; TwCBDA; WebAB
74, 79; WhAm 1; WhDW; WorAl;
WorAlBi; WorInv*

**Westlake, Donald E(dwin)
Edmund**
American. Author
Subjects include mystery, crime, humor,
satire; wrote *Nobody's Perfect*, 1977.
b. Jul 12, 1933 in New York, New York
Source: *AmAu&B; BioIn 14; ConAu
13AS, 16NR, 17R; ConLC 7, 33;
CrtSuMy; DcLP 87A; EncMys; HalFC
84, 88; IntAu&W 91; NewYTBS 80;
TwCCr&M 85, 91; WhoAm 82, 84, 86,
90; WhoEnt 92; WhoUSWr 88;
WhoWrEP 89, 92, 95; WorAu 1975;
WrDr 86, 92*

Westley, Helen
[Henrietta Meserole Manney]
American. Actor
Helped found the Theater Guild, 1918-
36.
b. Mar 28, 1879 in New York, New
York
d. Dec 12, 1942 in Franklin County,
New Jersey
Source: *CurBio 43; DcAmB S3; FilmEn;
FilmgC; ForYSC; HalFC 80, 84, 88;
InWom; MovMk; NotAW; NotNAT B;
ObitOF 79; OxCAmT 84; PIP&P; ThFT;
Vers B; WhoHol B; WhScrn 74, 77, 83;
WhThe*

Westmore, Perc(ival)
American. Cosmetics Executive
Hollywood make-up artist; founded
House of Westmore; developed make-
up studio at Warner Brothers Studios.
b. Oct 29, 1904 in Canterbury, England
d. Sep 30, 1970
Source: *BioIn 9, 10; CurBio 45, 70;
FilmgC; HalFC 84; IntDcF 1-4, 2-4;
NewYTBE 70*

Westmoreland, William Childs
American. Military Leader
Commanded US forces in Vietnam,
1964-68; Army chief of staff, 1968-72.
b. Mar 16, 1914 in Spartanburg, South
Carolina
Source: *BioIn 5, 6, 7, 8, 9, 10, 11, 12,
13, 14, 15, 16; BioNews 74; BlueB 76;
CamBiEn; CamDcAB; ChamBiD;
ColdWar 2; ConAu 101; CurBio 61;
DcAmMiB; EncAB-H 1974, 1996;
EncGuW; EncVieW; EncWB, 98;
FacFETw; HarEnMi; IntWW 74, 75, 76,
77, 78, 79, 80, 81, 82, 83, 89, 91, 93,
97, 98, 2000; LinLib S; McGEWB;
NewYTBS 84; PolProf J, NF; SmATA
63; WebAB 74, 79; WebAMB; WhoAm
74, 76; WhoGov 72; WhoWor 74; WorAl*

Weston, Edward

American. Photographer
One of most influential photographers of
20th c; was subject of film *The
Photographer,* 1948.
b. Mar 24, 1886 in Highland Park,
Illinois
d. Jan 1, 1958 in Carmel, California
Source: *AmNatBi; Benet 87, 96; BioIn 1,
2, 4, 5, 6, 7, 8, 9, 10, 11, 12, 13, 14, 15,
16, 19, 20, 21, 22, 24; BriEAA;
CamBiEn; CamDcAB; ChamBiD;
CmCal; ConPhot 82, 88; DcAmArt;
DcArts; DcTwDes; EncWB 2-19;
FacFETw; ICPEnP; LegTOT; MacBEP;
ObitOF 79; WebAB 79; WhAm 3;
WhAmArt 85; WorAl; WorAlBi*

Weston, Edward F

American. Manufacturer
Joined Western Electric, 1900; pres.,
1925; chm., 1944-71.
b. Oct 24, 1879 in Newark, New Jersey
d. Jul 27, 1971
Source: *BioIn 9; NewYTBE 71; WhAm 5*

Weston, Jack

[Morris Weinstein]
American. Actor
Supporting actor in films *The Four
Seasons,* 1981; *High Road to China,*
1983.
b. Aug 21, 1925 in Cleveland, Ohio
d. May 3, 1996 in New York, New York
Source: *BioIn 12; ConTFT 8; DcPseud;
EncAFC; FilmEn; FilmgC; HalFC 84;
IntMPA 86, 88; ObitPA 96; WhoAm 86;
WhoThe 81*

Westover, Russell (Channing)

American. Cartoonist
Created popular working-girl comic strip
Tillie the Toiler, 1921-50s.
b. Aug 3, 1886 in Los Angeles,
California
d. Mar 6, 1966 in San Rafael, California
Source: *BioIn 7; ObitOF 79; WhAm 4,
7; WhAmArt 85; WorECom*

Westphal, Paul Douglas

American. Basketball Player
Three-time all-star guard, 1972-84, with
several NBA teams; named comeback
player of yr., 1983.
b. Nov 30, 1950 in Torrance, California
Source: *BiDAmSp Sup; BioIn 13;
WhoAm 80, 82; WhoBbl 73*

Westrup, J(ack) A(llan), Sir

English. Musician, Lecturer, Educator
Music professor, Oxford U., from 1947;
edited *New Oxford History of Music;*
knighted, 1960.
b. Jul 26, 1904 in London, England
d. Apr 21, 1975 in Headley, England
Source: *Au&Wr 71; BakBD 78, 84, 92;
BakBDTw; ConAu 115; DcNaB 1971;
IntWW 74; NewGrDM 80; NewGrDO;
NewOxM; OxCMus; WhoAm 74;
WhoMus 72*

Westwick, Harry

"Rat"
Canadian. Hockey Player
Goalie-rover, Ottawa Silver Sevens,
1895-1908; Hall of Fame, 1962.
b. Apr 23, 1876 in Ottawa, Ontario,
Canada
d. Apr 3, 1957 in Ottawa, Ontario,
Canada
Source: *WhoHcky 73*

Westwood, Jean Miles

American. Politician
Dem. delegate, committeewoman;
campaign director for presidential
candidates.
b. Nov 22, 1923 in Price, Utah
d. Aug 18, 1997 in American Fork, Utah
Source: *BioIn 9, 75, 77, 91; WhoWest
74, 76*

Westwood, Vivienne

British. Fashion Designer
Known for her satirical style and
subversive chic, she is credited with
being the creator of punk fashion,
among other trend-setting styles.
b. 1941 in Tinwhistle, England
Source: *BioIn 20, 23, 24; CamBiEn;
ChamBiD; ConFash; CurBio 97; DcArts;
EncFash; EncWB 98; IntWW 98, 2000;
IntWWW 2; LegTOT; News 98, 98-3;
ThHDFas; WhoFash 88*

Wettig, Patricia

American. Actor
Played Nancy Weston on TV series
Thirty Something, 1987-1991.
b. Dec 4, 1951 in Grove City,
Pennsylvania
Source: *BioIn 16, 20; ConTFT 9;
IntMPA 94, 96; LegTOT; WhoAm 90, 95,
96, 97, 98; WhoAmW 91; WhoEnt 92,
98; WhoHol 92*

Wexler, Haskell

American. Director, Filmmaker
Won Oscars for cinematography for
Who's Afraid of Virginia Woolf? 1966;
Bound for Glory 1976.
b. 1926 in Chicago, Illinois
Source: *BioIn 11, 15, 16, 19, 24;
ConTFT 7; FilmEn; FilmgC; HalFC 80,
84, 88; IntDcF 1-4, 2-4; IntMPA 75, 76,
77, 78, 79, 80, 81, 82, 84, 86, 88, 92,
94; MiSFD 9; NewYTBE 73; OxCFilm;
WhoAm 86, 90; WhoEnt 92; WorEFlm*

Wexler, Nancy Sabin

American. Psychologist
Pres. Hereditary Disease Foundation;
research led to development of test
which determines whether one will
develop Huntington's disease.
b. Jul 19, 1945 in Washington, District
of Columbia
Source: *AmMWSc 98; AmWomSc 1950;
AZWoSci; ConAu 161; CurBio 94; News
92; WhoAm 96; WhoAmW 95;
WhoMedH 99, 2000*

Wexler, Norman

American. Screenwriter
Films include *Joe,* 1970; *Saturday Night
Fever,* 1977.
b. Aug 16, 1926 in New Bedford,
Massachusetts
d. Aug 23, 1999 in Washington, District
of Columbia
Source: *ConAu 116, 154; VarWW 85;
WhoAm 80, 82, 84; WhoE 91; WhoUSWr
88; WhoWrEP 89, 92, 95*

Wexler, Peter John

American. Designer
Noted for Broadway stage, costume
designs: *The Happy Time,* 1968; *On A
Clear Day You Can See Forever,*
1966.
b. Oct 31, 1936 in New York, New York
Source: *BioIn 10; BlueB 76; ConTFT 5,
6; MetOEnc; NotNAT; VarWW 85;
WhoAm 74, 76, 78, 80, 82, 84, 86, 88,
90, 92, 94, 95, 96, 97, 98, 99, 2000;
WhoE 95; WhoEnt 92, 98; WhoOp 76;
WhoThe 81*

Wexley, John

American. Dramatist
Wrote film *Hangmen Also Die,* 1943;
blacklisted by studio.
b. Sep 14, 1907 in New York, New
York
d. Feb 4, 1985 in Doylestown,
Pennsylvania
Source: *AmAu&B; AmNatBi; BenetAL
91; BioIn 14; CnMD; ConAmA; ConAu
115; ModWD; OxCAmL 65, 83, 95;
PenC AM; REn; REnAL; WhoThe 77A*

Wexner, Leslie

American. Businessman
Founded The Limited, a women's
clothing store, 1963.
b. Sep 8, 1937 in Dayton, Ohio
Source: *ConAmBL; CurBio 94*

Weyden, Rogier van der

[Roger de la Pasture]
Flemish. Artist
Religious, portrait painter; noted for
color, emotion, *Descent From the
Cross,* 1435.
b. 1399 in Tournai, Belgium
d. Jun 16, 1464 in Brussels, Belgium
Source: *AtlBL; DcArts; McGDA;
McGEWB; OxCArt; OxDcArt; REn;
WhDW*

Weyerhaeuser, Frederick

"Lumber King"
American. Business Executive
Lumber tycoon; acquired over two
million acres of forest land from WI
to Pacific NW at time of death.
b. Nov 21, 1834 in Mainz, Germany
d. Apr 4, 1914 in Pasadena, California
Source: *ApCAB X; BiDAmBL 83; BioIn
3, 5, 11, 14, 15, 23; NatCAB 14; WebAB
74, 79; WhAm 1*

Weyerhaeuser, Frederick Edward

American. Business Executive
Son of Frederick Weyerhaeuser,
  reportedly largest owner of forest land
  in US.
b. Jan 16, 1895 in Rock Island, Illinois
d. Oct 18, 1945 in Saint Paul, Minnesota
Source: *BiDAmBL 83; CurBio 45;*
DcAmB S3; EncAB-A 21; NatCAB 37;
WhAm 2

Weygand, Maxime

French. Military Leader
Supreme allied commander, 1939, known
  for unsuccessful attempt to create new
  front.
b. Jan 21, 1867 in Brussels, Belgium
d. Jan 28, 1965 in Paris, France
Source: *BiDFrPL; BioIn 1, 3, 7, 17;*
CamBiEn; ChamBiD; CurBio 40, 65;
DcTwHis; EncTR 91; FacFETw;
HarEnMi; HisEWW; WhoMilH 76;
WhWW-II

Whale, James

English. Director
Films include *Frankenstein,* 1931;
  Invisible Man, 1933.
b. Jul 22, 1896 in Dudley, England
d. May 29, 1957 in Hollywood,
  California
Source: *BiDFilm, 94; BioIn 4, 10, 11;*
CmMov; DcFM; FacFETw; FanAl;
FilmEn; FilmgC; IlWWWHD 1; MiSFD
9N; OxCFilm; PenEncH; TwCLC 63;
WhThe; WorEFlm

Whalen, Grover (Michael) A(loysius)

American. Merchant
Pres. of NY World's Fair, 1939-40; NY
  Police commissioner, 1928-30.
b. Jun 2, 1886 in New York, New York
d. Apr 20, 1962 in New York, New
  York
Source: *CamDcAB; DcAmB S7; WhAm 4*

Whalen, Michael

[Joseph Kenneth Shovlin]
American. Actor
Leading man of B-films, 1936-60,
  including *Sing, Baby, Sing; Poor Little*
  Rich Girl.
b. Jun 30, 1902 in Wilkes-Barre,
  Pennsylvania
d. Apr 14, 1974 in Woodland Hills,
  California
Source: *FilmEn; FilmgC; MovMk; What*
5; WhoHol B; WhScrn 77, 83

Wham!

[George Michael; Andrew Ridgeley]
English. Music Group
Childhood friends who formed group,
  1982-86; had three number one hits,
  including "Everything She Wants,"
  1985.
Source: *BiIEnR; BioIn 14, 15, 16, 17,*
18; EncPR&S 89; EncRk 88; EncRkSt;
HarEnR 86; PenEncP; RkOn 85;
WhoAm 92; WhoEnt 92

Wharton, Clifton Reginald, Jr.

American. University Administrator
Pres. of MI State U, 1970-78; chancellor,
  SUNY System, 1978-87.
b. Sep 13, 1926 in Boston,
  Massachusetts
Source: *AmMWSc 73S; BiDMoAE; BioIn*
9, 10, 11, 12, 13, 15; BlueB 76; ConAu
41R; CurBio 58, 87; Ebony 1; InB&W
85; IntWW 83, 91; LEduc 74; NewYTBS
77; SelBAAf; SelBAAu; St&PR 91;
WhoAm 74, 76, 78, 80, 82, 84, 86, 90,
92, 94, 95, 96, 97; WhoBlA 4, 7; WhoE
79, 81, 83, 85, 86, 93; WhoFI 89, 92,
94; WhoIns 92; WhoMW 74, 76, 78;
WhoUSWr 88; WhoWrEP 89, 92, 95

Wharton, Edith

[Edith Newbold Jones]
American. Author
Won Pulitzer, 1921, for *The Age of*
  Innocence; noted for *Ethan Frome,*
  1911, and novels of NY society.
b. Jan 24, 1862 in New York, New York
d. Aug 11, 1937 in Paris, France
Source: *AmBi; AmCulL; AmDec 1900;*
AmNatBi; AmWomWr 92; AmWr RS1;
ApCAB X; ArtclWW 2; AtlBL; Au&Arts
25; BeaEPF; Benet 87; BenetAL 91;
BiCoLiE; BioAmW; BioIn 14, 15, 16, 17,
18, 19, 20, 21, 22, 23, 24; BlmGWL;
CamGEL; CamGLE; CamHAL; CasWL;
ChhPo S3; ConAu 104, 132; ContDcW
89; CyWA 89, 97; DcAmB S2; DcLB 4,
9, 12, 78, 189, DS13; EncAB-H 1974;
EncALit; EncSF; EncWL 2, 2S, 3;
FacFETw; FemiCLE; GayN; GoodHs;
GrLiveH; GrWomW; HanAmWH; HerW,
84; IdentIs; IntDcWB; LegTOT; LibW;
LinLib L; LiveWoA; MagSAmL;
MajTwCW 1; MakMC; ModAL 4S1, 4S2,
4S3, 5; ModAWWr; ModWoWr; MorMA;
NatCAB 14; NotAW; NotNAT B; Novels;
OnHuYeA; OxCAmL 65, 83; OxCEng 67,
85; OxCWoWr 95; PenC AM; PenEncH;
RAdv 1, 13-1; RComAH; RealN; REn;
REnAL; RfGAmL 87; RfGShF 1, 2;
ScF&FL 1; ShSCr 6; ShSWr; SocPrL;
SupFW; TwCA SUP; TwCBDA; TwCLC
3, 9, 27, 53; TwCRHW 94; TwCWr;
WcbAB 74, 79; WhAm 1; WhDW;
WhE&EA; WhLit; WhoHr&F;
WhoTwCL; WomWWA 14; WorAlBi;
WorLitC; WrPh

Wharton, Joseph

American. Manufacturer
First to produce nickel in US, 1873;
  founded Bethlehem Steel, 1873,
  Wharton School of Finance, 1881.
b. Mar 3, 1826 in Philadelphia,
  Pennsylvania
d. Jan 11, 1909
Source: *AmNatBi; ApCAB; BiDAmBL*
83; BiInAmS; BioIn 4, 15, 24; DcAmB;
EncABHB 3; NatCAB 13; TwCBDA;
WhAm 1; WorAl; WorAlBi

Wheat, Alan (Dupree)

American. Politician
Known for building bridges between
  blacks and whites, served as
  Democratic congressman representing
  the 5th District of Missouri, 1983-94,

and president of Congressional Black
  Caucus Foundation; lost a bid for the
  U.S. Senate in 1994.
b. Oct 16, 1951 in San Antonio, Texas
Source: *BiDrUSC 89; BlkAmsC; WhoAm*
84, 86, 88, 90, 92, 94, 95; WhoE 95;
WhoMW 84, 86, 88, 90, 92, 93

Wheat, Zack

[Zachariah Davis Wheat]
"Buck"
American. Baseball Player
Outfielder, 1909-27, mostly with
  Brooklyn; led NL in batting, 1918;
  had .317 lifetime batting average; Hall
  of Fame, 1959.
b. May 23, 1888 in Hamilton, Missouri
d. Mar 11, 1972 in Sedalia, Missouri
Source: *AmNatBi; BioIn 14, 15;*
CulEncB; DcAmB S9; WhoProB 73;
WhoSpor

Wheatley, Phillis

American. Poet
Ex-slave; first black woman to have
  poetry published, 1770.
b. 1753, Senegal
d. Dec 5, 1784 in Boston, Massachusetts
Source: *AfrA; AfrAmAl 6, 8; AfrAmW;*
Alli; AmAu; AmAu&B; AmNatBi;
AmWomWr; ApCAB; ArtclWW 2; Benet
87, 96; BenetAL 91; BiCoLiE; BioAmW;
BioIn 1, 2, 3, 4, 6, 7, 8, 9, 10, 11, 12,
14, 15, 16, 17, 18, 19, 20, 21, 22, 23,
24; BlkAmW 1; BlkAWP; BlkLC;
BlkWrNE; BlmGEL; BlmGWL;
CamBiEn; CamDcAB; CamGLE;
ChamBiD; ChhPo; ColARen; ConAu 1R;
ContDcW 89; CyAL 1; CyWA 97;
DcAmAu; DcAmB; DcAmNB;
DcBrAmW; DcLEL; Drake; EncWB 98;
FemiCLE; GoodHs; GrWomW; GrWrEL
P; HanAmWH; HarEnUS; HerW, 84;
InB&W 80, 85; IntDcWB; InWom, SUP;
LegTOT; LibW; LitC 3, 50; McGEWB;
NegAl 76, 83, 89; NotAW; NotBlAW 1;
OxCAfAL; OxCAmL 65, 83, 95; OxCEng
67; OxCWoWr 95; PoeCrit 3; PorAmW;
RAdv 13-1; REn; REnAL; RfGAmL 4,
87, 94; SchCGBL; SelBAAf; SelBAAu;
WebAB 74, 79; WhAm HS; WhAmRev;
WomFir; WorAl; WorAlBi; WorLitC

Wheatstone, Charles, Sir

English. Scientist, Inventor
Invented the concertina, 1829; electric
  telegram, 1837; Wheatstone bridge for
  measuring electrical resistances, 1843.
b. Feb 6, 1802 in Gloucester, England
d. Oct 19, 1875 in Paris, France
Source: *Alli, SUP; AsBiEn; BiDPsy;*
BiESc; BioIn 2, 7, 8, 9, 10, 14, 15;
CamBiEn; CamDcSc; CelCen;
ChamBiD; DcArts; DcBiPP; DcInv;
DcNaB; DcScB; ICPEnP; InSci;
LarDcSc; MacBEP; McGCEnS;
NamesHP; NewGrDM 80; OxCMus;
RanHWDS; WhDW; WorAl; WorAlBi;
WorInv

Wheeler, Bert
[Wheeler and Woolsey; Albert Jerome
　Wheeler]
American. Comedian
Teamed with Robert Woolsey in over 30
　films, including *On Again, Off Again*,
　1937.
b. Apr 7, 1895 in Paterson, New Jersey
d. Jan 18, 1968 in New York, New York
Source: *BiE&WWA; BioIn 7, 8, 20;*
EncVaud; Film 2; FilmEn; FilmgC;
ForYSC; HalFC 80, 84, 88; JoeFr;
MovMk; NotNAT B; QDrFCA 92;
TelevWe; What 1; WhoHol B; WhScrn
74, 77, 83

Wheeler, Burton Kendall
American. Politician
Dem. politician from MT, 1923-47.
b. Feb 27, 1882 in Hudson,
　Massachusetts
d. Jan 6, 1975 in Washington, District of
　Columbia
Source: *AmNatBi; AmPolLe; ApCAB X;*
BiDrAC; BiDrUSC 89; BioIn 1, 6, 7, 10;
CamDcAB; ConAu 53; CurBio 40, 75;
DcAmB S9; EncAAH; WhAm 6; WhAmP;
Who 74

Wheeler, Candace Thurber
American. Designer
Pioneer in textile design; worked with
　Tiffany, 1879.
b. Mar 24, 1827 in Delaware County,
　New York
d. Aug 5, 1923 in New York, New York
Source: *AmNatBi; BiCAW; InWom SUP;*
NotAW

Wheeler, Earle G
American. Government Official
Served as Army chief of staff, 1962-64;
　confirmed in 1973 that Nixon ordered
　secret attacks over Cambodia, 1969.
b. Jan 13, 1908 in Washington, District
　of Columbia
d. Dec 18, 1975 in Frederick, Maryland
Source: *CurBio 65, 76N; EncVieW;*
IntWW 74, 76N; NewYTBS 75; PolProf
J, NF; WebAMB; WhAm 6; WhoAm 74

Wheeler, Hugh Callingham
English. Writer
Won Tonys for plays based on his
　books: *A Little Night Music*, 1973;
　Candide, 1974; *Sweeney Todd*, 1979.
b. Mar 19, 1912 in London, England
d. Jul 27, 1987 in Pittsfield,
　Massachusetts
Source: *AmNatBi; BioIn 10, 14, 15;*
BlueB 76; ConAu 59NR; ConDr 93;
ConTFT 5; EncMys; NewGrDO;
NewYTBS 87; VarWW 85; WhAm 9;
WhE&EA; WhoAm 74, 76, 78, 80, 82,
84, 86; WorAu 1950

Wheeler, Joseph
American. Military Leader
Resigned from US army to join
　Confederate army, 1861; tried to
　reconcile North, South.
b. Sep 10, 1836 in Augusta, Georgia
d. Jan 25, 1906 in New York, New York

Source: *Alli SUP; AmBi; AmNatBi;*
ApCAB; BiDConf; BiDrAC; BiDrUSC
89; BiDSA; BioIn 3, 5, 6, 7, 17;
CamDcAB; ChhPo S1; CivWDc;
DcAmAu; DcAmB; DcAmMiB; DcNAA;
EncSoH; GenMudB; HarEnMi;
HarEnUS; NatCAB 9; SpAmWar;
TwCBDA; WebAB 74, 79; WebAMB;
WebBD 83; WhAm 1; WhAmP;
WhCiWar; WorAl; WorAlBi

Wheeler, Mortimer
[Robert Eric Mortimer Wheeler]
British. Archaeologist
His book *Alms for Oblivion*, 1966,
　credited with increased interest in
　archaeology.
b. Sep 10, 1890 in Edinburgh, Scotland
d. Jul 22, 1976 in Leatherhead, England
Source: *BioIn 1, 3, 4, 5, 6, 8, 11, 12, 13,*
14, 21; BlueB 76; ConAu 32NR, 65, 77;
CurBio 56, 76N; DcNaB 1971; GrBr;
InSci; IntAu&W 77; IntWW 74, 75, 76;
LngCTC; NewYTBS 76; ObitOF 79;
WhDW; WhE&EA; Who 74; WhoWor
74; WorAl

Wheeler, Roger Milton
American. Business Executive
Pres., American Magnesium Co., 1968-
　81; chm., Telex, Inc., 1965-81.
b. Feb 27, 1926 in Boston,
　Massachusetts
d. May 27, 1981 in Tulsa, Oklahoma
Source: *BioIn 12; BlueB 76; WhAm 8;*
WhoAm 74, 76, 78, 80, 82; WhoSSW 73

Wheeler, Schuyler Skaats
American. Inventor
Invented the electric fan.
b. May 17, 1860
d. 1923
Source: *AmBi; BioIn 4; DcAmB; InSci;*
NatCAB 10, 41; WhAm 1

Wheeler, William Alrnon
American. US Vice President
Served under Rutherford B Hayes, 1877-
　81.
b. Jun 30, 1819 in Malone, New York
d. Jun 4, 1887 in Malone, New York
Source: *BiAUS; HarEnUS; WebAB 79*

Wheeler, William Morton
American. Zoologist
A leading expert on ants; books:*Ants:*
Their Structure, Development, and
Behavior, 1910 and *Social Life among*
the Insects, 1923, are classic reference
　works.
b. Mar 19, 1865 in Milwaukee,
　Wisconsin
d. Apr 19, 1937 in Cambridge,
　Massachusetts
Source: *AmBi; AmLY; AmNatBi;*
BiDAmCa; BioIn 3, 4, 9, 22, 23;
CamDcAB; DcAmB S2; DcNAA; DcScB;
InSci; NamesHP; NatCAB 27; TwCA;
WhAm 1; WorAu 1900

Wheelock, Eleazar
American. Clergy, Educator
Founded Dartmouth College; served as
　first pres., 1770-79.
b. Apr 22, 1711 in Windham,
　Connecticut
d. Apr 24, 1779 in Hanover, New
　Hampshire
Source: *Alli; AmBi; AmNatBi; AmWrBE;*
ApCAB; BenetAL 91; BiDAmEd;
BiDChrM; BioIn 1, 3, 9, 17, 19;
CamDcAB; CyAL 1; CyEd; DcAmB;
DcAmReB 1, 2; DcNAA; EncCRAm;
EncNAR; EncWB 98; HarEnUS;
McGEWB; OxCAmH; OxCAmL 65, 83,
95; TwCBDA; WebAB 74, 79; WhAm
HS; WhNaAH; WorAl; WorAlBi

Wheelock, John Hall
American. Poet
First book of poetry was *The Human*
Fantasy, 1911.
b. Sep 9, 1886 in Far Rockaway, New
　York
d. Mar 22, 1978 in New York, New
　York
Source: *AmAu&B; AmLY; AmNatBi;*
AnMV 1926; Au&Wr 71; BenetAL 91;
BioIn 4, 5, 9, 10, 11, 15, 22; BlueB 76;
ChhPo, S1, S2, S3; CnDAL; ConAmA;
ConAmL; ConAu 13R, 14NR, 77; ConLC
14; ConPo 70, 75; DcAmB S10; DcLB
45; DcLEL; DrAP 75; EncALit;
IntAu&W 77; IntWW 74, 75, 76, 77;
ModAL 4, 5; NewYTBS 78; OxCAmL 65,
83, 95; OxCTwCP; RAdv 1; REn;
REnAL; TwCA, SUP; WhAm 7; WhNAA;
WhoAm 74, 76, 78; WhoWor 74; WorAu
1900; WrDr 76

Wheelwright, William
American. Entrepreneur
Pioneered South American steamship,
　railroad, and telegraph construction.
b. Mar 18, 1798 in Newburyport,
　Massachusetts
d. Sep 26, 1873 in London, England
Source: *AmBi; AmNatBi; ApCAB; BioIn*
1; DcAmB; EncLatA; EncWB 98;
McGEWB; WhAm HS

Whelchel, Lisa
American. Actor
Played Blair on TV series "Facts of
　Life," 1979-88.
b. May 29, 1963 in Fort Worth, Texas
Source: *BioIn 13; ConTFT 3, 21;*
LegTOT; VarWW 85; WhoHol 92

Whicker, Alan Donald
English. Broadcast Journalist
Host of "Whicker's World," 1959-67;
　winner of numerous awards for his
　documentaries.
b. Aug 2, 1925 in Cairo, Egypt
Source: *CamBiEn; ChamBiD; IntAu&W*
91; IntWW 91, 97, 98, 2000; Who 92,
98, 99, 2000; WrDr 98, 99, 2000

Whiffen, Marcus
English. Author, Educator
Wrote *American Architecture, 1607-*
1976, 1981.

b. Mar 4, 1916 in Weston-under-
Penyard, England
Source: *ConAu 12NR, 61, 102; IntAu&W 82*

Whipple, George Hoyt
American. Physician, Educator
Shared 1934 Nobel Prize for discovering
treatment for once incurable anemia.
b. Aug 28, 1879 in Ashland, New
Hampshire
d. Feb 1, 1976 in Rochester, New York
Source: *AmMWSc 73P; IntWW 74;
WebAB 74; WebBD 83; WhAm 6;
WhDW; Who 74; WhoAm 82; WhoNob;
WhoWor 82*

Whipple, William
American. Continental Congressman,
Soldier
Spirited patriot; led militia contingents;
signed Declaration of Independence,
1776.
b. Jan 14, 1730 in Kittery, Maine
d. Nov 28, 1785 in Portsmouth, New
Hampshire
Source: *AmBi; AmNatBi; AmRev;
ApCAB; BiAUS; BiDrAC; BiDrUSC 89;
BioIn 7, 8, 9, 23; DcAmB; Drake;
EncAR; EncCRAm; HarEnUS; HisDcAR;
NatCAB 4; TwCBDA; WebBD 83; WhAm
HS; WhAmP; WhAmRev; WorAl;
WorAlBi*

Whistler, Anna Matilda McNeill
"Whistler's Mother"
American.
Best known as subject of son James'
painting.
b. 1804
d. 1881
Source: *BioIn 3, 9, 10; InWom, SUP*

Whistler, James Abbott McNeill
American. Artist, Author
Famous for *Arrangement in Gray and
Black No.1: The Artist's Mother*, 1872
or, "Whistler's Mother."
b. Jul 10, 1834 in Lowell, Massachusetts
d. Jul 17, 1903 in London, England
Source: *Alli SUP; AmAu; AmAu&B;
AmBi; AmCulL; ApCAB; ArtsNiC;
AtlBL; BiD&SB; BioIn 1, 2, 3, 4, 5, 6, 7,
8, 9, 10, 11, 12, 13; BriEAA; CamBiEn;
ChamBiD; Chambr 3; DcAmArt;
DcAmAu; DcAmB; DcArts; DcBrAr 1;
DcLEL; DcNAA; DcNaB S2; DcSeaP;
DcTwArt; DcVicP, 2; EncAB-H 1974,
1996; EncWB 98; GayN; LinLib S;
McGDA; McGEWB; NatCAB 9;
NewCBEL; NewYHSD; OxCAmH;
OxCAmL 65; OxCArt; OxCBrHi;
OxCEng 67, 85, 95; OxDcArt; REn;
REnAL; ThHElm; TwCBDA; WebAB 74,
79; WhAm 1; WhAmArt 85; WorAl;
WorAlBi*

Whistler, Rex
[Reginald John Whistler]
English. Illustrator
Designed posters, prestigious books,
stage settings.
b. Jun 24, 1905 in Eltham, England

d. Jul 18, 1944 in Normandy, France
Source: *BioIn 1, 2, 5, 11, 14, 15; ChhPo
S3; DancEn 78; DcNaB 1941; DcTwArt;
McGDA; NotNAT B; OxCArt; OxDcArt;
SmATA 30; TwCPaSc; WhThe*

Whitaker, Forest
American. Actor, Director
Films include *Bird*, 1988; *A Rage in
Harlem*, 1990; won Cannes Film
Festival award best actor for *Bird*,
1988; directed *Waiting to Exhale*,
1995.
b. Jul 15, 1961 in Longview, Texas
Source: *BioIn 16; ConTFT 8,
16, 27; CurBio 97; DcTwCCu 5; IntMPA
92, 94, 96; LegTOT; News 96, 96-2;
WhoAfA 9, 10, 11, 12; WhoAm 94, 95,
96, 97, 99, 2000; WhoBlA 7, 8; WhoEnt
98; WhoHol 92; WhoWor 95, 96, 97, 98,
99, 2000*

Whitaker, Jack
[John Francis Whitaker]
American. Sportscaster
Covered variety of sports for CBS;
commentator, ABC News, Sports since
1982.
b. May 18, 1924 in Philadelphia,
Pennsylvania
Source: *LesBEnT 92; WhoAm 76, 78, 80,
82, 84, 86, 88, 90; WhoTelC*

Whitaker, Johnny
American. Actor
Played Jody on TV series "Family
Affair," 1966-71.
b. Dec 13, 1959 in Van Nuys, California
Source: *BioIn 20; WhoHol 92, A*

Whitaker, Lou(is Rodman)
"Sweet Lou"
American. Baseball Player
Second baseman, Detroit, 1977-95; AL
rookie of year, 1978; with Alan
Trammell, formed MLs longest
standing double play combination.
b. May 12, 1957 in New York, New
York
Source: *Ballpl 90; BaseReg 86, 87;
BiDAmSp Sup; BioIn 13, 14, 16; InB&W
80; WhoAfA 9, 10, 11, 12; WhoAm 90,
92; WhoBlA 4, 5, 6, 7, 8; WhoMW 90*

Whitaker, Pernell
American. Boxer
WBC welterweight champion, 1993-96.
b. Jan 2, 1964 in Norfolk, Virginia
Source: *BioIn 14, 19; BlkOlyM;
ChamBiD; ConBlB 10; WhoAm 99,
2000; WhoWor 99, 2000*

**Whitaker, Rogers E(rnest)
M(alcolm)**
[E M Frimbo]
American. Author, Journalist
With *New Yorker* mag. one yr. after its
inception, 1926-81; cowrote *All
Aboard With E M Frimbo*, 1974.
b. Jan 15, 1899 in Arlington,
Massachusetts

d. May 11, 1981 in New York, New
York
Source: *AnObit 1981; BioIn 10; ConAu
103; NewYTBS 81*

Whitcroft, Fred(rick)
Canadian. Hockey Player
Amateur player with several teams,
1907-10; Hall of Fame, 1962.
b. 1880? in Fort Perry, Ontario, Canada
d. 1931 in Vancouver, British Columbia,
Canada
Source: *WhoHcky 73*

White, Andrew Dickson
American. Educator, University
Administrator
Founded, Cornell U, 1865; author of
many books on historical subjects.
b. Nov 7, 1832 in Homer, New York
d. Nov 4, 1918 in Ithaca, New York
Source: *Alli, SUP; AmAu; AmAu&B;
AmBi; AmNatBi; ApCAB, X; BiDAmEd;
BiD&SB; BiDInt; BioIn 1, 2, 3, 5, 6, 7,
12, 14, 15, 16, 23; CamDcAB;
ChamBiD; Chambr 3; CyAL 2;
DcAmAu; DcAmB; DcAmBC; DcAmDH
80, 89; DcLB 47; DcNAA; Drake;
EncAB-A 1; EncAB-H 1974, 1996;
EncWB 98; HarEnUS; LinLib L, S;
McGEWB; MorMA; NatCAB 4;
OxCAmH; OxCAmL 65, 83, 95; REnAL;
TwCBDA; WebAB 74, 79; WhAm 1;
WorAl; WorAlBi*

White, Antonia
English. Author
Translated over 30 French works; wrote
four novels.
b. Mar 31, 1899 in London, England
d. Apr 10, 1980 in London, England
Source: *AnObit 1980; ArtclWW 2;
Au&Wr 71; Benet 87, 96; BioIn 3, 4, 7,
10, 12, 13, 14, 15, 16, 18; BkC 5;
CamBiEn; CamGLE; CathA 1952;
ConAu 97, 104; ConNov 72, 76;
DcPseud; EncBrWW; FemiCLE;
IntAu&W 76, 77; InWom SUP; LegTOT;
LngCTC; ModWoWr; NewC; OxCEng
85, 95; OxCTwCL; REn; RGTwCWr;
Who 74; WorAu 1950; WrDr 76, 80*

White, Barry
American. Singer, Songwriter
Hits include "Never, Never Gonna Give
You Up," 1973; "My First, My Last,
My Everything," 1974.
b. Sep 12, 1944 in Galveston, Texas
Source: *BiDAfM; BillEnR; BioIn 12;
BkPepl; ConBlB 13; ConMus 6; DrBlPA,
90; EncRk 88; EncRkSt; IlEncRk;
InB&W 85; LegTOT; NewGrDA 86;
PenEncP; RkOn 74, 78; RolSEnR 83;
Songw; SoulM; WhoAfA 9, 10, 11, 12;
WhoAm 80, 82; WhoBlA 4, 5, 6, 7, 8;
WhoHol 92; WhoRock 81; WorAl;
WorAlBi*

White, Betty
American. Actor
Played Sue Ann Nevins on "The Mary
Tyler Moore Show," 1970-77; Rose
on "Golden Girls," 1985-92; plays

same character on CBS' "Golden
Palace," 1992-93.
b. Jan 17, 1922 in Oak Park, Illinois
Source: *BioIn 14, 15, 16; CelR 90;
ConTFT 3, 13; CurBio 87; IntMPA 92;
InWom SUP; LegTOT; LesBEnT 92;
WhoAm 82, 86, 88, 90, 92, 94, 95, 96,
97, 98, 99, 2000; WhoAmW 89, 93;
WhoCom; WhoEnt 92, 98; WhoHol 92,
A; WhoWest 00, 96, 98; WorAlBi*

White, Bill
[William Dekova White]
American. Baseball Player, Baseball
Executive
All-Star first baseman, 1956-69;
succeeded Bart Giamatti as president
of NL, 1989-94; first black to head a
major US pro sports league.
b. Jan 28, 1934 in Lakewood, Florida
Source: *AfrAmAl 6, 8; AfrAmSG; Ballpl
90; BaseEn 88; BiDAmSp Sup; BioIn 13,
16; ConBlB 1; InB&W 85; NegAl 89;
News 89-3; NewYTBS 91; WhoAfA 9, 10,
11, 12; WhoAm 94, 95, 96, 97; WhoBlA
7, 8; WhoWor 96*

White, Byron Raymond
American. Supreme Court Justice
Served on the Supreme Court from
1962-93.
b. Jun 8, 1917 in Fort Collins, Colorado
Source: *AmBench 79, 97; BiDAmSp FB;
BioIn 5, 6, 7, 8, 9, 10, 11, 12, 13, 14,
15; BlueB 76; CamDcAB; CngDr 74, 77,
79, 81, 83, 85, 87, 89, 91, 93, 95;
CriJuSA; CurBio 62; DrAS 82P;
EncWB; FacFETw; NewYTBE 72;
OxCSupC; PeoHis; SupCtJu; WebAB 74,
79; Who 85, 92, 98, 99, 2000; WhoAm
86, 90; WhoAmL 85, 92; WhoAmP 85,
91; WhoE 91; WhoGov 77; WorAl;
WorAlBi*

White, Charles Raymond
American. Football Player
Running back, won Heisman Trophy,
1979; in NFL with Cleveland, 1980-
84, LA Rams, 1985-88.
b. Jan 22, 1958 in Los Angeles,
California
Source: *BiDAmSp FB; FootReg 87*

White, Chris(topher Taylor)
[The Zombies]
English. Musician
Bass player with rock group, 1962-67;
hits include "She's Not There," 1964.
b. Mar 7, 1943 in Barnet, England
Source: *WhoRocM 82*

White, Dan(iel James)
American. Police Officer
Murdered San Francisco mayor George
Moscone, supervisor Harvey Milk,
Dec, 1978.
b. 1946?
d. Oct 21, 1985 in San Francisco,
California
Source: *BioIn 11, 12, 13*

White, Deacon
[James Laurie White]
American. Baseball Player
Catcher-infielder, 1876-90; won NL
batting title, 1877; first catcher to
crouch directly behind batter.
b. Dec 7, 1847 in Canton, New York
d. Jul 7, 1939 in Aurora, Illinois
Source: *Ballpl 90; BiDAmSp BB; BioIn
15; WhoProB 73*

White, E(lwyn) B(rooks)
American. Author
Wrote children's classics *Charlotte's
Web*, 1952; *Stuart Little*, 1945;
awarded Laura Wilder Medal, 1970.
b. Jul 11, 1899 in Mount Vernon, New
York
d. Oct 1, 1985 in North Brooklin, Maine
Source: *AmAu&B; AmPeW; AmWr S1;
Au&ICB; AuBYP 2, 3; AuNews 2; Benet
96; BioIn 1, 3, 4, 5, 6, 7, 8, 9, 10, 11,
12, 13, 14, 15, 16, 17, 18, 19, 20, 23;
BkCL; BlueB 76; CamBiEn; CamHAL;
CelR; ChamBiD; ChhPo, S1, S2, S3;
ChlLR 1; CnDAL; ConAu 13R, 16NR,
37NR; ConLC 10; ConPopW; CurBio
60, 85; DcAmChF 1960; DcArts; DcLB
11, 22; DcLEL; EncAB-H 1996; EncAJ;
EncALit; EncWL 2S, 3; EvLB; IntAu&W
76, 77; IntWW 74, 75, 76, 77, 78, 79,
80, 81, 82, 83; JrnUS; LinLib L, S;
LngCTC; MajAl; MajTwCW 2; ModAL
4; MorBMP; MorJA; OxCAmH;
OxCAmL 65, 83, 95; OxCChiL;
OxCTwCL; PenC AM; PiP; RAdv 1, 14;
REn; REnAL; RfGAmL 4, 94; ScrEAmL
1; SJGFanW; SmATA 2, 4, 29, 100;
TwCA, SUP; TwCChW 1, 2, 4; TwCWr;
WebAB 74, 79; WhAm 10; Who 74, 82,
83, 85; WhoAm 74, 76, 78, 80, 82, 84;
WhoChL; WhoWor 74, 84; WorAl;
WorAu 1900; WrDr 76, 80, 82, 84*

White, Ed(ward Higgins, III)
American. Astronaut
First American to exit orbiting
spacecraft, also first to control
movements while in space; died in
flash fire during *Apollo* flight
simulation.
b. Nov 14, 1930 in San Antonio, Texas
d. Jan 27, 1967 in Cape Canaveral,
Florida
Source: *CurBio 65, 67; WhAm 4*

White, Edmund
American. Author
Gay writer and activist; first novel,
Forgetting Elena, 1973; co-author of
The Joy of Gay Sex, 1977; Book
Critics Circle award, 1994.
b. Jan 13, 1940 in Cincinnati, Ohio
Source: *Au&Arts 7; BenetAL 91; BioIn
13, 15, 16, 17, 18, 19, 20, 24; CamBiEn;
CamGLE; CamHAL; CmpQue; ConAu
3NR, 19NR, 36NR, 45; ConGAN; ConLC
27, 110; ConNov 91; CurBio 91; DrAPF
80, 91; EncALit; GayLesB; IdentIs;
IntAu&W 91, 93; IntWW 93, 97, 98,
2000; MajTwCW 1; OxCTwCL; PostFic;
ScF&FL 92; WhoUSWr 88; WorAu
1980; WrDr 84, 86, 88, 90, 92, 94, 96,
98, 99, 2000*

White, Edward Douglass
American. Supreme Court Justice
Appointed to court by Pres. Cleveland,
1894; served as chief justice, 1910-21;
known for "rule of reason" practices.
b. Nov 3, 1845 in Lafourche, Louisiana
d. May 19, 1921 in Washington, District
of Columbia
Source: *AmBi; AmJust; AmNatBi;
AmPolLe; ApCAB; BiDFedJ; BiDrAC;
BiDrUSC 89; BioIn 2, 3, 5, 6, 7, 10, 11,
12, 15; CamDcAB; ChamBiD; DcAmB;
DcAmC; EncAB-H 1974, 1996; EncSoH;
EncWB 98; FacFETw; HarEnUS;
McGEWB; OxCAmH; OxCLaw;
OxCSupC; SupCtJu; TwCBDA; WebAB
74, 79; WebBD 83; WhAm 1; WhAmP*

White, Ellen Gould Harmon
American. Religious Leader
Co-founder, Seventh-Day Adventists,
1860; claimed 2000 visions.
b. Nov 26, 1827 in Gorham, Maine
d. Jul 16, 1915 in Saint Helena,
California
Source: *Alli SUP; AmDec 1900;
AmNatBi; AmPeW; AmRef; AmWomWr;
BiDAmCu; BiDChrM; BioIn 15, 18, 19;
CmCal; DcAmB; DcAmMeB 84;
DcAmReB 1, 2; GoodHs; InWom SUP;
LibW; NewCol 75; NotAW; RelLAm 1, 2;
WhAm 4, HSA; WorAl*

White, Frank, Jr.
American. Baseball Player
Second baseman, KC, 1973-90; only AL
second baseman to win six gold
gloves.
b. Sep 4, 1950 in Greenville, Mississippi
Source: *Ballpl 90; BaseReg 86, 87;
BiDAmSp Sup; BioIn 12, 14; ConTFT 6;
EncAFC; IntMPA 92; LesBEnT 92;
WhoAfA 9, 10, 11, 12; WhoBlA 2, 3, 4,
5, 6, 7, 8*

White, George
[George Weitz]
American. Actor, Director, Producer
Produced rival of *Ziegfeld Follies*,
George White's Scandals, 1919-31.
b. 1890 in Toronto, Ontario, Canada
d. Oct 11, 1968 in Los Angeles,
California
Source: *AmNatBi; BiDD; BiE&WWA;
BioIn 8; CamGWoT; DcAmB S8;
DcPseud; EncMT; EncVaud; Ent;
NewCBMT; NotNAT B; OxCAmT 84;
OxCPMus; WhoHol B; WhScrn 74, 77,
83; WhThe*

White, Gilbert
English. Naturalist
Wrote classic, *The Natural History and
Antiquities of Selborne*, 1789.
b. Jul 18, 1720 in Selborne, England
d. Jun 26, 1793 in Selborne, England
Source: *Alli; Benet 87, 96; BiCoLiE;
BiD&SB; BiESc; BioIn 1, 2, 3, 4, 6, 8,
9, 10, 11, 12, 14, 15, 16, 17; BlmGEL;
BritAu; CamBiEn; CamDcSc; CamGEL;
CamGLE; CasWL; ChamBiD; Chambr
2; DcArts; DcBiPP; DcEnA; DcEnL;
DcEuL; DcLEL; DcNaB; DcScB;*

EnvEnc; EvLB; InSci; LarDcSc; LinLib L, S; LngCEL; NewC; NewCBEL; OxCBrHi; OxCEng 67, 85, 95; PenC ENG; RanHWDS; REn; WebE&AL; WhDW

White, Helen Magill
American. Educator
First American woman to earn Ph.D. degree, 1877.
b. Nov 28, 1853 in Providence, Rhode Island
d. Oct 28, 1944 in Kittery Point, Maine
Source: *AmNatBi; BioIn 16; InWom SUP; LibW; NotAW; WomFir; WomWWA 14*

White, Jaleel
American. Actor
Played Steve Urkel on TV series "Family Matters," 1989-98.
b. Nov 27, 1976 in Los Angeles, California
Source: *ConTFT 17; LegTOT; News 92, 92-3*

White, Jesse
[Jesse Marc Weidenfeld]
American. Actor, Comedian
TV spokesman for Maytag Co., 1967-89; coined slogan "the loneliest man in the world."
b. Jan 3, 1919 in Buffalo, New York
d. Jan 9, 1997 in Los Angeles, California
Source: *BiE&WWA; BioIn 22, 24; ConTFT 6, 17; EncAFC; FilmEn; FilmgC; ForYSC; HalFC 84; IntMPA 75, 76, 77, 78, 79, 80, 81, 82, 84, 86, 88, 92; LegTOT; MovMk; NotNAT; Vers A; WhoAm 82; WorAl*

White, Jo Jo
[Joseph Henry White]
American. Basketball Player
Guard, 1969-81, mostly with Boston; MVP, 1976 playoffs; member, US Olympic team, 1968.
b. Nov 16, 1946 in Saint Louis, Missouri
Source: *BasBi; BiDAmSp BK; BioIn 15; NewYTBS 87; OfNBA 87; WhoAfA 9, 10, 11, 12; WhoBbl 73; WhoBlA 2, 3, 4, 6, 7, 8*

White, Josh(ua Daniel)
American. Singer
Folk singer who recorded, performed internationally, 1930s-60s; known for ballads: "Ballad of John Henry."
b. Feb 11, 1908 in Greenville, South Carolina
d. Sep 5, 1969 in Manhasset, New York
Source: *ASCAP 66; BiDAfM; BiDAmM; BioIn 13, 14, 15; CmpEPM; CurBio 44, 69; DrBlPA, 90; EncFCWM 69, 83; EncJzS; InB&W 85; LegTOT; NotNAT B; PenEncP; WhAm 5; WhoRocM 82*

White, Kevin Hagan
American. Politician
Mayor of Boston, 1967-84.
b. Sep 25, 1929 in Boston, Massachusetts

Source: *AmCath 80; BioIn 8, 9, 10, 11, 12, 13, 14; BlueB 76; CurBio 74; EncWB; PeoHis; WhoAm 74, 76, 78, 80, 82, 84; WhoAmP 73, 75, 77, 79, 81, 83, 85, 87, 89, 91, 93, 95, 97, 1999; WhoE 74, 75, 77, 79, 81, 83; WhoGov 72, 75, 77; WhoWor 74, 76*

White, Leslie A(lvin)
American. Anthropologist, Educator
Known for his fieldwork among the Keresan-speaking Indians, his "culturological" theory of human behavior, and his energy theory of cultural evolution.
b. Jan 19, 1900 in Salida, Colorado
d. 1975 in Death Valley, California
Source: *AmMWSc 73S; AmNatBi; BioIn 5, 10, 11; CamBiEn; CamDcAB; ChamBiD; IntEnSS 79; RAdv 14; WhAm 6; WhoAm 74*

White, Lois Jean
American. Organization Executive
Committed to parent involvement in children's education, elected president of the National Parent Teachers Association (PTA), 1997.
b. Mar 12, 1938 in Nashville, Tennessee
Source: *ConBlB 20*

White, Mark Wells, Jr.
American. Politician
Dem. governor of TX, 1983-87; known for improvements in public education.
b. Mar 17, 1940 in Henderson, Texas
Source: *CurBio 83, 89, 91, 93; WhoAm 78, 80, 82, 84, 86; WhoAmL 78, 83, 85, 87; WhoAmP 85, 91; WhoEmL 87; WhoGov 77; WhoSSW 84, 86; WhoWor 87*

White, Michael R(eed)
American. Politician
Mayor of Cleveland, 1990—.
b. Aug 13, 1951 in Cleveland, Ohio
Source: *BioIn 19; ConBlB 5; WhoAfA 9, 10, 11, 12; WhoAm 90, 92, 94, 95, 96, 97, 98, 99, 2000; WhoAmP 93, 95; WhoBlA 4, 5, 6, 7, 8; WhoMW 88, 90, 92, 93, 96, 98*

White, Michael Simon
Scottish. Producer
Won Tony for *Sleuth,* 1971; films include *The Rocky Horror Picture Show,* 1975.
b. Jan 16, 1936 in Scotland
Source: *ConTFT 5; IntWW 89, 91, 93, 97, 98, 2000; NotNAT; VarWW 85; Who 85, 88, 90, 92, 94, 98, 99, 2000; WhoThe 72, 77, 81*

White, Miles
American. Costume Designer
Won Tonys for costumes in *Bless You All,* 1951; *Hazel Flagg,* 1953.
b. Jul 27, 1914 in Oakland, California
d. Feb 17, 2000 in New York, New York
Source: *OxCAmT 84; VarWW 85; WhoThe 72, 77, 81*

White, Minor
American. Photographer
One of the most important photographers of the post-WWII era; founder, with Ansel Adams and others, of *Aperture.*
b. Jul 9, 1908 in Minneapolis, Minnesota
d. Jun 24, 1976 in Cambridge, Massachusetts
Source: *AmNatBi; BioIn 9, 10, 11, 12, 13, 14, 18, 24; BriEAA; CamBiEn; CamDcAB; ChamBiD; ConAu 10NR, 17R, 65; ConPhot 82, 88; DcAmArt; DcTwCCu 1; ICPEnP; ModArCr 2; NewYTBS 76; ObitOF 79; WhAmArt 85; WhoAmA 78N, 80N, 82N, 84N, 86N, 89N, 91N, 93N*

White, Neva
American. Basketball Player
Led Nashville based AAU team to ten national championships; one of first two women inducted into Basketball Hall of Fame.
b. Nov 15, 1935 in Macon County, Tennessee
Source: *BiDAmSp BK*

White, Patrick Victor Martindale
Australian. Author
Novels express religious philosophies, isolation themes; and contain complex symbols, myths, and allegories; won Nobel Prize, 1973, for *The Eye of the Storm.*
b. May 28, 1912 in London, England
d. Sep 30, 1990 in Sydney, Australia
Source: *Au&Wr 71; Benet 87, 96; BioIn 13, 14, 15; CamBiEn; CamGEL; CamGLE; CamGWoT; CasWL; ChamBiD; ConAu 43NR, 81; ConDr 82, 88, 93; ConNov 86; DcArts; DcLEL; EncWB 98; EncWL 1; GayLL 1; IntAu&W 89; IntDcT 2; IntvTCA 2; IntWW 83; LngCTC; MakMC; McGEWB; NewC; NewYTBE 73; NobelP; OxCAusL; OxCEng 67, 85, 95; OxCTwCL; PenC ENG; RAdv 1, 13-1; REn; RfGShF 1, 2; RGTwCWr; TwCA, SUP; TwCRHW 94; WebE&AL; Who 74, 82, 83, 85, 88, 90, 92N; WhoAm 88; WhoNob, 90, 95; WhoWor 87, 89; WorAl; WrDr 86, 88*

White, Paul Dudley
American. Physician
Helped found American Heart Association; personal doctor to FDR.
b. Jun 6, 1886 in Roxbury, Massachusetts
d. Oct 31, 1973 in Boston, Massachusetts
Source: *AmMWSc 73P; AmNatBi; BioIn 2, 3, 4, 5, 6, 7, 9, 10, 12, 15, 23; CamBiEn; CamDcAB; ChamBiD; ConAu 45; CurBio 55, 73, 73N; DcAmB S9; DcAmMeB 84; InSci; LinLib S; NatCAB 58; NewYTBE 73; ObitT 1971; OxCAmH; OxCMed 86; WhAm 6; WhoAm 74; WhoE 74; WhoWor 74*

White, Pearl
"Queen of Silent Serials"
American. Actor
Serial star in *The Perils of Pauline*, 1914.
b. Mar 4, 1889 in Green Ridge, Missouri
d. Aug 4, 1938 in Paris, France
Source: *AmNatBi; BioAmW; BioIn 4, 8, 9; DcAmB S2; DcPseud; EncAFC; Film 1, 2; FilmEn; FilmgC; HalFC 80, 84, 88; IntDcF 1-3, 2-3; InWom, SUP; LibW; MotPP; MovMk; NotAW; NotNAT B; OxCAmH; OxCFilm; REnAL; SilFlmP; TwYS; WhAm 4, HSA; WhoHol B; WhoHrs 80; WhScrn 74, 77, 83; WorAl; WorAlBi; WorEFlm*

White, Randy Lee
American. Football Player
Eight-time all-pro defensive tackle, Dallas, 1975-88.
b. Jan 15, 1953 in Wilmington, Delaware
Source: *BiDAmSp FB; BioIn 13, 14, 16; FootReg 87; WhoAm 88; WhoSSW 86; WorAlBi*

White, Reggie
[Reginald Howard White]
American. Football Player
Defensive end, Philadelphia, 1985-93; Green Bay, 1993—.
b. Dec 19, 1961 in Chattanooga, Tennessee
Source: *AfrAmSG; ConBlB 6; CurBio 95; News 93; WhoAfA 9; WhoAm 94, 95, 96, 97, 98, 99, 2000; WhoBlA 5, 6, 7, 8; WhoMW 93, 96, 98; WhoSpor*

White, Richard Grant
American. Author, Critic
Co-editor of humorous piece *Yankee Doodle*, 1846; with *NY Enquirer*, several other mags.
b. May 23, 1821 in New York, New York
d. Apr 8, 1885 in New York, New York
Source: *Alli, SUP; AmAu; AmAu&B; AmBi; ApCAB; BbD; BenetAL 91; BiD&SB; BioIn 8, 16; ChambBiD; Chambr 3; CyAL 2; DcAmAu; DcAmB; DcEnL; DcLB 64; DcNAA; Dis&D; EvLB; OxCAmL 65, 83, 95; REnAL; TwCBDA; WhAm HS*

White, Ryan
American. Victim
Hemophiliac; contracted AIDS from tainted blood transfusion, 1985; waged five-ye ar battle against the disease and influenced public opinion.
b. Dec 6, 1971 in Kokomo, Indiana
d. Apr 8, 1990 in Indianapolis, Indiana
Source: *AmDec 1980; BioIn 15, 16; ConAu 141; ConHero 2; EncWB 2-19; FacFETw; News 90-3; NewYTBS 90; ScrEAmL 2*

White, Slappy
[Melvin White]
American. Comedian
Popular on screen, 1970s; films include *Amazing Grace*, 1974.
b. 1921? in Baltimore, Maryland

---

d. Nov 7, 1995 in Brigantine, New Jersey
Source: *DrBlPA 90; InB&W 80, 85; WhoAfA 10N; WhoHol A*

White, Stan(ley Ray)
American. Football Player
Linebacker, 1972-84, mostly with Baltimore; first NFL player to sign with USFL, 1983.
b. Oct 24, 1949 in Dover, Ohio
Source: *BioIn 13; FootReg 81*

White, Stanford
American. Architect
Killed by Harry Thaw over alleged affair with Thaw's wife, showgirl Evelyn Nesbit.
b. Nov 9, 1853 in New York, New York
d. Jun 25, 1906 in New York, New York
Source: *AmBi; AmCulL; AmNatBi; ApCAB; AtlBL; BioIn 2, 5, 6, 7, 8, 9, 11, 12, 13, 16, 19, 22, 23, 24; BriEAA; CamBiEn; CamDcAB; ChambBiD; ChhPo; DcAmB; DcArch; DcArts; DcTwDes; EncAB-H 1974, 1996; EncWB 98; GayN; HarEnUS; IntDcAr; LegTOT; LinLib S; LngCTC; MacEA; McGDA; McGEWB; NatCAB 11, 23; OxCAmH; OxCAmL 65; REnAL; TwCBDA; WebAB 74, 79; WhAm 1; WorAl; WorAlBi*

White, Stephen
American. Writer
Wrote report "Public Television: A Program for Action;" helped to start Public TV Network.
b. Nov 22, 1915 in Boston, Massachusetts
d. Mar 27, 1993 in Bethesda, Maryland
Source: *BioIn 18; WhAm 12; WhoAm 78, 80, 82, 84, 86, 88, 90, 92*

White, Stewart Edward
American. Author
Wrote on his adventures, spiritualism; books include *African Camp Fires*, 1913.
b. Mar 12, 1873 in Grand Rapids, Michigan
d. Sep 18, 1946 in San Francisco, California
Source: *AmAu&B; AmNatBi; ArizL; BenetAL 91; BiDPara; BioIn 1, 4, 17, 22; CarSB; CmCal; CnDAL; ConAmA; ConAmL; CurBio 46; DcAmAu; DcAmB S4; DcLEL; DcNAA; EncFWF; EncO&P 1, 2, 3; EncSF, 93; LinLib L; LngCTC; NatCAB 13; NewEAmW; OxCAmL 65, 83, 95; REnAL; REnAW; ScF&FL 1; TwCA, SUP; TwCBDA; TwCWW 82, 91; WhAm 2; WhLit; WhNAA; WhoSpyF; WorAu 1900*

White, T(erence) H(anbury)
Irish. Author
Fantasy writer, known for Arthurian epics; *The Sword in the Stone*, 1939 was filmed as *Camelot*, 1961.
b. May 29, 1906 in Bombay, India
d. Jan 17, 1964 in Piraeus, Greece
Source: *Benet 96; BiCoLiE; BioIn 4, 5, 6, 7, 8, 10, 11, 15, 19; CamBiEn;*

CasWL; ChambiD; CnMWL; ConAu 37NR, 73; DcArts; DcIrL 96; DcLEL; DcNaB MP; EncSF 93; EngPo; LngCTC; MajAl; ModBrL; NewCBEL; OxCEng 67, 95; OxCTwCL; PenC ENG; RAdv 1; REn; RGTwCWr; SJGFanW; SJGYouA 2; SmATA 12; TwCA, SUP; TwCWr; TwCYAW 1; WhAm 4; WhDW; WhoChL; WorAu 1900

White, Theodore Harold
"Teddy"
American. Author
Won Pulitzer for *The Making of the President, 1960*, 1961.
b. May 6, 1915 in Boston, Massachusetts
d. May 15, 1986 in New York, New York
Source: *AmAu&B; Au&Wr 71; BioIn 1, 2, 3, 4, 5, 7, 8, 9, 10, 11, 12, 13; ConAu 64NR; CurBio 86; DcLEL 1940; HisDcWJ; IntAu&W 77, 82, 86; IntWW 74; LinLib L; MajTwCW 2; OxCAmL 65; REn; REnAL; ScrEAmL 2; WhAm 9; WhoAm 74, 76, 78, 80, 82, 84; WhoWor 74, 78, 80, 82, 84; WorAl; WorAu 1950; WrDr 76*

White, Vanna Marie
American. Model, TV Personality
Hostess of TV game show "Wheel of Fortune," 1982—; wrote autobiography: *Vanna Speaks*, 1987.
b. Feb 18, 1957 in Conway, South Carolina
Source: *BioIn 14, 15, 16; CelR 90; CurBio 88; LesBEnT 92; WhoHisp 91, 92, 94*

White, Walter Francis
American. Author, Civil Rights Leader
Active in NAACP, other civil liberties organizations; consultant to UN, 1945, 1948.
b. Jul 1, 1893 in Atlanta, Georgia
d. Mar 21, 1955 in New York, New York
Source: *AmAu&B; AmNatBi; AmSocL; BiDSocW; BioIn 11, 12, 14, 15, 17, 19, 22, 23; BlkAWP; CamDcAB; CivRSt; CurBio 42, 55; DcAmB S3, S5; DcLB 51; EncAACR; EncAB-H 1974; EncSoH; EncWB, 98; FacFETw; HisDCRM; InB&W 80, 85; MorMA; NatCAB 40; ObitOF 79; REn; REnAL; SelBAAf; SelBAAu; SouWr; TwCA, SUP; WebAB 74, 79; WhAm 3; WhLit; WhNAA; WorAl; WorAu 1900*

White, William Alanson
American. Physician, Writer, Psychiatrist, Hospital Administrator
He made Saint Elizabeth's Hospital the best-known institution of its kind and was integral in the development of modern psychiatry.
b. Jan 24, 1870 in New York, New York
d. Mar 7, 1937 in Washington, District of Columbia
Source: *AmBi; AmLY; AmNatBi; BiDPsy; BiDSocW; BioIn 3, 4; DcAmB S2; DcAmMeB 84; DcNAA; EncWB 98;*

InSci; McGEWB; NamesHP; NatCAB
38; WhAm 1; WhNAA

White, William Allen
"Sage of Emporia"
American. Journalist
World-famous, small-town newsman;
won Pulitzers, 1922, 1946.
b. Feb 10, 1868 in Emporia, Kansas
d. Jan 29, 1944 in Emporia, Kansas
Source: ABCMeAm; AmAu&B; AmDec
1900; AmLY; AmNatBi; AmPeW;
AmSocL; ApCAB X; BenetAL 91;
BiDAmJo; BiDInt; BioIn 1, 2, 3, 4, 5, 7,
8, 9, 10, 11, 12, 13, 14, 16, 17, 19, 22,
23; CamBiEn; CamDcAB; ChamBiD;
ChhPo, S1; CnDAL; ConAu 108; CurBio
40, 44; DcAmAu; DcAmB S3; DcAmSR;
DcLB 9, 25; DcLEL; DcNAA; EncAAH;
EncAB-H 1974, 1996; EncAJ; EncALit;
EncTwCJ; EncWB 98; GayN; JrnUS;
LegTOT; LinLib L, S; LngCTC;
McGEWB; MemAm; NatCAB 11;
NewEAmW; OxCAmH; OxCAmL 65, 83,
95; PeoHis; PolPar; REn; REnAL;
REnAW; TwCA, SUP; WebAB 74, 79;
WhAm 2; WhNAA; WhoPul; WorAl;
WorAlBi; WorAu 1900

White, William Lindsay
American. Editor, Publisher
Best known for *Journey for Margaret*,
1941.
b. Jun 17, 1900 in Emporia, Kansas
d. Jul 26, 1973 in Emporia, Kansas
Source: AmAu&B; AmNatBi; BiDAmJo;
BioIn 1, 4, 10, 12, 16, 22, 23, 24;
CnDAL; ConAu 101; EncTwCJ; NatCAB
58; OxCAmL 65; REnAL; TwCA SUP;
WhAm 5, 6, 7; WhoAm 74, 76; WorAu
1900

White, William S(mith)
American. Journalist
Nationally syndicated columnist, 1958-
74; won Pulitzer for *The Taft Story*,
1955.
b. Feb 5, 1907 in De Leon, Texas
d. Apr 30, 1994 in Louisville, Kentucky
Source: AmAu&B; BioIn 15; ConAu 5R,
145; CurBio 55; IntWW 74, 75, 76, 77,
78, 79, 80, 81, 82, 83, 89, 91; OxCAmL
65, 83; WhoAm 74, 76, 82; WhoSSW 73,
75, 76

Whitechurch, Victor Lorenzo
English. Clergy, Author
Mystery tales include *Murder at
Exbridge*, 1932.
b. Mar 12, 1868 in Norham, England
d. May 1933
Source: ChhPo, S1; ConAu 116, 160;
EncMys; MnBBF; TwCCr&M 80;
WhoLA

Whitefield, George
English. Religious Leader
Joined Methodists, 1732; adapted
Calvinist views to Methodism, 1741.
b. Dec 27, 1714 in Gloucester, England
d. Sep 30, 1770 in Newburyport,
Massachusetts

Source: Alli; AmAu&B; AmBi; AmNatBi;
AmOrN; AmWrBE; ApCAB; BbD;
BenetAL 91; BiDAmM; BiD&SB;
BiDChrM; BiDSA; BioIn 1, 2, 3, 4, 5, 6,
8, 9, 11, 12, 14, 15, 16, 17, 19; BritAu;
CamBiEn; CamDcAB; ChamBiD;
Chambr 2; DcAmB; DcAmReB 1, 2;
DcBiPP; DcEnL; DcNaB; Drake;
EncAB-H 1974, 1996; EncAR; EncARH;
EncCRAm; EncRelA; EncSoB; EncWB
98; EncWM; HarEnUS; LuthC 75;
McGEWB; NatCAB 5; NewC;
NewCBEL; OxCAmH; OxCAmL 65, 83,
95; OxCBrHi; OxCEng 67, 85, 95;
OxCMus; TwCBDA; WebE&AL; WhDW;
WhoChr

Whitehead, Alfred North
English. Philosopher, Mathematician
Author of popular books on philosophy;
also *Principia Mathematica*, with
Bertrand Russell, 1910-13.
b. Feb 15, 1861 in Ramsgate, England
d. Dec 30, 1947 in Cambridge,
Massachusetts
Source: AmAu&B; AmNatBi; AsBiEn;
Benet 87, 96; BenetAL 91; BiDPsy;
BiESc; BioIn 1, 2, 3, 4, 5, 6, 8, 9, 10,
12, 13, 14, 15, 17, 20, 22; CamBiEn;
ChamBiD; Chambr 3; ConAu 117, 165;
DcAmB S4; DcLB 100; DcLEL; DcNAA;
DcNaB 1941; DcScB; EncAB-H 1974,
1996; EncWB 98; FacFETw; GrBr;
InSci; LarDcSc; LegTOT; LinLib L, S;
LngCTC; LuthC 75; MakMC;
McGCEnS; McGEWB; NamesHP;
NatCAB 37; NewC; NewCBEL; NotMat;
NotTwCS 1; OxCAmH; OxCAmL 65, 83,
95; OxCEng 67; OxCPhil; OxCTwCL;
RAdv 14, 13-4; RanHWDS; REn;
REnAL; ThTwC 87; TwCA, SUP; WebAB
74, 79; WhAm 2; WhoChr; WorAlBi;
WorAu 1900; WorScD

Whitehead, Don(ald Ford)
American. Journalist
Won two Pulitzers for international,
1950, domestic reporting, 1952; with
Knoxville newspaper, 1957-81.
b. Apr 8, 1908 in Inman, Virginia
d. Jan 12, 1981 in Knoxville, Tennessee
Source: AmAu&B; AnObit 1981; BioIn 3,
5, 9, 12; ConAu 9R, 102; CurBio 53, 81,
81N; EncTwCJ; NewYTBS 81; SmATA 4;
WhAm 7; WhoAm 74, 76, 78, 80

Whitehead, (Walter) Edward
"Commander Whitehead"
English. Business Executive
Chairman, Schweppes, Ltd., 1967-71;
known in US for promoting
"Schweppervescence."
b. May 20, 1908 in Aldershot, England
d. Apr 16, 1978 in Petersfield, England
Source: BioIn 7, 8, 11; BlueB 76; CelR;
ConAu 77, 81; CurBio 78, 78N; DcAmB
S10; Who 74; WhoWor 76

Whitehead, Edwin C(arl)
American. Business Executive
Vice chm., Revlon, Inc., 1980-84;
founded own research institute.
b. Jun 1, 1919 in New York, New York

d. Feb 2, 1992 in Greenwich,
Connecticut
Source: BioIn 15; St&PR 75, 84, 87;
WhoAm 74, 76, 78, 80, 82, 84; WhoE
74; WhoFI 74; WhoWor 74

Whitehead, Robert
Canadian. Producer
Plays include *Member of the Wedding*,
1950; won Tony for *A Man for All
Seasons*, 1962.
b. Mar 3, 1916 in Montreal, Quebec,
Canada
Source: BiE&WWA; BioIn 1, 2, 15;
CamGWoT; CanWW 70, 79, 80, 81, 83,
89, 96, 97, 98, 1999; ConTFT 2;
NotNAT; OxCAmT 84; OxCCanT;
PIP&P; WhoAm 74, 76, 78, 80, 82, 84,
86, 88, 90, 92, 94, 95, 96, 97, 98, 99,
2000; WhoE 74; WhoEnt 98; WhoThe
72, 77, 81

Whitehead, William
British. Poet
Wrote play *A Charge to Poets*, 1762, in
reply to hostile comments on his
appointment as poet laureate, 1757.
b. 1715
d. 1785
Source: Alli; BiD&SB; BioIn 3, 12, 15,
17; BritAu; CamBiEn; CamGLE;
ChamBiD; ChhPo, S1; DcBiPP; DcEnA;
DcEnL; DcEuL; DcLB 84, 109; DcLEL;
DcNaB; EvLB; GrWrEL DR; LegTOT;
NewC; NewCBEL; OxCEng 67, 85, 95;
PoLE; RfGEnL 91

Whitehill, Clarence Eugene
American. Opera Singer
Bass with NY Met., 1914-32; Wagnerian
soloist.
b. Nov 5, 1871 in Marengo, Iowa
d. Dec 19, 1932 in New York, New
York
Source: AmBi; BakBD 84; BakBDTw;
DcAmB; WhAm 1

Whitelaw, Billie
English. Actor
Films include *Charlie Bubbles*, 1968;
The Omen, 1976.
b. Jun 6, 1932 in Coventry, England
Source: BioIn 14; CamBiEn; CamGWoT;
ChamBiD; ConTFT 2; FilmEn; FilmgC;
HalFC 80, 84, 88; IIWWBF; IntMPA 77,
80, 84, 92, 94, 96; IntWW 82, 83, 89,
91, 93, 97, 98, 2000; IntWWW 2;
NewYTBS 84; OxCThe 83; Who 74, 82,
83, 85, 88, 90, 92, 94, 98, 99, 2000;
WhoHol 92, A; WhoThe 77, 81

Whiteman, Paul
"King of Jazz"; "Pops"
American. Bandleader
Popularized jazz music, 1920s-30s;
commissioned, introduced George
Gershwin's *Rhapsody in Blue*, 1924;
had radio show, 1930s-40s.
b. Mar 28, 1891 in Denver, Colorado
d. Dec 29, 1967 in Doylestown,
Pennsylvania
Source: BiE&WWA; BioIn 1, 2, 4, 8, 9,
11, 12; ChamBiD; CmpEPM; CurBio 45,

68; *FacFETw; FilmgC; OxCAmH;*
WebAB 74, 79; WhAm 4A; WhoJazz 72;
WhScrn 74, 77; WorAlBi

Whiteman, Roberta Hill
American. Poet
Published *Star Quilt,* 1984.
b. Feb 17, 1947 in Baraboo, Wisconsin
Source: *AZNatAW; BioIn 21; DcNAL;*
NatAL; NatNAL; NotNaAm

Whitesnake
[David Coverdale; Aynsley Dunbar; John
Sykes; Steve Vai; Adrian Vandenburg]
English. Music Group
British heavy metal band; album
Whitesnake, 1987 sold over six million
copies.
Source: *Alli; BillEnR; BioIn 15; ConMus*
5; EncRk 88; EncRkSt; GrMetD;
PenEncP; RkOn 85; Who 92, 94;
WhoRocM 82

Whitestone, Heather
American. Beauty Contest Winner
Miss America, 1995; first deaf Miss
America.
b. c. 1973 in Dothan, Alabama
Source: *BioIn 20, 21, 22, 23; DeafPAS;*
News 95, 95-1

Whitfield, Lynn
American. Actor
Television, stage, and film actor known
for Emmy-award winning performance
in cable-TV movie "The Josephine
Baker Story," 1991, and for leading
role in the film *A Thin Line Between*
Love and Hate, 1996.
b. Feb 15, 1954 in Baton Rouge,
Louisiana
Source: *ConBlB 18; ConTFT 11*

Whitfield, Malvin
American. Track Athlete
Middle distance runner; won gold medals
in 880 yds., 1948, 1952 Olympics.
b. Oct 11, 1924 in Bay City, Texas
Source: *BiDAmSp OS; BioIn 2, 3, 4, 6,*
8, 11; BlkOlyM; WhoTr&F 73

Whitfield, Mark
American. Jazz Musician
Jazz guitarist who played with the Blue
Note jazz club in NYC, 1987; released
debut album, *The Marksman,* 1990;
also recorded *True Blue,* 1994 and *7th*
Ave., 1995.
b. Oct 1966 in Long Island, New York
Source: *ConMus 18*

Whiting, Leonard
British. Actor
Film debut as Romeo in *Romeo and*
Juliet, 1968.
b. 1950
Source: *BioIn 8, 9; FilmgC; ForYSC;*
HalFC 80, 84, 88; ItaFilm; MotPP;
WhoHol 92, A

Whiting, Margaret
American. Singer
Popular pop vocalist, 1940s-50s;
daughter of Richard.
b. Jul 22, 1924 in Detroit, Michigan
Source: *BioIn 2, 4, 11, 12, 15; CelR 90;*
CmpEPM; FacFETw; ForYSC; InWom,
SUP; LegTOT; NewAmDM; PenEncP;
RadStar; RkOn 74; WhoHol 92, A;
WomPO 76; WorAl; WorAlBi

Whiting, Richard Armstrong
American. Composer
Leading composer for 1930s movies; hits
include "Sleepy Time Gal," 1925.
b. Nov 12, 1891 in Peoria, Illinois
d. Feb 10, 1938 in Beverly Hills,
California
Source: *ASCAP 66; BioIn 4, 5, 6, 10;*
NatCAB 28

Whitington, Dick
[Richard Whitington]
English. Politician
Legendary figure who rose from poverty
to knighthood, public office; thrice
lord mayor of London.
b. 1358
d. 1423
Source: *NewCol 75*

Whitlam, Edward Gough
Australian. Diplomat
Prime minister of Australia, 1972-75;
representaive to UNESCO, 1983-86.
b. Jul 11, 1916 in Melbourne, Australia
Source: *BioIn 8, 9, 10, 11, 12; BlueB 76;*
CamBiEn; ChamBiD; ConAu 109;
CurBio 74; EncWB, 98; FacFETw;
FarE&A 81; IntWW 74, 75, 76, 91, 97,
2000; IntYB 78, 79, 80, 81, 82;
NewYTBE 72; WhDW; Who 85, 92, 98,
99, 2000; WhoWor 74, 76, 78; WrDr 86,
92, 98, 99, 2000

Whitley, Keith
American. Singer, Songwriter
Country, bluegrass singer and songwriter;
Country Music Association Award for
best single "I'm No Stranger to the
Rain," 1989.
b. Jul 1, 1956 in Sandy Hook, Kentucky
d. May 9, 1989 in Nashville, Tennessee
Source: *BioIn 16; ConMus 7; WhoNeCM*

Whitlock, Albert
English. Special Effects Technician
Won Oscars for *Earthquake,* 1974; *The*
Hindenburg, 1975.
b. 1915 in London, England
Source: *BioIn 11, 12; ConDes 84, 90,*
97; ConTFT 10; HalFC 84, 88; IntDcF
1-4, 2-4; VarWW 85; WhAm 8

Whitlock, Brand
American. Author, Diplomat
Wrote novels *13th District,* 1902;
Uprooted, 1926; minister to Belgium,
1911-22.
b. Mar 4, 1869 in Urbana, Ohio
d. May 24, 1934 in Cannes, France

Source: *AmAu&B; AmBi; AmNatBi;*
ApCAB X; BenetAL 91; BioIn 8, 9, 13,
16, 22; CamDcAB; ConAu 110, 162;
DcAmAu; DcAmB; DcAmDH 80, 89;
DcAmSR; DcLB 12; DcLEL; DcNAA;
HarEnUS; LinLib L, S; NatCAB 14;
OhA&B; OxCAmH; OxCAmL 65, 83, 95;
REnAL; TwCA; WebAB 74, 79; WhAm
1; WorAu 1900

Whitman, Alden
Canadian. Author, Journalist
With *NY Times,* 1951-76; books include
The End of a Presidency, 19 74.
b. Oct 27, 1913 in New Albany, Nova
Scotia, Canada
d. Sep 4, 1990 in Monte Carlo, Monaco
Source: *AmNatBi; BioIn 7, 8, 9, 12, 17,*
18; ConAu 17R, 29NR, 132; DcLB
Y91N; IntAu&W 76, 77; NewYTBS 90;
WhoE 74

Whitman, Charles Joseph
American. Murderer
Shooting spree on Texas U campus left
18 dead, 30 wounded.
b. Jun 24, 1941 in Fort Worth, Texas
d. Jun 24, 1966 in Austin, Texas
Source: *BioIn 7*

Whitman, Christine Todd
American. Politician
Governor of NJ, 1994—.
b. Sep 26, 1946 in New York
Source: *AlmAP 96, 2000; BiDrGov*
1988; CurBio 95; EncWoAP; IntWW
2000; IntWWW 2; NewYTBS 97; WhoAm
97, 98, 99, 2000; WhoAmP 1999;
WhoAmW 97, 99; WhoE 97, 99

Whitman, Marcus
American. Missionary, Physician
Opened part of Oregon Trail; mission
taught Indians farming, ranching, c.
1840.
b. Sep 4, 1802 in Rushville, New York
d. Nov 29, 1847 in Fort Walla Walla,
Washington
Source: *AmAu&B; AmBi; AmNatBi;*
ApCAB; BiDChrM; BioIn 1, 2, 3, 4, 5, 6,
7, 8, 10, 11, 14, 17, 18, 19, 20;
CamDcAB; DcAmB; DcAmMeB, 84;
DcAmReB 1, 2; Dis&D; EncAAH;
EncNAR; EncWB 98; HarEnUS; LuthC
75; McGEWB; MorMA; NatCAB 11;
NewEAmW; OxCAmH; OxCAmL 65, 83,
95; REnAW; TwCBDA; WebAB 74, 79;
WhAm HS; WhNaAH; WhWE; WorAl;
WorAlBi

Whitman, Marina VonNeumann
American. Economist
VP in charge of economics, GM, 1979-
85; group exec. VP for Public Affairs,
1991—.
b. Mar 6, 1935 in New York, New York
Source: *AmMWSc 73S, 78S; AmWomM;*
BioIn 16; ConAu 17R; CurBio 73;
Dun&B 90; IntAu&W 77; IntWW 74, 75,
76, 77, 78, 79, 80, 81, 82, 83, 91;
InWom SUP; NewYTBE 72; WhoAm 74,
76, 78, 80, 82, 84, 88; WhoAmW 68, 70,

83, 85, 87, 89, 91; WhoE 74, 75, 77;
WhoFI 87; WrDr 76, 86, 90

Whitman, Sarah Helen Power
American. Poet, Essayist
Once engaged to Edgar Allan Poe, ca.
  1848; wrote *Poe and His Critics*,
  1860.
b. Jan 19, 1803 in Providence, Rhode
  Island
d. Jun 27, 1878 in Providence, Rhode
  Island
Source: *NewCol 75; NotAW*

Whitman, Stephen F
American. Candy Manufacturer
Began candy co. in Philadelphia, 1842;
  famous for Whitman's Sampler, which
  is still sold today.
b. 1823
d. 1888
Source: *Entr*

Whitman, Stuart
American. Actor
Oscar nominee for *The Mark*, 1961.
b. Feb 1, 1926 in San Francisco,
  California
Source: *ConTFT 9; FilmEn; FilmgC;
  HalFC 80, 84, 88; IntMPA 84, 86, 88,
  92; ItaFilm; LegTOT; MotPP; MovMk;
  OsStAZ; WhoHol A; WorAl*

Whitman, Walt(er)
American. Poet
Used free verse style in *Leaves of Grass*,
  1855; became inspiration to other
  poets with his innovative style.
b. May 31, 1819 in West Hills, New
  York
d. Mar 26, 1892 in Camden, New Jersey
Source: *Alli, SUP; AmAu; AmAu&B;
  AmBi; AmCulL; AmRef; AmWr; AnCL;
  ApCAB, X; AtlBL; BbD; Benet 87, 96;
  BenetAL 91; BiCoLiE; BiDAmJo;
  BiDAmM; BiD&SB; BiDTran; BioIn 1,
  2, 3, 4, 5, 6, 7, 8, 9, 10, 11, 12, 13, 14,
  15, 16, 17, 18, 19, 20, 21; CamBiEn;
  CamGEL; CamGLE; CamHAL; CasWL;
  CelCen; ChamBiD; Chambr 3; ChhPo,
  S1, S3; CnDAL; CnE&AP; ColARen;
  CrtT 3, 4; CyWA 58; DcAmAu; DcAmB;
  DcAmSR; DcArts; DcEnA, A; DcEnL;
  DcLB 3, 64; DcLEL; DcNAA; Dis&D;
  Drake; EncAAH; EncAB-H 1974, 1996;
  EncARH; EncUnb; EvLB; GayLesB;
  GrWrEL P; HarEnUS; IlEncMy; JrnUS;
  LegTOT; LinLib L, S; MagSAmL;
  McGEWB; MemAm; MouLC 4; NatCAB
  1; NewGrDA 86; NinCLC 4, 31;
  OxCAmH; OxCAmL 65, 83, 95;
  OxCAusL; OxCCan; OxCEng 67, 85, 95;
  PenC AM; PoeCrit 3; RadHan; RAdv 1,
  14, 13-1; RComAH; RComWL; REn;
  REnAL; RfGAmL 4, 87, 94; RGFAP;
  SmATA 20; Str&VC; TwCBDA; WebAB
  74, 79; WebE&AL; WhAm HS;
  WhCiWar; WhDW; WorAl; WorAlBi;
  WorLitC; WrPh*

Whitmire, Kathy
[Kathryn Jean Niederhofer]
American. Politician
First woman mayor of Houston, TX,
  1981-91.
b. Aug 15, 1946 in Houston, Texas
Source: *AmWomM; BioIn 14, 15, 16;
  CurBio 88; News 88-2; NewYTBS 81,
  88; WhoAm 86, 90; WhoAmP 87, 91;
  WhoAmW 87, 91; WhoSSW 86, 91*

Whitmore, James Allen
American. Actor
Famous for one-man shows *Will Rogers,
  USA*, and *Give 'Em Hell, Harry*.
b. Oct 1, 1921 in White Plains, New
  York
Source: *BiE&WWA; BioIn 10, 11;
  ConTFT 7; FilmgC; HalFC 88; IntMPA
  84, 92; MotPP; MovMk; WhoAm 74, 76,
  78, 80, 82, 84, 86, 88, 90, 92, 94, 95,
  96, 97, 98; WhoEnt 98; WhoHol A;
  WhoThe 81; WorAl; WorAlBi*

Whitney, C(ornelius) V(anderbilt)
American. Businessman, Producer
Founder, board director, Pan Am
  Airways, 1927-41; co-produced *Gone
  With the Wind*, 1939.
b. Feb 20, 1899 in New York, New
  York
d. Dec 13, 1992 in Saratoga Springs,
  New York
Source: *AnObit 1992; BiDAmBL 83;
  BioIn 1, 4, 6, 13, 18, 19; CelR, 90;
  ConAu 85; IntWW 74; LegTOT;
  NewYTBS 92; St&PR 84, 87; WhAm 10;
  WhoAm 74, 76, 78, 80, 82, 84, 86, 88,
  90, 92; WhoE 74, 75, 77*

Whitney, Eli
American. Inventor
Invented cotton gin, 1793; first to use
  assembly line in industry, 1801.
b. Dec 8, 1765 in Westboro,
  Massachusetts
d. Jan 8, 1825 in New Haven,
  Connecticut
Source: *ABCWHCa; AmBi; AmNatBi;
  ApCAB; AsBiEn; BiDAmBL 83;
  BiInAmS; BioIn 1, 2, 3, 4, 5, 6, 7, 8, 9,
  10, 11, 12, 13, 14, 15, 17, 18, 20, 21;
  CamBiEn; CamDcAB; ChambiD;
  DcAmB; DcBiPP; DcInv; Drake;
  EncAAH; EncAB-H 1974, 1996; EncWB
  98; HarEnUS; InSci; LegTOT; LinLib S;
  MacEWoS; McGEWB; MemAm; NatCAB
  4; OxCAmH; RanHWDS; RComAH;
  SciMath; TwCBDA; WebAB 74, 79;
  WhAm 1, HS; WhDW; WorAl; WorAlBi;
  WorInv*

Whitney, Gertrude Vanderbilt
[Mrs. William Collins Whitney]
American. Sculptor, Art Patron
Founded Whitney Museum of American
  Art, NYC; opened, 1931.
b. Apr 19, 1877 in New York, New
  York
d. Apr 18, 1942 in New York, New
  York

Source: *BiCAW; CurBio 42; DcAmB S3;
  InWom; McGDA; NotAW; ObitOF 79;
  OxCAmH; WhAm 2; WorAl; WorAlBi*

Whitney, Harry Payne
American. Businessman, Impresario
Active in banking, mining, railroad
  concerns; organized "Big Four" polo
  team.
b. Apr 29, 1872 in New York, New
  York
d. Oct 26, 1930 in New York, New York
Source: *AmNatBi; BiDAmBL 83; BioIn
  16; DcAmB; NatCAB 21; OxCAmH;
  WhAm 1*

Whitney, John Hay
"Jock"
American. Diplomat, Publisher
Published *NY Herald Tribune*, 1957-66;
  ambassador to Great Britain, 1957-66;
  joined with David O Selznick to form
  Selznick International Pictures, which
  made *Gone With the Wind*, 1939.
b. Aug 17, 1904 in Ellsworth, Maine
d. Feb 8, 1982 in Manhasset, New York
Source: *AmNatBi; WhoWor 74*

Whitney, Josiah Dwight
American. Geologist, Educator
Measured California's highest peak,
  1864, later named Mt. Whitney.
b. Nov 23, 1819 in Northampton,
  Massachusetts
d. Aug 19, 1896 in Lake Sunapee, New
  Hampshire
Source: *Alli, SUP; AmBi; AmNatBi;
  ApCAB; BiDAmS; BiInAmS; BioIn 7;
  CamBiEn; ChamBiD; CmCal; CyAL 1;
  DcAmAu; DcAmB; DcNAA; DcScB;
  Drake; EncWB 98; LarDcSc; McGEWB;
  NatCAB 9; OxCAmH; TwCBDA; WebAB
  74, 79; WhAm HS*

Whitney, Phyllis Ayame
American. Author
Won Edgar for *Mystery of the Hidden
  Hand*, 1964; other books include
  Flaming Trees, 1986; Grand Master,
  1988.
b. Sep 9, 1903 in Yokohama, Japan
Source: *AmAu&B; AmWomWr; AuBYP
  2, 3; AuNews 2; BioIn 1, 2, 7, 9, 11, 12,
  14; ChlLR 59; ConAu 1R, 3NR, 25NR,
  60NR; ConLC 42; CurBio 48; EncMys;
  ForWC 70; IntAu&W 91; IntWWW 2;
  InWom, SUP; JBA 51; LibW; MajTwCW
  2; SJGYouA 2; SmATA 1, 30; ThrtnMM;
  TwCChW 1, 2, 3; TwCCr&M 85, 91;
  TwCRGW; TwCRHW 90; WhoAm 74,
  76, 78, 80, 82, 84, 86, 88, 90, 92, 94,
  95, 98, 99, 2000; WhoAmW 58, 61, 64,
  66, 68, 70, 72, 74, 75, 89, 91, 93, 95,
  97, 99; WhoEnt 98; WorAl; WorAlBi;
  WrDr 76, 80, 86, 92, 98, 99, 2000*

Whitney, Richard
American. Business Executive
Pres. of NY Stock Exchange, 1930-35.
b. Aug 1, 1888 in Beverly,
  Massachusetts
d. Dec 5, 1974 in Far Hills, New Jersey

Source: *BioIn 10, 16, 21; DcAmB S9;
NewYTBS 74; ObitOF 79; ObitT 1971;
WhAm 6*

Whitney, William Collins
American. Government Official
Secretary of US Navy, 1885-89; noted
sportsman, horsebreeder.
b. Jul 5, 1841 in Conway, Massachusetts
d. Feb 2, 1904 in New York, New York
Source: *AmBi; AmNatBi; ApCAB;
BiDAmBL 83; BiDrUSE 71, 89; BioIn 1,
8, 10, 12; CamDcAB; DcAmB; DcNAA;
EncAB-H 1974, 1996; HarEnUS;
NatCAB 2; OxCAmH; TwCBDA; WebAB
74, 79; WhAm 1; WorAl*

Whitney, William Dwight
American. Linguist
Wrote classic, *Sanskrit Grammar*, 1879;
brother of Josiah Dwight.
b. Feb 8, 1827 in Northampton,
Massachusetts
d. Jun 7, 1894 in New Haven,
Connecticut
Source: *Alli, SUP; AmAu; AmAu&B;
AmBi; AmNatBi; ApCAB; BbD;
BiD&SB; BioIn 7, 12; CamBiEn;
CamDcAB; ChamBiD; Chambr 3; CyAL
2; CyEd; DcAmAu; DcAmB; DcInB;
DcNAA; Drake; EvLB; HarEnUS;
NatCAB 2; OxCAmH; REnAL; TwCBDA;
WebAB 74, 79; WhAm HS; WhDW*

Whittaker, Charles Evans
American. Jurist
Named to the U.S. Supreme Court by
President Dwight Eisenhower, he
resigned after serving only five years.
b. Feb 22, 1901 in Troy, Kansas
d. Nov 26, 1973 in Kansas City,
Missouri
Source: *BioIn 4, 5, 9, 10, 11, 15;
CamDcAB; CurBio 74N; DcAmB S9;
EncWB 98; OxCSupC; SupCtJu; WebAB
74, 79; WhAm 6*

Whittemore, Arthur Austin
[Whittemore and Lowe]
''Buck''
American. Pianist
With Jack Lowe, member of two-piano
team popular, 1940s-60s.
b. Oct 23, 1916 in Vermillion, South
Dakota
d. Oct 23, 1984 in Long Island, New
York
Source: *CurBio 54; NewYTBS 84; WhAm
8; WhoAm 74, 76, 78, 80, 82, 84*

Whittier, John Greenleaf
American. Poet, Essayist
Popular rural poet who devoted life to
social causes and reform; wrote poem
Snow-Bound, 1866.
b. Dec 17, 1807 in Haverhill,
Massachusetts
d. Sep 7, 1892 in Hampton Falls, New
Hampshire
Source: *Alli, SUP; AmAu; AmAu&B;
AmBi; AmCulL; AmNatBi; AmPeW;
AmRef; AmWr S1; AnCL; ApCAB;
AtlBL; BbD; Benet 87, 96; BenetAL 91;*

*BiCoLiE; BiDAmM; BiD&SB;
BiDMoPL; BiDTran; BioIn 1, 2, 3, 4, 5,
6, 7, 8, 9, 10, 11, 12, 13, 15, 16, 19, 22,
23; CamBiEn; CamDcAB; CamGEL;
CamGLE; CamHAL; CarSB; CasWL;
CelCen; ChamBiD; Chambr 3; ChhPo,
S1, S2, S3; CnDAL; ColARen; CrtT 3, 4;
CyAL 2; CyWA 58, 97; DcAmAu;
DcAmB; DcAmSR; DcArts; DcBiPP;
DcEnA; DcEnL; DcLB 1; DcLEL;
DcNAA; Dis&D; Drake; EncAAH;
EncAB-H 1974, 1996; EncALit;
EncFoLi; EncWB 98; EvLB; GrWrEL P;
HarEnUS; LegTOT; LinLib L, S;
McGEWB; MouLC 4; NatCAB 1;
NewGrDA 86; NinCLC 8, 59; OxCAmH;
OxCAmL 65, 83, 95; OxCChiL; OxCEng
67, 85, 95; PenC AM; RAdv 1, 14, 13-1;
REn; REnAL; RfGAmL 4, 87, 94;
Str&VC; TwCBDA; WebAB 74, 79;
WebE&AL; WhAm HS; WhCiWar;
WhDW; WorAl; WorAlBi*

Whittingham, Charlie
American. Horse Trainer
Horse trainer, whose horses have won
more money than any other
thoroughbred trainer's.
b. Apr 13, 1913 in San Diego, California
d. Apr 20, 1999 in Pasadena, California
Source: *BiDAmSp OS; BioIn 15, 16, 21;
NewYTBS 86, 89; WhoAm 88; WhoSpor*

Whittington, Dick
[Richard Whittington]
English. Politician
Lord mayor of London, intermittently,
1397-1420; subject of nursery rhyme
legends.
b. 1358?
d. 1423?
Source: *Alli SUP; BioIn 2, 6, 9, 10;
CamBiEn; ChamBiD; LngCEL; NewC;
OxCChiL; OxCEng 67; WhDW*

Whittle, Christopher
American. Publisher
Maverick entrepreneur founded Whittle
Communications; introduced
commercial sponsorship of classroom
television; originator of Edison
Project, national private school system.
b. Aug 23, 1947 in Etowah, Tennessee
Source: *BioIn 14, 16; CurBio 91; News
89-3; NewYTBS 89; WhoAm 92, 94*

Whittle, Frank, Sir
English. Inventor
Invented the jet engine, 1937.
b. Jun 1, 1907 in Coventry, England
d. Aug 8, 1996 in Columbia, Maryland
Source: *AmMWSc 92, 95; BiEsc; BioIn
1, 2, 3, 4, 6, 7, 8, 9, 12, 15, 20, 22;
BlueB 76; CamBiEn; CamDcSc;
ChamBiD; ConAu 162; CurBio 96N;
DcInv; EncWB 98; HisEWW; InSci;
IntWW 74, 75, 76, 77, 78, 79, 80, 81, 82,
83, 89, 91, 93; LarDcSc; McGEWB;
McGMS 80; NewYTBS 96; NotTwCS 1,
1S; OxCBrHi; RanHWDS; WhDW; Who
74, 82, 83, 85, 88, 90, 92, 94; WhoAm
92; WhoScEn 94; WhoWor 96; WorInv*

Whittredge, Thomas Worthington
American. Artist
Painted Western scenes, romantic
landscapes; posed as Washington in
Leutze's *Washington Crossing the
Delaware*.
b. May 22, 1820 in Springfield, Ohio
d. Feb 25, 1910 in Summit, New Jersey
Source: *BioIn 15; CamDcAB; DcAmArt;
DcAmB; EarABI; IIBEAAW; McGDA;
NewEAmW; NewYHSD; WhAm 1*

Whitty, May, Dame
English. Actor
Oscar nominee for *Night Must Fall*,
1937.
b. Jun 19, 1865 in Liverpool, England
d. May 29, 1948 in Beverly Hills,
California
Source: *BioIn 1, 5, 9, 10; CurBio 45, 48;
Film 1; FilmAG WE; FilmEn; FilmgC;
ForYSC; HalFC 80, 84, 88; HolCA;
InWom, SUP; LegTOT; MGM; MotPP;
MovMk; NewC; NotNAT A, B; OxCThe
67, 83; ThFT; Vers A; WhoHol B;
WhScrn 74, 77, 83; WhThe; WorAl;
WorAlBi*

Whitworth, Kathy
[Kathrynne Ann Whitworth]
American. Golfer
Turned pro, 1959; greatest woman golfer
in modern times; leading money
winner eight times; first woman to win
$1 million on tour; inducted into
LPGA Hall of Fame.
b. Sep 27, 1939 in Monahans, Texas
Source: *BiDAmSp OS; BioIn 13, 14, 17;
CamBiEn; CelR; CurBio 76; EncWomS;
EncWoSp; GoodHs; HerW, 84; InWom
SUP; LegTOT; LibW; NewYTBS 81, 82;
OutWomA; WhoAm 76, 78, 80, 82, 84,
86, 88, 90, 92, 94, 95, 96, 97; WhoAmW
75, 77, 79, 81, 83, 85, 87, 89, 91, 93,
95, 97; WhoGolf; WhoSpor; WorAl;
WorAlBi*

Who, The
[Roger Daltry; John Entwistle; Kenny
Jones; Keith Moon; Peter Towshend]
English. Music Group
Leading rock band, 1960s-70s; hits
ranged from hard rock and country to
rock opera *Tommy*, 1969.
Source: *ABCCoAm; BakDcM; BillEnR;
BioIn 11; ConMuA 80A, 80B; ConMus
3; DcArts; EncPR&S 74, 89; EncRk 88;
EncRkSt; FacFETw; GrMetD; HarEnR
86; IlEncRk; NewAmDM; NewGrDM 80;
ObitOF 79; OxCPMus; PenEncP; RkOn
78; RkWho 96; RolSEnR 83; WhoHol
92; WhoRock 81; WhoRocM 82*

Whodini
[Ecstacy; Jalil; Grandmaster Dee]
American. Music Group
Brooklyn group with hit singles ''Funky
Beat,'' 1986; ''Fugitive,'' 1986.

Whorf, Richard
American. Actor, Director
Films include *Love from a Stranger*,
1947; *The Burning Hills*, 1956.

b. Jun 4, 1906 in Winthrop,
Massachusetts
d. Dec 14, 1966 in Santa Monica,
California
Source: *BiE&WWA; BioIn 2, 6, 7;
FilmEn; FilmgC; ForYSC; HalFC 80,
84, 88; MiSFD 9N; MotPP; MovMk;
NotNAT B; ObitOF 79; OxCAmT 84;
PlP&P; WhAm 4; WhoHol B; WhScrn
74, 77, 83; WhThe*

Whymper, Edward
English. Artist, Explorer
Wrote, illustrated book on mountain
climbing: *Scrambles Amongst the
Stars,* 1871.
b. Apr 27, 1840 in London, England
d. Sep 16, 1911 in Chamonix, France
Source: *Alli; BbD; BiD&SB; BioIn 1, 4,
5, 7, 8, 9, 13, 23, 24; BritAu 19;
CamBiEn; ChamBiD; Chambr 3;
DcBiPP; DcNaB, S2; EvLB; ExplAnT;
InSci; NewCBEL; OxCEng 67; WhDW;
WhLit*

Whyte, William H(ollingsworth)
American. Author
Writings include *The Last Landscape,*
1968; active in natural resources
conservation.
b. Oct 1, 1917 in West Chester,
Pennsylvania
d. Jan 12, 1999 in New York, New York
Source: *AmAu&B; Au&Wr 71; BioIn 5,
8, 16; BlueB 76; CamBiEn; CamDcAB;
ConAu 9R, 174; CurBio 59; DcLEL
1940; IntAu&W 76, 77, 82, 89; IntWW
74, 75, 76, 77, 78, 79, 80, 81, 82, 83,
89, 91, 93; NatLAC; REnAL; WhoAm 74,
76, 78, 80, 82, 84, 86, 88, 90, 92, 94,
95; WhoUSWr 88; WhoWor 74, 76, 78;
WhoWrEP 89, 92, 95*

Wibberley, Leonard Patrick O'Connor
[Leonard Holton; Christopher Webb]
Irish. Author, Journalist
Author of *The Mouse That Roared,*
1955; filmed, 1959.
b. Apr 9, 1915 in Dublin, Ireland
d. Nov 22, 1983 in Santa Monica,
California
Source: *AuBYP 2; ChhPo; ConAu 3NR,
5R, 111, X; CrtSuMy; EncMys; IntAu&W
76, 77, 82; MorJA; NewYTBS 83; REn;
SmATA 2; TwCChW 2; TwCCr&M 80,
85, 91; WhoAm 76, 78, 80, 82; WorAu
1950; WrDr 84*

Wick, Charles Z
[Charles Zwick]
American. Government Official
Member Ronald Reagan's "kitchen
cabinet"; director, US Information
Agency, 1981-89.
b. Oct 12, 1917 in Cleveland, Ohio
Source: *BioIn 13, 14, 15, 16; CurBio 85;
IntWW 91, 97, 98; NewYTBS 86, 88;
WhoAm 84, 86, 88*

Wickens, Aryness Joy
American. Economist
Research assistant Federal Reserve
Board, fundamental in development of
consumer price index, 1928.
b. Jan 5, 1901 in Bellingham,
Washington
d. Feb 2, 1991 in Jackson, Mississippi
Source: *AmMWSc 73S; BioIn 2, 6, 17;
CurBio 91N; InWom; NewYTBS 91;
WhAm 10; WhoAm 74, 76, 78, 80, 82,
84, 86, 88, 90; WhoAmW 58, 61, 64, 66,
68, 70, 72, 74, 75, 77; WhoGov 72*

Wicker, Ireene Seaton
"Lady with a Thousand Voices";
"Singing Lady"
American. TV Personality
Children's storyteller on TV, radio,
1931-75; won over 30 awards.
b. Nov 24, 1905 in Quincy, Illinois
d. Nov 17, 1987 in West Palm Beach,
Florida
Source: *AuBYP 2S; CmpEPM; ConAu
69; CurBio 43, 88; LegTOT*

Wicker, Tom
[Paul Connelly; Thomas Grey Wicker]
American. Journalist, Author
Washington bureau chief, *NY Times,*
1964-68; author *Kennedy Without
Tears: The Man Behind the Myth,*
1964.
b. Jun 18, 1926 in Hamlet, North
Carolina
Source: *AmAu&B; AuSpks; BiDAmNC;
BioIn 3, 4, 8, 9, 10, 11, 13, 16; BlueB
76; CelR, 90; ConAu 21NR, 46NR, 65,
X; ConLC 7; CurBio 73; DcLP 87A;
EncTwCJ; IntWW 91, 93; JrnUS;
LiJour; WhoAm 74, 76, 78, 80, 82, 84,
86, 88, 90, 92, 94, 95, 96, 97; WhoE 89,
91, 93; WhoSSW 73; WhoWor 74;
WorAu 1985; WrDr 76, 80, 82, 84, 86,
88, 90, 92, 94, 96, 98, 99, 2000*

Widal, Fernand Isidore
[Georges Fernand Isidore Widal]
French. Bacteriologist, Physician
Work involved many diseases; many
contributions; to diagnosis and
treatment.
b. Mar 9, 1862 in Dellys, Algeria
d. Jan 14, 1929 in Paris, France
Source: *BioIn 5, 9; InSci; OxCMed 86*

Widdemer, Margaret
American. Author, Poet
Award-winning works include poem,
"Lullaby," 1937; book series,
"Winona," 1915-23.
b. Sep 30, 1897? in Doylestown,
Pennsylvania
d. Jul 31, 1978 in Gloversville, New
York
Source: *AmAu&B; AmLY; AmNov;
Au&Wr 71; ConAmL; ConAu 4NR, 5R,
77; DcLEL; EvLB; IntWW 74; OxCAmL
65; REn; REnAL; TwCA; TwCWr;
WhAm 7*

Widdoes, James
American. Actor
Best known for film debut in *Animal
House,* 1977.
b. Nov 15, 1953 in Pittsburgh,
Pennsylvania
Source: *ConTFT 3*

Widdoes, Kathleen Effie
American. Actor
TV performances include "Much Ado
about Nothing"; "Edith Wharton:
Looking Back."
b. Mar 21, 1939 in Wilmington,
Delaware
Source: *BiE&WWA; ConTFT 5; FilmgC;
HalFC 88; NewYTBE 73; NotNAT;
WhoHol A; WhoThe 81*

Wideman, John Edgar
American. Author, Educator
Fiction deals with the struggles of blacks
in modern society; novel *Sent For You
Yesterday* won PEN/Faulkner Award,
1984.
b. Jun 14, 1941 in Washington, District
of Columbia
Source: *AfrAmAl 8; AfrAmW; BeaEPF;
Benet 96; BenetAL 91; BioIn 14, 15;
BlkLC; BlkWr 1, 2, 3; CamDcAB;
ConAfAN; ConAu 14NR, 42NR, 67NR,
85; ConBlB 5; ConLC 5, 34, 36, 67,
122; ConNov 86, 91, 96; CurBio 91;
CyWA 89, 97; DcLB 33, 143; DcTwCCu
5; EncALit; IdentIs; InB&W 85;
IntAu&W 91, 93; MagSAmL; MajTwCW
2; ModAL 5; ModBlW 2; NegAl 76, 83,
89; NotBlAM; OxCAfAL; OxCAmL 95;
OxCTwCL; RfGAmL 4, 94; RfGShF 2;
SchCGBL; SelBAAf; WhoAfA 9, 10, 11,
12; WhoAm 86, 90, 92, 94, 95, 96, 97,
98, 99, 2000; WhoBlA 7, 8; WorAu
1980; WrDr 88, 90, 92, 94, 96, 98, 99,
2000*

Widener, George D
American. Horse Owner
Race horse owner and breeder whose
horses won over $25 million, 1915-70.
b. Mar 11, 1889 in Philadelphia,
Pennsylvania
d. Dec 8, 1971 in Philadelphia,
Pennsylvania
Source: *NatCAB 57; NewYTBE 71;
ObitOF 79; WhAm 5*

Widerberg, Bo
Swedish. Director
Films include *Adalen 31,* 1969; *Joe Hill,*
1971.
b. Jun 8, 1930 in Malmo, Sweden
d. May 1, 1997 in Angelholm, Sweden
Source: *BiDFilm, 81, 94; BioIn 11, 12,
16, 22, 23, 24; DcFM; EncEurC;
FilmEn; FilmgC; HalFC 80, 84, 88;
IntDcF 1-2; IntWW 74, 75, 76, 77, 78,
79, 80, 81, 82, 83, 89, 91, 93; MiSFD 9;
MovMk; OxCFilm; WhAm 12; WhoWor
89, 95, 96; WorEFlm; WorFDir 2*

Widgery, John Passmore, Baron
English. Judge
Lord Chief Justice, 1971-80, known for
   1972 inquiry into killing of 13
   Catholic demonstrators by British
   paratroopers in Londonderry.
b. Jul 24, 1911 in Devonshire, England
d. Jul 25, 1981 in London, England
Source: *AnObit 1981; BioIn 12;
ChamBiD; DcNaB 1981; IntWW 82N;
IntYB 78, 79, 81; NewYTBS 81; Who
82N*

Widmark, Richard
American. Actor
Starred in *Judgment at Nuremberg*, 1961;
   Murder on the Orient Express, 1974.
b. Dec 26, 1914 in Sunrise City,
   Minnesota
Source: *BiDFilm; BioIn 6, 9, 11, 14, 15,
16, 17, 19; BlueB 76; CmMov; ConTFT
3, 20; CurBio 63; DcArts; FilmEn;
FilmgC; ForYSC; GangFlm; HalFC 80,
84, 88; IntDcF 1-3, 2-3; IntMPA 82, 84,
86, 88, 92, 94, 96; IntWW 79, 80, 81,
82, 83, 89, 91, 93, 97, 98; LegTOT;
MotPP; MovMk; NewYTBE 71; OsStAZ;
OxCFilm; RadStar; SaTiSS; VarWW 85;
WhoAm 74, 76, 78, 80, 82, 84, 86, 88,
90, 92, 94, 95, 96, 97, 98, 99, 2000;
WhoEnt 92, 98; WhoHol 92, A; WhoWor
78; WorAl; WorAlBi; WorEFlm*

Widnall, Sheila E.
American. Government Official
Secretary of the Air Force, 1993—.
b. Jul 13, 1938
Source: *CurBio 97; EncWB 98;
EncWoAv; NotTwCS 1; WhoEng 80, 88;
WhoTech 89, 95*

**Widor, Charles Marie Jean
Albert**
French. Composer, Organist
Best known for organ "symphonies";
   collaborated with Albert Schweitzer on
   J S Bach's works.
b. Feb 24, 1844 in Lyons, France
d. Mar 12, 1937 in Paris, France
Source: *BakBD 84; BakDcM; BriBkM
80; CamBiEn; MusMk; NewGrDM 80;
OxCMus*

Wieghorst, Olaf
Danish. Artist
Drew horses, Navajo portraits; a painting
   sold for $1 million, highest price ever
   paid to living American artist at the
   time.
b. Apr 30, 1899 in Jutland, Denmark
d. Apr 27, 1988 in La Mesa, California
Source: *AmArt; ArtsAmW 1; BioIn 4, 8,
9, 15, 16; IlBEAAW; OfPGCP 86;
WhAmArt 85; WhoAmA 82, 84, 86*

Wieland, Christoph Martin
German. Poet, Author
Sometimes called the German Voltaire,
   he was a typical stylist of the German
   rococo period.
b. Sep 5, 1733 in Wurttemberg, Germany
d. Jan 20, 1813

Source: *BbD; BioIn 1, 2, 3, 6, 7, 9, 10,
11, 12, 13, 14, 17; BlkwCE; CamBiEn;
CelCen; ChamBiD; DcArts; DcBiPP;
DcEnL; DcEuL; DcLB 97; EncEnl;
EncLitE; EncWB 98; EncWT; Ent;
EuAu; EuWr 4; EvEuW; LuthC 75;
McGEWB; McGEWD 72, 84; NewC;
NewCBEL; NewGrDM 80; NewGrDO;
NinCLC 17; OxCEng 67, 85, 95;
OxCGer 76, 86, 97; OxDcOp; PenC
EUR; REn; RfGWoL 95*

Wieland, Heinrich Otto
German. Chemist
Won Nobel Prize, 1927; noted for
   contributions to study of bile acids; set
   ground for steroid research.
b. Jun 4, 1877 in Pforzheim, Germany
d. Aug 5, 1957 in Starnberg, Germany
Source: *AsBiEn; BiESc; BioIn 3, 4, 5, 6,
14, 15, 19, 20; CamDcSc; ChamBiD;
ConAu 167; DcScB; InSci; LarDcSc;
RanHWDS; WhAm 3; WhoNob, 90, 95;
WorAl; WorAlBi*

Wieman, Henry Nelson
American. Philosopher, Theologian
Developed an "empirical theology"
   which opposed both orthodoxy and
   humanism, and claimed that one could
   discover God through the scientific
   method.
b. Aug 19, 1884 in Richhill, Missouri
d. Jun 19, 1975
Source: *AmAu&B; AmNatBi; BioIn 10,
19; ConAu 57, 61; DcAmReB 1, 2;
EncWB, 98; RelLAm 1, 2; WhAm 6, 7;
WhE&EA; WhoAm 74*

**Wien, Wilhelm Carl Werner Otto
Fritz Franz**
German. Scientist
Won 1911 Nobel Prize in physics;
   researched laws of the radiation of
   heat.
b. Jan 13, 1864 in Gaffken, Prussia
d. Aug 30, 1928 in Munich, Germany
Source: *CamBiEn; ChamBiD; DcScB;
LarDcSc; RanHWDS; WhoNob, 95*

Wiener, Leigh Auston
American. Photographer
Known for photographs of celebrities,
   historical moments.
b. Aug 28, 1929 in New York, New
   York
d. May 11, 1993 in Los Angeles,
   California
Source: *ConAu 47NR, 108, 141;
IntAu&W 89*

Wiener, Norbert
American. Mathematician
Professor, MIT, 1932-60; developed
   science of communication, cybernetics;
   contributed to development of
   calculators, computers.
b. Nov 26, 1894 in Columbia, Missouri
d. Mar 18, 1964 in Stockholm, Sweden
Source: *AmAu&B; AmNatBi; AmSocL;
AsBiEn; BenetAL 91; BiDPsy; BiESc;
BioIn 1, 2, 3, 4, 5, 6, 7, 8, 10, 11, 12,
14, 15, 17, 18, 19, 20, 21, 24; CamBiEn;*

*CamDcAB; CamDcSc; ChamBiD; ConAu
107, 157; CurBio 64; DcAmB S7;
DcScB; EncAB-H 1974, 1996; EncSF,
93; EncWB 98; FacFETw; FrTalk;
HisDcDP; InSci; LarDcSc; LinLib L, S;
MakMC; McGCEnS; McGEWB; McGMS
80; NamesHP; NotMat; NotTwCS 1;
OxCAmH; RAdv 14; RanHWDS; REnAL;
ThTwC 87; WebAB 74, 79; WhAm 4;
WorAl; WorAlBi; WorScD*

Wieniawski, Henri
[Henryk Wieniawski]
Polish. Violinist, Composer
Virtuoso; toured US with Anton
   Rubinstein, 1870s; wrote violin
   classics.
b. Jul 10, 1835 in Lublin, Poland
d. Apr 2, 1880 in Moscow, Russia
Source: *BakBD 78, 84, 92; BioIn 1, 2, 7,
14; BriBkM 80; ChamBiD; CmpBCM;
GrComp; MusMk; NewAmDM;
NewGrDM 80; OxCMus; PenDiMP;
PolBiDi*

Wierwille, Victor Paul
American. Religious Leader, Clergy
Founder, director of religious group The
   Way, 1942-82.
b. Dec 31, 1916 in New Knoxville, Ohio
d. May 20, 1985
Source: *BioIn 14, 23; ConAu 2NR, 5R,
116; IntAu&W 76; OhA&B; RelLAm 1,
2; WhoAm 84; WhoMW 76, 78, 80, 82*

Wiese, Kurt
American. Children's Author, Illustrator
Illustrated 300 books by other authors;
   writings include *Buddy the Bear*,
   1936.
b. Apr 22, 1887 in Minden, Germany
d. May 27, 1974 in Idell, New Jersey
Source: *AmAu&B; AuBYP 2, 3; BenetAL
91; BioIn 1, 2, 4, 5, 7, 8, 9, 10, 13, 14,
19; ChhPo; ChlBkCr; ConAu 9R, 49,
77NR; ConICB; IlsCB 1744, 1946, 1957;
JBA 34, 51; LinLib L; MajAI; OxCChiL;
REnAL; SmATA 3, 24N, 36; TwCChW 1;
WhAmArt 85*

Wiesel, Elie(zer)
American. Journalist, Author
Auschwitz concentration camp survivor
   whose books deal with Holocaust;
   won Nobel Peace Prize, 1986.
b. Sep 30, 1928 in Sighet, Transylvania
Source: *AmAu&B; Au&Arts 7; Au&Wr
71; AuNews 1; Benet 87, 96; BenetAL
91; BioIn 8, 9, 10, 11, 12, 13, 14, 15,
16, 17, 18, 19, 20, 21; CamDcAB;
ChamBiD; ConAu 4AS, 5R, 8NR, 40NR,
65NR; ConHero 1; ConIsC 1; ConLC 3,
5, 11, 37; ConWorW 93; CurBio 86;
CyWA 89; DcLB 83, Y87B; DcTwCCu 2;
DrAF 76; DrAPF 80, 91; EncWB;
EncWL 1, 2S; FacFETw; HeroCon;
IntAu&W 89, 91, 93; IntWW 89, 91, 93;
InWom SUP; JeAmHC; LegTOT;
LiExTwC; LinLib L; MagSWL;
MajTwCW 1, 2; NewYTBS 83, 86;
NobelP; RAdv 14, 13-2; SJGYouA 2;
SmATA 56; TwCYAW 1; Who 88, 90, 92,
94; WhoAm 74, 76, 78, 80, 82, 84, 86,*

88, 90, 92, 94, 95, 96, 97; WhoAmJ 80;
WhoE 74, 86, 89, 91, 93, 95, 97;
WhoNob 90, 95; WhoRel 92; WhoUSWr
88; WhoWor 89, 91, 93, 95, 96, 97;
WhoWorJ 72, 78; WhoWrEP 89, 92, 95;
WorAl; WorAlBi; WorAu 1950; WrDr
86, 88, 90, 92, 94, 96

Wiesel, Torsten Nils
American. Scientist, Educator
Shared 1981 Nobel Prize in medicine for
  vision research.
b. Jun 3, 1924 in Uppsala, Sweden
Source: AmMWSc 76P, 79, 82, 86, 89,
92, 95, 98; BioIn 12, 13, 14, 15, 19, 20;
CamBiEn; ChamBiD; LarDcSc;
McGCEnS; NewYTBS 81; NobelP; Who
83, 85, 88, 90, 92, 94, 98, 99, 2000;
WhoAm 80, 82, 84, 86, 88, 90, 92, 94,
95, 96, 97, 98, 99, 2000; WhoE 83, 85,
86, 89, 91, 93, 95, 97, 99; WhoFrS 84;
WhoMedH 96, 99, 2000; WhoNob, 90;
WhoScEn 94, 96, 2000; WhoWor 84, 87,
89, 91, 93, 95, 96, 97, 98, 99, 2000;
WorAlBi

Wiesenthal, Simon
Austrian. Author
Survivor of Nazi death camps who
  founded Jewish Documentation Center;
  wrote The Murderers Among Us,
  1967.
b. Dec 31, 1908 in Buczacz, Poland
Source: BioIn 6, 7, 9, 10, 11, 12, 13, 15,
16; CamBiEn; ConAu 13NR, 21R;
ConHero 2; CurBio 75; EncTR, 91;
EncWB, 98; FacFETw; IntAu&W 77, 89,
91, 93; IntMPA 84; IntWW 77, 78, 79,
80, 81, 82, 83, 89, 91, 93, 97, 98, 2000;
LegTOT; SpyCS; WhoIntA 2; WhoWor
74, 76, 78, 80, 82, 84, 87, 89, 91, 93,
95, 98, 99, 2000; WhoWorJ 78

Wiesner, Jerome B(ert)
American. Engineer
Expert on microwave theory; presidential
  assistant for science and technology,
  1961-63.
b. May 30, 1915
d. Oct 21, 1994 in Watertown,
  Massachusetts
Source: AmAu&B; AmNatBi; BioIn 5, 6,
9, 11, 12; BlueB 76; ConAu 13R, 147;
CurBio 95N; InSci; IntWW 74, 75, 76,
77, 78, 79, 80, 81, 82, 83, 89, 91, 93;
LElec; PolProf K; WhAm 11; Who 74,
82, 83, 85, 88, 90, 92, 94; WhoAm 74,
76, 78, 80, 82, 84, 86, 88, 90, 92, 94;
WhoAmJ 80; WhoE 74, 77, 79, 81, 83,
85, 86, 89, 91, 93, 95; WhoEng 80, 88;
WhoFrS 84; WhoScEn 94; WhoWor 87,
89, 91; WhoWorJ 72, 78

Wiest, Dianne
American. Actor
Won Oscar, best supporting actress, for
  Hannah and Her Sisters, 1986, and for
  Bullets Over Broadway, 1995.
b. Mar 28, 1948 in Kansas City,
  Missouri
Source: BioIn 14, 15, 21, 22, 23;
ConTFT 5, 12, 22; CurBio 97; HalFC
88; IntMPA 86, 92, 94, 96; IntWWW 2;

LegTOT; News 95, 95-2; OsStAZ;
VarWW 85; WhoAm 88, 90, 92, 94, 95,
96, 97, 99, 2000; WhoAmW 91, 93, 95,
97, 99; WhoEnt 92, 98; WhoHol 92;
WorAlBi

Wigg, George (Edward Cecil)
English. Politician, Author
Exposed 1963 Profumo scandal.
b. Nov 28, 1900
d. Aug 11, 1983 in London, England
Source: AnObit 1983; BioIn 7, 13; BlueB
76; ConAu 115; DcNaB 1981; IntWW
83; NewYTBS 83; Who 74

Wiggin, Kate Douglas
American. Children's Author
Wrote Rebecca of Sunnybrook Farm,
  1903.
b. Sep 28, 1856 in Philadelphia,
  Pennsylvania
d. Aug 24, 1923 in Harrow, England
Source: Alli SUP; AmAu&B; AmBi;
AmNatBi; AuBYP 2S, 3; BbD; BenetAL
91; BiDAmEd; BiD&SB; BioAmW; BioIn
1, 2, 3, 4, 6, 8, 10, 11, 12; CamBiEn;
CamGLE; CarSB; ChamBiD; Chambr 3;
ChhPo, S1, S2, S3; ChlBkCr; CmCal;
CnDAL; ConAmL; ConAu 111;
DcAmAu; DcAmB; DcArts; DcLB 42;
DcLEL; DcNAA; EncALit; EvLB;
FamAYP; FamSYP; FemiCLE; HerW,
84; JBA 34; LinLib L, S; LngCTC;
NatCAB 6; NotAW; OxCAmL 65, 83, 95;
OxCChiL; REn; REnAL; SJGChWr 5;
TwCA, SUP; TwCChW 1, 2, 3, 4;
WebAB 74, 79; WhAm 1; WhoChL;
WomWWA 14; WorAl; WorAlBi; WrChl;
YABC 1

Wiggins, Charles Edward
American. Politician
Congressman, 1967-79; defended Nixon
  during impeachment hearings, 1974.
b. Dec 3, 1927 in El Monte, California
d. Mar 2, 2000 in Las Vegas, Nevada
Source: AlmAP 78; BiDrAC; BiDrUSC
89; BioNews 74; PolProf NF; WhoAm
80, 88, 90, 92, 94, 95, 96, 97, 98, 99,
2000; WhoAmL 79, 83, 87, 90, 92, 94,
96, 98, 2000; WhoAmP 79; WhoGov 72,
75, 77; WhoWest 00, 74, 76, 78, 89, 94,
96, 98

Wiggins, J(ames) R(ussell)
American. Journalist, Diplomat
US ambassador to UN, 1968; editor,
  exec. vp, Washington Post, 1961-68.
b. Dec 4, 1903 in Luverne, Minnesota
Source: AuNews 2; BiDAmNC; BioIn 8,
11, 15, 16; BlueB 76; ConAu 86NR, 133;
CurBio 69; EncTwCJ; IntWW 74, 75, 76,
77, 78, 79, 80, 81, 82, 83, 89, 91, 93,
97, 98, 2000; JrnUS; PeoHis; PolProf J;
WhoAm 74, 76, 78, 80, 82, 84, 86, 88,
90, 92, 94, 95, 96, 97, 98, 99, 2000;
WhoE 91; WhoWor 74; WrDr 94, 96

Wigglesworth, Michael
American. Poet, Clergy, Physician
Known for morally instructive writings;
  long verse Day of Doom, 1662.
b. Oct 18, 1631 in Hedon, England

d. May 27, 1705 in Malden,
  Massachusetts
Source: Alli; AmAu; AmAu&B; AmBi;
AmNatBi; AmWrBE; ApCAB; Benet 87,
96; BenetAL 91; BiCoLiE; BiD&SB;
BioIn 1, 6, 7, 8, 12, 14; CamDcAB;
CamGEL; CamGLE; CamHAL; CasWL;
ChamBiD; CnDAL; CyAL 1; DcAmAu;
DcAmB; DcLB 24; DcLEL; DcNAA;
Drake; EncALit; EncApL; EncCRAm;
EncWB 98; GrWrEL P; HarEnUS;
LinLib L; McGEWB; NatCAB 8;
NewCBEL; OxCAmH; OxCAmL 65, 83,
95; OxCEng 67, 85, 95; PenC AM; REn;
REnAL; RfGAmL 4, 87, 94; WebAB 74,
79; WebE&AL; WhAm HS; WorAl;
WorAlBi; WrCNE

**Wightman, Hazel Virginia
  Hotchkiss**
American. Tennis Player
Won 44 nat. tennis titles, beginning
  1909; launched volleying technique.
b. Dec 20, 1886 in Healdsburg,
  California
d. Dec 5, 1974 in Newton, Massachusetts
Source: BiDAmSp OS; CamDcAB;
DcAmB S9; InWom SUP; NotAW MOD

Wigle, Ernest Douglas
Canadian. Physician, Educator
Pres., Canadian Cardiovascular Society,
  1984—.
b. Oct 30, 1928 in Windsor, Ontario,
  Canada
Source: AmMWSc 73P, 76P, 79, 82, 86,
89, 92, 95, 98; BiDrACP 79; WhoAm 76,
78, 80, 82, 84

Wigler, Michael (H.)
American. Biologist
Cancer researcher and molecular
  biologist, isolated a human gene that
  causes healthy cells to turn cancerous.
b. c. 1948

Wigman, Mary
German. Dancer, Choreographer,
  Educator
Considered one of the founders of
  modern dance, she established a dance
  school that influenced the movement.
b. Nov 13, 1886 in Hanover, Germany
d. 1973 in Berlin, Germany
Source: BiDD; BioIn 1, 3, 4, 7, 8, 10,
12, 19, 23; CamBiEn; ChamBiD;
CnOxB; CurBio 73N; DancEn 78;
DcArts; DcPseud; EncTR 91; EncWB,
98; IntDcMo; InWom, SUP; NewGrDM
80; WomThRe

Wigner, Eugene P(aul)
Hungarian. Physicist
Won Nobel Prize, 1963, for extensive
  work on quantum mechanics.
b. Nov 17, 1902 in Budapest, Hungary
d. Jan 1, 1995 in Princeton, New Jersey
Source: AmMWSc 76P, 79, 82, 86, 89,
92, 95; AmNatBi; AsBiEn; BiESc; BioIn
3, 5, 6, 7, 9, 10, 11, 12, 14, 15, 18;
BlueB 76; CamBiEn; CamDcAB;
CamDcSc; ChamBiD; ConAu 147, P-2;
CurBio 95N; EncWB 98; FacFETw;

InSci; IntAu&W 77, 82; IntWW 74, 75, 76, 77, 78, 79, 80, 81, 82, 83, 89, 91, 93; LarDcSc; McGCEnS; McGEWB; McGMS 80; NobelP; NotTwCS 1, 1S; OxCAmH; RAdv 14; RanHWDS; ThTwC 87; WebAB 74, 79; WhAm 11; Who 92, 94; WhoAm 74, 76, 78, 80, 82, 84, 86, 88, 90, 92, 94; WhoE 77, 79, 81, 85, 86, 89, 91, 93, 95; WhoFrS 84; WhoNob, 90, 95; WhoScEn 94; WhoWor 74, 80, 82, 84, 87, 89, 91, 93, 95; WorAl; WorAlBi; WrDr 76, 80, 82, 84, 86, 88

Wijdenbosch, Jules Albert
Surinamese. Political Leader
Closely associated with former military dictator Desi Bouterse and the 1990 Christmas Eve coup, he was elected president of Suriname in 1996 and promised economic development and more democratic practices and institutions.
b. May 2, 1941 in Paramaribo, Suriname
Source: *IntWW 2000*

Wilander, Mats
Swedish. Tennis Player
Winner of three French Open tournaments and three Australian Opens; known for his sense of good sportsmanship.
b. Aug 24, 1964 in Vaxjo, Sweden
Source: *BioIn 13, 15, 16; BuCMET; CelR 90; IntWW 91, 2000; NewYTBS 82*

Wilberforce, William
English. Abolitionist
Humanitarian who devoted much of his life to social reform; MP, won abolition of British slave trade, 1807.
b. Aug 24, 1759 in Hull, England
d. Jul 29, 1833 in London, England
Source: *Alli; BiD&SB; BiDChrM; BiDLA; BioIn 1, 2, 3, 4, 5, 6, 7, 8, 10, 11, 12, 13, 14, 16, 18, 22; BlkwCE; BlmGEL; BritAu 19; CamBiEn; CelCen; ChamBiD; Chambr 2; DcAfL; DcAmC; DcAmSR; DcBiPP; DcEnL; DcEuL; DcLB 158; DcLEL; DcNaB, C; EncWB 98; EncWM; EvLB; HisDBrE; LegTOT; LinLib S; LngCEL; LuthC 75; MacEWoS; McGEWB; NewC; NewCBEL; OxCBrHi; OxCEng 67, 85, 95; OxCMus; WhDW; WhoChr*

Wilbur, Dwight L(ocke)
American. Physician
Pres., AMA, 1968-69; founded San Francisco Society of Internal Medicine and California Society of Internal Medicine.
b. Sep 18, 1903
d. Mar 9, 1997 in San Francisco, California
Source: *AmMWSc 79, 82, 86, 89, 92, 95; BiDrACP 79; BioIn 8, 22, 23; BlueB 76; CurBio 97N; WhAm 12; WhoAm 74, 76, 78, 97; WhoMedH 96*

Wilbur, Richard Purdy
American. Author, Poet, Educator
Skilled writer who won 1957 Pulitzer for *Poems;* translated many of Moliere's works to English.
b. Mar 1, 1921 in New York, New York
Source: *AuBYP 3; Benet 87; BenetAL 91; BioIn 13, 14, 15; CamBiEn; CamDcAB; CamGEL; CamGLE; CamHAL; CasWL; ConAu 2BS, 2NR, 29NR, 76NR; ConLC 14, 53; ConPo 75, 91; ConTFT 3; CroCAP; CurBio 66; DrAP 75; DrAPF 91; DrAS 82E; EncALit; EncWB, 98; EncWL 1; IntAu&W 91; IntvTCA 2; IntWW 74, 91, 97; MajTwCW 1, 2; ModAL 4, 4S2; NewYTBS 87; OxCAmL 65; OxCTwCL; PenC AM; RAdv 13-1; REn; REnAL; RfGAmL 4, 87; SmATA 108; WebE&AL; WhoAm 86, 90, 98, 99, 2000; WhoE 99; WhoEnt 92, 98; WhoWor 98, 99, 2000; WhoWrEP 89; WorAlBi; WrDr 92, 98, 99, 2000*

Wilcock, John
English. Author, Newspaper Editor
One of the founders of *The Village Voice,* NYC; noted for one-dollar-a-day travel books.
b. 1927 in Shackhill, England
Source: *BioIn 10; ConAu 1R, 2NR; IntAu&W 86; MugS; NewYTBE 73; WhoAm 84; WhoEnt 98; WhoMedi 98; WhoUSWr 88; WhoWest 96, 98; WhoWor 89; WhoWrEP 89*

Wilcox, Ella Wheeler
American. Poet
Wrote almost 40 vols. of sentimental verse; most famous lines from ''Solitude'': ''Laugh, and the World laughs with you; weep, and you weep alone.''
b. Nov 5, 1850 in Johnstown, Wisconsin
d. Oct 31, 1919 in Short Beach, Connecticut
Source: *Alli SUP; AmAu; AmAu&B; AmBi; AmLY; AmNatBi; AmWom; AmWomPl; AmWomWr; ArtclWW 2; BbD; BenetAL 91; BiD&SB; BioAmW; CamDcAB; CasWL; ChamBiD; Chambr 3; ChhPo, S1, S2; DcAmAu; DcAmB; DcAmTB; DcLEL; DcNAA; EncAWoR; EvLB; InWom SUP; LibW; LngCTC; NotAW; OxCAmL 65, 83, 95; OxCEng 67, 85, 95; OxCTwCP; PenC AM; RelLam 1, 2; REnAL; WebAB 74, 79; WhAm 1; WisWr*

Wilcox, Francis (Orlando)
American. Political Scientist, Government Official
Director general, Atlantic Council, from 1975.
b. Apr 9, 1908 in Columbus Junction, Iowa
d. Feb 20, 1985 in Washington, District of Columbia
Source: *AmMWSc 73S, 78S; BioIn 6, 14; ConAu 37R, 115; CurBio 62, 85; LEduc 74; WhAm 8; WhoAm 74, 76, 78, 80, 82, 84; WhoWor 78*

Wilcox, Herbert
English. Producer
Films include *No, No, Nanette,* 1940; *Heart of a Man,* 1959.
b. Apr 19, 1891 in Cork, Ireland
d. May 15, 1977 in London, England
Source: *BioIn 8, 11; ConAu 57, 118; CurBio 77; DcFM; EncEurC; FilmgC; HalFC 80; IntDcF 1-2, 2-2; IntMPA 77; MovMk; NewYTBS 77; ObitOF 79; OxCFilm; TwYS A; Who 74; WhoThe 81N; WorEFlm*

Wilcox, Larry Dee
American. Actor
Played Officer Jon Baker on TV series ''CHIPS,'' 1977-82.
b. Aug 8, 1947 in San Diego, California
Source: *ConTFT 8; WhoAm 80, 82, 84, 86, 88; WhoWest 82; WhoWor 80, 82, 84*

Wilcoxon, Henry
[Harry Wilcoxon]
British. Actor, Producer
Starred in Cecil B. DeMille films, *Cleopatra,* 1934; *The Crusades,* 1935.
b. Sep 8, 1905, Dominica
d. Mar 6, 1984 in Burbank, California
Source: *BioIn 13, 17; CmMov; FilmEn; FilmgC; ForYSC; HalFC 80, 84, 88; IlWWBF; IntMPA 75, 76, 77, 78, 79, 80, 81, 82, 84; MotPP; MovMk; WhoHol A; WhThe*

Wild, Earl
American. Pianist, Composer
Pianist with NBC Orchestra; performed first piano recital on TV.
b. Nov 26, 1915 in Pittsburgh, Pennsylvania
Source: *BakBD 84, 92; BakBDTw; BioIn 14, 15, 16, 21; CamDcAB; CurBio 88; IntWW 74, 75, 76, 77, 78, 79, 80, 81, 82, 83, 89, 91, 93, 97, 98, 2000; IntWWM 77, 80, 90; NewAmDM; NewGrDA 86; NotTwCP; PenDiMP; WhoAmM 83*

Wild, Jack
English. Actor
Oscar nominee for debut in movie *Oliver,* 1968, as the Artful Dodger.
b. Sep 30, 1952 in Manchester, England
Source: *FilmgC; HalFC 80, 84, 88; IntMPA 75, 76, 77, 78, 79, 80, 81, 82, 84, 86; OsStAZ; WhoHol 92, A*

Wilde, Cornel
American. Actor, Producer, Director
Oscar nominee for role of Chopin in *A Song to Remember,* 1945.
b. Oct 13, 1915 in New York, New York
d. Oct 16, 1989 in Los Angeles, California
Source: *AnObit 1989; ASCAP 66; BiDFilm, 81, 94; BiE&WWA; BioIn 11, 16, 17, 22, 23; CmMov; ConTFT 8; FilmEn; FilmgC; ForYSC; GangFlm; HalFC 80, 84, 88; IntDcF 2-3; IntMPA 84, 88; ItaFilm; LegTOT; MiSFD 9N; MotPP; NewYTBS 89; OsStAZ; WhoAm 84, 90; WhoHol A; WorAl; WorAlBi; WorEFlm*

Wilde, Jimmy

"Mighty Atom"
Welsh. Boxer
Flyweight champion, 1916-23; Hall of
Fame, 1959.
b. May 15, 1892 in Pontypridd, Wales
d. Mar 10, 1969 in Cardiff, Wales
Source: *BioIn 7, 8, 14, 15; BoxReg, 2;*
ObitT 1961; OxCLiW 86; WhoBox 74

Wilde, Kim

English. Singer
Hit singles include "Kids in America,"
1981; "Rage To Love," 1985.
b. Nov 18, 1960 in London, England
Source: *BillEnR; BioIn 15; DcPseud;*
EncRk 88; EncRkSt; HarEnR 86;
LegTOT; NewWmR; RkOn 85; WhoEnt
98

Wilde, Oscar (Fingal O'Flahertie Wills)

Irish. Poet, Dramatist, Author
Flamboyant wit; wrote *The Importance*
of Being Earnest, 1895; imprisoned for
sodomy, 1890s.
b. Oct 16, 1856 in Dublin, Ireland
d. Nov 30, 1900 in Paris, France
Source: *AtlBL; BiDIrW; BlmGEL;*
CasWL; CnOxB; CnThe; CrtT 4;
DcAmSR; DcLEL; DcPup; Dis&D;
FilmgC; GayLesB; LngCTC; McGEWD
72; ModWD; MouLC 4; NewC; NewEOp
71; OxCEng 67; OxCFilm; OxCFr;
OxCThe 67; PenC ENG; PIP&P; REn;
REnWD; WebE&AL; WhoChL; WhoHrs
80

Wilde, Patricia

[Patricia Lorrain-Ann White]
American. Choreographer
Dir. American Ballet Theatre School,
1977-82; artistic director, Pittsburgh
Ballet Theatre, 1982—; ballerina,
NYC Ballet, 1950-65.
b. Jul 16, 1928 in Ottawa, Ontario,
Canada
Source: *BiDD; BioIn 7, 8, 9, 11, 14;*
CanWW 70; CnOxB; CurBio 68;
IntDcB; InWom; WhoAm 74, 76, 78, 80,
82, 84, 86, 88, 92, 94, 95, 96, 97, 98,
99, 2000; WhoAmW 87, 91, 93, 95, 97,
99; WhoE 85, 86, 93, 95, 97, 99;
WhoEnt 92, 98; WhoWor 74, 95, 96, 97,
98, 99, 2000

Wilder, Alec

[Alexander Lafayette Chew Wilder]
American. Composer
Writer of lyrical pop, jazz, classical
works; arranged for Frank Sinatra,
Judy Garland, Jimmy Dorsey, others.
b. Feb 17, 1907 in Rochester, New York
d. Dec 24, 1980 in Gainesville, Florida
Source: *AmNatBi; AnObit 1980; AuBYP*
2, 3; BakBD 78, 84, 92; BakBDTw;
BiE&WWA; BioIn 1, 8, 9, 10, 12, 16, 17,
18, 21, 22; CmpEPM; CndCPOM;
ConAmC 76, 82; ConAu 102, 104;
CpmDNM 80, 81; CurBio 80, 81N;
DcAmB S10; DcCM; NewAmDM;
NewGrDA 86; NewGrDM 80; NotNAT
A; OxCPMus; PenEncP; RAdv 14;

Songw; WhAm 7, 8; WhoAm 74, 76, 78,
82; WhoHol A; WhoWor 74

Wilder, Amos Niven

American. Scholar, Poet, Clergy, Critic
New Testament scholar and minister was
a seminal interpreter of biblical
language.
b. Sep 18, 1895 in Madison, Wisconsin
d. 1993
Source: *AmAu&B; BioIn 15, 18, 19, 20;*
ConAu 47NR, 81, 141; DrAS 74P;
EncWB 98; WhE&EA; WhoAm 74, 76,
78

Wilder, Billy (Samuel)

American. Director, Producer
Has over 50 films, six Oscars to credit;
films include *Double Indemnity,* 1944;
Some Like It Hot, 1959; won Lifetime
Achievement Award, 1986; Thalberg
Award, 1988.
b. Jun 22, 1906 in Sucha, Hungary
Source: *AmCulL; AmFD; BenetAL 91;*
BiDFilm, 81, 94; BioIn 2, 5, 6, 7, 8, 9,
10, 11, 12, 13, 14, 15, 16, 17, 18, 19,
20, 21; BlueB 76; CelR, 90; CmMov;
ConDr 77A, 82A, 88A; ConLC 20;
ConTFT 1, 4; CurBio 51, 84; DcArts;
DcFM; DcLB 26; DcTwCCu 1; EncAFC;
FacFETw; FilmEn; FilmgC; GangFlm;
HalFC 80, 84, 88; IlWWHD 1; IntAu&W
76, 77, 89, 91; IntDcF 1-2, 2-2; IntMPA
75, 76, 77, 78, 79, 80, 81, 82, 84, 86,
88, 92, 94, 96; IntWW 74, 75, 76, 77,
78, 79, 80, 81, 82, 83, 89, 91, 93;
ItaFilm; LegTOT; MiSFD 9; MovMk;
NewYTBS 86; OxCFilm; WhoAm 74, 76,
78, 80, 82, 84, 86, 88, 90, 92, 94, 95,
96, 97; WhoEnt 92; WhoWest 74;
WhoWor 74; WorAl; WorAlBi;
WorEFlm; WorFDir 1

Wilder, Clinton

American. Producer
Plays produced include *The Little Foxes,*
Visit to a Small Planet.
b. Jul 7, 1921 in Warren, Pennsylvania
d. Feb 14, 1986 in Bedford, New York
Source: *BiE&WWA; NewYTBS 86;*
NotNAT; WhoThe 81

Wilder, Douglas

[Lawrence Douglas Wilder]
American. Politician
Democratic governor of VA, 1990-94;
first elected black governor in US.
b. Jan 17, 1931 in Richmond, Virginia
Source: *AfrAmAl 6; AfrAmBi 1;*
AfrAmOr; BiDrGov 1988; CurBio 90;
Ebony 1; EncAACR; IntWW 91, 93;
NegAl 76, 83, 89A; NewYTBS 85, 91;
WhoAfA 9; WhoAm 86, 88, 90, 92, 94,
95; WhoAmP 73, 75, 77, 79, 81, 83, 85,
87, 89, 91, 93, 95; WhoBlA 5, 6, 7, 8;
WhoSSW 82, 84, 86, 91, 93, 95;
WhoWor 93

Wilder, Gene

[Jerome Silberman]
American. Actor
Starred in *Blazing Saddles,* 1974; *Young*
Frankenstein, 1974; *Stir Crazy,* 1980.

b. Jun 11, 1934 in Milwaukee,
Wisconsin
Source: *BiE&WWA; BioIn 10, 11, 12,*
16; CelR 90; ConAu X; ConTFT 7;
CurBio 78; EncAFC; FilmgC; HalFC
80, 84, 88; IntMPA 86, 92; MovMk;
NotNAT; QDrFCA 92; VarWW 85;
WhoAm 86, 90; WhoEnt 92; WhoHol A;
WorAlBi

Wilder, Joseph

American. Psychiatrist, Editor
Founder, first pres., Assn. of
Advancement of Psychotherapy;
originated "Wilder's Law."
b. Feb 13, 1895 in Drohobycz, Austria-
Hungary
d. Oct 31, 1976 in West Hartford,
Connecticut
Source: *BioIn 11, 12; BlueB 76; ConAu*
116; NatCAB 60; WhoWorJ 72, 78

Wilder, Laura Elizabeth Ingalls

[Mrs. Almanzo James Wilder]
American. Author
Published *Little House in the Big Woods,*
1932; books basis for TV series
"Little House on the Prairie," 1974-
82.
b. Feb 7, 1867 in Pepin, Wisconsin
d. Feb 10, 1957 in Mansfield, Missouri
Source: *AnCL; AuBYP 2; BkCL; CasWL;*
ChlLR 2; CurBio 57; DcLB 22; EncALit;
HerW; MajTwCW 2; OxCAmL 83;
REnAL; SJGChWr 5; SmATA 100;
Str&VC; TwCChW 2; WhoChL; WorAl

Wilder, Robert Ingersoll

American. Author, Journalist
Writings include *Flamingo Road,* 1942;
An Affair of Honor, 1969.
b. Jan 25, 1901 in Richmond, Virginia
d. Aug 22, 1974 in La Jolla, California
Source: *AmAu&B; AmNov; Au&Wr 71;*
BioIn 2, 4, 10; ConAu 53, P-2; LngCTC;
TwCA SUP; WhAm 6; WhoAm 74;
WorAu 1900

Wilder, Thornton (Niven)

American. Author, Dramatist
Won Pulitzers for novel, *The Bridge of*
San Luis Rey, 1928; plays, *Our Town,*
1938; *Skin of Our Teeth,* 1942.
b. Apr 17, 1897 in Madison, Wisconsin
d. Dec 7, 1975 in Hamden, Connecticut
Source: *AmAu&B; AmCulL; AmNov;*
AmWr; Au&Wr 71; AuNews 2; Benet 87,
96; BenetAL 91; BiDAmM; BiE&WWA;
BioIn 1, 2, 3, 4, 5, 6, 7, 8, 9, 10, 11, 12,
13, 14, 15, 16, 17, 19, 20; BlueB 76;
CamBiEn; CamDcAB; CamGEL;
CamGLE; CamGWoT; CamHAL;
CasWL; CelR; ChamBiD; Chambr 3;
CnDAL; CnMD; CnMWL; CnThe;
ConAmA; ConAmD; ConAmL; ConAu
13R, 40NR, 61; ConDr 73, 77, 93;
ConLC 1, 5, 6, 10, 15, 35, 82; ConNov
72; CroCD; CrtSuDr; CurBio 43, 71,
76N; CyWA 58, 89; DcAmB S9; DcArts;
DcLB 4, 7, 9; DcLEL; DramC 1;
EncAB-H 1974, 1996; EncWB 98;
EncWL 1, 2, 2S; EncWT; Ent; EvLB;
FacFETw; FilmEn; FilmgC; GrWrEL

DR, N; HalFC 80, 84, 88; IntAu&W 76; IntDcT 2; IntWW 74, 75; LegTOT; LinLib L, S; LngCTC; MagSAmL; MajMD 1; MajTwCW 1, 2; McGEWB; McGEWD 84; MemAm; ModAL 4, 4S1, 4S2; ModWD; NewEOp 71; NewYTBS 75; NotNAT A, B; Novels; ObitT 1971; OxCAmL 65, 83, 95; OxCAmT 84; OxCEng 67, 85, 95; OxCThe 67, 83; OxCTwCL; PenC AM; PiP; PlP&P; RAdv 1, 14, 13-1, 13-2; RComWL; REn; REnAL; REnWD; RfGAmL 4, 87, 94; RGTwCWr; TwCA, SUP; TwCRHW 90, 94; TwCWr; WebAB 74, 79; WebE&AL; WhAm 6; WhDW; WhE&EA; WhLit; WhNAA; Who 74; WhoAm 74; WhoTwCL; WhoWor 74; WhThe; WisWr; WorAl; WorAlBi; WorAu 1900; WorEFlm; WorLitC; WrDr 76; WrPh

Wilding, Michael

American. Actor
Son of Elizabeth Taylor, Michael
  Wilding; stars in TV soap opera
  "Guiding Light," 1985—.
Source: *IntvTCA 2; WhoHol 92; WhoThe 81N*

Wilding, Michael

English. Actor
Married to Elizabeth Taylor, 1952-57;
  debonair leading man of British films,
  1933-73.
b. Jul 28, 1912 in Westcliff-on-Sea,
  England
d. Jul 9, 1979 in Chichester, England
Source: *BioIn 10, 78, 79; ItaFilm; LegTOT; MotPP; MovMk; NewYTBS 79; OxCFilm; What 5; Who 74; WhoHol A; WhoThe 81N; WhScrn 83; WhThe; WorAl; WorAlBi*

Wilding, Michael

Australian. Author
Writer of postmodern Australian
  literature; wrote *Aspects of the Dying Process,* 1972.
b. Jan 5, 1942 in Worcester, England
Source: *BiCoLiE; CamGLE; ConAu 24NR, 49NR, 104; ConNov 86, 91, 96; IntAu&W 76, 77, 82, 89, 91, 93; OxCAusL; OxCTwCL; RfGShF 1, 2; ScF&FL 92; WhoEnt 98; WhoWor 78, 97, 98; WrDr 76, 80, 82, 84, 86, 88, 90, 92, 94, 96, 98, 99, 2000*

Wildmon, Donald Ellis

American. Religious Leader, Social
  Reformer
Conservative minister, founder of Nat.
  Federation of Decency; launched
  crusade to rid media of sexually
  explicit material.
b. Jan 18, 1938 in Dumas, Mississippi
Source: *BioIn 13, 16; ConAu 61; CurBio 92; LesBEnT 92; News 88; NewYTBS 90; RelLAm 2; WhoRel 77*

Wildsmith, Brian

English. Illustrator, Children's Author
Self-illustrated works include prize-
  winning, *Brian Wildsmith's ABC,* 1962.

b. Jan 22, 1930 in Penistone, England
Source: *AuBYP 3; BioIn 6, 8, 9, 11, 12, 14, 16, 18, 19; BritCA; ChlBkCr; ChlLR 2, 52; ConAu 35NR, 85; IntAu&W 91; MajAl; OxCChiL; SmATA 5AS, 16, 18, 69; ThrBJA; Who 92*

Wiles, Andrew J.

English. Mathematician
Professor, Princeton University, 1982—;
  proved Fermat's Last Theorem, 1993.
b. c. Apr 11, 1953 in Cambridge,
  England
Source: *CurBio 96; NotMat; NotTwCS 1; WhoAm 98, 99, 2000; WhoScEn 2000*

Wiley, George A

American. Educator, Civil Rights Leader
Founded National Welfare Rights
  Organization, 1966; nat. coordinator,
  Movement for Economic Justice.
b. Feb 26, 1931 in Bayonne, New Jersey
d. Aug 8, 1973 in Maryland
Source: *BioIn 8, 10, 11; InB&W 80, 85; NewYTBE 73*

Wiley, Harvey Washington

American. Chemist, Social Reformer
Wrote books on chemistry including
  Foods and Their Adulteration, 1917.
b. Oct 18, 1844 in Kent, Indiana
d. Jun 30, 1930 in Washington, District
  of Columbia
Source: *AmBi; AmLY; AmNatBi; AmRef; AmRef&R; ApCAB, X; BiDAmS; BioIn 1, 2, 3, 4, 5, 6, 7, 12, 17, 21, 22; CamBiEn; CamDcAB; ChamBiD; CopCroC; DcAmAu; DcAmB; DcAmMeB 84; DcAmSR; DcAmTB; DcNAA; DcScB; EncAAH; EncAB-A 4; EncAB-H 1974, 1996; EncWB 98; HarEnUS; IndAu 1816; InSci; LinLib S; McGEWB; NatCAB 9, 21; TwCBDA; WebAB 74, 79; WhAm 1; WhNAA*

Wiley, Ralph

American. Author
Author of *Why Black People Tend to Shout,* 1991.
b. Apr 12, 1952 in Memphis, Tennessee
Source: *ConAu 136; ConBlB 8; WhoAfA 9, 10, 11, 12; WrDr 94, 96, 98, 99*

Wiley, W(illiam) Bradford

American. Publisher
Chm., John Wiley & Sons, Inc., 1956-
  93.
b. Nov 17, 1910 in Orange, New Jersey
d. Feb 3, 1998 in Summit, New Jersey
Source: *AmAu&B; BioIn 4; Dun&B 88; St&PR 87; WhAm 11; WhoAm 74, 76, 78, 80, 82, 84, 86, 88, 90; WhoFI 79, 81, 89*

Wilhelm, Gale

American. Author
Novels include *No Letters for the Dead,*
  1936; *The Time Between,* 1942; other
  novels feature lesbian relationships.
b. Apr 26, 1908 in Eugene, Oregon
d. Jul 11, 1991

Source: *AmAu&B; AmNov; FemiCLE; GayLesB; GayLL 2; InWom*

Wilhelm, Hellmut

German. Scholar
Authority on Chinese history, literature;
  wrote many books on subject.
b. Dec 10, 1905 in Qingdao, China
Source: *ConAu 5R; DrAS 74H, 78H, 82H*

Wilhelm, Hoyt

[James Hoyt Wilhelm]
American. Baseball Player
Pitcher, 1952-72, known for knuckleball;
  Hall of Fame, 1985.
b. Jul 26, 1923 in Huntersville, North
  Carolina
Source: *Ballpl 90; BiDAmSp BB; BioIn 5, 7, 9, 10, 13, 14, 15; CulEncB; CurBio 71; LegTOT; NewYTBS 84; WhoProB 73; WhoSpor*

Wilhelm II

[Friedrich Wilhelm Viktor Albert;
  William II]
German. Ruler
Emperor of Germany, king of Prussia,
  1888-1918, whose aggressive colonial
  policy, expansion of navy contributed
  to WW I outbreak.
b. Jan 27, 1859 in Berlin, Germany
d. Jun 4, 1941 in Doorn, Netherlands
Source: *BioIn 23; ChamBiD; CurBio 41; IntWW 2000; NewCol 75; OxCGer 76, 97; REn; SpAmWar*

Wilhelmina

[Wilhelmina Helena Pauline Maria]
Dutch. Ruler
Constitutional monarch, 1890-1948;
  symbol of Dutch resistance, WW II;
  established govt. in exile in England;
  abdicated to daughter Juliana.
b. Aug 31, 1880 in The Hague,
  Netherlands
d. Nov 28, 1962 in Het Loo, Netherlands
Source: *BioIn 1, 5, 6, 8, 16; ContDcW 89; CurBio 63; DcTwHis; Dis&D; EncWB 98; HisWorL; IntDcWB; InWom; LegTOT; LinLib S; McGEWB; ObitT 1961; WhAm 4; WhWW-II; WomFir; WomWR*

Wilkens, Lenny

[Leonard Randolph Wilkens]
American. Basketball Player, Basketball
  Coach
Guard, 1960-76, mostly with St. Louis;
  led NBA in assists, 1970; coach,
  Seattle 1969-72, gen. mgr., 1978-86;
  Cleveland 1986-93; Atlanta Hawks
  1993—; won NBA championship with
  Seattle, 1979; Hall of Fame, 1989.
b. Oct 28, 1937 in New York, New York
Source: *AfrAmBi 2; AfrAmSG; BasBi; BiDAmSp BK; BioIn 16; BlkWrNE A; ConBlB 11; CurBio 96; InB&W 85; News 95, 95-2; OfNBA 87; WhoAm 82, 84, 86, 88, 90, 92, 94, 95, 96, 97; WhoBbl 73; WhoBlA 4, 7; WhoMW 88, 92; WhoSpor; WhoSSW 95, 97*

Wilkes, Charles
American. Explorer, Naturalist
Circled the globe, 1838-42; explored
unknown parts of Antarctica.
b. Apr 3, 1798 in New York, New York
d. Feb 8, 1877 in Washington, District of
Columbia
Source: *Alli; AmAu&B; AmBi; AmNatBi;
ApCAB; BiDAmS; BiD&SB; BiInAmS;
BioIn 1, 3, 4, 6, 7, 8, 9, 10, 12, 13, 14,
15, 17, 18, 20, 23, 24; CamBiEn;
CamDcAB; ChamBiD; CivWDc; CmCal;
DcAmAu; DcAmB; DcAmMiB; DcLB
183; DcNAA; EarABI; EncNaHi; EncWB
98; Expl 93; ExplAnT; HarEnMi;
HarEnUS; InSci; IntDcAn; LinLib S;
McGEWB; NatCAB 2; NewYHSD;
OxCAmH; OxCShps; TwCBDA; WebAB
74, 79; WebAMB; WhAm HS; WhCiWar;
WhWE; WorAl; WorAlBi*

Wilkes, Jamaal
[Jackson Keith Wilkes]
American. Basketball Player
Forward, 1974-85, mostly with LA;
NBA rookie of yr., 1975.
b. May 2, 1953 in Berkeley, California
Source: *BasBi; BiDAmSp Sup; BioIn 12,
14, 15; LegTOT; NewYTBS 85; OfNBA
86; WhoAfA 9, 10, 11, 12; WhoAm 84;
WhoBlA 2, 3, 4, 5, 6, 7*

Wilkes, John
English. Social Reformer
Radical critic of govt. policies who
became MP, lord mayor of London;
helped secure many political rights.
b. Oct 17, 1727 in London, England
d. Dec 26, 1797 in London, England
Source: *Alli; Benet 87, 96; BioIn 2, 3, 4,
6, 7, 8, 9, 10, 12, 14, 17, 19, 22;
BlkwCE; BlmGEL; BritAu; CamBiEn;
CamGEL; CamGLE; CasWL; ChamBiD;
Chambr 2; DcAmSR; DcBiPP; DcEnA;
DcEnL; DcNaB; EncAR; EncCRAm;
EncWB 98; EvLB; HarEnUS; HisDcAR;
LngCEL; NewC; NewCBEL; OxCEng 67,
85, 95; OxCLaw; REn; WebE&AL;
WhAmRev; WhDW*

Wilkie, David, Sir
Scottish. Artist
Influenced by Spanish art, Flemish
realists; pioneered English school of
anecdotal or ''subject'' painting.
b. Nov 18, 1785 in Cults, Scotland
d. Jun 1, 1841
Source: *Alli; ArtsNiC; BioIn 1, 2, 5, 8,
9, 10, 13; CamBiEn; CelCen; ChamBiD;
ChhPo, S1; ClaDrA; CmScLit; DcArts;
DcBiPP; DcBrBI; DcBrWA; DcNaB;
DcVicP, 2; IntDcAA 90; McGDA;
OxCArt; OxCBrHi; OxDcArt; WhDW*

Wilkins, Dominique
[Jacques Dominique Wilkins]
American. Basketball Player
Forward, Atlanta Hawks 1982-94, Boston
Celtics 1994—.
b. Jan 12, 1960 in Washington, North
Carolina
Source: *AfrAmSG; BiDAmSp Sup; BioIn
12, 15, 16; CurBio 95; OfNBA 87;*

*WhoAfA 9, 10, 11, 12; WhoAm 92, 94,
95, 96, 97, 98, 99, 2000; WhoBlA 5, 6,
7; WhoSpor; WhoWor 97, 98, 99, 2000;
WorAlBi*

Wilkins, Ernest Hatch
American. Educator
Pres., Oberlin College, 1927-46; wrote
The College and Society, 1932.
b. Sep 14, 1880 in Newton Centre,
Massachusetts
d. Jan 2, 1966
Source: *AmAu&B; BioIn 5, 7, 9;
NatCAB 53; OhA&B; WhAm 4; WhLit;
WhNAA*

Wilkins, George Hubert, Sir
American. Explorer
One of first to use submarines for polar
studies; commanded *Nautilus*, 1931,
on trip under Arctic Ocean.
b. Oct 31, 1888 in Mount Bryan,
Australia
d. Dec 1, 1958 in Framingham,
Massachusetts
Source: *CamBiEn; ChamBiD; EncWB
98; ExplAnT; InSci; LinLib L, S;
McGEWB; OxCShps; REn; WhWE;
WorAl; WorAlBi*

Wilkins, Mac
American. Track Athlete
Won gold medal, 1976 Olympics for
discus throwing.
b. Nov 15, 1950 in Eugene, Oregon
Source: *BiDAmSp OS; BioIn 11;
WhoSpor*

Wilkins, Maurice Hugh Frederick
New Zealander. Scientist
Won Nobel Prize in medicine, 1962, for
research on DNA.
b. Dec 15, 1916 in Pongaroa, New
Zealand
Source: *AmMWSc 95, 98; AsBiEn;
BiESc; BioIn 5, 6, 14, 15, 16, 20; BlueB
76; CamBiEn; ChamBiD; CurBio 63;
EncWB 99; IntWW 74, 75, 76, 77, 78,
79, 80, 81, 82, 83, 89, 91, 93, 97, 98,
2000; LarDcSc; McGCEnS; McGMS 80;
NobelP; NotTwCS 1; RAdv 14;
RanHWDS; Who 74, 82, 83, 85, 88, 90,
92, 94, 98, 99, 2000; WhoAm 99;
WhoMedH 99; WhoNob, 90; WhoNob, 90,
95; WhoScEn 94, 96, 2000; WhoWor 74,
76, 78, 80, 82, 84, 87, 89, 91, 93, 95,
96, 97, 98, 99, 2000; WorAl; WorAlBi;
WorScD*

Wilkins, Roger (Wood)
American. Author, Educator
Chronicled life as an American black
male in book *A Man's Life*, 1982.
b. Mar 25, 1932 in Kansas City,
Missouri
Source: *BioIn 12, 13, 16; BlkWr 1;
ConAu 109, 117; ConBlB 2; CurBio 94;
SchCGBL; SelBAAf; WhoAfA 9, 10, 11,
12; WhoAm 74, 76, 86, 88, 90; WhoBlA
6, 7, 8*

Wilkins, Roy
American. Social Reformer, Civil Rights
Leader
Moderate exec. secretary of NAACP,
1955-77.
b. Aug 30, 1901 in Saint Louis, Missouri
d. Sep 8, 1981 in New York, New York
Source: *AfrAmAl 6, 8; AmNatBi; AmRef;
AmSocL; AnObit 1981; BiDAmNC; BioIn
2, 5, 6, 7, 8, 9, 10, 11, 12, 13, 14, 15,
16, 19, 20, 23, 24; BlkWr 1; BlueB 76;
CelR; ChamBiD; CivR 74; CivRSt;
ConAu 104; ConBlB 4; ConHero 1;
CurBio 64, 81N; DcTwHis; Ebony 1;
EncAACR; EncAB-H 1974, 1996;
EncSoH; EncWB 98; FacFETw;
HisWorL; InB&W 80, 85; IntWW 74, 75,
76, 77, 78, 79, 80, 81; McGEWB; NegAl
76, 89; NewYTBS 81; NotBlAM; PeoHis;
PolProf E, J, K, NF; SchCGBL;
ScrEAmL 1; SelBAAf; WebAB 74, 79;
WhAm 8; WhoAm 74, 76, 78, 80;
WhoAmP 73, 75, 77, 79; WhoBlA 1, 2,
3; WhoWor 74, 76; WorAl; WorAlBi*

Wilkinson, Bud
[Charles Burnham Wilkinson]
American. Football Coach
Head coach, U of Oklahoma, 1947-63,
with 145-29-4 record; won nat.
championship three times.
b. Apr 23, 1916 in Minneapolis,
Minnesota
Source: *BiDAmSp FB; BioIn 3, 4, 5, 6,
7, 8, 10, 11, 14, 19, 20; ConAu 105;
CurBio 62, 94N; WhoAmP 73, 75, 77,
79; WhoFtbl 74; WhoGov 72; WhoSSW
73; WhoTelC*

Wilkinson, Charles (Burnham)
American. Football Coach
Head coach, Univ. of Oklahoma, 1947-
63; team won 47 consecutive games,
1953-57, an NCAA record.
b. Apr 23, 1916
d. Feb 9, 1994 in Saint Louis, Missouri
Source: *BioIn 2, 3, 4, 5, 6, 7, 8, 10, 11,
19, 20; CurBio 94N; WhoAmP 73, 75,
77, 79; WhoGov 72; WhoSSW 73*

Wilkinson, Ellen
English. Politician
Lifelong socialist, feminist, and Labour
politician, she was a crusader for the
unemployed during the Depression,
part of the World War II coalition
government, and minister of education
from 1945 to 1947.
b. 1891 in Manchester, England
d. 1947
Source: *BiDBrF 1; BioIn 14, 15;
ContDcW 89; EncWB, 98; IntDcWB;
OxCBrHi*

Wilkinson, Geoffrey
English. Educator
Won Nobel Prize in chemistry, 1973.
b. Jul 14, 1921 in Todmorden, England
Source: *AmMWSc 89, 92, 95; BiESc;
BioIn 4, 7, 9, 10, 14, 15, 19, 20, 22, 23;
BlueB 76; CamBiEn; CamDcSc;
ChamBiD; IntWW 74, 75, 76, 77, 78, 79,
80, 81, 82, 83, 89, 91, 93; LarDcSc;*

*McGCEnS; McGMS 80; NobelP;
NotTwCS 1; RanHWDS; WhAm 12; Who
74, 82, 83, 85, 88, 90, 92, 94; WhoAm
76, 78, 88, 90, 92, 94, 95; WhoNob, 90,
95; WhoScEn 94, 96; WhoWor 74, 76,
78, 80, 82, 84, 87, 89, 91, 93, 95, 96,
97; WorAl; WorAlBi*

Wilkinson, J(ohn) Burke
American. Author
Books include *By Sea and by Stealth*,
1956; *Night of the Short Knives*, 1964.
b. Aug 24, 1913 in New York, New
York
Source: *AmAu&B; Au&Wr 71; BioIn 9;
BlueB 76; ConAu 9R; IntAu&W 76, 77,
82; SmATA 4; WhoAm 74, 76, 78, 80,
82, 84, 86, 88, 90, 92, 94, 95, 96, 97;
WhoAmA 91N; WhoWor 74, 76, 78, 80,
82; WrDr 76, 80*

Wilkinson, James
American. Army Officer
General and frontier adventurer was
involved in western land intrigues with
Spain and in Aaron Burr's scheme to
disrupt the Union.
b. 1757 in Calvert County, Maryland
d. Dec 28, 1825 in Mexico City, Mexico
Source: *Alli; AmAu&B; AmBi; AmNatBi;
AmRev; ApCAB; BenetAL 91; BiAUS;
BiDrATG; BiDSA; BioIn 1, 3, 5, 8, 9,
10, 11, 15; CamDcAB; CmdGen 1991;
DcAmAu; DcAmB; DcAmMeB;
DcAmMiB; DcNAA; Drake; EncAB-H
1974, 1996; EncAR; EncSoH; EncWar;
EncWB 98; HarEnMi; HarEnUS;
McGEWB; NatCAB 1; NewEAmW;
OxCAmH; PeoHis; REnAL; REnAW;
TwCBDA; WebAB 74, 79; WebAMB;
WhAm HS; WhAmRev; WorAl; WorAlBi*

Will, George F(rederick)
American. Journalist, TV Personality
Conservative political syndicated
columnist; won Pulitzer, 1977;
commentator, ABC News; syndicated
columnist, *Washington Post*, 1974—;
contributing editor, *Newsweek*
magazine, 1976—.
b. May 4, 1941 in Champaign, Illinois
Source: *BiDAmNC; BioIn 10, 12, 13, 14,
15, 16; CamDcAB; CelR 90; ConAu
32NR, 67NR, 77; ConPopW; CurBio 81;
EncTwCJ; EncWB 98; FacFETw;
IntAu&W 91, 93; WhoAm 86, 90, 92, 94,
95, 96, 97, 98, 99, 2000; WhoAmP 91;
WhoE 91; WhoPul; WhoUSWr 88;
WhoWrEP 89; WorAu 1985; WrDr 92*

Willaert, Adrian
Flemish. Composer
Choir director of St. Mark's in Venice,
he founded the Venetian school of
composers.
b. c. 1480 in Bruges, Belgium
d. 1562
Source: *EncWB 98; LuthC 75;
McGEWB; OxCMus*

Willard, Archibald MacNeal
American. Artist
Painted *The Spirit of '76*.

b. Aug 22, 1836 in Bedford, Ohio
d. Oct 11, 1918 in Cleveland, Ohio
Source: *BioIn 4, 5, 6, 11; NatCAB 24;
NewYHSD; WhAm 4, HSA*

Willard, Daniel
American. Railroad Executive
Pres., chm., Baltimore and Ohio
Railroad, from 1910.
b. Jan 28, 1861 in North Hartland,
Vermont
d. Jul 6, 1942 in Baltimore, Maryland
Source: *AmNatBi; BiDAmBL 83; BioIn
1; DcAmB S3; EncABHB 1; NatCAB 18,
30; WhAm 2; WorAl; WorAlBi*

Willard, Emma Hart
American. Educator
Pioneer in women's education; founded
Troy (NY) Female Seminary, 1821,
forerunner of Emma Willard School.
b. Feb 23, 1787 in Berlin, Connecticut
d. Apr 15, 1870 in Troy, New York
Source: *Alli; AmAu; AmAu&B; AmBi;
AmNatBi; BiD&SB; CamDcAB; CyAL 2;
DcAmB; EncAB-H 1974, 1996; EncWB
98; EncWHA; EncWoAP; FemiWr;
McGEWB; NatCAB 1; NotAW; OxCAmL
83; REn; REnAL; WebAB 79; WhAm
HS; WomFir*

Willard, Frances Elizabeth Caroline
American. Social Reformer
President, Women's Christian
Temperance Union, 1879-98; toured
US, speaking on temperance, women's
suffrage.
b. Sep 28, 1839 in Churchville, New
York
d. Feb 18, 1898 in New York, New
York
Source: *Alli SUP; AmAu; AmAu&B;
AmBi; AmNatBi; AmRef; AmSocL;
AmWom; AmWomWr; ApCAB; BbD;
BiDAmEd; BiD&SB; CamBiEn;
CamDcAB; ChamBiD; ChhPo, S1;
DcAmAu; DcAmB; DcAmReB 1, 2;
DcAmTB; DcNAA; Drake; EncAB-H
1974, 1996; EncARH; EncAWoR;
EncRelA; EncWB 98; EncWHA;
EncWoAP; GayN; InWom, SUP; LibW;
LuthC 75; McGEWB; NatCAB 1;
NotAW; OhA&B; OxCAmL 65; REn;
REnAL; TwCBDA; WebAB 74, 79;
WhAm HS; WhAmP; WorAl*

Willard, Frank Henry
American. Cartoonist
Created "Moon Mullins," "Kitty
Higgins" cartoons.
b. Sep 21, 1893 in Chicago, Illinois
d. Jan 12, 1958 in Los Angeles,
California
Source: *ArtsAmW 2; BioIn 1, 3, 4, 5, 6;
DcAmB S6; LegTOT; NatCAB 46;
WhAm 3, 4; WhAmArt 85; WorECom*

Willard, Jess
"Pottawatomie Giant"
American. Boxer, Actor
World heavyweight champ, 1915-16, lost
to Jack Dempsey; starred in film *The
Heart Punch*, 1919.
b. Dec 29, 1881 in Pottawatomie County,
Kansas
d. Dec 15, 1968 in Los Angeles,
California
Source: *BiDAmSp BK; BioIn 10, 11;
Film 1; WhoBox 74; WhScrn 77, 83*

Wille, Frank
American. Government Official, Banker
Chm., Federal Deposit Insurance Corp.,
1970-76.
b. Feb 27, 1931 in New York, New
York
Source: *BioIn 9, 16; NewYTBS 88;
St&PR 84, 87; WhAm 9; WhoAm 74, 76,
78, 80, 82, 84, 86, 88; WhoAmP 75, 77;
WhoE 83, 85, 86; WhoGov 72, 75;
WhoSSW 73, 75, 76*

Wille, Lois Jean
American. Journalist
Associate editor, *Chicago Sun-Times*,
1978-83; associate editorial page
editor, *Chicago Tribune*, 1984-87;
editor, 1987-91.
b. Sep 19, 1932 in Arlington Heights,
Illinois
Source: *InWom SUP; WhoAm 82, 84, 86,
88, 90, 92, 94; WhoAmW 91, 93;
WhoMW 84, 86, 90, 92*

Willeford, Charles Ray, II
[Will Charles]
American. Author
Noted for series of works on Miami
detective, Hoke Moseley: *Miami
Blues*, 1984.
b. Jan 2, 1919 in Little Rock, Arkansas
d. Mar 27, 1988 in Miami, Florida
Source: *BioIn 9; ConAu 15NR;
OxCTwCL; WrDr 86*

William
[William the Lion]
Scottish. Ruler
Founded Arbroath Abbey, 1178, during
reign, 1165-1214.
b. 1143
d. 1214
Source: *BioIn 6, 9; ChamBiD; DcCathB;
NewCol 75; WebBD 83*

William, I
German. Emperor
First Hohenzollern ruler of the German
Empire, reigned as king of Prussia
beginning in 1861 and emperor of
Germany from 1871, with Otto von
Bismarck as minister president.
b. Mar 22, 1791 in Berlin, Germany
d. Mar 9, 1888

William, II
German. Emperor
Last of the Hohenzollern emperors,
reigned as emperor of Germany and

king of Prussia from 1888 until he was forced to abdicate in 1918; before World War I, the authoritarian ruler was the most powerful figure in Europe.
b. Jan 27, 1859
d. Jun 4, 1941 in Doorn, Netherlands
Source: *BioIn 1, 2, 3, 4, 6, 7, 8, 9, 10, 11, 12, 13, 14, 15, 16, 17, 18, 19, 20, 22, 23, 24; CamBiEn; DcTwHis; DicTyr; Dis&D; EncWB 98; LegTOT; LinLib S; McGEWB; REn; WhDW*

William, IV
English. King
Called the "Sailor King" and "Silly Billy," ruled as king of Great Britain and Ireland from 1830 to 1837; he was committed to his role as a constitutional monarch.
b. Aug 21, 1765 in London, England
d. Jun 20, 1837, England
Source: *BioIn 1, 2, 5, 6, 7, 9, 10, 12, 15, 17; CamBiEn; CelCen; ChamBiD; DcBiPP; DcNaB, C; Dis&D; EncNaHi; EncWB 98; HisDBrE; LegTOT; McGEWB; NewC; OxCBrHi; OxCShps; WhDW*

William, Warren
[Warren Krech]
American. Actor
Played sleuths in 1930s thrillers.
b. Dec 2, 1895 in Aitkin, Minnesota
d. Sep 24, 1948 in Encino, California
Source: *BioIn 21; DcPseud; Film 2; FilmEn; FilmgC; ForYSC; GangFlm; HalFC 80, 84, 88; MotPP; MovMk; NotNAT B; WhScrn 74, 77, 83; WhThe*

William II
English. Ruler
King of England, 1087-1100, succeeding father William the Conqueror; died in hunting accident possibly arranged by brother, Henry I, who succeeded him to throne.
b. 1056?
d. Aug 2, 1100
Source: *CamBiEn*

William III
Dutch. Ruler
Stadtholder, 1672-1702; ruled England, 1689-1702; signed many treaties, passed Act of Settlement, 1701.
b. Nov 4, 1650 in The Hague, Netherlands
d. Mar 8, 1702 in London, England
Source: *CamBiEn; ChamBiD; EncWB 98; NewCol 75; OxCBrHi; WebBD 83; WhAm HS; WhDW*

William of Malmesbury
English. Historian
Monk and librarian was the leading English historian of his day and was representative of the clerical humanism of the 12th century.
b. c. 1090
d. 1142
Source: *Alli; BbD; Benet 87, 96; BiB N; BiD&SB; BritAu; CamBiEn; CasWL;*

ChamBiD; Chambr 1; DcEnL; DcEuL; EncHiCA; EncWB 98; EvLB; LuthC 75; McGEWB; NewC; OxCEng 67; PenC ENG; REn

William of Ockham
"Doctor Invincibilis"; "Venerabilis Inceptor"
English. Philosopher
Joined the Franciscans, later became general of the order, 1342; wrote *Dialogus*, 1343.
b. 1290? in Surrey, England
d. 1349? in Munich, Bavaria
Source: *Alli; BiD&SB; BritAu; CasWL; DcEnL; EvLB; NewC; NewCol 75; OxCEng 67; REn; WebBD 83*

William of Tyre
Religious Leader, Historian
Official historian of the Latin Kingdom of Jerusalem, named chancellor of the kingdom and Archbishop of Tyre.
b. c. 1130 in Jerusalem
d. 1184
Source: *BiD&SB; CamBiEn; CasWL; ChamBiD; DcCathB; DcSpL; EncWB 98; GloEncH; McGEWB; OxDcByz; PenC EUR*

William of Wales
[William Arthur Philip Louis]
"Wills"
English. Prince
First son of Prince Charles and Princess Diana; second in line to British throne.
b. Jun 21, 1982 in London, England
Source: *BioIn 13, 16*

William of Waynflete
[William Patyn]
English. Religious Leader
Bishop of Winchester, 1447-86; founded Magdalen College, Oxford, 1448.
b. 1395
d. Aug 11, 1486
Source: *Alli; CamBiEn; ChamBiD; NewCol 75; WebBD 83*

Williams, Andy
[Howard Andrew Williams]
American. Singer
Award-winning crooner known for easygoing style; hits include "Where Do I Begin?", 1971; "Lonely Street," 1959.
b. Dec 3, 1930 in Wall Lake, Iowa
Source: *BakBD 84, 92; BioIn 5, 6, 7, 8, 9, 10, 11, 12, 15; BioNews 74; BkPepl; BlueB 76; ConMus 2; ConTFT 21; CurBio 60; DcPseud; NewGrDA 86; OxCPMus; PenEncP; WhoAm 74, 76, 78, 80, 82, 84, 86, 88, 92, 94, 95, 96, 97, 98; WhoEnt 92, 98; WhoHol 92, A; WorAl; WorAlBi*

Williams, Anson
[Anson William Heimlick]
American. Actor, Singer
Played Potsie on TV series "Happy Days," 1974-83.

b. Sep 25, 1949 in Los Angeles, California
Source: *BioIn 11, 24; ConTFT 9; LegTOT; VarWW 85; WhoHol 92*

Williams, Barry
American. Actor
Played Greg on TV series "The Brady Bunch," 1969-74.
b. Sep 30, 1954 in Santa Monica, California
Source: *ConTFT 8; WhoAm 74, 76, 78, 80; WhoHol 92, A*

Williams, Ben Ames
American. Journalist, Author
Writings include *Crucible*, 1937; *The Unconquered*, 1953.
b. Mar 7, 1889 in Macon, Mississippi
d. Feb 4, 1953 in Brookline, Massachusetts
Source: *AmAu&B; AmNatBi; AmNov; BenetAL 91; BioIn 1, 2, 3, 4, 17, 22; CnDAL; DcAmB S5; DcLB 102; LiveMA; OhA&B; OxCAmL 65, 83, 95; SouWr; TwCA, SUP; TwCLC 89; WhAm 3; WhE&EA; WhLit; WhNAA; WorAu 1900*

Williams, Bert
[Egbert Austin Williams]
American. Actor, Comedian
Best known as star comedian of Ziegfeld Follies, 1909-19, where his most famous song was "Nobody."
b. Nov 12, 1874 in New Providence Island, Bahamas
d. Mar 4, 1922 in New York, New York
Source: *AfrAmAl 8; AmAu&B; AmDec 1900; AmNatBi; BiDAfM; BioIn 18, 20, 23; BlkAWP; CamGWoT; CmCal; CmpEPM; ConBlB 18; DcAmB; DrBlPA, 90; EncMT; EncVaud; Ent; FamA&A; Film 1; JoeFr; NewAmDM; NewGrDA 86; OxCPMus; OxCThe 67; REnAL; Songw; SpreRhy; WebAB 74; WhAm 4; WhoHol B; WhScrn 74, 77*

Williams, Betty Smith
Irish. Social Reformer
With Mairead Corrigan, won Nobel Peace Prize for forming N Ireland Peace Movement, 1976.
b. May 22, 1943 in Andersontown, Northern Ireland
Source: *BioIn 14, 15, 16; ConHero 1; ContDcW 89; CurBio 79; FacFETw; InB&W 80; IntWW 91; InWom SUP; LadLa 86; NobelP; Who 88, 92; WhoBlA 3, 7; WhoWor 91*

Williams, Billy
English. Filmmaker
Won Oscar for cinematography of *Gandhi*, 1982.
b. Jun 3, 1929 in Walthamstow, England
Source: *BioIn 15; ConTFT 12; HalFC 80, 84, 88; VarWW 85*

Williams, Billy Dee

American. Actor
Best known for playing Gale Sayers in
TV movie "Brian's Song," 1971,
Louis McKay in film *Lady Sings the
Blues*, 1972.
b. Apr 6, 1937 in New York, New York
Source: *AfrAmAl 6, 8; AfrAmBi 1;
BiE&WWA; BioIn 13, 14, 16; BlksAmF;
CelR 90; ConBlB 8; ConTFT 2, 8, 16,
27; CurBio 84; DcTwCCu 5; DrBlPA,
90; FilmEn; HalFC 80, 84, 88; IntMPA
75, 76, 77, 78, 79, 80, 81, 82, 84, 86,
88, 92, 94, 96; LegTOT; NegAl 89;
NewYTBS 76; WhoAfA 9, 10, 11, 12;
WhoAm 78, 80, 82, 84, 86, 88, 90, 92,
94, 95, 96, 97, 99, 2000; WhoBlA 2, 4,
5, 6, 7, 8; WhoEnt 92; WhoHol 92, A;
WhoThe 77, 81; WorAlBi*

Williams, Billy Leo

American. Baseball Player
Outfielder, Chicago Cubs, 1959-76; set
record for most consecutive games
played in NL, 1963-70; Hall of Fame,
1987.
b. Jun 15, 1938 in Whistler, Alabama
Source: *BaseReg 87; BiDAmSp BB;
BioIn 8, 9, 10, 11; InB&W 80; WhoAfA
9, 10, 11, 12; WhoAm 74, 88, 90, 92, 94,
95, 96, 97; WhoBlA 3, 4, 5, 6, 7, 8;
WhoProB 73*

Williams, Carroll Milton

American. Biologist
Harvard biologist; worked out
fundamental principles of insect
development.
b. Dec 2, 1916 in Richmond, Virginia
d. Oct 11, 1991 in Watertown,
Massachusetts
Source: *AmMWSc 76P, 79, 82, 86, 89,
92; BioIn 2; BlueB 76; ConAu 65;
IntWW 74, 75, 76, 77, 78, 79, 80, 81, 82,
83, 89, 91; McGMS 80; NewYTBS 91;
WhAm 10; WhoAm 74, 76, 78, 80, 82,
84, 86, 88, 90; WhoFrS 84*

Williams, Charles

[K C and the Sunshine Band]
American. Musician
Trombone player with Sunshine Band
since 1973.
b. Nov 18, 1954 in Rockingham, North
Carolina
Source: *WhsWeAm 98*

Williams, Charles Linwood

"Buck"
American. Basketball Player
Forward, NJ, 1981-89; Portland, 1989—.
b. Mar 8, 1960 in Rocky Mount, North
Carolina
Source: *OfNBA 87; WhoAm 84, 86, 88,
90, 92, 96, 97, 98, 99, 2000; WhoWest
96*

Williams, Cindy

American. Actor
Starred in TV series "Laverne and
Shirley," 1976-82.
b. Aug 22, 1948 in Van Nuys, California

Source: *BioIn 13, 16; BkPepl; ConTFT
3; HalFC 80, 84, 88; IntMPA 77, 86,
92; InWom SUP; MovMk; WhoAm 82;
WhoEmL 91; WhoEnt 92; WhoHol A;
WorAl; WorAlBi*

Williams, Clarence, III

American. Actor
Starred in TV series "The Mod Squad,"
1968-73.
b. Aug 21, 1939 in New York, New
York
Source: *ConTFT 7, 15, 26; DrBlPA, 90;
InB&W 80; IntMPA 96; NotNAT;
WhoHol 92, A; WhoThe 72, 77, 81*

Williams, Cliff

English. Musician
Bass guitarist with rock band AC-DC,
replacing Mark Evans, 1977.
b. Dec 14, 1949 in Rumford, England

Williams, Cootie

[Charles Melvin Williams]
American. Jazz Musician
Last surviving member of Duke
Ellington Orchestra of 1920s; known
for growling, muted trumpet.
b. Jul 24, 1908? in Mobile, Alabama
d. Sep 15, 1985 in Long Island, New
York
Source: *ASCAP 66, 80; BakDcM;
BiDAfM; BiDAmM; BiDJaz; BioIn 6, 14,
15, 16, 20, 22; CmpEPM; DrBlPA, 90;
EncJzS; InB&W 80, 85; LegTOT;
NewGrDM 80; OxCPMus; PenEncP;
WhoJazz 72; WorAl*

Williams, Curtis

[Kool and the Gang]
American. Musician
Keyboardist with Kool and the Gang
since 1980.
b. Dec 11, 1962 in Buffalo, New York

Williams, Daniel Hale

American. Surgeon, Educator
Performed first successful surgical
closure of heart wound; successful in
stopping hemorrhage from spleen.
b. Jan 18, 1858 in Hollidaysburg,
Pennsylvania
d. Aug 4, 1931 in Idlewild, Michigan
Source: *BioIn 2, 3, 5, 6, 7, 8, 9, 10, 11,
12, 13; CamDcAB; DcAmB; DcAmMeB
84; InSci; NegAl 83; NotBlAS; NotTwCS
1; SciMath; WebAB 74, 79; WhAm 1;
WhoColR; WorInv*

Williams, Darnell

American. Actor
Won Emmy for role as Jesse Hubbard on
soap opera "All My Children," 1983.
b. Mar 3, in London, England
Source: *BioIn 13; DrBlPA 90; InB&W
85; VarWW 85; WhoMW 86*

Williams, Deniece

[June Deniece Williams]
American. Singer
Number one hits "Too Much, Too Little,
Too Late," with Johnny Mathis, 1978;
"Let's Hear It for the Boy," 1984.
b. Jun 3, 1951 in Gary, Indiana
Source: *BioIn 14, 15, 16; ConMus 1;
DcPseud; DrBlPA 90; EncRk 88;
EncRkSt; InB&W 80, 85; IntWWW 2;
LegTOT; RkOn 85; SoulM; WhoAfA 9,
10, 11, 12; WhoAmW 91; WhoBlA 8*

Williams, Dick

[Richard Hirshfield Williams]
American. Baseball Player, Baseball
Manager
Infielder-outfielder, 1951-64; has
managed six different teams, won four
pennants, two World Series.
b. May 7, 1928 in Saint Louis, Missouri
Source: *Ballpl 90; BaseEn 88; BaseReg
88; BiDAmSp BB; BioIn 13, 14, 15, 17,
18, 19; CurBio 73; WhoAm 84, 88;
WhoE 81; WhoProB 73; WhoSSW 84;
WhoWest 84, 92*

Williams, Don

American. Musician, Singer
Guitarist; laid-back style in hits *Cafe
Carolina*, 1984.
b. May 27, 1939 in Floydada, Texas
Source: *AllMGCo; ASCAP 80;
BgBkCoM; BioIn 14, 15; ConMus 4;
EncFCWM 83; HarEnCM 87; HarEnR
86; IlEncCM; LegTOT; PenEncP; RkOn
85; Songw*

Williams, Doug(las Lee)

American. Football Player
Quarterback, Tampa Bay, 1978-82,
USFL, 1984-85, Washington, 1986-89;
first black quarterback in Super Bowl,
1988; MVP Super Bowl, 1988.
b. Aug 9, 1955 in Zachary, Louisiana
Source: *AfrAmBi 1; BioIn 11, 12, 13, 14,
15; FootReg 87; InB&W 80; News 88,
88-2; NewYTBS 88; WhoBlA 3, 4, 5, 6,
7; WorAlBi*

Williams, Edward Bennett

American. Lawyer, Baseball Executive
Trial lawyer with many well-known
clients; owner, president, Baltimore
Orioles.
b. May 31, 1920 in Hartford,
Connecticut
d. Aug 13, 1988 in Washington, District
of Columbia
Source: *AmNatBi; BioIn 4, 5, 6, 7, 10,
11, 13; CamDcAB; CelR; ConAu 1R,
126; CopCroC; CurBio 65, 88, 88N;
EncMcCE; FacFETw; MafEnc; News 88;
NewYTBS 83, 88; ScrEAmL 2; WebAB
74, 79; WhAm 9; WhoAm 74, 76, 78, 80,
82, 84, 86, 88; WhoAmL 78, 79, 87;
WhoAmP 75, 77, 79; WhoE 79, 81, 83,
85, 86; WhoFI 74; WhoSSW 73, 75, 76;
WorAl; WorAlBi*

Williams, Edward Porter

American. Manufacturer
Cofounded Sherwin-Williams paint co.,
  first to offer money-back guarantee.
b. May 10, 1843 in Cleveland, Ohio
d. May 4, 1903 in Glenville, Ohio
Source: *Entr; NatCAB 21*

Williams, Elizabeth Betty Smyth

[Mrs. J T Perkins]
Irish. Civil Rights Leader
Shared 1976 Nobel Peace Prize with
  Mairead Corrigan; co-founded Peace
  People to end fighting in N Ireland.
b. May 22, 1943 in Belfast, Northern
  Ireland
Source: *CurBio 79; IntWW 81, 91; Who
85, 92; WhoAm 88; WhoAmW 91;
WhoNob, 90*

Williams, Emlyn

[George Emlyn Williams]
Welsh. Dramatist, Actor
Wrote, starred in *The Corn Is Green*,
  1930s; best known for one-man show
  on Charles Dickens.
b. Nov 26, 1905 in Mostyn, Wales
d. Sep 25, 1987 in London, England
Source: *AnObit 1987; Au&Wr 71; Benet
87; BiE&WWA; BioIn 1, 2, 3, 4, 5, 6, 8,
10, 12, 13, 15, 17, 22; BlueB 76;
CamGWoT; CasWL; CnMD; CnThe;
ConAu 36NR, 93, 104, 123; ConDr 73,
77, 82; ConLC 15; ConTFT 5; CroCD;
CrtSuDr; CurBio 41, 52, 87, 87N; CyWA
97; DcLB 10, 77; DcLEL; EncMys;
EncWT; Ent; EvLB; FamA&A; FilmAG
WE; FilmEn; FilmgC; ForYSC; GrWrEL
DR; HalFC 80, 84, 88; IlWWBF, A;
IntAu&W 76, 77; IntMPA 75, 76, 77, 78,
79, 80, 81, 82, 84, 86; IntWW 74, 75,
76, 77, 78, 79, 80, 81, 82, 83; LegTOT;
LngCTC; MajTwCW 1; McGEWD 72,
84; ModBrL, 2; ModWD; MotPP;
MovMk; NewC; NewCBEL; NewYTBS
81, 87; NotNAT, A; OxCAmT 84;
OxCLiW 86; OxCThe 67, 83; PenC
ENG; PIP&P; REn; TwCA, SUP;
TwCWr; WhAm 9; WhE&EA; Who 74,
82, 83, 85; WhoAm 74, 76, 78, 80, 82,
84, 86; WhoHol A; WhoThe 72, 77, 81;
WhoWor 74, 76, 78; WorAl; WorAlBi;
WorEFlm; WrDr 76, 80, 82, 84, 86*

Williams, Eric Eustace

Trinidadian. Politician, Educator,
  Historian, Author
First prime minister of Trinidad and
  Tobago, 1962-80; widely recognized
  authority on Caribbean.
b. Sep 25, 1911 in Port of Spain,
  Trinidad and Tobago
d. Mar 29, 1981 in Port of Spain,
  Trinidad and Tobago
Source: *AnObit 1981; BioIn 4, 7, 8, 9,
10, 23; ConAu 103; CurBio 66, 81;
DcPol; InB&W 80; IntWW 74, 75, 76,
77, 78, 79, 80; WhoGov 72; WhoWor 74,
76, 78, 80*

Williams, Esther

[Mrs. Fernando Lamas]
American. Actor, Swimmer
Olympic swimmer who starred in MGM
  aquatic musicals *Neptune's Daughter*,
  1949; *Dangerous When Wet*, 1953.
b. Aug 8, 1923 in Los Angeles,
  California
Source: *BiDFilm, 81, 94; BiE&WWA;
BioIn 3, 4, 8, 11, 14; CmMov; CurBio
55; EncAFC; FilmEn; FilmgC; ForYSC;
HalFC 80, 84, 88; IntDcF 1-3, 2-3;
IntMPA 75, 76, 77, 78, 79, 80, 81, 82,
84, 86, 88, 92, 94, 96; InWom, SUP;
LegTOT; McGEWD 84; MotPP; MovMk;
OxCFilm; What 2; WhoAmW 58;
WhoHol A; WorAl; WorAlBi; WorEFlm*

Williams, Evelyn

American. Lawyer
Defense attorney for members of the
  Black Liberation Army, 1973-79;
  wrote autobiography, *Inadmissible
  Evidence*, 1993.
b. c. 1922 in North Carolina
Source: *AfrAmaL 8; ConBlB 10*

Williams, G(erhard) Mennen

"Soapy"
American. Politician, Diplomat, Judge
Six-term Dem. governor of MI, 1949-60;
  ambassador to Africa, 1961-66.
b. Feb 23, 1911 in Detroit, Michigan
d. Feb 2, 1988 in Detroit, Michigan
Source: *AmBench 79; BiDrGov 1789;
BioIn 1, 2, 3, 4, 5, 6, 7, 8, 11, 15, 16;
BlueB 76; ConAu 124; CurBio 63, 88,
88N; IntWW 74, 75, 76, 77, 78, 79, 80,
81, 82, 83; News 88-2; NewYTBS 86, 88;
PolProf E, K, T; St&PR 87; WhAm 9;
WhoAm 74, 76, 78, 80, 82, 84, 86;
WhoAmL 83, 85; WhoAmP 73, 75, 77,
79, 81, 83, 85, 87; WhoGov 72, 75, 77;
WhoMW 74, 76, 78, 80, 82, 84, 86, 88*

Williams, Garth Montgomery

American. Illustrator
Illustrator of children's books: "Little
  House" series, *Stuart Little*, 1945,
  Charlotte's Web, 1952.
b. Apr 16, 1912 in New York, New
  York
d. May 8, 1996 in Guanajuato, Mexico
Source: *AmAu&B; AuBYP 2, 3; BenetAL
91; BioIn 14, 16; ChlLR 57; ConAu 134;
FacFETw; IlsCB 1744, 1946, 1957;
MajAI SUP; MorJA; REnAL; SmATA 18,
66; Str&VC; WhAmArt 85; WhoAm 86,
90; WrDr 98N*

Williams, George Washington

American. Historian, Clergy, Journalist,
  Politician
First important historian to record the
  African American experience, author
  of *History of the Negro Race*, 1883;
  also a soldier in the Civil War, a
  member of the Ohio legislature, a
  preacher, a lawyer, a publisher and
  journalist, and a political activist
  against colonialism in Africa.
b. Oct 16, 1849 in Bedford, Pennsylvania
d. Aug 2, 1891 in London, England

Source: *Alli SUP; AmAu; AmAu&B;
AmNatBi; ApCAB; BiD&SB; BioIn 1, 5,
6, 8, 9, 12, 13, 14, 15, 16, 17, 24;
BlkAWP; BlkWrNE; ConBlB 18;
DcAmAu; DcAmB; DcAmNB; DcLB 47;
DcNAA; EncAACR; HarEnUS; InB&W
80, 85; NatCAB 10; NegAl 76, 83, 89;
NotBlAM; OhA&B; OxCAfAL; PeoHis;
SelBAAf; SelBAAu; USGovLe; WhAm HS*

Williams, Gluyas

American. Cartoonist
Satirized middle-class America in *The
  New Yorker*, 1928-53.
b. Jul 23, 1888 in San Francisco,
  California
d. Feb 13, 1982 in Boston,
  Massachusetts
Source: *AmAu&B; AmNatBi; AuNews 2;
BioIn 1, 2, 3, 5, 11, 13, 14; ChhPo, S1;
ConAu 108; CurBio 46, 82, 82N;
REnAL; WhAm 9; WhAmArt 85;
WhoAmA 73, 76; WorECar*

Williams, Gregory (Howard)

American. Educator, University
  Administrator
Dean and professor, Ohio State
  University College of Law, 1993—.
b. Nov 12, 1943 in Muncie, Indiana
Source: *ConAu 155; ConBlB 11; DrAS
99P; WhoAfA 9, 10, 11, 12; WhoAm 86,
88, 90, 92, 94, 95, 96, 97, 98, 99, 2000;
WhoAmL 96, 98, 2000; WhoBlA 3, 4, 5,
6, 7, 8; WrDr 99, 2000*

Williams, Gus

American. Actor
Comedian at Tony Pastor's theatre,
  1868-79, starred in *Our German
  Senator*.
b. Jul 19, 1847 in New York, New York
d. Jan 16, 1915 in Yonkers, New York
Source: *NewGrDA 86; NotNAT B;
WhoStg 1906*

Williams, Gus

American. Basketball Player
Guard, 1975-87, mostly with Seattle; set
  NBA record for steals in career;
  named comeback player of yr., 1982.
b. Oct 10, 1953 in Mount Vernon, New
  York
Source: *BasBi; BioIn 12; LegTOT;
OfNBA 87; WhoAfA 9, 10, 11, 12;
WhoAm 84; WhoBlA 4, 5, 6, 7, 8*

Williams, Hank

[Hiram King Williams]
"The Drifting Cowboy"; "The Hillbilly
  Shakespeare"
American. Singer, Songwriter
Instrumental in popularizing country-
  western music; hits include "Your
  Cheatin' Heart" and "Jambalaya."
b. Sep 15, 1923 in Georgiana, Alabama
d. Jan 1, 1953 in Oak Hill, West
  Virginia
Source: *AllMGCo; AmNatBi; AmSong;
BakBD 84, 92; BakDcM; BgBkCoM;
BiDAmM; BillEnR; BioIn 3, 4, 6, 8, 9,
10, 12, 13, 14, 15, 17, 19, 20, 21, 22;
CamBiEn; CmpEPM; ConMus 4;*

CounME 74, 74A; DcAmB S3, S5; EncFCWM 69, 83; EncRk 88; EncRkSt; FacFETw; HarEnCM 87; HarEnR 86; IlEncCM; IlEncRk; LegTOT; NewAmDM; NewGrDA 86; NewGrDM 80; OxCPMus; PenEncP; PopAmC SUP; RolSEnR 83; Songw; TwCLC 81; WhoRock 81; WhScrn 77; WorAl; WorAlBi

Williams, Hank, Jr.
[Randall Hank Williams]
American. Singer
Country-western star since 1960s; hits include "Texas Women," 1981; Country Music Entertainer of the Year, 1987, 1988.
b. May 26, 1949 in Shreveport, Louisiana
Source: *AllMGCo; BgBkCoM; BillEnR; BioIn 11, 12, 14, 16, 22, 23, 24; ConAu 117; ConMus 1; CounME 74, 74A; CurBio 98; EncFCWM 69, 83; HarEnCM 87; IlEncCM; LegTOT; NewAmDM; NewGrDA 86; OxCPMus; PenEncP; RolSEnR 83; Songw; WhoAm 82, 84, 86, 88, 90, 92, 94, 95, 96, 97; WhoEnt 92; WhoHol 92, A; WhoNeCM; WhoRock 81; WorAlBi*

Williams, Harrison Arlington, Jr.
American. Lawyer, Politician
Dem. senator from NJ, 1959-82; convicted in Abscam bribery scandal, 1981.
b. Dec 10, 1919 in Plainfield, New Jersey
Source: *AlmAP 80; BiDrAC; BiDrUSC 89; BioIn 3, 5, 6, 7, 9, 10, 11, 12, 13, 14; BlueB 76; CngDr 74, 77, 79, 81; CurBio 60; IntWW 74, 75, 76, 77, 78, 79, 80, 81, 82, 83, 89, 91, 93; IntYB 78, 79, 80, 81, 82; NewYTBE 73; NewYTBS 80, 82, 86; PolProf E, NF; WhoAm 74, 76, 78, 80, 82; WhoAmP 73, 75, 77, 79, 81, 83; WhoE 74, 75, 77, 79, 81; WhoGov 72, 75, 77; WhoWor 80, 82*

Williams, Henry Sylvester
Trinidadian. Lawyer
Promoter of pan-African solidarity, he organized the First Pan-African Conference in London in 1900.
b. Feb 15, 1869, Trinidad
d. Mar 26, 1911, Trinidad
Source: *BioIn 10, 11; EncWB 98; InB&W 80; McGEWB*

Williams, Hosea Lorenzo
American. Civil Rights Leader, Clergy, Author
Nat. program director, SCLC, 1971.
b. Jan 5, 1926 in Attapulgis, Georgia
Source: *AfrAmBi 2; BioIn 11; BlueB 76; ConAu 49; ConBlB 15; EncAACR; HisDCRM; InB&W 85; WhoAmP 75, 77, 79, 81, 83, 85, 87, 89, 91, 93, 95, 97; WhoBlA 7; WhoSSW 73, 84*

Williams, J(ames) R(obert)
American. Cartoonist
Created comic strip "Out Our Way, With the Willits."

---

b. Aug 18, 1888 in Halifax, Nova Scotia, Canada
d. Jun 18, 1957 in Pasadena, California
Source: *ArtsAmW 1; BioIn 1, 2, 3, 4, 7, 8, 11; IlBEAAW; NatCAB 47; WhAm 3; WhAmArt 85; WorECom*

Williams, Jay
[Michael Delving]
American. Children's Author
Wrote *Danny Dunn* series of books for children.
b. May 31, 1914 in Buffalo, New York
d. Jul 12, 1978 in London, England
Source: *AuBYP 2S, 3; BioIn 4, 7, 9, 10, 11, 13, 14, 15, 19; ChlLR 8; ConAu 1R, 2NR, 39NR, 81; CurBio 55, 78N; FourBJA; IntAu&W 76, 77; MajAI; NatCAB 61; ObitOF 79; ScF&FL 1, 2, 92; SmATA 3, 24N, 41; TwCChW 1, 2, 3, 4; TwCCr&M 80, 85; WhScrn 83; WorAu 1950; WrDr 76*

Williams, Jimy
[James Francis Williams]
American. Baseball Manager
Toronto, coach, 1980-85, manager, 1986-89; manager, Boston, 1997—.
b. Oct 14, 1943 in Santa Maria, California
Source: *Ballpl 90; BaseReg 86, 87; BioIn 16; WhoAm 86, 88, 2000; WhoE 89; WhoMW 88; WhoWor 89*

Williams, JoBeth
[Margaret JoBeth Williams]
American. Actor
Films include *The Big Chill*, 1983; *Murder Ordained*, 1987.
b. 1953 in Houston, Texas
Source: *BioIn 13, 14, 15; ConTFT 6; HalFC 84, 88; IntMPA 92; LegTOT; WhoAm 95, 96, 97, 99; WhoAmW 95; WhoEnt 98*

Williams, Joe
[Joseph Goreed]
American. Singer
Blues, jazz, ballads singer, known for hits with Count Basie, including "Everyday I Have the Blues," 1955.
b. Dec 12, 1918 in Cordele, Georgia
d. Mar 29, 1999 in Las Vegas, Nevada
Source: *AllMGBl 1, 2; AllMGJa; BiDAfM; BiDAmM; BiDJaz; BioIn 4, 11, 12, 14, 15, 16; BluesWW; CmpEPM; ConBlB 5; ConMus 11; CurBio 85, 1999; DcPseud; DcTwCCu 5; DrBlPA, 90; EncJzS; GuBlues; LegTOT; NewAmDM; NewGrDJ 88, 94; News 1999; NewYTBS 89, 99; PenEncP; WhoAfA 9, 10, 11, 12; WhoAm 82, 84, 86, 88, 90, 92, 94, 95, 96, 97; WhoBlA 4, 5, 6, 7, 8; WhoHol 92; WorAlBi*

Williams, John
Australian. Musician
Classical guitarist; solo album *Echoes of London*, 1986.
b. Apr 24, 1941 in Melbourne, Australia
Source: *BakBD 84; BakDcM; BiDJaz; BioIn 11, 12, 13, 14; BlueB 76; BriBkM 80; CmpEGui; ConMus 9; CurBio 83;*

IntWW 74, 75, 76, 77, 78, 79, 80, 81, 82, 83, 89, 91, 93, 97, 98, 2000; IntWWM 77, 90; MusSN; NewGrDJ 88; NewYTBS 86; OnThGG; PenDiMP; PenEncP; Who 74, 82, 83, 85, 88, 90, 92, 94, 98, 99, 2000; WhoAm 80, 82; WhoEnt 98; WhoMus 72; WhoWor 84, 87, 89, 91, 93, 95; WhsWeAm 98

Williams, John A(lfred)
American. Writer
Wrote *One for New York*, 1960; *The Man Who Cried I Am*, 1967.
b. Dec 5, 1925 in Jackson, Mississippi
Source: *AmAu&B; Au&Wr 71; Benet 96; BioIn 8, 9, 10, 11, 12, 14, 15, 17, 20; BlkAmP; BlkAWP; BlkAmP; BlkWr 2, 3; CamDcAB; ConAu 51NR, 53; ConLC 5; ConNov 72, 76, 96; CurBio 94; DcLB 2; DrAF 76; DrAPF 80; DrAS 99E; EncALit; EncSF 93; InB&W 80, 85; IntAu&W 93; LiveMA; LivgBAA; OxCAmL 95; OxCTwCL; PenC AM; RAdv 1; RfGAmL 4, 94; SelBAAf; SelBAAu; SouWr; TwCSFW 81; WhoAfA 9, 10, 11, 12; WhoBlA 3, 4, 5, 6, 7, 8; WorAu 1950; WrDr 76, 94, 96, 98, 99, 2000*

Williams, John James
"Conscience of the Senate"
American. Politician
Rep. senator from DE, 1947-71; led investigation to expose fraud in IRS, early 1950s.
b. May 17, 1904 in Frankford, Delaware
d. Jan 11, 1988 in Lewes, Delaware
Source: *BiDrAC; BiDrUSC 89; BioIn 2, 3, 4, 6, 7, 8, 11, 12; BlueB 76; CurBio 88; PolProf E, J, K, NF, T; ScrEAmL 2; WhoAmP 73, 75, 77, 79, 81, 83, 85, 87*

Williams, John Towner
American. Composer, Conductor
Conductor, Boston Pops, 1980—; won Oscars for scores of *Jaws*, 1975; *Star Wars*, 1977.
b. Feb 8, 1932 in Flushing, New York
Source: *BakBD 92; BakBDTw; BioIn 12; CamDcAB; CelR 90; ConTFT 3; FacFETw; HalFC 88; IntMPA 92; OxCPMus; PenDiMP; PenEncP; VarWW 85; Who 82, 83, 85, 88, 90, 92, 94, 98, 99, 2000; WhoAm 86, 88, 92, 94, 95, 96, 97, 98, 99, 2000; WhoAmM 83; WhoE 89, 91, 97; WhoEnt 92, 98; WhoWor 87, 89, 91, 93, 95; WorAlBi*

Williams, Kit
English. Author, Artist
Wrote *Masquerade*, 1979, which sparked one of most exciting treasure hunts ever held on British soil.
b. 1947 in Romney Marshes, England
Source: *BioIn 13, 15; ConAu 107; NewYTBS 80, 81; SmATA 44; TwCPaSc; WrDr 84*

Williams, Lucinda
American. Singer, Songwriter
Sings short-story like songs marked with a country and blues music influence; recorded debut album, *Rambling on*

My Mind, 1979; later released *Lucinda Williams*, 1988 and *Passionate Kisses*, 1992.
b. 1953 in Lake Charles, Louisiana
Source: *AllMGCo; BgBkCoM; ConMus 10, 24; CurBio 1999; WhoAm 95, 96, 97*

Williams, Lynn Russell
Canadian. Labor Union Official
President of United Steelworkers of America, 1983.
b. Jul 21, 1924 in Springfield, Ontario, Canada
Source: *ConNews 86-4; IntWW 89, 91, 93, 97, 98, 2000; NewYTBS 84; WhoAm 86, 88, 92, 94, 95, 96, 97; WhoFI 94, 96*

Williams, Maggie
[Margaret Ann Williams]
American. Government Official
Assistant to the President and Chief of Staff to the First Lady, Clinton Administration, 1993—.
b. Dec 25, 1954 in Kansas City, Missouri
Source: *BioIn 19, 20, 21; ConBlB 7; NewYTBS 93; WhoAfA 9; WhoAmP 95*

Williams, Mary Lou
"Queen of Jazz"
American. Composer, Musician
Contributed to growth of bebop style, 1940s; wrote for Benny Goodman, Duke Ellington.
b. May 8, 1910 in Pittsburgh, Pennsylvania
d. May 28, 1981 in Durham, North Carolina
Source: *AfrAmAl 6, 8; AllMGJa; AmNatBi; AnObit 1981; ASCAP 66, 80; BakBD 84, 92; BakDcM; BiDAfM; BiDAmM; BiDJaz; BioIn 2, 4, 6, 7, 9, 10, 11, 12, 13, 14, 16, 17, 18, 19, 20, 22, 23, 24; BlkWAB; BlkWAm; CamBiEn; CamDcAB; ChamBiD; CmpBPM; ConAmC 76, 82; BakDcM; BiDAfM; ContDcW 89; CurBio 81N; DcTwCCu 5; DrBlPA, 90; EncJzS; FacFETw; GrLiveH; IlEncJ; InB&W 85; IntDcWB; InWom, SUP; NegAl 89; NewGrDA 86; NewGrDJ 88, 94; NewGrDM 80; NewYTBS 81; NotBlAW 1; OxCPMus; PenEncP; ScrEAmL 1; WhoBlA 3; WhoJazz 72; WomFir*

Williams, Mason
American. Composer, Musician, Author
Won Grammy, 1969, for "Classical Gas."
b. Aug 24, 1938 in Abilene, Texas
Source: *BiDAmM; BioIn 8; ConAu 25R; ConTFT 16; RkOn 74, 78; WhoAm 74, 76, 78, 80, 82; WhoRock 81*

Williams, Matt
American. Writer
Created television show *Roseanne*, co-created *Home Improvement*.
Source: *BioIn 18, 20, 21; LesBEnT 92*

Williams, Milan
[The Commodores]
American. Musician, Singer
Drummer since group's founding, 1971; wrote hit instrumental "Machine Gun," 1974.
b. 1947 in Mississippi
Source: *BkPepl*

Williams, Montel B
American. TV Personality
Known as talk show host on TV's "Montel Williams Show," 1991—.
b. Jul 3, 1956 in Baltimore, Maryland

Williams, O(swald) S.
[Ozzie Williams]
American. Aeronautical Engineer
Inventor and engineer managed the development of the control rocket systems for National Aeronautics and Space Administration (NASA) Apollo missions, and was responsible for the rocket that saved the lives of the Apollo 13 astronauts in 1970.
b. Sep 2, 1921 in Washington, District of Columbia

Williams, Patricia J(oyce)
American. Educator, Lawyer
Professor of law, Columbia University, 1992—; wrote *The Alchemy of Race and Rights: Diary of a Law Professor*, 1991.
b. Aug 28, 1951 in Boston, Massachusetts
Source: *ConAu 154; WrDr 99, 2000*

Williams, Patrick
American. Composer
Won Emmys for theme songs for TV shows "Lou Grant," 1980; "The Princess and the Cabbie," 1982.
b. Apr 23, 1939 in Bonne Terre, Missouri
Source: *ConTFT 12, 25; IntWWM 85; VarWW 85; WhoAm 86, 90; WhoE 85; WhoEnt 92*

Williams, Paul Hamilton
American. Singer, Songwriter
Won 1976 Oscar for best song: "Evergreen."
b. Sep 19, 1940 in Omaha, Nebraska
Source: *BioIn 16; BkPepl; ConMus 5; ConTFT 4; CurBio 83; EncFCWM 83; HalFC 84, 88; IntMPA 92; RkOn 74; Who 88; WhoAm 74, 76, 78, 80, 82, 84, 86, 88, 90, 92, 94, 95, 96, 97; WhoEnt 92, 98; WhoHol A; WorAlBi*

Williams, Paul R(evere)
American. Architect
One of America's first black architects; designed thousands of homes, commercial, public buildings.
b. Feb 18, 1894 in Los Angeles, California
d. Jan 23, 1980 in Los Angeles, California
Source: *AfrAmAl 6, 8; AfroAA; AmNatBi; AnObit 1980; BioIn 1, 8, 9,*

12, 15; *CamDcAB; CurBio 41, 80N; Ebony 1; InB&W 80; IntWW 78; NewYTBS 80; NotBlAS; WhoAm 76; WhoBlA 2*

Williams, Randy
American. Track Athlete
Long jumper; won gold medal, 1972 Olympics.
b. Aug 23, 1953 in Fresno, California
Source: *BlkOlyM; WhoTr&F 73*

Williams, Robert F(ranklin)
American. Civil Rights Activist
Advocated "meeting (racist) violence with violence," 1959; founder and publisher *Crusader* magazine, 1959-66.
b. Feb 26, 1925 in Monroe, North Carolina
Source: *InB&W 80, 85; WhoAfA 9, 10N*

Williams, Robin
American. Comedian, Actor
Starred in TV's "Mork and Mindy," 1978-82; won Grammy, 1979, for album, *Reality, What a Concept*; films include *Good Morning, Vietnam*, 1987 and *The Birdcage*, 1996; won best supporting actor Oscar for 1997's *Good Will Hunting*.
b. Jul 21, 1951 in Chicago, Illinois
Source: *BioIn 13, 14, 15, 16; BkPepl; CelR 90; ChamBiD; ConTFT 3, 10, 17; CurBio 79; EncAFC; HalFC 84, 88; IntMPA 86, 92, 94, 96; IntWW 91, 93, 97, 98, 2000; LesBEnT 92; News 88; NewYTBS 78, 84, 89, 90; Who 92; WhoAm 86, 90, 92, 94, 95, 96, 97, 98, 99, 2000; WhoEnt 92, 98; WhoTech 89; WorAlBi*

Williams, Roger
American. Clergy
Founded RI colony and Providence, RI, 1636; first to advocate complete religious tolerance in America.
b. 1603? in London, England
d. 1683 in Providence, Rhode Island
Source: *Alli; AmAu; AmAu&B; AmBi; AmNatBi; AmPolLe; AmRef; AmSocL; AmWrBE; BbD; Benet 87, 96; BenetAL 91; BiD&SB; BiDChrM; BiDrACR; BioIn 1; CamDcAB; CamGLE; CamHAL; CasWL; CnDAL; CyAG; CyAL 1; DcAmAu; DcAmB; DcAmReB 1, 2; DcHerTr; DcLB 24; DcLEL; DcNAA; EncAAH; EncAB-H 1974, 1996; EncAInd; EncALit; EncARH; EncCRAm; EncNAB; EncNAR; EncRelA; EncSoB; EncWB 98; HisWorL; LuthC 75; McGEWB; OxCAmH; OxCAmL 65, 83, 95; OxCBrHi; PenC AM; RComAH; REn; REnAL; WebAB 74, 79; WebE&AL; WhAm HS; WhAmP; WhDW; WhNaAH; WorAl; WorAlBi*

Williams, Roger
American. Pianist
Popular hits include "Autumn Leaves," 1955; "Born Free," 1966.
b. Oct 1, 1926 in Omaha, Nebraska

Source: *ASCAP 66, 80; BiDAmM; BioIn 5, 8; ForYSC; IntMPA 80, 84, 86, 88, 92, 94, 96; LegTOT; PenEncP; WhoAm 90; WorAl*

Williams, Roger J
American. Biochemist
Discovered growth promoting vitamin, pantothenic acid (B Complex); wrote *Introduction to Organic Chemistry*, 1928.
b. Aug 14, 1893 in Ootacamund, India
d. Feb 20, 1988 in Austin, Texas
Source: *AmMWSc 73P, 82; BioIn 15, 16; ConAu 7NR; CurBio 88, 88N; FacFETw; IntAu&W 77, 82; IntWW 74, 75, 76, 77, 78, 80, 81, 82, 83; NewYTBS 88; WhoAm 86; WrDr 86*

Williams, Roy Lee
American. Labor Union Official
Pres. of Teamsters, 1981-83; resigned following attempted bribery conviction.
b. Mar 22, 1915 in Ottumwa, Iowa
d. Apr 28, 1989 in Leeton, Missouri
Source: *BiDAmL; BioIn 12, 13, 15, 16; NewYTBS 81, 89; WhoAm 82*

Williams, Samm-Art
American. Actor, Dramatist
Plays include *Home*, 1979; *The Sixteenth Round*, 1980.
b. Jan 20, 1946 in Burgaw, North Carolina
Source: *BioIn 14, 15; BlkWr 1; ConAu X; ConBlAP 88; ConBlB 21; ConTFT 8; DcLB 38; DrBlPA 90; McGEWD 84; NatPD 81; OxCAfAL; SchCGBL; WhoAfA 9, 10, 11, 12; WhoBlA 6, 7, 8*

Williams, Serena
American. Tennis Player
With older sister Venus, drew attention as a brash, talented young African American tennis star, turned professional in 1995; lost to sister at the Australian Open in 1998, ranked thirty-first in the world.
b. Sep 26, 1981 in Saginaw, Michigan
Source: *ConBlB 20; News 1999; WhoAm 2000; WhoAmW 99*

Williams, Sherley Anne
American. Author
Author of *Dessa Rose*, 1986, about the life of an escaped slave.
b. Aug 25, 1944 in Bakersfield, California
d. Jul 6, 1999 in San Diego, California
Source: *AmWomWr SUP; BioIn 13, 15, 19, 20, 21; BlkLC; BlkWAm; BlkWr 1, 2, 3; ConAfAN; ConAu 25NR, 73, 82NR; ConLC 89; CyWA 97; DcLB 41; DcTwCCu 5; FemiCLE; InB&W 85; ModWoWr; OxCAfAL; OxCTwCL; OxCWoWr 95; SchCGBL; SelBAAf; SmATA 78; WhoAfA 9, 10, 11, 12; WhoAmW 79; WhoBlA 6, 7, 8*

Williams, Shirley
English. Politician
Paymaster-General, 1976-79; member of Labour Party National Exec. Com., 1970.
b. Jul 27, 1930 in London, England
Source: *BioIn 20, 21; BlkWr 1; BlueB 76; ConAu X; ContDcW 89; CurBio 76; DcWomA; FacFETw; IntAu&W 89; IntDcWB; IntWW 74, 75, 76, 77, 78, 79, 80, 81, 82, 83, 89, 91; InWom SUP; Who 92; WhoWor 91*

Williams, Simon
English. Actor
Played James Bellamy in PBS series "Upstairs, Downstairs."
b. Jun 16, 1946 in Windsor, England
Source: *ConAu 133; ConTFT 22; HalFC 84, 88; WhoHol 92, A*

Williams, Ted
[Theodore Samuel Williams]
"The Splendid Sprinter"; "The Thumper"
American. Baseball Player
Outfielder, Boston, 1939-42, 1946-60; won Triple Crown twice; last player to bat over .400; had .344 lifetime batting average; Hall of Fame, 1966.
b. Aug 30, 1918 in San Diego, California
Source: *Ballpl 90; BiDAmSp BB; BioIn 1, 2, 3, 4, 5, 6, 7, 8, 9, 10, 11, 12, 13, 14, 15, 16, 17, 18, 19, 20, 21, 22, 23, 24; CamBiEn; CelR; CmCal; CulEncB; CurBio 47; EncWB 2-19; FacFETw; LegTOT; NewYTBS 88; WebAB 74, 79; WhoAm 76, 78, 80, 82, 84, 86, 88, 90, 92, 94, 95, 96, 97, 98; WhoHol A; WhoProB 73; WhoSpor; WorAl; WorAlBi*

Williams, Tennessee
[Thomas Lanier Williams]
American. Dramatist, Author
Won Pulitzers for classic plays *A Streetcar Named Desire*, 1947; *Cat on a Hot Tin Roof*, 1955.
b. Mar 26, 1911 in Columbus, Mississippi
d. Feb 25, 1983 in New York, New York
Source: *AmAu&B; AmCulL; AmNatBi; AmWr; AnObit 1983; Au&Arts 31; Au&Wr 71; AuNews 2; Benet 87, 96; BenetAL 91; BiCoLiE; BiDConC; BiE&WWA; BioIn 9, 10, 11, 12, 13, 14, 15, 16, 17, 18, 19, 20, 21, 22, 23, 24; BioNews 74; BlueB 76; CamBiEn; CamDcAB; CamGEL; CamGLE; CamGWoT; CamHAL; CasWL; CelR; ChamBiD; CmpQue; CnMWL; CnThe; ConAmD; ConAu 3BS, 31NR, 108; ConDr 73, 77, 82, 93; ConLC 1, 2, 5, 7, 8, 11, 15, 19, 30, 39, 45, 71, 111; ConNov 72, 76, 82; ConTFT 1; CroCD; CrtSuDr; CurBio 72, 83N; CyWA 89, 97; DcArts; DcLB 7, DS4, Y83N; DcPseud; DcTwCCu 1; DrAF 76; DramC 4; EncAB-H 1974, 1996; EncALit; EncSoH; EncSoL; EncWL 1, 2, 2S, 3; EncWT; Ent; FacFETw; FifSWrA; GayLesB; GayLL 1; GrWrEL DR; HalFC 84, 88; IdentIs; IntAu&W 76, 77, 82; IntDcT 2; IntWW 76, 77, 78, 79, 80,*

81, 82, 2000; *LegTOT; LinLib L, S; LiveMA; LiveWoA; LngCTC; MagSAmL; MajMD 1; MajTwCW 1, 2; McGEWB; McGEWD 72, 84; ModAL 4S1, 4S2, 4S3, 5; ModWD; NatPD 77, 81; NewCon; NewYTBS 83; NotNAT; Novels; OxCAmL 83, 95; OxCAmT 84; OxCEng 85, 95; OxCThe 83; OxCTwCL; OxCTwCP; RAdv 14, 13-2; RComAH; REnWD; RfGAmL 4, 87, 94; RGTwCWr; ScF&FL 92; SouWr; TwCA SUP; WebAB 74, 79; WebE&AL; Who 74, 82, 83; WhoPul; WhoThe 72, 77, 81; WhoTwCL; WorAl; WorAlBi; WorAu 1900; WorLitC; WrDr 76, 80, 82; WrPh*

Williams, Tex
American. Musician, Actor
Country-western singer popular in films, 1930s-50s; best-selling hit singles include "Smoke! Smoke! Smoke!"
b. Aug 23, 1917 in Ramsey, Illinois
d. Oct 11, 1985 in Newhall, California
Source: *AllMGCo; AmNatBi; BgBkCoM; BioIn 14; CounME 74, 74A; EncFCWM 69, 83; HarEnCM 87; IlEncCM; NewYTBS 85; PenEncP*

Williams, Tiger
[David James Williams]
Canadian. Hockey Player
Left wing, 1974-88; holds NHL record for career penalty minutes (over 3,800); wrote autobiography *Tiger: A Hockey Story*, 1986.
b. Feb 3, 1954 in Weyburn, Saskatchewan, Canada
Source: *HocEn; HocReg 87*

Williams, Tommy
[Thomas Mark Williams]
American. Hockey Player
Center, 1961-76, mostly with Boston; held all NHL scoring records by American-born player until broken by Reed Larson; youngest gold medalist US Olympic hockey team, 1960.
b. Apr 17, 1940 in Duluth, Minnesota
d. Feb 8, 1992 in Hudson, Massachusetts
Source: *BiDAmSp BK; HocEn; WhoAdv 90; WhoE 89; WhoHcky 73*

Williams, Tony
[Anthony Williams]
American. Composer, Musician
Drummer; prime influence on jazz styles of the 1970s.
b. Dec 12, 1945 in Chicago, Illinois
d. Feb 23, 1997 in Daly City, California
Source: *AllMGJa; BiDJazz; BioIn 12, 13, 16, 22, 23, 24; ConMus 6; DcTwCCu 5; EncJzS; InB&W 80, 85; NewGrDA 86; NewGrDJ 88, 94; PenEncP; WhAm 12; WhoAm 82, 84, 86, 88, 92, 94, 95, 96, 97; WhoEnt 92*

Williams, Treat
[Richard Treat Williams]
American. Actor
Starred in films *Hair*, 1979, *Prince of the City*, 1981, *Dead Heat*, 1988.
b. Dec 1, 1951 in Stamford, Connecticut

Source: *BioIn 13; CelR 90; ConTFT 8, 16, 27; HalFC 84, 88; HolBB; IntMPA 88, 92; LegTOT; NewYTBS 79, 80, 81; WhoAm 86, 88, 90, 92, 94, 95, 96, 97, 99, 2000; WhoEnt 92, 98*

Williams, Ursula Moray
English. Children's Author
Writings include *The Noble Hawks,* 1959; *The Three Toymakers,* 1946.
b. Apr 19, 1911 in Petersfield, England
Source: *Au&Wr 71; AuBYP 2S; BioIn 8, 9, 14, 19, 22; ConAu 10NR, 13R, X; DcLB 160; FourBJA; IntAu&W 76, 77, 82, 86; IntWWP 77; NewCBEL; OxCChiL; ScF&FL 1, 2, 92; SmATA 3; TwCChW 1, 2, 3; WhoChL; WhoWor 76; WrDr 86, 92*

Williams, Vanessa
American. Actor, Beauty Contest Winner, Singer
First black crowned Miss America, 1983; first to give up title for violating pageant's morals code; was in film *The Pick-Up Artist,* 1987; *Eraser,* 1996.
b. Mar 18, 1963 in New York, New York
Source: *AfrAmAl 8; AfrAmBi 1; AmDec 1980; BioIn 13, 14, 15, 16; CelR 90; ConBlB 4; ConMus 10; ConTFT 14; CurBio 84; DcTwCCu 5; DrBlPA 90; InB&W 85; InWom SUP; LegTOT; NewYTBS 84; WhoAfA 9, 10; WhoAm 94, 95, 96, 97, 98; WhoAmW 95, 97, 99; WhoBlA 7; WhoEnt 98; WhoHol 92*

Williams, Venus (Ebone Starr)
American. Tennis Player
Unorthodox professional tennis player, debuted as a prodigy in 1994; the African American player found success at Wimbledon and U.S. Open tournaments in 1997, and the Italian Open and the Lipton Championship in 1999; sister Serena Williams is also a professional tennis player.
b. Jun 17, 1980 in Los Angeles, California
Source: *WhoAfA 9, 10, 11, 12*

Williams, Victoria
American. Singer, Songwriter
Released album *Happy Come Home,* which includes songs "Frying Pan" and "Opelousas," 1987; later recorded *Loose,* 1994 and *This Moment: Live in Toronto,* 1995.
b. 1959 in Forbing, Louisiana
Source: *ConMus 17*

Williams, Walter Edward
American. Economist
Conservative author of numerous books and articles; blames government programs for many social ills.
b. Mar 31, 1936 in Philadelphia, Pennsylvania
Source: *AfrAmOr; AmMWSc 78S; BiDAmNC; ConAu 123; WhoBlA 2, 3, 4, 5; WrDr 92, 98, 99, 2000*

Williams, Wayne Bertram
American. Murderer
Freelance photographer convicted of Atlanta's child killings, 1982.
b. May 27, 1958 in Atlanta, Georgia
Source: *BioIn 12, 13, 15; InB&W 85; MurCaTw; NewYTBS 81*

Williams, Wendy O(rlean)
[The Plasmatics]
American. Entertainer
Lead singer known for outrageous appearance and stage antics.
b. 1946? in Rochester, New York
d. Apr 6, 1998 in Storrs, Connecticut
Source: *BioIn 12, 13; NewWmR; WhoRocM 82*

Williams, William
American. Merchant, Judge
Signed Declaration of Independence, 1776; member, Continental Congress, 1776-78, 1783-84.
b. Apr 23, 1731 in Lebanon, Connecticut
d. Aug 2, 1811 in Lebanon, Connecticut
Source: *AmBi; AmNatBi; ApCAB; BiAUS; BiDrAC; BiDrUSC 89; BioIn 7, 8, 9, 10, 23; DcAmB; Drake; EncAR; EncCRAm; HarEnUS; HisDcAR; NatCAB 10; TwCBDA; WhAm HS; WhAmP; WhAmRev*

Williams, William Carlos
American. Author, Poet
Revolutionized American poetry; won 1963 Pulitzer for *Pictures From Brueghel.*
b. Sep 17, 1883 in Rutherford, New Jersey
d. Mar 4, 1963 in Rutherford, New Jersey
Source: *AmAu&B; AmCulL; AmNatBi; AmWr, RS1; AtlBL; Benet 87, 96; BenetAL 91; BiCoLiE; BiDAmM; BiDHisA; BioIn 1, 2, 4, 5, 6, 7, 8, 9, 10, 11, 12, 13, 14, 15, 16, 17, 19, 20, 22, 24; CamBiEn; CamDcAB; CamGEL; CamGLE; CamHAL; CasWL; ChamBiD; ChhPo; CnDAL; CnE&AmP; CnMD; CnMWL; ConAmA; ConAmL; ConAu 34NR, 89; ConLC 1, 2, 5, 9, 13, 22, 42, 67; CyWA 58, 89, 97; DcAmB S7; DcAmMeB 84; DcArts; DcLB 4, 16, 54, 86; DcLEL; DcTwCCu 1; EncAB-H 1996; EncALit; EncLitE; EncWB 98; EncWL 1, 2, 2S, 3; EvLB; FacFETw; GrWrEL P; InSci; LinLib L, S; LngCTC; MagSAmL; MajTwCW 1, 2; MakMC; McGEWB; ModAL 4, 4S1, 4S2, 4S3, 5; ModWD; NewGrDA 86; NotPoe; Novels; OxCAmL 65, 83, 95; OxCEng 67, 85, 95; OxCTwCL; OxCTwCP; PenC AM; PlP&P; PoeCrit 7; RAdv 1, 14, 13-1; RComAH; REn; REnAL; RfGAmL 4, 87, 94; RfGShF 1, 2; RGFAP; RGTwCWr; ShSCr 31; SixAP; Tw; TwCA, SUP; TwCWr; WebAB 74, 79; WebE&AL; WhAm 4; WhDW; WhLit; WhNAA; WhoPul; WhoTwCL; WorAl; WorAlBi; WorAu 1900; WorLitC*

Williams, William T(homas)
American. Painter
First black artist to be included in *History of Art,* H. W. Janson's widely used art textbook; professor of art, Brooklyn College, 1971—.
b. Jul 17, 1942 in Cross Creek, North Carolina
Source: *SJGBlA; WhoAfA 9, 10, 11, 12; WhoAm 82, 84, 86, 88, 90, 92, 94, 95, 96, 97, 98; WhoAmA 80, 82, 84, 86, 89, 91, 93, 1999; WhoBlA 2, 3, 4, 5, 6, 7, 8*

Williams, Willie Lawrence
American. Police Chief
Succeeded Daryl Gates as chief of police, Los Angeles, CA, 1992-97.
b. Oct 1, 1943 in Philadelphia, Pennsylvania
Source: *News 93-1*

Williamson, Cris
[Mary Cristine Williamson]
American. Musician
Recorded album *The Changer and the Changed,* 1974, the best-selling women's music album of all time.
b. 1947 in Deadwood, South Dakota
Source: *BakBD 92; GayLesB*

Williamson, David
Australian. Screenwriter
Films include *The Year of Living Dangerously,* 1983.
b. Feb 24, 1942 in Melbourne, Australia
Source: *AuLitCr; BiCoLiE; CamGLE; ConDr 77, 82, 88; ConLC 56; CrtSuDr; CyWA 97; IntLitE; IntvTCA 2; McGEWD 84; OxCAusL; OxCThe 83; OxCTwCL; RAdv 14; VarWW 85; WhoThe 77, 81; WrDr 82, 84, 86, 88, 90, 92*

Williamson, Marianne
American. Lecturer, Author
Founder of spiritual organizations Los Angeles Center for Living and Manhattan Center for Living, 1987; author of spiritual guide *Return to Love,* 1992.
b. Jul 8, 1952 in Houston, Texas
Source: *ConAu 141; CurBio 93; News 91*

Williamson, Nicol
Scottish. Actor
Films include *The Seven-Percent Solution,* 1976; *Excaliber,* 1980.
b. Sep 14, 1938 in Hamilton, Scotland
Source: *BioIn 7, 8, 9, 13, 24; CamGWoT; CelR, 90; CnThe; ConTFT 2, 8; CurBio 70; Ent; FilmEn; FilmgC; HalFC 84, 88; IntDcF 1-3; IntDcT 3; IntMPA 86, 88, 92, 94, 96; IntWW 79, 80, 81, 82, 83, 89, 91, 93, 97, 98, 2000; ItaFilm; LegTOT; MovMk; NewYTBE 73; NotNAT; Who 82, 83, 85, 88, 90, 92, 94, 98, 99, 2000; WhoAm 80, 82, 84, 86, 88, 90, 92; WhoEnt 92; WhoHol A; WhoThe 72, 77, 81; WhoWor 84, 87, 89, 91, 93, 95, 96, 97, 98, 99, 2000; WorAl; WorAlBi*

Williamson, Robin
[Incredible String Band]
Scottish. Musician
Sang, played many instruments for rock
   band, 1967, then began solo career;
   albums include *Journey's Edge*, 1977.
b. Nov 24, 1943 in Glasgow, Scotland
Source: *ConAu 102; IntAu&W 91, 93;
IntWWP 77, 82; WhoRocM 82; WrDr
84, 86, 88, 90, 92*

Williamson, Sonny Boy
[Aleck Ford; Rice Miller]
"Little Boy Blue"; "The One Man
   Band"
American. Singer, Musician
Singer and harmonica player; an early
   contributor in the formation of electric
   blues and rock and roll.
b. Dec 5, 1899 in Glendora, Mississippi
d. Mar 25, 1965 in Helena, Arkansas
Source: *AfrAmAl 8; AllMGBl 1, 2;
AmNatBi; BluesWW; CamDcAB;
ConMuA 80A; ConMus 9; DcPseud;
EncRk 88; GuBlues; NewAmDM;
NewGrDA 86; PenEncP; RolSEnR 83*

William the Conqueror
[William the Norman]
English. Ruler
Conquered England, 1066, replacing
   English nobility with Norman
   followers; King of England, 1066-87,
   succeeded by son, William II.
b. 1027 in Falaise, France
d. 1087 in Rouen, France
Source: *Benet 87, 96; BioIn 24;
ChamBiD; DcNaB; HisWorL; MilitOn;
NewC; REn; WorAl*

William the Silent
Dutch. Nobleman
Prince of Orange and Count of Nassau
   was considered the Father of the
   Dutch Fatherland; led a Low Countries
   revolt against Spain, which resulted in
   the creation of the independent United
   Provinces.
b. 1533
d. 1584
Source: *EncRev; EncWB 98; HarEnMi;
HisWorL; McGEWB; OxCGer 86, 97;
WhDW; WhoMilH 76*

Willig, George
American. Actor, Stunt Performer
Became instant celebrity when he
   climbed World Trade Center, NYC,
   1977; wrote *Going It Alone*, 1979.
b. Jun 11, 1949 in New York, New York
Source: *BioIn 11, 17, 18; ConAu 102;
NewYTBS 77*

Willingham, Calder Baynard, Jr.
American. Writer
His first novel, *End As a Man*, 1947,
   became film, play; wrote screenplay
   for *The Graduate*, 1967.
b. Dec 23, 1922 in Atlanta, Georgia
d. Feb 19, 1995 in Laconia, New
   Hampshire
Source: *Benet 87; BenetAL 91;
BiE&WWA; BioIn 15; CnMD; ConAu*

*3NR, 5R; ConLC 5, 51; ConNov 86, 91;
DcLB 2, 44; DcLEL 1940; DrAPF 91;
EncWL 1; NotNAT; OxCAmL 83;
OxCAmT 84; REnAL; TwCA SUP;
TwCWr; WhAm 11; WhoAm 74, 76, 78,
80, 82, 84, 86, 88, 95; WhoUSWr 88;
WhoWrEP 89, 92, 95; WorAu 1900;
WrDr 86, 92*

Willis, Bill
[William Willis]
American. Football Player
Guard, Cleveland, 1946-53; first black
   player in pro football after WW II;
   Hall of Fame, 1977.
Source: *BiDAmSp FB; BioIn 9, 16;
CabMA; ProFbHF; WhoFtbl 74*

Willis, Bruce
[Walter Bruce Willis]
"Bruno"
American. Actor
Played David Addison on TV series
   "Moonlighting," 1985-89; won 1987
   Emmy; starred in film *Die Hard*,
   1988, *Die Harder*, 1990.
b. Mar 19, 1955 in Idar-Oberstein,
   Germany
Source: *BiDFilm 94; BioIn 14, 15, 16;
CamBiEn; CelR 90; ChamBiD; ConNews
86-4; ConTFT 3, 9, 17; CurBio 87;
DcPseud; HalFC 88; HolBB; IntMPA
92, 94, 96; IntWW 91; LegTOT; WhoAm
90; WhoEnt 92; WhoHol 92*

Willis, Gordon
American. Filmmaker
Cinematographer whose major films
   include *Klute*, 1971; *Annie Hall*, 1983.
Source: *BioIn 11, 12, 15; ConTFT 7;
FilmEn; FilmgC; HalFC 80, 84, 88;
IntMPA 76, 77, 78, 79, 80, 81, 82, 84,
86, 88, 92, 94, 96; MiSFD 9; VarWW
85; WhoAm 82, 84, 86, 88, 90, 92, 94,
95, 96, 97; WhoEnt 92, 98*

Willis, Mary
American. Designer
Won Oscar for costumes in *The
   Wonderful World of the Brothers
   Grimm*, 1963.
b. Jul 4, 1919 in Prescott, Arizona
Source: *InWom SUP; VarWW 85*

Willis, Nathaniel Parker
American. Journalist
Foreign correspondent for *NY Mirror*,
   1832-36; cofounded weekly *Corsair*,
   1839-40.
b. Jan 20, 1806 in Portland, Maine
d. Jan 20, 1867 in Tarrytown, New York
Source: *Alli; AmAu; AmAu&B; AmBi;
AmNatBi; ApCAB; BbD; BenetAL 91;
BiD&SB; BiDTran; BioIn 1, 3, 4, 6, 7,
8, 9, 12, 16, 23; CamDcAB; CamGWoT;
CasWL; ChamBiD; Chambr 3; ChhPo,
S1, S2; CnDAL; CyAL 2; DcAmAu;
DcAmB; DcEnL; DcLB 3, 59, 73, 74,
183; DcLEL; DcNAA; EncAJ; EncALit;
EvLB; GrWrEL N; HarEnUS; JrnUS;
LinLib L; McGEWD 72, 84; NatCAB 3;
NotNAT B; OxCAmL 65; OxCCan;
OxCEng 67; OxCThe 67; REn; REnAL;*

*RfGAmL 4, 87, 94; TwCBDA; WebAB
74, 79; WhAm HS*

Willis, Paul S
American. Business Executive
President, Grocery Manufacturers of
   America, 1932-65; coordinated food
   supplies sent to US troops, WW II.
b. Nov 8, 1890 in Hallettsville, Texas
d. Jun 5, 1987 in New Rochelle, New
   York
Source: *BioIn 2; CurBio 51, 87*

Willkie, Wendell Lewis
[Lewis Wendell Willkie]
American. Politician, Business Executive
Critic of New Deal programs; Rep.
   nominee for pres., 1940, defeated by
   FDR.
b. Feb 18, 1892 in Elwood, Indiana
d. Oct 8, 1944 in New York, New York
Source: *AmAu&B; AmNatBi; AmPolLe;
BioIn 1, 2, 3, 4, 5, 6, 7, 8, 9, 13, 14, 17,
18, 22, 24; ChhPo S1; CurBio 40, 44;
DcAmB S3; DcNAA; EncAB-A 19;
EncAB-H 1974, 1996; IndAu 1917;
LinLib S; NatCAB 32; OhA&B;
OxCAmH; OxCAmL 65; REnAL; WebAB
74, 79; WhAm 2; WhAmP; WhWW-II;
WorAl*

Willmar 8
[Glennis Andresen; Doris Boshart; Sylvia
   Erickson; Jane Harguth; Teren
   Novotny; Shirley Solyntjes; Sandi
   Treml; Irene Wallin]
American. Social Reformers
Women employees of Citizens National
   Bank, Willmar, MN; staged strike,
   1976, over sexual discrimination.

Willners, Hal
American. Producer
Music director of NBC's "Saturday
   Night Live," 1980—; produced
   compilations *Stay Awake: Various
   Interpretations of Music From Vintage
   Disney Films*, 1988 and *Weird
   Nightmare: Meditations on Mingus*,
   1992.
b. 1948 in Philadelphia, Pennsylvania

Wills, Bob
[James Robert Wills]
American. Musician, Songwriter
Pioneered Western swing music; best
   known for song "San Antonio Rose,"
   1940.
b. Mar 6, 1905 in Limestone County,
   Texas
d. May 13, 1975 in Fort Worth, Texas
Source: *AllMGCo; AmNatBi; ASCAP 80;
BakBD 84, 92; BakDcM; BgBands 74;
BgBkCoM; BioIn 1, 10, 11, 12, 14, 15,
16, 20, 21, 22, 23; ChamBiD; CmpEPM;
ConMus 6; DcAmB S9; DcArts;
EncFCWM 69, 83; HarEnCM 87;
IlEncCM; LegTOT; NewAmDM;
NewGrDA 86; NewGrDJ 88, 94;
NewYTBS 75; OxCPMus; PenEncP;
Songw; WhAm 6; WhoAm 74; WhoHol
C; WhoRock 81; WhScrn 77, 83*

Wills, Chill
American. Actor
Voice of Francis the Talking Mule in
  film series, 1940s-50s.
b. Jul 18, 1903 in Seagoville, Texas
d. Dec 15, 1978 in Encino, California
Source: *BioNews 74; LegTOT; MotPP;
MovMk; OsStAZ; Vers A; WhoHol A;
WhScrn 83; WorAl*

Wills, Frank
American. Guard
Security guard at Watergate Hotel who
  reported burglary of Dem.
  headquarters, Jun 17, 1972.
b. 1948?
Source: *BioIn 9, 10, 12, 14; InB&W 80;
NewYTBS 74*

Wills, Garry
American. Author, Journalist
Syndicated political columnist since
  1970; books include *Bare Ruined
  Choirs, 1972; The Kennedy
  Imprisonment, 1982.*
b. May 22, 1934 in Atlanta, Georgia
Source: *AmAu&B; AmCath 80; AmSocL;
BiDAmNC; BioIn 8, 9, 11, 12, 13, 19,
22; ConAu 1NR, 1R; CurBio 82;
DcAmC; DrAS 74F, 78F, 82H; EncAJ;
EncTwCJ; FacFETw; LiJour; PeoHis;
WhoAm 78, 80, 82, 84, 86, 88, 90, 92,
94, 95, 96, 97, 98, 99, 2000; WhoE 74;
WhoMW 92, 93, 96, 98; WhoPul;
WhoRel 92; WhoUSWr 88; WhoWrEP
89, 92, 95; WorAu 1975; WrDr 76, 80,
82, 84, 86, 88, 90, 92, 94, 96, 98, 99,
2000*

Wills, Harry
''Black Panther''
American. Boxer
Heavyweight champion, 1919-22; Hall of
  Fame, 1970.
b. May 15, 1892 in New Orleans,
  Louisiana
d. Dec 21, 1958 in New York, New
  York
Source: *BioIn 1, 5; InB&W 80; WhoBox
74*

Wills, Maury
[Maurice Morning Wills]
American. Baseball Player
Shortstop, 1959-72, mostly with
  Dodgers; NL MVP, 1962; had 586
  career stolen bases.
b. Oct 2, 1932 in Washington, District of
  Columbia
Source: *Ballpl 90; BiDAmSp BB; BioIn
6, 7, 8, 9, 10, 11, 12, 15; CmCal; ConAu
105; CurBio 66; InB&W 85; LegTOT;
NewYTBE 72; WhoHol A; WhoProB 73;
WhoSpor*

Willson, Meredith
American. Composer
Best known for Broadway hits *The
  Music Man, 1957; The Unsinkable
  Molly Brown, 1960.*
b. May 18, 1902 in Mason City, Iowa
d. Jun 15, 1984 in Santa Monica,
  California

Source: *AmAu&B; AmNatBi; AmSong;
ASCAP 66, 80; BakBD 78, 84; BakDcM;
BestMus; BiDAmM; BiE&WWA; BioIn 1,
2, 3, 4, 5, 6, 7, 10, 11, 12, 14, 15, 24;
CamDcAB; CmpEPM; ConAmC 76, 82;
ConAu 49, 113; ConDr 73, 77D;
ConTFT 21; CurBio 58, 84, 84N;
DcPseud; EncMT; HalFC 80, 84, 88;
IntWWM 77, 80; LegTOT; LinLib L, S;
Music; NewAmDM; NewCBMT;
NewGrDA 86; NewGrDM 80; NewYTBS
80, 84; NotNAT, A; OxCAmT 84;
OxCPMus; PenEncP; PopAmC, SUP;
RadStar; SaTiSS; WhAm 9; WhoAm 74,
76, 78, 80, 82, 84, 86; WhoMus 72;
WorAl; WorAlBi*

Willson, S. Brian
American. Political Activist, Veterans'
  Leader
Head of Veterans Peace Action Team;
  lost legs when struck by a train during
  demonstration opposing government
  aid to Nicaraquan contras, 1988.
b. 1942

Willstater, Richard Martin
German. Chemist
Won Nobel Prize, 1915, for research on
  chlorophyll; developed techniques of
  partition chromatography.
b. Aug 13, 1872 in Karlsruhe, Germany
d. Aug 3, 1942 in Locarno, Switzerland
Source: *AsBiEn; BiESc; CurBio 42;
DcScB; Dis&D; ObitOF 79; WhDW;
WhoNob, 90, 95*

Willys, John North
American. Industrialist
Bought automobile plant, 1907;
  manufactured Willys-Overland cars;
  pres., 1907-29, 1935; chm., 1929-35.
b. Oct 25, 1873 in Canandaigua, New
  York
d. Aug 26, 1935 in Riverdale, New York
Source: *AmNatBi; ApCAB X; CamDcAB;
DcAmB S1; EncABHB 4; NatCAB 28;
WebAB 74, 79; WebBD 83; WhAm 1;
WorAl*

Wilmerding, John
American. Author
American art expert who wrote *Genius
  of American Painting,* 1973.
b. Apr 28, 1938 in Boston,
  Massachusetts
Source: *ConAu 111; DrAS 78H, 82H;
WhoAm 74, 76, 78, 80, 82, 84, 86, 88,
90, 92, 94, 95, 96, 97, 98, 99, 2000;
WhoAmA 78, 80, 82, 84, 86, 89, 91, 93,
1999; WrDr 90, 92, 94*

Wilmot, David
American. Politician
Wrote *Wilmot Proviso,* 1846, prohibiting
  slavery in territory purchased from
  Mexico.
b. Jan 20, 1814 in Bethany, Pennsylvania
d. 1868
Source: *AmBi; AmNatBi; AmPolLe;
ApCAB; BiAUS; BiDFedJ; BiDrAC;
BiDrUSC 89; BioIn 7; CamDcAB;
DcAmB; Drake; EncAAH; EncAB-H*

1974, 1996; *EncWB 98; HarEnUS;
McGEWB; NatCAB 3; NewCol 75;
PolPar; TwCBDA; WebAB 74, 79;
WhAm HS; WhAmP; WhCiWar*

Wilmut, Ian
English. Scientist
Cloned a lamb at Scotland's Roslin
  Institute, 1996.
b. Jul 7, 1944 in Hampton Lucey,
  England
Source: *CurBio 97; News 97, 97-3;
NotTwCS 1S; Who 99, 2000; WhoScEn
2000; WhoWor 99, 2000*

Wilson, A(ndrew) N(orman)
English. Critic, Writer
Wrote *The Life of John Milton,* 1983; *C.
  S. Lewis: A Biography,* 1990; won the
  Whitbread Award for *Tolstoy,* 1988.
b. Oct 27, 1950 in Stone, England
Source: *Benet 96; BiCoLiE; BioIn 16,
17, 18, 19; CamBiEn; ChamBID;
ConNov 96; CurBio 93; IntAu&W 86,
93; MajTwCW 2; OxCEng 95;
OxCTwCL; RGTwCWr*

Wilson, Alexander
American. Explorer, Naturalist, Poet
Wrote *American Ornithology,* 1808-14;
  preceded Audubon's work by 20 yrs.
b. Jul 6, 1766 in Paisley, Scotland
d. Aug 23, 1813 in Philadelphia,
  Pennsylvania
Source: *Alli; AmAu; AmAu&B; AmBi;
AmNatBi; ApCAB; BenetAL 91;
BiDAmCa; BiDAmS; BiD&SB; BiESc;
BiInAmS; BioIn 2, 3, 4, 5, 6, 7, 8, 9, 10,
11, 13, 23; CamBiEn; CamDcAB;
CelCen; ChamBID; ChhPo, S1; CyAL 1;
DcAmAu; DcAmB; DcBiPP; DcBrBI;
DcEnL; DcNAA; DcNaB; DcScB; Drake;
EncWB 98; EvLB; GrBII; HarEnUS;
InSci; LinLib L, S; McGEWB; NatCAB
7; NewCBEL; NewYHSD; OxCAmH;
OxCAmL 65, 83, 95; REnAL; TwCBDA;
WebAB 74, 79; WhAm HS*

Wilson, Allan C
American. Biochemist
Responsible for African Eve theory of
  evolution in which all humans
  descended from a single woman who
  lived in Africa 200,000 years ago.
b. Oct 18, 1934 in Ngaruawahia, New
  Zealand
d. Jul 21, 1991 in Seattle, Washington
Source: *AmMWSc 92; NewYTBS 91;
Who 92N; WhoAm 90; WhoTech 89;
WhoWest 89*

Wilson, Angus
[Sir Frank Johnstone]
English. Author
Writings include *As If By Magic,* 1973;
  Setting the World on Fire, 1980.
b. Aug 11, 1913 in Bexhill, England
d. May 31, 1991 in Bury Saint Edmunds,
  England
Source: *AnObit 1991; Au&Wr 71; Benet
87, 96; BiCoLiE; BioIn 4, 5, 8, 11, 12,
13, 14, 15, 16; BlmGEL; BlueB 76;
BritWr S1; CamGEL; CamGLE; CasWL;*

ConAu 5R, 21NR, 134; ConLC 2, 3, 5, 25; ConNov 72, 76, 82, 86; CurBio 59, 91N; CyWA 89, 97; DcLB 15, 139, 155; EncSF; EncWL 1, 2, 2S, 3; GrWrEL N; IntAu&W 76, 77, 82, 89, 91; IntvTCA 2; IntWW 74, 75, 76, 77, 78, 79, 80, 81, 82, 83, 89, 91; LegTOT; LngCEL; LngCTC; MajTwCW 1; ModBrL, 2, S1, S2; NewC; NewCBEL; NewYTBS 80, 91; Novels; OxCEng 85; PenC ENG; RAdv 1, 14, 13-1; REn; RfGEnL 91; ScF&FL 1, 2, 92; ScFSB; ShSCr 21; TwCA SUP; TwCWr; WebE&AL; WhAm 10; WhDW; Who 82, 83, 85, 88, 90, 92N; WhoTwCL; WhoWor 89, 91; WorAu 1900; WrDr 76, 80, 82, 84, 86, 88, 90

Wilson, Ann

American. Singer, Musician
Lead singer of Heart since 1972.
b. Jun 19, 1951 in San Diego, California
Source: *LegTOT; Songw; WhoRocM 82; WhoWest 82*

Wilson, August

[Frederick August Kittel]
American. Dramatist
Won 1987 Pulitzer, Tony for drama: *Fences*, about a 1950s black American family.
b. Apr 27, 1945 in Pittsburgh, Pennsylvania
Source: *AfrAmL 6, 8; AmDec 1980; Au&Arts 16; Benet 96; BenetAL 91; BioIn 14, 15, 16; BlkAWP; BlkLC; BlkWr 1, 2, 3; CamBiEn; CamDcAB; CamGWoT; ChamBiD; ConAmD; ConAu 42NR, 54NR, 76NR, 115, 122; ConBlAP 88; ConBlB 7; ConDr 88, 93; ConLC 39, 50, 63, 118; ConTFT 5, 10; CrtSuDr; CurBio 87; CyWA 89, 97; DcTwCCu 1, 5; DramC 2; DrBlPA 90; EncALit; EncWB 8; EncWL 2S, 3; IdentIs; IntAu&W 91; IntDcT 2; IntWW 91, 93, 97, 98, 2000; LegTOT; MajTwCW 1, 2; ModAL 4S3, 5; ModBlW 2; NegAl 89; NewYTBS 84, 87, 90; NotBlAM; OxCAfAL; OxCAmL 95; OxCTwCL; RAdv 14; RfGAmL 4, 94; SchCGBL; WhoAfA 9, 10, 11, 12; WhoAm 90, 92, 94, 95, 96, 97, 98, 99, 2000; WhoBlA 7, 8; WhoE 95, 97, 99; WhoEnt 98; WhoMW 90, 92; WhoPul; WorAlBi; WorAu 1980; WorLitC SUP; WrDr 88, 90, 92, 94, 96, 98, 99, 2000*

Wilson, Bertha

Canadian. Supreme Court Justice
First woman named to Supreme Court of Canada, 1982.
b. Sep 18, 1923 in Kirkcaldy, Scotland
Source: *BioIn 12, 15; CanWW 89, 96, 97, 98, 1999; ConNews 86-1; IntWWW 2; WhoAm 84, 86, 88, 90, 92, 94, 95, 96; WhoAmW 87, 89, 91, 93; WhoE 86, 91; WomLaw*

Wilson, Brian Douglas

[The Beach Boys]
American. Singer, Songwriter
Vocalist, bassist, pianist with CA rock group; hits include "Help Me,

Rhonda," 1965; wrote *Wouldn't It Be Nice: My Own Story*, 1991.
b. Jun 20, 1942 in Hawthorne, California
Source: *BakBD 84; BioIn 15; BkPepl; BlueB 76; ConLC 12; CurBio 88; EncPR&S 74; IlEncRk; NewYTBS 88; WhoAm 78, 80, 82, 84, 86, 90, 92, 94, 95, 96, 97, 98; WhoEnt 92, 98*

Wilson, Carl (Dean)

[The Beach Boys]
American. Singer
Vocalist, guitarist with the Beach Boys from 1961; famous CA rock hits include "Surfin USA," 1963.
b. Dec 21, 1946 in Hawthorne, California
d. Feb 6, 1998 in Los Angeles, California
Source: *BkPepl; EncPR&S 74; RkOn 85; WhoAm 76, 78, 80, 82, 84*

Wilson, Cassandra

American. Singer
Recorded first solo album,*Point of View*, 1986; *New Moon Daughter*, 1996.
b. 1955 in Jackson, Mississippi
Source: *AllMGJa; ConBlB 16; ConMus 12, 26; CurBio 98; DcTwCCu 5; News 96, 96-3; WhoAfA 11, 12; WhoAmW 97, 99; WhoEnt 98*

Wilson, Charles Edward

American. Business Executive
Pres., General Electric Co., 1940-42, 1944-50; board of governors, NY Stock Exchange, 1955-72.
b. Nov 18, 1886 in New York, New York
d. Jan 3, 1972 in Scarsdale, New York
Source: *AmNatBi; BiDAmBL 83; BioIn 1, 2, 3, 4, 5, 9, 11; CamBiEn; CamDcAB; CurBio 43, 51, 72; DcAmB S9; InSci; NatCAB 56; NewYTBE 72; WhAm 5*

Wilson, Charles Erwin

American. Government Official, Business Executive
Secretary of Defense, 1953-57; pres., General Motors, 1941-53.
b. Jul 18, 1890 in Minerva, Ohio
d. Sep 26, 1961 in Norwood, Louisiana
Source: *AmNatBi; AmPolLe; BiDAmBL 83; BiDrUSE 71, 89; BioIn 1, 2, 3, 4, 6, 7, 10, 11, 12; CamBiEn; CurBio 41, 50, 61; DcAmB S7; EncABHB 5; EncWB 98; InSci; NatCAB 57; WebAB 74, 79; WhAm 4; WorAl*

Wilson, Charles Thomson Rees

Scottish. Scientist
Won 1927 Nobel Prize for work on condensation of vapour.
b. Feb 14, 1869 in Glencorse, Scotland
d. Nov 15, 1959 in Carlops, Scotland
Source: *AsBiEn; BiESc; BioIn 3, 5, 6, 8, 14, 15, 20; CamBiEn; CamDcSc; ChamBiD; DcNaB 1951; DcScB; EncWB 98; FacFETw; GrBr; InSci; LarDcSc; McGCEnS; McGEWB; ObitOF 79; RanHWDS; WhoNob, 90, 95; WorAl*

Wilson, Colin Henry

English. Author
Books include *Ritual in the Dark*, 1960; *The Space Vampires*, 1975.
b. Jun 26, 1931 in Leicester, England
Source: *Au&Wr 71; Benet 87; BioIn 13, 14, 15, 16; CamBiEn; CamGLE; CasWL; ConAu 1NR, 1R, 5AS, 22NR, 33NR; ConLC 14; ConNov 86, 91; EncO&P 2, 3; FacFETw; IntAu&W 91; IntWW 83, 91, 97, 98, 2000; LngCTC; ModBrL S1; NewC; NewEScF; OxCEng 85; OxCTwCL; PenEncH; RAdv 1, 13-1; ScFSB; SJGHorW; TwCCr&M 91; TwCSFW 91; TwCWr; Who 85, 92, 98, 99, 2000; WhoAm 86, 90, 98, 99, 2000; WhoEnt 98; WhoWor 91, 98, 99, 2000; WorAu 1950; WrDr 86, 92, 98, 99, 2000*

Wilson, Demond

American. Actor
Starred in "Sanford and Son," 1972-77; "The New Odd Couple," 1982-83.
b. Oct 13, 1946 in Valdosta, Georgia
Source: *BioIn 14; BlksAmF; DrBlPA, 90; LegTOT; NegAl 89; WhoBlA 4, 7; WhoHol 92, A*

Wilson, Dennis

[The Beach Boys]
American. Musician, Singer
Drummer, keyboardist, singer; only member to release solo album, *Pacific Ocean Blue*.
b. Dec 4, 1944 in Hawthorne, California
d. Dec 28, 1983 in Marina del Rey, California
Source: *AnObit 1983; BioIn 11, 12, 13; BkPepl; EncPR&S 74; IlEncRk; LegTOT; NewYTBS 83; WhoHol A; WhoRock 81; WhoRocM 82*

Wilson, Don(ald Harlow)

American. Radio Performer, TV Personality
Jack Benny's announcer, foil on TV, radio shows over 40 yrs.
b. Sep 1, 1900 in Lincoln, Nebraska
d. Apr 25, 1982 in Palm Springs, California
Source: *BioIn 12, 13, 17; CurBio 44, 91N; LegTOT; NewYTBS 82; RadStar; WhAm 8; WhoHol A; WorAl*

Wilson, Dooley

[Arthur Wilson]
American. Actor, Musician
Played Sam, the piano player, in *Casablanca*, 1943.
b. Apr 3, 1894 in Tyler, Texas
d. May 30, 1953 in Los Angeles, California
Source: *BioIn 10; BlksAmF; DrBlPA, 90; EncAFC; FilmEn; FilmgC; HalFC 80, 84, 88; HolP 40; LegTOT; WhE&EA; WhoHol B; WhScrn 74, 77, 83*

Wilson, Dorothy Clarke

American. Author
Religious writings include over 70 plays; books include *Climb Every Mountain*, 1976.
b. May 9, 1904 in Gardiner, Maine

Source: *AmAu&B; AmNov; AmWomPl; Au&Wr 71; BioIn 2; ConAu 1R, 6NR; CurBio 51; ForWC 70; IntAu&W 76, 77, 82, 86, 89, 91; InWom; SmATA 16; WhoAm 74, 76, 78, 80, 82, 84, 86, 88, 90, 92, 94, 95, 96, 97, 98, 99, 2000; WhoAmW 58, 70, 72, 74; WhoEnt 98; WrDr 76, 80, 82, 84, 86, 88, 90, 92, 94, 96, 98, 99, 2000*

Wilson, Earl
[Harvey Earl Wilson]
American. Journalist
Best known for syndicated gossip column, "It Happened Last Night," 1943-83.
b. May 3, 1907 in Rockford, Ohio
d. Jan 16, 1987 in Yonkers, New York
Source: *AmAu&B; AnObit 1987; ASCAP 66, 80; BiDAmJo; BiDAmNC; BioIn 1, 2, 4, 10, 13; CelR; ConAu 69, 121; EncTwCJ; IntAu&W 91; LegTOT; NewYTBS 87; OhA&B; REnAL; ScrEAmL 2; WhAm 9; WhAmP; WhE&EA; WhoAm 74, 76, 78, 80, 82, 84, 86; WhoE 74; WhoHol A; WorAl; WrDr 80, 82, 84, 86, 88*

Wilson, Edith Bolling (Galt)
American. First Lady
Married US pres. Woodrow Wilson, 1915; nursed him after his 1919 stroke, virtually running country until his term expired.
b. Oct 15, 1872 in Wytheville, Virginia
d. Dec 28, 1961 in Washington, District of Columbia
Source: *AmNatBi; BioIn 16, 17, 18, 19, 21, 22, 23; DcAmB S7; EncWoAP; FacPr 89; InWom, SUP; NotAW MOD; ObitT 1961*

Wilson, Edmund
American. Author, Critic
Considered among this century's finest literary critics; wrote *Axel's Castle*, 1931.
b. May 8, 1895 in Red Bank, New Jersey
d. Jun 12, 1972 in Talcottville, New York
Source: *AmAu&B; AmCulL; AmNatBi; AmWr; Au&Wr 71; Benet 87, 96; BenetAL 91; BiCoLiE; BiE&WWA; BioIn 1, 3, 4, 5, 6, 7, 8, 9, 10, 11, 12, 13, 14, 15, 16, 17, 18, 19, 20, 21, 22, 23, 24; CamBiEn; CamDcAB; CamGEL; CamGLE; CamHAL; CasWL; ChamBiD; ChhPo S1; CnDAL; CnMD; ConAmA; ConAu 1NR, 1R, 37R, 46NR; ConLC 1, 2, 3, 8, 24; ConLCrt 77, 82; ConNov 72; CurBio 72N; CyWA 89, 97; DcAmB S9; DcArts; DcLB 63; DcLEL; EncAB-H 1974, 1996; EncAJ; EncALit; EncWB 98; EncWL 1, 2, 2S, 3; EvLB; FacFETw; GrWrEL N; JrnUS; LegTOT; LiJour; LinLib L, S; LngCTC; MajTwCW 1, 2; MakMC; McGEWB; ModAL 4, 4S1, 4S2, 4S3, 5; ModWD; NotNAT A; Novels; ObitT 1971; OxCAmL 65, 83, 95; OxCCan; OxCEng 67, 85, 95; OxCTwCL; OxCTwCP; PenC AM; PolProf T; RAdv 1, 14, 13-1; REn; REnAL; RfGAmL 4, 87, 94; RGTwCWr;*

ScF&FL 1, 2; ThTwC 87; TwCA, SUP; TwCWr; WebAB 74, 79; WebE&AL; WhAm 5; WhoTwCL; WorAl; WorAlBi; WorAu 1900

Wilson, Edward Arthur
American. Artist, Illustrator
Noted woodcut illustrator of sea adventures: *The Pirate's Treasure*, 1926.
b. Mar 4, 1886 in Glasgow, Scotland
d. Oct 2, 1970 in Dobbs Ferry, New York
Source: *BioIn 1, 3, 4, 5, 9; ChhPo, S1, S2; ConAu 116; IlrAm 1880, B; IlsBYP; IlsCB 1744, 1946; WhAm 5, 7*

Wilson, Edward Foss
American. Business Executive
President, Wilson & Co., 1934-56, the third-largest meatpacker in the US.
b. Jan 6, 1905
d. Mar 19, 1994 in Washington, District of Columbia
Source: *BioIn 4, 5, 19, 20; CurBio 94N; St&PR 75; WhoAm 74, 76*

Wilson, Edward Osborne
American. Biologist
His book, *On Human Nature*, won the 1979 Pulitzer Prize; one of the world's authorities on ants.
b. Jun 10, 1929 in Birmingham, Alabama
Source: *AmMWSc 76P, 79, 82, 86, 89, 92, 95, 98; BiESc; BioIn 9, 11, 12, 13, 14, 16; CamBiEn; CamDcAB; CamDcSc; ChamBiD; ConAu 16NR, 58NR, 61; CurBio 79; EncWB, 98; EnvEnc; FacFETw; IntAu&W 91, 93; IntWW 81, 82, 83, 89, 91, 93, 97, 98, 2000; LarDcSc; MajTwCW 1, 2; McGMS 80; RanHWDS; ThTwC 87; Who 98, 99, 2000; WhoAm 74, 76, 78, 80, 82, 84, 86, 88, 90, 92, 94, 95, 96, 97, 98, 99, 2000; WhoE 86, 89, 93, 95, 97, 99; WhoFrS 84; WhoScEn 94, 96, 2000; WhoTech 89; WhoThSc 1996; WhoWor 95, 96, 97, 98, 99, 2000; WorWWEn; WrDr 88, 92, 98, 99, 2000*

Wilson, Ellen Axson
American. First Lady
Prodded Congress to improve Washington, DC, slums; first wife of Woodrow Wilson.
b. May 15, 1860 in Savannah, Georgia
d. Aug 6, 1914 in Washington, District of Columbia
Source: *AmNatBi; BioAmW; EncWoAP; FacPr 89; NatCAB 19; NotAW; WhAm 1; WomWWA 14*

Wilson, Erica
English. Author
Owner, Erica Wilson Needle Works retail stores; wrote *Erica Wilson's Embroidery*, 1979.
b. 1929? in Shropshire, England
Source: *BioIn 14, 16; ConAu 7NR, 23NR, 53; InWom SUP; NewYTBE 71; SmATA 51*

Wilson, Flip
[Clerow Wilson]
American. Actor, Comedian
Star of TV series "The Flip Wilson Show," 1970-75; best known character, Geraldine.
b. Dec 8, 1933 in Jersey City, New Jersey
d. Nov 25, 1998 in Malibu, California
Source: *AfrAmAl 6, 8; BioIn 8, 9, 10, 16, 24; BkPepl; BlksAmF; BlueB 76; CelR; ConBlB 21; ConTFT 3, 24; CurBio 69, 1999; DcTwCCu 5; DrBlPA, 90; Ebony 1; EncAFC; HalFC 80, 84, 88; InB&W 80, 85; IntMPA 77, 80, 84, 86, 88, 92, 94, 96; JoeFr; LegTOT; NegAl 76, 83, 89; News 99-2, 1999; NewYTBE 71; NewYTBS 98; VarWW 85; WhoAfA 9, 10, 11, 12; WhoAm 74, 76, 78, 80, 82, 84, 86, 88, 92, 94; WhoBlA 1, 2, 3, 4, 5, 6, 7; WhoCom; WhoEnt 92; WhoHol 92, A; WorAl; WorAlBi*

Wilson, Gahan
American. Author, Cartoonist
Known for macabre cartoons in magazines, books; collections include *Is Nothing Sacred?*, 1982; *Gahan Wilson's America*, 1985.
b. Feb 18, 1930 in Evanston, Illinois
Source: *BiDScF; BioIn 12, 13, 14, 15; ConAu 19NR, 25R, 84NR; ConGrA 2; IlsBYP; IntvTCA 2; LegTOT; PenEncH; PrintW 85; ScF&FL 92; SmATA 27, 35; WhoAm 78, 80, 82, 84, 86, 88, 92, 94, 95, 96, 97; WhoEnt 98; WorECar*

Wilson, Hack
[Lewis Robert Wilson]
American. Baseball Player
Outfielder, 1923-34; holds ML record for RBIs in season, 190, 1930; had .307 lifetime batting average; Hall of Fame, 1979.
b. Apr 26, 1900 in Ellwood City, Pennsylvania
d. Nov 23, 1948 in Baltimore, Maryland
Source: *AmNatBi; Ballpl 90; BiDAmSp BB; BioIn 1, 3, 11, 14, 15, 17; CulEncB; LegTOT; WhoProB 73; WhoSpor*

Wilson, (James) Harold, Sir
English. Statesman
British Prime Minister, 1964-70, 1974-76.
b. Mar 11, 1916 in Huddersfield, England
d. May 24, 1995 in London, England
Source: *BioIn 1, 2, 5, 6, 7, 8, 9, 10, 11, 12, 14, 15, 16, 18, 19, 20, 21; BlueB 76; ColdWar 1, 2; ConAu 16NR, 53, 148; CopCroC; CurBio 63, 78, 95N; DcPol; DcTwHis; EncCW; EncWB 98; FacFETw; HisDBrE; HisWorL; IntAu&W 91, 93; IntWW 74, 75, 76, 77, 78, 79, 80, 81, 82, 83, 91; IntYB 78, 79, 80, 81, 82; LinLib L, S; McGEWB; NewYTBE 70, 72; NewYTBS 74, 76, 95; PolLCWE; WhDW; Who 74, 83, 90; WhoAm 74; WhoWor 74, 76, 78; WorAl; WorAlBi; WrDr 80, 82, 84, 86, 88, 90, 92, 94, 96*

Wilson, Harriet E. (Adams)
American. Author
Considered the first African American woman to publish a novel in English, she was also the first black to publish a novel in the United States; her work, *Our Nig,* was rediscovered by scholars in the 1980s.
b. c. 1827 in New Hampshire
d. 1863
Source: *NotBlAW 1*

Wilson, Hazel Hutchins
American. Children's Author
Series on Herbert character includes *Herbert's Space Trip,* 1965; *Herbert's Stilts,* 1972.
b. Apr 8, 1898 in Portland, Maine
d. Aug 20, 1992 in Bethesda, Maryland
Source: *ArtsAmW 2; AuBYP 2; BioIn 19; ConAu 1R, 6NR, 139; DcWomA; SmATA 3, 73; WrDr 86, 88*

Wilson, Henry
American. US Vice President
VP under U S Grant, 1873-77.
b. Feb 16, 1812 in Farmington, New Hampshire
d. Nov 10, 1875 in Washington, District of Columbia
Source: *Alli, SUP; AmAu&B; AmBi; AmNatBi; AmPolLe; ApCAB; BiAUS; BiD&SB; BiDrAC; BiDrUSC 89; BiDrUSE 71, 89; BioIn 1, 4, 7, 8, 9, 10, 14, 16, 22, 23; CamBiEn; CamDcAB; ChamBiD; CyAL 2; DcAmAu; DcAmB; DcAmSR; DcAmTB; DcBiPP; DcNAA; DcPseud; Dis&D; Drake; EncAAH; EncWB 98; HarEnUS; LegTOT; McGEWB; NatCAB 4; PolPar; TwCBDA; VicePre; WebAB 74, 79; WhAm HS; WhAmP; WhCiWar*

Wilson, Henry Braid
American. Naval Officer
Led patrol force of Atlantic fleet, 1917-18; commander in chief, 1919-21.
b. Feb 23, 1861 in Camden, New Jersey
d. Jan 30, 1954 in New York, New York
Source: *BioIn 3; EncNaHi; WebAMB; WebBD 83; WhAm 3*

Wilson, Jackie
"Mr. Excitement"
American. Singer
Hits include "Lonely Teardrops," 1959; "Higher and Higher," 1967.
b. Jun 9, 1932 in Detroit, Michigan
d. Jan 21, 1984 in Mount Holly, New Jersey
Source: *BiDAmM; BioIn 12; EncPR&S 74; InB&W 80; LegTOT; NewYTBS 84; WhoRock 81*

Wilson, James
American. Supreme Court Justice, Continental Congressman
Served 1789-98; appointed by Washington; signed Declaration of Independence, 1776.
b. Sep 14, 1742 in Fifeshire, Scotland
d. Aug 21, 1798 in Edenton, North Carolina

Source: *Alli; AmAu&B; AmBi; AmJust; AmNatBi; AmWrBE; ApCAB, X; BenetAL 91; BiAUS; BiDFedJ; BiDrAC; BiDrUSC 89; BioIn 2, 3, 4, 5, 7, 8, 9, 10, 11, 12, 15, 16, 23; BlkwCE; BlkwEAR; CamBiEn; CamDcAB; ChamBiD; CyAG; DcAmB; DcNAA; Drake; EncAB-H 1974, 1996; EncAR; EncCRAm; EncRelA; EncWB 98; HarEnUS; HisDcAR; McGEWB; NatCAB 1; OxCAmH; OxCAmL 65, 83, 95; OxCLaw; OxCSupC; REnAL; SupCtJu; TwCBDA; USGovLe; WebAB 74, 79; WhAm HS; WhAmP; WhAmRev*

Wilson, Jerry
American. Inventor
Took over open market area of home exercise equipment with Soloflex, Inc., 1978.
b. 1944?
Source: *BioIn 15; ConNews 86-2*

Wilson, John Johnston
American. Lawyer
Represented Haldeman, Ehrlichman in Watergate hearings, 1973.
b. Jul 25, 1901 in Washington, District of Columbia
d. May 18, 1986 in Washington, District of Columbia
Source: *BioIn 9, 10, 14, 15; WhoAm 74, 76, 78, 80, 82, 84; WhoAmL 78, 79*

Wilson, Joseph Chamberlain
American. Business Executive
Manager of the Haloid Company, which bought the rights to developing the process later called xerography and became the Xerox Corporation in 1961.
b. Dec 19, 1909 in Rochester, New York
d. Nov 22, 1971
Source: *AmNatBi; BiDAmBL 83; BioIn 7, 9, 12; CamDcAB; DcAmB S9; EncWB, 98*

Wilson, Julie
American. Singer, Actor
NYC cabaret performer.
b. Oct 21, 1924 in Omaha, Nebraska
Source: *BioIn 15; CelR 90; ConTFT 9; WhoHol 92*

Wilson, Kemmons
American. Hotel Executive
Opened first Holiday Inn, 1952; formed Holiday Inns of America, 1953; chm., CEO until 1979.
b. Jan 5, 1913 in Osceola, Arkansas
Source: *BiDAmBL 83; BioIn 7, 9, 10, 12, 14, 16; BlueB 76; CamBiEn; CelR; CurBio 73; Dun&B 79, 86, 88, 90; St&PR 75, 84, 87, 91, 93, 96, 97, 98, 99, 2000; WhoAm 74, 76, 78, 80, 82, 84; WhoFI 74, 79; WhoSSW 73; WhsWeAm 98; WorAl; WorAlBi*

Wilson, Kenneth Geddes
American. Physicist
Developed renormalization method for physical systems; won Nobel Prize, 1982.
b. Jun 8, 1936 in Waltham, Massachusetts
Source: *AmMWSc 73P, 76P, 79, 82, 86, 89, 92, 95, 98; BioIn 10, 12, 13, 15, 20; CamBiEn; CamDcAB; CamDcSc; ChamBiD; CurBio 83; IntWW 93, 97, 98; LarDcSc; McGCEnS; NewYTBS 82; NobelP; Who 85, 88, 90, 92, 94, 98, 99, 2000; WhoAm 84, 86, 88, 90, 92, 94, 95, 96, 97, 98, 99, 2000; WhoCanF 86; WhoE 83, 85, 89; WhoFrS 84; WhoMW 90, 92, 93, 96, 98; WhoNob, 90, 95; WhoScEn 94, 96, 2000; WhoTech 89; WhoWor 84, 87, 89, 91, 93, 95, 96, 97, 98, 99, 2000; WorAlBi*

Wilson, Lanford
American. Dramatist
Won Pulitzer Prize, 1980, for *Talley's Folly.*
b. Apr 13, 1937 in Lebanon, Missouri
Source: *Benet 87, 96; BenetAL 91; BioIn 10, 11, 12, 13, 15, 16, 18; CamBiEn; CamDcAB; CamGWoT; CelR 90; ConAu 3BS, 17R, 45NR; ConDr 73, 77, 82, 88; ConLC 7, 14, 36; ConTFT 1, 3, 21; CrtSuDr; CurBio 79; CyWA 89, 97; DcLB 7; DcTwCCu 1; EncALit; EncWL 2S, 3; IntAu&W 91, 93; LegTOT; McGEWD 84; ModAL 4S2, 5; NatPD 77, 81; NotNAT; OxCAmL 83, 95; OxCAmT 84; OxCTwCL; RAdv 14, 13-2; WhoAm 74, 76, 78, 80, 82, 84, 86, 88, 90, 92, 94, 95, 96, 97, 98, 99, 2000; WhoEnt 92, 98; WhoPul; WhoThe 72, 77, 81; WorAlBi; WorAu 1975; WrDr 76, 80, 82, 84, 86, 88, 90, 92, 94, 96, 98, 99, 2000*

Wilson, Larry
[Lawrence Frank Wilson]
American. Football Player
Defensive back, St. Louis Cardinals, 1960-72; known for safety blitz; Hall of Fame, 1978.
b. Mar 24, 1938 in Rigby, Idaho
Source: *BiDAmSp FB; BioIn 16, 17; Law&B 89B; LegTOT; WhoAm 84, 86, 88, 92, 94, 95, 96, 97; WhoFtbl 74; WhoSpor; WhoWest 92*

Wilson, Logan
American. Educator, Sociologist
Educational innovator; introduced first racial integration in higher learning systems as pres. of the U of Texas, 1954-61.
b. Mar 6, 1907 in Huntsville, Texas
d. Nov 7, 1990 in Austin, Texas
Source: *AmMWSc 73S; BiDMoAE; BioIn 4, 5, 6, 12, 17, 22, 24; ConAu 45; CurBio 91N; LEduc 74; NewYTBS 90; ScrEAmL 2; WhAm 10; WhE&EA; WhoAm 74, 76; WhoSSW 80, 82, 84; WhoWor 78*

Wilson, Louis Hugh
American. Army Officer
Marine Corps commandant, 1975-79.
b. Feb 11, 1920 in Brandon, Mississippi
Source: *BioIn 10, 17, 19; IntWW 76, 77, 78, 79, 80, 81, 82, 83, 91, 93, 97, 98, 2000; MedHR, 94; NewYTBS 75; St&PR 91; WebAMB; WhoAm 74, 76, 78, 80, 82; WhoGov 77; WhoWor 78; WorDWW*

Wilson, Lyle Campbell
American. Journalist
Washington general mgr., UPI, 1943-64.
b. Aug 2, 1899 in Topeka, Kansas
d. May 23, 1967 in Stuart, Florida
Source: *BiDAmNC; BioIn 6, 7; EncAB-A 40; EncTwCJ; WhAm 4*

Wilson, Malcolm
[Charles Malcolm Wilson]
American. Politician
Rep. lt. governor of NY, 1959-73; assumed governorship after Nelson Rockefeller's resignation, 1973; defeated by Hugh Carey, 1974.
b. Feb 26, 1914 in New York, New York
d. Mar 13, 2000 in New Rochelle, New York
Source: *AmCath 80; BiDrGov 1789; BioIn 5, 10; BlueB 76; CurBio 74; NewYTBE 72, 73; NewYTBS 76; St&PR 84, 87, 91, 93; WhoAm 74, 76, 80, 82, 84, 86, 88, 90, 92, 94, 95; WhoAmP 73, 75, 77, 79; WhoE 74, 75, 77, 79, 89; WhoFI 85, 87, 89; WhoGov 72, 75*

Wilson, Margaret
American. Author, Missionary
Novels from women's perspective include 1924 Pulitzer winner, *The Able McLaughlins.*
b. Jan 16, 1882 in Traer, Iowa
d. Oct 6, 1973 in Droitwich, England
Source: *AmAu&B; BenetAL 91; BioIn 12, 22; ConAu 113; DcLB 9; FacFETw; FemiCLE; InWom SUP; LegTOT; OxCAmL 65, 83; REnAL; TwCA; WhoPul; WorAu 1900*

Wilson, Marie (Katherine Elizabeth)
American. Actor
Starred on film, radio, TV, as ''My Friend Irma.''
b. Aug 19, 1916 in Anaheim, California
d. Nov 23, 1972 in Hollywood Hills, California
Source: *BioIn 1, 2, 9, 15; DcAmB S9; EncAFC; FilmEn; FilmgC; FunnyW; HalFC 80, 84, 88; InWom, SUP; LegTOT; MotPP; MovMk; NewYTBE 72; SaTiSS; ThFT; What 3; WhoHol B; WhScrn 77, 83; WorAl*

Wilson, Mary
[The Supremes]
American. Singer
Original member of 1960s-70s pop group; hits include ''Where Did Our Love Go?,'' 1964.
b. Mar 6, 1944 in Greenville, Mississippi

Source: *AfrAmAl 6, 8; BioIn 13, 15, 17, 20; ConTFT 4; DcLP 87B; DcWomA; DrBlPA, 90; Ebony 1; InB&W 80, 85; InWom SUP; LegTOT; PenNWW A; WhoBlA 1, 2, 3, 4, 5, 6, 7; WhoRocM 82; WrDr 86, 92*

Wilson, Michael (Holcombe)
Canadian. Politician, Businessman
Canadian finance minister 1984-91.
b. Nov 4, 1937 in Toronto, Ontario, Canada
Source: *BioIn 15; CanParl 1998; CanWW 89, 96, 97, 98, 1999; CurBio 90; IntWW 89, 91, 93; NewYTBS 86; WhoAm 80, 82, 84, 86, 88, 92; WhoCan 77, 82, 84; WhoCanF 86; WhoE 86, 89, 91, 93; WhoFI 00, 85, 96, 98; WhoWor 87, 89, 91, 93, 95, 96, 97, 98, 99, 2000*

Wilson, Mitchell A
American. Author
Novels about scientists were popular in USSR: *Live with Lightning,* 1949.
b. Jul 17, 1913 in New York, New York
d. Feb 26, 1973 in New York, New York
Source: *AmAu&B; AmNov; BioIn 2, 5, 6, 9; ConAu 1R, 3NR; ConNov 72; NewYTBE 72, 73; OxCAmL 83*

Wilson, Nancy
American. Singer
Hit singles since 1963 include ''Tell Me the Truth,'' 1963; ''Face It Girl, It's Over,'' 1968.
b. Feb 20, 1937 in Chillicothe, Ohio
Source: *AfrAmAl 8; AllMGJa; BakBD 84; BiDAfM; BiDAmM; BiDJaz; BioIn 9, 10, 12, 15; BlkWAm; CelR; ConBlB 10; ConMus 14; DcTwCCu 5; DrBlPA, 90; EncJzS; IlEncBM 82; InWom, SUP; LegTOT; NewGrDA 86; NewGrDJ 88; NotBlAW 1; PenEncP; RkOn 82; WhoAfA 9, 10, 11, 12; WhoAm 74, 76, 78, 80, 82, 84, 86, 88, 90, 92, 94, 95, 96, 97, 98; WhoAmW 68, 70, 72, 74, 81, 83; WhoBlA 1, 2, 3, 4, 5, 6, 7, 8; WhoEnt 92, 98*

Wilson, Nancy
American. Singer, Musician
Featured guitarist with Heart since 1972.
b. Mar 16, 1954 in San Francisco, California
Source: *BioIn 13; LegTOT; OnThGG; WhoRocM 82*

Wilson, Pete Barton
American. Politician
Rep governor, CA, 1991-99; senator, 1983-91; mayor of San Diego, 1971-83.
b. Aug 23, 1933 in Lake Forest, Illinois
Source: *AlmAP 88, 92; BiDrUSC 89; BioIn 13, 16; CngDr 87, 89; CurBio 91; IntWW 91; News 92; PolsAm 84; WhoAm 86, 90; WhoAmL 87; WhoAmP 87, 91; WhoWest 92; WhoWor 91; WorAlBi*

Wilson, Peter Cecil
English. Business Executive
Chm., Sotheby auction house, 1958-80.
b. Mar 8, 1913 in Yorkshire, England
d. Jun 3, 1984 in Paris, France
Source: *BioIn 6, 7, 8, 12; BlueB 76; ConAu 113; ConNews 85-2; CurBio 68, 84; DcNaB 1981; IntWW 74, 75, 76, 77, 78, 79, 80, 81, 82, 83; NewYTBS 79; WhAm 9; Who 74, 82, 83; WhoAm 78, 80, 82, 84; WhoWor 74*

Wilson, Phill
American. AIDS Activist
Director of public policy, AIDS Project Los Angeles, 1992—.
b. Apr 22, 1956 in Chicago, Illinois
Source: *AfrAmAl 8; ConBlB 9*

Wilson, Ransom
American. Musician
Flutist; founder of Solisti New York, 1981; performs as a soloist with world's leading chamber orchestras.
b. Oct 25, 1951 in Tuscaloosa, Alabama
Source: *BakBD 84, 92; BakBDTw; BioIn 12, 13, 15; ConMus 5; WhoAmM 83*

Wilson, Richard
American. Producer, Director
Founded Mercury Theater in 1930s with Orson Welles and John Houseman; worked on Welles' films, radio shows until 1951; directed film *Three in the Attic,* 1968.
b. Dec 25, 1915 in McKeesport, Pennsylvania
d. Aug 21, 1991 in Santa Monica, California
Source: *BioIn 17, 19; FilmEn; FilmgC; GangFlm; HalFC 80, 84, 88; IntMPA 75, 76, 77, 78, 79, 80, 81, 82, 84, 86, 88; MiSFD 9N; NewYTBS 91; WorEFlm*

Wilson, Robert M
American. Dramatist, Producer
Won special Obie for *The Life and Times of Joseph Stalin,* 1974; has won many awards for contributions to theater.
b. Oct 4, 1944 in Waco, Texas
Source: *BenetAL 91; ConArt 83, 89; ConAu 2NR, 49; ConDr 82, 88; ConTFT 5; CurBio 79; IntvTCA 2; MajTwCW 1; NotNAT; WhoAm 86, 90; WhoE 86; WhoEnt 92; WrDr 82*

Wilson, Robert R(athbun)
American. Physicist
Designer of Fermi National Accelerator Laboratory.
b. Mar 4, 1914 in Frontier, Wyoming
d. Jan 16, 2000 in Ithaca, New York
Source: *AmMWSc 92, 98; BioIn 9, 10, 11, 13, 14, 16; ConAu 162; CurBio 89; IntWW 89; WhoAm 86, 98, 99, 2000; WhoScEn 2000; WhoTech 89*

Wilson, Robert Woodrow

American. Physicist
With Arno Penzias, shared 1978 Nobel
  Prize in physics for researching "big
  bang" theory of creation.
b. Jan 10, 1936 in Houston, Texas
Source: *AmMWSc 73P, 76P, 79, 82, 86,
  89, 92, 95, 98; BiESc; BioIn 11, 12, 14,
  15, 20; CamBiEn; CamDcAB; CamDcSc;
  ChamBiD; InnAst; IntWW 79, 80, 81, 82,
  83, 89, 91, 93, 97, 98, 2000; LarDcSc;
  McGCEnS; McGMS 80; NotTwCS 1;
  RanHWDS; Who 82, 83, 85, 88, 90, 92,
  94, 98, 99, 2000; WhoAm 78, 80, 82, 84,
  86, 88, 90, 92, 94, 95, 96, 97, 98, 99,
  2000; WhoE 79, 81, 83, 85, 86, 89, 91,
  93, 95, 97, 99; WhoFrS 84; WhoNob,
  90, 95; WhoScEn 94, 96, 2000; WhoWor
  80, 82, 84, 87, 89, 91, 93, 95, 96, 97,
  98, 99, 2000; WorAlBi*

Wilson, Samuel

"Uncle Sam"
American. Merchant
Meat packer whose nickname became
  synonymous with US during War of
  1812; inspected, stamped meat barrels
  for govt.
b. Sep 16, 1766 in Arlington,
  Massachusetts
d. Jul 31, 1854 in Troy, New York
Source: *BioIn 2, 4, 5, 6, 11, 12;
  CamDcAB; DcAmB; WebAB 74, 79;
  WebBD 83; WhAm HS; WhAmRev*

Wilson, Sandy

[Alexander Galbraith Wilson]
American. Dramatist, Composer
Wrote play *The Boy Friend*, 1953.
b. May 19, 1924 in Sale, England
Source: *Au&Wr 71; BestMus;
  BiE&WWA; BioIn 3, 10, 12; BlueB 76;
  ConDr 73, 77D, 82D, 88D; DcLEL
  1940; EncMT; EncWT; HalFC 80, 84,
  88; IntAu&W 76, 77, 82, 89, 91, 93;
  IntWW 74, 75, 76, 77, 78, 79, 80, 81, 82,
  83, 89, 91, 93; IntWWM 90; Music;
  NewGrDM 80; NewOxM; NotNAT, A;
  OxCPMus; ScF&FL 1; Who 74, 82, 83,
  85, 88, 90, 92, 94, 98, 99, 2000;
  WhoThe 72, 77, 81; WhoWor 74, 76, 78;
  WrDr 76, 80, 82, 84, 86, 88, 90, 92, 94,
  96, 98, 99, 2000*

Wilson, Sarah

[Marchioness de Waldegrave]
English. Imposter
Escaped US indentured servitude to pose
  as sister of Queen Charlotte of
  England.
b. 1750 in Staffordshire, England
Source: *CarSB; DcCanB 6; FolkA 87;
  InWom SUP; NotAW*

Wilson, Sloan

American. Author
Best known for novels *The Man in the
  Gray Flannel Suit*, I and II, 1955,
  1983.
b. May 8, 1920 in Norwalk, Connecticut
Source: *AmAu&B; Benet 87; BenetAL
  91; BioIn 4, 5, 7, 10, 11; ConAu 1NR,
  1R, 44NR; ConLC 32; ConNov 72, 76,*

*82, 86, 91, 96; CurBio 59; DcLEL 1940;
  IntAu&W 76, 77; LegTOT; Novels; PenC
  AM; PolProf E; REnAL; WhoAm 74, 76,
  78, 80, 82, 84, 86, 88, 90, 92, 94, 95,
  96, 97, 98, 99, 2000; WhoEnt 98;
  WorAl; WorAu 1950; WrDr 76, 80, 82,
  84, 86, 88, 90, 92, 94, 96, 98, 99*

Wilson, Sunnie

[William Nathaniel Wilson]
American. Entertainer, Entrepreneur,
  Impresario
Promoter of stage shows and boxing
  matches, 1950s; political consultant for
  the mayoral campaigns of Detroit
  Mayor Coleman A. Young, 1972-88.
b. Oct 7, 1908 in Columbia, South
  Carolina
Source: *BioIn 20, 24; ConBlB 7*

Wilson, Teddy

[Theodore Wilson]
American. Jazz Musician
Pianist who played with Benny
  Goodman, 1935-39; one of first blacks
  to be accepted playing with white
  musicians.
b. Nov 24, 1912 in Austin, Texas
d. Jul 31, 1986 in New Britain,
  Connecticut
Source: *AfrAmAl 6, 8; AllMGJa;
  AmNatBi; AnObit 1986; ASCAP 66, 80;
  BakBD 84, 92; BgBands 74; BiDAfM;
  BiDAmM; BiDJazz; BioIn 4, 10, 11, 12,
  13, 14, 15, 16, 23, 24; CamBiEn;
  ChamBiD; CmpEPM; DcArts; DcTwCCu
  5; DrBlPA, 90; EncJzS; FacFETw;
  IlEncJ; NegAl 89; NewAmDM;
  NewGrDA 86; NewGrDJ 88, 94;
  NewGrDM 80; NewYTBS 74, 86;
  OxCPMus; PenEncP; WhoBlA 1, 2, 3, 4;
  WhoHol A; WhoJazz 72*

Wilson, Theodore Roosevelt

American. Actor
Has had supporting roles in films: *The
  River Niger*, 1976; TV shows include
  That's My Mama, 1974-75.
b. Dec 10, 1943 in New York, New
  York
d. Jul 21, 1991 in Los Angeles,
  California
Source: *VarWW 85; WhoBlA 3, 4*

Wilson, Tom

American. Cartoonist
Created "Ziggy" comic strip; syndicated
  since 1971.
b. Aug 1, 1931 in Grant Town, West
  Virginia
Source: *BioIn 14; ConAu 106; SmATA
  30, 33; WhoAm 74, 76, 78, 80, 82, 84,
  86, 88, 92, 94, 95, 96, 97, 98; WhoAmA
  86, 89, 91, 93, 1999; WhoEnt 98*

Wilson, William Griffith

[Bill W.]
American. Social Reformer
Co-founder with Dr. Robert H. Smith
  (Dr. Bob) of Alcoholics Anonymous
  (AA).
b. Nov 26, 1895 in East Dorset, Vermont
d. Jan 24, 1971 in Miami Beach, Florida

Source: *AmSocL; BioIn 9, 15, 16, 17, 18,
  19, 20; CamBiEn; CamDcAB; ConHero
  2; DcAmB S9; DcAmTB; WorAl;
  WorAlBi*

Wilson, William Julius

American. Sociologist
Author of *Power, Racism, and Privilege*,
  1973; *When Work Disappears*, 1987.
b. Dec 20, 1935 in Derry Township,
  Pennsylvania
Source: *AmMWSc 73S; CamDcAB;
  ConBlB 22; CurBio 99; News 97, 97-1;
  RAdv 14; SelBAAf; WhoAfA 9, 10, 11,
  12; WhoAm 80, 82, 84, 86, 88, 90, 92,
  94, 95, 96, 97, 98, 99, 2000; WhoBlA 3,
  4, 5, 6, 7, 8; WhoScEn 2000; WrDr 92,
  94, 96, 98, 99*

Wilson, Willie James

American. Baseball Player
Outfielder, KC, 1976-90; Oakland, 1991-
  92; Chicago Cubs, 1992—; led AL in
  runs scored, 1980, in batting, 1982;
  jailed three mos. on cocaine charges.
b. Jul 9, 1955 in Montgomery, Alabama
Source: *Ballpl 90; BaseReg 86, 87;
  BiDAmSp BB; BioIn 13, 14, 15; InB&W
  85; WhoAfA 9, 10, 11, 12; WhoBlA 4, 8*

Wilson, Woodrow

[Thomas Woodrow Wilson]
American. US President
Dem., 28th pres., 1913-21; WW I leader
  awarded Nobel Peace Prize for
  Versailles Treaty, 1919; domestic
  reforms included 1914 creation of
  Federal Researve.
b. Dec 28, 1856 in Staunton, Virginia
d. Feb 3, 1924 in Washington, District of
  Columbia
Source: *Alli SUP; AmAu&B; AmBi;
  AmDec 1910; AmJust; AmLY; AmNatBi;
  AmOrTwC; AmPeW; AmPolLe; ApCAB,
  X; BbD; Benet 87; BenetAL 91;
  BiDAmEd; BiD&SB; BiDInt; BiDrAC;
  BiDrGov 1789; BiDrUSE 71, 89;
  BiDSA; BioIn 1, 2, 3, 4, 5, 6, 7, 8, 9, 10,
  11, 12, 13, 14, 15, 16, 17, 18, 19, 20,
  21, 22, 23, 24; Chambr 3; CopCroC;
  CyAG; DcAmAu; DcAmB; DcAmC;
  DcAmSR; DcLB 47; DcLEL; DcNAA;
  DcTwHis; Dis&D; EncAAH; EncAB-H
  1974, 1996; EncAPar; EncRelA;
  EncSoH; EvLB; FacFETw; FacPr 89,
  93; HarEnUS; HealPre; HisEAAC;
  HisWorL; LegTOT; LinLib L, S;
  LngCTC; McGEWB; MemAm; NatCAB
  19; NobelP; OxCAmH; OxCAmL 65, 83;
  OxCLaw; PolPar; Pres 96; RAdv 13-3;
  RComAH; REn; REnAL; TwCBDA;
  TwCLC 73, 79; USGovLe; WebAB 74,
  79; WebBD 83; WhAm 1, 4A, HSA;
  WhAmP; WhDW; WhoNob, 90, 95;
  WorAl; WorAlBi*

Wilson Phillips

[Chynna Phillips; Carnie Wilson; Wendy
  Wilson]
American. Music Group
Pop singing trio, first album *Wilson
  Phillips*, 1990 contains *Hold On*, a

Reason to Believe, and *Eyes Like Twins.*
Source: *BioIn 15, 16, 17, 18, 20, 21; ConMus 5; EncRkSt*

Wilt, Fred(erick Loren)
American. Track Athlete
Won several NCAA titles and set many American records; National Track and Field Hall of Fame, 1981.
b. Dec 14, 1920
d. Aug 31, 1994 in Anderson, Indiana
Source: *BiDAmSp Sup; BioIn 2, 3, 20; ConAu 9NR, 57; CurBio 94N; IndAu 1967*

Wimsatt, William Kurtz, Jr.
American. Author, Critic, Educator
Yale U English professor, 1955-75; wrote *Literary Criticism, Idea and Act,* 1974.
b. Nov 17, 1907 in Washington, District of Columbia
d. Dec 17, 1975 in New Haven, Connecticut
Source: *AmAu&B; BioIn 1, 5, 10, 11; BlueB 76; CasWL; CathA 1930; ConAu 1R, 3NR, 61; DcAmB S9; DrAS 74E; NewYTBS 75; PenC AM; RAdv 14; WhAm 6, 7; WhoAm 74, 76; WhoTwCL; WorAu 1950; WrDr 76*

Winans, BeBe and CeCe
[Benjamin Winans; Priscilla Winans]
American. Singers
Gospel singers who have found crossover success in the pop music market; the brother and sister duo released several records beginning in 1987, won numerous Dove and Grammy Awards, and received the NAACP Image Award.

Winans, Marvin L.
American. Clergy, Musician
One of a family of Gospel musicians, singer, lyracist, and composer has recorded many albums and won Dove and Grammy Awards; combines religious music with preaching in services held at his 2000-member Perfecting Church in Detroit, MI; travels the world preaching and performing.
b. Mar 5, 1958 in Detroit, Michigan
Source: *ConBlB 17; WhoAfA 9, 10, 11, 12*

Wincelberg, Shimon
German. Writer
TV shows include "Gunsmoke"; "Star Trek"; "Police Woman."
b. Sep 26, 1924 in Kiel, Germany
Source: *BiE&WWA; ConAu 45, 46NR; NatPD 77, 81; NotNAT; VarWW 85; WhoWorJ 72, 78*

Winchell, Paul
American. Ventriloquist, Actor
Had TV show with dummy, "The Paul Winchell-Jerry Mahoney Show,"

1950-54; voice of "Smurfs" cartoon show.
b. Dec 21, 1922 in New York, New York
Source: *BioIn 1, 24; ConTFT 9; IntMPA 92, 96; LegTOT; VarWW 85; WhoAm 74, 76, 78, 80, 82, 84, 86, 88, 92; WhoEnt 92; WhoHol 92, A; WorAl*

Winchell, Walter
American. Journalist
First of modern gossip columnists; had popular syndicated column, radio show, 1930s-50s; known for aggressive style, use of slang.
b. Apr 7, 1897 in New York, New York
d. Feb 20, 1972 in Los Angeles, California
Source: *AmAu&B; AmDec 1920, 1930; AmNatBi; ASCAP 66; BiDAmJo; BiDAmNC; BiDD; BioIn 1, 2, 3, 4, 5, 8, 9, 10, 11, 12, 16, 17, 18, 20, 21, 22, 23, 24; CamDcAB; ConAu 33R, 101; CopCroC; CurBio 43, 72N; DcAmB S9; DcLB 29; EncAJ; EncTwCJ; FacFETw; FilmgC; HalFC 80, 84, 88; HisDcAR; JrnUS; LegTOT; LinLib L, S; MafEnc; NewYTET; NotNAT, A, B; ObitT 1971; OxCAmT 84; PIP&P; PolCom; PolProf T; RadStar; REnAL; WebAB 74, 79; WhAm 5; WhJnl; WhoHol B; WhScrn 77, 83; WhThe; WorAl; WorAlBi; WorAu 1900*

Winchester, Jesse (James Ridout)
Canadian. Singer, Songwriter
Wrote pop songs, 1970s, that became hits for others: "Brand New Tennessee Waltz," "Isn't That So"; moved to Canada to avoid draft, 1967.
b. May 17, 1944 in Bossier City, Louisiana
Source: *BioIn 11, 14; EncFCWM 83; IlEncRk; PenEncP; RkOn 85; RolSEnR 83; WhoAm 82*

Winchester, Oliver Fisher
American. Industrialist
Bought arms manufacturing co., 1857; name associated with co.'s repeating rifle, Winchester 73.
b. Nov 30, 1810 in Boston, Massachusetts
d. Dec 11, 1880 in New Haven, Connecticut
Source: *AmBi; AmNatBi; ApCAB; BioIn 18; CamBiEn; CamDcAB; DcAmB; EncAAH; HarEnUS; LegTOT; NatCAB 11; VioAm; WebAB 74, 79; WebBD 83; WhAm HS; WhCiWar*

Winckelmann, Johann Joachim
German. Archeologist
Scholar redefined archeology as a history of ancient art. His regard for Greek art influenced German classical literature and stimulated classicism. *
b. Dec 9, 1717 in Stendal, Prussia
d. Jun 8, 1768 in Trieste, Italy
Source: *Benet 87, 96; BiD&SB; BioIn 1, 2, 6, 7, 9, 10, 13, 14, 15, 17, 18, 19, 20, 21; BlkwCE; CamBiEn; CasWL; ChamBiD; CmpQue; DcArch; DcArts;*

DcBiPP; DcCathB; DcEuL; DcLB 97; EncEnl; EncHiCA; EncWB 98; EuAu; EvEuW; GloEncH; InSci; LuthC 75; McGDA; McGEWB; NewCBEL; OxCArt; OxCEng 67, 85, 95; OxCGer 76, 86, 97; OxDcArt; PenC EUR; REn

Wind, Herbert Warren
American. Journalist, Author
On staff of *New Yorker* mag., 1947-54, 1962-90; has written numerous books on golf.
b. Aug 11, 1916 in Brockton, Massachusetts
Source: *ConAu 1R, 6NR, 62NR; DcLB 171; WhoAm 80, 82, 90, 92, 94, 95, 96, 97, 98, 99, 2000; WhoEnt 98; WhoGolf*

Windaus, Adolf Otto Reinhold
German. Chemist
Won Nobel Prize in chemistry, 1928, for research of sterols; discovered histamine; worked in chemotherapy.
b. Dec 25, 1876 in Berlin, Germany
d. Jun 9, 1959 in Gottingen, Germany (West)
Source: *AsBiEn; BiESc; ChamBiD; DcScB; Dis&D; RanHWDS; WhoNob, 90, 95*

Windgassen, Wolfgang Friedrich Hermann
German. Opera Singer
Leading post-War Heldentenor; at Bayreuth Festival, 1951-70.
b. Jun 26, 1914 in Annemasse, Germany
d. Sep 8, 1974 in Stuttgart, Germany (West)
Source: *BakBD 84; IntWW 74; MusSN; NewYTBS 74; WhAm 6; WhoWor 74*

Winding, Kai Chresten
American. Jazz Musician
Instrumental in creating Be-Bop style of jazz; leading trombonist, 1940s-50s'; with World's Greatest Jazz Band, 1960s.
b. May 18, 1922 in Aarhus, Denmark
d. May 6, 1983 in Yonkers, New York
Source: *ASCAP 80; BiDAmM; BiDJaz; EncJzS; NewYTBS 83; RkOn 78; WhoAm 74*

Windom, William
American. Actor
Starred in "The Farmer's Daughter," 1962-65; "My World and Welcome to It," 1969-70.
b. Sep 28, 1923 in New York, New York
Source: *BiDrUSC 89; BiDrUSE 89; BiE&WWA; ConTFT 2, 7, 26; FilmgC; ForYSC; HalFC 80, 84, 88; IntMPA 92, 94, 96; LegTOT; NotNAT; PeoHis; WhoAm 74, 76, 78, 80, 82, 84, 86, 88, 92, 94, 99, 2000; WhoEnt 92, 98; WhoHol 92, A; WorAl; WorAlBi*

Windsor, Claire
[Claire Viola Cronk]
American. Actor
Starred in 45 silent films, 1920-29.

b. Apr 14, 1897 in Coffee City, Kansas
d. Oct 24, 1972 in Los Angeles,
California
Source: *BioIn 8, 9, 10; Film 1, 2;*
FilmEn; ForYSC; FrSilen; HalFC 84;
InWom SUP; MovMk; NewYTBE 72;
SilFlmP; SmATA X; TwYS; What 2;
WhScrn 77, 83

Windsor, Marie
[Emily Marie Bertelson]
American. Actor
Known for supporting roles in films:
Outpost in Morocco, 1949; *Support*
Your Local Gunfighter, 1971.
b. Dec 11, 1924 in Marysvale, Utah
Source: *FilmgC; HalFC 84, 88; IntMPA*
75, 76, 77, 78, 79, 80, 81, 82, 84, 86,
88; MotPP; MovMk; WhoHol 92, A

Wine, Sherwin T(heodore)
American. Clergy
Founded Humanistic Judaism, 1963;
rabbi, Birmingham (MI) Temple,
1964—.
b. Jan 25, 1928 in Detroit, Michigan
Source: *ConAu 93; WhoAm 74, 76, 78,*
80, 82, 84, 86, 88, 90, 92, 94, 95, 96,
97, 98, 99, 2000; WhoAmJ 80; WhoMW
88; WhoRel 85, 92

Winebrenner, John
American. Clergy
Organized church, 1830; published
Church Advocate, 1846-47; wrote
religious books.
b. Mar 25, 1797 in Walkerville,
Maryland
d. Sep 12, 1860 in Harrisburg,
Pennsylvania
Source: *AmBi; AmNatBi; ApCAB;*
BiDAmCu; BiDSA; BioIn 10; DcAmAu;
DcAmB; DcNAA; Drake; LuthC 75;
NatCAB 1; WhAm HS

Winfield, Dave
[David Mark Winfield]
American. Baseball Player
Outfielder, 1973—; led NL in RBIs,
1979; also drafted by pro basketball,
football teams; commentator, Fox
Broadcasting Co., 1996—.
b. Oct 3, 1951 in Saint Paul, Minnesota
Source: *AfrAmSG; Ballpl 90; BaseReg*
86, 87; BiDAmSp BB; BioIn 12, 13, 14,
15, 16, 17, 18, 19, 20, 21; CelR 90;
ConBlB 5; CurBio 84; InB&W 85;
LegTOT; NegAl 89; NewYTBS 80, 81,
85, 90; WhoAfA 9; WhoAm 82, 84, 86,
88, 90, 92, 94, 95, 96, 97; WhoBlA 5, 7,
8; WhoE 86, 89; WhoMW 93, 96;
WhoSpor; WhoWest 92

Winfield, Paul Edward
American. Actor
Oscar nominee for *Sounder,* 1973;
Emmy nominee for *King,* 1978; *Roots*
II, 1980.
b. May 22, 1941 in Los Angeles,
California
Source: *BioIn 16; BlksAmF; ConBlB 2;*
ConTFT 6; DrBlPA 90; HalFC 84, 88;
InB&W 80, 85; IntMPA 92; MovMk;

WhoAfA 9, 10, 11, 12; WhoAm 78, 80,
82, 84, 86, 88, 92, 94, 95, 96, 97, 98,
99, 2000; WhoBlA 7, 8; WhoEnt 92, 98;
WhoHol A; WorAl; WorAlBi

Winfrey, Oprah Gail
American. TV Personality, Actor
Nationally syndicated talk show has won
three daytime Emmy Awards; received
Oscar nomination for role of Sophia in
The Color Purple, 1985.
b. Jan 29, 1954 in Kosciusko,
Mississippi
Source: *AfrAmBi 1; BioIn 14, 15, 16;*
CamDcAB; ChamBiD; ConBlB 2;
ConNews 86-4; ConTFT 3, 9; CurBio
87; DrBlPA 90; EncWB 98; HalFC 88;
IntMPA 92; IntWW 91; LesBEnT;
NewYTBS 86, 89; NotBlAW 1; WhoAmW
89; WhoBlA 5, 7; WhoEnt 92; WhoMW
92

Wingate, Orde Charles
English. Army Officer
Expert on mobile tactics; active in China,
Burma campaigns, WW II.
b. Feb 26, 1903 in Naini Tal, India
d. Mar 24, 1944 in Assam, Burma
Source: *BioIn 1, 2, 4, 5, 6, 8, 9, 12, 13,*
14, 21; CamBiEn; ChamBiD; CurBio 44;
DcNaB 1941; DcTwHis; EncGuW; GrBr;
HarEnMi; HisDBrE; HisEAAC;
HisEWW; ObitOF 79; WhBriIn;
WhoMilH 76; WhThe; WhWW-II; WorAl;
WorAlBi

Winger, Debra
[Mary Debra Winger]
American. Actor
Oscar nominee for *Terms of Endearment,*
1983; also starred in *Urban Cowboy,*
1980; *An Officer and a Gentleman,*
1982; *Shadowlands,* 1994.
b. May 17, 1955 in Cleveland, Ohio
Source: *BiDFilm 94; BioIn 12, 13, 14,*
15, 16; CelR 90; ConTFT 2, 6, 13, 25;
CurBio 84; HalFC 84, 88; HolBB;
IntMPA 88, 92, 94, 96; IntWW 91, 93,
97, 98, 2000; IntWWW 2; InWom SUP;
LegTOT; News 94, 94-3; NewYTBS 86;
OsStAZ; VarWW 85; WhoAm 88, 90, 92,
94, 95, 96, 97, 98, 99, 2000; WhoAmW
87, 89, 91, 93, 95; WhoEnt 92, 98;
WhoHol 92; WorAlBi

Wingler, Hans Maria
German. Author
Expert in field of graphic design,
architecture; wrote, edited many books
on subject.
b. Jan 5, 1920 in Constance, Germany
Source: *BioIn 14; ConAu 14NR;*
WhoWor 78

Wingti, Paias
Papua New Guinean. Political Leader
Founder of the People's Democratic
Movement, which emphasized private
investment, universal education, equal
opportunities for women, freedom of
religion, and the rule of law, he was
elected prime minister of Papua New
Guinea in 1985.

b. 1951 in Moika, Papua New Guinea
Source: *ChamBiD; IntWW 89, 91, 93,*
97, 98, 2000; WhoAsAP 91

Winkelmann, Hermann
German. Opera Singer
Brilliant tenor of Vienna Opera, 1880-
1900; excelled in Wagnerian roles.
b. Mar 8, 1849 in Brunswick, Germany
d. Jan 18, 1912 in Vienna, Austria
Source: *BakBD 78, 84, 92; CmOp;*
MetOEnc; NewEOp 71; NewGrDM 80;
NewGrDO; OxDcOp

Winkler, Henry Franklin
American. Actor
Played Fonzie on TV series "Happy
Days," 1974-84.
b. Oct 30, 1945 in New York, New York
Source: *BkPepl; CelR 90; ConTFT 2;*
CurBio 76; EncAFC; HalFC 88; IntMPA
86, 92; NewYTBS 77; VarWW 85;
WhoAm 78, 80, 82, 84, 86, 88, 90, 92,
94, 95, 96, 97, 98, 99, 2000; WhoEnt 92,
98; WhoHol A; WhoWor 80; WorAl;
WorAlBi

Winkler, Irwin
American. Producer
Films include *They Shoot Horses Don't*
They?, 1969; *Raging Bull,* 1980; *The*
Right Stuff, 1983.
b. May 28, 1931 in New York, New
York
Source: *BioIn 16; ConTFT 3, 10, 17;*
HalFC 84, 88; IntDcF 2-4; IntMPA 92,
94, 96; MiSFD 9; WhoAm 78, 80, 82,
84, 86, 88, 90, 92, 94, 95, 96, 97;
WhoEnt 92; WhoWest 82, 84, 87, 89, 92

Winnemucca, Sarah
American. Translator
Served as an interpreter for her father,
Chief Winnemucca, during meetings
with Native American agents, army
officers, and inter-tribal councils.
b. 1844? in Nevada
d. Oct 16, 1891 in Henry's Lake, Idaho
Source: *ABCNaAm; AmIndBi; AmNatBi;*
AZNatAW; BioAmW; BioIn 4, 7, 10, 11,
12, 13, 16, 17, 18, 19, 20; CamDcAB;
ChamBiD; ContDcW 89; DcAmB; DcLB
175; DcNAL; EncAInd; EncFrLi;
EncNoAI; EncWB 98; EncWHA; GayN;
GoodHs; GrLiveH; HerW 84; HisWorL;
IntDcWB; InWom SUP; LibW; NatNAL;
NinCLC 79; NotAW; NotNaAm;
OxCWoWr 95; RfGAmL 4, 94; WhAm
HS; WhNaAH; WomFir; WorAl;
WorAlBi

Winninger, Charles
American. Actor
Played Cap'n Andy in original Broadway
production of *Show Boat,* 1927-30.
b. May 26, 1884 in Athens, Wisconsin
d. Jan 1969 in Palm Springs, California
Source: *BiE&WWA; BioIn 8; CmpEPM;*
EncAFC; EncMT; Film 1, 2; FilmEn;
FilmgC; ForYSC; FrSilen; HalFC 80,
84, 88; HolCA; LegTOT; MotPP;
MovMk; NotNAT B; OxCAmT 84;
OxCPMus; PIP&P; RadStar; Vers A;

WhoHol B; WhScrn 74, 77, 83; WhThe; WorAl; WorAlBi

Winograd, Arthur
American. Conductor
Founder, member, Julliard String Quartet, 1946-55; staff conductor, MGM Records, 1954-58.
b. Apr 22, 1920 in New York, New York
Source: *BakBD 78, 84, 92; BakBDTw; NewAmDM; NewGrDA 86; PenDiMP; WhoAm 74, 76, 78, 80, 82, 84, 86, 88; WhoAmM 83; WhoE 74, 83, 85, 86*

Winpisinger, William W(ayne)
"Wimp"; "Wimpy"
American. Labor Union Official
Joined International Assn. of Machinists and Aerospace Workers, 1947; president, 1968-89.
b. Dec 10, 1924 in Cleveland, Ohio
d. Dec 11, 1997 in Howard County, Maryland
Source: *BioIn 14; CurBio 80, 98N; WhoAm 86, 88; WhoE 81, 83; WhoFI 87*

Winship, Elizabeth
American. Author
Books on sex education for adolescents include *Masculinity and Femininity,* 1978.
b. May 17, 1921 in Pittsfield, Massachusetts
Source: *ConAu 41R; PenNWW A; WhoAmW 77*

Winslow, Edward
English. Colonial Figure
Mayflower passenger who governed Plymouth Colony, 1633, 1636, 1644.
b. Oct 18, 1595 in Droitwich, England
d. May 8, 1655
Source: *Alli; AmAu; AmAu&B; AmBi; AmNatBi; AmWrBE; ApCAB; BenetAL 91; BiD&SB; BiDrACR; BioIn 2, 3; CamBiEn; CamDcAB; ChamBiD; DcAmAu; DcAmB; DcNaB; Drake; EncCRAm; EncWB 98; HarEnUS; LinLib L; McGEWB; NatCAB 1, 7; NewCBEL; OxCAmH; OxCAmL 65, 83, 95; REnAL; TwCBDA; WebAB 74, 79; WhAm HS; WhNaAH; WhWE; WrCNE*

Winslow, Kellen Boswell
American. Football Player
Tight end, San Diego, 1979-87; led NFL in pass receptions, 1980, 1981.
b. Nov 5, 1957 in Saint Louis, Missouri
Source: *BiDAmSp FB; BioIn 13, 15; FootReg 87; NewYTBS 82; WhoAfA 9, 10, 11, 12; WhoAm 84, 86, 88; WhoBlA 4, 5, 6, 7, 8*

Winslow, Ola Elizabeth
American. Author, Educator
Colonial history expert who won Pulitzer for *Johnathan Edwards, 1703-1758,* 1940.
b. 1885 in Grant City, Missouri
d. Sep 27, 1977 in Damariscotta, Maine

Source: *AmNatBi; AmWomHi; AmWomWr; BioIn 11, 22, 23; ConAu 1R, 3NR, 73; DcAmB S10; DrAS 74H; InWom SUP; OxCAmL 65, 83; REnAL; TwCA, SUP; WhoAm 74; WhoPul; WorAu 1900*

Winsor, Justin
American. Historian, Librarian
Founder, first president of American Library Assn., 1876-88; edited eight-vol. *Narrative and Critical History of America,* 1884-89.
b. Jan 22, 1831 in Boston, Massachusetts
d. Oct 22, 1897 in Cambridge, Massachusetts
Source: *Alli, SUP; AmAu; AmAu&B; AmBi; ApCAB; BenetAL 91; BiD&SB; BioIn 1, 2, 3, 6, 10, 11, 12, 13, 15; CamDcAB; ChamBiD; DcAmAu; DcAmB; DcAmLiB; DcLB 47; DcNAA; Drake; HarEnUS; LibrCom; NatCAB 1; OxCAmH; OxCAmL 65, 83, 95; REnAL; TwCBDA; WebAB 74, 79; WhAm HS*

Winsor, Kathleen
American. Author
Writings include historical novel that took five years, *Forever Amber,* 1944; *Calais,* 1979.
b. Oct 16, 1916 in Olivia, Minnesota
Source: *AmAu&B; AmNov; BenetAL 91; BioIn 14; ConAu 97; CurBio 46; InWom, SUP; LngCTC; REn; REnAL; TwCRHW 90; TwCWr; WhoAm 86, 88, 90; WhoUSWr 88; WhoWrEP 89; WrDr 88, 92*

Winsten, Archer
American. Critic
Movie critic, *NY Post,* 1936-86; documentary script writer, 1944-48.
b. Sep 18, 1904 in Seattle, Washington
d. Feb 21, 1997 in Moreau, New York
Source: *BioIn 22; BlueB 76; IntMPA 75, 76, 77, 78, 79, 80, 81, 82; WhAm 12; WhoAm 74, 76, 78, 80, 82, 84, 86, 88, 90, 92, 94, 95, 96, 97*

Winston, George
American. Composer, Pianist
Known for acoustic solo piano music; albums include *Autumn,* 1980.
b. 1949 in Hart, Michigan
Source: *BioIn 13, 15, 16; ConMus 9; ConNews 87-1; NewAgMG; WhoAm 94, 95, 96, 97, 98, 99, 2000; WhoEnt 98*

Winston, Harry
American. Jeweler
Known for stunning purchases of estate jewelry.
b. Mar 1, 1896 in New York, New York
d. Dec 1978 in New York, New York
Source: *BioIn 5, 7, 11, 12, 14, 23; BlkAWP; CurBio 65, 79N; DcAmB S10; NatCAB 60; NewYTBS 78; WhoAm 74, 76; WhoWor 74; WorAl; WorAlBi*

Winter, Alice Vivian Ames
American. Writer
Pres., General Federation of Women's Clubs, 1920-24; contributing editor, *Ladies Home Journal,* 1924-28.
b. Nov 28, 1865 in Albany, New York
d. Apr 5, 1944 in Pasadena, California
Source: *AmNatBi; BiCAW; InWom SUP; NotAW; WhAm 2; WomWWA 14*

Winter, Edgar Holand
[Edgar Winter Group; White Trash]
American. Singer, Musician
Album *They Only Come Out at Night,* 1973, had hit "Frankenstein."
b. Dec 28, 1946 in Beaumont, Texas
Source: *BkPepl; EncPR&S 89; EncRk 88; HarEnR 86; IllEncRk; NewGrDA 86; PenEncP; RkOn 74, 84; WhoAm 82, 84; WhoRocM 82*

Winter, Johnny
[John Dawson Winter, III]
American. Singer, Musician
Noted blues guitarist; produced albums for Muddy Waters.
b. Feb 23, 1944 in Beaumont, Texas
Source: *AllMGBl 1, 2; BillEnR; BioIn 11, 14; Blues; BluesWW; CmpEGui; ConMuA 80A; EncPR&S 74, 89; EncRk 88; GuBlues; HarEnR 86; IllEncRk; LegTOT; NewGrDA 86; OnThGG; PenEncP; RkOn 74, 78; RkWho 96; RolSEnR 83; WhoAm 76, 78, 80, 82, 84, 86, 88, 90, 92, 94, 95, 96, 97; WhoEnt 92A; WhoRock 81; WhoRocM 82*

Winter, Paul Theodore
American. Musician
Leader of Paul Winter Sextet, 1961-65; first jazz group to perform at White House, 1962.
b. Aug 31, 1939 in Altoona, Pennsylvania
Source: *BiDJaz; BioIn 15; CamDcAB; CurBio 87; EncJzS; NewAgE 90; NewAgMG; NewGrDJ 88; News 90-2; WhoAm 78, 80, 82, 84, 86, 88, 90, 92, 94, 95, 96, 97, 98; WhoEnt 92; WhoMus 72*

Winter, William Forrest
American. Politician
Dem. governor of MS, 1980-84.
b. Feb 21, 1923 in Grenada, Mississippi
Source: *BiDrGov 1978, 1983; BioIn 12; CamDcAB; IntWW 97, 98, 2000; WhoAm 74, 76, 78, 80, 82, 84, 86, 88, 90, 92, 94, 95, 96, 97, 98, 99, 2000; WhoAmL 78, 79; WhoAmP 73, 75, 77, 83, 85, 87, 89, 91, 93, 95, 97, 1999; WhoGov 75, 77; WhoSSW 76, 80, 82, 84, 95; WhoWor 82*

Winterhalter, Hugo
American. Bandleader
Arranger of 11 gold records, 1950s; songs performed by Perry Como, Doris Day.
b. Aug 15, 1909 in Wilkes-Barre, Pennsylvania

d. Sep 17, 1973 in Greenwich,
Connecticut
Source: *ASCAP 66, 80; BiDAmM; BioIn
10; CmpEPM; CndCPOM; DcAmB S9;
NewYTBE 73; OxCPMus; PenEncP*

Winterich, John Tracy
American. Author, Editor
Wrote on book collecting, literary
history: *American Books and Printing*,
1935.
b. May 25, 1891 in Middletown,
Connecticut
d. Aug 15, 1970 in Springfield,
Massachusetts
Source: *AmAu&B; BioIn 1, 4, 8, 9, 10;
ChhPo, S1, S2, S3; NatCAB 55;
NewYTBE 70; OxCAmL 65; REnAL;
TwCA, SUP; WorAu 1900*

**Winters, Jonathan (Harshman,
III)**
American. Comedian, Actor
Known for characterizations,
improvisations; films since 1963
include *The Loved One*, 1965; won
Mark Twain Prize for humor, 1999.
b. Nov 11, 1925 in Dayton, Ohio
Source: *BioIn 4, 5, 6, 7, 8, 9, 12, 15, 16,
17, 21; BkPepl; CelR, 90; ConTFT 5,
12; CurBio 65; EncAFC; FilmEn;
FilmgC; ForYSC; HalFC 80, 84, 88;
IntMPA 75, 76, 77, 78, 79, 80, 81, 82,
84, 86, 88, 92, 94, 96; JoeFr; LegTOT;
MotPP; MovMk; VarWW 85; WhoAm
74, 76, 78, 80, 82, 84, 86, 88, 90, 92,
94, 95, 96, 97; WhoCom; WhoEnt 92;
WhoHol 92, A; WhoWest 74, 76;
WhoWor 74; WorAl; WorAlBi*

Winters, Shelley
[Shirley Schrift]
American. Actor
Won Oscars for *The Diary of Anne
Frank*, 1959; *A Patch of Blue*, 1966.
b. Aug 18, 1922 in Saint Louis, Missouri
Source: *BiDFilm, 81, 94; BiE&WWA;
BioIn 1, 2, 3, 6, 7, 8, 9, 10, 11, 12, 16;
BkPepl; CamBiEn; CelR, 90; ConAu
110, 113, X; ConTFT 4, 13; CurBio 52;
DcPseud; EncAFC; FemmeNo; FilmEn;
FilmgC; ForYSC; GangFlm; GoodHs;
HalFC 80, 84, 88; IntDcF 1-3, 2-3;
IntMPA 75, 76, 77, 78, 79, 80, 81, 82,
84, 86, 88, 92, 94, 96; IntWW 74, 75,
76, 77, 78, 79, 80, 81, 82, 83, 89, 91,
93, 97, 98, 2000; IntWWW 2; InWom,
SUP; LegTOT; MotPP; MovMk;
NewYTBE 71; NewYTBS 80; NotNAT;
OsStAZ; OxCFilm; VarWW 85; WhoAm
74, 76, 78, 80, 82, 84, 86, 88, 90, 92,
94, 95, 96, 97, 99, 2000; WhoAmW 58,
61, 64, 66, 68, 70, 72, 74, 91, 95;
WhoEnt 92, 98; WhoHol 92, A; WhoHrs
80; WhoThe 72, 77, 81; WhoWor 74;
WorAl; WorAlBi; WorEFlm*

Winterson, Jeanette
English. Author
Oranges Are Not the Only Fruit, won the
Whitbread Prize for best first novel,
1985.
b. 1959 in Lancashire, England

Source: *BioIn 16, 18, 19, 20, 21, 24;
BlmGWL; BritWr S4; CamBiEn;
CmpQue; ConAu 58NR, 136; ConLC 64;
ConNov 91, 96; ConPopW; CyWA 97;
DcArts; DcLB 207; FemiCLE; FemiWr;
GayLesB; GayLL 1; IntWW 91, 93, 97,
98, 2000; IntWWW 2; MajTwCW 2;
ModBrL 2; OxCEng 95; OxCTwCL;
RGTwCWr; ScF&FL 92; SJGFanW;
TwCRHW 94; Who 94, 98, 99, 2000;
WorAu 1985; WrDr 94*

Winthrop, John
English. Politician
Governor, Massachusetts Bay Colony, 12
times, 1629-48; helped banish Ann
Hutchinson.
b. Jan 12, 1588 in Suffolk, England
d. Mar 26, 1649 in Boston,
Massachusetts
Source: *Alli; AmAu; AmAu&B; AmBi;
AmNatBi; AmPolLe; AmWrBE; ApCAB;
Benet 87, 96; BenetAL 91; BiD&SB;
BiDrACR; BioIn 1, 2, 3, 4, 6, 7, 8, 10,
11, 14, 15, 17, 19, 24; CamBiEn;
CamGEL; CamGLE; CamHAL; CasWL;
ChamBiD; CyAL 1; DcAmAu; DcAmB;
DcAmReB 1, 2; DcLB 24, 30; DcNAA;
DcNaB; Drake; EncAB-A 31; EncAB-H
1974, 1996; EncALit; EncARH;
EncCRAm; EncRelA; EncWB 98; EvLB;
HarEnUS; HisWorL; LegTOT; LinLib L,
S; LitC 31; McGEWB; NatCAB 6;
NewCBEL; OxCAmH; OxCAmL 65, 83,
95; OxCBrHi; PenC AM; RComAH;
REn; REnAL; TwCBDA; USGovLe;
WebAB 74, 79; WebE&AL; WhAm HS;
WhDW; WorAl; WorAlBi; WrCNE*

Wintle, Justin Beecham
[Justin Beecham]
English. Author
Non-fiction writings include *Makers of
Modern Culture*, 1981.
b. May 24, 1949 in London, England
Source: *ConAu 13NR, 77*

Winton, Alexander
American. Auto Manufacturer
Formed the Winton Motor Carriage Co.,
1897.
b. Jun 20, 1860 in Grangemouth,
Scotland
d. Jun 21, 1932 in Cleveland, Ohio
Source: *AmNatBi; BiDAmBL 83; BioIn
1, 23; DcAmB; EncABHB 4; NatCAB
12; WebAB 74, 79; WhAm 1*

Wintour, Anna
English. Editor
Editor American Vogue 1988—.
b. Nov 3, 1949 in London, England
Source: *BioIn 15; CurBio 90; IntWW 91,
93, 97, 98, 2000; IntWWW 2; LegTOT;
News 90; Who 88, 90, 92, 94, 98, 99,
2000; WhoAm 90, 92, 94, 95, 96, 97, 98,
99, 2000; WhoAmW 89, 91, 93, 95, 97,
99; WhoE 95*

Winwar, Frances
[Francesca Vinciguerra Winwar]
American. Author, Critic
Writes romantic novels, biographies; won
Edgar for *The Haunted Palace*, 1959.
b. May 3, 1900 in Taormina, Sicily, Italy
d. Jul 24, 1985
Source: *AmAu&B; AmWomWr; Au&Wr
71; AuBYP 2, 3; BioIn 2, 4, 7, 22;
ConAu 89; DcLP 87B; DcPseud; InWom
SUP; LinLib L; OxCAmL 65, 83, 95;
PenNWW B; REn; REnAL; TwCA, SUP;
WhAm 9; WhE&EA; WhoAm 74, 76, 78,
80, 82, 84; WhoAmW 58, 61, 64, 66, 72,
74; WorAu 1900*

Winwood, Estelle
[Estelle Goodwin]
‘‘Cow Eyes’’
English. Actor
Character actress whose career spanned
90 years; played the fairy godmother
in *The Glass Slipper*, 1955.
b. Jan 24, 1883 in Leeds, England
d. Jun 20, 1984 in Los Angeles,
California
Source: *AnObit 1984; BiE&WWA; BioIn
7, 10, 11, 13, 14; FamA&A; FilmEn;
FilmgC; ForYSC; HalFC 80; InWom,
SUP; LegTOT; MovMk; NewYTBS 83,
84; NotNAT; OxCAmT 84; Vers A;
WhoHol A; WhoThe 72, 77A; WhThe;
WorAl*

Winwood, Steve
[Blind Faith; The Spencer Davis Group;
Traffic; Stephen Lawrence Winwood]
English. Musician, Singer
R&B vocalist; performed with several
groups before solo career; hit songs
include ‘‘While You See a Chance,’’
1982.
b. May 12, 1948 in Birmingham,
England
Source: *BakBD 84; BillEnR; BioIn 8, 12,
13, 15, 16; CelR 90; ConMuA 80A;
ConMus 2; EncPR&S 89; EncRk 88;
EncRkSt; HarEnR 86; IllEncRk; LegTOT;
NewYTBS 81; OnThGG; PenEncP; RkOn
85; RolSEnR 83; Songw; WhoAm 84, 86,
88, 90, 92, 94, 95, 96, 97; WhoEnt 92;
WhoRock 81; WhoRocM 82; WorAlBi*

Wirth, Timothy E
American. Politician
Dem. senator from Colorado 1987-93;
counselor, US State Dept., 1993-94.
b. Sep 22, 1939 in Santa Fe, New
Mexico
Source: *AlmAP 78, 80, 82, 84, 88, 92;
BiDrUSC 89; CngDr 77, 79, 81, 83, 85,
87, 89, 91; CurBio 91; IntWW 91;
NewYTBS 84, 93; PolsAm 84; St&PR
75; WhoAm 90; WhoAmP 75, 77, 79, 81,
83, 85, 87, 89, 91, 93, 95, 97, 1999;
WhoWest 92; WhoWor 91*

Wirtz, Arthur Michael
American. Businessman, Hockey
Executive
Owner, Detroit Red Wings, 1931-54,
Chicago Blackhawks, 1954-83; owned
several NHL arenas, including

Madison Square Garden; Hall of
Fame, 1971.
b. Jan 23, 1901 in Chicago, Illinois
d. Jul 21, 1983 in Chicago, Illinois
Source: *AnObit 1983; NewYTBS 83;
St&PR 84; WhAm 8; WhoAm 74, 76, 78,
80, 82; WhoFI 83; WhoHcky 73;
WhoMW 82; WhoWor 82*

Wirtz, William Willard
American. Government Official
Secretary of Labor, 1962-69.
b. Mar 14, 1912 in De Kalb, Illinois
Source: *BiDrUSE 71, 89; BioIn 1, 2, 5,
6, 7, 8, 10, 11; ConAu 101; IntWW 74,
75, 76, 77, 78, 79, 80, 81, 82, 83, 89;
WhoAm 74, 76, 78, 80, 82, 84, 86, 88,
90, 92, 94, 95, 96, 97, 98, 99, 2000;
WhoMW 90*

Wisdom, Norman
English. Actor, Comedian
Starred in plays *Where's Charley*, 1960;
Walking Happy, 1970.
b. Feb 4, 1925 in London, England
Source: *BlueB 76; ConTFT 20; EncMT;
FilmgC; HalFC 84, 88; IntMPA 84, 86,
92; NotNAT; Who 74, 85, 92; WhoHol
A; WhoThe 81*

Wise, Isaac Mayer
American. Religious Leader
Founded Reform Judaism in US; pres.,
Hebrew Union College, Cincinnati,
1875-1900.
b. Mar 29, 1819 in Steingrub, Bohemia
d. Mar 26, 1900 in Cincinnati, Ohio
Source: *Alli, SUP; AmAu&B; AmBi;
AmNatBi; AmRef; AmSocL; ApCAB;
BenetAL 91; BiDAmEd; BiDAmJo;
BiD&SB; BioIn 1, 2, 3, 4, 5, 7, 8, 10,
11, 14, 15, 16, 17, 18, 19, 22, 23, 24;
CamDcAB; DcAmAu; DcAmB;
DcAmReB 1, 2; DcNAA; EncAB-H 1974,
1996; EncARH; EncWB 98; JeAmHC;
McGEWB; NatCAB 10; OhA&B;
OxCAmH; OxDcJeR; RelLAm 1, 2;
REnAL; WebAB 74, 79; WhAm HS;
WorAl; WorAlBi*

Wise, John
American. Clergy
Congregational minister defended the
autonomy of individual congregations;
his advocacy of religious and civil
democracy foreshadowed the logic of
the Declaration of Independence.
b. Aug 1652 in Roxbury, Massachusetts
d. Apr 8, 1725 in Ipswich, Massachusetts
Source: *Alli; AmAu; AmAu&B; AmBi;
AmNatBi; AmWrBE; ApCAB; BenetAL
91; BioIn 2, 3, 5, 8, 14, 17, 19;
CamDcAB; CamGEL; CamGLE;
CamHAL; DcAmAu; DcAmB; DcAmReB
1, 2; DcAmSR; DcLB 24; DcLEL;
DcNAA; Drake; EncCRAm; EncWB 98;
McGEWB; NatCAB 1; OxCAmH;
OxCAmL 65, 83, 95; PenC AM; REnAL;
WebAB 74, 79; WhAm HS; WrCNE*

Wise, Robert
American. Director, Producer
Won Oscars for direction of *West Side
Story*, 1961; *Sound of Music*, 1965.
b. Sep 10, 1914 in Winchester, Indiana
Source: *BiDFilm, 81, 94; BioIn 15, 16,
17, 18, 20; CmMov; CurBio 89; DcArts;
DcFM; EncSF, 93; FilmEn; FilmgC;
GangFlm; HalFC 80, 84, 88; HorFD;
IlWWHD 1; IntDcF 1-2, 2-2; IntMPA
75, 76, 77, 78, 79, 80, 81, 82, 84, 86,
88, 92, 94, 96; ItaFilm; LegTOT; MiSFD
9; MovMk; NewEScF; OxCFilm;
PenEncH; WhoAm 74, 76, 78, 80, 82,
84, 86, 88, 90, 92, 94, 95, 96, 97, 98,
99, 2000; WhoEnt 92, 98; WhoHrs 80;
WhoWest 74, 76, 78; WhoWor 78, 80,
82, 84, 87, 89, 91, 93, 95, 96, 97, 98,
99, 2000; WorAl; WorAlBi; WorEFlm;
WorFDir 1*

Wise, Stephen Samuel
American. Religious Leader
Zionist spokesman; founded Federation
of American Zionists, 1898, Jewish
Institute of Religion, 1922; worked to
establish Palestine as national home
for Jews.
b. Mar 17, 1874 in Budapest, Austria-
Hungary
d. Apr 19, 1949 in New York, New
York
Source: *AmAu&B; AmDec 1930;
AmNatBi; BiDMoPL; BiDSocW; BioIn 1,
2, 4, 5, 6, 7, 8, 9, 11, 12, 14, 16, 17, 19;
CamDcAB; CurBio 41, 49; DcAmB S4;
DcAmReB 1, 2; DcPseud; EncAB-A 2;
EncAB-H 1974, 1996; EncWB 98;
McGEWB; NatCAB 41; OxCAmH;
RelLAm 1, 2; REnAL; WebAB 74, 79;
WhAm 2; WhNAA*

Wise, Thomas J
English. Bibliographer
Highly esteemed bookman, collector who
was later exposed as forger.
b. Oct 7, 1859 in Gravesend, England
d. May 13, 1937 in London, England
Source: *CasWL; DcLEL; DcNaB 1931;
EvLB; LngCTC; NewC; OxCEng 67;
TwCA, SUP; WhE&EA*

Wise, William H
American. Author
Writings for juveniles include *The
Cowboy Surprise*, 1961; *The Terrible
Trumpet*, 1969.
b. Jul 21, 1923 in New York, New York
Source: *AuBYP 2; ConAu 13R; Dun&B
90; SmATA 4; WhoEng 88*

Wise, Winifred E
American. Children's Author
Biographies for juveniles include
Lincoln's Secret Weapon, 1962; *Fanny
Kemble*, 1966.
Source: *AuBYP 2, 3; ForWC 70; SmATA
2; WrDr 86, 88*

Wiseman, Frederick
American. Filmmaker
Known for "cinema verite"
documentaries; specializes in

examining US institutions for public
TV.
b. Jan 1, 1930 in Boston, Massachusetts
Source: *BiDFilm 81, 94; BioIn 9, 10, 11,
12, 13, 16; CamDcAB; ConAu 159;
ConLC 20; ConTFT 8; CurBio 74;
EncAJ; EncWB, 98; HalFC 80, 84, 88;
IntDcF 1-2, 2-2; IntMPA 92, 94, 96;
LesBEnT, 92; MiSFD 9; OxCFilm;
WhoAm 82, 84, 86, 88, 90, 92, 94, 95,
96, 97, 98, 99, 2000; WhoEnt 92, 98;
WorFDir 2; WrDr 2000*

Wiseman, Joseph
Canadian. Actor
Played villainous title role in first James
Bond film *Dr. No*, 1962.
b. May 15, 1918 in Montreal, Quebec,
Canada
Source: *BiE&WWA; BioIn 5; ConTFT 9;
FilmEn; FilmgC; ForYSC; HalFC 88;
IntMPA 80, 81, 82, 84, 86, 88, 92, 94,
96; ItaFilm; MotPP; NotNAT; WhoHol
92, A; WhoThe 72, 77, 81; WhoWorJ 72,
78*

**Wiseman, Nicholas Patrick
Stephen**
English. Religious Leader
First archbishop of Westminister, 1850.
b. Aug 2, 1802 in Seville, Spain
d. Feb 15, 1865 in London, England
Source: *Alli; BbD; BiD&SB; BioIn 2;
BritAu 19; CamBiEn; ChamBiD;
DcBiPP; DcCathB; DcEnL; DcEuL;
DcNaB; LuthC 75; NewC; NewCBEL;
PoIre; VicBrit; WebBD 83; WhoChr*

Wister, Owen
American. Author
Novel, *The Virginian*, 1902, has been the
basis for long-running stage play, three
movies.
b. Jul 14, 1860 in Germantown,
Pennsylvania
d. Jul 21, 1938 in North Kingstown,
Rhode Island
Source: *Alli SUP; AmAu&B; AmBi;
AmLY; AmNatBi; ApCAB SUP; ArizL;
BeaEPF; BenetAL 91; BiD&SB; BioIn 1,
3, 4, 5, 7, 9, 10, 12, 13, 14, 16, 17, 21,
22, 23, 24; CamBiEn; CamDcAB;
CamGEL; CamGLE; CamHAL; CarSB;
CasWL; ChamBiD; Chambr 3; ChhPo,
S2; CnDAL; ConAmA; ConAmL; ConAu
108, 162; CyWA 58, 97; DcAmAu;
DcAmB; DcArts; DcLB 9, 78, 186;
DcLEL; DcNAA; EncAAH; EncAB-H
1974, 1996; EncALit; EncFrLi;
EncFWF; FifWWr; GayN; GrWrEL N;
HalFC 84, 88; HarEnUS; LegTOT;
LinLib L, S; LngCTC; MemAm; NatCAB
13; NewEAmW; Novels; OxCAmL 65,
83, 95; OxCTwCL; PenC AM; PeoHis;
RAdv 1, 14, 13-1; REn; REnAL;
REnAW; RfGAmL 4, 87, 94; ScF&FL 1;
SmATA 62; TwCA, SUP; TwCLC 21;
TwCWW 82, 91; WebAB 74, 79;
WebE&AL; WhAm 1; WhE&EA; WhLit;
WhNAA; WorAlBi; WorAu 1900*

Witcover, Walt
[Walter Witcover Scheinman]
American. Director, Actor
Won best actor Obies for *Maedchen in Uniform*, 1955; *Exiles*, 1957.
b. Aug 24, 1924 in New York, New York
Source: *BiE&WWA; ConTFT 4; NotNAT; WhoEnt 92, 98*

Withers, Bill
American. Singer, Songwriter
Hits include "Ain't No Sunshine," 1971; "Lean On Me," 1972; "Lovely Day," 1978.
b. Jul 4, 1938 in Slab Fork, West Virginia
Source: *BillEnR; DrBlPA, 90; EncJzS; EncPR&S 89; EncRk 88; EncRkSt; HarEnR 86; IlEncBM 82; IlEncRk; InB&W 80; LegTOT; NewGrDA 86; NewYTBE 72; PenEncP; RkOn 78; RolSEnR 83; Songw; SoulM; WhoEnt 98; WhoRock 81; WhoRocM 82*

Withers, Googie
[Georgina McCallum]
English. Actor
British films include *Miranda; Lady Vanishes*.
b. Mar 12, 1917 in Karachi, Pakistan
Source: *BioIn 12, 14, 19; ConTFT 9; DcPseud; EncEurC; FilmAG WE; FilmEn; FilmgC; HalFC 80, 84, 88; IlWWBF; IntDcF 2-3; IntMPA 75, 76, 77, 78, 79, 80, 81, 82, 84, 86, 88, 92, 94, 96; IntWWW 2; MovMk; OxCFilm; OxCThe 83; Who 74, 82, 83, 85, 88, 90, 92, 94, 98, 99, 2000; WhoHol 92, A; WhoThe 72, 77, 81; WhoWor 74, 76*

Withers, Jane
American. Actor
Child star of 1930s films; TV commercials as Josephine the Plumber.
b. Apr 12, 1926 in Atlanta, Georgia
Source: *BioIn 7, 8, 9, 11, 15, 17; EncAFC; FilmEn; FilmgC; HalFC 80, 84, 88; HolP 30; IntMPA 77, 86, 92; InWom, SUP; LegTOT; MotPP; MovMk; ThFT; WhoHol 92, A; WorAlBi*

Witherspoon, Herbert
American. Opera Singer
First basso; NY Met., 1908-16; director of Met., 1935.
b. Jul 21, 1873 in Buffalo, New York
d. May 10, 1935 in New York, New York
Source: *AmBi; BakBD 78, 84, 92; BakBDTw; BiDAmM; BioIn 1, 11; DcAmB S1; MetOEnc; MusSN; NatCAB 29; NewAmDM; NewEOp 71; NewGrDA 86; NewGrDO; NotNAT B; WhAm 1*

Witherspoon, John
American. Educator, Religious Leader, Continental Congressman
Only clergyman in first Continental Congress; signed Declaration of Independence; president, Princeton College; coined term "Americanism."
b. Feb 5, 1723? in Gifford, Scotland

d. Nov 15, 1794 in Princeton, New Jersey
Source: *Alli; AmAu; AmAu&B; AmBi; AmNatBi; AmSocL; AmWrBE; ApCAB; BenetAL 91; BiAUS; BiD&SB; BiDrAC; BiDrUSC 89; BioIn 1, 3, 7, 8, 9, 10, 11, 14, 15, 16, 18, 19, 23; BlkwEAR; CamBiEn; CamDcAB; ChamBiD; CyAL 1; DcAmB; DcAmReB 1, 2; DcEnL; DcLB 31, 31B; DcNaB; Drake; EncAR; EncCRAm; EncRelA; EncWB 98; HisDcAR; HisWorL; LuthC 75; McGEWB; NewCBEL; OxCAmH; OxCAmL 83, 95; REnAL; TwCBDA; WebAB 74, 79; WhAm HS; WhAmP; WhAmRev; WorAl; WorAlBi*

Witkin, Joel-Peter
American. Photographer
Photographer since the 1950s; works collected in *Forty Photographs*, 1985; *Gods of Earth and Heaven*, 1989.
b. Sep 13, 1939 in New York, New York
Source: *BioIn 15, 19, 22, 23; ConPhot 88, 95; ICPEnP A; MacBEP; News 96, 96-1; WhoAm 82, 84, 86, 88, 90, 92, 94, 95, 96, 97, 98, 99, 2000; WhoAmA 80, 82, 84, 86, 89, 91, 93, 1999; WhoWest 00, 84, 94, 96, 98*

Witmark, Isidore
American. Music Executive, Publisher
Internationally known music publisher, 1880s-1920s; big promoter of ragtime music.
b. Jun 15, 1869 in New York, New York
d. Apr 9, 1941 in New York, New York
Source: *BioIn 16; DcAmB S3*

Witt, Johan de
Dutch. Political Leader
Chief minister of the States of Holland from 1653 to 1672, he led the Dutch Republic after the end of its war of independence.
b. Sep 24, 1625 in Dordrecht, Netherlands
d. Aug 20, 1672 in The Hague, Netherlands
Source: *BioIn 3, 10, 11, 15, 16, 24; EncWB 98; McGEWB; WhoMilH 76*

Witt, Katarina
German. Skater
Three-time world champion figure skater; won gold medals, 1984, 1988 Olympics; first woman to win two gold medals in sport since Sonja Henie.
b. Dec 1965 in Karl-Marx-Stadt, German Democratic Republic
Source: *BioIn 14, 15, 16; CurBio 88; EncFiS; IntWWW 2; LegTOT; News 91-3; NewYTBS 91; WorAlBi*

Witt, Mike
[Michael Atwater Witt]
American. Baseball Player
Pitcher, California, 1981-90; NY Yankees 1990—; threw first perfect game in MLs since Len Barker in 1981, 1984.

b. Jul 20, 1960 in Fullerton, California
Source: *Ballpl 90; BaseReg 86, 87; BioIn 14*

Witt, Paul Junger
American. Producer, Director
TV shows include "The Rookies," 1972-76; won Emmy for "Brian's Song," 1972.
b. Mar 20, 1943 in New York, New York
Source: *BioIn 16, 22; ConTFT 3; IntMPA 94; LesBEnT, 92; VarWW 85; WhoAm 86, 88; WhoEnt 92*

Witte, Edwin Emil
American. Economist
Exec. director of FDR's Committee on Economic Security which resulted in Social Security Act, 1934-35.
b. Jan 4, 1887 in Jefferson County, Wisconsin
d. May 20, 1960
Source: *BioIn 1, 4, 5, 6, 8; DcAmB S6; NatCAB 45; WhAm 4; WorAl*

Witte, Erich
German. Opera Singer, Producer
Berlin Opera dramatic tenor, originally Spieltenor, 1945-60.
b. Mar 19, 1911 in Bremen, Germany
Source: *CmOp; IntWWM 90; NewEOp 71; NewGrDM 80; NewGrDO; PenDiMP*

Witte, Sergey Yulyevich
Russian. Statesman
Negotiated treaty ending Russo-Japanese War, 1905; first constitutional Russian premier, 1905.
b. 1849 in Tiflis, Russia
d. Mar 12, 1915 in Saint Petersburg, Russia
Source: *McGEWB; REn; WebBD 83*

Witten, Edward
American. Physicist
Works on "string theory," searching for a set of equations that would explain all of the universe's matter and energy.
b. Aug 26, 1951 in Baltimore, Maryland
Source: *AmMWSc 92, 95, 98; CamBiEn; CurBio 97; IntWW 93, 97, 98, 2000; NotTwCS 1; WhoAm 96, 99, 2000; WhoScEn 96, 2000*

Wittenmyer, Annie Turner
American. Social Reformer
First president, Woman's Christian Temperance Union; known for church, charity work.
b. Aug 26, 1827 in Sandy Springs, Ohio
d. Feb 2, 1900 in Sanatoga, Pennsylvania
Source: *AmNatBi; AmWom; DcAmTB; EncAWoR; InWom SUP; LibW; NatCAB 12; NotAW; RelLAm 1, 2; WomFir; WorAl; WorAlBi*

Wittgenstein, Ludwig
Austrian. Philosopher, Educator
Wrote *Tractatus Logico-Philosophicus,*
  1922, which attempted to prove all
  metaphysical propositions to be
  nonsense.
b. Apr 26, 1889 in Vienna, Austria
d. Apr 29, 1951 in Cambridge, England
Source: *Benet 87, 96; BioIn 2, 4, 5, 7,
8, 9, 10, 11, 12, 13, 14, 15, 16, 17, 20,
21, 24; ConAu 113; CyWA 89, 97;
DcNaB 1951; EncWB 98; LegTOT;
LngCTC; LuthC 75; ObitT 1951;
OxCEng 67; OxCGer 76, 86, 97; REn;
ThTwC 87; TwCLC 59; WhAm 4;
WorAl; WorAu 1950*

Wittgenstein, Paul
American. Pianist
One-armed virtuoso who played left-hand
  concertos; brother of Ludwig.
b. Nov 5, 1887 in Vienna, Austria
d. Mar 3, 1961 in Long Island, New
  York
Source: *BakBD 78, 84, 92; BakBDTw;
BakDcM; BioIn 1, 5, 6, 21; DcArts;
MusMk; NewAmDM; NewGrDA 86;
NewGrDM 80; OxCMus; PenDiMP*

Wittig, Georg Friedrich Karl
German. Educator
Won Nobel Prize in chemistry, 1979;
  discovered Wittig reaction.
b. Jun 16, 1897 in Berlin, Germany
d. Aug 26, 1987 in Heidelberg, Germany
  (West)
Source: *AmMWSc 89, 92; BiESc; WhAm
9; Who 85; WhoNob, 90, 95; WhoWor
74, 76, 78, 80, 82, 84, 87*

Wittig, Monique
French. Writer
One of her many feminist theories is that
  lesbians are not women because the
  latter is a term meaningful only in the
  heterosexual community; wrote *The
  Straight Mind,* 1992.
b. 1935, France
Source: *BioIn 17; CmpQue; ConAu 116,
135; ConLC 22; ContDcW 89;
ConWorW 93; DcLB 83; DcTwCCu 2;
EncSF, 93; EncWL 2S, 3; FemiCLE;
FemiWr; FrenWW; GayLesB; GayLL 1;
ModWoWr; PostFic; ScF&FL 92;
WomFir; WorAu 1970*

Wittop, Freddy
Dutch. Designer
Won Tony for costumes in *Hello Dolly!*
  1964.
b. Jul 26, 1921 in Bussum, Netherlands
Source: *BiE&WWA; NotNAT; VarWW
85; WhoThe 77, 81*

Witz, Konrad
Swiss. Artist
Among first to use realistic landscapes in
  religious scenes: *Christ Walking on the
  Waters.*
b. 1400 in Rottweil, Germany
d. 1447 in Basel, Switzerland
Source: *AtlBL; CamBiEn; ChamBiD;
DcArts; IntDcAA 90; McGDA;*

*McGEWB; NewCol 75; OxCArt;
OxDcArt*

Wodehouse, P(elham) G(renville)
English. Author
Created characters Bertie Wooster and
  Jeeves; *The Inimitable Jeeves,* 1924.
b. Oct 15, 1881 in Guildford, England
d. Feb 14, 1975 in Long Island, New
  York
Source: *AmPS; ASCAP 66, 80; Au&Wr
71; AuNews 2; Benet 96; BestMus;
BiCoLiE; BiDAmM; BioIn 1, 2, 3, 4, 5,
6, 7, 8, 9, 10, 11, 12, 13, 14, 16, 17, 18,
19; CamBiEn; CasWL; ChamBiD;
Chambr 3; CmpEPM; ConAu 57; ConLC
22; ConPopW; CurBio 71; DcAmB S9;
DcArts; DcLEL; DcNaB 1971; EncSF
93; EncWL 1, 2S, 3; Ent; EvLB; GrBr;
IntWW 74; LinLib S; MajTwCW 2;
MakMC; McGEWD 72; MnBBF;
ModBrL, S1; NewC; NewCBEL;
NewCBMT; NotNAT A; Novels; OxCEng
67, 95; OxCTwCL; PenC ENG; PlP&P;
RAdv 1; REn; RfGShF 1, 2; RGTwCWr;
SmATA 22; TwCA, SUP; WebE&AL;
WhAm 6; WhDW; WhLit; Who 74;
WhoAm 74; WhoChL; WhoWor 74;
WorAu 1900*

Woffington, Margaret
"Peg"
Irish. Actor
Best role as male in *Constant Couple.*
b. Oct 18, 1714 in Dublin, Ireland
d. Mar 28, 1760 in London, England
Source: *BioIn 2, 3, 5, 8, 9, 11, 17;
BlmGEL; CamGWoT; DcBiPP; DcIrB 1,
2, 3; DcNaB, C; EncWT; InWom SUP;
NewC; NewGrDM 80; WhDW*

Wohler, Friedrich
German. Chemist
First to synthesize an organic compound,
  urea, 1828; isolated aluminum; devised
  process of manufacturing nickel.
b. Jul 31, 1800 in Eschershelm, Germany
d. Sep 23, 1882 in Gottingen, Germany
Source: *AsBiEn; BiESc; BioIn 2, 3, 5, 6,
11, 12, 14; CamBiEn; CamDcSc;
CelCen; ChamBiD; DcBiPP; DcInv;
DcScB; InSci; LarDcSc; LinLib S;
McGCEnS; RAdv 14; RanHWDS;
SciMath; WebBD 83; WhDW; WorScD*

Woiwode, Larry
American. Author
Work includes *What I'm Going to Do, I
  Think,* 1969; *Beyond the Bedroom
  Wall,* 1975; *Born Brothers,* 1988.
b. Oct 30, 1941 in Carrington, North
  Dakota
Source: *BenetAL 91; BioIn 8, 10, 16;
ConAu 16NR, 73; ConLC 6, 10; ConNov
82, 86, 91; CurBio 89; CyWA 89, 97;
DcLB 6; DrAF 76; DrAP 75; DrAPF 80,
91; IntvTCA 2; MagSAmL; OxCAmL 83;
WhoAm 97, 98; WorAu 1975; WrDr 80,
82, 84, 86, 88, 90, 92*

Wojciechowicz, Alex(ander)
"Wojie"
American. Football Player
Center-linebacker, Detroit, 1938-45,
  Philadelphia, 1946-50; Hall of Fame,
  1968.
b. Aug 12, 1915 in South River, New
  Jersey
d. Jul 13, 1993 in South River, New
  Jersey
Source: *BiDAmSp FB; BioIn 8, 9, 17,
18; LegTOT; WhoFtbl 74*

Wo-jen
Chinese. Government Official
Conservative Confucian official was the
  principal opponent of Western learning
  and modernization in China
b. 1804 in Honan Province, China
d. Jun 8, 1871
Source: *EncWB 98; McGEWB*

Wojnilower, Albert Martin
American. Economist
Chief economist, First Boston Corp.,
  NYC, 1964-86; wrote *The Quality of
  Business Loans,* 1960.
b. Feb 3, 1930 in Vienna, Austria
Source: *BioIn 13; St&PR 75, 84, 87;
WhoAm 84, 86, 88, 90, 92, 94, 95, 96,
97, 98, 99, 2000; WhoFI 83; WhoSecI
86*

Wolcott, Oliver, Sr.
American. Judge, Military Leader,
  Continental Congressman
Signed Declaration of Independence,
  1776; governor of CT, 1796.
b. Nov 26, 1726 in Windsor, Connecticut
d. Dec 1, 1797 in Litchfield, Connecticut
Source: *AmBi; AmNatBi; ApCAB;
BiAUS; BiDrAC; BiDrGov 1789;
BiDrUSC 89; BioIn 3, 5, 7, 8, 9, 23;
DcAmB; DcAmMeB; Dis&D; Drake;
EncAR; EncCRAm; HarEnUS; HisDcAR;
NatCAB 10; TwCBDA; WebAB 74, 79;
WhAmP; WhAmRev; WorAlBi*

Wolcott, Roger
American. Colonial Figure
Governor of CT, 1750-54; wrote epic
  poem about John Winthrop.
b. Jan 4, 1679 in Windsor, Connecticut
d. May 17, 1767 in East Windsor,
  Connecticut
Source: *Alli; AmAu&B; AmBi; AmNatBi;
AmWrBE; ApCAB; BenetAL 91;
BiDrACR; BioIn 14; CyAL 1; DcAmAu;
DcAmB; DcLB 24; DcLEL; DcNAA;
Drake; HarEnUS; NatCAB 10; OxCAmL
65, 83, 95; REnAL; TwCBDA; WebAB
74, 79; WhAm HS; WhAmP; WrCNE*

Wolf, Friedrich August
German. Scholar, Philologist
Laid the foundations for modern
  philology through his scientific
  treatment of the classical period.
b. Feb 15, 1759 in Hagenrode, Germany
d. Aug 8, 1824 in Marseilles, France
Source: *BiD&SB; BioIn 7, 12, 13;
BlkwCE; CasWL; DcBiPP; DcEuL;
EncEnl; EncHiCA; EncWB 98; EuAu;*

GloEncH; McGEWB; OxCClL; OxCGer 76, 86, 97; REn

Wolf, Hugo
Austrian. Composer
Wrote *Italienische Serenade,* 1893; died in an asylum for the insane.
b. Mar 13, 1860 in Windischgraez, Austria
d. Feb 22, 1903 in Vienna, Austria
Source: *AtlBL; BakBD 78, 84; BioIn 1, 2, 3, 4, 5, 6, 7, 8, 9, 11, 12, 14, 15, 16, 20, 23; BriBkM 80; ChamBiD; CmOp; CmpBCM; DcCom 77; DcCom&M 79; Dis&D; GrComp; IntDcOp; MetOEnc; MusMk; NewAmDM; NewEOp 71; NewGrDM 80; NewOxM; OxCEng 85, 95; OxCGer 76, 86, 97; OxCMus; OxDcOp; WhDW; WorAlBi*

Wolf, Naomi
American. Author
Author of *The Beauty Myth,* 1991; *Fire With Fire,* 1993.
b. 1963 in San Francisco, California
Source: *CurBio 93; LegTOT; News 94, 94-3*

Wolf, Peter
[J. Geils Band]
American. Singer
Lead vocalist, J Geils Band until 1984; solo single ''I Need You Tonight,'' 1984.
b. Mar 7, 1946 in Boston, Massachusetts
Source: *BioIn 12, 24; DcPseud; LegTOT; RkOn 85; Songw; WhoRocM 82*

Wolf, Stephen M
American. Airline Executive
Revived two finacially troubled airlines; pres. and CEO Allegis Corp. 1987-92; chm., CEO, UAL Corp. and United Airlines, 1992-94; adviser, air France, 1994-96; chm., CEO, USAIR Inc., 1996—.
b. Aug 7, 1941 in Oakland, California
Source: *BioIn 15, 16; Dun&B 90, 98; IntWW 91, 97, 98, 2000; News 89-3; St&PR 87, 98, 99, 2000; WhoAm 88, 99, 2000; WhoFI 00, 92, 98; WhoMW 92; WhoSSW 99; WhoWor 98, 99, 2000*

Wolfe, Digby
English. Writer
Emmy winner for writing TV specials, shows including ''Laugh-In,'' 1968.
b. Jun 4, 1932, England
Source: *ASCAP 80; VarWW 85; WhoUSWr 88*

Wolfe, George C.
American. Director, Dramatist, Producer
Head of New York Shakespeare Festival, 1993—.
b. Sep 23, 1954 in Frankfort, Kentucky
Source: *AfrAmAl 8; BlkLC SUP; ConAmD; ConAu 149; ConBlB 6; ConDr 93; ConLC 49; CurBio 94; WhoAm 95, 96, 97, 98, 99, 2000; WhoE*

95, 99; WhoEnt 98; WhoWor 2000; WrDr 98, 99, 2000

Wolfe, James
English. Military Leader
British commander who captured Quebec from French on Plains of Abraham, 1759; killed in battle.
b. Jan 2, 1727 in Westerham, England
d. Sep 13, 1759 in Quebec, Canada
Source: *Alli; ApCAB; BbtC; Benet 87, 96; BioIn 1, 2, 3, 4, 5, 6, 7, 8, 9, 10, 16, 17, 22, 24; CamBiEn; ChamBiD; DcAmMiB; DcCanB 3; DcNaB; Dis&D; Drake; EncAR; EncCRAm; EncWB 98; GenMudB; HarEnMi; HarEnUS; HisDBrE; LinLib S; MacDCB 78; McGEWB; NatCAB 1; OxCAmH; OxCBrHi; OxCCan; REn; WebBD 83; WhAm HS; WhDW; WhNaAH; WhoMilH 76; WorAl; WorAlBi*

Wolfe, Thomas (Clayton)
American. Author
Wrote *Look Homeward, Angel,* 1929; *You Can't Go Home Again,* 1940.
b. Oct 3, 1900 in Asheville, North Carolina
d. Sep 15, 1938 in Baltimore, Maryland
Source: *AgeMat; AmAu&B; AmBi; AmCulL; AmWr; ASCAP 66, 80; AtlBL; Benet 87, 96; BenetAL 91; BioIn 1, 2, 3, 4, 5, 6, 7, 8, 9, 10, 11, 12, 13, 14, 15, 16, 17, 19; CamBiEn; CamDcAB; CamGEL; CamGLE; CamHAL; CasWL; ChamBiD; CnDAL; CnMD; CnMWL; ConAmA; ConAu 104, 132; CyWA 58; DcAmB S2; DcArts; DcLB 9, 102, DS2, Y85A; DcLEL; DcNAA; EncAB-H 1974, 1996; EncSoH; EncWB 98; EncWL 1, 2, 2S; EncWT; EvLB; FacFETw; FifSWrA; GrWrEL N; LegTOT; LinLib L, S; LngCTC; MagSAmL; MajTwCW 1, 2; MakMC; McGEWB; ModAL 4, 4S2; ModWD; Novels; OxCAmH; OxCAmL 65, 83, 95; OxCEng 67, 85, 95; OxCTwCL; PenC AM; PeoHis; PlP&P; RAdv 1, 14, 13-1; REn; REnAL; RfGAmL 4, 87, 94; RGTwCWr; SouWr; TwCA, SUP; TwCLC 4, 13, 29; TwCWr; WebAB 74, 79; WebBD 83; WebE&AL; WhAm 1; WhDW; WhoTwCL; WorAl; WorAlBi; WorLitC; WrPh*

Wolfe, Tom
[Thomas Kennerly Wolfe, Jr.]
American. Author
Wrote *The Electric Kool-Aid Acid Test,* 1968; *The Right Stuff,* 1979.
b. Mar 2, 1931 in Richmond, Virginia
Source: *AmAu&B; AmSocL; AmWr S3; Au&Arts 8; AuNews 2; BeaEPF; Benet 87, 96; BenetAL 91; BestSel 89-1; BiCoLiE; BioIn 7, 8, 9, 10, 11, 12, 13, 16, 20; BlueB 76; CamBiEn; CelR, 90; ChamBiD; CmCal; ConAu 9NR, 13R, 33NR; ConLC 1, 2, 9, 15, 35, 51; ConNov 91; CurBio 71; CyWA 89, 97; DcAmC; DcArts; DcLB 152, 185; DcLEL 1940; EncAJ; EncALit; EncTwCJ; FacFETw; IdentIs; IntAu&W 91; IntWW 89, 91, 93; JrnUS; LegTOT; LiJour; MagSAmL; MajTwCW 1; MakMC; NewYTBS 81; OxCAmL 83, 95;*

OxCTwCL; PenC AM; PostFic; RGTwCWr; SourALJ; SouWr; WebE&AL; Who 94; WhoAm 74, 76, 78, 80, 82, 84, 86, 88, 90, 92, 94, 95, 96, 97; WhoE 91, 93, 95, 97; WhoTwCL; WhoUSWr 88; WhoWor 74, 95, 96, 97; WhoWrEP 89, 92, 95; WorAl; WorAlBi; WorAu 1970; WrDr 86, 92

Wolfe, Willie
[S(ymbionese) L(iberation) A(rmy); William Lawton Wolfe]
American. Revolutionary
Member of terrorist group that kidnapped Patricia Hearst, 1974.
b. 1952?
d. May 24, 1974 in Los Angeles, California
Source: *BioIn 10*

Wolfenden, John Frederick, Sir
English. Museum Director
Director, British Museum, 1969-73; led com. which recommended liberalizing nation's homosexuality laws, 1967.
b. Jun 26, 1906 in Swindon, England
d. Jan 18, 1985 in London, England
Source: *ChamBiD; ConAu 106, 114; CurBio 70, 85; DcNaB 1981; IntWW 83; IntYB 79; NewYTBS 85; Who 85*

Wolfensohn, James David
American. Business Executive
Chm. of John F. Kennedy Center for the Performing Arts, 1990-95; pres., World Bank, 1995—.
b. Dec 1, 1933 in Sydney, Australia
Source: *BioIn 12, 16, 17, 18, 19, 20, 21, 22; DrAS 99H; IntWW 82, 83, 89, 91; NewYTBS 93; St&PR 75, 84, 87, 91, 93, 96, 97, 98, 99, 2000; Who 98, 99, 2000; WhoAm 74, 76, 78, 80, 82, 88, 92, 94, 95, 96, 97, 2000; WhoE 93, 95; WhoEnt 92; WhoFI 00, 83, 98; WhoIntA 2; WhoWor 97, 98, 99, 2000*

Wolfert, Ira
American. Journalist
War correspondent; won Pulitzer, 1943; writings collected in *Battle for the Solomons,* 1943.
b. Nov 1, 1908 in New York, New York
Source: *AmAu&B; AmNov; BioIn 1, 2, 3, 4, 22, 23, 24; CurBio 43, 98N; EncAJ; HisDcWJ; OxCAmL 65, 83; TwCA SUP; WhoPul; WhoWorJ 72; WorAu 1900*

Wolff, Albert Louis
French. Conductor
Led Opera-Comique, 1920s; wrote opera *Oiseau Bleu,* 1919.
b. Jan 19, 1884 in Paris, France
d. Feb 1970 in Paris, France
Source: *BakBD 84; BakBDTw; NewEOp 71*

Wolff, Christian von, Baron
German. Philosopher
Known for his broad concept of philosophy, he systematized the doctrines of Leibniz.

b. Jan 24, 1679 in Breslau, Silesia,
   Germany
d. Apr 9, 1754 in Halle, Germany
Source: *BiDPsy; BioIn 8, 11; CasWL;
   ChamBiD; DcBiPP; DcEuL; DcScB;
   EvEuW; LuthC 75; McGEWB;
   NamesHP; OxCGer 76; OxCLaw*

Wolff, Fritz
German. Opera Singer
Tenor, admired for Wagner roles;
   Bayreuth, 1925-41.
b. Oct 28, 1894 in Munich, Germany
d. Jan 18, 1957 in Munich, Germany
   (West)
Source: *BakBD 84, 92; BakBDTw;
   NewEOp 71; NewGrDM 80; NewGrDO*

Wolff, Geoffrey (Ansell)
American. Author
Wrote memoir *The Duke of Deception,*
   1979; novel *The Age on Consent,*
   1995.
b. Nov 5, 1937 in Los Angeles,
   California
Source: *BenetAL 91; BioIn 15, 16, 17,
   19; ConAu 29NR, 29R, 43NR, 78NR;
   ConLC 41; DcLEL 1940; DrAPF 80;
   IntAu&W 76, 93; OxCAmL 95; WhoAm
   74, 76, 78, 80, 82, 84, 90, 92, 94, 96,
   97, 98, 99, 2000; WhoEnt 98; WhoUSWr
   88; WhoWrEP 89, 92, 95; WorAu 1975;
   WrDr 80, 82, 84, 86, 88, 90, 92, 94, 96*

Wolff, Helen
[Mrs. Kurt Wolff]
American. Publisher
Founded Pantheon Books, 1942-61;
   introduced European writer to US.
b. Jul 27, 1906 in Veskueb, Yugoslavia
Source: *ArtclWW 2; BioIn 9, 13, 19, 21;
   ConAu 113, 117, 144; DcLB Y94N;
   NewYTBS 94*

Wolff, Hugh (MacPherson)
American. Conductor
Achieved a national reputation as a
   conductor and in the 1990s and was
   considered one of a handful of
   Americans who would lead the major
   orchestras of the future.
b. 1953 in Paris, France
Source: *BakBD 92; BakBDTw; WhoAm
   88, 90, 94, 99, 2000; WhoE 89, 91;
   WhoEnt 98; WhoMW 92*

Wolff, Mary Evaline
[Sister Mary Madalena]
American. Religious Figure, Educator
Pres., St. Mary's College, Notre Dame,
   1934-61; wrote *Chaucer's Nuns.*
b. May 24, 1887 in Cumberland,
   Wisconsin
d. Jul 25, 1964 in Boston, Massachusetts
Source: *AmAu&B; BenetAL 91; BioIn 1,
   2, 4, 5, 7, 8, 12; ConAu 116; CurBio 42,
   64; IndAu 1917; PenNWW A; REnAL;
   TwCA, SUP*

Wolff, Tobias (Jonathan Ansell)
American. Writer
Writer of short stories and memoirs;
   wrote *Garden of the North American
   Martyrs,* 1981; *In Pharaoh's Army:
   Memoirs of the Lost War,* 1994.
b. Jun 19, 1945 in Birmingham, Alabama
Source: *Au&Arts 16; BenetAL 91;
   BestSel 90-2; BioIn 16, 17, 18, 19, 20,
   21; ConAu 22AS, 54NR, 76NR, 114,
   117; ConLC 39, 64; ConNov 91, 96;
   CurBio 96; CyWA 89; DcLB 130;
   EncALit; IntAu&W 89, 91, 93; IntWW
   91; LegTOT; MajTwCW 2; OxCAmL 95;
   RfGAmL 4; RfGShF 2; RGTwCWr;
   WhoAm 94, 95, 96, 97; WhoUSWr 88;
   WhoWrEP 89, 92, 95; WrDr 90, 92, 94,
   96, 98, 99, 2000*

Wolf-Ferrari, Ermanno
German. Composer
Comic operas include *L'Amore Medico,*
   1913.
b. Jan 12, 1876 in Venice, Italy
d. Jan 21, 1948 in Venice, Italy
Source: *BakBD 78, 84, 92; BakBDTw;
   BakDcM; BioIn 1, 3, 4, 7, 8, 11; BriBkM
   80; CamBiEn; ChamBiD; CmOp;
   CompSN; DcArts; DcCom&M 79;
   IntDcOp; MetOEnc; MusMk;
   NewAmDM; NewEOp 71; NewGrDM 80;
   NewGrDO; NewOxM; NotNAT B;
   OxCMus; OxDcOp; PenDiMP A*

Wolfgang, Myra K
American. Labor Union Official
Helped organize Coalition of Labor
   Union Women, 1974.
b. 1914?
d. Apr 12, 1976 in Detroit, Michigan
Source: *BioIn 10, 12; ObitOF 79;
   WhoAmW 74; WomPO 76*

Wolfington, Iggie
American. Actor
Tony nominee for *The Music Man,* 1958.
b. Oct 14, 1920 in Philadelphia,
   Pennsylvania
Source: *BiE&WWA; NotNAT; WhoHol
   92, A*

Wolfit, Donald, Sir
English. Actor
Knighted, 1957, for achievements in
   presenting plays in England.
b. Apr 20, 1902 in Newark, England
d. Feb 17, 1968 in London, England
Source: *BioIn 3, 7, 8, 9, 10, 11;
   CamBiEn; CamGWoT; ChamBiD;
   CnThe; CurBio 65, 68; DcArts; DcNaB
   1961; DcPseud; EncWT; Ent; FilmEn;
   FilmgC; ForYSC; HalFC 80, 84, 88;
   IlWWBF, A; IntDcT 3; MotPP; MovMk;
   NotNAT A, B; ObitOF 79; ObitT 1961;
   OxCFilm; OxCThe 67, 83; WhAm 4, 4A,
   5; WhoHol B; WhoHrs 80; WhScrn 74,
   77, 83; WhThe; WorEFlm*

Wolfman Jack
[Robert Smith]
American. Radio Performer
Best known for wild, jive-talking radio
   program, 1970s; in film *American
   Graffiti,* 1973.
b. Jan 21, 1938 in New York, New York
d. Jul 1, 1995 in Belvidere, North
   Carolina
Source: *AmNatBi; BioIn 10, 16, 21, 22;
   BkPepl; CanWW 79, 80, 81, 83, 89;
   CmCal; DcPseud; HisDcAR; LegTOT;
   News 96, 96-1; NewYTBS 95; RadMoSP;
   VarWW 85; WhAm 11; WhoAm 80, 90,
   92, 94, 95, 96, 97; WhoCan 73, 75, 77,
   80, 82, 84; WhoCanB 86; WhoEnt 92;
   WhoHol 92*

Wolfram von Eschenbach
German. Author, Poet
Regarded as one of the greatest poets of
   the Middle Ages, he was the author of
   chivalric romances; best known is his
   Parzival, about man's relationship to
   God.
b. c. 1170
Source: *BbD; Benet 87, 96; BiD&SB;
   BioIn 5, 7, 13; CamBiEn; CasWL;
   ChamBiD; ClMLC 5; CnDWLB 2;
   CyWA 58, 97; DcCathB; DcEuL; DcLB
   138; EncLitE; EuAu; EuWr 1; EvEuW;
   LuthC 75; OxCEng 67; OxCGer 76, 86,
   97; OxDcOp; PenC EUR; RAdv 14, 13-
   2; RComWL; REn; WorAlBi*

Wolfson, Erwin Service
American. Businessman
NYC leading builder; constructed Pan
   Am Building, completed 1963.
b. Mar 27, 1902
d. Jun 26, 1962
Source: *AmNatBi; BioIn 5, 6, 7; DcAmB
   S7; NatCAB 48; WhAm 4*

Wolfson, Harry Austryn
American. Educator, Scholar
Leading historian of medieval philosophy
   of Islam, Judaism and Christianity, he
   was Harvard University's Littauer
   Professor of Hebrew Literature and
   Philosophy for more than 50 years.
b. Nov 2, 1887 in Austryn, Lithuania
d. 1974
Source: *AmAu&B; AmNatBi; BioIn 4, 5,
   6, 10, 11, 15, 16, 17; ConAu 53, P-2;
   DcAmB S9; DrAS 74F; EncWB 98;
   McGEWB; OxDcJeR; PeoHis; WhAm 6*

Wolfson, Louis Elwood
American. Industrialist
Known for financial manipulations,
   attempted takeovers of Montgomery
   Ward, AMC, 1950s-60s; jailed for
   conspiracy, 1969.
b. Jan 28, 1912 in Saint Louis, Missouri
Source: *BioIn 3, 4, 5, 6, 8, 11; IntWW
   74, 75, 76, 77, 78, 79, 80, 81, 82, 83;
   PolProf E; WhoFI 83, 85, 87*

Wolheim, Louis
American. Actor
Character actor, 1917-31, in films *Dr.
   Jekyll and Mr. Hyde; America.*

b. Mar 23, 1880 in New York, New
York
d. Feb 18, 1931 in Los Angeles,
California
Source: *DcAmB S1; Film 1, 2; FilmEn;
FilmgC; FrSilen; HalFC 80, 84, 88;
MotPP; MovMk; OxCThe 67; SilFlmP;
TwYS; WhoHol B; WhScrn 74, 77, 83*

Wolpe, Stefan
American. Composer
Known for his ability to absorb the
divergent styles and ideas of the
Modernist movements and for
producing out of them music of great
originality.
b. Aug 25, 1902 in Berlin, Germany
d. Apr 4, 1972
Source: *AmComp; ASCAP 66, 80;
BakBD 78, 84, 92; BakBDTw; BakDcM;
BiDAmM; BioIn 1, 2, 9; BriBkM 80;
CamDcAB; ConAmC 76, 82; DcCM;
EncWB 98; NewAmDM; NewGrDA 86;
NewGrDM 80; NewGrDO; NewOxM;
WhAm 5; WhoMus 72*

Wolper, David Lloyd
"Mr. Documentary"
American. Producer, Business Executive
Produces documentaries, TV shows,
including "Roots," 1976; won 11
Emmys, one special Oscar.
b. Jan 11, 1928 in New York, New York
Source: *BioIn 14, 15, 16; CamDcAB;
ConTFT 1, 2, 4; CurBio 86; FilmgC;
HalFC 88; IntMPA 92; IntWW 89, 91,
93, 97, 98, 2000; LesBEnT, 92; VarWW
85; WhoAm 74, 76, 78, 80, 82, 84, 86,
88, 90, 92, 94, 95, 96, 97, 98, 99, 2000;
WhoEnt 92, 98; WhoWest 74; WhoWor
74, 76, 78, 91, 93*

Wolsey, Thomas, Cardinal
English. Religious Figure
Cardinal and lord chancellor with papal
ambitions; Henry VIII's ally in attempt
to secure divorce from Catherine of
Aragon.
b. 1475 in Ipswich, England
d. Nov 29, 1530 in Leicester, England
Source: *Alli; Benet 87, 96; BioIn 1, 2, 3,
4, 5, 6, 7, 9, 10, 11, 12, 13, 14, 15, 17,
20, 23; BlmGEL; CamBiEn; ChamBiD;
DcCathB; DcNaB; Dis&D; EncWB 98;
LegTOT; LinLib S; LngCEL; LuthC 75;
McGEWB; NewC; REn; WhDW;
WorAlBi*

Wolsky, Albert
French. Designer
Won Oscar for costumes in *All That
Jazz,* 1979; *Bugsy,* 1992; designed for
Sophie's Choice, 1982; *Moscow on the
Hudson,* 1984.
b. Nov 24, 1930 in Paris, France
Source: *BioIn 13; VarWW 85*

Woltman, Frederick Enos
American. Journalist
Reporter, staff writer, *NY World-
Telegram,* 1927-70; won Pulitzers,
1946, 1947.
b. Mar 16, 1905 in York, Pennsylvania

d. Mar 5, 1970 in Sarasota, Florida
Source: *ConAu 89; CurBio 47, 70;
NewYTBE 70; WhAm 5; WhoPul*

Womack, Bobby
American. Singer, Songwriter
Prolific songwriter; protege of Sam
Cooke; no. 1 soul album *The Poet,*
1982.
b. Mar 4, 1944 in Cleveland, Ohio
Source: *BillEnR; BioIn 12, 16; ConMuA
80A; ConMus 5; DrBlPA, 90; EncPR&S
89; EncRk 88; EncRkSt; IlEncRk;
LegTOT; OnThGG; PenEncP; RkOn 78;
RolSEnR 83; Songw; SoulM; WhoBlA 5;
WhoRock 81; WhoRocM 82*

Wonder, Stevie
[Steveland Morris Hardaway]
American. Singer, Musician, Songwriter
Hits include "My Cherie Amour,"
"You Are the Sunshine of My Life;"
album *Innervisions,* won 1974
Grammy; inducted into Rock and Roll
Hall of Fame, 1989.
b. May 13, 1950 in Saginaw, Michigan
Source: *AfrAmAl 6, 8; AfrAmBi 1;
AmDec 1970; AmSong; BakBD 78, 84,
92; BakDcM; BiDAfM; BiDJaz; BillEnR;
BioIn 9, 10, 11, 12, 13, 14, 15, 16;
BioNews 74; BkPepl; CamDcAB; CelR
90; ChamBiD; ConAu X; ConBlB 11;
ConHero 2; ConLC 12; ConMus 2, 17;
ConTFT 21; CurBio 75; DcArts;
DcPseud; DcTwCCu 5; DrBlPA, 90;
Ebony 1; EncPR&S 89; EncRk 88;
EncRkSt; EncWB 2-19; FacFETw;
HarEnR 86; IlEncRk; InB&W 80, 85;
IntWW 78, 79, 80, 81, 82, 83, 89, 91, 93,
97, 98, 2000; LegTOT; NegAl 83, 89;
NewAmDM; NewGrDA 86; NewYTBE
71; NewYTBS 75, 85; OxCPMus;
PenEncP; RkOn 74, 78; RkWho 96;
RolSEnR 83; Songw; SoulM; WhoAfA 9,
10, 11, 12; WhoAm 76, 78, 80, 82, 84,
86, 88, 90, 92, 94, 95, 96, 97, 98, 2000;
WhoBlA 1, 2, 3, 4, 5, 6, 7, 8; WhoEnt
92, 98; WhoRock 81; WhoRocM 82;
WhoWor 84, 87, 89, 91, 93, 95, 96, 97,
98; WorAl; WorAlBi*

Wong, Anna May (Lu Tsong)
American. Actor
Star in 1920s-30s as mysterious Oriental
in *Shanghai Express; Thief of Bagdad.*
b. Jan 3, 1907 in Los Angeles, California
d. Feb 3, 1961 in Santa Monica,
California
Source: *AsAmAlm; BioIn 7, 11, 16, 20;
DcAmB S7; DcAmNB; Film 1, 2;
FilmEn; FilmgC; ForYSC; GangFlm;
HalFC 80, 84, 88; HolP 30; IntDcF 1-3,
2-3; InWom, SUP; ItaFilm; LegTOT;
MotPP; MovMk; NotAsAm; NotNAT B;
ObitOF 79; ThFT; TwYS; WhoHol B;
WhScrn 74, 77, 83; WhThe; WorAl;
WorAlBi*

Wong, B. D
American. Actor
Films include *The Karate Kid.*
b. Oct 24, 1962 in San Francisco,
California

Source: *BioIn 24; CelR 90; ConTFT 7;
WhoAm 2000; WhoEnt 92*

Woo, John
Chinese. Director
Directed *From Rags to Riches,* 1979;
Hard Target, 1993.
b. c. 1945 in Guangchou, China
Source: *News 94, 94-2*

Woo, Merle
American. Writer
Work has been published in many
different kinds of periodicals and
anthologies; wrote "Letter to Ma,"
1981.
b. Oct 24, 1941 in San Francisco,
California
Source: *GayLesB*

Wood, Anthony
English. Antiquarian
Noted for *Athenae Oxonienses,* 1692,
containing biographies of famous
Oxford graduates.
b. Dec 17, 1632 in Oxford, England
d. Nov 28, 1695 in Oxford, England
Source: *Alli; BbD; BiD&SB; BritAu;
CasWL; Chambr 1; DcEnA; DcNaB;
EvLB; NewC; NewGrDM 80; NewOxM;
OxCEng 67, 85, 95; OxCMus; PenC
ENG; REn; WebE&AL*

Wood, Chris
English. Musician
Hit LP's include *When the Eagle Flies,*
1974; *Traffic,* 1968.
b. Jun 24, 1944 in Birmingham, England
d. Jul 12, 1983 in Birmingham, England
Source: *WhoRocM 82*

Wood, Craig Ralph
American. Golfer
Touring pro, 1930s-40s; won US Open,
Masters, 1941.
b. Nov 18, 1901 in Lake Placid, New
York
d. May 8, 1968 in Palm Beach, Florida
Source: *BiDAmSp OS; BioIn 6, 8, 13;
DcAmB S8; ObitOF 79; WhoGolf*

Wood, Edward D., Jr.
American. Filmmaker
B-movie producer; received the "Worst
Director of All Time" award from the
Golden Turkey awards, 1980.
b. Oct 10, 1924 in Poughkeepsie, New
York
d. Dec 10, 1978 in Los Angeles,
California
Source: *HalFC 84; HorFD; MiSFD 9N;
ScF&FL 92*

Wood, Elijah
American. Actor
Appeared in *Back to the Future II,* 1989.
b. Jan 28, 1981 in Cedar Rapids, Iowa
Source: *BioIn 22, 23, 24; ConTFT 19;
IntMPA 94, 96; WhoAm 95, 96, 97, 99,
2000; WhoEnt 98*

Wood, Evelyn

American. Educator
Founded the Evelyn Wood Reading
   Dynamics Institute, 1959, to teach
   high-speed reading.
b. Jan 9, 1909 in Ogden, Utah
d. Aug 26, 1995 in Tucson, Arizona
Source: *BioIn 14, 21; NatCAB 63N;*
NewYTBS 95; WhoAm 90; WhoAmW 91

Wood, Fernando

American. Politician
Dem. congressman, NY, 1863-71; NYC
   mayor, 1854-56 and 59.
b. Jun 14, 1812 in Philadelphia,
   Pennsylvania
d. Feb 14, 1881 in Hot Springs,
   Arkansas
Source: *AmBi; AmNatBi; ApCAB;*
BiAUS; BiDrAC; BiDrUSC 89; BioIn 1,
2, 7, 17; CamDcAB; CopCroC; DcAmB;
Drake; EncWB 98; HarEnUS;
McGEWB; NatCAB 3; PolPar; WebAB
74, 79; WhAm HS; WhAmP; WhCiWar

Wood, Gar(field A)

American. Boat Racer
Powerboat champion of 1920s-30s with
   boat *Miss America.*
b. Dec 4, 1880 in Mapleton, Iowa
d. Jun 19, 1971 in Miami, Florida
Source: *BioIn 3, 5, 6, 7, 9, 10; BioNews*
74; NewYTBE 71

Wood, Grant

American. Artist
Depicted rural life in Midwest: *American*
Gothic, 1930.
b. Feb 13, 1892 in Anamosa, Iowa
d. Feb 12, 1942 in Iowa City, Iowa
Source: *ArtsAmW 3; AtlBL; Benet 87,*
96; BioIn 1, 2, 4, 6, 7, 9, 10, 12, 13, 14,
15, 17, 19, 21, 22; BriEAA; CamDcAB;
ChamBiD; CurBio 40, 42; DcAmArt;
DcAmB S3; DcArts; DcCAA 71;
DcTwArt; EncAAH; LegTOT; LinLib S;
McGDA; NatCAB 35; OxCAmH;
OxCAmL 65; OxCArt; OxCTwCA;
OxDcArt; PhDcTCA 77; REn; WebAB
74, 79; WhAm 1; WhAmArt 85; WorAl;
WorAlBi

Wood, Henry, Mrs.

[Ellen Price]
English. Author
Wrote successful melodrama *East Lynne,*
   1861.
b. Jan 17, 1814 in Worcester, England
d. Feb 10, 1887 in London, England
Source: *Alli; ArtclWW 2; Benet 87;*
BiD&SB; BioIn 16; BlmGWL; CamGEL;
CamGLE; ChamBiD; Chambr 3;
ContDcW 89; DcArts; DcEnA; DcEnL;
DcLB 18; DcLEL; DcNaB; HalFC 84,
88; HsB&A; NewC; NewCBEL; Novels;
OxCEng 67; PenC ENG; REn; StaCVF;
SupFW; TwCCr&M 80A, 85A, 91A

Wood, Henry Joseph, Sir

English. Conductor, Composer
Led London's popular promenade
   concerts, 1897-1944; introduced
   unknown composers.

---

b. Mar 3, 1869 in London, England
d. Aug 19, 1944 in London, England
Source: *BakBD 84; BakBDTw; BioIn 1,*
3, 5, 8, 9, 11, 14; CamBiEn; ChamBiD;
CurBio 44; DcNaB 1941; GrBr;
OxCMus; WhDW

Wood, James Rushmore

American. Surgeon
A founder, Bellevue Hospital, NYC,
   1847; began first hospital ambulance
   service in US, 1869; developed first
   training school for nurses in US, 1873.
b. Sep 14, 1816 in Mamaroneck, New
   York
d. May 4, 1882 in New York, New York
Source: *AmBi; ApCAB; BioIn 1; DcAmB;*
NatCAB 9; WebAB 74; WhAm HS

Wood, Joe

[Joseph Wood]
"Smokey Joe"
American. Baseball Player
Pitcher-outfielder, 1908-15, 1917, 1919-
   20, mostly with Red Sox; led AL in
   wins, 1912, in ERA, 1915.
b. Oct 25, 1889 in Kansas City, Missouri
Source: *Ballpl 90; BiDAmSp BB; BioIn*
7, 11, 14, 15; NewYTBS 85; WhoProB
73

Wood, John

English. Actor
Won 1976 Tony for *Travesties.*
b. 1930? in Derbyshire, England
Source: *BioIn 10, 11, 13; ChamBiD;*
ConTFT 5; CurBio 83; VarWW 85; Who
88; WhoHol 92

Wood, John Howland, Jr.

"Maximum John"
American. Judge
Appointed 1970-79; only federal judge
   assassinated in this century.
b. Mar 31, 1916 in Rockport, Texas
d. May 29, 1979 in San Antonio, Texas
Source: *BiDFedJ A*

Wood, John the Elder

English. Architect
England's first great town planner;
   creator of Bath.
b. 1705?
d. May 23, 1754?
Source: *Alli; McGDA; WhoArch*

Wood, Leonard

American. Physician, Army Officer
Governor general, Philippines, 1921-27;
   ran for US Rep. presidential
   nomination, 1920.
b. Oct 9, 1860 in Winchester, New
   Hampshire
d. Aug 7, 1927 in Boston, Massachusetts
Source: *AmBi; AmLY; AmNatBi; ApCAB*
SUP, X; BioIn 2, 5, 7, 9, 11, 16, 24;
CamDcAB; CmdGen 1991; CyAG;
DcAmB; DcAmDH 80, 89; DcAmMiB;
DcNAA; EncAB-H 1974, 1996; EncLatA;
EncWB 98; GayN; HarEnMi; HarEnUS;
LinLib S; McGEWB; MedHR 94;
NatCAB 9, 28; NewEAmW; OxCAmH;

PolPar; REnAW; SpAmWar; TwCBDA;
WebAB 74, 79; WebAMB; WhAm 1;
WorAl; WorAlBi

Wood, Louise Aletha

American. Social Reformer
Nat. exec. director, Girl Scouts of the
   USA, 1961-72; recreational supervisor,
   Federal Works Agency, 1934-42; won
   Medal of Freedom, 1947.
b. Feb 19, 1910 in Mankato, Minnesota
d. May 16, 1988 in Aurora, California
Source: *BioIn 5, 6, 15, 16; CurBio 61,*
88; InWom; WhoAm 74, 76; WhoAmW
64, 66, 68, 70, 72, 74

Wood, Natalie

[Natasha Gurdin; Mrs. Robert Wagner]
American. Actor
Starred in *Miracle on 34th Street,* 1946;
   Rebel Without a Cause, 1955; *West*
   Side Story, 1961.
b. Jul 20, 1939 in San Francisco,
   California
d. Nov 29, 1981 in Catalina Island,
   California
Source: *BiDFilm; BioAmW; CurBio 82;*
FilmgC; ForWC 70; GoodHs; IntMPA
82; MotPP; MovMk; OxCFilm; WhoAm
80; WhoAmW 72, 74; WhoHol A;
WorEFlm

Wood, Peggy

American. Actor, Author
Played in TV show "Mama," 1949-57;
   Oscar nominee for *Sound of Music,*
   1965.
b. Feb 9, 1892 in New York, New York
d. Mar 18, 1978 in Stamford,
   Connecticut
Source: *AmWomPl; BiE&WWA; BioIn 3,*
5, 6, 10, 11, 16; CmpEPM; ConAu 77;
CurBio 42, 53, 78, 78N; DcAmB S10;
EncAFC; EncMT; FamA&A; Film 1, 2;
FilmEn; FilmgC; ForYSC; HalFC 80,
84; IntMPA 77; InWom, SUP; LegTOT;
MotPP; NewYTBS 78; NotNAT;
NotWoAT; OsStAZ; OxCAmT 84;
OxCPMus; WhAm 9; What 4; WhoAmW
58, 61, 64, 66, 68, 70, 72, 74; WhoE 74;
WhoHol A; WhoThe 72, 77; WhScrn 83;
WorAl

Wood, Robert Dennis

American. TV Executive
Pres., CBS, 1969-76; introduced
   comedies "The Mary Tyler Moore
   Show"; "All in the Family";
   "M*A*S*H."
b. Apr 17, 1925 in Boise, Idaho
d. May 20, 1986 in Santa Monica,
   California
Source: *BioIn 10, 14, 15, 24; BlueB 76;*
CurBio 86; LesBEnT; ScrEAmL 2;
WhoAm 82

Wood, Robert Elkington

American. Business Executive
Pres., Sears Roebuck and Co., 1928-39;
   chm., 1939-54.
b. Jun 13, 1879 in Kansas City, Missouri
d. Nov 6, 1969 in Lake Forest, Illinois

Source: *AmNatBi; BiDAmBL 83; BioIn 1, 2, 3, 4, 6, 7, 8, 9, 10, 11, 14; CamDcAB; CurBio 41, 69; DcAmB S8; EncWB 98; McGEWB; NatCAB 55; WebAB 74, 79; WhAm 5; WorAl*

Wood, Robert Williams
American. Physicist
Known for work in atomic, molecular radiation, diffraction method in color photography.
b. May 2, 1868 in Concord, Massachusetts
d. Aug 11, 1955 in Amityville, New York
Source: *AmNatBi; BiESc; BioIn 2, 4, 6, 8, 12; CamBiEn; CamDcAB; ChamBiD; DcScB; InSci; LarDcSc; NatCAB 14, 46; NewCol 75; OxCAmH; ScF&FL 1; WhAm 3; WhLit*

Wood, Ron(ald)
[The Rolling Stones]
English. Musician
Guitarist with rock band since 1975; hits include "Going to a Go-Go," 1982.
b. Jun 1, 1947 in London, England
Source: *BioIn 13, 14, 15; ConMuA 80A; OnThGG; WhoAm 80, 82, 84, 86, 88, 90, 92, 94, 95, 96, 97, 98, 99, 2000; WhoEnt 92, 98; WhoRock 81; WhoRocM 82; WhoWor 98*

Wood, Samuel Grosvenor
American. Director
Directed Marx Brothers film *A Night at the Opera*, 1935.
b. Jul 10, 1884 in Philadelphia, Pennsylvania
d. Sep 22, 1949 in Hollywood, California
Source: *BiDFilm; BioIn 2; CurBio 49; DcFM; Film 1; FilmgC; MovMk; OxCFilm; TwYS; WhAm 2; WhoHol B; WhScrn 74, 77; WorEFlm*

Wood, Sarah Sayward Barrell Keating
American. Author
Published anonymous gothic romances: *Amelia, or Influence of Virtue*, 1802.
b. Oct 1, 1759 in York, Maine
d. Jan 6, 1855 in Kennebunk, Maine
Source: *AmAu; AmAu&B; BiD&SB; BlmGWL; DcAmAu; DcAmB; NotAW; OxCAmL 65, 83, 95; REnAL; WhAm HS*

Wood, Sharon
Canadian. Mountaineer
First North American woman to reach the top of Mt. Everest, 1986.
b. May 18, 1957 in Halifax, Nova Scotia, Canada
Source: *BioIn 15; ConNews 88-1; WhoAm 94, 95, 96, 97, 98, 99; WhoAmW 89, 91, 93, 95, 97, 99*

Wood, Stuart
[Bay City Rollers]
"Woody"
Scottish. Musician, Singer
Guitarist with rock group; albums include *Strangers in the Wild*, 1978.

b. Feb 25, 1957 in Edinburgh, Scotland
Source: *BkPepl*

Wood, Tim
American. Skater
Three-time US champion, 1968-70, two-time world champion, 1969-70, figure skater.
b. 1949?
Source: *BiDAmSp BK; BioIn 9*

Wood, Wilbur Forrester
American. Baseball Player
Knuckleball pitcher, 1961-78; led AL in wins, 1972, 1973, in losses, 1975.
b. Oct 22, 1941 in Cambridge, Massachusetts
Source: *Ballpl 90; BiDAmSp Sup; BioIn 9; WhoProB 73*

Woodall, Mary
English. Museum Director
First female director of major British provincial museum, Birmingham Museum and Art Gallery, 1956-64.
b. Mar 6, 1901
d. Mar 1, 1988
Source: *ConAu 125; Who 74, 82, 83, 85, 88; WhoArt 80, 82, 84; WhoWor 74*

Woodard, Alfre
American. Actor
Award-winning TV roles include "St. Elsewhere," "L.A. Law," "Hill Street Blues"; cable TV film *Mandela*, 1987.
b. Nov 8, 1953 in Tulsa, Oklahoma
Source: *BiDFilm 94; BioIn 14, 15, 16; BlksAmF; ConBlB 9; ConTFT 5, 9, 16, 27; CurBio 95; DrBlPA 90; FacFEBW TA; HalFC 88; InB&W 85; IntMPA 92, 94, 96; LegTOT; OsStAZ; VarWW 85; WhoAm 92, 94, 95, 96, 97, 99, 2000; WhoAmW 91, 95, 99; WhoBlA 4, 7; WhoEnt 92; WhoHol 92*

Woodard, Lynette
American. Basketball Player
Won gold medal, 1984 Olympics; first female member, Harlem Globetrotters, 1985-87; 1993 Flo Hyman award winner.
b. 1959? in Wichita, Kansas
Source: *BasBi; BiDAmSp BK; BioIn 14, 15; BlkOlyM; BlkWAm; ConNews 86-2; EncWomS; FacFEBW DS; InB&W 85; NewYTBS 86; OutWomA; WhoAfA 10, 11, 12; WhoSpor; WomFir*

Woodbridge, Frederick James Eugene
American. Educator
U. professor who wrote *The Purpose of History*, 1916; *Nature and Mind*, 1937.
b. Mar 26, 1867 in Windsor, Ontario, Canada
d. Jun 1, 1940 in New York, New York
Source: *AmAu&B; AmNatBi; BiDAmEd; BioIn 2, 4; CamDcAB; CurBio 40; DcAmB S2; DcNAA; REnAL; WebAB 74, 79; WhAm 1*

Woodbury, Levi
American. Supreme Court Justice, Politician
Supreme Court Justice 1846-51; advocate of states' rights; held various positions of power at both the state and national level.
b. Dec 22, 1789 in Francestown, New Hampshire
d. Sep 4, 1851 in Portsmouth, New Hampshire
Source: *Alli; AmBi; AmNatBi; ApCAB; BiAUS; BiDFedJ; BiDrAC; BiDrGov 1789; BiDrUSC 89; BiDrUSE 71, 89; BioIn 2, 5, 10, 15, 23; CamDcAB; CyAL 1; DcAmB; DcNAA; Drake; EncABHB 6; HarEnUS; NatCAB 2; OxCSupC; SupCtJu; TwCBDA; WebAB 74, 79; WhAm HS; WhAmP*

Woodcock, Amos Walter Wright
American. Government Official, Lawyer
Dist. attorney, MD, 1922-30; prosecuted Japanese war criminals for US, 1945-46.
b. Oct 29, 1883 in Salisbury, Maryland
d. Jan 17, 1964 in Salisbury, Maryland
Source: *BiDWWGF; BioIn 6; EncAB-A 22; ObitOF 79; WhAm 4*

Woodcock, Leonard Freel
American. Labor Union Official, Diplomat
Pres., UAW, 1970-77; ambassador to China, 1979-81.
b. Feb 15, 1911 in Providence, Rhode Island
Source: *BiDAmL; BiDAmLL; CurBio 70; EncABHB 5; FacFETw; IntWW 83, 91; NewYTBE 70; NewYTBS 79; PolProf NF; Ward 77C; WhoAm 84, 90; WhoAmP 85, 91; WhoGov 77; WhoMW 74; WhoWor 80; WorAl; WorAlBi*

Wooden, John Robert
American. Basketball Coach
Head coach, UCLA, 1949-75; won 10 NCAA championships; Hall of Fame, 1970.
b. Oct 14, 1910 in Martinsville, Indiana
Source: *BiDAmSp BK; BioIn 6, 9, 10, 11, 12, 14, 15, 16; CamBiEn; CamDcAB; CmCal; CurBio 76; IndAu 1917; NewYTBE 72, 73; NewYTBS 75; WhoAm 76, 78, 80, 82, 84, 86, 88, 90, 92, 94, 95, 96, 97, 98, 99, 2000; WhoWest 00, 94, 96, 98; WorAl; WorAlBi*

Woodhouse, Barbara Blackburn
English. TV Personality
Hosted popular dog training show on BBC, 1980; wrote *Dog Training My Way*, 1981; *No Bad Dogs: The Woodhouse Way*, 1982.
b. May 9, 1910 in Rathfarnham, Ireland
d. Jul 9, 1988 in Buckinghamshire, England
Source: *Au&Wr 71; ConAu 13NR; CurBio 85, 88; NewYTBS 88*

Woodhull, Victoria Claflin
American. Social Reformer
With sister, Tennessee Claflin, founded
Woodhull and Claflin's Weekly, 1870,
which advocated equal rights for
women; Equal Rights Party
presidential candidate, 1872.
b. Sep 23, 1838 in Homer, Ohio
d. Jun 10, 1927 in Norton Park, England
Source: *ABCAmRe; Alli SUP; AmAu;
AmAu&B; AmBi; AmNatBi; Benet 96;
CamDcAB; ConAu 180; DcAmB; EncAB-
H 1996; EncAWoR; EncWHA;
EncWoAP; NotAW; OhA&B; OxCAmL
65; RelLAm 2; REn; REnAL; WebAB 74;
WhAm 4; WhAmP; WomFir*

Woodiwiss, Kathleen (Erin)
American. Author
Best-selling novels include *Shanna*,
1977; *Ashes in the Wind*, 1979.
b. Jun 3, 1939 in Alexandria, Louisiana
Source: *ArtclWW 2; BioIn 12, 13, 14;
ConAu 23NR, 76NR, 89; MajTwCW 1, 2;
NewYTBS 79; RAdv 14; TwCRHW 90;
WhoAm 78, 80, 82, 84, 86, 88;
WhoAmW 81; WhoUSWr 88; WhoWrEP
89, 92, 95; WrDr 86, 92*

Woodruff, Hale (Aspacio)
American. Artist
Created mural series for the Atlanta
University library, *The Art of the
Negro*, tracing the history of African
art and showed its influence on
modern art.
b. Aug 26, 1900 in Cairo, Illinois
d. Sep 1980 in New York, New York
Source: *AfrAmAl 6; BioIn 9, 11, 12, 16,
19; ConBlB 9; DcAmArt; DcTwCCu 5;
InB&W 80, 85; NegAl 76, 83, 89;
NewYTBS 80; SJGBlA; WhAm 7;
WhAmArt 85; WhoAm 76, 78, 80*

Woodruff, John
American. Track Athlete
Middle-distance runner; won gold medal
in 800-meters, 1936 Olympics.
b. Jul 5, 1915 in Connellsville,
Pennsylvania
Source: *BiDAmSp OS; BlkOlyM;
WhoTr&F 73*

Woodruff, Judy Carline
American. Broadcast Journalist, Author
White House correspondent, NBC News,
1977-82.
b. Nov 20, 1946 in Tulsa, Oklahoma
Source: *BioIn 13; ConAu 13NR, 73;
CurBio 86; EncTwCJ; IntWW 89, 91, 93,
97, 98, 2000; IntWWW 2; InWom SUP;
WhoAm 80, 82, 84, 86, 88, 90, 92, 94,
95, 96, 97, 98, 99, 2000; WhoAmW 74,
75, 81, 85, 95, 97, 99; WhoE 89, 91*

Woodruff, Robert Winship
American. Business Executive
Pres., Coca-Cola, 1923-39; innovations
included vending machines, six-pack
cartons, large bottles.
b. Dec 6, 1889 in Columbus, Georgia
d. Mar 7, 1985 in Atlanta, Georgia

Source: *BiDAmBL 83; BioIn 1, 2, 4, 7,
8, 11, 12, 13; ConNews 85-1; FacFETw;
IntYB 78, 79, 80, 81, 82; ScrEAmL 1;
WhAm 8*

Woods, Donald
[Ralph L Zink]
American. Actor, Real Estate Executive
Appeared in over 40 films, including
True Grit, 1969.
b. Dec 2, 1904 in Brandon, Manitoba,
Canada
Source: *BiE&WWA; DcPseud; FilmEn;
FilmgC; ForYSC; HalFC 84, 88;
IntMPA 84, 86, 92; MotPP; MovMk;
NotNAT; SaTiSS; WhoHol A*

Woods, Donald
South African. Journalist, Author
Active against apartheid; relationship
with Steven Biko is subject of first
major anti-apartheid film, *Cry
Freedom*, 1987.
b. Dec 15, 1933 in Elliotdale, South
Africa
Source: *BioIn 11, 12, 13, 15, 16, 17;
ConAu 78NR, 114, 121; CurBio 82;
WhoEng 88*

Woods, Granville T
American. Inventor
Invented electric incubator, railroad
telegraph system.
b. Apr 23, 1856 in Columbus, Ohio
d. Jan 30, 1910 in New York, New York
Source: *BioIn 6, 8, 9, 10; CamDcAB;
NotBlAM; NotBlAS*

Woods, James
American. Actor
Films include *Against All Odds*, 1984;
Salvador, 1986; won Emmy, 1987.
b. Apr 18, 1947 in Vernal, Utah
Source: *BiDFilm 94; BioIn 12, 13, 15;
ConTFT 5, 12, 23; CurBio 89;
GangFlm; HalFC 88; HolBB; IntMPA
86, 88, 92, 94, 96; IntWW 91, 93, 97,
98, 2000; LegTOT; News 88-3; OsStAZ;
VarWW 85; WhoAm 86, 88; WhoHol 92,
A; WorAlBi*

Woods, Robert Archey
American. Social Worker
Founded South End House, the first
settlement house in Boston, and
pioneered surveys of ethnic
communities.
b. Dec 9, 1865 in Pittsburgh,
Pennsylvania
d. Feb 18, 1925 in Boston,
Massachusetts
Source: *AmBi; AmNatBi; AmSetPR;
BiDSocW; BioIn 9, 11; DcAmAu;
DcAmB; DcNAA; EncAB-H 1974;
EncWB 98; McGEWB; OxCAmH; WhAm
1*

Woods, Rose Mary
American. Secretary
Exec. secretary to Nixon, 1969-75;
erased portions of Watergate tapes.
b. Dec 26, 1917 in Sebring, Ohio

Source: *BioIn 5, 8, 10, 12, 13; InWom
SUP; NewYTBE 73; PolProf NF;
WhoAm 74, 76, 78, 80, 82, 84, 86, 88,
90, 92, 94, 95, 96, 97, 98, 99; WhoAmW
74, 95, 97, 99; WhoGov 72; WhoSSW 73*

Woods, Tiger
[Eldrick Woods]
American. Golfer
Golfweek/Titleist, Jr. Golfer of the Year,
1991; youngest player to compete in
the Masters, 1995; won Las Vegas
Invitational at age 20, 1996; youngest
player to win Masters, 1997.
b. Dec 30, 1975 in Cypress, California
Source: *AfrAmAl 8; ConBlB 14;
ConHero 3; CurBio 97; EncWB 99;
IntWW 98, 2000; News 95; NewYTBS
95; NotBlAM; WhoAfA 9, 10, 11, 12;
WhoAm 98, 99, 2000; WhoBlA 8;
WhoWor 98, 99, 2000*

Woodson, Carter Godwin
American. Editor, Author
Wrote *The African Background Outlined*,
1936; *The Rural Negro*, 1930; won
Spingarn, 1926.
b. Dec 19, 1875 in New Canton, Virginia
d. Apr 3, 1950 in Washington, District of
Columbia
Source: *AfrAmAl 8; AmAu&B; AmDec
1910, 1920; AmNatBi; AmSocL; BenetAL
91; BiDAmEd; BiDAmNC; BioIn 1, 2, 3,
4, 5, 6, 7, 8, 9, 10, 11, 12, 13, 14, 15,
16, 17, 18, 19, 23, 24; CamBiEn;
CamDcAB; CurBio 44; DcAmB S4;
DcAmNB; EncAACR; EncAB-H 1974,
1996; EncSoH; EncWB 98; FacFETw;
GloEncH; InB&W 80, 85; NatCAB 38;
REnAL; SelBAAf; SelBAAu; WebAB 74,
79; WhAm 3; WorAl*

Woodson, Robert L.
American. Sociologist
Founder and president, National Center
for Neighborhood Enterprise, 1981—.
b. Apr 8, 1937 in Philadelphia,
Pennsylvania
Source: *ConAu 127; ConBlB 10;
WhoAfA 9, 10, 11, 12; WhoBlA 3, 4, 5,
6, 7, 8*

Woodson, Rod(erick Kevin)
American. Football Player
Cornerback, Pittsburgh Steelers, 1987—.
b. Mar 10, 1965 in Fort Wayne, Indiana
Source: *News 96; WhoAfA 9, 11, 12;
WhoAm 94, 95, 96, 97, 98, 99, 2000;
WhoBlA 8*

Woodsworth, James Shaver
Canadian. Clergy, Politician
Leader, Cooperative Commonwealth
Federation Party, 1932 until WW II;
member, House of Commons.
b. Jul 29, 1874 in Toronto, Ontario,
Canada
d. Mar 21, 1942 in Vancouver, British
Columbia, Canada
Source: *BiDMoPL; BioIn 2, 3, 5, 10, 11,
13; CamBiEn; ChamBiD; DcNAA;
DcTwHis; EncWB 98; EncWM; MacDCB
78; McGEWB; ObitOF 79; OxCCan*

Woodville, Richard Caton
American. Artist
Painted genre themes of life in
   Baltimore, MD; known for humorous
   manner in technique.
b. 1825 in Baltimore, Maryland
d. 1855 in London, England
Source: ApCAB; BioIn 7, 11; BriEAA;
CamDcAB; DcAmArt; DcBrBI; Drake;
McGDA; NewYHSD; PeoHis

Woodward, Bob
[Robert Upshur Woodward]
American. Journalist
With Carl Bernstein uncovered
   Watergate scandal; wrote All the
   President's Men, 1974.
b. Mar 26, 1943 in Geneva, Illinois
Source: AmDec 1970; AuNews 1; BioIn
10, 11, 12, 13, 14, 15, 16, 17, 18, 19,
20, 21, 22, 23; BioNews 74; BkPepl;
ConAu 31NR, 69; CurBio 76; EncAJ;
EncTwCJ; IntAu&W 89, 91, 93; JrnUS;
LegTOT; LiJour; MajTwCW 1;
NewYTBS 82, 92; PolProf NF; WhoAm
74, 76, 78, 80, 82, 84, 86, 88, 90, 92,
94, 95, 96, 97; WhoE 93, 95, 97;
WhoUSWr 88; WhoWrEP 89, 92, 95;
WorAl; WrDr 80, 82, 84, 86, 88, 90, 92,
94, 96, 98, 99, 2000

Woodward, C(omer) Vann
American. Historian
Known for studies of history of
   American South; wrote The Strange
   Career of Jim Crow, 1955; Mary
   Chestnut's War earned him 1982
   Pulitzer Prize.
b. Nov 13, 1908 in Vanndale, Arkansas
d. Dec 17, 1999 in Hamden, Connecticut
Source: AmAu&B; AmSocL; Au&Wr 71;
BioIn 9, 11, 13, 14, 15, 16, 17, 19;
BlueB 76; CamDcAB; ChambID; ConAu
2NR, 5R, 17NR, 44NR; CurBio 86; DrAS
74H, 78H, 82H, 99H; EncAAH; EncSoH;
EncWB 98; GloEncH; IntAu&W 82;
IntWW 83, 91, 93, 97, 98, 2000;
McGEWB; OxCAmL 95; PeoHis; RAdv
14, 13-3; ThTwC 87; WebAB 74, 79;
WhNAA; Who 92; WhoAm 74, 78, 84,
86, 88, 90, 2000; WhoPul; WhoUSWr 88; WhoWor 84, 87;
WhoWrEP 89, 92, 95; WorAu 1970;
WrDr 84, 92, 94, 96

Woodward, Edward
English. Actor
Starred in Shakespearean roles, British
   TV, films; featured in US TV series
   "The Equalizer."
b. Jun 1, 1930 in Croydon, England
Source: BiE&WWA; BioIn 15; CelR 90;
ConTFT 6, 17; FilmgC; HalFC 80, 84;
IlWWBF; IntMPA 75, 76, 77, 80, 88, 92,
94, 96; IntWW 82, 83, 89, 91, 93, 97,
98, 2000; LegTOT; NotNAT; Who 82,
83, 85, 88, 90, 92, 94, 98, 99, 2000;
WhoAm 90, 92; WhoHol 92, A; WhoThe
72, 77, 81

Woodward, Ellen S.
American. Government Official
Advocate for economic security for
   women and children was the director
   of work relief programs for women
   during the New Deal in the 1930s.
b. Jul 11, 1887 in Oxford, Mississippi
d. Sep 23, 1971 in Washington, District
   of Columbia
Source: EncWB, 98

Woodward, Joanne Gignilliat
[Mrs. Paul Newman]
American. Actor
Won Oscar, 1957, for The Three Faces
   of Eve.
b. Feb 27, 1930 in Thomasville, Georgia
Source: BiDFilm; BioIn 13, 15, 16;
BkPepl; CelR 90; ConTFT 3; CurBio 58;
FilmgC; HalFC 84, 88; IntMPA 86, 92;
IntWW 77, 78, 79, 80, 81, 82, 83, 89, 91,
93, 97, 98, 2000; IntWWW 2; InWom
SUP; MotPP; MovMk; OxCFilm;
WhoAm 74, 76, 78, 80, 82, 84, 86, 88,
90, 92, 94, 95, 96, 97, 99, 2000;
WhoAmW 61, 64, 66, 68, 70, 72, 83, 85,
89, 91, 93, 95; WhoEnt 92, 98; WhoHol
A; WhoWor 74, 78, 95, 96, 97, 98, 99,
2000; WorAl; WorAlBi; WorEFlm

Woodward, Robert Burns
American. Educator
Won Nobel Prize in chemistry, 1965, for
   contributing to art of chemical
   synthesis.
b. Apr 10, 1917 in Boston,
   Massachusetts
d. Jul 8, 1979 in Cambridge,
   Massachusetts
Source: AmMWSc 76P, 79; AmNatBi;
AsBiEn; BiESc; BioIn 1, 2, 3, 4, 5, 6, 7,
8, 12, 13, 14, 15, 18, 19, 20; CamBiEn;
CamDcAB; CamDcSc; ChamBiD; ConAu
161; CurBio 52; DcAmB S10; InSci;
IntWW 74, 75, 76, 77, 78; LarDcSc;
McGCEnS; McGMS 80; NewYTBS 79;
OxCAmH; RAdv 14; RanHWDS; WebAB
74, 79; WhAm 7; WhDW; WhoAm 74,
76, 78; WhoE 74, 77, 79; WhoNob, 90,
95; WhoWor 74, 76, 78; WorAl; WorScD

Woodward, William E
American. Author
Wrote Lottery, 1924; A New American
   History, 1936.
b. Oct 2, 1874 in Ridge Spring, South
   Carolina
d. Sep 27, 1950 in Augusta, Georgia
Source: AmAu&B; BioIn 22; ConAmL;
OxCAmL 65; REn; REnAL; TwCA, SUP;
WhAm 3; WhE&EA; WhNAA; WorAu
1900

Woodwell, George M(asters)
American. Biologist
Outspoken ecologist known for
   comments on carbon dioxide and the
   "greenhouse effect"; founded Woods
   Hole Research Center, 1985.
b. Oct 23, 1928 in Cambridge,
   Massachusetts
Source: AmMWSc 76P, 79, 82, 86, 89,
92, 95, 98; BioIn 7, 13; ConNews 87-2;

NatLAC; WhoAm 74, 76, 78, 80, 82, 84,
86, 88, 90, 92, 94, 95, 96, 97, 98, 99,
2000; WhoE 95; WhoOcn 78; WhoScEn
94, 96, 2000

Woodworth, Samuel
American. Journalist, Author
Editor, NY Mirror, 1823-24; best known
   novel The Forest Rose, 1825.
b. Jan 13, 1784 in Scituate,
   Massachusetts
d. Dec 9, 1842 in New York, New York
Source: Alli; AmAu; AmAu&B; AmBi;
ApCAB; BenetAL 91; BiDAmM;
BiD&SB; BioIn 1, 5; DcAmB; DcLEL;
Drake; EncALit; EvLB; JrnUS;
McGEWD 72, 84; OxCAmL 65; OxCThe
67; PenC AM; REnAL; TwCBDA; WhAm
HS

Woody, Elizabeth
American. Poet
Published poetry collection Hand into
   Stone, 1988; co-founder of the
   Northwest Native American Writers
   Association.
b. 1959 in Ganado, Arizona
Source: AZNatAW; BioIn 21; ConAu
152; NotNaAm; SJGNNAA; WrDr 99,
2000

Woody, Regina Llewellyn Jones
American. Children's Author
Writings include Starlight, 1946; One
   Day at a Time, 1968.
b. Jan 4, 1894 in Boston, Massachusetts
Source: AuBYP 2, 3; ConAu 3NR, 5R;
ForWC 70; MorJA; SmATA 3; WhoE 74;
WrDr 76

Wooley, Sheb
American. Singer, Musician, Actor
Films include Giant, 1956; High Noon,
   1952.
b. Apr 10, 1921 in Erick, Oklahoma
Source: AllMGCo; ASCAP 66, 80;
BgBkCoM; BioIn 12, 14, 15; CounME
74, 74A; EncFCWM 69, 83; EncFWF;
HarEnCM 87; IlEncCM; LegTOT;
PenEncP; RkOn 74; TelevWe; WhoHol
92, A; WhoRock 81; WhoRocM 82

Woolf, Leonard Sidney
English. Author, Publisher
Wrote novel The Village in the Jungle,
   1913; play Hotel, 1939; founded
   Hogarth Press, 1917, with wife
   Virginia.
b. Nov 25, 1880 in London, England
d. Aug 14, 1969 in Rodmell, England
Source: BiDInt; BioIn 4, 5, 6, 7, 8, 9,
10, 11, 12, 13; CamBiEn; CamGEL;
ChamBiD; ConAu 5R; CurBio 65, 69;
DcLEL; DcNaB 1961; EvLB; GrBr;
LngCTC; ModBrL, S1; NewC;
NewCBEL; OxCEng 85, 95; OxCTwCL;
PenC ENG; RAdv 1; REn; TwCA, SUP;
TwCWr; WhE&EA; WhLit; WhoLA;
WorAu 1900

Woolf, Virginia
[Adeline Virginia Stephen Woolf]
English. Author, Critic
Wrote *To the Lighthouse*, 1927; member, the "Bloomsburys."
b. Jan 25, 1882 in London, England
d. Mar 28, 1941 in Lewes, England
Source: *ArtclWW 2; AtlBL; BeaEPF; Benet 87; BiDBrF 2; BioIn 1, 2, 3, 4, 5, 6, 7, 8, 9, 10, 11, 12, 13, 14, 15, 16, 17, 18, 19, 20, 21, 22, 23, 24; BlmGEL; BlmGWL; BritWr 7; CamGEL; CasWL; Chambr 3; CmpQue; CnDBLB 6; CnMWL; ConAu 104, 130; ConLCrt 77, 82; ContDcW 89; CurBio 41; CyWA 58, 89, 97; DcArts; DcLB 36, 100, 162, DS10; DcLEL; DcNaB 1941; EncBrWW; EncSF, 93; EncWL 1, 2, 2S, 3; EvLB; FacFETw; FemiCLE; GayLesB; GoodHs; GrWomW; GrWrEL N; HalFC 84, 88; IntDcWB; InWom, SUP; LegTOT; LinLib L, S; LiveWoA; LngCEL; LngCTC; MagSWL; MajTwCW 1; ModBrL, 2, S1, S2; ModWoWr; NewC; Novels; OxCBrHi; OxCEng 67, 85; OxCWoWr 95; PenC ENG; RadHan; RAdv 1, 14, 13-1; RComWL; REn; RfGEnL 91; ScF&FL 1; ScFSB; ShScr 7; TwCA, SUP; TwCLC 1, 5, 20, 43; TwCWr; WebE&AL; WhDW; WhoTwCL; WomFir; WomWrGB; WorAl; WorAlBi; WorLitC; WrPh*

Woollcott, Alexander Humphreys
"Town Crier"
American. Author, Critic
Model for egotist in Kaufman and Hart's *The Man Who Came to Dinner*.
b. Jan 19, 1887 in Phalanx, New Jersey
d. Jan 23, 1943 in New York, New York
Source: *AmNatBi; CasWL; ChamBiD; ConAu 161; DcAmB S3; EvLB; LngCTC; ModWD; OxCAmL 65; OxCThe 67; PIP&P; REn; REnAL; TwCA, SUP; WebAB 74; WhAm 2; WhoHol B; WhScrn 74, 77*

Woolley, Catherine
[Jane Thayer]
American. Author
Juvenile books include *Gus Was a Real Dumb Ghost*, 1982.
b. Aug 11, 1904 in Chicago, Illinois
Source: *Au&Wr 71; AuBYP 2, 3; BioIn 6, 7, 9; ConAu 1R, 6NR; DcLP 87A; ForWC 70; MorJA; PenNWW A, B; SmATA 3; WhoAm 78, 80, 82, 84, 86, 88, 90, 92, 94, 95, 96, 97, 98, 99, 2000; WhoAmW 64, 66, 68, 70, 72, 74, 75, 77, 79, 81, 83, 85, 87, 89, 91, 93, 95, 97, 99; WhoE 75, 77, 95; WhoWor 93, 95*

Woolley, Charles Leonard, Sir
English. Archaeologist
Best known for discovery of Royal Graves of Ur in ancient land of Sumer.
b. Apr 17, 1880 in London, England
d. Feb 20, 1960 in London, England
Source: *BioIn 3, 21; CamBiEn; ChamBiD; CurBio 54, 60; DcLEL; DcScB; LngCTC; LuthC 75; NewCBEL; REn; WhE&EA; Who 74*

Woolley, Monty
[Edgar Montillion Woolley]
"Mr. Beard"
American. Actor
Best known for stage, screen title role in *The Man Who Came to Dinner*.
b. Aug 17, 1888 in New York, New York
d. May 6, 1962 in Albany, New York
Source: *AmNatBi; BioIn 6, 13; CurBio 63; DcAmB S7; EncAFC; EncMT; FilmEn; FilmgC; HalFC 80, 84, 88; LegTOT; MotPP; MovMk; NatCAB 62; NotNAT B; ObitOF 79; OsStAZ; OxCAmT 84; RadStar; WhAm 4; WhoHol B; WhScrn 74, 77, 83; WhThe; WorAl*

Woolman, John
American. Religious Leader
Quaker preacher, 1743-72; best known for his journal, first published in 1774.
b. Oct 19, 1720 in Ancochs, New Jersey
d. Oct 7, 1772 in New York, New York
Source: *Alli; AmAu; AmAu&B; AmBi; AmNatBi; AmRef; AmWrBE; ApCAB; BenetAL 91; BiD&SB; BiDSocW; BioIn 1, 2, 3, 4, 5, 6, 7, 8, 9, 14, 15, 19; CamBiEn; CamDcAB; CasWL; ChamBiD; CnDAL; CyAL 1; DcAmAu; DcAmB; DcAmReB 1, 2; DcAmSR; DcBiPP; DcLB 31; DcNaB; Drake; EncAB-H 1974; EncALit; EncAnRW; EncARH; EncCRAm; EncWB 98; EvLB; IlEncMy; LinLib L; LuthC 75; MacEWoS; McGEWB; NatCAB 1; NewCBEL; OxCAmH; OxCAmL 65, 83, 95; OxCEng 67, 85, 95; PenC AM; RAdv 13-3; RComAH; REn; REnAL; WebAB 74, 79; WebBD 83; WebE&AL; WhAm HS; WhNaAH*

Woolpert, Phil
American. Basketball Coach
Inducted into Basketball Hall of Fame, 1992.
b. Dec 19, 1915 in Los Angeles, California
Source: *BioIn 8, 12, 21; NewYTBS 81; WhoBbl 73*

Woolrich, Cornell
[George Hopley; Cornell George Hopley-Woolrich; William Irish]
American. Author
Wrote novels *Cover Charge*, 1926; *The Bride Wore Black*, 1940.
b. Dec 4, 1903 in New York, New York
d. Sep 25, 1968 in New York, New York
Source: *AmAu&B; AmNatBi; Benet 96; BenetAL 91; BioIn 8, 14, 16, 18, 22, 24; ConAu P-1, X; ConLC 77; CrtSuMy; DcArts; EncMys; HalFC 80, 84, 88; LegTOT; MysSW; Novels; REnAL; ScF&FL 1, 2, 92; TwCA SUP; TwCCr&M 80, 85, 91*

Woolsey, Janette
American. Author
Wrote *It's Time for Thanksgiving*, 1957; *It's Time For Easter*, 1961, with Elizabeth Hough Sechrist.

b. Dec 11, 1904 in Livingston, New York
Source: *AuBYP 2, 3; BioIn 7, 9; ConAu 1R, 2NR; ForWC 70; ScF&FL 1, 2, 92; SmATA 3; WhoAmW 68*

Woolsey, R. James
American. Government Official
Director, CIA, 1995-95.
b. Sep 21, 1941 in Tulsa, Oklahoma
Source: *IntWW 97, 98, 2000; WhoAm 84, 98; WhoAmP 91, 97, 1999; WhoGov 77*

Woolsey, Robert
[Wheeler and Woolsey]
American. Actor, Comedian
Teamed with Bert Wheeler in Broadway musical, film *Rio Rita*, 1929; vaudeville and comedy film stars, 1927-38.
b. Aug 14, 1889 in Oakland, California
d. Oct 31, 1938 in Malibu Beach, California
Source: *BioIn 20; Film 2; FilmEn; FilmgC; HalFC 80, 84, 88; JoeFr; MovMk; NotNAT B; WhoHol B; WhScrn 74, 77; WhThe*

Woolsey, Sarah Chauncey
[Susan Coolidge]
American. Author
Best known for Katy Did series for children: *What Katy Did*, 1872.
b. Jan 29, 1835 in Cleveland, Ohio
d. Apr 9, 1905 in Newport, Rhode Island
Source: *Alli SUP; AmAu; AmAu&B; AmBi; AmWom; AmWomPl; AmWomWr; ApCAB; BbD; BenetAL 91; BiD&SB; BioIn 15; CarSB; Chambr 3; ChhPo, S2; ConAu 115; DcAmAu; DcAmB; DcLB 42; DcLEL; DcNAA; EvLB; InWom SUP; JBA 34; LibW; LinLib L; NatCAB 11; NotAW; OhA&B; OxCChiL; PenNWW A, B; REnAL; TwCBDA; TwCChW 1A, 2A, 3A, 4A; WhAm 1; WhoChL; WomNov*

Woolworth, Frank Winfield
American. Merchant
Founded F W Woolworth Co., 1879; sold only five and ten cent items.
b. Apr 13, 1852 in Rodman, New York
d. Apr 8, 1919 in Glen Cove, New York
Source: *AmBi; AmNatBi; BiDAmBL 83; BioIn 3, 5, 6, 7, 9, 11, 12, 16, 18, 21, 24; CamBiEn; CamDcAB; ChamBiD; DcAmB; EncAB-H 1974, 1996; EncWB 98; LinLib S; McGEWB; NatCAB 11, 23; OxCAmH; WebAB 74, 79; WhAm 1; WhDW; WorAl*

Wootton, Barbara (Frances) Adam
English. Social Scientist, Economist, Educator
Student of social policy, especially of welfare and social deviance; she was one of the first "Life Peers" in Parliament and the first woman to chair that assembly.
b. 1897 in Cambridge, England
d. 1988, England

Wopat, Tom

American. Actor
Co-star of TV series "The Dukes of
Hazzard," 1979-85.
b. Sep 9, 1951 in Lodi, Wisconsin
Source: *BioIn 12, 13, 15; ConTFT 7, 19;
IntMPA 86, 88, 92, 94, 96; LegTOT*

Worcester, Joseph Emerson

American. Lexicographer
His *Comprehensive Pronouncing
Dictionary of the English Language*,
1830 caused plagiarism charge from
Noah Webster, resulting in "War of
the Dictionaries."
b. Aug 24, 1784 in Bedford, New
Hampshire
d. Oct 27, 1865
Source: *Alli; AmAu; AmAu&B; AmBi;
AmNatBi; ApCAB; BbD; BenetAL 91;
BiDAmEd; BiD&SB; BiInAmS; BioIn 3,
6, 11, 13; CamBiEn; CamDcAB;
ChamBiD; CyEd; DcAmAu; DcAmB;
DcBiPP; DcLB 1; DcNAA; Drake;
HarEnUS; NatCAB 6; OxCAmH;
OxCAmL 65, 83, 95; REnAL; TwCBDA;
WebAB 74, 79; WebBD 83; WhAm HS*

Worden, Alfred Merrill

American. Astronaut
With NASA, 1966-72; command module
pilot of *Apollo 15*, 1971.
b. Feb 7, 1932 in Jackson, Michigan
Source: *BlueB 76; ConAu 101; IntWW
74; NewYTBE 71; WhoAm 74, 76, 78,
80, 82, 84, 86, 88, 90, 92, 94, 95, 96,
97, 98; WhoSpc; WhoSSW 73; WhoWest
76, 78; WorDWW*

Worden, John Lorimer

American. Naval Officer
Union commander of the *Monitor* in its
fight against the *Virginia*, the first such
battle of ironclads, 1862.
b. Mar 12, 1818 in Westchester County,
New York
d. Oct 18, 1897 in Washington, District
of Columbia
Source: *AmBi; AmNatBi; ApCAB; BioIn
4; CamDcAB; CivWDc; DcAmB;
DcAmMiB; Drake; EncNaHi; HarEnUS;
OxCShps; TwCBDA; WebAMB; WhAm
HS; WhCiWar*

Wordsworth, William

English. Poet
Wrote *Lyrical Ballads*, 1798, with
Coleridge; poet laureate, 1843-50.
b. Apr 7, 1770 in Cockermouth, England
d. Apr 23, 1850 in Grasmere, England
Source: *Alli; AnCL; AtlBL; BbD; Benet
87, 96; BiCoLiE; BiD&SB; BiDLA;
BiDTran; BioIn 1, 2, 3, 4, 5, 6, 7, 8, 9,
10, 11, 12, 13, 14, 15, 16, 17, 18, 19,
20, 21, 22, 23, 24; BlkwCE; BlmGEL;
BritAu 19; BritWr 4; CamBiEn;
CamGEL; CamGLE; CasWL; CelCen;
ChamBiD; Chambr 3; ChhPo, S1, S2,
S3; CnDBLB 3; CnE&AP; CrtT 2, 4;
CyEd; CyWA 58, 97; DcArts; DcBiPP;
DcEnA; DcEnL; DcEuL; DcLB 93, 107;
DcLEL; DcNaB; DcPup; Dis&D;
EncWB 98; EvLB; GrWrEL P; IlEncMy;*

*LegTOT; LinLib L, S; LiveWoA;
LngCEL; LuthC 75; MagSWL;
McGEWB; MouLC 3; NewC; NewCBEL;
NinCLC 12, 38; NotPoe; OxCBrHi;
OxCEng 67, 85, 95; OxCMus; PenC
ENG; PoeCrit 4; PoLE; RAdv 1, 14, 13-
1; RComWL; REn; RfGEnL 91; RGFBP;
Str&VC; WebE&AL; WhDW; WorAl;
WorAlBi; WorLitC; WrPh*

Work, Monroe (Nathan)

American. Sociologist
Published the *Negro Year Book* and a
bibliography on African Americans.
Was active in the anti-lynching
campaign and the Negro Health Week
movement.
b. Aug 15, 1866 in Iredell County, North
Carolina
d. May 2, 1945
Source: *AmNatBi; BioIn 2, 5, 9, 12, 23;
DcAmNB; EncAACR; InB&W 80, 85;
NotBlAM; PeoHis; SelBAAf; SelBAAu;
WhAm 2; WhNAA; WhoColR*

Workman, Fanny Bullock

American. Explorer
Pioneer Himalayan explorer.
b. 1859 in Worcester, Massachusetts
d. Jan 22, 1925 in Cannes, France
Source: *AmAu&B; AmBi; AmNatBi;
BenetAL 91; BiD&SB; BioIn 3, 7, 11,
12, 14, 18, 20, 24; DcAmAu; DcAmB;
DcLB 189; DcNAA; Expl 93; GrLiveH;
IntDcWB; InWom, SUP; LibW; NotAW;
REnAL; WhAm 1; WhWE; WomFir;
WomWWA 14*

Worl, Rosita

American. Anthropologist
Publisher, editor, and founder, *Alaska
Native News*, 1982-87; special staff
assistant for Native affairs to Alaska
governor Steve Cowper, 1987-89; won
Gloria Steinem Award for
Empowerment, 1989.
Source: *BioIn 21; NotNaAm*

Worley, Jo Anne

American. Comedian, Actor, Singer
Starred on TV series "Laugh-In," 1968-
73.
b. Sep 6, 1937 in Lowell, Indiana
Source: *BiE&WWA; IntMPA 96;
LegTOT; NotNAT; WhoEnt 92; WhoHol
92*

Worner, Manfred

German. Statesman
First German secretary-general of
NATO, 1988-94; W German defense
minister, 1982-88.
b. Sep 24, 1934 in Stuttgart, Germany
d. Aug 13, 1994 in Brussels, Belgium
Source: *BioIn 13, 15, 16; CamBiEn;
ChamBiD; CurBio 88, 94N; EncWB 98;
IntWW 83, 89, 91, 93; NewYTBS 87, 94;
WhAm 11; Who 90, 92, 94; WhoWor 84,
87, 89, 91, 93*

Worrell, Todd Roland

American. Baseball Player
Pitcher, St. Louis, 1985-92; LA Dodgers,
1992—; led NFL in saves, 1986;
rookie of year, 1986.
b. Sep 28, 1959 in Arcadia, California
Source: *Ballpl 90; BaseEn 88; BaseReg
87, 88; BioIn 15; NewYTBS 87*

Worrill, Conrad (W.)

American. Educator, Journalist, Political
Activist
Influential African American activist
contributed to the Civil Rights
movement in the 1960s and helped
mobilize the Million Man March in
the 1990s; journalist for the *Chicago
Defender* and host of radio talk show.
b. Aug 15, 1941 in Pasadena, California
Source: *DrAS 99H; WhoAfA 9, 10, 11,
12; WhoBlA 6, 7, 8*

Worsham, Lew(is Elmer)

American. Golfer
National Open champion, 1947; leading
money winner in 1952 tournaments.
b. Oct 5, 1917 in Altavista, Virginia
d. Oct 19, 1990 in Poquoson, Virginia
Source: *BiDAmSp Sup; BioIn 3, 7, 10,
17; CurBio 54, 91N; WhoGolf*

Worsley, Gump

[Lorne John Worsley]
Canadian. Hockey Player
Goalie, 1952-74, with three NHL teams;
won Vezina Trophy twice; Hall of
Fame, 1980.
b. May 14, 1929 in Montreal, Quebec,
Canada
Source: *BioIn 10, 12; ConAu 111;
HocEn; LegTOT; NewYTBE 72;
WhoHcky 73; WhoSpor*

Worters, Roy

"Shrimp"
Canadian. Hockey Player
Goalie, 1925-37, mostly with NY
Americans; won Hart Trophy, 1929,
Vezina Trophy, 1931; Hall of Fame,
1969.
b. Oct 19, 1900 in Toronto, Ontario,
Canada
d. Nov 7, 1957 in Toronto, Ontario,
Canada
Source: *HocEn; WhoHcky 73*

Worth, Charles Frederick

English. Fashion Designer
Founded House of Worth, Paris, 1858;
began Parisian haute couture.
b. Oct 13, 1825 in Bourne, England
d. Mar 10, 1895 in Paris, France
Source: *BioIn 2, 3, 5, 6, 12, 13;
CamBiEn; ChamBiD; DcArts; DcNaB;
EncFash; ThHDFas; WhoFash, 88;
WorAl; WorAlBi; WorFshn*

Worth, Irene

American. Actor
Won Tony for *Sweet Bird of Youth*,
1976.
b. Jun 23, 1916 in Nebraska

Source: *BiE&WWA; BioIn 8, 16, 22;*
BlueB 76; CamBiEn; CamDcAB;
CamGWoT; ChamBiD; CnThe; ConTFT
3, 10, 17; CurBio 68; EncWT; Ent;
FacFETw; FilmgC; HalFC 80, 84, 88;
IntDcT 3; IntMPA 81, 82, 84, 86, 88, 92,
94, 96; IntWW 74, 75, 76, 77, 78, 79,
80, 81, 82, 83, 89, 91, 93, 97, 98, 2000;
IntWWW 2; InWom, SUP; ItaFilm;
LegTOT; NotNAT; NotWoAT; OxCAmT
84; OxCThe 83; PlP&P; Who 74, 82,
83, 85, 88, 90, 92, 94, 98, 99, 2000;
WhoAm 74, 76, 78, 80, 82, 84, 86, 88,
90, 92, 94, 95, 96, 97, 98, 99, 2000;
WhoAmW 74, 81, 83, 93, 95, 97, 99;
WhoE 93, 95, 97, 99; WhoEnt 92, 98;
WhoHol 92, A; WhoThe 72, 77, 81;
WhoWor 74; WorAl; WorAlBi

Worthy, James Ager

American. Basketball Player
Forward, LA Lakers, 1982-94; won three
  NBA championships; MVP, 1988
  playoffs.
b. Feb 27, 1961 in Gastonia, New York
Source: *BiDAmSp Sup; BioIn 13, 15;*
News 91; NewYTBS 83; OfNBA 87;
WhoAm 90, 96, 97; WhoBlA 4, 7;
WhoWest 92, 96; WorAlBi

Wortman, Denys

American. Cartoonist
Worked for *NY World,* 1924-30; *NY*
  World-Telegram; Sun, 1930-54; proofs
  collected in Metropolitan Museum of
  Art, NYC.
b. May 1, 1887 in Saugerties, New York
d. Sep 20, 1958 in Massachusetts
Source: *BioIn 1, 3, 5; EncACom; IlrAm*
1880, D; ObitOF 79; WhAm 3;
WhAmArt 85; WhoAmA 84N; WorECar

Wortman, Sterling

American. Geneticist
Work at Rockefeller Foundation included
  "miracle grains."
b. Apr 3, 1923 in Quinlan, Oklahoma
d. May 26, 1981 in Greenwich,
  Connecticut
Source: *AmMWSc 82; AmNatBi; AnObit*
1981; ConAu 108; FacFETw; NewYTBS
81; WhAm 7, 8; WhoAm 74, 76, 78, 80,
82; WhoWor 74, 80

Woss, Kurt

Austrian. Conductor
Directed Tokyo's Fumiwara Opera,
  1970s.
b. May 2, 1914 in Linz, Austria
Source: *BakBD 78, 84, 92; BakBDTw;*
PenDiMP

Wottle, Dave

[David J. Wottle]
American. Track Athlete
Middle-distance runner; won gold medal
  in 800-meters, 1972 Olympics; known
  for running in golf cap.
b. Aug 7, 1950 in Canton, Ohio
Source: *BiDAmSp OS; BioIn 10;*
NewYTBS 74; WhoSpor; WhoTr&F 73

Wouk, Herman

American. Author, Dramatist
Wrote *The Caine Mutiny; The Winds of*
  War, 1971; *War and Remembrance,*
  1978; won Pulitzer for *The Caine*
  Mutiny.
b. May 27, 1915 in New York, New
  York
Source: *AmAu&B; AmNov; Au&Wr 71;*
BeaEPF; Benet 87, 96; BenetAL 91;
BiCoLiE; BiE&WWA; BioIn 1, 2, 3, 4, 5,
8, 9, 13, 17, 22, 24; BlueB 76;
CamBiEn; CamDcAB; CelR 90;
ChamBiD; CnMD; ConAu 5R, 6NR,
33NR, 67NR; ConJeAN; ConLC 1, 9, 38;
ConNov 72, 76, 82, 86, 91, 96;
ConPopW; ConTFT 1; CroCD; CurBio
52; CyWA 89, 97; DcLB Y82B; DcLEL
1940; EncALit; EncSF, 93; EncWL 1;
EncWT; FilmgC; HalFC 80, 84, 88;
IntAu&W 76, 77, 82, 89, 91, 93; IntWW
74, 75, 76, 77, 78, 79, 80, 81, 82, 83,
89, 91, 93, 97, 98, 2000; JeAmFiW;
JeAmHC; LegTOT; LinLib L; LngCTC;
MajTwCW 1, 2; ModAL 4, 5; ModWD;
ModWr; NatPD 81; NotNAT; Novels;
OxCAmL 65, 83, 95; OxCTwCL; PenC
AM; REn; REnAL; ScF&FL 1; ScFSB;
TwCA SUP; TwCWr; WebAB 74, 79;
Who 74, 82, 83, 85, 88, 90, 92, 94, 98,
99, 2000; WhoAm 74, 76, 78, 80, 82, 84,
86, 88, 90, 92, 94, 95, 96, 97, 98, 99,
2000; WhoAmJ 80; WhoE 83, 99;
WhoEnt 98; WhoPul; WhoRel 92;
WhoUSWr 88; WhoWor 74, 76, 78, 80,
82, 84, 87, 89, 91, 93, 95, 96, 97, 98,
99, 2000; WhoWorJ 72, 78; WhoWrEP
89, 92, 95; WorAl; WorAlBi; WorAu
1900; WrDr 76, 80, 82, 84, 86, 88, 90,
92, 94, 96, 98, 99, 2000

Wovoka

[Jack Wilson]
American. Religious Leader, Mystic
Originator of "Ghost Dance," 1890-91
  regarded as messiah by followers.
b. 1856 in Esmeralda County, Nevada
d. Sep 29, 1932 in Schurz, Nevada
Source: *ABCNaAm; BioIn 7, 11, 12;*
CamBiEn; DcAmB; DcAmReB 1, 2;
EncAInd; EncARH; EncNAB; EncNAR;
EncWB 98; NotNaAm; OxCAmH;
RelLAm 1, 2; TwCSAPR; WebAB 74, 79;
WhAm 4, HSA; WhNaAH

Wozniak, Steven

"Rocky Raccoon Clark"
American. Computer Executive
Co-founder, Apple Computers, Inc; had
  sales of $583 million in 1982.
b. 1950? in Sunnyvale, California
Source: *BioIn 12, 13; LElec*

Wragge, Sidney

American. Designer
Uniform, understated sportswear for men,
  women sold under B H Wragge label
  since 1935.
b. Mar 10, 1908 in New York, New
  York
d. Mar 28, 1978 in Boca Raton, Florida
Source: *WorFshn*

Wrangel, Ferdinand Petrovich, Baron

Russian. Explorer
Governor of Russian America (Alaska);
  promoted civilization of area, 1827-34.
b. Jan 9, 1797 in Pskov, Russia
d. Jun 6, 1870 in Tartu, Estonia
Source: *Drake*

Wrangel, Pietr Nikolayevich

Russian. Army Officer
General; served in Russo-Japanese War,
  1904-05, WW I, 1914-17; commanded
  volunteer army, 1920.
b. Aug 27, 1878 in Novo-Aleksandrovsk,
  Lithuania
d. Apr 25, 1928 in Brussels, Belgium
Source: *REn; WebBD 83*

Wrather, William Embry

American. Geologist, Government
  Official
Petroleum expert; director, US
  Geological Survey, 1943-56.
b. Jan 20, 1883 in Meade County,
  Kentucky
d. Nov 28, 1963 in Washington, District
  of Columbia
Source: *AmNatBi; BioIn 1, 3, 6, 7, 9;*
DcAmB S7; EncAB-A 36; NatCAB 52;
WhAm 4

Wray, Fay

Canadian. Actor
Starred in *King Kong,* 1933.
b. Sep 10, 1907 in Cardston, Alberta,
  Canada
Source: *BiDFilm 94; BioIn 8, 11, 12, 14,*
16, 17, 18, 20; ChamBiD; CmMov;
ConTFT 8; DcArts; Film 2; FilmEn;
FilmgC; ForYSC; FrSilen; GangFlm;
HalFC 80, 84, 88; HolP 30; IntDcF 1-3,
2-3; IntMPA 75, 76, 77, 78, 79, 80, 81,
82, 84, 86, 88, 92, 94, 96; InWom SUP;
LegTOT; MotPP; MovMk; NewYTBS 89;
OxCFilm; ThFT; TwYS; What 2;
WhoHol 92, A; WhoHrs 80; WomHorF
1930; WorAl; WorAlBi

Wray, Link

[Lincoln Wray]
American. Musician, Singer, Songwriter
Recorded instrumental hit single
  "Rumble," 1958; released debut
  album *Link Wray and the Wraymen,*
  1960; later recorded *Beans and*
  Fatback, 1973 and *Indian Child,* 1993.
b. May 2, 1935 in Dunn, North Carolina
Source: *ConMus 17; PenEncP; WhoRock*
81

Wren, Christopher, Sir

English. Architect
Built 52 London churches; helped rebuild
  London after 1666 fire.
b. Oct 20, 1632 in East Knoyle, England
d. Feb 25, 1723 in London, England
Source: *Alli; AsBiEn; AtlBL; Benet 87,*
96; BiDBrA; BiHiMed; BioIn 1, 2, 3, 4,
5, 6, 7, 8, 9, 10, 11, 12, 13, 14, 17, 20,
23; BlmGEL; CamBiEn; ChamBiD;
DcArch; DcArts; DcBiPP; DcD&D;
DcLB 213; DcNaB, C; DcScB; Dis&D;

EncEnl; EncUrb; EncWB 98; InSci;
IntDcAr; LegTOT; LinLib S; LngCEL;
MacEA; McGDA; McGEWB; NewC;
NewCBEL; NotNAT B; OxCArt;
OxCBrHi; OxCCAA; OxCEng 95;
OxCMed 86; OxCThe 67; RAdv 14, 13-
3; REn; WhDW; WhoArch; WhoChr;
WorAl; WorAlBi

Wright, Almroth Edward, Sir
English. Physician, Bacteriologist
One of founders of modern immunology;
    caricatured in Shaw's The Doctor's
    Dilemma.
b. Aug 10, 1861 in Richmond, England
d. Apr 30, 1947 in Cliveden, England
Source: BiESc; BioIn 7, 14, 20;
CamBiEn; ChamBiD; DcNaB 1941;
DcScB; GrBr; InSci; LarDcSc; LinLib S;
McGCEnS; NewCol 75; NotTwCS 1;
ObitOF 79; OxCMed 86; RanHWDS;
WhLit; WorScD

Wright, Bruce McMarion
American. Government Official
NY State Supreme Court justice, 1983—
    ; book Black Robes, White Justice,
    addressed the issue of racism in law,
    1987.
b. Dec 19, 1918 in Princeton, New
    Jersey
Source: BlkAWP; ConBlB 3; InB&W 80,
85; NewYTBS 79; WhoBlA 7

Wright, Carroll Davidson
American. Statistician, Economist
Organized the Bureau of Labor Statistics
    and encouraged and produced
    objective research on labor problems.
b. Jul 25, 1840 in Dunbarton, New
    Hampshire
d. Feb 20, 1909 in Worcester,
    Massachusetts
Source: Alli SUP; AmAu&B; AmBi;
AmSocL; ApCAB, X; BbD; BiD&SB;
BiInAmS; BioIn 3, 4, 5, 19; DcAmAu;
DcAmB; DcAmSR; DcNAA; EncAB-H
1974, 1996; EncWB 98; HarEnUS;
McGEWB; NatCAB 19; TwCBDA;
WebAB 74, 79; WhAm 1

Wright, Cobina
American. Journalist, Singer
Had leading roles in several operas;
    columnist for Hearst Newspapers.
b. Aug 14, 1921 in Lakeview, Oregon
d. Apr 9, 1970 in Hollywood, California
Source: BioIn 15; InWom SUP;
NewYTBE 70; WhAm 5; WhoHol 92, A

Wright, Elizur
American. Social Reformer, Abolitionist,
    Suffragist
Activist worked for the abolition of
    slavery, women's suffrage, and
    conservation.
b. Feb 12, 1804 in Connecticut
d. Nov 21, 1885
Source: Alli, SUP; AmNatBi; AmRef;
ApCAB; BbD; BiD&SB; BiInAmS; BioIn
15, 16; CamDcAB; ChhPo S1; DcAmAu;
DcAmB; DcAmSR; DcNAA; Drake;
EncWB 98; HarEnUS; McGEWB;

NatCAB 2; OhA&B; OxCAmH; PeoHis;
TwCBDA; WebAB 74, 79; WhAm HS

Wright, Frances
[Fanny Wright]
American. Social Reformer, Author
Scandalized America by lecturing on
    birth control, woman's rights; co-
    founded colony for freed slaves, 1827.
b. Sep 6, 1795 in Dundee, Scotland
d. Dec 13, 1852 in Cincinnati, Ohio
Source: Alli; AmAu; AmAu&B; AmBi;
AmNatBi; AmPeW; AmRef; AmSocL;
ApCAB; ArtclWW 2; BenetAL 91;
BiDAmJo; BiDAmLf; BiD&SB; BiDBrF
1; BioIn 3, 4, 6, 7, 9, 10, 11, 12, 13, 14,
15, 16, 18, 19, 20, 21; CamDcAB;
ChamBiD; ContDcW 89; DcAmAu;
DcAmB; DcAmSR; DcLB 73; DcNaB;
Drake; EncAB-H 1974, 1996; EncAWoR;
EncBrWW; EncUnb; EncWB 98;
EncWoAP; FemiCLE; GoodHs;
HarEnUS; HerW, 84; IntDcWB; InWom
SUP; LibW; McGEWB; NatCAB 2;
NinCLC 74; NotAW; OhA&B; OxCAmH;
OxCAmL 65, 83, 95; PenNWW A;
PeoHis; RadHan; RComAH; REnAL;
WebAB 74, 79; WhAm HS; WhAmP;
WorAl; WorAlBi

Wright, Frank Lloyd
American. Architect
Designer of homes of functional,
    dramatic simplicity who helped
    develop skyscrapers, 1912-36.
b. Jun 8, 1869 in Richland Center,
    Wisconsin
d. Apr 9, 1959 in Phoenix, Arizona
Source: AmAu&B; AmDec 1950; AtlBL;
Benet 87, 96; BenetAL 91; BioIn 1, 2, 3,
4, 5, 6, 7, 8, 9, 10, 11, 12, 13; BriEAA;
CmCal; ConHero 1; CurBio 59; DcArch;
DcArts; DcD&D; DcLEL; EncAAH;
EncAB-H 1974, 1996; EncUrb; EncWB
98; GayN; LinLib L, S; LngCTC;
MakMC; McGDA; McGEWB; MemAm;
ModArCr 1; ObitT 1951; OxCAmH;
OxCAmL 65, 83, 95; OxCArt; OxCDecA;
PlP&P; REn; REnAL; TwCA SUP;
WebAB 74, 79; WhAm 3; WhAmArt 85;
WhDW; WhFla; WhLit; WorAl; WorAu
1900

Wright, Gary
[Spooky Tooth]
American. Musician
Left rock band Spooky Tooth, 1970, for
    solo career; hit albums include Dream
    Weaver, 1976; Really Wanna Know
    You, 1981.
b. Apr 26, 1943 in Englewood, New
    Jersey
Source: ASCAP 80; ConMuA 80A;
IlEncRk; LegTOT; RkOn 78; RolSEnR
83; WhoRock 81

Wright, George
American. Baseball Player
Shortstop, 1876-82; first batter in NL
    history; Hall of Fame, 1937.
b. Jan 28, 1847 in New York, New York
d. Aug 31, 1937 in Boston,
    Massachusetts

Source: AmNatBi; Ballpl 90; BiDAmSp
BB; BioIn 3, 4, 7, 14, 15; CamDcAB;
CulEncB; DcAmB S2; WhoProB 73;
WhoSpor

Wright, Harold Bell
American. Author
Best known novels The Shepherd of the
    Hills, 1907; The Winning of Barbara
    Worth, 1911; works popular for moral
    lessons.
b. May 4, 1872 in Rome, New York
d. May 24, 1944 in La Jolla, California
Source: AmAu&B; AmLY; AmNatBi;
ArizL; BeaEPF; BenetAL 91; BioIn 1, 2,
4, 10, 12, 15, 20, 22; CamDcAB;
CmCal; ConAu 110; CurBio 44; DcAmB
S3; DcLB 9; DcLEL; DcNAA; Dis&D;
EncALit; EncFWF; EncSF 93; EvLB;
LinLib L; LngCTC; NatCAB 34;
OxCAmL 65, 83, 95; PeoHis; REnAL;
ScF&FL 1; TwCA, SUP; TwCSFW 81;
TwCWW 91; WebAB 74, 79; WhAm 2;
WhE&EA; WhNAA; WorAu 1900

Wright, Harry
[William Henry Wright]
American. Baseball Manager
Organized, managed baseball's first pro
    team, Cincinnati Red Stockings, 1866;
    Hall of Fame, 1953.
b. Jan 10, 1835 in Sheffield, England
d. Oct 3, 1895 in Atlantic City, New
    Jersey
Source: Ballpl 90; BiDAmSp BB; BioIn
3, 7, 14, 15, 21; CulEncB; LegTOT;
WhoProB 73; WhoSpor

Wright, Henry
American. Architect
Landscape designer, town planner; wrote
    Rehousing Urban America, 1935.
b. Jul 2, 1878 in Lawrence, Kansas
d. Jul 9, 1936 in Newton, New Jersey
Source: AmNatBi; BiDAmAr; BioIn 3, 4,
5; DcAmB S2; EncUrb; MacEA; NatCAB
27; WebAB 74, 79

Wright, Horatio Gouverneur
American. Army Officer, Engineer
Civil War Union general who led
    defense of Washington, DC, 1864.
b. May 5, 1820 in Clinton, Connecticut
d. Jul 2, 1899 in Washington, District of
    Columbia
Source: AmBi; AmNatBi; ApCAB;
BakBD 84; BioIn 7; CivWDc; DcAmB;
HarEnMi; HarEnUS; TwCBDA;
WebAMB; WhAm HS; WhCiWar

Wright, James Arlington
American. Poet
Writings include The Green Wall, 1957;
    Shall We Gather at the River, 1968.
b. Dec 13, 1927 in Martins Ferry, Ohio
d. Mar 25, 1980 in New York, New
    York
Source: AmAu&B; AmNatBi; AuNews 2;
BiCoLiE; BioIn 10, 11, 22; ChhPo, S1;
CnE&AP; ConAu 4NR, 49, 64NR, 97;
ConLC 3, 5, 10; ConPo 70, 75;
CroCAP; DcLEL 1940; DrAP 75;
EncALit; IntWWP 77; MajTwCW 2;

ModAL 4, 4S1; PenC AM; RAdv 1;
RfGAmL 4; WebE&AL; WhoAm 74, 76,
78, 80; WhoTwCL; WorAu 1950; WrDr
76

Wright, Jane Cooke
American. Physician
Pioneered in cancer chemotheraphy
research.
b. Nov 30, 1919 in New York, New
York
Source: AmMWSc 76P, 79, 82, 86, 89;
AZWoSci; BioIn 8, 11, 20, 22; BlksScM;
CurBio 68; InB&W 80, 85; InWom,
SUP; NegAl 83, 89; NotBlAS; NotBlAW
1; NotTwCS 1; NotWoLS; SciMath;
WhoAm 74, 76, 78, 80, 82, 84, 86, 88,
90, 92, 94, 95, 96, 97, 98, 99, 2000;
WhoAmW 58, 61, 64, 66, 68, 70, 72, 74,
75, 77; WhoBlA 4, 7

Wright, Jerauld
American. Naval Officer, Diplomat
Commanded US naval forces in the
eastern Atlantic and Mediterranean,
1952-54; ambassador to Taiwan, 1963-
65.
b. Jun 4, 1898
d. Apr 27, 1995 in Washington, District
of Columbia
Source: BioIn 3, 4, 5, 20, 21; CurBio
95N; WhAm 10; Who 74, 82, 83, 85, 88,
90, 92, 94; WhoAmP 73, 75, 77, 79

Wright, Jim
[James Claud Wright, Jr.]
American. Politician
Dem. con. from TX, 1955-87; succeeded
Tip O'Neill as Speaker of House,
1987.
b. Dec 22, 1922 in Fort Worth, Texas
Source: AlmAP 78, 80, 82, 84, 88;
AmPolLe; BiDAmNC; BiDrUSC 89;
BioIn 12, 14, 15, 16, 19, 22; CngDr 87,
89; ConAu 49, 127; CurBio 79; IntWW
91; NewYTBS 87; PolsAm 84; Who 92;
WhoAm 86, 90; WhoAmP 87, 91;
WhoSSW 91; WhoWor 91; WorAlBi

Wright, John Joseph
American. Religious Leader
Cardinal who was highest ranking
American in Vatican, 1967-79; author,
The Christian and the Law, 1962.
b. Jul 18, 1909 in Boston, Massachusetts
d. Aug 10, 1979 in Cambridge,
Massachusetts
Source: AmCath 80; AmNatBi; BioIn 6,
11, 12; CamDcAB; ConAu 2NR; CurBio
79; DcAmB S10; IntWW 74, 75, 76, 77,
78, 79; NewYTBS 79; RelLAm 1, 2;
WhoAm 78; WhoWor 74, 78

Wright, John Lloyd
American. Architect, Engineer
Son of Frank Lloyd Wright; established
own practice, 1926.
b. Dec 12, 1892 in Oak Park, Illinois
d. Dec 20, 1972
Source: BioIn 3, 4, 10, 12, 13; McGDA;
WhAm 5

Wright, Lloyd
[Frank Lloyd Wright, Jr.]
American. Architect
Best known for cleaning up slum areas;
designed Wayfarer's Chapel in LA,
CA.
b. Mar 31, 1890 in Oak Park, Illinois
d. May 31, 1978 in Santa Monica,
California
Source: BioIn 10, 11; ConArch 80, 87;
MacEA; NewYTBS 78; ObitOF 79;
WhoAmA 80N, 82N, 84N, 86N, 89N,
91N, 93N; WhoArch

Wright, Louis Booker
American. Educator, Library
Administrator
Director, Folger Shakespeare Library,
1948-68.
b. Mar 1, 1899 in Greenwood, South
Carolina
d. Feb 26, 1984 in Chevy Chase,
Maryland
Source: AmAu&B; AnObit 1984; Au&Wr
71; BioIn 1, 2, 3, 8, 13; BlueB 76;
ChhPo S1, S3; ConAu 1NR, 1R, 112;
CurBio 50, 84; DrAS 74H, 78H, 82H;
IntAu&W 77, 82; IntWW 74, 75, 76, 77,
78, 79, 80, 81, 82, 83; REnAL; ScrEAmL
1; WhAm 8; WhE&EA; Who 74, 82, 83;
WhoAm 74, 76, 78, 80, 82, 84; WrDr 76,
80, 82, 84

Wright, Louis Tompkins
American. Surgeon
One of the first US African-American
surgeons; many accomplishments as a
doctor and researcher.
b. Jul 23, 1891 in La Grange, Georgia
d. Oct 8, 1952 in New York, New York
Source: AmNatBi; BioIn 3, 6, 8, 9, 11,
19, 20; BlksScM; ConBlB 4; DcAmMeB
84; DcAmNB; InB&W 80, 85; InSci;
NatCAB 43; NegAl 83, 89; NotBlAM;
NotBlAS; NotTwCS 1; RanHWDS;
WhAm 3; WorScD

Wright, Martha
American. Singer, Actor
Replaced Mary Martin in South Pacific,
1951; played Nellie Forbush role
1,080 times.
b. Mar 23, 1926 in Seattle, Washington
Source: BiE&WWA; BioIn 3, 4; CurBio
55; InWom; NotNAT; WhoE 89; WhoEnt
92

Wright, Mickey
[Mary Kathryn Wright]
American. Golfer
Turned pro, 1954; has 82 career wins,
including record 14, 1963; LPGA
leading money winner, 1961-64.
b. Feb 14, 1935 in San Diego, California
Source: BiDAmSp OS; BioIn 5, 6, 7, 9,
12, 14, 17; CmCal; CurBio 65;
EncWomS; EncWoSp; GoodHs; InWom,
SUP; LegTOT; LibW; NewYTBS 76;
OutWomA; WhoGolf; WhoSpor; WorAl;
WorAlBi

Wright, Orville
[The Wright Brothers]
American. Inventor, Aviator
Designed engine and flew first flight in
power-driven airplane, 1903.
b. Aug 19, 1871 in Dayton, Ohio
d. Jan 30, 1948 in Dayton, Ohio
Source: AmDec 1900; AsBiEn; BenetAL
91; BioIn 1, 2, 3, 4, 5, 6, 7, 8, 9, 10, 11,
12, 13, 14, 15, 16, 17, 18, 20, 21, 23,
24; ChambiD; ConHero 3; CurBio 46,
48; DcAmB S4; DcScB; DcTwDes;
EncAB-H 1974, 1996; FacFETw; InSci;
LarDcSc; LegTOT; McGEWB; MemAm;
NatCAB 14; OxCAmH; RComAH; REn;
REnAL; SciMath; WebAB 74, 79; WhAm
2; WhDW; WorAl; WorAlBi; WorInv

Wright, Peter (Maurice)
English. Author, Spy
Memoirs of his yrs. as British
counterintelligence officer, Spycatcher,
became int'l. best seller, 1987.
b. 1916 in Chesterfield, England
d. Apr 27, 1995 in Sydney, Australia
Source: ConAu 128, 148; CurBio 88,
95N; FacFETw

Wright, Richard (Nathaniel)
American. Author
Became country's leading black author
with publication of Native Son, 1940.
b. Sep 4, 1908 in Natchez, Mississippi
d. Nov 28, 1960 in Paris, France
Source: AfrAmAl 6; AfrAmW; AgeMat;
AmAu&B; AmCulL; AmDec 1940;
AmNov; AmWr; Au&Arts 5; Benet 87,
96; BenetAL 91; BioIn 1, 2, 3, 4, 5, 6, 7,
8, 9, 10, 11, 12, 13, 14, 15, 16, 17, 18,
19, 20, 21; BlkAmP; BlkAmW 2;
BlkAWP; BlkLC; BlkWr 1; CamDcAB;
CamGEL; CamGLE; CamHAL; CasWL;
ChambiD; CnDAL; ConAu 64NR, 108;
ConBlB 5; ConLC 1, 3, 4, 9, 14, 21, 48,
74; ConNov 76; CyWA 58, 89; DcAmB
S6; DcAmNB; DcAmSR; DcArts; DcLB
76, 102, DS2; DcLEL; DcTwCCu 5;
Dis&D; DrBlPA, 90; EncAACR; EncAB-
H 1974, 1996; EncAL; EncALit;
EncSoH; EncWL 1, 2, 2S; EvLB;
FacFETw; FifSWrA; GrWrEL N; InB&W
80, 85; LegTOT; LiExTwC; LinLib L;
LiveMA; LngCTC; MagSAmL;
MajTwCW 1, 2; McGEWB; ModAL 4,
4S1, 4S2; ModBlW; NegAl 76, 83, 89;
NotNAT A, B; Novels; ObitT 1951;
OxCAmL 65, 83, 95; OxCEng 85, 95;
OxCTwCL; PenC AM; PeoHis; PlP&P;
RAdv 1, 14, 13-1; RComAH; REn;
REnAL; RfGAmL 4, 87, 94; RfGShF 1,
2; RGTwCWr; SchCGBL; SelBAAf;
SelBAAu; ShSCr 2; SJGYouA 2;
SouBlCW; SouWr; TwCA, SUP; TwCWr;
TwCYAW 1; WebAB 74, 79; WebE&AL;
WhAm 4; WhDW; WhoTwCL; WorAl;
WorAlBi; WorLitC; WrPh

Wright, Rick
[Pink Floyd; Richard Wright]
English. Singer, Musician
Keyboard player with band on and off
since its formation.
b. Jul 28, 1945 in London, England
Source: WhoRocM 82

Wright, Robert C
American. TV Executive
Chm., CEO, NBC, 1986—.
b. Apr 23, 1943 in Hempstead, New
    York
Source: *BioIn 15; CurBio 89; Dun&B
90, 98; IntMPA 92; LesBEnT 92;
WhoAm 90; WhoE 91; WhoEmL 87;
WhoEnt 92; WhoFI 87*

Wright, Russel
American. Designer
Industrial designer who combined
    functional efficiency with ease,
    integrity of design; designed chair,
    1933, now in Museum of Modern Art.
b. Apr 3, 1904 in Lebanon, Ohio
d. Dec 22, 1976 in New York, New
    York
Source: *AmNatBi; BioIn 11, 13;
CamDcAB; ConAu 69; ConDes 84, 90,
97; CurBio 77; DcTwDes; McGDA;
PenDiDA 89; WhAm 7; WhoAm 74, 76,
78; WhoAmA 73, 76, 78N, 80N, 82N,
84N, 86N, 89N, 91N, 93N*

Wright, Steven
American. Comedian
Stand-up comic since 1979; films include
    Desperately Seeking Susan, 1985.
b. Dec 6, 1955 in New York, New York
Source: *BioIn 14, 15, 16; ConNews 86-
3; ConTFT 9; LegTOT; NewYTBS 85;
WhoCom; WhoEnt 98*

Wright, Syretta
American. Singer, Songwriter
Ex-wife of Stevie Wonder; had hit
    "With You I'm Born Again," 1980
    with Billy Preston.
b. 1946 in Pittsburgh, Pennsylvania
Source: *BioIn 10; InB&W 85; RolSEnR
83*

Wright, Teresa
American. Actor
Won 1941 Oscar for *Mrs. Miniver;*
    nominated in same year for *Pride of
    the Yankees.*
b. Oct 27, 1918 in New York, New York
Source: *BiDFilm, 94; BiE&WWA; BioIn
10, 17; ConTFT 3, 10, 17; CurBio 43;
FilmEn; FilmgC; ForYSC; HalFC 80,
84, 88; HolP 40; IntDcF 1-3, 2-3;
IntMPA 79, 80, 81, 82, 84, 86, 88, 92,
94, 96; InWom, SUP; LegTOT; MotPP;
MovMk; NotNAT; OsStAZ; PIP&P;
WhoHol 92, A; WhoThe 72, 77, 81;
WorAl; WorAlBi; WorEFlm*

Wright, Wilbur
[The Wright Brothers]
American. Inventor, Aviator
With brother, Orville, made first
    sustained, controlled flight in power-
    driven airplane, 1903.
b. Apr 16, 1867 in Millville, Indiana
d. May 30, 1912 in Dayton, Ohio
Source: *AmBi; AmDec 1900; AmNatBi;
ApCAB X; AsBiEn; BenetAL 91;
BiInAmS; BioIn 1, 2, 3, 4, 5, 6, 7, 8, 9,
10, 11, 12, 13, 14, 15, 16, 17, 18, 20,
21, 23, 24; CamDcAB; CamDcSc;*

*ConHero 3; DcAmB; DcScB; DcTwDes;
EncAB-H 1996; FacFETw; HarEnUS;
IndAu 1967; InSci; LarDcSc; LegTOT;
McGCEnS; McGEWB; MemAm; NatCAB
14; NotTwCS 1; OxCAmH; RComAH;
REn; REnAL; SciMath; WebAB 74, 79;
WhAm 1; WhDW; WorAl; WorAlBi;
WorInv*

Wrightsman, Charles Bierer
American. Business Executive,
    Philanthropist
Pres., Standard Oil Co., 1932-53;
    donated to NYC art museums.
b. Jun 13, 1895 in Pawnee, Oklahoma
d. May 27, 1986 in New York, New
    York
Source: *AnObit 1986; BioIn 7, 14, 15;
CelR; NewYTBS 86; WhAm 9; WhoAm
74, 76, 78, 80; WhoAmA 73, 76, 78, 80,
82*

Wrightson, Earl
American. Singer
Popular baritone; specialized in show
    tunes, 1940s-50s.
b. Jan 1, 1916 in Baltimore, Maryland
d. Mar 7, 1993 in New York, New York
Source: *AnObit 1993; BiDAmM; BioIn
18; CmpEPM; RadStar*

Wrightson, Patricia
Australian. Author
Wrote *The Crooked Snake,* 1955; *The Ice
    is Coming,* 1977.
b. Jun 19, 1921 in Lismore, Australia
Source: *Au&Arts 5; AuBYP 2, 3;
AuWomWr; BiCoLiE; BioIn 8, 11, 15,
17, 19, 22, 23; BlmGWL; CamGLE;
ChlBkCr; ChlLR 4, 14; ConAu 3NR,
19NR, 36NR, 45; FourBJA; OnHuMoP;
OxCAusL; OxCChiL; ScF&FL 1, 2, 92;
SenS; SmATA 4AS, 8, 66; TwCChW 1, 2,
3; WrDr 80, 82, 84, 86, 88, 90, 92*

Wrigley, Philip Knight
American. Business Executive, Baseball
    Executive
Son of William Jr; president, Wm
    Wrigley chewing gum co., 1925-61;
    owner, Chicago Cubs, 1932-77.
b. Dec 5, 1894 in Chicago, Illinois
d. Apr 12, 1977 in Elkhorn, Wisconsin
Source: *AmNatBi; BiDAmBL 83;
BiDAmSp BB; BioIn 10, 11, 15;
CamDcAB; CurBio 75, 77; DcAmB S10;
ObitOF 79; St&PR 75; WhAm 7;
WhoAm 74, 76; WhoFI 74; WhoMW 74*

Wrigley, William, Jr.
American. Business Executive, Baseball
    Executive
Founded Wm Wrigley chewing gum co.,
    1891; developed Catalina Island into
    major resort; bought Chicago Cubs,
    1916.
b. Sep 30, 1861 in Philadelphia,
    Pennsylvania
d. Jan 26, 1932 in Phoenix, Arizona
Source: *BiDAmBL 83; BioIn 1, 15, 18;
CamBiEn; CamDcAB; DcAmB S1; Entr;
GayN; LegTOT; NatCAB 23; WebAB 74,
79; WhAm 1; WorAl; WorAlBi*

Wrigley, William, III
American. Business Executive
Son of Philip Knight; pres., CEO, Wm
    Wrigley chewing gum co., 1961-99.
b. Jan 21, 1933 in Chicago, Illinois
d. Mar 8, 1999 in Chicago, Illinois
Source: *BiDAmBL 83; BioIn 12, 15;
Dun&B 79, 86, 88, 90, 98; IntYB 78, 79,
80, 81, 82; St&PR 75, 84, 87, 91, 93,
96, 97, 98, 99, 2000; WhoAm 74, 76, 78,
80, 82, 84, 86, 88, 90, 92, 94, 95, 96,
97; WhoFI 74, 75, 77, 79, 81, 83, 85,
87, 89, 92, 94; WhoMW 74, 76, 78, 80,
82, 84, 86, 88, 90, 92, 93; WhoWest 96;
WhoWor 74*

Wriston, Walter Bigelow
American. Banker
With Citibank since 1946; pres., 1967-
    70, chm., 1970-84; director, Citicorp
    until 1984.
b. Aug 3, 1919 in Middleton, Colorado
Source: *BioIn 7, 9, 10, 11, 12, 13, 14,
15; BlueB 76; CamDcAB; CurBio 77;
Dun&B 79, 86; EncABHB 7; IntWW 83,
91; IntYB 78; NewYTBS 85; PolProf NF;
St&PR 87, 91; WhoAm 74, 76, 78, 80,
82, 84, 86, 88, 90, 92, 94, 95, 96, 97,
98, 99, 2000; WhoE 74, 77, 79, 81, 83,
85, 86; WhoFI 74, 75, 79, 81, 83, 85;
WhoWor 74, 87; WorAl*

Wroth, Lawrence Counselman
American. Librarian, Historian
With John Carter Brown Library, 1923-
    57; wrote historical, biographical
    books.
b. Jan 14, 1884
d. Dec 25, 1970
Source: *AmAu&B; AmNatBi; BioIn 1, 9,
10, 23; ChhPo S3; ConAu 29R;
DcAmLiB; NewYTBE 70; OxCAmL 65,
83; REnAL; WhNAA*

Wroth, Mary, Lady
[Mary Sidney]
English. Author, Poet
Considered to be the first woman writer
    of English original prose fiction; wrote
    *The Countesse of Mountgomeries
    Urania,* 1621.
b. 1587, England
d. 1653?
Source: *BlmGWL; DcLB 121; FemiCLE;
LitC 30*

Wu, Chien Shiung
American. Physicist
Proved that the principle of left/right
    parity conservation does not apply to
    weak interactions of subatomic
    particles, 1957.
b. May 29, 1912, China
d. Feb 16, 1997 in New York, New
    York
Source: *AZWoSci; BioIn 5, 20, 22, 23,
24; CamBiEn; ChamBiD; ConAu 159;
CurBio 97N; EncWB 2-19; InSci;
InWom; NotTwCS 1S; NotWoPS;
SciMath; WhAm 12; WhoAm 96;
WhoScEn 96; WomFir*

Wu, Gordon (Ying Sheung)

Chinese. Entrepreneur
Founder, Hopewell Holdings Ltd., 1972;
  real estate developer in Hong Kong
  and China.
b. Dec 3, 1935, Hong Kong
Source: *BioIn 13; CurBio 96; IntWW 91,
93*

Wu, Harry

[Wu Hongda]
Chinese. Political Activist
Political prisoner in China, 1957-79;
  founder and executive director,
  Laoghai Research Foundation, 1992—
  ; exposed human rights abuses in
  China.
b. Feb 8, 1937 in Shanghai, China
Source: *ConAu 145; ConHero 3; CurBio
96; HeroCon; News 96, 96-1; WrDr 98,
99, 2000*

Wulff, Lee

American. Sports Fisherman
Sports fisherman; popularized dry fly
  fishing for salmon; designed Short
  Wading vest for fly fishermen in early
  1930s.
b. Feb 10, 1905 in Valdez, Alaska
d. Apr 28, 1991 in Hancock, New York
Source: *AnObit 1991; BioIn 13, 14, 17,
18; ConAu 61, 134; IntAu&W 89;
NewYTBS 83, 91*

Wummer, John

American. Musician
First flutist, NY Philharmonic Orchestra,
  1942-65; original member of NBC
  Orchestra under Arturo Toscanini,
  1937.
b. Dec 31, 1899 in Philadelphia,
  Pennsylvania
d. Sep 6, 1977 in San Francisco,
  California
Source: *BioIn 2, 11; NewGrDA 86;
NewGrDM 80; NewYTBS 77*

Wunder, George S

American. Cartoonist
Succeeded Caniff as artist for comic strip
  "Terry and the Pirates," 1947-73.
b. Apr 24, 1912 in New York, New
  York
d. Dec 13, 1987 in New Milford,
  Connecticut
Source: *BioIn 15; WorECom*

Wunderlich, Fritz

German. Opera Singer
Tenor who appeared in *The Silent
  Woman*, 1959; died before scheduled
  US debut at Metropolitan Opera.
b. Sep 26, 1930 in Kassel, Germany
d. Sep 17, 1966 in Heidelberg, Germany
  (West)
Source: *BakBD 84, 92; BakBDTw;
BakDcM; BioIn 7, 21; FacFETw;
IntDcOp; MetOEnc; NewAmDM;
NewGrDM 80; NewGrDO; ObitT 1961;
OxDcOp; PenDiMP; WhAm 4; WhoMus
72*

Wundt, Wilhelm Max

German. Psychologist, Philosopher
The founder of experimental psychology,
  he edited the first journal and
  established the first laboratory
  dedicated to the discipline.
b. Aug 16, 1832 in Baden, Germany
d. Aug 31, 1920 in Leipzig, Germany
Source: *AsBiEn; BbD; BiD&SB;
BiDcPsy; BioIn 2, 7, 13, 18, 23;
CamBiEn; ChamBiD; DcScB; EncWB
98; LinLib L, S; LuthC 75; McGCEnS;
McGEWB; REn; WorAlBi*

Wuorinen, Charles (Peter)

American. Composer
Leading contemporary musician known
  for achieving new heights of lyricism,
  richness, and subtlety; awarded the
  Pulitzer Prize in 1970.
b. Jun 9, 1938 in New York, New York
Source: *BakBDTw; WhoAm 97, 98, 99,
2000; WhoEnt 98*

Wu P'ei-fu

Chinese. Ruler
Considered a relatively progressive
  warlord, he controlled much of central
  and northern China during the 1920s
  as head of the Chihli clique.
b. 1874 in Shantung, China
d. Dec 4, 1939
Source: *CamBiEn; EncWB 98; ModChi*

Wurdemann, Audrey May

American. Poet
Won 1935 Pulitzer for verse *Bright
  Ambush.*
b. Jan 1, 1911 in Seattle, Washington
d. May 18, 1960 in Miami, Florida
Source: *AmAu&B; ChhPo; ConAmA;
ConAu 116; DcLEL; InWom; OxCAmL
65; REn; REnAL; TwCA, SUP; WhAm 4;
WhNAA*

Wurf, Jerry

[Jerome Wurf]
American. Labor Union Official
Pres., AFSCME, 1964-81.
b. May 18, 1919 in New York, New
  York
d. Dec 10, 1981 in Washington, District
  of Columbia
Source: *AmDec 1960; AnObit 1981;
BiDAmL; BiDAmLL; BioIn 5, 9, 10, 11,
12, 13, 24; CurBio 79, 82, 82N;
NewYTBS 74, 76, 78, 79, 81; PolProf J,
NF; WhAm 8; WhoAm 74, 76, 78, 80;
WhoAmP 73, 75, 77, 79, 81, 83; WhoE
79, 81; WhoLab 76; WhoSSW 73, 75,
76; WorAl*

Wurlitzer, Rudolph

American. Manufacturer
Introduced first automatically played,
  electric instruments, 1892.
b. Jan 31, 1831 in Schoneck, Germany
d. Jan 14, 1914 in Cincinnati, Ohio
Source: *BakBD 92; CamBiEn; Entr;
NatCAB 16; NewAmDM; WorAl;
WorAlBi*

Wurster, William

American. Architect
Designs include Ghirardelli Square, San
  Francisco; Cowell College, U of CA,
  Berkeley.
b. Oct 20, 1895 in Stockton, California
d. Sep 19, 1973
Source: *AmArch 70; CmCal; CurBio 46,
73; WhAm 6; WhoAm 74; WhoGov 72;
WhoWor 74*

Wu Tao-tzu

Chinese. Painter
Most highly regarded figure painter in
  Chinese history, style is marked by the
  kinesthetic speed of his brush.
b. c. 689 in Yang-ti, Honan Province,
  China
d. 758
Source: *EncWB 98*

Wu-ti, Han

Chinese. Emperor
Han ruler enlarged China's frontiers,
  instituted new means of income for
  the state, and made Confucianism the
  state orthodoxy.
b. 157BC
d. 87BC

Wu Tse-t'ien

Chinese. Empress
Known for her strong will and capability
  as a leader, she was the only female
  ruler of China.
b. 623, China
d. 705, China
Source: *EncWB 98*

Wu wang

Chinese. Ruler
Led the overthrow of the Shang dynasty,
  and founded the Chou dynasty.
d. 1116BC
Source: *EncWB 98*

Wyant, Alexander Helwig

American. Painter
An outstanding American landscape
  painter of the late 19th century, his
  work is characterized by luminous
  atmospheric effects.
b. Jan 11, 1836 in Port Washington,
  Ohio
d. Nov 29, 1892
Source: *AmBi; AmNatBi; ApCAB;
ArtsAmW 1, 3; BioIn 1, 15, 22; BriEAA;
DcAmArt; DcAmB; EncWB 98; McGDA;
McGEWB; NatCAB 10; NewYHSD;
OxCAmL 65; WhAmArt 85; WhAm HS*

Wyatt, Jane

American. Actor
Starred in TV series "Father Knows
  Best," 1954-62.
b. Aug 13, 1912 in Campgaw, New York
Source: *BiE&WWA; BioIn 4, 9, 11, 18,
21; ConTFT 3; CurBio 57; FilmgC;
HalFC 80, 84, 88; HolP 30; IntMPA 86,
92; InWom SUP; MotPP; MovMk;
NotNAT; SmATA X; ThFT; WhoAm 74,
76, 78, 80, 82; WhoAmW 58, 61, 64, 66,*

68, 70, 72, 74; WhoHol A; WhoThe 72, 77A; WhThe; WorAl; WorAlBi

Wyatt, Thomas, Sir
English. Poet
Introduced sonnet ending with a rhymed couplet; wrote three satire couplets.
b. 1503 in Kent, England
d. Oct 11, 1542 in Sherbourne, England
Source: *AtlBL; BbD; Benet 87, 96; BiCoLiE; BiD&SB; BiDRP&D; BioIn 1, 3, 5, 6, 7, 8, 9, 10, 11, 12, 13, 19, 20, 24; BlmGEL; BritAu; CamBiEn; CamGEL; CamGLE; CasWL; ChambID; Chambr 1; ChhPo; CnE&AP; CroE&S; CrtT 1, 4; CyWA 97; DcArts; DcBiPP; DcEnA; DcEnL; DcEuL; DcLB 132; DcLEL; DcNaB, C; EncWB 98; EvLB; GrWrEL P; LinLib L; LngCEL; McGEWB; MouLC 1; NewC; NewCBEL; NotPoe; OxCEng 67, 85, 95; PenC ENG; PoeCrit 27; RAdv 1, 13-1; REn; RfGEnL 91; RGFBP; WebBD 83; WebE&AL; WhDW*

Wyatt, Wilson W(atkins)
American. Politician
Mayor, Louisville, KY, 1941-45.
b. Nov 21, 1905
d. Jun 11, 1996 in Louisville, Kentucky
Source: *BioIn 1, 3, 5, 11, 14; CurBio 96N; WhAm 11; WhoAm 74, 76, 78, 80, 82, 84, 86, 88, 90, 92, 94, 95, 96; WhoAmP 73, 75, 77, 79, 81, 83, 85, 87, 89, 91, 93, 95; WhoFI 81, 83; WhoSSW 73, 75, 76, 78, 80, 82, 95*

Wycherley, Margaret
American. Actor
1941 Oscar nominee for *Sergeant York*.
b. 1881 in London, England
d. Jun 6, 1966 in New York, New York
Source: *ObitOF 79; PIP&P*

Wycherley, William
English. Dramatist
Known for his Restoration comedies, including *The Country Wife*, that ridiculed the manners and morals of sophisticates who delighted in illicit intrigue.
b. c. 1640 in Clive, Shropshire, England
d. Jan 1, 1716
Source: *Alli; AtlBL; Benet 87, 96; BiCoLiE; BiD&SB; BioIn 1, 2, 3, 5, 7, 8, 9, 12, 18; BlmGEL; BritAu; CamBiEn; CamGLE; CasWL; ChamBiD; Chambr 2; ChhPo; CnThe; CrtT 2; CyWA 58; DcArts; DcBiPP; DcEnA; DcEnL; DcEuL; DcLEL; DcNaB; EncWB 98; EncWT; Ent; EvLB; GrWrEL DR; LitC 8, 21; LngCEL; McGEWB; McGEWD 72, 84; MouLC 2; NewC; NotNAT A, B; OxCEng 67; OxCThe 67, 83; PenC ENG; PIP&P; RAdv 14, 13-2; REn; REnWD; WebE&AL; WhDW*

Wyclif, John
English. Theologian, Social Reformer, Author
Most influential English ecclesiastical writer in the late 14th century, he denied the doctrine of transubstantiation, believed in the sole authority of Scripture, and supported the right of the laity to confiscate Church property.
b. c. 1330, England
d. 1384, England
Source: *CrtT 4; EncWB 98; McGEWB; MediEng; OxCEng 85, 95; OxCPhil; RAdv 14, 13-4*

Wycliffe, John
English. Social Reformer, Theologian
Involved in rejection of formalism; major force behind Protestant Reformation; compiled English translation of Bible.
b. Dec 31, 1320 in Richmond, England
d. Dec 31, 1384 in Lutterworth, England
Source: *Alli; AmAu&B; BiD&SB; BioIn 1, 2, 3, 4, 5, 6, 7, 8, 9, 10, 11, 12, 13; BlmGEL; BritAu; CamGLE; CasWL; Chambr 1; CrtT 1; DcEnA; DcEnL; DcLEL; EvLB; HisWorL; LngCEL; LuthC 75; NewC; OxCEng 67; PenC ENG; REn; WebBD 83; WebE&AL; WorAl; WorAlBi*

Wyden, Ron
American. Politician
Dem. senator, OR, 1996—.
b. May 3, 1949
Source: *AlmAP 82, 84, 88, 92, 96, 2000; CngDr 89, 91, 93, 95; PolsAm 84; WhoAm 98, 99, 2000; WhoWest 00, 98*

Wyeth, Andrew
American. Artist
Son of Newell Convers Wyeth; subjects are people, places of northeastern states; best-known painting: *Christina's World*.
b. Jul 12, 1917 in Chadds Ford, Pennsylvania
Source: *AmArt; Benet 87; BenetAL 91; BioIn 1, 2, 3, 4, 5, 6, 7, 8, 9, 10, 11, 12, 13, 14, 15, 16, 17, 19, 22, 23, 24; BkPepl; BlueB 76; BriEAA; CelR, 90; ConArt 77, 83, 89; CurBio 81; DcAmArt; DcCAA 71, 77, 88, 94; DcCAr 81; DcTwArt; DcTwCCu 1; EncAB-H 1974; FacFETw; IntWW 83, 91; LegTOT; McGEWB; OxCAmH; OxCAmL 65; OxCTwCA; OxDcArt; PhDcTCA 77; REn; WebAB 79; WhAmArt 85; Who 3, 92; WhoAm 74, 76, 78, 80, 82, 84, 86, 88, 90, 92, 94, 95, 96, 97, 98, 99, 2000; WhoAmA 84, 91; WhoE 74; WhoWor 74, 78, 80, 82, 84; WorAlBi; WorArt 1950*

Wyeth, Henriette (Zirngiebel)
[Mrs. Peter Hurd]
American. Artist
Specialized in portraits, murals; sister of Andrew.
b. Oct 22, 1907 in Wilmington, Delaware
d. Apr 3, 1997 in Roswell, New Mexico
Source: *BioIn 17; GrLiveH; IlBEAAW; PrintW 83, 85; WhAmArt 85; WhoAmA 73, 76, 78, 80, 82, 84, 86, 89, 91, 93; WhoAmW 58, 61, 85; WhoWest 84, 87, 89, 92*

Wyeth, Jamie
[James Browning Wyeth]
American. Artist
Called most commercially successful artist of his generation; son of Andrew, grandson of N.C.
b. Jul 6, 1946 in Wilmington, Delaware
Source: *AmArt; BioIn 14, 15, 22, 23; BioNews 75; BkPepl; CelR 90; CurBio 77; LegTOT; PrintW 83, 85; WhoAm 74, 76, 78, 80, 82, 84, 86, 88, 90, 92, 94, 95, 96, 97; WhoAmA 73, 76, 78, 80, 82, 84, 86, 89, 91, 93; WhoWor 78; WorAlBi*

Wyeth, N(ewell) C(onvers)
American. Illustrator, Artist
Illustrated popular children's novels; father of Andrew, grandfather of Jamie.
b. Oct 22, 1882 in Needham, Massachusetts
d. Oct 19, 1945 in Chadds Ford, Pennsylvania
Source: *AmAu&B; AntBDN B; ArtsAmW 3; BioIn 1, 2, 4, 5, 7, 8, 9, 10, 12, 13, 15, 17, 19, 23; ChhPo, S2, S3; ConICB; CurBio 45; DcAmB S3; FacFETw; IlBEAAW; IlrAm 1880, B, G; IlsBYP; JBA 34, 51; MajAl; NewEAmW; OxCAmH; OxDcArt; REnAL; SmATA 17; WebAB 74, 79; WhAm 2; WhAmArt 85*

Wyle, Noah
American. Actor
Plays Dr. John Carter on TV's "ER," 1994—.
b. Jun 2, 1971 in Los Angeles, California
Source: *ConTFT 16, 27; News 97, 97-3; WhoAm 99, 2000; WhoWor 2000*

Wyler, Gretchen
[Gretchen Wienecke]
American. Actor
Stage performances include *Silk Stockings*, 1955; *Damn Yankees*, 1956.
b. Feb 16, 1932 in Oklahoma City, Oklahoma
Source: *BiE&WWA; ConTFT 1, 6; DcPseud; ForWC 70; LegTOT; NotNAT; VarWW 85; WhoEnt 92; WhoHol A; WhsWeAm 98*

Wyler, William
American. Director, Producer
Won Oscars for *Mrs. Miniver*, 1942; *The Best Years of Our Lives*, 1946; *Ben Hur*, 1959.
b. Jul 1, 1902 in Muhlhausen, Germany
d. Jul 27, 1981 in Beverly Hills, California
Source: *AmFD; AmNatBi; AnObit 1981; BiDFilm, 81, 94; BioIn 2, 5, 7, 10, 11, 12, 15, 16, 18, 21, 24; BioNews 74; BlueB 76; CamBiEn; CamDcAB; CelR; ChamBiD; CmMov; ConAu 108; ConTFT 26; CurBio 81, 81N; DcArts; DcFM; FacFETw; FilmEn; FilmgC; GangFlm; HalFC 80, 84, 88; IlWWHD 1; IntDcF 1-2, 2-2; IntMPA 75, 76, 77, 78, 79, 80, 81; IntWW 74, 75, 76, 77, 78, 79, 80, 81, 82N; ItaFilm; LegTOT; MiSFD 9N; MovMk; OnHuYAF; OxCFilm; ScrEAmL 1; TwYS A; WhAm*

8; Who 74, 82N; WhoAm 74, 76, 78, 80; WhoWor 74, 78; WorAl; WorAlBi; WorEFlm; WorFDir 1

Wylie, Elinor Hoyt
American. Author
Wrote *The Orphan Angel*, 1927; *Mr. Hodge and Mr. Hazard*, 1928.
b. Sep 5, 1885 in Somerville, New Jersey
d. Dec 16, 1928 in New York, New York
Source: *AtlBL; BioIn 22; CasWL; ChamBiD; DcAmB; NotAW; OxCAmL 65; OxCEng 67; PenC AM; RAdv 1; REn; REnAL; SixAP; Str&VC; TwCA, SUP; TwCWr; WebAB 74; WhAm 1; WorAu 1900*

Wylie, Paul
American. Skater
Source: *BioIn 15, 18; WhoAm 94*

Wylie, Philip Gordon
American. Author
Critic of US society known for attack on "momism" in *Generation of Vipers*, 1942.
b. May 12, 1902 in Beverly, Massachusetts
d. Oct 25, 1971 in Miami, Florida
Source: *AmAu&B; AmNatBi; AmNov; ChhPo S2; CnDAL; ConAu P-2; ConNov 72; DcAmB S9; EncMys; EncSF 93; EvLB; LinLib S; NewYTBE 71; OxCTwCL; REn; REnAL; RGSF; SpyFic; TwCA, SUP; TwCCr&M 85; TwCSFW 81, 86; TwCWr; WebAB 74, 79; WhAm 5; WhFla*

Wyman, Bill
[The Rolling Stones; William George Wyman]
English. Musician
Bass player with The Rolling Stones; hits include *Paint It Black*, 1966; *Hang Fire*, 1982.
b. Oct 24, 1941 in London, England
Source: *BioIn 12, 13, 16; IntWW 91, 93, 98, 2000; LegTOT; WhoAm 80, 82, 84, 86, 88, 90, 92, 94, 95, 96; WhoEnt 92; WhoRocM 82*

Wyman, Jane
[Sarah Jane Fulks]
American. Actor
Won Oscar, 1948, for *Johnny Belinda*; starred in TV series "Falcon Crest," 1982-90; first wife of Ronald Reagan.
b. Jan 4, 1914 in Saint Joseph, Missouri
Source: *BiDFilm, 81, 94; BioAmW; BioIn 1, 2, 3, 4, 7, 8, 11, 12, 13, 14, 15, 16; CelR 90; ChamBiD; CmMov; ConTFT 3, 20; CurBio 49; DcPseud; EncAFC; FilmEn; FilmgC; ForYSC; GangFlm; GoodHs; HalFC 80, 84, 88; IntMPA 75, 76, 77, 78, 80, 81, 82, 84, 86, 88, 92; IntWW 91, 93, 98, 2000; IntWWW 2; InWom, SUP; LegTOT; MotPP; MovMk; NewYTBS 81; OsStAZ; ThFT; WhoAm 74, 76, 84, 86, 88, 90, 92, 94, 95, 96, 97; WhoAmW 74, 91, 93,*

95; WhoEnt 92; WhoHol 92, A; WhoTelC; WorAl; WorAlBi; WorEFlm

Wyman, Thomas Hunt
American. TV Executive
President, CEO of CBS, 1980-86.
b. Nov 30, 1929 in Saint Louis, Missouri
Source: *BioIn 10, 11, 12, 13; BlueB 76; CurBio 83; Dun&B 79, 88; IntMPA 92; IntWW 82, 83, 89; LesBEnT, 92; St&PR 84, 87, 91; WhoAm 74, 76, 78, 80, 82, 84, 86; WhoE 83, 85, 86; WhoFI 74, 77, 79, 81, 83, 85; WhoWor 82, 84, 87*

Wyman, Willard Gordon
American. Military Leader
First chief of staff for US Army, 1947-50; honored with many medals including Bronze Star.
b. Mar 21, 1898 in Augusta, Maine
d. Mar 29, 1969 in Bethesda, Maryland
Source: *BiDWWGF; BioIn 3, 4, 8, 9; EncAInt; ObitOF 79; WhAm 5*

Wynette, Tammy
[Virginia Wynette Pugh]
American. Singer
CMA female vocalist of year, 1968, 1969, 1970; autobiography *Stand by Your Man*, 1979.
b. May 5, 1942 in Itawamba County, Mississippi
d. Apr 6, 1998 in Nashville, Tennessee
Source: *AllMGCo; BakBD 84, 92; BakDcM; BgBkCoM; BiDAmM; BioIn 9, 10, 11, 12, 13, 14, 15, 16, 23, 24; BioNews 74; BkPepl; CelR 90; ChamBiD; ConAu X; ConMus 2, 24; ContDcW 89; ConTFT 23; CounME 74, 74A; CurBio 95, 98N; DcPseud; EncFCWM 69, 83; EncRk 88; GoodHs; HarEnCM 87; HarEnR 86; IlEncCM; IlEncRk; IntDcWB; IntWW 93, 97; IntWWW 2; InWom SUP; LegTOT; NewGrDA 86; News 98, 98-3; NewYTBS 98; OxCPMus; PenEncP; PeoHis; RkOn 78; WhoAm 74, 76, 78, 80, 82, 84, 86, 88, 90, 92, 94, 95, 96, 97, 98; WhoAmW 81, 83, 95, 97; WhoEnt 92, 98; WhoHol 92; WhoRock 81; WorAl; WorAlBi*

Wynn, Early
"Gus"
American. Baseball Player
Pitcher, 1939, 1941-44, 1946-63; had 300 career wins; won Cy Young Award, 1959; Hall of Fame, 1971.
b. Jan 6, 1920 in Hartford, Alabama
d. Apr 4, 1999 in Venice, Florida
Source: *Ballpl 90; BiDAmSp BB; BioIn 3, 5, 6, 10, 11, 14, 15, 17; CulEncB; FacFETw; LegTOT; WhoAm 99; WhoProB 73; WhoSpor; WorAl; WorAlBi*

Wynn, Ed
[Isiah Edwin Leopold]
American. Comedian
Ziegfeld Follies star; won Emmy for "Requiem for a Heavyweight," 1956; films include *Mary Poppins*, 1964.
b. Nov 9, 1886 in Philadelphia, Pennsylvania

d. Jun 19, 1966 in Beverly Hills, California
Source: *AmNatBi; ASCAP 66, 80; BiE&WWA; BioIn 1, 2, 3, 4, 5, 7, 8, 11, 15, 16; CamGWoT; CurBio 45, 66; DcAmB S8; DcPseud; EncAFC; EncMT; EncVaud; Ent; FamA&A; Film 2; FilmEn; FilmgC; Funs; HalFC 80, 84, 88; JoeFr; LegTOT; MotPP; MovMk; NewYTET; NotNAT B; OxCAmH; OxCAmT 84; OxCPMus; QDrFCA 92; RadStar; WebAB 74, 79; WebBD 83; WhAm 4; WhoCom; WhoHol B; WhScrn 74, 77, 83; WhThe; WorAl; WorAlBi*

Wynn, Keenan
[Francis Xavier Aloysius Wynn]
American. Actor
Mustachioed character actor best remembered for film roles in *Dr. Strangelove*, 1963; *Kiss Me Kate*, 1953; son of comedian Ed.
b. Jul 27, 1916 in New York, New York
d. Oct 14, 1986 in Brentwood, California
Source: *AnObit 1986; BiE&WWA; BioIn 1, 2, 4, 5, 10, 15, 16, 17; BioNews 75; ConAu 120; ConNews 87-1; ConTFT 4; EncAFC; FilmEn; FilmgC; ForYSC; HalFC 80, 84, 88; IntDcF 1-3; IntMPA 75, 76, 77, 78, 79, 80, 81, 82, 84, 86; ItaFilm; LegTOT; MGM; MotPP; MovMk; NotNAT A; SaTiSS; WhAm 9; WhoAm 74, 76, 78, 80, 82, 84, 86; WhoHol A; WorAl; WorAlBi*

Wynn, Stephen A.
American. Businessman
Chairman and president of Mirage Resorts Inc. (formerly Golden Nugget, Inc.), 1973-2000.
b. Jan 27, 1942 in New Haven, Connecticut
Source: *News 94, 94-3; St&PR 93, 96, 97, 98, 99, 2000*

Wynn, Tracy Keenan
American. Writer
Won Emmys for "Tribes," 1971; "The Autobiography of Miss Jane Pittman," 1974.
b. Feb 28, 1945 in Los Angeles, California
Source: *ConTFT 1, 8; HalFC 84, 88; IntMPA 86, 88, 92, 94, 96; LesBEnT, 92; MiSFD 9; VarWW 85; WhoEnt 92, 98; WhoHol 92; WrDr 96, 98, 99, 2000*

Wynonna
[The Judds; Christina Ciminella; Wynonna Judd; Mrs. Arch Kelley, III]
American. Singer, Musician
The daughter in the mother-daughter country duo 1984-91; first solo album, *Wynonna*, 1992; album *Revelations*, 1996.
b. May 30, 1964 in Ashland, Kentucky
Source: *BillEnR; BioIn 24; CelR 90; ConMus 2, 11; CurBio 96; LegTOT; News 93-3; NewYTBS 84; WhoAm 90, 92, 94, 95, 96, 97; WhoAmW 91, 93, 95, 97; WhoEnt 92*

Wynter, Dana
[Dagmar Spencer-Marcus]
English. Actor
Appeared in many TV shows including "Gunsmoke," 1969; films include *Airport,* 1970.
b. Jun 8, 1932 in London, England
Source: *BioIn 3, 4; ConTFT 7; FilmEn; FilmgC; HalFC 84, 88; IntMPA 86, 92; InWom; MotPP; MovMk; WhoAm 86, 90; WhoHol A*

Wynyard, Diana
[Dorothy Isobel Cox]
English. Actor
Oscar nominee for *Cavalcade,* 1933.
b. Jan 16, 1906 in London, England
d. May 13, 1964 in London, England
Source: *BioIn 5, 6, 9; DcNaB 1961; DcPseud; EncWT; FilmAG WE; FilmEn; FilmgC; ForYSC; HalFC 80, 84, 88; InWom, SUP; MotPP; MovMk; NotNAT B; ObitT 1961; OsStAZ; OxCFilm; OxCThe 67, 83; ThFT; WhoHol B; WhScrn 83; WhThe*

Wyss, Johann David
Swiss. Author
Wrote classic shipwreck, adventure novel, *Swiss Family Robinson* 1812-27; translated by son Johann Rudolf.
b. 1743 in Bern, Switzerland
d. 1818 in Bern, Switzerland
Source: *AuBYP 2S; BioIn 1, 3, 8, 13, 19; CarSB; CasWL; ChlBkCr; DcArts; NinCLC 10; OxCGer 76, 86, 97; Str&VC; WhoChL*

Wyss, Johann Rudolf
Swiss. Author
Wrote Swiss national anthem, 1811; translated father's novel *Swiss Family Robinson* to English, making it adventure classic.
b. Mar 13, 1782 in Bern, Switzerland
d. Mar 21, 1830 in Bern, Switzerland
Source: *BioIn 5, 8; CyWA 97; NewCBEL; WebBD 83*

Wyszynski, Stefan
Polish. Religious Leader
Responsible for peaceful co-existence of Roman Catholic church and socialist state in Poland.
b. Aug 3, 1901 in Zuzela, Russia
d. May 28, 1981 in Warsaw, Poland
Source: *AnObit 1981; BioIn 3, 4, 5, 6, 7, 11, 12, 13, 18; CamBiEn; ChamBiD; ColdWar 1, 2; ConAu 108; CurBio 81N; DcPol; EncCW; EncyDCo; FacFETw; HisDcPo; IntWW 74, 75, 76, 77, 78, 79, 80, 81, 81N; NewYTBS 81; PolBiDi; WhAm 7; WhoSocC 78; WhoWor 74, 78, 80*

Wythe, George
American. Judge, Lawyer, Continental Congressman
Singed Declaration of Independence, 1776; first law professor, William and Mary College, 1779-89; poisoned by grandnephew.
b. 1726 in Elizabeth City, Virginia
d. Jun 8, 1806 in Richmond, Virginia
Source: *Alli; AmBi; AmNatBi; ApCAB; BiDAmEd; BiDrAC; BiDrUSC 89; BiDSA; BioIn 3, 4, 6, 7, 8, 9, 10, 11, 15, 16, 23, 24; BlkwEAR; CamDcAB; CyAL 1; DcAmAu; DcAmB; Drake; EncAB-H 1974; EncAR; EncCRAm; EncSoH; EncWB 98; HarEnUS; HisDcAR; McGEWB; NatCAB 3; OxCAmH; OxCLaw; TwCBDA; WebAB 74, 79; WhAm HS; WhAmP; WhAmRev; WorAl; WorAlBi*

X

X
[D(on) J Bonebrake; Christine "Exene" Cervenka; John Doe; Billy Zoom]
American. Music Group
Group formed 1977; influenced by punk, heavy metal, rockabilly, country music.
Source: *BillEnR; ConMus 11; DcLP 87B; DcNAA; EncCoWW; EncPR&S 89; EvLB; NewAmDM; NewGrDA 86; NewYHSD; OnThGG; PenEncP; RkWho 96; RolSEnR 83; ScF&FL 1; TwCCr&M 91; WhCiWar; WhLit; WhNAA; WhoMus 72; WhoRocM 82; WhsNW 85; WomNov*

Xenakis, Iannis
French. Composer
Avant-garde musical theorist who developed computerized music; wrote compositions for all media including "Kottos," 1977.
b. May 29, 1922 in Braila, Romania
Source: *BakBD 78, 84, 92; BakBDTw; BakDcM; BioIn 7, 8, 9, 15; BriBkM 80; CamBiEn; ChamBiD; CnOxB; CompSN SUP; ConCom 92; CurBio 94; DcArts; DcCM; DcTwArt; EncWB 98; IntWW 74, 75, 76, 77, 78, 79, 80, 81, 82, 83, 89, 91, 93; IntWWM 77, 80, 90; McGEWB; MusMk; NewAmDM; NewGrDM 80; NewOxM; NewYTBS 76; OxCTwCA; PenDiMP A; PenEncH; RAdv 14, 13-3; Who 90, 92, 94, 98, 99, 2000; WhoMus 72; WhoWor 74, 78, 82, 84, 89, 91*

Xenophanes
Greek. Philosopher
Founder of Eleatic philosophy who rejected anthropomorphic gods.
b. 570BC in Colophon, Asia Minor

d. 480BC
Source: *AsBiEn; BbD; BiD&SB; CamBiEn; CasWL; ChamBiD; EncClPh; Grk&L; InSci; LinLib L, S; LuthC 75; NewC; OxCEng 67; PenC CL*

Xenophon
Greek. Historian, Essayist
Wrote *Memorabilia,* recollections of his teacher Socrates; *Hellenica,* which continued the history begun in Herodotus's *History of the Peloponnesian War.*
b. c. 430BC in Athens, Greece
d. c. 354BC in Corinth, Greece
Source: *AtlBL; BbD; Benet 87, 96; BiCoLiE; BiD&SB; BlmGEL; CasWL; ClMLC 17; CyEd; CyWA 58; DcEnL; DcLB 176; EncClPh; EncWB 98; GenMudB; HarEnMi; McGEWB; NewC; OxCClC; OxCClL; OxCEng 67; PenC CL; RAdv 14, 13-4; RComWL; REn; WhDW; WhWE; WorAl*

Xerxes I
Persian. Ruler
Son, successor of Darius I, 486-465 BC.
b. 519BC
d. 465BC
Source: *BioIn 24; CamBiEn; ChamBiD; DcBiPP; LngCEL; McGEWB; REn*

Xiang Jingyu
Chinese. Feminist, Political Activist
Women's rights activist founded China Women's Federation and initiated the national women's movement.
b. Sep 4, 1895 in Xupu, Hunan, China
d. May 1, 1928, China

Source: *EncWB 98; HisWorL; RadHan*

Xuan Thuy
Vietnamese. Politician
Secretary, Central Committee, 1976; Vice-chm., Socialist Republic of Vietnam, 1976—; minister of foreign affairs, 1963-65.
b. Sep 2, 1912 in Hanoi, Vietnam
d. Jun 18, 1985 in Hanoi, Vietnam (North)
Source: *AnObit 1985; BioIn 8; EncVieW; FarE&A 78, 79, 80, 81; IntWW 74, 76, 77, 78, 79, 80, 81, 82, 83; WhoSocC 78*

Xu Guangqi
[Kuang-ch'i Hsu]
Chinese. Scholar, Politician
High-ranking scholar-official in the Ming dynasty, he introduced Western science and technology into China and was one of the "Three Pillars of the Catholic Religion in China" during the 17th century.
b. 1562
d. Nov 8, 1633
Source: *EncWB 98; HisWorL*

Xuxa
[Maria da Graca Meneghel]
Brazilian. Entertainer
Host of children's program in Brazil; syndicated to South America and the United States.
b. c. 1963, Brazil
Source: *LatAmLi; News 94, 94-2*

Y

Yablans, Frank
American. Producer
Films include *The Other Side of Midnight*, 1977; *Mommie Dearest*, 1982.
b. Aug 27, 1935 in New York, New York
Source: *BioIn 13; ConTFT 1, 8; HalFC 84, 88; IntMPA 75, 76, 77, 78, 79, 80, 81, 82, 84, 86, 88, 92, 94, 96; VarWW 85; WhoAm 74, 76, 78, 80, 82, 84, 86, 88, 92, 94, 95, 96, 97, 98; WhoEnt 92A, 98*

Yablonski, Joseph
"Jock"
American. Labor Union Official
Lost UMW presidency to Tony Boyle, 1969; Boyle convicted of his murder.
b. 1910 in Pittsburgh, Pennsylvania
d. Jan 5, 1969 in Clarksville, Pennsylvania
Source: *FacFETw; PolProf NF; WorAl*

Yadin, Yigael
Israeli. Archaeologist
Organized digs at Masada, Dead Sea caves, published many scholarly works.
b. Mar 21, 1917
d. Jun 28, 1984 in Hadera, Israel
Source: *AnObit 1984; BioIn 6, 7, 8, 9, 10, 11, 14, 16, 19, 21, 23; CamBiEn; ConAu 6NR, 9R, 113; CurBio 66, 84N; DcPseud; FacFETw; HisEAAC; IntAu&W 77, 82; IntWW 74, 75, 76, 77, 78, 79, 80, 81, 82, 83; MidE 78, 79, 80, 81, 82; NewYTBS 84; SmATA 55; WhoAm 74, 76, 78; WhoWor 74, 76, 78, 80, 82; WhoWorJ 72, 78*

Yahya Khan, Agha Muhammad
Pakistani. Political Leader
Pres., Pakistan, 1969-71; sentenced to five yrs. house arrest after forced resignation.
b. Feb 4, 1917 in Peshawar, Pakistan
d. Aug 8, 1980 in Rawalpindi, India
Source: *ChamBiD; FacFETw; FarE&A 78, 79; IntWW 74, 75, 76, 77, 78, 79, 80; NewYTBE 71; Who 74*

Yakovlev, Aleksandr Sergeyevich
Russian. Aircraft Designer
Well-known for designing Soviet fighter aircraft used during WWII.
b. Apr 1, 1906 in Moscow, Russia
d. Aug 22, 1989 in Moscow, Union of Soviet Socialist Republics
Source: *BioIn 2, 14, 15, 16; DcRusLS; FacFETw; IntWW 77, 78, 79, 80, 81, 82, 83, 89; NewYTBS 89; WhoWor 89*

Yakub al-Mansur, Abu Yusuf
Moroccan. Ruler
Reigned as third caliph of the Almohad dynasty from 1184 to 1199 and was victorious against the Spanish Christians at the battle of Alarcos.
b. fl. 1184

Yale, Elihu
American. Colonial Figure, Philanthropist
Yale U named in his honor, 1718; governor, Fort St. George at Madras, 1687-92.
b. Apr 5, 1649 in Boston, Massachusetts
d. Jul 8, 1721, England
Source: *Alli; AmAu&B; AmBi; AmNatBi; ApCAB; BioIn 8, 11; CamBiEn; CamDcAB; ChamBiD; CyAL 1; CyEd; DcAmB; Drake; EncCRAm; LinLib S; NatCAB 1; TwCBDA; WhAm HS; WhBriIn; WhDW; WorAl; WorAlBi*

Yale, Linus
American. Manufacturer
Developed lock for banker's safes, 1865; basic principle still used today.
b. Apr 4, 1821 in Salisbury, New York
d. Dec 25, 1868 in New York, New York
Source: *AmBi; AmNatBi; ApCAB; BioIn 21; CamBiEn; CamDcAB; ChamBiD; DcAmB; Entr; NatCAB 9; OxCDecA; WebAB 74, 79; WhAm HS*

Yalow, Rosalyn Sussman
American. Physicist
Developed technique for measuring amounts of biological substances in body, radioimmunoassay (RIA);
second woman to win Nobel Prize in medicine, 1977.
b. Jul 19, 1921 in New York, New York
Source: *AmDec 1970; AmMWSc 76P, 79, 82, 86, 89, 92, 95, 98; AmWomSc; AZWoSci; BiESc; BioIn 13, 14, 15; CamBiEn; ConAu 157; CurBio 78; EncWB; EncWHA; FacFETw; IntWW 78, 79, 80, 81, 82, 83, 89, 91, 93, 97, 98, 2000; IntWWW 2; InWom SUP; LadLa 86; LibW; McGCEnS; McGMS 80; NewYTBS 77; NobelP; NotTwCS 1; NotWoLS; RanHWDS; SciMath; Who 82, 83, 85, 88, 90, 92, 94, 98, 99, 2000; WhoAm 74, 76, 78, 80, 82, 84, 86, 88, 90, 92, 94, 95, 96, 97, 98, 99, 2000; WhoAmJ 80; WhoAmW 64, 66, 68, 70, 72, 74, 75, 79, 81, 83, 85, 87, 89, 91, 93, 95, 97, 99; WhoE 79, 81, 83, 85, 86, 89, 91, 95, 97, 99; WhoFrS 84; WhoMedH 96, 99, 2000; WhoNob, 90, 95; WhoScEn 94, 96, 2000; WhoTech 89; WhoWor 78, 80, 82, 84, 87, 89, 91, 93, 95, 96, 97, 98, 99, 2000; WomBioS; WorAlBi*

Yamagata, Aritomo
Japanese. Military Leader
General and a member of the oligarchy which dominated Meiji Japan, he helped build a modern army, strengthen the power of the civil and military bureaucracy, and check the development of popular influences on the government.
b. Apr 22, 1838 in Hagi, Japan
d. Feb 22, 1922, Japan
Source: *BioIn 9; CamBiEn; EncWB 98; HarEnMi; LegTOT; McGEWB; WhDW; WhoMilH 76; WorAl; WorAlBi*

Yamaguchi, Kristi Tsuya
American. Skater
Winner of gold medal in the 1992 Olympics.
b. Jul 12, 1971 in Hayward, California
Source: *CurBio 92; News 92; WhoAm 94, 95, 96, 97, 98, 99, 2000; WhoAmW 93, 95, 97, 99*

Yamamoto, Isoroku
Japanese. Military Leader
Admiral who planned attack on Pearl
    Harbor, 1941.
b. Apr 4, 1884 in Nagaoka, Japan
d. Apr 18, 1943, Solomon Islands
Source: *BioIn 1, 2, 7, 8, 11, 12, 17, 24;
CamBiEn; EncNaHi; EncWB 98;
GenMudB; HarEnMi; HisEWW;
HisWorL; MilitOn; OxCShps; WhDW;
WhWW-II; WorAl; WorAlBi*

Yamamoto, Kenichi
Japanese. Auto Executive
Automotive Industries Man of the Year,
    1986; Chairman Mazda Motoe Corp.,
    1987-92; exec. advisor, 1992—.
b. Sep 16, 1922 in Hiroshima, Japan
Source: *BioIn 12, 14, 16; IntWW 89, 91,
93, 97, 98; News 89-1; WhoFI 96;
WhoWor 89, 93, 95, 96*

Yamani, Ahmad Zaki, Sheik
Saudi. Government Official
Minister of state, 1960-62; minister of
    Petroleum and Mineral Resources
    1962-86; influential OPEC spokesman,
    Western ally.
b. 1930 in Mecca, Saudi Arabia
Source: *BioIn 13, 14, 15, 16; CurBio 75;
DcMidEa; EncWB; IntWW 83, 91; MidE
82; NewYTBS 86; WhoWor 87*

Yamasaki, Minoru
American. Architect
His more than 300 designs include
    World Trade Center, NYC; Westin
    Century Plaza Hotel, LA.
b. Dec 1, 1912 in Seattle, Washington
d. Feb 6, 1986 in Detroit, Michigan
Source: *AmArch 70; AmDec 1970;
AmNatBi; AnObit 1986; AsAmAlm; BioIn
4, 5, 6, 7, 8, 9, 12, 14, 15, 20, 21, 24;
BriEAA; CelR; ConArch 80, 87, 94;
ConAu 118, 155; ConNews 86-2; CurBio
86N; DcArch; DcD&D; EncAAr 1, 2;
EncMA; FacFETw; IntDcAr; IntWW 74,
75, 76, 77, 78, 79, 80, 81, 82, 83;
MacEA; McGDA; NotAsAm; ScrEAmL 2;
WebAB 74, 79; WhAm 9; WhoAm 74, 76,
78, 80, 82, 84; WhoWor 74*

Yamashita, Kazuhito
Japanese. Musician
Clasical guitarist; as a teenager won
    three international competitions.
b. 1961, Japan
Source: *BioIn 11; ConMus 4*

Yamashita, Tomoyuki
Japanese. Army Officer
Led Japanese troops in Philippines, 1944;
    executed for war atrocities.
b. Nov 8, 1885 in Kochi, Japan
d. Feb 23, 1946 in Luzon, Philippines
Source: *BioIn 1, 2, 3, 8, 9, 10, 12, 15,
18, 24; CamBiEn; EncWB 98;
GenMudB; McGEWB; WebBD 83;
WhDW; WhWW-II; WorAl; WorAlBi*

Yancey, Jimmy
[James Edward Yancey]
American. Jazz Musician
Pianist who helped develop boogie
    woogie, 1930s-40s.
b. Feb 20, 1898 in Chicago, Illinois
d. Sep 17, 1951 in Chicago, Illinois
Source: *BiDAfM; BiDAmM; BioIn 1, 2;
Blues; BluesWW; CmpEPM; GuBlues;
IlEncJ; InB&W 85; NewGrDM 80;
OxCPMus; PenEncP; WhoJazz 72*

Yancey, William Lowndes
American. Politician
Democratic U.S. congressman known for
    his excellent oratorical abilities and as
    a spokesman of Southern interests.
b. Aug 10, 1814 in Warren County,
    Georgia
d. Jul 27, 1863 in Montgomery, Alabama
Source: *AmBi; AmNatBi; AmPolLe;
ApCAB; BiAUS; BiDAmJo; BiDConf;
BiDrAC; BiDrUSC 89; BioIn 4, 5, 9, 15,
16; CamDcAB; CivWDc; DcAmB;
DcAmDH 80, 89; Drake; EncSoH;
EncWB 98; HarEnUS; McGEWB;
NatCAB 4; OxCAmH; TwCBDA; WebAB
74, 79; WhAm HS; WhAmP; WhCiWar*

Yang, Chen Ning
American. Physicist
Won Nobel Prize, 1957, with Lee for
    disproving principle of parity.
b. Sep 22, 1922 in Hefei, China
Source: *AmMWSc 76P, 79, 82, 86, 89,
92, 95, 98; AsBiEn; BiESc; BioIn 4, 5,
6, 13, 14; CamBiEn; CamDcAB;
CamDcSc; ChamBiD; ConAu 157;
CurBio 58; EncWB 98; InSci; IntWW 74,
75, 76, 77, 78, 79, 80, 81, 82, 83, 91;
McGCEnS; McGEWB; McGMS 80;
NobelP; NotAsAm; NotTwCS 1; RAdv
14; RanHWDS; WebAB 74, 79; Who 74,
82, 83, 85, 88, 90, 92, 94, 98, 99, 2000;
WhoAm 74, 76, 78, 80, 82, 84, 86, 88,
90, 92, 94, 95, 97, 98; WhoAsA 94;
WhoE 77, 79, 81, 83, 85, 89, 91, 93, 95;
WhoNob, 90, 95; WhoPRCh 87;
WhoScEn 94, 96, 2000; WhoWor 74, 76,
78, 80, 82, 84, 87, 89, 91, 93, 95, 2000;
WorAl; WorAlBi*

Yang, Jerry
Chinese. Entrepreneur
With David Filo created the World Wide
    Web search engine Yahoo!, arguably
    the most popular such site on the
    Internet; Yahoo! stock was publicly
    offered in 1996, and both men became
    multimillionaires.
b. 1968, Taiwan
Source: *CurBio 97*

Yankelovich, Daniel
American. Sociologist
Pres., Public Agenda Foundation; wrote
    The Changing Values on Campus
    1972.
b. Dec 29, 1924 in Boston,
    Massachusetts
Source: *BioIn 12, 13, 14; CamDcAB;
ConAu 105; CurBio 82; Dun&B 79;
Future; PolPar; St&PR 75, 84; WhoAm*

74, 76, 78, 80, 82, 84, 86, 88, 90, 92,
94, 95, 96

Yankovic, Weird Al
[Alfred Matthew Yankovic]
American. Singer, Comedian
Best known for satirizing rock hits:
    "Like a Surgeon," 1985; "I'm Fat,"
    1988.
b. Oct 23, 1959 in Los Angeles,
    California
Source: *BioIn 15; ConMus 7; ConNews
85-4; CurBio 1999; PenEncP; RkOn 85;
WhoCom; WhoEnt 92; WorAlBi*

Yanni
[Yanni Chryssomallis]
Greek. Musician
Debut album *Optimystique*, 1986.
b. Nov 4, 1954 in Kalamata, Greece
Source: *ConMus 11; DcPseud; LegTOT*

Yarborough, Cale
[William Caleb Yarborough]
American. Auto Racer
Stock car racer; has won Daytona 500
    four times, second only to Richard
    Petty.
b. Mar 27, 1939 in Timminsville, South
    Carolina
Source: *BiDAmSp OS; BioIn 8, 10, 11,
13, 15, 21; BioNews 74; CelR 90;
CurBio 87; LegTOT; WhoAm 78, 80, 82,
84, 86, 88, 92, 94, 95, 96, 97; WhoSpor;
WhoSSW 95; WorAlBi*

Yarborough, Ralph W(ebster)
American. Politician, Lawyer
Dem. senator from TX, 1957-71.
b. Jun 8, 1903 in Chandler, Texas
d. Jan 27, 1996 in Austin, Texas
Source: *BiDrAC; BiDrUSC 89; BioIn 4,
5, 6, 8, 9, 11, 13; BlueB 76; CurBio 60,
96N; DcAmImH; IntWW 74, 75, 76, 77,
78, 79, 80, 81; IntYB 78, 79, 80, 81;
PolProf E, J, K; WhAm 11; WhoAm 74,
76, 78, 80, 82, 84, 86, 88, 92; WhoAmL
85; WhoAmP 73, 75, 77, 79, 81, 83, 85,
87, 89, 91, 93, 95; WhoSSW 73;
WhoWor 87*

Yarbrough, Glenn
American. Singer, Musician
Best known for top-ten hit "Baby, the
    Rain Must Fall," from 1965 film.
b. Jan 12, 1930 in Milwaukee, Wisconsin
Source: *ASCAP 66, 80; BiDAmM; BioIn
6, 8; EncFCWM 69; LegTOT; RkOn 78,
84; WhoRock 81; WorAlBi*

Yarbrough, Lee Roy
American. Auto Racer
Stock car racer who was top driver,
    1969; won $188,609, then a record,
    for Grand National stock race, 1969.
b. Sep 17, 1938
d. Dec 7, 1984 in Jacksonville, Florida
Source: *BioIn 8, 10; NewYTBS 84*

Yard, Molly
[Mary Alexander Yard]
American. Political Activist
President of NOW, 1987-91.
b. 1910? in Shanghai, China
Source: *BioIn 15, 16; CurBio 88; News 91; NewYTBS 87; WhoAmW 91*

Yardbirds
[Jeff Beck; Eric Clapton; Chris Dreja; James McCarty; Jimmy Page; Keith Relf; Paul Samwell-Smith; Anthony Sopham]
English. Music Group
Blues-based rock band, formed 1963; albums include *Little Games*, 1967.
Source: *AllMGBI 1, 2; BillEnR; BioIn 14, 15, 16, 17, 18, 19, 20, 21; ConMuA 80A, 80B; ConMus 10; EncPR&S 74, 89; EncRk 88; EncRkSt; HarEnR 86; IlEncRk; NewAgMG; NewAmDM; PenEncP; RkOn 78, 84; RkWho 96; RolSEnR 83; WhoAm 74, 76, 78; WhoRock 81; WhoRocM 82; WhoWor 78*

Yardley, George Harry
American. Basketball Player
Forward, 1953-60, mostly with Ft. Wayne-Detroit; first NBA player to score over 2,000 pts. in season, led league in scoring, 1958.
b. Nov 23, 1928 in Hollywood, California
Source: *BiDAmSp BK; BioIn 5, 14; NewYTBS 75, 85; OfNBA 87*

Yardley, Jonathan
American. Journalist
Book critic, *Washington Post*, 1981—.
b. Oct 27, 1939 in Pittsburgh, Pennsylvania
Source: *BiDAmNC; BioIn 13, 16; ConAu 73; IntAu&W 89, 91, 93; WhoAm 80, 82, 84, 86, 88, 90, 92, 94, 95, 96, 97, 98, 99, 2000; WhoE 93, 95; WhoPul; WhoSSW 73; WhsWeAm 98*

Yarmon, Betty
American. Journalist, Author
Contributing editor, *Good Housekeeping*; books include *Getting the Most for Your Money When You Buy a Home.*
b. Nov 14, in Plainfield, New Jersey
Source: *ForWC 70; WhoAdv 90; WhoAm 80, 82, 84, 86, 88, 90, 92, 94; WhoAmW 81; WhoE 89*

Yarnell, Bruce
American. Actor
Appeared on stage with Ethel Merman in revival of *Annie Get Your Gun.*
b. Dec 28, 1938 in Los Angeles, California
d. Nov 30, 1973 in California
Source: *NewYTBE 73; ObitOF 79; WhoHol B; WhScrn 77, 83*

Yarnell, Harry Ervin
American. Naval Officer
Commander, Pearl Harbor Naval Station, 1933-36; commander-in-chief of Asiatic fleet, 1936-39.

b. Oct 18, 1875 in Independence, Iowa
d. Jul 7, 1959 in Newport, Rhode Island
Source: *BiDWWGF; BioIn 1, 5, 7; NatCAB 48; OxCShps; WhAm 3*

Yarrow, Peter
[Peter, Paul, and Mary]
American. Composer, Author, Singer
With group Peter, Paul and Mary, 1962-70, 1978—; won Grammy 1963; solo albums include *That's Enough for Me.*
b. May 31, 1938 in New York, New York
Source: *ASCAP 66, 80; BakBD 84, 92; BiDAmM; BioIn 12, 14, 21, 24; EncFCWM 69; LegTOT; NewAmDM; WhoAm 74, 76, 78, 80, 82, 84, 86, 88, 90, 92, 94, 95, 96, 97, 98; WhoEnt 98; WhoHol 92, A; WorAl; WorAlBi*

Yastrzemski, Carl Michael
"Yaz"
American. Baseball Player
Outfielder, Boston, 1961-83; only player in AL with 400 home runs, 3,000 hits; won Triple Crown, 1967; Hall of Fame, 1989.
b. Aug 22, 1939 in Southampton, New York
Source: *Ballpl 90; BiDAmSp BB; BioIn 5, 6, 8, 9, 10, 11, 12, 13, 14, 15, 16; CamDcAB; CelR 90; ConAu 104; CurBio 68; NewYTBS 83, 86; PeoHis; WhoAm 74, 76, 78, 80, 82, 84, 86, 88, 90, 92, 94, 95, 96, 97, 98, 99, 2000; WhoE 95; WhoProB 73; WorAl; WorAlBi*

Yasui, Minoru
American. Lawyer
Activist argued about the unconstitutionality of the internment camps and fought for the civil rights of Japanese Americans during World War II.
b. 1917 in Hood River, Oregon
d. 1987
Source: *EncWB 98*

Yates, Bill
[Floyd Buford Yates]
American. Cartoonist
Drew comic strip "Professor Phumble," 1960-78; comics feature editor of King Features Syndicate, 1978-88.
b. Jul 5, 1921? in Samson, Alabama
Source: *BioIn 5, 12; EncACom; WorECar*

Yates, Elizabeth
[Mrs. William McGreal]
American. Children's Author
Won 1951 Newbery for *Amos Fortune, Free Man.*
b. Dec 6, 1905 in Buffalo, New York
Source: *AmAu&B; AmNov; AmWomWr; Au&ICB; Au&Wr 71; AuBYP 2, 3; BenetAL 91; BioIn 1, 2, 3, 4, 5, 7, 9, 10, 12, 14, 17, 19, 22, 24; ChhPo; ChlBkCr; ConAu 1R, 6NR, 13R, 21NR; CurBio 48; HerW 84; IntAu&W 77, 91; InWom; SUP; JBA 51; MajAl; MorBMP; NewbMB 1922; OxCChiL; REnAL;*

SJGYouA 2; SmATA 4, 6AS, 68; TwCA SUP; TwCChW 1, 2, 3; TwCYAW 1; WhoAm 74, 76, 78, 80, 82, 84, 86, 88, 90, 98, 99, 2000; WhoAmW 58, 61, 64, 66, 68, 70, 72, 74, 97, 99; WhoEnt 98; WhoProB 73; WorAu 1900; WrDr 80, 82, 84, 86, 88, 90, 92, 94, 96, 98, 99, 2000

Yates, Peter
English. Director
Oscar nominee for *Breaking Away*, 1979; other films include *The Deep*, 1977.
b. Jul 24, 1929 in Aldershot, England
Source: *BiDFilm, 81, 94; BioIn 12; ConTFT 6; FilmEn; FilmgC; GangFlm; HalFC 80, 84, 88; IlWWBF; IntDcF 1-2, 2-2; IntMPA 75, 76, 77, 78, 79, 80, 81, 82, 84, 86, 88, 92, 94, 96; IntWW 89, 91, 93, 97, 98, 2000; MiSFD 9; MovMk; OxCFilm; Who 85, 88, 90, 92; WhoAm 86, 88, 90, 92, 94, 95, 96, 97, 98, 99, 2000; WhoEnt 92, 98; WhoWor 89, 91, 93, 95, 96; WorEFlm; WorFDir 2*

Yates, Richard
American. Author
Writings include *Revolutionary Road*, 1961; *Liars in Love*, 1981.
b. Feb 3, 1926 in Yonkers, New York
d. Nov 7, 1992 in Birmingham, Alabama
Source: *AmAu&B; BenetAL 91; BioIn 10, 13, 18, 19; ConAu 5R, 10NR, 43NR, 139; ConLC 7, 8, 23, 76; ConNov 72, 76, 82, 86, 91; DcLB 2, Y81A, Y92N; DcLEL 1940; DrAF 76; DrAPF 80; IntAu&W 76, 77; LinLib L; WorAu 1950; WrDr 76, 80, 82, 84*

Yates, Sidney R(ichard)
American. Politician
Dem. congressman from IL, 1949—.
b. Aug 27, 1909 in Chicago, Illinois
Source: *BiDrAC; BiDrUSC 89; BioIn 11, 13; CurBio 93; WhoAm 74, 76, 78, 80, 82, 84, 86, 88, 90, 92, 94, 95, 96, 97, 98, 99, 2000; WhoAmJ 80; WhoMW 88, 90, 92, 93, 96, 98; WhoScEn 96, 2000*

Yawkey, Thomas Austin
American. Baseball Executive
Owner, Boston Red Sox, 1933-76.
b. Feb 21, 1903 in Detroit, Michigan
d. Jul 9, 1976 in Boston, Massachusetts
Source: *BiDAmSp BB; BioIn 2, 11; CamDcAB; DcAmB S10; WhoAm 76*

Ydigoras Fuentes Miguel
Guatemalan. Political Leader
President of Guatemala, 1958-63; overthrown in coup.
b. Oct 17, 1895
d. Oct 6, 1982 in Guatemala City, Guatemala
Source: *BioIn 4, 13; CurBio 58; IntWW 83N; NewYTBS 82*

Yeager, Chuck
[Charles Elwood Yeager]
American. Pilot
First man to break sound barrier;
  featured in Tom Wolfe's book, movie
  The Right Stuff.
b. Feb 13, 1923 in Myra, West Virginia
Source: *AmMWSc 95; BioIn 13, 14, 15,
16, 18, 20, 23, 24; CamBiEn; ChamBiD;
ConAu 154; ConHero 1; CurBio 54;
EncWB 98; FacFETw; InSci; LegTOT;
News 98, 98-1; NewYTBS 85; PeoHis;
WebAMB; WhoAm 76, 86, 88, 90, 94,
95, 96; WhoHol 92; WhoScEn 94;
WhoWest 94; WorAlBi*

Yeager, Jeana
American. Pilot
With Dick Rutan, made longest flight
  without refueling, flying *Voyager*
  around the world, Dec 1986.
b. 1952 in Texas
Source: *BioIn 14, 15, 16; ConAu 158;
ConHero 1; ContDcW 89; CurBio 87;
EncWoAv; WomStre*

Yearwood, Trisha
American. Singer, Songwriter
Country music singer; released *Trisha
  Yearwood,* 1991 and *Hearts in Armor,*
  1992, both became platinum records;
  received best new artist award from
  Academy of Country Music; recorded
  The Song Remembers When in 1993.
b. 1964 in Monticello, Georgia
Source: *BgBkCoM; ConMus 10, 25;
CurBio 98; LegTOT; News 99-1, 1999;
WhoAm 94, 95, 96, 97, 98, 99, 2000;
WhoAmW 95, 99; WhoEnt 98*

Yeats, William Butler
Irish. Poet, Dramatist
Leader, Irish literary renaissance;
  founded Abbey Theater, Dublin; won
  Nobel Prize for literature, 1923.
b. Jun 13, 1865 in Dublin, Ireland
d. Jan 28, 1939 in Menton, France
Source: *Alli SUP; AnCL; ArizL; BbD;
Benet 87, 96; BiCoLiE; BiD&SB;
BiDIrW; BioIn 1, 2, 3, 4, 5, 6, 7, 8, 9,
10, 11, 12, 13, 14, 15, 16, 17, 18, 19,
20, 23; BritWr 6; CamBiEn; CamGEL;
CamGLE; CamGWoT; CasWL;
ChamBiD; Chambr 3; ChhPo, S1, S2,
S3; CnDBLB 5; CnE&AP; CnMD;
CnMWL; CnThe; ConAu 45NR, 104,
127; CrtSuDr; CyWA 58, 97; DcEnA, A;
DcIrB 1, 2, 3; DcIrL, 96; DcIrW 1;
DcLB 10, 19, 98, 156; DcLEL; DcNaB
1931; Dis&D; EncApL; EncFoLi;
EncPaPR 91; EncWB 98; EncWL 1, 2,
2S, 1; EncWT; Ent; EvLB; FacFETw;
GrBr; GrWrEL DR, P; HisDcIr; IntWW
2000; IriPla; LegTOT; LinLib L, S;
LngCTC; MagSWL; MajMD 1;
MajTwCW 1, 2; MakMC; McGEWB;
McGEWD 72, 84; ModBrL, 2, S1, S2;
ModIrL; ModIrLi; ModWD; NewC;
NewCBEL; NewEOp 71; NobelP;
NotNAT A, B; NotPoe; OxCEng 67, 85,
95; OxCThe 67, 83; OxCTwCL;
OxDcOp; PenC ENG; PenEncH;
PlP&P; PoeCrit 20; PoIre; RAdv 1, 14,
13-1, 13-2; RComWL; REn; REnWD;*

*RfGEnL 91; TwCA, SUP; TwCLC 1, 11,
18, 31; TwCWr; VicBrit; WebE&AL;
WhDW; WhE&EA; WhoNob, 90, 95;
WhoTwCL; WhThe; Wiz; WorAl;
WorAlBi; WorAu 1900; WorLitC; WrPh*

**Yeats-Brown, F(rancis Charles
  Claypon)**
English. Author, Army Officer
Best known for autobiographical *Lives of
  a Bengal Lancer,* 1930.
b. Aug 15, 1886 in Genoa, Italy
d. Dec 19, 1944 in London, England
Source: *ConAu 119; CurBio 45; DcLEL;
EvLB; LngCTC; REn; TwCA, SUP;
TwCWr; WhE&EA; WorAu 1900*

Yegorov, Boris (Borisovitch)
Russian. Cosmonaut, Physician
Made 16 orbits of Earth in Voshkod I,
  the first multi-passenger spacecraft,
  becoming the first physician to
  practice medicine in outer space, 1964.
b. Nov 26, 1937
d. Sep 12, 1994 in Moscow, Russia
Source: *BioIn 8, 15, 20; CurBio 94N;
FacFETw; WhoSpc*

Yeh-lu Ch'u-ts'ai
Chinese. Government Official,
  Astrologer, Author
Secretary-astrologer to Genghis Khan
  and later chief of the Secretariat, he is
  known for his administrative reforms
  that centralized the government and
  restored order during the Mongol
  conquest North China.
b. 1189
d. 1243
Source: *EncWB 98*

Ye Jianying
Chinese. Political Leader
A founder, People's Liberation Army;
  one of leaders of the "Long March,"
  1934-35.
b. May 14, 1897 in Meixien, China
d. Oct 22, 1986 in Beijing, China
Source: *AnObit 1986; ConNews 87-1;
EncChi; EncRev; FacFETw*

Yekuno Amlak
Ethiopian. King
Restored the Solomonic dynasty to the
  throne of Ethiopia during his rule from
  c. 1268 to 1283.
b. fl. 1268

Yellen, Jack
American. Author, Songwriter
Wrote "Happy Days Are Here Again,"
  1929, which became campaign theme
  song for Franklin Delano Roosevelt,
  1932.
b. Jul 6, 1892 in Razcki, Poland
d. Apr 17, 1991 in Springville, New
  York
Source: *AmPS; AmSong; ASCAP 66, 80;
BiDAmM; BiE&WWA; BioIn 4, 15, 17;
CmpEPM; NewCBMT; NotNAT;
OxCPMus; Songw; Sw&Ld C; WhAm
10; WhoEnt 92; WorAl; WorAlBi*

Yellow Robe, Rosebud
American. Author
Published stories she learned from her
  father in *Tonweya and the Eagles, and
  Other Lakota Indian Tales,* 1979.
b. Feb 26, 1907
d. Oct 5, 1992
Source: *AZNatAW; BioIn 21; NotNaAm*

Yeltsin, Boris (Nikolayevich)
Russian. Political Leader
First popularly elected pres. in Russia's
  history, 1991-99.
b. Feb 1, 1931 in Sverdlovsk, Union of
  Soviet Socialist Republics
Source: *BioIn 15, 16, 18; CamBiEn;
ChamBiD; ConAu 140; CurBio 89;
EncCW; FacFETw; IntWW 89, 91, 93,
97, 98, 2000; News 91, 91-1; NewYTBS
90, 91; Who 94, 98, 99, 2000; WhoIntA
2; WhoRus; WhoWor 91, 93, 95, 96, 97,
98, 99, 2000; WorAlBi; WrDr 96, 98,
99, 2000*

Yen, Samuel
Chinese. Endocrinologist
Known for studies on growth hormone
  Dehydroepiandrosterone.
b. Feb 22, 1927 in Beijing, China
Source: *News 96*

Yen Fu
Chinese. Scholar, Translator
Introduced European political theory and
  sociological ideas to China through his
  influential translations and annotations.
b. 1853 in Fukien Province, China
d. 1921, China
Source: *EncWB 98*

Yen Hsi-shan
Chinese. Ruler
Warlord ruled northwestern province of
  Shansi from 1911 to 1949; under his
  reforms the region was called a model
  province.
b. 1883 in Ho-pien, China
d. May 24, 1960, Taiwan
Source: *EncWB 98; HarEnMi*

Yen Li-pen
Chinese. Painter
Regarded as the greatest painter of the
  early T'ang dynasty, artist was
  generally a figure painter known for
  his confident, expressive style and fine,
  even brushwork.
d. 673, China
Source: *EncWB 98*

Yeon, John B
American. Architect
Mostly self-taught; noted for
  manipulation of landscape in designs:
  Visitors Information Center, Portland,
  1948.
b. 1910 in Portland, Oregon
Source: *MacEA; McGDA*

Yepremian, Garo
[Garabed Sarkis Yepremian]
American. Football Player
Kicker, 1966-67, 1970-81, mostly with
  Miami; led NFL in scoring, 1971.
b. Jun 2, 1944 in Larnaca, Cyprus
Source: *BioIn 13, 14; NewYTBE 72;*
NewYTBS 80; WhoAm 82; WhoFtbl 74

Yerby, Frank (Garvin)
American. Author
Popular historical romances include
  Foxes of Harrow, 1946; *McKenzie's*
  Hundred, 1986.
b. Sep 5, 1916 in Augusta, Georgia
d. Nov 29, 1991 in Madrid, Spain
Source: *AmAu&B; AmNov; AnObit 1992;*
Au&Wr 71; Benet 87, 96; BenetAL 91;
BioIn 1, 2, 3, 4, 5, 7, 9, 12, 14, 17, 18,
19; BlkAWP; BlkLC; BlkWr 1, 3; BlueB
76; CamDcAB; CamGLE; CamHAL;
CivR 74; ConAfAN; ConAu 9R, 16NR;
ConLC 1, 7, 70; ConNov 72, 82, 86, 91;
CurBio 46, 92N; DcEnL; DcLB 76;
DcLEL 1940; DcTwCCu 5; EarBlAP;
EncSoH; GrWrEL N; InB&W 80, 85;
IntAu&W 76, 77, 82, 89, 91, 93; IntWW
74, 75, 76, 77, 78, 79, 80, 81, 82, 83,
89, 91; LegTOT; LinLib L; LivgBAA;
LngCTC; MajTwCW 1; NegAl 76, 89;
Novels; OxCAmL 65, 83, 95; OxCTwCL;
PenC AM; RAdv 14; RfGAmL 4, 87, 94;
ScF&FL 92; SchCGBL; SelBAAf;
SelBAAu; SouBlCW; SouWr; TwCA
SUP; TwCRGW; TwCRHW 90, 94;
WebAB 74, 79; WhAm 10; Who 74, 82,
83, 85, 88, 90, 92; WhoAm 74, 76, 78,
80, 82, 84, 86, 88, 90; WhoBlA 1, 2, 3,
4, 6, 7, 8N; WhoUSWr 88; WhoWrEP
89, 92; WorAl; WrDr 76, 80, 82, 84, 86,
88, 90, 92, 94N

Yergin, Daniel
American. Author
Winner of Pulitzer Prize for general non
  fiction, *The Prize: The Epic Quest for*
  Oil, Money and Power, 1992.
b. Feb 6, 1947 in Los Angeles,
  California
Source: *ConAu 103; CurBio 1999; RAdv*
14; WhoAm 90; WhoPul

Yerkes, Robert Mearns
American. Psychologist
Leader in the development of psychology
  in America, he helped establish
  important new areas of both research
  and practice.
b. May 26, 1876 in Bucks County,
  Pennsylvania
d. Feb 3, 1956
Source: *AmNatBi; ApCAB X; BiDcPsy;*
BiDPsy; BioIn 1, 4, 6, 7, 9, 19;
CamDcAB; DcAmB S6; DcScB; EncWB
98; FacFETw; InSci; LinLib L, S;
McGEWB; NamesHP; NatCAB 43;
OxCAmH; WebAB 74, 79; WhAm 3;
WhNAA; WorAlBi

Yermolova, Maria Nikolayevna
Russian. Actor
Dramatic actress; career spanned 50
  years; first person in Soviet Union to

be named People's Artist of the
  Republic, 1920.
b. Jul 3, 1853 in Moscow, Russia
d. Mar 12, 1928 in Moscow, Union of
  Soviet Socialist Republics
Source: *ContDcW 89; EncWT; IntDcWB;*
NotNAT B

Yes
[Jon Anderson; Peter Banks; Bill
  Bruford; Geoff Downes; Trevor Horn;
  Steve Howe; Tony Kaye; Patrick
  Moraz; Trevor Rabin; Chris Squire;
  Rick Wakeman; Alan White]
English. Music Group
Biggest hit single "Owner of a Lonely
  Heart," 1983.
Source: *Au&Wr 71; BillEnR; BioIn 11,*
14, 15, 16, 17, 18; ConAu 3NR, 45;
ConMuA 80A; ConMus 8; DcLEL 1940;
DcLP 87A; DrAPF 80, 83, 85, 87, 89,
91, 93, 97; EncPR&S 74, 89; EncRk 88;
EncRkSt; HarEnR 86; IlEncRk; MotPP;
NewAgMG; NewAmDM; NewYTBS 85;
OxCPMus; PenEncP; RkOn 78; RkWho
96; RolSEnR 83; St&PR 96, 97; WhoAm
76, 78, 80, 82, 84, 86, 88, 90; WhoEnt
92; WhoHol 92; WhoRock 81; WhoRocM
82; WhoScEu 91-1; WrDr 76, 80, 82, 84,
86, 88

Yeshurun, Avot
[Yehiel Perlmutter]
Israeli. Poet
Poetry collections include *The Wisdom of*
  the Road, 1942 (*Al Hahmot Derahim*);
  one of the first Israeli poets to discuss
  the establishment of a Palestinian
  homeland.
b. Sep 1904 in Niskish, Poland
d. Feb 22, 1992 in Jerusalem, Israel
Source: *ConAu 132, 136; ConLC 76;*
WhoWorJ 72, 78

Yetnikoff, Walter
American. Music Executive
Pres. CBS/Records Group, 1975—; vp,
  director, CBS Inc.
b. Aug 11, 1933 in New York, New
  York
Source: *BioIn 15, 16; ConNews 88-1;*
Dun&B 88; WhoAm 90; WhoEnt 92

Yeutter, Clayton Keith
American. Government Official
US trade representative, 1985-1989; US
  Secretary of Agriculture, 1989-1993.
b. Dec 10, 1930 in Eustis, Nebraska
Source: *BiDrUSE 89; BioIn 14, 15, 16;*
CngDr 89; CurBio 88; IntWW 91;
NewYTBS 85, 86; WhoAm 74, 76, 82,
86, 88, 90, 92, 95, 96; WhoAmL 79;
WhoAmP 73, 75, 77, 79, 81, 83, 85, 87,
89, 91, 93, 95, 97, 1999; WhoE 91, 93,
95; WhoFI 81, 85, 87, 89, 92; WhoGov
72, 75, 77; WhoWor 91, 93, 95

Yevtushenko, Yevgeny
Russian. Poet
Wrote poems critical of Stalin's legacy;
  wrote "Babiy Yar," 1961, attacking
  anti-Semitism, and "Stalin's Heirs,"
  1962.

b. Jul 18, 1933 in Zima Junction, Union
  of Soviet Socialist Republics
Source: *ConAu 33NR, 81; ConLC 26,*
51; CurBio 94; CyWA 97; LegTOT;
LinLib L; MagSWL; MajTwCW 1;
MakMC; NotPoe; RAdv 14, 13-2;
SocPrL; WhoHol 92; WorAlBi

Yezierska, Anzia
American. Author
Wrote of NY's Jewish immigrants:
  Hungry Hearts, 1920.
b. 1885 in Sukovoly, Russia
d. Nov 21, 1970 in Ontario, California
Source: *AmAu&B; ArtclWW 2; BenetAL*
91; BioIn 2, 4, 7, 9, 12, 14, 15, 17, 19,
20, 21, 22; BlmGWL; CamDcAB;
CamGLE; CamHAL; ConAu 89, 126;
ConLC 46; DcAmImH; DcLB 28;
InWom, SUP; JeAmFiW; LinLib L;
MajTwCW 1; NotAW MOD; OxCAmL
65, 83, 95; OxCTwCL; REnAL; TwCA,
SUP; WhAm 7; WomNov; WorAu 1900

Yi Hwang
Korean. Philosopher, Poet, Scholar
One of the leading Confucian
  philosophers in Korea, poet-scholar is
  best known for his studies of the Neo-
  Confucian philosopher Chu Hsi.
b. 1501, Republic of Korea
d. 1570 in Andong, Republic of Korea

Yilmaz, Mesut
Turkish. Political Leader
Leader of the center-right Motherland
  Party (ANAP), he served as prime
  minister of Turkey three times, the last
  beginning in 1997.
b. 1947 in Istanbul, Turkey
Source: *ChamBiD; PolEnME; ProfiWG*
98; WhoIntA 2; WhoWor 95, 98, 99,
2000

Yi Sng-gye
Korean. Military Leader, Ruler
Skilled military leader unified Korea
  under Chinese suzerainty, and founded
  the pro-Ming, anti-Buddhist Yi
  dynasty.
b. 1335 in Ynghung, Republic of Korea
d. Jun 18, 1408, Republic of Korea

Yi Sunsin
Korean. Military Leader
Naval hero and military strategist
  remembered for his spectacular
  victories in the naval battles of the
  Japanese invasions of Korea.
b. Apr 18, 1545 in Seoul, Republic of
  Korea
d. Dec 15, 1598

Yngjo
Korean. King
Brilliant king of the Yi dynasty, ruled
  from 1724 to 1776 and restored
  political order to Korea.
b. Oct 31, 1694, Republic of Korea
d. Apr 22, 1776 in Seoul, Republic of
  Korea

Yoakam, Dwight

American. Singer
Country singer's hits include *Honky Tonk Man,* 1987; named best new male vocalist 1987 by the American Academy of Country Music.
b. Oct 23, 1956 in Pikeville, Kentucky
Source: *AllMGCo; BgBkCoM; BillEnR; BioIn 16; CelR 90; ChamBiD; ConMus 1, 21; ConTFT 17; EncRkSt; LegTOT; News 92; Songw; WhoAm 92, 94, 95, 96, 97, 98; WhoEnt 92, 98; WhoNeCM*

Yoba, Malik

[Abdul-Malik Kashie Yoba]
American. Actor
Appeared in films *Cool Runnings,* 1992; *Smoke,* 1995.
b. Sep 17, 1967 in New York, New York
Source: *ConBlB 11; ConTFT 17; WhoAfA 9, 10, 11, 12*

Yo Fei

[Yo P'eng-chu]
Chinese. Military Leader
General became a symbol of nationalist resistance to foreign aggression by leading the Chinese army against the invading Chin; canonized as the Saint of War.
b. 1103 in T'ang-yin, Honan, China
d. 1141, China

Yogananda, Paramahansa, Swami

[Mukunda Lal Ghosh]
Indian. Mystic
Founder, Self-Realization Fellowship, 1950; taught Kriya yoga.
b. Jan 5, 1893 in Gorakhpur, India
d. Mar 7, 1952 in Los Angeles, California
Source: *AmNatBi; BiDAmCu; EncO&P 1, 2, 3; NewAgE 90; ObitOF 79; RelLAm 2*

Yokich, Stephen P.

American. Labor Union Official
President of the International Union of United Automobile, Aerospace, and Agricultural Implement Workers of America (UAW), 1995—.
b. Aug 20, 1935 in Detroit, Michigan
Source: *BioIn 13; CurBio 98; News 95; WhoAm 99, 2000; WhoFI 00*

Yon, Pietro Alessandro

American. Organist, Composer
Organist, musical director, NY's St. Patrick's Cathedral since 1926.
b. Aug 8, 1886 in Turin, Italy
d. Nov 22, 1943 in Long Island, New York
Source: *AmNatBi; ASCAP 66, 80; BakBD 78, 84, 92; BakBDTw; BioIn 1, 4, 6; ConAmC 76, 82; CurBio 44; DcAmB S3; DcCathB; NewGrDA 86; WhAm 2*

Yonge, Charlotte Mary

English. Author
Writings include *The Heir of Redclyffe,* 1853; *The Daisy Chain,* 1856.
b. Aug 11, 1823 in Otterbourne, England
d. Mar 24, 1901 in Elderfield, England
Source: *Alli; BiCoLiE; BiD&SB; BioIn 22; CamBiEn; CasWL; ChamBiD; ConAu 163; DcBiA; DcBiPP; DcEnA, A; DcEnL; DcEuL; DcLB 163; DcLEL; EvLB; FamSYP; JBA 34; NewC; OxCEng 67; PenC ENG; REn; SJGChWr 5A; WhoChL; WhoChr; WomWrGB*

Yonger Brothers, The

[Bob Younger; Cole Younger; Jim Younger]
American. Criminals
Famous gang of robbers, murderers; rode with James brothers.
Source: *BioIn 2, 4, 7, 8, 9, 10; DrInf; REnAW*

Yordan, Philip

American. Screenwriter
Won Oscar for *Broken Lance,* 1954; films include *God's Little Acre,* 1958.
b. 1913 in Chicago, Illinois
Source: *BiDFilm 94; CmMov; ConAu 116, 129; FilmEn; FilmgC; GangFlm; HalFC 80, 84, 88; IntMPA 77, 86, 92, 94; ItaFilm; NotNAT; OxCAmT 84; OxCFilm; VarWW 85; WorEFlm*

York, David

American. Social Worker
Founded Toughlove to help parents solve problems with children through strict discipline.
b. 1929? in Long Island, New York
Source: *BioIn 12*

York, Dick

[Richard Allen York]
American. Actor
Played the first Darrin in TV series "Bewitched," 1964-69.
b. Sep 4, 1928 in Fort Wayne, Indiana
d. Feb 20, 1992 in Grand Rapids, Michigan
Source: *AnObit 1992; BioIn 16, 19; EncAFC; FilmgC; ForYSC; HalFC 80, 84, 88; IntMPA 75, 76, 77, 78, 79, 80, 81, 82, 84, 86, 88, 92; LegTOT; MotPP; News 92; NewYTBS 92; RadStar; WhoHol 92, A*

York, Edward Palmer

American. Architect
Designs include post office, customs house, courts bldg., Honolulu, HI.
b. 1865 in Wellsville, New York
d. Dec 30, 1928
Source: *BiDAmAr; BioIn 2; BriEAA; MacEA; WhAm 1*

York, Michael

[Michael York-Johnson]
English. Actor
Starred in *The Island of Dr. Moreau,* 1977; on tour in *Cyrano de Bergerac,* 1981.

b. Mar 27, 1942 in Fulmer, England
Source: *BioIn 8, 10, 11, 18; BkPepl; CamBiEn; CelR, 90; ConTFT 1, 6, 13, 24; CurBio 76; DcPseud; FilmAG WE; FilmEn; FilmgC; HalFC 80, 84, 88; IlWWBF; IntDcF 1-3; IntMPA 75, 76, 77, 78, 79, 80, 81, 82, 84, 86, 88, 92, 94, 96; IntWW 82, 83, 89, 91, 93, 98, 2000; ItaFilm; LegTOT; MotPP; MovMk; OxCFilm; Who 85, 88, 90, 92, 94, 98, 99, 2000; WhoAm 76, 78, 80, 82, 84, 86, 88, 90, 92, 94, 98, 99, 2000; WhoEnt 92, 98; WhoHol 92, A; WhoHrs 80; WorAl; WorAlBi*

York, Rudy

[Rudolph Preston York]
American. Baseball Player
First baseman, 1934, 1937-48, mostly with Detroit; led AL in home runs, RBIs, 1943.
b. Aug 17, 1913 in Ragland, Alabama
d. Feb 5, 1970 in Rome, Georgia
Source: *Ballpl 90; BioIn 1, 4, 6, 8; WhoProB 73; WhoSpor*

York, Sergeant

[Alvin Cullum York]
American. Soldier
WW I hero; autobiography *Sergeant York* was filmed, 1941; won 50 medals including Congressional Medal of Honor.
b. Dec 13, 1887 in Pall Mall, Tennessee
d. Dec 2, 1964 in Nashville, Tennessee
Source: *BioIn 1, 2, 4, 5, 6, 7, 8, 9, 12, 14, 15; DcAmB S7; DcAmMiB; NewCol 75; WebAB 74, 79; WebAMB; WorAl*

York, Susannah

[Susannah Yolande Fletcher]
English. Actor
1969 Oscar nominee for *They Shoot Horses, Don't They?*
b. Jan 9, 1941 in London, England
Source: *BiDFilm, 81, 94; BioIn 5, 6, 9, 10, 11, 16; CelR; ChamBiD; ConAu 130; ConTFT 5; DcPseud; FilmEn; FilmgC; HalFC 84, 88; IlWWBF; IntMPA 86, 88, 92, 94, 96; IntWW 77, 78, 79, 80, 81, 82, 83, 89, 91, 93; IntWWW 2; InWom SUP; LegTOT; MotPP; MovMk; OsStAZ; OxCFilm; Who 85, 92; WhoAm 76, 86, 90; WhoEnt 92; WhoHol A; WhoWor 87, 91; WorAlBi; WrDr 94, 96, 98*

Yorty, Sam(uel William)

American. Politician
Mayor of Los Angeles, 1961-73.
b. Oct 1, 1909 in Lincoln, Nebraska
d. Jun 5, 1998 in Los Angeles, California
Source: *BiDrAC; BiDrUSC 89; BioIn 5, 7, 8, 9, 10, 11, 12; BlueB 76; CmCal; CurBio 98N; IntWW 74, 75, 76, 77, 78, 79, 80, 81, 82, 83; PolProf J, K, NF; WhoAm 74, 76, 78, 80, 82, 84, 86, 90; WhoAmP 73, 75, 77, 79, 81, 83, 85, 87, 89, 91, 93, 95; WhoGov 72; WhoWor 74*

Yoshida, Shigeru
Japanese. Political Leader
Prime minister of Japan, 1946-47, 1948-49; signed peace treaty with Allied Nations, 1951.
b. Sep 22, 1878 in Tokyo, Japan
d. Oct 20, 1967 in Oisi, Japan
Source: *Au&Wr 71; BioIn 1, 2, 3, 8, 12, 13, 14, 16, 23; CamBiEn; ConAu 113; CurBio 46, 68; FacFETw; HisEWW; McGEWB; ObitT 1961; REn; WhAm 4A; WhDW*

Yoshihito
Japanese. Ruler
Father of Hirohito; reigned as emperor, 1912-26.
b. Aug 31, 1879 in Tokyo, Japan
d. Dec 25, 1926 in Hayama, Japan
Source: *ChamBiD*

Yoshimoto, Banana
[Mahoko Yoshimoto]
Japanese. Author
Wrote novels *Tugumi,* 1989; *NP,* 1991.
b. 1964 in Tokyo, Japan
Source: *BioIn 21, 23; ConAu 144; ConLC 84; DcPseud; IntWWW 2; WrDr 96, 98, 99, 2000*

Yoshimune, Tokugawa
Japanese. Ruler
Shogun attempted to revitalize the Tokugawa shogunate after the economic and other difficulties of the late 17th and early 18th centuries.
b. 1684, Japan
d. 1751, Japan
Source: *EncWB 98*

Yost, Charles Woodruff
"The Gray Ghost"
American. Diplomat
One of founders of UN; chief American delegate, 1969-71.
b. Nov 6, 1907 in Watertown, New York
d. May 21, 1981 in Washington, District of Columbia
Source: *BioIn 4, 5, 8, 10, 11, 12, 16, 24; BlueB 76; ConAu 3NR, 9R, 104; CurBio 59, 81; DcAmDH 80, 89; IntWW 74, 75, 76, 77, 78, 79, 80, 81, 81N; PolProf K; ScrEAmL 1; WhAm 8, 10; Who 74; WhoAm 74, 76, 78, 80, 82; WhoGov 72, 75; WhoWor 74*

Yost, Fielding Harris
"Hurry Up"
American. Football Coach
Head coach, U of MI, 1901-25; won first Rose Bowl, 1902.
b. Apr 30, 1871 in Fairview, West Virginia
d. Aug 20, 1946 in Ann Arbor, Michigan
Source: *AmNatBi; BiDAmSp FB; BioIn 1, 4, 10; CamDcAB; CurBio 46; DcAmB S4; WhAm 2; WhoFtbl 74*

Yothers, Tina
American. Actor
Played Jennifer Keaton on TV comedy "Family Ties," 1982-89.

b. May 5, 1973 in Whittier, California
Source: *BioIn 14, 15; ConTFT 21; LegTOT; WhoHisp 91, 92, 94; WhoHol 92*

Youlou, Fulbert
Congolese. Clergy, Political Leader
Priest rose to the presidency of the Republic of the Congo.
b. Jul 9, 1917 in Brazzaville, Congo
d. May 5, 1972 in Madrid, Spain
Source: *BioIn 5, 6, 7, 9, 10, 21; CurBio 72N; DcAfHiB 86; EncWB 98; FacFETw; McGEWB*

Youmans, Vincent
American. Composer
Wrote song "Tea for Two," 1926; Broadway scores include *No, No, Nanette,* 1925.
b. Sep 27, 1898 in New York, New York
d. Apr 5, 1946 in Denver, Colorado
Source: *AmNatBi; AmPS; AmSong; ASCAP 66, 80; BakBD 78, 84; BakDcM; BestMus; BioIn 1, 3, 4, 5, 6, 9, 10, 12, 14, 15, 16; CmpEPM; CndCPOM; ConAmC 76, 82; CurBio 44, 46; DcAmB S4; EncMT; EncWT; FacFETw; HalFC 80, 84, 88; LegTOT; Music; NewAmDM; NewCBMT; NewGrDA 86; NewGrDM 80; NotNAT B; OxCAmT 84; OxCPMus; PenEncP; PlP&P; PopAmC, SUP; Songw; Sw&Ld C; WorAlBi*

Young, Alan (Angus)
American. Comedian, Actor
Starred in TV series "Mister Ed," 1961-65.
b. Nov 19, 1919 in North Shields, England
Source: *BioIn 2, 3, 18, 21; CurBio 53; EncAFC; FilmEn; FilmgC; ForYSC; HalFC 80, 84, 88; IntMPA 75, 76, 77, 78, 79, 80, 81, 82, 84, 86, 88, 92, 94, 96; JoeFr; LegTOT; RadStar; VarWW 83; Who 92; WhoHol 92, A; WhoHrs 80; WorAl; WorAlBi*

Young, Andrew
Scottish. Author
Writings include *Burning as Light,* 1967.
b. Apr 29, 1885 in Elgin, Scotland
d. Nov 26, 1971 in Bognor Regis, England
Source: *Au&Wr 71; BiCoLiE; BioIn 3, 4, 5, 6, 10; CamGLE; CmScLit; CnE&AP; CnMWL; ConAu 5R, 7NR, 29NR; ConBlB 3; ConLC 5; ConPo 70; DcLEL; EngPo; EvLB; LngCTC; NewC; OxCEng 67; PenC ENG; RfGEnL 91; TwCWr; WebE&AL; WhE&EA; WhoTwCL; WorAu 1950*

Young, Andrew Jackson, Jr.
American. Politician
Ambassador to UN, 1977-79; mayor of Atlanta, 1982-90; awarded Spingarn Medal, 1980; French Legion of Honor, 1982-89; chm., Law Cos. International Group Inc., 1990—.
b. Mar 12, 1932 in New Orleans, Louisiana

Source: *AfrAmBi 1; AfrAmOr; AmDec 1970; AmPolLe; BiDrUSC 89; BioNews 74; BkPepl; BlkAmsC; CamBiEn; CamDcAB; ChamBiD; DcAmDH 80, 89; DiAAPGL; Ebony 1; EncWB, 98; HisDCRM; InB&W 80, 85; NewYTBS 76, 77, 79; PolProf NF; Who 85; WhoAm 86; WhoAmP 87; WhoBlA 4; WhoSSW 97; WhoWor 84*

Young, Angus
Scottish. Musician
Knickers-clad guitarist with AC-DC since 1973.
b. Mar 31, 1959 in Glasgow, Scotland
Source: *AmPolLe; BiDrUSC 89; BioIn 14, 15; BlkAmsC; DcAmDH 89; LegTOT; OnThGG; Who 88; WhoAm 88; WhoAmP 87; WhoBlA 7; WhoSSW 88*

Young, Ann Eliza Webb
American. Author, Lecturer
An ex-wife of Brigham Young, 1869; exposed Mormon polygamy: *Life in Mormon Bondage,* 1876.
b. Sep 13, 1844 in Nauvoo, Illinois
d. 1908?
Source: *AmWomWr; InWom, SUP; LibW; NotAW*

Young, Art(hur Henry)
American. Cartoonist, Author
Contributed cartoons to *Life; Puck; Colliers* magazines.
b. Jan 14, 1866 in Orangeville, Illinois
d. Dec 29, 1943 in Bethel, Connecticut
Source: *AmAu&B; AmNatBi; BenetAL 91; BiDAmJo; BioIn 11, 12, 16; BriEAA; ChhPo S3; CurBio 40, 44; DcAmB S3; DcAmSR; DcNAA; EncAJ; EncAL; OxCAmL 65, 83; REnAL; WhAm 2; WhNAA*

Young, Brigham
American. Religious Leader
Baptized into Mormon faith, 1832; emigrated church to Utah, 1848, governor, 1850-58; had 27 wives, 47 children.
b. Jun 1, 1801 in Whitingham, Vermont
d. Aug 29, 1877 in Salt Lake City, Utah
Source: *AmAu&B; AmBi; AmNatBi; AmSocL; ApCAB; BenetAL 91; BiAUS; BiDAmCu; BiDrATG; BioIn 1, 2, 3, 4, 5, 6, 7, 8, 9, 10, 11, 12, 13, 14, 15, 17, 18, 19, 20, 21, 22, 23, 24; CamBiEn; CamDcAB; CelCen; ChamBiD; CyAG; DcAmB; DcAmReB 1, 2; DcBiPP; Drake; EncAAH; EncAB-H 1974, 1996; EncARH; EncRelA; EncWB 98; HarEnUS; HisWorL; LegTOT; LinLib L, S; LuthC 75; McGEWB; MemAm; NatCAB 7, 16; NewEAmW; OxCAmH; OxCAmL 65, 83, 95; PeoHis; RComAH; REn; REnAL; REnAW; TwCBDA; WebAB 74, 79; WhAm HS; WhNaAH; WhoChr; WhWE; WorAl; WorAlBi*

Young, Burt
American. Actor, Screenwriter
Oscar nominee for *Rocky,* 1976.
b. Apr 30, 1940 in New York, New York

Source: *BioIn 15; ConTFT 5; EncAFC; HalFC 84, 88; IntMPA 84, 86, 88, 92, 94, 96; ItaFilm; LegTOT; OsStAZ; WhoAm 80, 82, 84, 86, 88, 90, 92, 94, 99, 2000; WhoEnt 92A, 98; WhoHol 92, A*

Young, Candy
[Canzetta Young]
American. Track Athlete
b. 1963?
Source: *BioIn 12; InB&W 80*

Young, Charles Augustus
American. Astronomer
Discovered solar reversing layer, 1870.
b. Dec 15, 1834 in Hanover, New Hampshire
d. Jan 4, 1908 in Hanover, New Hampshire
Source: *Alli SUP; AmBi; AmNatBi; ApCAB; BbD; BiDAmEd; BiDAmS; BiD&SB; BiInAmS; BioIn 1, 11, 14; DcAmAu; DcAmB; DcNAA; DcScB; InSci; NatCAB 6; RanHWDS; TwCBDA; WhAm 1*

Young, Chic
[Murat Bernard Young]
American. Cartoonist
Created comic strip "Blondie," 1930.
b. Jan 9, 1901 in Chicago, Illinois
d. Mar 14, 1973 in Saint Petersburg, Florida
Source: *AmNatBi; BioIn 1, 3, 9; CamBiEn; ChamBiD; ConAu 41R; EncACom; EncTwCJ; LegTOT; LinLib L; NewYTBE 73; WebAB 74, 79; WhAm 5, 6; WhoAm 74; WhoAmA 76, 78N, 80N, 82N, 84N, 86N, 89N, 91N, 93N*

Young, Clara Kimball
American. Actor
Starred in Vitagraph films, 1909-15.
b. Sep 1890 in Chicago, Illinois
d. Oct 15, 1960 in Woodland Hills, California
Source: *EncAFC; Film 1, 2; FilmEn; FilmgC; FrSilen; HalFC 80, 84, 88; InWom SUP; LegTOT; MotPP; MovMk; NotNAT B; ObitOF 79; OxCFilm; SilFlmP; TwYS; WhAm 4; WhoHol B; WhScrn 74, 77, 83; WomWMM; WorAl*

Young, Coleman A(lexander)
American. Politician
First black mayor of Detroit, 1974-93; served longer than any other mayor in city's history; won Spingarn, 1980.
b. May 24, 1918 in Tuscaloosa, Alabama
d. Nov 29, 1997 in Detroit, Michigan
Source: *BiDAmL; BioIn 10, 11, 12, 13, 14, 16; BioNews 74; BlueB 76; CamDcAB; ConAu 156, 162; ConBlB 1; CurBio 77, 98N; EncWB, 98; InB&W 80, 85; NegAl 89A; WhAm 12; WhoAm 76, 78, 80, 82, 84, 86, 88, 90, 92, 94; WhoAmP 85, 87, 91; WhoBlA 4, 7; WhoGov 75, 77; WhoMW 80, 82, 84, 86, 88, 90, 92, 93; WorAl; WorAlBi*

Young, Cy
[Denton True Young]
American. Baseball Player
Pitcher, 1890-1911; holds many ML records, including most wins, 511, most losses, 313; Hall of Fame, 1937.
b. Mar 29, 1867 in Gilmore, Ohio
d. Nov 4, 1955 in Peoli, Ohio
Source: *AmNatBi; Ballpl 90; BiDAmSp BB; BioIn 2, 3, 4, 5, 6, 7, 8, 9, 10, 14, 15, 17, 22; CamBiEn; ChamBiD; CulEncB; DcAmB S5; FacFETw; LegTOT; WebAB 74, 79; WhAm 4, HSA; WhoProB 73; WhoSpor; WorAl; WorAlBi*

Young, Edward
English. Author
"Graveyard School" poet; wrote blank verse *Complaint, or Night Thoughts,* 1742-44.
b. Jun 1683 in Upham, England
d. Apr 5, 1765 in Welwyn Garden City, England
Source: *Alli; AtlBL; BbD; Benet 87, 96; BiCoLiE; BiD&SB; BioIn 1, 2, 3, 6, 8, 9, 10, 16, 17; BlkwCE; BlmGEL; BritAu; CamBiEn; CamGEL; CamGLE; CasWL; ChamBiD; ChhPo, S2, S3; CnE&AP; CrtT 2, 4; CyWA 97; DcArts; DcEnA; DcEnL; DcEuL; DcLB 95; DcLEL; DcNaB; EvLB; GrWrEL P; LinLib L; LitC 3, 40; LngCEL; MouLC 2; NewC; NewCBEL; OxCEng 67, 85, 95; OxCFr; OxCGer 76; PenC ENG; REn; RfGEnL 91; WebE&AL*

Young, Faron
"The Sheriff"
American. Singer, Musician
Recorded over 60 albums, 105 singles, including 32 number-one hits; wrote "I Miss You Already," 1957.
b. Feb 25, 1932 in Shreveport, Louisiana
d. Dec 10, 1996 in Nashville, Tennessee
Source: *AllMGCo; BakBD 84, 92; BgBkCoM; BiDAmM; BioIn 14, 22, 23; ConMus 7; CounME 74; EncFCWM 69, 83; HarEnCM 87; IlEncCM; LegTOT; ObitPA 96; OxCPMus; PenEncP; RkOn 74; WhAm 12; WhoAm 82, 84, 86, 88; WhoHol 92, A*

Young, George
American. Track Athlete
Long-distance runner; first American runner on four Olympic teams, 1960-72; won bronze medal in steeplechase, 1968 Olympics.
b. Jul 24, 1937 in Roswell, New Mexico
Source: *WhoTr&F 73*

Young, Gig
[Bryon Ellsworth Barr; Roland Reed]
American. Actor
Won Oscar for *They Shoot Horses, Don't They?,* 1969.
b. Nov 4, 1913 in Saint Cloud, Minnesota
d. Oct 19, 1978 in New York, New York
Source: *BiE&WWA; BioIn 9, 10, 11; CelR; DcPseud; EncAFC; FilmEn; FilmgC; HalFC 80, 84, 88; HolP 40; IntDcF 1-3; IntMPA 77; ItaFilm;*

MotPP; MovMk; ObitOF 79; OsStAZ; WhAm 7; WhoAm 74; WhoHol A; WhoThe 81N; WhScrn 83

Young, Jean Childs
American. Civil Rights Activist, Educator
Teacher and civil rights activist also worked for improvement in education and children's welfare; chairperson of the International Year of the Child, 1978; wife of civil rights leader Andrew Young.
b. Jul 1, 1933 in Marion, Alabama
d. Sep 16, 1994 in Atlanta, Georgia
Source: *BioIn 20; ConBlB 14; NotBlAW 2; WhoAfA 9; WhoBlA 3, 4, 5, 6, 7, 8*

Young, John Alan
American. Business Executive
President, Hewlett-Packard Co., electronics and computer firm, 1977-92.
b. Apr 24, 1932 in Nampa, Idaho
Source: *AmMWSc 98; BioIn 13; CurBio 86; Dun&B 90; WhoAm 76, 78, 80, 82, 84, 86, 88, 90, 92, 94, 95, 96, 97, 98, 99, 2000; WhoFI 00, 75, 77, 79, 81, 83, 85, 87, 89, 92, 94, 96, 98; WhoScEn 94, 96, 2000; WhoWest 00, 82, 84, 87, 89, 92, 94, 96, 98; WhoWor 84, 87, 89*

Young, John Watts
American. Astronaut
On maiden voyage of space shuttle *Columbia,* 1981.
b. Sep 24, 1930 in San Francisco, California
Source: *AmMWSc 92; BioIn 7, 8, 9, 10, 12, 13; IntWW 74; RanHWDS; WhoAm 80, 82, 84, 86, 88, 90, 92, 94, 95, 96, 97, 98, 99, 2000; WhoScEn 94, 2000; WhoSSW 73, 95, 97, 99; WhoWor 74; WorAl*

Young, Kevin
American. Track Athlete
Won gold medal, 400-meter hurdle, 1992; first person to break 47 seconds in the 400-meter hurdle.
b. Sep 16, 1966 in Los Angeles, California
Source: *AfrAmSG; BioIn 15; Law&B 89A; WhoAm 2000; WhoEmL 89; WhoMW 90*

Young, Lester Willis
"Prez"
American. Jazz Musician
Leading tenor saxist, prominent 1930s-40s; pioneered modern "cool" style.
b. Aug 27, 1909 in Woodville, Mississippi
d. Mar 15, 1959 in New York, New York
Source: *AfrAmAl 8; ASCAP 66; BiDAmM; CamBiEn; CamDcAB; ChamBiD; CmpEPM; EncWB 98; IlEncJ; MusMk; NewGrDM 80; WhAm 5; WhoJazz 72*

Young, Loretta Gretchen
American. Actor
Won Oscar for *The Farmer's Daughter*,
1947; star of TV series "The Loretta
Young Show," 1953-61.
b. Jan 6, 1913 in Salt Lake City, Utah
Source: *BiDFilm; BioIn 14, 15; CurBio
48; EncAFC; Film 1; FilmgC; HalFC
84; IntMPA 86, 88; MotPP; MovMk;
OxCFilm; ThFT; TwYS; WhoAm 82, 88;
WhoAmW 89; WhoHol A; WorEFlm*

Young, Lyman
American. Cartoonist
Best known for comic strip "Tim
Tyler," 1940s-50s.
Source: *EncACom; WorECom*

Young, Mahonri Mackintosh
American. Sculptor
Executed Mormon statues, Indian groups;
first prize for sculpture, 1932 Olympic
Games.
b. Aug 9, 1877 in Salt Lake City, Utah
d. Nov 2, 1957 in New York, New York
Source: *AmNatBi; BioIn 4, 7;
CamDcAB; DcAmArt; DcAmB S6;
GrAmP; IlBEAAW; McGDA; WhAm 3;
WhAmArt 85*

Young, Malcolm
Scottish. Musician
Guitarist, who helped form AC-DC,
1973.
b. Jan 6, 1953 in Glasgow, Scotland

Young, Margaret Ann Buckner
American. Children's Author
Writings include *Black American
Leaders*, 1969; *The Picture Life of
Thurgood Marshall*, 1970.
b. Mar 20, 1922 in Campbellsville,
Kentucky
Source: *BioIn 16; BkP; BlkAuII; InB&W
85; SelBAAf; SmATA 2; WhoAmW 91;
WhoBlA 4, 7; WhoE 91; WhoWor 87, 91*

Young, Marguerite (Vivian)
American. Author
Wrote epic novel *Miss MacIntosh, My
Darling*, 1965.
b. 1909 in Indianapolis, Indiana
Source: *AmAu&B; AmWomWr; ArtclWW
2; BenetAL 91; BioIn 7, 10, 11, 14;
ChhPo, S2; ConAu 150, P-1; ConLC 82;
ConNov 72, 76, 82, 86, 91, 96; DrAF
76; DrAPF 80; FemiCLE; Focus; IndAu
1917; IntAu&W 76, 77; ModWoWr;
WorAu 1950; WrDr 76, 80, 82, 84, 86,
88, 90, 92, 94, 96, 98N*

Young, Marian
[Martha Deane]
American. Radio Performer
Noted for hosting daily radio program,
1941-73; editor of daily newspapers.
b. Nov 21, 1908 in Star Lake, New York
d. Dec 9, 1973 in New York
Source: *BiDrLUS 70; BioIn 10, 11;
CurBio 52, 74; DcPseud; ForWC 70;
InWom SUP; NewYTBE 73; RadStar;
WhoAm 74*

Young, Neil
[Buffalo Springfield; Crosby, Stills,
Nash, and Young]
Canadian. Musician
Albums include *Rust Never Sleeps*, 1979;
Freedom, 1989; *Ragged Glory*, 1990.
b. Nov 12, 1945 in Toronto, Ontario,
Canada
Source: *ABCCoAm; AllMGCo; BakBD
84, 92; BakDcM; BgBkCoM; BillEnR;
BioIn 12, 13, 14, 16; CanWW 89, 96, 97,
98, 1999; ChamBiD; CmpEGui; ConAu
110; ConCaAu 1; ConLC 17; ConMuA
80A; ConMus 2, 15; ConTFT 21; CurBio
80, 98; DcArts; EncFCWM 83;
EncPR&S 89; EncRk 88; EncRkSt;
HarEnCM 87; HarEnR 86; IlEncRk;
LegTOT; NewAmDM; NewGrDA 86;
News 91, 91-2; NewYTBS 92; OnThGG;
PenEncP; RkWho 96; RolSEnR 83;
Songw; Who 92; WhoAm 78, 80, 82, 84,
86, 88, 90, 92, 94, 95, 96, 97, 98, 2000;
WhoEnt 92, 98; WhoHol 92, A;
WhoRock 81; WhoRocM 82; WorAl;
WorAlBi*

Young, Owen D
American. Lawyer, Diplomat
Founded RCA, 1919; chm., German
Reparations Commission, 1929.
b. Oct 27, 1874 in Van Hornesville, New
York
d. Jul 11, 1962 in Saint Augustine,
Florida
Source: *AmNatBi; BiDInt; BioIn 13, 16;
CamDcAB; DcAmBC; DcAmB S7;
DcAmDH 89; EncABHB 7; EncWB 98;
PeoHis*

Young, Paul
[Q-Tips; Streetband]
English. Singer
Lead singer turned soloist who had hit
single "Everytime You Go Away,"
1985.
b. Jan 17, 1956 in Bedfordshire, England
Source: *BillEnR; BioIn 14, 15;
EncPR&S 89; EncRk 88; EncRkSt;
HarEnR 86; LegTOT; PenEncP; RkOn
85; WhoHisp 92*

Young, Philip
American. Government Official
Ambassador to Netherlands, 1957-60;
director of International Chamber of
Commerce, 1960-65.
b. May 9, 1910 in Lexington,
Massachusetts
d. Jan 15, 1987 in Arlington, Virginia
Source: *AnObit 1987; BioIn 2, 3, 15;
CurBio 51, 87, 87N; NewYTBS 87;
WhAm 9; WhoAm 74, 76, 78, 80*

Young, Ralph
[Sandler and Young]
American. Singer
Partner with Tony Sandler, 1960s-70s;
albums include *More and More*.
Source: *CmpEPM*

Young, Robert (George)
American. Actor
Starred in TV series "Father Knows
Best," 1954-60; "Marcus Welby,
MD," 1969-76.
b. Feb 22, 1907 in Chicago, Illinois
d. Jul 21, 1998 in Westlake Village,
California
Source: *BiDFilm; CmMov; FilmgC;
HalFC 84; IntMPA 86; MovMk;
OxCFilm; WhoAm 74, 78, 86; WorEFlm*

Young, Roland
English. Actor
Oscar nominee for *Topper*, 1937.
b. Nov 11, 1887 in London, England
d. Jun 5, 1953 in New York, New York
Source: *BioIn 2, 3, 4, 7, 9, 21; ChhPo;
EncAFC; Film 2; FilmEn; FilmgC;
ForYSC; HalFC 80, 84, 88; HolCA;
LegTOT; MotPP; MovMk; NatCAB 40;
NotNAT B; OlFamFa; OsStAZ; OxCAmT
84; OxCFilm; PIP&P; QDrFCA 92;
Vers A; WhAm 3; WhoHol B; WhoHrs
80; WhScrn 74, 77, 83; WhThe; WorAlBi*

Young, Sean
American. Actor
Films include, *Bladerunner*, 1982; *No
Way Out*, 1987.
b. Nov 20, 1959 in Louisville, Kentucky
Source: *BioIn 14, 15, 16; ConTFT 7, 14,
24; HalFC 88; IntMPA 92, 94, 96;
IntWWW 2; LegTOT; NewYTBS 87;
WhoEnt 92*

Young, Sheila
[Mrs. Jim Ochowicz]
American. Skater
Speed skater; first American to win three
medals in single Olympics, 1976; is
also champion cyclist.
b. Oct 14, 1950 in Birmingham,
Michigan
Source: *BiDAmSp OS; BioIn 10, 11, 12,
17; ChamBiD; CurBio 77; EncWomS;
EncWoSp; InWom SUP; LegTOT;
NewYTBS 74, 76; OutWomA; WorAl*

Young, Stark
American. Author
Best known for *So Red the Rose*.
b. Oct 11, 1881 in Como, Mississippi
d. Jan 6, 1963 in New York, New York
Source: *AmAu&B; AmNatBi; BenetAL
91; BioIn 1, 2, 4, 5, 6, 8, 9, 11, 12, 17,
22; CamDcAB; CamGWoT; CasWL;
CnDAL; ConAmA; ConAmL; ConAu
60NR, 89, 105; CyWA 58, 97; DcAmB
S7; DcLB 9, 102, DS16; EncAJ;
EncSoH; EncWB, 98; EncWT; FifSWrA;
JrnUS; LiveMA; LngCTC; ModAL 4, 5;
NatCAB 52; NotNAT B; OxCAmL 65,
83, 95; OxCAmT 84; OxCThe 67; PenC
AM; REnAL; SouWr; TexWr; TwCA,
SUP; TwCRHW 90, 94; WhAm 4;
WhE&EA; WhNAA; WhThe; WorAu
1900*

Young, Stephen
Canadian. Actor
Starred in TV series "Judd for the
Defense," 1967-69.

b. May 19, 1939 in Toronto, Ontario,
Canada
Source: *DcPseud; FilmgC; HalFC 88;*
ItaFilm; WhoHol 92, A

Young, Steve
[Jon Steven Young]
American. Football Player
Quarterback, signed biggest contract in
pro sports history, $36 million with
USFL LA Express, 1984; Tampa Bay
1985-86; San Francisco, 1987—;
Superbowl MVP, 1994.
b. Oct 11, 1961 in Salt Lake City, Utah
Source: *BioIn 13, 14; CurBio 93;*
FootReg 87; News 95, 95-2; WhoSpor

Young, Terence
American. Director
Noted for James Bond films *Dr. No,*
1963; *From Russia With Love,* 1965;
Thunderball, 1967.
b. Jun 20, 1915 in Shanghai, China
Source: *BiDFilm, 81; BioIn 20, 22;*
CmMov; ConTFT 7, 13; FilmEn;
FilmgC; HalFC 80, 84, 88; IlWWBF;
IntMPA 75, 76, 77, 78, 79, 80, 81, 82,
84, 86, 88, 92, 94; ItaFilm; LegTOT;
MiSFD 9; MovMk; OxCFilm; WhAm 11;
WhoAm 74, 76, 78, 80, 82, 84, 86, 88,
90, 92, 94, 95; WhoHrs 80; WorEFlm

Young, Thomas
English. Physicist
Scientist is best known for his double-slit
interference experiment which
validated the wave theory of light, and
for the elastic modulus named for him.
b. Jun 16, 1773 in Milverton, England
d. May 10, 1829
Source: *Alli; AsBiEn; BiDLA; BiDPsy;*
BiEsc; BiHiMed; BioIn 2, 3, 4, 5, 9, 11,
12, 14, 17, 19; CamBiEn; CamDcSc;
CelCen; ChamBiD; DcBiPP; DcInv;
DcNaB; DcScB; EncWB 98; ICPEnP;
InSci; LarDcSc; LinLib L, S; McGCEnS;
McGEWB; NamesHP; NewCBEL;
OxCMed 86; RanHWDS; WhDW;
WorAl; WorAlBi; WorScD

Young, Trummy
[James Osborne Young]
American. Jazz Musician
Brash trumpeter; prominent, 1930s-50s.
b. Jan 12, 1912 in Savannah, Georgia
Source: *AllMGJa; AmNatBi; AnObit*
1984; BioIn 16; CmpEPM; EncJzS;
InB&W 85; NewGrDJ 88, 94;
OxCPMus; WhoJazz 72

Young, Victor
American. Songwriter, Conductor
Won Oscar for scoring *Around the*
World in Eighty Days, 1956; wrote
words for "Sweet Sue—Just You,"
1928.
b. Aug 8, 1900 in Chicago, Illinois
d. Nov 11, 1956 in Palm Springs,
California
Source: *AmNatBi; AmPS; ASCAP 66, 80;*
BakBD 78, 84, 92; BiDAmM; BioIn 1, 4,
6, 14; CamDcAB; CmMov; CmpEPM;
CndCPOM; ConAmC 76, 82; FacFETw;

FilmEn; FilmgC; HalFC 80, 84, 88;
IntDcF 1-4, 2-4; LegTOT; NewAmDM;
NewGrDA 86; NewGrDM 80; NotNAT
B; OxCFilm; OxCPMus; PenEncP;
PopAmC; RadStar; RkOn 74; Songw;
WhAm 3; WorEFlm

Young, Whitney Moore, Jr.
American. Civil Rights Leader
Director, National Urban League, 1961-
71; wrote *Beyond Racism,* 1969.
b. Jul 31, 1921 in Lincoln Ridge,
Kentucky
d. Mar 11, 1971 in Lagos, Nigeria
Source: *AmNatBi; AmRef; AmSocL;*
BiDSocW; BioIn 6, 7, 8, 9, 10, 11, 12,
15, 16, 19, 23, 24; CamBiEn; ChamBiD;
ConAu P-1; CurBio 65, 71; DcAmB S9;
EncAACR; EncAB-H 1974, 1996;
EncSoH; EncWB 98; HisDCRM; InB&W
80, 85; McGEWB; NatCAB 57;
NewYTBE 70, 71; SelBAAf; SelBAAu;
WebAB 74, 79; WhAm 5; WorAl

Youngblood, Jack
[Herbert Jackson Youngblood, III]
American. Football Player
Seven-time all-pro defensive end, LA
Rams, 1971-84.
b. Jan 26, 1950 in Jacksonville, Florida
Source: *BiDAmSp Sup; BioIn 13, 14, 16,*
22; FootReg 85; LegTOT; NewYTBS 84;
WhoAm 78, 80, 82; WhoFtbl 74; WorAl

Youngblood, Johnny Ray
American. Clergy
Senior pastor, St. Paul Community
Baptist Church, Brooklyn, NY; played
a leading role in developing the
Nehemiah Housing Project in
Brooklyn.
b. Jun 23, 1948 in New Orleans,
Louisiana
Source: *BioIn 20; ConBlB 8; News 94,*
94-1

Youngdahl, Luther Wallace
American. Politician, Judge
District of Columbia Federal judge,
1951-66; dismissed indictments against
Owen Lattimore in McCarthy witch-
hunt; three-term Rep. governor of MN.
b. May 29, 1896 in Minneapolis,
Minnesota
d. Jun 21, 1978 in Washington, District
of Columbia
Source: *AmAu&B; WhoSSW 73*

Younger, Bob
[Younger Brothers; Robert Younger]
American. Outlaw
Started life of crime with brothers at age
12; died in jail.
b. 1853 in Lee's Summit, Missouri
d. 1889 in Minnesota
Source: *BioIn 17, 24; REnAW; WhCiWar*

Younger, Cole
[Younger Brothers; Thomas Coleman
Younger]
American. Outlaw
Known for famous Northfield, MN, bank
raid, 1876; wrote *The Story of Cole*
Younger, 1903.
b. Jan 15, 1844 in Jackson County,
Missouri
d. Mar 21, 1916 in Jackson County,
Missouri
Source: *AmNatBi; BioIn 2, 4, 7, 8, 9, 10,*
17, 18, 20, 24; DcAmB; DcNAA;
NewCol 75; REnAW; WebAB 74, 79;
WhAm 4, HS, HSA; WhCiWar

Younger, Jim
[Younger Brothers; James Younger]
American. Outlaw
Famous for raids with brothers.
b. Jan 15, 1850 in Lee's Summit,
Missouri
d. Oct 19, 1902 in Saint Paul, Minnesota
Source: *REnAW*

Youngerman, Jack
American. Artist
Abstract paintings include "Dive,"
1980; "Ohio," 1977.
b. Mar 25, 1926 in Webster Groves,
Missouri
Source: *BioIn 6, 7, 8, 15; BlueB 76;*
BriEAA; CamDcAB; ConArt 77, 83, 89,
96; CurBio 86; DcCAA 71, 77, 88, 94;
DcCAr 81; DcTwArt; OxCTwCA;
PhDcTCA 77; PrintW 83, 85; WhoAm
74, 76, 78, 80, 84, 86, 88, 90, 92, 94,
95, 96, 97, 98, 99, 2000; WhoAmA 73,
76, 78, 82, 84, 86, 89, 91, 93, 1999;
WhoWor 74, 76; WorArt 1950

Younghusband, Francis Edward
English. Soldier, Explorer
Enthusiastic adventurer led an expedition
to Lhasa and served as president of
the Royal Geographical Society. He
also a crusade for worldwide religious
unity and founded the World
Fellowship of Faiths.
b. 1863
d. 1942
Source: *BioIn 1, 3, 5, 8, 14, 18, 22, 24;*
CamBiEn; ChamBiD; DcInB; DcNaB
1941; EncWB 98; ExplAnT; GrBr;
HisDBrE; InSci; LinLib L, S; McGEWB;
NewCBEL; REn; WhBriIn; WhDW;
WhLit; WhWE

Youngman, Henny
[Henry Youngman]
American. Comedian
Best known for line "Take my wife,
please!"
b. Mar 16, 1906 in Liverpool, England
d. Feb 24, 1998 in New York, New
York
Source: *BioIn 15; CelR; ConAu 107,*
134; ConTFT 23; CurBio 86, 98N;
EncAFC; EncVaud; JoeFr; LegTOT;
News 98, 98-3; NewYTBS 98; NotNAT
A; WhoAm 86, 88; WhoCom; WhoHol
92, A; WorAl; WorAlBi; WrDr 94, 96,
99

Young Man Afraid of His Horses
[Tasunka Kokipapi]
American. Native American Chief
Chief of the Ogala Sioux of the great
plains; signed the Fort Laramie Treaty,
1868.
b. 1830
d. 1900
Source: *AmIndBi; BioIn 11; NotNaAm*

Young MC
[Marvin Young]
American. Rapper
Rap artist; album *Stone Cold Rhymin'*,
1989 went platinum; won rap
Grammy, 1990.
b. 1968 in London, England
Source: *ConMus 4*

Youngs, Ross Middlebrook
''Pep''
American. Baseball Player
Outfielder, NY Giants, 1917-26, known
for fielding; had .322 lifetime batting
average; Hall of Fame, 1972.
b. Apr 10, 1897 in Shiner, Texas
d. Oct 22, 1927 in San Antonio, Texas
Source: *BiDAmSp BB; WhoProB 73*

Yount, Robin (R.)
American. Baseball Player
Shortstop-outfielder, Milwaukee, 1974-
93; AL MVP, 1982, 1989; led AL in
hits, 1982; 17th player in history to
reach 3,000 hits; Hall of Fame, 1999.
b. Sep 16, 1955 in Woodland Hills,
California
Source: *Ballpl 90; BaseReg 86, 87;
BiDAmSp BB; BioIn 12, 13, 14, 15, 16;
CurBio 93; LegTOT; WhoSpor; WorAlBi*

Yourcenar, Marguerite
[Marguerite Antoinette Jeanne Marie
Ghislaine C. de Crayencour]
French. Author
First woman ever admitted to Academie
Francaise, 1980; masterpiece novel:
Memoires d'Hadrien, 1951.
b. Jun 8, 1903 in Brussels, Belgium
d. Dec 17, 1987 in Bar Harbor, Maine
Source: *AmNatBi, 2S, 3; EuWr 12;
ForWC 70; FrenWW; GayLesB; GayLL
1; GrWomW; GuFrLit 1; IntAu&W 76,
77, 82, 89; IntDcWB; IntWW 74, 75, 76,
77, 78, 79, 80, 81, 82, 83; InWom SUP;
LegTOT; LiExTwC; LinLib L; MajTwCW
1, 2; ModFrL; ModWoWr; NewYTBS 79,
81, 87; RAdv 14, 13-2; REn; RfGWoL
95; ScF&FL 92; WhAm 9; WhoAm 74,
76, 78, 82, 84, 86; WhoAmW 61, 68, 70,
72, 74, 75, 81; WhoFr 79; WhoWor 74,
82, 84, 87; WomFir; WomWrGB; WorAu
1950*

Youskevitch, Igor
Russian. Dancer
Debuted in US at NY Met., 1938; starred
in film *Invitation to the Dance*, 1956.
b. Mar 13, 1912 in Kiev, Russia
d. Jun 13, 1994 in New York, New York

Source: *BiDD; BioIn 3, 4, 5, 12, 13, 20,
21, 22; BlueB 76; CnOxB; CurBio 56,
94N; DancEn 78; IntDcB; NewYTBS 94;
WhAm 11; WhoAm 94; WhoHol 92, A;
WhoWor 74*

Ysaye, Eugene
Belgian. Conductor, Violinist
Violin virtuoso, 1880s-90s; led
Cincinnati Symphony, 1920s; formed
own orchestra in Brussels.
b. Jul 16, 1858 in Liege, Belgium
d. May 13, 1931 in Brussels, Belgium
Source: *BakBD 78, 84; BioIn 1, 2, 5, 11,
12, 14; BriBkM 80; ChamBiD; MusSN;
NewAmDM; NewGrDA 86; NewGrDM
80; NewGrDO; NewOxM; OxCMus;
OxDcOp; PenDiMP; WhAm 1*

Yuan, Shih-Kai
Chinese. Political Leader
Pres. of China, 1913-16; sought to be
dictator, suppressing Sun Yat-sen,
1914.
b. 1859 in Henan Province, China
d. Jun 6, 1916
Source: *BioIn 1, 6, 9, 10, 11; McGEWB;
NewCol 75*

Yuan Mei
Chinese. Author
Critic and one of the great poets of the
Ch'ing dynasty, known for his
naturalness and individuality.
b. 1716
d. 1798
Source: *Benet 96; BioIn 19; EncWB 98*

Yukawa, Hideki
Japanese. Physicist, Educator
Won Nobel Prize in physics, 1949;
discovered meson particles.
b. Jan 23, 1907 in Tokyo, Japan
d. Sep 8, 1981 in Kyoto, Japan
Source: *AnObit 1981; AsBiEn; BiESc;
BioIn 1, 2, 3, 12, 13, 20; CamBiEn;
CamDcSc; ChamBiD; ConAu 108, 163;
CurBio 81, 81N; DcScB S2; EncWB 98;
FacFETw; FarE&A 78, 79, 80, 81;
InSci; IntWW 74, 75, 76, 77, 78, 79, 80,
81, 82N; LarDcSc; McGCEnS;
McGEWB; McGMS 80; NewCol 75;
NewYTBS 81; NobelP; NotTwCS 1;
RAdv 14, 13-5; RanHWDS; SciMath;
WhDW; Who 74, 82N; WhoNob, 90, 95;
WhoWor 74, 80; WorAl; WorAlBi;
WorScD*

Yung, Victor Sen
American. Actor
Played Hop Sing on TV series
''Bonanza,'' 1959-73.
b. Oct 18, 1915 in San Francisco,
California
d. Nov 9, 1980 in North Hollywood,
California
Source: *HalFC 84; TelevWe; WhAm 7;
WhoAm 80; WhoHol A*

Yung-lo
Chinese. Emperor
Third emperor of the Ming dynasty
known for his innovative institutional
reforms and military victories; his
reign marked the height of Ming
power.
b. 1360
d. Aug 2, 1424 in Yu-mu-ch'uan, Jehol,
China
Source: *DicTyr; EncWB 98; McGEWB*

Yunich, David Lawrence
American. Merchant, Businessman
Pres., Macy's, NY, 1962-71.
b. May 21, 1917 in Albany, New York
Source: *Dun&B 90; IntWW 74, 75, 76,
77, 78, 79, 80, 81, 82, 83, 89, 91, 93;
NewYTBE 73; St&PR 87, 91; WhoAm
74, 76, 78, 80, 82, 84, 86, 88, 90, 92,
94, 95, 96; WhoE 75, 77, 79, 81, 83, 85,
86, 89; WhoFI 74, 75, 77, 79, 81, 83,
85, 87; WhoWor 78, 82, 84, 87, 89, 95*

Yun Sondo
Korean. Poet
Major poet of the sijo form, helped
popularize the Korean vernacular.
b. 1587 in Seoul, Republic of Korea
d. 1671
Source: *EncWB 98*

Yurka, Blanche
American. Actor
Numerous classical roles included 130
performances of *Hamlet* with John
Barrymore, 1922.
b. Jun 19, 1887 in Saint Paul, Minnesota
d. Jun 6, 1974 in New York, New York
Source: *AmNatBi; BiE&WWA; BioIn 12,
16; ConAu 9R, 120; DcPseud; FamA&A;
FilmEn; FilmgC; GangFlm; HalFC 80,
84, 88; HolCA; MotPP; MovMk;
NewYTBS 74; NotAW MOD; NotNAT A,
B; NotWoAT; OxCThe 83; ThFT; Vers
A; WhAm 6; What 4; WhoHol B;
WhoThe 72; WhScrn 77, 83; WhThe*

Yust, Walter
American. Editor
Editor-in-chief of the *Encyclopedia
Britannica*, 1938-1960.
b. May 16, 1894 in Philadelphia,
Pennsylvania
d. Feb 29, 1960 in Evanston, Illinois
Source: *AmAu&B; BioIn 5; CurBio 60;
ObitOF 79; WhAm 3*

Yzerman, Steve
Canadian. Hockey Player
Center, Detroit, 1983—; youngest player
ever to play in NHL All-Star game,
1984; Stanley Cup, 1997.
b. May 9, 1965 in Cranbrook, British
Columbia, Canada
Source: *BioIn 16, 23, 24; HocReg 87;
News 91, 91-2; WhoAm 92, 94, 95, 96,
97, 98, 99, 2000; WhoMW 93, 96, 98;
WhoWor 99; WorAlBi*

Z

Zabach, Florian
American. Violinist
Noted for sometimes whistling while
  performing in concert; mastered classic
  music then turned to pop.
b. Aug 15, 1921 in Chicago, Illinois
Source: *ASCAP 66, 80; BioIn 4;*
CmpEPM; CurBio 55; PenEncP

Zabaleta, Nicanor
Spanish. Musician
Known as king of the harpists; harp
  works written for him include *Aria*
  and Passepied, 1965.
b. Jan 7, 1907 in San Sebastian, Spain
Source: *BakBD 78, 84, 92; BakDcM;*
BioIn 3, 9, 11; BriBkM 80; CamBiEn;
CurBio 71; IntWW 89, 91; IntWWM 77,
80, 90; MusSN; NewAmDM; NewGrDM
80; PenDiMP; WhoMus 72; WhoSSW
73, 75; WhoWor 76, 89

Zablocki, Clement John
American. Politician
Congressman from WI, 1949-83; chm.,
  House Foreign Affairs Committee,
  1977-83.
b. Nov 18, 1912 in Milwaukee,
  Wisconsin
d. Dec 3, 1983 in Washington, District
  of Columbia
Source: *AlmAP 84; AmCath 80;*
AmNatBi; BiDrAC; BiDrUSC 89; BioIn
4, 5, 11, 12; CngDr 83; CurBio 84;
IntWW 83; PolProf J, NF; WhAm 8;
WhoAm 74, 76, 78, 80, 82; WhoAmP 73,
75, 77, 79, 81, 83; WhoGov 72, 75, 77;
WhoMW 74, 76, 78, 80, 82

Zabolotskii, Nikolai Alekseevich
Russian. Poet
Now regarded as one of Soviet's finest
  poets; wrote verse *Stolbtsy,* 1929.
b. May 7, 1903 in Kazan, Russia
d. Oct 14, 1958 in Moscow, Union of
  Soviet Socialist Republics
Source: *BiDSovU; BioIn 5, 8, 9, 10;*
ConAu 116; PenC ENG; WorAu 1950

Zacharias, Jerrold R(einarch)
American. Engineer, Physicist
Director of engineering, Manhattan
  Project, which developed first atomic
  bomb.
b. Jan 23, 1905 in Jacksonville, Florida
d. Jul 16, 1986 in Belmont,
  Massachusetts
Source: *AmMWSc 73P, 82; CurBio 64,*
86; IntWW 83; NewYTBS 86; WhoAtom
77

Zadkine, Ossip
Russian. Artist
Sculptures include *The Destroyed City;*
  Musicians.
b. Jul 14, 1890 in Smolensk, Russia
d. Nov 25, 1967 in Paris, France
Source: *BioIn 2, 4, 5, 7, 8, 9, 12, 14, 17;*
CamBiEn; ChamBiD; ConArt 77, 83;
CurBio 57, 68; DcArts; DcTwArt;
DcTwCCu 2; IntDcAA 90; McGDA;
ObitT 1961; OxCArt; OxCTwCA;
OxDcArt; PhDcTCA 77; WhAm 4A;
WorArt 1950

Zadora, Pia
[Mrs. Jonathan Kaufer]
American. Actor, Singer
Had successful first album *Pia and Phil,*
  1985.
b. May 4, 1955 in New York, New York
Source: *BioIn 12, 14, 16; ConTFT 9;*
HalFC 84, 88; IntMPA 88; LegTOT;
RkOn 85

Zaentz, Saul
American. Producer
Won Oscars for *Amadeus,* 1984; *One*
  Flew Over the Cuckoo's Nest, 1975.
b. Feb 28, 1921 in Passaic, New Jersey
Source: *BioIn 14, 22, 23; ConTFT 9;*
CurBio 97; IntMPA 84, 86, 92; VarWW
85; WhoAm 90; WhoEnt 92

Zafrulla Khan, Muhammad, Sir
Pakistani. Diplomat
Long time diplomat; positions included:
  Pakistani UN delegate, 1947-54, 1961-
  64; pres. UN General Assembly 1962-
  63.

b. Feb 6, 1893 in Sialkot, India
d. Sep 1, 1985 in Lahore, Pakistan
Source: *BioIn 1, 6; CurBio 47; FarE&A*
78, 79, 80, 81; IntWW 74, 75, 76, 77,
78, 79, 80, 81, 82, 83; IntYB 80, 82;
Who 83, 85; WhoUN 75; WhoWor 74,
76

Zafy, Albert
Political Leader, Physician
Founder of the National Union for the
  Defense of Democracy and leader of
  the opposition to President Ratsiraka,
  he was elected president of
  Madagascar in 1993.
b. May 1, 1927 in Betsiaka, Antsiranana,
  Madagascar

Zaghlul Pasha, Saad
Egyptian. Political Leader
Founded the Wafd, Egypt's most
  important political party, and in 1919
  led the second Egyptian revolution for
  independence from Britain.
b. 1859 in Ibyana, Egypt
d. Aug 23, 1927
Source: *EncWB 98; McGEWB*

Zah, Peterson
American. Native American Leader
First president of the Navajo Nation,
  1990-94.
b. Dec 2, 1937 in Low Mountain,
  Arizona
Source: *BioIn 13, 21; CamDcAB;*
EncWB 98; NewYTBS 83; NotNaAm;
WhoAm 86, 92, 94, 95, 96; WhoWest 84,
92

Zaharias, Babe Didrikson
[Mildred Ella Didrickson; Mildred Ella
  Didrickson Zaharias; Mrs. George
  Zaharias]
American. Golfer
Outstanding female athlete, especially in
  track, golf; won two gold medals,
  1932 Olympics; won US Women's
  Open three times.
b. Jun 26, 1914 in Port Arthur, Texas
d. Sep 27, 1956 in Galveston, Texas

Source: *ConAu 117; CurBio 47, 56; DcAmB S6; GayLesB; GrLiveH; NotAW MOD; OxCAmH; WebAB 79; WhAm 4; WhoGolf; WhoTr&F 73*

Zaharias, George
"The Crying Greek from Cripple Creek"
American. Wrestler
World-class wrestler; husband, manager of Babe Didrickson.
b. 1908?
d. May 22, 1984 in Tampa, Florida
Source: *BiDProW; BioIn 13*

Zaharoff, Basil, Sir
[Basileios Zacharias]
"Mystery Man of Europe"
English. Financier
Considered world's greatest armament salesman; allied intelligence agent, WW I.
b. Oct 6, 1849 in Mugla, Turkey
d. Nov 27, 1936 in Monte Carlo, Monaco
Source: *BioIn 7; CamBiEn; DcNaB MP; DcPseud; WebBD 83*

Zahir Shah, Mohammad
Afghan. Ruler
Afghan king, 1933-73; deposed by his brother-in-law, General Mohammad Daud Khan; abdicated on Aug. 24, 1973.
b. Oct 15, 1914 in Kabul, Afghanistan
Source: *BioIn 15, 16; CurBio 56; IntWW 91; NewYTBE 73; NewYTBS 79, 88*

Zahn, Paula
American. Broadcast Journalist
Co-anchor "CBS This Morning," 1990-95.
b. Feb 24, 1956 in Naperville, Illinois
Source: *BioIn 16; LegTOT; News 92, 92-3; WhoAm 96, 97, 99, 2000; WhoAmW 95, 97, 99*

Zaitsev, Aleksandr
[Rodnina and Zaitsev]
Russian. Skater
With Irina Rodnina, won gold medals in pairs figure skating, 1976, 1980 Olympics.
b. 1952, Union of Soviet Socialist Republics
Source: *BiDSovU; BioIn 11, 12*

Zal, Roxana
American. Actor
Won Emmy for title role in *Something About Amelia*, 1984.
b. Nov 8, 1969 in Los Angeles, California
Source: *BioIn 13, 14, 16; ConTFT 4*

Zale, Tony
[Anthony Florian Zaleski]
"Man of Steel"
American. Boxer
Middleweight champion; known for fight to defend title against Rocky Graziano,

1946; lost, 1947, regained 11 months later.
b. May 29, 1913 in Gary, Indiana
d. Mar 20, 1997 in Portage, Indiana
Source: *BiDAmSp BK; BioIn 13, 22; BoxReg, 2; DcPseud; NewYTBS 82, 97; WhoBox 74; WhoMW 92; WhoSpor*

Zaleski, August
Polish. Statesman
Pres., Polish Democratic Committee, 1914-18; minister of foreign affairs, 1926-32.
b. 1883
d. Apr 7, 1972 in London, England
Source: *BioIn 9, 17; FacFETw; HisDcPo; PolBiDi*

Zambelli, Joseph
"The Grandfather of Fireworks"
American. Special Effects Technician
Pyrotechnics were used in six presidential inaugurations and at Statue of Liberty centennial, 1986.
d. May 4, 1988 in Castle, California
Source: *BioIn 12, 15*

Zamboni, Frank J
American. Inventor
Invented ice resurfacing machine that bears his name, 1947.
b. 1901? in Eureka, Utah
d. Jul 27, 1988 in Long Beach, California
Source: *ConNews 86-4*

Zamenhof, Ludwik Lazar
Polish. Linguist
Developed artificial language, Esperanto, 1887.
b. Dec 15, 1859 in Bialystok, Poland
d. Apr 14, 1917 in Warsaw, Poland
Source: *BiDInt; BioIn 5; Dis&D; LinLib L, S; WorAl*

Zamora, Bernice
American. Poet
Published poetry collection *Restless Serpents*, 1976.
b. 1938 in Aguilar, Colorado
Source: *ConLC 89; DcHiB; DcLB 82; HispLC; HispWr; NotHsAW 1; NotLatA; OxCTwCP*

Zamora, Pedro
Cuban. AIDS Activist
Educated teenagers about AIDS after contracting it at age 17.
b. 1972, Cuba
d. Nov 11, 1994 in Miami, Florida
Source: *BioIn 20, 21, 22; News 95, 95-2*

Zamora, Ruben
Salvadoran. Politician
Member of El Salvador's democratic left; after an exile of nearly 8 years, his return was considered the most important development in the country since civil war erupted in 1980.
b. 1942, El Salvador
Source: *CurBio 91; LatAmLi*

Zampa, Luigi
Italian. Director
Films include *A Yank in Rome*, 1945; *Difficult Years*, 1948; *Anyone Can Play*, 1967.
b. Jan 2, 1905 in Rome, Italy
d. Aug 15, 1991 in Rome, Italy
Source: *AnObit 1991; BioIn 5, 14, 15, 16, 17, 18; CelR 90; ConAu 157; ConTFT 7; DcFM; EncEurC; FilmEn; FilmgC; HalFC 80, 84, 88; IntDcF 1-2; IntMPA 75, 76, 77, 78, 79, 80, 81, 82, 84, 86, 88, 92; IntWW 91; ItaFilm; OxCFilm; St&PR 91; WhoAm 90; WhoEnt 92; WorEFlm*

Zanardi, Alex
Italian. Auto Racer
1997 PPG Championship Auto Racing Teams (CART) champion, winning five races and more than $2 million in prize money; *Automobile* magazine's Man of the Year, 1998, he is known for his "victory spin," spinning the race car and leaving a skid mark doughnut on the track.
b. Oct 23, 1966 in Bologna, Italy
Source: *News 98, 98-2*

Zander, Robin
[Cheap Trick]
American. Singer, Musician
b. Jan 23, 1953
Source: *WhoRocM 82*

Zandonai, Riccardo
Italian. Composer
Wrote operas *Francesca da Rimini*, 1914; *Giuliette e Romeo*, 1922; *I Cavalieri di Ekebu*, 1925.
b. May 28, 1883 in Sacco, Italy
d. Jun 5, 1944 in Pesaro, Italy
Source: *BakBD 78, 84, 92; BakBDTw; BakDcM; BioIn 13, 14; CmOp; CurBio 44; IntDcOp; ItaFilm; MetOEnc; NewAmDM; NewEOp 71; NewGrDM 80; NewGrDO; NewOxM; OxCMus; OxDcOp; WebBD 83*

Zane, Ebenezer
American. Pioneer
Established first permanent site on Ohio river, 1770, known as Wheeling, VA.
b. Oct 7, 1747 in Berkeley County, Virginia
d. 1811 in Wheeling, Virginia
Source: *AmBi; AmNatBi; ApCAB; DcAmB; Drake; EncAAH; EncAR; EncSoH; HarEnUS; LinLib S; NatCAB 11; WhAm HS; WhAmRev*

Zanelli, Renato
[Renato Morales]
Chilean. Opera Singer
Tenor, originally baritone; noted for Othello role; NY Met., 1919-23.
b. Apr 1, 1892 in Valparaiso, Chile
d. Mar 25, 1935 in Santiago, Chile
Source: *BakBD 84; BioIn 10, 12, 14; CmOp; MetOEnc; NewEOp 71; NewGrDM 80; OxDcOp; PenDiMP*

Zangara, Joseph
[Guiseppe Zangara]
American. Assassin
Shot mayor of Chicago, in attempt to kill FDR, Feb 15, 1933.
b. 1900, Italy
d. Mar 21, 1933
Source: *BioIn 9; EncACr; MafEnc*

Zangwill, Israel
English. Dramatist, Author
Popularized term "melting pot" in play of same name, 1908; wrote novels on Jewish themes.
b. Feb 14, 1864 in London, England
d. Aug 1, 1926 in London, England
Source: *BbD; BiCoLiE; BiD&SB; BiDBrF 2; BioIn 4, 5, 6, 7, 8, 9, 12, 13, 14, 16, 17, 20, 22, 24; CamBiEn; CamGLE; ChamBiD; Chambr 3; ChhPo S2; ConAu 109, 167; CrtSuMy; CyWA 58, 97; DcAmImH; DcAmSR; DcBiA; DcEnA A; DcEuL; DcLB 10, 135, 197; DcLEL; DcNaB 1922; EncMys; EncWB 98; EncWL 1; EvLB; GrWrEL N; LegTOT; LinLib L; LngCTC; McGEWB; ModWD; NewC; NewCBEL; NotNAT A; OxCEng 67, 85, 95; OxCThe 67, 83; OxCTwCL; PenC ENG; RfGEnL 91; ScFEYrs; SocPrL; StaCVF; TwCA; TwCCr&M 80, 85, 91A; TwCLC 16; TwCWr; VicBrit; WhLit; WhoStg 1906; WhThe; WorAu 1900*

Zanker, Bill
American. Business Executive
Founder of the Learning Annex, a for-profit enterprise offering short, inexpensive adult education classes in everything from white-water rafting to understanding computers; he describes the business as "the McDonald's of education."
b. c. 1954
Source: *ConNews 87-3*

Zanuck, Darryl Francis
American. Film Executive, Producer
Produced first sound film, 1927; co-founded 20th Century Pictures, 1933; won three special Oscars.
b. Sep 5, 1902 in Wahoo, Nebraska
d. Dec 22, 1979 in Palm Springs, California
Source: *BiDFilm; BioIn 2, 3, 6, 7, 8, 9, 10, 12, 13; BlueB 76; CamBiEn; CamDcAB; ChamBiD; CmMov; ConAu 93; CurBio 80N; DcAmB S10; DcFM; FilmgC; IntMPA 77; IntWW 74, 75, 76, 77, 78, 79; OxCFilm; WebAB 74, 79; WhAm 7; Who 74; WhoAm 74, 76, 78; WhoWor 74, 78; WorAl; WorEFlm*

Zanuck, Lili Fini
American. Director, Producer
Co-produced *Driving Miss Daisy*, 1989.
b. 1954 in Massachusetts
Source: *ConTFT 21; IntMPA 94, 96; News 94, 94-2; WhoAmW 97, 99; WhoEnt 98*

Zanuck, Richard Darryl
American. Film Executive, Producer
Produced two of the biggest box office draws in film history: *The Sting*, 1973, *Jaws*, 1975; won Oscar for *Driving Miss Daisy*, 1990; son of Darryl.
b. Dec 13, 1934 in Los Angeles, California
Source: *BioIn 8, 9; BkPepl; FilmEn; FilmgC; HalFC 80, 84; IntMPA 75, 76, 78, 79, 80, 81, 82, 84, 86, 88, 92, 94, 96; IntWW 89, 91, 93, 97, 98, 2000; OxCFilm; St&PR 84, 87; WhoAm 74, 76, 78, 80, 82, 84, 86, 88, 90, 92, 94, 95, 96, 97, 98, 99, 2000; WhoEnt 92, 98*

Zao-Wou-Ki
French. Artist
Known for imaginative landscapes, animals; brushstrokes resemble a type of calligraphy.
b. Feb 13, 1921 in Beijing, China
Source: *BioIn 16; McGDA; WhoArt 84*

Zapata, Emiliano
Mexican. Revolutionary
Guerilla leader of Mexican Aqarian Movement; helped Madero overthrow Porfiro Diaz, 1911; assassinated.
b. Aug 8, 1879? in Anenecuilco, Mexico
d. Apr 10, 1919 in Chinameca, Mexico
Source: *BiDLAmC; BioIn 9, 10, 16, 17, 19, 20, 22, 23; CamBiEn; ChamBiD; DcHiB; DcMexR; DcTwHis; EncLatA; EncWB 98; FacFETw; HarEnUS; HisWorL; LatAmLi; LegTOT; McGEWB; RadHan; REn; WorAl*

Zapf, Hermann
German. Type Designer
Expert on printing, book design; designed numerous type faces.
b. Nov 8, 1918 in Nuremberg, Germany
Source: *BioIn 6, 7, 15; ConDes 84, 90, 97; CurBio 65; DcTwDes; Who 2000; WhoAm 78, 80, 82, 84, 86, 88, 90, 92, 94, 95, 96, 97, 98, 99, 2000; WhoGrA 62, 82; WhoWor 78, 80, 82, 87, 93, 95, 96, 97, 98, 99, 2000*

Zappa, Dweezil
American. Musician, Actor
Solo albums *Havin' a Bad Day*, 1987; film *Running Man*, 1987; son of Frank.
b. Sep 5, 1969 in Los Angeles, California
Source: *BioIn 15, 16; ConTFT 21; GrMetD; LegTOT; WhoHol 92*

Zappa, Frank
[The Mothers of Invention; Francis Vincent Zappa, Jr.]
American. Musician, Singer
Early leader of hard-rock style; founded Mothers of Invention, 1964.
b. Dec 21, 1940 in Baltimore, Maryland
d. Dec 4, 1993 in Los Angeles, California
Source: *ABCCoAm; AmCulL; AnObit 1993; ASCAP 80; BakBD 78, 84, 92; BakBDTw; BiDAmM; BiDJaz; BillEnR; BioIn 8, 9, 10, 11, 12, 13, 14, 15, 16;*

BioNews 74; CamBiEn; CamDcAB; ChamBiD; CmCal; CmpEGui; ConAu 108, 143; ConLC 17; ConMuA 80A; ConMus 1, 17; ConTFT 21; CurBio 90, 94N; DcArts; DcTwCCu 1; EncJzS; EncPR&S 89; EncRk 88; EncRkSt; FacFETw; FreeExC; HarEnR 86; IlEncRk; IntWW 89, 91, 93; LegTOT; MiSFD 9; NewAmDM; NewGrDA 86; NewGrDJ 88, 94; News 94, 94-2; NewYTBS 93; OnThGG; OxCPMus; PenEncP; RkOn 78; RkWho 96; RolSEnR 83; Songw; WhAm 11; WhoAm 78, 80, 82, 84, 90, 92, 94; WhoEnt 92; WhoHol 92, A; WhoRocM 82; WorAl; WorAlBi

Zappa, Moon Unit
American. Singer
Daughter of Frank Zappa; had hit song "Valley Girl," 1982.
b. Sep 28, 1968? in Hollywood, California
Source: *BioIn 16*

Zaragosa, Federico Mayor
Spanish. Biochemist
Biochemist became director-general of United Nations Educational, Scientific, and Cultural Organization (UNESCO) in 1987.
b. Jan 27, 1934 in Barcelona, Spain

Zarlino, Gioseffo
Italian. Composer
Music theorist wrote the most lucid and comprehensive exposition of 16th-century counterpoint, and was a conservative composer.
b. 1517 in Chioggia, Italy
d. 1590
Source: *BakBD 78, 84, 92; BakDcM; BriBkM 80; EncWB 98; McGEWB; NewAmDM; NewGrDM 80; NewOxM; OxCMus*

Zaslofsky, Max
American. Basketball Player
Guard, 1946-56, with five NBA teams; led league in scoring, 1948.
b. Dec 7, 1925 in New York, New York
d. Oct 15, 1985
Source: *AnObit 1985; BiDAmSp BK; BioIn 8, 14; OfNBA 87; WhoBbl 73*

Zaslow, Jeff
American. Journalist
Co-winner of nationwide search for Ann Landers' advice column replacement, 1986.
b. 1959?
Source: *BioIn 15, 16; NewYTBS 89; WhoAm 90*

Zatopek, Emil
Czech. Track Athlete
Long distance runner; won one gold medal, 1948 Olympics, three gold medals, 1952 Olympics.
b. Sep 19, 1922 in Koprivnice, Moravia
Source: *BioIn 2, 3, 5, 8, 9, 10, 12, 13, 22; CamBiEn; ChamBiD; CurBio 53;*

IntWW 81, 82, 83, 89, 91, 93, 97, 98, 2000; LegTOT; WhoSoCE 89; WhoTr&F 73; WhoWor 91; WorAl

Zaturenska, Marya
[Mrs. Horace Gregory]
American. Poet
Won Pulitzer, 1938, for *Cold Morning Sky*.
b. Sep 12, 1902 in Kiev, Russia
d. Jan 19, 1982 in Shelburne Falls, Massachusetts
Source: *AmWomWr; AnObit 1982; ArtclWW 2; BenetAL 91; BioIn 4, 11, 12, 17, 22; CamDcAB; CamGLE; CamHAL; ChhPo, S3; CnDAL; ConAu 13R, 22NR, 105; ConLC 6, 11; ConPo 70, 75, 80; DrAP 75; DrAPF 80; FemiCLE; ForWC 70; InWom SUP; OxCAmL 65, 83, 95; OxCTwCL; PenC AM; REn; REnAL; SixAP; TwCA, SUP; WhAm 8; WhoAm 74, 76, 78, 80; WhoAmW 68, 70, 72, 74, 75, 77; WhoPolA; WhoPul; WrDr 76, 80, 82*

Zayak, Elaine
American. Skater
World champion figure skater, 1982.
b. Apr 12, 1965 in Paramus, New Jersey
Source: *BiDAmSp Sup; BioIn 12, 13, 14; EncFiS; NewYTBS 83, 84; WhoSpor*

Zayid bin Sultan Al-Nahyan, Shaykh
Arab. Ruler, Political Leader
Became the first president of the United Arab Emirates (U.A.E.) when it was formed in 1971; previously served as governor of the Buraimi Oasis and ruler of the emirate of Abu Dhabi, one of the Trucial States.
b. 1923

Zeami, Kanze
[Zeami Motokiyo]
Japanese. Actor, Dramatist, Critic
Celebrated for both his theoretical works on the art of the No and his dramas.
b. 1364
d. 1444
Source: *EncWB 98; McGEWB*

Zech, Lando William, Jr.
American. Government Official
Chairman of Nuclear Regulatory Commission, 1984-89.
b. Jun 29, 1923 in Astoria, Oregon
Source: *BioIn 16; ConNews 87-4; WhoAm 78, 80; WhoAmP 91*

Zedillo Ponce de Leon, Ernesto
Mexican. Political Leader
Pres., of Mexico, 1994—.
b. Dec 27, 1951 in Mexico City, Mexico
Source: *ChamBiD; CurBio 96; DcMexR; EncWB 98; IntWW 97, 98, 2000; WhoAm 96, 97, 98, 99, 2000; WhoIntA 2; WhoWor 95, 96, 97, 98, 99, 2000*

Zeeman, Pieter
Dutch. Scientist
Shared Nobel Prize in physics, 1902; researched effect of magnetism on radiation.
b. May 25, 1865 in Zonnemaire, Netherlands
d. Oct 9, 1943 in Amsterdam, Netherlands
Source: *AsBiEn; BiESc; BioIn 3, 7, 14, 15, 20; CamBiEn; CamDcSc; ChamBiD; CurBio 43; DcInv; DcScB; InSci; LarDcSc; McGCEnS; NobelP; NotTwCS 1; ObitOF 79; RanHWDS; WhDW; WhoNob, 90, 95; WorAl; WorAlBi*

Zeffirelli, Franco
Italian. Director
Films include *Taming of the Shrew*, 1967; *Romeo and Juliet*, 1968; TV work includes mini-series *Jesus of Nazareth*, 1977.
b. Feb 12, 1923 in Florence, Italy
Source: *BakBD 92; BakBDTw; BiE&WWA; BioIn 6, 7, 8, 9, 12, 13, 15, 16; CamBiEn; CamGWoT; CelR, 90; ChamBiD; CmOp; ConDes 84, 90; ConTFT 4; CurBio 64; DcArts; DcPseud; EncWB 99; EncWT; Ent; FacFETw; FilmEn; FilmgC; GayLesB; HalFC 84, 88; IntDcF 1-2, 2-2; IntDcOp; IntMPA 86, 88, 92, 94, 96; IntWW 74, 75, 76, 77, 78, 79, 80, 81, 82, 83, 91; IntWWM 90; ItaFilm; LegTOT; MetOEnc; MiSFD 9; MovMk; NewEOp 71; NewGrDA 86; NewGrDM 80; NewGrDO; News 91, 91-3; NewYTBE 72; OxCFilm; OxCThe 67, 83; OxDcOp; TheaDir; Who 92; WhoAm 80, 82, 84, 86, 88, 90, 92, 94, 95, 96, 97, 98; WhoEnt 92, 98; WhoHol 92, A; WhoWor 80, 82, 84, 87, 89, 91, 93, 95; WorAl; WorAlBi; WorEFlm*

Zeiss, Carl
German. Manufacturer
Founded optical instruments co., 1846.
b. Sep 11, 1816 in Weimar, Germany
d. Dec 3, 1888 in Jena, Germany
Source: *BioIn 2, 12; CamBiEn; ChamBiD; DcInv; DcTwDes; ICPEnP; InSci; LinLib S; MacBEP; OxCMed 86; WebBD 83*

Zeitlin, Zvi
American. Musician
Toured with major symphonies; known for furthering relations between Israel, US.
b. Feb 21, 1923 in Dubrowna, Union of Soviet Socialist Republics
Source: *BakBD 84, 92; BakBDTw; IntWWM 77, 80, 85, 90; NewAmDM; NewGrDA 86; NewGrDM 80; PenDiMP; WhoAm 76, 78, 80, 82, 84, 86, 88, 90; WhoAmJ 80; WhoAmM 83; WhoEnt 92; WhoMus 72; WhoWorJ 72, 78*

Zelaya, Jose Santos
Nicaraguan. Political Leader
Tyrannical president of Nicaragua made improvements in education and transportation in his country; his ambition and conflict with United States policy led to his downfall.
b. Oct 31, 1853 in Managua, Nicaragua
d. May 17, 1919 in New York, New York
Source: *BiDLAmC; BioIn 16; DicTyr; EncLatA; EncWB 98; LatAmLi; McGEWB*

Zelazny, Roger
American. Author
Science fiction writer of the New Wave school.
d. Jun 14, 1995 in Santa Fe, New Mexico
Source: *BioIn 15, 16, 17, 21, 22; ConSFF; DcLB Y95N; DcLP 87A; DrAPF 83, 85, 87, 89, 91, 93, 97, 1999; IntvTCA 2; NewYTBS 95; WhoSciF*

Zellerbach, William Joseph
American. Manufacturer
Pres., Crown Zellerbach Corp., 1946-85.
b. Sep 15, 1920 in San Francisco, California
Source: *BioIn 11; Dun&B 90; IntMPA 82; IntWW 74, 75, 76, 77, 78, 79, 80, 81, 82, 83, 89, 91, 93; IntYB 78, 79, 80, 81, 82; St&PR 84; WhoAm 74, 76, 78, 80, 82, 84, 86, 88, 90, 92, 94, 95, 96, 97, 98, 99, 2000; WhoFI 74*

Zemeckis, Robert
American. Director
Films include *Back to the Future*, 1985, *Who Framed Roger Rabbit*, 1988.
b. May 14, 1951 in Chicago, Illinois
Source: *BioIn 14, 16; ConTFT 7; HalFC 88; IntDcF 2-2; IntMPA 92; WhoAm 90; WhoEnt 92*

Zemlinsky, Alexander von
Austrian. Composer, Conductor
Led Berlin State Opera, 1927-32; fled to US, 1938; taught Arthur Schoenberg.
b. Oct 4, 1872 in Vienna, Austria
d. Mar 16, 1942 in New York, New York
Source: *BioIn 2, 11, 18, 23; CurBio 42; DcCM; WhAm 4A*

Zemurray, Samuel
American. Entrepreneur
Fruit importer built the United Fruit Company into a powerful international corporation and played a major economic and political role Central American states during the mid-20th century.
b. Jan 18, 1877 in Kishinev, Russia
d. Nov 30, 1961 in New Orleans, Louisiana
Source: *BiDAmBL 83; BioIn 1, 2, 4, 6, 14, 16; DcAmDH 80, 89; EncWB, 98; WhAm 4*

Zenatello, Giovanni
Italian. Opera Singer
Sang with Manhattan Opera Company, NYC, 1907-09; Boston Opera, 1909-14.
b. Feb 22, 1876 in Verona, Italy

d. Feb 11, 1949 in New York, New
  York
Source: *BakBD 78, 84, 92; BakBDTw;
BiDAmM; BioIn 1, 14; CmOp; IntDcOp;
MetOEnc; NewEOp 71; NewGrDM 80;
NewGrDO; OxDcOp; PenDiMP*

Zenger, John Peter
German. Printer, Publisher, Journalist
His acquittal in famous libel trial, 1735,
  helped establish freedom of press in
  US.
b. 1697, Germany
d. Jul 28, 1746 in New York, New York
Source: *Alli; AmAu; AmAu&B; AmBi;
AmNatBi; AmRef; AmSocL; AmWrBE;
Benet 87, 96; BiDAmJo; BioIn 2, 3, 4, 5,
6, 7, 8, 9, 10, 11, 14, 15, 16, 19, 20, 23;
CamDcAB; CriJuSA; DcAmB; DcAmSR;
DcLB 24, 43; Drake; EncAJ; EncCRAm;
EncWB 98; FreeExC; JrnUS; LegTOT;
McGEWB; NatCAB 23; OxCAmH;
OxCAmL 65, 83, 95; REn, REnAL;
TwCBDA; WebAB 74, 79; WhAm HS;
WorAl; WorAlBi*

Zeno, Apostolo
Italian. Poet, Librettist
Wrote libretti for melodrama, with
  subjects taken from classical history,
  mythology, 1600s-1700s.
b. Dec 11, 1668 in Venice, Italy
d. Nov 11, 1750 in Venice, Italy
Source: *BakBD 78, 84, 92; BiD&SB;
BlkwCE; BriBkM 80; CasWL; DcBiPP;
DcEuL; EvEuW; IntDcOp; MetOEnc;
NewEOp 71; NewGrDM 80; NewGrDO;
NotNAT B; OxCThe 67; OxDcOp*

Zenobia
Syrian. Queen
Warrior queen of Palmyra declared
  independence from Rome and sought
  to establish her own kingdom in the
  East.
b. 3rd cent.
Source: *Benet 87, 96; BioIn 1, 4, 7, 9,
11, 16, 21; CamBiEn; ChamBiD;
ContDcW 89; DcBiPP; DcCathB;
Dis&D; EncWB 98; GoodHs; HisWorL;
IntDcWB; InWom, SUP; LinLib S;
NewC; OxCCIL, 89; REn; WomWR*

Zeno of Citium
Greek. Philosopher
Founded Stoicism, which emphasized
  practical ethics.
b. 334BC, Cyprus
d. 262BC
Source: *BiD&SB; CasWL; ChamBiD;
DcScB; LuthC 75; McGEWB; OxCPhil;
PenC CL; REn*

Zeno of Elea
Greek. Philosopher
Student of Parmenides, known as an
  inventor of paradoxes.
b. 490BC
d. 430BC
Source: *BiESc; CamBiEn; ChamBiD;
DcScB; EncWB 98; InSci; LarDcSc;
McGCEnS; McGEWB; NewCol 75;
NotMat; OxCCIL 89; REn*

Zepeda, Ofelia
American. Linguist
Became co-director of the American
  Indian Language Development
  Institute, 1989.
b. Mar 24, 1954 in Stanfield, Arizona
Source: *AZNatAW; ConAu 114;
NatNAFi; NotNaAm*

**Zeppelin, Ferdinand Adolf
  August Heinrich von, Count**
German. Soldier, Aircraft Designer
Built first rigid airship, 1900.
b. Jul 8, 1838 in Konstanz, Germany
d. Mar 8, 1917 in Charlottenburg,
  Germany
Source: *AsBiEn; InSci; LinLib S;
NewCol 75; REn; WorAl*

Zerbe, Anthony
American. Actor
Won Emmy, 1976, for "Harry-O."
b. May 20, 1936 in Long Beach,
  California
Source: *ConTFT 6; FilmgC; HalFC 88;
IntMPA 92, 94, 96; WhoAm 84, 86, 90;
WhoEnt 92; WhoHol A*

Zernial, Gus Edward
"Ozark Ike"
American. Baseball Player
Outfielder, 1949-59; led AL in home
  runs, RBIs, 1951.
b. Jun 27, 1923 in Beaumont, Texas
Source: *Ballpl 90; BiDAmSp Sup; BioIn
3; WhoProB 73*

Zernike, Frits
Dutch. Physicist, Educator
Won Nobel Prize, 1953, for invention of
  phase-control microscope.
b. Jul 16, 1888 in Amsterdam,
  Netherlands
d. Mar 10, 1966 in Naarden, Netherlands
Source: *BiESc; BioIn 3, 4, 7, 8, 15, 20;
CamBiEn; ChamBiD; DcScB; LarDcSc;
McGMS 80; NobelP; NotTwCS 1; ObitT
1961; RanHWDS; WhAm 4; WhoNob,
90, 95*

Zeroual, Liamine
Algerian. Political Leader
President of Algeria, 1994—.
b. 1951
Source: *News 96, 96-2*

Zetkin, Clara
German. Political Activist
Distinguished member of Socialist and
  Communist organizations in Europe,
  she focused on the liberation of
  women in society through Marxist
  reforms of the capitalist system. She
  was a founder of the German
  Communist Party and a political ally
  of Vladimir Lenin.
b. May 5, 1857 in Wiederau, Germany
d. Jun 20, 1933 in Moscow, Russia
Source: *BiDMarx; BlmGWL; CamBiEn;
ChamBiD; ConAu 154; ContDcW 89;
EncTR 91; EncWB 98; FemiWr;
IntDcWB; RadHan; WomWrGe*

Zetterling, Mai (Elisabeth)
Swedish. Actor, Director
Pursued successful careers on both stage,
  screen; directed several feature films in
  Sweden including *Night Games,* 1966.
b. May 24, 1925 in Vasteras, Sweden
d. Mar 15, 1994
Source: *Au&Wr 71; BiDFilm, 81, 94;
BioIn 7, 10, 15, 16, 19; ConAu 111, 126,
144; ConLC 86; ContDcW 89; ConTFT
13; EncEurC; FilmEn; FilmgC; ForYSC;
HalFC 80, 84, 88; IlWWBF; IntAu&W
91, 93; IntDcF 1-2, 2-2; IntDcWB;
IntMPA 75, 76, 77, 78, 79, 80, 81, 82,
84, 86, 88, 92, 94; IntWW 74, 75, 76,
77, 78, 79, 80, 81, 82, 83, 89, 91, 93;
InWom SUP; LegTOT; MiSFD 9;
MotPP; MovMk; OxCFilm; ReelWom;
WhAm 11; Who 83, 92; WhoHol 92, A;
WhoWor 84, 87, 89, 91, 93; WhThe;
WomWMM; WorAl; WorEFlm; WorFDir
2; WrDr 80, 82, 84, 86, 88, 90, 92, 94,
96*

Zevin, B(enjamin) D(avid)
American. Publisher
Pres., World Publishing Co., 1945-62;
  founded Tower Books, 1939.
b. May 16, 1901? in New York, New
  York
d. Dec 27, 1984 in Miami Beach, Florida
Source: *BioIn 3; CurBio 43, 85, 85N*

Zevon, Warren
American. Singer, Songwriter
Known for his hit song "Werewolves of
  London," 1978.
b. Jan 24, 1947 in Chicago, Illinois
Source: *BillEnR; BioIn 11, 12, 13, 16;
ConMus 9; EncPR&S 89; LegTOT;
NewGrDA 86; PenEncP; RkOn 85;
RolSEnR 83; Songw; WhoAm 80, 82, 84,
86, 88, 90, 92, 95, 96, 97, 98; WhoEnt
92, 98; WhoRocM 82*

Zhang Yimou
Chinese. Filmmaker
Most celebrated filmmaker in China;
  films include *Red Sorghum,* 1987 and
  Operation Cougar, 1989.
b. 1951 in Xi'an, China
Source: *BioIn 16; CurBio 92; EncChi;
IntWW 89, 91, 93, 97, 98, 2000*

Zhao Kuang-yin
Chinese. Ruler
Founder of the Song dynasty centralized
  the country, reestablished the "civilian
  empire," and ended the military coups
  and civil wars of the previous 200
  years.
b. 927 in Lo-yang, China
d. 976 in Kai Feng, China
Source: *EncWB 98; HisWorL*

Zhao Ziyang
Chinese. Political Leader
Premier, 1980-87; replaced Deng
  Ziaoping as chief of Chinese
  Communist Party, 1987-89.
b. Oct 17, 1919 in Hunan, China
Source: *BioIn 13, 14, 15; ColdWar 2;
CurBio 84; EncChi; EncWB 98; FarE&A*

79, 80, 81; IntWW 80, 81, 82, 83, 89, 91, 93; LegTOT; ModChi; News 89-1; NewYTBS 80, 84, 87; Who 88, 90, 92, 94, 98, 99, 2000; WhoAsAP 91; WhoPRCh 81, 87, 91; WhoWor 91, 93

Zhdanov, Andrei Alexandrovich
Russian. Political Leader, Army Officer
Pres., foreign affairs com., 1943; received Order of Lenin, 1945; Order of Suvorov, 1944.
b. Feb 26, 1896 in Mariupol, Ukraine
d. Aug 31, 1948 in Moscow, Union of Soviet Socialist Republics
Source: *ColdWar 1; ConAu 167; FacFETw; REn; WhAm 2; WorAl*

Zhirinovsky, Vladimir
Russian. Politician
Founded Liberal Democratic Party of Russia, 1990.
b. Apr 25, 1946 in Alma-Ata, Union of Soviet Socialist Republics
Source: *CurBio 95; DcPseud; News 94, 94-2*

Zhivkov, Todor Khristov
Bulgarian. Politician
Prime minister, 1962-71; pres., 1971-89; Communist Party Leader of Bulgaria, 1954-89.
b. Sep 7, 1911 in Pravets, Bulgaria
d. Aug 5, 1998 in Sofia, Bulgaria
Source: *ColdWar 1; CurBio 76; EncRev; FacFETw; IntWW 83, 91; WhoWor 87, 89, 91*

Zhukov, Georgi Alexandrovich
Russian. Journalist, Politician
Pres., USSR-France Society who wrote *Three Months in Geneva*, 1954.
b. Apr 23, 1908 in Almazny, Russia
Source: *CurBio 60; IntWW 74, 75; Who 74, 82, 83, 85, 88, 90, 92, 94, 98, 99, 2000; WhoWor 74*

Zhukov, Georgi Konstantinovich
"The Eisenhower of Russia"
Russian. Military Leader
WW II hero; led defense of Moscow, Leningrad, capture of Berlin; minister of Defense, 1955-57.
b. Dec 2, 1896 in Stelkovka, Russia
d. Jun 18, 1974 in Moscow, Union of Soviet Socialist Republics
Source: *ChamBiD; ColdWar 1; CurBio 42, 55, 74; DcTwHis; EncCW; EncTR 91; EncWB 98; FacFETw; HarEnMi; HisEWW; LinLib S; McGEWB; MilitOn; NewYTBS 74; WhAm 6; Who 74; WhoWor 74; WorAl*

Zia, Helen
American. Political Activist, Journalist, Consultant
Advocated against racism and hate crimes that affected the Asian American community and was involved with gay and lesbian and feminist issues.
b. 1952 in Newark, New Jersey
Source: *EncWB 99*

Zia(ur) Rahman
Bangladeshi. Political Leader
Military leader declared the country independent from Pakistan in 1971, became president in 1975, and brought economic and political stability to the newly-formed state.
b. Jan 19, 1936 in Calcutta, India
d. May 31, 1981 in Cittagong, Bangladesh
Source: *AnObit 1981; BioIn 11, 12; CurBio 81; EncWB, 98; FacFETw; IntWW 81, 81N; IntYB 79, 80, 81; NewYTBS 78; WhoWor 78*

Zia-ul-Haq, Mohammad
[Mohammad Zia Al-Haq]
Pakistani. Political Leader
Overthrew Bhutto government, pres., 1978-88; died in plane crash.
b. Aug 12, 1924 in Jullunder, British India
d. Aug 17, 1988 in Bahawalpur, Pakistan
Source: *BioIn 11; ColdWar 1; CurBio 80, 88; EncWB 98; FarE&A 78, 79; IntWW 83; IntYB 79; NewYTBS 77; WhoWor 87*

Zieff, Howard
American. Director
Films include *Private Benjamin*, 1980; *Unfaithfully Yours*, 1984.
b. 1943 in Los Angeles, California
Source: *ConTFT 10; HalFC 84, 88; IntMPA 84, 86, 88, 92, 94, 96; MiSFD 9; NewYTBE 73*

Ziegfeld, Flo(renz)
American. Producer
Produced lavish, musical revues, "Ziegfeld Follies," 1907-30.
b. Mar 21, 1867 in Chicago, Illinois
d. Jul 22, 1932 in Hollywood, California
Source: *AmBi; AmDec 1910; AmNatBi; BiDD; CamDcAB; DcAmB; EncAB-H 1974; EncMT; EncVaud; FilmgC; HalFC 80, 84, 88; NewAmDM; NewGrDA 86; NotNAT B; OxCAmL 65; OxCAmT 84; OxCPMus; OxCThe 67, 83; PIP&P; RComAH; REn; WebAB 74; WhAm 1; WhDW; WhThe*

Ziegler, Edward
American. Critic, Manager
Music, drama critic for *NY Herald*, 1908-16; GM, consultant for Met. Opera House, 1920-47.
b. Mar 25, 1870 in Baltimore, Maryland
d. Oct 25, 1947 in New York, New York
Source: *AmAu&B; BiDAmM; BioIn 1, 13; MetOEnc; NewEOp 71; NotNAT B; WhAm 2*

Ziegler, John Augustus, Jr.
American. Hockey Executive
Succeeded Clarence Campbell as president of NHL, 1977-92.
b. Feb 9, 1934 in Grosse Pointe, Michigan
Source: *St&PR 75, 84, 87; WhoAm 76, 78, 80, 82, 84, 86, 88, 90, 92, 94, 95, 96, 97, 98, 99, 2000; WhoE 81, 83, 85, 86, 89*

Ziegler, Karl
German. Scientist
Won 1963 Nobel Prize in chemistry with Giulio Natta; studied polymerization.
b. Nov 26, 1898 in Helsa, Germany
d. Aug 12, 1973 in Mulheim, Germany (West)
Source: *AsBiEn; BiESc; BioIn 4, 5, 6, 10, 14, 15, 19, 20; CamBiEn; ChamBiD; LarDcSc; McGCEnS; McGMS 80; NobelP; NotTwCS 1; RanHWDS; WhAm 6; WhoNob, 90, 95; WhoWor 74; WorInv*

Ziegler, Ron(ald Louis)
American. Government Official
Press secretary to Richard Nixon, 1969-74.
b. May 12, 1939 in Covington, Kentucky
Source: *BioIn 13, 16; BioNews 74; CurBio 71; Dun&B 90; IntWW 74, 75, 76; NewYTBE 71, 73; WhoAm 74, 76, 78, 80, 82, 84, 86, 88, 90, 92, 94, 95, 96, 97, 98, 99, 2000; WhoAmP 73, 75, 77, 79, 81, 83, 85, 87, 89, 91, 93, 95, 97, 1999; WhoFI 00, 85, 87; WhoGov 72; WhoSSW 73, 95, 97, 99; WhoWor 91, 93, 95, 96, 97, 98*

Ziff, William B(ernard), Jr.
American. Publishing Executive
Media magnate and founder of Ziff Corp., dominated the magazine industry with 12 business publications and 12 general interest magazines, and owned six television stations; sold of most of his interests in 1984 for enormous profits.
b. 1930
Source: *AmAu&B; WhoAm 90, 92, 94, 95, 96, 97, 98, 99*

Ziff, William Bernard
American. Publisher
Publications include *Photography*, *Modern Bride* mags.
b. Aug 1, 1898 in Chicago, Illinois
d. Dec 20, 1953 in New York, New York
Source: *AmAu&B; AmNatBi; BioIn 1, 3; CurBio 46, 54; DcAmB S5; WhAm 3*

Zigler, Edward
American. Psychologist
Co-founder of Project Head Start, 1965.
b. Mar 1, 1930 in Kansas City, Missouri
Source: *AmMWSc 92, 95, 98; BiDcPsy; News 94, 94-1*

Zim, Herbert S(pencer)
American. Author
Science books include *Life and Death*, 1970; *The Universe*, 1973.
b. Jul 12, 1909 in New York, New York
d. Dec 5, 1994 in Plantation Key, Florida
Source: *AmAu&B; Au&Wr 71; AuBYP 2, 3; BioIn 2, 3, 4, 7, 9, 14, 15; BkP; ChhPo S3; ChlLR 2; ConAu 13R, 17NR, 147; CurBio 56, 95N; JBA 51; LinLib L; MajAl, SUP; SmATA 1, 2AS, 30, 85; WhAm 11; WhoAm 74, 76, 78, 80, 82, 84, 86, 88, 90, 92, 94, 95, 96; WrDr 86, 92, 94*

Zimbalist, Efrem

American. Violinist, Composer
Performances contained high technical
    polish, emotional understatement;
    composer of chamber music, opera
    Landara.
b. Apr 1890 in Rostov-on-Don, Russia
d. Feb 22, 1985 in Reno, Nevada
Source: *ASCAP 80; BakBD 84;
    BiDAmM; BioIn 14; CurBio 85;
    FacFETw; IntWW 83; LegTOT;
    NewAmDM; NewGrDM 80; NewYTBS
    85; Who 85*

Zimbalist, Efrem, Jr.

American. Actor, Composer
Played Lewis Erskine on TV series "The
    FBI," 1965-74.
b. Nov 30, 1923 in New York, New
    York
Source: *BiE&WWA; BioIn 5, 6, 14;
    ConTFT 3, 21; CurBio 60; FilmEn;
    FilmgC; ForYSC; HalFC 84, 88;
    IntMPA 75, 76, 77, 78, 79, 80, 81, 82,
    84, 86, 88, 92, 94, 96; MovMk; NotNAT;
    VarWW 85; WhoAm 74, 76, 78, 80, 82;
    WorAl; WorAlBi*

Zimbalist, Stephanie

American. Actor
Daughter of Efrem Zimbalist, Jr; starred
    in TV series "Remington Steele,"
    1982-87.
b. Oct 8, 1956 in Encino, California
Source: *BioIn 13, 14; CelR 90; ConTFT
    6; IntMPA 92, 94, 96; InWom SUP;
    LegTOT; VarWW 85; WhoHol 92;
    WhoTelC*

Zimmer, Don(ald William)

American. Baseball Player, Baseball
    Manager
Infielder, 1954-65; manager of four
    different teams including Chicago
    Cubs, 1988 -1991.
b. Jan 17, 1931 in Cincinnati, Ohio
Source: *Ballpl 90; BioIn 5, 15, 16, 17,
    19; LegTOT; WhoAm 78, 80, 82, 84, 86,
    88, 90, 92, 94, 95, 98, 99, 2000; WhoE
    79, 99; WhoMW 90, 92, 93, 96, 98;
    WhoSSW 82, 84, 95, 97; WhoWest 94,
    96, 98; WhoWor 80*

Zimmerman, Paul L

American. Author
Senior writer *Sports Illustrated*, 1979-83;
    wrote *The Last Season of Weeb
    Ewbank*, 1974.
b. Oct 23, 1932 in Philadelphia,
    Pennsylvania
Source: *ConAu 10NR, 25R*

Zimmerman, Udo

German. Composer
Composer of opera *Die Weisse Rose*
    which has enjoyed tremendous
    international acclaim since its premier
    in 1986.
b. Oct 6, 1943 in Dresden, Germany
Source: *ConMus 5*

Zimmermann, Bernd Alois

German. Composer
Musician remained independent of
    various 20th-century musical doctrines
    and established an original style of
    composition that was profoundly
    involved with music history.
b. 1918 in Bliesheim, Germany
d. 1970
Source: *BakBD 78, 84, 92; BakBDTw;
    BakDcM; BioIn 9, 23; CnOxB; DcCM;
    EncWB, 98; IntDcOp; MetOEnc;
    NewAmDM; NewGrDM 80; NewGrDO;
    NewOxM; Opera; OxCGer 76, 86, 97;
    OxDcOp; PenDiMP A*

Zimmermann, Johann Baptist and Domenikus

Artists
Brothers were a stucco worker and
    painter and an architect; their work
    epitomizes the Bavarian rococo style
    and their masterpiece is the church of
    Die Wies.
b. fl. 1730

Zindel, Paul

American. Author, Dramatist
Won 1971 Pulitzer for *The Effects of
    Gamma Rays on Man-in-the-Moon
    Marigolds*.
b. May 15, 1936 in New York, New
    York
Source: *Au&Arts 2; AuBYP 2, 3;
    BenetAL 91; BioIn 9, 10, 11, 12, 15;
    CamGWoT; CelR; ChlBkCr; ChlLR 3,
    45; CnThe; ConAmD; ConAu 31NR,
    65NR, 73; ConDr 73, 77, 82, 88, 93;
    ConLC 6, 26; ConTFT 3, 20; CrtSuDr;
    CurBio 73; DcAmChF 1960; DcLB 7,
    52; DcLEL 1940; DramC 5; EncWB 99;
    FifBJA; IntAu&W 91, 93; LegTOT;
    MagSAmL; MajAI; MajTwCW 1, 2;
    McGEWD 72, 84; ModWr; NatPD 77,
    81; NotNAT; OnHuMoP; OxCAmL 83,
    95; OxCAmT 84; OxCChiL; RAdv 14;
    SJGYouA 2; SmATA 16, 58, 102;
    TwCChW 1, 2, 3; TwCYAW 1; WhoAm
    74, 76, 78, 80, 82, 84, 86, 88, 90, 92,
    94, 95, 96; WhoPul; WhoThe 72, 77, 81;
    WhoUSWr 88; WhoWrEP 89, 92, 95;
    WorAl; WorAlBi; WorAu 1970; WrDr
    76, 80, 82, 84, 86, 88, 90, 92, 94, 96,
    98, 99, 2000; WrYoAd*

Zine el Abidine Ben Ali

Tunisian. Political Leader
Active in the movement for Tunisian
    independence, became prime minister
    in 1987, then removed the aging
    President Habib Bourguiba from office
    and assumed the title of president.
b. 1936
Source: *EncWB 98*

Zingarelli, Nicola Antonio

Italian. Composer, Musician
Wrote 34 operas including comic opera,
    Berenice, 1811.
b. Apr 4, 1752 in Naples, Italy
d. May 5, 1837 in Torre del Greco, Italy
Source: *BakBD 78, 84, 92; NewAmDM;
    OxCMus*

Zinn, Howard

American. Historian
Historical, political writings include *A
    People's History of the United States*,
    1980.
b. Aug 24, 1922 in New York, New
    York
Source: *AmAu&B; AmMWSc 73S, 78S;
    BioIn 10, 11, 20, 22, 23; CamDcAB;
    ConAu 1R, 2NR, 33NR; CurBio 1999;
    DrAS 74H, 78H, 82H; EncWB, 98;
    MugS; PolProf J; WhoAm 74, 76, 78,
    80, 82, 84, 86, 88, 90; WhoWor 74;
    WrDr 76, 80, 82, 84, 86, 88, 90, 92, 94,
    96, 98, 99, 2000*

Zinn, Walter Henry

American. Physicist
Member of the Manhattan Project; built
    first breeder reactor, 1951.
b. Dec 10, 1906 in Kitchener, Ontario,
    Canada
d. Feb 14, 2000 in Clearwater, Florida
Source: *AmMWSc 76P, 79, 82, 86, 89,
    92, 95, 98; BiESc; BioIn 4, 5; BlueB 76;
    CanWW 70, 79, 80; FacFETw; IntWW
    74; NotTwCS 1S; WorAlBi*

Zinnemann, Fred

American. Director
Won Oscars for *From Here to Eternity*,
    1953; *A Man for All Seasons*, 1966.
b. Apr 25, 1907 in Vienna, Austria
d. Mar 14, 1997 in London, England
Source: *AmFD; BiDFilm, 81, 94; BioIn
    2, 3, 4, 5, 7, 8, 11, 12, 13, 14, 15, 17,
    21, 22, 23, 24; BlueB 76; CamBiEn;
    CamDcAB; ChamBiD; CmMov; ConTFT
    1, 7, 17; CurBio 53, 97N; DcFM;
    FilmEn; FilmgC; HalFC 80, 84, 88;
    IlWWHD 1; IntDcF 1-2, 2-2; IntMPA
    75, 76, 77, 78, 79, 80, 81, 82, 84, 92, 94,
    96; IntWW 74, 75, 76, 77, 78, 79, 80,
    81, 82, 83, 89, 91, 93; LegTOT; MiSFD
    9; MovMk; News 97, 97-3; NewYTBS
    97; OxCFilm; WhAm 12; Who 74, 82,
    83, 85, 88, 90, 92, 94; WhoAm 74, 76,
    78, 80, 82, 84, 86, 88, 90, 92, 94, 95,
    96, 97; WhoEnt 92; WhoWest 74, 76;
    WhoWor 74, 82, 84, 96; WorAl;
    WorAlBi; WorEFlm; WorFDir 1*

Zinoviev, Grigori Evseevich

[Hirsch Apfelbaum]
Russian. Political Leader
Associate of Lenin accused of conspiring
    with Trotsky, 1927; expelled from
    party.
b. Sep 1883 in Elisavetgrad, Russia
d. Aug 25, 1936 in Moscow, Union of
    Soviet Socialist Republics
Source: *BlkwERR; DcPol; EncWB 98;
    McGEWB; NewCol 75; REn; WhDW;
    WorAl*

Zinzendorf, Nikolaus Ludwig von, Count

German. Clergy
Moravian clergyman tried to unite the
    German religious groups in
    Pennsylvania into one spiritual
    community.
b. May 26, 1700 in Dresden, Germany

d. May 6, 1760 in Pennsylvania
Source: *AmNatBi; BiDChrM; BiGAW;
DcEuL; DcLB 168; Dis&D; EncWB 98;
LinLib L; LuthC 75; NewCBEL;
NewGrDM 80; OxCAmL 65; PoChrch;
REn*

Ziolkowski, Korczak
American. Sculptor
Spent 35 years blasting Thunderhead Mt.
creating monument to Crazy Horse.
b. Sep 6, 1908 in Boston, Massachusetts
d. Oct 20, 1982 in Sturgis, South Dakota
Source: *AnObit 1982; BioIn 1, 2, 4, 7, 8,
9, 11, 12, 13, 14, 16, 24; CamDcAB;
CelR; NewYTBS 82; WhAm 8; WhAmArt
85; WhoAm 76, 78, 80, 82; WhoAmA 73,
76, 78, 80, 82, 84N, 86N, 89N, 91N,
93N; WhoPolA*

Zipprodt, Patricia
American. Designer
Won Tony for costume designs in
Fiddler on the Roof, 1965; films
include *The Graduate,* 1967.
b. Feb 25, 1925 in Evanston, Illinois
d. Jul 17, 1999 in New York, New York
Source: *BioIn 16; CamGWoT; ConDes
84, 90, 97; ConTFT 2, 7; MetOEnc;
NotNAT; NotWoAT; VarWW 85; WhoAm
74, 76, 86, 88; WhoAmW 72, 74, 91;
WhoEnt 92; WhoThe 77, 81*

Zirato, Bruno
American. Secretary, Manager
Private secretary to Enrico Caruso, 1915-
21; director, NY Philharmonic, 1956-
59.
b. Sep 27, 1884 in Calabria, Italy
d. Nov 28, 1972 in New York, New
York
Source: *BioIn 4, 5, 8, 9, 10; CurBio 73,
73N; NewYTBE 72; WhAm 5; WhoMus
72*

Zita of Bourbon-Parma
Italian. Consort
Wife of Karl I; last empress of Austria
and queen of Hungary; crowned on
death of Franz Josef, 1916, reigned
two years.
b. Mar 9, 1892 in Viareggio, Italy
d. Mar 14, 1989 in Zizers, Switzerland
Source: *NewCol 75*

Zmed, Adrian
American. Actor
Made Broadway debut as Danny Zuko in
Grease, 1977; played Johnny Nogeril
li in film *Grease 2,* 1982, Vince
Romano on TV series "T J Hooker,"
1982-85.
b. Mar 14, 1954 in Chicago, Illinois
Source: *BioIn 13, 14; ConTFT 8;
LegTOT; VarWW 85; WhoHol 92*

Znaniecki, Florian
American. Sociologist, Educator
Professor advocated a responsible
emphasis on the subjective aspects of
social behavior.
b. 1882 in Swiatniki, Poland

d. 1958
Source: *AmNatBi; BioIn 19, 22;
DcAmImH; DcSoc; EncWB 98; PolBiDi;
WhoPolA*

Zodiac Killer
American. Murderer
Killed at least six in CA beginning 1966;
letters, cryptograms sent to papers;
nothing heard since mid-1970s; never
caught.
Source: *EncACr*

Zoe
Macedonian. Empress
Byzantine empress was, with her sister,
the last representative of the
Macedonian dynasty; a beloved but
frivolous ruler, her dynasty crumbled
with the end of her reign.
b. c. 978
d. 1050
Source: *EncWB 98; McGEWB; OxDcByz*

Zoeller, Fuzzy
[Frank Urban Zoeller]
American. Golfer
Touring pro, beginning 1970s; won
Masters, 1979, US Open, 1984.
b. Nov 11, 1951 in New Albany, Indiana
Source: *BiDAmSp Sup; BioIn 11, 12;
LegTOT; NewYTBS 79, 85*

Zog I
[Ahmed Bey Zogu]
Albanian. Ruler
King of Albania, 1928-39; formally
deposed, 1946.
b. Oct 8, 1895 in Burgayeti, Albania
d. Apr 9, 1961 in Suresnes, France
Source: *CamBiEn; ChamBiD; CurBio
44, 61; EncWB 98; WebBD 83*

Zola, Emile (Edouard Charles)
French. Author, Journalist
Leader of French naturalism; defended
Dreyfus, 1898; wrote novel, *Nana,*
1880.
b. Apr 2, 1840 in Paris, France
d. Sep 29, 1902 in Paris, France
Source: *AtlBL; BbD; Benet 87, 96;
BiD&SB; BiDFrPL; BioIn 1, 2, 3, 4, 5,
6, 7, 8, 9, 10, 11, 12, 13, 14, 15, 16, 17,
18, 19, 20, 21; CamGWoT; CasWL;
CelCen; ClDMEL 47, 80; CnThe; ConAu
104; CyWA 58; DcAmSR; DcBiA;
DcEuL; DcLB 123; Dis&D; EncWL 1;
EncWT; EuAu; EuWr 7; EvEuW;
FilmgC; GrFLW; GuFrLit 1; HalFC 80,
84, 88; IntDcT 2; LegTOT; LinLib L, S;
MagSWL; McGEWB; McGEWD 72, 84;
ModWD; NewC; NewCBEL; NewEOp
71; NewGrDO; NotNAT A, B; Novels;
OxCEng 67, 85, 95; OxCFr; OxCThe
67; OxDcOp; PenC EUR; RAdv 14, 13-
2; RComWL; REn; REnWD; RfGWoL
95; ScF&FL 92; ThHEIm; TwCLC 1, 6,
21, 41; WhDW; WhoTwCL; WorAl;
WorAlBi; WorLitC*

Zolotow, Charlotte Shapiro
American. Children's Author
Writings include *Big Brother,* 1960; *Say
It!* 1980.
b. Jun 26, 1915 in Norfolk, Virginia
Source: *AmWomWr; ArtclWW 2; AuBYP
2, 3; BioIn 13, 14, 15; BkP; ChlLR 2;
ConAu 3NR, 5R, 18NR; DcLB 52;
ForWC 70; IntAu&W 91; IntWWW 2;
MorJA; OxCChiL; PenNWW A; PiP;
SmATA 1, 35; St&PR 91; TwCChW 2, 3;
WhoAm 76, 78, 80, 82, 84, 86, 88, 90,
92, 94, 95, 96, 97, 98, 99, 2000;
WhoAmW 66, 68, 70, 72, 74, 75, 77, 79,
81, 83, 85, 87, 89, 91, 93, 95, 97, 99;
WhoEnt 98; WhoUSWr 88; WhoWrEP
89, 92, 95; WrDr 76, 86, 88, 92*

Zolotow, Maurice
"The Boswell of Broadway"
American. Author
Writings include *Never Whistle in a
Dressing Room,* 1944; *A Gift of
Laughter,* 1965.
b. Nov 23, 1913 in New York, New
York
d. Mar 14, 1991 in Los Angeles,
California
Source: *AmAu&B; Au&Wr 71; BenetAL
91; BioIn 2, 4, 15, 17; ConAu 1NR, 1R,
133; CurBio 57, 91N; NewYTBS 91;
REnAL; WhAm 10; WhoAm 74, 76, 78,
80, 82, 84, 86, 88, 90, 92; WhoWorJ 72,
78; WrDr 76, 80, 82, 84, 86, 88, 90, 92,
94, 96, 98N*

Zombies, The
[Rod Argent; Paul Atkinson; Colin
Blunstone; Hugh Grundy; Chris Taylor
White]
English. Music Group
Formed, 1963; hits include "Tell Her
No," 1964; "Time of the Season,"
1968.
Source: *BillEnR; BioIn 9, 15; ConMuA
80A; ConMus 23; EncPR&S 74, 89;
EncRk 88; EncRkSt; HarEnR 86;
IlEncRk; PenEncP; RkOn 78; RolSEnR
83; WhoRock 81; WhoRocM 82*

Zondervan, Peter
American. Publishing Executive
Founder of Zondervan Publishing, 1931,
one of the world's largest publishers
of religious material.
b. Apr 2, 1909 in Paterson, New Jersey
d. May 10, 1993 in Boca Raton, Florida
Source: *Dun&B 86; St&PR 91; WhoAm
90; WhoFI 92; WhoMW 92; WhoWor 89*

Zorach, William
American. Artist, Sculptor
Sculptures include post office in
Washington, DC; facade for Mayo
Clinic Building.
b. Feb 28, 1887 in Eurburg, Lithuania
d. Nov 15, 1967 in Bath, Maine
Source: *ArtsAmW 3; CurBio 43, 63, 67;
DcAmArt; DcCAA 71, 77, 88, 94;
EncWB 98; FacFETw; IlBEAAW;
McGDA; McGEWB; OxCAmH;
OxCTwCA; OxDcArt; PhDcTCA 77;
WebAB 74, 79; WhAm 4; WhAmArt 85;*

WhoAmA 78N, 80N, 82N, 84N, 86N, 89N, 91N, 93N; WorArt 1950

Zorbaugh, Geraldine B(one)
American. Broadcasting Executive, Lawyer
Attorney, ABC, 1943-57; CBS, 1957-68.
b. May 1, 1905
d. Jun 29, 1996 in Pinehurst, North Carolina
Source: *BioIn 22; CurBio 96N; InWom; WhoAmW 58, 64, 66*

Zorina, Vera
[Eva Brigitta Hartwig]
German. Dancer, Actor
Appeared on Broadway in *On Your Toes,* 1954; films include *The Goldwyn Follies,* 1938.
b. Jan 2, 1917 in Berlin, Germany
Source: *BiDD; BiE&WWA; BioIn 6, 8, 9, 11, 12, 15, 21; CnOxB; CurBio 41; DancEn 78; DcPseud; EncAFC; EncMT; FilmEn; FilmgC; ForYSC; HalFC 80, 84, 88; IntDcB; InWom, SUP; LegTOT; MotPP; MovMk; NotNAT; ThFT; What 3; WhoAm 74, 76, 78; WhoAmW 58, 70, 72, 74; WhoHol 92, A; WhoThe 72, 77, 81*

Zorinsky, Edward
American. Politician
Dem. senator from NE, 1977-87.
b. Nov 11, 1928 in Omaha, Nebraska
d. Mar 6, 1987 in Omaha, Nebraska
Source: *AlmAP 78, 80, 82, 84; BiDrUSC 89; BioIn 11; CngDr 77, 79, 81, 83, 85; PolsAm 84; WhAm 9; WhoAm 78, 80, 82, 84, 86; WhoAmJ 80; WhoAmP 77, 79, 81, 83, 85; WhoGov 77; WhoMW 80, 82, 84, 86; WhoWor 80, 82, 87*

Zorn, Anders Leonard
Swedish. Artist
Paintings are usually Swedish subjects, nudes, portraits including *Portrait of the Artist and His Wife.*
b. Feb 18, 1860 in Mora, Sweden
d. Aug 22, 1920 in Mora, Sweden
Source: *BioIn 1, 2, 5, 6; ClaDrA; McGDA; NewCol 75; OxCArt*

Zoroaster
Persian. Religious Leader, Prophet
Founded Zoroastrianism, circa 575 BC, which replaced Persian polytheism.
b. 628BC, Persia
d. 551BC
Source: *BbD; CasWL; DcOrL 3; LegTOT; NewC; PenC CL; RComWL; REn; WhDW; WorAl*

Zorrilla de San Martin, Juan
Uruguayan. Poet
Known for his patriotic passion and for his great sentiment for a romanticized past, the newspaperman was declared his country's national poet.
b. Dec 28, 1855 in Montevideo, Uruguay
d. Dec 4, 1931 in Montevideo, Uruguay

Source: *BioIn 16; CasWL; DcCathB; DcSpL; EncWB 98; LatAmLi; LatAmWr; McGEWB; OxCSpan; PenC AM*

Zoser
Egyptian. Ruler
First pharaoh of the Third Dynasty and founder of the Old Kingdom, Egypt's first golden age; credited with building the Step Pyramid at Saqqara.
b. fl. 2686BC

Zsigmond, Vilmos
Hungarian. Filmmaker
Won Oscar for cinematography for *Close Encounters of the Third Kind,* 1977.
b. Jun 16, 1930 in Czeged, Hungary
Source: *BioIn 12, 13, 14, 15, 17; ConTFT 2, 8, 16, 27; CurBio 1999; FilmEn; HalFC 80, 84, 88; IntDcF 1-4, 2-4; IntMPA 80, 86, 92, 94, 96; MiSFD 9; VarWW 85; WhoAm 80, 82, 84, 86, 88, 90, 92, 94, 95, 96, 97, 98, 99, 2000; WhoEnt 92, 98*

Zsigmondy, Richard Adolf
Austrian. Chemist
Co-invented ultramicroscope; studied colloidal soultions; won Nobel Prize, 1925.
b. Apr 1, 1865 in Vienna, Austria
d. Sep 24, 1929 in Gottingen, Germany
Source: *AsBiEn; BiESc; BioIn 3, 6, 14, 15, 19, 20; CamBiEn; CamDcSc; ChamBiD; DcInv; DcScB; Dis&D; InSci; LarDcSc; RanHWDS; WhDW; WhoNob, 90, 95; WorAl*

Zucco, George
English. Actor
Had villainous supporting roles in over 100 films, 1931-51.
b. Jan 11, 1886 in Manchester, England
d. May 28, 1960 in Hollywood, California
Source: *BioIn 17, 21; FilmEn; FilmgC; ForYSC; HalFC 80, 84, 88; HolCA; MovMk; NotNAT B; ObitOF 79; ObitT 1951; OlFamFa; Vers A; WhoHol B; WhoHrs 80; WhScrn 74, 77, 83; WhThe*

Zucker, Jeff
American. TV Executive
Highly dedicated, mercurial producer was named executive producer of NBC-TV's "Today" show—a two hour long live television news program—in 1991, when he was only 26 years old.
b. c. 1965 in Miami, Florida
Source: *News 93-3*

Zuckerman, Ben
American. Fashion Designer, Manufacturer
Zuckerman suit was considered status symbol, 1950s-60s; won three Cotys; Hall of Fame, 1961.
b. Jul 29, 1890, Romania
d. Aug 9, 1979 in New York, New York
Source: *BioIn 12; NewYTBS 79; WhAm 7; WorFshn*

Zuckerman, Mortimer Benjamin
American. Publisher
Owner, editor-in-chief, *US News & World Report,* 1984—.
b. Jun 4, 1937 in Montreal, Quebec, Canada
Source: *BioIn 14, 15, 16; ConNews 86-3; CurBio 90; EncTwCJ; IntWW 97, 98, 2000; NewYTBS 85; WhoAm 82, 84, 86, 88, 90, 92, 94, 95, 96, 97, 98, 99, 2000; WhoE 95, 99; WhoMedi 98; WhoWor 96*

Zuckerman, Solly, Lord
English. Scientist, Author
Chief scientific adviser to British Govt., 1964-71; wrote *The Social Life of Monkeys and Apes,* 1931.
b. May 30, 1904 in Cape Town, South Africa
d. Apr 1, 1993 in London, England
Source: *AnObit 1993; Au&Wr 71; BioIn 14, 15, 16, 18, 19; ConAu 28NR, 65; HisPhAn; IntAu&W 82, 89; LarDcSc; RanHWDS; WhE&EA; WhoWor 74, 78, 80, 82, 84, 87; WrDr 76, 80, 82, 84, 86, 88, 90, 92, 94N*

Zuckmayer, Carl
German. Dramatist
Best known for satire *The Captain of Kopenick;* wrote film *The Blue Angel,* 1930.
b. Dec 27, 1896 in Nackenheim, Germany
d. Jan 18, 1977 in Visp, Switzerland
Source: *Au&Wr 71; Benet 87, 96; BiGAW; BioIn 9, 10, 11, 13, 16, 17, 19, 22; CamBiEn; CamGWoT; CasWL; ChamBiD; ClDMEL 47, 80; CnMD; ConAu 69; ConLC 18; CroCD; DcLB 56, 124; EncGRNM; EncTR, 91; EncWL 1, 2, 2S, 3; EncWT; Ent; EvEuW; FilmEn; HalFC 84, 88; IntAu&W 76; IntDcT 2; IntWW 74, 75, 76; LegTOT; LiExTwC; MajMD 1; McGEWD 72, 84; ModGL; ModWD; OxCGer 76, 86, 97; OxCThe 67, 83; PenC EUR; REn; REnWD; RfGWoL 95; TwCWr; WhAm 7; WhDW; WhoThe 72, 77; WhoTwCL; WhoWor 74; WorEFlm*

Zukerman, Pinchas
Israeli. Violinist
International concertist, 1968—; known for playing late-German romantics.
b. Jul 16, 1948 in Tel Aviv, Israel
Source: *BakBD 78, 84, 92; BakBDTw; BakDcM; BioIn 12, 14, 21, 24; BriBkM 80; CamBiEn; CelR 90; ChamBiD; ConMus 4; CurBio 78; IntWW 74, 75, 76, 77, 78, 79, 80, 81, 82, 83, 89, 91, 93, 97, 98, 2000; IntWWM 90; MidE 78, 79, 80, 81, 82; MusSN; NewAmDM; NewGrDA 86; NewGrDM 80; NewYTBE 72; NewYTBS 79, 81; PenDiMP; Who 82, 83, 88, 90, 92, 94, 98, 99, 2000; WhoAm 78, 80, 82, 84, 86, 88, 90, 92, 94, 95, 96, 97, 98; WhoAmM 83; WhoEnt 92, 98; WhoMW 86, 88; WhoWor 74, 82, 87, 89, 91, 93, 95*

Zukofsky, Louis
American. Author
Translated works of poet Catullus, 1971;
wrote "A-24."
b. Jan 23, 1904 in New York, New York
d. May 12, 1978 in Port Jefferson, New
York
Source: *AmAu&B; AmNatBi; AmWr S3;
Benet 87, 96; BenetAL 91; BioIn 8, 10,
11, 12, 16, 17, 22; CamBiEn;
CamDcAB; CamGLE; CamHAL;
ChamBiD; ConAu 9R, 39NR, 77; ConLC
1, 2, 4, 7, 11, 18; ConPo 70, 75, 80A,
85A; CyWA 97; DcAmB S10; DcArts;
DcLB 5, 165; DcLEL 1940; DrAF 76;
DrAP 75; EncALit; EncLitE; EncWL 2,
2S, 3; GrWrEL P; IntWWP 77;
MajTwCW 1; ModAL 4S1, 4S2, 4S3, 5;
OxCAmL 83, 95; OxCTwCL; OxCTwCP;
PenC AM; PoeCrit 11; RAdv 1, 14, 13-
1; RfGAmL 4, 87, 94; RGFAP;
RGTwCWr; WebE&AL; WhAm 7; WhLit;
WhoAm 76, 78; WhoTwCL; WorAu
1950; WrDr 76*

Zukor, Adolph
American. Film Executive, Producer
Founded Famous Players Lasky Corp.,
1916; Paramount Pictures, 1927.
b. Jan 7, 1873 in Riese, Austria-Hungary
d. Jun 10, 1976 in Los Angeles,
California
Source: *AmCulL; AmNatBi; ApCAB X;
BiDAmBL 83; BiDFilm 81, 94; BioIn 2,
3, 4, 5, 9, 10, 11, 15, 19; BlueB 76;
BusPN; CelR; ChamBiD; CmCal;
CurBio 50, 76N; DcAmB S10; DcFM;
EncWB 2-19; FacFETw; FilmEn;
FilmgC; HalFC 80, 84, 88; IntDcF 2-4;
IntMPA 75, 76; IntWW 74, 75, 76;
LegTOT; NatCAB 15; NewYTBE 73;
NewYTBS 76; OxCFilm; WhAm 6, 7;
Who 74; WhoAm 74; WorAl; WorAlBi;
WorEFlm*

Zumarraga, Juan de
Spanish. Clergy
Franciscan was the first bishop and first
archbishop of Mexico, he combined
missionary zeal, a sensitive social
conscience, and love of learning.
b. c. 1468
d. Jun 3, 1548 in Mexico City, Mexico
Source: *ApCAB; BiDChrM; BioIn 2, 5,
8; DcCathB; EncLatA; EncWB 98;
HisDcSE; LatAmLi; McGEWB*

Zumwalt, Elmo R(ussell), Jr.
American. Naval Officer
Youngest four-star admiral in US naval
history; commanded US forces in
Vietnam, 1968-70; ordered use of
Agent Orange, now believed to cause
cancer; wrote of son's illness in *My
Father, My Son*, 1986.
b. Nov 24, 1920 in San Francisco,
California
d. Jan 2, 2000 in Durham, North
Carolina
Source: *BioIn 8, 9, 10, 11, 12, 16;
CamDcAB; ColdWar 2; ConAu 85;
DcAmMiB; EncNaHi; EncWB, 98;
HarEnMi; IntWW 74, 75, 76, 77, 78, 79,
80, 81, 82, 83, 89, 91, 93, 97, 98, 2000;*

*IntYB 78, 79, 80, 81, 82; LinLib S;
NewYTBE 70; NewYTBS 86; St&PR 84,
87, 91, 93, 96, 97, 98, 99, 2000;
WebAMB; WhoAm 74, 76, 78, 80, 82,
84, 86, 88, 90, 92, 94, 95, 96, 97, 98,
99, 2000; WhoFI 85; WhoGov 72;
WhoSSW 73; WhoWor 78; WorAl;
WorAlBi; WorDWW*

Zumwalt, Elmo Russell, III
American. Author, Soldier, Victim
Believed to have contracted cancer from
exposure to chemical Agent Orange,
ordered used in Vietnam by father;
with father, wrote *My Father, My Son*,
1986.
b. Jul 30, 1946? in Tulare, California
d. Aug 13, 1988 in Fayetteville, North
Carolina
Source: *ConAu 126*

Zuniga, Daphne
American. Actor
Appreared in *The Sure Thing*, 1985.
b. 1962 in Berkeley, California
Source: *BiHaHis; ConTFT 16; IntMPA
94, 96; WhoHol 92*

Zunz, Leopold
German. Scholar
Enlightenment thinker founded the
modern historical and philological
study of Judaism.
b. Aug 10, 1794 in Lippe, Germany
d. Mar 18, 1886 in Berlin, Germany
Source: *BbD; BiD&SB; BioIn 3, 5, 6,
15, 22, 23; DcEuL; EncWB 98;
McGEWB; OxDcJeR*

Zuppke, Robert Carl
"Rembrandt of the Prairies"; "Zupp"
American. Football Coach
Head coach, U of IL, 1913-41, compiling
131-81-12 record; introduced onside
kick, screen pass, among others.
b. Jul 12, 1879 in Berlin, Germany
d. Dec 22, 1957 in Champaign, Illinois
Source: *AmNatBi; BiDAmSp FB; BioIn
4, 5, 6, 10; CamDcAB; DcAmB S6;
WhAm 3; WhoFtbl 74*

Zurbaran, Francisco
Spanish. Artist
Baroque painter known for religious,
monastic work: *Immaculate
Conception*, 1616.
b. Nov 7, 1598 in Fuentes de Cantos,
Spain
d. Aug 27, 1664 in Madrid, Spain
Source: *AtlBL; ChamBiD; DcBiPP;
DcCathB; LinLib S; McGEWB; OxCArt;
OxDcArt; WhDW; WorAl*

Zurbriggen, Pirmin
Swiss. Skier
Won gold medal in downhill, 1988
Olympics.
b. 1964? in Saas-Almagell, Switzerland
Source: *BioIn 15, 16; NewYTBS 87*

Zweig, Arnold
German. Author, Dramatist
Best known for novel *Case of Sergeant
Grischa*, 1927.
b. Nov 10, 1887, Prussia
d. Nov 26, 1968 in Berlin, German
Democratic Republic
Source: *Benet 87, 96; BioIn 1, 4, 5, 7, 8,
9, 10, 11, 15, 16, 22; CamBiEn; CasWL;
ChamBiD; CIDMEL 47, 80; CnMD;
ConAu 115; CyWA 58, 97; DcArts;
DcLB 66; EncGRNM; EncTR, 91;
EncWL 1, 2, 2S, 3; EvEuW; LiExTwC;
LinLib L, S; LngCTC; ModGL; ModWD;
ObitT 1961; OxCEng 67; OxCGer 76,
86, 97; PenC EUR; REn; TwCA, SUP;
TwCWr; WorAu 1900*

Zweig, Stefan
Austrian. Author
Wrote psychological biographies of
literary, historical figures: *Paul
Verlaine*, 1913.
b. Nov 28, 1881 in Vienna, Austria
d. Feb 22, 1942 in Petropolis, Brazil
Source: *Benet 87, 96; BiDMoPL; BioIn
1, 2, 3, 6, 7, 9, 10, 11, 12, 13, 14, 17,
18, 21, 22; CamBiEn; CasWL;
ChamBiD; CIDMEL 47, 80; CnMD;
CnMWL; ConAu 112, 170; CurBio 42;
DcArts; DcLB 81, 118; Dis&D; EncTR,
91; EncWL 1, 2, 2S, 3; Ent; EvEuW;
FacFETw; LegTOT; LiExTwC; LinLib L,
S; LngCTC; MakMC; McGEWD 72, 84;
ModGL; ModWD; NewGrDM 80;
NewGrDO; NotNAT A, B; Novels;
OxCGer 76, 86, 97; OxCThe 83;
OxDcOp; PenC EUR; PlP&P; RAdv 14,
13-2; REn; REnWD; TwCA, SUP;
TwCLC 17; TwCWr; WhAm 2; WhDW;
WorAu 1900*

Zwicky, Fritz
Swiss. Astronomer, Inventor
Expert on jet propulsion whose
inventions included the aeropulse,
hydroturbojet, monopropellants.
b. Feb 14, 1898 in Varna, Bulgaria
d. Feb 8, 1974 in Pasadena, California
Source: *AmMWSc 73P; AmNatBi;
AsBiEn; BiESc; BioIn 3, 4, 10, 14;
BlueB 76; CamBiEn; ChamBiD; ConAu
49; CurBio 74, 74N; DcAmB S9; DcScB
S2; InnAst; InSci; LarDcSc; LinLib L, S;
ObitOF 79; RanHWDS; WhAm 6;
WhoWor 74; WorAl; WorAlBi; WorScD*

Zwilich, Ellen Taaffe
American. Composer
First woman to win Pulitzer for music,
1983, for *Three Movements for
Orchest ra*.
b. Apr 30, 1939 in Miami, Florida
Source: *BakBD 78, 84, 92; BakBDTw;
BakDcM; BioIn 13, 14, 15, 16, 17, 18,
24; ChamBiD; ConAmC 76, 82;
ConCom 92; CpmDNM 80, 81, 82;
CurBio 86; DcTwCCu 1; EncWB, 98;
GrLiveH; IntWWM 85, 90; IntWWW 2;
InWom SUP; NewAmDM; NewGrDA 86;
News 90; NewYTBS 85; WhoAm 86, 88,
90, 92, 94, 95, 96, 97, 98, 99, 2000;
WhoAmM 83; WhoAmW 85, 87, 89, 91,*

93, 95, 97, 99; WhoE 85, 86, 89;
WhoEnt 92, 98; WhoPul; WomFir

Zwingli, Huldreich
Swiss. Social Reformer
Sermons criticizing the Mass started
   Reformation in Switzerland.
b. Jan 1, 1484 in Wildhause, Germany
d. Oct 10, 1531 in Kappel, Switzerland
Source: *CasWL; ChamBiD; CyEd;*
DcBiPP; Dis&D; EncWB 98; LuthC 75;
McGEWB; NewGrDM 80; REn; WhDW

Zworykin, Vladimir K(osma)
"Father of Television"
American. Engineer, Physicist
Invented the iconoscope, a television
   camera tube; later developed first all-
   electronic television system.
b. Jul 30, 1889 in Mourom, Russia
d. Jul 29, 1982 in Princeton, New Jersey

Source: *AmMWSc 76P, 79, 82;*
AmNatBi; AsBiEn; BiESc; BioIn 2, 3, 4,
6, 8, 9, 10, 12, 13, 24; CamBiEn;
CamDcAB; ChamBiD; ConAu 107, 157;
CurBio 82; EncWB 98; FacFETw;
FrTalk; ICPEnP; IntWW 74, 75, 76, 77,
78, 79, 80, 81, 82; LarDcSc; LElec;
LesBEnT; McGCEnS; McGEWB;
McGMS 80; NewYTBS 82; OxCAmH;
RanHWDS; ScrEAmL 1; WebAB 74, 79;
WhAm 8; WhoAm 74, 76, 78, 80;
WhoEng 80, 88; WhoWor 74, 78;
WorAl; WorInv

Zylis-Gara, Teresa
Polish. Opera Singer
Soprano with NY Met. since 1969.
b. Jan 23, 1937 in Vilna, Poland
Source: *BakBD 84; BioIn 13; IntWW 91;*
IntWWM 90; MetOEnc; MusSN;
NewAmDM; NewEOp 71; NewGrDM 80;
NewYTBS 74; PenDiMP; WhoAm 86, 90;
WhoAmW 83; WhoSoCE 89

Zyuganov, Gennadi A(ndreyevich)
Russian. Political Leader
Leader of the Russian Communist Party,
   1991—.
b. 1944 in Mymrino, Union of Soviet
   Socialist Republics
Source: *CurBio 96; WhoRus*

ZZ Top
[Frank Beard; Billy Gibbons; Dusty Hill]
American. Music Group
Texan group, formed 1970; frequent
   tours have made all albums gold or
   platinum.
Source: *Alli SUP; AllMGBl 1, 2;*
ApCAB; BillEnR; BioIn 11; ChhPo;
ConMuA 80A; ConMus 2; CurBio 70;
DcNAA; EncPR&S 89; EncRk 88;
GrMetD; HarEnR 86; IlEncRk; LinLib
LP; OhA&B; PenEncP; RkOn 78;
RkWho 96; RolSEnR 83; WhoRock 81;
WhoRocM 82

Chronological Index by Year

3400BC

b. Menes

3000BC

b. Imhotep

2950BC

d. Imhotep

2686BC

b. Zoser

2334BC

b. Sargon of Agade

2279BC

d. Sargon of Agade

1991BC

b. Amenemhet, I

1900BC

b. Sarah

1860BC

b. Rebecca

1838BC

b. Jacob

1792BC

b. Hammurabi

1753BC

b. Rachel

1750BC

d. Hammurabi

1689BC

d. Jacob

1575BC

b. Miriam

1540BC

b. Hatshepsut

1504BC

b. Thutmose, III

1481BC

d. Hatshepsut

1450BC

d. Thutmose, III

1417BC

b. Amenhotep, III

1392BC

b. Moses

1390BC

b. Nefertiti

1360BC

d. Nefertiti

1358BC

b. Tutankhamen

1354BC

d. Ikhnaton, Pharaoh

1340BC

d. Tutankhamen

14th CENTURY BC

b. Ikhnaton, Pharaoh

1272BC

d. Moses

13th CENTURY BC

b. Ramses II

1146BC

b. Nebuchadnezzar I

1123BC

d. Nebuchadnezzar I

1116BC

b. Chou Kung
d. Wu wang

1040BC

b. Bathsheba

1015BC

d. Bathsheba

11th CENTURY BC

b. Samuel

1000BC

b. David
b. Ruth

973BC

b. Solomon

960BC

d. David

950BC

b. Sheba

933BC

d. Solomon

10th CENTURY BC

b. Jeroboam, I

875BC

b. Elijah

9th CENTURY BC

b. Jezebel

750BC

b. Amos
b. Homer

745BC

d. Daniel

741BC

b. Piankhi

731BC

d. Tiglath-pileser, III

712BC

b. Shabaka
d. Piankhi

705BC

b. Sennacherib
d. Sargon, II

8th CENTURY BC

b. Isaiah
b. Micah

681BC

d. Sennacherib

662BC

d. Taharqa

650BC

b. Jeremiah
d. Draco

630BC

b. Nebuchadnezzar II

628BC

b. Zoroaster

620BC

b. Aesop

612BC

b. Sappho

611BC

b. Anaximander

600BC

b. Cyrus the Great
b. Thales

599BC

b. Mahavira

582BC

b. Pythagoras

572BC

b. Anacreon

570BC

b. Anaximenes of Miletus
b. Cleisthenes
b. Lao-Tzu
b. Xenophanes
d. Jeremiah

563BC

April 8, 563BC
b. Buddha

562BC

d. Nebuchadnezzar II

560BC

b. Croesus
d. Aesop

558BC

b. Darius I

551BC

d. Zoroaster

August 27, 551BC
b. Confucius

549BC

b. Miltiades

547BC

d. Anaximander

546BC

d. Croesus

540BC

b. Heraclitus of Ephesus
d. Thales

539BC

d. Bellshazzar

530BC

b. Aristides

529BC

d. Cyrus the Great

527BC

d. Mahavira

524BC

b. Aeschylus
b. Themistocles

522BC

d. Cambyses, II

520BC

b. Cleomenes, I

519BC

b. Vashti
b. Xerxes I

518BC

September 4, 518BC
b. Pindar

516BC

b. Bacchylides

515BC

b. Parmenides

507BC

d. Pythagoras

6th CENTURY BC

b. Coriolanus, Gaius
b. Scopas
b. Thespis

500BC

b. Anaxagoras
b. Phidias
d. Anaximenes of Miletus
d. Cleisthenes

496BC

b. Sophocles

495BC

b. Pericles

493BC

b. Empedocles

490BC

b. Polygnotus
b. Protagoras
b. Zeno of Elea
d. Lao-Tzu

488BC

d. Anacreon
d. Miltiades

486BC

d. Darius I

485BC

b. Herodotus

484BC

September 23, 484BC
b. Euripides

483BC

February 25, 483BC
d. Buddha

480BC

b. Antiphon of Rhamnus
b. Gorgias
b. Myron
d. Heraclitus of Ephesus
d. Leonidas I
d. Xenophanes

479BC

November 21, 479BC
d. Confucius

475BC

b. Cleon
b. Esther

470BC

b. Socrates

468BC

d. Aristides

465BC

d. Xerxes I

460BC

b. Democritus
b. Hippocrates
b. Thucydides
d. Themistocles

456BC

d. Aeschylus

450BC

b. Alcibiades
d. Bacchylides

448BC

b. Aristophanes

445BC

b. Eupolis

444BC

b. Agesilaus, II
b. Antisthenes

442BC

d. Pindar

441BC

d. Eupolis

440BC

d. Myron

436BC

b. Isocrates

433BC

d. Empedocles

432BC

d. Phidias

430BC

b. Dionysius the Elder
b. Xenophon
d. Zeno of Elea

429BC

d. Pericles

428BC

d. Anaxagoras

427BC

May 21, 427BC
b. Plato

425BC

d. Herodotus
d. Polygnotus

422BC

d. Cleon

421BC

d. Protagoras

412BC

b. Diogenes

411BC

d. Antiphon of Rhamnus

410BC

b. Epaminondas

408BC

b. Apollodorus
b. Eudoxus of Cnidus

406BC

d. Sophocles

November 30, 406BC
d. Euripides

404BC

d. Alcibiades

5th CENTURY BC

b. Alcamenes
b. Ictinus
b. Polycletus the Elder

400BC

b. Apelles
b. Nehemiah

399BC

d. Socrates
d. Thucydides

395BC

d. Lysander

390BC

b. Shang Yang

389BC

b. Hyperides

388BC

b. Heraclides of Pontus

385BC

d. Aristophanes

384BC

b. Aristotle
b. Demosthenes

382BC

b. Antigonus, I
b. Philip II

377BC

d. Hippocrates

376BC

d. Gorgias

371BC

b. Mencius
d. Antisthenes

370BC

b. Damocles
b. Praxiteles
d. Democritus

369BC

b. Chuang Tzu

367BC

d. Dionysius the Elder

366BC

b. Ptolemy (Soter), I

364BC

d. Pelopidas

362BC

d. Epaminondas

360BC

d. Agesilaus, II

358BC

b. Seleucus, I

356BC

September 20, 356BC
b. Alexander the Great

355BC

d. Eudoxus of Cnidus

354BC

d. Xenophon

353BC

d. Mausolus

350BC

d. Artemisia

347BC

January 14, 347BC
d. Plato

342BC

b. Epicurus
b. Menander

338BC

d. Isocrates
d. Shang Yang

337BC

b. Demetrius I

336BC

d. Philip II

334BC

b. Zeno of Citium

330BC

d. Praxiteles

323BC

b. Euclid
d. Diogenes
d. Hyperides

June 13, 323BC
d. Alexander the Great

322BC

d. Aristotle
d. Demosthenes

320BC

b. Chares

312BC

b. Hsun-tzu

311BC

d. Roxana

310BC

b. Aristarchus of Samos
b. Theocritus
d. Heraclides of Pontus

308BC

b. Ptolemy, II

305BC

b. Callimachus

304BC

b. Erasistratus

4th CENTURY BC

b. Kautilya
b. Lysippus
b. Parrhasius
b. Tsou Yen

301BC

d. Antigonus, I

300BC

b. Asoka the Great
b. Phryne

298BC

d. Chandragupta Maurya

292BC

d. Menander

290BC

b. Berosus

289BC

d. Mencius

287BC

b. Archimedes

286BC

d. Chuang Tzu

285BC

b. Hamilcar Barca

284BC

b. Livius Andronicus

283BC

d. Demetrius I
d. Euclid
d. Ptolemy (Soter), I

281BC

d. Seleucus, I

280BC

b. Chrysippus
b. Han Fei Tzu
b. Li Ssu

276BC

b. Euphorion

275BC

b. Eratosthenes

271BC

b. Aratus

270BC

d. Epicurus

262BC

b. Agis, IV
b. Appollonius of Perga
d. Zeno of Citium

260BC

b. Cleomenes, III

259BC

b. Quin Shi Huang-Di

256BC

b. Liu Pang

254BC

b. Plautus, Titus Maccius

250BC

d. Erasistratus
d. Theocritus

247BC

b. Han Kao-tsu
b. Hannibal

246BC

d. Ptolemy, II

241BC

b. Antiochus, III
d. Agis, IV

240BC

b. Masinissa
d. Callimachus

239BC

b. Ennius, Quintus

237BC

b. Philip V

235BC

d. Hsun-tzu

234BC

b. Cato, Marcus Porcius Censorius
b. Scipio Africanus, Publius Cornelius

233BC

d. Han Fei Tzu

232BC

d. Asoka the Great

230BC

b. Flamininus, Titus Quinctius
d. Aristarchus of Samos

229BC

d. Hamilcar Barca

219BC

d. Cleomenes, III

215BC

b. Antiochus, IV

213BC

b. Carneades
d. Aratus

212BC

d. Archimedes

210BC

b. Apollonius of Perga
d. Quin Shi Huang-Di

208BC

d. Li Ssu

206BC

d. Chrysippus

204BC

d. Livius Andronicus

3rd CENTURY BC

b. Sostratus

200BC

b. Polybius
d. Appollonius of Perga

195BC

d. Eratosthenes
d. Han Kao-tsu
d. Liu Pang

187BC

d. Antiochus, III

185BC

b. Terence

184BC

d. Plautus, Titus Maccius

183BC

d. Hannibal
d. Scipio Africanus, Publius Cornelius

180BC

b. Lucilius, Gaius

179BC

b. Ssu-ma Hsiang-ju
b. Tung Chung-shu
d. Philip V

175BC

d. Flamininus, Titus Quinctius

170BC

b. Jesus ben Sira

169BC

b. Gracchus, Tiberius Sempronius
d. Ennius, Quintus

163BC

d. Antiochus, IV

160BC

b. Hipparchus

159BC

d. Terence

157BC

b. Han Wu-ti
b. Marius, Gaius
b. Wu-ti, Han

153BC

b. Gracchus, Gaius Sempronius

149BC

d. Cato, Marcus Porcius Censorius

148BC

d. Masinissa

145BC

b. Ssu-ma Ch'ien

138BC

b. Sulla, Lucius C

128BC

d. Carneades

127BC

d. Hipparchus

124BC

b. Drusus, Marcus Livius

121BC

d. Gracchus, Gaius Sempronius

118BC

d. Polybius

117BC

d. Ssu-ma Hsiang-ju

116BC

b. Varro, Marcus Terentius

115BC

b. Crassus, Marcus Licinius Dives

110BC

b. Lucullus, Lucius Licinius

108BC

b. Catiline, Lucius

106BC

January 3, 106BC
b. Cicero, Marcus Tullius

September 30, 106BC
b. Pompey the Great

104BC

d. Tung Chung-shu

102BC

d. Lucilius, Gaius

100BC

July 12, 100BC
b. Caesar, Julius

99BC

b. Lucretius

95BC

b. Cato, Marcus Porcius Uticensis

91BC

d. Drusus, Marcus Livius

90BC

d. Ssu-ma Ch'ien

87BC

d. Han Wu-ti
d. Wu-ti, Han

86BC

d. Marius, Gaius

85BC

b. Brutus, Marcus Junius

84BC

b. Catullus, Gaius Valerius

83BC

b. Antony, Marc

78BC

d. Sulla, Lucius C

75BC

b. Vercingetorix

73BC

b. Herod the Great

71BC

d. Spartacus

70BC

b. Vitruvius

October 15, 70BC
b. Vergil

69BC

b. Cleopatra VII
b. Octavia

65BC

December 8, 65BC
b. Horace

63BC

b. Agrippa, Marcus Vipsanius
b. Strabo

September 23, 63BC
b. Augustus

62BC

d. Catiline, Lucius

60BC

b. Mariamne the Hasmonaean

59BC

b. Calpurnia
b. Livy

58BC

b. Livia

57BC

d. Lucullus, Lucius Licinius

55BC

b. Propertius, Sextus
d. Lucretius

54BC

d. Catullus, Gaius Valerius

53BC

June 6, 53BC
d. Crassus, Marcus Licinius Dives

52BC

d. Pulcher, Publius Clodius

48BC

September 29, 48BC
d. Pompey the Great

46BC

d. Cato, Marcus Porcius Uticensis
d. Vercingetorix

45BC

b. Wang Mang

44BC

March 15, 44BC
d. Caesar, Julius

43BC

d. Brutus Albinus, Decimus Junius

March 20, 43BC
b. Ovid

December 7, 43BC
d. Cicero, Marcus Tullius

42BC

d. Cassius

October 24, 42BC
d. Brutus, Marcus Junius

November 16, 42BC
b. Tiberius Julius Caesar Augustus

35BC

d. Sallust

30BC

b. Dionysius of Halicarnassus

d. Antony, Marc

August 30, 30BC
d. Cleopatra VII

29BC

d. Mariamne the Hasmonaean

27BC

d. Varro, Marcus Terentius

20BC

b. Philo Judaeus

19BC

September 21, 19BC
d. Vergil

16BC

d. Propertius, Sextus
d. Vitruvius

15BC

b. Phaedrus

12BC

b. Deborah
d. Agrippa, Marcus Vipsanius

11BC

d. Octavia

10BC

August 1, 10BC
b. Claudius I

8BC

November 27, 8BC
d. Horace

7BC

d. Dionysius of Halicarnassus

6BC

b. Kuang-wu-ti

4BC

b. Herod Antipas
b. Jesus Christ
b. Seneca, Lucius Annaeus, the
  Younger
d. Herod the Great

1st CENTURY BC

b. Joseph, Saint
b. Mary, The, Virgin Mother
b. Shammai

1st CENTURY

b. Androcles
b. Clement I, Saint
b. John the Apostle, Saint
b. John the Baptist
b. Jude, Saint
b. Luke, Saint
b. Mark, Saint
d. Mary, The, Virgin Mother

8

November 17, 8
b. Vespasian

9

d. Hillel

12

August 31, 12
b. Caligula

14

b. Salome

August 19, 14
d. Augustus

15

b. Vitellius, Aulus

16

b. Agrippina

17

d. Livy

January 2, 17
d. Ovid

22

d. Strabo

23

b. Pliny the Elder

October 6, 23
d. Wang Mang

26

b. Pilate, Pontius

27

b. Wang Ch'ung

28

b. Berenice

29

d. Jesus Christ
d. Livia

30

b. Joseph of Arimathea, Saint
d. Judas Iscariot
d. Lazarus

31

October 18, 31
d. Sejanus, Lucius Aelius

32

b. Pan Ku

34

December 4, 34
b. Persius

35

b. Frontinus, Sextus Julius

b. Quintilian Marcus Fabius

37

b. Josephus, Flavius

March 16, 37
d. Tiberius Julius Caesar Augustus

December 15, 37
b. Nero

39

d. Herod Antipas

June 3, 39
b. Lucan

40

b. Dioscorides, Pedanius

December 30, 40
b. Titus

41

January 24, 41
d. Caligula

43

b. Martial

44

d. James the Greater, Saint

46

b. Plutarch

50

b. Akiba ben Joseph
b. Ts'ai, Lun
d. Gamaliel the Elder
d. Phaedrus
d. Philo Judaeus

51

October 24, 51
b. Domitian

53

d. Thomas, Saint

127

d. Juvenal

129

b. Galen

133

d. Gracchus, Tiberius Sempronius

135

b. Judah, I
d. Akiba ben Joseph
d. Bar Kokhba, Simon
d. Epictetus

138

July 10, 138
d. Hadrian

140

d. Suetonius

146

b. Septimius Severus, Lucius

150

b. Clement of Alexandria
b. Ptolemy

155

b. Ts'ao Ts'ao

160

b. Tertullian, Quintus Septimus
Florens

161

d. Maccabeus, Judas

March 7, 161
d. Antoninus Pius

165

d. Justin Martyr

170

b. Hippolytus, Saint
d. Ptolemy, Claudius

175

b. Abba Arika

180

March 17, 180
d. Marcus Aurelius Antoninus

184

d. Chang Chueh

185

b. Origen Adamantius

186

April 4, 186
b. Caracalla, Marcus Aurelius
Antonius

199

d. Galen

200

b. Valerian
d. Apuleius, Lucius
d. Lucian

3rd CENTURY

b. Christopher, Saint
b. George, Saint
b. Longus
b. Zenobia

204

b. Heliogabalus
b. Plotinus

210

b. Longinus

211

d. Septimius Severus, Lucius

215

d. Clement of Alexandria

216

April 24, 216
b. Mani

217

April 8, 217
d. Caracalla, Marcus Aurelius
Antonius

220

d. Judah, I

March 15, 220
d. Ts'ao Ts'ao

222

d. Heliogabalus

226

b. Wang Pi

228

d. Ulpian, Domitius

230

d. Cecelia, Saint
d. Tertullian, Quintus Septimus
Florens

235

d. Hippolytus, Saint

236

d. Pontian, Saint

245

b. Diocletian

247

d. Abba Arika

249

d. Wang Pi

251

b. Anthony, Saint

254

d. Origen Adamantius

256

b. Arius

258

September 14, 258
d. Cyprianus, Thascius Caecilianus

260

d. Valerian

261

b. Lu Chi

264

b. Eusebius of Caearea

270

d. Plotinus

274

b. Shih Le

276

d. Mani

280

February 27, 280
b. Constantine I

291

b. Agnes, Saint

293

b. Athanasius, Saint

4th CENTURY

b. Ezana
b. Nicholas, Saint

303

d. Damian, Saint
d. Lu Chi

April 23, 303
d. George, Saint

304

d. Agnes, Saint

307

d. Catherine of Alexandria, Saint

310

b. Shahpur, II

311

b. Ulfilas

312

b. Tao-an

313

d. Diocletian

316

d. Blaise, Saint

330

b. Basil, Saint

331

November 17, 331
b. Julian

333

d. Shih Le

334

b. Hui-yuan

336

d. Arius

337

March 22, 337
d. Constantine I

340

b. Ambrose, Saint
d. Eusebius of Caearea

344

b. Kumarajiva

345

b. Chrysostom, John, Saint
b. Jerome, Saint
b. Ku K'ai-chih

December 6, 345
d. Nicholas, Saint

346

b. Theodosius

January 11, 346
b. Thedosius I

350

b. Samudragupta
d. Anthony, Saint

354

November 13, 354
b. Augustine, Saint

355

d. Donatus

359

April 19, 359
b. Gratian

363

June 26, 363
d. Julian

365

b. Claudian
b. T'ao Ch'ien

370

b. Alaric I

373

d. Athanasius, Saint

375

b. Kwanggaet'o

376

b. Cyril of Alexandria, Saint

379

d. Shahpur, II

January 1, 379
d. Basil, Saint

380

b. Eutyches

382

d. Ulfilas

383

August 25, 383
d. Gratian

385

b. Hsieh Ling-yun, Duke of K'ang-lo
b. Patrick, Saint
d. Tao-an

389

b. Nestorius

390

b. Simeon Stylites, Saint

395

January 17, 395
d. Thedosius I
d. Theodosius

397

April 4, 397
d. Ambrose, Saint

400

b. Kalidasa
b. Leo, I, St.

406

b. Attila
d. Ku K'ai-chih

407

September 14, 407
d. Chrysostom, John, Saint

408

d. Claudian

August 22, 408
d. Stilicho, Flavius

409

d. Kumarajiva

410

b. Proclus Diadochus
d. Alaric I

413

d. Kwanggaet'o

415

d. Hypatia

416

September 13, 416
d. Hui-yuan

420

d. Jerome, Saint

422

b. Genevieve, Saint

427

d. T'ao Ch'ien

430

d. Pelagius

August 28, 430
d. Augustine, Saint

November 5, 430
b. Apollinaris Sidonius, Gaius Sollius

433

b. Odoacer
d. Hsieh Ling-yun, Duke of K'ang-lo

444

June 27, 444
d. Cyril of Alexandria, Saint

451

d. Nestorius

453

b. Brigid of Kildare
b. Theodoric the Great
d. Attila

455

d. Eutyches

459

d. Simeon Stylites, Saint

461

d. Patrick, Saint

November 10, 461
d. Leo, I, St.

464

b. Liang Wu-ti

465

b. Liu Hsieh

466

b. Clovis I

467

October 13, 467
b. Wei Hsiao-Wen-ti

472

August 18, 472
d. Ricimer

477

d. Gaiseric

480

b. Benedict, Saint
b. Boethius
b. Cassiodorus, Flavius Magnus
   Aurelius

483

May 11, 483
b. Justinian I

484

b. Brendan of Clonfert, Saint

485

d. Proclus Diadochus

487

August 21, 487
d. Apollinaris Sidonius, Gaius Sollius

493

d. Odoacer

495

b. David, Saint

499

April 26, 499
d. Wei Hsiao-Wen-ti

500

b. Procopius of Caesarea
d. Genevieve, Saint

505

b. Belisarius

508

b. Theodora

511

November 27, 511
d. Clovis I

521

b. Columba, Saint

522

d. Liu Hsieh

523

d. Brigid of Kildare

524

d. Boethius

526

d. Theodoric the Great

531

b. Khosrow, I

538

b. Chih-i

November 30, 538
b. Gregory of Tours, St.

540

February 3, 540
b. Gregory the Great, Saint

541

b. Sui, Yang Chien
b. Sui Wen-ti

543

b. Columban, Saint

547

March 21, 547
d. Benedict, Saint

548

d. Theodora

549

June 7, 549
d. Liang Wu-ti

554

b. Suiko

560

b. Isidore of Seville, St.

565

d. Procopius of Caesarea
d. Belisarius

November 14, 565
d. Justinian I

570

January 30, 570
b. Mohammed

573

b. Abu Bakr
b. Shotoku Taishi

575

b. Heraclius
d. Cassiodorus, Flavius Magnus
Aurelius

576

d. Khosrow, I

577

d. Brendan of Clonfert, Saint

581

b. Omar I

589

d. David, Saint

590

b. Harsha

594

b. Solon

November 17, 594
d. Gregory of Tours, St.

596

b. Tao-hsuan

597

d. Chih-i

June 8, 597
d. Columba, Saint

600

b. Ali
b. T'ai-tsung, T'ang

602

b. Hsuan Tsang

604

d. Sui, Yang Chien
d. Sui Wen-ti

March 12, 604
d. Gregory the Great, Saint

May 26, 604
d. Augustine of Canterbury, Saint

606

b. Fatima

614

b. Ayesha
b. Fujiwara Kamatari

615

November 23, 615
d. Columban, Saint

621

d. Shotoku Taishi

623

b. Wu Tse-t'ien

628

d. Suiko

632

d. Fatima

June 8, 632
d. Mohammed

634

d. Abu Bakr

636

d. Isidore of Seville, St.

641

February 11, 641
d. Heraclius

644

d. Omar I

646

b. Abd al-Malik

647

d. Harsha

649

d. T'ai-tsung, T'ang

650

b. Caedmon, Saint

655

b. Hubert, Saint

661

d. Ali

664

d. Hsuan Tsang

667

d. Tao-hsuan

669

d. Fujiwara Kamatari

673

d. Yen Li-pen

May 26, 673
b. Bede the Venerable, Saint

675

b. Boniface, Saint

678

d. Ayesha

680

b. John of Damascus, St.
b. Leo, III
b. Sol Ch'ong
d. Caedmon, Saint
d. Muawiya ibn Abu Sufyan

685

b. T'ang Hsuan-tsung

689

b. Charles Martel
b. Wu Tao-tzu

693

b. Makibi, Kibi-no

699

b. Wang Wei

700

b. Hesiod
b. Sankara

8th CENTURY

b. Anan ben David
b. Cynewulf
b. Jabir ibn Hayyan

701

b. Li Po

703

b. An Lu-shan

705

d. Abd al-Malik
d. Wu Tse-t'ien

712

b. Mansur, (Abu Jafar Ibn
    Muhammad), Al
b. Tu, Fu

715

b. Pepin III

718

b. Constantine V

727

d. Hubert, Saint

731

b. Abd al-Rahman, I

735

b. Alcuin
d. Bede the Venerable, Saint

737

b. Kammu

741

d. Charles Martel

June 18, 741
d. Leo, III

742

April 2, 742
b. Charlemagne

750

d. John of Damascus, St.
d. Sankara
d. Sol Ch'ong

752

b. Irene of Athens

754

June 5, 754
d. Boniface, Saint

756

b. Abu Nuwas

757

d. An Lu-shan

758

d. Wu Tao-tzu

759

d. Wang Wei

762

d. Li Po
d. T'ang Hsuan-tsung

764

b. Harun-Al-Rashid

767

b. Saicho

768

b. Han Yu
d. Pepin III

770

January 14, 770
b. Constantine VI

772

February 28, 772
b. Po Chu-i

773

b. Liu Tsung-yuan

774

July 27, 774
b. Kukai

775

d. Makibi, Kibi-no

September 14, 775
d. Constantine V
d. Mansur, (Abu Jafar Ibn
    Muhammad), Al

777

d. Tu, Fu

778

b. Louis I

786

b. Mamun, Abdallah al-

788

b. Shankara

September 30, 788
d. Abd al-Rahman, I

792

b. Adrian II

794

b. Ennin

797

August 15, 797
d. Constantine VI

803

August 15, 803
d. Irene of Athens

804

May 19, 804
d. Alcuin

806

d. Kammu

809

March 24, 809
d. Harun-Al-Rashid

810

b. Bukhari, Muhammad ibn Ismail al-
b. Erigena, John Scotus

812

b. Basil, I

813

d. Abu Nuwas

814

January 28, 814
d. Charlemagne

819

June 10, 819
b. Courbet, (Jean Desire) Gustave

820

b. Photius
d. Shankara

822

d. Saicho

823

June 13, 823
b. Charles II

824

d. Han Yu

830

b. Junayd, Abu al-Qasim ibn
Muhammad al

833

d. Mamun, Abdallah al-

835

April 20, 835
d. Kukai

839

b. Tabari, Muhammad ibn Jarir al-

840

b. Edmund, Saint
b. Harold, I
b. Notker Balbulus
d. Nazzam, Ibrahim ibn Sayyar al-

June 20, 840

d. Louis I

846

d. Chang Po-go
d. Po Chu-i

849

b. Alfred the Great

850

d. Khwarizmi, Muhammad ibn Musa
al-

853

d. Achab

857

b. Hallaj, Al-Husayn ibn Mansur al-

860

b. Rollo

864

d. Ennin

865

b. Razi

870

d. Edmund, Saint

August 1, 870
d. Bukhari, Muhammad ibn Ismail al-

872

d. Adrian II

873

b. Ashari, Abu al-Hasan Ali al-
d. Kindi, Abu-Yusuf Yaqub ibn-Ishaq
al-
d. Rurik

877

b. Wang Kon

October 6, 877
d. Charles II

882

b. Saadia ben Joseph al-Fayumi

884

d. Huang Ch'ao

886

August 29, 886
d. Basil, I

891

b. Abd-Al-Rahman, III
d. Erigena, John Scotus
d. Photius

October 27, 891
d. Liu Tsung-yuan

901

October 28, 901
d. Alfred the Great

909

b. Dunstan, St.

910

d. Junayd, Abu al-Qasim ibn
Muhammad al

912

b. Otto, I
d. Notker Balbulus

922

d. Hallaj, Al-Husayn ibn Mansur al-

923

February 15, 923
d. Tabari, Muhammad ibn Jarir al-

924

July 17, 924
d. Edward the Elder

925

b. Kwangjong

October 26, 925
d. Razi

926

b. Brian Boru

927

b. Sung T'ai-tsu
b. Zhao Kuang-yin

932

d. Rollo

933

d. Harold, I

935

b. Firdausi
d. Ashari, Abu al-Hasan Ali al-

938

b. Hugh Capet

January 11, 938
b. Scargill, Arthur

939

b. Tai-Tsung

942

d. Saadia ben Joseph al-Fayumi

943

b. Edgar
d. Wang Kon

949

b. Simeon

950

b. Eric the Red
b. Gershom ben Judah

955

b. Aelfric

956

b. Vladimir, I
d. Masudi, Ali ibn al-Husayn al-

958

b. Basil, II

959

d. Edwy

961

d. Abd-Al-Rahman, III

966

b. Abu 'Ali al-Hasan ibn al-Haytham
b. Fujiwara Michinaga

968

b. Ethelred the Unready
b. Olaf I Tryggvason

971

b. Mahmud of Ghazni

973

b. Abu-L-Ala al-Maarri
b. Stephen, I
d. Otto, I

September 4, 973
b. Biruni, Abu Rayhan al-

975

b. Ericson, Leif
d. Edgar
d. Kwangjong

976

d. Sung T'ai-tsu

d. Zhao Kuang-yin

978

b. Murasaki, Shikibu, Lady
b. Zoe

980

b. Avicenna
b. Otto, III

988

May 19, 988
d. Dunstan, St.

989

b. Fan Chung-yen

990

b. Guido d'Arezzo
b. Olaf, II

994

b. ibn Hazm, Abu Muhammad Ali

995

b. Canute

996

d. Hugh Capet

997

d. Tai-Tsung

1000

b. Berengar of Tours
b. Rajaraja, I
d. Eric the Red
d. Olaf I Tryggvason

1002

b. Edward the Confessor
d. Otto, III

June 21, 1002
b. Leo, IX, St.

1007

b. Ou-yang Hsiu

1010

b. Godiva, Lady
b. Lanfranc

1012

d. Aelfric

1014

April 23, 1014
d. Brian Boru

1015

b. Harold, III
b. Robert Guiscard
d. Vladimir, I

1016

April 23, 1016
d. Ethelred the Unready

1017

b. Henry, III

1019

November 17, 1019
b. Ssu-ma kuang

1020

b. Gregory, VII
b. Saul
d. Firdausi
d. Meinong, Alexius, Ritter von
   Handschuchsheim

1021

b. ibn Gabirol, Solomon ben Judah

December 18, 1021
b. Wang An-shih

1022

b. Harold II
d. Simeon

1025

December 15, 1025
d. Basil, II

1026

b. Alp Arslan

1027

b. William the Conqueror
d. Fujiwara Michinaga

1028

d. Gershom ben Judah

1030

d. Mahmud of Ghazni
d. Olaf, II

1031

d. Murasaki, Shikibu, Lady

1033

b. Anselm, Saint

1035

b. Urban II

November 12, 1035
d. Canute

1036

b. Su Shih

1037

d. Avicenna

1038

d. Stephen, I

1039

d. Abu 'Ali al-Hasan ibn al-Haytham

1040

b. Alfonso, VI
b. Cid, El
b. Laszlo, I
b. Rashi
d. Duncan I

1045

b. Margaret of Scotland

1046

b. Matilda of Tuscany

1048

b. Alexius Comnenus
b. Omar Khayyam

1050

b. Callistus II, Pope
b. Henry, IV
d. Biruni, Abu Rayhan al-
d. Guido d'Arezzo
d. Zoe

1051

b. Mi Fei

1052

d. Fan Chung-yen

1053

b. Toba Sojo

1054

d. Leo, IX, St.

1056

b. William II
d. Henry, III

1057

August 15, 1057
d. Macbeth

1058

b. Baldwin, I

b. Ghazali, al
b. Godfrey of Bouillon
d. Abu-L-Ala al-Maarri
d. ibn Gabirol, Solomon ben Judah

1059

d. Abdullah ibn Yasin

1064

d. ibn Hazm, Abu Muhammad Ali

1065

b. Bohemund, I

1066

d. Harold, III

January 5, 1066
d. Edward the Confessor

October 15, 1066
d. Harold II

1067

d. Godiva, Lady

1069

b. Henry I

1072

d. Ou-yang Hsiu

November 24, 1072
d. Alp Arslan

1075

b. Ha-Levi, Judah
b. Kim Pusik

1079

b. Abelard, Pierre

1080

b. ibn Tumart, Muhammad

1081

b. Henry, V

b. Louis, VI
d. Bernard De Menthon, Saint

1082

b. Hui-Tsung

1083

b. Comnena, Anna

1084

b. David, I

1085

d. Robert Guiscard

May 25, 1085
d. Gregory, VII

1086

May 21, 1086
d. Wang An-shih

October 11, 1086
d. Ssu-ma kuang

1087

d. William the Conqueror

1088

d. Berengar of Tours

1089

May 24, 1089
d. Lanfranc

1090

b. Bernard of Clairvaux
b. Bernard of Clairvaux, Saint
b. Ch'in Kuei
b. William of Malmesbury

1093

d. Malcolm, III
d. Margaret of Scotland

1094

b. Abd al-Mumin

1095

b. Roger, II

July 29, 1095
d. Laszlo, I

1096

b. Stephen

1098

b. Heloise
b. Hildegard of Bingen, Saint

1099

July 10, 1099
d. Cid, El

October 29, 1099
d. Urban II

1100

b. Arnold of Brescia
b. Bernard of Cluny
b. Geoffrey of Monmouth
b. Idrisi, Muhammad ibn Muhammad
al-
b. Lombard, Peter

July 18, 1100
d. Godfrey of Bouillon

August 2, 1100
d. William II

12th CENTURY

b. Hsia Kuei
b. Marie de France

1101

d. Su Shih

1103

b. Yo Fei

1105

July 13, 1105
d. Rashi

1106

b. Chong Chung-bu

d. Henry, IV
d. ibn Tashufin, Yusuf

1107

b. Dandolo, Enrico
b. Kao-tsung
d. Mi Fei

1109

b. Alfonso, I

April 21, 1109
d. Anselm, Saint

June 30, 1109
d. Alfonso, VI

1110

b. ibn Tufayl, Abu Bakr Muhammad

1111

d. Bohemund, I

December 18, 1111
d. Ghazali, al

1114

b. Otto of Freising

1115

July 24, 1115
d. Matilda of Tuscany

1118

d. Baldwin, I

February 21, 1118
b. Nureddin

August 15, 1118
d. Alexius Comnenus

December 21, 1118
b. A'Becket, Thomas, Saint

1120

b. John of Salisbury
b. Louis, VII

1122

b. Eleanor of Aquitaine

1123

b. Frederick I
b. Manuel, I

1124

December 14, 1124
d. Callistus II, Pope

1125

b. Lu, Yu
d. Henry, V

1126

b. Averroes

1127

b. Goshirakawa

1130

b. Benjamin of Tudela
b. Chretien de Troyes
b. William of Tyre
d. Bernard De Chartres
d. ibn Tumart, Muhammad
b. Chu Hsi

1131

d. Omar Khayyam

1132

b. Joachim of Fiore

1133

b. Honen

March 5, 1133
b. Henry II

1134

d. Harding, Stephen

1135

March 30, 1135
b. Maimonides, Moses

June 4, 1135
d. Hui-Tsung

December 1, 1135
d. Henry I

1137

d. Louis, VI

1138

b. Saladin Yusuf ibn Ayyub

1139

b. Lu Chiu-yuan

1140

b. Attar, Farid ed-Din
d. Toba Sojo

1141

b. Eisai
d. Yo Fei
d. Ha-Levi, Judah

1142

d. William of Malmesbury

April 21, 1142
d. Abelard, Pierre

1143

b. William

1147

b. Minamoto Yoritomo

1148

d. Comnena, Anna

1149

b. Ch'oe Ch'ung-hn

1150

b. Bitruji, Nur al-Din Abu Ishaq al
b. Villehardouin, Geffroi de

1151

d. Kim Pusik

1153

d. Bernard of Clairvaux
d. David, I

August 20, 1153
d. Bernard of Clairvaux, Saint

1154

d. Geoffrey of Monmouth

February 26, 1154
d. Roger, II

October 25, 1154
d. Stephen

1155

b. Langton, Stephen
d. Arnold of Brescia
d. Ch'in Kuei

1156

d. Bernard of Cluny

1157

September 8, 1157
b. Richard I

1158

September 22, 1158
d. Otto of Freising

1160

b. Innocent, III, Pope
d. Lombard, Peter

1161

d. Eric IX

1162

b. Genghis Khan

1163

d. Abd al-Mumin

1164

May 15, 1164
d. Heloise

1165

b. Ibn al-Arabi, Muhyi al-Din
b. Leonin
d. Idrisi, Muhammad ibn Muhammad al-

July 21, 1165
b. Philip II

1167

December 24, 1167
b. John, King of England

1170

b. Dominic, Saint
b. Gottfried von Strassburg
b. Hartmann von Aue
b. Vogelweide, Walther von der
b. Wolfram von Eschenbach

December 29, 1170
d. A'Becket, Thomas, Saint

1173

b. Shinran
d. Benjamin of Tudela

1174

May 15, 1174
d. Nureddin

1175

b. Grosseteste, Robert

1178

b. Snorri, Sturluson

1179

September 17, 1179
d. Hildegard of Bingen, Saint

October 18, 1179
d. Chong Chung-bu

1180

b. Carpini, Giovanni de Piano
b. Fibonacci, Leonardo (Pisano)
b. John of Piano Carpini
d. Louis, VII

September 24, 1180
d. Manuel, I

October 25, 1180
d. John of Salisbury

1182

b. Francis of Assisi, Saint

1183

d. Chretien de Troyes

1184

b. Yakub al-Mansur, Abu Yusuf
d. William of Tyre

1185

b. Alexander of Hales
b. Perotin
d. ibn Tufayl, Abu Bakr Muhammad

December 6, 1185
d. Alfonso, I

1187

d. Kao-tsung

1189

b. Sordello
b. Yeh-lu Ch'u-ts'ai

July 6, 1189
d. Henry II

1190

b. Ma Yuan
d. Frederick I

1192

d. Goshirakawa

1193

b. Albert the Great
d. Lu Chiu-yuan
d. Saladin Yusuf ibn Ayyub

1194

b. Nahmanides

July 16, 1194
b. Clare of Assisi, Saint

December 26, 1194
b. Frederick II

1195

b. Gonzalo de Berceo

August 15, 1195
b. Anthony of Padua, Saint

1198

December 10, 1198
d. Averroes

1199

February 9, 1199
d. Minamoto Yoritomo

April 6, 1199
d. Richard I

1200

b. Layamon
b. Matthew Paris
b. Sa'di
d. Bitruji, Nur al-Din Abu Ishaq al
d. Chu Hsi

13th CENTURY

b. Guido of Sienna

1201

May 30, 1201
b. Thibaut, IV

1202

d. Joachim of Fiore

1204

April 1, 1204
d. Eleanor of Aquitaine

December 13, 1204
d. Maimonides, Moses

1205

June 14, 1205
d. Dandolo, Enrico

1207

b. Elizabeth of Hungary, Saint
b. Rumi, Jalai ed-Din

October 1, 1207
b. Henry III

1208

b. Montfort, Simon de

1210

b. Celestine V, Saint
b. Guillaume de Lorris
b. Sundiata Keita
d. Hartmann von Aue
d. Lu, Yu

May 5, 1210
b. Alfonso, III

1213

d. Villehardouin, Geffroi de

August 23, 1213
b. Chia Ssu-tao

1214

b. Bacon, Roger
d. William

1215

d. Eisai
d. Gottfried von Strassburg

April 25, 1215
b. Louis IX

1216

b. Kublai Khan

July 16, 1216
d. Innocent, III, Pope

October 29, 1216
d. John, King of England

1217

b. Hulagu Khan

1218

b. Rudolf, I
d. Waldo, Peter

1219

d. Ch'oe Ch'ung-hn

1220

b. Nevski, Alexander, Saint
b. Pisano, Nicola

1221

b. Bonaventure, Saint
d. Dominic, Saint

November 23, 1221
b. Alfonso, X

1222

b. Nichiren

1223

July 14, 1223
d. Philip II

1224

b. Joinville, Jean de
b. Michael, VIII

1225

b. Thomas Aquinas, Saint

1226

October 3, 1226
d. Francis of Assisi, Saint

1227

August 18, 1227
d. Genghis Khan

1228

July 9, 1228
d. Langton, Stephen

1229

d. Ma Yuan
d. Vogelweide, Walther von der

1230

b. Guinizzelli, Guido

1231

b. Montreuil, Pierre de
d. Elizabeth of Hungary, Saint

June 13, 1231
d. Anthony of Padua, Saint

1232

b. Lull, Raymond

1234

d. Attar, Farid ed-Din

1235

b. Boniface, VIII
b. Llull, Ramon

1236

b. Jacopone da Todi

June 6, 1236
b. Wen T'ien-hsiang

1237

d. Guillaume de Lorris

1239

b. Peter, III
b. Rama Khamhaeng

June 17, 1239
b. Edward I

1240

b. Adam de la Halle
b. Cimabue, Giovanni
b. Jean de Meun
d. Ibn al-Arabi, Muhyi al-Din

1241

d. Snorri, Sturluson

1243

d. Yeh-lu Ch'u-ts'ai

1245

b. Arnolfo di Cambio

August 21, 1245
d. Alexander of Hales

1250

b. Cavallini, Pietro
b. Franco of Cologne
b. Moses de Leon
b. Pisano, Giovanni
d. Fibonacci, Leonardo (Pisano)

December 13, 1250
d. Frederick II

1252

d. Carpini, Giovanni de Piano
d. Gonzalo de Berceo

August 1, 1252
d. John of Piano Carpini

1253

July 7, 1253
d. Thibaut, IV

August 11, 1253
d. Clare of Assisi, Saint

October 9, 1253
d. Grosseteste, Robert

1254

b. Chao Meng-fu
b. Polo, Marco

1255

b. Cavalcanti, Guido
d. Batu Khan

1256

January 6, 1256
b. Gertrude the Great, Saint

1259

b. Osman I
d. Matthew Paris

1260

b. Eckhart, Johannes
d. Sundiata Keita

1261

b. Peregrinus, Petrus

1262

d. Shinran

1263

d. Nevski, Alexander, Saint

1264

b. Clement, V

1265

b. Lorenzetti, Ambrogio
b. Luzzi, Mondino de'
d. Hulagu Khan

May 27, 1265
b. Dante Alighieri

August 4, 1265
d. Montfort, Simon de

1266

b. Duns Scotus, John
b. Giotto di Bondone
d. Montreuil, Pierre de
d. Savelli, Luca

1268

b. Philip, IV
b. Yekuno Amlak
d. Bracton, Henry de

1269

d. Peregrinus, Petrus
d. Sordello

1270

b. Villani, Giovanni
b. Wallace, William
d. Nahmanides

August 25, 1270
d. Louis IX

1272

November 16, 1272
d. Henry III

1273

d. Rumi, Jalai ed-Din

1274

b. Henry, VII

March 7, 1274
d. Thomas Aquinas, Saint

March 21, 1274
b. Robert I

July 15, 1274
d. Bonaventure, Saint

1275

b. Marsilius of Padua

1276

d. Guinizzelli, Guido

1278

b. Duccio di Buoninsegna

1279

February 16, 1279
d. Alfonso, III

1280

November 15, 1280
d. Albert the Great

1281

January 24, 1281
b. Aungervyle, Richard

1282

b. Tell, William
d. Nichiren

October 3, 1282
d. Llewelyn ap Gruffydd

December 11, 1282
d. Michael, VIII

1283

b. Ruiz, Juan
d. Pisano, Nicola
d. Wen T'ien-hsiang

1284

b. Martini, Simone

April 4, 1284
d. Alfonso, X

April 25, 1284
b. Edward II

1285

d. Francesca da Rimini

November 11, 1285
d. Peter, III

1287

d. Adam de la Halle

1288

b. Daigo, II
b. Levi ben Gershon

1290

b. Eulenspiegel, Till
b. Muhammad bin Tughluq
b. Pisano, Andrea
b. Rolle of Hampole, Richard
b. William of Ockham

1291

b. Vitry, Philippe de
d. Sa'di

July 15, 1291
d. Rudolf, I

1292

d. Bacon, Roger

1293

b. Philip VI
b. Ruysbroeck, Jan van

1294

d. Kublai Khan

1295

b. Guy de Chauliac

March 21, 1295
b. Suso, Heinrich

1296

May 19, 1296
d. Celestine V, Saint
b. Palamas, Gregory, Saint

1299

d. Rama Khamhaeng

1300

b. Machaut, Guillaume de
b. Mandeville, John, Sir

August 29, 1300
d. Cavalcanti, Guido

1301

b. Ni Tsan

1302

d. Cimabue, Giovanni

March 8, 1302
d. Arnolfo di Cambio

1303

d. Boniface, VIII

1304

b. ibn Battuta, Muhammad
b. Ibn Batutah

July 20, 1304
b. Petrarch, Francesco

1305

b. Ashikaga, Takauji
d. Jean de Meun
d. Moses de Leon
d. Wallace, William

1306

December 25, 1306
d. Jacopone da Todi

1307

July 7, 1307
d. Edward I

1308

b. Orcagna

November 8, 1308
d. Duns Scotus, John

1311

November 17, 1311
d. Gertrude the Great, Saint

1312

November 13, 1312
b. Edward III

1313

b. Boccaccio, Giovanni
b. Rienzi, Cola di

August 24, 1313
d. Henry, VII

1314

d. Pisano, Giovanni

April 14, 1314
d. Clement, V

November 29, 1314
d. Philip, IV

1316

b. Barbour, John
b. Robert, II
d. Llull, Ramon
d. Lull, Raymond
d. Ala-ud-din

May 14, 1316
b. Charles, IV

1317

d. Joinville, Jean de

1318

b. Urban, VI

1319

b. John, II
d. Duccio di Buoninsegna

1320

b. Du Guesclin, Bertrand
b. Hafiz, Shams-al-Din Muhammad
b. Nicholas of Oresme

December 31, 1320
b. Wycliffe, John

1321

September 14, 1321
d. Dante Alighieri

1322

d. Chao Meng-fu

1324

January 9, 1324
d. Polo, Marco

1326

d. Luzzi, Mondino de'
d. Osman I

1327

b. Gregory, XII
d. Eckhart, Johannes

September 21, 1327
d. Edward II

1328

b. Ming, T'ai-Tsu

October 21, 1328
b. Hung-Wu

1329

June 7, 1329
d. Robert I

1330

b. Gower, John
b. Wyclif, John
d. Cavallini, Pietro

June 15, 1330
b. Edward the Black Prince

1332

b. Langland, William
b. Lopez de Ayala, Pero

May 27, 1332
b. Ibn Khaldun

1333

b. Froissart, Jean

1335

b. Landini, Francesco
b. Yi Sng-gye

1336

b. Tamerlane

1337

b. Robert, III
d. Musa Mansa

January 8, 1337
d. Giotto di Bondone

January 21, 1337
b. Charles, V

1339

d. Daigo, II

1340

b. Chaucer, Geoffrey
b. Groote, Gerhard
b. John of Gaunt

1342

b. Julian of Norwich
d. Marsilius of Padua

1344

d. Levi ben Gershon
d. Martini, Simone

1345

d. Aungervyle, Richard

1346

b. Deschamps, Eustache

1347

March 25, 1347
b. Catherine of Siena, Saint

1348

d. Lorenzetti, Ambrogio
d. Pisano, Andrea
d. Villani, Giovanni

1349

d. Rolle of Hampole, Richard
d. William of Ockham

1350

b. Ailly, Pierre d'
b. Sluter, Claus
d. Eulenspiegel, Till
d. Philip VI
d. Ruiz, Juan

1351

d. Muhammad bin Tughluq

1353

b. Margaret of Denmark

1354

October 8, 1354
d. Rienzi, Cola di

1358

b. Whitington, Dick
b. Whittington, Dick

June 7, 1358
d. Ashikaga, Takauji

1359

b. Glendower, Owen
d. Palamas, Gregory, Saint

1360

b. Clement VIII
b. Yung-lo
d. Vitry, Philippe de

1361

b. Wenceslaus

1363

December 13, 1363
b. Gerson, Jean

1364

b. Christine de Pisan
b. Zeami, Kanze
d. Gajah Mada
d. John, II

May 20, 1364
b. Percy, Henry, Sir

1366

January 25, 1366
d. Suso, Heinrich

March 11, 1366
b. Anne of Bohemia

1367

January 6, 1367
b. Richard II

April 3, 1367
b. Henry IV

1368

d. ibn Battuta, Muhammad
d. Orcagna

February 15, 1368
b. Sigismund

February 20, 1368
b. Martin, V
d. Guy de Chauliac

December 3, 1368
b. Charles, VI

1369

b. Hus, Jan

1370

b. Gentile da Fabriano
b. Lydgate, John
b. Van Eyck, Hubert

1371

b. Cauchon, Pierre
b. Cheng Ho
b. Van Eyck, Jan

1372

d. Mandeville, John, Sir

1374

b. Quercia, Jacopo della
d. Ni Tsan

July 19, 1374
d. Petrarch, Francesco

1375

b. Campin, Robert

December 21, 1375
d. Boccaccio, Giovanni

1376

June 8, 1376
d. Edward the Black Prince

1377

b. Brunelleschi, Filippo
d. Machaut, Guillaume de

June 21, 1377
d. Edward III

1378

b. Fastolf, John, Sir
b. Feltre, Vittorino da
b. Ghiberti, Lorenzo
d. Ibn Batutah

November 29, 1378
d. Charles, IV

1380

b. Thomas a Kempis

April 29, 1380
d. Catherine of Siena, Saint

July 13, 1380
d. Du Guesclin, Bertrand

September 8, 1380
b. Bernardine of Siena, Saint

September 16, 1380
d. Charles, V

1381

d. Ruysbroeck, Jan van
d. Tyler, Wat

1382

July 11, 1382
d. Nicholas of Oresme

1384

d. Wyclif, John

August 20, 1384
d. Groote, Gerhard

December 31, 1384
d. Wycliffe, John

1385

b. Hunyadi, Janos
b. Hunyadi, John
d. Walworth, William, Sir

1386

b. Donatello

1387

b. Angelico, Fra

August 9, 1387
b. Henry V

1389

d. Hafiz, Shams-al-Din Muhammad

September 27, 1389
b. Medici, Cosimo de

October 15, 1389
d. Urban, VI

1390

b. Dunstable, John
b. Montezuma I
d. Robert, II

1391

b. Gloucester, Duke of

1392

b. Chartier, Alain

1394

b. Orleans, Charles d'

March 4, 1394
b. Henry the Navigator

June 7, 1394
d. Anne of Bohemia

July 25, 1394
b. James I

1395

b. Coeur, Jacques
b. Pisano, Antonio
b. Sassetta
b. William of Waynflete

March 13, 1395
d. Barbour, John

1396

b. Conti, Niccolo de'
b. Michelozzo
b. Uccello, Paolo

July 31, 1396
b. Philip the Good

1397

d. Landini, Francesco

May 7, 1397
b. Sejong

1398

d. Ming, T'ai-Tsu

June 24, 1398
d. Hung-Wu

August 19, 1398
b. Santillana, Inigo Lopez de Mendoza

1399

b. Limbourg Brothers, The
b. Weyden, Rogier van der

February 3, 1399
d. John of Gaunt

1400

b. Bellini, Jacopo
b. Dufay, Guillaume
b. Fust, Johann
b. Witz, Konrad
d. Froissart, Jean

d. Langland, William

February 14, 1400
d. Richard II

February 23, 1400
b. Gutenberg, Johann Gensfleischzur
Laden Zum

October 25, 1400
d. Chaucer, Geoffrey

December 22, 1400
b. DellaRobbia, Lucia

1401

b. Nicholas of Cusa

October 27, 1401
b. Catherine of Valois

December 21, 1401
b. Masaccio

1403

b. Giovanni di Paolo

February 22, 1403
b. Charles, VII

July 21, 1403
d. Percy, Henry, Sir

1404

February 14, 1404
b. Alberti, Leon Battista

1405

b. Pius, II
d. Tamerlane

February 7, 1405
b. Constantine XI Palaeologus

1406

b. Lippi, Filippo, Fra
d. Deschamps, Eustache
d. Robert, III
d. Sluter, Claus

March 17, 1406
d. Ibn Khaldun

1407

b. Valla, Lorenzo
d. Lopez de Ayala, Pero

1408

d. Gower, John

June 18, 1408
d. Yi Sng-gye

1410

b. Charonton, Enguerrand
b. Christus, Petrus
b. Coster, Laurens Janszoon
b. Lochner, Stephan
b. Veneziano, Domenico

1411

b. Richard, Duke of York

1412

d. Margaret of Denmark

January 6, 1412
b. Joan of Arc, Saint

1413

March 20, 1413
d. Henry IV

1414

b. Jami

1415

July 6, 1415
d. Hus, Jan

September 20, 1415
d. Glendower, Owen

September 21, 1415
b. Frederick, III

1416

d. Julian of Norwich
d. Limbourg Brothers, The

1417

October 18, 1417
d. Gregory, XII

November 7, 1417
b. Sejo

1418

b. Agostino di Duccio

1419

August 19, 1419
d. Wenceslaus

1420

b. Bertoldo di Giovanni
b. Bouts, Dierick C
b. Fouquet, Jean
b. Gozzoli, Benozzo
b. Piero della Francesca
b. Sesshu, Toyo
b. Torquemada, Tomas de
d. Ailly, Pierre d'

1421

b. Castagno, Andrea del

December 6, 1421
b. Henry VI

1422

August 13, 1422
b. Caxton, William

August 31, 1422
d. Henry V

October 21, 1422
d. Charles, VI

1423

d. Whitington, Dick
d. Whittington, Dick

July 3, 1423
b. Louis XI

1424

August 2, 1424
d. Yung-lo

1425

b. Ockeghem, Johannes

1426

d. Van Eyck, Hubert

1427

d. Gentile da Fabriano

October 14, 1427
b. Baldovinetti, Alesso

1428

b. da Settignano, Desiderio
d. Masaccio

November 22, 1428
b. Warwick and of Salisbury, Earl of

1429

b. Bellini, Gentile

July 12, 1429
d. Gerson, Jean

1430

b. Antonello da Messina
b. Bellini, Giovanni
b. Memling, Hans
b. Tura, Cosme
d. Chartier, Alain
d. Christine de Pisan

March 23, 1430
b. Margaret of Anjou

October 16, 1430
b. James II

1431

b. Dracula
b. Mantegna, Andrea
b. Pollaiuolo, Antonio
b. Villon, Francois

January 1, 1431
b. Alexander VI

February 20, 1431
d. Martin, V

May 30, 1431
d. Joan of Arc, Saint

1432

b. Cadamosto, Alvise Luigi da
b. Mohammed, II

March 30, 1432
b. Mehmed the Conqueror

August 15, 1432
b. Pulci, Luigi

1433

d. Cheng Ho

October 19, 1433
b. Ficino, Marsilio

1435

b. Crivelli, Carlo
b. DellaRobbia, Andrea
b. Pacher, Michael
b. Verrocchio, Andrea del

1436

June 6, 1436
b. Regiomontanus

1437

b. Abarbanel, Isaac Ben Jehudah
b. Abravanel, Isaac ben Judah

January 3, 1437
d. Catherine of Valois

February 20, 1437
d. James I

December 19, 1437
d. Sigismund

1438

b. Domenico, Veneziano
d. Quercia, Jacopo della

1439

b. Giorgio, Francesco di

1440

b. Goes, Hugo van der
b. Josquin des Prez
b. Manrique, Jorge
b. Pedrarias
d. Van Eyck, Jan

January 22, 1440
b. Ivan III

1441

b. Beaufort, Margaret, Countess of
Richmond
b. Boiardo, Matteo Maria
b. Signorelli, Luca

1442

April 28, 1442
b. Edward IV

December 18, 1442
d. Cauchon, Pierre

1443

b. Muhammad Ture, Askia

February 24, 1443
b. Matthias Corvinus

December 5, 1443
b. Julius II, Pope

1444

b. Botticelli, Sandro
b. Bramante, Donata d'Agnolo
d. Campin, Robert
d. Zeami, Kanze

May 20, 1444
d. Bernardine of Siena, Saint

1445

b. Comines, Philippe de
b. DesPres, Josquin
b. Perugino
b. Stoss, Veit

1446

b. Colet, John
d. Feltre, Vittorino da

April 16, 1446
d. Brunelleschi, Filippo

December 28, 1446
d. Clement VIII

1447

b. Catherine of Genoa, Saint
d. Witz, Konrad

February 23, 1447
d. Gloucester, Duke of

1449

b. Ghirlandaio, Domenico
d. Lydgate, John

January 1, 1449
b. Medici, Lorenzo de

1450

b. Bertinoro, Obadiah ben Abraham
  Yare
b. Bosch, Hieronymous
b. Dias, Bartholomew
b. Hiawatha
b. Isaac, Heinrich
b. Manutius, Aldus
b. Obrecht, Jacob
b. Roberti, Ercole
b. Schongauer, Martin
b. Warham, William
d. Sassetta

March 30, 1450
d. Sejong

June 24, 1450
b. Cabot, John

1451

b. Columbus, Christopher
d. Lochner, Stephan

March 9, 1451
b. Vespucci, Amerigo

April 22, 1451
b. Isabella I

May 10, 1451
b. James III

July 27, 1451
b. Sforza, Ludovico

1452

March 10, 1452
b. Ferdinand V

April 15, 1452
b. Leonardo da Vinci

September 21, 1452
b. Savonarola, Girolamo

October 2, 1452
b. Richard III

1453

b. Albuquerque, Affonso de

May 29, 1453
d. Constantine XI Palaeologus

December 24, 1453
d. Dunstable, John

1454

b. Pintuicchio

July 14, 1454
b. Poliziano, Angelo

1455

b. Carpaccio, Vittore
b. Covilhao, Pedro de
b. Reuchlin, Johann
d. Pisano, Antonio

March 18, 1455
d. Angelico, Fra

December 1, 1455
d. Ghiberti, Lorenzo

1456

d. Hunyadi, John

November 25, 1456
d. Coeur, Jacques

1457

b. Brant, Sebastian
d. Valla, Lorenzo

January 28, 1457
b. Henry VII

August 19, 1457
d. Castagno, Andrea del

1458

March 25, 1458
d. Santillana, Inigo Lopez de Mendoza

October 5, 1458
b. Casimir, Saint

1459

b. Fugger, Jacob
b. Hofhaimer, Paul
b. Lippi, Filippino

March 22, 1459
b. Maximilian I

November 5, 1459
d. Fastolf, John, Sir

1460

b. Abarbanel, Judah
b. Affonso, I
b. Berengario da Carpi, Jacopo
b. Cabral, Pedro Alvarez
b. DaGama, Vasco
b. David, Gerard
b. Dunbar, William
b. Froben, Johann

b. Geertgen tot Sint Jans
b. Linacre, Thomas
b. Riemenschneider, Tilman
b. Sansovino, Andrea
b. Skelton, John
d. Richard, Duke of York

April 8, 1460
b. Ponce de Leon, Juan

August 3, 1460
d. James II

November 13, 1460
d. Henry the Navigator

1461

d. Domenico, Veneziano
d. Veneziano, Domenico

July 22, 1461
d. Charles, VII

1462

b. Cosimo, Piero di

June 27, 1462
b. Louis, XII

September 16, 1462
b. Pomponazzi, Pietro

1463

b. Pico della Mirandola, Giovanni
d. Villon, Francois

1464

d. da Settignano, Desiderio
d. Montezuma I

June 16, 1464
d. Weyden, Rogier van der

August 1, 1464
d. Medici, Cosimo de

August 11, 1464
d. Nicholas of Cusa

August 15, 1464
d. Pius, II

1465

b. Holbein, Hans, the Elder
b. Leo Africanus
b. Velazquez de Cuellar, Diego
b. Vicente, Gil
d. Hunyadi, Janos
d. Orleans, Charles d'

1466

b. Massys, Quentin

October 30, 1466
d. Fust, Johann

November 30, 1466
b. Doria, Andrea

December 13, 1466
d. Donatello

1467

January 25, 1467
b. Bude, Guillaume

June 15, 1467
d. Philip the Good

1468

b. Encina, Juan del
b. Nino, Pedro Alonzo
b. Zumarraga, Juan de

February 3, 1468
d. Gutenberg, Johann Gensfleischzur
Laden Zum

February 29, 1468
b. Paul III

September 22, 1468
d. Sejo

1469

b. DellaRobbia, Giovanni
b. Fisher, John
d. Conti, Niccolo de'

April 15, 1469
b. Nanak

May 3, 1469
b. Machiavelli, Niccolo

May 31, 1469
b. Manuel I

October 9, 1469
d. Lippi, Filippo, Fra

October 27, 1469
b. Erasmus, Desiderius

1470

b. Bembo, Pietro
b. Pizarro, Francisco
b. Riccio, Andrea
b. Selim I
b. Solis, Juan Diaz de
b. Varthema, Ludovico di
b. Waldseemuller, Martin

d. Bellini, Jacopo

November 2, 1470
b. Edward V

1471

March 12, 1471
d. Malory, Thomas, Sir

April 14, 1471
d. Warwick and of Salisbury, Earl of

May 21, 1471
b. Durer, Albrecht
d. Henry VI

July 25, 1471
d. Thomas a Kempis

1472

b. Wang Yang-ming
d. Christus, Petrus
d. Michelozzo

April 25, 1472
d. Alberti, Leon Battista

October 4, 1472
b. Cranach, Lucas

1473

b. Bayard, Pierre du Terrail
b. Norfolk, 3d Duke of

February 19, 1473
b. Copernicus, Nicolaus

March 17, 1473
b. James IV

1474

b. Almagro, Diego de
b. Bermejo, Bartolome
b. Douglas, Gavin
b. Las Casas, Bartolome de

March 21, 1474
b. Angela Merici, Saint

September 8, 1474
b. Ariosto, Ludovico

November 27, 1474
d. Dufay, Guillaume

1475

b. Ayllon, Lucas Vasquez de
b. Balboa, Vasco Nunez de
b. Barclay, Alexander
b. Borgia, Cesare

b. Cordoba, Francisco Fernandez
b. Rojas, Fernando de
b. Wolsey, Thomas, Cardinal
d. Bouts, Dierick C

March 6, 1475
b. Michelangelo (Buonarroti)

March 28, 1475
b. Bartolommeo, Fra

December 10, 1475
d. Uccello, Paolo

December 14, 1475
b. Leo, X

1476

b. Cabot, Sebastian
d. Dracula

June 28, 1476
b. Paul, IV

July 6, 1476
d. Regiomontanus

August 28, 1476
b. Kano, Motonobu

1477

b. Giorgione
b. Titian

1478

b. Fracastoro, Gerolamo
b. Mabuse, Jan de
b. Narvaez, Panfilo de
d. Manrique, Jorge

February 7, 1478
b. More, Thomas, Sir

May 26, 1478
b. Clement VII

December 3, 1478
b. Castiglione, Baldassare, Conte

1479

b. Colon, Diego
b. Gioconda, Lisa Gherardini
b. Grolier, Jean
b. Vasily III

February 15, 1479
d. Antonello da Messina

1480

b. Altdorfer, Albrecht
b. Berlichingen, Gotz von

b. Biringuccio, Vannoccio
b. Cajetan, St.
b. Faust, Johann
b. Grunewald, Matthias
b. Karlstadt, Andreas Bodenheim von
b. Lotto, Lorenzo
b. Luini, Bernardino
b. Magellan, Ferdinand
b. Montezuma II
b. Pedersen, Christiern
b. Willaert, Adrian
d. Fouquet, Jean

April 18, 1480
b. Borgia, Lucrezia

1481

d. Agostino di Duccio
d. Mohammed, II

May 3, 1481
d. Mehmed the Conqueror

1482

d. Giovanni di Paolo
d. Goes, Hugo van der

February 23, 1482
d. DellaRobbia, Lucia

April 25, 1482
d. Margaret of Anjou

1483

b. Vitoria, Francisco de

February 14, 1483
b. Babur

March 6, 1483
b. Guicciardini, Francesco

March 28, 1483
b. Raphael

April 9, 1483
d. Edward IV

July 1, 1483
d. Edward V

August 30, 1483
d. Louis XI

November 10, 1483
b. Luther, Martin

1484

b. Baldung(-Grien), Hans
b. Sanmicheli, Michele
b. Tyndale, William

January 1, 1484
b. Zwingli, Huldreich

March 4, 1484
d. Casimir, Saint
d. Pulci, Luigi

1485

b. Bandello, Matteo
b. Cleve, Joos van
b. Clouet, Jean
b. Cortez, Hernando
b. Cromwell, Thomas
b. Latimer, Hugh
b. Lyndsay, David
b. Verrazano, Giovanni da

August 22, 1485
d. Richard III

December 16, 1485
b. Catherine of Aragon

1486

b. Alvarado, Pedro de
b. Berruguete, Alonso (Gonzalez)
b. Sansovino, Jacopo
b. Senfl, Ludwig

July 16, 1486
b. Sarto, Andrea del

August 11, 1486
d. William of Waynflete

September 14, 1486
b. Agrippa, Heinrich Cornelius

November 13, 1486
b. Eck, Johann Maier von

1487

September 10, 1487
b. Julius III, Pope

1488

b. Caro, Joseph
b. Coverdale, Miles
b. Hutten, Ulrich von

June 11, 1488
d. James III

July 18, 1488
d. Cadamosto, Alvise Luigi da

October 7, 1488
d. Verrocchio, Andrea del

1489

b. Schwenckfeld, Kasper von

April 15, 1489
b. Sinan, Kodja Mimar

July 2, 1489
b. Cranmer, Thomas

1490

b. Cabeza de Vaca, Alvar Nunez
b. Elyot, Thomas, Sir
b. Mendoza, Antonio de
b. Muntzer, Thomas
d. Geertgen tot Sint Jans

April 6, 1490
d. Matthias Corvinus

1491

b. Orley, Bernard van
d. Bertoldo di Giovanni
d. Caxton, William

February 2, 1491
d. Schongauer, Martin

June 28, 1491
b. Henry VIII

December 24, 1491
b. Ignatius of Loyola, Saint

December 31, 1491
b. Cartier, Jacques

1492

d. Ali, Sunni
d. Jami

April 8, 1492
d. Medici, Lorenzo de

April 11, 1492
b. Marguerite d'Angouleme

April 20, 1492
b. Aretino, Pietro

October 12, 1492
d. Piero della Francesca

1493

d. Crivelli, Carlo

August 19, 1493
d. Frederick, III

November 10, 1493
b. Paracelsus, Philippus Aureolus

1494

b. Bonivard, Francois

March 12, 1507
d. Borgia, Cesare

October 1, 1507
b. Vignola, Giacomo da

October 29, 1507
b. Alba, Duke of

1508

d. Abarbanel, Isaac Ben Jehudah
d. Abravanel, Isaac ben Judah

May 27, 1508
d. Sforza, Ludovico

November 30, 1508
b. Palladio, Andrea

1509

b. John of Leiden
b. Mendes Pinto, Fernao
b. Quesada, Gonzalo Jimenez de
b. Seymour, Jane
b. Telesio, Bernardino

April 21, 1509
d. Henry VII

June 29, 1509
d. Beaufort, Margaret, Countess of
Richmond

July 10, 1509
b. Calvin, John

1510

b. Aguirre, Lope de
b. Bassano, Jacopo
b. Cabezon, Antonio
b. Clemens non Papa, Jacobus
b. Clouet, Francois
b. Eustachio, Bartolomeo
b. Goujon, Jean
b. Lopez de Legaspi, Miguel
b. l'Orme, Philibert de
b. Pare, Ambroise
b. Recorde, Robert
d. Giorgione

February 25, 1510
b. Coronado, Francisco Vasquez de

May 17, 1510
d. Botticelli, Sandro

September 14, 1510
d. Catherine of Genoa, Saint

October 6, 1510
b. Caius, John

1511

b. Orellana, Francisco de
b. Velasco, Luis de
d. Comines, Philippe de

July 30, 1511
b. Vasari, Giorgio

September 29, 1511
b. Servetus, Michael

1512

b. Parr, Catherine

February 22, 1512
d. Vespucci, Amerigo

March 5, 1512
b. Mercator, Gerhardus

April 10, 1512
b. James V

1513

February 21, 1513
d. Julius II, Pope

September 9, 1513
d. James IV

October 30, 1513
b. Amyot, Jacques

December 11, 1513
d. Pintuicchio

1514

b. Goudimel, Claude
b. Plantin, Christophe

March 11, 1514
d. Bramante, Donata d'Agnolo

December 31, 1514
b. Vesalius, Andreas

1515

b. Ramus, Petrus
b. Tallis, Thomas
b. Toledo, Francisco de
d. Bertinoro, Obadiah ben Abraham
Yare

January 1, 1515
d. Louis, XII

February 3, 1515
d. Manutius, Aldus

March 28, 1515
b. Theresa, Saint

b. Theresa, St.

July 10, 1515
b. Toledo, Fernando Alvarez de

July 21, 1515
b. Neri, Philip

September 22, 1515
b. Anne of Cleves

December 16, 1515
d. Albuquerque, Affonso de

1516

d. Solis, Juan Diaz de

January 23, 1516
d. Ferdinand V

February 18, 1516
b. Mary I

March 26, 1516
b. Gesner, Konrad von

August 9, 1516
d. Bosch, Hieronymous

November 29, 1516
d. Bellini, Giovanni

1517

b. Zarlino, Gioseffo
d. Varthema, Ludovico di

March 26, 1517
d. Isaac, Heinrich

October 31, 1517
d. Bartolommeo, Fra

1518

b. Gresham, Thomas, Sir
d. Waldseemuller, Martin

September 29, 1518
b. Tintoretto

1519

b. Morales, Luis de
d. Colet, John

January 12, 1519
d. Balboa, Vasco Nunez de
d. Maximilian I

February 15, 1519
b. Menendez de Aviles, Pedro

February 16, 1519
b. Coligny, Gaspard de Chatillon

March 12, 1519
d. Borgia, Lucrezia

April 13, 1519
b. Catherine de Medici

May 2, 1519
d. Leonardo da Vinci

1520

b. Burghley, William Cecil, Baron
b. Cabrillo, Juan Rodriguez
b. Howard, Catherine
d. Dunbar, William

April 6, 1520
d. Raphael

June 30, 1520
d. Montezuma II

September 22, 1520
d. Selim I

December 13, 1520
b. Sixtus, V

1521

d. Cosimo, Piero di
d. Josquin des Prez
d. Ponce de Leon, Juan

April 27, 1521
d. Magellan, Ferdinand

May 8, 1521
b. Canisius, Peter

May 10, 1521
d. Brant, Sebastian

August 27, 1521
d. DesPres, Josquin

December 1, 1521
d. Leo, X

December 13, 1521
d. Manuel I

1522

b. du Bellay, Joachim
d. Douglas, Gavin
d. Reuchlin, Johann

1523

d. Bernard, Andrew Milroy
d. Hutten, Ulrich von
d. Perugino
d. Velazquez de Cuellar, Diego

August 13, 1523
d. David, Gerard

October 16, 1523
d. Signorelli, Luca

1524

b. Camoes, Luis de
d. Holbein, Hans, the Elder
d. Solari, Andrea

March 17, 1524
b. Landa, Diego de

April 30, 1524
d. Bayard, Pierre du Terrail

September 11, 1524
b. Ronsard, Pierre de

October 20, 1524
d. Linacre, Thomas

December 24, 1524
d. DaGama, Vasco

1525

b. Bruegel, Pieter, the El
b. Chang Chu-cheng
b. Moroni, Giovanni Battista
d. Carpaccio, Vittore
d. DellaRobbia, Andrea
d. Fugger, Jacob

February 26, 1525
d. Cuauhtemoc

May 18, 1525
d. Pomponazzi, Pietro

May 27, 1525
d. Muntzer, Thomas

December 27, 1525
b. Palestrina, Giovanni

1526

d. Ayllon, Lucas Vasquez de
d. Cabral, Pedro Alvarez
d. Cordoba, Francisco Fernandez

February 23, 1526
d. Colon, Diego

1527

b. Philip II

April 4, 1527
b. Ortelius, Abraham
b. Guerrero, Francisco

June 22, 1527
d. Machiavelli, Niccolo

July 13, 1527
b. Dee, John

July 31, 1527
b. Maximilian II
d. Froben, Johann

1528

b. Veronese, Paolo
d. Narvaez, Panfilo de

April 6, 1528
d. Durer, Albrecht
d. Grunewald, Matthias
d. Verrazano, Giovanni da

1529

b. Bodin, Jean
b. Giovanni da Bologna
d. DellaRobbia, Giovanni
d. Encina, Juan del
d. Sansovino, Andrea
d. Wang Yang-ming

February 2, 1529
d. Castiglione, Baldassare, Conte

June 21, 1529
d. Skelton, John

1530

b. Burbage, James
b. Herrera, Juan de
b. Le Jeune, Claude
b. Nicot, Jean
b. Walsingham, Francis, Sir
d. Behzad
d. Berengario da Carpi, Jacopo
d. Covilhao, Pedro de
d. Massys, Quentin

August 25, 1530
b. Ivan IV

November 29, 1530
d. Wolsey, Thomas, Cardinal

December 26, 1530
d. Babur

1531

b. Estienne, Henri

May 30, 1531
d. Pedrarias

July 7, 1531
d. Riemenschneider, Tilman

September 29, 1531
d. Sarto, Andrea del

October 10, 1531
d. Zwingli, Huldreich

1532

b. Hawkins, John, Sir
b. Lassus, Orlandus de
b. Leicester, Earl of
b. Vos, Martin de
d. Luini, Bernardino
d. Riccio, Andrea

August 22, 1532
d. Warham, William

1533

b. Merulo, Claudio
b. William the Silent
d. Mabuse, Jan de
d. Stoss, Veit
d. Van Leyden, Lucas

February 28, 1533
b. Montaigne, Michel Eyquem de

July 6, 1533
d. Ariosto, Ludovico

August 7, 1533
b. Ercilla y Zuniga, Alonso de

August 29, 1533
d. Atahualpa

September 7, 1533
b. Elizabeth I

December 3, 1533
d. Vasily III

1534

b. Luria, Isaac ben Solomon
b. Nobunaga, Oda

March 5, 1534
d. Correggio, Antonio Allegri da

September 25, 1534
d. Clement VII

1535

b. Frobisher, Martin
b. Lautaro
b. Pilon, Germain
b. Porta, Giambattista della
d. Abarbanel, Judah

February 18, 1535
d. Agrippa, Heinrich Cornelius

June 22, 1535
d. Fisher, John

July 6, 1535
d. More, Thomas, Sir

1536

b. Bothwell, James Hepburn, Earl of
b. Mariana, Juan de
b. Toyotomi Hideyoshi
d. Vicente, Gil

January 7, 1536
d. Catherine of Aragon

January 22, 1536
d. John of Leiden

May 19, 1536
d. Boleyn, Anne

July 12, 1536
d. Erasmus, Desiderius

October 6, 1536
d. Tyndale, William

1537

b. Fabricius, Hieronymus ab
    Aquapendente
b. Hilliard, Nicholas
b. Porta, Giacomo della
d. Hofhaimer, Paul
b. Grey, Jane, Lady

October 12, 1537
b. Edward VI

October 24, 1537
d. Seymour, Jane

1538

d. Muhammad Ture, Askia

February 12, 1538
d. Altdorfer, Albrecht
d. Almagro, Diego de

October 2, 1538
b. Borromeo, Charles, Saint

October 10, 1538
d. Nanak

1539

b. Gilbert, Humphrey, Sir
d. Biringuccio, Vannoccio

April 12, 1539
b. Garcilaso de la Vega, Inca

December 5, 1539
b. Socinus, Faustus

1540

b. Drake, Francis, Sir
b. Elzevir, Louis
b. Hatton, Christopher, Sir

d. Cleve, Joos van
d. Clouet, Jean
d. Estevanico
d. Faust, Johann
d. Rosso, Il

January 27, 1540
d. Angela Merici, Saint

May 22, 1540
d. Guicciardini, Francesco

July 28, 1540
d. Cromwell, Thomas

August 4, 1540
b. Scaliger, Joseph Justus

August 22, 1540
d. Bude, Guillaume

August 24, 1540
d. Parmigano

1541

b. Charron, Pierre
b. Greco, El
b. Mendana de Neyra, Alvaro de
d. Alvarado, Pedro de
d. Karlstadt, Andreas Bodenheim von

March 25, 1541
b. Medici, Francesco de
d. Rojas, Fernando de

June 26, 1541
d. Pizarro, Francisco

September 24, 1541
d. Paracelsus, Philippus Aureolus

1542

b. Byrd, William
b. Ieyasu, Tokugawa
d. Howard, Catherine

January 6, 1542
d. Orley, Bernard van

May 21, 1542
d. DeSoto, Hernando

June 15, 1542
b. Grenville, Richard, Sir

June 24, 1542
b. John of the Cross, Saint

October 4, 1542
b. Bellarmine, Robert, Saint

October 11, 1542
d. Wyatt, Thomas, Sir

October 14, 1542
b. Akbar

February 12, 1554
d. Grey, Jane, Lady
b. Hooker, Richard

August 25, 1554
d. Norfolk, 3d Duke of

September 22, 1554
d. Coronado, Francisco Vasquez de

November 30, 1554
b. Sidney, Philip, Sir

1555

b. Cavendish, Thomas
b. Malherbe, Francois de
b. Tung Ch'i-ch'ang
d. Lyndsay, David

March 23, 1555
d. Julius III, Pope

April 21, 1555
b. Carracci, Lodovico

May 1, 1555
d. Marcellus II, Pope

October 16, 1555
d. Latimer, Hugh

1556

b. Maderno, Carlo
b. Opechancanough
d. Clemens non Papa, Jacobus
d. Gombert, Nicolas

March 21, 1556
d. Cranmer, Thomas

July 31, 1556
d. Ignatius of Loyola, Saint

September 1, 1556
d. Lotto, Lorenzo

October 21, 1556
d. Aretino, Pietro

November 10, 1556
d. Chancellor, Richard
d. Pontormo, Jacopo da
d. Udall, Nicholas

1557

b. Accoramboni, Vittoria
b. Gabrieli, Giovanni
b. Hathaway, Anne
b. Morley, Thomas
d. Cabeza de Vaca, Alvar Nunez
d. Cabot, Sebastian
d. Francis Xavier, Saint
d. Lautaro

July 16, 1557
d. Anne of Cleves

September 1, 1557
d. Cartier, Jacques

December 13, 1557
d. Tartaglia, Niccolo (Fontana)

1558

b. Lodge, Thomas
b. Peele, George
d. Fernel, Jean Francois
d. Recorde, Robert

March 25, 1558
d. Marcos de Niza

July 11, 1558
b. Greene, Robert

September 21, 1558
d. Charles V

November 6, 1558
b. Kyd, Thomas

November 17, 1558
d. Mary I

1559

d. Sanmicheli, Michele

February 8, 1559
b. Casaubon, Isaac

August 18, 1559
d. Paul, IV

September 25, 1559
b. Borromini, Francesco

November 5, 1559
d. Kano, Motonobu

1560

b. Bathory, Elizabeth
b. Chapman, George
b. Corsi, Jacopo
b. Gesualdo, Carlo
b. Sully, Maximilien de Bethune, Duc
d. Gustavus, I

January 1, 1560
d. du Bellay, Joachim

April 19, 1560
d. Melanchthon, Philipp

August 19, 1560
b. Crichton, James

October 10, 1560
b. Arminius, Jacobus

November 3, 1560
b. Carracci, Annibale

November 25, 1560
d. Doria, Andrea

1561

d. Aguirre, Lope de
d. Berruguete, Alonso (Gonzalez)
d. Garamond, Claude
d. Milan, Luis
d. Schwenckfeld, Kasper von

January 22, 1561
b. Bacon, Francis, Sir

January 31, 1561
d. Menno Simonsz(con)

March 29, 1561
b. Sanctorius

July 11, 1561
b. Gongora y Argote, Luis de

August 20, 1561
b. Peri, Jacopo
b. Babington, Anthony

December 9, 1561
b. Sandys, Edwin, Sir

1562

b. Bull, John
b. Daniel, Samuel
b. Sweelinck, Jan Pieterszoon
b. Xu Guangqi
d. Scorel, Jan van
d. Willaert, Adrian

January 20, 1562
b. Rinuccini, Ottavio

July 9, 1562
b. Gentileschi, Orazio

July 23, 1562
d. Berlichingen, Gotz von

September 13, 1562
d. Bandello, Matteo

November 25, 1562
b. Lope de Vega

1563

b. Drayton, Michael
b. Dowland, John

1564

b. Adams, William
b. Pacheco, Francisco

February 15, 1564
b. Galileo

February 18, 1564
d. Michelangelo (Buonarroti)

February 26, 1564
b. Marlowe, Christopher

April 23, 1564
b. Shakespeare, William

May 27, 1564
d. Calvin, John

July 21, 1564
d. Sousa, Martim Afonso de

July 25, 1564
d. Ferdinand I

July 31, 1564
d. Velasco, Luis de

October 15, 1564
d. Vesalius, Andreas

1565

b. Ribalta, Francisco

January 29, 1565
b. Meres, Francis

October 22, 1565
d. Grolier, Jean

December 9, 1565
d. Pius, IV, Pope

December 13, 1565
d. Gesner, Konrad von

1566

b. Brewster, William
b. Gorges, Ferdinando, Sir
d. Cabezon, Antonio
d. Diane de Poitiers
d. Las Casas, Bartolome de

June 19, 1566
b. James I

July 2, 1566
d. Nostradamus

September 5, 1566
d. Suleiman I

September 22, 1566
d. Agricola, Georgius

November 19, 1566
b. Devereaux, Robert

1567

b. Burbage, Richard
b. Nash, Thomas
d. Gasca, Pedro de la

February 9, 1567
d. Darnley, Henry Stuart, Lord

February 12, 1567
b. Campion, Thomas

May 15, 1567
b. Monteverdi, Claudio

July 3, 1567
b. Champlain, Samuel de

August 21, 1567
b. Francis of Sales, St.

November 14, 1567
b. Maurice of Nassau

1568

b. Bruegel, Jan
d. Goujon, Jean
d. Coverdale, Miles

September 5, 1568
b. Campanella, Tommaso

1569

b. Lanyer, Aemilia
d. Bruegel, Pieter, the El

August 30, 1569
b. Jahangir

1570

b. Fawkes, Guy
b. Sotatsu, Tawaraya
d. Bonivard, Francois
d. l'Orme, Philibert de
d. Walter, Johann
d. Yi Hwang
d. Primaticcio, Francesco

October 4, 1570
b. Pazmany, Peter

October 20, 1570
d. Barros, Joao de

November 27, 1570
d. Sansovino, Jacopo

1571

d. Animuccia, Giovanni

January 27, 1571
b. Abbas I

February 14, 1571
d. Cellini, Benvenuto

February 15, 1571
b. Praetorius, Michael

December 27, 1571
b. Kepler, Johannes

1572

b. Dekker, Thomas
d. Clouet, Francois
d. Lopez de Legaspi, Miguel

January 12, 1572
d. Sa, Mem de

April 24, 1572
d. Ramus, Petrus

May 1, 1572
d. Pius, V, Pope

June 11, 1572
b. Jonson, Ben(jamin)

August 5, 1572
d. Luria, Isaac ben Solomon

August 24, 1572
d. Coligny, Gaspard de Chatillon

August 28, 1572
d. Goudimel, Claude

November 13, 1572
b. Lucaris, Cyril

November 23, 1572
d. Bronzino, Il
d. Bronzino, Agnolo

November 24, 1572
d. Knox, John

1573

b. Donne, John

March 13, 1573
d. L'Hopital, Michel de

April 26, 1573
b. Marie de Medicis

July 7, 1573
d. Vignola, Giacomo da

July 15, 1573
b. Jones, Inigo

July 29, 1573
d. Caius, John

September 8, 1573
b. Caravaggio, Michelangelo da

October 6, 1573
b. Southampton, Henry Wriothesley, Earl

October 7, 1573
b. Laud, William

1574

b. Day, John
b. Heywood, Thomas

June 27, 1574
d. Vasari, Giorgio
d. Eustachio, Bartolomeo

September 17, 1574
d. Menendez de Aviles, Pedro

1575

b. Marston, John
b. Tourneur, Cyril

March 5, 1575
b. Oughtred, William

March 24, 1575
d. Caro, Joseph

April 24, 1575
b. Boehme, Jakob

September 12, 1575
b. Hudson, Henry

November 4, 1575
b. Reni, Guido

1576

b. Carver, John
b. Dudley, Thomas

January 19, 1576
d. Sachs, Hans

August 27, 1576
d. Titian

September 21, 1576
d. Cardano, Geronimo

October 12, 1576
d. Maximilian II

1577

February 6, 1577
b. Cenci, Beatrice

February 8, 1577
b. Burton, Robert

April 12, 1577
b. Christian IV

June 29, 1577
b. Rubens, Peter Paul, Sir

1578

b. Ravaillac, Francois
d. Bothwell, James Hepburn, Earl of
d. Lescot, Pierre
d. Sinan, Kodja Mimar

February 5, 1578
d. Moroni, Giovanni Battista

March 18, 1578
b. Elsheimer, Adam

April 1, 1578
b. Harvey, William

April 4, 1578
b. Philip, III

July 9, 1578
b. Ferdinand II

1579

d. Quesada, Gonzalo Jimenez de

April 29, 1579
d. Landa, Diego de

November 21, 1579
d. Gresham, Thomas, Sir

December 20, 1579
b. Fletcher, John

1580

b. Alarcon y Mendoza, Juan Ruiz de
b. Baltimore, George Calvert, Baron
b. Lopez de Segura Ruy
b. Minuit, Peter
b. Schouten, William Cornelius
b. Van Rensselaer, Kiliaen
b. Webster, John
d. Camoes, Luis de
d. Holinshed, Raphael
b. Smith, John

January 12, 1580
b. Helmont, Jan Baptista van

April 18, 1580
b. Middleton, Thomas

July 26, 1580
b. Claver, Peter

August 19, 1580
b. Vernier, Pierre
d. Palladio, Andrea

September 17, 1580
b. Quevado y Villegas, Francisco Gomez de

December 1, 1580
b. Peiresc, Nicholas-Claude Fabri de

1581

b. Hals, Frans

January 4, 1581
b. Ussher, James

March 16, 1581
b. Hooft, Pieter Corneliszoon

April 24, 1581
b. Vincent de Paul, Saint

October 21, 1581
b. Domenichino, Il

1582

b. Allegri, Gregorio
d. Chang Chu-cheng
d. Nobunaga, Oda

April 21, 1582
d. Toledo, Fernando Alvarez de

July 3, 1582
d. Crichton, James

September 28, 1582
d. Buchanan, George

October 4, 1582
d. Theresa, Saint

October 15, 1582
d. Theresa, St.

December 11, 1582
d. Alba, Duke of

1583

b. Beaumont, John, Sir
b. Frescobaldi, Girolamo
b. Gibbons, Orlando
b. Massinger, Philip

March 3, 1583
b. Herbert, Edward, 1st Baron Herbert of Cherbury

April 10, 1583
b. Grotius, Hugo

June 16, 1583
b. Oxenstierna, Axel Gustafsson

July 8, 1583
d. Mendes Pinto, Fernao

September 9, 1583
d. Gilbert, Humphrey, Sir

September 24, 1583
b. Wallenstein, Albrecht Wenzel
Eusebius von

1584

b. Baffin, William
b. Beaumont, Francis
b. Pym, John
b. Standish, Miles
b. Tirso de Molina
b. Vos, Cornelis de
d. Castillo, Bernal Diaz del
d. Toledo, Francisco de
d. William the Silent

March 17, 1584
d. Ivan IV

November 3, 1584
d. Borromeo, Charles, Saint

December 4, 1584
b. Cotton, John

December 10, 1584
b. Selden, John

1585

b. Cary, Elizabeth Tanfield
b. Rolfe, John
b. Squanto

April 10, 1585
d. Gregory XIII

September 9, 1585
b. Richelieu, Armand Jean du Plessis,
Cardinal

October 8, 1585
b. Schutz, Heinrich

October 28, 1585
b. Jansen, Cornelis Otto

November 23, 1585
d. Tallis, Thomas

December 13, 1585
b. Drummond of Hawthornden,
William

December 22, 1585
d. Accoramboni, Vittoria

December 26, 1585
d. Ronsard, Pierre de

1586

b. Ford, John
b. Mason, John
d. Morales, Luis de

July 7, 1586
b. Hooker, Thomas

August 7, 1586
b. Andrae, Johann Valentin

September 20, 1586
d. Babington, Anthony

October 17, 1586
d. Sidney, Philip, Sir

1587

b. Wroth, Mary, Lady
b. Yun Sondo
d. Dare, Virginia

January 8, 1587
b. Coen, Jan Pieterszoon

February 8, 1587
d. Mary, Queen of Scots

August 18, 1587
b. Dare, Virginia

October 19, 1587
d. Medici, Francesco de

November 17, 1587
b. Vondel, Joost van den

1588

b. Endecott, John
b. Terbrugghen, Hendrick
d. Granjon, Robert
d. Telesio, Bernardino

January 12, 1588
b. Winthrop, John

April 5, 1588
b. Hobbes, Thomas

April 9, 1588
d. Veronese, Paolo

September 3, 1588
d. Tarlton, Richard

September 4, 1588
d. Leicester, Earl of

1589

b. Cutpurse, Moll
b. Fetti, Domenico
d. Plantin, Christophe

January 5, 1589
d. Catherine de Medici

1590

b. Bradford, William
b. Eaton, Theophilus
b. Massasoit
b. Samoset

d. Eitoku, Kano
d. Zarlino, Gioseffo

January 9, 1590
b. Vouet, Simon

February 3, 1590
d. Pilon, Germain

February 17, 1590
b. Ribera, Jusepe (Jose) de

April 6, 1590
d. Walsingham, Francis, Sir

August 27, 1590
d. Sixtus, V

December 22, 1590
d. Pare, Ambroise

1591

b. Herrick, Robert
b. Hutchinson, Anne

February 8, 1591
b. Guercino, Il
d. Grenville, Richard, Sir

November 20, 1591
d. Hatton, Christopher, Sir

December 14, 1591
d. John of the Cross, Saint

1592

b. Brule, Etienne
b. Buckingham, 1st Duke of
b. Callot, Jacques
b. Cavendish, William, Duke of
Newcastle
b. DeVries, David Pietersen
b. Gorton, Samuel

January 5, 1592
b. Shah Jahan

February 13, 1592
d. Bassano, Jacopo

March 28, 1592
b. Comenius, Johann Amos
d. Cavendish, Thomas

September 3, 1592
d. Greene, Robert

September 13, 1592
d. Montaigne, Michel Eyquem de

December 3, 1592
d. Farnese, Alessandro

1593

b. Gentileschi, Artemisia

b. La Tour, George de
b. Mumtaz Mahal
b. Van Diemen, Anthony Meuza

February 6, 1593
d. Amyot, Jacques

March 19, 1593
b. La Tour, Georges Dumesnil de

March 25, 1593
b. Brebeuf, Jean de

April 3, 1593
b. Herbert, George

April 13, 1593
b. Strafford, 1st Earl of

May 19, 1593
b. Jordaens, Jacob

May 30, 1593
d. Marlowe, Christopher

August 9, 1593
b. Walton, Izaak

1594

b. Daye, Stephen
b. Hampden, John
d. Kyd, Thomas

February 2, 1594
d. Palestrina, Giovanni

May 31, 1594
d. Tintoretto
b. Poussin, Nicolas

June 14, 1594
d. Lassus, Orlandus de

November 22, 1594
d. Frobisher, Martin

November 29, 1594
d. Ercilla y Zuniga, Alonso de
b. Cuyp, Jacob Gerritsz(oon)

December 2, 1594
d. Mercator, Gerhardus

December 9, 1594
b. Gustavus Adophus

1595

b. Carew, Thomas
b. Chmielnicki, Bogdan
b. Pocahontas

April 25, 1595
d. Tasso, Torquato

May 26, 1595
d. Neri, Philip

June 8, 1595
b. Parker, Thomas

October 18, 1595
b. Winslow, Edward
d. Mendana de Neyra, Alvaro de

November 12, 1595
d. Hawkins, John, Sir

1596

b. Hamen y Leon, Juan van der
b. Keyser, Thomas De
b. Mogila, Peter
d. Bodin, Jean

January 13, 1596
b. Goyen, Jan Josephszoon van

January 28, 1596
d. Drake, Francis, Sir

March 31, 1596
b. Descartes, Rene

September 18, 1596
b. Shirley, James

November 1, 1596
b. Cortona, Pietro da

December 3, 1596
b. Amati, Nicolo

1597

b. Davenport, John
b. Underhill, John
b. Waller, William, Sir
d. Burbage, James
d. Peele, George

January 15, 1597
d. Herrera, Juan de

June 9, 1597
d. Anchieta, Jose de

June 20, 1597
d. Barents, Willem

December 21, 1597
d. Canisius, Peter

1598

b. Choiseul, Cesar, Comte Du Plessis-
Praslin, duc de
b. Nicolet, Jean
b. Rossi, Luigi
d. Burghley, William Cecil, Baron
d. Estienne, Henri
d. Philip II
d. Toyotomi Hideyoshi

January 23, 1598
b. Mansart, Francois

June 28, 1598
d. Ortelius, Abraham

November 7, 1598
b. Zurbaran, Francisco

December 7, 1598
b. Bernini, Giovanni Lorenzo

December 15, 1598
d. Yi Sunsin

1599

b. Alden, John

January 13, 1599
d. Spenser, Edmund

March 22, 1599
b. Van Dyck, Anthony, Sir

April 25, 1599
b. Cromwell, Oliver

June 6, 1599
b. Velazquez, Diego Rodriguez de
Silva
b. Blake, Robert

August 22, 1599
d. Marenzio, Luca

September 11, 1599
d. Cenci, Beatrice

November 8, 1599
d. Guerrero, Francisco

1600

b. Brent, Margaret
b. Lorrain, Claude
b. Van Cortlandt, Oloff Stevenszen
b. Vlieger, Simon Jacobsz de
d. Deganawida
d. Deloney, Thomas

January 17, 1600
b. Calderon de la Barca, Pedro

February 17, 1600
d. Bruno, Giordano

May 5, 1600
d. Nicot, Jean

September 26, 1600
d. Le Jeune, Claude

November 2, 1600
d. Hooker, Richard

November 19, 1600
b. Charles I

17

b. Anokye, Okomfo

1601

b. Coddington, William
b. Gracian y Morales, Baltasar
  Jeronimo
d. Nash, Thomas

February 25, 1601
d. Devereaux, Robert

August 17, 1601
b. Fermat, Pierre de

September 16, 1601
b. Louis, XIII

October 24, 1601
d. Brahe, Tycho

1602

d. Morley, Thomas
d. Porta, Giacomo della

February 14, 1602
b. Cavalli, Francesco
b. Cavalli, Pietro Francesco

July 14, 1602
b. Mazarin, Jules, Cardinal

October 20, 1602
b. Guericke, Otto Von

1603

b. Tasman, Abel Janszoon
b. Williams, Roger

March 24, 1603
d. Elizabeth I

July 11, 1603
b. Digby, Kenelm, Sir

November 16, 1603
d. Charron, Pierre

December 4, 1603
d. Vos, Martin de

December 10, 1603
d. Gilbert, William

1604

b. Alden, Priscilla Mullens
b. Charnisay, Charles de Menou,
  Seigneur d'Aulnay
b. Manasseh ben Israel
d. Corsi, Jacopo
d. Merulo, Claudio

March 3, 1604
d. Socinus, Faustus

June 17, 1604
b. John Maurice of Nassau

August 5, 1604
b. Eliot, John

1605

b. Carissimi, Giacomo
b. Nikon, Nikita Minov

April 8, 1605
b. Philip, IV

April 23, 1605
d. Godunov, Boris Fedorovich

September 12, 1605
b. Dugdale, William, Sir

October 15, 1605
d. Akbar

October 19, 1605
b. Browne, Thomas

December 29, 1605
d. Davis, John

1606

b. Berkeley, William, Sir
b. Brouwer, Adriaen C
b. Heem, Jan Davidsz(oon) de
b. Li Tzu-Ch'eng
d. Lyly, John

January 31, 1606
d. Fawkes, Guy
b. Davenant, William, Sir

March 3, 1606
b. Waller, Edmund

June 6, 1606
b. Corneille, Pierre

1607

b. Jogues, Isaac
b. Rojas Zorrilla, Francisco de
d. Fontana, Domenico

March 12, 1607
b. Gerhardt, Paul(us)
d. Dyer, Edward, Sir

July 15, 1607
b. Rembrandt (Harmenszoon van Rijn)

November 15, 1607
b. Scudery, Madeleine de

November 26, 1607
b. Harvard, John

1608

February 6, 1608
b. Vieira, Antonio

March 16, 1608
d. Sonjo

July 13, 1608
b. Ferdinand, III

August 13, 1608
d. Giovanni da Bologna

October 15, 1608
b. Torricelli, Evangelista
d. Dee, John

December 6, 1608
b. Monck, George, 1st Duke of
  Albemarle

December 9, 1608
b. Milton, John

1609

b. Cooper, Samuel
b. Dunster, Henry

January 21, 1609
d. Scaliger, Joseph Justus
b. Suckling, John

February 18, 1609
b. Clarendon, Edward Hyde, Earl of

July 15, 1609
d. Carracci, Annibale

October 8, 1609
b. Clarke, John

October 19, 1609
d. Arminius, Jacobus

1610

b. Huang Tsung-hsi
b. Stuyvesant, Peter
d. Cueva de Garoza, Juan de la

May 11, 1610
d. Ricci, Matteo

May 14, 1610
d. Henry, IV

May 27, 1610
d. Ravaillac, Francois

July 18, 1610
d. Caravaggio, Michelangelo da
d. Elsheimer, Adam

December 10, 1610
b. Ostade, Adriaen van

December 14, 1610
b. Teniers, David, the Younger

1611

b. Harrington, James
d. Victoria, Tomas Luis de

January 28, 1611
b. Hevelius, Johannes

May 19, 1611
b. Innocent XI, Pope

June 23, 1611
d. Hudson, Henry

September 11, 1611
b. Turenne, Henri de La Tour
    Auvergne, Viscount

1612

b. Bradstreet, Anne
b. Le Vau, Louis
b. Maisoneuve, Sieur de

January 17, 1612
b. Fairfax, Thomas

January 20, 1612
d. Rudolf II
d. Gerard, John

February 7, 1612
b. Killigrew, Thomas

February 14, 1612
b. Butler, Samuel

August 12, 1612
d. Gabrieli, Giovanni

1613

b. Crashaw, Richard
b. Vane, Henry

January 28, 1613
d. Bodley, Thomas, Sir

March 12, 1613
b. LeNotre, Andre

April 7, 1613
b. Dou, Gerard
b. Taylor, Jeremy
b. Gondi, Cardinal

September 8, 1613
d. Gesualdo, Carlo

September 15, 1613
b. LaRochefoucauld, Francois, Duc de

September 25, 1613
b. Perrault, Claude

1614

b. Lilburne, John
b. Sarasin, Jean Francois
d. Bathory, Elizabeth

April 6, 1614
d. Greco, El

July 1, 1614
d. Casaubon, Isaac

1615

b. Biddle, John
b. Fouquet, Nicolas
d. Aleman, Mateo
d. Porta, Giambattista della

January 25, 1615
b. Flinck, Govert

June 20, 1615
b. Rosa, Salvator

November 12, 1615
b. Baxter, Richard

1616

b. Culpeper, Nicholas
b. Froberger, Johann Jakob
d. Ieyasu, Tokugawa
d. Scamozzi, Vincenzo

January 6, 1616
d. Henslowe, Philip

March 6, 1616
d. Beaumont, Francis
d. Garcilaso de la Vega, Inca

April 23, 1616
d. Cervantes (Saavedra), Miguel (de)
d. Shakespeare, William

May 24, 1616
b. Maitland, John

May 25, 1616
b. Dolci, Carlo

November 23, 1616
d. Hakluyt, Richard

1617

b. Cudworth, Ralph
b. Horrocks, Jeremiah
b. Ter Borch, Gerard

February 4, 1617
d. Elzevir, Louis
d. Pocahontas

April 4, 1617
d. Napier, John

May 7, 1617
d. Thou, Jacques Auguste de

September 25, 1617
d. Suarez, Francisco

1618

b. Blood, Thomas
b. Lovelace, Richard
b. Moronobu, Hishikawa

January 1, 1618
b. Murillo, Bartolome Esteban
d. Powhatan

July 24, 1618
b. Cowley, Abraham

October 14, 1618
b. Lely, Peter, Sir

October 24, 1618
b. Aurangzeb

October 29, 1618
d. Raleigh, Walter, Sir

December 10, 1618
d. Caccini, Giulio

1619

b. Kalf, Willem
d. Fabricius, Hieronymus ab
    Aquapendente

January 7, 1619
d. Hilliard, Nicholas

February 24, 1619
b. Le Brun, Charles
d. Burbage, Richard

March 6, 1619
b. Cyrano de Bergerac, Savinien de

April 21, 1619
b. Riebeeck, Jan Anthonisz van

May 13, 1619
d. Oldenbarnevelt, Johan van

August 29, 1619
b. Colbert, Jean-Baptiste

October 7, 1619
b. Wang Fu-chih

October 14, 1619
d. Daniel, Samuel

November 13, 1619
d. Carracci, Lodovico

1620

b. Cuyp, Aelbert Jacobsz(oon)
b. Frederick William
d. Stevin, Simon

January 17, 1620
b. Bourgeoys, Marguerite

March 1, 1620
d. Campion, Thomas

May 16, 1620
d. Adams, William

July 21, 1620
b. Picard, Jean

October 16, 1620
b. Puget, Pierre

October 31, 1620
b. Evelyn, John

November 10, 1620
b. Lenclos, Ninon de

1621

b. Grimmelshausen, Hans Jakob
Christoffel von
b. Tonge, Israel

February 15, 1621
d. Praetorius, Michael

February 26, 1621
b. Cooper, Anthony Ashley, 1st Earl
of Shaftesbury

March 28, 1621
d. Rinuccini, Ottavio

March 31, 1621
b. Marvell, Andrew
d. Philip, III

April 5, 1621
d. Carver, John

July 8, 1621
b. LaFontaine, Jean de

August 19, 1621
b. Eeckhout, Gerbrand van den

September 8, 1621
b. Conde, Prince de

September 17, 1621
d. Bellarmine, Robert, Saint

October 16, 1621
d. Sweelinck, Jan Pieterszoon

1622

b. Fabritius, Carel
b. Sidney, Algernon

b. Stoffels, Hendrijke
b. Valdes-Leal, Juan de
d. Rolfe, John
d. Squanto

January 15, 1622
b. Moliere

January 23, 1622
d. Baffin, William

April 17, 1622
b. Vaughan, Henry

May 22, 1622
b. Frontenac, Louis de Buade de

December 28, 1622
d. Francis of Sales, St.

1623

b. Cavendish, Margaret
d. Fetti, Domenico
d. Sarpi, Paolo

April 30, 1623
b. Laval, Francois Xavier de

May 26, 1623
b. Petty, William, Sir

June 19, 1623
b. Pascal, Blaise

July 4, 1623
d. Byrd, William

July 8, 1623
d. Gregory XV

August 5, 1623
b. Cesti, Pietro

August 6, 1623
d. Hathaway, Anne

1624

d. Onate, Juan de

January 17, 1624
b. Guarini, Guarino

February 16, 1624
d. Mariana, Juan de
b. Fox, George

August 17, 1624
b. Sobieski, John, III

September 10, 1624
b. Sydenham, Thomas

November 10, 1624
d. Southampton, Henry Wriothesley,
Earl

November 17, 1624
d. Boehme, Jakob

1625

d. Bruegel, Jan
d. Florio, John
d. Lodge, Thomas
d. Schouten, William Cornelius

March 27, 1625
d. James I

April 23, 1625
d. Maurice of Nassau

June 5, 1625
d. Gibbons, Orlando

June 23, 1625
b. Fell, John

August 29, 1625
d. Fletcher, John

September 24, 1625
b. Witt, Johan de

1626

b. Sabbatai Zevi
b. Steen, Jan

January 8, 1626
b. Talon, Jean

February 5, 1626
b. Sevigne, Marie de Rabutin-Chantal,
Marquise de

February 18, 1626
b. Redi, Francesco

February 28, 1626
d. Tourneur, Cyril

March 10, 1626
b. Malpighi, Marcello

March 12, 1626
b. Aubrey, John

April 7, 1626
d. Dowland, John

April 9, 1626
d. Bacon, Francis, Sir

October 4, 1626
b. Cromwell, Richard

December 8, 1626
b. Christina

1627

January 25, 1627
b. Boyle, Robert

April 6, 1627
b. Sivaji

April 19, 1627
d. Beaumont, John, Sir

May 24, 1627
d. Gongora y Argote, Luis de

July 4, 1627
d. Middleton, Thomas

September 27, 1627
b. Bossuet, Jacques Benigne

November 7, 1627
d. Jahangir

November 29, 1627
b. Ray, John

1628

b. Cambert, Robert
b. Girardon, Francois
b. Meer, Jan van der
b. Ruysdael, Jacob van

January 12, 1628
b. Perrault, Charles
d. Ribalta, Francisco

January 30, 1628
b. Villers, George

June 29, 1628
b. Molinos, Miguel de

October 16, 1628
d. Malherbe, Francois de

November 27, 1628
d. Buckingham, 1st Duke of

November 28, 1628
b. Bunyan, John

December 13, 1628
d. Bull, John

1629

d. Terbrugghen, Hendrick

January 19, 1629
d. Abbas I

January 30, 1629
d. Maderno, Carlo

March 10, 1629
b. Romanov, Alexis Mikhailovich

April 14, 1629
b. Huygens, Christian

September 21, 1629
d. Coen, Jan Pieterszoon
d. Sandys, Edwin, Sir

December 20, 1629
b. Hooch, Pieter de

1630

b. Richer, Jean
b. Tao-chi
d. Billington, John

April 28, 1630
b. Cotton, Charles

May 29, 1630
b. Charles II

November 15, 1630
d. Kepler, Johannes

1631

d. Hamen y Leon, Juan van der
d. Mumtaz Mahal

March 31, 1631
d. Donne, John

June 21, 1631
d. Smith, John

July 15, 1631
b. Cumberland, Richard

August 9, 1631
b. Dryden, John

October 18, 1631
b. Wigglesworth, Michael

December 23, 1631
d. Drayton, Michael

1632

b. Danby, Thomas Osborne
b. Philips, Katherine
d. Dekker, Thomas

January 8, 1632
b. Pufendorf, Samuel von

April 15, 1632
d. Baltimore, George Calvert, Baron

August 29, 1632
b. Locke, John

October 18, 1632
b. Giordano, Luca

October 20, 1632
b. Wren, Christopher, Sir

October 24, 1632
b. Leeuwenhoek, Antonie van

October 30, 1632
b. Vermeer, Jan

November 6, 1632
d. Gustavus Adophus

November 23, 1632
b. Mabillon, Jean

November 24, 1632
b. Spinoza, Baruch (Benedictus de)

November 28, 1632
b. Lully, Jean-Baptiste

December 17, 1632
b. Wood, Anthony

1633

b. Velde, Willem van de

February 23, 1633
b. Pepys, Samuel

March 1, 1633
d. Herbert, George

May 15, 1633
b. Vauban, Sebastien LePrestre de
d. Brule, Etienne

August 12, 1633
d. Peri, Jacopo

October 14, 1633
b. James II

November 8, 1633
d. Xu Guangqi

1634

b. Charpentier, Marc-Antoine
b. La Fayette, Comtesse de
b. Ochterveldt, Jacob Lucasz
d. Webster, John

February 25, 1634
d. Wallenstein, Albrecht Wenzel
Eusebius von

May 12, 1634
d. Chapman, George

June 25, 1634
d. Marston, John

September 3, 1634
d. Coke, Edward, Sir

1635

b. Etherege, George, Sir
b. Koprulu, Ahmed
b. Morgan, Henry, Sir

January 23, 1635
b. Spener, Philipp Jakob

March 24, 1635
d. Callot, Jacques

July 18, 1635
b. Hooke, Robert
b. Betterton, Thomas

August 27, 1635
d. Lope de Vega

November 27, 1635
b. Maintenon, Francoise d'Aubigne,
Marquise de
d. Mason, John

December 25, 1635
d. Champlain, Samuel de

1636

b. Beauchamp, Pierre
b. Duluth, Daniel (Greysolon)
b. Radisson, Pierre Espirit
d. Tung Ch'i-ch'ang

February 22, 1636
d. Sanctorius

July 19, 1636
b. Monnoyer, Jean-Baptiste

November 1, 1636
b. Boileau(-Despreaux), Nicolas

1637

b. Buxtehude, Dietrich

February 12, 1637
b. Swammerdam, Jan

February 15, 1637
d. Ferdinand II

March 19, 1637
d. Pazmany, Peter

April 6, 1637
d. Jonson, Ben(jamin)
d. Lucaris, Cyril

June 1, 1637
b. Marquette, Jacques, Pere

June 24, 1637
d. Peiresc, Nicholas-Claude Fabri de

August 27, 1637
b. Calvert, Charles

September 14, 1637
d. Vernier, Pierre

December 6, 1637
b. Andros, Edmund, Sir

1638

b. Hobbema, Meindert
b. Malebranche, Nicolas
d. Brouwer, Adriaen C

January 10, 1638
b. Steno, Nicolaus

May 6, 1638
d. Jansen, Cornelis Otto
d. Minuit, Peter

September 14, 1638
d. Harvard, John

September 16, 1638
b. Louis XIV

1639

d. Cary, Elizabeth Tanfield

February 7, 1639
d. Gentileschi, Orazio

March 22, 1639
d. Carew, Thomas

May 8, 1639
b. Gaulli, Giovanni Battista

May 21, 1639
d. Campanella, Tommaso

June 21, 1639
b. Mather, Increase

August 4, 1639
d. Alarcon y Mendoza, Juan Ruiz de
b. Racine, Jean Baptiste

1640

b. Leisler, Jacob
b. Metacom
b. Wycherley, William
d. Day, John
d. Ford, John

January 25, 1640
d. Burton, Robert
d. Massinger, Philip

April 7, 1640
b. Hennepin, Louis

May 30, 1640
d. Rubens, Peter Paul, Sir

July 10, 1640
b. Behn, Aphra

September 29, 1640
b. Coysevox, Antoine

1641

b. Grew, Nehemiah
b. Le Nain, Antoine, Louis, and
Mathieu
d. Sully, Maximilien de Bethune, Duc

January 3, 1641
d. Horrocks, Jeremiah

April 6, 1641
d. Domenichino, Il

May 12, 1641
d. Strafford, 1st Earl of

August 16, 1641
d. Heywood, Thomas

December 9, 1641
d. Van Dyck, Anthony, Sir

1642

b. Shadwell, Thomas
b. Taylor, Edward
d. Suckling, John

January 8, 1642
d. Galileo

July 3, 1642
d. Marie de Medicis

August 18, 1642
d. Reni, Guido

October 1, 1642
b. Stradella, Alessandro

November 1, 1642
d. Nicolet, Jean

November 11, 1642
b. Boulle, Andre Charles

December 4, 1642
d. Richelieu, Armand Jean du Plessis,
Cardinal

December 25, 1642
b. Newton, Isaac, Sir

1643

d. Sotatsu, Tawaraya
d. Van Rensselaer, Kiliaen

May 7, 1643
b. Van Cortlandt, Stephanus

May 14, 1643
d. Louis, XIII

June 24, 1643
d. Hampden, John
d. Hutchinson, Anne
b. Stoddard, Solomon

September 8, 1643
b. Burnet, Gilbert

November 22, 1643
b. La Salle, Rene Robert Cavelier de

November 29, 1643
d. Monteverdi, Claudio

December 15, 1643
d. Pym, John

1644

b. Basho
b. Mazepa, Ivan Stepanovich
b. Štradivari, Antonio
d. Shih Ko-fa

March 2, 1644
d. Frescobaldi, Girolamo

April 10, 1644
d. Brewster, William

October 14, 1644
b. Penn, William

December 30, 1644
d. Helmont, Jan Baptista van

1645

b. Jolliet, Louis
b. Kidd, William, Captain
d. Lanyer, Aemilia
d. Li Tzu-Ch'eng

January 10, 1645
d. Laud, William
b. Mansart, Jules Hardouin

May 19, 1645
d. Van Diemen, Anthony Meuza

June 15, 1645
b. Godolphin, Sidney

August 10, 1645
b. Kino, Eusebio Francisco

August 16, 1645
b. LaBruyere, Jean de

August 28, 1645
d. Grotius, Hugo

September 8, 1645
d. Quevado y Villegas, Francisco
Gomez de

1646

d. Jogues, Isaac
d. Opechancanough

June 15, 1646
b. La Fosse, Charles de

July 1, 1646
b. Leibniz, Gottfried Wilhelm von

August 8, 1646
b. Kneller, Godfrey, Sir

August 19, 1646
b. Flamsteed, John

December 31, 1646
d. Mogila, Peter

1647

d. Gorges, Ferdinando, Sir

January 2, 1647
b. Bacon, Nathaniel

January 29, 1647
d. Meres, Francis

May 21, 1647
d. Hooft, Pieter Corneliszoon

July 19, 1647
d. Hooker, Thomas

October 25, 1647
d. Torricelli, Evangelista

November 18, 1647
b. Bayle, Pierre

1648

d. Rojas Zorrilla, Francisco de
d. Tirso de Molina

February 28, 1648
d. Christian IV

April 4, 1648
b. Gibbons, Grinling

April 5, 1648
b. Franceschini, Marcantonio

August 20, 1648
d. Herbert, Edward, 1st Baron Herbert
of Cherbury
b. Juana Ines de la Cruz, Sor

December 12, 1648
b. Rogers, John

1649

January 30, 1649
d. Charles I

February 23, 1649
b. Blow, John

March 16, 1649
d. Brebeuf, Jean de

March 26, 1649
d. Winthrop, John

April 5, 1649
b. Yale, Elihu

April 9, 1649
b. Monmouth, James Scott, Duke

June 30, 1649
d. Vouet, Simon

August 21, 1649
d. Crashaw, Richard

September 15, 1649
b. Oates, Titus

December 4, 1649
d. Drummond of Hawthornden,
William

1650

b. Aulnoy, Marie-Catherine Jumel de
Berneville
b. Savery, Thomas

February 2, 1650
b. Gwyn, Nell

February 11, 1650
d. Descartes, Rene
d. Charnisay, Charles de Menou,
Seigneur d'Aulnay

May 26, 1650
b. Marlborough, John Churchill, Duke

November 4, 1650
b. William III

1651

d. Gentileschi, Artemisia
d. Vos, Cornelis de

February 2, 1651
b. Phips, William, Sir

August 6, 1651
b. Fenelon, Francois de Salignac

October 21, 1651
b. Bart, Jean

1652

d. Cuyp, Jacob Gerritsz(oon)
d. La Tour, George de

January 30, 1652
d. La Tour, Georges Dumesnil de

February 17, 1652
d. Allegri, Gregorio

March 3, 1652
b. Otway, Thomas

March 28, 1652
b. Sewall, Samuel
b. Dampier, William

June 21, 1652
d. Jones, Inigo
b. Wise, John

September 2, 1652
d. Ribera, Jusepe (Jose) de

September 12, 1652
b. Tate, Nahum

December 23, 1652
d. Cotton, John

1653

b. Chikamatsu, Monzaemon
b. D'Urfey, Thomas
d. Filmer, Robert
d. Samoset
d. Vlieger, Simon Jacobsz de
d. Wroth, Mary, Lady

February 17, 1653
b. Corelli, Arcangelo

February 19, 1653
d. Rossi, Luigi

June 22, 1653
b. Fleury, Andre Hercule de

July 31, 1653
d. Dudley, Thomas

September 1, 1653
b. Pachelbel, Johann

1654

b. Livingston, Robert
d. Culpeper, Nicholas
d. Pacheco, Francisco

January 27, 1654
d. Andrae, Johann Valentin

April 27, 1654
b. Blount, Charles

May 4, 1654
b. K'ang-hsi

July 25, 1654
b. Steffani, Agostino

August 28, 1654
d. Oxenstierna, Axel Gustafsson

September 8, 1654
d. Claver, Peter

October 12, 1654
d. Fabritius, Carel

November 30, 1654
d. Selden, John

December 5, 1654
d. Sarasin, Jean Francois

December 10, 1654
b. Rottmayr, Johann Michael

1655

b. Blair, James
d. DeVries, David Pietersen

January 1, 1655
b. Thomasius

May 4, 1655
b. Cristofori, Bartolomeo di Francesco

May 8, 1655
d. Winslow, Edward

July 28, 1655
d. Cyrano de Bergerac, Savinien de

August 13, 1655
b. Denner, Johann Christoph

November 12, 1655
b. Nicholson, Francis

1656

b. Tekakwitha, Kateri, Saint

March 21, 1656
d. Ussher, James

April 27, 1656
d. Goyen, Jan Josephszoon van

June 3, 1656
b. Tournefort, Joseph Pitton de

July 18, 1656
b. Fischer von Erlach, Johann
   Bernhard

October 3, 1656
d. Standish, Miles

November 8, 1656
b. Halley, Edmund

1657

d. Manasseh ben Israel

April 2, 1657
d. Ferdinand, III

May 9, 1657
d. Bradford, William

June 3, 1657
d. Harvey, William

August 6, 1657
d. Chmielnicki, Bogdan

August 7, 1657
d. Blake, Robert

August 29, 1657
d. Lilburne, John

1658

b. Korin, Ogata
b. Makemie, Francis
b. Purcell, Henry
b. Saint-Pierre, Abbe de
d. Lovelace, Richard

January 7, 1658
d. Eaton, Theophilus

March 5, 1658
b. Cadillac, Antoine de la Mothe

June 20, 1658
b. Brattle, Thomas

September 3, 1658
d. Cromwell, Oliver

December 6, 1658
d. Gracian y Morales, Baltasar
   Jeronimo

1659

d. Dunster, Henry
d. Tasman, Abel Janszoon

July 28, 1659
b. Rigaud, Hyacinthe

1660

b. Fux, Johann Joseph
b. Schluter, Andreas

February 2, 1660
d. Flinck, Govert

April 16, 1660
b. Sloane, Hans, Sir

April 26, 1660
b. Defoe, Daniel

May 2, 1660
b. Scarlatti, Alessandro

May 28, 1660
b. George I

June 30, 1660
d. Oughtred, William
b. Prandtauer, Jakob

August 6, 1660
d. Velazquez, Diego Rodriguez de Silva

September 27, 1660
d. Vincent de Paul, Saint

October 21, 1660
b. Stahl, Georg Ernst

1661

b. Hawksmoor, Nicholas
d. Massasoit

March 9, 1661
d. Mazarin, Jules, Cardinal

July 20, 1661
b. Iberville, Pierre Le Moyne, Sieur d'

November 6, 1661
b. Charles, II

December 5, 1661
b. Harley, Robert, 1st Earl of Oxford and Earl Mortimer

1662

b. Mary, II
d. Cutpurse, Moll
d. Vane, Henry

January 27, 1662
b. Bentley, Richard

August 19, 1662
d. Pascal, Blaise

September 22, 1662
d. Biddle, John

1663

b. Byng, George Torrington, Viscount
b. DeLancey, Stephen
d. Stoffels, Hendrijke

February 12, 1663
b. Mather, Cotton

February 24, 1663
b. Newcomen, Thomas

October 18, 1663
b. Eugene of Savoy

November 14, 1663
b. Hildebrandt, Johann Lucas von

1664

d. Philips, Katherine

January 24, 1664
b. Vanbrugh, John, Sir

July 21, 1664
b. Prior, Matthew

August 27, 1664
d. Zurbaran, Francisco

1665

b. Churriguera, Jose Benito de

January 12, 1665
d. Fermat, Pierre de

February 6, 1665
b. Anne

February 17, 1665
b. Camerarius, Rudolf Jakob

March 15, 1665
d. Endecott, John

June 11, 1665
d. Digby, Kenelm, Sir
d. Philip, IV

November 19, 1665
d. Poussin, Nicolas

1666

January 22, 1666
d. Shah Jahan

May 14, 1666
b. Victor Amadeus, II

September 1, 1666
d. Hals, Frans

September 23, 1666
d. Mansart, Francois

October 29, 1666
d. Shirley, James

December 22, 1666
d. Guercino, Il

1667

b. Arbuthnot, John
b. Boffrand, Gabriel Germain
b. Kelsey, Henry
b. Magnasco, Alessandro Lissandrino
b. Pepusch, Johann Christoph

d. Froberger, Johann Jakob

May 26, 1667
b. De Moivre, Abraham

June 7, 1667
d. Keyser, Thomas De

July 28, 1667
d. Cowley, Abraham

August 13, 1667
d. Taylor, Jeremy

November 30, 1667
b. Swift, Jonathan

1668

April 7, 1668
d. Davenant, William, Sir

May 8, 1668
b. Lesage, Alain-Rene

June 23, 1668
b. Vico, Giovanni Battista

September 19, 1668
d. Waller, William, Sir

November 10, 1668
b. Couperin, Francois

December 11, 1668
b. Zeno, Apostolo

December 22, 1668
d. Daye, Stephen

December 31, 1668
b. Boerhaave, Hermann

1669

May 16, 1669
d. Cortona, Pietro da

October 4, 1669
d. Rembrandt (Harmenszoon van Rijn)

October 14, 1669
d. Cesti, Pietro

1670

b. Doggett, Thomas
b. Mandeville, Bernard
d. Le Vau, Louis

January 3, 1670
d. Monck, George, 1st Duke of Albemarle

January 24, 1670
b. Congreve, William

May 12, 1670
b. Augustus II

May 30, 1670
d. Davenport, John

July 18, 1670
b. Bononcini, Giovanni Battista

November 15, 1670
d. Comenius, Johann Amos

November 30, 1670
b. Toland, John

1671

d. Brent, Margaret
d. Yun Sondo

February 26, 1671
b. Shaftesbury, Anthony Ashley
Cooper, Earl

April 21, 1671
b. Law, John

June 14, 1671
b. Albinoni, Tommaso

November 6, 1671
b. Cibber, Colley

November 12, 1671
d. Fairfax, Thomas

1672

b. Hoyle, Edmond
d. Cooper, Samuel
d. Stuyvesant, Peter
b. Steele, Richard, Sir

May 1, 1672
b. Addison, Joseph

May 30, 1672
b. Peter the Great

August 20, 1672
d. Witt, Johan de

September 16, 1672
d. Bradstreet, Anne

September 21, 1672
d. Underhill, John

October 21, 1672
b. Muratori, Lodovico Antonio

November 6, 1672
d. Schutz, Heinrich

1673

b. Beverley, Robert

b. Clarke, Jeremiah
d. Cavendish, Margaret

February 17, 1673
d. Moliere

March 15, 1673
d. Rosa, Salvator
b. Nicolini

1674

b. Bracegirdle, Anne
b. Orleans, Philippe II d'

January 9, 1674
b. Keiser, Reinhard

January 12, 1674
d. Carissimi, Giacomo

March 28, 1674
b. Byrd, William

June 20, 1674
b. Rowe, Nicholas

July 17, 1674
b. Watts, Isaac

September 29, 1674
d. Eeckhout, Gerbrand van den
d. Herrick, Robert

October 20, 1674
b. Logan, James

November 8, 1674
d. Milton, John

December 9, 1674
d. Clarendon, Edward Hyde, Earl of

1675

b. Twining, Thomas
d. Choiseul, Cesar, Comte Du Plessis-
Praslin, duc de

January 16, 1675
b. Saint-Simon, Duc de
d. Dou, Gerard

February 28, 1675
b. Delisle, Guillaume

May 18, 1675
d. Marquette, Jacques, Pere

July 27, 1675
d. Turenne, Henri de La Tour
Auvergne, Viscount

October 7, 1675
b. Carriera, Rosalba Giovanna

October 11, 1675
b. Clarke, Samuel

December 15, 1675
d. Vermeer, Jan

1676

b. Cadogan, William, Earl
b. Hamilton, Andrew
b. Selkirk, Alexander
b. Spotswood, Alexander
d. Maisoneuve, Sieur de
d. Metacom
d. Sabbatai Zevi

January 14, 1676
d. Cavalli, Francesco
d. Cavalli, Pietro Francesco

January 29, 1676
d. Romanov, Alexis Mikhailovich

March 9, 1676
b. Boylston, Zabdiel

April 28, 1676
d. Clarke, John

May 27, 1676
d. Gerhardt, Paul(us)

August 17, 1676
d. Grimmelshausen, Hans Jakob
Christoffel von

August 26, 1676
b. Walpole, Robert

October 26, 1676
d. Bacon, Nathaniel

October 30, 1676
d. Koprulu, Ahmed

December 25, 1676
d. Cavendish, William, Duke of
Newcastle

1677

d. Cambert, Robert
d. Gorton, Samuel

January 18, 1677
d. Riebeeck, Jan Anthonisz van

February 20, 1677
d. Spinoza, Baruch (Benedictus de)

April 24, 1677
d. Parker, Thomas

July 9, 1677
d. Berkeley, William, Sir

August 3, 1677
d. Borromini, Francesco

September 11, 1677
d. Harrington, James

September 17, 1677
b. Hales, Stephen

1678

b. Caffieri, Jacques
b. Farquhar, George

March 4, 1678
b. Vivaldi, Antonio (Lucio)

March 27, 1678
b. Juvara, Filippo

July 26, 1678
b. Joseph I

August 18, 1678
d. Marvell, Andrew

October 1, 1678
b. Bolingbroke, Henry St. John,
Viscount

October 18, 1678
d. Jordaens, Jacob

November 1, 1678
d. Coddington, William

1679

b. Psalmanazar, George

January 4, 1679
b. Wolcott, Roger

January 24, 1679
b. Wolff, Christian von, Baron

February 3, 1679
d. Steen, Jan

February 5, 1679
d. Vondel, Joost van den

August 24, 1679
d. Gondi, Cardinal

November 20, 1679
d. John Maurice of Nassau

December 4, 1679
d. Hobbes, Thomas

1680

b. Bering, Vitus Jonassen
b. Blackbeard
b. Senesino
d. Alden, Priscilla Mullens
d. Tonge, Israel

February 17, 1680
d. Swammerdam, Jan

February 22, 1680
d. Deshayes, Catherine

February 23, 1680
b. Bienville, Sieur de

March 16, 1680
d. LaRochefoucauld, Francois, Duc de

March 23, 1680
d. Fouquet, Nicolas

April 3, 1680
d. Sivaji

April 17, 1680
d. Tekakwitha, Kateri, Saint

August 24, 1680
d. Blood, Thomas

September 25, 1680
d. Butler, Samuel

November 28, 1680
d. Bernini, Giovanni Lorenzo

December 7, 1680
d. Lely, Peter, Sir

1681

March 14, 1681
b. Telemann, Georg Philipp

May 25, 1681
d. Calderon de la Barca, Pedro

August 27, 1681
d. Nikon, Nikita Minov

November 28, 1681
b. Cavalier, Jean

December 8, 1681
d. Ter Borch, Gerard

1682

b. Laurie, Annie
d. Browne, Thomas

February 4, 1682
b. Bottger, Johann Friedrich

February 25, 1682
b. Morgagni, Giovanni Battista

February 28, 1682
d. Stradella, Alessandro

March 14, 1682
d. Ruysdael, Jacob van

April 3, 1682
d. Murillo, Bartolome Esteban

June 17, 1682
b. Charles XII
d. Maitland, John

October 12, 1682
d. Picard, Jean

October 29, 1682
b. Charlevoix, Pierre Francis Xavier de

November 21, 1682
d. Lorrain, Claude

December 23, 1682
b. Gibbs, James

1683

b. Catesby, Mark
d. Hooch, Pieter de
d. Williams, Roger

February 15, 1683
d. Cooper, Anthony Ashley, 1st Earl
of Shaftesbury

March 6, 1683
d. Guarini, Guarino

May 19, 1683
d. Killigrew, Thomas
b. Young, Edward

September 6, 1683
d. Colbert, Jean-Baptiste

September 25, 1683
b. Rameau, Jean-Philippe

November 10, 1683
b. George II

December 7, 1683
d. Sidney, Algernon

December 15, 1683
d. Walton, Izaak

December 19, 1683
b. Philip, V

1684

b. Miller, Joe
b. Vernon, Edward, Sir
b. Yoshimune, Tokugawa

March 31, 1684
b. Durante, Francesco

April 5, 1684
d. Van Cortlandt, Oloff Stevenszen

April 6, 1684
d. Heem, Jan Davidsz(oon) de

April 12, 1684
d. Amati, Nicolo

October 1, 1684
d. Corneille, Pierre

October 10, 1684
b. Watteau, Jean Antoine

1685

b. Kent, William
b. la Verendrye, Sieur de

February 6, 1685
d. Charles II

February 23, 1685
b. Handel, George Frideric

March 12, 1685
b. Berkeley, George

March 17, 1685
b. Nattier, Jean Marc

March 21, 1685
b. Bach, Johann Sebastian

April 14, 1685
d. Otway, Thomas

May 2, 1685
d. Ostade, Adriaen van

June 23, 1685
b. Bernacchi, Antonio Maria

June 30, 1685
b. Gay, John

July 25, 1685
d. Monmouth, James Scott, Duke
b. Taylor, Brook

October 26, 1685
b. Scarlatti, Domenico Girolamo

1686

b. Law, William
d. Conde, Prince de

January 17, 1686
d. Dolci, Carlo

February 11, 1686
d. Dugdale, William, Sir

March 17, 1686
b. Oudry, Jean-Baptiste

May 11, 1686
d. Guericke, Otto Von

May 14, 1686
b. Fahrenheit, Gabriel Daniel

July 10, 1686
d. Fell, John

July 24, 1686
b. Marcello, Benedetto

August 19, 1686
b. Porpora, Niccolo

October 15, 1686
b. Ramsay, Allan

November 26, 1686
d. Steno, Nicolaus

1687

b. Carey, Henry
b. Neumann, Balthasar

January 28, 1687
d. Hevelius, Johannes

February 5, 1687
b. Geminiani, Francesco

February 16, 1687
d. Cotton, Charles

March 19, 1687
d. La Salle, Rene Robert Cavelier de

March 22, 1687
d. Lully, Jean-Baptiste

April 16, 1687
d. Villers, George

June 8, 1687
b. Guarneri, Giuseppe Antonio

September 12, 1687
d. Alden, John

October 21, 1687
d. Waller, Edmund

November 13, 1687
d. Gwyn, Nell

December 16, 1687
d. Petty, William, Sir

1688

b. Eusden, Laurence
b. Smibert, John
d. Frederick William

January 29, 1688
b. Swedenborg, Emanuel

February 4, 1688
b. Marivaux, Pierre Carlet de

February 7, 1688
b. Colden, Cadwallader

April 4, 1688
b. Delisle, Joseph-Nicolas

April 15, 1688
b. Fasch, Johann Friedrich

May 21, 1688
b. Pope, Alexander

June 26, 1688
d. Cudworth, Ralph

August 15, 1688
b. Frederick William I

August 25, 1688
d. Morgan, Henry, Sir

August 31, 1688
d. Bunyan, John

October 9, 1688
d. Perrault, Claude

October 22, 1688
b. Nadir Shah

1689

January 18, 1689
b. Montesquieu, Charles Louis de
Secondat, Baron

April 16, 1689
d. Behn, Aphra

April 19, 1689
d. Christina

May 26, 1689
b. Montagu, Mary Wortley, Lady

July 31, 1689
b. Richardson, Samuel

August 12, 1689
d. Innocent XI, Pope

December 29, 1689
d. Sydenham, Thomas

1690

b. Ged, William
d. Valdes-Leal, Juan de

January 22, 1690
b. Lancret, Nicolas

February 22, 1690
d. Le Brun, Charles
b. Beissel, Johann Conrad

April 25, 1690
d. Teniers, David, the Younger

May 20, 1690
d. Eliot, John

1691

b. Frelinghuysen, Theodorus Jacobus
b. Pannini, Giovanni Paolo
d. Etherege, George, Sir
d. Meer, Jan van der

January 13, 1691
d. Fox, George

May 16, 1691
d. Leisler, Jacob
d. Cuyp, Aelbert Jacobsz(oon)

December 8, 1691
d. Baxter, Richard

December 30, 1691
d. Boyle, Robert

1692

b. Mottley, John
b. Read, Mary
d. Bishop, Bridget
d. Wang Fu-chih

January 23, 1692
b. Caslon, William

April 5, 1692
b. Lecouvreur, Adrienne

April 8, 1692
b. Tartini, Giuseppe

May 18, 1692
b. Butler, Joseph

November 20, 1692
d. Shadwell, Thomas

1693

b. Cartouche, Louis Dominique
b. Dinwiddie, Robert
b. Haywood, Eliza
d. Kalf, Willem

January 29, 1693
b. Anna Ivanovna
b. Bradley, James

May 24, 1693
b. Donner, Georg Raphael

May 25, 1693
d. La Fayette, Comtesse de
d. Blount, Charles

September 3, 1693
b. Locatelli, Pietro Antonio

1694

April 25, 1694
b. Burlington, Richard Boyle, Earl

June 4, 1694
b. Quesnay, Francois

August 5, 1694
b. Leo, Leonardo

August 8, 1694
b. Hutcheson, Francis

September 22, 1694
b. Chesterfield, Philip Dormer, Earl

October 26, 1694
d. Pufendorf, Samuel von

October 31, 1694
b. Yngjo

November 21, 1694
b. Voltaire

November 24, 1694
d. Talon, Jean

November 28, 1694
d. Basho

November 30, 1694
d. Malpighi, Marcello

December 2, 1694
b. Shirley, William
d. Puget, Pierre

December 28, 1694
d. Mary, II

1695

b. Braddock, Edward
b. Pater, Jean-Baptiste
d. Huang Tsung-hsi

February 18, 1695
d. Phips, William, Sir

April 13, 1695
d. LaFontaine, Jean de

April 17, 1695
d. Juana Ines de la Cruz, Sor

April 23, 1695
d. Vaughan, Henry

June 8, 1695
d. Huygens, Christian

October 23, 1695
b. Cuvillies, Francois

November 21, 1695
d. Purcell, Henry

November 28, 1695
d. Wood, Anthony

1696

b. Richelieu, Louis Francois Armand de
d. Richer, Jean

March 5, 1696
b. Tiepolo, Giambattista

April 17, 1696
d. Sevigne, Marie de Rabutin-Chantal, Marquise de

May 10, 1696
d. LaBruyere, Jean de

June 17, 1696
d. Sobieski, John, III

June 27, 1696
b. Pepperell, William, Sir

October 28, 1696
b. Saxe, Maurice

December 22, 1696
b. Oglethorpe, James Edward

1697

b. Mabuchi, Kamo
b. Savage, Richard
b. Zenger, John Peter

January 1, 1697
b. Dupleix, Joseph Francois

April 1, 1697
b. Prevost d'Exiles, Antoine Francois, Abbe

April 23, 1697
b. Anson, George
d. Aubrey, John

July 11, 1697
b. Anville, Jean Baptiste Bourguignon d'

August 6, 1697
b. Charles VII

August 18, 1697
d. Vieira, Antonio

October 18, 1697
b. Canaletto, Antonio

November 10, 1697
b. Hogarth, William

1698

January 3, 1698
b. Metastasio, Pietro

March 1, 1698
d. Redi, Francesco

March 19, 1698
b. Calas, Jean

July 19, 1698
b. Bodmer, Johann Jakob
b. Logroscino, Nicola

October 23, 1698
b. Gabriel, Ange-Jacques

October 30, 1698
b. Troger, Paul

November 22, 1698
b. Vaudreuil-Cavagnal, Marquis de

November 28, 1698
d. Frontenac, Louis de Buade de

1699

February 16, 1699
d. Monnoyer, Jean-Baptiste

March 23, 1699
b. Bartram, John

March 25, 1699
b. Hasse, Johann Adolph

April 26, 1699
d. Racine, Jean Baptiste

May 13, 1699
b. Pombal, Marques de

August 17, 1699
b. Jussieu, Bernard de

November 2, 1699
b. Chardin, Jean Baptiste Simeon

1700

b. Ba'al Shem Tov, Israel
b. Bonny, Anne
b. Bordoni, Faustina
b. Cuzzoni, Francesca
b. Diver, Jenny
b. Vincennes, Francois Marie Bissot
d. Bourgeoys, Marguerite

February 8, 1700
b. Bernoulli, Daniel
d. Jolliet, Louis

May 1, 1700
d. Dryden, John

May 26, 1700
b. Zinzendorf, Nikolaus Ludwig von,
Count

June 20, 1700
b. Faneuil, Peter

September 11, 1700
b. Thomson, James

September 15, 1700
d. LeNotre, Andre

November 1, 1700
d. Charles, II

November 25, 1700
d. Van Cortlandt, Stephanus

1701

d. Hennepin, Louis

May 23, 1701
d. Kidd, William, Captain

June 2, 1701
d. Scudery, Madeleine de

September 16, 1701
d. James II

November 27, 1701
b. Celsius, Anders

December 1, 1701
d. Clarke, Jeremiah

1702

b. Sheppard, Jack

March 8, 1702
d. William III

April 27, 1702
d. Bart, Jean

December 22, 1702
b. Liotard, Jean-Etienne

1703

d. Moronobu, Hishikawa

February 5, 1703
b. Tennent, Gilbert

February 13, 1703
b. Dodsley, Robert

March 3, 1703
d. Hooke, Robert

May 16, 1703
d. Perrault, Charles

May 26, 1703
d. Pepys, Samuel

June 28, 1703
b. Wesley, John

September 29, 1703
b. Boucher, Francois

October 5, 1703
b. Edwards, Jonathan

1704

February 24, 1704
d. Charpentier, Marc-Antoine

April 12, 1704
d. Bossuet, Jacques Benigne

October 28, 1704
d. Locke, John

1705

b. Chauncy, Charles
b. Wood, John the Elder
d. Aulnoy, Marie-Catherine Jumel de
Berneville
d. Beauchamp, Pierre

January 3, 1705
d. Giordano, Luca

January 17, 1705
d. Ray, John

January 24, 1705
b. Farinelli

February 5, 1705
d. Spener, Philipp Jakob

May 27, 1705
d. Wigglesworth, Michael

July 12, 1705
d. Oates, Titus

August 8, 1705
b. Hartley, David

October 17, 1705
d. Lenclos, Ninon de

October 31, 1705
b. Clement XIV, Pope

1706

b. Gist, Christopher
b. Turpin, Dick

January 17, 1706
b. Franklin, Benjamin

January 28, 1706
b. Baskerville, John

February 27, 1706
d. Evelyn, John

March 3, 1706
d. Pachelbel, Johann

October 18, 1706
b. Galuppi, Baldassare

December 28, 1706
d. Bayle, Pierre

1707

b. Crebillon, Claude Prosper Jolyot de
b. LaPlace, Pierre-Antoine de
b. Luzzato, Moses Hayyim
d. Velde, Willem van de

January 20, 1707
b. Frederick Louis

February 20, 1707
d. Aurangzeb

February 25, 1707
b. Goldoni, Carlo

March 7, 1707
b. Hopkins, Stephen

March 30, 1707
d. Vauban, Sebastien LePrestre de

April 15, 1707
b. Euler, Leonhard

April 20, 1707
d. Denner, Johann Christoph

April 22, 1707
b. Fielding, Henry

April 29, 1707
d. Farquhar, George

May 9, 1707
d. Buxtehude, Dietrich

May 23, 1707
b. Linnaeus, Carolus

September 7, 1707
b. Buffon, Georges Louis Leclerc

December 18, 1707
b. Wesley, Charles

December 27, 1707
d. Mabillon, Jean

1708

b. Pitt, William, the Elder
d. Makemie, Francis
d. Ochterveldt, Jacob Lucasz

May 6, 1708
d. Laval, Francois Xavier de

May 11, 1708
d. Mansart, Jules Hardouin

July 22, 1708
b. Ames, Nathaniel

October 1, 1708
d. Blow, John

October 16, 1708
b. Haller, Albrecht von

November 28, 1708
d. Tournefort, Joseph Pitton de

1709

b. Cleland, John
d. Mazepa, Ivan Stepanovich

April 2, 1709
d. Gaulli, Giovanni Battista

July 5, 1709
b. Silhouette, Etienne de

September 18, 1709
b. Johnson, Samuel

December 7, 1709
d. Hobbema, Meindert

December 18, 1709
b. Elizabeth Petrovna

December 25, 1709
b. La Mettrie, Julien Offray de

1710

b. Boyce, William
b. Forbes, John
d. Radisson, Pierre Espirit

January 4, 1710
b. Pergolesi, Giovanni Battista

February 15, 1710
b. Louis XV

February 27, 1710
d. Duluth, Daniel (Greysolon)

March 12, 1710
b. Arne, Thomas Augustine

April 12, 1710
b. Carver, Jonathan
b. Majorano, Gaetano

April 15, 1710
b. Camargo, Marie Anne de Cupis de

April 26, 1710
b. Reid, Thomas

April 27, 1710
d. Betterton, Thomas

June 10, 1710
b. Short, James

October 12, 1710
b. Trumbull, Jonathan

October 24, 1710
b. Butler, Alban

November 13, 1710
b. Favart, Charles Simon

November 22, 1710
b. Bach, Wilhelm Friedemann

1711

b. Hart, John
d. Kino, Eusebio Francisco

March 13, 1711
d. Boileau(-Despreaux), Nicolas

April 17, 1711
d. Joseph I

April 22, 1711
b. Wheelock, Eleazar

April 26, 1711
b. Hume, David

May 18, 1711
b. Boscovich, Ruggiero Giuseppe

September 6, 1711
b. Muhlenberg, Heinrich Melchior

September 9, 1711
b. Hutchinson, Thomas

September 25, 1711
b. Ch'ien Lung

November 19, 1711
b. Lomonosov, Mikhail Vasilyevich

1712

b. Frederick II
d. Danby, Thomas Osborne

January 24, 1712
b. Frederick the Great

February 29, 1712
b. Montcalm, Louis Joseph de

March 25, 1712
d. Grew, Nehemiah

June 28, 1712
b. Rousseau, Jean Jacques
b. Bernard, Francis, Sir

July 13, 1712
d. Cromwell, Richard

September 15, 1712
d. Godolphin, Sidney

October 5, 1712
b. Guardi, Francesco

February 19, 1719
b. Rodney, George Brydges, Baron

March 13, 1719
d. Bottger, Johann Friedrich

April 15, 1719
d. Maintenon, Francoise d'Aubigne,
Marquise de

June 17, 1719
d. Addison, Joseph

November 14, 1719
b. Mozart, Leopold

December 31, 1719
d. Flamsteed, John

1720

b. Elijah Ben Solomon
b. Hammon, Jupiter
b. Hargreaves, James
b. Lewis, Andrew
b. Pontiac
d. Bonny, Anne

January 2, 1720
b. Galvez, Jose de

January 27, 1720
b. Foote, Samuel

January 30, 1720
b. Bellotto, Bernardo

May 11, 1720
b. Munchhausen, Hieronymus Karl
Friedrich von, Baron

June 12, 1720
b. Pinto, Isaac

July 18, 1720
b. White, Gilbert

August 12, 1720
b. Ekhof, Konrad

October 4, 1720
b. Piranesi, Giovanni Battista

October 8, 1720
b. Mayhew, Jonathan

October 10, 1720
d. Coysevox, Antoine

October 19, 1720
b. Woolman, John

December 4, 1720
d. Read, Mary

December 31, 1720
b. Charles Edward Louis Philip
Casimir Stuart
b. Stuart, Charles Edward Louis Philip

1721

b. Gage, Thomas
b. Haidar Ali
b. Turgot, A(nne) R(obert) J(acques),
Baron de l'Aulne
d. Doggett, Thomas
d. Selkirk, Alexander

January 21, 1721
b. Murray, James
b. Smollett, Tobias George

April 13, 1721
b. Hanson, John

April 19, 1721
b. Sherman, Roger

June 29, 1721
b. Kalb, Johann de

July 8, 1721
d. Yale, Elihu

July 18, 1721
d. Watteau, Jean Antoine

August 3, 1721
d. Gibbons, Grinling
b. Randolph, Peyton

September 9, 1721
b. Pendleton, Edmund

September 11, 1721
d. Camerarius, Rudolf Jakob

September 17, 1721
b. Hopkins, Samuel

September 18, 1721
d. Prior, Matthew

September 19, 1721
b. Robertson, William

October 28, 1721
d. Rogers, John

November 28, 1721
d. Cartouche, Louis Dominique

December 25, 1721
b. Collins, William

December 29, 1721
b. Pompadour, Jeanne Antoinette
Poisson

1722

February 24, 1722
b. Burgoyne, John, Sir

March 11, 1722
d. Toland, John
b. Warton, Joseph

April 21, 1722
d. Beverley, Robert

April 22, 1722
b. Smart, Christopher

June 16, 1722
d. Marlborough, John Churchill, Duke

September 13, 1722
b. Grasse, Francois Joseph Paul de,
Count

September 27, 1722
b. Adams, Samuel

December 20, 1722
d. K'ang-hsi

1723

b. Attucks, Crispus
b. Chambers, William, Sir
b. Ferguson, Adam
b. Occom, Samson
b. Portola, Gaspar de

February 5, 1723
b. Witherspoon, John

February 17, 1723
b. Mayer, Johann Tobias

February 25, 1723
d. Wren, Christopher, Sir

February 26, 1723
d. D'Urfey, Thomas

April 5, 1723
d. Fischer von Erlach, Johann
Bernhard

June 5, 1723
b. Smith, Adam

July 10, 1723
b. Blackstone, William, Sir

July 11, 1723
b. Marmontel, Jean Francois

July 16, 1723
b. Reynolds, Joshua, Sir

August 23, 1723
d. Mather, Increase

August 26, 1723
d. Leeuwenhoek, Antonie van

November 7, 1723
d. Kneller, Godfrey, Sir
b. Holbach, Baron d'

December 2, 1723
d. Orleans, Philippe II d'

December 22, 1723
b. Abel, Karl Friedrich

1724

b. Laclede, Pierre
b. Michell, John
b. Morton, John
b. Queensberry, William Douglas, Duke
d. Kelsey, Henry

January 9, 1724
b. Backus, Isaac

March 26, 1724
b. Laurens, Henry

April 12, 1724
b. Hall, Lyman

April 22, 1724
b. Kant, Immanuel

May 24, 1724
d. Harley, Robert, 1st Earl of Oxford and Earl Mortimer

June 8, 1724
b. Maulbertsch, Franz Anton
b. Smeaton, John

July 2, 1724
b. Klopstock, Friedrich Gottlieb

August 24, 1724
b. Stubbs, George

September 3, 1724
b. Carleton, Guy

September 11, 1724
b. Basedow, Johann Bernhard

September 27, 1724
b. Busching, Anton Friedrich

November 16, 1724
d. Sheppard, Jack

1725

b. Guadagni, Gaetano
b. Mason, George
d. Churriguera, Jose Benito de

January 6, 1725
d. Chikamatsu, Monzaemon

January 16, 1725
b. Piccinni, Nicola

January 28, 1725
d. Peter the Great

February 5, 1725
b. Otis, James

March 19, 1725
b. Howe, Richard

April 5, 1725
b. Casanova (de Seingalt), Giovanni Giacomo

April 8, 1725
d. Wise, John

July 1, 1725
b. Rochambeau, Jean Baptiste Donatien de Vimeur, Comte

July 24, 1725
b. Newton, John

August 21, 1725
b. Greuze, Jean-Baptiste

September 29, 1725
b. Clive, Robert

November 22, 1725
b. Gunther, Ignaz

November 24, 1725
d. Scarlatti, Alessandro

1726

b. Alexander, William
b. Stirling, Lord
b. Wythe, George

January 25, 1726
d. Delisle, Guillaume

February 15, 1726
b. Clark, Abraham

March 16, 1726
d. Vanbrugh, John, Sir

April 5, 1726
b. Harrison, Benjamin

April 7, 1726
b. Burney, Charles

April 8, 1726
b. Morris, Lewis

June 3, 1726
b. Hutton, James
b. Otterbein, Philip William

July 17, 1726
d. Cadogan, William, Earl

August 7, 1726
b. Bowdoin, James

September 7, 1726
b. Philidor, Francois Andre Danican

September 16, 1726
d. Prandtauer, Jakob

November 26, 1726
b. Wolcott, Oliver, Sr.

1727

b. Tiepolo, Giovanni Domenico

January 2, 1727
b. Wolfe, James

February 8, 1727
b. Deluc, Jean Andre

March 20, 1727
d. Newton, Isaac, Sir

March 30, 1727
b. Traetta, Tommaso

May 14, 1727
b. Gainsborough, Thomas

June 12, 1727
d. George I

October 17, 1727
b. Wilkes, John

December 22, 1727
b. Ellery, William

1728

b. Hesselius, John
d. Livingston, Robert

January 9, 1728
b. Warton, Thomas

February 7, 1728
d. Iberville, Pierre Le Moyne, Sieur d'

February 11, 1728
d. Stoddard, Solomon

February 12, 1728
d. Steffani, Agostino

February 13, 1728
b. Hunter, John
d. Mather, Cotton

February 16, 1728
b. Shippen, Edward

March 5, 1728
d. Nicholson, Francis

March 22, 1728
b. Mengs, Anton Raphael

April 16, 1728
b. Black, Joseph

April 23, 1728
b. Wallis, Samuel

July 3, 1728
b. Adam, Robert

July 26, 1728
b. Gates, Horatio

August 28, 1728
b. Stark, John

September 3, 1728
b. Boulton, Matthew

September 14, 1728
b. Warren, Mercy Otis

September 23, 1728
d. Thomasius

October 7, 1728
b. Rodney, Caesar

October 28, 1728
b. Cook, James, Captain

November 10, 1728
b. Goldsmith, Oliver
b. Herkimer, Nicholas

December 2, 1728
b. Galiani, Ferdinando

December 25, 1728
b. Hiller, Johann Adam

1729

b. Tryon, William

January 12, 1729
b. Burke, Edmund
b. Spallanzani, Lazzaro

January 19, 1729
d. Congreve, William

January 22, 1729
b. Lessing, Gotthold Ephraim

March 21, 1729
d. Law, John

May 2, 1729
b. Catherine the Great

May 13, 1729
b. Stiegel, Henry William

May 17, 1729
d. Clarke, Samuel

June 24, 1729
d. Taylor, Edward

August 3, 1729
b. Caswell, Richard

August 5, 1729
d. Newcomen, Thomas

August 10, 1729
b. Howe, William, Viscount

September 1, 1729
d. Steele, Richard, Sir

September 6, 1729
b. Mendelssohn, Moses

October 17, 1729
b. Monsigny, Pierre-Alexandre

November 11, 1729
b. Bougainville, Louis-Antoine de

November 21, 1729
b. Bartlett, Josiah

November 25, 1729
b. Suvorov, Aleksandr V

November 28, 1729
b. Estaing, Charles Henri Hector,
Comte d'

November 30, 1729
b. Seabury, Samuel

December 1, 1729
b. Sarti, Giuseppe

December 14, 1729
d. Franceschini, Marcantonio

1730

b. Christie, James
b. Fairfax, Sally
b. Hutchins, Thomas
b. Mason, Charles
b. Zimmermann, Johann Baptist and
Domenikus

January 1, 1730
d. Sewall, Samuel

January 6, 1730
b. Chittenden, Thomas

January 14, 1730
b. Whipple, William

January 23, 1730
b. Hewes, Joseph

March 10, 1730
b. Ross, George

March 20, 1730
d. Lecouvreur, Adrienne

May 13, 1730
b. Rockingham, 2nd Marquess of

June 14, 1730
b. Sacchini, Antonio

July 1, 1730
b. Sears, Isaac

July 12, 1730
b. Wedgwood, Josiah

July 21, 1730
b. Adam, James

August 27, 1730
b. Hamann, Johann Georg

September 17, 1730
b. Steuben, Friedrich Wilhelm Ludolf
Gerhard Augustin, Baron

September 27, 1730
d. Eusden, Laurence

October 1, 1730
b. Stockton, Richard

October 15, 1730
d. Cadillac, Antoine de la Mothe

October 28, 1730
d. Rottmayr, Johann Michael

December 4, 1730
b. Moultrie, William

December 8, 1730
b. Ingenhousz, Jan

December 14, 1730
b. Bruce, James

1731

b. Franklin, William
b. Galloway, Joseph
b. Lee, Charles
d. Taylor, Brook

January 27, 1731
d. Cristofori, Bartolomeo di Francesco
b. Churchill, Charles

March 11, 1731
b. Paine, Robert Treat

April 23, 1731
b. Williams, William

April 26, 1731
d. Defoe, Daniel

July 3, 1731
b. Huntington, Samuel

October 10, 1731
b. Cavendish, Henry

November 7, 1731
b. Rogers, Robert

November 9, 1731
b. Banneker, Benjamin

November 15, 1731
b. Cowper, William

December 12, 1731
b. Darwin, Erasmus

1732

b. Cornplanter

b. Dunmore, 4th Earl of
b. Marion, Francis
b. McDougall, Alexander

January 1, 1732
d. Nicolini

January 20, 1732
b. Lee, Richard Henry

January 24, 1732
b. Beaumarchais, Pierre Augustin
Caron de

February 19, 1732
b. Cumberland, Richard

February 22, 1732
b. Washington, George

February 29, 1732
d. Boulle, Andre Charles

March 31, 1732
b. Haydn, Joseph

April 5, 1732
b. Fragonard, Jean-Honore
b. Rittenhouse, David

April 6, 1732
b. Mutis, Jose Celestino

April 13, 1732
b. North, Frederick North, Baron

April 18, 1732
b. Colman, George

June 2, 1732
b. Washington, Martha (Dandridge
Custis)

July 11, 1732
b. Lalande, Joseph Jerome Lefrancais
de

September 30, 1732
b. Necker, Jacques

October 6, 1732
b. Maskelyne, Nevil

October 31, 1732
d. Victor Amadeus, II

November 8, 1732
b. Dickinson, John

December 4, 1732
d. Gay, John

December 17, 1732
b. Hastings, Warren

December 23, 1732
b. Arkwright, Richard, Sir

1733

b. Robert, Hubert
d. Mandeville, Bernard

January 17, 1733
d. Byng, George Torrington, Viscount

January 24, 1733
b. Lincoln, Benjamin

February 1, 1733
d. Augustus II

March 13, 1733
b. Priestley, Joseph

July 3, 1733
b. Copley, John Singleton

August 9, 1733
b. Clinton, James

August 22, 1733
b. Ducis, Jean Francois

September 5, 1733
b. Wieland, Christoph Martin

September 12, 1733
d. Couperin, Francois

September 18, 1733
b. Read, George

November 20, 1733
b. Schuyler, Philip John

1734

b. Heck, Barbara Ruckle

January 17, 1734
b. Gossec, Francois Joseph

January 31, 1734
b. Morris, Robert

May 14, 1734
d. Stahl, Georg Ernst

May 23, 1734
b. Mesmer, Franz Anton

August 14, 1734
b. Sumter, Thomas

October 7, 1734
b. Abercromby, Ralph, Sir

October 14, 1734
b. Lee, Francis Lightfoot

November 2, 1734
b. Boone, Daniel

December 15, 1734
b. Romney, George

December 17, 1734
b. Floyd, William

1735

b. Anza, Juan Bautista de
b. Gwinnett, Button
b. Handsome Lake
b. Raikes, Robert

January 1, 1735
b. Revere, Paul

January 8, 1735
b. Carroll, John

January 31, 1735
b. Crevecoeur, Michel-Guillaume Jean
de
b. Crevecoeur, (Hector) St. John de

February 27, 1735
b. Conway, Thomas
d. Arbuthnot, John

March 30, 1735
b. McKean, Thomas

April 20, 1735
b. Henderson, Richard

September 3, 1735
b. Bach, Johann Christian

October 16, 1735
b. Morgan, John

October 30, 1735
b. Adams, John

November 10, 1735
b. Sharp, Granville

November 22, 1735
b. Stewart, Dugald

1736

b. Brant, Molly
b. Morgan, Daniel
d. Pater, Jean-Baptiste

January 19, 1736
b. Watt, James

January 25, 1736
b. Lagrange, Joseph-Louis

January 31, 1736
d. Juvara, Filippo

February 29, 1736
b. Lee, Ann

March 16, 1736
d. Pergolesi, Giovanni Battista

March 21, 1736
b. Ledoux, Claude Nicolas

March 23, 1736
b. Saint Clair, Arthur
b. St. Clair, Arthur

March 25, 1736
d. Hawksmoor, Nicholas
d. Vincennes, Francois Marie Bissot

April 20, 1736
d. Eugene of Savoy

May 29, 1736
b. Henry, Patrick

June 14, 1736
b. Coulomb, Charles Augustin de

September 10, 1736
b. Braxton, Carter

September 15, 1736
b. Bailly, Jean Sylvain

September 16, 1736
d. Fahrenheit, Gabriel Daniel

October 27, 1736
b. Macpherson, James

December 2, 1736
b. Montgomery, Richard

1737

b. Abington, Fanny

January 12, 1737
b. Hancock, John

January 29, 1737
b. Paine, Thomas

March 2, 1737
b. Heath, William

May 8, 1737
b. Gibbon, Edward

September 9, 1737
b. Galvani, Luigi

September 19, 1737
b. Carroll, Charles

September 21, 1737
b. Hopkinson, Francis

December 17, 1737
b. Almon, John
d. Stradivari, Antonio

December 24, 1737
b. Deane, Silas

1738

b. Aleijadinho, O
b. Brown, Moses
b. Chang Hsueh-ch'eng

b. Clinton, Henry, Sir
b. Ward, Nancy
d. Miller, Joe

January 21, 1738
b. Allen, Ethan

March 15, 1738
b. Beccaria, Cesare

May 28, 1738
b. Guillotin, Joseph Ignace

June 4, 1738
b. George III

September 23, 1738
d. Boerhaave, Hermann

October 10, 1738
b. West, Benjamin

October 11, 1738
b. Phillip, Arthur

November 15, 1738
b. Herschel, William Frederick, Sir

December 20, 1738
b. Clodion

December 26, 1738
b. Nelson, Thomas, Jr.

December 31, 1738
b. Cornwallis, Charles, Marquis

1739

b. Boone, Rebecca B
b. Butler, Eleanor, Lady
b. Chalgrin, Francois
b. Walter, John, I

February 9, 1739
b. Bartram, William

March 16, 1739
b. Clymer, George

April 10, 1739
d. Turpin, Dick

July 24, 1739
d. Marcello, Benedetto

July 26, 1739
b. Clinton, George

August 31, 1739
b. Eberhard, Johann August
b. Rutledge, John

September 12, 1739
d. Keiser, Reinhard

September 13, 1739
b. Potemkin, Grigori Alexsandrovich

September 14, 1739
b. DuPont de Nemours, Pierre Samuel

November 2, 1739
b. Ditters, Karl

1740

b. Cort, Henry
b. Lee, Arthur
b. Leonard, Daniel
b. Revillagigedo, Conde de
b. Salomon, Haym
b. Schweppe, Jacob
b. Tandy, James Napper

February 4, 1740
b. Bellman, Carl Michael

February 16, 1740
b. Bodoni, Giambattista

February 17, 1740
b. Sullivan, John

March 18, 1740
d. Diver, Jenny
b. Pacchierotti, Gasparo

May 8, 1740
b. Paisiello, Giovanni

May 17, 1740
d. Cavalier, Jean

May 31, 1740
d. Frederick William I

June 2, 1740
b. Sade, Marquis (Donatien Alphonse Francoise) de

June 7, 1740
d. Spotswood, Alexander

August 14, 1740
b. Pius, VII

August 15, 1740
b. Claudius, Matthias

August 26, 1740
b. Montgolfier, Joseph Michel

August 31, 1740
b. Oberlin, Johann Friedrich

October 17, 1740
d. Anna Ivanovna

October 18, 1740
b. Boswell, James

October 23, 1740
b. Dalzel, Archibald

October 31, 1740
b. DeLoutherbourg, Philip James
b. Paca, William

November 4, 1740
b. Toplady, Augustus Montague

1741

b. Ali Pasha
b. Combe, William
b. Girty, Simon
b. Kirkland, Samuel
b. Pugachev, Yemelyan I
b. Walton, George
d. DeLancey, Stephen
d. Twining, Thomas

January 14, 1741
b. Arnold, Benedict

January 16, 1741
b. Piozzi, Hester Lynch Salisbury

February 7, 1741
b. Fuseli, Henry

February 10, 1741
b. Gretry, Andre Ernest Modeste

February 14, 1741
d. Fux, Johann Joseph

February 15, 1741
d. Donner, Georg Raphael

March 13, 1741
b. Joseph II

March 20, 1741
b. Houdon, Jean Antoine

April 15, 1741
b. Peale, Charles Willson

April 17, 1741
b. Chase, Samuel

May 17, 1741
b. Penn, John

June 11, 1741
b. Warren, Joseph

June 26, 1741
b. Langdon, John

July 27, 1741
d. Vivaldi, Antonio (Lucio)

August 4, 1741
d. Hamilton, Andrew

October 4, 1741
b. Malone, Edmund

October 18, 1741
b. Laclos, Pierre (Ambroise Francois)
Choderlos de

October 30, 1741
b. Kauffmann, Angelica

November 15, 1741
b. Lavater, Johann Casper

December 10, 1741
b. Murray, John

December 19, 1741
d. Bering, Vitus Jonassen

1742

b. Brant, Joseph
b. Bushnell, David
b. Johnson, John
b. Tupac Amaru

January 14, 1742
d. Halley, Edmund

May 13, 1742
b. Cutler, Manasseh

June 17, 1742
b. Hooper, William

June 26, 1742
b. Middleton, Arthur

July 14, 1742
d. Bentley, Richard

August 7, 1742
b. Greene, Nathanael

September 14, 1742
b. Wilson, James

December 9, 1742
b. Scheele, Karl Wilhelm

December 16, 1742
b. Blucher, Gebhard Leberecht von

1743

b. Stone, Thomas
b. Wyss, Johann David
d. Saint-Pierre, Abbe de

January 21, 1743
b. Fitch, John

January 25, 1743
b. Jacobi, Friedrich Heinrich

January 29, 1743
d. Fleury, Andre Hercule de

February 13, 1743
b. Banks, Joseph

February 19, 1743
b. Boccherini, Luigi

February 23, 1743
b. Rothschild, Mayer Amschel

February 28, 1743
b. Hauy, Rene Just

March 3, 1743
d. Faneuil, Peter

April 13, 1743
b. Jefferson, Thomas

April 18, 1743
d. Blair, James

April 24, 1743
b. Cartwright, Edmund

May 20, 1743
b. Toussaint l'Ouverture, Pierre
Dominique

May 24, 1743
b. Marat, Jean Paul

June 2, 1743
b. Cagliostro, Alessandro, Conte di

June 17, 1743
b. Lowell, John
b. Paley, William

August 1, 1743
d. Savage, Richard

August 11, 1743
b. Roentgen, David

August 13, 1743
b. Lavoisier, Antoine Laurent

September 14, 1743
d. Lancret, Nicolas

September 17, 1743
b. Condorcet, Marie-Jean-Antoine

October 5, 1743
b. Gazzaniga, Giuseppe
d. Carey, Henry

November 18, 1743
b. Ewald, Johannes

November 23, 1743
b. LaTour D'Auvergne, Theophile de

December 29, 1743
d. Rigaud, Hyacinthe

1744

b. Charlotte Sophia

January 23, 1744
d. Vico, Giovanni Battista

April 25, 1744
d. Celsius, Anders

May 30, 1744
d. Pope, Alexander

May 31, 1744
b. Edgeworth, Richard Lovell

July 17, 1744
b. Gerry, Elbridge

August 1, 1744
b. Lamarck, Jean Baptiste Pierre

August 25, 1744
b. Herder, Johann Gottfried von

August 26, 1744
d. Byrd, William
b. Reeve, Tapping

October 6, 1744
b. McGill, James

October 31, 1744
d. Leo, Leonardo

November 11, 1744
b. Adams, Abigail (Smith)

1745

b. Barry, John
b. Equiano, Olaudah
b. Hearne, Samuel
d. Guarneri, Giuseppe Antonio

January 1, 1745
b. Wayne, Anthony

January 7, 1745
b. Montgolfier, Jacques Etienne

January 20, 1745
d. Charles VII

February 18, 1745
b. Volta, Alessandro Giuseppe Antonio
Anastasio

February 20, 1745
b. Pye, Henry

March 4, 1745
b. Dibdin, Charles

March 14, 1745
b. Frank, Johann Peter

March 18, 1745
d. Walpole, Robert

April 6, 1745
b. Dawes, William

April 20, 1745
b. Pinel, Philippe

April 29, 1745
b. Ellsworth, Oliver

July 17, 1745
b. Pickering, Timothy

August 20, 1745
b. Asbury, Francis

August 26, 1745
b. Mackenzie, Henry

September 5, 1745
b. Kutuzov, Mikhail Ilarionovich

September 23, 1745
b. Sevier, John

October 7, 1745
b. Rutgers, Henry

October 19, 1745
d. Swift, Jonathan

October 29, 1745
b. Lee, Thomas Sim

December 12, 1745
b. Jay, John

December 16, 1745
d. Hildebrandt, Johann Lucas von

December 24, 1745
b. Paterson, William
b. Rush, Benjamin

1746

b. Azara, Felix de
b. Billings, William
b. Grattan, Henry
d. Hutcheson, Francis

January 12, 1746
b. Pestalozzi, Johann Heinrich

January 24, 1746
b. Gustavus, III

February 12, 1746
b. Kosciuszko, Thaddeus

February 25, 1746
b. Pinckney, Charles Cotesworth

March 30, 1746
b. Goya y Lucientes, Francisco Jose
de

May 10, 1746
b. Monge, Gaspard

June 10, 1746
b. Fouquier-Tinville, Antoine Quentin

July 9, 1746
d. Philip, V

July 23, 1746
b. Galvez, Bernardo de

July 28, 1746
b. Heyward, Thomas, Jr.
d. Zenger, John Peter

August 19, 1746
b. Du Barry, Marie Jeanne Gomard de
Vaubernier, Comtesse

November 12, 1746
b. Charles, Jacques-Alexandre-Cesar

November 27, 1746
b. Livingston, Robert R

1747

b. Shays, Daniel
d. Luzzato, Moses Hayyim

January 10, 1747
b. Breguet, Abraham Louis

March 4, 1747
b. Pulaski, Kazimierz

April 16, 1747
b. Baranov, Aleksandr Andreievich

May 5, 1747
b. Leopold, II

June 19, 1747
d. Nadir Shah

June 24, 1747
b. O'Keeffe, John

July 6, 1747
b. Jones, John Paul

July 9, 1747
d. Bononcini, Giovanni Battista

October 7, 1747
b. Zane, Ebenezer

October 9, 1747
d. Brainerd, David

November 17, 1747
d. Lesage, Alain-Rene

December 12, 1747
b. Seward, Anna

1748

d. Frelinghuysen, Theodorus Jacobus

February 9, 1748
b. Martin, Luther

February 15, 1748
b. Bentham, Jeremy

March 19, 1748
b. Hicks, Elias

April 12, 1748
d. Kent, William

April 13, 1748
b. Bramah, Joseph

May 3, 1748
b. Sieyes, Emmanuel Joseph

June 22, 1748
b. Day, Thomas

August 27, 1748
d. Thomson, James

August 30, 1748
b. David, Jacques Louis

September 1, 1748
b. Schikaneder, Emanuel

September 15, 1748
d. Bracegirdle, Anne

October 19, 1748
b. Jefferson, Martha (Wayles Skelton)

November 11, 1748
b. Charles, IV

November 12, 1748
b. Tiradentes

November 25, 1748
d. Watts, Isaac

1749

b. Brackenridge, H(ugh) H(enry)
b. Hickey, William
b. Peale, James
b. Stevens, John
d. Catesby, Mark

January 16, 1749
b. Alfieri, Vittorio

January 24, 1749
b. Fox, Charles James

March 9, 1749
b. Mirabeau, Honore Gabriel Riquetti

March 10, 1749
b. DaPonte, Lorenzo

March 12, 1749
d. Magnasco, Alessandro Lissandrino

March 23, 1749
b. Laplace, Pierre Simon, Marquis de

April 2, 1749
b. Ramsay, David

May 17, 1749
b. Jenner, Edward

August 5, 1749
b. Lynch, Thomas, Jr.

August 28, 1749
b. Goethe, Johann Wolfgang von

September 25, 1749
b. Werner, Abraham Gottlob

October 8, 1749
b. Levasseur, Rosalie

October 19, 1749
d. Ged, William

October 27, 1749
b. Strutt, Joseph

November 17, 1749
b. Appert, Nicolas

November 23, 1749
b. Rutledge, Edward

December 5, 1749
d. la Verendrye, Sieur de

December 9, 1749
b. Berthollet, Claude Louis, Comte

December 17, 1749
b. Cimarosa, Domenico

1750

b. Crosby, Enoch
b. DuSable, Jean Baptiste
b. Fergusson, Robert
b. Ho-shen
b. Salem, Peter
b. Tipu Sultan
b. Wilson, Sarah
d. Senesino

January 23, 1750
d. Muratori, Lodovico Antonio

January 30, 1750
b. Thomas, Isaiah

March 28, 1750
b. Miranda, Francisco de

April 24, 1750
b. Trumbull, John

May 2, 1750
b. Andre, John

May 20, 1750
b. Girard, Stephen

May 31, 1750
b. Hardenberg, Karl August von

June 24, 1750
b. Dolomieu, Deodat Guy Gratet de

July 25, 1750
b. Knox, Henry

July 28, 1750
d. Bach, Johann Sebastian

August 18, 1750
b. Salieri, Antonio

August 24, 1750
b. Bonaparte, Letizia

October 3, 1750
d. Mottley, John

October 13, 1750
b. Pitcher, Molly

November 11, 1750
d. Zeno, Apostolo

November 30, 1750
d. Saxe, Maurice

1751

b. Sheraton, Thomas
d. Smibert, John
d. Yoshimune, Tokugawa

January 17, 1751
d. Albinoni, Tommaso

February 23, 1751
b. Dearborn, Henry

March 16, 1751
b. Madison, James

March 20, 1751
d. Frederick Louis

April 3, 1751
b. Lemoyne, Jean-Baptiste

May 11, 1751
b. Earle, Ralph

June 17, 1751
b. Humphreys, Joshua

August 19, 1751
b. Prescott, Samuel

October 5, 1751
b. Iredell, James

October 30, 1751
b. Sheridan, Richard Brinsley

October 31, 1751
d. Logan, James

November 11, 1751
d. La Mettrie, Julien Offray de

November 12, 1751
b. Corbin, Margaret Cochran

December 12, 1751
d. Bolingbroke, Henry St. John, Viscount

December 16, 1751
b. Cabot, George

1752

b. Debrett, John
b. Nash, John
b. Repton, Humphry

January 1, 1752
b. Ross, Betsy

January 2, 1752
b. Freneau, Philip Morin

January 24, 1752
b. Clementi, Muzio

January 31, 1752
b. Morris, Gouverneur

February 21, 1752
b. Rochester, Nathaniel

February 25, 1752
b. Simcoe, John Graves

April 4, 1752
b. Zingarelli, Nicola Antonio

May 11, 1752
b. Blumenbach, Johann Friedrich

May 14, 1752
b. Dwight, Timothy

June 13, 1752
b. Burney, Fanny

June 16, 1752
d. Butler, Joseph
d. Washington, Lawrence

July 7, 1752
b. Jacquard, Joseph Marie

July 20, 1752
d. Pepusch, Johann Christoph

September 18, 1752
b. Legendre, Adrien Marie

October 28, 1752
b. Chongjo

November 19, 1752
b. Clark, George Rogers

November 20, 1752
b. Chatterton, Thomas

November 25, 1752
b. Reichardt, Johann Friedrich

1753

b. Leroy
b. Utamaro, Kitagawa
b. Wheatley, Phillis

November 12, 1753
b. Taylor, John

January 11, 1753
d. Sloane, Hans, Sir

January 14, 1753
d. Berkeley, George

March 9, 1753
b. Kleber, Jean Baptiste

March 26, 1753
b. Rumford, Count

March 27, 1753
b. Bell, Andrew

April 1, 1753
b. Maistre, Joseph de

April 28, 1753
b. Achard, Franz Karl

May 8, 1753
b. Hidalgo y Costilla, Miguel

May 13, 1753
b. Carnot, Lazare

May 23, 1753
b. Viotti, Giovanni Battista

June 11, 1753
b. Kamehameha I

June 24, 1753
b. Hull, William

July 4, 1753
b. Blanchard, Francois

July 18, 1753
d. Neumann, Balthasar

August 10, 1753
b. Randolph, Edmund Jennings

August 12, 1753
b. Bewick, Thomas

September 10, 1753
b. Soane, John, Sir

October 18, 1753
b. Cambaceres, Jean Jacques Regis de

November 5, 1753
b. Glover, John

December 3, 1753
d. Burlington, Richard Boyle, Earl

1754

d. Boffrand, Gabriel Germain

January 18, 1754
b. Martin y Soler, Vicente

January 29, 1754
b. Cleaveland, Moses

February 13, 1754
b. Talleyrand-Perigord, Charles
   Maurice de

March 4, 1754
b. Waterhouse, Benjamin

March 17, 1754
b. Roland (de La Platiere), Jeanne-
   Marie

March 24, 1754
b. Barlow, Joel

April 9, 1754
d. Wolff, Christian von, Baron

May 23, 1754
d. Wood, John the Elder

July 11, 1754
b. Bowdler, Thomas

July 16, 1754
b. Spode, Josiah

August 2, 1754
b. L'Enfant, Pierre Charles

August 5, 1754
d. Gibbs, James

August 21, 1754
b. Tarleton, Banastre, Sir

August 23, 1754
b. Louis XVI

September 9, 1754
b. Bligh, William, Captain

September 20, 1754
b. Paul, I

September 26, 1754
b. Proust, Joseph Louis

October 8, 1754
d. Fielding, Henry

November 27, 1754
d. De Moivre, Abraham

December 24, 1754
b. Crabbe, George

1755

b. Dixon, George
b. Louis, XVIII
b. Mackenzie, Alexander, Sir
b. Ponsonby, Sarah
b. Uthman don Fodio
d. Caffieri, Jacques

January 11, 1755
b. Hamilton, Alexander

February 10, 1755
d. Montesquieu, Charles Louis de
   Secondat, Baron

March 2, 1755
d. Saint-Simon, Duc de

March 24, 1755
b. King, Rufus

April 1, 1755
b. Brillat-Savarin, Jean Anthelme

April 10, 1755
b. Hahnemann, Samuel

April 11, 1755
b. Parkinson, James

April 16, 1755
b. Vigee-Lebrun, Marie-Louise-Elisabeth

April 30, 1755
d. Oudry, Jean-Baptiste

May 10, 1755
b. Gray, Robert

May 22, 1755
b. Coxe, Tench

June 6, 1755
b. Hale, Nathan

June 30, 1755
b. Barras, Paul Francois Jean Nicolas, Comte de

July 5, 1755
b. Siddons, Sarah Kemble

July 6, 1755
b. Flaxman, John

July 13, 1755
d. Braddock, Edward

August 13, 1755
b. Unanue, Jose Hipolito
d. Durante, Francesco

August 29, 1755
b. Dabrowski, Jan Henryk

September 13, 1755
b. Evans, Oliver

September 24, 1755
b. Marshall, John

October 2, 1755
b. Adams, Hannah

November 2, 1755
b. Marie Antoinette

November 12, 1755
b. Scharnhorst, Gerhard Johann David von

December 3, 1755
b. Stuart, Gilbert Charles

December 22, 1755
b. Couthon, Georges

1756

b. Red Jacket

January 27, 1756
b. Mozart, Wolfgang Amadeus

January 29, 1756
b. Lee, Henry

February 6, 1756
b. Burr, Aaron

February 25, 1756
d. Haywood, Eliza

March 3, 1756
b. Godwin, William

March 4, 1756
b. Raeburn, Henry, Sir

March 13, 1756
d. Bernacchi, Antonio Maria

June 4, 1756
b. Chaptal, Jean Antoine, Comte de Chanteloup

June 6, 1756
b. Trumbull, John
b. Rowlandson, Thomas

July 5, 1756
b. Rush, William

August 13, 1756
b. Gillray, James

September 21, 1756
b. McAdam, John Loudoun

1757

b. Alison, Archibald
b. Cugoano, Ottobah
b. Hebert, Jacques Rene
b. McIntire, Samuel
b. Pinckney, Charles
b. Tyler, Royall
b. Wilkinson, James
d. Vernon, Edward, Sir

February 1, 1757
b. Kemble, John Philip

February 3, 1757
b. Volney, (Constantin) Francois Chasseboeuf, Comte de

April 9, 1757
b. Boguslawski, Wojciech

April 15, 1757
d. Carriera, Rosalba Giovanna

June 22, 1757
b. Vancouver, George

July 23, 1757
d. Scarlatti, Domenico Girolamo

August 28, 1757
d. Hartley, David

September 6, 1757
b. Lafayette, Marie Joseph Paul, Marquis

October 26, 1757
b. Stein, Heinrich Friedrich Karl vom und zum, Baron

November 1, 1757
b. Canova, Antonio
b. Rapp, George

November 28, 1757
b. Blake, William

December 12, 1757
d. Cibber, Colley

1758

b. Dessalines, Jean Jacques

January 7, 1758
d. Ramsay, Allan

January 22, 1758
b. Watson, Elkanah

March 9, 1758
b. Gall, Franz Joseph

March 22, 1758
d. Edwards, Jonathan

April 4, 1758
b. Hoppner, John
b. Prud'hon, Pierre Paul
b. Prudhon, Pierre-Paul

April 9, 1758
b. Ames, Fisher

April 28, 1758
b. Monroe, James

May 6, 1758
b. Robespierre, Maximilien Francois de

September 29, 1758
b. Nelson, Horatio Nelson, Viscount

October 11, 1758
b. Olbers, Heinrich Wilhelm Matthaus

October 16, 1758
b. Webster, Noah

December 5, 1758
d. Fasch, Johann Friedrich

December 17, 1758
b. Macon, Nathaniel

1759

b. McGillivray, Alexander
d. Gist, Christopher

January 11, 1759
b. Lunardi, Vincenzo

January 17, 1759
b. Cuffe, Paul

January 25, 1759
b. Burns, Robert

February 15, 1759
b. Wolf, Friedrich August

March 11, 1759
d. Forbes, John

April 14, 1759
d. Handel, George Frideric

April 27, 1759
b. Godwin, Mary Wollstonecraft

May 21, 1759
b. Fouche, Joseph

May 28, 1759
b. Pitt, William, the Younger

June 12, 1759
d. Collins, William

July 6, 1759
d. Pepperell, William, Sir

August 24, 1759
b. Wilberforce, William

September 13, 1759
d. Wolfe, James

September 14, 1759
d. Montcalm, Louis Joseph de

September 29, 1759
b. Beckford, William

October 1, 1759
b. Weems, Mason Locke
b. Wood, Sarah Sayward Barrell
   Keating

October 22, 1759
b. Cooper, Thomas

October 28, 1759
b. Danton, Georges Jacques

November 10, 1759
b. Schiller, Friedrich von

1760

b. Delaware Prophet
b. Francisco, Peter
b. Shippen, Margaret
d. Alaungpaya
d. Ba'al Shem Tov, Israel

January 28, 1760
b. Carey, Mathew

February 14, 1760
b. Allen, Richard

February 15, 1760
b. Lesueur, Jean-Francois

March 2, 1760
b. Desmoulins, Camille

March 28, 1760
b. Clarkson, Thomas
d. Woffington, Margaret

May 6, 1760
d. Zinzendorf, Nikolaus Ludwig von,
   Count

May 10, 1760
b. Rouget de Lisle, Claude Joseph

June 20, 1760
b. Wellesley, Richard Colley, 1st
   Marquess Wellesley

September 14, 1760
b. Cherubini, Luigi Carlo Zenobio
   Salvadore Maria
b. Hokusai, Katsushika

October 17, 1760
b. Saint-Simon, Claude-Henri de
   Rouvroy

October 25, 1760
d. George II

October 27, 1760
b. Gneisenau, August Neithardt von

November 25, 1760
b. Babeuf, Francois-Noel

December 2, 1760
b. Breckinridge, John

December 7, 1760
b. Tussaud, Marie Gresholtz, Madame

December 17, 1760
b. Gannett, Deborah Sampson
b. Sampson, Deborah

1761

d. Law, William

January 4, 1761
d. Hales, Stephen

January 17, 1761
b. Hall, James, Sir

January 29, 1761
b. Gallatin, Albert

February 1, 1761
d. Charlevoix, Pierre Francis Xavier de

April 5, 1761
b. Ludington, Sybil

April 26, 1761
b. Hamilton, Emma, Lady

May 3, 1761
b. Kotzebue, August Friedrich
   Ferdinand von

June 3, 1761
b. Shrapnel, Henry

July 4, 1761
d. Richardson, Samuel

August 17, 1761
b. Carey, William

August 23, 1761
b. Morse, Jedidiah

November 26, 1761
b. Savage, Edward

December 24, 1761
b. Selim, III

December 25, 1761
d. Elizabeth Petrovna

1762

b. Chenier, Andre Marie de
b. Hoban, James
d. Troger, Paul

January 31, 1762
b. Macquarie, Lachlan

February 2, 1762
b. Crescentini, Girolamo

February 20, 1762
d. Mayer, Johann Tobias

March 10, 1762
d. Calas, Jean

March 19, 1762
b. Cobbett, William

May 19, 1762
b. Fichte, Johann Gottlieb

June 6, 1762
d. Anson, George

July 13, 1762
d. Bradley, James

August 9, 1762
b. Randolph, Mary

August 12, 1762
b. George IV

August 21, 1762
d. Montagu, Mary Wortley, Lady

September 17, 1762
d. Geminiani, Francesco

October 21, 1762
b. Colman, George

October 30, 1762
b. Chenier, Marie-Andre de

December 25, 1762
b. Kelly, Michael

1763

b. Bowles, William Augustus
b. Chavis, John
b. Tone, Theobald Wolfe

January 8, 1763
b. Genet, Edmond Charles Edouard

January 15, 1763
b. Talma, Francois Joseph

January 26, 1763
b. Bernadotte, Jean Baptiste

February 12, 1763
d. Marivaux, Pierre Carlet de

March 21, 1763
b. Richter, Jean Paul F
b. Richter, Johann Paul Friedrich

May 3, 1763
d. Psalmanazar, George

June 13, 1763
b. Andrada e Silva, Jose Bonifacio de

June 22, 1763
b. Mehul, Etienne Nicolas

June 24, 1763
b. Josephine

June 26, 1763
b. Morland, George

July 17, 1763
b. Astor, John Jacob

July 22, 1763
b. Geddes, James

July 30, 1763
b. Rogers, Samuel

July 31, 1763
b. Kent, James

August 8, 1763
b. Bulfinch, Charles

November 10, 1763
d. Dupleix, Joseph Francois

November 23, 1763
d. Prevost d'Exiles, Antoine Francois, Abbe

1764

b. Brown, Alexander
b. Christian, Fletcher
b. Jouy, Victor (Joseph-Etienne) de
b. Molson, John
b. Pushmataha
d. Laurie, Annie

March 13, 1764
b. Grey, Charles

March 17, 1764
b. Pinkney, William

March 30, 1764
d. Locatelli, Pietro Antonio

April 8, 1764
b. Rezanov, Nikolay Petrovich

April 15, 1764
d. Pompadour, Jeanne Antoinette Poisson

May 1, 1764
b. Latrobe, Benjamin Henry

May 2, 1764
b. Gentz, Friedrich Von

May 20, 1764
b. Schadow, Gottfried

May 26, 1764
b. Livingston, Edward

June 19, 1764
b. Artigas, Jose Gervasio

July 9, 1764
b. Radcliffe, Ann

July 11, 1764
d. Ames, Nathaniel

July 23, 1764
d. Tennent, Gilbert

September 12, 1764
d. Rameau, Jean-Philippe

September 23, 1764
d. Dodsley, Robert

October 26, 1764
d. Hogarth, William

November 1, 1764
b. Van Rensselaer, Stephen

November 4, 1764
d. Churchill, Charles

December 3, 1764
b. Lamb, Mary Ann

1765

b. Bagration, Petr Ivanovich

b. Johnston, Joshua
b. Smithson, James (Louis Macie)
d. Logroscino, Nicola
d. Pannini, Giovanni Paolo

March 7, 1765
b. Niepce, Joseph Nicephore

April 5, 1765
d. Young, Edward

April 9, 1765
b. Narino, Antonio

April 15, 1765
d. Lomonosov, Mikhail Vasilyevich

August 21, 1765
b. William, IV

September 2, 1765
d. Bouquet, Henry

September 30, 1765
b. Morelos y Pavon, Jose Maria

October 8, 1765
b. Otis, Harrison Gray

November 14, 1765
b. Fulton, Robert

December 1, 1765
b. Brown, William Hill

December 8, 1765
b. Whitney, Eli

1766

b. Fritchie, Barbara
b. Walker, Adam

January 23, 1766
d. Caslon, William
d. Porpora, Niccolo

February 11, 1766
b. Dunlap, William

February 17, 1766
b. Malthus, Thomas Robert

March 1, 1766
d. Boylston, Zabdiel

April 22, 1766
b. Stael-Holstein, Anne Louise Germaine Necker, Baroness de

April 24, 1766
b. Thomas, Robert B

May 11, 1766
b. D'Israeli, Isaac

July 6, 1766
b. Wilson, Alexander

July 9, 1766
b. Perkins, Jacob
d. Mayhew, Jonathan

July 20, 1766
b. Elgin, Thomas Bruce

September 2, 1766
b. Forten, James

September 6, 1766
b. Dalton, John

September 16, 1766
b. Wilson, Samuel

November 7, 1766
d. Nattier, Jean Marc

November 16, 1766
b. Kreutzer, Rodolphe

December 1, 1766
b. Karamzin, Nikolai Mikhailovich

December 3, 1766
b. Bloomfield, Robert

December 29, 1766
b. Macintosh, Charles

1767

b. Black Hawk
b. Macarthur, John
b. Vesey, Denmark
d. Silhouette, Etienne de

January 1, 1767
b. Edgeworth, Maria

January 5, 1767
b. Say, Jean Baptiste

March 12, 1767
b. Godoy y Alvarez de Faria, Manuel de

March 15, 1767
b. Jackson, Andrew

March 25, 1767
b. Murat, Joachim

May 17, 1767
d. Wolcott, Roger

June 15, 1767
b. Jackson, Rachel (Donelson Robards)

June 22, 1767
b. Humboldt, Wilhelm Freiherr von

June 25, 1767
d. Telemann, Georg Philipp

July 11, 1767
b. Adams, John Quincy

August 25, 1767
b. Saint-Just, Louis Antoine Leon de

October 6, 1767
b. Christophe, Henri

October 14, 1767
b. Saussure, Nicolas Thoedore de

October 15, 1767
b. Richard, Gabriel

October 25, 1767
b. Constant de Rebeque, (Henri) Benjamin

November 11, 1767
b. Romberg, Bernhard

November 22, 1767
b. Hofer, Andreas

December 22, 1767
d. Newbery, John

1768

b. Bateman, Mary
b. Billington, Elizabeth
b. Phyfe, Duncan
d. Beissel, Johann Conrad

January 7, 1768
b. Bonaparte, Joseph

February 12, 1768
b. Francis, II

February 14, 1768
b. Krylov, Ivan Andreyevich
b. Tecumseh

March 7, 1768
d. Bienville, Sieur de

March 18, 1768
d. Sterne, Laurence

March 21, 1768
b. Fourier, Jean Baptiste Joseph

April 14, 1768
d. Cuvillies, Francois

April 20, 1768
d. Canaletto, Antonio

May 20, 1768
b. Madison, Dolly (Payne Todd)

June 8, 1768
d. Winckelmann, Johann Joachim

June 9, 1768
b. Slater, Samuel

June 12, 1768
d. Delisle, Joseph-Nicolas

June 14, 1768
d. Short, James

June 30, 1768
b. Monroe, Elizabeth (Kortright)

July 27, 1768
b. Corday d'Armount, Charlotte

August 23, 1768
b. Cooper, Astley Paston, Sir

September 4, 1768
b. Chateaubriand, Francois Rene de

November 21, 1768
b. Schleiermacher, Friedrich Ernst Daniel

December 22, 1768
b. Crome, John

1769

b. Jumel, Eliza
b. Mohammed Ali

January 10, 1769
b. Ney, Michel de la Moskova, Prince

March 2, 1769
b. Clinton, DeWitt

March 23, 1769
b. Smith, William

April 20, 1769
d. Pontiac

April 25, 1769
b. Brunel, Marc Isambard, Sir

May 1, 1769
b. Wellington, Arthur Wellesley, Duke

May 4, 1769
b. Lawrence, Thomas, Sir

June 11, 1769
b. Royall, Anne Newport

June 18, 1769
b. Castlereagh, Robert Stewart, Viscount

August 15, 1769
b. Napoleon I

August 23, 1769
b. Cuvier, Georges, Baron

August 29, 1769
d. Hoyle, Edmond

September 14, 1769
b. Humboldt, Alexander, Freiherr von
b. Humboldt, Friedrich Heinrich Alexander von

October 6, 1769
b. Brock, Isaac, Sir

October 31, 1769
d. Mabuchi, Kamo

1770

b. Brooks, Henry Sands
b. Codrington, Edward, Sir
b. Fink, Mike
b. Frederick William, III
b. Hogg, James
b. Matamoros, Mariano
b. Sequoyah
b. Thorvaldsen, Albert Bertel
d. Cuzzoni, Francesca
d. Harunobu, Suzuki

February 26, 1770
d. Tartini, Giuseppe

March 5, 1770
d. Attucks, Crispus

March 20, 1770
b. Holderlin, Friedrich

March 27, 1770
d. Tiepolo, Giambattista

April 7, 1770
b. Wordsworth, William

April 9, 1770
b. Seebeck, Thomas Johann

April 11, 1770
b. Canning, George

April 28, 1770
d. Camargo, Marie Anne de Cupis de

April 30, 1770
b. Thompson, David

May 4, 1770
b. Gerard, Francois

May 10, 1770
b. Davout, Louis Nicholas

May 30, 1770
d. Boucher, Francois

June 3, 1770
b. Belgrano, Manuel

June 7, 1770
b. Liverpool, 2nd Earl of

July 27, 1770
d. Dinwiddie, Robert

August 1, 1770
b. Clark, William

August 25, 1770
d. Chatterton, Thomas

August 27, 1770
b. Hegel, Georg Wilhelm Friedrich

September 30, 1770
d. Whitefield, George

December 16, 1770
b. Beethoven, Ludwig van

December 22, 1770
b. Gallitzin, Demetrius Augustine

1771

January 17, 1771
b. Brown, Charles Brockden

February 24, 1771
b. Cramer, Johann Baptist

March 16, 1771
b. Gros, Antoine Jean

March 21, 1771
b. Dibdin, Thomas Pitt

March 24, 1771
d. Shirley, William

April 13, 1771
b. Trevithick, Richard

May 14, 1771
b. Owen, Robert
b. Wedgwood, Thomas

May 21, 1771
d. Smart, Christopher

June 1, 1771
b. Paer, Ferdinando

June 6, 1771
b. Smith, Sydney

June 20, 1771
b. Selkirk, 5th Earl of

June 24, 1771
b. DuPont, Eleuthere Irenee

July 30, 1771
d. Gray, Thomas

August 15, 1771
b. Scott, Walter, Sir

September 10, 1771
b. Park, Mungo

September 17, 1771
d. Smollett, Tobias George

October 3, 1771
b. Place, Francis

November 6, 1771
b. Senefelder, Aloys

November 11, 1771
b. Bichat, Marie Francois Xavier
b. McDowell, Ephraim

December 6, 1771
d. Morgagni, Giovanni Battista

December 26, 1771
d. Helvetius, Claude Adrien

December 27, 1771
b. Johnson, William

1772

b. Speransky, Mikhail

February 20, 1772
b. Chauncey, Isaac

February 24, 1772
b. Crawford, William Harris

March 10, 1772
b. Schlegel, Friedrich von

March 29, 1772
d. Swedenborg, Emanuel

April 7, 1772
b. Fourier, Francois Marie Charles

April 15, 1772
b. Geoffroy Saint-Hilaire, Etienne

April 19, 1772
b. Ricardo, David

May 2, 1772
b. Novalis

May 22, 1772
b. Roy, Ram Mohun

September 27, 1772
b. Jefferson, Martha

September 30, 1772
d. Brindley, James

October 7, 1772
d. Woolman, John

October 21, 1772
b. Coleridge, Samuel Taylor

1773

b. Chaka
b. Hemings, Sally
b. Rodgers, John

January 29, 1773
b. Mohs, Friedrich

February 9, 1773
b. Harrison, William Henry

March 9, 1773
b. Hull, Isaac

March 24, 1773
d. Chesterfield, Philip Dormer, Earl

March 26, 1773
b. Bowditch, Nathaniel

April 6, 1773
b. Mill, James

May 5, 1773
b. Tieck, (Johann) Ludwig

May 9, 1773
b. Sismondi, Jean Charles Leonard
Simonde de

May 15, 1773
b. Metternich-Winneburg, Clemens
d. Butler, Alban

June 2, 1773
b. Randolph, John

June 15, 1773
b. Benjamin, Asher

June 16, 1773
b. Young, Thomas

August 23, 1773
b. Fries, Jakob Friedrich

October 6, 1773
b. Louis Phillippe

October 23, 1773
b. Jeffrey, Francis Jeffrey, Lord

December 21, 1773
b. Brown, Robert

December 27, 1773
b. Cayley, George, Sir

1774

b. Coats, James
d. Fergusson, Robert

February 16, 1774
b. Rode, Jacques Pierre Joseph

February 17, 1774
b. Peale, Raphael

March 16, 1774
b. Flinders, Matthew

April 4, 1774
d. Goldsmith, Oliver

April 28, 1774
b. Baily, Francis

May 7, 1774
b. Bainbridge, William

May 10, 1774
d. Louis XV

June 21, 1774
b. Tompkins, Daniel D

July 11, 1774
d. Johnson, William, Sir

August 12, 1774
b. Southey, Robert

August 18, 1774
b. Lewis, Meriwether

August 25, 1774
d. Jommelli, Niccolo

August 28, 1774
b. Seton, Elizabeth Ann Bayley, Saint

September 5, 1774
b. Friedrich, Caspar David

September 14, 1774
b. Bentinck, William Henry
Cavendish, Lord

September 22, 1774
d. Clement XIV, Pope

September 26, 1774
b. Appleseed, Johnny
b. Bell, Charles

November 14, 1774
b. Spontini, Gasparo

November 22, 1774
d. Clive, Robert

December 16, 1774
d. Quesnay, Francois

1775

b. Clairborne, William Charles Coles
b. Colter, John
b. Feuerbach, Paul Johann Anselm
b. Gabriel
b. Secord, Laura Ingersoll
d. Pugachev, Yemelyan I

January 8, 1775
d. Baskerville, John

January 22, 1775
b. Ampere, Andre Marie
b. Garcia, Manuel del Popolo Vincente

January 27, 1775
b. Schelling, Friedrich Wilhelm Joseph
von

January 30, 1775
b. Landor, Walter Savage

February 10, 1775
b. Lamb, Charles

February 12, 1775
b. Adams, Louisa Catherine

February 18, 1775
b. Girtin, Thomas

April 7, 1775
b. Lowell, Francis Cabot

April 21, 1775
b. Anderson, Alexander

April 23, 1775
b. Turner, Joseph Mallord William

April 30, 1775
d. Harrison, Peter

May 6, 1775
b. Sherwood, Mary Martha

May 9, 1775
b. Brown, Jacob Jennings

May 21, 1775
b. Bonaparte, Lucien

June 17, 1775
d. Warren, Joseph

June 26, 1775
d. Gunther, Ignaz

July 9, 1775
b. Lewis, Matthew Gregory

July 25, 1775
b. Harrison, Anna (Tuthill Symmes)

August 6, 1775
b. O'Connell, Daniel

August 20, 1775
b. Tucker, George

September 14, 1775
b. Hobart, John Henry

October 12, 1775
b. Beecher, Lyman

October 15, 1775
b. Vanderlyn, John

October 22, 1775
d. Randolph, Peyton

November 25, 1775
b. Kemble, Charles

December 14, 1775
b. Chase, Philander

December 16, 1775
b. Austen, Jane
b. Boieldieu, Francois Adrien

December 31, 1775
d. Montgomery, Richard

1776

b. Dibdin, Thomas Frognall
b. Fernandez de Lizardi, Jose Joaquin
b. Fraser, Simon
b. Niebuhr, Barthold Georg

January 24, 1776
b. Hoffmann, E(rnst) T(heodor)
A(madeus)

February 28, 1776
b. Boyer, Jean Pierre

April 22, 1776
d. Yngjo

May 4, 1776
b. Herbart, Johann Friedrich

June 9, 1776
b. Avogadro, Amedeo

June 11, 1776
b. Constable, John

August 25, 1776
d. Hume, David

September 22, 1776
d. Hale, Nathan

September 28, 1776
d. Colden, Cadwallader

1777

b. Ireland, William Henry
d. Crebillon, Claude Prosper Jolyot de
d. Dixon, Jeremiah
d. Morton, John
d. Prescott, Samuel

February 8, 1777
b. Courtois, Bernard

March 17, 1777
b. Taney, Roger Brooke

April 12, 1777
b. Clay, Henry

April 30, 1777
b. Gauss, Carl Friedrich

May 16, 1777
d. Gwinnett, Button

August 14, 1777
b. Oersted, Hans Christian

August 16, 1777
d. Herkimer, Nicholas

August 27, 1777
b. Campbell, Thomas

September 16, 1777
b. Rothschild, Nathan Meyer

September 22, 1777
d. Bartram, John

October 18, 1777
b. Kleist, Heinrich von

October 21, 1777
d. Foote, Samuel

December 4, 1777
b. Recamier, Julie, Madame

December 6, 1777
d. Jussieu, Bernard de

December 12, 1777
d. Haller, Albrecht von

December 23, 1777
b. Alexander I

1778

b. Barbaja, Domenico
b. Foscolo, (Niccolo) Ugo
b. Lavalleja, Juan Antonio
d. Vaudreuil-Cavagnal, Marquis de

January 4, 1778
b. Buel, Jesse

January 10, 1778
d. Linnaeus, Carolus

February 4, 1778
b. Candolle, Augustin Pyrame de

February 13, 1778
b. Sor, Fernando

February 22, 1778
b. Peale, Rembrandt

February 25, 1778
b. San Martin, Jose de

March 5, 1778
d. Arne, Thomas Augustine

March 24, 1778
b. Gourlay, Robert

March 26, 1778
b. Ashley, William Henry

April 3, 1778
b. Bretonneau, Pierre Fidele

April 9, 1778
d. Hesselius, John

April 10, 1778
b. Hazlitt, William

April 12, 1778
b. Strachan, John

April 22, 1778
d. Hargreaves, James

May 10, 1778
b. Ladd, William

May 11, 1778
d. Pitt, William, the Elder

May 30, 1778
d. Voltaire

June 7, 1778
b. Brummell, Beau

June 12, 1778
d. Livingston, Philip

June 16, 1778
d. Ekhof, Konrad

June 20, 1778
d. Laclede, Pierre

July 2, 1778
d. Rousseau, Jean Jacques

August 1, 1778
b. Jefferson, Mary

August 11, 1778
b. Jahn, Friedrich Ludwig
d. Toplady, Augustus Montague

August 20, 1778
b. O'Higgins, Bernardo

September 2, 1778
b. Bonaparte, Louis

September 8, 1778
b. Brentano, Clemens Maria

September 20, 1778
b. Emmet, Robert

September 28, 1778
b. Douvillier, Suzanne Theodore
Vaillande

October 5, 1778
b. Champollion-Figeac, Jacques-Joseph

November 1, 1778
d. Piranesi, Giovanni Battista

November 5, 1778
b. Ritchie, Thomas

November 14, 1778
b. Hummel, Johann Nepomuk

November 25, 1778
b. Lancaster, Joseph

December 6, 1778
b. Gay-Lussac, Joseph-Louis

December 17, 1778
b. Davy, Humphrey, Sir

December 18, 1778
b. Grimaldi, Joseph

1779

d. Karim Khan Zand
d. Lynch, Thomas, Jr.

January 5, 1779
b. Decatur, Stephen

January 18, 1779
b. Roget, Peter Mark

January 20, 1779
d. Garrick, David

January 21, 1779
b. Savigny, Friedrich Karl von

February 5, 1779
b. Pike, Zebulon Montgomery

February 7, 1779
d. Boyce, William

February 14, 1779
d. Cook, James, Captain

March 2, 1779
b. Poinsett, Joel Roberts

March 15, 1779
b. Melbourne, William Lamb,
Viscount

April 6, 1779
d. Traetta, Tommaso

April 24, 1779
d. Wheelock, Eleazar

May 2, 1779
b. Galt, John

May 11, 1779
d. Hart, John

May 28, 1779
b. Moore, Thomas

June 16, 1779
d. Bernard, Francis, Sir

June 29, 1779
d. Mengs, Anton Raphael

July 14, 1779
d. Ross, George

July 15, 1779
b. Moore, Clement Clarke

August 1, 1779
b. Key, Francis Scott

August 8, 1779
b. Silliman, Benjamin

August 17, 1779
b. Ritter, Karl

August 29, 1779
b. Berzelius, Jons Jacob, Baron

August 30, 1779
b. Bellinghausen, Fabian Gottlieb von

September 18, 1779
b. Story, Joseph

October 6, 1779
b. Appleton, Nathan

October 11, 1779
d. Pulaski, Kazimierz
d. Chippendale, Thomas

November 5, 1779
b. Allston, Washington

November 10, 1779
d. Hewes, Joseph

December 6, 1779
d. Chardin, Jean Baptiste Simeon

1780

b. Keokuk
b. Ranjit Singh
b. Rossi, Gaetano

January 27, 1780
b. Alvarez, Juan

January 28, 1780
b. Velluti, Giovanni Battista

January 31, 1780
d. Carver, Jonathan

February 14, 1780
d. Blackstone, William, Sir

March 8, 1780
b. Bigge, John Thomas

March 10, 1780
b. Trollope, Frances

March 17, 1780
b. Chalmers, Thomas

April 4, 1780
b. Hicks, Edward

April 7, 1780
b. Channing, William Ellery

May 20, 1780
b. Rivadavia, Bernardino

May 21, 1780
b. Fry, Elizabeth Gurney

June 1, 1780
b. Clausewitz, Karl (Philipp Gottlieb)
von

June 3, 1780
b. Hone, William
d. Hutchinson, Thomas

July 11, 1780
b. Flint, Timothy

August 2, 1780
d. Condillac, Etienne Bonnot de

August 19, 1780
b. Beranger, Pierre-Jean de
d. Kalb, Johann de

August 29, 1780
b. Ingres, Jean Auguste Dominique
b. Laffite, Jean
d. Soufflot, Jacques Germain

September 20, 1780
b. Borghese, Maria Paolina

October 2, 1780
d. Andre, John

October 17, 1780
d. Bellotto, Bernardo

November 12, 1780
b. Retief, Pieter

November 29, 1780
d. Maria Theresa

December 14, 1780
b. Nesselrode, Karl Robert

December 15, 1780
b. Dobereiner, Johann Wolfgang

1781

b. Jarvis, John Wesley
d. Tupac Amaru
d. Turgot, A(nne) R(obert) J(acques),
Baron de l'Aulne

January 9, 1781
b. Shaw, Lemuel

January 17, 1781
b. Hare, Robert

January 26, 1781
b. Arnim, Achim von (Ludwig
Joachim)

February 15, 1781
d. Lessing, Gotthold Ephraim

February 17, 1781
b. Laennec, Rene Theophile Hyacinthe

February 22, 1781
d. Taylor, George

February 28, 1781
d. Stockton, Richard

March 4, 1781
b. Gratz, Rebecca

March 11, 1781
b. Heinrich, Anthony Philip

March 13, 1781
b. Schinkel, Karl Friedrich

March 17, 1781
b. Elliott, Ebenezer
d. Ewald, Johannes

April 7, 1781
b. Chantrey, Francis Legatt, Sir

June 9, 1781
b. Stephenson, George

July 5, 1781
b. Raffles, Thomas Stamford, Sir

August 12, 1781
b. Mills, Robert

September 26, 1781
d. Lewis, Andrew

October 1, 1781
b. Lawrence, James

October 17, 1781
b. Johnson, Richard Mentor

November 4, 1781
d. Bordoni, Faustina

November 29, 1781
b. Bello y Lopez, Andres

December 11, 1781
b. Brewster, David, Sir

1782

b. Atkinson, Henry
b. Guthrie, Samuel
d. Haidar Ali
d. Anville, Jean Baptiste Bourguignon d'

January 1, 1782
d. Bach, Johann Christian

January 4, 1782
d. Gabriel, Ange-Jacques

January 18, 1782
b. Webster, Daniel

January 19, 1782
b. Auber, Daniel Francois Esprit

January 20, 1782
b. Bibaud, Michel

February 15, 1782
b. Miller, William

March 13, 1782
b. Wyss, Johann Rudolf

March 14, 1782
b. Benton, Thomas Hart

March 17, 1782
d. Bernoulli, Daniel

March 18, 1782
b. Calhoun, John Caldwell

April 12, 1782
d. Metastasio, Pietro

April 21, 1782
b. Froebel, Friedrich Wilhelm August

May 8, 1782
d. Pombal, Marques de

June 19, 1782
b. Lamennais, Hugues Felicite Robert de

June 30, 1782
b. Taylor, Ann

July 1, 1782
d. Rockingham, 2nd Marquess of

July 15, 1782
d. Farinelli

July 26, 1782
b. Field, John

August 10, 1782
b. Napier, Charles James, Sir

August 16, 1782
b. Cotman, John Sell

September 6, 1782
d. Jefferson, Martha (Wayles Skelton)

October 2, 1782
d. Lee, Charles

October 9, 1782
b. Cass, Lewis

October 27, 1782
b. Paganini, Niccolo

November 3, 1782
b. Warrington, Lewis

December 5, 1782
b. Van Buren, Martin

1783

b. Deb, Radhakant
b. Ram Camul Sen

January 2, 1783
d. Bodmer, Johann Jakob

January 15, 1783
d. Alexander, William

January 23, 1783
b. Stendhal

January 25, 1783
b. Colgate, William

January 31, 1783
d. Majorano, Gaetano

February 6, 1783
d. Brown, Lancelot

February 28, 1783
b. Rossetti, Gabriele Pasquale Giuseppe

March 8, 1783
b. Van Buren, Hannah (Hoes)

March 30, 1783
d. Hunter, William

April 3, 1783
b. Irving, Washington

April 21, 1783
b. Heber, Reginald

April 29, 1783
b. Cox, David

May 22, 1783
b. Sturgeon, William

May 23, 1783
d. Otis, James

June 8, 1783
b. Sully, Thomas

June 21, 1783
b. Alston, Theodosia Burr

July 24, 1783
b. Bolivar, Simon

August 10, 1783
b. Guerrero, Vicente

September 15, 1783
d. Stirling, Lord

September 18, 1783
d. Euler, Leonhard

September 23, 1783
b. Cornelius, Peter von

September 26, 1783
b. Taylor, Jane

September 27, 1783
b. Iturbide, Augustin de

October 29, 1783
d. Alembert, Jean le Rond d'

November 22, 1783
d. Hanson, John

December 16, 1783
d. Hasse, Johann Adolph

December 31, 1783
b. MacDonough, Thomas

1784

b. Burckhardt, Johann Ludwig
d. Portola, Gaspar de
d. Ramsay, Allan

January 3, 1784
d. Galuppi, Baldassare

January 13, 1784
b. Woodworth, Samuel

January 21, 1784
b. DeWint, Peter

January 28, 1784
b. Aberdeen, 4th Earl of

February 5, 1784
b. Hanks, Nancy

March 12, 1784
b. Buckland, William

March 25, 1784
b. Fetis, Francois Joseph

April 5, 1784
b. Spohr, Louis Ludwig

May 3, 1784
d. Benezet, Anthony

May 12, 1784
b. Knowles, James Sheridan

June 13, 1784
b. McCoy, Isaac

June 29, 1784
d. Rodney, Caesar

July 1, 1784
d. Bach, Wilhelm Friedemann

July 22, 1784
b. Bessel, Friedrich Wilhelm

July 30, 1784
d. Diderot, Denis
d. Serra, Junipero

August 17, 1784
b. Feijo, Diogo Antonio

August 24, 1784
b. Worcester, Joseph Emerson

September 8, 1784
d. Lee, Ann

October 14, 1784
b. Ferdinand, VII

October 15, 1784
b. Bugeaud de la Piconnerie, Thomas Robert

October 19, 1784
b. Hunt, Leigh
b. McLoughlin, John

October 20, 1784
b. Palmerston, Henry John Temple, Viscount

October 24, 1784
b. Montefiore, Moses Haim, Sir

November 15, 1784
b. Bonaparte, Jerome

November 24, 1784
b. Taylor, Zachary

December 1, 1784
b. Castil-Blaze, Francois-Joseph

December 5, 1784
d. Wheatley, Phillis

December 13, 1784
d. Johnson, Samuel

December 30, 1784
b. Long, Stephen H

1785

b. Guemes, Martin
b. Ricordi, Giovanni
d. Henderson, Richard
d. Whitehead, William

January 4, 1785
b. Grimm, Jakob Ludwig Karl

January 6, 1785
d. Salomon, Haym

January 10, 1785
d. Stiegel, Henry William

January 30, 1785
b. Metcalfe, Charles Theophilus

February 2, 1785
b. Colbran, Isabella

February 6, 1785
b. Bonaparte, Elizabeth Patterson

February 12, 1785
b. Dulong, Pierre-Louis

February 17, 1785
b. Krochmal, Nachman Kohen

March 7, 1785
b. Manzoni, Alessandro (Antonio)

March 11, 1785
b. McLean, John

April 26, 1785
b. Audubon, John James

June 9, 1785
b. Thayer, Sylvanus, General

June 30, 1785
d. Oglethorpe, James Edward

July 6, 1785
b. Hooker, William Jackson, Sir

July 13, 1785
d. Hopkins, Stephen

July 20, 1785
b. Mahmud, II

August 15, 1785
b. DeQuincey, Thomas

August 17, 1785
d. Trumbull, Jonathan

August 19, 1785
b. Thomas, Seth

August 20, 1785
b. Perry, Oliver Hazard, Admiral

August 26, 1785
d. Germain, George Sackville

August 30, 1785
b. Lin Tse-hsu

September 1, 1785
b. Cartwright, Peter

September 28, 1785
b. Walker, David

October 15, 1785
b. Carrera, Jose Miguel

October 18, 1785
b. Peacock, Thomas Love

October 20, 1785
b. Drake, Daniel

October 21, 1785
b. Shreve, Henry Miller

November 13, 1785
b. Lamb, Caroline Ponsonby, Lady

November 18, 1785
b. Wilkie, David, Sir

November 21, 1785
b. Beaumont, William

November 28, 1785
d. Whipple, William

December 10, 1785
b. Appleton, Daniel

December 13, 1785
b. Milder-Hauptmann, Pauline Anna

1786

b. Aubert de Gaspe, Philippe(-Joseph)
b. Ch'i-ying
d. Hepplewhite, George

January 4, 1786
d. Mendelssohn, Moses

January 8, 1786
b. Biddle, Nicholas

January 26, 1786
b. Haydon, Benjamin Robert

February 24, 1786
b. Grimm, Wilhelm Karl

February 26, 1786
b. Arago, Dominque Francois Jean

April 7, 1786
b. King, William Rufus de Vane

April 15, 1786
b. Channing, Walter

April 16, 1786
b. Franklin, John, Sir

May 8, 1786
b. Vianney, Jean (Marie) Baptiste

May 26, 1786
d. Scheele, Karl Wilhelm

June 9, 1786
d. McDougall, Alexander

June 13, 1786
b. Scott, Winfield

June 19, 1786
d. Greene, Nathanael

August 17, 1786
b. Crockett, Davy
d. Frederick II
d. Frederick the Great

August 31, 1786
b. Chevreul, Michel Eugene

September 23, 1786
b. England, John

October 6, 1786
d. Sacchini, Antonio

October 7, 1786
b. Papineau, Louis-Joseph
d. Muhlenberg, Heinrich Melchior

October 26, 1786
b. Deringer, Henry

October 28, 1786
d. Sears, Isaac

November 18, 1786
b. Weber, Carl Maria von

November 30, 1786
d. Galvez, Bernardo de

December 8, 1786
b. Charpentier, Johann von

December 12, 1786
b. Marcy, William Learned

1787

b. Gruber, Franz-Xaver
b. Louis, Pierre Charles Alexandre
b. Moshweshwe
b. Sacagawea
b. Shaka
d. Chauncy, Charles
d. Galvez, Jose de

January 1, 1787
d. Middleton, Arthur
d. Mason, Charles

February 13, 1787
d. Boscovich, Ruggiero Giuseppe

February 23, 1787
b. Willard, Emma Hart

March 6, 1787
b. Fraunhofer, Joseph von

March 10, 1787
b. Etty, William

March 16, 1787
b. Ohm, Georg Simon

March 17, 1787
b. Kean, Edmund

March 28, 1787
b. Rich, Claudius James

April 2, 1787
d. Gage, Thomas

May 28, 1787
d. Mozart, Leopold

June 20, 1787
d. Abel, Karl Friedrich

August 24, 1787
b. Weddell, James

September 10, 1787
b. Crittenden, John Jordan

October 4, 1787
b. Guizot, Francois Pierre Guillaume

October 5, 1787
d. Stone, Thomas

October 18, 1787
b. Stevens, Robert Livingston

October 30, 1787
d. Galiani, Ferdinando

November 5, 1787
b. Richardson, John, Sir

November 12, 1787
b. Burke, John

November 15, 1787
b. Cunard, Samuel, Sir
b. Leslie, Eliza
d. Gluck, Christoph

November 18, 1787
b. Daguerre, Louis Jacques Mande

November 21, 1787
b. Procter, Bryan Waller

December 10, 1787
b. Gallaudet, Thomas Hopkins

December 16, 1787
b. Mitford, Mary Russell

December 30, 1787
b. Kotzebue, Otto von

1788

b. Holbrook, Josiah
b. Quiroga, Juan Facundo
b. Rivera, Fructuoso
b. Seattle
d. Anza, Juan Bautista de
d. Richelieu, Louis Francois Armand de
d. Stuart, James

January 1, 1788
b. Cabet, Etienne

January 11, 1788
d. Grasse, Francois Joseph Paul de, Count

January 22, 1788
b. Byron, George Gordon, Baron
b. Schopenhauer, Arthur

January 27, 1788
d. Tryon, William

January 31, 1788
b. Romani, Felice
d. Charles Edward Louis Philip Casimir Stuart
d. Stuart, Charles Edward Louis Philip

February 5, 1788
b. Peel, Robert, Sir

February 6, 1788
b. Kisfaludy, Karoly

March 7, 1788
b. Becquerel, Antoine-Cesar

March 8, 1788
b. Hamilton, William, Sir

March 10, 1788
b. Eichendorff, Joseph Karl Benedict
Freiherr von

March 12, 1788
b. David d'Angers

March 29, 1788
d. Wesley, Charles

April 16, 1788
d. Buffon, Georges Louis Leclerc

May 8, 1788
b. Clapperton, Hugh

May 10, 1788
b. Fresnel, Augustin-Jean

May 15, 1788
b. Gadsden, James

May 16, 1788
b. Ruckert, Friedrich

June 21, 1788
d. Hamann, Johann Georg

June 24, 1788
b. Blanchard, Thomas

June 25, 1788
b. Pellico, Silvio

August 2, 1788
d. Gainsborough, Thomas

August 9, 1788
b. Judson, Adoniram

September 12, 1788
b. Campbell, Alexander

September 14, 1788
d. Penn, John

September 21, 1788
b. Taylor, Margaret (Smith)

September 22, 1788
b. Hook, Theodore Edward

September 30, 1788
b. Raglan, Fitzroy James Henry
Somerset, Baron

October 21, 1788
b. Combe, George

October 24, 1788
b. Hale, Sarah Josepha Buell

December 14, 1788
d. Charles, III

December 15, 1788
d. Bach, Carl Philipp Emanuel

1789

b. Ibrahim Pasha
d. Holbach, Baron d'

January 4, 1789
b. Lundy, Benjamin
d. Nelson, Thomas, Jr.

January 23, 1789
d. Cleland, John

February 11, 1789
d. Allen, Ethan

March 16, 1789
b. Chesney, Francis Rawdon

April 28, 1789
d. Hutchins, Thomas

May 10, 1789
b. Sparks, Jared

June 11, 1789
b. Jay, William

June 12, 1789
d. Liotard, Jean-Etienne

June 15, 1789
b. Henson, Josiah

August 6, 1789
b. List, Georg Friedrich

August 16, 1789
b. Kendall, Amos

August 21, 1789
b. Cauchy, Augustin Louis
b. Garrett, Thomas

September 1, 1789
b. Blessington, Marguerite Gardiner,
Countess

September 15, 1789
b. Cooper, James Fenimore

September 23, 1789
d. Deane, Silas

September 28, 1789
b. Bright, Richard
d. Day, Thomas

October 5, 1789
b. Scoresby, William

October 15, 1789
d. Morgan, John

November 10, 1789
d. Caswell, Richard

December 22, 1789
b. Woodbury, Levi

December 23, 1789
d. Epee, Charles-Michel

December 28, 1789
b. Sedgwick, Catherine Maria

1790

b. Bartlett, John Sherren
b. Coloradas, Mangas
b. Joseph, Chief
b. Kanaris, Constantine
b. Said, Seyyid
b. Wentworth, William Charles
d. Basedow, Johann Bernhard

February 4, 1790
b. Bachman, John

February 20, 1790
d. Joseph II

February 24, 1790
b. Kelley, Hall Jackson

March 12, 1790
b. Daniell, John Frederic

March 29, 1790
b. Tyler, John

April 17, 1790
d. Franklin, Benjamin

April 29, 1790
d. Cochin, Charles Nicholas

May 21, 1790
d. Warton, Thomas

May 23, 1790
b. Dumont d'Urville, Jules Sebastian
Cesar

May 29, 1790
d. Putnam, Israel

June 13, 1790
b. Paez, Jose Antonio

June 18, 1790
b. Eaton, John Henry

June 19, 1790
b. Gibson, John

July 4, 1790
b. Everest, George, Sir

July 8, 1790
b. Halleck, Fritz-Greene

July 17, 1790
d. Smith, Adam

August 10, 1790
b. McDuffie, George

October 2, 1790
b. Ross, John

October 14, 1790
d. Hooper, William

October 19, 1790
d. Hall, Lyman

October 21, 1790
b. Lamartine, Alphonse Marie Louis de Prat de

November 4, 1790
b. Lipinski, Carl

November 6, 1790
d. Bowdoin, James

November 12, 1790
b. Tyler, Letitia Christian

November 17, 1790
b. Mobius, August Ferdinand

December 8, 1790
b. Carlile, Richard

December 16, 1790
b. Leopold, I

December 19, 1790
b. Parry, William Edward, Sir

December 23, 1790
b. Champollion, Jean Francois

1791

b. Knight, Charles
b. Said ibn Sultan
b. Scribe, (Augustin) Eugene

January 15, 1791
b. Grillparzer, Franz

January 17, 1791
d. Pinto, Isaac

January 24, 1791
d. Falconet, Etienne Maurice

January 28, 1791
b. Herold, Ferdinand

February 1, 1791
b. Sax, Charles Joseph

February 12, 1791
b. Cooper, Peter

February 20, 1791
b. Czerny, Karl

March 3, 1791
d. Wesley, John

March 9, 1791
b. Levasseur, Nicolas Prosper

March 10, 1791
b. Saavedra, Angel de

March 22, 1791
b. William, I

April 2, 1791
d. Mirabeau, Honore Gabriel Riquetti

April 3, 1791
b. Lister, Anne

April 23, 1791
b. Buchanan, James

April 24, 1791
d. Harrison, Benjamin

April 27, 1791
b. Morse, Samuel Finley Breese

May 9, 1791
d. Hopkinson, Francis

June 9, 1791
b. Payne, John Howard

July 26, 1791
b. Robinson, John Beverley

August 1, 1791
b. Ticknor, George

September 1, 1791
b. Sigourney, Lydia Howard

September 5, 1791
b. Meyerbeer, Giacomo

September 20, 1791
b. Aksakov, Sergei Timofeyevich

September 22, 1791
b. Faraday, Michael

September 26, 1791
b. Gericault, Jean Louis Andre Theodore

October 5, 1791
d. Potemkin, Grigori Alexsandrovich

November 10, 1791
b. Hayne, Robert Young

December 5, 1791
d. Mozart, Wolfgang Amadeus

December 12, 1791
b. Marie Louise

1792

b. Burke, William
b. Hare, William
b. Santander, Francisco de Paula
d. Bute, 3d Earl of
d. Lee, Arthur

January 8, 1792
b. Mason, Lowell

January 30, 1792
b. Hopkins, John Henry

February 4, 1792
b. Birney, James Gillespie

February 18, 1792
b. Gorham, Jabez

February 19, 1792
b. Baer, Karl Ernst von
b. Murchison, Roderick Impey

February 23, 1792
d. Reynolds, Joshua, Sir

February 29, 1792
b. Rossini, Gioacchino Antonio

March 1, 1792
d. Leopold, II

March 3, 1792
d. Adam, Robert

March 7, 1792
b. Herschel, John Frederick William, Sir

March 12, 1792
d. Favart, Charles Simon

March 29, 1792
d. Gustavus, III

April 4, 1792
b. Stevens, Thaddeus

April 7, 1792
b. Drexel, Francis Martin

April 12, 1792
b. Durham, 1st Earl of

April 21, 1792
d. Tiradentes

April 22, 1792
b. Levy, Uriah Phillips

April 25, 1792
b. Keble, John

April 29, 1792
b. Vassar, Matthew

April 30, 1792
d. Sandwich, John Montagu

May 13, 1792
b. Pius IX

May 24, 1792
d. Rodney, George Brydges, Baron

June 4, 1792
d. Burgoyne, John, Sir

June 21, 1792
b. Baur, Ferdinand Christian

July 10, 1792
b. Dallas, George Mifflin
b. Marryat, Frederick

July 14, 1792
d. Occom, Samson

July 18, 1792
d. Jones, John Paul

August 3, 1792
d. Arkwright, Richard, Sir

August 4, 1792
b. Irving, Edward
b. Shelley, Percy Bysshe

August 5, 1792
d. North, Frederick North, Baron

August 18, 1792
b. Russell, John, Lord

August 29, 1792
b. Finney, Charles Grandison

September 1, 1792
b. Harding, Chester

September 17, 1792
b. Smith, Seba

September 27, 1792
b. Cruikshank, George

October 3, 1792
b. Morazan, Jose Francisco

October 7, 1792
d. Mason, George

October 18, 1792
b. Alaman, Lucas

October 20, 1792
b. Clyde, Colin Campbell, Baron

October 28, 1792
d. Smeaton, John
d. Guadagni, Gaetano
d. Hearne, Samuel

November 4, 1792
b. Lopez, Carlos Antonio

November 13, 1792
b. Trelawny, Edward John

November 26, 1792
b. Grimke, Sarah Moore

November 28, 1792
b. Cousin, Victor

December 2, 1792
b. Lobachevskii, Nikolai Ivanovich

December 5, 1792
b. Santa Cruz, Andres de

December 8, 1792
d. Laurens, Henry

December 16, 1792
b. Lawrence, Abbott

December 18, 1792
b. Howitt, William

December 26, 1792
b. Babbage, Charles

1793

b. Slidell, John
d. Christian, Fletcher
d. LaPlace, Pierre-Antoine de
d. Slidell, John

January 1, 1793
d. Guardi, Francesco

January 3, 1793
b. Mott, Lucretia Coffin

January 21, 1793
d. Louis XVI

February 6, 1793
d. Goldoni, Carlo

February 17, 1793
d. McGillivray, Alexander

March 2, 1793
b. Houston, Sam(uel)

March 28, 1793
b. Schoolcraft, Henry Rowe

March 30, 1793
b. Rosas, Juan Manuel de
b. Addison, Thomas

April 3, 1793
b. Lardner, Dionysius

April 4, 1793
b. Delavigne, Jean Francois Casimir

April 15, 1793
b. Struve, Friedrich Georg Wilhelm
von

April 20, 1793
b. Laing, David

April 21, 1793
d. Michell, John

May 10, 1793
b. Baylor, Robert Emmet Bledsoe

May 24, 1793
b. Hitchcock, Edward

May 28, 1793
d. Busching, Anton Friedrich

June 11, 1793
d. Robertson, William

June 26, 1793
b. Portales, Diego (Jose Victor)
d. White, Gilbert

July 13, 1793
b. Clare, John
d. Marat, Jean Paul

July 17, 1793
d. Corday d'Armount, Charlotte

July 23, 1793
d. Sherman, Roger

August 19, 1793
b. Goodrich, Samuel Griswold

September 2, 1793
d. Brown, William Hill

September 25, 1793
b. Hemans, Felicia Dorothea Browne

September 26, 1793
b. Hobson, William

October 8, 1793
d. Hancock, John

October 16, 1793
d. Hunter, John
d. Marie Antoinette

October 27, 1793
b. Remington, Eliphalet

November 3, 1793
b. Austin, Stephen Fuller

November 8, 1793
d. Roland (de La Platiere), Jeanne-
Marie

November 12, 1793
d. Bailly, Jean Sylvain

November 17, 1793
b. Eastlake, Charles Lock, Sir

November 25, 1793
b. Havell, Robert, Jr.

December 7, 1793
d. Du Barry, Marie Jeanne Gomard de
Vaubernier, Comtesse

December 15, 1793
b. Carey, Henry Charles

December 27, 1793
b. Laing, Alexander Gordon

1794

b. Brooks, Maria Gowen
b. Duff, Mary Ann Dyke
b. Ogden, Peter Skene
b. Santa Anna, Antonio Lopez de
d. Chenier, Andre Marie de

January 5, 1794
b. Ruffin, Edmund

January 7, 1794
b. Mitscherlich, Eilhardt

January 16, 1794
d. Gibbon, Edward

March 4, 1794
b. Couper, James Hamilton

March 5, 1794
b. Grier, Robert Cooper

March 15, 1794
b. Diez, Friedrich Christian

March 24, 1794
d. Hebert, Jacques Rene

March 25, 1794
d. Condorcet, Marie-Jean-Antoine

April 5, 1794
d. Danton, Georges Jacques
d. Desmoulins, Camille

April 7, 1794
b. Rubini, Giovanni-Battista

April 10, 1794
b. Perry, Matthew Calbraith, Commodore
b. Robinson, Edward

April 11, 1794
b. Everett, Edward

April 21, 1794
b. Ashmun, Jehudi

April 23, 1794
b. Wei Yuan

April 27, 1794
d. Bruce, James

April 28, 1794
d. Estaing, Charles Henri Hector, Comte d'

May 8, 1794
d. Lavoisier, Antoine Laurent

May 27, 1794
b. Vanderbilt, Cornelius

May 30, 1794
b. Moscheles, Ignaz

June 18, 1794
d. Murray, James

June 19, 1794
d. Lee, Richard Henry

July 5, 1794
b. Graham, Sylvester

July 14, 1794
b. Lockhart, John Gibson

July 25, 1794
d. Chenier, Marie-Andre de

July 28, 1794
d. Couthon, Georges
d. Robespierre, Maximilien Francois de
d. Saint-Just, Louis Antoine Leon de

July 29, 1794
b. Corwin, Thomas

August 10, 1794
b. Zunz, Leopold

August 14, 1794
d. Colman, George

August 30, 1794
b. Kearny, Stephen Watts

September 15, 1794
d. Clark, Abraham

October 20, 1794
d. Adam, James

November 3, 1794
b. Bryant, William Cullen

November 15, 1794
d. Witherspoon, John

November 17, 1794
b. Grote, George

November 28, 1794
d. Beccaria, Cesare
d. Steuben, Friedrich Wilhelm Ludolf Gerhard Augustin, Baron

December 6, 1794
b. Lablache, Luigi

December 14, 1794
b. Corning, Erastus

1795

b. Bourdonnais, Louis Charles de la
b. Bransfield, Edward
b. Budding, Edwin
b. Dingane
b. Mzilikazi
b. Oshkosh
b. Scott, Dred
b. Sucre, Antonio J de
b. Thierry, Augustin

January 3, 1795
d. Wedgwood, Josiah

January 6, 1795
b. Payen, Anselme

January 21, 1795
d. Wallis, Samuel

January 23, 1795
d. Sullivan, John

February 11, 1795
d. Bellman, Carl Michael

February 18, 1795
b. Peabody, George

February 27, 1795
d. Marion, Francis

March 12, 1795
b. Mackenzie, William Lyon

April 13, 1795
b. Harper, James

April 19, 1795
b. Ehrenberg, Christian Gottfried

April 28, 1795
b. Sturt, Charles

May 7, 1795
d. Fouquier-Tinville, Antoine Quentin

May 18, 1795
d. Rogers, Robert

May 19, 1795
b. Hopkins, Johns
d. Bartlett, Josiah
d. Boswell, James

May 23, 1795
b. Barry, Charles, Sir

June 13, 1795
b. Arnold, Thomas

June 28, 1795
b. Hitchcock, Lambert

August 16, 1795
b. Marschner, Heinrich August

August 17, 1795
b. Drake, Joseph Rodman

August 20, 1795
b. Stockton, Robert Field

August 24, 1795
b. Wallack, James William
d. Philidor, Francois Andre Danican

August 26, 1795
d. Cagliostro, Alessandro, Conte di

September 1, 1795
b. Bennett, James Gordon

September 6, 1795
b. Wright, Frances

September 17, 1795
b. Mercadante, Saverio

October 6, 1795
b. Giddings, Joshua Reed

October 15, 1795
b. Frederick William, IV

October 25, 1795
b. Kennedy, John Pendleton

October 31, 1795
b. Keats, John

November 2, 1795
b. Polk, James Knox

December 3, 1795
b. Hill, Rowland, Sir

December 4, 1795
b. Carlyle, Thomas

December 8, 1795
b. Hansen, Peter Andreas

December 10, 1795
b. Baldwin, Matthias William

December 21, 1795
b. Ranke, Leopold von

December 23, 1795
d. Clinton, Henry, Sir

1796

b. Becknell, William
b. Bowie, Jim
b. Johnson, Joshua
d. Brant, Molly

January 5, 1796
d. Huntington, Samuel

January 17, 1796
b. Fairbanks, Thaddeus

February 17, 1796
b. Pacini, Giovanni
d. Macpherson, James

February 22, 1796
b. Quetelet, Lambert Adolphe Jacques

February 25, 1796
d. Seabury, Samuel

March 8, 1796
d. Chambers, William, Sir

March 11, 1796
b. Wayland, Francis

March 20, 1796
b. Wakefield, Edward Gibbon

April 2, 1796
b. Pickering, William

April 14, 1796
b. Bonneville, Benjamin Louie Eulalie
de

April 30, 1796
b. Cremieux, Isaac-Adolphe

May 1, 1796
b. Booth, Junius Brutus

May 4, 1796
b. Mann, Horace
b. Prescott, William Hickling

May 21, 1796
b. Johnson, Reverdy

June 1, 1796
b. Carnot, Nicolas Leonard Sadi

June 8, 1796
d. Giardini, Felice di

June 26, 1796
d. Rittenhouse, David

July 6, 1796
b. Nicholas I

July 15, 1796
b. Bulfinch, Thomas

July 16, 1796
b. Corot, Jean Baptiste Camille

July 21, 1796
d. Burns, Robert

July 24, 1796
b. Clayton, John Middleton

July 26, 1796
b. Catlin, George

July 29, 1796
b. Hunt, Walter

August 8, 1796
d. Maulbertsch, Franz Anton

August 21, 1796
b. Durand, Asher Brown

August 27, 1796
b. Smith, Sophia

September 16, 1796
b. Muhlenberg, William Augustus

September 19, 1796
b. Coleridge, Hartley

October 7, 1796
d. Reid, Thomas

November 6, 1796
b. Back, George, Sir
d. Catherine the Great

December 15, 1796
d. Wayne, Anthony

December 17, 1796
b. Haliburton, Thomas Chandler

December 25, 1796
b. Caballero, Fernan

December 30, 1796
d. Lemoyne, Jean-Baptiste

1797

b. Hiroshige, Ando
b. Kamehameha II
b. Omar ibn Said Tal, Al-Hajj
b. Petalesharo
b. Truth, Sojourner
d. Elijah Ben Solomon

January 3, 1797
b. Vestris, Lucia Elizabeth, Madame

January 9, 1797
b. Wrangel, Ferdinand Petrovich,
Baron

January 11, 1797
d. Lee, Francis Lightfoot

January 22, 1797
b. Harper, John

January 30, 1797
b. Sumner, Edwin V
d. Glover, John

January 31, 1797
b. Schubert, Franz Peter

February 15, 1797
b. Bell, John
b. Steinway, Henry Engelhard

February 18, 1797
b. Pierce, John Davis

February 22, 1797
d. Munchhausen, Hieronymus Karl
Friedrich von, Baron

February 28, 1797
b. Lyon, Mary Mason

March 2, 1797
d. Walpole, Horace

March 6, 1797
b. Smith, Gerrit

March 24, 1797
b. Rosmini-Serbati, Antonio

March 25, 1797
b. Winebrenner, John

March 26, 1797
d. Hutton, James

March 27, 1797
b. Vigny, Alfred Victor, Comte de

April 15, 1797
b. Thiers, Adolphe

April 27, 1797
d. Babeuf, Francois-Noel

July 9, 1797
d. Burke, Edmund

July 17, 1797
b. Delaroche, Hippolyte

July 29, 1797
b. Drew, Daniel

August 3, 1797
d. Amherst, Jeffrey

August 25, 1797
d. Chittenden, Thomas

August 27, 1797
b. James, Edwin

August 30, 1797
b. Shelley, Mary Wollstonecraft

August 31, 1797
b. Castilla, Ramon

September 10, 1797
d. Godwin, Mary Wollstonecraft

September 16, 1797
b. Panizzi, Anthony, Sir

October 10, 1797
d. Braxton, Carter

October 13, 1797
b. Motherwell, William

October 16, 1797
b. Cardigan, James Thomas Brudenell, Earl of

November 2, 1797
b. Power, Tyrone William Grattan

November 14, 1797
b. Lyell, Charles, Sir

November 15, 1797
b. Weed, Thurlow

November 29, 1797
b. Donizetti, Gaetano

December 1, 1797
d. Wolcott, Oliver, Sr.

December 13, 1797
b. Heine, Heinrich

December 17, 1797
b. Henry, Joseph

December 26, 1797
d. Wilkes, John

1798

b. Douglas, David
d. Tone, Theobald Wolfe
d. Yuan Mei

January 19, 1798
b. Comte, Auguste

January 22, 1798
d. Morris, Lewis

January 31, 1798
b. Apess, William

March 13, 1798
b. Fillmore, Abigail (Powers)

March 18, 1798
b. Lieber, Franz
b. Wheelwright, William

April 3, 1798
b. Wilkes, Charles

April 5, 1798
b. Chickering, Jonas

April 9, 1798
b. Pasta, Giuditta Negri

April 20, 1798
b. Logan, William Edmond

April 26, 1798
b. Beckwourth, James Pierson
b. Delacroix, (Ferdinand Victor) Eugene

April 27, 1798
b. Clairmont, Claire

May 10, 1798
d. Vancouver, George

June 4, 1798
d. Casanova (de Seingalt), Giovanni Giacomo

June 14, 1798
b. Palacky, Frantisek

June 29, 1798
b. Haring, Georg Wilhelm Heinrich
b. Leopardi, Giacomo

June 30, 1798
b. Dyce, Alexander

July 12, 1798
d. Fitch, John

July 24, 1798
b. Dix, John Adams

August 10, 1798
b. LaFever Minard

August 21, 1798
b. Michelet, Jules
d. Wilson, James

September 13, 1798
b. Lopez, Narciso

September 21, 1798
d. Read, George

September 26, 1798
b. Mosquera, Tomas Cipriano de

October 12, 1798
b. Charles Albert
b. Pedro I

October 28, 1798
b. Coffin, Levi

November 3, 1798
b. Mason, James Murray

November 27, 1798
b. Pretorius, Andries

December 4, 1798
d. Galvani, Luigi

December 13, 1798
b. Walker, Joseph Reddeford

December 27, 1798
b. Corcoran, William Wilson

1799

b. Belcher, Edward, Sir
b. Calvert, Edward
b. Catherwood, Frederick
b. Fellows, Charles, Sir
b. Fitzpatrick, Thomas
b. Landseer, Charles
b. Sublette, William L
d. Ho-shen
d. Pius, VI
d. Tipu Sultan

January 6, 1799
b. Smith, Jedediah Strong

February 7, 1799
d. Ch'ien Lung

February 11, 1799
d. Spallanzani, Lazzaro

February 25, 1799
d. Dawes, William

February 28, 1799
b. Dollinger, J(ohannes) J(osef) I(gnaz) von

March 8, 1799
b. Cameron, Simon

March 12, 1799
b. Howitt, Mary

March 20, 1799
d. Bard, John

March 22, 1799
b. Argelander, Friedrich Wilhelm August

April 22, 1799
b. Poiseuille, Jean Louis Marie

May 12, 1799
d. Revillagigedo, Conde de

May 16, 1799
b. Emmons, Ebenezer

May 18, 1799
d. Beaumarchais, Pierre Augustin
Caron de

May 20, 1799
b. Balzac, Honore de

May 23, 1799
b. Hood, Thomas

May 27, 1799
b. Halevy, Jacques Francois Fromental
Elie

May 31, 1799
d. Lemonnier, Pierre Charles

June 6, 1799
b. Pushkin, Aleksandr Sergeyevich
d. Henry, Patrick

July 25, 1799
b. Little, Charles Coffin

August 2, 1799
d. Montgolfier, Jacques Etienne

August 5, 1799
d. Howe, Richard

August 8, 1799
b. Palmer, Nathaniel Brown

August 9, 1799
b. James, G(eorge) P(ayne) R(ainsford)

September 7, 1799
d. Ingenhousz, Jan

September 13, 1799
b. Sydenham, Baron

October 1, 1799
b. Choate, Rufus
b. Russwurm, John Brown

October 2, 1799
d. Iredell, James

October 13, 1799
d. Paca, William

October 18, 1799
b. Schonbein, Christian Friedrich

November 9, 1799
b. Mahan, Asa

November 10, 1799
d. Black, Joseph

November 17, 1799
b. Peale, Titian Ramsay

November 19, 1799
b. Caillie, Rene Auguste

November 29, 1799
b. Alcott, Amos Bronson

December 14, 1799
d. Washington, George

December 24, 1799
d. Ditters, Karl

December 31, 1799
d. Marmontel, Jean Francois

1800

b. Aga Khan, I
d. Billings, William
d. Conway, Thomas
d. Corbin, Margaret Cochran
d. Cort, Henry
d. Dixon, George
d. Hammon, Jupiter

January 7, 1800
b. Beach, Moses Yale
b. Fillmore, Millard

January 17, 1800
b. Cushing, Caleb

January 23, 1800
d. Rutledge, Edward

January 24, 1800
b. Chadwick, Edwin

February 2, 1800
b. Gregg, William

February 11, 1800
b. Talbot, William Henry Fox

February 23, 1800
d. Warton, Joseph

March 14, 1800
b. Bogardus, James

March 18, 1800
b. Smithson, Harriet Constance

March 22, 1800
b. Pusey, Edward Bouverie

March 28, 1800
b. Tamburini, Antonio

April 15, 1800
b. Ross, James Clark, Sir
d. Shippen, Edward

April 25, 1800
d. Cowper, William

May 7, 1800
d. Piccinni, Nicola

May 9, 1800
b. Brown, John

May 17, 1800
d. Suvorov, Aleksandr V

May 19, 1800
b. Brown, James

June 2, 1800
b. Trist, Nicholas Philip

June 14, 1800
d. Kleber, Jean Baptiste

June 17, 1800
b. Parsons, William
b. Rosse, William Parsons, 3rd Earl of

June 27, 1800
d. LaTour D'Auvergne, Theophile de

July 14, 1800
b. Dumas, Jean Baptiste Andre

July 18, 1800
d. Rutledge, John

July 31, 1800
b. Wohler, Friedrich

August 17, 1800
b. Rogers, Isaiah

August 18, 1800
d. Chongjo
d. Gabriel

September 6, 1800
b. Beecher, Catharine (Esther)

September 22, 1800
b. Bentham, George
b. Locke, Richard Adams

September 23, 1800
b. McGuffey, William Holmes

September 30, 1800
b. Peach, Charles William

October 2, 1800
b. Turner, Nat

October 3, 1800
b. Bancroft, George

October 23, 1800
b. Lawrence, William Beach

October 25, 1800
b. Macaulay, Thomas Babington
Macaulay, Baron

October 26, 1800
b. Moltke, Helmuth Karl Bernhard von

October 27, 1800
b. Wade, Benjamin Franklin

December 21, 1800
b. Rhett, Robert Barnwell

December 29, 1800
b. Goodyear, Charles

1801

b. Bradshaw, George
b. Cadbury, John
b. Rylands, John
b. Santana, Pedro
d. Chang Hsueh-ch'eng
d. Equiano, Olaudah

January 2, 1801
d. Lavater, Johann Casper

January 11, 1801
b. Kirkland, Caroline Matilda
Stansbury
d. Cimarosa, Domenico

January 26, 1801
b. Quidor, John

January 30, 1801
b. Smet, Pierre Jean de

February 1, 1801
b. Cole, Thomas

February 21, 1801
b. Newman, John Henry, Cardinal

February 24, 1801
b. Maclean, George

March 11, 1801
d. Paul, I

March 21, 1801
d. Abercromby, Ralph, Sir

March 25, 1801
d. Novalis

April 13, 1801
b. Carnot, Hippolyte

April 19, 1801
b. Fechner, Gustav Theodor

April 28, 1801
b. Cooper, Anthony Ashley, 7th Earl
of Shaftesbury

May 9, 1801
b. Cousins, Samuel

May 10, 1801
b. Tulane, Paul

May 11, 1801
b. Labrouste, Pierre Francois Henri

May 15, 1801
b. Lartet, Edouard Armand Isidore
Hippolyte

May 16, 1801
b. Seward, William Henry

June 1, 1801
b. Young, Brigham

June 14, 1801
d. Arnold, Benedict

June 16, 1801
b. Plucker, Julius

June 19, 1801
b. Flores, Juan Jose

July 5, 1801
b. Farragut, David Glasgow

July 14, 1801
b. Muller, Johannes Peter

July 23, 1801
b. Walker, Robert James

July 27, 1801
b. Airy, George Biddell, Sir

August 28, 1801
b. Cournot, Antoine Augustin

August 31, 1801
b. Soule, Pierre

September 4, 1801
b. D'Orsay, Alfred Guillaume, Count

September 17, 1801
b. Lane, Edward William

October 18, 1801
b. Urquiza, Justo Jose

October 23, 1801
b. Lortzing, Gustav Albert

October 28, 1801
b. Inman, Henry

November 3, 1801
b. Baedeker, Karl
b. Bellini, Vincenzo

November 7, 1801
b. Saint Georges, Jules

November 8, 1801
b. Owen, Robert Dale

November 9, 1801
b. Borden, Gail

November 18, 1801
b. Butterfield, John

November 24, 1801
d. Earle, Ralph

November 26, 1801
d. Dolomieu, Deodat Guy Gratet de

December 25, 1801
b. Harper, Joseph Wesley

1802

b. Jones, Peter
b. Richardson, Benjamin
b. Traill, Catharine Parr
d. Bowles, William Augustus

January 22, 1802
b. Upjohn, Richard

February 2, 1802
b. Boussingault, Jean Baptiste

February 4, 1802
b. Hopkins, Mark

February 6, 1802
b. Wheatstone, Charles, Sir

February 11, 1802
b. Child, Lydia Maria Francis

February 19, 1802
b. Bacon, Leonard Woolsey

February 26, 1802
b. Hugo, Victor Marie
d. Hopkins, Esek

March 3, 1802
b. Nourrit, Adolphe

March 7, 1802
b. Landseer, Edwin Henry, Sir

April 4, 1802
b. Dix, Dorothea Lynde

April 14, 1802
b. Bushnell, Horace

April 18, 1802
d. Darwin, Erasmus

May 6, 1802
d. Lowell, John

May 12, 1802
b. Lacordaire, Jean Baptiste Henri

May 22, 1802
d. Washington, Martha (Dandridge
Custis)

June 12, 1802
b. Martineau, Harriet

July 1, 1802
b. Welles, Gideon

July 6, 1802
d. Morgan, Daniel

July 10, 1802
b. Chambers, Robert

July 19, 1802
b. Davenport, Thomas

July 22, 1802
d. Bichat, Marie Francois Xavier

July 24, 1802
b. Dumas, Alexandre Dumas Davy de
la Pailleterie

July 28, 1802
d. Sarti, Giuseppe

August 2, 1802
b. Wiseman, Nicholas Patrick Stephen

August 5, 1802
b. Abel, Niels Henrik
b. Collins, Edward Knight

September 4, 1802
b. Whitman, Marcus

September 14, 1802
b. Buckstone, John Baldwin

September 16, 1802
b. Larkin, Thomas Oliver

September 19, 1802
b. Kossuth, Lajos

September 30, 1802
b. Balard, Antoine-Jerome

October 3, 1802
b. Ripley, George

October 16, 1802
d. Strutt, Joseph

October 25, 1802
b. Bonington, Richard Parkes

November 9, 1802
b. Lovejoy, Elijah Parish
d. Girtin, Thomas

November 10, 1802
b. Howe, Samuel Gridley

November 15, 1802
d. Romney, George

November 29, 1802
b. Hauff, Wilhelm

November 30, 1802
b. Trendelenburg, Friedrich Adolf

December 5, 1802
b. Dew, Thomas Roderick

December 18, 1802
b. Prentice, George Denison

December 24, 1802
b. Cockburn, Alexander James
Edmund, Sir

December 30, 1802
d. Lewis, Francis

1803

b. Black Kettle
b. Boudinot, Elias
b. Cullen, Paul, Cardinal
b. Labatt, John Kinder
b. Stewart, Maria W. Miller
d. Cugoano, Ottobah
d. Hopkins, Samuel

January 2, 1803
b. Thurber, Charles

January 9, 1803
b. Memminger, Christopher Gustavus

January 19, 1803
b. Whitman, Sarah Helen Power

February 2, 1803
b. Johnston, Albert Sidney

February 15, 1803
b. Sutter, John Augustus

February 20, 1803
b. Nevin, John Williamson

March 3, 1803
b. Decamps, Alexandre Gabriel

March 14, 1803
d. Klopstock, Friedrich Gottlieb

March 24, 1803
b. Ryerson, Adolphus Egerton

April 7, 1803
d. Toussaint l'Ouverture, Pierre
Dominique

April 24, 1803
d. Tandy, James Napper

April 29, 1803
b. Brooke, James, Sir

May 12, 1803
b. Liebig, Justus von

May 15, 1803
b. Lytton, Edward George Earle
Lytton Bulwer-Lytton, 1st Baron
Lytton

May 25, 1803
b. Emerson, Ralph Waldo

June 10, 1803
b. Darcy, Henri Philibert Gaspard

June 18, 1803
b. Weir, Robert W

June 23, 1803
b. Lee, Jason

June 24, 1803
d. Thornton, Matthew

July 5, 1803
b. Borrow, George Henry

July 24, 1803
b. Adam, Adolphe Charles
b. Davis, Alexander Jackson

July 25, 1803
b. Maverick, Samuel Augustus

July 31, 1803
b. Ericsson, John

August 3, 1803
b. Paxton, Joseph, Sir

August 15, 1803
b. Douglas, James, Sir

August 18, 1803
b. Clifford, Nathan

August 25, 1803
b. Caxias, Duque de

August 29, 1803
d. Galloway, Joseph

September 3, 1803
b. Crandall, Prudence

September 4, 1803
b. Polk, Sarah Childress

September 13, 1803
b. Gerard, Jean Ignace Isidore
b. Grandville
d. Barry, John

September 16, 1803
b. Brownson, Orestes Augustus

September 20, 1803
d. Emmet, Robert

September 27, 1803
b. DuPont, Samuel Francis

September 28, 1803
b. Merimee, Prosper

September 29, 1803
b. Sturm, Charles Francois

October 2, 1803
d. Adams, Samuel

October 3, 1803
b. Gorrie, John

October 6, 1803
b. Dove, Heinrich Wilhelm

October 8, 1803
d. Alfieri, Vittorio

October 12, 1803
b. Stewart, Alexander Turney

October 17, 1803
b. Deak, Francis

October 26, 1803
b. Hansom, Joseph Aloysius
d. Pendleton, Edmund

October 28, 1803
b. Unger, Caroline

November 5, 1803
d. Laclos, Pierre (Ambroise Francois)
Choderlos de

November 8, 1803
d. Christie, James

November 15, 1803
b. Abbott, Jacob

November 23, 1803
b. Weld, Theodore Dwight

November 30, 1803
b. Doppler, Christian Johann

December 6, 1803
b. Moodie, Susanna

December 11, 1803
b. Berlioz, Hector

December 18, 1803
d. Herder, Johann Gottfried von

1804

b. Canot, Theodore
b. Osceola
b. Vickers, Edward
b. Washakie
b. Whistler, Anna Matilda McNeill
b. Wo-jen
d. Shippen, Margaret
d. Tiepolo, Giovanni Domenico

January 10, 1804
b. Ames, Oakes

January 13, 1804
b. Gavarni, Paul

January 20, 1804
b. Sue, Eugene Joseph Marie

February 2, 1804
d. Walton, George

February 5, 1804
b. Runeberg, Johan Ludwig

February 6, 1804
d. Priestley, Joseph

February 7, 1804
b. Deere, John

February 8, 1804
b. Lander, Richard Lemon

February 12, 1804
b. Wright, Elizur
d. Kant, Immanuel

February 28, 1804
b. Foote, Henry Stuart

March 14, 1804
b. Strauss, Johann, Sr.

March 17, 1804
b. Bridger, James

March 20, 1804
b. Dow, Neal

March 30, 1804
b. Sulzer, Salomon

April 4, 1804
d. Necker, Jacques

April 5, 1804
b. Schleiden, Matthias Jakob

April 17, 1804
d. Jefferson, Mary

April 23, 1804
b. Taglioni, Maria

May 12, 1804
b. Baldwin, Robert

May 13, 1804
b. Manin, Daniele

May 16, 1804
b. Peabody, Elizabeth Palmer

June 1, 1804
b. Glinka, Mikhail Ivanovich

June 3, 1804
b. Cobden, Richard

June 6, 1804
b. Godey, Louis Antoine

June 16, 1804
d. Hiller, Johann Adam

July 4, 1804
b. Hawthorne, Nathaniel

July 12, 1804
d. Hamilton, Alexander

July 20, 1804
b. Owen, Richard, Sir

July 28, 1804
b. Feuerbach, Ludwig Andreas

August 17, 1804
d. Heck, Barbara Ruckle

September 1, 1804
b. Sand, George

September 4, 1804
b. Walter, Thomas Ustick

September 5, 1804
b. Graham, William Alexander

September 8, 1804
b. Morike, Eduard Friedrich

September 18, 1804
b. Forbes, Robert Bennet

October 1, 1804
b. Stokes, William

October 3, 1804
b. Harris, Townsend

October 18, 1804
b. Mongkut

October 24, 1804
b. Weber, Wilhelm Eduard

October 29, 1804
d. Morland, George

November 18, 1804
d. Schuyler, Philip John

November 23, 1804
b. Pierce, Franklin

December 5, 1804
b. Cantu, Cesare

December 6, 1804
b. Schroder-Devrient, Wilhelmine

December 7, 1804
b. Swayne, Noah Haynes

December 10, 1804
b. Jacobi, Carl Gustav Jacob

December 13, 1804
b. Howe, Joseph

December 19, 1804
b. Lane, Fitz Hugh

December 21, 1804
b. Disraeli, Benjamin

December 23, 1804
b. Sainte-Beuve, Charles Augustin

1805

b. Aldridge, Ira Frederick
b. Baltard, Victor
b. Chisholm, Jesse
b. Head, Edmund Walker, Sir

February 1, 1805
b. Blanqui, Auguste

February 4, 1805
b. Ainsworth, W(illiam) H(arrison)

February 13, 1805
b. Field, David Dudley

February 18, 1805
b. Goldsborough, Louis Malesherbes

February 20, 1805
b. Grimke, Angelina Emily

March 17, 1805
b. Garcia, Manuel Patricio Rodriguez

March 21, 1805
d. Greuze, Jean-Baptiste

March 25, 1805
b. Evans, George Henry

April 2, 1805
b. Andersen, Hans Christian

May 9, 1805
d. Schiller, Friedrich von

May 17, 1805
b. Surtees, Robert Smith

May 25, 1805
d. Paley, William

May 28, 1805
d. Boccherini, Luigi

June 14, 1805
b. Anderson, Robert

June 21, 1805
b. Jackson, Charles Thomas

June 22, 1805
b. Mazzini, Giuseppe

June 27, 1805
b. Stanton, Henry Brewster

July 8, 1805
b. Gross, Samuel Daniel

July 11, 1805
d. Wedgwood, Thomas

July 26, 1805
b. Brumidi, Constantino

July 29, 1805
b. Powers, Hiram
b. Tocqueville, Alexis, Comte de

August 4, 1805
b. Hamilton, William Rowan, Sir

August 29, 1805
b. Brownlow, William Gannaway
b. Maurice, Frederick Denison

August 31, 1805
b. Sotheby, Samuel Leigh

September 2, 1805
b. Echeverria, Jose Esteban (Antonino)

September 6, 1805
b. Greenough, Horatio

September 27, 1805
d. Moultrie, William

October 5, 1805
d. Cornwallis, Charles, Marquis

October 21, 1805
d. Nelson, Horatio Nelson, Viscount

October 23, 1805
b. Bartlett, John Russell

November 7, 1805
b. Brassey, Thomas

November 19, 1805
b. Lesseps, Ferdinand Marie de

November 28, 1805
b. Stephens, John Lloyd

November 30, 1805
b. Ballivian, Jose

December 6, 1805
b. Houdin, Jean Eugene Robert

December 12, 1805
b. Garrison, William Lloyd
b. Wells, Henry
d. Almon, John

December 20, 1805
b. Graham, Thomas

December 23, 1805
b. Smith, Joseph

December 31, 1805
b. Agoult, Marie Catherine Sophie d'

1806

b. Bird, Robert Montgomery
b. Dewar, John
b. Rillieux, Norbert
b. Taqi Khan Amir-e Kabir, Mirza
b. Watie, Stand
d. Gray, Robert
d. Park, Mungo
d. Utamaro, Kitagawa

January 3, 1806
b. Sontag, Henriette

January 14, 1806
b. Maury, Matthew Fontaine

January 20, 1806
b. Willis, Nathaniel Parker

January 23, 1806
d. Pitt, William, the Younger

January 25, 1806
b. Maclise, Daniel

January 30, 1806
d. Martin y Soler, Vicente

January 31, 1806
b. Harper, Fletcher

February 7, 1806
b. Hoffman, Charles Fenno

March 6, 1806
b. Browning, Elizabeth Barrett

March 9, 1806
b. Forrest, Edwin

March 12, 1806
b. Pierce, Jane (Means)

March 21, 1806
b. Juarez, Benito Pablo

April 2, 1806
b. Antonelli, Giacomo

April 9, 1806
b. Brunel, Isambard Kingdom

April 10, 1806
d. Gates, Horatio

April 11, 1806
b. Le Play, Guillaume Frederic

April 17, 1806
b. Simms, William Gilmore

April 25, 1806
b. Duff, Alexander

May 4, 1806
b. Cooke, William Fothergil, Sir

May 7, 1806
d. Morris, Robert

May 20, 1806
b. Mill, John Stuart

June 8, 1806
d. Wythe, George

June 12, 1806
b. Roebling, John Augustus

June 27, 1806
b. De Morgan, Augustus

July 10, 1806
d. Stubbs, George

July 11, 1806
d. Smith, James

July 19, 1806
b. Bache, Alexander Dallas

July 31, 1806
d. Lunardi, Vincenzo

August 22, 1806
d. Fragonard, Jean-Honore

August 23, 1806
d. Coulomb, Charles Augustin de

September 9, 1806
d. Paterson, William

September 12, 1806
b. Foote, Andrew Hull

September 13, 1806
d. Fox, Charles James

September 19, 1806
b. Dyce, William

October 9, 1806
d. Banneker, Benjamin

October 16, 1806
b. Fessenden, William Pitt

October 17, 1806
d. Dessalines, Jean Jacques

October 22, 1806
d. Sheraton, Thomas

October 25, 1806
b. Stirner, Max
d. Knox, Henry

October 26, 1806
d. Simcoe, John Graves
b. Merriam, Charles

November 4, 1806
b. Fitzhugh, George

November 16, 1806
d. Cleaveland, Moses

November 19, 1806
d. Ledoux, Claude Nicolas

November 20, 1806
d. Backus, Isaac

December 6, 1806
b. DuPrez, Gilbert

December 14, 1806
d. Breckinridge, John

1807

b. Diaz de la Pena, Narciso Virgilio
b. McClure, Robert (John Le
  Mesurier)
d. Sotheby, John

January 11, 1807
b. Cornell, Ezra

January 19, 1807
b. Lee, Robert E(dward)

February 3, 1807
b. Johnston, Joseph Eggleston

February 6, 1807
b. Sibley, Hiram

February 12, 1807
d. Roentgen, David

February 27, 1807
b. Longfellow, Henry Wadsworth

March 13, 1807
d. Rezanov, Nikolay Petrovich

April 4, 1807
d. Lalande, Joseph Jerome Lefrancais
  de
b. Abd el-Kadir

May 10, 1807
d. Rochambeau, Jean Baptiste
  Donatien de Vimeur, Comte

May 28, 1807
b. Agassiz, Louis

June 1, 1807
b. Floyd, John Buchanan

June 22, 1807
b. Hildreth, Richard

July 4, 1807
b. Garibaldi, Giuseppe

July 11, 1807
b. Tichatschek, Joseph

August 11, 1807
b. Atchison, David R

August 15, 1807
b. Grevy, Francois Paul Jules

August 18, 1807
b. Adams, Charles Francis, Sr.

September 5, 1807
b. Trench, Richard Chenevix

September 25, 1807
b. Vail, Alfred Lewis

September 28, 1807
b. Guyot, Arnold Henry
b. LaFontaine, Louis Hippolyte, Sir

October 30, 1807
b. Wadsworth, James Samuel

November 5, 1807
d. Kauffmann, Angelica

November 15, 1807
b. Petrov, Ossip

November 17, 1807
b. Hammond, James Henry

November 24, 1807
d. Brant, Joseph

November 26, 1807
b. Mount, William Sidney
d. Ellsworth, Oliver

December 3, 1807
b. Bailey, Gamaliel

December 17, 1807
b. Whittier, John Greenleaf

December 21, 1807
d. Newton, John

1808

b. Crowther, Samuel Adjai
b. Jaeger, Gustav, Dr.
d. Kirkland, Samuel
d. Robert, Hubert

January 13, 1808
b. Chase, Salmon Portland

January 27, 1808
b. Strauss, David Friedrich

February 5, 1808
b. Spitzweg, Carl

February 14, 1808
d. Dickinson, John

February 26, 1808
b. Daumier, Honore Victorin

March 24, 1808
b. Malibran, Maria Felicita

April 20, 1808
b. Napoleon III
b. Chisholm, Caroline

May 15, 1808
b. Balfe, Michael William

May 20, 1808
b. Rice, Thomas Dartmouth

May 22, 1808
b. Nerval, Gerard de

June 3, 1808
b. Davis, Jefferson

July 4, 1808
d. Ames, Fisher

July 11, 1808
b. Reed, Henry Hope

July 15, 1808
b. Manning, Henry Edward

July 28, 1808
d. Selim, III

August 3, 1808
b. Fish, Hamilton

August 9, 1808
b. Bowditch, Henry Ingersoll

August 19, 1808
b. Nasmyth, James

September 11, 1808
d. Mutis, Jose Celestino

October 21, 1808
b. Smith, Samuel Francis

October 24, 1808
b. Sartain, John

October 28, 1808
b. Smith, Horace

November 10, 1808
d. Carleton, Guy

November 22, 1808
b. Cook, Thomas
b. Rothschild, Lionel Nathan
   Rothschild, Baron

December 7, 1808
b. McCulloch, Hugh

December 29, 1808
b. Johnson, Andrew

1809

b. Babbitt, Benjamin Talbot
b. Feng Kuei-fen
b. Garneau, Francois-Xavier
b. Haussmann, Georges Eugene
b. Montt Torres, Manuel
b. Semmes, Raphael

January 4, 1809
b. Braille, Louis

January 6, 1809
d. Eberhard, Johann August

January 15, 1809
b. Proudhon, Pierre Joseph

January 19, 1809
b. Poe, Edgar Allan

February 3, 1809
b. Mendelssohn, Felix

February 6, 1809
b. Bodmer, Karl

February 7, 1809
b. Paludan-Muller, Frederik

February 12, 1809
b. Darwin, Charles Robert
b. Lincoln, Abraham

February 15, 1809
b. McCormick, Cyrus Hall

March 5, 1809
d. Dunmore, 4th Earl of

March 6, 1809
d. Heyward, Thomas, Jr.

March 7, 1809
d. Blanchard, Francois

March 20, 1809
d. Bateman, Mary

March 24, 1809
b. Flandrin, Hippolyte Jean

March 25, 1809
d. Seward, Anna

March 31, 1809
b. FitzGerald, Edward
b. Gogol, Nikolai Vasilievich

April 4, 1809
b. Peirce, Benjamin

April 7, 1809
b. Glaisher, James

May 5, 1809
b. Barnard, Frederick Augustus Porter

May 12, 1809
b. Giusti, Giuseppe

May 31, 1809
d. Haydn, Joseph

June 1, 1809
b. Hoffmann, Heinrich

June 8, 1809
d. Paine, Thomas

June 28, 1809
b. Borel d'Hauterive, Petrus

August 5, 1809
b. Kinglake, Alexander William

August 6, 1809
b. Tennyson, Alfred, Lord

August 9, 1809
b. Travis, William Barret

August 17, 1809
d. Boulton, Matthew

August 22, 1809
b. Brisbane, Albert
b. Burton, John Hill, Sir

August 27, 1809
b. Hamlin, Hannibal

August 29, 1809
b. Holmes, Oliver Wendell, Sr.

September 11, 1809
b. Price, Sterling

October 4, 1809
b. Schenck, Robert Cumming

October 6, 1809
b. Griffiths, John Willis

October 11, 1809
b. Fowler, Orson Squire
d. Lewis, Meriwether

November 4, 1809
b. Curtis, Benjamin Robbins

November 9, 1809
b. Bledsoe, Albert Taylor

November 10, 1809
b. Einhorn, David

November 13, 1809
b. Dahlgren, John Adolphus Bernard

November 27, 1809
b. Kemble, Fanny

November 30, 1809
b. Lemon, Mark

December 24, 1809
b. Carson, Kit
b. Porter, William Trotter

December 29, 1809
b. Gladstone, William Ewart

1810

b. Bowlegs, Billy
b. Geiger, Abraham
b. Staunton, Howard

January 2, 1810
b. Miller, Alfred Jacob

January 12, 1810
b. Ferdinand, II

January 15, 1810
b. Foster, Abigail Kelley

January 23, 1810
d. Hoppner, John

February 1, 1810
b. Remond, Charles Lennox

February 5, 1810
b. Bull, Ole Bornemann

February 20, 1810
d. Hofer, Andreas

February 22, 1810
b. Chopin, Frederic Francois
d. Brown, Charles Brockden

February 24, 1810
d. Cavendish, Henry

March 2, 1810
b. Leo XIII

March 10, 1810
b. McCloskey, John

April 4, 1810
b. Clarke, James Freeman

April 10, 1810
b. Day, Benjamin Henry

April 13, 1810
b. David, Felicien Cesar

April 14, 1810
b. Morrill, Justin Smith

April 15, 1810
b. Montalembert, Comte de

May 2, 1810
b. Brewer, Ebenezer Cobham

May 9, 1810
d. Lincoln, Benjamin

May 10, 1810
b. Shields, James

May 18, 1810
b. Piave, Francesco Maria

May 23, 1810
b. Fuller, Margaret

May 30, 1810
b. Stephens, Ann Sophia

May 31, 1810
b. Seymour, Horatio

June 8, 1810
b. Schumann, Robert Alexander

June 9, 1810
b. Nicolai, Carl Otto Ehrenfried

June 23, 1810
b. Elssler, Fanny

June 26, 1810
d. Montgolfier, Joseph Michel

July 2, 1810
b. Toombs, Robert Augustus

July 5, 1810
b. Barnum, P(hineas) T(aylor)

July 20, 1810
b. Regnault, Henri Victor

August 4, 1810
b. Purvis, Robert

August 10, 1810
b. Cavour, Camillo Benso, Conte di

August 18, 1810
b. Troyon, Constant

August 24, 1810
b. Parker, Theodore

August 29, 1810
b. Alberdi, Juan Bautista

September 3, 1810
b. Kane, Paul

September 4, 1810
b. McKay, Donald

September 29, 1810
b. Gaskell, Elizabeth Cleghorn

October 4, 1810
b. Johnson, Eliza (McCardle)

October 17, 1810
b. Mario, Giovanni Matteo

October 19, 1810
b. Clay, Cassius Marcellus

November 4, 1810
b. Allen, John

November 18, 1810
b. Gray, Asa

November 30, 1810
b. Winchester, Oliver Fisher

December 1, 1810
b. Gungl, Joseph

December 6, 1810
b. Napier, Robert Cornelis

December 7, 1810
b. Schwann, Theodor

December 11, 1810
b. Musset, Alfred de

December 23, 1810
d. Queensberry, William Douglas, Duke

December 25, 1810
b. Langstroth, Lorenzo Lorraine

1811

b. Cinque, Joseph
b. Spokane Garry
d. Dalzel, Archibald
d. Fairfax, Sally
d. McIntire, Samuel
d. Raikes, Robert
d. Zane, Ebenezer

January 6, 1811
b. Sumner, Charles

January 18, 1811
b. Laboulaye, Edouard Rose

January 20, 1811
d. Chalgrin, Francois

January 24, 1811
b. Barnard, Henry

February 2, 1811
b. Bacon, Delia Salter

February 3, 1811
b. Greeley, Horace

February 9, 1811
d. Maskelyne, Nevil

February 15, 1811
b. Sarmiento, Domingo Faustino

February 17, 1811
b. A'Beckett, Gilbert Abbott

March 17, 1811
b. Gutzkow, Karl Ferdinand

March 20, 1811
b. Bingham, George Caleb
b. Bonaparte, Francois Charles Joseph

March 28, 1811
b. Neumann, John Nepomucene, Saint

March 31, 1811
b. Bunsen, Robert Wilhelm Eberhard

April 1, 1811
b. McCosh, James

April 14, 1811
b. Fisher, Clara

May 5, 1811
b. Draper, John William

May 7, 1811
d. Cumberland, Richard

May 11, 1811
b. Chang and Eng
b. LeVerrier, Urbain Jean Joseph
b. Scranton, George Whitfield

May 30, 1811
b. Belinsky, Vissarion Grigoryevich

June 3, 1811
b. James, Henry, Sr.

June 7, 1811
b. Simpson, James Young, Sir

June 14, 1811
b. Stowe, Harriet (Elizabeth) Beecher

June 18, 1811
b. Osgood, Frances Sargent Locke

June 19, 1811
d. Chase, Samuel

July 5, 1811
b. Applegate, Jesse

July 7, 1811
b. Meiggs, Henry

July 9, 1811
b. Parton, Sara Payson Willis

July 11, 1811
b. Grove, William Robert, Sir

July 13, 1811
b. Scott, George Gilbert, Sir

July 18, 1811
b. Thackeray, William Makepeace

July 20, 1811
b. Elgin, James Bruce

July 28, 1811
b. Grisi, Giulia

July 30, 1811
d. Hidalgo y Costilla, Miguel

August 2, 1811
d. Williams, William

August 3, 1811
b. Otis, Elisha Graves

August 5, 1811
b. Thomas, (Charles Louis) Ambroise

August 11, 1811
b. Benjamin, Judah Philip

August 21, 1811
b. Kelly, William

August 23, 1811
b. Bravais, Auguste

August 29, 1811
b. Bergh, Henry

August 31, 1811
b. Gautier, Theophile
d. Bougainville, Louis-Antoine de

September 3, 1811
b. Noyes, John Humphrey

September 6, 1811
b. Gilliss, James Melville

September 12, 1811
b. Hall, James

October 22, 1811
b. Liszt, Franz (Ferencz)

October 25, 1811
b. Galois, Evariste

October 27, 1811
b. Singer, Isaac Merrit

October 29, 1811
b. Blanc, Louis

November 16, 1811
b. Bright, John

November 21, 1811
d. Kleist, Heinrich von

November 26, 1811
b. Tseng Kuo-fan

November 29, 1811
b. Phillips, Wendell

December 5, 1811
b. Van Nostrand, David

1812

b. Grey, George
b. Lerdo de Tejada, Miguel
b. Lohman, Ann Trow
b. Mallory, Stephen R
b. Rousseau, Theodore

January 25, 1812
b. Page, Charles Grafton

February 7, 1812
b. Dickens, Charles (John Huffam)

February 11, 1812
b. Stephens, Alexander Hamilton

February 15, 1812
b. Tiffany, Charles Lewis

February 16, 1812
b. Wilson, Henry

March 1, 1812
b. Pugin, A(ugustus) W(elby)
N(orthmore)

March 11, 1812
d. DeLoutherbourg, Philip James

April 2, 1812
b. Forster, John

April 6, 1812
b. Herzen, Aleksandr Ivanovich

April 15, 1812
b. Rousseau, (Pierre Etienne) Theodore

April 20, 1812
d. Clinton, George

April 22, 1812
b. Dalhousie, James Andrew Broun
Ramsay, Marquess of

April 26, 1812
b. Flotow, Friedrich von, Baron
b. Krupp, Alfred

May 6, 1812
b. Delany, Martin Robinson

May 7, 1812
b. Browning, Robert

May 12, 1812
b. Lear, Edward

May 25, 1812
d. Malone, Edmund

June 14, 1812
b. Wood, Fernando

June 18, 1812
b. Goncharov, Ivan Aleksandrovich

June 26, 1812
b. Palmer, Frances Flora Bond

July 4, 1812
b. Jasper, John J

August 9, 1812
b. Judson, Egbert Putnam

August 31, 1812
b. Thompson, William Tappan

September 12, 1812
b. Hoe, Richard March

September 19, 1812
d. Rothschild, Mayer Amschel

September 21, 1812
d. Schikaneder, Emanuel

September 24, 1812
d. Bagration, Petr Ivanovich

October 4, 1812
b. Persiani, Fanny

October 12, 1812
b. Elliott, Charles Loring
b. Sobrero, Ascanio

October 13, 1812
d. Brock, Isaac, Sir

October 20, 1812
b. Flint, Austin

October 22, 1812
b. Clevenger, Shobal Vail

November 10, 1812
b. Tso Tsung-t'ang

November 16, 1812
d. Walter, John, I

December 2, 1812
d. Sacagawea

December 7, 1812
b. Linton, William James

December 8, 1812
b. Burritt, Elihu

December 14, 1812
b. Canning, Charles John, Earl

December 15, 1812
b. Levy, Joseph Moses

December 22, 1812
d. Clinton, James

December 24, 1812
d. Barlow, Joel

1813

b. Jacobs, Harriet Ann
b. Varesi, Felice
d. Boone, Rebecca B
d. Crevecoeur, (Hector) St. John de

January 1, 1813
d. Alston, Theodosia Burr

January 4, 1813
b. Bonaparte, Louis Lucien
b. Pitman, Isaac

January 18, 1813
b. Glidden, Joseph Farwell

January 19, 1813
b. Bessemer, Henry, Sir

January 20, 1813
d. Wieland, Christoph Martin

January 21, 1813
b. Fremont, John Charles

January 24, 1813
d. Clymer, George

January 25, 1813
b. Sims, James Marion

February 11, 1813
b. Ludwig, Otto

February 12, 1813
b. Dana, James Dwight
b. Lossing, Benson John

February 14, 1813
b. Dargomijsky, Alexander

February 26, 1813
d. Livingston, Robert R

March 2, 1813
b. Macfarren, George Alexander, Sir

March 7, 1813
b. Kamehameha III

March 11, 1813
b. Lamperti, Francesco

March 13, 1813
b. Delmonico, Lorenzo

March 14, 1813
b. Bradley, Joseph P

March 18, 1813
b. Hebbel, Friedrich
b. Lippincott, Joshua Ballinger

March 19, 1813
b. Livingstone, David

March 22, 1813
b. Crawford, Thomas

March 27, 1813
b. Currier, Nathaniel

March 29, 1813
b. Letcher, John

April 10, 1813
d. Lagrange, Joseph-Louis

April 14, 1813
b. Morgan, Junius Spencer

April 16, 1813
d. Kutuzov, Mikhail Ilarionovich

April 19, 1813
d. Rush, Benjamin

April 23, 1813
b. Douglas, Stephen Arnold
b. Ozanam, (Antoine) Frederic

April 27, 1813
d. Pike, Zebulon Montgomery

May 5, 1813
b. Kierkegaard, Soren Aabye

May 9, 1813
b. Matteson, Tompkins Harrison

May 10, 1813
b. Blair, Montgomery

May 22, 1813
b. Wagner, Richard

June 1, 1813
d. Lawrence, James

June 8, 1813
b. Porter, David Dixon

June 21, 1813
b. Aytoun, William Edmonstoune

June 24, 1813
b. Beecher, Henry Ward

June 28, 1813
d. Scharnhorst, Gerhard Johann David von

July 6, 1813
d. Sharp, Granville

July 12, 1813
b. Bernard, Claude

July 15, 1813
b. Healy, George Peter Alexander

August 10, 1813
b. Fry, William Henry

August 11, 1813
d. Pye, Henry

August 23, 1813
d. Wilson, Alexander

August 28, 1813
b. Very, Jones

September 12, 1813
d. Randolph, Edmund Jennings

September 13, 1813
b. MacMillan, Daniel
b. Sedgwick, John

September 24, 1813
d. Gretry, Andre Ernest Modeste

October 5, 1813
d. Tecumseh

October 10, 1813
b. Verdi, Giuseppe Fortunino Francesco

October 12, 1813
b. Trumbull, Lyman

October 17, 1813
b. Buchner, Georg

October 21, 1813
b. Fillmore, Caroline Carmichael McIntosh
d. Colter, John

November 12, 1813
d. Crevecoeur, Michel-Guillaume Jean de

November 13, 1813
b. Phelps, John Wolcott

November 16, 1813
d. Franklin, William

November 17, 1813
d. Otterbein, Philip William

November 20, 1813
d. Bodoni, Giambattista

December 10, 1813
b. Chandler, Zachariah

December 19, 1813
d. McGill, James

December 25, 1813
b. Roach, John

1814

b. Nestle, Henri
d. Aleijadinho, O

January 1, 1814
b. Hung Hsiu-ch'uan

January 10, 1814
b. DeVere, Aubrey Thomas

January 11, 1814
b. Paget, James, Sir

January 17, 1814
b. Wood, Henry, Mrs.

January 20, 1814
b. Wilmot, David

January 24, 1814
d. Heath, William

January 27, 1814
b. Appleton, William Henry
b. Viollet le Duc, Eugene Emmanuel
d. Fichte, Johann Gottlieb

February 3, 1814
d. Matamoros, Mariano

February 6, 1814
b. Sorin, Edward Frederick

February 7, 1814
b. Colton, Gardner Quincy

February 9, 1814
b. Tilden, Samuel Jones

March 9, 1814
b. Evans, John
b. Shevchenko, Taras

March 26, 1814
d. Guillotin, Joseph Ignace

March 28, 1814
d. Clodion

April 2, 1814
b. Bigelow, Erastus Brigham

April 12, 1814
d. Burney, Charles

April 15, 1814
b. Motley, John Lothrop

April 25, 1814
d. Dibdin, Charles

May 12, 1814
d. Paine, Robert Treat

May 29, 1814
d. Josephine

May 30, 1814
b. Bakunin, Mikhail Aleksandrovich

June 8, 1814
b. Reade, Charles

June 11, 1814
b. Bellows, Henry Whitney

June 27, 1814
d. Reichardt, Johann Friedrich

July 12, 1814
d. Howe, William, Viscount

July 19, 1814
b. Colt, Samuel
d. Flinders, Matthew

August 10, 1814
b. Pemberton, John Clifford
b. Yancey, William Lowndes

August 13, 1814
b. Angstrom, Anders Jonas

August 19, 1814
b. Pleasant, Mary Ellen

August 24, 1814
d. Rumford, Count

August 28, 1814
b. LeFanu, Joseph Sheridan

August 31, 1814
d. Phillip, Arthur

September 3, 1814
b. Sylvester, James Joseph

September 6, 1814
b. Cartier, Georges Etienne, Sir

September 7, 1814
b. Butterfield, William

October 4, 1814
b. Millet, Jean Francois

October 14, 1814
b. Lamy, Jean Baptist

October 15, 1814
b. Lermontov, Mikhail

October 19, 1814
d. Warren, Mercy Otis

October 25, 1814
b. Carrera, Jose Rafael

November 6, 1814
b. Sax, Adolphe (Antoine-Joseph)

November 13, 1814
b. Hooker, Joseph

November 23, 1814
d. Gerry, Elbridge

December 2, 1814
d. Sade, Marquis (Donatien Alphonse
Francoise) de

December 9, 1814
d. Bramah, Joseph

December 18, 1814
b. Bolton, Sarah Tittle Barrett

December 19, 1814
b. Stanton, Edwin McMasters

December 27, 1814
b. Simon, Jules Francois

1815

b. Christy, Edwin P.
b. Cochise
b. Gimbel, Adam
b. Jenner, William, Sir
b. Krieghoff, Cornelius
b. Sloan, Samuel
b. Smohalla

January 11, 1815
b. MacDonald, John Alexander

January 15, 1815
d. Hamilton, Emma, Lady

January 16, 1815
b. Halleck, Henry Wager

January 18, 1815
b. De La Rue, Warren

January 21, 1815
b. Wells, Horace
d. Claudius, Matthias

February 7, 1815
b. Beatty, Alfred Chester, Sir

February 12, 1815
b. Forbes, Edward

February 13, 1815
b. Stoltz, Rosine

February 21, 1815
b. Meissonier, Jean Louis Ernest

February 23, 1815
d. Fulton, Robert

March 1, 1815
b. Thorpe, Thomas Bangs

March 4, 1815
d. Abington, Fanny

March 5, 1815
d. Mesmer, Franz Anton

March 9, 1815
b. Davis, David

March 15, 1815
b. Brown, William Wells

March 29, 1815
b. Frere, Henry Bartle Edward

April 1, 1815
b. Bismarck, Otto Edward Leopold
von

April 24, 1815
b. Trollope, Anthony

May 8, 1815
d. Ramsay, David

May 9, 1815
b. Blythe, David Gilmour

May 18, 1815
b. Francis, James Bicheno

May 27, 1815
b. Parkes, Henry, Sir

June 1, 1815
d. Gillray, James

June 5, 1815
b. Curry, Jabez Lamar Monroe

June 15, 1815
b. Browne, Phiz

August 1, 1815
b. Dana, Richard Henry, Jr.

August 5, 1815
b. Eyre, Edward John

August 10, 1815
d. Handsome Lake

August 13, 1815
b. Phelps, Elizabeth Stuart Ward

August 29, 1815
b. Carroll, Anna Ella

September 3, 1815
d. Murray, John

September 9, 1815
d. Copley, John Singleton

September 18, 1815
b. Strepponi, Giuseppina

September 24, 1815
d. Sevier, John

October 12, 1815
b. Hardee, William Joseph

October 13, 1815
d. Murat, Joachim

October 16, 1815
b. Lubbock, Francis Richard

October 29, 1815
b. Emmett, Daniel Decatur

October 30, 1815
b. Comstock, Elizabeth L
b. Downing, Andrew Jackson

November 1, 1815
b. Long, Crawford Williamson

November 2, 1815
b. Boole, George

November 12, 1815
b. Stanton, Elizabeth Cady

November 17, 1815
b. Farnham, Eliza Wood Burhans

December 3, 1815
d. Carroll, John

December 7, 1815
d. Ney, Michel de la Moskova, Prince

December 10, 1815
b. Lovelace, Ada Byron

December 22, 1815
d. Morelos y Pavon, Jose Maria

December 23, 1815
b. Garnet, Henry Highland

December 31, 1815
b. Meade, George Gordon

1816

b. Allen, Macon B
b. Bacardi, Don Facundo
b. Freytag, Gustav
b. Heavysege, Charles
b. Lafarge, Marie
b. Ram Singh
b. Rutledge, Ann
b. Varnhagen, Francisco Adolfo de
d. Brackenridge, H(ugh) H(enry)
d. Ferguson, Adam
d. Salem, Peter
d. Uthman don Fodio

February 20, 1816
b. Rimmer, William

March 22, 1816
b. Kensett, John Frederick

March 31, 1816
d. Asbury, Francis
d. Ducis, Jean Francois

April 5, 1816
b. Miller, Samuel Freeman

April 13, 1816
b. Bennett, William Sterndale, Sir

April 21, 1816
b. Bronte, Charlotte

May 2, 1816
b. Egg, Augustus Leopold

May 3, 1816
b. Meigs, Montgomery Cunningham

May 24, 1816
b. Leutze, Emanuel

June 1, 1816
b. Monk, Maria

June 2, 1816
b. Aguilar, Grace

June 5, 1816
d. Paisiello, Giovanni

July 4, 1816
b. Walker, Hiram

July 7, 1816
d. Sheridan, Richard Brinsley

July 14, 1816
b. Gobineau, Joseph Arthur, Comte de
d. Miranda, Francisco de

July 21, 1816
b. Reuter, Paul Julius Von

July 23, 1816
b. Cushman, Charlotte Saunders

July 31, 1816
b. Thomas, George Henry

August 4, 1816
b. Sage, Russell

August 21, 1816
b. Gerhardt, Charles Frederic

September 9, 1816
b. Fee, John Gregg

September 11, 1816
b. Zeiss, Carl

September 14, 1816
b. Wood, James Rushmore

October 7, 1816
b. Hargraves, Edward Hammond

October 10, 1816
b. Simon, John, Sir

October 14, 1816
b. Huntington, Daniel

October 30, 1816
b. Dawes, Henry Laurens

November 3, 1816
b. Early, Jubal Anderson

November 4, 1816
b. Alcorn, James Lusk
b. Field, Stephen Johnson

November 6, 1816
d. Morris, Gouverneur

November 23, 1816
b. Duyckinck, Evert Augustus

November 25, 1816
b. Rutherfurd, Lewis Morris

November 29, 1816
b. Waite, Morrison Remick

December 8, 1816
b. Belmont, August

December 13, 1816
b. Siemens, (Ernst) Werner von

December 28, 1816
b. Packard, Elizabeth Parsons Ware

December 29, 1816
b. Ludwig, Karl Friedrich Wilhelm

1817

b. Campbell, Joseph
b. Duncanson, Robert Scott
b. Watts, George Frederic

January 11, 1817
d. Dwight, Timothy

January 14, 1817
d. Monsigny, Pierre-Alexandre

February 14, 1817
b. Douglass, Frederick

February 15, 1817
b. Daubigny, Charles Francois

February 22, 1817
b. Gade, Niels Vilhelm

February 26, 1817
b. Wallace, Horace Binney

March 5, 1817
b. Layard, Austen Henry, Sir

March 22, 1817
b. Bragg, Braxton

March 26, 1817
b. Haupt, Herman

March 28, 1817
b. DeSanctis, Francesco

April 2, 1817
b. Palmer, Erastus Dow

April 15, 1817
b. Jowett, Benjamin

April 18, 1817
b. Lewes, George Henry

April 28, 1817
b. Curtin, Andrew Gregg

May 21, 1817
b. Lotze, Rudolf Hermann

June 13, 1817
d. Edgeworth, Richard Lovell

June 24, 1817
d. McKean, Thomas

June 26, 1817
b. Bronte, Patrick Branwell

June 30, 1817
d. Werner, Abraham Gottlob

July 6, 1817
d. Savage, Edward

July 12, 1817
b. Thoreau, Henry David

July 14, 1817
d. Stael-Holstein, Anne Louise
Germaine Necker, Baroness de

July 18, 1817
d. Austen, Jane

July 19, 1817
b. Bickerdyke, Mary Ann Ball

July 21, 1817
b. Gilbert, John, Sir

August 7, 1817
d. DuPont de Nemours, Pierre Samuel

August 10, 1817
d. Lowell, Francis Cabot

August 16, 1817
b. Davis, Henry Winter

August 22, 1817
b. Judson, Emily Chubbock

August 29, 1817
b. Leech, John

September 6, 1817
b. Galt, Alexander Tilloch

September 9, 1817
d. Cuffe, Paul

September 14, 1817
b. Storm, (Hans) Theodor (Woldsen)

October 15, 1817
d. Burckhardt, Johann Ludwig

October 17, 1817
b. Syed Ahmed Khan

October 18, 1817
d. Mehul, Etienne Nicolas

October 23, 1817
b. Denver, James William
b. Larousse, Pierre Athanase

October 31, 1817
b. Graetz, Heinrich Hirsch

November 7, 1817
d. Deluc, Jean Andre

November 12, 1817
b. Baha'u'llah

November 15, 1817
d. Kosciuszko, Thaddeus

November 23, 1817
d. Clairborne, William Charles Coles

November 25, 1817
b. Bigelow, John

November 30, 1817
b. Mommsen, Theodor

December 2, 1817
b. Marmol, Jose

December 7, 1817
d. Bligh, William, Captain

December 25, 1817
b. Van Camp, Gilbert C

December 31, 1817
b. Fields, James Thomas

1818

b. Burckhardt, Jacob (Christoph)
b. Copway, George
b. Eastman, Mary Henderson
b. Keckley, Elizabeth Hobbs
b. Little Wolf
b. Mandelbaum, Fredericka
b. Manuelito
b. Montez, Lola
b. Secchi, Pietro Angelo
b. Tewodros II
d. Wyss, Johann David

January 23, 1818
b. Boutwell, George Sewall

February 1, 1818
d. Gazzaniga, Giuseppe

February 6, 1818
b. Evarts, William Maxwell
b. Litolff, Henri Charles

February 13, 1818
d. Clark, George Rogers

February 18, 1818
d. Girty, Simon

March 3, 1818
b. Ingersoll, Simon

March 11, 1818
b. LeClear, Thomas
b. Sainte-Clair Deville, Henri Etienne

March 12, 1818
b. Worden, John Lorimer

March 23, 1818
b. Buell, Don Carlos

March 24, 1818
d. Repton, Humphry

March 25, 1818
d. Lee, Henry

March 28, 1818
b. Hampton, Wade

April 8, 1818
b. Hofmann, August Wilhelm von

April 21, 1818
b. Billings, Josh

April 23, 1818
b. Froude, James Anthony

April 29, 1818
b. Alexander II

May 5, 1818
b. Marx, Karl Heinrich

May 8, 1818
b. Tilley, Samuel Leonard, Sir

May 10, 1818
d. Revere, Paul

May 14, 1818
d. Lewis, Matthew Gregory

May 20, 1818
b. Fargo, William George

May 27, 1818
b. Bloomer, Amelia Jenks

May 28, 1818
b. Beauregard, Pierre Gustav Toutant de

May 31, 1818
b. Andrew, John Albion

June 3, 1818
b. Faidherbe, Louis Leon Cesar

June 6, 1818
d. Dabrowski, Jan Henryk

June 11, 1818
b. Bain, Alexander

June 17, 1818
b. Gounod, Charles Francois

June 21, 1818
b. Wallace, Richard, Sir

July 1, 1818
b. Gorgas, Josiah
b. Semmelweis, Ignaz Philipp

July 11, 1818
b. Forster, William Edward

July 14, 1818
b. Lyon, Nathaniel

July 28, 1818
d. Monge, Gaspard

July 30, 1818
b. Bronte, Emily Jane

August 1, 1818
b. Mitchell, Maria

August 6, 1818
b. Anderssen, Adolf

August 13, 1818
b. Stone, Lucy

August 15, 1818
b. Mason, Biddy

August 22, 1818
d. Hastings, Warren

August 25, 1818
d. Billington, Elizabeth

August 28, 1818
d. DuSable, Jean Baptiste

August 31, 1818
d. Saint Clair, Arthur
d. St. Clair, Arthur

September 12, 1818
b. Gatling, Richard Jordan

September 14, 1818
b. Congreve, Richard

September 16, 1818
b. Haden, Francis Seymour, Sir

October 3, 1818
b. MacMillan, Alexander

October 5, 1818
d. Hanks, Nancy

October 15, 1818
b. McDowell, Irvin

October 17, 1818
b. Van Lew, Elizabeth

October 18, 1818
b. Ord, Edward Otho Cresap
b. Wen-hsiang

October 22, 1818
b. Leconte de Lisle, Charles Marie Rene

October 28, 1818
d. Adams, Abigail (Smith)

November 1, 1818
b. Renwick, James, Jr.

November 5, 1818
b. Butler, Benjamin Franklin

November 7, 1818
b. Du Bois-Reymond, Emil

November 9, 1818
b. Turgenev, Ivan Sergeevich

November 17, 1818
d. Charlotte Sophia

November 21, 1818
b. Morgan, Lewis Henry

November 24, 1818
b. Agnew, David Hayes

December 13, 1818
b. Lincoln, Mary Todd

December 24, 1818
b. Joule, James Prescott

1819

b. Tate, Henry, Sir

January 1, 1819
b. Clough, Arthur Hugh
b. Schaff, Philip

January 9, 1819
b. Frith, William Powell

January 29, 1819
d. Charles, IV

February 5; 1819
d. Van Buren, Hannah (Hoes)

February 8, 1819
b. Ruskin, John

February 12, 1819
b. Story, William Wetmore

February 14, 1819
b. Sholes, Christopher Latham

February 19, 1819
b. Pinkham, Lydia Estes

February 22, 1819
b. Lowell, James Russell
b. Crummell, Alexander

March 2, 1819
b. Brannan, Samuel

March 10, 1819
d. Jacobi, Friedrich Heinrich

March 23, 1819
d. Kotzebue, August Friedrich Ferdinand von

March 29, 1819
b. Drake, Edwin Laurentine
b. Wise, Isaac Mayer

April 11, 1819
b. Halle, Charles, Sir

April 15, 1819
d. Evans, Oliver

April 18, 1819
b. Cespedes, Carlos Manuel de

b. Suppe, Franz von

April 23, 1819
b. Quaritch, Bernard

April 28, 1819
d. Baranov, Aleksandr Andreievich

May 5, 1819
b. Moniuszko, Stanislaus
d. Kamehameha I

May 15, 1819
b. Crittendon, Thomas Leonidas

May 24, 1819
b. Victoria, Queen

May 27, 1819
b. Howe, Julia Ward

May 31, 1819
b. Whitman, Walt(er)

June 3, 1819
b. Ball, Thomas
b. Jongkind, Johan Barthold

June 5, 1819
b. Adams, John Couch

June 10, 1819
b. Courbet, Gustave

June 11, 1819
b. Thayer, Eli

June 12, 1819
b. Kingsley, Charles

June 20, 1819
b. Offenbach, Jacques

June 26, 1819
b. Doubleday, Abner

June 28, 1819
b. Harpignies, Henri

June 30, 1819
b. Wheeler, William Alrnon

July 4, 1819
b. Squibb, Edward Robinson

July 8, 1819
b. McClintock, Francis Leopold, Sir

July 9, 1819
b. Howe, Elias

July 11, 1819
b. Warner, Susan Bogert

July 19, 1819
b. Keller, Gottfried

August 1, 1819
b. Melville, Herman

August 5, 1819
b. Bidwell, John
b. Tait, Arthur Fitzwilliam

August 8, 1819
b. Dana, Charles Anderson

August 9, 1819
b. Morton, William Thomas Green

August 11, 1819
b. Heade, Martin Johnson

August 13, 1819
b. Stokes, George Gabriel, Sir

August 19, 1819
d. Watt, James

August 23, 1819
d. Perry, Oliver Hazard, Admiral

August 25, 1819
b. Pinkerton, Allan

August 26, 1819
b. Albert, Prince

September 6, 1819
b. Rosecrans, William Starke

September 7, 1819
b. Hendricks, Thomas Andrews

September 12, 1819
d. Blucher, Gebhard Leberecht von

September 13, 1819
b. Schumann, Clara Josephine Wieck

September 15, 1819
b. Pasdeloup, Jules Etienne

September 17, 1819
b. Pretorius, Marthinus Wessel

September 18, 1819
b. Foucault, Jean Bernard Leon
d. Langdon, John

September 23, 1819
b. Fizeau, Armand Hippolyte Louis

October 4, 1819
b. Crispi, Francesco

October 10, 1819
b. Monck, Charles Stanley, Sir

November 9, 1819
d. Lee, Thomas Sim

November 14, 1819
b. Rodgers, Christopher Raymond
Perry

November 22, 1819
b. Eliot, George

November 23, 1819
b. Whitney, Josiah Dwight

November 30, 1819
b. Field, Cyrus West

December 18, 1819
b. Hecker, Isaac Thomas

December 26, 1819
b. Southworth, Emma Dorothy Eliza
Nevitte

December 30, 1819
b. Fontane, Theodor

1820

b. Barboncito
b. Burke, Robert O'Hara
b. Comstock, Henry Tompkins Paige
b. Farmer, Moses Gerrish
b. Ja Ja of Opobo
b. Mahal, Hazrat
b. Phillips, Charles
b. Rogers, Mary Cecilia
b. Satanta
b. Taewon'gun, Hungson
b. Victorio
d. Banks, Joseph
d. Grattan, Henry

January 10, 1820
b. Drew, Louisa Lane

January 17, 1820
b. Bronte, Anne

January 24, 1820
b. Raymond, Henry Jarvis

January 29, 1820
d. George III

February 3, 1820
b. Kane, Elisha Kent

February 6, 1820
b. Durant, Thomas Clark

February 8, 1820
b. Sherman, William Tecumseh

February 15, 1820
b. Anthony, Susan B(rownell)
d. Ellery, William

February 20, 1820
b. Vieuxtemps, Henri Francois Joseph

February 23, 1820
b. Stampfli, Jakob

February 28, 1820
b. Rachel
b. Tenniel, John, Sir

March 9, 1820
b. Blatchford, Samuel

March 11, 1820
d. Mackenzie, Alexander, Sir
d. West, Benjamin

March 14, 1820
b. Victor Emmanuel II

March 16, 1820
b. Tamberlik, Enrico

March 17, 1820
b. Ingelow, Jean

March 22, 1820
d. Decatur, Stephen

March 24, 1820
b. Crosby, Fanny

March 26, 1820
b. Upchurch, John Jorden

March 30, 1820
b. Sewell, Anna

April 5, 1820
b. Nadar

April 8, 1820
d. Selkirk, 5th Earl of

April 14, 1820
b. Ballou, Maturin Murray

April 17, 1820
b. Cartwright, Alexander Joy, Jr.

April 25, 1820
d. Volney, (Constantin) Francois Chasseboeuf, Comte de

April 26, 1820
b. Cary, Alice

April 27, 1820
b. Spencer, Herbert
b. Surratt, Mary Eugenia Jenkins

May 4, 1820
b. Tyler, Julia Gardiner

May 5, 1820
b. Soloviev, Sergei Mikhailovich
b. Wright, Horatio Gouverneur

May 15, 1820
b. Nightingale, Florence

May 22, 1820
b. Whittredge, Thomas Worthington

May 23, 1820
b. Eads, James Buchanan

June 6, 1820
b. Durrie, George Henry

June 14, 1820
b. Bartlett, John

June 20, 1820
d. Belgrano, Manuel

July 20, 1820
b. De Bow, James Dunwoody Brownson
b. Keene, Laura

July 25, 1820
b. Doulton, Henry, Sir

July 29, 1820
b. Vallandigham, Clement Laird

July 31, 1820
b. Garrett, John Work

August 2, 1820
b. Tyndall, John

August 6, 1820
b. Smith, Donald Alexander

August 13, 1820
b. Grove, George, Sir

August 31, 1820
b. Creighton, Edward

September 2, 1820
b. Hale, Lucretia Peabody

September 3, 1820
b. Hearst, George
d. Latrobe, Benjamin Henry

September 21, 1820
d. Drake, Joseph Rodman

September 26, 1820
d. Boone, Daniel

October 5, 1820
d. Rich, Claudius James

October 6, 1820
b. Lind, Jenny

October 8, 1820
d. Christophe, Henri

October 24, 1820
b. Fromentin, Eugene

October 30, 1820
b. Dawson, John William, Sir

November 14, 1820
b. Burlingame, Anson

November 28, 1820
b. Engels, Friedrich

December 19, 1820
b. Livermore, Mary Ashton Rice

December 25, 1820
d. Fouche, Joseph

December 26, 1820
b. Boucicault, Dion Lardner

1821

b. Hall, Charles Francis
b. Mitre, Bartolome
d. Maistre, Joseph de
d. Schweppe, Jacob
d. Walker, Adam

January 4, 1821
d. Seton, Elizabeth Ann Bayley, Saint

January 8, 1821
b. Longstreet, James

January 14, 1821
b. Mosenthal, Salomon Hermann von

January 21, 1821
b. Breckinridge, John Cabell

February 3, 1821
b. Blackwell, Elizabeth

February 16, 1821
b. Barth, Heinrich

February 19, 1821
b. Blair, Francis Preston, Jr.

February 21, 1821
b. Scribner, Charles

February 23, 1821
d. Keats, John

March 19, 1821
b. Burton, Richard Francis, Sir

March 21, 1821
b. Leslie, Frank

April 4, 1821
b. Yale, Linus

April 9, 1821
b. Baudelaire, Charles Pierre

April 11, 1821
b. Bergmann, Carl

April 15, 1821
b. Brown, Joseph Emerson

April 20, 1821
d. Achard, Franz Karl

April 22, 1821
d. Crome, John

April 24, 1821
d. Frank, Johann Peter

May 2, 1821
d. Piozzi, Hester Lynch Salisbury

May 5, 1821
d. Napoleon I

May 8, 1821
b. A.L.O.E.
b. Vanderbilt, William Henry

May 23, 1821
b. White, Richard Grant

June 7, 1821
d. Guemes, Martin

June 8, 1821
b. Baker, Samuel White, Sir

June 28, 1821
b. Maretzek, Max

July 2, 1821
b. Tupper, Charles

July 11, 1821
b. Feuillet, Octave

July 13, 1821
b. Forrest, Nathan Bedford

July 16, 1821
b. Eddy, Mary Baker Morse

July 18, 1821
b. Viardot-Garcia, Pauline

August 3, 1821
b. Stephens, Uriah

August 4, 1821
d. Floyd, William

August 10, 1821
b. Cooke, Jay

August 16, 1821
b. Cayley, Arthur

August 31, 1821
b. Helmholtz, Hermann Ludwig
Ferdinand von

September 4, 1821
d. Carrera, Jose Miguel

September 11, 1821
b. Beadle, Erastus Flavel

October 2, 1821
b. Stewart, Alexander Peter

October 7, 1821
b. Still, William

October 17, 1821
b. Gardner, Alexander

October 20, 1821
d. Azara, Felix de

October 22, 1821
b. Huntington, Collis Potter

October 28, 1821
d. Pacchierotti, Gasparo

October 31, 1821
b. Virchow, Rudolf

November 11, 1821
b. Dostoyevsky, Fyodor Mikhailovich

November 24, 1821
b. Buckle, Henry Thomas

December 10, 1821
b. Nekrasov, Nikolay Alexeyevich

December 12, 1821
b. Flaubert, Gustave

December 24, 1821
b. Moreno, Gabriel Garcia
b. Poole, William Frederick

December 25, 1821
b. Barton, Clara Harlowe

1822

b. Macy, R(owland) H(ussey)
b. Red Cloud, Chief
b. Stroh, Bernard
d. Ali Pasha
d. Debrett, John

January 2, 1822
b. Clausius, Rudolf Julius Emmanuel

January 6, 1822
b. Schliemann, Heinrich

January 17, 1822
b. Fuller, George

January 28, 1822
b. Mackenzie, Alexander

February 9, 1822
b. Parton, James

February 16, 1822
b. Galton, Francis, Sir

February 21, 1822
b. Gibbs, Oliver Wolcott

March 7, 1822
b. Masse, Victor

March 8, 1822
b. Avery, Samuel Putnam
b. Johnston, Richard Malcolm

March 11, 1822
b. Bertrand, Joseph Louis Francois
b. Petipa, Marius

March 12, 1822
b. Read, Thomas Buchanan

March 16, 1822
b. Bonheur, Rosa

March 25, 1822
b. Ritschl, Albrecht Benjamin

April 3, 1822
b. Hale, Edward Everett

April 27, 1822
b. Grant, Ulysses Simpson
b. Olmsted, Frederick Law

April 30, 1822
b. Goodwin, Hannibal Williston

May 8, 1822
d. Stark, John

May 20, 1822
b. Passy, Frederic

May 26, 1822
b. Goncourt, Edmond Louis Antoine
Huot de

June 1, 1822
d. Hauy, Rene Just

June 23, 1822
b. Darley, Felix Octavius Carr
d. Vesey, Denmark

June 25, 1822
d. Hoffmann, E(rnst) T(heodor)
A(madeus)

July 8, 1822
d. Shelley, Percy Bysshe

July 22, 1822
b. Arditi, Luigi
b. Mendel, Gregor Johann

July 30, 1822
b. Adams, William Taylor

July 31, 1822
b. Hewitt, Abram Stevens

August 1, 1822
b. Grant, James

August 8, 1822
b. Stoneman, George

August 12, 1822
d. Castlereagh, Robert Stewart,
Viscount

August 15, 1822
b. Maine, Henry James Sumner

August 25, 1822
d. Herschel, William Frederick, Sir

September 16, 1822
b. Crocker, Charles

September 20, 1822
b. Miller, Elizabeth Smith

October 4, 1822
b. Hayes, Rutherford B(irchard)

October 9, 1822
b. Sykes, George

October 13, 1822
d. Canova, Antonio

October 20, 1822
b. Hughes, Thomas

November 6, 1822
d. Berthollet, Claude Louis, Comte
d. Hardenberg, Karl August von

December 5, 1822
b. Agassiz, Elizabeth Cabot Cary

December 10, 1822
b. Franck, Cesar Auguste

December 11, 1822
b. Cummins, George David

December 24, 1822
b. Arnold, Matthew

December 25, 1822
d. Pinkney, William

December 27, 1822
b. Pasteur, Louis

1823

b. Fowler, Lydia Folger
b. French, Robert T
b. Looking Glass
b. Pfizer, Charles
b. Spotted Tail
b. Whitman, Stephen F
d. Fink, Mike

January 8, 1823
b. Wallace, Alfred Russell

January 15, 1823
b. Brady, Mathew B

January 26, 1823
d. Jenner, Edward

January 27, 1823
b. Lalo, Edouard Victor Antoine
b. Renan, (Joseph) Ernest

February 3, 1823
b. Baird, Spencer Fullerton

February 7, 1823
d. Radcliffe, Ann

February 14, 1823
b. Powell, William Henry

February 15, 1823
b. Li Hung-Chang

February 16, 1823
d. Prud'hon, Pierre Paul
d. Prudhon, Pierre-Paul

February 18, 1823
b. Cropsey, Jasper Francis

February 26, 1823
d. Kemble, John Philip

February 27, 1823
b. Franklin, William Buel

March 3, 1823
b. Andrassy, Gyula, Count

March 10, 1823
b. Dykes, John Bacchus

March 18, 1823
b. Seiss, Joseph Augustus

March 20, 1823
b. Judson, Edward Zane Carroll

March 23, 1823
b. Colfax, Schuyler

March 31, 1823
b. Chesnut, Mary Boykin (Miller)

April 1, 1823
b. Buckner, Simon Bolivar

April 3, 1823
b. Tweed, Boss

April 4, 1823
b. Siemens, William, Sir

April 6, 1823
b. Medill, Joseph

April 7, 1823
d. Charles, Jacques-Alexandre-Cesar

April 12, 1823
b. Ostrovsky, Aleksandr Nikolaevich

April 30, 1823
b. Bradford, William
b. Houghton, Henry Oscar

May 10, 1823
b. Sherman, John

May 13, 1823
b. McArthur, John

June 1, 1823
d. Davout, Louis Nicholas

June 19, 1823
d. Combe, William

June 27, 1823
b. Eaton, Dorman Bridgman

July 8, 1823
d. Raeburn, Henry, Sir

July 22, 1823
d. Bartram, William

July 23, 1823
b. Patmore, Coventry Kersey Dighton

July 28, 1823
d. Cutler, Manasseh

August 2, 1823
d. Carnot, Lazare

August 4, 1823
b. Morton, Oliver Hazard Perry
Throck

August 10, 1823
b. Keene, Charles Samuel

August 11, 1823
b. Yonge, Charlotte Mary

August 13, 1823
b. Smith, Goldwin

August 19, 1823
d. Bloomfield, Robert

August 20, 1823
d. Pius, VII

August 28, 1823
b. Oliver, James

September 9, 1823
b. Leidy, Joseph

September 11, 1823
d. Ricardo, David

September 14, 1823
b. Hill, Benjamin Harvey

September 16, 1823
b. Parkman, Francis

September 17, 1823
d. Breguet, Abraham Louis

October 23, 1823
b. Naudin, Emilio

October 30, 1823
d. Cartwright, Edmund

December 1, 1823
b. Reyer, (Louis) Ernest (Etienne)

December 13, 1823
d. Narino, Antonio
d. Reeve, Tapping

December 22, 1823
b. Fabre, Jean Henri
b. Higginson, Thomas Wentworth
Storrow

December 26, 1823
b. Cairnes, John Elliott

December 27, 1823
b. Bowell, Mackenzie, Sir

December 28, 1823
b. Scott, Thomas Alexander

1824

b. Dayananda Saraswati, Swami

b. Miller, Frederic
b. Palmer, William
b. Slade, Jack
b. Valera y Alcala Galiano, Juan
d. Bushnell, David
d. Coxe, Tench
d. Johnson, Joshua
d. Pinckney, Charles
d. Ward, Nancy

January 8, 1824
b. Collins, Wilkie

January 15, 1824
b. Duplessis, Marie

January 17, 1824
b. Harvey, Hayward Augustus

January 21, 1824
b. Jackson, Stonewall

January 26, 1824
d. Gericault, Jean Louis Andre
   Theodore

January 27, 1824
b. Israels, Josef

February 7, 1824
b. Huggins, William, Sir

February 10, 1824
b. Plimsoll, Samuel

February 14, 1824
b. Hancock, Winfield Scott

February 22, 1824
b. Janssen, Pierre Jules Cesar

February 24, 1824
b. Curtis, George William

February 28, 1824
b. Blondin, Jean Francois Gravelet

March 2, 1824
b. Smetana, Bedrich

March 3, 1824
d. Viotti, Giovanni Battista

March 5, 1824
b. Ives, James Merritt
b. Larcom, Lucy

March 6, 1824
b. Skinner, Halcyon

March 8, 1824
d. Cambaceres, Jean Jacques Regis de

March 9, 1824
b. Stanford, Leland

March 12, 1824
b. Kirchhoff, Gustav Robert
b. Prang, Louis

March 15, 1824
b. Chevalier, Jules

March 19, 1824
b. Allingham, William

March 27, 1824
b. Hittorf, Johann Wilhelm

March 31, 1824
b. Hunt, William Morris

April 5, 1824
b. Dobell, Sydney Thompson

April 12, 1824
d. Taylor, Jane

April 19, 1824
d. Byron, George Gordon, Baron

May 8, 1824
b. Walker, William

May 11, 1824
b. Gerome, Jean Leon

May 16, 1824
b. Morton, Levi Parsons
b. Smith, Edmund Kirby

May 23, 1824
b. Burnside, Ambrose Everett

June 12, 1824
b. Carrier-Belleuse, Albert Ernest

June 20, 1824
b. Street, George Edmund

June 26, 1824
b. Kelvin, William Thomson, Baron

July 1, 1824
d. Macquarie, Lachlan

July 10, 1824
b. King, Richard

July 12, 1824
b. Boudin, Eugene Louis

July 14, 1824
d. Kamehameha II

July 19, 1824
d. Iturbide, Augustin de

July 21, 1824
b. Matthews, Stanley

July 27, 1824
b. Dumas, Alexandre

July 29, 1824
b. Johnson, Eastman
b. Johnson, Jonathan Eastman

August 8, 1824
d. Wolf, Friedrich August

August 15, 1824
b. Chisum, John Simpson
b. Leland, Charles Godfrey

August 21, 1824
d. Taylor, John
b. Doyle, Richard

September 4, 1824
b. Bruckner, Joseph Anton
b. Cary, Phoebe

September 16, 1824
d. Louis, XVIII

October 5, 1824
b. Chadwick, Henry

December 10, 1824
b. MacDonald, George

December 14, 1824
b. Puvis de Chavannes, Pierre Cecile

December 17, 1824
b. King, Thomas Starr

December 20, 1824
b. Vaux, Calvert

December 21, 1824
d. Parkinson, James

December 23, 1824
d. Pushmataha

December 24, 1824
b. Cornelius, Peter

1825

b. Bean, Roy
b. Big Foot
b. Cain, Richard H
b. Durkee, Eugene R
b. Manning, Maria
b. Maywood, Augusta
b. Naoroji, Dadabhai
b. Welch, Thomas B
b. Woodville, Richard Caton
d. Evans, George Henry
d. Laffite, Jean

January 8, 1825
d. Whitney, Eli

January 11, 1825
b. Taylor, Bayard

January 15, 1825
b. Strakosch, Maurice

January 25, 1825
b. Pickett, George Edward

February 2, 1825
b. Dalton, John Call

February 8, 1825
b. Bates, Henry Walter

b. Robinson, Harriet Jane Hanson

February 24, 1825
d. Bowdler, Thomas

March 4, 1825
d. Peale, Raphael

March 8, 1825
b. Barbier, Jules

March 12, 1825
b. Manns, August, Sir

April 5, 1825
b. Holmes, Mary Jane Hawes

April 11, 1825
b. Lassalle, Ferdinand

April 13, 1825
b. McGee, Thomas D'Arcy

April 16, 1825
d. Fuseli, Henry

April 18, 1825
d. Cabot, George

April 25, 1825
b. Lerdo de Tejada, Sebastian

May 1, 1825
b. Inness, George

May 4, 1825
b. Huxley, Thomas Henry

May 7, 1825
d. Salieri, Antonio

May 19, 1825
d. Saint-Simon, Claude-Henri de
   Rouvroy

May 20, 1825
b. Blackwell, Antoinette Louisa Brown

May 23, 1825
d. Weems, Mason Locke

May 25, 1825
b. Wesson, Daniel Baird

June 7, 1825
b. Blackmore, Richard Doddridge

June 9, 1825
d. Borghese, Maria Paolina

June 11, 1825
d. Tompkins, Daniel D

June 14, 1825
d. L'Enfant, Pierre Charles

July 6, 1825
b. Rogers, Randolph

July 12, 1825
b. Stoddard, Richard Henry

July 29, 1825
b. Pendleton, George Hunt

August 8, 1825
b. Mould, Jacob Wrey

August 16, 1825
d. Pinckney, Charles Cotesworth

August 27, 1825
b. Baikie, William Balfour

August 28, 1825
b. Ulrichs, Karl Heinrich

September 5, 1825
b. Mills, Darius Ogden

September 9, 1825
b. Lea, Henry Charles

September 11, 1825
b. Hanslick, Eduard

September 13, 1825
b. Rinehart, William H

September 15, 1825
b. Iwakura, Tomomi

September 17, 1825
b. Lamar, Lucius Quintus Cincinnatus

September 24, 1825
b. Harper, Frances Ellen Watkins

September 29, 1825
d. Shays, Daniel

October 4, 1825
b. Wales, Salem Howe

October 10, 1825
b. Kruger, Paul

October 13, 1825
b. Worth, Charles Frederick

October 20, 1825
b. Sickles, Daniel Edgar

October 25, 1825
b. Strauss, Johann, Jr.

October 31, 1825
b. Lavigerie, Charles Martel Allemand

November 5, 1825
b. Jackson, John Adams

November 6, 1825
b. Gardner, Jean Louis Charles
b. Garnier, Jean Louis Charles

November 9, 1825
b. Hill, Ambrose Powell

November 10, 1825
d. MacDonough, Thomas

November 14, 1825
d. Richter, Jean Paul F
d. Richter, Johann Paul Friedrich

November 29, 1825
b. Charcot, Jean Martin
d. Hull, William

December 1, 1825
d. Alexander I

December 2, 1825
b. Pedro II

December 28, 1825
d. Wilkinson, James

December 29, 1825
d. David, Jacques Louis

1826

b. Blackwell, Emily
b. Cetshwayo
b. Craft, Ellen
b. Dun, Robert Graham
b. Judah, Theodore Dehone
b. Kelley, Oliver Hudson
b. Tubman, Harriet Ross
d. Tyler, Royall

January 26, 1826
b. Grant, Julia Dent

February 2, 1826
d. Brillat-Savarin, Jean Anthelme

February 3, 1826
b. Bagehot, Walter

February 9, 1826
b. Bowles, Samuel, II
b. Logan, John Alexander

February 15, 1826
b. Stoney, George Johnstone

February 24, 1826
b. Hollyer, Samuel

March 3, 1826
b. Wharton, Joseph

March 4, 1826
b. Buford, John

March 24, 1826
b. Gage, Matilda Joslyn

March 29, 1826
b. Liebknecht, Wilhelm

April 1, 1826
b. Sothern, Edward Askew

April 3, 1826
d. Heber, Reginald

April 4, 1826
b. Gramme, Zenobe Theophile

April 6, 1826
b. Moreau, Gustave

April 20, 1826
b. Craik, Dinah Maria Mulock

April 25, 1826
b. Deering, William

May 4, 1826
b. Church, Frederick Edwin

May 5, 1826
b. Eugenie

May 6, 1826
d. Levasseur, Rosalie

May 20, 1826
b. Palmer, Potter

May 22, 1826
b. Langdell, Christopher Columbus
d. Karamzin, Nikolai Mikhailovich

May 28, 1826
b. Brown, Benjamin Gratz

May 29, 1826
b. Butterick, Ebenezer

June 1, 1826
d. Oberlin, Johann Friedrich

June 5, 1826
b. Hallstrom, Ivar
d. Weber, Carl Maria von

June 7, 1826
d. Fraunhofer, Joseph von

June 9, 1826
d. Morse, Jedidiah

June 19, 1826
b. Brace, Charles Loring

July 4, 1826
b. Foster, Stephen Collins
d. Adams, John
d. Jefferson, Thomas

July 5, 1826
d. Proust, Joseph Louis
d. Raffles, Thomas Stamford, Sir

July 8, 1826
b. Chrysander, Karl Franz Friedrich

July 10, 1826
d. Martin, Luther

July 13, 1826
b. Cannizzaro, Stanislao

July 21, 1826
b. Loomis, Mahlon

July 24, 1826
b. Lopez, Francisco Solano

August 13, 1826
d. Laennec, Rene Theophile Hyacinthe

August 30, 1826
d. Douvillier, Suzanne Theodore
Vaillande

September 1, 1826
b. Beach, Alfred Ely

September 13, 1826
b. Drexel, Anthony Joseph

September 17, 1826
b. Riemann, Georg Friedrich

September 26, 1826
d. Laing, Alexander Gordon

September 29, 1826
b. Chesney, Charles Cornwallis

October 1, 1826
b. Hotchkiss, Benjamin Berkeley

October 9, 1826
d. Kelly, Michael

October 19, 1826
d. Talma, Francois Joseph

October 20, 1826
b. George, James Zachariah

October 26, 1826
d. Pinel, Philippe

November 18, 1826
b. Newberry, John Stoughton

November 24, 1826
b. Collodi, Carlo

December 1, 1826
b. Mahone, William

December 3, 1826
b. McClellan, George Brinton

December 7, 1826
d. Flaxman, John

1827

b. Cuypers, Petrus Josephus Hubertus
b. Wilson, Harriet E. (Adams)
d. Fernandez de Lizardi, Jose Joaquin
d. Sampson, Deborah
d. Spode, Josiah

January 7, 1827
b. Fleming, Sandford

February 7, 1827
b. Saigo, Takamori

February 8, 1827
b. Whitney, William Dwight

February 17, 1827
b. Cooke, Rose Terry
d. Pestalozzi, Johann Heinrich

February 22, 1827
d. Peale, Charles Willson

February 28, 1827
b. Lacombe, Albert

March 5, 1827
d. Laplace, Pierre Simon, Marquis de

March 19, 1827
b. Ridge, John Rollin

March 24, 1827
b. Wheeler, Candace Thurber

March 26, 1827
d. Beethoven, Ludwig van

April 2, 1827
b. Hunt, Holman

April 5, 1827
b. Lister, Joseph

April 10, 1827
b. Wallace, Lew(is)

April 13, 1827
d. Clapperton, Hugh

April 22, 1827
d. Rowlandson, Thomas

April 29, 1827
d. Gannett, Deborah Sampson
d. King, Rufus

May 1, 1827
b. Breton, Jules Adolphe

May 4, 1827
b. Speke, John Hanning

May 7, 1827
d. Volta, Alessandro Giuseppe Antonio
Anastasio

May 11, 1827
b. Carpeaux, Jean Baptiste

May 16, 1827
b. Colman, Norman Jay

May 21, 1827
b. Pobedonostsev, Konstantin
Petrovich

June 12, 1827
b. Spyri, Johanna Heuser

July 14, 1827
d. Fresnel, Augustin-Jean

August 5, 1827
b. Fonseca, Manuel Deodoro da

August 8, 1827
d. Canning, George

August 12, 1827
d. Blake, William

August 20, 1827
b. Decoster, Charles Theodore Henri

August 26, 1827
b. Wittenmyer, Annie Turner

September 10, 1827
d. Foscolo, (Niccolo) Ugo

September 18, 1827
b. Trowbridge, John Townsend

September 27, 1827
b. Revels, Hiram Rhodes

October 8, 1827
b. Sarcey, Francisque

October 16, 1827
b. Bocklin, Arnold

October 27, 1827
b. Berthelot, Marcellin

November 8, 1827
b. Cremazie, Octave

November 10, 1827
b. Terry, Alfred Howe

November 16, 1827
b. Norton, Charles Eliot

November 18, 1827
d. Hauff, Wilhelm

November 26, 1827
b. White, Ellen Gould Harmon

1828

b. Dull Knife
b. Parker, Ely Samuel
d. Ashmun, Jehudi

January 23, 1828
d. Randolph, Mary

January 24, 1828
b. Cohn, Ferdinand Julius
d. Lamb, Caroline Ponsonby, Lady

January 26, 1828
b. Sylvis, William (H.)

February 1, 1828
b. Edmunds, George Franklin
b. Guggenheim, Meyer

February 2, 1828
b. Meredith, George

February 8, 1828
b. Verne, Jules

February 11, 1828
d. Clinton, DeWitt

February 14, 1828
b. About, Edmond-Francois-Valentin

February 24, 1828
d. Brown, Jacob Jennings

March 20, 1828
b. Ibsen, Henrik Johan

March 22, 1828
b. Kimball, William Wallace

March 24, 1828
b. Gray, Horace

April 4, 1828
b. Oliphant, Margaret

April 16, 1828
d. Goya y Lucientes, Francisco Jose
de

April 21, 1828
b. Taine, Hippolyte Adolphe

April 24, 1828
b. Nuitter, Charles Louis

April 26, 1828
b. Finley, Martha

May 8, 1828
b. Dunant, Jean Henri

May 9, 1828
b. Cramp, Charles Henry

May 12, 1828
b. Rossetti, Dante Gabriel

May 22, 1828
b. Grafe, Albrecht Friedrich Wilhelm
Ernst von

May 29, 1828
b. Massey, Gerald

June 11, 1828
d. Stewart, Dugald

July 1, 1828
b. Chernyshevsky, Nikolai Gavrilovich

July 9, 1828
b. Spreckels, Claus
d. Stuart, Gilbert Charles

July 15, 1828
d. Houdon, Jean Antoine

July 29, 1828
b. Pillsbury, John Sargent

August 6, 1828
b. Still, Andrew Taylor

August 22, 1828
d. Gall, Franz Joseph

d. Chaka

September 8, 1828
b. Sage, Margaret Olivia

September 9, 1828
b. Tolstoy, Leo Nikolayevich

September 10, 1828
b. Simmons, Zalmon G

September 22, 1828
d. Shaka

September 23, 1828
d. Bonington, Richard Parkes

October 10, 1828
b. Randall, Samuel J

October 27, 1828
b. Cox, Jacob Dolson

October 29, 1828
b. Bayard, Thomas Francis

October 31, 1828
b. Hunt, Richard Morris
b. Swan, Joseph Wilson, Sir

November 8, 1828
d. Bewick, Thomas

November 10, 1828
b. Wang T'ao

November 14, 1828
b. McPherson, James Birdseye

November 19, 1828
d. Schubert, Franz Peter

November 24, 1828
b. Sala, George Augustus

December 4, 1828
d. Liverpool, 2nd Earl of

December 8, 1828
b. Timrod, Henry

December 13, 1828
b. Savage, John

December 16, 1828
b. Clarke, Alexander Ross

December 22, 1828
d. Jackson, Rachel (Donelson Robards)

December 23, 1828
b. Wesendonck, Mathilde Luckemeyer

December 25, 1828
b. DeVinne, Theodore Low

1829

b. Blanco, Antonio Guzman
b. Oliphant, Laurence

b. Standing Bear
b. Strauss, Levi
d. Butler, Eleanor, Lady
d. Leonard, Daniel
d. Leroy

January 7, 1829
b. Angell, James Burrill

January 12, 1829
d. Schlegel, Friedrich von

January 17, 1829
b. Booth, Catherine Mumford

January 28, 1829
d. Burke, William

January 29, 1829
d. Barras, Paul Francois Jean Nicolas,
    Comte de
d. Pickering, Timothy

February 15, 1829
b. Mitchell, Silas Weir

February 16, 1829
d. Gossec, Francois Joseph

February 20, 1829
b. Jefferson, Joseph

February 24, 1829
b. Spielhagen, Friedrich von

March 2, 1829
b. Allison, William Boyd
b. Schurz, Carl

March 4, 1829
b. Gardiner, Samuel Rawson

March 5, 1829
b. Henner, Jean Jacques

April 6, 1829
d. Abel, Niels Henrik

April 10, 1829
b. Booth, William

April 26, 1829
b. Billroth, Theodore

May 8, 1829
b. Gottschalk, Louis Moreau

May 10, 1829
d. Young, Thomas

May 12, 1829
b. Childs, George William

May 17, 1829
d. Jay, John

May 29, 1829
d. Davy, Humphrey, Sir
b. Geronimo

June 4, 1829
d. Dearborn, Henry

June 8, 1829
b. Millais, John Everett, Sir

June 27, 1829
d. Smithson, James (Louis Macie)

July 23, 1829
d. Boguslawski, Wojciech

July 26, 1829
b. Beernaert, Auguste Marie Francois

August 19, 1829
b. Moran, Edward

September 7, 1829
b. Kekule, Friedrich August

September 11, 1829
b. Hill, Thomas

September 12, 1829
b. Warner, Charles Dudley

September 15, 1829
b. Tamayo y Baus, Manuel

September 19, 1829
b. Schirmer, Gustave

September 22, 1829
b. Belknap, William Worth

September 23, 1829
b. Crook, George

September 25, 1829
b. Rossetti, William Michael

October 3, 1829
b. Holly, James Theodore

October 15, 1829
b. Hall, Asaph

October 30, 1829
b. Conkling, Roscoe
b. Rogers, John

November 14, 1829
b. Feuerbach, Paul Johann Anselm von

November 28, 1829
b. Rubinstein, Anton Gregorovitch

December 14, 1829
b. Langston, John Mercer

December 18, 1829
d. Lamarck, Jean Baptiste Pierre

December 19, 1829
b. Croly, Jane Cunningham

December 21, 1829
b. Bridgman, Laura Dewey

December 25, 1829
b. Gilmore, Patrick Sarsfield

December 27, 1829
b. Helper, Hinton Rowan

1830

b. Crowfoot
b. Diaz, Jose de la Cruz Porfirio
b. Ismail Pasha
b. Kennedy, John Stewart
b. Leotard, Jules
b. Roman Nose
b. Samory Toure
b. Young Man Afraid of His Horses
d. Hickey, William
d. Johnson, John
d. Johnston, Joshua

January 2, 1830
b. Flagler, Henry Morrison
b. Kingsley, Henry

January 7, 1830
b. Bierstadt, Albert
d. Lawrence, Thomas, Sir

January 8, 1830
b. Bulow, Hans Guido von

January 20, 1830
d. Red Jacket

January 31, 1830
b. Blaine, James Gillespie
b. Rochefort, Henri

February 3, 1830
b. Salisbury, Robert Arthur Talbot, 3rd
    Marquess

February 17, 1830
d. Rutgers, Henry

February 25, 1830
b. Carter, William

February 27, 1830
d. Hicks, Elias

March 5, 1830
b. Thomson, Charles Wyville, Sir

March 8, 1830
b. Deus, Joao de

March 15, 1830
b. Heyse, Paul Johann Ludwig von

March 18, 1830
b. Fustel de Coulanges, Numa Denis

March 21, 1830
d. Wyss, Johann Rudolf

April 9, 1830
b. Muybridge, Eadweard

May 1, 1830
b. Jones, Mary Harris

May 4, 1830
b. Mapleson, James Henry

May 5, 1830
b. Stetson, John Batterson

May 6, 1830
b. Jacobi, Abraham

May 13, 1830
b. Vance, Zebulon Baird

May 16, 1830
d. Fourier, Jean Baptiste Joseph

May 18, 1830
b. Goldmark, Karl

June 4, 1830
d. Sucre, Antonio J de

June 25, 1830
d. George IV
d. McDowell, Ephraim

June 28, 1830
d. Walker, David

June 29, 1830
b. Ward, J(ohn) Q(uincy) A(dams)

July 17, 1830
b. Remenyi, Eduard

July 25, 1830
b. Bausch, John Jacob

July 30, 1830
b. Hugo, Adele

August 6, 1830
b. Carpenter, Francis Bicknell

August 10, 1830
b. Okubo, Toshimichi

August 18, 1830
b. Francis Joseph, (I)
b. Franz Joseph I

September 8, 1830
b. Mistral, Frederic

September 12, 1830
d. Hobart, John Henry

September 15, 1830
b. Diaz, Porfirio

September 18, 1830
d. Hazlitt, William

September 23, 1830
d. Monroe, Elizabeth (Kortright)

September 27, 1830
b. Hazen, William Babcock

October 2, 1830
b. Pratt, Charles

October 5, 1830
b. Arthur, Chester A(lan)

October 9, 1830
b. Hosmer, Harriet Goodhue

October 10, 1830
b. Isabella II

October 24, 1830
b. Lockwood, Belva Ann Bennett

November 3, 1830
b. Cooke, John Esten

November 8, 1830
b. Howard, Oliver Otis

November 21, 1830
d. Kisfaludy, Karoly

November 25, 1830
d. Rode, Jacques Pierre Joseph

November 26, 1830
b. Tabor, Horace Austin Warner

December 5, 1830
b. Rossetti, Christina Georgina

December 8, 1830
d. Constant de Rebeque, (Henri)
   Benjamin

December 10, 1830
b. Dickinson, Emily (Elizabeth)

December 11, 1830
b. Kamehameha V

December 16, 1830
b. Tisza, Kalman

December 17, 1830
b. Goncourt, Jules Alfred Huot de
d. Bolivar, Simon

December 31, 1830
b. Smith, Alexander

1831

b. Libby, Arthur
b. Malkam Khan, Mirza
b. Sitting Bull
d. Francisco, Peter
d. Ponsonby, Sarah

January 1, 1831
d. Niebuhr, Barthold Georg

January 3, 1831
b. Fenn, George Manville

January 4, 1831
b. Dutton, E(dward) P(ayson)

January 6, 1831
d. Kreutzer, Rodolphe

January 14, 1831
d. Mackenzie, Henry

January 15, 1831
b. Niemann, Albert

January 21, 1831
d. Arnim, Achim von (Ludwig
   Joachim)

January 22, 1831
b. Winsor, Justin

January 26, 1831
b. DeBary, Heinrich Anton
b. Dodge, Mary Elizabeth Mapes

January 31, 1831
b. Wurlitzer, Rudolph

February 13, 1831
b. Rawlins, John A

February 14, 1831
d. Guerrero, Vicente

February 16, 1831
b. Leskov, Nikolai Semyonovich

February 22, 1831
b. Byers, William Newton

February 23, 1831
b. Meilhac, Henri

March 3, 1831
b. Pullman, George Mortimer

March 6, 1831
b. Sheridan, Philip Henry

March 12, 1831
b. Studebaker, Clement

March 20, 1831
b. Burton, Isabel Arundel

March 21, 1831
b. Beale, Dorothea

March 26, 1831
d. Allen, Richard

March 29, 1831
b. Barr, Amelia Edith Huddleston

March 31, 1831
b. Couper, Archibald Scott

April 4, 1831
d. Thomas, Isaiah

April 12, 1831
b. Dodge, Grenville Mellen

April 19, 1831
b. Echegaray y Eizaguirre, Jose

April 28, 1831
  b. Tait, Peter Guthrie

April 29, 1831
  b. Lemoyne, W(illiam) J

May 11, 1831
  d. Trumbull, John

May 17, 1831
  d. Rochester, Nathaniel

May 24, 1831
  d. Peale, James

May 27, 1831
  d. Smith, Jedediah Strong

June 1, 1831
  b. Hood, John Bell

June 8, 1831
  d. Siddons, Sarah Kemble

June 24, 1831
  b. Davis, Rebecca Blaine Harding

June 25, 1831
  b. Miller, Olive Thorne

June 28, 1831
  b. Joachim, Joseph

June 29, 1831
  d. Stein, Heinrich Friedrich Karl vom und zum, Baron

July 4, 1831
  d. Monroe, James

July 5, 1831
  b. Shaw, Richard Norman

July 6, 1831
  b. Gilman, Daniel Coit

July 9, 1831
  b. His, Wilhelm

July 10, 1831
  b. Pissarro, Camille Jacob

July 26, 1831
  b. Florence, William Jermyn

July 30, 1831
  b. Blavatsky, Helena Petrovna

August 16, 1831
  b. Timken, Henry

August 23, 1831
  d. Gneisenau, August Neithardt von

August 28, 1831
  b. Hayes, Lucy Webb

September 7, 1831
  b. Sardou, Victorien

September 29, 1831
  b. Schofield, John McAllister

October 2, 1831
  b. Godkin, E(dwin) L(awrence)

October 15, 1831
  b. Bishop, Isabella Lucy Bird

October 18, 1831
  b. Frederick III
  b. Jackson, Helen Maria Hunt Fiske

October 19, 1831
  b. Hunter, Thomas

October 29, 1831
  b. Marsh, Othniel Charles

October 31, 1831
  b. Butterford, Daniel

November 3, 1831
  b. Donnelly, Ignatius

November 8, 1831
  b. Lytton, Edward Robert Bulwer-Lytton, Earl

November 11, 1831
  d. Turner, Nat

November 13, 1831
  b. Maxwell, James Clerk

November 14, 1831
  d. Hegel, Georg Wilhelm Friedrich

November 16, 1831
  d. Clausewitz, Karl (Philipp Gottlieb) von

November 19, 1831
  b. Garfield, James Abram

November 28, 1831
  b. Mackay, John William

December 8, 1831
  d. Hoban, James

December 10, 1831
  d. Seebeck, Thomas Johann

December 15, 1831
  d. Adams, Hannah

December 26, 1831
  d. Girard, Stephen

December 31, 1831
  b. Terhune, Mary Virginia

1832

  d. Carnot, Nicolas Leonard Sadi
  d. Petalesharo

January 6, 1832
  b. Dore, Gustave

January 7, 1832
  b. Talmadge, Thomas de Witt

January 13, 1832
  b. Alger, Horatio

January 22, 1832
  d. Pitcher, Molly

January 23, 1832
  b. Manet, Edouard

January 24, 1832
  b. Choate, Joseph Hodges

January 26, 1832
  b. Shiras, George, Jr.

January 27, 1832
  b. Carroll, Lewis
  b. Hughes, Arthur
  d. Bell, Andrew

February 3, 1832
  d. Crabbe, George

February 6, 1832
  b. Gordon, John Brown

February 18, 1832
  b. Chanute, Octave

February 23, 1832
  b. Vincent, John Heyl

February 26, 1832
  b. Nicolay, John George

March 4, 1832
  b. Colman, Samuel
  d. Champollion, Jean Francois

March 5, 1832
  b. Hayes, Isaac Israel

March 10, 1832
  d. Clementi, Muzio

March 12, 1832
  b. Boycott, Charles Cunningham
  b. Friedel, Charles

March 17, 1832
  b. Conway, Moncure Daniel

March 22, 1832
  d. Goethe, Johann Wolfgang von

April 5, 1832
  b. Ferry, Jules Francois Camille

April 13, 1832
  b. Montalvo, Juan Maria

April 15, 1832
  b. Busch, Wilhelm

April 19, 1832
  b. Garfield, Lucretia (Rudolph)

April 22, 1832
b. Morton, Julius Sterling

May 5, 1832
b. Bancroft, Hubert Howe

May 10, 1832
b. Grace, William Russell

May 13, 1832
d. Cuvier, Georges, Baron

May 16, 1832
b. Armour, Philip Danforth

May 31, 1832
d. Galois, Evariste

June 1, 1832
d. Sumter, Thomas

June 2, 1832
d. Garcia, Manuel del Popolo Vincente

June 6, 1832
d. Bentham, Jeremy

June 9, 1832
d. Gentz, Friedrich Von

June 10, 1832
b. Otto, Nikolaus August

June 14, 1832
b. Mitchell, Margaret Julia

June 17, 1832
b. Crookes, William, Sir

June 20, 1832
b. Bristow, Benjamin Helm

June 21, 1832
b. Rainey, Joseph Hayne

June 23, 1832
d. Hall, James, Sir

July 6, 1832
b. Maximilian

July 10, 1832
b. Arnold, Edwin
b. Clark, Alvin Graham

July 22, 1832
d. Bonaparte, Francois Charles Joseph

July 29, 1832
b. Cesnola, Luigi Palma di

July 30, 1832
d. Chaptal, Jean Antoine, Comte de
Chanteloup

August 2, 1832
b. Olcott, Henry Steel

August 3, 1832
b. Blyden, Edward Wilmot

August 16, 1832
b. Wundt, Wilhelm Max

September 13, 1832
d. Richard, Gabriel

September 21, 1832
d. Scott, Walter, Sir

September 25, 1832
b. Jenney, William LeBaron

September 30, 1832
b. Roberts, Frederick Sleigh

October 1, 1832
b. Harrison, Caroline (Lavinia Scott)

October 2, 1832
b. Tylor, Edward Bennett, Sir

October 9, 1832
b. Allen, Elizabeth Ann Chase Akers

October 12, 1832
b. Watts-Dunton, Theodore

October 22, 1832
b. Damrosch, Leopold

November 7, 1832
b. White, Andrew Dickson

November 14, 1832
d. Carroll, Charles

November 15, 1832
d. Say, Jean Baptiste

November 18, 1832
b. Nordenskiold, Nils Adolph Erik,
Baron

November 26, 1832
b. Walker, Mary Edwards

November 28, 1832
b. Stephen, Leslie, Sir

November 29, 1832
b. Alcott, Louisa May

December 8, 1832
b. Bjornson, Bjornstjerne Martinius
b. Henty, George Alfred

December 15, 1832
b. Eiffel, Alexandre Gustave

December 18, 1832
d. Freneau, Philip Morin

1833

b. Bannister, Edward Mitchell
b. Johnson, Samuel C
b. Ouray
d. Brooks, Henry Sands
d. Feuerbach, Paul Johann Anselm

January 10, 1833
d. Legendre, Adrien Marie

January 12, 1833
b. Duhring, Eugen Karl

January 17, 1833
d. Rush, William

January 19, 1833
d. Herold, Ferdinand

January 25, 1833
d. Tarleton, Banastre, Sir

January 28, 1833
b. Gordon, Charles George

February 4, 1833
d. O'Keeffe, John

February 6, 1833
b. Pereda, Jose Marie de
b. Stuart, Jeb

February 7, 1833
b. Palma, Ricardo

February 19, 1833
b. Ducommun, Elie

February 20, 1833
b. Crittenton, Charles Nelson

February 22, 1833
b. Clarke, Rebecca Sophia

February 28, 1833
b. Schlieffen, Alfred, Graf von

March 10, 1833
b. Alarcon, Pedro Antonio de

March 14, 1833
b. Taylor, Lucy Beaman Hobbs

March 20, 1833
b. Home, Daniel Douglas

April 5, 1833
d. Niepce, Joseph Nicephore

April 22, 1833
d. Trevithick, Richard

May 2, 1833
b. Heenan, John Carmel

May 5, 1833
b. Richthofen, Ferdinand Paul Wilhelm

May 7, 1833
b. Brahms, Johannes

May 15, 1833
d. Kean, Edmund

May 24, 1833
d. Randolph, John

May 26, 1833
b. Godwin, Edward William

June 1, 1833
b. Harlan, John Marshall, I

June 10, 1833
b. Cushman, Pauline

June 12, 1833
b. Weaver, James Baird

July 15, 1833
b. Platt, Thomas Collier
d. Unanue, Jose Hipolito

July 27, 1833
d. Bainbridge, William

July 29, 1833
d. Wilberforce, William

August 11, 1833
b. Ingersoll, Robert Green

August 20, 1833
b. Harrison, Benjamin

August 23, 1833
b. Burne-Jones, Edward Coley, Sir

August 26, 1833
b. Fawcett, Henry

September 5, 1833
b. Hartford, George Huntington

September 11, 1833
b. Hatch, William Henry

September 20, 1833
b. Locke, David Ross
b. Moneta, Ernesto Teodora

September 26, 1833
b. Bradlaugh, Charles

September 27, 1833
d. Roy, Ram Mohun

September 29, 1833
d. Ferdinand, VII

September 30, 1833
b. Quay, Matthew Stanley

October 7, 1833
b. Fox, Margaret

October 8, 1833
b. Stedman, Edmund Clarence

October 10, 1833
b. Studebaker, John Mohler

October 13, 1833
b. Lorillard, Pierre

October 21, 1833
b. Nobel, Alfred Bernhard

November 6, 1833
b. Lie, Jonas Laurite Idemil

November 9, 1833
b. Tompkins, Sally Louisa

November 12, 1833
b. Borodin, Alexander Profirevich

November 13, 1833
b. Booth, Edwin Thomas

November 19, 1833
b. Dilthey, Wilhelm Christian Ludwig

December 1, 1833
b. Andrews, Jane

December 3, 1833
b. Finlay, Carlos Juan

December 6, 1833
b. Mosby, John Singleton

December 16, 1833
b. Knapp, Seaman Asahel

December 20, 1833
b. Mudd, Samuel Alexander

1834

b. Crow Dog
b. Eaton, Timothy
b. Siddal, Elizabeth Eleanor
b. Walras, Marie Esprit Leon
d. Brown, Alexander
d. Douglas, David

January 1, 1834
b. Halevy, Ludovic

January 10, 1834
b. Acton, John Emerich Edward
    Dalberg-Acton, Baron

January 12, 1834
b. Marty, Martin

January 17, 1834
b. Weismann, August Friedrich
    Leopold

January 28, 1834
b. Baring-Gould, Sabine

February 1, 1834
b. Turner, Henry McNeal

February 3, 1834
b. Adams, Edwin

February 6, 1834
b. Klebs, Edwin
d. Lander, Richard Lemon

February 7, 1834
b. Mendeleev, Dmitri Ivanovich

February 9, 1834
b. Kamehameha IV

February 12, 1834
d. Schleiermacher, Friedrich Ernst
    Daniel

February 15, 1834
b. Haeckel, Ernst Heinrich Philipp
    August

February 18, 1834
b. Ramakrishna, Sri

February 26, 1834
d. Senefelder, Aloys

March 6, 1834
b. DuMaurier, George Louis P B

March 17, 1834
b. Daimler, Gottlieb (Wilhelm)

March 20, 1834
b. Eliot, Charles William
b. Orton, Arthur

March 24, 1834
b. Morris, William
b. Powell, John Wesley

April 1, 1834
b. Fisk, Jim

April 2, 1834
b. Bartholdi, Auguste

April 5, 1834
b. Stockton, Frank

April 11, 1834
d. Macarthur, John

April 23, 1834
b. Depew, Chauncey Mitchell

April 26, 1834
b. Ward, Artemus

May 20, 1834
d. Lafayette, Marie Joseph Paul,
    Marquis

May 31, 1834
b. Burns, Anthony

June 2, 1834
b. Stolz, Teresa

June 9, 1834
d. Carey, William

June 25, 1834
b. Potter, Henry Codman

July 10, 1834
b. Whistler, James Abbott McNeill

July 14, 1834
d. Genet, Edmond Charles Edouard

July 19, 1834
b. Degas, (Hilaire Germain) Edgar

July 23, 1834
b. Gibbons, James, Cardinal

July 25, 1834
d. Coleridge, Samuel Taylor

August 4, 1834
d. Johnson, William

August 7, 1834
d. Jacquard, Joseph Marie

August 18, 1834
b. Field, Marshall

August 22, 1834
b. Langley, Samuel Pierpont

August 31, 1834
b. Ponchielli, Amilcare

September 9, 1834
b. Shorthouse, Joseph Henry
d. Weddell, James

September 15, 1834
b. Treitschke, Heinrich Gotthard von
d. Crawford, William Harris

September 24, 1834
d. Pedro I

September 28, 1834
b. Lamoureux, Charles

October 8, 1834
d. Boieldieu, Francois Adrien

October 22, 1834
b. Duniway, Abigail Jane Scott

October 31, 1834
d. DuPont, Eleuthere Irenee

November 3, 1834
b. Fleischmann, Charles Louis

November 5, 1834
b. Leonowens, Anna Harriette
    Crawford

November 10, 1834
b. Hernandez, Jose

November 21, 1834
b. Green, Hetty
b. Weyerhaeuser, Frederick

November 23, 1834
b. Thomson, James

December 7, 1834
d. Irving, Edward

December 15, 1834
b. Young, Charles Augustus

December 23, 1834
d. Malthus, Thomas Robert

December 27, 1834
d. Lamb, Charles

1835

b. Bozeman, John M
b. Burberry, Thomas
b. Datsolalee
b. Folger, James A
b. Kicking Bird
b. Olney, Richard
b. Rain-in-the-Face
b. Smith, Madeline Hamilton
d. Crosby, Enoch
d. Hemings, Sally
d. Ireland, William Henry
d. Quiroga, Juan Facundo
d. Slater, Samuel

January 10, 1835
b. Wright, Harry

January 18, 1835
b. Cui, Cesar Antonovich

January 29, 1835
b. Woolsey, Sarah Chauncey

February 13, 1835
b. Ahmad, Mirza Ghulam Hazat

February 15, 1835
b. Dabney, Virginius

February 24, 1835
b. Vogel, Julius

February 27, 1835
b. Garnett, Richard

March 2, 1835
d. Francis, II

March 12, 1835
b. Newcomb, Simon

March 14, 1835
b. Schiaparelli, Giovanni

March 25, 1835
b. Nachbaur, Franz

March 31, 1835
b. LaFarge, John

April 4, 1835
b. Jackson, John Hughlings

April 8, 1835
d. Humboldt, Wilhelm Freiherr von

April 9, 1835
b. Leopold II

April 10, 1835
b. Villard, Henry

May 13, 1835
d. Nash, John

May 16, 1835
d. Hemans, Felicia Dorothea Browne

May 27, 1835
b. Adams, Charles Francis, Jr.

May 30, 1835
b. Austin, Alfred

June 2, 1835
b. Pius X

June 7, 1835
b. Hill, George Birkbeck Norman

June 10, 1835
b. Felton, Rebecca Ann Latimer

June 15, 1835
b. Menken, Adah Isaacs

June 18, 1835
d. Cobbett, William

June 26, 1835
d. Gros, Antoine Jean

June 27, 1835
b. Harvey, Fred(erick Henry)

June 29, 1835
b. Thaxter, Celia

July 6, 1835
d. Marshall, John

July 9, 1835
b. Estrada Palma, Tomas

July 10, 1835
b. Wieniawski, Henri

July 19, 1835
b. Barrios, Justo Rufino

July 20, 1835
b. Giles, Ernest

July 27, 1835
b. Carducci, Giosue Alessandro
    Guiseppe

July 31, 1835
b. Du Chaillu, Paul Belloni

August 2, 1835
b. Gray, Elisha
b. Tyler, Moses Coit

August 19, 1835
b. Bland, Richard Parks

August 25, 1835
d. Rutledge, Ann

September 5, 1835
b. Carlisle, John Griffin

September 23, 1835
d. Bellini, Vincenzo

October 9, 1835
b. Saint-Saens, (Charles) Camille

October 11, 1835
b. Thomas, Theodore

October 16, 1835
b. Shafter, William Rufus

October 23, 1835
b. Stevenson, Adlai Ewing

October 30, 1835
b. Patti, Carlotta

October 31, 1835
b. Ames, Adelbert
b. Baeyer, Adolf Johann Friedrich
Wilhelm, von

November 1, 1835
b. Jevons, William Stanley
d. Motherwell, William

November 16, 1835
b. Beltrami, Eugenio

November 19, 1835
b. Lee, Fitzhugh

November 21, 1835
d. Hogg, James

November 25, 1835
b. Carnegie, Andrew

November 29, 1835
b. Tz'u Hsi

November 30, 1835
b. Twain, Mark

December 4, 1835
b. Butler, Samuel

December 13, 1835
b. Brooks, Phillips

December 17, 1835
b. Agassiz, Alexander Emmanuel
Rodolphe

December 18, 1835
b. Abbott, Lyman

December 28, 1835
b. Geikie, Archibald, Sir

1836

b. Anderson, Elizabeth Garrett
b. Armstrong, Thomas M
b. Johannes, IV
b. Leslie, Miriam Florence Folline
d. Brown, Moses

January 8, 1836
b. Alma-Tadema, Lawrence, Sir

January 11, 1836
b. Wyant, Alexander Helwig
d. Molson, John

January 14, 1836
b. Fantin-Latour, (Ignace) Henri

January 27, 1836
b. Sacher-Masoch, Leopold von

January 30, 1836
d. Ross, Betsy

February 2, 1836
d. Bonaparte, Letizia

February 11, 1836
b. Gladden, Washington

February 17, 1836
b. Becquer, Gustavo Adolfo
Dominguez

February 18, 1836
d. Cornplanter

February 21, 1836
b. Delibes, Leo

February 24, 1836
b. Homer, Winslow

February 26, 1836
b. Vedder, Elihu

March 2, 1836
b. Brown, Henry Billings

March 5, 1836
b. Goodnight, Charles

March 6, 1836
d. Bowie, Jim
d. Crockett, Davy
d. Travis, William Barret

March 8, 1836
b. Butler, Matthew Calbraith

March 14, 1836
b. Beeton, Isabella Mary Mayson

March 19, 1836
b. Wallace, Henry

March 28, 1836
b. Pabst, Frederick

April 7, 1836
d. Godwin, William

April 19, 1836
b. Juilliard, Augustus D

April 21, 1836
b. Sonzogno, Edoardo

May 7, 1836
b. Cannon, Joseph Gurney

May 17, 1836
b. Lockyer, Joseph Norman, Sir
b. Steinitz, Wilhelm

May 23, 1836
d. Livingston, Edward

May 27, 1836
b. Gould, Jay

June 10, 1836
d. Ampere, Andre Marie

June 16, 1836
b. Merritt, Wesley

June 20, 1836
d. Rouget de Lisle, Claude Joseph
d. Sieyes, Emmanuel Joseph

June 23, 1836
d. Mill, James

June 28, 1836
d. Madison, James

July 2, 1836
b. Schnorr, Ludwig von Carolsfeld

July 8, 1836
b. Chamberlain, Joseph

July 28, 1836
d. Rothschild, Nathan Meyer

August 9, 1836
b. Gamble, James Norris

August 14, 1836
b. Besant, Walter, Sir

August 22, 1836
b. Willard, Archibald MacNeal

August 25, 1836
b. Harte, (Francis) Bret

September 7, 1836
b. Campbell-Bannerman, Henry, Sir

September 10, 1836
b. Wheeler, Joseph

September 11, 1836
b. Ludlow, Fitz Hugh

September 14, 1836
d. Burr, Aaron

September 23, 1836
d. Malibran, Maria Felicita

October 4, 1836
b. Adam, Juliette Lamber

October 10, 1836
d. Jefferson, Martha

October 15, 1836
b. Tissot, James Joseph Jacques

October 17, 1836
d. Colman, George

November 6, 1836
b. Lombroso, Cesare

November 8, 1836
b. Bradley, Milton

November 11, 1836
b. Alden, Henry M
b. Aldrich, Thomas Bailey

November 16, 1836
b. Kalakaua, David

November 18, 1836
b. Gilbert, William S(chwenck), Sir
b. Gomez, Maximo

November 26, 1836
d. McAdam, John Loudoun

November 28, 1836
b. Martin, Homer Dodge

December 13, 1836
b. Kerr, Orpheus C

December 27, 1836
d. Austin, Stephen Fuller

1837

b. Bell, Joseph
b. Bowie, Walter
b. Captain Jack
b. Cardozo, Francis Louis
b. Coup, W(illiam) C(ameron)
b. Crapper, Thomas
b. Dumont, Gabriel
b. Grass, John
b. Hitotsubashi
b. Tippu Tib

January 2, 1837
b. Balakirev, Mili Alekseyevich

January 9, 1837
b. Chesebrough, Robert Augustus

January 11, 1837
d. Field, John
d. Gerard, Francois

January 12, 1837
b. Jensen, Adolph

January 17, 1837
b. Browning, Oscar

January 19, 1837
b. Keen, William Williams

January 20, 1837
d. Soane, John, Sir

January 22, 1837
b. Moran, Thomas

February 5, 1837
b. Moody, Dwight Lyman

February 7, 1837
b. Murray, James Augustus Henry, Sir

February 10, 1837
d. Pushkin, Aleksandr Sergeyevich

February 19, 1837
d. Buchner, Georg

March 1, 1837
b. Ebers, Georg Moritz
b. Howells, William Dean

March 18, 1837
b. Cleveland, Grover

March 30, 1837
d. Constable, John

April 1, 1837
b. Isaacs, Jorge

April 3, 1837
b. Burroughs, John

April 5, 1837
b. Swinburne, Algernon Charles

April 17, 1837
b. Morgan, J(ohn) P(ierpont)

April 21, 1837
b. Bajer, Fredrik

April 24, 1837
b. Polk, Leonidas Lafayette

April 29, 1837
b. Boulanger, Georges Ernest Jean Marie

May 5, 1837
d. Zingarelli, Nicola Antonio

May 10, 1837
b. Pinchback, P(inckney) B(enton) S(tewart)

May 13, 1837
b. Brinton, Daniel Garrison

May 26, 1837
b. Roebling, Washington Augustus

May 27, 1837
b. Hickok, Wild Bill

May 28, 1837
b. Pastor, Tony

May 31, 1837
d. Grimaldi, Joseph

June 6, 1837
d. Portales, Diego (Jose Victor)

June 14, 1837
d. Leopardi, Giacomo

June 20, 1837
b. Brewer, David Josiah
d. William, IV

June 22, 1837
b. Morphy, Paul Charles

June 29, 1837
d. Macon, Nathaniel

July 14, 1837
b. Douglas, Amanda Minnie

July 31, 1837
b. Quantrill, William Clarke

August 17, 1837
b. Grimke, Charlotte Lottie Forten

August 30, 1837
b. Arthur, Ellen (Lewis) Herndon

September 2, 1837
b. Chang Chih-tung

September 8, 1837
b. Miller, Joaquin

September 24, 1837
b. Hanna, Mark

October 6, 1837
d. Lesueur, Jean-Francois

October 8, 1837
d. Fourier, Francois Marie Charles

October 9, 1837
b. Parker, Francis Wayland

October 10, 1837
b. Shaw, Robert Gould

October 17, 1837
d. Hummel, Johann Nepomuk

October 25, 1837
b. Harkness, Anna M Richardson

October 27, 1837
b. Reid, Whitelaw

November 7, 1837
d. Lovejoy, Elijah Parish

November 20, 1837
b. Waterman, Lewis Edson

November 23, 1837
b. Waals, Johannes Diderik van der

December 10, 1837
b. Eggleston, Edward

December 12, 1837
b. Green, John Richard

December 21, 1837
b. McCoy, Joseph Geiting

December 25, 1837
b. Gerry, Elbridge Thomas
b. Wagner, Cosima Liszt

December 26, 1837
b. Bulkeley, Morgan G
b. Dewey, George

1838

b. Libby, Charles
b. Mutesa I
d. Caillie, Rene Auguste

January 4, 1838
b. Tom Thumb, General

January 6, 1838
b. Bruch, Max

January 12, 1838
d. Humphreys, Joshua

January 16, 1838
b. Brentano, Franz Clemens

January 30, 1838
d. Osceola

February 6, 1838
b. Irving, Henry, Sir
d. Retief, Pieter

February 12, 1838
b. Howland, Alfred Cornelius

February 16, 1838
b. Adams, Henry Brooks
b. Okuma, Shigenobu

February 18, 1838
b. Mach, Ernst

February 22, 1838
b. Sangster, Margaret Elizabeth

March 3, 1838
b. Hill, George William

March 6, 1838
d. Stevens, John

March 7, 1838
b. Roe, Edward Payson

March 9, 1838
b. Gumplowicz, Ludwig

March 12, 1838
b. Perkin, William Henry, Sir

March 15, 1838
b. Fletcher, Alice Cunningham

March 16, 1838
d. Bowditch, Nathaniel

March 18, 1838
b. Cremer, William Randal, Sir

March 26, 1838
b. Lecky, William Edward Hartpole
d. Ashley, William Henry

April 3, 1838
b. Gambetta, Leon

April 5, 1838
b. Hyatt, Alpheus

April 6, 1838
d. Andrada e Silva, Jose Bonifacio de

April 22, 1838
b. Yamagata, Aritomo

April 29, 1838
b. Asser, Tobias Michael Carel

May 2, 1838
b. Tourgee, Albion Winegar

May 10, 1838
b. Booth, John Wilkes
b. Bryce, James Bryce, Viscount

May 17, 1838
d. Talleyrand-Perigord, Charles
   Maurice de

May 29, 1838
d. Milder-Hauptmann, Pauline Anna

May 31, 1838
b. Sidgwick, Henry

June 13, 1838
d. Chavis, John

June 24, 1838
b. Schmoller, Gustav Friedrich von

June 26, 1838
b. Chatterji, Bankimchandra

July 8, 1838
b. Zeppelin, Ferdinand Adolf August
   Heinrich von, Count

July 10, 1838
b. Allen, Joel Asaph

July 11, 1838
b. Wanamaker, John

July 18, 1838
d. Dulong, Pierre-Louis

July 20, 1838
b. Daly, Augustin

July 21, 1838
b. Muir, John

July 23, 1838
b. Colonne, Edouard

August 6, 1838
b. Symons, George James

August 10, 1838
d. Rodgers, John

August 17, 1838
d. DaPonte, Lorenzo

August 18, 1838
b. Neumann, Angelo

August 19, 1838
d. Geddes, James

September 1, 1838
d. Clark, William

September 2, 1838
b. Liliuokalani, Queen

September 16, 1838
b. Hill, James Jerome

September 23, 1838
b. Woodhull, Victoria Claflin

September 27, 1838
d. Courtois, Bernard

September 29, 1838
b. Richardson, Henry Hobson

October 1, 1838
b. Field, Kate

October 3, 1838
d. Black Hawk

October 8, 1838
b. Hay, John Milton

October 24, 1838
d. Lancaster, Joseph

October 25, 1838
b. Bizet, Georges (Alexandre Cesar
   Leopold)

November 14, 1838
b. Richards, William Trost

November 22, 1838
b. Hartmann, Franz

December 3, 1838
b. Abbe, Cleveland

December 24, 1838
b. Morley, John, Viscount

1839

b. Corrigan, Michael Augustine
b. Edenshaw, Charles
b. Fox, Kate
b. Machado de Assis, Joaquim Maria
d. Buel, Jesse
d. Ranjit Singh
d. Speransky, Mikhail

January 1, 1839
b. Ouida

January 9, 1839
b. Paine, John Knowles

January 11, 1839
b. Hostos (y Bonilla), Eugenio Maria de
b. Simmons, Franklin

January 14, 1839
d. Jarvis, John Wesley

January 19, 1839
b. Cezanne, Paul

January 26, 1839
d. Van Rensselaer, Stephen

January 30, 1839
b. Armstrong, Samuel Chapman

February 11, 1839
b. Gibbs, J(osiah) Willard

February 26, 1839
d. Ludington, Sybil

March 3, 1839
b. Tata, Jamshedji Nusserwanji

March 8, 1839
b. Crafts, James Mason
d. Nourrit, Adolphe

March 10, 1839
b. Buck, Dudley

March 16, 1839
b. Sully Prudhomme

March 21, 1839
b. Mussorgsky, Modest Petrovich
d. Apess, William

April 5, 1839
b. Smalls, Robert

April 6, 1839
b. Przhevalsky, Nikolai Mikhailovich

April 11, 1839
d. Galt, John

April 30, 1839
b. Peixoto, Floriano

May 1, 1839
b. Chardonnet, Louis Marie Hilaire Bernigaud

May 3, 1839
d. Paer, Ferdinando

May 8, 1839
b. Beard, George Miller

May 11, 1839
d. Cooper, Thomas

May 17, 1839
d. Alison, Archibald

June 17, 1839
d. Bentinck, William Henry Cavendish, Lord

June 22, 1839
d. Boudinot, Elias

June 23, 1839
b. Mueller, Christian F

June 24, 1839
b. Swift, Gustavus Franklin

July 1, 1839
d. Mahmud, II

July 8, 1839
b. Rockefeller, John D(avison)
d. Sor, Fernando

July 10, 1839
b. Busch, Adolphus

July 25, 1839
b. Garnier, Francis

August 5, 1839
b. Pater, Walter (Horatio)

August 7, 1839
b. Dryden, John Fairfield

August 8, 1839
b. Miles, Nelson Appleton

August 22, 1839
d. Lundy, Benjamin

August 24, 1839
b. Napravnik, Eduard

August 28, 1839
d. Smith, William

August 31, 1839
b. Denison, George Taylor

September 2, 1839
b. George, Henry, Sr.

September 10, 1839
b. Funk, Isaac Kauffman
b. Peirce, Charles Sanders

September 16, 1839
d. Carey, Mathew

September 24, 1839
d. Hayne, Robert Young

September 28, 1839
b. Willard, Frances Elizabeth Caroline
d. Dunlap, William

September 29, 1839
d. Mohs, Friedrich

October 2, 1839
b. Thoma, Hans

October 9, 1839
b. Schley, Winfield Scott

October 18, 1839
b. Reed, Thomas Brackett

October 30, 1839
b. Sisley, Alfred

November 7, 1839
b. Levi, Hermann

November 16, 1839
b. De Morgan, William Frend
b. Frechette, Louis-Honore

November 21, 1839
b. Keith, William

December 5, 1839
b. Custer, George Armstrong

December 22, 1839
b. Maskelyne, John Nevil

1840

b. Allison, Clay
b. Balmaceda Fernandez, Jose Manuel
b. Gall
b. Joseph, Chief
b. Lee, Rebecca
b. O'Sullivan, Timothy H
d. Bourdonnais, Louis Charles de la
d. Dingane
d. Frederick William, III
d. Santander, Francisco de Paula

January 3, 1840
b. Damien, Father
b. Holt, Henry

January 6, 1840
d. Burney, Fanny

January 18, 1840
b. Dobson, Henry Austin

January 22, 1840
d. Blumenbach, Johann Friedrich

January 23, 1840
b. Abbe, Ernst

January 27, 1840
d. Chauncey, Isaac

February 5, 1840
b. Dunlop, John Boyd
b. Maxim, Hiram Stevens, Sir

February 9, 1840
b. Sampson, William T

February 10, 1840
b. Cleve, Per Teodor

February 16, 1840
b. Watterson, Henry

February 22, 1840
b. Bebel, August

March 2, 1840
d. Olbers, Heinrich Wilhelm Matthaus

March 8, 1840
b. Emin Pasha

March 27, 1840
b. Baker, George Fisher

March 30, 1840
b. Booth, Charles
d. Brummell, Beau

April 2, 1840
b. Zola, Emile (Edouard Charles)

April 12, 1840
b. Haberl, Franz Xaver

April 14, 1840
b. Gardner, Isabella Stewart

April 22, 1840
b. Redon, Odilon

April 27, 1840
b. Whymper, Edward

April 28, 1840
b. Cox, Palmer

May 6, 1840
d. Gallitzin, Demetrius Augustine

May 7, 1840
b. Tchaikovsky, Peter Ilyich
d. Friedrich, Caspar David

May 13, 1840
b. Daudet, Leon

May 23, 1840
b. Appleby, John Francis

May 27, 1840
d. Paganini, Niccolo

June 2, 1840
b. Hardy, Thomas

June 7, 1840
b. Carlota

June 30, 1840
d. Bonaparte, Lucien

July 12, 1840
b. Altman, Benjamin

July 25, 1840
b. Wright, Carroll Davidson

July 28, 1840
b. Cope, Edward Drinker
d. Durham, 1st Earl of

July 31, 1840
d. Krochmal, Nachman Kohen

August 6, 1840
b. Bandelier, Adolph Francis Alphonse

August 14, 1840
b. Krafft-Ebing, Richard von

August 16, 1840
d. Flint, Timothy

August 17, 1840
b. Blunt, Wilfrid Scawen

August 31, 1840
b. Verga, Giovanni
d. Lister, Anne

September 7, 1840
b. Crowell, Luther Childs

September 27, 1840
b. Mahan, Alfred Thayer
b. Nast, Thomas

September 28, 1840
b. Peck, George Wilbur

October 5, 1840
b. Symonds, John Addington

October 12, 1840
b. Modjeska, Helena

October 26, 1840
b. Keene, Thomas Wallace

October 30, 1840
b. Sumner, William Graham
b. Galli-Marie, Marie Celestine

November 12, 1840
b. Rodin, Auguste

November 14, 1840
b. Monet, Claude-Oscar

December 2, 1840
b. Cobden-Sanderson, Thomas James

1841

b. Dugdale, Richard Louis
b. Fisher, John Arbuthnot
b. Le Bon, Gustave
b. Klyuchevsky, Vasily Osipovich

January 10, 1841
b. Melville, George Wallace

January 11, 1841
b. Gierke, Otto von

January 12, 1841
b. Henry, Edward Lamson

January 14, 1841
b. Corson, Juliet
b. Morisot, Berthe

January 15, 1841
b. Stanley, Frederick Arthur, Earl of Derby

January 18, 1841
b. Chabrier, Emmanuel

January 23, 1841
b. Coquelin, Benoit Constant

January 28, 1841
b. Nessler, Victor E

January 30, 1841
b. Faure, Francois Felix
b. Townsend, George Alfred

January 31, 1841
b. Loyd, Sam(uel)
b. Stanley, Henry Morton, Sir

February 4, 1841
b. Ader, Clement

February 12, 1841
d. Cooper, Astley Paston, Sir

February 24, 1841
b. Holland, John Philip

February 25, 1841
b. Renoir, (Pierre) Auguste

February 26, 1841
b. Cromer, 1st Earl of
d. Power, Tyrone William Grattan

March 1, 1841
b. Bruce, Blanche Kelso

March 3, 1841
b. Murray, John, Sir

March 7, 1841
b. Nelson, William Rockhill

March 8, 1841
b. Holmes, Oliver Wendell, Jr.

April 4, 1841
d. Harrison, William Henry

April 9, 1841
d. Ladd, William

April 25, 1841
b. Lucca, Pauline

April 29, 1841
b. Sill, Edward Rowland

May 10, 1841
b. Bennett, James Gordon, Jr.

May 22, 1841
b. Mendes, Catulle

May 31, 1841
b. Rockefeller, William

June 1, 1841
d. Wilkie, David, Sir

June 2, 1841
d. Appert, Nicolas

June 18, 1841
b. Ward, Lester Frank

July 5, 1841
b. Whitney, William Collins

July 13, 1841
b. Wagner, Otto

July 25, 1841
d. Rogers, Mary Cecilia

July 27, 1841
d. Lermontov, Mikhail

August 3, 1841
b. Ewing, Julianna Horatia (Gatty)

August 4, 1841
b. Hudson, William Henry

August 11, 1841
d. Herbart, Johann Friedrich

August 13, 1841
d. Romberg, Bernhard

August 24, 1841
d. Hook, Theodore Edward

August 25, 1841
b. Kocher, Emil Theodor

August 28, 1841
b. Weir, John F(erguson)

September 2, 1841
b. Ito, Hirobumi

September 8, 1841
b. Dvorak, Anton

September 9, 1841
d. Candolle, Augustin Pyrame de

September 16, 1841
d. Dibdin, Thomas Pitt

September 19, 1841
d. Sydenham, Baron

September 28, 1841
b. Clemenceau, Georges Eugene
   Benjamin

October 9, 1841
d. Schinkel, Karl Friedrich

October 16, 1841
d. Barbaja, Domenico

November 3, 1841
b. Alden, Isabella Macdonald

November 4, 1841
b. Goodrich, Benjamin Franklin
b. Tausig, Karl

November 6, 1841
b. Aldrich, Nelson Wilmarth

November 9, 1841
b. Edward VII

November 14, 1841
d. Elgin, Thomas Bruce

November 20, 1841
b. Laurier, Wilfrid, Sir

November 23, 1841
b. Croker, Boss

November 25, 1841
d. Chantrey, Francis Legatt, Sir
b. Edmonds, Emma E

December 5, 1841
b. Daly, Marcus

December 7, 1841
b. Cudahy, Michael

December 20, 1841
b. Buisson, Ferdinand Edouard

December 27, 1841
b. Spitta, Philipp

1842

b. Crazy Horse
b. Hennebique, Francois
b. Poundmaker
b. Shinburn, Mark
b. Sorel, Albert
d. Watson, Elkanah

January 6, 1842
b. King, Clarence

January 11, 1842
b. James, William

January 15, 1842
b. Breuer, Josef
b. MacKillop, Mary

January 19, 1842
b. Ladd, George Trumbull

January 26, 1842
b. Coppee, Francois Edouard Joachim

February 3, 1842
b. Lanier, Sidney

February 4, 1842
b. Brandes, Georg Morris Cohen

February 15, 1842
b. Quad, M

February 24, 1842
b. Boito, Arrigo
b. Habberton, John

February 25, 1842
b. Flammarion, Camille
b. Lewis, Ida
b. May, Karl Friedrich

March 3, 1842
b. Burnaby, Frederick Gustavus

March 4, 1842
d. Forten, James

March 7, 1842
b. Hyndman, Henry Mayers

March 13, 1842
d. Shrapnel, Henry

March 15, 1842
d. Cherubini, Luigi Carlo Zenobio
   Salvadore Maria

March 18, 1842
b. Mallarme, Stephane

March 21, 1842
b. Rosa, Carl

March 23, 1842
d. Stendhal

March 24, 1842
b. Krauss, Gabrielle

March 25, 1842
b. Fogazzaro, Antonio

March 30, 1842
b. Fiske, John
d. Vigee-Lebrun, Marie-Louise-
   Elisabeth

April 8, 1842
b. Custer, Elizabeth Bacon

April 11, 1842
d. England, John

April 14, 1842
b. Chaffee, Adna Romanza

April 17, 1842
b. Parkhurst, Charles Henry

April 24, 1842
b. Schindler, Solomon

April 28, 1842
d. Bell, Charles

May 8, 1842
d. Dumont d'Urville, Jules Sebastian
   Cesar

May 12, 1842
b. Massenet, Jules Emile Frederic

May 14, 1842
b. Sullivan, Arthur Seymour, Sir

June 6, 1842
b. Mackaye, James Morrison Steele

June 12, 1842
d. Arnold, Thomas

June 14, 1842
d. Atkinson, Henry

June 24, 1842
b. Bierce, Ambrose Gwinett

June 25, 1842
b. Alfaro, Jose Eloy
d. Sismondi, Jean Charles Leonard
　Simonde de

July 4, 1842
b. Cohen, Hermann

July 12, 1842
b. Kellogg, Clara Louise

July 26, 1842
b. Marshall, Alfred

July 28, 1842
d. Brentano, Clemens Maria

August 11, 1842
b. Elliott, Robert Brown

August 31, 1842
b. Jacobi, Mary Corinna Putnam

September 9, 1842
b. Coues, Elliott

September 10, 1842
d. Hobson, William
d. Tyler, Letitia Christian

September 15, 1842
d. Morazan, Jose Francisco

September 16, 1842
b. Castlemon, Harry

September 20, 1842
b. Dewar, James, Sir

September 21, 1842
b. Abdul-Hamid, II
b. Abdulhamid II

September 26, 1842
d. Wellesley, Richard Colley, 1st
　Marquess Wellesley

September 27, 1842
b. Sherwin, Henry Alden

October 2, 1842
d. Channing, William Ellery

October 7, 1842
b. Bateman, Kate Josephine
b. Howard, Bronson Crocker

October 22, 1842
b. Cary, Anne Louise
b. Giolitti, Giovanni

October 24, 1842
d. O'Higgins, Bernardo

October 26, 1842
b. Vereshchagin, Vasily Vasilyevich

November 4, 1842
b. Cushing, William Barker

November 6, 1842
d. Hone, William

November 12, 1842
b. Rayleigh, John William Strutt,
　Baron

November 21, 1842
b. Packer, Alfred G

November 25, 1842
b. Visscher, William Lightfoot

December 3, 1842
b. Pillsbury, Charles Alfred
b. Richards, Ellen Henrietta Swallow

December 9, 1842
d. Woodworth, Samuel

December 17, 1842
b. Lavisse, Ernest

December 21, 1842
b. Kropotkin, Peter Alekseyevich,
　Prince

December 22, 1842
b. Bloomingdale, Joseph Bernard

1843

b. Bass, Henry
d. Fries, Jakob Friedrich
d. Sequoyah

January 6, 1843
b. Spooner, John Coit

January 10, 1843
b. James, Frank

January 11, 1843
d. Key, Francis Scott

January 13, 1843
b. Ferrier, David, Sir

January 20, 1843
b. Cambon, Pierre Paul

January 29, 1843
b. McKinley, William

February 3, 1843
b. Van Horne, William Cornelius, Sir

February 10, 1843
d. Carlile, Richard

February 16, 1843
b. Leland, Henry Martyn

February 17, 1843
b. Ward, Montgomery

February 19, 1843
b. Patti, Adelina Juana Maria

March 12, 1843
b. Tarde, Gabriel

March 17, 1843
b. Lawton, Henry Ware

March 21, 1843
d. Southey, Robert

April 4, 1843
b. Jackson, William Henry
b. Richter, Hans

April 15, 1843
b. James, Henry, (Jr.)

May 6, 1843
b. Gilbert, Grove Karl

May 8, 1843
b. Boyd, Belle

May 10, 1843
b. Kohler, Kaufmann
b. Perez Galdos, Benito
b. Williams, Edward Porter

May 14, 1843
b. Walker, Henry Oliver

May 21, 1843
b. Gobat, Charles Albert
b. Renault, Louis

May 24, 1843
b. Blaikie, William

May 28, 1843
d. Webster, Noah

June 7, 1843
b. Blow, Susan Elizabeth
d. Holderlin, Friedrich

June 9, 1843
b. Suttner, Bertha Felicie Sophie
　Kinsky von

June 13, 1843
b. Neuendorff, Adolf

June 15, 1843
b. Grieg, Edvard Hagerup

July 2, 1843
d. Hahnemann, Samuel

July 7, 1843
b. Golgi, Camillo

July 9, 1843
d. Allston, Washington

July 17, 1843
b. Roca, Julio Argentino

July 18, 1843
b. Earp, Virgil W

July 24, 1843
b. Abney, William de Wiveleslie, Sir

July 25, 1843
d. Macintosh, Charles

July 31, 1843
b. Rossegger, Peter

August 1, 1843
b. Lincoln, Robert Todd

August 19, 1843
b. Doughty, Charles Montagu

August 20, 1843
b. Nilsson, Christine

September 13, 1843
b. Furphy, Joseph

September 18, 1843
b. Riley, Charles Valentine

September 23, 1843
d. Clevenger, Shobal Vail

September 24, 1843
b. Wagnalls, Adam Willis

September 25, 1843
b. Bissell, Melville Reuben
b. Chamberlin, Thomas Chrowder

October 22, 1843
b. Babcock, Stephen Moulton

November 10, 1843
d. Feijo, Diogo Antonio
d. Trumbull, John

November 27, 1843
b. Vanderbilt, Cornelius

December 7, 1843
b. Perky, Henry D

December 11, 1843
b. Koch, Robert
d. Delavigne, Jean Francois Casimir

December 13, 1843
d. Hull, Isaac

December 16, 1843
b. Kendal, William Hunter
b. Lowell, Josephine Shaw

December 22, 1843
d. Bigge, John Thomas

1844

b. Mahdi, Mohammed Ahmed
b. Ringo, John(ny)
b. Surratt, John Harrison
b. Winnemucca, Sarah
d. Thorvaldsen, Albert Bertel
b. Breshkovsky, Catherine

January 7, 1844
b. Bernadette of Lourdes, Saint

January 15, 1844
b. Younger, Cole

January 31, 1844
b. L'Hermitte, Leon Augustin

February 1, 1844
b. Hall, G(ranville) Stanley
b. Strasburger, Eduard Adolf

February 3, 1844
b. Lanston, Tolbert

February 20, 1844
b. Boltzmann, Ludwig
b. Slocum, Joshua

February 24, 1844
b. Widor, Charles Marie Jean Albert

February 26, 1844
b. Lurton, Horace Harmon

February 27, 1844
d. Biddle, Nicholas

February 29, 1844
b. Chadwick, French Ensor

March 7, 1844
b. Comstock, Anthony

March 8, 1844
d. Bernadotte, Jean Baptiste

March 10, 1844
b. Sarasate, Pablo de

March 18, 1844
b. Rimsky-Korsakov, Nikolai
Andreevich

March 20, 1844
b. Dollar, Robert

March 25, 1844
b. Engler, Adolph Gustav Heinrich

March 27, 1844
b. Greely, Adolphus Washington

March 30, 1844
b. Verlaine, Paul (Marie)

March 31, 1844
b. Lang, Andrew

April 15, 1844
d. Bulfinch, Charles

April 16, 1844
b. France, Anatole

April 23, 1844
b. Dole, Sanford Ballard

May 2, 1844
b. McCoy, Elijah
d. Beckford, William

May 3, 1844
b. Carte, Richard d'Oyly

May 16, 1844
b. Hare, John, Sir
b. Reinhart, Charles S

May 21, 1844
b. Rousseau, Henri

May 22, 1844
b. Cassatt, Mary Stevenson

May 23, 1844
b. Abdu'l-Baha

June 3, 1844
b. Hobart, Garret Augustus
b. Liliencron, Detlev von

June 10, 1844
b. Hagenbeck, Carl

June 15, 1844
d. Campbell, Thomas

June 19, 1844
d. Geoffroy Saint-Hilaire, Etienne

June 22, 1844
b. Lothrop, Harriet Mulford Stone

June 27, 1844
d. Smith, Joseph

June 28, 1844
b. Hopkins, Gerard Manley

July 1, 1844
b. Cameron, Verney Lovett

July 3, 1844
b. Adler, Dankmar

July 8, 1844
b. Lincoln, Mary Johnson Bailey

July 10, 1844
b. Materna, Amalia

July 11, 1844
b. Peter, I

July 20, 1844
b. Queensberry, John Sholto Douglas

July 22, 1844
b. Spooner, William Archibald

July 25, 1844
b. Eakins, Thomas

July 27, 1844
d. Dalton, John

July 28, 1844
d. Bonaparte, Joseph
d. Ram Camul Sen

August 5, 1844
b. Repin, Ilya Yefimovich

August 17, 1844
b. Menelik II

August 22, 1844
b. DeLong, George Washington

August 29, 1844
b. Carpenter, Edward

August 30, 1844
b. Ratzel, Friedrich
d. Baily, Francis

September 8, 1844
b. Guiteau, Charles Julius

September 13, 1844
b. Young, Ann Eliza Webb

October 3, 1844
b. Manson, Patrick, Sir

October 6, 1844
b. Davis, Sam(uel)

October 11, 1844
b. Heinz, Henry John

October 12, 1844
b. Cable, George Washington

October 15, 1844
b. Nietzsche, Friedrich Wilhelm

October 18, 1844
b. Wiley, Harvey Washington

October 22, 1844
b. Bernhardt, Sarah

October 23, 1844
b. Bridges, Robert Seymour
b. Riel, Louis David, Jr.

October 27, 1844
b. Arnoldson, Klas Pontus

October 28, 1844
b. Ezekiel, Moses Jacob

November 10, 1844
b. Thompson, John S(parrow) D(avid),
Sir

November 21, 1844
d. Krylov, Ivan Andreyevich

November 25, 1844
b. Benz, Karl Friedrich
b. Coffin, Charles Albert

December 1, 1844
b. Alexandra Caroline Mary Charlotte

December 16, 1844
b. Villard, Helen Francis Garrison

1845

b. Cipriani, Amilcare
b. Courtright, Jim
b. Mehta, Pherozeshah (Merwanji)
b. Quanah
b. Rio Branco, Barao do

January 6, 1845
b. Lee-Hamilton, Eugene Jacob

January 15, 1845
b. Vogl, Heinrich

January 21, 1845
b. Mallinckrodt, Edward

January 22, 1845
b. Vidal de la Blache, Paul

February 6, 1845
b. Straus, Isidor

February 15, 1845
b. Root, Elihu

February 17, 1845
b. McBurney, Charles

February 22, 1845
d. Smith, Sydney

March 3, 1845
b. Cantor, Georg Ferdinand Ludwig
Philipp

March 7, 1845
b. Palmer, Daniel David

March 10, 1845
b. Alexander III

March 12, 1845
d. Lee, Jason

March 13, 1845
d. Daniell, John Frederic

March 22, 1845
b. Tabb, John Banister

March 27, 1845
b. Roentgen, Wilhelm Konrad

April 18, 1845
d. Saussure, Nicolas Thoedore de

April 24, 1845
b. Spitteler, Karl Friedrich Georg

April 27, 1845
b. Freshfield, Douglas William

May 1, 1845
b. Mifflin, George Harrison

May 3, 1845
d. Hood, Thomas

May 7, 1845
b. Mahoney, Mary Eliza

May 12, 1845
b. Faure, Gabriel Urbain

May 15, 1845
b. Metchnikoff, Elie

June 2, 1845
b. MacArthur, Arthur

June 7, 1845
b. Auer, Leopold
b. Goucher, John Franklin

June 8, 1845
d. Jackson, Andrew

June 14, 1845
b. Maceo, Antonio

June 18, 1845
b. Colvin, Sidney, Sir
b. Laveran, Charles Louis Alphonse

June 21, 1845
b. Griffith, Samuel Walker

June 22, 1845
b. Seddon, Richard John

July 4, 1845
b. Barnardo, Thomas John
b. Lewis, Edmonia

July 9, 1845
b. Darwin, George Howard, Sir

July 16, 1845
b. Vail, Theodore Newton

July 17, 1845
d. Grey, Charles

July 18, 1845
b. Corbiere, Tristan (Edouard Joachim)

July 23, 1845
d. Sublette, William L

July 26, 1845
d. Benjamin, Asher

August 6, 1845
b. Fillmore, Myrtle Page

August 15, 1845
b. Crane, Walter

August 16, 1845
b. Lippmann, Gabriel Jonas

August 25, 1845
b. Ludwig II

September 2, 1845
d. Rivadavia, Bernardino

September 10, 1845
d. Story, Joseph

October 7, 1845
d. Colbran, Isabella

October 10, 1845
b. Saintsbury, George Edward Bateman

October 12, 1845
d. Fry, Elizabeth Gurney

October 16, 1845
b. Hanes, Pleasant H

October 21, 1845
b. Carleton, Will

October 26, 1845
b. Harrigan, Edward

November 3, 1845
b. White, Edward Douglass

November 11, 1845
d. Brooks, Maria Gowen

December 3, 1845
b. Bradley, Henry

1846

b. Bissell, Anna
b. Goldie, George Dashwood Taubman
b. Harjo, Chitto
b. Scott, Edward Irvin
d. Budding, Edwin

January 5, 1846
b. Eucken, Rudolf Christoph

January 17, 1846
d. Inman, Henry

January 26, 1846
b. Keith, Benjamin Franklin

January 30, 1846
b. Bradley, Francis Herbert

February 2, 1846
b. Smith, Francis Marion

February 10, 1846
b. Remsen, Ira

February 15, 1846
d. Kotzebue, Otto von

February 23, 1846
b. Horlick, William

February 26, 1846
b. Cody, Buffalo Bill

March 2, 1846
b. Roze, Marie

March 17, 1846
b. Greenaway, Kate
d. Bessel, Friedrich Wilhelm

March 22, 1846
b. Caldecott, Randolph

March 25, 1846
b. Davitt, Michael

April 4, 1846
b. Lautreamont, Comte de
b. Pictet, Raoul-Pierre

April 7, 1846
b. Tosti, Francesco Paolo

April 24, 1846
b. Clarke, Marcus (Andrew Hislop)
d. Crescentini, Girolamo

April 27, 1846
b. Van Depoele, Charles Joseph

May 5, 1846
b. Sienkiewicz, Henryk Adam Aleksander Pius

May 8, 1846
b. Galle, Emile
b. Hammerstein, Oscar

May 18, 1846
b. Faberge, Peter Carl

May 19, 1846
d. Thomas, Robert B

May 22, 1846
b. Hay, Oliver Perry

May 23, 1846
b. Mansfield, Arabella

June 21, 1846
d. McCoy, Isaac

June 22, 1846
b. Hawthorne, Julian
d. Haydon, Benjamin Robert

June 27, 1846
b. Abbey, Henry Eugene
b. Parnell, Charles Stewart

July 11, 1846
b. Bloy, Leon Marie

July 19, 1846
b. Pickering, Edward Charles

July 25, 1846
d. Bonaparte, Louis

August 6, 1846
d. Dew, Thomas Roderick

August 8, 1846
b. Jones, Samuel Milton

August 18, 1846
b. Evans, Robley Dunglison

August 20, 1846
b. Mead, William Rutherford

September 4, 1846
b. Burnham, Daniel H(udson)
d. Jouy, Victor (Joseph-Etienne) de

September 5, 1846
d. Metcalfe, Charles Theophilus

September 14, 1846
b. Selden, George Baldwin

September 26, 1846
d. Clarkson, Thomas

October 2, 1846
d. Waterhouse, Benjamin

October 6, 1846
b. Westinghouse, George

October 8, 1846
b. Gary, Elbert Henry

October 9, 1846
b. Drachmann, Holger Henrik Herholdt

October 17, 1846
b. Hudson, Joseph Lowthian

October 21, 1846
b. Amicis, Edmond de

October 26, 1846
b. Claflin, Tennessee Celeste
b. Scott, Charles Prestwich

October 28, 1846
b. Escoffier, Georges Auguste

November 11, 1846
b. Green, Anna Katharine

November 23, 1846
b. Schuch, Ernst von

November 25, 1846
b. Nation, Carry A(melia Moore)

November 30, 1846
d. List, Georg Friedrich

1847

b. Bonfanti, Marie
b. Coors, Adolph
b. Forrest, John, 1st Baron Forrest of Bunbury
b. Sorel, Georges
d. Cespedes, Carlos Manuel de
d. Maclean, George

January 10, 1847
b. Schiff, Jacob Henry

January 19, 1847
b. Strong, Josiah

January 26, 1847
b. Clark, John Bates

January 28, 1847
b. Wright, George

February 1, 1847
b. Kearney, Denis

February 3, 1847
d. Duplessis, Marie

February 11, 1847
b. Edison, Thomas Alva

February 14, 1847
b. Shaw, Anna Howard

February 17, 1847
b. Mallinger, Mathilde

March 3, 1847
b. Bell, Alexander Graham

March 6, 1847
b. Hagen, Johann Georg

March 11, 1847
d. Appleseed, Johnny

March 14, 1847
b. Castro Alves, Antonio de

March 17, 1847
d. Gerard, Jean Ignace Isidore
d. Grandville

March 19, 1847
b. Ryder, Albert Pinkham

March 27, 1847
b. Wallach, Otto

April 2, 1847
b. Steel, Flora Annie Webster

April 7, 1847
b. Jacobsen, Jens Peter

April 10, 1847
b. Pulitzer, Joseph

May 1, 1847
b. Lloyd, Henry Demarest

May 7, 1847
b. Rosebery, Archibald Philip
Primrose, Earl

May 15, 1847
d. O'Connell, Daniel

May 20, 1847
d. Lamb, Mary Ann

May 25, 1847
b. Dowie, John Alexander

May 31, 1847
d. Chalmers, Thomas

June 8, 1847
b. McKinley, Ida Saxton

June 11, 1847
b. Fawcett, Millicent Garrett, Dame
d. Franklin, John, Sir

July 4, 1847
b. Bailey, James Anthony

July 19, 1847
b. Williams, Gus

July 20, 1847
b. Liebermann, Max

August 7, 1847
d. Rapp, George

August 11, 1847
b. Tillman, Benjamin Ryan

August 22, 1847
b. Mackenzie, Alexander Campbell,
Sir

August 24, 1847
b. McKim, Charles Follen

September 5, 1847
b. James, Jesse Woodson

September 16, 1847
d. Aguilar, Grace

September 22, 1847
b. Meynell, Alice Christina Gertrude

October 1, 1847
b. Besant, Annie Wood

October 2, 1847
b. Hindenburg, Paul Ludwig Hans
Anton von Beneckendorff und

October 6, 1847
b. Hildebrand, Adolf von

October 14, 1847
b. O'Neill, James

October 15, 1847
b. Blakelock, Ralph Albert

October 16, 1847
b. Mueller, Otto

October 28, 1847
b. Thompson, J(ames) Walter

October 31, 1847
b. Ferraris, Galileo

November 4, 1847
d. Mendelssohn, Felix

November 6, 1847
b. Meggendorfer, Lothar

November 7, 1847
b. Crabtree, Lotta

November 8, 1847
b. Stoker, Bram

November 10, 1847
b. Bridgman, Frederic Arthur

November 18, 1847
d. Dibdin, Thomas Frognall

November 29, 1847
d. Whitman, Marcus

December 1, 1847
b. Ladd-Franklin, Christine
b. Moore, Julia A Davis

December 7, 1847
b. White, Deacon

December 12, 1847
d. Kent, James

December 14, 1847
b. Lassale, Jean

December 17, 1847
d. Marie Louise

December 30, 1847
b. Altgeld, John Peter

1848

b. Hump
b. Latimer, Lewis Howard
b. Plenty Coups
b. Scott, Clarence

January 6, 1848
b. Gonzalez Prada, Manuel

January 18, 1848
b. Graydon, James Weir

January 19, 1848
b. Keith, Minor Cooper
d. D'Israeli, Isaac

January 22, 1848
b. Laffan, William Mackay

January 24, 1848
d. Wells, Horace

January 26, 1848
b. Sierra, Justo

January 30, 1848
b. Mannlicher, Ferdinand

January 31, 1848
b. Straus, Nathan

February 1, 1848
b. Howard, Cordelia

February 4, 1848
b. Ayer, Francis Wayland

February 5, 1848
b. Huysmans, Joris Karl
b. Mancinelli, Luigi
b. Starr, Belle

February 11, 1848
d. Cole, Thomas

February 16, 1848
b. DeVries, Hugo

February 18, 1848
b. Tiffany, Louis Comfort

February 23, 1848
b. Ritz, Cesar
d. Adams, John Quincy

February 25, 1848
b. Harriman, Edward Henry

February 27, 1848
b. Parry, Charles Hubert Hastings, Sir
b. Terry, Ellen Alicia, Dame

March 1, 1848
b. Saint Gaudens, Augustus

March 15, 1848
b. Kendal, Madge, Dame
b. Reichmann, Theodor

March 17, 1848
b. Morris, Clara

March 19, 1848
b. Earp, Wyatt Berry Stapp

March 25, 1848
b. Brooks, William Keith

March 27, 1848
d. Burke, John

March 29, 1848
d. Astor, John Jacob

March 31, 1848
b. Astor, William Waldorf Astor,
Viscount

April 8, 1848
d. Donizetti, Gaetano

May 1, 1848
b. Rhodes, James Ford

May 23, 1848
b. Lilienthal, Otto

May 26, 1848
d. Belinsky, Vissarion Grigoryevich
d. Keokuk

June 7, 1848
b. Gauguin, Paul

June 14, 1848
b. Bosanquet, Bernard

June 17, 1848
b. Maurel, Victor

June 24, 1848
b. Adams, Brooks
b. Adams, Peter Chardon Brooks

July 3, 1848
b. Presser, Theodore

July 4, 1848
d. Chateaubriand, Francois Rene de

July 25, 1848
b. Balfour, Arthur James

July 31, 1848
b. Planquette, Jean(-Robert)

August 1, 1848
b. Gailhard, Pierre

August 5, 1848
b. Taylor, Susie Baker King

August 7, 1848
d. Berzelius, Jons Jacob, Baron

August 9, 1848
d. Marryat, Frederick

August 10, 1848
b. Harnett, William Michael
b. Scott, Austin

August 12, 1848
d. Stephenson, George

August 15, 1848
b. Pareto, Vilfredo

August 16, 1848
b. Holland, William Jacob
b. Sukhomlinov, Vladimir
Aleksandrovich

August 22, 1848
b. Stone, Melville Elijah

September 4, 1848
b. Bowker, R(ichard) R(ogers)

September 26, 1848
b. Walters, Henry
d. Bronte, Patrick Branwell

October 5, 1848
b. O'Connor, Thomas Power
b. Trudeau, Edward Livingston

October 9, 1848
b. Duveneck, Frank

October 12, 1848
b. Leggett, William

b. Valleria, Alwina

October 17, 1848
b. Cummings, Candy

October 19, 1848
d. Guthrie, Samuel

October 28, 1848
d. Otis, Harrison Gray

October 31, 1848
d. Kearny, Stephen Watts
d. Ibrahim Pasha

November 6, 1848
b. Jeffries, Richard

November 8, 1848
b. Frege, (Friedrich Ludwig) Gottlob
b. Gould, George Milbry

November 10, 1848
b. Banerjee, Surendranath

November 24, 1848
b. Lehmann, Lilli
d. Melbourne, William Lamb,
Viscount

November 27, 1848
b. Rowland, Henry Augustus

December 9, 1848
b. Harris, Joel Chandler

December 15, 1848
b. Blashfield, Edwin Howland
b. Coryell, John Russell

December 19, 1848
d. Bronte, Emily Jane

December 22, 1848
b. Togo, Heihachiro

December 24, 1848
b. Lyons, Sophie Levy

December 29, 1848
b. Cheney, John Vance

1849

b. Abduh ibn Hasan Khayr Allah,
Muhammad
b. Hoover, William K
b. Lee, Henry D
b. Lewisohn, Adolph
b. Witte, Sergey Yulyevich

January 6, 1849
d. Coleridge, Hartley

January 17, 1849
b. Carriere, Eugene

January 18, 1849
b. Barton, Edmund

January 22, 1849
b. Powderly, Terence Vincent
b. Strindberg, August

January 30, 1849
d. DeWint, Peter

February 7, 1849
b. Mallock, William Hurrell

February 13, 1849
b. Churchill, Randolph Henry Spencer,
Lord

February 26, 1849
b. McDowell, Katharine Sherwood
Bonner

March 5, 1849
d. Lyon, Mary Mason

March 7, 1849
b. Burbank, Luther

March 8, 1849
b. Winkelmann, Hermann

March 17, 1849
b. Brush, Charles Francis

March 19, 1849
b. Tirpitz, Alfred von

March 24, 1849
d. Dobereiner, Johann Wolfgang

March 27, 1849
d. Appleton, Daniel

April 17, 1849
b. Day, William Rufus

April 24, 1849
b. Gallieni, Joseph-Simon

May 3, 1849
b. Bulow, Bernhard H M
b. Riis, Jacob August

May 6, 1849
b. Eaton, Wyatt

May 10, 1849
d. Hokusai, Katsushika

May 11, 1849
d. Nicolai, Carl Otto Ehrenfried
d. Recamier, Julie, Madame

May 21, 1849
b. Stuart, Ruth McEnery

May 22, 1849
d. Edgeworth, Maria

May 24, 1849
b. Munroe, Charles Edward

May 25, 1849
b. Bethune, Thomas Greene

May 28, 1849
d. Bronte, Anne

June 1, 1849
b. Stanley, Francis Edgar
b. Stanley, Freelan O

June 4, 1849
d. Blessington, Marguerite Gardiner,
Countess

June 15, 1849
d. Polk, James Knox

June 18, 1849
d. Bugeaud de la Piconnerie, Thomas
Robert

June 27, 1849
b. Ayer, Harriet Hubbard

July 12, 1849
b. Osler, William, Sir
d. Madison, Dolly (Payne Todd)

July 19, 1849
b. Aulard, Francois Victor Alphonse

July 22, 1849
b. Lazarus, Emma

July 28, 1849
d. Charles Albert

July 30, 1849
d. Perkins, Jacob

August 1, 1849
b. Dawson, George Mercer

August 12, 1849
b. Thayer, Abbott Handerson
d. Gallatin, Albert

August 13, 1849
b. Barry, Leonora Marie Kearney

August 14, 1849
b. Godard, Benjamin Louis Paul

August 17, 1849
b. Grimke, Archibald H(enry)

August 19, 1849
b. Nabuco de Araujo, Joaquim Aurelio

August 23, 1849
b. Henley, William Ernest
d. Hicks, Edward

August 24, 1849
b. Comstock, John Henry

September 3, 1849
b. Jewett, Sarah Orne

September 4, 1849
d. Monk, Maria

September 14, 1849
b. Pavlov, Ivan Petrovich

September 21, 1849
b. Barrymore, Maurice
b. Gosse, Edmund William, Sir

September 25, 1849
d. Strauss, Johann, Sr.

September 29, 1849
b. Schwatka, Frederik

October 1, 1849
b. DeYoung, Michel Harry

October 2, 1849
d. Mohammed Ali

October 6, 1849
b. Zaharoff, Basil, Sir

October 7, 1849
b. Riley, James Whitcomb
d. Poe, Edgar Allan

October 16, 1849
b. Williams, George Washington

October 17, 1849
d. Chopin, Frederic Francois

October 23, 1849
b. Saionji, Kimmochi

November 1, 1849
b. Chase, William Merritt

November 5, 1849
b. Barbosa, Ruy

November 13, 1849
d. Etty, William
d. Manning, Maria

November 24, 1849
b. Burnett, Frances Eliza Hodgson

November 29, 1849
b. Fleming, John Ambrose, Sir
b. Schechter, Solomon

December 1, 1849
d. Elliott, Ebenezer

December 7, 1849
b. Fischer, Carl

December 12, 1849
b. Vanderbilt, William Kissam
d. Brunel, Marc Isambard, Sir

December 19, 1849
b. Frick, Henry Clay

December 20, 1849
b. Eminescu, Mihail
d. Miller, William

December 21, 1849
b. Allen, James Lane

1850

b. Bamba, Amadou
b. Grasselli, Caesar Augustin
b. Hanes, John Wesley
b. Irigoyen, Hipolito
b. Reyes, Rafael
d. Lin Tse-hsu

January 2, 1850
d. Peel, Robert, Sir

January 6, 1850
b. Bernstein, Eduard

January 10, 1850
b. Root, John Wellborn

January 11, 1850
b. Arthur, Joseph Charles

January 13, 1850
b. Ray, Charlotte E.

January 14, 1850
b. DeReszke, Jean
b. Loti, Pierre

January 15, 1850
b. Younger, Jim

January 18, 1850
b. Low, Seth

January 19, 1850
b. Birrell, Augustine

January 22, 1850
b. Brookings, Robert Somers

January 24, 1850
b. Ebbinghaus, Hermann
b. Murfree, Mary Noailles

January 26, 1850
d. Jeffrey, Francis Jeffrey, Lord

January 27, 1850
b. Genung, John Franklin
b. Gompers, Samuel
d. Schadow, Gottfried

January 29, 1850
b. Hargrave, Lawrence
b. Howard, Ebenezer, Sir

February 12, 1850
b. Davis, William Morris

February 27, 1850
b. Huntington, Henry Edwards
b. Richards, Laura Elizabeth Howe

March 7, 1850
b. Clark, Champ
b. Masaryk, Tomas Garrigue

March 24, 1850
b. Hocking, Silas

March 26, 1850
b. Bellamy, Edward

March 31, 1850
d. Calhoun, John Caldwell
d. Giusti, Giuseppe

April 2, 1850
b. Laughlin, James Laurence

April 8, 1850
b. Welch, William Henry

April 10, 1850
b. Davenport, Fanny Lily Gypsy

April 12, 1850
d. Judson, Adoniram

April 15, 1850
d. Tussaud, Marie Gresholtz, Madame

April 16, 1850
b. Adams, Herbert Baxter
b. Thomas, Sidney Gilchrist

April 20, 1850
b. French, Daniel Chester

April 23, 1850
d. Wordsworth, William

May 7, 1850
b. Seidl, Anton

May 9, 1850
d. Gay-Lussac, Joseph-Louis

May 10, 1850
b. Lipton, Thomas Johnstone, Sir

May 12, 1850
b. Lodge, Henry Cabot
d. Osgood, Frances Sargent Locke

May 24, 1850
b. Grady, Henry Woodfin

May 26, 1850
b. Lopez-Portillo y Rojas, Jose

May 28, 1850
b. Maitland, Frederic William

June 5, 1850
b. Garrett, Pat(rick Floyd)

June 6, 1850
b. Braun, Karl Ferdinand

June 9, 1850
b. Roux, Wilhelm
b. Stillman, James

June 14, 1850
b. Kitchener, Horatio Herbert

June 18, 1850
b. Curtis, Cyrus Hermann Kotszchmar

June 21, 1850
b. Beard, Dan(iel Carter)
b. Cecchetti, Enrico

June 24, 1850
b. Gummere, William Stryker

June 27, 1850
b. Hearn, Lafcadio

July 8, 1850
b. Lanman, Charles Rockwell

July 9, 1850
d. Boyer, Jean Pierre
d. Taylor, Zachary

July 15, 1850
b. Cabrini, Frances Xavier, Saint

July 19, 1850
d. Fuller, Margaret

July 26, 1850
b. Henry, Edward Richard, Sir

August 5, 1850
b. Maupassant, Guy de

August 17, 1850
d. San Martin, Jose de

August 18, 1850
d. Balzac, Honore de

August 25, 1850
b. Nye, Edgar Wilson

August 26, 1850
b. Richet, Charles Robert
d. Louis Phillippe

August 30, 1850
b. Del Pilar, Marcelo Hilario

September 2, 1850
b. Field, Eugene
b. Spalding, Albert Goodwill

September 9, 1850
b. Lawson, Victor Fremont

September 23, 1850
d. Artigas, Jose Gervasio

October 8, 1850
b. Le Chatelier, Henry-Louis

November 5, 1850
b. Wilcox, Ella Wheeler

November 13, 1850
b. Evans, Charles
b. Stevenson, Robert Louis (Balfour)

November 19, 1850
d. Johnson, Richard Mentor

November 29, 1850
b. Scalchi, Sofia

December 4, 1850
d. Sturgeon, William

December 10, 1850
b. Brownscombe, Jennie Augusta
b. Hinrichs, Gustav

December 16, 1850
b. Bates, Arlo

December 20, 1850
b. Anderson, Elizabeth Milbank

December 23, 1850
b. Straus, Oscar Solomon

December 28, 1850
b. Tamagno, Francesco

1851

b. Bulova, Joseph
b. Hills, Austin H
b. Holliday, Doc
b. Kim Ok-kyun
b. Lever, William Hesketh
b. Min
d. Codrington, Edward, Sir

January 17, 1851
b. Frost, Arthur Burdett

January 19, 1851
b. Jordan, David Starr
b. Kapteyn, Jacobus Cornelis
d. Echeverria, Jose Esteban (Antonino)

January 21, 1851
d. Lortzing, Gustav Albert

January 24, 1851
d. Spontini, Gasparo

January 27, 1851
d. Audubon, John James

January 31, 1851
b. Webb, William Seward

February 1, 1851
d. Shelley, Mary Wollstonecraft

February 8, 1851
b. Chopin, Kate

February 12, 1851
b. Bohm von Bawerk, Eugene

February 18, 1851
d. Jacobi, Carl Gustav Jacob

February 26, 1851
b. Booth, Joseph

March 6, 1851
d. Shreve, Henry Miller

March 9, 1851
d. Oersted, Hans Christian

March 11, 1851
d. McDuffie, George

March 18, 1851
b. Coghlan, Rose

March 26, 1851
b. Bradley, Andrew Cecil

March 27, 1851
b. Indy, Paul (Marie Theodore Vincent d')

April 2, 1851
b. Walker, Emery, Sir

April 17, 1851
b. Anson, Cap

April 20, 1851
b. Acevedo Diaz, Eduardo

April 24, 1851
b. Earp, Morgan

April 27, 1851
b. Earle, Alice Morse

May 2, 1851
b. Taylor, Graham

May 4, 1851
b. Dewing, Thomas Wilmer

May 7, 1851
b. Harnack, Adolf von

May 18, 1851
b. Peretz, Isaac Loeb

May 20, 1851
b. Berliner, Emile
b. Lathrop, Rose Hawthorne

May 29, 1851
b. Bourgeois, Leon-Victor Auguste

June 3, 1851
b. Baker, Theodore

June 12, 1851
b. Lodge, Oliver Joseph, Sir

June 17, 1851
d. Russwurm, John Brown

June 23, 1851
b. Eddy, Clarence

July 6, 1851
d. Davenport, Thomas

July 8, 1851
b. Evans, Arthur John, Sir

July 12, 1851
d. Daguerre, Louis Jacques Mande

July 21, 1851
b. Bass, Sam

August 3, 1851
b. Fitzgerald, George Francis

August 13, 1851
b. Adler, Felix

August 16, 1851
b. Harvey, William Hope

August 19, 1851
b. Hires, Charles E

August 22, 1851
b. Frohman, Daniel

September 1, 1851
d. Lopez, Narciso

September 4, 1851
d. Woodbury, Levi

September 10, 1851
d. Gallaudet, Thomas Hopkins

September 11, 1851
d. Graham, Sylvester

September 13, 1851
b. Reed, Walter

September 14, 1851
d. Cooper, James Fenimore

September 22, 1851
d. Sherwood, Mary Martha

October 2, 1851
b. Foch, Ferdinand

October 4, 1851
d. Godoy y Alvarez de Faria, Manuel de

October 12, 1851
d. Warrington, Lewis

October 17, 1851
b. Ryan, Thomas Fortune

November 6, 1851
b. Dow, Charles Henry

November 16, 1851
b. Hauk, Minnie

November 20, 1851
b. Coulter, John Merle

November 21, 1851
b. Spy

December 10, 1851
b. Dewey, Melvil

December 12, 1851
d. Poinsett, Joel Roberts

December 19, 1851
d. Turner, Joseph Mallord William

December 30, 1851
b. Candler, Asa Griggs

1852

b. Calamity Jane
b. De Leon, Daniel
b. Edwardes, George
b. Forain, Jean-Louis
b. Harris, Augustus, Sir
b. Jergens, Andrew
b. King, Grace Elizabeth
b. Kojong
b. Matzeliger, Jan Ernest
b. Parker, Quanah
b. Stokely, Anna
b. Tewfik Pasha
b. Upton, Francis Robbins
d. Bransfield, Edward
d. Cinque, Joseph
d. Drake, Daniel
d. Hitchcock, Lambert
d. Lafarge, Marie
d. Taqi Khan Amir-e Kabir, Mirza

January 12, 1852
b. Joffre, Joseph Jacques Cesaire

January 25, 1852
d. Bellinghausen, Fabian Gottlieb von

January 26, 1852
b. Brazza, Pierre Paul Francois
Camille Savorgnan de

February 6, 1852
b. Morgan, C(onwy) Lloyd

February 13, 1852
b. Dreyer, Johan Ludwig Emil

February 16, 1852
b. Russell, Charles Taze

February 24, 1852
b. Moore, George Augustus

February 25, 1852
d. Moore, Thomas

February 26, 1852
b. Kellogg, John Harvey

March 1, 1852
b. Delcasse, Theophile

March 4, 1852
d. Gogol, Nikolai Vasilievich

March 5, 1852
b. Gregory, Isabella Augusta Persse,
Lady

March 28, 1852
d. Braille, Louis

April 1, 1852
b. Abbey, Edwin Austin

April 6, 1852
b. Cole, Timothy

April 9, 1852
d. Payne, John Howard

April 13, 1852
b. Woolworth, Frank Winfield

April 23, 1852
b. Markham, Edwin

April 25, 1852
b. Cannon, James W

May 1, 1852
b. Patten, Simon Nelson
b. Ramon y Cajal, Santiago

May 5, 1852
b. von Hugel, Friedrich, Baron

May 11, 1852
b. Fairbanks, Charles Warren

May 14, 1852
b. Parker, Alton Brooks
d. Adams, Louisa Catherine

May 15, 1852
b. Goldsmith, Fred Ernest

May 23, 1852
b. Chirol, Valentine, Sir

May 24, 1852
b. Cunninghame-Graham, Robert
Bontine

June 3, 1852
b. Robinson, Theodore

June 21, 1852
d. Froebel, Friedrich Wilhelm August

June 24, 1852
b. Adler, Victor

June 25, 1852
b. Gaudi y Cornet, Antonio

June 29, 1852
b. McMaster, John Bach
d. Clay, Henry

July 10, 1852
b. Chalmers, William James

July 28, 1852
d. Downing, Andrew Jackson

August 4, 1852
d. D'Orsay, Alfred Guillaume, Count

August 12, 1852
b. McGivney, Michael Joseph

August 18, 1852
d. Taylor, Margaret (Smith)

August 24, 1852
b. O'Rourke, Jim

August 30, 1852
b. Hoff, Jacobus Henricus van't
b. Van't Hoff, Jacobus Henricus
b. Weir, Julian Alden

September 2, 1852
b. Bourget, Paul (Charles Joseph)

September 9, 1852
b. Poynting, John Henry

September 12, 1852
b. Asquith, Herbert Henry

September 14, 1852
d. Wellington, Arthur Wellesley, Duke

September 15, 1852
b. Bouchet, Edward Alexander

September 20, 1852
d. Chase, Philander

September 23, 1852
b. Halsted, William Stewart
d. Vanderlyn, John

September 28, 1852
b. Moissan, Ferdinand Frederick Henri

September 30, 1852
b. Stanford, Charles Villiers, Sir

October 2, 1852
b. Ramsay, William, Sir

October 9, 1852
b. Fischer, Emil Herman

October 12, 1852
d. Stephens, John Lloyd

October 15, 1852
d. Jahn, Friedrich Ludwig

October 16, 1852
d. Ballivian, Jose

October 24, 1852
d. Webster, Daniel

October 31, 1852
b. Freeman, Mary E Wilkins

November 3, 1852
b. Mutsuhito

November 10, 1852
b. Vandyke, Henry Jackson, Jr.

November 14, 1852
d. Pugin, A(ugustus) W(elby)
N(orthmore)

November 22, 1852
b. D'Estournelles, Paul Henri
Benjamin Balleut de Constant,
Baron

November 27, 1852
d. Lovelace, Ada Byron

November 30, 1852
d. Booth, Junius Brutus
d. Phelps, Elizabeth Stuart Ward

December 13, 1852
d. Wright, Frances

December 14, 1852
b. Cheyne, William Watson, Sir

December 15, 1852
b. Becquerel, Antoine Henri

December 16, 1852
d. Wallace, Horace Binney

December 18, 1852
d. Greenough, Horatio

December 19, 1852
b. Michelson, Albert Abraham

December 20, 1852
b. Kitasato Shibasaburo

1853

b. Chang Chien
b. Lease, Mary Elizabeth Clyens
b. Meinong, Alexius, Ritter von
  Handschuchsheim
b. Michelin, Andre
b. Yen Fu
b. Younger, Bob
d. Bradshaw, George
d. Ricordi, Giovanni

January 12, 1853
b. Ricci-Curbastro, Gregorio

January 16, 1853
b. Forbes-Robertson, Johnston, Sir
b. Hamilton, Ian Standish Monteith,
  Sir

January 17, 1853
b. Belmont, Alva Erskine Smith
  Vanderbilt

January 22, 1853
b. Gore, Charles

January 28, 1853
b. Marti (y Perez), Jose Julian
b. Soloviev, Vladimir Sergeevich

February 3, 1853
b. Jameson, Leander Starr, Sir
b. Maxim, Hudson

February 18, 1853
b. Belmont, August, Jr.
b. Fenollosa, Ernest Francisco

March 5, 1853
b. Foote, Arthur William
b. Pyle, Howard

March 14, 1853
b. Hodler, Ferdinand

March 16, 1853
b. Kayser, Heinrich Gustav Johannes

March 17, 1853
d. Doppler, Christian Johann

March 29, 1853
b. Thomson, Elihu

March 30, 1853
b. Van Gogh, Vincent Willem
d. Fillmore, Abigail (Powers)

April 18, 1853
d. King, William Rufus de Vane

April 23, 1853
b. Page, Thomas Nelson

April 24, 1853
b. Bertillon, Alphonse

April 25, 1853
b. Stevens, John Frank
d. Beaumont, William

April 28, 1853
d. Tieck, (Johann) Ludwig

May 3, 1853
b. Howe, Edgar Watson

May 6, 1853
b. Knox, Philander Chase

May 14, 1853
b. Caine, Hall

May 26, 1853
b. Hardin, John Wesley

May 28, 1853
b. Larsson, Carl Olof

June 2, 1853
d. Alaman, Lucas

June 3, 1853
b. Petrie, (William Matthew) Flinders,
  Sir

July 3, 1853
b. Yermolova, Maria Nikolayevna

July 5, 1853
b. Rhodes, Cecil John

July 13, 1853
b. Bonvalot, Pierre Gabriel Edouard

July 18, 1853
b. Lorentz, Hendrick Antoon

July 23, 1853
d. Pretorius, Andries

July 24, 1853
b. Gillette, William Hooker

July 25, 1853
b. Belasco, David

July 27, 1853
b. Korolenko, Vladimir Galaktionovich

August 4, 1853
b. Twachtman, John Henry

August 21, 1853
b. Wellcome, Henry Solomon, Sir

August 29, 1853
d. Napier, Charles James, Sir

September 2, 1853
b. Ostwald, Friedrich Wilhelm

September 8, 1853
d. Ozanam, (Antoine) Frederic

September 13, 1853
b. Dellenbaugh, Frederick Samuel
b. Gram, Hans Christian Joachim

September 16, 1853
b. Kossel, Karl Martin Leonhard
  Albrecht

September 20, 1853
b. Chulalongkorn

September 21, 1853
b. Kamerlingh Onnes, Heike

October 2, 1853
d. Arago, Dominque Francois Jean

October 4, 1853
b. Palacio Valdes, Armando

October 13, 1853
b. Langtry, Lillie

October 22, 1853
d. Lavalleja, Juan Antonio

October 31, 1853
b. Zelaya, Jose Santos

November 9, 1853
b. White, Stanford

November 13, 1853
b. Drew, John

November 24, 1853
b. Masterson, Bat

November 28, 1853
b. White, Helen Magill

December 8, 1853
d. Chickering, Jonas

December 17, 1853
b. Tree, Herbert Beerbohm

December 22, 1853
b. DeReszke, Edouard

December 26, 1853
b. Bazin, Rene

December 30, 1853
b. Messager, Andre Charles Prosper

December 31, 1853
b. Bliss, Tasker Howard

1854

b. Ayrton, Hertha
b. Gilbert, Alfred, Sir
b. Horn, Alfred Aloysius
b. Husein ibn Ali
b. Kautsky, Karl Johann
b. LaFlesche Tibbles, Susette
b. Maherero, Samuel
b. Mayo-Smith, Richmond
b. Tabor, Elizabeth Bonduel McCourt
    Doe
d. Catherwood, Frederick
d. Rivera, Fructuoso

January 1, 1854
b. Frazer, James George, Sir
d. Place, Francis

January 9, 1854
b. Churchill, Jennie Jerome

January 12, 1854
b. Marquis, Albert Nelson

January 25, 1854
b. Shaw, Mary

January 31, 1854
d. Pellico, Silvio

February 7, 1854
d. Fitzpatrick, Thomas

February 9, 1854
b. Carson, Edward Henry

February 27, 1854
d. Lamennais, Hugues Felicite Robert
    de

March 2, 1854
d. Rubini, Giovanni-Battista

March 3, 1854
d. Smithson, Harriet Constance

March 14, 1854
b. Ehrlich, Paul Ralph
b. Marshall, Thomas Riley

March 15, 1854
b. Behring, Emil Adolph von

March 23, 1854
b. Milner, Alfred, Viscount

March 26, 1854
b. Furniss, Harry

March 27, 1854
b. Grassi, Giovanni Battista

April 13, 1854
b. Drummond, William Henry
b. Ely, Richard Theodore

April 16, 1854
b. Coxey, Jacob Sechler

April 22, 1854
b. La Fontaine, Henri Marie

April 24, 1854
d. Rossetti, Gabriele Pasquale
    Giuseppe

April 27, 1854
d. Pickering, William

April 29, 1854
b. Poincare, Jules Henri

May 11, 1854
b. Mergenthaler, Ottmar
b. Small, Albion W(oodbury)

May 21, 1854
b. Peto, John Frederick

May 22, 1854
b. Schurman, Jacob Gould

May 24, 1854
b. Mansfield, Richard
b. Love, Nat

June 1, 1854
d. Judson, Emily Chubbock

June 10, 1854
b. Curel, Francois de

June 12, 1854
b. Plancon, Pol-Henri

June 13, 1854
b. Parsons, Charles Algernon, Sir

June 17, 1854
d. Holbrook, Josiah
d. Sontag, Henriette

June 18, 1854
b. Scripps, Edward Wyllis

June 19, 1854
b. Catalani, Alfredo

June 26, 1854
b. Borden, Robert Laird, Sir

July 3, 1854
b. Janacek, Leos

July 7, 1854
d. Ohm, Georg Simon

July 11, 1854
b. Barrymore, Georgiana Emma Drew

July 12, 1854
b. Eastman, George

July 24, 1854
b. Takahashi, Korekiyo

July 31, 1854
d. Wilson, Samuel

August 2, 1854
b. Crawford, Francis Marion

August 12, 1854
b. Thomas, Edith Matilda

August 16, 1854
d. Phyfe, Duncan

August 18, 1854
b. Hyslop, James Hervey

August 20, 1854
d. Schelling, Friedrich Wilhelm Joseph
    von

August 21, 1854
b. Munsey, Frank Andrew

August 23, 1854
b. Moszkowski, Moritz

August 29, 1854
b. Jacobs, Joseph

September 1, 1854
b. Humperdinck, Engelbert

September 11, 1854
b. Holabird, William

September 17, 1854
b. Buick, David Dunbar
b. Ellsler, Effie

September 22, 1854
b. Finck, Henry Theophilus

September 26, 1854
b. Bausch, Edward
d. LaFever Minard

September 27, 1854
d. Ogden, Peter Skene
d. Reed, Henry Hope

September 28, 1854
b. Sedgwick, Adam

October 1, 1854
d. Royall, Anne Newport

October 2, 1854
b. Geddes, Patrick, Sir

October 3, 1854
b. Gorgas, William Crawford

October 18, 1854
b. Andree, Salomon August

October 20, 1854
b. Rimbaud, (Jean Nicolas) Arthur

October 26, 1854
b. Post, Charles William

November 3, 1854
b. Takamine, Jokichi

November 5, 1854
b. Sabatier, Paul

November 6, 1854
b. Sousa, John Philip

November 12, 1854
d. Kemble, Charles

November 13, 1854
b. Chadwick, George Whitefield

November 14, 1854
b. Parsons, Frank

November 17, 1854
b. Lyautey, Louis Hubert Gonzalve

November 18, 1854
d. Forbes, Edward

November 21, 1854
b. Benedict XV

November 25, 1854
d. Lockhart, John Gibson

November 28, 1854
b. Haberlandt, Gottlieb

December 1, 1854
b. Vinogradoff, Paul Gavrilovitch

December 3, 1854
d. Ritchie, Thomas

December 11, 1854
b. Radbourn, Old Hoss

December 15, 1854
d. Kamehameha III

December 16, 1854
b. Fels, Joseph

December 23, 1854
b. Huerta, Victoriano

December 26, 1854
b. Tappan, Eva March

1855

b. Adler, Jacob Pavlovitch
b. Corelli, Marie
b. Enhsaihan, M.
b. Inukai, Tsuyoshi
b. Thomas, Samuel Bath
d. Woodville, Richard Caton

January 1, 1855
b. Sverdrup, Otto

January 4, 1855
b. Brann, William Cowper

January 5, 1855
b. Gillette, King Camp

January 6, 1855
d. Wood, Sarah Sayward Barrell Keating

January 10, 1855
d. Mitford, Mary Russell

January 21, 1855
b. Browning, John Moses

January 25, 1855
d. Nerval, Gerard de

January 27, 1855
d. Rossi, Gaetano

January 28, 1855
b. Burroughs, William Seward

February 5, 1855
b. Merriam, Clinton Hart

February 21, 1855
b. Palmer, Alice Elvira Freeman

February 23, 1855
d. Gauss, Carl Friedrich

March 2, 1855
d. Nicholas I

March 3, 1855
d. Mills, Robert

March 10, 1855
d. Brown, James

March 13, 1855
b. Lowell, Percival

March 23, 1855
b. Giddings, Franklin Henry

March 24, 1855
b. Mellon, Andrew William

March 31, 1855
d. Bronte, Charlotte

April 9, 1855
b. Osgood, Herbert Levi

April 27, 1855
b. Duke, Benjamin Newton

May 8, 1855
b. Gates, John Warne

May 12, 1855
b. Isham, Samuel

May 15, 1855
b. Bamberger, Louis

May 17, 1855
b. Healy, T(imothy) M(ichael)

May 25, 1855
b. Pinero, Arthur Wing, Sir

May 29, 1855
b. Bruce, David, Sir
b. Kelly, Ned

June 1, 1855
b. Angle, Edward Hartley

June 14, 1855
b. LaFollette, Robert Marion

June 16, 1855
d. Gorrie, John

June 21, 1855
b. Chausson, Ernest

June 28, 1855
d. Raglan, Fitzroy James Henry Somerset, Baron

July 1, 1855
d. Rosmini-Serbati, Antonio

July 2, 1855
b. Barron, Clarence Walker

July 8, 1855
d. Parry, William Edward, Sir

July 26, 1855
b. Tonnies, Ferdinand

August 3, 1855
b. Bunner, Henry Cuyler

August 5, 1855
b. Dines, William Henry

August 15, 1855
b. Page, Walter Hines

August 18, 1855
d. Lawrence, Abbott

September 7, 1855
b. Friese-Greene, William Edward

September 9, 1855
b. Chamberlain, Houston Stewart

September 12, 1855
b. Sharp, William

September 19, 1855
b. Klafsky, Katharina

September 21, 1855
b. Roosevelt, Sara Delano

September 27, 1855
b. Morton, Joy

September 28, 1855
b. Brush, George

October 12, 1855
b. Nikisch, Arthur

October 21, 1855
b. Ball, Edmund B

October 24, 1855
b. Sherman, James Schoolcraft

November 1, 1855
b. Adler, Guido

November 5, 1855
b. Debs, Eugene Victor
b. Teisserenc de Bort, Leon-Philippe

November 6, 1855
b. Kalisch, Paul

November 7, 1855
b. Hall, Edwin Herbert

November 10, 1855
b. Darracq, Alexandre

November 11, 1855
d. Kierkegaard, Soren Aabye

November 20, 1855
b. Royce, Josiah

December 12, 1855
d. Charpentier, Johann von

December 18, 1855
d. Rogers, Samuel
d. Sturm, Charles Francois

December 28, 1855
b. Zorrilla de San Martin, Juan

December 31, 1855
b. Pascoli, Giovanni

1856

b. Ahad Haam
b. Bethmann Hollweg, Theobald von
b. Dockstader, Lew
b. Gordon, Aaron David
b. Haam, Ahad
b. Hara, Kei
b. Hills, Reuben W
b. Major, Charles
b. Michelin, Edouard
b. Peters, Carl
b. Wovoka
d. Bird, Robert Montgomery
d. Palmer, William
d. Thierry, Augustin
d. Wei Yuan

January 4, 1856
d. David d'Angers

January 9, 1856
b. Reese, Lizette Woodworth

January 11, 1856
b. Sinding, Christian

January 12, 1856
b. Sargent, John Singer

January 20, 1856
b. Blatch, Harriot Eaton Stanton

February 14, 1856
b. Harris, Frank

February 17, 1856
b. Ives, Frederic Eugene
d. Heine, Heinrich

February 19, 1856
b. Stammler, Rudolf

February 21, 1856
b. Berlage, Hendrik Petrus

February 24, 1856
d. Lobachevskii, Nikolai Ivanovich

February 25, 1856
b. Freer, Charles Lang
b. Lamprecht, Karl

February 27, 1856
b. Battistini, Mattia
b. Lavery, John, Sir

March 9, 1856
b. Acheson, Edward Goodrich
b. Foy, Eddie

March 15, 1856
b. Hara Takashi

March 20, 1856
b. Taylor, Frederick Winslow

March 21, 1856
b. Flipper, Henry Ossian

March 26, 1856
b. Massey, William Ferguson

April 5, 1856
b. Washington, Booker T(aliafero)

April 7, 1856
b. Fuller-Maitland, John Alexander

April 15, 1856
b. Daniels, Frank
b. Hubert, Conrad

April 20, 1856
d. Stevens, Robert Livingston

April 23, 1856
b. Woods, Granville T

April 24, 1856
b. Petain, Henri Philippe

April 25, 1856
b. Hadley, Arthur Twining

April 26, 1856
b. Morgenthau, Henry

May 2, 1856
b. Rozanov, Vasili Vasilyevich

May 3, 1856
b. Alvary, Max
d. Adam, Adolphe Charles

May 5, 1856
b. Denslow, W(illiam) W(allace)

May 6, 1856
b. Freud, Sigmund
b. Peary, Robert Edwin
d. Hamilton, William, Sir

May 13, 1856
b. Emerson, Peter Henry

May 15, 1856
b. Baum, L(yman) Frank

May 21, 1856
b. Batlle y Ordonez, Jose
b. Dodge, Grace Hoadley

June 15, 1856
b. Channing, Edward Perkins

June 19, 1856
b. Hubbard, Elbert Green

June 22, 1856
b. Haggard, Henry Rider, Sir

June 24, 1856
b. Mercer, Henry Chapman

June 26, 1856
d. Stirner, Max

June 29, 1856
d. Jones, Peter

July 9, 1856
b. Guggenheim, Daniel
d. Avogadro, Amedeo

July 10, 1856
b. Tesla, Nikola

July 21, 1856
b. Bethune, Louise Blanchard

July 24, 1856
b. Picard, Charles Emile

July 26, 1856
b. Harper, William Rainey
b. Shaw, George Bernard

July 29, 1856
d. Schumann, Robert Alexander

August 3, 1856
b. Deakin, Alfred

August 8, 1856
d. Vestris, Lucia Elizabeth, Madame

August 10, 1856
b. Doheny, Edward Lawrence

August 12, 1856
b. Brady, Diamond Jim

August 14, 1856
d. Buckland, William

August 15, 1856
b. Hardie, James Keir

August 19, 1856
b. Frederic, Harold
d. Gerhardt, Charles Frederic

August 24, 1856
b. Mottl, Felix

August 30, 1856
d. A'Beckett, Gilbert Abbott

September 3, 1856
b. Sullivan, Louis Henri

September 5, 1856
b. Watson, Thomas Edward

September 28, 1856
b. Thompson, Edward Herbert
b. Wiggin, Kate Douglas

October 3, 1856
b. Fortune, Timothy Thomas
b. Hare, James Henry

October 16, 1856
b. Wilde, Oscar (Fingal O'Flahertie Wills)

October 19, 1856
d. Said, Seyyid
d. Said ibn Sultan

October 27, 1856
b. Cox, Kenyon

November 1, 1856
b. Saunders, William Laurence

November 8, 1856
d. Cabet, Etienne

November 9, 1856
d. Clayton, John Middleton

November 10, 1856
b. Todd, Mabel Loomis

November 13, 1856
b. Brandeis, Louis Dembitz

November 17, 1856
d. Eaton, John Henry

November 25, 1856
b. Taneyev, Sergey Ivanovich

December 5, 1856
b. Brown, Alice

December 13, 1856
b. Lowell, Abbott Lawrence

December 18, 1856
b. Thomson, Joseph John, Sir

December 20, 1856
b. Blomfield, Reginald Theodore, Sir

December 22, 1856
b. Kellogg, Frank Billings

December 23, 1856
b. Duke, James Buchanan

December 25, 1856
b. Galvin, Pud
b. Thomas, Brandon

December 28, 1856
b. Wilson, Woodrow

1857

b. Bekhterev, Vladimir Mikhailovich
b. Dodge, Henry Chee
b. Gomez, Juan Vicente
b. Goodwin, Nat C
d. Coats, James

January 1, 1857
b. Cline, Maggie
b. Keefe, Tim(othy John)

January 2, 1857
b. Opper, Frederick Burr
b. Thomas, Martha Carey

January 9, 1857
b. Fuller, Henry Blake

January 17, 1857
b. Kienzl, Wilhelm

February 6, 1857
b. Flagg, Ernest

February 10, 1857
d. Thompson, David

February 12, 1857
b. Atget, Eugene

February 15, 1857
d. Glinka, Mikhail Ivanovich

February 16, 1857
d. Kane, Elisha Kent

February 17, 1857
b. McClure, Samuel Sidney

February 18, 1857
b. Klinger, Max

February 22, 1857
b. Baden-Powell, Robert Stephenson Smyth Baden-Powell, Baron
b. Hertz, Heinrich Rudolph
b. Stanton, Frank Lebby

February 23, 1857
b. Deland, Margaret Wade

February 26, 1857
b. Coue, Emile
b. Lawson, Thomas William
b. Sheldon, Charles M(onroe)

February 28, 1857
b. Loisy, Alfred Firmin

March 4, 1857
b. Kobbe, Gustav

March 7, 1857
b. Wagner-Jaurregg, Julius, von

March 22, 1857
d. Scoresby, William

March 23, 1857
b. Farmer, Fannie Merritt

March 25, 1857
d. Colgate, William

April 10, 1857
b. Levy-Bruhl, Lucien

April 11, 1857
b. Davidson, John

April 12, 1857
b. Underwood, John Thomas

April 14, 1857
b. Kelley, Edgar Stillman

April 16, 1857
b. Pritchett, Henry S

April 18, 1857
b. Darrow, Clarence Seward

April 30, 1857
b. Bleuler, Eugen

May 2, 1857
d. Musset, Alfred de

May 5, 1857
b. Zetkin, Clara

May 9, 1857
b. Kidman, Sidney

May 12, 1857
b. Dunning, William Archibald

May 13, 1857
b. Ross, Ronald, Sir

May 15, 1857
b. Fleming, Williamina Paton Stevens

May 19, 1857
b. Abel, John Jacob

May 20, 1857
b. Rice, Joseph Mayer

May 23, 1857
d. Cauchy, Augustin Louis

May 28, 1857
b. Hilliard, Robert Cochran

May 30, 1857
b. Peabody, Endicott

May 31, 1857
b. Pius XI

June 2, 1857
b. Elgar, Edward William, Sir
b. Gjellerup, Karl Adolf

June 10, 1857
b. Potthast, Edward Henry

June 18, 1857
b. Folger, Henry Clay

June 27, 1857
d. MacMillan, Daniel

July 1, 1857
b. Connor, Roger

July 3, 1857
d. Bibaud, Michel

July 4, 1857
d. Marcy, William Learned

July 8, 1857
b. Binet, Alfred

July 15, 1857
d. Czerny, Karl

July 16, 1857
d. Beranger, Pierre-Jean de

July 23, 1857
b. Shaw, Albert

July 24, 1857
b. Pontoppidan, Henrik

July 25, 1857
b. Sprague, Frank Julian

July 27, 1857
b. Budge, Ernest Alfred Thompson
Wallis, Sir

July 30, 1857
b. Veblen, Thorstein Bunde

August 3, 1857
d. Sue, Eugene Joseph Marie

August 8, 1857
b. McIntyre, James
b. Osborn, Henry Fairfield

September 3, 1857
d. McLoughlin, John

September 5, 1857
d. Comte, Auguste
d. Duff, Mary Ann Dyke

September 6, 1857
b. Nuttall, Zelia Maria Magdalena

September 9, 1857
b. Hervieu, Paul-Ernest

September 10, 1857
b. Keeler, James Edward

September 13, 1857
b. Hershey, Milton Snavely

September 15, 1857
b. Taft, William (Howard)

September 17, 1857
b. Tsiolkovsky, Konstantin
Eduardovich

September 22, 1857
d. Manin, Daniele

September 30, 1857
b. Sudermann, Hermann

October 6, 1857
b. Dickman, Joseph Theodore

October 8, 1857
b. Albee, Edward Franklin

October 10, 1857
d. Crawford, Thomas

October 14, 1857
b. Haynes, Elwood
b. Lamar, Joseph Rucker

October 30, 1857
b. Atherton, Gertrude Franklin

November 5, 1857
b. Tarbell, Ida Minerva

November 18, 1857
b. Knox, Rose Markward

November 21, 1857
b. Estrada Cabrera, Manuel

November 22, 1857
b. Gissing, George Robert

November 24, 1857
b. Ball, Frank

November 25, 1857
d. Birney, James Gillespie

November 26, 1857
b. Plekhanov, Georgi Valentinovich
d. Eichendorff, Joseph Karl Benedict
Freiherr von

November 27, 1857
b. Sherrington, Charles Scott, Sir

December 3, 1857
b. Conrad, Joseph

December 11, 1857
d. Castil-Blaze, Francois-Joseph

December 13, 1857
b. Nieman, Lucius William

December 15, 1857
d. Cayley, George, Sir

December 16, 1857
b. Barnard, Edward Emerson

December 25, 1857
b. LaFlesche, Francis

December 27, 1857
b. Manners, Charles

December 31, 1857
b. Kelly, King

1858

b. Abrahams, Israel
b. Antoine, Andre
b. Chona, Maria
b. Davenport, Eva
b. Eastman, Charles Alexander
b. Rosso, Medardo
b. Smucker, Jerome
b. Smyth, Ethel, Dame
b. Taylor, Walter
b. Wallas, Graham
d. Ch'i-ying

January 1, 1858
d. Leslie, Eliza

January 3, 1858
d. Darcy, Henri Philibert Gaspard
d. Rachel

January 4, 1858
b. Glass, Carter

January 7, 1858
b. Ben-Yehuda, Eliezer

January 11, 1858
b. Selfridge, Harry Gordon

January 13, 1858
b. Minkowski, Oskar

January 14, 1858
b. Solomon, Hannah Greenebaum

January 15, 1858
b. Segantini, Giovanni

January 18, 1858
b. Williams, Daniel Hale

January 19, 1858
b. Brieux, Eugene

January 22, 1858
b. Lugard, Frederick John Dealtry
b. Webb, Beatrice Potter

January 23, 1858
d. Lablache, Luigi

January 28, 1858
b. Adams, Herbert Samuel
b. Dubois, Eugene

February 10, 1858
b. McDougall, Walt(er)

February 15, 1858
b. Pickering, William Henry

February 18, 1858
b. Sembrich, Marcella

February 24, 1858
b. Dolmetsch, Arnold

March 1, 1858
b. Simmel, Georg

March 4, 1858
d. Perry, Matthew Calbraith,
    Commodore

March 8, 1858
b. Leoncavallo, Ruggiero

March 9, 1858
b. Stickley, Gustav

March 10, 1858
b. Fowler, Henry Watson

March 12, 1858
b. Ochs, Adolph Simon

March 15, 1858
b. Bailey, Liberty Hyde

March 18, 1858
b. Diesel, Rudolf Christian Karl

March 19, 1858
b. K'ang Yu-wei

March 23, 1858
b. Chapais, Thomas, Sir
b. Quidde, Ludwig

March 24, 1858
b. Adamowski, Timothee

March 26, 1858
b. Delano, Jane Arminda

March 30, 1858
b. Hopper, De Wolfe

April 1, 1858
b. King, Frederic Truby
b. Repplier, Agnes

April 4, 1858
b. Gourmont, Remy (-Marie-Charles)
    de

April 5, 1858
b. Burpee, W(ashington) Atlee

April 8, 1858
b. Keenan, Frank

April 10, 1858
d. Benton, Thomas Hart

April 15, 1858
b. Durkheim, Emile

April 16, 1858
d. Cramer, Johann Baptist

April 19, 1858
b. Robson, May

April 23, 1858
b. Planck, Max Karl Ernst Ludwig

April 28, 1858
d. Muller, Johannes Peter

April 30, 1858
b. Harrison, Mary Scott Lord
    Dimmick

May 2, 1858
b. Somerville, Edith Anna OEnone

May 8, 1858
b. Brouthers, Dan

May 15, 1858
d. Hare, Robert

June 10, 1858
d. Brown, Robert

June 12, 1858
b. Johnston, Henry Hamilton

June 20, 1858
b. Chesnutt, Charles Waddell

June 28, 1858
b. Skinner, Otis

June 29, 1858
b. Goethals, George Washington

July 1, 1858
b. Metcalf, Willard Leroy
b. Stephens, Alice Barber

July 6, 1858
b. Hobson, John Atkinson

July 9, 1858
b. Boas, Franz

July 14, 1858
b. Pankhurst, Emmeline Goulden

July 16, 1858
b. Ysaye, Eugene

July 19, 1858
d. Porter, William Trotter

July 21, 1858
b. Corinth, Lovis

July 24, 1858
b. Kapp, Wolfgang

July 26, 1858
b. Boole, Ella Alexander
b. House, Edward Mandell

August 10, 1858
b. Cooper, Annie

August 11, 1858
b. Eijkman, Christiaan

August 14, 1858
d. Combe, George

August 15, 1858
b. Calve, Emma

August 19, 1858
b. Nesbit, Edith

August 20, 1858
d. Oshkosh

August 21, 1858
b. Rudolf of Hapsburg

August 27, 1858
b. Peano, Giuseppe

September 1, 1858
b. Welsbach, Carl Auer von, Baron

September 14, 1858
b. Hubay, Jeno

September 16, 1858
b. Law, Andrew Bonar

September 17, 1858
b. Vonnoh, Robert William
d. Scott, Dred

September 29, 1858
b. Mugnone, Leopoldo

October 3, 1858
b. Duse, Eleanora

October 4, 1858
b. Pupin, Michael Idvorsky

October 7, 1858
b. Eigenmann, Rosa Smith

October 12, 1858
b. Lewis, Isaac Newton
d. Hiroshige, Ando

October 14, 1858
d. Jay, William

October 15, 1858
b. Coulton, George Gordon
b. Sims, William Sowden
b. Sullivan, John L(awrence)

October 27, 1858
b. Roosevelt, Theodore
d. Larkin, Thomas Oliver

November 1, 1858
b. Tyrrell, Joseph Burr

November 3, 1858
b. Wellman, Walter

November 4, 1858
b. Benson, Frank Robert, Sir

November 17, 1858
d. Owen, Robert

November 20, 1858
b. Lagerlof, Selma Ottiliana Lovisa

November 26, 1858
b. Drexel, Mary Katherine

November 30, 1858
b. Bose, Jagadis Chandra, Sir
b. Coolidge, Charles Allerton

December 4, 1858
b. Greenwood, Chester

December 9, 1858
d. Baldwin, Robert

December 16, 1858
d. Bright, Richard

December 22, 1858
b. Puccini, Giacomo

December 23, 1858
b. Nemirovich-Danchenko, Vladimir I

December 26, 1858
d. Gadsden, James

1859

b. Brach, Emil J
b. Calvert, Louis
b. Chadwick, Cassie L
b. Curly
b. Hewitt, J(ohn) N(apoleon) B(rinton)
b. Jefferson, Thomas
b. Lenox, Walter S
b. Luden, William H
b. Lummis, Charles Fletcher
b. Masson, Paul
b. Palmer, Austin Norman
b. Samsonov, Aleksandr Vasilievich
b. Workman, Fanny Bullock
b. Yuan, Shih-Kai
b. Zaghlul Pasha, Saad
d. Bowlegs, Billy

January 1, 1859
b. Owens, Michael Joseph

January 6, 1859
b. Alexander, Samuel

January 8, 1859
b. Palamas, Kostes

January 9, 1859
b. Catt, Carrie Chapman

January 10, 1859
b. U'Ren, William Simon

January 11, 1859
b. Curzon of Kedleston, George
Nathaniel Curzon, Marquis

January 15, 1859
b. Britton, Nathaniel, Lord

January 18, 1859
d. Vail, Alfred Lewis

January 20, 1859
b. Lindbergh, Charles Augustus

January 27, 1859
b. Miliukov, Pavel Nikolayevich
b. Wilhelm II
b. William, II

January 28, 1859
d. Prescott, William Hickling

January 29, 1859
d. Thomas, Seth

February 1, 1859
b. Herbert, Victor

February 2, 1859
b. Ellis, Havelock

February 3, 1859
b. Junkers, Hugo

February 7, 1859
b. Nevada, Emma

February 14, 1859
b. Ferris, George Washington Gale

February 18, 1859
b. Aleichem, Sholom

February 19, 1859
b. Arrhenius, Svante August

February 21, 1859
b. Bentley, Charles Edwin

March 5, 1859
b. Durand, William F.

March 8, 1859
b. Grahame, Kenneth

March 16, 1859
b. Popov, Aleksandr Stepanovich

March 21, 1859
b. Savage, Henry Wilson

March 26, 1859
b. Housman, A(lfred) E(dward)

March 29, 1859
b. Mayer, Oscar Ferdinand

April 7, 1859
b. Camp, Walter Chauncey

b. Loeb, Jacques

April 8, 1859
b. Husserl, Edmund

April 11, 1859
b. Crowder, Enoch Herbert

April 13, 1859
b. Allen, Henry Tureman

April 16, 1859
d. Tocqueville, Alexis, Comte de

April 17, 1859
b. Van Devanter, Willis

April 29, 1859
d. Lardner, Dionysius

April 30, 1859
d. Aksakov, Sergei Timofeyevich

May 2, 1859
b. Jerome, Jerome Klapka

May 3, 1859
b. Adams, Andy

May 6, 1859
b. Drago, Luis Maria
d. Humboldt, Alexander, Freiherr von
d. Humboldt, Friedrich Heinrich
Alexander von

May 12, 1859
b. Nordica, Lillian

May 15, 1859
b. Curie, Pierre

May 19, 1859
b. Melba, Nellie, Dame

May 22, 1859
b. Doyle, Arthur Conan, Sir
d. Ferdinand, II

May 28, 1859
b. Janet, Pierre Marie Felix

June 5, 1859
d. Bailey, Gamaliel

June 7, 1859
d. Cox, David

June 8, 1859
d. Hunt, Walter

June 11, 1859
d. Metternich-Winneburg, Clemens

June 12, 1859
b. Walsh, Thomas James

June 21, 1859
b. Tanner, Henry Ossawa

June 22, 1859
b. Damrosch, Frank Heino

July 4, 1859
b. Welch, Mickey

July 6, 1859
b. Heidenstam, Carl Gustaf Verner von

July 13, 1859
b. Webb, Sidney James

July 14, 1859
d. Borel d'Hauterive, Petrus

July 15, 1859
d. Choate, Rufus

July 17, 1859
b. Rhys, Ernest Percival
b. Rivera, Luis Munoz

July 22, 1859
b. Glasscock, Jack

July 26, 1859
b. Bunau-Varilla, Philippe Jean

July 28, 1859
b. Anderson, Mary Antoinette
b. Booth, Ballington

July 31, 1859
b. Smith, Theobald

August 2, 1859
d. Mann, Horace

August 4, 1859
b. Hamsun, Knut
d. Vianney, Jean (Marie) Baptiste

August 12, 1859
b. Bates, Katharine Lee

August 15, 1859
b. Comiskey, Charlie

August 28, 1859
d. Hunt, Leigh

September 2, 1859
d. Bacon, Delia Salter

September 3, 1859
b. Jaures, Jean Leon
b. Pregl, Fritz

September 12, 1859
b. Kelley, Florence

September 15, 1859
d. Brunel, Isambard Kingdom

September 18, 1859
b. Hitchcock, Gilbert Monell

September 23, 1859
b. Osborne, Thomas Mott

September 26, 1859
b. Bacheller, Irving Addison

September 28, 1859
d. Ritter, Karl

September 29, 1859
b. Biggs, Hermann Michael

October 4, 1859
d. Baedeker, Karl

October 6, 1859
b. Seiberling, Frank Augustus

October 7, 1859
b. Wise, Thomas J

October 9, 1859
b. Dreyfus, Alfred

October 17, 1859
b. Hassam, Childe

October 18, 1859
b. Bergson, Henri Louis

October 20, 1859
b. Dewey, John

October 22, 1859
b. Muck, Karl
d. Spohr, Louis Ludwig

October 27, 1859
b. Ewing, Buck

October 29, 1859
b. Ebbets, Charles Hercules

November 1, 1859
b. Hunt, George Wylie Paul

November 4, 1859
d. Delaroche, Hippolyte

November 9, 1859
b. Ippolitov-Ivanov, Mikhail
   Mikhailovich

November 11, 1859
b. Insull, Samuel

November 23, 1859
b. Billy the Kid

November 24, 1859
b. Gilbert, Cass

November 28, 1859
d. Irving, Washington

December 2, 1859
b. Seurat, Georges Pierre
d. Brown, John

December 5, 1859
b. Jellicoe, John Rushworth
b. Lee, Sidney, Sir

December 6, 1859
b. Sothern, Edward Hugh

December 8, 1859
d. DeQuincey, Thomas

December 15, 1859
b. Zamenhof, Ludwik Lazar

December 16, 1859
d. Grimm, Wilhelm Karl

December 18, 1859
b. Thompson, Francis Joseph

December 28, 1859
b. Taussig, Frank William
d. Macaulay, Thomas Babington
   Macaulay, Baron

December 29, 1859
b. Carranza, Venustiano

December 30, 1859
b. Foerster, Josef Bohuslav

1860

b. Andrews, Mary Raymond Shipman
b. Chato, Alfred
b. Ford, Bob
b. Horn, Tom
b. McCarthy, Justin Huntly
b. Nampeyo
b. Omar al-Mukhtar
b. Schwinn, Ignaz
b. Sickert, Walter Richard
b. Smith, Amanda W
b. Tappan, William J
b. Vazquez, Horacio
d. Canot, Theodore

January 5, 1860
d. Neumann, John Nepomucene, Saint

January 8, 1860
b. Katayama, Sen

January 10, 1860
b. Roberts, Charles George Douglas,
   Sir

January 17, 1860
b. Chekhov, Anton Pavlovich
b. Hyde, Douglas

January 24, 1860
b. Kroger, Bernard Henry

January 25, 1860
b. Curtis, Charles Brent

January 26, 1860
d. Schroder-Devrient, Wilhelmine

January 29, 1860
b. Robertson, William Robert, Sir

January 31, 1860
b. Huneker, James Gibbons

February 1, 1860
b. Miller, Henry John

February 14, 1860
b. Lillie, Gordon William

February 16, 1860
b. Fels, Samuel Simeon

February 18, 1860
b. Zorn, Anders Leonard

February 20, 1860
b. Howell, William H(enry)

February 24, 1860
b. Updike, Daniel Berkeley

February 28, 1860
b. Berger, Victor Louis
b. Kittredge, G(eorge) L(yman)

February 29, 1860
b. Hollerith, Herman

March 3, 1860
b. Ward, Monte

March 5, 1860
b. Thompson, Sam(uel Luther)

March 11, 1860
b. Hastings, Thomas

March 13, 1860
b. Wolf, Hugo

March 18, 1860
b. Bryan, William Jennings

April 6, 1860
b. Lalique, Rene

April 7, 1860
b. Kellogg, Will Keith

April 13, 1860
b. Ensor, James Sydney, Baron

April 20, 1860
b. Curtis, Charles Gordon

April 22, 1860
b. Rehan, Ada

April 27, 1860
b. Copeland, Charles Townsend

April 29, 1860
b. Taft, Lorado

May 2, 1860
b. Bayliss, William Maddock, Sir
b. Herzl, Theodor

May 3, 1860
b. Eeden, Fredrik Willem van
b. Haldane, John Scott

May 4, 1860
b. Reznicek, Emil von

May 6, 1860
b. Sherman, Frank Dempster

May 9, 1860
b. Barrie, James Matthew, Sir
d. Goodrich, Samuel Griswold
d. James, G(eorge) P(ayne) R(ainsford)

May 10, 1860
d. Parker, Theodore

May 12, 1860
d. Barry, Charles, Sir

May 14, 1860
b. Mudgett, Herman Webster

May 15, 1860
b. Wilson, Ellen Axson

May 17, 1860
b. Wheeler, Schuyler Skaats

May 19, 1860
b. Orlando, Vittorio Emanuele

May 20, 1860
b. Buchner, Eduard

May 22, 1860
b. Einthoven, Willem

May 25, 1860
b. Cattell, James McKeen

May 29, 1860
b. Albeniz, Isaac Manuel Francisco

June 6, 1860
b. Inge, William Ralph

June 17, 1860
b. Frohman, Charles

June 20, 1860
b. Winton, Alexander

June 24, 1860
d. Bonaparte, Jerome

June 25, 1860
b. Charpentier, Gustave

June 29, 1860
d. Addison, Thomas

July 1, 1860
d. Goodyear, Charles

July 3, 1860
b. Gilman, Charlotte Anna Perkins

July 4, 1860
b. Pennell, Joseph Stanley

July 7, 1860
b. Cahan, Abraham
b. Mahler, Gustav

July 14, 1860
b. Wister, Owen

July 19, 1860
b. Borden, Lizzie Andrew

July 21, 1860
b. Olcott, Chauncey

July 22, 1860
b. Corvo, Baron

July 24, 1860
b. Mucha, Alphonse Marie

July 31, 1860
b. Walcott, Mary Morris Vaux

August 7, 1860
b. Moses, Grandma

August 11, 1860
b. Melchers, Gari

August 13, 1860
b. Oakley, Annie

August 14, 1860
b. Seton, Ernest Thompson

August 15, 1860
b. Harding, Florence Kling (De Wolfe)

August 16, 1860
b. Laforgue, Jules

August 19, 1860
b. Kane, John

August 20, 1860
b. Poincare, Raymond

August 22, 1860
d. Decamps, Alexandre Gabriel

September 3, 1860
b. Filene, Edward Albert

September 6, 1860
b. Addams, Jane

September 12, 1860
d. Walker, William
d. Winebrenner, John

September 13, 1860
b. Pershing, John J(oseph)

September 14, 1860
b. Garland, Hamlin

September 19, 1860
d. Rice, Thomas Dartmouth

September 20, 1860
d. Schopenhauer, Arthur

September 24, 1860
b. Crockett, S(amuel) R(utherford)

September 25, 1860
b. Russell, Charles Edward

October 3, 1860
d. Peale, Rembrandt

October 9, 1860
b. Wood, Leonard

October 10, 1860
b. Reading, 1st Marquess of

October 11, 1860
b. Litvinne, Felia

October 12, 1860
b. Sperry, Elmer Ambrose

October 13, 1860
b. Allan, Montagu, Sir

October 31, 1860
b. Low, Juliette Gordon
b. Volstead, Andrew J

November 1, 1860
b. Penrose, Boies

November 8, 1860
d. Fellows, Charles, Sir

November 18, 1860
b. Paderewski, Ignace Jan

November 23, 1860
b. Branting, Karl Hjalmar

November 25, 1860
b. Perry, Bliss

December 2, 1860
d. Baur, Ferdinand Christian

December 3, 1860
b. Moore, John Bassett

December 4, 1860
b. Hormel, George Albert

December 14, 1860
d. Aberdeen, 4th Earl of

December 15, 1860
b. Finsen, Niels Ryberg

December 19, 1860
d. Dalhousie, James Andrew Broun
   Ramsay, Marquess of

December 21, 1860
b. Szold, Henrietta

December 23, 1860
b. Monroe, Harriet

December 27, 1860
b. Bergey, David Hendricks

December 31, 1860
b. Thompson, John Taliaferro

1861

b. Andreas-Salome, Lou
b. Bates, Daisy Mae
b. Guiney, Louise Imogene

d. Appleton, Nathan
d. Burke, Robert O'Hara
d. Scribe, (Augustin) Eugene

January 1, 1861
b. Boule, Marcellin
b. Long, John Luther

January 2, 1861
d. Frederick William, IV

January 12, 1861
b. Baldwin, James Mark

January 14, 1861
b. Wesson, David

January 15, 1861
b. Bullard, Robert Lee

January 17, 1861
d. Montez, Lola

January 18, 1861
b. Kemble, Edward W(indsor)

January 22, 1861
d. Velluti, Giovanni Battista

January 25, 1861
b. Bobbs, William Conrad

January 26, 1861
b. Lowden, Frank O(rren)

January 27, 1861
b. Modjeski, Ralph

January 28, 1861
b. Willard, Daniel

January 30, 1861
b. Loeffler, Charles Martin Tornow

February 2, 1861
b. Guggenheim, Solomon Robert

February 6, 1861
b. Tyrrell, George

February 13, 1861
b. Curran, Charles Courtney

February 15, 1861
b. Guillaume, Charles Edouard
b. Mackinder, Halford John, Sir
b. Whitehead, Alfred North

February 23, 1861
b. Wilson, Henry Braid

February 25, 1861
b. Bates, Mary Elizabeth

February 27, 1861
b. Steiner, Rudolf

March 10, 1861
b. Johnson, Emily Pauline
b. Sifton, Clifford
d. Shevchenko, Taras

March 22, 1861
d. Lerdo de Tejada, Miguel

March 24, 1861
d. Scranton, George Whitfield

March 30, 1861
d. Shaw, Lemuel

April 3, 1861
b. DeKoven, (Henry Louis) Reginald

April 4, 1861
d. McLean, John

April 8, 1861
d. Otis, Elisha Graves

April 10, 1861
d. Tucker, George

April 15, 1861
b. Carman, Bliss

April 23, 1861
b. Allenby, Edmund Henry Hynman

April 25, 1861
b. Seligman, Edwin Robert Anderson

May 3, 1861
d. Heinrich, Anthony Philip

May 5, 1861
b. Hewitt, Peter Cooper

May 6, 1861
b. Nehru, Motilal
b. Tagore, Rabindranath, Sir

May 20, 1861
b. Smith, Christopher Columbus

June 2, 1861
b. Taft, Helen Herron

June 3, 1861
d. Douglas, Stephen Arnold

June 6, 1861
d. Cavour, Camillo Benso, Conte di

June 9, 1861
b. Duhem, Pierre Maurice Marie
b. Tammann, Gustav Heinrich Johann
   Apollon

June 15, 1861
b. Schumann-Heink, Ernestine Rossler

June 19, 1861
b. Haig, Douglas
b. Rizal, Jose
d. Sotheby, Samuel Leigh

June 29, 1861
b. Mayo, William James
d. Browning, Elizabeth Barrett

June 30, 1861
b. Hopkins, Frederick Gowland, Sir

July 1, 1861
b. Clarkson, John Gibson

July 3, 1861
b. Jackson, Peter B

July 7, 1861
b. Stevens, Nettie Maria

July 10, 1861
b. Paine, Albert Bigelow

July 11, 1861
b. Norris, George William

July 24, 1861
b. Renaud, Maurice

July 29, 1861
b. Roosevelt, Alice Lee

August 8, 1861
b. Bateson, William
b. Chaminade, Cecile

August 10, 1861
b. Wright, Almroth Edward, Sir
d. Lyon, Nathaniel

August 11, 1861
b. Herrick, James Bryan

August 16, 1861
b. Roosevelt, Edith Kermit (Carow)

August 25, 1861
b. Fawcett, George

August 28, 1861
d. Mackenzie, William Lyon

September 2, 1861
b. Crosman, Henrietta

September 5, 1861
b. Raleigh, Walter Alexander, Sir

September 13, 1861
b. Waugh, Frederick Judd

September 18, 1861
b. Seaman, Owen, Sir

September 23, 1861
b. Bosch, Robert August
b. Coleridge, Mary Elizabeth

September 30, 1861
b. Wrigley, William, Jr.
b. Prendergast, Maurice Brazil

October 4, 1861
b. Rauschenbusch, Walter
b. Remington, Frederic

October 8, 1861
b. Van Zandt, Marie

October 10, 1861
b. Nansen, Fridtjof

October 16, 1861
b. Bury, John Bagnell

October 19, 1861
b. Burns, William John

October 23, 1861
b. Converse, Marquis M

October 25, 1861
d. Savigny, Friedrich Karl von

October 26, 1861
b. Sears, Richard Dudley

October 28, 1861
d. James, Edwin

October 30, 1861
b. Bourdelle, Emile-Antoine

November 6, 1861
b. Naismith, James A

November 9, 1861
b. Bache, Jules Sermon

November 13, 1861
d. Clough, Arthur Hugh

November 14, 1861
b. Turner, Frederick Jackson

November 15, 1861
b. Haley, Margaret A(ngela)

November 17, 1861
b. Lampman, Archibald
b. Nutting, Wallace

November 21, 1861
d. Lacordaire, Jean Baptiste Henri

November 22, 1861
b. Dallin, Cyrus Edwin

November 26, 1861
b. Fall, Albert Bacon

December 4, 1861
b. Russell, Lillian

December 8, 1861
b. Durant, William Crapo
b. Maillol, Aristide
b. Melies, Georges

December 13, 1861
d. Albert, Prince

December 14, 1861
d. Marschner, Heinrich August

December 16, 1861
d. Lipinski, Carl

December 18, 1861
b. MacDowell, Edward Alexander

December 19, 1861
b. Garnett, Constance

b. Svevo, Italo

1862

b. Barres, (Auguste) Maurice
b. Dalton, Gratton
b. Ishi
b. Meinecke, Friedrich
b. Tweedale, Violet Chambers
d. Buckle, Henry Thomas
d. Christy, Edwin P.
d. Fritchie, Barbara

January 1, 1862
b. Coubertin, Pierre de, Baron

January 8, 1862
b. Doubleday, Frank Nelson

January 10, 1862
d. Colt, Samuel

January 15, 1862
b. Fuller, Loie

January 18, 1862
d. Tyler, John

January 23, 1862
b. Hilbert, David

January 24, 1862
b. Wharton, Edith

January 29, 1862
b. Delius, Frederick

January 30, 1862
b. Damrosch, Walter Johannes

February 4, 1862
b. Hammarskjold, Hjalmar

February 7, 1862
b. Maybeck, Bernard Ralph

February 10, 1862
d. Siddal, Elizabeth Eleanor

February 18, 1862
b. Schwab, Charles Michael
d. Bretonneau, Pierre Fidele

March 9, 1862
b. Widal, Fernand Isidore

March 13, 1862
b. Crippen, Hawley Harvey

March 14, 1862
b. Bjerknes, Vilhelm (Frimann Koren)

March 17, 1862
d. Halevy, Jacques Francois Fromental
Elie

March 22, 1862
d. Levy, Uriah Phillips

March 23, 1862
d. Nesselrode, Karl Robert

March 24, 1862
b. Benson, Frank Weston

March 28, 1862
b. Briand, Aristide

April 2, 1862
b. Butler, Nicholas Murray

April 6, 1862
d. Johnston, Albert Sidney

April 10, 1862
b. Cross, Wilbur Lucius

April 11, 1862
b. Campbell, William Wallace
b. Freeman, R(ichard) Austin
b. Hughes, Charles Evans

April 14, 1862
b. Stolypin, Piotr Arkadevich

April 24, 1862
b. Benson, Arthur Christopher

April 25, 1862
b. Grey of Fallodon, Edward, Viscount

April 29, 1862
b. Altsheler, Joseph Alexander

May 1, 1862
b. Prevost, Marcel

May 6, 1862
b. Underwood, Oscar Wilder
d. Thoreau, Henry David

May 15, 1862
b. Schnitzler, Arthur

May 16, 1862
d. Wakefield, Edward Gibbon

May 18, 1862
b. Daniels, Josephus

June 1, 1862
b. Patino, Simon Iturri

June 4, 1862
b. Fitzsimmons, Bob
b. Jewett, Henry

June 5, 1862
b. Gullstrand, Allvar

June 7, 1862
b. Lenard, Philipp Edward Anton

June 10, 1862
b. Carter, Caroline Louise Dudley
b. Carter, Leslie, Mrs.

June 17, 1862
d. Canning, Charles John, Earl

June 27, 1862
b. Irwin, May

July 2, 1862
b. Bragg, William Henry, Sir

July 4, 1862
b. Klimt, Gustav

July 8, 1862
b. Bloor, Mother

July 14, 1862
b. Bascom, Florence

July 16, 1862
b. Wells-Barnett, Ida Bell

July 24, 1862
d. Van Buren, Martin

July 27, 1862
d. Burns, Anthony

August 1, 1862
b. James, Montague Rhodes

August 2, 1862
b. Scott, Duncan Campbell

August 5, 1862
b. Merrick, Joseph Carey

August 11, 1862
b. Bond, Carrie Jacobs

August 12, 1862
b. Rosenwald, Julius

August 16, 1862
b. Stagg, Amos Alonzo

August 18, 1862
d. Fraser, Simon

August 22, 1862
b. Debussy, Claude Achille

August 25, 1862
b. Procter, William Cooper

August 29, 1862
b. Fisher, Andrew
b. Maeterlinck, Maurice

September 1, 1862
b. Appia, Adolphe

September 4, 1862
b. Kerr, Alexander H

September 10, 1862
d. Lopez, Carlos Antonio

September 11, 1862
b. Byng, Julian Hedworth George, Viscount
b. Henry, O

September 21, 1862
d. Ross, James Clark, Sir

September 24, 1862
b. Brooke, L Leslie

September 26, 1862
b. Davies, Arthur Bowen

September 27, 1862
b. Botha, Louis

October 4, 1862
b. Stratemeyer, Edward L

October 6, 1862
b. Beveridge, Albert Jeremiah

October 13, 1862
b. Commons, John Rogers

October 19, 1862
b. Lumiere, Auguste Marie Louis

November 3, 1862
b. George, Henry, Jr.

November 4, 1862
b. Phillpotts, Eden

November 7, 1862
b. Welch, Herbert

November 15, 1862
b. Hauptmann, Gerhart Johann Robert

November 18, 1862
b. Sunday, Billy

November 20, 1862
b. Westermarck, Edward Alexander

November 23, 1862
b. Parker, Gilbert, Sir

November 25, 1862
b. Nevin, Ethelbert Woodbridge

November 30, 1862
d. Knowles, James Sheridan

December 5, 1862
b. Atkinson, William Walker

December 7, 1862
b. Adam, Paul

December 8, 1862
b. Feydeau, Georges

December 12, 1862
b. Ismay, Joseph Bruce

December 15, 1862
b. Duryea, Charles Edgar

December 18, 1862
b. Rosenthal, Moriz

December 22, 1862
b. Mack, Connie

December 23, 1862
b. Pirenne, Jean Henri Otto Lucien
Marie

December 25, 1862
b. Meriwether, Lee

1863

b. Beaux, Cecilia
b. Bernard, Sam
b. Black Elk
b. Carder, Frederick
b. Cavafy, C(onstantine) P(eter)
b. Marchand, Jean-Baptiste
b. Serusier, Paul
b. Vivekananda
b. Wanamaker, Lewis Rodman
b. Younghusband, Francis Edward
d. Wilson, Harriet E. (Adams)
d. Coloradas, Mangas

January 7, 1863
b. Lloyd George of Dwyfor, David
Lloyd George Earl

January 10, 1863
d. Beecher, Lyman

January 14, 1863
b. Outcault, Richard Felton

January 17, 1863
b. Stanislavsky, Konstantin
Sergeyevich

January 19, 1863
b. Sombart, Werner

January 25, 1863
b. Jones, Rufus Matthew

January 27, 1863
d. Robinson, Edward

January 31, 1863
d. Robinson, John Beverley

February 7, 1863
b. Hope-Hawkins, Anthony, Sir

February 11, 1863
b. Fitzgerald, John Francis

February 19, 1863
b. Leguia y Salcedo, Augusto
Bernardino

February 20, 1863
b. Pissaro, Lucien

February 22, 1863
b. Andrews, Charles McLean

February 25, 1863
b. Bannerman, Helen

February 27, 1863
b. Mead, George Herbert

March 3, 1863
b. Machen, Arthur

March 12, 1863
b. D'Annunzio, Gabriele

March 13, 1863
b. Tokutomi Soho

March 20, 1863
b. Locke, William John

March 21, 1863
d. Sumner, Edwin V

March 22, 1863
b. Pattee, Fred Lewis

March 26, 1863
d. Egg, Augustus Leopold

March 27, 1863
b. Royce, Frederick Henry, Sir

March 30, 1863
b. Caillaux, Joseph Marie Auguste
d. Bravais, Auguste

April 3, 1863
b. van de Velde, Henry

April 7, 1863
b. Green, Thomas Hill

April 9, 1863
b. Kitson, Henry Hudson

April 10, 1863
b. Heroult, Paul Louis Toussaint

April 17, 1863
b. Love, Augustus Edward Hough

April 18, 1863
b. Berchtold, Leopold von

April 29, 1863
b. Hearst, William Randolph

May 10, 1863
d. Jackson, Stonewall

May 15, 1863
b. Johnston, Annie Fellows

May 18, 1863
b. Heinemann, William

May 24, 1863
b. Barnard, George Grey

May 27, 1863
b. Schalk, Franz

June 2, 1863
b. Weingartner, Felix

June 5, 1863
d. Drexel, Francis Martin

June 7, 1863
d. Gruber, Franz-Xaver

June 10, 1863
b. Couperius, Louis (Marie Anne)

June 19, 1863
b. Brady, William Aloysius

June 21, 1863
b. Sauveur, Albert

June 26, 1863
d. Foote, Andrew Hull

June 29, 1863
b. Robinson, James Harvey

July 4, 1863
b. Juch, Emma

July 7, 1863
b. Noyes, Frank B(rett)

July 10, 1863
d. Moore, Clement Clarke

July 11, 1863
b. Kilgour, Joseph

July 12, 1863
b. Calmette, Albert Leon Charles

July 13, 1863
b. Murray, Margaret Alice

July 18, 1863
d. Shaw, Robert Gould

July 21, 1863
b. Smith, C Aubrey

July 23, 1863
b. Kress, Samuel Henry

July 26, 1863
d. Crittenden, John Jordan
d. Houston, Sam(uel)

July 27, 1863
d. Yancey, William Lowndes

July 30, 1863
b. Ford, Henry

August 1, 1863
d. Gourlay, Robert

August 4, 1863
b. McAdie, Alexander George

August 8, 1863
b. Bailey, Florence Augusta Merriam

August 13, 1863
b. Thomas, W(illiam) I(saac)
d. Delacroix, (Ferdinand Victor)
Eugene

August 14, 1863
b. Thayer, Ernest L

d. Clyde, Colin Campbell, Baron

August 16, 1863
b. Pierne, Gabriel

August 23, 1863
b. Rives, Amelie Louise
d. Bartlett, John Sherren

August 26, 1863
d. Floyd, John Buchanan

August 27, 1863
b. Hepbron, George

August 28, 1863
d. Mitscherlich, Eilhardt
b. Smith, Jessie Wilcox

September 8, 1863
b. Jacobs, W(illiam) W(ymark)

September 13, 1863
b. Adler, Cyrus
b. Henderson, Arthur

September 15, 1863
b. Parker, Horatio William

September 17, 1863
d. Vigny, Alfred Victor, Comte de

September 20, 1863
d. Grimm, Jakob Ludwig Karl

September 21, 1863
b. Bunny, John
b. Howell, Clark

September 23, 1863
b. Terrell, Mary Church

September 28, 1863
b. MacMonnies, Fred W

October 1, 1863
d. Emmons, Ebenezer

October 6, 1863
d. Trollope, Frances

October 9, 1863
b. Bok, Edward William
b. Bradford, Gamaliel

October 11, 1863
b. Leroux, Xavier

October 14, 1863
b. Black, Winifred Sweet

October 15, 1863
d. Durrie, George Henry

October 16, 1863
b. Chamberlain, Austen, Sir

October 19, 1863
b. Finley, John Huston

October 26, 1863
b. Statler, Ellsworth Milton

October 31, 1863
b. McAdoo, William Gibbs

November 1, 1863
b. Parker, George Safford

November 2, 1863
d. Judah, Theodore Dehone

November 11, 1863
b. Signac, Paul

November 14, 1863
b. Baekeland, Leo Hendrik

November 20, 1863
d. Elgin, James Bruce

November 21, 1863
b. Quiller-Couch, Arthur Thomas, Sir

November 22, 1863
b. Ch'i Pai-Shih

November 24, 1863
b. Conklin, Edwin Grant

November 27, 1863
d. Davis, Sam(uel)

November 30, 1863
b. Bonifacio, Andres
d. Kamehameha IV

December 1, 1863
b. Herford, Oliver

December 2, 1863
b. Ringling, Charles
d. Pierce, Jane (Means)

December 6, 1863
b. Hall, Charles Martin

December 7, 1863
b. Mascagni, Pietro
b. Sears, Richard Warren

December 11, 1863
b. Cannon, Annie Jump

December 12, 1863
b. Munch, Edvard

December 13, 1863
b. Park, William Hallock
d. Hebbel, Friedrich

December 16, 1863
b. Cram, Ralph Adams
b. Fox, John W, Jr.
b. Santayana, George
d. Buford, John

December 18, 1863
b. Francis Ferdinand
b. Franz Ferdinand

December 19, 1863
b. Ternina, Milka

December 24, 1863
d. Thackeray, William Makepeace

December 25, 1863
b. Pathe, Charles

1864

b. Alzheimer, Alois
b. Beam, James B
b. Beresford, Harry
b. Clark, David L
b. Johnson, Marietta Louise Pierce
b. Lucile
b. Macaulay, Herbert
b. Mack, John M
d. Bowie, Walter
d. Hung Hsiu-ch'uan
d. Omar ibn Said Tal, Al-Hajj

January 1, 1864
b. Stieglitz, Alfred

January 5, 1864
b. Carver, George Washington
b. Hodge, Frederick Webb

January 8, 1864
b. Johnson, Ban

January 9, 1864
b. Roebuck, Alvah Curtis

January 12, 1864
b. Russell, Annie
b. Schoen-Rene, Anna

January 13, 1864
b. Wien, Wilhelm Carl Werner Otto
Fritz Franz
d. Foster, Stephen Collins

January 15, 1864
b. Johnston, Frances Benjamin

January 16, 1864
b. Bacon, Frank

January 20, 1864
b. Taylor, Charles Alonzo

February 2, 1864
b. Asquith, Emma Alice Margot

February 4, 1864
b. Eilshemius, Louis Michel

February 10, 1864
b. Roller, Alfred

February 14, 1864
b. Park, Robert Ezra
b. Zangwill, Israel
d. Dyce, William

February 16, 1864
b. Harvey, George Brinton M

February 17, 1864
b. Paterson, A(ndrew) B(arton)

February 22, 1864
b. Renard, Jules

February 25, 1864
d. Harrison, Anna (Tuthill Symmes)

February 26, 1864
d. LaFontaine, Louis Hippolyte, Sir

February 27, 1864
d. Hitchcock, Edward

March 4, 1864
b. Mannix, Daniel
d. King, Thomas Starr

March 9, 1864
b. Dawson, Bertrand Edward

March 10, 1864
d. Slade, Jack

March 13, 1864
b. Jawlensky, Alexej von

March 14, 1864
b. Jones, Casey

March 16, 1864
d. Surtees, Robert Smith

March 19, 1864
b. Russell, Charles Marion

March 21, 1864
d. Flandrin, Hippolyte Jean

April 6, 1864
d. Kirkland, Caroline Matilda
Stansbury

April 7, 1864
b. Hassan, Muhammad Abdille

April 10, 1864
b. D'Albert, Eugene

April 13, 1864
b. Marshall, Tully

April 16, 1864
d. Blanchard, Thomas

April 18, 1864
b. Davis, Richard Harding

April 21, 1864
b. Weber, Max

April 22, 1864
b. May, Phil(ip William)

May 1, 1864
b. Jarvis, Anna

May 2, 1864
d. Meyerbeer, Giacomo

May 4, 1864
b. Hovey, Richard

May 8, 1864
d. Wadsworth, James Samuel

May 9, 1864
d. Sedgwick, John

May 12, 1864
d. Stuart, Jeb

May 19, 1864
b. Akeley, Carl Ethan
d. Hawthorne, Nathaniel

May 20, 1864
d. Clare, John

May 27, 1864
d. Giddings, Joshua Reed

June 2, 1864
b. Robinson, Wilbert
b. Webster, Ben(jamin)

June 3, 1864
b. Olds, Ranson E(li)

June 9, 1864
b. Nielsen, Carl August

June 11, 1864
b. Strauss, Richard Georg

June 12, 1864
b. Chapman, Frank Michler

June 14, 1864
d. Santana, Pedro

June 18, 1864
b. Casey, Edward Pearce

June 22, 1864
d. McPherson, James Birdseye

June 25, 1864
b. Nernst, Walther Hermann

July 1, 1864
b. Russell, James Earl

July 15, 1864
b. Tempest, Marie

July 18, 1864
b. Huch, Ricarda (Octavia)

July 20, 1864
b. Karlfeldt, Erik Axel

July 21, 1864
b. Cleveland, Frances Folsom

July 22, 1864
b. Mabini, Apolinario

July 24, 1864
b. McCarthy, Tommy
b. Wedekind, Frank

August 1, 1864
b. Smith, Ellison DuRant

August 17, 1864
b. Cooley, Charles Horton
b. Eberle, Edward Walter

August 23, 1864
b. Venizelos, Eleutherios Kyriakos

August 28, 1864
d. Lassalle, Ferdinand

August 29, 1864
b. Dalton, Charles

September 1, 1864
b. Casement, Roger David

September 2, 1864
b. Ruef, Abraham

September 4, 1864
b. Ittner, William Butts
d. Long, Stephen H

September 8, 1864
b. Hobhouse, Leonard Trelawny

September 14, 1864
b. Cecil, Edgar Algernon Robert

September 17, 1864
d. Landor, Walter Savage

September 18, 1864
d. Speke, John Hanning

September 24, 1864
b. Booth, George Gough

September 25, 1864
b. Hughes, William Morris

September 27, 1864
b. Dharmapala, Anagarika

September 29, 1864
b. Unamuno (y Jugo), Miguel de
d. Anderson, William

October 1, 1864
d. Flores, Juan Jose

October 5, 1864
b. Lumiere, Louis Jean

October 12, 1864
d. Taney, Roger Brooke

October 17, 1864
b. Glyn, Elinor Sutherland
b. Lansing, Robert

October 24, 1864
b. Leoni, Franco

October 25, 1864
b. Dodge, John Francis
b. Gretchaninov, Aleksandr
Tikhonovich

October 29, 1864
d. Leech, John

October 31, 1864
b. Benediktsson, Einar
b. Lang, William Cosmo Gordon,
Baron

November 7, 1864
b. Hartford, George Ludlum

November 11, 1864
b. Crile, George Washington
b. Fried, Alfred Hermann

November 13, 1864
d. Hammond, James Henry

November 23, 1864
d. Struve, Friedrich Georg Wilhelm
von

November 24, 1864
b. Toulouse-Lautrec (Monfa), (Henri
Marie Raymond de)
d. Silliman, Benjamin

December 8, 1864
d. Boole, George

December 9, 1864
b. Homer, Sidney

December 10, 1864
d. Schoolcraft, Henry Rowe

December 12, 1864
b. Brisbane, Arthur
b. More, Paul Elmer
d. Baikie, William Balfour

December 15, 1864
d. Farnham, Eliza Wood Burhans

December 19, 1864
b. Leblanc, Maurice

December 21, 1864
d. Fry, William Henry

December 25, 1864
b. Maher, George Washington
d. Wallack, James William

December 31, 1864
b. Aitkin, Robert Grant
b. Ritchey, George Willis
d. Dallas, George Mifflin

1865

b. Ferdinand
b. Kuk, Abraham Isaac
b. Leverson, Ada
b. Rai, Lala Lajpat
b. Robins, Elizabeth
b. Rondon, Candido Mariano da Silva
b. Schildkraut, Rudolph
b. Troeltsch, Ernst
b. York, Edward Palmer
d. Santa Cruz, Andres de

January 2, 1865
b. Phelps, William Lyon

January 11, 1865
b. Dixon, Thomas

January 15, 1865
d. Everett, Edward

January 16, 1865
d. Proudhon, Pierre Joseph

January 24, 1865
b. Bartlett, Paul Wayland

January 26, 1865
b. Bauer, Louis Agricola

January 28, 1865
b. Stahlberg, Kaarlo Juho
d. Romani, Felice

February 4, 1865
b. Abe, Isao

February 6, 1865
d. Beeton, Isabella Mary Mayson

February 9, 1865
b. Campbell, Patrick, Mrs.
d. Gilliss, James Melville

February 14, 1865
b. Anderson, Carl Thomas

February 15, 1865
d. Wiseman, Nicholas Patrick Stephen

February 19, 1865
b. Hedin, Sven Anders

February 21, 1865
d. Troyon, Constant

February 25, 1865
d. Ludwig, Otto

February 28, 1865
b. Grenfell, Wilfred Thomason, Sir
b. Symons, Arthur William

March 8, 1865
b. Goudy, Frederic William

March 19, 1865
b. Wheeler, William Morton

March 21, 1865
b. Fisher, Herbert Albert Laurens

March 23, 1865
b. Cawein, Madison Julius
b. Ford, Paul Leicester

March 27, 1865
b. Graves, William Sidney

March 29, 1865
b. Bonsal, Stephen

April 1, 1865
b. Zsigmondy, Richard Adolf
d. Pasta, Giuditta Negri

April 2, 1865
d. Cobden, Richard
d. Hill, Ambrose Powell

April 5, 1865
b. Filene, Lincoln

April 9, 1865
b. Ludendorff, Erich Friedrich
Wilhelm
b. Steinmetz, Charles Proteus

April 10, 1865
b. Miner, Jack

April 11, 1865
b. Ovington, Mary White

April 14, 1865
d. Carrera, Jose Rafael

April 15, 1865
d. Lincoln, Abraham

April 16, 1865
b. Hill, Grace Livingstone

April 26, 1865
d. Booth, John Wilkes
d. Sax, Charles Joseph

April 28, 1865
d. Cunard, Samuel, Sir

April 30, 1865
d. Becknell, William

May 2, 1865
b. Fitch, (William) Clyde

May 6, 1865
b. Christie, John Walter

May 9, 1865
b. Jordan, Elizabeth Garver

May 15, 1865
d. Blythe, David Gilmour

May 17, 1865
b. Bennett, John

May 25, 1865
b. Mott, John Raleigh
b. Zeeman, Pieter

May 26, 1865
b. Chambers, Robert W

June 3, 1865
b. George V

June 5, 1865
d. Richardson, John, Sir

June 6, 1865
d. Quantrill, William Clarke

June 8, 1865
d. Paxton, Joseph, Sir

June 10, 1865
b. Cook, Frederick Albert
d. Sigourney, Lydia Howard

June 13, 1865
b. Yeats, William Butler

June 17, 1865
b. LaFlesche Picotte, Susan

June 18, 1865
d. Ruffin, Edmund

June 19, 1865
b. Whitty, May, Dame

June 22, 1865
d. Saavedra, Angel de

June 23, 1865
d. DuPont, Samuel Francis

June 25, 1865
b. Henri, Robert

June 26, 1865
b. Berenson, Bernard
b. Scheidemann, Philipp

June 27, 1865
b. Monash, John

June 29, 1865
b. Borah, William Edgar

July 2, 1865
b. Braun, Lily von Kretschman

July 6, 1865
b. Jaques-Dalcroze, Emile

July 7, 1865
d. Surratt, Mary Eugenia Jenkins

July 11, 1865
d. Hildreth, Richard

July 14, 1865
b. Capper, Arthur

July 15, 1865
b. Northcliffe, Alfred Charles William
Harmsworth, Viscount

July 16, 1865
d. Jumel, Eliza

July 18, 1865
b. Housman, Laurence

July 19, 1865
b. Mayo, Charles Horace

July 21, 1865
d. Schnorr, Ludwig von Carolsfeld

July 24, 1865
d. Cotman, John Sell

August 2, 1865
b. Babbitt, Irving
b. Merezhkovsky, Dmitry Sergeyevich

August 4, 1865
d. Aytoun, William Edmonstoune

August 10, 1865
b. Glazunov, Alexander
Constantinovich
b. Morrice, James Wilson

August 11, 1865
b. Pinchot, Gifford

August 12, 1865
d. Hooker, William Jackson, Sir

August 13, 1865
b. Eames, Emma Hayden
d. Lane, Fitz Hugh
d. Semmelweis, Ignaz Philipp

August 14, 1865
b. Merejkowski, Dmitri Sergeyevich

August 19, 1865
b. Berdichevsky, Micah Joseph

August 27, 1865
b. Breasted, James Henry
b. Dawes, Charles Gates
d. Haliburton, Thomas Chandler

September 2, 1865
d. Hamilton, William Rowan, Sir

September 23, 1865
b. Orczy, Emmuska, Baroness

September 30, 1865
d. Wayland, Francis

October 1, 1865
b. Dukas, Paul Abraham

October 2, 1865
b. Casey, Dan(iel Maurice)

October 12, 1865
b. Harden, Arthur, Sir

October 15, 1865
d. Bello y Lopez, Andres

October 18, 1865
d. Palmerston, Henry John Temple,
Viscount

October 22, 1865
b. Hitchcock, Raymond

October 27, 1865
d. Worcester, Joseph Emerson

November 2, 1865
b. Harding, Warren G(amaliel)

November 4, 1865
b. Jackson, Chevalier

November 9, 1865
b. Funston, Frederick

November 12, 1865
d. Gaskell, Elizabeth Cleghorn

November 28, 1865
b. Winter, Alice Vivian Ames

December 4, 1865
b. Cavell, Edith Louisa
b. Gulick, Luther (Halsey)

December 7, 1865
b. Sanderson, Sybil

December 8, 1865
b. Hadamard, Jacques Salomon
b. Sibelius, Jean

December 9, 1865
b. Woods, Robert Archey

December 10, 1865
d. Leopold, I

December 18, 1865
d. Corwin, Thomas

December 19, 1865
b. Fiske, Minnie Maddern

December 20, 1865
b. Mendl, Lady Elsie de Wolfe

December 22, 1865
b. Merriam, Frank Finley

December 24, 1865
d. Eastlake, Charles Lock, Sir

December 25, 1865
b. Booth, Evangeline Cory
b. Templeton, Fay
d. Barth, Heinrich

December 30, 1865
b. Kipling, Rudyard
b. Shirley, Ralph
d. Davis, Henry Winter

1866

b. Bassett, John D
b. Berry, Martha McChesney
b. Cullen, Maurice Galbraith
b. Deterding, Henri Wilhelm August,
Sir
b. Gonne, Maud
b. Hrushevsky, Mykhailo
b. Kinney, George Romanta
b. Kronold, Selma
b. Mwanga
b. Valle Inclan, Ramon Maria del
d. Campbell, Alexander
d. Couper, James Hamilton
d. Garneau, Francois-Xavier
d. Labatt, John Kinder

January 2, 1866
b. Murray, Gilbert

January 14, 1866
b. MacCameron, Robert L
b. Young, Art(hur Henry)

January 15, 1866
b. Soderblom, Nathan

January 20, 1866
b. Cunha, Euclides (Rodrigues Pimenta) da
b. LeGallienne, Richard

January 22, 1866
b. Barton, George

January 23, 1866
d. Peacock, Thomas Love

January 25, 1866
b. Scotti, Antonio
b. Vandervelde, Emile

January 27, 1866
d. Gibson, John

January 29, 1866
b. Rolland, Romain

January 30, 1866
b. Burgess, Gelett

January 31, 1866
b. Shestov, Lev
d. Ruckert, Friedrich

February 5, 1866
b. Keith, Arthur

February 9, 1866
b. Ade, George

February 10, 1866
b. Altamira Y Crevea, Rafael

February 16, 1866
b. Hamilton, Billy
b. Mannes, David

February 21, 1866
b. Wassermann, August von

February 24, 1866
b. Pearson, Cyril Arthur, Sir

February 25, 1866
b. Croce, Benedetto

February 26, 1866
b. Dow, Herbert Henry

February 27, 1866
b. MacNeil, Hermon Atkins

March 7, 1866
b. Ernst, Paul Karl Friedrich

March 14, 1866
d. Sparks, Jared

March 16, 1866
b. Chambers, Edmund Kerchever, Sir

March 21, 1866
b. Maury, Antonia Caetana De Paiua Pereira

March 24, 1866
b. McAuliffe, Jack B

March 27, 1866
d. Keble, John

April 1, 1866
b. Breckinridge, Sophonisba Preston
b. Busoni, Ferruccio Benvenuto
d. Harding, Chester

April 3, 1866
b. Hertzog, James Barry Munnik

April 6, 1866
b. Cassidy, Butch
b. Steffens, Lincoln

April 13, 1866
b. Davenport, Charles Benedict

April 14, 1866
b. Sullivan, Anne

April 17, 1866
b. Starling, Ernest Henry

April 22, 1866
b. Seeckt, Hans von

May 2, 1866
b. Lazear, Jesse William

May 4, 1866
b. Corey, William Ellis

May 9, 1866
b. Gokhale, Gopal Krishna

May 17, 1866
b. Satie, Erik

May 25, 1866
b. Schultze, Carl Emil

May 29, 1866
d. Scott, Winfield

May 31, 1866
b. Rebikov, Vladimir Ivanovich

June 7, 1866
b. Hornung, Ernest William
d. Seattle

June 17, 1866
d. Cass, Lewis

June 26, 1866
b. Herbert, George Edward Stanhope Molyneux

July 6, 1866
b. Potter, Beatrix

July 14, 1866
b. Frost, Edwin Brant

July 20, 1866
d. Riemann, Georg Friedrich

July 26, 1866
b. Cilea, Francesco
b. McCutcheon, George Barr

August 1, 1866
d. Ross, John

August 6, 1866
b. Schmedes, Erik

August 8, 1866
b. Henson, Matthew Alexander

August 12, 1866
b. Benavente y Martinez, Jacinto

August 13, 1866
b. Agnelli, Giovanni

August 15, 1866
b. Work, Monroe (Nathan)

August 17, 1866
b. Marlowe, Julia

August 22, 1866
b. Graham, Ernest Robert

September 1, 1866
b. Corbett, James John

September 2, 1866
b. Johnson, Hiram Warren

September 4, 1866
b. Lake, Simon

September 7, 1866
d. Baldwin, Matthias William

September 18, 1866
b. Talbert, Mary Morris Burnett

September 21, 1866
b. Nicolle, Charles Jules Henri
b. Wells, H(erbert) G(eorge)

September 25, 1866
b. Morgan, Thomas Hunt

September 28, 1866
b. Tschirky, Oscar

September 29, 1866
b. Hayford, J(oseph) E(phraim)Casely

October 6, 1866
b. Fessenden, Reginald Aubrey

October 7, 1866
d. Stockton, Robert Field

October 9, 1866
b. Loeb, William

October 12, 1866
b. MacDonald, James Ramsay

October 15, 1866
b. Upshaw, William David

October 25, 1866
b. Patten, Gilbert

November 2, 1866
b. Door, Rheta Childe

November 5, 1866
b. Milne, George Francis, Baron

November 8, 1866
b. Austin, Herbert

November 12, 1866
b. Collier, William, Sr.
b. Sun Yat-Sen

November 13, 1866
b. Flexner, Abraham

November 18, 1866
b. Guerin, Jules

November 20, 1866
b. Landis Kenesaw, Mountain, Judge

November 23, 1866
d. Gavarni, Paul

November 26, 1866
b. Duffy, Hugh

November 28, 1866
b. Bacon, Henry
b. Warfield, David

December 1, 1866
d. Everest, George, Sir

December 2, 1866
b. Burleigh, Harry Thacker

December 4, 1866
b. Kandinsky, Wassily

December 12, 1866
b. Parker, George Swinnerton
b. Ross, Edward Alsworth
b. Werner, Alfred

December 14, 1866
b. Fry, Roger Eliot

December 17, 1866
b. Menocal, Mario Garcia

December 20, 1866
d. Taylor, Ann

December 31, 1866
b. Harding, Chester

1867

b. Andrews, Fannie Fern Phillips
b. Capone, Teresa
b. Dalton, Robert
b. Lanvin, Jeanne

b. Lewis, Rosa
b. Montezuma, Carlos
b. Natsume, Soseki
b. Polk, Willis Jefferson
b. Rathenau, Walter
b. Ts'ai Yuan-p'ei
d. Beckwourth, James Pierson
d. Cousin, Victor
d. Deb, Radhakant
d. Rousseau, Theodore

January 1, 1867
b. Fields, Lew Maurice

January 3, 1867
b. Lytton, Henry Alfred, Sir

January 5, 1867
d. Smith, Alexander

January 7, 1867
b. Maginnis, Charles Donagh

January 8, 1867
b. Balch, Emily G

January 11, 1867
b. Titchener, Edward Bradford

January 13, 1867
b. Townsend, Francis Everett
d. Ingres, Jean Auguste Dominique

January 17, 1867
b. Laemmle, Carl, Sr.

January 18, 1867
b. Dario, Ruben

January 20, 1867
b. Guilbert, Yvette
d. Willis, Nathaniel Parker

January 21, 1867
b. Weygand, Maxime

January 24, 1867
b. Mayo, Katherine

January 29, 1867
b. Blasco-Ibanez, Vicente

February 2, 1867
b. Saunders, Charles E, Sir

February 7, 1867
b. Wilder, Laura Elizabeth Ingalls

February 17, 1867
d. Bache, Alexander Dallas

February 21, 1867
b. Kahn, Otto Hermann

February 27, 1867
b. Fisher, Irving
d. De Bow, James Dunwoody
Brownson

March 3, 1867
b. Rogers, James Gamble

March 6, 1867
d. Cornelius, Peter von
d. Ward, Artemus

March 8, 1867
b. Davenport, Homer Calvin

March 10, 1867
b. Guimard, Hector Germain
b. Wald, Lillian D

March 15, 1867
b. Johnson, Lionel Pigot

March 20, 1867
b. Myers, Jerome

March 21, 1867
b. Ziegfeld, Flo(renz)

March 25, 1867
b. Borglum, John Gutzon de la Mothe
b. Toscanini, Arturo

March 26, 1867
b. Woodbridge, Frederick James
Eugene

March 27, 1867
b. Walker, Edyth

March 29, 1867
b. Young, Cy

April 1, 1867
b. Roper, Daniel C(alhoun)

April 8, 1867
b. Streeton, Arthur Ernest

April 10, 1867
b. Russell, George William
b. Sandow, Eugene

April 16, 1867
b. Wright, Wilbur

April 20, 1867
d. Bozeman, John M

April 23, 1867
b. Fibiger, Johannes Andreas Grib

May 2, 1867
b. Reymont, Wladyslaw Stanislaw

May 5, 1867
b. Bly, Nellie

May 9, 1867
d. Champollin-Figeac, Jacques-Joseph

May 13, 1867
b. Brangwyn, Frank, Sir

May 14, 1867
b. Eisner, Kurt
b. Gillmore, Frank

May 21, 1867
b. Densmore, Frances

May 25, 1867
d. Castilla, Ramon

May 26, 1867
b. Mary

May 27, 1867
b. Bennett, Arnold
d. Bulfinch, Thomas

May 30, 1867
b. Davis, Arthur Vining

June 4, 1867
b. Mannerheim, Carl Gustav Emil,
Baron

June 10, 1867
b. Meier-Graefe, Julius

June 11, 1867
b. Fabry, Charles

June 17, 1867
b. Gregg, John Robert
b. Lawson, Henry (Archibald
Hertzberg)

June 19, 1867
d. Maximilian

June 28, 1867
b. Pirandello, Luigi

July 4, 1867
b. Mather, Stephen Tyng

July 7, 1867
b. Douglass, Andrew Ellicott

July 8, 1867
b. Kollwitz, Kathe Schmidt

July 10, 1867
b. Dunne, Finley Peter

July 15, 1867
b. Charcot, Jean Baptiste Etienne
Auguste
b. Walker, Maggie Lena

July 24, 1867
b. Benson, Edward Frederic

July 27, 1867
b. Granados, Enrique

July 28, 1867
b. Perrine, Charles Dillon

July 30, 1867
b. Beck, Martin

July 31, 1867
b. Kresge, Sebastian Spering
d. Sedgwick, Catherine Maria

August 2, 1867
b. Dowson, Ernest Christopher

August 3, 1867
b. Baldwin, Stanley

August 4, 1867
b. Beckley, Jake

August 6, 1867
b. Loeb, James Morris

August 7, 1867
b. Nolde, Emil

August 10, 1867
d. Aldridge, Ira Frederick

August 11, 1867
b. Bosworth, Hobart van Zandt
b. Weber, Joseph M

August 12, 1867
b. Hamilton, Edith

August 13, 1867
b. Luks, George Benjamin

August 14, 1867
b. Galsworthy, John

August 21, 1867
d. Alvarez, Juan

August 22, 1867
b. Powell, Maud

August 23, 1867
b. Schwob, Marcel

August 25, 1867
d. Faraday, Michael

August 27, 1867
b. Giordano, Umberto

August 31, 1867
d. Baudelaire, Charles Pierre

September 5, 1867
b. Beach, H H A, Mrs.

September 7, 1867
b. Morgan, J(ohn) P(ierpont), Jr.

September 13, 1867
d. Gregg, William

September 14, 1867
b. Gibson, Charles Dana

September 19, 1867
b. Rackham, Arthur

September 21, 1867
b. Stimson, Henry Lewis

September 23, 1867
b. Lomax, John Avery

September 29, 1867
d. Price, Sterling

October 3, 1867
d. Howe, Elias

October 5, 1867
d. Ridge, John Rollin

October 6, 1867
d. Timrod, Henry

October 13, 1867
b. Ripley, William Zebina
d. Parsons, William

October 14, 1867
b. Masaoka, Tsunenori

October 17, 1867
b. Magonigle, Harold Van Buren

October 27, 1867
b. Allen, Viola Emily

October 28, 1867
b. Driesch, Hans Adolf Eduard

October 30, 1867
b. Bonnard, Pierre
d. Andrew, John Albion

October 31, 1867
d. Delahanty, Ed(ward James)
b. Philips, David Graham
d. Rosse, William Parsons, 3rd Earl of

November 1, 1867
d. Strachan, John

November 3, 1867
d. Persiani, Fanny

November 5, 1867
b. Reisner, George Andrew

November 7, 1867
b. Curie, Marie

November 16, 1867
b. Daudet, Leon

November 19, 1867
d. Halleck, Fritz-Greene

November 20, 1867
b. Hayes, Patrick Joseph, Cardinal

December 5, 1867
b. Pilsudski, Jozef

December 6, 1867
b. Bitter, Karl Theodore Francis
d. Pacini, Giovanni

December 11, 1867
b. Pratt, Bela Lyon

December 20, 1867
b. Heffelfinger, Pudge
b. Lowes, John Livingston

December 22, 1867
b. Olbrich, Joseph Maria

d. Rousseau, (Pierre Etienne) Theodore

December 23, 1867
b. Walker, C. J., Madame
b. Walker, Sarah Breedlove
McWilliams

December 27, 1867
b. Benda, Julien

1868

b. Amiet, Cuno
b. Apache Kid
b. Aucherlonie, Laurie
b. Bernard, Emile
b. Edeson, Robert
b. Little Tich
b. Lowndes, Marie Adelaide Belloc
b. Maurer, Alfred Henry
b. Maurras, Charles Marie Photius
b. Olivetti, Camillo
b. Warburg, Paul Moritz
d. Deringer, Henry
d. Mzilikazi
d. Roman Nose
d. Wilmot, David

January 8, 1868
b. Dyson, Frank Watson, Sir

January 9, 1868
d. Hopkins, John Henry

January 28, 1868
d. Head, Edmund Walker, Sir

January 31, 1868
b. Richards, Theodore William

February 4, 1868
b. Markievicz, Constance Georgine,
Countess

February 10, 1868
b. White, William Allen
d. Brewster, David, Sir

February 11, 1868
d. Foucault, Jean Bernard Leon

February 12, 1868
b. Faversham, William Alfred

February 19, 1868
b. Curtis, Edward Sheriff

February 23, 1868
b. DuBois, W(illiam) E(dward)
B(urghardt)

March 3, 1868
b. Alain

March 4, 1868
d. Chisholm, Jesse

March 11, 1868
d. Moshweshwe

March 12, 1868
b. Whitechurch, Victor Lorenzo

March 22, 1868
b. Millikan, Robert Andrews

March 25, 1868
b. Calkins, Earnest Elmo

March 26, 1868
b. Fuad, I

March 27, 1868
b. Hill, Patty Smith
d. Cardigan, James Thomas Brudenell,
Earl of

March 28, 1868
b. Gorky, Maxim
b. Hapgood, Norman
b. Jaegers, Albert

April 1, 1868
b. Rostand, Edmond Alexis

April 7, 1868
d. McGee, Thomas D'Arcy

April 10, 1868
b. Arliss, George

April 13, 1868
d. Tewodros II

April 14, 1868
b. Behrens, Peter

April 19, 1868
b. Schillings, Max von

April 26, 1868
b. Harmsworth, Harold Sidney
b. Rothermere, Harold Sidney
Harmsworth

May 2, 1868
b. Wood, Robert Williams

May 5, 1868
d. Page, Charles Grafton

May 6, 1868
b. LeRoux, Gaston

May 10, 1868
b. Barrow, Ed(ward Grant)
b. Hart, George Overbury

May 12, 1868
b. Shean, Al

May 14, 1868
b. Hirschfeld, Magnus

May 17, 1868
b. Dodge, Horace Elgin

May 18, 1868
b. Nicholas II

May 19, 1868
b. Hayford, John Fillmore

May 21, 1868
b. Cabot, Richard C

May 22, 1868
d. Plucker, Julius

May 23, 1868
d. Carson, Kit

May 30, 1868
b. Dillingham, Charles Bancroft

June 1, 1868
d. Buchanan, James

June 2, 1868
b. Hope, John

June 3, 1868
b. Agramonte y Simoni, Aristides

June 6, 1868
b. Cubberley, Ellwood Patterson
b. Scott, Robert Falcon

June 7, 1868
b. Mackintosh, Charles Rennie
b. Townsend, John Sealy Edward, Sir

June 11, 1868
d. Brooke, James, Sir

June 18, 1868
b. Horthy de Nagybanya, Nicholas

June 23, 1868
d. Vassar, Matthew

June 29, 1868
b. Hale, George Ellery

July 7, 1868
b. Gilbreth, Frank Bunker

July 12, 1868
b. George, Stefan

July 14, 1868
b. Bell, Gertrude Margaret
b. Landsteiner, Karl

July 15, 1868
d. Morton, William Thomas Green

July 18, 1868
d. Leutze, Emanuel

July 19, 1868
b. Nitti, Francesco Saverio
d. Beach, Moses Yale

July 28, 1868
d. Smith, Seba

August 6, 1868
b. Claudel, Paul Louis Charles

August 7, 1868
b. Bantock, Granville, Sir

August 10, 1868
b. Eckener, Hugo
d. Menken, Adah Isaacs

August 11, 1868
d. Stevens, Thaddeus

August 12, 1868
b. Chelmsford, Frederic John Napier
  Thesiger, 1st Viscount Chelmsford

August 16, 1868
b. Macfadden, Bernarr Adolphus

August 17, 1868
b. Porter, Gene Stratton

August 25, 1868
d. Elliott, Charles Loring

August 29, 1868
d. Schonbein, Christian Friedrich

September 1, 1868
b. Bourassa, Henri
b. Hubbard, Kin

September 6, 1868
b. Bolden, Buddy

September 9, 1868
b. Austin, Mary Hunter

September 26, 1868
d. Mobius, August Ferdinand

October 1, 1868
b. Ozaki, Koyo

October 12, 1868
b. Greene, Charles Sumner

October 15, 1868
d. Mongkut

October 17, 1868
d. Secord, Laura Ingersoll

October 19, 1868
b. Landes, Bertha Ethel

October 21, 1868
b. Swinton, Ernest Dunlop, Sir

October 24, 1868
b. David-Neel, Alexandra

October 28, 1868
b. Connolly, James B

November 11, 1868
b. Vuillard, (Jean) Edouard

November 13, 1868
d. Rossini, Gioacchino Antonio

November 18, 1868
b. Dehmel, Richard

November 19, 1868
d. Mount, William Sidney

November 22, 1868
b. Garner, John Nance

November 24, 1868
b. Joplin, Scott

November 26, 1868
d. Black Kettle

November 30, 1868
b. Newman, Ernest

December 2, 1868
b. Jammes, Francis

December 8, 1868
b. Douglas, Norman

December 9, 1868
b. Haber, Fritz

December 13, 1868
b. Sammarco, Mario

December 19, 1868
b. Porter, Eleanor H

December 20, 1868
b. Alessandri Palma, Arturo
b. Firestone, Harvey Samuel
b. Quinn, Edmond T

December 22, 1868
b. Borglum, Solon Hannibal

December 24, 1868
b. Lasker, Emanuel

December 25, 1868
d. Yale, Linus

1869

b. Bad Heart Bull, Amos
b. Bell, Donald J
b. Dargan, Olive Tilford
b. Farnham, Sally James
b. Gottschalk, Ferdinand
b. Gulbenkian, Calouste S
b. Heath, Lawrence S
b. Landru, Henri Desire
b. Nexo, Martin Andersen
b. Otto, Louis Karl Rudolf
d. Sylvis, William (H.)
d. Copway, George

January 5, 1869
b. Jones, Matilda Sissieretta Joyner

January 6, 1869
b. Wagner, Siegfried (Helferich)

January 8, 1869
b. Genthe, Arnold

January 17, 1869
d. Dargomijsky, Alexander

January 23, 1869
b. Croly, Herbert David

January 27, 1869
b. Cook, Will Marion

February 2, 1869
b. Child, Charles Manning

February 3, 1869
b. Gatti-Casazza, Giulio

February 4, 1869
b. Haywood, William Dudley

February 10, 1869
b. Cortissoz, Royal

February 14, 1869
b. Wilson, Charles Thomson Rees

February 15, 1869
b. Williams, Henry Sylvester

February 26, 1869
b. Krupskaya, Nadezhda
  Konstantinovna

February 27, 1869
b. Cowles, Henry Chandler
b. Hamilton, Alice
d. Lamartine, Alphonse Marie Louis
  de Prat de

March 3, 1869
b. Wood, Henry Joseph, Sir

March 4, 1869
b. Whitlock, Brand

March 8, 1869
d. Berlioz, Hector

March 13, 1869
b. Menendez Pidal, Ramon

March 14, 1869
b. Blackwood, Algernon Henry

March 18, 1869
b. Chamberlain, Neville

March 21, 1869
b. Kahn, Albert

March 22, 1869
b. Aguinaldo, Emilio

March 24, 1869
d. Gorham, Jabez

March 27, 1869
d. Harper, James

March 29, 1869
b. Hrdlicka, Ales
b. Lutyens, Edwin Landseer, Sir
b. Neilson, William A(llan)

April 2, 1869
b. Berryman, Clifford Kennedy

April 5, 1869
b. Roussel, Albert

April 6, 1869
b. Raemaekers, Louis

April 7, 1869
b. Fairchild, David Grandison

April 8, 1869
b. Cushing, Harvey Williams

April 11, 1869
b. Vigeland, Gustav

April 13, 1869
d. Rogers, Isaiah

April 14, 1869
b. Van Heusen, John

April 20, 1869
b. Chase, Mary Agnes

April 28, 1869
b. Goodhue, Bertram G(rosvenor)

May 2, 1869
b. Power, Tyrone

May 5, 1869
b. Pfitzner, Hans

May 8, 1869
b. Angell, James Rowland

May 13, 1869
b. Danforth, William

May 15, 1869
d. Dyce, Alexander

June 1, 1869
b. Breitenstein, Ted

June 2, 1869
b. Foerster, Friedrich Wilhelm

June 8, 1869
b. Wright, Frank Lloyd

June 15, 1869
b. Witmark, Isidore

June 16, 1869
d. Sturt, Charles

June 18, 1869
b. Wells, Carolyn
d. Raymond, Henry Jarvis

June 19, 1869
b. Addison, Christopher, Viscount

June 27, 1869
b. Goldman, Emma
b. Spemann, Hans

July 7, 1869
b. Atterbury, Grosvenor

July 8, 1869
b. Moody, William Vaughn

July 20, 1869
b. Thurston, Howard

July 22, 1869
d. Roebling, John Augustus

July 29, 1869
b. Tarkington, Booth

July 31, 1869
b. Brasher, Rex

August 1, 1869
b. Hillquit, Morris

August 9, 1869
b. Malone, Annie Minerva Turnbo
  Pope
d. Little, Charles Coffin

August 10, 1869
b. Binyon, Laurence

August 15, 1869
b. Michael, Moina Belle

August 20, 1869
b. Anderson, George Everett

August 23, 1869
b. Masters, Edgar Lee

August 27, 1869
b. Haushofer, Karl Ernst

August 29, 1869
d. Gratz, Rebecca

September 2, 1869
b. Maxim, Hiram Percy

September 6, 1869
b. Davies, Henry Walford, Sir
b. Salten, Felix
d. Rawlins, John A

September 8, 1869
d. Fessenden, William Pitt

September 10, 1869
d. Bell, John

September 12, 1869
d. Roget, Peter Mark

September 14, 1869
b. Nichols, Kid

September 16, 1869
d. Graham, Thomas

September 17, 1869
b. Lange, Christian Louis
b. Turpin, Ben

September 20, 1869
b. Robey, George, Sir

September 23, 1869
b. Valadon, Suzanne

September 26, 1869
b. McCay, Winsor

October 2, 1869
b. Gandhi, Mahatma

October 5, 1869
b. Morrison, Cameron

October 8, 1869
b. Duryea, J(ames) Frank
d. Pierce, Franklin

October 13, 1869
d. Sainte-Beuve, Charles Augustin

October 14, 1869
b. Duveen, Joseph, Sir

October 15, 1869
b. Largo Caballero, Francisco

October 21, 1869
b. Dodd, William Edward

October 23, 1869
b. Heisman, John William
b. Rutherford, Joseph Franklin

November 4, 1869
d. Peabody, George

November 8, 1869
b. Hartmann, Sadakichi

November 9, 1869
b. Dressler, Marie

November 11, 1869
b. Victor Emmanuel III
d. Walker, Robert James

November 12, 1869
d. Kendall, Amos

November 14, 1869
d. Butterfield, John

November 15, 1869
b. Mew, Charlotte Mary

November 20, 1869
b. Griffith, Clark Calvin

November 22, 1869
b. Gide, Andre (Paul Guillaume)

November 25, 1869
b. Lindsey, Benjamin Barr

November 29, 1869
d. Grisi, Giulia

November 30, 1869
b. Dalen, Nils Gustaf

December 1, 1869
b. Sterling, George

December 6, 1869
b. Lavigne, Kid
b. Nordenskold, Nils Otto Gustaf

December 16, 1869
b. Pollard, Albert Frederick

December 18, 1869
d. Gottschalk, Louis Moreau

December 20, 1869
b. Grapewin, Charley

December 22, 1869
b. Robinson, Edwin Arlington

December 24, 1869
d. Stanton, Edwin McMasters

December 26, 1869
d. Poiseuille, Jean Louis Marie

December 28, 1869
b. Trumbauer, Horace

December 30, 1869
b. Leacock, Stephen Butler

December 31, 1869
b. Matisse, Henri Emile Benoit

1870

b. Bentley, Arthur F.
b. Boltwood, Bertram Borden
b. Coleman, William
b. Farnum, Dustin Lancy
b. Fish, Albert
b. Teggart, Frederick J.
b. Typhoid Mary
d. Hare, William
d. Leotard, Jules

January 1, 1870
b. Van Rooy, Anton

January 2, 1870
b. Barlach, Ernst Heinrich
b. Rickard, Tex

January 3, 1870
b. Richardson, Henry Handel

January 4, 1870
b. Pitt, Percy

January 8, 1870
b. Holmes, Burton
b. Primo de Rivera (y Orbaneja),
Miguel

January 9, 1870
b. Strauss, Joseph Baermann

January 11, 1870
b. Rice, Alice Caldwell Hegan

January 12, 1870
b. Richman, Charles

January 15, 1870
b. DuPont, Pierre Samuel

January 18, 1870
b. Nethersole, Olga
d. Anderson, Alexander

January 21, 1870
d. Herzen, Aleksandr Ivanovich

January 22, 1870
d. Prentice, George Denison

January 23, 1870
b. Greene, Henry Mather

January 24, 1870
b. White, William Alanson

January 25, 1870
b. Ratana, Taupotiki Wiremu

January 29, 1870
b. Bordeaux, Henry

February 3, 1870
b. Haines, Robert Terrel

February 4, 1870
b. Mitchell, John

February 6, 1870
b. Braid, James

February 7, 1870
b. Adler, Alfred

February 10, 1870
b. Bonci, Alessandro

February 11, 1870
b. Dube, John Langalibalele

February 12, 1870
b. Burkett, Jesse Cail
b. Lloyd, Marie

February 13, 1870
b. Godowsky, Leopold
b. Lincoln, Joseph C(rosby)

February 14, 1870
d. Harper, Joseph Wesley

February 22, 1870
b. Reiss, Albert

February 23, 1870
d. Burlingame, Anson

March 1, 1870
d. Lopez, Francisco Solano

March 5, 1870
b. Norris, Frank(lin)

March 10, 1870
d. Moscheles, Ignaz

March 13, 1870
b. Glackens, William James

d. Montalembert, Comte de

March 25, 1870
b. Ziegler, Edward

March 26, 1870
d. Soule, Pierre

March 28, 1870
d. Thomas, George Henry

March 31, 1870
b. Cox, James Middleton, Sr.
b. Ryan, Tommy
d. Urquiza, Justo Jose

April 2, 1870
b. Jennings, Hugh(ey Ambrose)

April 6, 1870
b. Straus, Oskar

April 15, 1870
d. Willard, Emma Hart

April 17, 1870
b. Baker, Ray Stannard

April 21, 1870
b. Porter, Edwin

April 22, 1870
b. Lenin, Vladimir Ilyich

April 24, 1870
b. Quinn, John

April 25, 1870
d. Maclise, Daniel

April 30, 1870
b. Lehar, Franz

May 6, 1870
b. Giannini, A(madeo) P(eter)
b. McCutcheon, John Tinney
d. Simpson, James Young, Sir

May 7, 1870
b. Loew, Marcus

May 9, 1870
b. Vardon, Harry

May 14, 1870
b. Rogers, Bruce

May 23, 1870
d. Lemon, Mark

May 24, 1870
b. Cardozo, Benjamin Nathan
b. Smuts, Jan Christian

June 6, 1870
d. Wrangel, Ferdinand Petrovich,
Baron

June 9, 1870
d. Dickens, Charles (John Huffam)

June 11, 1870
d. Simms, William Gilmore

June 12, 1870
d. Smith, Sophia

June 13, 1870
b. Bordet, Jules Jean Baptiste Vincent

June 20, 1870
d. Goncourt, Jules Alfred Huot de

June 25, 1870
b. Childers, Erskine

July 3, 1870
b. Bennett, Richard Bedford

July 4, 1870
b. Moffatt, James

July 12, 1870
d. Dahlgren, John Adolphus Bernard

July 18, 1870
b. Kornilov, Lavr Georgyevich

July 20, 1870
d. Grafe, Albrecht Friedrich Wilhelm
   Ernst von

July 25, 1870
b. Journet, Marcel
b. Parrish, Maxfield
b. Skipworth, Alison

July 27, 1870
b. Belloc, Hilaire

July 29, 1870
b. Dixon, George

August 4, 1870
b. Lauder, Harry MacLennan, Sir

August 13, 1870
b. Levy, Florence

August 14, 1870
d. Farragut, David Glasgow

August 17, 1870
b. Hobson, Richmond Pearson

August 18, 1870
d. Kennedy, John Pendleton

August 19, 1870
b. Baruch, Bernard Mannes

August 31, 1870
b. Montessori, Maria

September 2, 1870
d. Maverick, Samuel Augustus

September 6, 1870
b. Halevy, Elie

September 7, 1870
b. Kuprin, Aleksandr Ivanovich

September 9, 1870
b. Pears, Charles

September 10, 1870
b. Danforth, William H

September 12, 1870
d. Ludlow, Fitz Hugh

September 15, 1870
b. Bragg, Mabel Caroline

September 22, 1870
b. Pryor, Arthur W

September 23, 1870
d. Merimee, Prosper

September 24, 1870
b. Claude, Georges

September 25, 1870
d. Grier, Robert Cooper

September 26, 1870
b. Christian X

September 27, 1870
d. Comstock, Henry Tompkins Paige

September 30, 1870
b. Lamont, Thomas William
b. Perrin, Jean Baptiste

October 3, 1870
b. Kraus, Felix von

October 12, 1870
d. Lee, Robert E(dward)

October 18, 1870
b. Suzuki, Daisetz Teitaro

October 20, 1870
d. Balfe, Michael William

October 21, 1870
b. Douglas, Alfred Bruce, Lord

October 22, 1870
b. Bunin, Ivan Alekseevich

October 27, 1870
b. Pound, Roscoe

November 5, 1870
b. Das, Chitta Ranjan

November 10, 1870
b. Rostovtzeff, Michael Ivanovich

November 18, 1870
b. Dix, Dorothy

November 21, 1870
b. Berkman, Alexander

November 24, 1870
d. Lautreamont, Comte de

November 25, 1870
b. Denis, Maurice

November 26, 1870
b. Knote, Heinrich

November 27, 1870
b. Paasikivi, Juho Kusti

November 29, 1870
b. Friganza, Trixie

December 5, 1870
b. Novak, Vitezslav
b. Pickett, Bill
d. Dumas, Alexandre Dumas Davy de
   la Pailleterie

December 6, 1870
b. Hart, William Surrey

December 8, 1870
d. Brassey, Thomas

December 10, 1870
b. Loos, Adolf
b. Louys, Pierre

December 11, 1870
b. Weinman, Adolph A

December 14, 1870
b. Renner, Karl

December 15, 1870
b. Hoffmann, Josef

December 17, 1870
d. Mercadante, Saverio

December 18, 1870
b. Saki

December 20, 1870
b. Cahill, Marie

December 21, 1870
b. Haskins, Charles Homer

December 22, 1870
d. Becquer, Gustavo Adolfo
   Dominguez

December 25, 1870
b. Rubinstein, Helena

December 28, 1870
b. Hendrick, Burton Jesse

December 31, 1870
b. Connolly, Tommy

1871

b. Baker, Newton D(iehl)
b. Booth, Hubert Cecil
b. Dalton, Emmett
b. DePriest, Oscar Stanton
b. Kuang-hsu
b. Pitney, Arthur

b. Ukrainka, Lesia
d. Aubert de Gaspe, Philippe(-Joseph)
d. Jaeger, Gustav, Dr.
d. Joseph, Chief
d. Lartet, Edouard Armand Isidore
   Hippolyte

January 1, 1871
b. Dalmores, Charles

January 5, 1871
b. Converse, Frederick Shepherd

January 7, 1871
b. Horder, Thomas Jeeves

January 11, 1871
b. Eddy, Sherwood

January 14, 1871
b. Howe, Louis McHenry
b. Warburg, Felix Moritz

January 17, 1871
b. Beatty, David Beatty, Earl

January 23, 1871
b. Rasputin, Grigori Efimovich

January 24, 1871
b. Jaggar, Thomas Augustus

January 25, 1871
b. Park, Maud May Wood
d. Garrett, Thomas

January 26, 1871
b. Adams, Samuel Hopkins
d. Ticknor, George

January 28, 1871
b. Lukeman, Henry A

February 1, 1871
b. Thaw, Harry Kendall

February 4, 1871
b. Ebert, Friedrich

February 5, 1871
b. Gardner, Mary Sewall

February 9, 1871
b. Ricketts, Howard T

February 12, 1871
d. Cary, Alice

February 15, 1871
b. Nordstrom, John

February 16, 1871
d. Locke, Richard Adams

February 20, 1871
d. Kane, Paul

February 28, 1871
b. Irving, Isabel

March 5, 1871
b. Luxemburg, Rosa

March 6, 1871
b. Harney, Benjamin Robertson

March 15, 1871
b. McIlwain, Charles Howard

March 16, 1871
d. Barboncito

March 17, 1871
d. Chambers, Robert

March 18, 1871
d. De Morgan, Augustus

March 19, 1871
b. McGinnity, Joe
b. Taylor, J(ohn) H(enry)

March 26, 1871
d. Fetis, Francois Joseph

March 27, 1871
b. Mann, Heinrich Ludwig

March 28, 1871
b. Jones, William
b. Mengelberg, Willem

April 5, 1871
b. Warner, Pop

April 12, 1871
b. Metaxas, John

April 16, 1871
b. Stephenson, Henry
b. Synge, John Millington

April 21, 1871
b. Blech, Leo

April 28, 1871
b. Homer, Louise
d. Mason, James Murray

April 30, 1871
b. Yost, Fielding Harris

May 2, 1871
b. Duffy, Francis Patrick

May 3, 1871
b. Dietz, Angel DeCora

May 6, 1871
b. Grignard, Francois Auguste Victor

May 11, 1871
b. Fortuny
b. Schlesinger, Frank
d. Herschel, John Frederick William,
   Sir

May 12, 1871
d. Auber, Daniel Francois Esprit
d. Payen, Anselme

May 19, 1871
b. Daly, Reginald Aldworth

May 27, 1871
b. Rouault, Georges

May 28, 1871
b. Daly, Thomas Augustine

May 31, 1871
b. Rusie, Amos Wilson

June 8, 1871
d. Wo-jen

June 13, 1871
d. Houdin, Jean Eugene Robert

June 17, 1871
b. Johnson, James Weldon
d. Vallandigham, Clement Laird

June 18, 1871
b. Andreyev, Leonid Nikolayevich
b. Breese, Edmund
d. Grote, George

June 22, 1871
b. McDougall, William
b. Raine, William MacLeod

July 6, 1871
d. Castro Alves, Antonio de

July 7, 1871
b. Carle, Richard

July 10, 1871
b. Proust, Marcel

July 17, 1871
b. Feininger, Lyonel
b. Litvinov, Maxim
d. Tausig, Karl

July 18, 1871
b. Balla, Giacomo

July 21, 1871
b. Ferrero, Guglielmo

July 23, 1871
b. Verrill, Alpheus Hyatt

July 31, 1871
d. Cary, Phoebe

August 2, 1871
b. Sloan, John F

August 3, 1871
b. Parrington, Vernon L(ouis)

August 9, 1871
d. Marmol, Jose

August 13, 1871
b. Liebknecht, Karl

August 19, 1871
b. Wright, Orville

August 26, 1871
d. Scribner, Charles

August 27, 1871
b. Dreiser, Theodore

August 29, 1871
b. Lebrun, Albert

August 30, 1871
b. Rutherford, Ernest, Baron

September 3, 1871
b. Kupka, Frank

September 9, 1871
d. Watie, Stand

September 19, 1871
b. Schaudinn, Fritz Richard

September 23, 1871
b. Kupka, Frank

September 25, 1871
d. Papineau, Louis-Joseph

September 28, 1871
b. Badoglio, Pietro

September 29, 1871
b. Machado y Morales, Gerardo

October 2, 1871
b. Hull, Cordell

October 11, 1871
b. Hawes, Harriet Ann Boyd

October 18, 1871
d. Babbage, Charles

October 19, 1871
b. Cannon, Walter Bradford

October 22, 1871
d. Murchison, Roderick Impey

October 24, 1871
b. Shrady, Henry M

October 27, 1871
d. Anderson, Robert

October 30, 1871
b. Valery, Paul Ambroise

November 1, 1871
b. Crane, Stephen

November 5, 1871
b. Whitehill, Clarence Eugene

November 8, 1871
d. Hall, Charles Francis

November 9, 1871
b. Sabin, Florence Rena

November 10, 1871
b. Churchill, Winston

November 14, 1871
b. Coulter, Ernest Kent
b. Russell, Henry

November 18, 1871
b. Bonstelle, Jessie

November 20, 1871
b. Guiterman, Arthur
b. Kilpatrick, William H(eard)

November 25, 1871
b. Ames, Winthrop

November 26, 1871
b. McIntyre, John Thomas

November 27, 1871
b. Giorgi, Giovanni

December 7, 1871
d. Levasseur, Nicolas Prosper

December 9, 1871
b. Kelley, Joe

December 12, 1871
b. Carr, Emily

December 16, 1871
d. Haring, Georg Wilhelm Heinrich

December 20, 1871
b. Hadley, Henry Kimball

December 21, 1871
b. Irving, Laurence Sidney

1872

b. Alexandra Feodorovna
b. Barker, Ma
b. Bean, L(eon) L(eonwood)
b. Blinn, Holbrook
b. Chicherin, Georgi Vasilyevich
b. Cruz, Oswaldo Goncalves
b. Denikin, Anton Ivanovich
b. Diagne, Blaise
b. Fry, Charles Burgess
b. Ghose, Aurobindo
b. Gurdjieff, George Ivanovitch
b. Keyes, Roger John Brownlow,
    Baron
b. Mizner, Addison
b. Scott, Walter
b. Smith, Alex
d. Louis, Pierre Charles Alexandre

January 6, 1872
b. Scriabin, Alexander Nicholaevich

January 7, 1872
d. Fisk, Jim

January 9, 1872
d. Halleck, Henry Wager

January 11, 1872
b. Pierce, George Washington

January 15, 1872
b. Davis, John Staige

January 16, 1872
b. Craig, Gordon

January 21, 1872
d. Grillparzer, Franz

January 24, 1872
d. Trendelenburg, Friedrich Adolf

January 26, 1872
b. Morgan, Julia

January 27, 1872
b. Hand, Learned

January 29, 1872
b. Rothenstein, William, Sir

January 30, 1872
d. Chesney, Francis Rawdon

January 31, 1872
b. Grey, Zane
b. Hughes, Rupert

February 3, 1872
b. Harris, Sam Henry
b. Meiklejohn, Alexander

February 10, 1872
b. Hartford, John Augustine

February 14, 1872
b. Grove, Frederick Philip

February 17, 1872
b. Duane, William

March 6, 1872
b. Bojer, Johan

March 7, 1872
b. Mondrian, Piet(er Cornelis)

March 9, 1872
d. Krieghoff, Cornelius

March 10, 1872
d. Mazzini, Giuseppe

March 12, 1872
d. Tseng Kuo-fan

March 13, 1872
b. Keeler, Wee Willie
b. Villard, Oswald (Garrison)

March 19, 1872
b. Diaghilev, Sergei (Pavlovich)

March 20, 1872
d. Wentworth, William Charles

March 23, 1872
b. Savage, Michael Joseph

March 24, 1872
b. Birch, Stephen

March 30, 1872
b. Vassilenko, Sergei

March 31, 1872
b. Griffith, Arthur

April 1, 1872
b. Kollontai, Alexandra Mikhailovna
(Domantovich)
d. Maurice, Frederick Denison

April 2, 1872
d. Morse, Samuel Finley Breese

April 7, 1872
b. Trotter, Monroe

April 9, 1872
b. Blum, Leon
d. Corning, Erastus

April 10, 1872
b. Hirshfield, Morris

April 19, 1872
b. Salomon, Alice

April 21, 1872
b. Bitzer, George William

April 24, 1872
b. Ring, Blanche

April 28, 1872
b. Esposito, Joseph

April 29, 1872
b. Whitney, Harry Payne

May 4, 1872
b. Palmer, Alexander Mitchell
b. Wright, Harold Bell

May 6, 1872
b. Bowie, William
b. Sitter, Willem de

May 10, 1872
b. Mauss, Marcel

May 11, 1872
d. Read, Thomas Buchanan

May 12, 1872
b. Rathbone, Eleanor

May 16, 1872
b. Holmes, Taylor

May 18, 1872
b. Russell, Bertrand Arthur William

May 26, 1872
b. Urban, Joseph Maria

May 31, 1872
b. Abbot, C(harles) G(reeley)
b. Robinson, W Heath

June 1, 1872
d. Bennett, James Gordon

June 4, 1872
d. Moniuszko, Stanislaus

June 15, 1872
b. Gadski, Johanna

June 19, 1872
b. Farrand, Beatrix Jones

June 24, 1872
b. Crowninshield, Francis Welch

June 27, 1872
b. Curtis, Heber Doust
b. Dunbar, Paul Laurence

June 30, 1872
b. Pound, Louise

July 1, 1872
b. Bleriot, Louis

July 2, 1872
b. Mundelein, George William

July 4, 1872
b. Coolidge, Calvin

July 5, 1872
b. Herriot, Edouard

July 8, 1872
b. VonTilzer, Harry

July 15, 1872
b. Hertz, Alfred
b. Rodo, Jose Enrique

July 16, 1872
b. Amundsen, Roald Engelbregt

July 18, 1872
d. Juarez, Benito Pablo

July 22, 1872
b. Pendergast, Thomas Joseph

August 3, 1872
b. Haakon VII

August 11, 1872
b. Fuller, Solomon Carter, Jr.
d. Mason, Lowell

August 13, 1872
b. Willstater, Richard Martin

August 21, 1872
b. Beardsley, Aubrey Vincent

August 24, 1872
b. Beerbohm, Max

August 27, 1872
b. Anderson, Mary

September 7, 1872
d. Thayer, Sylvanus, General

September 13, 1872
d. Feuerbach, Ludwig Andreas

September 20, 1872
b. Gamelin, Maurice Gustave

September 22, 1872
b. Rothwell, Walter Henry

September 25, 1872
b. Cochran, C(harles) B(lake)
b. Sforza, Carlo
d. Cartwright, Peter

September 29, 1872
b. Murchison, Kenneth MacKenzie

October 2, 1872
d. Lieber, Franz

October 3, 1872
b. Clarke, Fred Clifford

October 4, 1872
b. Blood, Ernest
b. Zemlinsky, Alexander von

October 8, 1872
b. Powys, John Cowper

October 10, 1872
d. Parton, Sara Payson Willis
d. Seward, William Henry

October 11, 1872
b. Stone, Harlan Fiske

October 12, 1872
b. Vaughan Williams, Ralph

October 14, 1872
b. Hess, Sol

October 15, 1872
b. Wilson, Edith Bolling (Galt)

October 23, 1872
d. Gautier, Theophile

November 5, 1872
d. Sully, Thomas

November 6, 1872
d. Meade, George Gordon

November 10, 1872
b. Moisseiff, Leon Solomon

November 11, 1872
b. Adams, Maude
b. Stock, Frederick A

November 13, 1872
b. Hupp, Louis Gorham

November 18, 1872
b. Marsh, Edward Howard, Sir

November 23, 1872
b. Ward, Fannie

November 29, 1872
b. Mildenburg, Anna von
d. Greeley, Horace

November 30, 1872
b. McCrae, John

December 1, 1872
b. Swope, Gerard

December 7, 1872
b. Huizinga, Johan
b. Rice, Cale Young

December 11, 1872
d. Kamehameha V

December 12, 1872
d. Forrest, Edwin

December 14, 1872
d. Kensett, John Frederick

December 21, 1872
b. Terhune, Albert Payson
d. Duncanson, Robert Scott

December 22, 1872
b. Guerin, Camille

December 23, 1872
b. Marin, John
d. Catlin, George

December 28, 1872
b. Baroja (y Nessi), Pio

1873

b. Bialik, Hayyim Nahman
b. Chang Tso-Lin
b. Clapham, John Harold
b. Coffroth, Jimmy
b. Czolgosz, Leon F
b. Dalton, William
b. Drinkwater, Charles Graham
b. Kell, Vernon, Sir
b. Kolchak, Aleksandr Vasilievich
b. Nash, George Frederick
b. Reed, Austin Leonard
b. Santos-Dumont, Alberto
b. Terra, Gabriel
b. Upjohn, Lawrence Northcote
d. McClure, Robert (John Le Mesurier)

January 1, 1873
b. Azuela, Mariano

January 2, 1873
b. Therese of Lisieux, Saint

January 7, 1873
b. Zukor, Adolph

January 9, 1873
b. Bialik, Chaim Nachman
d. Napoleon III

January 10, 1873
b. Christy, Howard Chandler

January 11, 1873
b. Morrow, Dwight Whitney

January 16, 1873
b. Collins, Jimmy

January 18, 1873
d. Lytton, Edward George Earle
Lytton Bulwer-Lytton, 1st Baron
Lytton

January 19, 1873
b. Dupree, Minnie

January 28, 1873
b. Colette

January 29, 1873
b. Abruzzi, Luigi Amedeo
b. Palmer, Frederick

January 30, 1873
b. Jensen, Johannes Vilhelm

February 1, 1873
d. Maury, Matthew Fontaine

February 2, 1873
b. Neurath, Konstantin von

February 3, 1873
b. Trenchard, Hugh Montague, First
Viscount

February 5, 1873
b. Elliott, Maxine
b. Heiser, Victor George

February 7, 1873
d. LeFanu, Joseph Sheridan

February 13, 1873
b. Chaliapin, Feodor Ivanovitch, Jr.

February 15, 1873
b. Euler-Chelpin, Hans Karl August
Simon von

February 19, 1873
b. Feuillade, Louis

February 20, 1873
b. Judd, Charles Hubbard

February 22, 1873
b. Upton, Florence Kate

February 23, 1873
b. Liang Ch'i-ch'ao

February 25, 1873
b. Caruso, Enrico

March 3, 1873
b. Green, William

March 6, 1873
b. Ferguson, Homer Lenoir

March 8, 1873
b. Held, Anna

March 9, 1873
d. Knight, Charles

March 10, 1873
b. Wassermann, Jakob

March 12, 1873
b. White, Stewart Edward

March 17, 1873
b. Bondfield, Margaret Grace

March 19, 1873
b. Reger, Max

March 24, 1873
b. Coolidge, Dane

March 26, 1873
b. DuMaurier, Gerald Hubert, Sir

March 28, 1873
b. Sedgwick, Anne Douglas

April 1, 1873
b. Rachmaninoff, Sergei Vasilyevich

April 4, 1873
b. Faure, Elie

April 7, 1873
b. McGraw, John Joseph

April 12, 1873
b. Duncan, Augustin

April 13, 1873
b. Davis, John Williams

April 18, 1873
d. Liebig, Justus von

April 22, 1873
b. Glasgow, Ellen Anderson Gholson

April 25, 1873
b. DeLaMare, Walter
b. Garis, Howard Roger
b. Herelle, Felix d'

April 28, 1873
b. Bauer, Harold
d. Manzoni, Alessandro (Antonio)

May 1, 1873
d. Livingstone, David

May 4, 1873
d. McGuffey, William Holmes

May 6, 1873
d. Paez, Jose Antonio

May 7, 1873
d. Chase, Salmon Portland

May 8, 1873
d. Ames, Oakes
d. Mill, John Stuart

May 9, 1873
b. Cermak, Anton Joseph

May 12, 1873
b. MacDonald, J(ames) E(dward)
H(ervey)

May 14, 1873
b. Tcherepnin, Nicholas

May 17, 1873
b. Richardson, Dorothy Miller

May 18, 1873
b. Silverman, Sime

May 21, 1873
b. Bennett, Richard
b. Berger, Hans
d. Cartier, Georges Etienne, Sir

May 23, 1873
b. Baeck, Leo
d. Smet, Pierre Jean de

June 1, 1873
d. Howe, Joseph

June 3, 1873
b. Loewi, Otto
b. Smith, Alfred

June 7, 1873
b. Ronald, Landon, Sir
b. Weidenreich, Franz

June 8, 1873
b. Ruiz, Jose Martinez

June 17, 1873
b. Bloomingdale, Samuel

June 21, 1873
b. Tomlinson, Henry Major

June 27, 1873
d. Powers, Hiram

June 28, 1873
b. Carrel, Alexis

July 1, 1873
b. Guy-Blache, Alice

July 21, 1873
b. Witherspoon, Herbert

August 1, 1873
b. Hocking, William Ernest

August 3, 1873
b. Posey, Alexander Lawrence

August 4, 1873
b. Paul-Boncour, Joseph

August 7, 1873
b. Peguy, Charles Pierre

August 18, 1873
b. Harbach, Otto Abels

August 19, 1873
b. Stone, Fred Andrew

August 25, 1873
b. Bates, Blanche Lyon

August 26, 1873
b. DeForest, Lee

August 28, 1873
b. Saarinen, Eliel

September 1, 1873
b. Standing, Guy, Sir

September 6, 1873
b. Coffin, Howard Earle

September 7, 1873
b. Becker, Carl Lotus

September 8, 1873
b. McKay, David O
b. Salvemini, Gaetano

September 9, 1873
b. Reinhardt, Max

September 10, 1873
b. Onions, Charles Talbut

September 14, 1873
b. Irwin, Will(iam Henry)

September 22, 1873
b. Day, Joseph Paul

September 26, 1873
d. Wheelwright, William

September 27, 1873
b. Chatfield, Alfred E Montacute,
Baron

October 1, 1873
d. Landseer, Edwin Henry, Sir

October 3, 1873
b. Horlick, Alexander James
b. Post, Emily (Price)
d. Captain Jack

October 6, 1873
b. Sonneck, Oscar George Theodore

October 8, 1873
b. Hertzsprung, Ejnar
b. Jarry, Alfred

October 9, 1873
b. Flesch, Karl
b. Walgreen, Charles Rudolph

October 10, 1873
b. Lovejoy, Arthur Oncken
(Schauffler)

October 13, 1873
b. McCoy, Charles

October 14, 1873
b. Ewry, Ray C

October 20, 1873
b. Kellor, Frances (Alice)
b. McClung, Nellie Letitia Mooney

October 23, 1873
b. Coolidge, William David

October 24, 1873
b. Bode, Boyd Henry

October 25, 1873
b. Willys, John North

October 28, 1873
d. Heenan, John Carmel

October 29, 1873
b. Kelly, Walter C

October 30, 1873
b. Madero, Francisco Indalecio

November 4, 1873
b. Moore, George Edward
d. Keene, Laura

November 6, 1873
d. Hardee, William Joseph

November 9, 1873
b. Thyssen, Fritz

November 10, 1873
b. Rabaud, Henri

November 15, 1873
b. Baker, Sara Josephine

November 16, 1873
b. Handy, W(illiam) C(hristopher)

November 19, 1873
d. Mallory, Stephen R

November 20, 1873
b. Mason, Daniel Gregory

November 23, 1873
b. Ross, Donald James

November 27, 1873
b. Christophers, S(amuel) Rickard, Sir

November 28, 1873
b. Ginzberg, Louis
b. Mantle, (Robert) Burns

December 1, 1873
b. Chernov, Viktor Mikhailovich

December 3, 1873
b. Kent, Arthur Atwater

December 7, 1873
b. Cather, Willa (Sibert)

December 11, 1873
d. Beadle, William

December 12, 1873
b. Ridge, Lola

d. Agassiz, Louis

December 17, 1873
b. Ford, Ford Madox
b. Goldin, Horace

December 21, 1873
d. Garnier, Francis

December 22, 1873
d. Remond, Charles Lennox

December 23, 1873
d. Grimke, Sarah Moore

December 24, 1873
b. Brittain, Harry Ernest, Sir
d. Hopkins, Johns

December 28, 1873
b. Harkins, William Draper

December 30, 1873
b. Smith, Alfred Emanuel
d. Baylor, Robert Emmet Bledsoe

1874

b. Bain, Dan
b. Crump, Edward Hull
b. Divine, Father Major Jealous
b. Elliott, Gertrude
b. Fort, Charles Hoy
b. Johnson, Alvin Saunders
b. Reilly, Sidney George
b. Sebastiani, Samuele
b. Wu P'ei-fu
d. Feng Kuei-fen

January 1, 1874
b. Knox, Frank

January 4, 1874
b. Suk, Josef

January 5, 1874
b. Erlanger, Joseph

January 6, 1874
b. Niblo, Fred

January 10, 1874
b. Mathiez, Albert

January 11, 1874
d. Borden, Gail

January 13, 1874
d. Baltard, Victor

January 14, 1874
b. Burgess, Thornton Waldo

January 16, 1874
b. Service, Robert William

January 17, 1874
d. Chang and Eng

January 20, 1874
d. Kelley, Hall Jackson

January 22, 1874
b. Harkness, Edward Stephen

January 24, 1874
b. Schomburg, Arthur Alfonso

January 25, 1874
b. Johnson, Hewlett
b. Maugham, W(illiam) Somerset

January 28, 1874
b. Meyerhold, Vsevolod Emilievich

January 29, 1874
b. Davis, Owen
b. Rockefeller, John D(avison), Jr.

February 1, 1874
b. Hofmannsthal, Hugo von

February 3, 1874
b. Stein, Gertrude

February 6, 1874
b. Medary, Milton B

February 7, 1874
b. Fuertes, Louis Agassiz

February 9, 1874
b. Lowell, Amy
d. Michelet, Jules

February 11, 1874
d. Trist, Nicholas Philip

February 12, 1874
b. Perret, Auguste

February 14, 1874
b. Boon, Dickie

February 15, 1874
b. Shackleton, Ernest Henry, Sir

February 17, 1874
b. Watson, Thomas J(ohn), Sr.
d. Quetelet, Lambert Adolphe Jacques

February 18, 1874
b. Dewson, Mary Williams

February 20, 1874
b. Bottomley, Gordon
b. Garden, Mary

February 22, 1874
b. Klem, Bill
b. Takahama Kyoshi

February 24, 1874
b. Wagner, Honus

February 25, 1874
d. Bachman, John

February 28, 1874
d. Strauss, David Friedrich

March 6, 1874
b. Berdyayev, Nikolay Aleksandrovich

March 8, 1874
d. Fillmore, Millard

March 11, 1874
d. Sumner, Charles

March 15, 1874
b. Bagley, William Chandler
b. Ickes, Harold LeClair

March 16, 1874
b. Matthes, Francois-Emile

March 17, 1874
b. Wise, Stephen Samuel

March 23, 1874
b. Leyendecker, Joseph Christian

March 24, 1874
b. Einaudi, Luigi
b. Houdini, Harry

March 26, 1874
b. Frost, Robert Lee
b. Nast, Conde

March 28, 1874
d. Hansen, Peter Andreas

April 1, 1874
b. Barnes, Ernest William

April 5, 1874
b. Jones, Jesse Holman

April 12, 1874
b. Bankhead, William Brockman

April 13, 1874
d. Bogardus, James

April 15, 1874
b. Shull, George Harrison
b. Stark, Johannes

April 17, 1874
b. Mackay, Clarence Hungerford

April 24, 1874
b. Pope, John Russell

April 25, 1874
b. Marconi, Guglielmo

April 27, 1874
b. Baring, Maurice

April 28, 1874
b. Toler, Sidney

May 1, 1874
b. Brooks, Romaine

May 3, 1874
b. Coty, Francois Marie Joseph
Spoturno

May 4, 1874
b. Conrad, Frank

May 9, 1874
b. Baylis, Lilian Mary
b. Carter, Howard

May 18, 1874
b. Tharaud, Jerome

May 22, 1874
b. Malan, Daniel Francois

May 28, 1874
b. Cockrell, Ewing

May 29, 1874
b. Chesterton, G(ilbert) K(eith)

May 30, 1874
b. Peabody, Josephine Preston

June 5, 1874
b. Chesbro, Jack

June 9, 1874
d. Cochise

June 12, 1874
b. McNary, Charles Linza

June 13, 1874
b. Bowes, Major

June 16, 1874
b. Meighen, Arthur

June 21, 1874
d. Angstrom, Anders Jonas

June 22, 1874
d. Staunton, Howard

June 25, 1874
b. O'Neill, Rose Cecil

June 26, 1874
d. Miller, Alfred Jacob

June 27, 1874
b. Golden, John

June 28, 1874
b. Speaks, Oley

June 29, 1874
b. Tetrazzini, Luisa

July 3, 1874
b. Andersson, Johan Gunnar
b. Ngata, Apirana Turupa

July 16, 1874
b. Goldberger, Joseph

July 23, 1874
b. Fitzsimmons, James E

July 26, 1874
b. Koussevitzky, Serge Alexandrovich

July 28, 1874
b. Cassirer, Ernst
b. Miller, Alice Duer

July 29, 1874
b. Woodsworth, James Shaver

August 1, 1874
b. Spaulding, Charles Clinton

August 5, 1874
b. Mitchell, Wesley Clair

August 6, 1874
b. Lefebvre, Georges
b. Shotwell, James Thomson

August 10, 1874
b. Hoover, Herbert C(lark)

August 22, 1874
d. Dobell, Sydney Thompson

August 26, 1874
b. Gale, Zona

August 27, 1874
b. Bosch, Carl

August 29, 1874
b. Machado (y Ruiz), Manuel

August 31, 1874
b. Pierce, Edward Allen
b. Thorndike, Edward L(ee)

September 3, 1874
b. Stormer, Fredrik (Carl Mulertz)

September 10, 1874
b. Sullivan, Mark

September 13, 1874
b. Schoenberg, Arnold

September 15, 1874
d. Curtis, Benjamin Robbins

September 21, 1874
b. Holst, Gustav Theodore

September 22, 1874
b. Mendenhall, Dorothy Reed

September 23, 1874
b. Barker, Ernest, Sir

September 26, 1874
b. Hine, Lewis Wickes

September 27, 1874
b. Reed, Myrtle
d. Geiger, Abraham

October 2, 1874
b. Woodward, William E

October 4, 1874
d. Procter, Bryan Waller

October 12, 1874
b. Brill, Abraham Arden
d. Guizot, Francois Pierre Guillaume

October 20, 1874
b. Ives, Charles Edward

October 25, 1874
b. Dawson, Geoffrey

October 26, 1874
b. Rockefeller, Abby Aldrich
d. Cornelius, Peter

October 27, 1874
b. Young, Owen D

October 28, 1874
d. Rinehart, William H

November 4, 1874
b. Avery, Sewell
b. Wallace, Bobby

November 5, 1874
d. Creighton, Edward

November 7, 1874
b. Blair, William Richards

November 10, 1874
b. MacMillan, Donald Baxter

November 12, 1874
b. Williams, Bert

November 15, 1874
b. Krogh, Schack August Steenberg

November 18, 1874
b. Day, Clarence Shepard, Jr.

November 20, 1874
b. Curley, James Michael

November 22, 1874
b. Horne, Herman Harrell

November 25, 1874
b. Gans, Joe
b. Spence, Lewis

November 27, 1874
b. Beard, Charles Austin
b. Walter, Eugene
b. Weizmann, Chaim

November 29, 1874
b. Egas Moniz, Antonio C A F

November 30, 1874
b. Churchill, Winston Leonard
   Spencer, Sir
b. Montgomery, Lucy Maud

December 3, 1874
b. Lhevinne, Josef

December 9, 1874
d. Cornell, Ezra

July 23, 1875
d. Singer, Isaac Merrit

July 26, 1875
b. Jung, Carl Gustav
b. Machado (y Ruiz), Antonio

July 27, 1875
b. Fisher, Harrison

July 30, 1875
d. Pickett, George Edward

July 31, 1875
d. Johnson, Andrew

August 4, 1875
b. Montemezzi, Italo
d. Andersen, Hans Christian

August 5, 1875
b. Briggs, Clare A
b. Craig, Malin

August 6, 1875
d. Moreno, Gabriel Garcia

August 8, 1875
b. Hamilton, Charles Harold St. John

August 11, 1875
d. Graham, William Alexander

August 12, 1875
b. Panizza, Ettore

August 15, 1875
b. Bartlett, Robert Abram
b. Coleridge-Taylor, Samuel

August 16, 1875
d. Finney, Charles Grandison

August 18, 1875
b. Slezak, Leo

August 20, 1875
b. Tchernichowski, Saul Gutmanovich

August 24, 1875
b. Craven, Frank

August 26, 1875
b. Buchan, John, Sir

August 31, 1875
b. Plank, Eddie

September 1, 1875
b. Burroughs, Edgar Rice

September 3, 1875
b. Porsche, Ferdinand

September 5, 1875
b. Lajoie, Nap(oleon)

September 6, 1875
b. Fuller, Ida
b. Train, Arthur Cheney

September 16, 1875
b. Penney, J(ames) C(ash)

September 20, 1875
b. Erzberger, Matthias

September 26, 1875
b. Gwenn, Edmund

September 27, 1875
b. Deledda, Grazia

September 30, 1875
b. Fisher, Fred
b. Voelker, Paul Frederick

October 4, 1875
b. Daly, Arnold

October 12, 1875
b. Crowley, Aleister (Edward Alexander)
d. Carpeaux, Jean Baptiste

October 18, 1875
b. Leonard, Eddie
b. Yarnell, Harry Ervin

October 19, 1875
d. Wheatstone, Charles, Sir

October 23, 1875
b. Lewis, Gilbert Newton

October 28, 1875
b. Grosvenor, Gilbert Hovey

October 29, 1875
b. Marie Alexandra Victoria

November 6, 1875
b. Dixon, Roland Burrage

November 10, 1875
d. Wilson, Henry

November 11, 1875
b. Slipher, Vesto Melvin

November 13, 1875
b. Kling, Johnny
b. Swinnerton, James Guilford

November 15, 1875
b. Kurz, Selma

November 19, 1875
b. Bingham, Hiram

November 20, 1875
b. Kalinin, Mikhail (Ivanovich)

November 27, 1875
b. Parsons, Elsie Clews
b. Wallace, Edgar

December 1, 1875
b. Mqhayi, S(amuel) E(dward) K(rune Loliwe)

December 5, 1875
b. Currie, Arthur William

December 6, 1875
b. Underhill, Evelyn

December 12, 1875
b. Rundstedt, Karl Rudolf Gerd von

December 19, 1875
b. Woodson, Carter Godwin

December 20, 1875
b. Powys, Theodore Francis

December 23, 1875
b. Waldron, Charles D
d. Saint Georges, Jules

1876

b. Burchenal, Elizabeth
b. Churchill, May
b. Cohan, Josephine
b. Hellmann, Richard
b. John, Gwendolyn Mary
b. Royden, Agnes Maude
b. Scullin, James Henry
b. Stokely, John
d. American Horse
d. Diaz de la Pena, Narciso Virgilio
d. Heavysege, Charles
d. Wen-hsiang

January 3, 1876
b. Pieck, Wilhelm

January 5, 1876
b. Adenauer, Konrad

January 9, 1876
b. Michels, Robert
d. Howe, Samuel Gridley

January 11, 1876
b. Flick, Elmer Harrison

January 12, 1876
b. London, Jack
b. Wolf-Ferrari, Ermanno

January 15, 1876
d. Johnson, Eliza (McCardle)

January 17, 1876
b. Hague, Frank

January 20, 1876
b. Hofmann, Josef Casimir
d. Dykes, John Bacchus

January 23, 1876
b. Diels, Otto Paul Herman

January 25, 1876
b. Leonard, William Ellery

January 28, 1876
d. Deak, Francis

January 31, 1876
b. Spargo, John

February 1, 1876
d. Forster, John

February 4, 1876
b. Cleghorn, Sarah Norcliffe
b. Dickey, Herbert Spencer

February 8, 1876
b. Modersohn-Becker, Paula

February 10, 1876
d. Johnson, Reverdy

February 15, 1876
b. Everleigh, Ada

February 16, 1876
b. Trevelyan, George Macaulay

February 17, 1876
d. Bushnell, Horace
d. Cushman, Charlotte Saunders

February 21, 1876
b. Brancusi, Constantin

February 22, 1876
b. Bonnin, Gertrude Simmons
b. Zenatello, Giovanni

February 24, 1876
b. Moore, Victor

February 26, 1876
b. Justo, Agustin Pedro

February 28, 1876
b. Carpenter, John Alden

March 2, 1876
b. Pius XII

March 5, 1876
b. Belin, Edouard
d. Agoult, Marie Catherine Sophie d'
d. Piave, Francesco Maria

March 11, 1876
b. Ruggles, Carl

March 15, 1876
b. Carias Andino, Tiburcio

March 19, 1876
d. Chesney, Charles Cornwallis

March 23, 1876
b. Bone, Muirhead, Sir

March 26, 1876
b. Ammann, Othmar Hermann

March 27, 1876
b. Thompson, Mary

March 30, 1876
b. Beers, Clifford Whittingham
b. Tikhomirov, Vasily Dmitrievich

d. Balard, Antoine-Jerome

April 3, 1876
b. Anglin, Margaret Mary

April 4, 1876
b. Vlaminck, Maurice de

April 5, 1876
b. Dinneen, Bill

April 10, 1876
d. Stewart, Alexander Turney

April 17, 1876
d. Brownson, Orestes Augustus

April 22, 1876
b. Barany, Robert
b. Rolvaag, Ole Edvart

April 23, 1876
b. Westwick, Harry

April 24, 1876
b. Raeder, Erich
b. Tallmadge, Thomas Eddy

April 27, 1876
b. Farrere, Claude

May 1, 1876
b. Swanson, Carl A

May 13, 1876
b. Laparra, Raoul

May 16, 1876
b. West, James Edward

May 24, 1876
d. Kingsley, Henry

May 26, 1876
b. Root, Jack
b. Yerkes, Robert Mearns
d. Palacky, Frantisek

May 29, 1876
d. Diez, Friedrich Christian

June 7, 1876
b. Cantacuzene, Princess
b. Nielsen, Alice

June 8, 1876
d. Sand, George

June 11, 1876
b. Kroeber, Alfred Louis

June 13, 1876
b. Franklin, Irene

June 17, 1876
b. Crerar, Thomas Alexander

June 20, 1876
b. Ditmars, Raymond Lee
d. Santa Anna, Antonio Lopez de

June 21, 1876
b. Keesom, Willem Hendrik

June 23, 1876
b. Cobb, Irvin Shrewsbury

June 25, 1876
d. Cummins, George David
d. Custer, George Armstrong

June 27, 1876
d. Ehrenberg, Christian Gottfried
d. Martineau, Harriet

July 1, 1876
d. Bakunin, Mikhail Aleksandrovich

July 3, 1876
b. Perry, Ralph Barton

July 4, 1876
b. Farnum, William
b. Loeb, Sophia Irene Simon

July 6, 1876
b. Cobb, Will D
b. Sinclair, Harry Ford

July 11, 1876
b. Jacob, Max

July 16, 1876
b. Dent, Edward Joseph

July 19, 1876
b. Smith, Joseph Fielding

July 22, 1876
b. Rosenbach, Abraham Simon Wolf
b. Ufer, Walter

July 24, 1876
b. Webster, Jean

July 26, 1876
b. Schelling, Ernest Henry

July 27, 1876
d. Channing, Walter

July 29, 1876
b. Ouspenskaya, Maria

August 2, 1876
d. Hickok, Wild Bill

August 5, 1876
b. Beard, Mary Ritter

August 7, 1876
b. Mata Hari

August 10, 1876
d. Lane, Edward William

August 12, 1876
b. Rinehart, Mary Roberts

August 16, 1876
b. Bilibin, Ivan Iakolevich
d. Bergmann, Carl

August 17, 1876
b. Perth, 16th Earl of

August 20, 1876
d. Palmer, Frances Flora Bond

August 26, 1876
b. Couzens, James Joseph, Jr.

August 27, 1876
d. Fromentin, Eugene

August 29, 1876
b. Kettering, Charles Franklin
b. Muratore, Lucien
d. David, Felicien Cesar

September 4, 1876
b. Kirby, Rollin

September 6, 1876
b. MacLeod, John James Rickard
b. Robinson, Boardman

September 7, 1876
b. Darwin, Bernard Richard Meirion

September 8, 1876
b. Thomas, Elmer

September 13, 1876
b. Anderson, Sherwood
b. Marcosson, Isaac Frederick

September 14, 1876
d. Rhett, Robert Barnwell

September 15, 1876
b. Altrock, Nick
b. Gannett, Frank Ernest
b. Walter, Bruno

September 16, 1876
b. Huntington, Ellsworth

September 20, 1876
b. Ellis, Carleton

September 21, 1876
b. Gonzalez, Julio

September 24, 1876
b. Cossart, Ernest

September 26, 1876
b. Abbott, Edith

September 27, 1876
d. Bragg, Braxton

October 9, 1876
b. Warwick, Robert

October 13, 1876
b. Waddell, Rube

October 14, 1876
b. Ironside, Henry Allan

October 18, 1876
b. Adams, Charles Francis

October 19, 1876
b. Brown, Mordecai Peter Centennial

October 21, 1876
b. Darling, Jay Norwood

October 23, 1876
b. Cret, Paul P(hilippe)

October 26, 1876
b. Loftus, Cissie

October 27, 1876
d. Walker, Joseph Reddeford

October 31, 1876
b. Barney, Natalie Clifford

November 3, 1876
d. Maywood, Augusta

November 4, 1876
b. Fraser, James Earle

November 5, 1876
b. Duchamp-Villon, Raymond

November 6, 1876
d. Antonelli, Giacomo

November 7, 1876
b. Shinn, Everett

November 9, 1876
d. Tamburini, Antonio

November 17, 1876
b. Lea, Homer

November 19, 1876
b. Ehrenfest-Afanaseva, Tatiana

November 23, 1876
b. Dufresne, Charles
b. Falla, Manuel de

November 24, 1876
b. Griffin, Walter Burley

November 26, 1876
b. Carrier, Willis Haviland

November 28, 1876
d. Baer, Karl Ernst von

November 29, 1876
b. Davies, Joseph Edward
b. Ross, Nellie Taylor

December 1, 1876
b. Creel, George Edward

December 4, 1876
b. Rilke, Rainer Maria

December 6, 1876
b. Duesenberg, Frederick S

December 11, 1876
b. Comstock, Ada Louise

December 12, 1876
b. Kraenzlein, Alvin C

December 20, 1876
b. Adams, Walter Sydney

December 21, 1876
b. Lang, John Thomas

December 22, 1876
b. Elmen, Gustav Waldemar
b. Marinetti, Filippo Tommaso Emilio
b. Mofolo, Thomas (Mokopu)

December 25, 1876
b. Hughan, Jessie Wallace
b. Jinnah, Mohammed Ali
b. Windaus, Adolf Otto Reinhold

December 28, 1876
d. Paludan-Muller, Frederik

December 29, 1876
b. Casals, Pablo (Pau Carlos Salvador)
b. DeLuca, Giuseppe

1877

b. Calder, Frank
b. Factor, Max
b. Goldmark, Josephine
b. Hutton, Edward F
b. Renault, Louis
b. Schwimmer, Rosika
b. Spilsbury, Bernard Henry, Sir
b. Sutton, Walter Stanborough
d. Allison, Clay
d. Muhlenberg, William Augustus
d. Semmes, Raphael

January 4, 1877
b. Hartley, Marsden
d. Vanderbilt, Cornelius

January 5, 1877
b. Coffin, Henry Sloane

January 10, 1877
b. Cottrell, Frederick Gardner

January 15, 1877
b. Terman, Lewis Madison

January 18, 1877
b. Zemurray, Samuel

January 20, 1877
b. St. Denis, Ruth
b. Saint Denis, Ruth

January 22, 1877
b. Schacht, Hjalmar Horace Greeley

January 26, 1877
b. Dongen, Kees van

February 2, 1877
b. Towne, Charles Hanson

February 4, 1877
b. Pickard, Greenleaf Whittier

February 7, 1877
b. Hardy, Godfrey Harold

February 8, 1877
d. Wilkes, Charles

February 13, 1877
b. Smith, (Robert) Sidney

February 16, 1877
b. Gougelman, Pierre

February 17, 1877
b. Maginot, Andre Louis Rene
d. Mosenthal, Salomon Hermann von

February 20, 1877
d. Goldsborough, Louis Malesherbes

February 21, 1877
b. Garrigou-Lagrange, Reginald Marie

February 22, 1877
b. Costello, Maurice

February 24, 1877
b. Ganz, Rudolph
b. Rider-Kelsey, Corinne

February 26, 1877
b. Dirks, Rudolph

February 27, 1877
b. Briggs, Walter Owen

February 28, 1877
b. Breuil, Henri Abbe

March 3, 1877
b. Frick, Wilhelm

March 4, 1877
b. Morgan, Garrett Augustus

March 12, 1877
b. Adams, Annette Abbott

March 14, 1877
b. Chase, Edna Woolman
b. Marshall, Jack
d. Rosas, Juan Manuel de

March 16, 1877
b. Pahlevi, Riza

March 17, 1877
b. Gardner, George

March 18, 1877
b. Cayce, Edgar
d. Belcher, Edward, Sir

March 23, 1877
d. Unger, Caroline

March 24, 1877
d. Bagehot, Walter

March 25, 1877
d. Chisholm, Caroline

March 28, 1877
b. Ray, Edward

March 29, 1877
d. Macy, R(owland) H(ussey)

March 30, 1877
d. Cournot, Antoine Augustin

April 7, 1877
d. Caballero, Fernan

April 16, 1877
b. Turner, Thomas Wyatt

April 19, 1877
b. Evinrude, Ole
b. Whitney, Gertrude Vanderbilt

April 26, 1877
b. Taylor, William Desmond

April 29, 1877
b. Dorgan, Thomas Aloysius
d. Brownlow, William Gannaway

April 30, 1877
b. Toklas, Alice B(abette)

May 6, 1877
d. Runeberg, Johan Ludwig

May 9, 1877
b. Tharaud, Jean

May 16, 1877
b. McCormick, Joseph Medill

May 19, 1877
b. Girdler, Tom Mercer

May 20, 1877
b. MacCarthy, Desmond Charles Otto, Sir

May 26, 1877
b. Araki Sadao

May 28, 1877
b. Deeping, (George) Warwick

May 29, 1877
d. Harper, Fletcher
d. Motley, John Lothrop

June 3, 1877
b. Dufy, Raoul (Ernest Joseph)

June 4, 1877
b. Wieland, Heinrich Otto

June 5, 1877
b. Breck, John Henry

June 8, 1877
b. Wagner, Robert F(erdinand)

June 9, 1877
b. Ruffo, Titta

June 12, 1877
b. Marcoux, Vanni

June 17, 1877
b. Cady, (Walter) Harrison

June 18, 1877
b. Flagg, James Montgomery

June 19, 1877
b. Coburn, Charles Douville

June 21, 1877
d. Palmer, Nathaniel Brown

June 22, 1877
b. Vionnet, Madeleine

June 24, 1877
d. Owen, Robert Dale

June 27, 1877
b. Barkla, Charles Glover
b. McLaughlin, Frederic
b. Scholes, Percy Alfred

July 1, 1877
b. Davis, Benjamin Oliver, Sr.

July 2, 1877
b. Hesse, Hermann

July 4, 1877
b. Tozzer, Alfred Marston

July 6, 1877
b. Alcala Zamora, Niceto

July 16, 1877
b. Schick, Bela

July 23, 1877
b. Glass, Montague (Marsden)

July 27, 1877
b. Dohnanyi, Erno von
d. Nekrasov, Nikolay Alexeyevich

July 29, 1877
b. Beebe, William

August 2, 1877
d. Douglas, James, Sir

August 4, 1877
b. Thomson, Tom

August 9, 1877
b. Young, Mahonri Mackintosh

August 10, 1877
b. Marshall, Frank James

August 19, 1877
b. Connally, Tom

August 22, 1877
b. Coomaraswamy, Ananda Kentish

August 27, 1877
b. Douglas, Lloyd Cassel

b. Rolls, Charles Stewart

August 29, 1877
d. Young, Brigham

September 1, 1877
b. Aston, Francis William

September 2, 1877
b. Soddy, Frederick

September 3, 1877
d. Thiers, Adolphe

September 5, 1877
d. Crazy Horse

September 7, 1877
b. Stone, George Robert

September 9, 1877
b. Agate, James Evershed
b. Chance, Frank Leroy

September 11, 1877
b. Dzerzhinsky, Felix Edmundovich
b. Jeans, James Hopwood, Sir

September 16, 1877
b. Schick, Jacob
d. Coffin, Levi

September 17, 1877
d. Talbot, William Henry Fox

September 23, 1877
b. Kaempffert, Waldemar (Bernhard)

September 24, 1877
d. Saigo, Takamori

September 25, 1877
b. Calles, Plutarco Elias
d. LeVerrier, Urbain Jean Joseph

September 26, 1877
b. Cortot, Alfred-Denis

September 27, 1877
b. Dole, James

September 29, 1877
d. Meiggs, Henry

October 2, 1877
b. Hayden, Carl Trumball

October 3, 1877
b. Gildersleeve, Virginia Crocheron

October 4, 1877
b. Gerould, Gordon Hall

October 5, 1877
d. Looking Glass

October 10, 1877
b. Morris, William Richard
b. Nuffield, William Richard Morris

October 13, 1877
b. Bilbo, Theodore Gilmore

October 16, 1877
b. Helland-Hansen, Bjorn
b. Lawrie, Lee

October 21, 1877
b. Avery, Oswald T

October 24, 1877
b. Hutton, Bouse

October 25, 1877
b. Russell, Henry Norris
d. Adams, Edwin

October 26, 1877
b. Mason, Max

October 29, 1877
d. Forrest, Nathan Bedford

October 30, 1877
b. Rombauer, Irma von Starkloff

November 1, 1877
d. Morton, Oliver Hazard Perry
   Throck

November 2, 1877
b. Aga Khan III

November 3, 1877
b. Ibanez del Campo, Carlos

November 5, 1877
b. Mead, George Houk

November 6, 1877
b. Dillon, William A

November 9, 1877
b. Iqbal, Mahomed, Sir

November 12, 1877
b. Austin, Warren R(obinson)

November 18, 1877
b. Mayr, Richard
b. Pigou, Arthur Cecil

November 22, 1877
b. Ady, Endre

November 24, 1877
b. Barkley, Alben William

November 25, 1877
b. Granville-Barker, Harley

November 27, 1877
b. Anthony, Katharine Susan
b. Nomura, Kichisaburo

December 1, 1877
b. Beach, Rex Ellingwood

December 8, 1877
d. Bledsoe, Albert Taylor

December 20, 1877
b. Cooper, Emil

December 25, 1877
b. Trihey, Harry

December 31, 1877
d. Courbet, Gustave
d. Courbet, (Jean Desire) Gustave

1878

b. Carr, Alexander
b. Cartier, Pierre C
b. Hart, Pearl
b. MacDonagh, Thomas
b. Plaatje, Sol(omon) T(shekisho)
b. Uspenskii, Petr Dem'yanovich
d. Collins, Edward Knight
d. Cullen, Paul, Cardinal
d. Mindon Min
d. Varnhagen, Francisco Adolfo de

January 1, 1878
b. Goldman, Edwin Franko

January 4, 1878
b. Coppard, A(lfred) E(dgar)
b. John, Augustus Edwin

January 6, 1878
b. Sandburg, Carl (August)

January 9, 1878
b. Watson, John Broadus
d. Victor Emmanuel II

January 10, 1878
d. Stokes, William

January 12, 1878
b. Kahles, Charles William
b. Molnar, Ferenc

January 13, 1878
b. Reid Dick, William, Sir

January 16, 1878
b. Carey, Harry
d. Bowles, Samuel, II

January 18, 1878
d. Becquerel, Antoine-Cesar

January 19, 1878
b. Corwin, Edward Samuel
d. Regnault, Henri Victor

January 20, 1878
b. Currie, Finlay

January 21, 1878
b. Garrod, Heathcote William

January 22, 1878
b. Collier, Constance
b. Fairfax, Beatrice

January 25, 1878
b. Alexanderson, Ernst Frederik
   Werner

January 26, 1878
b. Gabrilowitsch, Ossip Salomonovich

January 29, 1878
b. Akeley, Mary Lee Jobe
b. George, Walter Franklin
b. Oldfield, Barney

February 1, 1878
b. Bailey, H(enry) C(hristopher)
b. Caraway, Hattie Wyatt
d. Cruikshank, George

February 4, 1878
b. Copeau, Jacques
b. Schaefer, Germany

February 5, 1878
b. Citroen, Andre Gustave

February 6, 1878
b. Pitkin, Walter Boughton

February 7, 1878
d. Pius IX

February 8, 1878
b. Buber, Martin

February 10, 1878
b. Farnol, Jeffery
d. Bernard, Claude

February 11, 1878
d. Welles, Gideon

February 12, 1878
b. Howard, Joseph Edgar
d. Duff, Alexander

February 18, 1878
b. Ames, Blanche

February 19, 1878
d. Daubigny, Charles Francois

February 25, 1878
d. Harris, Townsend

February 26, 1878
b. Destinn, Emmy
b. Malevich, Kasimir Severinovich
d. Secchi, Pietro Angelo

March 2, 1878
d. Wade, Benjamin Franklin

March 3, 1878
b. Lindsay, David
b. Thomas, Edward

March 8, 1878
b. Currie, Barton Wood

March 9, 1878
d. Anderssen, Adolf

March 14, 1878
d. Petrov, Ossip

March 16, 1878
b. Walthall, Henry B

March 21, 1878
b. Amato, Pasquale

March 23, 1878
b. Schreker, Franz

March 27, 1878
d. Scott, George Gilbert, Sir

March 28, 1878
b. Lehman, Herbert Henry
b. Spingarn, Arthur Barnett

March 29, 1878
b. Von Tilzer, Albert

March 31, 1878
b. Johnson, Jack

April 1, 1878
d. Lohman, Ann Trow

April 6, 1878
b. Eberle, Mary Abastenia St. Leger

April 12, 1878
d. Tweed, Boss

April 22, 1878
b. Gordon, Kitty

April 25, 1878
d. Sewell, Anna

April 28, 1878
b. Barrymore, Lionel Blythe

May 7, 1878
b. Heruy Walda-Sellase

May 8, 1878
b. Aitken, Robert

May 9, 1878
b. Gallo, Fortune

May 10, 1878
b. Stresemann, Gustav

May 12, 1878
d. Beecher, Catharine (Esther)

May 13, 1878
d. Henry, Joseph

May 14, 1878
d. Okubo, Toshimichi

May 21, 1878
b. Curtiss, Glenn Hammond
b. Desmond, William

May 24, 1878
b. Fosdick, Harry Emerson
b. Gilbreth, Lillian Moller

May 25, 1878
b. Robinson, Bill

May 27, 1878
b. Duncan, Isadora

May 28, 1878
d. Russell, John, Lord

June 1, 1878
b. Masefield, John

June 3, 1878
b. Henderson, Lawrence Joseph

June 4, 1878
b. Buchman, Frank Nathan Daniel

June 5, 1878
b. Villa, Pancho

June 12, 1878
b. Curwood, James Oliver
d. Bonneville, Benjamin Louie Eulalie de
d. Bryant, William Cullen

June 15, 1878
b. Abbott, Margaret I.

June 16, 1878
b. Torrence, Ernest
d. Long, Crawford Williamson

June 20, 1878
b. Morgan, Arthur

June 23, 1878
d. Back, George, Sir

June 27, 1878
d. Whitman, Sarah Helen Power

July 2, 1878
b. Wright, Henry

July 4, 1878
b. Cohan, George M(ichael)

July 5, 1878
b. Everleigh, Minna
b. Gilman, Lawrence
b. Holbrooke, Josef

July 9, 1878
b. Kaltenborn, H(ans) V(on)

July 10, 1878
b. Partridge, Bellamy

July 12, 1878
b. Bloch, Claude Charles

July 13, 1878
b. Sterne, Maurice

July 21, 1878
d. Bass, Sam

July 22, 1878
b. Ball, Ernest

July 24, 1878
b. Dunsany, Edward J M Plunkett,
Baron

July 27, 1878
b. Cline, Genevieve Rose

July 29, 1878
b. Marquis, Don Robert Perry

August 1, 1878
b. Tanguay, Eva

August 13, 1878
d. Duyckinck, Evert Augustus

August 17, 1878
b. Gogarty, Oliver St. John
d. Upjohn, Richard

August 19, 1878
b. Quezon (y Molina), Manuel Luis

August 27, 1878
b. Wrangel, Pietr Nikolayevich

September 6, 1878
b. Canby, Henry Seidel

September 9, 1878
b. Crapsey, Adelaide
b. Osmena, Sergio, Jr.

September 11, 1878
d. Satanta

September 14, 1878
b. Carey, William F

September 20, 1878
b. Sinclair, Upton Beall
d. Thorpe, Thomas Bangs

September 22, 1878
b. Yoshida, Shigeru

October 2, 1878
b. Gibson, Wilfred Wilson

October 4, 1878
b. Hopkins, Arthur

October 7, 1878
d. Mosquera, Tomas Cipriano de

October 8, 1878
b. Munnings, Alfred James, Sir

October 11, 1878
b. Hofer, Karl

October 15, 1878
b. Reynaud, Paul

October 18, 1878
b. Adams, James Truslow
b. Artsybashev, Mikhail Petrovich
d. Laing, David

October 19, 1878
b. Sanborn, Pitts

November 1, 1878
b. Cisneros, Eleanora
b. Saavdedra, Lamas Carlos

November 4, 1878
b. Schwartz, Jean

November 7, 1878
b. Meitner, Lise

November 10, 1878
b. Ubico y Castaneda, Jorge

November 11, 1878
d. Havell, Robert, Jr.

November 17, 1878
b. Abbott, Grace

November 20, 1878
b. Bowers, Claude Gernade
b. Gilpin, Charles Sidney

November 23, 1878
b. King, Ernest Joseph

November 25, 1878
b. Kaiser, Georg

November 27, 1878
b. Orpen, William Newneham, Sir

November 28, 1878
d. Lewes, George Henry

November 29, 1878
d. Godey, Louis Antoine

December 2, 1878
b. Candler, Charles Howard

December 6, 1878
b. Braithwaite, William Stanley
Beaumont
b. Pillsbury, John Sargent

December 8, 1878
b. Serafin, Tullio

December 10, 1878
d. Wells, Henry

December 12, 1878
b. Crothers, Rachel

December 16, 1878
d. Gutzkow, Karl Ferdinand

December 19, 1878
d. Taylor, Bayard

December 25, 1878
b. Chevrolet, Louis Joseph
b. Schenck, Joseph M

December 26, 1878
b. Bowman, Isaiah

December 30, 1878
b. Aberhart, William

December 31, 1878
b. Quiroga, Horacio

1879

b. Arber, Agnes
b. Bauersfeld, Walther
b. Ch'en Tu-hsiu
b. Connelly, One-Eyed
b. Duesenberg, August S
b. Fairbank, Janet Ayer
b. Han Yongun
b. Martin, Mungo
b. May, Edna
b. McIntyre, Frank J
b. Rajagopalachari, Chakravarti
b. Reese, Harry B
b. Rodia, Simon
b. Tsankov, Aleksandur
d. Dull Knife
d. Landseer, Charles
d. Mahal, Hazrat

January 1, 1879
b. Forster, E(dward) M(organ)
b. Fox, William
b. Jones, Ernest Alfred

January 2, 1879
d. Cushing, Caleb

January 3, 1879
b. Coolidge, Grace (Anne Goodhue)

January 5, 1879
b. Norworth, Jack

January 6, 1879
b. Patterson, Joseph Medill

January 12, 1879
b. Harroun, Ray

January 13, 1879
b. Harrison, Ross Granville

January 18, 1879
b. Giraud, Henri Honore
d. Cremazie, Octave

January 22, 1879
b. Picabia, Francis

January 23, 1879
d. Jensen, Adolph

January 26, 1879
d. Fowler, Lydia Folger

February 1, 1879
b. Chretien, Henri

February 6, 1879
b. Friesz, Othon

February 8, 1879
b. Slye, Maud

February 11, 1879
d. Daumier, Honore Victorin

February 13, 1879
b. Naidu, Sarojini

February 17, 1879
b. Fisher, Dorothy Frances Canfield

February 22, 1879
b. Bronsted, Johannes Nicolaus

February 26, 1879
b. Bridge, Frank
b. Luhan, Mabel (Ganson) Dodge

March 1, 1879
b. Stambuliski, Aleksandr

March 3, 1879
b. McCollum, Elmer Verner
d. Howitt, William

March 5, 1879
b. Beveridge, William Henry, Lord

March 6, 1879
d. Burritt, Elihu

March 8, 1879
b. Hahn, Otto

March 14, 1879
b. Einstein, Albert
b. Monro, Harold Edward

March 15, 1879
b. Catto, Thomas Sivewright, Baron

March 16, 1879
b. Sykes, Mark, Sir

March 17, 1879
b. Grauman, Sid(ney Patrick)

March 19, 1879
b. Raskob, John J
d. Clairmont, Claire

March 22, 1879
b. Teschner, Richard

March 25, 1879
b. Knudsen, William Signius

March 27, 1879
b. Huggins, Miller James
b. MacSwiney, Terence
b. Steichen, Edward Jean

March 28, 1879
b. Westley, Helen

April 4, 1879
d. Bonaparte, Elizabeth Patterson
d. Dove, Heinrich Wilhelm

April 6, 1879
b. Prouty, Jed

April 8, 1879
b. Schauffler, Robert Haven
d. Panizzi, Anthony, Sir

April 9, 1879
b. Meighan, Thomas

April 10, 1879
b. Hertz, John Daniel

April 12, 1879
b. Melcher, Frederic Gershon

April 14, 1879
b. Cabell, James Branch

April 16, 1879
d. Bernadette of Lourdes, Saint

April 17, 1879
b. Howell, Albert S

April 20, 1879
b. Poiret, Paul

April 21, 1879
d. Dix, John Adams

April 26, 1879
b. Richardson, Owen Williams, Sir

April 29, 1879
b. Beecham, Thomas, Sir

April 30, 1879
b. Resor, Stanley Burnett
d. Hale, Sarah Josepha Buell

May 2, 1879
b. Byrnes, James Francis

May 3, 1879
b. Pollack, Egon

May 7, 1879
d. Decoster, Charles Theodore Henri

May 15, 1879
d. Stampfli, Jakob

May 19, 1879
b. Astor, Nancy Witcher Langhorne
b. Bestor, Arthur Eugene

May 24, 1879
d. Garrison, William Lloyd

May 25, 1879
b. Beaverbrook, William Maxwell
Aitken, Baron

May 30, 1879
b. Bell, Vanessa
b. Crofts, Freeman Willis

June 1, 1879
d. Shields, James

June 3, 1879
d. Rothschild, Lionel Nathan
Rothschild, Baron

June 4, 1879
b. Lubbock, Percy
b. Nazimova, Alla

June 5, 1879
b. Mayer, Robert, Sir

June 7, 1879
b. Rasmussen, Knud Johan Victor

June 11, 1879
b. Bresnaham, Roger Philip
b. Pulitzer, Ralph

June 13, 1879
b. Wood, Robert Elkington

June 25, 1879
d. Cooke, William Fothergil, Sir

June 30, 1879
b. Hampden, Walter

July 1, 1879
b. Jouhaux, Leon

July 3, 1879
b. Korzybski, Alfred Habdank

July 5, 1879
b. Davis, Dwight Filley
b. Jadlowker, Hermann
b. Landowska, Wanda Louise

July 7, 1879
d. Bingham, George Caleb

July 9, 1879
b. Respighi, Ottorino

July 12, 1879
b. Zuppke, Robert Carl

July 13, 1879
b. Freyssinet, Eugene

July 15, 1879
b. Arguedas, Alcides

July 19, 1879
b. Laviolette, Jack
b. Mitchel, John Purroy

July 28, 1879
b. Ferrer, Gabriel (Francisco Victor)
Miro

August 8, 1879
b. Smith, Robert H
b. Zapata, Emiliano

August 11, 1879
b. Lawrence, Frieda

August 13, 1879
b. Ireland, John Nicholson

August 15, 1879
b. Barrymore, Ethel Mae Blythe

August 16, 1879
b. Bell, James Ford

August 18, 1879
b. Edwards, Gus

August 20, 1879
b. Budd, Ralph
d. Rimmer, William

August 27, 1879
d. Hill, Rowland, Sir

August 28, 1879
b. Whipple, George Hoyt

August 30, 1879
b. Scheff, Fritzi
d. Hood, John Bell
d. Jackson, John Adams

August 31, 1879
b. Yoshihito

September 5, 1879
b. Jewett, Frank Baldwin
b. Rogers, Will(iam Penn Adair)

September 8, 1879
d. Hunt, William Morris

September 15, 1879
b. Lyons, Joseph Aloysius

September 17, 1879
b. Foster, Rube
d. Viollet le Duc, Eugene Emmanuel

September 18, 1879
b. Fisher, Welthy (Blakesley
Honsinger)
d. Drew, Daniel

September 19, 1879
b. Drum, Hugh A
b. Vance, Louis Joseph
b. Westheimer, Irvin Ferdinand

September 20, 1879
b. Banning, Kendall
b. Cromwell, Dean Bartlett
b. Sjostrom, Victor

September 27, 1879
b. Scott, Cyril (Meir)

October 2, 1879
b. Stevens, Wallace

October 3, 1879
b. Bigelow, Henry Bryant

October 4, 1879
b. East, Edward Murray
d. Soloviev, Sergei Mikhailovich

October 5, 1879
b. Erskine, John
b. Rous, Francis Peyton

October 6, 1879
d. Powell, William Henry

October 7, 1879
b. Hill, Joe

October 9, 1879
b. Laue, Max Theodor Felix von

October 13, 1879
d. Carey, Henry Charles

October 14, 1879
b. Franklin, Miles

October 15, 1879
b. Darwell, Jane

October 24, 1879
b. Weston, Edward F

October 26, 1879
d. Grimke, Angelina Emily

October 29, 1879
b. Papen, Franz von

October 31, 1879
d. Abbott, Jacob
d. Buckstone, John Baldwin
d. Hooker, Joseph

November 1, 1879
b. Barnack, Oskar
d. Chandler, Zachariah

November 2, 1879
d. Einhorn, David

November 3, 1879
b. Stefansson, Vihjalmur

November 5, 1879
b. Hays, Will Harrison
d. Maxwell, James Clerk

November 8, 1879
b. Trotsky, Leon

November 9, 1879
b. Holmes, John Haynes

November 10, 1879
b. Lindsay, Vachel
b. Pearse, Padraic

November 15, 1879
b. Cape, Herbert Jonathan
b. Stone, Lewis

November 17, 1879
b. Heggie, O P

November 22, 1879
b. Hawtrey, Ralph George, Sir
d. Stewart, Maria W. Miller

December 1, 1879
b. Bryant, Lane

December 3, 1879
b. Nagai, Sokichi

December 5, 1879
b. Cessna, Clyde Vernon

December 6, 1879
d. Bigelow, Erastus Brigham

December 7, 1879
b. Friml, Rudolf

December 10, 1879
b. Norris, James, Sr.
b. Shepard, Ernest Howard

December 12, 1879
b. Crews, Laura Hope

December 13, 1879
b. Belmont, Eleanor Robson

December 15, 1879
b. Laban, Rudolf von

December 18, 1879
b. Klee, Paul

December 21, 1879
b. Stalin, Joseph

December 25, 1879
b. George, Grace

December 27, 1879
b. Greenstreet, Sydney Hughes
b. Johnson, Bunk

December 29, 1879
b. Mitchell, Billy

1880

b. Bailey, Alice A(nne La Trobe-
Bateman)
b. Bhashani, Maulana Abdul Hamid
Khan
b. Hahn, Archie
b. Hemon, Louis
b. Ibn Saud
b. Jackson, Aunt Molly
b. McGee, Frank
b. Mossadegh, Mohammed
b. Premchand
b. Richardson, George Taylor
b. Sargent, George
b. Stuart, Hod
b. Whitcroft, Fred(rick)
d. Dewar, John
d. Montt Torres, Manuel

January 1, 1880
b. Cwiklinska, Mieczyslawa

January 2, 1880
b. Breguet, Louis Charles

January 5, 1880
b. Sachse, Leopold

January 6, 1880
b. Mix, Tom

January 7, 1880
b. Rollins, Carl Purington

January 10, 1880
b. Azana y Diaz, Manuel
b. Bayes, Nora
b. Grock

d. Leslie, Frank

January 12, 1880
d. Arthur, Ellen (Lewis) Herndon

January 14, 1880
b. Beach, Joseph Warren

January 18, 1880
b. Ehrenfest, Paul

January 23, 1880
b. Poole, Ernest

January 26, 1880
b. MacArthur, Douglas

January 28, 1880
b. Boland, Mary

January 29, 1880
b. Fields, W C

February 1, 1880
b. Pratella, Francesco Balilla

February 3, 1880
b. Price, Nancy

February 8, 1880
b. Faust, Lotta
b. Marc, Franz
d. Sykes, George

February 10, 1880
d. Cremieux, Isaac-Adolphe

February 12, 1880
b. Lewis, John L(lewellyn)

February 15, 1880
b. Davidson, J Brownlee
b. Hergesheimer, Joseph

February 17, 1880
b. Obregon, Alvaro

February 19, 1880
d. Brumidi, Constantino

February 22, 1880
b. Europe, James Reese

February 23, 1880
b. Chapin, Roy Dikeman

February 24, 1880
b. Hoare, Samuel John Gurney, Sir

February 27, 1880
b. Grimke, Angelina Emily Weld

March 1, 1880
b. Strachey, (Giles) Lytton

March 2, 1880
b. Kreuger, Ivar

March 4, 1880
b. Pollock, Channing
b. Walker, Stuart Armstrong

March 9, 1880
b. McGovern, Terry

March 10, 1880
b. Jacobs, Michael S
b. Thorek, Max

March 12, 1880
b. Ataturk, Kemal

March 16, 1880
b. Stout, William Bushnell

March 21, 1880
b. Hofmann, Hans

March 22, 1880
b. Cooper, Kent

March 23, 1880
b. Wolheim, Louis

March 26, 1880
b. Hines, Duncan

March 29, 1880
b. Lhevinne, Rosina L

March 30, 1880
b. O'Casey, Sean
b. Short, Walter Campbell

March 31, 1880
b. Birley, Oswald Hornby Joseph, Sir

April 2, 1880
d. Wieniawski, Henri

April 4, 1880
b. Flint, William Russell, Sir

April 12, 1880
b. Joss, Addie

April 13, 1880
b. Leginska

April 15, 1880
b. Wertheimer, Max

April 17, 1880
b. Woolley, Charles Leonard, Sir

April 18, 1880
b. Crawford, Sam(uel Earl)
b. Crisp, Donald

April 23, 1880
b. Norden, Carl Lukas

April 25, 1880
b. Mellor, Walter

April 26, 1880
b. Fokine, Michel
b. Anderson, Willie

May 1, 1880
b. Lasker, Albert D(avis)

May 6, 1880
b. Ironside, William Edmund
b. Kirchner, Ernst Ludwig

May 7, 1880
d. Caxias, Duque de

May 8, 1880
d. Flaubert, Gustave
d. Very, Jones

May 11, 1880
b. Haynes, George Edmund

May 12, 1880
b. Ellsworth, Lincoln

May 14, 1880
b. Forbes, Bertie

May 20, 1880
b. Fields, Stanley
b. Theodorescu, Ion N
d. Foote, Henry Stuart

May 21, 1880
b. Arghezi, Tudor

May 22, 1880
b. Phillips, Tommy

May 27, 1880
b. DuPont, Henry Francis
b. Grew, Joseph Clark

May 29, 1880
b. Spengler, Oswald
d. Feuerbach, Paul Johann Anselm von

June 1, 1880
b. Lahey, Frank Howard

June 2, 1880
b. Gowers, Ernest Arthur, Sir

June 6, 1880
b. Cosgrave, William Thomas

June 7, 1880
b. McGimsie, Billy

June 9, 1880
b. Digges, Dudley

June 10, 1880
b. Derain, Andre

June 13, 1880
b. Rose, Vincent
b. Stella, Joseph

June 15, 1880
b. Nagano, Osami

June 17, 1880
b. Van Vechten, Carl

June 18, 1880
d. Sutter, John Augustus

June 19, 1880
b. Dwiggins, William Addison

June 21, 1880
b. Gesell, Arnold

June 27, 1880
b. Keller, Helen Adams

June 29, 1880
b. Beck, Ludwig August Theoder

July 4, 1880
b. Rooney, Pat
d. Ripley, George

July 5, 1880
b. Kubelik, Jan

July 11, 1880
b. Rankin, Jeannette

July 14, 1880
b. Meek, Donald

July 16, 1880
b. Norris, Kathleen Thompson

July 20, 1880
b. Keyserling, Hermann Alexander
Graf Von

July 21, 1880
b. Stefanik, Milan Rastislav

July 24, 1880
b. Bloch, Ernest

July 25, 1880
b. Cohen, Morris Raphael

July 26, 1880
b. Lincoln, G(eorge) Gould

July 27, 1880
b. Tinker, Joe
b. Vynnychenko, Volodymyr

July 30, 1880
b. McCormick, Robert Rutherford

August 2, 1880
b. Dove, Arthur Garfield

August 5, 1880
b. Sawyer, Ruth

August 6, 1880
b. Carrillo, Leo

August 12, 1880
b. Hall, Radclyffe
b. Mathewson, Christy

August 15, 1880
b. Shubert, Jacob J

August 17, 1880
d. Bull, Ole Bornemann

August 18, 1880
b. Cleland, Thomas Maitland

August 22, 1880
b. Herriman, George

August 24, 1880
b. Bowie, Russell

August 25, 1880
b. Cowen, Joshua Lionel

August 26, 1880
b. Apollinaire, Guillaume
b. Moeller, Philip

August 27, 1880
d. Ouray

August 28, 1880
d. Jackson, Charles Thomas

August 31, 1880
b. Wilhelmina

September 12, 1880
b. Mencken, H(enry) L(ouis)

September 13, 1880
b. Lasky, Jesse L(ouis)

September 14, 1880
b. Wilkins, Ernest Hatch

September 16, 1880
b. Noyes, Alfred

September 17, 1880
b. Russell, Blair

September 20, 1880
b. Pizzetti, Ildebrando
d. McKay, Donald

September 22, 1880
b. Pankhurst, Christabel Harriette,
Dame

September 23, 1880
b. Boyd-Orr, John, Baron
b. Orr, John Boyd, 1st Baron of
Brechin

September 28, 1880
b. Flanders, Ralph Edward

October 3, 1880
b. Oland, Warner

October 4, 1880
d. Offenbach, Jacques

October 6, 1880
d. Peirce, Benjamin

October 7, 1880
b. Holme, Constance

October 12, 1880
b. Kyne, Peter Bernard

October 14, 1880
b. Bely, Andrey

October 15, 1880
b. Stopes, Marie Charlotte Carmichael
d. Victorio

October 18, 1880
b. Jabotinsky, Vladimir Evgenevich

October 22, 1880
b. Carr, Joe
d. Child, Lydia Maria Francis

October 27, 1880
b. Kuhn, Walt

October 28, 1880
b. Evans, Edward Ratcliffe Garth
Russell

October 31, 1880
b. Peterkin, Julia Mood

November 1, 1880
b. Asch, Sholem
b. Rice, Grantland
b. Wegener, Alfred Lothar

November 2, 1880
b. Hooker, Brian
b. Merivale, Philip

November 3, 1880
b. Sterling, Ford

November 6, 1880
b. Musil, Robert Edler Von

November 8, 1880
d. Drake, Edwin Laurentine

November 10, 1880
b. Epstein, Jacob, Sir

November 11, 1880
d. Kelly, Ned
d. Mott, Lucretia Coffin

November 12, 1880
b. Stark, Harold Raynsford

November 21, 1880
d. Cockburn, Alexander James
Edmund, Sir

November 25, 1880
b. Flynn, John
b. Woolf, Leonard Sidney

November 28, 1880
b. Blok, Aleksandr Aleksandrovich

November 30, 1880
b. Tawney, Richard Henry

December 4, 1880
b. Wood, Gar(field A)

December 5, 1880
b. Hern, Riley

June 1, 1881
b. Matzenauer, Margaret

June 5, 1881
b. Wenner-Gren, Axel (Lenard)

June 6, 1881
d. Vieuxtemps, Henri Francois Joseph

June 9, 1881
b. Luckner, Felix von, Count

June 10, 1881
b. Gruenberg, Sidonie Matsner

June 11, 1881
b. Kaplan, Mordecai

June 13, 1881
b. Weber, Lois

June 15, 1881
b. McFee, William

June 17, 1881
b. Burns, Tommy

June 19, 1881
b. Walker, Jimmy

June 23, 1881
d. Schleiden, Matthias Jakob

June 24, 1881
b. Randall, James Garfield
b. Tietjen, Heinz

June 26, 1881
b. Shambaugh, Jessie Field

July 1, 1881
d. Lotze, Rudolf Hermann
d. Sainte-Clair Deville, Henri Etienne

July 3, 1881
b. Errol, Leon

July 5, 1881
b. Landis, Walter Savage

July 10, 1881
b. Richberg, Donald R(andall)

July 11, 1881
b. Kelland, Clarence Budington

July 13, 1881
d. Pemberton, John Clifford

July 14, 1881
d. Billy the Kid

July 17, 1881
d. Bridger, James

July 21, 1881
b. Evers, Johnny

July 22, 1881
b. Bianco, Margery Williams

July 23, 1881
b. Gallatin, Albert Eugene

July 25, 1881
d. Clifford, Nathan

July 26, 1881
d. Borrow, George Henry

July 27, 1881
b. Fischer, Hans

July 29, 1881
d. Fitzhugh, George

August 1, 1881
b. Macaulay, (Emilie) Rose, Dame

August 2, 1881
d. Clarke, Marcus (Andrew Hislop)

August 3, 1881
d. Fargo, William George

August 5, 1881
b. Reynolds, Richard S
d. Spotted Tail

August 6, 1881
b. Fleming, Alexander, Sir
b. Parsons, Louella Oettinger

August 7, 1881
b. Darlan, Jean Louis Xavier Francois

August 10, 1881
b. Bynner, Harold Witter
d. Burton, John Hill, Sir

August 11, 1881
d. Fillmore, Caroline Carmichael McIntosh

August 12, 1881
b. DeMille, Cecil B(lount)

August 13, 1881
d. Trelawny, Edward John

August 19, 1881
b. Enesco, Georges

August 20, 1881
b. Guest, Edgar A(lbert)

August 26, 1881
b. Irvin, Rea

September 3, 1881
d. Delmonico, Lorenzo

September 7, 1881
d. Lanier, Sidney

September 13, 1881
d. Burnside, Ambrose Everett

September 15, 1881
b. Bugatti, Ettore Arco Isidoro
b. Grant, Harry Johnston
b. Phillips, Lena Madesin

September 16, 1881
b. Bell, Clive
b. Shinichiro Imaoka

September 19, 1881
d. Garfield, James Abram

September 28, 1881
b. DeCordoba, Pedro
b. Sears, Eleonora Randolph

September 29, 1881
b. von Mises, Ludwig (Edler)

October 1, 1881
b. Boeing, William Edward

October 4, 1881
b. Brauchitsch, Heinrich Alfred

October 11, 1881
b. Kelsen, Hans
b. Richardson, Lewis Fry
b. Young, Stark

October 15, 1881
b. Wodehouse, P(elham) G(renville)

October 16, 1881
b. Harridge, Will(iam)

October 17, 1881
b. Chinard, Gilbert

October 22, 1881
b. Davisson, Clinton Joseph

October 23, 1881
b. O'Connor, Una

October 25, 1881
b. Picasso, Pablo Ruiz y

October 30, 1881
d. DeLong, George Washington

November 4, 1881
b. Tucker, Rosina

November 8, 1881
b. Speck, Frank Gouldsmith

November 9, 1881
b. Kalmus, Herbert Thomas

November 14, 1881
b. Schenck, Nicholas Michael

November 15, 1881
b. Adams, Franklin P(ierce)

November 18, 1881
b. LeSueur, Percy

November 23, 1881
b. Enver Pasha

November 25, 1881
b. John, XXIII
b. John XXIII

November 28, 1881
b. Zweig, Stefan

December 4, 1881
b. Cadman, Charles Wakefield

December 8, 1881
b. Colum, Padraic
b. Gleizes, Albert L

December 12, 1881
b. Warner, Harry Morris

December 13, 1881
d. Quidor, John

December 17, 1881
d. Hayes, Isaac Israel
d. Morgan, Lewis Henry

December 18, 1881
d. Street, George Edmund

December 20, 1881
b. Rickey, Branch

December 24, 1881
b. Jimenez, Juan Ramon
d. Bacon, Leonard Woolsey

December 25, 1881
b. Dill, John Greer, Sir

December 29, 1881
b. Willard, Jess

December 31, 1881
b. Pechstein, Max

1882

b. Abd el-Krim el-Khatabi, Mohamed
ben
b. Abdullah Ibn Hussein
b. Bowes, Walter
b. Brown, Charlotte (Eugenia)
Hawkins
b. Clay, Jacob
b. Cuong De
b. Dodd, John Bruce, Mrs.
b. Feng Yu-hsiang
b. Huntington, Henry S, Jr.
b. Moran, George
b. Nadelman, Elie
b. Stephens, James
b. Stuart, Bruce
b. Znaniecki, Florian
d. Bellows, Henry Whitney
d. Green, Thomas Hill
d. Jevons, William Stanley
d. Phillips, Charles
d. Stroh, Bernard

January 3, 1882
d. Ainsworth, W(illiam) H(arrison)

January 4, 1882
d. Draper, John William

January 5, 1882
b. Swope, Herbert Bayard

January 6, 1882
b. Pecora, Ferdinand
b. Rayburn, Sam(uel Taliaferro)
d. Dana, Richard Henry, Jr.

January 8, 1882
b. Milne, David Brown

January 10, 1882
b. Sills, Milton

January 11, 1882
d. Schwann, Theodor

January 14, 1882
b. Van Loon, Hendrik Willem
d. O'Sullivan, Timothy H

January 16, 1882
b. Wilson, Margaret

January 18, 1882
b. Milne, A(lan) A(lexander)

January 24, 1882
b. Babcock, Harold Delos
b. Rothstein, Arnold

January 25, 1882
b. Woolf, Virginia

January 27, 1882
b. Pew, J(ohn) Howard

January 28, 1882
b. Hobart, Alice Tisdale Nourse

January 30, 1882
b. Roosevelt, Franklin D(elano)
b. Torrio, Johnny

February 1, 1882
b. St. Laurent, Louis Stephen
b. Saint Laurent, Louis Stephen
b. Tobias, Channing Heggie

February 2, 1882
b. Joyce, James Augustus Aloysius

February 3, 1882
b. Bailey, Frederick Marshman

February 5, 1882
b. Lattuada, Felice

February 8, 1882
b. Selfridge, Thomas Etholen

February 13, 1882
d. Garnet, Henry Highland
d. Stephens, Uriah

February 14, 1882
b. Nathan, George Jean

February 15, 1882
b. Barrymore, John

February 19, 1882
d. Ryerson, Adolphus Egerton

February 22, 1882
b. Gill, Eric

February 23, 1882
b. Fischer, Anton Otto
b. Traven, B.

February 26, 1882
b. Kimmel, Husband Edward

February 27, 1882
b. Stevens, Emily A
b. Vasconcelos (Calderon), Jose
b. Wheeler, Burton Kendall

February 28, 1882
b. Farrar, Geraldine
b. Schlick, Friedrich Albert Moritz

March 3, 1882
b. Ludikar, Pavel

March 4, 1882
b. Titulescu, Nicolae

March 5, 1882
b. VanAlstyne, Egbert Anson

March 6, 1882
b. Kibbee, Guy

March 10, 1882
d. Thomson, Charles Wyville, Sir

March 18, 1882
b. Malipiero, Gian Francesco
d. Earp, Morgan

March 19, 1882
b. Lachaise, Gaston

March 20, 1882
b. Coty, Rene (Jules Gustave)

March 21, 1882
b. Anderson, Gilbert M

March 23, 1882
b. Noether, (Amalie) Emmy

March 24, 1882
b. Marinuzzi, Giuseppe (Gino)
d. Longfellow, Henry Wadsworth
d. Thompson, William Tappan

March 30, 1882
b. Klein, Melanie
d. Griffiths, John Willis

March 31, 1882
b. Chukovsky, Korney Ivanovich

April 3, 1882
d. James, Jesse Woodson

April 5, 1882
b. Hall, Joe
b. Sung Chiao-jen
d. Le Play, Guillaume Frederic
d. Pierce, John Davis

April 6, 1882
b. Schneiderman, Rose

April 7, 1882
b. Schleicher, Kurt von

April 9, 1882
d. Rossetti, Dante Gabriel

April 10, 1882
b. Perkins, Frances

April 17, 1882
b. MacIver, Robert Morrison
b. Schnabel, Artur

April 18, 1882
b. Stokowski, Leopold (Anton
Stanislaw Boleslawawicz)

April 19, 1882
d. Darwin, Charles Robert

April 20, 1882
b. Smith, Holland McTeire

April 21, 1882
b. Bridgman, Percy Williams

April 22, 1882
b. Brawley, Benjamin Griffith
b. Dowding, Hugh Caswell
Tremenheere, Baron

April 23, 1882
b. Coates, Albert

April 24, 1882
b. Maude, Cyril
b. Sarg, Tony

April 25, 1882
b. McLeod, Fred(erick)

April 27, 1882
b. Fauset, Jessie Redmon
d. Emerson, Ralph Waldo

May 3, 1882
b. Dale, Chester

May 4, 1882
d. Wood, James Rushmore

May 5, 1882
b. Mawson, Douglas, Sir
b. Pankhurst, Sylvia

May 9, 1882
b. Kaiser, Henry John

May 13, 1882
b. Braque, Georges

May 16, 1882
b. Hayes, Carlton Joseph Huntley
b. Reid, Ogden Mills

May 17, 1882
b. Lehman, Adele Lewisohn

May 20, 1882
b. Undset, Sigrid

May 24, 1882
b. Oppenheim, James

May 28, 1882
b. Hopwood, Avery

May 30, 1882
b. Lewisohn, Ludwig

June 1, 1882
b. Drinkwater, John

June 2, 1882
d. Garibaldi, Giuseppe

June 3, 1882
d. Thomson, James

June 5, 1882
b. Nelson, Battling

June 15, 1882
b. Antonescu, Ion

June 17, 1882
b. Herne, Chrystal Katharine
b. Stravinsky, Igor Fedorovich

June 18, 1882
b. Dimitrov, Georgi Mikhailovich

June 19, 1882
b. Stein, Clarence S

June 21, 1882
b. Kent, Rockwell

June 22, 1882
b. Bercovici, Konrad
b. Scholl, William M

June 29, 1882
d. Hansom, Joseph Aloysius

June 30, 1882
d. Guiteau, Charles Julius

July 1, 1882
b. Glaspell, Susan Keating

July 8, 1882
b. Grainger, Percy Aldridge
d. Browne, Phiz

July 10, 1882
b. Hogg, Ima

July 12, 1882
b. Browning, Tod

July 14, 1882
d. Ringo, John(ny)

July 16, 1882
b. Hearst, Millicent Veronica Willson
d. Lincoln, Mary Todd

July 18, 1882
b. Hagedorn, Hermann

July 22, 1882
b. Hopper, Edward

July 24, 1882
b. Thorndike, Lynn

July 27, 1882
b. DeHavilland, Geoffrey, Sir

July 31, 1882
b. Ives, Herbert Eugene

August 5, 1882
b. Johnson, Hugh Samuel

August 8, 1882
b. Samaroff, Olga

August 9, 1882
b. Guion, Connie Myers

August 11, 1882
b. Graziani, Rodolfo
b. Kallen, Horace M(eyer)

August 12, 1882
b. Bellows, George Wesley
b. Bendix, Vincent

August 13, 1882
b. Mercer, Beryl

August 16, 1882
d. Hill, Benjamin Harvey

August 17, 1882
b. Kearns, Jack

August 19, 1882
b. Chanel, Coco

August 24, 1882
b. Pogany, Willy

August 26, 1882
b. Franck, James

August 27, 1882
b. Goldwyn, Samuel

September 4, 1882
b. Knerr, H(arold) H

September 6, 1882
b. Marks, Charles

September 9, 1882
b. McCarthy, Clem

September 14, 1882
d. Pusey, Edward Bouverie

September 22, 1882
b. Keitel, Wilhelm

September 23, 1882
b. Evans, Herbert McLean
d. Wohler, Friedrich

September 30, 1882
b. Bancroft, George
b. Geiger, Hans

October 3, 1882
b. Jackson, A(lexander) Y(oung)

October 5, 1882
b. Dresser, Louise
b. Goddard, Robert Hutchings

October 6, 1882
b. Szymanowski, Karol Maciej

October 10, 1882
b. Traphagen, Ethel Leigh

October 11, 1882
b. Dett, Robert Nathaniel

October 13, 1882
d. Gobineau, Joseph Arthur, Comte de

October 14, 1882
b. DeValera, Eamon

October 16, 1882
b. Buttenheim, Edgar Joseph

October 18, 1882
b. Burt, Maxwell Struthers

October 19, 1882
b. Boccioni, Umberto

October 20, 1882
b. Lugosi, Bela

October 22, 1882
b. Dulac, Edmund
b. Guggenheimer, Minnie
b. Wyeth, N(ewell) C(onvers)

October 24, 1882
b. Thorndike, Sybil, Dame

October 27, 1882
b. Rogers, Mary Joseph(ine)

October 29, 1882
b. Giraudoux, Jean
b. Martinez, Maximiliano Hernandez

October 30, 1882
b. Halsey, William Frederick, Jr.

November 6, 1882
b. Ince, Thomas H(arper)
b. Wallerstein, Lothar

November 10, 1882
b. Dewey, Charles Schuveldt

November 11, 1882
b. Gustaf Adolf VI

November 13, 1882
b. Bartlett, Francis Alonzo

November 15, 1882
b. Frankfurter, Felix

November 18, 1882
b. Galli-Curci, Amelita
b. Maritain, Jacques

November 22, 1882
d. Weed, Thurlow

November 23, 1882
b. Reid, Helen Rogers

November 26, 1882
d. LeClear, Thomas

December 4, 1882
b. Reulbach, Ed(ward Marvin)

December 6, 1882
d. Blanc, Louis
d. Trollope, Anthony

December 10, 1882
b. Neurath, Otto

December 11, 1882
b. Born, Max
b. La Guardia, Fiorello Henry

December 12, 1882
d. Gardner, Alexander

December 14, 1882
b. Christie, John

December 16, 1882
b. Kodaly, Zoltan

December 18, 1882
d. James, Henry, Sr.

December 19, 1882
b. Huberman, Bronislaw

December 27, 1882
b. Hidalgo, Elvira de

December 28, 1882
b. Eddington, Arthur Stanley, Sir

December 31, 1882
b. Jones, Benjamin Allyn
d. Gambetta, Leon

1883

b. Blackburn, Jack
b. Clarke, Edith
b. Hare, Ernie
b. Jantzen, Carl
b. Kamenev, Lev Borisovich
b. McCullough, Paul
b. Metzinger, Jean
b. Ricci, Nina
b. Schutzendorf, Gustav
b. Sparks, Ned
b. Wang Ching-wei
b. Yen Hsi-shan
b. Zaleski, August
d. Calvert, Edward
d. Dayananda Saraswati, Swami
b. Ayres, Ruby Mildred

January 1, 1883
b. Clark, Charles Badger
b. Donovan, William Joseph
b. Hatoyama Ichiro
b. Howard, Roy Wilson

January 3, 1883
b. Adler, David
b. Attlee, Clement Richard Attlee, Earl

January 4, 1883
b. Eastman, Max Forrester

January 6, 1883
b. Gibran, Kahlil

January 7, 1883
b. Cunningham, Andrew Browne,
Viscount

January 8, 1883
b. Hurley, Patrick Jay

January 10, 1883
b. Bushman, Francis X(avier)
b. Tolstoy, Alexey Nikolaevich
d. Mudd, Samuel Alexander

January 17, 1883
b. Mackenzie, Compton

January 20, 1883
b. Wrather, William Embry

January 21, 1883
b. Hackett, Francis

January 23, 1883
d. Beard, George Miller
d. Dore, Gustave

January 24, 1883
b. Winwood, Estelle
d. Flotow, Friedrich von, Baron

January 27, 1883
b. Toye, Francis

February 2, 1883
b. McCulley, Johnston
b. Sakall, S Z
b. Smith, Howard Worth

February 3, 1883
b. Mulford, Clarence Edward

February 4, 1883
b. Pratt, Edwin John

February 7, 1883
b. Blake, Eubie

February 8, 1883
b. Schumpeter, Joseph Alois

February 9, 1883
b. Carter, John Garnet

February 11, 1883
b. Klenau, Paul von

February 13, 1883
d. Wagner, Richard

February 15, 1883
b. Rohmer, Sax

February 23, 1883
b. Fleming, Victor
b. Jaspers, Karl

February 25, 1883
b. Alice

March 4, 1883
d. Stephens, Alexander Hamilton

March 7, 1883
d. Green, John Richard

March 8, 1883
b. Starch, Daniel

March 10, 1883
b. Barrientos, Maria

March 13, 1883
b. Holland, Clifford Milburn

March 14, 1883
d. Marx, Karl Heinrich

March 15, 1883
b. Bernhard, Lucian

March 19, 1883
b. Graham, Evarts Ambrose
b. Haworth, Walter Norman, Sir
b. Stilwell, Joseph Warren

March 20, 1883
b. Funk, Wilfred John
b. Ridder, Bernard Herman

March 23, 1883
b. Burt, Cyril Lodowic, Sir

March 30, 1883
b. Davidson, Jo

April 1, 1883
b. Chaney, Lon

April 2, 1883
b. Radin, Paul

April 4, 1883
d. Cooper, Peter

April 5, 1883
b. Speicher, Eugene Edward

April 7, 1883
b. Severini, Gino

April 9, 1883
b. King, Frank

April 12, 1883
b. Cunningham, Imogen
b. Lewis, Clarence Irving

April 15, 1883
b. Bruce of Melbourne, 1st Viscount

April 19, 1883
b. Vargas, Getulio Dornelles

April 20, 1883
b. Sloane, John
d. Manet, Edouard

April 25, 1883
b. Ford, Russ(ell William)

April 30, 1883
b. Hasek, Jaroslav

May 5, 1883
b. Wavell, Archibald Percival Wavell,
Earl

May 7, 1883
b. Berry, James Gomer

May 9, 1883
b. Ortega y Gasset, Jose

May 13, 1883
b. Papanicolaou, George Nicholas

May 14, 1883
b. Eltinge, Julian

May 15, 1883
d. Gorgas, Josiah
d. Henson, Josiah

May 17, 1883
d. Pinkham, Lydia Estes

May 18, 1883
b. Gropius, Walter Adolf

May 20, 1883
b. Faisal, I

May 23, 1883
b. Fairbanks, Douglas

May 24, 1883
b. Maxwell, Elsa

May 25, 1883
d. Laboulaye, Edouard Rose

May 26, 1883
d. Abd el-Kadir

May 28, 1883
b. Zandonai, Riccardo

May 29, 1883
b. Dafoe, Allan Roy

May 31, 1883
b. Alda, Frances

June 5, 1883
b. Keynes, John Maynard, Baron

June 9, 1883
b. Fosdick, Raymond Blaine

June 12, 1883
b. Lowie, Robert Harry

June 14, 1883
d. FitzGerald, Edward

June 17, 1883
b. Gordon, C Henry

June 23, 1883
b. Taylor, Cyclone

June 24, 1883
b. Hess, Victor Francis

June 28, 1883
b. Laval, Pierre
b. Moran, Polly

June 30, 1883
b. Wachter, Ed(ward)

July 2, 1883
b. Kafka, Franz

July 4, 1883
b. Goldberg, Rube

July 6, 1883
b. Morgan, Ralph

July 7, 1883
b. Adams, Frank Ramsay

July 10, 1883
b. Flick, Friedrich

July 15, 1883
d. Tom Thumb, General

July 16, 1883
b. Sheeler, Charles

July 17, 1883
b. Lazare, Kaplan
b. Stiller, Mauritz

July 18, 1883
b. Chiang K'ang-Hu

July 19, 1883
b. Fleischer, Max

July 20, 1883
d. Iwakura, Tomomi

July 22, 1883
d. McDowell, Katharine Sherwood
Bonner
d. Ord, Edward Otho Cresap

July 23, 1883
b. Alanbrooke, Alan Francis Brooke,
1st Viscount
d. Dugdale, Richard Louis

July 27, 1883
d. Blair, Montgomery

July 29, 1883
b. Mussolini, Benito Amilcare Andrea

July 31, 1883
b. Heckel, Erich

August 2, 1883
b. Black, Samuel Duncan

August 6, 1883
b. Bolton, Isabel
b. Nearing, Scott

August 9, 1883
b. Lampkin, Daisy

August 14, 1883
b. Just, Ernest Everett

August 15, 1883
b. Mestrovic, Ivan

August 23, 1883
b. Wainwright, Jonathan Mayhew
b. Zinoviev, Grigori Evseevich

September 3, 1883
b. Arnold, Harold De Forest
d. Turgenev, Ivan Sergeevich

September 5, 1883
b. Petri, Angelo

September 11, 1883
b. Miller, Olive Beaupre

September 13, 1883
b. Lawes, Lewis Edward

September 14, 1883
b. Sanger, Margaret

September 16, 1883
b. Hulme, Thomas Ernest

September 17, 1883
b. Williams, William Carlos

September 18, 1883
b. Maytag, Elmer Henry

September 30, 1883
b. Doesburg, Theo van

October 8, 1883
b. Warburg, Otto Heinrich

October 11, 1883
b. Stiedry, Fritz

October 15, 1883
b. Ghormley, Robert Lee

October 17, 1883
b. Neill, A(lexander) S(utherland)

October 21, 1883
b. Russell, Ernie

October 29, 1883
b. Woodcock, Amos Walter Wright

October 30, 1883
b. Jones, Bob

October 31, 1883
b. Allgood, Sara

November 2, 1883
b. Ames, Jessie Daniel
b. Flavin, Martin Archer

November 6, 1883
b. Brophy, John

November 8, 1883
b. Bax, Arnold Edward Trevor, Sir
b. Demuth, Charles

November 9, 1883
b. Oliver, Edna May

November 10, 1883
b. Ficke, Arthur Davidson

November 11, 1883
b. Ansermet, Ernest Alexandre

November 13, 1883
d. Sims, James Marion

November 15, 1883
b. Rawlinson, Herbert

November 18, 1883
b. Vinson, Carl
d. Siemens, William, Sir

November 23, 1883
b. Orozco, Jose Clemente

November 24, 1883
b. Hooper, Tom

November 26, 1883
d. Truth, Sojourner

November 29, 1883
b. Hunter, Dard

December 2, 1883
b. Kazantzakis, Nikos

December 3, 1883
b. Webern, Anton Friedrich Ernst von

December 4, 1883
b. Bellison, Simeon

December 6, 1883
b. Braniff, Thomas Elmer

December 10, 1883
b. Kreymborg, Alfred
b. Vyshinsky, Andrei Yanuarievich

December 11, 1883
d. Doyle, Richard
d. Mario, Giovanni Matteo

December 12, 1883
b. Sterrett, Cliff

December 13, 1883
b. Greene, Belle da Costa

December 15, 1883
b. Hinton, William Augustus
b. Kemp, Harry (Hibbard)

December 17, 1883
b. Raimu

December 18, 1883
b. Teague, Walter Dorwin

December 19, 1883
d. DeSanctis, Francesco

December 22, 1883
b. Varese, Edgar

December 25, 1883
b. Utrillo, Maurice

December 27, 1883
b. Eaton, Cyrus Stephen

December 30, 1883
b. Patrick, Lester B

1884

b. Ahmed Hasim
b. Brady, St. Elmo
b. Clark, John Maurice
b. Graham, Stephen
b. Halide Edip Adivar
b. Kennedy, Tom
b. Mountain Wolf Woman
b. Pitre, Didier
d. Cetshwayo
d. Dumas, Jean Baptiste Andre

January 1, 1884
b. Jones, Eli Stanley
b. Seymour, Charles

January 2, 1884
b. Micheaux, Oscar

January 3, 1884
b. Hull, Josephine

January 4, 1884
b. DuBois, Guy Pene

January 6, 1884
d. Mendel, Gregor Johann

January 7, 1884
b. Giovannitti, Arturo

January 11, 1884
b. Fitch, Aubrey

January 12, 1884
b. Horst, Louis

January 13, 1884
b. Hathaway, Sibyl Collings
b. Tucker, Sophie

January 14, 1884
b. Wroth, Lawrence Counselman

January 16, 1884
b. Decker, Alonzo G

January 17, 1884
b. Beery, Noah
b. Sennett, Mack

January 18, 1884
b. Ransome, Arthur Mitchell

January 19, 1884
b. Wolff, Albert Louis

January 20, 1884
b. Merritt, Abraham

January 21, 1884
b. Baldwin, Roger Nash

January 23, 1884
b. De Palma, Ralph
b. McManus, George

January 25, 1884
b. Kilenyi, Edward, Sr.

January 26, 1884
b. Andrews, Roy Chapman
b. Sapir, Edward
d. Letcher, John

January 28, 1884
b. Piccard, Auguste
b. Piccard, Jean Felix

February 2, 1884
d. Matteson, Tompkins Harrison
d. Phillips, Wendell

February 3, 1884
b. Andrews, Frank M(axwell)

February 8, 1884
d. Guyot, Arnold Henry

February 10, 1884
b. Evans, Billy

February 12, 1884
b. Beckmann, Max
b. Longworth, Alice Roosevelt

February 14, 1884
d. Roosevelt, Alice Lee

February 15, 1884
b. Gilbert, A(lfred) C(arleton)

February 16, 1884
b. Flaherty, Robert Joseph
b. Kalmar, Bert

February 17, 1884
b. Smith, Joe

February 18, 1884
b. Laidler, Harry Wellington
b. McIntyre, O(scar) O(dd)

February 22, 1884
b. Attell, Abe B

February 23, 1884
b. Funk, Casimir

February 24, 1884
b. Bustamante, William Alexander
Clarke, Sir

March 3, 1884
b. Fox, Fontaine Talbot, Jr.

March 13, 1884
b. Walpole, Hugh Seymour, Sir

March 17, 1884
b. Buck, Frank

March 21, 1884
b. Birkhoff, George David
d. Baez, Buenaventura
d. Fuller, George

March 22, 1884
b. Vandenberg, Arthur Hendrick

March 23, 1884
b. Allen, Florence Ellinwood

March 24, 1884
b. Debye, Peter Joseph William

March 26, 1884
b. Backhaus, Wilhelm

March 28, 1884
b. Sikelianos, Angelos

April 2, 1884
b. Courboin, Charles
b. Hoagland, Dennis Robert

April 4, 1884
b. Yamamoto, Isoroku

April 6, 1884
b. Huston, Walter

April 7, 1884
b. Dodd, Charles Harold
b. Malinowski, Bronislaw Kasper

April 11, 1884
d. Reade, Charles

April 12, 1884
b. Meyerhof, Otto Fritz

April 15, 1884
b. Lloyd, John Henry

April 21, 1884
b. Frankau, Gilbert
b. Liebling, Estelle

April 22, 1884
b. Enskog, David
b. Rank, Otto

April 24, 1884
d. Taglioni, Maria

April 26, 1884
b. Norena, Eide

May 1, 1884
b. Quimby, Harriet

May 4, 1884
b. Collier, John

May 5, 1884
b. Bender, Chief

May 6, 1884
d. Gross, Samuel Daniel

May 8, 1884
b. Truman, Harry S
d. Benjamin, Judah Philip

May 11, 1884
b. Gluck, Alma

May 12, 1884
d. Smetana, Bedrich

May 13, 1884
d. McCormick, Cyrus Hall

May 14, 1884
b. Dornier, Claude

May 24, 1884
b. Hull, Clark Leonard
b. Odum, Howard Washington

May 25, 1884
b. Duranty, Walter

May 26, 1884
b. Winninger, Charles

May 27, 1884
b. Brod, Max

May 28, 1884
b. Benes, Eduard

May 29, 1884
d. Frere, Henry Bartle Edward

May 31, 1884
b. Bottome, Phyllis

June 7, 1884
d. Hoffman, Charles Fenno

June 8, 1884
d. Swayne, Noah Haynes

June 13, 1884
b. Crohn, Burrill Bernard
b. Gilson, Etienne Henry

June 14, 1884
b. McCormack, John

June 15, 1884
b. Langdon, Harry

June 18, 1884
b. Daladier, Edouard

b. Reynolds, Robert Rice
d. Alberdi, Juan Bautista

June 21, 1884
b. Auchinleck, Claude, Sir

June 30, 1884
b. Duhamel, Georges

July 1, 1884
d. Pinkerton, Allan

July 3, 1884
b. Miller, Gilbert Heron

July 4, 1884
b. Trendle, George Washington

July 5, 1884
d. Masse, Victor

July 6, 1884
b. Dunoyer de Segonzac, Andre
b. Vanderbilt, Harold Stirling

July 7, 1884
b. Feuchtwanger, Lion

July 10, 1884
b. Wood, Samuel Grosvenor
d. Morphy, Paul Charles

July 12, 1884
b. Modigliani, Amedeo

July 14, 1884
b. Cecchi, Emilio

July 15, 1884
b. Myers, Garry Cleveland

July 19, 1884
d. Sloan, Samuel

July 22, 1884
b. Adler, Elmer
b. Alvarez, Walter Clement
b. Shepard, Odell

July 23, 1884
b. Krauss, Werner
b. Warner, Albert

July 25, 1884
b. Black, Davidson

July 29, 1884
b. Tietjens, Eunice

July 31, 1884
b. Goerdeler, Karl Friedrich

August 2, 1884
b. Gallegos, Romulo
b. Larsen-Todsen, Nanny

August 3, 1884
b. Gruenberg, Louis

August 8, 1884
b. Teasdale, Sara

August 9, 1884
d. Elliott, Robert Brown

August 12, 1884
b. Swinnerton, Frank Arthur

August 13, 1884
b. Powys, Llewelyn

August 16, 1884
b. Gernsback, Hugo

August 19, 1884
b. Wieman, Henry Nelson

August 20, 1884
b. Bultmann, Rudolf

August 23, 1884
b. Cuppy, Will(iam Jacob)
b. Mills, Ogden Livingston

August 24, 1884
b. Melford, Austin

August 25, 1884
b. Auriol, Vincent

August 26, 1884
b. Biggers, Earl Derr

August 27, 1884
b. Arbuthnot, May Hill

August 28, 1884
b. Fraser, Peter

August 30, 1884
b. Svedberg, Theodor H E

August 31, 1884
b. Cates, Clifton Bledsoe
b. Sarton, George
b. Scott, Austin Wakeman

September 10, 1884
d. Bentham, George

September 14, 1884
b. Pile, Frederick Alfred

September 17, 1884
b. Griffes, Charles Tomlinson

September 20, 1884
b. Brightman, Edgar Sheffield
b. Perkins, Maxwell Evarts
b. Perkins, William Maxwell Evarts

September 21, 1884
b. Andrus, Ethel Percy
b. Price, Irving L
b. Ray, Shorty

September 23, 1884
b. Chaffee, Adna Romanza
b. Talmadge, Eugene

September 24, 1884
b. Inonu, Ismet

September 26, 1884
d. Garrett, John Work

September 27, 1884
b. Zirato, Bruno
d. Mutesa I

October 4, 1884
b. Runyon, Damon

October 8, 1884
b. Agus Salim, Hadji

October 9, 1884
b. Deutsch, Helene R(osenbach)
b. Johnson, Martin Elmer

October 11, 1884
b. Bergius, Friedrich Karl Rudolph
b. Roosevelt, Eleanor
b. Rumann, Sig(fried)

October 20, 1884
b. Senanayake, Don Stephen

October 21, 1884
b. Beecher, Janet

October 22, 1884
b. Hill, George Washington

October 25, 1884
b. Easton, Florence Gertrude

October 30, 1884
b. Lea, Fanny Heaslip

November 3, 1884
b. Martin, Joseph William, Jr.

November 4, 1884
b. Douglas, Robert L
b. Ferguson, Harry George

November 6, 1884
d. Brown, William Wells
d. Fawcett, Henry

November 7, 1884
b. Patterson, Eleanor Medill

November 8, 1884
b. Rorschach, Hermann

November 18, 1884
b. Lewis, Wyndham

November 20, 1884
b. Thomas, Norman Mattoon

November 23, 1884
b. Bolton, Guy Reginald

November 25, 1884
b. Cadogan, Alexander George
  Montague, Sir

November 27, 1884
b. DeCreeft, Jose
d. Elssler, Fanny

November 30, 1884
b. Poling, Daniel A

December 1, 1884
b. Schmidt-Rottluf, Karl

December 2, 1884
b. Draper, Ruth

December 3, 1884
b. Prasad, Rajendra

December 6, 1884
b. Kroll, Leon

December 14, 1884
b. Cowl, Jane

December 16, 1884
b. Bobst, Elmer Holmes

December 17, 1884
b. Peirce, Waldo
b. Uttley, Alice Jane Taylor

December 19, 1884
b. Unwin, Stanley, Sir

December 20, 1884
b. Mennen, William Gerhard

December 23, 1884
d. Chisum, John Simpson

December 30, 1884
b. Tojo, Hideki

December 31, 1884
b. Arden, Elizabeth
b. Reed, Stanley Forman
b. Viereck, George Sylvester

1885

b. Fyffe, Will
b. Hsiung Shih-Li
b. Laurens, Henri
b. Matchabelli, Georges, Prince
b. Matteotti, Giacomo
b. Moore, Tom
b. Mourning Dove
b. Philby, Harold St. John Bridger
b. Radek, Karl Bernhardovich
b. Revel, Bernard
b. Sale, Charles Partlow
b. Winslow, Ola Elizabeth
b. Yezierska, Anzia
d. Brown, Benjamin Gratz
d. Ram Singh

January 8, 1885
b. Curtin, John Joseph
b. Muste, A(braham) J(ohannes)

January 10, 1885
b. Gifford, Walter Sherman

January 11, 1885
b. Paul, Alice

January 12, 1885
b. Fuess, Claude Moore

January 13, 1885
b. Fuller, Alfred Carl
d. Colfax, Schuyler

January 15, 1885
b. Burr, Henry
b. DeLaRoche, Mazo

January 16, 1885
b. Chou Tso-Jen
d. About, Edmond-Francois-Valentin

January 17, 1885
b. Kern, Jerome David
d. Burnaby, Frederick Gustavus

January 21, 1885
b. Grant, Duncan (James Corrowr)
b. Leadbelly
b. Nobile, Umberto

January 22, 1885
b. Doherty, Robert Ernest

January 24, 1885
b. Biddle, George
d. Delany, Martin Robinson

January 26, 1885
d. Gordon, Charles George

January 30, 1885
b. Towers, John Henry

January 31, 1885
b. Pavlova, Anna

February 1, 1885
b. Chautemps, Camille
d. Thomas, Sidney Gilchrist

February 2, 1885
b. Frunze, Mikhail Vasilievich
d. Phelps, John Wolcott

February 7, 1885
b. Lewis, Sinclair

February 9, 1885
b. Berg, Alban

February 12, 1885
b. Streicher, Julius

February 13, 1885
b. Truman, Bess

February 14, 1885
d. Hotchkiss, Benjamin Berkeley

February 15, 1885
d. Damrosch, Leopold

February 17, 1885
b. Guardini, Romano

February 21, 1885
b. Guitry, Sacha

February 24, 1885
b. Lytell, Bert
b. Nimitz, Chester William

March 1, 1885
b. Atwill, Lionel

March 4, 1885
b. Foyle, William Alfred

March 6, 1885
b. Lardner, Ring(gold Wilmer), Sr.

March 9, 1885
b. Karsavina, Tamara (Platonova)

March 11, 1885
b. Campbell, Malcolm, Sir

March 13, 1885
d. Peale, Titian Ramsay

March 16, 1885
b. Holloway, Emory

March 17, 1885
b. Chaplin, Sydney Dryden
d. Warner, Susan Bogert

March 21, 1885
b. Gilmour, Billy
b. Pulitzer, Joseph, II

March 29, 1885
b. Bolton, Frances Payne

April 1, 1885
b. Beery, Wallace Fitzgerald
b. Churchill, Clementine Ogilvy
(Hozier) Spencer, Baroness
b. Lilly, Eli

April 2, 1885
d. Barrios, Justo Rufino

April 3, 1885
b. Dwan, Allan
b. Fisher, Bud

April 8, 1885
d. Moodie, Susanna
d. White, Richard Grant

April 10, 1885
b. Gimbel, Bernard Feustman
b. Spaeth, Sigmund Gottfried

April 12, 1885
b. Delaunay, Robert
b. Kuykendall, Ralph Simpson

April 13, 1885
b. Lukacs, Gyorgy

April 14, 1885
b. Janncy, Russell Dixon
b. Ochs, Adolph Shelby, II
d. King, Richard

April 17, 1885
b. Blixen, Karen Christentze, Baroness

April 29, 1885
b. Riegger, Wallingford
b. Young, Andrew

April 30, 1885
b. Sayre, Francis Bowes

May 4, 1885
d. McDowell, Irvin

May 7, 1885
b. Hayes, Gabby

May 8, 1885
b. Costain, Thomas Bertram

May 11, 1885
b. Oliver, Joe

May 12, 1885
b. Sironi, Mario

May 13, 1885
d. Ewing, Julianna Horatia (Gatty)

May 14, 1885
b. Klemperer, Otto

May 15, 1885
b. Daubert, Jake

May 16, 1885
b. Pool, David de Sola

May 17, 1885
b. Stakman, Elvin Charles

May 18, 1885
b. Dutra, Eurico Gaspar

May 22, 1885
d. Hugo, Victor Marie

May 26, 1885
b. DeCuevas, Marquis

May 30, 1885
d. Jacobsen, Jens Peter

June 5, 1885
b. Mandel, Georges

June 6, 1885
b. Coanda, Henri Marie
b. Walker, A'lelia

June 13, 1885
b. Igoe, Hype
b. Schumann, Elisabeth

June 16, 1885
b. Howard, Tom

June 22, 1885
d. Mahdi, Mohammed Ahmed

June 24, 1885
b. Tairov, Aleksandr Yakovlevich

June 26, 1885
b. Hempel, Frieda

June 27, 1885
b. Lismer, Arthur

July 4, 1885
b. Mayer, L(ouis) B(urt)

July 7, 1885
b. Bloch, Ernst

July 8, 1885
b. Brinkley, John Romulus

July 10, 1885
b. O'Hara, Mary

July 19, 1885
b. Muir, Malcolm

July 21, 1885
b. Keyes, Frances Parkinson

July 23, 1885
d. Grant, Ulysses Simpson

July 26, 1885
b. Maurois, Andre

July 28, 1885
d. Montefiore, Moses Haim, Sir

August 1, 1885
b. Hevesy, George Charles von

August 12, 1885
b. Frederick, Pauline
d. Jackson, Helen Maria Hunt Fiske

August 15, 1885
b. Burton, Montague Maurice, Sir

August 17, 1885
b. Fleischmann, Raoul H(erbert)

August 19, 1885
b. Ferguson, Elsie

August 20, 1885
b. Campana, Dino

August 23, 1885
b. Tizard, Henry Thomas, Sir

August 26, 1885
b. Romains, Jules

August 27, 1885
b. Pabst, Georg Wilhelm

August 31, 1885
b. Heyward, (Edwin) DuBose
b. Ohrbach, Nathan M

September 5, 1885
b. Defauw, Desire
b. Wylie, Elinor Hoyt
d. Tso Tsung-t'ang

September 6, 1885
b. Kruger, Otto

September 9, 1885
b. Sheridan, Clare Consuelo

September 10, 1885
b. Van Doren, Carl Clinton

September 11, 1885
b. Lawrence, D(avid) H(erbert)

September 13, 1885
b. Ribeiro, Aquilino Gomez

September 14, 1885
b. Gui, Vittorio
b. Hilberseimer, Ludwig Karl

September 16, 1885
b. Horney, Karen Danielson

September 20, 1885
b. Morton, Jelly Roll

September 21, 1885
b. Webster, H(arold) T(ucker)

September 22, 1885
b. Asplund, Erik Gunnar
b. Chifley, Joseph Benedict
b. VonStroheim, Erich

September 23, 1885
d. Spitzweg, Carl

September 27, 1885
b. Blackstone, Harry
b. Smith, Tommy
b. Dasgupta, S(urendra) N(ath)

October 1, 1885
b. Untermeyer, Louis
d. Cooper, Anthony Ashley, 7th Earl of Shaftesbury

October 2, 1885
b. Rohde, Ruth Bryan Owen

October 5, 1885
d. Durant, Thomas Clark

October 7, 1885
b. Bohr, Niels Henrik David

October 10, 1885
b. Britton, Jack
d. McCloskey, John

October 11, 1885
b. Mauriac, Francois
b. Sherman, Lowell

October 13, 1885
b. Hershfield, Harry

October 14, 1885
d. Billings, Josh

October 19, 1885
b. Merrill, Charles Edward

October 21, 1885
b. Wellesz, Egon

October 22, 1885
b. Martinelli, Giovanni

October 23, 1885
b. Harris, Lauren

October 27, 1885
b. Lehman, Hughie

October 29, 1885
b. Kidder, Alfred Vincent
d. McClellan, George Brinton

October 30, 1885
b. Pound, Ezra Loomis

October 31, 1885
b. Laurencin, Marie

November 1, 1885
b. Cherrington, Ben Mark

November 2, 1885
b. Aldrich, Winthrop Williams
b. Shapley, Harlow T

November 4, 1885
b. Covici, Pascal

November 5, 1885
b. Durant, Will(iam James)

November 7, 1885
b. Crawford, Rusty
b. Knight, Frank Hyneman

November 8, 1885
b. Yamashita, Tomoyuki

November 11, 1885
b. Patton, George Smith, Jr.

November 14, 1885
b. Delaunay-Terk, Sonia
b. Rourke, Constance Mayfield

November 15, 1885
b. Page, Frederick Handley, Sir

November 16, 1885
d. Riel, Louis David, Jr.

November 18, 1885
b. Allen, Forrest Claire

November 19, 1885
b. Crommelynck, Fernand

November 20, 1885
b. Kesselring, Albert

November 21, 1885
d. Wright, Elizur

November 24, 1885
b. Strong, Anna Louise

November 25, 1885
d. Hendricks, Thomas Andrews

December 1, 1885
b. Hunt, Frazier

December 2, 1885
b. Minot, George Richards

December 3, 1885
b. Lasker, Edward

December 4, 1885
b. Magnin, Grover Arnold

December 8, 1885
b. Roberts, Kenneth Lewis
d. Vanderbilt, William Henry

December 14, 1885
b. Pemberton, Brock

December 15, 1885
d. Toombs, Robert Augustus

December 21, 1885
b. Patrick, Frank A

December 22, 1885
b. Taylor, (Joseph) Deems

December 23, 1885
b. Sardi, Vincent, Sr.

December 25, 1885
b. Manship, Paul
b. Nesbit, Evelyn

December 26, 1885
b. Eboue, Adolphe Felix Sylvestre

December 28, 1885
b. Allen, Arthur Augustus
b. Tatlin, Vladimir Yevgrapovich

December 31, 1885
b. Leslie, Edgar

1886

b. Baer, Bugs
b. Benn, Gottfried
b. Carr-Saunders, Alexander Morris
b. Cherwell, Frederick Alexander L, Viscount
b. Johnson, Moose
b. Roberts, Elizabeth Madox
b. Russell, Morgan
b. Tuthill, Harry J
d. Bacardi, Don Facundo

January 2, 1886
b. Lawrence, Florence

January 3, 1886
b. Fletcher, John Gould

January 5, 1886
d. Lippincott, Joshua Ballinger

January 9, 1886
b. Brooks, Walter R(ollin)
b. Guthrie, Edwin Ray

b. Holt, Ivan Lee
b. Rosenthal, Ida Cohen

January 11, 1886
b. Zucco, George

January 13, 1886
b. Druzhinin, Nicolai Mikhailovich
b. Ross, Art(hur Howie)

January 14, 1886
b. Lofting, Hugh

January 15, 1886
b. Howe, Clarence Decatur
b. Newell, Edward Theodore

January 16, 1886
d. Ponchielli, Amilcare

January 17, 1886
b. Firbank, Ronald
b. Martin, Glenn Luther
b. Rugg, Harold

January 18, 1886
b. Pevsner, Antoine
d. Tichatschek, Joseph

January 19, 1886
b. Davenport, Harry George Bryant

January 25, 1886
b. Furtwangler, Wilhelm

January 27, 1886
b. Downes, Olin

February 2, 1886
b. Benet, William Rose

February 9, 1886
d. Hancock, Winfield Scott

February 12, 1886
d. Caldecott, Randolph
d. Seymour, Horatio

February 13, 1886
b. Guiraldes, Ricardo (Guillermo)

February 16, 1886
b. Brooks, Van Wyck

February 20, 1886
b. Freuchen, Peter
b. Kun, Bela

February 22, 1886
b. Markey, Enid

February 27, 1886
b. Black, Hugo LaFayette

February 28, 1886
d. Peach, Charles William

March 1, 1886
b. Kokoschka, Oskar

March 2, 1886
b. O'Brien, Willis Harold

March 4, 1886
b. Langford, Sam
b. Wilson, Edward Arthur

March 6, 1886
b. Baillie, John

March 8, 1886
b. Kendall, Edward C(alvin)

March 9, 1886
b. Eichelberger, Robert Lawrence
b. Foyle, Gilbert Samuel

March 10, 1886
b. Laubenthal, Rudolf
b. Waller, Fred(erick)

March 13, 1886
b. Baker, Frank
b. Stevens, Albert William
b. Untermeyer, Jean Starr
d. Flint, Austin

March 18, 1886
b. Koffka, Kurt
d. Zunz, Leopold

March 19, 1886
b. Bellanca, Giuseppe Mario

March 24, 1886
b. Weston, Edward

March 25, 1886
b. Athenagoras I

March 27, 1886
b. Kirov, Sergei Mironovich
b. Mies van der Rohe, Ludwig

March 28, 1886
d. Trench, Richard Chenevix

March 29, 1886
b. Krupp von Bohlen und Halbach,
Bertha

March 30, 1886
b. Cornford, Frances Crofts Darwin

April 3, 1886
b. Gumilev, Nikolai

April 4, 1886
b. Mott, Frank Luther

April 6, 1886
d. Forster, William Edward

April 8, 1886
b. Barnes, Margaret Ayer

April 12, 1886
d. Fairbanks, Thaddeus

April 13, 1886
b. Howard, Willie

d. Noyes, John Humphrey

April 14, 1886
b. McFee, Henry Lee
b. Tolman, Edward Chace

April 15, 1886
b. Ozenfant, Amedee

April 16, 1886
b. Thalmann, Ernst

April 19, 1886
b. Bandeira, Manuel

April 23, 1886
b. Coveleski, Harry Frank

April 26, 1886
b. Dawson, William L(evi)
b. Rainey, Gertrude

April 27, 1886
d. Richardson, Henry Hobson

May 3, 1886
b. DuPre, Marcel

May 6, 1886
b. Karfiol, Bernard

May 9, 1886
b. Biddle, Francis Beverley

May 10, 1886
b. Ahearn, Frank
b. Barth, Karl
b. Stapledon, Olaf

May 15, 1886
b. Lambert, Gerard Barnes
d. Dickinson, Emily (Elizabeth)

May 16, 1886
b. Freeman, Douglas S

May 17, 1886
b. Alfonso XIII
d. Deere, John

May 18, 1886
b. Thorarensen, Jakob

May 19, 1886
b. Schmitt, Bernadotte Everly

May 23, 1886
b. Gleason, James
d. Ranke, Leopold von

May 24, 1886
b. Paray, Paul

May 25, 1886
b. Murray, Philip

May 26, 1886
b. Jolson, Al

May 28, 1886
b. Mayer, Arthur Loeb

d. Bartlett, John Russell
d. Ostrovsky, Aleksandr Nikolaevich

May 29, 1886
b. Khodasevich, Vladislav

May 30, 1886
b. Bourne, Randolph Silliman
b. Eustis, Dorothy Leib Harrison
Wood

June 2, 1886
b. Whalen, Grover (Michael)
A(loysius)

June 5, 1886
b. Keaney, Frank

June 6, 1886
b. White, Paul Dudley
d. Nevin, John Williamson

June 7, 1886
d. Hoe, Richard March

June 9, 1886
b. Gorman, Tommy

June 10, 1886
b. Hayakawa, Sessue (Kintaro)

June 11, 1886
b. Gordon, Vera
b. Steinman, David Barnard

June 13, 1886
d. Ludwig II

June 14, 1886
d. Mould, Jacob Wrey
d. Van Nostrand, David

June 18, 1886
b. Mallory, George Leigh

June 21, 1886
d. Home, Daniel Douglas

June 25, 1886
b. Arnold, Henry Harley
b. McIntyre, James Francis Aloysius,
Cardinal

June 26, 1886
d. Atchison, David R
d. Davis, David

June 29, 1886
b. Cheney, Sheldon Warren
b. Ogburn, W(illiam) F(ielding)
b. Schuman, Robert
b. VanDerZee, James

July 3, 1886
b. Spruance, Raymond Ames

July 4, 1886
d. Poundmaker

July 5, 1886
b. Drees, Willem
b. Timmermans, Felix

July 6, 1886
b. Bloch, Marc

July 12, 1886
b. Bax, Clifford
b. Hersholt, Jean

July 13, 1886
b. Flanagan, Edward Joseph, Father

July 16, 1886
d. Judson, Edward Zane Carroll

July 18, 1886
b. Buckner, Simon Bolivar, Jr.

July 23, 1886
b. Brown, Arthur Whitten, Sir
b. Madariaga (y Rojo), Salvador de

July 24, 1886
b. Tanizaki Jun'ichiro

July 26, 1886
b. Jannings, Emil

July 31, 1886
d. Liszt, Franz (Ferencz)

August 1, 1886
b. McLean, Evalyn Walsh

August 2, 1886
b. Sodero, Cesare

August 3, 1886
b. Westover, Russell (Channing)

August 4, 1886
d. Tilden, Samuel Jones

August 5, 1886
b. Barton, Bruce

August 7, 1886
b. Burke, Billie
b. Hazeltine, (Louis) Alan

August 8, 1886
b. Buck, Gene
b. Yon, Pietro Alessandro

August 14, 1886
b. Dempster, Arthur Jeffrey

August 15, 1886
b. Yeats-Brown, F(rancis Charles
    Claypon)

August 16, 1886
d. Ramakrishna, Sri

August 19, 1886
b. Heger, Robert

August 20, 1886
b. Tillich, Paul Johannes
d. Stephens, Ann Sophia

August 24, 1886
b. Gibbs, William Francis

August 25, 1886
b. Stolz, Robert

August 26, 1886
b. Hunsaker, Jerome Clarke
b. McNamara, George

August 28, 1886
b. Higgins, Andrew J

September 1, 1886
b. Schoech, Othmar

September 8, 1886
b. Sassoon, Siegfried

September 9, 1886
b. Wheelock, John Hall

September 12, 1886
b. Ryden, Ernest Edwin

September 13, 1886
b. Locke, Alain Leroy
b. Robinson, Robert, Sir

September 14, 1886
b. Masaryk, Jan Garrigue

September 17, 1886
d. Durand, Asher Brown

September 18, 1886
b. Crosley, Powel, Jr.
b. Sullivan, C(harles) Gardner

September 19, 1886
b. Doolittle, Hilda
b. O'Sheel, Shaemas

September 20, 1886
b. Anderson, John Murray
b. Kenny, Sister Elizabeth

September 26, 1886
b. Hill, Archibald Vivian

September 27, 1886
b. Moley, Raymond Charles
d. Cooke, John Esten

October 3, 1886
b. Alain-Fournier

October 4, 1886
b. Robinson, Lennox

October 6, 1886
d. Godwin, Edward William

October 13, 1886
d. Loomis, Mahlon

October 16, 1886
b. Ben-Gurion, David

October 17, 1886
b. Goodpasture, E(rnest) W(illiam)

October 21, 1886
d. Hernandez, Jose

October 22, 1886
b. Bartlett, F(rederic) C(harles)

October 24, 1886
b. Agustini, Delmira

October 25, 1886
b. Polanyi, Karl

October 26, 1886
b. Starrett, Vincent

October 30, 1886
b. Akins, Zoe

October 31, 1886
b. Chiang Kai-Shek
b. Burke, Thomas

November 2, 1886
b. Giesler, Jerry

November 6, 1886
b. Kahn, Gus

November 7, 1886
b. Barnard, Chester Irving
d. Thurber, Charles

November 9, 1886
b. Wynn, Ed

November 10, 1886
b. Stavisky, Serge Alexandre

November 12, 1886
b. Travers, Ben

November 13, 1886
b. Wigman, Mary

November 16, 1886
b. Krock, Arthur Bernard

November 17, 1886
b. Stace, W(alter) T(erence)

November 18, 1886
b. Kemper, James S(cott)
b. Rand, James Henry
b. Wilson, Charles Edward
d. Arthur, Chester A(lan)

November 20, 1886
b. Frisch, Karl von
b. Hammond, Bray

November 21, 1886
b. Nicolson, Harold George, Sir
d. Adams, Charles Francis, Sr.

November 22, 1886
d. Chesnut, Mary Boykin (Miller)

November 24, 1886
b. Anderson, Margaret (Carolyn)

November 30, 1886
b. Struss, Karl

December 1, 1886
b. Stout, Rex Todhunter

December 3, 1886
b. Siegbahn, Karl Manne Georg

December 5, 1886
b. Lane, Rose Wilder
b. Spry, Constance

December 6, 1886
b. Kilmer, Joyce

December 8, 1886
b. Rivera, Diego

December 9, 1886
b. Birdseye, Clarence Frank

December 10, 1886
b. Liveright, Horace Brisbin

December 11, 1886
b. McLaglen, Victor

December 18, 1886
b. Chu Te
b. Cobb, Ty(rus Raymond)
b. Watkins, Arthur V(ivian)

December 20, 1886
b. Wightman, Hazel Virginia
Hotchkiss

December 21, 1886
b. Papi, Genarro

December 25, 1886
b. Barker, Elliott
b. Ory, Kid
b. Rosenzweig, Franz

December 26, 1886
d. Logan, John Alexander

December 28, 1886
b. Cloud, Henry Roe

1887

b. Barnes, Jim
b. Benefield, Barry
b. Brauer, Max Julius Friedrich
b. Cavanaugh, Hobart
b. Church, George W
b. Clayton, Lou
b. Kahn, Ben
b. Koo, V(i) K(yuin) Wellington
b. Martinez, Maria Montoya
b. Nagumo, Chuichi
b. Patou, Jean
b. Schwitters, Kurt (Hermann Edward
Karl Julius)
d. Cain, Richard H
d. Kanaris, Constantine
d. Richardson, Benjamin
b. Vezina, Georges

January 1, 1887
b. Canaris, Wilhelm

January 2, 1887
d. Newberry, John Stoughton

January 3, 1887
b. Macke, August

January 4, 1887
b. Witte, Edwin Emil

January 5, 1887
b. Hodges, Courtney

January 6, 1887
b. Kelly, George Edward

January 7, 1887
d. Stanton, Henry Brewster

January 10, 1887
b. Jeffers, (John) Robinson
d. Roach, John

January 12, 1887
b. Helburn, Theresa

January 14, 1887
d. Foster, Abigail Kelley

January 16, 1887
d. Hazen, William Babcock

January 18, 1887
d. Upchurch, John Jorden

January 19, 1887
b. Hunter, Clementine
b. Woollcott, Alexander Humphreys

January 21, 1887
b. Kohler, Wolfgang

January 22, 1887
b. Olds, Irving S

January 23, 1887
b. Wenrich, Percy

January 26, 1887
b. Mitscher, Marc Andrew

January 27, 1887
b. Blegen, Carl William

January 28, 1887
b. Rubinstein, Arthur

February 1, 1887
b. Nordhoff, Charles Bernard
b. Scherman, Harry

February 4, 1887
b. Kaye-Smith, Sheila

February 6, 1887
b. Frings, Joseph Richard

February 8, 1887
d. Courtright, Jim

February 10, 1887
b. Sawyer, Charles

b. Ungaretti, Giuseppe
d. Wood, Henry, Mrs.

February 11, 1887
b. Hanfstaengl, Ernst Franz Sedgwick
b. Hewitt, Henry Kent

February 15, 1887
b. Bateman, Henry Mayo

February 17, 1887
b. Bech, Joseph

February 19, 1887
b. Terry, Paul H

February 20, 1887
b. Ebert, Carl
b. Massey, Vincent

February 22, 1887
b. Clark, Marguerite
b. Cody, Lew

February 24, 1887
b. Chase, Mary Ellen
d. Eastman, Mary Henderson

February 25, 1887
b. McNaughton, Andrew

February 26, 1887
b. Alexander, Grover Cleveland

February 27, 1887
d. Borodin, Alexander Profirevich
d. Sill, Edward Rowland

February 28, 1887
b. Zorach, William

March 4, 1887
b. Edgell, George Harold

March 5, 1887
b. Villa-Lobos, Heitor

March 7, 1887
b. Parkhurst, Helen

March 8, 1887
d. Beecher, Henry Ward
d. Eads, James Buchanan

March 11, 1887
b. Moran, Paddy
b. Walsh, Raoul

March 13, 1887
b. Vandegrift, Alexander Archer

March 14, 1887
b. Beach, Sylvia

March 15, 1887
b. Post, Marjorie Merriweather

March 18, 1887
b. Horton, Edward Everett

March 21, 1887
b. Mendelsohn, Eric
b. Van Dyke, W(oodbridge) S(trong)

March 22, 1887
b. Lualdi, Adriano

March 23, 1887
b. Gris, Juan
b. Hillman, Sidney (Simcha)

March 24, 1887
b. Arbuckle, Fatty

March 25, 1887
b. Swing, Raymond Gram

March 27, 1887
d. Tulane, Paul

March 29, 1887
b. Read, Albert Cushing

April 1, 1887
b. Bloomfield, Leonard
b. Taylor, Laurette

April 8, 1887
b. Connolly, Walter

April 9, 1887
b. Adair, Frank E(arl)

April 10, 1887
b. Houssay, Bernardo Alberto

April 14, 1887
b. Foerster, Norman

April 15, 1887
b. Bonham Carter, Violet

April 20, 1887
b. Lazzari, Virgilio

April 21, 1887
b. McCarthy, Joe

April 22, 1887
b. Hall, James Norman
b. Wiese, Kurt

May 1, 1887
b. Cunningham, Alan Gordon, Sir
b. Wortman, Denys

May 2, 1887
b. Castle, Vernon
b. Collins, Eddie
b. Griffis, Stanton

May 5, 1887
d. Grant, James

May 7, 1887
d. Cousins, Samuel

May 12, 1887
d. Boussingault, Jean Baptiste

May 15, 1887
b. Muir, Edwin

May 16, 1887
b. Montana, Bull

May 19, 1887
b. Travers, Jerry

May 21, 1887
b. Gladstone, James

May 24, 1887
b. Wolff, Mary Evaline

May 25, 1887
b. Pio da Pietrelcina, Francesco
Forgione, Father

May 26, 1887
b. Bacon, Leonard

May 29, 1887
b. Thurstone, Louis Leon

May 30, 1887
b. Archipenko, Alexander Porfirievich

May 31, 1887
b. Leger, Alexis St. Leger

June 1, 1887
b. Brook, Clive

June 3, 1887
b. Hayes, Roland
d. Carrier-Belleuse, Albert Ernest

June 4, 1887
d. Wheeler, William Alrnon

June 5, 1887
b. Benedict, Ruth (Fulton)

June 8, 1887
b. Balaban, Barney

June 10, 1887
b. Byrd, Harry Flood

June 13, 1887
b. Frank, Bruno

June 15, 1887
b. Hoffman, Malvina

June 16, 1887
b. Lauro, Achille

June 17, 1887
d. Hopkins, Mark

June 19, 1887
b. Yurka, Blanche

June 21, 1887
b. Ismay, Hastings Lionel, Baron

June 22, 1887
b. Huxley, Julian Sorell, Sir

June 24, 1887
b. Watson, Mark Skinner

June 25, 1887
b. Abbott, George (Francis)

June 28, 1887
b. Dell, Floyd

July 7, 1887
b. Chagall, Marc

July 9, 1887
b. Chapin, James Ormsbee
b. Morison, Samuel Eliot
d. Merriam, Charles

July 11, 1887
b. Woodward, Ellen S.

July 14, 1887
b. Mowrer, Paul Scott
d. Krupp, Alfred

July 15, 1887
d. Andrews, Jane

July 16, 1887
b. Gibbons, Floyd Phillips

July 17, 1887
b. Conway, Jack
d. Dix, Dorothea Lynde

July 18, 1887
b. Quisling, Vidkun Abraham

July 22, 1887
b. Hertz, Gustav Ludwig

July 28, 1887
b. Duchamp, Marcel

July 29, 1887
b. Mara, Tim(othy James)
b. Romberg, Sigmund

July 30, 1887
b. Meinesz, Felix Andries Vening

August 2, 1887
d. Rainey, Joseph Hayne

August 3, 1887
b. Brooke, Rupert Chawner

August 5, 1887
b. Owen, (John) Reginald

August 7, 1887
b. McKechnie, Bill

August 10, 1887
b. Herbert, Hugh
b. Thompson, Oscar
b. Warner, Sam(uel Louis)

August 12, 1887
b. Schroedinger, Erwin

August 13, 1887
d. Pasdeloup, Jules Etienne

August 14, 1887
d. Jeffries, Richard

August 15, 1887
b. Campbell, Walter Stanley
b. Ferber, Edna

August 17, 1887
b. Garvey, Marcus Moziah

August 18, 1887
d. Fowler, Orson Squire

August 19, 1887
d. Baird, Spencer Fullerton

August 20, 1887
d. Laforgue, Jules

August 21, 1887
b. Snow, Carmel White

August 22, 1887
b. Sanderson, Julia

August 23, 1887
b. Hansen, Alvin Harvey

August 24, 1887
b. Hooper, Harry Bartholomew

August 31, 1887
b. Paneth, Friedrich Adolf

September 2, 1887
b. Bruce Lockhart, Robert Hamilton,
Sir

September 7, 1887
b. Sitwell, Edith, Dame

September 8, 1887
b. Devers, Jacob Loucks

September 9, 1887
b. Landon, Alf(red Mossman)
b. Walburn, Raymond

September 10, 1887
b. Gronchi, Giovanni

September 13, 1887
b. Grau San Martin, Ramon
b. Roosevelt, Theodore, Jr.
b. Ruzicka, Leopold Stephen

September 14, 1887
b. Compton, Karl Taylor
b. Ketchel, Stanley

September 16, 1887
b. Arp, Hans
b. Boulanger, Nadia Juliette
b. Boyd, Louise Arner
b. Davis, Marguerite

September 19, 1887
b. Overman, Lynne

September 26, 1887
b. Wallis, Barnes Neville, Sir

September 28, 1887
b. Brundage, Avery

October 4, 1887
b. Armour, Norman

October 5, 1887
b. Cassin, Rene-Samuel

October 6, 1887
b. Jeritza, Maria
b. LeCorbusier

October 9, 1887
d. Strakosch, Maurice

October 11, 1887
b. Hoppe, Willie

October 12, 1887
d. Craik, Dinah Maria Mulock

October 17, 1887
d. Kirchhoff, Gustav Robert

October 22, 1887
b. Reed, John Silas

October 30, 1887
d. Walter, Thomas Ustick

October 31, 1887
d. Macfarren, George Alexander, Sir

November 1, 1887
b. Lowry, Lawrence Stephen

November 2, 1887
b. Wolfson, Harry Austryn
d. Lind, Jenny

November 3, 1887
b. Fleischer, Nat(haniel Stanley)

November 5, 1887
b. Wittgenstein, Paul

November 6, 1887
b. Johnson, Walter Perry

November 8, 1887
d. Holliday, Doc

November 10, 1887
b. Zweig, Arnold

November 11, 1887
b. Young, Roland

November 15, 1887
b. Moore, Marianne Craig
b. O'Keeffe, Georgia

November 17, 1887
b. Montgomery of Alamein, Bernard
Law Montgomery, Viscount

November 18, 1887
d. Fechner, Gustav Theodor

November 19, 1887
b. Sumner, James Batcheller
d. Lazarus, Emma

November 20, 1887
b. Hooton, Earnest Albert

November 23, 1887
b. Karloff, Boris

November 25, 1887
b. Vavilov, Nikolai Ivanovich

November 28, 1887
b. Rohm, Ernst

November 5, 1887
b. Baillie, D(onald) M(acpherson)

December 5, 1887
b. Daryush, Elizabeth Bridges

December 6, 1887
b. Fontanne, Lynn

December 7, 1887
b. Toch, Ernst

December 12, 1887
b. Jones, Robert Edmond

December 13, 1887
b. Polya, George
b. York, Sergeant

December 16, 1887
b. Bodanzky, Artur

December 22, 1887
b. Ramanujan Aiyangar, Srinivasa

December 23, 1887
b. Blore, Eric
b. Cromwell, John

December 24, 1887
b. Jouvet, Louis

December 25, 1887
b. Hilton, Conrad Nicholson

December 26, 1887
b. Booth, Charles Brandon

December 30, 1887
b. Broad, C(harlie) D(unbar)

December 31, 1887
b. Lalonde, Newsy

1888

b. Bonestell, Chesley
b. Brinkley, Nell
b. Bugbee, Emma
b. Chapin, F(rancis) Stuart
b. Dane, Clemence

b. DeMar, Clarence
b. Kurusu, Saburo
b. Marcus, Luis J
b. McCall, Dorothy Lawson
b. Nelson, Erik Henning
b. Nowlan, Phil
b. Nuri al-Sa'id
b. Radhakrishnan, Sarvepalli
b. Rivera, Jose Eustasio
b. Schlemmer, Oskar
b. Skaggs, M(arion) B
d. Hecker, Isaac Thomas
d. Miller, Frederic
d. Rylands, John
d. Whitman, Stephen F

January 1, 1888
b. Garand, John Cantius

January 3, 1888
b. Bridie, James
b. Morrison of Lambeth, Herbert
    Stanley Morrison, Baron

January 8, 1888
b. Courant, Richard

January 11, 1888
b. Conklin, Chester

January 18, 1888
b. Sopwith, Thomas O M, Sir

January 19, 1888
d. DeBary, Heinrich Anton

January 24, 1888
b. Baum, Vicki
b. Heinkel, Ernst Heinrich

January 27, 1888
b. Goldschmidt, Victor Moritz

January 29, 1888
b. Chapman, Sydney
d. Lear, Edward

January 30, 1888
d. Gray, Asa
d. Howitt, Mary

February 1, 1888
b. Caton-Thompson, Gertrude

February 2, 1888
b. Lloyd, Frank

February 3, 1888
d. Maine, Henry James Sumner

February 5, 1888
b. Fraser, Bruce Austin, Sir

February 6, 1888
b. Gleason, Lucille

February 8, 1888
b. Evans, Edith Mary Booth, Dame

February 11, 1888
b. Persinger, Louis
d. Kelly, William

February 12, 1888
b. Coulter, John William

February 13, 1888
b. Papandreou, George
d. Lamy, Jean Baptist

February 15, 1888
d. Locke, David Ross

February 16, 1888
b. Medina, Harold Raymond

February 17, 1888
b. Knox, Ronald Arbuthnott
b. Stern, Otto

February 18, 1888
b. Sheil, Bernard James, Archbishop

February 20, 1888
b. Bernanos, Georges
b. Rambert, Marie, Dame

February 22, 1888
b. Brewster, (Ralph) Owen
b. Pippin, Horace

February 24, 1888
d. Corcoran, William Wilson

February 25, 1888
b. Dulles, John Foster
b. Ferguson, Homer

February 27, 1888
b. Lehmann, Lotte

March 4, 1888
b. Rockne, Knute Kenneth
d. Alcott, Amos Bronson

March 6, 1888
d. Alcott, Louisa May

March 8, 1888
b. Chase, Stuart

March 9, 1888
d. William, I

March 10, 1888
b. Fitzgerald, Barry
b. Mayer, Oscar Gottfried

March 12, 1888
b. Johnson, Hall
b. Knappertsbusch, Hans
d. Bergh, Henry

March 16, 1888
d. Carnot, Hippolyte

March 19, 1888
b. Albers, Josef

March 20, 1888
b. Stevenson, Coke Robert

March 21, 1888
b. Ball, Edward

March 23, 1888
d. Waite, Morrison Remick

March 27, 1888
d. Darley, Felix Octavius Carr

March 29, 1888
b. Casey, James E

March 30, 1888
b. Nilsson, Anna Q(uerentia)

March 31, 1888
b. Rockwell, Willard F

April 1, 1888
b. Batchelor, Clarence Daniel

April 2, 1888
b. Ahearn, Daniel F.

April 3, 1888
b. Webb, Walter Prescott

April 4, 1888
b. Speaker, Tris(tram E)

April 6, 1888
b. Richter, Hans

April 8, 1888
b. Price, Florence Beatrice Smith

April 9, 1888
b. Hurok, Sol(omon Isaievich)

April 13, 1888
b. Hammond, John Hays, Jr.

April 15, 1888
b. Bates, Florence
d. Arnold, Matthew

April 17, 1888
b. Teyte, Maggie, Dame

April 18, 1888
b. Chavez, Dennis
b. Leider, Frida
b. Lunn, Arnold Henry Moore, Sir
d. Conkling, Roscoe

April 22, 1888
d. Applegate, Jesse

April 26, 1888
b. Risdon, Elizabeth

April 30, 1888
b. Ransom, John Crowe

May 6, 1888
b. Celler, Emanuel
b. Stover, Russell

May 10, 1888
b. Steiner, Max

May 11, 1888
b. Berlin, Irving

May 12, 1888
b. Reik, Theodor
b. Stabile, Mariano

May 14, 1888
b. Alexander, Archie Alphonso

May 16, 1888
b. Sarett, Lew R

May 19, 1888
b. Simpson, William Hood

May 23, 1888
b. Wheat, Zack

May 26, 1888
d. Sobrero, Ascanio

May 28, 1888
b. Lambert, Piggy
b. Lambert, Ward L
b. Thorpe, Jim

May 30, 1888
b. Farley, James A(loysius)

May 31, 1888
b. Holt, Jack

June 8, 1888
d. Clarke, James Freeman

June 11, 1888
b. Akhmatova, Anna
b. Vanzetti, Bartolomeo

June 15, 1888
b. D'Arcy, Martin Cyril
d. Frederick III

June 16, 1888
b. Clark, Bobby

June 17, 1888
b. Guderian, Heinz Wilhelm

June 18, 1888
b. Burger, Carl Victor

June 19, 1888
b. Johnston, Frank H

June 21, 1888
b. Upson, Ralph Hazlett

June 22, 1888
b. Namier, Lewis Bernstein
b. Seeger, Alan

June 24, 1888
b. Rietveld, Gerrit Thomas

June 27, 1888
b. Perry, Antoinette

July 2, 1888
b. Boyd, James

July 4, 1888
b. Armetta, Henry

d. Storm, (Hans) Theodor (Woldsen)

July 5, 1888
b. Gasser, Herbert Spencer

July 6, 1888
b. Kellerman, Annette

July 9, 1888
b. Bairnsfather, Bruce
b. Marks, Simon

July 10, 1888
b. Chirico, Giorgio de
b. McNamee, Graham

July 12, 1888
d. Sibley, Hiram

July 16, 1888
b. Jackson, Joe
b. Kilbride, Percy
b. Zernike, Frits

July 17, 1888
b. Agnon, S(hmuel) Y(osef)

July 18, 1888
b. Cowdry, Edmund Vincent

July 19, 1888
d. Roe, Edward Payson

July 20, 1888
b. McMurtrie, Douglas C

July 22, 1888
b. Waksman, Selman Abraham

July 23, 1888
b. Chandler, Raymond Thornton
b. Williams, Gluyas

July 30, 1888
b. Jaeger, Werner Wilhelm

August 1, 1888
b. Whitney, Richard

August 3, 1888
d. Goodrich, Benjamin Franklin

August 5, 1888
d. Sheridan, Philip Henry

August 6, 1888
b. Schlusnus, Heinrich

August 12, 1888
b. Lorne, Marion

August 13, 1888
b. Baird, John Logie

August 14, 1888
d. Crocker, Charles

August 15, 1888
b. Lawrence, T(homas) E(dward)
b. Spalding, Albert

August 17, 1888
b. Woolley, Monty

August 18, 1888
b. Williams, J(ames) R(obert)

August 20, 1888
b. Thang, Ton Duc

August 24, 1888
b. Jagendorf, Moritz Adolf
d. Clausius, Rudolf Julius Emmanuel
b. Grey Owl

September 2, 1888
b. Schorr, Friedrich

September 3, 1888
b. Rivers, Thomas Milton

September 6, 1888
b. Faber, Red
b. Kennedy, Joseph Patrick, Sr.

September 9, 1888
d. Savage, John

September 10, 1888
b. Fleming, Ian

September 11, 1888
d. Sarmiento, Domingo Faustino

September 12, 1888
b. Chevalier, Maurice Auguste

September 16, 1888
b. Bentley, Walter Owen
b. Sillanpaa, Frans E

September 19, 1888
b. Alexander, James Waddell, II

September 20, 1888
b. Petersham, Miska

September 26, 1888
b. Dobie, J(ames) Frank
b. Eliot, T(homas) S(tearns)

September 27, 1888
b. Dean, Basil

September 28, 1888
b. McNeile, Herman Cyril

September 30, 1888
b. Poor, Henry Varnum, III

October 7, 1888
b. Wallace, Henry Agard

October 9, 1888
b. Bukharin, Nikolai Ivanovich

October 12, 1888
d. Levy, Joseph Moses

October 14, 1888
b. Mansfield, Katherine
b. Turnbull, Agnes Sligh

October 15, 1888
b. Van Dine, S S

October 16, 1888
b. O'Neill, Eugene Gladstone

October 18, 1888
b. Waymack, W(illiam) W(esley)

October 25, 1888
b. Byrd, Richard Evelyn, Admiral
b. Crosby, Elizabeth Caroline

October 30, 1888
b. Kirk, Alan Goodrich

October 31, 1888
b. Wilkins, George Hubert, Sir

November 1, 1888
d. Przhevalsky, Nikolai Mikhailovich

November 4, 1888
b. O'Brien, John J

November 7, 1888
b. Raman, Chandrasekhara Venkata,
Sir

November 9, 1888
b. Monnet, Jean Omer Marie Gabriel

November 10, 1888
b. Tupolev, Andrei Nikolaevich

November 12, 1888
b. Parrish, Anne

November 15, 1888
b. Sverdrup, H(arald) U(lrik)

November 18, 1888
b. Marion, Frances

November 19, 1888
b. Capablanca, Jose Raoul

November 20, 1888
d. Currier, Nathaniel

November 24, 1888
b. Carnegie, Dale
b. Huebner, Clarence R

November 28, 1888
b. Walker, Jack

November 30, 1888
b. LeTourneau, Robert Gilmour

December 3, 1888
d. Zeiss, Carl

December 6, 1888
b. Hyman, Libbie Henrietta

December 7, 1888
b. Broun, (Matthew) Heywood
(Campbell)
b. Cary, Joyce
b. Fish, Hamilton, III

December 8, 1888
b. Kimball, Fiske

December 10, 1888
b. Reiner, Fritz

December 15, 1888
b. Anderson, Maxwell

December 16, 1888
b. Alexander of Yugoslavia
b. Juin, Alphonse Pierre

December 18, 1888
b. Cooper, Gladys, Dame
b. Moses, Robert

December 23, 1888
b. Rank, J(oseph) Arthur
d. Oliphant, Laurence

December 24, 1888
b. Curtiz, Michael

December 25, 1888
b. Henderson, Robert W
b. Lawrence, David
b. Stravinsky, Vera de Bossett

December 28, 1888
b. Branner, Martin Michael

1889

b. Ben Badis, Abd al-Hamid
b. Carnegie, Hattie
b. Case, Anna
b. Craig, May
b. Crater, Joseph Force
b. Darrow, Charles Brace
b. Dick, Lena Frank
b. Guinan, Texas
b. Horsbrugh, Florence
b. Humphrey, Elliott S
b. Irwin, Margaret
b. Kaufmann, Ezekiel
b. Li Ta-chao
b. Lyttle, Hulda Margaret
b. Marshall, Laurence
b. Morin, Paul
b. Mowrer, Lilian Thomson
b. Norton, Jack
b. O'Hanlon, Virginia
b. Rockwell, Doc
b. Sukenik, Eliazer Lipa
d. Burberry, Thomas
d. Cadbury, John
d. Dalton, John Call
d. Folger, James A
d. Forbes, Robert Bennet
d. Fustel de Coulanges, Numa Denis
d. Mandelbaum, Fredericka
d. Matzeliger, Jan Ernest
d. Younger, Bob

January 1, 1889
b. Bickford, Charles Ambrose
b. Smallens, Alexander

January 2, 1889
b. Hyland, Harry
b. Schipa, Tito

January 6, 1889
b. Craven, Thomas

January 10, 1889
b. Held, John, Jr.

January 11, 1889
b. Bridges, Calvin Blackman

January 17, 1889
d. Montalvo, Juan Maria

January 19, 1889
b. Taeuber-Arp, Sophie

January 20, 1889
b. Toffenetti, Dario Louis

January 21, 1889
b. Sorokin, Pitirim A(lexandrovitch)

January 22, 1889
b. Baumeister, Willi

January 28, 1889
d. Crandall, Prudence

January 30, 1889
d. Rudolf of Hapsburg

January 31, 1889
b. Deloria, Ella Clara
d. Gungl, Joseph

February 2, 1889
b. Lattre de Tassigny, Jean de (Marie
Gabriel) de

February 3, 1889
b. Dreyer, Carl Theodore
d. Starr, Belle

February 4, 1889
b. Catlett, Walter

February 7, 1889
b. Muzio, Claudia

February 11, 1889
b. Mills, John

February 14, 1889
b. Auerbach-Levy, William

February 17, 1889
b. Hunt, H(aroldson) L(afayette)

February 20, 1889
b. Gomez Castro, Laureano Eleuterio

February 22, 1889
b. Baden-Powell, Olave St. Claire,
Lady
b. Collingwood, Robin George

February 28, 1889
b. Dietrich, Noah

March 3, 1889
b. Rentner, Maurice

March 4, 1889
b. White, Pearl

March 7, 1889
b. Williams, Ben Ames

March 8, 1889
d. Ericsson, John

March 10, 1889
d. Johannes, IV

March 11, 1889
b. Widener, George D

March 12, 1889
b. Bucher, Walter Herman
b. Guedalla, Philip

March 13, 1889
d. Tamberlik, Enrico
d. Varesi, Felice

March 14, 1889
b. DeAngeli, Marguerite Lofft

March 15, 1889
b. Jones, Billy
d. Bissell, Melville Reuben

March 16, 1889
b. Janis, Elsie

March 20, 1889
d. Ritschl, Albrecht Benjamin

March 22, 1889
d. Matthews, Stanley

March 27, 1889
d. Bright, John

March 29, 1889
b. Lindsay, Howard

April 2, 1889
b. Cardus, Neville, Sir

April 4, 1889
d. Mahan, Asa
d. Remington, Eliphalet

April 8, 1889
b. Boult, Adrian Cedric, Sir

April 9, 1889
d. Chevreul, Michel Eugene

April 10, 1889
b. Murray, Mae

April 14, 1889
b. Toynbee, Arnold Joseph

April 15, 1889
b. Benton, Thomas Hart
b. Holmes, Hap
b. Randolph, Asa Philip
d. Damien, Father

April 16, 1889
b. Chaplin, Charlie

April 17, 1889
b. Boussac, Marcel

April 19, 1889
d. De La Rue, Warren

April 20, 1889
b. Hitler, Adolf
b. Kohler, Fred, Sir

April 21, 1889
b. Harrison, G(eorge) Donald
b. Karrar, Paul
b. Prado Ugarteche, Manuel
d. Lerdo de Tejada, Sebastian

April 24, 1889
b. Cripps, Stafford, Sir
b. Popova, Liubov Sergeevna

April 26, 1889
b. Wittgenstein, Ludwig

April 27, 1889
d. Barnard, Frederick Augustus Porter

April 28, 1889
b. Salazar, Antonio de Oliveira

April 30, 1889
d. Rosa, Carl

May 1, 1889
d. Weir, Robert W

May 4, 1889
b. Spellman, Francis Joseph

May 5, 1889
d. Brannan, Samuel

May 11, 1889
b. Nash, Paul

May 17, 1889
b. Mackay, John Alexander
b. Reyes, Alfonso

May 18, 1889
b. Midgeley, Thomas

May 23, 1889
b. Niekisch, Ernest

May 24, 1889
d. Bridgman, Laura Dewey

May 25, 1889
b. Sikorsky, Igor Ivanovich

May 29, 1889
b. Blackwell, Basil Henry, Sir

June 1, 1889
b. Daugherty, James Henry

June 8, 1889
d. Hopkins, Gerard Manley

June 9, 1889
b. Jerger, Alfred

June 13, 1889
b. Henry, George William

June 14, 1889
b. Lincoln, Elmo

June 15, 1889
d. Eminescu, Mihail

June 16, 1889
b. Doubleday, Nelson
b. Hamlin, Talbot Faulkner

June 23, 1889
b. Bishop, Katharine Scott

June 25, 1889
d. Hayes, Lucy Webb

June 26, 1889
d. Cameron, Simon

June 27, 1889
d. Patti, Carlotta

June 28, 1889
b. Aqqad, Abbas Mahmud al-
b. Dodds, Harold Willis
d. Mitchell, Maria

June 30, 1889
b. Dean, Man Mountain

July 4, 1889
b. Chotzinoff, Samuel

July 5, 1889
b. Cocteau, Jean

July 8, 1889
b. Pallette, Eugene

July 9, 1889
b. Dandurand, Leo

July 10, 1889
b. Sissle, Noble
d. Tyler, Julia Gardiner

July 12, 1889
b. Friedman, Max

July 13, 1889
b. Coveleski, Stanley Anthony

July 15, 1889
b. Rambeau, Marjorie

July 17, 1889
b. Gardner, Erle Stanley

July 20, 1889
b. Reith, John Charles Walsham

July 22, 1889
b. Fishbein, Morris

July 23, 1889
b. Bonnet, Georges Etienne

July 27, 1889
b. Bliven, Bruce

July 29, 1889
b. Reuter, Ernst

July 30, 1889
b. Haldeman-Julius, Emanuel
b. Wellesley, Dorothy Violet
b. Zworykin, Vladimir K(osma)

August 2, 1889
b. Lawrence, Margaret

August 5, 1889
b. Aiken, Conrad Potter

August 6, 1889
b. Kenney, George Churchill
b. Murry, John Middleton

August 12, 1889
b. Sharp, Zerna A

August 14, 1889
b. Woolsey, Robert

August 15, 1889
b. Crowley, Leo Thomas

August 19, 1889
b. Waley, Arthur David

August 23, 1889
b. Faber, Geoffrey Cust, Sir

August 24, 1889
b. Gowdy, Hank

August 25, 1889
b. Frank, Waldo

September 8, 1889
b. Taft, Robert A(lphonso)

September 15, 1889
b. Benchley, Robert Charles
b. McKay, Claude
b. McKay, Festus Claudius

September 19, 1889
b. Delany, Sarah Louise

September 22, 1889
b. Dauss, George August

September 23, 1889
b. Lippmann, Walter
d. Collins, Wilkie

September 25, 1889
b. Cole, George Douglas Howard

September 26, 1889
b. Heidegger, Martin

September 29, 1889
d. Faidherbe, Louis Leon Cesar

October 1, 1889
b. Sockman, Ralph W

October 3, 1889
b. Ossietzky, Carl von

October 6, 1889
b. Dabrowska, Maria Szumska
b. Heard, Gerald

October 9, 1889
b. Marquard, Rube

October 10, 1889
b. Roosevelt, Kermit

October 11, 1889
b. Lelong, Lucien
d. Joule, James Prescott

October 19, 1889
b. Hurst, Fannie
b. Satherly, Arthur Edward

October 20, 1889
b. Dumont, Margaret
d. Babbitt, Benjamin Talbot

October 22, 1889
b. Balderston, John Lloyd

October 23, 1889
b. Saerchinger, Cesar Victor Charles

October 25, 1889
b. Gance, Abel
b. Wood, Joe

October 27, 1889
b. Bagnold, Enid

October 29, 1889
d. Chernyshevsky, Nikolai Gavrilovich

November 1, 1889
b. Noel-Baker, Philip John

November 4, 1889
b. Husayn, Taha

November 9, 1889
b. Rains, Claude

November 10, 1889
b. Hinton, Walter

November 12, 1889
b. Wallace, DeWitt

November 14, 1889
b. Nehru, Jawaharlal
b. Taha Hussein

November 16, 1889
b. Kaufman, George S(imon)

November 18, 1889
d. Allingham, William

November 20, 1889
b. Hubble, Edwin Powell

November 22, 1889
b. Beer, Thomas
b. Draper, Dorothy Tuckerman

November 23, 1889
b. Patch, Alexander M(c Carrell)

November 24, 1889
b. Nesbitt, Cathleen Mary
b. Shazar, Zalman
d. Pendleton, George Hunt

November 26, 1889
b. Phillips, Harry Irving

November 27, 1889
b. Hatch, Carl A

November 28, 1889
b. Walker, Ralph Thomas

November 30, 1889
b. Adrian, Edgar Douglas, Baron

December 2, 1889
b. Althouse, Paul Shearer

December 3, 1889
b. Bern, Paul

December 6, 1889
b. Lipman, Clara
b. Woodruff, Robert Winship
d. Davis, Jefferson

December 7, 1889
b. Marcel, Gabriel Honore

December 8, 1889
b. Allen, Hervey

December 9, 1889
b. Counts, George S(ylvester)
b. Kolehmainen, Hannes

December 10, 1889
b. Collins, Ray

December 11, 1889
b. Knott, Walter

December 12, 1889
d. Browning, Robert

December 21, 1889
d. Day, Benjamin Henry

December 23, 1889
b. Brunner, Emil
d. Grady, Henry Woodfin

December 24, 1889
b. Craig, May
b. Sauer, Carl Ortwin

December 25, 1889
b. Wallace, Lila Bell Acheson

1890

b. Abu Madi, Iliya
b. Bell, Herbert A
b. Bolitho, William
b. Cleghorn, Sprague
b. Cook, Joe
b. Erickson, Eric
b. Focke, Heinrich Karl Johann
b. Frisco, Joe
b. Immelmann, Max
b. Langsdorff, Hans
b. Melnikov, Konstantin Stepanovich
b. Mussolini, Rachele Guidi
b. Romanoff, Mike
b. Stroud, Robert Franklin
b. Washburn, Charles
b. White, George
d. Chadwick, Edwin
d. Nestle, Henri

January 5, 1890
b. Kauff, Benny

January 8, 1890
b. Clark, Bennett Champ
d. McArthur, John

January 9, 1890
b. Capek, Karel

January 10, 1890
d. Dollinger, J(ohannes) J(osef) I(gnaz) von

January 11, 1890
b. Blue, Monte
b. Carey, Max George

January 12, 1890
b. Johnson, Mordecai Wyatt

January 13, 1890
b. Davis, Elmer Holmes

January 14, 1890
b. Harger, Rolla
b. Holmes, Arthur
d. Napier, Robert Cornelis

January 15, 1890
b. Hayden, Palmer

January 16, 1890
b. Ackerman, Carl William

January 17, 1890
d. Sulzer, Salomon

January 20, 1890
b. Owsley, Frank Lawrence

January 22, 1890
b. Vinson, Frederick Moore

January 28, 1890
b. Fergusson, Harvey

February 1, 1890
b. Lubin, Germaine

February 2, 1890
b. Correll, Charles J

February 3, 1890
b. MacPhail, Larry

February 6, 1890
b. Cameron, Harry

February 8, 1890
b. Menjou, Adolphe Jean
b. Recto, Claro M.

February 9, 1890
b. Oud, Jacobus Johannes Pieter

February 11, 1890
b. Pasternak, Boris Leonidovich

February 15, 1890
b. Ley, Robert

February 17, 1890
b. Fisher, R(onald) A(ylmer)
b. Lesser, Sol
d. Sholes, Christopher Latham

February 18, 1890
b. Arnold, Edward
d. Andrassy, Gyula, Count

February 22, 1890
b. Gerard, Eddie
b. Norwich, Alfred Duff Cooper, Viscount

February 24, 1890
b. Main, Marjorie

February 25, 1890
b. Hess, Myra, Dame

February 26, 1890
b. Vought, Chance Milton

February 27, 1890
b. Staupers, Mabel K.

February 28, 1890
b. Malone, Joe
b. Nijinsky, Vaslav

March 2, 1890
b. DeKruif, Paul Henry

March 3, 1890
b. Bethune, Norman
b. Lowe, Edmund Dante

March 7, 1890
b. Danforth, Dave

March 8, 1890
b. Fowler, Gene
b. Humphrey, George Magoffin
b. Keogan, George

March 9, 1890
b. Molotov, Vyacheslav Mikhaylovich

March 11, 1890
b. Bush, Vannevar

March 13, 1890
b. Busch, Fritz
b. Idris I

March 17, 1890
b. Clarke, Harry

March 20, 1890
b. Gigli, Beniamino
b. Melchior, Lauritz

March 21, 1890
d. Crook, George

March 23, 1890
d. Schenck, Robert Cumming

March 24, 1890
b. Rock, John

March 25, 1890
b. Brendel, El(mer)

March 31, 1890
b. Bragg, William Lawrence, Sir
b. Wright, Lloyd
b. Zimbalist, Efrem

April 6, 1890
b. Danjon, Andre Louis
b. Fokker, Anthony Herman Gerard
b. Tydings, Millard Evelyn

April 7, 1890
b. Douglas, Marjory (Stoneman)

April 11, 1890
d. Merrick, Joseph Carey

April 13, 1890
d. Randall, Samuel J

April 14, 1890
d. Morgan, Junius Spencer

April 15, 1890
b. DeBeck, Billy

April 20, 1890
b. Duplessis, Maurice le Noblet

April 23, 1890
b. Murphy, Frank

April 25, 1890
d. Crowfoot

April 26, 1890
b. Kennedy, Edgar

May 1, 1890
d. Brisbane, Albert

May 3, 1890
b. Fairless, Benjamin F

May 4, 1890
b. Carmichael, Franklin

b. Rosenfeld, Paul

May 5, 1890
b. Morley, Christopher (Darlington)
d. Naudin, Emilio

May 7, 1890
d. Nasmyth, James

May 10, 1890
b. Brown, Clarence

May 15, 1890
b. McNaughton, F(oye) F(isk)

May 17, 1890
b. James, Philip

May 19, 1890
b. Ho Chi Minh
b. Maxwell, Steamer

May 20, 1890
b. Nevins, Allan

May 23, 1890
b. Marshall, Herbert
b. Robertson, Dennis Holme

May 26, 1890
b. Croft, Arthur C

May 27, 1890
b. Harsh, Vivian Gordon

May 28, 1890
d. Nessler, Victor E

May 30, 1890
b. Langer, Lawrence

May 31, 1890
b. Townsend, William H(enry)

June 2, 1890
b. Hopper, Hedda

June 7, 1890
b. Lashley, Karl Spencer

June 9, 1890
b. Banks, Leslie
b. Dashwood, Elizabeth Monica

June 12, 1890
b. Schiele, Egon

June 16, 1890
b. Laurel, Stan

June 18, 1890
b. Schwartz, Maurice

June 19, 1890
b. Eberstadt, Ferdinand

June 23, 1890
b. Buckley, Charles Anthony

June 29, 1890
b. MacFarlane, Willie

July 1, 1890
b. Morgan, Frank

July 5, 1890
b. Allen, Frederick Lewis

July 6, 1890
b. Mukerji, Dham Gopal

July 8, 1890
b. MacDonald-Wright, Stanton

July 11, 1890
b. O'Dwyer, William
b. Tedder, Arthur William Tedder, Baron

July 13, 1890
d. Fremont, John Charles

July 14, 1890
b. Zadkine, Ossip

July 16, 1890
b. Ed, Carl Frank Ludwig
d. Keller, Gottfried

July 17, 1890
b. France, Harry Clinton

July 18, 1890
b. Evans, Chick
b. Wilson, Charles Erwin

July 20, 1890
b. Felton, Verna
b. George II
b. Morandi, Giorgio
d. Wallace, Richard, Sir

July 22, 1890
b. Kennedy, Rose (Fitzgerald)

July 27, 1890
b. Lowry, Judith Ives

July 29, 1890
b. Zuckerman, Ben
d. Van Gogh, Vincent Willem

July 30, 1890
b. Stengel, Casey

August 4, 1890
b. Luque, Dolf

August 5, 1890
b. Gabo, Naum
b. Kleiber, Erich
b. Petersham, Maud

August 6, 1890
b. Johnson, Gerald White

August 7, 1890
b. Flynn, Elizabeth Gurley

August 8, 1890
b. Lord, Pauline

August 10, 1890
b. Hart, Frances Noyes

August 11, 1890
d. Brace, Charles Loring
d. Newman, John Henry, Cardinal

August 14, 1890
d. McGivney, Michael Joseph

August 15, 1890
b. Ibert, Jacques (Francois Antoine)
b. Jellinek, Elvin Morton

August 17, 1890
b. Hopkins, Harry Lloyd

August 18, 1890
b. Clark, Sydney
b. Funk, Walther
b. Podoloff, Maurice

August 20, 1890
b. Lovecraft, H(oward) P(hillips)

August 21, 1890
b. Henry, William M
b. Liston, Emil

August 23, 1890
b. Guggenheim, Harry Frank

August 24, 1890
b. Kahanamoku, Duke Paoa
b. Kendrick, Pearl Luella

August 26, 1890
b. Clark, Barrett H

August 27, 1890
b. Flanagan, Hallie Mae Ferguson
b. Ray, Man
b. Young, Clara Kimball

September 6, 1890
b. Chennault, Claire Lee
b. Weldon, John

September 7, 1890
b. Komroff, Manuel

September 9, 1890
b. Eccles, Marriner Stoddard
b. Lewin, Kurt
b. Sanders, Colonel

September 10, 1890
b. Schiaparelli
b. Werfel, Franz
b. Wheeler, Mortimer

September 15, 1890
b. Christie, Agatha Mary Clarissa Miller, Dame
b. Martin, Frank

September 17, 1890
b. Heatter, Gabriel

September 18, 1890
d. Boucicault, Dion Lardner

September 19, 1890
b. Truex, Ernest

September 22, 1890
b. McCormick, Cyrus Hall

September 23, 1890
b. Paulus, Friedrich von

September 24, 1890
b. Ellender, Allen Joseph
b. Herbert, A(lan) P(atrick), Sir

September 25, 1890
b. Sackheim, Maxwell Byron

October 1, 1890
b. Holloway, Stanley
b. Joyce, Alice

October 2, 1890
b. Marx, Groucho

October 3, 1890
b. Hull, Henry
b. Obolensky, Serge

October 4, 1890
b. Breen, Joseph Ignatius
b. Kelly, John Brenden
d. Booth, Catherine Mumford

October 5, 1890
b. Schmid, Eduard

October 8, 1890
b. Hoffenstein, Samuel Goodman
b. Rickenbacker, Eddie

October 9, 1890
b. McPherson, Aimee Semple

October 13, 1890
d. Belknap, William Worth
d. Miller, Samuel Freeman

October 14, 1890
b. Conroy, Frank
b. Eisenhower, Dwight D(avid)

October 15, 1890
b. Compton, Wilson Martindale
b. James, Art

October 16, 1890
b. Collins, Michael
b. Strand, Paul

October 20, 1890
b. Minton, Sherman
d. Burton, Richard Francis, Sir

October 22, 1890
b. Welch, Joseph Nye

October 23, 1890
b. Baillie, Hugh
b. Littlejohn, Robert McGowan

October 24, 1890
b. Mainbocher

October 25, 1890
b. Bennett, Floyd

October 26, 1890
b. Eckstein, Gustav
d. Collodi, Carlo

October 29, 1890
b. Ottaviani, Alfredo, Cardinal

November 1, 1890
b. Barton, James

November 6, 1890
b. Quirino, Elpidio
b. Sherrill, Henry Knox

November 7, 1890
b. Spitalny, Phil

November 8, 1890
b. Willis, Paul S
d. Franck, Cesar Auguste

November 13, 1890
b. Richter, Conrad Michael

November 14, 1890
b. Egan, Raymond B

November 15, 1890
b. Lamburn, Richmal Crompton
b. Nygren, Anders T(heodor) S(amuel)
b. Ornitz, Samuel

November 16, 1890
b. Seldes, George (Henry)

November 20, 1890
b. Armstrong, Robert

November 22, 1890
b. DeGaulle, Charles Andre Joseph Marie
b. Pollitt, Harry

November 24, 1890
b. Stratemeyer, George E, General
d. Belmont, August

November 25, 1890
b. Rosenberg, Issac

December 4, 1890
b. Darragh, Jack

December 5, 1890
b. Bomberg, Dave
b. Lang, Fritz

December 8, 1890
b. Martinu, Bohuslav

December 11, 1890
b. Tobey, Mark

December 12, 1890
b. Song Sisters, The

December 13, 1890
b. Connelly, Marc(us Cook)

December 15, 1890
b. Babcock, Harry
d. Sitting Bull

December 16, 1890
d. Terry, Alfred Howe

December 20, 1890
b. Heyrovsky, Jaroslav

December 21, 1890
b. Muller, Hermann Joseph
d. Gade, Niels Vilhelm

December 26, 1890
d. Schliemann, Heinrich

December 29, 1890
d. Big Foot
d. Feuillet, Octave

December 30, 1890
b. Ruiz Cortines, Adolfo

1891

b. Ambedkar, Bhimrao Ramji
b. Calvert, Catherine
b. Daniel, Dan(iel)
b. Goodrich, Frances
b. Gorbatov, Aleksandr Vassil'evich
b. Gueye, Lamine
b. Jameson, Margaret Storm
b. Juan, Don
b. Kauffer, Edward McKnight
b. Khan, Abdul Ghaffar
b. Kline, Otis Adelbert
b. Kuwatli, Shukri al-
b. Rutherfurd, Lucy Page Mercer
b. Skelly, Hal
b. Wilkinson, Ellen
d. Haussmann, Georges Eugene
d. Ja Ja of Opobo

January 2, 1891
d. Kinglake, Alexander William

January 4, 1891
d. Keene, Charles Samuel

January 8, 1891
b. Kiplinger, W(illard) M(onroe)
b. Nijinska, Bronislava

January 9, 1891
b. Stone, Grace Zaring

January 15, 1891
b. Mandelstam, Osip Emilyevich
b. Mandelstam, Osip Emilyevich
d. Mason, Biddy
d. Root, John Wellborn

January 16, 1891
d. Delibes, Leo

January 17, 1891
d. Bancroft, George

January 21, 1891
b. Elman, Mischa

January 22, 1891
b. Alexander, Franz Gabriel
b. Gramsci, Antonio

January 25, 1891
b. Bullitt, William Christian

January 26, 1891
b. Costello, Frank
b. Penfield, Wilder Graves
d. Otto, Nikolaus August

January 27, 1891
b. Ehrenburg, Ilya Grigoryevich

January 28, 1891
b. Doak, Bill
b. Sedran, Barney

January 30, 1891
b. Beech, Walter Herschel
d. Bradlaugh, Charles
d. Kalakaua, David

January 31, 1891
d. Meissonier, Jean Louis Ernest

February 1, 1891
b. Johnson, James Price
b. Kipnis, Alexander

February 2, 1891
b. Foyston, Frank C
b. Segni, Antonio

February 9, 1891
b. Colman, Ronald
b. Nenni, Pietro Sandro
d. Jongkind, Johan Barthold

February 12, 1891
b. Mathews, Mitford M

February 13, 1891
b. Paul, Elliot Harold
d. Porter, David Dixon

February 14, 1891
d. Sherman, William Tecumseh

February 16, 1891
b. Gunther, Hans F K

February 21, 1891
d. Johnston, Joseph Eggleston

February 26, 1891
b. Baugh, Albert Croll

February 27, 1891
b. Moore, Roy W
b. Sarnoff, David

February 28, 1891
d. Hearst, George

March 1, 1891
b. Kalish, Max

March 4, 1891
b. Bronfman, Samuel
b. Vance, Dazzy

March 5, 1891
b. Fitzpatrick, Daniel R
b. Johnson, Chic

March 6, 1891
b. Kilian, Victor
b. Tanner, Marion

March 10, 1891
b. Wang Shih-chieh

March 11, 1891
b. Polanyi, Michael

March 15, 1891
b. Ray, Charles

March 18, 1891
b. Banning, Margaret Culkin

March 19, 1891
b. Crawford, Frederick C(oolidge)
b. Guptill, Arthur Leighton
b. Monaghan, (James) Jay, (IV)
b. Warren, Earl

March 20, 1891
b. Goulding, Edmund

March 22, 1891
b. Gibbons, Tom
b. List, Emanuel
b. Marx, Chico

March 25, 1891
b. Price, Byron

March 28, 1891
b. Whiteman, Paul

March 29, 1891
b. Baxter, Warner
d. Seurat, Georges Pierre

April 2, 1891
b. Buchanan, Jack
b. Ernst, Max
b. Howes, Frank Stewart

April 7, 1891
b. Eliot, Martha May
b. Low, David Alexander Cecil, Sir
d. Barnum, P(hineas) T(aylor)

April 9, 1891
b. Szenkar, Eugen

April 10, 1891
b. McCoy, Tim(othy John Fitzgerald)

April 12, 1891
b. Anderson, C(larence) W(illiam)

April 13, 1891
b. Larsen, Nella

April 15, 1891
b. Reid, Wallace Eugene

April 19, 1891
b. Bacchelli, Riccardo
b. Kennedy, Madge

b. Rosay, Francoise
b. Wilcox, Herbert

April 21, 1891
b. Harkness, Georgia (Elma)

April 22, 1891
b. Gilpin, Laura
b. Jeffreys, Harold
b. Sacco, Nicola

April 23, 1891
b. Prokofiev, Sergei Sergeevich

April 24, 1891
d. Moltke, Helmuth Karl Bernhard von

April 25, 1891
b. Richardson, Sid

April 26, 1891
b. Hoffman, Paul Gray

April 30, 1891
b. Walsh, James Edward
d. Leidy, Joseph

May 3, 1891
b. Rixey, Eppa Jephtha

May 4, 1891
d. Pratt, Charles

May 8, 1891
b. Gardiner, Herb(ert Martin)
d. Blavatsky, Helena Petrovna

May 11, 1891
b. Morgenthau, Henry, Jr.

May 15, 1891
b. Bulgakov, Mikhail Afanasyevich

May 18, 1891
b. Carnap, Rudolf

May 20, 1891
b. Browder, Earl Russell

May 22, 1891
b. Sproul, Robert Gordon

May 23, 1891
b. Lagerkvist, Par Fabian

May 24, 1891
b. Albright, William Foxwell

May 25, 1891
b. Winterich, John Tracy

May 30, 1891
b. Bernie, Ben

June 1, 1891
b. Onegin, Sigrid

June 2, 1891
b. Arnold, Thurman Wesley

June 3, 1891
d. Lossing, Benson John

June 6, 1891
d. MacDonald, John Alexander

June 8, 1891
b. Bothe, Walter Wilhelm Georg

June 10, 1891
b. Dubin, Al
b. Levinsky, Battling

June 18, 1891
b. Conrad, Con

June 20, 1891
b. Costello, John Aloysius

June 21, 1891
b. Nervi, Pier Luigi
b. Scherchen, Hermann

June 23, 1891
d. Weber, Wilhelm Eduard

June 26, 1891
b. Cohen, Octavus Roy
b. Howard, Sidney Coe

June 28, 1891
b. Spaatz, Carl Andrew

June 30, 1891
b. Spencer, Stanley, Sir

July 4, 1891
d. Hamlin, Hannibal

July 5, 1891
b. Northrop, John Howard

July 6, 1891
b. O'Neill, Steve

July 7, 1891
b. Abercrombie, James Smither
b. Ross, David

July 10, 1891
b. Quimby, Edith H.
b. Tugwell, Rexford Guy

July 17, 1891
b. Budenz, Louis Francis

July 18, 1891
b. Lockhart, Gene
b. McNutt, Paul Vories

July 20, 1891
b. Allyn, Stanley Charles
d. Alarcon, Pedro Antonio de

July 21, 1891
b. Ripley, Elmer Horton

July 22, 1891
b. Culbertson, Ely

July 23, 1891
b. Cohn, Harry
b. Wright, Louis Tompkins

July 27, 1891
b. Thompson, Ruth Plumly

July 28, 1891
b. Gallagher, Richard

August 1, 1891
b. Streeter, Edward

August 2, 1891
b. Bliss, Arthur, Sir
d. Williams, George Washington

August 3, 1891
d. Comstock, Elizabeth L

August 6, 1891
b. Slim, William Joseph
d. Litolff, Henri Charles

August 10, 1891
b. Donovan, Arthur

August 11, 1891
b. Broderick, Helen

August 12, 1891
b. McDermott, Johnny
d. Lowell, James Russell

August 14, 1891
b. Oxnam, G(arfield) Bromley
d. Polk, Sarah Childress

August 17, 1891
b. Kardiner, Abram

August 22, 1891
b. Lipchitz, Jacques

August 28, 1891
b. Chekhov, Michael

September 1, 1891
b. Asbury, Herbert

September 3, 1891
b. Delany, Annie Elizabeth

September 5, 1891
b. Molyneux, Edward H
b. Roberts, Gordon

September 6, 1891
b. Thomas, John Charles

September 7, 1891
d. Graetz, Heinrich Hirsch

September 9, 1891
b. Marks, Percy

September 10, 1891
b. Burckhardt, Carl Jacob

September 12, 1891
b. Sulzberger, Arthur Hays

September 16, 1891
b. Doenitz, Karl C

September 18, 1891
d. Balmaceda Fernandez, Jose Manuel

September 19, 1891
d. Grevy, Francois Paul Jules

September 22, 1891
b. Flynn, Edward Joseph
b. Thomas, Alma (Woodsy)

September 24, 1891
b. Branzell, Karin
b. Friedman, William Frederick

September 26, 1891
b. Munch, Charles

September 27, 1891
d. Goncharov, Ivan Aleksandrovich

September 28, 1891
d. Melville, Herman

September 29, 1891
b. James, Marquis
b. Sevitzky, Fabien

September 30, 1891
d. Boulanger, Georges Ernest Jean Marie

October 1, 1891
b. McLean, Robert

October 3, 1891
b. Gannett, Lewis Stiles

October 6, 1891
d. Parnell, Charles Stewart

October 9, 1891
b. Schnering, Otto

October 11, 1891
b. Ault, George Christian
b. Dickinson, Edwin W

October 12, 1891
b. Konoye, Fumimaro, Prince
b. Mesta, Perle Skirvin
b. Stein, Edith

October 14, 1891
b. Gray, James, Sir

October 16, 1891
d. Winnemucca, Sarah

October 17, 1891
b. Banting, Frederick Grant, Sir
d. Parton, James

October 20, 1891
b. Bemis, Samuel Flagg
b. Kenyatta, Jomo

October 21, 1891
b. Burnett, Leo

b. Knaths, Karl
b. Shawn, Ted

October 22, 1891
b. Chadwick, James, Sir

October 24, 1891
b. Trujillo (Molina), Rafael Leonidas

October 25, 1891
b. Coughlin, Charles Edward, Father

October 26, 1891
b. Schlink, Frederick John

October 29, 1891
b. Brice, Fanny
d. Hargraves, Edward Hammond

October 30, 1891
b. Goddard, Calvin Hooker

November 3, 1891
d. Bonaparte, Louis Lucien

November 5, 1891
b. Neale, Greasy

November 6, 1891
b. Buitoni, Giovanni

November 7, 1891
b. Howard, Guy Wesley

November 9, 1891
b. Geiger, Theodor Julius

November 10, 1891
d. Rimbaud, (Jean Nicolas) Arthur

November 11, 1891
b. Ivogun, Maria
b. Maranville, Rabbit

November 12, 1891
b. Nicholson, Seth Barnes
b. Whiting, Richard Armstrong

November 15, 1891
b. Astor, William Vincent
b. Harriman, W(illiam) Averell
b. Rommel, Erwin Johannes Eugin

November 18, 1891
b. Ponti, Gio(vanni)

November 19, 1891
b. Webb, Clifton
d. Florence, William Jermyn

November 20, 1891
b. Denny, Reginald Leigh
b. Murphy, Jimmy

November 21, 1891
b. Ellsberg, Edward
b. Sturtevant, Alfred Henry

November 22, 1891
b. Bernays, Edward L.

November 23, 1891
b. Rodchenko, Alexander Mikhailovich

November 24, 1891
b. Ospina Perez, Mariano
d. Lytton, Edward Robert Bulwer-
Lytton, Earl

November 26, 1891
b. Nichols, Anne

November 27, 1891
b. Salinas (y Serrano), Pedro

December 2, 1891
b. Dix, Otto
b. Merida, Carlos
b. Wesley, Charles Harris

December 4, 1891
b. Jones, Buck

December 5, 1891
d. Pedro II

December 7, 1891
b. Bainter, Fay Okell

December 8, 1891
b. Crosby, Percy L

December 10, 1891
b. Alexander of Tunis
b. Sachs, Nelly (Leonie)

December 13, 1891
b. Kurath, Hans

December 17, 1891
b. Hu Shih

December 18, 1891
b. Armstrong, Edwin Howard
b. Izac, Edouard V(ictor Michel)
d. Owen, Richard, Sir

December 21, 1891
b. McCormack, John William

December 22, 1891
b. Gitlow, Benjamin

December 23, 1891
b. Kaplan, Jacob Merrill

December 24, 1891
b. Rojankovsky, Feodor Stepanovich

December 26, 1891
b. Miller, Henry (Valentine)

December 29, 1891
b. Hall, Joyce Clyde

December 30, 1891
b. Pinay, Antoine

December 31, 1891
d. Crowther, Samuel Adjai

1892

b. Benedictos I
b. Broyhill, James E
b. Cassidy, Marshall
b. Converse, Frederick J
b. Davidson, Scotty
b. Epstein, Abraham
b. Falconetti, Renee Maria
b. Haggar, Joseph M(arion)
b. Hickok, Lorena A
b. Husted, Marjorie Child
b. Jodl, Alfred
b. Kalmus, Natalie Mabelle Dunfee
b. Khalil, Sayyid Abdullah
b. Kulish, Mykola
b. Kuo Mo-jo
b. Laurie, Joe, Jr.
b. Leitzel, Lillian
b. Makonnen Endalkacaw
b. Mallory, Molla
b. Nungesser, Charles Eugene Jules
Marie
b. Smith, Thorne
b. Villa, Luz Corral de
b. Walker, Cyril
b. Walker, Joseph
d. Couper, Archibald Scott
d. Emin Pasha
d. Tewfik Pasha
b. Baker, Hobey
b. Cotten, Libba

January 1, 1892
b. Roxas, Manuel

January 2, 1892
d. Airy, George Biddell, Sir
d. Meigs, Montgomery Cunningham

January 3, 1892
b. Tolkien, J(ohn) R(onald) R(euel)

January 8, 1892
b. O'Connor, Basil
d. Rodgers, Christopher Raymond
Perry

January 10, 1892
b. Malone, Dumas

January 12, 1892
d. Spokane Garry

January 14, 1892
b. Niemoller, Martin
b. Roach, Hal
d. Bowditch, Henry Ingersoll
d. Davis, Alexander Jackson
d. Manning, Henry Edward

January 15, 1892
d. Rogers, Randolph

January 17, 1892
b. Bennett, Harry Herbert
b. Gulick, Luther (Halsey)

January 18, 1892
b. Hardy, Oliver

January 21, 1892
d. Adams, John Couch

January 22, 1892
b. Dassault, Marcel
d. Bradley, Joseph P

January 28, 1892
b. Lubitsch, Ernst

January 31, 1892
b. Cantor, Eddie

February 4, 1892
b. Betti, Ugo

February 6, 1892
b. Murphy, William Parry

February 7, 1892
b. Behrens, Earl Charles

February 8, 1892
b. Ruggles, Charles

February 9, 1892
b. Wood, Peggy

February 10, 1892
b. Hale, Alan

February 13, 1892
b. Jackson, Robert Houghwout
b. Wood, Grant

February 15, 1892
b. Forrestal, James Vincent

February 16, 1892
d. Bates, Henry Walter

February 17, 1892
b. Neyland, Robert Reese

February 18, 1892
b. Willkie, Wendell Lewis

February 19, 1892
b. Lucas, Scott Wike

February 20, 1892
b. Rice, Sam

February 21, 1892
b. Sullivan, Harry Stack

February 22, 1892
b. Dubinsky, David
b. Millay, Edna St. Vincent

February 23, 1892
b. Tabouis, Genevieve

February 24, 1892
b. Fedin, Konstantin Aleksandrovich

February 25, 1892
b. Madden, Ray John

February 27, 1892
b. Demarest, William

February 29, 1892
b. Savage, Augusta Christine

March 1, 1892
b. Akutagawa Ryunosuke

March 6, 1892
b. Shaughnessy, Clark Daniel

March 8, 1892
b. Hurt, Mississippi John
b. Mowrer, Edgar Ansel
d. Allen, John

March 9, 1892
b. Garnett, David
b. Sackville-West, Vita
b. Zita of Bourbon-Parma

March 10, 1892
b. Honegger, Arthur
b. Turner, Eva, Dame

March 11, 1892
b. Handy, Thomas Troy

March 13, 1892
b. Flanner, Janet

March 14, 1892
b. Rakosi, Matyas

March 16, 1892
b. Petrillo, James Caesar
b. Vallejo, Cesar Abraham

March 18, 1892
b. Cochrane, Edward Lull
b. Coffin, Robert Peter Tristram
d. Van Depoele, Charles Joseph

March 19, 1892
b. Van Fleet, James Alward

March 20, 1892
b. Dixon, Mort

March 22, 1892
d. Agnew, David Hayes

March 23, 1892
b. Buttrick, George Arthur

March 25, 1892
b. Clyde, Andy
b. Orr, Douglas William

March 26, 1892
b. Douglas, Paul Howard
d. Whitman, Walt(er)

March 27, 1892
b. Grofe, Ferde

March 28, 1892
b. Heymans, Corneille Jean Francois

March 29, 1892
b. Mindszenty, Jozsef, Cardinal

March 30, 1892
b. Odlum, Floyd Bostwick
b. Panofsky, Erwin

April 1, 1892
b. Shippen, Katherine Binney
b. Zanelli, Renato

April 6, 1892
b. Douglas, Donald Willis
b. Thomas, Lowell Jackson

April 8, 1892
b. Neutra, Richard Joseph

April 10, 1892
b. DeSabata, Victor

April 12, 1892
b. Dodds, Johnny

April 13, 1892
b. Harris, Arthur Travers, Sir
b. Watson-Watt, Robert Alexander, Sir

April 14, 1892
b. Childe, Vere Gordon

April 15, 1892
b. Ten Boom, Corrie

April 16, 1892
b. Jones, Howard Mumford

April 17, 1892
d. Mackenzie, Alexander

April 18, 1892
b. Bierut, Boleslaw
b. Houdry, Eugene Jules

April 19, 1892
b. Tailleferre, Germaine

April 20, 1892
b. Bancroft, Dave

April 22, 1892
d. Lalo, Edouard Victor Antoine

April 24, 1892
b. Hulbert, Jack

April 25, 1892
d. Bradford, William

April 27, 1892
b. Levy, David Mordecai

April 28, 1892
b. Niles, John Jacob

April 30, 1892
b. Clapper, Raymond Lewis

May 1, 1892
b. Barlow, Howard
d. Lamperti, Francesco

May 2, 1892
b. Richthofen, Manfred von, Baron
d. Hofmann, August Wilhelm von

May 3, 1892
b. Bondi, Beulah

b. Thomson, George Paget, Sir

May 5, 1892
b. Bloch, Bertram
b. Garrod, Dorothy Annie Elizabeth

May 7, 1892
b. MacLeish, Archibald

May 11, 1892
b. Rutherford, Margaret

May 15, 1892
b. Wilde, Jimmy
b. Wills, Harry

May 16, 1892
b. Perkins, Osgood
b. Tauber, Richard

May 18, 1892
b. Pinza, Ezio

May 19, 1892
b. Foster, Pops

May 20, 1892
b. Anslinger, Harry Jacob
b. Russell, Sydney Gordon, Sir

May 24, 1892
b. Lewis, Elizabeth Foreman

May 25, 1892
b. Tito

May 27, 1892
b. Crosthwait, David Nelson, Jr.

May 29, 1892
b. Faust, Frederick Schiller
d. Baha'u'llah

May 30, 1892
b. Amorsolo, Fernando
d. Rutherfurd, Lewis Morris
b. Madden, Owen Victor

June 1, 1892
b. Amanollah Khan

June 5, 1892
b. Compton-Burnett, Ivy, Dame
b. Sugiura, Kanematsu

June 6, 1892
b. James, Will(iam Roderick)

June 7, 1892
b. Ponselle, Carmela

June 9, 1892
b. Lewis, Ted
b. Porter, Cole

June 11, 1892
b. Maney, Richard
d. Polk, Leonidas Lafayette

June 12, 1892
b. Barnes, Djuna

June 13, 1892
b. Rathbone, Basil

June 14, 1892
b. Reed, Peter Hugh

June 16, 1892
b. Grossinger, Jennie
b. Rubicam, Raymond

June 20, 1892
b. Jung, Leo

June 21, 1892
b. Niebuhr, Reinhold
b. Rosenberg, Hilding

June 23, 1892
b. Butler, Paul

June 24, 1892
b. Daringer, Helen Fern
d. Ford, Bob

June 26, 1892
b. Buck, Pearl S(ydenstricker)

June 28, 1892
b. Campbell, Clifford, Sir
b. Gordon, Max

July 1, 1892
b. Cain, James M(allahan)
b. Lurcat, Jean Marie

July 2, 1892
b. Seyss-Inquart, Artur von
d. Fox, Kate

July 4, 1892
b. Gaston, Arthur George

July 6, 1892
b. Yellen, Jack

July 8, 1892
b. Aldington, Richard (Edward Godfree)

July 11, 1892
b. Mitchell, Thomas

July 12, 1892
b. Clarke, Gilmore David
d. Cartwright, Alexander Joy, Jr.
d. Field, Cyrus West

July 13, 1892
b. Broadbent, Punch

July 16, 1892
b. Seeley, Blossom

July 18, 1892
d. Cooke, Rose Terry

July 19, 1892
b. Irvin, Dick
d. Cook, Thomas

July 20, 1892
b. Bara, Theda

July 23, 1892
b. Haile Selassie, I

July 24, 1892
b. Jones, Thomas Hudson

July 26, 1892
b. Jones, Sam(uel Pond)
b. Leonard, Dutch

July 28, 1892
b. Brown, Joe E(van)

July 29, 1892
b. Powell, William

July 31, 1892
b. Armstrong, Herbert W

August 2, 1892
b. Kieran, John Francis
b. Warner, Jack Leonard

August 4, 1892
b. Swigert, Ernest Goodnough

August 6, 1892
b. Gibson, Hoot
b. Suckow, Ruth

August 9, 1892
d. Denver, James William

August 11, 1892
b. Anders, Wladyslaw
b. MacDiarmid, Hugh

August 12, 1892
b. Olczewska, Maria
b. Rea, Gardner
b. Schalk, Ray(mond William)

August 15, 1892
b. Broglie, Louis Prince De

August 16, 1892
b. Braslau, Sophie
b. Foster, Hal
b. Messmer, Otto

August 19, 1892
b. Lunt, Alfred

August 20, 1892
b. Aiken, George David

August 23, 1892
d. Fonseca, Manuel Deodoro da

August 29, 1892
b. Norwich, Diana (Manners) Cooper, Viscountess

August 31, 1892
d. Curtis, George William
b. Piastro, Michel

September 1, 1892
b. Lamb, Harold Albert
b. Saltonstall, Leverett

September 2, 1892
b. Szigeti, Joseph

September 4, 1892
b. Milhaud, Darius
b. Smith, Pete

September 6, 1892
b. Appleton, Edward Victor, Sir

September 7, 1892
d. Whittier, John Greenleaf

September 10, 1892
b. Compton, Arthur Holly

September 12, 1892
b. Knopf, Alfred Abraham

September 18, 1892
d. Francis, James Bicheno

September 22, 1892
b. Kiesler, Frederick John
b. Sullivan, Frank

September 24, 1892
d. Gilmore, Patrick Sarsfield

September 26, 1892
b. Lynd, Robert Staughton
b. Tsvetayeva, Marina Ivanovna

September 28, 1892
b. Rice, Elmer

October 2, 1892
d. Renan, (Joseph) Ernest

October 4, 1892
b. Dollfuss, Engelbert
b. Lawson, Robert

October 5, 1892
d. Dalton, Gratton
d. Dalton, Robert

October 6, 1892
d. Tennyson, Alfred, Lord

October 8, 1892
b. Smith, Lowell Herbert

October 10, 1892
b. Andric, Ivo
b. Dickson, Earle Ensign

October 12, 1892
b. Dalla Rizza, Gilda

October 14, 1892
b. Welles, Sumner

October 18, 1892
b. Carroll, Leo G

October 21, 1892
b. Boni, Albert
b. Lopokova, Lydia Vasilievna

October 22, 1892
b. Rascoe, Burton

October 25, 1892
b. Dolly, Jenny
b. Dolly, Rosie
d. Harrison, Caroline (Lavinia Scott)

October 28, 1892
b. Johnson, Dink

October 29, 1892
d. Harnett, William Michael
b. Guo Moruo

November 1, 1892
b. Alekhine, Alexander

November 2, 1892
d. Schwatka, Frederik

November 3, 1892
b. Chao, Yuen Ren

November 5, 1892
b. Haldane, J(ohn) B(urdon)
S(anderson)

November 6, 1892
b. Alcock, John William, Sir
b. Olsen, Ole
b. Ross, Harold Wallace

November 11, 1892
b. Schacht, Al(exander)

November 23, 1892
b. Erte

November 26, 1892
b. Brackett, Charles
b. Guyon, Joe
d. Lavigerie, Charles Martel Allemand

November 29, 1892
d. Wyant, Alexander Helwig

December 2, 1892
d. Gould, Jay

December 3, 1892
b. Adler, Julius Ochs

December 4, 1892
b. Franco, Francisco

December 6, 1892
b. Lawless, Theodore K(enneth)
b. Sitwell, Osbert, Sir
d. Siemens, (Ernst) Werner von

December 8, 1892
b. Mooney, Tom

December 10, 1892
b. Johnson, Eleanor M

December 11, 1892
b. Adams, Harriet Stratemeyer
b. Bloom, Ursula
b. Larson, John Augustus

December 12, 1892
b. Wright, John Lloyd

December 15, 1892
b. Getty, J(ean) Paul
b. Guion, David Wendel Fentress

December 17, 1892
b. Cohn, Edwin Joseph

December 19, 1892
b. Nye, Gerald Prentice

December 20, 1892
b. May, Mortimer

December 21, 1892
b. Hagen, Walter Charles

December 23, 1892
b. Greene, Ward

December 25, 1892
b. West, Rebecca, Dame

December 31, 1892
b. Robards, Jason

1893

b. Bajor, Gizi
b. Brown, A Roy
b. Culligan, Emmett J
b. Dali, Gala
b. Davis, Tobe
b. de Acosta, Mercedes
b. Donlon, Mary Honor
b. Fitzgerald, Ed(ward)
b. Husseini, Haj Amin
b. Joyce, Peggy Hopkins
b. Lightner, Theodore
b. Martin, James, Sir
b. Moran, Bugs
b. Pennington, Ann
b. Peters, Brandon
b. Peterson, Lorraine Collett
d. Dalton, William
d. Farmer, Moses Gerrish
d. French, Robert T

January 1, 1893
b. Gorman, Herbert Sherman

January 3, 1893
b. Seldes, Gilbert Vivian

January 5, 1893
b. Yogananda, Paramahansa, Swami

January 7, 1893
b. Wayman, Dorothy

January 8, 1893
b. Kindler, Hans

January 9, 1893
d. Judson, Egbert Putnam

January 11, 1893
b. Pasero, Tancredi
d. Butler, Benjamin Franklin

January 12, 1893
b. Goering, Hermann Wilhelm
b. Rosenberg, Alfred

January 15, 1893
b. Novello, Ivor
d. Kemble, Fanny
d. Smith, Horace

January 16, 1893
b. Bordoni, Irene

January 17, 1893
b. Scott, Evelyn
d. Hayes, Rutherford B(irchard)

January 18, 1893
b. Guillen, Jorge

January 21, 1893
b. Barnaby, Ralph S

January 22, 1893
b. Oursler, (Charles) Fulton
b. Veidt, Conrad

January 23, 1893
b. Carlson, Frank
b. Pangborn, Franklin
d. Brooks, Phillips
d. Lamar, Lucius Quintus Cincinnatus

January 26, 1893
b. Coleman, Bessie
b. Nighbor, Frank
d. Doubleday, Abner

January 27, 1893
b. Sun Yat-Sen, Chingling Soong, Madame
d. Blaine, James Gillespie

January 28, 1893
b. Silver, Abba Hillel

February 4, 1893
b. Dart, Raymond Arthur

February 6, 1893
b. Pudovkin, Vsevolod
b. Zafrulla Khan, Muhammad, Sir

February 8, 1893
b. Ba Maw

February 10, 1893
b. Durante, Jimmy
b. Tilden, Bill

February 11, 1893
b. Kovalev, Mikhail Aleksandrovich

February 12, 1893
b. Bradley, Omar Nelson
b. Shannon, Fred Albert

February 14, 1893
b. Smith, Dora

February 15, 1893
b. Baxter, James Phinney, III
b. Donaldson, Walter

February 16, 1893
b. Tukhachevski, Mikhail Nikolayevich

February 17, 1893
b. Pipp, Wally

February 19, 1893
b. Hardwicke, Cedric Webster, Sir
d. Carroll, Anna Ella

February 20, 1893
b. Crouse, Russel
d. Beauregard, Pierre Gustav Toutant de

February 22, 1893
b. O'Donnell, Peadar

February 26, 1893
b. Frawley, William
b. Richards, Ivor Armstrong

February 27, 1893
b. Dobrowen, Issai
b. Linton, Ralph

February 28, 1893
b. Hecht, Ben
b. Thomason, John William, Jr.
b. Tannenbaum, Frank

March 5, 1893
b. Sands, Dorothy

March 6, 1893
b. Jones, Barry

March 7, 1893
b. Avery, Milton Clark

March 8, 1893
b. Jaffe, Sam
d. Fox, Margaret
d. Smith, Edmund Kirby

March 9, 1893
b. Marston, William Moulton
d. Taine, Hippolyte Adolphe

March 15, 1893
b. Lyttleton, Oliver

March 17, 1893
b. Garrett, Eileen Jeanette Lyttle
d. Ferry, Jules Francois Camille

March 18, 1893
b. Owen, Wilfred

March 19, 1893
b. Velasco Ibarra, Jose Maria

March 24, 1893
b. Baade, (Wilhelm Heinrich) Walter

b. Sisler, George Harold

March 26, 1893
b. Conant, James Bryant
b. Togliatti, Palmiro

March 27, 1893
b. Mannheim, Karl
b. Mihajlovic, Dragoliub

March 28, 1893
b. Skouras, Spyros Panagiotes

March 31, 1893
b. Krauss, Clemens

April 1, 1893
b. Courtneidge, Cicely, Dame
b. Wells, Linton

April 3, 1893
b. Howard, Leslie

April 5, 1893
b. Burpee, David
b. DePaolis, Alessio

April 7, 1893
b. Armstrong, Hamilton Fish
b. Castle, Irene Foote
b. Dulles, Allen Welsh

April 9, 1893
b. Burchfield, Charles Ephraim
b. Fineman, Irving
b. Gollancz, Victor, Sir

April 10, 1893
b. Mompou, Federico

April 11, 1893
b. Acheson, Dean Gooderham

April 15, 1893
b. Paul, Prince

April 17, 1893
b. Grant, Bruce
d. Larcom, Lucy

April 19, 1893
d. Symonds, John Addington

April 20, 1893
b. Lloyd, Harold
b. Miro, Joan
b. Ratoff, Gregory

April 21, 1893
b. Christaller, Walter

April 23, 1893
b. Borzage, Frank

April 26, 1893
b. Loos, Anita

April 27, 1893
b. Geddes, Norman Bel

April 29, 1893
b. Urey, Harold Clayton

April 30, 1893
b. Ribbentrop, Joachim von
b. Pearlroth, Norbert

May 7, 1893
b. Atwood, Francis Clarke
b. Selke, Frank J, Sr.

May 8, 1893
b. Ku Chieh-kang
b. Ouimet, Francis de Sales
b. Roush, Edd J

May 9, 1893
b. Barclay, McClelland

May 10, 1893
b. Rau, Dhanvanthi Rama, Lady

May 11, 1893
b. Gag, Wanda
b. Graham, Martha
d. Armstrong, Samuel Chapman

May 12, 1893
b. Black, Walter J

May 13, 1893
b. Kelly, Shipwreck

May 15, 1893
b. Ichikawa, Fusae

May 17, 1893
b. Shields, Larry

May 19, 1893
b. VonSchmidt, Harold

May 23, 1893
b. Bodenheim, Maxwell

May 26, 1893
b. Goossens, Eugene, Sir

May 30, 1893
b. Raisa, Rosa

May 31, 1893
b. Coatsworth, Elizabeth Jane

June 1, 1893
b. Stanley, Barney

June 2, 1893
b. Martin, John

June 7, 1893
b. Feis, Herbert
d. Booth, Edwin Thomas

June 8, 1893
b. Scobie, Ronald Mackenzie

June 9, 1893
b. Behrman, S(amuel) N(athaniel)

June 12, 1893
b. Hodge, John Reed

June 13, 1893
b. Sayers, Dorothy Leigh

June 15, 1893
b. Weeks, Sinclair

June 17, 1893
b. Helck, Peter

June 21, 1893
d. Stanford, Leland

June 23, 1893
b. Davison, Frank Dalby

June 24, 1893
b. Disney, Roy O(liver)

June 25, 1893
b. Greenwood, Charlotte

June 26, 1893
b. Broonzy, Big Bill

June 30, 1893
b. Laski, Harold Joseph
b. Ulbricht, Walter
d. Drexel, Anthony Joseph

July 1, 1893
b. Parker, Daniel Francis
b. White, Walter Francis

July 2, 1893
d. Barrymore, Georgiana Emma Drew

July 6, 1893
d. Maupassant, Guy de

July 7, 1893
d. Blatchford, Samuel

July 11, 1893
b. McCabe, Thomas Bayard

July 12, 1893
b. Brain, Aubrey

July 15, 1893
b. Dieterle, William

July 19, 1893
b. Mayakovsky, Vladimir

July 21, 1893
b. Fallada, Hans

July 22, 1893
b. Haines, Jesse Joseph

July 23, 1893
b. Menninger, Karl Augustus

July 24, 1893
b. Johnson, Charles Spurgeon

July 25, 1893
b. Confalonieri, Carlo, Cardinal

July 26, 1893
b. Grosz, George Ehrenfried

August 2, 1893
b. Burns, Bob

August 4, 1893
d. Bolton, Sarah Tittle Barrett

August 6, 1893
b. McClintic, Guthrie
b. Patman, (John Williams) Wright
d. Schirmer, Gustave

August 7, 1893
d. Catalani, Alfredo

August 9, 1893
b. Bedells, Phyllis

August 10, 1893
b. Moore, Douglas Stuart

August 14, 1893
b. Leibowitz, Samuel Simon
b. Williams, Roger J

August 15, 1893
b. Curtice, Harlow Herbert

August 16, 1893
d. Charcot, Jean Martin

August 17, 1893
b. West, Mae

August 18, 1893
b. Davidson, Donald Grady
b. Grimes, Burleigh Arland
b. MacMillan, Ernest Campbell, Sir

August 22, 1893
b. Holbrook, Stewart Hall
b. Kellaway, Cecil
b. Parker, Dorothy Rothschild

August 25, 1893
b. Dean, Henry Trendley

August 27, 1893
b. Henderson, Arthur

August 28, 1893
b. Arnold, Leslie Philip
d. Harvey, Hayward Augustus

August 30, 1893
b. Long, Huey Pierce

August 31, 1893
b. Laskin, Lily

September 1, 1893
b. Blythe, Betty
b. Kappel, Gertrude
b. Kuniyoshi, Yasuo

September 5, 1893
b. Rosenberg, Jakob
b. Sokolsky, George E

September 6, 1893
b. Bricker, John William
d. Fish, Hamilton

September 7, 1893
b. Hore-Belisha, Leslie, Baron
b. Karns, Roscoe

September 12, 1893
b. Hershey, Lewis Blaine

September 16, 1893
b. Carroll, Earl
b. Korda, Alexander, Sir
b. Szent-Gyorgyi, Albert (von Nagyrapolt)

September 18, 1893
b. Benjamin, Arthur
b. Campbell, William Edward March

September 19, 1893
d. Galt, Alexander Tilloch

September 21, 1893
b. Willard, Frank Henry

September 26, 1893
b. Rosenstein, Nettie

September 28, 1893
b. Field, Marshall, III

October 1, 1893
b. Baldwin, Faith
d. Jowett, Benjamin

October 4, 1893
b. Ljungberg, Gota

October 5, 1893
b. Hibberd, Andrew Stuart

October 6, 1893
b. Ager, Milton

October 7, 1893
b. Dalgleish, Alice

October 14, 1893
b. Gish, Lillian (Diana)
b. Lenski, Lois

October 15, 1893
b. Lewis, Saunders

October 16, 1893
b. Carmer, Carl Lamson
b. Carol II

October 17, 1893
b. Byington, Spring
d. Gounod, Charles Francois

October 18, 1893
d. Stonc, Lucy

October 20, 1893
b. Chase, Charley
d. Schaff, Philip

October 23, 1893
b. Marx, Gummo
d. Crittendon, Thomas Leonidas

October 28, 1893
b. Ingold, Christopher Kelk, Sir

October 30, 1893
d. Bodmer, Karl

October 31, 1893
b. Strode, Hudson
d. Sorin, Edward Frederick

November 2, 1893
b. Brady, Alice

November 4, 1893
b. Coste, Dieudonne

November 5, 1893
b. Loewy, Raymond Fernand

November 6, 1893
b. Ford, Edsel Bryant
d. Tchaikovsky, Peter Ilyich

November 7, 1893
b. Joy, Leatrice
b. Leech, Margaret Kernochan

November 8, 1893
d. Parkman, Francis

November 10, 1893
b. Marquand, John Phillips

November 11, 1893
b. Finletter, Thomas Knight

November 13, 1893
b. Beals, Carleton
b. Doisy, Edward Adelbert, Sr.
b. Rubin, Reuven

November 17, 1893
b. Christison, (Alexander Frank) Philip

November 22, 1893
b. Dundee, Johnny
b. Kaganovich, Lazar M(oiseevich)

November 23, 1893
b. Marx, Harpo
b. Schram, Emil

November 25, 1893
b. Krutch, Joseph Wood

November 26, 1893
b. Vaughan, Harry Hawkins

November 28, 1893
b. Downey, Fairfax Davis

December 1, 1893
b. Toller, Ernst

December 2, 1893
b. Gaxton, William
d. A.L.O.E.

d. Cushman, Pauline

December 4, 1893
b. Read, Herbert, Sir
d. Tyndall, John

December 6, 1893
b. Little, Lou(is)
b. Warner, Sylvia Townsend

December 7, 1893
b. Kirkus, Virginia

December 9, 1893
b. Brett, George Platt, Jr.

December 10, 1893
b. Brown, Lew

December 12, 1893
b. Robinson, Edward G

December 15, 1893
b. Fruehauf, Harvey Charles

December 23, 1893
b. Douglas, Sholto

December 24, 1893
b. Chatterton, Ruth
b. Warren, Harry

December 25, 1893
b. Ripley, Robert Leroy

December 26, 1893
b. Golschmann, Vladimir
b. Mao Zedong

December 30, 1893
d. Baker, Samuel White, Sir

1894

b. Bane, Frank B
b. Barker, Herman
b. Beck, Dave
b. Benedict, Clint(on Stephen)
b. Berwind, Charles G
b. Epperson, Frank W
b. Ertz, Susan
b. Fleischmann, Gisi
b. Fonck, Rene
b. Innis, Harold Adams
b. Kiam, Omar
b. Lewis, Dominic Bevan Wyndham
b. MacDonald, Elizabeth G.
b. Merrill, Henry Tindall
b. Munn, Frank
b. Pauker, Ana
b. Perls, Frederick Salomon
b. Smedley, Agnes
b. Soutine, Chaim
b. Treptow, Martin A
b. Varipapa, Andy
d. Apache Kid
d. Gall
d. Kim Ok-kyun
d. Lobengula
d. Manuelito
d. Rillieux, Norbert

January 1, 1894
b. Bose, Satyendranath
d. Hertz, Heinrich Rudolph

January 2, 1894
b. Nathan, Robert
b. Rodzinski, Artur

January 3, 1894
d. Peabody, Elizabeth Palmer

January 4, 1894
b. Woody, Regina Llewellyn Jones

January 8, 1894
b. Kolbe, Maximilian Maria, Saint

January 9, 1894
b. Markel, Lester

January 11, 1894
b. Ballinger, Margaret

January 12, 1894
b. Carpentier, Georges

January 16, 1894
b. Chamberlin, B Guy
b. Mills, Irving

January 18, 1894
b. Berlin, Richard E

January 20, 1894
b. Gray, Harold Lincoln
b. Piston, Walter

January 22, 1894
b. Morgan, Charles Langbridge
b. Ponselle, Rosa

January 27, 1894
b. Pollard, Fritz

January 31, 1894
b. Jones, Isham

February 3, 1894
b. Negrin, Juan
b. Rockwell, Norman
d. Childs, George William

February 4, 1894
d. Sax, Adolphe (Antoine-Joseph)

February 5, 1894
b. Morgan, Frederick, Sir

February 6, 1894
b. Bonelli, Richard
b. Partridge, Eric Honeywood
. d. Billroth, Theodore

February 8, 1894
b. Bishop, Billy
b. Vidor, King Wallis

February 10, 1894
b. MacMillan, Harold
b. Pennock, Herb(ert Jefferis)

February 12, 1894
d. Bulow, Hans Guido von

February 14, 1894
b. Benny, Jack

February 15, 1894
b. Aranha, Osvaldo

February 18, 1894
b. Nicolson, Marjorie Hope
b. Segovia, Andres
b. Williams, Paul R(evere)

February 20, 1894
b. Richter, Curt Paul

February 23, 1894
b. Schilt, Jan

February 25, 1894
b. Hansberry, William Leo
d. Mackaye, James Morrison Steele

February 26, 1894
b. Harmon, Ernest N(ason)

February 27, 1894
b. Close, Upton

March 1, 1894
d. Poole, William Frederick

March 2, 1894
b. Oparin, Aleksandr Ivanovich
d. Early, Jubal Anderson

March 5, 1894
b. Daniell, Henry

March 12, 1894
b. Meyer, Joseph

March 13, 1894
b. Braden, Spruille

March 14, 1894
b. Johnson, Osa Helen Leighty

March 17, 1894
b. Green, Paul Eliot

March 19, 1894
b. Mabley, Moms
b. Wambsganss, Bill

March 20, 1894
d. Kossuth, Lajos

March 25, 1894
b. Best, Oswald Herbert

March 27, 1894
d. Cameron, Verney Lovett

March 28, 1894
b. Carlson, Wally

March 30, 1894
b. Bainton, Roland Herbert

March 31, 1894
b. Ilyushin, Sergei Vladimirovich

April 3, 1894
b. Wilson, Dooley

April 5, 1894
b. Bell, Lawrence Dale

April 7, 1894
b. Brenan, Gerald

April 8, 1894
b. Pickford, Mary
d. Chatterji, Bankimchandra

April 9, 1894
b. Manville, Tommy

April 10, 1894
b. Nicholson, Ben

April 12, 1894
b. Gold, Michael

April 13, 1894
d. Field, David Dudley
d. Spitta, Philipp

April 14, 1894
d. Vance, Zebulon Baird

April 15, 1894
b. Smith, Bessie

April 17, 1894
b. Khrushchev, Nikita Sergeyevich

April 19, 1894
b. Dudley, George S

April 24, 1894
b. Ehmke, Howard Jonathan

April 26, 1894
b. Austral, Florence Wilson
b. Hess, Rudolf

April 27, 1894
b. Slonimsky, Nicolas

April 30, 1894
b. Bartlett, Vernon
b. Evatt, Herbert Vere

May 6, 1894
b. Cobham, Alan John, Sir

May 11, 1894
b. Bunker, Ellsworth

May 14, 1894
b. Folsom, Frank M

May 15, 1894
b. Porter, Katherine Anne

May 16, 1894
b. Yust, Walter

May 18, 1894
b. Sandino, Augusto C(esar Calderon)

May 19, 1894
b. Busse, Henry

May 20, 1894
b. Saint Johns, Adela Rogers

May 21, 1894
b. MacKay, Mickey

May 22, 1894
b. Davis, Clyde Brion

May 26, 1894
b. Lukas, Paul

May 27, 1894
b. Celine, Louis-Ferdinand
b. Destouches, Louis-Ferdinand
b. Hammett, Dashiell

May 29, 1894
b. VonSternberg, Josef

May 31, 1894
b. Allen, Fred

June 2, 1894
d. Dabney, Virginius

June 3, 1894
b. Szyk, Arthur

June 4, 1894
b. Pascal, Gabriel

June 5, 1894
b. Thomson, Roy Herbert

June 6, 1894
b. Greb, Harry

June 7, 1894
b. DeSeversky, Alexander Procofieff
d. Whitney, William Dwight

June 13, 1894
b. Kanner, Leo
b. Lartique, Jacques-Henri Charles
   Auguste
b. Van Doren, Mark

June 15, 1894
b. Bennett, Robert Russell

June 17, 1894
b. Bache, Harold Leopold

June 19, 1894
b. Cicotte, Eddie

June 20, 1894
b. Delacorte, George Thomas, Jr.
b. Hall, Lloyd Augustus

June 22, 1894
b. Eliot, George Fielding
b. Luboshutz, Pierre

June 23, 1894
b. Edward VIII
b. Kinsey, Alfred Charles
b. Weiss, George Martin

June 24, 1894
d. Healy, George Peter Alexander

June 25, 1894
b. Oberth, Hermann Julius
b. Sturtzel, Howard Allison

June 26, 1894
b. Eagels, Jeanne
b. Kapitsa, Pyotr Leonidovich
b. Lovejoy, Clarence Earle

June 28, 1894
b. Forbes, Esther
b. Nicoll, (John Ramsay) Allardyce

July 2, 1894
b. Kertesz, Andre
b. Treacher, Arthur

July 4, 1894
b. Carlson, Doc

July 5, 1894
d. Layard, Austen Henry, Sir

July 9, 1894
b. Spencer, Percy Le Baron
b. Thompson, Dorothy

July 10, 1894
b. McHugh, Jimmy

July 11, 1894
b. Wanger, Walter

July 12, 1894
b. Stromberg, Hunt

July 13, 1894
b. Babel, Isaac Emmanuelovich

July 14, 1894
b. Dixon, Jean

July 16, 1894
b. Toledano, Vicente Lombardo

July 17, 1894
b. Lemaitre, Georges
d. Leconte de Lisle, Charles Marie
   Rene

July 18, 1894
b. Dix, Richard

July 21, 1894
b. Ulric, Lenore

July 22, 1894
b. Totheroh, Dan

July 23, 1894
b. Stronge, Norman, Sir

July 24, 1894
d. Ingersoll, Simon

July 25, 1894
b. Brennan, Walter Andrew

July 26, 1894
b. Huxley, Aldous (Leonard)

July 30, 1894
b. Knopf, Blanche Wolf
d. Pater, Walter (Horatio)

August 1, 1894
b. Mays, Benjamin E(lijah)

August 2, 1894
b. Pegler, Westbrook

August 3, 1894
b. Heilmann, Harry Edwin
d. Inness, George

August 9, 1894
b. Starkie, Walter Fitzwilliam

August 14, 1894
b. Bricktop

August 16, 1894
b. Meany, George

August 23, 1894
b. Secunda, Sholom

August 24, 1894
b. Rhys, Jean

August 26, 1894
d. Thaxter, Celia

August 28, 1894
b. Bohm, Karl

September 3, 1894
b. Niebuhr, Helmut Richard

September 5, 1894
d. Stoneman, George

September 8, 1894
d. Helmholtz, Hermann Ludwig
   Ferdinand von

September 9, 1894
b. Freed, Arthur

September 11, 1894
b. Dovzhenko, Alexander

September 12, 1894
b. Gilbert, Billy

September 13, 1894
b. Priestley, (J)ohn (B)oynton
d. Chabrier, Emmanuel

September 15, 1894
b. Renoir, Jean

September 17, 1894
b. McKinney, Bill

September 18, 1894
b. Compton, Fay

September 19, 1894
b. Field, Rachel Lyman

September 20, 1894
b. Collinge, Patricia
d. Hoffmann, Heinrich

September 22, 1894
b. Rethberg, Elizabeth

September 23, 1894
b. Cohen, Benjamin Victor

September 25, 1894
b. Briscoe, Robert

October 3, 1894
b. Sharett, Moshe

October 6, 1894
b. McNair, Malcolm Perrine

October 7, 1894
b. Mulhall, Jack
d. Curtin, Andrew Gregg
d. Holmes, Oliver Wendell, Sr.

October 9, 1894
b. Bullard, Eugene
b. McFarland, Ernest William

October 10, 1894
d. Allen, Macon B

October 11, 1894
b. Lubke, Heinrich
b. Stoessel, Albert

October 13, 1894
b. Corey, Lewis

October 14, 1894
b. Cummings, E(dward) E(stlin)
b. Pate, Maurice

October 20, 1894
d. Froude, James Anthony

October 21, 1894
b. Purviance, Edna

October 24, 1894
b. Lewis, Ted

October 25, 1894
b. Phillips, Marjorie Acker

October 26, 1894
b. Knight, John Shivley

October 28, 1894
b. Murphy, Robert Daniel
b. Pangborn, Clyde Edward
b. Wolff, Fritz

October 30, 1894
b. Atlas, Charles
b. Heseltine, Philip Arnold

October 31, 1894
b. King, Charles

November 1, 1894
b. Smith, Chard Powers
d. Alexander III

November 5, 1894
b. Ruml, Beardsley

November 7, 1894
b. Blanding, Don

November 8, 1894
d. Kelly, King

November 10, 1894
b. Normand, Mabel

November 13, 1894
b. Moten, Bennie

November 16, 1894
b. Potofsky, Jacob Samuel
d. McCosh, James

November 18, 1894
b. Denny, Ludwell

November 19, 1894
b. Thomaz, Americo

November 20, 1894
b. Humphries, Rolfe
d. Rubinstein, Anton Gregorovitch

November 22, 1894
b. Bayne, Beverly Pearl

November 23, 1894
b. Folsom, Marion Bayard

November 25, 1894
b. Stallings, Laurence

November 26, 1894
b. Papanin, Ivan D
b. Wiener, Norbert

November 27, 1894
b. Matsushita, Konosuke

November 28, 1894
b. Atkinson, Brooks
b. Taggard, Genevieve

November 29, 1894
d. Monck, Charles Stanley, Sir

November 30, 1894
b. Stewart, Donald Ogden
d. Brown, Joseph Emerson

December 2, 1894
d. Thompson, John S(parrow) D(avid), Sir

December 3, 1894
d. Stevenson, Robert Louis (Balfour)

December 4, 1894
b. Soong, T V

December 5, 1894
b. Swart, Charles Robberts
b. Wrigley, Philip Knight

December 6, 1894
b. Lynch, J(ohn) Joseph

December 7, 1894
b. Davis, Stuart
d. Lesseps, Ferdinand Marie de

December 8, 1894
b. Segar, Elzie Crisler
b. Thurber, James Grover

December 11, 1894
b. Dowling, Eddie
b. Lauri-Volpi, Giacoma

December 12, 1894
b. Drinker, Philip

December 13, 1894
b. Ronning, Chester A

December 17, 1894
b. Fiedler, Arthur

December 18, 1894
b. Healey, Ed(ward)
d. Beadle, Erastus Flavel

December 19, 1894
b. Dessau, Paul
b. Frick, Ford Christopher

December 20, 1894
b. Menzies, Robert Gordon, Sir
d. Alcorn, James Lusk

December 24, 1894
b. Guynemer, Georges Marie

December 26, 1894
b. Toomer, Jean

December 28, 1894
b. Matthews, Burnita S(helton)
b. Romer, Alfred Sherwood

December 29, 1894
b. Hill, Lester
d. Rossetti, Christina Georgina

December 30, 1894
b. Bakeless, John Edwin
d. Bloomer, Amelia Jenks

December 31, 1894
b. Negri, Pola

1895

b. Abdullah al-Salim al-Sabah

b. Baker, Belle
b. Blaisdell, George G
b. Calkins, Dick
b. Cierva, Juan de la
b. Cord, E(rret) L(obban)
b. Crowder, Henry
b. Dahl-Wolfe, Louise
b. Edwards, India Moffett
b. Frederickson, Frank
b. Gluck
b. Husayni, Al-Hajj Amin al-
b. Jennings, Talbot
b. La Follette, Suzanne
b. Mitchell, Reginald Joseph
b. Morgana, Nina
b. Neff, Wallace
b. Rees, Lloyd Frederic
b. Sanapia
b. Sorge, Richard
b. Thuku, Harry
b. Volpi, Alfredo
b. Wallace-Johnson, Isaac Theophilus
   Akunna
b. Wertham, Fredric
d. Coup, W(illiam) C(ameron)
d. Ismail Pasha
d. Libby, Charles
d. Smohalla

January 1, 1895
b. Hoover, J(ohn) Edgar

January 2, 1895
b. Bernadotte, Folke, Count
b. Leonidoff, Leon

January 3, 1895
d. Ives, James Merritt

January 4, 1895
b. Grumman, Leroy Randle

January 5, 1895
b. Piccard, Jeannette Ridlon

January 9, 1895
b. Farr, Wanda K.

January 10, 1895
b. Davis, Meyer
d. Godard, Benjamin Louis Paul

January 11, 1895
b. Hammond, Laurens

January 15, 1895
b. Virtanen, Artturi Llmari

January 16, 1895
b. Weyerhaeuser, Frederick Edward

January 21, 1895
b. Balenciaga, Cristobal

January 22, 1895
b. Alley, Norman William

January 24, 1895
d. Churchill, Randolph Henry Spencer,
   Lord

January 25, 1895
b. Mills, Florence

January 26, 1895
d. Cayley, Arthur

January 27, 1895
b. Rosenstock, Joseph
b. Ruby, Harry

January 29, 1895
b. Berle, Adolf Augustus, Jr.

February 1, 1895
b. Ford, John Sean O'Feeney
b. Smythe, Conn

February 2, 1895
b. Halas, George Stanley

February 3, 1895
b. Kenny, Nick
d. Weld, Theodore Dwight

February 4, 1895
b. Bruce, Nigel

February 6, 1895
b. Camerini, Mario
b. Ruth, Babe

February 7, 1895
b. Van Paassen, Pierre

February 8, 1895
b. Samuel, Maurice

February 9, 1895
b. Vargas, Alberto

February 13, 1895
b. Wilder, Joseph

February 15, 1895
b. Thomson, Earl

February 18, 1895
b. Gipp, George

February 19, 1895
b. Calhern, Louis
b. Timoshenko, Semen
   Konstantinovich

February 20, 1895
d. Douglass, Frederick

February 21, 1895
b. Dam, (Carl Peter) Henrik
b. Esenin, Sergei Aleksandrovich
b. Fields, Joseph

February 22, 1895
b. Haya de la Torre, Victor Raul

February 25, 1895
b. Bell, Bert

February 28, 1895
b. Novaes (Pinto), Guiomar

March 1, 1895
b. Keats, Duke

March 2, 1895
b. Aurell, Tage
b. Frisch, Ragnar Anton Kittil
d. Morisot, Berthe

March 3, 1895
b. Ridgway, Matthew Bunker

March 4, 1895
b. Gross, Milt

March 5, 1895
d. Leskov, Nikolai Semyonovich

March 9, 1895
b. Chase, William Curtis
d. Sacher-Masoch, Leopold von

March 10, 1895
d. Worth, Charles Frederick

March 11, 1895
d. Cantu, Cesare

March 23, 1895
b. Rudhyar, Dane

March 26, 1895
b. Carney, Robert Bostwick

March 27, 1895
d. Ballou, Maturin Murray

March 28, 1895
b. Herter, Christian Archibald
b. Kimball, Spencer Woolley

March 29, 1895
b. Juenger, Ernst

March 30, 1895
b. Giono, Jean

March 31, 1895
b. Fisher, Vardis
b. McCloy, John Jay

April 1, 1895
b. Hunter, Alberta

April 3, 1895
b. Castelnuovo-Tedesco, Mario
b. Confrey, Zez
b. Mischakoff, Mischa
b. Strang, Ruth May

April 4, 1895
b. Boylston, Helen Dore
b. Murray, Arthur

April 6, 1895
b. Craig, Cleo F
b. Robin, Leo

April 7, 1895
b. Flannagan, John Bernard
b. Wheeler, Bert

April 10, 1895
b. Russell, Edward Frederick Langley,
   Baron of Liverpool

April 11, 1895
b. Murchison, Clint(on Williams, Sr.)

April 14, 1895
d. Dana, James Dwight

April 17, 1895
d. Isaacs, Jorge

April 18, 1895
b. Pagnol, Marcel Paul

April 23, 1895
b. Noone, Jimmie
d. Ludwig, Karl Friedrich Wilhelm

April 26, 1895
b. Lengyel, Emil

April 29, 1895
b. Sargent, Malcolm, Sir

April 30, 1895
d. Freytag, Gustav
b. Chevallier, Gabriel

May 1, 1895
b. Sowerby, Leo

May 2, 1895
b. Bacon, Peggy
b. Hart, Lorenz
b. Holman, Eugene

May 3, 1895
b. Mark, Herman Francis

May 6, 1895
b. Valentino, Rudolph

May 8, 1895
b. Sheen, Fulton John, Bishop
b. Wilson, Edmund

May 9, 1895
b. Barthelmess, Richard
b. Blaga, Lucien

May 11, 1895
b. Brugnon, Jacques
b. Still, William Grant

May 12, 1895
b. Giauque, William Francis
b. Olsen, Harold G
b. Slotta, Karl Heinrich

May 14, 1895
b. Lehr, Lew

May 17, 1895
b. Davis, James Curran
b. Derby, Jane
b. Hauser, Gayelord

May 19, 1895
d. Marti (y Perez), Jose Julian

May 21, 1895
b. Cardenas, Lazaro
d. Suppe, Franz von

May 22, 1895
b. Krishnamurti, Jiddu

May 24, 1895
b. Newhouse, Samuel Irving
d. McCulloch, Hugh

May 26, 1895
b. Baron, Salo Wittmayer
b. Henderson, Leon
b. Hull, John Edwin
b. Lange, Dorothea Nutzhorn

May 29, 1895
b. Grant, Jane

May 31, 1895
b. Stewart, George Rippey

June 1, 1895
b. Dulles, Eleanor Lansing

June 3, 1895
b. Hillyer, Robert

June 4, 1895
b. Grandi, Dino
b. Waln, Nora

June 9, 1895
b. DeGraff, Robert F(air)

June 10, 1895
b. McDaniel, Hattie

June 11, 1895
b. Bulganin, Nikolai Aleksandrovich

June 13, 1895
b. Wrightsman, Charles Bierer

June 14, 1895
b. Adams, Jack
b. Edwards, Cliff
b. Finkelstein, Louis, Dr.
b. Mariategui, Jose Carlos

June 15, 1895
b. Herrick, Elinore Morehouse

June 16, 1895
b. Pitz, Henry Clarence

June 20, 1895
b. Price, Gwilym Alexander

June 21, 1895
b. Snyder, John Wesley

June 23, 1895
b. Noble, Reg
d. Renwick, James, Jr.

June 24, 1895
b. Dempsey, Jack

June 26, 1895
b. Hainsworth, George

June 29, 1895
d. Huxley, Thomas Henry

d. Peixoto, Floriano

July 4, 1895
b. Caesar, Irving

July 7, 1895
b. Hoffman, Julius Jennings

July 8, 1895
b. Rattner, Abraham
b. Tamm, Igor Evgenevich

July 10, 1895
b. Goldmann, Nahum
b. Orff, Carl

July 12, 1895
b. Flagstad, Kirsten
b. Fuller, Richard Buckminster
b. Hammerstein, Oscar, II

July 13, 1895
b. Blackmer, Sidney Alderman

July 14, 1895
b. Leavis, F(rank) R(aymond)
d. Ulrichs, Karl Heinrich

July 17, 1895
b. Kelly, Machine Gun

July 20, 1895
b. Corum, Martene Windsor
b. Moholy-Nagy, Laszlo

July 21, 1895
b. Barnes, Leonard John
b. Maynard, Ken

July 22, 1895
b. Rosbaud, Hans

July 23, 1895
b. Poulson, Norris
b. Pringle, Aileen
b. Vidor, Florence

July 25, 1895
b. Princip, Gavrilo

July 26, 1895
b. Graves, Robert von Ranke

August 4, 1895
b. Anthony, Edward

August 5, 1895
b. Flowers, Tiger
d. Engels, Friedrich

August 6, 1895
b. Reichelderfer, Francis Wylton

August 10, 1895
b. Richman, Harry
b. Vertes, Marcel

August 12, 1895
b. Lawler, Richard Harold

August 13, 1895
b. Lahr, Bert

August 19, 1895
d. Hardin, John Wesley

August 20, 1895
d. Min

August 24, 1895
b. Cushing, Richard James, Cardinal

August 25, 1895
d. Houghton, Henry Oscar

August 26, 1895
b. Long, Earl Kemp

August 29, 1895
b. Dial, Morris Grant

August 31, 1895
d. Parker, Ely Samuel

September 1, 1895
b. Schillinger, Joseph

September 3, 1895
b. Houston, Charles Hamilton

September 4, 1895
b. Xiang Jingyu

September 6, 1895
b. Dornberger, Walter Robert

September 7, 1895
b. Harrison, William Kelly, Jr.
b. Horrocks, Brian Gwynne, Sir

September 10, 1895
b. Herskovits, Melville Jean
b. Kelly, George Lange

September 11, 1895
b. Bhave, Acharya Vinoba
b. Stillman, Irwin Maxwell

September 13, 1895
b. McDevitt, Ruth

September 14, 1895
b. Lovett, Robert A(bercrombie)
d. Riley, Charles Valentine

September 16, 1895
b. Bidwell, Charles W

September 18, 1895
b. Diefenbaker, John George
b. Wilder, Amos Niven

September 22, 1895
b. Deutsch, Babette
b. Janssen, Herbert
b. Meek, Samuel Williams
b. Muni, Paul

September 24, 1895
b. Armour, Tommy
b. Cournand, Andre Frederic

September 25, 1895
b. Lawson, John Howard

September 26, 1895
b. Holden, Fay
b. Raft, George

September 27, 1895
b. Arends, Leslie Cornelius

September 28, 1895
b. Harrison, Wallace Kirkman
b. Petrie, Charles Alexander, Sir
d. Pasteur, Louis

September 29, 1895
b. Rhine, J(oseph) B(anks)
b. Turner, Roscoe Wilson

September 30, 1895
b. Milestone, Lewis

October 1, 1895
b. Liaquat Ali, Khan

October 2, 1895
b. Streeter, Ruth

October 3, 1895
d. Wright, Harry

October 4, 1895
b. Keaton, Buster

October 5, 1895
b. Smith, Walter Bedell

October 6, 1895
b. Gordon, Caroline
d. Langstroth, Lorenzo Lorraine

October 7, 1895
d. Story, William Wetmore

October 8, 1895
b. Peron, Juan
b. Zog I
d. Mahone, William

October 10, 1895
b. Lin, Yutang

October 13, 1895
b. Schumacher, Kurt

October 14, 1895
b. Baldwin, Horace

October 15, 1895
b. Claire, Ina

October 17, 1895
b. Humphrey, Doris
b. Ydigoras Fuentes Miguel

October 18, 1895
b. DelRuth, Roy

October 19, 1895
b. Mumford, Lewis

October 20, 1895
b. Ingram, Rex
b. Ryskind, Morrie
b. Wurster, William

October 22, 1895
b. Beckman, Johnny

October 23, 1895
b. Anderson, Clint(on Presba)
b. Maverick, Maury

October 25, 1895
b. Eshkol, Levi
d. Halle, Charles, Sir

October 27, 1895
b. Scripps, Robert Paine

October 28, 1895
b. Boles, John
b. Chamberlain, Samuel

October 29, 1895
b. Pearl, Jack

October 30, 1895
b. Domagk, Gerhard
b. Richards, Dickinson Woodruff

October 31, 1895
b. Liddell Hart, Basil Henry, Sir

November 1, 1895
b. Hecht, George Joseph
b. Jones, David

November 3, 1895
b. Arvey, Jacob Meyer

November 4, 1895
d. Field, Eugene

November 5, 1895
b. Garber, Jan
b. Gieseking, Walter Wilhelm
b. MacArthur, Charles

November 9, 1895
b. Hay, George Dewey

November 10, 1895
b. Northrop, John Knudsen

November 14, 1895
b. Lausche, Frank John
b. Lewis, Wilmarth Sheldon

November 16, 1895
b. Arlen, Michael
b. Hindemith, Paul
b. Mathews, John Joseph
d. Smith, Samuel Francis

November 17, 1895
b. Bakhtin, Mikhail (Mikhailovich)

November 18, 1895
b. Smith, Loring

November 19, 1895
b. Marsh, Mae

d. Vaux, Calvert

November 21, 1895
b. Gerhardi, William Alexander

November 22, 1895
b. Dehn, Adolf Arthur
b. Enoch, Kurt

November 24, 1895
b. Maison, Rene

November 25, 1895
b. Kempff, (Wilhelm) Walter Friedrich
b. Mikoyan, Anastas Ivanovich
b. Santmyer, Helen Hooven
b. Svoboda, Ludvik

November 26, 1895
b. Wilson, William Griffith

November 27, 1895
d. Dumas, Alexandre

November 28, 1895
b. Iturbi, Jose

November 29, 1895
b. Berkeley, Busby
b. Canutt, Yakima
b. Rocca, Lodovico
b. Tubman, William Vacanarat
   Shadrach
b. Danquah, Joseph (Kwame
   Kyeretwi) B(oakye)

December 2, 1895
b. William, Warren

December 3, 1895
b. Freud, Anna

December 4, 1895
b. Townsend, Willard Saxby

December 7, 1895
b. Margai, Milton Augustus Striery

December 8, 1895
d. Sala, George Augustus

December 9, 1895
b. Ibarruri, Dolores Gomez

December 12, 1895
b. Burman, Ben Lucien

December 14, 1895
b. Eluard, Paul
b. George VI

December 15, 1895
b. Razaf, Andy

December 16, 1895
b. Ets, Marie Hall

December 20, 1895
b. Langer, Suzanne K

December 24, 1895
b. Harriman, E(dward) Roland (Noel)
b. Robinson, M(aurice) R(ichard)

December 28, 1895
b. Brink, Carol Ryrie

December 30, 1895
b. Hartley, L(eslie) P(oles)
b. Lopez, Vincent

1896

b. Barker, Lloyd
b. Boucher, Buck
b. Brittain, Vera Mary
b. Cheyney, Peter
b. Diamond, Legs
b. Doubrovska, Felia
b. Dunhill, Alfred Henry
b. Ford, Arthur A
b. Greer, Howard
b. Johnson, Howard Deering
b. Kadalie, Clements
b. Lupescu, Magda (Elena)
b. Nelson, Christian
b. Nick the Greek
b. Pesotta, Rose
b. Price, Garrett
b. Raushenbush, Stephen
b. Robeson, Eslanda Cardoza Goode
b. Savo, Jimmy
b. Townsend, William Cameron
d. Gimbel, Adam

January 1, 1896
b. Kinugasa, Teinosuke
d. Beach, Alfred Ely

January 4, 1896
b. Dirksen, Everett McKinley
b. Masson, Andre (Aime Rene)

January 6, 1896
b. Pritzker, Abram Nicholas

January 8, 1896
b. Weinberger, Jaromir
d. Verlaine, Paul (Marie)

January 10, 1896
b. Lockridge, Frances Louise

January 11, 1896
b. Driscoll, Paddy
b. Stephenson, William
d. Deus, Joao de

January 12, 1896
b. Wechsler, David

January 14, 1896
b. Dos Passos, John (Roderigo)

January 15, 1896
d. Brady, Mathew B

January 17, 1896
b. Davis, Loyal

January 18, 1896
b. Ritola, Ville

January 20, 1896
b. Burns, George

January 23, 1896
b. Charlotte Aldegonde E M
   Wilhelmine

January 24, 1896
b. King, Henry

January 26, 1896
d. MacMillan, Alexander

January 27, 1896
b. DeSylva, Buddy

January 31, 1896
b. Strauss, Lewis Lichtenstein

February 1, 1896
b. Lane, Frank C
b. Somoza, Anastasio

February 7, 1896
b. Paludan, Jacob

February 9, 1896
b. Parks, Floyd Lavinius

February 12, 1896
d. Thomas, (Charles Louis) Ambroise

February 16, 1896
b. Brailowsky, Alexander

February 17, 1896
b. Hicks, Ursula Kathleen Webb
b. Stewart, Anita

February 18, 1896
b. Breton, Andre
b. Harris, Joseph Pratt
b. Mitropoulos, Dimitri

February 21, 1896
b. Redman, Ben Ray

February 22, 1896
b. Brown, Nacio Herb
d. Nye, Edgar Wilson

February 25, 1896
b. Farrar, John Chipman
b. McClellan, John Little

February 26, 1896
b. Carlson, Evans Fordyce
b. Zhdanov, Andrei Alexandrovich

February 27, 1896
b. Radford, Arthur William

February 28, 1896
b. Hench, Philip Showalter

February 29, 1896
b. Desai, Morarji (Ranchhodji)
b. Fischer, Louis

b. Wellman, William Augustus

March 1, 1896
b. Little, Royal
b. Winston, Harry

March 5, 1896
b. Marcus, Jacon R(ader)

March 17, 1896
b. Lynd, Helen Merrell

March 21, 1896
d. Burton, Isabel Arundel

March 22, 1896
b. Cone, Russell Glenn
b. Schildkraut, Joseph
d. Hughes, Thomas

March 27, 1896
b. Gribble, Harry Wagstaff Graham
b. Lescaze, William

March 29, 1896
b. Kleberg, Robert Justus, Jr.

March 30, 1896
b. Raphaelson, Samson

March 31, 1896
b. Nolan, Jeannette Covert

April 2, 1896
d. Robinson, Theodore

April 3, 1896
b. Traglia, Luigi, Cardinal

April 4, 1896
b. Sherwood, Robert Emmet
b. Tzara, Tristan

April 7, 1896
b. Fairchild, Sherman Mills
b. Leonard, Benny

April 8, 1896
b. Harburg, E(dgar) Y(ipsel)

April 13, 1896
b. Eaker, Ira Clarence

April 15, 1896
b. Bean, Louis H(yman)
b. Chinn, May (Edward)

April 16, 1896
b. Semenov, Nikolai Nikolaevich

April 22, 1896
b. Ethridge, Mark Foster

April 23, 1896
b. Kennedy, Margaret

April 26, 1896
b. Stein, Jules Caesar
b. Udet, Ernst

April 27, 1896
b. Carothers, Wallace Hume
b. Hornsby, Rogers
d. Parkes, Henry, Sir

April 28, 1896
b. Dunninger, Joseph
d. Treitschke, Heinrich Gotthard von

April 30, 1896
b. Davis, Gary, Reverend

May 1, 1896
b. Clark, Mark Wayne
b. Collins, Joseph Lawton, General

May 2, 1896
b. Van Doren, Dorothy Graffe

May 3, 1896
b. Menon, (Vengalil Krishnan) Krishna
b. Smith, Dodie

May 4, 1896
b. Baxter, Frank Condie
b. Ochsner, Alton

May 7, 1896
d. Mudgett, Herman Webster

May 9, 1896
b. Clarke, Austin

May 11, 1896
b. Pisis, Filippo Tibertelli de
d. Bunner, Henry Cuyler

May 16, 1896
b. Sullavan, Margaret

May 17, 1896
b. Donnelly, Ruth

May 19, 1896
b. Alessandri, Jorge
b. Balcon, Michael Elias, Sir
b. Thorborg, Kerstin
d. Field, Kate

May 20, 1896
d. Schumann, Clara Josephine Wieck

May 26, 1896
b. Munson, Gorham B(ert)

May 28, 1896
b. Giles, Warren Crandall

May 29, 1896
b. Youngdahl, Luther Wallace

May 30, 1896
b. Hawks, Howard Winchester

June 2, 1896
b. Gulbenkian, Nubar Sarkis

June 5, 1896
b. Cox, Allyn

June 6, 1896
b. Balbo, Italo
b. Ford, Eleanor Clay
b. Sherriff, Robert Cedric

June 7, 1896
b. Kellems, Vivien
b. Mulliken, Robert Sanderson
b. Nagy, Imre
d. Eaton, Wyatt

June 8, 1896
d. Simon, Jules Francois

June 9, 1896
b. Gunnison, Foster

June 13, 1896
b. Crown, Henry

June 15, 1896
b. Jacobs, Walter L

June 17, 1896
b. Lupino, Stanley

June 18, 1896
b. Barry, Philip
b. Goldstein, Israel
b. Sweet, Blanche

June 19, 1896
b. Simpson, Wallis (Bessie Wallis
   Warfield)

June 20, 1896
b. Pelletier, Wilfrid

June 21, 1896
b. Stickney, Dorothy

June 22, 1896
d. Bristow, Benjamin Helm
d. Harris, Augustus, Sir

June 23, 1896
b. Ferril, Thomas Hornsby

June 25, 1896
d. Tilley, Samuel Leonard, Sir
d. Trumbull, Lyman

July 1, 1896
d. Stowe, Harriet (Elizabeth) Beecher

July 4, 1896
d. Del Pilar, Marcelo Hilario

July 8, 1896
b. Janis, Sidney

July 10, 1896
b. Summerville, Slim

July 13, 1896
d. Kekule, Friedrich August

July 16, 1896
b. Lie, Trygve Halvdan
d. Goncourt, Edmond Louis Antoine
   Huot de

July 17, 1896
b. Andresen, Ivar
b. Green, Wilf(red Thomas)

July 18, 1896
b. O'Boyle, Patrick Aloysius, Cardinal

July 19, 1896
b. Breeskin, Adelyn Dohme
b. Cronin, A(rchibald) J(oseph)

July 21, 1896
b. Hickenlooper, Bourke B

July 22, 1896
b. Whale, James

July 25, 1896
b. Gale, Richard Nelson, Sir

July 28, 1896
b. LaMarr, Barbara

July 29, 1896
b. Catlin, George Edward Gordon, Sir
b. Menzies, William Cameron

July 31, 1896
d. Hunt, Richard Morris

August 1, 1896
d. Grove, William Robert, Sir

August 2, 1896
b. Hughes, Sarah Tilghman

August 7, 1896
b. Bergen, John Joseph

August 8, 1896
b. Rawlings, Marjorie Kinnan

August 9, 1896
b. Massine, Leonide Fedorovich
b. Piaget, Jean
b. Sullivan, A(loysius) M(ichael)

August 10, 1896
b. Sobol, Louis
d. Lilienthal, Otto

August 13, 1896
d. Millais, John Everett, Sir

August 15, 1896
b. Cori, Gerty Theresa (Radnitz)
b. Glueck, Sheldon

August 17, 1896
b. Groves, Leslie Richard
b. Larkin, Oliver Waterman

August 18, 1896
b. Pickford, Jack
b. Warburg, James Paul

August 19, 1896
d. Whitney, Josiah Dwight

August 20, 1896
b. Gersten, Berta

August 21, 1896
b. Bradford, Roark Whitney Wickliffe

August 22, 1896
b. Gould, Laurence M(cKinley)

August 24, 1896
b. Baker, Phil

August 28, 1896
b. O'Flaherty, Liam

August 30, 1896
b. Massey, Raymond Hart
d. Reinhart, Charles S

September 1, 1896
b. Bhaktivedanta, A(bhay)
    C(haranaravinda)

September 4, 1896
b. Artaud, Antonin

September 5, 1896
b. VonDoderer, Heimito

September 6, 1896
b. Praz, Mario

September 8, 1896
b. Dietz, Howard M

September 10, 1896
b. Ryan, Sylvester James

September 11, 1896
b. Hoopes, Darlington
b. Kerr, Robert Samuel

September 14, 1896
b. Powers, John Robert
b. Sample, Paul Starrett

September 16, 1896
b. Granger, Lester

September 18, 1896
d. Fizeau, Armand Hippolyte Louis

September 19, 1896
d. Marty, Martin

September 21, 1896
b. Kelsey, Alice Geer

September 22, 1896
b. King, Charles Glen
b. Segrave, Henry O'Neal de Hane,
    Sir
d. Klafsky, Katharina

September 23, 1896
d. DuPrez, Gilbert

September 24, 1896
b. Fitzgerald, F(rancis) Scott (Key)

September 25, 1896
b. Pertini, Sandro

September 27, 1896
b. Ervin, Sam(uel James Jr.)

September 30, 1896
b. Forbes, Ralph

October 1, 1896
b. Healy, Ted

October 2, 1896
b. Duclos, Jacques

October 3, 1896
d. Morris, William

October 7, 1896
b. Lasser, Jacob Kay

October 8, 1896
b. Duvivier, Julien
d. DuMaurier, George Louis P B

October 9, 1896
b. Cook, Bill

October 10, 1896
b. Germer, Lester Halbert

October 11, 1896
b. Firpo, Luis Angel
b. Jakobson, Roman
b. Marshall, George Preston
d. Bruckner, Joseph Anton

October 12, 1896
b. Charleston, Oscar McKinley
b. Montale, Eugenio

October 14, 1896
b. Cummings, Nathan

October 15, 1896
b. Charoux, Siegfried
b. Cooper, Melville

October 17, 1896
d. Abbey, Henry Eugene

October 18, 1896
b. Davis, Harold Lenoir
b. Holman, Nat(han)

October 24, 1896
b. Gray, Gilda

October 28, 1896
b. Hanson, Howard

October 30, 1896
b. Dooley, Rae
b. Gordon, Ruth

October 31, 1896
b. Chace, Marian
b. Waters, Ethel

November 1, 1896
b. Blunden, Edmund Charles

November 3, 1896
b. Tenggren, Gustaf Adolf

November 4, 1896
b. Garcia, Carlos Polestico

November 8, 1896
b. Harris, Bucky
b. Hough, Henry Beetle

November 10, 1896
b. Dykes, Jimmy

November 12, 1896
b. Ali, Salim A

November 13, 1896
b. Beard, Myron Gould
b. Kishi, Nobusuke

November 14, 1896
b. Eisenhower, Mamie (Geneva) Doud

November 16, 1896
b. Jordan, Jim
b. Mosley, Oswald Ernald, Sir
b. Tibbett, Lawrence Mervil

November 22, 1896
b. Mays, David John
d. Ferris, George Washington Gale

November 23, 1896
b. Gottwald, Klement

November 24, 1896
b. Griffith, Corinne

November 25, 1896
b. Thomson, Virgil Garnett

November 26, 1896
d. Patmore, Coventry Kersey Dighton

November 28, 1896
b. Black, Frank J.
b. Griffith, Ernest S(tacey)

November 30, 1896
d. Steinway, Henry Engelhard

December 1, 1896
b. Henderson, Ray
b. Shutta, Ethel

December 2, 1896
b. Zhukov, Georgi Konstantinovich

December 5, 1896
b. Cori, Carl Ferdinand

December 6, 1896
b. Gershwin, Ira
b. Trafton, George

December 7, 1896
b. Crossley, Archibald Maddock
d. Maceo, Antonio

December 10, 1896
d. Nobel, Alfred Bernhard

December 13, 1896
b. Balderston, William

December 14, 1896
b. Doolittle, James H(arold)
b. Markey, Lucille (Parker) Wright

December 15, 1896
b. Dempsey, Miles Christopher, Sir

December 16, 1896
b. Clinchy, Everett Ross

December 17, 1896
b. Biddle, Anthony Joseph

December 20, 1896
b. Browning, Frederick A(rthur)
M(ontague), Sir
b. Hobbs, Leonard Sinclair

December 21, 1896
b. Rokossovsky, Konstantin
Konstantinovich

December 23, 1896
b. Tomasi di Lampedusa, Guiseppe
d. Hatch, William Henry

December 24, 1896
b. Powdermaker, Hortense

December 26, 1896
d. Du Bois-Reymond, Emil

December 27, 1896
b. Bromfield, Louis Brucker
b. Zuckmayer, Carl

December 28, 1896
b. Sessions, Roger Huntington

December 29, 1896
b. Siqueiros, David A

December 30, 1896
d. Rizal, Jose

1897

b. Andrew, Prince of Russia
b. Auchincloss, Hugh D
b. Avila Camacho, Manuel
b. Ben-Haim, Paul
b. Boiardi, Hector
b. Buchalter, Lepke
b. Carney, Don
b. Dejongh, Peter
b. Dewar, James A
b. Foley, Martha
b. Hunter, Glenn
b. Johnson, Henry
b. Julian, Hubert Fauntleroy
b. Lawrence, Josephine
b. Parks, Lillian (Adele) Rogers
b. Reard, Louis
b. Ross, Ishbel
b. Seagrave, Gordon Stifler
b. Tey, Josephine
b. Walters, Lou
b. Wootton, Barbara (Frances) Adam
d. Burckhardt, Jacob (Christoph)
d. Craft, Ellen
d. Vickers, Edward
d. Wang T'ao

January 1, 1897
b. Bowen, Catherine Drinker
b. Greaza, Walter N

January 3, 1897
b. Davies, Marion

January 5, 1897
b. Jessup, Philip Caryl

January 9, 1897
b. Gautier, Felisa Rincon de

January 11, 1897
b. DeVoto, Bernard Augustine
b. Morinigo, Higinio
b. Thuilier, Raymond

January 12, 1897
d. Pitman, Isaac

January 15, 1897
b. Barr, Stringfellow

January 23, 1897
b. Bose, Subhas Chandra

January 28, 1897
b. Katayev, Valentin Petrovich

January 29, 1897
b. O'Meara, Walter (Andrew)

February 1, 1897
b. Robins, Denise Naomi

February 4, 1897
b. Erhard, Ludwig

February 5, 1897
d. Radbourn, Old Hoss

February 6, 1897
b. Cavalcanti, Alberto

February 7, 1897
b. Porter, Quincy
d. Ferraris, Galileo

February 8, 1897
b. Husain, Zakir
b. Rubens, Alma

February 9, 1897
b. Kingsford-Smith, Charles Edward,
Sir

February 10, 1897
b. Enders, John Franklin

February 11, 1897
b. Darden, Colgate Whitehead

February 12, 1897
d. Martin, Homer Dodge

February 15, 1897
b. Blaik, Red

February 17, 1897
b. Chamberlin, William Henry

February 19, 1897
d. Blondin, Jean Francois Gravelet

February 20, 1897
b. Albright, Ivan Le Lorraine
b. Albright, Malvin Marr

February 24, 1897
b. Breech, Ernest Robert
b. Grede, William John

February 27, 1897
b. Anderson, Marian
b. Lyot, Bernard Ferdinand

March 2, 1897
b. Schuster, Max Lincoln

March 3, 1897
b. Poulter, Thomas Charles

March 5, 1897
b. Herbst, Josephine Frey

March 6, 1897
b. MacArthur, John Donald
d. Brewer, Ebenezer Cobham

March 7, 1897
d. Jacobs, Harriet Ann

March 10, 1897
b. Hoyt, Palmer

March 11, 1897
b. Cowell, Henry Dixon

March 15, 1897
b. Scholz, Jackson Volney
d. Sylvester, James Joseph

March 16, 1897
b. Nagel, Conrad

March 18, 1897
b. Jenkins, Ray Howard

March 20, 1897
b. Sheed, Frank

March 23, 1897
b. Farrar, Margaret (Petherbridge)

March 24, 1897
b. Kroeber, Theodora Kracaw
b. Reich, Wilhelm

March 27, 1897
b. Swanson, Gloria May Josephine
d. Adams, William Taylor

April 1, 1897
b. Derricotte, Juliette Aline

April 3, 1897
b. Aadlberg, John O.
d. Brahms, Johannes

April 6, 1897
b. Coates, Robert Myron

April 7, 1897
b. Winchell, Walter

April 8, 1897
b. Skidmore, Louis

April 9, 1897
b. Gambling, John Bradley

April 10, 1897
b. Youngs, Ross Middlebrook

April 12, 1897
d. Cope, Edward Drinker

April 13, 1897
b. Braestrup, Carl Bjorn

April 14, 1897
b. McCoy, Horace
b. Windsor, Claire

April 15, 1897
b. Jordan, Marian Driscoll

April 16, 1897
b. Cross, Milton John
b. Glubb, John Bagot, Sir

April 17, 1897
b. Wilder, Thornton (Niven)

April 19, 1897
b. Segal, Vivienne
b. Swift, Kay

April 23, 1897
b. Clay, Lucius du Bignon
b. Pearson, Lester B(owles)

April 25, 1897
b. Pratt, Fletcher

April 26, 1897
b. Canfield, Cass

May 1, 1897
b. Cabot, Thomas D(udley)

May 2, 1897
b. Coots, J Fred

May 3, 1897
b. Krishna Menon, V(engalil) K(rishnan)

May 5, 1897
b. Burke, Kenneth

May 6, 1897
b. Purtell, William Arthur

May 7, 1897
b. Jacobs, Joe B

May 8, 1897
b. Hillenkoetter, Roscoe H(enry)

May 9, 1897
b. Fisher, Rudolph

May 10, 1897
b. Allen of Hurtwood, Lady
b. Gerhardsen, Einar Henry
b. Lowenfels, Walter
d. Bonifacio, Andres

May 11, 1897
b. Gross, Robert Ellsworth

May 14, 1897
b. Bechet, Sidney
b. Ye Jianying
d. Maretzek, Max

May 17, 1897
b. Hassel, Odd

May 18, 1897
b. Capra, Frank
b. LaFollete, Philip Fox
b. Swerling, Jo

May 21, 1897
b. McGraw, Donald Cushing

May 26, 1897
b. Talmadge, Norma

May 27, 1897
b. Cockcroft, John Douglas, Sir

May 28, 1897
b. Bolitho, Henry Hector

May 29, 1897
b. Korngold, Erich Wolfgang

June 2, 1897
b. Mueller, Reuben Herbert

June 5, 1897
b. Chiang Mei-Ling
b. Hartshorne, Charles

June 6, 1897
b. Capehart, Homer Earl

June 7, 1897
b. Szell, George

June 9, 1897
d. Clark, Alvin Graham

June 10, 1897
b. Jagel, Frederick

June 12, 1897
b. Eden, Anthony
b. Goossens, Leon Jean

June 13, 1897
b. Nurmi, Paavo Johannes

June 16, 1897
b. Wittig, Georg Friedrich Karl

June 18, 1897
d. Corson, Juliet

June 19, 1897
b. Hinshelwood, Cyril Norman, Sir

b. Howard, Moe

June 20, 1897
b. Keyhoe, Donald E(dward)

June 24, 1897
b. Ludwig, Daniel Keith

June 25, 1897
d. Oliphant, Margaret

June 28, 1897
b. Dana, Viola

July 1, 1897
b. Barry, Tom
b. Bickerman, Elias Joseph

July 3, 1897
d. Evans, John

July 6, 1897
b. Damon, Ralph Shepard
d. Meilhac, Henri

July 9, 1897
b. Cassou, Jean
b. Lyons, Enid Muriel
b. Wedemeyer, Albert Coady

July 10, 1897
b. Brosio, Manilo Giovanni
b. Gilbert, John
b. Goodrich, Lloyd

July 11, 1897
b. Connor, Bull
b. Jefferson, Blind Lemon

July 14, 1897
b. Phibun Songkhram, Luang

July 17, 1897
b. Banks, Monty

July 18, 1897
b. Spottswood, Stephen Gill

July 19, 1897
d. Boycott, Charles Cunningham

July 20, 1897
b. Reichstein, Tadeus
d. Ingelow, Jean

July 23, 1897
b. Cloete, Stuart

July 25, 1897
d. Packard, Elizabeth Parsons Ware

July 26, 1897
b. Butterworth, Charles
b. Gallico, Paul William

July 28, 1897
b. Martin, Kingsley

July 29, 1897
b. Shaver, Dorothy

August 2, 1897
b. Soupault, Philippe

August 4, 1897
b. Lyman, Abe

August 9, 1897
b. Galbreath, John Wilmer

August 10, 1897
b. Nakian, Reuben

August 11, 1897
b. Blyton, Enid Mary
b. Bogan, Louise

August 12, 1897
b. Struve, Otto

August 13, 1897
b. Bronk, Detlev Wulf

August 14, 1897
d. George, James Zachariah

August 18, 1897
b. Mowbray, Alan
b. Rinehart, Stanley Marshall, Jr.

August 19, 1897
b. Vishniac, Roman

August 21, 1897
b. Green, Constance Windsor
McLaughlin

August 22, 1897
b. Lucas, Nick

August 24, 1897
b. Rose, Fred

August 26, 1897
b. Roland, Ruth

August 29, 1897
b. Roswaenge, Helge
b. Singmaster, Elsie

August 31, 1897
b. March, Fredric
d. Drew, Louisa Lane

September 5, 1897
b. Carnovsky, Morris
b. Nielsen, Arthur Charles

September 8, 1897
b. Rodgers, Jimmie

September 12, 1897
b. Gibson, Walter B(rown)
b. Joliot-Curie, Irene

September 14, 1897
b. Rudkin, Margaret Fogarty

September 15, 1897
b. Curti, Merle Eugene

September 16, 1897
b. Gopallawa, William

September 19, 1897
b. Knight, George Wilson

September 20, 1897
b. Barea, Arturo
b. Taft, Charles Phelps

September 24, 1897
b. Frazier, Edward Franklin

September 25, 1897
b. Faulkner, William

September 26, 1897
b. Paul VI
b. Telva, Marion

September 28, 1897
b. Fraenkel, Heinrich

September 29, 1897
b. Agar, Herbert Sebastian
b. Queeny, Edgar Monsanto

September 30, 1897
b. Dagover, Lil
b. Widdemer, Margaret
d. Therese of Lisieux, Saint

October 2, 1897
d. Andree, Salomon August
d. Dow, Neal

October 3, 1897
b. Aragon, Louis Marie Antoine
Alfred

October 4, 1897
b. Stoopnagle, Lemuel Q, Colonel

October 5, 1897
b. DeLue, Donald Harcourt
d. Gilbert, John, Sir

October 6, 1897
b. Cowan, Jerome
b. Dietz, David
b. Seibert, Florence B(arbara)

October 7, 1897
b. Freeman, Joseph

October 8, 1897
b. Cisler, Walker (Lee)
b. Mamoulian, Rouben (Zachary)
b. Stoodard, George Dinsmore
b. Throckmorton, Cleon

October 10, 1897
b. Muhammad, Elijah

October 11, 1897
b. Auslander, Joseph
b. Twining, Nathan F(arragut)

October 13, 1897
b. Rich, Irene

October 14, 1897
b. Liebes, Dorothy Katherine Wright
b. Warburg, Frederick Marcus

October 17, 1897
d. Dana, Charles Anderson

October 18, 1897
d. Worden, John Lorimer

October 19, 1897
d. Pullman, George Mortimer

October 20, 1897
b. Deutsch, Adolph

October 22, 1897
d. Winsor, Justin

October 25, 1897
d. Sartain, John

October 26, 1897
b. Lemnitz, Tiana

October 28, 1897
b. Speidel, Hans

October 29, 1897
b. Goebbels, Joseph
d. George, Henry, Sr.

October 31, 1897
b. Henry, Pete

November 1, 1897
b. Mitchison, Naomi Margaret
(Haldane)

November 2, 1897
b. Bjerknes, Jacob
b. King, Dennis
b. Russell, Richard Brevard, Jr.

November 4, 1897
b. Van Niel, Cornelius B(ernardus)

November 7, 1897
b. Sperry, Armstrong W

November 8, 1897
b. Day, Dorothy

November 9, 1897
b. Norrish, Ronald George Wreyford

November 11, 1897
b. Allport, Gordon William

November 13, 1897
b. Edinger, Tilly
d. Giles, Ernest

November 14, 1897
b. Curry, John Steuart
b. Ricca, Paul

November 15, 1897
b. Bevan, Aneurin
b. McCord, David (Thompson Watson)
b. Sitwell, Sacheverell, Sir

d. Langston, John Mercer
d. Strepponi, Giuseppina

November 17, 1897
b. Fay, Frank

November 18, 1897
b. Blackett, Patrick Maynard Stuart
d. Doulton, Henry, Sir

November 19, 1897
b. Garrison, Lloyd K(irkham)
b. Roosevelt, Quentin

November 23, 1897
b. Etting, Ruth
b. Smith, William

November 24, 1897
b. Luciano, Lucky

November 26, 1897
b. Odria Amoretti, Manuel Apolinario

November 27, 1897
b. Genovese, Vito

December 1, 1897
b. Ritchard, Cyril

December 2, 1897
b. Alley, Rewi
b. Bagramian, Ivan Christofovorich
b. Hoving, Walter

December 3, 1897
b. Gropper, William

December 4, 1897
b. Redfield, Robert
d. Neuendorff, Adolf

December 5, 1897
b. Johnson, Nunnally
b. Scholem, Gershom Gerhard

December 8, 1897
b. Tunis, Edwin Burdett

December 9, 1897
b. Gingold, Hermione Ferdinanda
b. Hurley, Jack B

December 10, 1897
b. LaFarge, Christopher
d. Fleischmann, Charles Louis

December 11, 1897
b. Van Dusen, Henry Pitney

December 12, 1897
b. Smith, Lillian

December 13, 1897
b. Pearson, Drew

December 14, 1897
b. Schuschnigg, Kurt von
b. Smith, Margaret (Madeline) Chase
b. Thill, Georges

December 16, 1897
d. Daudet, Leon

December 18, 1897
b. Henderson, Fletcher

December 23, 1897
b. Denneny, Cy(ril)

December 27, 1897
b. Konev, Ivan Stepanovich

December 29, 1897
b. Mayer, Albert
d. Linton, William James

December 31, 1897
b. Orry-Kelly

1898

b. Azhari, Sayyid Ismail al-
b. Boardman, Eleanor
b. Born, Ernest Alexander
b. Brodovitch, Alexey
b. Chou En-Lai
b. Cosio Villegas, Daniel
b. DeMarco, Tony
b. Fischer, Herman G
b. Fishbein, Harry J
b. Forsythe, Albert E
b. Gaines, Clarence F
b. Garst, Roswell
b. Gelb, Lawrence
b. Gimbel, Sophie Haas
b. Goldman, Sylvan N
b. Gould, Beatrice Blackmar
b. Holm, Hanya
b. Ingersoll, Stuart H
b. Kalthoum, Um
b. Larsen, Emmanuel
b. Lehand, Missy
b. Liu Shao-Ch'i
b. Luthuli, Albert John Mvumbi
b. Maserati, Ernesto
b. Moore, Audley
b. Pelkey, Edward
b. Prestes, Luiz Carlos
b. Sande, Earl
b. Stern, Max
b. Touhy, Roger
b. Traikov, Georgi
b. Vollmer, Lula

January 1, 1898
b. Fuchs, Marta

January 3, 1898
b. Loder, John
b. Ryan, T(ubal) Claude

January 9, 1898
b. Fields, Gracie

January 10, 1898
b. Blodgett, Katherine Burr
b. Hay, George W

January 12, 1898
b. Watts, Richard, Jr.

January 13, 1898
b. Tagliabue, Carlo

January 14, 1898
d. Carroll, Lewis

January 15, 1898
b. Fox, Uffa

January 22, 1898
b. Barnett, Ross Robert

January 23, 1898
b. Eisenstein, Sergei Mikhailovich
b. Gaitan, Jorge Eliecer
b. Granick, Harry
b. Scott, Randolph
b. Utley, Freda

January 25, 1898
b. Tarasova, Alla Konstantinovna

January 26, 1898
b. Hickerson, John Dewey

January 29, 1898
b. Muller, Maria
b. Banda, Hastings Kamuzu
d. Taewon'gun, Hungson

February 2, 1898
b. Brinton, Clarence Crane

February 3, 1898
b. Aalto, Alvar Henrik Hugo

February 4, 1898
b. Monroe, Marion

February 5, 1898
b. McGill, Ralph Emerson

February 7, 1898
b. Charlot, Jean

February 10, 1898
b. Anderson, Judith, Dame
b. Brecht, Bertolt (Eugen Friedrich)

February 11, 1898
b. Szilard, Leo

February 12, 1898
b. Bruce, David Kirkpatrick Estes
b. Ford, Wallace
b. Harris, Roy

February 14, 1898
b. Zwicky, Fritz

February 15, 1898
b. Ibuse, Masuji

February 16, 1898
b. Cornell, Katharine

February 18, 1898
b. Ferrari, Enzo
b. Hadden, Briton
b. Munoz Marin, Luis
d. Willard, Frances Elizabeth Caroline

February 20, 1898
b. Yancey, Jimmy

February 25, 1898
b. Astbury, William

February 27, 1898
b. Smith, Gerald Lyman Kenneth

March 3, 1898
b. Artin, Emil

March 6, 1898
b. Conzelman, Jimmy
b. Flippen, Jay C

March 9, 1898
b. Hodges, Luther Hartwell

March 10, 1898
b. Bacharach, Bert(ram Mark)

March 11, 1898
b. Gish, Dorothy
d. Rosecrans, William Starke

March 13, 1898
b. Hathaway, Henry

March 14, 1898
b. Marsh, Reginald
b. Strout, Richard Lee

March 15, 1898
d. Bessemer, Henry, Sir

March 16, 1898
b. Messali Hadj
d. Beardsley, Aubrey Vincent

March 17, 1898
d. Bruce, Blanche Kelso

March 18, 1898
d. Gage, Matilda Joslyn

March 20, 1898
b. Pales Matos, Luis

March 21, 1898
b. Wyman, Willard Gordon

March 23, 1898
b. Dawn, Hazel

March 24, 1898
b. Alpert, George

March 27, 1898
d. Syed Ahmed Khan

March 28, 1898
d. Seidl, Anton

April 1, 1898
d. Orton, Arthur

April 2, 1898
d. Brann, William Cowper

April 3, 1898
b. Esau, Katherine
b. Ghelderode, Michel de
b. Jessel, George Albert
b. Luce, Henry Robinson

April 4, 1898
b. Tracy, Lee

April 5, 1898
b. Dehnert, Henry

April 8, 1898
b. Bowra, Maurice, Sir
b. Wilson, Hazel Hutchins

April 9, 1898
b. Lambeau, Curly
b. Patzak, Julius
b. Robeson, Paul Leroy

April 10, 1898
b. Gregory, Horace Victor

April 11, 1898
b. Holtz, Lou

April 15, 1898
d. Purvis, Robert

April 16, 1898
b. Dykstra, John

April 18, 1898
d. Moreau, Gustave

April 20, 1898
b. Firestone, Harvey Samuel, Jr.

April 21, 1898
b. Owen, Steve

April 26, 1898
b. Aleixandre, Vicente
b. Grierson, John

April 27, 1898
b. Bemelmans, Ludwig

April 28, 1898
b. Soutar, William

April 30, 1898
b. Towle, Katherine Amelia
b. Vanderbilt, Cornelius, Jr.

May 3, 1898
b. Clark, Septima
b. Meir, Golda

May 6, 1898
b. Gerber, Daniel Frank

May 8, 1898
b. Stepinac, Alojzije

May 10, 1898
b. Durant, Ariel

May 11, 1898
b. Billings, John Shaw

May 13, 1898
b. Dye, Babe

May 14, 1898
b. Singleton, Zutty

May 15, 1898
b. Arletty
b. Skulnik, Menasha
d. Remenyi, Eduard

May 16, 1898
b. Mizoguchi, Kenji

May 19, 1898
d. Gladstone, William Ewart

May 21, 1898
b. Hammer, Armand

May 22, 1898
d. Bellamy, Edward

May 23, 1898
b. Grivas, Georgios Theodoros
b. McHugh, Frank

May 24, 1898
b. Taussig, Helen Brooke

May 25, 1898
b. Cerf, Bennett Alfred
b. Tunney, Gene

May 29, 1898
b. Lillie, Beatrice Gladys
b. Rothermere, Esmond Cecil
Harmsworth, Viscount

May 30, 1898
b. Farrington, Elizabeth Pruett (Mary)

May 31, 1898
b. Peale, Norman Vincent
b. Ferragamo, Salvatore
b. Goetz, Delia

June 1, 1898
b. Picon, Molly
d. Keene, Thomas Wallace

June 3, 1898
d. Plimsoll, Samuel

June 4, 1898
b. Crosby, Harry
b. Wright, Jerauld

June 5, 1898
b. Boyd, William
b. Garcia Lorca, Federico

June 6, 1898
b. Abel, Walter Charles
b. DeValois, Ninette, Dame

June 9, 1898
b. Malaparte, Curzio

June 10, 1898
b. Brokenshire, Norman

June 13, 1898
b. O'Neil, James F(rancis)

June 17, 1898
b. Escher, M(aurits) C(ornelis)
d. Burne-Jones, Edward Coley, Sir

June 19, 1898
b. Seifert, Elizabeth
b. Tharp, Louise Hall

June 20, 1898
d. Tamayo y Baus, Manuel

June 21, 1898
b. Peattie, Donald Culross

June 22, 1898
b. Remarque, Erich Maria

June 25, 1898
b. Ascoli, Max
b. Ross, Roy G
d. Cohn, Ferdinand Julius

June 26, 1898
b. Messerschmitt, Willy

July 1, 1898
b. Lyons, Eugene

July 2, 1898
b. McAuliffe, Anthony Clement

July 5, 1898
b. Condie, Richard P

July 8, 1898
b. Gero, Erno
b. Waugh, Alec

July 10, 1898
b. Malott, Deane W(aldo)

July 14, 1898
b. Brook, Alexander
b. Chandler, Happy
b. Watson, Moose

July 17, 1898
b. Abbott, Berenice

July 19, 1898
b. Marcuse, Herbert

July 22, 1898
b. Benet, Stephen Vincent
b. Calder, Alexander
b. Roy, Ross

July 23, 1898
b. Dutton, Red

July 24, 1898
b. Earhart, Amelia (Mary)

July 25, 1898
b. Printemps, Yvonne

July 26, 1898
b. Gimbel, Richard

July 28, 1898
b. Gould, Charles Bruce

July 29, 1898
b. Arkell, Anthony John
b. Rabi, Isidor Isaac

July 30, 1898
b. Moore, Henry Spencer
d. Bismarck, Otto Edward Leopold
von

August 1, 1898
b. Stotz, Charles Morse
b. Ziff, William Bernard

August 3, 1898
d. Gardner, Jean Louis Charles
d. Garnier, Jean Louis Charles

August 4, 1898
b. O'Connell, Hugh

August 7, 1898
d. Ebers, Georg Moritz
d. Hall, James

August 8, 1898
d. Boudin, Eugene Louis

August 9, 1898
b. Hays, Brooks
d. Colton, Gardner Quincy

August 10, 1898
b. Haley, Jack

August 13, 1898
b. Borotra, Jean Robert
b. Toomey, Regis

August 14, 1898
b. Bullard, Dexter Means

August 15, 1898
b. Carter, Lillian

August 16, 1898
b. Rodale, Jerome Irving

August 20, 1898
b. Infeld, Leopold
b. Moberg, Vihelm

August 23, 1898
b. Claude, Albert
b. Papashvily, George

August 24, 1898
b. Cowley, Malcolm
b. Duffy, Clinton Truman

August 25, 1898
b. Dutton, Ralph Stawell

August 26, 1898
b. Guggenheim, Peggy

August 29, 1898
b. Sturges, Preston
d. Crummell, Alexander

September 1, 1898
b. Anthony, John J(ason)
b. Arlen, Richard
b. Berger, Meyer
b. Hatlo, Jimmy
b. Miller, Marilyn

September 2, 1898
b. Archibald, Joe

September 3, 1898
b. Parker, Cecil

September 4, 1898
b. Ayres, Agnes
b. Rankin, K(arl) L(ott)

September 5, 1898
b. Carlson, William Hugh
d. Edmonds, Emma E

September 7, 1898
b. Robinson, Henry Morton

September 9, 1898
b. Bridges, Styles
b. Frisch, Frankie
b. Nichols, Beverley
d. Mallarme, Stephane

September 10, 1898
b. Astaire, Adele

September 12, 1898
b. Shahn, Ben(jamin)

September 14, 1898
d. Burroughs, William Seward

September 15, 1898
b. Gottlieb, Eddie

September 16, 1898
b. Rey, Hans Augustus

September 19, 1898
b. Love, Bessie
b. Saragat, Giuseppe
d. Grey, George

September 20, 1898
b. Dressen, Chuck
d. Fontane, Theodor

September 21, 1898
b. Tchelitchew, Pavel

September 22, 1898
b. Wasson, R(obert) Gordon

September 23, 1898
b. Pidgeon, Walter
d. Johnston, Richard Malcolm

September 24, 1898
b. Behn, Harry
b. Florcy, Howard Walter
b. Moore, Charlotte E(mma)

September 25, 1898
b. Brackman, Robert
b. Judd, Walter H(enry)

September 26, 1898
b. Gershwin, George
b. Lockridge, Richard
d. Davenport, Fanny Lily Gypsy

September 27, 1898
b. Youmans, Vincent

September 28, 1898
b. Carter, Boake
d. Bayard, Thomas Francis

September 29, 1898
b. Lysenko, Trofim Denisovich

September 30, 1898
b. Adoree, Renee
b. D'Aulaire, Edgar Parin

October 2, 1898
b. Profaci, Joe
b. Wank, Roland A

October 3, 1898
b. McCarey, Leo

October 7, 1898
b. Wallenstein, Alfred Franz

October 9, 1898
b. Sewell, Joe

October 10, 1898
d. Puvis de Chavannes, Pierre Cecile

October 14, 1898
b. Wellman, Paul Iselin

October 16, 1898
b. Dean, Arthur H(obson)
b. Douglas, William Orville

October 17, 1898
b. Suzuki, Shin'ichi

October 19, 1898
d. Frederic, Harold

October 21, 1898
b. Walker, Stanley

October 22, 1898
b. Alonso, Damaso
b. Rickword, Edgell

October 26, 1898
b. Oliver, Harry

October 29, 1898
b. Emerson, Hope

October 30, 1898
b. Terry, Bill

November 1, 1898
b. Wallace, Sippie

November 7, 1898
d. Alvary, Max

November 11, 1898
b. Clair, Rene
b. Eberle, Irmengarde

November 12, 1898
d. Fisher, Clara

November 13, 1898
b. Bennett, Wallace F(oster)

November 18, 1898
b. Ivens, Joris

November 19, 1898
b. Sheldon, William Herbert
d. Buell, Don Carlos

November 21, 1898
b. Magritte, Rene Francois Ghislain

November 22, 1898
b. Blanding, Sarah Gibson

November 23, 1898
b. Brown, Rachel Fuller
b. Malinovsky, Rodion Yakovlevich

November 26, 1898
b. Ziegler, Karl

November 29, 1898
b. LaRocque, Rod
b. Lewis, C(live) S(taples)

November 30, 1898
b. Lyman, Link
b. Lynch, Joe
b. Gidlow, Elsa

December 6, 1898
b. Eisenstaedt, Alfred
b. Myrdal, Karl Gunnar
b. Shumlin, Herman Elliott

December 7, 1898
b. Johnson, Ching
d. Jenner, William, Sir

December 8, 1898
b. Burchard, John Ely

December 9, 1898
b. Kelly, Emmett Lee

December 14, 1898
b. Cowles, John, Sr.

December 20, 1898
b. Dunne, Irene Marie
b. Votipka, Thelma

December 24, 1898
b. Dodds, Baby

December 28, 1898
b. Franken, Rose
d. Morrill, Justin Smith

December 29, 1898
b. Bledsoe, Jules
b. Cooke, Samuel

1899

b. Barker, Doc
b. Brunhoff, Jean de
b. Copeland, Jo
b. Disney, Lillian
b. Drew, Richard G
b. Freyse, William
b. Haas, Walter A(braham), Sr.
b. Hill, Howard
b. Ho, Ying-Chin
b. Hoffman, Robert C
b. Hokinson, Helen
b. Kang, Sheng
b. Kern, Harold G
b. Lao She
b. Ortega, Santos
b. Peret, Benjamin
b. Scott, F(rancis) R(eginald)
b. Shearer, Douglas
b. Stiffel, Theodopholous
b. Sumner, Jessie
d. Blanco, Antonio Guzman
d. Bland, Richard Parks
d. Libby, Arthur
d. Tate, Henry, Sir
d. Traill, Catharine Parr

January 1, 1899
b. Cottam, Clarence
b. Pacciardi, Randolfo

January 7, 1899
b. Lee, J(oseph) Bracken
b. Poulenc, Francis

January 8, 1899
b. Adams, Sherman Llewellyn
b. Bandaranaike, S(olomon) W(est)
R(idgeway) D(ias)

January 11, 1899
b. Le Gallienne, Eva

January 12, 1899
b. Crisler, Fritz
b. Muller, Paul Hermann
d. Walker, Hiram

January 13, 1899
b. DeRochemont, Louis

January 15, 1899
b. Ace, Goodman
b. Whitaker, Rogers E(rnest)
M(alcolm)

January 17, 1899
b. Capone, Al(phonse)
b. Harris, Abram Lincoln, Jr.
b. Hutchins, Robert Maynard
b. Shute, Nevil

January 20, 1899
b. Tcherepnin, Alexander Nikolayevich

January 23, 1899
b. Bogart, Humphrey de Forest
b. Denning, Alfred Thompson
b. Kane, Joseph Nathan

January 24, 1899
b. Vandenberg, Hoyt Sanford

January 25, 1899
b. Spaak, Paul-Henri

January 27, 1899
b. Strong, Philip Duffield

January 29, 1899
d. Sisley, Alfred

January 30, 1899
b. Theiler, Max

February 2, 1899
b. Caudill, Rebecca
b. Rubin, Benny

February 3, 1899
b. Trotter, Mildred

February 6, 1899
b. Novarro, Ramon

February 8, 1899
b. Johnson, Lonnie

February 9, 1899
b. Donlevy, Brian
b. Langer, Walter C
b. Miller, Max (Carlton)

February 10, 1899
d. Lampman, Archibald

February 12, 1899
b. Tokatyan, Armand

February 15, 1899
b. Auric, Georges
b. Josephson, Matthew
b. Keppard, Freddie
b. Sondergaard, Gale (Edith Holm)

February 16, 1899
d. Faure, Francois Felix

February 18, 1899
b. Bryant, Arthur W M, Sir

February 20, 1899
b. Whitney, C(ornelius) V(anderbilt)

February 23, 1899
b. Kastner, Erich
b. Taurog, Norman

February 24, 1899
d. Nuitter, Charles Louis

February 25, 1899
d. Reuter, Paul Julius Von

February 26, 1899
b. Petitpierre, Max

February 27, 1899
b. Best, Charles Herbert
b. Keith, Ian

March 1, 1899
b. Duffy, Edmund
b. Wright, Louis Booker

March 3, 1899
b. DeBernardi, Forrest S
b. Gruenther, Alfred Maximillian

March 6, 1899
b. Simon, Richard Leo

March 11, 1899
b. Douglas, James Henderson, Jr.
b. Frederick IX

March 12, 1899
b. Iturbi, Amparo
d. Vogel, Julius

March 13, 1899
b. Van Vleck, John Hasbrouck

March 14, 1899
b. Irving, Kenneth Colin
b. Laver, James

March 16, 1899
b. Millis, Walter
d. Medill, Joseph

March 17, 1899
b. Summerfield, Arthur Ellsworth

March 18, 1899
d. Marsh, Othniel Charles

March 22, 1899
b. Page, Ruth

March 23, 1899
b. Adamic, Louis

March 24, 1899
b. Saunders, Allen

March 25, 1899
b. Audiberti, Jacques
b. Spewack, Bella Cohen

March 26, 1899
b. Ursuleac, Viorica

March 27, 1899
b. Kaufman, Joseph William

March 28, 1899
b. Busch, August Anheuser, Jr.

March 29, 1899
b. Beria, Lavrenti Pavlovich

March 31, 1899
b. White, Antonia
d. Thayer, Eli

April 1, 1899
b. Naldi, Nita

April 4, 1899
b. Belbenoit, Rene Lucien
b. Hannagan, Steve

April 5, 1899
b. Anderson, Elda Emma
b. Blalock, Alfred

April 7, 1899
b. Casadesus, Robert
b. Mistral, Gabriela

April 8, 1899
b. Christie, John Reginald Halliday
b. Meyerhoff, Joseph

April 9, 1899
b. McDonnell, James Smith
d. Field, Stephen Johnson

April 10, 1899
d. Tabor, Horace Austin Warner

April 11, 1899
b. Julian, Percy Lavon

April 12, 1899
b. Taber, Gladys Bagg
b. Thompson, Randall

April 13, 1899
b. Butts, Alfred M(osher)

April 14, 1899
b. Romulo, Carlos Pena

April 16, 1899
b. Neyman, Jerzy

April 18, 1899
b. Dole, Charles Minot

April 19, 1899
b. Coghill, Nevill Henry Kendall
  Aylmer
b. Douglas, Emily Taft

April 20, 1899
b. Larsen, Roy Edward
d. Friedel, Charles

April 21, 1899
b. Day, James Wentworth
b. Fritzsche, Hans

April 22, 1899
b. Green, Martyn

April 23, 1899
b. Marsh, Ngaio, Dame
b. Nabokov, Vladimir
b. Ohlin, Bertil Gotthard

April 27, 1899
b. Diegel, Leo

April 29, 1899
b. Angell, Robert Cooley
b. Ellington, Duke

April 30, 1899
b. Wieghorst, Olaf

May 3, 1899
b. MacMahon, Aline Laveen

May 5, 1899
b. Gosden, Freeman Fisher

May 8, 1899
b. Hayek, Friedrich August von
b. Heim, Jacques

May 10, 1899
b. Astaire, Fred
b. Tiomkin, Dimitri

May 11, 1899
b. Ewing, Alfred Cyril

May 14, 1899
b. Combs, Earle Bryan

May 15, 1899
d. Sarcey, Francisque

May 20, 1899
b. Harlan, John Marshall, II
b. Taylor, Estelle

May 24, 1899
b. Lenglen, Suzanne
b. Michaux, Henri
b. Thorp, Willard Long

May 25, 1899
b. Artzybasheff, Boris Mikhailovich
d. Bonheur, Rosa

May 26, 1899
b. Douglas, Aaron

May 30, 1899
b. Thalberg, Irving Grant

May 31, 1899
b. Leonov, Leonid Maximovich

June 1, 1899
b. Janssen, Werner

June 2, 1899
b. Teale, Edwin Way

June 3, 1899
b. Von Bekesy, Georg
d. Strauss, Johann, Jr.

June 7, 1899
b. Bowen, Elizabeth Dorthea Cole
d. Daly, Augustin

June 10, 1899
d. Chausson, Ernest

June 11, 1899
b. Kawabata, Yasunari

June 12, 1899
b. Lipmann, Fritz Albert

June 13, 1899
b. Chavez (y Ramirez), Carlos Antonio
  de Pauda

June 17, 1899
b. Fazenda, Louise

June 19, 1899
b. Mellon, Richard King

June 20, 1899
b. Traubel, Helen

June 21, 1899
b. Gard, Wayne

June 24, 1899
b. George, Dan, Chief

June 27, 1899
b. Trippe, Juan Terry

June 28, 1899
b. Meland, Bernard Eugene

June 30, 1899
b. Gross, H(arold) R(oyce)
d. Southworth, Emma Dorothy Eliza
  Nevitte

July 1, 1899
b. Laughton, Charles
b. Tsatsos, Constantinos

July 2, 1899
d. Wright, Horatio Gouverneur

July 4, 1899
b. Warren, Austin

July 5, 1899
d. Congreve, Richard

July 6, 1899
b. Eberhart, Mignon Good
b. Magnin, Cyril Isaac

July 7, 1899
b. Cukor, George (Dewey)

July 8, 1899
b. Lilienthal, David Eli

July 10, 1899
b. Conkle, Ellsworth Prouty

July 11, 1899
b. Solomon, Samuel Joseph
b. White, E(lwyn) B(rooks)

July 12, 1899
b. Fellig, Arthur
b. Nixon, E(dgar) D(aniel)

July 14, 1899
b. Breit, Gregory
b. Hill, Billy

July 17, 1899
b. Cagney, James

July 18, 1899
d. Alger, Horatio

July 21, 1899
b. Crane, Hart
b. Hemingway, Ernest (Miller)
d. Ingersoll, Robert Green

July 22, 1899
b. Sobhuza II

July 23, 1899
b. Heinemann, Gustav Walter

July 24, 1899
b. Loeb, Gerald Martin

July 25, 1899
b. Dumke, Ralph

July 26, 1899
b. Walker, Danton MacIntyre

July 27, 1899
b. Houghton, Amory
b. McDonald, Harl

July 30, 1899
b. Binns, Archie Fred
b. Moore, Gerald

July 31, 1899
b. Stevens, Robert Ten Broeck
d. Brinton, Daniel Garrison

August 1, 1899
b. Dean, William Frishe
b. Steinberg, William

August 2, 1899
b. Fry, E Maxwell
b. Szabolcsi, Bence
b. Wilson, Lyle Campbell

August 8, 1899
b. Markert, Russell

August 9, 1899
b. Kelly, Paul
b. Pendleton, Nat

August 11, 1899
b. Hirshhorn, Joseph Herman

August 12, 1899
b. DeLeeuw, Adele Louise

August 13, 1899
b. Hitchcock, Alfred Joseph, Sir

August 14, 1899
b. Burnett, Whit

August 16, 1899
d. Bunsen, Robert Wilhelm Eberhard

August 17, 1899
b. Lewis, Janet

August 18, 1899
b. Belluschi, Pietro

August 19, 1899
b. Baclanova, Olga
b. Tomlin, Bradley Walker

August 20, 1899
b. Bochner, Salomon

August 24, 1899
b. Borges, Jorge Luis

August 26, 1899
b. Tamayo, Rufino

August 27, 1899
b. Forester, Cecil Scott
b. Torroja (y Miret), Eduardo

August 28, 1899
b. Boyer, Charles
b. Grimm, Charlie
b. Howe, James Wong

August 29, 1899
b. Lemnitzer, Lyman Louis
b. Streibert, Theodore Cuyler

August 30, 1899
b. Cuyler, Kiki

August 31, 1899
b. Riggs, Lynn

September 2, 1899
b. Maury, Reuben

September 3, 1899
b. Benson, Ezra Taft
b. Burnet, F(rank) MacFarlane, Sir

September 4, 1899
b. Kaminska, Ida

September 6, 1899
b. Rose, Billy

September 9, 1899
b. Brassai
b. Hamilton, Neil
b. Hoyt, Waite Charles
b. Smith, Cyrus Rowlett

September 12, 1899
d. Vanderbilt, Cornelius

September 14, 1899
b. Chandler, Norman
b. Wallis, Hal Brent

September 15, 1899
b. Eisenhower, Milton Stover

September 16, 1899
b. Spewack, Samuel

September 17, 1899
d. Pillsbury, Charles Alfred

September 19, 1899
b. Cortez, Ricardo

September 20, 1899
b. Nugent, Elliott
b. Strauss, Leo

September 22, 1899
b. Allen, Elsie
b. Harlan, Veit

September 23, 1899
b. Clark, Tom
b. Nevelson, Louise Berliawsky

September 24, 1899
b. Dobell, William
b. Doriot, Georges Frederic

September 25, 1899
b. Buck, Paul Herman
b. Landis, James McCauley

September 26, 1899
b. Dawson, William Levi

September 27, 1899
b. Eiseman, Florence

September 28, 1899
d. Segantini, Giovanni

September 29, 1899
b. Butlin, William Heygate Edmund, Sir

October 1, 1899
b. Patterson, William Allan

October 3, 1899
b. Berg, Gertrude

October 4, 1899
b. Jonas, Franz

October 5, 1899
b. Bidault, Georges
b. Wallenberg, Marcus

October 9, 1899
b. Catton, Bruce

October 11, 1899
b. Ewen, Frederic

October 12, 1899
b. Collins, Ted

October 15, 1899
b. Menninger, William C

October 17, 1899
b. Kempner, Robert M(aximilian) W(asilii)

October 19, 1899
b. Asturias, Miguel Angel
b. Bauer, Eddie
d. Appleton, William Henry

October 20, 1899
b. Brent, Evelyn

October 21, 1899
b. Hussey, Christopher Edward Clive

October 22, 1899
b. Morris, William, Jr.

October 23, 1899
b. Balchen, Bernt
b. Kimbrough, Emily
b. Tashman, Lilyan

October 24, 1899
b. Abbas, Ferhat

October 25, 1899
b. MacLiammoir, Michael

October 26, 1899
b. Johnson, Judy

October 28, 1899
d. Mergenthaler, Ottmar

October 31, 1899
b. Mandelstam, Nadezhda Yakovlevna

November 2, 1899
b. Klineberg, Otto

November 4, 1899
b. Berman, Eugene

November 7, 1899
b. Shear, Murray Jacob

November 9, 1899
b. Mezzrow, Mezz

November 10, 1899
b. Seredy, Kate
b. Stowe, Leland

November 11, 1899
b. Green, Anne
b. O'Brien, Pat
b. Traynor, Pie

November 15, 1899
b. Johnson, Herbert Fisk

November 16, 1899
b. McBride, Mary Margaret

November 18, 1899
b. Ormandy, Eugene

November 19, 1899
b. Tate, Allen (John Orley)

November 20, 1899
d. Dawson, John William, Sir

November 21, 1899
b. Borgmann, Benny
d. Hobart, Garret Augustus

November 22, 1899
b. Berndt, Walter
b. Carmichael, Hoagy

November 24, 1899
b. Morehouse, Ward

November 25, 1899
b. Burnett, W(illiam) R(iley)

November 26, 1899
b. Hauptmann, Bruno Richard

November 27, 1899
b. Abramson, Harold A(lexander)

November 29, 1899
b. Artukovic, Andrija
b. Ulreich, Nura Woodson

December 1, 1899
b. Briggs, Ellis O(rmsbee)
b. Welch, Robert Henry Winborne, Jr.

December 2, 1899
b. Adler, Peter Herman
b. Barbirolli, John, Sir
b. Benary-Isbert, Margot
b. Cobb, John Rhodes

December 5, 1899
b. Conroy, Jack
b. Sheean, (James) Vincent
b. Williamson, Sonny Boy

December 6, 1899
b. Conlan, Jocko

December 8, 1899
b. Qualen, John Mandt
b. Supervia, Conchita

December 9, 1899
b. Adams, Leonie Fuller

December 12, 1899
b. Crosby, Floyd Delafield

December 15, 1899
b. Abrahams, Harold

December 16, 1899
b. Coward, Noel Pierce, Sir

December 17, 1899
d. Quaritch, Bernard

December 19, 1899
b. Hinkle, Paul
b. King, Martin Luther, Sr.
d. Lawton, Henry Ware

December 20, 1899
b. Ronne, Finn
b. Sparkman, John Jackson

December 21, 1899
d. Lamoureux, Charles

December 22, 1899
d. Moody, Dwight Lyman

December 23, 1899
d. Eaton, Dorman Bridgman

December 25, 1899
b. Power, Donald Clinton
b. Soyer, Moses
b. Soyer, Raphael
d. Coues, Elliott

December 26, 1899
b. Mannes, Leopold Damrosch

December 28, 1899
b. Murnau, Friedrich W
b. Poage, W(illiam) R(obert)

December 30, 1899
b. Ingstad, Helge Marcus
d. Paget, James, Sir

December 31, 1899
b. Mearns, David Chambers
b. Wummer, John

1900

b. Cassidy, Claudia
b. Gadamer, Hans-Georg
b. Goldie, Grace Wyndham
b. Golenpaul, Dan
b. Jaabari, Mohammed Ali, Sheik
b. Jewtraw, Charlie
b. Khrushchev, Nina Petrovna
b. Louiseboulanger
b. Mitchell, Millard
b. Plumb, Charles
b. Van Westerborg, Edward
b. Weems, Ted
b. Zangara, Joseph
d. Campbell, Joseph
d. Cropsey, Jasper Francis
d. Dun, Robert Graham
d. Washakie
d. Young Man Afraid of His Horses

January 1, 1900
b. Cugat, Xavier
b. Haines, William

January 3, 1900
b. Arzner, Dorothy
b. Pitts, Zasu
b. Russell, Donald Joseph

January 4, 1900
b. Bond, James

January 5, 1900
b. Tanguy, Yves

January 6, 1900
b. Hulme, Kathryn Cavarly

January 9, 1900
b. Halliburton, Richard

January 13, 1900
b. Straus, Jack Isidor

January 15, 1900
b. Kuhn, Irene

January 17, 1900
b. Rosenman, Dorothy
b. Sperti, George Speri

January 19, 1900
b. Christians, Mady
b. White, Leslie A(lvin)

January 20, 1900
b. Clive, Colin
d. Blackmore, Richard Doddridge
d. Ruskin, John

January 21, 1900
b. Naish, J(oseph) Carrol

January 25, 1900
b. Dobzhansky, Theodosius
(Grigorievich)

January 27, 1900
b. Clark, Georgia Neese
b. Rickover, Hyman George

January 28, 1900
b. Neel, Alice Hartley
b. Perkins, Milo Randolph

January 30, 1900
b. Hunt, Martita

January 31, 1900
b. Parsons, Betty Pierson
d. Queensberry, John Sholto Douglas

February 1, 1900
b. Busoni, Rafaello
b. Mercer, Mabel
b. Potter, Stephen

February 2, 1900
b. Righter, Carroll
d. Wittenmyer, Annie Turner

February 4, 1900
b. Impellitteri, Vincent R(ichard)

February 5, 1900
b. Stevenson, Adlai Ewing, II

February 8, 1900
b. Kredel, Fritz

February 10, 1900
b. Sunay, Cevdet

February 11, 1900
b. Hitchcock, Tommy

February 12, 1900
b. Boothby, Robert John Graham, Lord
b. Chuikov, Vasili Ivanovitch
b. Fenton, Carroll Lane

February 15, 1900
b. Thomas, Charles Allen

February 16, 1900
b. Hackett, Albert
b. Switzer, Mary E.

February 18, 1900
d. Beltrami, Eugenio

February 20, 1900
b. Kabotie, Fred

February 22, 1900
b. Bunuel, Luis
b. Kollsman, Paul
b. O'Faolain, Sean
b. Seferiades, Giorgos Styljanou

February 23, 1900
d. Butterfield, William
d. Dowson, Ernest Christopher

February 24, 1900
d. Hovey, Richard

February 25, 1900
b. Harris, Jed

February 29, 1900
b. Negulesco, Jean

March 1, 1900
b. Bunting, Basil
b. Rathbone, Monroe Jackson

March 2, 1900
b. Bee, Clair Francis
b. Weill, Kurt

March 3, 1900
b. Best, Edna

March 4, 1900
b. Biberman, Herbert

March 6, 1900
b. Cigna, Gina
b. Grove, Lefty
d. Daimler, Gottlieb (Wilhelm)

March 8, 1900
b. Aiken, Howard Hathaway

March 10, 1900
b. Billingsley, Sherman
b. Brayman, Harold
b. DeRose, Peter
d. Symons, George James

March 12, 1900
b. Rojas Pinilla, Gustavo

March 13, 1900
b. Seferis, George
b. Soss, Wilma Porter

March 15, 1900
b. Freyre, Gilberto (de Mello)

March 16, 1900
b. Burns, Eveline Mabel

March 17, 1900
b. Howard, Shemp

March 18, 1900
b. Delaney, Jack

March 19, 1900
b. Joliot(-Curie), (Jean) Frederic
b. Muccio, John Joseph

March 20, 1900
b. Cordiner, Ralph Jarron

March 21, 1900
b. Leontovich, Eugenie

March 22, 1900
b. Robinson, Claude Everett

March 23, 1900
b. Fromm, Erich

March 25, 1900
b. Boettiger, John

March 26, 1900
d. Wise, Isaac Mayer

March 27, 1900
b. Scott, Arleigh Winston, Sir

March 29, 1900
b. Elton, Charles Sutherland

March 31, 1900
b. Henry William Frederick Albert

April 1, 1900
b. Benton, William

April 2, 1900
d. Church, Frederick Edwin

April 3, 1900
b. Brownell, Samuel Miller
b. Chamoun, Camille N(imer)

April 4, 1900
d. Bidwell, John
d. Van Camp, Gilbert C

April 5, 1900
b. Bayer, Herbert
b. Tracy, Spencer Bonaventure
d. Bertrand, Joseph Louis Francois

April 9, 1900
b. Jenkins, Allen

April 10, 1900
b. Beckman, Arnold (Orville)

April 12, 1900
b. Lapchick, Joe
b. Leighton, Clare Veronica Hope

April 14, 1900
b. Baccaloni, Salvatore

April 15, 1900
b. Taubes, Frederic

April 16, 1900
b. Adler, Polly
d. Adler, Dankmar

April 19, 1900
b. Hughes, Richard Arthur Warren
b. Michener, Roland
b. O'Brien, George
b. Talmadge, Constance

April 20, 1900
b. Norell, Norman

April 21, 1900
d. Vogl, Heinrich

April 23, 1900
b. Bottomley, Jim

April 24, 1900
b. Goudge, Elizabeth

April 25, 1900
b. Halpert, Edith Gregor

b. Pauli, Wolfgang Ernst

April 26, 1900
b. Fuchs, Joseph (Philip)
b. Richter, Charles Francis
b. Sirk, Douglas
b. Wilson, Hack

April 27, 1900
b. Lantz, Walter

April 28, 1900
b. Gielgud, Val Henry
b. Oort, Jan Hendrik
b. Thorez, Maurice

April 30, 1900
d. Jones, Casey

May 1, 1900
b. Caples, John
b. Silone, Ignazio

May 3, 1900
b. Frank, Hans
b. LaRue, Jack
b. Winwar, Frances

May 5, 1900
b. Schmidt-Isserstedt, Hans

May 6, 1900
b. Mattingley, Garrett

May 10, 1900
b. Payne-Gaposchkin, Cecilia (Helena)

May 11, 1900
b. Cotton, Norris
b. Sandoz, Mari

May 12, 1900
b. Macy, George
b. McAfee, Mildred H(elen)

May 13, 1900
d. Levi, Hermann

May 14, 1900
b. Borland, Hal
b. Finch, Robert Duer Clayton

May 15, 1900
b. Gordon, John F

May 17, 1900
b. Khomeini, Ruhollah Musavi,
   Ayatollah

May 18, 1900
b. Keating, Kenneth B

May 22, 1900
b. Tolson, Clyde Anderson

May 23, 1900
d. Carpenter, Francis Bicknell

May 28, 1900
b. Abel, Taffy
b. Ladnier, Tommy
b. Little, Little Jack

d. Grove, George, Sir

May 30, 1900
b. Villanueva, Carlos Raul

June 2, 1900
d. Samory Toure

June 3, 1900
b. Edwards, Alan
b. Green, Abel
b. Mundt, Karl Earl
b. Sinclair, Gordon

June 4, 1900
b. Glueck, Nelson

June 5, 1900
b. Gabor, Dennis
d. Crane, Stephen

June 6, 1900
b. Stouffer, Samuel A.

June 9, 1900
b. Waring, Fred Malcolm

June 11, 1900
b. Kresge, Stanley Sebastian
b. Spivak, Lawrence E(dmund)
d. Boyd, Belle

June 12, 1900
d. Hale, Lucretia Peabody

June 13, 1900
b. Hunter, Ian

June 15, 1900
b. Feingold, Benjamin Franklin
b. Luening, Otto

June 17, 1900
b. Bormann, Martin Ludwig
b. White, William Lindsay

June 19, 1900
b. Hobson, Laura Zametkin

June 20, 1900
b. Levi, Julian Edwin

June 23, 1900
b. Noyes, Blanche Wilcox
b. Steelman, John Roy

June 24, 1900
b. Austin, Gene

June 25, 1900
b. Chapman, John (Arthur)
b. Mountbatten of Burma, Louis
   Mountbatten, Earl

June 26, 1900
b. Crooks, Richard Alexander

June 29, 1900
b. Saint-Exupery, Antoine (Jean
   Baptiste Marie Roger) de

July 1, 1900
b. Dorsey, Thomas Andrew

July 2, 1900
b. Guthrie, Tyrone, Sir

July 3, 1900
b. Brown, John Mason

July 4, 1900
b. Armstrong, Louis
b. Baddeley, Angela
b. Lawrence, Gertrude

July 5, 1900
b. Achard, Marcel
b. Alfrink, Bernard (Jan), Cardinal
b. Gaunt, William
d. Barnard, Henry

July 8, 1900
b. Antheil, George

July 9, 1900
b. Schaefer, Rudolph Jay

July 10, 1900
b. Cole, Kenneth Stewart
b. Parish, Mitchell

July 14, 1900
b. Allen, Robert Sharon

July 15, 1900
b. Francis, Thomas, Jr.

July 18, 1900
b. Marshall, S(amuel) L(yman)
   A(twood)
b. Sarraute, Nathalie

July 19, 1900
b. Rosenberg, Anna Marie

July 20, 1900
b. Arnold, Oren

July 22, 1900
b. Braceland, Francis J(ames)
b. Dahlberg, Edward

July 24, 1900
b. Fitzgerald, Zelda

July 26, 1900
b. Mortimer, Charles Greenough

July 27, 1900
b. Haug, Hans

July 28, 1900
b. Maxon, Lou Russell

July 29, 1900
b. Johnson, Eyvind Olof Verner
b. Lattimore, Owen
b. Redman, Don

July 31, 1900
b. Roper, Elmo Burns, Jr.

August 2, 1900
b. Holling, Holling C(lancy)
b. Morgan, Helen Riggins

August 3, 1900
b. Kekkonen, Urho Kaleva
b. Pyle, Ernie
b. Scopes, John Thomas
b. Sprague, R(obert) C(hapman)

August 4, 1900
b. Elizabeth, Queen Mother
b. Illia, Arturo Umberto

August 6, 1900
b. Hillcourt, William

August 7, 1900
d. Liebknecht, Wilhelm

August 8, 1900
b. Young, Victor
d. Cox, Jacob Dolson

August 9, 1900
b. Tully, Grace George

August 10, 1900
b. Levine, Philip
b. Porritt, Arthur Espie, Sir
b. Shearer, Norma

August 11, 1900
b. Brogan, Denis William, Sir
b. Dunn, Alan
b. Mayes, Herbert Raymond

August 12, 1900
d. Keeler, James Edward
d. Steinitz, Wilhelm

August 13, 1900
d. Huntington, Collis Potter
d. Soloviev, Vladimir Sergeevich

August 14, 1900
b. Bauer, Helen

August 15, 1900
b. Parr, A(lbert) E(ide)
b. Tworkov, Jack

August 17, 1900
b. Howe, Quincy

August 18, 1900
b. O'Keefe, Walter
b. Pandit, Vijaya Lakshmi (Nehru)

August 19, 1900
b. Ryle, Gilbert

August 22, 1900
b. Bergner, Elisabeth
b. Halleck, Charles Abraham
b. Motley, Arthur Harrison

August 23, 1900
b. Krenek, Ernst

August 24, 1900
b. Chervenkov, Vulko

b. Fidler, Jimmie
b. Foster, Preston

August 25, 1900
b. Kober, Arthur
b. Krebs, Hans Adolf, Sir
d. Nietzsche, Friedrich Wilhelm

August 26, 1900
b. Woodruff, Hale (Aspacio)

August 28, 1900
d. Sidgwick, Henry

August 29, 1900
b. Dollard, John
b. Kazee, Buell Hilton

August 30, 1900
b. Fry, Franklin Clark
b. Rankin, Arthur

September 1, 1900
b. Allen, William McPherson
b. Wilson, Don(ald Harlow)

September 3, 1900
b. Beinum, Eduard van
b. Benson, Sally

September 4, 1900
b. Love, George Hutchinson

September 6, 1900
b. Bennett, W(illiam) A(ndrew) C(ecil)
b. Green, Julian (Hartridge)
b. Harand, Irene

September 7, 1900
b. Caldwell, Taylor

September 8, 1900
b. Pepper, Claude Denson

September 9, 1900
b. Hilton, James

September 10, 1900
b. Stern, Philip Van Doren

September 13, 1900
b. Linder, Harold Francis

September 17, 1900
b. Marriott, John Willard
b. Ostenso, Martha

September 18, 1900
b. Ramgoolam, Seewoosagur, Sir

September 20, 1900
b. Castello Branco, Humberto
b. DeParis, Wilbur
b. Visser T Hooft, Willem Adolf

September 21, 1900
b. O'Brien, Leo W

September 24, 1900
b. Bechtel, Stephen Davison
b. Fisher, Ham(mond Edward)

September 25, 1900
d. Lazear, Jesse William
d. Van Lew, Elizabeth

September 27, 1900
b. Paddleford, Clementine Haskin

September 29, 1900
b. Gabor, Jolie

October 2, 1900
b. Abbott, Bud

October 3, 1900
b. Wolfe, Thomas (Clayton)

October 7, 1900
b. Butterfield, Herbert, Sir
b. Himmler, Heinrich

October 8, 1900
b. Chermayeff, Serge (Ivan)

October 9, 1900
b. Sim, Alastair

October 10, 1900
b. Hayes, Helen

October 11, 1900
b. Hartmann, Rudolph
b. Hubbard, Cal

October 14, 1900
b. Deming, W(illiam) Edwards

October 15, 1900
b. Aronson, Boris
b. Feld, Fritz
b. Leroy, Mervyn

October 16, 1900
b. Ardizzone, Edward Jeffrey Irving
b. Goslin, Goose

October 18, 1900
b. Lenya, Lotte

October 19, 1900
b. Worters, Roy

October 20, 1900
b. Morse, Wayne Lyman
d. Warner, Charles Dudley

October 22, 1900
b. Stettinius, Edward R, Jr.
d. Sherman, John

October 25, 1900
d. Squibb, Edward Robinson

October 26, 1900
b. Abboud, (El Ferik) Ibrahim

October 30, 1900
b. Granit, Ragnar Arthur
b. Axis Sally

November 4, 1900
b. Lucioni, Luigi

November 5, 1900
b. Dies, Martin, Jr.

November 7, 1900
b. Kurtz, Efrem

November 8, 1900
b. Frey-Wyssling, Albert F
b. Gleason, Thomas W(illiam)
b. Mitchell, Margaret

November 11, 1900
b. Scott, Hugh (Doggett), Jr.

November 12, 1900
d. Daly, Marcus
d. Villard, Henry

November 13, 1900
b. Allison, Samuel King
b. King, Alexander
b. Miner, Worthington C

November 14, 1900
b. Copland, Aaron

November 15, 1900
b. Hamilton, Hamish

November 16, 1900
b. Barrett, William Edmund

November 18, 1900
b. Alajalov, Constantin
b. Kistiakowsky, George Bogdan
b. Thurman, Howard

November 19, 1900
b. Walbrook, Anton

November 20, 1900
b. Burch, Billy
b. Gould, Chester

November 22, 1900
b. Pantaleoni, Helenka (Tradeusa
　Adamowski)
b. Post, Wiley
d. Sullivan, Arthur Seymour, Sir

November 25, 1900
b. Douglas, Helen Mary Gahagan
b. Hoess, Rudolf Franz
b. Schwartz, Arthur

November 27, 1900
b. Barzin, Leon Eugene

November 28, 1900
b. Wigg, George (Edward Cecil)
d. Skinner, Halcyon

November 30, 1900
b. Household, Geoffrey Edward West
b. Lasker, Mary (Woodward)
d. Wilde, Oscar (Fingal O'Flahertie
　Wills)

December 3, 1900
b. Daugherty, Carroll Roop
b. Kuhn, Richard

December 6, 1900
b. Arciniegas, German

December 7, 1900
b. Plimpton, Francis Taylor Pearson

December 8, 1900
b. Ingersoll, Ralph McAllister

December 9, 1900
b. Needham, Joseph

December 10, 1900
b. Lebrun, Rico

December 12, 1900
b. Telkes, Maria (de)
b. Trueblood, D(avid) Elton

December 16, 1900
b. Lortel, Lucille
b. Pritchett, V(ictor) S(awdon), Sir

December 17, 1900
b. Paxinou, Katina

December 19, 1900
b. Giannini, Dusolina
b. Mildmay, Audrey

December 20, 1900
b. Fiorito, Ted
b. Hartnett, Gabby

December 22, 1900
b. Brinig, Myron
b. Bush, Alan (Dudley)

December 23, 1900
b. Soglow, Otto

December 24, 1900
b. Smallwood, Joey

December 25, 1900
b. MacLane, Barton

December 28, 1900
b. Lyons, Ted
d. Tyler, Moses Coit

December 29, 1900
b. Corcoran, Thomas Gardiner

December 30, 1900
b. Barnhart, Clarence L(ewis)

December 31, 1900
b. Burke, Selma (Hortense)
d. Goodwin, Hannibal Williston

1901

b. Arliss, Leslie
b. Blumenfeld, Isadore
b. Braun, Otto
b. Campagnolo, Gitullio
b. Chen Yi
b. Cushman, Austin Thomas
b. Dassler, Adolf

b. Dempster, Carol
b. Dhlomo, R(olfus) R(eginald)
　R(aymond)
b. Eaton, Mary
b. Friedrich, Carl Joachim
b. Godfrey, Isadore
b. Hampton, Hope
b. Harris, William Bliss
b. Herzog, Arthur, Jr.
b. Hoyt, Lawrence W
b. Johnson, Guy Benton
b. Kunhardt, Dorothy (Meserve)
b. Lazarsfeld, Paul F(elix)
b. Manoogian, Alex
b. Moore, Don W
b. Peller, Clara
b. Pridi Phanomyong
b. Segal, Henry
b. Shankar, Uday
b. Zamboni, Frank J
d. Bannister, Edward Mitchell
d. Mayo-Smith, Richmond
d. Mwanga

January 1, 1901
d. Donnelly, Ignatius

January 2, 1901
b. Ralf, Torsten

January 3, 1901
b. Ngo-Dinh-Diem
b. Voegelin, Eric (Herman Wilhelm)

January 4, 1901
b. Berger, Raoul

January 5, 1901
b. Wickens, Aryness Joy

January 6, 1901
d. Armour, Philip Danforth

January 7, 1901
b. Brownlee, John
b. Page, Irvine H
b. Schwarzhaupt, Elisabeth

January 8, 1901
b. Malenkov, Georgi Maximilianovich

January 9, 1901
b. Young, Chic

January 11, 1901
b. Lloyd-Jones, Esther McDonald
d. Fee, John Gregg

January 12, 1901
b. Johnson, Arno Hollock
b. Jooss, Kurt

January 13, 1901
b. Guthrie, A(lfred) B(ertram), Jr.

January 14, 1901
b. Daniels, Bebe

January 16, 1901
b. Batista y Zaldivar, Fulgencio
b. Jackson, Laura Riding
b. Matthews, T(homas) S(tanley)
b. Riding, Laura

d. Barbier, Jules
d. Bocklin, Arnold
d. Revels, Hiram Rhodes

January 17, 1901
b. Asther, Nils
b. Dutra, Olin

January 20, 1901
d. Gramme, Zenobe Theophile

January 21, 1901
d. Gray, Elisha

January 22, 1901
d. Victoria, Queen

January 23, 1901
b. Wirtz, Arthur Michael

January 24, 1901
b. Romm, Mikhail

January 25, 1901
b. Dunnock, Mildred
b. Wilder, Robert Ingersoll

January 27, 1901
b. Rooney, Art(hur Joseph)
d. Verdi, Giuseppe Fortunino
   Francesco

January 28, 1901
b. Barthe, Richmond

January 29, 1901
b. DuMont, Allen Balcom

January 31, 1901
b. Fabian, Robert Honey

February 1, 1901
b. Gable, Clark

February 2, 1901
b. Heifetz, Jascha
b. Husch, Gerhard
b. Kahn, Louis I(sadore)
b. Kuekes, Edward Daniel

February 3, 1901
b. Floyd, Pretty Boy
b. Lehmann, Rosamond Nina

February 4, 1901
b. Werth, Alexander

February 5, 1901
b. Sheekman, Arthur

February 6, 1901
b. Lyon, Ben

February 8, 1901
b. Dabney, Virginius

February 9, 1901
d. Harvey, Fred(erick Henry)

February 11, 1901
b. Hulman, Tony, Jr.

February 13, 1901
b. Gibbon, Lewis Grassic
b. Kuznetzov, Vassili Vasilyevich

February 15, 1901
b. Bracken, Brendan Rendall, Viscount
b. Humphreys, Christmas

February 16, 1901
b. King, Wayne
b. Morris, Chester
b. Pei, Mario Andrew

February 17, 1901
d. Nevin, Ethelbert Woodbridge

February 18, 1901
b. Berlenbach, Paul

February 20, 1901
b. Dubos, Rene Jules
b. Naguib, Mohammed

February 21, 1901
b. Peyre, Henri Maurice
d. Fitzgerald, George Francis

February 22, 1901
b. Lorant, Stefan
b. Whittaker, Charles Evans

February 23, 1901
b. Nichols, Ruth Rowland

February 24, 1901
b. Parry, Albert

February 25, 1901
b. Marx, Zeppo

February 27, 1901
b. Marini, Marino

February 28, 1901
b. Pauling, Linus C(arl)
d. Evarts, William Maxwell

March 2, 1901
d. Dawson, George Mercer

March 3, 1901
b. Cordier, Andrew Wellington

March 4, 1901
b. Goren, Charles Henry
b. Rabearivelo, Jean Joseph

March 6, 1901
b. Woodall, Mary

March 10, 1901
b. Calderone, Frank Anthony

March 13, 1901
d. Harrison, Benjamin

March 17, 1901
b. Catledge, Turner
b. Newman, Alfred

March 18, 1901
b. Hall, Manly Palmer
b. Johnson, William Henry

March 19, 1901
b. Mielziner, Jo

March 20, 1901
b. Groves, Wallace

March 21, 1901
b. Weintal, Edward

March 24, 1901
b. Iwerks, Ub(be)
d. Yonge, Charlotte Mary

March 25, 1901
b. Begley, Ed(ward James)
b. Fetzer, John Earl

March 27, 1901
b. Barks, Carl
b. Sato, Eisaku

March 28, 1901
d. Jasper, John J

March 29, 1901
b. Montagu, Ewen

April 1, 1901
b. Chambers, Whittaker
b. Farrell, Johnny

April 3, 1901
b. Hare, Raymond A(rthur)
d. Carte, Richard d'Oyly

April 5, 1901
b. Alexander, Hattie Elizabeth
b. Bowles, Chester Bliss
b. Douglas, Melvyn
b. Johnson, Raynor Carey
b. Julian, Doggie

April 7, 1901
b. Paton, Richard

April 9, 1901
b. Kotsching, Walter Maria

April 10, 1901
b. Kavan, Anna

April 11, 1901
b. Olivetti, Adriano
b. Wescott, Glenway
d. Hallstrom, Ivar

April 13, 1901
b. Dennison, Robert Lee
b. Lacan, Jacques (Marie Emile)

April 14, 1901
b. Stulberg, Louis

April 15, 1901
b. Davis, Joe
b. Pleven, Rene Jean

April 16, 1901
b. Akimov, Nikolay Pavlovich
d. Rowland, Henry Augustus

April 17, 1901
b. Prebisch, Raul

April 19, 1901
b. Summerskill, Edith Clara, Baroness

April 22, 1901
b. Maxwell, Vera (Huppe)

April 23, 1901
b. Coxe, George Harmon

April 29, 1901
b. Hirohito

April 30, 1901
b. Kuznets, Simon Smith

April 31, 1901
b. Magee, Harry L

May 1, 1901
b. Brown, Sterling (Allen)
b. Gill, Amory Tingle
d. Waterman, Lewis Edson

May 5, 1901
b. Blind Willie McTell

May 7, 1901
b. Coggeshall, L(owell) T(helwell)
b. Cooper, Gary

May 12, 1901
b. Hinton, Christopher, Sir

May 15, 1901
b. Anderson, Dorothy Hansine
b. Spanel, Abram N

May 16, 1901
b. Justus, Roy Braxton
b. Zevin, B(enjamin) D(avid)

May 17, 1901
b. Egk, Werner
b. Lorenz, Max
b. Schonfield, Hugh J

May 18, 1901
b. DuVigneaud, Vincent
b. Sauguet, Henri
b. Stratton, Julius A(dams)

May 19, 1901
b. Chandler, Dorothy (Buffum)
d. Pretorius, Marthinus Wessel

May 20, 1901
b. Euwe, Max
b. Fleeson, Doris

May 21, 1901
b. Drewry, Guy Carleton
b. Heidt, Horace Murray
b. Nolan, Thomas Brennan

May 24, 1901
b. Conacher, Lionel Pretoria
b. Haley, William John, Sir

May 27, 1901
b. Godowsky, Leopold, Jr.

May 30, 1901
b. Felsenstein, Walter
b. Skinner, Cornelia Otis
b. Trumbauer, Frank(ie)

June 1, 1901
b. Carr, William G(eorge)
b. Day, Hap
b. Denny-Brown, Derek Ernest
b. Sukarno, Achmed
b. Van Druten, John William

June 2, 1901
b. Andrews, Bert

June 3, 1901
b. Evans, Maurice

June 5, 1901
b. Rifkind, Simon H(irsch)
b. Romanov, Anastasia

June 6, 1901
b. Struther, Jan

June 9, 1901
b. Price, George
d. Besant, Walter, Sir
d. Moran, Edward

June 10, 1901
b. Loewe, Frederick

June 12, 1901
b. Hartnell, Norman Bishop, Sir

June 13, 1901
b. Erlander, Tage Fritiof

June 24, 1901
b. Partch, Harry
b. Penney, William George

June 26, 1901
b. Symington, Stuart

June 27, 1901
b. Tuve, Merle Antony

June 28, 1901
b. Bruce, Ailsa Mellon

June 29, 1901
b. Eddy, Nelson
b. Inescort, Frieda

June 30, 1901
b. Sutton, Willie
d. Kerr, Orpheus C

July 1, 1901
b. Phillips, Irna

July 4, 1901
d. Fiske, John

d. Tait, Peter Guthrie

July 7, 1901
b. DeSica, Vittorio
d. Lorillard, Pierre
d. Spyri, Johanna Heuser

July 9, 1901
b. Cartland, Barbara Hamilton

July 13, 1901
b. Benjamin, Curtis G
b. Lewis, (Myrtle) Tillie
b. Walker, Mickey
d. Jackson, Peter B

July 14, 1901
b. Tobias, George

July 16, 1901
b. Mahler, Fritz

July 17, 1901
d. Butterford, Daniel

July 19, 1901
b. Beals, Ralph Leon
b. Damita, Lily

July 20, 1901
b. Manush, Heinie

July 22, 1901
b. Weidman, Charles Edward, Jr.

July 23, 1901
b. Hibbs, Ben

July 25, 1901
b. Wilson, John Johnston

July 28, 1901
b. Vallee, Rudy

July 29, 1901
b. Bridges, Harry Renton

July 30, 1901
d. Adams, Herbert Baxter

July 31, 1901
b. Dubuffet, Jean
b. Slansky, Rudolf Salzmann
b. Boyce, Westray Battle

August 1, 1901
b. Villa, Pancho

August 3, 1901
b. Stennis, John C(ornelius)
b. Wyszynski, Stefan

August 7, 1901
b. Heiden, Konrad

August 8, 1901
b. Berberova, Nina Nikolaevna
b. Lawrence, Ernest Orlando

August 9, 1901
b. Casadesus, Gaby (Lhote)

b. Farrell, Charles

August 11, 1901
d. Crispi, Francesco

August 12, 1901
d. Nordenskiold, Nils Adolph Erik,
Baron

August 14, 1901
b. Konwitschny, Franz
b. Pitman, James

August 15, 1901
b. Arias Madrid, Arnulfo

August 17, 1901
b. MacDonald, Malcolm John

August 18, 1901
b. Keller, Arthur C

August 20, 1901
b. Quasimodo, Salvatore

August 21, 1901
b. Rogell, Albert S

August 22, 1901
b. Caston, Saul
b. Stouffer, Vernon B

August 23, 1901
b. Bush, Guy Terrell
b. Cooper, John Sherman

August 25, 1901
b. Engstrom, Elmer William

August 26, 1901
b. DeQuay, Jan E
b. Genaro, Frankie
b. Taylor, Maxwell Davenport

August 27, 1901
b. Pryor, Roger
b. Ritz, Al

August 28, 1901
b. Lang, Paul Henry

August 29, 1901
b. Joliat, Aurel

August 30, 1901
b. Gunther, John
b. Wilkins, Roy

September 1, 1901
d. Chrysander, Karl Franz Friedrich

September 2, 1901
b. Rupp, Adolph Frederick

September 4, 1901
b. Lyons, William, Sir
b. Osborn, Paul

September 5, 1901
b. Bailey, Donald Coleman, Sir
b. Eldridge, Florence

September 6, 1901
b. Jonsson, John Erik
b. Weber, Ernst

September 8, 1901
b. McAvoy, May
b. Verwoerd, Hendrik F

September 9, 1901
b. Hicks, Granville
d. Toulouse-Lautrec (Monfa), (Henri
Marie Raymond de)

September 11, 1901
b. Bates, Ted
b. Sebrell, W(illiam) H(enry), Jr.

September 12, 1901
b. Blue, Ben

September 14, 1901
d. McKinley, William

September 17, 1901
b. Chichester, Francis Charles, Sir

September 18, 1901
b. Clurman, Harold Edgar

September 19, 1901
b. Pasternak, Joe

September 20, 1901
b. Edson, Gus

September 21, 1901
b. Constantine, Learie Nicholas
Constantine, Baron
b. Dubridge, L(ee) A(lvin)

September 22, 1901
b. Alexander, Katherine
b. Huggins, Charles B(renton)

September 23, 1901
b. Brace, Gerald Warner
b. Seifert, Jaroslav

September 25, 1901
b. Bresson, Robert
b. Houser, Clarence

September 26, 1901
b. Cook, Donald
d. Nicolay, John George

September 28, 1901
b. Paley, William Samuel

September 29, 1901
b. Fermi, Enrico

October 2, 1901
b. Campbell, Roy
b. Draper, Charles Stark

October 6, 1901
b. Deloria, Vine (Victor), Sr.

October 7, 1901
b. Boucher, Frank
b. Souvanna, Phouma

October 9, 1901
b. Jemison, Alice Mae

October 10, 1901
b. Giacometti, Alberto
b. Patterson, Frederick Douglass

October 12, 1901
b. Hebert, F(elix) Edward

October 13, 1901
b. Sampson, Edith Spurlock
b. Shirley-Smith, Hubert

October 14, 1901
b. Stuhldreher, Harry A

October 15, 1901
b. Abs, Hermann J(osef)

October 17, 1901
b. Arthur, Jean
b. Collins, Lee

October 18, 1901
d. Pillsbury, John Sargent

October 19, 1901
b. Burke, Arleigh A(lbert)

October 21, 1901
b. Clark, Joseph Sill
b. von Rad, Gerhard

October 24, 1901
b. Eichenberg, Fritz

October 26, 1901
b. Evergood, Philip (Howard Francis
Dixon)

October 29, 1901
b. Amfiteatrof, Daniele
b. Tamiroff, Akim
d. Czolgosz, Leon F

November 2, 1901
b. Ford, Paul

November 3, 1901
b. Leopold III
b. Malraux, Andre Georges

November 4, 1901
b. Morrison, Theodore

November 5, 1901
b. Moten, Etta

November 6, 1901
b. Hall, Juanita
b. Katona, George
d. Greenaway, Kate

November 7, 1901
d. Li Hung-Chang

November 8, 1901
b. Gheorghiu-Dej, Gheorghe
d. Bickerdyke, Mary Ann Ball

November 11, 1901
b. Lindner, Richard
b. Mason, F(rancis) van Wyck

November 12, 1901
b. Adams, James Luther

November 13, 1901
b. Sackville-West, Edward Charles

November 14, 1901
d. Mapleson, James Henry

November 16, 1901
b. Nagel, Ernest

November 17, 1901
b. Hallstein, Walter
b. Strasberg, Lee

November 18, 1901
b. Gallup, George Horace
b. Wood, Craig Ralph

November 19, 1901
b. Kraushaar, Otto

November 22, 1901
b. Crane, Roy(ston Campbell)

November 23, 1901
b. Gardiner, Muriel

November 26, 1901
b. Grosvenor, Melville Bell

November 27, 1901
b. Husing, Ted
d. Studebaker, Clement

November 28, 1901
b. Havighurst, Walter Edwin
b. Mountbatten, Edwina

November 30, 1901
d. Eyre, Edward John

December 1, 1901
b. Moore, Grace

December 5, 1901
b. Disney, Walt(er Elias)
b. Heisenberg, Werner Karl

December 6, 1901
b. Porter, Eliot Furness

December 8, 1901
b. Urrutia Lleo, Manuel

December 11, 1901
b. Cabot, John Moors
b. Oakeshott, Michael Joseph

December 12, 1901
b. Menken, Helen

December 13, 1901
b. Perlea, Jonel

December 14, 1901
b. Cochet, Henri
b. Michalowski, Kazimierz
b. Paul I

December 16, 1901
b. Mead, Margaret

December 19, 1901
b. LaFarge, Oliver

December 22, 1901
b. Kostelanetz, Andre

December 23, 1901
d. Croly, Jane Cunningham

December 24, 1901
d. King, Clarence

December 26, 1901
b. Lipsig, Harry H(avon)

December 27, 1901
b. Dietrich, Marlene
b. Hayter, Stanley William

December 30, 1901
b. Delaney, Beauford

1902

b. Abel, Rudolf Ivanovich
b. Aylward, Gladys May
b. Barker, Fred
b. Barragan, Luis
b. Barrows, Marjorie (Ruth)
b. Breneman, Tom
b. Costa, Lucio
b. Day, Frank
b. Donner, Frederic Garrett
b. Evans-Pritchard, Edward Evan
b. Gao Gang
b. Gibbs, Woolcott
b. Gucci, Rodolfo
b. Heaton, Leonard
b. Johnson, Wallace Edward
b. Korjus, Miliza
b. Kressy, Edmund
b. Lackey, Kenneth
b. Lauck, Chester H
b. Lewis, Tom
b. Licavoli, Peter Joseph, Sr.
b. Liddell, Eric
b. Mahin, John Lee
b. McDonald, Maurice James
b. Miller, Don
b. Namatjira, Albert
b. Olympio, Sylvanus E.
b. Padmore, George
b. Pitseolak, Peter
b. Politz, Alfred
b. Pollock, Charles
b. Pomerantz, Fred P
b. Powolny, Frank
b. Sharietmadari, Ayatollah Seyed
b. Turkus, Burton B
b. Waters, Frank (Joseph)
d. Corrigan, Michael Augustine
d. Durkee, Eugene R
d. Hitotsubashi
d. Still, William
d. Strauss, Levi

d. Vivekananda
d. Wales, Salem Howe

January 2, 1902
b. Merritt, Hiram Houston

January 4, 1902
b. McCone, John Alex

January 5, 1902
b. Beuve-Mery, Hubert
b. Gibbons, Stella (Dorothea)

January 8, 1902
b. Rogers, Carl Ransom
b. Smith, Kenneth Danforth

January 9, 1902
b. Bing, Rudolf (Franz Josef), Sir
b. Escriva de Balaguer, Josemarie

January 10, 1902
b. Minsky, Morton

January 11, 1902
b. Lahey, Edwin A(loysius)

January 12, 1902
b. Lewis, Joe E

January 13, 1902
b. Drummond, Roscoe

January 14, 1902
b. Kappel, Frederick R(ussell)
b. Tarski, Alfred

January 15, 1902
b. Saud (Ibn Abdul Aziz al Saud)
d. Hyatt, Alpheus

January 21, 1902
b. Duffy, Ben
d. DeVere, Aubrey Thomas

January 23, 1902
b. Klopfer, Donald Simon

January 24, 1902
b. Kiernan, Walter

January 25, 1902
b. Hass, H(enry) B(ohn)

January 26, 1902
b. Brent, Romney

January 28, 1902
b. Barr, Alfred Hamilton, Jr.

January 30, 1902
b. Pevsner, Nikolaus Bernhard Leon, Sir

January 31, 1902
b. Bankhead, Tallulah Brockman
b. Myrdal, Alva Reimer
b. Steward, Julian Haynes

February 1, 1902
b. Gosho Heinosuke

b. Hughes, Langston

February 2, 1902
b. Morris, Newbold

February 3, 1902
b. Armstrong, Lil(lian Hardin)
b. Pusey, Merlo John
b. Sender, Ramon Jose

February 4, 1902
b. Lindbergh, Charles A(ugustus)

February 5, 1902
b. Kaper, Bronislau

February 6, 1902
b. Brunis, George
b. Nizer, Louis

February 8, 1902
b. Connell, Alex
b. Talbot, Lyle

February 9, 1902
b. Harman, Fred

February 10, 1902
b. Adler, Stella
b. Brattain, Walter Houser
b. Webb, Chick

February 11, 1902
b. Jacobsen, Arne

February 13, 1902
b. Lasswell, Harold Dwight

February 14, 1902
b. Erwin, Stuart

February 18, 1902
d. Bierstadt, Albert
d. Tiffany, Charles Lewis

February 19, 1902
b. Boyle, Kay
b. Bubbles, John
b. Matthiessen, Francis Otto
b. Peabody, Eddie

February 20, 1902
b. Adams, Ansel Easton

February 22, 1902
b. Strassmann, Fritz

February 24, 1902
d. Gardiner, Samuel Rawson

February 27, 1902
b. Sarazen, Gene
b. Steinbeck, John (Ernst)

March 1, 1902
b. Thayer, Tiffany Ellsworth

March 2, 1902
b. Condon, Edward Uhler
b. Monroney, Mike (Aimer Stillwell)
d. Parker, Francis Wayland

March 3, 1902
b. Bishop, Isabel
b. Dandridge, Ruby Jean

March 7, 1902
b. Oenslager, Donald Mitchell
d. Galvin, Pud

March 8, 1902
b. Beavers, Louise
b. Randolph, Jennings

March 9, 1902
b. Geer, Will
b. Gibbs, Anthony
b. Saint John, Robert
b. Stone, Edward Durell

March 11, 1902
b. Rains, Albert McKinley

March 12, 1902
b. Fenton, Leslie
d. Altgeld, John Peter

March 13, 1902
b. Fix, Paul

March 14, 1902
b. Hickey, Margaret A.

March 15, 1902
b. De La Torre(-Bueno), Lillian

March 17, 1902
b. Carusi, Ugo
b. Jones, Bobby

March 21, 1902
b. House, Son
d. Nachbaur, Franz

March 22, 1902
b. Berlin, Ellin (Mackay)

March 23, 1902
b. Dodge, Bertha Sanford
b. Ober, Philip (Nott)
d. Tisza, Kalman

March 24, 1902
b. Dewey, Thomas Edmund
b. Scheuer, Philip K(latz)

March 25, 1902
b. Amsterdam, Birdie

March 26, 1902
d. Rhodes, Cecil John

March 27, 1902
b. Wolfson, Erwin Service

March 28, 1902
b. Ayme, Marcel
b. Lamont, Corliss
b. Robson, Flora McKenzie, Dame

March 29, 1902
b. Walton, William Turner, Sir

March 30, 1902
b. Heath, Ted

April 1, 1902
b. Felton, Harold W

April 2, 1902
b. Peugeot, Rodolphe

April 3, 1902
b. Gehlen, Reinhard

April 8, 1902
b. Krips, Josef

April 9, 1902
b. Cecil, Edward Christian David
Gascoyne

April 11, 1902
b. Reynolds, Quentin James
d. Hampton, Wade

April 12, 1902
d. Talmadge, Thomas de Witt

April 13, 1902
b. Henry, Marguerite
b. Rothschild, Philippe de, Baron

April 14, 1902
b. Loeffler, Ken(neth D)
b. Mantha, Sylvio

April 18, 1902
b. Owens, Harry
b. Pella, Giuseppe
b. Schneerson, Menachem M(endel)

April 19, 1902
b. Latham, Jean Lee

April 20, 1902
b. Wolfit, Donald, Sir
d. Stockton, Frank

April 22, 1902
b. Angoff, Charles
b. Tyler, Ralph W(infred)
b. Vandercook, John Womack

April 23, 1902
b. Laxness, Halldor (Kiljan)

April 24, 1902
b. Tamiris, Helen

April 26, 1902
b. Daniels, Jonathan Worth

April 27, 1902
d. Morton, Julius Sterling

April 29, 1902
b. Ford, Corey

April 30, 1902
b. Schultz, Theodore W(illiam)

May 2, 1902
b. Aherne, Brian de Lacy

May 3, 1902
  b. Barbanell, Maurice
  b. Kastler, Alfred
  b. Slezak, Walter

May 4, 1902
  b. Dexter, Al
  b. Stone, W Clement
  d. Palmer, Potter

May 5, 1902
  d. Harte, (Francis) Bret

May 6, 1902
  b. Ophuls, Max
  d. Sampson, William T

May 8, 1902
  b. Lwoff, Andre Michel
  d. Ford, Paul Leicester

May 10, 1902
  b. Selznick, David O(liver)

May 11, 1902
  b. Sayao, Bidu

May 12, 1902
  b. Wylie, Philip Gordon

May 14, 1902
  b. Chidsey, Donald Barr
  b. Dunbar, Helen Flanders

May 15, 1902
  b. Daley, Richard Joseph

May 16, 1902
  b. Kiepura, Jan Wiktor

May 17, 1902
  b. Cleva, Fausto

May 18, 1902
  b. Bein, Albert
  b. Willson, Meredith

May 21, 1902
  b. Averill, Earl
  b. Litvak, Anatole
  d. Godkin, E(dwin) L(awrence)

May 22, 1902
  b. Breuer, Marcel Lajos

May 24, 1902
  b. Chapman, Gilbert Whipple

May 27, 1902
  b. Marshall, Peter

May 30, 1902
  b. Fetchit, Stepin

June 1, 1902
  b. Lindtberg, Leopold

June 2, 1902
  b. Davis, Frederick C(lyde)

June 4, 1902
  b. Drewry, John Eldridge

June 6, 1902
  b. Lunceford, Jimmy

June 9, 1902
  b. James, Skip

June 14, 1902
  b. Eurich, Alvin C(hristian)

June 15, 1902
  b. Erikson, Erik H(omburger)
  b. Rudolf, Max

June 16, 1902
  b. McClintock, Barbara
  b. Simpson, George Gaylord

June 17, 1902
  b. Fain, Sammy

June 18, 1902
  d. Butler, Samuel

June 19, 1902
  b. Lombardo, Guy Albert

June 21, 1902
  b. Kesselring, Joseph Otto
  b. Morenz, Howie

June 22, 1902
  b. Burns, David

June 25, 1902
  b. Rubloff, Arthur

June 26, 1902
  b. Brico, Antonia
  b. Lear, William Powell

June 27, 1902
  d. Agassiz, Elizabeth Cabot Cary

June 28, 1902
  b. Dillinger, John Herbert
  b. Smith, Joe

June 30, 1902
  b. Whalen, Michael

July 1, 1902
  b. Cohen, Myron
  b. Sert, Jose Luis
  b. Wyler, William

July 4, 1902
  b. Dwyer, Florence Price
  b. Lansky, Meyer
  b. Murphy, George Lloyd

July 5, 1902
  b. Lodge, Henry Cabot, Jr.
  b. Trudeau, Arthur G(ilbert)

July 10, 1902
  b. Adler, Kurt
  b. Alder, Kurt
  b. Guillen (y Batista), Nicolas
  (Cristobal)

July 11, 1902
  b. Goudsmit, Samuel Abraham

July 12, 1902
  b. Julesberg, Elizabeth Rider
  Montgomery

July 13, 1902
  b. Endacott, Paul
  b. Lord, Phillips H

July 14, 1902
  b. Haenigsen, Harry William

July 15, 1902
  b. Hackett, Raymond

July 17, 1902
  b. Stead, Christina (Ellen)

July 18, 1902
  b. West, Jessamyn

July 19, 1902
  d. Acton, John Emerich Edward
  Dalberg-Acton, Baron

July 20, 1902
  d. Mackay, John William

July 22, 1902
  b. Bennett, John C(oleman)
  b. Bitter, Francis

July 23, 1902
  b. Cowles, William Hutchinson, Jr.
  b. Schneirla, Theodore Christian

July 25, 1902
  b. Hoffer, Eric
  b. Lee, Lila

July 28, 1902
  b. Fearing, Kenneth Flexner
  b. Popper, Karl R(aimund), Sir
  b. Rodgers, Richard

August 1, 1902
  b. Latzo, Pete

August 3, 1902
  b. Bloch, Raymond A
  b. DeWitt, William Orville, Sr.

August 5, 1902
  b. Liebman, Max

August 6, 1902
  b. Heyer, Georgette
  b. Schultz, Dutch

August 8, 1902
  b. Dirac, Paul Adrien Maurice
  d. Tissot, James Joseph Jacques
  d. Twachtman, John Henry

August 9, 1902
  b. Francescatti, Zino Rene
  b. Solomon

August 10, 1902
  b. Siodmark, Curt

b. Tiselius, Arne Wilhelm Kaurin

August 11, 1902
b. Nolan, Lloyd
b. Shoemaker, Vaughn Richard

August 12, 1902
b. Hatta, Mohammad

August 13, 1902
b. Wankel, Felix

August 16, 1902
b. Thurman, Wallace (Henry)

August 17, 1902
b. Aldrich, Richard Stoddard

August 19, 1902
b. Moore, Colleen
b. Nash, Ogden Frederick

August 21, 1902
b. Kennon, Robert Floyd
b. Tully, Tom

August 22, 1902
b. Riefenstahl, Leni

August 23, 1902
d. Stolz, Teresa

August 24, 1902
b. Brandel, Fernand Paul
b. Braudel, Fernand (Paul)

August 25, 1902
b. Wolpe, Stefan

August 27, 1902
b. Christensen, William

August 31, 1902
d. Wesendonck, Mathilde Luckemeyer

September 1, 1902
b. Gambino, Carlo

September 2, 1902
b. Dalrymple, Jean
b. Illingworth, Leslie Gilbert
b. Taylor, Henry Junior

September 4, 1902
d. Eggleston, Edward

September 5, 1902
b. Zanuck, Darryl Francis

September 6, 1902
b. Beatty, Morgan

September 8, 1902
b. Kaplan, Joseph

September 10, 1902
b. Crowley, Jim

September 12, 1902
b. Hamilton, Margaret Brainard
b. Kubitschek (de Oliveira), Juscelino

b. Zaturenska, Marya

September 13, 1902
b. Hayward, Leland

September 14, 1902
b. Mullin, Willard

September 15, 1902
d. Gray, Horace

September 17, 1902
b. Ralston, Esther

September 19, 1902
b. Leon, Henry Cecil
d. Masaoka, Tsunenori

September 21, 1902
b. Lane, Allen, Sir

September 22, 1902
b. Houseman, John
b. Jarvis, Howard Arnold

September 23, 1902
b. Maurer, Ion Gheorghe
d. Powell, John Wesley

September 24, 1902
b. Coy, Harold
b. Crawford, Cheryl

September 25, 1902
b. Hoffman, Al

September 26, 1902
b. Anastasia, Albert

September 28, 1902
b. Okada, Kenzo
b. Sullivan, Ed(ward Vincent)

September 29, 1902
d. Zola, Emile (Edouard Charles)

October 3, 1902
b. Costa e Silva, Arthur da

October 4, 1902
d. Johnson, Lionel Pigot

October 5, 1902
b. Fine, Larry
b. Kroc, Ray(mond) Albert

October 6, 1902
b. Block, Joseph L(eopold)
b. Sharkey, Jack

October 8, 1902
b. Currie, Lauchlin (Bernard)

October 9, 1902
b. Hannah, John Alfred

October 10, 1902
b. Davis, (William) Allison

October 11, 1902
b. Ilg, Frances Lillian

b. Narayan, Jayaprakash
b. Tully, Alice

October 13, 1902
b. Bontemps, Arna Wendell

October 18, 1902
b. Hopkins, Miriam

October 19, 1902
b. Grattan, Clinton Hartley
d. Younger, Jim

October 22, 1902
b. Spedding, Frank Harold

October 25, 1902
b. Commager, Henry Steele
b. Lang, Eddie
d. Norris, Frank(lin)

October 26, 1902
b. Markham, Beryl
d. Stanton, Elizabeth Cady

October 27, 1902
b. Dinwiddie, John Ekin

October 28, 1902
b. Lanchester, Elsa

October 30, 1902
b. Overstreet, Bonaro Wilkinson

October 31, 1902
b. Drummond de Andrade, Carlos
b. Franz, Eduard
b. Shaw, Wilbur

November 1, 1902
b. Grieg, Nordahl Brun

November 2, 1902
b. Jochum, Eugen
b. Wells, James Lesesne

November 5, 1902
b. Schafer, Natalie

November 7, 1902
b. Dodd, Ed(ward) Benton

November 8, 1902
b. Smith, A(rthur) J(ames) M(arshall)

November 9, 1902
b. Asquith, Anthony

November 14, 1902
b. Downey, Morton

November 15, 1902
b. Losch, Tilly

November 16, 1902
d. Henty, George Alfred

November 17, 1902
b. Spofford, Charles M(erville)
b. Wigner, Eugene P(aul)

November 21, 1902
b. Omlie, Phoebe Jane Fairgrave
b. Suslov, Mikhail Andreevich

November 22, 1902
b. Adonis, Joe
b. Feuermann, Emanuel
b. McDonald, David John
d. Reed, Walter

November 23, 1902
b. Jory, Victor

November 24, 1902
b. Vanderbilt, William Henry

November 25, 1902
b. Lapidus, Morris
b. Shore, Eddie

November 28, 1902
b. Leclerc, Jacques-Philippe

November 29, 1902
b. Levi, Carlo
b. Loughran, Tommy

December 1, 1902
b. Crittenden, Christopher

December 2, 1902
b. Bernhard, Arnold
b. Hildreth, Horace A(ugusta)

December 4, 1902
d. Dow, Charles Henry

December 5, 1902
b. Thurmond, Strom

December 6, 1902
d. Palmer, Alice Elvira Freeman

December 7, 1902
b. Edwards, Willard
d. Nast, Thomas
d. Reed, Thomas Brackett

December 8, 1902
b. Jacoby, Oswald

December 9, 1902
b. Beebe, Lucius Morris
b. Butler of Saffron Walden, Richard
    Austen, Baron

December 10, 1902
b. Marcantonio, Vito Anthony

December 13, 1902
b. Parsons, Talcott

December 14, 1902
b. Burke, Billy
b. Feigl, Herbert
d. Grant, Julia Dent

December 15, 1902
b. Machlup, Fritz

December 16, 1902
b. Alberti, Rafael

December 17, 1902
b. Jameson, House

December 19, 1902
b. Richardson, Ralph David, Sir

December 20, 1902
b. George Edward Alexander Edmund
b. Hook, Sidney
b. Lerner, Max

December 22, 1902
d. Krafft-Ebing, Richard von

December 23, 1902
b. Maclean, Norman (Fitzroy)

December 26, 1902
b. Lytle, Andrew Nelson

December 28, 1902
b. Adler, Mortimer J(erome)

December 29, 1902
b. Stewart, Nels(on Robert)

1903

b. Astor, Brooke Marshall
b. Beemer, Brace
b. Bergeron, Victor J
b. Block, Martin
b. Busch, Niven
b. Carmichael, John P
b. Fadil al-Jamali, Muhammad
b. Halstead, William S
b. Harman, Hugh
b. Holman, Bill
b. Jacobs, Lou
b. Jacuzzi, Candido
b. Johnson, Amy
b. Koruturk, Fahri S
b. Lame Deer
b. Loo, Richard
b. Lucchese, Thomas
b. Mawdudi, Abu-I A'la
b. O'Connor, Frank
b. Phinney, Archie
b. Portinari, Candido
b. Primo de Rivera, Jose A
b. Rinehart, Frederick Roberts
b. Robinson, Joan Violet Maurice
b. Rose, Carl
b. Sack, Erna
b. Shihab, Fu'ad
b. Siskind, Aaron
b. Smart, Jack Scott
b. Soloveitchik, Joseph Baer
b. Stone, Sidney
b. Thayer, Mary Van Rensselaer
b. Tucker, Mary Bradham
b. Vreeland, Diana (Dalziel)
d. Cardozo, Francis Louis
d. Hanes, John Wesley
d. Lloyd, Henry Demarest
d. Welch, Thomas B

January 5, 1903
b. Gianninoto, Frank Anthony

January 6, 1903
b. Abravanel, Maurice

b. Sullivan, Francis Loftus

January 7, 1903
b. Hurston, Zora Neale
b. Pauley, Edwin Wendell

January 9, 1903
b. Banky, Vilma

January 10, 1903
b. Hepworth, Barbara, Dame
b. Roos, Frank John, Jr.

January 11, 1903
b. Paton, Alan Stewart

January 12, 1903
b. Kurchatov, Igor Vasilyevich

January 13, 1903
b. Francis, Kay

January 17, 1903
b. Hull, Warren

January 18, 1903
d. Hewitt, Abram Stevens

January 19, 1903
b. Nyiregyhazi, Ervin

January 20, 1903
b. Ames, Leon

January 22, 1903
b. Jacobs, Al(bert T)
b. Sutton, Margaret Beebe

January 23, 1903
b. Galamian, Ivan

January 24, 1903
b. DeWohl, Louis
b. Gwathmey, Robert

January 27, 1903
b. Eccles, John C(arew), Sir

January 28, 1903
b. Lonsdale, Kathleen (Yardley)
d. Planquette, Jean(-Robert)

January 30, 1903
b. Gassner, John Waldhorn

January 31, 1903
b. Cowles, Gardner, Jr.

February 1, 1903
d. Stokes, George Gabriel, Sir

February 4, 1903
b. Takehara Han

February 5, 1903
b. Owings, Nathaniel Alexander
b. Payson, Joan Whitney
d. Dawes, Henry Laurens

February 6, 1903
b. Arrau, Claudio

February 8, 1903
b. Rahman, Abdul, Prince
d. Glaisher, James

February 9, 1903
b. Gibbs, Frederic A

February 11, 1903
b. MacDougall, Curtis Daniel

February 12, 1903
b. Duncan, Todd
b. Hafey, Chick
d. Curry, Jabez Lamar Monroe

February 13, 1903
b. Simenon, Georges

February 16, 1903
b. Bergen, Edgar John

February 17, 1903
b. Hidayat, Sadiq

February 18, 1903
b. Podgorny, Nikolai Viktorovich

February 19, 1903
b. Slobodkin, Louis

February 21, 1903
b. Cone, Fairfax Mastick
b. Nin, Anais
b. Renaud, Madeleine
b. Yawkey, Thomas Austin

February 22, 1903
b. Ramsey, Frank Plumpton
b. Weede, Robert
d. Wolf, Hugo

February 23, 1903
b. Alexandrov, Grigori

February 25, 1903
b. Clancy, King

February 26, 1903
b. Natta, Giulio
b. Wingate, Orde Charles
d. Gatling, Richard Jordan

February 27, 1903
b. Gardiner, Reginald
d. Hill, George Birkbeck Norman

March 3, 1903
b. Adrian

March 4, 1903
b. Boyd, William Clouser
b. Scarne, John
d. Shorthouse, Joseph Henry

March 6, 1903
b. Nagako, Empress

March 8, 1903
b. Ciano (di Cortellazzo), Galeazzo
d. Franklin, William Buel

March 10, 1903
b. Beiderbecke, Bix
b. Luce, Clare Boothe

March 11, 1903
b. Schiff, Dorothy
b. Welk, Lawrence

March 14, 1903
b. Beall, Lester Thomas
b. Gottlieb, Adolph

March 16, 1903
b. Mansfield, Mike
d. Bean, Roy

March 17, 1903
b. Britain, Radie
b. Childs, Marquis William

March 19, 1903
b. Ehrlich, Bettina Bauer

March 20, 1903
b. Buchanan, Edgar
d. Leland, Charles Godfrey

March 21, 1903
b. Hellinger, Mark

March 22, 1903
b. Baldwin, Hanson Weightman

March 24, 1903
b. Butenandt, Adolf Fredrick Johann
b. Muggeridge, Malcolm

March 25, 1903
b. Carle, Frankie
d. Byers, William Newton

March 28, 1903
b. Serkin, Rudolph

March 29, 1903
d. Swift, Gustavus Franklin

March 31, 1903
d. Butterick, Ebenezer

April 2, 1903
b. Chevrier, Lionel
b. Hubbard, Orville Liscum

April 3, 1903
b. Bailey, Ace

April 4, 1903
b. Nabokov, Nicolas

April 6, 1903
b. Cochrane, Mickey
b. Edgerton, Harold Eugene
b. Jackson, Charles Reginald

April 8, 1903
b. Roberts, Dennis J(oseph)

April 9, 1903
b. Bond, Ward
b. Pincus, Gregory

April 10, 1903
b. Graf, Herbert

April 11, 1903
b. Gaither, Jake

April 12, 1903
b. Tinbergen, Jan

April 16, 1903
b. Pillsbury, Philip Winston
b. Waner, Paul Glee

April 17, 1903
b. Piatigorsky, Gregor

April 19, 1903
b. Ness, Eliot

April 20, 1903
d. Du Chaillu, Paul Belloni

April 21, 1903
b. Hedtoft (-Hansen), Hans Christian

April 23, 1903
b. Kolmogorov, Andrey Nikolayevich

April 24, 1903
b. Michalske, Mike

April 28, 1903
b. Fitts, Dudley
d. Gibbs, J(osiah) Willard

April 30, 1903
b. Lewis, Fulton, Jr.

May 1, 1903
d. Arditi, Luigi

May 2, 1903
b. Spock, Benjamin (McLane)

May 4, 1903
b. Adler, Luther
b. Layden, Elmer Francis
d. Williams, Edward Porter

May 5, 1903
b. Beard, James Andrews
b. Stanford, Sally

May 6, 1903
b. Banks, William (Venoid)
b. Golden, Harry Lewis

May 7, 1903
b. Zabolotskii, Nikolai Alekseevich

May 8, 1903
b. Fernandel
d. Gauguin, Paul

May 10, 1903
b. Jonas, Hans

May 11, 1903
b. Gehringer, Charlie

May 12, 1903
b. Hyde-White, Wilfrid
d. Stoddard, Richard Henry

May 13, 1903
d. Mabini, Apolinario

May 15, 1903
b. MacTaggart, William, Sir
d. Sanderson, Sybil

May 17, 1903
b. Bell, Cool Papa
b. Norton, Elliot

May 19, 1903
b. Chiang, Yee
b. Samuels, Ernest

May 21, 1903
b. Aramburu, Pedro Eugenio

May 22, 1903
b. Bonsal, Philip Wilson
b. Simmons, Al(oysius Harry)
d. Reichmann, Theodor

May 23, 1903
b. O'Dell, Scott

May 25, 1903
b. Nu Thakin

May 26, 1903
d. LaFlesche Tibbles, Susette

May 27, 1903
b. Kiesling, Walt(er)

May 29, 1903
b. Hope, Bob

May 30, 1903
b. Baldwin, Billy
b. Conklin, Gladys Plemon
b. Cullen, Countee (Porter)

May 31, 1903
b. Russell, Honey

June 1, 1903
b. Hardy, Porter, Jr.

June 3, 1903
b. Hitchcock, Henry Russell

June 4, 1903
b. McKeen, John Elmer
b. Mravinsky, Eugene

June 6, 1903
b. Khachaturian, Aram
b. Paasio, Rafael

June 8, 1903
b. Yarborough, Ralph W(ebster)
b. Yourcenar, Marguerite

June 9, 1903
b. Davenport, Marcia

June 11, 1903
b. Nevers, Ernie

June 13, 1903
b. Bennett, Willard Harrison
b. Grange, Red

June 14, 1903
b. Rich, Louise Dickinson

June 19, 1903
b. Gehrig, Lou

June 20, 1903
b. Croft-Cooke, Rupert
b. Vare, Glenna Collett

June 21, 1903
b. Hirschfeld, Al(bert)
b. Sjoberg, Alf

June 22, 1903
b. Hubbell, Carl Owen
b. Sturtzel, Jane Levington

June 23, 1903
b. Darling, Frank Fraser, Sir

June 25, 1903
b. Orwell, George
b. Revere, Anne
b. Tracy, Arthur

June 26, 1903
b. Herman, Babe

June 27, 1903
b. Cox, James Middleton, Jr.

June 29, 1903
b. Voelker, John Donaldson

July 1, 1903
b. Emerson, Gladys Anderson

July 2, 1903
b. Douglas-Home, Alexander
   Frederick, Sir
b. Harris, Harwell Hamilton
b. Olav V
d. Delahanty, Ed(ward James)

July 4, 1903
b. Saperstein, Abe
b. Trohan, Walter

July 6, 1903
b. Theorell, (Axel) Hugh Teodor

July 10, 1903
b. Stoneham, Horace

July 11, 1903
d. Henley, William Ernest

July 13, 1903
b. Clark, Kenneth MacKenzie, Sir
b. Portman, Eric

July 14, 1903
b. Clark, Thomas Dionysius
b. Murray, Ken

b. Prio Socarras, Carlos
b. Stone, Irving

July 15, 1903
b. Edmonds, Walter D(umaux)
b. Kamaraj, Kumaraswami

July 16, 1903
b. Lombardo, Carmen

July 17, 1903
d. Whistler, James Abbott McNeill

July 18, 1903
b. Gruen, Victor
b. Wills, Chill

July 19, 1903
b. Haskell, Arnold Lionel

July 20, 1903
d. Leo XIII

July 22, 1903
d. Clay, Cassius Marcellus

July 26, 1903
b. Kefauver, Estes
b. Voorhees, Donald

July 28, 1903
d. Stoltz, Rosine

August 1, 1903
b. Horgan, Paul
d. Calamity Jane

August 3, 1903
b. Bourguiba, Habib Ben Ali
b. Hopkins, Claude

August 5, 1903
b. Autant-Lara, Claude

August 6, 1903
b. Morse, Philip McCord

August 7, 1903
b. Leakey, Louis Seymour Bazett

August 11, 1903
b. Seagram, Joseph Edward Frowde
d. Hayford, J(oseph) E(phraim)Casely
d. Hostos (y Bonilla), Eugenio Maria
   de

August 12, 1903
b. Homolka, Oscar

August 14, 1903
b. North, John Ringling

August 17, 1903
b. Chasins, Abram

August 19, 1903
b. Barton, Robert B(rown) M(orison)
b. Cozzens, James Gould
b. Dauphin, Claude Le Grand Maria
   Eugene

August 22, 1903
b. Hathaway, Starke R
b. Wellek, Rene
d. May, Phil(ip William)
d. Salisbury, Robert Arthur Talbot, 3rd Marquess

August 23, 1903
b. Millikan, Clark Blanchard
b. Semenenko, Serge

August 24, 1903
b. Sutherland, Graham Vivian

August 26, 1903
b. Dalrymple, Ian (Murray)
b. Miller, Caroline
b. Rushing, Jimmy

August 28, 1903
b. Bettelheim, Bruno
b. Wagner-Regeny, Rudolf
d. Olmsted, Frederick Law

August 31, 1903
b. Godfrey, Arthur Michael

September 3, 1903
b. Bolz, Lothar

September 6, 1903
b. Sananikone, Phoui

September 7, 1903
b. Landon, Margaret (Dorothea Mortenson)

September 9, 1903
b. Whitney, Phyllis Ayame

September 10, 1903
b. Connolly, Cyril Vernon

September 11, 1903
b. Adorno, Theodor Wiesengrund

September 13, 1903
b. Colbert, Claudette

September 15, 1903
b. Acuff, Roy (Claxton)

September 16, 1903
d. Crowell, Luther Childs

September 18, 1903
b. Washington, Val J.
b. Wilbur, Dwight L(ocke)
d. Bain, Alexander

September 19, 1903
b. Saltzman, Charles E(skridge)

September 20, 1903
b. Smith, Stevie

September 21, 1903
b. Tucker, Preston Thomas

September 22, 1903
b. Callaghan, Morley Edward

September 23, 1903
b. Villiers, Alan John

September 25, 1903
b. Beech, Olive Ann (Mellor)
b. Rothko, Mark

September 28, 1903
b. Billington, Ray Allen
b. Hansell, Haywood Shepherd, Jr.

September 29, 1903
b. Aleman, Miguel
b. Garson, Greer
b. Harnwell, Gaylord Probasco
b. Neher, Fred

October 1, 1903
b. Coulouris, George

October 4, 1903
b. Lehmann-Haupt, Hellmut Emil

October 6, 1903
b. McMahon, Brien
b. Walton, Ernest Thomas Sinton

October 9, 1903
b. O'Malley, Walter Francis

October 10, 1903
b. Duke, Vernon

October 11, 1903
b. Weatherford, Teddy

October 12, 1903
b. Kirk, Grayson Louis

October 15, 1903
b. Bettmann, Otto L(udwig)

October 16, 1903
b. Washington, Buck

October 17, 1903
b. Birdwell, Russell Juarez
b. Grechko, Andrei Antonovick
b. Ryan, Irene Noblette
b. West, Nathanael

October 19, 1903
b. Giannini, Vittorio

October 22, 1903
b. Beadle, George Wells
b. Howard, Curly
d. Lecky, William Edward Hartpole

October 24, 1903
b. Purvis, Melvin

October 28, 1903
b. Chamberlain, John Rensselaer
b. Waugh, Evelyn Arthur St. John

October 30, 1903
d. Ozaki, Koyo

November 1, 1903
d. Mommsen, Theodor

November 2, 1903
b. Berman, Emile Zola
b. Jackson, Travis Calvin

November 3, 1903
b. Boyd, Julian Parks
b. Evans, Walker

November 7, 1903
b. Jagger, Dean
b. Lorenz, Konrad Zacharias

November 12, 1903
b. Oakie, Jack

November 13, 1903
d. Pissarro, Camille Jacob

November 17, 1903
b. Walters, Charles

November 20, 1903
b. Onsager, Lars
d. Horn, Tom

November 21, 1903
b. Hewitt, Foster

November 23, 1903
d. Ayer, Harriet Hubbard

November 24, 1903
b. Popper, Hans

November 29, 1903
b. Autori, Franco
b. Rooney, John (James)

November 30, 1903
b. Gres, Alix

December 3, 1903
b. Fuchida, Mitsuo
b. Holifield, Chet
b. Von Neumann, John

December 4, 1903
b. Merrill, Frank Dow
b. Rowse, A(lfred) L(eslie)
b. Wiggins, J(ames) R(ussell)
b. Woolrich, Cornell

December 5, 1903
b. Gingrich, Arnold
b. Powell, Cecil Frank

December 8, 1903
b. George, Zelma W(atson)
b. Shera, Jesse Hauk
b. Simpson, Adele (Smithline)
d. Spencer, Herbert

December 10, 1903
b. Merkel, Una
b. Norton, Mary
b. Plomer, William Charles Franklyn
b. Sargeant, Winthrop

December 11, 1903
b. Edwards, Willard Eldridge
b. Jensen, Alfred Julio
b. Mumford, Lawrence Quincy

December 13, 1903
b. Baker, Ella
b. Darrell, R(obert) D(onaldson)
b. De Rochemont, Richard Guertis
b. Foster, Norman
b. Greer, Sonny
b. Montoya, Carlos

December 16, 1903
b. Hawes, Elizabeth

December 17, 1903
b. Caldwell, Erskine Preston
b. Noble, Ray

December 19, 1903
b. Darlington, Cyril Dean
b. Snell, George D(avis)

December 21, 1903
b. Stroup, Thomas Bradley
b. Treat, Lawrence

December 22, 1903
b. Hartline, Haldan Keffer

December 23, 1903
b. Kalatozov, Mikhail
b. Washington, Fredi

December 24, 1903
b. Cornell, Joseph

December 25, 1903
b. Bromberg, J Edward
b. Cobleigh, Ira Underwood
b. Samstag, Nicholas

December 26, 1903
b. Lazzeri, Tony

December 28, 1903
d. Gissing, George Robert

December 29, 1903
b. McCoy, Clyde

1904

b. Bailey, Raymond
b. Bazna, Elyesa
b. Benoit, Jehane
b. Black, William
b. Bond, Horace Mann
b. Cicero
b. Coulomb, Jean (Marie)
b. Dache, Lilly
b. Diemer, Walter
b. Gunzberg, Nicolas de, Baron
b. Horikoshi, Jiro
b. Hurrell, George
b. King, Alberta Christine Williams
b. Lewis, David
b. Licavoli, Thomas
b. Lubin, Charles W
b. Mars, Forrest
b. Pa Chin
b. Pedersen, Charles J
b. Piper, H(enry) Beam
b. Richier, Germaine
b. Rose, Helen Bronberg
b. Royle, Selena

b. Tieri, Frank
b. Vlasic, Joseph
b. Wang Ming
d. Kimball, William Wallace
d. Little Wolf
d. Quay, Matthew Stanley
d. Vereshchagin, Vasily Vasilyevich
d. Watts, George Frederic

January 1, 1904
b. Allen, Ethan (Nathan)
d. Pabst, Frederick

January 2, 1904
b. Melton, James
b. Rand, Sally
d. Longstreet, James

January 5, 1904
b. Morini, Erica

January 8, 1904
b. Arno, Peter

January 9, 1904
d. Gordon, John Brown

January 10, 1904
b. Bolger, Ray(mond Wallace)
b. Burck, Jacob
d. Gerome, Jean Leon

January 11, 1904
d. Pleasant, Mary Ellen

January 13, 1904
b. Addinsell, Richard

January 14, 1904
b. Beaton, Cecil (Walter Hardy), Sir
b. Siebert, Babe

January 18, 1904
b. Grant, Cary
b. McNickle, D'Arcy

January 19, 1904
b. Blough, Roger Miles

January 20, 1904
b. Brameld, Theodore
b. Danilova, Alexandra
d. Mannlicher, Ferdinand

January 21, 1904
b. Blackmur, Richard Palmer
b. Crawford, John Edmund

January 22, 1904
b. Balanchine, George

January 23, 1904
b. Quarles, Benjamin Arthur
b. Zukofsky, Louis

January 26, 1904
b. Keys, Ancel Benjamin
b. MacBride, Sean

February 1, 1904
b. Perelman, S(idney) J(oseph)

February 2, 1904
b. Gruber, Frank
d. Whitney, William Collins

February 3, 1904
b. Canham, Erwin Dain
b. Dallapiccola, Luigi
b. Makins, Roger (Mellor), Sir

February 4, 1904
b. Covarrubias, Miguel
b. Kantor, Mackinlay

February 7, 1904
b. Dorne, Albert
b. Nugent, Edward

February 11, 1904
b. Holyoake, Keith Jacka, Sir
b. Labouisse, Henry Richardson

February 12, 1904
b. Mack, Ted

February 13, 1904
b. Manone, Wingy

February 15, 1904
d. Hanna, Mark

February 16, 1904
b. Kennan, George Frost

February 17, 1904
b. Morgenthau, Hans Joachim

February 20, 1904
b. Brownell, Herbert, Jr.
b. Kosygin, Aleksei Nikolaevich

February 21, 1904
b. Fergusson, Francis

February 22, 1904
b. Hurd, Peter
b. Sidarouss, Stephanos, Cardinal
d. Stephen, Leslie, Sir

February 23, 1904
b. Fisher, Terence
b. Shirer, William L(awrence)

February 25, 1904
b. Davis, Adelle
b. Goody, Sam

February 27, 1904
b. Farrell, James Thomas

February 29, 1904
b. Dorsey, Jimmy
b. Martin, Pepper
b. Russell, Solveig Paulson

March 1, 1904
b. Baker, Rachel
b. Hartman, Paul
b. Miller, Glenn

March 2, 1904
b. Dreyfuss, Henry
b. Seuss, Doctor

March 4, 1904
b. Alikhanov, Abram Isaakovich
b. Gamow, George

March 5, 1904
b. Rahner, Karl

March 9, 1904
b. Heydrich, Reinhard Tristan Eugen
d. Palmer, Erastus Dow

March 10, 1904
b. Fishback, Margaret

March 15, 1904
b. Brent, George
b. O'Malley, J Pat

March 16, 1904
b. Myer, Buddy

March 17, 1904
b. Gross, Chaim
b. Hamilton, Patrick

March 18, 1904
b. Conze, Edward J D

March 19, 1904
b. Sirica, John Joseph

March 20, 1904
b. Elsasser, Walter M, Dr.
b. Skinner, B(urrhus) F(rederic)

March 21, 1904
d. Grace, William Russell

March 22, 1904
b. Anderson, Jack Zuinglius

March 24, 1904
b. Morrison, Hobe
d. Arnold, Edwin

March 26, 1904
b. Campbell, Joseph
b. Fernandez, Emilio

April 3, 1904
b. Wright, Russel

April 4, 1904
b. Afinogenov, Aleksandr Nikolaevich

April 5, 1904
b. Eberhart, Richard (Ghormley)

April 6, 1904
b. Kiesinger, Kurt Georg

April 8, 1904
b. Hicks, John Richard, Sir

April 12, 1904
b. Cockburn, Claud
b. Pons, Lily

April 14, 1904
b. Gielgud, (Arthur) John, Sir

April 16, 1904
b. Case, Clifford Philip
b. D'Orsay, Fifi

April 17, 1904
b. Chodorov, Edward

April 18, 1904
b. Markham, Pigmeat

April 19, 1904
b. Pough, Richard Hooper
d. Isabella II

April 20, 1904
b. Cabot, Bruce

April 21, 1904
b. Helion, Jean
b. Mallory, L(ester) D(ewitt)

April 22, 1904
b. Appley, Lawrence A(sa)
b. Oppenheimer, J(ulius) Robert

April 23, 1904
b. Renaldo, Duncan

April 24, 1904
b. Davidson, Garrison H(olt)
b. deKooning, Willem

April 27, 1904
b. Burns, Arthur Frank
b. Day-Lewis, Cecil

April 29, 1904
b. Martin, Fletcher
b. Morgan, Russ

April 30, 1904
b. Logan, Harlan (De Braun)

May 1, 1904
b. Valentina
d. Dvorak, Anton
d. His, Wilhelm

May 2, 1904
b. Crosby, Bing
b. Haury, Emil W

May 3, 1904
b. Brandt, Bill
b. DeErdely, Francis

May 4, 1904
b. Saito, Yoshishige

May 5, 1904
b. Becker, B Jay

May 6, 1904
b. Mallowan, Max Edgar Lucien, Sir

May 7, 1904
b. Lewton, Val Ivan
b. Walker, Harold Blake

May 8, 1904
d. Muybridge, Eadweard

May 9, 1904
b. Bateson, Gregory
b. Wilson, Dorothy Clarke

May 10, 1904
d. Stanley, Henry Morton, Sir

May 11, 1904
b. Dali, Salvador

May 13, 1904
b. Birney, Earle
d. Tarde, Gabriel

May 15, 1904
b. Fadiman, Clifton (Paul)

May 16, 1904
b. Peterson, Virgilia

May 17, 1904
b. Gabin, Jean
b. Williams, John James

May 18, 1904
b. Javits, Jacob Koppel

May 19, 1904
b. Bushell, Anthony
b. Creighton, Thomas H(awk)
d. Tata, Jamshedji Nusserwanji

May 20, 1904
b. Allingham, Margery

May 21, 1904
b. Montgomery, Robert Henry
b. Waller, Fats

May 22, 1904
b. Greene, Balcomb

May 26, 1904
b. O'Konski, Alvin E(dward)

May 29, 1904
b. Toland, Gregg

May 30, 1904
b. Zuckerman, Solly, Lord

June 2, 1904
b. Weissmuller, Johnny

June 3, 1904
b. Drew, Charles Richard
b. Peerce, Jan

June 4, 1904
b. Bessie, Alvah
b. Potok, Anna Maximilian Apfelbaum

June 5, 1904
b. Ellingson, Mark

June 7, 1904
b. Deutsch, Harold C(harles)

June 9, 1904
b. Arkell, William Joscelyn

June 11, 1904
b. Smith, Clarence

June 14, 1904
b. Bourke-White, Margaret

June 17, 1904
b. Bellamy, Ralph

June 18, 1904
b. Buehrig, Gordon
b. Hafstad, Lawrence R(andolph)
b. Luke, Keye

June 20, 1904
d. Seiss, Joseph Augustus

June 22, 1904
b. Wallmann, Margherita

June 23, 1904
b. Coon, Carleton Stevens

June 24, 1904
b. Harris, Phil

June 25, 1904
b. Muller-Munk, Peter

June 26, 1904
b. Carroll, Gladys Hasty
b. Lorre, Peter

June 28, 1904
b. Rollini, Adrian
d. Emmett, Daniel Decatur

June 30, 1904
b. Farrell, Glenda

July 1, 1904
b. Calderone, Mary Steichen

July 2, 1904
b. Lacoste, Rene
d. Chekhov, Anton Pavlovich

July 3, 1904
d. Herzl, Theodor

July 4, 1904
b. Keane, Mary Nesta

July 5, 1904
b. Mayr, Ernst Walter
b. Stone, Milburn

July 6, 1904
b. Suenens, Leon Joseph, Cardinal

July 11, 1904
b. Haworth, Leland John

July 12, 1904
b. Neruda, Pablo
d. Jones, Samuel Milton

July 14, 1904
b. Griswold, Erwin N(athaniel)
b. Reisenberg, Nadia
b. Singer, Isaac Bashevis

d. Kruger, Paul

July 20, 1904
b. Hammon, William McDowell

July 23, 1904
d. Simon, John, Sir

July 24, 1904
b. Killian, James Rhyne, Jr.
b. Morris, Richard Brandon

July 26, 1904
b. Link, Edwin Albert
b. Roark, Garland
b. Westrup, J(ack) A(llan), Sir
d. Rogers, John

July 27, 1904
b. Christiansen, Arthur
b. Divine, Arthur Durham
b. Dolin, Anton, Sir
b. Rudenko, Lyudmila

July 28, 1904
b. Lloyd, Selwyn

July 29, 1904
b. Tata, J(ehangir) R(atanji) D(adbhoy)

July 31, 1904
b. Carberry, John J(oseph)
b. Daley, Arthur (John)
b. Dresser, Davis

August 3, 1904
b. Halper, Albert
b. Simak, Clifford Donald

August 4, 1904
b. Hobson, Harold

August 6, 1904
b. Desses, Jean
b. Iba, Hank
b. Renault, Gilbert (Leon Etienne Theodore)
d. Hanslick, Eduard

August 7, 1904
b. Bunche, Ralph Johnson

August 9, 1904
b. Adams, Weston W, Sir
b. Shannon, James A(ugustine)
d. Ratzel, Friedrich

August 11, 1904
b. Woolley, Catherine

August 13, 1904
b. Rogers, Buddy
b. Waldock, Humphrey Meredith, Sir

August 14, 1904
b. Singher, Martial
d. Avery, Samuel Putnam

August 15, 1904
b. Baird, Bil
b. Sammartino, Peter

August 16, 1904
b. Hruska, Roman L(ee)
b. Stanley, Wendell Meredith

August 17, 1904
b. Harding, Ann
b. Whitney, John Hay

August 18, 1904
b. Cole, Sterling W(illiam)
b. Factor, Max, Jr.

August 21, 1904
b. Basie, Count

August 22, 1904
b. Deng Xiaoping
d. Chopin, Kate

August 23, 1904
b. Primrose, William

August 24, 1904
b. Castroviejo, Ramon
b. Mendez, Aparicio
b. Thompson, Llewellyn E, Jr.

August 25, 1904
d. Fantin-Latour, (Ignace) Henri

August 26, 1904
b. Isherwood, Christopher (William)

August 27, 1904
b. Lofts, Norah Robinson

August 28, 1904
b. Duvoisin, Roger Antoine

August 29, 1904
b. Forssmann, Werner Theodor Otto

August 30, 1904
b. Bohlen, Charles Eustis
b. Yeshurun, Avot

September 1, 1904
b. Brown, Johnny Mack
b. Flaherty, Ray(mond)

September 2, 1904
b. Svanholm, Set
b. Trevino, Elizabeth Borton de

September 4, 1904
b. Carr, Sabin
b. Christian-Jacque
b. Gombrowicz, Witold
d. Heade, Martin Johnson

September 5, 1904
b. Basso, Hamilton

September 6, 1904
b. Rosenbloom, Maxie

September 7, 1904
b. Colby, Carroll Burleigh

September 8, 1904
b. Cousins, Frank

September 10, 1904
b. Arevalo, Juan Jose

September 13, 1904
b. George, Gladys

September 14, 1904
b. Germi, Pietro

September 15, 1904
b. Conway, Tom
b. Umberto II

September 18, 1904
b. DeRivera, Jose Ruiz
b. Winsten, Archer

September 19, 1904
b. Evans, Bergen Baldwin

September 21, 1904
b. Hartung, Hans
b. Riddleberger, James Williams
d. Joseph, Chief

September 22, 1904
b. Valachi, Joe

September 23, 1904
b. Schapiro, Meyer
d. Galle, Emile

September 24, 1904
d. Finsen, Niels Ryberg

September 26, 1904
d. Hearn, Lafcadio

September 29, 1904
b. Eiermann, Egon

October 1, 1904
b. Frisch, O(tto) R(obert)
b. Haider, Michael Lawrence
b. Horowitz, Vladimir

October 2, 1904
b. Greene, Graham (Henry)
b. Shastri, Lal Badahur

October 4, 1904
d. Bartholdi, Auguste
d. Bishop, Isabella Lucy Bird

October 6, 1904
b. DeLiagre, Alfred

October 7, 1904
b. Klein, Chuck

October 8, 1904
b. Taishoff, Sol Joseph

October 12, 1904
b. Cobb, William Montague

October 14, 1904
b. Pineau, Christian (Paul Francis)

October 18, 1904
b. Liebling, Abbot Joseph

October 20, 1904
b. Douglas, Thomas Clement
b. Neagle, Anna, Dame

October 21, 1904
b. Kavanagh, Patrick

October 23, 1904
b. Lincoln, Victoria Endicott

October 24, 1904
b. Hart, Moss

October 25, 1904
b. Gorky, Arshile
b. Shute, Denny

October 26, 1904
b. Osborn, Robert C(hesley)

October 28, 1904
b. Dangerfield, George Bubb

October 29, 1904
b. Westmore, Perc(ival)

October 30, 1904
b. Foster, Joseph C
b. McElroy, Neil Hosler
b. Still, Clyfford

October 31, 1904
b. Taylor, Sydney Brenner

November 1, 1904
b. LaPlante, Laura

November 3, 1904
b. Lee, Jennie

November 4, 1904
b. Delano, Isaac O
b. Holm, John Cecil

November 5, 1904
b. Weiland, Cooney

November 6, 1904
b. Gilpatric, Roswell L(eavitt)

November 10, 1904
b. Geray, Steven

November 11, 1904
b. Hiss, Alger
b. Penner, Joe
b. Spiegel, Sam

November 13, 1904
b. Caspary, Vera
b. Terris, Norma

November 14, 1904
b. Lord, Mary Pillsbury
b. Mannes, Marya
b. Ramsey, Arthur Michael, Lord

November 16, 1904
b. Azikiwe, Nnamdi

November 17, 1904
b. Bernstein, Theodore Menline
b. Diederichs, Nicholaas
b. Hastie, William Henry
b. Noguchi, Isamu

November 19, 1904
b. Leopold, Nathan Freudenthal

November 20, 1904
d. Cesnola, Luigi Palma di

November 21, 1904
b. Gross, Courtlandt Sherrington
b. Hawkins, Bean
b. Hawkins, Coleman
d. Bloomingdale, Joseph Bernard

November 22, 1904
b. Neel, Louis Eugene Felix

November 24, 1904
b. Powell, Dick
b. Rogell, Billy

November 25, 1904
b. Landis, Jessie Royce

November 26, 1904
b. Flood, Daniel J(ohn)

November 27, 1904
b. McNally, John Victor

November 28, 1904
b. Cherenkov, Pavel Alekseyevich
b. Eastland, James Oliver
b. Mili, Gjon
b. Mitford, Nancy Freeman

December 1, 1904
b. Boyle, Tony

December 2, 1904
b. Woods, Donald

December 4, 1904
b. Holt, A(ndrew) D(avid, Jr.)

December 6, 1904
b. Curie, Eve
b. Landi, Elissa
d. Blaikie, William

December 8, 1904
b. Abrams, Harry Nathan

December 9, 1904
b. Kronenberger, Louis

December 10, 1904
b. Novotny, Antonin

December 11, 1904
b. Davies, Ronald N(orwood)
b. Woolsey, Janette

December 12, 1904
b. Carter, Wilf

December 15, 1904
b. Bloomgarden, Kermit

b. Legg, W(illiam) Dorr
b. Smith, Betty

December 17, 1904
b. Cadmus, Paul
b. Lonergan, Bernard J F

December 18, 1904
b. Stevens, George (Cooper)

December 25, 1904
b. Christensen, Harold
b. Herzberg, Gerhard
b. Swarthout, Gladys

December 26, 1904
b. Stern, James
b. Stribling, Young

December 27, 1904
b. D'Aulaire, Ingri Mortenson

December 30, 1904
b. Kabalevsky, Dmitri Borisovich

December 31, 1904
b. Gardiner, Chuck
b. Milstein, Nathan

1905

b. Albrecht, Duke
b. Blackwell, Betsy Talbot
b. Boswell, Martha
b. Chiari, Roberto
b. Fabrizi, Aldo
b. Fuller, S(amuel) B.
b. Haydn, Richard
b. Karume, Abeid Amani
b. Khaikin, Boris
b. Mann, Erika
b. May, Robert Lewis
b. Mikoyan, Artem Ivanovich
b. Miller, Howard
b. Morton, Nelle Katherine
b. Musial, Joe
b. O'Neal, Frederick
b. Sharp, Margery
b. Wakefield, Ruth G
d. Abduh ibn Hasan Khayr Allah,
　Muhammad
d. Earp, Virgil W
d. Lubbock, Francis Richard
d. Valera y Alcala Galiano, Juan

January 1, 1905
b. Price, Melvin

January 2, 1905
b. Tippett, Michael Kemp, Sir
b. Zampa, Luigi

January 3, 1905
b. Milland, Ray(mond Alton)

January 4, 1905
b. Holloway, Sterling Price
d. Thomas, Theodore

January 6, 1905
b. Wilson, Edward Foss

January 7, 1905
b. Dent, Alan Holmes
b. Smith, Hooley

January 11, 1905
b. Kluckhohn, Clyde
b. Kluckhorn, Clyde Kay Maben
b. Lee, Manfred B(ennington)

January 13, 1905
b. Messel, Oliver

January 14, 1905
b. Bavier, Frances
b. Fukuda, Takeo
b. Hahn, Emily
d. Abbe, Ernst

January 17, 1905
b. Salam, Saeb

January 18, 1905
b. Bonanno, Joseph

January 19, 1905
b. Hobby, Oveta Culp

January 21, 1905
b. Dior, Christian
b. Wallenda, Karl

January 23, 1905
b. Zacharias, Jerrold R(einarch)

January 26, 1905
b. Cousins, (Sue) Margaret
b. Trapp, Maria Augusta von

January 28, 1905
b. Fairclough, Ellen Louks

January 29, 1905
b. Delmar, Vina Croter
b. Judd, Winnie Ruth McKinnell
b. Newman, Barnett

January 31, 1905
b. O'Hara, John Henry

February 1, 1905
b. Berkner, Lloyd Viel
b. Lee, Doris Emrick
b. Segre, Emilio Gino

February 2, 1905
b. Hayward, John Davy
b. Rand, Ayn

February 4, 1905
b. Foy, Eddie, Jr.

February 6, 1905
b. Gomulka, Wladyslaw

February 7, 1905
b. Von Euler, Ulf

February 10, 1905
b. Brown, Walter Augustine
b. Chaney, Lon, Jr.
b. Livingston, J(oseph) A(rnold)
b. Troy, Hannah

b. Wulff, Lee

February 13, 1905
b. McKelway, St. Clair

February 14, 1905
b. Ritter, Thelma

February 15, 1905
b. Arlen, Harold
d. Wallace, Lew(is)

February 16, 1905
b. Franks, Oliver (Shewell), Sir
b. Waterhouse, Ellis Kirkham, Sir

February 18, 1905
d. Cooke, Jay

February 23, 1905
b. Victor, Sally Josephs

February 25, 1905
b. Carter, Katherine Jones
b. Miller, Perry Gilbert Eddy

February 26, 1905
d. Schwob, Marcel

February 27, 1905
b. Tone, Franchot
d. Boutwell, George Sewall

February 28, 1905
b. Jones, (Morgan) Glyn

March 2, 1905
b. Blitzstein, Marc
b. Grigson, Geoffrey Edward Harvey

March 6, 1905
b. Wills, Bob

March 8, 1905
b. Cooper, Louise Field

March 9, 1905
b. Quennell, Peter (Courtney)
b. Renick, Marion Lewis

March 10, 1905
b. Masserman, Jules H(oman)

March 12, 1905
b. Suits, C(hauncey) G(uy)

March 14, 1905
b. Aron, Raymond Claude Ferdinand

March 15, 1905
b. Hill, Chippie
b. Ross, Joe E
b. Webster, Margaret
d. Guggenheim, Meyer

March 16, 1905
b. Woltman, Frederick Enos

March 18, 1905
b. Donat, Robert
b. Parnis, Mollie

March 19, 1905
b. Speer, Albert

March 21, 1905
b. Konetzni, Hilde
b. McGinley, Phyllis

March 24, 1905
d. Verne, Jules

March 25, 1905
b. Argentinita
b. Barnes, Binnie

March 26, 1905
b. Cluytens, Andre
b. Frankl, Viktor E(mil)
d. Barrymore, Maurice

March 28, 1905
b. Berman, Pandro Samuel
b. Hague, Raoul (Heukelekian)
b. Perkins, Marlin

March 31, 1905
b. Stevenson, Robert

April 1, 1905
b. Eyskens, Gaston, Viscount
b. Hale, Clara (McBride)
b. Hasluck, Paul Meernaa, Sir
b. Moore, George Stevens

April 2, 1905
b. Adler, Kurt Herbert
b. Lifar, Serge

April 3, 1905
b. Halliday, Richard

April 4, 1905
b. Manero, Tony

April 6, 1905
b. Cardozo, W. Warrick

April 8, 1905
b. Chase, Ilka
b. Joseph, Helen

April 9, 1905
b. Fulbright, J(ames) William
d. Woolsey, Sarah Chauncey

April 10, 1905
b. Fletcher, Joseph Francis (III)

April 11, 1905
b. Jozsef, Attila
b. Root, Lynn

April 12, 1905
b. Magnuson, Warren Grant

April 13, 1905
b. Agle, Nan Hayden
b. Padover, Saul Kussiel

April 17, 1905
b. Lake, Arthur

April 18, 1905
b. Hitchings, George H(erbert)

April 20, 1905
b. Hochoy, Solomon, Sir
b. Marcus, Stanley

April 21, 1905
b. Brown, Edmund G.

April 22, 1905
b. Choquette, Robert Guy

April 23, 1905
b. Knorr, Nathan Homer
d. Jefferson, Joseph

April 24, 1905
b. Warren, Robert Penn

April 25, 1905
d. Paine, John Knowles

April 26, 1905
b. Vigo, Jean

April 28, 1905
d. Lee, Fitzhugh
d. Tait, Arthur Fitzwilliam

May 1, 1905
b. Cagle, Red
b. Zorbaugh, Geraldine B(one)

May 2, 1905
b. Armstrong, Charlotte

May 5, 1905
b. Caniglia, Maria
b. Ruffing, Red
b. Skolsky, Sidney

May 6, 1905
b. Irish, Ned
b. Martinson, Harry Edmund
b. Shor, Toots

May 7, 1905
b. Stoll, George E

May 8, 1905
b. Nichols, Red

May 10, 1905
b. Kaufman, Louis

May 13, 1905
b. Ahmed, Fakhruddin Ali

May 14, 1905
b. O'Callahan, Joseph Timothy

May 15, 1905
b. Cotten, Joseph

May 16, 1905
b. Bates, H(erbert) E(rnest)
b. Fonda, Henry Jaynes
b. Lichty, George

May 17, 1905
b. Patrick, John

May 19, 1905
b. Copeland, Lammot du Pont

May 20, 1905
b. Achterberg, Gerrit

May 21, 1905
d. Tourgee, Albion Winegar

May 23, 1905
b. Fleming, Donald M(ethuen)
d. Livermore, Mary Ashton Rice

May 24, 1905
b. Dihigo, Martin
b. McCardell, Claire
b. Sholokhov, Mikhail Aleksandrovich

May 25, 1905
b. Harsch, Joseph Close
b. Livingston, M(ilton) Stanley
b. Wesley, Dorothy Porter

May 26, 1905
b. Guffey, Burnett
b. Uris, Harold David

May 27, 1905
b. Corbett, Young, III

May 28, 1905
b. Grucci, Felix
b. Kuter, Laurence S(herman)

May 31, 1905
b. Schneider, Herman
b. Thompson, Tiny

June 1, 1905
b. Newton, Robert

June 3, 1905
b. Goddard, Paulette
b. Stone, Dorothy

June 4, 1905
b. Power, Eugene Barnum

June 6, 1905
b. Halasz, Laszlo

June 9, 1905
b. DeJong, David Cornel

June 11, 1905
b. Loeb, Richard A

June 12, 1905
b. Flemming, Arthur S(herwood)
b. Wadsworth, James Jeremiah

June 13, 1905
b. Cheatham, Adolphus
b. Colbert, Lester L(um)

June 14, 1905
d. Tippu Tib

June 15, 1905
b. Justice, James Robertson

June 17, 1905
d. Gomez, Maximo

June 18, 1905
b. Power, Thomas S(arsfield)
d. Cleve, Per Teodor

June 19, 1905
b. Voskovec, George

June 20, 1905
b. Hellman, Lillian

June 21, 1905
b. Sartre, Jean-Paul

June 24, 1905
b. Whistler, Rex

June 26, 1905
b. Ward, Lynd

June 28, 1905
b. Binns, Joseph Patterson
b. Montagu, (Montague Francis)
Ashley

June 29, 1905
b. Gardner, Ed(ward Francis)

July 1, 1905
d. Hay, John Milton

July 4, 1905
b. Trilling, Lionel

July 9, 1905
b. Campbell, Clarence Sutherland

July 10, 1905
b. Anderson, Ivie
b. Gomez, Thomas

July 11, 1905
b. Lipman, Howard W

July 13, 1905
b. Crowther, Bosley

July 15, 1905
b. Fields, Dorothy

July 17, 1905
b. Gargan, William

July 19, 1905
b. Kentner, Louis Philip
b. Neel, (Louis) Boyd
b. Snow, Edgar Parks

July 21, 1905
b. Joslyn, Allyn Morgan
b. Kennedy, David M(atthew)
b. Trilling, Diana (Rubin)

July 23, 1905
d. Henner, Jean Jacques

July 25, 1905
b. Canetti, Elias

July 27, 1905
b. Broudy, Harry Samuel

July 29, 1905
b. Hammarskjold, Dag (Hjalmar Agne
Carl)
b. Kunitz, Stanley Jasspon
b. Todd, Thelma

July 30, 1905
b. Ballard, Harold
b. Ellis, John Tracy

August 2, 1905
b. Loy, Myrna

August 3, 1905
b. DelRio, Dolores
b. Kuhn, Maggie

August 5, 1905
b. Leontief, Wassily W

August 6, 1905
b. Allers, Franz
b. Klose, Margarete

August 8, 1905
b. Martini, Nino
b. Smith, Carleton Sprague

August 9, 1905
b. Gaud, William Steen, Jr.
b. Genn, Leo
b. Nix, Robert N(elson) C(ornelius),
Sr.

August 11, 1905
b. Chargaff, Erwin

August 12, 1905
b. Ferrell, Rick
b. Isbell, Marion William

August 18, 1905
b. Lewis, Boyd de Wolf

August 20, 1905
b. Naruse, Mikio
b. Schoonmaker, Frank Musselman
b. Teagarden, Jack

August 21, 1905
d. Dodge, Mary Elizabeth Mapes

August 23, 1905
b. Bushmiller, Ernie
b. Lambert, Constant

August 24, 1905
b. Stevens, Siaka Probyn

August 25, 1905
b. Bow, Clara Gordon

August 27, 1905
b. Ward, Mary Jane

August 28, 1905
b. Levene, Sam

August 31, 1905
b. Meisner, Sanford
b. Schary, Dore
d. Tamagno, Francesco

September 2, 1905
b. Warne, William E(lmo)

September 3, 1905
b. Anderson, Carl David

September 4, 1905
b. Lewis, Meade Anderson Lux
b. Renault, Mary

September 5, 1905
b. Koestler, Arthur
d. Virchow, Rudolf

September 7, 1905
b. Priest, Ivy (Maude) Baker
b. Sommer, Frederick

September 8, 1905
b. Elder, Ruth
b. Glennan, T(homas) Keith
b. Quill, Mike
b. Wilcoxon, Henry

September 9, 1905
b. Levine, Joseph Edward

September 12, 1905
b. DeMille, Agnes (George)

September 14, 1905
d. Brazza, Pierre Paul Francois
Camille Savorgnan de
d. Rain-in-the-Face

September 17, 1905
b. Colonna, Jerry
b. Costello, Dolores

September 18, 1905
b. Anderson, Eddie
b. Garbo, Greta
d. MacDonald, George

September 19, 1905
b. Hawley, Cameron
b. Jaworski, Leon
d. Barnardo, Thomas John

September 20, 1905
b. Bouche, Rene Robert

September 21, 1905
b. Stuart, Kenneth James

September 22, 1905
d. Galli-Marie, Marie Celestine

September 23, 1905
b. Hardy, Harriet

September 24, 1905
b. Ochoa, Severo

September 25, 1905
b. Smith, Red

September 28, 1905
b. Rivers, L(ucius) Mendel
b. Schmeling, Max(imilian)

September 29, 1905
b. La Barba, Fidel

September 30, 1905
b. Mott, Nevill Francis, Sir
b. Powell, Michael Latham

October 2, 1905
b. Seper, Franjo

October 5, 1905
b. Fodor, Eugene
b. Ritz, Jimmy

October 6, 1905
b. Moody, Helen Wills
d. Richthofen, Ferdinand Paul Wilhelm

October 7, 1905
b. Devine, Andy

October 8, 1905
b. Levin, Meyer

October 9, 1905
b. Saint John, Howard
b. Ward, Paul W

October 11, 1905
b. Alexander, Leo

October 12, 1905
b. Ace, Jane Sherwood
d. Lowell, Josephine Shaw

October 13, 1905
d. Irving, Henry, Sir

October 14, 1905
b. Bernhard, Ruth

October 15, 1905
b. Snow, C(harles) P(ercy), Sir

October 18, 1905
b. Houphouet-Boigny, Felix

October 20, 1905
b. Dannay, Frederic

October 21, 1905
b. Henry, David D(odds)

October 22, 1905
b. Bennett, Constance Campbell

October 23, 1905
b. Bloch, Felix

October 29, 1905
b. Green, Henry

October 31, 1905
b. Sour, Robert B(andler)

November 1, 1905
b. Borduas, Paul-Emile
b. Gemayel, Pierre, Sheikh

November 2, 1905
b. Clark, Colin Grant
b. Dunn, James Howard
b. Keyserlingk, Robert Wendelin Henry

November 3, 1905
b. Ball, Joseph H(urst)
b. Jones, Lois Mailou

November 5, 1905
b. Bangor, Edward Henry Harold Ward, Viscount
b. Mantovani, Annunzio
b. McCrea, Joel
b. Thomson, Vernon Wallace

November 6, 1905
d. Lemoyne, W(illiam) J

November 8, 1905
d. Richards, William Trost

November 16, 1905
b. Condon, Eddie

November 17, 1905
b. Auer, Mischa

November 18, 1905
b. Carlson, William S(amuel)

November 19, 1905
b. Dorsey, Tommy
b. Kashdan, Isaac

November 21, 1905
b. Fernald, John Bailey
b. Lindstrom, Freddie
b. Wyatt, Wilson W(atkins)

November 22, 1905
b. Burnham, James

November 24, 1905
b. Wicker, Ireene Seaton

November 26, 1905
b. Williams, Emlyn

November 29, 1905
b. Lefebvre, Marcel Francois

December 3, 1905
b. Murphy, Thomas F(rancis)
d. Bartlett, John

December 4, 1905
b. Leaf, Munro

December 5, 1905
b. Abdullah, Mohammad, Sheik
b. Magnante, Charles

December 6, 1905
b. Braddock, Jim
b. DuPont, Clifford Walter
b. Yates, Elizabeth

December 7, 1905
b. Goldenson, Leonard H(arry)
b. Kuiper, Gerard Peter
b. Nash, Clarence

December 8, 1905
b. Barry, Marty

December 9, 1905
b. Trumbo, Dalton

December 10, 1905
b. Wilhelm, Hellmut

December 11, 1905
b. Childers, Erskine Hamilton
b. Lorentz, Pare
b. Roland, Gilbert

December 12, 1905
b. Anand, Mulk Raj
d. Sharp, William

December 13, 1905
b. McWilliams, Carey

December 14, 1905
d. Haupt, Herman

December 17, 1905
b. McLarnin, Jimmy
b. Verissimo, Erico Lopes

December 20, 1905
b. Dekker, Albert

December 21, 1905
b. Powell, Anthony Dymoke

December 22, 1905
b. Gerasimov, Innokentii Petrovich
b. Porter, James A(mos)
b. Rexroth, Kenneth

December 23, 1905
b. Derthick, L(awrence) G(ridley)

December 24, 1905
b. Hughes, Howard Robard

December 26, 1905
b. Loeb, William

December 27, 1905
b. Coslow, Sam

December 28, 1905
b. Arquette, Cliff
b. Dean, Gordon Evans
b. Hines, Fatha

December 31, 1905
b. Mollet, Guy
b. Styne, Jule

1906

b. Abu Salma
b. Adamson, George
b. Carvel, Thomas A

b. Chinh, Truong
b. Eastern Jewel
b. Farina, Giuseppe
b. Frick, Gottlob
b. Gibbs, Erna Leonhardt
b. Hibbert, Eleanor Alice Burford
b. Issigonis, Alec Arnold Constantine,
  Sir
b. Loper, Don
b. Martin, John C
b. Mattei, Enrico
b. Messick, Dale
b. Montor, Henry
b. Sayyid Qutb
b. Welchman, Gordon
d. Dumont, Gabriel
d. Mitre, Bartolome
d. Pfizer, Charles
d. Sorel, Albert
d. Wesson, Daniel Baird
b. Levinas, Emmanuel

January 2, 1906
b. Campbell, E Simms

January 5, 1906
b. Davison, Wild Bill

January 6, 1906
d. Krauss, Gabrielle

January 10, 1906
d. Harper, William Rainey

January 13, 1906
d. Popov, Aleksandr Stepanovich

January 14, 1906
b. Bendix, William

January 15, 1906
b. Onassis, Aristotle Socrates

January 16, 1906
b. Wynyard, Diana
d. Field, Marshall

January 18, 1906
b. Aeschbacher, Hans

January 19, 1906
b. Ross, Lanny

January 20, 1906
b. McNeill, Robert Edward, Jr.

January 21, 1906
b. Johansen, Gunnar
b. Moiseyev, Igor Alexandrovich

January 22, 1906
b. Cox, Gardner
b. Howard, Robert Ervin
b. Levy, Julien

January 23, 1906
b. Steele, Bob

January 24, 1906
b. Primeau, Joe

January 25, 1906
b. Custin, Mildred
d. Wheeler, Joseph

January 31, 1906
b. Sykes, Roosevelt

February 1, 1906
b. Hildegarde, Loretta Sell

February 2, 1906
b. Gordon, Gale

February 3, 1906
b. Doherty, Brian

February 4, 1906
b. Bonhoeffer, Dietrich
b. Tombaugh, Clyde W(illiam)

February 5, 1906
b. Carradine, John

February 6, 1906
b. Catherall, Arthur

February 7, 1906
b. Amrouche, Jean

February 8, 1906
b. Balsam, Artur
b. Carlson, Chester Floyd
b. Roth, Henry

February 9, 1906
d. Dunbar, Paul Laurence

February 10, 1906
b. Bingham, Barry
b. Farrow, John Villiers
b. Rhodes, Erik

February 11, 1906
b. Malik, Charles Habib
b. Malik, Yakov (Alexandrovich)
b. Pu-Yi, Henry

February 16, 1906
b. Menchik-Stevenson, Vera Francevna

February 17, 1906
b. Plaza Lasso, Galo
b. Spivak, Charlie

February 18, 1906
d. Stetson, John Batterson

February 20, 1906
b. Fletcher, Bramwell

February 22, 1906
b. Henderson, Leon N(esbit)

February 24, 1906
b. Coombs, Herbert Cole

February 26, 1906
b. Romano, Umberto

February 27, 1906
d. Langley, Samuel Pierpont

February 28, 1906
b. Siegel, Bugsy

March 1, 1906
b. Curran, Joseph Edwin
b. Pham van Dong
b. Powell, Teddy
d. Pereda, Jose Marie de

March 3, 1906
b. Bigard, Albany Barney Leon
b. Lundkvist, Artur Nils

March 4, 1906
b. Davis, Phil
b. Dejong, Meindert
b. Fisher, Avery
b. Macdonald, Eleanor Josephine
b. Walgreen, Charles Rudolph, Jr.
d. Schofield, John McAllister

March 6, 1906
b. Costello, Lou

March 9, 1906
b. Smith, David

March 13, 1906
d. Anthony, Susan B(rownell)

March 14, 1906
b. John, John P(ico)
b. Teschemacher, Frank

March 16, 1906
b. Waner, Lloyd James
b. Youngman, Henny

March 17, 1906
b. O'Shea, Michael

March 18, 1906
b. Chiang Ching-Kuo

March 19, 1906
b. Eichmann, Adolf

March 20, 1906
b. Beame, Abraham David
b. Nelson, Ozzie

March 21, 1906
b. Deutsch, Helen
b. Rockefeller, John D(avison), III

March 22, 1906
b. Laeri, J(ohn) Howard

March 23, 1906
b. Evans, Richard Louis

March 24, 1906
b. MacDonald, Dwight

March 25, 1906
b. Pyle, Howard
b. Sablon, Jean Georges
b. Taylor, A(lan) J(ohn) P(ercivale)

March 27, 1906
b. Russell, Pee Wee
d. Carriere, Eugene

March 29, 1906
b. Allred, Rulon Clark
b. Bausch, James
b. Biggs, Edward George Power
b. Stevens, Onslow

March 31, 1906
b. Tomonaga Shinichiro

April 1, 1906
b. Yakovlev, Aleksandr Sergeyevich

April 4, 1906
b. Benaderet, Bea
b. Reynolds, R(ichard) J(oshua), Jr.
b. Swayze, John Cameron, Sr.

April 5, 1906
d. Johnson, Eastman
d. Johnson, Jonathan Eastman

April 8, 1906
b. Jobin, Raoul

April 9, 1906
b. Dorati, Antal
b. Faisal (Ibn Abdul-Aziz al Saud)
b. Gaitskell, Hugh (Todd Naylor)

April 10, 1906
b. Darvas, Lili
b. Gates, Thomas Sovereign, Jr.

April 11, 1906
d. Bailey, James Anthony

April 13, 1906
b. Beckett, Samuel (Barclay)
b. Freeman, Bud
d. Garnett, Richard

April 16, 1906
b. Gimpel, Jakob

April 18, 1906
d. Huntington, Daniel

April 19, 1906
d. Curie, Pierre

April 22, 1906
b. Dixon, Robert Ellington

April 25, 1906
b. Brennan, William Joseph, Jr.

April 26, 1906
b. Joyce, William

April 27, 1906
b. Maeght, Aime

April 28, 1906
b. Bok, Bart J(an)
b. Godel, Kurt
b. Sacher, Paul

May 1, 1906
b. Hobart, Rose

May 2, 1906
b. Halsman, Philippe

May 3, 1906
b. Astor, Mary
b. Roosevelt, Anna Eleanor

May 6, 1906
b. Lattimore, Richmond Alexander

May 7, 1906
b. Corle, Edwin

May 8, 1906
b. Rossellini, Roberto

May 9, 1906
b. Estes, Eleanor Ruth Rosenfeld

May 11, 1906
b. Higginbotham, Jack

May 12, 1906
b. Ewing, William Maurice
b. Jones, Gorilla

May 13, 1906
b. McConnell, Joseph H(oward)

May 14, 1906
d. Schurz, Carl

May 16, 1906
b. Rey, Margret (Elizabeth)

May 17, 1906
b. McIntire, Carl
b. Milanov, Zinka Kunc

May 21, 1906
b. Buddhadasa Bhikkhu
b. Gerasimov, Sergei Appolinarievich
b. Lane, Lola

May 22, 1906
b. Howe, Mark De Wolfe
b. Ritz, Harry

May 23, 1906
b. Holman, Libby
d. Ibsen, Henrik Johan

May 24, 1906
b. Vishnevsky, Alexandr
Alekandrovich

May 25, 1906
b. Greenaway, Emerson

May 28, 1906
b. Hills, Lee
b. Regan, Phil

May 29, 1906
b. White, T(erence) H(anbury)

May 31, 1906
d. Davitt, Michael

June 3, 1906
b. Baker, Josephine (Carson)

June 4, 1906
b. Whorf, Richard

June 7, 1906
b. Dane, Maxwell
b. Gray, Glen

June 10, 1906
b. Crosby, Alexander L
d. Jacobi, Mary Corinna Putnam
d. Seddon, Richard John

June 14, 1906
b. Lamb, Gil

June 15, 1906
b. Taeuber, Conrad F.

June 16, 1906
b. Munson, Ona

June 18, 1906
b. Kyser, Kay (James King Kern)

June 19, 1906
b. Chain, Ernest Boris, Sir

June 20, 1906
b. Burnshaw, Stanley
b. Jones, Robert Trent

June 21, 1906
b. Elson, Robert Truscott
b. Elting, Mary Letha

June 22, 1906
b. Highet, Gilbert (Arthur)
b. Wilder, Billy (Samuel)
d. Schaudinn, Fritz Richard

June 24, 1906
b. Fournier, Pierre

June 25, 1906
b. Livesey, Roger
d. White, Stanford

June 26, 1906
b. Wolfenden, John Frederick, Sir

June 28, 1906
b. Mayer, Maria Goeppert

June 29, 1906
d. Perky, Henry D

July 1, 1906
b. Calder, Peter Ritchie
d. Garcia, Manuel Patricio Rodriguez

July 2, 1906
b. Bethe, Hans Albrecht

July 3, 1906
b. Lleras Camargo, Alberto
b. Sanders, George
b. Steegmuller, Francis

July 4, 1906
b. Schaefer, Vincent Joseph

July 5, 1906
d. Breton, Jules Adolphe

July 6, 1906
d. Langdell, Christopher Columbus

July 7, 1906
b. Paige, Satchel

July 8, 1906
b. Johnson, Philip Cortelyou

July 10, 1906
b. Icaza (Coronel), Jorge

July 11, 1906
b. Von Zell, Harry

July 13, 1906
b. Sosnik, Harry

July 15, 1906
b. Armour, Richard Willard

July 16, 1906
b. Barnes, Lee
b. Sherman, Vincent

July 18, 1906
b. Hayakawa, S(amuel) I(chiye)
b. Odets, Clifford

July 23, 1906
b. Prelog, Vladimir

July 25, 1906
b. Hodges, Johnny
b. Wengenroth, Stow

July 26, 1906
b. Allen, Gracie Ethel Cecil Rosaline

July 27, 1906
b. Durocher, Leo Ernest
b. Wolff, Helen

July 29, 1906
b. Roebling, Mary G(indhart)

August 3, 1906
b. Trauner, Alexander

August 5, 1906
b. Huston, John

August 6, 1906
b. Sterling, John Ewart Wallace
b. Strong, Ken(neth E)

August 8, 1906
b. Thon, William

August 9, 1906
b. Travers, P(amela) L(yndon)
b. Wallace, Ed(ward Tatum)

August 10, 1906
d. Clarke, Rebecca Sophia

August 14, 1906
b. Horst, Horst P(aul)

August 16, 1906
b. Franz Joseph II

August 17, 1906
b. Bishop, Hazel
b. Caetano, Marcello

August 19, 1906
b. Farnsworth, Philo Taylor

August 20, 1906
b. Tuttle, Lurene

August 21, 1906
b. Freleng, Friz

August 23, 1906
b. Ragland, Rags

August 24, 1906
b. Kaufman, Boris

August 25, 1906
b. Panter-Downes, Mollie

August 26, 1906
b. Bloom, Mickey
b. Sabin, Albert Bruce

August 27, 1906
b. Gein, Ed

August 28, 1906
b. Betjeman, John, Sir

August 29, 1906
b. Gerold, Karl

September 1, 1906
b. Schioetz, Aksel

September 3, 1906
b. Powell, Lawrence Clark

September 4, 1906
b. Delbruck, Max

September 5, 1906
d. Boltzmann, Ludwig

September 6, 1906
b. Leloir, Luis Federico

September 8, 1906
b. Prescott, Orville

September 10, 1906
b. Lyons, Leonard

September 15, 1906
b. Becker, Jacques
b. Murray, Kathryn (Hazel)
b. O'Donnell, Emmett, Jr.

September 17, 1906
b. Ashton, Frederick William, Sir
b. Jayewardene, J(unius) R(ichard)

September 18, 1906
b. Gellhorn, Walter

September 19, 1906
b. Reifel, Ben

September 21, 1906
b. Farago, Ladislas
b. Fitzgerald, Albert J

September 22, 1906
b. Koch, Ilse

September 23, 1906
b. Tarsis, Valery Yakovlevich

September 25, 1906
b. Figueres Ferrer, Jose
b. Shostakovich, Dmitri Dmitryevich

September 27, 1906
b. Empson, William, Sir

September 28, 1906
b. Miller, Paul

September 30, 1906
b. Stewart, J(ohn) I(nnes)
M(ackintosh)

October 2, 1906
b. Ley, Willy

October 4, 1906
b. Frankfurter, Alfred Moritz
b. Kepes, Gyorgy

October 5, 1906
b. Frankenstein, Alfred Victor
b. Jones, R(enato) William

October 6, 1906
b. Gaynor, Janet

October 7, 1906
b. Webb, James Edwin

October 9, 1906
b. Senghor, Leopold Sedar
d. Glidden, Joseph Farwell

October 10, 1906
b. Creston, Paul
b. Narayan, R(asipuram)
K(rishnaswami)

October 11, 1906
b. Clark, Dutch
b. Revson, Charles Haskell

October 12, 1906
b. Cronin, Joe

October 13, 1906
b. Morgan, Thomas E(llsworth)
b. Redding, Jay Saunders

October 14, 1906
b. Arendt, Hannah

October 16, 1906
b. Brooks, Cleanth

October 17, 1906
b. Cassidy, Harold Gomes

October 18, 1906
b. Kingsley, Sidney

October 20, 1906
b. Johnson, Crockett
d. Ewing, Buck

October 22, 1906
d. Cezanne, Paul

October 23, 1906
b. Ederle, Gertrude Caroline
b. Monroe, Lucy

October 24, 1906
b. Gelfond, Aleksandr Osipovich

October 26, 1906
b. Carnera, Primo

October 27, 1906
b. Blume, Peter
b. Griswold, Alfred Whitney

October 29, 1906
b. Schottland, Charles I(rwin)

October 30, 1906
b. Smith, Paul Joseph

November 2, 1906
b. Visconti, Luchino

November 4, 1906
b. Considine, Bob
b. Herberg, Will
b. North, Sterling
b. Stevens, S(tanley) S(mith)
b. Strouse, Norman H(ulbert)
d. Sage, Russell

November 6, 1906
b. Charriere, Henri
b. Lederer, Francis
b. Norris, James D

November 7, 1906
b. Blake, Eugene Carson

November 9, 1906
b. Spanier, Muggsy
d. Beale, Dorothea

November 10, 1906
b. Model, Lisette

November 12, 1906
b. Dillon, George
b. Saidenberg, Daniel
d. Shafter, William Rufus

November 13, 1906
b. Baddeley, Hermione Clinton

November 14, 1906
b. Brooks, Louise
b. Dwinell, Lane

November 15, 1906
b. LeMay, Curtis Emerson
b. Niwano, Nikkyo
b. Stein, Aaron Marc

November 16, 1906
b. Dowling, Dan(iel Blair)

November 17, 1906
b. Bronson, Betty
b. Honda, Soichiro

November 18, 1906
b. Mann, Klaus
b. Wald, George

November 19, 1906
b. Carroll, Nancy

November 22, 1906
b. Patrick, Lee

November 25, 1906
b. Jepson, Helen

November 27, 1906
b. Morton, Digby
b. Scheffer, Victor B(lanchard)

November 30, 1906
b. Carr, John Dickson

December 1, 1906
b. Sommers, Ben

December 2, 1906
b. Goldmark, Peter Carl
b. Harrar, J(acob) George

December 5, 1906
b. Preminger, Otto Ludwig

December 6, 1906
b. Moorehead, Agnes
b. Spychalski, Marian

December 7, 1906
d. Ducommun, Elie

December 8, 1906
b. Llewellyn, Richard

December 9, 1906
b. Hopper, Grace Brewster Murray
b. Martin, Freddy
d. Maitland, Frederic William

December 10, 1906
b. Zinn, Walter Henry

December 11, 1906
b. Diop, Birago

December 12, 1906
b. Meng, John Joseph
b. Mosley, Zack Terrell
b. Pahlmann, William Carroll

December 13, 1906
b. Marina
b. Van Der Post, Laurens (Jan), Sir

December 14, 1906
b. Soby, James Thrall

December 17, 1906
b. Martin, William McChesney, Jr.

December 19, 1906
b. Brezhnev, Leonid Ilyich
b. Thompson, Paul W(illiams)

December 20, 1906
b. Krick, Irving P(arkhurst)

December 23, 1906
b. Elson, Edward L(ee) R(oy)

December 24, 1906
b. Hoffner, Joseph, Cardinal
b. Walker, John
b. Waxman, Franz

December 25, 1906
b. Barnes-Taeuber, Irene
b. Clifford, Clark M(cAdams)
b. Grade, Lew, Sir
b. Ruska, Ernst

December 26, 1906
b. Cook, Elisha, Jr.

December 27, 1906
b. Feininger, Andreas (Bernhard Lyonel)
b. Levant, Oscar

December 28, 1906
b. Bridges, Tommy

December 30, 1906
b. Bruce, Louis R., Jr.
b. Reed, Carol, Sir

1907

b. Ammons, Albert C
b. Avery, R Stanton
b. Cannon, Poppy
b. Claytor, Helen (Natalie Jackson)
b. Cornell, Douglas B
b. Desjardins, Pete
b. Fitzgerald, John Dennis
b. Frank, Gerold
b. Freeman, Paul Lamar
b. Gerber, John
b. Hartman, Grace
b. Heschel, Abraham Joshua
b. Hughes, George
b. Hunter, Howard
b. Jaffee, Irving
b. Manheim, Ralph
b. Mayer, Edward Newton, Jr.
b. Miles, Bernard, Sir
b. Paz Estenssoro, Victor
b. Shuttlesworth, Dorothy Edwards
b. Weng, Will
d. Chadwick, Cassie L

January 1, 1907
b. Carzou, Jean

January 3, 1907
b. Wong, Anna May (Lu Tsong)

January 5, 1907
b. Marsala, Joe

January 7, 1907
b. Zabaleta, Nicanor

January 11, 1907
b. Mendes-France, Pierre

January 12, 1907
b. Ritter, Tex

January 15, 1907
b. Nitze, Paul Henry

January 16, 1907
b. Knox, Alexander

January 17, 1907
b. Badings, Henk

January 18, 1907
b. Ferencsik, Janos

January 20, 1907
b. Welensky, Roy

January 22, 1907
b. Corrigan, Douglas

January 23, 1907
b. Duryea, Dan
b. Yukawa, Hideki

January 24, 1907
b. Couve de Murville, (Jacques) Maurice

January 26, 1907
b. Cotton, Henry, Sir
b. Selye, Hans

January 27, 1907
b. Compton, Joyce

January 29, 1907
b. Becker, Ralph E(lihu)
b. Bernstein, Sid(ney Ralph)

January 31, 1907
d. Eaton, Timothy

February 1, 1907
b. Canaday, John (Edwin John)

February 2, 1907
d. Mendeleev, Dmitri Ivanovich

February 3, 1907
b. Michener, James A(lbert)
b. Morey, Walt(er Nelson)

February 4, 1907
b. Spivakovsky, Tossy

February 5, 1907
b. Bender, Hans
b. Simon, Norton Winfred
b. White, William S(mith)

February 8, 1907
b. Cole, Charles Woolsey
b. Middleton, Ray

February 9, 1907
b. Clapper, Dit

February 10, 1907
b. Hamilton, Grace Towns

February 11, 1907
b. Levitt, William J(aird)

February 13, 1907
b. Goodman, Andrew

February 14, 1907
b. Longden, Johnny

February 15, 1907
b. Romero, Cesar

February 16, 1907
b. Anstey, Edgar Harold McFarlane
b. Previtali, Fernando
d. Carducci, Giosue Alessandro Guiseppe

February 17, 1907
b. Wilder, Alec
d. Olcott, Henry Steel

February 18, 1907
b. DeWolfe, Billy

February 19, 1907
b. Bosley, Harold A

February 20, 1907
d. Moissan, Ferdinand Frederick Henri

February 21, 1907
b. Auden, W(ystan) H(ugh)
b. Pletcher, Stew

February 22, 1907
b. Leonard, Sheldon
b. Young, Robert (George)

February 25, 1907
b. Chase, Mary Coyle

February 26, 1907
b. Yellow Robe, Rosebud

February 27, 1907
b. Bailey, Mildred
b. Traube, Shepard

February 28, 1907
b. Caniff, Milt(on Arthur)
b. Cox, Herald Rea

March 2, 1907
d. Manns, August, Sir

March 4, 1907
b. Targ, William

March 5, 1907
b. Rosenbloom, Carroll D

March 6, 1907
b. Tyler, Parker
b. Wilson, Logan

March 8, 1907
b. Karamanlis, Constantine

March 9, 1907
b. Eliade, Mircea
d. Dowie, John Alexander

March 10, 1907
b. Frissell, Toni

March 11, 1907
b. Matthews, Jessie
b. Moltke, Helmuth James, Graf von

March 15, 1907
b. McPartland, Jimmy
b. Osborne, John Franklin

March 17, 1907
b. Miki Takeo
b. Pastore, John Orlando

March 18, 1907
d. Berthelot, Marcellin

March 19, 1907
b. Smith, Kent
d. Aldrich, Thomas Bailey

March 20, 1907
b. Arnall, Ellis (Gibbs)
b. MacLennan, Hugh

March 21, 1907
b. Sweet, John Howard

March 22, 1907
b. Gavin, James Maurice

March 23, 1907
b. Bovet, Daniele
d. Pobedonostsev, Konstantin Petrovich

March 24, 1907
b. Norstad, Lauris

March 26, 1907
b. Lasch, Robert

March 27, 1907
b. Chase, Lucia

March 28, 1907
b. Lazar, Irving Paul

March 31, 1907
b. Quillan, Eddie

April 2, 1907
b. Appling, Luke
b. Selznick, Irene Mayer

April 4, 1907
b. Pusey, Nathan Marsh

April 6, 1907
b. Day, Chon
d. Drummond, William Henry

April 7, 1907
b. Gordon-Walker of Leyton, Patrick
Chrestien Gordon-Walker, Baron
b. Liebman, Joshua Loth
b. Shimkin, Leon

April 9, 1907
b. Goodfellow, Ebbie

April 10, 1907
b. Murphy, Charles

April 12, 1907
b. Gramatky, Hardie

April 13, 1907
b. Stassen, Harold Edward

April 14, 1907
b. Duvalier, Francois

April 15, 1907
b. Tinbergen, Nikolaas

April 18, 1907
b. Lampman, Evelyn Sibley
b. Roa (y Garcia), Raul
b. Rozsa, Miklos

April 20, 1907
b. Soyer, Isaac

April 21, 1907
b. Baker, Dorothy Dodds

April 24, 1907
d. Kearney, Denis
d. Packer, Alfred G

April 25, 1907
b. Matter, Herbert
b. Zinnemann, Fred

April 28, 1907
b. Sunderland, Thomas E(lbert)

May 1, 1907
b. Roszak, Theodore
b. Smith, Kate

May 3, 1907
b. Lee, Canada
b. Wilson, Earl

May 4, 1907
b. Kirstein, Lincoln (Edward)

May 6, 1907
b. Ewbank, Weeb

May 9, 1907
b. Kuhlman, Kathryn

May 10, 1907
b. Hunt, Pee Wee

May 11, 1907
b. Taylor, Kent

May 12, 1907
b. Charteris, Leslie

b. Hepburn, Katharine (Houghton)
d. Huysmans, Joris Karl

May 13, 1907
b. DuMaurier, Daphne

May 14, 1907
b. Ayub Khan, Mohammad
b. Enrique Tarancon, Vicente, Cardinal

May 15, 1907
b. Appel, James Ziegler
b. Dodd, Thomas Joseph

May 17, 1907
b. McMahon, Horace

May 18, 1907
b. Curzon, Clifford Michael, Sir
b. Dohanos, Stevan

May 20, 1907
b. Mydans, Carl M

May 21, 1907
b. Ivanov, Konstantin Konstantinovich

May 22, 1907
b. Olivier, Laurence Kerr, Sir

May 24, 1907
b. Jones, Gwynn

May 25, 1907
b. Nu, U

May 26, 1907
b. Wayne, John
d. Keckley, Elizabeth Hobbs
d. McKinley, Ida Saxton

May 27, 1907
b. Carson, Rachel (Louise)

May 28, 1907
b. Gilmore, Eddy Lanier King

May 29, 1907
b. Molson, Hartland de Montarville

May 31, 1907
b. Alphand, Herve

June 1, 1907
b. Hecht, Harold
b. Whittle, Frank, Sir

June 2, 1907
b. Lehmann, John Frederick
b. West, Dorothy

June 3, 1907
b. Rotha, Paul

June 6, 1907
b. Dickey, Bill
b. Rickey, George Warren

June 7, 1907
b. Chalk, O(scar) Roy
b. Clarke, Thomas Ernest Bennett

June 10, 1907
b. Porter, Fairfield

June 11, 1907
b. Mellon, Paul

June 12, 1907
b. Warner, Roger Sherman, Jr.

June 14, 1907
b. Char, Rene (Emile)
b. Hansen, Julia Butler

June 15, 1907
d. Jenney, William LeBaron

June 16, 1907
b. Pilkington, Francis Meredyth

June 17, 1907
b. Britt, Steuart Henderson
b. Eames, Charles
b. Murphy, W(illiam) B(everly)

June 18, 1907
b. MacDonald, Jeanette
b. Shalamov, Varlam Tikhonovich

June 20, 1907
b. Driftwood, Jimmy

June 21, 1907
b. Prestopino, Gregorio
b. Shea, William Alfred

June 22, 1907
b. Lindbergh, Anne Spencer Morrow

June 23, 1907
b. Meade, James Edward
d. Stuart, Hod

June 24, 1907
b. Schlumberger, Jean

June 25, 1907
b. Jensen, Johannes Hans Daniel
b. Six, Robert Forman

June 27, 1907
b. McIntire, John
b. Tucker, Lorenzo

June 28, 1907
b. Bull, Odd
b. Victor, Paul-Emile

June 29, 1907
b. Davis, Joan
b. O'Dwyer, Paul

June 30, 1907
b. Vandenberg, Arthur Hendrick, Jr.

July 1, 1907
b. Bolotowsky, Ilya
b. Stern, Bill

July 4, 1907
b. Taubman, (Hyman) Howard

July 6, 1907
b. Kahlo, Frida

July 7, 1907
b. Heinlein, Robert Anson

July 8, 1907
b. Rankin, J(ames) Lee
b. Romney, George (Wilcken)

July 9, 1907
b. Klutznick, Philip M.

July 10, 1907
b. Stignani, Ebe

July 11, 1907
b. Lea, Tom

July 14, 1907
d. Perkin, William Henry, Sir

July 16, 1907
b. Calmer, Ned
b. Redenbacher, Orville
b. Stanwyck, Barbara

July 20, 1907
b. Lincoln, George A
b. Simpson, Cedric Keith

July 23, 1907
b. Cunningham, Harry Blair
b. Huxley, Elspeth Josceline Grant

July 25, 1907
b. Gilford, Jack

July 28, 1907
b. Tupper, Earl Silas

July 29, 1907
b. Belli, Melvin M(ouron)
b. Butterfield, Roger Place

August 3, 1907
b. Staggers, Harley O(rrin)
d. Saint Gaudens, Augustus

August 7, 1907
b. Dart, Justin Whitlock

August 8, 1907
b. Carter, Benny
b. Stuart, Jesse Hilton

August 11, 1907
b. Newsom, Bobo

August 12, 1907
b. Bentley, Gladys
b. Besser, Joe
b. Sheares, Benjamin Henry

August 13, 1907
b. Spence, Basil Urwin, Sir

August 14, 1907
b. Adams, Stanley
b. Dichter, Ernest
b. Topolski, Feliks

August 15, 1907
b. Trotta, Maurice S
d. Joachim, Joseph

August 16, 1907
b. Clarke, Mae

August 17, 1907
b. Peyrefitte, Roger

August 18, 1907
b. Bolinger, Dwight Lemerton
b. Light, Enoch Henry

August 19, 1907
b. Morton, Thruston Ballard
b. Singh, (Sardar) Swaran

August 20, 1907
b. Reed, Alan

August 25, 1907
d. Coleridge, Mary Elizabeth

August 28, 1907
b. Hart-Davis, Rupert

August 29, 1907
b. Wechsberg, Joseph

August 30, 1907
b. Booth, Shirley
b. Keogh, Eugene James
b. Mauchly, John William
d. Mansfield, Richard

August 31, 1907
b. Hawkins, Gus
b. Magsaysay, Ramon
b. Shawn, William

September 1, 1907
b. Balaguer, Joaquin
b. Emery, Anne (McGuigan)
b. Reuther, Walter Philip

September 3, 1907
b. Eiseley, Loren Corey
b. Mizener, Arthur Moore

September 4, 1907
b. Griffin, Marvin
d. Grieg, Edvard Hagerup

September 5, 1907
b. Blough, Glenn Orlando
b. Douglass, Lathrop

September 7, 1907
b. Neddermeyer, Seth H
d. Lee-Hamilton, Eugene Jacob
d. Sully Prudhomme

September 8, 1907
b. Leonard, Buck

September 9, 1907
b. Edel, Leon

September 10, 1907
b. Landrum, Phil(lip) M(itchell)
b. Wray, Fay

September 12, 1907
b. MacNeice, Louis
b. McMillan, Edwin Mattison

September 14, 1907
b. Brown, Cecil B
b. Wexley, John

September 15, 1907
b. Bailey, Jack
b. Wallington, Jimmy

September 17, 1907
b. Burger, Warren E(arl)
b. Vinson, Helen

September 19, 1907
b. Powell, Lewis F(ranklin), Jr.

September 21, 1907
b. Bird, Junius Bouton
b. Bullard, Edward Crisp, Sir
b. Roskolenko, Harry

September 22, 1907
b. Strudwick, Shepperd

September 23, 1907
b. Moscona, Nicola
b. Novotna, Jarmila

September 24, 1907
b. Dunning, John Ray
b. McArthur, Edwin Douglas

September 26, 1907
b. Blunt, Anthony Frederick

September 28, 1907
b. Edwards, Turk

September 29, 1907
b. Autry, Gene

September 30, 1907
b. Kramm, Joseph

October 1, 1907
b. Fong, Hiram Leong
b. Lawrenson, Helen Brown

October 2, 1907
b. Todd, Alexander (Robertus), Sir

October 5, 1907
b. Gorman, Carl Nelson
b. Louis, Jean

October 6, 1907
d. Holmes, Mary Jane Hawes

October 7, 1907
b. MacInnes, Helen

October 12, 1907
b. Delaplane, Stanton Hill
b. Jarring, Gunnar Valfrid
b. Kraus, Hans Peter
d. Massey, Gerald

October 13, 1907
b. Allegret, Yves

January 7, 1908
b. Allen, Red
b. Gibberd, Frederick, Sir

January 8, 1908
b. Frankau, Pamela

January 9, 1908
b. Beauvoir, Simone de
b. Trefflich, Henry Herbert Frederick
d. Busch, Wilhelm

January 10, 1908
b. Henreid, Paul
b. Lee, Bernard
d. Spreckels, Claus

January 12, 1908
b. Delannoy, Jean
b. Hurd, Clement
b. Limon, Jose Arcadio
b. Lowinsky, Edward Elias
b. Ludwig, Leopold

January 13, 1908
b. Wheeler, Earle G

January 14, 1908
d. Drachmann, Holger Henrik Herholdt

January 15, 1908
b. Teller, Edward

January 18, 1908
b. Bronowski, Jacob
b. Callender, John Hancock
b. Morano, Albert Paul
d. Stedman, Edmund Clarence

January 21, 1908
b. Gary, Raymond
b. Stromgren, Bengt Georg Daniel

January 22, 1908
b. Keyserling, Leon Hirsch
b. Landau, Lev Davidovich

January 23, 1908
d. MacDowell, Edward Alexander

January 24, 1908
b. Duncan-Sandys, Edwin, Lord
b. Ford, Alexander

January 25, 1908
d. Ouida

January 26, 1908
b. Esmond, Jill
b. Grappelli, Stephane

January 27, 1908
b. Burtin, Will
b. Hearst, William Randolph, Jr.
b. Page, Hot Lips

January 31, 1908
b. Cantwell, Robert Emmett

February 1, 1908
b. Booth, Albie
b. Pal, George

February 2, 1908
b. Ferrell, Wes(ley Cheek)
b. Rossellini, Renzo
b. Tinney, Cal(vin Lawrence)

February 3, 1908
b. Jones, Roger W(arren)
b. Miller, William Ernest

February 5, 1908
b. Gervasi, Frank Henry
b. Hilton, Daisy
b. Hilton, Violet

February 6, 1908
b. Fanfani, Amintore
b. Lansdale, Edward Geary

February 8, 1908
b. McCormick, Myron

February 11, 1908
b. Fuchs, Vivian (Ernest), Sir
b. White, Josh(ua Daniel)

February 13, 1908
b. Dozier, William
b. Frederick, Pauline
b. Goode, Mal
b. Hayton, Lennie

February 14, 1908
b. Scribner, Fred C(lark), Jr.

February 17, 1908
b. Barber, Red
b. Cotsworth, Staats
b. Crabbe, Buster

February 20, 1908
b. Kingsbury-Smith, Joseph

February 21, 1908
d. Hosmer, Harriet Goodhue

February 22, 1908
b. Betancourt, Romulo
b. Kolodin, Irving
b. Mills, John, Sir

February 23, 1908
b. McMahon, William

February 25, 1908
b. Slaughter, Frank Gill

February 26, 1908
b. Avery, Tex
b. Groth, John August
b. LeFleming, Christopher Kaye

February 28, 1908
b. Brown, Dee (Alexander)
d. Lucca, Pauline

February 29, 1908
b. Balthus
b. Hasegawa, Kazuo
d. Garrett, Pat(rick Floyd)

March 2, 1908
d. Oliver, James

March 4, 1908
b. Kraus, Lili

March 5, 1908
b. Harrison, Rex, Sir

March 10, 1908
b. Wragge, Sidney

March 12, 1908
b. Conley, Eugene
d. Amicis, Edmond de

March 13, 1908
b. Annenberg, Walter Hubert
b. Key, Valdimer Orlando, Jr.
b. Stewart, Paul

March 14, 1908
b. Heinemann, Edward H
b. Merleau-Ponty, Maurice

March 15, 1908
b. Baum, Kurt

March 16, 1908
b. Rossen, Robert

March 20, 1908
b. Redgrave, Michael Scudamore, Sir
b. Stanton, Frank Nicholas

March 22, 1908
b. L'Amour, Louis Dearborn
b. Stans, Maurice H(ubert)

March 24, 1908
b. Beam, Jacob D(yneley)

March 25, 1908
b. Kautner, Helmut
b. Lean, David, Sir

March 26, 1908
b. Stangl, Franz Paul

March 27, 1908
b. Fleming, Joan Margaret

March 28, 1908
b. Crawford, Joan

March 29, 1908
b. O'Connell, Arthur

March 31, 1908
b. Kitchell, Iva
b. Norvo, Red

April 1, 1908
b. Maslow, Abraham Harold

April 2, 1908
b. Ebsen, Buddy

April 4, 1908
b. Tudor, Antony

April 5, 1908
b. Carey, Ernestine Moller Gilbreth
b. Davis, Bette

b. Hemingway, Mary Welsh
b. Karajan, Herbert von
b. Ram, Jagjivan

April 6, 1908
b. Lombardi, Ernie

April 7, 1908
b. Faith, Percy
b. Fitzsimmons, Frank Edward
b. Le Duan

April 8, 1908
b. Whitehead, Don(ald Ford)

April 9, 1908
b. Allan, Elizabeth
b. Krumgold, Joseph (Quincy)
b. Vasarely, Victor
b. Wilcox, Francis (Orlando)

April 10, 1908
b. Feather, Victor

April 11, 1908
b. Ancerl, Karel
b. Rosten, Leo C(alvin)

April 12, 1908
b. Lleras Restrepo, Carlos

April 13, 1908
b. Bresler, Jerry

April 19, 1908
b. Keilberth, Joseph

April 20, 1908
d. Chadwick, Henry

April 22, 1908
b. Albert, Eddie
d. Campbell-Bannerman, Henry, Sir

April 23, 1908
b. Camilli, Dolph
b. Zhukov, Georgi Alexandrovich

April 24, 1908
b. Oppen, George

April 25, 1908
b. Murrow, Edward R

April 26, 1908
b. Bugas, John Stephen
b. Tough, Dave
b. Wilhelm, Gale

April 28, 1908
b. Schindler, Oskar

May 1, 1908
b. Kline, Morris

May 2, 1908
b. Bakewell, William
b. O'Brien-Moore, Erin

May 6, 1908
b. Hale, Nancy

May 8, 1908
b. Graham, John
d. Halevy, Ludovic

May 9, 1908
b. Newhall, Nancy Wynne
b. Sillman, Leonard

May 10, 1908
b. Albert, Carl Bert
b. Barraclough, Geoffrey

May 11, 1908
b. Morris, Ernest Brougham

May 17, 1908
b. Prokosch, Frederic
b. Schorer, Mark

May 18, 1908
b. Tucker, Tommy

May 20, 1908
b. Stewart, James (Maitland)
b. Whitehead, (Walter) Edward

May 21, 1908
b. McSpaden, Byron

May 22, 1908
b. Smith, Horton

May 23, 1908
b. Abramovitz, Max
b. Bardeen, John
d. Coppee, Francois Edouard Joachim

May 25, 1908
b. Roethke, Theodore (Huebner)

May 26, 1908
b. Morley, Robert
d. Ahmad, Mirza Ghulam Hazat

May 27, 1908
b. Rome, Harold J(acob)
d. Posey, Alexander Lawrence

May 28, 1908
b. Fleming, Ian Lancaster

May 30, 1908
b. Alfven, Hannes Olof Gosta
b. Blanc, Mel(vin Jerome)

May 31, 1908
b. Ameche, Don
b. Coates, Edith
d. Frechette, Louis-Honore

June 2, 1908
b. Grauer, Ben(jamin Franklin)

June 4, 1908
b. Barbour, Walworth

June 5, 1908
b. Bickmore, Lee Smith
b. Randolph, Georgiana Ann
b. Rice, Craig

June 7, 1908
b. Goldovsky, Boris
b. Goodall, John Strickland

June 9, 1908
b. Cummings, Bob
b. Gilbertson, Mildred Geiger
b. McCracken, Branch

June 12, 1908
b. Semyonova, Marina

June 13, 1908
b. Abbott, L(enwood) B(allard)
b. Vieira Da Silva, Maria Helena
d. Bethune, Thomas Greene

June 14, 1908
b. Trotter, John Scott
d. Stanley, Frederick Arthur, Earl of Derby

June 15, 1908
b. Anderson, Vernon Ellsworth
b. Giancana, Sam

June 16, 1908
b. Sarit Thanarat

June 18, 1908
b. Collyer, Bud

June 19, 1908
b. Burdick, Quentin Northrop
b. Natwick, Mildred

June 20, 1908
b. Barr, Murray Llewellyn

June 21, 1908
d. Rimsky-Korsakov, Nikolai Andreevich

June 22, 1908
b. Livingstone, Mary

June 24, 1908
d. Cleveland, Grover

June 25, 1908
b. Quine, W(illard) V(an Orman)

June 26, 1908
b. Knowland, William Fife

June 29, 1908
b. Anderson, Leroy

July 1, 1908
b. Ali, Ahmed
b. Lauder, Estee

July 2, 1908
b. Marshall, Thurgood

July 3, 1908
b. Fisher, M(ary) F(rances) K(ennedy)
d. Harris, Joel Chandler

July 4, 1908
b. Pennell, Joseph Stanley

July 5, 1908
b. Greeley, Dana McLean
d. Lie, Jonas Laurite Idemil

July 7, 1908
b. Arnow, Harriette Louisa Simpson

July 8, 1908
b. Jordan, Louis
b. Rockefeller, Nelson A(ldrich)

July 9, 1908
b. Brown, Paul
b. White, Minor

July 10, 1908
b. Heinz, Henry John, II

July 11, 1908
b. Schell, Orville H, Jr.

July 12, 1908
b. Berle, Milton
b. Runyan, Paul Scott

July 13, 1908
b. Todd, Garfield

July 14, 1908
b. Murphy, Johnny (John Joseph)
b. Raphael, Chaim

July 21, 1908
b. Jenner, William Ezra
d. Potter, Henry Codman

July 22, 1908
b. Vanderbilt, Amy
d. Cremer, William Randal, Sir

July 23, 1908
b. Vittorini, Elio

July 24, 1908
b. Williams, Cootie

July 25, 1908
b. Peary, Harold

July 26, 1908
b. Allende Gossens, Salvador

July 27, 1908
b. Hamilton, Nancy
b. Mitchell, Joseph

July 28, 1908
b. Kerby, William Frederick

July 29, 1908
b. Kaiser, Edgar Fosburgh

July 30, 1908
b. Suhl, Yuri

July 31, 1908
b. Hagen, John Peter

August 2, 1908
b. Moore, Harry Thornton

August 3, 1908
b. Geisel, Ernesto

August 4, 1908
b. Kane, Helen
b. Lancaster, Osbert, Sir
d. Allison, William Boyd
d. Howard, Bronson Crocker

August 5, 1908
b. Holt, Harold Edward
b. Rothschild, Miriam Louisa

August 6, 1908
b. Jacobs, Helen (Hull)
b. Keener, Jefferson Ward
b. Lee, Will

August 8, 1908
b. Goldberg, Arthur Joseph
b. Morton, Arthur
d. Olbrich, Joseph Maria

August 9, 1908
b. Landolfi, Tommaso

August 10, 1908
b. Thornhill, Claude

August 11, 1908
b. Abel, I(orwith) W(ilbur)

August 13, 1908
b. Ennis, Skinnay
b. Raymond, Gene

August 15, 1908
b. Kerner, Otto

August 16, 1908
b. Maxwell, William

August 18, 1908
b. Faure, Edgar Jean

August 19, 1908
b. Knowles, Warren Perley

August 20, 1908
b. Davis, Kingsley
b. Lopez, Al(fonso Ramon)

August 21, 1908
b. Kaye, Mary Margaret Mollie

August 22, 1908
b. Cartier-Bresson, Henri

August 23, 1908
b. Adamov, Arthur

August 25, 1908
b. Heindorf, Ray
d. Becquerel, Antoine Henri

August 26, 1908
d. Pastor, Tony

August 27, 1908
b. Bradman, Donald George
b. Johnson, Lyndon B(aines)
b. Leahy, Frank

August 28, 1908
b. Peterson, Roger Tory

August 30, 1908
b. Brown, Frank Arthur, Jr.
b. Fini, Leonor
b. MacMurray, Fred(erick Martin)
d. Stewart, Alexander Peter

August 31, 1908
b. Saroyan, William
b. Sears, Robert Richardson
b. Graham, Sheilah
d. Standing Bear

September 4, 1908
b. Dmytryk, Edward
b. Wright, Richard (Nathaniel)

September 6, 1908
b. Essen, Louis
b. Lavalle, Paul
b. Ziolkowski, Korczak

September 7, 1908
b. DeBakey, Michael Ellis
b. Kaminsky, Max

September 8, 1908
b. Briggs, Austin Eugene

September 9, 1908
b. Lorjou, Bernard Joseph Pierre
b. Pavese, Cesare
b. Tomlin, Pinky

September 10, 1908
b. Adams, Eva Bertrand

September 13, 1908
b. Devereux, George

September 14, 1908
b. Gaddis, Thomas (Eugene)

September 15, 1908
b. Singleton, Penny

September 17, 1908
b. Creasey, John
d. Selfridge, Thomas Etholen

September 18, 1908
b. Ambartsumyan, Viktor
  Amazaspovich
b. Courlander, Harold

September 19, 1908
b. Waltari, Mika

September 20, 1908
b. Bestor, Arthur (Eugene)
b. Manning, Ernest (Charles)
b. Mitscherlich, Alexander
d. Sarasate, Pablo de

September 21, 1908
b. Corcos, Lucille
d. Fenollosa, Ernest Francisco

September 26, 1908
b. Marlowe, Sylvia

d. Parsons, Frank

September 27, 1908
b. Chappell, William

September 28, 1908
b. Frondizi, Arturo

October 3, 1908
b. Burke, Johnny

October 5, 1908
b. Logan, Josh(ua Lockwood)

October 6, 1908
b. Lombard, Carole
b. Price, Sammy

October 7, 1908
b. Wilson, Sunnie

October 8, 1908
b. Maltz, Albert

October 9, 1908
b. Folsom, James E(lisha)
b. Tati, Jacques

October 10, 1908
b. Chang, M(in) C(heuh), Dr.
b. Green, Johnny

October 11, 1908
b. Rolfe, Red

October 12, 1908
b. Engle, Paul (Hamilton)

October 13, 1908
d. Gilman, Daniel Coit

October 14, 1908
b. Castle, Frederick W
b. Rowley, James Joseph

October 15, 1908
b. Castagna, Bruna
b. Galbraith, John Kenneth
b. Trout, Robert

October 16, 1908
b. Ardrey, Robert
b. Hoxha, Enver

October 17, 1908
b. Johnson, U(ral) Alexis

October 19, 1908
b. Allen, Larry

October 20, 1908
b. Francis, Arlene

October 21, 1908
b. Ferguson, Howard
b. Schneider, Alexander
d. Norton, Charles Eliot

October 22, 1908
b. Sutton, John

October 23, 1908
b. Frank, Ilya Mikaylovich
b. Oistrakh, David Fyodorovich

October 26, 1908
b. Gorin, Igor

October 27, 1908
b. Krasner, Lee

October 28, 1908
b. Oppenheimer, Harry Frederick

October 29, 1908
b. Ames, Louise (Bates)

October 30, 1908
b. Ustinov, Dmitri Fedorovich

November 1, 1908
b. Wolfert, Ira

November 3, 1908
b. Leone, Giovanni
b. Nagurski, Bronko

November 4, 1908
d. Estrada Palma, Tomas

November 6, 1908
b. Canzoneri, Tony
b. Klassen, Elmer Theodore

November 8, 1908
b. Fowlie, Wallace
d. Sardou, Victorien

November 9, 1908
b. Kilgore, Bernard

November 12, 1908
b. Blackmun, Harry A(ndrew)
d. Brooks, William Keith

November 13, 1908
b. Thibault, Conrad
b. Woodward, C(omer) Vann

November 14, 1908
b. McCarthy, Joe
b. Salisbury, Harrison Evans
d. Kuang-hsu
d. Tz'u Hsi

November 16, 1908
b. Burns, John L(awrence)

November 17, 1908
b. Park, Thomas

November 19, 1908
b. Coca, Imogene Fernandez y

November 20, 1908
b. Cooke, (Alfred) Alistair

November 21, 1908
b. Politi, Leo
b. Richards, Paul Rapier
b. Speare, Elizabeth George
b. Young, Marian

November 24, 1908
b. Kemelman, Harry

November 26, 1908
b. Forte, Charles, Sir
b. Spigelgass, Leonard

November 27, 1908
b. Howells, William White

November 28, 1908
b. Levi-Strauss, Claude Gustave

November 29, 1908
b. Debus, Kurt Heinrich
b. Powell, Adam Clayton, Jr.

December 2, 1908
b. Gardner, Hy

December 3, 1908
b. Balchin, Nigel Marlin

December 4, 1908
b. Hershey, Alfred D(ay)

December 6, 1908
b. Nelson, Baby Face

December 8, 1908
b. Volpe, John A(nthony)

December 9, 1908
d. Gibbs, Oliver Wolcott

December 10, 1908
b. DeSapio, Carmine Gerard
b. Messiaen, Olivier (Eugene Prosper Charles)

December 11, 1908
b. Carter, Elliott Cook, Jr.

December 12, 1908
b. Babin, Victor

December 17, 1908
b. Ashton-Warner, Sylvia Constance
b. Libby, Willard Frank

December 18, 1908
b. Johnson, Celia, Dame
b. Siple, Paul Allman

December 21, 1908
b. Barzini, Luigi Giorgio, Jr.
b. Weaver, Pat

December 22, 1908
b. Bill, Max
b. Manzu, Giacomo

December 23, 1908
b. Karsh, Yousuf

December 25, 1908
b. Crisp, Quentin
b. Twelvetrees, Helen

December 28, 1908
b. Ayres, Lew

b. Mielke, Erich

December 31, 1908
b. Kirby, John
b. Lewyt, Alexander Milton
b. Rothmuller, Marko A
b. Wiesenthal, Simon

1909

b. Anello, John David
b. Aranason, H Harvard
b. Bello, (Alhaji Sir) Ahmadu
b. Bird, Vere Cornwall, Sr.
b. Bowen, Billy
b. Brannigan, Owen
b. Buckmaster, Henrietta
b. Cramm, Gottfried von, Baron
b. Gies, Miep
b. Harshaw, Margaret
b. Henkle, Henrietta
b. Hoving, Jane Pickens
b. Klein, Abraham Moses
b. Maddow, Ben
b. Maskell, Dan
b. Music, Antonio Zoran
b. Pious, Minerva
b. Reuther, Roy
b. Riesman, David
b. Rubirosa, Porfirio
b. Sapir, Pinchas
b. Stuckey, Williamson Sylvester
b. Walter, Marie Therese
b. Wells, George
b. Young, Marguerite (Vivian)
d. Gumplowicz, Ludwig
d. Howland, Alfred Cornelius
d. Jones, William
d. Kennedy, John Stewart
d. Red Cloud, Chief
d. Sundance Kid, The

January 1, 1909
b. Andrews, (Carver) Dana
b. Goldwater, Barry M(orris)
b. Shaaban Robert

January 3, 1909
b. Borge, Victor
b. Crankshaw, Edward

January 5, 1909
b. Aumont, Jean-Pierre
b. Kurnitz, Harry

January 6, 1909
d. Dixon, George

January 9, 1909
b. Miller, Otto Neil
b. Wood, Evelyn

January 11, 1909
b. Stander, Lionel (Jay)
d. Wharton, Joseph

January 14, 1909
b. Losey, Joseph Walton

January 15, 1909
b. Krupa, Gene
b. Siegmeister, Elie
d. Reyer, (Louis) Ernest (Etienne)

January 16, 1909
b. Greenberg, Clement
b. Merman, Ethel

January 19, 1909
b. Hotter, Hans
b. Pudney, John Sleigh

January 20, 1909
b. Eckert, William Dole

January 22, 1909
b. Sothern, Ann
b. Thant, U

January 24, 1909
b. Cassandre, A(dolphe) M(ouron)
b. Kagel, Sam
b. Todd, Ann

January 27, 1909
b. Eklund, Carl Robert
d. Coquelin, Benoit Constant

January 29, 1909
b. Marshal, Alan
b. Masur, Harold Q

January 30, 1909
b. Alinsky, Saul David
d. Finley, Martha

February 2, 1909
b. Albertson, Frank
b. Randhawa, Mohinder Singh

February 3, 1909
b. Cayatte, Andre
b. Weil, Simone

February 4, 1909
b. Coote, Robert
d. Clarkson, John Gibson

February 6, 1909
b. Blassingale, Wyatt Rainey

February 8, 1909
b. Sherrod, Robert (Lee)
d. Mendes, Catulle

February 9, 1909
b. Angel, Heather Grace
b. Rusk, (David) Dean

February 11, 1909
b. Baer, Max
b. Mankiewicz, Joseph (Leo)

February 14, 1909
b. Moss, Carlton

February 16, 1909
b. Beaumont, Hugh

February 17, 1909
b. Lawrence, Marjorie Florence
d. Geronimo

February 18, 1909
b. Stegner, Wallace (Earle)

February 19, 1909
b. Rodman, Selden

February 20, 1909
b. Alvary, Lorenzo
d. Wright, Carroll Davidson

February 21, 1909
b. Dickens, Helen Octavia

February 22, 1909
b. MacIver, Loren

February 24, 1909
b. Derleth, August (William)

February 26, 1909
b. Carroll, Madeleine
d. Ebbinghaus, Hermann

February 28, 1909
b. LaBern, Arthur Joseph
b. Soule, Olan
b. Spender, Stephen (Harold)

March 2, 1909
b. Ott, Mel(vin Thomas)

March 4, 1909
b. Helmsley, Harry B(rakmann)

March 6, 1909
b. Awolowo, Obafemi Awo

March 7, 1909
b. Magnani, Anna
b. Revelle, Roger Randall

March 8, 1909
b. Trevor, Claire

March 9, 1909
b. Tromp, Solco Walle
d. Helper, Hinton Rowan

March 10, 1909
b. Galento, Tony

March 12, 1909
b. Vila, George Raymond

March 14, 1909
b. Stern, Arthur Cecil

March 16, 1909
b. Dean, Patrick (Henry), Sir
d. Timken, Henry

March 19, 1909
b. Hayward, Louis

March 20, 1909
b. Forbes, Kathryn
b. Knipling, Edward Fred

March 22, 1909
b. Roy, Gabrielle

March 23, 1909
d. Davidson, John

March 24, 1909
d. Synge, John Millington

March 25, 1909
b. Blackton, Jay S
b. Leonard, Dutch
b. Livingston, Jerry

March 26, 1909
b. Campora, Hector Jose
b. Rafferty, Chips

March 28, 1909
b. Algren, Nelson
b. Warneke, Lon(nie)

April 1, 1909
b. Duchin, Eddy

April 2, 1909
b. Marsala, Marty
b. Zondervan, Peter

April 7, 1909
b. Jones, Joe
b. Snow, Dorothea Johnston

April 9, 1909
b. Helpmann, Robert Murray, Sir
d. Crawford, Francis Marion
d. Modjeska, Helena

April 10, 1909
b. Cannon, Jimmy
d. Swinburne, Algernon Charles

April 13, 1909
b. Welty, Eudora

April 14, 1909
d. Butler, Matthew Calbraith

April 16, 1909
b. McCoy, Charles B(relsford)

April 21, 1909
b. Coker, Elizabeth Boatwright
b. May, Rollo (Reece)

April 22, 1909
b. Levi-Montalcini, Rita

April 23, 1909
b. Hawkins, Erick

April 24, 1909
b. Grzimek, Bernhard

April 25, 1909
b. Pereira, William Leonard

April 26, 1909
b. Connor, William Neil, Sir

April 27, 1909
b. Matlock, Matty

April 29, 1909
b. Ewell, Tom

April 30, 1909
b. Juliana

May 1, 1909
b. Melachrino, George Miltiades

May 4, 1909
b. DaSilva, Howard

May 5, 1909
b. Baker, Carlos Heard

May 6, 1909
b. Christensen, Lew Farr

May 7, 1909
b. Land, Edwin Herbert

May 8, 1909
b. Fitch, James Marston

May 9, 1909
b. Bunshaft, Gordon
b. Hagerty, James Campbell

May 10, 1909
b. Carter, Mother Maybelle

May 13, 1909
b. Darby, Ken

May 15, 1909
b. Mason, James Neville

May 16, 1909
b. Luckman, Charles
b. Ward, Deighton Harcourt Lisle, Sir

May 18, 1909
b. Gidal, Tim
d. Meredith, George

May 20, 1909
b. Kunz, Erich

May 21, 1909
b. Hummel, Berta
b. Rothschild, Guy Edouard Alphonse
Paul de, Baron

May 24, 1909
b. Barrow, Clyde
b. Blaiberg, Philip
b. Mills, Wilbur Daigh

May 26, 1909
b. Anderson, Eugenie M(oore)
b. Busby, Matthew, Sir
b. Gucci, Aldo

May 27, 1909
b. Hansen, William Webster

May 28, 1909
b. Horner, Red

May 30, 1909
b. Frank, Jerome David
b. Goodman, Benny
b. Gray, Gordon

May 31, 1909
b. Coulter, Art(hur Edmund)
b. Schmitt, Gladys

June 1, 1909
b. Rowe, James Henry, Jr.

June 3, 1909
b. Lay, Herman Warden

June 4, 1909
b. Batten, William Milfred

June 6, 1909
b. Berlin, Isaiah, Sir

June 7, 1909
b. Rodino, Peter Wallace, Jr.
b. Tandy, Jessica
b. Walker, A Maceo, Sr.

June 9, 1909
b. Kutner, Luis

June 10, 1909
d. Hale, Edward Everett

June 12, 1909
b. Bleyer, Archie

June 14, 1909
b. Ives, Burl (Icle Ivanhoe)
d. Prang, Louis

June 16, 1909
b. Beilenson, Edna Rudolph
d. Albeniz, Isaac Manuel Francisco

June 18, 1909
b. Gerard, Dave

June 20, 1909
b. Flynn, Errol
b. Harrison, Joan (Mary)

June 22, 1909
b. Adler, Buddy
b. Todd, Mike

June 23, 1909
b. Li Xiannian
b. Parks, Sam(uel McLaughlin)

June 24, 1909
b. Cavanna, Betty
b. Katims, Milton
d. Jewett, Sarah Orne

June 25, 1909
b. Fuchs, Daniel

June 28, 1909
b. Ambler, Eric

June 30, 1909
b. Bosch Gavino, Juan

July 1, 1909
b. Evans, Madge
b. Onetti, Juan Carlos

July 3, 1909
b. Butz, Earl Lauer
b. Niarchos, Stavros (Spyros)

July 7, 1909
b. Apgar, Virginia
b. Herman, Billy

July 11, 1909
d. Newcomb, Simon

July 12, 1909
b. DeRita, Joe
b. Zim, Herbert S(pencer)

July 15, 1909
d. Tyrrell, George

July 16, 1909
b. Saunders, Stuart T(homas)

July 17, 1909
b. Amies, Hardy
b. Strasfogel, Ignace

July 18, 1909
b. Gromyko, Andrei Andreevich
b. Wright, John Joseph

July 20, 1909
b. Miller, William Mosley

July 22, 1909
d. Liliencron, Detlev von

July 24, 1909
b. Curtis, Alan (Harold Neberroth)

July 26, 1909
b. Thorneycroft, (George Edward)
    Peter

July 28, 1909
b. Lowry, Malcolm

July 29, 1909
b. Baker, Samm Sinclair
b. Crosby, Sumner McKnight
b. Himes, Chester Bomar

July 30, 1909
b. Parkinson, C(yril) Northcote

August 3, 1909
b. Clark, Walter van Tilburg
b. Jones, Edward Vason

August 4, 1909
b. Cunningham, Glenn Clarence

August 6, 1909
b. Craig, George N(orth)
b. Schnabel, Karl Ulrich

August 8, 1909
b. Butterfield, Lyman Henry
b. Service, John S(tewart)
d. MacKillop, Mary

August 9, 1909
b. Baur, John I(reland) H(owe)

August 10, 1909
b. Crockett, George (William), Jr.
b. Fender, Leo
b. Hughes, Richard J(oseph)

August 13, 1909
b. Beal, John

August 15, 1909
b. Winterhalter, Hugo
d. Cunha, Euclides (Rodrigues
    Pimenta) da

August 16, 1909
b. Chute, Marchette (Gaylord)
b. Koch, John

August 17, 1909
b. Clinton, Larry
b. McNally, Andrew, III

August 18, 1909
b. Carne, Marcel Albert

August 19, 1909
b. Andrzejewski, Jerzy

August 21, 1909
b. Dillon, (Clarence) Douglas

August 22, 1909
b. Darrow, Whitney, Jr.
b. Epstein, Julius
b. Epstein, Philip G
b. Hein, Mel(vin John)
b. Vronsky, Vitya

August 25, 1909
b. Keeler, Ruby

August 26, 1909
d. Fenn, George Manville

August 27, 1909
b. George, Don
b. Sexton, Leo
b. Yates, Sidney R(ichard)
b. Young, Lester Willis

August 29, 1909
b. Macready, George
b. Rennie, Michael

August 30, 1909
b. Burton, Virginia Lee

September 3, 1909
b. Bazelon, David L(ionel)

September 4, 1909
d. Fitch, (William) Clyde

September 6, 1909
b. Gordon, Michael

September 7, 1909
b. Kazan, Elia
d. Lassale, Jean

September 9, 1909
d. Harriman, Edward Henry

September 10, 1909
b. Bacon, Selden D(askam)
b. Brioni, Gaetano Savini, Marquis
b. Scott, Raymond

September 11, 1909
b. Seymour, Anne Eckert

September 12, 1909
b. Chandler, Spud
b. Howard, Eddy
b. Kintner, Robert Edmonds

September 13, 1909
b. Rhodes, James Allen

September 14, 1909
b. Eklund, John M(anly)
b. Scott, Peter Markham, Sir
d. McKim, Charles Follen

September 15, 1909
b. Batten, Jean Gardner
b. Katayama, Yutaka

September 17, 1909
b. Cole, Edward Nicholas
b. Enright, Elizabeth
b. Hightower, John Marmann

September 18, 1909
b. Darken, Lawrence Stamper

September 19, 1909
b. Porsche, Ferdinand

September 21, 1909
b. Gordon-Lazareff, Helene
b. Nkrumah, Kwame

September 22, 1909
b. Slobodkina, Esphyr

September 25, 1909
b. Glasspole, Florizel Augustus

September 27, 1909
b. Hauser, Philip M(orris)

September 28, 1909
b. Capp, Al

October 1, 1909
b. Sloane, Everett
b. Yorty, Sam(uel William)

October 2, 1909
b. Fielding, Lewis J
b. Hosking, Eric J
b. Raymond, Alex(ander Gillespie)
d. Schley, Winfield Scott

October 4, 1909
d. Chang Chih-tung

October 6, 1909
b. Carson, Robert
d. Buck, Dudley

October 7, 1909
b. Corning, Erastus, III
b. Genet, Arthur Samuel

October 8, 1909
b. Hewitt, Bill
b. Jaroszewicz, Piotr

October 9, 1909
b. Beatty, Robert
b. Coggan, Frederick Donald, Baron

October 10, 1909
b. Friebus, Florida

October 12, 1909
b. Livesay, Dorothy (Kathleen)
b. Petry, Ann (Lane)

October 13, 1909
b. Herblock

October 15, 1909
b. Patterson, Alicia

October 17, 1909
b. Cole, Cozy

October 19, 1909
b. Mott, William Penn, Jr.
d. Lombroso, Cesare

October 20, 1909
d. Lea, Henry Charles

October 25, 1909
b. Draper, Paul (Nathaniel Saltonstall)
b. Nash, Philleo

October 26, 1909
b. Lewis, Allen Montgomery, Sir
d. Howard, Oliver Otis
d. Ito, Hirobumi

October 28, 1909
b. Bacon, Francis
b. Gingold, Josef

October 30, 1909
b. Bassett, Ben
b. Bhabha, Homi Jehangir

November 1, 1909
b. Arthur, Robert

November 2, 1909
b. Berigan, Bunny
d. Frith, William Powell

November 3, 1909
b. Reston, James (Barrett)

November 4, 1909
b. Alegria, Ciro
b. Graves, Alvin Cushman

November 7, 1909
b. Krasna, Norman

November 10, 1909
b. Marks, Johnny

November 15, 1909
b. Manning, Timothy, Cardinal

November 16, 1909
d. Crittenton, Charles Nelson

November 18, 1909
b. Mercer, Johnny

November 19, 1909
b. Drucker, Peter Ferdinand
d. Laffan, William Mackay
d. Tabb, John Banister

November 20, 1909
b. Bible, Alan

November 24, 1909
b. Gerstenberg, Richard Charles

November 26, 1909
b. Gomez, Lefty
b. Ionesco, Eugene

November 27, 1909
b. Agee, James Rufus

November 28, 1909
b. Bampton, Rose Elizabeth
b. Bleeker, Sonia

December 2, 1909
b. Lash, Joseph P

December 6, 1909
b. Oboler, Arch

December 7, 1909
b. Kainen, Jacob

December 9, 1909
b. Fairbanks, Douglas, Jr.

December 10, 1909
b. Kirstein, George G

December 12, 1909
b. Moores, Dick

December 14, 1909
b. Tatum, Edward Lawrie

December 15, 1909
b. Glassco, John Stinson

December 17, 1909
d. Leopold II

December 18, 1909
b. Barrie, Mona

December 19, 1909
b. Wilson, Joseph Chamberlain

December 21, 1909
b. Ball, George W(ildman)

December 24, 1909
b. Rapacki, Adam

December 25, 1909
b. Mazurki, Mike

December 26, 1909
b. Wakeman, Frederic
d. Remington, Frederic

December 27, 1909
b. Holland, Charles
b. Jablonski, Henryk

December 31, 1909
b. Jones, Jonah

1910

b. Aarons, Ruth Hughes
b. Aflaq, Michel
b. Biossat, Bruce
b. Brousse, Amy Elizabeth Thorpe
b. Carr, Joe
b. Carre, Mathilde
b. Fagunwa, D(aniel) O(lorunfemi)
b. Gallo, Ernest
b. Gold, Harry
b. Goodman, Johnny
b. Grizodubova, Valentina
  (Stepanovna)
b. Harris, Thomas Anthony
b. Hatem, George
b. Jordan, Fred
b. Kasavubu, Joseph
b. Lauder, Joseph H
b. Lester, Jerry
b. Logan, Onnie Lee
b. Lowe, Edwin S
b. Olson, Johnny
b. Parker, Tom, Colonel
b. Passarella, Art
b. Potter, David M(orris)
b. Reddick, L(awrence) D(unbar)
b. Robinson, Joan Mary Gale Thomas
b. Sharaff, Irene
b. Sheppard, Eugenia Benbow
b. Stone, Louis
b. Tal, Josef
b. Thomas, Vivien
b. Yablonski, Joseph
b. Yard, Molly
b. Yeon, John B
d. Anderson, Willie
d. Cudahy, Michael
d. Slocum, Joshua
d. Walras, Marie Esprit Leon
d. Ward, J(ohn) Q(uincy) A(dams)

January 4, 1910
b. Crawford, James Strickland
b. Paul, Gabe

January 5, 1910
b. Brannum, Hugh

January 6, 1910
b. Kid Chocolate
b. Morris, Wright Marion

January 7, 1910
b. Faubus, Orval E(ugene)
b. Rothschild, Alain de, Baron

January 9, 1910
b. Hitch, Charles J(ohnston)

January 10, 1910
b. Allal al-Fassi, Mohamed

b. Martinon, Jean
b. Ulanova, Galina

January 11, 1910
b. Bratteli, Trygve Martin
b. Solomon, Izler

January 12, 1910
b. Kelly, Patsy

January 17, 1910
b. Catlett, Big Sid
b. Green, Edith S(tarrett)
b. Rush, (David) Kenneth
d. Crapper, Thomas
d. Nabuco de Araujo, Joaquim Aurelio

January 18, 1910
b. Boulding, Kenneth E(wart)

January 20, 1910
b. Adamson, Joy Friederike Victoria Gessner
b. Johnson, Josephine Winslow

January 23, 1910
b. Price, Don K.
b. Reinhardt, Django (Jean Baptiste)

January 25, 1910
d. Faust, Lotta

January 27, 1910
b. Candela, Felix

January 30, 1910
d. Woods, Granville T

February 4, 1910
b. Ellison, Virginia Howell

February 9, 1910
b. Monod, Jacques Lucien

February 10, 1910
b. Cebotari, Maria
b. Grenfell, Joyce Irene
b. Pire, Dominique

February 11, 1910
d. Simmons, Zalmon G

February 13, 1910
b. Cowles, Fleur Fenton
b. Halsey, Margaret (Frances)
b. Shockley, William B(radford)

February 14, 1910
b. Dragonette, Jessica

February 15, 1910
b. Aitken, Max

February 19, 1910
b. Wood, Louise Aletha

February 21, 1910
b. Bader, Douglas Robert Steuart, Sir

February 25, 1910
b. Fenwick, Millicent Hammond
d. Whittredge, Thomas Worthington

February 26, 1910
b. Gorshkov, Sergei

February 27, 1910
b. Bennett, Joan
b. DeVries, Peter
b. Johnson, Clarence Leonard
b. Sloane, Eric

February 28, 1910
b. Falter, John

March 1, 1910
b. Martin, Archer John Porter
b. Niven, David

March 4, 1910
b. Boothroyd, John Basil

March 6, 1910
d. Platt, Thomas Collier

March 9, 1910
b. Barber, Samuel
b. Gault, William Campbell

March 12, 1910
b. Stevens, Roger L(acey)

March 17, 1910
b. Rustin, Bayard
b. Werblin, Sonny

March 18, 1910
b. Tarnower, Herman

March 21, 1910
b. Gallo, Julio
d. Nadar

March 22, 1910
b. Monsarrat, Nicholas John Turney

March 23, 1910
b. Kurosawa, Akira

March 24, 1910
b. Conte, Richard

March 27, 1910
b. Pierce, John Robinson
d. Agassiz, Alexander Emmanuel Rodolphe

March 28, 1910
b. O'Keefe, Dennis
d. Brewer, David Josiah
d. Colonne, Edouard

April 1, 1910
b. Carney, Harry Howell
b. Lidz, Theodore

April 2, 1910
b. Herber, Arnie

April 6, 1910
b. Teague, Olin E

April 9, 1910
b. Ribicoff, Abraham A(lexander)

April 10, 1910
b. Wauneka, Annie Dodge

April 11, 1910
b. Clapp, Margaret Antoinette
b. Spinola, Antonio (Sebastiao Ribeiro) de

April 12, 1910
d. Sumner, William Graham

April 19, 1910
b. Walters, Bucky

April 20, 1910
b. Wagner, Robert Ferdinand, Jr.

April 21, 1910
d. Twain, Mark

April 24, 1910
b. Joseph, Richard

April 25, 1910
b. Hirsch, Joseph

April 26, 1910
b. Tanaka, Tomoyuki
d. Bjornson, Bjornstjerne Martinius

April 27, 1910
b. Fischer, John

April 28, 1910
b. Borch, Fred J.
b. Robinson, Francis Arthur

April 29, 1910
b. Walker, Eric A(rthur)

May 1, 1910
b. Battles, Cliff(ord Franklin)
b. Hynek, J(oseph) Allen
b. Rockefeller, Mary French

May 3, 1910
b. Corwin, Norman
b. Massey, D Curtis
d. Ricketts, Howard T

May 5, 1910
b. Burton, Glenn W(illard)
b. Lionni, Leo

May 6, 1910
d. Edward VII

May 8, 1910
b. Williams, Mary Lou

May 9, 1910
b. Woodhouse, Barbara Blackburn
b. Young, Philip

May 10, 1910
b. Berne, Eric Lennard
b. Demaret, Jimmy
d. Cannizzaro, Stanislao

May 11, 1910
b. Cochran, Jacqueline

May 12, 1910
b. Hodgkin, Dorothy Mary Crowfoot
b. Jenkins, Gordon
d. Huggins, William, Sir

May 14, 1910
b. Pully, B S

May 15, 1910
b. Cummings, Constance

May 18, 1910
b. Taylor, Phoebe Atwood
d. Viardot-Garcia, Pauline

May 22, 1910
d. Renard, Jules

May 23, 1910
b. Brown, Margaret Wise
b. Crothers, Scatman
b. Shaw, Artie

May 26, 1910
b. Lopez Mateos, Adolfo
b. Rockefeller, Laurance Spelman

May 28, 1910
b. Kempson, Rachel
b. Takhtadzhian, Armen Leonovich
b. Walker, T-Bone
d. Balakirev, Mili Alekseyevich
d. Koch, Robert

May 30, 1910
b. Metcalfe, Ralph H

May 31, 1910
d. Blackwell, Elizabeth

June 1, 1910
b. Heatherton, Ray(mond Joseph)
d. Haden, Francis Seymour, Sir

June 2, 1910
d. Petipa, Marius

June 3, 1910
b. Hollowood, Albert Bernard

June 4, 1910
b. Cockerell, Christopher (Sydney), Sir

June 5, 1910
d. Henry, O

June 7, 1910
b. Annigoni, Pietro
d. Smith, Goldwin

June 8, 1910
b. Beck, C(harles) C(larence)
b. Bombal, Maria Luisa
b. Campbell, John W

June 10, 1910
b. Haydon, Julie
b. Howlin' Wolf

June 11, 1910
b. Coppola, Carmine
b. Cousteau, Jacques (Yves)

b. Geneen, Harold S(ydney)

June 13, 1910
b. Christ-Janer, Albert

June 14, 1910
b. Kempe, Rudolf

June 15, 1910
b. Rose, David

June 16, 1910
b. Albertson, Jack
b. Massey, Ilona
b. Velasco Alvarado, Juan

June 17, 1910
b. Foley, Red

June 18, 1910
b. Foran, Dick John Nicholas
b. Long, Avon
b. Marshall, E(dda) G(unnar)
b. McKinley, Ray
b. Tourel, Jennie

June 19, 1910
b. Flory, Paul John
b. Fortas, Abe

June 22, 1910
b. Dunham, Katherine
b. Hunt, John, Baron
b. Pears, Peter, Sir

June 23, 1910
b. Anouilh, Jean Marie Lucien Pierre
b. Little, Lawson
b. Morgan, Edward P

June 24, 1910
b. Kaufman, Irving R(obert)

June 26, 1910
b. Mellon, William Larimer, Jr.
b. Nowicki, Matthew

June 29, 1910
b. Loesser, Frank Henry

June 30, 1910
b. Graham, Winston Mawdesley
b. Allard, Sydney

July 1, 1910
b. Piret, Edgar L

July 2, 1910
b. Robinson, Earl Hawley

July 3, 1910
b. Barrett, Edward Ware

July 4, 1910
b. Hayes, Alfred
b. Larson, (Lewis) Arthur
b. Templeton, Alec
d. Schiaparelli, Giovanni

July 5, 1910
b. Arran, Arthur Kattendyke Strange
David Archibald Gore, Earl of

b. Merton, Robert King

July 6, 1910
b. Kirsten, Dorothy

July 7, 1910
b. Tunnard, Christopher

July 10, 1910
b. Bunting, Mary Ingraham
b. Nguyen Huu Tho

July 11, 1910
b. Blane, Sally

July 12, 1910
b. Faye, Joey
d. Rolls, Charles Stewart

July 14, 1910
b. Annabella
b. Hanna, William Denby

July 18, 1910
b. Baker, Elbert Hall, II
b. Velez, Lupe

July 20, 1910
b. Wedgwood, C(icely) V(eronica)

July 22, 1910
b. Moorehead, Alan
b. Stevens, Edmund William

July 24, 1910
b. Horner, Harry
b. Vera

July 28, 1910
b. Goodwin, Bill

July 31, 1910
d. Carlisle, John Griffin

August 4, 1910
b. Birnie, William Alfred Hart
b. Schuman, William Howard

August 6, 1910
b. Crichton, Charles

August 8, 1910
b. Sidney, Sylvia

August 9, 1910
b. Tobin, Richard L(ardner)

August 10, 1910
b. Mohammed V
d. Gans, Joe

August 11, 1910
b. Homans, George Caspar

August 12, 1910
b. Ishak, Yusof bin
b. Sutermeister, Heinrich

August 13, 1910
b. Said bin Taimur
b. Spectorsky, Auguste Compte

d. Nightingale, Florence

August 15, 1910
b. Kuchel, Thomas H(enry)

August 20, 1910
b. Saarinen, Eero

August 23, 1910
b. Cromley, Raymond Avolon

August 26, 1910
b. Wells, Edward
d. James, William

August 27, 1910
b. Teresa, Mother

August 28, 1910
b. Graves, Morris Cole
b. Koopmans, Tjalling (Charles)

August 30, 1910
b. Fisk, James Brown

August 31, 1910
b. Baker, Charlotte

September 2, 1910
d. Rousseau, Henri

September 3, 1910
b. Maynor, Dorothy

September 4, 1910
b. Celebrezze, Anthony J(oseph)

September 5, 1910
d. Haberl, Franz Xaver

September 7, 1910
b. Stahl, Ben(jamin Albert)
d. Blackwell, Emily
d. Hunt, Holman

September 8, 1910
b. Barrault, Jean-Louis

September 10, 1910
b. Reeves, Rosser

September 11, 1910
b. Schroder, Gerhard

September 12, 1910
b. Engel, Lehman
b. Fields, Shep

September 13, 1910
b. Berry, Chu

September 14, 1910
b. Hawkins, Jack
b. Liebermann, Rolf

September 19, 1910
b. Lasky, Jesse Louis, Jr.
b. Lindsay, Margaret

September 23, 1910
b. Roosevelt, Elliott

September 24, 1910
b. Walker, Dixie

September 25, 1910
d. Mills, Darius Ogden

September 28, 1910
b. Macapagal, Diosdado P(angan)

September 29, 1910
b. Boyd, Bill
b. Bruce, Virginia
b. Frankovich, Mike J
d. Davis, Rebecca Blaine Harding
d. Homer, Winslow

October 1, 1910
b. Parker, Bonnie

October 2, 1910
b. Carmichael, James Vinson

October 3, 1910
b. Hines, John E(lbridge)
d. Taylor, Lucy Beaman Hobbs

October 8, 1910
b. Hall, Gus

October 9, 1910
b. Graham, Wallace H(arry)
b. Robert, Paul

October 10, 1910
b. Daniel, Price

October 11, 1910
b. Alsop, Joseph Wright, Jr.

October 12, 1910
b. Fitzgerald, Robert Stuart
b. Funston, George Keith

October 13, 1910
b. Gann, Ernest Kellogg
b. McCrary, Tex
b. Tatum, Art(hur)

October 14, 1910
b. Guinan, Matthew
b. Wooden, John Robert

October 15, 1910
d. Ketchel, Stanley

October 17, 1910
b. Cherberg, John A(ndrew)
d. Howe, Julia Ward
d. Moody, William Vaughn

October 19, 1910
b. Chandrasekhar, Subrahmanyan

October 23, 1910
b. Fredericks, Carlton
b. Rorke, Hayden
d. Chulalongkorn

October 25, 1910
b. Higinbotham, William A(lfred)
b. Lichine, David

October 26, 1910
b. Krol, John (Joseph), Cardinal

October 27, 1910
b. Carson, Jack
b. DeCordova, Frederick Timmins

October 28, 1910
b. Kamp, Irene Kittle

October 29, 1910
b. Ayer, Alfred Jules, Sir

October 30, 1910
d. Dunant, Jean Henri

November 8, 1910
b. Kane, Harnett T(homas)
b. Voit, Willard Darby

November 13, 1910
b. Huie, William Bradford

November 14, 1910
b. Arnon, Daniel I(srael)
b. DeCamp, Rosemary
d. LaFarge, John

November 15, 1910
b. Greene, Hugh (Carleton), Sir

November 17, 1910
b. Wiley, W(illiam) Bradford

November 20, 1910
b. Murray, Pauli
d. Tolstoy, Leo Nikolayevich

November 22, 1910
b. Smith, Ethel

November 23, 1910
d. Chanute, Octave
d. Crippen, Hawley Harvey

November 24, 1910
b. Fitzgerald, Pegeen

November 26, 1910
b. Cusack, Cyril
b. Kahane, Melanie

December 1, 1910
b. Markova, Alicia, Dame

December 2, 1910
b. Lynes, Joseph Russell, Jr.
b. Paige, Robert (John Arthur)

December 3, 1910
d. Eddy, Mary Baker Morse
d. Merritt, Wesley

December 4, 1910
b. North, Alex
b. Venkataraman, Ramaswamy

December 7, 1910
b. Furtseva, Ekaterina Alexeyevna
b. Goldman, Richard Franko

December 11, 1910
b. Sauer, George (Henry)

December 12, 1910
b. Leser, Tina

December 13, 1910
b. Grene, Marjorie
b. Heflin, Van Emmett Evan
b. Roth, Lillian

December 15, 1910
b. Hammond, John Henry, Jr.

December 17, 1910
b. Oliver, Sy

December 18, 1910
b. Burrows, Abe

December 19, 1910
b. Genet, Jean

December 20, 1910
b. Conacher, Charlie
d. Neumann, Angelo

December 24, 1910
b. Ayres, Mitchell

December 25, 1910
b. Leiber, Fritz (Reuter), Jr.

December 27, 1910
b. Olson, Charles John

December 30, 1910
b. Bowles, Paul (Frederick)

December 31, 1910
b. Kollmar, Richard

1911

b. Armstrong, Jack Lawrence
b. Bannon, Jim
b. Bernstein, Allan
b. Boswell, Vet
b. Bourgeois, Louise
b. Burgess, Guy Francis de Moncy
b. Delmar, Kenny
b. Finney, Jack
b. Gluckman, Max
b. Imam, Alhadji Abubakar
b. McIlhenny, Walter S
b. Musso, George Francis
b. Rempp, Adolph
b. Shils, Edward Albert
b. Stone, Harold J
b. Thomas, Michel
d. Bell, Joseph
d. Bigelow, John
d. Crow Dog
d. Holly, James Theodore
d. Klyuchevsky, Vasily Osipovich
d. Lewis, Edmonia
d. Richards, Ellen Henrietta Swallow

January 1, 1911
b. DuPont, Pierre Samuel, III
b. Greenberg, Hank

b. Wurdemann, Audrey May

January 2, 1911
b. Glass, David Victor

January 3, 1911
b. Hazam, Lou(is J)
b. Rauh, Joseph Louis, Jr.

January 4, 1911
d. Ray, Charlotte E.

January 6, 1911
b. Adams, Joey

January 7, 1911
b. Baker, Laura Nelson
b. McQueen, Butterfly
b. Thompson, Vivian Laubach

January 8, 1911
b. Hadley, Reed
b. Watt, George Willard

January 10, 1911
b. Kirkpatrick, Ralph Leonard

January 11, 1911
b. Suzuki, Zenko

January 12, 1911
b. Almond, Gabriel Abraham
b. Bjelke-Petersen, Johannes

January 13, 1911
b. Mecom, John Whitfield

January 15, 1911
b. Feuer, Cy

January 16, 1911
b. Dean, Dizzy
b. Frei, Eduardo

January 17, 1911
b. McCain, John Sidney, Jr.
b. Nickerson, Albert L(indsay)
d. Galton, Francis, Sir

January 18, 1911
b. Arguedas, Jose Maria

January 19, 1911
b. Jackson, Busher

January 20, 1911
b. Hill, Abram

January 22, 1911
b. Kreisky, Bruno
b. Powell, Gordon George

January 23, 1911
b. Eifert, Virginia Snider

January 24, 1911
b. Mathieson, Muir
d. Philips, David Graham

January 26, 1911
b. Kusch, P(olycarp)

January 27, 1911
b. Venuta, Benay

January 28, 1911
b. Metcalf, Lee
b. Miller, Max
b. Moss, Arnold

January 29, 1911
b. Eldridge, Roy

January 30, 1911
b. Foyle, Christina Agnes Lilian
b. Sanderson, Ivan Terence

January 31, 1911
b. Ivan, Tommy

February 2, 1911
b. Bjoerling, Jussi

February 3, 1911
b. Creavy, Tom

February 6, 1911
b. Gage, Harlow W
b. Reagan, Ronald (Wilson)

February 8, 1911
b. Bishop, Elizabeth

February 9, 1911
b. Snively, William Daniel, Jr.
b. Walker, David Harry

February 11, 1911
b. Cairncross, Alexander Kirkland, Sir

February 12, 1911
b. Guzman, Antonio
b. O'Dalaigh, Cearbhall

February 13, 1911
b. Muir, Jean

February 14, 1911
b. Kolff, Willem Johan
b. Porter, Bernard H

February 15, 1911
b. Woodcock, Leonard Freel

February 16, 1911
b. Porter, Hal
d. Earle, Alice Morse

February 17, 1911
b. Hunnicutt, Arthur
b. Tucker, Orrin

February 19, 1911
b. Oberon, Merle

February 20, 1911
b. Grahame, Margot

February 21, 1911
b. Boyle, Harold Vincent

February 22, 1911
d. Harper, Frances Ellen Watkins

February 23, 1911
b. Allen, Walter Ernest
b. Williams, G(erhard) Mennen
d. Quanah

February 25, 1911
d. Parker, Quanah
d. Spielhagen, Friedrich von

March 1, 1911
d. Hoff, Jacobus Henricus van't
d. Van't Hoff, Jacobus Henricus

March 3, 1911
b. Harlow, Jean

March 7, 1911
d. Fogazzaro, Antonio

March 8, 1911
b. Hovhaness, Alan
b. Mitchell, Clarence M

March 10, 1911
b. Anderson, Warner

March 11, 1911
b. Mitchell, Howard (Bundy)

March 12, 1911
b. Diaz Ordaz, Gustavo
b. Moats, Alice-Leone

March 13, 1911
b. Hubbard, L(afayette) Ron(ald)

March 14, 1911
b. Bode, Carl

March 15, 1911
b. Allen, Ivan, Jr.

March 16, 1911
b. Bedford, Sybille
b. La Tour du Pin, Patrice de
b. Mengele, Josef

March 17, 1911
b. Gilbreth, Frank Bunker, Jr.

March 18, 1911
b. Burnette, Smiley

March 19, 1911
b. Colonius, Lillian
b. Witte, Erich

March 20, 1911
b. Garcia Robles, Alfonso

March 21, 1911
b. Hawkins, Walter Lincoln

March 22, 1911
b. Barron, Blue

March 23, 1911
b. Ruby, Jack

March 24, 1911
b. Barbera, Joseph Roland

b. Jorda, Enrique

March 25, 1911
b. Thompson, Bradbury James

March 26, 1911
b. Austin, John Langshaw
b. Katz, Bernard, Sir
b. Williams, Tennessee
d. Williams, Henry Sylvester

March 31, 1911
b. Golden, William
b. Hamer, Robert
b. Kingman, Dong Moy Shu
b. Liebow, Averill A(braham)

April 1, 1911
d. Knapp, Seaman Asahel

April 3, 1911
b. DiDonato, Pietro
b. Walsh, Stella

April 5, 1911
b. Revolta, Johnny

April 6, 1911
b. Lynen, Feodor Felix Konrad

April 8, 1911
b. Calvin, Melvin

April 10, 1911
b. Schumann, Maurice
d. Loyd, Sam(uel)

April 11, 1911
b. Saudek, Robert
d. Harjo, Chitto

April 13, 1911
d. Keith, William

April 14, 1911
d. Joss, Addie

April 16, 1911
b. Roueche, Berton

April 17, 1911
b. Elisofon, Eliot
b. Hayes, Alfred
b. Seaton, George

April 18, 1911
b. Goldhaber, Maurice
b. Hartford, Huntington

April 19, 1911
b. Williams, Ursula Moray

April 20, 1911
b. Kukrit Pramoj, Momrajawong
(M.R.)

April 21, 1911
b. Warren, Leonard

April 22, 1911
b. Atwater, Edith

April 23, 1911
b. Cyrankiewicz, Josef

April 24, 1911
b. Leonard, Jack E
b. Schiller, Karl (August Fritz)

April 26, 1911
b. Raskin, A(braham) H(enry)

May 3, 1911
b. Lawson, Yank
b. Margolius, Sidney Senier

May 5, 1911
b. Loveless, Herschel C(ellel)

May 6, 1911
b. Ballantrae, Lord

May 8, 1911
b. Flesch, Rudolf (Franz)
b. Johnson, Robert

May 9, 1911
b. Simeone, Harry
d. Higginson, Thomas Wentworth
Storrow

May 11, 1911
b. Silvers, Phil

May 13, 1911
b. Sullivan, Maxine

May 14, 1911
b. Curtis, Thomas B(radford)

May 15, 1911
b. Frisch, Max

May 17, 1911
b. Kerr, Clark
b. O'Sullivan, Maureen
b. Rosenfeld, Henry J

May 18, 1911
b. Gurie, Sigrid
b. Turner, Joe
d. Mahler, Gustav

May 21, 1911
b. Haviland, Virginia
b. Hurkos, Peter
d. Fleming, Williamina Paton Stevens

May 22, 1911
d. Miller, Elizabeth Smith

May 24, 1911
b. Ne Win, U

May 25, 1911
b. Barnet, Will

May 26, 1911
b. Alexander, Ben

May 27, 1911
b. Hirschfelder, Joseph Oakland
b. Humphrey, Hubert Horatio, Jr.
b. Kollek, Teddy

b. Price, Vincent

May 28, 1911
b. Churchill, Randolph Frederick
Edward Spencer

May 29, 1911
d. Gilbert, William S(chwenck), Sir

May 30, 1911
d. Bradley, Milton

May 31, 1911
b. Allais, Maurice

June 4, 1911
b. Carlson, Edward Elmer
b. Russell, Rosalind

June 6, 1911
b. Aardema, Verna Norberg
b. Laing, Hugh
d. Harrigan, Edward

June 9, 1911
b. McCarty, Maclyn
b. Terra, Daniel J(ames)
d. Nation, Carry A(melia Moore)

June 10, 1911
b. Rattigan, Terence Mervyn, Sir

June 11, 1911
b. Miles, Josephine
b. Nebel, Long John

June 12, 1911
b. Djilas, Milovan

June 13, 1911
b. Agyeman, Jaramogi Abebe
b. Alvarez, Luis W(alter)
b. Hays, Wayne Levere
b. Mueller, Erwin Wilhelm
b. Root, Oren

June 15, 1911
b. Awdry, W(ilbert Vere)

June 17, 1911
b. Stigler, George Joseph

June 19, 1911
b. Senanayake, Dudley Shelton

June 20, 1911
b. Patrick, Gail

June 23, 1911
b. Ogilvy, David Mackenzie

June 24, 1911
b. Fangio, Juan Manuel
b. Sabato, Ernesto

June 25, 1911
b. Stein, William Howard

June 26, 1911
b. Levi, Edward Hirsch

June 29, 1911
b. Bernhard, Prince
b. Herrmann, Bernard
b. Josefsberg, Milt

June 30, 1911
b. Milosz, Czeslaw

July 1, 1911
b. Rey, Alvino

July 2, 1911
d. Mottl, Felix

July 4, 1911
b. Miller, Mitch(ell William)
b. Moninari-Pradelli, Francesco

July 5, 1911
b. Pompidou, Georges Jean Raymond
d. Stoney, George Johnstone

July 7, 1911
b. Menotti, Gian Carlo

July 8, 1911
b. Ball, John Dudley, Jr.

July 9, 1911
b. Peake, Mervyn Laurence

July 14, 1911
b. Terry-Thomas

July 16, 1911
b. Rogers, Ginger
b. Tufts, Sonny

July 18, 1911
b. Cronyn, Hume

July 21, 1911
b. McLuhan, (Herbert) Marshall
b. Polk, Ralph Lane

July 24, 1911
b. Martinson, Joseph Bertram
b. Widgery, John Passmore, Baron

July 25, 1911
b. Krauss, Ruth Ida

July 29, 1911
b. Furcolo, (John) Foster
b. Iakovos, Demetrios A Coucouzis,
Archbishop

July 31, 1911
b. Liberace, George J

August 1, 1911
d. Abbey, Edwin Austin

August 2, 1911
d. Mansfield, Arabella

August 5, 1911
b. Taylor, Robert

August 6, 1911
b. Ball, Lucille (Desiree)

August 7, 1911
b. Ray, Nicholas
d. Allen, Elizabeth Ann Chase Akers

August 9, 1911
b. Fowler, William A(lfred)
d. Gates, John Warne

August 10, 1911
b. Chodorov, Jerome
b. Elkin, Benjamin

August 11, 1911
b. Kittikachorn, Thanom
b. McCormick, Robert K

August 12, 1911
b. Cantinflas
b. Downes, Edward Olin Davenport
d. Israels, Josef

August 13, 1911
b. Bernbach, William
b. Parsons, James

August 16, 1911
b. Schumacher, E(rnst) F(riedrich)

August 17, 1911
b. Botvinnik, Mikhail (Moisseyevich)
b. Rosenfeld, Harry N(athan)
d. Reed, Myrtle

August 24, 1911
b. Lay, James Selden, Jr.

August 26, 1911
b. Lanin, Lester

August 28, 1911
b. Luns, Joseph Marie Antoine Hubert

August 29, 1911
b. Charnley, John, Sir
b. Conover, Harry

September 2, 1911
b. Harrah, Bill

September 6, 1911
b. Lipsky, Eleazar

September 7, 1911
b. Haughton, Daniel Jeremiah
b. Zhivkov, Todor Khristov

September 8, 1911
b. Gibbons, Euell

September 9, 1911
b. Goodman, Paul
b. Gorton, John Grey, Sir

September 10, 1911
b. Grubert, Carl Alfred

September 13, 1911
b. Monroe, Bill

September 14, 1911
d. Stolypin, Piotr Arkadevich

September 15, 1911
b. Terry, Luther Leonidas

September 16, 1911
b. Wald, Jerry
d. Whymper, Edward

September 18, 1911
b. LePoer Trench, Brinsley

September 19, 1911
b. Golding, William (Gerald), Sir

September 21, 1911
b. Engle, Clair

September 23, 1911
b. Moss, Frank Edward

September 24, 1911
b. Chernenko, Konstantin Ustinovich

September 25, 1911
b. Williams, Eric Eustace

September 28, 1911
b. Howe, Syd(ney Harris)
b. Vines, Ellsworth

October 1, 1911
b. Boland, Edward P(atrick)
b. Hickman, Herman Michael, Jr.
b. Knebel, Fletcher

October 3, 1911
b. Hordern, Michael
d. Dilthey, Wilhelm Christian Ludwig

October 6, 1911
b. Castle, Barbara Anne Betts

October 7, 1911
b. Jones, Jo(nathan)
b. Monroe, Vaughn
d. Jackson, John Hughlings

October 8, 1911
d. Binet, Alfred

October 9, 1911
b. Morgan, Russell H(edley)
b. Rosenthal, Joe

October 11, 1911
b. Cherkassky, Shura
b. Hunter, Ivory Joe

October 14, 1911
b. Le Duc Tho
d. Harlan, John Marshall, I

October 18, 1911
b. Mahesh Yogi, Maharishi

October 21, 1911
b. Graves, Peter

October 24, 1911
b. Kelley, Clarence Marion
b. Terry, Sonny
d. Lewis, Ida

October 25, 1911
b. Jackson, Mahalia

October 26, 1911
b. Chern, Shiing-shen
b. Gillman, Sidney

October 27, 1911
b. Erickson, Leif

October 29, 1911
d. Pulitzer, Joseph

November 1, 1911
b. Jones, Jenkin Lloyd
b. Kerst, Donald W(illiam)
b. Troyat, Henri

November 2, 1911
b. Elytis, Odysseus

November 3, 1911
b. Lubell, Samuel
b. Ussachevsky, Vladimir Alexis
d. Colman, Norman Jay

November 4, 1911
b. Lee, Dixie
b. Medwick, Joe

November 5, 1911
b. Rogers, Roy
b. Stader, Maria

November 6, 1911
b. Bosustow, Stephen

November 9, 1911
d. Pyle, Howard

November 10, 1911
b. Andrews, Harry

November 11, 1911
b. Knowles, Patric
b. Matta, Roberto Sebastian Antonio
  Echaurren

November 12, 1911
b. Clayton, Buck

November 13, 1911
b. O'Neil, Buck

November 18, 1911
b. McKenney, Ruth

November 20, 1911
b. Hanfmann, George Maxim Anossov

November 22, 1911
b. Cacers, Ernest

November 24, 1911
b. Grant, Kirby
d. Dryden, John Fairfield

November 25, 1911
b. Hogarth, Burne

November 26, 1911
b. Reshevsky, Samuel

November 30, 1911
b. Schriner, Sweeney

December 1, 1911
b. Alston, Walter Emmons

December 3, 1911
b. Suesse, Dana Nadine

December 4, 1911
b. Payne, Robert

December 5, 1911
b. Manessier, Alfred

December 6, 1911
b. Berger, Samuel David

December 7, 1911
b. Seibert, Earl Walter

December 9, 1911
b. Cobb, Lee J
b. Crawford, Broderick

December 10, 1911
b. Huntley, Chet
b. Pan, Hermes

December 11, 1911
b. Mahfouz, Naguib
d. Ball, Thomas

December 12, 1911
b. Dassin, Jules

December 13, 1911
b. Haavelmo, Trygve Magnus
b. Patchen, Kenneth

December 14, 1911
b. Jones, Spike

December 15, 1911
b. Dallis, Nicholas Peter

December 16, 1911
b. Jacobson, Leon Orris

December 17, 1911
b. Sale, Richard Bernard

December 20, 1911
b. Calisher, Hortense

December 21, 1911
b. Gibson, Josh(ua)

December 22, 1911
b. Reber, Grote
b. Treece, Henry
d. Robinson, Harriet Jane Hanson

December 23, 1911
b. Gregory, James
b. Jerne, Niels Kaj

December 25, 1911
b. Langley, Noel

December 27, 1911
b. Russell, Anna

December 28, 1911
b. Levenson, Sam(uel)

December 29, 1911
b. Fuchs, Klaus

December 30, 1911
b. Friendly, Alfred
b. Nolan, Jeanette

1912

b. August, Jan
b. Beale, Betty
b. Bernard, Bruno
b. Honda, Ishiro
b. Hovland, Carl I.
b. Ising, Rudolf C
b. Mackendrick, Alexander
b. McCulloch, Robert P
b. Morgan, Rose Meta
b. Odinga, Ajuma Jaramogi
b. Popov, Dusko
b. Porter, Don
b. Siad Barre, Mohamed
b. Sisulu, Walter Max Ulyate
b. Smith, Tony
b. Souphanouvong, Prince
b. Sullivan, Daniel P
b. Tanny, Vic
d. Scott, Clarence

January 1, 1912
b. Philby, Kim

January 3, 1912
d. Evans, Robley Dunglison

January 4, 1912
b. Helmore, Tom

January 6, 1912
b. Manfred, Frederick Feikema

January 7, 1912
b. Addams, Charles Samuel
b. Bundy, Robert F.

January 8, 1912
b. Ferrer, Jose Vicente
b. Walsh, Lawrence E

January 11, 1912
b. Lewis, Roger
b. Rowe, Schoolboy

January 12, 1912
b. Rainer, Luise
b. Young, Trummy

January 14, 1912
b. Olsen, Tillie

January 15, 1912
b. Debre, Michel (Jean Pierre)

January 16, 1912
b. Dennis, Nigel Forbes

January 17, 1912
b. Landis, Frederick

January 18, 1912
b. Sansom, William
d. Winkelmann, Hermann

January 19, 1912
b. Kantorovich, Leonid Vital'evich

January 21, 1912
b. Bloch, Konrad Emil

January 26, 1912
b. Baird, Cora Eisenberg
b. Cannon, Howard Walter
b. Sheinwold, Alfred

January 28, 1912
b. Pollock, Jackson
b. Wolfson, Louis Elwood
d. Alfaro, Jose Eloy

January 30, 1912
b. Tuchman, Barbara Wertheim

February 2, 1912
b. Lane, Burton

February 3, 1912
b. Carlisle, Mary
b. Patrick, Lynn
b. Soustelle, Jacques

February 4, 1912
b. Leinsdorf, Erich
b. Nelson, Byron
b. Richardson, Scovel

February 6, 1912
b. Braun, Eva
b. Scott, Adrian

February 7, 1912
b. Drysdale, George Russell
d. Blyden, Edward Wilmot

February 9, 1912
b. Moorer, Thomas H(inman)

February 10, 1912
b. Baum, Herbert (M.)
d. Lister, Joseph
d. Rio Branco, Barao do

February 11, 1912
b. Faiz, Faiz Ahmad
b. Firkusny, Rudolf
b. Fuller, Roy Broadbent

February 12, 1912
b. Delderfield, Ronald Frederick

February 14, 1912
b. Harrington, Oliver W(endell)

February 17, 1912
b. Norton, Andre
b. Sorensen, Virginia

February 19, 1912
b. Buttigieg, Anton
b. Chaplin, Saul
b. Chapman, Ceil
b. Kenton, Stan(ley Newcomb)

February 20, 1912
b. Boulle, Pierre Francois Marie-Louis
b. Humphrey, Muriel Fay Buck

February 24, 1912
b. Trnka, Jiri

February 25, 1912
b. Frobe, Gerd

February 26, 1912
b. Hunter, Floyd

February 27, 1912
b. Durrell, Lawrence (George)

February 28, 1912
b. Petacci, Claretta
b. Walsh, Michael Patrick

March 4, 1912
b. Leitner, Ferdinand

March 9, 1912
b. Vaughan, Arky

March 12, 1912
b. Brown, Les(ter Raymond)
b. Spyropoulos, Jannis

March 13, 1912
b. Youskevitch, Igor

March 14, 1912
b. Claytor, W(illiam) Graham, Jr.
b. Millett, John D(avid)
b. Wirtz, William Willard

March 15, 1912
b. Hopkins, Lightnin'

March 16, 1912
b. Nixon, Patricia
b. Rosenthal, Jean E

March 17, 1912
b. Stydahar, Joe
d. Melville, George Wallace

March 18, 1912
b. Lawrence, Robert

March 19, 1912
b. Galland, Adolf
b. Wheeler, Hugh Callingham

March 21, 1912
b. Bull, Peter

March 22, 1912
b. Brambell, Wilfrid
b. Martin, Agnes
b. Modl, Martha

March 23, 1912
b. Cameron, Eleanor Frances

b. VonBraun, Wernher

March 24, 1912
b. Height, Dorothy Irene

March 27, 1912
b. Callaghan, James
d. Scott, Robert Falcon

March 28, 1912
b. Damas, Leon-Gontran
b. Taoka Kazuo

March 29, 1912
b. Reitsch, Hanna

March 30, 1912
d. May, Karl Friedrich

March 31, 1912
b. Lederer, William Julius
b. Lee, Robert E(mmet)

April 2, 1912
b. Mills, Herbert

April 3, 1912
b. Eden, Dorothy

April 4, 1912
b. Chorell, Walentin
d. Funk, Isaac Kauffman

April 6, 1912
d. Pascoli, Giovanni

April 7, 1912
b. Hay, Harry
b. Lawrence, Jack

April 8, 1912
b. Brunner, Alois
b. Henie, Sonja

April 9, 1912
b. Borglum, James Lincoln Delamothe

April 10, 1912
b. Hinkle, W Clarke
b. Hofheinz, Roy Mark

April 11, 1912
b. George, Graham Elias

April 12, 1912
d. Barton, Clara Harlowe

April 15, 1912
b. Kim Il Sung
d. Futrelle, Jacques
d. Straus, Isidor

April 16, 1912
b. Williams, Garth Montgomery

April 18, 1912
b. Barrie, Wendy

April 19, 1912
b. Seaborg, Glenn T(heodore)

April 20, 1912
b. Chipperfield, Joseph Eugene
d. Stoker, Bram

April 21, 1912
b. Camus, Marcel

April 22, 1912
b. Ferrier, Kathleen

April 24, 1912
b. Kane, Robert Joseph
b. Wunder, George S

April 25, 1912
b. Blitch, Iris F(aircloth)

April 28, 1912
b. Sansom, Odette Marie Celine

April 29, 1912
b. Carlson, Richard

April 30, 1912
b. Arden, Eve

May 1, 1912
b. Rockefeller, Winthrop

May 2, 1912
b. Springer, Axel Caesar
d. Davenport, Homer Calvin

May 3, 1912
b. Bay, Howard
b. Fox, Virgil Keel
b. Sarton, May

May 4, 1912
d. Stevens, Nettie Maria

May 5, 1912
b. Dolbier, Maurice (Wyman)

May 8, 1912
b. Lev, Ray

May 9, 1912
b. Armendariz, Pedro

May 10, 1912
b. Viscardi, Henry, Jr.

May 11, 1912
b. Brooks, Foster Murrell

May 13, 1912
b. Evans, Gil

May 14, 1912
d. Strindberg, August

May 15, 1912
b. Berger, Arthur

May 16, 1912
b. Terkel, Studs (Louis)

May 17, 1912
b. Cox, Archibald

May 18, 1912
b. Brooks, Richard
b. Como, Perry
b. Crosby, John Campbell
d. Strasburger, Eduard Adolf

May 20, 1912
b. Drachler, Norman
b. Sellars, Wilfred

May 21, 1912
b. Schwarzschild, Martin
b. Soria, Dario
b. Stratton, Monty Franklin Pierce

May 22, 1912
b. Brown, Herbert Charles
b. Dodington, Sven H(enry Marriott)

May 23, 1912
b. Francaix, Jean
b. Goring, Marius
b. Payne, John

May 24, 1912
b. Anthony, Joseph

May 26, 1912
b. Ephron, Henry
b. Kadar, Janos

May 27, 1912
b. Cheever, John
b. Snead, Sam(uel Jackson)

May 28, 1912
b. White, Patrick Victor Martindale

May 29, 1912
b. Johnson, Pamela Hansford
b. Schweitzer, Pierre-Paul
b. Wu, Chien Shiung

May 30, 1912
b. Axelrod, Julius
b. Griffith, Hugh Emrys
b. Stein, Joseph
b. Symons, Julian (Gustave)
d. Wright, Wilbur

May 31, 1912
b. Deller, Alfred George
b. Jackson, Henry Martin

June 1, 1912
d. Burnham, Daniel H(udson)

June 2, 1912
b. Berelson, Bernard (Reuben)

June 3, 1912
b. Home, William Douglas

June 4, 1912
d. Sangster, Margaret Elizabeth

June 8, 1912
b. Kennedy, Walter

June 9, 1912
b. Clapp, Patricia

June 10, 1912
b. Lesage, Jean

June 11, 1912
b. Baziotes, William
b. Montgomery, Ruth Shick
b. Pham Hung
b. Topping, Dan(iel Reid)

June 12, 1912
b. Cowley, Bill
b. Crane, Eva
b. Hayden, Russell
d. Passy, Frederic

June 13, 1912
b. Taylor, Samuel (Albert)

June 14, 1912
b. Hammond, E(dward) Cuyler

June 16, 1912
b. Powell, Enoch

June 17, 1912
b. Gillis, Don

June 18, 1912
b. Morris, Glenn

June 19, 1912
b. Gabel, Martin

June 20, 1912
b. Linen, James A(lexander), III

June 21, 1912
b. McCarthy, Mary Therese

June 23, 1912
b. Turing, Alan (Mathison)

June 24, 1912
b. Cousins, Norman

June 25, 1912
b. Cahill, William T(homas)
b. Shapp, Milton J(errold)
d. Alma-Tadema, Lawrence, Sir

June 27, 1912
b. Christie, Audrey

June 28, 1912
b. Celibidache, Sergiu
b. Coons, Albert Hewett

June 29, 1912
b. Toland, John Willard

June 30, 1912
b. Reeves, Dan(iel F)

July 1, 1912
b. Brower, David Ross
b. Matheson, Murray
d. Quimby, Harriet

July 2, 1912
b. Mitchell, William Leroy

July 4, 1912
b. Dunton, Davidson
b. Graham, Virginia

July 5, 1912
b. David, Mack
b. Pace, Frank, Jr.

July 8, 1912
b. McCarthy, Frank

July 11, 1912
b. Barry, Donald
d. Shaw, Richard Norman

July 12, 1912
b. Bradley, Will
b. Deutsch, Karl Wolfgang
b. Rugambwa, Laurean

July 14, 1912
b. Frye, (Herman) Northrop
b. Guthrie, Woody
b. Motley, Willard Francis

July 15, 1912
d. Hudson, Joseph Lowthian

July 17, 1912
b. Belaunde-Terry, Fernando
b. Linkletter, Art(hur Gordon)
d. Poincare, Jules Henri

July 18, 1912
b. Levin, Harry Tuchman
b. Nelson, Harriet
b. Roy, Mike

July 20, 1912
d. Lang, Andrew

July 23, 1912
b. Miller, Carl S

July 26, 1912
b. Vance, Vivian

July 27, 1912
b. Markevitch, Igor

July 28, 1912
b. Wilding, Michael

July 29, 1912
b. Corey, Irwin

July 30, 1912
b. McLaughlin, Leo (Plowden)
d. Mutsuhito

July 31, 1912
b. Friedman, Milton
b. Kupcinet, Irv

August 1, 1912
b. Jones, Henry

August 2, 1912
b. Dvorak, Ann

August 4, 1912
b. Wallenberg, Raoul Gustav

August 7, 1912
b. Dorman, Maurice Henry, Sir
d. Hartmann, Franz

August 10, 1912
b. Amado, Jorge

August 11, 1912
b. Harvey, Frank Laird
b. Parker, Jean

August 12, 1912
b. Fuller, Samuel
b. Sullivan, Barry
b. Timmerman, George Bell, Jr.

August 13, 1912
b. Hogan, Ben
b. Luria, Salvador Edward
b. Wyatt, Jane
d. Massenet, Jules Emile Frederic

August 14, 1912
b. Abercrombie, Michael
b. Oppenheimer, Frank F

August 15, 1912
b. Child, Julia McWilliams
b. Hiller, Wendy, Dame

August 16, 1912
b. Price, H(enry) Ryan

August 20, 1912
d. Booth, William

August 21, 1912
b. Blake, Toe
b. Donovan, Robert John
b. Fish, Robert Lloyd

August 22, 1912
b. Peel, Ronald Francis (Edward Waite)

August 23, 1912
b. Kelly, Gene
b. Knutson, Coya

August 24, 1912
b. Kirby, Durward

August 25, 1912
b. Honecker, Erich
b. Key, Ted

August 27, 1912
b. Dorsey, Bob Rawls

August 30, 1912
b. Blondell, Joan
b. Purcell, Edward M(ills)

August 31, 1912
b. Vinay, Ramon

September 1, 1912
b. Giap, Vo Nguyen
d. Coleridge-Taylor, Samuel

September 2, 1912
b. Daiches, David

b. Xuan Thuy

September 3, 1912
b. Fisher, James Maxwell McConnell

September 4, 1912
b. Hoff, Sydney
b. Liberman, Alexander
(Semeonovitch)

September 5, 1912
b. Cage, John
d. MacArthur, Arthur

September 6, 1912
b. DiMaggio, Vince(nt Paul)

September 7, 1912
b. Packard, David

September 8, 1912
b. Cherne, Leo

September 10, 1912
b. Everson, William Oliver

September 12, 1912
b. Fath, Jacques

September 13, 1912
b. Babcock, Horace Welcome
d. Furphy, Joseph
d. Sierra, Justo

September 15, 1912
b. Welsh, Matthew E(mpson)

September 19, 1912
b. Daniel, Clifton, Jr.

September 21, 1912
b. Jones, Chuck
b. MacGregor, Ian Kinloch, Sir

September 22, 1912
b. Vanderbilt, Alfred G(wynne)

September 23, 1912
b. Bloom, Julius

September 24, 1912
b. Serraillier, Ian Lucien

September 25, 1912
b. Cooke, Jack Kent

September 26, 1912
b. Cloud, Preston (Ercelle)

September 29, 1912
b. Antonioni, Michelangelo

September 30, 1912
b. Baker, Kenny

October 2, 1912
b. Knudsen, Semon E(mil)

October 6, 1912
d. Beernaert, Auguste Marie Francois

October 7, 1912
b. Benn, Anthony
b. Waddles, Charleszetta, Mother

October 8, 1912
b. Gardner, John William

October 12, 1912
b. Rogers, Will, Jr.
d. Taylor, Susie Baker King

October 13, 1912
b. Weisgall, Hugo (David)

October 15, 1912
b. Conger, Clement Ellis
b. Perkins, Carl Dewey

October 16, 1912
b. Hansen, Clifford Peter
b. Norman, Maidie (Ruth)
b. Siegel, Don

October 17, 1912
b. John Paul I

October 18, 1912
b. Tsiranana, Philibert

October 19, 1912
b. Ghezzi, Vic(tor)

October 21, 1912
b. Solti, Georg, Sir

October 22, 1912
b. Callahan, Harry (Morey)

October 24, 1912
b. Gellhorn, Peter
b. Lundberg, Daniel

October 25, 1912
b. Pearl, Minnie

October 27, 1912
b. Sulzberger, C(yrus) L(eo)

October 30, 1912
b. Haynsworth, Clement Furman, Jr.
b. Parks, Gordon Alexander Buchanan
d. Sherman, James Schoolcraft

October 31, 1912
b. Evans, Dale

November 1, 1912
d. Lea, Homer

November 2, 1912
b. Conklin, Peggy

November 3, 1912
b. Donohue, Jack
b. Stroessner, Alfredo

November 4, 1912
b. Trigere, Pauline

November 6, 1912
b. Brasch, Rudolph

b. Cakobau, Ratu George, Sir

November 8, 1912
b. Dryfoos, Orvil Eugene
b. Ronan, William John

November 9, 1912
b. Fedorenko, Nikolai Trofimovich
b. Thompson, Kay

November 10, 1912
b. Tebbetts, Birdie

November 14, 1912
b. Hutton, Barbara Woolworth

November 15, 1912
b. Baez, Albert V.

November 16, 1912
b. Bennett, Robert LaFollette
b. Tebbel, John William

November 17, 1912
b. Ackerman, Harry S
b. Burgess, John Lawrie, Sir
b. Rebozo, Bebe

November 18, 1912
b. Martin, Louis E.
b. Zablocki, Clement John

November 19, 1912
b. Palade, George Emil

November 21, 1912
b. Joyce, Eileen
b. Powell, Eleanor

November 22, 1912
b. Duke, Doris
b. Guldahl, Ralph

November 24, 1912
b. Kanin, Garson
b. Wilson, Teddy

November 25, 1912
b. Nikolais, Alwin
b. Sengstacke, John H(erman Henry)
b. Smith, Austin E(dward)

November 26, 1912
b. Sevareid, Eric

November 27, 1912
b. Merrick, David

November 28, 1912
b. Louis, Morris

December 1, 1912
b. Yamasaki, Minoru

December 2, 1912
b. Sukman, Harry

December 4, 1912
b. Boyington, Pappy

December 7, 1912
b. Cameron, Rod
b. Prima, Louis
d. Darwin, George Howard, Sir

December 9, 1912
b. O'Neill, Thomas P(hilip), Jr.

December 10, 1912
b. Hart, Philip Aloysius

December 12, 1912
b. Armstrong, Henry
b. Balewa, Abubakar Tafawa, Sir

December 15, 1912
d. Reid, Whitelaw

December 18, 1912
b. Davis, Benjamin Oliver, Jr.
b. Mazia, Daniel
d. Carleton, Will

December 22, 1912
b. Johnson, Lady Bird

December 24, 1912
b. Llewelyn-Davies, Richard

December 29, 1912
b. Glanville-Hicks, Peggy
d. MacCameron, Robert L

December 30, 1912
b. Curry, Peggy Simson

1913

b. Barrett, John L
b. Baskin, Burton
b. Bechi, Gino
b. Bloom, Harry
b. Chiang, Ching
b. Dandridge, Ray(mond)
b. Dreyfus, Jack Jonas
b. Erdos, Paul
b. Espriu, Salvador
b. Evelyn, Judith
b. Green, Guy
b. Huang Hua
b. Khalid Ibn Abdul Azia Al-Saud
b. LaRose, Rose
b. Lembede, Anton
b. Lennon, Jimmy, Sr.
b. Lund, John
b. Minnesota Fats
b. Moraes, Vinicius de
b. Oppenheim, Meret
b. Ortiz, Peter J(ulien)
b. Washkansky, Louis
b. Yordan, Philip
d. Bad Heart Bull, Amos
d. Kelley, Oliver Hudson
d. Lanston, Tolbert
d. Ukrainka, Lesia

January 1, 1913
b. Janeway, Eliot

January 2, 1913
d. Teisserenc de Bort, Leon-Philippe

January 3, 1913
b. Chute, Beatrice Joy

January 4, 1913
d. Schlieffen, Alfred, Graf von

January 5, 1913
b. Wilson, Kemmons

January 6, 1913
b. Brown, Tom
b. Gierek, Edward
b. Young, Loretta Gretchen

January 7, 1913
b. Mize, Johnny

January 9, 1913
b. Donahue, Woolworth
b. Nixon, Richard M(ilhous)
b. Tatum, Donn B

January 10, 1913
b. Husak, Gustav
b. Shehu, Mehmet

January 13, 1913
b. Millner, Wayne E

January 15, 1913
b. Bridges, Lloyd

January 17, 1913
b. Musso, Vido

January 18, 1913
b. Graham, Gwethalyn
b. Kaye, Danny

January 24, 1913
b. Dello Joio, Norman Joseph

January 25, 1913
b. Lutoslawski, Witold

January 26, 1913
b. Prince, William
b. Van Heusen, Jimmy

January 29, 1913
b. Mature, Victor (John)
b. Schneider, Nina

January 31, 1913
b. Hutson, Don(ald M)

February 4, 1913
b. Parks, Rosa Lee McCauley
b. Stevenson, Janet

February 6, 1913
b. Leakey, Mary (Douglas)
d. Weaver, James Baird

February 10, 1913
b. Smith, Merriman

February 11, 1913
b. Mosley, Leonard O(swald)

February 13, 1913
b. Agostini, Peter
d. Major, Charles

February 14, 1913
b. Allen, Mel
b. Hayes, Woody
b. Hoffa, Jimmy
b. Pike, James Albert, Bishop

February 17, 1913
b. Leibowitz, Rene
b. Nye, Russel Blaine
d. Miller, Joaquin

February 18, 1913
b. Clark, Dane

February 20, 1913
b. Conner, Nadine
b. Henrich, Tommy

February 22, 1913
d. Madero, Francisco Indalecio

February 25, 1913
b. Backus, Jim

February 26, 1913
b. Barker, George Granville

February 27, 1913
b. Ricoeur, Paul
b. Shaw, Irwin
d. Sedgwick, Adam

February 28, 1913
b. Minnelli, Vincente

March 3, 1913
b. Henry, Charlotte

March 4, 1913
b. Garfield, John

March 6, 1913
b. Logan, Ella

March 7, 1913
d. Johnson, Emily Pauline

March 8, 1913
b. Wilson, Peter Cecil

March 9, 1913
b. Placzek, Adolf K(urt)

March 10, 1913
d. Tubman, Harriet Ross

March 12, 1913
b. Mikhalkov, Sergei Vladimirovich

March 13, 1913
b. Casey, William Joseph
b. Kaye, Sammy

March 15, 1913
b. Carey, Macdonald
b. Wasserman, Lew(is Robert)
b. Wasserman, Lew R

March 17, 1913
b. Karpin, Fred Leon

March 18, 1913
b. Amerasinghe, Hamilton Shirley
b. Clement, Rene
b. Crawford, William Hulfish

March 22, 1913
b. Dederich, Charles (Edwin)
b. Malden, Karl
b. McCall, Thomas Lawson
d. Sung Chiao-jen

March 23, 1913
b. Escobar, Sixto

March 24, 1913
b. Porter, Richard William

March 29, 1913
b. Thomas, Ronald Stuart

March 30, 1913
b. Helms, Richard McGarrah
b. Laine, Frankie

March 31, 1913
d. Morgan, J(ohn) P(ierpont)

April 2, 1913
b. Blofeld, John

April 4, 1913
b. Langford, Frances
b. Leger, Jules
b. Weidman, Jerome

April 5, 1913
b. Clave, Antoni

April 6, 1913
b. Ruchlis, Hy(man)

April 7, 1913
b. Vanik, Charles Albert

April 8, 1913
b. Apithy, Sourou Migan

April 10, 1913
b. Heym, Stefan

April 11, 1913
b. Cassini, Oleg Loiewski

April 12, 1913
b. Hampton, Lionel Leo

April 13, 1913
b. Albritton, David
b. Hingson, Robert A(ndrew)
b. Whittingham, Charlie

April 14, 1913
d. Hagenbeck, Carl

April 16, 1913
b. Tremayne, Les

April 18, 1913
d. Ward, Lester Frank

April 19, 1913
b. Carpenter, Ken(neth)

April 21, 1913
b. Li, C(hoh) H(ao)
b. Parkinson, Norman

April 23, 1913
b. Meyerowitz, Jan
b. Simon, Simone

April 26, 1913
b. Burcham, Lester Arthur

April 27, 1913
b. Abelson, Philip Hauge
b. Adler, Irving

May 1, 1913
b. Russell, Elizabeth Shull
b. Susskind, Walter

May 3, 1913
b. Blackwell, (Samuel) Earl, Jr.
b. Inge, William Motter
b. Kohut, Heinz

May 6, 1913
b. Cavallaro, Carmen
b. Granger, Stewart

May 7, 1913
b. Glazer, David
b. Powers, Anne

May 8, 1913
b. Clampett, Bob
b. Dole, Vincent P(aul)

May 10, 1913
b. Gemmell, Alan

May 13, 1913
b. Reddy, N(eelam) Sanjeeva
b. Tolbert, William Richard, Jr.

May 14, 1913
b. Doxiadis, Constantinos Apostolos
b. Terry, Walter

May 16, 1913
b. Herman, Woody

May 17, 1913
b. Parker, Ace

May 18, 1913
b. Trenet, Charles

May 20, 1913
b. Hewlett, William
d. Flagler, Henry Morrison

May 21, 1913
b. Bachauer, Gina
b. Shulman, Irving

May 24, 1913
b. Chaudhuri, Haridas

May 25, 1913
b. Grace, J(oseph) Peter, Jr.
b. Maclean, Donald Duart

May 26, 1913
b. Cushing, Peter

May 29, 1913
b. Zale, Tony

May 30, 1913
b. Erwin, Pee Wee

June 2, 1913
b. Pym, Barbara Mary Crampton
d. Austin, Alfred

June 3, 1913
b. Cope, Jack
b. Corby, Ellen

June 4, 1913
d. Davison, Emily Wilding

June 5, 1913
b. Ellis, Effie O'Neal
b. Marca-Relli, Conrad

June 6, 1913
d. Cramp, Charles Henry

June 7, 1913
b. Nash, N Richard

June 8, 1913
b. Diamand, Peter

June 9, 1913
b. Steptoe, Patrick Christopher

June 10, 1913
b. Cohen, Wilbur Joseph
b. Khrennikov, Tikhon Nikolaevich

June 11, 1913
b. Lombardi, Vince(nt Thomas)
b. Stevens, Rise

June 13, 1913
b. Edwards, Ralph Livingstone
b. Martin, David Stone

June 15, 1913
b. Huddleston, Trevor

June 18, 1913
b. Cahn, Sammy
b. Mondavi, Robert Gerald
b. Porter, Sylvia Field

June 20, 1913
b. Juan Carlos, Count of Barcelona
b. Torrance, Jack

June 21, 1913
b. Mosconi, Willie

June 23, 1913
b. Humes, Helen
b. Rogers, William Pierce

June 25, 1913
b. Cesaire, Aime Fernand

June 27, 1913
b. Bissell, Richard Pike
b. Guston, Philip

June 29, 1913
b. Meadows, Earle

June 30, 1913
d. Rochefort, Henri
d. Hemon, Louis

July 1, 1913
b. Sinclair, Jo

July 3, 1913
b. Kilgallen, Dorothy

July 6, 1913
b. Clark, Eleanor
b. Thomas, Gwyn

July 8, 1913
b. Kerr, Walter F(rancis)

July 10, 1913
b. Welitsch, Ljuba

July 11, 1913
b. Busia, Kofi A(brefa)
b. Ironside, Christopher

July 12, 1913
b. Cohn, Mildred
b. Lamb, Willis Eugene, Jr.
b. Oursler, Will(iam Charles)

July 13, 1913
b. Garroway, Dave

July 14, 1913
b. Ford, Gerald R(udolph)

July 15, 1913
b. Innes, Hammond

July 17, 1913
b. Goldberg, Bertrand
b. Wilson, Mitchell A

July 18, 1913
b. Rolvaag, Karl Fritjof
b. Skelton, Red

July 19, 1913
b. Teagarden, Charles

July 22, 1913
b. Albanese, Licia
b. Thornton, Charles Bates

July 23, 1913
b. Browne, Coral Edith
b. Foot, Michael

July 24, 1913
b. Byroade, Henry A(lfred)
b. Chance, Britton
b. Davis, Burke

July 27, 1913
b. Corbett, Scott

July 28, 1913
b. Ryder, James Arthur

July 29, 1913
b. Grimond, Jo(seph)
d. Asser, Tobias Michael Carel

July 31, 1913
b. Hextall, Bryan Aldwyn

August 4, 1913
b. Addy, Wesley
b. Hayden, Robert Earl

August 8, 1913
b. Stafford, Robert Theodore

August 9, 1913
b. Talmadge, Herman Eugene

August 10, 1913
b. Paul, Wolfgang

August 11, 1913
b. Crane, Nathalia Clara Ruth
b. Oliver, Edith
b. Wilson, Angus

August 13, 1913
b. Kasznar, Kurt
b. Makarios III, Archbishop
b. Newell, Pete
d. Bebel, August

August 14, 1913
b. Dean, Daffy
b. Tagliavini, Ferrucio

August 16, 1913
b. Begin, Menachem (Wolfovitch)
b. Hawkins, Osie Penman, Jr.

August 17, 1913
b. York, Rudy

August 18, 1913
b. Cornelius, Henry

August 19, 1913
b. Mills, Harry

August 20, 1913
b. Sperry, Roger W(olcott)

August 21, 1913
b. Boehm, Edward M
b. Churchill, Diana Josephine
b. Faulk, John Henry
b. Johnson, Cornelius

August 23, 1913
b. Crosby, Bob

August 24, 1913
b. Knowles, Malcolm Shepherd
b. Wilkinson, J(ohn) Burke

August 25, 1913
b. Kelly, Walt(er Crawford)

b. Rostow, Eugene Victor

August 27, 1913
b. Kamen, Martin David

August 28, 1913
b. Cudlipp, Hugh
b. Davies, (William) Robertson
b. Irving, Robert Augustine
b. Tucker, Richard

August 29, 1913
b. Fine, Sylvia

August 30, 1913
b. Stone, John Richard Nicholas, Sir

August 31, 1913
b. Lovell, Bernard, Sir

September 3, 1913
b. Ladd, Alan

September 4, 1913
b. Cohen, Mickey
b. Moore, Stanford
b. Savitt, Jan
b. Tange, Kenzo
d. Brown, Henry Billings

September 5, 1913
b. Andrews, Wayne

September 7, 1913
b. Crowe, Colin Tradescant, Sir
b. Quayle, (John) Anthony, Sir

September 10, 1913
b. Mein, John Gordon

September 11, 1913
b. Bryant, Bear
b. Lamarr, Hedy

September 12, 1913
b. Owens, Jesse
b. Toyoda, Eiji

September 14, 1913
b. Arbenz Guzman, Jacobo

September 15, 1913
b. Mitchell, John Newton

September 16, 1913
b. Heckscher, August

September 27, 1913
b. Ellis, Albert (Isaac)

September 28, 1913
b. Marble, Alice
b. Peters, Ellis

September 29, 1913
b. Dixon, Paul Rand
b. Kramer, Stanley E
d. Diesel, Rudolf Christian Karl

October 3, 1913
b. Pitt, David Thomas

October 4, 1913
b. Janson, Horst Woldemar

October 6, 1913
b. Dyer-Bennet, Richard

October 7, 1913
b. Janeway, Elizabeth Hall
d. Altman, Benjamin

October 8, 1913
b. Fielding, Temple Hornaday
b. Gilruth, Robert Rowe
b. Schumann, Walter

October 10, 1913
b. Downs, Johnny
b. Pressman, David
b. Simon, Claude Eugene Henri
d. Busch, Adolphus

October 14, 1913
b. Casey, Hugh Thomas

October 19, 1913
b. Jennings, Robert Yewdall

October 20, 1913
b. Jones, Grandpa
d. Palmer, Daniel David

October 22, 1913
b. Bao Dai
b. Capa, Robert

October 23, 1913
b. Gorkin, Jess
d. Klebs, Edwin

October 25, 1913
b. Barbie, Klaus
b. Fletcher, Grant

October 26, 1913
b. Barnet, Charlie
b. Scanlon, Hugh Parr
d. Corvo, Baron

October 27, 1913
b. Whitman, Alden

November 2, 1913
b. Lancaster, Burt(on Stephen)

November 3, 1913
b. Chapman, Leonard F., Jr.

November 4, 1913
b. Young, Gig

November 5, 1913
b. Leigh, Vivien
b. McGiver, John

November 7, 1913
b. Camus, Albert
d. McBurney, Charles
d. Wallace, Alfred Russell

November 8, 1913
b. Ambers, Lou
b. Strauss, Robert

November 10, 1913
b. Shapiro, Karl Jay

November 11, 1913
b. MacLeod, Iain Norman
b. Ryan, Robert (Bushnell)

November 13, 1913
b. Nol, Lon
b. Scourby, Alexander

November 14, 1913
b. Smathers, George Armistead

November 15, 1913
b. Cameron, Roderick W

November 21, 1913
b. Boulting, John
b. Boulting, Roy
b. Unkelbach, Kurt

November 22, 1913
b. Berlitz, Charles L Frambach
b. Britten, (Edward) Benjamin

November 23, 1913
b. Zolotow, Maurice

November 25, 1913
b. Thomas, Lewis

November 29, 1913
b. Guyer, Tennyson

December 1, 1913
b. Martin, Mary

December 3, 1913
b. Lichine, Alexis

December 6, 1913
b. Holm, Eleanor

December 7, 1913
b. Linowitz, Sol Myron
d. Ward, Montgomery

December 8, 1913
b. Schwartz, Delmore (David)
b. Thomas, Caitlin Macnamara
d. Simmons, Franklin

December 9, 1913
d. Deering, William

December 10, 1913
b. Gould, Morton

December 11, 1913
b. Marais, Jean
b. Ponti, Carlo

December 12, 1913
b. Burdett, Winston M.
d. Menelik II

December 13, 1913
b. Moore, Archie

December 15, 1913
b. Rukeyser, Muriel

December 16, 1913
b. Parker, Buddy

December 18, 1913
b. Bari, Lynn
b. Bester, Alfred
b. Brandt, Willy
b. Meyer, Ray(mond Joseph)
d. Bethune, Louise Blanchard

December 24, 1913
b. Erteszek, Jan
b. Hamilton, Charles
b. Reinhardt, Ad(olph Frederick)

December 25, 1913
b. Martin, Tony
b. Moczar, Mieczyslaw

December 28, 1913
b. Jacobi, Lou

December 29, 1913
b. Werner, Pierre

December 30, 1913
b. Barrett, William Christopher

1914

b. Bakr, Ahmad Hasan al
b. Barrymore, Elaine Jacobs
b. Collazo, Oscar
b. Corio, Ann
b. Daniels, Mickey
b. Finlay, Virgil
b. Hays, Lee
b. Jonathan, Leabua, Chief
b. Kutschmann, Walter
b. Loring, Eugene
b. Lubachivsky, Myroslav Ivan,
  Cardinal
b. Madison, Helene
b. Mann, Jack
b. Mattus, Reuben
b. May, Morton David
b. Mellinger, Frederick
b. Mercader, Ramon
b. O'Brian, Patrick
b. Ortese, Anna Maria
b. Roloff, Lester
b. Smith, Hazel Brannon
b. Unsworth, Geoffrey
b. Wolfgang, Myra K
d. Bierce, Ambrose Gwinett
d. De Leon, Daniel

January 1, 1914
b. Oliver, James A(rthur)
b. Rosten, Norman

January 3, 1914
b. Bodard, Lucien (Albert)

January 4, 1914
b. Wyman, Jane
d. Mitchell, Silas Weir

January 5, 1914
b. Stael, Nicolas de

January 6, 1914
b. Reeves, George
b. Thomas, Danny

January 8, 1914
b. Watson, Thomas J(ohn), Jr.
d. Buckner, Simon Bolivar

January 9, 1914
b. Clarke, Kenny

January 11, 1914
b. Jeakins, Dorothy

January 12, 1914
b. Gurney, Edward John
b. McMurrin, Sterling M(oss)

January 13, 1914
b. Cory, John Mackenzie

January 14, 1914
b. Randall, Dudley
b. Russell, Harold
d. Wurlitzer, Rudolph

January 15, 1914
b. Trevor-Roper, Hugh Redwald

January 16, 1914
b. Wagner, Roger Frances

January 17, 1914
b. Stafford, William Edgar

January 19, 1914
d. Leonowens, Anna Harriette
  Crawford

January 20, 1914
b. Plomley, Roy
b. Watt, Douglas Benjamin

January 21, 1914
d. Smith, Donald Alexander

January 25, 1914
b. Flora, James (Royer)

January 26, 1914
b. DeManio, Jack

January 29, 1914
b. Prudden, Bonnie

January 30, 1914
b. Marlowe, Hugh
b. Wayne, David

January 31, 1914
b. Addonizio, Hugh Joseph
b. Walcott, Joe

February 2, 1914
b. Apostoli, Fred
b. Dedijer, Vladimir

February 5, 1914
b. Burroughs, William S(eward)
b. Hodgkin, Alan Lloyd, Sir

February 6, 1914
b. Towns, Forrest

February 9, 1914
b. Lee, Gypsy Rose
b. Tubb, Ernest
b. Veeck, Bill

February 10, 1914
b. Adler, Larry

February 11, 1914
d. Clarke, Alexander Ross

February 12, 1914
b. Beneke, Tex

February 13, 1914
d. Bertillon, Alphonse

February 15, 1914
b. Boggs, Hale
b. McCarthy, Kevin

February 16, 1914
b. Wakely, Jimmy
d. DeVinne, Theodore Low

February 17, 1914
b. Kennedy, Arthur
b. Morris, Wayne

February 20, 1914
b. Daly, John Charles, Jr.
b. MacKellar, William
b. Slavenska, Mia

February 21, 1914
b. Kondrashin, Kiril Petrovich

February 22, 1914
b. Dulbecco, Renato
d. Fels, Joseph

February 24, 1914
b. Scott, Zachary

February 25, 1914
b. Bonham, Frank
d. Tenniel, John, Sir

February 26, 1914
b. Alda, Robert
b. Wilson, Malcolm

February 27, 1914
b. Davis, Hal Charles

March 1, 1914
b. Ellison, Ralph (Waldo)

March 3, 1914
b. Fuller, Edmund

March 4, 1914
b. Cooper, Mort(on Cecil)
b. Wilson, Robert R(athbun)

March 7, 1914
b. DaCosta, Morton
b. Hauge, Gabriel
b. Sann, Paul

March 9, 1914
b. Clark, Fred
b. Ullman, Al(bert Conrad)

March 10, 1914
b. Harper, Chandler
b. Mitchell, Corinne

March 12, 1914
b. Farr, Tommy B
d. Westinghouse, George

March 13, 1914
b. Bottel, Helen Alfea
b. Haggart, Bob
b. Mitchell, W(illiam) O(rmond)
b. Weiskopf, Bob

March 14, 1914
b. Hess, Leon

March 16, 1914
b. Mayer, Oscar Gottfried, II
b. Westmoreland, William Childs
d. Gobat, Charles Albert
d. Murray, John, Sir

March 17, 1914
b. Baugh, Sammy

March 19, 1914
b. Berwanger, J Jay
b. Morison, Patricia
b. Siles Zuazo, Hernan
d. Bandelier, Adolph Francis Alphonse

March 20, 1914
b. Corey, Wendell

March 21, 1914
b. Tortelier, Paul

March 22, 1914
b. Miller, William E
b. Stokes, Donald Gresham Stokes,
  Baron

March 25, 1914
b. Borlaug, Norman Ernest
b. Olivero, Magda
b. Rounseville, Robert Field
b. Saarinen, Aline Bernstein
d. Mistral, Frederic

March 26, 1914
d. Keith, Benjamin Franklin

March 27, 1914
b. Denning, Richard
b. Lanson, Snooky
b. Schulberg, Budd Wilson

March 28, 1914
b. Anhalt, Edward
b. Hrabal, Bohumil
b. Lovejoy, Frank
b. Muskie, Edmund S(ixtus)

March 29, 1914
b. Foster, Phil

March 30, 1914
d. Poynting, John Henry

March 31, 1914
b. Paz, Octavio
d. Lurton, Horace Harmon

April 1, 1914
d. Waddell, Rube

April 2, 1914
b. Guinness, Alec, Sir
d. Heyse, Paul Johann Ludwig von

April 4, 1914
b. Duras, Marguerite
b. Kopal, Zdenek
b. Lane, Rosemary
d. Weyerhaeuser, Frederick

April 8, 1914
b. Giroux, Robert

April 11, 1914
b. Bernstein, Dorothy Lewis
b. McLaren, Norman

April 14, 1914
b. Salant, Richard S

April 15, 1914
b. Manso, Leo
d. Townsend, George Alfred

April 16, 1914
b. Hodiak, John
b. Jensen, Oliver Ormerod
d. Hill, George William

April 19, 1914
d. Peirce, Charles Sanders

April 21, 1914
b. Gaines, Lee
b. Lachs, Manfred
b. Panama, Norman
d. Crockett, S(amuel) R(utherford)

April 22, 1914
b. DeHartog, Jan
b. Sisson, Charles Hubert

April 24, 1914
b. Bingham, Jonathan Brewster
b. Castle, William
b. Conniff, Frank

April 25, 1914
b. Lockridge, Ross Franklin, Jr.
b. Mauriac, Claude
b. Perez Jimenez, Marcos

April 26, 1914
b. Malamud, Bernard
b. Rouse, James W(ilson)

April 27, 1914
b. Cole, Jack

April 30, 1914
b. Royster, Vermont C(onnecticut)

May 2, 1914
b. Woss, Kurt

May 3, 1914
d. Sickles, Daniel Edgar

May 4, 1914
b. Muller, Hilgard
b. Smith, Gerard C(oad)

May 5, 1914
b. Power, Tyrone, Jr.

May 6, 1914
b. Jarrell, Randall

May 8, 1914
b. Gary, Romain

May 9, 1914
b. Giulini, Carlo Maria
b. Kheel, Theodore Woodrow
b. Salter, Andrew
b. Snow, Hank
d. Heroult, Paul Louis Toussaint
d. Post, Charles William

May 10, 1914
b. Walsh, Chad
d. Nordica, Lillian
d. Schuch, Ernst von

May 11, 1914
b. Severn, William Irving
b. Weaver, Doodles

May 12, 1914
b. Smith, Howard K(ingsbury)

May 13, 1914
b. Louis, Joe

May 15, 1914
b. Broda, Turk
b. Tenzing Norgay

May 17, 1914
b. Alsop, Stewart Johonnot Oliver
b. Ongania, Juan Carlos

May 18, 1914
b. Balmain, Pierre Alexandre

May 19, 1914
b. Perutz, M(ax) F(erdinand)

May 22, 1914
b. Hartt, Frederick
b. Packard, Vance (Oakley)
b. Sun Ra

May 23, 1914
b. Ward, Barbara Mary

May 24, 1914
b. Donovan, Hedley Williams
b. Palmer, Lilli

May 26, 1914
b. Baker, Shorty
b. Elman, Ziggy
d. Riis, Jacob August

May 27, 1914
d. Swan, Joseph Wilson, Sir

May 29, 1914
b. Keach, Stacy, Sr.
d. Irving, Laurence Sidney

May 31, 1914
b. Valtman, Edmund Siegfried
b. Williams, Jay

June 5, 1914
b. Cahners, Norman Lee
b. Dunlop, John Thomas

June 7, 1914
d. Watts-Dunton, Theodore

June 12, 1914
b. Lundigan, William
d. Isham, Samuel

June 13, 1914
b. Franklin, Frederic

June 14, 1914
b. Peers, William Raymond
d. Stevenson, Adlai Ewing

June 15, 1914
b. Andropov, Yuri Vladimirovich
b. Steinberg, Saul

June 17, 1914
b. Hersey, John (Richard)

June 18, 1914
b. Allen, Jack

June 19, 1914
b. Cranston, Alan MacGregor
d. Thomas, Brandon

June 21, 1914
b. Vickrey, William
d. Suttner, Bertha Felicie Sophie
Kinsky von

June 22, 1914
b. Lucas, Jim Griffing

June 24, 1914
b. Peterson, Edith R.

June 26, 1914
b. Lee, Laurie
b. Maltby, Richard E
b. Spitzer, Lyman, Jr.
b. Windgassen, Wolfgang Friedrich
Hermann
b. Zaharias, Babe Didrikson

June 27, 1914
b. Almirante, Giorgio
b. Coombs, Charles Ira

June 28, 1914
b. Arieti, Silvano
b. Flatt, Lester Raymond
b. Seymour, Dan
b. Trifa, Valerian
d. Francis Ferdinand
d. Franz Ferdinand

June 29, 1914
b. Kubelik, Rafael (Jeronym)

June 30, 1914
b. Houser, Allan

July 1, 1914
b. Linh, Nguyen Van

July 2, 1914
b. Bok, Hannes Vajn
b. Fennell, Frederick
b. Hamburger, Philip
d. Chamberlain, Joseph

July 3, 1914
b. MacGrath, Leueen (Emily)

July 6, 1914
b. Abbas, Khwaja Ahmad
d. Agustini, Delmira

July 7, 1914
b. Mayehoff, Eddie

July 8, 1914
b. Eckstine, Billy
b. Sellinger, Frank

July 9, 1914
b. Carlson, Curtis L.

July 10, 1914
b. Shuster, Joe
d. Jacobi, Abraham

July 20, 1914
b. Uhde, Hermann

July 21, 1914
b. Aries, Philippe

July 22, 1914
b. Farber, Edward Rolke

July 23, 1914
b. Foreman, Carl
d. Grimke, Charlotte Lottie Forten

July 24, 1914
b. Clark, Kenneth Bancroft
b. Mirvish, Edwin
b. Silvera, Frank

July 25, 1914
b. Strode, Woody

July 26, 1914
b. Hawkins, Erskine (Ramsey)

July 27, 1914
b. Horan, James David
b. White, Miles

July 28, 1914
b. Dragon, Carmen

July 29, 1914
b. Bich, Marcel

July 30, 1914
b. Killanin, Michael Morris, Lord

July 31, 1914
b. Head, Howard
d. Jaures, Jean Leon

August 1, 1914
b. Mangrum, Lloyd

August 2, 1914
b. Crocker, Fay
b. Merrill, Gary Franklin

August 4, 1914
b. Colville, Neil McNeil

August 5, 1914
b. Brian, David
b. Colby, Anita

August 6, 1914
d. Wilson, Ellen Axson

August 10, 1914
b. Corey, Jeff
b. Malcuzynski, Witold

August 11, 1914
d. Plancon, Pol-Henri

August 12, 1914
d. Holland, John Philip

August 15, 1914
b. Rand, Paul

August 16, 1914
b. DeRegniers, Beatrice Schenk

August 17, 1914
b. Downs, William Randall, Jr.
b. Roosevelt, Franklin Delano, Jr.

August 20, 1914
d. Pius X

August 26, 1914
b. Cortazar, Julio

August 27, 1914
d. Bohm von Bawerk, Eugene

August 29, 1914
d. Samsonov, Aleksandr Vasilievich

August 30, 1914
b. Bishop, Julie

August 31, 1914
b. Basehart, Richard

September 1, 1914
b. Porter, William James

September 2, 1914
b. Bearden, Romare Howard
b. Brown, George Alfred

September 3, 1914
b. Ray, Dixy Lee

September 4, 1914
b. Hutson, Jean Blackwell

September 5, 1914
b. Parra, Nicanor
d. Peguy, Charles Pierre

September 7, 1914
b. Van Allen, James Alfred

September 8, 1914
b. Albrand, Martha
b. Brooke, Hillary
b. Dimitrios I, Patriarch

September 10, 1914
b. O'Neill, Terence Marne
b. Wise, Robert

September 13, 1914
b. Feather, Leonard Geoffrey

September 14, 1914
b. Armstrong, William H(oward)
b. Moore, Clayton

September 15, 1914
b. Abrams, Creighton Williams
b. Bioy Casares, Adolfo
b. McCloskey, Robert

September 16, 1914
b. Funt, Allen
b. Ready, William Bernard

September 18, 1914
d. Leslie, Miriam Florence Folline

September 19, 1914
b. Farmer, Frances
b. Morton, Rogers Clark Ballard

September 20, 1914
b. More, Kenneth Gilbert

September 21, 1914
b. Kluge, John Werner
b. Stewart, Slam

September 22, 1914
b. Scott, Martha Ellen
d. Alain-Fournier

September 25, 1914
b. Osborne, Leone Neal

September 26, 1914
b. LaLanne, Jack
d. Macke, August

September 27, 1914
b. Marshall, Catherine

September 28, 1914
d. Sears, Richard Warren

September 29, 1914
b. Condit, Carl Wilbur

October 1, 1914
b. Boorstin, Daniel J(oseph)

October 4, 1914
b. Gill, Brendan

October 6, 1914
b. Heyerdahl, Thor

October 7, 1914
b. Churchill, Sarah
b. Drake, Alfred
b. Golub, William Weldon
b. Keiser, Herman

October 8, 1914
b. Schocken, Theodore
d. Crapsey, Adelaide

October 11, 1914
b. Day, J(ames) Edward

October 12, 1914
b. Chase, Richard Volney

October 14, 1914
b. Brecheen, Harry David
b. Davis, Raymond, Jr.

October 15, 1914
b. Zahir Shah, Mohammad

October 17, 1914
b. Siegel, Jerry

October 18, 1914
b. Salt, Waldo

October 19, 1914
d. Roca, Julio Argentino

October 20, 1914
b. Davies, Leslie Purnell

October 21, 1914
b. Gardner, Martin

October 23, 1914
b. Drillon, Gordie
b. Kinard, Frank M

October 25, 1914
b. Berryman, John

October 26, 1914
b. Coogan, Jackie
b. Masters, John

October 27, 1914
b. Thomas, Dylan Marlais

October 28, 1914
b. Salk, Jonas E(dward)
b. Synge, Richard Laurence Millington

October 30, 1914
b. Jonathan, Joseph Leabua
b. Laughlin, James, IV

b. Mohammed Zahir Shah
b. Montana, Patsy

November 2, 1914
b. Guerard, Albert Joseph
b. Vander Meer, Johnny

November 3, 1914
b. Shamir, Yitzhak

November 4, 1914
b. Cowan, Peter Wilkinshaw

November 5, 1914
b. Nsubuga, Emmanuel, Cardinal

November 6, 1914
b. Gerson, Noel Bertram
d. Weismann, August Friedrich
Leopold

November 7, 1914
b. Lafferty, Raphael Aloysius

November 11, 1914
b. Elias, Taslim Olawale
b. Fast, Howard Melvin

November 12, 1914
b. Schillebeeckx, Edward (Cornelis
Florentius Alfons)

November 13, 1914
b. Gibson, William

November 14, 1914
b. Crozier, Eric John
d. Chaffee, Adna Romanza
d. Roberts, Frederick Sleigh

November 15, 1914
b. Bolet, Jorge

November 16, 1914
b. Dunham, Sonny

November 20, 1914
b. Pucci, Emilio Marchese di Barsento

November 21, 1914
b. Grant, Michael
b. Kassem, Abdul Karim (el)

November 22, 1914
b. Townsend, Peter Wooldridge

November 24, 1914
b. Chadwick, Lynn Russell
b. DiMaggio, Joe
b. Fitzgerald, Geraldine

November 27, 1914
b. Begle, Edward G(riffith)

November 28, 1914
b. Dodson, Owen (Vincent)
d. Hittorf, Johann Wilhelm

November 29, 1914
b. Du Bois, Raoul Pene
b. McIntyre, Hal

December 1, 1914
d. Mahan, Alfred Thayer

December 2, 1914
b. Sauter, Eddie

December 3, 1914
b. Parks, Larry

December 5, 1914
b. Magyar, Gabriel

December 7, 1914
d. Cawein, Madison Julius

December 8, 1914
b. Garrigue, Jean

December 9, 1914
b. Turnesa, Jim

December 10, 1914
b. Lamour, Dorothy

December 13, 1914
b. Bullock, Alan Louis Charles

December 14, 1914
b. Amsterdam, Morey
b. Carstens, Karl Walter
b. Tureck, Rosalyn

December 16, 1914
b. Link, O(gle) Winston

December 20, 1914
b. Byrd, Harry Flood, Jr.

December 23, 1914
b. Coe, Frederick H

December 24, 1914
b. Cushman, Robert Everton, Jr.
b. Marterie, Ralph
d. Muir, John

December 25, 1914
b. Lewis, Oscar
b. Mabee, Carleton

December 26, 1914
b. Widmark, Richard

December 27, 1914
d. Dodge, Grace Hoadley
d. Hall, Charles Martin

December 28, 1914
b. Bowman, Lee

December 30, 1914
b. Parks, Bert

December 31, 1914
b. Brady, Pat

1915

b. Ameche, Jim
b. Bond, George Foote

b. Burri, Alberto
b. Cashin, Bonnie
b. Cordero, Helen Quintana
b. Dio, Johnny
b. Falk, Lee Harrison
b. Freeman, Cynthia
b. Leemans, Tuffy
b. Lundahl, Arthur Charles
b. Manning, Olivia
b. Minsky, Harold
b. Noziere, Violette
b. Perry, Eleanor Bayer
b. Pierre, Andre
b. Tibbets, Paul Warfield
b. Whitlock, Albert
d. Alzheimer, Alois
d. Edwardes, George
d. LaFlesche Picotte, Susan
d. Mehta, Pherozeshah (Merwanji)

January 1, 1915
b. Clarke, John Henrik

January 2, 1915
b. Franklin, John Hope
d. Goldmark, Karl

January 3, 1915
b. Dempsey, John Noel
b. Levine, Jack

January 5, 1915
b. Robinson, Arthur H(oward)

January 6, 1915
b. Lilly, John C
b. Watts, Alan Wilson

January 8, 1915
b. Apps, Syl
b. Cooper, Walker

January 9, 1915
b. Mikkelsen, Henning Dahl

January 10, 1915
b. Dixon, Dean

January 12, 1915
b. Agronsky, Martin Zama
b. Schultes, Richard Evans

January 13, 1915
b. Stewart, Potter

January 15, 1915
b. Borg, Veda Ann
b. Lomax, Alan
d. Farmer, Fannie Merritt

January 16, 1915
d. Williams, Gus

January 17, 1915
b. Angott, Sammy
b. Smith, Mayo

January 19, 1915
b. Ruder, Melvin

January 20, 1915
b. Marek, Kurt W

January 21, 1915
b. Hewitt, Alan
b. Sefton, William

January 23, 1915
b. Lewis, William Arthur, Sir

January 24, 1915
b. Goodson, Mark
b. Motherwell, Robert Burns

January 25, 1915
b. Deiss, Joseph Jay
b. Maccoll, Ewan

January 26, 1915
b. Hopper, William

January 27, 1915
b. Brymer, Jack

January 30, 1915
b. Ireland, John
b. Profumo, John Dennis

January 31, 1915
b. Hackett, Bobby
b. Merton, Thomas
b. Moore, Garry

February 1, 1915
b. Matthews, Stanley, Sir

February 2, 1915
b. Eban, Abba

February 4, 1915
b. Evans, Ray
b. Talman, William

February 5, 1915
b. Hofstadter, Robert
b. Millar, Margaret (Ellis)
b. Sanderlin, George William

February 8, 1915
b. Jenkins, Newell
b. Lustig, Alvin

February 9, 1915
b. Miranda, Carmen

February 12, 1915
b. Goodpaster, Andrew Jackson
b. Greene, Lorne
d. Crosby, Fanny

February 13, 1915
b. Aung San
b. Bettger, Lyle

February 14, 1915
b. Austin, John Paul

February 15, 1915
d. Gokhale, Gopal Krishna

February 18, 1915
b. Calvert, Phyllis
b. Gordon, Joe
b. Landowski, Marcel
d. James, Frank

February 20, 1915
b. Harbert, Chick

February 21, 1915
b. Sheridan, Ann

February 22, 1915
b. Lesnevich, Gus
b. Munshin, Jules
b. Seymour, Dan

February 23, 1915
b. Weingarten, Violet Brown

February 24, 1915
b. Ferrier, Jim

February 28, 1915
b. Frings, Ketti
b. Medawar, Peter Brian, Sir
b. Mostel, Zero

March 6, 1915
b. Hudson, Rochelle

March 7, 1915
b. Chaban-Delmas, Jacques Pierre
Michel

March 8, 1915
b. Kitagawa, Joseph Mitsuo

March 10, 1915
b. Bertoia, Harry
b. Groves, Charles Barnard, Sir

March 12, 1915
b. Mucha, Jiri
d. Witte, Sergey Yulyevich

March 15, 1915
b. Schoenbach, Sol Israel
b. Schoenbrun, David
d. Crane, Walter

March 17, 1915
b. Arbib, Robert Simeon, Jr.
b. McGee, Gale William

March 18, 1915
b. Condon, Richard (Thomas)

March 20, 1915
b. Kirchschlager, Rudolf
b. Richter, Sviatoslav Theofilovich
d. Adams, Charles Francis, Jr.

March 21, 1915
d. Taylor, Frederick Winslow

March 22, 1915
b. Williams, Roy Lee

March 24, 1915
b. Cox, John Rogers

March 27, 1915
b. Lockwood, Robert, Jr.

March 28, 1915
b. Knauer, Virginia Harrington Wright

March 29, 1915
   d. Denslow, W(illiam) W(allace)

March 31, 1915
   b. Morgan, Henry

April 1, 1915
   b. Conreid, Hans
   b. Hemingway, Leicester

April 3, 1915
   b. Cody, Iron Eyes
   d. Peretz, Isaac Loeb

April 4, 1915
   b. Ahlin, Lars
   b. Waters, Muddy

April 7, 1915
   b. Holiday, Billie

April 8, 1915
   b. Higbe, Kirby

April 9, 1915
   b. Wibberley, Leonard Patrick
   O'Connor

April 10, 1915
   b. DeButts, John Dulany
   b. Morgan, Harry
   d. Bitter, Karl Theodore Francis

April 13, 1915
   b. DeJong, Petrus
   d. Nelson, William Rockhill

April 15, 1915
   b. Washington, Walter Edward

April 16, 1915
   d. Aldrich, Nelson Wilmarth

April 17, 1915
   b. Foss, Joe
   b. Harkness, Rebekah West

April 19, 1915
   b. Kennedy, Joseph Patrick, Jr.

April 21, 1915
   d. Hugo, Adele

April 22, 1915
   b. Barnes, Edward Larrabee

April 23, 1915
   d. Brooke, Rupert Chawner

April 24, 1915
   b. Goyen, William

April 25, 1915
   b. Tajo, Italo

April 26, 1915
   b. Kubly, Herbert (Oswald)
   d. Bunny, John

April 27, 1915
   d. Scriabin, Alexander Nicholaevich

April 29, 1915
   b. Mills, Donald

April 30, 1915
   b. Henderson, Bruce

May 3, 1915
   b. Comden, Betty
   b. Lippold, Richard

May 5, 1915
   b. Faye, Alice
   b. Rovere, Richard Halworth
   d. Schindler, Solomon

May 6, 1915
   b. Perle, George
   b. Welles, Orson
   b. White, Theodore Harold

May 7, 1915
   b. Elliot, Win
   d. Frohman, Charles
   d. Hubbard, Elbert Green

May 8, 1915
   d. Turner, Henry McNeal

May 10, 1915
   b. Dickens, Monica Enid
   d. Lamprecht, Karl

May 11, 1915
   b. Philbrick, Herbert Arthur

May 12, 1915
   b. Engel, Lyle Kenyon

May 13, 1915
   b. Howe, Oscar

May 15, 1915
   b. Monicelli, Mario
   b. Samuelson, Paul Anthony

May 16, 1915
   b. Hosmer, Craig

May 20, 1915
   b. Dayan, Moshe

May 22, 1915
   b. Baker, George

May 27, 1915
   b. Wouk, Herman

May 28, 1915
   b. McKay, Scott

May 29, 1915
   b. Buketoff, Igor
   b. Munchinger, Karl

May 30, 1915
   b. Blair, Frank
   b. Kelley, Larry
   b. Lang, Daniel
   b. Manulis, Martin
   b. Wiesner, Jerome B(ert)

June 2, 1915
   b. del Ray, Lester (Ramon Alvarez)

June 3, 1915
   b. Gorcey, Leo

June 4, 1915
   b. Keita, Modibo

June 5, 1915
   b. Branley, Franklyn Mansfield
   b. Kazin, Alfred

June 6, 1915
   b. Persichetti, Vincent

June 12, 1915
   b. Gorman, Mike
   b. Rockefeller, David

June 13, 1915
   b. Budge, Don

June 15, 1915
   b. Weller, Thomas Huckle

June 16, 1915
   b. Rumor, Mariano

June 17, 1915
   b. Cadieux, Marcel (Joseph David
   Romeo)
   b. Goldman, Eric Frederick

June 18, 1915
   b. Adair, Red
   b. DeFrank, Vincent

June 19, 1915
   d. Taneyev, Sergey Ivanovich

June 20, 1915
   b. Young, Terence

June 22, 1915
   b. Warmerdam, Dutch

June 23, 1915
   b. Price, Dennis

June 24, 1915
   b. Hoyle, Fred, Sir

June 25, 1915
   b. Hayes, Peter Lind

June 26, 1915
   b. Zolotow, Charlotte Shapiro

June 27, 1915
   b. Johnson, Walter

June 29, 1915
   b. Trout, Dizzy
   b. Warrick, Ruth

June 30, 1915
   b. Litvinoff, Emanuel

July 1, 1915
   b. Dixon, Willie (James)

b. Stafford, Jean

July 2, 1915
d. Diaz, Jose de la Cruz Porfirio
d. Diaz, Porfirio

July 5, 1915
b. Paley, Barbara Cushing
b. Woodruff, John

July 6, 1915
b. Andrews, LaVerne
d. Hargrave, Lawrence

July 7, 1915
b. Dominick, Peter Hoyt
b. Ford, Ruth Elizabeth
b. Walker, Margaret (Abigail)

July 9, 1915
b. Diamond, David

July 10, 1915
b. Bellow, Saul
b. Connolly, Mike

July 12, 1915
b. Brynner, Yul

July 14, 1915
b. Lawrence, Jerome

July 16, 1915
b. Hughes, Barnard
d. White, Ellen Gould Harmon

July 17, 1915
b. Jarman, John
b. Rothstein, Arthur

July 22, 1915
d. Fleming, Sandford

July 23, 1915
b. Sardi, Vincent, Jr.

July 26, 1915
d. Murray, James Augustus Henry, Sir

July 27, 1915
b. DelMonaco, Mario

July 28, 1915
b. Townes, Charles Hard

July 31, 1915
b. Aptheker, Herbert

August 3, 1915
b. Peterson, Helen White

August 4, 1915
b. Martin, John Bartlow

August 5, 1915
b. Lisagor, Peter Irvin

August 8, 1915
b. Elliott, Jumbo

August 12, 1915
b. Wojciechowicz, Alex(ander)

August 14, 1915
b. Santamaria, Bartholomew Augustine

August 15, 1915
b. Hasso, Signe Eleonora Cecilia
b. Turkle, Brinton Cassaday

August 16, 1915
b. Hibbler, Al

August 19, 1915
b. Lardner, Ring(gold Wilmer), Jr.

August 20, 1915
d. Ehrlich, Paul Ralph
d. Finlay, Carlos Juan

August 22, 1915
b. Dellinger, David T
b. Hillier, James
b. McNamara, Margaret Craig
d. Castlemon, Harry

August 24, 1915
b. Sheldon, Alice Hastings Bradley

August 25, 1915
b. Trampler, Walter

August 26, 1915
b. Davis, Jim
b. Murphy, Arthur Richard, Jr.

August 27, 1915
b. Heller, Walter Wolfgang
b. Ramsey, Norman

August 29, 1915
b. Bergman, Ingrid
b. Pritikin, Nathan

September 1, 1915
b. Adams, John

September 3, 1915
b. Carlisle, Kitty

September 6, 1915
b. Strauss, Franz Josef

September 7, 1915
b. Gardner, Isabella

September 8, 1915
b. Daugherty, Duffy

September 9, 1915
d. Spalding, Albert Goodwill

September 10, 1915
b. O'Brien, Edmond

September 11, 1915
d. Van Horne, William Cornelius, Sir

September 12, 1915
b. Daniels, Billy
b. Kronhausen, Eberhard Wilhelm

September 13, 1915
b. Frank, Clinton Edward
b. Heiskell, Andrew
b. Sullivan, William Hallisey, Jr.

September 15, 1915
b. Brodie, Fawn McKay
b. Cassini, Igor Loiewski
b. Krag, Jens Otto

September 16, 1915
b. Praeger, Frederick A(mos)

September 20, 1915
b. Lee-Smith, Hughie

September 21, 1915
b. Chapin, Roy Dikeman, Jr.
d. Comstock, Anthony

September 23, 1915
b. Baker, Julius

September 24, 1915
b. Gates, Larry
b. Montoya, Joseph Manuel

September 25, 1915
b. Sperling, Godfrey, Jr.
d. Hervieu, Paul-Ernest

September 26, 1915
b. Brimsek, Frankie
d. Hardie, James Keir

September 27, 1915
d. Gourmont, Remy (-Marie-Charles) de

September 28, 1915
b. Rosenberg, Ethel Greenglass

September 29, 1915
b. Handlin, Oscar
b. Marshall, Brenda

September 30, 1915
b. Clark, Peggy
b. Maddox, Lester Garfield

October 1, 1915
b. Bruner, Jerome Seymour

October 8, 1915
b. Vaughan, Bill

October 9, 1915
b. Andrews, Edward
b. Crockett, James Underwood

October 11, 1915
d. Duniway, Abigail Jane Scott
d. Fabre, Jean Henri

October 12, 1915
d. Cavell, Edith Louisa

October 13, 1915
b. Wilde, Cornel

October 14, 1915
d. Hunter, Thomas

October 15, 1915
b. Medeiros, Humberto, Cardinal

October 16, 1915
b. Holdren, Judd Clifton

October 17, 1915
b. Miller, Arthur

October 18, 1915
b. Mosley, J(ohn) Brooke
b. Yung, Victor Sen

October 19, 1915
d. McCoy, Joseph Geiting

October 20, 1915
b. Ginsberg, Mitchell I(rving)

October 24, 1915
b. Gobbi, Tito
b. Laski, Marghanita

October 25, 1915
b. Cox, Constance

October 28, 1915
b. Soo, Jack

October 30, 1915
b. Carnevale, Ben
b. Friendly, Fred W.
b. Hussey, Ruth Carol
d. Tupper, Charles

October 31, 1915
b. Wechsler, James Arthur

November 4, 1915
b. Feifel, Herman

November 5, 1915
b. Biller, Moe

November 6, 1915
b. Oldfield, Maurice, Sir

November 7, 1915
b. Morrison, Philip

November 9, 1915
b. Shriver, (Robert) Sargent

November 11, 1915
b. Proxmire, William

November 12, 1915
b. Barthes, Roland (Gerard)

November 13, 1915
b. Benchley, Nathaniel Goddard

November 14, 1915
b. Trafficante, Santo, Jr.
d. Washington, Booker T(aliafero)

November 15, 1915
d. Trudeau, Edward Livingston

November 16, 1915
b. Fritz, Jean Guttery

November 19, 1915
b. Halaby, Najeeb E(lias)
b. Sutherland, Earl Wilbur, Jr.
d. Hill, Joe

November 20, 1915
b. Hu Yaobang
d. Schechter, Solomon

November 22, 1915
b. White, Stephen

November 23, 1915
b. Dehner, John Forkum

November 25, 1915
b. Pinochet Ugarte, Augusto

November 26, 1915
b. Wild, Earl
d. Burpee, W(ashington) Atlee

November 27, 1915
b. Adonias (Aguiar) Filho
b. Alessandro, Victor Nicholas

November 28, 1915
b. Simonov, Konstantin (Kirill)
   Mikhailovich

November 29, 1915
b. Schonberg, Harold C
b. Strayhorn, Billy

November 30, 1915
b. Duke, Angier Biddle
b. Taube, Henry
b. Piaf, Edith

December 1, 1915
b. Johnston, Johnny

December 2, 1915
b. Gentry, Minnie Lee
b. Green, Adolf
b. Hearst, Randolph Apperson

December 3, 1915
b. Hodgson, James Day

December 4, 1915
b. Heywood, Eddie, Jr.

December 7, 1915
b. Wallach, Eli

December 9, 1915
b. Schwarzkopf, Elisabeth

December 10, 1915
b. Murphy, Thomas Aquinas
b. Ode, Robert C

December 12, 1915
b. Jurgens, Curt
b. Sinatra, Frank

December 13, 1915
b. MacDonald, Ross
b. Vorster, Balthazar Johannes

December 14, 1915
b. Dailey, Dan

December 16, 1915
b. Murphy, Turk

December 19, 1915
b. Woolpert, Phil

December 20, 1915
b. Mann, Paul

December 22, 1915
d. Hughes, Arthur

December 25, 1915
b. Wilson, Richard

December 27, 1915
b. Masters, William Howell

December 29, 1915
b. Ruark, Robert Chester

1916

b. Aptidon, Hassan Gouled
b. Bakhtiar, Shahpur
b. Batchler, Amelia
b. Caldera Rodriguez, Rafael
b. Campanis, Al
b. Caselotti, Adriana
b. Coors, William K
b. Dadie, Bernard Binlin
b. Davies, Rupert
b. Eames, Ray
b. Farah, James
b. Handler, Elliot
b. Hunter, Madeline Cheek
b. Lamizana, Sangoule
b. Lasswell, Fred
b. Lee, Pinky
b. Leokum, Arkady
b. Littlewood, Joan
b. McWilliams, Alden S
b. Scherr, Max
b. Seton, Anya Chase
b. Wright, Peter (Maurice)
d. Natsume, Soseki
d. Shinburn, Mark
d. Stokely, Anna

January 1, 1916
b. Wrightson, Earl

January 2, 1916
b. Neumann, Robert Gerhard
d. Lamar, Joseph Rucker

January 3, 1916
b. Furness, Betty
b. King, Warren Thomas
b. Rice, Gregory
d. Dodge, Grenville Mellen

January 6, 1916
b. Maleska, Eugene T.

January 7, 1916
b. Estes, E(lliott) M(arantette)
b. Estes, Pete
b. Pratt, Babe

January 8, 1916
d. Rehan, Ada

January 9, 1916
b. Holland, Jerome Heartwell

January 10, 1916
b. Bergstrom, Sune
b. Hamilton, Bob

January 12, 1916
b. Botha, Pieter Willem
b. Wehrwein, Austin Carl

January 16, 1916
b. Rothschild, Edmund Leopold de
d. Huerta, Victoriano

January 20, 1916
b. Stone, Paula

January 22, 1916
b. Durnan, Bill
b. Teichmann, Howard Miles

January 23, 1916
b. Duncan, David Douglas

January 24, 1916
b. Haas, Walter A(braham), Jr.

January 29, 1916
b. Murphy, Franklin D(avid)

January 30, 1916
d. Jacobs, Joseph

January 31, 1916
b. Parker, Frank

February 6, 1916
b. Doggett, Bill
d. Dario, Ruben

February 9, 1916
d. Richardson, George Taylor

February 11, 1916
b. Kennedy, Florynce

February 12, 1916
b. Alioto, Joseph L(awrence)
d. Trowbridge, John Townsend

February 15, 1916
b. Ballantine, Ian (Keith)
b. Seton-Watson, Hugh

February 18, 1916
b. Drapeau, Jean
b. Lawrence, Lawrence Shubert, Jr.
b. New, Lloyd Kiva

February 19, 1916
b. Arcaro, Eddie
b. Duong Van Minh
d. Mach, Ernst

February 20, 1916
b. Tripp, Paul
d. Arnoldson, Klas Pontus

February 22, 1916
d. Smalls, Robert
d. Wallace, Henry

February 26, 1916
b. Gleason, Jackie

February 28, 1916
d. James, Henry, (Jr.)

March 3, 1916
b. Hutton, Ina Ray
b. Whitehead, Robert

March 4, 1916
b. Miller, Arjay Ray
b. Whiffen, Marcus
d. Marc, Franz

March 8, 1916
b. McBride, Lloyd

March 9, 1916
b. Brandon, Henry Oscar

March 11, 1916
b. Clemo, Jack
b. Keats, Ezra Jack
b. Wilson, (James) Harold, Sir

March 13, 1916
b. Boggs, Lindy
b. Roosevelt, John Aspinal

March 14, 1916
b. Eysenck, Hans J(urgen)
b. Foote, Horton

March 15, 1916
b. James, Harry

March 19, 1916
b. Wallace, Irving

March 20, 1916
b. Fingesten, Peter

March 21, 1916
b. Duke, Robin (Anthony Hare)
d. Younger, Cole

March 22, 1916
b. Kline, Nathan Schellenberg

March 24, 1916
d. Granados, Enrique

March 25, 1916
b. Fielding, Gabriel
d. Ishi

March 26, 1916
b. Anfinsen, Christian Boehmer
b. Hayden, Sterling Relyea Walter
b. Stokely, Alfred Jehu
d. Blow, Susan Elizabeth

March 27, 1916
b. Warner, Jack, Jr.

March 29, 1916
b. McCarthy, Eugene Joseph

March 31, 1916
b. Mayer, Norman D
b. Oldenbourg, Zoe
b. Wood, John Howland, Jr.

April 1, 1916
d. Angell, James Burrill

April 3, 1916
b. Caen, Herb

April 4, 1916
b. Owen, Mickey

April 5, 1916
b. Peck, Gregory

April 9, 1916
b. Leonard, Bill

April 11, 1916
b. Fortmann, Danny
b. Ginastera, Alberto Evaristo
d. Davis, Richard Harding

April 12, 1916
b. Cleary, Beverly (Atlee Bunn)

April 14, 1916
b. Buckley, Emerson

April 15, 1916
b. Bloomingdale, Alfred S

April 16, 1916
b. Keppel, Francis
d. Peck, George Wilbur

April 17, 1916
b. Bandaranaike, Sirimavo Ratwatte
   Dias
b. Eggerth, Marta

April 18, 1916
b. Kolchin, Ellis Robert

April 19, 1916
b. Carnegie, Mary Elizabeth Lancaster
b. Moos, Malcolm Charles

April 20, 1916
b. Lowery, Robert O

April 21, 1916
b. Quinn, Anthony Rudolph Oaxaca
d. Surratt, John Harrison

April 22, 1916
b. Menuhin, Yehudi

April 23, 1916
b. Dozier, Edward P.
b. Wilkinson, Bud
b. Wilkinson, Charles (Burnham)

April 24, 1916
b. Kauffmann, Stanley Jules

April 25, 1916
b. Barber, Jerry

April 26, 1916
  b. West, Morris L(anglo)

April 27, 1916
  b. Slaughter, Enos Bradsher

April 28, 1916
  d. Strong, Josiah

April 30, 1916
  b. Shannon, Claude Elwood
  b. Shaw, Robert Lawson

May 1, 1916
  b. Ford, Glenn

May 3, 1916
  b. Gonzalez, Henry Barbosa
  b. Mathieu, Noel Jean
  d. MacDonagh, Thomas
  d. Pearse, Padraic

May 9, 1916
  b. Du Bois, William Pene

May 10, 1916
  b. Babbitt, Milton Byron

May 11, 1916
  b. Cela (Trulock), Camilo Jose
  d. Reger, Max

May 12, 1916
  b. Murray, Albert L(ee)
  b. Simionato, Guilietta

May 13, 1916
  d. Aleichem, Sholom
  d. Kellogg, Clara Louise

May 14, 1916
  b. Harper, Marion, Jr.

May 15, 1916
  b. Singh, Giani Zail

May 17, 1916
  b. Maugham, Robin

May 19, 1916
  b. Bloom, Murray Teigh
  b. Jack, Homer A(lexander)

May 20, 1916
  b. Chadwick, William Owen

May 21, 1916
  b. Robbins, Harold

May 25, 1916
  b. Simms, Ginny

May 26, 1916
  b. Hardin, Louis Thomas

May 27, 1916
  d. Gallieni, Joseph-Simon

May 28, 1916
  b. Percy, Walker

May 29, 1916
  d. Hill, James Jerome

May 30, 1916
  d. Mosby, John Singleton

June 1, 1916
  b. Aldrich, Ki

June 4, 1916
  b. Nelson, Gaylord Anton

June 5, 1916
  b. Rosen, Sidney
  d. Kitchener, Horatio Herbert

June 6, 1916
  d. Yuan, Shih-Kai

June 7, 1916
  b. Darcy, Tom

June 8, 1916
  b. Crick, Francis Harry Compton

June 9, 1916
  b. Hightower, Florence Josephine Cole
  b. McNamara, Robert S(trange)
  b. Paul, Les

June 11, 1916
  d. Webster, Jean

June 12, 1916
  b. Allen, Irwin
  b. Tors, Ivan

June 13, 1916
  b. Conway, Shirl

June 15, 1916
  b. Field, Marshall, IV
  b. Simon, Herbert Alexander

June 16, 1916
  b. Luisetti, Hank

June 17, 1916
  b. Atkinson, Ted

June 18, 1916
  b. Turbay Ayala, Julio Cesar

June 21, 1916
  b. Friedman, Herbert
  b. O'Connor, Buddy

June 23, 1916
  b. Worth, Irene

June 24, 1916
  b. Ciardi, John Anthony

June 25, 1916
  b. Saxbe, William Bart
  b. Toynbee, Philip
  d. Eakins, Thomas

June 26, 1916
  b. Taddei, Giuseppe
  d. Sherwin, Henry Alden

July 1, 1916
  b. DeHavilland, Olivia Mary
  b. Shklovsky, Iosif Samvilovitch
  b. Stanford-Tuck, Robert Roland

July 2, 1916
  b. Gray, Barry

July 3, 1916
  b. Kundla, John
  d. Green, Hetty

July 4, 1916
  b. Tokyo Rose
  b. Toon, Malcolm
  d. Seeger, Alan

July 6, 1916
  d. Redon, Odilon

July 7, 1916
  b. Robbie, Joe

July 9, 1916
  b. Heath, Edward Richard George

July 10, 1916
  b. Provensen, Martin

July 11, 1916
  b. Prokhorov, Alexander Mikhailovich
  b. Whitlam, Edward Gough

July 12, 1916
  b. Curtis, Ken
  d. Cohan, Josephine

July 14, 1916
  b. Ginzburg, Natalia
  b. Harmon, Claude

July 16, 1916
  d. Metchnikoff, Elie

July 17, 1916
  b. Steber, Eleanor

July 18, 1916
  b. Armitage, Kenneth
  b. Gray, Louis Patrick
  d. Immelmann, Max

July 19, 1916
  b. Cavarretta, Phil(ip Joseph)
  b. Merriam, Eve

July 22, 1916
  b. Cerdan, Marcel B
  d. Riley, James Whitcomb

July 23, 1916
  d. Ramsay, William, Sir

July 24, 1916
  b. Eberle, Bob
  b. MacDonald, John Dann

July 25, 1916
  d. Tompkins, Sally Louisa

July 27, 1916
  b. Ashmore, Harry Scott

b. Hardwick, Elizabeth
b. Wynn, Keenan

July 28, 1916
b. Brown, David
b. Cregar, Laird

July 29, 1916
b. Christian, Charlie

July 31, 1916
b. Todman, Bill

August 3, 1916
d. Casement, Roger David

August 5, 1916
b. Chubak, Sadeq-i
b. Viereck, Peter Robert Edwin

August 6, 1916
b. Burke, Mike
b. Cooney, Barbara
b. Gerstacker, Carl A(llan)
b. Hofstadter, Richard

August 9, 1916
d. Braun, Lily von Kretschman

August 10, 1916
b. Beery, Noah, Jr.

August 11, 1916
b. Harlow, Bryce Nathaniel
b. Wind, Herbert Warren

August 12, 1916
b. Nelson, Ralph

August 14, 1916
b. Mara, Wellington T

August 16, 1916
d. Boccioni, Umberto

August 17, 1916
b. Toledano, Ralph de

August 18, 1916
b. Lympany, Moura

August 19, 1916
b. Wilson, Marie (Katherine Elizabeth)

August 20, 1916
b. Goldfinger, Nathaniel

August 21, 1916
b. Gagne, Robert Mills

August 25, 1916
b. Johnson, Van
b. Robbins, Fredrick Chapman

August 26, 1916
b. Hill, Virginia

August 27, 1916
b. Raye, Martha
b. Stein, Herbert

August 28, 1916
b. Mills, C(harles) Wright
d. Harpignies, Henri

August 29, 1916
b. Montgomery, George

August 31, 1916
b. Schorr, Daniel Louis

September 3, 1916
b. Bentley, Doug(las Wagner)
b. Knight, Arthur
b. Memphis Slim
b. Stanky, Eddie

September 4, 1916
b. Lowndes, Robert A(ugustine)
W(ard)

September 5, 1916
b. Shuster, Frank
b. Yerby, Frank (Garvin)

September 10, 1916
b. McCarten, John
b. Sebelius, Keith George

September 12, 1916
b. Anderson, Cat

September 13, 1916
b. Dahl, Roald

September 14, 1916
b. Bentley, Eric
d. Duhem, Pierre Maurice Marie
d. Royce, Josiah

September 15, 1916
b. Lockwood, Margaret Mary
d. Echegaray y Eizaguirre, Jose

September 16, 1916
d. McGee, Frank

September 17, 1916
b. Stewart, Mary (Florence Elinor)
b. Tsedenbal, Yumzahgin
d. Low, Seth

September 18, 1916
b. Brazzi, Rossano
b. Rhodes, John Jacob

September 19, 1916
b. Tiller, Rogers
d. Sherman, Frank Dempster

September 21, 1916
b. Giroud, Francoise
b. Kauffman, Ewing Marion

September 23, 1916
b. Moro, Aldo

September 24, 1916
b. Alpert, Hollis

September 27, 1916
b. Fischetti, John
b. Stratton, Samuel S(tuddiford)

September 28, 1916
b. Finch, Peter

September 29, 1916
b. Buero Vallejo, Antonio
b. Howard, Trevor Wallace

October 3, 1916
b. Alvarino (de Leira), Angeles
b. Herriot, James

October 4, 1916
b. Sidney, George

October 6, 1916
b. Ellin, Stanley
b. Sneider, Vernon John

October 7, 1916
b. Burns, John Horne
b. Rostow, Walt Whitman

October 8, 1916
b. Matsunaga, Spark Masayuki

October 9, 1916
b. Perry, Harold R

October 10, 1916
b. Gascoyne, David Emery

October 11, 1916
b. Marshak, Robert E(ugene)

October 14, 1916
b. Koop, C(harles) Everett

October 16, 1916
b. Winsor, Kathleen

October 17, 1916
b. Marley, John
b. Partch, Virgil Franklin, II

October 19, 1916
b. Blum, Stella
b. Dausset, Jean (Baptiste Gabriel
Joachim)
b. Gilels, Emil Grigoyevich

October 23, 1916
b. Whittemore, Arthur Austin

October 25, 1916
d. Chase, William Merritt

October 26, 1916
b. Mitterrand, Francois (Maurice
Marie)

October 28, 1916
b. Harris, Willard Palmer
d. Abbe, Cleveland

October 29, 1916
b. Keogh, James

October 31, 1916
b. Barnett, Marvin Robert
d. Russell, Charles Taze

November 1, 1916
b. Mack, Peter

November 4, 1916
b. Cronkite, Walter Leland, Jr.
b. Handler, Ruth

November 6, 1916
b. Bushkin, Joe
b. Conniff, Ray

November 8, 1916
b. Havoc, June
b. Weiss, Peter Ulrich

November 10, 1916
b. May, Billy
d. Sutton, Walter Stanborough

November 11, 1916
b. Foote, Shelby

November 13, 1916
b. Ashford, Emmett Littleton
b. Elam, Jack
d. Lowell, Percival
d. Saki

November 14, 1916
d. George, Henry, Jr.

November 15, 1916
b. Barrow, Ruth Nita, Dame
b. Davis, Edward Michael
d. Rivera, Luis Munoz
d. Sienkiewicz, Henryk Adam
Aleksander Pius

November 16, 1916
b. Butler, Daws

November 17, 1916
b. Silk, George

November 20, 1916
b. Canova, Judy

November 21, 1916
b. Luckman, Sid(ney)
d. Francis Joseph, (I)
d. Franz Joseph I

November 22, 1916
b. Ross, Percy Nathan
d. London, Jack

November 23, 1916
d. Booth, Charles
d. Napravnik, Eduard

November 24, 1916
b. Ackerman, Forest J
d. Maxim, Hiram Stevens, Sir

November 28, 1916
b. Theriault, Yves
b. Tregaskis, Richard William

December 1, 1916
b. Stoutenburg, Adrien Pearl

December 2, 1916
b. Bentley, John
b. Hearst, David W(hitmire)
b. Ventura, Charlie
b. Williams, Carroll Milton

December 4, 1916
b. Kahn, E(ly) J(acques), Jr.

December 5, 1916
d. Richter, Hans

December 6, 1916
b. Eldjarn, Kristjan
d. Tosti, Francesco Paolo

December 9, 1916
b. Douglas, Kirk
b. Hildesheimer, Wolfgang

December 12, 1916
d. Lacombe, Albert

December 14, 1916
b. Priscilla of Boston

December 15, 1916
b. Wilkins, Maurice Hugh Frederick

December 16, 1916
b. Weiss, Theodore (Russell)

December 18, 1916
b. Fraser, Douglas Andrew
b. Grable, Betty

December 20, 1916
b. Smith, Courtney Craig

December 22, 1916
b. Boswell, Charles Albert

December 31, 1916
b. Boller, Paul Franklin, Jr.
b. Wierwille, Victor Paul
d. Rasputin, Grigori Efimovich

1917

b. Angleton, James J(esus)
b. Avakian, Aram A
b. Barker, Bernard L
b. Brown, Rosemary
b. Constantine, Eddie
b. Francis, Freddie
b. Goodlad, John Inkster
b. Haworth, Ted
b. Heard, J.C.
b. Justin, John, Jr.
b. Kornman, Mary
b. Lamborghini, Ferruccio
b. McCobb, Paul Winthrop
b. Monroe, Phil
b. Nkomo, Joshua (Mqabuko
Nyongolo)
b. Patton, Edward L
b. Rabin, Yehuda L
b. Robbins, Irvine
b. Seiler, James, W
b. Thao, Tran Duc
b. Yasui, Minoru
d. Borochov, Dov Ber

d. Cruz, Oswaldo Goncalves
d. Naoroji, Dadabhai
d. Olney, Richard

January 1, 1917
b. Cott, Ted

January 2, 1917
b. Zorina, Vera
d. Tylor, Edward Bennett, Sir

January 3, 1917
b. Straus, Roger W(illiams), Jr.
b. Walters, Vernon Anthony

January 5, 1917
b. Wagner, Wieland Adolf Gottfried

January 6, 1917
b. Jumblatt, Kamal Fouad

January 7, 1917
b. Kay, Ulysses Simpson

January 8, 1917
b. Riad, Mahmoud
b. Taylor, Peter (Hillsman)

January 9, 1917
b. Lom, Herbert
b. Louise, Anita

January 10, 1917
d. Cody, Buffalo Bill

January 11, 1917
b. Robarts, John Parmenter

January 13, 1917
d. Niemann, Albert

January 14, 1917
b. Butterfield, Billy

January 15, 1917
d. De Morgan, William Frend

January 16, 1917
b. Hartley, Fred Lloyd
d. Dewey, George

January 19, 1917
b. Nicolson, Nigel
b. Raitt, John Emmet

January 24, 1917
b. Borgnine, Ernest

January 25, 1917
b. Prigogine, Ilya

January 26, 1917
b. Verity, C(alvin) William, Jr.

January 29, 1917
d. Cromer, 1st Earl of

January 30, 1917
b. Darion, Joseph

February 2, 1917
b. Muoi, Do

February 4, 1917
b. Yahya Khan, Agha Muhammad

February 5, 1917
b. Edelmann, Otto

February 11, 1917
b. DeSantis, Giuseppe
b. Sheldon, Sidney

February 12, 1917
b. Cervi, Al
b. DiMaggio, Dom(inic Paul)
b. Scherman, Thomas Kielty

February 14, 1917
b. Hauptman, Herbert Aaron
b. Hauptman, Herbert Aaron

February 19, 1917
b. McCullers, Carson (Smith)
d. Funston, Frederick

February 22, 1917
b. Bowles, Jane Sydney
b. Leek, Sybil

February 24, 1917
b. Long, Scott
b. Raedler, Dorothy (Florence)

February 25, 1917
b. Burgess, Anthony
b. Raymond, James C

February 26, 1917
b. Taft, Robert A(lphonso), Jr.

February 27, 1917
b. Connally, John B.

February 28, 1917
b. Malcolm, George

March 1, 1917
b. Gleason, Ralph Joseph
b. Lowell, Robert Trail Spence, Jr.
b. Shore, Dinah

March 2, 1917
b. Arnaz, Desi
b. Collins, Janet Faye

March 5, 1917
b. Kirbo, Charles H(ughes)

March 6, 1917
b. Eisner, Will(iam E.)
b. Gray, Pete(r)

March 8, 1917
b. Fiedler, Leslie Aaron
d. Zeppelin, Ferdinand Adolf August
   Heinrich von, Count

March 9, 1917
b. Fascell, Dante B(runo)

March 10, 1917
b. Hare, David
b. Merrill, John Putnam

March 12, 1917
b. Withers, Googie

March 16, 1917
d. Studebaker, John Mohler

March 17, 1917
b. Brisson, Frederick
d. Brentano, Franz Clemens

March 19, 1917
b. Lipatti, Dinu

March 21, 1917
b. Barnetson, William Denholm
b. Yadin, Yigael

March 22, 1917
b. Grey, Virginia
b. Shaplen, Robert Modell

March 23, 1917
b. Guarnieri, Johnny

March 24, 1917
b. Ehricke, Krafft Arnold
b. Kendrew, John Cowdery, Sir

March 26, 1917
b. Thomas, Rufus

March 27, 1917
b. Vance, Cyrus Roberts
d. Ezekiel, Moses Jacob

March 28, 1917
b. Meloy, Francis Edward, Jr.
b. Rountree, William M(anning)
d. Ryder, Albert Pinkham

March 29, 1917
b. Holmes, Tommy

March 31, 1917
d. Behring, Emil Adolph von

April 1, 1917
b. Baker, Bonnie
b. Janney, Leon
d. Joplin, Scott

April 3, 1917
b. Clements, William Perry, Jr.

April 5, 1917
b. Bloch, Robert Albert

April 6, 1917
b. Macy, John Williams, Jr.

April 7, 1917
b. Armstrong, R G

April 8, 1917
d. Bateman, Kate Josephine

April 9, 1917
b. Hewes, Henry
d. Thomas, Edward

April 10, 1917
b. Woodward, Robert Burns

April 11, 1917
b. Sobell, Morton

April 12, 1917
b. Bijedic, Dzemal
b. Tree, Marietta Endicott Peabody

April 13, 1917
b. Anderson, Robert Orville
d. Brady, Diamond Jim

April 14, 1917
b. Hobson, Valerie Babette
b. Luboff, Norman
b. Miller, Marvin Julian
d. Zamenhof, Ludwik Lazar

April 16, 1917
b. Salomon, Charlotte

April 17, 1917
b. Campos, Roberto de Oliveira

April 18, 1917
b. Frederika Louise

April 21, 1917
b. Lambert, J(ack) W(alter)

April 22, 1917
b. Chauvire, Yvette
b. Nolan, Sidney, Sir

April 25, 1917
b. Fitzgerald, Ella

April 26, 1917
b. Maglie, Sal(vatore Anthony)
b. Pei, I(eoh) M(ing)

April 28, 1917
b. Anderson, Robert Woodruff

April 29, 1917
b. Deren, Maya

April 30, 1917
b. Wain, Bea

May 1, 1917
b. Beradino, John
b. Darrieux, Danielle
d. Rodo, Jose Enrique

May 3, 1917
b. Gligorov, Kiro

May 5, 1917
b. Sawyer, John E(dward)

May 6, 1917
b. Stewart, Black Jack
d. Stuart, Ruth McEnery

May 7, 1917
b. Rafferty, Max(well Lewis, Jr.)

May 12, 1917
b. Kay, Mary

May 14, 1917
d. Choate, Joseph Hodges

May 15, 1917
b. Barnes, Wade

May 17, 1917
b. Creach, Papa
b. Lescoulie, Jack

May 18, 1917
b. Donald, James
d. Maskelyne, John Nevil
d. Pratt, Bela Lyon

May 19, 1917
d. Lockwood, Belva Ann Bennett

May 20, 1917
b. Lawson, Donald Elmer

May 21, 1917
b. Burr, Raymond (William Stacy)
b. Day, Dennis
b. Yunich, David Lawrence

May 23, 1917
b. Squires, James Radcliffe

May 25, 1917
b. Cochran, Steve
b. Cooper, Joseph D
b. Hesburgh, Theodore Martin
d. DeReszke, Edouard

May 26, 1917
b. Singer, Jane Sherrod

May 28, 1917
b. Commoner, Barry

May 29, 1917
b. Kennedy, John F(itzgerald)

June 1, 1917
b. McNellis, Maggi

June 3, 1917
b. Saint Cyr, Lillian

June 4, 1917
b. Collingwood, Charles Cummings
b. Metzenbaum, Howard M(orton)

June 6, 1917
b. Kerkorian, Kirk

June 7, 1917
b. Brooks, Gwendolyn Elizabeth
b. Cooke, David Coxe

June 8, 1917
b. Romney, Seymour Leonard
b. White, Byron Raymond

June 9, 1917
b. Reed, John Shedd

June 12, 1917
b. Lane, Priscilla

June 14, 1917
b. Monash, Paul
b. Rootes, William Edward Rootes, Baron

June 15, 1917
b. Payne, Leon

June 16, 1917
b. Graham, Katharine Meyer
b. Penn, Irving

June 17, 1917
b. Martin, Dean

June 18, 1917
b. Boone, Richard

June 19, 1917
b. Buttram, Pat

June 20, 1917
d. Crafts, James Mason

June 22, 1917
b. O'Brien, Davey

June 27, 1917
b. Riles, Wilson Camanza
d. Schmoller, Gustav Friedrich von

June 30, 1917
b. Hayward, Susan
b. Horne, Lena Calhoun
b. Rich, Buddy

July 2, 1917
d. Tree, Herbert Beerbohm

July 3, 1917
b. Davis, Lorenzo

July 5, 1917
b. Manolete

July 7, 1917
b. O'Brien, Larry

July 8, 1917
b. Brown, Pamela
b. Emerson, Faye Margaret
b. Langan, Glenn
b. Powers, James Farl
d. Thomson, Tom

July 9, 1917
b. Youlou, Fulbert

July 11, 1917
b. Suzman, Helen

July 12, 1917
b. Wyeth, Andrew

July 13, 1917
b. Hill, Morton A(nthony)

July 14, 1917
b. Eastlake, William (Derry)
b. Edwards, Douglas

July 15, 1917
b. Conquest, Robert

July 17, 1917
b. Boudreau, Lou(is)
b. Diller, Phyllis

July 19, 1917
b. Scranton, William Warren

July 22, 1917
b. McGarity, Lou

July 23, 1917
b. Arriola, Gus
b. Deming, Barbara
b. Kreuger, Kurt

July 24, 1917
b. Brickman, Morrie

July 27, 1917
d. Kocher, Emil Theodor

August 5, 1917
b. Reedy, George E(dward)

August 6, 1917
b. Mitchum, Robert
b. Tyne, George

August 10, 1917
b. Tomes, Margot

August 11, 1917
b. Browne, Dik

August 13, 1917
b. McNeil, Claudia Mae
d. Buchner, Eduard

August 15, 1917
b. Romero y Galdamez, Oscar Arnulfo

August 16, 1917
b. Christopher, Matt(hew F.)

August 18, 1917
b. Weinberger, Caspar Willard

August 20, 1917
b. Sanford, Terry
d. Baeyer, Adolf Johann Friedrich Wilhelm, von

August 22, 1917
b. Hooker, John Lee

August 23, 1917
b. Williams, Tex

August 24, 1917
b. Causley, Charles Stanley
b. James, Dennis

August 25, 1917
b. DeFore, Don
b. Ferrer, Mel(chor Gaston)

August 26, 1917
b. Smith, William French

August 28, 1917
b. Kirby, Jack

August 29, 1917
d. Hartford, George Huntington

August 30, 1917
b. Gates, Pop

August 31, 1917
b. Jordy, William H(enry)

September 2, 1917
b. Almeida, Laurindo
b. Amory, Cleveland

September 4, 1917
b. Ford, Henry, II

September 6, 1917
b. Smith, (Charles) Page

September 7, 1917
b. Cornforth, John Warcup, Sir

September 9, 1917
b. Robbins, Frank

September 10, 1917
b. Gentele, Goeran

September 11, 1917
b. Forsythe, Henderson
b. Marcos, Ferdinand Edralin
b. Mitford, Jessica
d. Guynemer, Georges Marie

September 12, 1917
b. Han Suyin

September 13, 1917
b. Haymes, Dick
b. Ward, Robert Eugene

September 14, 1917
b. Harris, Sydney J(ustin)

September 15, 1917
b. Gueden, Hilde

September 17, 1917
b. Lawrence, Jacob Armstead

September 20, 1917
b. Auerbach, Red
b. Rey, Fernando

September 22, 1917
b. Hottelet, Richard C(urt)

September 24, 1917
b. Bundy, William Putnam

September 26, 1917
b. Rico, Don(ato)

September 27, 1917
b. Auchincloss, Louis
d. Degas, (Hilaire Germain) Edgar

September 28, 1917
b. Davison, Frederic Ellis
b. Somes, Michael (George)
d. Hulme, Thomas Ernest

September 29, 1917
b. Luce, Charles (Franklin)

September 30, 1917
b. Lyubimov, Yuri Petrovich
b. Park, Chung Hee

October 1, 1917
b. Whyte, William H(ollingsworth)

October 2, 1917
b. DeDuve, Christian Rene Marie
Joseph

October 4, 1917
b. Murray, Jan

October 5, 1917
b. Worsham, Lew(is Elmer)

October 6, 1917
b. Hamer, Fannie Lou Townsend

October 7, 1917
b. Allyson, June
b. Dantine, Helmut
b. Smythe, Reg(inald)

October 8, 1917
b. Conn, Billy
b. Lord, Walter
b. Porter, Rodney Robert

October 12, 1917
b. Marshall, William
b. Wick, Charles Z

October 13, 1917
b. Stark, Ray
b. Tillstrom, Burr

October 14, 1917
b. Bibby, Thomas Geoffrey

October 15, 1917
b. Fabri, Zoltan
b. Schlesinger, Arthur M(eier), Jr.
d. Mata Hari

October 17, 1917
b. Kahn, Alfred Edward
b. Monk, Thelonious Sphere, Jr.

October 20, 1917
b. Melville, Jean-Pierre

October 21, 1917
b. Gillespie, Dizzy

October 22, 1917
b. Fontaine, Joan
d. Fitzsimmons, Bob

October 25, 1917
b. MacPhail, Lee

October 26, 1917
b. Biaggi, Mario

October 27, 1917
b. Tambo, Oliver

October 28, 1917
b. Page, Joe

October 30, 1917
b. Dobozy, Imre
b. Ogarkov, Nikolai

October 31, 1917
b. McNeill, William Hardy

November 1, 1917
b. Burroughs, Margaret Taylor

November 2, 1917
b. Rutherford, Ann
b. Wasserman, Dale

November 3, 1917
b. O'Brien, Conor Cruise
d. Bloy, Leon Marie

November 5, 1917
b. Auriol, Jacqueline Douet

November 6, 1917
b. Rashidov, Sharaf Rashidovich
d. Kendal, William Hunter

November 7, 1917
b. Cobb, Joe

November 8, 1917
d. Appleby, John Francis

November 11, 1917
d. Liliuokalani, Queen

November 12, 1917
b. Coors, Joseph

November 13, 1917
b. LaTouche, John
b. Sterling, Robert

November 14, 1917
b. Field, Virginia (Margaret Cynthia
St. John)

November 15, 1917
b. Begay, Harrison
d. Durkheim, Emile

November 17, 1917
b. Orr, Robert Dunkerson
d. Rodin, Auguste

November 18, 1917
b. DePinies, Jaime

November 19, 1917
b. Gandhi, Indira Priyadarshini Nehru

November 20, 1917
b. Locke, Bobby

November 21, 1917
b. Chung, Il-Kwon

November 22, 1917
b. Huxley, Andrew Fielding, Sir

November 24, 1917
b. Duff, Howard

November 25, 1917
b. Chestnut, Harold

November 26, 1917
b. Jergens, Adele
d. Jameson, Leander Starr, Sir

November 27, 1917
b. Smith, Bob

November 29, 1917
b. Travis, Merle Robert

December 1, 1917
b. Marion, Marty

December 2, 1917
b. Stone, Ezra (Chaim)
b. Syms, Sylvia

December 5, 1917
b. Resor, Stanley Rogers

December 8, 1917
b. Cantrick, Robert

December 9, 1917
b. Rainwater, James

December 10, 1917
d. Bowell, Mackenzie, Sir

December 12, 1917
b. Schneider, Alan
b. Warner, Denis Ashton
d. Still, Andrew Taylor

December 13, 1917
b. Frankel, Charles

December 16, 1917
b. Clarke, Arthur C(harles)
b. Kempton, (James) Murray

December 17, 1917
b. Dike, Kenneth (Onwuka)
d. Anderson, Elizabeth Garrett

December 18, 1917
b. Davis, Ossie
b. Vinson, Cleanhead

December 21, 1917
b. Boll, Heinrich (Theodor)
b. Eglevsky, Andre

December 22, 1917
b. Darro, Frankie
b. Rayburn, Gene
d. Cabrini, Frances Xavier, Saint

December 25, 1917
b. Lowe, Jack (Warren)

December 26, 1917
b. Woods, Rose Mary

December 28, 1917
b. Clarke, Ellis Emmanuel Innocent,
Sir

December 29, 1917
b. Bradley, Tom

1918

b. Arias, Roberto Emilio
b. Blanton, Jimmy
b. Coxe, Louis Osborne
b. Dall, John
b. Donald, Peter
b. Ernst, Kenneth
b. Evren, Kenan
b. Gibson, Guy
b. Kane, Henry
b. Kell, Reginald George
b. Kinnick, Nile
b. Leboyer, Frederick
b. Lewis, Robert Alvin
b. McAfee, George A
b. McCord, James Walter
b. Mokhehle, Ntsu
b. Nahayan, Zayed bin al-, Sultan
b. Nakai, Raymond
b. Ney, Richard
b. O'Day, Dawn
b. Pao, Y(ue) K(ong), Sir
b. Redman, Joyce
b. Salem, Mamdouh
b. Sisulu, Nontsikelelo Albertina
b. Szabo, Violette Bushell
b. TallMountain, Mary
b. Taylor, June
b. Zimmermann, Bernd Alois
d. Cipriani, Amilcare
d. Forrest, John, 1st Baron Forrest of
Bunbury
d. Peters, Carl

January 3, 1918
b. Andrews, Maxene

January 5, 1918
b. Dixon, Jeane (Pinckert)

January 6, 1918
d. Cantor, Georg Ferdinand Ludwig
Philipp

January 7, 1918
b. Lasky, Victor

January 9, 1918
b. Chaikin, Sol Chick

January 10, 1918
b. Chung, Arthur
b. McGraw, Harold Whittlesey, Jr.

January 12, 1918
b. Sullivan, Walter

January 15, 1918
b. Byrd, Robert C(arlyle)
b. Figueiredo, Joao Baptista de
Oliveira
b. Nasser, Gamal Abdel

January 16, 1918
b. Silliphant, Stirling Dale

January 17, 1918
b. Barr, Joseph W(alker)
b. Joseph, Keith (Sinjohn)

January 18, 1918
b. Chaney, Norman
b. Roudebush, Richard L(owell)
d. Materna, Amalia

January 19, 1918
b. Cleveland, James Harlan
b. Johnson, John Harold

January 20, 1918
b. Esquivel, Juan

January 21, 1918
b. Janigo, Antonio

January 22, 1918
b. Lach, Elmer James

January 23, 1918
b. Elion, Gertrude B(ell)

January 24, 1918
b. Einem, Gottfried von
b. Roberts, Oral

January 25, 1918
b. Donovan, King
b. Harwell, Ernie

January 26, 1918
b. Ceausescu, Nicolae
b. Farmer, Philip Jose

January 27, 1918
b. Henderson, Skitch
b. Heyns, Roger W(illiam)
b. James, Elmore

January 28, 1918
d. McCrae, John

January 29, 1918
b. Barber, Bernard
b. Forsythe, John

January 30, 1918
b. Opatoshu, David

February 1, 1918
b. Spark, Muriel Sarah

February 2, 1918
d. Sullivan, John L(awrence)

February 3, 1918
b. Bishop, Joey

b. Stephens, Helen

February 4, 1918
b. Lupino, Ida

February 5, 1918
b. Holt, Tim

February 6, 1918
d. Klimt, Gustav

February 7, 1918
b. Sager, Ruth

February 8, 1918
b. Field, Betty
d. Renault, Louis

February 10, 1918
d. Abdul-Hamid, II
d. Abdulhamid II
d. Moneta, Ernesto Teodora

February 12, 1918
b. Schwinger, Julian (Seymour)

February 13, 1918
b. Berg, Patty
b. Smith, Oliver

February 15, 1918
d. Castle, Vernon

February 17, 1918
b. Vallone, Raf(faele)

February 18, 1918
b. Gillenson, Lewis W
b. Saint-Subber, Arnold

February 22, 1918
b. Abel, Sid(ney Gerald)
b. Finley, Charles O(scar)

February 25, 1918
b. Riggs, Bobby

February 26, 1918
b. Bowen, Otis Ray
b. Sturgeon, Theodore Hamilton
d. McGovern, Terry

February 28, 1918
b. Dinkeloo, John Gerard

March 1, 1918
b. Goulart, Joao

March 2, 1918
d. Bancroft, Hubert Howe

March 3, 1918
b. Kornberg, Arthur
b. Newman, Arnold Abner

March 4, 1918
b. Andreas, Dwayne Orville

March 5, 1918
b. Schmidt, Milt(on Conrad)
b. Tobin, James

March 6, 1918
b. Von Eckardt, Wolf

March 8, 1918
b. Donahue, Sam Koontz
b. Hale, Alan, Jr.

March 9, 1918
b. Rockwell, George Lincoln
b. Spillane, Mickey
d. Wedekind, Frank

March 10, 1918
b. Broun, Heywood Hale

March 11, 1918
b. Gordon, Thomas

March 12, 1918
b. Gottschalk, Robert

March 13, 1918
b. O'Shea, Tessie

March 14, 1918
b. Chapelle, Dickey
d. Garfield, Lucretia (Rudolph)

March 15, 1918
b. Ellmann, Richard David
b. Imlach, Punch
d. Stillman, James

March 17, 1918
b. Lubalin, Herbert Frederick
b. McCambridge, Mercedes

March 18, 1918
b. Pett, Saul

March 19, 1918
b. Jennings, Paul Joseph

March 20, 1918
b. Barry, Jack
b. McPartland, Margaret Marian

March 21, 1918
b. Lucey, Patrick Joseph

March 22, 1918
b. Jagan, Cheddi (Berret)
d. Mitchell, Margaret Julia

March 24, 1918
d. Cui, Cesar Antonovich

March 25, 1918
b. Condon, Jackie
d. Debussy, Claude Achille

March 27, 1918
d. Adams, Henry Brooks

March 29, 1918
b. Bailey, Pearl Mae
b. Walton, Sam Moore

March 30, 1918
b. Evans, Bob

March 31, 1918
b. Bolt, Tommy

April 1, 1918
b. Klein, Herbert George

April 3, 1918
b. Ehrling, Sixten
d. Tillman, Benjamin Ryan

April 4, 1918
b. Ashbrook, Joseph
d. Cohen, Hermann

April 6, 1918
b. Ovando Candia, Alfredo

April 7, 1918
b. Doerr, Bobby

April 8, 1918
b. Ford, Betty
b. Swarthout, Glendon (Fred)

April 9, 1918
b. Utzon, Jorn

April 11, 1918
d. Wagner, Otto

April 12, 1918
b. Forrest, Helen

April 13, 1918
d. Kornilov, Lavr Georgyevich

April 14, 1918
b. Healy, Mary

April 16, 1918
b. Milligan, Spike

April 17, 1918
b. Holden, William
b. Shirley, Anne

April 18, 1918
b. Bazin, Andre
b. Hillegrass, C(lifton) K(eith)

April 19, 1918
b. Capa, Cornell
d. Rosenberg, Issac

April 20, 1918
b. Siegbahn, Kai Manne Boerje
d. Braun, Karl Ferdinand

April 21, 1918
d. Richthofen, Manfred von, Baron

April 22, 1918
b. Smith, William Jay
b. Vernon, Mickey

April 23, 1918
b. Richards, Stanley

April 24, 1918
b. Kaplan, Henry Seymour

April 25, 1918
b. Varnay, Astrid

April 26, 1918
b. Blankers-Koen, Fanny

April 27, 1918
b. Scali, John (Alfred)

April 30, 1918
d. Princip, Gavrilo

May 1, 1918
b. Paar, Jack
d. Gilbert, Grove Karl

May 3, 1918
b. Simoneau, Leopold

May 4, 1918
b. Tanaka, Kakuei

May 5, 1918
d. Vidal de la Blache, Paul

May 9, 1918
b. Feld, Irvin
b. Freeman, Orville Lothrop
b. Wallace, Mike

May 10, 1918
b. Brazelton, T(homas) Berry
b. Margo
d. Grass, John

May 11, 1918
b. Burnford, Sheila
b. Feynman, Richard Phillips

May 12, 1918
b. Ash, Mary Kay
b. Rosenberg, Julius

May 14, 1918
d. Bennett, James Gordon, Jr.

May 15, 1918
b. Arnold, Eddy
b. Wiseman, Joseph

May 16, 1918
b. Rulfo, Juan

May 17, 1918
b. Hunt, Jack Reed
b. Nilsson, Birgit

May 18, 1918
b. Christoff, Boris

May 19, 1918
b. Pais, Abraham
d. Hodler, Ferdinand

May 20, 1918
b. Harlech, William David Ormsby-
Gore, Baron

May 23, 1918
b. Bate, Walter Jackson

May 24, 1918
b. Brennan, Peter J(oseph)
b. Young, Coleman A(lexander)

May 25, 1918
b. Akins, Claude

May 27, 1918
b. Nakasone, Yasuhiro
b. Sheehan, Joseph Green

May 28, 1918
b. Birch, John
b. Wayne, Johnny

May 29, 1918
b. Corona, Bert
b. Shriner, Herb

May 30, 1918
d. Plekhanov, Georgi Valentinovich

May 31, 1918
b. Quarterman, Lloyd Albert

June 1, 1918
b. Astor, Gavin

June 3, 1918
b. Drucker, Daniel Charles

June 4, 1918
b. De Cuir, John
d. Fairbanks, Charles Warren

June 6, 1918
b. Krebs, Edwin Gerhard
b. Montez, Maria

June 8, 1918
b. Esslin, Martin Julius
b. Preston, Robert

June 10, 1918
b. Morse, Barry
d. Boito, Arrigo

June 12, 1918
b. Arkoff, Samuel Z

June 13, 1918
b. Joanis, John W

June 14, 1918
b. Aluko, Timothy Mofolorunso
b. McGuire, Dorothy Hackett
b. Walker, LeRoy Tashreau

June 15, 1918
b. Tombalbaye, Nagarta Francois

June 16, 1918
b. Elliott, George Paul

June 18, 1918
b. Karle, Jerome
b. Modigliani, Franco

June 19, 1918
b. Abram, Morris Berthold

June 21, 1918
b. Lopat, Ed(mund Walter)
b. Roosa, Robert V(incent)

June 25, 1918
d. Beckley, Jake

June 26, 1918
d. Rossegger, Peter

June 29, 1918
b. Lyng, Richard E

July 2, 1918
b. Sarnoff, Robert W(illiam)
d. Gladden, Washington

July 4, 1918
b. Landers, Ann
b. Tupou, IV
b. Van Buren, Abigail

July 5, 1918
b. Rochberg, George

July 6, 1918
b. Cabot, Sebastian
b. List, Eugene
d. Mitchel, John Purroy

July 7, 1918
b. Paulucci, Jeno Francisco

July 13, 1918
b. Ascari, Alberto
b. Brown, Marcia

July 14, 1918
b. Bergman, Ingmar (Ernst)
b. Forrester, Jay Wright
b. Laurents, Arthur
d. Roosevelt, Quentin

July 15, 1918
b. Boehm, Eric Hartzell

July 16, 1918
d. Alexandra Feodorovna
d. Carter, William
d. Nicholas II
d. Romanov, Anastasia

July 17, 1918
b. Manning, Irene

July 18, 1918
b. Mandela, Nelson (Rolihlahla)
d. Douglas, Amanda Minnie

July 22, 1918
d. Gonzalez Prada, Manuel

July 23, 1918
b. Reese, Pee Wee

July 24, 1918
b. Ricci, Ruggiero

July 25, 1918
b. Amen, Irving
d. Rauschenbusch, Walter

July 26, 1918
b. Thompson, Frank, Jr.

July 27, 1918
b. Rose, Leonard
d. Kobbe, Gustav

July 28, 1918
d. Treptow, Martin A

July 29, 1918
b. O'Connor, Edwin Greene

July 30, 1918
d. Kilmer, Joyce

July 31, 1918
b. Rowen, Hobart
d. Stanley, Francis Edgar

August 2, 1918
b. Straight, Beatrice Whitney

August 3, 1918
b. Burns, James MacGregor
b. Elgart, Les

August 4, 1918
b. Iceberg Slim

August 5, 1918
b. Drake, Tom

August 6, 1918
b. Granz, Norman

August 9, 1918
b. Aldrich, Robert
b. Cooper, Giles (Stannus)

August 10, 1918
b. Cobb, Arnett Cleophus

August 12, 1918
d. Held, Anna

August 13, 1918
b. Sanger, Frederick
d. Gulick, Luther (Halsey)

August 14, 1918
b. Provensen, Alice Rose Twitchell

August 17, 1918
b. Ankers, Evelyn
b. Brown, George Scratchley
b. Howe, Harold, II

August 18, 1918
b. Shelepin, Aleksandr (Nikolaevich)

August 22, 1918
b. McGrory, Mary

August 24, 1918
d. Bates, Arlo

August 25, 1918
b. Bernstein, Leonard
b. Greene, Richard

August 27, 1918
b. Lowrey, Peanuts

August 28, 1918
b. Lanusse, Alejandro Agustin

August 30, 1918
b. Bentley, Alvin Morell
b. Williams, Ted

August 31, 1918
b. Lerner, Alan Jay

September 2, 1918
b. Drury, Allen (Stuart)
b. Fenelon, Fania
b. Mitchell, Martha Elizabeth Beall

September 4, 1918
b. Harvey, Paul

September 7, 1918
b. Swearingen, John Eldred

September 8, 1918
b. Barton, Derek H(arold) R(ichard),
Sir

September 9, 1918
b. Scalfaro, Oscar Luigi

September 11, 1918
b. Martin, Robert Bernard
d. Osgood, Herbert Levi

September 13, 1918
b. Charles, Ray

September 15, 1918
b. Chandler, Alfred Du Pont, Jr.
b. Sain, Johnny

September 17, 1918
b. Herzog, Chaim

September 19, 1918
b. Kiplinger, Austin Huntington
b. Velarde, Pablita

September 23, 1918
b. Sinclair, Mary

September 24, 1918
b. Daddario, Emilio Quincy
b. Lindley, Audra

September 25, 1918
b. Rizzuto, Phil(ip Francis)

September 26, 1918
b. Morley, Eric Douglas
d. Simmel, Georg

September 27, 1918
b. Ryle, Martin, Sir

October 3, 1918
b. Cone, Molly Lamken

October 4, 1918
b. Fukui, Kenichi

b. Kantrowitz, Adrian

October 5, 1918
b. Ludden, Allen Ellsworth

October 7, 1918
d. Parry, Charles Hubert Hastings, Sir

October 9, 1918
b. Burkemo, Walter
b. Hunt, E(verette) Howard

October 10, 1918
b. Allon, Yigal
b. King, John W(illiam)

October 11, 1918
b. Bodsworth, Charles Frederick
b. Robbins, Jerome
d. Willard, Archibald MacNeal

October 12, 1918
d. Gailhard, Pierre

October 13, 1918
b. Walker, Robert

October 15, 1918
b. Lee, Robert E(dwin)

October 16, 1918
b. Althusser, Louis

October 17, 1918
b. Hayworth, Rita
d. Duchamp-Villon, Raymond

October 18, 1918
b. Mitsotakis, Constantine
b. Troup, Bobby

October 19, 1918
b. Kirk, Russell (Amos)
b. Strauss, Robert Schwarz

October 20, 1918
b. Ash, Roy Lawrence

October 23, 1918
b. Daly, James
b. Rudolph, Paul Marvin

October 27, 1918
b. Falkner, Frank T(ardrew)
b. Wright, Teresa

October 28, 1918
d. Bouchet, Edward Alexander

October 31, 1918
b. Bell, Griffin Boyette
d. Schiele, Egon

November 1, 1918
d. Ritz, Cesar

November 2, 1918
b. Adams, John Hanly

November 3, 1918
b. Boullioun, E(rnest) H(erman Jr.)

b. Feller, Bob
b. Long, Russell Billiu

November 4, 1918
b. Carney, Art
b. Mitchell, Cameron
d. Owen, Wilfred
d. Sage, Margaret Olivia
d. White, Andrew Dickson

November 6, 1918
b. Scott, Ken

November 7, 1918
b. Graham, Billy

November 8, 1918
b. Kirby, Robert E(mory)
b. Zapf, Hermann

November 9, 1918
b. Agnew, Spiro T(heodore)
b. Chadwick, Florence (May)

November 10, 1918
b. Fischer, Ernst Otto
d. Apollinaire, Guillaume

November 11, 1918
b. Kaye, Stubby
d. Adler, Victor

November 12, 1918
b. Stafford, Jo

November 14, 1918
b. Madeira, Jean

November 20, 1918
b. Kent, Corita

November 22, 1918
b. Pell, Claiborne DeBorda
b. Walston, Ray

November 24, 1918
b. Sandburg, Helga

November 25, 1918
b. Opie, Peter Mason

November 26, 1918
b. Aylwin (Azocar), Patricio

November 27, 1918
b. Beard, Dita Davis

November 29, 1918
b. L'Engle, Madeleine

December 2, 1918
b. DeLugg, Milton
d. Rostand, Edmond Alexis

December 6, 1918
b. Hamilton, Denis, Sir

December 7, 1918
b. Hatfield, Hurd
b. Maier, Henry W

December 11, 1918
b. Solzhenitsyn, Aleksandr (Isayevich)

December 12, 1918
b. Burdick, Eugene Leonard
b. Williams, Joe

December 14, 1918
b. Aubrey, James (Thomas), Jr.

December 15, 1918
b. Chandler, Jeff

December 18, 1918
b. Kanter, Hal

December 19, 1918
b. Byrd, Henry
b. Professor Longhair
b. Wright, Bruce McMarion

December 20, 1918
b. Totter, Audrey

December 21, 1918
b. Hampson, Frank
b. Regan, Donald Thomas
b. Waldheim, Kurt
d. Baker, Hobey
d. Page, Walter Hines

December 22, 1918
d. Bourne, Randolph Silliman

December 23, 1918
b. Greco, Jose
b. Schmidt, Helmut Heinrich
   Waldemar

December 25, 1918
b. Ben Bella, Ahmed
b. Sadat, Anwar el
d. Miller, Olive Thorne

December 30, 1918
b. Smith, W(illiam) Eugene

December 31, 1918
b. Hagg, Gunder

1919

b. Abdallah, Ahmed
b. Anielewicz, Mordecai
b. Bordes, Francois
b. Canadeo, Tony
b. Farah, William F.
b. Frailberg, Selma
b. Fraser, Gretchen Kunigh
b. Giacalone, Anthony
b. Hua Guofeng
b. Korda, Michael
b. Laszlo, Magda
b. Lorillard, Louis Livingston
b. Ly, Abdoulaye
b. Maag, Peter
b. McCarthy, William J.
b. Meredith, Sidney
b. Orwell, Sonia
b. Shorr, Kehat
b. Siegel, Owen R
b. Stokes, Doris

d. Europe, James Reese
d. Hollyer, Samuel
d. Johnson, Samuel C
d. Kinney, George Romanta
d. Kojong
d. Stokely, John
d. Thomas, Samuel Bath

January 1, 1919
b. Landis, Carole
b. Salinger, J(erome) D(avid)

January 2, 1919
b. Willeford, Charles Ray, II

January 3, 1919
b. White, Jesse
d. Duveneck, Frank

January 5, 1919
b. Gazzelloni, Severino
b. Ryder, Alfred

January 6, 1919
b. Cleaver, Vera Allen
d. Roosevelt, Theodore

January 7, 1919
b. Brown, Dorothy Lavinia
b. Duncan, Robert Edward

January 8, 1919
d. O'Rourke, Jim

January 11, 1919
b. McCurdy, Ed

January 13, 1919
b. Archerd, Army
b. Stack, Robert Langford

January 14, 1919
b. Andreotti, Giulio
b. Rooney, Andy

January 15, 1919
d. Liebknecht, Karl
d. Luxemburg, Rosa

January 16, 1919
b. Cochran, Roy

January 18, 1919
d. Astor, William Waldorf Astor,
   Viscount

January 19, 1919
b. Eberle, Ray

January 20, 1919
b. Cooper, Lester Irving

January 21, 1919
b. Falkenburg, Jinx

January 22, 1919
d. Larsson, Carl Olof

January 23, 1919
b. Kovacs, Ernie

January 25, 1919
b. Newman, Edwin Harold

January 27, 1919
b. Seville, David
d. Ady, Endre
d. Chadwick, French Ensor

January 31, 1919
b. Robinson, Jackie
d. Goodwin, Nat C

February 1, 1919
b. DellaCasa, Lisa

February 2, 1919
b. Fogarty, Anne
d. Leroux, Xavier

February 3, 1919
d. Pickering, Edward Charles

February 5, 1919
b. Buttons, Red
b. Papandreou, Andreas (George)
d. Rossetti, William Michael
d. Rozanov, Vasili Vasilyevich

February 6, 1919
b. Gabor, Zsa Zsa
b. Gold, Arthur
d. Dietz, Angel DeCora

February 7, 1919
b. Iwama, Kazuo
b. Mahoney, Jock

February 8, 1919
b. Morrow, Buddy

February 9, 1919
b. Gilkey, Langdon Brown

February 10, 1919
b. Reynolds, Allie
b. Smith, Mary Carter

February 11, 1919
b. Bannister, Constance Gibbs

February 12, 1919
b. Tucker, Forrest Meredith

February 13, 1919
b. Edwards, Joan
b. Ford, Tennessee Ernie
b. Robinson, Eddie

February 16, 1919
d. Sykes, Mark, Sir

February 17, 1919
d. Laurier, Wilfrid, Sir

February 18, 1919
b. Hoveyda, Amir Abbas

February 21, 1919
d. Eisner, Kurt
d. Walker, Mary Edwards

February 25, 1919
b. Bendick, Jeanne
b. Irvin, Monte

February 26, 1919
b. Adams, Mason

February 27, 1919
d. Edmunds, George Franklin

February 28, 1919
b. Urquhart, Brian Edward

March 2, 1919
b. Jones, Jennifer
b. Toumanova, Tamara

March 5, 1919
b. Boles, Paul Darcy

March 7, 1919
b. Stout, Juanita Kidd

March 10, 1919
d. Barr, Amelia Edith Huddleston

March 11, 1919
b. Ellington, Mercer

March 12, 1919
b. Szmuness, Wolf

March 14, 1919
b. Shulman, Max

March 15, 1919
b. Avakian, George
b. Gregson, John

March 16, 1919
b. Lang, Eugene M

March 17, 1919
b. Cole, Nat King
b. Reiser, Pete
d. Cox, Kenyon

March 19, 1919
b. Abrahams, Peter Henry
b. Tristano, Leonard Joseph

March 24, 1919
b. Burrenchobay, Dayendranath
b. Ferlinghetti, Lawrence Monsanto

March 25, 1919
b. Cagney, Jeanne
d. Lehmbruck, Wilhelm

March 26, 1919
b. Martin, Strother

March 27, 1919
b. Amery, Julian
b. Furgol, Ed(ward)

March 28, 1919
b. Doktor, Paul Karl

March 29, 1919
b. Heckart, Eileen

March 30, 1919
b. Bundy, McGeorge

April 1, 1919
b. Murray, Joseph

April 3, 1919
b. Edwards, Sherman

April 4, 1919
d. Crookes, William, Sir
d. Stefanik, Milan Rastislav

April 5, 1919
d. Hall, Joe

April 8, 1919
b. Smith, Ian Douglas
d. Woolworth, Frank Winfield

April 9, 1919
b. Eckert, John Presper, Jr.
b. Moncreiffe, Iain

April 10, 1919
d. Zapata, Emiliano

April 11, 1919
b. Carey, Hugh Leo

April 13, 1919
b. Keel, Howard
b. O'Hair, Madalyn Murray

April 15, 1919
b. Catlett, Elizabeth
d. Delano, Jane Arminda

April 16, 1919
b. Cunningham, Merce

April 21, 1919
b. Cornell, Don

April 22, 1919
b. Cram, Donald James

April 24, 1919
b. Clerides, Glafcos (John)

April 25, 1919
d. Juilliard, Augustus D

April 28, 1919
b. Frasconi, Antonio
b. Muses, Charles Arthur

April 29, 1919
b. Holm, Celeste

May 1, 1919
b. O'Herlihy, Dan

May 3, 1919
b. Seeger, Pete(r)

May 4, 1919
b. Heloise

May 5, 1919
b. Papadopoulos, George

May 6, 1919
d. Baum, L(yman) Frank

May 7, 1919
b. Peron, Eva Duarte

May 8, 1919
b. Barker, Lex

May 9, 1919
d. Henry, Edward Lamson

May 10, 1919
b. Bell, Daniel
b. Grasso, Ella

May 11, 1919
b. Hayes, John Michael

May 12, 1919
b. Townsend, Lynn Alfred

May 13, 1919
b. Kelly, Stephen Eugene

May 14, 1919
d. Heinz, Henry John

May 15, 1919
b. Charles, Mary Eugenia

May 16, 1919
b. Liberace
d. Schaefer, Germany

May 17, 1919
b. Cassill, R(onald) V(erlin)
b. DeBartolo, Edward J(ohn), Sr.
b. Miller, Merle
b. Sutton, Horace (Ashley)
d. Zelaya, Jose Santos

May 18, 1919
b. Fonteyn, Margot, Dame
b. Wurf, Jerry

May 20, 1919
b. Gobel, George Leslie

May 22, 1919
b. Boeynants, Paul Vanden

May 23, 1919
b. Garrett, Betty
b. Kline, Franz Joseph

May 25, 1919
d. Walker, C. J., Madame
d. Walker, Sarah Breedlove
   McWilliams

May 26, 1919
b. Silverheels, Jay

May 28, 1919
b. Swenson, May

May 30, 1919
b. Barrientos Ortuno, Rene

May 31, 1919
b. Hartke, Vance

June 1, 1919
b. Whitehead, Edwin C(arl)

June 3, 1919
b. Koontz, Elizabeth Duncan

June 4, 1919
b. Merrill, Robert

June 5, 1919
b. Scarry, Richard (McClure)
d. Altsheler, Joseph Alexander
d. Coors, Adolph

June 6, 1919
b. Carrington, Peter Alexander Rupert,
   Baron

June 7, 1919
b. Scherer, Ray(mond Lewis)

June 8, 1919
b. Fitzgibbon, Constantine

June 11, 1919
b. Todd, Richard
d. Spooner, John Coit

June 12, 1919
b. Hagen, Uta Thyra

June 14, 1919
b. Wanamaker, Sam

June 17, 1919
b. Brewster, Kingman, Jr.
b. DePaul, Gene Vincent

June 19, 1919
b. Kael, Pauline
b. Reisman, Simon

June 21, 1919
b. Soleri, Paolo

June 23, 1919
b. Gmeiner, Hermann

June 24, 1919
b. Molinaro, Al

June 26, 1919
b. Lasker, Joe

June 27, 1919
b. Macquarrie, John

June 29, 1919
b. Jordan, Joseph
b. Pickens, Slim

June 30, 1919
d. Rayleigh, John William Strutt,
   Baron

July 2, 1919
b. George, Jean Craighead
d. Shaw, Anna Howard

July 4, 1919
b. Willis, Mary

July 7, 1919
b. Kunstler, William M(oses)

July 8, 1919
b. Scheel, Walter
d. Fox, John W, Jr.

July 9, 1919
b. Van Slyke, Helen Lenore Vogt

July 10, 1919
b. Gabor, Magda

July 12, 1919
b. Ralston, Vera

July 14, 1919
b. Attwood, William Hollingsworth

July 15, 1919
b. Murdoch, Iris
d. Fischer, Emil Herman

July 17, 1919
b. Cottrell, Alan Howard, Sir

July 20, 1919
b. Collins, John F(rederick)
b. Ford, Benson
b. Hillary, Edmund Percival, Sir
b. Stevens, K T

July 26, 1919
b. Gilmore, Virginia
b. Lovelock, James

July 27, 1919
b. Harman, Jeanne Perkins

July 31, 1919
b. Conley, Renie
b. Gowdy, Curt(is)
b. Levi, Primo
b. Morgenthau, Robert Morris

August 1, 1919
d. Hammerstein, Oscar

August 3, 1919
b. Wriston, Walter Bigelow

August 6, 1919
b. Betz, Pauline

August 7, 1919
b. Borg, Kim

August 8, 1919
b. DeLaurentiis, Dino
d. Haeckel, Ernst Heinrich Philipp
   August

August 9, 1919
b. Den Uyl, Joop
b. Houk, Ralph George
d. Blakelock, Ralph Albert
d. Leoncavallo, Ruggiero

August 11, 1919
d. Carnegie, Andrew

August 12, 1919
b. Kidd, Michael

August 13, 1919
b. Humbard, Rex
b. Shearing, George Albert

August 15, 1919
b. Arundel, Honor Morfydd
b. Goheen, Robert Francis
b. Kiely, Benedict

August 18, 1919
b. Hickel, Wally

August 19, 1919
b. Forbes, Malcolm Stevenson

August 22, 1919
b. Bauer, Erwin Adam

August 25, 1919
b. Urban, Matt
b. Wallace, George C(orley)

August 26, 1919
b. Graham, Ronny

August 27, 1919
d. Botha, Louis

August 28, 1919
b. Hounsfield, Godfrey Newbold, Sir

August 30, 1919
b. Wagner, Wolfgang
b. Wells, Kitty
b. Sousa, Henrique Teixeira de

September 4, 1919
b. Morris, Howard

September 8, 1919
b. Bowker, Albert Hosmer

September 9, 1919
b. Snyder, Jimmy the Greek
d. Mitchell, John

September 10, 1919
b. Leighton, Robert B(enjamin)

September 12, 1919
d. Andreyev, Leonid Nikolayevich

September 13, 1919
b. Midgely, Mary Burton

September 15, 1919
b. Cambra, Jessie G.

September 16, 1919
b. Peter, Laurence Johnston

September 18, 1919
b. Losonczi, Pal

September 19, 1919
b. Thebom, Blanche

September 21, 1919
b. Ulibarri, Sabine (Reyes)

September 24, 1919
b. Ford, Anne McDonnell

September 25, 1919
d. Freer, Charles Lang

September 26, 1919
b. Britton, Barbara

September 27, 1919
b. Percy, Charles Harting
d. Patti, Adelina Juana Maria

September 28, 1919
b. Harmon, Tom

September 30, 1919
b. Neway, Patricia

October 2, 1919
b. Buchanan, James McGill

October 5, 1919
b. Pleasence, Donald

October 6, 1919
d. Palma, Ricardo

October 7, 1919
b. Cowen, Zelman, Sir
b. Dell, Gabriel
d. Alden, Henry M
d. Deakin, Alfred

October 8, 1919
b. Miyazawa, Kiichi
b. Ramsbotham, Peter, Sir

October 9, 1919
b. Plain, Belva
b. Seefried, Irmgard Maria Theresia

October 10, 1919
d. Genung, John Franklin

October 11, 1919
b. Blakey, Art
d. Gjellerup, Karl Adolf

October 12, 1919
b. Miller, Dorie

October 16, 1919
b. Pearce, Alice

October 17, 1919
b. Zhao Ziyang

October 18, 1919
b. O'Day, Anita
b. Trudeau, Pierre Elliott

October 20, 1919
b. Mathison, Richard Randolph

October 22, 1919
b. Janowitz, Morris
b. Lessing, Doris May

October 26, 1919
b. Bourgholtzer, Frank
b. Brooke, Edward William, III
b. Gronouski, John A(ustin)
b. Pahlevi, Mohammed Riza

October 31, 1919
b. Sisco, Joseph John
d. Wilcox, Ella Wheeler

November 1, 1919
b. Bondi, Hermann, Sir

November 3, 1919
b. Freed, Bert

November 4, 1919
b. Balsam, Martin Henry
b. Broyhill, Joel Thomas

November 5, 1919
b. Floren, Myron

November 6, 1919
b. Harris, Jonathan

November 10, 1919
b. Fenneman, George
b. Tshombe, Moise

November 12, 1919
b. Lefever, Ernest Warren

November 14, 1919
b. Desmond, Johnny
b. Lake, Veronica

November 15, 1919
b. Bruce, Carol
b. Wapner, Joseph A
d. Werner, Alfred

November 16, 1919
b. Dobrynin, Anatoly Fedorovich

November 17, 1919
b. Kay, Hershy

November 19, 1919
b. Pontecorvo, Gillo
b. Young, Alan (Angus)

November 20, 1919
b. Gray, Dulcie
b. Keyes, Evelyn Louise

November 25, 1919
b. Brodie, Steve

November 26, 1919
b. Pohl, Frederik

November 29, 1919
b. Kermode, (John) Frank
b. Primus, Pearl

November 30, 1919
b. Wright, Jane Cooke

December 1, 1919
b. Chambers, Anne Cox
b. Gilbert, Alfred Carlton, Jr.

December 2, 1919
d. Frick, Henry Clay

December 8, 1919
b. Robinson, Julia (Bowman)
d. Weir, Julian Alden

December 9, 1919
b. DeCarava, Roy
b. Lipscomb, William Nunn

December 10, 1919
b. Williams, Harrison Arlington, Jr.

December 14, 1919
b. Jackson, Shirley (Hardie)

December 17, 1919
b. Mphahlele, Ezekiel
d. Renoir, (Pierre) Auguste

December 18, 1919
d. Alcock, John William, Sir
d. Parker, Horatio William

December 19, 1919
b. Kalem, T(heodore) E(ustace)

December 20, 1919
b. Bettis, Valerie

December 23, 1919
b. Heggen, Thomas Orls, Jr.

December 24, 1919
b. Soulages, Pierre

December 29, 1919
b. Murray, Jim
d. Osler, William, Sir

December 30, 1919
b. Van Fleet, Jo

December 31, 1919
d. Van Zandt, Marie

1920

b. Bald, Kenneth
b. Balopoulos, Michael
b. Bates, Daisy Lee Gatson
b. Bell, William Holden
b. Ben Barka, Mehdi
b. Bernier, Rosamond Margaret
b. Christine, Virginia
b. ElMallakh, Kamal
b. Fleischmann, Sid
b. Freij, Elias
b. Keylor, Arthur W
b. McMullen, Mary
b. Memmi, Albert
b. Morgan, Jane
b. Perdue, Frank
b. Sanders, Lawrence
b. Saubel, Katherine Siva
b. Shaughnessy, Mickey

b. Slovik, Eddie
b. Springer, Ya'acov
b. Wallace, Phyllis A(nn)
d. Edenshaw, Charles
d. Fisher, John Arbuthnot
d. Lenox, Walter S
d. Okuma, Shigenobu
d. Reyes, Rafael

January 2, 1920
b. Asimov, Isaac
d. Adam, Paul
d. Powell, Maud

January 4, 1920
b. Colby, William E(gan)
d. Perez Galdos, Benito

January 5, 1920
b. Michelangeli, Arturo Benedetti
b. Wingler, Hans Maria

January 6, 1920
b. Cabral de Melo Neto, Joao
b. Moon, Sung Myung
b. Wynn, Early

January 7, 1920
d. Barton, Edmund

January 8, 1920
b. Preus, Jacob A(all) O(ttesen)

January 12, 1920
b. Farmer, James
b. Reid, William Ronald
b. Uppman, Theodor

January 14, 1920
b. Herman, George Edward
d. Dodge, John Francis

January 15, 1920
b. Davies, Bob
b. O'Connor, John Joseph, Cardinal

January 16, 1920
b. Reid, Elliott
d. DeKoven, (Henry Louis) Reginald

January 17, 1920
b. Kaye, Nora

January 19, 1920
b. Bolte, Charles G(uy)
b. Perez de Cuellar, Javier
b. Sundlun, Bruce George

January 20, 1920
b. Douglas, Keith Castellain
b. Fellini, Federico
b. Kelley, DeForest
b. Landau, Ely A
b. Lasky, Melvin Joseph

January 21, 1920
b. Barrow, Errol Walton

January 22, 1920
b. Kristol, Irving
b. Stavropoulos, George Peter
b. Volkov, Leon
b. Warfield, William Caesar

January 24, 1920
b. Saddler, Donald

January 25, 1920
d. Modigliani, Amedeo

January 27, 1920
b. Albert, Frank C.
b. Box, John

January 29, 1920
b. Allsop, Kenneth

January 30, 1920
b. Anderson, Michael
b. Hightower, Rosella

January 31, 1920
b. Udall, Stewart Lee
b. Warnke, Paul Culliton

February 3, 1920
b. Heimlich, Henry Jay
b. Osterwald, Bibi

February 4, 1920
b. Beebe, Burdetta Faye

February 6, 1920
b. Jovanovich, William Iliya

February 7, 1920
b. Bracken, Eddie
b. Brand, Oscar
b. Wang, An
d. Kolchak, Aleksandr Vasilievich

February 8, 1920
b. Smith, Bruce P
b. Turner, Lana
d. Dehmel, Richard

February 10, 1920
b. Comfort, Alexander

February 11, 1920
b. Farouk I
b. Halop, Billy
b. James, Daniel, Jr.
b. Wilson, Louis Hugh

February 13, 1920
b. Bryant, Boudleaux
b. Farrell, Eileen

February 16, 1920
b. Andrews, Patti

February 18, 1920
b. Cullen, Bill
b. Palance, Jack

February 19, 1920
b. Guest, C. Z.
b. Mayer, Jean
b. Rose, George Walter

February 20, 1920
d. Peary, Robert Edwin

February 23, 1920
b. Netsch, Walter Andrew, Jr.

February 25, 1920
b. Habib, Philip Charles
b. Justice, William Wayne
b. Travis, Dempsey Jerome

February 26, 1920
b. Baunsgaard, Hilmar Tormod Ingolf
b. Greenhill, Basil

February 27, 1920
b. Melis, Jose

February 29, 1920
b. Franz, Arthur
b. Morgan, Michele

March 1, 1920
b. Bentley, Max(well Herbert Lloyd)
b. Caray, Harry
b. Fernandez-Muro, Jose Antonio
b. Nemerov, Howard (Stanley)
b. Swann, Michael Meredith, Sir

March 2, 1920
b. Ritt, Martin

March 3, 1920
b. Boros, Julius (Nicholas)
b. Doohan, James Montgomery
b. Searle, Ronald William Fordham

March 5, 1920
b. Kelly, Leontine Turpeau Current

March 6, 1920
b. Dickason, Olive Patricia
b. Price, Roger Taylor

March 8, 1920
b. Batchelor, George (Keith)
b. Herlie, Eileen
b. Wallop, Douglass

March 9, 1920
b. Betz, Carl

March 10, 1920
b. Kent, Jack

March 11, 1920
b. Bloembergen, Nicolaas
b. Enright, Dennis Joseph

March 12, 1920
b. DeKooning, Elaine Marie Catherine Fried
b. Monroe, Rose Will

March 14, 1920
b. Ketcham, Hank
d. Sonzogno, Edoardo

March 15, 1920
b. Thomas, E Donall

March 16, 1920
b. Addison, John
b. McKern, Leo

March 17, 1920
b. Rahman, Mujibur, Sheik

March 19, 1920
b. Andrews, Tige

March 20, 1920
b. Cleaver, William Joseph
b. Harriman, Pamela
b. Hershey, Lenore

March 22, 1920
b. Klemperer, Werner
b. Martin, Ross

March 24, 1920
b. Nelson, Gene

March 25, 1920
b. Cosell, Howard
b. Scott, Paul Mark

March 27, 1920
b. Hayman, Richard
d. Colman, Samuel

March 29, 1920
b. Duerk, Alene B(ertha)

March 30, 1920
b. Bey, Turhan

April 1, 1920
b. Lund, Art(hur Earl, Jr.)
b. Mifune, Toshiro

April 2, 1920
b. Webb, Jack Randolph

April 5, 1920
b. Hailey, Arthur

April 6, 1920
b. Fischer, Edmond

April 7, 1920
b. Shankar, Ravi

April 8, 1920
d. Griffes, Charles Tomlinson

April 11, 1920
b. Colombo, Emilio
b. O'Donnell, Peter

April 12, 1920
b. Fizdale, Robert

April 14, 1920
b. Saint Clair, James Draper

April 15, 1920
b. Simms, Hilda
b. Szasz, Thomas Stephen
b. Weizsacker, Richard Freiherr von

April 16, 1920
b. Nelson, Barry
d. Vail, Theodore Newton

April 19, 1920
b. Fontaine, Frank
b. Mandel, Marvin
d. Mallinger, Mathilde

April 20, 1920
b. Stevens, John Paul

April 22, 1920
b. March, Hal
b. Winograd, Arthur

April 26, 1920
b. Walsh, William B(ertalan)
d. Ramanujan Aiyangar, Srinivasa

April 27, 1920
b. Morgan, Edwin George

April 28, 1920
b. Merriman, Nan

April 29, 1920
b. Guenther, Charles John

April 30, 1920
b. Cosgrave, Liam

May 2, 1920
b. Hutt, William Ian Dewitt

May 3, 1920
b. Bankhead, Dan(iel Robert)
b. Lewis, John Aaron
b. Schaffner, Franklin James

May 4, 1920
b. Schreiber, Hermann Otto Ludwig

May 6, 1920
b. Hunter, Ross

May 7, 1920
b. Post, Elizabeth Lindley

May 8, 1920
b. Bass, Saul
b. Wilson, Sloan

May 9, 1920
b. Adams, Richard
d. Vincent, John Heyl

May 10, 1920
d. Howells, William Dean

May 11, 1920
b. Pyle, Denver

May 12, 1920
b. Murphy, Patrick Vincent

May 13, 1920
b. Mara, Ratu Sir Kamisese

May 15, 1920
b. Audiard, Michel

May 16, 1920
d. Morton, Levi Parsons

May 17, 1920
b. Van Horne, Harriet

May 18, 1920
b. John Paul II

b. Storr, (Charles) Anthony

May 20, 1920
b. Menuhin, Hephzibah
b. Smith, Owen Guinn

May 21, 1920
b. Bachrach, Howard L.
b. Steel, Anthony
d. Carranza, Venustiano
d. Porter, Eleanor H

May 22, 1920
b. Gold, Thomas

May 24, 1920
b. Kalmanoff, Martin
b. Valdengo, Giuseppe

May 26, 1920
b. Lee, Peggy

May 30, 1920
b. London, George

May 31, 1920
b. Williams, Edward Bennett
b. Adhikary, Man Mohan

June 2, 1920
b. Schramm, Tex(as Edward)
b. Waldman, Max

June 4, 1920
b. Barbieri, Fedora
b. Obregon, Alejandro
b. Train, Russell Errol

June 5, 1920
b. Motley, Marion
b. Ryan, Cornelius John
d. Moore, Julia A Davis

June 7, 1920
b. Marchais, Georges (Rene Louis)

June 9, 1920
d. Griffith, Samuel Walker

June 11, 1920
b. Howe, Irving
b. Hutton, Robert
b. Mahendra, Bir Bikram Shah Dev
b. Manne, Shelly
b. Patterson, Tom
b. Scott, Hazel Dorothy

June 13, 1920
b. Evans, Clifford
b. Johnson, Ben

June 14, 1920
d. Weber, Max

June 15, 1920
b. Clampitt, Amy

June 16, 1920
b. Griffin, John Howard

June 17, 1920
b. Jacob, Francois

b. Reid, Beryl
d. Hyslop, James Hervey

June 18, 1920
b. Carmichael, Ian

June 19, 1920
b. Jourdan, Louis

June 20, 1920
b. Mondlane, Eduardo Chivambo
b. Tutuola, Amos

June 21, 1920
b. Martin, James Slattin, Jr.

June 24, 1920
b. Ernst, Jimmy

June 25, 1920
b. Harkless, Necia Desiree

June 26, 1920
b. Farley, Walter Lorimer
b. Hambro, Leonid

June 27, 1920
b. Diamond, I(sidore) A L
b. McEntee, Peter Donovan

June 28, 1920
b. Hotchner, Aaron Edward

June 29, 1920
b. Harryhausen, Ray

June 30, 1920
b. Bagdikian, Ben Haig
b. Ginsburg, Charles P

July 3, 1920
b. Allbritton, Louise
b. McCree, Wade Hampton, Jr.
d. Gorgas, William Crawford

July 4, 1920
b. Garraty, John Arthur
b. Helmsley, Leona Mindy Rosenthal

July 5, 1920
d. Klinger, Max

July 7, 1920
b. Coleman, William T, Jr.
b. Hechinger, Fred Michael

July 10, 1920
b. Brinkley, David (McClure)
b. Chamberlain, Owen
b. Lowe, Edward
b. Shriver, Eunice Mary Kennedy

July 11, 1920
d. Eugenie

July 12, 1920
b. Andes, Keith
b. Berton, Pierre

July 16, 1920
b. Lopez Portillo (y Pacheco), Jose

July 17, 1920
b. Bell, Arthur Donald
b. Monroe, Bill
b. Samaranch, Juan Antonio

July 18, 1920
b. Redhead, Hugh McCulloch

July 19, 1920
b. Gould, Gordon
b. Medina, Patricia

July 20, 1920
b. Richardson, Elliot L(ee)

July 21, 1920
b. Sithole, Ndabaningi
b. Stern, Isaac

July 22, 1920
d. Vanderbilt, William Kissam

July 24, 1920
b. Abzug, Bella (Savitsky)
b. Cohen, Alexander H
b. Ter-Arutunian, Rouben

July 25, 1920
b. Franklin, Rosalind Elsie

July 26, 1920
b. Waterfield, Bob

July 30, 1920
b. Tharp, Marie

August 1, 1920
b. Cole, Maria

August 2, 1920
b. Coleman, Lonnie William

August 3, 1920
b. Hegan, Jim
b. James, P(hyllis) D(orothy)

August 4, 1920
b. Thomas, Helen A.

August 5, 1920
b. Diamond, Selma

August 9, 1920
b. Hoskins, Allen Clayton

August 10, 1920
b. Holzman, Red
d. O'Neill, James

August 11, 1920
b. Masselos, William
b. Rayner, Chuck

August 14, 1920
b. Persoff, Nehemiah

August 15, 1920
b. Hall, Huntz

August 16, 1920
b. Bukowski, Charles

d. Lockyer, Joseph Norman, Sir

August 19, 1920
b. Kibbee, Robert Joseph

August 20, 1920
b. Kovel, Ralph Mallory

August 21, 1920
b. Milne, Christopher Robin

August 22, 1920
b. Bradbury, Ray Douglas
b. Cooley, Denton Arthur
d. Zorn, Anders Leonard

August 24, 1920
b. Colville, Alex

August 26, 1920
b. Parker, Brant (Julian)
b. Prem Tinsulanonda

August 29, 1920
b. Boykin, Otis Frank
b. Parker, Charlie

August 31, 1920
d. Wundt, Wilhelm Max

September 1, 1920
b. Carpenter, Liz
b. Farnsworth, Richard

September 3, 1920
b. Higgins, Marguerite

September 4, 1920
b. Claiborne, Craig

September 9, 1920
b. Aldridge, Michael

September 11, 1920
b. Bouchard, Butch

September 12, 1920
b. Dailey, Irene

September 14, 1920
b. Calderon, Alberto P(edro)
b. Klein, Lawrence Robert
b. Medford, Kay

September 15, 1920
b. Zellerbach, William Joseph

September 18, 1920
b. Warden, Jack

September 19, 1920
b. Angell, Roger

September 20, 1920
b. Mitchell, Peter Dennis

September 21, 1920
b. Ward, Jay

September 22, 1920
b. Lemon, Bob

September 23, 1920
b. Rooney, Mickey

September 24, 1920
b. Bong, Richard Ira
d. Faberge, Peter Carl

September 25, 1920
d. Schiff, Jacob Henry

September 26, 1920
b. Anthony, Michael

September 27, 1920
b. Conrad, William
b. Stommel, Henry Melson

September 28, 1920
b. Davie, Alan

September 29, 1920
b. Butler, John

October 1, 1920
b. Matthau, Walter

October 2, 1920
d. Bruch, Max

October 5, 1920
d. Heinemann, William

October 8, 1920
b. Herbert, Frank (Patrick)

October 9, 1920
d. Kronold, Selma

October 10, 1920
b. Sinkwich, Frank

October 11, 1920
b. Hickey, James Aloysius, Cardinal

October 12, 1920
b. Childress, Alice
b. Soames, Christopher

October 13, 1920
b. Day, Laraine
b. Hague, Albert

October 14, 1920
b. Wolfington, Iggie

October 15, 1920
b. Economaki, Chris(topher
    Constantine)
b. Monteux, Claude
b. Puzo, Mario

October 17, 1920
b. Abel, Elie
b. Clift, Montgomery
b. Kilbracken, John Raymond Godley,
    Baron

October 19, 1920
d. Reed, John Silas

October 20, 1920
b. Jagan, Janet

October 21, 1920
b. Eckart, William Joseph

October 22, 1920
b. Green, Mitzi
b. Leary, Timothy (Francis)

October 23, 1920
b. Montana, Bob
b. Rizzo, Frank Lazzaro

October 24, 1920
d. MacSwiney, Terence

October 27, 1920
b. Fabray, Nanette

October 28, 1920
b. Robitscher, Jonas Bondi, Jr.
b. Swados, Harvey

October 29, 1920
b. Benacerraf, Baruj

October 31, 1920
b. Danielian, Leon
b. Francis, Dick
b. Newton, Helmut

November 1, 1920
b. Kilpatrick, James J(ackson), Jr.

November 2, 1920
d. Guiney, Louise Imogene

November 6, 1920
b. Rossi-Lemeni, Nicola

November 7, 1920
b. Kampelman, Max M

November 8, 1920
b. Rolle, Esther

November 11, 1920
b. Jenkins, Roy Harris
b. Tierney, Gene

November 12, 1920
b. Quine, Richard

November 13, 1920
b. Saxon, Charles David

November 15, 1920
b. Bufalino, Gesualdo
b. Thiebaud, (Morton) Wayne

November 16, 1920
b. Viertel, Peter

November 18, 1920
b. Khalil, Mustafa

November 20, 1920
b. Thaxter, Phyllis

November 21, 1920
b. Meeker, Ralph
b. Musial, Stan(ley Frank)

November 23, 1920
b. Celan, Paul

November 24, 1920
b. Zumwalt, Elmo R(ussell), Jr.

November 25, 1920
b. Montalban, Ricardo

November 29, 1920
b. Ligachev, Yegor (Kuzmich)

November 30, 1920
b. Mayo, Virginia

December 1, 1920
b. Rohmer, Eric
d. Rebikov, Vladimir Ivanovich

December 3, 1920
b. Canfield, Francis X(avier)
d. Abney, William de Wiveleslie, Sir

December 6, 1920
b. Brubeck, Dave
b. Dimmock, Peter
b. Porter, George, Sir

December 8, 1920
b. DiCamerino, Roberta
b. Souzay, Gerard

December 10, 1920
b. Menard, H William
b. Morgan, Dennis
d. Dodge, Horace Elgin

December 13, 1920
b. Kaysone Phomvihan
b. Shultz, George Pratt

December 14, 1920
b. Cary, Frank Taylor
b. Wilt, Fred(erick Loren)
d. Gipp, George

December 15, 1920
b. Anderson, Roy A(rnold)

December 18, 1920
b. Fryer, Robert
b. Streich, Rita

December 19, 1920
b. Susskind, David Howard

December 20, 1920
b. Pitrone, Jean Maddern
b. Thomas, Gerald

December 21, 1920
b. Nagle, Kel(vin David George)
d. Hassan, Muhammad Abdille

December 22, 1920
b. Henle, Guy

December 26, 1920
b. Gendron, Maurice
b. Hughes, Emmet John

December 28, 1920
b. Van Buren, Steve W

December 29, 1920
b. Lindfors, Viveca

December 30, 1920
b. Lord, Jack

1921

b. Beregovoi, Georgi
b. Bernstein, Felicia Montealegre
b. Colemon, Johnnie
b. Coplon, Judith
b. Douglas, Mary Tew
b. Ewonwu, Benedict Chuka
b. Freire, P(aulo)
b. Huxtable, Ada Louise
b. Iceman
b. Ilizarov, Gavril A
b. Jaffe, Herb
b. Leiber, Judith
b. Martin, Del
b. Massamba-Debat, Alphonse
b. Piazzola, Astor
b. Schmemann, Alexander
b. Senesh, Hannah
b. Stone, Toni
b. Thorpe, Grace F.
b. Unruh, Howard B
b. White, Slappy
d. Bethmann Hollweg, Theobald von
d. Cuypers, Petrus Josephus Hubertus
d. Dunlop, John Boyd
d. Hennebique, Francois
d. Love, Nat
d. Yen Fu

January 1, 1921
b. Highsmith, Patricia

January 5, 1921
b. Durrenmatt, Friedrich
b. Jean, Prince

January 6, 1921
b. Harris, Louis
b. Middlecoff, Cary

January 7, 1921
b. Loloma, Charles

January 11, 1921
b. Kreps, Juanita Morris

January 13, 1921
b. Franey, Pierre

January 15, 1921
b. Barker, Cliff

January 18, 1921
d. Hildebrand, Adolf von

January 21, 1921
b. Clark, Barney Bailey

January 24, 1921
b. Connolly, Sybil
b. Mintz, Beatrice

January 25, 1921
d. Bonfanti, Marie

January 26, 1921
b. Morita, Akio

January 27, 1921
b. Reed, Donna

January 31, 1921
b. Agar, John
b. Jones, Fay
b. Lanza, Mario

February 1, 1921
b. Blount, Winton Malcolm

February 2, 1921
d. Mancinelli, Luigi

February 4, 1921
b. Friedan, Betty (Naomi Goldstein)

February 5, 1921
b. Adam, Ken
b. Pritchard, John Michael, Sir

February 8, 1921
b. Jakobovits, Immanuel
d. Kropotkin, Peter Alekseyevich,
    Prince

February 9, 1921
d. Huneker, James Gibbons

February 11, 1921
b. Bentsen, Lloyd Millard, Jr.
b. Gabor, Eva

February 13, 1921
b. Warner, Rawleigh, Jr.
b. Zao-Wou-Ki

February 14, 1921
b. Downs, Hugh (Malcolm)

February 17, 1921
b. Manuel, George

February 18, 1921
b. Faulkner, Brian

February 19, 1921
b. Treurnicht, Andries Petrus

February 21, 1921
b. Bokassa I
b. Rawls, John (Bordley)

February 22, 1921
b. Bokassa, Jean-Bedel
d. Anderson, Elizabeth Milbank

February 24, 1921
b. Vigoda, Abe
d. Habberton, John

February 26, 1921
b. Hutton, Betty

February 28, 1921
b. Diener, Theodor Otto
b. Zaentz, Saul

March 1, 1921
b. Clayton, Jack
b. Cooke, Terence James
b. Wilbur, Richard Purdy

March 2, 1921
b. Haas, Ernst
d. Clark, Champ

March 3, 1921
b. Barrymore, Diana

March 4, 1921
b. Greenwood, Joan

March 6, 1921
b. Bealer, Alex W(inkler III)
b. Rudel, Julius

March 10, 1921
d. Upton, Francis Robbins

March 12, 1921
b. Agnelli, Giovanni
b. MacRae, Gordon
b. McCafferty, Don
b. Shapey, Ralph

March 13, 1921
b. Jaffee, Allan

March 14, 1921
b. Carr, Harold Noflet

March 15, 1921
b. Daly, Maureen Patricia

March 16, 1921
b. Truitt, Anne

March 19, 1921
b. Turner, Donald F(rank)

March 20, 1921
b. M'Bow, Mahtar-Amadou

March 22, 1921
b. Carter, Dorothy Sharp
b. Gilligan, John Joyce
b. Masina, Giulietta
d. Hornung, Ernest William

March 23, 1921
b. Campbell, Donald Malcolm
b. Smyslov, Vasili Vasil'evich

March 24, 1921
d. Gibbons, James, Cardinal

March 25, 1921
b. Kelly, Nancy
b. Signoret, Simone Henrietta
  Charlotte
d. Burroughs, John

March 27, 1921
b. Markle, Fletcher

March 28, 1921
b. Bogarde, Dirk
b. Daubeny, Peter Lauderdale, Sir

April 1, 1921
b. Reardon, Ken(neth Joseph)

April 3, 1921
b. Demjanjuk, John
b. Landers, Harry
d. Cary, Anne Louise

April 5, 1921
b. Lewis, Robert Q
d. Mifflin, George Harrison

April 6, 1921
b. Thompson, Moose

April 8, 1921
b. Bass, Alfie

April 10, 1921
b. Connors, Chuck
b. Risling, David
b. Wooley, Sheb

April 13, 1921
b. Griese, Arnold
b. Thyssen-Bornemisza de Kaszan,
  Hans Heinrich, Baron

April 16, 1921
b. Mollenhoff, Clark Raymond
b. Ustinov, Peter Alexander

April 19, 1921
b. Navon, Yitzhak

April 23, 1921
b. Blair, Janet
b. Spahn, Warren Edward

April 25, 1921
b. Appel, Karel Christian

April 26, 1921
b. Costello, Robert E
b. Giuffre, James Peter

April 28, 1921
b. Evans, Rowland, Jr.

April 29, 1921
b. Durslag, Melvin

May 2, 1921
b. Gottlieb, Morton Edgar
b. Ray, Satyajit

May 3, 1921
b. Robinson, Sugar Ray

May 5, 1921
b. Schawlow, Arthur L(eonard)
d. Friese-Greene, William Edward

May 6, 1921
b. Wakefield, Dick

d. Fried, Alfred Hermann

May 7, 1921
b. Davies, Rodger Paul
b. Rebuffat, Gaston Louis Simon

May 9, 1921
b. Berrigan, Daniel J
b. Van Duyn, Mona

May 10, 1921
b. Walker, Nancy

May 11, 1921
b. Hamm-Brucher, Hildegard

May 12, 1921
b. Beuys, Joseph
b. Mowat, Farley McGill

May 17, 1921
b. Brain, Dennis
b. Winship, Elizabeth

May 18, 1921
b. Dennis, Patrick

May 19, 1921
d. White, Edward Douglass

May 20, 1921
b. Kume, Yutaka
b. Newhouser, Hal

May 21, 1921
b. Benelli, Giovanni, Cardinal
b. Sakharov, Andrei Dmitrievich

May 22, 1921
b. Alexander, Donald Crichton

May 23, 1921
b. Blish, James Benjamin
b. Chukrai, Grigori
b. De Larrocha, Alicia
b. O'Connell, Helen

May 25, 1921
b. David, Hal
b. Steinberger, Jack

May 27, 1921
b. Chessman, Caryl Whittier

May 29, 1921
d. Thayer, Abbott Handerson

May 31, 1921
b. Valli, Alida

June 1, 1921
b. Riddle, Nelson

June 2, 1921
b. Speight, Johnny

June 4, 1921
b. Wanzer, Bobby

June 5, 1921
b. Bosin, Blackbear

June 6, 1921
d. Feydeau, Georges

June 8, 1921
b. Smith, Alexis
b. Soeharto
b. Southall, Ivan Francis
b. Suharto

June 9, 1921
b. Frazier, Brenda Diana Dudd
b. Hertzberg, Arthur
d. Drago, Luis Maria

June 10, 1921
b. Philip, Prince

June 12, 1921
b. Houston, James Archibold

June 15, 1921
b. Garner, Erroll

June 17, 1921
b. Anderson, William Robert
b. Scott, Tony

June 18, 1921
b. Bertelli, Angelo B.

June 19, 1921
b. Heflin, Howell Thomas
b. Wrightson, Patricia

June 20, 1921
b. Segura, Pancho

June 21, 1921
b. Emanuel, James A
b. Russell, Jane

June 22, 1921
b. Champion, Gower
b. Papp, Joseph

June 25, 1921
b. Franca, Celia

June 28, 1921
b. Rao, P V Narasimha

June 29, 1921
d. Churchill, Jennie Jerome

July 1, 1921
b. Khama, Seretse M., Sir

July 3, 1921
b. Peters, Susan

July 4, 1921
b. Debreu, Gerard

July 5, 1921
b. Merrifield, R(obert) Bruce
b. Yates, Bill

July 6, 1921
b. Reagan, Nancy (Davis)

July 7, 1921
b. Charles, Ezzard
b. Wilder, Clinton

July 9, 1921
b. Jones, David Charles

July 10, 1921
b. Donnell, Jeff
b. LaMotta, Jake

July 12, 1921
b. Douglas, Ellen

July 13, 1921
b. Scribner, Charles, Jr.
d. Lippmann, Gabriel Jonas

July 14, 1921
b. Garfield, Leon
b. Wilkinson, Geoffrey

July 15, 1921
b. Reiss, Stuart

July 16, 1921
b. Rogers, Bernard William

July 17, 1921
b. Isaacs, Alick

July 18, 1921
b. Glenn, John Herschel, Jr.

July 19, 1921
b. O'Hearn, Robert Raymond
b. Yalow, Rosalyn Sussman

July 22, 1921
b. Roth, William Victor, Jr.

July 24, 1921
b. DiStefano, Giuseppe
b. Taylor, Billy

July 26, 1921
b. Wittop, Freddy

July 29, 1921
b. Marker, Chris

July 30, 1921
b. Johannesen, Grant

July 31, 1921
b. Young, Whitney Moore, Jr.

August 1, 1921
b. Kramer, Jack

August 2, 1921
d. Caruso, Enrico

August 3, 1921
b. Adler, Richard
b. Carruth, Hayden
b. Maxwell, Marilyn

August 4, 1921
b. Ellis, Herb
b. Richard, Maurice

August 6, 1921
b. Raines, Ella

August 7, 1921
b. Covington, Warren
d. Blok, Aleksandr Aleksandrovich

August 8, 1921
d. Ladd, George Trumbull

August 9, 1921
b. Exon, (John) James, (Jr.)

August 11, 1921
b. Graff, Henry Franklin
b. Haley, Alex (Murray Palmer)

August 12, 1921
b. Monty, Gloria
b. Reynolds, Marjorie

August 13, 1921
b. Brand, Neville

August 14, 1921
b. Bartlett, Charles Leffingwell
b. Strehler, Giorgio
b. Wright, Cobina

August 15, 1921
b. Banner, Bob
b. Zabach, Florian

August 16, 1921
b. O'Brian, Jack
d. Peter, I

August 17, 1921
b. O'Hara, Maureen

August 19, 1921
b. Roddenberry, Gene

August 20, 1921
b. Susann, Jacqueline

August 21, 1921
b. Hunthausen, Raymond Gerhardt

August 22, 1921
b. Corn, Ira George, Jr.

August 23, 1921
b. Arrow, Kenneth Joseph
b. Brown, Charles Lee

August 25, 1921
b. Moore, Brian
b. Oduber (Quiros), Daniel
d. Gumilev, Nikolai
d. Hewitt, Peter Cooper

August 26, 1921
b. Begelman, David
b. Bradlee, Ben(jamin Crowninshield)
d. Erzberger, Matthias

August 28, 1921
b. Kulp, Nancy Jane

August 29, 1921
b. Wendell Oliver, Scott, Sr.

d. Allen, Joel Asaph

August 30, 1921
b. Dundee, Angelo Mirena, Jr.

August 31, 1921
b. Feeney, Chub
b. Pike, Otis Grey

September 2, 1921
b. Williams, O(swald) S.
d. Dobson, Henry Austin

September 3, 1921
b. Bellmon, Henry Louis
b. Dart, Thurston
b. Orkin, Ruth

September 5, 1921
b. Valenti, Jack Joseph

September 6, 1921
b. Laforet (Diaz), Carmen

September 7, 1921
b. Ferrante, Arthur
b. Harris, MacDonald

September 8, 1921
b. Secombe, Harry

September 9, 1921
b. Prather, Richard Scott

September 11, 1921
b. Jobert, Michel

September 12, 1921
b. McGee, Frank

September 14, 1921
b. Motley, Constance Baker
b. Rudd, Hughes Day

September 15, 1921
b. Gordon, Richard
b. Lewis, Elma Ina

September 16, 1921
b. Brauer, Jerald C(arl)

September 17, 1921
b. Barco Vargas, Virgilio

September 19, 1921
b. Chapman, Christian Addison
b. Conerly, Charlie

September 21, 1921
b. McHale, John Joseph
d. Duhring, Eugen Karl

September 22, 1921
b. Szeryng, Henryk

September 23, 1921
b. Bogart, Leo
b. Nestingen, Ivan Arnold

September 24, 1921
b. McKay, Jim

September 25, 1921
b. Muldoon, Robert David, Sir

September 26, 1921
b. Ekwensi, Cyprian Odiatu Duaka

September 27, 1921
d. Humperdinck, Engelbert

September 30, 1921
b. Kerr, Deborah

October 1, 1921
b. Hillis, Margaret
b. Whitmore, James Allen

October 2, 1921
b. Crispin, Edmund

October 4, 1921
b. Hills, Argentina (Schifano)
b. Morales Bermudez, Francisco
b. Poe, James

October 5, 1921
b. Tabbert, William

October 6, 1921
b. Biro, Val

October 9, 1921
b. Nader, George

October 10, 1921
d. Gierke, Otto von

October 12, 1921
d. Knox, Philander Chase

October 13, 1921
b. Montand, Yves
b. Thomas, Bill

October 15, 1921
b. Benzer, Seymour

October 17, 1921
b. Brown, George Mackay

October 18, 1921
b. Helms, Jesse Alexander, Jr.

October 19, 1921
b. Kalmbach, Herbert Warren
b. Power, Jules

October 21, 1921
b. Arnold, Malcolm, Sir
b. Runcie, Robert Alexander Kennedy

October 22, 1921
b. Brassens, Georges

October 24, 1921
b. Jurinac, Sena

October 25, 1921
b. Michael V
d. Masterson, Bat

October 26, 1921
b. Fulks, Joe

October 29, 1921
b. Mauldin, Bill

November 2, 1921
b. Mosienko, Bill
b. Schaefer, William Donald

November 3, 1921
b. Bronson, Charles

November 4, 1921
d. Hara, Kei
d. Hara Takashi

November 5, 1921
d. Blackwell, Antoinette Louisa Brown

November 6, 1921
b. Jones, James

November 8, 1921
b. Mirisch, Walter Mortimer
b. Saks, Gene

November 9, 1921
b. Chukarin, Viktor Ivanovich
b. Drake, Stan(ley Albert)
b. Hines, Jerome
b. Paine, Thomas Otten

November 11, 1921
b. Bell, T(errel) H(oward)

November 14, 1921
b. Keith, Brian

November 18, 1921
d. Berdichevsky, Micah Joseph

November 19, 1921
b. Anda, Geza
b. Campanella, Roy

November 20, 1921
b. Garrison, Jim C.

November 22, 1921
b. Atherton, Alfred LeRoy, Jr.
b. Dangerfield, Rodney
d. Hyndman, Henry Mayers
d. Nilsson, Christine

November 24, 1921
b. Lindsay, John Vliet

November 26, 1921
b. Gilot, Francoise

November 27, 1921
b. Dubcek, Alexander

November 28, 1921
d. Abdu'l-Baha

December 2, 1921
b. Karle, Isabella (L.)
d. Lincoln, Mary Johnson Bailey

December 3, 1921
b. Doar, John Michael

December 4, 1921
b. Durbin, Deanna

December 6, 1921
b. Graham, Otto Everett, Jr.

December 8, 1921
b. Morgan, Terence

December 9, 1921
b. Ellis, Harry Bearse
d. Pearson, Cyril Arthur, Sir

December 12, 1921
b. Demara, Ferdinand Waldo, Jr.

December 16, 1921
d. Saint-Saens, (Charles) Camille

December 19, 1921
d. Cannon, James W

December 21, 1921
b. Alonso, Alicia
d. Pinchback, P(inckney) B(enton) S(tewart)

December 22, 1921
b. Garvin, Clifton Canter, Jr.
d. Watterson, Henry

December 23, 1921
b. Johnson, Robert Willard

December 24, 1921
b. Dudley, Bill

December 25, 1921
d. Korolenko, Vladimir Galaktionovich

December 26, 1921
b. Allen, Steve

December 27, 1921
b. Lipshutz, Robert Jerome
b. Rossi, Peter Henry
b. Wallerstein, Jusith S.

December 28, 1921
d. Hare, John, Sir

December 30, 1921
b. Karami, Rashid Abdul Hamid

December 31, 1921
d. Penrose, Boies

1922

b. Alexandre
b. Black, Eli M
b. Boehm, Helen
b. Clokey, Art
b. Duran Ballen, Sixto
b. Fahd ibn Abdul Aziz, King
b. Greenglass, David
b. Hamilton, Guy

b. Kemal, Yashar
b. Kuhn, Thomas Samuel
b. Ling, James J
b. Loloma, Otellie
b. Lonsdale, Gordon Arnold
b. Martinez, Eugenio R
b. Onoda, Hiroo
b. Richards, Lloyd George
b. Robinson, Rachel
b. Smith, Frances Scott Fitzgerald Lanahan
b. Thorne, Jim
b. Toulmin, Stephen Edelston
b. Toure, Sekou
b. Vo Van Kiet
b. Williams, Evelyn
d. Gordon, Aaron David
d. Sorel, Georges
d. Stokely, James

January 1, 1922
b. Hollings, Ernest Frederick

January 3, 1922
b. Travers, Bill

January 4, 1922
b. Battelle, Phyllis Marie

January 5, 1922
d. Shackleton, Ernest Henry, Sir

January 7, 1922
b. Gardenia, Vincent
b. Rampal, Jean-Pierre

January 9, 1922
b. Khorana, Har Gobind
b. Toure, Ahmed Sekou

January 15, 1922
b. Marcinkus, Paul Casimir

January 17, 1922
b. Echeverria Alvarez, Louis
b. Katzenbach, Nicholas de Belleville
b. White, Betty
d. Selden, George Baldwin

January 18, 1922
b. Moore, Constance

January 19, 1922
b. Madison, Guy

January 20, 1922
b. Anthony, Ray

January 21, 1922
b. Scofield, Paul

January 22, 1922
b. Moss, Howard
d. Bajer, Fredrik
d. Benedict XV
d. Bryce, James Bryce, Viscount

January 23, 1922
b. Golub, Leon Albert
d. Nikisch, Arthur

January 27, 1922
b. Fleischmann, Peter F(rancis)

d. Bly, Nellie
d. Verga, Giovanni

January 28, 1922
b. Holley, Robert W(illiam)

January 29, 1922
b. Richman, Milton

January 31, 1922
d. Borglum, Solon Hannibal

February 1, 1922
b. Tebaldi, Renata

February 2, 1922
d. Taylor, William Desmond

February 6, 1922
b. MacNee, Patrick

February 8, 1922
b. Glanzman, Louis S

February 10, 1922
b. Hughes, Harold E(verett)
b. Patterson, Neva

February 13, 1922
b. Pym, Francis Leslie

February 14, 1922
b. Kaufman, Murray

February 15, 1922
b. Anderson, John Bayard
b. Kahn, Herman

February 16, 1922
b. Evans, Geraint Llewellyn, Sir

February 18, 1922
b. Brown, Helen Gurley
b. Gairy, Eric Matthew, Sir

February 20, 1922
b. Carpenter, Leslie

February 21, 1922
b. Gunning, Lucille C

February 22, 1922
d. Yamagata, Aritomo

February 23, 1922
b. Komer, Robert William

February 25, 1922
d. Landru, Henri Desire

February 26, 1922
b. Lawe, John Edward
b. Leighton, Margaret

February 27, 1922
b. McGill, William James
b. Nyerere, Julius Kambarage

March 1, 1922
b. Flanders, Michael
b. Gaines, William M(axwell)

b. Rabin, Yitzhak

March 2, 1922
b. Quackenbush, Bill

March 3, 1922
b. Allen, Jay Presson

March 4, 1922
b. O'Driscoll, Martha
d. Williams, Bert

March 5, 1922
b. Pasolini, Pier Paolo

March 7, 1922
b. Phillip, Andy

March 8, 1922
b. Croft, Michael
b. Furillo, Carl Anthony

March 9, 1922
b. McKissick, Floyd Bixler

March 10, 1922
b. Mason, Pamela Helen

March 11, 1922
b. Carroll, Vinnette

March 12, 1922
b. Kerouac, Jack
b. Kirkland, Lane

March 13, 1922
b. Byers, Walter

March 14, 1922
b. Baxter, Les

March 15, 1922
b. Brinsmead, Hesba Fay

March 18, 1922
b. Bahr, Egon
b. Lipset, Seymour Martin
b. Shuttlesworth, Fred Lee

March 20, 1922
b. Goulding, Ray(mond Walter)
b. Reiner, Carl
b. Young, Margaret Ann Buckner

March 21, 1922
b. Casewit, Curtis
b. Meyer, Russ
b. Nederlander, James Morton

March 22, 1922
b. Stern, Stewart

March 25, 1922
b. Ford, Eileen

March 26, 1922
b. Milliken, William Grawn

March 27, 1922
b. Agase, Alexander A.
b. Olderman, Murray

b. Olitski, Jules

March 29, 1922
b. Fain, Ferris Roy

March 31, 1922
b. Kiley, Richard (Paul)
b. May, John L.

April 2, 1922
d. Rorschach, Hermann

April 4, 1922
b. Bernstein, Elmer
b. Manchester, William Raymond

April 5, 1922
b. Chatichai Choonhavan
b. Storm, Gale

April 6, 1922
b. Donegan, Dorothy

April 8, 1922
b. Friendly, Ed
b. Green, Gerald
b. McRae, Carmen

April 9, 1922
d. Manson, Patrick, Sir

April 10, 1922
b. Simonetta

April 12, 1922
b. Tiny Tim
d. Shrady, Henry M

April 13, 1922
b. Braine, John Gerard

April 14, 1922
b. Fradon, Dana
b. Khan, Ali Akbar
d. Anson, Cap

April 15, 1922
b. Washington, Harold

April 16, 1922
b. Amis, Kingsley (William)
b. Tindemans, Leo(nard)

April 18, 1922
b. Hale, Barbara

April 22, 1922
b. Diebenkorn, Richard C.
b. Lafontant-Mankarious, Jewel
(Stradford)
b. Mingus, Charles

April 26, 1922
b. Kellin, Mike
b. Sauve, Jeanne Mathilde Benoit

April 27, 1922
b. Klugman, Jack

April 28, 1922
b. MacLean, Alistair (Stuart)

April 29, 1922
b. Allen, George Herbert
d. Croker, Boss
b. Kiwanuka, Benedicto Kagima
Mugumba

May 1, 1922
b. Goodman, Julian B
b. Mosel, Tad
d. Cheney, John Vance

May 2, 1922
b. Rosenthal, Abraham Michael

May 3, 1922
b. Svetlova, Marina

May 4, 1922
b. Hambleton, Hugh George

May 7, 1922
b. McGavin, Darren

May 11, 1922
b. Chylak, Nestor

May 14, 1922
b. Clark, Robert Edward
b. Deacon, Richard
b. Tudjman, Franjo

May 15, 1922
d. Spy

May 16, 1922
b. Carol, Martine

May 18, 1922
b. Macy, Bill
b. Winding, Kai Chresten
d. Laveran, Charles Louis Alphonse
d. Raleigh, Walter Alexander, Sir

May 20, 1922
b. Johnson, James Ralph

May 21, 1922
b. Covey, Cyclone

May 22, 1922
b. Crist, Judith Klein

May 23, 1922
b. Conwell, Esther Marly

May 24, 1922
b. McKenna, Siobhan

May 25, 1922
b. Berlinguer, Enrico

May 27, 1922
b. Lee, Christopher Frank Carandini

May 28, 1922
b. Craveirinha, Jose

May 29, 1922
b. Xenakis, Iannis

May 30, 1922
b. Coit, Margaret Louise

May 31, 1922
b. Elliott, Denholm Mitchell

June 1, 1922
b. Caulfield, Joan
b. Spencer, William

June 2, 1922
b. Sifford, Charlie

June 3, 1922
b. Resnais, Alain
d. Terhune, Mary Virginia

June 4, 1922
b. Barry, Gene
b. Gravely, Samuel Lee, Jr.

June 6, 1922
d. Russell, Lillian

June 7, 1922
b. Graziano, Rocky

June 9, 1922
b. Axelrod, George

June 10, 1922
b. Garland, Judy
b. Mofford, Rose

June 11, 1922
b. Bromfield, John
b. Cacoyannis, Michael
b. Campbell, Douglas
b. Charmoli, Tony

June 12, 1922
d. Kapp, Wolfgang

June 14, 1922
b. Roche, Kevin

June 15, 1922
b. Udall, Morris K(ing)

June 17, 1922
b. Herrera Lane, Felipe

June 18, 1922
b. Keene, Donald Lawrence
d. Kapteyn, Jacobus Cornelis

June 19, 1922
b. Bohr, Aage Niels

June 21, 1922
b. Holliday, Judy

June 22, 1922
b. Blass, Bill

June 24, 1922
d. Rathenau, Walter
d. Rockefeller, William

June 26, 1922
b. Parker, Eleanor

June 27, 1922
b. Campbell, Donald Guy

June 29, 1922
b. Vessey, John William, Jr.

July 2, 1922
b. Henry, Aaron
b. Rowan, Dan

July 3, 1922
b. Corneille

July 4, 1922
b. Keith, Damon (Jerome)

July 7, 1922
b. Cardin, Pierre

July 9, 1922
b. Pollard, Jim

July 11, 1922
b. TerHorst, Jerald Franklin

July 12, 1922
b. Hatfield, Mark Odom
b. MacGregor, Clark

July 13, 1922
b. Harlan, Louis R
b. Jorgensen, Anker Henrik

July 15, 1922
b. Lederman, Leon Max

July 17, 1922
b. Davie, Donald Alfred

July 18, 1922
b. Chayes, Abram J(oseph)

July 19, 1922
b. McGovern, George Stanley
d. Goucher, John Franklin

July 22, 1922
b. Robards, Jason, Jr.
d. Takamine, Jokichi

July 24, 1922
b. Mathias, Charles McCurdy, Jr.
d. Patten, Simon Nelson

July 26, 1922
b. Edwards, Blake
b. Lord, Marjorie

July 27, 1922
b. Lear, Norman Milton

July 28, 1922
b. Piccard, Jacques Ernest Jean

July 29, 1922
b. Popa, Vasko

July 30, 1922
b. Bloch, Henry W(ollman)

July 31, 1922
b. Axelson, Kenneth Strong
b. Bauer, Hank
d. Murfree, Mary Noailles

August 1, 1922
b. Hill, Arthur
b. McColough, C(harles Peter)

August 2, 1922
b. Laxalt, Paul
d. Bell, Alexander Graham

August 3, 1922
b. Eisenhower, John Sheldon Doud

August 4, 1922
b. Aponte-Martinez, Luis, Cardinal
d. Enver Pasha

August 5, 1922
b. Ginott, Haim
d. McCarthy, Tommy

August 6, 1922
b. Cardus, David
b. Laingen, (Lowell) Bruce
b. Laker, Freddie, Sir
b. Lomax, Louis
b. Walker, Daniel

August 8, 1922
b. Calhoun, Rory
b. Gernreich, Rudi
b. Himmelfarb, Gertrude
d. Gould, George Milbry

August 9, 1922
b. Larkin, Philip Arthur

August 10, 1922
b. von Mehren, Robert Brandt

August 11, 1922
b. Gallant, Mavis
b. Stuart, Lyle

August 12, 1922
b. Jakes, Milos
d. Griffith, Arthur

August 14, 1922
b. Messick, Hank
d. Northcliffe, Alfred Charles William
    Harmsworth, Viscount

August 15, 1922
b. Baskin, Leonard
b. Foss, Lukas
d. Dunning, William Archibald

August 16, 1922
b. Alfred, William
d. Scott, Austin

August 18, 1922
b. Robbe-Grillet, Alain
b. Winters, Shelley
d. Hudson, William Henry
d. Lavisse, Ernest

August 20, 1922
b. Resnik, Regina

August 22, 1922
b. Presle, Micheline
d. Collins, Michael
d. Scalchi, Sofia

August 23, 1922
b. Dumas, Roland
b. Kell, George (Clyde)

August 24, 1922
b. Levesque, Rene
b. Zinn, Howard

August 26, 1922
b. Levine, Irving R(askin)

August 28, 1922
b. Oakland, Simon

September 1, 1922
b. DeCarlo, Yvonne
b. Gassman, Vittorio
b. Laird, Melvin Robert

September 2, 1922
d. Lawson, Henry (Archibald Hertzberg)

September 7, 1922
d. Cobden-Sanderson, Thomas James
d. Halsted, William Stewart

September 8, 1922
b. Caesar, Sid
b. Larouche, Lyndon Hermyle, Jr.
b. Pierce, Samuel Riley, Jr.

September 9, 1922
b. Dehmelt, Hans Georg

September 10, 1922
d. Blunt, Wilfrid Scawen

September 15, 1922
b. Cooper, Jackie

September 16, 1922
b. Yamamoto, Kenichi

September 17, 1922
b. Bourjaily, Vance
b. Neto, Agostinho

September 19, 1922
b. Pep, Willie
b. Zatopek, Emil

September 20, 1922
b. Kapell, William

September 22, 1922
b. Yang, Chen Ning

September 23, 1922
b. Gidal, Sonia

September 25, 1922
b. Bondarchuk, Sergei (Fedorovich)

September 26, 1922
d. Watson, Thomas Edward

September 27, 1922
b. Jancso, Miklos
b. Newman, Joe Dwight
b. Penn, Arthur Hiller

September 28, 1922
b. Sedney, Jules

September 29, 1922
b. Scott, Lizabeth

September 30, 1922
b. Pettiford, Oscar
b. Unruh, Jesse Marvin

October 4, 1922
b. Baldrige, Malcolm
b. Heston, Charlton

October 5, 1922
b. Keane, Bil

October 7, 1922
d. Lloyd, Marie

October 8, 1922
b. Barnard, Christiaan Neethling

October 10, 1922
b. Holladay, Wilhelmina Cole

October 12, 1922
b. McDonnell, Sanford N
b. Sullivan, William Healy

October 16, 1922
b. Sullivan, Leon H

October 17, 1922
b. Juneau, Pierre
d. Upton, Florence Kate

October 18, 1922
b. Stankiewicz, Richard Peter

October 19, 1922
b. Anderson, Jack Northman

October 22, 1922
b. Chafee, John H(ubbard)
d. Abbott, Lyman

October 23, 1922
b. Gray, Coleen
b. Gray, Nicholas Stuart

October 27, 1922
b. Kiner, Ralph McPherran
b. Perez, Carlos Andres

October 28, 1922
b. Glenn, Carroll

October 29, 1922
b. Hefti, Neal Paul

October 30, 1922
b. Costa Mendez, Nicanor

October 31, 1922
b. Geddes, Barbara Bel
b. Jacquet, Illinois (Robert Russell)
b. Sihanouk, Norodom

November 1, 1922
b. Irving, George Steven
d. Page, Thomas Nelson

November 2, 1922
b. Conable, Barber B., Jr.

November 6, 1922
d. Bulkeley, Morgan G

November 7, 1922
b. Hirt, Al(ois Maxwell)
d. Thompson, Sam(uel Luther)

November 9, 1922
b. Dandridge, Dorothy
b. Lakatos, Imre

November 11, 1922
b. Vonnegut, Kurt, Jr.

November 12, 1922
b. Hunter, Kim

November 13, 1922
b. Werner, Oskar

November 14, 1922
b. Boutros-Ghali, Boutros

November 16, 1922
b. Amdahl, Gene M(yron)

November 17, 1922
b. Cohen, Stanley
b. Schulberg, Stuart

November 18, 1922
d. Proust, Marcel

November 19, 1922
b. Harris, Mark
d. Bacon, Frank

November 24, 1922
d. Childers, Erskine

November 25, 1922
b. Duggan, Maurice Noel
b. McCloskey, Robert James

November 26, 1922
b. Schulz, Charles M(onroe)

November 27, 1922
d. Meynell, Alice Christina Gertrude

November 29, 1922
b. Gibran, Kahlil George
b. Minoso, Minnie

December 2, 1922
b. Diggs, Charles C(oles), Jr.

December 3, 1922
b. Grunwald, Henry Anatole

b. Nykvist, Sven Vilhem

December 4, 1922
b. Philipe, Gerard
d. Peabody, Josephine Preston

December 5, 1922
b. Robertson, Don

December 6, 1922
b. McGivern, William Peter

December 8, 1922
b. Freud, Lucian
b. Ritchie, Jean

December 9, 1922
b. Foxx, Redd

December 11, 1922
b. Westermann, H(orace) C(lifford)

December 12, 1922
d. Wanamaker, John

December 13, 1922
b. Stevens, Mark

December 14, 1922
b. Basov, Nikolai Gennadievich
b. Hewitt, Don S.
b. Trippi, Charlie

December 15, 1922
b. Freed, Alan

December 16, 1922
d. Ben-Yehuda, Eliezer

December 18, 1922
b. Brooks, Jack Bascom
b. Valletti, Cesare

December 19, 1922
b. Andrews, Eamonn

December 20, 1922
b. Hill, George Roy

December 21, 1922
b. Winchell, Paul

December 22, 1922
b. Billingsley, Barbara
b. Wright, Jim

December 23, 1922
b. Willingham, Calder Baynard, Jr.

December 24, 1922
b. Gardner, Ava

December 25, 1922
b. Lahbabi, Mohammed Aziz

December 28, 1922
b. Lee, Stan

December 29, 1922
b. Gaddis, William (Thomas)

December 31, 1922
b. Bookout, John Frank, Jr.
b. McCracken, Joan
b. Stamos, Theodoros

1923

b. Abplanalp, Robert H
b. Aliyev, Heydar
b. Bastianini, Ettore
b. Bjorn-Larsen, Knut
b. Crean, Robert
b. DeForest, Calvert
b. Dixon, Margaret (A.)
b. Favaloro, Rene Geronimo
b. Fraker, William A
b. Graham, Barbara
b. Grese, Irma
b. Haykal, Muhammad Husain
b. Horvath, Leslie
b. Jordan, Bobby
b. Jumper, Betty Mae Tiger
b. Keating, Charles H, Jr.
b. Kelley, Virginia
b. Kordich, Jay
b. Lavelli, Dante
b. Lazarus, Charles P
b. Lewis, Flora
b. McCarty, Mary
b. Ngala, Ronald Gideon
b. Schoellkopf, Caroline Rose Hunt
b. Zayid bin Sultan Al-Nahyan,
   Shaykh
d. Maherero, Samuel
d. Troeltsch, Ernst
d. Wheeler, Schuyler Skaats

January 1, 1923
b. Jackson, Milt(on)
b. Sembene, Ousmane
d. Keeler, Wee Willie

January 3, 1923
d. Hasek, Jaroslav

January 5, 1923
b. Bernstein, Robert L(ouis)
b. Phillips, Sam

January 6, 1923
b. Timerman, Jacobo

January 7, 1923
b. Dark, Alvin Ralph

January 8, 1923
b. Storch, Larry
b. Tozzi, Giorgio

January 9, 1923
d. Mansfield, Katherine

January 11, 1923
b. Ashley, Thomas William Ludlow
b. Shelby, Carroll (Hall)

January 12, 1923
b. Hayes, Ira Hamilton

January 14, 1923
b. Korinetz, Yuri

January 15, 1923
b. Lee, Teng-Hui
b. Lee Teng-hui

January 16, 1923
b. Hecht, Anthony Evan

January 18, 1923
d. Claflin, Tennessee Celeste
d. Reid, Wallace Eugene

January 19, 1923
b. Moyes, Patricia
b. Schonhuber, Franz Xaver
b. Stapleton, Jean

January 21, 1923
b. Savalas, Telly

January 23, 1923
b. Ashenfelter, Nip
b. Halop, Florence
b. Logan, John

January 24, 1923
b. Rama Rau, Santha

January 25, 1923
b. Galamison, Milton Arthur
b. Rinkoff, Barbara Jean

January 26, 1923
b. Jeffreys, Anne

January 29, 1923
b. Burke, Jack, Jr.
b. Chayefsky, Paddy
d. Vedder, Elihu

January 30, 1923
b. Dropo, Walt(er)
b. Martin, Dick

January 31, 1923
b. Channing, Carol
b. Dru, Joanne
b. Mailer, Norman (Kingsley)
d. Montezuma, Carlos

February 2, 1923
b. Dickey, James (Lafayette)
b. Granville, Bonita
b. Schoendienst, Red
b. Smith, Liz

February 4, 1923
b. Bain, Conrad Stafford
b. Betancur, Belisario
d. Fischer, Carl

February 6, 1923
d. Barnard, Edward Emerson

February 7, 1923
b. Banks, Harvey Washington
b. Brasselle, Keefe
b. Harewood, George Henry Hubert
   Lascelles, Earl

February 8, 1923
d. Bosanquet, Bernard

February 9, 1923
b. Behan, Brendan (Francis)
b. Grayson, Kathryn

February 10, 1923
b. Henderson, Vivian Wilson
b. Siepi, Cesare
d. Roentgen, Wilhelm Konrad

February 12, 1923
b. Dugan, Alan
b. Zeffirelli, Franco

February 13, 1923
b. Abdnor, James S
b. Bilandic, Michael Anthony
b. Chapin, Schuyler Garrison
b. Shafran, Daniel
b. Yeager, Chuck

February 14, 1923
b. Hebert, Jay

February 15, 1923
b. Bonner, Yelena

February 17, 1923
b. Allegro, John Marco
b. Clausen, A(lden) W(inship)
b. DeFranco, Buddy

February 19, 1923
b. Hillings, Patrick J(ohn)

February 20, 1923
b. Burnham, Forbes

February 21, 1923
b. Winter, William Forrest
b. Zeitlin, Zvi

February 22, 1923
b. Ogilvie, Richard Buell
d. Delcasse, Theophile

February 24, 1923
b. Soyer, David

February 25, 1923
b. Glazer, Nathan

February 27, 1923
b. Gordon, Dexter Keith

February 28, 1923
b. Durning, Charles
b. Obata, Gyo

March 1, 1923
d. Barbosa, Ruy

March 2, 1923
b. Michel, Robert H(enry)
b. Perlmutter, Nathan
b. Watson, Doc

March 4, 1923
b. King, Francis Henry

March 5, 1923
b. Irsay, Robert
d. Ayer, Francis Wayland

March 6, 1923
b. McMahon, Ed(ward Lee)

March 8, 1923
b. Charisse, Cyd

March 9, 1923
b. Buckley, James Lane
b. Courreges, Andre
d. Waals, Johannes Diderik van der

March 10, 1923
b. Fitch, Val Logsdon

March 11, 1923
b. Brough, Louise Althea

March 12, 1923
b. Schirra, Wally

March 13, 1923
b. Bolger, William Frederick

March 14, 1923
b. Arbus, Diane

March 15, 1923
b. Cony, Edward Roger
b. Tisch, Laurence Alan

March 18, 1923
b. Granatelli, Andy

March 19, 1923
b. Morgentaler, Henry

March 21, 1923
b. Lindsey, Mort

March 22, 1923
b. Marceau, Marcel

March 23, 1923
b. Weinmesiter, Arnie

March 24, 1923
b. Hamilton, Murray

March 26, 1923
b. Elliott, Bob
d. Bernhardt, Sarah

March 27, 1923
b. Endo, Shusaku
b. Simpson, Louis
d. Dewar, James, Sir

March 28, 1923
b. Jones, Thad(deus Joseph)

April 2, 1923
b. Schiess, Betty Bone
d. Jefferson, Thomas

April 3, 1923
b. Sterling, Jan
b. Wortman, Sterling

April 5, 1923
b. Nguyen Van Thieu
b. Rothstein, Ruth

d. Mallock, William Hurrell

April 6, 1923
d. Fletcher, Alice Cunningham
d. Herbert, George Edward Stanhope
   Molyneux

April 8, 1923
b. Corelli, Franco
b. Moorhead, William Singer
b. Mulhare, Edward

April 9, 1923
b. Levy, Leonard Williams

April 10, 1923
b. Old Coyote, Barney
b. Popovi Da

April 11, 1923
b. Rubin, Theodore Isaac

April 12, 1923
b. Engle, Eloise Katherine
b. Miller, Ann

April 14, 1923
b. DeVicenzo, Roberto
b. Holt, John Caldwell

April 15, 1923
b. Aziz, Philip John Andrew Ferris
b. DePugh, Robert Bolivar
b. Lembeck, Harvey

April 16, 1923
b. Moore, Arch Alfred, Jr.

April 17, 1923
b. Anderson, Lindsay (Gordon)
b. McCallister, Lon
b. Reasoner, Harry

April 20, 1923
b. Puente, Tito

April 21, 1923
b. Mortimer, John Clifford

April 22, 1923
b. Spelling, Aaron

April 23, 1923
b. Briscoe, Dolph

April 25, 1923
b. Healy, Timothy S(tafford)
b. King, Albert
b. Miller, Arnold Ray

May 1, 1923
b. Heller, Joseph

May 2, 1923
b. Hillery, Patrick John

May 7, 1923
b. Baxter, Anne
b. Roche, John P

May 8, 1923
b. Cairns, John, Jr.

May 10, 1923
b. Parseghian, Ara (Raoul)

May 15, 1923
b. Avedon, Richard
b. Poussaint, Alvin F.

May 17, 1923
b. Mahoney, David Joseph, Jr.
b. Mennin, Peter

May 19, 1923
b. Arbatov, Georgi

May 20, 1923
b. Fellows, Edith
b. Selvon, Samuel Dickson

May 22, 1923
b. Lobel, Arnold Stark
b. Namgyal, Palden Thondup
d. Lopez-Portillo y Rojas, Jose

May 23, 1923
b. Larrocha, Alicia de
d. Bradley, Henry

May 25, 1923
b. Weitz, John

May 26, 1923
b. Arness, James

May 27, 1923
b. Kissinger, Henry Alfred
b. Redstone, Sumner (Murray)

May 28, 1923
b. Ligeti, Gyorgy (Sandor)

May 30, 1923
b. Lydon, James

May 31, 1923
b. Kelly, Ellsworth
b. Rainier III, Prince

June 6, 1923
b. Hyams, Joe

June 8, 1923
b. Boyd, Malcolm
b. Kirby, George
b. Rosenthal, Benjamin Stanley

June 10, 1923
b. Maxwell, Robert Ian Charles
d. Loti, Pierre

June 12, 1923
d. Stambuliski, Aleksandr

June 13, 1923
b. Mazzola, Anthony T

June 15, 1923
b. Benarde, Melvin Albert

June 16, 1923
b. Colombo, Joseph Anthony

June 17, 1923
b. Bevilacqua, Anthony Joseph, Cardinal
b. Hirsch, Crazylegs

June 19, 1923
b. Rodriguez, Andres

June 20, 1923
b. Gay, Peter Jack

June 24, 1923
b. Carter, Jack
b. Romiti, Cesare

June 25, 1923
b. Francis, Sam(uel Lewis)
b. Gilman, Dorothy
b. Mosley, Nicholas

June 27, 1923
b. Zernial, Gus Edward

June 28, 1923
d. Biggs, Hermann Michael

June 29, 1923
b. Zech, Lando William, Jr.

July 2, 1923
d. Calvert, Louis

July 5, 1923
b. McKay, John Harvey

July 6, 1923
b. Jaruzelski, Wojciech Witold
b. McDonald, Marie

July 7, 1923
b. Ciulei, Liviu

July 8, 1923
b. Dillard, Harrison

July 9, 1923
d. Day, William Rufus

July 10, 1923
b. Hamner, Earl Henry, Jr.
b. Kerr, Jean

July 11, 1923
b. Barry, Daniel

July 12, 1923
b. Fields, Freddie
b. Jenkins, Paul

July 14, 1923
b. Lear, Frances
b. Robertson, Dale
b. Steele, Willie

July 15, 1923
b. Jackson, Cordell

July 16, 1923
b. Laroche, Guy
d. Couperius, Louis (Marie Anne)

July 17, 1923
b. Purdy, James

July 19, 1923
b. Hannum, Alex(ander Murray)
b. Hansen, Joseph
b. Rusher, William Allen
d. Holabird, William

July 20, 1923
d. Villa, Pancho

July 21, 1923
b. Marcus, Rudolph A
b. Wise, William H

July 22, 1923
b. Armstrong, Charles B
b. Dole, Robert Joseph

July 24, 1923
b. Weaver, William

July 25, 1923
b. Getty, Estelle

July 26, 1923
b. Wilhelm, Hoyt

July 29, 1923
b. Egan, Richard

July 31, 1923
b. Ertegun, Ahmet (Munir)

August 1, 1923
b. Brown, Carter
b. Sando, Joe

August 2, 1923
d. Harding, Warren G(amaliel)

August 3, 1923
b. Hagen, Jean
b. Klein, Anne

August 5, 1923
b. Kleindienst, Richard Gordon
d. Wheeler, Candace Thurber

August 8, 1923
b. Williams, Esther

August 10, 1923
b. Fleming, Rhonda

August 12, 1923
b. Gannett, Ruth

August 16, 1923
b. Peres, Shimon

August 17, 1923
b. Rivers, Larry

August 19, 1923
d. Pareto, Vilfredo

August 20, 1923
b. Granville, Joseph E(nsign)
b. Shattuck, Roger Whitney

August 24, 1923
b. Cater, Douglass
b. Jensen, Arthur Robert
d. Wiggin, Kate Douglas

August 27, 1923
d. Ayrton, Hertha

August 29, 1923
b. Attenborough, Richard Samuel, Sir
b. Gershon, Karen

September 1, 1923
b. Marciano, Rocky
b. Thomson, Ken(neth Roy)

September 2, 1923
b. Champion, Marge Celeste

September 3, 1923
b. Walker, Mort

September 6, 1923
b. Peter II
d. Dutton, E(dward) P(ayson)

September 7, 1923
b. Lawford, Peter
b. Suggs, Louise

September 9, 1923
b. Gajdusek, D(aniel) Carleton

September 11, 1923
b. Drake, Betsy
b. Evers, James Charles
b. Kotzky, Alex Sylvester
b. Schultz, Harry D

September 13, 1923
b. Correia, Natalia

September 14, 1923
b. Rollins, Kenny
b. Rubin, Vitalii

September 15, 1923
b. Williams, Hank

September 16, 1923
b. Lee Kuan Yew
b. Paige, Janis

September 18, 1923
b. Wilson, Bertha

September 22, 1923
b. Abse, Dannie

September 23, 1923
d. Morley, John, Viscount

September 24, 1923
b. MacRae, Sheila
b. Navarro, Fats

September 25, 1923
b. DeRoburt, Hammer, Sir

September 28, 1923
b. Windom, William

September 29, 1923
b. Phillips, Bum

September 30, 1923
b. Swann, Donald (Ibrahim)

October 3, 1923
b. Skrowaczewski, Stanislaw

October 4, 1923
b. Martin, Harold Eugene

October 5, 1923
b. Berrigan, Philip Francis
b. Johns, Glynis

October 6, 1923
b. Thomas, Lowell Jackson, Jr.
d. Browning, Oscar

October 7, 1923
b. Riopelle, Jean-Paul

October 9, 1923
b. Sinden, Donald (Alfred)

October 11, 1923
b. Hatathli, Ned

October 12, 1923
b. Nidetch, Jean

October 15, 1923
b. Calvino, Italo
d. Talbert, Mary Morris Burnett

October 16, 1923
b. Darnell, Linda (Monetta Eloyse)
b. Hicks, Louise Day
b. Kaempfert, Bert
b. Ponnamperuma, Cyril (Andrew)

October 20, 1923
b. Craft, Robert

October 22, 1923
b. Pihos, Pete(r L)
d. Maurel, Victor

October 23, 1923
b. Mardian, Robert Charles
b. Rorem, Ned

October 24, 1923
b. Levertov, Denise

October 25, 1923
b. Thomson, Bobby

October 26, 1923
d. Steinmetz, Charles Proteus

October 27, 1923
b. Lichtenstein, Roy

October 29, 1923
b. Djerassi, Carl

October 30, 1923
b. Bernardi, Hershel
d. Law, Andrew Bonar

October 31, 1923
b. Waldron, Hicks Benjamin

November 1, 1923
b. Angeles, Victoria de los
b. Dickson, Gordon Rupert

November 5, 1923
b. Sheppard, Sam(uel)

November 6, 1923
b. Griffin, Bob

November 9, 1923
b. Coachman, Alice
b. Schuyler, James Marcus

November 13, 1923
b. Christian, Linda

November 15, 1923
b. Schapiro, Miriam

November 17, 1923
b. Garcia, Mike

November 18, 1923
b. Gregor, Arthur
b. Shepard, Alan B(artlett), Jr.
b. Stevens, Ted

November 20, 1923
b. Gordimer, Nadine
b. Sprinkel, Beryl Wayne

November 22, 1923
b. Hiller, Arthur
b. Westwood, Jean Miles

November 23, 1923
b. Haughton, Billy

November 24, 1923
b. Meredith, Scott

November 25, 1923
b. Koivisto, Mauno Henrik
b. Wall, Art(hur Jonathan), Jr.

November 29, 1923
b. Reynolds, Frank

November 30, 1923
b. Gowans, Alan
b. Zimbalist, Efrem, Jr.
d. Barres, (Auguste) Maurice

December 1, 1923
b. Turner, Stansfield

December 2, 1923
b. Riklis, Meshulam

December 3, 1923
b. Callas, Maria
b. Fears, Tom
b. Guarrera, Frank
b. Keller, George Matthew

December 5, 1923
d. Phillips, Tommy

December 7, 1923
b. Knight, Ted

December 11, 1923
b. Blair, Betsy
b. Turner, Morrie

December 12, 1923
b. Barker, Bob

December 13, 1923
b. Anderson, Philip Warren
b. Goodman, Mitchell

December 14, 1923
b. McNair, Robert Evander

December 15, 1923
b. Carter, Jimmy
b. Dyson, Freeman John

December 17, 1923
b. Pelikan, Jaroslav

December 18, 1923
b. Cruz, Arturo

December 19, 1923
b. Jackson, Gordon Cameron
b. Lopez Bravo, Gregorio

December 21, 1923
b. Tucker, Sterling

December 22, 1923
b. Corena, Fernando

December 23, 1923
b. Diop, Cheikh Anta
b. Frankel, Gene
b. Masursky, Harold
b. Okun, Milton Theodore
b. Roman, Ruth
b. Stern, Leonard B
b. Stockdale, James

December 26, 1923
b. Artschwager, Richard (Ernst)

December 27, 1923
d. Owens, Michael Joseph

December 28, 1923
b. Duggan, Andrew
d. Eiffel, Alexandre Gustave

1924

b. Adzhubei, Aleksei I(vanovich)
b. Berrill, Jack
b. Boyle, Gertrude
b. Cates, Joseph
b. Egan, Eddie
b. Ford, Constance
b. Furman, Roger
b. Gennaro, Peter
b. Harris, Jean Witt Struven
b. Jacobs, Raymond
b. Jaffe, Sam(uel Anderson)
b. Jawara, Dauda Kairaba
b. Jones, Arthur A

b. Kamen, Milt
b. Khamtay Siphandone
b. Lawford, Pat(ricia Kennedy)
b. Liedtke, William C, Jr.
b. Lyon, Phyllis Ann
b. Magee, Patrick
b. Marshall, Lois
b. McMurray, Bette Clair
b. Merritt, Justine
b. Most, Johnny
b. Murchison, Clint(on Williams, Jr.)
b. Ngo dinh Nhu, Madame
b. Pennington, John Selman
b. Romero, Carlos Humberto
b. Schoenfeld, Gerald
b. Van der Klugt, Cor
d. Mack, John M
d. McLaughlin, John J
d. Polk, Willis Jefferson
d. Powderly, Terence Vincent
d. Quinn, John

January 1, 1924
b. Danto, Arthur C(oleman)

January 2, 1924
d. Baring-Gould, Sabine

January 6, 1924
b. Kim Dae Jung
b. Rubenstein, Richard L(owell)
b. Scruggs, Earl Eugene

January 8, 1924
b. Moody, Ron

January 10, 1924
b. Chillida, Eduard
b. Roach, Max(well Lemuel)

January 11, 1924
b. Guillemin, Roger Charles Louis

January 13, 1924
b. Heckert, Richard Edwin
b. Petit, Roland

January 17, 1924
b. Cobb, Jewel Plummer

January 19, 1924
b. Colasanto, Nicholas
b. Revel, Jean Francois

January 20, 1924
b. Josey, E. J.

January 21, 1924
b. Hill, Benny
d. Lenin, Vladimir Ilyich

January 22, 1924
b. Johnson, J J

January 23, 1924
b. Lautenberg, Frank R
d. Morrice, James Wilson

January 24, 1924
b. Hill, Herbert

January 25, 1924
b. Groza, Lou(is)

January 27, 1924
b. Denktash, Rauf

January 29, 1924
b. Nono, Luigi

January 30, 1924
b. Alexander, Lloyd Chudley

February 1, 1924
d. Prendergast, Maurice Brazil

February 2, 1924
b. Stitt, Sonny

February 3, 1924
b. Gelb, Arthur
b. Stevens, Leslie
d. Wilson, Woodrow

February 7, 1924
b. Bryan, Dora

February 8, 1924
b. Meadows, Audrey

February 10, 1924
d. Visscher, William Lightfoot

February 11, 1924
d. Loeb, Jacques

February 13, 1924
b. Servan-Schreiber, Jean-Jacques

February 16, 1924
b. MacKenzie, Warren
d. Bacon, Henry

February 17, 1924
b. Truman, Margaret

February 19, 1924
b. Marvin, Lee
b. Norris, Bruce A

February 20, 1924
b. Fraser, Donald Mackay
b. Terzi, Zehdi Labib
b. Vanderbilt, Gloria Morgan

February 21, 1924
b. Buzhardt, J(oseph) Fred, Jr.
b. Estrin, Thelma (Austern)
b. Hathaway, William Dodd
b. Mugabe, Robert (Gabriel)

February 23, 1924
b. Cormack, Allan MacLeod

February 24, 1924
b. Arison, Ted

February 26, 1924
b. Randall, Tony
b. Stone, Marvin Lawrence
b. Takeshita, Noboru
b. Varviso, Silvio

February 28, 1924
b. Kraft, Chris(topher Columbus, Jr.)

March 1, 1924
b. Slayton, Donald Kent

March 3, 1924
b. Murayama, Tomiichi
b. Nolte, Henry R, Jr.

March 4, 1924
b. O'Donnell, Kenneth P

March 5, 1924
b. Bernhard, Harvey

March 6, 1924
b. Caldwell, Sarah
b. Webster, William Hedgcock

March 7, 1924
b. Abe, Kobo

March 8, 1924
b. Caro, Anthony, Sir

March 9, 1924
b. Gold, Herbert

March 12, 1924
d. Chardonnet, Louis Marie Hilaire Bernigaud

March 15, 1924
b. Sabu

March 16, 1924
b. Ludwig, Christa

March 22, 1924
b. Fussell, Paul
b. Neuharth, Allen Harold

March 24, 1924
b. Fell, Norman

March 27, 1924
b. Holloman, Bobo
b. Vaughan, Sarah Lois

March 28, 1924
b. Bartholomew, Freddie

March 29, 1924
b. Mathers, Frank
d. Stanford, Charles Villiers, Sir

April 1, 1924
b. Byrne, Brendan Thomas

April 2, 1924
b. Avila, Bobby

April 3, 1924
b. Brando, Marlon, Jr.
b. Day, Doris

April 4, 1924
b. Hodges, Gil(bert Raymond)

April 5, 1924
b. Chew, Peter

April 6, 1924
b. Benzell, Mimi
b. King, Bruce
b. Mita, Katsushige

April 10, 1924
b. Noland, Kenneth Clifton

April 12, 1924
b. Barre, Raymond

April 13, 1924
b. Biggers, John (Thomas)
b. Donen, Stanley

April 14, 1924
b. Rogers, Shorty
b. Warnock, (Helen) Mary (Wilson)
d. Sullivan, Louis Henri

April 15, 1924
b. Hazan, Marcella Maddalena
b. Marriner, Neville

April 16, 1924
b. Mancini, Henry

April 17, 1924
b. Gallant, Roy Arthur
b. Simmons, Althea T L

April 18, 1924
b. Hyde, Henry J(ohn)

April 20, 1924
b. Foch, Nina

April 21, 1924
d. Corelli, Marie

April 22, 1924
b. Longley, James Bernard
b. Putch, William Henry
b. Weber, Robert Maxwell

April 23, 1924
d. Duse, Eleanora
d. Goodhue, Bertram G(rosvenor)

April 24, 1924
b. Bevan, Brian
d. Hall, G(ranville) Stanley

April 26, 1924
b. Nype, Russell

April 28, 1924
b. Kaunda, Kenneth D(avid)

April 29, 1924
b. Jeanmaire, Renee Marcelle

April 30, 1924
b. Harnick, Sheldon Mayer

May 1, 1924
b. Granville, Evelyn Boyd
b. Kayibanda, Gregoire
b. Southern, Terry

May 2, 1924
b. Bikel, Theodore Meir

May 3, 1924
b. Roderick, David Milton

May 4, 1924
d. Nesbit, Edith

May 5, 1924
b. Torre-Nilsson, Leopoldo

May 8, 1924
d. Lyons, Sophie Levy

May 11, 1924
b. Garment, Leonard
b. Hewish, Antony

May 12, 1924
b. Alegria, Claribel
b. Mecham, Evan

May 13, 1924
b. Mann, Theodore

May 14, 1924
b. Babb, Howard Selden

May 15, 1924
d. D'Estournelles, Paul Henri Benjamin Balleut de Constant, Baron

May 16, 1924
b. Jawara, Alhaji Dawda Kairaba, Sir
b. Mankiewicz, Frank Fabian

May 17, 1924
d. Cummings, Candy

May 18, 1924
b. Edmonson, Munro Sterling
b. Justice, Choo Choo
b. Whitaker, Jack

May 19, 1924
b. Wilson, Sandy

May 22, 1924
b. Aznavour, Charles

May 24, 1924
d. Lindbergh, Charles Augustus

May 25, 1924
d. Popova, Liubov Sergeevna

May 27, 1924
b. Lusinchi, Jaime
d. Herbert, Victor

May 29, 1924
d. Cambon, Pierre Paul

May 30, 1924
b. Powell, Maxine

May 31, 1924
b. Harris, Patricia Roberts

June 1, 1924
b. Coffin, William Sloan, Jr.

June 2, 1924
b. DeMott, Benjamin Haile

June 3, 1924
b. Van Andel, Jay
b. Wiesel, Torsten Nils
d. Kafka, Franz

June 4, 1924
b. Alesana, Tofilau Eti

June 5, 1924
b. Brissie, Lou
b. Chew, Geoffrey Foucar

June 6, 1924
b. Andrews, V(irginia) C(leo)

June 7, 1924
b. Gray, Dolores

June 8, 1924
b. Nofziger, Lyn
d. Mallory, George Leigh

June 11, 1924
d. Matteotti, Giacomo

June 12, 1924
b. Bush, George (Herbert Walker)

June 14, 1924
b. Black, James Whyte, Sir
b. Erickson, Arthur Charles
d. Gilbreth, Frank Bunker

June 15, 1924
b. Weizman, Ezer

June 16, 1924
b. Shah, Indries

June 18, 1924
b. Mikan, George Lawrence, Jr.
d. Acevedo Diaz, Eduardo

June 19, 1924
b. Nomelleni, Leo Joseph

June 20, 1924
b. Atkins, Chet
b. Murphy, Audie

June 21, 1924
b. Bleiberg, Robert Marvin

June 22, 1924
b. Barber, Jesse B., Jr.

June 23, 1924
b. Premadasa, Ranasinghe

June 25, 1924
b. Lumet, Sidney
d. Darragh, Jack

June 26, 1924
b. Haack, Morton R

June 27, 1924
b. Conrad, Paul Francis

June 28, 1924
b. Dolci, Danilo

June 29, 1924
b. Walford, Roy L(ee, Jr.)

July 2, 1924
b. Riccardo, John Joseph
b. Swinburne, Laurence

July 4, 1924
b. Saint, Eva Marie

July 5, 1924
b. Starker, Janos

July 6, 1924
b. Royal, Darrell K

July 7, 1924
b. Ford, Mary

July 9, 1924
b. Pennario, Leonard

July 13, 1924
b. Bergonzi, Carlo
d. Marshall, Alfred

July 15, 1924
b. Denton, Jeremiah Andrew, Jr.
d. Coryell, John Russell

July 16, 1924
b. Myerson, Bess

July 17, 1924
d. Gardner, Isabella Stewart

July 19, 1924
b. Hathaway, Stanley Knapp
b. Hingle, Pat

July 20, 1924
b. Albright, Lola Jean
b. Berger, Thomas Louis
b. Sarkis, Elias

July 21, 1924
b. Knotts, Don
b. Starr, Kay
b. Stone, Chuck
b. Williams, Lynn Russell

July 22, 1924
b. Whiting, Margaret

July 24, 1924
d. Cox, Palmer

July 25, 1924
b. Church, Frank

July 27, 1924
b. Canby, Vincent
b. Taktakishvili, Otar Vasilevich
d. Busoni, Ferruccio Benvenuto

July 29, 1924
b. Bochner, Lloyd
b. Ethridge, Mark Foster, Jr.
b. Horton, Robert

July 30, 1924
b. Gallen, Hugh J
b. Gass, William Howard

August 1, 1924
b. Medicine, Beatrice A.

August 2, 1924
b. Baldwin, James (Arthur)
b. O'Connor, Carroll
d. Lothrop, Harriet Mulford Stone

August 3, 1924
b. Campeau, Robert Joseph
b. Uris, Leon Marcus
d. Conrad, Joseph

August 6, 1924
b. Jenkins, Ella (Louise)

August 9, 1924
b. Quaison-Sackey, Alex(ander)

August 10, 1924
b. Hyer, Martha

August 12, 1924
b. Zia-ul-Haq, Mohammad

August 15, 1924
b. Bolt, Robert (Oxton)
b. Schlafly, Phyllis Stewart

August 17, 1924
b. Connell, Evan Shelby, Jr.

August 19, 1924
b. Marshall, William

August 20, 1924
b. Reeves, Jim

August 21, 1924
b. Janov, Arthur
b. Schenkel, Chris(topher Eugene)

August 23, 1924
b. Solow, Robert Merton

August 24, 1924
b. Ahidjo, Ahmadou
b. Ikle, Fred Charles
b. Teicher, Louis
b. Witcover, Walt

August 25, 1924
b. Hall, Monty

August 27, 1924
d. Bayliss, William Maddock, Sir

August 28, 1924
b. Ryan, Peggy

August 29, 1924
b. Mayer, Dick
b. Washington, Dinah

August 31, 1924
b. Hackett, Buddy

September 2, 1924
b. Moi, Daniel arap
d. Shiras, George, Jr.

September 3, 1924
d. Wagnalls, Adam Willis

September 4, 1924
b. Aiken, Joan Delano
b. Kraft, Joseph

September 6, 1924
b. Melcher, John

September 7, 1924
b. Aitken, Hugh
b. Inouye, Daniel Ken

September 8, 1924
b. Ford, Wendell Hampton
b. Metalious, Grace de Repentigny

September 9, 1924
b. Greer, Jane

September 10, 1924
b. Kluszewski, Ted

September 11, 1924
b. Akaka, Daniel Kahikina
b. Landry, Tom

September 12, 1924
b. Cabral, Amilcar Lopes
b. Morse, Ella Mae

September 13, 1924
b. Brady, Scott
b. Jarre, Maurice

September 14, 1924
d. Chance, Frank Leroy

September 15, 1924
d. Roux, Wilhelm

September 16, 1924
b. Bacall, Lauren
b. Benton, Nelson

September 18, 1924
b. Fichandler, Zelda Diamond
d. Bradley, Francis Herbert

September 20, 1924
b. Galanos, James
b. Grant, Gogi
b. Meara, Anne

September 21, 1924
d. Quad, M

September 22, 1924
b. Middendorf, John William, II

September 23, 1924
b. Russell, Gail

September 24, 1924
b. Bardis, Panos Demetrios
d. Estrada Cabrera, Manuel

September 25, 1924
d. Crabtree, Lotta

September 26, 1924
b. Wincelberg, Shimon

September 27, 1924
b. Powell, Earl

September 28, 1924
b. Mastroianni, Marcello

September 30, 1924
b. Capote, Truman

October 1, 1924
b. Carter, Jimmy
b. Rehnquist, William Hubbs

October 3, 1924
b. Kurtzman, Harvey

October 5, 1924
b. Dana, Bill
b. Donoso, Jose
b. Morton, Frederic

October 6, 1924
b. Demirel, Suleyman
b. Lowery, Joseph E

October 9, 1924
d. Daubert, Jake

October 10, 1924
b. Clavell, James (Edmund Du Maresq)
b. Wood, Edward D., Jr.

October 11, 1924
b. Whitfield, Malvin

October 12, 1924
d. France, Anatole

October 13, 1924
b. Gibbs, Terry
b. Russell, Nipsey

October 14, 1924
b. Kogan, Leonid Borisovich

October 15, 1924
b. Hesse, Mary B(renda)
b. Iacocca, Lee
b. Quintero, Jose (Benjamin)

October 17, 1924
b. Coryell, Don(ald David)

October 19, 1924
b. Strougal, Lubomir

October 21, 1924
b. Wilson, Julie

October 22, 1924
b. Levine, Albert Norman

October 25, 1924
b. Brown, Bobby

b. Elliott, Osborn
d. Gokalp, Mehmet Ziya

October 26, 1924
d. Dockstader, Lew

October 27, 1924
b. Avallone, Michael Angelo, Jr.
b. Dee, Ruby
d. Holland, Clifford Milburn

October 29, 1924
d. Burnett, Frances Eliza Hodgson

November 4, 1924
b. Anson, Jay
b. Meeker, Howie
d. Faure, Gabriel Urbain

November 7, 1924
b. Mankowitz, Wolf
d. Thoma, Hans

November 8, 1924
b. Bower, Johnny

November 9, 1924
b. Frank, Robert
d. Lodge, Henry Cabot

November 10, 1924
d. Geikie, Archibald, Sir

November 17, 1924
b. Heath, Catherine
b. Pereira, Aristides

November 19, 1924
b. Mutesa II
d. Ince, Thomas H(arper)

November 20, 1924
b. Allison, Fran(ces)
b. Mandelbrot, Benoit B.

November 21, 1924
b. Blaine, Vivian
b. Planinc, Milka
d. Harding, Florence Kling (De Wolfe)

November 22, 1924
b. Page, Geraldine

November 25, 1924
b. Desmond, Paul Breitenfeld
b. Markovic, Ante
b. Turnbull, Collin M(acmillan)

November 26, 1924
b. Hoffman, Irwin
b. Segal, George

November 28, 1924
b. Brutus, Dennis Vincent

November 29, 1924
b. Freilicher, Jane
d. Puccini, Giacomo

November 30, 1924
b. Chisholm, Shirley Anita St. Hill
b. Sherman, Allan

December 2, 1924
b. Haig, Alexander Meigs, Jr.

December 3, 1924
b. Backus, John

December 4, 1924
b. Portman, John Calvin, Jr.

December 5, 1924
b. Sobukwe, Robert Mangaliso

December 6, 1924
b. Cox, Wally
b. Foster, Susanna
d. Porter, Gene Stratton

December 7, 1924
b. Soares, Mario Alberto Nobre Lopes

December 10, 1924
b. Manley, Michael (Norman)
b. Winpisinger, William W(ayne)
d. Belmont, August, Jr.

December 11, 1924
b. Blanchard, Doc
b. Windsor, Marie

December 12, 1924
b. Koch, Ed(ward Irwin)
b. Schultze, Charles Louis

December 13, 1924
b. Doby, Larry
d. Gompers, Samuel

December 15, 1924
b. McGee, Charles

December 19, 1924
b. Harvey, Doug(las Norman)
b. Roney, William Chapoton, Jr.
b. Tournier, Michel

December 20, 1924
b. LaMarsh, Judy

December 22, 1924
b. Bhattarai, Krishna Prasad
b. Fletcher, Arthur Allen

December 23, 1924
b. Devine, Dan(iel John)
b. Kalber, Floyd
b. Kurland, Bob

December 24, 1924
b. Haney, Carol

December 25, 1924
b. Daddah, Moktar Ould
b. Serling, Rod

December 26, 1924
b. Davis, Glenn W

December 27, 1924
b. McClure, James A

December 28, 1924
b. Obote, Milton

d. Spitteler, Karl Friedrich Georg

December 29, 1924
b. Yankelovich, Daniel

December 30, 1924
b. Brill, Yvonne Claeys

December 31, 1924
b. Allen, Rex E., Sr.
b. Brown, Pamela Beatrice
b. Kelley, Frank Joseph

1925

b. Abercrombie, Josephine
b. Avedon, Doe
b. Averback, Hy
b. Burbidge, Margaret
b. Cartier, Claude
b. Chandler, Colby H
b. Elazar, David
b. Estes, Billie Sol
b. First, Ruth
b. Fleming, Art
b. Fomon, Robert
b. Fonseca, Rubem
b. Habash, Georges
b. Hugel, Max
b. Kilburn, Peter
b. Kilroy, James, Jr.
b. Koirala, Girija Prasad
b. Liss, Alan R
b. Liuzzo, Viola
b. Montenegro, Hugh
b. Moore, Charles Willard
b. Nunn, Bobby
b. Pyne, Joe
b. Rodriguez Pedotti, Andres
b. Spicer, Jack
d. Bass, Henry
d. Datsolalee
d. Flammarion, Camille
d. Hart, Pearl
d. Lever, William Hesketh
d. Meggendorfer, Lothar
d. Reilly, Sidney George

January 1, 1925
b. Amin, Idi
b. Beard, Matthew, Jr.
b. Connor, George
b. Cortesa, Valentina
b. Jessup, Richard

January 2, 1925
b. Crowe, William James, Jr.

January 4, 1925
b. Lujack, John(ny)

January 5, 1925
b. Opel, John Roberts

January 6, 1925
b. DeLorean, John Zachary

January 7, 1925
b. Durrell, Gerald (Malcolm)

January 8, 1925
d. Bellows, George Wesley

January 9, 1925
b. Bloch, Eric
b. Lamas, Fernando
b. Van Cleef, Lee

January 13, 1925
b. Verdon, Gwen

January 14, 1925
b. Mishima, Yukio
d. Furniss, Harry

January 15, 1925
b. Slenczynska, Ruth

January 16, 1925
b. Schwartz, Felice N(ierenberg)

January 17, 1925
b. Hanson, Duane (Elwood)

January 19, 1925
b. Bawden, Nina Mary Mabey

January 20, 1925
b. Bloustein, Edward J.
b. Cardenal, Ernesto

January 22, 1925
d. Workman, Fanny Bullock

January 23, 1925
b. Arnold, Danny

January 24, 1925
b. Tallchief, Maria

January 25, 1925
b. Carnesseca, Lou

January 26, 1925
b. Leslie, Joan
b. Newman, Paul
b. Ryan, Claude

January 27, 1925
d. von Hugel, Friedrich, Baron

January 29, 1925
b. Abrahams, Doris Cole
b. Crichton, Robert

January 30, 1925
b. Malone, Dorothy

January 31, 1925
b. Hooks, Benjamin Lawson
b. Taubman, A(dolph) Alfred
d. Cable, George Washington

February 4, 1925
b. Hoban, Russell
b. Wisdom, Norman

February 8, 1925
b. Lemmon, Jack
d. Lawson, Thomas William

February 9, 1925
d. Kerr, Alexander H

February 11, 1925
b. Johnson, Virginia E
b. Stanley, Kim

February 12, 1925
b. Finney, Joan Marie McInroy

February 14, 1925
b. Lawrence, Elliot
d. Bausch, John Jacob

February 15, 1925
b. Gardner, Edward George
d. DeYoung, Michel Harry

February 17, 1925
b. Holbrook, Hal
d. Valleria, Alwina

February 18, 1925
b. Kennedy, George
d. Allen, James Lane
d. Woods, Robert Archey

February 20, 1925
b. Altman, Robert B

February 21, 1925
b. Peckinpah, Sam
b. Ramsay, Jack
b. Rigby, Harry

February 22, 1925
b. Gorey, Edward St. John

February 23, 1925
b. Stokes, Louis

February 24, 1925
b. Owen, Guy, Jr.
d. Branting, Karl Hjalmar

February 25, 1925
b. Kirk, Lisa
b. Zipprodt, Patricia
d. McCormick, Joseph Medill

February 26, 1925
b. Williams, Robert F(ranklin)
d. Feuillade, Louis

February 27, 1925
b. Dash, Samuel
b. Koch, Kenneth Jay
b. Toyoda, Shoichiro

February 28, 1925
b. Burke, James Edward
d. Ebert, Friedrich

March 1, 1925
b. Rosen, Al(bert Leonard)

March 4, 1925
b. Albers, Hans
d. Moszkowski, Moritz
d. Ward, Monte

March 6, 1925
b. Montgomery, Wes

March 8, 1925
d. Ball, Edmund B

March 9, 1925
b. Miller, G(eorge) William
b. Orfilo, Alejandro
d. Metcalf, Willard Leroy

March 10, 1925
d. Hayford, John Fillmore

March 12, 1925
b. Delerue, Georges
b. Esaki, Leo
d. Sun Yat-Sen

March 13, 1925
b. Vyvyan, Jennifer Brigit

March 14, 1925
b. Ford, William Clay
b. Wain, John Barrington
d. Camp, Walter Chauncey

March 15, 1925
d. Wassermann, August von

March 17, 1925
b. Addabbo, Joseph Patrick
b. Rees, Ennis (Samuel, Jr.)

March 19, 1925
b. Scowcroft, Brent

March 20, 1925
b. Ehrlichman, John D(aniel)
d. Curzon of Kedleston, George
Nathaniel Curzon, Marquis

March 21, 1925
b. Brook, Peter Stephen Paul
b. Jones, Madison Percy, Jr.

March 25, 1925
b. O'Connor, Flannery

March 26, 1925
b. Boulez, Pierre
d. Vezina, Georges

March 29, 1925
b. Tunnell, Em(len)

March 30, 1925
d. Steiner, Rudolf

March 31, 1925
b. Buscaglia, Leo
b. Shagari, Alhaji Shehu Usman Aliyu

April 2, 1925
b. Fraser, George MacDonald
b. Owen, Lewis James
b. Shulman, Morton
b. Stautner, Ernie

April 3, 1925
b. Benn, Tony
d. DeReszke, Jean

April 9, 1925
b. Goodman, Linda

April 13, 1925
b. Irving, Jules
d. Haynes, Elwood

April 14, 1925
b. Ammons, Jug
b. Muzorewa, Abel Tendekai
b. Steiger, Rod
b. Traub, Marvin Stuart

April 15, 1925
d. Sargent, John Singer

April 17, 1925
b. Wood, Robert Dennis

April 18, 1925
d. Ebbets, Charles Hercules

April 22, 1925
b. Cole, George
b. MacNutt, Francis, Father

April 23, 1925
b. Hoppe, Arthur Watterson

April 25, 1925
b. Sohappy, David, Sr.
b. Stacton, David Derek

April 27, 1925
b. Baron, Samuel

April 29, 1925
b. Elkins, Stanley Maurice

April 30, 1925
b. Calvet, Corinne
b. Leachman, Cloris
b. Ghorbal, Ashraf A

May 1, 1925
b. Bednarik, Chuck
b. Blair, Clay, Jr.
b. Carpenter, Scott

May 2, 1925
b. Browne, Roscoe Lee
b. Neville, John

May 4, 1925
b. Herrera Campins, Luis
d. Grassi, Giovanni Battista

May 5, 1925
b. Ryan, Leo Joseph

May 7, 1925
b. Kirk, Ruth Kratz

May 8, 1925
b. Mwinyi, Ali Hassan

May 9, 1925
b. Neville, Kris Ottman

May 10, 1925
b. Bechtel, Stephen Davison, Jr.
d. Massey, William Ferguson

May 12, 1925
b. Berra, Yogi

b. Pierson, Frank R(omer)
b. Simon, John Ivan
d. Lowell, Amy

May 13, 1925
d. Milner, Alfred, Viscount

May 14, 1925
b. Munsel, Patrice Beverly
d. Haggard, Henry Rider, Sir

May 15, 1925
b. Bolin, Bert (Richard Johannes)
d. Miles, Nelson Appleton

May 16, 1925
b. Pierpoint, Robert Charles

May 17, 1925
b. Luckenbach, Edgar Frederick, Jr.

May 19, 1925
b. Malcolm X
b. Pol Pot

May 21, 1925
b. Cass, Peggy
b. Kameny, Frank(lin Edward)

May 22, 1925
b. King, James Ambros
b. Tinguely, Jean

May 23, 1925
b. Lederberg, Joshua

May 24, 1925
b. Epstein, Alvin
b. Zetterling, Mai (Elisabeth)

May 25, 1925
b. Crain, Jeanne

May 27, 1925
b. Hillerman, Tony

May 28, 1925
b. Ecevit, Bulent
b. Fischer-Dieskau, Dietrich
b. Vickers, Martha

May 31, 1925
b. Beck, Julian

June 1, 1925
d. Marshall, Thomas Riley

June 3, 1925
b. Curtis, Tony

June 4, 1925
b. Dumas, Jean Baptiste Andre
b. Weaver, Dennis
d. Louys, Pierre

June 5, 1925
b. Donovan, Art(hur, Jr.)

June 6, 1925
b. Kumin, Maxine Winokur
d. Denison, George Taylor

June 8, 1925
b. Bush, Barbara (Pierce)
b. Ennis, Del(mer)
b. Gaedel, Eddie
b. McNerney, Walter James

June 9, 1925
d. Hanes, Pleasant H

June 10, 1925
b. Costa, Don
b. Hentoff, Nat(han Irving)

June 11, 1925
b. Styron, William Clark, Jr.

June 14, 1925
b. Salinger, Pierre Emil George

June 16, 1925
d. Das, Chitta Ranjan

June 17, 1925
d. Benson, Arthur Christopher

June 18, 1925
d. LaFollette, Robert Marion

June 19, 1925
b. Nzo, Alfred (Baphethuxolo)

June 20, 1925
d. Breuer, Josef

June 21, 1925
b. Stapleton, Maureen

June 23, 1925
b. Blyden, Larry
b. Chennault, Anna Chan
b. Modell, Art(hur B)

June 25, 1925
b. Briley, John Richard
b. Chenier, Clifton
b. Lockhart, June
b. Venturi, Robert

June 26, 1925
b. Brenner, Barbara Johnes
b. Burch, Robert Joseph

June 28, 1925
b. Klebe, Giselher

July 1, 1925
b. Granger, Farley
d. Satie, Erik

July 2, 1925
b. Lumumba, Patrice

July 3, 1925
b. Jamison, Philip Duane, Jr.

July 6, 1925
b. Griffin, Merv(yn Edward)
b. Haley, Bill
b. O'Donnell, Cathy
b. Rich, John

July 8, 1925
b. Brathwaite, Nicholas A(lexander)

July 11, 1925
b. Aldecoa, Ignacio
b. Dobbs, Mattiwilda
b. Gedda, Nicolai

July 12, 1925
b. Smith, Roger Bonham
d. Corinth, Lovis

July 14, 1925
d. Villa, Pancho

July 15, 1925
b. Carey, Phil(ip)

July 16, 1925
b. Braly, Malcolm
b. Shapiro, Stanley
b. Tjader, Cal(len Radcliffe, Jr.)

July 19, 1925
b. Evers, Medgar Wiley

July 20, 1925
b. Delors, Jacques Lucien Jean
b. Fanon, Frantz (Omar)

July 22, 1925
d. Jaegers, Albert

July 23, 1925
b. DeHaven, Gloria
b. Masire, Quett (Ketumile Jonny)

July 24, 1925
b. Addison, Adele

July 25, 1925
b. Newquist, Roy
b. Paris, Jerry
d. L'Hermitte, Leon Augustin

July 26, 1925
d. Bryan, William Jennings
d. Frege, (Friedrich Ludwig) Gottlob

July 28, 1925
b. Blumberg, Baruch Samuel

July 29, 1925
b. Lindsay, Ted
b. Theodorakis, Mikis

August 2, 1925
b. Dexter, John
b. Videla, Jorge Rafael
b. Whicker, Alan Donald

August 3, 1925
b. Hargis, Billy James
b. Touraine, Alain (Louis)

August 6, 1925
d. Banerjee, Surendranath
d. Ricci-Curbastro, Gregorio

August 7, 1925
b. Bryant, Felice

b. Swaminathan, M(onkombu)
S(ambisivan)
b. Weber, Carl

August 8, 1925
b. Izetbegovic, Alija

August 11, 1925
b. Douglas, Mike
b. Rowan, Carl Thomas

August 12, 1925
b. Bumpers, Dale Leon
b. McWhirter, A(lan) Ross
b. McWhirter, Norris Dewar

August 14, 1925
b. Baker, Russell Wayne

August 15, 1925
b. Connors, Mike
b. Khaleda Zia
b. Peterson, Oscar Emanuel
b. Rose-Marie

August 17, 1925
b. Hawkes, John

August 18, 1925
b. Aldiss, Brian Wilson

August 19, 1925
d. Lawson, Victor Fremont

August 21, 1925
b. Weston, Jack

August 24, 1925
b. Hufstedler, Shirley (Ann) M(ount)

August 25, 1925
d. Goldie, George Dashwood Taubman

August 26, 1925
b. Clayton, Jan(e Byral)

August 28, 1925
b. Davis, Marvin
b. O'Connor, Donald
b. Trifonov, Yuri Valentinovich

August 30, 1925
b. Brunhoff, Laurent de

August 31, 1925
b. Schwinden, Ted

September 1, 1925
b. Pepper, Art(hur Edward)

September 3, 1925
b. Thompson, Hank

September 4, 1925
b. Hrawi, Elias

September 5, 1925
b. Kaplan, Justin

September 7, 1925
b. Ashley, Laura Mountney

b. Jastrow, Robert

September 8, 1925
b. Darcel, Denise
b. Sellers, Peter

September 9, 1925
b. Poirier, Richard
b. Robertson, Cliff

September 10, 1925
b. Dennison, George

September 11, 1925
b. Bergman, Alan

September 12, 1925
b. Moore, Dick(ie)

September 13, 1925
b. Torme, Mel(vin Howard)
d. Thomas, Edith Matilda

September 16, 1925
b. Byrd, Charlie
b. Haughey, Charles James
b. King, B. B.
b. Walter, Cyril

September 20, 1925
d. Bartlett, Paul Wayland

September 24, 1925
b. Burbidge, Geoffrey
b. Guyer, David Leigh

September 26, 1925
b. Robbins, Marty

September 27, 1925
b. Edwards, Robert Geoffrey

September 28, 1925
b. Cray, Seymour R.
b. Stang, Arnold

September 29, 1925
b. Forrest, Steve
b. Mac Cready, Paul Beattie
b. Tower, John Goodwin
d. Bourgeois, Leon-Victor Auguste

October 1, 1925
b. Biebuyck, Daniel Prosper

October 3, 1925
b. Vidal, Gore
b. Wein, George Theodore

October 4, 1925
b. Schindler, Alexander Moshe

October 5, 1925
b. Miller, Walter Dale
b. Morgan, Robert Burren

October 6, 1925
b. Alexander, Shana

October 7, 1925
d. Mathewson, Christy

October 8, 1925
b. Dalis, Irene
b. Magana, Alvaro (Alfredo)
b. Sinyavsky, Andrei D(onatovich)

October 9, 1925
b. Finch, Robert H(utchison)

October 10, 1925
d. Duke, James Buchanan

October 11, 1925
b. Leonard, Elmore John, Jr.

October 12, 1925
b. Gordone, Charles Edward
b. Skelton, Robin

October 13, 1925
b. Bruce, Lenny
b. Gilroy, Frank Daniel
b. Thatcher, Margaret (Hilda Roberts)

October 14, 1925
b. Poling, Harold Arthur
d. Sandow, Eugene

October 16, 1925
b. Evans, Daniel Jackson
b. Lansbury, Angela Brigid

October 18, 1925
b. Alia, Ramiz
b. Mercouri, Melina

October 20, 1925
b. Buchwald, Art(hur)

October 22, 1925
b. Martin, Slater
b. Previn, Dory Langdon
b. Rauschenberg, Robert

October 23, 1925
b. Carson, Johnny

October 24, 1925
b. Berio, Luciano

October 26, 1925
b. DeMoss, Arthur S

October 27, 1925
b. Christopher, Warren M(inor)
d. Presser, Theodore

October 28, 1925
d. Leggett, William

October 29, 1925
b. Brooks, Geraldine
b. Dunne, Dominick
b. Siegel, Larry
b. Sims, Zoot

October 31, 1925
d. Frunze, Mikhail Vasilievich

November 8, 1925
b. Flynn, Joe

November 10, 1925
b. Burton, Richard

November 11, 1925
b. Winters, Jonathan (Harshman, III)

November 14, 1925
b. Medvedev, Zhores Aleksandrovich

November 15, 1925
b. Baker, Howard Henry, Jr.

November 17, 1925
b. Hudson, Rock
b. Mackerras, Charles

November 18, 1925
b. Mauch, Gene William

November 20, 1925
b. Kennedy, Robert Francis
b. Plisetskaya, Maya Mikhailovna
d. Alexandra Caroline Mary Charlotte
d. Morris, Clara

November 21, 1925
b. Garrett, Lila

November 22, 1925
b. Schuller, Gunther

November 24, 1925
b. Buckley, William Frank, Jr.
b. Cohn, Al
b. Meer, Simon van der
b. Van der Meer, Simon

November 26, 1925
b. Hunt, Lois
b. Istomin, Eugene George

November 27, 1925
b. Boley, Forrest Irving

November 28, 1925
b. Grahame, Gloria

December 2, 1925
b. Harris, Julie

December 3, 1925
b. Olson, James E(lias)

December 5, 1925
b. Nizami, Khaliq Ahmad
b. Somoza Debayle, Anastasio
b. Williams, John A(lfred)
d. Reymont, Wladyslaw Stanislaw

December 7, 1925
b. Zaslofsky, Max

December 8, 1925
b. Davis, Sammy, Jr.

December 10, 1925
b. Kizer, Carolyn (Ashley)
b. Lispector, Clarice

December 12, 1925
b. Kennedy, Ted

December 13, 1925
b. Van Dyke, Dick

December 15, 1925
b. Pollock, Sam

December 18, 1925
b. Stewart, Paul Wilbur

December 19, 1925
b. Dickens, Little Jimmy
d. Vinogradoff, Paul Gavrilovitch

December 20, 1925
b. Mahathir Bin Mohamad

December 22, 1925
b. Corsaro, Frank
d. Munsey, Frank Andrew

December 23, 1925
b. Beregovoy, Pierre (Eugene)
b. Guardino, Harry

December 24, 1925
b. Sherrill, Robert Glenn

December 27, 1925
b. Arens, Moshe

December 28, 1925
b. Neff, Hildegarde
d. Esenin, Sergei Aleksandrovich

December 29, 1925
b. Merrill, Dina

December 31, 1925
b. Jones, Candy

1926

b. Brown, Charlie
b. Chiepe, Gaositwe Keagakwa Tibe
b. Compton, John (George M.)
b. Cooper, Chuck
b. Dedman, Robert H
b. Douglas, Emmitt
b. Erbakan, Necmettin
b. Goulet, Leo D
b. Hale, Lorraine
b. Kendall, Kay
b. Maxwell, Hamish
b. Moltmann, Juergen (Dankwart)
b. Morrow, Richard Martin
b. Pierce, Charles
b. Rosenbloom, Georgia
b. Slovo, Joe
b. Spethmann, Dieter
b. Stompanato, Johnny
b. Wexler, Haskell
d. Chang Chien

January 2, 1926
b. Bush-Brown, Albert

January 3, 1926
b. Anglund, Joan Walsh
b. Blumenthal, W Michael
b. Martin, George

January 4, 1926
d. Mahoney, Mary Eliza

January 5, 1926
b. Schell, Maria Margarethe
b. Snodgrass, W(illiam) D(eWitt)
b. Williams, Hosea Lorenzo

January 6, 1926
b. Branca, Ralph Theodore Joseph
b. Gault, Stanley Carleton
b. Gavilan, Kid

January 7, 1926
b. Kirk, Claude Roy, Jr.
d. Mueller, Christian F

January 8, 1926
b. Geschwind, Norman
b. Mori, Hanae

January 11, 1926
b. Tinker, Grant Almerin

January 12, 1926
b. Feldman, Morton
b. Price, Ray

January 13, 1926
b. Heilbrun, Carolyn Gold

January 14, 1926
b. Tryon, Thomas

January 15, 1926
b. Berry, Chuck
b. MacLeish, Rod(erick)

January 17, 1926
b. Minow, Newton Norman
b. Shearer, Moira

January 19, 1926
b. Weaver, Fritz William

January 20, 1926
b. Neal, Patricia

January 21, 1926
b. Mikva, Abner Joseph
b. Reeves, Steve
d. Golgi, Camillo

January 25, 1926
b. Kedourie, Elie
b. McGuire, Dick

January 28, 1926
d. Kohler, Kaufmann

January 29, 1926
b. Salam, Abdus

January 30, 1926
d. Doughty, Charles Montagu
d. LaMarr, Barbara
b. Parbo, Arvi (Hillar)

February 1, 1926
b. Whitman, Stuart

February 2, 1926
b. Giscard d'Estaing, Valery
b. Obando (y Bravo), Miguel
d. Sukhomlinov, Vladimir
Aleksandrovich

February 3, 1926
b. Berman, Shelley
b. Vogel, Hans-Jochen
b. Yates, Richard

February 4, 1926
b. Tassell, Gustave
b. Welch, Ken

February 5, 1926
b. Sulzberger, Arthur O(chs)

February 6, 1926
b. Gelb, Barbara Stone
b. Long, Dale

February 7, 1926
b. Feoktistov, Konstantin Petrovich
b. Hoest, Bill

February 8, 1926
b. Cassady, Neal
d. Bateson, William

February 9, 1926
b. FitzGerald, Garret Michael

February 11, 1926
b. Bocuse, Paul
b. Nielsen, Leslie
d. Bobbs, William Conrad

February 12, 1926
b. Garagiola, Joe
b. Mitchell, Joan
b. Van Doren, Charles Lincoln

February 13, 1926
d. Holt, Henry

February 14, 1926
b. Sleet, Moneta, Jr.

February 16, 1926
b. Mohieddin, Ahmed Faud
b. Schlesinger, John Richard
b. Vera-Ellen

February 17, 1926
b. Hoiby, Lee
b. Kohlmeier, Louis Martin, Jr.

February 18, 1926
b. Ford, Len
b. Gorr, Rita

February 19, 1926
b. Thomas, Ross (Elmore)

February 20, 1926
b. Matheson, Richard Burton
b. Olsen, Kenneth Harry
b. Richards, Bob

February 21, 1926
d. Kamerlingh Onnes, Heike

February 22, 1926
b. Hunt, Nelson Bunker

February 24, 1926
b. Dean, John Gunther
d. Plank, Eddie

February 27, 1926
b. Hubel, David Hunter
b. Wheeler, Roger Milton

February 28, 1926
b. Stalin, Svetlana Alliluyeva

March 1, 1926
b. Clary, Robert
b. Rozelle, Pete
b. Stanley, Allan Herbert

March 3, 1926
b. Merrill, James (Ingram)
d. Lee, Sidney, Sir

March 4, 1926
b. DeVos, Richard Marvin

March 5, 1926
d. Ader, Clement

March 6, 1926
b. Curtis, Ann
b. Greenspan, Alan
b. Wajda, Andrzej

March 10, 1926
b. Haynes, Marques Oreole

March 11, 1926
b. Abernathy, Ralph David
b. Starzl, Thomas Earl

March 12, 1926
b. Holmes, John Clellon
d. Scripps, Edward Wyllis

March 13, 1926
b. Reina, Carlos Roberto

March 14, 1926
b. Hemion, Dwight

March 15, 1926
b. Van Brocklin, Norm (an Mack)

March 16, 1926
b. Goodell, Charles Ellsworth
b. Lewis, Jerry

March 18, 1926
b. Graves, Peter

March 20, 1926
b. Rosen, Harold A.

March 23, 1926
b. Wright, Martha

March 24, 1926
b. Fo, Dario
b. Porter, Bill
d. Small, Albion W(oodbury)

March 25, 1926
b. Papp, Laszlo
b. Youngerman, Jack

March 26, 1926
b. Hinde, Thomas, Sir

March 27, 1926
d. Harkness, Anna M Richardson

March 29, 1926
b. Adams, Diana

March 30, 1926
b. Chaplin, Sydney

March 31, 1926
b. Alfonsin Foulkes, Raul Ricardo
b. Fowles, John (Robert)

April 1, 1926
d. Adler, Jacob Pavlovitch

April 2, 1926
b. Brabham, Jack
b. Duffy, James Edson

April 3, 1926
b. Grissom, Virgil Ivan

April 5, 1926
b. Corman, Roger William

April 6, 1926
b. Butterfield, Alexander Porter
b. Paisley, Ian Richard Kyle

April 8, 1926
b. Greene, Shecky
d. Weir, John F(erguson)

April 9, 1926
b. Hefner, Hugh Marston
d. Miller, Henry John

April 10, 1926
b. Nossiter, Bernard Daniel

April 11, 1926
d. Burbank, Luther

April 12, 1926
b. Withers, Jane

April 14, 1926
b. Calvo Sotelo (y Bustelo), Leopoldo

April 15, 1926
b. Huddleston, Walter Darlington

April 19, 1926
b. Adams, Don

April 20, 1926
b. Verdugo, Elena

April 21, 1926
b. Elizabeth II
b. Leigh, Carolyn

April 22, 1926
b. Rae, Charlotte
b. Stirling, James

April 23, 1926
b. Donleavy, James Patrick
d. Pennell, Joseph Stanley

April 24, 1926
b. Falldin, Thorbjorn Nils Olof

April 26, 1926
b. Linn, Bambi

April 27, 1926
b. LaHaye, Tim
b. Paterson, Basil Alexander

April 28, 1926
b. Dearie, Blossom
b. Lee, Harper

April 29, 1926
b. Meek, Carrie

April 30, 1926
d. Coleman, Bessie

May 3, 1926
b. Davis, Ann Bradford
b. O'Horgan, Tom
d. Straus, Oscar Solomon

May 6, 1926
b. Piazza, Marguerite

May 8, 1926
b. Attenborough, David Frederick
b. Rickles, Don

May 10, 1926
d. Parker, Alton Brooks

May 12, 1926
b. Coleman, James S(amuel)

May 13, 1926
b. Arthur, Beatrice

May 15, 1926
b. Shaffer, Anthony
b. Shaffer, Peter Levin

May 16, 1926
b. Sinatra, Barbara Marx Spencer

May 19, 1926
b. Andrews, Mark N

May 20, 1926
b. Hurst, George
b. Jorgensen, Christine

May 21, 1926
b. Creeley, Robert (White)
b. Jason, Rick
b. Robinson, Forbes
b. Toren, Marta
d. Firbank, Ronald

May 23, 1926
b. Hernandez, Aileen Clark

May 25, 1926
b. Davis, Miles Dewey, III
b. Kallen, Kitty
b. Sharman, Bill

May 26, 1926
b. McCowen, Alec

May 31, 1926
b. Kemeny, John G(eorge)

June 1, 1926
b. Burton, Phillip
b. Griffith, Andy
b. Monroe, Marilyn
b. Schweiker, Richard Schultz

June 2, 1926
b. O'Shea, Milo

June 3, 1926
b. Dewhurst, Colleen
b. Ginsberg, Allen

June 4, 1926
b. Malina, Judith

June 6, 1926
b. Ryan, Tom Kreusch
b. Schlein, Miriam
b. Tennstedt, Klaus

June 8, 1926
b. Stiller, Jerry

June 9, 1926
b. Rockefeller, Happy
d. Dole, Sanford Ballard

June 10, 1926
b. Haver, June
b. Jeffries, Lionel Charles
b. Low, George M(ichael)
d. Gaudi y Cornet, Antonio

June 11, 1926
b. Floyd, Carlisle Sessions

June 13, 1926
b. Lynde, Paul Edward

June 14, 1926
b. Newcombe, Don(ald)
d. Cassatt, Mary Stevenson

June 15, 1926
b. Fox, Carol

June 16, 1926
b. Rios Montt, Jose Efrain

June 18, 1926
b. Bartok, Eva
b. Wicker, Tom

June 21, 1926
b. Anders, Edward
b. Ubell, Earl
d. Roze, Marie

June 27, 1926
b. O'Hara, Frank

June 28, 1926
b. Booth, George
b. Brooks, Mel

June 29, 1926
b. Jaber Al-Sabah, Jaber Al-Ahmad Al-
b. Jabir al-Ahmad al-Jabir Al Sabah, Sheikh

June 30, 1926
b. Berg, Paul

July 1, 1926
b. Hahn, Carl Horst
b. Henze, Hans Werner

July 2, 1926
d. Coue, Emile

July 3, 1926
b. Michelin, Francois

July 5, 1926
b. Jorge Blanco, Salvador
b. Taft, Henry Waters, II

July 7, 1926
b. Rushmore, Robert (William)

July 8, 1926
b. Dingell, John David, Jr.
b. Kubler-Ross, Elisabeth

July 9, 1926
b. Dale, Alan
b. Krim, Mathilde Galland
b. Mottelson, Benjamin Roy
d. Lathrop, Rose Hawthorne

July 10, 1926
b. Banzer-Suarez, Hugo
b. Gwynne, Fred

July 11, 1926
b. Buechner, Frederick
d. Bell, Gertrude Margaret

July 12, 1926
b. Crosby, John

July 14, 1926
b. Jones, Wallace

July 15, 1926
b. Chraibi, Driss
b. Galtieri, Leopoldo Fortunato

July 16, 1926
b. Carson, Mindy

July 18, 1926
b. Jennings, Elizabeth Joan
b. Laurence, Margaret

July 19, 1926
b. Gallagher, Helen

July 20, 1926
d. Dzerzhinsky, Felix Edmundovich

July 21, 1926
b. Burke, Paul
b. Jewison, Norman
b. Premice, Josephine
b. Reisz, Karel
d. Roebling, Washington Augustus

July 22, 1926
b. Forbes, Bryan

July 26, 1926
d. Lincoln, Robert Todd

July 27, 1926
b. Priestly, Jack

July 29, 1926
b. Carter, Don(ald James)

July 30, 1926
b. Bookspan, Martin

August 1, 1926
d. Zangwill, Israel

August 2, 1926
b. Bloomingdale, Betsy

August 3, 1926
b. Bennett, Tony
b. Murphy, John Michael

August 4, 1926
b. Goscinny, Rene

August 5, 1926
b. Jolas, Betsy
b. Omarr, Sydney
b. Wahloo, Per

August 6, 1926
b. Finlay, Frank
b. Presser, Jackie

August 7, 1926
b. Freberg, Stan
b. Kaufman, Sue

August 8, 1926
b. Anderson, Richard Norman
b. Pierce, Webb

August 10, 1926
b. Ward, Benjamin

August 11, 1926
b. Klug, Aaron, Sir
b. Von Bulow, Claus

August 12, 1926
b. Derek, John

August 14, 1926
b. Adams, Alice
b. Ghostley, Alice
b. Greco, Buddy

August 15, 1926
b. Silber, John Robert

August 16, 1926
b. Wexler, Norman

August 17, 1926
b. Jiang Zemin

August 19, 1926
b. Rock, Arthur

August 20, 1926
b. Vickrey, Robert (Remsen)

August 22, 1926
b. Blackman, Honor
d. Eliot, Charles William

August 23, 1926
b. Geertz, Clifford James
d. Valentino, Rudolph

August 25, 1926
d. Moran, Thomas

August 26, 1926
b. Gibbs, Georgia

August 29, 1926
b. Lewenthal, Raymond

August 30, 1926
b. Gates, Daryl F

September 3, 1926
b. Flemming, Bill
b. Jackson, Anne
b. Lurie, Alison
b. Papas, Irene

September 4, 1926
b. Illich, Ivan
b. Keough, Donald Raymond
b. Olmstead, Bert
b. Petersen, Donald Eugene

September 9, 1926
b. Duncan, Charles William, Jr.

September 10, 1926
b. Fuller, Hoyt William

September 11, 1926
b. Richardson, Lee

September 12, 1926
d. Maher, George Washington

September 13, 1926
b. Brimmer, Andrew Felton
b. Francis, Emile Percy
b. Sonnenfeldt, Helmut
b. Wharton, Clifton Reginald, Jr.

September 14, 1926
b. Butor, Michel
d. Dreyer, Johan Ludwig Emil

September 15, 1926
b. Derwinski, Edward Joseph
b. Short, Bobby
d. Eucken, Rudolf Christoph

September 16, 1926
b. Knowles, John
b. Schuller, Robert Harold

September 19, 1926
b. Snider, Duke
b. Wallace, Lurleen Burns

September 20, 1926
b. Bluhdorn, Charles G

September 21, 1926
b. Glaser, Donald Arthur

September 25, 1926
b. Ray, Aldo

September 26, 1926
b. Coltrane, Trane
b. London, Julie

September 27, 1926
b. Meadows, Jayne Cotter

September 28, 1926
b. Bressani, Ricardo

September 30, 1926
b. Roberts, Robin Evan

October 1, 1926
b. Morath, Max Edward
b. Williams, Roger
d. Finck, Henry Theophilus

October 2, 1926
b. Farenthold, Frances T(arlton)
b. Morris, Jan

October 6, 1926
b. Jahoda, Gloria (Adelaide Love)

October 7, 1926
b. Groza, Alex John
b. Lynn, Diana

October 9, 1926
b. Russell, Franklin Alexander

October 10, 1926
b. Brown, Oscar, Jr.

October 11, 1926
b. Hyman, Earle

October 12, 1926
b. Pelli, Cesar

October 13, 1926
b. Herbert, John
b. Lamb, Lawrence Edward

October 15, 1926
b. Foucault, Michel
b. Hunter, Evan
b. Peters, Jean
b. Richter, Karl
b. Stumpf, Richard J

October 17, 1926
b. Adams, Julie
b. Garland, Beverly
b. Henize, Karl G(ordon)

October 18, 1926
b. Kinski, Klaus

October 19, 1926
b. Wallant, Edward Lewis

October 20, 1926
d. Debs, Eugene Victor
d. Osborne, Thomas Mott

October 21, 1926
b. Rosburg, Bob

October 22, 1926
d. Greb, Harry

October 24, 1926
b. Tittle, Y(elberton) A(braham)
d. Russell, Charles Marion

October 25, 1926
b. Butcher, Willard C(arlisle)
b. McGuire, Biff
b. Vishnevskaya, Galina (Pavlovna)

October 26, 1926
b. Jaeckel, Richard (Hanley)

October 27, 1926
b. Haldeman, H(arry) R(obbins)

October 28, 1926
b. Kuhn, Bowie Kent

October 29, 1926
b. Vickers, Jon
d. Webb, William Seward

October 31, 1926
d. Houdini, Harry

November 1, 1926
b. Knight, Hilary
b. Palmer, Betsy

November 2, 1926
d. Oakley, Annie

November 3, 1926
b. Adamkus, Valdas (V.)

November 5, 1926
b. Berger, John

November 9, 1926
b. Leonard, Hugh
d. Coffin, Charles Albert

November 11, 1926
b. Fall, Bernard B
b. Lumley, Harry

November 12, 1926
b. Rysanek, Leonie
d. Cannon, Joseph Gurney

November 16, 1926
b. Cohn, Zanvil (Alexander)

November 17, 1926
d. Akeley, Carl Ethan

November 18, 1926
b. Collins, Dorothy

d. Sterling, George

November 19, 1926
b. Kirkpatrick, Jeane Duane Jordan

November 20, 1926
b. Ballard, Kaye
b. Luz, Arturo Rogerio

November 21, 1926
b. Baum, William Wakefield, Cardinal

November 22, 1926
b. Burdette, Lew

November 23, 1926
b. Duarte (Fuentes), Jose Napoleon
b. Hunter, Jeffrey

November 24, 1926
b. Lee, Tsung-Dao

November 25, 1926
b. Drexler, Rosalyn
b. Schisgal, Murray Joseph

November 26, 1926
b. Butler, Michael
b. Lebowsky, Stanley Richard
d. Browning, John Moses

November 27, 1926
b. Thompson, Marshall

November 28, 1926
b. Kops, Bernard

November 29, 1926
b. Dagmar

November 30, 1926
b. Schally, Andrew Victor

December 1, 1926
b. McLerie, Allyn Ann
b. Rakowski, Mieczyslaw Franciszek

December 3, 1926
d. Ringling, Charles

December 5, 1926
d. Monet, Claude-Oscar

December 7, 1926
b. Kiam, Victor Kermit, II

December 9, 1926
b. Dominguin, Luis Miguel
b. Kendall, Henry Way

December 10, 1926
b. Rich, Lee

December 11, 1926
b. Barnet, Sylvan M., Jr.
b. Cooper, Edward S(awyer)
b. Thornton, Willie Mae

December 12, 1926
b. Baulieu, Etienne-Emile
b. Kasper, Herbert

December 13, 1926
b. Erskine, Carl Daniel

December 16, 1926
b. Brinegar, Claude Stout
b. McCracken, James (Eugene)
b. Robinson, A(rthur) N(apoleon)
R(aymond)

December 18, 1926
b. Cummins, Peggy

December 19, 1926
b. Layne, Bobby
b. Purdom, Edmund

December 20, 1926
b. Howe, Geoffrey Richard Edward,
Sir
b. Lambsdorff, Otto
b. Levine, David

December 21, 1926
b. Paterno, Joe

December 22, 1926
b. Peters, Charles

December 23, 1926
b. Bly, Robert Elwood

December 24, 1926
b. Gunn, Hartford Nelson, Jr.

December 25, 1926
b. Vajpayee, Atal Behari
d. Yoshihito

December 26, 1926
b. Brown, Earle
b. Lilly, Doris

December 27, 1926
b. Carazo (Odio), Rodrigo
b. Salk, Lee

December 29, 1926
d. Rilke, Rainer Maria

December 31, 1926
b. Riley, Helen Caldwell Day

1927

b. Baldridge, Letitia Katherine
b. Ellis, Ruth
b. Ford, Christina
b. Furman, Rosemary
b. Hill, Jesse, Jr.
b. Hilton, William Barron
b. Konitz, Lee
b. Martin, Jimmy
b. Nguyen Khanh
b. Nguyen thi Binh, Madame
b. Pendleton, Don
b. Ransohoff, Martin
b. Reed, Susan
b. Roberts, Edward Glenn
b. Vernon, Lillian
b. Wilcock, John
d. Ahad Haam

d. Bamba, Amadou
d. Bekhterev, Vladimir Mikhailovich
d. Boltwood, Bertram Borden
d. Ferdinand
d. Grasselli, Caesar Augustin
d. Haam, Ahad
d. Johnston, Henry Hamilton
d. Palmer, Austin Norman

January 1, 1927
b. Baxley, Barbara
b. Bejart, Maurice
b. Walker, Doak

January 2, 1927
b. Evers, Jason
b. Grigorovich, Yuri Nikolaevich
b. Marchetti, Gino

January 4, 1927
b. Cavazos, Lauro F(red, Jr.)

January 7, 1927
d. Stanton, Frank Lebby

January 9, 1927
d. Chamberlain, Houston Stewart

January 10, 1927
b. MacKenzie, Gisele
b. Ray, Johnnie

January 12, 1927
d. Daly, Arnold

January 13, 1927
b. Adams, Brock(man)
b. Brenner, Sydney
b. Murphy, Rosemary
b. Pope, Generoso
d. Bridgman, Frederic Arthur

January 15, 1927
b. Badura-Skoda, Paul

January 16, 1927
b. Jurado, Katy

January 17, 1927
b. Dooley, Thomas Anthony, III
b. Mathews, Harlan

January 18, 1927
b. Lubic, Ruth Watson
d. Low, Juliette Gordon

January 19, 1927
d. Carlota

January 21, 1927
b. Butler, Robert N(eil)

January 22, 1927
d. Rhodes, James Ford

January 24, 1927
b. Burns, Jerry
b. Hawkins, Paula Fickes

January 25, 1927
b. Jobim, Antonio Carlos

January 26, 1927
b. Azcona Hoyo, Jose Simon

January 27, 1927
b. Barnes, Billy
b. Dickerson, Nancy Hanschman
b. Fulton, Richard Harmon
b. Perry, Joe

January 28, 1927
b. Teshigahara, Hiroshi

January 29, 1927
b. Abbey, Edward

January 30, 1927
b. Palme, Olof

February 1, 1927
b. Kinnell, Galway

February 2, 1927
b. Getz, Stan
b. Kaplow, Herbert Elias

February 4, 1927
b. Cummings, Sam

February 5, 1927
b. Davis, Martin S.

February 6, 1927
b. Burgess, Smoky
b. Haynie, Hugh
b. O'Neill, Gerard Kitchen

February 10, 1927
b. Lind, Jakov
b. Price, Leontyne
b. Weidenbaum, Murray Lew

February 13, 1927
d. Adams, Brooks
d. Adams, Peter Chardon Brooks

February 15, 1927
b. Dunlop, Frank
b. Korman, Harvey Herschel

February 18, 1927
b. Snelling, Richard
b. Warner, John William
d. Gerry, Elbridge Thomas

February 19, 1927
d. Brandes, Georg Morris Cohen

February 20, 1927
b. Cohn, Roy (Marcus)
b. Poitier, Sidney

February 21, 1927
b. Bombeck, Erma (Louise)
b. Givenchy, Hubert James Marcel
  Taffin de

February 22, 1927
b. Yen, Samuel

February 24, 1927
b. Lane, Mark

February 25, 1927
b. Stanley, Ralph Edmond

February 27, 1927
b. Herlihy, James Leo
b. Mitchell, Guy

March 1, 1927
b. Abell, George O(gden)
b. Amara, Lucine
b. Belafonte, Harry, Jr.
b. Bork, Robert Heron

March 2, 1927
b. Brademas, John

March 3, 1927
b. Freeling, Nicolas
b. Kurelek, William
b. McLaughlin, John (Joseph)
d. Artsybashev, Mikhail Petrovich

March 5, 1927
b. Cassidy, Jack
d. Remsen, Ira

March 6, 1927
b. Cooper, Gordon
b. Fairchild, John Burr

March 7, 1927
b. Broderick, James Joseph
b. Watkins, James (David)

March 8, 1927
b. Kania, Stanislaw

March 9, 1927
b. Jensen, Jackie
d. Potthast, Edward Henry

March 11, 1927
b. Mosbacher, Robert Adam

March 12, 1927
d. Rothwell, Walter Henry

March 16, 1927
b. Braff, Ruby
b. Courtney, Clint(on Dawson)
b. Komarov, Vladimir Mikhaylovich
b. Moynihan, Daniel Patrick

March 17, 1927
b. Newell, Allen
b. Suazo Cordova, Roberto

March 18, 1927
b. Kander, John
b. Katz, Lillian
b. Plimpton, George Ames

March 19, 1927
b. Ashburn, Richie

March 21, 1927
b. Genscher, Hans-Dietrich

March 23, 1927
b. Crespin, Regine

March 25, 1927
  b. Wasserburg, Gerald Joseph

March 27, 1927
  b. Lewis, Anthony
  b. Ostin, Mo

March 29, 1927
  b. Vane, John Robert, Sir

March 31, 1927
  b. Becker, Stephen David
  b. Chavez, Cesar (Estrada)
  b. Daniels, William
  d. K'ang Yu-wei

April 1, 1927
  b. Jump, Gordon
  b. Shekhar, Chandra

April 2, 1927
  b. Basilio, Carmen
  b. Callaway, Howard Hollis
  b. Tynan, Kenneth Peacock

April 6, 1927
  b. Mulligan, Gerry

April 8, 1927
  b. Thomas, Jess

April 10, 1927
  b. Brandon, Brumsic, Jr.
  b. Nirenberg, Marshall Warren
  b. Samples, Junior

April 12, 1927
  b. Sargent, Alvin
  b. Shanks, Michael

April 15, 1927
  b. Carritt, David Graham
  b. Goldman, Albert
  d. LeRoux, Gaston

April 16, 1927
  b. Ratzinger, Joseph Alois, Cardinal

April 18, 1927
  b. Mazowiecki, Tadeusz

April 19, 1927
  b. Kenneth

April 20, 1927
  b. Hill, Phil(ip Toll)
  b. Muller, Karl Alex(ander)

April 21, 1927
  b. Brustein, Robert Sanford

April 26, 1927
  b. Gallatin, Harry J

April 27, 1927
  b. King, Coretta Scott
  d. Beveridge, Albert Jeremiah

April 28, 1927
  d. Li Ta-chao

April 30, 1927
  b. Horton, Johnny
  d. Nungesser, Charles Eugene Jules Marie

May 1, 1927
  b. Bertini, Gary
  b. Cordtz, Dan
  b. Person, Waverly
  b. Zafy, Albert

May 2, 1927
  b. Unger, Irwin
  d. Starling, Ernest Henry

May 3, 1927
  b. Lazarus, Mell
  d. Ball, Ernest

May 5, 1927
  b. Carroll, Pat(ricia Ann Angela Bridgit)

May 6, 1927
  d. Maxim, Hudson

May 7, 1927
  b. Jhabvala, Ruth Prawer
  b. Soderstrom, Elisabeth Anna

May 9, 1927
  b. Eigen, Manfred

May 11, 1927
  b. Sahl, Mort (Lyon)
  d. Colvin, Sidney, Sir
  d. Gris, Juan

May 12, 1927
  b. Crosby, James Morris

May 13, 1927
  b. Barnes, Clive Alexander
  b. Castro, Raul
  b. Hellerman, Fred
  b. Rhodes, Dusty
  b. Ross, Herbert David

May 16, 1927
  b. Graves, John Earl
  d. Bernard, Sam

May 20, 1927
  b. Grant, Bud

May 22, 1927
  b. Constantine, Michael
  b. Martin, Quinn

May 23, 1927
  d. Huntington, Henry Edwards

May 24, 1927
  b. Kelly, John Brenden, Jr.

May 25, 1927
  b. Ludlum, Robert

May 26, 1927
  b. Bergerac, Jacques

May 28, 1927
  b. Levy, Allan

May 29, 1927
  b. Toms, Carl

May 30, 1927
  b. Walker, Clint

June 1, 1927
  d. Borden, Lizzie Andrew
  d. Bury, John Bagnell

June 3, 1927
  b. Randolph, Boots

June 5, 1927
  b. Anhava, Tuomas

June 6, 1927
  b. Spier, Peter Edward
  d. Hilliard, Robert Cochran

June 8, 1927
  b. Neiman, LeRoy

June 10, 1927
  d. Woodhull, Victoria Claflin

June 12, 1927
  b. Slesar, Henry

June 13, 1927
  b. Ableman, Paul

June 14, 1927
  d. Jerome, Jerome Klapka

June 15, 1927
  b. Hinderas, Natalie Leota Henderson

June 16, 1927
  b. Johnson, George E(llis)

June 21, 1927
  b. Stokes, Carl B(urton)

June 23, 1927
  b. Fosse, Bob

June 24, 1927
  b. Edwards, James Burrows

June 25, 1927
  b. Freedman, Gerald

June 26, 1927
  b. Schaltzberg, Jerry Ned
  d. Horn, Alfred Aloysius

June 27, 1927
  b. Keeshan, Bob

June 28, 1927
  b. Levy, Raymond

June 30, 1927
  b. Goldman, James

July 3, 1927
  b. Russell, Ken

July 4, 1927
b. Simon, Neil

July 5, 1927
d. Kossel, Karl Martin Leonhard
Albrecht

July 6, 1927
b. Cabot, Susan
b. Leigh, Janet
b. Paulsen, Pat

July 7, 1927
b. Casadesus, Jean
b. Dixon, Alan John
b. Severinsen, Doc

July 9, 1927
b. Ames, Ed(mund Dantes)
b. Diop, David
b. Kelly, Red
d. Drew, John

July 10, 1927
b. Dinkins, David Norman

July 11, 1927
b. Maiman, Theodore Harold
b. Somers, Brett

July 13, 1927
b. Veil, Simone Annie Jacob

July 14, 1927
b. Chancellor, John (William)
b. Parish, Peggy

July 15, 1927
b. Jellicoe, Ann
d. Markievicz, Constance Georgine,
Countess

July 16, 1927
b. Llewellyn, James Bruce

July 18, 1927
b. Masur, Kurt

July 19, 1927
b. Myrdal, Jan

July 24, 1927
b. Howard, James John
b. Katz, Alex
d. Akutagawa Ryunosuke

July 25, 1927
b. Dancer, Stanley
b. Decter, Midge

July 27, 1927
b. Peters, Brock

July 28, 1927
b. Ashbery, John (Lawrence)

July 30, 1927
b. Johnson, Richard

July 31, 1927
b. Nichols, Peter

August 1, 1927
b. Smale, John Gray

August 3, 1927
b. Scott, Gordon
b. Silverstein, Elliot
d. Titchener, Edward Bradford

August 4, 1927
d. Atget, Eugene

August 6, 1927
b. Warhol, Andy

August 7, 1927
b. Busbee, George Dekle
b. Edwards, Edwin Washington
b. Switzer, Carl
d. Wood, Leonard

August 8, 1927
b. Gadsby, Bill

August 9, 1927
b. Keyes, Daniel
b. Minsky, Marvin Lee
b. Shaw, Robert

August 11, 1927
b. Dahl, Arlene
b. Leppard, Raymond John
b. Rubin, William Stanley

August 12, 1927
b. Rostropovich, Mstislav
Leopoldovich
b. Wagoner, Porter

August 13, 1927
b. Castro (Ruz), Fidel
d. Curwood, James Oliver

August 15, 1927
b. Cranko, John
d. Gary, Elbert Henry

August 16, 1927
b. Parker, Fess
b. Strawser, Neil Edward

August 17, 1927
b. Cornfeld, Bernard

August 18, 1927
b. Carter, Rosalynn

August 21, 1927
b. Marcum, John Arthur

August 22, 1927
d. Fuertes, Louis Agassiz

August 23, 1927
b. Berger, Melvin H
b. Boumedienne, Houari
b. Kaprow, Allan
b. Solal, Martial
d. Sacco, Nicola
d. Vanzetti, Bartolomeo
d. Zaghlul Pasha, Saad

August 24, 1927
b. Shannon, William Vincent

August 25, 1927
b. Gibson, Althea

August 30, 1927
b. Beene, Geoffrey

September 1, 1927
b. Bucher, Lloyd Mark
b. Rosovsky, Henry

September 3, 1927
b. Sidey, Hugh Swanson

September 4, 1927
b. McCarthy, John

September 5, 1927
b. Volcker, Paul Adolph
d. Loew, Marcus

September 8, 1927
b. Altizer, Thomas J(onathan)
J(ackson)

September 9, 1927
b. Jones, Elvin

September 11, 1927
b. Nipon, Albert
b. Schine, G(erard) David

September 14, 1927
b. Caidin, Martin
b. Szoka, Edmund Casimir, Cardinal
d. Duncan, Isadora

September 15, 1927
b. Belli, Carlos German
b. Crosby, Norm(an Lawrence)

September 16, 1927
b. Bond, Tommy
b. Falk, Peter
b. Kelly, Jack
b. Ogata, Sadako (Nakamura)

September 17, 1927
b. Blanda, George Frederick
b. Weiss, Ted

September 18, 1927
b. Green, Paula
b. Greenspan, Bud

September 19, 1927
b. Brown, Harold
b. Ross, Steven J
d. Barker, Herman

September 20, 1927
b. Dankworth, John Philip William
b. Roberts, Rachel

September 21, 1927
b. Jensen, Virginia Allen
b. Sherman, Harry R

September 22, 1927
b. Lasorda, Tommy

September 23, 1927
* b. Breitschwerdt, Werner
b. Daily, Thomas V, Bishop

September 24, 1927
b. Corman, Gene
b. Kraus, Alfredo

September 25, 1927
b. Davis, Colin Rex, Sir

September 26, 1927
b. O'Neal, Patrick

September 27, 1927
b. Gellis, Roberta Leah Jacobs

September 28, 1927
d. Einthoven, Willem

September 29, 1927
b. McCloskey, Paul Norton, Jr.
b. Mertz, Barbara Louise Gross

September 30, 1927
b. Merwin, W(illiam) S(tanley)
b. Reiffel, Leonard

October 1, 1927
b. Bosley, Tom

October 2, 1927
b. Clarke, Shirley
d. Arrhenius, Svante August

October 3, 1927
b. Kenojuak

October 4, 1927
b. Tucker, C(ynthia) DeLores
(Nottage)

October 5, 1927
d. Warner, Sam(uel Louis)

October 6, 1927
d. Serusier, Paul

October 7, 1927
b. Laing, R(onald) D(avid)

October 8, 1927
b. Milstein, Cesar
d. Guiraldes, Ricardo (Guillermo)

October 11, 1927
b. Perry, William J(ames)
b. Tiffeau, Jacques Emile

October 13, 1927
b. Ozal, Turgut

October 16, 1927
b. Conrad, Michael
b. Grass, Gunter (Wilhelm)

October 17, 1927
b. Bailey, Martin Jean
b. Boolootian, Richard Andrew
b. Poston, Tom

October 18, 1927
b. Fanning, Katherine Woodruff
b. Scott, George C(ampbell)

October 19, 1927
b. Alechinsky, Pierre
b. Tallchief, Marjorie

October 20, 1927
b. Kaufman, Henry

October 21, 1927
b. Blucker, Robert Olof
b. Jordan, Charles Morrell

October 22, 1927
d. Youngs, Ross Middlebrook

October 23, 1927
b. Kienholz, Edward
b. Kolakowski, Leszek
b. Lamantia, Philip
d. Dickman, Joseph Theodore

October 24, 1927
b. Becaud, Gilbert (Francois Silly)

October 25, 1927
b. Cook, Barbara
b. Shagan, Steve

October 28, 1927
b. Laine, Cleo

October 29, 1927
b. Sedgman, Frank

October 31, 1927
b. Kahn, Roger
d. Long, John Luther

November 1, 1927
b. Ophuls, Marcel
d. Mills, Florence

November 3, 1927
b. Nordli, Odvar

November 5, 1927
b. Abernethy, Robert Gordon

November 7, 1927
b. Martino, Al

November 8, 1927
b. Newhouse, S(amuel) I(rving), Jr.
b. Page, Patti

November 11, 1927
b. Allison, Mose
b. Roose-Evans, James

November 12, 1927
b. Secunda, Arthur

November 16, 1927
b. Butler, Robert
d. Flowers, Tiger

November 20, 1927
b. Parsons, Estelle

November 21, 1927
b. Campanella, Joseph Mario

November 23, 1927
b. Chandler, Otis

November 24, 1927
b. Diemer, Emma Lou

November 27, 1927
b. Rowling, Wallace Edward
b. Simon, William E(dward)

November 29, 1927
b. Scully, Vin(cent Edward)
d. Savage, Henry Wilson

November 30, 1927
b. Crenna, Richard
b. Guillaume, Robert

December 1, 1927
b. Beard, Ralph Milton
b. Mann, Abby

December 3, 1927
b. Curtin, Phyllis Smith
b. Hall, Adrian
b. Husky, Ferlin
b. Wiggins, Charles Edward

December 5, 1927
b. Bhumibol, Adulyadej

December 6, 1927
b. Mink, Patsy Takemoto

December 7, 1927
b. Mahoney, James P(atrick)

December 8, 1927
b. Luhmann, Niklas

December 10, 1927
b. McGowan, William George

December 12, 1927
b. Blocker, Dan
b. Noyce, Robert Norton

December 13, 1927
b. Wright, James Arlington

December 14, 1927
b. Feldman, Alvin Lindbergh

December 17, 1927
b. Ivask, Ivar Vidrik
b. Long, Richard

December 18, 1927
b. Clark, Ramsey
b. Stroh, Peter W

December 19, 1927
b. Kilgore, Al

December 20, 1927
b. Burch, Dean
b. Kim Young Sam
b. Simpson, Jim

December 22, 1927
b. Castle, Peggie

December 24, 1927
b. Simon, Norma Feldstein
b. Stich-Randall, Teresa
d. Dines, William Henry

December 25, 1927
b. Besse, Georges Noel
b. Fox, Nellie

December 26, 1927
b. King, Alan

December 27, 1927
b. Armstrong, Anne Legendre

December 28, 1927
b. Babiuch, Edward

December 29, 1927
b. Stanfield, Andy

December 31, 1927
b. Hanks, Nancy

1928

b. Bolles, Don F
b. Cantrell, Ed
b. Christopher, Sybil Williams Burton
b. Cook, Lowdrick M
b. Gerussi, Bruno
b. Hill, Jimmy
b. Holland, Leland James
b. Kolvenbach, Peter-Hans
b. Larue, Frederick Chaney
b. Maki, Fumihiko
b. Mitchell, Willie
b. Monteilhet, Hubert
b. Sadr, Musa al-
b. Saw Maung
b. Schwarz-Bart, Andre
b. Serrault, Michel
b. Sharon, Ariel
b. Sylbert, Paul
b. Thompson, Mickey
b. Vernon, Jackie
d. Latimer, Lewis Howard
d. Lee, Henry D
d. Mackintosh, Charles Rennie
d. Rai, Lala Lajpat
d. Rivera, Jose Eustasio
d. Rosso, Medardo

January 1, 1928
b. Edley, Christopher Fairfield
b. Laye, Camara
b. Sissman, L(ouis) E(dward)
b. Smith, Iain Crichton
b. Tidyman, Ernest

January 2, 1928
b. Beals, Vaughn LeRoy, Jr.
b. Ikeda, Daisaku
b. Rostenkowski, Daniel David
d. Fuller, Loie
d. Stevens, Emily A

January 5, 1928
b. Bhutto, Zulfikar Ali

b. Mondale, Walter F(rederick)

January 6, 1928
b. Behn, Noel
d. Kraenzlein, Alvin C

January 7, 1928
b. Blatty, William Peter
b. Snow, Clyde Collins

January 8, 1928
b. Gorton, Slade
b. Vanocur, Sander

January 9, 1928
b. Krantz, Judith

January 10, 1928
b. Brooks, Donald Marc
b. Levine, Philip

January 11, 1928
b. Wolper, David Lloyd
d. Hardy, Thomas

January 14, 1928
b. Faircloth, Lauch
b. Mayer, Martin Prager

January 16, 1928
b. Kennedy, William (Joseph)
b. Kitt, Eartha Mae
b. Lorengar, Pilar

January 17, 1928
b. Sassoon, Vidal

January 20, 1928
b. Hebert, Lionel

January 21, 1928
b. Bignone, Reynaldo Benito Antonio
d. Goethals, George Washington

January 22, 1928
b. Bayh, Birch Evans, Jr.

January 23, 1928
b. Moreau, Jeanne

January 24, 1928
b. Morris, Desmond

January 25, 1928
b. Shevardnadze, Eduard
   Amvrosiyevich
b. Wine, Sherwin T(heodore)

January 26, 1928
b. Vadim, Roger

January 28, 1928
d. Blasco-Ibanez, Vicente

January 29, 1928
d. Haig, Douglas

January 30, 1928
b. Leigh, Mitch
b. Meskill, Thomas J
b. Prince, Hal
d. Fibiger, Johannes Andreas Grib

February 1, 1928
d. Jennings, Hugh(ey Ambrose)
d. Mallinckrodt, Edward

February 2, 1928
b. Stritch, Elaine

February 4, 1928
d. Lorentz, Hendrick Antoon

February 5, 1928
b. Greeley, Andrew Moran
b. Marty, Martin Emil

February 6, 1928
b. Jones, Weyman

February 9, 1928
b. Frazetta, Frank
b. Mudd, Roger Harrison

February 10, 1928
b. Lagardere, Jean-Luc
d. Little Tich

February 11, 1928
b. Garfinkle, Louis
b. Janis, Conrad

February 13, 1928
b. Fried, Gerald

February 14, 1928
b. Allain, William A
b. Gimbel, Peter Robin
d. Hubert, Conrad

February 15, 1928
d. Asquith, Herbert Henry

February 16, 1928
d. Foy, Eddie

February 17, 1928
b. Jones, Tom
b. Peck, Robert Newton

February 18, 1928
b. Johnson, Tom

February 20, 1928
b. Face, Roy

February 24, 1928
b. Harrington, Michael

February 25, 1928
b. Gelbart, Larry
b. Higginbotham, A(loysius) Leon, Jr.
b. Stern, Richard Gustave

February 26, 1928
b. Domino, Fats

February 28, 1928
b. Ackerman, Bettye
b. Baker, Stanley, Sir
b. Tevis, Walter

February 29, 1928
b. Ackland, Joss
d. Appia, Adolphe

March 4, 1928
b. Sillitoe, Alan

March 6, 1928
b. Garcia-Marquez, Gabriel Jose
b. Veronis, John James

March 7, 1928
b. Elegant, Robert Sampson

March 8, 1928
b. Segal, Lore Groszmann

March 9, 1928
d. Wanamaker, Lewis Rodman

March 10, 1928
b. Akins, Virgil B
b. Grebey, Ray
b. Ray, James Earl
b. Tennenbaum, Silvia

March 11, 1928
b. Salmi, Albert

March 12, 1928
b. Albee, Edward
d. Yermolova, Maria Nikolayevna

March 13, 1928
b. Raskin, Ellen

March 14, 1928
b. Borman, Frank

March 18, 1928
b. Ramos, Fidel V(aldez)

March 19, 1928
b. Kung, Hans
b. McGoohan, Patrick (Joseph)
d. Bayes, Nora
d. Ferrier, David, Sir

March 20, 1928
b. Rogers, Fred McFeely

March 21, 1928
b. Kinnear, James Wesley
b. Thapa, Surya Bahadur
d. Esposito, Joseph

March 22, 1928
b. Hammer, Richard
b. Hirsch, E(ric) D(onald), Jr.
b. Macauley, Ed

March 23, 1928
b. Phillips, Channing Emery

March 24, 1928
b. Brown, Vanessa
b. Janis, Byron
d. Mew, Charlotte Mary

March 25, 1928
b. Lovell, Jim

March 28, 1928
b. Brzezinski, Zbigniew Kazimierz

March 31, 1928
b. Costigan, James
b. Frizzell, Lefty
b. Howe, Gordie

April 1, 1928
b. Grizzard, George
b. Powell, Jane

April 2, 1928
b. Bernardin, Joseph L(ouis), Cardinal
b. Gam, Rita Elenore
d. Richards, Theodore William

April 3, 1928
b. Gibson, Don(ald)

April 4, 1928
b. Angelou, Maya

April 5, 1928
d. Depew, Chauncey Mitchell

April 6, 1928
b. Watson, James Dewey

April 7, 1928
b. Garner, James
b. Pakula, Alan J(ay)

April 8, 1928
b. Porter, Eric Richard

April 9, 1928
b. Arizin, Paul Joseph
b. Lehrer, Tom

April 11, 1928
b. Kennedy, Ethel Skakel

April 12, 1928
b. Kruger, Hardy
d. Smith, Madeline Hamilton

April 16, 1928
b. Lane, Dick
b. Sylbert, Richard
d. Statler, Ellsworth Milton

April 19, 1928
b. Garwin, Richard Lawrence
b. Korner, Alexis

April 23, 1928
b. Black, Shirley Temple

April 25, 1928
b. Clements, Vassar
b. Hayden, Melissa
d. Bennett, Floyd
d. Curel, Francois de
d. Wrangel, Pietr Nikolayevich

April 29, 1928
b. Singer, Burns James Hyman

May 1, 1928
d. Howard, Ebenezer, Sir
d. Xiang Jingyu

May 2, 1928
b. Falls, Joe

May 3, 1928
b. Brown, James
b. Eckstein, George

May 4, 1928
b. Ferguson, Maynard
b. Mubarak, (Mohammed) Hosni
b. Rawl, Lawrence G
b. Rawls, Betsy

May 7, 1928
b. Mitchelson, Marvin M(orris)
b. Williams, Dick

May 8, 1928
b. Sorensen, Ted

May 9, 1928
b. Gonzalez, Pancho
b. Scott, Barbara Ann

May 11, 1928
b. Agam, Yaacov

May 12, 1928
b. Lujan, Manuel, Jr.

May 16, 1928
b. Martin, Billy
d. Gosse, Edmund William, Sir

May 18, 1928
d. Haywood, William Dudley

May 19, 1928
b. Chapman, (Anthony) Colin (Bruce)
b. McDougald, Gil(bert James)
b. Schayes, Dolph

May 20, 1928
b. Hedison, David

May 22, 1928
b. Pickens, T(homas) Boone, Jr.

May 23, 1928
b. Clooney, Rosemary
b. Davenport, Nigel

May 24, 1928
b. Caras, Roger Andrew
b. Trevor, William

May 25, 1928
b. Lawrence, Mary Wells

May 26, 1928
b. Kevorkian, Jack

May 27, 1928
b. Musgrave, Thea

May 28, 1928
b. Stein, Horst

May 29, 1928
b. Rohatyn, Felix George
b. Sinner, George Albert

May 30, 1928
b. Varda, Agnes

May 31, 1928
b. Lateiner, Jacob

June 1, 1928
b. Dobrovolsky, Georgi Timofeyevich

June 2, 1928
d. Fortune, Timothy Thomas
d. Nordenskold, Nils Otto Gustaf

June 3, 1928
b. Judd, Donald (Clarence)
b. Simons, Howard

June 4, 1928
d. Chang Tso-Lin

June 5, 1928
b. Richardson, Tony

June 6, 1928
b. Deukmejian, George
b. Glossop, Peter

June 7, 1928
b. Ivory, James
b. Strouse, Charles

June 8, 1928
b. Gutierrez, Gustavo
b. Perkins, Edward Joseph

June 10, 1928
b. Sendak, Maurice Bernard

June 11, 1928
b. Cavanagh, Jerome Patrick
b. Fabiola, Queen

June 12, 1928
b. Damone, Vic
b. Sherman, Richard Morton

June 14, 1928
b. Guevara, Che
b. Udry, Janice May
d. Pankhurst, Emmeline Goulden

June 16, 1928
b. Comissiona, Sergiu

June 18, 1928
d. Amundsen, Roald Engelbregt

June 19, 1928
b. Marchand, Nancy

June 20, 1928
b. Le Pen, Jean-Marie
d. Mead, William Rutherford

June 21, 1928
b. Raskin, Judith

June 22, 1928
b. Hermannsson, Steingrimur
b. Waite, Ralph
d. Frost, Arthur Burdett

June 24, 1928
b. Foust, Larry
b. Selzer, Richard (Alan)

d. Blinn, Holbrook

June 25, 1928
b. Culliford, Peyo

June 26, 1928
b. Druckman, Jacob (Raphael)

June 27, 1928
b. Mercer, David
b. Perpich, Rudy George

June 28, 1928
b. Evans, Harold Matthew

June 29, 1928
b. Bannen, Ian

June 30, 1928
b. Marcus, Frank

July 1, 1928
b. Denoff, Sam
d. Hopwood, Avery

July 2, 1928
b. Kohout, Pavel

July 3, 1928
b. Anthony, Evelyn
b. Horchow, S(amuel) Roger

July 4, 1928
b. Berberian, Cathy
b. Boyd, Stephen
b. Lollobrigida, Gina

July 5, 1928
b. Mauroy, Pierre
b. Oates, Warren
d. Villard, Helen Francis Garrison

July 7, 1928
b. Edwards, Vince(nt)

July 9, 1928
b. Hall, Donald Joyce

July 10, 1928
b. Buffet, Bernard

July 11, 1928
b. Farquhar, Marilyn G(ist)

July 12, 1928
b. Corey, Elias James

July 13, 1928
b. Bond, Sudie
b. Crane, Bob

July 14, 1928
b. Olaf, Pierre
b. Olson, Nancy

July 15, 1928
b. Benko, Paul Charles

July 16, 1928
b. Brookner, Anita
b. Davidovich, Bella

b. Wilde, Patricia

July 17, 1928
b. Dyer, Charles (Raymond)
b. Guaraldi, Vince(nt Anthony)
b. Morello, Joseph A
d. Giolitti, Giovanni
d. Obregon, Alvaro

July 21, 1928
b. Keane, John Brendon
d. Terry, Ellen Alicia, Dame

July 22, 1928
b. Bean, Orson
b. Bergland, Bob

July 23, 1928
b. Fleisher, Leon
b. Selby, Hubert, Jr.

July 26, 1928
b. Cossiga, Francesco
b. Kubrick, Stanley
b. Lougheed, Peter

August 5, 1928
b. Maglich, Bogdan C

August 7, 1928
b. Byars, Betsy
b. Randi, James

August 9, 1928
b. Cousy, Bob
b. Johnson, Harold

August 10, 1928
b. Dean, Jimmy
b. Fisher, Eddie

August 12, 1928
d. Janacek, Leos

August 14, 1928
b. Wertmuller, Lina von Eigg

August 15, 1928
b. Roeg, Nicholas (Jack)

August 16, 1928
b. Blyth, Ann Marie

August 17, 1928
b. Rossant, James Stephane

August 18, 1928
b. Schott, Marge

August 19, 1928
b. Levin, Bernard
b. Stewart, Thomas

August 20, 1928
d. Harvey, George Brinton M

August 21, 1928
b. de Andrade, Mario
b. Farmer, Art(hur Stewart)

August 22, 1928
b. Marshall, Ray

August 23, 1928
b. Seldes, Marian

August 24, 1928
b. Brooks, Angie Elizabeth

August 25, 1928
b. Epstein, Jason

August 27, 1928
b. Buthelezi, Gatsha Mangosuthu

August 28, 1928
b. Stockhausen, Karlheinz

August 30, 1928
d. Wien, Wilhelm Carl Werner Otto
Fritz Franz

August 31, 1928
b. Coburn, James
b. Sin, Jaime L(achica)

September 1, 1928
b. Guy, Rosa Cuthbert

September 2, 1928
b. Stuart, Mel

September 3, 1928
b. Thorn, Gaston

September 4, 1928
b. Rausch, James Stevens
b. York, Dick

September 6, 1928
b. Pirsig, Robert M(aynard)
b. Svetlanov, Evgeni Fyodorovich

September 7, 1928
b. McGuire, Al

September 9, 1928
b. Adderley, Cannonball
b. LeWitt, Sol

September 10, 1928
b. Sumac, Yma

September 11, 1928
b. Askew, Reubin O'Donovan
b. Holliman, Earl
b. Kienzle, William X(avier)

September 12, 1928
b. Irwin, Robert

September 13, 1928
b. Boyer, Ernest L(eroy)
b. Indiana, Robert
d. Svevo, Italo

September 14, 1928
b. Shanker, Albert

September 17, 1928
b. McDowall, Roddy

September 18, 1928
b. Smith, Robert Lee

September 20, 1928
b. Hall, Donald Andrew
b. Jennings, Gary

September 21, 1928
b. Ashbrook, John Milan

September 22, 1928
b. Stone, Dick

September 24, 1928
b. Brown, Kelly

September 25, 1928
b. Gwaltney, John Langston
d. Outcault, Richard Felton

September 26, 1928
b. Ray, Robert D
b. Strenger, Hermann Josef

September 27, 1928
b. Neufeld, Elizabeth F(ondal)

September 28, 1928
b. Silver, Horace Ward Martin Tavares

September 30, 1928
b. Fries, Charles W
b. Thomas, Piri
b. Wiesel, Elie(zer)
b. Li Peng

October 1, 1928
b. Harvey, Laurence
b. Peppard, George

October 2, 1928
b. Felker, Clay S
b. McFarland, Spanky
b. Pannenberg, Wolfhart Ulrich
d. Barron, Clarence Walker

October 3, 1928
b. Bruhn, Erik Belton Evers
b. Ramphal, Shridath Surendranath

October 4, 1928
b. Forman, James
b. Toffler, Alvin

October 9, 1928
b. Solotaroff, Theodore

October 12, 1928
b. Held, Al

October 14, 1928
b. Graffman, Gary
b. Moore, Roger George

October 16, 1928
b. Daly, Mary
b. Flavin, Joseph B(ernard)
d. Thompson, J(ames) Walter

October 17, 1928
b. Bennett, Lerone, Jr.
b. Gilliam, Jim

October 20, 1928
b. Brothers, Joyce Diane Bauer

October 21, 1928
b. Ford, Whitey
b. Mikkelsen, Vern

October 22, 1928
d. Fisher, Andrew

October 23, 1928
b. Woodwell, George M(asters)
d. Aulard, Francois Victor Alphonse
d. McCutcheon, George Barr

October 24, 1928
d. Davies, Arthur Bowen

October 25, 1928
b. Franciosa, Anthony
b. Ross, Marion

October 27, 1928
b. Kovel, Terry Horvitz
b. Rote, Kyle
b. Smith, Perry Edward

October 30, 1928
b. Nathans, Daniel
b. Wigle, Ernest Douglas
d. Lansing, Robert
d. Sonneck, Oscar George Theodore

October 31, 1928
b. Romer, Roy R
b. Sarris, Andrew George

November 2, 1928
b. Cobbs, Price M(ashaw)
b. Hart, Leon J
b. Johnson, Paul (Bede)

November 6, 1928
d. Rothstein, Arnold

November 7, 1928
d. Battistini, Mattia

November 8, 1928
d. Stiller, Mauritz

November 9, 1928
b. Duke, Wayne
b. Sexton, Anne Harvey

November 11, 1928
b. Fuentes, Carlos
b. Zorinsky, Edward

November 12, 1928
b. Baker, Bobby
b. Muncey, Bill
b. Sharmat, Marjorie Weinman

November 15, 1928
b. Brady, James Winston
d. Chamberlin, Thomas Chrowder

November 16, 1928
b. Gulager, Clu
d. Cecchetti, Enrico

November 17, 1928
b. Arman
b. Kabua, Amata

November 18, 1928
b. Laurel, Salvador H(idalgo)

November 20, 1928
b. Cover, Franklin

November 21, 1928
b. Cook, Samuel DuBois
d. Sudermann, Hermann

November 23, 1928
b. Bock, Jerry
b. Yardley, George Harry
d. Ryan, Thomas Fortune

November 25, 1928
d. Lummis, Charles Fletcher

November 28, 1928
b. Costanza, Midge
b. Okun, Arthur Melvin

November 29, 1928
b. Crosse, Rupert
b. Simon, Paul M(artin)

November 30, 1928
b. Doi, Takako
b. Hall, Joe Beasman
b. Hecht, Chic
b. Scott, Norman

December 1, 1928
b. Michell, Keith

December 2, 1928
b. Demus, Joreg

December 7, 1928
b. Chomsky, Noam Avram

December 8, 1928
b. Caldwell, John Charles

December 9, 1928
b. Van Patten, Dick Vincent

December 10, 1928
b. Colicos, John

December 12, 1928
b. Aitmatov, Chingiz
b. Frankenthaler, Helen

December 15, 1928
b. Hundertwasser, Friedensreich

December 16, 1928
b. Ames, Bruce N(athan)
b. Dick, Philip K(indred)
b. MacDonald, Peter
d. Wylie, Elinor Hoyt

December 17, 1928
b. Beck, Marilyn (Mohr)

December 19, 1928
b. MacDermot, Galt

December 20, 1928
b. Brown, Les(ter Louis)
b. Christiansen, Jack L

December 21, 1928
b. Nelson, Ed(win Stafford)

December 23, 1928
b. Jepsen, Roger William
d. Coulter, John Merle

December 30, 1928
b. Diddley, Bo
d. York, Edward Palmer

December 31, 1928
b. McElhenny, Hugh

1929

b. Anderson, Gerry
b. Baniszewski, Gertrude Wright
b. Baudrillard, Jean
b. Bebey, Francis
b. Beheshti, Mohammad, Ayatollah
b. Bryant, Hugh
b. D'Alessio, Kitty
b. dos Santos, Marcelino
b. Duke, Red, Dr.
b. Kawawa, Rashidi Mfaume
b. Kloss, Henry E.
b. Mennen, Frederick
b. Naisbitt, John
b. Ramsey, Anne
b. Schluter, Poul (Holmskov)
b. Shukshin, Vasilii Makarovich
b. Walker, Albertina
b. Westheimer, Ruth
b. Wilson, Erica
b. York, David
d. Churchill, May
d. Cooley, Charles Horton
d. McCoy, Elijah
d. Jergens, Andrew

January 3, 1929
b. Leone, Sergio

January 4, 1929
b. Etzioni, Amitai Werner
b. Rush, Barbara

January 6, 1929
b. Hamilton, Joe
b. Karmal, Babrak
b. Tayback, Vic

January 8, 1929
d. Duke, Benjamin Newton

January 9, 1929
b. Friel, Brian
b. Grosbard, Ulu
b. Matheson, Scott Milne

January 10, 1929
b. Charlip, Remy

January 12, 1929
b. MacIntyre, Alasdair Chalmers

January 13, 1929
b. Pass, Joe
d. Earp, Wyatt Berry Stapp

January 14, 1929
b. Quilico, Louis
d. Walker, Henry Oliver
d. Widal, Fernand Isidore

January 15, 1929
b. King, Martin Luther, Jr.
b. Queen Ida

January 16, 1929
b. Lowenstein, Allard Kenneth
b. Scavullo, Francesco

January 17, 1929
d. Goldberger, Joseph

January 18, 1929
d. Loeb, Sophia Irene Simon

January 19, 1929
d. Liang Ch'i-ch'ao

January 21, 1929
b. Hinojosa, Rolando

January 23, 1929
b. Clarkson, Ewan
b. Polanyi, John C

January 25, 1929
b. Golson, Benny
d. Underwood, Oscar Wilder

January 26, 1929
b. Feiffer, Jules Ralph
b. Kronhausen, Phyllis Carmen

January 27, 1929
b. Thulin, Ingrid

January 28, 1929
b. Oldenburg, Claes Thure

January 29, 1929
b. Petri, Elio

January 30, 1929
b. Stevens, Morton

January 31, 1929
b. Mossbauer, Rudolf Ludwig
b. Simmons, Jean

February 3, 1929
b. Harris, Derek

February 4, 1929
b. Johnston, Neil

February 6, 1929
b. Waterhouse, Keith Spencer
d. Hauk, Minnie

February 10, 1929
b. Goldsmith, Jerry

February 12, 1929
d. Langtry, Lillie

February 13, 1929
b. Torrijos Herrera, Omar

February 14, 1929
b. Morrow, Vic

February 15, 1929
b. Hill, Graham
b. Schlesinger, James Rodney
d. Stone, Melville Elijah

February 17, 1929
b. Plante, Jacques
b. Potok, Chaim

February 18, 1929
b. Deighton, Len

February 22, 1929
b. Duren, Ryne
b. Nixon, Marni

February 23, 1929
b. Howard, Elston Gene

February 24, 1929
d. Keenan, Frank
d. Messager, Andre Charles Prosper

February 25, 1929
b. Biryukova, Aleksandra Pavlovna
b. George, Christopher

February 27, 1929
d. Hadden, Briton

February 28, 1929
b. Gehry, Frank Owen

March 1, 1929
b. James, Sonny

March 2, 1929
b. DiSabato, Giovanni

March 4, 1929
b. Haitink, Bernard

March 5, 1929
b. Murray, Allen Edward

March 6, 1929
b. Foley, Thomas S(tephen)
d. Buick, David Dunbar

March 7, 1929
b. Chouteau, Yvonne

March 8, 1929
b. Krainik, Ardis

March 9, 1929
b. Hoyte, Hugh Desmond

March 11, 1929
b. Browning, Edmond Lee
b. Jacobsen, Hugh Newell

March 12, 1929
d. Candler, Asa Griggs

March 14, 1929
d. Smith, Clarence

March 16, 1929
b. Foley, Tom

March 17, 1929
b. Howe, Florence Rosenfeld

March 19, 1929
b. Muczynski, Robert

March 20, 1929
d. Foch, Ferdinand

March 21, 1929
b. Andrews, Bert
b. Bergman, Jules Verne
b. Coco, James Emil

March 23, 1929
b. Bannister, Roger, Sir

March 25, 1929
b. Hicks, David (Nightingale)

March 26, 1929
b. Sorel, Edward

March 28, 1929
b. Exley, Frederick (Earl)
d. Bates, Katharine Lee

March 29, 1929
b. Meri, Lennart

March 30, 1929
b. Dysart, Richard (Allan)

March 31, 1929
b. Claiborne, Liz

April 1, 1929
b. Kundera, Milan
b. Schembechler, Bo

April 3, 1929
b. Khan, Fazlur Rahman
b. Umeki, Miyoshi

April 4, 1929
d. Benz, Karl Friedrich

April 5, 1929
b. Claus, Hugo
b. Giaever, Ivar

April 6, 1929
b. Previn, Andre

April 8, 1929
b. Berry, Walter
b. Brel, Jacques

April 9, 1929
b. Learned, Michael
b. Lichtenstein, Harvey
b. Marshall, Paule

April 10, 1929
b. VonSydow, Max Carl Adolf

April 12, 1929
d. Steel, Flora Annie Webster

April 13, 1929
b. McEwen, Terence Alexander
b. Old Person, Earl

April 14, 1929
b. Chadli, Bendjedid

April 15, 1929
b. Cadbury, George Adrian Hayhurst,
Sir

April 16, 1929
b. Adams, Edie
b. Hamilton, Roy

April 17, 1929
d. Sifton, Clifford

April 22, 1929
b. Cabrera Infante, Guillermo

April 25, 1929
b. Twombly, Cy

April 28, 1929
b. Bailey, Charles Waldo, II

April 29, 1929
b. Strong, Maurice Frederick
b. Thorpe, Jeremy

May 1, 1929
b. Weaver, Thomas

May 2, 1929
b. Balladur, Edouard
d. Dorgan, Thomas Aloysius

May 4, 1929
b. Hepburn, Audrey (Edda)
b. Lamb, Sydney MacDonald

May 8, 1929
b. Allen, Ethel D.

May 9, 1929
b. Franklin, Hardy R.

May 10, 1929
b. Newman, Peter Charles

May 12, 1929
b. Bacharach, Burt
b. Nujoma, Samuel Shafiihuma

May 13, 1929
b. Galvin, John Rogers

May 14, 1929
b. Thompson, George Selden
b. Worsley, Gump

May 16, 1929
b. Conyers, John, Jr.
b. Rich, Adrienne (Cecile)

May 17, 1929
b. Greenfield, Eloise
d. Lehmann, Lilli

May 18, 1929
d. Shaw, Mary

May 19, 1929
b. Cox, Harvey Gallagher, Jr.

May 21, 1929
d. Rosebery, Archibald Philip
Primrose, Earl

May 23, 1929
b. Chomsky, Marvin
b. Jacobsson, Ulla

May 25, 1929
b. Ruder, David Sturtevant
b. Sills, Beverly

June 1, 1929
b. Billington, James H(adley)

June 2, 1929
b. Barris, Chuck

June 3, 1929
b. Arber, Werner
b. Williams, Billy

June 5, 1929
b. Lansing, Robert
d. Rickard, Tex

June 7, 1929
b. Turner, John Napier

June 8, 1929
d. Carman, Bliss

June 9, 1929
b. Ace, Johnny
d. Lawrence, Margaret

June 10, 1929
b. McDivitt, Jim
b. Wilson, Edward Osborne

June 11, 1929
b. Garrett, George Palmer, Jr.

June 12, 1929
b. Brophy, Brigid Antonia
b. Frank, Anne

June 14, 1929
b. Coleman, Cy
d. Keith, Minor Cooper

June 15, 1929
b. Mansouri, Lotfi
d. Brush, Charles Francis

June 16, 1929
d. Parrington, Vernon L(ouis)

June 17, 1929
b. Petrosian, Tigran Vartanovich

June 18, 1929
b. Habermas, Juergen

June 20, 1929
b. Bronfman, Edgar Miles

June 21, 1929
d. Hobhouse, Leonard Trelawny

June 23, 1929
b. Carter, June
b. Lapidus, Ted

June 24, 1929
d. Hern, Riley

June 25, 1929
b. Carle, Eric
b. Eisner, Thomas

June 26, 1929
b. Glaser, Milton

June 27, 1929
b. Maas, Peter

June 28, 1929
d. Carpenter, Edward

July 1, 1929
b. Edelman, Gerald Maurice

July 2, 1929
d. Johnson, Henry

July 3, 1929
d. Farnum, Dustin Lancy

July 4, 1929
b. Davis, Al(len)

July 5, 1929
b. Carruthers, John(ny)

July 6, 1929
d. Eberle, Edward Walter

July 8, 1929
b. Grau, Shirley Ann

July 9, 1929
b. Hassan II
b. Hazelwood, Lee

July 11, 1929
b. Prey, Hermann

July 12, 1929
d. Henri, Robert

July 13, 1929
b. Johnston, Basil H.

July 15, 1929
d. Hofmannsthal, Hugo von

July 18, 1929
b. Button, Dick
b. Hawkins, Screamin' Jay

July 19, 1929
b. Hejduk, John

July 20, 1929
b. Ilitch, Mike

July 22, 1929
b. Merchant, Vivien

July 24, 1929
b. Yates, Peter

July 25, 1929
b. Farb, Peter

July 26, 1929
b. Lalonde, Marc
b. Shepherd, Jean Parker
b. Weissenberg, Alexis Sigismund

July 27, 1929
d. Pictet, Raoul-Pierre

July 28, 1929
b. Onassis, Jacqueline (Lee Bouvier
Kennedy)

July 29, 1929
d. Fuller, Henry Blake

July 30, 1929
b. Krofft, Sid

July 31, 1929
b. Murray, Don(ald Patrick)

August 1, 1929
b. Stewart, Michael

August 3, 1929
d. Berliner, Emile
d. Veblen, Thorstein Bunde

August 4, 1929
d. Welsbach, Carl Auer von, Baron

August 5, 1929
b. Alvarez, Alfred
d. Fawcett, Millicent Garrett, Dame

August 7, 1929
b. Larsen, Don(ald James)
b. Stapleton, Ruth Carter
d. Berger, Victor Louis
d. Medary, Milton B

August 8, 1929
b. Biggs, Ronald Arthur

August 10, 1929
b. Vagelos, P Roy

August 11, 1929
b. Bustamante, John H

August 12, 1929
b. Owens, Buck

August 13, 1929
b. Harrington, Pat

August 16, 1929
b. Evans, Bill
b. Kenny, Maurice (Francis)

August 17, 1929
b. Powers, Francis Gary

August 18, 1929
b. Kuznetsov, Anatoli Vasilievich
b. Sadik, Nafis

August 19, 1929
d. Diaghilev, Sergei (Pavlovich)

August 21, 1929
b. Badillo, Herman
b. Cox, Richard Joseph
b. Kennedy, X J

August 23, 1929
b. Thomson, Peter William

August 24, 1929
b. Arafat, Yasir

August 27, 1929
b. Cervantes, Alfonso Juan
b. Levin, Ira

August 28, 1929
b. Roker, Roxie
b. Wiener, Leigh Auston

August 29, 1929
b. Gunn, Thom(son William)
b. Kertesz, Istvan
b. Soelle, Dorothee

September 4, 1929
b. Eagleton, Thomas Francis

September 5, 1929
b. Nikolayev, Andriyan Grigoryevich
b. Schultz, Richard D(ale)

September 6, 1929
b. Finsterwald, Dow

September 7, 1929
b. Neal, James Foster

September 8, 1929
b. Dohnanyi, Christoph von

September 9, 1929
d. Quinn, Edmond T

September 10, 1929
b. Leonetti, Tommy
b. Palmer, Arnold Daniel

September 11, 1929
b. Broder, David S

September 13, 1929
b. Ghiaurov, Nicolai

September 14, 1929
b. Clark, Richard Clarence
b. Collins, Larry

September 15, 1929
b. Gell-Mann, Murray

September 17, 1929
b. Crowley, Pat
b. Moss, Stirling Crauford

September 23, 1929
b. Horrigan, Edward, Jr.

September 24, 1929
d. Zsigmondy, Richard Adolf

September 25, 1929
b. Barker, Ronnie
b. White, Kevin Hagan
d. Huggins, Miller James

September 26, 1929
b. Murray, Cecil (Leonard)

September 27, 1929
b. Harris, Leonard
b. Thompson, Sada Carolyn

September 29, 1929
b. Newhart, Bob

October 1, 1929
d. Bourdelle, Emile-Antoine

October 2, 1929
b. Gunn, Moses

October 3, 1929
b. Stern, Bert
d. Eagels, Jeanne
d. Stresemann, Gustav

October 5, 1929
b. Gordon, Richard Francis, Jr.

October 7, 1929
b. Westall, Robert Atkinson

October 8, 1929
b. Stahl, Franklin William

October 9, 1929
b. Morial, Ernest Nathan

October 10, 1929
b. Boutte, Alvin J

October 11, 1929
b. Freedman, Russell

October 12, 1929
b. Coles, Robert

October 13, 1929
d. Bentley, Charles Edwin

October 15, 1929
b. Dreyfus, Hubert L(ederer)

October 16, 1929
b. VonHoffman, Nicholas

October 18, 1929
b. Chamorro, Violeta Barrios de
b. Elkins, Hillard

October 20, 1929
d. Batlle y Ordonez, Jose

October 21, 1929
b. Cruz, Celia
b. LeGuin, Ursula K(roeber)

October 22, 1929
d. Chirol, Valentine, Sir
d. Hastings, Thomas

October 23, 1929
b. Darvi, Bella

October 24, 1929
b. Brosnan, Jim
b. Crumb, George Henry

October 28, 1929
b. Ginzburg, Ralph
b. Goodman, Dody
b. Hollander, John
b. Plowright, Joan Anne
d. Bulow, Bernhard H M

November 2, 1929
b. Bose, Amar Gopal
b. Taylor, Richard Edward

November 7, 1929
b. Abdul, Raoul
b. Sutherland, Joan, Dame

November 8, 1929
b. Bowden, Bobby

November 10, 1929
b. Bergman, Marilyn Keith

November 12, 1929
b. Kelly, Grace Patricia

November 14, 1929
b. Piersall, Jimmy
b. Stevenson, McLean
d. McGinnity, Joe

November 15, 1929
b. Asner, Ed(ward)

November 17, 1929
d. Hollerith, Herman

November 18, 1929
d. O'Connor, Thomas Power

November 20, 1929
b. Denenberg, Herbert Sidney
b. January, Don(ald)

November 21, 1929
b. French, Marilyn

November 22, 1929
b. Lynd, Staughton (Craig)

November 24, 1929
b. Johnson, John Henry
b. Moscone, George Richard
d. Clemenceau, Georges Eugene
　Benjamin

November 26, 1929
b. Saint John, Betta

November 28, 1929
b. Gordy, Berry, Jr.

November 30, 1929
b. Clark, Dick
b. Cooney, Joan Ganz
b. Wyman, Thomas Hunt

December 1, 1929
b. Doyle, David (Fitzgerald)
b. Shawn, Dick

December 2, 1929
b. Phillips, Harvey Gene

December 4, 1929
b. McGovern, Arthur F

December 6, 1929
b. Harnoncourt, Nikolaus
b. Tanner, Alain

December 9, 1929
b. Cassavetes, John
b. Hawke, Bob

December 10, 1929
d. Crosby, Harry
d. Rosenzweig, Franz

December 11, 1929
b. MacMillan, Kenneth, Sir

December 12, 1929
b. Osborne, John (James)
d. Goodnight, Charles

December 13, 1929
b. Plummer, (Arthur) Christopher

December 17, 1929
b. Safire, William L

December 18, 1929
b. Glemp, Jozef, Cardinal

December 19, 1929
b. Sackler, Howard Oliver

December 20, 1929
b. Panic, Milan

December 23, 1929
b. Weber, Dick

December 24, 1929
b. Clark, Mary Higgins
d. Hitchcock, Raymond

December 26, 1929
b. Regine

December 28, 1929
b. Bieber, Owen Frederick
b. Sawchuk, Terry

December 29, 1929
d. Jefferson, Blind Lemon

1930
b. Abu Musa
b. Allen, John Polk
b. Applewhite, Marshall Herff
b. Armstrong, Garner Ted
b. Beckett, Wendy
b. Boschwitz, Rudy
b. Capucci, Roberto
b. Contino, Dick
b. Cunningham, William T(homas)
b. Curtis, Charlotte Murray
b. De Ribes, Jacqueline
b. Famolare, Joseph P
b. Frankel, Emily
b. Garth, David
b. Halffter, Christobal
b. Herbert, Anthony B
b. Iglesias, Enrique V.
b. Laatasi, Kamuta
b. La Haye, Beverly
b. Lary, Yale
b. Lynch, David
b. Marchetti, Victor L
b. McCormick, Patricia Keller
b. Ogot, Grace Emily Akinyi
b. Patrick, Ted
b. Pulitzer, Peter
b. Riordan, Richard J
b. Schlamme, Martha
b. Sherman, Russell
b. Toomer, Ronald V
b. Wood, John
b. Yamani, Ahmad Zaki, Sheik
b. Ziff, William B(ernard), Jr.
d. Grimke, Archibald H(enry)
d. Spooner, William Archibald
b. Adonis
b. Ahmed, Shahabuddin

January 1, 1930
b. Nimeiry, Gaafar Mohammed al
b. Wiseman, Frederick

January 2, 1930
b. LaRosa, Julius

January 3, 1930
d. Briggs, Clare A

January 4, 1930
b. Booke, Sorrell
b. McMahon, Don(ald John)
b. Shula, Don(ald Francis)

January 6, 1930
b. Keniston, Kenneth

January 7, 1930
b. Kiker, Douglas

January 8, 1930
b. Sales, Soupy

January 9, 1930
b. Sloane, Dennis
d. Bok, Edward William

January 10, 1930
b. Disney, Roy E(dward)

January 11, 1930
b. Stacey, Thomas Charles Gerard
b. Taylor, Rod(ney)

January 12, 1930
b. Horton, Tim
b. Makihara, (Ben) Minoru
b. Yarbrough, Glenn

January 13, 1930
b. Lortz, Richard

January 16, 1930
b. Podhoretz, Norman

January 18, 1930
b. OhEithir, Breandan

January 19, 1930
d. Ramsey, Frank Plumpton

January 20, 1930
b. Aldrin, Edwin E(ugene), Jr.
d. Cobb, Will D

January 22, 1930
b. Wildsmith, Brian
d. Mather, Stephen Tyng

January 23, 1930
b. Pogue, William R(eid)
b. Walcott, Derek (Alton)

January 24, 1930
d. Felton, Rebecca Ann Latimer
d. Sammarco, Mario

January 26, 1930
b. Gumbleton, Thomas J

January 27, 1930
b. Bland, Bobby Blue

January 28, 1930
d. Destinn, Emmy

January 29, 1930
d. Tappan, Eva March

February 1, 1930
b. Ershad, Hussain Mohammad

February 3, 1930
b. Anger, Kenneth
b. Wojnilower, Albert Martin

February 7, 1930
b. Bar-Ilian, David Jacob

February 8, 1930
b. Rey, Alejandro

February 10, 1930
b. Wagner, Robert John, Jr.

February 11, 1930
b. Polshek, James Stewart

February 12, 1930
b. Specter, Arlen

February 15, 1930
b. Moore, Sara Jane

February 17, 1930
b. Rendell, Ruth

February 18, 1930
b. Wilson, Gahan

February 19, 1930
b. Frankenheimer, John Michael

February 23, 1930
b. Davis, Gerry
d. Normand, Mabel

February 26, 1930
b. Berman, Lazar
b. Janowicz, Vic(tor Felix)

February 27, 1930
b. Stone, Peter H
b. Woodward, Joanne Gignilliat

February 28, 1930
b. Cooper, Leon Neil
b. MacLeod, Gavin

March 1, 1930
b. Saint Jacques, Raymond
b. Zigler, Edward

March 2, 1930
b. Cullum, John
d. Lawrence, D(avid) H(erbert)

March 3, 1930
b. Aki, Keiiti
b. Iliescu, Ion

March 5, 1930
b. Crandall, Del(mar Wesley)
b. Maazel, Lorin Varencove
d. Ladd-Franklin, Christine

March 6, 1930
d. Hadley, Arthur Twining
d. Tirpitz, Alfred von

March 7, 1930
b. Armstrong-Jones, Antony Charles Robert
b. Marlowe, Marion

March 8, 1930
b. Hurd, Douglas
d. Taft, William (Howard)

March 9, 1930
b. Schippers, Thomas
d. Mercer, Henry Chapman

March 11, 1930
b. Jutra, Claude
b. Ruttman, Troy
d. Albee, Edward Franklin

March 12, 1930
b. Law, Vern(on Sanders)

March 13, 1930
d. Freeman, Mary E Wilkins

March 16, 1930
b. Flanagan, Tommy (Lee)

d. Primo de Rivera (y Orbaneja), Miguel

March 17, 1930
b. Allen, Betty (Lou)
b. Horn, Paul Joseph
b. Irwin, James Benson

March 18, 1930
b. Maida, Adam (Joseph)

March 19, 1930
b. Coleman, Ornette
d. Balfour, Arthur James

March 21, 1930
b. Fraser, John Malcolm

March 22, 1930
b. Bok, Derek Curtis
b. Pindling, Lynden Oscar
b. Robertson, Pat
b. Sondheim, Stephen (Joshua)

March 24, 1930
b. Dacko, David
b. McQueen, Steve

March 26, 1930
b. Corso, Gregory Nunzio
b. O'Connor, Sandra Day

March 28, 1930
b. Friedman, Jerome

March 29, 1930
b. Jugnauth, Anerood

March 30, 1930
b. Astin, John Allen
b. Jones, Robert C
b. Marshall, Peter

April 1, 1930
d. Wagner, Cosima Liszt

April 3, 1930
b. Chiles, Lawton Mainor, Jr.
b. Frankel, Max
b. Kohl, Helmut (Michael)

April 5, 1930
b. Cheshire, Maxine
b. Costa, Mary

April 6, 1930
b. Bristow, Lonnie
b. Lansing, Joi

April 8, 1930
b. Fenton, Thomas Trail
b. Reardon, John

April 10, 1930
b. Blanton, (Leonard) Ray
b. Huerta, Dolores (Fernandez)

April 11, 1930
b. Brady, Nicholas Frederick

April 12, 1930
b. Antonelli, John(ny August)

b. Landy, John

April 13, 1930
b. Dillman, Bradford

April 14, 1930
b. Robinson, Jay

April 15, 1930
b. Finnbogadottir, Vigdis

April 16, 1930
b. Mann, Herbie
d. Mariategui, Jose Carlos

April 18, 1930
b. Revill, Clive Selsby

April 19, 1930
b. O'Brian, Hugh

April 20, 1930
d. Smith, Alex

April 21, 1930
b. Mangano, Silvana
b. Tyson, Don
d. Bridges, Robert Seymour

April 24, 1930
b. Tahse, Martin

April 25, 1930
b. Mazursky, Paul

April 26, 1930
b. Friedman, Bruce Jay

April 28, 1930
b. Baker, James Addison, III

April 29, 1930
b. Humphry, Derek John

April 30, 1930
b. Guattari, Felix
b. Sarney, Jose

May 1, 1930
b. Hirsch, John Stephen
b. Matson, Ollie

May 2, 1930
b. Slade, Bernard

May 4, 1930
b. Peters, Roberta

May 5, 1930
b. Ward, Douglas Turner

May 6, 1930
b. Rykiel, Sonia
d. Gilpin, Charles Sidney

May 7, 1930
b. Fields, Totie

May 8, 1930
b. Atkins, Doug(las L)
b. Harper, Heather Mary

b. Scaasi, Arnold
b. Snyder, Gary Sherman

May 10, 1930
d. Stratemeyer, Edward L

May 11, 1930
b. Dijkstra, Edsger W(ybe)
b. Elkin, Stanley (Lawrence)

May 12, 1930
b. Kunene, Mazisi (Raymond)

May 13, 1930
b. Gravel, Mike

May 15, 1930
b. Johns, Jasper, (Jr.)
d. Locke, William John

May 16, 1930
b. Carter, Betty
b. Gulda, Friedrich

May 17, 1930
d. Croly, Herbert David

May 18, 1930
b. Roberts, Pernell
b. Rudman, Warren Bruce
b. Seed, Jenny

May 19, 1930
b. Hansberry, Lorraine

May 20, 1930
b. McEachin, James Elton

May 22, 1930
b. Lefall, LaSalle Doheny, Jr.
b. Marisol (Escobar)
b. Milk, Harvey

May 23, 1930
b. Anuszkiewicz, Richard Joseph
b. Kelman, Charles David

May 24, 1930
b. Meselson, Matthew Stanley

May 27, 1930
b. Barth, John (Simmons)
b. Sessions, William Steele
d. Ferrer, Gabriel (Francisco Victor)
   Miro

May 28, 1930
b. Drake, Frank Donald
b. Seaga, Edward Phillip George

May 30, 1930
b. Janklow, Morton Lloyd
d. Nansen, Fridtjof

May 31, 1930
b. Eastwood, Clint

June 1, 1930
b. Corley, Pat
b. Woodward, Edward

June 2, 1930
b. Conrad, Charles, Jr.
d. Bolitho, William

June 3, 1930
b. Bradley, Marion Zimmer

June 4, 1930
b. King, Morganna

June 8, 1930
b. Codron, Michael
b. Widerberg, Bo

June 9, 1930
b. Abruzzo, Ben(jamine Lou)
b. Kalb, Marvin Leonard

June 10, 1930
b. Mirabella, Grace
d. Harnack, Adolf von
d. Sperry, Elmer Ambrose

June 11, 1930
b. Gonzalez, Jose Ramon
b. Rangel, Charles Bernard
d. Folger, Henry Clay

June 12, 1930
b. Harris, Barbara Clementine

June 13, 1930
d. Segrave, Henry O'Neal de Hane,
   Sir

June 15, 1930
b. Pronovost, Marcel

June 16, 1930
b. Zsigmond, Vilmos

June 20, 1930
b. Craig, Wendy

June 21, 1930
b. Kaufman, Gerald Bernard
b. McCormack, Mike

June 22, 1930
b. Bonatti, Walter
b. Lindbergh, Charles Augustus

June 23, 1930
b. Dinitz, Simcha
b. Eisele, Donn Fulton

June 24, 1930
b. Chabrol, Claude
d. Jewett, Henry

June 27, 1930
b. Perot, H(enry) Ross

June 29, 1930
b. Evans, Bob
b. Fallaci, Oriana

June 30, 1930
b. Sowell, Thomas
d. Wiley, Harvey Washington

July 1, 1930
b. Menem, Carlos Saul

July 3, 1930
b. Fountain, Pete(r Dewey)
b. Kleiber, Carlos

July 4, 1930
b. Angelos, Peter
b. Steinbrenner, George Michael, III

July 6, 1930
b. Armstrong, George Edward
b. Mallet-Joris, Francoise
b. Skurzynski, Gloria

July 7, 1930
b. Jamal, Ahmad
d. Doyle, Arthur Conan, Sir

July 9, 1930
b. Iness, Sim

July 11, 1930
b. Bloom, Harold

July 12, 1930
b. Pinsent, Gordon Edward

July 14, 1930
b. Bergen, Polly
b. Simons, Elwyn L(aVerne)

July 15, 1930
b. Derrida, Jacques
d. Auer, Leopold
d. Barry, Leonora Marie Kearney

July 16, 1930
b. Giardello, Joey

July 19, 1930
b. Callahan, Daniel John

July 20, 1930
b. Daly, Chuck

July 21, 1930
b. Littler, Gene

July 23, 1930
b. Freed, James I(ngo)
b. Landrieu, Moon
d. Curtiss, Glenn Hammond

July 25, 1930
d. Vought, Chance Milton

July 27, 1930
b. Williams, Shirley

July 28, 1930
d. Gullstrand, Allvar

July 29, 1930
b. Perkoff, Stuart Z.
b. Taylor, Paul

July 30, 1930
d. Schildkraut, Rudolph

July 31, 1930
b. Popham, William James

August 1, 1930
b. Bart, Lionel
b. Eagleburger, Lawrence S.
b. Grosz, Karoly
b. Holder, Geoffrey

August 3, 1930
b. Popov, Oleg Konstantinovich

August 4, 1930
d. Wagner, Siegfried (Helferich)

August 5, 1930
b. Armstrong, Neil Alden
d. Alden, Isabella Macdonald

August 6, 1930
b. Duberman, Martin
b. Lincoln, Abbey

August 8, 1930
b. Mondale, Joan Adams
b. Talbot, Nita
b. Tarkanian, Jerry

August 9, 1930
b. Parizeau, Jacques

August 10, 1930
b. Goodman, George Jerome Waldo
b. Unsworth, Barry (Foster)

August 11, 1930
b. O'Neill, William Atchison
d. Angle, Edward Hartley

August 12, 1930
b. Borge Martinez, Tomas
b. Soros, George

August 13, 1930
b. Culp, Robert
b. Ho, Don

August 14, 1930
b. Weaver, Earl Sidney
d. Mayakovsky, Vladimir

August 15, 1930
b. Mboya, Tom

August 16, 1930
b. Gifford, Frank

August 17, 1930
b. Bennett, Harve
b. Hughes, Ted
b. Warren, Gerald Lee

August 19, 1930
b. McCourt, Frank

August 21, 1930
b. Margaret
b. Perry, Frank

August 22, 1930
b. Kirkwood, James

August 23, 1930
b. Miles, Vera
b. Rocard, Michel Louis Leon

August 25, 1930
b. Connery, Sean

August 26, 1930
d. Chaney, Lon

August 28, 1930
b. Gazzara, Ben
b. Rothwax, Harold

August 30, 1930
b. Buffett, Warren Edward
b. Clayton, Xernona
d. Allen, Henry Tureman

August 31, 1930
b. Donovan, Raymond James

September 1, 1930
b. Blumenthal, Monica David

September 5, 1930
d. Hagen, Johann Georg

September 7, 1930
b. Baudouin, I, King
b. Rollins, Sonny

September 8, 1930
b. Ky, Nguyen Cao

September 9, 1930
b. Morefield, Richard H

September 14, 1930
b. Bloom, Allan David

September 15, 1930
d. Sills, Milton

September 16, 1930
b. Francis, Anne
b. Trabert, Tony

September 17, 1930
b. Mitchell, Edgar Dean
b. Stafford, Thomas P(atten)

September 18, 1930
b. Kirk, Phyllis

September 19, 1930
b. Harris, Rosemary Ann

September 21, 1930
b. Addams, Dawn

September 22, 1930
b. Quint, Bert

September 23, 1930
b. Blakely, Colin (George Edward)
b. Charles, Ray
b. Weinberg, Chester

September 24, 1930
b. Langner, Nola

b. Young, John Watts
d. Mueller, Otto

September 26, 1930
b. Wunderlich, Fritz

September 27, 1930
b. Kipnis, Igor

September 28, 1930
d. Guggenheim, Daniel

September 29, 1930
b. Bonynge, Richard

October 1, 1930
b. Harris, Richard, Sir

October 3, 1930
b. Eden, Nicholas
b. Lee, Ming Cho

October 5, 1930
b. Popovich, Pavel Romanovich

October 6, 1930
b. Assad, Hafez al-

October 7, 1930
b. Dubinin, Yuri Vladimirovich

October 8, 1930
b. Ringgold, Faith
b. Takemitsu, Toru

October 9, 1930
b. Rounds, David

October 10, 1930
b. Pinter, Harold
b. Stevenson, Adlai Ewing, III
d. Engler, Adolph Gustav Heinrich

October 11, 1930
b. Bufman, Zev
b. Shevchenko, Arkady N(ikolayevich)

October 13, 1930
b. Geller, Bruce

October 14, 1930
b. Mobutu Sese Seko

October 15, 1930
b. McWherter, Ned Ray
d. Dow, Herbert Henry

October 17, 1930
b. Breslin, Jimmy

October 18, 1930
b. Carlucci, Frank Charles, III

October 20, 1930
b. Kountz, Samuel L(ee)

October 24, 1930
b. Big Bopper, The

October 25, 1930
b. Brodkey, Harold

b. Gray, Hanna (Holborn)

October 26, 1930
b. Arden, John
d. Whitney, Harry Payne

October 27, 1930
b. George, Bill

October 28, 1930
b. Fifield, Elaine
b. Morton, Bruce Alexander

October 29, 1930
d. Repin, Ilya Yefimovich

October 30, 1930
b. Almendros, Nestor
b. Pullein-Thompson, Diana

October 31, 1930
b. Collins, Mike
d. Wegener, Alfred Lothar

November 1, 1930
b. Gurney, A(lbert) R(amsdell), Jr.

November 2, 1930
d. Hay, Oliver Perry

November 3, 1930
b. Crane, Philip Miller

November 4, 1930
b. Groat, Dick
b. Reid, Kate
b. Roberts, Doris

November 5, 1930
b. Irving, Clifford Michael
b. Kennedy, Moorehead Cowell, Jr.
d. Eijkman, Christiaan

November 6, 1930
b. Bell, Derrick Albert, Jr.
b. McCormach, Mark Hume

November 7, 1930
b. Bell, Greg

November 8, 1930
b. Malavasi, Ray(mondo Guiseppi Giovanni Baptiste)

November 9, 1930
d. Bliss, Tasker Howard

November 10, 1930
b. Pendleton, Clarence McLane, Jr.
b. Watt, Richard Martin

November 11, 1930
b. Dresselhaus, Mildred S(piewak)

November 13, 1930
b. Harris, Fred Roy

November 14, 1930
b. Berge, Pierre (Vital Georges)
b. Ketelsen, James Lee
b. White, Ed(ward Higgins, III)

November 15, 1930
b. Ballard, J(ames) G(raham)

November 16, 1930
b. Achebe, Chinua
b. Groppi, James E

November 17, 1930
b. Amram, David Werner, III
b. Cook-Lynn, Elizabeth
b. Mathias, Bob

November 22, 1930
b. Garriott, Owen
b. Hall, Peter Reginald Frederick, Sir

November 23, 1930
b. Brock, Bill
b. Kazmaier, Richard W, Jr.

November 24, 1930
b. Friend, Bob
b. Wolsky, Albert

November 26, 1930
d. Sverdrup, Otto

November 30, 1930
b. Liddy, G(eorge) Gordon
d. Jones, Mary Harris

December 2, 1930
b. Becker, Gary S(tanley)
b. Silkin, Jon

December 3, 1930
b. Godard, Jean Luc
b. Williams, Andy

December 4, 1930
b. Kuenn, Harvey Edward

December 5, 1930
b. Estevez (de Galvez), Luis
b. Kert, Larry

December 6, 1930
b. Robustelli, Andy

December 8, 1930
b. Schell, Maximilian

December 9, 1930
b. Henry, Buck
b. Mejia Victores, Oscar Humberto
d. Foster, Rube

December 10, 1930
b. Yeutter, Clayton Keith

December 11, 1930
b. Trintignant, Jean-Louis Xavier

December 12, 1930
b. Beutel, Bill

December 13, 1930
b. Prosky, Robert Joseph
d. Pregl, Fritz

December 15, 1930
b. Sullivan, Haywood Cooper

December 17, 1930
b. Guccione, Bob
b. Meade, Julia
d. Heseltine, Philip Arnold

December 18, 1930
b. Skowron, Bill

December 24, 1930
b. De Patie, David H
b. Joffrey, Robert

December 26, 1930
b. Moffat, Donald
d. Hubbard, Kin

December 27, 1930
b. Greenfield, Meg
b. Sheed, Wilfrid John Joseph

December 31, 1930
b. Escalante, Jaime
b. Odetta

1931

b. Alcott, John
b. Blackburn, Molly
b. Bussotti, Sylvano
b. Cabral, Luis de Almeida
b. da Graca, Carlos Alberto Dias
b. Dwyer, Cynthia
b. Frank, Billy, Jr.
b. Gutfreund, Yosef
b. Japrisot, Sebastien
b. Keough, William Francis, Jr.
b. Lorring, Joan
b. Reichmann, Paul
b. Revard, Carter
b. Rhoades, Everett Ronald
b. Rorty, Richard (McKay)
b. Rozhdestvensky, Gennadi Nikolaevich
b. Rush, Richard
b. Russell, Herman J(erome)
b. Schaefer, Thomas E
b. Summerall, Pat
b. Tanen, Ned Stone
b. Van Eekelen, Willem Frederik
d. Clarke, Harry
d. Darracq, Alexandre
d. Forain, Jean-Louis
d. Henry, Edward Richard, Sir
d. Michelin, Andre
d. Scott, Edward Irvin
d. Whitcroft, Fred(rick)

January 2, 1931
b. Kaifu Toshiki
b. Kaifu Toshiki

January 4, 1931
d. Connor, Roger

January 5, 1931
b. Ailey, Alvin
b. Brendel, Alfred
b. Davis, Walter
b. Duvall, Robert (Selden)

January 6, 1931
b. Doctorow, E(dgar) L(aurence)

b. Moore, Dickie

January 7, 1931
b. Mattingly, Mack Francis
d. Channing, Edward Perkins

January 8, 1931
b. Graham, Bill

January 10, 1931
b. Barnes, Peter
b. Galella, Ron
b. Sanders, Marlene

January 11, 1931
b. Rodgers, Mary
d. Straus, Nathan

January 13, 1931
b. Hendry, Ian
b. Reilly, Charles Nelson
d. Joffre, Joseph Jacques Cesaire

January 15, 1931
b. Hoving, Thomas Pearsall Field

January 16, 1931
b. Rau, Johannes

January 17, 1931
b. Jones, James Earl
b. Wilder, Douglas
b. Zimmer, Don(ald William)

January 18, 1931
b. Lear, Evelyn

January 19, 1931
b. MacNeil, Robert Breckenridge Ware

January 20, 1931
b. Grant, Earl

January 21, 1931
d. Kahles, Charles William

January 22, 1931
b. Rayner, Claire Berenice

January 23, 1931
b. Chun Doo Hwan
d. Pavlova, Anna
d. Rubens, Alma

January 27, 1931
b. Richler, Mordecai

January 29, 1931
b. Bricusse, Leslie

January 30, 1931
b. Crosbie, John (Carnell)
b. Hackman, Gene
b. Hazzard, Shirley
b. McKinney, Stewart Brett

January 31, 1931
b. Banks, Ernie
b. Carbine, Patricia Theresa
b. Chataway, Christopher John

February 1, 1931
b. Yeltsin, Boris (Nikolayevich)

February 2, 1931
b. Agt, Andries Antonius Maria van
b. Viorst, Judith (Stahl)

February 3, 1931
b. Garner, Peggy Ann
b. Levitt, Arthur, Jr.

February 4, 1931
b. Peron, Isabel Martinez de

February 6, 1931
b. Torn, Rip
d. Nehru, Motilal

February 8, 1931
b. Dean, James Byron

February 9, 1931
b. Morris, Robert
d. Converse, Marquis M

February 11, 1931
b. Cooper, David (Graham)
d. Parsons, Charles Algernon, Sir

February 13, 1931
b. Klarsfeld, Beate

February 14, 1931
b. Geoffrion, Bernie

February 15, 1931
b. Bloom, Claire
b. Harris, LaDonna (Crawford)
b. Singer, Maxine (Frank)
d. Leitzel, Lillian

February 17, 1931
b. Craig, Roger Lee

February 18, 1931
b. Hart, Johnny
b. Morrison, Toni
b. St. Clair, Bob
d. Wolheim, Louis

February 20, 1931
b. Blake, Amanda
b. Paige, Emmett, Jr.

February 23, 1931
b. Wesselmann, Tom
d. Melba, Nellie, Dame

February 24, 1931
b. Abourezk, James George

February 26, 1931
b. Novak, Robert
b. Wiley, George A
d. Wallach, Otto

February 27, 1931
b. Wille, Frank

February 28, 1931
b. Smith, Dean Edwards

March 1, 1931
b. Dini, Lamberto

March 2, 1931
b. Gorbachev, Mikhail (Sergeyevich)
b. Wolfe, Tom

March 4, 1931
b. Cooper, Kenneth Hardy
b. Rivlin, Alice Mitchell

March 5, 1931
b. Cobb, Jerrie
b. Tuckwell, Barry Emmanuel

March 6, 1931
b. DeLavallade, Carmen
b. Needham, Hal

March 7, 1931
d. Doesburg, Theo van

March 8, 1931
b. McPhee, John (Angus)

March 9, 1931
b. Febres-Cordero, Leon
b. Hills, Roderick M

March 11, 1931
b. Eckert, Horst
b. Murdoch, Rupert
b. Walters, Peter Ingram, Sir
d. Murnau, Friedrich W

March 12, 1931
b. Kelleher, Herb(ert David)
b. Thomas, Billy

March 13, 1931
b. Berkowitz, Joan B.
b. Elias, Rosalind

March 14, 1931
b. Goalby, Bob

March 15, 1931
b. Mitchell, James

March 18, 1931
d. Johnson, Ban

March 20, 1931
b. Linden, Hal
d. Comstock, John Henry

March 22, 1931
b. Richter, Burton
b. Shatner, William
b. Vessels, Billy

March 23, 1931
d. Schmedes, Erik

March 24, 1931
d. Edeson, Robert

March 25, 1931
b. Haigh, Kenneth
d. Wells-Barnett, Ida Bell

March 26, 1931
b. Nimoy, Leonard
d. Healy, T(imothy) M(ichael)

March 27, 1931
b. Janssen, David
d. Bennett, Arnold

March 28, 1931
b. Rule, Jane

March 29, 1931
b. Tebbit, Norman Beresford

March 31, 1931
d. Rockne, Knute Kenneth

April 1, 1931
b. Hochhuth, Rolf

April 4, 1931
b. Inman, Bobby Ray

April 6, 1931
b. Dixon, Ivan

April 7, 1931
b. Barthelme, Donald
b. Ellsberg, Daniel
d. Chadwick, George Whitefield

April 8, 1931
b. Gavin, John Anthony Golenor
d. Karlfeldt, Erik Axel

April 9, 1931
b. Hatfield, Richard

April 10, 1931
b. Dozier, James Lee
b. Lary, Frank Strong
d. Gibran, Kahlil

April 13, 1931
b. Gurney, Dan

April 15, 1931
b. Gearhart, Sally (Miller)

April 19, 1931
b. Knight, Etheridge

April 20, 1931
b. Hamilton, Lee Herbert

April 22, 1931
b. Buchanan, John

April 23, 1931
b. Pettit, William Thomas

April 24, 1931
b. Riley, Bridget

April 26, 1931
b. Almond, Paul
d. Mead, George Herbert

April 27, 1931
b. Oistrakh, Igor Davidovich

April 29, 1931
b. Ball, William
b. Donegan, Lonnie
b. Gottlieb, Robert A(dams)

April 30, 1931
b. Clay, William Lacy

May 2, 1931
d. Baker, George Fisher

May 3, 1931
b. Layton, Joe

May 4, 1931
b. Kahng, Dawon

May 5, 1931
b. East, John Porter

May 6, 1931
b. Mays, Willie

May 7, 1931
b. Brewer, Teresa
b. Phelan, John Joseph

May 8, 1931
b. Scaasi, Arnold

May 9, 1931
b. Brand, Vance DeVoe
d. Michelson, Albert Abraham

May 11, 1931
d. Cole, Timothy

May 13, 1931
d. Ysaye, Eugene

May 14, 1931
d. Belasco, David

May 15, 1931
b. Califano, Joseph Anthony, Jr.
b. Venturi, Ken(neth)

May 16, 1931
b. Weicker, Lowell Palmer, Jr.

May 18, 1931
b. Morse, Robert Alan

May 20, 1931
b. Boyer, Ken(ton Lloyd)
b. Vassiliou, George (Vassos)

May 21, 1931
b. Frank, Anthony Melchior

May 23, 1931
b. Barrie, Barbara

May 26, 1931
b. Delblanc, Sven
b. Frey, Jim

May 27, 1931
b. Price, Kenny

May 28, 1931
b. Baker, Carroll
b. Birmingham, Stephen
b. Winkler, Irwin

May 29, 1931
b. Gordon, Ellen Rubin

May 31, 1931
b. Jones, Reverend Jim
b. Rossi, Aldo
b. Schrieffer, John Robert

June 3, 1931
b. Harvey, Anthony (Kesteven)
b. Lance, (Thomas) Bert(ram)

June 5, 1931
b. Demy, Jacques

June 6, 1931
b. Hickock, Richard Eugene

June 7, 1931
b. Driskell, David C(lyde)
b. McKenna, Virginia

June 11, 1931
d. Giddings, Franklin Henry

June 13, 1931
d. Kitasato Shibasaburo

June 14, 1931
b. Gibbs, Marla Bradley

June 16, 1931
b. Spong, John

June 17, 1931
b. Baldessari, John
b. Ing, Dean

June 18, 1931
b. Cardoso, Fernando Henrique

June 19, 1931
b. Lander, Toni

June 20, 1931
b. Dukakis, Olympia

June 21, 1931
b. Grossman, Lawrence K(ugelmass)
b. Heckler, Margaret Mary

June 22, 1931
b. Lipton, Martin

June 24, 1931
b. Casper, Billy

June 25, 1931
b. Singh, V(ishwanath) P(ratap)
d. Saunders, William Laurence

June 26, 1931
b. Wilson, Colin Henry

June 30, 1931
b. Davison, Ian Frederic Hay

July 1, 1931
b. Caron, Leslie Clare Margaret
b. Kountche, Seyni

July 2, 1931
b. Costello, Larry
b. Marcos, Imelda Romualdez
d. Babcock, Stephen Moulton

July 4, 1931
d. Husein ibn Ali

July 6, 1931
b. Reese, Della
d. Acheson, Edward Goodrich

July 8, 1931
b. Arledge, Roone Pinckney, Jr.
b. Ballard, Louis W.

July 10, 1931
b. Adams, Nick
b. Munro, Alice

July 11, 1931
b. Dalton, John Nichols
b. Hunter, Tab

July 12, 1931
d. Soderblom, Nathan

July 14, 1931
b. Stephens, Robert, Sir

July 15, 1931
b. Asencio, Diego Cortes

July 18, 1931
d. Minkowski, Oskar

July 23, 1931
b. Isozaki, Arata
b. Isozaki, Arata
b. Troell, Jan

July 25, 1931
b. Forrester, Maureen

July 26, 1931
b. Gorman, R(udolph) C(arl)

July 27, 1931
b. Van Dyke, Jerry

July 28, 1931
b. Hickman, Darryl

July 31, 1931
b. Ramsey, Frank Vernon, Jr.
b. Van Wachem, Lodewijk Christiaan

August 1, 1931
b. Connolly, Harold
b. Wilson, Tom

August 3, 1931
b. Cord, Alex

August 4, 1931
d. Williams, Daniel Hale

August 7, 1931
d. Beiderbecke, Bix

August 8, 1931
b. Penrose, Roger

August 9, 1931
b. Jackson, Hurricane

August 10, 1931
b. Perry, Carrie Saxon

August 12, 1931
b. Goldman, William

August 14, 1931
b. Raphael, Frederic Michael

August 15, 1931
b. Rule, Janice

August 16, 1931
b. Nettleton, Lois June
d. Walker, A'lelia

August 18, 1931
b. Chwast, Seymour
b. Kassorla, Irene Chamie

August 19, 1931
b. Shoemaker, Willie
d. Agramonte y Simoni, Aristides

August 20, 1931
b. King, Don(ald)

August 23, 1931
b. Smith, Hamilton Othanel

August 25, 1931
b. Andrus, Cecil D(ale)

August 26, 1931
d. Harris, Frank

August 27, 1931
b. Ghose, Sri Chinmoy Kumar
d. Smith, Francis Marion

August 28, 1931
b. Shirley-Quirk, John Stanton

August 30, 1931
b. Swigert, Jack

August 31, 1931
b. Beliveau, Jean (Marc A)
d. Caine, Hall

September 2, 1931
b. Simpson, Alan Kooi
d. Schalk, Franz

September 3, 1931
b. DeSalvo, Albert
b. Motta, Dick

September 4, 1931
b. Gaynor, Mitzi

September 8, 1931
b. Washam, Wisner McCamey

September 9, 1931
b. Tyzack, Margaret Maud

September 11, 1931
b. Damon, Cathryn
b. Moffett, Ken(neth Elwood)
d. Omar al-Mukhtar

September 12, 1931
b. Holm, Ian
b. Jones, George (Glenn)
b. Rogers, Adrian Pierce

September 13, 1931
b. Kennedy, Adrienne
b. Thomas, Elizabeth Marshall

September 14, 1931
b. Klima, Ivan

September 17, 1931
b. Bancroft, Anne

September 19, 1931
b. Benton, Brook
b. Calvet, Jacques
b. Danton, Ray(mond)
d. Jordan, David Starr

September 20, 1931
b. Palmer, Peter

September 21, 1931
b. Hagman, Larry

September 22, 1931
b. Weldon, Fay

September 23, 1931
b. Maunick, Edouard Joseph Marc
b. Suzuki, Pat

September 24, 1931
b. Adams, Tom
b. Collins, Cardiss (Hortense
   Robertson)
b. Newley, Anthony (George)

September 25, 1931
b. Cronin, James Watson
b. Walters, Barbara

September 29, 1931
b. Ekberg, Anita
d. Orpen, William Newneham, Sir

September 30, 1931
b. Dickinson, Angie

October 2, 1931
d. Lipton, Thomas Johnstone, Sir
d. Nielsen, Carl August

October 3, 1931
b. Hall, Glenn Henry

October 5, 1931
d. Johnston, Annie Fellows
d. Morrow, Dwight Whitney

October 6, 1931
b. Graham, Fred P(atterson)
d. Fillmore, Myrtle Page

October 7, 1931
b. Stewart, Ellen
b. Tutu, Desmond (Mpilo)
d. French, Daniel Chester

October 8, 1931
b. Kerr, Malcolm (Hooper)
d. Monash, John

October 13, 1931
b. Dennis, Jack B(onnell)
b. Mathews, Eddie

October 15, 1931
b. Foster, Paul

October 16, 1931
b. Colson, Chuck

October 18, 1931
d. Edison, Thomas Alva

October 19, 1931
b. LeCarre, John

October 20, 1931
b. Caliguiri, Richard
b. Mantle, Mickey (Charles)

October 21, 1931
b. Royer, William Blackburn, Jr.
d. Schnitzler, Arthur

October 22, 1931
b. Hanley, William

October 23, 1931
b. Bunning, Jim
b. Clark, William P(atrick Jr.)
b. Davis, Margaret B(ryan)
b. Dors, Diana

October 25, 1931
b. Girardot, Annie

October 26, 1931
d. Comiskey, Charlie

October 30, 1931
b. Araskog, Rand Vincent

October 31, 1931
b. Grant, Lee
b. Rather, Dan(iel Irvin)
b. Lissouba, Pascal

November 3, 1931
b. Lewis, Drew
b. Vitti, Monica

November 4, 1931
b. Hood, Darla Jean
b. Law, Bernard Francis, Cardinal
d. Bolden, Buddy

November 5, 1931
b. Pickering, Thomas (Reeve)
b. Turner, Ike

d. Rolvaag, Ole Edvart

November 6, 1931
b. Nichols, Mike
d. Chesbro, Jack

November 7, 1931
d. Derricotte, Juliette Aline

November 8, 1931
b. Safer, Morley

November 9, 1931
b. Herzog, Whitey
b. Lipscomb, Eugene
d. Lewis, Isaac Newton

November 12, 1931
b. Slotnick, Daniel Leonid

November 15, 1931
b. Kerr, John

November 16, 1931
b. Gibson, Bob

November 18, 1931
b. Goizueta, Roberto C(rispulo)

November 23, 1931
b. Keen, Sam

November 26, 1931
b. Perez Esquivel, Adolfo

November 27, 1931
d. Bruce, David, Sir

November 28, 1931
b. Ungerer, Tomi

November 30, 1931
b. Walsh, Bill
d. Walters, Henry

December 1, 1931
b. Sovern, Michael I(ra)

December 2, 1931
b. Calder, Nigel David Ritchie
b. Meese, Edwin, III
d. Indy, Paul (Marie Theodore Vincent d')

December 4, 1931
b. Delvecchio, Alex Peter
d. Zorrilla de San Martin, Juan

December 5, 1931
b. Cleveland, James
d. Lindsay, Vachel

December 7, 1931
b. Cottrell, Comer J(oseph), Jr.
b. Goodwin, Richard N(aradhof)

December 9, 1931
b. Hagan, Cliff(ord Oldham)
b. Reynolds, William

December 11, 1931
b. Moreno, Rita
b. Pilote, Pierre Paul
b. Rajneesh, Bhagwan Shree
b. Rothenberg, Jerome

December 13, 1931
b. Johnson, F(rederick) Ross
d. Le Bon, Gustave

December 14, 1931
b. Shrontz, Frank Anderson

December 15, 1931
b. O'Brien, Edna

December 18, 1931
b. Shue, Gene
d. Diamond, Legs
d. Van Heusen, John

December 19, 1931
b. Clark, J.E.

December 25, 1931
b. Castaneda, Carlos
b. Lewis, Byron E(ugene)

December 26, 1931
d. Dewey, Melvil

December 27, 1931
b. Phieu, Le Kha
b. Tomlinson, Jill

December 28, 1931
b. Milner, Martin Sam

December 30, 1931
b. Davis, Skeeter
d. Power, Tyrone

December 31, 1931
b. Baker, Gwendolyn Calvert

1932

b. Ahern, Thomas Leo, Jr.
b. al-Turabi, Hassan
b. Anders, Merry
b. Appelfeld, Aharon
b. Begay, Fred
b. Bell, Tom
b. Calero (Portocarrero), Adolfo
b. Carmel, Roger C
b. DeGennes, Pierre-Gilles
b. Downey, Morton, Jr.
b. Duncan, Sheena
b. Englund, Richard
b. Fry, Art
b. Garavani, Valentino
b. Hardwick, Billy
b. Houston, Cissy
b. Johnson, Norma L. Holloway
b. Lancetti, Pino
b. Lawrence, Andrea Mead
b. Makem, Tommy
b. Marvin, Michelle Triola
b. McTaggart, David
b. Morgan, Dodge
b. Obomsawin, Alanis

b. Okigbo, Christopher
(Ifenayichukwu)
b. Roth, Ann
b. Sanchez de Lozada, Gonzalo
b. Schily, Otto
b. Shalit, Gene
b. Shapira, Amitzur
b. Siebert, Muriel
b. Streithorst, Tom
b. Thani, Shiekh Khalifa Ben Hamad
al
d. Booth, Joseph
d. Duesenberg, Frederick S
d. Hoover, William K
d. Maurer, Alfred Henry
d. Santos-Dumont, Alberto
d. Wallas, Graham
d. Warburg, Paul Moritz

January 1, 1932
b. Carlino, Lewis John
b. Moore, Terry
d. Scott, Charles Prestwich

January 2, 1932
b. Little, (Flora) Jean

January 3, 1932
b. Coleman, Dabney W
b. Fenten, D X

January 4, 1932
b. Saura (Atares), Carlos

January 5, 1932
b. Eco, Umberto
b. Gorbachev, Raisa (Maksimovna
Titorenko)
b. Layden, Frank
b. Noll, Chuck

January 6, 1932
d. Rosenwald, Julius

January 7, 1932
d. Maginot, Andre Louis Rene

January 9, 1932
b. Casey, Robert P

January 12, 1932
d. King, Grace Elizabeth

January 14, 1932
b. Andersson, Harriet

January 16, 1932
b. Berry, Jim
b. Cox, Jean
b. Fossey, Dian

January 17, 1932
d. Gore, Charles

January 18, 1932
b. Schmidt, Joe

January 19, 1932
b. Lester, Richard
b. MacBeth, George Mann

January 20, 1932
b. Carr, Martin

January 21, 1932
b. Chaney, John
d. Strachey, (Giles) Lytton

January 22, 1932
b. Laurie, Piper

January 26, 1932
b. Clements, George Harold
d. Wrigley, William, Jr.

January 28, 1932
b. O'Brien, Parry

February 1, 1932
b. Hart, John Richard
b. Nott, John William Frederic, Sir

February 2, 1932
b. Mandan, Robert

February 4, 1932
b. Coover, Robert (Lowell)

February 5, 1932
b. Kalb, Bernard

February 6, 1932
b. Truffaut, Francois
d. Leguia y Salcedo, Augusto
Bernardino

February 7, 1932
b. Talese, Gay
b. Worden, Alfred Merrill

February 8, 1932
b. Williams, John Towner

February 9, 1932
b. Richter, Gerhard

February 10, 1932
b. Rockin' Dopsie
d. Wallace, Edgar

February 12, 1932
b. Lutz, Robert Anthony

February 13, 1932
b. Bergerac, Michel C

February 14, 1932
b. Schroeder, William J

February 16, 1932
b. Kabbah, (Alhaji) Ahmad Tejan
b. Wyler, Gretchen
d. Buisson, Ferdinand Edouard
d. Fiske, Minnie Maddern

February 17, 1932
d. Kelley, Florence

February 18, 1932
b. Forman, Milos
b. Michals, Duane Steven

February 19, 1932
b. Kerwin, Joseph Peter

February 20, 1932
b. Sidaris, Andy

February 22, 1932
b. Kennedy, Edward Moore
d. Gadski, Johanna

February 24, 1932
b. Legrand, Michel Jean
b. Miller, Zell (Bryan)
b. Okamura, Arthur
b. Sandrich, Jay H
b. Vernon, John

February 25, 1932
b. Young, Faron
d. Mathiez, Albert

February 26, 1932
b. Cash, Johnny

February 27, 1932
b. Solomon, Neil
b. Taylor, Elizabeth Rosemond

February 29, 1932
d. Teschemacher, Frank

March 1, 1932
d. Lindbergh, Charles Augustus

March 2, 1932
b. Bauer, Peggy

March 3, 1932
d. D'Albert, Eugene

March 4, 1932
b. Kapuscinski, Ryszard
b. Makeba, Miriam
d. Plenty Coups

March 6, 1932
d. Sousa, John Philip

March 7, 1932
b. Olter, Bailey
d. Briand, Aristide

March 9, 1932
b. Smith, Keely

March 11, 1932
b. Lawson, Nigel
d. Campana, Dino

March 12, 1932
b. Houbregs, Bob
b. Young, Andrew Jackson, Jr.
d. Kreuger, Ivar

March 14, 1932
b. Blyton, Carey
b. Morrisseau, Norval
d. Eastman, George
d. Turner, Frederick Jackson

March 15, 1932
b. Bean, Alan L

March 16, 1932
b. Cunningham, R Walter

d. Monro, Harold Edward

March 18, 1932
b. Updike, John (Hoyer)
d. Olcott, Chauncey

March 19, 1932
b. Brewer, Gay, Jr.

March 21, 1932
b. Gilbert, Walter

March 25, 1932
b. Gilliatt, Penelope (Ann Douglas Conner)
b. Marriott, John Willard, Jr.
b. Santee, Wes
b. Wilkins, Roger (Wood)

March 26, 1932
b. Harris, James Andrew
d. Leland, Henry Martyn

March 31, 1932
b. Jakes, John (William)
b. McCann, Elizabeth Ireland
b. Oshima, Nagisa

April 1, 1932
b. Reynolds, Debbie (Marie Frances)

April 2, 1932
d. Coghlan, Rose

April 3, 1932
b. Stevens, George, Jr.

April 4, 1932
b. Davis, Clive Jay
b. Lugar, Richard Green
b. Tarkovsky, Andrei (Arsenyich)
d. Ostwald, Friedrich Wilhelm

April 8, 1932
b. Antall, Jozsef, Jr.

April 9, 1932
b. Krassner, Paul
b. Perkins, Carl (Lee)

April 10, 1932
b. Rhodes, Hari
b. Sharif, Omar

April 11, 1932
b. Grey, Joel
d. Bradford, Gamaliel

April 12, 1932
b. Gelber, Jack
b. Rosen, Moishe Martin
d. Bauer, Louis Agricola

April 13, 1932
b. Letelier, Orlando

April 14, 1932
b. Bennett, William
b. Perkins, Anthony
d. Burns, William John

April 16, 1932
d. Geddes, Patrick, Sir

April 19, 1932
b. Botero, Fernando
b. Mansfield, Jayne
d. Cheyne, William Watson, Sir

April 20, 1932
d. Peano, Giuseppe

April 21, 1932
b. May, Elaine
b. Melnick, Daniel
d. Pickett, Bill

April 22, 1932
b. Lane, Kenneth Jay

April 23, 1932
b. Fixx, James Fuller
b. Halston

April 24, 1932
b. Rockefeller, Rodman C
b. Young, John Alan

April 25, 1932
b. Lemon, Meadowlark

April 27, 1932
b. Botha, Roelof Frederik
b. Knox, Chuck
d. Crane, Hart

May 3, 1932
d. Fort, Charles Hoy

May 5, 1932
b. Hutchins, Will

May 7, 1932
b. Domenici, Pete V(ichi)
b. Hogrogian, Nonny
b. Kingsley, Pat(ricia)
d. Crowder, Enoch Herbert

May 8, 1932
b. Liston, Sonny

May 10, 1932
b. Miles, Tichi Wilkerson

May 11, 1932
b. Valentino

May 12, 1932
b. Baby Leroy
b. Mitchell, David

May 14, 1932
b. Estes, Richard
b. Richards, Richard

May 15, 1932
b. Chavalit Yongchaiyudh
b. Gibson, Kenneth Allen
d. Inukai, Tsuyoshi

May 16, 1932
d. Dollar, Robert

May 19, 1932
b. Erdman, Paul E(mil)

May 21, 1932
b. Wakefield, Dan

May 22, 1932
d. Gregory, Isabella Augusta Persse, Lady

May 24, 1932
b. Malbin, Elaine
b. Wesker, Arnold
d. McMaster, John Bach

May 25, 1932
b. Bowen, Roger
b. Dunne, John Gregory
b. Jones, KC

May 26, 1932
b. Altobelli, Joe

May 29, 1932
b. Ehrlich, Paul
b. Guerin, Richard V

May 31, 1932
b. Briggs, Fred

June 1, 1932
b. Lasch, Christopher

June 2, 1932
b. Gayle, Addison, Jr.

June 4, 1932
b. Barrymore, John Blythe Drew, Jr.
b. McNamara, John Francis
b. Wolfe, Digby

June 5, 1932
b. Brown, Christy

June 6, 1932
b. Chermayeff, Ivan
b. Scott, David Randolph
b. Whitelaw, Billie

June 7, 1932
d. Keen, William Williams

June 8, 1932
b. Wynter, Dana

June 9, 1932
b. Wilson, Jackie

June 10, 1932
b. Johnston, J. Bennett, Jr.

June 11, 1932
b. Fugard, Athol

June 12, 1932
b. Jaffe, Rona
b. Nabors, Jim

June 15, 1932
b. Cuomo, Mario Matthew
b. Roberts, Gene

June 16, 1932
d. Eeden, Fredrik Willem van

June 17, 1932
b. Murtha, John Patrick

June 18, 1932
b. Herschbach, Dudley Robert
b. Hill, Geoffrey

June 19, 1932
b. Pavan, Marisa
d. Plaatje, Sol(omon) T(shekisho)

June 20, 1932
b. Baird, Bill

June 21, 1932
b. Schifrin, Lalo Claudio
b. Strong, James Matthew
d. Winton, Alexander

June 26, 1932
d. Duffy, Francis Patrick

June 28, 1932
b. Morita, Pat

June 30, 1932
b. Beti, Mongo
b. Biyidi, Alexandre

July 1, 1932
b. Duffey, Joseph Daniel

July 2, 1932
b. Thomas, Dave
d. Gamble, James Norris

July 5, 1932
b. Backe, John David
b. Horn, Gyula
b. Navasky, Victor Saul

July 6, 1932
d. Grahame, Kenneth

July 8, 1932
b. Vale, Jerry

July 9, 1932
b. Rumsfeld, Donald (Harold)
d. Gillette, King Camp

July 13, 1932
b. Commager, Steele
d. Stephens, Alice Barber

July 14, 1932
b. Grier, Rosey

July 16, 1932
b. Protopopov, Oleg Alekseevich
b. Thornburgh, Dick

July 17, 1932
b. Riney, Hal (Patrick)

July 20, 1932
b. Banharn Silpa-archa
b. Paik, Nam June

July 21, 1932
d. Bazin, Rene

July 22, 1932
b. DeLaRenta, Oscar
b. Terry, Megan
d. Fessenden, Reginald Aubrey
d. Ziegfeld, Flo(renz)

July 27, 1932
b. Blair, David

July 29, 1932
b. Kassebaum, Nancy Landon

July 31, 1932
b. Gittings, Barbara

August 1, 1932
b. Kahane, Meir David

August 2, 1932
b. Ben-Elissar, Eliahu
b. Boivin, Leo Joseph
b. Hunt, Lamar
b. O'Toole, Peter

August 3, 1932
d. Brouthers, Dan

August 4, 1932
d. Oppenheim, James

August 6, 1932
b. Carriere, Jean-Claude
b. Ford, Doug
b. Hodgkin, Howard

August 8, 1932
b. Culver, John Chester
b. Montagnier, Luc
b. Tillis, Mel(vin)

August 9, 1932
b. Halberstam, Michael Joseph

August 11, 1932
b. Arrabal (Teran), Fernando
b. Eisenman, Peter

August 14, 1932
b. Meehan, Thomas Edward

August 16, 1932
b. Gorme, Eydie
b. VonFurstenberg, Betsy

August 17, 1932
b. Kerr, Red
b. Naipaul, V(idiahar) S(urajprasad)

August 19, 1932
b. Cohen, Joan Lebold

August 20, 1932
b. Aksyonov, Vassily Pavlovich

August 21, 1932
b. Van Peebles, Melvin

August 22, 1932
b. Aldredge, Theoni (Athanasiou)
   V(achliotis)
b. Carr, Gerald Paul

August 23, 1932
b. Johnson, Howard Brennan
b. Russell, Mark

August 25, 1932
b. Goldberg, Bernard

August 26, 1932
b. Engle, Joe Henry

August 27, 1932
b. Fraser, Antonia Pakenham, Lady

August 28, 1932
b. Bathgate, Andy
d. Nougues, Jean

August 29, 1932
b. Valeriani, Richard Gerard
b. Bannon, Ann

September 1, 1932
b. Von Bulow, Sunny

September 4, 1932
d. Bern, Paul

September 5, 1932
d. LaFlesche, Francis

September 6, 1932
d. Parker, Gilbert, Sir

September 7, 1932
b. Bradbury, Malcolm Stanley

September 8, 1932
b. Cline, Patsy

September 9, 1932
b. Miles, Sylvia

September 10, 1932
b. Goldman, Bo

September 11, 1932
b. Packwood, Bob

September 13, 1932
b. Bain, Barbara

September 15, 1932
b. Bartlett, Neil

September 16, 1932
d. Ross, Ronald, Sir

September 17, 1932
b. Parker, Robert B(rown)

September 19, 1932
b. Royko, Mike
b. Wille, Lois Jean

September 22, 1932
b. Brazauskas, Algirdas (Mykolas)

b. Johansson, Ingemar

September 23, 1932
b. Manley, Joan Adele Daniels

September 24, 1932
b. Beriosova, Svetlana
b. Greenberg, Joanne

September 25, 1932
b. Gould, Glenn Herbert
b. Silverstein, Shel(by)
b. Suarez Gonsales, Adolfo

September 26, 1932
d. Davenport, Eva

September 29, 1932
b. Benton, Robert Douglass
b. Pfeiffer, Jane Cahill
d. Wovoka

September 30, 1932
b. Podres, Johnny

October 1, 1932
b. Collins, Albert

October 2, 1932
b. Wills, Maury

October 4, 1932
b. Davignon, Viscount
b. Farr, Felicia

October 5, 1932
b. Burke, Yvonne Watson Brathwaite

October 9, 1932
b. Plowden, David

October 11, 1932
b. Friedlander, Saul
b. West, Dottie

October 12, 1932
b. Garn, Jake
b. Gregory, Dick

October 14, 1932
b. Siegel, Bernie S(hepard)
d. Bonstelle, Jessie
d. Todd, Mabel Loomis

October 16, 1932
b. Lewis, Henry (Jay)

October 18, 1932
b. Landsbergis, Vytautas

October 19, 1932
b. Reed, Robert

October 20, 1932
b. Brown, Roosevelt
b. Christopher, William
b. McClure, Michael Thomas

October 23, 1932
b. Barfield, Velma
b. Zimmerman, Paul L

October 24, 1932
b. Covey, Stephen R.
b. Dorfman, Dan
b. Lattner, Johnny

October 27, 1932
b. Plath, Sylvia

October 28, 1932
b. Kyprianou, Spyros Achilles

October 29, 1932
b. Kitaj, R(onald) B(rooks)

October 30, 1932
b. Malle, Louis

November 1, 1932
b. Arbour, Al(ger Joseph)
b. Arinze, Francis Cardinal

November 2, 1932
b. Mazzoli, Romano L
b. Namphy, Henri
b. Schwartz, Melvin

November 3, 1932
b. Reynolds, Albert

November 4, 1932
b. Klestil, Thomas
b. Pitlik, Noam

November 5, 1932
b. Jacobs, Sally
b. Liman, Arthur L(awrence)

November 6, 1932
b. Castle, Wendell Keith

November 8, 1932
b. Aganbegyan, Abel Gezevich
b. Audran, Stephane
b. Bova, Ben(jamin William)

November 9, 1932
b. Christy, Marian

November 12, 1932
b. Forman, James Douglas

November 13, 1932
b. Connolly, Olga Fikotova
b. Mulligan, Richard

November 15, 1932
b. Clark, Petula
d. Brookings, Robert Somers
d. Chesnutt, Charles Waddell

November 16, 1932
b. Kelly, Thomas

November 20, 1932
b. Dawson, Richard

November 21, 1932
b. Ringo, Jim

November 22, 1932
b. Vaughn, Robert
d. Atkinson, William Walker

November 23, 1932
b. Toye, Clive Roy
d. Pitt, Percy

November 26, 1932
d. MacDonald, J(ames) E(dward)
H(ervey)

November 27, 1932
b. Aquino, Benigno Simeon, Jr.

November 28, 1932
d. Van Rooy, Anton

November 29, 1932
b. Chirac, Jacques (Rene)
b. Gary, John
b. Ladd, Diane

November 30, 1932
d. Melchers, Gari
b. Diggs-Taylor, Anna

December 3, 1932
b. Morgan, Jaye P

December 4, 1932
b. Cheek, James Edward
b. Roh Tae Woo

December 5, 1932
b. Glashow, Sheldon Lee

December 7, 1932
b. Burstyn, Ellen
d. Brieux, Eugene

December 9, 1932
b. Byrd, Donald
b. Hartack, Billy

December 12, 1932
b. Pettit, Bob

December 13, 1932
d. Holland, William Jacob

December 14, 1932
b. Lane, Abbe
b. Rich, Charlie

December 16, 1932
b. Blake, Quentin
b. Shchedrin, Rodion Konstantinovich

December 18, 1932
b. Smith, Roger
d. Bernstein, Eduard

December 19, 1932
d. Whitehill, Clarence Eugene

December 20, 1932
b. Hillerman, John Benedict

December 21, 1932
b. Hoagland, Edward Morley

December 24, 1932
b. Cowdrey, (Michael) Colin

December 28, 1932
b. Haber, Joyce
b. Howell, Harry
b. Puig, Manuel

December 29, 1932
b. Swenson, Inga

1933

b. Bradford, Barbara Taylor
b. Daniell, Robert F
b. Davidson, Bruce
b. Davis, (Thomas) Cullen
b. Deckers, Jeanine
b. Fairuz
b. Gibson, William F(rank)
b. Gilliam, Sam, (Jr.)
b. Itami, Juzo
b. Kasem, Casey (Kemal Amin)
b. Lai, Francis
b. Moore, William
b. Nichols, Nichelle
b. Rajai, Mohammed Ali
b. Reed, Frank H
b. Roszak, Theodore
b. Roxon, Lillian
b. Schneider, Bert
b. Scott, Charles Wesly
b. Shariati, Ali
b. Stempel, Robert
b. Uhnak, Dorothy
d. Bonvalot, Pierre Gabriel Edouard
d. Cavafy, C(onstantine) P(eter)
d. Hills, Austin H
d. Irigoyen, Hipolito
d. Lease, Mary Elizabeth Clyens
d. Pitney, Arthur

January 1, 1933
b. Orton, Joe

January 2, 1933
b. Riley, Richard W(ilson)

January 3, 1933
d. Pickford, Jack

January 4, 1933
b. Bangerter, Norman Howard

January 5, 1933
d. Coolidge, Calvin

January 7, 1933
b. Kneip, Richard F

January 8, 1933
b. Osgood, Charles

January 13, 1933
b. Gallo, Frank
b. Gola, Tom
b. Goulart, Ron(ald Joseph)

January 14, 1933
b. Brakhage, Stan

January 15, 1933
b. Gaines, Ernest J(ames)

January 16, 1933
b. Sontag, Susan

January 17, 1933
b. Aga Khan, Sadruddin, Prince
b. North, Sheree
d. Tiffany, Louis Comfort

January 18, 1933
b. Boorman, John
b. Dolby, Ray M(ilton)

January 21, 1933
b. Wrigley, William, III
d. Moore, George Augustus

January 23, 1933
b. Rivera, Chita

January 24, 1933
b. Beatty, Roger

January 25, 1933
b. Aquino, Corazon (Cojuangco)

January 26, 1933
d. Belmont, Alva Erskine Smith
Vanderbilt
d. Gummere, William Stryker

January 27, 1933
b. Buss, Jerry Hatten

January 28, 1933
d. Saintsbury, George Edward
Bateman
d. Teasdale, Sara

January 30, 1933
b. Brautigan, Richard
b. Rukeyser, Louis (Richard)
b. Sinkford, Jeanne C(raig)

January 31, 1933
d. Galsworthy, John

February 1, 1933
b. Anderson, Wendell Richard
b. Price, Reynolds

February 3, 1933
b. Sarbanes, Paul S(pyros)

February 5, 1933
b. King, Claude
d. Mizner, Addison

February 6, 1933
b. Fauntroy, Walter E(dward)
b. Van Doren, Mamie

February 10, 1933
b. Schickel, Richard

February 12, 1933
d. Robertson, William Robert, Sir

February 13, 1933
b. Costa-Gavras
b. Ungaro, Emanuel Matteotti

February 14, 1933
b. Cook, Michael

February 15, 1933
b. Adolfo

February 17, 1933
b. Thomas, Craig

February 18, 1933
b. Novak, Kim
b. Ono, Yoko
b. Ure, Mary
d. Corbett, James John

February 19, 1933
b. Biya, Paul

February 20, 1933
b. Christian, Mary Blount

February 21, 1933
b. Simone, Nina

February 23, 1933
b. Calhoun, Lee

February 24, 1933
b. Mazrui, Ali A(l'Amin)

February 26, 1933
b. Cambridge, Godfrey
b. Goldsmith, James (Michael), Sir

February 27, 1933
b. Berry, Raymond Emmett
b. Wallop, Malcolm

February 28, 1933
b. Furie, Sidney J

March 2, 1933
b. Dillon, Leo
d. Walsh, Thomas James

March 3, 1933
b. Irvin, Robert W
b. Radziwill, Lee Bouvier

March 6, 1933
d. Cermak, Anton Joseph

March 11, 1933
b. Rosen, Benjamin M(aurice)

March 13, 1933
b. Dillon, Diane Claire Sorber

March 14, 1933
b. Caine, Michael
b. Jones, Quincy Delight

March 15, 1933
b. DeBroca, Philippe Claude Alex
b. Ginsburg, Ruth Bader
b. Taylor, Cecil Percival

March 16, 1933
b. Weill, Sanford I.

March 17, 1933
b. Evers-Williams, Myrlie
b. Janifer, Laurence M(ark)
b. Lively, Penelope
b. Van Vooren, Monique

March 18, 1933
b. Blackwell, Unita
d. Abruzzi, Luigi Amedeo

March 19, 1933
b. Roth, Philip (Milton)

March 21, 1933
b. Heseltine, Michael Ray Dibdin
d. Zangara, Joseph

March 22, 1933
b. Bani-Sadr, Abolhassan
b. Britt, May
b. McCarthy, J(oseph) P(riestley)

March 23, 1933
b. Jenkins, Hayes Alan

March 26, 1933
b. Deloria, Vine (Victor), Jr.
d. Lang, Eddie

March 28, 1933
b. Murkowski, Frank Hughes

April 1, 1933
d. Chelmsford, Frederic John Napier
Thesiger, 1st Viscount Chelmsford

April 2, 1933
b. Konrad, Gyorgy

April 4, 1933
d. Custer, Elizabeth Bacon

April 5, 1933
d. Biggers, Earl Derr

April 6, 1933
b. Snyder, Richard Elliot

April 7, 1933
b. Rogers, Wayne

April 8, 1933
b. Ebb, Fred

April 9, 1933
b. Belmondo, Jean-Paul

April 10, 1933
d. Vandyke, Henry Jackson, Jr.

April 11, 1933
b. Brown, Tony

April 12, 1933
b. Caballe, Montserrat Folch
b. Lau, Charlie
d. Ames, Adelbert
d. Nuttall, Zelia Maria Magdalena

April 13, 1933
b. Campbell, Ben Nighthorse

April 15, 1933
b. Clark, Roy Linwood
b. Montgomery, Elizabeth

April 16, 1933
b. Pappas, Ike
b. Wallis, Shani

April 19, 1933
b. Sargent, Dick

April 20, 1933
d. Kilgour, Joseph

April 22, 1933
b. Kalfin, Robert
d. Royce, Frederick Henry, Sir

April 23, 1933
b. McKuen, Rod Marvin
d. Keefe, Tim(othy John)

April 24, 1933
b. Eagleson, Alan
d. Adler, Felix

April 25, 1933
b. Lukas, J(ay) Anthony

April 26, 1933
b. Burnett, Carol
b. Penzias, Arno Allan

April 28, 1933
b. Faas, Horst
b. Jones, Carolyn

April 29, 1933
d. Dharmapala, Anagarika

April 30, 1933
b. Nelson, Willie
b. Vendler, Helen Hennessy
d. Whitechurch, Victor Lorenzo

May 1, 1933
b. Camdessus, Michel (Jean)

May 3, 1933
b. Weinberg, Steven

May 7, 1933
b. Unitas, Johnny

May 8, 1933
b. El-Sayed, Mostafa Amr

May 10, 1933
d. Kurz, Selma

May 11, 1933
b. Farrakhan, Louis

May 13, 1933
b. Roseboro, Johnny
d. Ernst, Paul Karl Friedrich

May 15, 1933
d. Torrence, Ernest

May 18, 1933
b. Gowda, H(aradanahalli) D(odde)
Deve

May 19, 1933
b. Feelings, Tom
b. Poniatowska, Elena

May 23, 1933
b. Browning, John
b. Collins, Joan Henrietta

May 25, 1933
b. Panday, Basdeo

May 26, 1933
d. Rodgers, Jimmie

May 28, 1933
b. Karlen, John
d. Loeb, James Morris

May 30, 1933
b. Perryman, Jill

May 31, 1933
b. Sedelmaier, Joe
b. Verrett, Shirley Carter

June 1, 1933
b. Ameche, Alan Dante

June 4, 1933
b. al-Khalifa, Sheikh Isa Bin Sulman
d. Ahmed Hasim

June 6, 1933
b. Rohrer, Heinrich

June 7, 1933
b. Score, Herb(ert Jude)
d. Curtis, Cyrus Hermann Kotszchmar

June 10, 1933
b. Bailey, F(rancis) Lee
b. Fairbanks, Chuck

June 14, 1933
b. Kosinski, Jerzy (Nikodem)
d. Pollack, Egon

June 17, 1933
b. Hunt, Guy

June 19, 1933
b. Angeli, Pier
b. Patsayev, Viktor Ivanovich

June 20, 1933
b. Aiello, Danny Louis, Jr.
b. Landau, Martin
d. Zetkin, Clara

June 21, 1933
b. Kopell, Bernie

June 22, 1933
b. Feinstein, Dianne

June 24, 1933
b. Jones, Sam(uel)
d. Jones, Matilda Sissieretta Joyner

June 25, 1933
b. Meredith, James Howard
b. Siza, Alvaro (Joaquim Melo)

June 26, 1933
b. Abbado, Claudio

June 29, 1933
b. Bradshaw, John Elliot
b. Sutton, Carol
d. Arbuckle, Fatty

July 1, 1933
b. Young, Jean Childs

July 7, 1933
b. McCullough, David Gaub

July 8, 1933
b. Feldman, Marty
d. Hope-Hawkins, Anthony, Sir

July 9, 1933
b. Sacks, Oliver Wolf
b. Smith, Hedrick Laurence

July 10, 1933
b. De Gaetani, Jan
b. Hatcher, Richard Gordon
b. Herman, Jerry
d. Arnold, Harold De Forest
d. Urban, Joseph Maria

July 12, 1933
b. Westlake, Donald E(dwin) Edmund

July 13, 1933
b. Bourassa, (Jean) Robert
b. Storey, David Malcolm

July 15, 1933
b. Bream, Julian Alexander
d. Babbitt, Irving
d. Keppard, Freddie

July 18, 1933
b. Evtushenko, Evgeniy Alexandrovich
b. Yevtushenko, Yevgeny

July 20, 1933
b. Doubleday, Nelson

July 21, 1933
b. Gardner, John Champlin, Jr.

July 22, 1933
b. Trotman, Alexander J.
d. Walker, Emery, Sir

July 23, 1933
b. Convy, Bert
b. Rogers, Richard
d. Schillings, Max von

July 29, 1933
b. Reuben, David Robert

July 30, 1933
b. Byrnes, Edd

August 1, 1933
b. DeLuise, Dom

b. Love, Iris Cornelia

August 3, 1933
b. Martinelli, Elsa

August 5, 1933
b. Weldon, Joan

August 8, 1933
b. Tex, Joe

August 9, 1933
b. Kohan, Buz

August 10, 1933
b. Colavito, Rocky

August 11, 1933
b. Berger, Terry
b. Falwell, Jerry L
b. Grotowski, Jerzy
b. Yetnikoff, Walter

August 12, 1933
b. Jones, Parnelli

August 13, 1933
b. Elders, Joycelyn

August 16, 1933
b. Roosa, Stuart Allen

August 18, 1933
b. Polanski, Roman

August 20, 1933
b. Alexander, Sue
b. Mitchell, George John

August 21, 1933
b. Baker, Janet Abbott, Dame

August 23, 1933
b. Fraser, Ian
b. Wilson, Pete Barton
d. Cahill, Marie
d. Loos, Adolf

August 25, 1933
b. Philbin, Regis (Francis Xavier)
b. Shorter, Wayne
b. Skerritt, Tom

August 26, 1933
b. Chartoff, Robert
b. Wattenberg, Ben J

August 28, 1933
b. Seal, Elizabeth

August 29, 1933
b. Sanford, Isabel Gwendolyn

August 30, 1933
b. Getty, Donald

August 31, 1933
b. Wagner, Robin

September 1, 1933
b. Maharis, George

b. Richards, Ann
b. Twitty, Conway

September 2, 1933
b. Kerekou, Mathieu Ahmed

September 4, 1933
b. Castellano, Richard

September 5, 1933
d. Journet, Marcel

September 7, 1933
d. Grey of Fallodon, Edward, Viscount

September 8, 1933
b. Frayn, Michael
d. Chesebrough, Robert Augustus
d. Faisal, I
d. Parkhurst, Charles Henry

September 9, 1933
d. Hart, George Overbury

September 10, 1933
b. Khrunov, Evgeny Vasilievich

September 12, 1933
b. Throneberry, Marv(in Eugene)

September 13, 1933
b. Murphy, Warren B

September 14, 1933
b. Caldwell, Zoe
b. Presnell, Harve

September 15, 1933
b. Darrow, Henry

September 17, 1933
b. Grassley, Charles Ernest
b. Loudon, Dorothy

September 18, 1933
b. Bennett, Robert F.
b. Bowman, Scotty
b. DiSuvero, Mark
b. Rodgers, Jimmy F

September 19, 1933
b. McCallum, David
d. Kemble, Edward W(indsor)

September 20, 1933
d. Besant, Annie Wood

September 21, 1933
b. Alexander, Clifford L, Jr.
b. Oldenburg, Richard

September 22, 1933
d. Silverman, Sime

September 23, 1933
b. Viguerie, Richard A(rt)

September 24, 1933
d. Liveright, Horace Brisbin

September 25, 1933
b. Brown, Hubie
b. Darling, Erik
b. Tyson, Ian
d. Ehrenfest, Paul
d. Lardner, Ring(gold Wilmer), Sr.

September 27, 1933
b. Nolan, Kathy

September 28, 1933
b. Kunin, Madeleine May

September 29, 1933
b. Machel, Samora Moises

October 2, 1933
d. Stribling, Young

October 3, 1933
b. Thompson, Thomas

October 5, 1933
b. Cilento, Diane
d. Adoree, Renee
d. Katayama, Sen

October 7, 1933
d. Hillquit, Morris

October 8, 1933
b. Korda, Michael Vincent

October 9, 1933
b. Gottfried, Martin

October 10, 1933
b. Massey, Daniel (Raymond)
b. Sebring, Jay

October 14, 1933
b. Gordy, Robert

October 16, 1933
d. Renaud, Maurice

October 17, 1933
b. Anders, William Alison

October 18, 1933
b. Gregg, Forrest

October 21, 1933
b. Brown, Georgia

October 24, 1933
b. Bray, Charles William, III
b. Kray, Reggie
b. Kray, Ronnie

October 25, 1933
b. Haley, Jack, Jr.

October 27, 1933
b. Cramer, Floyd

October 28, 1933
b. Parker, Suzy
d. Sothern, Edward Hugh

October 29, 1933
d. Calmette, Albert Leon Charles
d. Luks, George Benjamin

October 30, 1933
b. Muhammad, Wallace D

November 3, 1933
b. Barry, John
b. Berry, Ken
b. Dukakis, Michael Stanley
b. Sullivan, Louis W(ade)

November 4, 1933
b. Grier, Barbara
b. McDaniel, Mildred
b. Ojukwu, Chukwuemeka Odumegwu

November 5, 1933
b. Edelman, Herb
b. Fornos, Werner H(orst)
b. Madden, Donald
d. Guinan, Texas

November 6, 1933
b. Krea, Henri

November 10, 1933
b. Bessmertnykh, Aleksandr
Aleksandrovich
b. Evans, Ronald Ellwin

November 12, 1933
d. Bowker, R(ichard) R(ogers)

November 13, 1933
b. Corri, Adrienne

November 14, 1933
b. Haise, Fred W(allace, Jr.)

November 15, 1933
b. Burns, Jack
b. McPhatter, Clyde

November 19, 1933
b. King, Larry

November 20, 1933
d. Birrell, Augustine

November 21, 1933
b. Bainbridge, Beryl

November 23, 1933
b. Penderecki, Krzysztof

November 25, 1933
b. Crosby, Kathryn
b. Moore, Lenny

November 26, 1933
b. Goulet, Robert Gerard
b. Pozsgay, Imre

November 28, 1933
b. Lange, Hope Elise Ross
d. Laughlin, James Laurence

November 29, 1933
b. Mayall, John Brumwell
b. Rosenquist, James Albert

November 30, 1933
b. Proctor, Barbara Gardner
d. Currie, Arthur William

December 1, 1933
b. Verdy, Violette
b. Wolfensohn, James David

December 2, 1933
d. Breasted, James Henry

December 4, 1933
b. Buchholz, Horst
d. George, Stefan

December 5, 1933
b. Hackney, (Francis) Sheldon

December 6, 1933
b. Gorecki, Henryk (Mikolaj)

December 7, 1933
b. Rogers, Rosemary

December 8, 1933
b. Wilson, Flip

December 9, 1933
b. Moody, Orville

December 12, 1933
b. Freeman, Charles Eldridge

December 15, 1933
b. Conway, Tim
b. Woods, Donald

December 16, 1933
d. Chambers, Robert W
d. Vance, Louis Joseph

December 20, 1933
b. Getty, Gordon Peter

December 21, 1933
d. Rasmussen, Knud Johan Victor

December 23, 1933
b. Akihito
b. Morgan, Frank

December 27, 1933
b. Marr, Dave
d. Fowler, Henry Watson

December 28, 1933
b. Brown, John Young, Jr.
b. Portis, Charles
d. Vonnoh, Robert William

December 30, 1933
b. Silverstein, Alvin

1934

b. Alter, Hobie
b. Anquetil, Jacques
b. Bron, Eleanor
b. Caesar, Adolph
b. Cardinal, Douglas

b. Chenoweth, Dean
b. Chikatilo, Andrei
b. Conte, Lansana
b. Corona, Juan
b. Field, Ron(ald)
b. French, Albert
b. Frye, David
b. Grist, Reri
b. Keegan, John
b. Kissinger, Nancy Maginnes
b. O'Doherty, Brian
b. Pierce, Frederick S
b. Plotkin, Jerry
b. Rafsanjani, Hashemi
b. Rense, Paige
d. Bell, Donald J
d. Bialik, Hayyim Nahman
d. Bissell, Anna
d. Breshkovsky, Catherine
d. Cullen, Maurice Galbraith
d. Diagne, Blaise
d. Gilbert, Alfred, Sir
d. Hills, Reuben W
d. Hrushevsky, Mykhailo
d. Marchand, Jean-Baptiste
d. Taylor, Walter

January 1, 1934
d. Wassermann, Jakob

January 3, 1934
b. Hills, Carla Anderson

January 7, 1934
b. Forbes, Jack D(ouglas)
b. Murphy, Reg

January 8, 1934
b. Ripley, Alexandra
d. Bely, Andrey
d. Stavisky, Serge Alexandre

January 9, 1934
b. Starr, Bart

January 10, 1934
b. Kravchuk, Leonid Makarovich

January 11, 1934
b. Chretien, Jean (Joseph-Jacques)
b. Exner, Judith Campbell
b. Rafshoon, Gerald Monroe

January 14, 1934
b. Harris, Alice

January 16, 1934
b. Brennan, Edward A.
b. Horne, Marilyn Berneice

January 17, 1934
b. Lewis, Shari
b. Schanberg, Sydney Hillel

January 19, 1934
d. Fisher, Harrison

January 20, 1934
b. Debost, Michel H
b. Johnson, Arte

January 22, 1934
b. Azenberg, Emanuel

b. Bixby, Bill
b. Kerr, Graham

January 24, 1934
b. Goldberg, Leonard

January 25, 1934
b. Allen, Elizabeth

January 27, 1934
b. Cresson, Edith Campion
b. Zaragosa, Federico Mayor

January 28, 1934
b. White, Bill
b. White, Bill

January 29, 1934
d. Haber, Fritz

January 30, 1934
b. Grimes, Tammy Lee
b. Markus, Robert
d. Doubleday, Frank Nelson

January 31, 1934
b. Franciscus, James Grover
d. Wellman, Walter

February 3, 1934
d. Cisneros, Eleanora
d. Glass, Montague (Marsden)
d. Hitchcock, Gilbert Monell

February 5, 1934
b. Aaron, Hank
b. Cherry, Don(ald Stewart)
d. Davis, William Morris

February 6, 1934
b. Lindauer, Lois L

February 7, 1934
b. Fenech-Adami, Eddie
b. King Curtis

February 9, 1934
b. Ziegler, John Augustus, Jr.
d. Freshfield, Douglas William

February 10, 1934
b. Fordice, Kirk

February 11, 1934
b. Carnahan, Mel Eugene
b. Quant, Mary
b. Surtees, John

February 12, 1934
b. Howard, Anthony
b. Russell, Bill

February 13, 1934
b. Segal, George

February 14, 1934
b. Henderson, Florence

February 17, 1934
b. Bates, Alan Arthur
b. Humphries, Barry
d. Albert I

February 18, 1934
b. Lorde, Audre (Geraldine)

February 19, 1934
b. Brown, William Melvin, Jr.

February 20, 1934
b. Unser, Bobby

February 21, 1934
d. Sandino, Augusto C(esar Calderon)

February 22, 1934
b. Anderson, Sparky

February 23, 1934
d. Elgar, Edward William, Sir

February 24, 1934
b. Craxi, Bettino
b. Scotto, Renata

February 25, 1934
b. Lema, Tony
d. McGraw, John Joseph

February 27, 1934
b. Momaday, N(avarre) Scott
b. Nader, Ralph

February 28, 1934
b. Lord, Shirley
d. Chato, Alfred

March 1, 1934
b. Folon, Jean-Michel
b. Hackett, Joan

March 2, 1934
b. Cassady, Howard
b. Waxman, Al

March 3, 1934
b. Kuron, Jacek
b. McManus, Jason Donald
b. Scala, Gia

March 5, 1934
b. Sikking, James B

March 7, 1934
b. Scott, Willard Herman, Jr.
b. Walker, Zena

March 9, 1934
b. Demmert, William G., Jr.
b. Gagarin, Yuri Alexseyevich
b. Van Patten, Joyce

March 10, 1934
b. Rechy, John Francisco

March 11, 1934
b. Donaldson, Sam(uel Andrew)

March 12, 1934
b. Ayala, Francisco J(ose)

March 13, 1934
b. Schnellenberger, Howard Leslie

March 14, 1934
b. Cernan, Eugene Andrew

March 15, 1934
d. Black, Davidson

March 16, 1934
b. Norrington, Roger Arthur Carver

March 20, 1934
b. Brown, Willie
b. Malouf, David

March 21, 1934
b. Freeman, Al(bert Cornelius), Jr.
b. Mehta, Ved (Parkash)
d. Schreker, Franz
d. Tashman, Lilyan

March 22, 1934
b. Hatch, Orrin G(rant)

March 25, 1934
b. Burnette, Johnny
b. Manley, Audrey Forbes
b. Steinem, Gloria

March 26, 1934
b. Arkin, Alan Wolf
b. Cappeletti, Gino

March 27, 1934
b. Mitchell, Arthur Adam

March 28, 1934
b. Brown, Lester Russell
b. Ruddy, Al(bert Stotland)

March 29, 1934
d. Kahn, Otto Hermann

March 30, 1934
b. Curran, Charles E(dward)

March 31, 1934
b. Hutton, Jim
b. Rubbia, Carlo

April 1, 1934
b. Brown, Jim Ed
b. Posner, Vladimir

April 3, 1934
b. Goodall, Jane
b. Mayhew, Richard
b. Parker, Jim

April 5, 1934
b. Gorshin, Frank John
b. Herzog, Roman

April 7, 1934
d. Trotter, Monroe

April 8, 1934
b. Gregorian, Vartan

April 10, 1934
b. Halberstam, David

April 11, 1934
b. Strand, Mark

d. DuMaurier, Gerald Hubert, Sir

April 16, 1934
b. Stigwood, Robert Colin

April 17, 1934
b. Kirshner, Don

April 18, 1934
b. Drury, James
b. Shirley, George Irving

April 21, 1934
b. Bailar, Benjamin Franklin

April 24, 1934
b. MacLaine, Shirley

April 26, 1934
b. McCloskey, John Michael

April 27, 1934
b. Aimee, Anouk

April 29, 1934
b. Aparicio, Luis Ernesto

April 30, 1934
d. Welch, William Henry

May 1, 1934
b. Cardenas Solorzano, Cuauhtemoc
b. Horn, Shirley

May 2, 1934
d. Procter, William Cooper

May 3, 1934
b. Cooper, Henry B

May 5, 1934
b. Sweeney, John J(oseph)

May 6, 1934
b. Shelby, Richard C.

May 9, 1934
b. Bennett, Alan
d. Morton, Joy

May 11, 1934
b. Jeffords, James Merrill
b. Twyman, Jack
d. Corey, William Ellis

May 13, 1934
b. Bell, Ralph S.

May 14, 1934
b. Phillips, Sian

May 15, 1934
b. Bedie, Henri Konan

May 16, 1934
b. Kerr, Roy Patrick

May 17, 1934
b. Morrall, Earl E
d. Gilbert, Cass

May 18, 1934
b. Hickman, Dwayne B

May 19, 1934
b. Fitch, Bill
b. Lehrer, Jim

May 21, 1934
b. Samuelsson, Bengt Ingemar

May 22, 1934
b. Nero, Peter
b. Wills, Garry
d. Wesson, David

May 23, 1934
b. Moog, Robert A
d. Barrow, Clyde
d. Parker, Bonnie

May 24, 1934
b. Byrne, Jane Margaret Burke
d. Whitlock, Brand

May 25, 1934
b. Nessen, Ron(ald Harold)
b. Samrin, Heng
d. Holst, Gustav Theodore

May 27, 1934
b. Ellison, Harlan Jay
b. Hess, Richard
b. Thomas, Franklin Augustine

May 28, 1934
b. Dionne, Emilie
b. Dionne, Marie
b. Dionne Sisters

May 29, 1934
b. Marino, Eugene Antonio
b. Vander Zalm, William

May 30, 1934
b. Leonov, Alexei Arkhipovich
d. Togo, Heihachiro

May 31, 1934
d. Cody, Lew

June 1, 1934
b. Boone, Pat

June 3, 1934
b. Polhill, Robert

June 5, 1934
b. Moyers, Bill

June 6, 1934
b. Albert, II
b. Andrews, Raymond
b. Cates, Gilbert
b. Innis, Roy Emile Alfredo

June 7, 1934
b. Blatchford, Joseph Hoffer
b. Entremont, Phillippe
b. Stewart, Wynn

June 8, 1934
b. Martin, Millicent

June 9, 1934
b. Mason, Jackie
b. Welch, Larry Dean

June 10, 1934
d. Delius, Frederick

June 11, 1934
b. Wilder, Gene
d. Cline, Maggie

June 12, 1934
b. Giago, Tim

June 13, 1934
b. Means, Marianne Hansen
d. Gardiner, Chuck

June 14, 1934
b. Lehmann-Haupt, Christopher
Charles Herbert

June 15, 1934
d. Britton, Nathaniel, Lord

June 16, 1934
d. Skelly, Hal

June 20, 1934
b. Podesta, Rossana

June 21, 1934
d. Smith, Thorne

June 22, 1934
b. Jordan, Don

June 23, 1934
b. Torrey, Bill

June 24, 1934
d. Rice, Joseph Mayer

June 26, 1934
b. Grusin, Dave
b. Raab, Selwyn
b. Tunney, John Varick

June 27, 1934
b. Moffo, Anna

June 28, 1934
b. Levin, Carl Milton

June 29, 1934
b. Kronstam, Henning

June 30, 1934
b. Blackstone, Harry, Jr.
d. Schleicher, Kurt von
b. Fletcher, Louise

July 1, 1934
b. Farr, Jamie
b. Langman, Claude Berel
b. Marsh, Jean
b. Pollack, Sydney

July 2, 1934
d. Rohm, Ernst

July 4, 1934
b. Welland, Colin
d. Bialik, Chaim Nachman
d. Curie, Marie

July 5, 1934
b. Helmond, Katherine

July 8, 1934
b. DiPrete, Edward Daniel

July 9, 1934
b. Graves, Michael

July 11, 1934
b. Armani, Giorgio

July 12, 1934
b. Cliburn, Van
d. Evinrude, Ole

July 13, 1934
b. Soyinka, Wole

July 14, 1934
b. Elder, Lee
d. Hawthorne, Julian

July 16, 1934
b. Ortega, Katherine Davalos
b. Payne, Donald M

July 17, 1934
b. Sutherland, Donald

July 18, 1934
b. Bond, Edward

July 20, 1934
b. Howes, Sally Ann

July 21, 1934
b. Miller, Jonathan (Wolfe)
b. Towns, Edolphus

July 22, 1934
d. Dillinger, John Herbert

July 24, 1934
b. Ruckelshaus, William Doyle

July 25, 1934
b. Calvo, Paul McDonald
d. Coty, Francois Marie Joseph
Spoturno
d. Dollfuss, Engelbert

July 26, 1934
d. McCay, Winsor

July 27, 1934
d. Lyautey, Louis Hubert Gonzalve

July 28, 1934
b. D'Amboise, Jacques
d. Dressler, Marie

July 29, 1934
b. Fuller, Robert
d. Pitre, Didier

July 30, 1934
b. Selig, Bud

July 31, 1934
b. De Vorzon, Barry
b. Jones, Shirley
b. Sadat, Jehan Raouf

August 2, 1934
b. Bykovsky, Valery Fyodorovich
d. Hindenburg, Paul Ludwig Hans
Anton von Beneckendorff und

August 3, 1934
b. Savimbi, Jonas Malheiro

August 4, 1934
b. Green, Dallas

August 5, 1934
b. Berry, Wendell
b. King, Cammie

August 7, 1934
b. Levinson, Richard Leighton

August 8, 1934
d. Robinson, Wilbert

August 10, 1934
d. Kane, John

August 12, 1934
d. Berlage, Hendrik Petrus

August 13, 1934
d. Austin, Mary Hunter

August 14, 1934
d. Hood, Raymond Matthewson

August 18, 1934
b. Bugliosi, Vincent T
b. Clemente, Roberto Walker
b. Levitin, Sonia

August 19, 1934
b. Bell, Gordon (Bennett)
b. Durenberger, David Ferdinand
b. Richards, Rene

August 22, 1934
b. Sands, Diana Patricia
b. Schwarzkopf, H Norman

August 23, 1934
b. Eden, Barbara
b. Jurgenson, Sonny

August 24, 1934
b. Baker, Kenny
b. Myers, Norman

August 26, 1934
b. Heinsohn, Tommy
b. Leach, Will

August 29, 1934
b. Pryor, David Hampton

August 30, 1934
b. Craig, Helen

d. Dillingham, Charles Bancroft

September 2, 1934
d. Columbo, Russ

September 3, 1934
b. King, Freddy

September 4, 1934
b. Sawyer, Eugene, Jr.

September 7, 1934
b. Cardona, Manuel

September 8, 1934
b. Davies, Peter Maxwell

September 9, 1934
b. Chandler, Don(ald G)
b. Sanchez, Sonia (Benita)
d. Fry, Roger Eliot

September 10, 1934
b. Anderson, Max(ie Leroy)
b. Kuralt, Charles (Bishop)
b. Maris, Roger (Eugene)

September 12, 1934
b. Davis, Glenn
b. Gebel-Williams, Gunther

September 13, 1934
b. Crystal, Lester M

September 14, 1934
b. Millett, Kate

September 16, 1934
b. Baylor, Elgin Gay
b. Chakiris, George
b. Clayton, Eva M.

September 17, 1934
b. Connolly, Maureen

September 18, 1934
b. Blake, Robert

September 19, 1934
b. Epstein, Brian

September 20, 1934
b. Loren, Sophia

September 21, 1934
b. Cohen, Leonard Norman

September 23, 1934
b. Johnson, Nicholas

September 24, 1934
b. Carlson, Arne Helge
b. Worner, Manfred

September 25, 1934
b. Comer, James P(ierpont)

September 26, 1934
b. Mandela, Winnie
b. Mihajlov, Mihajlo
b. Morris, Greg

September 27, 1934
b. Brimley, Wilford
b. Howar, Barbara
b. Jarman, Claude, Jr.
b. Schaap, Dick

September 28, 1934
b. Bardot, Brigitte

October 4, 1934
b. Huff, Sam

October 5, 1934
b. Taylor, Kenneth Douglas
d. Vigo, Jean

October 7, 1934
b. Baraka, Amiri
b. Meinhof, Ulrike Marie

October 8, 1934
b. Brown, John Carter

October 9, 1934
b. Conway, Jill Kathryn Ker
d. Alexander of Yugoslavia

October 12, 1934
b. Meier, Richard Alan

October 13, 1934
b. Davis, Tommy
d. Baker, Theodore

October 15, 1934
b. Fuisz, Robert E
d. Poincare, Raymond

October 18, 1934
b. Stevens, Inger
b. Wilson, Allan C
d. Ramon y Cajal, Santiago

October 19, 1934
b. Gowon, Yakubu

October 20, 1934
b. Dunn, Michael

October 22, 1934
b. Vizenor, Gerald
d. Floyd, Pretty Boy

October 23, 1934
b. Rodriguez, Chi-Chi

October 24, 1934
b. Walton, Tony

October 25, 1934
d. Sprague, Frank Julian

October 28, 1934
b. Beatty, Jim

October 31, 1934
b. Beaton, Norman
b. Humes, James Calhoun

November 1, 1934
b. Jensen, Mike

November 2, 1934
b. Rosewall, Ken(neth R)

November 5, 1934
b. Magruder, Jeb Stuart

November 8, 1934
d. Baldwin, James Mark

November 9, 1934
b. Carlsson, Ingvar Gosta
b. Sagan, Carl (Edward)

November 10, 1934
b. Cash, Norm(an Dalton)

November 11, 1934
b. Manson, Charles

November 13, 1934
b. Arnett, Peter Gregg
b. Densen-Gerber, Judianne
b. Marshall, Garry Kent

November 14, 1934
b. De Benedetti, Carlo

November 15, 1934
b. Barnes, Joanna

November 17, 1934
b. Inhofe, James M.

November 20, 1934
b. Apple, R(aymond) W(alter), Jr.
b. Peter, Valentine J
d. Sitter, Willem de

November 21, 1934
b. Pawley, Howard Russell
b. Tawley, Howard

November 23, 1934
b. Colwell, Rita R(ossi)
b. Hoad, Lew(is A.)
d. Budge, Ernest Alfred Thompson
  Wallis, Sir
d. Pinero, Arthur Wing, Sir

November 24, 1934
b. Charnin, Martin
b. Schnittke, Alfred

November 27, 1934
b. Jenco, Lawrence M
d. Nelson, Baby Face

November 29, 1934
b. Morris, Willie

December 1, 1934
d. Kirov, Sergei Mironovich

December 2, 1934
b. Bok, Sissela

December 3, 1934
b. Syms, Sylvia

December 4, 1934
b. French, Victor
b. Martindale, Wink

December 5, 1934
b. Didion, Joan

December 9, 1934
b. Wells, Junior

December 10, 1934
b. Temin, Howard Martin
d. Smith, Theobald

December 12, 1934
b. Dench, Judith Olivia
b. Limann, Hilla
b. Madrid Hurtado, Miguel de la

December 13, 1934
b. Zanuck, Richard Darryl

December 15, 1934
d. Walker, Maggie Lena

December 16, 1934
b. Jacob, John Edward

December 19, 1934
b. Kaline, Al(bert William)
d. Dixon, Roland Burrage

December 20, 1934
b. Gorman, Leon Arthur

December 21, 1934
d. Thurman, Wallace (Henry)

December 22, 1934
b. Pearson, David

December 24, 1934
d. Hunt, George Wylie Paul

December 25, 1934
b. Martinez, Bob

December 26, 1934
d. Fisher, Rudolph

December 27, 1934
b. Latynina, Larisa Semyonovna

December 28, 1934
b. Akers, John Fellows
b. Smith, Maggie Natalie
d. Sherman, Lowell

December 29, 1934
b. Flanders, Ed
b. Jarriel, Tom

December 30, 1934
b. Daniloff, Nicholas

1935

b. Berry, Richard
b. Clark, John Pepper
b. Delahanty, Thomas K
b. Fadlallah, Sayyid Muhammad
  Husayn
b. Genovese, Kitty
b. Glass, David (Dayne)

b. Hullinger, Charlotte
b. Kanokogi, Rusty
b. Kohoutek, Lubos
b. Levinger, Moshe
b. Miller, Nolan
b. Moss, Jerry
b. Sanders, Dori(nda)
b. Soglo, Nicephore (Dieudonne)
b. Sosa, Mercedes
b. Syberberg, Hans Jurgen
b. Taylor, KoKo
b. Wittig, Monique
d. Curly
d. Gilman, Charlotte Anna Perkins
d. Kuk, Abraham Isaac
d. Lucile
d. Matchabelli, Georges, Prince

January 3, 1935
b. Fuller, Millard (Dean)

January 4, 1935
b. Patterson, Floyd

January 6, 1935
b. Capucine

January 7, 1935
b. Kubasov, Valery Nikolaevich

January 8, 1935
b. Lapham, Lewis Henry
b. Presley, Elvis Aaron

January 9, 1935
b. Denver, Bob
b. Graves, Earl Gilbert

January 10, 1935
b. Hawkins, Ronnie
b. Milnes, Sherrill Eustace

January 11, 1935
b. Mears, Walter Robert
d. Sembrich, Marcella

January 12, 1935
b. Kreskin
d. Daniels, Frank

January 15, 1935
b. Goodman, Martin Wise
b. Silverberg, Robert

January 16, 1935
b. Foyt, A(nthony) J(oseph Jr.)
d. Barker, Fred
d. Barker, Ma

January 19, 1935
b. Hedren, Tippi

January 22, 1935
b. Cooke, Sam
b. DuPont, Pierre Samuel, IV

January 23, 1935
b. Moses, Robert Parris

January 25, 1935
b. Allen, Bob
b. Burns, Conrad Ray
b. Eanes, Antonio dos Santos Ramalho

b. Gerrard, Roy

January 26, 1935
b. Uecker, Bob
d. Ippolitov-Ivanov, Mikhail
  Mikhailovich

January 27, 1935
b. Thomas, D(onald) M(ichael)

January 28, 1935
b. Lodge, David (John)
b. Pryor, Nicholas

January 29, 1935
b. Payne, Roger S.
d. Dellenbaugh, Frederick Samuel

January 31, 1935
b. Oe, Kenzaburo

February 2, 1935
b. Wagner, Jane

February 3, 1935
b. Watson, Johnny "Guitar"
d. Junkers, Hugo

February 4, 1935
b. Talvela, Martti Olavi

February 7, 1935
b. Kohl, Herbert H.

February 8, 1935
d. Evans, Charles
d. Liebermann, Max

February 11, 1935
b. Vincent, Gene

February 12, 1935
b. Manzarek, Ray
d. Escoffier, Georges Auguste

February 13, 1935
b. Hanafi, Hassan

February 14, 1935
b. Wright, Mickey

February 15, 1935
b. Block, John Rusling
b. Brownmiller, Susan
b. Chaffee, Roger Bruce

February 16, 1935
b. Bedford, Brian
b. Bono, Sonny

February 17, 1935
b. Cohen, Stanley N(orman)

February 18, 1935
b. Richardson, Jack

February 21, 1935
d. Gibbon, Lewis Grassic

February 27, 1935
b. Freni, Mirella

March 1, 1935
b. Conrad, Robert

March 3, 1935
b. Moore, Bert C

March 6, 1935
b. Whitman, Marina VonNeumann
d. Holmes, Oliver Wendell, Jr.

March 7, 1935
b. DeVita, Vincent Theodore, Jr.
b. Donghia, Angelo R
d. Duane, William
d. Tabor, Elizabeth Bonduel McCourt
Doe

March 12, 1935
d. Pupin, Michael Idvorsky

March 13, 1935
b. Awoonor, Kofi
b. Uhlman, Wes(ley Carl)

March 15, 1935
b. Hirsch, Judd
b. Swaggart, Jimmy Lee

March 16, 1935
b. Berganza, Teresa
b. Park, Tongsun
d. MacLeod, John James Rickard

March 18, 1935
b. Welsing, Frances Cress

March 19, 1935
b. Newman, Phyllis

March 21, 1935
b. Kunzel, Erich

March 23, 1935
b. Slavitt, David R

March 25, 1935
d. Zanelli, Renato

March 27, 1935
b. Glover, Julian

March 31, 1935
b. Alpert, Herb
b. Chamberlain, Richard
b. Rossner, Judith

April 1, 1935
b. McDonald, Larry

April 2, 1935
b. Geyer, Georgie Anne
d. Moten, Bennie

April 3, 1935
b. Kushner, Harold S(amuel)
d. Lukeman, Henry A

April 6, 1935
d. Robinson, Edwin Arlington

April 7, 1935
b. Carter, Hodding

April 8, 1935
d. Ochs, Adolph Simon

April 9, 1935
b. Schreiber, Avery

April 10, 1935
b. Patterson, P(ercival Noel) J(ames)

April 11, 1935
d. Green, Anna Katharine

April 13, 1935
b. Waggoner, Lyle

April 14, 1935
b. Lynn, Loretta
b. VonDaeniken, Erich
d. Noether, (Amalie) Emmy

April 16, 1935
b. Vinton, Bobby

April 17, 1935
b. Lundy, Lamar

April 19, 1935
b. Moore, Dudley Stuart John

April 21, 1935
b. Grodin, Charles
b. Kean, Thomas Howard

April 22, 1935
b. Chambers, Paul
b. Cossotto, Fiorenza

April 24, 1935
b. Keith, Louis Gerald

April 28, 1935
b. Gyllenhammar, Pehr Gustaf
d. Mackenzie, Alexander Campbell,
Sir

April 29, 1935
b. Baxter, Keith

May 2, 1935
b. Faisal II
b. Wray, Link

May 3, 1935
d. Breitenstein, Ted
d. Manners, Charles
d. Smith, Jessie Wilcox

May 4, 1935
b. Howard, Jane Temple

May 5, 1935
b. Pivot, Bernard

May 8, 1935
b. Jens, Salome

May 10, 1935
b. Owens, Gary
d. Witherspoon, Herbert

May 11, 1935
b. McClure, Doug
d. Thompson, Edward Herbert

May 12, 1935
b. Alou, Felipe Rojas
b. Bucyk, John Paul
d. Pilsudski, Jozef

May 13, 1935
b. Benetton, Luciano

May 14, 1935
d. Frost, Edwin Brant
d. Hirschfeld, Magnus

May 15, 1935
b. Bragg, Don(ald)
d. Malevich, Kasimir Severinovich

May 17, 1935
b. Potter, Dennis (Christopher George)
d. Dukas, Paul Abraham

May 19, 1935
b. Hartman, David Downs
d. Lawrence, T(homas) E(dward)

May 20, 1935
b. Bessell, Ted
d. Loeffler, Charles Martin Tornow

May 21, 1935
b. Faust, Gerry
d. Addams, Jane
d. DeVries, Hugo

May 23, 1935
b. Hodel, Donald P(aul)

May 24, 1935
b. Mora, Jim

May 27, 1935
b. Lewis, Ramsey Emanuel, Jr.
b. Meriwether, Lee

May 28, 1935
b. Brooks, Ronald E.
b. Rogers, Darryl D

May 29, 1935
b. Brink, Andre Philippus
d. Suk, Josef

May 31, 1935
b. Bolger, Jim

June 1, 1935
b. Ike, Reverend

June 6, 1935
b. Crews, Harry Eugene
b. Kogawa, Joy (Nozomi)
b. Mitchell, Bobby
d. Byng, Julian Hedworth George,
Viscount

June 8, 1935
b. Shapiro, Harold Tafler

June 13, 1935
b. Christo

June 14, 1935
b. Evans, Jerry

June 16, 1935
b. Dine, Jim

June 18, 1935
b. Michaels, Al
b. Mirkin, Gabe

June 19, 1935
b. Borja Cevallos, Rodrigo
b. Taylor, John Russell

June 20, 1935
b. Dawson, Len

June 21, 1935
b. Markham, Monte
b. Sagan, Francoise
d. Roller, Alfred

June 23, 1935
b. Ferre, Maurice Antonio

June 24, 1935
b. Hamill, Pete

June 25, 1935
b. Kramer, Larry
d. Meier-Graefe, Julius

July 3, 1935
b. Schmitt, Harrison Hagan
d. Citroen, Andre Gustave

July 5, 1935
b. Geldzahler, Henry
d. Herford, Oliver

July 6, 1935
b. Dalai Lama, the 14th Incarnate
b. Taylor, Arthur Robert

July 8, 1935
b. Crow, John David
b. Lawrence, Steve

July 12, 1935
d. Dreyfus, Alfred

July 13, 1935
b. Kemp, Jack

July 15, 1935
b. Karras, Alex(ander G)
b. Kercheval, Ken
b. Prescott, Peter Sherwin

July 17, 1935
b. Carroll, Diahann
b. Civiletti, Benjamin Richard
b. Schickele, Peter
d. Russell, George William

July 18, 1935
b. Albright, Tenley Emma

July 19, 1935
b. Agee, Philip
d. Sedgwick, Anne Douglas

July 22, 1935
b. Dale, Grover

July 24, 1935
b. Oliphant, Patrick Bruce

July 25, 1935
b. Bullins, Ed
b. Harris, Barbara
b. Khashoggi, Adnan
b. Robinson, John Alexander

August 3, 1935
b. Lamm, Richard Douglas

August 5, 1935
b. Saxon, John

August 6, 1935
b. Benjamin, Adam, Jr.

August 7, 1935
b. Deer, Ada E(lizabeth)

August 13, 1935
b. Grant, Mudcat

August 14, 1935
b. Brodie, John Riley

August 15, 1935
b. Dale, Jim
b. Dalton, Abby
b. Jordan, Vernon Eulion, Jr.
d. Post, Wiley
d. Rogers, Will(iam Penn Adair)
d. Signac, Paul

August 16, 1935
b. Newmar, Julie

August 17, 1935
b. Dinning, Mark
b. Tsegaye, Gabre-Medhin

August 18, 1935
b. Fisher, Gail
b. Johnson, Rafer Lewis

August 19, 1935
b. Richardson, Bobby

August 20, 1935
b. Yokich, Stephen P.

August 22, 1935
b. Dean, Morton
b. Proulx, E(dna) Annie

August 23, 1935
b. Berger, Marilyn

August 26, 1935
b. Ferraro, Geraldine Anne
d. Willys, John North

August 27, 1935
b. Holroyd, Michael De Courcy Fraser

b. Yablans, Frank
d. Hassam, Childe

August 29, 1935
d. Magonigle, Harold Van Buren

August 30, 1935
b. Earle, Sylvia Alice
b. Phillips, John

August 31, 1935
b. Cleaver, Eldridge
b. Robinson, Frank

September 1, 1935
b. Ozawa, Seiji
b. Rodgers, Guy William, Jr.
d. Kidman, Sidney

September 2, 1935
d. Bradley, Andrew Cecil

September 3, 1935
b. Brennan, Eileen Regina

September 5, 1935
b. Erhard, Werner
b. Just, Ward
b. Lawrence, Carol

September 7, 1935
b. Diouf, Abdou

September 8, 1935
d. Doheny, Edward Lawrence

September 9, 1935
b. Topol, Chaim

September 10, 1935
d. Long, Huey Pierce

September 11, 1935
b. Part, Arvo
b. Titov, Gherman Stepanovich

September 12, 1935
b. Calloway, (David) Wayne
b. Hunt, Richard (Howard)

September 14, 1935
d. Kendal, Madge, Dame

September 16, 1935
b. Andre, Carl
b. Chaikin, Joseph

September 17, 1935
b. Kesey, Ken

September 19, 1935
b. Massi, Nick
d. Tsiolkovsky, Konstantin
   Eduardovich

September 20, 1935
b. Taylor, Jim

September 21, 1935
b. Freedman, James Oliver
b. Gibson, Henry

September 23, 1935
b. McCann, Les
d. Hopper, De Wolfe

September 25, 1935
b. Sjowall, Maj

September 26, 1935
d. Adams, Andy

September 28, 1935
b. Crampton, Bruce Sidney
b. Sears, Heather

September 30, 1935
b. Aoun, Michel
b. Mathis, Johnny

October 1, 1935
b. Andrews, Julie
b. Hermann, Jane Pomerance
d. Nieman, Lucius William

October 2, 1935
b. Lawrence, Robert (Henry), Jr.

October 3, 1935
b. Duke, Charles Moss, Jr.

October 7, 1935
b. Keneally, Thomas (Michael)

October 9, 1935
b. McCullin, Donald

October 12, 1935
b. Kubek, Tony
b. Moore, Sam(uel David)
b. Pavarotti, Luciano
b. Raspberry, William

October 15, 1935
b. Morrow, Bobby
b. O'Ree, Willie

October 18, 1935
b. Boyle, Peter
d. Lachaise, Gaston

October 19, 1935
b. Haynes, Lloyd

October 20, 1935
b. Buatta, Mario
b. Orbach, Jerry
d. Greely, Adolphus Washington
d. Henderson, Arthur
d. Smith, (Robert) Sidney

October 22, 1935
d. Carson, Edward Henry

October 23, 1935
d. Demuth, Charles

October 24, 1935
d. Pirenne, Jean Henri Otto Lucien
Marie
d. Schultz, Dutch

October 25, 1935
b. Schweickart, Russell L

November 1, 1935
b. Player, Gary Jim
b. Said, Edward W

November 3, 1935
b. Brett, Jeremy

November 6, 1935
d. Osborn, Henry Fairfield
d. Sunday, Billy

November 8, 1935
b. Delon, Alain
d. Kingsford-Smith, Charles Edward,
Sir

November 9, 1935
b. Gibson, Bob

November 10, 1935
b. Scheider, Roy Richard
b. Scott, Pippa

November 11, 1935
b. Andersson, Bibi
b. Walgreen, Charles Rudolph, III

November 12, 1935
b. Briand, Rena

November 13, 1935
b. Carey, George Leonard, Archbishop

November 14, 1935
b. Hussein, I, King

November 15, 1935
b. Coleman, John
b. White, Neva

November 16, 1935
b. Drew, Elizabeth Brenner
b. Rene, (France) Albert

November 18, 1935
d. Bulova, Joseph

November 19, 1935
b. Robertson, James D, III
b. Welch, John Francis, Jr.

November 20, 1935
d. Jellicoe, John Rushworth

November 22, 1935
b. Callan, Michael
b. Protopopov, Ludmilla Evgenievna
Belousova

November 23, 1935
b. Volkov, Vladislav Nikolayevich

November 24, 1935
b. Dellums, Ronald Vernie

November 25, 1935
b. Berner, Robert A(rbuckle)

November 26, 1935
b. Pringle, Laurence

November 28, 1935
b. Stow, (Julian) Randolph

November 29, 1935
b. Pozzi, Lucio

November 30, 1935
b. Sachs, Samuel, II

December 1, 1935
b. Allen, Woody
b. Goody, Joan
d. Mayr, Richard

December 2, 1935
b. Sample, Bill
d. Thomas, Martha Carey

December 3, 1935
b. Johnson, Eddie Bernice
b. Wu, Gordon (Ying Sheung)

December 4, 1935
b. Vesco, Robert Lee
d. Richet, Charles Robert

December 5, 1935
b. Donahue, Phil
b. Trillin, Calvin Marshall

December 6, 1935
b. Crandall, Robert Lloyd
b. Epstein, Edward Jay
b. Mathews, Forrest David

December 9, 1935
b. Bell, Steve
b. Pratt, Christopher

December 11, 1935
b. Martin, James Grubbs

December 13, 1935
b. Fernandez, Joseph
b. Koren, Edward Benjamin
d. Grignard, Francois Auguste Victor

December 14, 1935
b. Remick, Lee

December 15, 1935
b. Walton, Joe

December 17, 1935
b. Costa, Victor Charles
b. Ripken, Cal(vin Edwin, Sr.)
d. Gomez, Juan Vicente
d. Reese, Lizette Woodworth

December 18, 1935
d. Todd, Thelma

December 20, 1935
b. Wilson, William Julius

December 21, 1935
b. Schreyer, Edward Richard

December 22, 1935
d. Braslau, Sophie

December 23, 1935
b. Hornung, Paul Vernon
b. Phillips, Esther

December 24, 1935
b. Carlisle, Kevin
d. Berg, Alban

December 25, 1935
b. Hoge, James Fulton, Jr.
b. Little Richard
d. Bourget, Paul (Charles Joseph)

December 26, 1935
b. Humphries, Frederick (S.)
b. Ullman, Norm(an Victor Alexander)

December 27, 1935
b. Lanvin, Bernard

December 28, 1935
d. Day, Clarence Shepard, Jr.

December 30, 1935
b. Bongo, Albert-Bernard (Omar)
b. Koufax, Sandy
b. Tamblyn, Russ
d. Reading, 1st Marquess of

1936

b. Ashby, Hal
b. Aziz, Tariq Mikhayl
b. Ben-Gal, Avigdor
b. Biba
b. Brown, Dean
b. Cooper, Alexander
b. Dassler, Horst
b. Derr, Kenneth T
b. Eaton, Shirley
b. Farina, Richard
b. Freeman, Roland L(eon)
b. Ghotbzadeh, Sadegh
b. Gorbanevskaya, Natalya
b. Grove, Andrew S.
b. Helms, Bobby
b. Jordan, James
b. Kinmont, Jill
b. Kopits, Steven E
b. Lexcen, Ben
b. Lockhart, Calvin
b. Lukas, D. Wayne
b. Medina, Ernest L
b. Schwartz, David
b. Tal, Mikhail Nekhemyevich
b. Towne, Robert (Burton)
b. Westerman, Floyd
b. Zine el Abidine Ben Ali
d. Chona, Maria
d. Cierva, Juan de la
d. Kamenev, Lev Borisovich
d. Leverson, Ada
d. Premchand
d. Primo de Rivera, Jose A
d. Valle Inclan, Ramon Maria del
d. Vazquez, Horacio

January 1, 1936
b. Allen, Richard Vincent
b. Queler, Eve Rabin

January 2, 1936
b. Miller, Roger Dean

January 3, 1936
b. Einhorn, Eddie
b. Rollin, Betty
b. Ruppe, Loret Miller

January 6, 1936
b. Sanguinetti, Julio Maria

January 7, 1936
b. Davies, Hunter

January 9, 1936
d. Gilbert, John

January 10, 1936
b. Crane, Daniel B
b. Wilson, Robert Woodrow

January 11, 1936
b. Hesse, Eva

January 12, 1936
b. Brannigan, Bill

January 13, 1936
b. Madigan, Edward R.

January 15, 1936
b. Conroy, Frank

January 16, 1936
b. White, Michael Simon
d. Barnack, Oskar
d. Fish, Albert
d. Russell, Annie

January 18, 1936
d. Kipling, Rudyard

January 19, 1936
b. Zia(ur) Rahman

January 20, 1936
b. Feigenbaum, Edward A(lbert)
d. George V

January 22, 1936
b. Ong Teng Cheong

January 23, 1936
b. Golonka, Arlene
b. Stone, Edward C, Jr.

January 24, 1936
b. Kershaw, Doug(las James)

January 25, 1936
b. Hyland, Diana
b. Jones, Dean Carroll

January 26, 1936
b. Simitis, Costas
d. Ittner, William Butts

January 27, 1936
b. Donahue, Troy
b. Ting, Samuel Chao Chung

January 28, 1936
b. Alda, Alan
b. Kadare, Ismail
d. Loeb, Richard A

January 29, 1936
b. Harrison, Noel

February 2, 1936
b. LaFollette, Bronson Cutting
d. Seaman, Owen, Sir

February 3, 1936
b. Bridges, James

February 7, 1936
d. Heggie, O P

February 8, 1936
d. Curtis, Charles Brent

February 11, 1936
b. Reynolds, Burt
d. Harvey, William Hope

February 12, 1936
b. Baker, Joe Don
b. Fang Lizhi

February 16, 1936
b. Harris, Joe Frank
d. Chapin, Roy Dikeman
d. Robinson, James Harvey

February 17, 1936
b. Bartholomew, Reginald
b. Brown, Jim
d. Maxim, Hiram Percy

February 18, 1936
b. Auel, Jean Marie
b. Hemphill, Paul

February 19, 1936
d. Mitchell, Billy

February 20, 1936
b. Abdulkarim, Mohamed Taki
d. Hope, John

February 21, 1936
b. Jordan, Barbara C(harline)
b. McClanahan, Rue

February 22, 1936
b. Bishop, J(ohn) Michael

February 24, 1936
b. Cristal, Linda
b. Reventlow, Lance

February 26, 1936
d. Scotti, Antonio
d. Takahashi, Korekiyo

February 27, 1936
b. Johnson, Sonia
b. Mahony, Roger Michael
b. Poli, Robert E
d. Pavlov, Ivan Petrovich

February 28, 1936
d. Nicolle, Charles Jules Henri

February 29, 1936
b. Lousma, Jack
b. Richard, Henri

d. Ruef, Abraham
d. Patou, Jean

March 4, 1936
b. Clark, James

March 5, 1936
b. Stockwell, Dean

March 6, 1936
b. Barry, Marion S(hepilov), Jr.
d. Morgan, C(onwy) Lloyd

March 8, 1936
b. Cryer, David

March 9, 1936
b. Brown, Kenneth H
b. Gilley, Mickey Leroy
b. Ingels, Marty

March 11, 1936
b. Scalia, Antonin
d. Beatty, David Beatty, Earl

March 12, 1936
b. Cohen, Daniel
b. Dobyns, Lloyd Allen, Jr.

March 13, 1936
b. Hamilton, Virginia

March 14, 1936
b. Charles, Bob
d. Haldane, John Scott

March 18, 1936
b. De Klerk, F(rederik) W(illem)
d. Venizelos, Eleutherios Kyriakos

March 19, 1936
b. Andress, Ursula

March 20, 1936
b. Meader, Vaughn
b. Owen, Tobias Chant
b. Perry, Lee
d. Cunninghame-Graham, Robert
Bontine

March 21, 1936
b. Broadbent, Ed
d. Glazunov, Alexander
Constantinovich
d. McCarthy, Justin Huntly

March 22, 1936
b. Carey, Ron(ald Robert)

March 24, 1936
b. Suzuki, David T(akayoshi)

March 25, 1936
d. McCullough, Paul

March 26, 1936
b. Jofre, Eder

March 28, 1936
b. Vargas Llosa, Mario

March 29, 1936
b. Bennett, Richard Rodney
b. Guest, Judith Ann

March 30, 1936
d. Fuller-Maitland, John Alexander
d. Supervia, Conchita

March 31, 1936
b. German, Bruce W
b. Piercy, Marge
b. Williams, Walter Edward

April 1, 1936
b. Kovac, Michael
b. Perranoski, Ron(ald Peter)
d. Coolidge, Charles Allerton

April 2, 1936
b. Giovenco, John Vincent
b. Owens, Rochelle

April 3, 1936
d. Hauptmann, Bruno Richard

April 6, 1936
b. Thinnes, Roy
d. Breese, Edmund
d. Lavigne, Kid

April 7, 1936
b. Cordes, Eugene Harold
b. Jones, Preston St. Vrain
d. Miller, Marilyn

April 8, 1936
d. Barany, Robert

April 9, 1936
d. Tonnies, Ferdinand

April 10, 1936
b. Madden, John

April 12, 1936
b. Simmonds, Kennedy Alphonse

April 13, 1936
d. Thurston, Howard

April 14, 1936
b. Nichols, Bobby
b. Scheer, Robert
b. Serpico, Frank

April 18, 1936
d. Howe, Louis McHenry
d. Respighi, Ottorino

April 19, 1936
b. Martens, Wilfried

April 20, 1936
b. Roberts, Pat

April 22, 1936
b. Campbell, Glen Travis

April 23, 1936
b. Orbison, Roy

April 24, 1936
b. Crombie, David Edward
b. Ireland, Jill
b. Logan, Daniel
d. Dunne, Finley Peter

April 25, 1936
b. Arron, Henck Alphonsus Eugene
d. Fuad, I

April 29, 1936
b. Mehta, Zubin

April 30, 1936
d. Housman, A(lfred) E(dward)

May 2, 1936
b. Rabin, Michael

May 3, 1936
b. Humperdinck, Engelbert
d. Michels, Robert

May 4, 1936
b. Cordobes, El

May 5, 1936
b. DiSant'Angelo, Giorgio

May 7, 1936
b. O'Reilly, Anthony John Francis

May 8, 1936
b. Thompson, James Robert
d. Spengler, Oswald

May 9, 1936
b. Drinkwater, Terry
b. Finney, Albert
b. Jackson, Glenda

May 11, 1936
d. Palmer, Alexander Mitchell

May 12, 1936
b. Endara (Galimany), Guillermo
b. Snyder, Tom
b. Stella, Frank Philip
d. Emerson, Peter Henry

May 13, 1936
b. Lampert, Zohra

May 14, 1936
b. Darin, Bobby
b. Neuhaus, Richard John
d. Allenby, Edmund Henry Hynman

May 15, 1936
b. Alberghetti, Anna Maria
b. Zindel, Paul

May 16, 1936
b. DeMontebello, Guy-Philippe

May 17, 1936
b. Hopper, Dennis

May 19, 1936
b. Jenrette, John Wilson, Jr.

May 20, 1936
b. Zerbe, Anthony

May 22, 1936
b. Peck, M Scott

May 23, 1936
b. Van Itallie, Jean-Claude

May 24, 1936
d. Muzio, Claudia

May 25, 1936
b. Hall, Tom T
b. Lewis, David Levering

May 26, 1936
d. Black, Winifred Sweet

May 27, 1936
b. Edwards, Helen T(hom)
b. Gossett, Louis, Jr.
b. Green, Richard R(eginald)

May 28, 1936
b. Chappell, Fred (Davis)
b. Shabazz, Betty

May 30, 1936
b. Dullea, Keir
d. Chaney, Norman

June 3, 1936
b. McMurtry, Larry Jeff

June 4, 1936
b. Dern, Bruce MacLeish

June 6, 1936
b. Stubbs, Levi

June 8, 1936
b. Darren, James
b. Wilson, Kenneth Geddes

June 9, 1936
b. Manatt, Charles Taylor

June 10, 1936
b. Chesney, Marion
b. Freemantle, Brian Harry

June 11, 1936
b. Newton, Christopher

June 12, 1936
d. Howard, Robert Ervin
d. James, Montague Rhodes

June 13, 1936
b. Raven, Peter H(amilton)

June 14, 1936
d. Chesterton, G(ilbert) K(eith)
d. Gorky, Maxim

June 16, 1936
b. Karlin, Frederick James

June 17, 1936
b. Cattani, Richard J.

b. Loach, Ken(neth)
d. Walthall, Henry B

June 19, 1936
b. DeVito, Tommy
b. Rowlands, Gena (Catherine)

June 22, 1936
b. Kristofferson, Kris
d. Schlick, Friedrich Albert Moritz

June 23, 1936
b. Bach, Richard David

June 24, 1936
b. Predock, Antoine Samuel

June 25, 1936
b. Habibie, B(acharuddin) J(usuf)

June 26, 1936
b. Greer, Hal

June 27, 1936
b. Clifton, (Thelma) Lucille
b. Shalikashvili, John (Malchase
David)

June 28, 1936
b. Magliozzi, Tom
b. Owens, Major (Robert)
d. Berkman, Alexander

June 29, 1936
b. Killebrew, Harmon Clayton

June 30, 1936
b. Dussault, Nancy Elizabeth

July 1, 1936
b. Amos, Wally

July 2, 1936
b. Nemec, Jan
b. Newman, Joseph Westley

July 7, 1936
d. Chicherin, Georgi Vasilyevich

July 8, 1936
d. Meighan, Thomas

July 9, 1936
b. Hampton, James
b. Jordan, June
d. Wright, Henry

July 10, 1936
b. Boyer, Herbert Wayne

July 13, 1936
b. Stern, Sandor

July 14, 1936
b. Gordon, David
d. Mukerji, Dham Gopal

July 15, 1936
b. Penner, Rudolph Gerhard
b. Voinovich, George V(ictor)

July 20, 1936
b. Mikulski, Barbara Ann

July 22, 1936
b. DellaFemina, Jerry
b. Robbins, Tom

July 23, 1936
b. Drysdale, Don(ald Scott)
b. Kennedy, Anthony McLeod

July 24, 1936
b. Buzzi, Ruth Ann

July 25, 1936
d. Wellcome, Henry Solomon, Sir

July 28, 1936
b. Chuan Leekpai

July 29, 1936
b. Dole, Elizabeth Hanford

July 30, 1936
b. Guy, Buddy

August 1, 1936
b. Saint Laurent, Yves Mathieu

August 2, 1936
d. Andrews, Mary Raymond Shipman
d. Bleriot, Louis
d. Ufer, Walter

August 5, 1936
b. Dancy, John Albert
d. Brownscombe, Jennie Augusta

August 7, 1936
b. Kirk, Rahsaan Roland

August 8, 1936
b. Bowden, Don
b. Howard, Frank Oliver
d. Mourning Dove

August 9, 1936
d. Steffens, Lincoln

August 12, 1936
b. Haacke, Hans Christoph
b. Kolingba, Andre-Dieudonne
b. Poindexter, John Marlan

August 15, 1936
d. Lytton, Henry Alfred, Sir

August 16, 1936
d. Deledda, Grazia

August 19, 1936
b. Oerter, Al(fred A)
d. Garcia Lorca, Federico

August 20, 1936
b. Fracci, Carla

August 21, 1936
b. Chamberlain, Wilt(on Norman)
b. Gardner, Booth

August 22, 1936
b. Moritz, Charles Worthington

August 23, 1936
d. Adam, Juliette Lamber

August 24, 1936
b. Byatt, A S
b. Spikes, Dolores

August 25, 1936
d. Zinoviev, Grigori Evseevich

August 29, 1936
b. McCain, John Sidney, III

August 31, 1936
b. Collins, Marva Deloise Nettles

September 2, 1936
b. Werner, Helmut (Eberhard)

September 5, 1936
b. Danforth, John Claggett
b. Hastings, Alcee L
b. Kennedy, Joan Bennett
b. Kozol, Jonathan
b. Mazeroski, Bill

September 7, 1936
b. Holly, Buddy
d. Le Chatelier, Henry-Louis

September 10, 1936
b. Lovesey, Peter Harmer

September 14, 1936
b. Koenig, Walter
b. Samaras, Lucas
d. Gabrilowitsch, Ossip Salomonovich
d. Thalberg, Irving Grant

September 16, 1936
d. Charcot, Jean Baptiste Etienne
Auguste

September 19, 1936
b. Cowans, Adger W.

September 20, 1936
b. Church, Sam(uel Morgan Jr.)

September 21, 1936
b. Luzhkov, Yuri

September 24, 1936
b. Henson, Jim

September 25, 1936
b. Prowse, Juliet
b. Traore, Moussa
d. Horlick, William
d. Sims, William Sowden

September 26, 1936
d. Monroe, Harriet

September 27, 1936
b. Cornelius, Don

September 30, 1936
b. Haire, Bill Martin

b. Sasser, James R(alph)
d. Lu Hsun

October 1, 1936
b. Villella, Edward Joseph

October 3, 1936
b. Perry, Jim
b. Reich, Steve
d. Heisman, John William

October 5, 1936
b. Havel, Vaclav

October 6, 1936
b. Chambers, Julius LeVonne
b. Quayle, Anna

October 7, 1936
b. Dutoit, Charles

October 8, 1936
b. Andrews, James Frederick
b. Barrett, Rona

October 11, 1936
b. Fullerton, (Charles) Gordon

October 12, 1936
d. Blashfield, Edwin Howland
d. Litvinne, Felia

October 13, 1936
b. Gorman, Cliff

October 19, 1936
b. Bevel, James Luther
b. Cole, Johnnetta Betsch

October 20, 1936
b. Horse Capture, George, Sr.
b. Seale, Bobby G
d. Sullivan, Anne

October 21, 1936
b. Gray, Simon James Holliday

October 22, 1936
d. Couzens, James Joseph, Jr.

October 24, 1936
b. Hernandez-Colon, Rafael
b. Nelson, David

October 25, 1936
b. Gilbert, Martin John

October 27, 1936
b. Sheehan, Neil

October 28, 1936
b. Antes, Horst
b. Daniels, Charlie

October 29, 1936
b. Jayston, Michael

October 30, 1936
b. Caro, Robert A
b. Vermeil, Dick
d. Taft, Lorado

October 31, 1936
b. Wexler, Peter John
b. Bishara, Abdullah Yaccoub

November 2, 1936
b. Ruether, Rosemary Radford

November 3, 1936
b. Emerson, Roy

November 4, 1936
b. Ratsiraka, Didier

November 7, 1936
b. Attles, Al(vin A)
b. Jones, Gwyneth
b. McLaughlin, Audrey
d. Sale, Charles Partlow

November 8, 1936
b. Gibson, Edward George

November 9, 1936
b. Graham, Bob

November 11, 1936
b. Kohner, Susan
d. Harding, Chester

November 14, 1936
d. Howell, Clark

November 16, 1936
b. Callender, Clive O(rville)
d. Schumann-Heink, Ernestine Rossler

November 18, 1936
b. Ballard, Hank
b. Cherry, Don

November 19, 1936
b. Cavett, Dick

November 20, 1936
b. DeLillo, Don

November 21, 1936
b. DePreist, James Anderson
b. Ginzburg, Aleksandr Ilich

November 22, 1936
d. Graham, Ernest Robert

November 25, 1936
b. Brown, Trisha

November 27, 1936
d. Zaharoff, Basil, Sir

November 28, 1936
b. Gilligan, Carol
b. Hart, Gary Warren

November 29, 1936
b. Lee, Yuan Tseh

November 30, 1936
b. Hoffman, Abbie

December 1, 1936
b. Rawls, Lou(is Allen)

December 4, 1936
b. Giorno, John

December 5, 1936
b. Mitchell, Chad
b. Nkosi, Lewis

December 7, 1936
b. Belinsky, Bo
b. Collins, Martha Layne Hall

December 8, 1936
b. Carradine, David

December 10, 1936
d. Pirandello, Luigi
d. Tweedale, Violet Chambers

December 13, 1936
b. Aga Khan IV

December 14, 1936
b. Bach, Bert Coates

December 15, 1936
b. Palmieri, Eddie

December 16, 1936
b. Dees, Morris S(eligman), Jr.
b. Kicknosway, Faye

December 17, 1936
b. Steele, Tommy

December 21, 1936
b. Roberts, Barbara

December 22, 1936
b. Elizondo, Hector

December 23, 1936
b. Stacy, James

December 25, 1936
b. Merchant, Ismail
d. Brisbane, Arthur

December 26, 1936
b. Ross, Bobby

December 27, 1936
b. Trovoada, Miguel
d. Seeckt, Hans von

December 29, 1936
b. Moore, Mary Tyler
b. Nitschke, Ray(mond E.)

December 31, 1936
b. Anderson, W(illiam) French
b. Major, Clarence
d. Unamuno (y Jugo), Miguel de

1937

b. Abu Daoud
b. Assad, Rifaat al-
b. Bayer, Wolfgang
b. Carter, Hurricane
b. Clayton, Constance Elaine

b. Dahl, Gary
b. Daly, John
b. Dunlap, Albert J.
b. Fassett, Kaffe
b. Greene, Gael
b. Grettenberger, John O
b. Haddad, Saad
b. Haden, Charlie
b. Kelly, Dan
b. Mengistu Haile Mariam
b. Menguistu Haile Mariam
b. Molloy, John T
b. Panchen Lama
b. Penske, Roger
b. Pusser, Buford
b. Russo, Anthony J, Jr.
b. Schwab, Charles
b. Smaltz, Audrey
b. Snake, Reuben, Jr.
b. Sobchak, Anatoly Aleksandrovich
b. Toole, John Kennedy
b. Uhry, Alfred
b. Waddell, Tom
b. Wang Hung-Wen
d. Andreas-Salome, Lou
d. Cassidy, Butch
d. Crater, Joseph Force
d. Hewitt, J(ohn) N(apoleon) B(rinton)
d. Mitchell, Reginald Joseph
d. Otto, Louis Karl Rudolf
d. Tappan, William J

January 1, 1937
b. Stovall, Luther McKinley

January 2, 1937
b. Davis, Peter Frank

January 4, 1937
b. Bumbry, Grace Ann Jaeckel
b. Cannon, Dyan

January 6, 1937
b. Holkeri, Harri (Hermanni)
b. Holtz, Lou(is Leo)

January 8, 1937
b. Bassey, Shirley

January 9, 1937
b. Epstein, Joseph

January 10, 1937
b. Walinsky, Adam
d. Eddy, Clarence

January 13, 1937
d. Johnson, Martin Elmer

January 15, 1937
b. O'Brien, Margaret

January 18, 1937
b. Hume, John

January 19, 1937
b. Jeffries, Leonard

January 20, 1937
b. Howell, Bailey E
b. Provine, Dorothy Michele

January 22, 1937
b. Pastora (Gomez), Eden
b. Wambaugh, Joseph Aloysius, Jr.

January 23, 1937
b. Zylis-Gara, Teresa

January 24, 1937
b. Clark, Monte Dale

January 25, 1937
b. Maynard, Don(ald)

January 26, 1937
b. Momoh, Joseph (Saidu)

January 30, 1937
b. Redgrave, Vanessa
b. Spassky, Boris Vasilyevich

January 31, 1937
b. Glass, Philip
b. Pleshette, Suzanne

February 1, 1937
b. Everly, Don(ald)

February 2, 1937
b. Arroyo, Martina
b. Smothers, Tommy

February 4, 1937
b. Newman, David

February 5, 1937
b. Damon, Stuart

February 6, 1937
b. Breuer, Lee

February 7, 1937
b. Jay, Peter
d. Root, Elihu

February 8, 1937
b. Raposo, Joseph
b. Wu, Harry

February 9, 1937
d. Quiroga, Horacio

February 13, 1937
d. Griffin, Walter Burley

February 17, 1937
b. Mobley, Mary Ann

February 20, 1937
b. Huber, Robert
b. Wilson, Nancy

February 21, 1937
b. Clarke, Ron
b. Harald
b. Lockwood, Gary

February 22, 1937
b. Aaron, Tommy

February 24, 1937
b. Tiede, Tom Robert

d. Standing, Guy, Sir

February 25, 1937
b. Courtenay, Tom
b. Sarduy, Severo
b. Schieffer, Bob

March 2, 1937
b. Bouteflika, Abdelaziz
b. Crum, Denny

March 3, 1937
b. Driscoll, Bobby

March 4, 1937
b. Gelb, Leslie Howard
d. Hocking, Silas

March 6, 1937
b. Boesky, Ivan Frederick
b. Tereshkova-Nikolaeva, Valentina

March 7, 1937
d. White, William Alanson

March 8, 1937
d. Morenz, Howie

March 9, 1937
d. More, Paul Elmer

March 12, 1937
d. Hubay, Jeno
d. Widor, Charles Marie Jean Albert

March 13, 1937
d. Thomson, Elihu

March 15, 1937
b. Friedman, Stephen
b. Greenfield, Howard
d. Lovecraft, H(oward) P(hillips)

March 16, 1937
b. Armstrong, William L
d. Chamberlain, Austen, Sir
d. Hobson, Richmond Pearson

March 17, 1937
b. Smith, Lee

March 19, 1937
b. Henry, Clarence
b. Krenz, Egon

March 20, 1937
b. Reed, Jerry
d. Vardon, Harry

March 21, 1937
b. Flores, Tom

March 22, 1937
d. MacMonnies, Fred W

March 23, 1937
b. Gallo, Robert Charles

March 24, 1937
b. Sandiford, Lloyd Erskine

March 25, 1937
b. Monaghan, Tom
d. Drinkwater, John

March 26, 1937
b. Embry, Wayne Richard
b. Lee, James

March 29, 1937
b. Carter, Billy
d. Szymanowski, Karol Maciej

March 30, 1937
b. Beatty, Warren

March 31, 1937
b. Stoddard, Brandon

April 1, 1937
b. Tekere, Edgar Zivanai

April 3, 1937
b. Perret, Gene
b. Spuzich, Sandra Ann

April 5, 1937
b. Carter, Ron
b. Lelyveld, Joseph Salem
b. Powell, Colin (Luther)

April 6, 1937
b. Haggard, Merle Ronald
b. Williams, Billy Dee

April 8, 1937
b. Hersh, Seymour
b. Woodson, Robert L.
d. Foote, Arthur William

April 9, 1937
d. Paine, Albert Bigelow

April 12, 1937
b. Banks, Dennis J.

April 13, 1937
b. Fox, Edward
b. Wilson, Lanford

April 17, 1937
b. Piech, Ferdinand

April 18, 1937
b. Hooks, Robert

April 19, 1937
b. Donahue, Elinor
b. Estrada, Joseph (Marcelo Ejercito)
d. Parker, George Safford
d. Wheeler, William Morton

April 20, 1937
b. Takei, George

April 22, 1937
b. Joseph, Frederick
b. Nicholson, Jack

April 24, 1937
b. Henderson, Joe

April 27, 1937
b. Dennis, Sandy
b. Jones, Phil(ip Howard)
d. Gramsci, Antonio
d. Schutzendorf, Gustav

April 28, 1937
b. Hussein, Saddam (Al-Tikriti)
b. Redpath, Jean

April 29, 1937
d. Carothers, Wallace Hume
d. Gillette, William Hooker
d. Hapgood, Norman
b. Nidal, Abu

May 3, 1937
b. Valli, Frankie

May 4, 1937
b. Edwards, Melvin

May 5, 1937
b. Obasanjo, Olusegun

May 6, 1937
b. Terris, Susan

May 8, 1937
b. Cuellar, Mike
b. DeConcini, Dennis Webster
b. Pynchon, Thomas

May 9, 1937
b. Dalrymple, G. Brent
b. Moneo, Jose Rafael
b. Prater, Dave

May 10, 1937
b. Kopit, Arthur Lee
b. Press, Tamara

May 12, 1937
b. Carlin, George Dennis
b. Studds, Gerry E(astman)

May 13, 1937
b. Carrier, Roch
b. Somogi, Judith
d. Wise, Thomas J

May 14, 1937
b. Howser, Dick
d. Haskins, Charles Homer

May 15, 1937
b. Albright, Madeleine K(orbel)
b. Lopez, Trini(dad, III)

May 16, 1937
b. Hunt, James Baxter, Jr.

May 17, 1937
b. O'Leary, Hazel R(eid)

May 18, 1937
b. Barth, Roland Sawyer
b. Robinson, Brooks Calbert, Jr.
b. Santer, Jacques

May 20, 1937
b. Iveagh, Arthur Francis Benjamin
Guinness, Lord

May 23, 1937
d. Rockefeller, John D(avison)

May 25, 1937
d. Tanner, Henry Ossawa

May 26, 1937
b. Murphy, Jack R

May 27, 1937
d. Ives, Frederic Eugene

May 28, 1937
d. Adler, Alfred

May 29, 1937
b. Tung Chee-hwa

June 1, 1937
b. Freeman, Morgan
b. McCullough, Colleen

June 2, 1937
b. Grooms, Red
b. Kellerman, Sally Claire
b. Paul, Bob

June 4, 1937
b. Fender, Freddy
b. Fulghum, Robert
b. Zuckerman, Mortimer Benjamin

June 7, 1937
b. Bernstein, Jay
b. Jarvi, Neemi
d. Harlow, Jean

June 8, 1937
b. McCandless, Bruce, II
b. Rivers, Joan

June 10, 1937
b. Foreman, Richard
b. Howe, Susan
d. Borden, Robert Laird, Sir

June 11, 1937
b. Everett, Chad
b. Kearse, Amalya Lyle
b. Lewis, Shirley A(nn) R(edd)
d. Tukhachevski, Mikhail
Nikolayevich

June 12, 1937
b. Claybrook, Joan B

June 15, 1937
b. Jennings, Waylon

June 16, 1937
b. Busch, August Adolphus, III
b. Segal, Erich Wolf

June 17, 1937
b. Lupus, Peter
b. Maynard, Robert Clyve

June 18, 1937
b. Godwin, Gail
b. Rockefeller, John D(avison), IV

June 19, 1937
d. Barrie, James Matthew, Sir

June 22, 1937
d. Rabearivelo, Jean Joseph

June 25, 1937
b. Morgan, Marabel
d. Clive, Colin

June 27, 1937
b. Salinas, Luis Omar

June 28, 1937
b. Luciano, Ron(ald Michael)

June 29, 1937
b. Akalaitis, JoAnne

July 2, 1937
b. Holliday, Polly Dean
d. Earhart, Amelia (Mary)
d. Underwood, John Thomas

July 3, 1937
b. Shire, David (Lee)
b. Stoppard, Tom
d. Schick, Jacob

July 5, 1937
b. Hayward, Brooke
b. Knight, Shirley
d. Greenwood, Chester

July 6, 1937
b. Ashkenazy, Vladimir Davidovich
b. Beatty, Ned
b. Head, Bessie Emery

July 8, 1937
b. Loden, Barbara Ann

July 9, 1937
b. Hockney, David

July 10, 1937
b. Cho, Alfred Y(i)

July 11, 1937
d. Gershwin, George

July 12, 1937
b. Cosby, Bill
b. McFarlane, Robert Carl

July 13, 1937
b. Coody, Charles
d. Dalton, Emmett

July 16, 1937
b. Bryan, Richard H.

July 17, 1937
d. Pierne, Gabriel

July 18, 1937
b. Hoffmann, Roald

July 19, 1937
b. Jordan, Richard

July 20, 1937
d. Marconi, Guglielmo

July 21, 1937
b. Frederickson, H Gray

July 24, 1937
b. Young, George

July 25, 1937
b. Carmines, Al(vin Allison Jr.)
d. Saunders, Charles E, Sir

July 27, 1937
b. Galloway, Don

July 28, 1937
b. Duchin, Peter Oelrichs

July 29, 1937
b. Hashimoto, Ryutaro

July 31, 1937
d. Hires, Charles E
b. Crowe, J D

August 1, 1937
b. D'Amato, Alfonse Marcello
b. Plotnik, Arthur

August 2, 1937
b. Cannon, Billy

August 3, 1937
b. Habyarimana, Juvenal
b. Wakoski, Diane

August 5, 1937
b. Brooks, Herb(ert Paul)
b. Pinto da Costa, Manuel

August 7, 1937
b. Maples, William R.
b. Stern, Carl Leonard
d. Gerard, Eddie

August 8, 1937
b. Hoffman, Dustin (Lee)

August 11, 1937
b. Massey, Anna
b. Theodoracopulos, Taki
d. Wharton, Edith

August 12, 1937
b. Myers, Walter Dean

August 13, 1937
b. Weathers, Felicia

August 14, 1937
b. Lord, Winston
d. McNeile, Herman Cyril

August 18, 1937
b. Redford, Robert
d. McIntyre, James

August 21, 1937
b. Stone, Robert Anthony
d. Halevy, Elie

August 22, 1937
b. Kohl, Herbert R

August 23, 1937
d. Roussel, Albert

August 24, 1937
b. Abiola, Moshood

August 26, 1937
d. Mellon, Andrew William

August 27, 1937
b. Sands, Tommy
d. Pope, John Russell

August 28, 1937
d. Opper, Frederick Burr

August 29, 1937
b. Florio, James Joseph

August 30, 1937
b. McLaren, Bruce Leslie

August 31, 1937
b. Berlinger, Warren
d. Wright, George

September 1, 1937
b. Douglas-Home, Charles
b. Geiberger, Al(len L)
b. O'Neal, Ron
d. Coubertin, Pierre de, Baron

September 2, 1937
b. Ueberroth, Peter Victor

September 4, 1937
b. Fraser, Dawn

September 5, 1937
b. Neal, Larry
d. Bergey, David Hendricks

September 6, 1937
b. Worley, Jo Anne
d. Hadley, Henry Kimball

September 7, 1937
b. Law, John Phillip

September 8, 1937
b. Frum, Barbara
b. Lisi, Virna
b. Wexner, Leslie
d. Branch, Anna Hempstead

September 11, 1937
b. Crippen, Robert Laurel

September 12, 1937
b. Chuvalo, George

September 13, 1937
b. Silverman, Fred

September 14, 1937
d. Masaryk, Tomas Garrigue

September 17, 1937
b. Cepeda, Orlando Manuel

September 19, 1937
d. Loeb, William

September 22, 1937
b. McLellan, Diana
b. Metrano, Art
d. Roland, Ruth

September 23, 1937
d. Perkins, Osgood

September 24, 1937
b. Elvira, Pablo
b. Leland, Timothy

September 26, 1937
b. Weintraub, Jerry
d. Filene, Edward Albert
d. Smith, Bessie

September 28, 1937
b. Dickinson, Brian
b. Schul, Bob

September 29, 1937
d. Ewry, Ray C

October 1, 1937
b. Poons, Lawrence

October 2, 1937
b. Cochran, Johnnie

October 3, 1937
d. Howe, Edgar Watson

October 4, 1937
b. Brown, Lee P(atrick)
b. Vranitzky, Franz

October 5, 1937
b. Switzer, Barry

October 6, 1937
b. Maltby, Richard Eldridge, Jr.
b. Scholder, Fritz

October 8, 1937
b. Clodagh

October 11, 1937
b. Charlton, Bobby
b. Leibman, Ron
d. Mills, Ogden Livingston
d. Russell, Henry

October 15, 1937
b. Lavin, Linda

October 16, 1937
b. Anthony, Tony
d. Brunhoff, Jean de

October 17, 1937
d. Ismay, Joseph Bruce

October 18, 1937
b. Dowler, Boyd H

October 19, 1937
b. Bell, Marilyn
b. Max, Peter
d. Rutherford, Ernest, Baron

October 20, 1937
d. Warburg, Felix Moritz

October 22, 1937
b. Ladd, Alan Walbridge, Jr.
d. Damrosch, Frank Heino

October 28, 1937
b. Wilkens, Lenny

October 29, 1937
b. Heth, Charlotte

October 30, 1937
b. Gautier, Dick
b. LeLouch, Claude
d. Kraus, Felix von

October 31, 1937
b. Landon, Michael
b. Paxton, Tom
b. Pender, Mel(vin)
d. Faure, Elie

November 1, 1937
b. Anderson, Bill

November 3, 1937
b. Wayne, Paula
d. Ames, Winthrop

November 4, 1937
b. Wilson, Michael (Holcombe)

November 5, 1937
b. Wolff, Geoffrey (Ansell)
d. McAuliffe, Jack B

November 6, 1937
d. Forbes-Robertson, Johnston, Sir

November 7, 1937
b. Travers, Mary

November 9, 1937
d. MacDonald, James Ramsay

November 11, 1937
b. Celeste, Richard F
b. Lewis, Stephen Henry

November 12, 1937
b. Balin, Ina
b. Fisher, Jules Edward
b. Truly, Richard H
d. Carter, Leslie, Mrs.

November 13, 1937
d. Carter, Caroline Louise Dudley

November 17, 1937
b. Cook, Peter

November 19, 1937
b. Leach, Penelope

November 20, 1937
b. Laredo, Ruth

November 21, 1937
b. Howe, Tina
d. Coffin, Howard Earle

November 22, 1937
b. Idei, Nobuyuki

November 23, 1937
b. Kroll, Alexander S
d. Bose, Jagadis Chandra, Sir

November 25, 1937
b. Joseph, Stephen (Carl)
d. Baylis, Lilian Mary

November 26, 1937
b. Yegorov, Boris (Borisovitch)

November 27, 1937
b. Sheehy, Gail Henion

November 30, 1937
b. Chaudhari, Praveen
b. Threlkeld, Richard D

December 2, 1937
b. Dumas, Charles
b. Zah, Peterson
d. Smith, Joe

December 3, 1937
b. Allison, Bobby
d. Jozsef, Attila

December 4, 1937
b. Baer, Max, Jr.
b. Mott, Stewart Rawlings

December 7, 1937
b. Cochran, Thad

December 8, 1937
b. Berle, Peter A. A.
b. MacArthur, James
b. Shively, Charles

December 9, 1937
d. Dalen, Nils Gustaf

December 15, 1937
b. Goines, Donald

December 16, 1937
b. Ruscha, Edward

December 17, 1937
b. Harris, Bertha

December 20, 1937
d. Ludendorff, Erich Friedrich
   Wilhelm

December 21, 1937
b. Fonda, Jane
d. Healy, Ted
d. Kellogg, Frank Billings

December 25, 1937
b. Casper, Gerhard
d. Baker, Newton D(iehl)

December 26, 1937
b. Dukakis, Kitty
b. Eyadema, Etienne Gnassingbe

December 28, 1937
d. Ravel, Maurice Joseph

December 29, 1937
d. Marquis, Don Robert Perry

December 30, 1937
b. Hartford, John Cowan
b. Stookey, Paul

December 31, 1937
b. Hopkins, Anthony (Philip), Sir

1938

b. Abdel-Rahman, Omar
b. Anderson, Peggy
b. Auldridge, Mike
b. Barnes, Eddie, Jr.
b. Belk, William E
b. Berri, Nabih
b. Bohlem, Arndt von
b. Campo, John(ny)
b. Cousteau, Jean-Michel
b. Efron, Marshall
b. Estridge, Philip D
b. Freedman, Marcia
b. Gould, Lois
b. Gund, Agnes
b. Hasani, Ali Nasir Muhammad
b. Healey, Jack
b. James, Etta
b. Kennedy, Weldon
b. Laughlin, Tom
b. Levy, David
b. Mabuza, Lindiwe
b. Mello, Dawn
b. Mills, Billy
b. Murray, Les(lie) A(llan)
b. Niatum, Duane
b. Payton, Lawrence
b. Pedersen, William
b. Prime, Geoffrey Arthur
b. Ringer, Robert J
b. Schussler Fiorenza, Elisabeth
b. Tuck, Lily
b. Zamora, Bernice
d. Alexander, Samuel
d. Johnson, Marietta Louise Pierce
d. Kautsky, Karl Johann
d. Vallejo, Cesar Abraham

January 2, 1938
b. Conway, Lynn Ann
b. Smithson, Robert (Irving)

January 5, 1938
b. Agee, William McReynolds
b. Juan Carlos I
b. Ngugi, James Thiong'o
b. Otto, Jim

January 7, 1938
b. Graham, Lou
b. Watkins, Shirley R.

January 9, 1938
d. Gruelle, Johnny

January 10, 1938
b. Mahovlich, Frank
b. McCovey, Willie Lee

January 13, 1938
b. Nachman, Gerald Weil

January 14, 1938
b. Hosokawa, Morihiro

January 16, 1938
b. Lipsyte, Robert Mitchell Michael
d. Pickering, William Henry

January 17, 1938
b. Qoboza, Percy

January 18, 1938
b. Flood, Curt(is Charles)
b. Kirk, Paul G(rattan), Jr.
b. Wildmon, Donald Ellis

January 21, 1938
b. Wolfman Jack
d. Melies, Georges

January 22, 1938
b. Beard, Peter Hill

January 24, 1938
d. Barlach, Ernst Heinrich

January 25, 1938
b. Vysotsky, Vladimir Semyonovich

January 26, 1938
d. Bonnin, Gertrude Simmons

January 27, 1938
b. Cole, Kenneth Reese

January 30, 1938
b. Karimov, Islam Abduganievich

January 31, 1938
b. Beatrix
b. Watt, James Gaius
d. King, Frederic Truby

February 1, 1938
b. Hemsley, Sherman

February 2, 1938
b. Estes, Simon Lamont
b. Katz, Jonathan Ned

February 3, 1938
b. Buono, Victor
b. Griffith, Emile Alphonse
d. Palacio Valdes, Armando

February 4, 1938
b. Riegle, Donald Wayne, Jr.

February 5, 1938
b. Guare, John

February 7, 1938
b. Thomopoulos, Anthony Denis
d. Firestone, Harvey Samuel

February 8, 1938
b. Ameling, Elly

February 10, 1938
d. Whiting, Richard Armstrong

February 11, 1938
b. Louise, Tina

February 12, 1938
b. Blume, Judy Sussman

February 13, 1938
b. Reed, Oliver
d. McIntyre, O(scar) O(dd)

February 16, 1938
b. Corigliano, John (Paul)

February 17, 1938
b. Berry, Mary Frances
b. Henry, Martha

February 21, 1938
b. Bird, Lester
d. Hale, George Ellery

February 22, 1938
b. Reed, Ishmael Scott

February 23, 1938
b. Chase, Sylvia B
b. Menzel, Jiri
b. Varsi, Diane

February 24, 1938
b. Farentino, James
b. Knight, Phil
b. Knight, Philip H.

February 25, 1938
b. Baker, Diane
b. Elliott, Herb

March 1, 1938
d. D'Annunzio, Gabriele
d. Harney, Benjamin Robertson

March 2, 1938
d. Scripps, Robert Paine

March 4, 1938
d. McDougall, Walt(er)

March 5, 1938
b. Margulis, Lynn
b. Wainwright, James

March 7, 1938
b. Baltimore, David
b. Guthrie, Janet

March 8, 1938
b. Dawkins, Pete(r M)

March 10, 1938
b. Mix, Ron(ald J)

March 11, 1938
b. Gorman, Chester

March 12, 1938
b. Panov, Valery
b. White, Lois Jean

March 13, 1938
b. Bellino, Joe
b. Brunson, Dorothy
d. Darrow, Clarence Seward

March 14, 1938
d. Bukharin, Nikolai Ivanovich
d. Rykov, Aleksey Ivanovich

March 17, 1938
b. Nureyev, Rudolf (Hametovich)

March 18, 1938
b. McDonnell, John Finney
b. Pride, Charley

March 19, 1938
b. Kapp, Joe

March 21, 1938
d. Clark, John Bates

March 23, 1938
b. Breedlove, Craig
b. Jackson, Maynard Holbrook, Jr.

March 24, 1938
b. Wilson, Larry

March 25, 1938
b. Axton, Hoyt (Wayne)

March 28, 1938
b. Stern, Leonard Norman
d. House, Edward Mandell

March 31, 1938
b. Steel, David Martin Scott

April 1, 1938
b. MacGraw, Ali

April 4, 1938
b. Giamatti, A(ngelo) Bartlett
b. Parks, Michael

April 5, 1938
b. Massey, Walter E(ugene)

April 6, 1938
b. Smith, Jack

April 7, 1938
b. Brown, Jerry
b. Hubbard, Freddie
d. Valadon, Suzanne

April 8, 1938
b. Annan, Kofi (Atta)
b. Norton, Eleanor Holmes
d. Oliver, Joe

April 10, 1938
b. Meredith, Don

April 11, 1938
b. Deaver, Michael Keith

April 13, 1938
b. Rotimi, Ola
d. Grey Owl

April 14, 1938
b. Scott, Gloria Dean Randle

April 15, 1938
b. Cardinale, Claudia

April 18, 1938
b. Glasser, Ira

April 20, 1938
b. Cuthbert, Betty

April 21, 1938
d. Iqbal, Mahomed, Sir

April 22, 1938
b. Beman, Deane Randolph
b. Bond, Alan
b. Kipnis, Claude
b. Miyake, Issey

April 23, 1938
b. Symms, Steven Douglas

April 24, 1938
b. Dale, Carroll W
d. Barnard, George Grey

April 25, 1938
d. Stammler, Rudolf

April 26, 1938
b. Eddy, Duane

April 27, 1938
b. Anthony, Earl Roderick
d. Husserl, Edmund

April 28, 1938
b. Bennett, Ramona
b. Rosenfeld, Alvin Hirsch
b. Sinclair, Madge
b. Wilmerding, John

May 2, 1938
b. Moshoeshoe II

May 4, 1938
d. Ossietzky, Carl von

May 5, 1938
b. Wagner, Barbara

May 7, 1938
b. O'Connor, Kevin
b. Thurow, Lester C

May 9, 1938
b. Simic, Charles

May 10, 1938
b. Shostakovich, Maxim

May 11, 1938
b. Bley, Carla

May 12, 1938
b. Amalrik, Andrei Alekseyevich

May 13, 1938
b. Amato, Giuliano

May 16, 1938
d. Strauss, Joseph Baermann

May 17, 1938
b. Bortoluzzi, Paolo

May 21, 1938
b. Marlowe, Derek

May 22, 1938
b. Benjamin, Richard
b. Converse, Frank
b. Strasberg, Susan Elizabeth
d. Glackens, William James

May 24, 1938
b. Chong, Tommy

May 25, 1938
b. Carver, Raymond Clevie, Jr.
b. Thomas, Joyce Carol

May 26, 1938
b. Bolcom, William Elden
d. Abel, John Jacob

May 28, 1938
b. West, Jerry

May 29, 1938
b. Vincent, Fay

May 31, 1938
b. Yarrow, Peter

June 2, 1938
b. Brownlow, Kevin

June 8, 1938
b. Lee, Martin (Yongho)

June 9, 1938
b. Wuorinen, Charles (Peter)

June 10, 1938
b. Skinner, Sam
b. Skinner, Samuel K(nox)
d. Schomburg, Arthur Alfonso

June 13, 1938
d. Guillaume, Charles Edouard

June 14, 1938
b. Bluitt, Juliann S.
d. Campbell, William Wallace

June 15, 1938
b. Williams, Billy Leo
d. Kirchner, Ernst Ludwig

June 16, 1938
b. Oates, Joyce Carol

June 19, 1938
b. Gwathmey, Charles

June 21, 1938
b. Ely, Ron

June 26, 1938
d. Johnson, James Weldon

June 27, 1938
b. Babbitt, Bruce E(dward)

June 28, 1938
b. Panetta, Leon E(dward)

June 30, 1938
b. Moss, Geoffrey

July 2, 1938
b. Owen, David Anthony Llewellyn
b. Petty, Richard

July 4, 1938
b. Withers, Bill
d. Lenglen, Suzanne

July 5, 1938
b. Goldwater, Barry M(orris), Jr.

July 6, 1938
b. Franco

July 9, 1938
b. Dennehy, Brian
d. Cardozo, Benjamin Nathan

July 13, 1938
b. Widnall, Sheila E.

July 14, 1938
b. Rubin, Jerry
b. Safdie, Moshe

July 16, 1938
b. Vitale, Milly
d. Insull, Samuel

July 18, 1938
d. Marie Alexandra Victoria

July 20, 1938
b. Rigg, Diana

July 21, 1938
b. Allaire, Paul Arthur
b. Aspin, Les
b. Kuerti, Anton
b. Reno, Janet
d. Kroger, Bernard Henry
d. Wister, Owen

July 27, 1938
b. Deutch, John

July 28, 1938
b. Fujimori, Alberto
b. Hughes, Robert Studley Forrest

July 29, 1938
b. Jennings, Peter (Charles)

August 4, 1938
b. Coburn, D(onald) L(ee)
b. Jones, Hayes
d. White, Pearl

August 5, 1938
b. Cone, James H
d. Oland, Warner

August 6, 1938
b. Bonerz, Peter

August 7, 1938
b. Caldicott, Helen Broinowski
d. Stanislavsky, Konstantin
    Sergeyevich

August 8, 1938
b. Pinson, Vada Edward
b. Stevens, Connie
d. Dufresne, Charles

August 9, 1938
b. Laver, Rod(ney George)

August 10, 1938
b. Muldaur, Diana Charlton

August 11, 1938
b. Kent, Allegra

August 12, 1938
b. Marshall, Alan Peter

August 14, 1938
b. Sudarkasa, Niara
d. Ronald, Landon, Sir

August 15, 1938
b. Breyer, Stephen Gerald
b. Waters, Maxine

August 16, 1938
b. Masterton, Bill
b. Rodgers, Bob

August 17, 1938
d. Lewisohn, Adolph

August 19, 1938
b. Cobb, Vicki
b. Goode, Wilson
b. Graham, Robert
d. Frederick, Pauline

August 21, 1938
b. Cowper, Steve Cambreleng
b. Rogers, Kenny

August 24, 1938
b. Williams, Mason

August 25, 1938
b. Forsyth, Frederick

August 29, 1938
b. Gould, Elliott
b. Rubin, Robert E.

August 30, 1938
b. Collins, Gary
d. Factor, Max

November 22, 1938
b. Lee, Henry C.
d. Shestov, Lev

November 24, 1938
b. Robertson, Oscar Palmer
b. Starkweather, Charles

November 26, 1938
b. Goldsmith, Judith Ann Becker
b. Little, Rich(ard Caruthers)

November 28, 1938
d. McDougall, William

November 30, 1938
d. Kun, Bela

December 2, 1938
b. Valerio, James Robert

December 3, 1938
b. Martin, John

December 5, 1938
b. Cale, J J

December 7, 1938
d. Munroe, Charles Edward

December 8, 1938
b. Krause, Bernie

December 9, 1938
b. Jones, Deacon

December 10, 1938
d. Chalmers, William James

December 11, 1938
b. Tyner, McCoy Alfred
d. Lange, Christian Louis

December 12, 1938
b. Francis, Connie

December 13, 1938
b. Johnson, Gus, Jr.

December 14, 1938
b. Boff, Leonardo
b. Brand, Stewart

December 16, 1938
b. Deford, Frank
b. Ullmann, Liv (Johanne)
d. Murchison, Kenneth MacKenzie

December 17, 1938
b. Snell, Peter George
d. Tammann, Gustav Heinrich Johann
Apollon

December 20, 1938
b. Harbison, John Harris

December 22, 1938
b. Alou, Matty

December 24, 1938
d. Capek, Karel

December 26, 1938
b. Fakir, Abdul
b. Snyder, Solomon H(albert)

December 27, 1938
d. Bridges, Calvin Blackman
d. Gale, Zona
d. Lawrence, Florence
d. Mandelstam, Osip Emilyevich
d. Vandervelde, Emile

December 28, 1938
b. Yarnell, Bruce

December 29, 1938
b. Voight, Jon

December 30, 1938
b. Bologna, Joseph

1939

b. Agpaoa, Tony
b. Atkinson, Ti-Grace
b. Berrigan, Elizabeth McAlister
b. Burns, Charles R
b. Jones, Bobby
b. Kalp, Malcolm
b. Khamenei, (Sayed) Ali,
Hojatolislam
b. Koob, Kathryn L
b. Lewis, Thomas
b. Mayle, Peter
b. Miele, Jerry J
b. Mnouchkine, Ariane
b. Reed, Dean
b. Roberts, Roy S.
b. Scott, Ridley
b. Sorvino, Paul
b. Teannaki, Teatao
b. Wasmosy, Juan Carlos
d. Clark, David L
d. Deterding, Henri Wilhelm August,
Sir
d. Eastman, Charles Alexander
d. Hare, Ernie
d. Jantzen, Carl
d. John, Gwendolyn Mary
d. Langsdorff, Hans
d. Radek, Karl Bernhardovich
d. Seligman, Edwin Robert Anderson

January 2, 1939
b. Bakker, Jim
b. Orr, Kay Avonne

January 3, 1939
b. Hull, Bobby

January 5, 1939
d. Haley, Margaret A(ngela)

January 6, 1939
b. Rose, Murray
d. Kelly, Walter C

January 7, 1939
b. Povich, Maury

January 8, 1939
b. Herrera, Carolina
b. Mimieux, Yvette Carmen M

January 10, 1939
b. Horowitz, David Joel
b. Mineo, Sal(vatore)
b. Toomey, Bill

January 11, 1939
b. Posner, Richard Allen

January 12, 1939
b. Golden, William Lee

January 18, 1939
b. Janzen, Daniel Hunt
d. Schultze, Carl Emil

January 19, 1939
b. Everly, Phil

January 21, 1939
b. Norman, Pat

January 22, 1939
b. Smith, Jeff

January 24, 1939
b. Stevens, Ray

January 26, 1939
b. Garfield, Brian Wynne
d. Sauveur, Albert

January 27, 1939
b. Lester, Julius

January 28, 1939
b. Wallace, Cornelia Folsom
d. Yeats, William Butler

January 29, 1939
b. Coverdell, Paul
b. Greer, Germaine

February 1, 1939
d. Brawley, Benjamin Griffith

February 4, 1939
d. Sapir, Edward

February 5, 1939
b. Quinn, Jane Bryant

February 6, 1939
b. Farrell, Mike

February 7, 1939
b. Reed, John S(hepard)

February 9, 1939
b. Suzman, Janet

February 10, 1939
b. Flack, Roberta
b. Kolb, Barbara Anne
d. Pius XI

February 12, 1939
b. Dayan, Yael
b. Hancock, John D

February 17, 1939
b. Keeton, Kathy

February 21, 1939
b. Beymer, Richard

February 22, 1939
d. Machado (y Ruiz), Antonio

February 23, 1939
b. Castro, George (A.)

February 25, 1939
b. Leonard, John

February 27, 1939
b. Revson, Peter Jeffrey
b. Smith, Margaret
d. Krupskaya, Nadezhda
 Konstantinovna

February 28, 1939
b. Fahey, John
b. Tune, Tommy

March 2, 1939
d. Carter, Howard

March 4, 1939
b. Carner, Joanne Gunderson
b. McNair, Barbara
b. Prentiss, Paula

March 5, 1939
b. Fuller, Charles

March 6, 1939
b. Bond, Christopher Samuel
b. Osborne, Adam
b. Spielberg, David
d. Juch, Emma

March 8, 1939
b. Bouton, Jim
b. Lowry, Mike
b. Seymour, Lynn

March 9, 1939
b. Bricklin, Malcolm N

March 10, 1939
b. Press, Irina Natanovna

March 12, 1939
b. Feldon, Barbara

March 13, 1939
b. Sedaka, Neil
d. Levy-Bruhl, Lucien

March 14, 1939
b. Blier, Bertrand

March 15, 1939
b. Chand, Lokendra Bahadur

March 16, 1939
b. Sobieski, Carol

March 18, 1939
b. Burrell, Thomas Jason

March 20, 1939
b. Mulroney, Brian

March 21, 1939
b. Davis, Tommy, Jr.
b. Spann, Otis
b. Widdoes, Kathleen Effie

March 23, 1939
d. Halliburton, Richard

March 24, 1939
b. Nugent, Nelle

March 25, 1939
b. Bambara, Toni Cade

March 26, 1939
b. Jenifer, Franklyn Green

March 27, 1939
b. Yarborough, Cale

March 28, 1939
d. Goldsmith, Fred Ernest

March 29, 1939
d. Machado y Morales, Gerardo

March 31, 1939
b. Horovitz, Israel Arthur
b. Schlondorff, Volker
d. Park, William Hallock

April 1, 1939
b. Niekro, Phil(ip Henry)

April 2, 1939
b. Gaye, Marvin (Pentz)
b. Lake, Anthony

April 4, 1939
b. Bridges, Bill
b. Masekela, Hugh Ramapolo

April 6, 1939
b. Sculley, John

April 7, 1939
b. Coppola, Francis Ford
b. Frost, David
d. Lyons, Joseph Aloysius

April 9, 1939
b. Rogers, Lynn L(eroy)

April 10, 1939
b. Oliver, Daniel

April 11, 1939
b. Lasser, Louise
d. Van Dine, S S

April 12, 1939
b. Ayckbourn, Alan

April 13, 1939
b. Collins, Barbara-Rose
b. Heaney, Seamus (Justin)

April 15, 1939
b. Paz Zamora, Jaime

April 16, 1939
b. Springfield, Dusty

April 20, 1939
b. Brundtland, Gro Harlem

April 21, 1939
b. McCabe, John

April 22, 1939
b. Miller, Jason

April 23, 1939
b. Williams, Patrick

April 25, 1939
b. Lichfield, Patrick

April 27, 1939
b. Carne, Judy
b. Vieira, Joao (Bernardo)

April 30, 1939
b. Kleban, Edward Lawrence
b. Ortiz, Alfonso
b. Zwilich, Ellen Taaffe

May 1, 1939
b. Beard, Frank
b. Collins, Judy
b. Robinson, Max C

May 2, 1939
b. Shreve, Susan Richards

May 4, 1939
b. Abrams, George H. J.
b. Jackson, Mannie (L.)
b. Oz, Amos

May 5, 1939
b. Jones, James Robert

May 6, 1939
b. Levin, Gerald

May 7, 1939
b. Altman, Sidney
b. Clark, Joe
b. Lubbers, Ruud
b. Ruffin, Jimmy

May 8, 1939
d. Cabot, Richard C

May 9, 1939
b. Boston, Ralph

May 10, 1939
b. Darnton, Robert Choate

May 11, 1939
b. Pappas, Milt(on Steven)

May 12, 1939
b. Ziegler, Ron(ald Louis)

May 13, 1939
b. Keitel, Harvey

May 15, 1939
b. Hammer, Barbara J.

May 17, 1939
b. Purdy, Susan Gold

May 19, 1939
b. Fox, James
b. Kwan, Nancy Kashen
b. Scobee, Dick
b. Young, Stephen

May 20, 1939
d. Carr, Joe

May 21, 1939
b. Groh, David Lawrence
b. Holliger, Heinz

May 22, 1939
d. Toller, Ernst

May 25, 1939
b. Carter, Dixie
b. McKellen, Ian (Murray), Sir
d. Duveen, Joseph, Sir
d. Dyson, Frank Watson, Sir

May 26, 1939
b. Musburger, Brent Woody
b. Stratas, Teresa
d. Mayo, Charles Horace

May 27, 1939
b. Sigmund, Barbara Boggs
b. Williams, Don

May 29, 1939
b. Unser, Al, Sr.

May 30, 1939
b. Pollard, Michael J

May 31, 1939
b. Waite, Terry

June 1, 1939
b. Dodson, Howard, Jr.
b. Little, Cleavon Jake

June 2, 1939
b. Collier, Peter
b. Hamilton, William

June 3, 1939
b. Woodiwiss, Kathleen (Erin)

June 4, 1939
d. Ladnier, Tommy

June 5, 1939
b. Clark, Joe
b. Drabble, Margaret

June 6, 1939
b. Bonds, Gary U S
b. Edelman, Marian Wright
b. Giacomin, Eddie
d. Fawcett, George

June 8, 1939
b. Adderley, Herb(ert Anthony)

b. Rukeyser, William Simon

June 9, 1939
b. Cotrubas, Ileana
b. Vitale, Dick

June 11, 1939
b. Crawford, Christina
b. Purdie, Bernard
b. Stewart, Jackie

June 13, 1939
b. Froines, John Radford
d. Barker, Doc

June 14, 1939
b. Andrews, Michael Alford
d. Khodasevich, Vladislav
d. Pulitzer, Ralph

June 15, 1939
b. Connerly, Ward

June 16, 1939
d. Webb, Chick

June 18, 1939
b. Brock, Lou(is Clark)
b. Slotnick, Barry Ivan

June 19, 1939
d. Abbott, Grace

June 24, 1939
b. Garrett, Henry Lawrence, III

June 26, 1939
b. Chase-Riboud, Barbara
b. Robb, Charles Spittal
d. Ford, Ford Madox

June 27, 1939
b. Jones, Brereton C

July 2, 1939
b. Castle, Michael Newbold
b. Sununu, John Henry

July 3, 1939
b. Fassbaender, Brigitte

July 7, 1939
b. Obraztsova, Elena
d. White, Deacon

July 8, 1939
d. Ellis, Havelock

July 11, 1939
b. Laoretti, Larry

July 14, 1939
d. Mucha, Alphonse Marie

July 15, 1939
b. Cavaco Silva, Anibal Antonio
b. Wayne, Patrick
d. Bleuler, Eugen

July 16, 1939
b. Perry, Ruth (Sando)
b. Redgrave, Corin

July 18, 1939
b. Auger, Brian
b. Dion
b. Thompson, Hunter S(tockton)

July 20, 1939
b. Chicago, Judy
b. Wood, Natalie

July 22, 1939
b. Flynn, Ray
b. Flynn, Raymond (Leo)

July 23, 1939
b. Gage, Nicholas

July 24, 1939
b. Bellamy, Walt(er Jones)

July 26, 1939
b. Howard, John (Winston)
b. Lilly, Bob
d. Spingarn, Joel Elias

July 27, 1939
b. Costle, Douglas Michael

July 28, 1939
b. Horner, Matina Souretis
d. Mayo, William James
d. Mercer, Beryl

July 30, 1939
b. Bogdanovich, Peter
b. Smeal, Eleanor Marie Cutri

July 31, 1939
b. Nuyen, France

August 1, 1939
b. Waller, Robert James

August 2, 1939
b. Craven, Wes

August 3, 1939
b. Krogh, Egil, Jr.

August 5, 1939
b. Irene

August 7, 1939
b. Kantor, Mickey

August 8, 1939
b. Kuchma, Leonid Danylovich

August 9, 1939
b. Prodi, Romano

August 12, 1939
b. Gabor, Mark
b. Hamilton, George, IV

August 16, 1939
b. Shelley, Carole Augusta

August 17, 1939
b. Sanders, Ed

August 18, 1939
b. Bee, Molly

August 19, 1939
b. Baker, Alan

August 21, 1939
b. Burton, James
b. Mogae, Festus Gontebanye
b. Williams, Clarence, III

August 22, 1939
b. Milano, Fred
b. Yastrzemski, Carl Michael
d. Goldin, Horace

August 23, 1939
d. Howard, Sidney Coe

August 25, 1939
b. Canary, David
d. Siebert, Babe

August 27, 1939
b. Least Heat Moon, William

August 28, 1939
b. Fahrenkopf, Frank Joseph, Jr.
b. Mackin, Catherine Patricia
d. Pritchett, Henry S

August 29, 1939
b. Carruthers, Garrey E
b. Chan, Julius
b. Friedkin, William
b. Thornell, Jack Randolph

August 31, 1939
b. Stevens, Eileen
b. Winter, Paul Theodore
d. Rackham, Arthur

September 1, 1939
b. Carty, Rico
b. Tomlin, Lily

September 3, 1939
b. Nicholas, Nicholas John, Jr.
d. Westermarck, Edward Alexander

September 5, 1939
b. Devane, William
b. Stewart, John
b. Tonegawa, Susumu

September 6, 1939
b. Coe, David Allan
b. Mark, Norman (Barry)

September 8, 1939
d. Gilman, Lawrence

September 9, 1939
d. Smith, Christopher Columbus

September 10, 1939
b. Mullavey, Greg

September 12, 1939
b. Waxman, Henry Arnold
d. Cowles, Henry Chandler

September 13, 1939
b. Auger, Arleen
b. Kiel, Richard
b. Speakes, Larry Melvin
b. Ulmanis, Guntis
b. Witkin, Joel-Peter

September 16, 1939
b. Breytenbach, Breyten

September 17, 1939
b. Fey, Thomas Hossler
b. Souter, David Hackett

September 18, 1939
d. Ratana, Taupotiki Wiremu
d. Schwab, Charles Michael

September 21, 1939
b. Mas Canosa, Jorge

September 22, 1939
b. Wirth, Timothy E

September 23, 1939
b. Sullivan, Mike
d. Freud, Sigmund

September 24, 1939
b. Gillott, Jacky
d. Gibbons, Floyd Phillips
d. Laemmle, Carl, Sr.

September 25, 1939
b. Brittan, Leon

September 26, 1939
b. Douglas, Donna

September 27, 1939
b. Whitworth, Kathy

September 28, 1939
b. Luedtke, Kurt (Mamre)

September 29, 1939
b. Linville, Larry Lavon

September 30, 1939
b. Cariou, Len
b. Lehn, Jean-Marie

October 1, 1939
b. Archer, George
b. Carruthers, George Robert, Dr.

October 2, 1939
b. Reed, Rex
d. Mundelein, George William

October 3, 1939
d. Templeton, Fay

October 6, 1939
b. Bragg, Melvyn

October 7, 1939
d. Cushing, Harvey Williams

October 8, 1939
b. Hogan, Paul

October 11, 1939
b. Bueno, Maria Ester Audion

October 13, 1939
b. Colbert, Virgis William
d. Sterling, Ford

October 14, 1939
b. Feldman, Sandra
b. Lauren, Ralph

October 18, 1939
b. Cotti, Flavio
b. Ditka, Mike
b. Oswald, Lee Harvey

October 20, 1939
b. Slick, Grace Wing

October 22, 1939
b. Chissano, Joaquim Alberto
b. Roberts, Tony

October 23, 1939
d. Grey, Zane

October 24, 1939
b. Allen, Paula Gunn

October 27, 1939
b. Chatham, Russell
b. Cleese, John Marwood
b. Frazier, Dallas June
b. Yardley, Jonathan

October 28, 1939
b. Alexander, Jane
d. Brady, Alice

October 31, 1939
b. Dillon, Melinda
d. Rank, Otto
b. Flowers, Wayland Parrott, Jr.

November 1, 1939
b. Bosson, Barbara
b. Kouchner, Bernard

November 2, 1939
b. Serra, Richard Anthony

November 3, 1939
b. McNally, Terrence

November 4, 1939
b. Swit, Loretta

November 6, 1939
b. Bell, Arthur (Irving)

November 7, 1939
b. Egan, John Leopold, Sir

November 12, 1939
d. Bethune, Norman

November 13, 1939
b. Higgins, George V.
d. Weber, Lois

November 17, 1939
b. Waugh, Auberon

November 18, 1939
b. Atwood, Margaret (Eleanor)
b. Vaccaro, Brenda

November 19, 1939
b. Constantinescu, Emil
b. Harkin, Thomas R(ichard)
b. Utley, (Clifton) Garrick

November 23, 1939
d. Bodanzky, Artur

November 24, 1939
b. Northrup, Jim

November 25, 1939
b. Delaney, Shelagh
b. Feldstein, Martin Stuart

November 26, 1939
b. Turner, Tina

November 27, 1939
b. Giusti, Dave

November 28, 1939
d. Naismith, James A

November 29, 1939
b. Gilder, George
b. McAuliffe, Dick
d. Scheidemann, Philipp

November 30, 1939
b. Keyworth, George Albert

December 1, 1939
b. Lennon, Dianne
b. Trevino, Lee Buck

December 2, 1939
b. Reid, Harry
d. Powys, Llewelyn

December 4, 1939
b. Brady, Joan
d. Wu P'ei-fu

December 5, 1939
b. Berendt, John
b. Bofill, Ricardo

December 6, 1939
d. Dalmores, Charles

December 8, 1939
b. Galway, James
d. Schelling, Ernest Henry

December 11, 1939
b. Hayden, Tom
b. McGuane, Thomas Francis
d. Walgreen, Charles Rudolph

December 12, 1939
d. Fairbanks, Douglas

December 14, 1939
. b. Davis, Ernie

December 16, 1939
b. Gayoom, Maumoon Abdul

December 18, 1939
b. Varmus, Harold E(lliot)
b. Versalles, Zoilo Casanova
d. Broun, (Matthew) Heywood
(Campbell)

December 19, 1939
b. Tyson, Cicely

December 22, 1939
b. Pinkney, Jerry
d. Rainey, Gertrude

December 23, 1939
d. Fokker, Anthony Herman Gerard

December 25, 1939
b. James, Bob

December 26, 1939
b. Martin, Lynn

December 29, 1939
b. Huizenga, H(arry) Wayne

December 30, 1939
b. Shannon, Del

December 31, 1939
d. Benson, Frank Robert, Sir

1940

b. Alaia, Azzedine
b. Ali Mahdi Mohamed
b. Aoki, Hiroaki
b. Arnstein, Bobbie
b. Behrens, Hildegard
b. Ben-Israel, Ben Ami
b. Blyth, Chay
b. Brown, Marie Dutton
b. Burum, Stephen H
b. Canfield, Alan B.
b. Cisse, Souleymane
b. Crowley, Diane
b. Donath, Helen
b. Duel, Peter
b. Elizabeth Bagaaya Nyabongo of
Toro
b. France, Johnny
b. Gordon, Steve
b. Hamblin, Ken
b. Harper, Ken
b. Henriksen, Lance
b. Husseini, Faisal
b. Husseini, Faisal
b. Koch, Bill
b. Lewis, Vaughan Allen
b. LiPuma, Tommy
b. Lucinschi, Petru
b. McKay, Nellie Yvonne
b. Means, Russell
b. Micombero, Michel
b. Miranda, Ernesto
b. Muldowney, Shirley
b. Murray, Elizabeth
b. Nazarbayev, Nursultan (Abishevich)
b. Porter, Nyree Dawn
b. Rabani, Burhanuddin
b. Reggio, Godfrey
b. Robelo, Alfonso
b. Rodriguez, Miguel Angel
b. Roeder, David

b. Romano, Joseph
b. Romero, George A
b. Saibou, Ali
b. Schoonmaker, Thelma
b. Smith, Juane Quick-to-See
b. Snegur, Mircea Ion
b. Tabei, Junko
b. Treybig, James G
b. Warner, Emily Howell
b. Weinberg, Moshe
b. Welch, James
b. Wesley, Valerie Wilson
d. Ben Badis, Abd al-Hamid
d. Masson, Paul

January 1, 1940
b. Langella, Frank
d. Tallmadge, Thomas Eddy

January 2, 1940
d. Casey, Edward Pearce

January 4, 1940
b. Josephson, Brian David

January 5, 1940
b. O'Donoghue, Michael

January 7, 1940
b. Berkow, Ira Harvey

January 8, 1940
b. Hampton, Henry

January 11, 1940
d. Mellor, Walter

January 13, 1940
b. White, Edmund

January 14, 1940
b. Bond, Julian
b. Castle, John
b. Nunn, Trevor Robert
d. Benediktsson, Einar

January 17, 1940
b. Keino, Kip

January 19, 1940
b. Mills, Mary
d. Borah, William Edgar

January 20, 1940
b. Heiss, Carol Elizabeth
b. Jenkins, Carol Elizabeth Heiss

January 21, 1940
b. Nicklaus, Jack William

January 22, 1940
b. Hurt, John

January 24, 1940
b. Waissman, Kenneth

January 26, 1940
b. Cadoria, Sherian Grace
b. Reilly, William Kane

January 29, 1940
b. Diaz, Justino

d. Harkness, Edward Stephen

January 31, 1940
b. Margolin, Stuart

February 1, 1940
d. Nowlan, Phil

February 3, 1940
b. Hartz, James Leroy
b. Tarkenton, Fran(cis Asbury)

February 4, 1940
b. Bakke, Allan Paul
b. Broadhurst, Kent

February 6, 1940
b. Brokaw, Tom

February 8, 1940
b. Koppel, Ted

February 9, 1940
b. Bordeaux, Lionel R.
b. Coetzee, J(ohn) M
d. Dodd, William Edward

February 10, 1940
b. Toomey, Mary Rand

February 11, 1940
b. Ford, Kathleen DuRoss
b. Noriega (Moreno), Manuel Antonio
d. Buchan, John, Sir

February 12, 1940
b. Brown, Hank

February 13, 1940
b. Eaton, Robert James

February 19, 1940
b. Krementz, Jill
b. Robinson, Smokey

February 20, 1940
b. Eschenbach, Christoph

February 21, 1940
b. Caperton, Gaston
b. Lewis, John Robert

February 22, 1940
b. Walker, Chet

February 23, 1940
b. Fonda, Peter

February 25, 1940
b. Santo, Ron(ald Edward)

February 27, 1940
b. Hesseman, Howard
d. Behrens, Peter
d. Graves, William Sidney

February 28, 1940
b. Andretti, Mario Gabriel
b. Takada, Kenzo
d. Dolmetsch, Arnold

February 29, 1940
d. Benson, Edward Frederic

March 2, 1940
b. De Maiziere, Lothar

March 3, 1940
b. Ellis, Perry Edwin
d. Muck, Karl
d. Ts'ai Yuan-p'ei

March 4, 1940
d. Garland, Hamlin

March 5, 1940
b. Auletta, Robert
b. Eggar, Samantha
d. Elliott, Maxine

March 7, 1940
b. Travanti, Daniel J(ohn)
d. Finley, John Huston
d. Markham, Edwin

March 9, 1940
b. Julia, Raul

March 10, 1940
b. Norris, Chuck
b. Rabe, David William
d. Bulgakov, Mikhail Afanasyevich

March 12, 1940
b. Jarreau, Al(wyn Lopez)

March 15, 1940
b. Lesh, Phil

March 16, 1940
d. Barton, George
d. Lagerlof, Selma Ottiliana Lovisa

March 17, 1940
b. White, Mark Wells, Jr.
d. Anderson, George Everett

March 18, 1940
b. Medoff, Mark Howard

March 20, 1940
b. Mark, Mary Ellen

March 22, 1940
b. Keon, Dave
b. Ward, Phillip R

March 24, 1940
b. Mackie, Bob

March 25, 1940
b. Bryant, Anita Jane

March 26, 1940
b. Caan, James

March 27, 1940
b. Pendleton, Austin
d. Savage, Michael Joseph

March 28, 1940
b. Banks, Russell
b. Loughery, Kevin Michael

March 30, 1940
b. Lucas, Jerry Ray

March 31, 1940
b. Frank, Barney
b. Leahy, Patrick Joseph
b. Campbell, Maria
b. Holland, Robert, Jr.

April 1, 1940
b. Jahn, Helmut
b. Maathai, Wangari (Muta)
d. Hobson, John Atkinson

April 4, 1940
b. Bijan
b. Hailwood, Mike

April 7, 1940
d. Adler, Cyrus
d. Faversham, William Alfred

April 8, 1940
b. Havlicek, John
b. Lennon, Peggy

April 9, 1940
d. Campbell, Patrick, Mrs.

April 12, 1940
b. Hancock, Herbie

April 14, 1940
b. Christie, Julie

April 15, 1940
b. Archer, Jeffrey Howard
b. Davis, Willie

April 16, 1940
b. Margrethe II

April 17, 1940
b. Jerusalem, Siegfried
b. Williams, Tommy

April 18, 1940
b. Garvey, Ed(ward Robert)
b. Goldstein, Joseph Leonard
d. Beer, Thomas
d. Fisher, Herbert Albert Laurens
d. McCoy, Charles

April 23, 1940
b. Birney, David Edwin
b. Majors, Lee

April 24, 1940
d. Jacobs, Joe B

April 25, 1940
b. Pacino, Al(fredo James)

April 26, 1940
b. Cruikshank, Margaret
d. Bosch, Carl

April 28, 1940
d. Tetrazzini, Luisa

April 30, 1940
b. Young, Burt

b. Niyazov, Saparmurad Atayevich

May 1, 1940
b. Alcala, Jose (Ramon)
b. Cooper, Wilhelmina Behmenburg
b. Foxman, Abraham H
b. Mason, Bobbie Ann
b. Peretti, Elsa
d. Brooke, L Leslie

May 2, 1940
b. Esquivel, Manuel
b. Leghari, Sardar Farooq Ahmed
  Khan

May 3, 1940
b. Fagan, Garth
d. Flipper, Henry Ossian

May 4, 1940
b. Cook, Robin

May 5, 1940
b. Oh, Sadaharu
b. Rudd, Paul Ryan

May 7, 1940
b. Carter, Angela (Olive)

May 8, 1940
b. Benchley, Peter Bradford
b. Nelson, Rick

May 9, 1940
b. Brooks, James L.

May 10, 1940
b. Dyer, Wayne Walter

May 12, 1940
b. Nestle, Joan
b. Perkins, Millie

May 13, 1940
b. Chatwin, Bruce

May 14, 1940
d. Goldman, Emma

May 15, 1940
b. Ailes, Roger Eugene
b. Nelson, Don(ald Arvid)

May 18, 1940
d. Bunau-Varilla, Philippe Jean

May 19, 1940
b. Lorenzo, Frank

May 20, 1940
b. Mikita, Stan(ley)
b. Schell, Orville H(ickock), 3rd.
d. Heidenstam, Carl Gustaf Verner von

May 21, 1940
d. MacKay, Mickey

May 22, 1940
b. Sarrazin, Michael
b. Shaw, Bernard

May 24, 1940
b. Brodsky, Joseph (Alexandrovich)
b. Futrell, Mary Alice Franklin
  Hatwood

May 26, 1940
b. Bikoff, James L

May 27, 1940
b. Morris, Edmund

May 28, 1940
b. Binchy, Maeve
d. Connolly, Walter

May 29, 1940
d. Anderson, Mary Antoinette

May 30, 1940
b. Sayers, Gale Eugene

June 1, 1940
b. Auberjonois, Rene Murat
d. Loisy, Alfred Firmin
d. Woodbridge, Frederick James
  Eugene

June 2, 1940
b. Constantine XII

June 4, 1940
b. Sherwood, Frances

June 5, 1940
b. Patterson, Orlando
d. Love, Augustus Edward Hough

June 7, 1940
b. Jones, Tom

June 8, 1940
b. Sinatra, Nancy
d. Converse, Frederick Shepherd

June 10, 1940
d. Garvey, Marcus Moziah

June 11, 1940
b. Vidov, Oleg

June 16, 1940
b. Craddock, Crash
b. Goldschmidt, Neil Edward
d. Heyward, (Edwin) DuBose

June 17, 1940
b. Bell, Bobby
d. Harden, Arthur, Sir

June 19, 1940
d. Myers, Jerome

June 20, 1940
d. Chase, Charley
d. Nevada, Emma
d. Reiss, Albert

June 21, 1940
b. Cooke, Hope
b. Flaherty, Joe
b. Hartley, Mariette
d. Thompson, John Taliaferro

d. Vuillard, (Jean) Edouard

June 23, 1940
b. Faith, Adam
b. Rudolph, Wilma (Glodean)
b. Trask, Diana

June 26, 1940
b. Davis, Billy, Jr.
b. Valdez, Luis (Miguel)
d. Modjeski, Ralph

June 28, 1940
d. Balbo, Italo

June 29, 1940
d. Klee, Paul

July 1, 1940
b. Jones, Charles A, Jr.
d. Turpin, Ben

July 2, 1940
b. Clarke, Kenneth Harry

July 3, 1940
b. Alexander, Lamar
b. Sears, John Patrick

July 7, 1940
b. Armey, Richard K(eith)
b. Starr, Ringo

July 8, 1940
b. Baliles, Gerald L

July 10, 1940
d. Tovey, Donald Francis, Sir

July 13, 1940
b. Prudhomme, Paul
b. Stewart, Patrick

July 14, 1940
b. Howatch, Susan

July 18, 1940
b. Brolin, James
b. Faderman, Lillian
b. Torre, Joe

July 20, 1940
b. Oliva, Tony
d. Maytag, Elmer Henry

July 22, 1940
b. Stamp, Terence
b. Trebek, Alex

July 23, 1940
b. Goldin, Daniel S
b. Imus, Don

July 24, 1940
b. Campbell, Carroll Ashmore, Jr.
b. Moss, Cynthia Jane

July 25, 1940
b. Pennel, John (Thomas)

July 26, 1940
b. Kopechne, Mary Jo

July 27, 1940
b. Bausch, Pina
b. Mukherjee, Bharati
b. Perry, Troy D.

July 28, 1940
b. Grahn, Judy

July 30, 1940
b. Gourdine, Simon (Peter)
b. Schroeder, Patricia Scott

August 2, 1940
b. Rosenberg, Steven A

August 3, 1940
b. Alworth, Lance Dwight
b. Sheen, Martin
d. Jabotinsky, Vladimir Evgenevich

August 5, 1940
b. Gabriel, Roman, Jr.
d. Cook, Frederick Albert

August 7, 1940
b. Dehaene, Jean-Luc

August 8, 1940
d. Bonci, Alessandro
d. Coolidge, Dane
d. Dodds, Johnny

August 9, 1940
b. Saint John, Jill

August 10, 1940
b. Hatfield, Bobby

August 14, 1940
b. Crofts, Dash
b. Laffer, Arthur Betz
b. Royo, Aristides

August 16, 1940
b. Beresford, Bruce
b. Dobkin, Alix

August 18, 1940
d. Chrysler, Walter Percy

August 19, 1940
b. Baker, Ginger
b. Nash, Johnny

August 21, 1940
d. Thayer, Ernest L
d. Trotsky, Leon

August 22, 1940
b. Harper, Valerie
b. McCartney, Bill
d. Lodge, Oliver Joseph, Sir
d. Walcott, Mary Morris Vaux

August 23, 1940
b. Bill, Tony
b. Sanders, Richard Kinard

August 24, 1940
b. Grafton, Sue

August 25, 1940
d. Michelin, Edouard

August 28, 1940
b. Cohen, William S(ebastian)
d. Bowie, William

August 29, 1940
b. Brady, James Scott

August 30, 1940
d. Thomson, Joseph John, Sir

September 1, 1940
b. Ernaux, Annie
d. Wald, Lillian D

September 2, 1940
b. Debray, Regis
d. Gatti-Casazza, Giulio

September 3, 1940
b. Galeano, Eduardo (Hughes)

September 4, 1940
b. Tribble, Isreal, Jr.

September 5, 1940
b. Welch, Raquel

September 9, 1940
b. Smith, Dennis

September 10, 1940
b. Ayers, Roy
b. Buchanan, Buck

September 11, 1940
b. DePalma, Brian Russell
b. Rhodes, Zandra
d. Waugh, Frederick Judd

September 12, 1940
b. Gray, Linda
b. Lolich, Mickey
b. Solarz, Stephen Joshua

September 14, 1940
b. Brown, Larry

September 15, 1940
b. Olsen, Merlin Jay
d. Bankhead, William Brockman

September 18, 1940
b. Avalon, Frankie
b. Keohane, Nannerl Overholser

September 19, 1940
b. Medley, Bill
b. Tyson, Sylvia Fricker
b. Williams, Paul Hamilton

September 21, 1940
b. Kurtis, Bill

September 22, 1940
b. Schuler, Mike
b. Stanton, Robert

September 23, 1940
b. Peters, C(larence) J(ames), (Jr.)

September 25, 1940
d. Clark, Marguerite

September 27, 1940
d. Wagner-Jaurregg, Julius, von

September 29, 1940
b. Lewis, Jerry Lee

October 1, 1940
b. Corben, Richard Vance

October 2, 1940
d. Stanley, Freelan O

October 3, 1940
b. Ferris, Barbara Gillian
b. Ratelle, Jean

October 5, 1940
d. Booth, Ballington

October 9, 1940
b. Humphrey, Gordon John
b. Lennon, John Winston
b. Pepitone, Joe
d. Grenfell, Wilfred Thomason, Sir
d. Mayo, Katherine

October 12, 1940
d. Mix, Tom

October 14, 1940
b. Richard, Cliff
d. Kayser, Heinrich Gustav Johannes

October 15, 1940
b. Moser, Barry

October 16, 1940
b. DeBusschere, Dave

October 21, 1940
b. FitzGerald, Frances

October 23, 1940
b. Pele

October 24, 1940
b. Abraham, F(ahrid) Murray

October 25, 1940
b. Knight, Bobby

October 27, 1940
b. Gotti, John
b. Kingston, Maxine Hong

October 29, 1940
b. Mack, Connie

October 30, 1940
b. Fox, Charles
d. Asplund, Erik Gunnar

October 31, 1940
d. Pulford, Harvey

November 1, 1940
b. Sloan, Hugh W

November 2, 1940
b. Bakken, Jim

November 3, 1940
d. Hine, Lewis Wickes

November 4, 1940
b. McClinton, Delbert
d. Azana y Diaz, Manuel

November 5, 1940
b. Roldos Aguilera, Jamie

November 7, 1940
d. Gardner, Jimmy

November 9, 1940
d. Chamberlain, Neville

November 10, 1940
b. Means, Russell C(harles)

November 11, 1940
b. Boxer, Barbara Levy
d. Taussig, Frank William

November 15, 1940
b. Waterston, Sam(uel Atkinson)

November 16, 1940
b. Bloch, Ivan Sol
d. Beck, Martin

November 18, 1940
b. Qaboos Bin Al Sai'id
b. Quabus bin Saud
d. Gill, Eric

November 20, 1940
b. Butala, Tony
b. Einstein, Bob
d. Blatch, Harriot Eaton Stanton

November 21, 1940
b. Makarova, Natalia

November 22, 1940
b. Gilliam, Terry (Vance)

November 23, 1940
b. Tiant, Luis Clemente
d. Jones, Billy

November 24, 1940
b. Tagliabue, Paul John
d. Saionji, Kimmochi

November 25, 1940
b. Gibbs, Joe Jackson

November 26, 1940
b. Kantrowitz, Arnie
d. Andresen, Ivar
d. Harmsworth, Harold Sidney
d. Rothermere, Harold Sidney
   Harmsworth

November 27, 1940
b. Lee, Bruce

November 29, 1940
b. Mangione, Chuck

November 30, 1940
b. Phillips, Kevin (Price)

December 1, 1940
b. Pryor, Richard (Franklin Lennox
   Thomas)
d. Richman, Charles

December 2, 1940
b. Brown, Willie
b. Chapin, Dwight Lee
d. Revel, Bernard

December 3, 1940
b. Swift, Elizabeth Ann
d. Gordon, C Henry

December 5, 1940
d. Kubelik, Jan

December 6, 1940
b. Edlund, Richard

December 7, 1940
b. Cheevers, Gerry
b. Simpson, Carole

December 10, 1940
b. Smitherman, Geneva

December 11, 1940
b. Gates, David

December 12, 1940
b. Warwick, Dionne

December 15, 1940
b. Buoniconti, Nick

December 16, 1940
d. Dubois, Eugene
d. Hamilton, Billy

December 17, 1940
b. Kendricks, Eddie
b. McIntyre, James Talmadge, Jr.

December 19, 1940
b. Ochs, Phil(ip David)

December 20, 1940
b. Goffstein, Marilyn

December 21, 1940
b. Fox, Matthew (Timothy James)
b. Zappa, Frank
d. Fitzgerald, F(rancis) Scott (Key)

December 22, 1940
d. West, Nathanael

December 23, 1940
b. Graves, Nancy (Stevenson)
b. Kauokenen, Jorma

December 24, 1940
b. Fauci, Anthony Stephen
d. Hill, Billy

December 25, 1940
b. Brown, Peter
d. Ayres, Agnes

December 26, 1940
b. Spector, Phil(lip Harvey)
d. Frohman, Daniel

December 29, 1940
b. Hansen, Fred Morgan
d. Birch, Stephen

December 30, 1940
b. Burrows, James
b. Cousteau, Philippe
b. Pentifallo, Kenny

1941

b. Anthony, Earl
b. Bayley, Corrine
b. Beals, Melba Patillo
b. Cash, Jim
b. Dijkstra, Sjoukje
b. Dr. John
b. Dubnov, Simon
b. Evora, Cesaria
b. Flynn, Sean
b. Gilmore, Gary Mark
b. Glancy, Diane
b. Hansen, Georges
b. Holbrooke, Richard
b. Holt, Fritz
b. Kharitonov, Yevgeni
b. Klein, Marty
b. Klepfisz, Irena
b. Korman, Maxime Carlot
b. Lyne, Adrian
b. McLaren, Wayne
b. Nakamura, Kuniwo
b. Parent, Elizabeth Anne
b. Roybal-Allard, Lucille
b. Sadler, Barry
b. Sharer, Donald A
b. Stewart, Martha
b. Westwood, Vivienne
d. Dubnov, Simon
d. Menocal, Mario Garcia

January 3, 1941
d. Bergson, Henri Louis

January 4, 1941
b. Reagan, Maureen Elizabeth

January 5, 1941
b. McKinley, Chuck
d. Johnson, Amy

January 7, 1941
b. Gregory, Frederick D(rew)

January 8, 1941
b. Chapman, Graham
d. Baden-Powell, Robert Stephenson
   Smyth Baden-Powell, Baron

January 9, 1941
b. Baez, Joan
b. Hands, Terry
b. York, Susannah

January 10, 1941
b. Caputo, Philip Joseph
d. Lavery, John, Sir
d. Penner, Joe

January 11, 1941
d. Bridge, Frank
d. Lasker, Emanuel

January 12, 1941
b. Howells, Anne Elizabeth

January 13, 1941
d. Ellis, Carleton
d. Joyce, James Augustus Aloysius

January 14, 1941
b. Dunaway, Faye
b. Kucan, Milan

January 15, 1941
b. Beefheart, Captain
b. Captain Beefheart
b. Farmer, Forest Jackson

January 18, 1941
b. Goldsboro, Bobby
b. Lopez de Arriortua, Jose Ignacio
b. Ruffin, David

January 21, 1941
b. Domingo, Placido
b. Havens, Richie

January 24, 1941
b. Diamond, Neil
b. Neville, Aaron

January 29, 1941
b. Morgan, Robin
d. Metaxas, John

January 30, 1941
b. Cheney, Dick

January 31, 1941
b. Gephardt, Richard Andrew
b. Mickelson, George Speaker

February 1, 1941
b. Shapiro, Arnold
d. McAdoo, William Gibbs

February 3, 1941
b. Mann, Carol Ann

February 4, 1941
b. Chavers, Dean

February 5, 1941
b. Laird, Rick
b. Selby, David
b. Villiger, Kaspar
d. Paterson, A(ndrew) B(arton)

February 6, 1941
b. Albert, Stephen Joel

February 8, 1941
b. Rush, Tom
d. Van Devanter, Willis

February 9, 1941
b. Kuehl, Sheila James

February 10, 1941
b. Apted, Michael

February 11, 1941
b. Mendes, Sergio

February 13, 1941
b. Polke, Sigmar

February 14, 1941
b. Freeman, Cliff(ord Lee)
b. Shalala, Donna Edna
b. Tsongas, Paul E(fthemios)

February 15, 1941
d. Adler, Guido

February 17, 1941
b. Pitney, Gene
b. Webb, Wellington

February 18, 1941
b. Chappell, Emma C(arolyn)
d. Newell, Edward Theodore

February 20, 1941
b. Sainte-Marie, Buffy
d. Lanman, Charles Rockwell

February 21, 1941
b. Reid, Irvin D.
d. Banting, Frederick Grant, Sir

February 25, 1941
b. Puttnam, David Terence

February 27, 1941
b. Ashdown, Paddy

February 28, 1941
b. Brock, Alice May
b. Sanders, Marty
d. Alfonso XIII

March 2, 1941
b. Finch, Jon
b. Satcher, David

March 3, 1941
d. Babel, Isaac Emmanuelovich

March 4, 1941
b. Johnson, Bob
b. Stargell, Willie

March 5, 1941
b. Sand, Paul
d. Quidde, Ludwig

March 6, 1941
d. Borglum, John Gutzon de la Mothe

March 7, 1941
b. Grimes, J William
b. Malone, John Charles Custer
b. Read, Piers Paul
d. Eltinge, Julian
d. Sanborn, Pitts

March 8, 1941
d. Anderson, Sherwood

March 10, 1941
b. Torrence, Dean

March 11, 1941
d. Davies, Henry Walford, Sir

March 13, 1941
b. Babe, Thomas
d. Roberts, Elizabeth Madox
d. Walker, Stuart Armstrong

March 14, 1941
b. Bartlett, Jennifer Losch
b. Petersen, Wolfgang

March 15, 1941
b. Love, Mike
d. Jawlensky, Alexej von

March 16, 1941
b. Bertolucci, Bernardo

March 17, 1941
d. Titulescu, Nicolae

March 18, 1941
b. Pickett, Wilson

March 23, 1941
d. Rourke, Constance Mayfield

March 28, 1941
d. Woolf, Virginia

March 29, 1941
b. Hansen, James E(dward)

March 30, 1941
b. Smith, Robert C

April 2, 1941
b. Demento, Dr.
b. Ndungane, Winston N(jongonkulu)
b. Russell, Leon

April 3, 1941
b. Berry, Jan
b. Ford, Charlotte

April 5, 1941
b. Burdon, Eric
b. Moriarty, Michael

April 6, 1941
d. Burr, Henry

April 8, 1941
b. Smith, Joshua (Isaac)
d. Prevost, Marcel

April 9, 1941
d. Witmark, Isidore

April 10, 1941
b. Gleason, John James
b. Theroux, Paul Edward

April 11, 1941
b. Goodman, Ellen Holtz
b. Platt, Lewis E

April 13, 1941
b. Brown, Michael Stuart
b. Price, Margaret Berenice
d. Cannon, Annie Jump

April 14, 1941
b. Rose, Pete(r Edward)
b. Tomseth, Victor Lloyd

April 16, 1941
d. Bernard, Emile
d. Danforth, William

April 17, 1941
b. Fury, Billy
d. Driesch, Hans Adolf Eduard

April 20, 1941
b. Cook, Blanche Wiesen
b. O'Neal, Ryan

April 21, 1941
b. Boren, David (Lyle)

April 23, 1941
b. Lipponen, Paavo (T.)
d. Fields, Stanley
d. Russell, Charles Edward

April 24, 1941
b. Williams, John
d. Brush, George

April 25, 1941
b. Tavernier, Bertrand

April 26, 1941
b. Schroeder, Barbet

April 27, 1941
b. Blegen, Judith Eyer

April 28, 1941
b. Ann-Margret

April 29, 1941
b. Anaya, Toney

April 30, 1941
d. Porter, Edwin

May 2, 1941
b. Wijdenbosch, Jules Albert

May 3, 1941
b. Malloy, Edward Aloysius

May 4, 1941
b. Will, George F(rederick)

May 5, 1941
b. Baker, Terry Wayne

May 6, 1941
b. Brant, Beth
b. Dimitrova, Ghena

May 7, 1941
d. Frazer, James George, Sir

May 8, 1941
b. Burr, Donald Calvin

May 10, 1941
b. Aretsky, Ken
b. Rapp, Danny

May 11, 1941
b. Charney, Nicolas Herman

May 13, 1941
b. Berger, Senta
b. Field, Marshall, V
b. Valens, Ritchie
d. Sombart, Werner

May 17, 1941
b. Nelson, Ben

May 18, 1941
d. Ternina, Milka

May 19, 1941
b. Brody, Jane Ellen
b. Ephron, Nora
d. Ridge, Lola

May 20, 1941
b. Goh Chok Tong
b. Liberia-Peters, Maria Philomena

May 21, 1941
b. Cox, Bobby

May 22, 1941
b. Winfield, Paul Edward

May 23, 1941
b. Davis, Rennie
b. Puryear, Martin
d. Austin, Herbert

May 24, 1941
b. Dylan, Bob

May 27, 1941
b. Carr, Allan
b. Ortiz, Simon

May 28, 1941
b. Howland, Beth

May 30, 1941
b. Calasso, Robert

May 31, 1941
b. Paycheck, Johnny

June 1, 1941
b. Chance, Dean
b. DeWaart, Edo
d. Berger, Hans
d. Dolly, Jenny
d. Walpole, Hugh Seymour, Sir

June 2, 1941
b. Keach, Stacy, Jr.
b. Nanne, Lou(is Vincent)
b. Watts, Charlie
d. Gehrig, Lou

June 4, 1941
d. Wilhelm II
d. William, II

June 6, 1941
d. Chevrolet, Louis Joseph

June 7, 1941
b. Laredo, Jaime

June 8, 1941
b. Robison, Paula Judith

June 11, 1941
d. Beard, Dan(iel Carter)

June 12, 1941
b. Corea, Chick
b. Hobson, Geary

June 14, 1941
b. Wideman, John Edgar

June 15, 1941
b. Nilsson
d. Underhill, Evelyn

June 16, 1941
d. Franklin, Irene

June 17, 1941
b. Hensley, William L.

June 19, 1941
b. Klaus, Vaclav

June 20, 1941
b. Frears, Stephen Arthur

June 21, 1941
b. Foat, Ginny
b. Simmons, Adele Smith

June 22, 1941
b. Bradley, Ed(ward R.)

June 24, 1941
b. Kristeva, Julia
b. Whitman, Charles Joseph

June 25, 1941
b. Arcand, Denys

June 26, 1941
b. Apuzzo, Virginia M.

June 27, 1941
b. Kieslowski, Krzysztof
d. Holmes, Hap

June 28, 1941
d. Carle, Richard

June 29, 1941
b. Carmichael, Stokely
d. Paderewski, Ignace Jan

July 1, 1941
b. Gilbert, Rod(rigue Gabriel)
b. Gilman, Alfred G
b. Quinn, Sally
b. Tharp, Twyla

July 3, 1941
b. Allred, Gloria Rachel
d. Harris, Sam Henry

July 4, 1941
b. Phelps, Digger

July 8, 1941
b. Kidwell, Clara Sue

July 9, 1941
b. Aroldingen, Karin von

July 10, 1941
d. Morton, Jelly Roll

July 11, 1941
d. Evans, Arthur John, Sir

July 12, 1941
b. Lahr, John
b. Parsons, Benny

July 13, 1941
b. Antonini, Joseph

July 14, 1941
b. Karenga, Maulana

July 17, 1941
b. Bracey, John H(enry Jr.)
b. Oswald, Marina Nikolaevna

July 18, 1941
b. Masekela, Barbara
b. Reeves, Martha

July 19, 1941
b. Bessmertnova, Natalya (Igorevna)
b. Carr, Vikki
d. Nutting, Wallace

July 20, 1941
d. Fields, Lew Maurice

July 22, 1941
b. Berning, Susie Maxwell
b. Bode, Vaughn
b. Clinton, George
b. Turcotte, Ron

July 23, 1941
d. Kittredge, G(eorge) L(yman)

July 25, 1941
b. Thurmond, Nate
b. Till, Emmett (Louis)

July 28, 1941
b. Higgins, Colin
b. Muti, Riccardo

July 29, 1941
b. Stofflet, Ty(rone Earl)
b. Warner, David
d. Leonard, Eddie

July 30, 1941
b. Anka, Paul
d. Welch, Mickey

August 1, 1941
b. Brown, Ron(ald Harmon)

August 7, 1941
b. Wolf, Stephen M

d. Tagore, Rabindranath, Sir

August 9, 1941
b. Bandy, Way

August 10, 1941
d. Howard, Cordelia

August 11, 1941
b. Holtzman, Elizabeth

August 12, 1941
b. Ducharme, Rejean
b. Feulner, Edwin John, Jr.

August 13, 1941
b. Fleming, Erin
d. Blackton, James Stuart

August 14, 1941
b. Cheney, Lynne V
b. Crosby, David (Van Cortlandt)
b. Eyen, Tom
d. Kolbe, Maximilian Maria, Saint
d. Sabatier, Paul

August 15, 1941
b. Worrill, Conrad (W.)

August 16, 1941
d. Ripley, William Zebina

August 17, 1941
b. Babangida, Ibrahim Badamasi
b. Powell, Boog

August 18, 1941
b. Jones, Christopher

August 20, 1941
b. Gray, William H, III
b. Pfeiffer, Eckhard

August 22, 1941
b. Parcells, Bill
d. Chaffee, Adna Romanza

August 25, 1941
b. Bolt, Carol
b. Burden, Carter

August 26, 1941
b. Ehrenreich, Barbara
b. Tuttle, Merlin Devere

August 28, 1941
b. Plishka, Paul Peter

August 29, 1941
b. Days, Drew S(aunders), III
b. Leach, Robin
b. Milosevic, Slobodan

August 30, 1941
b. Ashley, Elizabeth

August 31, 1941
d. Tsvetayeva, Marina Ivanovna

September 2, 1941
b. Thompson, John

September 4, 1941
b. Harrelson, Ken(neth Smith)

September 5, 1941
b. Boudjedra, Rachid

September 7, 1941
d. Roosevelt, Sara Delano

September 8, 1941
b. Connelly, Christopher
b. Sanders, Bernard

September 9, 1941
b. Redding, Otis

September 10, 1941
b. Gould, Stephen Jay
b. Hogwood, Christopher

September 12, 1941
d. Spemann, Hans

September 13, 1941
b. Ando, Tadao
b. Arias Sanchez, Oscar

September 14, 1941
d. Cubberley, Ellwood Patterson

September 16, 1941
b. Perle, Richard Norman

September 17, 1941
b. Matsui, Robert T(akeo)
b. Segretti, Donald H

September 20, 1941
b. Chihuly, Dale (Patrick)

September 21, 1941
b. Woolsey, R James

September 23, 1941
b. Jackson, George

September 24, 1941
b. McCartney, Linda

September 26, 1941
d. Walter, Eugene

September 27, 1941
b. Richie, Leroy C.
b. Schopf, J(ames) William

October 3, 1941
b. Checker, Chubby
d. Kienzl, Wilhelm

October 4, 1941
b. Collins, Jackie
b. Rice, Anne
b. Saunders, Lori

October 5, 1941
d. Brandeis, Louis Dembitz

October 6, 1941
b. Fowler, Mark Stapleton

October 8, 1941
b. Jackson, Jesse Louis
b. Stevens, Shane
d. Kahn, Gus

October 9, 1941
b. Lamb, Brian (P.)
b. Lott, Trent
d. Morgan, Helen Riggins

October 10, 1941
b. Nena, Jacob
b. Saro-Wiwa, Ken
b. Tribe, Laurence Henry

October 11, 1941
b. Shyer, Charles

October 13, 1941
b. Simon, Paul

October 19, 1941
b. Ward, Simon

October 22, 1941
b. Wood, Wilbur Forrester

October 24, 1941
b. Woo, Merle
b. Wyman, Bill

October 25, 1941
b. Reddy, Helen
b. Tyler, Anne
d. Delaunay, Robert

October 27, 1941
d. Just, Ernest Everett

October 28, 1941
b. Hightower, Dennis F(owler)

October 29, 1941
b. Crocker, Chester Arthur

October 30, 1941
b. Hill, Bonnie Guiton
b. Woiwode, Larry

October 31, 1941
d. Berry, Chu

November 1, 1941
b. Foxworth, Robert
b. Payton-Wright, Pamela

November 2, 1941
b. Black, David (Jay)
b. Stockton, Dave

November 4, 1941
d. Afinogenov, Aleksandr Nikolaevich

November 5, 1941
b. Garfunkel, Art(hur)
b. Sommer, Elke

November 6, 1941
b. Clark, Guy
b. Stoddard, Alexandra
d. Leblanc, Maurice

November 9, 1941
b. Gossett, Bruce

November 13, 1941
b. Rambo, Dack
b. Stottlemyre, Mel(vin Leon)

November 15, 1941
b. Pinkwater, Daniel Manus

November 16, 1941
b. McLaughlin, Ann Dore

November 17, 1941
d. Udet, Ernst

November 18, 1941
b. Hemmings, David Leslie Edward
b. Pocklington, Peter H
d. Nernst, Walther Hermann

November 19, 1941
b. Haggerty, Dan
b. Johnson, Cletus Merlin
b. Thompson, Tommy George

November 21, 1941
b. Hough, John
b. Mills, Juliet

November 22, 1941
b. Conti, Tom
b. Dante, Nicholas
b. Laperriere, Jacques
b. Price, Hugh B.
d. Koffka, Kurt

November 23, 1941
b. Nero, Franco

November 24, 1941
b. Best, Peter

November 26, 1941
b. Torborg, Jeff(rey Allen)

November 27, 1941
b. Rabbitt, Eddie

November 29, 1941
b. Freehan, Bill
d. Papi, Genarro

December 2, 1941
b. Chu, Paul C W
d. Merezhkovsky, Dmitry Sergeyevich

December 3, 1941
b. Mary Alice
d. Sinding, Christian

December 6, 1941
b. Nauman, Bruce
b. Perkins, Ray
b. Speck, Richard Franklin

December 7, 1941
d. Fiske, Billy

December 8, 1941
b. Berenson, Red
d. Morganweck, Frank

December 9, 1941
b. Bridges, Beau
d. Merejkowski, Dmitri Sergeyevich

December 10, 1941
b. Considine, Tim

December 11, 1941
b. Baucus, Max Sieben
d. Conrad, Frank
d. Picard, Charles Emile

December 13, 1941
b. Dalton, John H.
b. Davidson, John

December 16, 1941
b. Stahl, Lesley (Rene)
b. Stahl, Leslie

December 18, 1941
d. Rand, Ellen Gertrude Emmet

December 19, 1941
d. Parsons, Elsie Clews

December 22, 1941
b. Langhart, Janet
d. Mugnone, Leopoldo

December 23, 1941
b. Hardin, Tim
b. Hartman, Elizabeth

December 25, 1941
d. Bates, Blanche Lyon

December 27, 1941
b. Amos, John
b. Richardson, Nolan

December 28, 1941
d. Updike, Daniel Berkeley

December 29, 1941
d. Eilshemius, Louis Michel

December 30, 1941
b. Renfro, Mel(vin Lacy)

December 31, 1941
d. Hess, Sol

1942

b. Allende, Isabel
b. Barak, Ehud
b. Bonga, Kuenda
b. Borofsky, Jonathan
b. Brooks, Charlie, Jr.
b. Cardiff, Gladys
b. Darwish, Mahmud
b. da Silva, Benedita
b. de Leon Carpio, Ramiro
b. Foster, Julia
b. Frizon, Maud
b. Gemayel, Amin
b. Gorbunovs, Anatolijs
b. Habre, Hissene
b. Hart, Josephine
b. Humphry, Ann Wickett

b. Ivins, Molly
b. Jarman, Derek
b. Junot, Philippe
b. Karolyi, Bela
b. Keeler, Christine
b. Lifshin, Lyn
b. Lini, Walter Hadye
b. Lyons, Henry (J.)
b. McHale, Tom
b. Nascimento, Milton
b. Oakes, Richard
b. Oslin, K(ay) T(oinette)
b. Parks, Van Dyke
b. Qadhafi, Muammar al-
b. Ragan, Regis
b. Ray, Elizabeth
b. Robinson, Randall
b. Rosenberg, Evelyn Edelson
b. Saleh, Ali Abdullah
b. Salih, Ali Abdallah
b. Schumacher, Joel
b. Toure, Ali Farka
b. von Praunheim, Rosa
b. Vrba, Elisabeth S.
b. Willson, S Brian
b. Zamora, Ruben
d. Kell, Vernon, Sir
d. Kulish, Mykola
d. Meyerhold, Vsevolod Emilievich
d. Sickert, Walter Richard
d. Stein, Edith
d. Terra, Gabriel
d. Younghusband, Francis Edward

January 1, 1942
b. Archer, Dennis W(ayne)
b. McDonald, Country Joe

January 4, 1942
b. McLaughlin, John
d. Skinner, Otis

January 5, 1942
b. Lacalle (Herrera), Luis Alberto
b. Rose, Charlie
b. Wilding, Michael

January 6, 1942
d. Calve, Emma
d. Flannagan, John Bernard

January 7, 1942
b. Alekseyev, Vasily Ivanovich

January 8, 1942
b. Hawking, Stephen William

January 9, 1942
d. Curtis, Heber Doust
d. Rutherford, Joseph Franklin

January 11, 1942
b. Clemons, Clarence
d. Nast, Conde

January 12, 1942
b. Dohrn, Bernadine Rae

January 14, 1942
d. Fisher, Fred

January 15, 1942
b. Lucas, Phil

January 16, 1942
d. Lombard, Carole

January 17, 1942
b. Ali, Muhammad

January 19, 1942
b. Crawford, Michael
b. Hassenfeld, Stephen David

January 21, 1942
b. Davis, Mac

January 23, 1942
b. Bogner, Willi

January 26, 1942
b. Glenn, Scott

January 27, 1942
b. Wynn, Stephen A.

January 29, 1942
b. Longet, Claudine Georgette

February 1, 1942
b. Jones, Terry

February 2, 1942
b. Diller, Barry Charles
b. Hopkins, Bo
b. Nash, Graham
b. Ulmer, James

February 3, 1942
d. Lillie, Gordon William

February 4, 1942
d. Calder, Frank

February 5, 1942
b. Staubach, Roger Thomas

February 6, 1942
b. Brady, Sarah Jane

February 7, 1942
d. Bilibin, Ivan Iakolevich

February 8, 1942
b. Klein, Robert
b. Nolte, Nick

February 9, 1942
b. King, Carole

February 10, 1942
d. Henderson, Lawrence Joseph
d. Rice, Alice Caldwell Hegan

February 12, 1942
b. Wegman, William George
d. Wood, Grant

February 13, 1942
b. Archambault, JoAllyn
b. Lynley, Carol

February 14, 1942
b. Bloomberg, Michael (R.)

February 15, 1942
b. Kim Jong Il

February 17, 1942
b. Newton, Huey P(ercy)

February 18, 1942
d. Terhune, Albert Payson

February 20, 1942
b. Esposito, Phil(ip Anthony)
b. McConnell, Mitch

February 21, 1942
b. Trotta, Margarethe Von
b. Von Wangenheim, Chris

February 22, 1942
d. Zweig, Stefan

February 23, 1942
b. Madhubuti, Haki R.

February 24, 1942
b. Lieberman, Joseph Isadore
b. Neumeier, John
b. Williamson, David

February 26, 1942
d. Eberle, Mary Abastenia St. Leger

February 27, 1942
b. Hunter-Gault, Charlayne
d. Berry, Martha McChesney

February 28, 1942
b. Bonner, Frank
b. Phillips, Robin
b. South, Joe

March 1, 1942
b. Gerstner, Lou
b. Gerstner, Louis Vincent, Jr.
b. Guber, Peter

March 2, 1942
b. Firbank, Louis
b. Irving, John
d. Christian, Charlie

March 5, 1942
b. Gonzalez Marquez, Felipe

March 6, 1942
b. Murphy, Ben(jamin Edward)
b. Purim, Flora
d. Mooney, Tom

March 7, 1942
b. Eisner, Michael Dammann
b. Messner, Tammy Faye
d. Sarg, Tony

March 8, 1942
b. Allen, Richie
d. Capablanca, Jose Raoul

March 9, 1942
b. Campaneris, Bert
d. Bosch, Robert August

March 12, 1942
b. Kantner, Paul
d. Bragg, William Henry, Sir

March 14, 1942
b. Tushingham, Rita

March 15, 1942
b. Adelman, Sybil
d. Field, Rachel Lyman

March 16, 1942
b. Crozier, Roger Allan
d. Zemlinsky, Alexander von

March 17, 1942
b. Gacy, John Wayne, Jr.

March 19, 1942
d. Merriam, Clinton Hart

March 20, 1942
b. Schmidt, Benno C(harles), Jr.
d. Taylor, Charles Alonzo

March 21, 1942
b. Dorleac, Francoise
d. Woodsworth, James Shaver

March 24, 1942
b. Cammermeyer, Margarethe

March 25, 1942
b. Blandiana, Ana
b. Franklin, Aretha
b. Glaser, Paul Michael

March 26, 1942
b. Jong, Erica (Mann)
d. Hinrichs, Gustav
d. Wells, Carolyn

March 27, 1942
b. York, Michael
d. Gonzalez, Julio

March 28, 1942
b. Kinnock, Neil Gordon
b. Ramey, Samuel Edward

March 29, 1942
b. Lane, Vincent
b. Pressler, Larry

April 1, 1942
b. Delany, Samuel R.

April 3, 1942
b. Haas, Robert D(ouglas)
b. Mason, Marsha
b. Newton, Wayne

April 4, 1942
b. Kelley, Kitty

April 5, 1942
b. Greenaway, Peter

April 6, 1942
b. Levinson, Barry (Michael)

April 8, 1942
b. Huff, Leon

April 9, 1942
b. DeWilde, Brandon
b. Fedoroff, Nina V(sevolod)

April 10, 1942
b. Evans, Joni

April 12, 1942
b. McDonald, Gabrielle (Anne) Kirk

April 13, 1942
b. Conti, Bill
b. Parkhurst, Michael Hus

April 15, 1942
b. Clarke, Allan
d. Johnson, Hugh Samuel
d. Musil, Robert Edler Von

April 16, 1942
b. Lonborg, Jim

April 17, 1942
d. Hertz, Alfred
d. Perrin, Jean Baptiste

April 18, 1942
b. Rindt, Jochen
d. Whitney, Gertrude Vanderbilt

April 19, 1942
b. Price, Alan

April 21, 1942
b. Burford, Anne McGill Gorsuch
d. Stickley, Gustav

April 23, 1942
b. Dee, Sandra
b. Hannah, Barry

April 24, 1942
b. Daley, Richard Michael
b. Streisand, Barbra (Joan)
d. Blackburn, Jack
d. Montgomery, Lucy Maud

April 25, 1942
b. Kyl, Jon
b. O'Sullivan, John

April 26, 1942
b. Rydell, Bobby

April 29, 1942
b. Walz, Ken

April 30, 1942
d. Arthur, Joseph Charles

May 3, 1942
b. Caslavska, Vera

May 4, 1942
b. Ashford, Nickolas

May 5, 1942
b. Wynette, Tammy

May 6, 1942
b. Dorfman, Ariel
b. Maestro, Giulio
b. Stilwell, Richard Dale

May 7, 1942
d. Weingartner, Felix

May 8, 1942
b. Cordero, Angel Tomas
b. Lamont, Norman

May 9, 1942
b. Ashcroft, John David
b. Gergen, David (Richmond)
b. Roe, Tommy
d. McNamee, Graham

May 10, 1942
d. Weber, Joseph M

May 12, 1942
b. Dury, Ian
b. Hampshire, Susan
d. Ditmars, Raymond Lee

May 13, 1942
b. Boudin, Kathy
b. Dzhanibekov, Vladimir
  Alexandrovich

May 14, 1942
b. Dorgan, Byron Leslie
b. Perez, Tony

May 15, 1942
b. Hilliard, David
b. Kazan, Lainie

May 16, 1942
d. Gest, Morris
d. Malinowski, Bronislaw Kasper

May 17, 1942
b. Taj Mahal

May 20, 1942
b. Morrison, Keith (Anthony)
d. Guimard, Hector Germain

May 22, 1942
b. Kaczynski, Theodore (John)
b. Parkins, Barbara

May 25, 1942
d. Feuermann, Emanuel

May 26, 1942
d. Brinkley, John Romulus

May 27, 1942
d. Ch'en Tu-hsiu

May 28, 1942
b. Prusiner, Stanley (Ben)

May 29, 1942
d. Barrymore, John

June 1, 1942
b. Frohnmayer, John Edward
b. Nagler, Eric

June 2, 1942
d. Berigan, Bunny

June 3, 1942
b. Mayfield, Curtis (Lee)

June 4, 1942
d. Heydrich, Reinhard Tristan Eugen

June 5, 1942
b. Burton, Nelson, Jr.
b. Obiang Nguema Mbasogo, Teodoro

June 6, 1942
b. Bowie, Norman Ernest
b. Kane, Howie
d. Reisner, George Andrew

June 8, 1942
b. Weil, Andrew (Thomas)

June 10, 1942
d. Lupino, Stanley

June 11, 1942
d. Baum, Herbert (M.)
d. Dalton, Charles

June 13, 1942
b. Abubakar, Abdulsalam (Alhaji)

June 14, 1942
b. Bush, Melinda
b. Walker, Junior

June 18, 1942
b. Ebert, Roger (Joseph)
b. Mbeki, Thabo Mvuyelwa
b. McCartney, Paul
d. Pryor, Arthur W

June 19, 1942
b. Kasten, Robert Walter, Jr.

June 20, 1942
b. Wilson, Brian Douglas

June 21, 1942
b. Reynolds, William Bradford
b. West, Togo D., Jr.

June 22, 1942
b. Deodato

June 24, 1942
b. Fleetwood, Mick
b. Frei Ruiz-Tagle, Eduardo
b. Lee, Michele

June 25, 1942
b. Miller, James Clifford, III
b. Reed, Willis, Jr.
b. Tremblay, Michel

June 28, 1942
b. Hani, Chris
b. Kopay, David

June 30, 1942
b. Ballard, Robert Duane
d. Jackson, William Henry

July 1, 1942
b. Black, Karen
b. Bujold, Genevieve
b. Crouch, Andrae Edward
d. Daudet, Leon

July 2, 1942
b. Ernst, Richard

July 4, 1942
b. Lanier, Hal
d. Boule, Marcellin

July 5, 1942
b. Feld, Eliot

July 6, 1942
d. Willard, Daniel

July 8, 1942
b. Gramm, (William) Phil(ip)

July 10, 1942
b. Millar, Jeff(rey) Lynn

July 12, 1942
b. Stoltzman, Richard Leslie

July 13, 1942
b. Ford, Harrison
b. Forster, Robert
b. McGuinn, Roger

July 15, 1942
b. Malone, Vivian

July 16, 1942
b. Court, Margaret

July 17, 1942
b. Davis, Spencer
b. Garnett, Gale
b. Hawkins, Connie
b. Williams, William T(homas)

July 20, 1942
b. Stanley, Mickey
d. Nampeyo

July 24, 1942
b. Sarandon, Chris

July 25, 1942
b. Rader, Dotson

July 26, 1942
b. Gray, Dobie
b. Meciar, Vladimir

July 27, 1942
b. Pleshette, John

July 28, 1942
d. Petrie, (William Matthew) Flinders, Sir

July 30, 1942
d. Blanton, Jimmy

August 1, 1942
b. Garcia, Jerry
b. Giannini, Giancarlo

August 2, 1942
b. Falco, Louis

August 3, 1942
d. Ferrero, Guglielmo
d. Willstater, Richard Martin

August 4, 1942
b. Lange, David Russell
b. Michelman, Kate

August 7, 1942
b. Comer, Anjanette
b. Keillor, Garrison
b. Thomas, B(illy) J(oe)

August 8, 1942
b. Blanchard, Jim
b. Ramo, Roberta Cooper
d. Genthe, Arnold

August 9, 1942
b. DeJohnette, Jack
b. Steinberg, David

August 10, 1942
b. Johnson, Betsey Lee

August 12, 1942
d. Amato, Pasquale

August 13, 1942
d. Schurman, Jacob Gould

August 14, 1942
b. Asante, Molefi Kete

August 17, 1942
b. Bereano, Nancy K(irp)

August 19, 1942
b. Monk, Allan James
b. Thompson, Fred

August 20, 1942
b. Hayes, Isaac
b. Moses, Gilbert, III

August 22, 1942
b. Lennon, Kathy
d. Fokine, Michel
d. Miller, Alice Duer

August 23, 1942
b. Barnett, Steve
b. McBride, Patricia

August 24, 1942
b. Cleland, Max
b. Uhlenbeck, Karen (Keskulla)

August 25, 1942
d. George Edward Alexander Edmund

August 27, 1942
b. Dragon, Daryl
b. Peckford, Brian

August 28, 1942
b. Santos, Jose Eduardo dos

August 29, 1942
b. Morrison, Sterling

August 31, 1942
b. Aoki, Isao

September 2, 1942
b. Chaudhry, Mahendra

September 3, 1942
b. Jardine, Al(lan)
d. James, Will(iam Roderick)

September 5, 1942
b. Herzog, Werner

September 7, 1942
b. Roundtree, Richard

September 10, 1942
b. Darden, Christine (Mann)

September 12, 1942
b. Goldsberry, Ronald (Eugene)

September 14, 1942
b. Floyd, Raymond Loran
b. Lehman, John Francis, Jr.

September 17, 1942
d. Beaux, Cecilia

September 21, 1942
b. McDowell, Sam(uel Edward)

September 22, 1942
b. Heyworth, James
b. Stern, David Joel
d. Cram, Ralph Adams

September 24, 1942
b. Marsden, Gerry

September 25, 1942
b. Bonavena, Oscar

September 26, 1942
b. Anzaldua, Gloria
b. McCord, Kent

September 27, 1942
b. Dith Pran
b. Weller, Michael

September 28, 1942
b. Taylor, Charley

September 29, 1942
b. Kahn, Madeline (Gail)
b. McShane, Ian
b. Ponty, Jean-Luc
b. Tesich, Steve

September 30, 1942
b. Lyman, Frankie

October 4, 1942
b. Reagon, Bernice Johnson

October 6, 1942
b. Ekland, Britt

October 8, 1942
b. Tomasson, Helgi
d. Ellsler, Effie

October 10, 1942
b. Marshall, James Edward

October 12, 1942
b. Franklin, Melvin

October 13, 1942
b. Jones, Jerry
b. Tiffin, Pamela Kimberley

October 15, 1942
b. Marshall, Penny
d. Tempest, Marie

October 16, 1942
b. Bruchac, Joseph, III

October 17, 1942
b. Seals, Jim

October 18, 1942
b. Horton, Willie

October 20, 1942
b. Nuesslein-Volhard, Christiane
d. Robson, May
d. Stock, Frederick A

October 21, 1942
b. Bishop, Elvin

October 22, 1942
b. Funicello, Annette

October 23, 1942
b. Crichton, Michael
b. Roddick, Anita Lucia Perella

October 26, 1942
b. Hoskins, Bob

October 27, 1942
b. Greenwood, Lee

October 31, 1942
b. McNally, Dave
b. Stiers, David Ogden
b. Honwana, Luis Bernardo

November 1, 1942
b. Flynt, Larry (Claxton)

November 2, 1942
b. Hite, Shere

November 3, 1942
b. Smith, Martin Cruz

November 5, 1942
d. Cohan, George M(ichael)

November 6, 1942
b. Shrimpton, Jean Rosemary

November 7, 1942
b. Peters, Tom
b. Rivers, Johnny

November 9, 1942
b. Weiskopf, Tom
d. Curran, Charles Courtney
d. Oliver, Edna May

November 11, 1942
d. DeBeck, Billy

November 13, 1942
d. Crews, Laura Hope
d. Schoen-Rene, Anna

November 14, 1942
b. Watson, Bryan Joseph

November 15, 1942
b. Barenboim, Daniel

November 16, 1942
b. McKechnie, Donna

November 17, 1942
b. Gaudio, Bob
b. Scorsese, Martin

November 18, 1942
b. Evans, Linda

November 19, 1942
b. Klein, Calvin
b. Olds, Sharon

November 20, 1942
b. Biden, Joe
b. Greenbaum, Norman
b. Monk, Meredith Jane

November 21, 1942
d. Berchtold, Leopold von
d. Hertzog, James Barry Munnik

November 22, 1942
b. Bluford, Guy
b. Edwards, Harry, Jr.

November 24, 1942
b. Fitzwater, Marlin
b. Thomas, Craig D

November 26, 1942
b. Cole, Olivia
b. Hauptman, William

November 27, 1942
b. Carr, Henry
b. Hacker, Marilyn
b. Hendrix, Jimi

November 28, 1942
b. Warfield, Paul Dryden

November 29, 1942
b. Grillo, John

November 30, 1942
d. Jones, Buck

December 1, 1942
b. Kalikow, Peter Stephen

December 4, 1942
b. Hillman, Chris

December 5, 1942
b. Cale, John

December 6, 1942
b. Handke, Peter
d. Rusie, Amos Wilson

December 7, 1942
b. Chapin, Harry Foster
b. Johnson, Alex(ander)
b. Lewis, Reginald F.
d. Solomon, Hannah Greenebaum

December 8, 1942
d. Kahn, Albert

December 9, 1942
b. Butkus, Dick
b. McGinniss, Joe
d. Trihey, Harry

December 12, 1942
b. Casablancas, John(ny)
d. Westley, Helen

December 15, 1942
b. Clark, Dave

December 17, 1942
b. Butterfield, Paul

December 20, 1942
b. Hayes, Bob

December 21, 1942
d. Boas, Franz

December 23, 1942
b. Lewis, Loida Nicolas
d. Cagle, Red

December 24, 1942
d. Darlan, Jean Louis Xavier Francois

December 26, 1942
b. Cerezo (Arevalo), Vinicio

December 27, 1942
b. Rothstein, Ron

December 28, 1942
b. Horowitz, Paul
d. Blomfield, Reginald Theodore, Sir

December 30, 1942
b. Bukovsky, Vladimir
b. Nesmith, Mike

December 31, 1942
b. Summers, Andy

1943

b. Adair, Peter
b. Baca-Barragan, Polly
b. Barksdale, James L(ove)
b. Brennan, Robert E
b. Carey, Peter (Philip)
b. Clarke, Hope
b. Debus, Sigurd Friedrich
b. Deisenhofer, Johann

b. Dukepoo, Frank C.
b. Ebbers, Bernie
b. Faye, Safi
b. Fugate, Caril Ann
b. Hohman, Donald
b. Hollander, Xaviera
b. Isaacson, Portia
b. Jordan, I(rving) King
b. Judkins, Reba
b. Kalpokas, Donald
b. Khatami, Mohammad
b. King, Micki
b. King, Thomas
b. Lerner, Michael
b. Lubovitch, Lar
b. Lucid, Shannon
b. Mamaloni, Solomon
b. Manigault, Earl
b. Mann, Michael
b. Martinez, Vilma Socorro
b. Melman, Richard
b. Nance, Jack
b. Numan, Eppo
b. Nyrup Rasmussen, Poul
b. Perelman, Ronald O
b. Petrossian, Christian
b. Raphael
b. Raskin, Jef
b. Reason, J. Paul
b. Rutan, Burt
b. Sabich, Spider
b. Sampson, Will, Jr.
b. Sassou-Nguesso, Denis
b. Stevens, James (Richard)
b. Taya, Maaouya Ould Sid'Ahmed
b. Tompkins, Susie
b. Veruschka
b. Zieff, Howard
d. Tschernichowsky, Saul

January 1, 1943
b. Britz, Jerilyn
b. Novello, Don

January 4, 1943
b. Kearns, Doris H

January 5, 1943
d. Carver, George Washington

January 6, 1943
d. Lowell, Abbott Lawrence

January 7, 1943
d. Crile, George Washington
d. Tesla, Nikola

January 8, 1943
b. Berresford, Susan Vail
b. Murray, Charles Alan

January 9, 1943
b. Moskowitz, J(ay)
d. Collingwood, Robin George

January 10, 1943
b. Annaud, Jean-Jacques
b. Croce, Jim

January 11, 1943
d. Guiterman, Arthur
d. Justo, Agustin Pedro

January 13, 1943
b. Church, Sandra
d. Taeuber-Arp, Sophie

January 14, 1943
b. Gantt, Harvey Bernard
d. Richards, Laura Elizabeth Howe

January 15, 1943
b. Moody, John

January 16, 1943
b. Harris, Marcelite Jordan

January 17, 1943
b. Preval, Rene

January 19, 1943
b. Joplin, Janis
d. O'Connell, Hugh

January 22, 1943
b. Carroll, James

January 23, 1943
b. Burton, Gary
b. Gerard, Gil
d. Rice, Cale Young
d. Woollcott, Alexander Humphreys

January 24, 1943
b. Tate, Sharon

January 26, 1943
b. Gutierrez, Cesar Dario
b. Hite, Robert Ernest, Jr.
b. Panek, LeRoy Lad
d. Vavilov, Nikolai Ivanovich

January 28, 1943
b. Howard, Susan

January 29, 1943
b. Quinn, Pat
b. Ross, Katharine

January 30, 1943
b. Balin, Marty
b. Deane, Sandy
b. Johnson, Davey

February 1, 1943
b. Jamieson, Bob

February 3, 1943
b. Bogart, Neil
b. Danner, Blythe Katharine
b. Edwards, Dennis

February 4, 1943
b. Lee, Gary Earl

February 5, 1943
b. Bushnell, Nolan Kay
b. Cannell, Stephen Joseph
b. Morton, Craig
d. Van Dyke, W(oodbridge) S(trong)

February 6, 1943
b. Fabian
b. Gray, C(layland) Boyden
b. Hunnicutt, Gayle

d. Coffroth, Jimmy

February 7, 1943
b. Robbins, Carrie Fishbein

February 8, 1943
d. Casey, Dan(iel Maurice)

February 9, 1943
b. Pesci, Joe

February 13, 1943
b. Pagels, Elaine

February 14, 1943
d. Hilbert, David

February 16, 1943
b. Dowell, Anthony James

February 17, 1943
b. Chappell, Tom
d. Keogan, George

February 19, 1943
b. Elliot, Cass
d. Overman, Lynne

February 20, 1943
b. Leigh, Mike

February 21, 1943
b. Ambrose, David Edwin
b. Geffen, David

February 22, 1943
b. Kaskey, Ray(mond John)

February 23, 1943
b. Biletnikoff, Fred(erick)

February 25, 1943
b. Harrison, George
b. Raphael, Sally Jessy

February 26, 1943
b. Duke, Bill
b. Jones, Brian

February 27, 1943
b. Frann, Mary

February 28, 1943
d. Palamas, Kostes

March 2, 1943
b. Brown, Elaine
b. Denneny, Michael (Leo)
b. Straub, Peter

March 6, 1943
d. Collins, Jimmy

March 7, 1943
b. White, Chris(topher Taylor)

March 8, 1943
b. Redgrave, Lynn
d. Nielsen, Alice

March 9, 1943
b. Fischer, Bobby
b. Gibson, Charles Dewolf

March 10, 1943
b. Limbert, John William, Jr.
d. Binyon, Laurence
d. Marshall, Tully

March 12, 1943
b. Mladic, Ratko
d. Vigeland, Gustav

March 13, 1943
b. Hirschorn, Joel
d. Benet, Stephen Vincent
d. Morgan, J(ohn) P(ierpont), Jr.

March 14, 1943
b. Jampolis, Neil Peter

March 15, 1943
b. Kanter, Rosabeth Moss
b. Schuman, Patricia Glass

March 17, 1943
b. Muluzi, Bakili

March 19, 1943
b. Wertheimer, Linda (Cozby)
d. Ball, Frank

March 20, 1943
b. Witt, Paul Junger
d. Lowden, Frank O(rren)

March 22, 1943
b. Baker, Houston A(lfred), Jr.
b. Benson, George

March 23, 1943
d. Schillinger, Joseph

March 24, 1943
b. Alou, Jesus Maria Rojas

March 26, 1943
b. Woodward, Bob
d. Lindsey, Benjamin Barr

March 27, 1943
b. Curtis, Mike

March 28, 1943
b. Ferrell, Conchata Galen
d. Rachmaninoff, Sergei Vasilyevich

March 29, 1943
b. Glover, Nathaniel, Jr.
b. Idle, Eric
b. Major, John (Roy)
b. Vangelis
d. Gillmore, Frank

March 30, 1943
b. Etchison, Dennis

March 31, 1943
b. Walken, Christopher
d. Miliukov, Pavel Nikolayevich
d. Schlemmer, Oskar

April 2, 1943
b. Coryell, Larry

April 3, 1943
d. Veidt, Conrad

April 4, 1943
d. Laparra, Raoul

April 5, 1943
b. Gail, Max(well Trowbridge, Jr.)

April 7, 1943
b. Dryden, Spencer

April 8, 1943
b. Bennett, Michael
b. Hiller, John Frederick
d. Sears, Richard Dudley

April 11, 1943
d. Roper, Daniel C(alhoun)

April 12, 1943
b. Ludlam, Charles

April 13, 1943
b. Kidd, William

April 17, 1943
b. Holmes, Anna Marie

April 18, 1943
d. Adamowski, Timothee
d. Yamamoto, Isoroku

April 20, 1943
b. Gardiner, John Eliot

April 22, 1943
b. Gluck, Louise

April 23, 1943
b. Goodrich, Gail Charles
b. Meriwether, W(ilhelm) Delano
b. Villechaize, Herve Jean Pierre
b. Wright, Robert C

April 24, 1943
b. Sterban, Richard

April 25, 1943
d. Nemirovich-Danchenko, Vladimir I

April 26, 1943
b. Wright, Gary

April 28, 1943
d. Farnham, Sally James

April 29, 1943
b. Allen, Duane David

April 30, 1943
b. Chiluba, Frederick Jacob Titus
b. Douglas, Cathleen Curran Heffernan
b. Vee, Bobby
d. Webb, Beatrice Potter

May 3, 1943
b. Snepp, Frank Warren, III

d. Andrews, Frank M(axwell)

May 4, 1943
b. Rice, Norm(an Blann)

May 5, 1943
b. Palin, Michael
b. Volner, Jill Wine

May 6, 1943
b. Baader, Andreas
d. Haines, Robert Terrel

May 8, 1943
b. Tennille, Toni

May 10, 1943
b. Darman, Richard G(ordon)
b. Donovan
b. Jamison, Judith
d. Anielewicz, Mordecai

May 11, 1943
b. Greene, Nancy Catherine

May 12, 1943
d. Stoessel, Albert

May 13, 1943
b. Wells, Mary

May 14, 1943
b. Bruce, Jack
b. Leon, Tania (Justina)
b. Urtain, Jose Manuel Ibar
d. La Fontaine, Henri Marie

May 15, 1943
b. Brosten, Harve
b. Cronenberg, David

May 16, 1943
b. Adams, Hank
b. Coats, Dan(iel R)

May 20, 1943
b. Kabua, Imata

May 22, 1943
b. John, Tommy
b. Williams, Betty Smith
b. Williams, Elizabeth Betty Smyth
d. Taft, Helen Herron

May 23, 1943
d. Aberhart, William

May 24, 1943
b. Burghoff, Gary

May 25, 1943
b. Uggams, Leslie (Marian Crayne)

May 26, 1943
b. Helm, Levon
d. Ford, Edsel Bryant

May 27, 1943
b. Weitz, Bruce Peter

May 31, 1943
b. Gless, Sharon

b. Namath, Joe

June 1, 1943
b. Goode, Richard Stephen

June 2, 1943
d. Dafoe, Allan Roy
d. Howard, Leslie
d. Kinnick, Nile
d. Stevens, John Frank

June 3, 1943
b. Cunningham, Billy

June 4, 1943
b. Haynie, Sandra
d. Roosevelt, Kermit

June 7, 1943
b. Giovanni, Nikki
b. Osmond, Ken

June 8, 1943
b. Calley, William Laws, Jr.
b. Davenport, Willie D

June 9, 1943
b. Saatchi, Charles

June 11, 1943
b. Sinclair, Iain

June 12, 1943
b. Albert, Marv(in Philip)

June 13, 1943
b. McDowell, Malcolm

June 15, 1943
b. Halliday, Johnny
b. Kissling, Frances

June 16, 1943
b. Arenas, Reinaldo
d. Onegin, Sigrid

June 17, 1943
b. Gingrich, Newt(on Leroy)

June 21, 1943
b. McKinnon, Isaiah
b. Serban, Andrei George

June 22, 1943
b. Hume, Brit
b. Malcolm, Andrew H(ogarth)

June 23, 1943
b. Levine, James Lawrence

June 26, 1943
b. Fame, Georgie
d. Landsteiner, Karl

June 27, 1943
b. Petrocelli, Rico (Americo Peter)

June 28, 1943
b. Johanson, Donald Carl
b. Klitzing, Klaus von
b. Laguna, Ismael
b. Von Klitzing, Klaus

June 30, 1943
b. Ballard, Florence

July 4, 1943
b. Rivera, Geraldo

July 5, 1943
b. French, Albert

July 6, 1943
- b. Matlovich, Leonard P., Jr.

July 9, 1943
b. Edmiston, Mark Morton
d. Beers, Clifford Whittingham

July 10, 1943
b. Ashe, Arthur
d. Schlesinger, Frank

July 11, 1943
b. Holland, Tom

July 12, 1943
b. McVie, Christine Perfect
b. Silas, Paul Theron
d. Loftus, Cissie

July 14, 1943
d. Bledsoe, Jules

July 15, 1943
b. Bell Burnell, Jocelyn

July 16, 1943
b. Johnson, Jimmy

July 18, 1943
b. Peete, Calvin
d. Barclay, McClelland

July 19, 1943
b. Cole, Dennis
b. Smith, Jerry

July 21, 1943
b. Herrmann, Edward

July 22, 1943
b. Hutchison, Kay Bailey

July 25, 1943
b. Margolin, Janet
b. McElligott, Thomas J

July 26, 1943
b. Crane, Cheryl
b. Jagger, Mick

July 28, 1943
b. Bradley, Bill

July 29, 1943
b. Jacobson, Michael Faraday

July 31, 1943
b. Bennett, William John

August 5, 1943
b. Smith, Sammi

August 6, 1943
b. Anderson, Michael, Jr.

August 7, 1943
b. Cantrell, Lana
b. Wattleton, Faye

August 9, 1943
d. Soutine, Chaim

August 11, 1943
b. Gamble, Kenny

August 13, 1943
b. Pascal-Trouillot, Ertha
b. Walley, Deborah

August 14, 1943
b. Snyder, Mitch
d. Kelley, Joe

August 16, 1943
b. Altman, Dennis

August 17, 1943
b. DeNiro, Robert

August 18, 1943
b. Mull, Martin

August 19, 1943
b. Violet, Arlene

August 21, 1943
b. Schell, Johnathan Edward
d. Phelps, William Lyon
d. Pontoppidan, Henrik

August 24, 1943
d. Weil, Simone

August 25, 1943
b. Eldredge, Niles

August 27, 1943
b. Axthelm, Pete(r Macrae)
b. Kerrey, Bob
b. Weld, Tuesday

August 28, 1943
b. LeVay, Simon
b. Piniella, Lou(is Victor)
d. Ray, Edward

August 30, 1943
b. Crumb, R(obert)
b. Killy, Jean-Claude
d. Merritt, Abraham

September 1, 1943
d. Jacobs, W(illiam) W(ymark)
d. Streeton, Arthur Ernest

September 2, 1943
b. Sather, Glen Cameron
b. Simon, Joe
d. Hartley, Marsden

September 3, 1943
b. McCoo, Marilyn
b. Perrine, Valerie
d. Moisseiff, Leon Solomon

d. Pallette, Eugene

September 5, 1943
d. Hrdlicka, Ales

September 9, 1943
d. Andrews, Charles McLean

September 11, 1943
b. Falana, Lola
b. Hart, Mickey

September 12, 1943
b. Muldaur, Maria

September 16, 1943
b. Conner, Dennis
b. Lafontaine, Oskar
b. McPherson, James Alan

September 19, 1943
b. Morgan, Joe (Leonard)

September 20, 1943
b. Abacha, Sani

September 23, 1943
b. Iglesias, Julio
d. Glyn, Elinor Sutherland

September 25, 1943
b. Gates, Robert M(ichael)
b. Walden, Robert

September 27, 1943
b. Bachman, Randy

September 29, 1943
b. Walesa, Lech

September 30, 1943
b. Deisenhofer, Johann
b. Ogilvy, Ian
b. Powell, Jody
d. Freeman, R(ichard) Austin
d. Salomon, Charlotte

October 1, 1943
b. Williams, Willie Lawrence

October 2, 1943
d. Dett, Robert Nathaniel

October 3, 1943
b. Bingaman, Jeff

October 4, 1943
b. Al-Amin, Jamil Abdullah
b. Brown, H(ubert) Rap
b. Roemer, Buddy
d. Ely, Richard Theodore

October 5, 1943
b. Miller, Steve

October 6, 1943
b. Zimmerman, Udo

October 7, 1943
b. North, Oliver Laurence, Jr.
d. Hall, Radclyffe

October 8, 1943
b. Chase, Chevy
b. Stine, R. L.

October 9, 1943
d. Zeeman, Pieter

October 12, 1943
d. Wertheimer, Max

October 14, 1943
b. Rentzel, Lance
b. Williams, Jimy
d. Tchernichowski, Saul Gutmanovich

October 15, 1943
d. Soutar, William

October 20, 1943
d. Bernie, Ben

October 21, 1943
b. Piccolo, Brian

October 22, 1943
b. Deneuve, Catherine

October 23, 1943
d. Antoine, Andre

October 24, 1943
b. Powell, Earl A, III

October 25, 1943
b. Smalls, Charlie
d. Hart, Frances Noyes

October 26, 1943
b. Swimmer, Ross

October 31, 1943
d. Reinhardt, Max

November 1, 1943
d. McAdie, Alexander George

November 3, 1943
b. Corinne, Tee A.

November 4, 1943
b. Graebner, Clark

November 5, 1943
b. Shepard, Sam

November 7, 1943
b. Mitchell, Joni

November 12, 1943
b. Hyland, Brian
b. Shawn, Wallace
b. Williams, Gregory (Howard)

November 13, 1943
d. Denis, Maurice

November 14, 1943
b. Callejas Romero, Rafael Leonardo

November 16, 1943
b. DeFreeze, Donald David

November 17, 1943
b. Hutton, Lauren

November 21, 1943
b. Laffite, Jacques Henry Sabin
b. Mahan, Larry

November 22, 1943
b. Courneyor, Yvan Serge
b. King, Billie Jean
d. Hart, Lorenz
d. Yon, Pietro Alessandro

November 23, 1943
d. Ray, Charles
d. Ullstein, Hermann

November 24, 1943
b. Williamson, Robin

November 25, 1943
b. Mortier, Gerard

November 26, 1943
b. Paltrow, Bruce
b. Stenerud, Jan
d. Roberts, Charles George Douglas, Sir

November 27, 1943
b. Sander, Jil

November 28, 1943
b. Newman, Randy

November 29, 1943
b. Bing, Dave
b. Galati, Frank
d. Landes, Bertha Ethel

November 30, 1943
b. Malick, Terence
d. Miller, Dorie

December 2, 1943
b. Allard, Wayne
d. Dashwood, Elizabeth Monica
d. Grieg, Nordahl Brun

December 4, 1943
d. Olivetti, Camillo

December 7, 1943
b. Isaacs, Susan
b. Parks, Bernard C.

December 8, 1943
b. Morrison, Jim
b. Tate, James

December 9, 1943
b. Martin, Pit
b. Ondaatje, Michael
b. Vance, Kenny

December 10, 1943
b. Wilson, Theodore Roosevelt

December 11, 1943
b. Kerry, John F(orbes)
b. Mills, Donna

December 12, 1943
b. Washington, Grover, Jr.

December 13, 1943
b. Jenkins, Ferguson Arthur

December 14, 1943
d. Kellogg, John Harvey

December 15, 1943
d. Waller, Fats

December 16, 1943
b. Bochco, Steven Ronald
b. Hicks, Tony

December 18, 1943
b. Richards, Keith

December 19, 1943
b. DeVries, William Castle

December 20, 1943
b. Barden, Don H.

December 21, 1943
d. Marquis, Albert Nelson

December 22, 1943
d. Potter, Beatrix

December 23, 1943
b. Silvia

December 27, 1943
b. Roberts, Cokie

December 28, 1943
b. Peterson, David Robert
d. Mandelstam, Osip Emilyevich

December 29, 1943
d. Young, Art(hur Henry)

December 30, 1943
d. Bosworth, Hobart van Zandt

December 31, 1943
b. Denver, John
b. Kingsley, Ben
b. Miles, Sarah

1944

b. Aadland, Beverly
b. Bandy, Moe
b. Barrett, Stan
b. Bean, Carl
b. Berger, David
b. Bowling, Roger
b. Bowser, Betty Ann
b. Bunch, Charlotte
b. Burnett, Charles
b. Clark, James H.
b. Copeland, Al
b. Dummar, Melvin
b. Ellis, Robin
b. Friedman, Ze'ev
b. Garretta, Michel
b. Gebbie, Kristine
b. Henderson, Wade J.

b. James, Edison
b. Jeffreys, Garland
b. Kickingbird, Kirke
b. Lindley, David
b. Lynch, Peter
b. Mazel, Judy
b. Meyer, Ron
b. Museveni, Yoweri Kaguta
b. Rice-Davies, Mandy
b. Rosen, Barry
b. Rubell, Steve
b. Salgado, Sebastiao
b. Sherrod, Clayton
b. Smith, Harold
b. Studi, Wes
b. Wilson, Jerry
b. Zyuganov, Gennadi A(ndreyevich)
d. Han Yongun
d. Sebastiani, Samuele
d. Sorge, Richard
d. Temple, William
d. Wang Ching-wei

January 1, 1944
d. Lutyens, Edwin Landseer, Sir

January 2, 1944
b. Rannaridh, Norodom, Prince

January 3, 1944
b. Lacey, Robert

January 5, 1944
b. McCarthy, Carolyn

January 6, 1944
b. Franklin, Bonnie Gail
b. Kravis, Henry R
b. McCoy, Van
d. Tarbell, Ida Minerva

January 7, 1944
d. Hoover, Lou Henry

January 9, 1944
b. Page, Jimmy

January 10, 1944
b. Cox, Geraldine V(ang)
b. Sinatra, Frank, Jr.

January 11, 1944
d. Christie, John Walter
d. Ciano (di Cortellazzo), Galeazzo
d. King, Charles

January 13, 1944
d. Collier, William, Sr.

January 14, 1944
b. Totenberg, Nina

January 16, 1944
b. Milsap, Ronnie
b. Stafford, Jim

January 17, 1944
b. Frazier, Joe

January 18, 1944
b. Keating, Paul John

January 19, 1944
b. Fabares, Shelley Michelle Marie
b. Reeves, Dan(iel Edward)

January 20, 1944
b. Parker, Pat
d. Cattell, James McKeen

January 21, 1944
b. Abbott, Jack

January 22, 1944
b. Noble, Elaine

January 23, 1944
b. Hauer, Rutger
d. Munch, Edvard

January 26, 1944
b. Davis, Angela (Yvonne)

January 27, 1944
b. Corrigan-Maguire, Mairead
b. Maguire, Mairead Corrigan

January 29, 1944
d. White, William Allen

January 30, 1944
b. Dixon, Sharon Pratt
b. Harrell, Lynn Morris
b. Kelly, Sharon Pratt

January 31, 1944
b. Walter, Jessica
d. Giraudoux, Jean

February 1, 1944
b. Enzi, Michael B.
d. Clapper, Raymond Lewis
d. Mondrian, Piet(er Cornelis)

February 3, 1944
d. Bestor, Arthur Eugene

February 4, 1944
b. Davis, Andrew Frank
d. Guilbert, Yvette

February 5, 1944
b. Kooper, Al

February 7, 1944
d. Park, Robert Ezra

February 8, 1944
d. Cavalieri, Lina

February 9, 1944
b. Walker, Alice

February 10, 1944
b. Allen, Peter Woolnough
b. Lappe, Francis Moore

February 12, 1944
b. Torrence, Jackie

February 13, 1944
b. Bando, Sal(vatore Leonard)
b. Channing, Stockard
b. Springer, Jerry

b. Tork, Peter

February 14, 1944
b. Bernstein, Carl
b. Fireman, Paul
b. Parker, Alan William
b. Threadgill, Henry

February 16, 1944
b. Ford, Richard
b. Mascarenhas Monteiro, Antonio

February 18, 1944
b. Bowlen, Patrick Dennis
d. Davenport, Charles Benedict

February 21, 1944
b. Daly, Tyne

February 22, 1944
b. Demme, Jonathan

February 23, 1944
b. Winter, Johnny
d. Baekeland, Leo Hendrik

February 25, 1944
b. Grassle, Karen Gene
d. Boyd, James
d. McNary, Charles Linza

February 28, 1944
b. Bishop, Kelly

February 29, 1944
b. Farina, Dennis
b. Frelich, Phyllis

March 1, 1944
b. Breaux, John B.
b. Daltrey, Roger Harry
b. Napier, John

March 2, 1944
b. Jones, Elaine R.
b. Reed, Lou

March 4, 1944
b. Brown, Judie
b. Womack, Bobby
d. Buchalter, Lepke

March 5, 1944
b. Gutman, Roy
d. Jacob, Max

March 6, 1944
b. Gilmour, Dave
b. Te Kanawa, Kiri, Dame
b. Wilson, Mary

March 7, 1944
b. Fiennes (Twisleton Wykeham),
Ranulph

March 8, 1944
b. Clark, Susan Nora Goulding

March 9, 1944
d. Brown, A Roy

March 10, 1944
d. Cobb, Irvin Shrewsbury
d. Lincoln, Joseph C(rosby)
d. Van Loon, Hendrik Willem

March 12, 1944
d. Thomason, John William, Jr.

March 15, 1944
b. Stone, Sly

March 16, 1944
b. Hayden, Mike

March 17, 1944
b. Gaston, Cito
b. Sebastian, John

March 18, 1944
b. Dobson, Kevin

March 19, 1944
b. Johnson, Lynda Bird
b. Sirhan, Sirhan Bishara

March 20, 1944
b. Neher, Erwin

March 21, 1944
b. Sanguillen, Manny

March 23, 1944
b. Scott, George Charles, Jr.

March 24, 1944
d. Bache, Jules Sermon
d. Wingate, Orde Charles

March 25, 1944
b. Bravo, Ellen

March 26, 1944
b. Ross, Diana

March 27, 1944
b. Brown, Jesse

March 28, 1944
b. Barry, Rick
b. Howard, Ken(neth Joseph, Jr.)
d. Leacock, Stephen Butler

March 29, 1944
b. McLain, Denny

April 1, 1944
b. Staub, Rusty

April 3, 1944
b. Orlando, Tony

April 4, 1944
b. Faisal ibn Musaed
b. Nelson, Craig T

April 5, 1944
d. Winter, Alice Vivian Ames

April 6, 1944
b. Dumurcq, Charles
b. Huarte, John G

July 19, 1944
b. Turnbull, Walter (J.)
d. Cook, Will Marion

July 20, 1944
b. Sheppard, T G
d. Beck, Ludwig August Theoder
d. Stauffenberg, Claus (Schenk Graf) Von

July 21, 1944
b. Emecheta, Buchi
b. Wellstone, Paul David

July 22, 1944
b. Lyle, Sparky

July 26, 1944
d. Pahlevi, Riza

July 27, 1944
b. Gentry, Bobbie

July 28, 1944
b. Bloomfield, Mike

July 30, 1944
b. Rader, Doug(las Lee)
d. Bausch, Edward

July 31, 1944
b. Chaplin, Geraldine
b. Flannery, Susan
b. Lansing, Sherry Lee
d. Lehand, Missy
d. Saint-Exupery, Antoine (Jean Baptiste Marie Roger) de

August 1, 1944
b. Berisha, Sali
d. Quezon (y Molina), Manuel Luis

August 2, 1944
b. Cassidy, Joanna
b. Healy, Bernadine

August 4, 1944
b. Belzer, Richard

August 8, 1944
b. Weir, Peter

August 9, 1944
b. Elliott, Sam

August 11, 1944
b. Coles, Joanna
b. Smith, Frederick Wallace

August 12, 1944
d. Kennedy, Joseph Patrick, Jr.

August 14, 1944
b. Smith, Robyn Caroline

August 15, 1944
b. Ellerbee, Linda
b. Ferre, Gianfranco

August 17, 1944
b. Drexler, Millard S

August 18, 1944
b. Moffett, Anthony Toby
d. Thalmann, Ernst

August 19, 1944
d. Wood, Henry Joseph, Sir

August 20, 1944
b. Gandhi, Rajiv Ratna
b. Nettles, Graig

August 21, 1944
b. DeShannon, Jackie

August 22, 1944
b. Lawrence-Lightfoot, Sara

August 23, 1944
b. D'Aubuisson, Roberto
b. Novello, Antonia Coello

August 24, 1944
b. Capaldi, Jim
b. Jarvis, Gregory

August 25, 1944
b. Black, Conrad Moffat
b. Demers, Jacques
b. Martino, Pat
b. Williams, Sherley Anne

August 27, 1944
b. Bogert, Tim

August 29, 1944
·b. Holland, Endesha Ida Mae

August 30, 1944
b. McGraw, Tug
d. Gibson, Guy

September 1, 1944
b. Slatkin, Leonard
d. Irving, Isabel

September 3, 1944
d. Norris, George William

September 4, 1944
b. Salt, Jennifer
d. Bianco, Margery Williams

September 6, 1944
b. Kurtz, Swoosie
d. Tietjens, Eunice

September 9, 1944
b. Rodin, Judith

September 10, 1944
b. Entwistle, John Alec
b. Fontaine, Philip

September 12, 1944
b. Peltier, Leonard
b. Puccio, Thomas Philip
b. Spivakov, Valdimir (Teodorovich)
b. White, Barry

September 13, 1944
b. Cetera, Peter
d. Robinson, W Heath

September 14, 1944
b. Heatherton, Joey

September 15, 1944
d. Landis, Walter Savage

September 16, 1944
b. Henning, Linda Kaye

September 17, 1944
b. Messner, Reinhold

September 19, 1944
b. Schenk, Ard

September 21, 1944
b. Flagg, Fannie
b. Jordan, Hamilton

September 25, 1944
b. Douglas, Michael Kirk

September 27, 1944
d. McPherson, Aimee Semple

September 29, 1944
b. Gibson, Michael
d. McMurtrie, Douglas C

October 4, 1944
b. LaBelle, Patti
b. LaRussa, Tony
b. Wilson, Robert M
d. Beresford, Harry
d. Smith, Alfred Emanuel

October 5, 1944
d. Maillol, Aristide

October 8, 1944
b. Browles, William Dodson, Jr.
d. Willkie, Wendell Lewis

October 9, 1944
b. Tosh, Peter

October 10, 1944
d. Gottschalk, Ferdinand

October 13, 1944
b. Lamm, Robert

October 15, 1944
b. Trimble, (William) David

October 16, 1944
b. Durcan, Paul

October 18, 1944
b. Kurtz, Katherine
d. Fleischmann, Gisi

October 21, 1944
d. Brinkley, Nell

October 22, 1944
d. Bennett, Richard

October 23, 1944
b. Leavell, Dorothy R.
d. Barkla, Charles Glover

October 24, 1944
d. Renault, Louis

October 25, 1944
b. Anderson, Jon
b. Carville, James

October 26, 1944
b. Cleaver, Emanuel, II

October 28, 1944
b. Coluche
b. Franz, Dennis
d. White, Helen Magill

October 31, 1944
d. Crosman, Henrietta

November 1, 1944
b. Emerson, Keith

November 2, 1944
b. Chereau, Patrice
d. Midgeley, Thomas

November 3, 1944
b. Collin, Frank
d. Miner, Jack

November 4, 1944
b. Niekro, Joe
d. Dill, John Greer, Sir

November 5, 1944
b. Rand, A(ddison) Barry
d. Carrel, Alexis

November 7, 1944
d. Dawson, Geoffrey
d. Senesh, Hannah

November 9, 1944
d. Marshall, Frank James

November 10, 1944
b. Akayev, Askar Akayevich
b. Neely, Mark E., Jr.
b. Rice, Tim(othy Miles Bindon)

November 12, 1944
b. Houston, Ken(neth Ray)
b. Jones, Booker T
d. Birkhoff, George David
d. Kelley, Edgar Stillman

November 14, 1944
d. Dallin, Cyrus Edwin

November 15, 1944
b. Kotto, Yaphet Frederick
d. Flesch, Karl

November 16, 1944
b. Pettet, Joanna

November 17, 1944
b. DeVito, Danny
b. Michaels, Lorne
b. Seaver, Tom
d. Peabody, Endicott
d. Smith, Ellison DuRant

November 18, 1944
b. Sullivan, Susan

November 21, 1944
b. Carsey, Marcy
b. Durbin, Richard J.
b. Monroe, Earl
d. Caillaux, Joseph Marie Auguste
d. Hartmann, Sadakichi

November 22, 1944
d. Eddington, Arthur Stanley, Sir

November 24, 1944
b. Dreifus, Claudia
b. Glickman, Daniel R.

November 25, 1944
d. Landis Kenesaw, Mountain, Judge

November 27, 1944
b. Leland, Mickey

November 28, 1944
b. Brown, Rita Mae

November 29, 1944
b. Cavaliere, Felix

November 30, 1944
d. Fall, Albert Bacon

December 1, 1944
b. Bloom, Eric

December 2, 1944
d. Lhevinne, Josef
d. Marinetti, Filippo Tommaso Emilio

December 4, 1944
b. Wilson, Dennis
d. Bresnaham, Roger Philip

December 7, 1944
b. Antoon, A(lfred) J(oseph)
b. Chorzempa, Daniel Walter

December 8, 1944
d. Cregar, Laird

December 10, 1944
b. Rockefeller, Sharon Percy

December 11, 1944
b. Lee, Brenda
d. Mendes, Chico

December 14, 1944
d. Velez, Lupe

December 15, 1944
b. Leyland, Jim
b. Mendes, Chico
d. Miller, Glenn

December 16, 1944
d. Guedalla, Philip

December 17, 1944
d. Kandinsky, Wassily
d. McLaughlin, Frederic

December 19, 1944
b. Christie, William Lincoln
b. Feigenbaum, Mitchell Jay
b. Leakey, Richard E(rskine Frere)
b. Reid, Tim
d. Yeats-Brown, F(rancis Charles Claypon)

December 21, 1944
b. Ben Jelloun, Tahar
b. Tilson Thomas, Michael

December 22, 1944
b. Carlton, Steve(n Norman)
d. Langdon, Harry

December 23, 1944
d. Gibson, Charles Dana

December 24, 1944
b. Curb, Mike
b. Gordy, Emory, Jr.
d. Castle, Frederick W

December 26, 1944
b. Lapotaire, Jane

December 27, 1944
d. Banning, Kendall
d. Beach, H H A, Mrs.

December 28, 1944
b. Faber, Sandra M(oore)
b. Mullis, Kary B(anks)

December 30, 1944
d. Rolland, Romain

December 31, 1944
b. Hackford, Taylor
d. Nash, George Frederick

1945

b. Ackerman, Robert Allan
b. Bakker, Robert T.
b. Bush, Barney Furman
b. Cosby, Camille (Olivia Hanks)
b. Craft, Christine
b. Dayan, Assaf
b. Foster, Vincent
b. Geiogamah, Hanay
b. Harjo, Susan Shown
b. Hay, John
b. Holmes, John C.
b. Jacobs, Joe
b. Karadzic, Radovan
b. Kroker, Arthur
b. Machel, Graca Simbine
b. McMahon, Vince, Jr.
b. Migenes, Julia
b. Peters, Jon
b. Serrano Elias, Jorge Antonio
b. Sheehan, Daniel P
b. Spheeris, Penelope
b. Spitzer, Andre
b. Steger, Will
b. Suu Kyi, Aung San
b. Tyner, Rob
b. Woo, John
d. Chiang K'ang-Hu
d. Epstein, Abraham

d. Lugard, Frederick John Dealtry
d. Macaulay, Herbert
d. Russell, James Earl

January 3, 1945
b. Stills, Stephen
d. Cayce, Edgar
d. Stone, George Robert

January 6, 1945
b. Freeman, Seth
b. Lopez, Barry (Holstun)

January 7, 1945
b. Conigliaro, Tony

January 9, 1945
b. Biondi, Frank J., Jr.
b. Ter-Petrosyan, Levon

January 10, 1945
b. Stewart, Rod(erick David)

January 13, 1945
d. Deland, Margaret Wade

January 14, 1945
b. Gortner, Marjoe (Hugh Ross)

January 16, 1945
d. Patten, Gilbert

January 20, 1945
b. Butler, Robert Olen
b. Rothenberg, Susan

January 22, 1945
b. Cristofer, Michael
b. Harris, William
b. Jackson, Isaiah Allen
d. Symons, Arthur William

January 23, 1945
b. Harris, Michael Wesley
d. Moltke, Helmuth James, Graf von

January 26, 1945
b. DuPre, Jacqueline
b. Jones, Thom
b. Kruger, Barbara
b. Rifkin, Jeremy
d. Pendergast, Thomas Joseph
d. Szabo, Violette Bushell

January 27, 1945
b. Cardinal, Harold
b. Ghiz, Joseph A
b. Mason, Nick

January 28, 1945
b. Keller, Marthe

January 29, 1945
b. Caponi, Donna
b. Selleck, Tom

January 30, 1945
b. Dorris, Michael (Anthony)
b. Flake, Floyd H(arold)
d. Haberlandt, Gottlieb

January 31, 1945
d. Slovik, Eddie

February 1, 1945
d. Huizinga, Johan

February 2, 1945
d. Goerdeler, Karl Friedrich

February 3, 1945
b. Griese, Bob

February 4, 1945
b. Brenner, David

February 6, 1945
b. Marley, Bob
d. Howell, William H(enry)

February 8, 1945
b. Clodumar, Kinza

February 9, 1945
b. Farrow, Mia

February 11, 1945
d. Dubin, Al
d. Igoe, Hype

February 12, 1945
b. Adams, Maud
b. De Young, Cliff

February 13, 1945
b. Schama, Simon
d. Szold, Henrietta

February 14, 1945
d. Rothenstein, William, Sir

February 15, 1945
b. Hans Adam, II

February 17, 1945
b. Brown, Les(lie Calvin)

February 18, 1945
b. Nader, Michael
b. Rankin, Judy

February 19, 1945
b. Taulbert, Clifton Lemoure

February 20, 1945
b. Haines, Randa
b. Smoot, George

February 21, 1945
d. Liddell, Eric

February 22, 1945
d. Baker, Sara Josephine
d. Tolstoy, Alexey Nikolaevich

February 23, 1945
b. Boesak, Allan Aubrey

February 24, 1945
b. Bostwick, Barry

February 26, 1945
b. Ryder, Mitch

February 28, 1945
b. Smith, Bubba
b. Wynn, Tracy Keenan
d. Frank, Anne

March 1, 1945
b. Benedict, Dirk

March 2, 1945
d. Carr, Emily

March 5, 1945
b. Matson, Randy

March 6, 1945
b. Grundy, Hugh

March 7, 1945
b. Heard, John
d. Dawson, Bertrand Edward

March 8, 1945
b. Dolenz, Mickey
b. Kiefer, Anselm Karl Albert

March 9, 1945
b. Trower, Robin
b. Van Devere, Trish

March 10, 1945
b. Houghton, Katharine

March 11, 1945
b. Ellis, Dock Phillip, Jr.

March 12, 1945
b. Anson, Robert Sam
b. Summers, Anne Fairhurst

March 14, 1945
b. Murphey, Michael Martin
b. Parazaider, Walter
b. Perry, Walt

March 15, 1945
b. Green, Mark J(oseph)

March 18, 1945
d. Kalish, Max

March 20, 1945
b. Riley, Pat(rick James)
d. Douglas, Alfred Bruce, Lord

March 22, 1945
b. Frahm, Sheila

March 23, 1945
b. Grisman, David

March 26, 1945
d. Lloyd George of Dwyfor, David
   Lloyd George Earl

March 27, 1945
b. Aquash, Anna Mae Pictou
d. Bendix, Vincent

March 29, 1945
b. Frazier, Walt(er Jr.)

March 30, 1945
b. Clapton, Eric
b. Miller, Bob

March 31, 1945
b. Kaplan, Gabe
d. Fischer, Hans
d. Hawes, Harriet Ann Boyd

April 2, 1945
b. Hunt, Linda
b. Sutton, Don(ald Howard)

April 3, 1945
b. Knight, John Shively, III
b. Parent, Bernie

April 9, 1945
d. Bonhoeffer, Dietrich
d. Canaris, Wilhelm

April 10, 1945
d. Becker, Carl Lotus

April 11, 1945
b. Koplovitz, Kay Smith

April 12, 1945
d. Roosevelt, Franklin D(elano)

April 13, 1945
b. Dow, Tony
d. Cassirer, Ernst

April 14, 1945
b. Blackmore, Ritchie

April 17, 1945
b. O'Neil, Roger

April 18, 1945
d. Fleming, John Ambrose, Sir
d. Pyle, Ernie

April 20, 1945
b. Spurrier, Steve(n Orr)

April 22, 1945
b. Graham, Donald Edward
d. Kollwitz, Kathe Schmidt

April 25, 1945
b. Ulvaeus, Bjorn
d. Bragg, Mabel Caroline
d. Weatherford, Teddy

April 27, 1945
b. Wilson, August

April 28, 1945
d. Mussolini, Benito Amilcare Andrea

April 29, 1945
b. Terrell, Tammi
d. Petacci, Claretta

April 30, 1945
b. Dillard, Annie Doak
b. Smith, Michael John

d. Braun, Eva
d. Hitler, Adolf

May 1, 1945
b. Coolidge, Rita
d. Goebbels, Joseph

May 2, 1945
d. Bormann, Martin Ludwig
d. Work, Monroe (Nathan)

May 5, 1945
d. Lalique, Rene

May 6, 1945
b. Seger, Bob

May 8, 1945
b. Jarrett, Keith

May 10, 1945
b. Greenberg, Stanley B

May 11, 1945
b. Adams, Floyd, Jr.
d. Commons, John Rogers

May 14, 1945
b. Cornish, Gene

May 18, 1945
b. Quarry, Jerry

May 19, 1945
b. Townshend, Peter Dennis Blandford

May 21, 1945
d. Adams, Herbert Samuel

May 23, 1945
d. Himmler, Heinrich

May 24, 1945
b. Presley, Priscilla Ann Beaulieu

May 28, 1945
b. Fogerty, John
b. Vera, Billy

June 1, 1945
b. Oldfield, Brian
b. VonStade, Frederica

June 2, 1945
b. Long, Richard

June 3, 1945
b. Irwin, Hale S

June 4, 1945
b. Waller, Gordon

June 5, 1945
b. Carlos, John
d. Kaiser, Georg

June 6, 1945
b. Dukes, David
d. Lindsay, David

June 7, 1945
b. Tannen, Deborah Frances

June 11, 1945
b. Barbeau, Adrienne

June 13, 1945
b. Watkins, Levi, Jr.

June 14, 1945
b. Argent, Rod(ney Terence)

June 15, 1945
b. Pagett, Nicola
b. Sawyer, Amos
d. Rives, Amelie Louise

June 16, 1945
b. Matthews, Ian

June 17, 1945
b. Kennedy, Paul (Michael)
b. Livingstone, Ken

June 18, 1945
d. Bascom, Florence
d. Buckner, Simon Bolivar, Jr.

June 19, 1945
b. Wolff, Tobias (Jonathan Ansell)

June 20, 1945
b. Murray, Anne
d. Frank, Bruno

June 23, 1945
d. Lake, Simon

June 24, 1945
b. Blunstone, Colin
b. Pataki, George E(lmer)
b. Stove, Betty

June 25, 1945
b. Kilpatrick, Carolyn Cheeks
b. Simon, Carly

June 26, 1945
d. Tcherepnin, Nicholas

June 27, 1945
b. Kamali, Norma
b. Lacoste, Catherine

June 29, 1945
b. Kumaratunga, Chandrika Bandaranaike
b. Little Eva

July 1, 1945
b. Harry, Deborah (Ann)

July 2, 1945
d. Thompson, Oscar

July 3, 1945
b. Cole, Michael
b. Simmons, Ruth J(ean)

July 5, 1945
d. Curtin, John Joseph

July 7, 1945
b. Rodford, Jim

July 9, 1945
b. Koontz, Dean R(ay)

July 10, 1945
b. Glass, Ron
b. Wade, Virginia

July 13, 1945
d. Nazimova, Alla

July 19, 1945
b. Wexler, Nancy Sabin

July 20, 1945
b. Craig, Larry Edwin
d. Valery, Paul Ambroise

July 21, 1945
b. Lawson, Leigh

July 22, 1945
b. Sherman, Bobby

July 23, 1945
b. Danelli, Dino

July 25, 1945
d. Craig, Malin

July 26, 1945
b. Martin, Kiel

July 28, 1945
b. Davis, Jim
b. Wright, Rick
d. Asquith, Emma Alice Margot

July 29, 1945
d. Mqhayi, S(amuel) E(dward) K(rune Loliwe)

July 30, 1945
b. Sanborn, David

July 31, 1945
b. Weld, William F(loyd)

August 2, 1945
b. McCabe, Jewell Jackson
d. Mascagni, Pietro
d. Reznicek, Emil von

August 6, 1945
b. Messersmith, Andy
d. Bong, Richard Ira
d. Johnson, Hiram Warren

August 7, 1945
b. Page, Alan Cedric

August 8, 1945
b. Bowles, Erskine B.

August 9, 1945
b. Norton, Ken(neth Howard)

August 10, 1945
d. Goddard, Robert Hutchings

August 11, 1945
b. Echohawk, John E.

August 12, 1945
b. Symington, J Fife, III

August 14, 1945
b. Benet, Brenda
b. Martin, Steve
b. Wenders, Wim

August 15, 1945
b. Upshaw, Gene
d. Lowes, John Livingston

August 16, 1945
b. Farrell, Suzanne

August 17, 1945
d. Marinuzzi, Giuseppe (Gino)

August 19, 1945
d. Bose, Subhas Chandra

August 21, 1945
b. Lanier, Willie E
b. McCormack, Patty

August 22, 1945
b. Chase, David
b. Kroft, Steve
d. Maraghi, Mustafa al-

August 25, 1945
d. Birch, John

August 26, 1945
d. Werfel, Franz

August 29, 1945
b. Tyus, Wyomia

August 31, 1945
b. Morrison, Van
b. Perlman, Itzhak
b. Shavers, Ernie

September 1, 1945
d. Craven, Frank

September 4, 1945
b. Edelin, Ramona Hoage

September 5, 1945
b. Stewart, Al

September 7, 1945
b. Lemaire, Jacques Gerald

September 8, 1945
b. Barney, Lem(uel Jackson)
b. Vachon, Rogie
d. Cret, Paul P(hilippe)

September 10, 1945
b. Feliciano, Jose

September 11, 1945
b. Kottke, Leo

September 13, 1945
b. Mongella, Gertrude

September 15, 1945
b. Norman, Jessye
d. Webern, Anton Friedrich Ernst von

September 16, 1945
d. McCormack, John

September 17, 1945
b. Jackson, Phil(ip D.)

September 19, 1945
b. Blalock, Jane
b. Bromberg, David
b. Christian-Green, Donna M.
b. Payne, Freda

September 22, 1945
d. Burke, Thomas

September 23, 1945
b. Boskin, Michael J(ay)
b. Petersen, Paul

September 24, 1945
d. Argentinita
d. Geiger, Hans

September 26, 1945
b. Ferry, Bryan

September 27, 1945
b. Dichter, Mischa

September 29, 1945
d. Bartok, Bela

October 1, 1945
b. Carew, Rod(ney Cline)
b. Hathaway, Donny
d. Cannon, Walter Bradford

October 2, 1945
b. McLean, Don

October 3, 1945
b. Saneyev, Viktor

October 4, 1945
b. Davis, Clifton

October 8, 1945
d. Salten, Felix

October 11, 1945
b. Gale, Robert Peter

October 13, 1945
d. Hershey, Milton Snavely

October 15, 1945
b. Palmer, Jim
d. Laval, Pierre

October 16, 1945
b. Monette, Paul

October 17, 1945
b. Cutler, Dave

October 18, 1945
d. Weyerhaeuser, Frederick Edward

October 19, 1945
b. Ireland, Patricia
b. Lithgow, John (Arthur)
b. Riley, Jeannie C
d. Calles, Plutarco Elias
d. Wyeth, N(ewell) C(onvers)

October 21, 1945
b. Mikhalkov, Nikita
d. Armetta, Henry

October 24, 1945
b. Dunn, Katherine (Karen)
b. Ward, David S
d. Carmichael, Franklin
d. Quisling, Vidkun Abraham

October 25, 1945
b. Borysenko, Joan
d. Ley, Robert

October 26, 1945
b. Conroy, Pat

October 28, 1945
b. Brett, Simon Anthony Lee

October 29, 1945
b. Moore, Melba
b. Simpson, Donald C

October 30, 1945
b. Winkler, Henry Franklin

October 31, 1945
b. Keefe, Barrie Colin

November 2, 1945
b. Souther, J(ohn) D(avid)

November 4, 1945
d. Ritchey, George Willis
d. Smith, Lowell Herbert

November 7, 1945
d. Edwards, Gus

November 11, 1945
b. Alexander, Denise
b. Martell, Vincent
b. Ortega Saavedra, Daniel
d. Kern, Jerome David

November 12, 1945
b. Powers, Stefanie
b. Young, Neil

November 15, 1945
b. Lyngstad-Fredriksson, Annifrid
d. Chapman, Frank Michler

November 16, 1945
b. Van Hamel, Martine

November 17, 1945
b. Hayes, Elvin Ernest

November 18, 1945
b. Mankiller, Wilma P(earl)

November 20, 1945
b. Hamel, Veronica
b. Johnstone, Jay
d. Aston, Francis William

November 21, 1945
b. Hawn, Goldie (Jean)
d. Benchley, Robert Charles
d. Glasgow, Ellen Anderson Gholson
d. Patch, Alexander M(c Carrell)

November 23, 1945
b. Anspach, Susan

November 25, 1945
b. Hagegard, Hakan

November 28, 1945
d. Davis, Dwight Filley
d. Fairfax, Beatrice

November 30, 1945
b. Hair, Jay D(ee)
b. Lupu, Radu
d. Ficke, Arthur Davidson

December 1, 1945
b. Densmore, John
b. Midler, Bette

December 2, 1945
b. Watson, Charles

December 3, 1945
b. Dean, Laura

December 4, 1945
d. Morgan, Thomas Hunt

December 5, 1945
b. Kemmis, Daniel (Orra)
d. Lang, William Cosmo Gordon, Baron

December 6, 1945
b. Bowa, Larry

December 8, 1945
b. Banville, John

December 9, 1945
b. Nouri, Michael

December 11, 1945
b. Preston, John
d. Fabry, Charles

December 12, 1945
b. Williams, Tony

December 13, 1945
b. Cain, Herman
d. Grese, Irma

December 14, 1945
b. Crouch, Stanley
d. Baring, Maurice

December 15, 1945
d. Konoye, Fumimaro, Prince

December 16, 1945
d. Agnelli, Giovanni

December 17, 1945
b. Cazenove, Christopher
b. Muske, Carol (Anne)

December 19, 1945
b. Joyce, Elaine

December 21, 1945
d. Patton, George Smith, Jr.

December 22, 1945
b. Sawyer, Diane (K.)
d. Neurath, Otto
d. Train, Arthur Cheney

December 24, 1945
b. Meyer, Nicholas

December 25, 1945
b. Stabler, Ken(neth Michael)

December 26, 1945
d. Keyes, Roger John Brownlow, Baron

December 27, 1945
b. Jones, Ingrid Saunders

December 28, 1945
b. Birendra Bir Bikram, Shah Dev
d. Dreiser, Theodore

December 30, 1945
b. Jones, Davy
d. Hunter, Glenn

December 31, 1945
b. Carrera, Barbara

1946

b. Arzu, Avaro
b. Ashrawi, Hanan
b. Blakeley, Ronee
b. Christian, Meg
b. Ciller, Tansu
b. Clark, C(arter) Blue
b. Cohn-Bendit, Daniel
b. Eden, Elizabeth Debbie
b. Escovedo, Alejandro
b. Fonseca, Harry
b. Fripp, Robert
b. Guy-Sheftall, Beverly
b. Hardin, Helen
b. Higgins, Bertie
b. Higgins, William R
b. Horner, Jack
b. Hunt, Marsha
b. Kallen, Jackie
b. Kim, Willyce
b. Kwoh, Yik San
b. Lewis, James W
b. Mansion, Gracie
b. Maura, Carmen
b. Milken, Michael
b. Netanyahu, Yonatan
b. Olmert, Ehud
b. Owen, Richard Lee, II
b. Perennou, Marie

b. Puller, Lewis B., Jr.
b. Russo, Vito
b. Sonnier, Jo-El
b. Trump, Donald John
b. Tyrrell, Susan
b. White, Dan(iel James)
b. Williams, Wendy O(rlean)
b. Wright, Syretta
d. Bagley, William Chandler
d. Clapham, John Harold
d. Falconetti, Renee Maria
d. Hirshfield, Morris
d. Nadelman, Elie
d. Sheldon, Charles M(onroe)
d. Teggart, Frederick J.
b. Layton, Larry

January 1, 1946
b. Steele, Claude Mason
b. Steele, Shelby

January 2, 1946
d. Rathbone, Eleanor

January 3, 1946
b. Jones, John Paul
d. Joyce, William

January 4, 1946
b. Barrett, Syd

January 5, 1946
b. Keaton, Diane

January 6, 1946
d. Summerville, Slim

January 7, 1946
b. Wenner, Jann

January 8, 1946
b. Krieger, Robby

January 10, 1946
b. O'Steen, Van
d. Cullen, Countee (Porter)
d. VonTilzer, Harry

January 11, 1946
b. Hale, Janet Campbell
b. Judd, Naomi (Diana)

January 15, 1946
b. Tennant, Veronica

January 17, 1946
d. Kalisch, Paul

January 18, 1946
b. Rodgers, Johnathan (Arlin)
b. Varnedoe, (John) Kirk (Train)

January 19, 1946
b. Barnes, Julian Patrick
b. Parton, Dolly (Rebecca)

January 20, 1946
b. Lynch, David K
b. Williams, Samm-Art

January 22, 1946
b. Savard, Serge A

January 23, 1946
b. Aleman, Arnoldo
b. Hilbert, Stephen C.
b. Taylor, Susan L.

January 24, 1946
b. Ontkean, Michael

January 26, 1946
b. Hampton, Christopher James
b. Siskel, Gene

January 28, 1946
b. Allen, Rick
b. Beck, John
b. Skolnick, Mark H(enry)

January 29, 1946
d. Hopkins, Harry Lloyd

January 30, 1946
b. Beesley, H(orace) Brent

January 31, 1946
b. Kath, Terry
b. Dowiyogo, Bernard

February 2, 1946
b. Konare, Alpha Oumar

February 3, 1946
b. Wachner, Linda

February 5, 1946
b. Rampling, Charlotte
d. Arliss, George

February 9, 1946
b. Webb, James H(enry), Jr.

February 13, 1946
d. Neilson, William A(llan)

February 14, 1946
b. Hines, Gregory Oliver

February 15, 1946
d. Johnson, Cornelius

February 19, 1946
b. Silkwood, Karen

February 20, 1946
b. Briles, Judith Joyce
b. Duncan, Sandy

February 21, 1946
b. Mungo, Raymond
b. Nixon, Tricia

February 23, 1946
d. Yamashita, Tomoyuki

February 27, 1946
b. King, Mary-Claire

March 2, 1946
b. Garrett, Joy

March 4, 1946
d. Waldron, Charles D

March 5, 1946
b. Bleier, Rocky
b. Warren, Michael

March 7, 1946
b. Wolf, Peter

March 8, 1946
b. Meisner, Randy
b. Rowland, Pleasant

March 9, 1946
b. Fuchs, Michael J(oseph)

March 10, 1946
b. Valvano, Jim

March 12, 1946
b. Minnelli, Liza
b. Schank, Roger C(arl)

March 13, 1946
d. Haushofer, Karl Ernst
d. Merivale, Philip

March 14, 1946
b. Kanaly, Steve(n Francis)
b. Unseld, Wes(tley Sissel)

March 15, 1946
b. Bonds, Bobby (Lee)

March 16, 1946
b. Knight, J. Z.

March 18, 1946
b. Reagan, Michael Edward

March 19, 1946
b. Pointer, Ruth

March 20, 1946
d. Richardson, Henry Handel

March 21, 1946
b. Dalton, Timothy

March 23, 1946
d. Largo Caballero, Francisco
d. Lewis, Gilbert Newton

March 24, 1946
b. Hall, Camilla Christine
d. Alekhine, Alexander

April 1, 1946
b. Lane, Ronnie
d. Beery, Noah

April 3, 1946
b. Suchocka, Hanna
d. Dixon, Thomas

April 5, 1946
d. Youmans, Vincent

April 8, 1946
b. Johnson, Robert Louis

April 11, 1946
b. Nuridsany, Claude

April 12, 1946
b. O'Neill, Ed

April 13, 1946
b. Green, Al(bert Leornes)

April 14, 1946
b. Monteleone, Thomas F(rancis)

April 17, 1946
b. Koehler, Georges J F

April 18, 1946
b. Hunter, Catfish
b. Mills, Hayley

April 20, 1946
b. Chia, Sandro

April 21, 1946
d. Keynes, John Maynard, Baron

April 22, 1946
b. Waters, John
d. Atwill, Lionel
d. Stone, Harlan Fiske

April 25, 1946
b. Shire, Talia Rose Coppola
b. Zhirinovsky, Vladimir

April 26, 1946
b. Jaffe, Harold W
d. Keyserling, Hermann Alexander
Graf Von

April 28, 1946
d. Bartlett, Robert Abram

April 30, 1946
b. Carl Gustaf XVI
b. Schollander, Don(ald Arthur)
d. Hepbron, George
b. Altea, Rosemary

May 2, 1946
b. Gore, Lesley
b. Henrit, Robert

May 3, 1946
b. Gumbel, Greg(ory)
b. Lopes, Davey

May 4, 1946
b. Watson, John

May 8, 1946
d. Arguedas, Alcides

May 9, 1946
b. Bergen, Candice

May 10, 1946
b. Blacque, Taurean
b. Mason, Dave
b. Pisier, Marie-France

May 11, 1946
b. Jarvik, Robert Koffler

May 16, 1946
d. Tarkington, Booth

May 18, 1946
b. Jackson, Reggie

May 19, 1946
b. Rudd, Phil(lip)
b. Waihee, John David, III

May 20, 1946
b. Cher
b. Murcer, Bobby Ray

May 21, 1946
b. Hatch, Richard Lawrence

May 22, 1946
b. Best, George

May 23, 1946
b. Graham, David

May 24, 1946
b. Roosevelt, Anna C(urtenius)
b. Szewinska, Irena Kirszenstein

May 25, 1946
b. Ginsburg, Douglas Howard
b. Hayes, James C.
b. Salhany, Lucie
d. Hill, Patty Smith
d. Rhys, Ernest Percival

May 26, 1946
d. Patterson, Joseph Medill

May 28, 1946
d. Glass, Carter

May 30, 1946
b. Lightner, Candy

May 31, 1946
b. Fassbinder, Rainer Werner

June 1, 1946
d. Antonescu, Ion
d. Slezak, Leo

June 3, 1946
b. Hunter, Ian
d. Kalinin, Mikhail (Ivanovich)

June 4, 1946
b. Gregory, Bettina Louise

June 5, 1946
d. Hormel, George Albert
d. Liggett, Louis Kroh

June 6, 1946
d. Hauptmann, Gerhart Johann Robert

June 7, 1946
b. Kreutzmann, Bill

June 8, 1946
b. Lawson, Jennifer Karen

June 9, 1946
b. Adelman, Kenneth Lee
b. Kelman, James

June 10, 1946
d. Johnson, Jack

June 13, 1946
b. Deuba, Sher Bahadur
d. Bowes, Major
d. Guerin, Jules

June 14, 1946
b. Ingersoll, Ralph McAllister, II
b. McLarty, Thomas F, III
d. Baird, John Logie
d. Butterworth, Charles
d. Ubico y Castaneda, Jorge

June 16, 1946
b. Sanderson, Derek Michael
b. Van Ark, Joan
b. Williams, Simon

June 17, 1946
b. Manilow, Barry

June 20, 1946
b. Vila, Bob
b. Watts, Andre

June 21, 1946
b. Merrill, Steve
b. Saatchi, Maurice

June 23, 1946
b. Shackelford, Ted
d. Hart, William Surrey

June 24, 1946
b. Onizuka, Ellison
b. Reich, Robert B(ernard)
d. Hare, James Henry

June 25, 1946
b. Lanier, Allen

June 26, 1946
b. Bellwood, Pamela

June 27, 1946
b. Priesand, Sally Jane
d. Gag, Wanda

June 28, 1946
b. Davison, Bruce
b. Martyn, John
b. Radner, Gilda
d. Perry, Antoinette

June 29, 1946
b. Furstenberg, Egon von
b. Perez Balladares, Ernesto

July 2, 1946
b. Silver, Ron

July 3, 1946
b. Lee, Johnny

July 4, 1946
b. Kovic, Ron

July 5, 1946
b. Johnson, Pierre Marc

July 6, 1946
  b. Bush, George W(alker)
  b. Dryer, Fred
  b. Singer, Peter
  b. Stallone, Sylvester (Enzio)
  b. Ward, Burt
  b. Wyeth, Jamie
  d. Lanvin, Jeanne
  d. Pippin, Horace

July 7, 1946
  b. Spano, Joe

July 8, 1946
  b. Fuller, Kathryn S(cott)
  b. Gregory, Cynthia Kathleen

July 10, 1946
  d. Hillman, Sidney (Simcha)

July 11, 1946
  d. Nash, Paul

July 12, 1946
  d. Baker, Ray Stannard

July 13, 1946
  b. Marin, Richard
  d. Stieglitz, Alfred

July 15, 1946
  b. Bolkiah, Muda Hassanal, Sir
  b. Ronstadt, Linda

July 17, 1946
  d. Mihajlovic, Dragoliub

July 18, 1946
  d. Judd, Charles Hubbard

July 19, 1946
  b. Nastase, Ilie

July 20, 1946
  b. Carnes, Kim

July 21, 1946
  b. Starr, Kenneth
  d. Rosenfeld, Paul

July 22, 1946
  b. Edgar, Jim
  b. Schrader, Paul Joseph

July 26, 1946
  b. Mirren, Helen

July 27, 1946
  d. Stein, Gertrude

July 28, 1946
  b. Kelsey, Linda

July 30, 1946
  b. Zumwalt, Elmo Russell, III

July 31, 1946
  b. Welch, Bob

August 5, 1946
  b. Anderson, Loni
  b. Beban, Gary Joseph

  b. Jackson, Shirley Ann
  b. Slezak, Erika

August 6, 1946
  b. Lynch, Benny
  d. Lazzeri, Tony

August 8, 1946
  d. Barrientos, Maria

August 9, 1946
  b. Kiick, Jim

August 11, 1946
  b. Savant, Marilyn vos

August 13, 1946
  d. Wells, H(erbert) G(eorge)

August 14, 1946
  b. Graham, Larry
  b. Saint James, Susan

August 15, 1946
  b. Webb, Jim
  b. Whitmire, Kathy

August 16, 1946
  b. Warren, Lesley Ann

August 17, 1946
  b. Manning, Patrick (Augustus
    Mervyn)
  d. Pollock, Channing

August 19, 1946
  b. Bolden, Charles F(rank), Jr.
  b. Clinton, Bill
  b. Steel, Dawn

August 20, 1946
  b. Chung, Connie
  b. Fabius, Laurent
  d. Ragland, Rags
  d. Yost, Fielding Harris

August 21, 1946
  b. Bazell, Robert Joseph

August 23, 1946
  b. Moon, Keith

August 25, 1946
  b. Fingers, Rollie

August 28, 1946
  b. Soul, David

August 29, 1946
  b. Bagaza, Jean-Baptiste
  b. Beamon, Bob
  d. Curry, John Steuart

August 31, 1946
  d. Granville-Barker, Harley
  d. Klenau, Paul von
  b. Ade, Sunny, King

September 1, 1946
  b. Gibb, Barry

September 2, 1946
  b. Avalos, Luis

September 3, 1946
  d. Rosenthal, Moriz

September 5, 1946
  b. Miles, Buddy

September 6, 1946
  b. Boone, Ron(ald Bruce)

September 7, 1946
  b. Rudi, Joe

September 8, 1946
  b. Forsch, Ken(neth Roth)
  b. McKernan, Ron
  b. Mercury, Freddie
  d. Eustis, Dorothy Leib Harrison
    Wood

September 9, 1946
  b. Preston, Billy

September 10, 1946
  b. Hines, Jim

September 12, 1946
  b. N'Namdi, George R(ichard)

September 13, 1946
  b. Bisset, Jacqueline Fraser
  d. Hill, George Washington

September 14, 1946
  b. Russell-McCloud, Patricia (A.)

September 15, 1946
  b. Jones, Tommy Lee
  b. Stone, Oliver

September 17, 1946
  d. Jeans, James Hopwood, Sir

September 18, 1946
  d. White, Stewart Edward

September 19, 1946
  d. Carr, Alexander

September 20, 1946
  d. Raimu

September 24, 1946
  b. Greene, Joe

September 25, 1946
  b. Kendal, Felicity

September 26, 1946
  b. Dworkin, Andrea
  b. Whitman, Christine Todd

September 28, 1946
  b. Vermeij, Geerat J(acobus)

September 30, 1946
  b. Moussa, Ibrahim

October 1, 1946
b. O'Brien, Tim

October 2, 1946
b. Cox, Edward Finch

October 3, 1946
b. Dotson, Bob

October 4, 1946
b. Hagel, Chuck
b. Sarandon, Susan
d. Oldfield, Barney
d. Pinchot, Gifford

October 7, 1946
b. MacKinnon, Catharine A(lice)
b. Soren, David

October 8, 1946
b. Kucinich, Dennis John

October 10, 1946
b. Mahovlich, Pete(r Joseph)
b. Prine, John
b. Tenace, Gene
b. Vereen, Ben(jamin Augustus)

October 11, 1946
b. Martins, Peter

October 12, 1946
d. Stilwell, Joseph Warren

October 13, 1946
b. Dalton, Lacy J
b. Wilson, Demond
d. Bannerman, Helen

October 14, 1946
b. Sloan, Michael
b. Venter, J. Craig

October 15, 1946
b. Banerjee, Victor
b. Carpenter, Richard Lynn
d. Goering, Hermann Wilhelm

October 16, 1946
b. Somers, Suzanne
d. Bantock, Granville, Sir
d. Frank, Hans
d. Frick, Wilhelm
d. Jodl, Alfred
d. Keitel, Wilhelm
d. Ribbentrop, Joachim von
d. Rosenberg, Alfred
d. Seyss-Inquart, Artur von
d. Streicher, Julius

October 17, 1946
b. Mackintosh, Cameron
b. Michnik, Adam
b. Seagren, Bob

October 19, 1946
b. Divine

October 20, 1946
b. Grizzard, Lewis M., Jr.

October 21, 1946
b. Loughname, Lee

October 22, 1946
b. Brigati, Eddie

October 23, 1946
d. Seton, Ernest Thompson

October 24, 1946
d. Kline, Otis Adelbert

October 26, 1946
b. Reitman, Ivan

October 27, 1946
b. Snodgress, Carrie

October 29, 1946
b. Green, Peter

November 1, 1946
b. Muren, Dennis

November 2, 1946
b. Carter, Mandy
b. Sinopoli, Giuseppe

November 4, 1946
b. Mapplethorpe, Robert

November 5, 1946
b. Parsons, Gram
d. Stella, Joseph

November 6, 1946
b. DeBartolo, Edward J, Jr.
b. Field, Sally Margaret
b. Penner, Fred
d. Hummel, Berta

November 7, 1946
b. Chrystos

November 10, 1946
b. Stockman, David Allen

November 11, 1946
b. Metrinko, Michael John

November 14, 1946
d. Falla, Manuel de

November 15, 1946
b. Lennon, Janet

November 16, 1946
b. Smith, Barbara
b. White, Jo Jo

November 17, 1946
b. Branstad, Terry Edward
d. Horne, Herman Harrell

November 18, 1946
b. Begiebing, Robert J.
d. Meek, Donald
d. Walker, Jimmy

November 20, 1946
b. Allman, Duane

b. Cook, Greg(ory Lynn)
b. Woodruff, Judy Carline

November 23, 1946
d. Dove, Arthur Garfield

November 24, 1946
b. Bundy, Ted
d. Moholy-Nagy, Laszlo

November 25, 1946
d. Morgenthau, Henry

November 26, 1946
b. Hill, Norbert S., Jr.
b. McVie, John
b. Shell, Art

November 29, 1946
b. Chaffee, Suzy

December 1, 1946
b. O'Sullivan, Gilbert

December 2, 1946
b. Versace, Gianni

December 5, 1946
b. Carreras, Jose

December 7, 1946
d. Taylor, Laurette

December 8, 1946
b. Rubinstein, John Arthur

December 10, 1946
b. Loring, Gloria Jean
d. Johnson, Walter Perry
d. Runyon, Damon

December 11, 1946
b. George, Lynda Day

December 12, 1946
b. Fittipaldi, Emerson

December 14, 1946
b. Botstein, Leon
b. Duke, Patty
b. Gandhi, Sanjay
b. Ovitz, Michael S.
b. Smith, Stan(ley Roger)

December 15, 1946
b. Appice, Carmine

December 16, 1946
b. Andersson, Benny
b. Pinnock, Trevor David

December 17, 1946
d. Garnett, Constance

December 18, 1946
b. Biko, Steven

December 19, 1946
b. Pinero, Miguel

December 20, 1946
b. Codrescu, Andrei
b. Geller, Uri

December 21, 1946
b. Keene, Christopher
b. Wilson, Carl (Dean)
d. Talmadge, Eugene

December 22, 1946
b. Garwood, Robert Russell

December 23, 1946
b. Lucci, Susan
d. Davis, John Staige

December 24, 1946
b. Sessions, Jeff

December 25, 1946
b. Buffett, Jimmy
b. Csonka, Larry
b. Sandy, Gary
d. Fields, W C

December 26, 1946
b. Krens, Thomas

December 28, 1946
b. Green, Hubie
b. Johnson, Tim
b. Winter, Edgar Holand
d. Bond, Carrie Jacobs
d. Hooker, Brian

December 29, 1946
b. Faithfull, Marianne
b. Pincay, Laffit, Jr.
b. Trible, Paul Seward, Jr.
d. Shirley, Ralph

December 30, 1946
b. Smith, Patti
b. Takei, Kei
d. Cadman, Charles Wakefield

December 31, 1946
b. Furstenberg, Diane Halfin von

1947

b. Anderson, Laurie
b. Barry, Dave
b. Benson, Renaldo
b. Bilon, Michael Patrick
b. Bondevik, Kjell (Magne)
b. Bremen, Barry
b. Buckwheat Zydeco
b. Carols
b. Clancy, Thomas L., Jr.
b. Curry, Tim
b. Danvers, Dennis
b. DeVarona, Donna
b. Dicciani, Nance K(atherine)
b. Dudley, Barbara
b. Englemann, Robert A
b. Faison, George
b. Foreman, Dave
b. Forne Molne, Marc
b. Garcia, Joe
b. Goetz, Bernhard
b. Guelleh, Ismael Omar

b. Howland, Michael
b. Ji Jaga, Geronimo
b. Kingsborough Donald
b. Komunyakaa, Yusef
b. Lauria, Dan
b. Laybourne, Geraldine
b. Marley, Rita
b. Mikhail-Ashrawi, Hanan
b. Mosbacher, Georgette
b. Najib Ahmadzi
b. Ongala, Remmy
b. Orange, Walter
b. Patterson, Melody
b. Rosendahl, Bruce R
b. Savitskaya, Svetlana Y
b. Schlessinger, Laura
b. Seddon, Rhea
b. Smith, Cathy Evelyn
b. Trudell, John
b. Warnes, Jennifer
b. Weed, Steven Andrew
b. Weill, Claudia
b. Williams, Kit
b. Williams, Milan
b. Williamson, Cris
b. Yilmaz, Mesut
d. Bakhita, Giuseppina
d. Coulton, George Gordon
d. Farber, Simon W
d. Smith, Amanda W
d. Uspenskii, Petr Dem'yanovich
d. Wilkinson, Ellen

January 2, 1947
b. Hill, Calvin

January 3, 1947
d. Reid, Ogden Mills

January 5, 1947
b. DeWine, Mike
b. Lange, Ted
b. Morris, Mercury
b. Switzer, Katherine Virginia
d. Nagano, Osami

January 7, 1947
d. Dodge, Henry Chee

January 8, 1947
b. Bowie, David

January 9, 1947
d. Mannheim, Karl

January 10, 1947
b. Morris, James Peppler

January 11, 1947
b. Calder-Marshall, Anna Lucia
d. Tanguay, Eva

January 12, 1947
b. Dempsey, Tom
d. Eigenmann, Rosa Smith

January 14, 1947
d. Hewitt, Bill

January 17, 1947
b. Dove, Ulysses

January 19, 1947
b. Compton, Ann (Woodruff)
d. Machado (y Ruiz), Manuel

January 20, 1947
d. Gibson, Josh(ua)
d. Volstead, Andrew J

January 21, 1947
b. Eikenberry, Jill

January 23, 1947
b. Carper, Thomas Richard
d. Bonnard, Pierre

January 24, 1947
b. Chinaglia, Giorgio
b. Zevon, Warren
d. Timmermans, Felix

January 25, 1947
d. Capone, Al(phonse)

January 26, 1947
b. Dewaere, Patrick
d. Moore, Grace

January 27, 1947
d. Mildenburg, Anna von

January 28, 1947
d. Cohen, Morris Raphael

January 31, 1947
b. Ryan, Nolan
d. Kling, Johnny

February 2, 1947
b. Fawcett, Farrah Leni

February 3, 1947
b. Auster, Paul
b. Davies, Dave
d. Mitscher, Marc Andrew

February 4, 1947
b. Quayle, Dan

February 5, 1947
b. Waltrip, Darrell Lee

February 6, 1947
b. Yergin, Daniel
d. Fallada, Hans

February 9, 1947
b. Ely, Joe

February 11, 1947
b. Harris, Emily Schwartz

February 12, 1947
d. Lewin, Kurt
d. Toler, Sidney

February 13, 1947
b. Krzyzewski, Mike

February 14, 1947
b. Gregg, Judd

February 15, 1947
b. Adams, John Coolidge
b. Hamer, Rusty

February 17, 1947
b. Buckley, Tim
b. Whiteman, Roberta Hill

February 18, 1947
b. Christina
b. DeYoung, Dennis

February 19, 1947
b. Curtis, Jackie

February 20, 1947
b. Strauss, Peter

February 21, 1947
b. Snowe, Olympia J(ean)

February 22, 1947
b. Jay, Karla
d. Thaw, Harry Kendall

February 23, 1947
d. Hill, Grace Livingstone
d. Janet, Pierre Marie Felix

February 24, 1947
b. Fratello, Mike
b. Holmes, Rupert
b. Olmos, Edward James
d. Glasscock, Jack
d. Jordan, Elizabeth Garver

February 25, 1947
b. Beatts, Anne
b. Evans, Lee

February 26, 1947
d. Webster, Ben(jamin)

February 27, 1947
b. Guth, Alan Harvey
b. Kremer, Gidon

February 28, 1947
b. Beacham, Stephanie

March 1, 1947
b. Thicke, Alan

March 2, 1947
d. Marston, William Moulton

March 5, 1947
b. Hodges, Eddie
b. Tekulve, Kent(on Charles)

March 6, 1947
b. Dee, Kiki
b. Fosbury, Dick
b. Reiner, Rob(ert)
d. Mackinder, Halford John, Sir

March 8, 1947
b. Sager, Carole Bayer

March 9, 1947
b. Kennerly, David Hume
d. Catt, Carrie Chapman

March 10, 1947
b. Campbell, Kim
b. Greene, Bob
b. Scholz, Tom

March 11, 1947
b. Stein, Mark

March 12, 1947
d. Churchill, Winston

March 13, 1947
b. St. James, Lyn

March 14, 1947
b. Crystal, Billy

March 15, 1947
b. Cooder, Ry(land Peter)
b. Pena, Federico F.

March 16, 1947
b. Roche, Joyce

March 18, 1947
d. Durant, William Crapo

March 19, 1947
b. Close, Glenn

March 20, 1947
b. Boswell, John (Eastburn)
d. Goldschmidt, Victor Moritz

March 21, 1947
b. Kylian, Jiri

March 23, 1947
d. Rankin, Arthur

March 25, 1947
b. John, Elton

March 27, 1947
b. Sullivan, Tom

March 28, 1947
b. Gilbert, Bruce
d. Evers, Johnny

March 31, 1947
b. Gaviria Trujillo, Cesar Augusto

April 1, 1947
b. Eisenhower, David
d. George II

April 2, 1947
b. Harris, Emmylou
b. Paglia, Camille

April 3, 1947
b. Namaliu, Rabbie Langanai

April 6, 1947
b. Ratzenberger, John Dezso

April 7, 1947
d. Ford, Henry

April 10, 1947
d. Flagg, Ernest

April 11, 1947
d. Nordhoff, Charles Bernard

April 12, 1947
b. Letterman, David

April 13, 1947
b. Batts, Deborah A.

April 15, 1947
d. Hoess, Rudolf Franz

April 16, 1947
b. Abdul-Jabbar, Kareem
b. Rafferty, Gerry

April 18, 1947
b. Woods, James
d. Leonard, Benny

April 19, 1947
b. Perahia, Murray
d. Bidwell, Charles W

April 20, 1947
b. Tobias, Andrew Previn
d. Christian X
d. Patino, Simon Iturri

April 21, 1947
b. Pop, Iggy

April 23, 1947
b. Devlin, Bernadette Josephine
d. Lawes, Lewis Edward

April 24, 1947
d. Cather, Willa (Sibert)

April 25, 1947
b. Cruyff, Johan

April 26, 1947
d. McLean, Evalyn Walsh

April 27, 1947
b. Magnuson, Keith Arlen

April 29, 1947
b. Miller, Johnny Laurence
b. Ryun, Jim
d. Fisher, Irving

April 30, 1947
d. Wright, Almroth Edward, Sir

May 1, 1947
b. Davis, Barbara

May 2, 1947
b. Oglesby, Zena, (Jr.)

May 3, 1947
b. Henning, Doug(las James)

May 6, 1947
d. Homer, Louise

May 8, 1947
d. Selfridge, Harry Gordon

May 9, 1947
b. Natori, Josie

May 11, 1947
b. Popcorn, Faith
b. Vonnegut, Mark
d. Goudy, Frederic William

May 13, 1947
b. Baxter, Charles (Morley)
b. Donaldson, Stephen Reeder
b. Watts, Pete
d. Gleason, Lucille

May 15, 1947
b. Boyd, T(heophilus) B(artholomew), III

May 16, 1947
b. Edwards, Bob
d. Hopkins, Frederick Gowland, Sir

May 18, 1947
b. Bruton, John (Gerard)

May 19, 1947
b. Brady, Paul Joseph
b. Helfgott, David

May 20, 1947
d. Lenard, Philipp Edward Anton

May 23, 1947
d. Dupree, Minnie

May 25, 1947
b. Colter, Jessie
b. Valentine, Karen

May 26, 1947
b. Evans, Darrell Wayne

May 27, 1947
d. Carlson, Evans Fordyce

May 28, 1947
b. Johnston, Lynn Beverley
b. Locke, Sondra

May 29, 1947
b. Geary, Anthony

June 1, 1947
b. Wood, Ron(ald)
d. Enskog, David

June 2, 1947
b. Page, Clarence
b. Rudd, Mark

June 4, 1947
b. Klima, Viktor

June 5, 1947
b. Hare, David

June 6, 1947
d. Agate, James Evershed

June 7, 1947
b. Munson, Thurman Lee

June 8, 1947
b. Paretsky, Sara

June 11, 1947
b. Cisneros, Henry G(abriel)
b. Gurganus, Allan

June 13, 1947
d. Marquet, Albert

June 14, 1947
b. Harwood, Vanessa Clare

June 16, 1947
d. Huberman, Bronislaw

June 17, 1947
b. Chavez, Linda
d. Perkins, Maxwell Evarts
d. Perkins, William Maxwell Evarts

June 18, 1947
b. McCashin, Constance Broman

June 19, 1947
b. Rushdie, Salman Ahmed

June 20, 1947
d. Siegel, Bugsy

June 21, 1947
b. Baxter, Meredith
b. Gross, Michael

June 22, 1947
b. Butler, Octavia E(stelle)
b. Rawlings, Jerry John

June 23, 1947
b. Brown, Bryan

June 25, 1947
d. Shaw, Albert

June 26, 1947
d. Bennett, Richard Bedford
d. Kitson, Henry Hudson

June 28, 1947
b. Helprin, Mark
b. Tyson, Laura D'Andrea

June 29, 1947
b. Lewis, Richard
d. Lembede, Anton

July 2, 1947
b. Johnson, Luci Baines

July 3, 1947
b. Buckley, Betty Lynn
b. Burton, Michael
b. Carter, Jack
b. Lomahaftewa, Linda

July 5, 1947
b. Ott, David Lee

July 9, 1947
b. Simpson, O(renthal) J(ames)

July 10, 1947
b. Guthrie, Arlo Davy
b. Schmiechen, Richard Kurt
d. Rider-Kelsey, Corinne

July 12, 1947
b. Gary, Willie E.

July 13, 1947
d. Lunceford, Jimmy

July 14, 1947
b. Ramgoolam, Navin

July 15, 1947
d. Donaldson, Walter

July 16, 1947
b. Boggs, Tom
b. Herman, Alexis M.
b. Hogan, Linda
b. Shakur, Assata

July 17, 1947
d. Wallenberg, Raoul Gustav

July 18, 1947
b. Forbes, Malcolm Stevenson, Jr.

July 19, 1947
b. Leadon, Bernie
b. May, Brian
d. Aung San

July 20, 1947
b. Binnig, Gerd
b. Santana, Carlos

July 22, 1947
b. Brooks, Albert (Lawrence Einstein)
b. Glover, Danny
b. Henley, Don

July 23, 1947
b. Christian, Spencer
b. Essex, David
b. Manetti, Larry

July 24, 1947
b. Hays, Robert
b. Serkin, Peter A(dolf)

July 28, 1947
b. Ebersol, Dick

July 29, 1947
b. Forsyth, Bill

July 30, 1947
b. Atherton, William
b. Schwarzenegger, Arnold Alois

August 1, 1947
b. Anderson, Rich

August 4, 1947
b. Derringer, Rick
b. Ingraham, Hubert

August 8, 1947
b. Dryden, Ken(neth Wayne)
b. Wilcox, Larry Dee
d. Denikin, Anton Ivanovich

August 10, 1947
b. Anderson, Ian

August 13, 1947
b. McDougall, Gay J.

August 14, 1947
b. Steel, Danielle Fernande

August 15, 1947
b. Costello, Chris

August 16, 1947
b. Moseley-Braun, Carol

August 17, 1947
b. Talley, Gary

August 19, 1947
b. Schwarz, Gerard

August 20, 1947
b. Pankow, James

August 21, 1947
d. Bilbo, Theodore Gilmore
d. Bugatti, Ettore Arco Isidoro

August 23, 1947
b. O'Hara, Jill
b. Whittle, Christopher

August 25, 1947
b. Archer, Anne
b. Castillo, Edward (Daniel)

August 27, 1947
b. Bach, Barbara
b. Reems, Harry

August 29, 1947
b. Grandin, Temple
b. Hunt, James
b. Lutz, Bob
d. Manolete

August 30, 1947
b. Gilles, D(onald) B(ruce)
b. Lipton, Peggy

September 1, 1947
b. Lazarus, Shelly

September 5, 1947
b. Wainwright, Loudon, III

September 6, 1947
b. Curtin, Jane (Therese)

September 7, 1947
b. Tilberis, Elizabeth

September 8, 1947
b. Beattie, Ann
b. Lavelle, Rita Marie

September 9, 1947
d. Coomaraswamy, Ananda Kentish

September 10, 1947
b. Nelson, Larry Gene

September 11, 1947
d. Bullard, Robert Lee

September 14, 1947
d. LeGallienne, Richard

September 17, 1947
b. MacNelly, Jeff(rey Kenneth)

September 18, 1947
d. Kalmar, Bert

September 19, 1947
b. Brown, Larry
b. Perry, Nancy Ling

September 20, 1947
d. La Guardia, Fiorello Henry

September 21, 1947
b. Felder, Don(ald William)
b. King, Stephen Edwin
b. Norman, Marsha Williams
d. Carey, Harry

September 23, 1947
b. Place, Mary Kay

September 25, 1947
b. Tiegs, Cheryl

September 26, 1947
b. Anderson, Lynn
d. Lofting, Hugh

September 28, 1947
b. Hasina Wajed

September 30, 1947
b. Lenska, Rula

October 1, 1947
b. Collins, Stephen
d. Martinez Sierra, Gregorio
d. Rogers, James Gamble

October 2, 1947
d. MacNeil, Hermon Atkins

October 3, 1947
b. Buckingham, Lindsey
d. Adams, Charles Francis

October 4, 1947
d. Planck, Max Karl Ernst Ludwig

October 6, 1947
d. Hoffenstein, Samuel Goodman

October 12, 1947
b. Wallace, Chris(topher)
d. Hamilton, Ian Standish Monteith, Sir

October 13, 1947
d. Webb, Sidney James

October 14, 1947
b. Joiner, Charlie

October 17, 1947
b. McKean, Michael
d. Huntington, Ellsworth

October 18, 1947
b. Morton, Joe
b. Nyro, Laura

October 22, 1947
b. Barbour, Haley (Reeves)

October 24, 1947
b. Kline, Kevin Delaney
d. Digges, Dudley

October 25, 1947
d. Ziegler, Edward

October 26, 1947
b. Clinton, Hillary Rodham
b. Sajak, Pat
b. Smith, Jaclyn

October 27, 1947
b. Anderson, Terry A
b. Maraldo, Pamela Jean

October 29, 1947
b. Dreyfuss, Richard (Stephan)
d. Brach, Emil J
d. Cleveland, Frances Folsom

October 30, 1947
b. Schmidt, Tim(othy B)

October 31, 1947
b. Ballard, Russ(ell)
b. Shorter, Frank C

November 1, 1947
b. Hendricks, Ted

November 3, 1947
b. Stevens, Shadoe

November 5, 1947
b. Noone, Peter

November 7, 1947
b. Bryant, Wayne R(ichard)

November 8, 1947
b. Allman, Gregg
b. Magaziner, Ira C(harles)

November 10, 1947
b. Gemayel, Bashir
b. Sneed, Paula A(nn)

November 11, 1947
b. Daugherty, Pat
b. Glaser, Elizabeth
d. Lowndes, Marie Adelaide Belloc

November 12, 1947
b. Roeser, Donald

d. Moore, John Bassett
d. Orczy, Emmuska, Baroness

November 13, 1947
b. Lovins, Amory B(loch)
b. Mantegna, Joe

November 14, 1947
b. O'Rourke, P J

November 15, 1947
b. Richardson, Bill
d. Levy, Florence

November 16, 1947
b. Giddings, Paula (Jane)
d. Carter, Boake

November 17, 1947
b. Vollbracht, Michaele J
d. Huch, Ricarda (Octavia)

November 19, 1947
b. Boone, Bob

November 20, 1947
b. Walsh, Joe

November 22, 1947
b. Buckard, Alfredo Cristiani
b. Cristiani, Alfredo
b. Reynolds, Jack

November 23, 1947
b. Landesberg, Steve

November 25, 1947
b. Larroquette, John (Bernard)

November 26, 1947
b. Hebner, Richie

November 28, 1947
b. Hasford, Jerry Gustav
d. Leclerc, Jacques-Philippe

November 29, 1947
b. Kelly, Petra (Karin)

November 30, 1947
b. Mamet, David Alan
d. Lubitsch, Ernst
b. De Lucia, Paco

December 1, 1947
b. Shanley, Kathryn W.
d. Crowley, Aleister (Edward Alexander)
d. Hardy, Godfrey Harold

December 2, 1947
b. Scharping, Rudolf

December 3, 1947
b. Krenwinkel, Patricia

December 4, 1947
d. Butler, Nicholas Murray

December 5, 1947
b. Messina, Jim
b. Plunkett, Jim

d. Thomas, W(illiam) I(saac)

December 7, 1947
b. Bench, Johnny Lee
b. Unger, Garry Douglas

December 8, 1947
b. Cech, Thomas Robert
b. Geller, Margaret J(oan)

December 9, 1947
b. Daschle, Thomas Andrew
b. Owens, Steve E

December 10, 1947
b. Kenney, Douglas C

December 13, 1947
b. Garver, Kathy
b. Gonzalez Macchi, Luis

December 14, 1947
b. Parkening, Christopher William
d. Baldwin, Stanley
d. Fyffe, Will

December 15, 1947
d. Machen, Arthur

December 16, 1947
b. Cross, Ben
b. Matthews, Vince(nt)
d. Sodero, Cesare

December 17, 1947
d. Bronsted, Johannes Nicolaus
d. Spilsbury, Bernard Henry, Sir

December 18, 1947
b. Spielberg, Steven

December 19, 1947
b. Urich, Robert
d. Scott, Duncan Campbell

December 20, 1947
b. Criss, Peter

December 21, 1947
d. Hellinger, Mark

December 23, 1947
b. Rodgers, Bill

December 26, 1947
b. Fisk, Carlton Ernest

December 27, 1947
d. Beam, James B

December 28, 1947
d. Crowninshield, Francis Welch
d. Victor Emmanuel III

December 29, 1947
b. Danson, Ted

December 30, 1947
b. Lynne, Jeff
d. Whitehead, Alfred North

December 31, 1947
b. Cummings, Burton

1948

b. Atkins, Susan Denise
b. Atwood, Angela
b. Brown, Blair
b. Buchanan, Angela Marie
b. Carlton, Larry
b. Charlemagne, Manno
b. Cimino, Michael
b. Cliff, Jimmy
b. Daugherty, William J
b. D'Emilio, John
b. DuBay, William Bryan
b. Dupuy, Diane
b. Ellroy, James
b. English, Diane
b. Fairstein, Linda
b. Feld, Kenneth Jeffrey
b. Gucci, Maurizio
b. Halfin, Eliezer
b. Hampton, Fred
b. Harris, Jay T(errence)
b. Hinton, S(usan) E(loise)
b. Hoffman, Rob
b. Kellner, Jamie
b. Kristiansen, Kjeld Kirk
b. Kupke, Frederick Lee
b. Levy, David H.
b. Morris, Dick
b. O'Donnell, Bill
b. O'Leary, Jean
b. Pipher, Mary
b. Sanda, Dominique
b. Sidney, Ivan
b. Stringer, C. Vivian
b. Sunshine, Linda
b. Taylor, Charles McArthur
b. Thalheimer, Richard
b. Thigpen Lynne
b. Tiburzi, Bonnie
b. Toure, Amadou Toumani
b. Trudeau, Garry
b. Wigler, Michael (H.)
b. Willners, Hal
b. Wills, Frank
d. Eastern Jewel
d. Rutherfurd, Lucy Page Mercer
d. Schwimmer, Rosika
d. Schwinn, Ignaz
d. Smucker, Jerome

January 1, 1948
d. May, Edna

January 5, 1948
d. Harrison, Mary Scott Lord Dimmick

January 7, 1948
b. Loggins, Kenny

January 8, 1948
b. Troutt, Kenny A.
d. Schwitters, Kurt (Hermann Edward Karl Julius)
d. Tauber, Richard

January 10, 1948
b. Fagen, Donald

January 11, 1948
b. Jackson, Madeline Manning

January 12, 1948
b. Andrews, Anthony Corin Gerald

January 14, 1948
b. Weathers, Carl

January 15, 1948
d. Daniels, Josephus

January 16, 1948
b. Carpenter, John Howard

January 17, 1948
b. Oddsson, David
b. Taylor, Mick

January 19, 1948
b. McKenna, Frank
d. Sobol, Louis

January 20, 1948
b. Shcharansky, Anatoly Borisovich
d. Aucherlonie, Laurie

January 21, 1948
b. Laiken, Deirdre Susan
d. Wolf-Ferrari, Ermanno

January 22, 1948
b. Chavis, Benjamin Franklin, Jr.

January 23, 1948
b. Pointer, Anita

January 24, 1948
b. Abrams, Elliott

January 26, 1948
d. Lomax, John Avery

January 28, 1948
b. Baryshnikov, Mikhail
b. Taylor, Charles

January 30, 1948
d. Gandhi, Mahatma
d. Pennock, Herb(ert Jefferis)
d. Wright, Orville

February 2, 1948
b. Savitch, Jessica Beth
d. Lamont, Thomas William

February 3, 1948
b. Melanie

February 4, 1948
b. Cooper, Alice
b. Grams, Rod

February 5, 1948
b. Hershey, Barbara
b. Wallechinsky, David

February 7, 1948
d. McKenzie, Red

February 8, 1948
b. Seals, Dan Wayland

February 9, 1948
b. Love, Susan M(argaret)

February 10, 1948
d. Eisenstein, Sergei Mikhailovich

February 12, 1948
b. Kurzweil, Raymond C

February 14, 1948
d. Brown, Mordecai Peter Centennial

February 15, 1948
b. Berenson, Marisa
b. Cey, Ron(ald Charles)
b. Spiegelman, Art

February 18, 1948
b. Johnson, Robert T.

February 23, 1948
d. Gregg, John Robert

February 24, 1948
d. Irwin, Will(iam Henry)

February 26, 1948
b. Edgar, David
b. Lopez, Priscilla

February 28, 1948
b. Peters, Bernadette
b. Sant, Alfred

February 29, 1948
b. Smith, Willi Donnell
d. Mantle, (Robert) Burns

March 2, 1948
d. Brill, Abraham Arden

March 3, 1948
b. Hundt, Reed

March 4, 1948
b. Squire, Chris
d. Artaud, Antonin

March 5, 1948
b. Grant, Eddy
b. Silko, Leslie Marmon

March 6, 1948
b. Schwartz, Stephen L(awrence)
d. Lockridge, Ross Franklin, Jr.

March 9, 1948
b. Fischl, Eric

March 10, 1948
d. Fitzgerald, Zelda
d. Masaryk, Jan Garrigue

March 12, 1948
b. Conrad, Kent
b. Mosely, Mark DeWayne
b. Taylor, James Vernon

March 15, 1948
b. Bornstein, Kate

March 17, 1948
b. Gibson, Bill
b. Stallings, George Augustus, Jr.

March 19, 1948
b. Bass, Robert M(use)

March 20, 1948
b. Orr, Bobby

March 22, 1948
b. Lloyd Webber, Andrew

March 23, 1948
d. Berdyayev, Nikolay Aleksandrovich
d. Milne, George Francis, Baron

March 25, 1948
b. Bedelia, Bonnie

March 26, 1948
b. Tyler, Steven

March 28, 1948
b. Wiest, Dianne

March 30, 1948
b. Mangrum, Jim Dandy
b. Sims, Naomi

March 31, 1948
b. Gore, Albert, Jr.
b. Perlman, Rhea
b. Ralphs, Mick

April 3, 1948
b. Salinas de Gortari, Carlos

April 4, 1948
b. Parsons, Richard Dean

April 6, 1948
b. Fisher, Mary

April 7, 1948
b. Oates, John William

April 9, 1948
d. Gaitan, Jorge Eliecer

April 10, 1948
b. Blount, Mel(vin Cornell)

April 14, 1948
b. Martin, Valerie
d. Roxas, Manuel

April 15, 1948
b. Bloodworth-Thomason, Linda Joyce
d. Rockefeller, Abby Aldrich

April 16, 1948
b. Tate, Eleanora E(laine)

April 17, 1948
b. Hammer, Jan

April 18, 1948
b. Archibald, Nate
b. Stephenson, Skip

April 20, 1948
b. Potts, Nadia

April 23, 1948
b. Johnson, Charles Richard

April 26, 1948
d. Ross, Donald James

April 27, 1948
d. Knudsen, William Signius

April 28, 1948
b. Strassman, Marcia
d. Breneman, Tom

April 30, 1948
b. King, Perry

May 2, 1948
b. Ben-Shalom, Miriam
b. Gatlin, Larry Wayne

May 7, 1948
b. Rose, Wendy

May 8, 1948
b. Bolan, Marc
d. Gordon, Vera

May 9, 1948
b. Mahaffey, John
b. Murphy, Calvin Jerome
d. Allen, Viola Emily

May 10, 1948
b. Galdikas, Birute M(arija)
F(ilomena)

May 12, 1948
b. Crouse, Lindsay Ann
b. Winwood, Steve

May 15, 1948
b. Eno, Brian
d. Flanagan, Edward Joseph, Father
d. West, James Edward

May 16, 1948
b. Langer, Jim
b. Legg, Adrian

May 17, 1948
d. Samaroff, Olga

May 18, 1948
b. Bonsall, Joe

May 20, 1948
b. McKernan, John Rettie, Jr.

May 21, 1948
b. Sayer, Leo

May 22, 1948
d. McKay, Claude

May 26, 1948
b. Nicks, Stevie

May 29, 1948
b. Raimondi, John
d. Whitty, May, Dame

May 31, 1948
b. Molina, Gloria

June 1, 1948
b. Sneva, Tom

June 2, 1948
b. Innaurato, Albert
b. Mathers, Jerry

June 4, 1948
b. Post, Sandra

June 6, 1948
d. Lumiere, Louis Jean

June 9, 1948
b. Rosen, Nathaniel
d. Liebman, Joshua Loth

June 14, 1948
d. Atherton, Gertrude Franklin

June 16, 1948
d. Jones, Rufus Matthew

June 17, 1948
d. Carroll, Earl

June 18, 1948
b. Drake, Nick
d. Roebuck, Alvah Curtis

June 19, 1948
b. Rashad, Phylicia

June 20, 1948
b. Sinatra, Christina

June 21, 1948
b. McEwan, Ian (Russell)
d. Brown, Alice
d. Matthes, Francois-Emile

June 22, 1948
b. Rundgren, Todd

June 23, 1948
b. Echo-Hawk, Walter R.
b. Thomas, Clarence
b. Youngblood, Johnny Ray

June 24, 1948
b. Calderon Sol, Armando

June 25, 1948
b. Walker, Jimmie

June 28, 1948
b. Bates, Kathy
b. Maravich, Pete(r Press)

June 29, 1948
b. Grandy, Fred(erick Lawrence)

July 1, 1948
b. Robinson, Tom

July 4, 1948
b. Arnoux, Rene Alexandre
b. Culvahouse, Art(hur Boggess, Jr.)
b. Dale, Clamma Churita
d. Teschner, Richard

July 5, 1948
b. Eisenhower, Julie Nixon
d. Bernanos, Georges
d. Landis, Carole

July 6, 1948
b. Park, Brad

July 7, 1948
b. Dalto, Jorge

July 8, 1948
b. Darby, Kim
b. Raffi

July 11, 1948
d. Weidenreich, Franz

July 12, 1948
b. Egan, Walter Lindsay
b. Simmons, Richard

July 15, 1948
b. Diaz, Henry F(rank)
d. Chapais, Thomas, Sir
d. Pershing, John J(oseph)

July 16, 1948
b. Blades, Ruben, Jr.
b. Zukerman, Pinchas

July 18, 1948
b. Fehr, Donald Martin
b. Michel, Hartmut

July 21, 1948
b. Richards, Michael
b. Stevens, Cat
d. Gorky, Arshile

July 23, 1948
b. Dell'Olio, Louis
d. Griffith, D(avid Lewelyn) W(ark)

July 24, 1948
b. Racicot, Marc F
d. Patterson, Eleanor Medill

July 25, 1948
b. Goodman, Steve(n Benjamin)

July 27, 1948
b. Fleming, Peggy Gale
b. Thomas, Betty
d. Glaspell, Susan Keating
d. Tinker, Joe

July 28, 1948
b. Engel, Georgia Bright
b. Struthers, Sally Anne

July 30, 1948
b. Burnley, James H, IV

d. Breckinridge, Sophonisba Preston

July 31, 1948
b. Loulan, JoAnn
b. Redig, Patrick

August 1, 1948
b. Branch, Cliff(ord)

August 2, 1948
b. Rae, Bob

August 3, 1948
d. Pollard, Albert Frederick
d. Ryan, Tommy

August 5, 1948
d. Walker, Cyril

August 8, 1948
b. Erasmus, Georges Henry
d. Door, Rheta Childe

August 9, 1948
b. Daley, William M.

August 10, 1948
b. Austin, Patti

August 13, 1948
b. Battle, Kathleen Deanne

August 16, 1948
d. Ruth, Babe

August 18, 1948
d. Grove, Frederick Philip

August 19, 1948
b. Gore, Tipper
b. McRaney, Gerald

August 20, 1948
b. Plant, Robert Anthony
b. Watkins, Perry

August 22, 1948
b. Williams, Cindy

August 23, 1948
b. Blomberg, Ron(ald Mark)

August 24, 1948
b. Jarre, Jean-Michel

August 25, 1948
d. Bottomley, Gordon

August 26, 1948
b. Simpson, Valerie

August 27, 1948
d. Hughes, Charles Evans
d. Speaks, Oley

August 28, 1948
b. Seraphine, Danny

August 30, 1948
d. Salomon, Alice

August 31, 1948
d. Zhdanov, Andrei Alexandrovich

September 1, 1948
d. Beard, Charles Austin
d. Feng Yu-hsiang

September 2, 1948
b. Bradshaw, Terry Paxton
b. McAuliffe, Christa

September 3, 1948
d. Benes, Eduard

September 5, 1948
d. Tolman, Richard C(hace)

September 6, 1948
b. Smith, Claydes

September 7, 1948
b. Blakely, Susan
b. Brockington, John Stanley

September 8, 1948
d. Mofolo, Thomas (Mokopu)

September 10, 1948
b. Geeson, Judy
b. Lanier, Bob
b. Trudeau, Margaret Joan Sinclair

September 11, 1948
b. Gomez, Jewelle
d. Jinnah, Mohammed Ali

September 13, 1948
b. Carter, Nell

September 14, 1948
b. Natividad, Irene
b. Rabuka, Sitiveni (Ligamamada)

September 16, 1948
b. Casals, Rosemary
b. Jones, Kenny
d. Everleigh, Minna

September 17, 1948
b. Ritter, John(athan Southworth)
d. Benedict, Ruth (Fulton)
d. Bernadotte, Folke, Count
d. Ludwig, Emil

September 19, 1948
b. Irons, Jeremy John

September 22, 1948
b. Phillips, Mark Anthony Peter
d. Bailey, Florence Augusta Merriam

September 24, 1948
b. Hartman, Phil
d. William, Warren

September 26, 1948
b. Hurt, Mary Beth Supinger
b. Newton-John, Olivia

September 27, 1948
b. Meat Loaf

September 28, 1948
d. Toland, Gregg

September 29, 1948
b. Gumbel, Bryant (Charles)

September 30, 1948
d. Roosevelt, Edith Kermit (Carow)

October 2, 1948
b. Karan, Donna Faske

October 4, 1948
d. Brown, Arthur Whitten, Sir
d. Daly, Thomas Augustine
d. Savitt, Jan

October 5, 1948
d. Cross, Wilbur Lucius

October 6, 1948
b. Adams, Gerald

October 7, 1948
b. Ackerman, Diane

October 8, 1948
b. Purcell, Sarah

October 9, 1948
b. Browne, Jackson
b. Osbourne, Jeffrey

October 10, 1948
d. Eaton, Mary

October 12, 1948
b. Engler, John Mathias

October 17, 1948
b. Kidder, Margot
b. Wendt, George (Robert)
d. Cortissoz, Royal

October 18, 1948
b. Shange, Ntozake
d. Brauchitsch, Heinrich Alfred

October 24, 1948
b. Griffin, Dale
b. Mfume, Kweisi
d. Lehar, Franz

October 25, 1948
b. Cowens, Dave
b. Issel, Dan(iel Paul)

October 28, 1948
b. Hopkins, Telma Louise
d. Dickey, Herbert Spencer

October 29, 1948
b. Reynolds, Ricky
d. Mitchell, Wesley Clair

October 31, 1948
b. Hall, Deidre
d. Landi, Elissa

November 3, 1948
b. Lulu
b. Shales, Tom

November 4, 1948
d. Anderson, Carl Thomas

November 5, 1948
b. Levy, Bernard-Henri

November 6, 1948
b. Frey, Glenn
b. McPhail, Sharon

November 8, 1948
b. Riperton, Minnie
d. Taggard, Genevieve

November 9, 1948
b. Bouchard, Joe
d. Kennedy, Edgar

November 10, 1948
b. Lake, Greg(ory)

November 11, 1948
d. Niblo, Fred

November 12, 1948
d. Giordano, Umberto

November 13, 1948
d. Bradford, Roark Whitney Wickliffe

November 14, 1948
b. Charles, Prince of Wales

November 16, 1948
d. Cottrell, Frederick Gardner

November 17, 1948
b. Agyeman-Rawlings, Nana Konadu
b. Dean, Howard

November 18, 1948
b. Tatum, Jack

November 20, 1948
b. Hendricks, Barbara

November 23, 1948
d. Wilson, Hack

November 24, 1948
d. Jarvis, Anna

November 25, 1948
b. Niezabitowska, Malgorzata

November 26, 1948
b. Blackburn, Elizabeth Helen
b. Sargent, Ben

November 27, 1948
d. Delaney, Jack

November 28, 1948
b. Lightman, Alan (Paige)
b. Bangs, Lester

December 1, 1948
d. Noyes, Frank B(rett)

December 2, 1948
b. Boyle, T. Coraghessan

December 3, 1948
b. Osbourne, Ozzy

December 4, 1948
b. Lyon, Southside Johnny

December 6, 1948
b. Nickles, Donald Lee
b. Rosberg, Keke
d. Tough, Dave

December 7, 1948
b. Cleage, Pearl (Michelle)

December 13, 1948
b. Nugent, Ted

December 15, 1948
b. Cowings, Patricia S.

December 17, 1948
b. Bonfanti, Jim Alexander

December 20, 1948
b. Uchida, Mitsuko
d. Smith, C Aubrey

December 21, 1948
b. Kingman, Dave

December 22, 1948
b. Garvey, Steve(n Patrick)
d. Brian, Donald

December 23, 1948
b. Ham, Jack Raphael
b. Sharif, Nawaz
d. Tojo, Hideki

December 25, 1948
b. Mandrell, Barbara Ann

December 26, 1948
b. Justiz, Manuel Jon

December 27, 1948
b. Depardieu, Gerard

December 30, 1948
d. Ault, George Christian

December 31, 1948
b. Matheson, Tim
b. Robert, Rene Paul
b. Summer, Donna

1949

b. Alexander, Joyce London
b. Ansa, Tina McElroy
b. Astorga, Nora Gadea
b. Bopp, Thomas
b. Brooks, Avery
b. Busby, Jheryl
b. Butts, Calvin O(tis), III
b. Buyoya, Pierre
b. Chopra, Deepak
b. Creed, Linda
b. Ford, Edsel Bryant, II
b. Fortune, Michele
b. Fournier, Rafael (Angel) Calderon

b. Franklin, Carl
b. Franklin, Carl
b. Gaines, Steve
b. Gigli, Romeo
b. Haney, Chris
b. Harper, Elijah
b. Heid, Bill
b. Jackson, Samuel L(eroy)
b. Jay, Ricky
b. Joyner, Tom
b. Jumblatt, Walid
b. Mainassara, Ibrahim Bare
b. Mathison, Melissa
b. Menken, Alan
b. Milford, Penny
b. Millington, June
b. Mosbacher, Dee
b. Newkirk, Ingrid
b. Ocasek, Ric
b. Pease-Windy Boy, Jeanine
b. Rebbot, Olivier
b. Robillard, Duke
b. Sakiestewa, Ramona
b. Schwinn, Edward R, Jr.
b. Spenkelink, John Arthur
b. Tebelak, John Michael
b. Winston, George
b. Wood, Tim
d. Bailey, Alice A(nne La Trobe-
   Bateman)
d. Barker, Lloyd
d. Phinney, Archie

January 1, 1949
b. Patrick, Jennie R.
d. Campbell, Malcolm, Sir

January 2, 1949
b. Durang, Christopher Ferdinand

January 3, 1949
d. Aitken, Robert

January 5, 1949
b. Brown, George

January 6, 1949
d. Fleming, Victor

January 8, 1949
b. Puck, Wolfgang

January 10, 1949
b. Foreman, George
d. Ahearn, Daniel F.

January 11, 1949
d. Doubleday, Nelson
d. Friesz, Othon

January 13, 1949
b. Tartikoff, Brandon

January 14, 1949
b. Kasdan, Lawrence Edward
d. Howard, Willie
d. Sullivan, Harry Stack

January 15, 1949
b. Van Zant, Ronnie

January 17, 1949
b. Kaufman, Andy

January 19, 1949
b. Palmer, Robert

January 20, 1949
b. Persson, Goran
b. Stanley, Paul
d. Sapru, Tej Bahadur

January 21, 1949
b. Browne, Walter Shawn

January 22, 1949
b. Perry, Steve

January 24, 1949
b. Belushi, John

January 25, 1949
d. Marshall, Peter

January 30, 1949
b. King, William

February 4, 1949
b. Beck, Michael

February 5, 1949
b. Holzer, Harold

February 6, 1949
b. Orantes, Manuel

February 8, 1949
b. Adams, Brooke
d. Leoni, Franco

February 10, 1949
d. Abe, Isao

February 11, 1949
b. Saint James, Synthia
d. Dube, John Langalibalele
d. Zenatello, Giovanni

February 12, 1949
b. Knight, Stan
d. Levinsky, Battling

February 15, 1949
b. Anderson, Ken(neth Allan)

February 17, 1949
b. Coleman, Leonard S., Jr.
b. Green, Dennis

February 18, 1949
d. Alcala Zamora, Niceto

February 20, 1949
b. O'Neill, Jennifer
b. Trump, Ivana Winkelmayr

February 22, 1949
b. Lauda, Niki
d. Herelle, Felix d'

February 23, 1949
b. Garneau, Marc

February 28, 1949
d. Towne, Charles Hanson

February 29, 1949
b. Herdt, Gilbert

March 1, 1949
b. Trafzer, Clifford Earl

March 2, 1949
b. Gallagher, Rory
d. Naidu, Sarojini

March 4, 1949
d. Angell, James Rowland

March 5, 1949
b. Gwilym, Mike

March 8, 1949
d. U'Ren, William Simon

March 10, 1949
b. Radocy, Robert

March 11, 1949
d. Giraud, Henri Honore

March 13, 1949
b. Kemp, Jan

March 16, 1949
b. Estrada, Erik

March 17, 1949
b. Duffy, Patrick

March 20, 1949
b. Brown, Zora Kramer

March 21, 1949
d. McClure, Samuel Sidney

March 23, 1949
d. Hendrick, Burton Jesse

March 25, 1949
b. Lowe, Nick

March 26, 1949
b. Lawrence, Vicki Ann
d. Stevens, Albert William

March 27, 1949
b. Steinberg, Leigh

March 28, 1949
b. Pendleton, Moses Robert Andrew

March 30, 1949
b. Magliozzi, Ray
d. Bergius, Friedrich Karl Rudolph

April 3, 1949
b. Alzado, Lyle Martin
b. Thompson, Richard

April 4, 1949
d. Kent, Arthur Atwater

April 5, 1949
b. Borders, James
b. Resnik, Judy

April 10, 1949
b. Fay, Michael, Sir

April 11, 1949
b. Allison, Dorothy E.
d. Booth, George Gough

April 12, 1949
b. Turow, Scott

April 14, 1949
b. Shea, John

April 15, 1949
d. Beery, Wallace Fitzgerald

April 16, 1949
b. Spooner, Bill

April 18, 1949
d. Bloomfield, Leonard

April 19, 1949
b. Picasso, Paloma
d. Wise, Stephen Samuel

April 20, 1949
b. Cranston, Toller
b. Lange, Jessica
b. Quill, Timothy E.

April 21, 1949
b. LuPone, Patti Ann

April 22, 1949
b. Haywood, Spencer

April 23, 1949
b. DeWitt, Joyce

April 26, 1949
b. Schaufuss, Peter

April 30, 1949
b. Guterres, Antonio Manuel de Oliveira

May 3, 1949
b. Wyden, Ron
d. Fortuny

May 6, 1949
b. Broumas, Olga
d. Maeterlinck, Maurice

May 8, 1949
d. Luden, William H

May 9, 1949
b. Joel, Billy
b. Kurzban, Ira Jay

May 11, 1949
b. Martin, Jerry Lindsey

May 14, 1949
b. Laurel, Alicia Bay

May 15, 1949
d. Antin, Mary

May 18, 1949
b. Wakeman, Rick
d. Adams, James Truslow

May 19, 1949
b. Manning, Archie
d. Heggen, Thomas Orls, Jr.

May 20, 1949
b. Thomas, Dave

May 21, 1949
b. Suarez, Xavier Louis
d. Mann, Klaus

May 22, 1949
d. Forrestal, James Vincent
d. Pfitzner, Hans

May 23, 1949
b. Garcia Perez, Alan
d. Hansen, William Webster

May 24, 1949
b. Wintle, Justin Beecham

May 25, 1949
b. Kincaid, Jamaica

May 26, 1949
b. Grier, Pam(ela Suzette)
b. Thomas, Philip Michael
b. Williams, Hank, Jr.

May 27, 1949
d. Ripley, Robert Leroy

May 31, 1949
b. Bonham, John Henry
b. Rubin, Gayle

June 1, 1949
b. Boothe, Powers

June 2, 1949
b. Vogelstein, Bert

June 3, 1949
d. Giannini, A(madeo) P(eter)

June 5, 1949
b. Follett, Ken(neth Martin)

June 6, 1949
b. Englund, Robert
b. Near, Holly

June 8, 1949
b. Ax, Emanuel
d. McIntyre, Frank J

June 9, 1949
d. Cebotari, Maria

June 10, 1949
d. McCutcheon, John Tinney
d. Undset, Sigrid

June 11, 1949
b. Willig, George

June 15, 1949
b. Baker, Dusty
b. Varney, Jim

June 16, 1949
b. Madison, Joseph E(dward)

June 18, 1949
b. Hearst, William Randolph, III
b. VanAllsburg, Chris

June 20, 1949
b. Richie, Lionel (Brockman)

June 21, 1949
b. Urquhart, Jane

June 22, 1949
b. Streep, Meryl
b. Wagner, Lindsay J

June 24, 1949
b. Allen, Nancy

June 25, 1949
b. George, Phyllis

June 27, 1949
b. Wang, Vera

June 28, 1949
b. Baylor, Don(ald Edward)
b. Otte, Ruth

June 29, 1949
b. Dierdorf, Dan(iel Lee)
b. Montana, Claude

July 1, 1949
d. Johnston, Frank H

July 2, 1949
b. Bittan, Roy
d. Dimitrov, Georgi Mikhailovich

July 3, 1949
b. Smithers, Jan

July 6, 1949
b. Hyman, Phyllis

July 7, 1949
b. Duvall, Shelley
d. Johnson, Bunk

July 8, 1949
d. Knerr, H(arold) H

July 10, 1949
b. Smalley, David Bruce

July 11, 1949
b. Boyd, Liona Maria
b. Misrach, Richard

July 12, 1949
d. Hyde, Douglas

July 13, 1949
d. Kuhn, Walt

July 15, 1949
b. Bildt, Carl

July 17, 1949
d. Murphy, Frank

July 18, 1949
b. Bryson, Wally Carter
d. Novak, Vitezslav

July 21, 1949
b. Byrd, Donald
b. Hrabosky, Al(an Thomas)

July 22, 1949
b. Viren, Lasse

July 24, 1949
b. Trumka, Richard Louis

July 27, 1949
b. McGovern, Maureen Therese

July 28, 1949
b. Blue, Vida Rochelle

July 29, 1949
b. Quayle, Marilyn Tucker

August 1, 1949
d. Moran, George

August 2, 1949
b. Fallows, James (Mackenzie)

August 4, 1949
b. Riggins, John

August 7, 1949
b. Novi, Carlo

August 8, 1949
b. Carradine, Keith Ian

August 9, 1949
d. Davenport, Harry George Bryant
d. Thorndike, Edward L(ee)

August 11, 1949
b. Carmen, Eric
b. Charleson, Ian
b. Hutchinson, Tim

August 12, 1949
b. Collor de Mello, Fernando Affonso
b. Knopfler, Mark
b. Ridgeway, Rick
d. Shean, Al

August 13, 1949
b. Clarke, Bobby
b. Petit, Philippe

August 16, 1949
b. Swift, Graham (Colin)
d. Mitchell, Margaret

August 22, 1949
b. Nyad, Diana

August 23, 1949
b. Springfield, Rick

August 24, 1949
b. Smith, Barbara
d. Dunne, John William

August 25, 1949
b. Amis, Martin (Louis)
b. Simmons, Gene
b. Watson, Elizabeth

August 30, 1949
d. Kindler, Hans

August 31, 1949
b. Gere, Richard

September 1, 1949
b. Maddox, Garry Lee

September 3, 1949
d. Short, Walter Campbell

September 4, 1949
b. Watson, Tom

September 5, 1949
d. Hoagland, Dennis Robert
d. Minsky, Abraham Bennett

September 7, 1949
b. Gaynor, Gloria
d. Orozco, Jose Clemente

September 8, 1949
d. Strauss, Richard Georg

September 9, 1949
b. Curry, John (Anthony)
b. Theismann, Joe

September 11, 1949
b. Liquori, Marty
d. Rabaud, Henri

September 12, 1949
b. Rodnina, Irina
d. Burleigh, Harry Thacker

September 13, 1949
b. Dempsey, Rick
d. Krogh, Schack August Steenberg

September 16, 1949
b. Begley, Ed, Jr.

September 18, 1949
d. Morgan, Frank

September 19, 1949
b. Twiggy
d. Cuppy, Will(iam Jacob)

September 20, 1949
d. Dix, Richard

September 21, 1949
b. Futter, Ellen Victoria
b. Futter, Ellen Victoria
b. Gilmore, Artis

September 22, 1949
b. Carmichael, Harold
d. Wood, Samuel Grosvenor

September 23, 1949
b. Springsteen, Bruce

September 25, 1949
b. Williams, Anson

September 26, 1949
b. Smiley, Jane (Graves)

September 27, 1949
b. Martinez, A(dolpe)
b. Schmidt, Mike
d. Adler, David

October 1, 1949
d. Villard, Oswald (Garrison)

October 2, 1949
b. Leibovitz, Annie

October 4, 1949
b. Adamle, Mike
b. Assante, Armand

October 5, 1949
b. Ackroyd, Peter

October 8, 1949
b. Weaver, Sigourney
d. Somerville, Edith Anna OEnone

October 9, 1949
b. Messing, Shep
d. Swanson, Carl A

October 11, 1949
b. Hall, Daryl

October 12, 1949
b. Price, Richard

October 13, 1949
b. Hagar, Sammy

October 14, 1949
b. Schultz, Dave

October 16, 1949
b. Weir, Bob

October 17, 1949
b. Arthur, Owen

October 20, 1949
b. Collett, Wayne
d. Copeau, Jacques

October 21, 1949
b. Keenan, Mike
b. Netanyahu, Benjamin

October 22, 1949
b. Goring, Butch

October 24, 1949
b. White, Stan(ley Ray)

October 26, 1949
d. Liston, Emil

October 27, 1949
b. Prichard, Diana Garcia
b. Tallent, Garry Wayne
b. Tsang, Daniel C.
d. Cerdan, Marcel B

October 28, 1949
b. Jenner, Bruce

October 29, 1949
b. Jackson, Kate
d. Gurdjieff, George Ivanovitch

October 31, 1949
d. Stettinius, Edward R, Jr.
b. Ackerman, Will

November 1, 1949
d. Hokinson, Helen

November 3, 1949
b. Epps, Jack, Jr.
b. Evans, Mike
b. Holmes, Larry
b. Wintour, Anna
d. Desmond, William
d. Guggenheim, Solomon Robert

November 6, 1949
b. Davis, Brad

November 8, 1949
b. Berger, Al
b. Mittermeier, Russell A
b. Raitt, Bonnie

November 10, 1949
b. Fargo, Donna
b. Reinking, Ann H

November 12, 1949
b. Reed, Jack

November 13, 1949
b. Goldberg, Whoopi
b. Steen, Roger
d. Wallerstein, Lothar

November 18, 1949
d. Jewett, Frank Baldwin

November 19, 1949
b. Rashad, Ahmad
d. Ensor, James Sydney, Baron

November 21, 1949
b. Rubin, Barbara Jo
b. Siegel, Morris J

November 25, 1949
d. Robinson, Bill

November 28, 1949
b. Godunov, Alexander
b. Shaffer, Paul

November 29, 1949
b. Shandling, Garry

December 1, 1949
b. Brett, Jan Churchill
b. Foster, George Arthur
b. Schmoke, Kurt L(idell)

December 2, 1949
b. Crosby, Cathy Lee
d. Ammons, Albert C

December 3, 1949
d. Barry, Philip
d. Ouspenskaya, Maria

December 4, 1949
b. Bridges, Jeff
b. Kemp, Barry

December 5, 1949
b. Wadkins, Lanny

December 6, 1949
d. Leadbelly

December 7, 1949
b. Waits, Tom
d. Beach, Rex Ellingwood

December 8, 1949
b. Gordon, Mary Catherine

December 9, 1949
b. Kite, Tom

December 11, 1949
b. Garr, Teri Ann
b. Martin, Jared
d. Berryman, Clifford Kennedy

December 14, 1949
b. Buckner, Bill
b. Williams, Cliff

December 15, 1949
b. Johnson, Don

December 19, 1949
b. Kolb, Claudia

December 20, 1949
b. Cooper, Cecil Celester

December 21, 1949
b. Sankara, Thomas

December 22, 1949
b. Fromme, Lynette Alice
b. Gibb, Maurice
b. Gibb, Robin
b. Guy, Ray

December 23, 1949
b. Bender, Ariel
b. Kostov, Ivan

December 25, 1949
b. Pastorini, Dan(te Anthony, Jr.)
b. Spacek, Sissy

December 28, 1949
d. Allen, Hervey
d. Anderson, Ivie

December 30, 1949
b. Forsythe, William

1950

b. Akerman, Chantal
b. Alvarez, Julia
b. Belew, Adrian
b. Brooks, Diana D
b. Burnison, Chantal Simone
b. Byrne, Gabriel
b. Campbell, Bebe Moore
b. Cardinal, Tantoo
b. Cedras, Raoul
b. Compaore, Blaise
b. Crew, Rudolph F.
b. Dixon, Rod
b. Edmonds, Terry
b. Flowers, Gennifer
b. Franklin, Joseph Paul
b. Galvin, Martin
b. Hall, Joseph M
b. Hamad bin Khalifa al-Thani, Sheikh
b. Harvard, Beverly
b. Hughes, John
b. Ito, Lance
b. Jagland, Thorbjoern
b. Katzenberg, Jeffrey
b. Khan, Princess Yasmin Aga
b. McGuinness, Martin
b. McNamer, Deirdre
b. Miller, Frankie
b. Moeller, Michael E
b. Montgomery, Belinda
b. Morrison, Trudi Michelle
b. Pang, May
b. Plater-Zyberk, Elizabeth
b. Powers, Brian M
b. Prada, Miuccia
b. Redfield, James
b. Schifter, Peter Mark
b. Siberry, Jane
b. Ulufa'alu, Bart
b. Whiting, Leonard
b. Wozniak, Steven
d. Andrews, Fannie Fern Phillips
d. Ghose, Aurobindo
d. Goldmark, Josephine
d. Patel, Vallabhbhai
d. Ulreich, Nura Woodson

January 3, 1950
b. Cannon, Katie
b. Principal, Victoria
d. Jannings, Emil

January 6, 1950
b. Freeh, Louis J(oseph)
d. Bowman, Isaiah
d. Brady, William Aloysius

January 7, 1950
d. Banks, Monty

January 8, 1950
d. Schumpeter, Joseph Alois

January 9, 1950
b. Johansen, David
b. Stein, James R

January 10, 1950
d. Poole, Ernest

January 12, 1950
b. Jones, Randy
b. Lee, Sheila Jackson

January 13, 1950
b. Forsch, Bob

January 15, 1950
d. Arnold, Henry Harley

January 16, 1950
b. Allen, Debbie

January 18, 1950
b. Sullivan, Pat(rick J)
b. Villeneuve, Gilles

January 20, 1950
b. Hamad, Sheikh
b. Ousmane, Mahamane

January 21, 1950
b. Ocean, Billy
d. Orwell, George

January 22, 1950
d. Hale, Alan

January 23, 1950
b. Anderson, Richard Dean
b. Cunningham, Bill
b. Federici, Daniel Paul
b. Simmons, Pat(rick)

January 24, 1950
d. Montana, Bull

January 25, 1950
b. Cotten, Michael
b. Johnson, Virginia (Alma Fairfax)
b. Naylor, Gloria

January 26, 1950
b. Youngblood, Jack

January 28, 1950
b. Benton, Barbie

February 3, 1950
b. Fairchild, Morgan

February 4, 1950
b. Franklin, Pamela
b. Hakuta, Ken

February 6, 1950
b. Cole, Natalie
d. Speck, Frank Gouldsmith

February 7, 1950
b. Abramson, Lyn

February 9, 1950
b. Light, Judith Ellen
d. Cloud, Henry Roe

February 10, 1950
b. Colosio Murrieta, Luis Donaldo
b. Spitz, Mark Andrew
d. Mauss, Marcel

February 11, 1950
d. Cuyler, Kiki

February 12, 1950
b. Hackett, Steve

February 13, 1950
d. Sabatini, Rafael

February 14, 1950
b. Dent, Phil

February 16, 1950
d. Walker, Jack

February 18, 1950
b. Shepherd, Cybill (Lynne)

February 19, 1950
d. Walker, Edyth

February 22, 1950
b. Erving, Julius Winfield
b. Walters, Julie

February 24, 1950
d. Bacheller, Irving Addison

February 25, 1950
b. Jordan, Neil
d. Minot, George Richards

February 26, 1950
d. Lauder, Harry MacLennan, Sir

March 1, 1950
b. Flores Facusse, Carlos Roberto

March 2, 1950
b. Carpenter, Karen (Anne)

March 3, 1950
b. Marinaro, Ed(ward Francis)
b. Styles, Re

March 5, 1950
b. Fodor, Eugene Nicholas
d. Grauman, Sid(ney Patrick)
d. Masters, Edgar Lee

March 6, 1950
d. Lebrun, Albert
d. Lehr, Lew

March 7, 1950
b. Harris, Franco
b. Richard, J(ames) R(odney)
d. Korzybski, Alfred Habdank

March 9, 1950
b. North, Andy
b. Sullivan, Danny

March 11, 1950
b. McFerrin, Bobby
d. Dempster, Arthur Jeffrey
d. Pemberton, Brock

March 12, 1950
d. Mann, Heinrich Ludwig

March 14, 1950
b. Ford, Michael Gerald

March 18, 1950
b. Dourif, Brad

March 19, 1950
d. Burroughs, Edgar Rice
d. Haworth, Walter Norman, Sir

March 20, 1950
b. Hurt, William

March 22, 1950
d. Hopkins, Arthur

March 24, 1950
d. Laski, Harold Joseph

March 25, 1950
d. Buck, Frank

March 26, 1950
b. Pendergrass, Teddy
b. Short, Martin

March 27, 1950
b. Banks, Tony
b. Ewing, Maria Louise

March 30, 1950
d. Blum, Leon

April 1, 1950
d. Drew, Charles Richard
d. Matthiessen, Francis Otto

April 3, 1950
b. West, Riff
d. Weill, Kurt
d. Woodson, Carter Godwin

April 4, 1950
b. Lahti, Christine

April 5, 1950
b. Faltskog, Agnetha

April 7, 1950
d. Huston, Walter

April 8, 1950
d. Nijinsky, Vaslav

April 10, 1950
b. Griffey, Ken

April 11, 1950
b. Irwin, Bill

April 12, 1950
b. Carter, Chip
b. Cassidy, David Bruce
b. Werner, Tom

April 13, 1950
b. Perlman, Ron

April 14, 1950
b. Collins, Francis S(ellers)

April 19, 1950
b. Guinier, Lani

April 20, 1950
b. Cartwright, Veronica
b. Lebed, Alexander
d. Deeping, (George) Warwick

April 22, 1950
b. Frampton, Peter Kenneth
d. Houston, Charles Hamilton

April 23, 1950
b. Leach, Reggie

April 25, 1950
b. Fulani, Lenora
b. Humphrey, Bobbi
b. Nussbaum, Karen

April 27, 1950
b. Simmons, Calvin
d. Cavanaugh, Hobart

April 28, 1950
b. Forche, Carolyn (Louise)
b. Golden, Marita
b. Leno, Jay

May 1, 1950
b. Foster, David

May 2, 1950
b. Jagger, Bianca Teresa

May 3, 1950
b. Hopkin, Mary

May 4, 1950
d. Benet, William Rose

May 6, 1950
b. Bond, Victoria
b. Hyatt, Joel
d. Pattee, Fred Lewis
d. Smedley, Agnes

May 7, 1950
b. Ian, Janis
b. Prince, Prairie
d. Hill, Chippie

May 9, 1950
b. Beroff, Michel
b. Graham, Jorie

May 10, 1950
d. Greene, Belle da Costa

May 11, 1950
b. Quaid, Randy

May 12, 1950
b. Squier, Billy

May 13, 1950
b. Gabriel, Peter
b. Marable, Manning
b. Wonder, Stevie

May 15, 1950
b. Berkowitz, Bob

May 16, 1950
b. Bednorz, J(ohannes) Georg

May 17, 1950
b. Lacroix, Christian
b. Soltysik, Patricia Michelle

May 18, 1950
b. Milburn, Rodney, Jr.

May 19, 1950
b. Caddell, Pat(rick Hayward)

May 20, 1950
b. Jingsheng, Wei
d. Fletcher, John Gould

May 22, 1950
b. Taupin, Bernie

May 23, 1950
b. Barr, William Pelham

May 24, 1950
d. Wavell, Archibald Percival Wavell,
  Earl

May 27, 1950
b. Bridgewater, Dee Dee

May 29, 1950
b. Dixon, Melvin
d. Stoopnagle, Lemuel Q, Colonel

May 31, 1950
b. Berenger, Tom
b. Harrison, Gregory

June 2, 1950
b. Gleason, Joanna

June 3, 1950
b. Quatro, Suzi

June 4, 1950
b. Golacinski, Alan Bruce

June 6, 1950
d. Horlick, Alexander James

June 8, 1950
b. Baker, Kathy

June 19, 1950
b. Shuster, Rosie

June 20, 1950
b. Longmuir, Alan

June 22, 1950
d. Cowl, Jane

June 23, 1950
d. Fels, Samuel Simeon

July 1, 1950
d. Jaques-Dalcroze, Emile
d. Saarinen, Eliel

July 7, 1950
d. Navarro, Fats

July 11, 1950
d. DeSylva, Buddy

July 12, 1950
d. Mendl, Lady Elsie de Wolfe

July 14, 1950
d. Ngata, Apirana Turupa

July 15, 1950
b. Huffington, Arianna

July 17, 1950
d. Booth, Evangeline Cory

July 18, 1950
b. Branson, Richard
d. Van Doren, Carl Clinton

July 20, 1950
b. Achtenberg, Roberta

July 22, 1950
d. King, William Lyon Mackenzie

July 26, 1950
b. George, Susan

July 29, 1950
b. Holzer, Jenny
d. Pavese, Cesare

August 3, 1950
b. Landis, John David
b. Samper Pizano, Ernesto

August 4, 1950
d. Coveleski, Harry Frank

August 5, 1950
b. Mittermaier, Rosi

August 7, 1950
b. Crowell, Rodney
b. Keyes, Alan L(ee)
b. Wottle, Dave

August 10, 1950
b. Buse, Don(ald R)

August 12, 1950
b. Kleinfield, Sonny
b. McGinnis, George

August 14, 1950
b. Larson, Gary

August 15, 1950
b. Anne
b. Harper, Tess
b. Kelly, Tom
b. Serrano, Andres

August 17, 1950
d. Black Elk

August 18, 1950
b. Ingrassia, Paul

August 19, 1950
d. Giorgi, Giovanni

August 21, 1950
b. Bremer, Arthur Herman

August 23, 1950
b. Long, Shelley

August 24, 1950
d. Alessandri Palma, Arturo

August 25, 1950
b. Savage, John

August 26, 1950
d. Olds, Ranson E(li)

August 27, 1950
d. DeLuca, Giuseppe

August 28, 1950
b. Guidry, Ron(ald Ames)
b. Miller, Bebe

September 4, 1950
b. LaPread, Ronald
b. White, Frank, Jr.

September 5, 1950
b. Guisewite, Cathy Lee

September 6, 1950
d. Stapledon, Olaf

September 7, 1950
b. Bradley, David Henry, Jr.
b. Noonan, Peggy

September 8, 1950
b. Richard, Zachary

September 11, 1950
d. Smuts, Jan Christian

September 12, 1950
d. Clayton, Lou

September 13, 1950
d. Allgood, Sara

September 16, 1950
b. Classen, Willie
b. Gates, Henry Louis, Jr.

September 17, 1950
b. Waybill, Fee
d. DeCordoba, Pedro

September 18, 1950
b. Sittler, Darryl Glen
b. Smith, Anna Deavere

September 19, 1950
b. Lunden, Joan (Elise)
d. Herne, Chrystal Katharine

September 21, 1950
b. Murray, Bill

September 22, 1950
b. Tyler, Richard

September 25, 1950
d. Tairov, Aleksandr Yakovlevich

September 27, 1950
d. Knox, Rose Markward
d. Woodward, William E

September 28, 1950
b. Hofsiss, Jack Bernard
b. Sayles, John
b. Tosovsky, Josef

October 2, 1950
b. Khambatta, Persis
b. Rutherford, Michael
d. Fitzgerald, John Francis

October 3, 1950
b. Hensley, Pamela Gail

October 5, 1950
b. Conaway, Jeff
b. Jones, Edward P.

October 7, 1950
d. Carrier, Willis Haviland

October 8, 1950
b. Bell, Kool

October 9, 1950
d. Hainsworth, George

October 11, 1950
b. Murray, Patty
d. Lord, Pauline

October 12, 1950
b. Anton, Susan
b. McNair, Ronald Ervin

October 13, 1950
b. Katzen, Mollie
b. Shanley, John Patrick

October 14, 1950
b. Lloyd, Robin
b. Young, Sheila
d. Raskob, John J

October 17, 1950
b. Rollins, Howard Ellsworth, Jr.

October 18, 1950
b. Wasserstein, Wendy

October 19, 1950
d. Doherty, Robert Ernest
d. Millay, Edna St. Vincent

October 20, 1950
b. Curtis, Isaac Fisher
b. Rhodes, Ray
d. Stimson, Henry Lewis

October 23, 1950
d. Jolson, Al

October 26, 1950
b. Foreman, Chuck

October 27, 1950
b. Lebowitz, Fran(ces Ann)
b. Wilson, A(ndrew) N(orman)

October 30, 1950
d. Costello, Maurice

October 31, 1950
b. Candy, John (Franklin)
b. Goodfriend, Lynda
b. Pauley, Jane
d. Boettiger, John

November 1, 1950
d. Torresola, Griselio

November 2, 1950
d. Shaw, George Bernard

November 4, 1950
d. Alexander, Grover Cleveland
d. Fulton, Maude

November 6, 1950
b. Thompson, Ernest
d. Tschirky, Oscar

November 7, 1950
b. Canady, Alexa I(rene)

November 11, 1950
b. Armstrong, Otis

November 12, 1950
d. Marlowe, Julia

November 13, 1950
b. Perreault, Gilbert

November 15, 1950
b. Wilkins, Mac

November 16, 1950
b. Martin, Harvey Banks
d. Smith, Robert H

November 17, 1950
b. Matthes, Roland

November 18, 1950
b. Parker, Graham
b. Parker, Jameson

November 19, 1950
b. Moffatt, Katy

November 20, 1950
d. Cilea, Francesco

November 21, 1950
b. Taylor, Livingston

November 22, 1950
b. Bostock, Lyman Wesley
b. Luzinski, Greg(ory Michael)

November 23, 1950
b. Schumer, Charles E(llis)

November 24, 1950
b. Livingston, Stanley

November 25, 1950
d. Jensen, Johannes Vilhelm

November 27, 1950
d. Braid, James

November 28, 1950
b. Harris, Ed

November 29, 1950
d. Beech, Walter Herschel

November 30, 1950
b. Westphal, Paul Douglas
d. Burch, Billy

December 2, 1950
b. Ashley, Merrill
d. Lipatti, Dinu

December 8, 1950
b. Baker, Rick

December 9, 1950
b. Armatrading, Joan

December 11, 1950
b. Onassis, Christina

December 12, 1950
b. Smith, Billy
d. Fraser, Peter

December 15, 1950
b. Gates, Sylvester James, Jr.
d. Repplier, Agnes

December 16, 1950
b. Tabai, Ieremia Tienang

December 18, 1950
b. Armstrong, Gillian (May)
b. Frickie, Janie
b. Maltin, Leonard

December 20, 1950
b. Dolan, Terry
b. Ferguson, Tom R

December 21, 1950
d. Caraway, Hattie Wyatt

December 22, 1950
d. Damrosch, Walter Johannes

December 24, 1950
d. Elliott, Gertrude

December 25, 1950
b. DiBello, Paul
b. Rote, Kyle, Jr.
d. Torrence, Ridgely

December 26, 1950
d. Stephens, James

December 27, 1950
d. Beckmann, Max

December 28, 1950
b. Chilton, Alex

b. Tutwiler, Margaret (DeBardeleben)

December 29, 1950
b. Kimbro, Dennis (Paul)

December 31, 1950
d. Renner, Karl

1951

b. Bizimungu, Pasteur
b. Braga, Sonia
b. Cohen, Ben(nett)
b. Doucet, Michael
b. Duke, David
b. Ferrare, Christina
b. Frazier, Ian
b. Fudge, Ann (Marie)
b. Graham, Stedman
b. Greenfield, Jerry
b. Highway, Thomson
b. Hilfiger, Tommy
b. Holder, Eric H., Jr.
b. Iger, Robert A
b. Kapor, Mitchell
b. Koon, Stacey C.
b. Kozyrev, Andrei Y
b. Lanois, Daniel
b. Larkin, Patty
b. Locklear, Arlinda Faye
b. Matuszak, John (Daniel)
b. Mboup, Souleymane
b. McDonnell, Joe
b. Moutoussamy-Ashe, Jeanne
b. Muhammad, Khallid Abdul
b. Naughton, David
b. Needham, Paul M, Jr.
b. Normandin, Jean-Louis
b. Perez, Anna
b. Pirro, Jeanine (Ferris)
b. Sapphire
b. Snider, Paul
b. Staller, Ilona
b. Staples, Brent
b. Sullivan, Kathryn D
b. Wingti, Paias
b. Zeroual, Liamine
b. Zhang Yimou
d. Kadalie, Clements
d. Ross, Edward Alsworth
d. Stephens, Charlotte Andrews

January 3, 1951
d. Howell, Albert S

January 4, 1951
b. Cochran, Barbara Ann

January 8, 1951
b. Anthony, Kenny

January 9, 1951
b. Gayle, Crystal
d. Nethersole, Olga

January 10, 1951
d. Lewis, Sinclair

January 12, 1951
b. Alley, Kirstie
b. Limbaugh, Rush Hudson, III
b. Madlock, Bill
b. Pearson, Drew

January 15, 1951
b. Charo
d. Ironside, Henry Allan
d. Swinton, Ernest Dunlop, Sir

January 18, 1951
d. Holt, Jack

January 21, 1951
d. Cossart, Ernest

January 22, 1951
b. Fixico, Donald L.

January 24, 1951
b. Smirnoff, Yakov

January 25, 1951
b. Prefontaine, Steve Roland

January 27, 1951
d. Mannerheim, Carl Gustav Emil,
   Baron

January 29, 1951
b. Jillian, Ann
d. Bridie, James

January 30, 1951
b. Collins, Phil(ip)
b. Dutton, Charles S
d. Porsche, Ferdinand

January 31, 1951
b. Casey, H(arry) W(ayne)
d. Cochran, C(harles) B(lake)

February 5, 1951
b. Swados, Elizabeth A

February 8, 1951
d. Thyssen, Fritz

February 9, 1951
b. Thomas, Dennis
d. Duchin, Eddy

February 11, 1951
b. Leavitt, Mike

February 12, 1951
d. Bajor, Gizi

February 13, 1951
d. Douglas, Lloyd Cassel

February 14, 1951
b. Gross, Terry

February 15, 1951
b. Jenkins, Beverly
b. Manchester, Melissa Toni
b. Seymour, Jane

February 18, 1951
b. Stockton, Dick

February 19, 1951
d. Gide, Andre (Paul Guillaume)

February 20, 1951
b. Albert, Edward Laurence
b. Cose, Ellis
b. Davis, Anthony
d. Maude, Cyril

February 21, 1951
b. Welnick, Vince(nt)

February 23, 1951
b. Dibbs, Eddie
b. Jones, Too Tall

February 24, 1951
b. Shaver, Helen
d. Carey, William F

February 27, 1951
b. Atwater, Lee

March 2, 1951
b. Thomson, Gordon

March 6, 1951
d. Novello, Ivor
d. Vynnychenko, Volodymyr

March 7, 1951
d. Harkins, William Draper

March 9, 1951
b. Kinsley, Michael (E.)

March 12, 1951
d. Bauer, Harold

March 13, 1951
d. Herbert, Hugh

March 14, 1951
d. Lewton, Val Ivan

March 16, 1951
b. Nelligan, Kate

March 17, 1951
b. Russell, Kurt (Von Vogel)

March 20, 1951
b. Miller, Nicole (Jacqueline)
b. Palmer, Carl

March 22, 1951
d. Mengelberg, Willem

March 23, 1951
b. Jaworski, Ron(ald Vincent)

March 24, 1951
b. Bradley, Pat(ricia Ellen)

March 25, 1951
b. Blondin-Andrew, Ethel
d. Catlett, Big Sid
d. Collins, Eddie

March 26, 1951
d. Micheaux, Oscar

March 28, 1951
b. Kain, Karen Alexandria

March 29, 1951
b. Cort, Bud
b. Ut, Huynh Cong
d. Travers, Jerry

March 31, 1951
d. Forbes, Ralph
b. Hun Sen

April 4, 1951
b. Hannah, John Allen

April 6, 1951
b. Blyleven, Bert
d. Cuong De

April 9, 1951
d. Bjerknes, Vilhelm (Frimann Koren)
d. Hidayat, Sadiq

April 10, 1951
b. Roth, Mark Stephan
b. Seagal, Steven

April 13, 1951
b. Bryson, Peabo
b. Weinberg, Max M

April 14, 1951
d. Bevin, Ernest

April 15, 1951
b. Evans, Heloise Cruse
b. Heloise

April 16, 1951
b. Bentley, John

April 17, 1951
b. Hussey, Olivia

April 18, 1951
d. Bates, Daisy Mae
d. Vandenberg, Arthur Hendrick

April 20, 1951
b. Vandross, Luther

April 21, 1951
b. Danza, Tony

April 22, 1951
b. Carrack, Paul

April 23, 1951
d. Dawes, Charles Gates

April 26, 1951
d. Carpenter, John Alden

April 27, 1951
b. Falkenberg, Nanette
b. Frehley, Ace

April 29, 1951
d. Wittgenstein, Ludwig

April 30, 1951
b. Lucas, Craig

May 3, 1951
b. Cross, Christopher
b. Lane, Stewart F

May 4, 1951
b. Jackson, Jackie

May 5, 1951
d. Flynn, John

May 6, 1951
b. Doe, Samuel Kanyon

May 7, 1951
b. Hegyes, Robert
b. Roehm, Carolyne Jane Smith
d. Baxter, Warner

May 8, 1951
b. Bailey, Philip
d. Diegel, Leo

May 9, 1951
b. Harjo, Joy

May 12, 1951
b. Boxleitner, Bruce
d. DePriest, Oscar Stanton

May 13, 1951
b. Kessler, David Aaron

May 14, 1951
b. Hubley, Season
b. Zemeckis, Robert

May 15, 1951
b. Palminteri, Chazz

May 18, 1951
b. Champagne, Duane (Willard)
b. Gregg, Eric
b. Sundburg, Jim
d. Coxey, Jacob Sechler

May 21, 1951
d. McIntyre, John Thomas

May 23, 1951
b. Barad, Jill E(likann)
b. Karpov, Anatoly Yevgenyevich

May 26, 1951
b. Ride, Sally K
d. Ellsworth, Lincoln

May 29, 1951
b. Hamer, Dean H.
d. Brice, Fanny
d. Foerster, Josef Bohuslav

June 1, 1951
d. Altamira Y Crevea, Rafael

June 2, 1951
b. Chenault, Kenneth I
b. Robinson, Larry
d. Alain
d. Erskine, John

June 3, 1951
b. Williams, Deniece

June 4, 1951
b. Stevenson, Parker
d. Koussevitzky, Serge Alexandrovich

June 8, 1951
d. Bonsal, Stephen

June 9, 1951
b. Parker, Dave

June 10, 1951
b. Fouts, Dan(iel Francis)

June 13, 1951
b. Thomas, Richard Earl
d. Chifley, Joseph Benedict

June 15, 1951
b. Amsterdam, Jane

June 16, 1951
b. Duran, Roberto

June 17, 1951
b. Piscopo, Joe
b. Starhawk

June 19, 1951
b. Wilson, Ann
d. Sikelianos, Angelos

June 20, 1951
b. Muldoon, Paul

June 21, 1951
b. Lofgren, Nils
d. Perrine, Charles Dillon

June 26, 1951
d. Cheyney, Peter

June 27, 1951
b. Duffy, Julia
b. Lavis, Gilson
d. Warfield, David

June 30, 1951
b. Clarke, Stanley Marvin

July 1, 1951
b. Anderson, Daryl

July 2, 1951
b. Ladd, Cheryl

July 3, 1951
b. Duvalier, Jean-Claude
b. Rigby, Bob
d. Casey, Hugh Thomas

July 5, 1951
b. Gossage, Goose
b. Lewis, Huey
b. Rodgers, Johnny

July 6, 1951
d. Hall, James Norman

July 8, 1951
b. Huston, Anjelica

July 9, 1951
b. Brown, Larry
d. Heilmann, Harry Edwin
d. VanAlstyne, Egbert Anson

July 11, 1951
b. Pointer, Bonnie

July 13, 1951
b. Lanting, Frans
d. Schoenberg, Arnold

July 15, 1951
d. Ovington, Mary White

July 17, 1951
b. Arnaz, Lucie Desiree

July 20, 1951
d. Abdullah Ibn Hussein

July 21, 1951
b. Williams, Robin

July 23, 1951
d. Flaherty, Robert Joseph
d. Petain, Henri Philippe

July 24, 1951
b. Carter, Lynda Jean

July 25, 1951
d. Leyendecker, Joseph Christian

July 26, 1951
b. Martin, Rick

July 31, 1951
b. Goolagong, Evonne
d. Haldeman-Julius, Emanuel

August 1, 1951
b. Carroll, Jim

August 2, 1951
b. Gold, Andrew

August 3, 1951
b. Dionne, Marcel Elphege

August 6, 1951
b. Harewood, Dorian

August 8, 1951
b. Shilts, Randy (Martin)

August 10, 1951
d. Bloor, Mother

August 13, 1951
b. Fogelberg, Dan(iel Grayling)
b. White, Michael R(eed)

August 14, 1951
d. Hearst, William Randolph

August 15, 1951
d. Schnabel, Artur

August 16, 1951
d. Jouvet, Louis

August 18, 1951
b. Pruitt, Greg(ory Donald)

August 19, 1951
d. Bomberg, Dave

August 20, 1951
b. Lynott, Phil(ip)

August 21, 1951
d. Lambert, Constant

August 23, 1951
b. Noor, Queen

August 24, 1951
b. Randisi, Robert Joseph

August 26, 1951
b. Torricelli, Robert G.
b. Witten, Edward

August 27, 1951
b. Bell, Buddy
b. Kavanaugh, Kevin

August 28, 1951
b. Williams, Patricia J(oyce)
d. Walker, Robert

August 30, 1951
b. Bottoms, Timothy

August 31, 1951
d. Cahan, Abraham
d. Nowicki, Matthew

September 1, 1951
b. Cunningham, Mary Elizabeth
d. McClung, Nellie Letitia Mooney

September 2, 1951
b. Harmon, Mark

September 4, 1951
b. Ivey, Judith
b. Reese, Don(ald Francis)
d. Adamic, Louis

September 7, 1951
b. Hynde, Chrissie
b. Jones, Bert(ram Hays)
b. Kavner, Julie Deborah
d. Montez, Maria

September 8, 1951
d. Hewitt, William Archibald
d. Sloan, John F

September 9, 1951
b. Keaton, Michael
b. Wopat, Tom

September 10, 1951
b. Rogers, Bill

September 12, 1951
b. Ahern, Bertie
b. Fontana, Tom

September 13, 1951
d. Szyk, Arthur

September 14, 1951
d. Busch, Fritz

September 16, 1951
d. Klem, Bill

September 17, 1951
b. Elvira
d. Yancey, Jimmy

September 18, 1951
b. Carson, Benjamin S.
b. Stingley, Darryl
d. Burgess, Gelett

September 20, 1951
b. Lafleur, Guy Damien
d. Hartford, John Augustine

September 22, 1951
b. Sulzberger, Arthur O(chs), Jr.

September 25, 1951
b. Almodovar, Pedro
b. McAdoo, Bob

September 26, 1951
b. Defeo, Ronald
d. Allan, Montagu, Sir
d. Bryant, Lane

September 30, 1951
b. Marshall, Barry J(ames)

October 2, 1951
b. Sting

October 3, 1951
b. Winfield, Dave
d. Drum, Hugh A

October 5, 1951
b. Allen, Karen Jane

October 6, 1951
d. Kellogg, Will Keith
d. Meyerhof, Otto Fritz

October 7, 1951
b. Mellencamp, John

October 11, 1951
b. Hawkins, Tramaine

October 12, 1951
b. Little, Sally
d. Errol, Leon

October 13, 1951
b. Garzarelli, Elaine Marie

October 15, 1951
b. Tanner, Roscoe

October 16, 1951
b. Wheat, Alan (Dupree)
d. Liaquat Ali, Khan

October 17, 1951
b. Hickman, Fred(erick Douglass)

October 18, 1951
b. Dawber, Pam
b. McMillan, Terry

October 25, 1951
b. Stemrick, Greg(ory Earl, Sr.)
b. Wilson, Ransom

October 26, 1951
b. Collins, Bootsy
b. Schnabel, Julian

October 27, 1951
b. Kennedy, Jayne Harrison

October 28, 1951
d. Christians, Mady

October 29, 1951
b. Barfield, Jesse Lee
b. Boone, Mary
b. Kempthorne, Dirk Arthur
d. Aitkin, Robert Grant

October 30, 1951
b. Hamlin, Harry Robinson

November 1, 1951
b. Bell, Ronald

November 7, 1951
b. Gilder, Nick

November 8, 1951
b. Hart, Mary

November 9, 1951
d. Romberg, Sigmund

November 11, 1951
b. Zoeller, Fuzzy

November 13, 1951
d. Medtner, Nicholas

November 14, 1951
b. Bishop, Stephen
d. Benson, Frank Weston

November 16, 1951
b. Long, Irene D.
b. Vogel, Paula (Anne)

November 17, 1951
b. Martin, Dean Paul

November 19, 1951
b. Jojola, Ted

November 20, 1951
b. Walters, David

November 25, 1951
b. Dent, Bucky
b. Tolliver, William (Mack)

December 1, 1951
b. Pastorius, Jaco
b. Williams, Treat

December 3, 1951
b. Juantorena, Alberto
b. Mears, Rick Ravon

December 4, 1951
b. Wettig, Patricia
d. Salinas (y Serrano), Pedro

December 5, 1951
b. Brittany, Morgan
d. Jackson, Joe

December 6, 1951
d. Bromberg, J Edward
d. Ross, Harold Wallace
d. Rothier, Leon

December 10, 1951
b. Rodriguez, Johnny
d. Blackwood, Algernon Henry

December 11, 1951
d. Addison, Christopher, Viscount

December 12, 1951
d. Bailey, Mildred

December 15, 1951
d. Perth, 16th Earl of

December 16, 1951
b. Flanagan, Mike
d. Dix, Dorothy

December 19, 1951
d. Capper, Arthur

December 22, 1951
b. Grosvenor, Gerald Cavendish
b. Manzi, Jim Paul
b. Stephenson, Jan Lynn

December 26, 1951
b. Scofield, John

December 27, 1951
b. Zedillo Ponce de Leon, Ernesto

December 28, 1951
d. Fairbank, Janet Ayer

December 31, 1951
b. Goytisolo, Fermin
d. Litvinov, Maxim

1952

b. Anderson, Ray
b. Bigelow, Kathryn
b. Buckley, Christopher (Taylor)
b. Burke, Glenn
b. Dash, Julie
b. Deby, Idriss
b. Dickerson, Ernest
b. Dlugacz, Judy
b. Draper, Sharon M(ills)
b. Engelbreit, Mary
b. Fortensky, Larry
b. Franken, Al
b. Gatien, Peter
b. Gay, John

b. Gray, John
b. Greene, Graham
b. Hiatt, John
b. Holum, Dianne
b. Klammer, Franz
b. Lauterbach, Steven
b. Lavin, Christine
b. Lee, Andrew Daulton
b. Lee, Mark
b. McDonnell, Mary
b. McKee, Lonette
b. Milla, Roger
b. Mistry, Rohinton
b. Morris, Bill
b. Nelson, Jill
b. Queen, Richard I
b. Reubens, Paul
b. Sagansky, Jeff
b. Sakamoto, Ryuichi
b. Salle, David
b. Sayles Belton, Sharon
b. Smith, Ronnie
b. Tsui, Kitty
b. Van Sant, Gus
b. Wolfe, Willie
b. Yeager, Jeana
b. Zaitsev, Aleksandr
b. Zia, Helen
d. Innis, Harold Adams
d. Kellor, Frances (Alice)
d. Lewis, Rosa
d. Maurras, Charles Marie Photius
d. Singleton, Penny

January 2, 1952
d. Davidson, Jo

January 4, 1952
b. Wallace, Michele Faith

January 8, 1952
b. Feltsman, Vladimir
d. Maury, Antonia Caetana De Paiua
Pereira

January 10, 1952
b. Benatar, Pat

January 11, 1952
b. Crenshaw, Ben Daniel
b. Ritenour, Lee
d. Lattre de Tassigny, Jean de (Marie
Gabriel) de

January 12, 1952
b. Mosley, Walter
b. Van Shelton, Ricky

January 13, 1952
b. Oliver, Stephanie Stokes

January 14, 1952
b. Dowd, Maureen (Brigid)

January 17, 1952
b. Porter, Darrell Ray
d. Briggs, Walter Owen

January 19, 1952
d. Howard, Curly

January 21, 1952
b. Johnson, Billy

January 25, 1952
d. Moran, Polly

January 27, 1952
b. Gottfried, Brian
d. Ward, Fannie

February 1, 1952
b. James, Rick

February 3, 1952
b. Lynn, Fred(ric Michael)
d. Ickes, Harold LeClair

February 4, 1952
b. Eichhorn, Lisa
b. Shipley, Jenny

February 6, 1952
d. George VI

February 7, 1952
d. Epstein, Philip G
d. Henry, Pete

February 9, 1952
d. Douglas, Norman

February 10, 1952
b. Lee Hsien Loong
b. Pulitzer, Roxanne

February 13, 1952
b. De Grassi, Alex
d. Einstein, Alfred
d. Tey, Josephine

February 15, 1952
b. Jones, Bill T.

February 18, 1952
b. Crawford, Randy
b. Newton, Juice

February 19, 1952
b. Tan, Amy
d. Hamsun, Knut

February 20, 1952
b. Bucaram, Abdala

February 22, 1952
b. Frist, Bill

February 28, 1952
b. Manion, Eddie
b. Clemente, Francesco

March 1, 1952
d. Azuela, Mariano

March 3, 1952
b. Gradishar, Randy Charles

March 4, 1952
d. Christy, Howard Chandler
d. Sherrington, Charles Scott, Sir

March 7, 1952
b. Boyd, William
b. Swann, Lynn Curtis
d. Yogananda, Paramahansa, Swami

March 9, 1952
d. Kollontai, Alexandra Mikhailovna (Domantovich)

March 10, 1952
d. McNamara, George

March 11, 1952
b. Adams, Douglas Noel
b. Rhone, Sylvia
b. Richardson, Susan

March 13, 1952
d. Boole, Ella Alexander

March 14, 1952
d. Ferguson, Homer Lenoir

March 16, 1952
b. Ford, Jack

March 17, 1952
d. Wenrich, Percy

March 18, 1952
b. Webster, Mike

March 19, 1952
b. Weinstein, Harvey

March 22, 1952
b. Costas, Bob
d. Senanayake, Don Stephen

March 23, 1952
b. Stevenson, Teofilo

March 25, 1952
b. Chang, Jung

March 27, 1952
b. Schneider, Maria

March 30, 1952
b. Byrd, Robert

April 1, 1952
d. Molnar, Ferenc

April 2, 1952
d. Lyot, Bernard Ferdinand

April 5, 1952
b. Mayer, Sandy

April 6, 1952
b. Larocque, Bunny

April 9, 1952
d. Tharaud, Jean

April 12, 1952
b. Arguello, Alexis
b. Soto, Gary
b. Wiley, Ralph

April 15, 1952
d. Chernov, Viktor Mikhailovich

April 16, 1952
b. Westbrook, Peter (J.)

April 21, 1952
b. Early, Gerald
d. Banks, Leslie
d. Cripps, Stafford, Sir

April 23, 1952
d. Schumann, Elisabeth

April 24, 1952
b. Gaultier, Jean-Paul

April 25, 1952
b. Tretiak, Vladislav

April 27, 1952
b. Gervin, George

April 29, 1952
b. Dunn, Nora

May 1, 1952
d. Coulter, Ernest Kent

May 2, 1952
b. Baranski, Christine

May 6, 1952
d. Birley, Oswald Hornby Joseph, Sir
d. Montessori, Maria

May 8, 1952
b. Henley, Beth
d. Fox, William
d. Kirby, Rollin
d. Robins, Elizabeth

May 9, 1952
d. Lee, Canada

May 10, 1952
b. Strait, George
d. Hull, Clark Leonard

May 14, 1952
b. Byrne, David

May 15, 1952
d. Montemezzi, Italo

May 16, 1952
d. Johnston, Frances Benjamin

May 19, 1952
b. Jones, Grace

May 21, 1952
b. T, Mr.
d. Garfield, John

May 23, 1952
b. Hagler, Marvelous Marvin

May 24, 1952
d. Oursler, (Charles) Fulton

May 25, 1952
b. Smith, Gordon H.

May 26, 1952
b. McMillen, Thomas

May 29, 1952
b. Cooney, Rory

May 30, 1952
d. Lasker, Albert D(avis)

May 31, 1952
b. Leary, Kathryn D.

June 1, 1952
d. Dewey, John

June 4, 1952
b. Weaver, Mike

June 7, 1952
b. Neeson, Liam

June 8, 1952
d. MacCarthy, Desmond Charles Otto, Sir

June 12, 1952
b. Abraham, Spencer
b. Knussen, Oliver

June 13, 1952
d. Eames, Emma Hayden

June 14, 1952
b. Mekka, Eddie
d. Kirby, John

June 15, 1952
d. Gallatin, Albert Eugene

June 16, 1952
b. Hadley, Jerry
b. LeFlore, Ron(ald)
b. Vannelli, Gino
d. Geiger, Theodor Julius

June 18, 1952
b. Gazda, Ricky
b. Kane, Carol
b. Rossellini, Isabella

June 19, 1952
d. Schlusnus, Heinrich

June 20, 1952
b. Goodman, John
b. Seth, Vikram

June 22, 1952
d. Lipman, Clara

June 25, 1952
d. Ross, Alex(ander)

June 27, 1952
d. Lincoln, Elmo

June 30, 1952
b. Garrison, David

July 1, 1952
b. Aykroyd, Dan(iel Edward)
b. Shutt, Steve
d. Rosenbach, Abraham Simon Wolf

July 5, 1952
d. Skipworth, Alison

July 6, 1952
b. Goodeve, Grant
b. Hack, Shelley
b. Hartke, Stephen Paul

July 8, 1952
b. Lambert, Jack
b. Williamson, Marianne

July 11, 1952
d. Leonard, Dutch

July 15, 1952
b. Ros-Lehtinen, Ileana
b. Stallworth, John(ny Lee)

July 16, 1952
b. Copeland, Stewart

July 17, 1952
b. Hasselhoff, David
b. Larson, Nicolette
b. Snow, Phoebe Laub

July 24, 1952
d. Copeland, Charles Townsend

July 26, 1952
d. Peron, Eva Duarte

July 27, 1952
b. Herman, Pee-Wee

July 28, 1952
d. McMahon, Brien

August 1, 1952
b. Berbick, Trevor
b. Lemon, Ralph
d. Higgins, Andrew J
d. Spaulding, Charles Clinton

August 3, 1952
b. North, Jay

August 4, 1952
b. Tabori, Kristoffer

August 8, 1952
d. Weinman, Adolph A

August 9, 1952
b. Cappelletti, John Raymond
b. Morgan, Vicki
d. Farnol, Jeffery

August 13, 1952
d. Sullivan, Mark

August 14, 1952
b. Meyer, Debbie

August 16, 1952
d. Karfiol, Bernard

August 17, 1952
b. Piquet, Nelson
b. Vilas, Guillermo

August 18, 1952
b. Boosler, Elayne
b. Carter, Jeff
b. Swayze, Patrick

August 21, 1952
d. Schumacher, Kurt

August 26, 1952
b. Rush, Billy
b. Shortz, Will(iam Frederic)

August 28, 1952
b. Dove, Rita (Frances)

August 30, 1952
b. Fibak, Wojtek
d. Vaughan, Arky

August 31, 1952
d. Bourassa, Henri

September 2, 1952
b. Connors, Jimmy

September 4, 1952
b. Romero Barcelo, Carlos Antonio
d. Sforza, Carlo

September 5, 1952
d. Robinson, Boardman

September 6, 1952
d. Lawrence, Gertrude

September 9, 1952
b. Cartwright, Angela

September 11, 1952
b. Saporta, Vicki

September 12, 1952
b. Silver, Franelle

September 15, 1952
b. Estleman, Loren D

September 17, 1952
b. Solomon, Harold Charles
d. Strong, Austin

September 18, 1952
d. Alda, Frances

September 19, 1952
b. Rodgers, Nile
b. Stewart, David

September 20, 1952
b. Jeter, Michael

September 21, 1952
b. Taylor, John
d. Burton, Montague Maurice, Sir

September 22, 1952
d. Stahlberg, Kaarlo Juho
d. Webster, H(arold) T(ucker)

September 24, 1952
b. Kennedy, Joseph Patrick, II

September 25, 1952
  b. Hamill, Mark
  b. Hooks, Bell
  b. Moraga, Cherrie
  b. Reeve, Christopher

September 26, 1952
  d. Parker, George Swinnerton
  d. Santayana, George

September 28, 1952
  b. Kristel, Sylvia

September 29, 1952
  d. Cobb, John Rhodes

September 30, 1952
  b. Wild, Jack
  b. Rakhmonov, Imomali

October 1, 1952
  b. James, Juanita (T.)

October 5, 1952
  b. Barker, Clive

October 7, 1952
  b. Turischeva, Ludmila

October 8, 1952
  b. Adams, Cliff
  b. Bell, John Kim
  d. Wright, Louis Tompkins

October 9, 1952
  d. Murray, Philip

October 10, 1952
  b. Nystrom, Bob

October 11, 1952
  d. Conway, Jack
  d. Kelly, Shipwreck

October 13, 1952
  b. Johnson, Beverly

October 14, 1952
  b. Anderson, Harry

October 19, 1952
  d. Curtis, Edward Sheriff

October 20, 1952
  b. Petty, Tom
  d. Rostovtzeff, Michael Ivanovich

October 22, 1952
  b. Davis, Patti
  b. Goldblum, Jeff

October 23, 1952
  d. Peters, Susan

October 26, 1952
  d. McDaniel, Hattie

October 27, 1952
  b. Fukuyama, Francis
  b. Vuckovich, Pete(r Dennis)

October 28, 1952
  b. Potts, Annie
  b. Tcherkassky, Marianna Alexsavena
  d. Hughes, William Morris

November 1, 1952
  d. Lee, Dixie

November 3, 1952
  b. Ho, David D.
  b. Roseanne

November 4, 1952
  d. Frankau, Gilbert

November 5, 1952
  b. Walton, Bill

November 8, 1952
  b. Denny, John Allen
  b. Hefner, Christie

November 9, 1952
  b. Ferrigno, Lou
  d. Weizmann, Chaim

November 12, 1952
  b. Bartkowski, Steve(n Joseph)
  b. Hayes, Robert Michael

November 13, 1952
  d. Brown, Margaret Wise
  d. Egan, Raymond B

November 14, 1952
  b. Sharkey, Ray

November 17, 1952
  b. Ramaphosa, Cyril

November 18, 1952
  b. Lindo, Delroy
  d. Eluard, Paul

November 20, 1952
  d. Croce, Benedetto

November 21, 1952
  b. Luft, Lorna
  d. Conklin, Edwin Grant
  d. Green, William
  d. Upshaw, William David

November 26, 1952
  b. Turnbull, Wendy

November 27, 1952
  b. Copps, Sheila Maureen

November 29, 1952
  d. Capone, Teresa

November 30, 1952
  b. Patinkin, Mandy
  d. Kenny, Sister Elizabeth

December 1, 1952
  d. Orlando, Vittorio Emanuele

December 2, 1952
  b. McDonald, Michael
  b. Roberts, Steven K

December 3, 1952
  b. Roland, Duane
  d. Slansky, Rudolf Salzmann

December 4, 1952
  d. Horney, Karen Danielson
  d. Norris, James, Sr.

December 7, 1952
  b. Collins, Susan M.

December 10, 1952
  b. Dey, Susan Hallock

December 11, 1952
  b. Seidelman, Susan

December 12, 1952
  b. Rigby, Cathy

December 16, 1952
  b. Estrich, Susan

December 18, 1952
  d. Dasgupta, S(urendra) N(ath)

December 20, 1952
  b. Agutter, Jenny

December 21, 1952
  b. Andujar, Joaquin

December 23, 1952
  b. Kristol, William

December 24, 1952
  d. Danforth, William H

December 26, 1952
  d. Hedin, Sven Anders

December 27, 1952
  b. Bonoff, Karla
  b. Feldshuh, Tovah

December 28, 1952
  b. Knight, Ray

December 29, 1952
  b. Kirkland, Gelsey
  d. Henderson, Fletcher

December 30, 1952
  b. Anderson, June

December 31, 1952
  b. Briscoe, Connie
  b. Ogletree, Charles (J.), Jr.

1953

  b. Boyce, Christopher John
  b. Burns, Robin
  b. Campbell, Bill
  b. Coghlan, Eamonn
  b. Coleman, Sheldon, Jr.
  b. Crow Dog, Mary
  b. Emanuel, David
  b. Harris, Robert Alton
  b. Hitchcock, Robyn

b. Horner, James
b. Hudlin, Warrington
b. Jarmusch, Jim
b. Kinison, Sam
b. Kitaro
b. Lipkis, Andy
b. Longo, Robert
b. Marshack, Megan
b. Naranjo-Morse, Nora
b. Ndadaye, Melchior
b. Parkerson, Michelle
b. Pinckney, Darryl
b. Quivers, Robin
b. Rahal, Bobby
b. Schultz, Howard M.
b. Steenburgen, Mary
b. Tapahonso, Luci
b. Vollenweider, Andreas
b. Walker, Cedric Ricky
b. Williams, JoBeth
b. Williams, Lucinda
b. Wolff, Hugh (MacPherson)
d. Black, Samuel Duncan
d. Bode, Boyd Henry
d. Brightman, Edgar Sheffield
d. Gonne, Maud
d. Gucci, Guccio

January 1, 1953
b. Dhlakama, Afonso
d. Williams, Hank

January 6, 1953
b. Young, Malcolm
d. Fuller, Solomon Carter, Jr.

January 7, 1953
d. Johnson, Osa Helen Leighty

January 8, 1953
b. Stastny, Marian
b. Sutter, Bruce

January 13, 1953
d. Marsh, Edward Howard, Sir

January 14, 1953
b. Douglas, Denzil

January 15, 1953
b. White, Randy Lee
d. Knote, Heinrich

January 17, 1953
d. Jaggar, Thomas Augustus

January 19, 1953
b. Arnaz, Desi(derio Alberto IV), J
d. Schnering, Otto

January 22, 1953
b. Chung, Myung-Whun

January 23, 1953
b. Haden, Pat(rick Capper)
b. Zander, Robin

January 25, 1953
d. Jacobs, Michael S
d. Pitkin, Walter Boughton

January 27, 1953
b. Augustyn, Frank Joseph

January 28, 1953
d. Scullin, James Henry
d. Tharaud, Jerome

February 1, 1953
d. Curtis, Alan (Harold Neberroth)

February 4, 1953
d. Williams, Ben Ames

February 5, 1953
d. Hannagan, Steve

February 7, 1953
b. Quisenberry, Dan(iel Raymond)

February 9, 1953
b. Franks, Gary A

February 11, 1953
b. Anglim, Philip

February 12, 1953
b. MacCorkindale, Simon

February 13, 1953
b. Shea, Lisa

February 15, 1953
b. Adams, Tony
b. Dallmeier, Francisco

February 16, 1953
b. McDonald, Lanny
b. St. Laurent, Andre
d. Kraft, James Lewis

February 20, 1953
b. Chailly, Riccardo
d. Nitti, Francesco Saverio
d. Randall, James Garfield

February 24, 1953
d. Rundstedt, Karl Rudolf Gerd von

February 25, 1953
b. Aznar, Jose Maria

February 26, 1953
b. Bolton, Michael

February 28, 1953
b. Raines, Cristina
d. Sukenik, Eliazer Lipa

March 2, 1953
b. Feingold, Russell D.

March 3, 1953
d. Jeffries, James Jackson

March 4, 1953
b. Lenz, Kay

March 5, 1953
d. Prokofiev, Sergei Sergeevich
d. Stalin, Joseph

March 8, 1953
b. Rice, Jim

March 10, 1953
b. Gareau, Jacqueline
d. Curtis, Charles Gordon

March 12, 1953
b. Hiassen, Carl

March 13, 1953
b. Bean, Andy
b. Raffin, Deborah

March 14, 1953
d. Gottwald, Klement

March 19, 1953
b. Schenkkan, Robert
d. Bordoni, Irene
d. McFee, Henry Lee

March 21, 1953
b. Johnson, Robert

March 23, 1953
b. Khan, Chaka
b. Velazquez, Nydia Margarita
d. Dufy, Raoul (Ernest Joseph)

March 24, 1953
d. Mary

March 25, 1953
d. Dulac, Edmund

March 27, 1953
b. Gatti, Gabriele
b. Proell Moser, Annemarie

March 28, 1953
d. Thorpe, Jim

April 3, 1953
b. Francis, Russ(ell Ross)

April 4, 1953
d. Carol II

April 6, 1953
b. Henner, Marilu
b. Lynn, Janet

April 11, 1953
b. Wiles, Andrew J.
d. Nichols, Kid

April 23, 1953
d. DeRose, Peter

April 24, 1953
b. Bogosian, Eric

May 1, 1953
d. Shinn, Everett

May 2, 1953
b. Wilkes, Jamaal

May 4, 1953
d. Bellison, Simeon
d. Wagner, Robert F(erdinand)

May 6, 1953
b. Blair, Tony

May 11, 1953
b. Gaines, Boyd
d. Tomlin, Bradley Walker

May 13, 1953
d. Jadlowker, Hermann

May 14, 1953
d. Kuniyoshi, Yasuo

May 15, 1953
b. Brett, George (Howard)
b. Oldfield, Mike

May 16, 1953
b. Brosnan, Pierce
d. Reinhardt, Django (Jean Baptiste)

May 26, 1953
b. LeBoutillier, John
d. Spalding, Albert

May 27, 1953
d. Burkett, Jesse Cail

May 29, 1953
b. Elfman, Danny
d. Dean, Man Mountain
d. Russell, Morgan

May 30, 1953
d. Wilson, Dooley

May 31, 1953
d. Mildmay, Audrey
d. Tatlin, Vladimir Yevgrapovich

June 1, 1953
b. Berkowitz, David

June 2, 1953
b. Canova, Diana
b. Stadler, Craig Robert
b. West, Cornel

June 3, 1953
d. Price, Florence Beatrice Smith

June 5, 1953
d. Farnum, William
d. Tilden, Bill
d. Young, Roland

June 8, 1953
b. Tyler, Bonnie

June 9, 1953
d. Betti, Ugo

June 10, 1953
b. Barrios, Francisco Javier
b. Ramirez, Raul

June 12, 1953
b. Farmer, Gary Dale

June 13, 1953
b. Allen, Tim
d. Freeman, Douglas S

June 15, 1953
b. Kunjufu, Jawanza
b. Purcell, Lee

June 16, 1953
d. Bondfield, Margaret Grace

June 18, 1953
b. Smith, Jerome
d. Fonck, Rene

June 19, 1953
d. Rosenberg, Ethel Greenglass
d. Rosenberg, Julius

June 20, 1953
b. Lauper, Cyndi

June 21, 1953
b. Bhutto, Benazir

June 23, 1953
d. Gleizes, Albert L

June 27, 1953
b. McDermott, Alice
d. Lahey, Frank Howard

June 30, 1953
d. Pudovkin, Vsevolod

July 3, 1953
b. Tanana, Frank Daryl

July 6, 1953
b. Griffith, Nanci
b. Knudson, Tom
d. Ruffo, Titta

July 8, 1953
b. Quindlen, Anna

July 9, 1953
b. Tesh, John

July 10, 1953
d. Homer, Sidney

July 11, 1953
b. Spinks, Leon

July 12, 1953
d. Rawlinson, Herbert

July 15, 1953
b. Aristide, Jean-Bertrand
d. Christie, John Reginald Halliday

July 16, 1953
b. Ornish, Dean
d. Belloc, Hilaire

July 17, 1953
d. Adams, Maude

July 20, 1953
b. Friedman, Thomas L(oren)
d. Struther, Jan

July 24, 1953
b. Grogan, Steve(n James)

July 27, 1953
b. Inatome, Rick
d. Gerould, Gordon Hall

July 29, 1953
b. Burns, Ken(neth Lauren)
b. Lee, Geddy

July 31, 1953
d. Taft, Robert A(lphonso)

August 1, 1953
b. Cray, Robert

August 4, 1953
b. Brand, Jack

August 5, 1953
b. Sang, Samantha
d. Clark, Barrett H

August 8, 1953
b. Most, Donny

August 10, 1953
d. Burns, John Horne

August 11, 1953
b. Hogan, Hulk

August 14, 1953
b. Claiborne, Loretta (Lynn)
d. Schorr, Friedrich

August 16, 1953
b. Gifford, Kathie Lee
b. Taylor, J T

August 18, 1953
d. Flynn, Edward Joseph

August 19, 1953
b. Matalin, Mary (Joe)

August 20, 1953
d. Morrison, Cameron

August 21, 1953
d. Andrews, Bert
d. Smith, Alfred

August 23, 1953
b. Williams, Randy

August 25, 1953
b. English, Doug
b. Tito, Teburoro

August 29, 1953
b. Downey, Rick

August 30, 1953
b. Harris, Robin
b. Parish, Robert L
d. Merola, Gaetano

September 2, 1953
b. Danelo, Joe
d. Wainwright, Jonathan Mayhew

September 8, 1953
d. Vinson, Frederick Moore

September 10, 1953
b. Irving, Amy

September 11, 1953
d. Stone, Lewis

September 13, 1953
b. Vanzant, Iyanla (Rhonda)

September 15, 1953
d. Mendelsohn, Eric

September 16, 1953
b. Pate, Jerry
d. Corey, Lewis

September 26, 1953
b. Skate, Bill

September 27, 1953
b. Abbott, Diane (Julie)
b. Watts, Heather
d. Fritzsche, Hans

September 28, 1953
d. Hubble, Edwin Powell

September 29, 1953
d. Reuter, Ernst

September 30, 1953
b. Allen, Deborah
d. Richardson, Lewis Fry

October 1, 1953
b. Waitz, Grete
d. Cohn, Edwin Joseph
d. Marin, John
d. Munn, Frank

October 3, 1953
d. Bax, Arnold Edward Trevor, Sir
d. Creel, George Edward
d. Sabin, Florence Rena

October 4, 1953
d. Lazzari, Virgilio

October 7, 1953
b. Norris, Christopher

October 8, 1953
d. Bruce, Nigel
d. Ferrier, Kathleen

October 10, 1953
b. Williams, Gus

October 11, 1953
d. Fraser, James Earle

October 12, 1953
b. Mallett, Conrad (LeRoy), Jr.
d. Hammarskjold, Hjalmar
d. Mitchell, Millard

October 13, 1953
b. Day, Pat

October 14, 1953
b. Evigan, Greg(ory Ralph)

October 15, 1953
b. Jackson, Tito

October 20, 1953
b. Hernandez, Keith
d. Cameron, Harry

October 23, 1953
d. Bone, Muirhead, Sir

October 27, 1953
b. Firth, Peter

October 29, 1953
b. Potvin, Denis Charles
d. Kapell, William
d. Olsen, Harold G

October 31, 1953
b. Clegg, Johnny
b. Lucas, John

November 3, 1953
b. Banks, Jeffrey (Laurence)
b. Miller, Dennis

November 6, 1953
b. Flynt, Althea Sue

November 8, 1953
b. Woodard, Alfre
d. Bunin, Ivan Alekseevich

November 9, 1953
d. Ibn Saud
d. Thomas, Dylan Marlais

November 11, 1953
d. Ginzberg, Louis

November 13, 1953
b. Tickner, Charlie
d. Ives, Herbert Eugene

November 15, 1953
b. D'Angelo, Beverly
b. Widdoes, James

November 19, 1953
b. Todd, Richard

November 21, 1953
b. Brown, Tina

November 22, 1953
d. Shields, Larry

November 27, 1953
b. Grebenshikov, Boris
d. O'Neill, Eugene Gladstone
d. Powys, Theodore Francis

November 28, 1953
b. Mbuende, Kaire (Munionganda)

November 29, 1953
d. Barnes, Ernest William
d. Gross, Milt

November 30, 1953
b. Espy, Mike
d. Picabia, Francis

December 4, 1953
d. Mason, Daniel Gregory

December 5, 1953
b. Lane, Charles

December 6, 1953
b. Hulce, Thomas
b. Stones, Dwight

December 8, 1953
b. Basinger, Kim
b. Firestone, Roy

December 9, 1953
b. Free, World B
b. Malkovich, John
d. Dobrowen, Issai

December 10, 1953
b. Schuur, Diane

December 11, 1953
b. Armstrong, Bess
d. Coates, Albert

December 13, 1953
b. Gainey, Bob

December 14, 1953
d. Rawlings, Marjorie Kinnan

December 15, 1953
d. Barrow, Ed(ward Grant)

December 17, 1953
b. Livingston, Barry

December 19, 1953
d. Millikan, Robert Andrews

December 20, 1953
d. Connelly, One-Eyed
d. Ziff, William Bernard

December 23, 1953
d. Beria, Lavrenti Pavlovich

December 24, 1953
d. Linton, Ralph

December 25, 1953
d. Shubert, Lee

December 26, 1953
b. Fernandez, Leonel
d. Milne, David Brown

December 27, 1953
b. Kent, Arthur

December 28, 1953
b. Clayderman, Richard
b. Pittman, Robert W(arren)

December 29, 1953
b. Elliman, Yvonne

December 31, 1953
b. Hedges, Michael

1954

b. Bronfman, Samuel
b. Califia, Pat
b. Campion, Jane
b. Carter, Stephen L(isle)
b. Chauncey, George
b. Clark, Marcia
b. Cooke, Janet
b. Crenshaw, Marshall
b. Emanuel, Elizabeth
b. Fabi, Teo
b. Gober, Robert
b. Griffin, Anthony P.
b. Holloway, Wanda
b. Jones, Cleve
b. Kamel, Hussein
b. Louie, David Wong
b. Luyendyk, Arie
b. McDonald, Erroll
b. McIntyre, Richard
b. McKeel, Johnny
b. Moore, Michael
b. Mueller, Peter
b. Nealon, Kevin
b. Ouedraogo, Idrissa
b. Ritts, Herb
b. Roker, Al
b. Ruiz, Rosie
b. Sachs, Jeffrey D(avid)
b. Slavin, Mark
b. Smith, Geoff
b. Stephens, Charlotte Andrews
b. Wanke, Daouda Malam
b. Zanker, Bill
b. Zanuck, Lili Fini
d. Bates, Mary Elizabeth
d. Crowder, Henry
d. Laurens, Henri
d. Meinecke, Friedrich
d. Nexo, Martin Andersen

January 1, 1954
d. Bacon, Leonard
d. Norwich, Alfred Duff Cooper, Viscount

January 5, 1954
b. English, Alex(ander)
b. Martin, Pamela Sue
d. Maranville, Rabbit
d. Scott, Walter

January 9, 1954
d. Braniff, Thomas Elmer

January 11, 1954
d. Straus, Oskar

January 12, 1954
b. Stern, Howard (Allan)

January 14, 1954
d. Carney, Don

January 16, 1954
b. Thompson, Starley

January 17, 1954
d. Benn, Ernest John Pickstone, Sir

January 19, 1954
b. Bichler, Joyce
b. Sherman, Cindy
d. Greenstreet, Sydney Hughes

January 21, 1954
d. Chambers, Edmund Kerchever, Sir

January 25, 1954
b. Finch, Rick

January 29, 1954
b. Galbreath, Tony
b. Winfrey, Oprah Gail

January 30, 1954
d. Anderson, John Murray
d. Wilson, Henry Braid

January 31, 1954
d. Bates, Florence

February 1, 1954
d. Armstrong, Edwin Howard

February 2, 1954
b. Brinkley, Christie
b. Tudor, John Thomas

February 3, 1954
b. Williams, Tiger

February 6, 1954
b. Prothrow-Stith, Deborah
d. Althouse, Paul Shearer
d. Bodenheim, Maxwell

February 7, 1954
d. Nelson, Battling

February 13, 1954
d. Allen, Frederick Lewis
d. Perry, Bliss

February 15, 1954
b. Groening, Matt
b. Whitfield, Lynn

February 18, 1954
b. Travolta, John

February 20, 1954
b. Hearst, Patty
d. Duncan, Augustin

February 22, 1954
b. Franklin, Robert M(ichael)

February 25, 1954
b. Brenly, Bob
d. Perret, Auguste

February 26, 1954
d. Inge, William Ralph

February 27, 1954
b. Falletta, JoAnn

March 1, 1954
b. Bach, Catherine
b. Howard, Ron(ald William)

March 2, 1954
b. Johnson, Pete

March 4, 1954
b. Ratushinskaya, Irina

March 7, 1954
d. Diels, Otto Paul Herman
d. Hays, Will Harrison
d. Herrick, James Bryan

March 8, 1954
d. Balderston, John Lloyd

March 9, 1954
b. Sands, Bobby

March 13, 1954
b. Bass, Randy William

March 14, 1954
b. Zmed, Adrian

March 16, 1954
b. Stacy, Hollis
b. Wilson, Nancy

March 17, 1954
b. Down, Lesley-Anne
b. Stocker, Wally

March 20, 1954
b. Simmer, Charlie

March 22, 1954
b. Browner, Ross

March 24, 1954
b. Carradine, Robert Reed
b. Pescow, Donna
b. Zepeda, Ofelia

March 26, 1954
b. Sliwa, Curtis

March 28, 1954
b. McEntire, Reba
d. Kiam, Omar

March 29, 1954
b. Quinlan, Karen Ann

March 31, 1954
b. Brock, Tony

April 2, 1954
b. Palillo, Ron
d. Heffelfinger, Pudge
d. O'Sheel, Shaemas
d. Vandenberg, Hoyt Sanford

April 5, 1954
d. DuPont, Pierre Samuel

April 7, 1954
b. Chan, Jackie
b. Dorsett, Tony
b. Gillies, Clark
d. Kurusu, Saburo

April 8, 1954
b. Carter, Gary Edmund

b. Schneider, John
d. Scheff, Fritzi

April 9, 1954
b. Quaid, Dennis William

April 10, 1954
d. Lumiere, Auguste Marie Louis

April 11, 1954
b. Difford, Chris

April 14, 1954
b. Sterling, Bruce

April 19, 1954
b. Francis, Trevor

April 22, 1954
b. Bottoms, Joseph

April 24, 1954
b. Abu-Jamal, Mumia

April 25, 1954
d. Hergesheimer, Joseph

April 27, 1954
d. Ralf, Torsten

April 28, 1954
d. Jouhaux, Leon

April 29, 1954
b. McKenzie, Kevin
d. Laurie, Joe, Jr.

May 1, 1954
b. Parker, Ray, Jr.

May 2, 1954
b. Bofill, Angela

May 3, 1954
d. Hooton, Earnest Albert

May 5, 1954
d. Reed, Austin Leonard

May 6, 1954
d. Forbes, Bertie

May 7, 1954
b. Heckerling, Amy

May 8, 1954
b. Keith, David Lemuel
b. Little, Joan
b. Talbot, John Michael
d. Edwards, Alan

May 9, 1954
b. Palligrosi, Tony

May 11, 1954
d. Ives, Charles Edward
d. Lasser, Jacob Kay
d. Stover, Russell

May 12, 1954
b. Borden, Barry

May 15, 1954
d. Campbell, William Edward March
d. Guderian, Heinz Wilhelm

May 16, 1954
d. Krauss, Clemens

May 17, 1954
b. Sullivan, Kathleen

May 18, 1954
d. Waller, Fred(erick)

May 20, 1954
b. Aho, Esko (Tapani)
b. Henderson, Jimmy

May 22, 1954
d. Bender, Chief

May 25, 1954
d. Capa, Robert

May 26, 1954
b. Devine, Michael
d. Conacher, Lionel Pretoria

May 27, 1954
b. Thompson, Tazewell (Alfred)

May 28, 1954
b. Egorov, Youri

May 29, 1954
d. McCormick, Anne (Elizabeth)
   O'Hare
d. Turing, Alan (Mathison)

June 3, 1954
b. Hill, Dan
b. Matola, Sharon Rose

June 6, 1954
b. Fierstein, Harvey (Forbes)

June 7, 1954
d. Maverick, Maury

June 9, 1954
d. Locke, Alain Leroy

June 15, 1954
b. Belushi, Jim
b. Gibbs, Terri

June 16, 1954
b. Nano, Fatos

June 19, 1954
b. Turner, Kathleen

June 22, 1954
b. Prinze, Freddie
d. Compton, Karl Taylor

June 27, 1954
b. Kirk, Ron

June 28, 1954
b. Krige, Alice

June 29, 1954
d. Edgell, George Harold

June 30, 1954
d. Riggs, Lynn

July 1, 1954
b. Hanauer, Chip

July 2, 1954
b. Amaya, Victor

July 3, 1954
d. Marsh, Reginald

July 6, 1954
b. Beasley, Allyce
b. Erdrich, Louise
b. Randolph, Willie
d. Pascal, Gabriel

July 7, 1954
b. O'Neill, Cherry Boone

July 8, 1954
d. Gardner, George

July 9, 1954
b. Sledge, Debbie

July 13, 1954
b. Mendoza, Mark
b. Thompson, David O'Neil
d. Clark, Bennett Champ
d. Kahlo, Frida
d. Rice, Grantland

July 14, 1954
d. Benavente y Martinez, Jacinto

July 16, 1954
d. Muratore, Lucien

July 17, 1954
d. Kelly, Machine Gun

July 18, 1954
b. Norwich, William
b. Skaggs, Ricky

July 20, 1954
b. Bosley, Freeman (Robertson), Jr.
b. French, Jay Jay

July 21, 1954
b. McKee, Lonette
d. Carter, John Garnet

July 22, 1954
b. DiMeola, Al

July 24, 1954
d. Terrell, Mary Church

July 25, 1954
b. Payton, Walter
d. Raine, William MacLeod

July 26, 1954
b. Gerulaitis, Vitas

July 29, 1954
b. Adams, Alvan Leigh

July 30, 1954
b. Olin, Ken

August 3, 1954
d. Aldrich, Bess Streeter
d. Colette

August 5, 1954
b. Ojeda, Eddie

August 6, 1954
d. Dionne, Emilie
d. Fairchild, David Grandison

August 7, 1954
b. Kemp, Steve(n F)

August 8, 1954
b. Mansell, Nigel

August 9, 1954
d. Marcantonio, Vito Anthony

August 11, 1954
b. Jackson, Joe

August 12, 1954
b. Metheny, Pat(rick Bruce)

August 14, 1954
b. Fidrych, Mark Steven
d. Eckener, Hugo

August 16, 1954
b. Cameron, James

August 17, 1954
b. Pastrana, Andres
d. Sarett, Lew R

August 18, 1954
b. Green, Rickey Anthony

August 19, 1954
d. De Gasperi, Alcide

August 21, 1954
b. Griffin, Archie Mason

August 23, 1954
b. Busch, Charles

August 24, 1954
d. Vargas, Getulio Dornelles

August 25, 1954
b. Costello, Elvis

August 27, 1954
b. Lloyd, John

August 28, 1954
d. Burt, Maxwell Struthers

August 30, 1954
b. Lukashenka, Alyaksandr
　Hrihoryevich

August 31, 1954
b. Kocharyan, Robert

September 7, 1954
d. Fisher, Bud
d. Warner, Pop

September 9, 1954
b. Davis, Walter Paul

September 10, 1954
d. Derain, Andre

September 13, 1954
b. Hurson, Martin

September 16, 1954
b. Klugh, Earl
b. McEwen, Mark

September 17, 1954
d. Slye, Maud

September 18, 1954
b. Johnson, Dennis Wayne

September 19, 1954
d. Franklin, Miles

September 22, 1954
b. Belafonte, Shari

September 23, 1954
b. Wolfe, George C.

September 24, 1954
b. Kelly, Patrick

September 27, 1954
b. Barrow, Keith E

September 28, 1954
b. Largent, Steve M
d. Lytell, Bert
d. Shull, George Harrison

September 30, 1954
b. Rushen, Patrice Louise
b. Williams, Barry

October 2, 1954
d. Greene, Henry Mather

October 3, 1954
b. Sharpton, Al(fred), Jr.
b. Vaughan, Stevie Ray

October 5, 1954
b. Geldof, Bob
d. Charleston, Oscar McKinley
d. Tozzer, Alfred Marston

October 7, 1954
b. Dawson, Andre (Nolan)
b. Eckersley, Dennis

October 9, 1954
d. Jackson, Robert Houghwout

October 11, 1954
b. Sanders, Joseph

October 12, 1954
b. Gomez-Preston, Cheryl

October 14, 1954
b. Aikens, Willie Mays

October 16, 1954
b. Carcaterra, Lorenzo
d. Crump, Edward Hull

October 18, 1954
b. Weinstein, Bob

October 19, 1954
d. Duffy, Hugh

October 20, 1954
b. Selmon, Lee Roy

October 22, 1954
d. Kauffer, Edward McKnight
d. McManus, George

October 23, 1954
b. Lee, Ang

October 25, 1954
b. Eruzione, Mike

October 27, 1954
b. McCurry, Michael D(emaree)

October 28, 1954
d. Gorman, Herbert Sherman

October 30, 1954
d. Shaw, Wilbur

October 31, 1954
d. Baillie, D(onald) M(acpherson)
b. Fenley, Molissa

November 3, 1954
b. Adam Ant
d. Matisse, Henri Emile Benoit

November 4, 1954
b. Yanni
d. Agus Salim, Hadji

November 5, 1954
d. Page, Hot Lips

November 8, 1954
b. Ishiguro, Kazuo
b. Jones, Rickie Lee
d. Odum, Howard Washington

November 13, 1954
b. McNealy, Scott (G.)
d. Fath, Jacques

November 14, 1954
b. Rice, Condoleezza
d. Verrill, Alpheus Hyatt

November 15, 1954
b. Kwasniewski, Aleksander
d. Barrymore, Lionel Blythe

November 18, 1954
b. Williams, Charles

November 19, 1954
b. Quinlan, Kathleen

November 20, 1954
d. Cessna, Clyde Vernon

November 22, 1954
d. Vyshinsky, Andrei Yanuarievich

November 23, 1954
b. Hornsby, Bruce

November 25, 1954
d. Coffin, Henry Sloane

November 26, 1954
d. Doak, Bill
d. Jones, Robert Edmond

November 28, 1954
d. Fermi, Enrico

November 29, 1954
d. Johnson, Dink
d. Robey, George, Sir

November 30, 1954
b. Pointer, June
d. Furtwangler, Wilhelm

December 1, 1954
d. Rose, Fred

December 5, 1954
b. Kureishi, Hanif

December 8, 1954
d. George, Gladys

December 9, 1954
b. Juncker, Jean-Claude

December 11, 1954
b. Jackson, Jermaine La Jaune

December 13, 1954
b. Anderson, John

December 14, 1954
b. Andersen, Ib Steen

December 15, 1954
b. Cox, Alex

December 19, 1954
d. Child, Charles Manning

December 20, 1954
b. Cisneros, Sandra
d. Hilton, James

December 21, 1954
b. Evert, Chris(tine Marie)

December 23, 1954
b. Teacher, Brian

December 24, 1954
b. Figueres Olsen, Jose Maria

December 25, 1954
b. Lennox, Annie
b. Wariner, Steve
b. Williams, Maggie
d. Ace, Johnny
d. Bailey, Liberty Hyde

December 26, 1954
b. Butcher, Susan
b. Smith, Ozzie

December 28, 1954
b. Washington, Denzel, Jr.

December 30, 1954
b. Beam, Joseph

1955

b. Alvin, Dave
b. Bailey, Xenobia
b. Berners-Lee, Tim
b. Brooks, David Owen
b. Burck, Wade
b. Callen, Michael
b. Chast, Roz
b. Coen, Joel
b. Cooke, Donald
b. Davis, Judy
b. DeLaurentiis, Federico
b. Devi, Phoolan
b. Eilberg, Amy
b. Goldman, Francisco
b. Grisham, John
b. Hagelstein, Peter
b. Harris, E. Lynn
b. Iwatani, Toro
b. Jen, Gish
b. Jones, Carl
b. Kennedy, David Anthony
b. Knight, Wayne
b. Koons, Jeff
b. McCall, Nathan
b. Ntaryamira, Cyprien
b. Plotkin, Mark
b. Shipp, E. R.
b. Sui, Anna
b. Wilson, Cassandra
d. Clay, Jacob
d. Gao Gang
d. Radcliffe-Brown, A(lfred)
R(eginald)

January 1, 1955
b. Hoyt, LaMarr
d. Parker, Arthur C(aswell)

January 7, 1955
d. Keith, Arthur

January 8, 1955
b. Reno, Mike

January 11, 1955
d. Graziani, Rodolfo

January 13, 1955
b. McInerney, Jay
d. Dinneen, Bill

d. Lea, Fanny Heaslip

January 14, 1955
d. Booth, Hubert Cecil

January 15, 1955
d. Tanguy, Yves

January 18, 1955
b. Costner, Kevin (Michael)
d. Duesenberg, August S

January 19, 1955
b. Rattle, Simon

January 20, 1955
b. Kenney, Bill

January 21, 1955
b. Fleming, Peter
d. Hahn, Archie

January 22, 1955
b. Hayes, Lester

January 24, 1955
d. Hayes, Ira Hamilton

January 29, 1955
d. Hedtoft (-Hansen), Hans Christian

January 30, 1955
b. Cromwell, Nolan Neil
b. Strange, Curtis

January 31, 1955
b. Ruzici, Virginia
d. Mott, John Raleigh
d. Washington, Buck

February 5, 1955
d. Blood, Ernest

February 7, 1955
b. Benirschke, Rolf Joachim

February 10, 1955
b. Beller, Kathleen
b. Norman, Greg
b. Stewart, Luisa Harris
d. McDonald, Harl

February 11, 1955
d. Munson, Ona

February 12, 1955
b. Hall, Arsenio
b. Kerns, Joanna
d. Moore, Tom
d. Sakall, S Z

February 15, 1955
d. Maginnis, Charles Donagh

February 16, 1955
b. Katt, William
b. McManus, Sean

February 19, 1955
b. Daniels, Jeff
b. Hemingway, Margaux
b. Hustvedt, Siri

February 20, 1955
d. Avery, Oswald T

February 21, 1955
b. Grammer, Kelsey

February 22, 1955
d. Goddard, Calvin Hooker

February 23, 1955
b. Jones, Howard
b. Slater, Rodney E.
d. Claudel, Paul Louis Charles

February 24, 1955
b. Jobs, Steven Paul
b. Prost, Alain Marie Pascal

February 27, 1955
d. Friganza, Trixie
d. Howard, Tom
b. Sinder, Dee

March 3, 1955
b. Schlessinger, David
d. Drexel, Mary Katherine
d. Spence, Lewis

March 5, 1955
b. Otto, Whitney
b. Warfield, Marsha

March 9, 1955
b. Bujones, Fernando
d. Henson, Matthew Alexander

March 10, 1955
b. DeBarge, Bunny
b. Hughes, Holly

March 11, 1955
d. Fleming, Alexander, Sir
d. Mayer, Oscar Ferdinand

March 12, 1955
d. Parker, Charlie

March 13, 1955
b. Tucker, Cynthia (Anne)

March 15, 1955
b. Snider, Dee

March 16, 1955
b. Huppert, Isabelle

March 17, 1955
b. Clark, Patrick
b. McKinney, Cynthia A(nn)
b. Sinise, Gary

March 19, 1955
b. Longmuir, Derek
b. Willis, Bruce

March 21, 1955
d. White, Walter Francis

March 22, 1955
d. Stael, Nicolas de

March 23, 1955
b. Malone, Moses Eugene

March 24, 1955
b. Jarvis, Doug(las)
d. Davis, John Williams
d. McNutt, Paul Vories

March 27, 1955
b. McCarron, Chris

March 29, 1955
b. Campbell, Earl Christian
b. Kay, Dianne

March 30, 1955
b. Lomawaima, K(imberly) Tsianina
d. Pulitzer, Joseph, II

April 1, 1955
b. Pohl, Dan(ny Joe)
d. McCormick, Robert Rutherford
d. Towers, John Henry

April 2, 1955
b. Carvey, Dana

April 3, 1955
d. Hofer, Karl

April 7, 1955
d. Bara, Theda

April 8, 1955
b. Bell, Ricky Lynn
b. Kingsolver, Barbara

April 10, 1955
d. Hughan, Jessie Wallace
d. Teilhard de Chardin, Pierre

April 11, 1955
b. Richardson, Micheal Ray

April 16, 1955
b. Barkin, Ellen

April 17, 1955
b. Moure, Erin
b. Runnels, Tom

April 18, 1955
d. Einstein, Albert

April 23, 1955
d. Busse, Henry

April 24, 1955
b. Vohor, (Rialuth) Serge

April 25, 1955
d. Collier, Constance
d. Merriam, Frank Finley

April 26, 1955
b. Scott, Mike

April 29, 1955
b. Seinfeld, Jerry

May 2, 1955
d. Vollmer, Lula

May 4, 1955
b. Zadora, Pia
d. Breguet, Louis Charles
d. Enesco, Georges

May 8, 1955
b. Van Halen, Alex
d. Park, Maud May Wood

May 9, 1955
b. Meles Zenawi
b. Otter, Anne Sofie von

May 10, 1955
b. Chapman, Mark David
d. Burns, Tommy

May 15, 1955
b. Horsley, Lee

May 16, 1955
b. Bronfman, Edgar Miles, Jr.
b. Korbut, Olga
d. Agee, James Rufus

May 17, 1955
b. Paxton, Bill
b. Winger, Debra

May 18, 1955
d. Bethune, Mary McLeod
d. Pratella, Francesco Balilla

May 21, 1955
b. Plotkin, Mark J.
d. Phillips, Lena Madesin

May 22, 1955
d. Gallagher, Richard

May 24, 1955
b. Cash, Roseanne

May 25, 1955
b. Sellecca, Connie

May 26, 1955
b. Walker, Wesley Darcel

May 27, 1955
d. Ascari, Alberto

May 28, 1955
b. Howe, Mark Steven

May 29, 1955
b. Hinckley, John Warnock, Jr.

June 3, 1955
d. Graham, Barbara

June 4, 1955
b. Verdi-Fletcher, Mary (Regina)

June 6, 1955
b. Bernhard, Sandra

June 7, 1955
b. Scarbury, Joey

June 8, 1955
b. Dunne, Griffin

June 10, 1955
b. Stevens, Andrew
d. Abbott, Margaret I.

June 11, 1955
d. Hampden, Walter

June 13, 1955
b. Sears-Collins, Leah J.

June 15, 1955
b. Metcalf, Laurie

June 16, 1955
b. Rollins, Wayne Monte

June 17, 1955
d. Golden, John
d. Holme, Constance

June 20, 1955
b. Anthony, Michael

June 28, 1955
b. Hampson, Thomas
d. Ljungberg, Gota

June 29, 1955
d. Pechstein, Max

June 30, 1955
b. Grier, David Allen

July 3, 1955
b. Corby, Mike
b. Wallace, Amy

July 4, 1955
b. Waite, John

July 7, 1955
b. Barker, Len

July 9, 1955
b. Dillon, Mia
b. Smits, Jimmy
b. Wilson, Willie James

July 13, 1955
d. Ellis, Ruth

July 17, 1955
b. Lansky, Aaron

July 22, 1955
b. Dafoe, Willem

July 23, 1955
d. Hull, Cordell

July 25, 1955
b. Iman

July 29, 1955
d. Reynolds, Richard S

July 30, 1955
b. Kenty, Hilmer
d. Pogany, Willy

August 2, 1955
b. Carr, Caleb
d. Stevens, Wallace

August 5, 1955
d. Miranda, Carmen

August 6, 1955
d. Beecher, Janet

August 8, 1955
d. Hartman, Grace

August 9, 1955
b. Ovett, Steve
b. Williams, Doug(las Lee)

August 11, 1955
d. Seiberling, Frank Augustus
d. Wood, Robert Williams

August 12, 1955
d. Mann, Thomas

August 13, 1955
d. Easton, Florence Gertrude
d. Horder, Thomas Jeeves

August 14, 1955
d. Kimball, Fiske

August 16, 1955
b. Gayle, Helene Doris

August 17, 1955
d. Leger, Fernand

August 19, 1955
d. Sumner, James Batcheller

August 22, 1955
d. Downes, Olin

August 24, 1955
b. Guyton, Tyree

August 25, 1955
b. Bell, Earl

August 28, 1955
d. Till, Emmett (Louis)

August 31, 1955
b. Moses, Edwin Corley
d. Baumeister, Willi

September 2, 1955
b. Gordon, Pamela (Felicity)
b. Purl, Linda

September 4, 1955
b. Schiavo, Mary (Fackler)

September 7, 1955
b. Bernsen, Corbin
d. Bernstein, Alice Frankau

September 10, 1955
b. Kudelka, James
d. Goodfellow, Ebbie

September 16, 1955
b. Yount, Robin (R.)

September 17, 1955
b. Simpson, Scott

September 18, 1955
b. Sims, Billy Ray

September 19, 1955
b. Dawkins, Wayne J(esse)
d. Milles, Carl Wilhelm Emil

September 21, 1955
d. Brain, Aubrey

September 22, 1955
d. Kress, Samuel Henry

September 26, 1955
b. Carter, Carlene

September 29, 1955
d. Thurstone, Louis Leon

September 30, 1955
d. Chekhov, Michael
d. Dean, James Byron

October 3, 1955
d. Adler, Julius Ochs

October 6, 1955
b. Dungy, Tony

October 7, 1955
b. Ma, Yo-Yo
d. Hempel, Frieda

October 9, 1955
b. Bakula, Scott
d. Joyce, Alice
d. Rogers, Mary Joseph(ine)

October 10, 1955
b. Roth, David Lee
d. Stracciari, Riccardo

October 12, 1955
d. Macfadden, Bernarr Adolphus

October 13, 1955
d. Avila Camacho, Manuel

October 17, 1955
b. Bottoms, Sam
b. Driver, David E.

October 18, 1955
d. Ortega y Gasset, Jose

October 19, 1955
d. Hodiak, John

October 20, 1955
d. Gulbenkian, Calouste S

October 21, 1955
b. Faulkner, Eric

October 22, 1955
b. Anderson, Bonnie Marie

October 24, 1955
b. Studer, Cheryl

October 27, 1955
b. Gates, William Henry, III
d. Griffith, Clark Calvin

October 31, 1955
b. Roberts, Xavier
b. Nye, Bill

November 1, 1955
d. Carnegie, Dale

November 3, 1955
b. Simms, Phil(ip)

November 4, 1955
d. Young, Cy

November 5, 1955
d. Utrillo, Maurice

November 6, 1955
b. Shriver, Maria (Owings)

November 10, 1955
b. Clark, Jack Anthony

November 11, 1955
b. Wangchuk, Jigme Singye

November 13, 1955
d. DeVoto, Bernard Augustine

November 14, 1955
b. Hernandez, Willie (Guillermo Villaneuva)
d. Ayres, Ruby Mildred
d. Sherwood, Robert Emmet
d. Tobin, Daniel Joseph

November 17, 1955
b. King, Yolanda Denise
d. Johnson, James Price

November 19, 1955
d. James, Marquis

November 21, 1955
b. Maxwell, Cedric Bryan

November 22, 1955
d. Howard, Shemp

November 23, 1955
b. Landrieu, Mary L.

November 27, 1955
d. Honegger, Arthur

November 29, 1955
b. Mandel, Howie

November 30, 1955
b. Idol, Billy

December 2, 1955
b. Christopher, Dennis

December 4, 1955
b. Taylor, Dave
d. Lustig, Alvin
d. Martin, Glenn Luther

December 6, 1955
b. Wright, Steven
d. Wagner, Honus

December 11, 1955
d. Merrill, Frank Dow

December 13, 1955
d. Egas Moniz, Antonio C A F

December 16, 1955
b. Browner, Carol M.

December 17, 1955
d. McCoy, Horace

December 18, 1955
b. Liotta, Ray

December 26, 1955
b. Bayh, Evan

December 27, 1955
d. Culbertson, Ely
d. Fisher, Ham(mond Edward)

December 31, 1955
d. Lewisohn, Ludwig

1956

b. Ballmer, Steve
b. Barry, Lynda
b. Benjamin, Regina (M.)
b. Buttafuoco, Joey
b. Cooke, Christopher M
b. Finley, Karen
b. Guccione, Bob, Jr.
b. Henning, Anne
b. Hughes, Mark
b. King, Betsy
b. King, Gayle
b. Kushner, Tony
b. McTear, Houston
b. Ntibantunganya, Sylvestre
b. Rourke, Mickey
b. Rudner, Rita
b. Sagal, Katey
b. Samara, Noah (Azmi)
b. Scott, Steve
b. Some, Malidoma Patrice
b. Stonesifer, Patty
b. Tharoor, Shashi
b. Thornton, Billy Bob
b. Toone, Bill
b. Vig, Butch
b. Washington, Laura S.
d. Baeck, Leo
d. Benefield, Barry
d. Benn, Gottfried
d. Church, George W

d. Heath, Lawrence S
d. Reese, Harry B
d. Royden, Agnes Maude

January 1, 1956
d. Hague, Frank

January 3, 1956
b. Gibson, Mel
b. Ribbs, Willy T
d. Gretchaninov, Aleksandr Tikhonovich

January 4, 1956
d. Damon, Ralph Shepard

January 5, 1956
d. LaFarge, Christopher
d. Mistinguett

January 7, 1956
b. Liut, Mike
d. Tucker, Preston Thomas

January 8, 1956
d. Pickard, Greenleaf Whittier

January 12, 1956
d. Langford, Sam

January 13, 1956
d. Feininger, Lyonel

January 14, 1956
b. Heppner, Ben
d. Kaye-Smith, Sheila

January 17, 1956
b. Caruso, David
b. Young, Paul

January 20, 1956
b. Maher, Bill
b. Naber, John

January 21, 1956
b. Benson, Robby

January 22, 1956
d. Greene, Ward

January 23, 1956
d. Evans, Billy
d. Korda, Alexander, Sir

January 26, 1956
b. Harris, Eddy L(ouis)

January 27, 1956
d. Kleiber, Erich

January 28, 1956
b. Schilling, Peter

January 29, 1956
d. Mencken, H(enry) L(ouis)

January 31, 1956
b. Lydon, John (Joseph)
d. Milne, A(lan) A(lexander)

February 2, 1956
d. Burns, Bob
d. Grapewin, Charley

February 3, 1956
b. Jefferson, John Larry
b. Lane, Nathan
d. Yerkes, Robert Mearns

February 5, 1956
b. Saar, Alison

February 6, 1956
b. Walmsley, Jon
d. Chretien, Henri

February 8, 1956
b. Johnson, Marques Kevin
d. Mack, Connie

February 9, 1956
b. Ford, Phil Jackson

February 10, 1956
d. Trenchard, Hugh Montague, First
Viscount

February 14, 1956
b. Dravecky, Dave

February 16, 1956
b. Ingram, James

February 18, 1956
d. Charpentier, Gustave

February 21, 1956
d. Goldman, Edwin Franko

February 22, 1956
b. Alcott, Amy Strum
d. Carnegie, Hattie

February 24, 1956
b. Murray, Eddie Clarence
b. Zahn, Paula

February 26, 1956
d. Janis, Elsie

February 27, 1956
d. Peters, Brandon

February 28, 1956
b. Dantley, Adrian (Delano)
b. Hughes, Francis

February 29, 1956
d. Guptill, Arthur Leighton
d. Quirino, Elpidio

March 1, 1956
b. Daly, Timothy

March 10, 1956
b. Aurre, Laura
b. Lang, Helmut
b. Myricks, Larry

March 11, 1956
d. Vassilenko, Sergei

March 12, 1956
b. Murphy, Dale Bryan
d. Bierut, Boleslaw

March 13, 1956
b. Delany, Dana

March 17, 1956
d. Allen, Fred
d. Joliot-Curie, Irene

March 18, 1956
b. Stenmark, Ingemar
d. Bromfield, Louis Brucker
d. Decker, Alonzo G

March 20, 1956
d. Stout, William Bushnell

March 22, 1956
b. Olin, Lena
d. Sarton, George

March 23, 1956
d. Dixon, Mort

March 24, 1956
b. Templeton, Garry Lewis
d. Keesom, Willem Hendrik

March 25, 1956
d. Newton, Robert

March 29, 1956
b. Thomas, Kurt

March 30, 1956
d. Bentley, Edmund Clerihew

March 31, 1956
d. De Palma, Ralph

April 2, 1956
d. Pisis, Filippo Tibertelli de

April 6, 1956
b. Darden, Christopher A.

April 9, 1956
d. Little, Little Jack

April 11, 1956
b. Mayer, Gene

April 12, 1956
b. Garcia, Andy

April 15, 1956
d. Nolde, Emil

April 16, 1956
d. Chaplin, Sydney Dryden

April 17, 1956
b. Sembello, Michael

April 18, 1956
b. James, John
b. Roberts, Eric

April 19, 1956
b. Barker, Sue
b. Carlyle, Randy

April 21, 1956
d. MacArthur, Charles

April 22, 1956
b. Wilson, Phill

April 24, 1956
d. Stephenson, Henry

April 26, 1956
d. Arnold, Edward

April 30, 1956
d. Barkley, Alben William

May 4, 1956
b. Guterson, David

May 7, 1956
d. Hoffmann, Josef

May 10, 1956
b. Paeniu, Bikenibeu
d. Mulford, Clarence Edward
d. Prouty, Jed

May 11, 1956
d. Adams, Walter Sydney

May 12, 1956
b. Federko, Bernie
d. Calhern, Louis

May 15, 1956
d. Rollini, Adrian

May 16, 1956
b. Morris, Jack

May 17, 1956
b. Leonard, Sugar Ray
b. Saget, Bob

May 19, 1956
b. Ford, Steven Meigs

May 20, 1956
d. Beerbohm, Max
d. Macy, George

May 21, 1956
b. Reinhold, Judge

May 24, 1956
d. Kibbee, Guy

May 25, 1956
b. Lynch, Kevin

May 26, 1956
d. Simmons, Al(oysius Harry)
b. Hockenberry, John (Charles)

June 1, 1956
b. Hartman, Lisa
d. Jones, Jesse Holman

June 2, 1956
b. Guerrero, Pedro
d. Hersholt, Jean

June 5, 1956
b. Kenny G

June 6, 1956
b. Borg, Bjorn Rune
b. Chan, June
d. Bingham, Hiram

June 7, 1956
d. Benda, Julien

June 8, 1956
d. Laurencin, Marie

June 9, 1956
b. Cornwell, Patricia (Daniels)

June 10, 1956
d. Pratt, Fletcher

June 11, 1956
b. Montana, Joe
d. Brangwyn, Frank, Sir
d. Corle, Edwin
d. Morgan, Ralph
d. Trumbauer, Frank(ie)

June 14, 1956
d. Harrison, G(eorge) Donald

June 15, 1956
b. Parrish, Lance Michael

June 19, 1956
b. Stone, Doug
d. Watson, Thomas J(ohn), Sr.

June 20, 1956
d. Tikhomirov, Vasily Dmitrievich

June 21, 1956
b. Sutcliffe, Rick

June 22, 1956
d. DeLaMare, Walter

June 23, 1956
d. Gliere, Reinhold Moritsevich

June 25, 1956
d. Arlen, Michael
d. King, Ernest Joseph

June 26, 1956
b. Isaak, Chris

July 1, 1956
b. Whitley, Keith

July 2, 1956
b. Hall, Jerry (Faye)

July 3, 1956
b. Williams, Montel B

July 8, 1956
d. Papini, Giovanni

July 9, 1956
b. Hanks, Tom

July 11, 1956
d. Cleghorn, Sprague
d. Wellesley, Dorothy Violet

July 12, 1956
b. Patti, Sandi
b. Soto, Mario Melvin

July 17, 1956
b. Trottier, Bryan John

July 20, 1956
b. Jausovec, Mima

July 26, 1956
b. Hamill, Dorothy Stuart
d. Raemaekers, Louis

July 29, 1956
b. Spinks, Michael

July 30, 1956
b. Burke, Delta
b. Hill, Anita Faye
b. Larson, Reed David

July 31, 1956
b. Patrick, Deval Laurdine

August 7, 1956
d. LaTouche, John

August 10, 1956
b. Fromholtz, Dianne

August 11, 1956
d. Lawrence, Frieda
d. Pollock, Jackson

August 14, 1956
d. Brecht, Bertolt (Eugen Friedrich)
d. Neurath, Konstantin von

August 20, 1956
b. Allen, Joan

August 21, 1956
b. Cattrall, Kim

August 22, 1956
b. Molitor, Paul Leo

August 24, 1956
b. Cooney, Gerry
d. Mizoguchi, Kenji

August 25, 1956
d. Kinsey, Alfred Charles
d. Pierce, George Washington

August 29, 1956
b. Morris, Mark

August 31, 1956
d. MacKaye, Percy Wallace

September 4, 1956
b. Gould, Shane

September 5, 1956
b. Denton, Steve

September 6, 1956
d. Raymond, Alex(ander Gillespie)

September 7, 1956
b. Feinstein, Michael Jay
d. Fry, Charles Burgess

September 9, 1956
d. Hughes, Rupert

September 11, 1956
b. Camp, Kimberly
d. Bishop, Billy

September 12, 1956
b. Brownback, Sam

September 13, 1956
b. Sledge, Joni

September 16, 1956
b. Copperfield, David
d. Lugosi, Bela
d. Ray, Shorty

September 18, 1956
b. Fields, Debbi
b. Stastny, Peter

September 19, 1956
b. Smith, Rex

September 22, 1956
b. Boone, Debby
d. Soddy, Frederick

September 26, 1956
b. Bulatovic, Momir

September 27, 1956
b. Handford, Martin
d. Zaharias, Babe Didrikson

September 28, 1956
d. Boeing, William Edward
d. Hodge, Frederick Webb

September 29, 1956
b. Coe, Sebastian Newbold
d. Somoza, Anastasio

September 30, 1956
b. Curtis-Hall, Vondie

October 1, 1956
d. Von Tilzer, Albert

October 2, 1956
d. Bancroft, George

October 6, 1956
b. Cefalo, Jimmy
d. Merrill, Charles Edward

October 7, 1956
d. Birdseye, Clarence Frank
d. Hamlin, Talbot Faulkner

October 8, 1956
b. Zimbalist, Stephanie

October 13, 1956
b. Hannah, Marc (Regis)
d. Davis, Owen

October 15, 1956
b. Hennard, George, Jr.

October 16, 1956
b. Belote, Melissa
b. Doherty, Kieran

October 17, 1956
b. Jemison, Mae C(arol)
b. Morrow, Ken(neth)

October 18, 1956
b. Navratilova, Martina
d. Atterbury, Grosvenor

October 19, 1956
d. Jones, Isham

October 20, 1956
d. Bell, Lawrence Dale

October 21, 1956
b. Fisher, Carrie Frances
d. Owsley, Frank Lawrence

October 23, 1956
b. Yoakam, Dwight

October 24, 1956
b. Gerstler, Amy

October 26, 1956
d. Adams, Annette Abbott
d. Gieseking, Walter Wilhelm

October 27, 1956
d. Johnson, Charles Spurgeon

October 28, 1956
b. Story, Liz

October 29, 1956
d. Coffin, Robert Peter Tristram

October 30, 1956
d. Baroja (y Nessi), Pio

October 31, 1956
d. Badoglio, Pietro

November 3, 1956
b. Welch, Bob
d. Metzinger, Jean

November 4, 1956
d. Tatum, Art(hur)

November 6, 1956
d. Kelly, Paul

November 8, 1956
d. Field, Marshall, III

November 10, 1956
b. Sinbad
d. Sinclair, Harry Ford

November 11, 1956
d. Young, Victor

November 14, 1956
d. Negrin, Juan

November 18, 1956
b. Moon, Warren (Harold)

November 19, 1956
b. Collins, Eileen
d. Sullivan, Francis Loftus

November 20, 1956
b. Derek, Bo
b. Gastineau, Mark

November 21, 1956
b. Fattah, Chaka
b. Simionescu, Mariana
d. Burchenal, Elizabeth

November 25, 1956
d. Dovzhenko, Alexander

November 26, 1956
d. Dorsey, Tommy

November 27, 1956
d. Kaempffert, Waldemar (Bernhard)

November 29, 1956
b. Baker, Bill
b. Cary, Lorene

November 30, 1956
b. Goodman, Robert O, Jr.
d. Schwartz, Jean

December 3, 1956
b. Bochner, Hart
d. Rodchenko, Alexander Mikhailovich

December 4, 1956
b. King, Bernard

December 6, 1956
d. Ambedkar, Bhimrao Ramji

December 7, 1956
b. Bird, Larry (Joe)

December 14, 1956
d. Paasikivi, Juho Kusti

December 20, 1956
b. Baker, Blanche
d. Risdon, Elizabeth

December 21, 1956
d. Terman, Lewis Madison

December 25, 1956
d. Dwiggins, William Addison

December 27, 1956
d. Marks, Percy

December 28, 1956
b. Kennedy, Nigel Paul
d. Bennett, John

December 30, 1956
b. Ralph, Sheryl Lee
d. Draper, Ruth

1957

b. Allen, Geri
b. Blumberg, Judy
b. Burns, Diane M.
b. Carrere, Emmanuel
b. Cave, Nicholas Edward
b. Childs, Toni
b. Cope, Julian
b. Cousins, Robin
b. Cruzan, Nancy
b. Ducksworth, Marilyn (Jacoby)
b. Eubanks, Kevin
b. Ford, Bill
b. George, Nelson
b. Gibbons, Leeza
b. Gillette, Duane
b. Harvey, Steve(n Patrick)
b. Hemphill, Essex
b. Henderson, Gordon
b. Judy, Steven
b. King, Martin Luther, III
b. Lasseter, John
b. Leary, Denis
b. Leon, Kenny
b. Lepage, Robert
b. Lewis, Paul Edward
b. Loveless, Patty
b. Nair, Mira
b. Ng, Fae Myenne
b. Nkoli, Simon
b. O'Hara, Patrick
b. Powter, Susan
b. Riggs, Marlon
b. Rudnick, Paul
b. Russell, Theresa
b. Sampson, Charles
b. Satriani, Joe
b. Stark, Koo
b. Subic, Joseph, Jr.
b. Teena Marie
b. Thomas, Pinklon
b. Ward, Rachel
b. Wenzel, Hanni
d. Abu Madi, Iliya
d. Bentley, Arthur F.
d. Coleman, William

January 6, 1957
b. Lopez, Nancy Marie

January 7, 1957
b. Baker, Nicholson
b. Couric, Katie
b. Janaszak, Steve

January 10, 1957
d. Mistral, Gabriela

January 11, 1957
b. Dawkins, Darryl

January 13, 1957
b. O'Meara, Mark
b. Snow, Don

d. Coppard, A(lfred) E(dgar)

January 14, 1957
b. Min, Anchee
d. Bogart, Humphrey de Forest

January 15, 1957
b. Van Peebles, Mario

January 16, 1957
d. Toscanini, Arturo

January 18, 1957
d. Wolff, Fritz

January 19, 1957
b. Anderson, O(ttis) J(erome)
b. Kennard, William Earl

January 20, 1957
d. Connolly, James B

January 21, 1957
b. Davis, Geena
d. Kupka, Frank

January 22, 1957
b. Bossy, Mike
d. Perry, Ralph Barton

January 23, 1957
b. Caroline, Princess

January 24, 1957
b. Eaton, Mark E

January 25, 1957
d. Tuthill, Harry J

January 26, 1957
b. McCourt, Dale Allen
b. Van Halen, Eddie

January 28, 1957
b. Price, Nick

January 31, 1957
b. Babashoff, Shirley

February 1, 1957
b. Adamek, Donna
d. Paulus, Friedrich von

February 2, 1957
d. Morgan, Julia

February 3, 1957
d. Townsend, Willard Saxby

February 6, 1957
b. Townsend, Robert
d. Covarrubias, Miguel

February 7, 1957
b. Garcia y Sanchez, Damaso
Domingo

February 8, 1957
d. Bothe, Walter Wilhelm Georg
d. Von Neumann, John

February 10, 1957
d. Wilder, Laura Elizabeth Ingalls

February 14, 1957
b. Wahl, Ken

February 16, 1957
b. Burton, LeVar(dis Robert Martyn
Jr.)
d. Hofmann, Josef Casimir
d. Hore-Belisha, Leslie, Baron
d. Townsend, John Sealy Edward, Sir

February 18, 1957
b. White, Vanna Marie
d. Russell, Henry Norris

February 19, 1957
b. Falco
b. Stewart, Dave
d. Toren, Marta

February 24, 1957
d. Buck, Gene

February 25, 1957
b. McCreesh, Raymond
b. Wood, Stuart
d. Moran, Bugs

February 26, 1957
b. Mullen, Joe

February 28, 1957
b. Turturro, John

March 2, 1957
d. Maybeck, Bernard Ralph

March 4, 1957
d. Graham, Evarts Ambrose

March 5, 1957
d. Menzies, William Cameron

March 7, 1957
d. Lewis, Wyndham

March 8, 1957
d. Schoech, Othmar

March 9, 1957
b. Lewis, Chris
d. Horthy de Nagybanya, Nicholas

March 11, 1957
d. Byrd, Richard Evelyn, Admiral
d. Ornitz, Samuel

March 12, 1957
b. Allen, Leslie
b. Jackson, Marlon David
d. Hull, Josephine

March 16, 1957
b. Samuelson, Joan
d. Brancusi, Constantin

March 17, 1957
d. Magsaysay, Ramon

March 19, 1957
d. Rascoe, Burton

March 20, 1957
b. Lee, Spike
d. Chase, Edna Woolman

March 22, 1957
b. Mills, Stephanie

March 23, 1957
b. Plummer, Amanda

March 26, 1957
d. Herriot, Edouard
d. Ophuls, Max

March 28, 1957
d. Morley, Christopher (Darlington)

March 29, 1957
b. Lambert, Christopher
d. Cary, Joyce

March 30, 1957
b. Reiser, Paul

March 31, 1957
d. Lockhart, Gene

April 2, 1957
d. Sparks, Ned

April 3, 1957
d. Westwick, Harry

April 9, 1957
b. Ballesteros, Seve(riano)
b. Macy, Kyle Robert

April 11, 1957
d. Crofts, Freeman Willis

April 12, 1957
b. Gill, Vince(nt Grant)
b. Janowitz, Tama

April 15, 1957
b. Ashford, Evelyn

April 16, 1957
d. Torrio, Johnny

April 22, 1957
d. Campbell, Roy

April 26, 1957
d. Strong, Philip Duffield

April 29, 1957
b. Day-Lewis, Daniel Michael Blake
b. Pfeiffer, Michelle
d. Baker, Belle

May 1, 1957
d. Mitchell, Grant

May 2, 1957
d. McCarthy, Joe

May 4, 1957
b. Kreiner, Kathy

May 7, 1957
d. Ness, Eliot

May 8, 1957
d. Davidson, J Brownlee

May 9, 1957
d. Pinza, Ezio

May 10, 1957
b. Mahre, Phil(lip)
b. Mahre, Steve(n Irving)
b. Vicious, Sid
d. Malone, Annie Minerva Turnbo
   Pope

May 12, 1957
b. Whitaker, Lou(is Rodman)
d. VonStroheim, Erich

May 13, 1957
d. Murry, John Middleton

May 16, 1957
b. Cousineau, Tom
d. Irvin, Dick

May 18, 1957
b. Wood, Sharon
d. Rogers, Bruce

May 19, 1957
b. Laimbeer, Bill

May 20, 1957
d. Murray, Gilbert

May 26, 1957
d. Lawson, Robert

May 28, 1957
b. Gibson, Kirk Harold

May 29, 1957
d. Whale, James

May 31, 1957
b. Craig, Jim
b. Adams, Scott

June 5, 1957
d. Densmore, Frances

June 9, 1957
b. Jakes, Thomas T.D.
d. Blanding, Don

June 11, 1957
d. Greene, Charles Sumner

June 12, 1957
b. Busfield, Timothy
d. Dorsey, Jimmy
d. Joyce, Peggy Hopkins

June 14, 1957
b. Simpson, Mona Elizabeth

June 15, 1957
b. Butler, Brett

June 17, 1957
d. Richardson, Dorothy Miller

June 18, 1957
d. Williams, J(ames) R(obert)

June 21, 1957
b. Breathed, Berke
d. Farrere, Claude
d. Stark, Johannes

June 23, 1957
b. McDormand, Frances

June 24, 1957
d. Bowes, Walter
d. Kupka, Frank

June 27, 1957
d. Lowry, Malcolm

June 29, 1957
b. Browne, Leslie

July 1, 1957
b. Patterson, Lorna

July 2, 1957
d. Cherwell, Frederick Alexander L,
   Viscount

July 3, 1957
b. Branigan, Laura
d. Luque, Dolf

July 6, 1957
b. Ford, Susan Elizabeth

July 8, 1957
d. Coolidge, Grace (Anne Goodhue)

July 9, 1957
b. McGillis, Kelly

July 10, 1957
d. Asch, Sholem

July 11, 1957
d. Aga Khan III

July 13, 1957
b. Crowe, Cameron

July 15, 1957
d. Cox, James Middleton, Sr.

July 18, 1957
b. Faldo, Nick

July 19, 1957
d. Malaparte, Curzio

July 20, 1957
b. Colmenares, Margarita (H.)

July 21, 1957
b. Lovitz, Jon
d. Roberts, Kenneth Lewis

July 22, 1957
b. Stieb, Dave

July 23, 1957
b. Cornell, Lydia
d. Sterne, Maurice

July 24, 1957
b. O'Callahan, Jack
b. Tillis, Pam
d. Guitry, Sacha

July 25, 1957
b. Billingsley, Ray

July 26, 1957
d. Tomasi di Lampedusa, Guiseppe

July 28, 1957
d. Abbott, Edith

July 30, 1957
b. Cartwright, Bill

July 31, 1957
d. Tchelitchew, Pavel

August 1, 1957
b. Peeters, Pete(r)

August 4, 1957
d. George, Walter Franklin

August 5, 1957
d. Wieland, Heinrich Otto

August 6, 1957
b. Horner, Bob

August 7, 1957
d. Hardy, Oliver

August 9, 1957
b. Griffith, Melanie

August 11, 1957
b. Hwang, David Henry

August 13, 1957
d. Beach, Joseph Warren
d. Stormer, Fredrik (Carl Mulertz)

August 14, 1957
b. Jackee

August 16, 1957
d. Langmuir, Irving

August 20, 1957
b. Donaldson, Simon (Kirwan)
b. Nicholas, Cindy
d. Evans, Edward Ratcliffe Garth
   Russell

August 21, 1957
b. Sledge, Kim
d. Stewart, Nels(on Robert)
d. Sverdrup, H(arald) U(lrik)

August 22, 1957
b. Dunn, Holly

d. Dent, Edward Joseph

August 23, 1957
b. Boddicker, Mike

August 24, 1957
d. Knox, Ronald Arbuthnott

August 26, 1957
d. Tyrrell, Joseph Burr

August 27, 1957
b. Langer, Bernhard
d. Filene, Lincoln

August 28, 1957
d. Randolph, Georgiana Ann
d. Rice, Craig

August 31, 1957
b. Tilbrook, Glenn

September 1, 1957
b. Estefan, Gloria
d. Brain, Dennis

September 2, 1957
d. Freuchen, Peter

September 3, 1957
b. Ancier, Garth

September 5, 1957
d. Parrish, Anne

September 6, 1957
d. Salvemini, Gaetano

September 7, 1957
d. Helland-Hansen, Bjorn

September 10, 1957
b. Burton, Kate

September 11, 1957
d. Watson, Moose

September 13, 1957
b. Black, Keith Lanier

September 16, 1957
d. Ch'i Pai-Shih

September 19, 1957
d. Childe, Vere Gordon
d. Daly, Reginald Aldworth

September 20, 1957
d. Sibelius, Jean

September 21, 1957
b. Moncrief, Sidney A
d. Haakon VII
d. Krupp von Bohlen und Halbach,
Bertha
d. Lowie, Robert Harry

September 22, 1957
b. Johnson, Mark
d. Gogarty, Oliver St. John

September 23, 1957
d. Hartford, George Ludlum

September 26, 1957
b. Hamilton, Linda
d. Clark, Charles Badger

September 30, 1957
b. Drescher, Fran

October 1, 1957
d. Candler, Charles Howard

October 2, 1957
b. Saint, Assotto

October 3, 1957
d. Duranty, Walter

October 4, 1957
b. Simmons, Russell

October 11, 1957
b. Sereno, Paul C.

October 12, 1957
b. Chasnoff, Debra

October 17, 1957
b. Van Patten, Vince(nt)

October 20, 1957
d. Buchanan, Jack

October 23, 1957
d. Lyman, Abe

October 24, 1957
d. Dior, Christian

October 25, 1957
d. Anastasia, Albert
d. Dunsany, Edward J M Plunkett,
Baron

October 26, 1957
d. Cori, Gerty Theresa (Radnitz)
d. Kazantzakis, Nikos

October 27, 1957
b. Honeyman-Scott, James
d. van de Velde, Henry

October 29, 1957
d. Mayer, L(ouis) B(urt)

October 30, 1957
b. Mintz, Shlomo

November 1, 1957
b. Lovett, Lyle

November 2, 1957
d. Young, Mahonri Mackintosh

November 3, 1957
b. Johnson, Steve
d. Reich, Wilhelm
d. Tokutomi Soho

November 5, 1957
b. Hexum, Jon-Erik
b. Winslow, Kellen Boswell

November 7, 1957
d. Worters, Roy

November 18, 1957
b. Watts, J(ulius) C(aesar), (Jr.)

November 20, 1957
d. Swope, Gerard

November 25, 1957
d. Kyne, Peter Bernard
d. Rivera, Diego

November 27, 1957
b. Kennedy, Caroline Bouvier

November 29, 1957
b. Napolitano, Janet
d. Korngold, Erich Wolfgang

November 30, 1957
b. McIlwee, Thomas
d. Gigli, Beniamino

December 1, 1957
b. Bissell, Patrick

December 3, 1957
b. Jordan, Kathy
d. Gannett, Frank Ernest

December 4, 1957
b. Smith, Lee (Arthur)

December 5, 1957
b. Monk, Art

December 6, 1957
b. Bedrosian, Steve
b. Cuomo, Andrew M.

December 9, 1957
b. Osmond, Donny

December 10, 1957
b. Arkadie, Kevin
b. Maharaj Ji, Guru
d. Elmen, Gustav Waldemar

December 12, 1957
b. Ana-Alicia

December 17, 1957
d. Sayers, Dorothy Leigh

December 19, 1957
b. McHale, Kevin (Edward)
d. Van Druten, John William

December 20, 1957
b. Bragg, Billy

December 22, 1957
d. Zuppke, Robert Carl

December 24, 1957
d. Barea, Arturo

d. Talmadge, Norma

December 25, 1957
b. Persinger, Gregory A
d. Campbell, Walter Stanley
d. Pathe, Charles

December 30, 1957
b. Lauer, Matt

1958

b. Amanpour, Christiane
b. Bass, Rick
b. Burton, Tim
b. Buscemi, Steve
b. Clay, Andrew Dice
b. Coen, Ethan
b. Daniels, Faith
b. Doyle, Roddy
b. Edmonds, Kenneth
b. Esposito, Giancarlo (Giusseppi)
b. Flatley, Michael
b. Gorka, John
b. Hooks, Jan
b. Jones, Anissa
b. Kirtley, Steven William
b. Krikalev, Sergei
b. Kulwicki, Alan
b. Mason, Belinda
b. McDuffie, Robert
b. McLish, Rachel Elizondo
b. Millard, Barbara J(eanne)
b. Park, Nick
b. Pizzolato, Orlando
b. Profet, Margie
b. Sellars, Peter
b. Sickmann, Rodney Virgil
b. Straw, Syd
b. Tilly, Jennifer
b. Torvill, Jayne
b. Vaid, Urvashi
b. Watterson, Bill
d. Znaniecki, Florian
d. Pears, Charles

January 1, 1958
b. Silk, Dave
d. Weston, Edward

January 3, 1958
b. Morial, Marc (Haydel)

January 4, 1958
d. Alexander, Archie Alphonso

January 5, 1958
b. Kittle, Ron(ald Dale)

January 7, 1958
d. Anglin, Margaret Mary

January 9, 1958
b. Agca, Mehmet Ali
b. McClanahan, Rob

January 12, 1958
d. Willard, Frank Henry

January 13, 1958
d. Lasky, Jesse L(ouis)
d. Purviance, Edna

January 19, 1958
d. Rondon, Candido Mariano da Silva

January 20, 1958
b. Lamas, Lorenzo
d. Lambert, Ward L

January 21, 1958
d. Bowers, Claude Gernade

January 22, 1958
b. White, Charles Raymond

January 23, 1958
b. Christoff, Steve

January 25, 1958
b. Manoff, Dinah

January 26, 1958
b. Baker, Anita
b. DeGeneres, Ellen
b. Lemon, Ted

January 29, 1958
b. Norton-Taylor, Judy

January 30, 1958
b. Butler, Brett
d. Heinkel, Ernst Heinrich

February 1, 1958
d. Davisson, Clinton Joseph
d. Jones, Ernest Alfred

February 5, 1958
d. Brown, Lew
d. Tomlinson, Henry Major

February 6, 1958
d. Morgan, Charles Langbridge

February 8, 1958
b. Miller, Barry

February 9, 1958
b. Lyle, Sandy

February 13, 1958
d. Rouault, Georges

February 14, 1958
d. Pankhurst, Christabel Harriette, Dame
d. Twelvetrees, Helen

February 15, 1958
b. McKegney, Tony

February 16, 1958
b. Ice-T
d. Frisco, Joe

February 19, 1958
b. Hewitt, Martin

February 21, 1958
b. Carpenter, Mary Chapin
b. Trammell, Alan Stuart

February 27, 1958
b. Price, Deb(orah Jane)
d. Cohn, Harry

February 28, 1958
b. Pavelich, Mark

March 1, 1958
d. Balla, Giacomo

March 2, 1958
b. Curren, Kevin
d. Held, John, Jr.

March 3, 1958
b. Richardson, Miranda

March 5, 1958
b. Gibb, Andy
b. Winans, Marvin L.

March 8, 1958
b. Numan, Gary

March 10, 1958
b. Howe, Steve
b. Stone, Sharon

March 13, 1958
b. Phillips, Caryl
d. Muller, Maria

March 14, 1958
b. Albert, Prince

March 20, 1958
b. Hunter, Holly

March 21, 1958
b. Oldman, Gary

March 22, 1958
b. Rice, Linda Johnson
d. McCardell, Claire
d. Todd, Mike

March 25, 1958
b. Bright, Susie

March 27, 1958
b. Molinari, Susan

March 28, 1958
d. Klein, Chuck

March 29, 1958
d. Handy, W(illiam) C(hristopher)
d. Pangborn, Clyde Edward

March 31, 1958
b. Rogers, John W., Jr.

April 3, 1958
b. Baldwin, Alec

April 4, 1958
d. Stompanato, Johnny

April 5, 1958
b. Kriek, Johann

April 7, 1958
d. Paul, Elliot Harold

April 8, 1958
d. Nathan, George Jean

April 10, 1958
b. Bronfman, Yefim

April 14, 1958
b. Millo, Aprile

April 15, 1958
d. Taylor, Estelle

April 16, 1958
d. Black, Walter J
d. Franklin, Rosalind Elsie

April 18, 1958
d. Arkell, William Joscelyn
d. Gamelin, Maurice Gustave

April 21, 1958
b. MacDowell, Andie

April 25, 1958
d. Hickman, Herman Michael, Jr.

April 28, 1958
b. Sutton, Hal Evan

April 29, 1958
b. Klass, Perri Elizabeth

May 3, 1958
d. Cornelius, Henry

May 4, 1958
b. Haring, Keith
b. Tway, Bob

May 5, 1958
b. Bening, Annette
d. Cabell, James Branch

May 8, 1958
d. Geddes, Norman Bel

May 9, 1958
d. Davies, Joseph Edward
d. Goodwin, Bill

May 10, 1958
b. Boucher, Gaetan
b. Ochoa, Ellen
b. Santorum, Rick
d. Connell, Alex

May 11, 1958
d. Lelong, Lucien

May 14, 1958
d. Dole, James

May 18, 1958
d. Davis, Elmer Holmes

May 19, 1958
d. Colman, Ronald

May 20, 1958
b. Reagan, Ronald Prescott

May 23, 1958
b. Carey, Drew

May 27, 1958
b. Williams, Wayne Bertram

May 29, 1958
d. Jimenez, Juan Ramon

June 3, 1958
b. Valentine, Scott

June 4, 1958
b. Velez, Eddie

June 7, 1958
b. Artist Formerly Known as Prince,
The

June 8, 1958
b. Wayans, Keenen Ivory

June 9, 1958
d. Donat, Robert
d. Hackett, Raymond

June 10, 1958
d. Grimke, Angelina Emily Weld

June 11, 1958
d. DeMar, Clarence

June 14, 1958
b. Heiden, Eric Arthur

June 15, 1958
b. Boggs, Wade (Anthony)

June 16, 1958
b. Griffith, Darrell Steven

June 17, 1958
d. Nagy, Imre
d. Pound, Louise

June 20, 1958
d. Adler, Kurt
d. Alder, Kurt
d. Swope, Herbert Bayard

June 21, 1958
d. Ghormley, Robert Lee

June 24, 1958
b. Chen, T.C.

June 27, 1958
b. Adjani, Isabelle

June 28, 1958
d. Noyes, Alfred

June 30, 1958
b. Froese, Bob

July 1, 1958
b. Lieberman, Nancy
d. Laban, Rudolf von

July 2, 1958
d. Boswell, Martha

July 5, 1958
d. Crothers, Rachel

July 7, 1958
d. Rentner, Maurice

July 8, 1958
b. Bacon, Kevin

July 10, 1958
b. Fleck, Bela

July 11, 1958
b. Lester, Mark

July 14, 1958
d. Faisal II
d. Nuri al-Sa'id

July 18, 1958
d. DuBois, Guy Pene

July 19, 1958
b. Olson, Billy Richard

July 20, 1958
d. Pangborn, Franklin

July 22, 1958
d. Holmes, Burton

July 24, 1958
b. Carroll, Joe Barry

July 25, 1958
d. Warner, Harry Morris

July 26, 1958
d. Rohde, Ruth Bryan Owen

July 27, 1958
d. Chennault, Claire Lee

July 28, 1958
b. Fox, Terry
b. Schulman, Sarah (Miriam)

July 30, 1958
b. Bush, Kate
b. Thompson, Daley

August 1, 1958
b. Vandeweghe, Kiki

August 2, 1958
d. Scholes, Percy Alfred

August 4, 1958
b. Decker Slaney, Mary

August 5, 1958
d. Holbrooke, Josef

August 6, 1958
b. DeBarge, Randy

August 7, 1958
b. Salazar, Alberto

d. Lashley, Karl Spencer
d. Lewis, Elizabeth Foreman

August 8, 1958
b. Norville, Deborah (Anne)
d. Bracken, Brendan Rendall, Viscount

August 9, 1958
b. Bearse, Amanda
d. Durand, William F.

August 14, 1958
d. Beard, Mary Ritter
d. Broonzy, Big Bill
d. Joliot(-Curie), (Jean) Frederic

August 15, 1958
b. Cowley, Joe
d. Dean, Gordon Evans

August 16, 1958
b. Bassett, Angela
b. Clerc, Jose-Luis
b. Madonna
d. Gibbs, Woolcott
d. Jackson, Chevalier

August 17, 1958
b. Carlisle, Belinda
d. Brooks, Walter R(ollin)

August 18, 1958
b. Stowe, Madeleine

August 21, 1958
b. Case, Steve
d. Schumann, Walter

August 22, 1958
d. Martin du Gard, Roger

August 24, 1958
b. Guttenberg, Steve
d. Blech, Leo

August 26, 1958
d. Vaughan Williams, Ralph

August 27, 1958
d. Lawrence, Ernest Orlando

August 28, 1958
b. Hamilton, Scott
b. Henry, Lenny

August 29, 1958
b. Jackson, Michael Joseph

September 2, 1958
d. Palmer, Frederick

September 6, 1958
b. Foxworthy, Jeff

September 10, 1958
b. Columbus, Chris

September 11, 1958
d. Service, Robert William

September 16, 1958
b. Hershiser, Orel Leonard, IV

September 17, 1958
b. Jahan, Marine
d. Paneth, Friedrich Adolf

September 19, 1958
b. Hooks, Kevin

September 20, 1958
d. Wortman, Denys

September 22, 1958
d. Rinehart, Mary Roberts

September 23, 1958
b. Mize, Larry

September 25, 1958
b. Hillis, W(illiam) Daniel, (Jr.)
d. Watson, John Broadus

September 27, 1958
b. Cassidy, Shaun Paul

September 30, 1958
b. Stuart, Marty
d. Singmaster, Elsie

October 2, 1958
b. Jackson, Freddie
d. Stopes, Marie Charlotte Carmichael

October 5, 1958
b. Tyson, Neil de Grasse

October 9, 1958
b. Singletary, Mike
d. Pius XII

October 10, 1958
b. Tucker, Tanya (Denise)

October 11, 1958
d. Vlaminck, Maurice de

October 13, 1958
b. Berliner, Ron

October 14, 1958
b. Daniel, Beth
b. Dolby, Thomas
d. Mawson, Douglas, Sir
d. Robinson, Lennox
d. Zabolotskii, Nikolai Alekseevich

October 15, 1958
d. Norton, Jack

October 16, 1958
b. Robbins, Tim(othy Francis)
d. Redfield, Robert

October 17, 1958
b. Jackson, Alan Eugene

October 18, 1958
b. Hearns, Thomas

October 20, 1958
b. Pogorelich, Ivo

October 23, 1958
b. Dyson, Michael Eric

October 24, 1958
d. Moore, George Edward

October 25, 1958
b. Ender, Kornelia

October 27, 1958
b. LeBon, Simon

October 29, 1958
d. Akins, Zoe

October 30, 1958
b. Delaney, Joe Alton
d. Macaulay, (Emilie) Rose, Dame

November 2, 1958
b. McGee, Willie Dean

November 9, 1958
b. Higuera, Teddy
d. Fisher, Dorothy Frances Canfield

November 11, 1958
d. Bazin, Andre

November 12, 1958
d. Curley, James Michael

November 15, 1958
d. Adams, Samuel Hopkins
d. Power, Tyrone, Jr.

November 16, 1958
b. Guerrero, Roberto
b. Shabazz, Attallah

November 17, 1958
d. Cooper, Mort(on Cecil)

November 19, 1958
b. McGinnis, Scott

November 21, 1958
d. Ott, Mel(vin Thomas)

November 22, 1958
b. Curtis, Jamie Lee

November 23, 1958
d. McCulley, Johnston
d. Moeller, Philip

November 24, 1958
d. Cecil, Edgar Algernon Robert

November 25, 1958
d. Kettering, Charles Franklin

November 27, 1958
d. Rodzinski, Artur

November 28, 1958
b. Righetti, Dave

December 1, 1958
b. Tilton, Charlene
d. Wilkins, George Hubert, Sir

December 2, 1958
b. Gardner, Randy

December 8, 1958
b. Rogers, George Washington, Jr.
d. Speaker, Tris(tram E)

December 15, 1958
d. Pauli, Wolfgang Ernst

December 16, 1958
d. Corum, Martene Windsor

December 17, 1958
b. Poulin, Dave

December 21, 1958
d. Feuchtwanger, Lion
d. Wills, Harry

December 25, 1958
b. Henderson, Rickey (Henley)

December 28, 1958
b. Diffie, Joe

December 29, 1958
d. Humphrey, Doris

1959

b. Araki, Gregg
b. Azali, Assoumani
b. Basia
b. Biafra, Jello
b. Dahmer, Jeffrey L
b. Dean, Christopher
b. Ford, Lita
b. Gallegos, William
b. Garcia, Cristina
b. Guerin, Veronica
b. Hall, Edd
b. Hall, Fawn
b. Johnson, Lynn-Holly
b. Kim, Duk Koo
b. Koresh, David
b. LaDuke, Winona
b. Lagasse, Emeril
b. Lopez, James Michael
b. Menchu, Rigoberta
b. Morrissey
b. Porter, Connie
b. Poundstone, Paula
b. Prince, Faith
b. Raines, Franklin (Delano)
b. Reid, Vernon
b. Seibert, Michael
b. Taylor, Regina
b. Treitel, Jonathan
b. Videnov, Zhan (Vassilev)
b. Vollmann, William T.
b. Williams, Victoria
b. Winterson, Jeanette
b. Woodard, Lynette
b. Woody, Elizabeth
b. Zaslow, Jeff
d. Clarke, Edith
d. Greg, Walter Wilson, Sir
d. Namatjira, Albert
d. Padmore, George
d. Peret, Benjamin
d. Richier, Germaine

January 3, 1959
d. Muir, Edwin

January 6, 1959
b. Sledge, Kathy
d. Cohen, Octavus Roy

January 13, 1959
b. von Lipsey, Roderick K.

January 14, 1959
d. Cole, George Douglas Howard

January 16, 1959
b. Sade

January 17, 1959
b. Hoffs, Susanna

January 21, 1959
d. DeMille, Cecil B(lount)
d. Switzer, Carl

January 22, 1959
b. Blair, Linda Denise

January 27, 1959
b. Collinsworth, Cris

February 1, 1959
d. Hoppe, Willie

February 2, 1959
b. Manley, Dexter

February 3, 1959
d. Astor, William Vincent
d. Big Bopper, The
d. Holly, Buddy
d. Valens, Ritchie

February 4, 1959
b. Taylor, Lawrence Julius
d. O'Connor, Una

February 5, 1959
b. Sanchez, Salvador

February 7, 1959
d. Lajoie, Nap(oleon)
d. Malan, Daniel Francois

February 8, 1959
d. Berger, Meyer
d. Donovan, William Joseph

February 10, 1959
b. O'Grady, Sean

February 12, 1959
d. Antheil, George

February 14, 1959
b. Fleming, Renee
d. Dodds, Baby
d. Irwin, Wallace (Admah)

February 15, 1959
d. Richardson, Owen Williams, Sir

February 16, 1959
b. McEnroe, John Patrick, Jr.
d. Mara, Tim(othy James)

February 17, 1959
b. Lomax, Neil Vincent

February 20, 1959
d. Housman, Laurence

February 21, 1959
d. Radin, Paul

February 22, 1959
b. Lloyd, Lewis Kevin
b. MacLachlan, Kyle

February 23, 1959
d. Pales Matos, Luis

February 26, 1959
d. Belbenoit, Rene Lucien

February 27, 1959
d. Farrand, Beatrix Jones

February 28, 1959
d. Anderson, Maxwell

March 1, 1959
d. Booth, Albie

March 2, 1959
d. Blore, Eric

March 3, 1959
d. Costello, Lou

March 6, 1959
b. Arnold, Tom
d. Stone, Fred Andrew

March 7, 1959
d. Hatoyama Ichiro
d. Pigou, Arthur Cecil

March 10, 1959
d. Parks, Floyd Lavinius

March 13, 1959
b. Lee, Helen Elaine
d. Gilmour, Billy

March 15, 1959
b. Baines, Harold Douglass
b. Okri, Ben
d. Hines, Duncan
d. Young, Lester Willis

March 17, 1959
b. Ainge, Danny
d. Ehmke, Howard Jonathan

March 18, 1959
b. Cara, Irene (Escalera)

March 22, 1959
b. Modine, Matthew

March 26, 1959
b. Taylor, Kristin Clark

d. Chandler, Raymond Thornton

March 31, 1959
b. Young, Angus

April 2, 1959
b. Goodell, Brian Stuart

April 3, 1959
b. Pierce, David Hyde

April 4, 1959
d. Cleghorn, Sarah Norcliffe

April 8, 1959
d. Bowie, Russell
d. Takahama Kyoshi

April 9, 1959
d. Wright, Frank Lloyd

April 12, 1959
d. Gleason, James

April 13, 1959
d. Beinum, Eduard van

April 15, 1959
b. Thompson, Emma

April 18, 1959
b. Faludi, Susan

April 20, 1959
b. Howard, Clint

April 23, 1959
d. Guthrie, Edwin Ray

April 25, 1959
b. Terry, Randall A.
d. Mannes, David

April 27, 1959
b. Easton, Sheena
d. Ogburn, W(illiam) F(ielding)

April 30, 1959
d. Nagai, Sokichi

May 4, 1959
b. Travis, Randy

May 5, 1959
d. McIntyre, Hal
d. Saavdedra, Lamas Carlos

May 7, 1959
d. Hoare, Samuel John Gurney, Sir

May 8, 1959
b. Lott, Ronnie

May 11, 1959
b. Quinn, Martha

May 12, 1959
b. Christian, Dave

May 14, 1959
b. Vaive, Rick Claude

d. Bechet, Sidney

May 16, 1959
d. Cook, Joe

May 19, 1959
b. Simpson, Nicole Brown

May 20, 1959
b. Pinchot, Bronson Alcott

May 24, 1959
b. Lindbergh, Pelle (Per-Eric)
d. Dulles, John Foster

May 26, 1959
d. Walsh, Ed(ward Augustine)

June 1, 1959
d. Rohmer, Sax

June 9, 1959
d. Windaus, Adolf Otto Reinhold

June 12, 1959
b. Harrison, Jenilee

June 16, 1959
d. Reeves, George

June 18, 1959
d. Barrymore, Ethel Mae Blythe

June 19, 1959
b. DeBarge, Mark

June 20, 1959
b. Ogrodnick, John Alexander

June 21, 1959
b. Chambers, Tom

June 23, 1959
b. Gustafson, Karin

June 24, 1959
d. Starkweather, Charles

June 27, 1959
b. Morgan, Lorrie

June 28, 1959
b. Balukas, Jean
b. Fraser, Brad
d. Shaver, Dorothy

June 30, 1959
d. Vasconcelos (Calderon), Jose

July 3, 1959
d. Bojer, Johan

July 6, 1959
d. Grosz, George Ehrenfried

July 7, 1959
b. Hahn, Jessica
d. Newman, Ernest
d. Yarnell, Harry Ervin

July 11, 1959
b. Vega, Suzanne

July 12, 1959
b. Watts, Rolonda

July 14, 1959
d. Grock

July 15, 1959
d. Bloch, Ernest

July 17, 1959
d. Holiday, Billie
d. Munnings, Alfred James, Sir
d. Tsankov, Aleksandur

July 18, 1959
b. Landers, Audrey

July 19, 1959
b. Treas, Terri

July 20, 1959
d. Leahy, William Daniel

July 26, 1959
b. Spacey, Kevin

July 31, 1959
b. Jordan, Stanley

August 1, 1959
b. Elliott, Joe

August 5, 1959
b. Stastny, Anton
d. Guest, Edgar A(lbert)

August 6, 1959
d. Sturges, Preston

August 8, 1959
d. Hinton, William Augustus

August 14, 1959
b. Johnson, Earvin, Jr.

August 16, 1959
d. Halsey, William Frederick, Jr.
d. Landowska, Wanda Louise

August 18, 1959
d. Helburn, Theresa

August 19, 1959
d. Blind Willie McTell
d. Epstein, Jacob, Sir

August 21, 1959
b. Kaplan, John
b. McMahon, Jim
d. Dunbar, Helen Flanders

August 23, 1959
b. Ricci, Nino
d. Catto, Thomas Sivewright, Baron
d. Thayer, Tiffany Ellsworth

August 28, 1959
d. Lefebvre, Georges

d. Martinu, Bohuslav

September 1, 1959
d. Norworth, Jack

September 6, 1959
d. Gwenn, Edmund
d. Kendall, Kay

September 7, 1959
d. Duplessis, Maurice le Noblet

September 11, 1959
d. Dinwiddie, John Ekin
d. Douglas, Paul

September 13, 1959
d. Adrian

September 14, 1959
b. Berry, John
b. Crosby, Mary Frances
d. Morris, Wayne

September 16, 1959
b. Raines, Tim(othy)

September 18, 1959
b. Sandberg, Ryne (Dee)

September 21, 1959
d. Flexner, Abraham

September 22, 1959
b. Renvall, Johan Bengt Erik
d. Ironside, William Edmund

September 23, 1959
b. Alexander, Jason

September 25, 1959
d. Broderick, Helen

September 26, 1959
b. Gedman, Rich(ard Leo, Jr.)
d. Bandaranaike, S(olomon) W(est)
R(idgeway) D(ias)

September 28, 1959
b. Worrell, Todd Roland

September 29, 1959
d. Bairnsfather, Bruce
d. Richardson, Sid

September 30, 1959
d. Harrison, Ross Granville
d. Holmes, Taylor

October 1, 1959
b. Ndour, Youssou

October 3, 1959
b. Couples, Fred
b. Wagner, Jack Peter

October 5, 1959
b. Lin, Maya Ying

October 6, 1959
d. Berenson, Bernard

October 7, 1959
d. Lanza, Mario

October 9, 1959
d. Tizard, Henry Thomas, Sir

October 10, 1959
d. Ed, Carl Frank Ludwig

October 11, 1959
d. Bell, Bert

October 13, 1959
b. Osmond, Marie

October 14, 1959
b. Pero, A J
d. Flynn, Errol

October 15, 1959
b. Ferguson, Sarah (Margaret)

October 16, 1959
d. Marshall, George Catlett

October 17, 1959
b. Flores, Francisco

October 20, 1959
d. Krauss, Werner

October 21, 1959
b. Bell, George Antonio

October 23, 1959
b. Yankovic, Weird Al
d. Golden, William

October 25, 1959
d. Cline, Genevieve Rose

October 28, 1959
d. Bauersfeld, Walther

October 29, 1959
b. Parsons, David

October 31, 1959
b. Nasland, Mats

November 3, 1959
b. Hartley, Hal

November 5, 1959
b. Adams, Bryan Guy

November 7, 1959
d. McLaglen, Victor

November 10, 1959
b. Phillips, MacKenzie

November 14, 1959
b. Stevenson, Bryan (Allen)
d. Cochrane, Edward Lull

November 15, 1959
d. Wilson, Charles Thomson Rees

November 16, 1959
b. Pavin, Corey

November 17, 1959
d. Villa-Lobos, Heitor

November 19, 1959
d. Tolman, Edward Chace

November 20, 1959
b. Dunne, Dominique
b. Young, Sean

November 21, 1959
d. Baer, Max

November 22, 1959
d. Mallory, Molla

November 23, 1959
b. Caulfield, Maxwell

November 27, 1959
d. Philipe, Gerard

November 28, 1959
d. DeErdely, Francis

November 29, 1959
b. Broten, Neal LaMoy

November 30, 1959
b. Hanika, Sylvia

December 8, 1959
b. Junior, E(ster) J(ames, III)

December 9, 1959
d. Canzoneri, Tony

December 10, 1959
b. Aguirre, Mark (Anthony)

December 11, 1959
d. Bottomley, Jim

December 12, 1959
b. Sheila E

December 13, 1959
b. Whitaker, Johnny

December 14, 1959
d. Spencer, Stanley, Sir

December 15, 1959
b. Bohay, Heidi

December 17, 1959
d. Touhy, Roger

December 21, 1959
b. Joyner, Florence Griffith

December 22, 1959
d. Gray, Gilda

December 23, 1959
d. Halifax, Edward Frederick Lindley
Wood

December 24, 1959
d. Goulding, Edmund

December 27, 1959
d. Reyes, Alfonso

December 28, 1959
b. Walls, Everson Collins

December 30, 1959
b. Ullman, Tracey

December 31, 1959
b. Kilmer, Val
d. Giovannitti, Arturo

1960

b. Berry, Bertice
b. Brandon, Barbara
b. Carruthers, Peter
b. Chuck D
b. Cooper, Douglas
b. Duvall, Camille
b. Eugenides, Jeffrey
b. Farrell, Perry
b. Gibbons, Kaye
b. Gordon, Ed
b. Graham, Nicholas
b. Grant, Rodney A
b. Hawkins, La-Van
b. Henson, Lisa
b. Hermening, Kevin Jay
b. Hoffmann, Jan
b. Jackson, George
b. Jenkins, Sally
b. Kostabi, Mark
b. Lover, Ed
b. Mathabane, Mark
b. Rowell, Victoria (Lynn)
b. RuPaul
b. Signorile, Michelangelo
b. Smith, Roger Guenveur
d. Becker, Jacques
d. Bentley, Gladys
d. Ibanez del Campo, Carlos
d. Rugg, Harold

January 1, 1960
d. Sullavan, Margaret

January 3, 1960
d. Everleigh, Ada
d. Sjostrom, Victor
d. Spry, Constance

January 4, 1960
b. Stipe, Michael
d. Camus, Albert
d. French, Albert

January 5, 1960
b. Kerr, Tim(othy)

January 6, 1960
b. Azinger, Paul

January 8, 1960
d. Haynes, George Edmund

January 10, 1960
d. Laviolette, Jack

January 12, 1960
b. Wilkins, Dominique

d. Shute, Nevil

January 15, 1960
d. Smart, Jack Scott

January 19, 1960
b. Joyner, Al(fred, Jr.)

January 22, 1960
b. Hutchence, Michael

January 23, 1960
d. Suckow, Ruth

January 24, 1960
b. Kinski, Nastassja
d. Ford, Russ(ell William)

January 25, 1960
d. Barrymore, Diana
d. Thorek, Max

January 27, 1960
d. Aranha, Osvaldo

January 28, 1960
d. Hurston, Zora Neale

January 29, 1960
b. Louganis, Greg(ory Efthimios)
b. Julien, Isaac

February 7, 1960
b. Spader, James
d. Henderson, Leon N(esbit)
d. Kurchatov, Igor Vasilyevich

February 8, 1960
d. Austin, John Langshaw

February 9, 1960
d. Dohnanyi, Erno von

February 10, 1960
d. Cape, Herbert Jonathan
d. Stepinac, Alojzije

February 11, 1960
d. Barker, Ernest, Sir

February 12, 1960
d. Clark, Bobby

February 14, 1960
b. Kelly, Jim

February 19, 1960
b. Andrew

February 20, 1960
d. Woolley, Charles Leonard, Sir

February 21, 1960
d. Mountbatten, Edwina

February 22, 1960
d. Borduas, Paul-Emile

February 28, 1960
b. Stratten, Dorothy
d. Olivetti, Adriano

February 29, 1960
d. Brasher, Rex
d. Purvis, Melvin
d. Yust, Walter

March 4, 1960
d. Warren, Leonard

March 7, 1960
b. Carter, Joe
b. Duchovny, David
b. Lendl, Ivan

March 8, 1960
b. Williams, Charles Linwood

March 9, 1960
b. Fiorentino, Linda

March 11, 1960
d. Andrews, Roy Chapman

March 12, 1960
b. Vance, Courtney B.

March 18, 1960
b. Carbonneau, Guy

March 21, 1960
b. Senna, Ayrton

March 22, 1960
d. Arber, Agnes

March 23, 1960
d. Adams, Franklin P(ierce)
d. Hooper, Tom

March 26, 1960
b. Allen, Marcus
b. Grey, Jennifer
d. Keith, Ian

March 27, 1960
b. Mowry, Jess

April 2, 1960
b. Christie, Linford

April 7, 1960
b. Douglas, Buster

April 10, 1960
d. Benjamin, Arthur

April 17, 1960
d. Cochran, Eddie

April 18, 1960
d. Ruml, Beardsley

April 19, 1960
b. Viola, Frank John, Jr.
d. Green, Wilf(red Thomas)

April 21, 1960
b. Goulet, Michel

April 23, 1960
b. Bertinelli, Valerie
b. Clark, Steve

April 24, 1960
d. Laue, Max Theodor Felix von

April 25, 1960
b. Schlicter, Art(hur E)
d. Amanollah Khan
d. Emerson, Hope

April 28, 1960
b. Browning, Tom

April 30, 1960
d. Polacco, Giorgio

May 1, 1960
b. Cauthen, Steve

May 2, 1960
d. Chessman, Caryl Whittier

May 3, 1960
b. Lanier, Jaron (Zepel)

May 8, 1960
d. Dudley, George S

May 9, 1960
b. Gwynn, Tony
b. Nanula, Richard D.

May 10, 1960
b. Bono
d. Schwartz, Maurice

May 11, 1960
d. Rockefeller, John D(avison), Jr.

May 15, 1960
d. Petersham, Miska

May 16, 1960
b. Noah, Yannick Simon Camille

May 18, 1960
b. Kurri, Jarri
d. Wurdemann, Audrey May

May 20, 1960
d. Witte, Edwin Emil

May 21, 1960
b. Hrbek, Kent Alan

May 23, 1960
d. Claude, Georges

May 24, 1960
d. Yen Hsi-shan

May 27, 1960
d. Flagg, James Montgomery

May 28, 1960
d. Zucco, George

May 29, 1960
d. Pasternak, Boris Leonidovich

May 31, 1960
d. Funk, Walther
d. Pauker, Ana

June 1, 1960
d. Patrick, Lester B

June 8, 1960
b. Hucknall, Mick

June 12, 1960
b. Calcavecchia, Mark
d. Tokatyan, Armand

June 18, 1960
d. Norris, Kathleen Thompson

June 20, 1960
d. Kelly, John Brenden

June 23, 1960
b. Deshaies, Jim

June 25, 1960
d. Baade, (Wilhelm Heinrich) Walter

June 27, 1960
b. Durie, Jo
d. Pollitt, Harry

June 28, 1960
b. Elway, John (Albert)

June 29, 1960
b. Hodges, Craig Anthony
d. Patrick, Frank A

July 1, 1960
b. King, Evelyn

July 2, 1960
d. Fowler, Gene

July 5, 1960
d. Partridge, Bellamy

July 6, 1960
d. Bevan, Aneurin

July 7, 1960
b. Sampson, Ralph Lee
d. Bennett, Hugh Hammond
d. Collins, Lee

July 10, 1960
b. Craig, Roger Timothy
b. Ellington, E. David

July 12, 1960
d. Adler, Buddy

July 15, 1960
b. Aames, Willie
b. Alexis, Kim
d. Tibbett, Lawrence Mervil

July 16, 1960
d. Kesselring, Albert
d. Marquand, John Phillips

July 17, 1960
b. Upshaw, Dawn

July 19, 1960
b. Egoyan, Atom

July 20, 1960
b. Witt, Mike

July 21, 1960
b. Mulhern, Matt
d. Hoffman, Al

July 25, 1960
d. Defauw, Desire

July 29, 1960
d. Kluckhohn, Clyde
d. Kluckhorn, Clyde Kay Maben
d. Simon, Richard Leo
d. Diop, David

August 2, 1960
b. Fratianne, Linda

August 5, 1960
d. Meighen, Arthur

August 6, 1960
d. Kemp, Harry (Hibbard)

August 7, 1960
d. Ferragamo, Salvatore
d. Firpo, Luis Angel

August 8, 1960
d. Walker, Danton MacIntyre

August 10, 1960
b. Arquette, Rosanna
b. Banderas, Antonio
d. Lloyd, Frank

August 13, 1960
b. Simpson, Lorna

August 14, 1960
d. Clarke, Fred Clifford

August 16, 1960
b. Hutton, Timothy James

August 17, 1960
b. Penn, Sean
d. Harsh, Vivian Gordon

August 19, 1960
b. Darling, Ron(ald Maurice), Jr.
b. Hebert, Bobby Joseph
d. Cornford, Frances Crofts Darwin
d. Namier, Lewis Bernstein

August 22, 1960
d. Hammerstein, Oscar, II
d. Steinman, David Barnard

August 24, 1960
b. Ripken, Cal(vin Edwin, Jr.)
d. Stouffer, Samuel A.

August 26, 1960
b. Marsalis, Branford

August 28, 1960
b. Samms, Emma

August 29, 1960
d. Baum, Vicki

September 1, 1960
d. Jackson, Aunt Molly
d. Townsend, Francis Everett

September 2, 1960
b. Dickerson, Eric Demetric

September 5, 1960
b. Gault, Willie James
d. Long, Earl Kemp

September 6, 1960
d. Savo, Jimmy

September 7, 1960
d. Pieck, Wilhelm

September 8, 1960
b. Casiraghi, Stefano
d. Pettiford, Oscar

September 9, 1960
b. Grant, Hugh
d. Bjoerling, Jussi

September 10, 1960
b. Bechdel, Alison
d. Rogers, Edith

September 15, 1960
b. Morris, Joe

September 17, 1960
b. Carter, Anthony Calvin

September 20, 1960
d. Goodpasture, E(rnest) W(illiam)

September 22, 1960
b. Babilonia, Tai (Reina)
b. Coleman, Vince(nt Maurice)
b. Jett, Joan
d. Klein, Melanie

September 25, 1960
d. Nichols, Ruth Rowland
d. Post, Emily (Price)

September 27, 1960
d. Pankhurst, Sylvia

September 29, 1960
b. Deer, Rob(ert George)
d. Baillie, John

September 30, 1960
d. Philby, Harold St. John Bridger

October 2, 1960
b. Anderson, Glenn Chris
d. Recto, Claro M.

October 5, 1960
d. Kroeber, Alfred Louis

October 6, 1960
d. Welch, Joseph Nye

October 15, 1960
d. Young, Clara Kimball

October 16, 1960
d. Quinn, Arthur Hobson

October 17, 1960
d. Boucher, Buck

October 18, 1960
b. Van Damme, Jean-Claude

October 19, 1960
b. Davis, Mark William
b. Holliday, Jennifer Yvette

October 25, 1960
d. Ferguson, Harry George

October 29, 1960
d. Andersson, Johan Gunnar

October 30, 1960
b. Maradona, Diego

October 31, 1960
b. Pahlevi, Riza Cyrus
d. Avery, Sewell
d. Davis, Harold Lenoir

November 1, 1960
b. Valenzuela, Fernando

November 2, 1960
b. Aouita, Said
d. Mitropoulos, Dimitri

November 3, 1960
d. Wallace, Bobby

November 5, 1960
d. Bond, Ward
d. Horton, Johnny
d. Sennett, Mack
d. Waymack, W(illiam) W(esley)

November 6, 1960
b. Kerwin, Lance
d. Raeder, Erich

November 9, 1960
d. Mountain Wolf Woman

November 13, 1960
d. Close, Upton

November 14, 1960
d. Catlett, Walter

November 16, 1960
d. Gable, Clark

November 18, 1960
b. Wilde, Kim

November 19, 1960
d. Cooper, Emil
d. Gibbons, Tom

November 20, 1960
d. Rollins, Carl Purington

November 23, 1960
b. Roberts, Robin

November 25, 1960
b. Grant, Amy
b. Kennedy, John F(itzgerald), Jr.

November 27, 1960
b. Nelson, Judd
d. Richberg, Donald R(andall)

November 28, 1960
b. Galliano, John
d. Wright, Richard (Nathaniel)

November 29, 1960
b. Moriarty, Cathy

December 1, 1960
b. Alt, Carol

December 2, 1960
b. Moore, Julianne
b. Savage, Rick

December 3, 1960
b. Hannah, Daryl
b. Ramsey, Mike

December 5, 1960
d. Teague, Walter Dorwin

December 10, 1960
b. Branagh, Kenneth (Charles)

December 13, 1960
d. Thomas, John Charles

December 14, 1960
d. Ratoff, Gregory

December 21, 1960
b. Van Slyke, Andy

December 22, 1960
b. Basquiat, Jean-Michel

December 25, 1960
d. Garrod, Heathcote William

December 26, 1960
d. Bellanca, Giuseppe Mario

December 28, 1960
b. Bourque, Ray(mond Jean)

December 29, 1960
d. Phillpotts, Eden

December 31, 1960
d. Howe, Clarence Decatur

1961

b. Baumgartner, Bruce
b. Butler, Paul D.
b. Campbell, Luther
b. Curry, Donald
b. D'Abo, Maryam
b. Daley, Rosie
b. Davidovich, Lolita
b. Ferrell, Rachelle
b. Harris, Leslie

b. Hill, Lynn
b. Johnson, Bill
b. Kevin, Clash
b. King, Dexter (Scott)
b. Kiraly, Karch
b. Kitaen, Tawny
b. Larson, Jonathan
b. Lemmons, Kasi
b. McNally, T. M.
b. Mould, Bob
b. Oldham, Todd
b. Perlman, Steve
b. Potzsch, Anett
b. Rhames, (Ir)ving
b. Sasway, Benjamin H
b. Sweat, Keith
b. Vai, Steve
b. Vassallo, Jesse
b. Walker, T. J.
b. Wayans, Damon
b. Yamashita, Kazuhito
d. Amiet, Cuno
d. Astbury, William
d. Brown, Charlotte (Eugenia)
  Hawkins
d. Bullard, Eugene
d. Hovland, Carl I.

January 3, 1961
b. Vanity

January 4, 1961
d. Fitzgerald, Barry
d. Schroedinger, Erwin

January 8, 1961
d. Rowe, Schoolboy

January 9, 1961
d. Balch, Emily G

January 10, 1961
b. Salerno-Sonnenberg, Nadja
d. Hammett, Dashiell

January 13, 1961
b. Louis-Dreyfus, Julia
d. Ring, Blanche
d. Robinson, Henry Morton

January 18, 1961
b. Messier, Mark (Douglas)
d. Dooley, Thomas Anthony, III
d. Lumumba, Patrice

January 21, 1961
d. Cone, Russell Glenn

January 23, 1961
d. Lawrie, Lee

January 24, 1961
d. Gilbert, A(lfred) C(arleton)

January 26, 1961
b. Gretzky, Wayne

January 30, 1961
b. Watley, Jody

January 31, 1961
b. Cole, Lloyd
d. Thompson, Dorothy

b. Cameron, David

February 3, 1961
d. Wong, Anna May (Lu Tsong)

February 4, 1961
b. Savard, Denis Joseph

February 9, 1961
b. Kruk, John
d. Tydings, Millard Evelyn

February 10, 1961
b. Stephanopoulos, George (Robert)

February 16, 1961
d. Vance, Dazzy

February 17, 1961
d. Naldi, Nita

February 20, 1961
b. Lundquist, Steve
d. Gardner, Mary Sewall
d. Grainger, Percy Aldridge

February 21, 1961
b. Atkins, Christopher

February 22, 1961
d. DeCuevas, Marquis

February 26, 1961
d. Mohammed V

February 27, 1961
b. Worthy, James Ager

March 1, 1961
b. Rozier, Mike

March 3, 1961
d. Wittgenstein, Paul

March 4, 1961
b. Mancini, Ray

March 8, 1961
b. Murphy, Larry
d. Beecham, Thomas, Sir

March 14, 1961
b. Puckett, Kirby
d. Marcosson, Isaac Frederick

March 15, 1961
b. Cummings, Terry
b. Fabio

March 18, 1961
b. Warner, Curt

March 20, 1961
b. Baker, Kathy
b. Gable, John Clark
b. Harrison, Kathryn

March 21, 1961
d. Arnold, Leslie Philip

March 23, 1961
d. Mason, Max

March 24, 1961
d. Bailey, H(enry) C(hristopher)

March 28, 1961
d. Crosley, Powel, Jr.

March 31, 1961
b. Brown, Ron(ald James)
d. Faber, Geoffrey Cust, Sir

April 2, 1961
d. Riegger, Wallingford

April 3, 1961
b. Murphy, Eddie

April 4, 1961
d. Sachse, Leopold

April 5, 1961
d. Canby, Henry Seidel

April 6, 1961
d. Bordet, Jules Jean Baptiste Vincent

April 7, 1961
d. Bell, Vanessa
d. Jordan, Marian Driscoll

April 8, 1961
d. Lehman, Hughie

April 9, 1961
d. Zog I

April 17, 1961
b. Esiason, Boomer
d. Anderson, Elda Emma

April 20, 1961
b. Mattingly, Don(ald Arthur)

April 21, 1961
d. Melton, James

April 22, 1961
b. Allen, Byron

April 27, 1961
d. DelRuth, Roy

April 28, 1961
d. Connolly, Tommy

April 30, 1961
b. Thomas, Isiah
d. Fauset, Jessie Redmon

May 3, 1961
d. Boon, Dickie
d. Merleau-Ponty, Maurice

May 4, 1961
b. McDonough, Mary Elizabeth
d. Stewart, Anita

May 5, 1961
b. Clooney, George

May 6, 1961
d. Blaga, Lucien

May 7, 1961
d. Bell, James Ford
d. Snow, Carmel White

May 13, 1961
b. Rodman, Dennis (Keith)
d. Cooper, Gary

May 14, 1961
b. Roth, Tim

May 15, 1961
d. Gorman, Tommy

May 19, 1961
d. George, Grace
d. Howard, Joseph Edgar

May 23, 1961
d. Davis, Joan

May 29, 1961
b. Etheridge, Melissa
d. Gesell, Arnold

May 30, 1961
d. Trujillo (Molina), Rafael Leonidas

June 1, 1961
b. Coffey, Paul (Douglas)

June 2, 1961
d. DeWohl, Louis
d. Kaufman, George S(imon)

June 3, 1961
b. Hart, Charles

June 4, 1961
b. DeBarge, El(dra)

June 6, 1961
d. Jung, Carl Gustav

June 7, 1961
d. Barnard, Chester Irving

June 9, 1961
b. Fox, Michael J.
d. Chambers, Whittaker
d. Guerin, Camille

June 13, 1961
d. Jones, Benjamin Allyn

June 14, 1961
b. Boy George

June 15, 1961
d. Torroja (y Miret), Eduardo

June 17, 1961
d. Chandler, Jeff

June 18, 1961
d. Gaedel, Eddie

June 24, 1961
b. Reed, Ralph

June 25, 1961
d. Ferguson, Miriam Amanda

June 26, 1961
b. LeMond, Greg(ory James)
d. Fearing, Kenneth Flexner

June 28, 1961
b. Schroeder, Jay Brian

June 30, 1961
d. DeForest, Lee

July 1, 1961
b. Diana, Princess of Wales
b. Lewis, Carl

July 2, 1961
b. McNichol, Jimmy
d. Hemingway, Ernest (Miller)

July 4, 1961
d. Celine, Louis-Ferdinand
d. Destouches, Louis-Ferdinand

July 8, 1961
b. Keith, Toby

July 9, 1961
d. Marshal, Alan

July 12, 1961
d. DeLaRoche, Mazo

July 15, 1961
b. Whitaker, Forest

July 17, 1961
d. Cobb, Ty(rus Raymond)
d. Reulbach, Ed(ward Marvin)

July 18, 1961
b. McGovern, Elizabeth

July 23, 1961
b. Harrelson, Woody

July 30, 1961
b. Fishburne, Laurence

August 1, 1961
d. Redman, Ben Ray

August 7, 1961
d. Buchman, Frank Nathan Daniel
d. Robinson, Claude Everett

August 9, 1961
d. Smith, Walter Bedell

August 10, 1961
d. Peterkin, Julia Mood

August 13, 1961
d. Sironi, Mario

August 14, 1961
d. Breuil, Henri Abbe

August 16, 1961
b. Okoye, Christian

August 18, 1961
d. Hand, Learned
d. MacFarlane, Willie

August 20, 1961
d. Bridgman, Percy Williams

August 25, 1961
b. Cyrus, Billy Ray

August 26, 1961
d. Russell, Gail

August 27, 1961
b. Adams, Yolanda

August 30, 1961
d. Coburn, Charles Douville

September 1, 1961
b. Myers, Dee Dee
d. Foster, William Zebulon
d. Saarinen, Eero

September 2, 1961
b. Lang, K(atherine) D(awn)

September 3, 1961
d. Gross, Robert Ellsworth

September 10, 1961
d. Carrillo, Leo

September 11, 1961
b. Washington, Patrice Clarke

September 15, 1961
b. Marino, Dan

September 18, 1961
d. Hammarskjold, Dag (Hjalmar Agne Carl)

September 21, 1961
b. Oxenberg, Catherine
d. Dickson, Earle Ensign

September 22, 1961
b. Baio, Scott Vincent
d. Davies, Marion

September 24, 1961
d. Welles, Sumner

September 25, 1961
b. Locklear, Heather
d. Fay, Frank

September 26, 1961
d. Eichelberger, Robert Lawrence
d. Wilson, Charles Erwin

September 27, 1961
d. Doolittle, Hilda

October 1, 1961
d. Cook, Donald
d. Reid Dick, William, Sir

October 2, 1961
d. Lewis, Essington

October 4, 1961
d. Petri, Angelo
d. Weber, Max

October 7, 1961
b. Landers, Judy

October 8, 1961
d. Hertz, John Daniel

October 11, 1961
b. Young, Steve
d. Marx, Chico

October 13, 1961
d. Deren, Maya

October 14, 1961
b. Mizrahi, Isaac

October 18, 1961
b. Marsalis, Wynton
b. Moran, Erin
d. Darwin, Bernard Richard Meirion

October 19, 1961
d. Gunnison, Foster
d. Jaeger, Werner Wilhelm
d. Osmena, Sergio, Jr.

October 22, 1961
d. Schenck, Joseph M

October 28, 1961
d. Stuart, Bruce

October 29, 1961
b. Crosby, Nathaniel
b. Jackson, Randy
d. McClintic, Guthrie

October 30, 1961
d. Einaudi, Luigi

October 31, 1961
d. John, Augustus Edwin
d. Vertes, Marcel

November 1, 1961
d. McCracken, Joan

November 2, 1961
d. Thurber, James Grover

November 5, 1961
d. Tobias, Channing Heggie

November 8, 1961
b. Garrett, Leif

November 12, 1961
b. Comaneci, Nadia

November 13, 1961
d. Biddle, Anthony Joseph

November 15, 1961
d. Ferguson, Elsie

November 16, 1961
d. Rayburn, Sam(uel Taliaferro)

November 17, 1961
b. VanKamp, Merete
d. Kauff, Benny

November 19, 1961
b. Ryan, Meg

November 21, 1961
b. Hemingway, Mariel

November 24, 1961
d. Chatterton, Ruth
d. Wenner-Gren, Axel (Lenard)

November 26, 1961
d. Bridges, Styles

November 30, 1961
d. Zemurray, Samuel

December 6, 1961
d. Fanon, Frantz (Omar)

December 7, 1961
d. Russell, Blair

December 10, 1961
d. Hupp, Louis Gorham

December 13, 1961
d. Moses, Grandma

December 18, 1961
b. Orser, Brian

December 19, 1961
b. White, Reggie

December 20, 1961
d. Hart, Moss

December 24, 1961
d. Hamilton, Charles Harold St. John
d. Hillyer, Robert

December 25, 1961
d. Brewster, (Ralph) Owen
d. Loewi, Otto

December 27, 1961
d. Bercovici, Konrad

December 28, 1961
d. Wilson, Edith Bolling (Galt)

December 30, 1961
b. Johnson, Ben

December 31, 1961
b. Coupland, Douglas

1962

b. Akin, Phil
b. Baldwin, Adam
b. Braugher, Andre
b. Carruthers, Kitty

b. Enke, Karin
b. Enya
b. Harrell, Andre (O'Neal)
b. Hudlin, Reginald
b. Jones, Star(let Marie)
b. Khanga, Yelena
b. Lee, Joie
b. Meinhold, Keith
b. Murray, Lenda
b. O'Donnell, Rosie
b. O'Malley, Susan
b. Payne, Allen
b. Zuniga, Daphne
d. Dewson, Mary Williams
d. Goncharova, Natalia
d. Mattei, Enrico
d. Mills, C(harles) Wright
d. Portinari, Candido

January 1, 1962
d. Fairless, Benjamin F
d. Giesler, Jerry

January 2, 1962
d. Dye, Babe

January 11, 1962
d. Adler, Elmer

January 13, 1962
b. Mitchell, Kevin (Darrell)
d. Kovacs, Ernie

January 16, 1962
d. Mestrovic, Ivan
d. Tawney, Richard Henry
d. Toffenetti, Dario Louis

January 17, 1962
b. Carrey, Jim
d. Achterberg, Gerrit

January 19, 1962
b. Sabo, Chris(topher Andrew)
d. Noble, Reg

January 20, 1962
d. Jeffers, (John) Robinson

January 21, 1962
d. Cockrell, Ewing

January 25, 1962
b. Chelios, Chris

January 26, 1962
d. Luciano, Lucky
d. O'Neill, Steve

January 27, 1962
d. LeSueur, Percy

January 29, 1962
d. Kreisler, Fritz
d. Johnson, Chic

February 2, 1962
d. Budd, Ralph

February 4, 1962
b. Black, Clint

February 5, 1962
b. Leigh, Jennifer Jason
d. Ibert, Jacques (Francois Antoine)

February 6, 1962
b. Rose, Axl

February 7, 1962
b. Brooks, Garth
b. McCrory, Milton

February 12, 1962
d. Darling, Jay Norwood

February 17, 1962
b. Phillips, Lou Diamond
d. Walter, Bruno

February 19, 1962
d. Barton, James
d. Papanicolaou, George Nicholas

February 24, 1962
d. Hu Shih

February 26, 1962
b. Gruber, Kelly

February 27, 1962
b. Show, Grant

March 1, 1962
d. Piccard, Auguste

March 2, 1962
b. Steinbach, Terry Lee
d. Kiesling, Walt(er)

March 3, 1962
b. Joyner-Kersee, Jackie
b. Walker, Herschel

March 12, 1962
b. Strawberry, Darryl (Eugene)

March 15, 1962
b. D'Arby, Terence Trent
d. Compton, Arthur Holly

March 17, 1962
d. Busoni, Rafaello

March 18, 1962
b. McMurtry, James Lawrence
d. Viereck, George Sylvester

March 21, 1962
b. Broderick, Matthew

March 26, 1962
b. Blab, Uwe Konstantine
b. Stockton, John (Houston)
d. Fischer, Anton Otto
d. Savage, Augusta Christine

March 27, 1962
d. Britton, Jack

March 28, 1962
d. Neyland, Robert Reese

April 1, 1962
d. Ghelderode, Michel de

April 9, 1962
d. Lamb, Harold Albert

April 11, 1962
d. Curtiz, Michael

April 12, 1962
d. Pevsner, Antoine

April 16, 1962
d. Amrouche, Jean

April 17, 1962
d. Fazenda, Louise

April 18, 1962
b. Marshall, Wilbur Buddyhia

April 19, 1962
b. Unser, Al, Jr.

April 20, 1962
d. Whalen, Grover (Michael)
A(loysius)

April 21, 1962
d. Page, Frederick Handley, Sir

April 24, 1962
d. Hackett, Francis

May 2, 1962
b. Bon Jovi, Jon

May 6, 1962
d. Grant, Gordon
d. Woolley, Monty

May 7, 1962
d. Currie, Barton Wood

May 11, 1962
d. Speicher, Eugene Edward

May 12, 1962
b. Estevez, Emilio
d. Rivers, Thomas Milton

May 13, 1962
d. Calkins, Dick
d. Dean, Henry Trendley
d. Kline, Franz Joseph

May 17, 1962
d. Frazier, Edward Franklin

May 23, 1962
b. Duffy, Karen

May 26, 1962
b. Francis, Genie
d. Gibson, Wilfred Wilson

May 28, 1962
b. Gift, Roland

May 29, 1962
b. Davis, Eric Keith

May 31, 1962
d. Eichmann, Adolf

June 2, 1962
d. Sackville-West, Vita

June 4, 1962
d. Beebe, William
d. McCarthy, Clem

June 6, 1962
d. Profaci, Joe

June 8, 1962
d. Braithwaite, William Stanley
Beaumont
d. Freyssinet, Eugene

June 9, 1962
d. Adler, Polly

June 12, 1962
d. Ireland, John Nicholson

June 13, 1962
b. Sheedy, Ally
d. Goossens, Eugene, Sir

June 15, 1962
d. Cortot, Alfred-Denis

June 16, 1962
b. Joyner, Wally

June 18, 1962
d. Sargent, George

June 19, 1962
d. Borzage, Frank

June 22, 1962
b. Drexler, Clyde
d. Shaaban Robert

June 26, 1962
d. Wolfson, Erwin Service

June 28, 1962
d. Cochrane, Mickey

July 3, 1962
b. Cruise, Tom

July 4, 1962
b. Shriver, Pam(ela Howard)
d. Christie, John

July 5, 1962
d. Niebuhr, Helmut Richard

July 6, 1962
d. Faulkner, William

July 8, 1962
b. Osborne, Joan

July 10, 1962
b. Hawkins, Steven (Wayne)

July 11, 1962
d. Hutton, Edward F

d. Young, Owen D

July 13, 1962
d. Wald, Jerry

July 15, 1962
d. Maison, Rene

July 18, 1962
d. Houdry, Eugene Jules

July 19, 1962
b. Edwards, Anthony
d. Davis, Clyde Brion

July 21, 1962
d. Trevelyan, George Macaulay

July 22, 1962
b. Robertson, Alvin

July 23, 1962
b. LaSalle, Eriq
d. Moore, Victor

July 25, 1962
b. Drabek, Doug(las Dean)

July 27, 1962
d. Aldington, Richard (Edward
  Godfree)
d. Konwitschny, Franz

July 29, 1962
d. Fisher, R(onald) A(ylmer)

July 30, 1962
d. McCormick, Myron

July 31, 1962
b. Murray, Troy
b. Snipes, Wesley

August 3, 1962
d. Cromwell, Dean Bartlett

August 4, 1962
b. Clemens, (William) Roger

August 5, 1962
b. Ewing, Patrick Aloysius
d. Monroe, Marilyn

August 9, 1962
d. Hesse, Hermann

August 10, 1962
d. Husing, Ted

August 11, 1962
d. Cardozo, W. Warrick

August 12, 1962
d. Holman, Eugene

August 13, 1962
d. Luhan, Mabel (Ganson) Dodge

August 15, 1962
d. Bain, Dan

August 16, 1962
d. Martin, Mungo

August 21, 1962
b. Weber, Pete(r)

August 23, 1962
d. Gibson, Hoot

August 24, 1962
b. Louis, Errol T.

August 25, 1962
b. Nasrin, Taslima

August 26, 1962
d. Chase, Richard Volney
d. Stefansson, Vihjalmur

August 29, 1962
b. DeMornay, Rebecca

September 2, 1962
d. Blair, William Richards

September 3, 1962
d. Cummings, E(dward) E(stlin)

September 7, 1962
d. Blixen, Karen Christentze, Baroness
d. Louis, Morris

September 9, 1962
b. McNichol, Kristy
d. Rooney, Pat

September 13, 1962
d. Duffy, Edmund

September 17, 1962
b. Rogers, Don(ald Lavert)

September 21, 1962
b. Morrow, Rob

September 23, 1962
d. Hamilton, Patrick

September 26, 1962
b. Anderson, Melissa Sue

September 27, 1962
d. Skidmore, Louis

September 28, 1962
b. Fuhr, Grant Scott

October 1, 1962
b. Morales, Esai
d. Bemelmans, Ludwig

October 2, 1962
b. Rypien, Mark
d. Lovejoy, Frank

October 6, 1962
d. Beach, Sylvia
d. Browning, Tod

October 10, 1962
d. Allen, Vivian Beaumont

d. Boswell, Connee

October 12, 1962
b. Fernandez, Sid

October 13, 1962
b. Rice, Jerry (Lee)

October 14, 1962
d. Rombauer, Irma von Starkloff

October 16, 1962
b. Bol, Manute

October 17, 1962
b. Judge, Mike

October 19, 1962
b. Holyfield, Evander

October 20, 1962
d. Douglass, Andrew Ellicott

October 22, 1962
d. Marcoux, Vanni

October 23, 1962
b. Flutie, Doug(las Richard)
d. Telva, Marion

October 24, 1962
b. Wong, B D

October 26, 1962
d. Beavers, Louise

October 27, 1962
d. Hutton, Bouse

October 29, 1962
d. Resor, Stanley Burnett

November 1, 1962
b. Kiedis, Anthony

November 2, 1962
d. Lattuada, Felice

November 3, 1962
d. Curtice, Harlow Herbert

November 4, 1962
b. Macchio, Ralph George, Jr.
d. Eklund, Carl Robert

November 5, 1962
d. Garis, Howard Roger

November 7, 1962
d. Roosevelt, Eleanor

November 8, 1962
d. O'Brien, Willis Harold

November 11, 1962
b. Moore, Demi

November 15, 1962
d. Irene

November 17, 1962
d. Ahearn, Frank
d. Davis, Arthur Vining

November 18, 1962
d. Bax, Clifford
d. Bohr, Niels Henrik David
d. Chavez, Dennis

November 19, 1962
b. Foster, Jodie

November 22, 1962
b. Fields, Cleo
d. Coty, Rene (Jules Gustave)

November 25, 1962
d. Walker, Stanley

November 28, 1962
d. Wilhelmina

November 30, 1962
b. Jackson, Bo
b. Turner, Janine

December 5, 1962
d. Wallant, Edward Lewis

December 7, 1962
d. Flagstad, Kirsten
d. Newsom, Bobo

December 11, 1962
b. Williams, Curtis

December 12, 1962
b. Austin, Tracy Ann

December 13, 1962
d. Sokolsky, George E

December 15, 1962
d. Laughton, Charles

December 16, 1962
b. Perry, William
d. Dale, Chester

December 17, 1962
b. Brown, Eddie Lee
d. Mitchell, Thomas

December 18, 1962
d. Mattingley, Garrett

December 22, 1962
b. Fiennes, Ralph

December 25, 1962
b. Graham, Lawrence Otis
d. Austin, Warren R(obinson)
d. Davis, Tobe

December 26, 1962
d. Langer, Lawrence

December 30, 1962
d. Lovejoy, Arthur Oncken
   (Schauffler)
d. Rosbaud, Hans

1963

b. Baldwin, William
b. Belle, Regina
b. Charles, Suzette
b. Cole, Holly
b. Cruz, Stevie
b. Elbegdorj, Tsahiagiyn
b. Holdereid, Kristine
b. Kaprisky, Valerie
b. Knievel, Robbie
b. Kool Moe Dee
b. Mallon, Meg
b. McCarthy, Andrew
b. Mc Kinney, Tamara
b. Norfolk, Lawrence
b. Quirot, Ana
b. Shocked, Michelle
b. Soderbergh, Steven
b. Stewart, Jon
b. Tripplehorn, Jean
b. Waitt, Tedd
b. Wolf, Naomi
b. Xuxa
b. Young, Candy
d. Brousse, Amy Elizabeth Thorpe
d. Burgess, Guy Francis de Moncy
d. Carder, Frederick
d. Clark, John Maurice
d. Harris, Abram Lincoln, Jr.
d. Kaufmann, Ezekiel
d. Morin, Paul
d. Sutton, John

January 1, 1963
d. Kerr, Robert Samuel
d. Mead, George Houk

January 2, 1963
d. Carson, Jack
d. Powell, Dick

January 5, 1963
d. Hornsby, Rogers

January 6, 1963
d. Vandercook, John Womack
d. Young, Stark

January 10, 1963
b. Leveille, Norm(and)

January 11, 1963
b. Caulkins, Tracy

January 18, 1963
d. Gaitskell, Hugh (Todd Naylor)

January 21, 1963
b. Olajuwon, Hakeem

January 24, 1963
d. Harbach, Otto Abels

January 26, 1963
b. Ridgeley, Andrew
d. Olsen, Ole

January 28, 1963
d. Farrow, John Villiers
d. Piccard, Jean Felix

January 29, 1963
d. Frost, Robert Lee

January 30, 1963
d. Poulenc, Francis

February 2, 1963
d. Gaxton, William

February 3, 1963
b. Berg, Matraca

February 4, 1963
d. Weldon, John

February 6, 1963
b. Griffith, Mark Winston
d. Abd el-Krim el-Khatabi, Mohamed
ben

February 9, 1963
b. Tritt, Travis
d. Kassem, Abdul Karim (el)

February 10, 1963
b. Dykstra, Lenny
d. Taylor, J(ohn) H(enry)

February 11, 1963
d. Plath, Sylvia

February 13, 1963
d. Reynolds, Robert Rice

February 14, 1963
d. Shannon, Fred Albert

February 17, 1963
b. Jordan, Michael (Jeffery)
d. Lockridge, Frances Louise

February 18, 1963
d. Blue, Monte

February 19, 1963
b. Mandlikova, Hana
b. Seal
d. Brophy, John

February 20, 1963
b. Barkley, Charles Wade

February 23, 1963
b. Bonilla, Bobby
d. Russell, Ernie

February 24, 1963
b. Vernon, Mike
d. Asbury, Herbert

February 25, 1963
d. Herskovits, Melville Jean

February 27, 1963
d. Makonnen Endalkacaw

February 28, 1963
d. Prasad, Rajendra
d. Rixey, Eppa Jephtha

March 3, 1963
d. Anderson, Dorothy Hansine
d. Eddy, Sherwood

March 4, 1963
d. Belin, Edouard
d. Olds, Irving S
d. Williams, William Carlos

March 5, 1963
d. Cline, Patsy

March 7, 1963
b. Dayne, Taylor

March 8, 1963
d. Webb, Walter Prescott

March 9, 1963
d. Melcher, Frederic Gershon

March 10, 1963
b. Rubin, Rick

March 12, 1963
d. Oxnam, G(arfield) Bromley

March 16, 1963
d. Beveridge, William Henry, Lord

March 18, 1963
b. Williams, Vanessa

March 25, 1963
d. Johnson, Moose

March 27, 1963
b. Cunningham, Randall
b. Tarantino, Quentin

March 28, 1963
b. King, Bernice Albertine
d. Templeton, Alec

March 29, 1963
b. Hammer
b. Hu Na

April 4, 1963
b. Green, Benny
b. Hawerchuk, Dale
d. Robards, Jason

April 5, 1963
d. Oud, Jacobus Johannes Pieter

April 6, 1963
d. Struve, Otto

April 8, 1963
b. Lennon, Julian

April 9, 1963
d. Jones, Joe

April 13, 1963
b. Kasparov, Garry Kimovich

April 14, 1963
b. Cooper, Cynthia

April 18, 1963
b. O'Brien, Conan

April 19, 1963
d. Griswold, Alfred Whitney

April 21, 1963
d. Robertson, Dennis Holme

April 29, 1963
d. Corwin, Edward Samuel
d. Traphagen, Ethel Leigh

May 2, 1963
d. Brooks, Van Wyck

May 6, 1963
b. Ferri, Alessandra Maria
d. Weems, Ted

May 7, 1963
d. Von Karman, Theodore

May 9, 1963
d. Kuykendall, Ralph Simpson

May 10, 1963
d. Lipscomb, Eugene

May 11, 1963
b. Richardson, Natasha
d. Gasser, Herbert Spencer

May 18, 1963
d. Davis, Ernie

May 19, 1963
d. Matzenauer, Margaret

May 23, 1963
d. Howard, Eddy

May 24, 1963
b. Dumars, Joe, III
d. James, Elmore

May 25, 1963
d. Dryfoos, Orvil Eugene

May 27, 1963
b. Dean, Laura
d. Ribeiro, Aquilino Gomez

May 29, 1963
b. Whelchel, Lisa

May 31, 1963
b. Orban, Viktor
d. Hamilton, Edith

June 1, 1963
d. Gougelman, Pierre

June 3, 1963
d. John, XXIII
d. John XXIII

June 4, 1963
b. McDaniel, Xavier Maurice

June 5, 1963
d. Baziotes, William
d. Ennis, Skinnay

June 7, 1963
d. Pitts, Zasu

June 9, 1963
b. Depp, Johnny

June 10, 1963
b. Shue, Elizabeth
d. Root, Jack

June 11, 1963
d. Kidder, Alfred Vincent

June 12, 1963
d. Cunningham, Andrew Browne,
   Viscount
d. Evers, Medgar Wiley

June 15, 1963
b. Hunt, Helen

June 17, 1963
d. Alanbrooke, Alan Francis Brooke,
   1st Viscount
d. Powys, John Cowper

June 18, 1963
b. Smith, Bruce (Bernard)
d. Armendariz, Pedro

June 19, 1963
b. Abdul, Paula (Julie)

June 25, 1963
b. Gilmour, Doug
b. Michael, George

June 28, 1963
d. Baker, Frank

June 29, 1963
b. Mutter, Anne-Sophie

July 1, 1963
d. Chautemps, Camille

July 2, 1963
d. Nicholson, Seth Barnes
d. Patterson, Alicia

July 3, 1963
d. Bouche, Rene Robert

July 4, 1963
d. Foyle, William Alfred

July 7, 1963
d. Kearns, Jack

July 11, 1963
d. Kalmus, Herbert Thomas

July 12, 1963
d. Grant, Harry Johnston

July 13, 1963
b. Carpenter, Bobby

b. Webb, Spud

July 14, 1963
d. Janney, Russell Dixon

July 16, 1963
b. Cates, Phoebe

July 17, 1963
b. Thigpen, Bobby

July 24, 1963
b. Krone, Julie
b. Malone, Karl

July 27, 1963
d. Dauss, George August
d. Morgan, Garrett Augustus

July 30, 1963
b. Kudrow, Lisa
d. Hurley, Patrick Jay

August 1, 1963
b. Coolio
d. Roethke, Theodore (Huebner)

August 2, 1963
d. LaFarge, Oliver

August 3, 1963
d. Scott, Evelyn

August 7, 1963
b. Kennedy, Patrick Bouvier
b. Roberts, Marcus

August 8, 1963
b. Lewis, Carol

August 9, 1963
b. Houston, Whitney
d. Kennedy, Patrick Bouvier

August 10, 1963
d. Kefauver, Estes

August 11, 1963
d. Seymour, Charles

August 14, 1963
d. Odets, Clifford

August 17, 1963
d. Barthelmess, Richard
d. Gardner, Ed(ward Francis)

August 19, 1963
b. Stamos, John

August 22, 1963
b. DeBarge, James
d. Morris, William Richard
d. Nuffield, William Richard Morris

August 23, 1963
d. Bottome, Phyllis
d. Gray, Glen

August 24, 1963
d. Smith, Hooley

August 27, 1963
d. DuBois, W(illiam) E(dward)
   B(urghardt)

August 31, 1963
d. Braque, Georges

September 3, 1963
d. MacNeice, Louis

September 4, 1963
b. Vanbiesbrouck, John
d. Schuman, Robert

September 7, 1963
b. Eazy-E

September 9, 1963
d. Fuess, Claude Moore

September 10, 1963
b. Johnson, Randy

September 11, 1963
d. Low, David Alexander Cecil, Sir

September 15, 1963
d. Hatch, Carl A

September 16, 1963
b. Marx, Richard

September 21, 1963
b. Brown, Donald
b. Fielder, Cecil Grant

September 24, 1963
d. Chase, Mary Agnes

September 26, 1963
d. Pennell, Joseph Stanley

September 27, 1963
d. Christiansen, Arthur

September 28, 1963
d. Raisa, Rosa

October 1, 1963
b. McGwire, Mark (David)
d. Nordstrom, John

October 4, 1963
d. Key, Valdimer Orlando, Jr.

October 7, 1963
d. Hadamard, Jacques Salomon

October 8, 1963
d. Adams, Frank Ramsay

October 11, 1963
d. Piaf, Edith

October 12, 1963
d. Cocteau, Jean

October 15, 1963
d. Kirk, Alan Goodrich
d. Smith, Horton

October 22, 1963
b. Boitano, Brian
d. Jellinek, Elvin Morton

October 25, 1963
b. Nelson, Tracy

October 26, 1963
b. Merchant, Natalie

October 28, 1963
d. Connally, Tom

October 29, 1963
d. Menjou, Adolphe Jean

October 31, 1963
b. McGriff, Fred(erick Stanley)
d. Daniell, Henry

November 1, 1963
b. Allen, Rick
d. Maxwell, Elsa

November 3, 1963
d. Ngo-Dinh-Diem

November 4, 1963
b. McArdle, Andrea

November 5, 1963
b. O'Neal, Tatum

November 6, 1963
d. Mannix, Daniel

November 10, 1963
b. Powell, Mike

November 12, 1963
d. Hodge, John Reed

November 13, 1963
b. Testaverde, Vinny
d. Murray, Margaret Alice

November 15, 1963
d. Reiner, Fritz

November 16, 1963
b. Garrison, Zina

November 18, 1963
b. Bias, Len

November 21, 1963
b. Sheridan, Nicollette
d. Bartlett, Francis Alonzo
d. Stroud, Robert Franklin

November 22, 1963
d. Huxley, Aldous (Leonard)
d. Kennedy, John F(itzgerald)
d. Lewis, C(live) S(taples)

November 24, 1963
d. Ostenso, Martha
d. Oswald, Lee Harvey

November 25, 1963
b. Kosar, Bernie, Jr.

November 26, 1963
d. Galli-Curci, Amelita

November 28, 1963
b. Weiss, Walt(er William, Jr.)
d. Silver, Abba Hillel
d. Wrather, William Embry

November 29, 1963
b. Auguste, Rose-Anne

November 30, 1963
d. Baker, Phil
d. Hatlo, Jimmy

December 2, 1963
d. Sabu

December 3, 1963
d. Bentley, Elizabeth Terrill

December 4, 1963
b. Bubka, Sergei (Nazarovich)
d. Hamer, Robert

December 5, 1963
b. Hamilton, Carrie
d. Lehman, Herbert Henry

December 8, 1963
d. Sarit Thanarat

December 9, 1963
d. Fagunwa, D(aniel) O(lorunfemi)
d. Miller, Perry Gilbert Eddy

December 14, 1963
d. Washington, Dinah

December 18, 1963
b. McNeil, Lori

December 19, 1963
b. Beals, Jennifer

December 24, 1963
d. Tzara, Tristan

December 26, 1963
d. Shubert, Jacob J

December 27, 1963
b. Cohen, Anthony

December 28, 1963
d. Hindemith, Paul
d. Liebling, Abbot Joseph

1964

b. Armstrong, Debbie
b. Bezos, Jeff
b. Biellmann, Denise
b. Cheadle, Don
b. Curren, Tommy
b. Curry, Mark
b. Henson, Brian
b. Hounsou, Djimon
b. Jones, Rosie
b. Kinnear, Greg
b. Malandro, Kristina

b. Mataya, Ewa
b. Miller, Cheryl
b. Myers, Mike
b. Owado, Masako
b. Perez, Rosie
b. Sister Souljah
b. Sullivan, Andrew
b. Tartt, Donna (Louise)
b. Yearwood, Trisha
b. Yoshimoto, Banana
b. Zurbriggen, Pirmin
d. Farah, James
d. Garrigou-Lagrange, Reginald Marie
d. Larionov, Mikhail

January 2, 1964
b. Whitaker, Pernell

January 4, 1964
d. Dumke, Ralph

January 7, 1964
b. Cage, Nicolas

January 9, 1964
d. Halide Edip Adivar

January 15, 1964
d. Teagarden, Jack

January 17, 1964
d. Allen, Arthur Augustus
d. White, T(erence) H(anbury)
d. Woodcock, Amos Walter Wright

January 20, 1964
b. Guillen, Ozzie

January 21, 1964
d. Schildkraut, Joseph

January 22, 1964
d. Blitzstein, Marc

January 23, 1964
d. Horst, Louis

January 27, 1964
b. Fonda, Bridget
b. Reagon, Toshi

January 29, 1964
d. Anderson, Mary
d. Ladd, Alan

February 3, 1964
d. Lewis, Clarence Irving

February 4, 1964
d. Conroy, Frank

February 6, 1964
d. Aguinaldo, Emilio

February 9, 1964
d. Chotzinoff, Samuel

February 11, 1964
b. Crow, Sheryl

February 15, 1964
b. Farley, Chris

February 18, 1964
b. Dillon, Matt
d. Kelland, Clarence Budington

February 25, 1964
d. Archipenko, Alexander Porfirievich
d. Burke, Johnny
d. Metalious, Grace de Repentigny

February 26, 1964
d. Orry-Kelly

February 27, 1964
d. Cooper, Annie

February 28, 1964
d. Lesnevich, Gus

February 29, 1964
d. Albertson, Frank
d. Jemison, Alice Mae

March 6, 1964
d. Paul I

March 7, 1964
b. Ellis, Bret Easton
b. Graves, Denyce (Antoinette)

March 8, 1964
b. Salt
d. Alexander, Franz Gabriel

March 9, 1964
d. DePaolis, Alessio

March 10, 1964
b. Edward
b. Guy, Jasmine

March 12, 1964
d. Aqqad, Abbas Mahmud al-

March 13, 1964
b. Clark, Will(iam Nuschler, Jr.)
d. Genovese, Kitty

March 15, 1964
b. Rockwell

March 17, 1964
b. Lowe, Rob(ert Hepler)

March 18, 1964
b. Blair, Bonnie Kathleen
d. O'Callahan, Joseph Timothy
d. Wiener, Norbert

March 20, 1964
d. Behan, Brendan (Francis)

March 24, 1964
d. Lorre, Peter

March 27, 1964
d. Bordeaux, Henry

March 30, 1964
b. Chapman, Tracy
d. Larsen, Nella

April 3, 1964
d. Holmes, John Haynes

April 5, 1964
d. MacArthur, Douglas

April 8, 1964
b. Markie, Biz

April 9, 1964
d. Brendel, El(mer)

April 11, 1964
b. Saberhagen, Bret (William)
d. Bok, Hannes Vajn

April 13, 1964
d. Harlan, Veit

April 14, 1964
d. Carson, Rachel (Louise)

April 16, 1964
b. Pirner, Dave

April 18, 1964
d. Hecht, Ben

April 20, 1964
b. Sumners, Rosalyn

April 22, 1964
b. Makepeace, Chris

April 23, 1964
d. Polanyi, Karl

April 24, 1964
d. Domagk, Gerhard

April 26, 1964
d. Pratt, Edwin John

April 28, 1964
b. Larkin, Barry
d. Margai, Milton Augustus Striery

May 2, 1964
d. Astor, Nancy Witcher Langhorne

May 3, 1964
b. Hextall, Ron(ald Jeffrey)

May 8, 1964
b. Gilbert, Melissa
d. Nomura, Kichisaburo

May 10, 1964
d. Haney, Carol
d. Lebrun, Rico

May 13, 1964
d. Basso, Hamilton
d. Wynyard, Diana

May 17, 1964
d. Owen, Steve

May 21, 1964
d. Franck, James

May 23, 1964
d. Henry, George William

May 24, 1964
d. Hazeltine, (Louis) Alan

May 26, 1964
b. Kravitz, Lenny

May 27, 1964
d. Collins, Ted
d. Nehru, Jawaharlal

May 30, 1964
b. Wynonna
d. Szilard, Leo

June 3, 1964
d. Sillanpaa, Frans E

June 4, 1964
b. Kistler, Darci Anna
d. Warwick, Robert

June 7, 1964
d. Lewis, Meade Anderson Lux

June 9, 1964
b. Tisdale, Wayman Lawrence
d. Beaverbrook, William Maxwell
Aitken, Baron
d. Gruenberg, Louis

June 11, 1964
d. Phibun Songkhram, Luang

June 15, 1964
b. Cox, Courteney

June 18, 1964
d. Morandi, Giorgio

June 21, 1964
b. Davis, Sammi

June 24, 1964
b. Suter, Gary
d. Davis, Stuart

June 25, 1964
d. Rietveld, Gerrit Thomas

June 26, 1964
d. Dandurand, Leo

June 27, 1964
b. Person, Chuck Connors
d. Gilbert, Alfred Carlton, Jr.

June 29, 1964
d. Auerbach-Levy, William

July 1, 1964
d. Monteux, Pierre
d. Pound, Roscoe

July 2, 1964
b. Canseco, Jose
b. Graver, Elizabeth

July 11, 1964
d. Thorez, Maurice

July 16, 1964
b. Indurain, Miguel

July 19, 1964
b. Edwards, Teresa

July 20, 1964
b. Cornell, Chris

July 24, 1964
b. Bonds, Barry (Lamar)
d. Roberts, Edward Glenn

July 25, 1964
d. Townsend, William H(enry)
d. Wolff, Mary Evaline

July 27, 1964
d. Hagedorn, Hermann

July 30, 1964
b. Fox, Vivica A.
d. Engle, Clair
d. Landis, James McCauley

July 31, 1964
d. Mendenhall, Dorothy Reed
d. Reeves, Jim

August 1, 1964
d. Abel, Taffy

August 3, 1964
d. O'Connor, Flannery

August 5, 1964
d. Ross, Art(hur Howie)

August 6, 1964
d. Hardwicke, Cedric Webster, Sir

August 9, 1964
b. Hull, Brett (A.)

August 10, 1964
b. Cherry, Neneh
d. Fox, Fontaine Talbot, Jr.

August 11, 1964
d. Mannes, Leopold Damrosch

August 12, 1964
d. Fleming, Ian Lancaster

August 14, 1964
d. Burnette, Johnny

August 16, 1964
b. Arias, Jimmy

August 21, 1964
d. Togliatti, Palmiro

August 22, 1964
b. Amos, Tori

August 24, 1964
b. Wilander, Mats

August 25, 1964
b. Underwood, Blair

August 27, 1964
d. Allen, Gracie Ethel Cecil Rosaline

September 3, 1964
d. Hayes, Carlton Joseph Huntley
d. Holbrook, Stewart Hall

September 4, 1964
b. Reeves, Keanu

September 5, 1964
d. Flynn, Elizabeth Gurley

September 7, 1964
d. Brown, Walter Augustine

September 8, 1964
d. Singer, Burns James Hyman

September 13, 1964
b. Smiley, Tavis
d. Honeywell, Mark Charles

September 15, 1964
d. Blalock, Alfred

September 16, 1964
d. Meiklejohn, Alexander

September 18, 1964
d. Bell, Clive
d. Dobie, J(ames) Frank
d. O'Casey, Sean

September 27, 1964
d. Waln, Nora

September 28, 1964
b. Garofalo, Janeane
d. Brown, Nacio Herb
d. Marx, Harpo

October 1, 1964
d. Toch, Ernst

October 4, 1964
d. Calkins, Earnest Elmo
d. Svanholm, Set

October 6, 1964
b. Sweet, Matthew

October 10, 1964
d. Cantor, Eddie

October 11, 1964
d. Herrick, Elinore Morehouse

October 14, 1964
d. Covici, Pascal

October 15, 1964
d. Porter, Cole

October 20, 1964
d. Hoover, Herbert C(lark)

October 23, 1964
d. Mott, Frank Luther

October 27, 1964
b. Meagher, Mary T
d. Cartier, Pierre C

October 31, 1964
d. Toye, Francis

November 1, 1964
d. Carlson, Doc

November 6, 1964
b. Keough, Danny
d. Euler-Chelpin, Hans Karl August
Simon von

November 7, 1964
b. McKerrow, Amanda

November 9, 1964
d. Cleland, Thomas Maitland

November 11, 1964
b. Flockhart, Calista
b. McKeon, Philip
d. Piper, H(enry) Beam

November 16, 1964
b. Gooden, Dwight Eugene
d. Peattie, Donald Culross

November 20, 1964
d. Howard, Roy Wilson

November 21, 1964
b. Vincent, Marjorie Judith

November 23, 1964
d. Buttenheim, Edgar Joseph

November 24, 1964
d. O'Dwyer, William
d. Schauffler, Robert Haven

November 27, 1964
b. Givens, Robin

November 30, 1964
d. Redman, Don

December 1, 1964
d. Haldane, J(ohn) B(urdon)
S(anderson)

December 2, 1964
d. York, Sergeant

December 4, 1964
b. Tomei, Marisa

December 8, 1964
b. Hatcher, Teri
d. Crosby, Percy L
d. Marks, Simon

December 9, 1964
d. Sitwell, Edith, Dame

December 11, 1964
d. Cooke, Sam
d. Kilbride, Percy

December 14, 1964
d. Bendix, William
d. Reynolds, R(ichard) J(oshua), Jr.

December 16, 1964
b. Ripken, Bill
d. Davis, Phil

December 17, 1964
d. Hess, Victor Francis

December 18, 1964
b. Pitt, Brad

December 21, 1964
d. Van Vechten, Carl

December 23, 1964
b. Klima, Petr
b. Vedder, Eddie

December 28, 1964
d. Sterrett, Cliff

1965

b. Bowser, Yvette Lee
b. Byrd, Michelle
b. Chandra, Sheila
b. Dr. Dre
b. Fletcher, Alfonso, Jr.
b. Gerardo
b. Golden, Thelma
b. KRS-One
b. Macpherson, Elle
b. Marcelo, (Edward) Jovy
b. Mathews, Dan
b. Rochon, Lela
b. Shimomura, Tsutomu
b. Slash
b. Twain, Shania
b. Wells, Sharlene
b. Zucker, Jeff
d. Abdullah al-Salim al-Sabah
d. Ben Barka, Mehdi
d. Lubbock, Percy
d. Pesotta, Rose
d. Rodia, Simon
d. Spicer, Jack

January 3, 1965
d. Avery, Milton Clark

January 4, 1965
b. Ormond, Julia (Karin)
d. Eliot, T(homas) S(tearns)

January 8, 1965
d. Onions, Charles Talbut

January 9, 1965
b. Bogues, Mugsy

January 11, 1965
d. Pipp, Wally

January 12, 1965
b. Doyle, Jill
d. Hansberry, Lorraine

January 14, 1965
d. MacDonald, Jeanette

January 19, 1965
d. Pate, Maurice

January 20, 1965
d. Altrock, Nick
d. Freed, Alan

January 22, 1965
b. Lane, Diane
d. Stuhldreher, Harry A

January 24, 1965
d. Churchill, Winston Leonard
    Spencer, Sir

January 28, 1965
d. Weygand, Maxime

January 29, 1965
b. Hasek, Dominik

January 31, 1965
d. Cooper, Kent
b. Dell, Michael

February 1, 1965
b. Fenn, Sherilyn
b. Lee, Brandon
b. Stephanie, Princess

February 2, 1965
d. Blackmur, Richard Palmer

February 4, 1965
d. Girdler, Tom Mercer

February 7, 1965
b. Otto, Kristin

February 8, 1965
d. Danquah, Joseph (Kwame
    Kyeretwi B(oakye)

February 12, 1965
d. Hammond, John Hays, Jr.

February 13, 1965
d. Kilpatrick, William H(eard)

February 15, 1965
d. Cole, Nat King

February 16, 1965
d. Breck, John Henry

February 17, 1965
d. Bucher, Walter Herman

February 21, 1965
d. Malcolm X

February 22, 1965
b. La Fontaine, Pat
d. Frankfurter, Felix

February 23, 1965
b. Guillem, Sylvie
d. Laurel, Stan

February 26, 1965
d. Bassett, John D
d. Dick, Lena Frank

March 1, 1965
d. Beemer, Brace

March 5, 1965
d. Martin, Pepper
d. Mayer, Oscar Gottfried
d. Motley, Willard Francis

March 6, 1965
d. Dumont, Margaret
d. Morrison of Lambeth, Herbert
    Stanley Morrison, Baron

March 9, 1965
b. Bosworth, Brian Keith
d. Murphy, Jimmy

March 10, 1965
b. Woodson, Rod(erick Kevin)
d. Lampkin, Daisy

March 11, 1965
b. Jackson, Jesse, Jr.

March 14, 1965
d. Browning, Frederick A(rthur)
    M(ontague), Sir

March 15, 1965
d. Phillips, Harry Irving

March 17, 1965
d. Reynolds, Quentin James
d. Stagg, Amos Alonzo

March 18, 1965
d. Farouk I
d. Lubin, Germaine

March 19, 1965
d. Gheorghiu-Dej, Gheorghe
d. Lloyd, John Henry

March 23, 1965
d. Murray, Mae

March 25, 1965
b. Parker, Sarah Jessica
d. Liuzzo, Viola
d. Williamson, Sonny Boy

March 28, 1965
d. Dane, Clemence
d. Seagrave, Gordon Stifler

March 30, 1965
d. Hench, Philip Showalter

March 31, 1965
b. Barrasso, Tom

April 1, 1965
b. Jackson, Mark
d. Rubinstein, Helena

April 4, 1965
b. Downey, Robert, Jr.
b. Downey, Robert, Jr.

April 6, 1965
b. Sharpe, Sterling

April 9, 1965
b. Porizkova, Paulina
d. Minton, Sherman

April 10, 1965
d. Darnell, Linda (Monetta Eloyse)

April 12, 1965
b. Zayak, Elaine

April 14, 1965
d. Ehrenfest-Afanaseva, Tatiana
d. Hickock, Richard Eugene
d. Smith, Perry Edward

April 16, 1965
b. Lawrence, Martin

April 21, 1965
d. Appleton, Edward Victor, Sir

April 22, 1965
d. Dundee, Johnny

April 24, 1965
d. Dresser, Louise
d. Madden, Owen Victor

April 27, 1965
d. Murrow, Edward R

May 1, 1965
d. Jones, Spike

May 4, 1965
d. Brokenshire, Norman

May 7, 1965
d. Sheeler, Charles

May 9, 1965
b. Yzerman, Steve

May 10, 1965
d. Wallace-Johnson, Isaac Theophilus
    Akunna

May 12, 1965
d. Frankfurter, Alfred Moritz

May 13, 1965
b. Rijo, Jose Antonio Abreu

May 14, 1965
d. Perkins, Frances

May 16, 1965
d. Breckinridge, Mary

May 17, 1965
b. Reznor, Trent

May 19, 1965
d. Dabrowska, Maria Szumska

May 21, 1965
d. DeHavilland, Geoffrey, Sir

May 22, 1965
d. Cooke, Samuel

May 23, 1965
d. Smith, David

May 25, 1965
b. Jammeh, Yahya A(bdulaziz)
J(emus) J.
d. Grew, Joseph Clark

May 27, 1965
b. Bridges, Todd
b. Cash, Pat(rick)

May 30, 1965
b. McBride, Bryant

May 31, 1965
b. Shields, Brooke

June 1, 1965
d. Funk, Wilfred John
d. Lambeau, Curly

June 3, 1965
d. Janssen, Herbert

June 4, 1965
b. Jaeger, Andrea

June 5, 1965
d. Babcock, Harry
d. Farjeon, Eleanor

June 7, 1965
d. Burgess, Thornton Waldo
d. Holliday, Judy

June 10, 1965
b. Evangelista, Linda
b. Hurley, Elizabeth

June 12, 1965
b. Torrence, Gwen(dolyn Lenna)

June 13, 1965
d. Buber, Martin

June 14, 1965
d. Kaltenborn, H(ans) V(on)

June 15, 1965
d. Cochran, Steve
d. Norden, Carl Lukas

June 17, 1965
b. Jansen, Dan

June 18, 1965
d. Melachrino, George Miltiades

June 20, 1965
d. Baruch, Bernard Mannes

June 22, 1965
d. Auslander, Joseph
d. Selznick, David O(liver)

June 23, 1965
d. Boland, Mary

June 28, 1965
d. Nichols, Red

June 29, 1965
b. Fonyo, Steve

June 30, 1965
b. Richmond, Mitch(ell James)

July 1, 1965
d. Ruark, Robert Chester
d. Thornhill, Claude

July 4, 1965
d. Bennett, Constance Campbell
d. Sackville-West, Edward Charles

July 5, 1965
d. Rubirosa, Porfirio

July 7, 1965
d. Gildersleeve, Virginia Crocheron
d. Sharett, Moshe

July 8, 1965
b. Walton, Jerome O'Terrell
d. Stribling, Thomas Sigismund

July 9, 1965
b. Love, Courtney

July 10, 1965
d. Audiberti, Jacques

July 11, 1965
d. Collins, Ray

July 13, 1965
d. Gomez Castro, Laureano Eleuterio

July 14, 1965
d. Stevenson, Adlai Ewing, II

July 15, 1965
d. Shotwell, James Thomson

July 16, 1965
b. Lemieux, Claude
d. Artzybasheff, Boris Mikhailovich

July 19, 1965
d. Gitlow, Benjamin
d. Rhee, Syngman

July 21, 1965
d. Conover, Harry

July 26, 1965
d. Burdick, Eugene Leonard

July 29, 1965
d. Graves, Alvin Cushman

July 30, 1965
d. Tanizaki Jun'ichiro

August 1, 1965
d. Howard, Eugene

d. Lynch, Joe

August 6, 1965
b. Robinson, David (Maurice)
d. Carroll, Nancy
d. Sloane, Everett

August 7, 1965
d. Derby, Jane
d. Marshall, Jack

August 8, 1965
d. Jackson, Shirley (Hardie)

August 9, 1965
d. Freeman, Joseph

August 11, 1965
d. Lehman, Adele Lewisohn

August 18, 1965
d. LaFollete, Philip Fox

August 24, 1965
b. Matlin, Marlee
b. Miller, Reggie

August 26, 1965
b. Burke, Christopher

August 27, 1965
d. LeCorbusier

August 28, 1965
b. Boykin, Keith (O.)

August 29, 1965
d. Waner, Paul Glee

September 3, 1965
b. Santiago, Benito
b. Sheen, Charlie

September 4, 1965
b. Boyd, John W., Jr.
d. Schweitzer, Albert

September 5, 1965
b. Nolan, Christopher
d. Sullivan, C(harles) Gardner

September 8, 1965
d. Cowen, Joshua Lionel
d. Dandridge, Dorothy

September 9, 1965
b. Majerle, Dan
d. Staudinger, Hermann

September 10, 1965
d. Divine, Father Major Jealous
d. Jordan, Bobby

September 11, 1965
b. Moby

September 15, 1965
d. Allison, Samuel King

September 17, 1965
d. Hayward, John Davy

September 18, 1965
b. Peete, Holly Robinson
d. Field, Marshall, IV

September 19, 1965
d. Thomas, Elmer

September 20, 1965
d. Holmes, Arthur

September 21, 1965
d. Larson, John Augustus

September 22, 1965
d. Ammann, Othmar Hermann

September 25, 1965
b. Pippen, Scottie

September 27, 1965
d. Bow, Clara Gordon

October 3, 1965
d. Scott, Zachary

October 5, 1965
b. Lemieux, Mario
b. Roy, Patrick

October 6, 1965
b. Sierra (Garcia), Ruben Angel
d. Kennedy, Tom

October 8, 1965
b. Biondi, Matt
d. Costain, Thomas Bertram

October 10, 1965
d. Uhde, Hermann

October 11, 1965
d. Lange, Dorothea Nutzhorn

October 12, 1965
d. Muller, Paul Hermann

October 14, 1965
d. Jarrell, Randall

October 21, 1965
d. McDonald, Marie

October 22, 1965
b. Harding, John Wesley
d. Tillich, Paul Johannes

October 23, 1965
d. Throckmorton, Cleon

October 25, 1965
d. Knappertsbusch, Hans

October 29, 1965
d. McKechnie, Bill

October 31, 1965
b. Annabella
b. Schneider, Rob

November 2, 1965
d. Evatt, Herbert Vere

November 3, 1965
d. Hansberry, William Leo

November 4, 1965
d. Chapelle, Dickey

November 6, 1965
d. Varese, Edgar

November 8, 1965
d. Kilgallen, Dorothy

November 12, 1965
d. Spaeth, Sigmund Gottfried

November 14, 1965
d. DeMarco, Tony

November 15, 1965
d. Kalmus, Natalie Mabelle Dunfee

November 16, 1965
d. Cosgrave, William Thomas
d. DuMont, Allen Balcom
d. King, Alexander

November 17, 1965
d. Blackstone, Harry

November 18, 1965
d. Wallace, Henry Agard

November 20, 1965
d. Anthony, Katharine Susan

November 21, 1965
b. Bjork

November 24, 1965
d. Graham, Gwethalyn

November 30, 1965
b. Stiller, Ben
b. Witt, Katarina

December 5, 1965
d. Erlanger, Joseph

December 7, 1965
d. Breen, Joseph Ignatius

December 9, 1965
d. Rickey, Branch

December 10, 1965
d. Cowell, Henry Dixon

December 12, 1965
d. Lovelace, William Randolph, II

December 13, 1965
d. Robeson, Eslanda Cardoza Goode

December 15, 1965
d. Dorne, Albert

December 16, 1965
d. Maugham, W(illiam) Somerset
d. Schipa, Tito

December 17, 1965
d. Ismay, Hastings Lionel, Baron

December 20, 1965
b. Utley, Mike

December 22, 1965
d. Ritz, Al

December 25, 1965
b. Webb, Veronica

December 26, 1965
d. Hess, Myra, Dame

December 27, 1965
d. Kiesler, Frederick John

December 28, 1965
d. Thorndike, Lynn

December 31, 1965
b. Gong Li

1966

b. Alexie, Sherman
b. Brickell, Edie
b. Buckley, Jeff
b. Chai Ling
b. Filo, David
b. Fox, Samantha
b. Gertz, Alison L.
b. Hardison, Kadeem
b. Healey, Jeff
b. King, Rodney G
b. Lewis, Reggie
b. Pilatus, Rob(ert)
b. Stewart, Alison
b. Sweet, Rachel
d. Campbell, Donald Fraser
d. Carr-Saunders, Alexander Morris
d. Genaro, Frankie
d. Martinez, Maximiliano Hernandez
d. McNaughton, Andrew
b. Gilstrap, Suzy
d. Bello, (Alhaji Sir) Ahmadu

January 1, 1966
d. Auriol, Vincent

January 2, 1966
d. Millikan, Clark Blanchard
d. Wilkins, Ernest Hatch

January 3, 1966
d. Higgins, Marguerite

January 6, 1966
d. Lurcat, Jean Marie

January 9, 1966
d. Foerster, Friedrich Wilhelm

January 11, 1966
d. Giacometti, Alberto
d. Kolehmainen, Hannes
d. Shastri, Lal Badahur

January 14, 1966
d. Moran, Paddy

January 15, 1966
d. Balewa, Abubakar Tafawa, Sir

January 16, 1966
d. Hodges, Courtney

January 19, 1966
b. Edberg, Stefan

January 22, 1966
d. Marshall, Herbert

January 24, 1966
d. Bhabha, Homi Jehangir
d. Foyston, Frank C

January 28, 1966
d. Quill, Mike

January 31, 1966
d. Manship, Paul

February 1, 1966
b. Akers, Michelle
d. Hopper, Hedda
d. Keaton, Buster

February 3, 1966
d. Gannett, Lewis Stiles

February 4, 1966
d. Beebe, Lucius Morris
d. Grosvenor, Gilbert Hovey

February 5, 1966
d. Binswanger, Ludwig

February 9, 1966
d. Tucker, Sophie

February 10, 1966
d. Dillon, William A
d. Rose, Billy

February 14, 1966
d. Vittorini, Elio

February 17, 1966
b. Robitaille, Luc
d. Hofmann, Hans
d. Sloan, Alfred Pritchard, Jr.

February 18, 1966
d. Rossen, Robert

February 19, 1966
b. Bateman, Justine

February 20, 1966
b. Crawford, Cindy
d. Hunter, Dard
d. Nimitz, Chester William

February 25, 1966
b. Leoni, Tea
d. Norris, James D

February 29, 1966
d. Severini, Gino

March 1, 1966
d. Baillie, Hugh

March 3, 1966
b. Tone-Loc
d. Fields, Joseph
d. Frawley, William
d. Pearce, Alice

March 4, 1966
b. Johnson, Kevin

March 5, 1966
b. Irvin, Michael (Jerome)
d. Akhmatova, Anna

March 6, 1966
b. Ashley, Maurice
d. Westover, Russell (Channing)

March 10, 1966
d. O'Connor, Frank
d. Sandoz, Mari
d. Zernike, Frits

March 11, 1966
d. Fitzsimmons, James E

March 12, 1966
d. Meriwether, Lee
d. Wachter, Ed(ward)

March 15, 1966
d. Saperstein, Abe

March 24, 1966
d. Hill, Virginia

March 25, 1966
d. Watson, Mark Skinner

March 27, 1966
d. Menken, Helen

March 30, 1966
d. Morris, Newbold
d. Parrish, Maxfield

April 2, 1966
d. Forester, Cecil Scott

April 3, 1966
d. Crouse, Russel

April 4, 1966
b. McKeon, Nancy

April 5, 1966
d. Gill, Amory Tingle

April 6, 1966
d. Brunner, Emil

April 10, 1966
d. Waugh, Evelyn Arthur St. John

April 11, 1966
b. Reese, Mason
b. Stansfield, Lisa

April 12, 1966
d. Allard, Sydney

April 13, 1966
d. Carra, Carlo
d. Duhamel, Georges
d. Luckner, Felix von, Count
d. Nighbor, Frank

April 14, 1966
b. Justice, David
b. Justice, David (Christopher)
b. Maddux, Greg(ory Alan)

April 16, 1966
d. Gowers, Ernest Arthur, Sir

April 19, 1966
b. Knight, Suge
d. Tanner, Valno Alfred

April 29, 1966
d. Orr, Douglas William

April 30, 1966
d. Farina, Richard

May 1, 1966
b. McGraw, Tim

May 4, 1966
d. Ozenfant, Amedee

May 7, 1966
d. Gifford, Walter Sherman

May 12, 1966
b. Baldwin, Stephen
d. Howard, Guy Wesley

May 13, 1966
b. Rucker, Darius

May 15, 1966
d. Forbes, Kathryn

May 16, 1966
b. Jackson, La Toya
b. Thomas, Thurman Lee

May 17, 1966
b. Manning, Danny

May 20, 1966
b. Cohn, Mindy

May 23, 1966
d. Guggenheimer, Minnie

May 24, 1966
d. Barnes, Jim

May 26, 1966
b. Bonham Carter, Helena

June 1, 1966
b. Tyson, Mike

June 2, 1966
b. Astley, Rick

June 4, 1966
b. Bartoli, Cecilia
d. Knopf, Blanche Wolf

June 6, 1966
d. Wycherley, Margaret

June 7, 1966
d. Arp, Hans

June 8, 1966
b. Margulies, Julianna

June 10, 1966
b. McKeon, Doug
d. Treece, Henry

June 11, 1966
d. Ford, Wallace

June 12, 1966
d. Hocking, William Ernest
d. Scherchen, Hermann

June 16, 1966
b. Jackson, Janet Damita
d. Eifert, Virginia Snider

June 19, 1966
d. Wynn, Ed

June 20, 1966
d. Lemaitre, Georges

June 24, 1966
d. Whitman, Charles Joseph

June 25, 1966
b. Mutombo, Dikembe
d. Jackson, Busher

June 27, 1966
d. Waley, Arthur David

June 28, 1966
b. Cusack, John

June 30, 1966
d. Allingham, Margery
d. Farina, Giuseppe

July 2, 1966
d. McFee, William

July 3, 1966
d. Taylor, (Joseph) Deems

July 5, 1966
d. Hevesy, George Charles von

July 6, 1966
d. Jones, Sam(uel Pond)

July 10, 1966
d. Hoffman, Malvina

July 11, 1966
d. Schwartz, Delmore (David)

July 12, 1966
d. Suzuki, Daisetz Teitaro

July 18, 1966
b. O'Brien, Dan
d. Heiden, Konrad

July 19, 1966
d. Akeley, Mary Lee Jobe

July 22, 1966
b. Brown, Tim

July 23, 1966
d. Clift, Montgomery

July 24, 1966
d. Lema, Tony

July 25, 1966
d. O'Hara, Frank

July 30, 1966
d. Craig, Gordon

July 31, 1966
b. Cain, Dean

August 1, 1966
d. Gowdy, Hank
d. Powell, Earl
d. Smith, Tommy

August 3, 1966
d. Bruce, Lenny

August 5, 1966
b. Silverman, Jonathan

August 10, 1966
d. Dressen, Chuck

August 12, 1966
d. Meinesz, Felix Andries Vening

August 14, 1966
d. Kreymborg, Alfred

August 15, 1966
d. Kiepura, Jan Wiktor

August 17, 1966
d. Spargo, John

August 21, 1966
d. Lewis, Fulton, Jr.

August 23, 1966
d. Bushman, Francis X(avier)

August 25, 1966
b. Belle, Albert
d. Sayyid Qutb
d. Tamiris, Helen

August 29, 1966
d. Cournos, John

August 31, 1966
d. Schmid, Eduard
d. Lao She

September 2, 1966
d. Roberts, Gordon

September 5, 1966
d. Cecchi, Emilio

September 6, 1966
d. Menninger, William C
d. Sanger, Margaret
d. Verwoerd, Hendrik F

September 8, 1966
b. Robinson, Patrick

September 9, 1966
b. Sandler, Adam

September 10, 1966
b. Nieuwendyk, Joe

September 12, 1966
d. Allen, Florence Ellinwood

September 14, 1966
d. Berg, Gertrude

September 15, 1966
b. Strasser, Valentine (E. M.)
d. Nichols, Anne

September 16, 1966
b. Young, Kevin

September 17, 1966
d. Wellman, Paul Iselin
d. Wunderlich, Fritz

September 21, 1966
d. Reynaud, Paul

September 26, 1966
d. Edson, Gus
d. Kane, Helen

September 28, 1966
d. Breton, Andre
d. Smith, Lillian

September 29, 1966
d. Gimbel, Bernard Feustman
b. Whitfield, Mark

October 4, 1966
d. Billingsley, Sherman

October 11, 1966
b. Olson, Gregg William
b. Perry, Luke

October 13, 1966
d. Webb, Clifton

October 16, 1966
d. Wagner, Wieland Adolf Gottfried

October 18, 1966
d. Arden, Elizabeth
d. Kresge, Sebastian Spering

October 20, 1966
d. Byrd, Harry Flood

October 22, 1966
d. Johnson, Hewlett

October 23, 1966
b. Zanardi, Alex

October 25, 1966
b. Clark, Wendel
d. Chou Tso-Jen

November 2, 1966
d. Araki Sadao
d. Debye, Peter Joseph William
d. Hurt, Mississippi John

November 8, 1966
d. Baker, Shorty

November 12, 1966
b. Schwimmer, David
d. Porter, Quincy

November 19, 1966
b. Devers, Gail
d. Connolly, Mike

November 21, 1966
b. Aikman, Troy (Kenneth)

November 25, 1966
b. Lattisaw, Stacy

November 28, 1966
d. Giannini, Vittorio

December 2, 1966
d. Cooper, Giles (Stannus)

December 7, 1966
d. Morehouse, Ward

December 8, 1966
b. O'Connor, Sinead

December 9, 1966
d. Barth, Karl

December 14, 1966
d. Felton, Verna
d. Whorf, Richard

December 15, 1966
d. Disney, Walt(er Elias)

December 19, 1966
b. Tomba, Alberto

December 21, 1966
b. Sutherland, Keifer

December 23, 1966
d. VonDoderer, Heimito

December 24, 1966
d. Peterson, Virgilia

December 25, 1966
d. Brady, St. Elmo
d. Nick the Greek

December 27, 1966
d. Rea, Gardner

December 30, 1966
d. Herter, Christian Archibald

December 31, 1966
d. Persinger, Louis

1967

b. Alvardo, Trini(dad)
b. Bellamy, Bill
b. Biehl, Amy
b. Bullock, Sandra
b. Carrere, Tia
b. Casella, Max
b. Davidson, Jaye
b. Dube, Lucky
b. Edmonds, Tracey
b. Gathers, Hank
b. Heavy D
b. Jean-Baptiste, Marianne
b. Kaas, Patricia
b. Randle, Theresa
b. Rock, Chris
b. Tricky
d. Baskin, Burton
d. Davis, Marguerite
d. Irwin, Margaret
d. Lucchese, Thomas
d. Okigbo, Christopher
  (Ifenayichukwu)

January 3, 1967
d. Ruby, Jack

January 4, 1967
d. Campbell, Donald Malcolm
d. Garden, Mary

January 8, 1967
d. Heim, Jacques

January 9, 1967
d. Frank, Waldo

January 10, 1967
d. Burchfield, Charles Ephraim

January 12, 1967
d. Holt, Ivan Lee
d. Smith, Holland McTeire

January 18, 1967
d. Nesbit, Evelyn
d. Ross, Barney

January 21, 1967
d. Sheridan, Ann

January 22, 1967
d. Buckley, Charles Anthony

January 25, 1967
d. Bastianini, Ettore

January 26, 1967
d. Isaacs, Alick

January 27, 1967
d. Chaffee, Roger Bruce
d. Grissom, Virgil Ivan
d. Juin, Alphonse Pierre

d. White, Ed(ward Higgins, III)

February 2, 1967
d. Roos, Frank John, Jr.
d. Sevitzky, Fabien

February 4, 1967
b. Grinkov, Sergei

February 5, 1967
d. Bean, L(eon) L(eonwood)

February 6, 1967
d. Carol, Martine
d. Morgenthau, Henry, Jr.

February 8, 1967
d. Gollancz, Victor, Sir

February 10, 1967
b. Dern, Laura Elizabeth

February 11, 1967
d. Muste, A(braham) J(ohannes)

February 12, 1967
d. Spanier, Muggsy

February 14, 1967
d. Rumann, Sig(fried)

February 15, 1967
d. Bullitt, William Christian
d. Duryea, J(ames) Frank

February 16, 1967
d. Burnette, Smiley

February 17, 1967
d. Alegria, Ciro

February 18, 1967
d. Oppenheimer, J(ulius) Robert

February 20, 1967
b. Cobain, Kurt
b. Shue, Andrew

February 21, 1967
d. Fall, Bernard B

February 24, 1967
d. Waxman, Franz

February 28, 1967
d. Howe, Mark De Wolfe
d. Luce, Henry Robinson

March 2, 1967
d. Ruiz, Jose Martinez

March 5, 1967
d. Auer, Mischa
d. Mossadegh, Mohammed

March 6, 1967
d. Eddy, Nelson
d. Kodaly, Zoltan

March 7, 1967
b. Bocca, Julio

d. Compton, Wilson Martindale
d. Toklas, Alice B(abette)

March 8, 1967
b. Harkes, John

March 11, 1967
d. Farrar, Geraldine

March 12, 1967
d. Muller-Munk, Peter

March 13, 1967
d. Malinovsky, Rodion Yakovlevich

March 14, 1967
d. Hobart, Alice Tisdale Nourse

March 19, 1967
b. Konstantinov, Vladimir

March 20, 1967
d. Morgan, Frederick, Sir

March 24, 1967
b. Rinaldi, Kathy

March 25, 1967
b. Thomas, Debi

March 27, 1967
d. Heyrovsky, Jaroslav

March 30, 1967
d. Toomer, Jean

April 2, 1967
d. Gassner, John Waldhorn

April 4, 1967
d. Chamberlin, B Guy

April 5, 1967
d. Elman, Mischa
d. Muller, Hermann Joseph

April 6, 1967
d. Connor, William Neil, Sir

April 17, 1967
b. Phair, Liz
d. Allen, Red
d. Bailey, Frederick Marshman

April 19, 1967
d. Adenauer, Konrad

April 21, 1967
d. Danjon, Andre Louis

April 22, 1967
d. Conway, Tom

April 24, 1967
d. Komarov, Vladimir Mikhaylovich

April 26, 1967
d. Charoux, Siegfried

May 6, 1967
d. Hilberseimer, Ludwig Karl

May 7, 1967
d. Evelyn, Judith

May 8, 1967
d. Andrews, LaVerne
d. Rice, Elmer

May 12, 1967
d. Masefield, John

May 14, 1967
d. Gold, Michael

May 15, 1967
b. Smoltz, John
d. Hopper, Edward

May 18, 1967
d. Clyde, Andy

May 20, 1967
d. Parker, Daniel Francis

May 22, 1967
d. Hughes, Langston

May 23, 1967
d. Niekisch, Ernest
d. Wilson, Lyle Campbell

May 27, 1967
d. Edinger, Tilly

May 29, 1967
d. Pabst, Georg Wilhelm

May 30, 1967
d. Rains, Claude

May 31, 1967
b. Lofton, Kenny
d. Strayhorn, Billy

June 1, 1967
d. Rudkin, Margaret Fogarty

June 2, 1967
d. Upjohn, Lawrence Northcote

June 3, 1967
d. Cluytens, Andre
d. Ransome, Arthur Mitchell
d. Tedder, Arthur William Tedder,
  Baron

June 4, 1967
d. Berkner, Lloyd Viel

June 7, 1967
d. Parker, Dorothy Rothschild

June 8, 1967
d. Frankau, Pamela

June 10, 1967
d. Tracy, Spencer Bonaventure

June 11, 1967
d. Kohler, Wolfgang

June 16, 1967
d. Denny, Reginald Leigh

June 20, 1967
b. Kidman, Nicole

June 21, 1967
d. List, Emanuel

June 24, 1967
b. Stringfield, Sherry

June 26, 1967
d. Dorleac, Francoise

June 29, 1967
d. Carnera, Primo
d. Mansfield, Jayne

June 30, 1967
d. Kuwatli, Shukri al-

July 1, 1967
b. Lee, Pamela

July 5, 1967
d. Barton, Bruce

July 7, 1967
d. Leigh, Vivien

July 13, 1967
b. Peck, Dale
d. Andrus, Ethel Percy

July 14, 1967
d. Arghezi, Tudor
d. Theodorescu, Ion N

July 17, 1967
b. Ashton, Susan
d. Coltrane, Trane

July 18, 1967
d. Castello Branco, Humberto

July 19, 1967
d. Shepard, Odell

July 21, 1967
d. Foxx, Jimmie
d. Luthuli, Albert John Mvumbi
d. Rathbone, Basil

July 22, 1967
d. Sandburg, Carl (August)

July 25, 1967
b. LeBlanc, Matt

July 26, 1967
d. Bitter, Francis

July 28, 1967
d. Julian, Doggie

July 31, 1967
d. Kennedy, Margaret

August 1, 1967
d. Kuhn, Richard

August 2, 1967
b. Krickstein, Aaron
d. Stace, W(alter) T(erence)

August 6, 1967
d. Kiplinger, W(illard) M(onroe)
d. Weinberger, Jaromir

August 9, 1967
b. Sanders, Deion (Luwynn)
d. Orton, Joe
d. Walbrook, Anton

August 10, 1967
b. Bowe, Riddick (Lamont)

August 12, 1967
d. Forbes, Esther

August 13, 1967
b. Cummings, Quinn
d. Darwell, Jane

August 14, 1967
d. Prado Ugarteche, Manuel

August 15, 1967
d. Magritte, Rene Francois Ghislain

August 19, 1967
b. Dillon, Kevin
b. Soren, Tabitha
d. Gernsback, Hugo

August 22, 1967
d. Pincus, Gregory

August 24, 1967
d. Kaiser, Henry John

August 25, 1967
d. Bruce of Melbourne, 1st Viscount
d. Muni, Paul
d. Rockwell, George Lincoln

August 27, 1967
d. Epstein, Brian

August 28, 1967
d. Smith, Bruce P

August 29, 1967
d. Darrow, Charles Brace

August 30, 1967
d. Reinhardt, Ad(olph Frederick)

August 31, 1967
d. Ehrenburg, Ilya Grigoryevich

September 1, 1967
d. Koch, Ilse
d. Sassoon, Siegfried

September 2, 1967
d. Ouimet, Francis de Sales

September 3, 1967
d. Dunn, James Howard

September 5, 1967
d. DeJong, David Cornel

September 6, 1967
d. Gibbs, William Francis

September 11, 1967
b. Connick, Harry, Jr.

September 13, 1967
b. Johnson, Michael

September 15, 1967
d. Haug, Hans

September 17, 1967
b. Yoba, Malik

September 18, 1967
d. Cockcroft, John Douglas, Sir

September 19, 1967
b. Abbott, Jim
d. Block, Martin

September 21, 1967
b. Hill, Faith

September 29, 1967
d. McCullers, Carson (Smith)

October 2, 1967
b. Muster, Thomas

October 3, 1967
d. Guthrie, Woody
d. Sargent, Malcolm, Sir

October 6, 1967
d. Bloch, Claude Charles
d. Gilmore, Eddy Lanier King

October 7, 1967
d. Angell, Norman

October 8, 1967
d. Attlee, Clement Richard Attlee, Earl
d. Guevara, Che
d. Manville, Tommy

October 9, 1967
d. Allport, Gordon William
d. Hinshelwood, Cyril Norman, Sir
d. Maurois, Andre

October 10, 1967
d. Keaney, Frank
d. Read, Albert Cushing

October 11, 1967
d. Pendleton, Nat

October 14, 1967
d. Ayme, Marcel

October 17, 1967
d. Pu-Yi, Henry

October 19, 1967
b. Carter, Amy Lynn

October 20, 1967
d. Yoshida, Shigeru

October 21, 1967
d. Hertzsprung, Ejnar

October 26, 1967
d. Barnes, Margaret Ayer

October 28, 1967
b. Roberts, Julia

October 29, 1967
d. Duvivier, Julien

October 31, 1967
b. Vanilla Ice

November 1, 1967
d. Tietjen, Heinz

November 5, 1967
d. Kesselring, Joseph Otto

November 7, 1967
d. Garner, John Nance

November 9, 1967
d. Bickford, Charles Ambrose

November 12, 1967
b. Moorer, Michael

November 13, 1967
d. Paddleford, Clementine Haskin

November 14, 1967
d. Kilgore, Bernard

November 15, 1967
d. Chatfield, Alfred E Montacute,
Baron
d. McCollum, Elmer Verner
d. Zorach, William

November 16, 1967
b. Bonet, Lisa

November 19, 1967
d. Funk, Casimir

November 22, 1967
b. Becker, Boris

November 25, 1967
d. Zadkine, Ossip

November 26, 1967
d. Warner, Albert

November 29, 1967
d. Panizza, Ettore

November 30, 1967
d. Kavanagh, Patrick

December 2, 1967
d. Spellman, Francis Joseph

December 4, 1967
d. Lahr, Bert

December 5, 1967
d. Kavan, Anna

December 6, 1967
d. Schick, Bela

December 7, 1967
d. Baird, Cora Eisenberg

December 8, 1967
d. Lawrence, Robert (Henry), Jr.
d. Mills, John

December 9, 1967
d. O'Brien, John J

December 10, 1967
d. Redding, Otis

December 11, 1967
d. Bigelow, Henry Bryant
d. DeSabata, Victor

December 15, 1967
b. Vaughn, Mo

December 17, 1967
d. Holt, Harold Edward

December 21, 1967
d. Erwin, Stuart
d. Washkansky, Louis

December 24, 1967
d. Hunt, Frazier

December 27, 1967
d. Flavin, Martin Archer
d. Miller, Max (Carlton)

December 29, 1967
d. Whiteman, Paul

December 30, 1967
d. Burger, Carl Victor
d. Conacher, Charlie
d. Massey, Vincent

1968

b. Bailey, Radcliffe
b. Bergalis, Kimberly
b. Bleeth, Yasmine
b. Braxton, Toni
b. Burns, Edward
b. Corgan, Billy
b. Horovitz, Adam
b. Kani, Karl
b. Lords, Traci
b. Lynne, Shelby
b. Marley, Ziggy
b. Phillips, Chynna
b. Sangare, Oumou
b. Tillman, George, Jr.
b. Yang, Jerry
b. Young MC
d. Cassandre, A(dolphe) M(ouron)
d. de Acosta, Mercedes
d. Gooch, George Peabody
d. Guy-Blache, Alice
d. Hsiung Shih-Li

d. Latzo, Pete
d. McIlwain, Charles Howard

January 2, 1968
b. Gooding, Cuba, Jr.

January 6, 1968
b. Singleton, John (Daniel)

January 8, 1968
b. Kelly, R(obert)
d. Van Paassen, Pierre

January 10, 1968
d. Reuther, Roy

January 11, 1968
d. Stabile, Mariano

January 14, 1968
b. LL Cool J

January 15, 1968
b. Lowe, Chad
d. Masterton, Bill

January 16, 1968
d. Infeld, Leopold
d. Jones, Bob

January 18, 1968
d. Vandenberg, Arthur Hendrick, Jr.
d. Wheeler, Bert

January 19, 1968
d. Harroun, Ray

January 20, 1968
d. Beatty, Alfred Chester, Sir
d. Stacton, David Derek

January 22, 1968
d. Dargan, Olive Tilford
d. Kahanamoku, Duke Paoa

January 24, 1968
b. Retton, Mary Lou

January 28, 1968
b. McLachlan, Sarah

January 29, 1968
d. Black, Frank J.

January 31, 1968
d. Pillsbury, John Sargent

February 1, 1968
b. Presley, Lisa Marie
d. Little, Lawson

February 2, 1968
d. Serafin, Tullio

February 4, 1968
d. Cassady, Neal

February 5, 1968
b. Alomar, Roberto
d. Adams, Nick

February 6, 1968
d. Berry, James Gomer

February 7, 1968
d. Poling, Daniel A

February 8, 1968
b. Coleman, Gary

February 10, 1968
d. Sorokin, Pitirim A(lexandrovitch)

February 11, 1968
d. Lindsay, Howard

February 13, 1968
d. Marsh, Mae
d. Pizzetti, Ildebrando

February 17, 1968
d. Mennen, William Gerhard
d. Wolfit, Donald, Sir

February 18, 1968
b. Ringwald, Molly

February 20, 1968
d. Asquith, Anthony

February 21, 1968
d. Florey, Howard Walter

February 22, 1968
d. Arno, Peter
d. Lucas, Scott Wike

February 23, 1968
d. Hurst, Fannie

February 28, 1968
d. Hall, Juanita
d. Lyman, Frankie
d. Stallings, Laurence

March 3, 1968
b. Leetch, Brian

March 6, 1968
d. Martin, Joseph William, Jr.

March 14, 1968
d. Bache, Harold Leopold
d. Panofsky, Erwin

March 15, 1968
d. Castelnuovo-Tedesco, Mario

March 17, 1968
d. Millis, Walter

March 18, 1968
d. Kurnitz, Harry

March 23, 1968
d. O'Connor, Edwin Greene

March 25, 1968
d. Miller, Olive Beaupre

March 26, 1968
d. Samstag, Nicholas

d. Sears, Eleonora Randolph

March 27, 1968
d. Gagarin, Yuri Alexseyevich

March 28, 1968
b. Lawless, Lucy
d. Dreyer, Carl Theodore

March 30, 1968
b. Dion, Celine
d. Driscoll, Bobby
d. Scholl, William M

April 2, 1968
d. Landau, Lev Davidovich

April 4, 1968
d. King, Martin Luther, Jr.

April 7, 1968
d. Clark, James

April 8, 1968
b. Arquette, Patricia
d. Babcock, Harold Delos

April 14, 1968
b. Hall, Anthony Thomas Charles

April 16, 1968
d. Bainter, Fay Okell
d. Ferber, Edna

April 19, 1968
b. Judd, Ashley
d. Bridges, Tommy

April 20, 1968
d. Dirks, Rudolph

April 25, 1968
d. Davidson, Donald Grady

May 1, 1968
d. Adams, Jack
d. Nicolson, Harold George, Sir

May 3, 1968
d. Hickok, Lorena A

May 5, 1968
d. Dekker, Albert

May 7, 1968
d. Wallace, Lurleen Burns

May 8, 1968
d. Collier, John
d. Wood, Craig Ralph

May 9, 1968
d. Currie, Finlay
d. Dillon, George
d. Gray, Harold Lincoln
d. Hay, George Dewey
d. Lorne, Marion

May 10, 1968
d. Bloomingdale, Samuel

May 15, 1968
d. Austral, Florence Wilson
d. Kimmel, Husband Edward

May 19, 1968
d. Dehn, Adolf Arthur

May 20, 1968
d. Lev, Ray

May 21, 1968
b. Buckmire, Ron

May 27, 1968
b. Thomas, Frank

May 28, 1968
d. Dongen, Kees van

June 1, 1968
d. Bynner, Harold Witter
d. Keller, Helen Adams

June 3, 1968
d. Rand, James Henry

June 4, 1968
d. Gish, Dorothy

June 6, 1968
d. Churchill, Randolph Frederick
Edward Spencer
d. Fry, Franklin Clark
d. Kennedy, Robert Francis

June 7, 1968
d. Duryea, Dan

June 8, 1968
d. Enright, Elizabeth

June 10, 1968
d. Gueye, Lamine

June 12, 1968
d. Read, Herbert, Sir

June 14, 1968
d. Quasimodo, Salvatore

June 15, 1968
d. Crawford, Sam(uel Earl)
d. Montgomery, Wes

June 18, 1968
d. Baker, Dorothy Dodds

June 21, 1968
d. Saint Denis, Ruth

June 22, 1968
d. Beckman, Johnny

June 24, 1968
d. Alexander, Hattie Elizabeth

June 26, 1968
d. Elman, Ziggy

June 29, 1968
d. Driscoll, Paddy

June 30, 1968
d. Maney, Richard

July 2, 1968
b. Goldman, Ronald Lyle

July 6, 1968
b. Scarpelli, Glenn

July 7, 1968
b. Knoblauch, Chuck
d. Keilberth, Joseph
d. Queeny, Edgar Monsanto
d. Sowerby, Leo

July 9, 1968
d. Cadogan, Alexander George
Montague, Sir
d. Fisher, Vardis

July 10, 1968
d. Fitts, Dudley

July 16, 1968
b. Sanders, Barry

July 18, 1968
d. Heymans, Corneille Jean Francois

July 19, 1968
b. Butler, LeRoy

July 20, 1968
b. Carson, Jimmy
d. Hammond, Bray

July 21, 1968
d. St. Denis, Ruth

July 23, 1968
d. Dale, Henry Hallett

July 24, 1968
b. Leighton, Laura

July 28, 1968
d. Hahn, Otto

July 29, 1968
b. Rippy, Rodney Allen

July 31, 1968
b. Ware, Andre

August 2, 1968
b. Harris, Monica

August 3, 1968
d. Rokossovsky, Konstantin
Konstantinovich

August 9, 1968
b. Anderson, Gillian
d. Stiedry, Fritz

August 13, 1968
d. Upson, Ralph Hazlett

August 14, 1968
b. Berry, Halle

August 15, 1968
d. Kilenyi, Edward, Sr.

August 18, 1968
d. Sande, Earl
d. Walter, Cyril

August 19, 1968
d. Gamow, George

August 20, 1968
d. Schneirla, Theodore Christian

August 23, 1968
d. Stromberg, Hunt

August 26, 1968
d. Francis, Kay

August 27, 1968
d. Marina

August 28, 1968
d. Henderson, Arthur
d. Mein, John Gordon

August 29, 1968
b. Me'Shell Ndegeocello

August 30, 1968
d. Talman, William

August 31, 1968
b. Nomo, Hideo
d. O'Keefe, Dennis

September 4, 1968
b. Piazza, Mike

September 6, 1968
d. Akimov, Nikolay Pavlovich
d. Sexton, Leo

September 7, 1968
d. Brinton, Clarence Crane

September 10, 1968
b. Kane, Big Daddy

September 11, 1968
d. Armour, Tommy

September 18, 1968
b. Kukoc, Toni
d. Tone, Franchot

September 19, 1968
d. Carlson, Chester Floyd
d. Foley, Red
d. Genet, Arthur Samuel

September 21, 1968
b. Lake, Ricki
d. Jackson, Charles Reginald

September 22, 1968
d. Scott, Norman

September 23, 1968
d. Pio da Pietrelcina, Francesco
Forgione, Father

September 25, 1968
b. Smith, Will
d. Gunther, Hans F K
d. Woolrich, Cornell

September 28, 1968
b. Zappa, Moon Unit

October 1, 1968
d. Duchamp, Marcel
d. Guardini, Romano

October 4, 1968
d. Biddle, Francis Beverley

October 11, 1968
d. White, George

October 12, 1968
b. Rich, Adam

October 13, 1968
d. Bandeira, Manuel
d. Benaderet, Bea
d. Unwin, Stanley, Sir

October 14, 1968
d. Fruehauf, Harvey Charles

October 15, 1968
d. Burton, Virginia Lee

October 18, 1968
d. Tracy, Lee

October 23, 1968
d. Cassidy, Marshall

October 28, 1968
d. McGimsie, Billy
d. Meitner, Lise

October 30, 1968
d. Kelton, Pert
d. Lane, Rose Wilder
d. Richter, Conrad Michael

October 31, 1968
d. Novarro, Ramon

November 1, 1968
d. Papandreou, George

November 6, 1968
d. Munch, Charles

November 7, 1968
d. Gelfond, Aleksandr Osipovich

November 9, 1968
d. Corey, Wendell

November 14, 1968
d. Menendez Pidal, Ramon

November 16, 1968
d. Toledano, Vicente Lombardo

November 17, 1968
d. Peake, Mervyn Laurence

November 18, 1968
b. Sheffield, Gary (Antonian)
d. Wanger, Walter

November 19, 1968
d. Norena, Eide

November 23, 1968
d. Bea, Augustinus

November 25, 1968
d. Sinclair, Upton Beall
d. Siple, Paul Allman

November 26, 1968
d. Zweig, Arnold

November 28, 1968
d. Blyton, Enid Mary

December 5, 1968
d. Clark, Fred

December 10, 1968
d. Merton, Thomas

December 11, 1968
d. Sulzberger, Arthur Hays

December 12, 1968
d. Bankhead, Tallulah Brockman

December 14, 1968
d. Klose, Margarete

December 15, 1968
d. Willard, Jess

December 18, 1968
d. Garrod, Dorothy Annie Elizabeth

December 19, 1968
d. Thomas, Norman Mattoon

December 20, 1968
d. Brod, Max
d. Steinbeck, John (Ernst)

December 22, 1968
d. Swing, Raymond Gram

December 26, 1968
d. Fellig, Arthur

December 30, 1968
d. Lie, Trygve Halvdan

1969

b. Campbell, Tisha
b. Chideya, Farai (Nduu)
b. Gray, F. Gary
b. Healy, Katherine
b. Parker, Trey
b. Rodriguez, Robert
b. Sorvino, Mira
b. Trenary, Jill
b. Walker, Kara
d. Carlson, Wally
d. Chevallier, Gabriel

d. Naruse, Mikio
d. Scobie, Ronald Mackenzie
b. Danticat, Edwidge
d. Winninger, Charles

January 1, 1969
d. Fleming, Ian
d. MacLane, Barton

January 2, 1969
b. Turlington, Christy
d. Miller, Gilbert Heron

January 3, 1969
b. Carter, James

January 4, 1969
d. Chambers, Paul
d. Hilton, Daisy
d. Hilton, Violet

January 5, 1969
d. Yablonski, Joseph

January 10, 1969
d. Brownlee, John
d. Lamburn, Richmal Crompton

January 14, 1969
b. Bateman, Jason
d. Sedran, Barney

January 16, 1969
d. Smith, Courtney Craig

January 17, 1969
d. Duke, Vernon

January 25, 1969
d. Castle, Irene Foote

January 28, 1969
d. Herbst, Josephine Frey

January 29, 1969
d. Boehm, Edward M
d. Dulles, Allen Welsh

January 30, 1969
d. Pire, Dominique

February 1, 1969
b. Redman, Joshua

February 2, 1969
d. Karloff, Boris
d. Martinelli, Giovanni

February 3, 1969
d. McGill, Ralph Emerson

February 5, 1969
b. Brown, Bobby
d. Ritter, Thelma

February 9, 1969
d. Hayes, Gabby
d. Lescaze, William

February 11, 1969
b. Aniston, Jennifer

February 14, 1969
d. Genovese, Vito

February 15, 1969
d. Russell, Pee Wee

February 16, 1969
d. Martin, Kingsley

February 19, 1969
d. Bonham Carter, Violet

February 20, 1969
d. Ansermet, Ernest Alexandre

February 23, 1969
d. Mondlane, Eduardo Chivambo
d. Saud (Ibn Abdul Aziz al Saud)

February 26, 1969
d. Eshkol, Levi
d. Jaspers, Karl

February 27, 1969
d. Boles, John
d. Craven, Thomas

March 1, 1969
d. Ames, Blanche

March 3, 1969
d. Freyse, William
d. Schenck, Nicholas Michael

March 4, 1969
b. Bono, Chastity

March 5, 1969
d. Werth, Alexander

March 9, 1969
d. Brackett, Charles
d. Christaller, Walter
d. Hawley, Cameron

March 10, 1969
d. Draper, Dorothy Tuckerman
d. McCobb, Paul Winthrop
d. Wilde, Jimmy

March 14, 1969
b. Johnson, Larry
d. Shahn, Ben(jamin)

March 16, 1969
d. Brown, John Mason

March 17, 1969
d. Magnin, Grover Arnold

March 19, 1969
b. Lopez, Josefina Maria

March 22, 1969
d. Schmitt, Bernadotte Everly

March 23, 1969
d. Lismer, Arthur

March 24, 1969
d. Kasavubu, Joseph

March 25, 1969
d. Eastman, Max Forrester
d. Mowbray, Alan

March 26, 1969
d. Toole, John Kennedy

March 27, 1969
d. Traven, B.

March 28, 1969
d. Eisenhower, Dwight D(avid)

March 29, 1969
d. Wyman, Willard Gordon

April 4, 1969
d. Gallegos, Romulo
d. Welch, Herbert

April 10, 1969
d. Bentley, Alvin Morell

April 11, 1969
d. DuPont, Henry Francis

April 21, 1969
d. Iturbi, Amparo

April 22, 1969
d. Humphries, Rolfe

April 26, 1969
d. Rinehart, Stanley Marshall, Jr.

April 27, 1969
d. Barrientos Ortuno, Rene

May 1, 1969
d. Logan, Ella
d. Rosenthal, Jean E

May 2, 1969
d. Papen, Franz von

May 3, 1969
d. Husain, Zakir

May 4, 1969
d. Sitwell, Osbert, Sir

May 5, 1969
d. Cicotte, Eddie

May 11, 1969
d. Fleischmann, Raoul H(erbert)

May 12, 1969
b. Fields, Kim

May 15, 1969
b. Smith, Emmitt
d. Malone, Joe

May 17, 1969
d. Baer, Bugs
d. Olczewska, Maria

May 18, 1969
d. Fitzpatrick, Daniel R

May 19, 1969
d. Hawkins, Bean
d. Hawkins, Coleman

May 21, 1969
d. Leiper, Robert Thomson

May 23, 1969
d. McHugh, Jimmy

May 24, 1969
d. Green, Mitzi

May 25, 1969
b. Heche, Ann

May 27, 1969
d. Hunter, Jeffrey

May 30, 1969
d. Briscoe, Robert

June 1, 1969
d. LeTourneau, Robert Gilmour
d. Tannenbaum, Frank

June 2, 1969
d. Gorcey, Leo

June 3, 1969
d. Warburg, James Paul

June 5, 1969
b. McKnight, Brian

June 6, 1969
d. Dempsey, Miles Christopher, Sir

June 8, 1969
d. Taylor, Robert

June 11, 1969
d. Lewis, John L(lewellyn)

June 13, 1969
d. Hunt, Martita

June 14, 1969
b. Graf, Steffi

June 15, 1969
b. Ice Cube

June 16, 1969
d. Alexander of Tunis

June 20, 1969
b. Washington, MaliVai
d. Beall, Lester Thomas
d. Murchison, Clint(on Williams, Sr.)

June 21, 1969
d. Connolly, Maureen

June 22, 1969
d. Garland, Judy

June 24, 1969
d. King, Frank
d. Ley, Willy
d. Pegler, Westbrook

June 25, 1969
d. Dix, Otto

June 28, 1969
b. Brisebois, Danielle

June 29, 1969
d. Tshombe, Moise

July 3, 1969
d. Jones, Brian

July 5, 1969
d. Alexander, Ben
d. Backhaus, Wilhelm
d. Gropius, Walter Adolf
d. Mboya, Tom
d. McCarey, Leo

July 6, 1969
d. Swarthout, Gladys

July 7, 1969
b. Sakic, Joe

July 8, 1969
d. Rolfe, Red
d. Sebring, Jay

July 17, 1969
d. Lahey, Edwin A(loysius)

July 18, 1969
d. Armstrong, Charlotte

July 19, 1969
d. Kopechne, Mary Jo

July 20, 1969
d. Hamilton, Roy

July 23, 1969
d. Dell, Floyd
d. Flanagan, Hallie Mae Ferguson

July 25, 1969
d. Gombrowicz, Witold
d. Moore, Douglas Stuart

July 26, 1969
d. Walburn, Raymond

July 27, 1969
d. Ford, Corey

July 28, 1969
d. Grau San Martin, Ramon
d. Loesser, Frank Henry

August 3, 1969
d. Hyman, Libbie Henrietta

August 6, 1969
d. Adorno, Theodor Wiesengrund

August 7, 1969
d. Morgan, Russ

August 8, 1969
d. Hyland, Harry

August 9, 1969
d. Marshall, George Preston
d. Powell, Cecil Frank
d. Stratemeyer, George E, General
d. Tate, Sharon

August 14, 1969
d. Gurie, Sigrid
d. Woolf, Leonard Sidney

August 15, 1969
d. Munson, Gorham B(ert)

August 17, 1969
b. Wahlberg, Donnie
d. Blaiberg, Philip
d. Stern, Otto

August 18, 1969
b. Slater, Christian
d. Mies van der Rohe, Ludwig

August 19, 1969
b. Perry, Matthew

August 25, 1969
d. Bruce, Ailsa Mellon

August 27, 1969
d. Compton-Burnett, Ivy, Dame
d. Mann, Erika

August 28, 1969
b. Priestly, Jason

August 31, 1969
d. Marciano, Rocky

September 1, 1969
d. Pearson, Drew

September 2, 1969
d. Pike, James Albert, Bishop

September 3, 1969
d. Ho Chi Minh

September 5, 1969
b. Zappa, Dweezil
d. Ayres, Mitchell
d. White, Josh(ua Daniel)

September 7, 1969
d. Dirksen, Everett McKinley

September 8, 1969
d. Collyer, Bud
d. David-Neel, Alexandra
d. Varley, F(rederick) H(orseman)

September 9, 1969
b. Pepa

September 11, 1969
d. Payne, Leon

September 12, 1969
d. Chamberlin, William Henry

September 13, 1969
d. Sheil, Bernard James, Archbishop

September 18, 1969
d. Wagner-Regeny, Rudolf

September 19, 1969
d. Ingram, Rex

September 22, 1969
d. Lopez Mateos, Adolfo

September 25, 1969
d. Reed, Peter Hugh

September 30, 1969
d. Bartlett, F(rederic) C(harles)

October 1, 1969
d. Francis, Thomas, Jr.

October 2, 1969
d. Arbuthnot, May Hill

October 3, 1969
d. James, Skip

October 5, 1969
b. Bissett, Josie
d. Fosdick, Harry Emerson
d. Hagen, Walter Charles

October 10, 1969
b. Favre, Brett (Lorenzo)

October 12, 1969
d. Henie, Sonja

October 13, 1969
b. Kerrigan, Nancy
d. Crittenden, Christopher

October 14, 1969
d. Herber, Arnie
d. McKinney, Bill

October 15, 1969
d. LaRocque, Rod

October 20, 1969
b. Gonzales, Juan (Alberto)

October 21, 1969
d. Kerouac, Jack

October 26, 1969
d. Azhari, Sayyid Ismail al-

October 28, 1969
b. Harper, Ben
d. Chukovsky, Korney Ivanovich

October 29, 1969
d. Douglas, Sholto

October 30, 1969
d. Foster, Pops

October 31, 1969
d. Pastor, Tony

November 2, 1969
d. Friedman, William Frederick

November 4, 1969
b. McConaughey, Matthew (David)
d. Jones, Thomas Hudson

November 6, 1969
d. Wood, Robert Elkington

November 7, 1969
d. Arnold, Thurman Wesley

November 8, 1969
b. Zal, Roxana
d. Slipher, Vesto Melvin

November 10, 1969
d. Torrance, Jack

November 11, 1969
d. Eberstadt, Ferdinand

November 12, 1969
d. Scherman, Harry

November 13, 1969
d. Liu Shao-Ch'i

November 15, 1969
d. Aldecoa, Ignacio

November 16, 1969
d. Fenton, Carroll Lane

November 18, 1969
b. Ismail, Raghib
d. Heath, Ted
d. Kennedy, Joseph Patrick, Sr.

November 19, 1969
d. Sardi, Vincent, Sr.

November 21, 1969
b. Griffey, Ken, Jr.
d. Mutesa II

November 23, 1969
d. Lewis, Dominic Bevan Wyndham

November 26, 1969
b. Kemp, Shawn

November 28, 1969
d. Arguedas, Jose Maria

December 2, 1969
d. Potter, Stephen
d. Voroshilov, Kliment Efremovich

December 4, 1969
d. Hampton, Fred

December 5, 1969
d. Dornier, Claude

December 6, 1969
d. Horsbrugh, Florence

December 7, 1969
d. Portman, Eric

December 9, 1969
b. Smith, Allison

d. Gruber, Frank

December 13, 1969
b. Fedorov, Sergei
d. Spruance, Raymond Ames

December 17, 1969
d. Costa e Silva, Arthur da

December 22, 1969
d. VonSternberg, Josef

December 23, 1969
d. Carias Andino, Tiburcio

December 27, 1969
d. Flint, William Russell, Sir

December 28, 1969
d. Molinos, Miguel de

December 30, 1969
d. Trnka, Jiri

December 31, 1969
d. Baccaloni, Salvatore
d. Reik, Theodor

1970

b. Cho, Margaret
b. Desormeaux, Kent
b. DiFranco, Ani
b. Franklin, Kirk
b. Gist, Carole Anne-Marie
b. Hargrove, Roy
b. Harvey, Polly Jean
b. Jackson, Sheneska
b. Jean, (Nel) Wyclef
b. Kiptanui, Moses
b. Kronberger, Petra
b. Meyers, Ari(adne)
b. Morceli, Noureddine
b. O'Donnell, Chris
b. Shante
b. Tikaram, Tanita
d. Bazna, Elyesa
d. Brooks, Romaine
d. Culligan, Emmett J
d. Flynn, Sean
d. Khalil, Sayyid Abdullah
d. Ludikar, Pavel
d. Scott, Cyril (Meir)
d. Thuku, Harry
d. Zimmermann, Bernd Alois

January 3, 1970
d. Aylward, Gladys May

January 5, 1970
d. Born, Max

January 10, 1970
d. Olson, Charles John

January 11, 1970
d. March, Hal

January 14, 1970
d. Murphy, Johnny (John Joseph)

January 15, 1970
d. Fischer, Louis
d. Piper, William Thomas

January 16, 1970
d. Breger, Dave

January 18, 1970
d. McKay, David O

January 20, 1970
d. Humphrey, George Magoffin

January 22, 1970
d. Folsom, Frank M

January 27, 1970
d. Heckel, Erich

January 29, 1970
d. Harris, Lauren
d. Liddell Hart, Basil Henry, Sir

January 31, 1970
d. Bell, Herbert A
d. Wolff, Albert Louis

February 1, 1970
d. Dolly, Rosie

February 2, 1970
d. Russell, Bertrand Arthur William

February 4, 1970
d. Bogan, Louise

February 5, 1970
d. York, Rudy

February 6, 1970
d. Attell, Abe B
d. Karns, Roscoe

February 8, 1970
b. Mourning, Alonzo

February 11, 1970
d. Bateman, Henry Mayo

February 14, 1970
b. Moe, Tommy

February 15, 1970
d. Dowding, Hugh Caswell
Tremenheere, Baron

February 16, 1970
d. Rous, Francis Peyton

February 17, 1970
d. Agnon, S(hmuel) Y(osef)
d. Newman, Alfred

February 19, 1970
d. Flanders, Ralph Edward
d. Munshin, Jules

February 20, 1970
b. Brando, Cheyenne

February 21, 1970
d. Nagel, Conrad

February 25, 1970
d. Rothko, Mark

February 26, 1970
d. Leginska

February 27, 1970
d. Bruce Lockhart, Robert Hamilton,
Sir
d. Dionne, Marie

February 28, 1970
d. Porter, James A(mos)

March 5, 1970
d. Woltman, Frederick Enos

March 6, 1970
d. Hopper, William

March 8, 1970
d. Peirce, Waldo

March 11, 1970
d. Gardner, Erle Stanley

March 14, 1970
d. Perls, Frederick Salomon

March 16, 1970
d. Adamov, Arthur
d. Terrell, Tammi

March 17, 1970
d. Crommelynck, Fernand

March 18, 1970
b. Latifah, Queen

March 20, 1970
d. Hussey, Christopher Edward Clive

March 22, 1970
b. CasSelle, Malcolm

March 23, 1970
d. Pyne, Joe

March 27, 1970
b. Carey, Mariah

March 28, 1970
d. Gallo, Fortune

March 29, 1970
d. Brittain, Vera Mary
d. Strong, Anna Louise

March 30, 1970
d. McCormick, Cyrus Hall

March 31, 1970
d. Price, Nancy
d. Timoshenko, Semen
Konstantinovich

April 1, 1970
d. Warburg, Otto Heinrich

April 5, 1970
d. Sturtevant, Alfred Henry

April 6, 1970
d. Sheppard, Sam(uel)
d. Tenggren, Gustaf Adolf

April 9, 1970
d. Wright, Cobina

April 10, 1970
d. Piastro, Michel

April 11, 1970
d. O'Donnell, Cathy
d. O'Hara, John Henry

April 12, 1970
d. Thorborg, Kerstin

April 13, 1970
b. Schroder, Rick
d. Henry, William M
d. Johnson, William Henry
d. Smith, Merriman

April 16, 1970
d. Neutra, Richard Joseph

April 22, 1970
d. Wank, Roland A

April 23, 1970
d. Shriner, Herb

April 24, 1970
d. Spann, Otis

April 25, 1970
d. Louise, Anita

April 26, 1970
d. Lee, Gypsy Rose

April 28, 1970
d. Begley, Ed(ward James)

April 29, 1970
b. Agassi, Andre
b. Thurman, Uma
d. DeBernardi, Forrest S

April 30, 1970
d. Johnson, Hall
d. Stevens, Inger

May 1, 1970
d. Celan, Paul

May 9, 1970
d. Nelson, Erik Henning

May 10, 1970
d. Reuther, Walter Philip

May 11, 1970
b. Ford, Harold E(ugene), Jr.
d. Hodges, Johnny

May 12, 1970
d. Anders, Wladyslaw

d. Sachs, Nelly (Leonie)

May 14, 1970
d. Burke, Billie
d. Dobell, William

May 15, 1970
b. Howard, Desmond
d. Shaughnessy, Clark Daniel

May 16, 1970
b. Sabatini, Gabriela

May 17, 1970
d. Balchin, Nigel Marlin

May 19, 1970
d. Branner, Martin Michael
d. Schalk, Ray(mond William)

May 20, 1970
b. Brandon, (Thomas) Terrell

May 22, 1970
b. Campbell, Naomi
d. Krutch, Joseph Wood

May 24, 1970
d. Davison, Frank Dalby

May 27, 1970
d. Gimbel, Richard

May 29, 1970
d. Gunther, John
d. Hesse, Eva

May 31, 1970
d. Sawchuk, Terry
d. Sheridan, Clare Consuelo

June 1, 1970
b. Lalas, Alexi
d. Ungaretti, Giuseppe

June 2, 1970
d. McLaren, Bruce Leslie

June 3, 1970
d. Mellon, Richard King
d. Sawyer, Ruth

June 4, 1970
d. McCracken, Branch
d. Schacht, Hjalmar Horace Greeley
d. Skulnik, Menasha

June 5, 1970
d. Tufts, Sonny

June 6, 1970
d. Cates, Clifton Bledsoe
d. Johnson, Lonnie

June 7, 1970
d. Forster, E(dward) M(organ)

June 8, 1970
d. Maslow, Abraham Harold

June 10, 1970
d. Grant, Earl

June 11, 1970
d. Kerensky, Alexander Fedorovitch
d. Silvera, Frank

June 15, 1970
d. MacIver, Robert Morrison
d. Powdermaker, Hortense

June 16, 1970
b. Jones, Cobi
d. Chapman, Sydney
d. Piccolo, Brian

June 21, 1970
d. Lucas, Jim Griffing
d. Sukarno, Achmed

June 23, 1970
d. Turner, Roscoe Wilson

July 3, 1970
b. Audra (Ann), McDonald
d. Keyes, Frances Parkinson
d. Newman, Barnett

July 4, 1970
d. Vanderbilt, Harold Stirling

July 7, 1970
d. Lane, Allen, Sir
d. Rambeau, Marjorie

July 10, 1970
d. Benediktsson, Bjarni

July 13, 1970
d. Groves, Leslie Richard

July 14, 1970
d. Foster, Preston
d. Laidler, Harry Wellington

July 15, 1970
d. Berne, Eric Lennard

July 16, 1970
d. Anthony, John J(ason)
d. Aramburu, Pedro Eugenio

July 20, 1970
d. Chace, Marian
d. Eiermann, Egon
d. MacLeod, Iain Norman

July 24, 1970
b. Lopez, Jennifer

July 27, 1970
d. Reid, Helen Rogers
d. Salazar, Antonio de Oliveira
d. Untermeyer, Jean Starr

July 28, 1970
d. Barbirolli, John, Sir
d. Caston, Saul

July 30, 1970
d. Lomax, Louis
d. Perlea, Jonel

d. Szell, George

July 31, 1970
d. Conzelman, Jimmy

August 1, 1970
d. Farmer, Frances
d. Fleeson, Doris

August 2, 1970
d. Desses, Jean

August 8, 1970
d. Goodman, Johnny

August 10, 1970
d. Lapchick, Joe

August 15, 1970
d. Winterich, John Tracy

August 17, 1970
b. Courier, Jim

August 18, 1970
b. Warner, Malcolm-Jamal

August 23, 1970
b. Phoenix, River

August 29, 1970
d. Sockman, Ralph W

September 1, 1970
d. Mauriac, Francois

September 3, 1970
d. Lombardi, Vince(nt Thomas)

September 5, 1970
d. Rindt, Jochen

September 7, 1970
d. MacMillan, Donald Baxter
d. Spencer, Percy Le Baron

September 10, 1970
d. Denneny, Cy(ril)

September 11, 1970
d. Morris, Chester

September 14, 1970
d. Carnap, Rudolf

September 16, 1970
d. Garrett, Eileen Jeanette Lyttle

September 18, 1970
d. Hendrix, Jimi

September 19, 1970
d. Danforth, Dave

September 22, 1970
d. Hamilton, Alice

September 25, 1970
d. Fisher, James Maxwell McConnell
d. Liebling, Estelle
d. Remarque, Erich Maria

September 28, 1970
d. Dos Passos, John (Roderigo)
d. Nasser, Gamal Abdel

September 29, 1970
d. Horton, Edward Everett
d. Seldes, Gilbert Vivian

September 30, 1970
d. Westmore, Perc(ival)

October 2, 1970
d. Wilson, Edward Arthur

October 3, 1970
d. Joplin, Janis

October 6, 1970
d. Halpert, Edith Gregor

October 9, 1970
d. Ackerman, Carl William
d. Giono, Jean
d. Lonsdale, Gordon Arnold

October 10, 1970
d. Daladier, Edouard
d. Rapacki, Adam

October 11, 1970
d. Spitalny, Phil

October 12, 1970
d. Denny, Ludwell

October 19, 1970
d. Cardenas, Lazaro

October 20, 1970
b. Cameron, Kirk
d. Lewis, Ted

October 21, 1970
d. Rojankovsky, Feodor Stepanovich
d. Scopes, John Thomas

October 24, 1970
d. Hofstadter, Richard

October 30, 1970
b. Long, Nia
d. Martinson, Joseph Bertram

October 31, 1970
d. Allyn, Stanley Charles

November 1, 1970
d. Lynd, Robert Staughton

November 2, 1970
d. Cushing, Richard James, Cardinal

November 4, 1970
d. Peter II

November 6, 1970
b. Hawke, Ethan

November 7, 1970
d. Peabody, Eddie

November 9, 1970
d. Dawson, William L(evi)
d. DeGaulle, Charles Andre Joseph Marie

November 21, 1970
d. Lalonde, Newsy
d. Raman, Chandrasekhara Venkata, Sir
d. Yezierska, Anzia

November 23, 1970
d. Ishak, Yusof bin

November 25, 1970
d. Madison, Helene
d. Mishima, Yukio

November 26, 1970
d. Davis, Benjamin Oliver, Sr.

November 29, 1970
d. Ricci, Nina

December 1, 1970
d. Pool, David de Sola

December 7, 1970
d. Goldberg, Rube
d. Power, Thomas S(arsfield)

December 8, 1970
d. Alikhanov, Abram Isaakovich
d. Ingold, Christopher Kelk, Sir
d. Poor, Henry Varnum, III

December 9, 1970
d. Cady, (Walter) Harrison
d. Mikoyan, Artem Ivanovich

December 14, 1970
d. Slim, William Joseph

December 16, 1970
d. Lewis, Oscar

December 19, 1970
b. Beckford, Tyson

December 20, 1970
d. Schuster, Max Lincoln

December 21, 1970
d. Cicero

December 22, 1970
b. Wasow, Omar

December 23, 1970
d. Benzell, Mimi
d. Ruggles, Charles

December 25, 1970
d. Wroth, Lawrence Counselman

December 28, 1970
d. Rivers, L(ucius) Mendel

December 29, 1970
d. Liston, Sonny

December 30, 1970
d. Ulric, Lenore

1971

b. Andreessen, Mark
b. Auermann, Nadja
b. Austin, Dallas
b. Beck
b. Combs, Sean
b. Lawrence, Ruth
b. McGregor, Ewan (Gordon)
b. MC Lyte
b. Pinkett, Jada
b. Rathbun-Nealy, Melissa
b. Shaham, Gil
b. Snoop Doggy Dogg
b. Stone, Matt
b. Wahlberg, Mark
d. Deloria, Ella Clara
d. Dhlomo, R(olfus) R(eginald) R(aymond)
d. Johnson, Alvin Saunders
d. Lawless, Theodore K(enneth)
d. Marks, Charles
d. McDonald, Maurice James
d. Stiffel, Theodopholous
d. Twitchell, Paul
d. Strang, Ruth May

January 1, 1971
d. Ford, Arthur A

January 2, 1971
d. Hall, Lloyd Augustus
d. Knox, E(dmund) G(eorge) V(alpy)

January 5, 1971
d. Shearer, Douglas

January 7, 1971
d. Kollmar, Richard

January 9, 1971
d. Flick, Elmer Harrison

January 10, 1971
d. Cacers, Ernest
d. Chanel, Coco

January 11, 1971
b. Blige, Mary J(ane)

January 15, 1971
d. Dall, John
d. Shambaugh, Jessie Field

January 18, 1971
d. Calvert, Catherine
d. Finlay, Virgil

January 20, 1971
d. Anderson, Gilbert M

January 21, 1971
d. Russell, Richard Brevard, Jr.

January 22, 1971
d. Guggenheim, Harry Frank

January 24, 1971
d. Wilson, William Griffith

January 27, 1971
d. Arbenz Guzman, Jacobo
d. Campbell, E Simms

February 2, 1971
d. Hellmann, Richard

February 3, 1971
d. Flippen, Jay C

February 5, 1971
d. Rakosi, Matyas

February 12, 1971
d. Glueck, Nelson
d. Penney, J(ames) C(ash)

February 17, 1971
d. Berle, Adolf Augustus, Jr.
d. Mays, David John

February 18, 1971
d. Potter, David M(orris)

February 25, 1971
d. Svedberg, Theodor H E

February 26, 1971
d. Fernandel

February 28, 1971
d. DeKruif, Paul Henry

March 5, 1971
d. Nevins, Allan

March 6, 1971
d. Broadbent, Punch
d. Dart, Thurston
d. Evans, Herbert McLean

March 7, 1971
d. Balaban, Barney
d. Smith, Stevie

March 8, 1971
d. Lloyd, Harold

March 9, 1971
b. Lewis, Emmanuel
d. Knaths, Karl

March 11, 1971
d. Broad, C(harlie) D(unbar)
d. Farnsworth, Philo Taylor
d. Young, Whitney Moore, Jr.

March 12, 1971
d. Burns, David

March 13, 1971
d. Kent, Rockwell

March 16, 1971
d. Daniels, Bebe
d. Dewey, Thomas Edmund

March 18, 1971
d. Hayward, Leland

March 24, 1971
d. Jacobsen, Arne

March 25, 1971
b. Swoopes, Sheryl

March 26, 1971
d. Anderson, C(larence) W(illiam)

March 28, 1971
d. Fairchild, Sherman Mills

April 1, 1971
d. Lonsdale, Kathleen (Yardley)

April 3, 1971
d. Kappel, Gertrude
d. Lee, Manfred B(ennington)
d. Valachi, Joe

April 5, 1971
d. Mowrer, Paul Scott

April 6, 1971
d. Stravinsky, Igor Fedorovich

April 9, 1971
b. Villeneuve, Jacques
d. Harridge, Will(iam)

April 12, 1971
b. Doherty, Shannen
d. Tamm, Igor Evgenevich

April 15, 1971
d. Brodovitch, Alexey
d. Reeves, Dan(iel F)
d. Stanley, Wendell Meredith

April 16, 1971
b. Selena
d. Eckert, William Dole

April 17, 1971
d. Lombardo, Carmen

April 18, 1971
d. Luboshutz, Pierre

April 19, 1971
d. Thomson, Earl

April 21, 1971
d. Duvalier, Francois
d. Eliot, George Fielding
d. Lowe, Edmund Dante
d. Parker, Cecil

April 23, 1971
d. Jameson, House

April 24, 1971
d. Hayton, Lennie
d. Soong, T V

April 29, 1971
d. Guion, Connie Myers

April 30, 1971
d. Roper, Elmo Burns, Jr.

May 1, 1971
d. Farrell, Glenda

May 2, 1971
d. Dozier, Edward P.

May 12, 1971
d. Manush, Heinie

May 13, 1971
d. O'Hanlon, Virginia

May 15, 1971
d. Goslin, Goose
d. Guthrie, Tyrone, Sir
d. Maxon, Lou Russell

May 16, 1971
d. Stanley, Barney

May 19, 1971
d. Nash, Ogden Frederick

May 20, 1971
d. Dihigo, Martin

May 21, 1971
d. King, Dennis

May 24, 1971
d. Dodd, Thomas Joseph

May 25, 1971
d. Conniff, Frank

May 27, 1971
d. Rafferty, Chips

May 28, 1971
d. Murphy, Audie

May 30, 1971
d. DuPre, Marcel

June 1, 1971
d. Niebuhr, Reinhold

June 2, 1971
b. Wyle, Noah

June 4, 1971
d. Lewis, Joe E
d. Lukacs, Gyorgy

June 7, 1971
d. Burnett, Leo
d. Rodale, Jerome Irving

June 10, 1971
d. Rennie, Michael

June 14, 1971
d. Garcia, Carlos Polestico

June 16, 1971
b. Shakur, Tupac
d. Reith, John Charles Walsham

June 18, 1971
d. Gomez, Thomas
d. Holman, Libby
d. Karrar, Paul

June 19, 1971
d. Wood, Gar(field A)

June 20, 1971
d. Ullman, James Ramsey

June 21, 1971
d. Rose, Carl

June 25, 1971
d. Boyd-Orr, John, Baron
d. Orr, John Boyd, 1st Baron of
Brechin

June 28, 1971
d. Binns, Archie Fred
d. Stangl, Franz Paul

June 29, 1971
d. Patsayev, Viktor Ivanovich

June 30, 1971
d. Biberman, Herbert
d. Dobrovolsky, Georgi Timofeyevich
d. Volkov, Vladislav Nikolayevich

July 1, 1971
d. Bragg, William Lawrence, Sir
d. Constantine, Learie Nicholas
Constantine, Baron

July 3, 1971
d. Morrison, Jim

July 4, 1971
d. Bowra, Maurice, Sir
d. Derleth, August (William)

July 6, 1971
d. Armstrong, Louis

July 7, 1971
d. Iwerks, Ub(be)

July 8, 1971
d. Dunhill, Alfred Henry

July 10, 1971
d. Bronfman, Samuel

July 11, 1971
d. Campbell, John W

July 12, 1971
b. Yamaguchi, Kristi Tsuya

July 16, 1971
b. Feldman, Corey

July 17, 1971
d. Edwards, Cliff
d. Nye, Gerald Prentice

July 18, 1971
b. Hardaway, Anfernee (Deon)

July 19, 1971
d. Myers, Garry Cleveland

July 22, 1971
d. Fiorito, Ted

July 23, 1971
b. Krauss, Alison (Maria)
d. Heflin, Van Emmett Evan
d. Tubman, William Vacanarat
Shadrach

July 26, 1971
d. Arbus, Diane

July 27, 1971
d. Weston, Edward F

August 1, 1971
d. McDermott, Johnny

August 3, 1971
d. Sloane, John

August 4, 1971
b. Gordon, Jeff

August 6, 1971
d. Cleva, Fausto

August 7, 1971
d. Evans, Orrin C

August 12, 1971
b. Sampras, Pete(r)
d. Cowles, William Hutchinson, Jr.

August 13, 1971
d. Bentley, Walter Owen

August 14, 1971
d. Heard, Gerald
d. King Curtis

August 15, 1971
d. Lukas, Paul

August 16, 1971
d. Anthony, Edward
d. Skouras, Spyros Panagiotes

August 17, 1971
d. McMahon, Horace

August 19, 1971
d. Melford, Austin

August 21, 1971
d. Jackson, George

August 24, 1971
b. Schiffer, Claudia
d. Blegen, Carl William
d. Fergusson, Harvey

August 25, 1971
d. Lewis, Ted

August 27, 1971
d. Armstrong, Lil(lian Hardin)
d. Bourke-White, Margaret

d. Cerf, Bennett Alfred
d. Turnesa, Jim

August 28, 1971
b. Evans, Janet
d. Leopold, Nathan Freudenthal
d. McGarity, Lou

August 31, 1971
b. Gibson, Deborah (Ann)

September 1, 1971
d. Romanoff, Mike

September 4, 1971
d. Gladstone, James
d. Hickenlooper, Bourke B

September 5, 1971
d. Trafton, George

September 6, 1971
d. Hawes, Elizabeth

September 7, 1971
d. Byington, Spring

September 10, 1971
d. Angeli, Pier
d. Darvi, Bella

September 11, 1971
d. Blotta, Anthony
d. Khrushchev, Nikita Sergeyevich

September 13, 1971
d. Lin, Piao (Yu-Yung)

September 18, 1971
b. Smith, Jada Pinkett

September 19, 1971
d. Albright, William Foxwell

September 20, 1971
d. Seferiades, Giorgos Styljanou
d. Seferis, George

September 21, 1971
b. David
b. Ribeiro, Alfonso
d. Houssay, Bernardo Alberto

September 23, 1971
d. Alexander, James Waddell, II
d. Gilbert, Billy
d. Woodward, Ellen S.

September 25, 1971
d. Black, Hugo LaFayette

September 26, 1971
d. Gipson, Lawrence Henry

September 29, 1971
d. Moore, Roy W

October 2, 1971
b. Tiffany
d. Laubenthal, Rudolf

October 3, 1971
d. Germer, Lester Halbert

October 9, 1971
b. Kissin, Evgeny

October 10, 1971
d. Burt, Cyril Lodowic, Sir
d. Saerchinger, Cesar Victor Charles

October 11, 1971
d. Conklin, Chester

October 12, 1971
d. Acheson, Dean Gooderham
d. Crawford, John Edmund
d. Vincent, Gene

October 14, 1971
d. Spewack, Samuel

October 16, 1971
d. Switzer, Mary E.

October 17, 1971
d. Popovi Da

October 21, 1971
d. Bronson, Betty

October 24, 1971
d. Ruggles, Carl

October 25, 1971
b. Midori
d. Terry, Paul H
d. Wylie, Philip Gordon

October 28, 1971
d. Foyle, Gilbert Samuel

October 29, 1971
b. Ryder, Winona
d. Allman, Duane
d. Tiselius, Arne Wilhelm Kaurin

October 31, 1971
d. von Rad, Gerhard

November 1, 1971
d. Evans, Richard Louis
d. Romm, Mikhail

November 2, 1971
d. Vickers, Martha

November 4, 1971
d. Pennington, Ann

November 10, 1971
d. Clark, Walter van Tilburg
d. Foster, Joseph C

November 11, 1971
d. Herbert, A(lan) P(atrick), Sir

November 13, 1971
d. Bleeker, Sonia

November 15, 1971
d. Abel, Rudolf Ivanovich

November 17, 1971
d. Cooper, Gladys, Dame

November 19, 1971
d. Stern, Bill

November 22, 1971
d. Confrey, Zez
d. Wilson, Joseph Chamberlain

November 26, 1971
d. Adonis, Joe
d. Young, Andrew

November 27, 1971
d. Guyon, Joe
d. Pew, J(ohn) Howard

November 29, 1971
d. Petersham, Maud

December 1, 1971
d. Spingarn, Arthur Barnett

December 6, 1971
b. White, Ryan

December 7, 1971
d. Pecora, Ferdinand

December 8, 1971
d. Widener, George D

December 9, 1971
d. Bunche, Ralph Johnson

December 12, 1971
d. Sarnoff, David

December 17, 1971
b. McCray, Nikki
d. Larkin, Oliver Waterman

December 18, 1971
b. Sanchez-Vicario, Arantxa
d. Jones, Bobby
d. Lynn, Diana

December 20, 1971
d. Crawford, Rusty
d. Disney, Roy O(liver)

December 26, 1971
d. O'Donnell, Emmett, Jr.

December 28, 1971
d. Steiner, Max

December 29, 1971
d. Harlan, John Marshall, II

December 31, 1971
d. Duel, Peter
d. Henderson, Ray

1972

b. Busta Rhymes
b. Cerovsek, Corey
b. Ferrell, Trevor

b. Gordeeva, Ekaterina
b. Martinez, Andrew
b. MC Breed
b. Rheaume, Manon
b. Sanders, Summer
b. Zamora, Pedro
d. Amorsolo, Fernando
d. Clay-Jolles, Tettje Clasina
d. Crooks, Richard Alexander
d. Kiwanuka, Benedicto Kagima
  Mugumba
d. Klein, Abraham Moses
d. Lawrence, Bill
d. Ngala, Ronald Gideon
d. Schneiderman, Rose
d. Thorarensen, Jakob
d. Tupolev, Andrei Nikolaevich
d. Washburn, Charles

January 1, 1972
d. Chevalier, Maurice Auguste

January 2, 1972
d. Gilbreth, Lillian Moller

January 3, 1972
d. Wilson, Charles Edward

January 6, 1972
d. Chen Yi
d. Pully, B S

January 7, 1972
d. Berryman, John

January 8, 1972
d. Patchen, Kenneth

January 9, 1972
d. Shawn, Ted

January 10, 1972
d. Gulbenkian, Nubar Sarkis

January 11, 1972
d. Gardiner, Herb(ert Martin)

January 12, 1972
d. Colum, Padraic

January 13, 1972
b. Shcherbo, Vitaly

January 14, 1972
d. Frederick IX

January 15, 1972
d. Ashford, Daisy

January 16, 1972
d. Seville, David

January 17, 1972
d. Hudson, Rochelle
d. Smith, Betty
d. Spectorsky, Auguste Compte

January 18, 1972
d. Burtin, Will
d. France, Harry Clinton

January 19, 1972
d. Chapman, John (Arthur)
d. Rabin, Michael

January 20, 1972
d. Casadesus, Jean

January 21, 1972
d. Lyttleton, Oliver

January 24, 1972
d. Austin, Gene
d. Cowan, Jerome

January 25, 1972
d. Hayden, Carl Trumball

January 27, 1972
d. Courant, Richard
d. Jackson, Mahalia
d. Weeks, Sinclair

January 31, 1972
d. Barlow, Howard
d. Boyce, Westray Battle
d. Mahendra, Bir Bikram Shah Dev

February 2, 1972
d. Barney, Natalie Clifford
d. Landis, Jessie Royce

February 5, 1972
d. Moore, Marianne Craig

February 6, 1972
d. Steward, Julian Haynes
d. Thompson, Llewellyn E, Jr.

February 8, 1972
d. Chinard, Gilbert

February 9, 1972
d. Craig, May

February 14, 1972
b. Bledsoe, Drew

February 15, 1972
b. Jagr, Jaromir
d. Snow, Edgar Parks

February 17, 1972
b. Armstrong, Billie Joe

February 19, 1972
d. Grierson, John

February 20, 1972
d. Mayer, Maria Goeppert
d. Winchell, Walter

February 21, 1972
d. Ames, Jessie Daniel
d. Nijinska, Bronislava

February 22, 1972
b. Chang, Michael

February 27, 1972
d. Brady, Pat
d. Heiser, Victor George

February 28, 1972
d. Trout, Dizzy

March 1, 1972
d. Babin, Victor
d. Golschmann, Vladimir

March 2, 1972
d. Dykstra, John
d. Feis, Herbert
d. Sack, Erna

March 6, 1972
b. O'Neal, Shaquille

March 9, 1972
d. O'Connor, Basil

March 11, 1972
d. Wheat, Zack

March 14, 1972
d. Ford, Len

March 16, 1972
d. Grant, Jane
d. Traynor, Pie

March 20, 1972
d. Maxwell, Marilyn

March 23, 1972
d. Balenciaga, Cristobal

March 27, 1972
d. Escher, M(aurits) C(ornelis)

March 28, 1972
d. Paul-Boncour, Joseph

March 29, 1972
d. Rank, J(oseph) Arthur
d. Sayre, Francis Bowes

March 30, 1972
d. Heatter, Gabriel

April 1, 1972
b. Hughes, Albert
b. Hughes, Allen

April 2, 1972
d. Hodges, Gil(bert Raymond)

April 3, 1972
d. Grofe, Ferde

April 4, 1972
d. Powell, Adam Clayton, Jr.
d. Wolpe, Stefan

April 5, 1972
d. Donahue, Woolworth
d. Donlevy, Brian

April 6, 1972
b. Hervey, Jason
d. Lubke, Heinrich

April 7, 1972
d. Blythe, Betty

d. Karume, Abeid Amani
d. Zaleski, August

April 9, 1972
d. Byrnes, James Francis

April 12, 1972
d. Marek, Kurt W

April 15, 1972
d. Crowley, Leo Thomas
d. Knight, Frank Hyneman

April 16, 1972
d. Kawabata, Yasunari

April 19, 1972
d. Burke, Billy

April 25, 1972
d. Sanders, George

April 26, 1972
d. Summerfield, Arthur Ellsworth

April 27, 1972
d. Budenz, Louis Francis
d. Nkrumah, Kwame

April 30, 1972
d. Scala, Gia

May 2, 1972
d. Hoover, J(ohn) Edgar

May 3, 1972
d. Cabot, Bruce

May 4, 1972
d. Kendall, Edward C(alvin)
d. Samuel, Maurice

May 5, 1972
d. Davis, Gary, Reverend
d. Youlou, Fulbert

May 11, 1972
d. Trendle, George Washington

May 13, 1972
d. Blocker, Dan

May 21, 1972
b. McBride, Christian

May 22, 1972
d. Day-Lewis, Cecil
d. Rutherford, Margaret

May 28, 1972
d. Edward VIII
d. Irvin, Rea

May 29, 1972
d. Bernhard, Lucian

May 30, 1972
d. Bates, Ted

June 8, 1972
d. Rushing, Jimmy

June 12, 1972
d. Alinsky, Saul David
d. Wilson, Edmund

June 13, 1972
d. McPhatter, Clyde
d. Von Bekesy, Georg

June 20, 1972
d. Johnson, Howard Deering

June 24, 1972
d. Delderfield, Ronald Frederick

June 25, 1972
d. Fleischer, Nat(haniel Stanley)
d. McKenney, Ruth

June 26, 1972
d. Lichine, David

June 29, 1972
b. Smith, Samantha

July 2, 1972
d. Smith, Joseph Fielding

July 6, 1972
d. Athenagoras I
d. DeWilde, Brandon

July 7, 1972
b. Leslie, Lisa

July 10, 1972
d. Madeira, Jean
d. Weede, Robert

July 13, 1972
d. Saarinen, Aline Bernstein

July 18, 1972
d. Fosdick, Raymond Blaine
d. Gentele, Goeran

July 19, 1972
d. Benson, Sally
d. Roswaenge, Helge

July 20, 1972
d. Flick, Friedrich

July 25, 1972
d. Reventlow, Lance

July 27, 1972
d. Ellender, Allen Joseph
d. LaRose, Rose

July 28, 1972
d. Cwiklinska, Mieczyslawa
d. Traubel, Helen

July 31, 1972
d. Spaak, Paul-Henri

August 2, 1972
d. Ganz, Rudolph
d. Goodman, Paul

August 5, 1972
d. Mezzrow, Mezz

August 7, 1972
d. Lansing, Joi

August 11, 1972
d. Theiler, Max

August 13, 1972
d. Weiss, George Martin

August 14, 1972
d. Levant, Oscar
d. Romains, Jules

August 20, 1972
d. Stark, Harold Raynsford

August 26, 1972
d. Chichester, Francis Charles, Sir

August 28, 1972
d. Gold, Harry
d. Leibowitz, Rene

September 1, 1972
d. Duffy, Ben

September 2, 1972
b. Mohajer, Dineh

September 5, 1972
d. Berger, David
d. Friedman, Ze'ev
d. Gutfreund, Yosef
d. Halfin, Eliezer
d. Romano, Joseph
d. Shapira, Amitzur
d. Shorr, Kehat
d. Slavin, Mark
d. Spitzer, Andre
d. Springer, Ya'acov
d. Weinberg, Moshe

September 8, 1972
b. Thomas, Henry

September 10, 1972
d. Gersten, Berta

September 11, 1972
d. Fleischer, Max

September 12, 1972
d. Boyd, William

September 14, 1972
d. Boyd, Louise Arner

September 15, 1972
d. Hewitt, Henry Kent

September 17, 1972
d. Tamiroff, Akim

September 19, 1972
d. Casadesus, Robert

September 20, 1972
d. Liebes, Dorothy Katherine Wright
d. Oakes, Richard

September 23, 1972
b. Dupri, Jermaine
d. Huebner, Clarence R

September 26, 1972
d. Correll, Charles J
d. Boggs, Hale

October 1, 1972
d. Leakey, Louis Seymour Bazett

October 3, 1972
d. Schmitt, Gladys

October 5, 1972
b. Hill, Grant
d. Dreyfuss, Henry

October 9, 1972
d. Bancroft, Dave
d. Hopkins, Miriam
d. Magee, Harry L

October 11, 1972
d. Ricca, Paul

October 16, 1972
d. Carroll, Leo G
d. Hatathli, Ned

October 17, 1972
d. Broda, Turk

October 19, 1972
d. Drinker, Philip
d. Said bin Taimur

October 20, 1972
d. Shapley, Harlow T

October 24, 1972
d. Robinson, Jackie
d. Votipka, Thelma
d. Windsor, Claire

October 25, 1972
d. Norell, Norman

October 26, 1972
d. Fox, Uffa
d. Perkins, Milo Randolph
d. Sikorsky, Igor Ivanovich

October 27, 1972
b. Mutola, Maria

October 28, 1972
b. Davis, Terrell

October 31, 1972
d. Durnan, Bill

November 1, 1972
b. McCarthy, Jenny
d. Pound, Ezra Loomis

November 3, 1972
d. Richman, Harry

November 5, 1972
d. Owen, (John) Reginald

November 9, 1972
d. Berwind, Charles G
d. James, Art

November 12, 1972
d. Friml, Rudolf

November 13, 1972
d. Webster, Margaret

November 14, 1972
d. Dies, Martin, Jr.

November 16, 1972
d. Hurley, Jack B

November 19, 1972
d. Ohrbach, Nathan M

November 20, 1972
d. Grossinger, Jennie

November 22, 1972
d. Loper, Don

November 23, 1972
d. Wilson, Marie (Katherine Elizabeth)

November 24, 1972
d. Bentley, Doug(las Wagner)
d. Smallens, Alexander

November 25, 1972
d. Coanda, Henri Marie

November 28, 1972
d. Carmichael, James Vinson
d. Zirato, Bruno

November 30, 1972
d. Mackenzie, Compton
d. McElroy, Neil Hosler
d. Bond, Horace Mann

December 1, 1972
d. Segni, Antonio

December 2, 1972
d. Limon, Jose Arcadio

December 9, 1972
d. Dieterle, William
d. Parsons, Louella Oettinger

December 10, 1972
d. Van Doren, Mark

December 11, 1972
d. Swados, Harvey

December 13, 1972
d. Hartley, L(eslie) P(oles)

December 14, 1972
d. Berman, Eugene

December 19, 1972
b. Milano, Alyssa

December 20, 1972
d. Hartnett, Gabby

d. Wright, John Lloyd

December 22, 1972
d. Wallington, Jimmy

December 23, 1972
d. Atlas, Charles
d. Heschel, Abraham Joshua

December 26, 1972
d. Truman, Harry S

December 27, 1972
d. Garrigue, Jean
d. Pearson, Lester B(owles)

December 29, 1972
d. Cornell, Joseph

December 31, 1972
d. Clemente, Roberto Walker

1973

b. Acosta, Carlos
b. Bonaly, Surya
b. Lopez, Mario
b. Notorious B.I.G.
b. Tucker, Chris
b. Whitestone, Heather
d. Bulgari, Constantine
d. Harris, Willard Palmer
d. Husayn, Taha
d. Pitseolak, Peter
d. Ruiz Cortines, Adolfo
d. Scott, Adrian
d. Strauss, Leo
d. von Mises, Ludwig (Edler)
d. Wigman, Mary
d. DeParis, Wilbur

January 10, 1973
d. Edwards, Turk

January 17, 1973
d. Walker, Ralph Thomas

January 18, 1973
d. Stevens, S(tanley) S(mith)

January 20, 1973
d. Cabral, Amilcar Lopes

January 21, 1973
d. Szabolcsi, Bence

January 22, 1973
d. Johnson, Lyndon B(aines)

January 23, 1973
d. Ory, Kid

January 24, 1973
d. Naish, J(oseph) Carrol
d. Weintal, Edward

January 26, 1973
d. Jones, Eli Stanley
d. Robinson, Edward G

January 31, 1973
d. Frisch, Ragnar Anton Kittil

February 1, 1973
b. Van Dyken, Amy
d. Brauer, Max Julius Friedrich
d. Costello, Frank

February 3, 1973
d. Razaf, Andy

February 4, 1973
b. De La Hoya, Oscar

February 7, 1973
b. Howard, Juwan (Antonio)

February 8, 1973
d. Coates, Robert Myron

February 11, 1973
d. Jensen, Johannes Hans Daniel
d. Lawrence, David

February 12, 1973
d. Maritain, Jacques

February 15, 1973
d. Cox, Wally
d. Holt, Tim

February 18, 1973
d. Hayden, Palmer
d. Mott, Charles Stewart

February 19, 1973
d. Sanderson, Ivan Terence

February 20, 1973
d. Szigeti, Joseph

February 22, 1973
d. Bowen, Elizabeth Dorthea Cole
d. Paxinou, Katina
d. Rockefeller, Winthrop

February 23, 1973
d. Richards, Dickinson Woodruff

February 26, 1973
d. Wilson, Mitchell A

February 28, 1973
b. Lindros, Eric (Bryan)
d. Gerold, Karl
d. Kellaway, Cecil

March 1, 1973
b. Webber, Chris

March 3, 1973
d. Halliday, Richard

March 5, 1973
d. Crosse, Rupert

March 6, 1973
d. Buck, Pearl S(ydenstricker)

March 8, 1973
d. Connor, Bull

d. McKernan, Ron

March 11, 1973
d. Evergood, Philip (Howard Francis Dixon)

March 12, 1973
d. Frisch, Frankie

March 14, 1973
d. Aiken, Howard Hathaway
d. Young, Chic

March 18, 1973
d. Benton, William
d. Melchior, Lauritz

March 19, 1973
d. Adams, Weston W, Sir

March 23, 1973
d. Maynard, Ken

March 25, 1973
d. Steichen, Edward Jean

March 26, 1973
d. Coward, Noel Pierce, Sir
d. Sisler, George Harold

March 28, 1973
d. Kalatozov, Mikhail
d. Rosenthal, Ida Cohen

March 29, 1973
d. Cooper, Melville
d. Graf, Herbert

April 5, 1973
d. Tarasova, Alla Konstantinovna

April 7, 1973
d. Elisofon, Eliot

April 8, 1973
d. Picasso, Pablo Ruiz y

April 11, 1973
d. Barker, Lex

April 12, 1973
d. Freed, Arthur
d. Senanayake, Dudley Shelton

April 13, 1973
d. Courboin, Charles

April 17, 1973
d. Kertesz, Istvan

April 18, 1973
d. Smith, William

April 19, 1973
d. Kelsen, Hans

April 20, 1973
d. Armstrong, Robert

April 22, 1973
d. Burnett, Whit

April 24, 1973
d. Armstrong, Hamilton Fish

April 25, 1973
d. Shihab, Fu'ad

April 26, 1973
d. Ryan, Irene Noblette
d. Ewing, Alfred Cyril

May 4, 1973
d. Bowles, Jane Sydney

May 5, 1973
b. Yothers, Tina

May 6, 1973
d. MacMillan, Ernest Campbell, Sir

May 8, 1973
d. Vandegrift, Alexander Archer

May 9, 1973
d. Brannigan, Owen
d. Leonard, Jack E

May 10, 1973
d. Green, Abel

May 12, 1973
b. Astin, Mackenzie Alexander
d. Marion, Frances

May 16, 1973
b. Spelling, Tori

May 18, 1973
d. Coste, Dieudonne
d. Rankin, Jeannette

May 21, 1973
d. Konev, Ivan Stepanovich
d. Monroe, Vaughn

May 23, 1973
b. Maxwell
d. Allsop, Kenneth

May 26, 1973
d. Higginbotham, Jack
d. Lipchitz, Jacques

May 28, 1973
d. Schmidt-Isserstedt, Hans

June 1, 1973
d. Firestone, Harvey Samuel, Jr.
d. Greaza, Walter N
d. Kornman, Mary
d. Parkhurst, Helen

June 4, 1973
d. Bontemps, Arna Wendell

June 8, 1973
d. Arundel, Honor Morfydd

June 9, 1973
d. Creasey, John

June 10, 1973
d. Inge, William Motter
d. Kredel, Fritz

June 13, 1973
d. Cott, Ted

June 15, 1973
b. Harris, Neil Patrick

June 18, 1973
d. Bonnet, Georges Etienne
d. Mahler, Fritz

June 21, 1973
b. Lewis, Juliette
d. Leahy, Frank

June 23, 1973
d. Holden, Fay

June 26, 1973
d. Cranko, John

June 27, 1973
d. Browder, Earl Russell
d. Truex, Ernest

June 30, 1973
d. Layden, Elmer Francis
d. Mitford, Nancy Freeman

July 1, 1973
d. Hammond, Laurens

July 2, 1973
d. Grable, Betty
d. Hafey, Chick
d. Macready, George

July 3, 1973
d. Ancerl, Karel

July 6, 1973
d. Brown, Joe E(van)
d. Klemperer, Otto

July 7, 1973
d. Lake, Veronica

July 10, 1973
d. Brown, Dean
d. Warburg, Frederick Marcus

July 11, 1973
d. Ryan, Robert (Bushnell)

July 12, 1973
d. Chaney, Lon, Jr.

July 18, 1973
d. Hawkins, Jack

July 20, 1973
d. Lee, Bruce
d. Smithson, Robert (Irving)

July 23, 1973
d. Rickenbacker, Eddie

July 24, 1973
d. Saint Laurent, Louis Stephen

July 26, 1973
d. White, William Lindsay

July 28, 1973
d. Chase, Mary Ellen

July 29, 1973
d. Charriere, Henri

August 1, 1973
b. Bledsoe, Tempestt Kenieth
d. Malipiero, Gian Francesco
d. Ulbricht, Walter

August 2, 1973
d. Melville, Jean-Pierre

August 3, 1973
d. Condon, Eddie

August 6, 1973
d. Batista y Zaldivar, Fulgencio

August 7, 1973
d. Tunis, Edwin Burdett

August 8, 1973
d. Wiley, George A

August 9, 1973
d. Behrman, S(amuel) N(athaniel)
d. Moberg, Vihelm
d. Roxon, Lillian

August 11, 1973
d. Castle, Peggie

August 12, 1973
d. Hess, Walter Rudolf
d. Ziegler, Karl

August 15, 1973
d. Tregaskis, Richard William

August 16, 1973
d. Borg, Veda Ann
d. Waksman, Selman Abraham

August 17, 1973
d. Aiken, Conrad Potter
d. Radford, Arthur William

August 22, 1973
d. MacDonald-Wright, Stanton

August 25, 1973
d. Corcos, Lucille

August 29, 1973
d. Dunn, Michael

August 31, 1973
b. Gooch, George Peabody
d. Ford, John Sean O'Feeney

September 1, 1973
d. Watkins, Arthur V(ivian)

September 2, 1973
d. Tolkien, J(ohn) R(onald) R(euel)

September 4, 1973
d. Behn, Harry

September 7, 1973
d. Holling, Holling C(lancy)

September 11, 1973
d. Allende Gossens, Salvador
d. Evans-Pritchard, Edward Evan

September 12, 1973
d. Post, Marjorie Merriweather

September 13, 1973
d. Field, Betty

September 15, 1973
d. Gustaf Adolf VI

September 16, 1973
d. Licavoli, Thomas

September 17, 1973
d. Winterhalter, Hugo

September 19, 1973
d. Parsons, Gram
d. Wurster, William

September 20, 1973
d. Croce, Jim

September 21, 1973
d. Plomer, William Charles Franklyn
d. Sands, Diana Patricia

September 22, 1973
d. Dodd, Charles Harold

September 23, 1973
d. Neruda, Pablo

September 24, 1973
d. Neill, A(lexander) S(utherland)

September 26, 1973
d. Bemis, Samuel Flagg
d. Magnani, Anna

September 28, 1973
b. Paltrow, Gwyneth
d. Auden, W(ystan) H(ugh)

October 2, 1973
d. Hartman, Paul
d. Nurmi, Paavo Johannes

October 3, 1973
b. Campbell, Neve

October 5, 1973
d. Blackmer, Sidney Alderman

October 6, 1973
d. Wilson, Margaret

October 7, 1973
d. Price, Dennis

October 9, 1973
d. Marcel, Gabriel Honore

October 13, 1973
d. Briggs, Austin Eugene

October 16, 1973
d. Krupa, Gene

October 17, 1973
d. Balchen, Bernt

October 18, 1973
d. Anderson, Margaret (Carolyn)
d. Kelly, Walt(er Crawford)

October 20, 1973
d. Chandler, Norman

October 21, 1973
d. Cobham, Alan John, Sir

October 22, 1973
d. Casals, Pablo (Pau Carlos Salvador)

October 28, 1973
d. Taha Hussein

October 31, 1973
d. White, Paul Dudley

November 1, 1973
d. Bowen, Catherine Drinker

November 2, 1973
d. Neale, Greasy

November 3, 1973
d. Neihardt, John Gneisenau

November 4, 1973
d. Ginott, Haim

November 5, 1973
d. Romer, Alfred Sherwood

November 6, 1973
d. Biddle, George

November 11, 1973
d. Virtanen, Artturi Llmari

November 13, 1973
d. Lee, Lila

November 14, 1973
d. Schiaparelli

November 15, 1973
d. Russell, Honey

November 16, 1973
d. Watts, Alan Wilson

November 17, 1973
d. Mangrum, Lloyd

November 19, 1973
b. Glover, Savion

November 20, 1973
d. Sherman, Allan

November 23, 1973
d. Talmadge, Constance
d. Tourel, Jennie

November 25, 1973
d. Harvey, Laurence

November 26, 1973
d. Haines, William
d. Whittaker, Charles Evans

November 29, 1973
d. Apostoli, Fred

November 30, 1973
d. Yarnell, Bruce
d. O'Shea, Michael

December 1, 1973
d. Ben-Gurion, David

December 2, 1973
b. Seles, Monica
d. Haydn, Hiram Collins

December 4, 1973
b. Banks, Tyra
d. Cordiner, Ralph Jarron
d. Fuller, Alfred Carl

December 5, 1973
d. Cannon, Jimmy
d. Watson-Watt, Robert Alexander, Sir

December 7, 1973
d. Gorbatov, Aleksandr Vassil'evich

December 9, 1973
d. Young, Marian

December 12, 1973
d. Christ-Janer, Albert
d. Comstock, Ada Louise

December 13, 1973
d. Green, Henry

December 17, 1973
d. Abbot, C(harles) G(reeley)

December 20, 1973
d. Darin, Bobby

December 22, 1973
d. Phillips, Irna

December 23, 1973
d. Kuiper, Gerard Peter

December 24, 1973
d. Korda, Michael

December 25, 1973
d. Inonu, Ismet

December 26, 1973
d. Geray, Steven

December 27, 1973
d. DeSalvo, Albert

1974

b. Grant, Charity
b. Marier, Rebecca
d. Bolitho, Henry Hector
d. Chapin, F(rancis) Stuart
d. Doherty, Brian
d. Fuchs, Marta
d. Harkness, Georgia (Elma)
d. Loeb, Gerald Martin
d. Melnikov, Konstantin Stepanovich
d. Morgan, Jane
d. Wolfson, Harry Austryn

January 2, 1974
d. Bohlen, Charles Eustis
d. Cord, E(rret) L(obban)
d. Ritter, Tex

January 3, 1974
d. Daley, Arthur (John)

January 4, 1974
d. Starrett, Vincent

January 5, 1974
d. Brogan, Denis William, Sir

January 6, 1974
d. Siqueiros, David A

January 13, 1974
d. Jobin, Raoul

January 16, 1974
b. Moss, Kate
d. Lovejoy, Clarence Earle

January 20, 1974
d. Blunden, Edmund Charles

January 21, 1974
d. Strauss, Lewis Lichtenstein

January 22, 1974
d. Volkov, Leon

January 26, 1974
d. Patzak, Julius

January 27, 1974
d. Grivas, Georgios Theodoros

January 29, 1974
d. Bates, H(erbert) E(rnest)

January 31, 1974
d. Goldwyn, Samuel
d. Morris, Glenn
d. Pryor, Roger

February 2, 1974
d. Lakatos, Imre

February 4, 1974
d. Bose, Satyendranath

February 7, 1974
d. McGraw, Donald Cushing

February 8, 1974
d. Zwicky, Fritz

February 11, 1974
d. Nilsson, Anna Q(uerentia)

February 13, 1974
d. Golenpaul, Dan

February 16, 1974
d. Garand, John Cantius
d. Kallen, Horace M(eyer)

February 17, 1974
d. Cole, Jack

February 18, 1974
d. Odria Amoretti, Manuel Apolinario

February 20, 1974
d. Strauss, Robert

February 21, 1974
d. Daugherty, James Henry
d. Horton, Tim

February 23, 1974
d. Knowland, William Fife
d. Ruby, Harry

February 24, 1974
d. Barnes-Taeuber, Irene
d. Leech, Margaret Kernochan

February 25, 1974
d. Aldrich, Winthrop Williams

February 26, 1974
d. Sample, Paul Starrett

March 3, 1974
d. Burckhardt, Carl Jacob

March 4, 1974
d. Gottlieb, Adolph

March 5, 1974
d. DeWolfe, Billy
d. Hurok, Sol(omon Isaievich)

March 9, 1974
d. Sutherland, Earl Wilbur, Jr.

March 11, 1974
d. Gruenberg, Sidonie Matsner
d. Holdren, Judd Clifton

March 13, 1974
d. Saint John, Howard

March 16, 1974
d. Gerber, Daniel Frank

March 17, 1974
d. Kahn, Louis I(sadore)

March 19, 1974
d. Klein, Anne

March 20, 1974
d. Clarke, Austin
d. Huntley, Chet

March 22, 1974
d. Revson, Peter Jeffrey

March 23, 1974
d. Molyneux, Edward H

March 26, 1974
d. Condon, Edward Uhler

March 27, 1974
d. Wang Ming

March 28, 1974
d. Fields, Dorothy
d. Rosay, Francoise

March 30, 1974
d. Cottam, Clarence

April 1, 1974
d. Boyle, Harold Vincent

April 2, 1974
d. Pompidou, Georges Jean Raymond

April 5, 1974
d. Crossman, Richard Howard Stafford
d. Vyvyan, Jennifer Brigit

April 6, 1974
d. Jackson, A(lexander) Y(oung)

April 10, 1974
d. Collinge, Patricia

April 12, 1974
d. Krock, Arthur Bernard

April 14, 1974
d. Whalen, Michael

April 17, 1974
d. Seeley, Blossom

April 18, 1974
d. Pagnol, Marcel Paul

April 19, 1974
d. Ayub Khan, Mohammad

April 20, 1974
d. Greer, Howard

April 24, 1974
d. Abbott, Bud
d. Jonas, Franz

April 30, 1974
d. Moorehead, Agnes

May 3, 1974
d. Clapp, Margaret Antoinette

May 4, 1974
d. Ewing, William Maurice

May 6, 1974
d. Crean, Robert

May 8, 1974
d. May, Mortimer

May 13, 1974
d. Shute, Denny

May 18, 1974
d. Topping, Dan(iel Reid)

May 19, 1974
d. Allal al-Fassi, Mohamed

May 20, 1974
d. Dunn, Alan

May 24, 1974
d. Atwood, Angela
d. DeFreeze, Donald David
d. Ellington, Duke
d. Perry, Nancy Ling
d. Soltysik, Patricia Michelle
d. Wolfe, Willie

May 25, 1974
d. Crisp, Donald

May 26, 1974
d. Alsop, Stewart Johonnot Oliver
d. Gordon, Kitty

May 27, 1974
d. Biossat, Bruce
d. Wiese, Kurt

May 29, 1974
d. Ochs, Adolph Shelby, II

May 31, 1974
d. Davis, Adelle

June 1, 1974
b. Morissette, Alanis

June 2, 1974
d. Lunn, Arnold Henry Moore, Sir

June 3, 1974
d. Messali Hadj

June 6, 1974
d. Yurka, Blanche

June 9, 1974
d. Asturias, Miguel Angel
d. Cornell, Katharine
d. Henry William Frederick Albert

June 11, 1974
d. Dutra, Eurico Gaspar

June 13, 1974
d. Secunda, Sholom

June 14, 1974
d. Perkoff, Stuart Z.

June 18, 1974
d. Kelly, George Edward

d. Zhukov, Georgi Konstantinovich

June 22, 1974
d. Milhaud, Darius

June 28, 1974
d. Bush, Vannevar

June 30, 1974
d. King, Alberta Christine Williams

July 1, 1974
d. Peron, Juan

July 4, 1974
d. Heyer, Georgette
d. Husayni, Al-Hajj Amin al-
d. Husseini, Haj Amin

July 5, 1974
d. Ransom, John Crowe

July 7, 1974
d. Newhall, Nancy Wynne
d. Vanderbilt, Cornelius, Jr.

July 9, 1974
d. Brittain, Harry Ernest, Sir
d. Warren, Earl

July 11, 1974
d. Lagerkvist, Par Fabian

July 13, 1974
d. Blackett, Patrick Maynard Stuart

July 14, 1974
d. Hathaway, Sibyl Collings
d. Spaatz, Carl Andrew

July 17, 1974
d. Dean, Dizzy

July 19, 1974
d. Flynn, Joe

July 20, 1974
d. Jenkins, Allen

July 22, 1974
d. Darvas, Lili
d. Morse, Wayne Lyman

July 24, 1974
d. Carpenter, Leslie
d. Chadwick, James, Sir
d. Kastner, Erich
d. Tyler, Parker

July 26, 1974
d. Stouffer, Vernon B

July 28, 1974
d. McCafferty, Don

July 29, 1974
d. Elliot, Cass
b. Fisher, Amy
d. Mantha, Sylvio

August 6, 1974
d. Ammons, Jug
d. Rounseville, Robert Field

August 7, 1974
d. Apgar, Virginia

August 9, 1974
d. Luckenbach, Edgar Frederick, Jr.

August 10, 1974
d. Massey, Ilona

August 15, 1974
d. Braun, Otto

August 16, 1974
d. Mundt, Karl Earl

August 19, 1974
d. Davies, Rodger Paul

August 21, 1974
d. Pusser, Buford

August 22, 1974
d. Bronowski, Jacob
d. Wilder, Robert Ingersoll

August 24, 1974
d. DeSeversky, Alexander Procofieff

August 26, 1974
d. Lindbergh, Charles A(ugustus)

August 29, 1974
d. Griffis, Stanton

September 2, 1974
d. Soyer, Moses

September 3, 1974
d. Partch, Harry

September 4, 1974
d. Abrams, Creighton Williams
d. Achard, Marcel

September 5, 1974
d. Swinnerton, James Guilford

September 6, 1974
d. Baclanova, Olga
d. Kruger, Otto

September 8, 1974
d. Windgassen, Wolfgang Friedrich
Hermann

September 11, 1974
d. Lenski, Lois

September 16, 1974
d. Allen, Forrest Claire

September 17, 1974
d. Dunoyer de Segonzac, Andre

September 18, 1974
d. Best, Edna

September 21, 1974
d. Hull, Warren
d. Susann, Jacqueline

September 22, 1974
d. Brennan, Walter Andrew

September 23, 1974
d. Arquette, Cliff

September 24, 1974
d. Stone, Dorothy

September 26, 1974
d. McCarten, John

September 28, 1974
d. Howes, Frank Stewart

October 2, 1974
d. Shukshin, Vasilii Makarovich

October 4, 1974
d. Sexton, Anne Harvey

October 5, 1974
d. Shazar, Zalman
d. Stignani, Ebe

October 6, 1974
d. Hodges, Luther Hartwell
d. Krishna Menon, V(engalil)
K(rishnan)
d. Menon, (Vengalil Krishnan) Krishna

October 8, 1974
d. Carney, Harry Howell
d. Hoffman, Paul Gray

October 9, 1974
d. Schindler, Oskar

October 12, 1974
d. Krips, Josef
d. Nolan, Jeannette Covert

October 13, 1974
d. Kleberg, Robert Justus, Jr.
d. Rice, Sam
d. Rubin, Reuven
d. Sullivan, Ed(ward Vincent)

October 20, 1974
d. Tabbert, William

October 21, 1974
d. Goines, Donald

October 24, 1974
d. Oistrakh, David Fyodorovich

October 25, 1974
d. Furtseva, Ekaterina Alexeyevna
d. Kroll, Leon

October 27, 1974
d. Cox, James Middleton, Jr.

October 28, 1974
d. Jones, David

October 31, 1974
d. Myer, Buddy

November 6, 1974
d. Farrar, John Chipman

November 8, 1974
d. Hunter, Ivory Joe

November 9, 1974
d. Wellesz, Egon

November 10, 1974
d. Counts, George S(ylvester)

November 11, 1974
b. DiCaprio, Leonardo
d. Ace, Jane Sherwood

November 13, 1974
d. DeSica, Vittorio
d. Silkwood, Karen

November 14, 1974
d. Brown, Johnny Mack

November 17, 1974
d. Childers, Erskine Hamilton

November 18, 1974
d. Brook, Clive

November 19, 1974
d. Brunis, George

November 21, 1974
d. Gambling, John Bradley
d. Martin, Frank

November 23, 1974
d. Hayakawa, Sessue (Kintaro)
d. Ryan, Cornelius John

November 24, 1974
d. Drake, Nick

November 25, 1974
d. Lane, Rosemary
d. Thant, U

November 26, 1974
d. Connolly, Cyril Vernon

November 29, 1974
d. Braddock, Jim
d. Hunt, H(aroldson) L(afayette)

December 1, 1974
d. Lincoln, G(eorge) Gould
d. Spottswood, Stephen Gill

December 5, 1974
d. Germi, Pietro
d. Whitney, Richard
d. Wightman, Hazel Virginia
Hotchkiss

December 6, 1974
d. Hearst, Millicent Veronica Willson

December 10, 1974
d. Komroff, Manuel

December 11, 1974
d. Hadley, Reed

December 14, 1974
d. Lippmann, Walter

December 15, 1974
d. Branzell, Karin
d. Hershfield, Harry
d. Litvak, Anatole

December 16, 1974
d. Pierce, Edward Allen

December 18, 1974
d. Hooper, Harry Bartholomew

December 21, 1974
d. North, Sterling

December 22, 1974
d. Long, Richard

December 25, 1974
d. Beard, Myron Gould

December 26, 1974
d. Benny, Jack

December 27, 1974
d. Vanderbilt, Amy

1975

b. DeCaprio, Leonardo
b. Faulkner, Shannon
b. Gilbert, Sara
b. Hill, Lauryn
b. Jones, Marion (Patrick)
b. Pierce, Mary
d. Fischer, Herman G
d. Gluckman, Max
d. White, Leslie A(lvin)
d. Arnstein, Bobbie
d. Duggan, Maurice Noel

January 1, 1975
d. Loeffler, Ken(neth D)

January 3, 1975
d. Cross, Milton John

January 4, 1975
d. Montana, Bob

January 5, 1975
d. Levi, Carlo

January 6, 1975
d. Wheeler, Burton Kendall

January 7, 1975
d. Abercrombie, James Smither

January 8, 1975
d. Gregson, John
d. Tucker, Richard

January 10, 1975
d. Chamberlain, Samuel

January 11, 1975
d. Lorenz, Max

January 14, 1975
d. Traikov, Georgi

January 17, 1975
d. Rojas Pinilla, Gustavo

January 19, 1975
d. Benton, Thomas Hart

January 20, 1975
d. Summersby, Kay

January 21, 1975
d. Bosley, Harold A

January 24, 1975
d. Fine, Larry

January 25, 1975
d. Kellems, Vivien

January 27, 1975
d. Fuller, Ida
d. Sanderson, Julia

January 28, 1975
d. Novotny, Antonin

February 3, 1975
d. Black, Eli M
d. Coolidge, William David
d. Harand, Irene
d. Kalthoum, Um

February 4, 1975
d. Hill, Howard
d. Jordan, Louis

February 7, 1975
d. Stein, Clarence S

February 8, 1975
d. Green, Martyn
d. Robinson, Robert, Sir

February 13, 1975
d. Van Dusen, Henry Pitney

February 14, 1975
d. Huxley, Julian Sorell, Sir
d. Wodehouse, P(elham) G(renville)

February 18, 1975
d. Moley, Raymond Charles
d. Rinkoff, Barbara Jean

February 19, 1975
d. Dallapiccola, Luigi

February 22, 1975 ·
b. Barrymore, Drew

February 24, 1975
d. Bulganin, Nikolai Aleksandrovich

February 25, 1975
d. Muhammad, Elijah

February 28, 1975
d. Cardus, Neville, Sir

March 2, 1975
d. Vionnet, Madeleine

March 7, 1975
d. Bakhtin, Mikhail (Mikhailovich)
d. Blue, Ben
d. Seredy, Kate

March 8, 1975
d. Bech, Joseph
d. Stevens, George (Cooper)

March 9, 1975
d. Dunninger, Joseph

March 11, 1975
d. Gibbs, Anthony

March 13, 1975
d. Andric, Ivo

March 14, 1975
d. Hayward, Susan

March 15, 1975
d. Graham, Stephen
d. Onassis, Aristotle Socrates
d. Sheean, (James) Vincent

March 16, 1975
d. Mesta, Perle Skirvin
d. Walker, T-Bone

March 20, 1975
d. Schocken, Theodore

March 21, 1975
d. Hawtrey, Ralph George, Sir
d. Medwick, Joe

March 25, 1975
d. Cooper, Joseph D
d. Faisal (Ibn Abdul-Aziz al Saud)

March 27, 1975
d. Bliss, Arthur, Sir

March 29, 1975
d. Hibbs, Ben

April 2, 1975
d. Cannon, Poppy

April 3, 1975
d. Soglow, Otto
d. Ure, Mary

April 5, 1975
d. Chiang Kai-Shek

April 10, 1975
d. Evans, Walker
d. Main, Marjorie

April 11, 1975
d. Crerar, Thomas Alexander

April 13, 1975
d. Bolton, Isabel
d. Parks, Larry
d. Tombalbaye, Nagarta Francois

April 14, 1975
d. Baker, Josephine (Carson)
d. Booth, Charles Brandon
d. Flanders, Michael
d. March, Fredric
d. Tolson, Clyde Anderson

April 15, 1975
d. Conte, Richard

April 17, 1975
d. McGee, Frank
d. Radhakrishnan, Sarvepalli

April 19, 1975
d. Julian, Percy Lavon
d. Schioetz, Aksel

April 20, 1975
d. Clark, Sydney

April 21, 1975
d. Westrup, J(ack) A(llan), Sir

April 25, 1975
d. Duclos, Jacques

April 27, 1975
d. Marsala, Marty

May 4, 1975
d. Howard, Moe

May 5, 1975
d. Keating, Kenneth B
d. Ridder, Bernard Herman

May 6, 1975
d. Mindszenty, Jozsef, Cardinal

May 7, 1975
d. Baker, George

May 8, 1975
d. Brundage, Avery
d. Slobodkin, Louis

May 12, 1975
d. Allen, Larry

May 13, 1975
d. Wills, Bob

May 14, 1975
d. Alexanderson, Ernst Frederik
Werner

May 18, 1975
d. Anderson, Leroy

May 20, 1975
d. Hepworth, Barbara, Dame

May 22, 1975
d. Grove, Lefty

May 23, 1975
d. Mabley, Moms

May 24, 1975
d. Lincoln, George A

May 28, 1975
d. Charles, Ezzard

May 30, 1975
d. Prefontaine, Steve Roland

June 3, 1975
d. Gleason, Ralph Joseph
d. Laver, James
d. Nelson, Ozzie
d. Sato, Eisaku

June 4, 1975
d. Leider, Frida

June 6, 1975
d. Blyden, Larry
d. Hansen, Alvin Harvey

June 7, 1975
d. Brent, Evelyn

June 10, 1975
d. Hull, John Edwin

June 12, 1975
d. Kober, Arthur

June 16, 1975
d. Courtney, Clint(on Dawson)

June 17, 1975
d. Baxter, James Phinney, III

June 18, 1975
d. Faisal ibn Musaed

June 19, 1975
d. Giancana, Sam
d. Wieman, Henry Nelson

June 20, 1975
d. Chaudhuri, Haridas

June 21, 1975
d. Oenslager, Donald Mitchell

June 22, 1975
d. Wahloo, Per

June 23, 1975
d. Priest, Ivy (Maude) Baker

June 25, 1975
d. Cowdry, Edmund Vincent

June 26, 1975
d. Escriva de Balaguer, Josemarie

June 27, 1975
d. Stolz, Robert

June 28, 1975
d. Doxiadis, Constantinos Apostolos
d. Serling, Rod
d. Stevenson, Coke Robert

June 29, 1975
d. Buckley, Tim

July 2, 1975
d. Justice, James Robertson

July 4, 1975
d. Beatty, Morgan

July 5, 1975
d. Dalla Rizza, Gilda

July 7, 1975
d. Bjerknes, Jacob

July 11, 1975
d. Cordier, Andrew Wellington
d. Johnson, Crockett

July 12, 1975
d. Chapin, James Ormsbee

July 13, 1975
d. Hay, George W

July 14, 1975
d. Singleton, Zutty

July 15, 1975
d. Craig, May
d. Weidman, Charles Edward, Jr.

July 17, 1975
d. Omlie, Phoebe Jane Fairgrave

July 18, 1975
d. Sauer, Carl Ortwin

July 19, 1975
d. Frizzell, Lefty

July 22, 1975
d. Tunnell, Em(len)

July 30, 1975
d. Blish, James Benjamin
d. Hoffa, Jimmy

August 2, 1975
d. Mathieson, Muir

August 6, 1975
d. Daubeny, Peter Lauderdale, Sir

August 8, 1975
d. Adderley, Cannonball

August 9, 1975
d. Shostakovich, Dmitri Dmitryevich
d. Shostakovich, Maxim

August 11, 1975
d. McAuliffe, Anthony Clement

August 12, 1975
d. Sapir, Pinchas

August 15, 1975
d. Edwards, Willard Eldridge
d. Rahman, Mujibur, Sheik

August 16, 1975
d. Villanueva, Carlos Raul

August 19, 1975
d. Hogg, Ima

August 24, 1975
d. Revson, Charles Haskell

August 25, 1975
d. Billings, John Shaw
d. Dunning, John Ray

August 27, 1975
d. Haile Selassie, I
d. Stillman, Irwin Maxwell

August 30, 1975
d. DeValera, Eamon

September 5, 1975
d. Evans, Alice (Catherine)

September 6, 1975
d. Croft, Arthur C

September 8, 1975
b. Tate, Larenz

September 9, 1975
d. McGiver, John

September 10, 1975
d. Sproul, Robert Gordon
d. Thomson, George Paget, Sir

September 12, 1975
d. Redhead, Hugh McCulloch

September 17, 1975
d. Moscona, Nicola

September 18, 1975
d. Brown, Pamela
d. Porter, Fairfield

September 20, 1975
d. Bishop, Katharine Scott
d. Leger, Alexis St. Leger
d. Lopez, Vincent

September 21, 1975
d. Ross, Ishbel

September 24, 1975
d. Hunter, Ian

September 25, 1975
d. Considine, Bob

September 26, 1975
d. Paludan, Jacob

September 27, 1975
d. Lang, John Thomas

September 29, 1975
d. Stengel, Casey

October 1, 1975
d. MacPhail, Larry

October 2, 1975
d. Kamaraj, Kumaraswami

October 3, 1975
d. Mollet, Guy

October 4, 1975
d. Payson, Joan Whitney

October 5, 1975
d. Cantacuzene, Princess

October 8, 1975
d. Felsenstein, Walter

October 16, 1975
d. Gui, Vittorio

October 19, 1975
d. Lord, Phillips H

October 22, 1975
d. Toynbee, Arnold Joseph

October 26, 1975
d. Rooney, John (James)

October 27, 1975
d. Carpentier, Georges
d. Stout, Rex Todhunter
d. Wayman, Dorothy

October 28, 1975
d. La Tour du Pin, Patrice de

October 29, 1975
d. Trotter, John Scott

October 30, 1975
d. Hertz, Gustav Ludwig
d. Kellerman, Annette

November 1, 1975
d. James, Philip

November 2, 1975
d. Pasolini, Pier Paolo

November 5, 1975
d. Tatum, Edward Lawrie
d. Trilling, Lionel

November 6, 1975
d. Hanfstaengl, Ernst Franz Sedgwick

November 11, 1975
d. Anderson, Clint(on Presba)

November 12, 1975
d. Morgan, Arthur
d. Ross, David

November 13, 1975
d. Sherriff, Robert Cedric

November 14, 1975
d. Anslinger, Harry Jacob

November 17, 1975
d. Bronk, Detlev Wulf

November 19, 1975
d. Vishnevsky, Alexandr
   Alekandrovich

November 20, 1975
d. Franco, Francisco

November 27, 1975
d. McWhirter, A(lan) Ross

November 28, 1975
d. Cartier, Claude
d. Verissimo, Erico Lopes

November 30, 1975
d. Hill, Graham

December 1, 1975
d. Fox, Nellie
d. Kenny, Nick
d. Mayer, Edward Newton, Jr.
d. Roosevelt, Anna Eleanor

December 2, 1975
d. Maserati, Ernesto

December 4, 1975
d. Arendt, Hannah

December 5, 1975
d. Green, Constance Windsor
   McLaughlin

December 7, 1975
d. Knight, John Shively, III
d. Wilder, Thornton (Niven)

December 9, 1975
d. Wellman, William Augustus

December 12, 1975
b. Bialik, Mayim

December 14, 1975
d. Gray, James, Sir
d. Treacher, Arthur

December 16, 1975
d. Kang, Sheng

December 17, 1975
d. Sissle, Noble
d. Wimsatt, William Kurtz, Jr.

December 18, 1975
d. Dobzhansky, Theodosius
   (Grigorievich)
d. Wheeler, Earle G

December 21, 1975
b. Herrera, Paloma
d. Lundigan, William

December 24, 1975
d. Herrmann, Bernard
d. Losch, Tilly

December 25, 1975
d. Burchard, John Ely

December 29, 1975
d. Gibbons, Euell

December 30, 1975
b. Woods, Tiger

1976

b. Cameron, Candace
b. Nieminen, Toni
d. Aquash, Anna Mae Pictou
d. Cosio Villegas, Daniel
d. Day, Frank
d. Inescort, Frieda
d. Jones, Anissa
d. Lame Deer
d. McKelway, St. Clair
d. Tomlinson, Jill
d. Totheroh, Dan

January 4, 1976
d. Leventhal, Albert Rice

January 5, 1976
d. Costello, John Aloysius

January 8, 1976
d. Chou En-Lai

January 9, 1976
d. Granger, Lester
d. Taylor, Phoebe Atwood

January 10, 1976
d. Howlin' Wolf

January 11, 1976
d. Schoonmaker, Frank Musselman

January 12, 1976
d. Christie, Agatha Mary Clarissa
Miller, Dame

January 13, 1976
d. Leighton, Margaret

January 18, 1976
d. August, Jan

January 22, 1976
d. Leslie, Edgar

January 23, 1976
d. Robeson, Paul Leroy

January 25, 1976
d. Henderson, Vivian Wilson

January 31, 1976
d. Miranda, Ernesto
d. Wells, Linton

February 1, 1976
d. Heisenberg, Werner Karl
d. Richter, Hans
d. Whipple, George Hoyt

February 5, 1976
d. Kahn, Ben
d. Livesey, Roger
d. Shutta, Ethel

February 6, 1976
d. Guaraldi, Vince(nt Anthony)

February 9, 1976
d. Faith, Percy

February 10, 1976
d. Kern, Harold G

February 11, 1976
d. Cobb, Lee J

February 12, 1976
d. Mineo, Sal(vatore)

February 13, 1976
d. Pons, Lily

February 18, 1976
d. Dowling, Eddie

February 19, 1976
d. Fishbein, Harry J
d. Sullivan, Frank

February 20, 1976
d. Aurell, Tage
d. Cassin, Rene-Samuel
d. Kuhlman, Kathryn

February 21, 1976
d. Briggs, Ellis O(rmsbee)

February 22, 1976
d. Baddeley, Angela
d. Ballard, Florence
d. Polanyi, Michael

February 23, 1976
d. Lowry, Lawrence Stephen

February 24, 1976
d. Smith, H(arry) Allen

February 25, 1976
d. Crosthwait, David Nelson, Jr.

February 26, 1976
d. Weil, Joseph R

February 29, 1976
d. Dwyer, Florence Price

March 1, 1976
d. Martinon, Jean

March 6, 1976
d. Rosenbloom, Maxie

March 7, 1976
d. Patman, (John Williams) Wright

March 8, 1976
d. Disney, Doris Miles

March 10, 1976
d. Sissman, L(ouis) E(dward)

March 14, 1976
d. Berkeley, Busby
d. Dole, Charles Minot

March 15, 1976
d. Mielziner, Jo

March 17, 1976
d. Visconti, Luchino

March 19, 1976
d. Cloete, Stuart

March 21, 1976
d. Fulks, Joe
d. Sabich, Spider

March 24, 1976
d. Shepard, Ernest Howard

March 25, 1976
d. Albers, Josef
d. Montgomery of Alamein, Bernard
Law Montgomery, Viscount

March 26, 1976
d. Lin, Yutang

March 28, 1976
d. Arlen, Richard

March 29, 1976
b. Capriati, Jennifer

March 31, 1976
d. Strand, Paul
d. Streeter, Edward

April 1, 1976
d. Blair, David
d. Ernst, Max

April 5, 1976
d. Davis, Meyer
d. Hughes, Howard Robard
d. Penfield, Wilder Graves

April 6, 1976
d. Thompson, Ruth Plumly

April 7, 1976
d. McBride, Mary Margaret

April 9, 1976
d. Ochs, Phil(ip David)

April 10, 1976
d. Ortega, Santos

April 12, 1976
d. Ford, Paul
d. Miller, William Ernest
d. Wolfgang, Myra K

April 14, 1976
d. Hastie, William Henry
d. Ospina Perez, Mariano

April 15, 1976
d. Elazar, David
d. Smith, Gerald Lyman Kenneth

April 16, 1976
d. Lackey, Kenneth

April 17, 1976
d. Dam, (Carl Peter) Henrik
d. Nicoll, (John Ramsay) Allardyce

April 20, 1976
d. Sansom, William

April 24, 1976
d. Tobey, Mark

April 25, 1976
b. Duncan, Tim(othy Theodore)
d. Brailowsky, Alexander
d. Reed, Carol, Sir

April 26, 1976
d. Grechko, Andrei Antonovick

April 28, 1976
d. Hughes, Richard Arthur Warren
d. Sperry, Armstrong W

May 2, 1976
d. Bankhead, Dan(iel Robert)

May 3, 1976
d. Nevers, Ernie

May 7, 1976
d. Uttley, Alice Jane Taylor

May 8, 1976
d. McLeod, Fred(erick)
d. Skaggs, M(arion) B

May 9, 1976
d. Kerner, Otto
d. Meinhof, Ulrike Marie

May 11, 1976
d. Aalto, Alvar Henrik Hugo
d. Kempe, Rudolf

May 15, 1976
d. Morison, Samuel Eliot

May 19, 1976
b. Garnett, Kevin

May 21, 1976
d. Geller, Bruce
d. Leon, Henry Cecil

May 22, 1976
d. Bonavena, Oscar
d. Fitch, Aubrey

May 26, 1976
d. Heidegger, Martin

May 27, 1976
d. McDevitt, Ruth
d. Teyte, Maggie, Dame

May 30, 1976
d. Carey, Max George
d. Fuchida, Mitsuo
d. Ghezzi, Vic(tor)

May 31, 1976
d. Mitchell, Martha Elizabeth Beall
d. Monod, Jacques Lucien

June 6, 1976
d. Getty, J(ean) Paul
d. Rethberg, Elizabeth

June 7, 1976
d. Hackett, Bobby

June 9, 1976
d. Farley, James A(loysius)
d. Thorndike, Sybil, Dame

June 10, 1976
d. Zukor, Adolph

June 13, 1976
d. Anda, Geza
d. Bolles, Don F

June 15, 1976
d. Dykes, Jimmy

June 16, 1976
d. Meloy, Francis Edward, Jr.

June 17, 1976
d. Odlum, Floyd Bostwick

June 23, 1976
d. Warneke, Lon(nie)

June 24, 1976
d. Cunningham, Imogen
d. White, Minor

June 25, 1976
d. Mercer, Johnny

June 26, 1976
d. Roy, Mike

June 28, 1976
d. Baker, Stanley, Sir

July 3, 1976
d. Netanyahu, Yonatan

July 7, 1976
d. Foster, Norman
d. Heinemann, Gustav Walter
d. Lowenfels, Walter

July 9, 1976
b. Savage, Fred
d. Gingrich, Arnold
d. Yawkey, Thomas Austin

July 11, 1976
d. Trotta, Maurice S

July 12, 1976
d. Howe, James Wong
d. Mack, Ted

July 15, 1976
d. Gallico, Paul William

July 17, 1976
d. Weingarten, Violet Brown

July 21, 1976
b. Nall, Anita

July 22, 1976
d. Goldfinger, Nathaniel
d. Wheeler, Mortimer

July 28, 1976
d. Feather, Victor

July 29, 1976
d. Cohen, Mickey

July 30, 1976
d. Bultmann, Rudolf

August 2, 1976
d. Lang, Fritz
d. Rathbone, Monroe Jackson

August 3, 1976
d. Warner, Roger Sherman, Jr.

August 4, 1976
d. Thomson, Roy Herbert

August 6, 1976
d. Chu Te
d. Piatigorsky, Gregor

August 9, 1976
d. Schmidt-Rottluf, Karl
d. Scott, Arleigh Winston, Sir

August 11, 1976
d. May, Robert Lewis

August 19, 1976
d. Sim, Alastair

August 22, 1976
d. Bachauer, Gina
d. Kubitschek (de Oliveira), Juscelino

August 25, 1976
d. Johnson, Eyvind Olof Verner

August 26, 1976
d. Anderson, Warner
d. Lehmann, Lotte

August 31, 1976
d. Kazee, Buell Hilton

September 9, 1976
d. Mao Zedong

September 10, 1976
d. Johnson, Mordecai Wyatt
d. Trumbo, Dalton

September 11, 1976
d. Carmer, Carl Lamson

September 14, 1976
d. Paul, Prince

September 20, 1976
d. Bloomgarden, Kermit

September 21, 1976
d. Letelier, Orlando

September 22, 1976
d. Strode, Hudson

September 24, 1976
d. Brent, Romney
d. Douglas, Paul Howard

September 25, 1976
d. Faber, Red

September 26, 1976
d. Ruzicka, Leopold Stephen

September 27, 1976
d. Fishbein, Morris

September 28, 1976
d. Folsom, Marion Bayard

September 30, 1976
d. Joseph, Richard

October 3, 1976
d. Smith, Howard Worth

October 4, 1976
b. Silverstone, Alicia

October 5, 1976
d. Onsager, Lars

October 6, 1976
d. Ryle, Gilbert

October 7, 1976
d. Lyons, Leonard

October 10, 1976
d. Wallace, Ed(ward Tatum)

October 14, 1976
d. Evans, Edith Mary Booth, Dame

October 15, 1976
d. Gambino, Carlo

October 19, 1976
d. Ford, Eleanor Clay

October 31, 1976
d. Wilder, Joseph

November 2, 1976
d. Starkie, Walter Fitzwilliam

November 3, 1976
d. Dixon, Dean

November 6, 1976
d. Dennis, Patrick

November 8, 1976
d. Cramm, Gottfried von, Baron

November 9, 1976
d. Halop, Billy
d. Lhevinne, Rosina L

November 11, 1976
d. Calder, Alexander

November 12, 1976
b. Campbell, Tevin
d. Piston, Walter

November 13, 1976
d. Benedict, Clint(on Stephen)

November 14, 1976
d. Pile, Frederick Alfred

November 15, 1976
d. Gabin, Jean

November 17, 1976
d. Bhashani, Maulana Abdul Hamid Khan

November 18, 1976
d. Jerger, Alfred
d. Ray, Man
d. Spence, Basil Urwin, Sir

November 20, 1976
b. Dawes, Dominique (Margaux)
d. Auchincloss, Hugh D
d. D'Arcy, Martin Cyril
d. Lysenko, Trofim Denisovich
d. Millner, Wayne E

November 22, 1976
d. Davies, Rupert

November 23, 1976
d. Malraux, Andre Georges
d. Price, Irving L

November 24, 1976
d. Ward, Paul W

November 26, 1976
d. Pitz, Henry Clarence

November 27, 1976
b. White, Jaleel
d. Alessandro, Victor Nicholas

November 28, 1976
d. Russell, Rosalind

November 29, 1976
d. Cambridge, Godfrey
d. Lowry, Judith Ives

December 4, 1976
d. Britten, (Edward) Benjamin

December 6, 1976
d. Goulart, Joao

December 9, 1976
d. Ferrell, Wes(ley Cheek)
d. Martini, Nino

December 10, 1976
d. Lisagor, Peter Irvin

December 12, 1976
d. Cassidy, Jack

December 20, 1976
d. Daley, Richard Joseph

December 21, 1976
d. Leaf, Munro

December 22, 1976
d. Wright, Russel

December 25, 1976
d. Darro, Frankie

December 26, 1976
d. Hart, Philip Aloysius

December 27, 1976
d. Mainbocher

December 28, 1976
d. King, Freddy

December 31, 1976
d. Hayes, Roland

1977

b. Wek, Alek
d. Bloch, Ernst
d. Davis, Frederick C(lyde)
d. Ponselle, Carmela
d. Shariati, Ali
d. Wakefield, Ruth G
d. Walter, Marie Therese
d. Walters, Lou

January 2, 1977
d. Garner, Erroll

January 5, 1977
d. Stevens, Onslow

January 6, 1977
d. Gropper, William

January 7, 1977
d. Stuckey, Williamson Sylvester

January 12, 1977
d. Clouzot, Henri-George

January 14, 1977
d. Eden, Anthony
d. Finch, Peter

January 18, 1977
d. Bijedic, Dzemal
d. Gilmore, Gary Mark
d. Printemps, Yvonne
d. Zuckmayer, Carl

January 24, 1977
d. Lilly, Eli
d. Shor, Toots

January 29, 1977
d. Prinze, Freddie

February 4, 1977
d. Dresser, Davis

February 9, 1977
d. Ilyushin, Sergei Vladimirovich

February 11, 1977
d. Ahmed, Fakhruddin Ali

February 17, 1977
d. Howe, Quincy

February 18, 1977
d. Devine, Andy

February 24, 1977
d. Kamen, Milt

February 25, 1977
d. McCulloch, Robert P

February 26, 1977
d. Vaughan, Bill

February 27, 1977
d. Carr, John Dickson
d. Dahlberg, Edward

February 28, 1977
d. Anderson, Eddie

March 1, 1977
d. Levy, David Mordecai

March 2, 1977
d. Bothwell, Jean
d. Mowrer, Edgar Ansel

March 3, 1977
d. Faulkner, Brian

March 5, 1977
d. Donlon, Mary Honor

March 8, 1977
d. Hull, Henry

March 9, 1977
d. Bolton, Frances Payne

March 10, 1977
b. Miller, Shannon (Lee)
d. Biggs, Edward George Power

March 14, 1977
d. Hamer, Fannie Lou Townsend

March 16, 1977
d. Jumblatt, Kamal Fouad

March 23, 1977
d. Stydahar, Joe

March 25, 1977
d. Johnson, Nunnally
d. Massamba-Debat, Alphonse

March 27, 1977
d. Herberg, Will
d. Hyland, Diana

March 28, 1977
d. Szenkar, Eugen

April 5, 1977
d. Prio Socarras, Carlos

April 7, 1977
d. Daryush, Elizabeth Bridges

April 9, 1977
d. Grant, Bruce

April 12, 1977
d. Wrigley, Philip Knight

April 21, 1977
d. Marx, Gummo

April 30, 1977
d. Lewis, (Myrtle) Tillie

May 2, 1977
d. Cole, Edward Nicholas

May 4, 1977
d. Bissell, Richard Pike

May 7, 1977
d. Erhard, Ludwig

May 9, 1977
d. Jones, James

May 10, 1977
d. Allred, Rulon Clark
d. Crawford, Joan

May 14, 1977
d. Hutchins, Robert Maynard
d. Victor, Sally Josephs

May 15, 1977
d. Wilcox, Herbert

May 17, 1977
d. Keita, Modibo
d. Mueller, Erwin Wilhelm

May 20, 1977
d. Hershey, Lewis Blaine

May 27, 1977
d. Bliven, Bruce

May 28, 1977
d. Ba Maw
d. Cortez, Ricardo

May 30, 1977
d. Desmond, Paul Breitenfeld

May 31, 1977
d. Castle, William
d. Grauer, Ben(jamin Franklin)
d. VonBraun, Wernher

June 2, 1977
d. Boyd, Stephen

June 3, 1977
d. Hill, Archibald Vivian
d. Rossellini, Roberto

June 6, 1977
d. Musial, Joe

June 13, 1977
d. Clark, Tom

June 14, 1977
d. Reed, Alan

June 15, 1977
d. Knorr, Nathan Homer

June 19, 1977
d. Brooks, Geraldine

June 20, 1977
d. Cone, Fairfax Mastick

June 25, 1977
d. Kaufman, Sue

June 26, 1977
d. Baden-Powell, Olave St. Claire, Lady
d. Kennedy, Walter

June 29, 1977
d. Lupescu, Magda (Elena)

July 1, 1977
b. Tyler, Liv

July 2, 1977
d. Nabokov, Vladimir

July 4, 1977
b. Victoria Ingrid Alice Desiree

July 5, 1977
d. Gerhardi, William Alexander

July 7, 1977
d. Crane, Roy(ston Campbell)

July 9, 1977
d. Eiseley, Loren Corey
d. Paul, Alice

July 15, 1977
d. Fedin, Konstantin Aleksandrovich

July 17, 1977
d. Malcuzynski, Witold

July 30, 1977
d. Holloway, Emory

August 1, 1977
d. Powers, Francis Gary

August 2, 1977
d. Lunt, Alfred
d. Makarios III, Archbishop

August 4, 1977
d. Adrian, Edgar Douglas, Baron

August 6, 1977
d. Bustamante, William Alexander
Clarke, Sir

August 9, 1977
d. Kenney, George Churchill

August 11, 1977
d. Schorer, Mark

August 12, 1977
d. Lawson, John Howard

August 16, 1977
b. Mingxia, Fu
d. Presley, Elvis Aaron

August 19, 1977
d. Marx, Groucho
d. Powers, John Robert

August 23, 1977
d. Cabot, Sebastian
d. Gabo, Naum

August 25, 1977
d. Arvey, Jacob Meyer

August 26, 1977
d. Rey, Hans Augustus

August 29, 1977
d. Hagen, Jean

September 1, 1977
d. Waters, Ethel

September 4, 1977
d. Schumacher, E(rnst) F(riedrich)

September 5, 1977
d. Batchelor, Clarence Daniel
d. Foley, Martha

September 6, 1977
d. Wummer, John

September 8, 1977
d. Mostel, Zero

September 9, 1977
d. O'Donnell, Kenneth P

September 12, 1977
d. Biko, Steven
d. Godfrey, Isadore
d. Lowell, Robert Trail Spence, Jr.

September 13, 1977
d. Stokowski, Leopold (Anton
Stanislaw Boleslawawicz)

September 16, 1977
d. Bolan, Marc
d. Callas, Maria
d. Sheldon, William Herbert

September 26, 1977
d. Lombardi, Ernie
d. Shankar, Uday

September 27, 1977
d. Winslow, Ola Elizabeth

September 29, 1977
d. Tcherepnin, Alexander Nikolayevich

September 30, 1977
d. Ford, Mary

October 5, 1977
d. Garber, Jan

October 9, 1977
d. Elder, Ruth

October 11, 1977
d. Kantor, Mackinlay

October 13, 1977
d. Condon, Jackie

October 14, 1977
d. Crosby, Bing
d. Nin, Anais

October 17, 1977
d. Balcon, Michael Elias, Sir
d. Chiang, Yee
d. Hubbard, Cal

October 18, 1977
d. Baader, Andreas

October 20, 1977
d. Gaines, Steve
d. Van Zant, Ronnie

October 23, 1977
d. Markel, Lester

October 27, 1977
d. Cain, James M(allahan)
d. Hulman, Tony, Jr.

October 31, 1977
d. Colby, Carroll Burleigh
d. Smith, Chard Powers

November 1, 1977
d. Hobbs, Leonard Sinclair

November 3, 1977
d. Kurelek, William
d. Vidor, Florence

November 5, 1977
d. Garst, Roswell
d. Goscinny, Rene
d. Lombardo, Guy Albert

November 8, 1977
d. Harris, Bucky

November 10, 1977
d. Pudney, John Sleigh

November 14, 1977
d. Bhaktivedanta, A(bhay)
C(haranaravinda)

November 15, 1977
d. Addinsell, Richard

November 16, 1977
b. Baiul, Oksana

November 18, 1977
d. O'Brien, Davey
d. Schuschnigg, Kurt von

November 19, 1977
b. Strug, Kerri

November 22, 1977
d. Traglia, Luigi, Cardinal

November 24, 1977
d. Smith, Mayo

November 25, 1977
d. Carlson, Richard

November 27, 1977
d. McClellan, John Little

November 30, 1977
d. Rattigan, Terence Mervyn, Sir
d. McNickle, D'Arcy

December 4, 1977
d. Eglevsky, Andre

December 5, 1977
d. Gaud, William Steen, Jr.
d. Kirk, Rahsaan Roland

December 7, 1977
d. Goldmark, Peter Carl

December 8, 1977
d. Solomon, Samuel Joseph

December 9, 1977
d. Lispector, Clarice

December 10, 1977
d. Rupp, Adolph Frederick

December 12, 1977
d. Boucher, Frank
d. Churchill, Clementine Ogilvy
(Hozier) Spencer, Baroness

December 13, 1977
d. Petrie, Charles Alexander, Sir

December 14, 1977
b. Hall, Bridget
d. Stulberg, Louis

December 15, 1977
d. Birdwell, Russell Juarez

December 16, 1977
d. Schippers, Thomas

December 17, 1977
d. Marshall, S(amuel) L(yman)
A(twood)

December 18, 1977
d. Eccles, Marriner Stoddard
d. Ritchard, Cyril
d. Untermeyer, Louis

December 19, 1977
d. Ross, Nellie Taylor

December 24, 1977
d. Velasco Alvarado, Juan

December 25, 1977
d. Chaplin, Charlie

December 26, 1977
d. Hawks, Howard Winchester

December 28, 1977
d. Heloise
d. Minsky, Harold

1978

b. Genet, Taras
b. Jones, Stormie
d. Blaisdell, George G
d. Gluck
d. Nygren, Anders T(heodor) S(amuel)
d. Sadr, Musa al-
d. Sobukwe, Robert Mangaliso
d. Unsworth, Geoffrey

January 1, 1978
d. Ascoli, Max
d. Davis, Hal Charles

January 6, 1978
d. Gordon, John F
d. MacArthur, John Donald

January 7, 1978
d. Flanner, Janet

January 8, 1978
d. Kiernan, Walter
d. Ross, Roy G

January 10, 1978
d. Braden, Spruille
d. Gillis, Don

January 11, 1978
d. Leibowitz, Samuel Simon

January 12, 1978
d. Metcalf, Lee
d. Sheekman, Arthur

January 13, 1978
d. Humphrey, Hubert Horatio, Jr.
d. McCarthy, Joe

January 14, 1978
d. Abrahams, Harold
d. Godel, Kurt
d. Heger, Robert

January 18, 1978
d. Betz, Carl
d. Greenwood, Charlotte

January 20, 1978
d. Clapper, Dit
d. Highet, Gilbert (Arthur)

January 21, 1978
d. Utley, Freda

January 22, 1978
d. Wengenroth, Stow

January 23, 1978
d. Damas, Leon-Gontran
d. Kath, Terry
d. Oakie, Jack

January 26, 1978
d. Genn, Leo

January 27, 1978
d. Homolka, Oscar

January 29, 1978
d. McCoy, Tim(othy John Fitzgerald)
d. Eliot, Martha May

February 2, 1978
d. Barrie, Wendy

February 4, 1978
d. Evans, Bergen Baldwin

February 6, 1978
d. Cole, Charles Woolsey

February 9, 1978
d. King, Warren Thomas

February 11, 1978
d. Conant, James Bryant
d. Martinson, Harry Edmund

February 12, 1978
d. Taylor, Sydney Brenner

February 14, 1978
d. Rattner, Abraham

February 15, 1978
d. Chase, Ilka

February 16, 1978
d. Harriman, E(dward) Roland (Noel)

February 19, 1978
d. Christophers, S(amuel) Rickard, Sir

February 22, 1978
d. Borland, Hal
d. Lawrence, Josephine
d. McGinley, Phyllis

February 23, 1978
d. McKeen, John Elmer

February 24, 1978
d. Thomas, Alma (Woodsy)

February 25, 1978
d. James, Daniel, Jr.

March 1, 1978
d. Scott, Paul Mark

March 2, 1978
d. Begle, Edward G(riffith)
d. Pei, Mario Andrew

March 3, 1978
d. Balopoulos, Michael
d. Marsala, Joe
d. Rockwell, Doc

March 6, 1978
d. MacLiammoir, Michael

March 13, 1978
d. Josephson, Matthew

March 18, 1978
d. Wood, Peggy

March 19, 1978
d. Baldwin, Faith

March 20, 1978
d. Brugnon, Jacques

March 21, 1978
d. O'Dalaigh, Cearbhall

March 22, 1978
d. Dodd, John Bruce, Mrs.
d. Wallenda, Karl
d. Wheelock, John Hall

March 25, 1978
d. Hulbert, Jack

March 28, 1978
d. Wragge, Sidney

March 29, 1978
d. Papashvily, George

March 31, 1978
d. Best, Charles Herbert

April 2, 1978
d. Noble, Ray

April 5, 1978
d. Tagliabue, Carlo

April 6, 1978
d. Kelly, Stephen Eugene
d. Nabokov, Nicolas

April 8, 1978
d. Frick, Ford Christopher

April 10, 1978
d. Nebel, Long John

April 14, 1978
d. Leavis, F(rank) R(aymond)

April 16, 1978
d. Clay, Lucius du Bignon

d. Lindner, Richard
d. Tsiranana, Philibert
d. Whitehead, (Walter) Edward

April 19, 1978
d. Koch, John

April 21, 1978
d. Craig, Cleo F
d. Turner, Thomas Wyatt

April 22, 1978
d. Dean, Basil
d. Geer, Will

April 24, 1978
d. Nestingen, Ivan Arnold

May 1, 1978
d. Khachaturian, Aram
d. Warner, Sylvia Townsend

May 3, 1978
d. Downs, William Randall, Jr.

May 8, 1978
d. Grant, Duncan (James Corrowr)
d. Rubicam, Raymond

May 9, 1978
d. Moro, Aldo

May 11, 1978
d. Khaikin, Boris

May 12, 1978
d. Zukofsky, Louis

May 14, 1978
d. Kipnis, Alexander
d. Lear, William Powell
d. Menzies, Robert Gordon, Sir

May 16, 1978
d. Steinberg, William

May 17, 1978
d. Lloyd, Selwyn

May 23, 1978
d. Colombo, Joseph Anthony

May 26, 1978
d. Icaza (Coronel), Jorge
d. Karsavina, Tamara (Platonova)

May 31, 1978
d. Liebow, Averill A(braham)
d. Purtell, William Arthur
d. Wright, Lloyd

June 5, 1978
d. Montoya, Joseph Manuel

June 7, 1978
d. Darken, Lawrence Stamper
d. Gordon, Joe
d. Norrish, Ronald George Wreyford

June 9, 1978
d. Murphy, Robert Daniel

June 12, 1978
d. Cushman, Austin Thomas
d. Guo Moruo
d. Kuo Mo-jo

June 14, 1978
d. Fabian, Robert Honey
d. Matlock, Matty
d. Poulter, Thomas Charles

June 16, 1978
d. Bernstein, Felicia Montealegre

June 18, 1978
d. Alvarez, Walter Clement

June 21, 1978
d. Youngdahl, Luther Wallace

June 22, 1978
d. Krag, Jens Otto

June 24, 1978
d. Babb, Howard Selden

June 28, 1978
d. DuPont, Clifford Walter

June 29, 1978
d. Crane, Bob

June 30, 1978
d. Harrah, Bill

July 3, 1978
d. Breech, Ernest Robert
d. Daly, James

July 6, 1978
d. Paley, Barbara Cushing

July 7, 1978
d. Baker, Rachel
d. Trefflich, Henry Herbert Frederick

July 10, 1978
d. Davis, Joe
d. Rockefeller, John D(avison), III

July 12, 1978
d. Rothermere, Esmond Cecil
  Harmsworth, Viscount
d. Williams, Jay

July 14, 1978
d. Messel, Oliver

July 20, 1978
d. Brace, Gerald Warner

July 25, 1978
b. Brown, Louise Joy

July 27, 1978
d. Ford, Benson

July 29, 1978
d. Nobile, Umberto

July 31, 1978
d. Light, Enoch Henry

d. Widdemer, Margaret

August 2, 1978
d. Bobst, Elmer Holmes
d. Chavez (y Ramirez), Carlos Antonio
  de Pauda
d. Fields, Totie

August 4, 1978
d. Fontaine, Frank

August 5, 1978
d. Clark, Dutch
d. Haines, Jesse Joseph

August 6, 1978
d. Paul VI
d. Stone, Edward Durell

August 8, 1978
d. Bakeless, John Edwin

August 9, 1978
d. Cozzens, James Gould

August 18, 1978
d. Fischer, John

August 19, 1978
d. Mallowan, Max Edgar Lucien, Sir

August 21, 1978
d. Diederichs, Nicholaas
d. Eames, Charles
d. Lord, Mary Pillsbury

August 22, 1978
d. Kenyatta, Jomo
d. Silone, Ignazio

August 23, 1978
b. Bryant, Kobe

August 24, 1978
d. Prima, Louis

August 26, 1978
d. Boyer, Charles

August 28, 1978
d. Busia, Kofi A(brefa)
d. Catton, Bruce
d. Mason, F(rancis) van Wyck
d. Shaw, Robert

August 30, 1978
d. Lazarsfeld, Paul F(elix)

September 7, 1978
d. Moon, Keith

September 8, 1978
d. Torre-Nilsson, Leopoldo

September 9, 1978
d. MacDiarmid, Hugh
d. Warner, Jack Leonard

September 15, 1978
d. Crispin, Edmund
d. Messerschmitt, Willy

September 18, 1978
d. Dassler, Adolf

September 19, 1978
d. Gilson, Etienne Henry

September 24, 1978
d. Bostock, Lyman Wesley
d. Etting, Ruth

September 26, 1978
d. Siegbahn, Karl Manne Georg

September 27, 1978
d. Johnston, Neil

September 28, 1978
d. John Paul I

September 29, 1978
d. Obolensky, Serge

September 30, 1978
d. Bergen, Edgar John
d. Coons, Albert Hewett

October 8, 1978
d. Gilliam, Jim

October 9, 1978
d. Brel, Jacques

October 10, 1978
d. Metcalfe, Ralph H

October 15, 1978
d. Smith, W(illiam) Eugene

October 16, 1978
d. Rockwell, Willard F

October 17, 1978
d. Dailey, Dan
d. Gronchi, Giovanni

October 18, 1978
d. Mercader, Ramon

October 19, 1978
d. Young, Gig

October 22, 1978
d. Mikoyan, Anastas Ivanovich

October 23, 1978
d. Carter, Mother Maybelle

November 2, 1978
d. Gordon, Max

November 6, 1978
d. Bertoia, Harry

November 7, 1978
d. Tunney, Gene

November 8, 1978
d. Fischetti, John
d. Rockwell, Norman

November 11, 1978
d. Borgmann, Benny

November 15, 1978
d. Mead, Margaret

November 17, 1978
d. Dauphin, Claude Le Grand Maria Eugene

November 18, 1978
d. Jones, Reverend Jim
d. Tristano, Leonard Joseph

November 19, 1978
d. Ryan, Leo Joseph

November 20, 1978
d. Chirico, Giorgio de

November 27, 1978
d. Milk, Harvey
d. Moscone, George Richard
d. Dent, Alan Holmes
d. Winston, Harry

December 2, 1978
d. Dickinson, Edwin W

December 3, 1978
d. Still, William Grant

December 4, 1978
d. Bruce, David Kirkpatrick Estes
d. Goudsmit, Samuel Abraham

December 5, 1978
d. Brown, George Scratchley

December 8, 1978
d. Cantwell, Robert Emmett
d. Meir, Golda

December 10, 1978
d. Wood, Edward D., Jr.

December 11, 1978
d. DuVigneaud, Vincent

December 12, 1978
d. Compton, Fay

December 13, 1978
d. Johnson, Herbert Fisk

December 14, 1978
d. Madariaga (y Rojo), Salvador de

December 15, 1978
d. Wills, Chill

December 16, 1978
d. Buzhardt, J(oseph) Fred, Jr.

December 17, 1978
d. Frings, Joseph Richard

December 18, 1978
d. Lasswell, Harold Dwight

December 21, 1978
d. Mullin, Willard

December 23, 1978
d. Buck, Paul Herman
d. DeRochemont, Louis

December 25, 1978
d. Mortimer, Charles Greenough

December 27, 1978
d. Boumedienne, Houari

1979

d. Banks, Harvey Washington
d. Berelson, Bernard (Reuben)
d. Dio, Johnny
d. Frisch, O(tto) R(obert)
d. Ludwig, Leopold
d. Simonov, Konstantin (Kirill) Mikhailovich

January 3, 1979
d. Hilton, Conrad Nicholson

January 4, 1979
d. Bennett, Harry Herbert

January 5, 1979
d. Mingus, Charles

January 9, 1979
d. Merritt, Hiram Houston
d. Nervi, Pier Luigi

January 11, 1979
d. Soo, Jack

January 12, 1979
d. Smith, Pete

January 13, 1979
d. Buitoni, Giovanni
d. Hathaway, Donny
d. Lawrence, Marjorie Florence

January 19, 1979
d. Leemans, Tuffy

January 22, 1979
d. Stakman, Elvin Charles

January 26, 1979
d. Rockefeller, Nelson A(ldrich)

January 29, 1979
d. Soby, James Thrall

January 30, 1979
d. Muir, Malcolm

February 2, 1979
d. Douglas, Aaron
d. Vicious, Sid

February 7, 1979
d. Giles, Warren Crandall
d. Mengele, Josef

February 8, 1979
d. Catlin, George Edward Gordon, Sir
d. Gabor, Dennis
d. Starch, Daniel

February 9, 1979
d. Tate, Allen (John Orley)

February 11, 1979
b. Brandy

February 12, 1979
d. Renoir, Jean

February 14, 1979
d. Tunnard, Christopher

February 16, 1979
d. Allbritton, Louise
d. Gargan, William

February 23, 1979
d. Bennett, W(illiam) A(ndrew) C(ecil)

February 25, 1979
d. Focke, Heinrich Karl Johann

February 27, 1979
d. Eberle, Irmengarde

March 1, 1979
d. Costello, Dolores

March 3, 1979
d. Creavy, Tom

March 5, 1979
d. Haworth, Leland John

March 7, 1979
d. Novaes (Pinto), Guiomar

March 11, 1979
d. Kilian, Victor
d. Power, Donald Clinton

March 15, 1979
d. Britt, Steuart Henderson

March 16, 1979
d. Massine, Leonide Fedorovich
d. Monnet, Jean Omer Marie Gabriel
d. Pious, Minerva

March 17, 1979
d. Lauri-Volpi, Giacoma

March 20, 1979
d. Charlot, Jean

March 22, 1979
d. Lyon, Ben

March 26, 1979
d. Stafford, Jean

March 28, 1979
d. Kelly, Emmett Lee

March 29, 1979
d. Delaney, Beauford

March 30, 1979
d. Velasco Ibarra, Jose Maria

April 2, 1979
d. Rosenbloom, Carroll D

April 4, 1979
d. Bhutto, Zulfikar Ali
d. Buchanan, Edgar

April 7, 1979
d. Hoveyda, Amir Abbas
d. Sawyer, Charles

April 8, 1979
d. Price, Garrett

April 9, 1979
b. Pulliam, Keisha Knight
d. Cotsworth, Staats

April 12, 1979
b. Danes, Claire

April 15, 1979
d. Caniglia, Maria

April 19, 1979
d. Morton, Rogers Clark Ballard

April 20, 1979
d. Dehnert, Henry
d. Donald, Peter

April 29, 1979
d. Coe, Frederick H
d. Gramatky, Hardie

May 2, 1979
d. Natta, Giulio

May 3, 1979
d. Angoff, Charles
d. O'Brien-Moore, Erin

May 6, 1979
d. Ager, Milton

May 8, 1979
d. Parsons, Talcott

May 9, 1979
d. Eaton, Cyrus Stephen

May 10, 1979
d. Frankel, Charles

May 11, 1979
d. Flatt, Lester Raymond
d. Hutton, Barbara Woolworth

May 14, 1979
d. Rhys, Jean
d. Scherman, Thomas Kielty

May 16, 1979
d. Randolph, Asa Philip

May 22, 1979
d. Jooss, Kurt

May 25, 1979
d. Spenkelink, John Arthur

May 26, 1979
d. Brent, George

May 28, 1979
d. Abercrombie, Michael
d. Little, Lou(is)

May 29, 1979
d. Pickford, Mary
d. Wood, John Howland, Jr.

May 30, 1979
d. Martin, Fletcher

June 1, 1979
d. Forssmann, Werner Theodor Otto
d. Mulhall, Jack
d. Partridge, Eric Honeywood

June 2, 1979
d. Hutton, Jim

June 6, 1979
d. Haley, Jack

June 8, 1979
d. Gehlen, Reinhard
d. Hartnell, Norman Bishop, Sir

June 10, 1979
d. Croft-Cooke, Rupert
d. Taylor, Cyclone

June 11, 1979
d. Dalgleish, Alice
d. Mathews, John Joseph
d. Wayne, John

June 13, 1979
d. Hood, Darla Jean
d. Kuznetsov, Anatoli Vasilievich

June 14, 1979
d. Shumlin, Herman Elliott

June 16, 1979
d. Johnson, Ching
d. Ray, Nicholas

June 17, 1979
d. Saltonstall, Leverett

June 25, 1979
d. Halsman, Philippe
d. Hoyt, Palmer

June 26, 1979
d. Beals, Carleton

June 27, 1979
d. Bernstein, Theodore Menline

June 28, 1979
d. Cousteau, Philippe
d. Dessau, Paul
d. Schulberg, Stuart

July 3, 1979
d. Van Slyke, Helen Lenore Vogt

July 4, 1979
d. Kroeber, Theodora Kracaw

July 6, 1979
d. McCoy, Van

July 7, 1979
d. Landolfi, Tommaso

July 8, 1979
d. Tomonaga Shinichiro
d. Woodward, Robert Burns

July 9, 1979
d. Skinner, Cornelia Otis
d. Wilding, Michael

July 10, 1979
d. Fiedler, Arthur

July 11, 1979
d. Crockett, James Underwood

July 12, 1979
d. Riperton, Minnie

July 13, 1979
d. Chapman, Ceil
d. Griffith, Corinne

July 15, 1979
d. Diaz Ordaz, Gustavo

July 16, 1979
d. Deller, Alfred George
d. Douglas, Robert L
d. McIntyre, James Francis Aloysius, Cardinal

July 21, 1979
d. Tugwell, Rexford Guy

July 22, 1979
d. Galento, Tony

July 28, 1979
d. Irving, Jules
d. Miller, Don
d. Seaton, George

July 29, 1979
d. Marcuse, Herbert
d. Todman, Bill

August 2, 1979
d. Haya de la Torre, Victor Raul
d. Munson, Thurman Lee

August 3, 1979
d. Ohlin, Bertil Gotthard
d. Ottaviani, Alfredo, Cardinal

August 5, 1979
d. Potofsky, Jacob Samuel

August 6, 1979
d. Kasznar, Kurt
d. Lynen, Feodor Felix Konrad

August 7, 1979
d. Monsarrat, Nicholas John Turney

August 8, 1979
d. McDonald, David John

August 9, 1979
d. O'Malley, Walter Francis
d. Zuckerman, Ben

August 10, 1979
d. Foran, Dick John Nicholas
d. Wright, John Joseph

August 12, 1979
d. Chain, Ernest Boris, Sir
d. Karpis, Alvin

August 13, 1979
d. Berndt, Walter

August 16, 1979
d. Diefenbaker, John George

August 17, 1979
d. Vance, Vivian

August 22, 1979
d. Farrell, James Thomas

August 24, 1979
d. Reitsch, Hanna

August 25, 1979
d. Kenton, Stan(ley Newcomb)

August 26, 1979
d. Waltari, Mika

August 27, 1979
d. Mountbatten of Burma, Louis Mountbatten, Earl

August 29, 1979
d. Newhouse, Samuel Irving

August 31, 1979
d. Rand, Sally
d. Seberg, Jean
d. Mawdudi, Abu-I A'la

September 3, 1979
d. Capehart, Homer Earl

September 5, 1979
d. Bolton, Guy Reginald

September 7, 1979
d. Richards, Ivor Armstrong

September 9, 1979
d. Larsen, Roy Edward

September 10, 1979
d. Neto, Agostinho

September 15, 1979
d. Leonetti, Tommy
d. Ponti, Gio(vanni)

September 19, 1979
d. Birnie, William Alfred Hart
d. Jones, Preston St. Vrain

September 20, 1979
d. Svoboda, Ludvik

September 26, 1979
d. Cromwell, John

September 27, 1979
d. Fields, Gracie
d. Hunnicutt, Arthur

October 1, 1979
d. Arzner, Dorothy
d. Harris, Roy

October 5, 1979
d. Strong, Ken(neth E)

October 6, 1979
d. Bishop, Elizabeth

October 7, 1979
d. Lewis, Wilmarth Sheldon

October 8, 1979
d. Narayan, Jayaprakash
d. Sampson, Edith Spurlock

October 10, 1979
d. Paray, Paul

October 15, 1979
d. Devers, Jacob Loucks

October 17, 1979
d. Perelman, S(idney) J(oseph)

October 21, 1979
d. Sugiura, Kanematsu

October 22, 1979
d. Boulanger, Nadia Juliette

October 24, 1979
d. Belmont, Eleanor Robson

October 25, 1979
d. Darling, Frank Fraser, Sir

October 26, 1979
d. Park, Chung Hee

October 27, 1979
d. Coughlin, Charles Edward, Father

October 30, 1979
d. Mussolini, Rachele Guidi
d. Wallis, Barnes Neville, Sir

November 1, 1979
d. Eisenhower, Mamie (Geneva) Doud

November 5, 1979
d. Capp, Al

November 6, 1979
d. Evans, Chick

November 8, 1979
d. Ardizzone, Edward Jeffrey Irving

November 11, 1979
d. Tiomkin, Dimitri

November 13, 1979
d. Harmon, Ernest N(ason)

November 14, 1979
d. Harris, Jed

November 23, 1979
d. Oberon, Merle
d. Rovere, Richard Halworth

November 25, 1979
d. Abrams, Harry Nathan

November 27, 1979
d. Cavanagh, Jerome Patrick

November 28, 1979
d. Classen, Willie
d. Seagram, Joseph Edward Frowde

November 30, 1979
d. Gilpin, Laura
d. Grenfell, Joyce Irene
d. Kuter, Laurence S(herman)
d. Marx, Zeppo

December 5, 1979
d. Delaunay-Terk, Sonia

December 7, 1979
d. Gottlieb, Eddie
d. Haas, Walter A(braham), Sr.
d. Payne-Gaposchkin, Cecilia (Helena)

December 10, 1979
d. Blodgett, Katherine Burr
d. Dvorak, Ann
d. Sheen, Fulton John, Bishop

December 16, 1979
d. Chapman, Gilbert Whipple

December 20, 1979
d. Illingworth, Leslie Gilbert

December 22, 1979
d. Zanuck, Darryl Francis

December 23, 1979
d. Guggenheim, Peggy
d. Kunhardt, Dorothy (Meserve)

December 25, 1979
d. Blondell, Joan

December 29, 1979
d. Hebert, F(elix) Edward

December 30, 1979
d. Rodgers, Richard

1980

b. Chang, Sarah Yong-chu
b. Kingsley, Gregory
d. Aarons, Ruth Hughes
d. Catherall, Arthur

d. Chinn, May (Edward)
d. Martinez, Maria Montoya
d. McMurray, Bette Clair
d. Moraes, Vinicius de

January 1, 1980
d. Deutsch, Adolph
d. Nenni, Pietro Sandro

January 3, 1980
d. Adamson, Joy Friederike Victoria
  Gessner

January 8, 1980
d. Mauchly, John William

January 10, 1980
d. Meany, George

January 11, 1980
d. Pym, Barbara Mary Crampton

January 12, 1980
d. Ronne, Finn

January 13, 1980
d. Jahoda, Gloria (Adelaide Love)
d. Kostelanetz, Andre

January 14, 1980
d. Ardrey, Robert
d. Brown, Rachel Fuller

January 15, 1980
d. Fogarty, Anne

January 18, 1980
d. Beaton, Cecil (Walter Hardy), Sir
d. Britton, Barbara

January 19, 1980
d. Douglas, William Orville
d. Goldman, Richard Franko

January 21, 1980
d. Hidalgo, Elvira de

January 23, 1980
d. Buttrick, George Arthur
d. Williams, Paul R(evere)

January 24, 1980
d. Poe, James

January 25, 1980
d. Harsh, George

January 26, 1980
d. Patrick, Lynn

January 28, 1980
d. Durante, Jimmy

January 30, 1980
d. Byrd, Henry
d. Dagover, Lil
d. Margolius, Sidney Senier
d. Papanin, Ivan D
d. Professor Longhair

January 31, 1980
d. Crosby, Alexander L

d. Voit, Willard Darby

February 1, 1980
d. Bailey, Jack

February 2, 1980
d. Stein, William Howard

February 3, 1980
d. Heindorf, Ray

February 4, 1980
d. Laye, Camara
d. Summerskill, Edith Clara, Baroness

February 7, 1980
d. Ballinger, Margaret

February 11, 1980
d. Malik, Yakov (Alexandrovich)

February 12, 1980
d. Berger, Samuel David
d. Rukeyser, Muriel

February 13, 1980
d. Janssen, David
d. Monroney, Mike (Aimer Stillwell)

February 14, 1980
d. Gruen, Victor

February 17, 1980
d. Sutherland, Graham Vivian

February 20, 1980
d. Longworth, Alice Roosevelt
d. Rhine, J(oseph) B(anks)
d. Shippen, Katherine Binney

February 21, 1980
d. Lauck, Chester H

February 22, 1980
d. Kokoschka, Oskar

February 25, 1980
d. Hayden, Robert Earl

February 26, 1980
d. Arkell, Anthony John
d. Brook, Alexander
d. Shukairy, Ahmed

February 27, 1980
b. Clinton, Chelsea Victoria
d. Tobias, George

February 29, 1980
d. Allon, Yigal

March 1, 1980
d. Ashford, Emmett Littleton
d. Cooper, Wilhelmina Behmenburg
d. Niles, John Jacob

March 5, 1980
d. Silverheels, Jay

March 7, 1980
d. Patterson, William Allan

March 10, 1980
d. Glueck, Sheldon
d. Tarnower, Herman

March 11, 1980
d. Taber, Gladys Bagg

March 12, 1980
d. Anson, Jay
d. Gero, Erno

March 13, 1980
d. Rosenstein, Nettie

March 14, 1980
d. Brosio, Manilo Giovanni
d. Dennison, Robert Lee
d. Hatta, Mohammad
d. Lowenstein, Allard Kenneth

March 17, 1980
d. Bealer, Alex W(inkler III)

March 18, 1980
d. Dragonette, Jessica
d. Fromm, Erich

March 23, 1980
d. Johnson, Gerald White
d. Okun, Arthur Melvin

March 24, 1980
d. Romero y Galdamez, Oscar Arnulfo

March 25, 1980
d. Barthes, Roland (Gerard)
d. Susskind, Walter
d. Wright, James Arlington

March 28, 1980
d. Haymes, Dick
d. Soria, Dario

March 29, 1980
d. Watt, George Willard

March 30, 1980
d. Mantovani, Annunzio
d. Thang, Ton Duc

March 31, 1980
d. Boussac, Marcel
d. Owens, Jesse
d. Henry, Charlotte

April 2, 1980
d. Reed, Stanley Forman

April 3, 1980
d. Bullard, Edward Crisp, Sir

April 5, 1980
d. McCarty, Mary

April 7, 1980
d. Braly, Malcolm
d. Rosenberg, Jakob

April 8, 1980
d. Farb, Peter

April 10, 1980
d. Medford, Kay
d. White, Antonia

April 12, 1980
d. Tolbert, William Richard, Jr.

April 15, 1980
d. Bailey, Raymond
d. Sartre, Jean-Paul

April 17, 1980
d. Sjoberg, Alf

April 20, 1980
d. Kautner, Helmut
d. Konetzni, Hilde

April 21, 1980
d. Oparin, Aleksandr Ivanovich
d. Paasio, Rafael
d. Page, Joe

April 22, 1980
d. Froman, Jane
d. Strassmann, Fritz

April 23, 1980
d. Hecht, George Joseph

April 24, 1980
d. Finletter, Thomas Knight
d. Semenenko, Serge

April 26, 1980
d. Courtneidge, Cicely, Dame

April 29, 1980
d. Hitchcock, Alfred Joseph, Sir

April 30, 1980
d. Kronenberger, Louis
d. Munoz Marin, Luis

May 2, 1980
d. Pal, George

May 3, 1980
d. Elliott, George Paul

May 4, 1980
d. Cherrington, Ben Mark
d. Tito

May 6, 1980
d. Bombal, Maria Luisa

May 12, 1980
d. Jones, Howard Mumford
d. Roth, Lillian
d. Sherrill, Henry Knox

May 14, 1980
d. Ebert, Carl
d. Griffith, Hugh Emrys
d. Robinson, Francis Arthur

May 21, 1980
d. Boyd, Julian Parks
d. Kaminska, Ida

May 24, 1980
d. Gaunt, William

May 29, 1980
d. Jaabari, Mohammed Ali, Sheik

June 1, 1980
d. Marquard, Rube
d. Nielsen, Arthur Charles

June 7, 1980
d. Bonelli, Richard
d. Guston, Philip
d. Miller, Henry (Valentine)
d. Spychalski, Marian

June 10, 1980
d. Sullivan, A(loysius) M(ichael)

June 12, 1980
d. Butlin, William Heygate Edmund, Sir
d. Stone, Milburn

June 13, 1980
d. Lampman, Evelyn Sibley

June 16, 1980
d. Nolan, Bob

June 17, 1980
b. Williams, Venus (Ebone Starr)

June 18, 1980
d. Fisher, Terence

June 23, 1980
d. Gandhi, Sanjay
d. Still, Clyfford

June 24, 1980
d. Burpee, David
d. Kaufman, Boris

June 25, 1980
d. Grattan, Clinton Hartley

June 27, 1980
d. Bigard, Albany Barney Leon
d. Dornberger, Walter Robert
d. McWilliams, Carey

June 28, 1980
d. Douglas, Helen Mary Gahagan
d. Iturbi, Jose

June 30, 1980
d. Duvoisin, Roger Antoine

July 1, 1980
d. Snow, C(harles) P(ercy), Sir

July 2, 1980
d. Barry, Tom

July 4, 1980
d. Bateson, Gregory

July 6, 1980
d. Patrick, Gail

July 7, 1980
d. Gardiner, Reginald
d. Schary, Dore

July 10, 1980
d. Krumgold, Joseph (Quincy)

July 13, 1980
d. Khama, Seretse M., Sir

July 16, 1980
d. Brackman, Robert

July 17, 1980
d. Barry, Donald
d. Roskolenko, Harry

July 19, 1980
d. Morgenthau, Hans Joachim

July 23, 1980
d. Manning, Olivia

July 24, 1980
d. Sellers, Peter

July 25, 1980
d. Vysotsky, Vladimir Semyonovich

July 26, 1980
d. Hoskins, Allen Clayton
d. Richards, Stanley
d. Tynan, Kenneth Peacock

July 27, 1980
d. Pahlevi, Mohammed Riza

August 1, 1980
d. Martin, Strother

August 2, 1980
d. Stewart, Donald Ogden

August 4, 1980
d. Ashbrook, Joseph

August 6, 1980
d. Marini, Marino

August 8, 1980
d. Mercer, David
d. Yahya Khan, Agha Muhammad

August 9, 1980
d. Cochran, Jacqueline
d. Nugent, Elliott

August 11, 1980
d. Robert, Paul

August 14, 1980
d. Snider, Paul
d. Stratten, Dorothy

August 15, 1980
d. Simpson, William Hood

August 16, 1980
d. Longley, James Bernard

August 22, 1980
d. McDonnell, James Smith
d. Stewart, George Rippey

August 25, 1980
d. Champion, Gower

August 26, 1980
b. Culkin, Macaulay
d. Korjus, Miliza

August 27, 1980
d. Avery, Tex
d. Kenney, Douglas C
d. Levenson, Sam(uel)
d. Woodruff, Hale (Aspacio)

September 1, 1980
d. Donovan, Arthur
d. Evans, Bill

September 3, 1980
d. Renaldo, Duncan

September 5, 1980
d. Loden, Barbara Ann

September 8, 1980
d. Libby, Willard Frank

September 9, 1980
d. Clurman, Harold Edgar
d. Griffin, John Howard

September 10, 1980
d. Kirkus, Virginia

September 11, 1980
d. Sands, Dorothy

September 13, 1980
d. Abu Salma

September 16, 1980
d. Piaget, Jean

September 17, 1980
d. Somoza Debayle, Anastasio

September 18, 1980
d. Porter, Katherine Anne

September 19, 1980
d. Gillott, Jacky
d. Lesser, Sol

September 25, 1980
d. Bonham, John Henry
d. Milestone, Lewis

September 27, 1980
d. Gelb, Lawrence

September 29, 1980
d. Abramson, Harold A(lexander)

October 1, 1980
d. Jones, Edward Vason

October 7, 1980
d. Russell, Sydney Gordon, Sir

October 8, 1980
d. Dollard, John
d. Kendrick, Pearl Luella

October 10, 1980
d. Cheney, Sheldon Warren
d. Thomas, Billy

October 15, 1980
d. Farago, Ladislas
d. O'Hara, Mary

October 18, 1980
d. Teale, Edwin Way

October 19, 1980
d. Andrews, James Frederick

October 21, 1980
d. Chervenkov, Vulko

October 24, 1980
d. D'Aulaire, Ingri Mortenson

October 25, 1980
d. Dodds, Harold Willis
d. Fox, Virgil Keel

October 26, 1980
d. Caetano, Marcello

October 27, 1980
d. LaMarsh, Judy

October 28, 1980
d. Janney, Leon

November 2, 1980
d. Sutton, Willie

November 4, 1980
d. Langley, Noel

November 5, 1980
d. Lortz, Richard
d. Marshall, Laurence

November 6, 1980
d. Coghill, Nevill Henry Kendall
Aylmer

November 7, 1980
d. McQueen, Steve

November 9, 1980
d. Yung, Victor Sen

November 11, 1980
d. Amalrik, Andrei Alekseyevich

November 14, 1980
d. Haskell, Arnold Lionel

November 15, 1980
d. Fleming, Joan Margaret

November 16, 1980
d. Aronson, Boris

November 18, 1980
d. Smythe, Conn

November 21, 1980
d. Smith, A(rthur) J(ames) M(arshall)

November 22, 1980
d. Leger, Jules
d. McCormack, John William
d. West, Mae

November 23, 1980
d. Binns, Joseph Patterson
d. Pennington, John Selman

November 24, 1980
d. Agar, Herbert Sebastian
d. Raft, George

November 26, 1980
d. Roberts, Rachel

November 28, 1980
d. Ballantrae, Lord
d. Van Vleck, John Hasbrouck

November 29, 1980
d. Day, Dorothy

December 1, 1980
d. Coulter, John William
d. Irvin, Robert W

December 2, 1980
d. Gary, Romain
d. Gordon-Walker of Leyton, Patrick
Chrestien Gordon-Walker, Baron
d. Mosley, Oswald Ernald, Sir

December 4, 1980
d. Amerasinghe, Hamilton Shirley
d. Walsh, Stella

December 5, 1980
d. Halberstam, Michael Joseph
d. McLean, Robert

December 7, 1980
d. Drew, Richard G

December 8, 1980
d. Lennon, John Winston

December 10, 1980
d. Benedictos I

December 11, 1980
d. Bergen, John Joseph
d. Lesage, Jean
d. Orwell, Sonia

December 14, 1980
d. Howard, Elston Gene

December 16, 1980
d. Fisher, Welthy (Blakesley
Honsinger)
d. Sanders, Colonel

December 18, 1980
d. Travers, Ben

December 19, 1980
d. Campora, Hector Jose
d. Kosygin, Aleksei Nikolaevich

December 20, 1980
d. Kintner, Robert Edmonds

December 21, 1980
d. Connelly, Marc(us Cook)

December 24, 1980
d. Doenitz, Karl C
d. Neville, Kris Ottman
d. Wilder, Alec

December 25, 1980
d. Ku Chieh-kang

December 26, 1980
d. Dewey, Charles Schuveldt
d. Jenkins, Ray Howard
d. Smith, Tony

December 28, 1980
d. Levene, Sam

December 29, 1980
d. Hardin, Tim
d. Mandelstam, Nadezhda Yakovlevna
d. Westheimer, Irvin Ferdinand

December 31, 1980
d. McLuhan, (Herbert) Marshall
d. Walsh, Raoul

1981

d. Bickerman, Elias Joseph
d. Blumenfeld, Isadore
d. Bosustow, Stephen
d. Chiari, Roberto
d. Chidsey, Donald Barr
d. DeLaurentiis, Federico
d. Drysdale, George Russell
d. Imam, Alhadji Abubakar
d. Jones, Barry
d. Monaghan, (James) Jay, (IV)
d. Noyes, Blanche Wilcox

January 1, 1981
d. Menuhin, Hephzibah
d. Michalowski, Kazimierz
d. Ryden, Ernest Edwin

January 2, 1981
d. Keener, Jefferson Ward
d. Lynch, David
d. Watts, Richard, Jr.

January 3, 1981
d. Alice

January 4, 1981
d. Rabin, Yehuda L

January 5, 1981
d. Martin, James, Sir

January 6, 1981
d. Cronin, A(rchibald) J(oseph)
d. Neal, Larry
d. Urey, Harold Clayton

January 8, 1981
d. Beard, Matthew, Jr.

d. Jagendorf, Moritz Adolf

January 9, 1981
d. MacTaggart, William, Sir

January 10, 1981
d. Boone, Richard
d. Brodie, Fawn McKay

January 11, 1981
d. MacDonald, Malcolm John

January 12, 1981
d. Bondi, Beulah
d. Whitehead, Don(ald Ford)

January 14, 1981
d. Lilienthal, David Eli

January 15, 1981
d. Celler, Emanuel

January 16, 1981
d. Lee, Bernard

January 19, 1981
d. Evans, Clifford

January 21, 1981
d. Douglass, Lathrop
d. Joslyn, Allyn Morgan
' d. Strong, James Matthew
d. Stronge, Norman, Sir

January 23, 1981
d. Barber, Samuel
d. Teague, Olin E

January 25, 1981
d. Astaire, Adele

January 28, 1981
b. Wood, Elijah
d. Gerber, John
d. Gribble, Harry Wagstaff Graham

January 29, 1981
d. Cole, Cozy
d. Glassco, John Stinson

January 30, 1981
d. Gopallawa, William

January 31, 1981
d. Butterfield, Roger Place

February 1, 1981
d. Douglas, Donald Willis
d. Mischakoff, Mischa

February 2, 1981
d. Addonizio, Hugh Joseph

February 3, 1981
d. McNamara, Margaret Craig

February 5, 1981
d. Grasso, Ella

February 6, 1981
d. Camerini, Mario

d. Frederika Louise
d. Montenegro, Hugh

February 8, 1981
d. Kipnis, Claude

February 9, 1981
d. Anderson, Jack Zuinglius
d. Haley, Bill
d. Thompson, Tiny

February 10, 1981
d. Levy, Julien
d. Rebbot, Olivier
d. Shirley-Smith, Hubert

February 11, 1981
d. Frings, Ketti
d. Ichikawa, Fusae

February 12, 1981
d. Dixon, Jean
d. Fraser, Bruce Austin, Sir

February 13, 1981
d. Kaufman, Joseph William

February 15, 1981
d. Bloomfield, Mike

February 16, 1981
d. Huntington, Henry S, Jr.
d. Richter, Karl

February 17, 1981
d. Garnett, David

February 18, 1981
d. Northrop, John Knudsen

February 19, 1981
d. Streithorst, Tom

February 20, 1981
d. Gunzberg, Nicolas de, Baron

February 21, 1981
d. Houghton, Amory

February 22, 1981
d. Padover, Saul Kussiel
d. Smith, Joe

February 23, 1981
d. Allen, Robert Sharon
d. Cabot, John Moors
d. Fields, Shep

February 24, 1981
d. Fish, Robert Lloyd

February 26, 1981
d. Hanson, Howard

February 28, 1981
d. Beilenson, Edna Rudolph

March 1, 1981
d. Waldman, Max

March 5, 1981
d. Harburg, E(dgar) Y(ipsel)

March 6, 1981
d. Hightower, Florence Josephine Cole

March 7, 1981
d. Billington, Ray Allen
d. Crowther, Bosley
d. Kondrashin, Kiril Petrovich

March 9, 1981
d. Delbruck, Max
d. Judy, Steven
d. Nicolson, Marjorie Hope
d. Von Wangenheim, Chris

March 10, 1981
d. Oldfield, Maurice, Sir

March 12, 1981
d. Barnetson, William Denholm

March 13, 1981
d. Brown, Kelly
d. Maugham, Robin

March 14, 1981
d. Perry, Eleanor Bayer

March 15, 1981
d. Clair, Rene

March 16, 1981
d. Blumenthal, Monica David

March 17, 1981
d. Dean, Daffy
d. Gray, Nicholas Stuart

March 18, 1981
d. Dominick, Peter Hoyt

March 19, 1981
d. Cadieux, Marcel (Joseph David Romeo)
d. Lane, Frank C

March 20, 1981
d. Jaffee, Irving

March 21, 1981
d. Baugh, Albert Croll
d. Trifonov, Yuri Valentinovich

March 22, 1981
d. Elliott, Jumbo
d. McCain, John Sidney, Jr.

March 23, 1981
d. Auchinleck, Claude, Sir
d. Hailwood, Mike
d. Lasker, Edward

March 25, 1981
d. Douglas, Emmitt
d. Robitscher, Jonas Bondi, Jr.

March 26, 1981
d. Darlington, Cyril Dean

March 28, 1981
d. Hollowood, Albert Bernard
d. Kovalev, Mikhail Aleksandrovich

March 29, 1981
d. Tieri, Frank
d. Williams, Eric Eustace

March 30, 1981
d. Edwards, Sherman
d. Wallace, DeWitt

March 31, 1981
d. Bagnold, Enid
d. Wang Shih-chieh

April 1, 1981
d. Alley, Norman William

April 3, 1981
d. Kanner, Leo
d. Trippe, Juan Terry

April 4, 1981
d. Jensen, Alfred Julio

April 5, 1981
d. Ethridge, Mark Foster
d. Hite, Robert Ernest, Jr.

April 7, 1981
d. Taurog, Norman

April 8, 1981
d. Bradley, Omar Nelson
d. Russell, Edward Frederick Langley, Baron of Liverpool

April 9, 1981
d. Scott, Austin Wakeman

April 10, 1981
d. Ryan, Sylvester James
d. Thurman, Howard

April 11, 1981
d. Gordon, Caroline
d. Hagerty, James Campbell
d. Moore, Harry Thornton

April 12, 1981
d. Guyer, Tennyson
d. Louis, Joe

April 13, 1981
d. Thomas, Gwyn

April 14, 1981
d. Galamian, Ivan
d. Mayer, Arthur Loeb
d. Vanderbilt, William Henry

April 16, 1981
d. Debus, Sigurd Friedrich

April 20, 1981
d. Denny-Brown, Derek Ernest

April 21, 1981
d. Sauter, Eddie

April 23, 1981
d. Maury, Reuben

April 26, 1981
d. Davis, Jim
d. Evans, Madge

April 27, 1981
d. Battles, Cliff(ord Franklin)
d. Roosevelt, John Aspinal

April 28, 1981
d. Walker, Mickey

April 29, 1981
d. Stein, Jules Caesar

April 30, 1981
d. Anderson, Cat
d. Bordes, Francois

May 1, 1981
d. Gosho Heinosuke
d. Sneider, Vernon John

May 2, 1981
d. Osborne, John Franklin
d. Wechsler, David

May 4, 1981
d. Green, Paul Eliot
d. McNeill, Robert Edward, Jr.

May 5, 1981
d. Sands, Bobby

May 6, 1981
d. Fitzsimmons, Frank Edward

May 8, 1981
d. Andrew, Prince of Russia
d. Lindsay, Margaret

May 9, 1981
d. Algren, Nelson
d. Lincoln, Victoria Endicott

May 11, 1981
d. Fuller, Hoyt William
d. Hassel, Odd
d. Marley, Bob
d. Whitaker, Rogers E(rnest) M(alcolm)

May 12, 1981
d. Hughes, Francis
d. Sheares, Benjamin Henry

May 17, 1981
d. Piccard, Jeannette Ridlon

May 18, 1981
d. Rausch, James Stevens
d. Saroyan, William

May 19, 1981
d. O'Connell, Arthur

May 20, 1981
d. Vaughan, Harry Hawkins

May 21, 1981
d. McCreesh, Raymond
d. Mearns, David Chambers
d. O'Hara, Patrick
d. Yost, Charles Woodruff

May 24, 1981
d. Jessel, George Albert
d. Lubalin, Herbert Frederick
d. Roldos Aguilera, Jamie

May 25, 1981
d. Ponselle, Rosa

May 26, 1981
d. Wortman, Sterling

May 27, 1981
d. Wheeler, Roger Milton

May 28, 1981
d. Williams, Mary Lou
d. Wyszynski, Stefan

May 29, 1981
d. Sun Yat-Sen, Chingling Soong, Madame

May 31, 1981
d. Pella, Giuseppe
d. Ward, Barbara Mary
d. Zia(ur) Rahman

June 1, 1981
d. Vinson, Carl

June 3, 1981
d. Coon, Carleton Stevens

June 6, 1981
d. Humphrey, Elliott S

June 7, 1981
d. Gorman, Chester

June 8, 1981
d. Lopokova, Lydia Vasilievna

June 9, 1981
d. Darden, Colgate Whitehead
d. Hayden, Russell
d. Ludden, Allen Ellsworth

June 15, 1981
d. Dinkeloo, John Gerard
d. Rinehart, Frederick Roberts
d. Toynbee, Philip

June 16, 1981
d. Knight, John Shivley

June 17, 1981
d. Sharp, Zerna A

June 18, 1981
d. Johnson, Pamela Hansford
d. Katona, George

June 20, 1981
d. Erwin, Pee Wee

June 21, 1981
d. Taubes, Frederic

June 22, 1981
d. Frankenstein, Alfred Victor
d. Harris, William Bliss
d. Lane, Lola
d. Linder, Harold Francis

June 24, 1981
d. Albrand, Martha
d. Ball, Edward
d. Butler, Paul

June 28, 1981
d. Beheshti, Mohammad, Ayatollah
d. Fox, Terry

June 29, 1981
d. Kharitonov, Yevgeni

July 1, 1981
d. Breuer, Marcel Lajos
d. Daniel, Dan(iel)
d. Voskovec, George

July 3, 1981
d. Berman, Emile Zola
d. Martin, Ross

July 4, 1981
d. Langer, Walter C

July 5, 1981
d. Urrutia Lleo, Manuel

July 6, 1981
d. Villa, Luz Corral de

July 7, 1981
d. Brasselle, Keefe
d. Gardner, Isabella

July 8, 1981
d. McDonnell, Joe
d. Smith, Loring
d. Soyer, Isaac

July 9, 1981
d. Levin, Meyer

July 12, 1981
d. Little, Edward Herman

July 13, 1981
d. Hurson, Martin

July 16, 1981
d. Chapin, Harry Foster

July 17, 1981
d. Barbanell, Maurice

July 20, 1981
d. Kardiner, Abram

July 21, 1981
d. Fox, Carol
d. Liebman, Max

July 23, 1981
d. Owen, Guy, Jr.

July 24, 1981
d. Hauge, Gabriel

July 25, 1981
d. Widgery, John Passmore, Baron

July 26, 1981
d. Ilg, Frances Lillian

July 27, 1981
d. Wyler, William

July 28, 1981
d. Bloom, Harry
d. O'Neil, James F(rancis)
d. Pauley, Edwin Wendell

July 29, 1981
d. Moses, Robert
d. Walsh, James Edward

July 30, 1981
d. Taoka Kazuo

July 31, 1981
d. Boni, Albert
d. Torrijos Herrera, Omar

August 1, 1981
d. Chayefsky, Paddy
d. Lynch, Kevin

August 2, 1981
d. Doherty, Kieran

August 4, 1981
d. Douglas, Melvyn

August 5, 1981
d. Neyman, Jerzy

August 6, 1981
d. Bliss, Ray C(harles)
d. Price, Byron

August 7, 1981
d. Arieti, Silvano

August 8, 1981
d. McIlwee, Thomas

August 9, 1981
d. Feldman, Alvin Lindbergh
d. Lawrence, Robert

August 10, 1981
d. Fisk, James Brown

August 14, 1981
d. Bohm, Karl
d. Curran, Joseph Edwin

August 15, 1981
d. Barr, Alfred Hamilton, Jr.
d. Brink, Carol Ryrie
d. Meek, Samuel Williams
d. Waldock, Humphrey Meredith, Sir

August 17, 1981
d. Keylor, Arthur W

August 18, 1981
d. Bennett, Robert Russell
d. Loos, Anita

August 19, 1981
d. Matthews, Jessie

August 20, 1981
d. Cleaver, William Joseph
d. Devine, Michael

August 21, 1981
d. Popov, Dusko

August 24, 1981
d. Dean, William Frishe

August 25, 1981
d. Hulme, Kathryn Cavarly

August 26, 1981
d. Baldwin, Roger Nash
d. Hays, Lee

August 27, 1981
d. Edwards, Joan

August 29, 1981
d. Thomas, Lowell Jackson

August 30, 1981
d. Rajai, Mohammed Ali
d. Vera-Ellen

August 31, 1981
d. Appel, James Ziegler
d. Hirshhorn, Joseph Herman

September 1, 1981
d. Harding, Ann
d. Speer, Albert

September 2, 1981
d. Lyons, Enid Muriel

September 3, 1981
d. Roszak, Theodore
d. Waugh, Alec

September 5, 1981
d. Maeght, Aime

September 6, 1981
d. Brown, Christy

September 7, 1981
d. Link, Edwin Albert

September 8, 1981
b. Thomas, Jonathan Taylor
d. Wilkins, Roy
d. Yukawa, Hideki

September 9, 1981
d. Lacan, Jacques (Marie Emile)

September 11, 1981
d. McHugh, Frank

September 12, 1981
d. Montale, Eugenio

September 13, 1981
d. Breit, Gregory
d. Humes, Helen
d. Loeb, William

September 15, 1981
d. DiSalle, Michael Vincent

September 17, 1981
d. Kemper, James S(cott)

September 18, 1981
d. Doubrovska, Felia

September 21, 1981
d. Hirsch, Joseph

September 22, 1981
d. Warren, Harry

September 23, 1981
d. Eckstein, Gustav
d. George, Dan, Chief

September 24, 1981
d. Kelly, Patsy
d. Ochsner, Alton

September 26, 1981
b. Williams, Serena

September 27, 1981
d. Montgomery, Robert Henry

September 28, 1981
d. Betancourt, Romulo
d. Hinton, Walter

September 30, 1981
d. Neel, (Louis) Boyd
d. Passarella, Art

October 2, 1981
d. Golden, Harry Lewis
d. La Barba, Fidel
d. Scott, Hazel Dorothy

October 4, 1981
d. Lindstrom, Freddie

October 5, 1981
d. Bullard, Dexter Means
d. Grahame, Gloria

October 6, 1981
d. Bugbee, Emma
d. Sadat, Anwar el

October 8, 1981
d. Kohut, Heinz

October 11, 1981
d. Hays, Brooks

October 12, 1981
d. Mecom, John Whitfield

October 13, 1981
d. Asther, Nils
d. Horan, James David

October 14, 1981
d. Mayer, Albert
d. Raymond, James C

October 16, 1981
d. Dayan, Moshe

October 17, 1981
d. Guion, David Wendel Fentress

October 18, 1981
d. Muncey, Bill
d. Rubin, Vitalii

October 20, 1981
d. Chase, Mary Coyle

October 21, 1981
d. Dixon, Robert Ellington

October 24, 1981
d. Head, Edith
d. Holm, John Cecil

October 25, 1981
d. Durant, Ariel
d. Reiser, Pete

October 26, 1981
d. Llewelyn-Davies, Richard

October 30, 1981
d. Brassens, Georges

October 31, 1981
d. Scherr, Max

November 1, 1981
d. DeGraff, Robert F(air)

November 3, 1981
d. Westermann, H(orace) C(lifford)

November 6, 1981
d. Daniels, Jonathan Worth

November 7, 1981
d. Durant, Will(iam James)

November 10, 1981
d. Gance, Abel

November 15, 1981
d. Markey, Enid

November 16, 1981
d. Holden, William

November 17, 1981
d. Eberle, Bob
d. Lang, Daniel

November 18, 1981
d. Wertham, Fredric

November 20, 1981
d. Sheed, Frank

November 21, 1981
d. Bolotowsky, Ilya
d. Von Zell, Harry

November 22, 1981
d. Krebs, Hans Adolf, Sir
d. Lightner, Theodore

November 24, 1981
d. Thornton, Charles Bates

November 25, 1981
d. Albertson, Jack

November 26, 1981
d. Euwe, Max

November 27, 1981
d. Lenya, Lotte

November 28, 1981
d. Gimbel, Sophie Haas

November 29, 1981
d. Wood, Natalie

November 30, 1981
d. Gielgud, Val Henry

December 2, 1981
d. Harrison, Wallace Kirkman
d. Kay, Hershy
d. Oliver, James A(rthur)

December 3, 1981
b. Filipovic, Zlata
d. Knott, Walter

December 6, 1981
d. Corcoran, Thomas Gardiner

December 10, 1981
d. Kieran, John Francis
d. Marlowe, Sylvia
d. Wurf, Jerry

December 11, 1981
d. Kaiser, Edgar Fosburgh

December 13, 1981
d. Markham, Pigmeat

December 14, 1981
d. Benchley, Nathaniel Goddard

December 15, 1981
d. Cockburn, Claud

December 16, 1981
d. Allen, Ethel D.
d. Struss, Karl

December 17, 1981
d. Shehu, Mehmet

December 18, 1981
d. Conley, Eugene

December 19, 1981
d. Frailberg, Selma

December 20, 1981
d. Goodman, Martin Wise

December 21, 1981
d. Dwan, Allan

December 23, 1981
d. Kountz, Samuel L(ee)

December 27, 1981
d. Carmichael, Hoagy

December 28, 1981
b. Carr, Elizabeth Jordan
d. Davis, James Curran
d. Stoodard, George Dinsmore

December 29, 1981
d. McNaughton, F(oye) F(isk)

December 31, 1981
d. Adair, Frank E(arl)
d. Seper, Franjo

1982

d. First, Ruth
d. Gottschalk, Robert
d. Moos, Malcolm Charles
d. Quarterman, Lloyd Albert

January 1, 1982
d. Buono, Victor
d. Grahame, Margot

January 2, 1982
d. Hampton, Hope
d. Harman, Fred

January 3, 1982
d. Canham, Erwin Dain

January 4, 1982
d. Banning, Margaret Culkin

January 5, 1982
d. Conreid, Hans
d. Lembeck, Harvey

January 6, 1982
d. Crawford, William Hulfish

January 9, 1982
d. Lynde, Paul Edward
d. Musso, Vido
d. Schilt, Jan

January 11, 1982
d. Horikoshi, Jiro

January 13, 1982
d. Camus, Marcel

January 15, 1982
d. Jarman, John
d. Sender, Ramon Jose
d. Smith, Red

January 17, 1982
d. Shalamov, Varlam Tikhonovich

January 19, 1982
d. Plumb, Charles

d. Zaturenska, Marya

January 20, 1982
d. Baxter, Frank Condie

January 21, 1982
d. Irish, Ned

January 22, 1982
d. Farber, Edward Rolke
d. Frei, Eduardo

January 23, 1982
d. Sillman, Leonard

January 24, 1982
d. Ovando Candia, Alfredo

January 26, 1982
d. Suslov, Mikhail Andreevich

January 29, 1982
d. Namgyal, Palden Thondup

January 30, 1982
d. Holloway, Stanley
d. Hopkins, Lightnin'
d. Lynd, Helen Merrell

January 31, 1982
d. Calder, Peter Ritchie
d. Turnbull, Agnes Sligh
d. Campagnolo, Gitullio

February 2, 1982
d. Stanford, Sally

February 3, 1982
d. Barr, Stringfellow

February 5, 1982
d. Opie, Peter Mason

February 6, 1982
d. Nicholson, Ben

February 7, 1982
d. Robinson, M(aurice) R(ichard)

February 8, 1982
d. Whitney, John Hay

February 11, 1982
d. Powell, Eleanor

February 12, 1982
d. Jory, Victor

February 13, 1982
d. Williams, Gluyas

February 14, 1982
d. Jackson, Hurricane

February 15, 1982
d. Dietrich, Noah
d. Enoch, Kurt

February 17, 1982
d. Chylak, Nestor
d. Monk, Thelonious Sphere, Jr.

d. Strasberg, Lee

February 18, 1982
d. Marsh, Ngaio, Dame

February 20, 1982
d. Cornell, Douglas B
d. Dubos, Rene Jules
d. Scholem, Gershom Gerhard

February 21, 1982
d. Kaufman, Murray

February 24, 1982
d. Bruce, Virginia
d. Chao, Yuen Ren

February 26, 1982
d. Kinugasa, Teinosuke

February 28, 1982
d. Levi, Julian Edwin

March 1, 1982
d. Spivak, Charlie

March 2, 1982
d. Dick, Philip K(indred)

March 3, 1982
d. DeWitt, William Orville, Sr.
d. Villiers, Alan John

March 4, 1982
d. Eden, Dorothy

March 5, 1982
d. Belushi, John
d. Case, Clifford Philip
d. Patton, Edward L

March 6, 1982
d. Rand, Ayn

March 8, 1982
d. Shera, Jesse Hauk

March 9, 1982
d. Butler of Saffron Walden, Richard
  Austen, Baron

March 11, 1982
d. Gregory, Horace Victor

March 15, 1982
d. Rickword, Edgell

March 18, 1982
d. Chuikov, Vasili Ivanovitch

March 20, 1982
d. Copeland, Jo

March 22, 1982
d. Fitzgerald, Ed(ward)
d. Parker, Buddy

March 23, 1982
d. Feingold, Benjamin Franklin
d. Greer, Sonny
d. Praz, Mario

March 24, 1982
d. Gorin, Igor

March 25, 1982
d. Ace, Goodman

March 27, 1982
d. Adams, Harriet Stratemeyer
d. Khan, Fazlur Rahman

March 28, 1982
d. Uris, Harold David

March 29, 1982
d. Bloch, Raymond A
d. Deutsch, Helene R(osenbach)
d. Giauque, William Francis
d. Hallstein, Walter
d. Orff, Carl
d. Twining, Nathan F(arragut)

March 30, 1982
d. McHale, Tom
d. Richardson, Scovel
d. Thomas, Charles Allen
d. Boykin, Otis Frank

April 2, 1982
d. Bird, Junius Bouton
d. Coslow, Sam
d. McCall, Dorothy Lawson

April 3, 1982
d. Oates, Warren

April 5, 1982
d. Fortas, Abe
d. Lawrenson, Helen Brown

April 7, 1982
d. Benet, Brenda

April 9, 1982
d. Barrios, Francisco Javier
d. Pelletier, Wilfrid

April 14, 1982
d. Handy, Thomas Troy

April 15, 1982
d. Montor, Henry

April 18, 1982
d. Harnwell, Gaylord Probasco
d. Harrar, J(acob) George

April 20, 1982
d. MacLeish, Archibald

April 22, 1982
d. Grosvenor, Melville Bell

April 23, 1982
d. Townsend, William Cameron
d. Walsh, Michael Patrick

April 24, 1982
d. Ashbrook, John Milan
d. Ritola, Ville

April 25, 1982
d. Burnett, W(illiam) R(iley)

d. Butterfield, Lyman Henry
d. Cody, John Patrick
d. Johnson, Celia, Dame
d. Wilson, Don(ald Harlow)

April 27, 1982
d. Tully, Tom

April 28, 1982
d. Corn, Ira George, Jr.

April 29, 1982
d. Ripley, Elmer Horton

April 30, 1982
d. Bangs, Lester

May 1, 1982
d. Fitzgerald, Albert J
d. Primrose, William

May 2, 1982
d. Bochner, Salomon
d. Marlowe, Hugh

May 3, 1982
d. Dantine, Helmut
d. Frazier, Brenda Diana Dudd

May 4, 1982
d. O'Brien, Leo W

May 5, 1982
d. Tjader, Cal(len Radcliffe, Jr.)

May 6, 1982
d. Littlejohn, Robert McGowan

May 8, 1982
d. Bogart, Neil
d. Villeneuve, Gilles

May 10, 1982
d. Sloane, Dennis
d. Weiss, Peter Ulrich

May 11, 1982
d. Burck, Jacob

May 14, 1982
d. Beaumont, Hugh
d. Rossellini, Renzo

May 17, 1982
d. Walker, Dixie

May 20, 1982
d. Stern, Max
d. Tuve, Merle Antony

May 22, 1982
d. Sunay, Cevdet

May 26, 1982
d. Larsen-Todsen, Nanny

May 27, 1982
d. McCabe, Thomas Bayard

May 29, 1982
d. Schneider, Romy

June 1, 1982
d. Mikkelsen, Henning Dahl

June 3, 1982
d. VonSchmidt, Harold

June 6, 1982
d. Rexroth, Kenneth
d. Szmuness, Wolf

June 7, 1982
d. Demara, Ferdinand Waldo, Jr.

June 8, 1982
d. Neff, Wallace
d. Paige, Satchel

June 10, 1982
b. Lipinski, Tara
d. Dali, Gala
d. Fassbinder, Rainer Werner

June 12, 1982
d. Frisch, Karl von
d. Rambert, Marie, Dame

June 13, 1982
d. Griffin, Marvin
d. Khalid Ibn Abdul Azia Al-Saud
d. Rafferty, Max(well Lewis, Jr.)

June 15, 1982
d. Pepper, Art(hur Edward)

June 16, 1982
d. Honeyman-Scott, James
d. Kibbee, Robert Joseph

June 17, 1982
d. Harkness, Rebekah West

June 18, 1982
d. Barnes, Djuna
d. Cheever, John
d. Hicks, Granville
d. Hillenkoetter, Roscoe H(enry)
d. Jurgens, Curt

June 19, 1982
d. Lockridge, Richard

June 21, 1982
b. William of Wales

June 26, 1982
d. Mitscherlich, Alexander

June 28, 1982
d. Mills, Harry

June 29, 1982
d. Balmain, Pierre Alexandre
d. King, Henry

July 4, 1982
d. Guzman, Antonio
d. Sullivan, Daniel P

July 5, 1982
d. Jagel, Frederick
d. Mueller, Reuben Herbert

July 6, 1982
d. Roa (y Garcia), Raul

July 7, 1982
d. Loughran, Tommy

July 9, 1982
d. Manone, Wingy

July 10, 1982
d. Jeritza, Maria

July 12, 1982
d. More, Kenneth Gilbert

July 14, 1982
d. Jensen, Jackie

July 16, 1982
d. Dewaere, Patrick
d. Gross, Courtlandt Sherrington
d. Swart, Charles Robberts

July 18, 1982
d. Jakobson, Roman

July 21, 1982
d. Barbour, Walworth
d. Garroway, Dave

July 22, 1982
d. Stitt, Sonny
d. Waner, Lloyd James

July 23, 1982
d. Morrow, Vic
d. Parsons, Betty Pierson

July 24, 1982
d. Lawler, Richard Harold
d. Markey, Lucille (Parker) Wright

July 25, 1982
d. Foster, Hal
d. Okada, Kenzo

July 27, 1982
d. Seymour, Dan

July 28, 1982
d. Lucas, Nick

July 29, 1982
d. Gale, Richard Nelson, Sir
d. Zworykin, Vladimir K(osma)

July 31, 1982
d. Atwood, Francis Clarke
d. Chenoweth, Dean

August 2, 1982
d. Nesbitt, Cathleen Mary

August 3, 1982
d. Carritt, David Graham

August 4, 1982
d. De Rochemont, Richard Guertis

August 6, 1982
d. Clarke, Gilmore David

August 8, 1982
d. Braestrup, Carl Bjorn

August 11, 1982
d. Drake, Tom

August 12, 1982
d. Charnley, John, Sir
d. Fonda, Henry Jaynes
d. Sanchez, Salvador

August 13, 1982
d. Coleman, Lonnie William
d. Ross, Joe E
d. Tex, Joe
d. Walters, Charles

August 14, 1982
d. Magee, Patrick
d. Morton, Thruston Ballard

August 15, 1982
d. Bushmiller, Ernie
d. Mumford, Lawrence Quincy
d. Taishoff, Sol Joseph
d. Theorell, (Axel) Hugh Teodor

August 18, 1982
d. Bayne, Beverly Pearl

August 19, 1982
d. Crisler, Fritz
d. Davis, Loyal

August 20, 1982
d. Bloomingdale, Alfred S

August 21, 1982
d. Simmons, Calvin
d. Sobhuza II

August 22, 1982
d. Jacobsson, Ulla

August 23, 1982
d. Cavalcanti, Alberto
d. Moore, Stanford

August 24, 1982
d. Iwama, Kazuo

August 28, 1982
b. Rimes, LeAnn

August 29, 1982
d. Bergman, Ingrid
d. Engel, Lehman
d. Goldmann, Nahum

August 30, 1982
d. Loring, Eugene

September 1, 1982
d. Curzon, Clifford Michael, Sir
d. Gomulka, Wladyslaw

September 2, 1982
d. Schaefer, Rudolph Jay

September 3, 1982
d. Dannay, Frederic

September 4, 1982
d. Tworkov, Jack

September 5, 1982
d. Bader, Douglas Robert Steuart, Sir
d. Sebelius, Keith George

September 7, 1982
d. Benjamin, Adam, Jr.
d. Boyer, Ken(ton Lloyd)

September 8, 1982
d. Abdullah, Mohammad, Sheik

September 10, 1982
d. DeCreeft, Jose

September 11, 1982
d. Ryan, T(ubal) Claude

September 13, 1982
d. Eldjarn, Kristjan
d. Hemingway, Leicester
d. Ober, Philip (Nott)
d. Wallenberg, Marcus

September 14, 1982
d. Gardner, John Champlin, Jr.
d. Gemayel, Bashir
d. Kelly, Grace Patricia

September 15, 1982
d. Ghotbzadeh, Sadegh

September 17, 1982
d. Dubinsky, David
d. Stravinsky, Vera de Bossett

September 20, 1982
d. Hughes, Emmet John

September 21, 1982
d. Bagramian, Ivan Christofovorich

September 23, 1982
d. Dobozy, Imre
d. Wakely, Jimmy

September 24, 1982
d. Churchill, Sarah

September 25, 1982
d. Poulson, Norris

September 26, 1982
d. Bettis, Valerie
d. Cox, Allyn
d. Kollsman, Paul

September 27, 1982
d. Armour, Norman
d. Bowen, Billy
d. Romano, Umberto

September 29, 1982
d. Stratton, Monty Franklin Pierce

September 30, 1982
d. George, Bill
d. Janson, Horst Woldemar

October 1, 1982
d. Bernbach, William

October 3, 1982
d. Merchant, Vivien

October 4, 1982
d. Bakr, Ahmad Hasan al
d. Dial, Morris Grant
d. Gould, Glenn Herbert
d. Grumman, Leroy Randle
d. Terry, Walter

October 6, 1982
d. Ydigoras Fuentes Miguel

October 8, 1982
d. Freud, Anna
d. Lamas, Fernando
d. Noel-Baker, Philip John

October 11, 1982
d. Duffy, Clinton Truman
d. Hosmer, Craig
d. Quimby, Edith H.

October 14, 1982
d. Sackler, Howard Oliver

October 16, 1982
d. DelMonaco, Mario
d. Selye, Hans

October 17, 1982
d. Riddleberger, James Williams
d. Rothschild, Alain de, Baron

October 18, 1982
d. Mendes-France, Pierre
d. Robarts, John Parmenter
d. Truman, Bess

October 20, 1982
d. Ziolkowski, Korczak

October 22, 1982
d. Jessup, Richard

October 26, 1982
d. Benelli, Giovanni, Cardinal
d. Leek, Sybil

October 29, 1982
d. Hall, Joyce Clyde
d. Thompson, Thomas

November 1, 1982
d. Broderick, James Joseph
d. Vidor, King Wallis

November 2, 1982
d. Roloff, Lester

November 4, 1982
d. Dunne, Dominique

November 5, 1982
d. Tati, Jacques

November 6, 1982
d. Swinnerton, Frank Arthur

November 8, 1982
d. Politz, Alfred

November 10, 1982
d. Brezhnev, Leonid Ilyich
d. Petri, Elio

November 13, 1982
d. Deutsch, Babette
d. Kim, Duk Koo

November 15, 1982
d. Bhave, Acharya Vinoba

November 16, 1982
d. Crosby, Sumner McKnight

November 17, 1982
d. Donnelly, Ruth

November 18, 1982
d. McGivern, William Peter

November 20, 1982
d. Mackin, Catherine Patricia

November 21, 1982
d. Hofheinz, Roy Mark
d. Patrick, Lee

November 22, 1982
d. Batten, Jean Gardner
d. Turkus, Burton B

November 25, 1982
d. Coote, Robert
d. Gray, Gordon

November 26, 1982
d. Harman, Hugh

November 27, 1982
d. Gordon, Steve

November 30, 1982
d. Merrill, Henry Tindall

December 2, 1982
d. Bugas, John Stephen
d. Feldman, Marty
d. Sackheim, Maxwell Byron

December 6, 1982
d. Lay, Herman Warden

December 7, 1982
d. Brooks, Charlie, Jr.
d. Kistiakowsky, George Bogdan
d. Lee, Will

December 8, 1982
d. Mayer, Norman D
d. Robbins, Marty

December 9, 1982
d. Jaworski, Leon

December 10, 1982
d. Gosden, Freeman Fisher

December 11, 1982
d. Miner, Worthington C

December 16, 1982
d. Chapman, (Anthony) Colin (Bruce)
d. Hubbard, Orville Liscum

December 17, 1982
d. Ferguson, Homer
d. Hoyt, Lawrence W
d. Kogan, Leonid Borisovich

December 19, 1982
d. MacDonald, Dwight

December 20, 1982
d. Rubinstein, Arthur

December 23, 1982
d. Webb, Jack Randolph

December 24, 1982
d. Aragon, Louis Marie Antoine
Alfred

December 25, 1982
d. Bowling, Roger
d. Pearl, Jack

December 27, 1982
d. Swigert, Jack

December 29, 1982
d. Gallen, Hugh J

1983

b. Kielburger, Craig
d. Day, James Wentworth
d. Pelkey, Edward
d. Robinson, Joan Violet Maurice
d. Bartlett, Vernon

January 2, 1983
d. Seiler, James, W

January 3, 1983
d. Bond, George Foote

January 4, 1983
d. Rosenthal, Benjamin Stanley

January 7, 1983
d. Coates, Edith
d. Hanks, Nancy

January 8, 1983
d. McCall, Thomas Lawson

January 11, 1983
d. Podgorny, Nikolai Viktorovich

January 15, 1983
d. Lansky, Meyer
d. Lauder, Joseph H
d. Strudwick, Shepperd
d. Weaver, Doodles

January 18, 1983
d. Illia, Arturo Umberto

January 19, 1983
d. Carson, Robert
d. Costa, Don

January 22, 1983
d. Madden, Donald

January 23, 1983
d. Bane, Frank B

January 24, 1983
d. Cukor, George (Dewey)
d. Ellsberg, Edward
d. Erickson, Eric

January 26, 1983
d. Bryant, Bear
d. Reichelderfer, Francis Wylton

January 27, 1983
d. Bidault, Georges
d. Bilon, Michael Patrick

January 29, 1983
d. Fury, Billy
d. Ingersoll, Stuart H

January 30, 1983
d. Cunningham, Alan Gordon, Sir
d. Machlup, Fritz
d. Stevens, Robert Ten Broeck

February 4, 1983
d. Ameche, Jim
d. Carpenter, Karen (Anne)

February 8, 1983
d. Wallenstein, Alfred Franz

February 10, 1983
d. Franz, Eduard

February 11, 1983
d. Drewry, John Eldridge
d. Kline, Nathan Schellenberg

February 12, 1983
d. Blake, Eubie

February 17, 1983
d. Pasero, Tancredi

February 18, 1983
d. Godowsky, Leopold, Jr.
d. Payne, Robert

February 19, 1983
d. Bluhdorn, Charles G
d. Boyd, William Clouser

February 23, 1983
d. Arran, Arthur Kattendyke Strange
David Archibald Gore, Earl of
d. Boult, Adrian Cedric, Sir

February 25, 1983
d. Cowles, John, Sr.
d. Williams, Tennessee
d. Von Euler, Ulf

March 3, 1983
d. Koestler, Arthur

d. Tarsis, Valery Yakovlevich

March 6, 1983
d. Berberian, Cathy
d. Maclean, Donald Duart

March 7, 1983
d. Black, William
d. Markevitch, Igor

March 8, 1983
d. Walton, William Turner, Sir

March 9, 1983
d. Emerson, Faye Margaret

March 12, 1983
d. Aldrich, Ki

March 15, 1983
d. Sert, Jose Luis
d. West, Rebecca, Dame

March 16, 1983
d. Godfrey, Arthur Michael

March 17, 1983
d. Hartline, Haldan Keffer
d. Tromp, Solco Walle

March 18, 1983
d. Marshall, Catherine
d. Umberto II

March 23, 1983
d. Fitzgibbon, Constantine

March 24, 1983
d. Clark, Barney Bailey

March 25, 1983
d. Gates, Thomas Sovereign, Jr.

March 26, 1983
d. Blunt, Anthony Frederick
d. Waterfield, Bob

March 27, 1983
d. Stankiewicz, Richard Peter

March 29, 1983
d. Barrows, Marjorie (Ruth)
d. Model, Lisette

March 30, 1983
d. Peterson, Lorraine Collett

March 31, 1983
d. Stead, Christina (Ellen)

April 4, 1983
d. Rapp, Danny
d. Swanson, Gloria May Josephine

April 10, 1983
d. Burton, Phillip
d. Wechsberg, Joseph

April 11, 1983
d. DelRio, Dolores

April 13, 1983
d. Humphreys, Christmas
d. May, Morton David

April 14, 1983
d. Pearlroth, Norbert

April 15, 1983
d. Ten Boom, Corrie

April 17, 1983
d. Leonard, Dutch

April 19, 1983
d. Andrzejewski, Jerzy

April 21, 1983
d. Slezak, Walter

April 22, 1983
d. Hines, Fatha

April 23, 1983
d. Crabbe, Buster
d. La Follette, Suzanne
d. Royle, Selena

April 25, 1983
d. Glenn, Carroll

April 26, 1983
d. Buckmaster, Henrietta

April 27, 1983
d. Catledge, Turner

April 30, 1983
d. Balanchine, George
d. Waters, Muddy
d. Kaper, Bronislau

May 2, 1983
d. Pridi Phanomyong
d. Van Brocklin, Norm (an Mack)

May 3, 1983
d. Skolsky, Sidney

May 5, 1983
d. Buttigieg, Anton
d. Dutra, Olin

May 6, 1983
d. Keats, Ezra Jack
d. Masters, John
d. Winding, Kai Chresten

May 9, 1983
d. Rosenberg, Anna Marie

May 14, 1983
d. Aleman, Miguel

May 15, 1983
d. Gucci, Rodolfo
d. VanDerZee, James

May 18, 1983
d. Fielding, Temple Hornaday

May 20, 1983
d. Bee, Clair Francis
d. Claude, Albert

May 21, 1983
d. Clark, Kenneth MacKenzie, Sir
d. Hoffer, Eric

May 25, 1983
d. Idris I

May 28, 1983
d. Corning, Erastus, III

May 30, 1983
d. Grubert, Carl Alfred
d. Gruenther, Alfred Maximillian
d. Guffey, Burnett

May 31, 1983
d. Dempsey, Jack

June 4, 1983
d. Tors, Ivan

June 6, 1983
d. Casey, James E

June 9, 1983
d. Mackay, John Alexander

June 10, 1983
d. Reisenberg, Nadia

June 12, 1983
d. Shearer, Norma

June 16, 1983
d. Lee, Doris Emrick

June 17, 1983
d. Mennin, Peter
d. Seifert, Elizabeth

June 18, 1983
d. Lewis, Robert Alvin

June 21, 1983
d. Dodson, Owen (Vincent)

June 22, 1983
d. Hinton, Christopher, Sir

June 23, 1983
d. Cervantes, Alfonso Juan

June 24, 1983
d. Miller, William E
d. Taft, Charles Phelps

June 25, 1983
d. Ginastera, Alberto Evaristo
d. Monroe, Marion

June 26, 1983
d. O'Keefe, Walter

June 27, 1983
d. Anderson, Max(ie Leroy)

June 29, 1983
d. Delaney, Joe Alton

June 30, 1983
d. Livingstone, Mary

July 1, 1983
d. Copeland, Lammot du Pont
d. Fuller, Richard Buckminster
d. Hoffman, Julius Jennings

July 5, 1983
d. Dejongh, Peter
d. James, Harry

July 7, 1983
d. Amfiteatrof, Daniele
d. Kahn, Herman
d. Morgan, Vicki

July 10, 1983
d. Castagna, Bruna
d. Egk, Werner

July 11, 1983
d. MacDonald, Ross

July 12, 1983
d. Wood, Chris

July 13, 1983
d. Roy, Gabrielle

July 15, 1983
d. Foy, Eddie, Jr.

July 16, 1983
d. Micombero, Michel
d. Raphaelson, Samson

July 18, 1983
d. Lichty, George

July 20, 1983
d. Reynolds, Frank

July 21, 1983
d. Wirtz, Arthur Michael

July 23, 1983
d. Auric, Georges
d. Traube, Shepard

July 25, 1983
d. Balderston, William

July 28, 1983
d. Crosby, Elizabeth Caroline

July 29, 1983
d. Bunuel, Luis
d. Crohn, Burrill Bernard
d. Massey, Raymond Hart
d. Niven, David

July 30, 1983
d. Dietz, Howard M
d. Fontanne, Lynn
d. Plimpton, Francis Taylor Pearson

August 1, 1983
d. Carter, Ernestine Marie

August 3, 1983
d. Jones, Carolyn

August 5, 1983
d. Bok, Bart J(an)
d. Canova, Judy

August 7, 1983
d. Lyttle, Hulda Margaret

August 8, 1983
d. Harger, Rolla

August 11, 1983
d. Wigg, George (Edward Cecil)

August 15, 1983
d. Cohen, Benjamin Victor
d. Kilgore, Al

August 16, 1983
d. Averill, Earl
d. Roy, Ross

August 17, 1983
d. Gershwin, Ira

August 18, 1983
d. Pevsner, Nikolaus Bernhard Leon, Sir

August 21, 1983
d. Aquino, Benigno Simeon, Jr.

August 24, 1983
d. Nearing, Scott

August 25, 1983
d. Keller, Arthur C

August 26, 1983
d. Kellin, Mike

August 28, 1983
d. Clayton, Jan(e Byral)

August 29, 1983
d. Goyen, William
d. Oakland, Simon
d. Carr, Sabin

September 1, 1983
d. Herzog, Arthur, Jr.
d. Jackson, Henry Martin
d. McDonald, Larry

September 6, 1983
d. Hazam, Lou(is J)

September 8, 1983
d. Abboud, (El Ferik) Ibrahim

September 10, 1983
d. Bloch, Felix
d. Lofts, Norah Robinson
d. Vorster, Balthazar Johannes

September 11, 1983
d. Heaton, Leonard
d. Wechsler, James Arthur

September 14, 1983
d. Albright, Malvin Marr

September 15, 1983
d. Bacharach, Bert(ram Mark)
d. Nichols, Beverley

September 17, 1983
d. Medeiros, Humberto, Cardinal

September 25, 1983
d. Leopold III

September 26, 1983
d. Stapleton, Ruth Carter

September 27, 1983
d. Shear, Murray Jacob

September 30, 1983
d. Drummond, Roscoe
d. Martin, Freddy
d. Moorehead, Alan

October 3, 1983
d. Tupper, Earl Silas

October 6, 1983
d. Cooke, Terence James

October 7, 1983
d. Abell, George O(gden)
d. Howe, Oscar

October 8, 1983
d. Hackett, Joan

October 10, 1983
d. Debus, Kurt Heinrich
d. Richardson, Ralph David, Sir

October 14, 1983
d. Fix, Paul

October 15, 1983
d. O'Brien, Pat

October 16, 1983
d. Liberace, George J

October 17, 1983
d. Aron, Raymond Claude Ferdinand

October 19, 1983
d. Bishop, Maurice Rupert

October 20, 1983
d. Theriault, Yves
d. Travis, Merle Robert

October 22, 1983
d. Barrow, Keith E

October 23, 1983
d. Savitch, Jessica Beth

October 25, 1983
d. Epperson, Frank W

October 26, 1983
d. Dike, Kenneth (Onwuka)

d. Tarski, Alfred

October 27, 1983
d. Baldwin, Horace

October 28, 1983
d. Messmer, Otto

October 30, 1983
d. Carter, Lillian

October 31, 1983
d. Halas, George Stanley
d. Rashidov, Sharaf Rashidovich
d. Hibberd, Andrew Stuart

November 5, 1983
d. Benjamin, Curtis G

November 6, 1983
d. McBride, Lloyd

November 7, 1983
d. Friendly, Alfred
d. Tailleferre, Germaine

November 8, 1983
d. Kaplan, Mordecai

November 13, 1983
d. Samples, Junior

November 14, 1983
d. Sheehan, Joseph Green

November 15, 1983
d. Grimm, Charlie

November 18, 1983
d. Albright, Ivan Le Lorraine

November 19, 1983
d. Kitchell, Iva
d. Leigh, Carolyn

November 20, 1983
d. Loo, Richard

November 21, 1983
d. Davis, (William) Allison

November 22, 1983
d. Conrad, Michael
d. Wibberley, Leonard Patrick
    O'Connor

November 23, 1983
d. Putch, William Henry

November 25, 1983
d. Baldwin, Billy
d. Dolin, Anton, Sir

November 27, 1983
d. Furman, Roger

November 29, 1983
d. George, Christopher

November 30, 1983
d. Llewellyn, Richard

December 2, 1983
d. D'Orsay, Fifi

December 3, 1983
d. Zablocki, Clement John

December 4, 1983
d. Sananikone, Phoui

December 5, 1983
d. Aldrich, Robert
d. Brown, Charlie
d. Morton, Digby

December 8, 1983
d. Holyoake, Keith Jacka, Sir
d. Pickens, Slim

December 9, 1983
d. Rounds, David

December 12, 1983
d. Thayer, Mary Van Rensselaer

December 13, 1983
d. Renault, Mary
d. Schmemann, Alexander

December 19, 1983
d. Alexandrov, Grigori

December 20, 1983
d. Brandt, Bill
d. Fenelon, Fania

December 21, 1983
d. Cameron, Rod

December 25, 1983
d. Miro, Joan

December 27, 1983
d. Demarest, William

December 28, 1983
d. Demaret, Jimmy
d. Wilson, Dennis

December 30, 1983
d. Vargas, Alberto

1984

d. Ben-Haim, Paul
d. Friedrich, Carl Joachim
d. Justus, Roy Braxton
d. Lauro, Achille
d. Nidal, Abu
d. Sanapia
d. Simpson, George Gaylord
d. Chorell, Walentin

January 1, 1984
d. Korner, Alexis

January 4, 1984
d. Geschwind, Norman

January 7, 1984
d. Case, Anna

d. Hunt, Jack Reed
d. Kastler, Alfred

January 9, 1984
d. Gibberd, Frederick, Sir
d. Ward, Deighton Harcourt Lisle, Sir

January 10, 1984
d. Souvanna, Phouma

January 11, 1984
d. LaRue, Jack
d. Licavoli, Peter Joseph, Sr.

January 13, 1984
d. Atkinson, Brooks
d. Shanks, Michael

January 14, 1984
d. Haddad, Saad
d. Kroc, Ray(mond) Albert

January 18, 1984
d. Kerr, Malcolm (Hooper)

January 19, 1984
d. Bentley, Max(well Herbert Lloyd)

January 20, 1984
d. Weissmuller, Johnny

January 21, 1984
d. Wilson, Jackie

January 24, 1984
d. Reeves, Rosser

January 26, 1984
d. Dart, Justin Whitlock

January 28, 1984
d. Dexter, Al
d. Dooley, Rae

January 29, 1984
d. Goodrich, Frances

January 30, 1984
d. Coxe, George Harmon

January 31, 1984
d. Bricktop
d. Cipullo, Aldo Massimo Fabrizio

February 4, 1984
d. Kaplan, Henry Seymour

February 5, 1984
d. Cooper, Chuck

February 6, 1984
d. Ernst, Jimmy
d. Guillen, Jorge

February 8, 1984
d. Aries, Philippe

February 9, 1984
d. Andropov, Yuri Vladimirovich
d. Polk, Ralph Lane

February 11, 1984
d. Brett, George Platt, Jr.

February 12, 1984
d. Bainton, Roland Herbert
d. Cortazar, Julio

February 14, 1984
d. Mili, Gjon

February 15, 1984
d. Long, Avon
d. Merman, Ethel

February 17, 1984
d. Stuart, Jesse Hilton

February 19, 1984
d. Hopkins, Claude
d. Hutton, Ina Ray

February 21, 1984
d. Sholokhov, Mikhail Aleksandrovich

February 22, 1984
d. David

February 25, 1984
d. West, Jessamyn

February 26, 1984
d. Lattimore, Richmond Alexander
d. Taylor, Henry Junior
d. Wright, Louis Booker

February 27, 1984
d. Paton, Richard

March 1, 1984
d. Coogan, Jackie

March 5, 1984
d. Powell, William

March 6, 1984
d. Niemoller, Martin
d. Wilcoxon, Henry

March 7, 1984
d. Rotha, Paul

March 13, 1984
d. Wadsworth, James Jeremiah

March 18, 1984
d. Lau, Charlie
d. Mitchell, Clarence M

March 20, 1984
d. Coveleski, Stanley Anthony

March 21, 1984
d. Mays, Benjamin E(lijah)

March 22, 1984
d. Webster, Paul Francois

March 24, 1984
d. Jaffe, Sam

March 26, 1984
d. Toure, Ahmed Sekou
d. Toure, Sekou

March 27, 1984
d. Donohue, Jack

March 28, 1984
d. Dragon, Carmen

March 30, 1984
d. Barzini, Luigi Giorgio, Jr.
d. Rahner, Karl

April 1, 1984
d. Gaye, Marvin (Pentz)
d. Goudge, Elizabeth

April 2, 1984
d. Commager, Steele

April 4, 1984
d. Merrill, John Putnam

April 5, 1984
d. Harris, Arthur Travers, Sir

April 6, 1984
d. Peers, William Raymond

April 7, 1984
d. Church, Frank

April 8, 1984
d. Kapitsa, Pyotr Leonidovich

April 9, 1984
d. Blackwell, Basil Henry, Sir

April 10, 1984
d. Middleton, Ray

April 13, 1984
d. Kirkpatrick, Ralph Leonard

April 15, 1984
d. Empson, William, Sir

April 17, 1984
d. Clark, Mark Wayne

April 18, 1984
d. Cole, Kenneth Stewart
d. Mahin, John Lee

April 20, 1984
d. Burnford, Sheila

April 21, 1984
d. Mercer, Mabel

April 22, 1984
d. Adams, Ansel Easton
d. Marley, John

April 25, 1984
d. Kennedy, David Anthony

April 26, 1984
d. Basie, Count
d. McAvoy, May

d. Roney, William Chapoton, Jr.

April 28, 1984
d. Ashton-Warner, Sylvia Constance

May 1, 1984
d. Barrett, John L
d. Jenkins, Gordon

May 2, 1984
d. Barry, Jack
d. Clampett, Bob

May 3, 1984
d. Schneider, Alan

May 4, 1984
d. Boles, Paul Darcy
d. Dors, Diana

May 5, 1984
d. Gobbi, Tito

May 8, 1984
d. Matter, Herbert
d. Wallace, Lila Bell Acheson

May 12, 1984
d. Angell, Robert Cooley

May 16, 1984
d. Kaufman, Andy
d. Shaw, Irwin

May 17, 1984
d. Sinclair, Gordon

May 19, 1984
d. Betjeman, John, Sir

May 20, 1984
d. Bull, Peter

May 22, 1984
d. Zaharias, George

May 26, 1984
d. Tucker, Mary Bradham

May 29, 1984
d. Motley, Arthur Harrison

June 2, 1984
d. Bell, Arthur (Irving)

June 3, 1984
d. Wilson, Peter Cecil

June 5, 1984
d. Mohieddin, Ahmed Faud

June 8, 1984
d. McFarland, Ernest William

June 9, 1984
d. Hardin, Helen

June 11, 1984
d. Berlinguer, Enrico
d. Farrar, Margaret (Petherbridge)

June 12, 1984
d. Ferencsik, Janos

June 13, 1984
d. Owings, Nathaniel Alexander

June 14, 1984
d. Pillsbury, Philip Winston

June 15, 1984
d. Tully, Grace George
d. Willson, Meredith

June 17, 1984
d. Hegan, Jim
d. Rowe, James Henry, Jr.

June 19, 1984
d. Krasner, Lee

June 20, 1984
d. Winwood, Estelle

June 24, 1984
d. Campbell, Clarence Sutherland

June 25, 1984
d. Foucault, Michel

June 26, 1984
d. Foreman, Carl
d. Hamilton, Floyd (Garland)

June 27, 1984
d. Jacoby, Oswald

June 28, 1984
d. Astor, Gavin
d. Yadin, Yigael

June 30, 1984
d. Hellman, Lillian

July 4, 1984
d. Hathaway, Starke R

July 5, 1984
d. Bloom, Julius

July 7, 1984
d. Oppen, George
d. Robson, Flora McKenzie, Dame

July 8, 1984
d. Brassai

July 9, 1984
d. Hurd, Peter
d. Thompson, Randall

July 14, 1984
d. Delmar, Kenny
d. Schacht, Al(exander)
d. Tidyman, Ernest

July 17, 1984
d. Low, George M(ichael)
d. Sykes, Roosevelt

July 20, 1984
d. Fixx, James Fuller

July 21, 1984
d. Farrington, Elizabeth Pruett (Mary)

July 22, 1984
d. Losey, Joseph Walton

July 24, 1984
d. Hextall, Bryan Aldwyn

July 25, 1984
d. Thornton, Willie Mae

July 26, 1984
d. Gallup, George Horace
d. Gein, Ed

July 27, 1984
d. Mason, James Neville

July 29, 1984
d. Waring, Fred Malcolm

July 30, 1984
d. Renault, Gilbert (Leon Etienne Theodore)

July 31, 1984
d. Stern, Philip Van Doren
d. Chukarin, Viktor Ivanovich

August 2, 1984
d. Deming, Barbara

August 3, 1984
d. Perkins, Carl Dewey

August 5, 1984
d. Burton, Richard

August 7, 1984
d. Phillips, Esther

August 8, 1984
d. Khrushchev, Nina Petrovna
d. Raskin, Ellen

August 9, 1984
d. Deacon, Richard
d. Tevis, Walter

August 10, 1984
d. Partch, Virgil Franklin, II

August 11, 1984
d. Knopf, Alfred Abraham

August 13, 1984
d. Petrosian, Tigran Vartanovich

August 14, 1984
d. Priestley, (J)ohn (B)oynton

August 25, 1984
d. Capote, Truman
d. Hoyt, Waite Charles
d. Varipapa, Andy

August 28, 1984
d. Naguib, Mohammed

August 30, 1984
d. Aadlberg, John O.
d. Gemayel, Pierre, Sheikh

September 3, 1984
d. Schwartz, Arthur

September 4, 1984
d. Kane, Harnett T(homas)

September 6, 1984
d. Feld, Irvin
d. Tubb, Ernest

September 7, 1984
d. Cronin, Joe
d. O'Flaherty, Liam

September 10, 1984
d. Hunsaker, Jerome Clarke

September 14, 1984
d. Gaynor, Janet

September 15, 1984
b. Henry of Wales

September 16, 1984
d. Reard, Louis

September 17, 1984
d. Basehart, Richard

September 20, 1984
d. Goodman, Steve(n Benjamin)

September 22, 1984
d. Mathieu, Noel Jean

September 24, 1984
d. Hamilton, Neil

September 25, 1984
d. Pidgeon, Walter

September 26, 1984
d. Manne, Shelly

September 27, 1984
d. Bunker, Ellsworth

September 29, 1984
d. Porter, Hal

September 30, 1984
d. Boylston, Helen Dore

October 1, 1984
d. Alston, Walter Emmons

October 6, 1984
d. Creighton, Thomas H(awk)

October 8, 1984
d. Brisson, Frederick

October 9, 1984
d. Christensen, Lew Farr

October 10, 1984
d. Gaddis, Thomas (Eugene)

October 11, 1984
d. Bergeron, Victor J

October 13, 1984
d. Kelly, George Lange
d. Neel, Alice Hartley

October 14, 1984
d. Ryle, Martin, Sir

October 17, 1984
d. Garner, Peggy Ann
d. Hunter, Alberta
d. Michaux, Henri
d. Thill, Georges

October 18, 1984
d. Hexum, Jon-Erik

October 20, 1984
d. Cori, Carl Ferdinand
d. Dirac, Paul Adrien Maurice

October 21, 1984
d. Truffaut, Francois

October 23, 1984
d. Petrillo, James Caesar
d. Werner, Oskar
d. Whittemore, Arthur Austin

October 25, 1984
d. Brautigan, Richard

October 29, 1984
d. Bloom, Ursula

October 30, 1984
d. Engstrom, Elmer William

October 31, 1984
d. Gandhi, Indira Priyadarshini Nehru

November 1, 1984
d. Krasna, Norman

November 2, 1984
d. Barfield, Velma

November 10, 1984
d. Bond, Sudie

November 11, 1984
d. King, Martin Luther, Sr.
d. Sheppard, Eugenia Benbow

November 12, 1984
d. Burman, Ben Lucien
d. Himes, Chester Bomar

November 16, 1984
d. Rose, Leonard

November 19, 1984
d. Aiken, George David

November 20, 1984
d. Bratteli, Trygve Martin
d. Faiz, Faiz Ahmad

November 21, 1984
d. Husch, Gerhard

November 25, 1984
d. Goldman, Sylvan N

November 26, 1984
d. Corena, Fernando
d. Lonergan, Bernard J F

November 27, 1984
d. Duke, Robin (Anthony Hare)

November 28, 1984
d. Bell, Ricky Lynn
d. Speidel, Hans

November 29, 1984
d. Crankshaw, Edward

December 2, 1984
d. Hauser, Gayelord
d. Sukman, Harry

December 4, 1984
d. Rock, John

December 7, 1984
d. Yarbrough, Lee Roy

December 8, 1984
d. Adler, Luther

December 9, 1984
d. Dietz, David

December 10, 1984
d. Teagarden, Charles

December 11, 1984
d. Ehricke, Krafft Arnold

December 14, 1984
d. Aleixandre, Vicente

December 15, 1984
d. Peerce, Jan
d. Spedding, Frank Harold

December 16, 1984
d. Prestopino, Gregorio

December 19, 1984
d. Seton-Watson, Hugh

December 20, 1984
d. Hill, Lester
d. Ustinov, Dmitri Fedorovich

December 21, 1984
d. Raskin, Judith

December 22, 1984
d. Merida, Carlos

December 24, 1984
d. Lawford, Peter

December 26, 1984
d. Barraclough, Geoffrey

December 27, 1984
d. Zevin, B(enjamin) D(avid)

December 28, 1984
d. Peckinpah, Sam

December 29, 1984
d. Robin, Leo

December 31, 1984
d. Ronning, Chester A

1985

b. Foster, Tabatha
d. Braudel, Fernand (Paul)
d. Morinigo, Higinio
d. Oppenheim, Meret
d. Scott, F(rancis) R(eginald)
d. Thomas, Vivien

January 1, 1985
d. Du Bois, Raoul Pene

January 2, 1985
d. Cushman, Robert Everton, Jr.

January 6, 1985
d. Horrocks, Brian Gwynne, Sir
d. Welch, Robert Henry Winborne, Jr.

January 7, 1985
d. Guarnieri, Johnny
d. Lyons, Eugene
d. Oursler, Will(iam Charles)

January 9, 1985
d. Mayer, Robert, Sir

January 11, 1985
d. Buzzell, Eddie

January 13, 1985
d. Holland, Jerome Heartwell

January 16, 1985
d. Fitzgerald, Robert Stuart
d. Orkin, Ruth

January 17, 1985
d. Rigby, Harry

January 18, 1985
d. Brambell, Wilfrid
d. Stoll, George E
d. Wolfenden, John Frederick, Sir

January 19, 1985
d. Voegelin, Eric (Herman Wilhelm)

January 22, 1985
d. Bryant, Arthur W M, Sir

January 23, 1985
d. Beard, James Andrews

January 25, 1985
d. Clarke, Kenny
d. Smith, Paul Joseph

January 26, 1985
d. Harlech, William David Ormsby-
   Gore, Baron

January 28, 1985
d. Saunders, Allen
d. Smith, Dora

February 2, 1985
d. Meyerhoff, Joseph

February 3, 1985
d. Oppenheimer, Frank F

February 4, 1985
d. Blackwell, Betsy Talbot
d. Wexley, John

February 6, 1985
d. Gardiner, Muriel

February 7, 1985
d. Jacobs, Walter L

February 8, 1985
d. Jaffe, Sam(uel Anderson)
d. Lyons, William, Sir

February 9, 1985
d. Roark, Garland

February 11, 1985
d. Abruzzo, Ben(jamine Lou)
d. Hathaway, Henry

February 12, 1985
d. Colasanto, Nicholas
d. Lengyel, Emil

February 13, 1985
d. Harris, Joseph Pratt
d. Jacobs, Al(bert T)

February 14, 1985
d. Mathews, Mitford M
d. Spigelgass, Leonard

February 18, 1985
d. Hamilton, Nancy
d. Scheuer, Philip K(latz)

February 19, 1985
d. Cummings, Nathan
d. Gorkin, Jess
d. Julesberg, Elizabeth Rider
   Montgomery
d. Lopez Bravo, Gregorio
d. Sutton, Carol

February 20, 1985
d. Kashdan, Isaac
d. Nash, Clarence
d. Wilcox, Francis (Orlando)

February 21, 1985
d. Claire, Ina
d. Hayward, Louis
d. Pritikin, Nathan

February 22, 1985
d. Espriu, Salvador
d. Scourby, Alexander

d. Zimbalist, Efrem

February 23, 1985
d. Braceland, Francis J(ames)

February 25, 1985
d. Weatherwax, Rudd B

February 26, 1985
d. Koopmans, Tjalling (Charles)

February 27, 1985
d. Lodge, Henry Cabot, Jr.
d. Moncreiffe, Iain
d. O'Malley, J Pat

March 1, 1985
d. Ethridge, Mark Foster, Jr.
d. List, Eugene

March 2, 1985
d. Kelly, John Brenden, Jr.

March 3, 1985
d. Blanding, Sarah Gibson
d. Shklovsky, Iosif Samvilovitch

March 5, 1985
d. Stotz, Charles Morse

March 6, 1985
d. Sloane, Eric
d. Sour, Robert B(andler)

March 7, 1985
d. Woodruff, Robert Winship

March 8, 1985
d. Andrews, Edward
d. Ingersoll, Ralph McAllister

March 9, 1985
d. Jenner, William Ezra

March 10, 1985
d. Chernenko, Konstantin Ustinovich
d. Van Niel, Cornelius B(ernardus)

March 12, 1985
d. Adams, Tom
d. Ormandy, Eugene

March 16, 1985
d. Sessions, Roger Huntington
d. Shore, Eddie
d. Stone, Louis

March 20, 1985
d. Knight, George Wilson

March 21, 1985
d. DeRivera, Jose Ruiz
d. Redgrave, Michael Scudamore, Sir

March 23, 1985
d. Harris, Patricia Roberts
d. Sims, Zoot

March 24, 1985
d. London, George

March 25, 1985
d. Armstrong, Charles B

March 27, 1985
d. Rico, Don(ato)

March 28, 1985
d. Chagall, Marc

March 29, 1985
d. Terry, Luther Leonidas

March 30, 1985
d. Gerasimov, Innokentii Petrovich
d. Peary, Harold
d. Spanel, Abram N

March 31, 1985
d. Deckers, Jeanine

April 1, 1985
d. Wallop, Douglass

April 2, 1985
d. Fernald, John Bailey
d. Tebelak, John Michael

April 8, 1985
d. Coots, J Fred

April 10, 1985
d. Donghia, Angelo R

April 11, 1985
d. Ertz, Susan
d. Hoxha, Enver

April 17, 1985
d. Brady, Scott
d. Bunting, Basil

April 18, 1985
d. Caton-Thompson, Gertrude

April 20, 1985
d. Dutton, Ralph Stawell

April 21, 1985
d. Gernreich, Rudi
d. Hewitt, Foster
d. Mills, Irving

April 23, 1985
d. Ervin, Sam(uel James Jr.)
d. Hughes, Sarah Tilghman
d. Smith, Kent

April 24, 1985
d. Weinberg, Chester

April 25, 1985
d. Haydn, Richard
d. Matheson, Murray

April 26, 1985
d. Maltz, Albert

April 30, 1985
d. Aitken, Max
d. Sommers, Ben

May 1, 1985
d. Crossley, Archibald Maddock
d. Robins, Denise Naomi

May 2, 1985
d. Bedells, Phyllis
d. Clinton, Larry
d. Eisenhower, Milton Stover

May 5, 1985
d. Bailey, Donald Coleman, Sir
d. Brown, Carter

May 6, 1985
d. Desjardins, Pete
d. Higbe, Kirby

May 7, 1985
d. Addams, Dawn

May 8, 1985
d. O'Brien, Edmond
d. Sturgeon, Theodore Hamilton

May 11, 1985
d. Gould, Chester

May 12, 1985
d. Dubuffet, Jean
d. Miles, Josephine

May 13, 1985
d. Behrens, Earl Charles
d. Diamond, Selma
d. Joy, Leatrice

May 16, 1985
d. Hamilton, Margaret Brainard
d. King, Wayne

May 17, 1985
d. Burrows, Abe

May 19, 1985
d. Lander, Toni
d. Martin, John

May 20, 1985
d. Wierwille, Victor Paul

May 25, 1985
d. Hecht, Harold
d. Nathan, Robert

May 29, 1985
d. Plomley, Roy

May 30, 1985
d. Jennings, Talbot

May 31, 1985
d. Rebuffat, Gaston Louis Simon

June 1, 1985
d. Greene, Richard
d. Price, Gwilym Alexander

June 2, 1985
d. Brown, George Alfred

June 4, 1985
d. North, John Ringling

June 6, 1985
d. Cooper, Lester Irving
d. Hough, Henry Beetle

June 10, 1985
d. Armstrong, Jack Lawrence

June 11, 1985
d. Quinlan, Karen Ann
d. Tanny, Vic

June 14, 1985
d. Johnson, Walter

June 15, 1985
d. Kamp, Irene Kittle

June 18, 1985
d. Xuan Thuy

June 19, 1985
d. Boulting, John
d. LeFleming, Christopher Kaye
d. Phillips, Marjorie Acker

June 21, 1985
d. Boiardi, Hector
d. Erlander, Tage Fritiof

June 23, 1985
d. Kotsching, Walter Maria
d. McIlhenny, Walter S

June 27, 1985
d. Sarkis, Elias

June 28, 1985
d. Ward, Lynd

June 30, 1985
d. Dewar, James A
d. Kresge, Stanley Sebastian

July 1, 1985
d. Murray, Pauli
d. Sterling, John Ewart Wallace

July 2, 1985
d. Bush, Guy Terrell

July 3, 1985
d. Kalem, T(heodore) E(ustace)

July 4, 1985
d. DeQuay, Jan E
d. Visser T Hooft, Willem Adolf
d. Weiland, Cooney

July 7, 1985
d. Scarne, John

July 8, 1985
d. Cowles, Gardner, Jr.
d. Foster, Phil
d. Hampson, Frank
d. Kuznets, Simon Smith

July 9, 1985
d. Charlotte Aldegonde E M
   Wilhelmine

July 10, 1985
d. Muller, Hilgard

July 12, 1985
d. Miller, Arnold Ray

July 16, 1985
d. Arends, Leslie Cornelius
d. Boll, Heinrich (Theodor)
d. Hicks, Ursula Kathleen Webb

July 17, 1985
d. Langer, Suzanne K
d. Margo
d. Stewart, Wynn

July 18, 1985
d. Hoffman, Robert C
d. Segal, Henry

July 19, 1985
d. Canaday, John (Edwin John)
d. Montagu, Ewen

July 20, 1985
d. Alexander, Leo
d. Johnson, Arno Hollock

July 21, 1985
d. Bessie, Alvah
d. Simpson, Cedric Keith

July 23, 1985
d. Kyser, Kay (James King Kern)
d. Shaughnessy, Mickey

July 24, 1985
d. Winwar, Frances

July 28, 1985
d. Audiard, Michel

July 30, 1985
d. Robinson, Julia (Bowman)

July 31, 1985
d. Blake, Eugene Carson
d. Blum, Stella

August 1, 1985
d. Walker, Joseph

August 2, 1985
d. Estridge, Philip D
d. Faylen, Frank

August 6, 1985
d. Burnham, Forbes

August 8, 1985
d. Brooks, Louise

August 10, 1985
d. Baker, Kenny

August 13, 1985
d. Marriott, John Willard

August 14, 1985
d. Hayes, Alfred
d. Sondergaard, Gale (Edith Holm)

August 17, 1985
d. Eden, Nicholas

August 19, 1985
d. Henderson, Robert W

August 24, 1985
d. Banks, William (Venoid)
d. Creston, Paul
d. Ryskind, Morrie

August 25, 1985
d. Smith, Samantha

August 26, 1985
d. Wakefield, Dick

August 27, 1985
b. Nechita, Alexandra

August 28, 1985
d. Gordon, Ruth

August 29, 1985
d. Ankers, Evelyn
d. Stein, Aaron Marc

August 30, 1985
d. Caldwell, Taylor

August 31, 1985
d. Burnet, F(rank) MacFarlane, Sir

September 1, 1985
d. Lewis, Saunders
d. Pitman, James
d. Zafrulla Khan, Muhammad, Sir

September 2, 1985
d. Burns, Eveline Mabel

September 3, 1985
d. Jones, Jo(nathan)
d. Marks, Johnny

September 4, 1985
d. McCormick, Robert K
d. O'Brien, George

September 5, 1985
d. Morse, Philip McCord

September 6, 1985
d. Desmond, Johnny
d. Porter, Rodney Robert

September 7, 1985
d. Polya, George
d. Waterhouse, Ellis Kirkham, Sir

September 8, 1985
d. Enders, John Franklin

September 9, 1985
d. Flory, Paul John
d. McNair, Malcolm Perrine

September 10, 1985
d. Overstreet, Bonaro Wilkinson

September 13, 1985
d. Rudhyar, Dane

September 14, 1985
d. Beck, Julian
d. Holt, John Caldwell

September 15, 1985
d. Williams, Cootie

September 17, 1985
d. Ashley, Laura Mountney

September 18, 1985
d. Cameron, Roderick W

September 19, 1985
d. Calvino, Italo
d. Straus, Jack Isidor

September 21, 1985
d. Peel, Ronald Francis (Edward Waite)

September 22, 1985
d. Nagel, Ernest
d. Springer, Axel Caesar
d. Tabouis, Genevieve

September 24, 1985
d. Mann, Paul

September 25, 1985
d. Fishback, Margaret

September 27, 1985
d. Kertesz, Andre
d. Nolan, Lloyd

September 28, 1985
d. Abbott, L(enwood) B(allard)

September 30, 1985
d. Bayer, Herbert
d. Crosby, Floyd Delafield
d. MacInnes, Helen
d. Richter, Charles Francis
d. Signoret, Simone Henrietta Charlotte

October 1, 1985
d. White, E(lwyn) B(rooks)

October 2, 1985
d. Caudill, Rebecca
d. Hudson, Rock

October 3, 1985
d. Collingwood, Charles Cummings

October 4, 1985
d. Buckley, William F

October 6, 1985
d. Riddle, Nelson
d. Schlamme, Martha

October 8, 1985
d. Bacchelli, Riccardo
d. Blough, Roger Miles
d. Welchman, Gordon

October 9, 1985
d. Snyder, John Wesley

October 10, 1985
d. Brynner, Yul
d. Welles, Orson

October 11, 1985
d. Lowinsky, Edward Elias
d. Williams, Tex

October 12, 1985
d. Olson, Johnny

October 14, 1985
d. Gilels, Emil Grigoyevich

October 15, 1985
d. Browning, Alice Crolley
d. Zaslofsky, Max

October 17, 1985
d. Rosenstock, Joseph

October 18, 1985
d. Kent, Jack

October 21, 1985
d. White, Dan(iel James)

October 25, 1985
d. Downey, Morton
d. Slotnick, Daniel Leonid

October 29, 1985
d. Allen, William McPherson
d. Douglas-Home, Charles

October 30, 1985
d. Grant, Kirby
d. Tanner, Marion

November 1, 1985
d. Silvers, Phil

November 4, 1985
d. Groppi, James E
d. Hill, Morton A(nthony)

November 5, 1985
d. Kimball, Spencer Woolley

November 9, 1985
d. Rose, Helen Bronberg

November 10, 1985
d. MacDougall, Curtis Daniel

November 11, 1985
d. Rothstein, Arthur

November 12, 1985
d. Lindbergh, Pelle (Per-Eric)

November 13, 1985
d. Pereira, William Leonard

November 14, 1985
d. Koo, V(i) K(yuin) Wellington

November 16, 1985
d. Sparkman, John Jackson

November 17, 1985
d. Chase, Stuart
d. Nol, Lon
d. Ritz, Jimmy

November 19, 1985
d. Fetchit, Stepin
d. Joanis, John W

November 24, 1985
d. Turner, Joe

November 25, 1985
d. Grigson, Geoffrey Edward Harvey
d. Podoloff, Maurice
d. Pusey, Merlo John

November 28, 1985
d. Brandel, Fernand Paul
d. Gerasimov, Sergei Appolinarievich
d. McNally, John Victor

November 29, 1985
d. Keough, William Francis, Jr.

December 2, 1985
d. Larkin, Philip Arthur

December 6, 1985
d. Gibson, Walter B(rown)
d. Tillstrom, Burr

December 7, 1985
d. Graves, Robert von Ranke
d. Stewart, Potter

December 8, 1985
d. Wambsganss, Bill

December 10, 1985
d. Grimes, Burleigh Arland

December 12, 1985
d. Baxter, Anne

December 13, 1985
d. Russell, Donald Joseph

December 14, 1985
d. Maris, Roger (Eugene)

December 15, 1985
d. Ramgoolam, Seewoosagur, Sir
d. Romulo, Carlos Pena

December 22, 1985
d. Condie, Richard P

December 24, 1985
d. Abbas, Ferhat

December 26, 1985
d. Austin, John Paul

December 27, 1985
d. Fossey, Dian

December 28, 1985
d. Blackburn, Molly

December 31, 1985
d. Nelson, Rick
d. Spiegel, Sam

1986

d. Gidlow, Elsa
d. Prebisch, Raul

January 1, 1986
d. Cecil, Edward Christian David
Gascoyne
d. Friedman, Max

January 2, 1986
d. Gaines, Clarence F
d. Gunn, Hartford Nelson, Jr.
d. Veeck, Bill

January 4, 1986
d. Isherwood, Christopher (William)
d. Lynott, Phil(ip)
d. Merkel, Una

January 7, 1986
d. Rulfo, Juan

January 8, 1986
d. Fournier, Pierre

January 9, 1986
d. Chase, Lucia
d. Powolny, Frank

January 10, 1986
d. Kraft, Joseph
d. Seifert, Jaroslav

January 13, 1986
d. Garcia, Mike

January 14, 1986
d. Reed, Donna

January 15, 1986
d. Crowley, Jim

January 16, 1986
d. Armstrong, Herbert W

January 22, 1986
d. Clinchy, Everett Ross

January 23, 1986
d. Beuys, Joseph
d. Leser, Tina

January 24, 1986
d. Hubbard, L(afayette) Ron(ald)
d. MacRae, Gordon

January 26, 1986
d. Lorjou, Bernard Joseph Pierre

January 27, 1986
d. Borglum, James Lincoln Delamothe
d. Palmer, Lilli

January 28, 1986
d. Berlin, Richard E
d. Jarvis, Gregory
d. McAuliffe, Christa
d. McNair, Ronald Ervin
d. Onizuka, Ellison
d. Resnik, Judy
d. Scobee, Dick
d. Smith, Michael John

January 30, 1986
d. Erickson, Leif

January 31, 1986
d. Allegret, Yves
d. Jessup, Philip Caryl

February 1, 1986
d. Myrdal, Alva Reimer

February 5, 1986
d. Rosenfeld, Henry J

February 6, 1986
d. Yamasaki, Minoru

February 7, 1986
d. Diop, Cheikh Anta

February 9, 1986
d. Menard, H William
d. Pritzker, Abram Nicholas

February 10, 1986
d. Aherne, Brian de Lacy
d. Satherly, Arthur Edward

February 11, 1986
d. Herbert, Frank (Patrick)

February 12, 1986
d. Lazare, Kaplan
d. Stone, Sidney

February 14, 1986
d. Wilder, Clinton

February 16, 1986
d. DaSilva, Howard

February 17, 1986
d. Krishnamurti, Jiddu
d. Ruffing, Red
d. Stewart, Paul

February 19, 1986
d. Eastland, James Oliver

February 21, 1986
d. Pomerantz, Fred P
d. Santmyer, Helen Hooven

February 24, 1986
d. Douglas, Thomas Clement
d. Morgan, Russell H(edley)

February 25, 1986
d. Lowe, Edwin S

February 27, 1986
d. Plante, Jacques

February 28, 1986
d. Hobson, Laura Zametkin
d. Palme, Olof

March 1, 1986
d. Archibald, Joe
d. Towle, Katherine Amelia

March 2, 1986
d. Rudenko, Lyudmila

March 3, 1986
d. Halleck, Charles Abraham
d. Randhawa, Mohinder Singh

March 4, 1986
d. Greenfield, Howard

March 5, 1986
d. Nelson, George H

March 6, 1986
d. Caesar, Adolph
d. O'Keeffe, Georgia

March 9, 1986
d. Calmer, Ned

March 10, 1986
d. Cohen, Myron
d. Milland, Ray(mond Alton)

March 11, 1986
d. Terry, Sonny

March 13, 1986
d. Hanfmann, George Maxim Anossov

March 14, 1986
d. Cahners, Norman Lee

March 17, 1986
d. Glubb, John Bagot, Sir

March 18, 1986
d. Malamud, Bernard

March 19, 1986
d. Atwater, Edith

March 22, 1986
d. Arnow, Harriette Louisa Simpson
d. Bricker, John William
d. Dinning, Mark

March 27, 1986
d. Canfield, Cass

March 28, 1986
d. Gilmore, Virginia

March 29, 1986
d. Ritz, Harry

March 30, 1986
d. Cagney, James

March 31, 1986
d. Aldrich, Richard Stoddard
d. Paris, Jerry

April 1, 1986
d. Bruhn, Erik Belton Evers
d. Ciardi, John Anthony

April 3, 1986
d. Kirstein, George G
d. Pears, Peter, Sir

April 7, 1986
d. Javits, Jacob Koppel
d. Kantorovich, Leonid Vital'evich
d. Moore, Don W

April 10, 1986
d. Addabbo, Joseph Patrick
d. Creed, Linda
d. Crosby, James Morris

April 11, 1986
d. Goldstein, Israel
d. Karpin, Fred Leon

April 12, 1986
d. Katayev, Valentin Petrovich

April 14, 1986
d. Beauvoir, Simone de

April 15, 1986
d. Genet, Jean

April 17, 1986
d. Head, Bessie Emery
d. Kilburn, Peter

April 18, 1986
d. Bauer, Eddie
d. Dassault, Marcel

April 19, 1986
d. Childress, Alvin

April 20, 1986
d. Miller, Carl S

April 22, 1986
d. Agron, Salvador
d. Eliade, Mircea
d. Moores, Dick

April 23, 1986
d. Arlen, Harold
d. Collett, Alec
d. Preminger, Otto Ludwig

April 24, 1986
d. Simpson, Wallis (Bessie Wallis
   Warfield)

April 26, 1986
d. Crawford, Broderick
d. Gmeiner, Hermann
d. Love, Bessie

April 27, 1986
d. Hynek, J(oseph) Allen

April 30, 1986
d. Stevenson, Robert

May 1, 1986
d. D'Aulaire, Edgar Parin

May 3, 1986
d. Alda, Robert

May 4, 1986
d. Richards, Paul Rapier

May 5, 1986
d. Cook, Bill

May 7, 1986
d. Forsythe, Albert E
d. Lovett, Robert A(bercrombie)

May 9, 1986
d. Bernardi, Hershel
d. Tenzing Norgay

May 11, 1986
d. Pollard, Fritz

May 12, 1986
d. Bergner, Elisabeth

May 13, 1986
d. Bohlem, Arndt von
d. Hearst, David W(hitmire)
d. O'Donnell, Peadar

May 15, 1986
d. White, Theodore Harold

May 18, 1986
d. Bubbles, John
d. Wilson, John Johnston

May 20, 1986
d. Taussig, Helen Brooke
d. Wood, Robert Dennis

May 22, 1986
d. Gabel, Martin

May 23, 1986
d. Hayden, Sterling Relyea Walter

May 24, 1986
d. Canutt, Yakima
d. Rubloff, Arthur

May 26, 1986
d. Bowles, Chester Bliss

May 27, 1986
d. Wrightsman, Charles Bierer

May 28, 1986
d. Aranason, H Harvard
d. Maclaughlin, Don
d. Tuttle, Lurene

May 29, 1986
d. Martin, John C

May 30, 1986
d. Ellis, Perry Edwin
d. Klopfer, Donald Simon

May 31, 1986
d. Rainwater, James

September 24, 1986
d. Gard, Wayne
d. Gordy, Robert

September 28, 1986
d. Helpmann, Robert Murray, Sir
d. Semenov, Nikolai Nikolaevich

September 30, 1986
d. Jameson, Margaret Storm

October 3, 1986
d. DiMaggio, Vince(nt Paul)

October 5, 1986
d. Flesch, Rudolf (Franz)
d. Wallis, Hal Brent

October 6, 1986
d. Hill, Abram
d. Six, Robert Forman

October 7, 1986
d. Crawford, Cheryl
d. Jacuzzi, Candido
d. Kressy, Edmund

October 10, 1986
d. Soss, Wilma Porter

October 11, 1986
d. Cash, Norm(an Dalton)
d. Ullman, Al(bert Conrad)

October 13, 1986
d. Angel, Heather Grace

October 14, 1986
d. Wynn, Keenan

October 15, 1986
d. Smith, Jerry

October 19, 1986
d. Henderson, Leon
d. Lebowsky, Stanley Richard
d. Machel, Samora Moises

October 22, 1986
d. Szent-Gyorgyi, Albert (von
   Nagyrapolt)
d. Ye Jianying

October 24, 1986
d. Doisy, Edward Adelbert, Sr.

October 25, 1986
d. Tucker, Forrest Meredith

October 26, 1986
d. Scholz, Jackson Volney

October 27, 1986
d. Adams, Sherman Llewellyn

October 28, 1986
d. Arthur, Robert
d. Braine, John Gerard

October 29, 1986
d. Schwarzhaupt, Elisabeth

October 31, 1986
d. Mulliken, Robert Sanderson

November 1, 1986
d. Moczar, Mieczyslaw
d. Wallace, Sippie

November 3, 1986
d. Hammond, E(dward) Cuyler

November 5, 1986
d. Lorillard, Louis Livingston
d. Nunn, Bobby

November 6, 1986
d. Kraus, Lili

November 7, 1986
d. Hewitt, Alan

November 8, 1986
d. Molotov, Vyacheslav Mikhaylovich
d. Suhl, Yuri

November 10, 1986
d. Clancy, King

November 11, 1986
d. Carmel, Roger C

November 15, 1986
d. Croft, Michael

November 16, 1986
d. McKenna, Siobhan

November 17, 1986
d. Besse, Georges Noel

November 21, 1986
d. Bay, Howard
d. Colonna, Jerry

November 22, 1986
d. Crothers, Scatman

November 23, 1986
d. Huie, William Bradford

November 27, 1986
d. Fielding, Gabriel
d. Hemingway, Mary Welsh

November 29, 1986
d. Grant, Cary

November 30, 1986
d. Swigert, Ernest Goodnough

December 1, 1986
d. Heidt, Horace Murray
d. Layne, Bobby
d. McCarthy, Frank

December 2, 1986
d. Arnaz, Desi

December 4, 1986
d. Nakian, Reuben

December 7, 1986
d. Harris, Sydney J(ustin)

December 10, 1986
d. Cabot, Susan

December 12, 1986
d. Owens, Harry

December 13, 1986
d. Baker, Ella

December 15, 1986
d. Lifar, Serge

December 17, 1986
d. DeButts, John Dulany

December 19, 1986
d. Andrews, V(irginia) C(leo)
d. Fergusson, Francis

December 22, 1986
d. Macy, John Williams, Jr.

December 23, 1986
d. Husted, Marjorie Child
d. Wasson, R(obert) Gordon

December 26, 1986
d. Lanchester, Elsa

December 27, 1986
d. Dangerfield, George Bubb
d. Malone, Dumas

December 28, 1986
d. Dolan, Terry
d. MacDonald, John Dann

December 29, 1986
d. Bolz, Lothar
d. MacMillan, Harold
d. Tarkovsky, Andrei (Arsenyich)

December 31, 1986
d. Fleming, Donald M(ethuen)
d. Haynes, Lloyd

1987

d. Avakian, Aram A
d. Carr, Martin
d. Doriot, Georges Frederic
d. Fedorenko, Fyodor
d. Johnson, Raynor Carey
d. Jonathan, Joseph Leabua
d. Jung, Leo
d. Sankara, Thomas
d. Yasui, Minoru

January 1, 1987
d. Castroviejo, Ramon

January 3, 1987
d. Martin, John Bartlow
d. Poage, W(illiam) R(obert)

January 4, 1987
d. Bacon, Peggy

January 5, 1987
d. Laurence, Margaret
d. Pantaleoni, Helenka (Tradeusa Adamowski)

January 9, 1987
d. Lake, Arthur

January 13, 1987
d. Kuekes, Edward Daniel

January 14, 1987
d. Sirk, Douglas

January 15, 1987
d. Bolger, Ray(mond Wallace)
d. Young, Philip

January 16, 1987
d. Brenan, Gerald
d. Wilson, Earl

January 18, 1987
d. Streibert, Theodore Cuyler

January 21, 1987
d. Goodell, Charles Ellsworth

January 24, 1987
d. Burcham, Lester Arthur

January 26, 1987
d. McLaren, Norman

January 28, 1987
d. Plaza Lasso, Galo
d. Trifa, Valerian

January 29, 1987
d. Impellitteri, Vincent R(ichard)

February 2, 1987
d. MacLean, Alistair (Stuart)

February 4, 1987
d. Liberace
d. Rogers, Carl Ransom

February 5, 1987
d. Burke, Mike

February 7, 1987
d. Dunton, Davidson
d. Saunders, Stuart T(homas)

February 9, 1987
d. Hightower, John Marmann

February 10, 1987
d. Burgess, John Lawrie, Sir
d. Calderone, Frank Anthony

February 12, 1987
d. Bergman, Jules Verne

February 13, 1987
d. Hass, H(enry) B(ohn)

February 17, 1987
d. Harlow, Bryce Nathaniel
d. Kabalevsky, Dmitri Borisovich

February 19, 1987
d. Greene, Hugh (Carleton), Sir
d. Hitchcock, Henry Russell

February 22, 1987
d. Susskind, David Howard
d. Warhol, Andy
d. Wescott, Glenway

February 23, 1987
d. Heinz, Henry John, II
d. Lansdale, Edward Geary

February 24, 1987
d. McArthur, Edwin Douglas

February 25, 1987
d. Coco, James Emil
d. Nixon, E(dgar) D(aniel)

February 27, 1987
d. Holman, Bill

February 28, 1987
d. Donner, Frederic Garrett
d. Kaye, Nora
d. Lewis, David

March 2, 1987
d. Greenwood, Joan
d. Scott, Randolph

March 3, 1987
d. Kaye, Danny
d. Tucker, Rosina

March 5, 1987
d. DeLiagre, Alfred

March 6, 1987
d. Zorinsky, Edward

March 9, 1987
d. Kneip, Richard F
d. Locke, Bobby
d. Salt, Waldo

March 11, 1987
d. Elson, Robert Truscott
d. Kilroy, James, Jr.

March 12, 1987
d. Hayes, Woody
d. Levinson, Richard Leighton

March 13, 1987
d. Grzimek, Bernhard
d. Moore, Gerald

March 15, 1987
d. Cole, Sterling W(illiam)
d. Dutton, Red

March 17, 1987
d. Trafficante, Santo, Jr.

March 18, 1987
d. Baird, Bil

March 19, 1987
d. Broglie, Louis Prince De
d. Oboler, Arch

March 21, 1987
d. Martin, Dean Paul
d. Preston, Robert

March 23, 1987
d. Minsky, Morton

March 25, 1987
d. Labouisse, Henry Richardson

March 26, 1987
d. Abel, Walter Charles
d. Jochum, Eugen

March 27, 1987
d. Goodrich, Lloyd
d. Provensen, Martin

March 28, 1987
d. Trapp, Maria Augusta von

March 30, 1987
d. Murchison, Clint(on Williams, Jr.)

April 1, 1987
d. Cochet, Henri

April 2, 1987
d. Davis, Tommy
d. Rich, Buddy

April 5, 1987
d. Jonathan, Leabua, Chief

April 7, 1987
d. Lehmann, John Frederick
d. Sullivan, Maxine

April 10, 1987
d. Dassler, Horst

April 11, 1987
d. Caldwell, Erskine Preston
d. Levi, Primo

April 13, 1987
d. Nyiregyhazi, Ervin
d. Taylor, Kent

April 16, 1987
d. Curtis, Charlotte Murray

April 17, 1987
d. Shawn, Dick
d. Smith, Willi Donnell

April 18, 1987
d. Baker, Carlos Heard

April 19, 1987
d. Brannum, Hugh
d. Taylor, Maxwell Davenport

April 20, 1987
d. Tudor, Antony

April 21, 1987
d. Green, Edith S(tarrett)

April 22, 1987
d. Potok, Anna Maximilian Apfelbaum

April 23, 1987
d. Jutra, Claude

April 28, 1987
d. Johnson, Gus, Jr.

May 5, 1987
d. Stanford-Tuck, Robert Roland

May 6, 1987
d. Casey, William Joseph
d. Damon, Cathryn

May 7, 1987
d. Blakely, Colin (George Edward)
d. McKinney, Stewart Brett

May 9, 1987
d. Awolowo, Obafemi Awo

May 11, 1987
d. Angleton, James J(esus)

May 13, 1987
d. Ellmann, Richard David

May 14, 1987
d. Hayworth, Rita
d. Lynch, J(ohn) Joseph

May 15, 1987
d. Baur, John I(reland) H(owe)

May 17, 1987
d. Myrdal, Karl Gunnar

May 18, 1987
d. Cohen, Wilbur Joseph

May 19, 1987
d. Sheldon, Alice Hastings Bradley

May 21, 1987
d. Rey, Alejandro

May 24, 1987
d. Gingold, Hermione Ferdinanda

May 25, 1987
d. Harrison, William Kelly, Jr.

May 27, 1987
d. Eurich, Alvin C(hristian)
d. Northrop, John Howard

May 28, 1987
d. Ludlam, Charles

May 30, 1987
d. Carlson, Frank
d. Murphy, Turk

June 1, 1987
d. Barrow, Errol Walton
d. Karami, Rashid Abdul Hamid

June 2, 1987
d. Kaye, Sammy
d. Sampson, Will, Jr.
d. Segovia, Andres

June 4, 1987
d. Bernard, Bruno

June 5, 1987
d. Willis, Paul S

June 10, 1987
d. Kennedy, Madge

June 11, 1987
d. Guldahl, Ralph
d. Hartman, Elizabeth

June 13, 1987
d. Caspary, Vera
d. Page, Geraldine

June 15, 1987
d. Heller, Walter Wolfgang

June 17, 1987
d. Howser, Dick
d. Schell, Orville H, Jr.

June 19, 1987
d. DeAngeli, Marguerite Lofft

June 20, 1987
d. Ali, Salim A

June 21, 1987
d. Bloch, Bertram
d. Chasins, Abram

June 22, 1987
d. Astaire, Fred
d. Nix, Robert N(elson) C(ornelius),
Sr.

June 24, 1987
d. Gleason, Jackie

June 26, 1987
d. Bryant, Boudleaux
d. Burns, Arthur Frank

June 27, 1987
d. Flynt, Althea Sue

June 28, 1987
d. Lay, James Selden, Jr.

June 29, 1987
d. Cotten, Libba

June 30, 1987
d. Donovan, King
d. Mompou, Federico

July 2, 1987
d. Bennett, Michael
d. Livingston, Jerry

July 4, 1987
d. Stromgren, Bengt Georg Daniel

July 5, 1987
d. Goulet, Leo D
d. Haughton, Daniel Jeremiah

July 7, 1987
d. Halstead, William S
d. Teichmann, Howard Miles

July 8, 1987
d. Chevrier, Lionel
d. O'Konski, Alvin E(dward)
d. Vila, George Raymond

July 10, 1987
d. Dana, Viola
d. Hammond, John Henry, Jr.

July 11, 1987
d. Waddell, Tom

July 12, 1987
d. Gimbel, Peter Robin
d. Perlmutter, Nathan

July 14, 1987
d. Holt, Fritz
d. Morton, Nelle Katherine

July 15, 1987
d. Bass, Alfie
d. Gaines, Lee

July 17, 1987
d. Slotta, Karl Heinrich

July 18, 1987
d. Freyre, Gilberto (de Mello)
d. Kaplan, Jacob Merrill

July 19, 1987
d. Rau, Dhanvanthi Rama, Lady

July 20, 1987
d. Arbib, Robert Simeon, Jr.
d. Egan, Richard

July 22, 1987
d. Hinderas, Natalie Leota Henderson
d. Lescoulie, Jack
d. McMahon, Don(ald John)

July 23, 1987
d. Bryant, Hugh
d. Gibbs, Erna Leonhardt

July 25, 1987
d. Baldrige, Malcolm
d. Draper, Charles Stark

July 26, 1987
d. Bishop, Jim

July 27, 1987
d. Jackson, Travis Calvin
d. Wheeler, Hugh Callingham

July 28, 1987
d. Burnham, James
d. Fredericks, Carlton

July 31, 1987
d. Levine, Joseph Edward

August 1, 1987
d. Negri, Pola
d. Thibault, Conrad

August 3, 1987
d. Moorhead, William Singer

August 4, 1987
d. Price, Kenny
d. Unruh, Jesse Marvin

August 6, 1987
d. Eaker, Ira Clarence

August 7, 1987
d. Chamoun, Camille N(imer)
d. Holt, A(ndrew) D(avid, Jr.)
d. Kishi, Nobusuke

August 9, 1987
d. Keyserling, Leon Hirsch

August 10, 1987
d. Abel, I(orwith) W(ilbur)
d. O'Boyle, Patrick Aloysius, Cardinal

August 11, 1987
d. Peller, Clara

August 14, 1987
d. Persichetti, Vincent

August 16, 1987
d. Lubell, Samuel
d. Wesley, Charles Harris

August 17, 1987
d. Andrews, Wayne
d. Brown, Clarence
d. Drummond de Andrade, Carlos
d. Hess, Rudolf

August 19, 1987
d. Rorke, Hayden

August 22, 1987
d. Lash, Joseph P

August 23, 1987
d. Sidarouss, Stephanos, Cardinal

August 24, 1987
d. Keeler, William Wayne
d. Rustin, Bayard

August 26, 1987
d. Wittig, Georg Friedrich Karl

August 27, 1987
d. Smalls, Charlie

August 28, 1987
d. Huston, John

August 29, 1987
d. Marvin, Lee
d. Murphy, Arthur Richard, Jr.
d. Schlumberger, Jean

August 30, 1987
d. McCree, Wade Hampton, Jr.

September 3, 1987
d. Feldman, Morton
d. Fry, E Maxwell

September 4, 1987
d. Marquand, Richard

September 5, 1987
d. Martin, Quinn

September 6, 1987
d. Chute, Beatrice Joy
d. Haley, William John, Sir

September 7, 1987
d. Jennings, Paul Joseph

September 9, 1987
d. Fingesten, Peter

September 11, 1987
d. Greene, Lorne
d. Tosh, Peter

September 12, 1987
d. Collins, Joseph Lawton, General
d. Qualen, John Mandt

September 13, 1987
d. Leroy, Mervyn

September 16, 1987
d. Moss, Howard
d. Soames, Christopher

September 18, 1987
d. Schram, Emil
d. Thomaz, Americo

September 19, 1987
d. Gerhardsen, Einar Henry

September 20, 1987
d. Bester, Alfred
d. Stewart, Michael

September 21, 1987
d. Pastorius, Jaco

September 22, 1987
d. Gross, H(arold) R(oyce)
d. Luboff, Norman
d. Rowan, Dan

September 23, 1987
d. Fosse, Bob

September 24, 1987
d. Meyer, Joseph

September 25, 1987
d. Astor, Mary
d. Daugherty, Duffy
d. Williams, Emlyn

September 26, 1987
d. Anstey, Edgar Harold McFarlane

September 28, 1987
d. Madden, Ray John

September 29, 1987
d. Eden, Elizabeth Debbie
d. Ford, Henry, II

October 2, 1987
d. Carroll, Madeleine
d. Medawar, Peter Brian, Sir
d. Piret, Edgar L

October 3, 1987
d. Anouilh, Jean Marie Lucien Pierre
d. Ivogun, Maria

October 7, 1987
d. Flavin, Joseph B(ernard)

October 8, 1987
d. Dennison, George
d. Johnson, Eleanor M
d. Tsatsos, Constantinos

October 9, 1987
d. Becker, B Jay
d. Converse, Frederick J
d. Luce, Clare Boothe
d. Murphy, William Parry

October 11, 1987
d. DiSabato, Giovanni

October 12, 1987
d. Koruturk, Fahri S
d. Landon, Alf(red Mossman)
d. Nash, Philleo

October 13, 1987
d. Brattain, Walter Houser
d. Monroe, Lucy

October 14, 1987
d. Bassett, Ben

October 16, 1987
d. Hoffner, Joseph, Cardinal
d. Suesse, Dana Nadine

October 17, 1987
d. Dandridge, Ruby Jean

October 18, 1987
d. Brameld, Theodore
d. Levine, Philip

October 19, 1987
d. DuPre, Jacqueline
d. Stahl, Ben(jamin Albert)

October 20, 1987
d. Kolmogorov, Andrey Nikolayevich

October 21, 1987
d. Ho, Ying-Chin

October 24, 1987
d. Alajalov, Constantin

October 25, 1987
d. Brown, Cecil B

October 27, 1987
d. Dalto, Jorge
d. Helion, Jean

October 28, 1987
d. Masson, Andre (Aime Rene)

October 29, 1987
d. ElMallakh, Kamal
d. Herman, Woody

October 30, 1987
d. Mayes, Herbert Raymond

October 31, 1987
d. Campbell, Joseph

November 1, 1987
d. Levesque, Rene

November 4, 1987
d. Soyer, Raphael

November 5, 1987
d. Andrews, Eamonn

November 6, 1987
d. Barnett, Ross Robert
d. Logan, John
d. Pahlmann, William Carroll

November 7, 1987
d. Holland, Charles

November 9, 1987
d. Bernstein, Allan

November 10, 1987
d. Kountche, Seyni
d. Vernon, Jackie

November 11, 1987
d. Coggeshall, L(owell) T(helwell)
d. Phillips, Channing Emery

November 12, 1987
d. Lewis, Roger

November 17, 1987
d. Wicker, Ireene Seaton

November 18, 1987
d. Anquetil, Jacques

November 21, 1987
d. Folsom, James E(lisha)

November 24, 1987
d. Benoit, Jehane

November 25, 1987
d. Washington, Harold

November 26, 1987
d. Duncan-Sandys, Edwin, Lord

November 27, 1987
d. Herman, Babe

November 28, 1987
d. Li, C(hoh) H(ao)

November 29, 1987
d. Pyle, Howard

November 30, 1987
d. Baldwin, James (Arthur)
d. Dean, Arthur H(obson)

December 1, 1987
d. Imlach, Punch

December 2, 1987
d. Eisele, Donn Fulton
d. Leloir, Luis Federico

December 4, 1987
d. Mamoulian, Rouben (Zachary)

December 6, 1987
d. Lobel, Arnold Stark

December 10, 1987
d. Heifetz, Jascha
d. Stewart, Slam

December 12, 1987
d. Chenier, Clifton

December 13, 1987
d. Wunder, George S

December 14, 1987
d. Josefsberg, Milt

December 15, 1987
d. Clark, Septima
d. Haggar, Joseph M(arion)
d. Malavasi, Ray(mondo Guiseppi
    Giovanni Baptiste)
d. Tomlin, Pinky

December 16, 1987
d. Morano, Albert Paul

December 17, 1987
d. Alfrink, Bernard (Jan), Cardinal
d. Yourcenar, Marguerite

December 21, 1987
d. Nelson, Ralph

December 22, 1987
d. Bernhard, Arnold
d. Cotton, Henry, Sir

December 24, 1987
d. Den Uyl, Joop

December 27, 1987
d. Alley, Rewi

December 28, 1987
d. Kleban, Edward Lawrence
d. Malik, Charles Habib

December 29, 1987
d. Bissell, Patrick

December 31, 1987
d. Arliss, Leslie

1988

d. Barker, Elliott
d. Paige, Robert (John Arthur)
d. Wootton, Barbara (Frances) Adam

January 1, 1988
d. Hunter, Clementine

January 3, 1988
d. Brayman, Harold
d. Eyskens, Gaston, Viscount

January 5, 1988
d. Laskin, Lily
d. Maravich, Pete(r Press)

January 6, 1988
d. Engellau, Gunnar Ludwig
d. Haviland, Virginia

January 7, 1988
d. Howard, Trevor Wallace

January 8, 1988
d. Eiseman, Florence
d. Pace, Frank, Jr.

January 11, 1988
b. L'Esperance Quintuplets
d. Boyington, Pappy
d. Kennon, Robert Floyd
d. Rabi, Isidor Isaac
d. Williams, John James

January 13, 1988
d. Chiang Ching-Kuo

January 14, 1988
d. Malenkov, Georgi Maximilianovich

January 15, 1988
d. MacBride, Sean

January 16, 1988
d. Artukovic, Andrija

January 17, 1988
d. Qoboza, Percy

January 20, 1988
d. Harper, Ken
d. Khan, Abdul Ghaffar
d. Mravinsky, Eugene
d. Rothschild, Philippe de, Baron

January 22, 1988
d. Fennelly, Parker W

January 24, 1988
d. King, Charles Glen
d. Schonfield, Hugh J

January 25, 1988
d. Moore, Colleen

January 28, 1988
d. Fuchs, Klaus

January 29, 1988
d. Killian, James Rhyne, Jr.

January 30, 1988
d. Groves, Wallace
d. Neddermeyer, Seth H

February 1, 1988
d. Linen, James A(lexander), III

February 2, 1988
d. Williams, G(erhard) Mennen

February 3, 1988
d. Duncan, Robert Edward

February 4, 1988
d. Miller, Otto Neil

February 5, 1988
d. Hurd, Clement

February 6, 1988
d. Laski, Marghanita

February 9, 1988
d. Adler, Kurt Herbert

February 11, 1988
d. Mizener, Arthur Moore

February 12, 1988
d. Goossens, Leon Jean

February 14, 1988
d. Astorga, Nora Gadea
d. Benton, Nelson
d. Cohn, Al
d. Loewe, Frederick

February 15, 1988
d. Feynman, Richard Phillips
d. Meng, John Joseph

February 16, 1988
d. Gordon-Lazareff, Helene

February 17, 1988
d. Allegro, John Marco

February 18, 1988
d. Lewyt, Alexander Milton

February 19, 1988
d. Bishop, Isabel
d. Char, Rene (Emile)
d. Cournand, Andre Frederic

February 20, 1988
d. Williams, Roger J

February 22, 1988
d. Solomon

February 24, 1988
d. Douglas, James Henderson, Jr.
d. Memphis Slim
d. Salem, Mamdouh

February 27, 1988
d. Boothroyd, John Basil
d. DePaul, Gene Vincent

February 28, 1988
d. Kuenn, Harvey Edward

March 1, 1988
d. Besser, Joe
d. Woodall, Mary

March 2, 1988
d. Redding, Jay Saunders

March 3, 1988
d. Szeryng, Henryk

March 4, 1988
d. Mosley, J(ohn) Brooke

March 7, 1988
d. Divine

March 8, 1988
d. Brubacher, John Seiler

March 9, 1988
d. Galamison, Milton Arthur
d. Kiesinger, Kurt Georg

March 10, 1988
d. Cunningham, Glenn Clarence
d. Gibb, Andy
d. Pham Hung

March 11, 1988
d. Bearden, Romare Howard

March 12, 1988
d. Holmes, John C.

March 15, 1988
d. Porter, William James

March 17, 1988
d. Memminger, Christopher Gustavus

March 18, 1988
d. Butterfield, Billy

March 20, 1988
d. Evans, Gil

March 21, 1988
d. Roush, Edd J
d. Steptoe, Patrick Christopher

March 23, 1988
d. Somogi, Judith
d. Thompson, Mickey

March 24, 1988
d. Estes, E(lliott) M(arantette)
d. Estes, Pete

March 25, 1988
d. Howard, James John
d. Joffrey, Robert

March 27, 1988
d. Willeford, Charles Ray, II

March 29, 1988
d. Kluszewski, Ted

March 30, 1988
d. Faure, Edgar Jean
d. Holmes, John Clellon

March 31, 1988
d. McMahon, William

April 1, 1988
d. Jordan, Jim

April 2, 1988
d. Thomson, Vernon Wallace

April 3, 1988
d. Caniff, Milt(on Arthur)

April 7, 1988
d. Hamilton, Denis, Sir
d. Rogell, Albert S

April 8, 1988
d. Gianninoto, Frank Anthony

April 9, 1988
d. Benton, Brook
d. DuPont, Pierre Samuel, III
d. Prater, Dave

April 11, 1988
d. Cory, John Mackenzie
d. Donnell, Jeff
d. Lasky, Jesse Louis, Jr.
d. Shinichiro Imaoka

April 12, 1988
d. Paton, Alan Stewart

April 15, 1988
d. Egorov, Youri

April 16, 1988
d. Reardon, John

April 17, 1988
d. Freeman, Paul Lamar
d. Frissell, Toni
d. Nevelson, Louise Berliawsky

April 18, 1988
d. Delaplane, Stanton Hill
d. Olson, James E(lias)

April 21, 1988
d. Diamond, I(sidore) A L
d. Rudensky, Morris

April 22, 1988
d. Price, Melvin

April 23, 1988
d. Ramsey, Arthur Michael, Lord
d. Rich, Irene

April 24, 1988
d. Jordan, Fred

April 25, 1988
d. Matthews, Burnita S(helton)
d. Simak, Clifford Donald

April 26, 1988
d. Patterson, Frederick Douglass
d. Rempp, Adolph
d. Ross, Lanny

April 27, 1988
d. Johnson, Wallace Edward
d. Wieghorst, Olaf

April 29, 1988
d. Cruickshank, Andrew John
d. Kolodin, Irving
d. Larsen, Emmanuel

April 30, 1988
d. McCracken, James (Eugene)
d. Righter, Carroll

May 1, 1988
d. Darrell, R(obert) D(onaldson)
d. Lexcen, Ben

May 3, 1988
d. Hansen, Julia Butler

May 4, 1988
d. Hayter, Stanley William
d. Zambelli, Joseph

May 5, 1988
d. Rose, George Walter

May 6, 1988
d. Caliguiri, Richard
d. Popper, Hans

May 7, 1988
d. Van Westerborg, Edward

May 8, 1988
d. Heinlein, Robert Anson
d. Pollock, Charles

May 10, 1988
d. Laing, Hugh
d. Ogilvie, Richard Buell

May 11, 1988
d. Daugherty, Carroll Roop
d. Foster, Tabatha
d. Philby, Kim

May 12, 1988
d. Osborn, Paul

May 13, 1988
d. Gorshkov, Sergei

May 14, 1988
d. Drees, Willem
d. Guyer, David Leigh

May 15, 1988
d. Duggan, Andrew
d. Shaplen, Robert Modell

May 16, 1988
d. Ortiz, Peter J(ulien)
d. Wood, Louise Aletha

May 18, 1988
d. Butler, Daws

May 20, 1988
d. Lewis, Tom

May 21, 1988
d. Fitzgerald, John Dennis
d. Grandi, Dino

May 22, 1988
d. Almirante, Giorgio

May 23, 1988
d. Schoenbrun, David

May 25, 1988
d. Hamilton, Hamish
d. Shimkin, Leon

May 27, 1988
d. Friebus, Florida
d. Oliver, Sy
d. Ruska, Ernst

May 29, 1988
d. Stevens, Siaka Probyn

May 30, 1988
d. Raines, Ella
d. Volpi, Alfredo
d. Mendez, Aparicio

June 1, 1988
d. Hurkos, Peter

June 2, 1988
d. Hildreth, Horace A(ugusta)

June 5, 1988
d. Pendleton, Clarence McLane, Jr.

June 8, 1988
d. Magnin, Cyril Isaac

June 10, 1988
d. L'Amour, Louis Dearborn

June 11, 1988
d. Saragat, Giuseppe

June 12, 1988
d. DeLeeuw, Adele Louise

June 14, 1988
d. Farrell, Johnny

June 16, 1988
d. Pinero, Miguel

June 20, 1988
d. Leach, Will

June 22, 1988
d. Day, Dennis
d. Franken, Rose
d. Matlovich, Leonard P., Jr.
d. Mitchell, Howard (Bundy)

June 25, 1988
d. Axis Sally

June 27, 1988
d. Adams, Leonie Fuller
d. Groth, John August

July 2, 1988
d. Vinson, Cleanhead

July 3, 1988
d. Dell, Gabriel

July 9, 1988
d. Presser, Jackie
d. Woodhouse, Barbara Blackburn

July 12, 1988
d. Logan, Josh(ua Lockwood)

July 14, 1988
d. Monroe, Phil

July 15, 1988
d. Estes, Eleanor Ruth Rosenfeld
d. Lubin, Charles W

July 20, 1988
d. Galbreath, John Wilmer

July 22, 1988
d. Lucioni, Luigi

July 27, 1988
d. Zamboni, Frank J

July 29, 1988
d. Berlin, Ellin (Mackay)

August 1, 1988
d. Dearden, John Francis, Cardinal
d. Eldridge, Florence

August 2, 1988
d. Carver, Raymond Clevie, Jr.

August 5, 1988
d. Higgins, Colin
d. Meeker, Ralph

August 8, 1988
b. Beatrice, Princess of York
d. Ameche, Alan Dante
d. Kid Chocolate

August 9, 1988
d. Fidler, Jimmie

August 10, 1988
d. Arias Madrid, Arnulfo
d. Saint Johns, Adela Rogers

August 11, 1988
d. Ramsey, Anne

August 12, 1988
d. Basquiat, Jean-Michel

August 13, 1988
d. Williams, Edward Bennett
d. Zumwalt, Elmo Russell, III

August 14, 1988
d. Ferrari, Enzo
d. Sweet, John Howard

August 15, 1988
d. Bingham, Barry

August 17, 1988
d. Roosevelt, Franklin Delano, Jr.
d. Zia-ul-Haq, Mohammad

August 18, 1988
d. Ashton, Frederick William, Sir

August 20, 1988
d. Robinson, Joan Mary Gale Thomas

August 21, 1988
d. Eames, Ray

August 25, 1988
d. Daniel, Price
d. Rooney, Art(hur Joseph)

August 26, 1988
d. DeLue, Donald Harcourt

August 28, 1988
d. Dawn, Hazel
d. Shulman, Max

August 30, 1988
d. Frey-Wyssling, Albert F

September 1, 1988
d. Alvarez, Luis W(alter)

September 5, 1988
d. Frobe, Gerd

September 11, 1988
d. Alpert, George

September 12, 1988
d. Bible, Alan
d. Norstad, Lauris

September 17, 1988
d. Gueden, Hilde

September 21, 1988
d. Gwathmey, Robert

September 24, 1988
d. Hale, Nancy

September 25, 1988
d. Carter, Billy

September 27, 1988
d. Shannon, William Vincent

September 29, 1988
d. Addams, Charles Samuel

September 30, 1988
d. Chinh, Truong

October 1, 1988
d. Sitwell, Sacheverell, Sir

October 2, 1988
d. Issigonis, Alec Arnold Constantine, Sir
d. Pope, Generoso

October 3, 1988
d. Hatem, George
d. Strauss, Franz Josef

October 4, 1988
d. Household, Geoffrey Edward West

October 7, 1988
d. Daniels, Billy

October 9, 1988
d. Chodorov, Edward
d. Wankel, Felix

October 10, 1988
d. Flowers, Wayland Parrott, Jr.

October 11, 1988
d. Granville, Bonita

October 12, 1988
d. Murray, Ken

October 15, 1988
d. Ball, John Dudley, Jr.

October 19, 1988
d. House, Son

October 20, 1988
d. Isbell, Marion William

October 22, 1988
d. Armstrong, Henry

October 24, 1988
d. Fuller, S(amuel) B.

October 27, 1988
d. Heard, J.C.

October 28, 1988
d. Annigoni, Pietro

October 31, 1988
d. Houseman, John

November 1, 1988
d. Kraus, Hans Peter

November 5, 1988
d. Freeman, Cynthia

November 7, 1988
d. Hoest, Bill
d. Janowitz, Morris

November 8, 1988
d. Brewster, Kingman, Jr.

November 9, 1988
d. Hinkle, W Clarke
d. Mitchell, John Newton

November 12, 1988
d. Boswell, Vet
d. Lemnitzer, Lyman Louis

November 13, 1988
d. Dorati, Antal
d. Miki Takeo

November 14, 1988
d. Hansell, Haywood Shepherd, Jr.

November 16, 1988
d. Lee, Jennie

November 17, 1988
d. Graham, Sheilah

November 18, 1988
d. Parish, Peggy

November 19, 1988
d. Hubbell, Carl Owen
d. Onassis, Christina

November 20, 1988
d. Gerson, Noel Bertram

November 21, 1988
d. Lewenthal, Raymond

November 22, 1988
d. Barragan, Luis
d. Dart, Raymond Arthur

November 24, 1988
d. Seefried, Irmgard Maria Theresia

November 27, 1988
d. Carradine, John
d. Morrison, Theodore

November 29, 1988
d. Keyhoe, Donald E(dward)
d. Rees, Lloyd Frederic
d. Richards, Richard

December 6, 1988
d. Orbison, Roy
d. Saxon, Charles David

December 7, 1988
d. Connelly, Christopher

December 8, 1988
d. Seymour, Anne Eckert

December 9, 1988
d. Peyre, Henri Maurice

December 10, 1988
d. Castellano, Richard

December 14, 1988
d. Symington, Stuart

December 16, 1988
d. Pratt, Babe

December 20, 1988
d. Robinson, Max C

December 21, 1988
d. Richter, Curt Paul
d. Steele, Bob
d. Tinbergen, Nikolaas

December 22, 1988
d. Kahane, Melanie

December 27, 1988
d. Ashby, Hal

December 28, 1988
d. Loder, John

December 30, 1988
d. Noguchi, Isamu

1989

b. Dubroff, Jessica
d. Bruce, Louis R., Jr.
d. Guillen (y Batista), Nicolas (Cristobal)
d. Livingston, J(oseph) A(rnold)
d. Manuel, George
d. Morris, William, Jr.
d. Sauguet, Henri
d. Sellars, Wilfred

January 1, 1989
d. Heywood, Eddie, Jr.

January 5, 1989
d. Lawe, John Edward

January 6, 1989
d. Koontz, Elizabeth Duncan

January 7, 1989
d. Hirohito

January 9, 1989
d. Terry, Bill

January 10, 1989
d. Voorhees, Donald

January 12, 1989
d. Little, Royal

January 18, 1989
d. Chatwin, Bruce
d. Hickerson, John Dewey

January 20, 1989
d. Cyrankiewicz, Josef
d. Lillie, Beatrice Gladys

January 21, 1989
d. Furillo, Carl Anthony

January 23, 1989
d. Dali, Salvador

January 24, 1989
d. Bundy, Ted

January 27, 1989
d. Sopwith, Thomas O M, Sir

January 28, 1989
d. Panchen Lama

January 29, 1989
d. DaCosta, Morton

January 30, 1989
d. Fitzgerald, Pegeen
d. Gould, Beatrice Blackmar

January 31, 1989
d. Stephenson, William

February 1, 1989
d. DeKooning, Elaine Marie Catherine Fried

February 3, 1989
d. Cassavetes, John
d. Vare, Glenna Collett

February 5, 1989
d. Raposo, Joseph

February 6, 1989
d. Field, Ron(ald)
d. Tuchman, Barbara Wertheim

February 10, 1989
d. Kelly, Dan

February 11, 1989
d. Clarke, Thomas Ernest Bennett
d. Kimbrough, Emily

February 14, 1989
d. Bond, James

February 17, 1989
d. Gomez, Lefty
d. Laroche, Guy

February 19, 1989
d. Goldman, Eric Frederick
d. Gorman, Mike

February 20, 1989
d. Christensen, Harold

February 24, 1989
d. Cotton, Norris

February 26, 1989
d. Eldridge, Roy

February 27, 1989
d. Lorenz, Konrad Zacharias

February 28, 1989
d. Armour, Richard Willard

March 3, 1989
d. Morris, Richard Brandon

March 6, 1989
d. Andrews, Harry
d. Barthe, Richmond

March 9, 1989
d. Mapplethorpe, Robert

March 11, 1989
d. McCloy, John Jay

March 12, 1989
d. Evans, Maurice
d. Gimpel, Jakob

March 14, 1989
d. Abbey, Edward
d. Bechtel, Stephen Davison
d. Zita of Bourbon-Parma

March 17, 1989
d. Kerby, William Frederick

March 18, 1989
d. Jeffreys, Harold

March 24, 1989
d. Cobb, Arnett Cleophus

March 27, 1989
d. Cowley, Malcolm

April 12, 1989
d. Hoffman, Abbie
d. Mills, Herbert
d. Robinson, Sugar Ray

April 15, 1989
d. Attwood, William Hollingsworth
d. Hu Yaobang

April 16, 1989
d. Conlan, Jocko

April 19, 1989
d. DuMaurier, Daphne

April 21, 1989
d. Kirkwood, James

April 22, 1989
d. Segre, Emilio Gino

April 25, 1989
d. Coulouris, George

April 26, 1989
d. Ball, Lucille (Desiree)

April 27, 1989
d. Matsushita, Konosuke

April 28, 1989
d. Williams, Roy Lee

April 30, 1989
d. Leone, Sergio

May 1, 1989
d. Janigo, Antonio

May 3, 1989
d. Jorgensen, Christine
d. Loveless, Herschel C(ellel)

May 6, 1989
d. Blaik, Red

May 9, 1989
d. Whitley, Keith

May 10, 1989
d. Green, Richard R(eginald)

May 14, 1989
d. Moats, Alice-Leone

May 15, 1989
d. Green, Johnny
d. Primeau, Joe

May 19, 1989
d. Muccio, John Joseph

May 20, 1989
d. Hicks, John Richard, Sir
d. Magnuson, Warren Grant
d. Radner, Gilda

May 22, 1989
d. Sears, Robert Richardson

May 24, 1989
d. McNellis, Maggi

May 26, 1989
d. Keogh, Eugene James

May 29, 1989
d. Homans, George Caspar

May 30, 1989
d. Milanov, Zinka Kunc
d. Pepper, Claude Denson

May 31, 1989
d. Drinkwater, Terry
d. Lattimore, Owen

June 1, 1989
d. Lichine, Alexis

June 2, 1989
d. Prokosch, Frederic

June 3, 1989
d. Browne, Dik
d. Khomeini, Ruhollah Musavi,
   Ayatollah

June 4, 1989
d. Parker, Pat

June 5, 1989
d. Grede, William John

June 9, 1989
d. Beadle, George Wells

June 10, 1989
d. Quine, Richard

June 13, 1989
d. Allison, Fran(ces)
d. Simons, Howard

June 14, 1989
d. Johnson, Judy

June 15, 1989
d. French, Victor

June 17, 1989
d. Gardner, Hy
d. Matuszak, John (Daniel)

June 18, 1989
d. Stone, I(sidor) F(einstein)

June 23, 1989
d. Aflaq, Michel
d. Manning, Timothy, Cardinal

June 25, 1989
d. Hassenfeld, Stephen David

June 27, 1989
d. Ayer, Alfred Jules, Sir

June 28, 1989
d. Ivens, Joris

June 30, 1989
d. Baunsgaard, Hilmar Tormod Ingolf
d. Higgins, William R

July 2, 1989
d. Gromyko, Andrei Andreevich
d. Schaffner, Franklin James

July 6, 1989
d. Kadar, Janos

July 10, 1989
d. Blanc, Mel(vin Jerome)
d. Tucker, Tommy

July 11, 1989
d. Olivier, Laurence Kerr, Sir

July 12, 1989
d. Hook, Sidney

July 15, 1989
d. Bradley, Will

July 16, 1989
d. Dempsey, John Noel
d. Karajan, Herbert von

July 19, 1989
d. Dennis, Nigel Forbes

July 22, 1989
d. Talvela, Martti Olavi
d. Thompson, Frank, Jr.

July 23, 1989
d. Barthelme, Donald
d. Harmon, Claude

July 25, 1989
d. Rubell, Steve

July 29, 1989
d. Leonidoff, Leon

July 31, 1989
d. Harrington, Michael

August 1, 1989
d. Hirsch, John Stephen

August 3, 1989
d. Brico, Antonia
d. Mellon, William Larimer, Jr.

August 6, 1989
d. Beuve-Mery, Hubert

August 7, 1989
d. Leland, Mickey

August 12, 1989
d. Shockley, William B(radford)

August 13, 1989
d. Brooks, Ronald E.

August 16, 1989
d. Blake, Amanda

August 20, 1989
d. Adamson, George

August 21, 1989
d. Bolger, William Frederick

August 22, 1989
d. Newton, Huey P(ercy)
d. Vreeland, Diana (Dalziel)
d. Yakovlev, Aleksandr Sergeyevich

August 23, 1989
d. Laing, R(onald) D(avid)

August 24, 1989
d. Topolski, Feliks

August 26, 1989
d. Stone, Irving

August 27, 1989
d. Gould, Charles Bruce

August 28, 1989
d. Alsop, Joseph Wright, Jr.

August 29, 1989
d. DiSant'Angelo, Giorgio
d. Scott, Peter Markham, Sir

August 30, 1989
d. Schiff, Dorothy

September 1, 1989
d. Giamatti, A(ngelo) Bartlett

September 4, 1989
d. Simenon, Georges

September 12, 1989
d. Miller, William Mosley

September 14, 1989
d. Valentina

September 15, 1989
d. De Gaetani, Jan
d. Olga
d. Warren, Robert Penn

September 18, 1989
d. Mitchell, William Leroy

September 19, 1989
d. Hammon, William McDowell

September 22, 1989
d. Berlin, Irving

September 23, 1989
d. Kraushaar, Otto

September 25, 1989
d. Hoopes, Darlington

September 28, 1989
d. Marcos, Ferdinand Edralin

September 29, 1989
d. Busch, August Anheuser, Jr.
d. O'Meara, Walter (Andrew)

September 30, 1989
d. Thomson, Virgil Garnett

October 4, 1989
d. Chapman, Graham

October 6, 1989
d. Davis, Bette

October 12, 1989
d. Franco
d. Ward, Jay

October 15, 1989
d. O'Dell, Scott

October 16, 1989
d. Wilde, Cornel

October 17, 1989
d. Farley, Walter Lorimer

October 18, 1989
b. Brubacher, John Seiler

October 20, 1989
d. Quayle, (John) Anthony, Sir

October 22, 1989
d. Hayes, Alfred
d. Maccoll, Ewan

October 23, 1989
d. Barrett, Edward Ware

October 25, 1989
d. Harper, Marion, Jr.
d. McCarthy, Mary Therese

October 26, 1989
d. Pedersen, Charles J
d. Baron, Salo Wittmayer
d. Hughes, George

November 5, 1989
d. Horowitz, Vladimir
d. Sadler, Barry

November 12, 1989
d. Apithy, Sourou Migan
d. Ibarruri, Dolores Gomez

November 13, 1989
d. Franz Joseph II

November 14, 1989
d. Davison, Wild Bill

November 15, 1989
d. Terris, Norma

November 18, 1989
d. Buckley, Emerson

November 20, 1989
d. Bari, Lynn

November 22, 1989
d. Arias, Roberto Emilio
d. Beck, C(harles) C(larence)

November 23, 1989
d. Janis, Sidney

November 25, 1989
d. Cakobau, Ratu George, Sir
d. Diop, Birago

November 27, 1989
d. Hoving, Walter

November 29, 1989
d. Staupers, Mabel K.

November 30, 1989
d. Ahidjo, Ahmadou

December 1, 1989
d. Ailey, Alvin

December 4, 1989
d. Pritchard, John Michael, Sir

December 5, 1989
d. Payne, John
d. Thompson, George Selden

December 6, 1989
d. Bavier, Frances
d. Fain, Sammy

December 7, 1989
d. Hartung, Hans

December 9, 1989
d. Bloustein, Edward J.

December 14, 1989
d. Sakharov, Andrei Dmitrievich

December 15, 1989
d. Moss, Arnold

December 16, 1989
d. Mangano, Silvana
d. Pringle, Aileen
d. Van Cleef, Lee

December 17, 1989
d. Wedemeyer, Albert Coady

December 19, 1989
d. Gibbons, Stella (Dorothea)

December 22, 1989
d. Beckett, Samuel (Barclay)

December 24, 1989
d. Morial, Ernest Nathan

December 25, 1989
d. Ceausescu, Nicolae

d. Martin, Billy

December 26, 1989
d. Harvey, Doug(las Norman)

December 27, 1989
d. Baum, Kurt

December 29, 1989
d. Oberth, Hermann Julius

December 31, 1989
d. Dache, Lilly
d. Schroder, Gerhard

1990

d. Allen, Elsie
d. Althusser, Louis
d. Bufalino, Gesualdo
d. Russo, Vito
d. Leighton, Clare Veronica Hope

January 1, 1990
d. Kelly, Patrick

January 2, 1990
d. Hale, Alan, Jr.
d. Reifel, Ben

January 3, 1990
d. Gold, Arthur

January 4, 1990
d. Edgerton, Harold Eugene
d. Lleras Camargo, Alberto
d. Ussachevsky, Vladimir Alexis

January 5, 1990
d. Kennedy, Arthur

January 6, 1990
d. Charleson, Ian
d. Cherenkov, Pavel Alekseyevich

January 7, 1990
d. Nagurski, Bronko
d. Robbie, Joe
d. Stoneham, Horace

January 8, 1990
d. Terry-Thomas

January 9, 1990
d. Chandler, Spud

January 11, 1990
d. McCoy, Clyde

January 12, 1990
d. Clark, Joseph Sill
d. Peter, Laurence Johnston

January 14, 1990
d. Edwards, India Moffett
d. Jackson, Gordon Cameron

January 18, 1990
d. Hamer, Rusty
d. Izac, Edouard V(ictor Michel)
d. Jones, Candy

January 19, 1990
d. Goldberg, Arthur Joseph
d. Gucci, Aldo
d. Rajneesh, Bhagwan Shree

January 20, 1990
d. Stanwyck, Barbara

January 21, 1990
d. Gervasi, Frank Henry

January 22, 1990
d. Buehrig, Gordon
d. Rumor, Mariano
d. Vishniac, Roman

January 24, 1990
d. Alonso, Damaso

January 25, 1990
d. Gardner, Ava

January 26, 1990
d. Mumford, Lewis
d. Day, Hap

February 7, 1990
d. Van Heusen, Jimmy

February 8, 1990
d. Shannon, Del

February 11, 1990
d. De Mestral, Georges

February 15, 1990
d. Parkinson, Norman

February 16, 1990
d. Haring, Keith

February 17, 1990
d. Rhodes, Erik

February 19, 1990
d. Keppel, Francis
d. Powell, Michael Latham

February 22, 1990
d. Lasky, Victor

February 23, 1990
d. Duarte (Fuentes), Jose Napoleon
d. Gavin, James Maurice

February 24, 1990
d. Conigliaro, Tony
d. Forbes, Malcolm Stevenson
d. Pertini, Sandro
d. Ray, Johnnie

February 26, 1990
d. Deloria, Vine (Victor), Sr.

February 27, 1990
d. Johnson, Josephine Winslow

February 28, 1990
d. Conroy, Jack
d. Marcus, Luis J

March 1, 1990
d. Landis, Frederick

March 3, 1990
d. Gathers, Hank
d. Moore, Charlotte E(mma)

March 6, 1990
d. Klassen, Elmer Theodore
d. Merrill, Gary Franklin
d. Sewell, Joe

March 7, 1990
d. Prestes, Luiz Carlos

March 10, 1990
d. Singher, Martial

March 11, 1990
d. Soupault, Philippe

March 12, 1990
d. Lehmann, Rosamond Nina

March 13, 1990
d. Bettelheim, Bruno
d. Munchinger, Karl

March 14, 1990
d. Medina, Harold Raymond

March 15, 1990
d. Harmon, Tom

March 17, 1990
d. Capucine

March 18, 1990
d. Harris, Robin

March 23, 1990
b. Eugenie, Princess of York
d. Dexter, John

March 24, 1990
d. Goulding, Ray(mond Walter)
d. Wang, An

March 26, 1990
d. Halston

March 30, 1990
d. Bridges, Harry Renton
d. Hirschfelder, Joseph Oakland

April 3, 1990
d. Carlson, Edward Elmer
d. Vaughan, Sarah Lois

April 4, 1990
d. Smith, Cyrus Rowlett

April 7, 1990
d. Evans, Ronald Ellwin

April 8, 1990
d. Greenaway, Emerson
d. White, Ryan

April 9, 1990
d. Faulk, John Henry

April 11, 1990
d. Ballard, Harold

April 15, 1990
d. Garbo, Greta
d. Matsunaga, Spark Masayuki

April 17, 1990
d. Abernathy, Ralph David

April 21, 1990
d. Erte
d. Lausche, Frank John

April 22, 1990
d. Salmi, Albert

April 23, 1990
d. Goddard, Paulette

April 25, 1990
d. Gordon, Dexter Keith

April 27, 1990
d. Spewack, Bella Cohen

May 4, 1990
d. Dawson, William Levi

May 6, 1990
d. Farrell, Charles

May 9, 1990
d. Frederick, Pauline
d. Nono, Luigi

May 10, 1990
d. Percy, Walker

May 16, 1990
d. Davis, Sammy, Jr.
d. Henson, Jim

May 18, 1990
d. Ireland, Jill

May 20, 1990
d. Seibert, Earl Walter

May 22, 1990
d. Graziano, Rocky

May 25, 1990
d. Tayback, Vic

May 31, 1990
d. Downey, Fairfax Davis

June 2, 1990
d. Harrison, Rex, Sir
d. Mellinger, Frederick

June 3, 1990
d. Noyce, Robert Norton

June 4, 1990
d. Gilford, Jack

June 5, 1990
d. Kuznetsov, Vassili Vasilyevich

June 6, 1990
d. Lund, Art(hur Earl, Jr.)

June 7, 1990
d. Baxley, Barbara

June 8, 1990
d. Figueres Ferrer, Jose

June 13, 1990
d. O'Neill, Terence Marne

June 16, 1990
d. Turner, Eva, Dame

June 20, 1990
d. Balin, Ina

June 22, 1990
d. Frank, Ilya Mikaylovich

June 25, 1990
d. Carney, Robert Bostwick
d. Glanville-Hicks, Peggy

June 29, 1990
d. Wallace, Irving

June 30, 1990
d. Childs, Marquis William

July 2, 1990
d. Lanson, Snooky

July 5, 1990
d. Snyder, Mitch

July 7, 1990
d. Cullen, Bill

July 9, 1990
d. Duff, Howard

July 15, 1990
d. Lockwood, Margaret Mary

July 18, 1990
d. Menninger, Karl Augustus
d. Wayne, Johnny

July 19, 1990
d. Quillan, Eddie

July 21, 1990
d. Shapiro, Stanley

July 22, 1990
d. Puig, Manuel

July 28, 1990
d. Esmond, Jill

July 29, 1990
d. Kreisky, Bruno
d. de Andrade, Mario

August 2, 1990
d. Maclean, Norman (Fitzroy)

August 6, 1990
d. Bunshaft, Gordon

August 7, 1990
d. Soustelle, Jacques

August 14, 1990
d. Crown, Henry
d. Donovan, Hedley Williams

August 17, 1990
d. Bailey, Pearl Mae

August 18, 1990
d. Skinner, B(urrhus) F(rederic)

August 19, 1990
d. Strout, Richard Lee

August 23, 1990
d. Rose, David

August 24, 1990
d. Masursky, Harold

August 25, 1990
d. Callaghan, Morley Edward

August 26, 1990
d. Hagen, John Peter

August 27, 1990
d. Saint Jacques, Raymond
d. Vaughan, Stevie Ray

August 29, 1990
d. Hall, Manly Palmer

September 4, 1990
d. Dunne, Irene Marie
d. Whitman, Alden

September 6, 1990
d. Fogerty, John

September 7, 1990
d. Taylor, A(lan) J(ohn) P(ercivale)

September 9, 1990
d. Doe, Samuel Kanyon

September 13, 1990
d. Mannes, Marya
d. Simmons, Althea T L
d. Stratton, Samuel S(tuddiford)

September 19, 1990
d. Pan, Hermes

September 21, 1990
d. Janssen, Werner

September 26, 1990
d. Moravia, Alberto

September 27, 1990
d. O'Brien, Larry

September 30, 1990
d. Mowrer, Lilian Thomson
d. Streeter, Ruth
d. White, Patrick Victor Martindale

October 1, 1990
d. LeMay, Curtis Emerson

October 2, 1990
d. Adler, Peter Herman
d. Holland, Leland James

October 3, 1990
d. Casiraghi, Stefano
d. Steber, Eleanor

October 6, 1990
d. Arevalo, Juan Jose

October 10, 1990
d. Selznick, Irene Mayer

October 11, 1990
d. Sigmund, Barbara Boggs

October 12, 1990
d. Brownell, Samuel Miller

October 13, 1990
d. Edwards, Douglas
d. Le Duc Tho

October 14, 1990
d. Bernstein, Leonard

October 16, 1990
d. Autori, Franco
d. Blakey, Art
d. Bolet, Jorge

October 19, 1990
d. Hartley, Fred Lloyd
d. Worsham, Lew(is Elmer)

October 20, 1990
d. McCrea, Joel

October 21, 1990
d. Carvel, Thomas A

October 22, 1990
d. Sinkwich, Frank

October 26, 1990
d. OhEithir, Breandan
d. Paley, William Samuel

October 27, 1990
d. Cugat, Xavier
d. Demy, Jacques
d. Roosevelt, Elliott

October 29, 1990
d. Smith, William French

October 31, 1990
d. Price, Roger Taylor

November 2, 1990
d. Porter, Eliot Furness

November 3, 1990
d. Martin, Mary

November 5, 1990
d. Kahane, Meir David

November 7, 1990
d. Durrell, Lawrence (George)
d. MacLennan, Hugh
d. Wilson, Logan

November 8, 1990
d. Seton, Anya Chase

November 11, 1990
d. Kirk, Lisa

November 12, 1990
d. Arden, Eve
d. Greene, Balcomb

November 14, 1990
d. Muggeridge, Malcolm

November 17, 1990
d. Hofstadter, Robert

November 18, 1990
d. Harris, Harwell Hamilton

November 19, 1990
d. Landrum, Phil(lip) M(itchell)

November 20, 1990
d. Cobb, William Montague

November 23, 1990
d. Dahl, Roald

November 24, 1990
d. Smith, Dodie

November 30, 1990
d. Cousins, Norman
d. Eichenberg, Fritz

December 1, 1990
d. Markert, Russell
d. Pandit, Vijaya Lakshmi (Nehru)

December 2, 1990
d. Copland, Aaron
d. Cummings, Bob

December 6, 1990
d. Rahman, Abdul, Prince

December 7, 1990
d. Arenas, Reinaldo
d. Bennett, Joan

December 8, 1990
d. Ritt, Martin

December 9, 1990
d. Mazurki, Mike

December 10, 1990
d. Hammer, Armand
d. Stavropoulos, George Peter

December 13, 1990
d. Marble, Alice

December 14, 1990
d. Durrenmatt, Friedrich

December 18, 1990
d. Revere, Anne
d. Tortelier, Paul

December 20, 1990
d. Rolvaag, Karl Fritjof

December 21, 1990
d. Johnson, Clarence Leonard

December 24, 1990
d. Wendell Oliver, Scott, Sr.

December 26, 1990
d. Cruzan, Nancy

December 28, 1990
d. Martin, Kiel

December 31, 1990
d. Allen, George Herbert

1991

d. Johnson, Guy Benton

January 3, 1991
d. Appling, Luke

January 4, 1991
d. Matthews, T(homas) S(tanley)

January 8, 1991
d. Clark, Steve

January 11, 1991
d. Anderson, Carl David

January 12, 1991
d. Luke, Keye

January 13, 1991
d. Rosenman, Dorothy

January 15, 1991
d. Rankin, K(arl) L(ott)

January 16, 1991
d. Cloud, Preston (Ercelle)

January 17, 1991
d. Manzu, Giacomo
d. Olav V
d. Walsh, Chad

January 18, 1991
d. Fish, Hamilton, III

January 22, 1991
d. Frye, (Herman) Northrop

January 24, 1991
d. Schaefer, Jack Warner

January 26, 1991
d. Langan, Glenn

January 27, 1991
d. Long, Dale

January 28, 1991
d. Grange, Red

January 29, 1991
d. Graham, John

January 30, 1991
d. Bardeen, John
d. McIntire, John

February 2, 1991
d. Axthelm, Pete(r Macrae)
d. Wickens, Aryness Joy

February 3, 1991
d. Ackerman, Harry S
d. Kulp, Nancy Jane

February 5, 1991
d. Jagger, Dean
d. Knight, James L

February 6, 1991
d. Luria, Salvador Edward
d. Thomas, Danny

February 9, 1991
d. Cleveland, James

February 12, 1991
d. Wagner, Robert Ferdinand, Jr.

February 14, 1991
d. McCone, John Alex

February 15, 1991
d. Englund, Richard

February 18, 1991
d. Fodor, Eugene

February 21, 1991
d. Cooper, John Sherman
d. Fetzer, John Earl
d. Fonteyn, Margot, Dame

February 23, 1991
d. Hannah, John Alfred

February 24, 1991
d. Daly, John Charles, Jr.
d. Gobel, George Leslie
d. Pierce, Webb

February 26, 1991
d. Scott, Ken

March 1, 1991
d. Land, Edwin Herbert
d. Liedtke, William C, Jr.
d. Smith, Kenneth Danforth
d. Sunderland, Thomas E(lbert)

March 2, 1991
d. Mollenhoff, Clark Raymond

March 3, 1991
d. Head, Howard
d. Murray, Arthur
d. Revolta, Johnny

March 6, 1991
d. Penney, William George

March 7, 1991
d. Bell, Cool Papa

March 10, 1991
d. Knight, Etheridge
d. Siegmeister, Elie

March 12, 1991
d. Granit, Ragnar Arthur
d. Rossi-Lemeni, Nicola

March 13, 1991
d. McPartland, Jimmy
d. Snelling, Richard

March 14, 1991
d. Ashman, Howard
d. Zolotow, Maurice

March 15, 1991
d. Sherman, George

March 18, 1991
d. Banky, Vilma
d. Taft, Henry Waters, II
d. Voelker, John Donaldson

March 19, 1991
d. Mennen, Frederick

March 21, 1991
d. Fender, Leo

March 22, 1991
d. Engle, Paul (Hamilton)
d. Rains, Albert McKinley

March 23, 1991
d. Spofford, Charles M(erville)

March 25, 1991
d. Joyce, Eileen
d. Lefebvre, Marcel Francois

March 27, 1991
d. Ray, Aldo

March 29, 1991
d. Atwater, Lee

April 1, 1991
d. Chaikin, Sol Chick
d. Graham, Martha

April 3, 1991
d. Goren, Charles Henry
d. Greene, Graham (Henry)

April 4, 1991
d. Frisch, Max
d. Heinz, John

April 5, 1991
d. Tower, John Goodwin

April 7, 1991
d. Page, Ruth

April 9, 1991
d. Rich, Louise Dickinson
d. Towns, Forrest

April 10, 1991
d. Schafer, Natalie

April 12, 1991
d. Schuyler, James Marcus

April 14, 1991
d. Pacciardi, Randolfo

April 16, 1991
d. Lean, David, Sir

April 17, 1991
d. Yellen, Jack

April 18, 1991
d. Walters, Bucky

April 20, 1991
d. Nsubuga, Emmanuel, Cardinal
d. O'Faolain, Sean
d. Siegel, Don

April 24, 1991
d. Dozier, William

April 26, 1991
d. Coppola, Carmine
d. Guthrie, A(lfred) B(ertram), Jr.

April 28, 1991
d. Curtis, Ken
d. McKissick, Floyd Bixler
d. Wulff, Lee

April 29, 1991
d. Sperti, George Speri

May 3, 1991
d. Kosinski, Jerzy (Nikodem)

May 4, 1991
d. Delacorte, George Thomas, Jr.
d. Gross, Chaim

May 6, 1991
d. Hyde-White, Wilfrid

May 7, 1991
d. Sohappy, David, Sr.

May 8, 1991
d. Serkin, Rudolph

May 13, 1991
d. Brinig, Myron

May 14, 1991
d. Chiang, Ching

May 19, 1991
d. Rice, Gregory

May 21, 1991
d. Dante, Nicholas
d. Gandhi, Rajiv Ratna

May 23, 1991
d. Kempff, (Wilhelm) Walter Friedrich
d. Markle, Fletcher

May 25, 1991
d. Johansen, Gunnar

May 26, 1991
d. Eyen, Tom

May 27, 1991
d. Dodd, Ed(ward) Benton

May 29, 1991
d. Browne, Coral Edith

May 31, 1991
d. Wilson, Angus

June 1, 1991
d. Ruffin, David

June 3, 1991
d. Le Gallienne, Eva

June 5, 1991
d. Chang, M(in) C(heuh), Dr.
d. Kert, Larry
d. Porter, Sylvia Field
d. Trudeau, Arthur G(ilbert)

June 6, 1991
d. Getz, Stan

June 9, 1991
d. Arrau, Claudio
d. Loloma, Charles

June 10, 1991
d. Page, Irvine H

June 11, 1991
d. Hamilton, Joe

June 14, 1991
d. Ashcroft, Peggy, Dame
d. Miles, Bernard, Sir

June 15, 1991
d. Chandler, Happy

June 16, 1991
d. Lewis, William Arthur, Sir

June 18, 1991
d. Caulfield, Joan

June 19, 1991
d. Arthur, Jean

June 22, 1991
d. O'Connor, Kevin

June 24, 1991
d. Tamayo, Rufino

June 25, 1991
d. Tomes, Margot

July 1, 1991
d. Landon, Michael

July 2, 1991
d. Remick, Lee

July 4, 1991
d. Raushenbush, Stephen

July 5, 1991
d. Dunnock, Mildred
d. Nemerov, Howard (Stanley)

July 6, 1991
d. Dallis, Nicholas Peter

July 9, 1991
d. Franciscus, James Grover

July 11, 1991
d. Wilhelm, Gale

July 15, 1991
d. Convy, Bert
d. Revelle, Roger Randall

July 16, 1991
d. Dejong, Meindert
d. Motherwell, Robert Burns
d. Rizzo, Frank Lazzaro

July 17, 1991
d. Parr, A(lbert) E(ide)
d. Perry, Harold R

July 20, 1991
d. Robinson, Earl Hawley

July 21, 1991
d. Wilson, Allan C
d. Wilson, Theodore Roosevelt

July 22, 1991
d. McLaren, Wayne

July 24, 1991
d. Singer, Isaac Bashevis

July 25, 1991
d. Kaganovich, Lazar M(oiseevich)
d. Knight, Arthur
d. Love, George Hutchinson

July 30, 1991
d. Ball, William

August 3, 1991
d. Drewry, Guy Carleton

August 4, 1991
d. Burch, Dean

August 5, 1991
d. Brown, Paul
d. Hess, Richard
d. Honda, Soichiro

August 6, 1991
d. Michener, Roland
d. Reasoner, Harry

August 7, 1991
d. Goody, Sam

August 8, 1991
d. Irwin, James Benson
d. Levine, Herbert

August 13, 1991
d. Roosevelt, James

August 14, 1991
d. Elias, Taslim Olawale
d. Kiker, Douglas
d. Suits, C(hauncey) G(uy)

August 15, 1991
d. Tree, Marietta Endicott Peabody
d. Zampa, Luigi

August 18, 1991
d. Shoemaker, Vaughn Richard

August 19, 1991
d. Maltby, Richard E

August 20, 1991
d. Staggers, Harley O(rrin)

August 21, 1991
d. Hildesheimer, Wolfgang
d. Miller, Paul
d. Wilson, Richard

August 22, 1991
d. Dewhurst, Colleen

August 23, 1991
d. Adams, Eva Bertrand
d. Seibert, Florence B(arbara)
d. Trotter, Mildred

August 25, 1991
d. Busch, Niven

August 30, 1991
d. Tinguely, Jean

September 2, 1991
d. Garcia Robles, Alfonso
d. Jackson, Laura Riding
d. Riding, Laura

September 3, 1991
d. Capra, Frank

September 4, 1991
d. Barnet, Charlie
d. Tryon, Thomas
d. West, Dottie

September 7, 1991
d. Crosby, John Campbell
d. McMillan, Edwin Mattison

September 8, 1991
d. Davis, Brad
d. North, Alex

September 9, 1991
d. Mason, Belinda

September 13, 1991
d. Irving, Robert Augustine
d. Pasternak, Joe

September 14, 1991
d. Lynes, Joseph Russell, Jr.

September 15, 1991
d. Baruch, Andre
d. Burgess, Smoky

September 17, 1991
d. Francescatti, Zino Rene
d. Tyner, Rob

September 21, 1991
d. Lang, Paul Henry

September 23, 1991
d. Pao, Y(ue) K(ong), Sir

September 24, 1991
d. Seuss, Doctor

September 25, 1991
d. Barbie, Klaus

September 27, 1991
d. Fuller, Roy Broadbent
d. Sprague, R(obert) C(hapman)

September 28, 1991
d. Davis, Miles Dewey, III

September 29, 1991
d. Stone, Grace Zaring

October 2, 1991
d. Dimitrios I, Patriarch
d. Garrison, Lloyd K(irkham)
d. Shea, William Alfred

October 3, 1991
d. Gayle, Addison, Jr.
d. Kaplan, Joseph

October 7, 1991
d. Durocher, Leo Ernest
d. Ginzburg, Natalia
d. Goerlich, John

October 8, 1991
d. Humphry, Ann Wickett

October 9, 1991
d. Lilly, Doris

October 11, 1991
d. Foxx, Redd
d. Williams, Carroll Milton

October 12, 1991
d. MacMahon, Aline Laveen
d. Toomey, Regis

October 14, 1991
d. Elsasser, Walter M, Dr.

October 16, 1991
d. Hennard, George, Jr.

October 17, 1991
d. Ford, Tennessee Ernie

October 20, 1991
d. Massey, D Curtis

October 24, 1991
d. Roddenberry, Gene

October 25, 1991
d. Graham, Bill

October 26, 1991
d. Sutton, Horace (Ashley)

October 27, 1991
d. Barker, George Granville

October 28, 1991
d. Fine, Sylvia
d. Fletcher, Joseph Francis (III)

October 30, 1991
d. Kolchin, Ellis Robert

October 31, 1991
d. Hartt, Frederick
d. Papp, Joseph

November 2, 1991
d. Allen, Irwin

November 5, 1991
d. MacMurray, Fred(erick Martin)
d. Maxwell, Robert Ian Charles

November 6, 1991
d. Tierney, Gene

November 9, 1991
d. Montand, Yves

November 13, 1991
d. Baldwin, Hanson Weightman

November 15, 1991
d. Richardson, Tony

November 18, 1991
d. Husak, Gustav

November 21, 1991
d. Dichter, Ernest
d. Lloyd-Jones, Esther McDonald
d. Werblin, Sonny

November 23, 1991
d. Kinski, Klaus

November 24, 1991
d. Furst, Anton
d. Mercury, Freddie

November 26, 1991
d. Andrews, Raymond
d. Heinemann, Edward H
d. Johnson, Bob

November 27, 1991
d. Heath, Catherine

November 29, 1991
d. Bellamy, Ralph
d. Finkelstein, Louis, Dr.

d. Yerby, Frank (Garvin)

December 1, 1991
d. Stigler, George Joseph

December 5, 1991
d. Speck, Richard Franklin
d. Welensky, Roy

December 6, 1991
d. Goodrich, Bert

December 7, 1991
d. Jaffe, Herb

December 8, 1991
d. Bergalis, Kimberly
d. Clayton, Buck

December 10, 1991
d. Abbott, Berenice
d. Tshabalala, Headman

December 11, 1991
d. Lewis, Robert Q
d. Lundkvist, Artur Nils

December 12, 1991
d. Boardman, Eleanor

December 14, 1991
d. Dyer-Bennet, Richard

December 17, 1991
d. Smallwood, Joey

December 19, 1991
d. Gann, Ernest Kellogg

December 22, 1991
d. Morris, Ernest Brougham

December 23, 1991
d. Krenek, Ernst

December 24, 1991
d. Hudson, Walter
d. Sorensen, Virginia

1992

d. Adams, James Luther
d. Brand, Neville
d. Hinkle, Paul
d. Loloma, Otellie
d. Oort, Jan Hendrik
d. Rootes, William Edward Rootes, Baron

January 1, 1992
d. Frankovich, Mike J
d. Hopper, Grace Brewster Murray

January 2, 1992
d. Field, Virginia (Margaret Cynthia St. John)

January 3, 1992
d. Anderson, Judith, Dame

January 12, 1992
d. Morey, Walt(er Nelson)

January 13, 1992
d. Dodington, Sven H(enry Marriott)

January 17, 1992
d. Ventura, Charlie

January 19, 1992
d. DiDonato, Pietro

January 22, 1992
d. Antoon, A(lfred) J(oseph)

January 23, 1992
d. Bartholomew, Freddie

January 24, 1992
d. Darby, Ken

January 25, 1992
d. Riad, Mahmoud

January 26, 1992
d. Ferrer, Jose Vicente

January 29, 1992
d. Dixon, Willie (James)

January 31, 1992
d. Hein, Mel(vin John)
d. D'Aubuisson, Roberto

February 1, 1992
d. Kaufman, Irving R(obert)

February 2, 1992
d. Parks, Bert
d. Whitehead, Edwin C(arl)

February 4, 1992
d. Dehner, John Forkum

February 8, 1992
d. Williams, Tommy

February 10, 1992
d. Haley, Alex (Murray Palmer)

February 11, 1992
d. Danton, Ray(mond)

February 15, 1992
d. Schuman, William Howard

February 16, 1992
d. Carter, Angela (Olive)

February 20, 1992
d. York, Dick

February 21, 1992
d. Hoving, Jane Pickens

February 22, 1992
d. Yeshurun, Avot

February 23, 1992
d. Bolinger, Dwight Lemerton

February 27, 1992
d. Hayakawa, S(amuel) I(chiye)

February 28, 1992
d. Maurer, Emilia Sherman

March 2, 1992
d. Dennis, Sandy

March 3, 1992
d. Beatty, Robert

March 4, 1992
d. Almendros, Nestor

March 5, 1992
d. Walker, David Harry

March 6, 1992
d. Klineberg, Otto
d. Martin, David Stone
d. Vieira Da Silva, Maria Helena

March 8, 1992
d. Nelson, Christian

March 9, 1992
d. Begin, Menachem (Wolfovitch)

March 11, 1992
d. Brooks, Richard
d. Lehmann-Haupt, Hellmut Emil

March 13, 1992
d. Hobson, Harold

March 15, 1992
d. Deutsch, Helen

March 20, 1992
d. Delerue, Georges

March 21, 1992
d. Ireland, John

March 23, 1992
d. Hayek, Friedrich August von

March 25, 1992
d. Walker, Nancy

March 26, 1992
d. Frum, Barbara

March 27, 1992
d. Colby, Anita
d. MacGrath, Leueen (Emily)
d. Webb, James Edwin

March 29, 1992
d. Henreid, Paul
d. Sammartino, Peter

March 30, 1992
d. Park, Thomas

April 3, 1992
d. Bohrod, Aaron

April 4, 1992
d. Reshevsky, Samuel

April 5, 1992
d. Walton, Sam Moore

April 6, 1992
d. Asimov, Isaac
d. Mark, Herman Francis
d. Picon, Molly

April 7, 1992
d. Ruffin, Clovis

April 8, 1992
d. Bovet, Daniele
d. Cherberg, John A(ndrew)

April 9, 1992
d. Ginsburg, Charles P
d. McGee, Gale William

April 10, 1992
d. Kinison, Sam
d. Mitchell, Peter Dennis

April 11, 1992
d. Merriam, Eve
d. Obregon, Alejandro

April 14, 1992
d. Hazelton, Nika
d. Price, Sammy

April 16, 1992
d. Russell, Andy

April 17, 1992
d. Stern, Arthur Cecil

April 20, 1992
d. Hill, Benny
d. Lennon, Jimmy, Sr.

April 22, 1992
d. Harris, Robert Alton

April 23, 1992
d. Ray, Satyajit

April 27, 1992
d. O'Neill, Gerard Kitchen

April 28, 1992
d. Bacon, Francis
d. Iceberg Slim
d. Messiaen, Olivier (Eugene Prosper Charles)

April 29, 1992
d. Clarke, Mae

May 2, 1992
d. Mills, Wilbur Daigh
d. Wallmann, Margherita

May 3, 1992
d. Murphy, George Lloyd

May 4, 1992
d. Paine, Thomas Otten
d. Parry, Albert
d. Salk, Lee

May 6, 1992
d. Dietrich, Marlene

May 10, 1992
d. Lund, John
d. Syms, Sylvia
d. Thorp, Willard Long

May 11, 1992
d. Henle, Guy
d. MacDonald, Elizabeth G.

May 12, 1992
d. Reed, Robert

May 13, 1992
d. Kahng, Dawon

May 14, 1992
d. Alzado, Lyle Martin

May 15, 1992
d. Funston, George Keith
d. Marcelo, (Edward) Jovy

May 17, 1992
d. Hurrell, George
d. Welk, Lawrence

May 22, 1992
d. David, Elizabeth

May 23, 1992
d. Falcone, Giovanni

May 24, 1992
d. Stevens, Edmund William

May 25, 1992
d. Thompson, Marshall

May 30, 1992
d. Carstens, Karl Walter

May 31, 1992
d. Kane, Robert Joseph

June 3, 1992
d. Gaines, William M(axwell)
d. Morley, Robert

June 5, 1992
d. Lerner, Max

June 6, 1992
d. Goodman, Martin

June 8, 1992
d. McGowan, William George

June 10, 1992
d. Kline, Morris

June 15, 1992
d. Lopat, Ed(mund Walter)

June 17, 1992
d. Exley, Frederick (Earl)
d. Hamilton, Grace Towns

June 18, 1992
d. Allen, Peter Woolnough
d. Iveagh, Arthur Francis Benjamin
  Guinness, Lord

June 21, 1992
d. Li Xiannian

June 22, 1992
d. Fisher, M(ary) F(rances) K(ennedy)

June 24, 1992
d. Nossiter, Bernard Daniel

June 25, 1992
d. Stirling, James

June 27, 1992
d. Jones, Allan

June 28, 1992
d. Tal, Mikhail Nekhemyevich

June 29, 1992
d. Kedourie, Elie

June 30, 1992
d. Ruchlis, Hy(man)

July 1, 1992
d. Meredith, Sidney

July 4, 1992
d. Newman, Joe Dwight
d. Piazzola, Astor

July 5, 1992
d. Brown, Georgia

July 7, 1992
d. Frank, Clinton Edward

July 9, 1992
d. Sevareid, Eric

July 12, 1992
d. Miller, Caroline

July 13, 1992
d. Ironside, Christopher

July 15, 1992
d. DeRoburt, Hammer, Sir

July 16, 1992
d. Buchanan, Buck

July 18, 1992
d. Ising, Rudolf C
d. Lawrence, Lawrence Shubert, Jr.
d. Parnis, Mollie

July 19, 1992
d. Newell, Allen

July 20, 1992
d. Henderson, Bruce

July 24, 1992
d. Ilizarov, Gavril A

July 25, 1992
d. Arletty
d. Drake, Alfred

July 26, 1992
d. Wells, Mary

July 29, 1992
d. Larocque, Bunny

July 30, 1992
d. Marshall, Brenda
d. Shuster, Joe

August 2, 1992
d. Nolan, Thomas Brennan

August 3, 1992
d. Costa Mendez, Nicanor

August 5, 1992
d. Muldoon, Robert David, Sir

August 8, 1992
d. Bakhtiar, Shahpur
d. Gertz, Alison L.

August 12, 1992
d. Cage, John

August 14, 1992
d. Jordan, Joseph
d. Sirica, John Joseph

August 15, 1992
d. Peterson, Edith R.

August 20, 1992
d. Hawkins, Walter Lincoln
d. Liss, Alan R
d. Wilson, Hazel Hutchins

August 25, 1992
d. O'Neal, Frederick

August 27, 1992
d. Ludwig, Daniel Keith

August 29, 1992
d. Guattari, Felix
d. Norton, Mary

September 1, 1992
d. Carnovsky, Morris

September 2, 1992
d. Harbert, Chick
d. Jaroszewicz, Piotr
d. McClintock, Barbara

September 3, 1992
d. Rauh, Joseph Louis, Jr.

September 4, 1992
d. Gillenson, Lewis W

September 5, 1992
d. Herman, Billy
d. Leiber, Fritz (Reuter), Jr.

September 6, 1992
d. Ephron, Henry

September 8, 1992
d. Barrett, William Christopher
d. Burdick, Quentin Northrop

September 11, 1992
d. Crile, George Washington, Jr.

September 12, 1992
d. Perkins, Anthony

September 13, 1992
d. Jacobs, Lou

September 14, 1992
d. Weiss, Ted

September 16, 1992
d. Fenwick, Millicent Hammond

September 17, 1992
d. Chaliapin, Feodor Ivanovitch, Jr.
d. Swanberg, William Andrew
d. Wagner, Roger Frances

September 18, 1992
d. Jacobson, Leon Orris

September 19, 1992
d. Evans, Geraint Llewellyn, Sir

September 23, 1992
d. Home, William Douglas
d. Ivask, Ivar Vidrik
d. Swarthout, Glendon (Fred)
d. Van Fleet, James Alward

September 26, 1992
d. Manheim, Ralph

September 29, 1992
d. Sebrell, W(illiam) H(enry), Jr.

October 5, 1992
d. Kendricks, Eddie
d. Yellow Robe, Rosebud

October 6, 1992
d. Elliott, Denholm Mitchell

October 7, 1992
d. Bloom, Allan David
d. Kitagawa, Joseph Mitsuo

October 8, 1992
d. Brandt, Willy

October 9, 1992
d. Cooper, Louise Field
d. Maddow, Ben

October 13, 1992
d. Marshall, James Edward
d. Rudd, Hughes Day

October 15, 1992
d. Franks, Oliver (Shewell), Sir

October 16, 1992
d. Ellis, John Tracy

October 17, 1992
d. Ter-Arutunian, Rouben

October 18, 1992
d. Gibbs, Frederic A
d. Lipman, Howard W

October 19, 1992
d. Golub, William Weldon
d. Kelly, Petra (Karin)

October 21, 1992
d. Garrison, Jim C.

October 22, 1992
d. Barber, Red
d. Little, Cleavon Jake

October 23, 1992
d. Masselos, William

October 24, 1992
d. Colwin, Laurie
d. Miller, Max
d. Moore, William

October 25, 1992
d. Klein, Marty
d. Miller, Roger Dean

October 26, 1992
d. Dixon, Melvin

October 29, 1992
d. MacMillan, Kenneth, Sir

October 30, 1992
d. Mitchell, Joan

November 1, 1992
d. Rowley, James Joseph

November 2, 1992
d. Deutsch, Karl Wolfgang
d. Roach, Hal

November 3, 1992
d. Holm, Hanya

November 7, 1992
d. Dubcek, Alexander
d. Yates, Richard

November 8, 1992
d. Kelly, Jack

November 9, 1992
d. Hillcourt, William

November 10, 1992
d. Connors, Chuck

November 11, 1992
d. Cunningham, Harry Blair
d. Jones, Stormie

November 12, 1992
d. Mayehoff, Eddie

November 16, 1992
d. Booth, Shirley

November 17, 1992
d. Block, Joseph L(eopold)
d. Lorde, Audre (Geraldine)

November 18, 1992
d. Kirsten, Dorothy

November 19, 1992
d. Varsi, Diane

November 21, 1992
d. Gazzelloni, Severino

November 22, 1992
d. Holloway, Sterling Price

November 23, 1992
d. Acuff, Roy (Claxton)

November 27, 1992
d. Nolan, Sidney, Sir

November 29, 1992
d. Pucci, Emilio Marchese di Barsento

November 30, 1992
d. Blume, Peter

December 4, 1992
d. Derthick, L(awrence) G(ridley)

December 5, 1992
d. Haury, Emil W

December 6, 1992
d. Bacon, Selden D(askam)

December 7, 1992
d. Hughes, Richard J(oseph)

December 8, 1992
d. Shawn, William

December 11, 1992
d. Gardenia, Vincent

December 13, 1992
d. Arnall, Ellis (Gibbs)
d. Irving, Kenneth Colin
d. Whitney, C(ornelius) V(anderbilt)

December 17, 1992
d. Andrews, (Carver) Dana
d. Craig, George N(orth)

December 18, 1992
d. Goodson, Mark
d. Hale, Clara (McBride)

December 20, 1992
d. Ross, Steven J

December 21, 1992
d. Adler, Stella
d. Hare, David
d. King, Albert
d. Milstein, Nathan

December 23, 1992
d. Marshak, Robert E(ugene)

December 24, 1992
d. Culliford, Peyo
d. Gleason, Thomas W(illiam)

December 25, 1992
d. Davidson, Garrison H(olt)
d. Dickens, Monica Enid
d. Joseph, Helen

December 26, 1992
d. Kemeny, John G(eorge)
d. Rajagopalachari, Chakravarti

December 27, 1992
d. Albert, Stephen Joel
d. Boyle, Kay

December 28, 1992
d. Maglie, Sal(vatore Anthony)
d. Quaison-Sackey, Alex(ander)

December 29, 1992
d. Segal, Vivienne

December 30, 1992
d. Healy, Timothy S(tafford)

1993

d. Andrews, Bert
d. Buddhadasa Bhikkhu
d. Meland, Bernard Eugene
d. Mott, William Penn, Jr.
d. Snake, Reuben, Jr.
d. Wells, James Lesesne
d. Wilder, Amos Niven

January 1, 1993
d. Mayer, Jean

January 3, 1993
d. Most, Johnny

January 5, 1993
d. Bode, Carl

January 6, 1993
d. Gillespie, Dizzy
d. Nureyev, Rudolf (Hametovich)

January 9, 1993
d. Gonzalez, Xavier

January 10, 1993
d. Adams, Diana
d. Curtis, Thomas B(radford)
d. Gulick, Luther (Halsey)
d. Wallace, Phyllis A(nn)

January 13, 1993
d. Pleven, Rene Jean

January 15, 1993
d. Cahn, Sammy
d. Iba, Hank

January 18, 1993
d. Hibbert, Eleanor Alice Burford

January 19, 1993
d. Lewis, Reginald F.
d. Strouse, Norman H(ulbert)

January 20, 1993
d. Anthony, Joseph
d. Hepburn, Audrey (Edda)
d. Rothmuller, Marko A

January 21, 1993
d. Gehringer, Charlie
d. Kelly, Bruce

January 22, 1993
d. Abe, Kobo
d. Pollard, Jim

January 23, 1993
d. Dorsey, Thomas Andrew

January 24, 1993
d. Marshall, Thurgood

January 26, 1993
d. Sauve, Jeanne Mathilde Benoit

January 28, 1993
d. Swift, Kay

January 29, 1993
d. Hasford, Jerry Gustav

February 4, 1993
d. Schneider, Alexander

February 5, 1993
d. Du Bois, William Pene
d. Jonas, Hans
d. Mankiewicz, Joseph (Leo)
d. Manso, Leo

February 6, 1993
d. Ashe, Arthur

February 8, 1993
d. Janeway, Eliot

February 11, 1993
d. Garrett, Joy
d. Holley, Robert W(illiam)
d. Meredith, Scott

February 12, 1993
d. Ellingson, Mark

February 14, 1993
d. Lipsky, Eleazar
d. Squires, James Radcliffe

February 16, 1993
d. Salant, Richard S

February 17, 1993
d. Hague, Raoul (Heukelekian)

February 18, 1993
d. Haworth, Ted

February 19, 1993
d. Bazelon, David L(ionel)

February 20, 1993
d. Lamborghini, Ferruccio

February 21, 1993
d. Kurtzman, Harvey
d. Van Doren, Dorothy Graffe

February 25, 1993
d. Constantine, Eddie

February 26, 1993
d. Ford, Constance
d. Knebel, Fletcher
d. Newhall, Beaumont

February 27, 1993
d. Gish, Lillian (Diana)
d. Stuart, Kenneth James

February 28, 1993
d. Honda, Ishiro
d. Keeler, Ruby

March 1, 1993
d. Kutner, Luis

March 3, 1993
d. Montoya, Carlos
d. Sabin, Albert Bruce

March 4, 1993
d. Sale, Richard Bernard

March 6, 1993
d. Rothschild, Judith

March 7, 1993
d. Reid, Kate
d. Wrightson, Earl

March 8, 1993
d. Eckstine, Billy

March 9, 1993
d. Parkinson, C(yril) Northcote

March 16, 1993
d. Correia, Natalia

March 17, 1993
d. Hayes, Helen
d. Jacobs, Raymond

March 19, 1993
d. Adzhubei, Aleksei I(vanovich)
d. Boulding, Kenneth E(wart)
d. McWilliams, Alden S

March 20, 1993
d. Kusch, P(olycarp)

March 23, 1993
d. Crichton, Robert

March 24, 1993
d. Gershon, Karen
d. Hersey, John (Richard)

March 26, 1993
d. Falco, Louis

March 27, 1993
d. Agostini, Peter
d. Larson, (Lewis) Arthur
d. White, Stephen

March 29, 1993
d. Tajo, Italo

March 30, 1993
d. Diebenkorn, Richard C.

March 31, 1993
d. Lee, Brandon
d. Parish, Mitchell

April 1, 1993
d. Juan Carlos, Count of Barcelona
d. Kulwicki, Alan
d. Zuckerman, Solly, Lord

April 2, 1993
d. Leontovich, Eugenie

April 3, 1993
d. Goodman, Andrew
d. Lee, Pinky
d. Plage, Dieter

April 4, 1993
d. Butts, Alfred M(osher)
d. Shirley, Anne

April 5, 1993
d. Lee, Robert E(mmet)

April 7, 1993
d. Rodham, Hugh
d. Schmiechen, Richard Kurt

April 8, 1993
d. Anderson, Marian
d. Soloveitchik, Joseph Baer

April 10, 1993
d. Hani, Chris

April 13, 1993
d. Stegner, Wallace (Earle)

April 15, 1993
d. Charteris, Leslie
d. Westall, Robert Atkinson

April 16, 1993
d. Velez, Clemente Soto

April 17, 1993
d. Fleischmann, Peter F(rancis)
d. Ozal, Turgut

April 18, 1993
d. Wayne, Bernie

April 19, 1993
d. Koresh, David
d. Mickelson, George Speaker
d. Sellinger, Joseph A

April 20, 1993
d. Brandon, Henry Oscar
d. Cantinflas

April 21, 1993
d. Mitchell, Corinne

April 23, 1993
d. Chavez, Cesar (Estrada)

April 24, 1993
d. Tambo, Oliver
d. Thao, Tran Duc

April 26, 1993
d. Henkle, Henrietta

April 28, 1993
d. Grizodubova, Valentina
  (Stepanovna)
d. Valvano, Jim

April 29, 1993
d. Gordon, Michael

May 1, 1993
d. Beregovoy, Pierre (Eugene)
d. Knowles, Warren Perley
d. Premadasa, Ranasinghe

May 2, 1993
d. Gallo, Julio
d. Weng, Will

May 5, 1993
d. Howe, Irving

May 6, 1993
d. Todd, Ann

May 8, 1993
d. Nikolais, Alwin

May 9, 1993
d. Gilliatt, Penelope (Ann Douglas
  Conner)

May 10, 1993
d. del Ray, Lester (Ramon Alvarez)
d. Zondervan, Peter

May 11, 1993
d. Gentry, Minnie Lee
d. Wiener, Leigh Auston

May 13, 1993
d. Garcia Vargas, Joaquin

May 14, 1993
d. Hearst, William Randolph, Jr.

May 19, 1993
d. Burdett, Winston M.

May 25, 1993
d. Coxe, Louis Osborne
d. Seymour, Dan

May 26, 1993
d. Priestly, Jack

May 28, 1993
d. Jones, Roger W(arren)

May 29, 1993
d. Bernstein, Sid(ney Ralph)
d. Conn, Billy

May 30, 1993
d. Sun Ra

May 31, 1993
d. Tatum, Donn B

June 2, 1993
d. Mize, Johnny
d. Simon, Norton Winfred

June 5, 1993
d. Twitty, Conway

June 6, 1993
d. Bridges, James

June 9, 1993
d. Smith, Alexis

June 10, 1993
d. Auger, Arleen

June 11, 1993
d. Sharkey, Ray

June 13, 1993
d. Slayton, Donald Kent

June 14, 1993
d. Pett, Saul

June 15, 1993
d. Connally, John B.
d. Hunt, James
d. Vera

June 19, 1993
d. Golding, William (Gerald), Sir
d. Parsons, James

June 20, 1993
d. Thuilier, Raymond

June 22, 1993
d. Nixon, Patricia
d. Troy, Hannah

June 23, 1993
d. Kopal, Zdenek

June 25, 1993
d. John, John P(ico)

June 26, 1993
d. Campanella, Roy

June 28, 1993
d. Christoff, Boris
d. Cohn, Zanvil (Alexander)

July 3, 1993
d. DeRita, Joe
d. Drysdale, Don(ald Scott)

July 5, 1993
d. Salisbury, Harrison Evans

July 6, 1993
d. Beech, Olive Ann (Mellor)

July 10, 1993
d. Ibuse, Masuji

July 13, 1993
d. Wojciechowicz, Alex(ander)

July 15, 1993
d. Brian, David

July 20, 1993
d. Corbett, Young, III

July 23, 1993
d. Jordan, James

July 24, 1993
d. Harris, MacDonald

July 25, 1993
d. Schaefer, Vincent Joseph

July 26, 1993
d. Fuchs, Daniel
d. Ridgway, Matthew Bunker

July 27, 1993
d. Dowling, Dan(iel Blair)
d. Lewis, Reggie

July 31, 1993
d. Baudouin, I, King
d. Sarduy, Severo

August 1, 1993
d. Kauffman, Ewing Marion
d. Manessier, Alfred

August 3, 1993
d. Donald, James
d. Maleska, Eugene T.

August 5, 1993
d. Jack, Homer A(lexander)

August 15, 1993
d. Kempner, Robert M(aximilian)
  W(asilii)

August 16, 1993
d. Beam, Jacob D(yneley)
d. Granger, Stewart
d. Philbrick, Herbert Arthur
d. Sharaff, Irene

August 17, 1993
d. Maynard, Robert Clyve

August 19, 1993
d. Blitch, Iris F(aircloth)
d. Kerst, Donald W(illiam)

August 21, 1993
d. Troyanos, Tatiana

August 25, 1993
d. Biehl, Amy
d. Elson, Edward L(ee) R(oy)

August 26, 1993
d. Rockin' Dopsie

August 27, 1993
d. Foster, Vincent

August 28, 1993
d. Stafford, William Edgar

August 30, 1993
d. Jordan, Richard

September 1, 1993
d. Coker, Elizabeth Boatwright

September 4, 1993
d. Villechaize, Herve Jean Pierre

September 10, 1993
d. O'Connell, Helen
d. Schifter, Peter Mark

September 11, 1993
d. Butler, John
d. Leinsdorf, Erich

September 12, 1993
d. Burr, Raymond (William Stacy)

September 13, 1993
d. De La Torre(-Bueno), Lillian

September 15, 1993
d. Allen, Ethan (Nathan)

September 20, 1993
d. Sulzberger, C(yrus) L(eo)

September 22, 1993
d. Abravanel, Maurice

September 26, 1993
d. Berberova, Nina Nikolaevna
d. Pennel, John (Thomas)

September 27, 1993
d. Doolittle, James H(arold)

September 28, 1993
d. DeVries, Peter

October 7, 1993
d. DeMille, Agnes (George)

October 9, 1993
d. Smith, Austin E(dward)

October 11, 1993
d. Thomas, Jess

October 12, 1993
d. Ames, Leon
d. Hafstad, Lawrence R(andolph)

October 13, 1993
d. Hardy, Harriet

October 16, 1993
d. Bortoluzzi, Paolo

October 20, 1993
d. Dolbier, Maurice (Wyman)

October 21, 1993
d. Herlihy, James Leo
d. Ndadaye, Melchior

October 24, 1993
d. Barnhart, Clarence L(ewis)
d. Grimond, Jo(seph)

October 25, 1993
d. Price, Vincent

October 26, 1993
d. Rome, Harold J(acob)

October 27, 1993
d. Quennell, Peter (Courtney)

October 28, 1993
d. Duke, Doris

October 31, 1993
d. Fellini, Federico
d. Phoenix, River

November 1, 1993
d. Ochoa, Severo

November 4, 1993
d. Landau, Ely A

November 11, 1993
d. Hawkins, Erskine (Ramsey)

November 12, 1993
d. Haldeman, H(arry) R(obbins)

November 14, 1993
d. Millett, John D(avid)

November 19, 1993
d. Burke, Kenneth

November 21, 1993
d. Bixby, Bill

November 22, 1993
d. Stern, James

November 24, 1993
d. Collins, Albert
d. Gres, Alix

November 25, 1993
d. Burgess, Anthony

November 28, 1993
d. Moore, Garry

November 29, 1993
d. Tata, J(ehangir) R(atanji) D(adbhoy)

December 3, 1993
d. Glaser, Elizabeth
d. Thomas, Lewis

December 4, 1993
d. Landon, Margaret (Dorothea Mortenson)

d. Zappa, Frank

December 6, 1993
d. Ameche, Don
d. Taft, Robert A(lphonso), Jr.

December 7, 1993
d. Houphouet-Boigny, Felix

December 10, 1993
d. Tully, Alice

December 11, 1993
d. Gary, Raymond
d. Raedler, Dorothy (Florence)

December 12, 1993
d. Antall, Jozsef, Jr.

December 14, 1993
d. Loy, Myrna

December 16, 1993
d. Moore, Charles Willard
d. Tanaka, Kakuei

December 17, 1993
d. Gunn, Moses

December 18, 1993
d. Ball, Joseph H(urst)

December 19, 1993
d. Bennett, Wallace F(oster)

December 20, 1993
d. Deming, W(illiam) Edwards

December 21, 1993
d. Christison, (Alexander Frank) Philip

December 22, 1993
d. Raskin, A(braham) H(enry)

December 23, 1993
d. Currie, Lauchlin (Bernard)
d. Roosa, Robert V(incent)

December 24, 1993
d. Peale, Norman Vincent

December 26, 1993
d. Beck, Dave

December 27, 1993
d. Callen, Michael

December 28, 1993
d. Shirer, William L(awrence)

December 30, 1993
d. Lazar, Irving Paul

December 31, 1993
d. Byroade, Henry A(lfred)
d. Watson, Thomas J(ohn), Jr.

1994

d. DeBartolo, Edward J(ohn), Sr.

d. Henize, Karl G(ordon)
d. Jarman, Derek
d. Judd, Donald (Clarence)
d. Riggs, Marlon
d. Saint, Assotto
d. Tyler, Ralph W(infred)
d. Odinga, Ajuma Jaramogi

January 1, 1994
d. Romero, Cesar

January 2, 1994
d. Ray, Dixy Lee
d. Schweitzer, Pierre-Paul

January 5, 1994
d. O'Neill, Thomas P(hilip), Jr.
d. Scribner, Fred C(lark), Jr.

January 6, 1994
d. Kelley, Virginia

January 8, 1994
d. Blackton, Jay S
d. Buttram, Pat

January 10, 1994
d. Aldridge, Michael
d. Feeney, Chub

January 13, 1994
d. Alphand, Herve

January 14, 1994
d. Ralston, Esther

January 16, 1994
d. Stowe, Leland

January 17, 1994
d. Stephens, Helen

January 22, 1994
d. Barrault, Jean-Louis
d. Busby, Matthew, Sir
d. Savalas, Telly

January 23, 1994
d. Dubridge, L(ee) A(lvin)
d. Smith, Oliver

January 27, 1994
d. Adams, Stanley
d. Akins, Claude

January 28, 1994
d. Douglas, Emily Taft
d. Levitt, William J(aird)

January 30, 1994
d. Boulle, Pierre Francois Marie-Louis
d. Fisher, Avery

February 1, 1994
d. Soule, Olan

February 5, 1994
d. Abs, Hermann J(osef)
d. Sauer, George (Henry)

February 6, 1994
d. Cotten, Joseph

d. Kirby, Jack
d. Simms, Hilda
d. Strasfogel, Ignace

February 7, 1994
d. Lutoslawski, Witold

February 8, 1994
d. Scott, Raymond

February 9, 1994
d. Hare, Raymond A(rthur)
d. Kaufman, Louis
d. Novotna, Jarmila
d. Wilkinson, Charles (Burnham)

February 11, 1994
d. Booke, Sorrell
d. Conrad, William

February 13, 1994
d. Judd, Walter H(enry)
d. Sherrod, Robert (Lee)

February 14, 1994
d. Belluschi, Pietro
d. Lasch, Christopher

February 17, 1994
d. Shilts, Randy (Martin)

February 18, 1994
d. Gaither, Jake

February 21, 1994
d. Lasker, Mary (Woodward)

February 24, 1994
d. Sablon, Jean Georges
d. Shore, Dinah

February 25, 1994
d. Walcott, Joe

March 3, 1994
d. Stone, Ezra (Chaim)

March 4, 1994
d. Candy, John (Franklin)

March 6, 1994
d. Mercouri, Melina

March 7, 1994
d. Bolte, Charles G(uy)

March 9, 1994
d. Bukowski, Charles
d. Rey, Fernando
d. Spivak, Lawrence E(dmund)

March 15, 1994
d. Zetterling, Mai (Elisabeth)

March 19, 1994
d. Wilson, Edward Foss

March 20, 1994
d. Grizzard, Lewis M., Jr.

March 21, 1994
d. Rambo, Dack

March 22, 1994
d. Lantz, Walter

March 23, 1994
d. Colosio Murrieta, Luis Donaldo
d. Masina, Giulietta
d. Swann, Donald (Ibrahim)

March 24, 1994
d. May, John L.

March 25, 1994
d. Petitpierre, Max

March 26, 1994
d. Millar, Margaret (Ellis)

March 28, 1994
d. Goldman, Albert
d. Ionesco, Eugene

April 2, 1994
d. Furness, Betty

April 4, 1994
d. Simms, Ginny

April 6, 1994
d. Habyarimana, Juvenal
d. Ntaryamira, Cyprien

April 8, 1994
d. Cobain, Kurt

April 15, 1994
d. Curry, John (Anthony)

April 16, 1994
d. Ellison, Ralph (Waldo)

April 17, 1994
d. Sperry, Roger W(olcott)

April 22, 1994
d. Nixon, Richard M(ilhous)

April 27, 1994
d. Preston, John

April 28, 1994
d. Roueche, Berton

April 29, 1994
d. Kirk, Russell (Amos)

April 30, 1994
d. Scarry, Richard (McClure)
d. White, William S(mith)

May 1, 1994
d. Senna, Ayrton

May 5, 1994
d. Layton, Joe

May 6, 1994
d. Chute, Marchette (Gaylord)

May 7, 1994
d. Greenberg, Clement

May 8, 1994
d. Carlson, William S(amuel)
d. Peppard, George

May 10, 1994
d. Brooks, Cleanth
d. Gacy, John Wayne, Jr.

May 12, 1994
d. Erikson, Erik H(omburger)

May 14, 1994
d. Albritton, David
d. Claytor, W(illiam) Graham, Jr.
d. Smith, Hazel Brannon

May 19, 1994
d. Morgan, Henry
d. Onassis, Jacqueline (Lee Bouvier
   Kennedy)

May 20, 1994
d. Shannon, James A(ugustine)

May 23, 1994
d. Pass, Joe

May 24, 1994
d. Wain, John Barrington

May 26, 1994
d. Ball, George W(ildman)

May 28, 1994
d. Boros, Julius (Nicholas)
d. Flood, Daniel J(ohn)
d. Kahn, E(ly) J(acques), Jr.
d. Praeger, Frederick A(mos)

May 29, 1994
d. Honecker, Erich
d. Murphy, W(illiam) B(everly)

May 30, 1994
d. Benson, Ezra Taft
d. Onetti, Juan Carlos

June 3, 1994
d. Everson, William Oliver

June 4, 1994
d. Thorneycroft, (George Edward)
   Peter

June 5, 1994
d. Kabibble, Ish

June 6, 1994
d. Downs, Johnny
d. Sullivan, Barry

June 7, 1994
d. Brown, William Melvin, Jr.
d. Potter, Dennis (Christopher George)

June 9, 1994
d. Tinbergen, Jan

June 10, 1994
d. Kienholz, Edward

June 11, 1994
d. Anderson, Herbert

June 12, 1994
d. Schneerson, Menachem M(endel)

June 13, 1994
d. Goldman, Ronald Lyle
d. Simpson, Nicole Brown
d. Youskevitch, Igor

June 14, 1994
d. Mancini, Henry

June 16, 1994
d. Murphy, Franklin D(avid)
d. Saltzman, Charles E(skridge)

June 21, 1994
d. Mallory, L(ester) D(ewitt)

June 22, 1994
d. Stratton, Julius A(dams)

June 28, 1994
d. Washington, Fredi

June 30, 1994
d. Roberts, Dennis J(oseph)

July 3, 1994
d. George, Zelma W(atson)
d. Hoad, Lew(is A.)

July 4, 1994
d. Smith, Gerard C(oad)

July 8, 1994
d. Kim Il Sung
d. Lee, Robert E(dwin)
d. Sargent, Dick

July 16, 1994
d. Schwinger, Julian (Seymour)

July 19, 1994
d. Firkusny, Rudolf
d. Turner, Donald F(rank)

July 20, 1994
d. Hillings, Patrick J(ohn)

July 21, 1994
d. Carusi, Ugo
d. Scott, Hugh (Doggett), Jr.

July 26, 1994
d. Legg, W(illiam) Dorr

July 28, 1994
d. Turnbull, Collin M(acmillan)

August 1, 1994
d. Cushing, Peter

August 5, 1994
d. Bean, Louis H(yman)

August 7, 1994
d. Nickerson, Albert L(indsay)

August 8, 1994
d. Leonov, Leonid Maximovich

August 10, 1994
d. Sumner, Jessie

August 13, 1994
d. Canetti, Elias
d. Preus, Jacob A(all) O(ttesen)
d. Worner, Manfred

August 14, 1994
d. Childress, Alice
d. Harrison, Joan (Mary)

August 16, 1994
d. Geldzahler, Henry

August 19, 1994
d. Pauling, Linus C(arl)

August 22, 1994
d. Houser, Allan

August 24, 1994
d. Becker, Ralph E(lihu)

August 30, 1994
d. Anderson, Lindsay (Gordon)

August 31, 1994
d. Wilt, Fred(erick Loren)

September 2, 1994
d. McAfee, Mildred H(elen)
d. TallMountain, Mary

September 3, 1994
d. Aubrey, James (Thomas), Jr.

September 6, 1994
d. Clavell, James (Edmund Du
   Maresq)

September 10, 1994
d. Clampitt, Amy

September 11, 1994
d. Tandy, Jessica

September 12, 1994
d. Ewell, Tom
d. Yegorov, Boris (Borisovitch)

September 16, 1994
d. Gautier, Felisa Rincon de
d. Young, Jean Childs

September 17, 1994
d. Popper, Karl R(aimund), Sir

September 18, 1994
d. Gerulaitis, Vitas

September 19, 1994
d. Smith, Carleton Sprague

September 20, 1994
d. Styne, Jule

September 23, 1994
d. Barber, Jerry
d. Bloch, Robert Albert
d. Renaud, Madeleine

September 27, 1994
d. Lleras Restrepo, Carlos

October 2, 1994
d. Nelson, Harriet

October 10, 1994
d. Raphael, Chaim

October 18, 1994
d. Cisler, Walker (Lee)

October 19, 1994
d. Raye, Martha

October 20, 1994
d. Lancaster, Burt(on Stephen)

October 21, 1994
d. Wiesner, Jerome B(ert)

October 22, 1994
d. May, Rollo (Reece)

October 23, 1994
d. Leonard, Bill

October 24, 1994
d. Julia, Raul
d. Shelepin, Aleksandr (Nikolaevich)

October 25, 1994
d. Natwick, Mildred
d. Roebling, Mary G(indhart)

October 29, 1994
d. Primus, Pearl

October 30, 1994
d. Singh, (Sardar) Swaran
d. Feld, Fritz

November 1, 1994
d. Beery, Noah, Jr.

November 2, 1994
d. Taylor, Peter (Hillsman)

November 4, 1994
d. Francis, Sam(uel Lewis)

November 5, 1994
d. Dean, Patrick (Henry), Sir

November 6, 1994
d. Masserman, Jules H(oman)

November 9, 1994
d. O'Donoghue, Michael

November 10, 1994
d. Higinbotham, William A(lfred)
d. Kappel, Frederick R(ussell)

d. McRae, Carmen
d. Nizer, Louis

November 11, 1994
d. Volpe, John A(nthony)
d. Zamora, Pedro

November 12, 1994
d. Rudolph, Wilma (Glodean)
d. Stewart, J(ohn) I(nnes) M(ackintosh)

November 15, 1994
d. Speare, Elizabeth George

November 18, 1994
d. Calloway, Cab
d. Somes, Michael (George)

November 19, 1994
d. Symons, Julian (Gustave)

November 21, 1994
d. Kuchel, Thomas H(enry)

November 23, 1994
d. Hawkins, Erick

November 24, 1994
d. Shapp, Milton J(errold)

November 28, 1994
d. Dahmer, Jeffrey L
d. Enrique Tarancon, Vicente, Cardinal
d. Rubin, Jerry
d. Serraillier, Ian Lucien

November 29, 1994
d. Griswold, Erwin N(athaniel)
d. Timmerman, George Bell, Jr.

November 30, 1994
d. Stander, Lionel (Jay)

December 5, 1994
d. Horner, Harry
d. Zim, Herbert S(pencer)

December 7, 1994
d. Hickey, Margaret A.
d. Madigan, Edward R.

December 8, 1994
d. Jobim, Antonio Carlos

December 9, 1994
d. Crawford, Frederick C(oolidge)

December 10, 1994
d. Joseph, Keith (Sinjohn)

December 11, 1994
d. Rush, (David) Kenneth

December 12, 1994
d. Roosa, Stuart Allen

December 13, 1994
d. Bestor, Arthur (Eugene)
d. Hauser, Philip M(orris)
d. Pinay, Antoine

December 14, 1994
d. Beaton, Norman
d. Faubus, Orval E(ugene)

December 16, 1994
d. Logan, Harlan (De Braun)

December 18, 1994
d. Pitt, David Thomas

December 20, 1994
d. Arnon, Daniel I(srael)
d. Osborn, Robert C(hesley)
d. Ponnamperuma, Cyril (Andrew)
d. Rusk, (David) Dean
d. Trueblood, D(avid) Elton

December 24, 1994
d. Boswell, John (Eastburn)
d. Brazzi, Rossano
d. Haydon, Julie
d. Osborne, John (James)

December 25, 1994
d. Dreyfus, Pierre
d. Singh, Giani Zail

December 26, 1994
d. Schiller, Karl (August Fritz)

December 27, 1994
d. Reynolds, Allie

December 31, 1994
d. Strode, Woody

1995

d. Washington, Val J.

January 1, 1995
d. Wigner, Eugene P(aul)

January 2, 1995
d. Kelly, Nancy
d. Siad Barre, Mohamed

January 4, 1995
d. Tax, Sol

January 6, 1995
d. Slovo, Joe

January 9, 1995
d. Cook, Peter
d. Souphanouvong, Prince

January 12, 1995
d. Price, George

January 13, 1995
d. Stibitz, George R.

January 14, 1995
d. Root, Oren

January 15, 1995
d. Maxwell, Vera (Huppe)
d. Schlink, Frederick John

January 16, 1995
d. McCoy, Charles B(relsford)

January 18, 1995
d. Butenandt, Adolf Fredrick Johann
d. Luciano, Ron(ald Michael)

January 21, 1995
d. Groza, Alex John

January 22, 1995
d. Kennedy, Rose (Fitzgerald)

January 23, 1995
d. Shils, Edward Albert

January 26, 1995
d. Allers, Franz

January 28, 1995
d. Roudebush, Richard L(owell)
d. Tagliavini, Ferrucio

January 30, 1995
d. Durrell, Gerald (Malcolm)

January 31, 1995
d. Abbott, George (Francis)

February 2, 1995
d. Pleasence, Donald

February 5, 1995
d. Highsmith, Patricia
d. Holifield, Chet
d. McClure, Doug

February 6, 1995
d. Merrill, James (Ingram)

February 7, 1995
d. Briggs, Fred
d. Sawyer, John E(dward)

February 9, 1995
d. Fulbright, J(ames) William
d. Wayne, David

February 10, 1995
d. Monette, Paul

February 12, 1995
d. Holman, Nat(han)

February 13, 1995
d. Burri, Alberto

February 14, 1995
d. Barton, Robert B(rown) M(orison)
d. Nu, U
d. Nu Thakin

February 17, 1995
d. Walker, Eric A(rthur)

February 18, 1995
d. Lawson, Yank

February 19, 1995
d. Willingham, Calder Baynard, Jr.

February 20, 1995
d. Bolt, Robert (Oxton)

February 22, 1995
d. Flanders, Ed

February 23, 1995
d. Franklin, Melvin
d. Herriot, James

February 25, 1995
d. Clayton, Jack

February 27, 1995
d. Cornfeld, Bernard

February 28, 1995
d. Allen, Walter Ernest

March 1, 1995
d. Blackwell, (Samuel) Earl, Jr.
d. Borch, Fred J.
d. Koehler, Georges J F
d. Rudolf, Max

March 2, 1995
d. Mahoney, James P(atrick)

March 3, 1995
d. Marker, Russell Earl

March 4, 1995
d. Urban, Matt

March 6, 1995
d. Anello, John David
d. Resnik, Muriel

March 7, 1995
d. Rosten, Norman

March 8, 1995
d. Horgan, Paul
d. Victor, Paul-Emile

March 9, 1995
d. Ballantine, Ian (Keith)
d. Bernays, Edward L.

March 13, 1995
d. Glasser, Melvin

March 14, 1995
d. Blair, Frank
d. Fowler, William A(lfred)

March 15, 1995
d. Chadwick, Florence (May)

March 16, 1995
d. Hackett, Albert

March 17, 1995
d. Kray, Ronnie

March 20, 1995
d. Kingsley, Sidney

March 22, 1995
d. Guinan, Matthew

March 23, 1995
d. Shulman, Irving

March 24, 1995
d. Lester, Jerry
d. Needham, Joseph

March 25, 1995
d. Coleman, James S(amuel)

March 26, 1995
d. Eazy-E

March 27, 1995
d. Gucci, Maurizio

March 30, 1995
d. Callender, John Hancock

March 31, 1995
d. Selena

April 1, 1995
d. Warner, Jack, Jr.

April 2, 1995
d. Alfven, Hannes Olof Gosta

April 4, 1995
d. Lane, Priscilla
d. Sinclair, Jo

April 5, 1995
d. Pineau, Christian (Paul Francis)

April 6, 1995
d. Harris, Derek

April 9, 1995
d. Chamberlain, John Rensselaer

April 10, 1995
d. Desai, Morarji (Ranchhodji)

April 11, 1995
d. Glennan, T(homas) Keith

April 13, 1995
d. Rowen, Hobart

April 14, 1995
d. Ives, Burl (Icle Ivanhoe)
d. Moses, Gilbert, III

April 16, 1995
d. Brando, Cheyenne

April 18, 1995
d. Frondizi, Arturo

April 19, 1995
d. Grace, J(oseph) Peter, Jr.
d. Hardy, Porter, Jr.

April 20, 1995
d. Djilas, Milovan

April 21, 1995
d. O'Shea, Tessie

April 22, 1995
d. Kuhn, Maggie

April 23, 1995
d. Cosell, Howard
d. Gerstacker, Carl A(llan)
d. Stennis, John C(ornelius)

April 24, 1995
d. Harp, Holly
d. Rainey, Melanie

April 25, 1995
d. Fleming, Art
d. Rogers, Ginger

April 26, 1995
d. Friedrich, Otto
d. Knox, Alexander
d. Lamont, Corliss

April 27, 1995
d. Bennett, John C(oleman)
d. Wright, Jerauld
d. Wright, Peter (Maurice)

April 30, 1995
d. Duke, Angier Biddle
d. Haire, Bill Martin

May 2, 1995
d. Hordern, Michael

May 4, 1995
d. Harris, Thomas Anthony

May 5, 1995
d. Botvinnik, Mikhail (Moisseyevich)

May 7, 1995
d. McKinley, Ray

May 14, 1995
d. Anfinsen, Christian Boehmer

May 15, 1995
d. Flores, Lola
d. Porter, Eric Richard

May 17, 1995
d. Blake, Toe

May 18, 1995
d. Cook, Elisha, Jr.
d. Godunov, Alexander
d. Harris, Robert
d. LePoer Trench, Brinsley
d. Montgomery, Elizabeth
d. Stone, Michael Patrick William

May 20, 1995
d. Kay, Ulysses Simpson

May 21, 1995
d. Aspin, Les
d. Parker, Albert

May 24, 1995
d. Wilson, (James) Harold, Sir

May 26, 1995
d. Freleng, Friz

May 28, 1995
d. Kronstam, Henning
d. Muir, Jean
d. Welsh, Matthew E(mpson)

May 29, 1995
d. Smith, Margaret (Madeline) Chase

May 31, 1995
d. Elkin, Stanley (Lawrence)
d. Burke, Glenn

June 2, 1995
d. Rosenfeld, Harry N(athan)

June 3, 1995
d. Eckert, John Presper, Jr.
d. Waters, Frank (Joseph)

June 8, 1995
d. Cabot, Thomas D(udley)
d. Ongania, Juan Carlos

June 9, 1995
d. Versalles, Zoilo Casanova

June 11, 1995
d. Cullinan, Thomas P.

June 14, 1995
d. Gallagher, Rory
d. Zelazny, Roger

June 17, 1995
d. Sterling, Claire

June 19, 1995
d. Townsend, Peter Wooldridge

June 20, 1995
d. Gould, Laurence M(cKinley)

June 21, 1995
d. Jones, Tristan

June 23, 1995
d. Grimsby, Roger
d. Salk, Jonas E(dward)

June 25, 1995
d. Burger, Warren E(arl)
d. Walton, Ernest Thomas Sinton

June 27, 1995
d. Kurtz, Efrem
d. Schottland, Charles I(rwin)

June 28, 1995
d. Bonsal, Philip Wilson

June 29, 1995
d. Turner, Lana

June 30, 1995
d. Gordon, Gale
d. Hyman, Phyllis

July 1, 1995
d. Smith, Robert Weston
d. Wolfman Jack

July 2, 1995
d. Seldes, George (Henry)

July 3, 1995
d. Gonzalez, Pancho

July 4, 1995
d. Gabor, Eva

July 5, 1995
d. Beregovoi, Georgi
d. Fukuda, Takeo
d. Furcolo, (John) Foster

July 10, 1995
d. Flatt, Ernie
d. Logan, Onnie Lee
d. Price, Don K.

July 16, 1995
d. Sarton, May
d. Spender, Stephen (Harold)

July 17, 1995
d. Fangio, Juan Manuel
d. Guardino, Harry

July 25, 1995
d. Rich, Charlie

July 26, 1995
d. Almeida, Laurindo
d. Romney, George (Wilcken)

July 27, 1995
d. Rozsa, Miklos

July 29, 1995
d. Elgart, Les

July 31, 1995
d. Morgan, Thomas E(llsworth)

August 2, 1995
d. Reddick, L(awrence) D(unbar)

August 3, 1995
d. Lupino, Ida

August 7, 1995
d. Begelman, David
d. Brophy, Brigid Antonia

August 9, 1995
d. Garcia, Jerry
d. Katz, Milton

August 11, 1995
d. Harris, Phil

August 12, 1995
d. Mantle, Mickey (Charles)

August 15, 1995
d. Swayze, John Cameron, Sr.

August 16, 1995
d. Hobby, Oveta Culp
d. McCarthy, J(oseph) P(riestley)

August 19, 1995
d. Arnold, Danny

August 21, 1995
d. Chandrasekhar, Subrahmanyan

August 23, 1995
d. Eisenstaedt, Alfred
d. Simpson, Adele (Smithline)

August 24, 1995
d. Crosby, Gary

August 26, 1995
d. Wood, Evelyn

August 27, 1995
d. Von Eckardt, Wolf

August 28, 1995
d. Smith, (Charles) Page

August 29, 1995
d. Burke, Selma (Hortense)
d. Perry, Frank

August 31, 1995
d. Jonsson, John Erik

September 4, 1995
d. Henry, David D(odds)
d. Kunstler, William M(oses)

September 8, 1995
d. Ode, Robert C

September 9, 1995
d. Douglas-Home, Alexander
Frederick, Sir

September 10, 1995
d. Tobin, Richard L(ardner)

September 11, 1995
d. Heyns, Roger W(illiam)
d. Hitch, Charles J(ohnston)

September 12, 1995
d. Brett, Jeremy
d. Goode, Mal

September 15, 1995
d. Cater, Douglass
d. Colbert, Lester L(um)

September 18, 1995
d. Davie, Donald Alfred

September 19, 1995
d. Redenbacher, Orville

September 20, 1995
d. Haas, Walter A(braham), Jr.

September 21, 1995
d. Perpich, Rudy George

September 25, 1995
d. Delany, Annie Elizabeth

September 30, 1995
d. Kirby, George
d. Kukrit Pramoj, Momrajawong
(M.R.)

October 4, 1995
d. Lowe, Edward

October 8, 1995
d. Keene, Christopher

October 9, 1995
d. Scali, John (Alfred)

October 10, 1995
d. Finch, Robert H(utchison)

October 13, 1995
d. Roth, Henry

October 15, 1995
d. Peters, Ellis
d. Walker, John

October 21, 1995
d. Andrews, Maxene
d. Goodman, Linda
d. Graves, Nancy (Stevenson)
d. Pinson, Vada Edward

October 22, 1995
d. Amis, Kingsley (William)
d. Boswell, Charles Albert

October 23, 1995
d. Pendleton, Don

October 25, 1995
d. Lindfors, Viveca
d. Riggs, Bobby

October 26, 1995
d. Clark, Georgia Neese
d. Murphy, Thomas F(rancis)

October 29, 1995
d. Southern, Terry

October 30, 1995
d. Morini, Erica

October 31, 1995
d. Bush, Alan (Dudley)
d. Campbell, James

November 1, 1995
d. Thompson, Bradbury James

November 3, 1995
d. Rountree, William M(anning)

November 4, 1995
d. Egan, Eddie
d. Rabin, Yitzhak

November 5, 1995
d. Hemphill, Essex

November 6, 1995
d. Hechinger, Fred Michael

November 7, 1995
d. Patrick, John
d. White, Slappy

November 10, 1995
d. Saro-Wiwa, Ken
d. Wellek, Rene

November 11, 1995
d. Scribner, Charles, Jr.

November 12, 1995
d. Mann, Jack
d. Stephens, Robert, Sir

November 14, 1995
d. Finney, Jack
d. Marcus, Jacon R(ader)
d. Rifkind, Simon H(irsch)

November 16, 1995
d. Horvath, Leslie

November 17, 1995
d. Gordone, Charles Edward

November 20, 1995
d. Grinkov, Sergei

November 21, 1995
d. Jeakins, Dorothy

November 23, 1995
d. Collins, John F(rederick)
d. Malle, Louis
d. Walker, Junior

December 1, 1995
d. Chalk, O(scar) Roy

December 2, 1995
d. Davies, (William) Robertson
d. Roker, Roxie
d. Telkes, Maria (de)

December 5, 1995
d. Washington, Thomas L.

December 6, 1995
d. Fizdale, Robert
d. Reston, James (Barrett)

December 8, 1995
d. Boyer, Ernest L(eroy)

December 9, 1995
d. Bambara, Toni Cade
d. Blaine, Vivian
d. Corrigan, Douglas
d. Gellhorn, Walter

December 12, 1995
d. Lytle, Andrew Nelson
d. Marshall, David (Saul)

December 17, 1995
d. Wesley, Dorothy Porter

December 18, 1995
d. Thomas, Ross (Elmore)

December 19, 1995
d. Barrow, Ruth Nita, Dame

December 20, 1995
d. Sinclair, Madge

December 22, 1995
d. Meade, James Edward
d. Pettit, William Thomas

December 23, 1995
d. Knowles, Patric
d. McQueen, Butterfly

December 25, 1995
d. Levinas, Emmanuel
d. Martin, Dean
d. Slonimsky, Nicolas

December 27, 1995
d. Cherkassky, Shura

December 28, 1995
d. Dabney, Virginius

December 30, 1995
d. Kuhn, Irene

1996

d. Herrera Lane, Felipe

January 1, 1996
d. Burke, Arleigh A(lbert)

January 4, 1996
d. Graham, Wallace H(arry)

January 5, 1996
d. Kirstein, Lincoln (Edward)

January 6, 1996
d. Gillette, Paul
d. Hanson, Duane (Elwood)
d. Johnston, Johnny

January 7, 1996
d. Gronouski, John A(ustin)
d. Grosz, Karoly

January 8, 1996
d. Mitterrand, Francois (Maurice Marie)
d. Taubman, (Hyman) Howard

January 10, 1996
d. Crozier, Roger Allan

January 15, 1996
d. Baxter, Les
d. Moshoeshoe II

January 16, 1996
d. Davenport, Marcia

January 17, 1996
d. Jordan, Barbara C(harline)
d. Minnesota Fats

January 18, 1996
d. Fini, Leonor

January 19, 1996
d. Gaston, Arthur George
d. Simpson, Donald C

January 20, 1996
d. Mulligan, Gerry

January 23, 1996
d. Burden, Carter

January 25, 1996
d. Larson, Jonathan

January 26, 1996
d. Brodkey, Harold
d. Jewtraw, Charlie
d. Lewis, Henry (Jay)

January 27, 1996
d. Yarborough, Ralph W(ebster)

January 28, 1996
d. Brodsky, Joseph (Alexandrovich)
d. Hogarth, Burne
d. Siegel, Jerry

February 2, 1996
d. Kelly, Gene

February 3, 1996
d. Meadows, Audrey

February 6, 1996
d. Madison, Guy

February 8, 1996
d. Ellington, Mercer
d. Ennis, Del(mer)
d. Schwartz, Felice N(ierenberg)

February 9, 1996
d. Galland, Adolf
d. Thompson, Paul W(illiams)

February 11, 1996
d. Regan, Phil

February 12, 1996
d. Samuels, Ernest

February 13, 1996
d. Balsam, Martin Henry
d. Conerly, Charlie

February 15, 1996
d. Stevenson, McLean
d. Weber, Ernst

February 16, 1996
d. Bowen, Roger
d. Brown, Edmund G.
d. Clark, Eleanor

February 19, 1996
d. Finley, Charles O(scar)
d. Manning, Ernest (Charles)
d. Maynor, Dorothy

February 20, 1996
d. Takemitsu, Toru

February 21, 1996
d. Gould, Morton

February 23, 1996
d. Barr, Joseph W(alker)

February 25, 1996
d. Ngor, Haing S

February 27, 1996
d. Janowicz, Vic(tor Felix)

February 29, 1996
d. Farrell, Wes

March 1, 1996
d. Carr, William G(eorge)

March 2, 1996
d. Ginsberg, Mitchell I(rving)

March 3, 1996
d. Duras, Marguerite
d. Krol, John (Joseph), Cardinal
d. Schapiro, Meyer
d. Talbot, Lyle

March 4, 1996
d. Pearl, Minnie

March 9, 1996
d. Burns, George
d. Curti, Merle Eugene
d. Warne, William E(lmo)

March 10, 1996
d. Hunter, Ross

March 11, 1996
d. Edwards, Vince(nt)

March 13, 1996
d. Kieslowski, Krzysztof
d. Watkins, Perry

March 14, 1996
d. Berrill, Jack

March 15, 1996
d. Courlander, Harold
d. Gilpatric, Roswell L(eavitt)

March 17, 1996
d. Clement, Rene

March 18, 1996
d. Elytis, Odysseus
d. Jorda, Enrique

March 19, 1996
d. Sullivan, Walter

March 25, 1996
d. Politi, Leo

March 26, 1996
d. Muskie, Edmund S(ixtus)
d. Packard, David

March 29, 1996
d. Ford, Anne McDonnell

April 3, 1996
d. Brown, Ron(ald Harmon)

April 4, 1996
d. Stokes, Carl B(urton)

April 6, 1996
d. Garson, Greer
d. McMurrin, Sterling M(oss)

April 8, 1996
d. Johnson, Ben

April 9, 1996
d. Condon, Richard (Thomas)
d. Rouse, James W(ilson)

April 11, 1996
d. Dubroff, Jessica

April 13, 1996
d. Brown, George Mackay

April 15, 1996
d. Niarchos, Stavros (Spyros)

April 18, 1996
d. Davies, Ronald N(orwood)

April 20, 1996
d. Milne, Christopher Robin

April 21, 1996
d. Snyder, Jimmy the Greek

April 22, 1996
d. Bombeck, Erma (Louise)
d. Keane, Mary Nesta

April 23, 1996
d. Travers, P(amela) L(yndon)

April 25, 1996
d. Bass, Saul

April 26, 1996
d. Silliphant, Stirling Dale

April 27, 1996
d. Colby, William E(gan)

April 28, 1996
d. Prescott, Orville

April 30, 1996
d. Opatoshu, David

May 1, 1996
d. Brownell, Herbert, Jr.
d. Kennedy, David M(atthew)

May 3, 1996
d. Weston, Jack

May 4, 1996
d. Montana, Patsy

May 6, 1996
d. Suenens, Leon Joseph, Cardinal

May 7, 1996
d. McNeill, Don(ald Thomas)

May 8, 1996
d. Chermayeff, Serge (Ivan)
d. Dominguin, Luis Miguel
d. Williams, Garth Montgomery

May 11, 1996
d. Azikiwe, Nnamdi

May 14, 1996
d. Gurney, Edward John

May 17, 1996
d. Smith, Ethel
d. Watson, Johnny "Guitar"

May 19, 1996
d. Beradino, John

May 24, 1996
d. Druckman, Jacob (Raphael)
d. Mitchell, Joseph

May 29, 1996
d. Toumanova, Tamara

May 31, 1996
d. Leary, Timothy (Francis)
d. Hemingway, Margaux

June 1, 1996
d. Reddy, N(eelam) Sanjeeva

June 2, 1996
d. Garfield, Leon
d. Lorengar, Pilar
d. Lowe, Jack (Warren)

June 3, 1996
d. Goodall, John Strickland

June 6, 1996
d. Plotkin, Jerry
d. Snell, George D(avis)

June 7, 1996
d. Factor, Max, Jr.

June 10, 1996
d. Van Fleet, Jo

June 11, 1996
d. Wyatt, Wilson W(atkins)

June 15, 1996
d. Fitzgerald, Ella

June 16, 1996
d. Allen, Mel

June 17, 1996
d. Kuhn, Thomas Samuel

June 19, 1996
d. Schine, G(erard) David

June 20, 1996
d. Krick, Irving P(arkhurst)

June 22, 1996
d. Bell, T(errel) H(oward)

June 23, 1996
d. Papandreou, Andreas (George)

June 26, 1996
d. Goetz, Delia
d. Guerin, Veronica
d. Rankin, J(ames) Lee

June 27, 1996
d. Adair, Peter
d. Howard, Jane Temple

June 28, 1996
d. Terra, Daniel J(ames)

June 29, 1996
d. Mason, Pamela Helen
d. Zorbaugh, Geraldine B(one)

June 30, 1996
d. Mazia, Daniel

July 1, 1996
d. Cahill, William T(homas)
d. Tesich, Steve

July 8, 1996
d. Albrecht, Duke
d. Amsterdam, Birdie

July 9, 1996
d. Belli, Melvin M(ouron)

July 10, 1996
d. Manoogian, Alex

July 12, 1996
d. Chancellor, John (William)
d. Einem, Gottfried von

July 13, 1996
d. Berman, Pandro Samuel

July 19, 1996
d. Jenco, Lawrence M

July 21, 1996
d. Cassidy, Claudia
d. Edelman, Herb

July 22, 1996
d. Royster, Vermont C(onnecticut)

July 23, 1996
d. Mitford, Jessica
d. Muir, Jean

July 24, 1996
d. Christine, Virginia

July 28, 1996
d. Peterson, Roger Tory

July 30, 1996
d. Colbert, Claudette

d. Cousins, (Sue) Margaret

August 1, 1996
d. Reichstein, Tadeus

August 2, 1996
d. Debre, Michel (Jean Pierre)

August 3, 1996
d. Thompson, Mary

August 4, 1996
d. Kubelik, Rafael (Jeronym)

August 5, 1996
d. Marcus, Frank

August 6, 1996
d. Ruppe, Loret Miller
d. Siles Zuazo, Hernan

August 7, 1996
d. Kubly, Herbert (Oswald)

August 8, 1996
d. Mott, Nevill Francis, Sir
d. Whittle, Frank, Sir

August 9, 1996
d. King, John W(illiam)

August 12, 1996
d. Ambartsumyan, Viktor
   Amazaspovich

August 13, 1996
d. Spinola, Antonio (Sebastiao
   Ribeiro) de

August 14, 1996
d. Celibidache, Sergiu

August 15, 1996
d. McLaughlin, Leo (Plowden)

August 26, 1996
d. Lanusse, Alejandro Agustin

August 27, 1996
d. Morris, Greg

September 1, 1996
d. Welitsch, Ljuba

September 2, 1996
d. Kirbo, Charles H(ughes)
d. Luening, Otto
d. Morrison, Sterling

September 7, 1996
d. Flemming, Arthur S(herwood)

September 8, 1996
d. Burns, John L(awrence)

September 9, 1996
d. Monroe, Bill

September 10, 1996
d. Dru, Joanne

September 11, 1996
d. Malott, Deane W(aldo)

September 12, 1996
d. Geisel, Ernesto

September 13, 1996
d. Shakur, Tupac

September 14, 1996
d. Prowse, Juliet

September 16, 1996
d. Bundy, McGeorge
d. Nelson, Gene

September 17, 1996
d. Agnew, Spiro T(heodore)

September 18, 1996
d. Annabella

September 20, 1996
d. Draper, Paul (Nathaniel Saltonstall)
d. Erdos, Paul

September 22, 1996
d. Lamour, Dorothy

September 26, 1996
d. Kotzky, Alex Sylvester

September 27, 1996
d. Najib Ahmadzi

September 29, 1996
d. Endo, Shusaku

September 30, 1996
d. Lear, Frances
d. Sleet, Moneta, Jr.

October 2, 1996
d. Bourassa, (Jean) Robert
d. Brennan, Peter J(oseph)

October 4, 1996
d. Friedman, Stephen

October 5, 1996
d. Cray, Seymour R.

October 6, 1996
d. Bessell, Ted
d. Porter, Richard William

October 7, 1996
d. Salter, Andrew

October 8, 1996
d. Eberhart, Mignon Good
d. Prince, William

October 9, 1996
d. Hingson, Robert A(ndrew)
d. Kerr, Walter F(rancis)

October 10, 1996
d. Knutson, Coya

October 11, 1996
d. Cameron, Eleanor Frances
d. Lacoste, Rene
d. Vickrey, William

October 13, 1996
d. Reid, Beryl

October 14, 1996
d. LaPlante, Laura

October 15, 1996
d. Franey, Pierre

October 20, 1996
d. Lee, J(oseph) Bracken

October 23, 1996
d. Trilling, Diana (Rubin)

October 24, 1996
d. Hughes, Harold E(verett)

October 28, 1996
d. Amsterdam, Morey

October 29, 1996
d. Day, J(ames) Edward

October 30, 1996
d. Dulles, Eleanor Lansing

October 31, 1996
d. Ames, Louise (Bates)
d. Carne, Marcel Albert

November 1, 1996
d. Jayewardene, J(unius) R(ichard)

November 3, 1996
d. Bokassa, Jean-Bedel

November 9, 1996
d. Makins, Roger (Mellor), Sir

November 10, 1996
d. Stone, Toni

November 13, 1996
d. Doggett, Bill

November 14, 1996
d. Bernardin, Joseph L(ouis), Cardinal

November 15, 1996
d. Hiss, Alger

November 16, 1996
d. Quarles, Benjamin Arthur

November 21, 1996
d. Salam, Abdus

November 22, 1996
d. Blanton, (Leonard) Ray

November 23, 1996
d. Shah, Indries

November 26, 1996
d. Rand, Paul

November 28, 1996
d. McCloskey, Robert James

November 30, 1996
d. Tiny Tim
d. Kabua, Amata

December 1, 1996
d. Karmal, Babrak

December 6, 1996
d. Rozelle, Pete

December 7, 1996
d. Donoso, Jose

December 8, 1996
d. Rollins, Howard Ellsworth, Jr.

December 9, 1996
d. Leakey, Mary (Douglas)

December 10, 1996
d. Young, Faron

December 11, 1996
d. Hamilton, Charles

December 12, 1996
d. Gates, Larry
d. Packard, Vance (Oakley)

December 13, 1996
d. Alvary, Lorenzo

December 15, 1996
d. Kemelman, Harry
d. Van Der Post, Laurens (Jan), Sir

December 17, 1996
d. Caesar, Irving

December 19, 1996
d. Mastroianni, Marcello

December 20, 1996
d. Sagan, Carl (Edward)

December 21, 1996
d. Gray, Barry
d. Rey, Margret (Elizabeth)

December 24, 1996
d. Jenkins, Newell

December 27, 1996
d. Walsh, William B(ertalan)

December 28, 1996
d. Carfagno, Edward

December 30, 1996
d. Ayres, Lew
d. Nance, Jack

December 31, 1996
d. Addy, Wesley

1997

d. Henry, Aaron
d. Rossi, Aldo
d. Martin, Louis E.

January 4, 1997
d. Helmsley, Harry B(rakmann)

January 5, 1997
d. Lane, Burton

January 8, 1997
d. Calvin, Melvin

January 9, 1997
d. White, Jesse

January 10, 1997
d. Huxley, Elspeth Josceline Grant
d. Leonard, Sheldon
d. Todd, Alexander (Robertus), Sir

January 11, 1997
d. Eklund, John M(anly)

January 12, 1997
d. Huggins, Charles B(renton)

January 14, 1997
d. Irsay, Robert

January 17, 1997
d. Griffith, Ernest S(tacey)
d. Tombaugh, Clyde W(illiam)

January 18, 1997
d. Krainik, Ardis
d. Tsongas, Paul E(fthemios)

January 19, 1997
d. Caselotti, Adriana
d. Dickey, James (Lafayette)

January 20, 1997
d. Flood, Curt(is Charles)
d. Fontaine, Marcel

January 21, 1997
d. Parker, Tom, Colonel

January 22, 1997
d. Panter-Downes, Mollie

January 23, 1997
d. Berry, Richard

January 25, 1997
d. Dixon, Jeane (Pinckert)

February 1, 1997
d. Caen, Herb
d. Goodman, Mitchell
d. Reynolds, Marjorie

February 2, 1997
d. Meisner, Sanford
d. Stamos, Theodoros

February 3, 1997
d. Hrabal, Bohumil

February 4, 1997
d. Halsey, Margaret (Frances)

February 5, 1997
d. Harriman, Pamela

February 11, 1997
d. Porter, Don

February 16, 1997
d. Wu, Chien Shiung

February 18, 1997
d. Hahn, Emily

February 19, 1997
d. Deng Xiaoping
d. Marshall, Lois
d. Rosten, Leo C(alvin)

February 21, 1997
d. Winsten, Archer

February 22, 1997
d. Sarnoff, Robert W(illiam)
d. Shanker, Albert

February 23, 1997
d. Williams, Tony

February 25, 1997
d. Sinyavsky, Andrei D(onatovich)

February 26, 1997
d. Doyle, David (Fitzgerald)

February 27, 1997
d. Davis, Kingsley
d. Maples, William R.

February 28, 1997
d. Dederich, Charles (Edwin)
d. Hershey, Lenore

March 3, 1997
d. McConnell, Joseph H(oward)

March 5, 1997
d. Baker, Samm Sinclair

March 6, 1997
d. Furgol, Ed(ward)
d. Jagan, Cheddi (Berret)
d. Manley, Michael (Norman)

March 7, 1997
d. Purcell, Edward M(ills)

March 8, 1997
d. Danielian, Leon
d. Sheinwold, Alfred

March 9, 1997
d. Leighton, Robert B(enjamin)
d. Notorious B.I.G.
d. Wedgwood, C(icely) V(eronica)
d. Wilbur, Dwight L(ocke)

March 10, 1997
d. Drake, Stan(ley Albert)

March 11, 1997
d. Weisgall, Hugo (David)

March 13, 1997
d. Saudek, Robert

March 14, 1997
d. Fuchs, Joseph (Philip)
d. Zinnemann, Fred

March 15, 1997
d. Vasarely, Victor

March 19, 1997
d. deKooning, Willem

March 20, 1997
d. Pritchett, V(ictor) S(awdon), Sir
d. Zale, Tony

March 21, 1997
d. Awdry, W(ilbert Vere)

March 24, 1997
d. Caidin, Martin
d. Johnson, U(ral) Alexis

March 25, 1997
d. Ryder, James Arthur

March 26, 1997
d. Applewhite, Marshall Herff

March 27, 1997
d. Custin, Mildred
d. Dwinell, Lane

March 29, 1997
d. Sager, Ruth

March 31, 1997
d. Anderson, Eugenie M(oore)
d. Spitzer, Lyman, Jr.

April 1, 1997
d. Gabor, Jolie

April 2, 1997
d. Tanaka, Tomoyuki

April 3, 1997
d. Wyeth, Henriette (Zirngiebel)

April 4, 1997
d. Appley, Lawrence A(sa)

April 5, 1997
d. Ginsberg, Allen
d. Heckscher, August

April 6, 1997
d. Cooke, Jack Kent

April 8, 1997
d. Nyro, Laura

April 10, 1997
d. Schwarzschild, Martin

April 11, 1997
d. Dorris, Michael (Anthony)

April 12, 1997
d. Wald, George

April 13, 1997
d. McCord, David (Thompson Watson)

April 17, 1997
d. Herzog, Chaim
d. Rockefeller, Mary French

April 20, 1997
d. Louis, Jean

April 21, 1997
d. Macapagal, Diosdado P(angan)
d. Rodriguez, Andres

April 25, 1997
d. May, Brian
d. Paulsen, Pat

April 26, 1997
d. Beal, John
d. Faye, Joey

April 28, 1997
d. Petry, Ann (Lane)

April 29, 1997
d. Royko, Mike

April 30, 1997
d. Picard, Henry

May 1, 1997
d. Widerberg, Bo

May 2, 1997
d. Eccles, John C(arew), Sir
d. Freire, P(aulo)
d. Moore, Audley

May 5, 1997
d. Kempton, (James) Murray

May 14, 1997
d. Blackstone, Harry, Jr.
d. Lee, Laurie

May 16, 1997
d. Baron, Samuel
d. DeSantis, Giuseppe

May 18, 1997
d. Saidenberg, Daniel

May 19, 1997
d. Ruttman, Troy

May 20, 1997
d. Barco Vargas, Virgilio

May 22, 1997
d. Davis, Lorenzo
d. Hershey, Alfred D(ay)

May 24, 1997
d. Mulhare, Edward

May 25, 1997
d. Hebert, Jay

May 26, 1997
d. Cunningham, William T(homas)

May 28, 1997
d. Sengstacke, John H(erman Henry)

May 29, 1997
d. Buckley, Jeff
d. Fenneman, George

May 31, 1997
d. Lafontant-Mankarious, Jewel
(Stradford)
d. Monroe, Rose Will

June 1, 1997
d. Eastlake, William (Derry)

June 2, 1997
d. Cheatham, Adolphus
d. Jacobs, Helen (Hull)

June 3, 1997
d. James, Dennis

June 4, 1997
d. Esau, Katherine

June 5, 1997
d. Lane, Ronnie
d. Lukas, J(ay) Anthony

June 6, 1997
d. Gabor, Magda

June 8, 1997
d. Tutuola, Amos

June 14, 1997
d. Jaeckel, Richard (Hanley)

June 20, 1997
d. Helms, Bobby
d. Payton, Lawrence

June 23, 1997
d. Shabazz, Betty

June 24, 1997
d. Keith, Brian

June 25, 1997
d. Cousteau, Jacques (Yves)

June 26, 1997
d. Hutson, Don(ald M)

July 1, 1997
d. Mitchum, Robert

July 2, 1997
d. Stewart, James (Maitland)

July 4, 1997
d. Kuralt, Charles (Bishop)

July 6, 1997
d. Chandler, Dorothy (Buffum)

July 13, 1997
d. Danilova, Alexandra

July 15, 1997
d. Versace, Gianni

July 17, 1997
d. Liman, Arthur L(awrence)
d. Weaver, Robert C(lifton)

July 18, 1997
d. Goldsmith, James (Michael), Sir

July 19, 1997
d. Hines, John E(lbridge)

July 21, 1997
d. Root, Lynn

July 24, 1997
d. Brennan, William Joseph, Jr.
d. Parker, Frank

July 25, 1997
d. Hogan, Ben

July 27, 1997
d. Saw Maung

July 31, 1997
d. Bao Dai

August 1, 1997
d. Richter, Sviatoslav Theofilovich

August 2, 1997
d. Burroughs, William S(eward)
d. Fela
d. Kuti, Fela Anikulapo

August 4, 1997
d. Calment, Jean

August 5, 1997
d. Gerrard, Roy
d. Kelley, Clarence Marion

August 8, 1997
d. Rudolph, Paul Marvin

August 10, 1997
d. Jordy, William H(enry)
d. Moss, Carlton

August 15, 1997
d. Heatherton, Ray(mond Joseph)

August 18, 1997
d. Westwood, Jean Miles

August 23, 1997
d. Gairy, Eric Matthew, Sir
d. Kendrew, John Cowdery, Sir

August 27, 1997
d. Blane, Sally
d. Tartikoff, Brandon

August 31, 1997
d. Diana, Princess of Wales

September 2, 1997
d. Bing, Rudolf (Franz Josef), Sir
d. Frankl, Viktor E(mil)

September 4, 1997
d. Eysenck, Hans J(urgen)

September 5, 1997
d. Edel, Leon
d. Solti, Georg, Sir
d. Teresa, Mother

September 7, 1997
d. Crockett, George (William), Jr.
d. Mobutu Sese Seko

September 9, 1997
d. Ashburn, Richie
d. Meredith, Burgess

September 16, 1997
d. Jepson, Helen

September 17, 1997
d. Skelton, Red

September 19, 1997
d. Keeton, Kathy

September 20, 1997
d. Christopher, Matt(hew F.)

September 23, 1997
d. Clarke, Shirley

September 27, 1997
d. Trampler, Walter

September 29, 1997
d. Lichtenstein, Roy

October 3, 1997
d. Rowse, A(lfred) L(eslie)

October 5, 1997
d. Marr, Dave
d. Tracy, Arthur

October 6, 1997
d. Vander Meer, Johnny

October 8, 1997
d. Goldberg, Bertrand

October 10, 1997
d. Malcolm, George

October 12, 1997
d. Denver, John

October 13, 1997
d. Compton, Joyce

October 14, 1997
d. Robbins, Harold

October 16, 1997
d. Lindley, Audra

October 18, 1997
d. Dickerson, Nancy Hanschman
d. Goizueta, Roberto C(rispulo)

October 19, 1997
d. McGill, William James

October 21, 1997
d. Camilli, Dolph

October 22, 1997
d. Rothwax, Harold

October 29, 1997
d. Coombs, Herbert Cole

October 30, 1997
d. Fuller, Samuel

November 2, 1997
d. Rothschild, Edmund Leopold de

November 3, 1997
d. Bleiberg, Robert Marvin

November 5, 1997
d. Berlin, Isaiah, Sir

November 6, 1997
d. Parks, Lillian (Adele) Rogers

November 7, 1997
d. Harshaw, Margaret

November 10, 1997
d. Wauneka, Annie Dodge

November 11, 1997
d. Milburn, Rodney, Jr.

November 12, 1997
d. Laughlin, James, IV

November 14, 1997
d. Arcaro, Eddie
d. Lorant, Stefan

November 15, 1997
d. Chaplin, Saul

November 16, 1997
d. Marchais, Georges (Rene Louis)

November 21, 1997
d. Geneen, Harold S(ydney)
d. Kirk, Grayson Louis

November 23, 1997
d. Hutchence, Michael
d. Mas Canosa, Jorge

November 25, 1997
d. Banda, Hastings Kamuzu

November 26, 1997
d. Henry, Marguerite

November 27, 1997
d. Knowles, Malcolm Shepherd
d. Leonard, Buck

November 29, 1997
d. Young, Coleman A(lexander)

December 1, 1997
d. Grappelli, Stephane

December 2, 1997
d. Hedges, Michael

December 8, 1997
d. Rugambwa, Laurean

December 9, 1997
d. Geva, Tamara

December 11, 1997
d. Winpisinger, William W(ayne)

December 12, 1997
d. Avery, R Stanton

December 14, 1997
d. Kaye, Stubby

December 16, 1997
d. Disney, Lillian
d. Larson, Nicolette

December 18, 1997
d. Farley, Chris

December 20, 1997
d. Itami, Juzo
d. Levertov, Denise
d. Steel, Dawn

December 24, 1997
d. Mifune, Toshiro

December 25, 1997
d. Pyle, Denver
d. Strehler, Giorgio

December 27, 1997
d. Gill, Brendan

December 30, 1997
d. Dolci, Danilo

December 31, 1997
d. Cramer, Floyd

1998

d. Ashmore, Harry Scott
d. Bunting, Mary Ingraham

January 2, 1998
d. Moody, Helen Wills

January 4, 1998
d. Gary, John

January 5, 1998
d. Bono, Sonny

January 7, 1998
d. Prelog, Vladimir
d. Treat, Lawrence

January 8, 1998
d. Diemer, Walter
d. Tippett, Michael Kemp, Sir

January 9, 1998
d. Fukui, Kenichi

January 11, 1998
d. Tennstedt, Klaus

January 15, 1998
d. Van Horne, Harriet
d. Wells, Junior

January 19, 1998
d. Perkins, Carl (Lee)

January 21, 1998
d. Lord, Jack

January 23, 1998
d. Limann, Hilla

January 24, 1998
d. Edmonds, Walter D(umaux)

January 26, 1998
d. Suzuki, Shin'ichi

January 29, 1998
d. Alioto, Joseph L(awrence)
d. Gorman, Carl Nelson

February 2, 1998
d. Stevens, Roger L(acey)

February 3, 1998
d. Wiley, W(illiam) Bradford

February 4, 1998
d. Hillis, Margaret

February 6, 1998
d. Wilson, Carl (Dean)

February 7, 1998
d. Falco
d. Sanders, Lawrence

February 8, 1998
d. Laxness, Halldor (Kiljan)
d. Powell, Enoch

February 10, 1998
d. Schumann, Maurice

February 15, 1998
d. Gellhorn, Martha Ellis

February 17, 1998
d. Juenger, Ernst

February 18, 1998
d. Caray, Harry

February 21, 1998
d. Jones, Grandpa

February 22, 1998
d. Ribicoff, Abraham A(lexander)

February 23, 1998
d. Oliver, Edith
d. Sullivan, William Hallisey, Jr.

February 24, 1998
d. Youngman, Henny

February 26, 1998
d. Schultz, Theodore W(illiam)

February 27, 1998
d. Hitchings, George H(erbert)

February 28, 1998
d. Duncan, Todd
d. Shevchenko, Arkady N(ikolayevich)

March 2, 1998
d. Bodard, Lucien (Albert)
d. Commager, Henry Steele

March 5, 1998
d. Friendly, Fred W.

March 7, 1998
d. Rysanek, Leonie

March 8, 1998
d. Nitschke, Ray(mond E.)

March 9, 1998
d. Farah, William F.

March 10, 1998
d. Bridges, Lloyd

March 13, 1998
d. Reid, William Ronald

March 15, 1998
d. Spock, Benjamin (McLane)

March 16, 1998
d. Barton, Derek H(arold) R(ichard), Sir

March 17, 1998
d. Barker, Cliff

March 19, 1998
d. Ali, Ahmed

March 21, 1998
d. Ulanova, Galina

March 25, 1998
d. Massey, Daniel (Raymond)

March 27, 1998
d. Porsche, Ferdinand

March 29, 1998
d. Freij, Elias
d. Hicks, David (Nightingale)

March 31, 1998
d. Abzug, Bella (Savitsky)

April 4, 1998
d. Pilatus, Rob(ert)

April 6, 1998
d. Lasch, Robert
d. Williams, Wendy O(rlean)
d. Wynette, Tammy

April 13, 1998
d. MacGregor, Ian Kinloch, Sir

April 14, 1998
d. Stans, Maurice H(ubert)

April 15, 1998
d. Pol Pot

April 16, 1998
d. Calderon, Alberto P(edro)

April 17, 1998
d. McCartney, Linda

April 18, 1998
d. Sanford, Terry

April 19, 1998
d. Paz, Octavio

April 20, 1998
d. Huddleston, Trevor

April 21, 1998
d. Hayes, Peter Lind

April 23, 1998
d. Aurre, Laura
d. Karamanlis, Constantine
d. Ray, James Earl

April 24, 1998
d. Stevens, Leslie

April 25, 1998
d. Morris, Wright Marion

April 26, 1998
d. Paul, Gabe

April 27, 1998
d. Castaneda, Carlos
d. Linh, Nguyen Van

May 1, 1998
d. Bettmann, Otto L(udwig)
d. Cleaver, Eldridge

May 2, 1998
d. Norman, Maidie (Ruth)

May 3, 1998
d. MacIver, Loren
d. Raymond, Gene

May 6, 1998
d. Chatichai Choonhavan
d. Connolly, Sybil

May 7, 1998
d. Cormack, Allan MacLeod
d. Rabbitt, Eddie

May 8, 1998
d. Randolph, Jennings
d. Rebozo, Bebe

May 9, 1998
d. Faye, Alice

May 14, 1998
d. Douglas, Marjory (Stoneman)
d. Sinatra, Frank

May 15, 1998
d. Hawkes, John

May 19, 1998
d. Donegan, Dorothy

May 20, 1998
d. Mankowitz, Wolf

May 22, 1998
d. Derek, John

May 28, 1998
d. Hartman, Phil

May 29, 1998
d. Goldwater, Barry M(orris)

June 1, 1998
d. Stickney, Dorothy

June 5, 1998
d. Kazin, Alfred
d. Nolan, Jeanette
d. Yorty, Sam(uel William)

June 8, 1998
d. Abacha, Sani

June 10, 1998
d. Innes, Hammond

June 12, 1998
d. Buscaglia, Leo

June 13, 1998
d. Costa, Lucio
d. Smythe, Reg(inald)

June 17, 1998
d. Carberry, John J(oseph)

June 21, 1998
d. Campanis, Al

June 22, 1998
d. O'Sullivan, Maureen

June 24, 1998
d. O'Dwyer, Paul

July 2, 1998
d. Thompson, Kay

July 5, 1998
d. Luckman, Sid(ney)

July 6, 1998
d. Knudsen, Semon E(mil)
d. Rogers, Roy

July 7, 1998
d. Abiola, Moshood

July 8, 1998
d. Calloway, (David) Wayne

July 9, 1998
d. Flora, James (Royer)

July 12, 1998
d. Driftwood, Jimmy

July 14, 1998
d. McDonald, Richard

July 16, 1998
d. Clarke, John Henrik

July 20, 1998
d. Spivakovsky, Tossy

July 21, 1998
d. Shepard, Alan B(artlett), Jr.
d. Young, Robert (George)

July 22, 1998
d. Prey, Hermann

July 27, 1998
d. Barnes, Binnie
d. Behn, Noel
d. Martin, William McChesney, Jr.

July 29, 1998
d. Robbins, Jerome

July 30, 1998
d. Smith, Bob

August 1, 1998
d. Bartok, Eva

August 2, 1998
d. Lewis, Shari

August 3, 1998
d. Schnittke, Alfred

August 5, 1998
d. Zhivkov, Todor Khristov

August 13, 1998
d. Green, Julian (Hartridge)

August 16, 1998
d. Fowlie, Wallace
d. Murray, Jim
d. West, Dorothy

August 18, 1998
d. Khambatta, Persis

August 21, 1998
d. Stout, Juanita Kidd

August 24, 1998
d. Diggs, Charles C(oles), Jr.
d. Marshall, E(dda) G(unnar)

August 25, 1998
d. Powell, Lewis F(ranklin), Jr.

September 1, 1998
d. Middlecoff, Cary

September 2, 1998
d. Drury, Allen (Stuart)

September 6, 1998
d. Kurosawa, Akira

September 11, 1998
d. Clark, Dane

September 13, 1998
d. Lumley, Harry
d. Wallace, George C(orley)

September 14, 1998
d. McEwen, Terence Alexander

September 17, 1998
d. Elliot, Win
d. Frank, Gerold

September 20, 1998
d. Humphrey, Muriel Fay Buck

September 21, 1998
d. Joyner, Florence Griffith

September 23, 1998
d. Frann, Mary

September 26, 1998
d. Carter, Betty

September 27, 1998
d. Walker, Doak

September 29, 1998
d. Bradley, Tom

September 30, 1998
d. Goring, Marius
d. Quisenberry, Dan(iel Raymond)

October 2, 1998
d. Autry, Gene

October 3, 1998
d. McDowall, Roddy

October 6, 1998
d. Weidman, Jerome

October 10, 1998
d. Cates, Joseph
d. Clifford, Clark M(cAdams)

October 11, 1998
d. Denning, Richard

October 14, 1998
d. Amory, Cleveland

October 15, 1998
d. Smith, Iain Crichton

October 21, 1998
d. Cairncross, Alexander Kirkland, Sir

October 22, 1998
d. Ambler, Eric

October 23, 1998
d. Judd, Winnie Ruth McKinnell

October 24, 1998
d. Calderone, Mary Steichen

October 28, 1998
d. Goldman, James
d. Hughes, Ted

October 30, 1998
d. Celebrezze, Anthony J(oseph)
d. Abdulkarim, Mohamed Taki

November 3, 1998
d. O'Driscoll, Martha

November 8, 1998
d. Godden, Rumer
d. Hunt, John, Baron
d. Marais, Jean

November 10, 1998
d. Beriosova, Svetlana
d. Newhouser, Hal

November 11, 1998
d. Brimsek, Frankie

November 13, 1998
d. Hobson, Valerie Babette
d. Holzman, Red

November 15, 1998
d. Carmichael, Stokely
d. Dalrymple, Jean

November 17, 1998
d. Ewbank, Weeb
d. Rolle, Esther

November 19, 1998
d. McCarthy, William J.
d. Pakula, Alan J(ay)

November 22, 1998
d. Hampton, Henry

November 25, 1998
d. Wilson, Flip

November 28, 1998
d. Fascell, Dante B(runo)

November 30, 1998
d. Lewis, Janet

December 2, 1998
d. Haggart, Bob

December 5, 1998
d. Bishop, Hazel
d. Gore, Albert Arnold

December 6, 1998
d. Bates, Peg Leg

December 9, 1998
d. Moore, Archie

December 12, 1998
d. Chiles, Lawton Mainor, Jr.
d. Udall, Morris K(ing)

December 13, 1998
d. Grade, Lew, Sir

December 14, 1998
d. Fell, Norman

December 15, 1998
d. Meyerowitz, Jan

December 16, 1998
d. Blair, Clay, Jr.
d. Gaddis, William (Thomas)

December 20, 1998
d. Hodgkin, Alan Lloyd, Sir

December 22, 1998
d. Graham, Virginia

December 24, 1998
d. Apps, Syl

December 25, 1998
d. Hatfield, Hurd

December 31, 1998
d. Kirby, Robert E(mory)

1999

January 2, 1999
d. Liebermann, Rolf

January 3, 1999
d. Quarry, Jerry

January 4, 1999
d. Cody, Iron Eyes

January 11, 1999
d. Mitchison, Naomi Margaret
  (Haldane)
d. Moore, Brian

January 12, 1999
d. Cherne, Leo
d. Whyte, William H(ollingsworth)

January 14, 1999
d. Grotowski, Jerzy

January 21, 1999
d. Strasberg, Susan Elizabeth

January 22, 1999
d. Batten, William Milfred

January 23, 1999
d. Sommer, Frederick

January 25, 1999
d. Shaw, Robert Lawson

January 26, 1999
d. Delany, Sarah Louise
d. Luckman, Charles

January 29, 1999
d. Saint Cyr, Lillian

January 30, 1999
d. Hall, Huntz

February 1, 1999
d. Mellon, Paul

February 3, 1999
d. Kingsbury-Smith, Joseph
d. Service, John S(tewart)

February 5, 1999
d. Leontief, Wassily W

February 7, 1999
d. Hussein, I, King
d. Troup, Bobby

February 8, 1999
d. Murdoch, Iris

February 13, 1999
d. Jennings, Gary

February 14, 1999
d. Ehrlichman, John D(aniel)

February 15, 1999
d. Kendall, Henry Way

February 18, 1999
d. Feininger, Andreas (Bernhard
    Lyonel)
d. Pitlik, Noam

February 19, 1999
d. Carlson, Curtis L.

February 20, 1999
d. Siskel, Gene

February 21, 1999
d. Elion, Gertrude B(ell)

February 25, 1999
d. Seaborg, Glenn T(heodore)

February 26, 1999
d. Quintero, Jose (Benjamin)

March 1, 1999
d. Corio, Ann

March 2, 1999
d. Springfield, Dusty

March 3, 1999
d. Herzberg, Gerhard

March 4, 1999
d. Blackmun, Harry A(ndrew)

March 5, 1999
d. Denning, Alfred Thompson
d. Kiley, Richard (Paul)

March 7, 1999
d. Kubrick, Stanley

March 8, 1999
d. Cass, Peggy
d. DiMaggio, Joe
d. Wrigley, William, III

March 12, 1999
d. Menuhin, Yehudi
d. Sayao, Bidu

March 13, 1999
d. Kanin, Garson

March 15, 1999
d. Callahan, Harry (Morey)

March 21, 1999
d. Reedy, George E(dward)

March 24, 1999
d. Tebbetts, Birdie

March 25, 1999
d. Ripken, Cal(vin Edwin, Sr.)

March 29, 1999
d. Williams, Joe

April 1, 1999
d. Carroll, Gladys Hasty

April 3, 1999
d. Bart, Lionel

April 4, 1999
d. Lortel, Lucille
d. Wynn, Early

April 6, 1999
d. Norvo, Red

April 11, 1999
d. Armstrong, William H(oward)

April 14, 1999
d. Corby, Ellen
d. Newley, Anthony (George)

April 20, 1999
d. Whittingham, Charlie

April 21, 1999
d. Rogers, Buddy
d. Tilberis, Elizabeth

April 25, 1999
d. Hruska, Roman L(ee)
d. Killanin, Michael Morris, Lord

April 27, 1999
d. Hirt, Al(ois Maxwell)

April 28, 1999
d. Calhoun, Rory
d. Schawlow, Arthur L(eonard)

April 29, 1999
d. Stader, Maria

May 2, 1999
d. Reed, Oliver

May 7, 1999
d. Hess, Leon

May 8, 1999
d. Bogarde, Dirk

May 9, 1999
d. Silverstein, Shel(by)

May 11, 1999
d. Fifield, Elaine

May 12, 1999
d. Steinberg, Saul

May 13, 1999
d. Greenfield, Meg
d. Sarazen, Gene

May 17, 1999
d. Jones, Henry

May 20, 1999
d. Alfred, William

May 21, 1999
d. Brown, Vanessa

May 25, 1999
d. Brooke, Hillary

May 26, 1999
d. Sacher, Paul

May 27, 1999
d. Adams, Alice

May 31, 1999
d. Pierce, Charles

June 1, 1999
d. Cockerell, Christopher (Sydney), Sir

June 5, 1999
d. Torme, Mel(vin Howard)

June 6, 1999
d. Stanky, Eddie

June 8, 1999
d. Foyle, Christina Agnes Lilian

June 11, 1999
d. Kelley, DeForest

June 12, 1999
d. Powers, James Farl

June 20, 1999
d. Fadiman, Clifton (Paul)

June 26, 1999
d. Bertelli, Angelo B.
d. Ivan, Tommy

June 27, 1999
d. Motley, Marion
d. Papadopoulos, George

June 29, 1999
d. Carr, Allan

July 1, 1999
d. Dmytryk, Edward
d. Mars, Forrest
d. Mitchell, Guy

d. Nkomo, Joshua (Mqabuko
   Nyongolo)
d. Polhill, Robert
d. Sidney, Sylvia

July 2, 1999
d. Puzo, Mario

July 4, 1999
d. Graham, Ronny

July 6, 1999
d. Williams, Sherley Anne

July 9, 1999
d. Farmer, James

July 11, 1999
d. Forrest, Helen

July 14, 1999
d. Steelman, John Roy

July 16, 1999
d. Kennedy, John F(itzgerald), Jr.

July 17, 1999
d. Zipprodt, Patricia

July 21, 1999
d. Ogilvy, David Mackenzie

July 22, 1999
d. Targ, William

July 23, 1999
d. Hassan II

July 25, 1999
d. Agronsky, Martin Zama

July 26, 1999
d. Bate, Walter Jackson

August 2, 1999
d. Morris, Willie

August 4, 1999
d. Mature, Victor (John)
d. Toms, Carl

August 6, 1999
d. Murray, Kathryn (Hazel)

August 10, 1999
d. Darrow, Whitney, Jr.

August 12, 1999
d. Drapeau, Jean

August 14, 1999
d. Kirkland, Lane
d. Klutznick, Philip M.
d. Reese, Pee Wee

August 23, 1999
d. Wexler, Norman

September 5, 1999
d. Funt, Allen

September 8, 1999
d. Hardin, Louis Thomas
d. Stein, Herbert

September 9, 1999
d. Hunter, Catfish
d. Roman, Ruth

September 10, 1999
d. Kraus, Alfredo

September 11, 1999
d. Taeuber, Conrad F.

September 12, 1999
d. Quackenbush, Bill

September 14, 1999
d. Crichton, Charles

September 20, 1999
d. Gorbachev, Raisa (Maksimovna
   Titorenko)

September 22, 1999
d. Scott, George C(ampbell)

September 24, 1999
d. Exner, Judith Campbell

September 26, 1999
d. Brauer, Jerald C(arl)

October 1, 1999
d. Arison, Ted

October 2, 1999
d. Richardson, Lee

October 3, 1999
d. Morita, Akio

October 4, 1999
d. Buffet, Bernard
d. Davis, Martin S.
d. Farmer, Art(hur Stewart)

October 9, 1999
d. Cabral de Melo Neto, Joao
d. Jackson, Milt(on)
d. West, Morris L(anglo)

October 11, 1999
d. Lionni, Leo

October 12, 1999
d. Chamberlain, Wilt(on Norman)

October 14, 1999
d. Nyerere, Julius Kambarage

October 16, 1999
d. Morse, Ella Mae
d. Shepherd, Jean Parker

October 20, 1999
d. Sarraute, Nathalie

October 24, 1999
d. Chafee, John H(ubbard)

October 26, 1999
d. Axton, Hoyt (Wayne)

October 28, 1999
d. Alberti, Rafael

October 31, 1999
d. Jakobovits, Immanuel

November 1, 1999
d. Payton, Walter

November 3, 1999
d. Bannen, Ian

November 4, 1999
d. Bates, Daisy Lee Gatson

November 6, 1999
d. Higgins, George V.
d. Messick, Hank

November 11, 1999
d. Fuchs, Vivian (Ernest), Sir
d. Timerman, Jacobo

November 12, 1999
d. Casadesus, Gaby (Lhote)
d. Vanderbilt, Alfred G(wynne)

November 13, 1999
d. Mills, Donald

November 16, 1999
d. Nathans, Daniel

November 18, 1999
d. Bowles, Paul (Frederick)
d. Horst, Horst P(aul)

November 19, 1999
d. Liberman, Alexander
   (Semeonovitch)

November 20, 1999
d. Fanfani, Amintore

November 21, 1999
d. Crisp, Quentin

November 23, 1999
d. Little, Robert Langdon

November 26, 1999
d. Haynie, Hugh
d. Montagu, (Montague Francis)
   Ashley

November 29, 1999
d. Arciniegas, German
d. Rayburn, Gene

December 1, 1999
d. Byrd, Charlie
d. Gates, Pop

December 2, 1999
d. Adams, Joey

December 3, 1999
d. Kahn, Madeline (Gail)

December 8, 1999
d. Hart-Davis, Rupert

December 10, 1999
d. Tudjman, Franjo

December 12, 1999
d. Cadmus, Paul
d. Heller, Joseph

December 17, 1999
d. Allen, Rex E., Sr.
d. Washington, Grover, Jr.
d. Woodward, C(omer) Vann

December 18, 1999
d. Bresson, Robert

December 20, 1999
d. Snow, Hank

December 24, 1999
d. Cattani, Richard J.
d. Couve de Murville, (Jacques) Maurice
d. Figueiredo, Joao Baptista de Oliveira

December 26, 1999
d. Mayfield, Curtis (Lee)

December 27, 1999
d. Goldenson, Leonard H(arry)

December 28, 1999
d. Moore, Clayton

December 31, 1999
d. Richardson, Elliot L(ee)

2000

d. Khrunov, Evgeny Vasilievich

January 2, 2000
d. O'Brian, Patrick
d. Zumwalt, Elmo R(ussell), Jr.

January 6, 2000
d. Chapman, Leonard F., Jr.

January 9, 2000
d. Cony, Edward Roger

January 11, 2000
d. Lemon, Bob

January 16, 2000
d. Wilson, Robert R(athbun)

January 19, 2000
d. Craxi, Bettino
d. Lamarr, Hedy

January 22, 2000
d. Claiborne, Craig
d. Morrison, Hobe

January 23, 2000
d. Salam, Saeb

January 24, 2000
d. Eckart, William Joseph

January 26, 2000
d. Budge, Don

January 27, 2000
d. Gulda, Friedrich

February 3, 2000
d. Cashin, Bonnie
d. Hills, Lee

February 4, 2000
d. Albert, Carl Bert
d. Kleindienst, Richard Gordon

February 5, 2000
d. Autant-Lara, Claude
d. Elvira, Pablo

February 7, 2000
d. Henning, Doug(las James)

February 8, 2000
d. Abel, Sid(ney Gerald)
d. Maurer, Ion Gheorghe

February 10, 2000
d. Varney, Jim

February 12, 2000
d. Auriol, Jacqueline Douet
d. Hawkins, Screamin' Jay
d. Landry, Tom
d. Schulz, Charles M(onroe)
d. Vadim, Roger

February 14, 2000
d. Zinn, Walter Henry

February 17, 2000
d. White, Miles

February 19, 2000
d. Hundertwasser, Friedensreich

February 20, 2000
d. Sobchak, Anatoly Aleksandrovich

February 21, 2000
d. Daniel, Clifton, Jr.

February 23, 2000
d. Matthews, Stanley, Sir

March 1, 2000
d. DeRegniers, Beatrice Schenk

March 2, 2000
d. Wiggins, Charles Edward

March 6, 2000
d. Colicos, John

March 7, 2000
d. Levi, Edward Hirsch

March 10, 2000
d. Cooney, Barbara

March 13, 2000
d. Wilson, Malcolm

March 15, 2000
d. Kirby, Durward

March 16, 2000
d. Abram, Morris Berthold

March 19, 2000
d. Placzek, Adolf K(urt)

March 23, 2000
d. McCurdy, Ed

March 26, 2000
d. Comfort, Alexander

March 27, 2000
d. Dury, Ian

March 28, 2000
d. Powell, Anthony Dymoke

March 30, 2000
d. Kirchschlager, Rudolf

April 6, 2000
d. Bourguiba, Habib Ben Ali

April 8, 2000
d. Trevor, Claire

April 9, 2000
d. Komer, Robert William

April 10, 2000
d. Fitch, James Marston
d. Linville, Larry Lavon

April 15, 2000
d. Gorey, Edward St. John
d. Morton, Arthur

April 16, 2000
d. Chayes, Abram J(oseph)

April 21, 2000
d. Moore, George Stevens

April 22, 2000
d. Cohen, Alexander H

April 26, 2000
d. Merrick, David

April 28, 2000
d. Buero Vallejo, Antonio

April 30, 2000
d. Jones, Jonah

May 1, 2000
d. Mahoney, David Joseph, Jr.
d. Reeves, Steve
d. Stone, Marvin Lawrence

May 3, 2000
d. O'Connor, John Joseph, Cardinal

May 7, 2000
d. Fairbanks, Douglas, Jr.

May 11, 2000
d. Aardema, Verna Norberg

May 12, 2000
d. Kingman, Dong Moy Shu

May 14, 2000
d. Rockefeller, Rodman C
d. Shapiro, Karl Jay

May 17, 2000
d. Coggan, Frederick Donald, Baron

May 18, 2000
d. Lederer, Francis

May 20, 2000
d. Drachler, Norman
d. Rampal, Jean-Pierre
d. Valletti, Cesare

May 21, 2000
d. Cartland, Barbara Hamilton
d. Gielgud, (Arthur) John, Sir
d. Mielke, Erich

May 26, 2000
d. Taylor, Samuel (Albert)

May 27, 2000
d. Richard, Maurice

May 28, 2000
d. Fryer, Robert

May 30, 2000
d. Beneke, Tex
d. Casey, Robert P
d. Thomas, Bill

May 31, 2000
d. Puente, Tito

June 3, 2000
d. Baskin, Leonard
d. Simon, William E(dward)

June 6, 2000
d. Kelly, Thomas

June 8, 2000
d. MacNelly, Jeff(rey Kenneth)
d. Moore, Bert C

June 9, 2000
d. Lawrence, Jacob Armstead
d. Segal, George

June 10, 2000
d. Assad, Hafez al-

June 14, 2000
d. Jones, Robert Trent

June 16, 2000
d. Nagako, Empress

June 18, 2000
d. Marchand, Nancy

June 19, 2000
d. Takeshita, Noboru

June 21, 2000
d. Hovhaness, Alan

June 27, 2000
d. Kelley, Larry

June 28, 2000
d. Weinmesiter, Arnie

June 29, 2000
d. Gassman, Vittorio

July 1, 2000
d. Matthau, Walter
d. Scherer, Ray(mond Lewis)

July 3, 2000
d. Hejduk, John

July 11, 2000
d. Runcie, Robert Alexander Kennedy

July 14, 2000
d. MacRae, Meredith

July 15, 2000
d. Pastore, John Orlando
d. Quilico, Louis

July 18, 2000
d. Coverdell, Paul

July 28, 2000
d. Pais, Abraham

July 31, 2000
d. Maxwell, William

August 2, 2000
d. Moyes, Patricia

August 5, 2000
d. Guinness, Alec, Sir

August 12, 2000
d. Ben-Elissar, Eliahu
d. Young, Loretta Gretchen

August 17, 2000
d. Gilruth, Robert Rowe
d. Townsend, Lynn Alfred

August 19, 2000
d. Oppenheimer, Harry Frederick

Chronological Index by Date

JANUARY

b. 1504 Pius, V, Pope
b. 1563 Dowland, John
b. 1580? Smith, John
b. 1841 Klyuchevsky, Vasily Osipovich
b. 1844 Breshkovsky, Catherine
b. 1883 Ayres, Ruby Mildred
b. 1887 Vezina, Georges
b. 1892 Baker, Hobey
b. 1892 Cotten, Libba
b. 1906 Levinas, Emmanuel
b. 1930 Adonis
b. 1930 Ahmed, Shahabuddin
b. 1946 Layton, Larry
b. 1966 Gilstrap, Suzy
b. 1969 Danticat, Edwidge
d. 1283 Wen T'ien-hsiang
d. 1316 Ala-ud-din
d. 1638 Brouwer, Adriaen C
d. 1782 Anville, Jean Baptiste Bourguignon d'
d. 1789 Holbach, Baron d'
d. 1854 Rivera, Fructuoso
d. 1863 Coloradas, Mangas
d. 1869 Copway, George
d. 1871 Lartet, Edouard Armand Isidore Hippolyte
d. 1929 Jergens, Andrew
d. 1958 Pears, Charles
d. 1966 Bello, (Alhaji Sir) Ahmadu
d. 1969 Winninger, Charles
d. 1971 Strang, Ruth May
d. 1973 DeParis, Wilbur

d. 1975 Arnstein, Bobbie
d. 1975 Duggan, Maurice Noel
d. 1983 Bartlett, Vernon
d. 1984 Chorell, Walentin
d. 1990 Leighton, Clare Veronica Hope
d. 1994 Odinga, Ajuma Jaramogi
d. 1997 Martin, Louis E.
d. 1998 Ashmore, Harry Scott
d. 1998 Bunting, Mary Ingraham

January 1
b. 1431 Alexander VI
b. 1449 Medici, Lorenzo de
b. 1484 Zwingli, Huldreich
b. 1618 Murillo, Bartolome Esteban
b. 1655 Thomasius
b. 1697 Dupleix, Joseph Francois
b. 1735 Revere, Paul
b. 1745 Wayne, Anthony
b. 1752 Ross, Betsy
b. 1767 Edgeworth, Maria
b. 1788 Cabet, Etienne
b. 1814 Hung Hsiu-ch'uan
b. 1819 Clough, Arthur Hugh
b. 1819 Schaff, Philip
b. 1834 Halevy, Ludovic
b. 1839 Ouida
b. 1854 Frazer, James George, Sir
b. 1855 Sverdrup, Otto
b. 1857 Cline, Maggie
b. 1857 Keefe, Tim(othy John)
b. 1859 Owens, Michael Joseph
b. 1861 Boule, Marcellin

b. 1861 Long, John Luther
b. 1862 Coubertin, Pierre de, Baron
b. 1864 Stieglitz, Alfred
b. 1867 Fields, Lew Maurice
b. 1870 Van Rooy, Anton
b. 1871 Dalmores, Charles
b. 1873 Azuela, Mariano
b. 1874 Knox, Frank
b. 1878 Goldman, Edwin Franko
b. 1879 Forster, E(dward) M(organ)
b. 1879 Fox, William
b. 1879 Jones, Ernest Alfred
b. 1880 Cwiklinska, Mieczyslawa
b. 1883 Clark, Charles Badger
b. 1883 Donovan, William Joseph
b. 1883 Hatoyama Ichiro
b. 1883 Howard, Roy Wilson
b. 1884 Jones, Eli Stanley
b. 1884 Seymour, Charles
b. 1887 Canaris, Wilhelm
b. 1888 Garand, John Cantius
b. 1889 Bickford, Charles Ambrose
b. 1889 Smallens, Alexander
b. 1892 Roxas, Manuel
b. 1893 Gorman, Herbert Sherman
b. 1894 Bose, Satyendranath
b. 1895 Hoover, J(ohn) Edgar
b. 1896 Kinugasa, Teinosuke
b. 1897 Bowen, Catherine Drinker

b. 1897 Greaza, Walter N
b. 1898 Fuchs, Marta
b. 1899 Cottam, Clarence
b. 1899 Pacciardi, Randolfo
b. 1900 Cugat, Xavier
b. 1900 Haines, William
b. 1904 Allen, Ethan (Nathan)
b. 1905 Price, Melvin
b. 1907 Carzou, Jean
b. 1909 Andrews, (Carver) Dana
b. 1909 Goldwater, Barry M(orris)
b. 1909 Shaaban Robert
b. 1911 DuPont, Pierre Samuel, III
b. 1911 Greenberg, Hank
b. 1911 Wurdemann, Audrey May
b. 1912 Philby, Kim
b. 1913 Janeway, Eliot
b. 1914 Oliver, James A(rthur)
b. 1914 Rosten, Norman
b. 1915 Clarke, John Henrik
b. 1916 Wrightson, Earl
b. 1917 Cott, Ted
b. 1919 Landis, Carole
b. 1919 Salinger, J(erome) D(avid)
b. 1921 Highsmith, Patricia
b. 1922 Hollings, Ernest Frederick
b. 1923 Jackson, Milt(on)
b. 1923 Sembene, Ousmane
b. 1924 Danto, Arthur C(oleman)
b. 1925 Amin, Idi
b. 1925 Beard, Matthew, Jr.
b. 1925 Connor, George
b. 1925 Cortesa, Valentina
b. 1925 Jessup, Richard
b. 1927 Baxley, Barbara

b. 1927 Bejart, Maurice
b. 1927 Walker, Doak
b. 1928 Edley,
Christopher Fairfield
b. 1928 Laye, Camara
b. 1928 Sissman,
L(ouis) E(dward)
b. 1928 Smith, Iain
Crichton
b. 1928 Tidyman,
Ernest
b. 1930 Nimeiry, Gaafar
Mohammed al
b. 1930 Wiseman,
Frederick
b. 1932 Carlino, Lewis
John
b. 1932 Moore, Terry
b. 1933 Orton, Joe
b. 1936 Allen, Richard
Vincent
b. 1936 Queler, Eve
Rabin
b. 1937 Stovall, Luther
McKinley
b. 1940 Langella, Frank
b. 1942 Archer, Dennis
W(ayne)
b. 1942 McDonald,
Country Joe
b. 1943 Britz, Jerilyn
b. 1943 Novello, Don
b. 1946 Steele, Claude
Mason
b. 1946 Steele, Shelby
b. 1949 Patrick, Jennie
R.
b. 1953 Dhlakama,
Afonso
b. 1955 Hoyt, LaMarr
b. 1958 Silk, Dave
d. 379 Basil, Saint
d. 1515 Louis, XII
d. 1560 du Bellay,
Joachim
d. 1716 Wycherley,
William
d. 1730 Sewall, Samuel
d. 1732 Nicolini
d. 1782 Bach, Johann
Christian
d. 1787 Middleton,
Arthur
d. 1793 Guardi,
Francesco
d. 1813 Alston,
Theodosia Burr
d. 1831 Niebuhr,
Barthold Georg
d. 1854 Place, Francis
d. 1858 Leslie, Eliza
d. 1881 Blanqui,
Auguste
d. 1894 Hertz, Heinrich
Rudolph
d. 1896 Beach, Alfred
Ely
d. 1901 Donnelly,
Ignatius
d. 1904 Pabst, Frederick
d. 1923 Keeler, Wee
Willie
d. 1932 Scott, Charles
Prestwich
d. 1934 Wassermann,
Jakob

d. 1940 Tallmadge,
Thomas Eddy
d. 1944 Lutyens, Edwin
Landseer, Sir
d. 1948 May, Edna
d. 1949 Campbell,
Malcolm, Sir
d. 1953 Williams, Hank
d. 1954 Bacon, Leonard
d. 1954 Norwich, Alfred
Duff Cooper,
Viscount
d. 1955 Parker, Arthur
C(aswell)
d. 1956 Hague, Frank
d. 1958 Weston,
Edward
d. 1960 Sullavan,
Margaret
d. 1962 Fairless,
Benjamin F
d. 1962 Giesler, Jerry
d. 1963 Kerr, Robert
Samuel
d. 1963 Mead, George
Houk
d. 1966 Auriol, Vincent
d. 1969 Fleming, Ian
d. 1969 MacLane,
Barton
d. 1971 Ford, Arthur A
d. 1972 Chevalier,
Maurice Auguste
d. 1975 Loeffler,
Ken(neth D)
d. 1978 Ascoli, Max
d. 1978 Davis, Hal
Charles
d. 1980 Deutsch,
Adolph
d. 1980 Nenni, Pietro
Sandro
d. 1981 Menuhin,
Hephzibah
d. 1981 Michalowski,
Kazimierz
d. 1981 Ryden, Ernest
Edwin
d. 1982 Buono, Victor
d. 1982 Grahame,
Margot
d. 1984 Korner, Alexis
d. 1985 Du Bois, Raoul
Pene
d. 1986 Cecil, Edward
Christian David
Gascoyne
d. 1986 Friedman, Max
d. 1987 Castroviejo,
Ramon
d. 1988 Hunter,
Clementine
d. 1989 Heywood,
Eddie, Jr.
d. 1990 Kelly, Patrick
d. 1992 Frankovich,
Mike J
d. 1992 Hopper, Grace
Brewster Murray
d. 1993 Mayer, Jean
d. 1994 Romero, Cesar
d. 1995 Wigner, Eugene
P(aul)
d. 1996 Burke, Arleigh
A(lbert)

January 2
b. 1647 Bacon,
Nathaniel
b. 1720 Galvez, Jose de
b. 1727 Wolfe, James
b. 1752 Freneau, Philip
Morin
b. 1803 Thurber,
Charles
b. 1810 Miller, Alfred
Jacob
b. 1822 Clausius,
Rudolf Julius
Emmanuel
b. 1830 Flagler, Henry
Morrison
b. 1830 Kingsley, Henry
b. 1837 Balakirev, Mili
Alekseyevich
b. 1857 Opper,
Frederick Burr
b. 1857 Thomas, Martha
Carey
b. 1865 Phelps, William
Lyon
b. 1866 Murray, Gilbert
b. 1870 Barlach, Ernst
Heinrich
b. 1870 Rickard, Tex
b. 1873 Therese of
Lisieux, Saint
b. 1880 Breguet, Louis
Charles
b. 1881 Varley,
F(rederick)
H(orseman)
b. 1884 Micheaux,
Oscar
b. 1886 Lawrence,
Florence
b. 1889 Hyland, Harry
b. 1889 Schipa, Tito
b. 1894 Nathan, Robert
b. 1894 Rodzinski,
Artur
b. 1895 Bernadotte,
Folke, Count
b. 1895 Leonidoff, Leon
b. 1901 Ralf, Torsten
b. 1902 Merritt, Hiram
Houston
b. 1904 Melton, James
b. 1904 Rand, Sally
b. 1905 Tippett,
Michael Kemp, Sir
b. 1905 Zampa, Luigi
b. 1906 Campbell, E
Simms
b. 1911 Glass, David
Victor
b. 1915 Franklin, John
Hope
b. 1916 Neumann,
Robert Gerhard
b. 1917 Zorina, Vera
b. 1919 Willeford,
Charles Ray, II
b. 1920 Asimov, Isaac
b. 1925 Crowe, William
James, Jr.
b. 1926 Bush-Brown,
Albert
b. 1927 Evers, Jason
b. 1927 Grigorovich,
Yuri Nikolaevich
b. 1927 Marchetti, Gino

b. 1928 Beals, Vaughn
LeRoy, Jr.
b. 1928 Ikeda, Daisaku
b. 1928 Rostenkowski,
Daniel David
b. 1930 LaRosa, Julius
b. 1931 Kaifu Toshiki
b. 1932 Little, (Flora)
Jean
b. 1933 Riley, Richard
W(ilson)
b. 1936 Miller, Roger
Dean
b. 1937 Davis, Peter
Frank
b. 1938 Conway, Lynn
Ann
b. 1938 Smithson,
Robert (Irving)
b. 1939 Bakker, Jim
b. 1939 Orr, Kay
Avonne
b. 1944 Rannaridh,
Norodom, Prince
b. 1947 Hill, Calvin
b. 1949 Durang,
Christopher Ferdinand
b. 1964 Whitaker,
Pernell
b. 1968 Gooding, Cuba,
Jr.
b. 1969 Turlington,
Christy
d. 17 Ovid
d. 1783 Bodmer, Johann
Jakob
d. 1801 Lavater, Johann
Casper
d. 1850 Peel, Robert,
Sir
d. 1861 Frederick
William, IV
d. 1879 Cushing, Caleb
d. 1887 Newberry, John
Stoughton
d. 1891 Kinglake,
Alexander William
d. 1892 Airy, George
Biddell, Sir
d. 1892 Meigs,
Montgomery
Cunningham
d. 1904 Longstreet,
James
d. 1913 Teisserenc de
Bort, Leon-Philippe
d. 1915 Goldmark, Karl
d. 1916 Lamar, Joseph
Rucker
d. 1917 Tylor, Edward
Bennett, Sir
d. 1920 Adam, Paul
d. 1920 Powell, Maud
d. 1924 Baring-Gould,
Sabine
d. 1928 Fuller, Loie
d. 1928 Stevens, Emily
A
d. 1940 Casey, Edward
Pearce
d. 1946 Rathbone,
Eleanor
d. 1952 Davidson, Jo
d. 1962 Dye, Babe
d. 1963 Carson, Jack
d. 1963 Powell, Dick

d. 1966 Millikan, Clark
Blanchard
d. 1966 Wilkins, Ernest
Hatch
d. 1969 Miller, Gilbert
Heron
d. 1971 Hall, Lloyd
Augustus
d. 1971 Knox,
E(dmund) G(eorge)
V(alpy)
d. 1972 Gilbreth, Lillian
Moller
d. 1974 Bohlen, Charles
Eustis
d. 1974 Cord, E(rret)
L(obban)
d. 1974 Ritter, Tex
d. 1977 Garner, Erroll
d. 1981 Keener,
Jefferson Ward
d. 1981 Lynch, David
d. 1981 Watts, Richard,
Jr.
d. 1982 Hampton, Hope
d. 1982 Harman, Fred
d. 1983 Seiler, James,
W
d. 1985 Cushman,
Robert Everton, Jr.
d. 1986 Gaines,
Clarence F
d. 1986 Gunn, Hartford
Nelson, Jr.
d. 1986 Veeck, Bill
d. 1990 Hale, Alan, Jr.
d. 1990 Reifel, Ben
d. 1992 Field, Virginia
(Margaret Cynthia St.
John)
d. 1994 Ray, Dixy Lee
d. 1994 Schweitzer,
Pierre-Paul
d. 1995 Kelly, Nancy
d. 1995 Siad Barre,
Mohamed
d. 1998 Moody, Helen
Wills
d. 1999 Liebermann,
Rolf
d. 2000 O'Brian, Patrick
d. 2000 Zumwalt, Elmo
R(ussell), Jr.

January 3
b. 106BC Cicero,
Marcus Tullius
b. 1698 Metastasio,
Pietro
b. 1793 Mott, Lucretia
Coffin
b. 1797 Vestris, Lucia
Elizabeth, Madame
b. 1806 Sontag,
Henriette
b. 1831 Fenn, George
Manville
b. 1840 Damien, Father
b. 1840 Holt, Henry
b. 1867 Lytton, Henry
Alfred, Sir
b. 1870 Richardson,
Henry Handel
b. 1876 Pieck, Wilhelm
b. 1879 Coolidge, Grace
(Anne Goodhue)
b. 1883 Adler, David

b. 1883 Attlee, Clement
Richard Attlee, Earl
b. 1884 Hull, Josephine
b. 1886 Fletcher, John
Gould
b. 1887 Macke, August
b. 1888 Bridie, James
b. 1888 Morrison of
Lambeth, Herbert
Stanley Morrison,
Baron
b. 1892 Tolkien, J(ohn)
R(onald) R(euel)
b. 1893 Seldes, Gilbert
Vivian
b. 1897 Davies, Marion
b. 1898 Loder, John
b. 1898 Ryan, T(ubal)
Claude
b. 1900 Arzner, Dorothy
b. 1900 Pitts, Zasu
b. 1900 Russell, Donald
Joseph
b. 1901 Ngo-Dinh-Diem
b. 1901 Voegelin, Eric
(Herman Wilhelm)
b. 1905 Milland,
Ray(mond Alton)
b. 1907 Wong, Anna
May (Lu Tsong)
b. 1909 Borge, Victor
b. 1909 Crankshaw,
Edward
b. 1911 Hazam, Lou(is
J)
b. 1911 Rauh, Joseph
Louis, Jr.
b. 1913 Chute, Beatrice
Joy
b. 1914 Bodard, Lucien
(Albert)
b. 1915 Dempsey, John
Noel
b. 1915 Levine, Jack
b. 1916 Furness, Betty
b. 1916 King, Warren
Thomas
b. 1916 Rice, Gregory
b. 1917 Straus, Roger
W(illiams), Jr.
b. 1917 Walters, Vernon
Anthony
b. 1918 Andrews,
Maxene
b. 1919 White, Jesse
b. 1922 Travers, Bill
b. 1926 Anglund, Joan
Walsh
b. 1926 Blumenthal, W
Michael
b. 1926 Martin, George
b. 1929 Leone, Sergio
b. 1932 Coleman,
Dabney W
b. 1932 Fenten, D X
b. 1934 Hills, Carla
Anderson
b. 1935 Fuller, Millard
(Dean)
b. 1936 Einhorn, Eddie
b. 1936 Rollin, Betty
b. 1936 Ruppe, Loret
Miller
b. 1939 Hull, Bobby
b. 1944 Lacey, Robert
b. 1945 Stills, Stephen

b. 1946 Jones, John
Paul
b. 1950 Cannon, Katie
b. 1950 Principal,
Victoria
b. 1956 Gibson, Mel
b. 1956 Ribbs, Willy T
b. 1958 Morial, Marc
(Haydel)
b. 1961 Vanity
b. 1969 Carter, James
d. 1437 Catherine of
Valois
d. 1543 Cabrillo, Juan
Rodriguez
d. 1641 Horrocks,
Jeremiah
d. 1670 Monck, George,
1st Duke of
Albemarle
d. 1705 Giordano, Luca
d. 1784 Galuppi,
Baldassare
d. 1795 Wedgwood,
Josiah
d. 1858 Darcy, Henri
Philibert Gaspard
d. 1858 Rachel
d. 1875 Larousse, Pierre
Athanase
d. 1882 Ainsworth,
W(illiam) H(arrison)
d. 1894 Peabody,
Elizabeth Palmer
d. 1895 Ives, James
Merritt
d. 1912 Evans, Robley
Dunglison
d. 1916 Dodge,
Grenville Mellen
d. 1919 Duveneck,
Frank
d. 1923 Hasek, Jaroslav
d. 1930 Briggs, Clare A
d. 1933 Pickford, Jack
d. 1941 Bergson, Henri
Louis
d. 1945 Cayce, Edgar
d. 1945 Stone, George
Robert
d. 1946 Joyce, William
d. 1947 Reid, Ogden
Mills
d. 1949 Aitken, Robert
d. 1950 Jannings, Emil
d. 1951 Howell, Albert
S
d. 1956 Gretchaninov,
Aleksandr
Tikhonovich
d. 1959 Muir, Edwin
d. 1960 Everleigh, Ada
d. 1960 Sjostrom,
Victor
d. 1960 Spry, Constance
d. 1965 Avery, Milton
Clark
d. 1966 Higgins,
Marguerite
d. 1967 Ruby, Jack
d. 1970 Aylward,
Gladys May
d. 1972 Wilson, Charles
Edward
d. 1974 Daley, Arthur
(John)

d. 1975 Cross, Milton
John
d. 1979 Hilton, Conrad
Nicholson
d. 1980 Adamson, Joy
Friederike Victoria
Gessner
d. 1981 Alice
d. 1982 Canham, Erwin
Dain
d. 1983 Bond, George
Foote
d. 1987 Martin, John
Bartlow
d. 1987 Poage,
W(illiam) R(obert)
d. 1988 Brayman,
Harold
d. 1988 Eyskens,
Gaston, Viscount
d. 1990 Gold, Arthur
d. 1991 Appling, Luke
d. 1992 Anderson,
Judith, Dame
d. 1993 Most, Johnny
d. 1999 Quarry, Jerry

January 4
b. 1581 Ussher, James
b. 1679 Wolcott, Roger
b. 1710 Pergolesi,
Giovanni Battista
b. 1778 Buel, Jesse
b. 1785 Grimm, Jakob
Ludwig Karl
b. 1789 Lundy,
Benjamin
b. 1809 Braille, Louis
b. 1813 Bonaparte,
Louis Lucien
b. 1813 Pitman, Isaac
b. 1831 Dutton,
E(dward) P(ayson)
b. 1838 Tom Thumb,
General
b. 1855 Brann, William
Cowper
b. 1858 Glass, Carter
b. 1870 Pitt, Percy
b. 1874 Suk, Josef
b. 1877 Hartley,
Marsden
b. 1878 Coppard,
A(lfred) E(dgar)
b. 1878 John, Augustus
Edwin
b. 1881 Lehmbruck,
Wilhelm
b. 1881 Merola,
Gaetano
b. 1883 Eastman, Max
Forrester
b. 1884 DuBois, Guy
Pene
b. 1887 Witte, Edwin
Emil
b. 1894 Woody, Regina
Llewellyn Jones
b. 1895 Grumman,
Leroy Randle
b. 1896 Dirksen, Everett
McKinley
b. 1896 Masson, Andre
(Aime Rene)
b. 1900 Bond, James
b. 1901 Berger, Raoul

b. 1902 McCone, John Alex
b. 1905 Holloway, Sterling Price
b. 1908 Columbo, Russ
b. 1910 Crawford, James Strickland
b. 1910 Paul, Gabe
b. 1912 Helmore, Tom
b. 1914 Wyman, Jane
b. 1920 Colby, William E(gan)
b. 1922 Battelle, Phyllis Marie
b. 1925 Lujack, John(ny)
b. 1927 Cavazos, Lauro F(red, Jr.)
b. 1929 Etzioni, Amitai Werner
b. 1929 Rush, Barbara
b. 1930 Booke, Sorrell
b. 1930 McMahon, Don(ald John)
b. 1930 Shula, Don(ald Francis)
b. 1932 Saura (Atares), Carlos
b. 1933 Bangerter, Norman Howard
b. 1935 Patterson, Floyd
b. 1937 Bumbry, Grace Ann Jaeckel
b. 1937 Cannon, Dyan
b. 1940 Josephson, Brian David
b. 1941 Reagan, Maureen Elizabeth
b. 1942 McLaughlin, John
b. 1943 Kearns, Doris H
b. 1946 Barrett, Syd
b. 1951 Cochran, Barbara Ann
b. 1952 Wallace, Michele Faith
b. 1960 Stipe, Michael
b. 1965 Ormond, Julia (Karin)
d. 1761 Hales, Stephen
d. 1782 Gabriel, Ange-Jacques
d. 1786 Mendelssohn, Moses
d. 1789 Nelson, Thomas, Jr.
d. 1821 Seton, Elizabeth Ann Bayley, Saint
d. 1856 David d'Angers
d. 1877 Vanderbilt, Cornelius
d. 1882 Draper, John William
d. 1891 Keene, Charles Samuel
d. 1905 Thomas, Theodore
d. 1908 Young, Charles Augustus
d. 1911 Ray, Charlotte E.
d. 1913 Schlieffen, Alfred, Graf von
d. 1914 Mitchell, Silas Weir

d. 1920 Perez Galdos, Benito
d. 1926 Mahoney, Mary Eliza
d. 1931 Connor, Roger
d. 1942 Skinner, Otis
d. 1956 Damon, Ralph Shepard
d. 1958 Alexander, Archie Alphonso
d. 1960 Camus, Albert
d. 1960 French, Albert
d. 1961 Fitzgerald, Barry
d. 1961 Schroedinger, Erwin
d. 1964 Dumke, Ralph
d. 1965 Eliot, T(homas) S(tearns)
d. 1967 Campbell, Donald Malcolm
d. 1967 Garden, Mary
d. 1969 Chambers, Paul
d. 1969 Hilton, Daisy
d. 1969 Hilton, Violet
d. 1974 Starrett, Vincent
d. 1975 Montana, Bob
d. 1976 Leventhal, Albert Rice
d. 1979 Bennett, Harry Herbert
d. 1981 Rabin, Yehuda L
d. 1982 Banning, Margaret Culkin
d. 1983 Rosenthal, Benjamin Stanley
d. 1984 Geschwind, Norman
d. 1986 Isherwood, Christopher (William)
d. 1986 Lynott, Phil(ip)
d. 1986 Merkel, Una
d. 1987 Bacon, Peggy
d. 1990 Edgerton, Harold Eugene
d. 1990 Lleras Camargo, Alberto
d. 1990 Ussachevsky, Vladimir Alexis
d. 1991 Matthews, T(homas) S(tanley)
d. 1995 Tax, Sol
d. 1996 Graham, Wallace H(arry)
d. 1997 Helmsley, Harry B(rakmann)
d. 1998 Gary, John
d. 1999 Cody, Iron Eyes

January 5
b. 1548 Suarez, Francisco
b. 1592 Shah Jahan
b. 1767 Say, Jean Baptiste
b. 1779 Decatur, Stephen
b. 1794 Ruffin, Edmund
b. 1846 Eucken, Rudolf Christoph
b. 1855 Gillette, King Camp
b. 1864 Carver, George Washington

b. 1864 Hodge, Frederick Webb
b. 1869 Jones, Matilda Sissieretta Joyner
b. 1871 Converse, Frederick Shepherd
b. 1874 Erlanger, Joseph
b. 1875 Blackton, James Stuart
b. 1876 Adenauer, Konrad
b. 1877 Coffin, Henry Sloane
b. 1879 Norworth, Jack
b. 1880 Sachse, Leopold
b. 1882 Swope, Herbert Bayard
b. 1887 Hodges, Courtney
b. 1890 Kauff, Benny
b. 1893 Yogananda, Paramahansa, Swami
b. 1895 Piccard, Jeannette Ridlon
b. 1897 Jessup, Philip Caryl
b. 1900 Tanguy, Yves
b. 1901 Wickens, Aryness Joy
b. 1902 Beuve-Mery, Hubert
b. 1902 Gibbons, Stella (Dorothea)
b. 1903 Gianninoto, Frank Anthony
b. 1904 Morini, Erica
b. 1906 Davison, Wild Bill
b. 1907 Marsala, Joe
b. 1909 Aumont, Jean-Pierre
b. 1909 Kurnitz, Harry
b. 1910 Brannum, Hugh
b. 1913 Wilson, Kemmons
b. 1914 Stael, Nicolas de
b. 1915 Robinson, Arthur H(oward)
b. 1917 Wagner, Wieland Adolf Gottfried
b. 1918 Dixon, Jeane (Pinckert)
b. 1919 Gazzelloni, Severino
b. 1919 Ryder, Alfred
b. 1920 Michelangeli, Arturo Benedetti
b. 1920 Wingler, Hans Maria
b. 1921 Durrenmatt, Friedrich
b. 1921 Jean, Prince
b. 1923 Bernstein, Robert L(ouis)
b. 1923 Phillips, Sam
b. 1925 Opel, John Roberts
b. 1926 Schell, Maria Margarethe
b. 1926 Snodgrass, W(illiam) D(eWitt)
b. 1926 Williams, Hosea Lorenzo

b. 1928 Bhutto, Zulfikar Ali
b. 1928 Mondale, Walter F(rederick)
b. 1931 Ailey, Alvin
b. 1931 Brendel, Alfred
b. 1931 Davis, Walter
b. 1931 Duvall, Robert (Selden)
b. 1932 Eco, Umberto
b. 1932 Gorbachev, Raisa (Maksimovna Titorenko)
b. 1932 Layden, Frank
b. 1932 Noll, Chuck
b. 1938 Agee, William McReynolds
b. 1938 Juan Carlos I
b. 1938 Ngugi, James Thiong'o
b. 1938 Otto, Jim
b. 1940 O'Donoghue, Michael
b. 1941 McKinley, Chuck
b. 1942 Lacalle (Herrera), Luis Alberto
b. 1942 Rose, Charlie
b. 1942 Wilding, Michael
b. 1944 McCarthy, Carolyn
b. 1946 Keaton, Diane
b. 1947 DeWine, Mike
b. 1947 Lange, Ted
b. 1947 Morris, Mercury
b. 1947 Switzer, Katherine Virginia
b. 1949 Brown, George
b. 1954 English, Alex(ander)
b. 1954 Martin, Pamela Sue
b. 1958 Kittle, Ron(ald Dale)
b. 1960 Kerr, Tim(othy)
d. 1066 Edward the Confessor
d. 1589 Catherine de Medici
d. 1796 Huntington, Samuel
d. 1860 Neumann, John Nepomucene, Saint
d. 1867 Smith, Alexander
d. 1886 Lippincott, Joshua Ballinger
d. 1922 Shackleton, Ernest Henry, Sir
d. 1933 Coolidge, Calvin
d. 1939 Haley, Margaret A(ngela)
d. 1941 Johnson, Amy
d. 1943 Carver, George Washington
d. 1947 Nagano, Osami
d. 1948 Harrison, Mary Scott Lord Dimmick
d. 1954 Maranville, Rabbit
d. 1954 Scott, Walter

d. 1956 LaFarge,
Christopher
d. 1956 Mistinguett
d. 1963 Hornsby,
Rogers
d. 1969 Yablonski,
Joseph
d. 1970 Born, Max
d. 1971 Shearer,
Douglas
d. 1974 Brogan, Denis
William, Sir
d. 1975 Levi, Carlo
d. 1976 Costello, John
Aloysius
d. 1977 Stevens,
Onslow
d. 1979 Mingus, Charles
d. 1981 Martin, James,
Sir
d. 1982 Conreid, Hans
d. 1982 Lembeck,
Harvey
d. 1987 Laurence,
Margaret
d. 1987 Pantaleoni,
Helenka (Tradeusa
Adamowski)
d. 1988 Laskin, Lily
d. 1988 Maravich,
Pete(r Press)
d. 1989 Lawe, John
Edward
d. 1990 Kennedy,
Arthur
d. 1993 Bode, Carl
d. 1994 O'Neill,
Thomas P(hilip), Jr.
d. 1994 Scribner, Fred
C(lark), Jr.
d. 1996 Kirstein,
Lincoln (Edward)
d. 1997 Lane, Burton
d. 1998 Bono, Sonny

January 6
b. 1256 Gertrude the
Great, Saint
b. 1367 Richard II
b. 1412 Joan of Arc,
Saint
b. 1730 Chittenden,
Thomas
b. 1795 Payen, Anselme
b. 1799? Smith,
Jedediah Strong
b. 1811 Sumner,
Charles
b. 1822 Schliemann,
Heinrich
b. 1832 Dore, Gustave
b. 1838 Bruch, Max
b. 1842 King, Clarence
b. 1843 Spooner, John
Coit
b. 1845 Lee-Hamilton,
Eugene Jacob
b. 1848 Gonzalez Prada,
Manuel
b. 1850 Bernstein,
Eduard
b. 1859 Alexander,
Samuel
b. 1869 Wagner,
Siegfried (Helferich)

b. 1872 Scriabin,
Alexander
Nicholaevich
b. 1874 Niblo, Fred
b. 1878 Sandburg, Carl
(August)
b. 1879 Patterson,
Joseph Medill
b. 1880 Mix, Tom
b. 1882 Pecora,
Ferdinand
b. 1882 Rayburn,
Sam(uel Taliaferro)
b. 1883 Gibran, Kahlil
b. 1887 Kelly, George
Edward
b. 1889 Craven, Thomas
b. 1896 Pritzker, Abram
Nicholas
b. 1900 Hulme, Kathryn
Cavarly
b. 1903 Abravanel,
Maurice
b. 1903 Sullivan,
Francis Loftus
b. 1905 Wilson, Edward
Foss
b. 1908 DiSalle,
Michael Vincent
b. 1910 Kid Chocolate
b. 1910 Morris, Wright
Marion
b. 1911 Adams, Joey
b. 1912 Manfred,
Frederick Feikema
b. 1913 Brown, Tom
b. 1913 Gierek, Edward
b. 1913 Young, Loretta
Gretchen
b. 1914 Reeves, George
b. 1914 Thomas, Danny
b. 1915 Lilly, John C
b. 1915 Watts, Alan
Wilson
b. 1916 Maleska,
Eugene T.
b. 1917 Jumblatt, Kamal
Fouad
b. 1919 Cleaver, Vera
Allen
b. 1920 Cabral de Melo
Neto, Joao
b. 1920 Moon, Sung
Myung
b. 1920 Wynn, Early
b. 1921 Harris, Louis
b. 1921 Middlecoff,
Cary
b. 1923 Timerman,
Jacobo
b. 1924 Kim Dae Jung
b. 1924 Rubenstein,
Richard L(owell)
b. 1924 Scruggs, Earl
Eugene
b. 1925 DeLorean, John
Zachary
b. 1926 Branca, Ralph
Theodore Joseph
b. 1926 Gault, Stanley
Carleton
b. 1926 Gavilan, Kid
b. 1928 Behn, Noel
b. 1929 Hamilton, Joe
b. 1929 Karmal, Babrak
b. 1929 Tayback, Vic

b. 1930 Keniston,
Kenneth
b. 1931 Doctorow,
E(dgar) L(aurence)
b. 1931 Moore, Dickie
b. 1935 Capucine
b. 1936 Sanguinetti,
Julio Maria
b. 1937 Holkeri, Harri
(Hermanni)
b. 1937 Holtz, Lou(is
Leo)
b. 1939 Rose, Murray
b. 1944 Franklin,
Bonnie Gail
b. 1944 Kravis, Henry
R
b. 1944 McCoy, Van
b. 1945 Freeman, Seth
b. 1945 Lopez, Barry
(Holstun)
b. 1950 Freeh, Louis
J(oseph)
b. 1953 Young,
Malcolm
b. 1957 Lopez, Nancy
Marie
b. 1959 Sledge, Kathy
b. 1960 Azinger, Paul
b. 1968 Singleton, John
(Daniel)
d. 1542 Orley, Bernard
van
d. 1616 Henslowe,
Philip
d. 1725 Chikamatsu,
Monzaemon
d. 1785 Salomon, Haym
d. 1809 Eberhard,
Johann August
d. 1831 Kreutzer,
Rodolphe
d. 1840 Burney, Fanny
d. 1849 Coleridge,
Hartley
d. 1855 Wood, Sarah
Sayward Barrell
Keating
d. 1882 Dana, Richard
Henry, Jr.
d. 1884 Mendel, Gregor
Johann
d. 1901 Armour, Philip
Danforth
d. 1906 Krauss,
Gabrielle
d. 1909 Dixon, George
d. 1918 Cantor, Georg
Ferdinand Ludwig
Philipp
d. 1919 Roosevelt,
Theodore
d. 1928 Kraenzlein,
Alvin C
d. 1932 Rosenwald,
Julius
d. 1939 Kelly, Walter C
d. 1942 Calve, Emma
d. 1942 Flannagan, John
Bernard
d. 1943 Lowell, Abbott
Lawrence
d. 1944 Tarbell, Ida
Minerva
d. 1946 Summerville,
Slim

d. 1949 Fleming, Victor
d. 1950 Bowman, Isaiah
d. 1950 Brady, William
Aloysius
d. 1953 Fuller, Solomon
Carter, Jr.
d. 1959 Cohen, Octavus
Roy
d. 1963 Vandercook,
John Womack
d. 1963 Young, Stark
d. 1966 Lurcat, Jean
Marie
d. 1972 Chen Yi
d. 1972 Pully, B S
d. 1974 Siqueiros,
David A
d. 1975 Wheeler,
Burton Kendall
d. 1977 Gropper,
William
d. 1978 Gordon, John F
d. 1978 MacArthur,
John Donald
d. 1981 Cronin,
A(rchibald) J(oseph)
d. 1981 Neal, Larry
d. 1981 Urey, Harold
Clayton
d. 1982 Crawford,
William Hulfish
d. 1985 Horrocks, Brian
Gwynne, Sir
d. 1985 Welch, Robert
Henry Winborne, Jr.
d. 1988? Engellau,
Gunnar Ludwig
d. 1988 Haviland,
Virginia
d. 1989 Koontz,
Elizabeth Duncan
d. 1990 Charleson, Ian
d. 1990 Cherenkov,
Pavel Alekseyevich
d. 1993 Gillespie, Dizzy
d. 1993 Nureyev,
Rudolf (Hametovich)
d. 1994 Kelley, Virginia
d. 1995 Slovo, Joe
d. 1996 Gillette, Paul
d. 1996 Hanson, Duane
(Elwood)
d. 1996 Johnston,
Johnny
d. 2000 Chapman,
Leonard F., Jr.

January 7
b. 1718 Putnam, Israel
b. 1745 Montgolfier,
Jacques Etienne
b. 1768 Bonaparte,
Joseph
b. 1794 Mitscherlich,
Eilhardt
b. 1800 Beach, Moses
Yale
b. 1800 Fillmore,
Millard
b. 1827 Fleming,
Sandford
b. 1829 Angell, James
Burrill
b. 1830 Bierstadt,
Albert
b. 1832 Talmadge,
Thomas de Witt

b. 1844 Bernadette of
Lourdes, Saint
b. 1858 Ben-Yehuda,
Eliezer
b. 1863 Lloyd George
of Dwyfor, David
Lloyd George Earl
b. 1867 Maginnis,
Charles Donagh
b. 1871 Horder, Thomas
Jeeves
b. 1873 Zukor, Adolph
b. 1880 Rollins, Carl
Purington
b. 1881 Gest, Morris
b. 1883 Cunningham,
Andrew Browne,
Viscount
b. 1884 Giovannitti,
Arturo
b. 1893 Wayman,
Dorothy
b. 1899 Lee, J(oseph)
Bracken
b. 1899 Poulenc,
Francis
b. 1901 Brownlee, John
b. 1901 Page, Irvine H
b. 1901 Schwarzhaupt,
Elisabeth
b. 1903 Hurston, Zora
Neale
b. 1903 Pauley, Edwin
Wendell
b. 1905 Dent, Alan
Holmes
b. 1905 Smith, Hooley
b. 1907 Zabaleta,
Nicanor
b. 1908 Allen, Red
b. 1908 Gibberd,
Frederick, Sir
b. 1910 Faubus, Orval
E(ugene)
b. 1910 Rothschild,
Alain de, Baron
b. 1911 Baker, Laura
Nelson
b. 1911 McQueen,
Butterfly
b. 1911 Thompson,
Vivian Laubach
b. 1912 Addams,
Charles Samuel
b. 1912 Bundy, Robert
F.
b. 1913 Mize, Johnny
b. 1916 Estes, E(lliott)
M(arantette)
b. 1916 Estes, Pete
b. 1916 Pratt, Babe
b. 1917 Kay, Ulysses
Simpson
b. 1918 Lasky, Victor
b. 1919 Brown, Dorothy
Lavinia
b. 1919 Duncan, Robert
Edward
b. 1921 Loloma,
Charles
b. 1922 Gardenia,
Vincent
b. 1922 Rampal, Jean-
Pierre
b. 1923 Dark, Alvin
Ralph

b. 1925 Durrell, Gerald
(Malcolm)
b. 1926 Kirk, Claude
Roy, Jr.
b. 1928 Blatty, William
Peter
b. 1928 Snow, Clyde
Collins
b. 1930 Kiker, Douglas
b. 1931 Mattingly,
Mack Francis
b. 1933 Kneip, Richard
F
b. 1934 Forbes, Jack
D(ouglas)
b. 1934 Murphy, Reg
b. 1935 Kubasov,
Valery Nikolaevich
b. 1936 Davies, Hunter
b. 1938 Graham, Lou
b. 1938 Watkins,
Shirley R.
b. 1939 Povich, Maury
b. 1940 Berkow, Ira
Harvey
b. 1941 Gregory,
Frederick D(rew)
b. 1942 Alekseyev,
Vasily Ivanovich
b. 1945 Conigliaro,
Tony
b. 1946 Wenner, Jann
b. 1948 Loggins, Kenny
b. 1956 Liut, Mike
b. 1957 Baker,
Nicholson
b. 1957 Couric, Katie
b. 1957 Janaszak, Steve
b. 1964 Cage, Nicolas
d. 1536 Catherine of
Aragon
d. 1619 Hilliard,
Nicholas
d. 1658 Eaton,
Theophilus
d. 1715 Fenelon,
Francois de Salignac
d. 1758 Ramsay, Allan
d. 1830 Lawrence,
Thomas, Sir
d. 1872 Fisk, Jim
d. 1887 Stanton, Henry
Brewster
d. 1920 Barton, Edmund
d. 1926 Mueller,
Christian F
d. 1927 Stanton, Frank
Lebby
d. 1931 Channing,
Edward Perkins
d. 1932 Maginot, Andre
Louis Rene
d. 1943 Crile, George
Washington
d. 1943 Tesla, Nikola
d. 1944 Hoover, Lou
Henry
d. 1947 Dodge, Henry
Chee
d. 1950 Banks, Monty
d. 1953 Johnson, Osa
Helen Leighty
d. 1955 Keith, Arthur
d. 1956 Tucker, Preston
Thomas

d. 1958 Anglin,
Margaret Mary
d. 1971 Kollmar,
Richard
d. 1972 Berryman, John
d. 1975 Abercrombie,
James Smither
d. 1977 Stuckey,
Williamson Sylvester
d. 1978 Flanner, Janet
d. 1983 Coates, Edith
d. 1983 Hanks, Nancy
d. 1984 Case, Anna
d. 1984 Hunt, Jack
Reed
d. 1984 Kastler, Alfred
d. 1985 Guarnieri,
Johnny
d. 1985 Lyons, Eugene
d. 1985 Oursler,
Will(iam Charles)
d. 1986 Rulfo, Juan
d. 1988 Howard, Trevor
Wallace
d. 1989 Hirohito
d. 1990 Nagurski,
Bronko
d. 1990 Robbie, Joe
d. 1990 Stoneham,
Horace
d. 1996 Gronouski, John
A(ustin)
d. 1996 Grosz, Karoly
d. 1998 Prelog,
Vladimir
d. 1998 Treat, Lawrence

January 8
b. 1587 Coen, Jan
Pieterszoon
b. 1626 Talon, Jean
b. 1632 Pufendorf,
Samuel von
b. 1735 Carroll, John
b. 1763 Genet, Edmond
Charles Edouard
b. 1786 Biddle,
Nicholas
b. 1792 Mason, Lowell
b. 1821 Longstreet,
James
b. 1823 Wallace, Alfred
Russell
b. 1824 Collins, Wilkie
b. 1830 Bulow, Hans
Guido von
b. 1836 Alma-Tadema,
Lawrence, Sir
b. 1859 Palamas, Kostes
b. 1860 Katayama, Sen
b. 1862 Doubleday,
Frank Nelson
b. 1864 Johnson, Ban
b. 1867 Balch, Emily G
b. 1868 Dyson, Frank
Watson, Sir
b. 1869 Genthe, Arnold
b. 1870 Holmes, Burton
b. 1870 Primo de
Rivera (y Orbaneja),
Miguel
b. 1881 Neihardt, John
Gneisenau
b. 1881 Piper, William
Thomas
b. 1882 Milne, David
Brown

b. 1883 Hurley, Patrick
Jay
b. 1885 Curtin, John
Joseph
b. 1885 Muste,
A(braham) J(ohannes)
b. 1888 Courant,
Richard
b. 1890 Clark, Bennett
Champ
b. 1891 Kiplinger,
W(illard) M(onroe)
b. 1891 Nijinska,
Bronislava
b. 1892 O'Connor, Basil
b. 1893 Kindler, Hans
b. 1894 Kolbe,
Maximilian Maria,
Saint
b. 1896 Weinberger,
Jaromir
b. 1899 Adams,
Sherman Llewellyn
b. 1899 Bandaranaike,
S(olomon) W(est)
R(idgeway) D(ias)
b. 1901 Malenkov,
Georgi
Maximilianovich
b. 1902 Rogers, Carl
Ransom
b. 1902 Smith, Kenneth
Danforth
b. 1904 Arno, Peter
b. 1908 Frankau,
Pamela
b. 1911 Hadley, Reed
b. 1911 Watt, George
Willard
b. 1912 Ferrer, Jose
Vicente
b. 1912 Walsh,
Lawrence E
b. 1914 Watson,
Thomas J(ohn), Jr.
b. 1915 Apps, Syl
b. 1915 Cooper, Walker
b. 1917 Riad, Mahmoud
b. 1917 Taylor, Peter
(Hillsman)
b. 1920 Preus, Jacob
A(all) O(ttesen)
b. 1923 Storch, Larry
b. 1923 Tozzi, Giorgio
b. 1924 Moody, Ron
b. 1926 Geschwind,
Norman
b. 1926 Mori, Hanae
b. 1928 Gorton, Slade
b. 1928 Vanocur,
Sander
b. 1930 Sales, Soupy
b. 1931 Graham, Bill
b. 1933 Osgood,
Charles
b. 1934 Ripley,
Alexandra
b. 1935 Lapham, Lewis
Henry
b. 1935 Presley, Elvis
Aaron
b. 1937 Bassey, Shirley
b. 1939 Herrera,
Carolina
b. 1939 Mimieux,
Yvette Carmen M

b. 1940 Hampton, Henry
b. 1941 Chapman, Graham
b. 1942 Hawking, Stephen William
b. 1943 Berresford, Susan Vail
b. 1943 Murray, Charles Alan
b. 1946 Krieger, Robby
b. 1947 Bowie, David
b. 1948 Troutt, Kenny A.
b. 1949 Puck, Wolfgang
b. 1951 Anthony, Kenny
b. 1952 Feltsman, Vladimir
b. 1953 Stastny, Marian
b. 1953 Sutter, Bruce
b. 1955 Reno, Mike
b. 1968 Kelly, R(obert)
d. 1337 Giotto di Bondone
d. 1642 Galileo
d. 1713 Corelli, Arcangelo
d. 1775 Baskerville, John
d. 1825 Whitney, Eli
d. 1890 McArthur, John
d. 1892 Rodgers, Christopher Raymond Perry
d. 1896 Verlaine, Paul (Marie)
d. 1914 Buckner, Simon Bolivar
d. 1916 Rehan, Ada
d. 1919 O'Rourke, Jim
d. 1925 Bellows, George Wesley
d. 1929 Duke, Benjamin Newton
d. 1934 Bely, Andrey
d. 1934 Stavisky, Serge Alexandre
d. 1941 Baden-Powell, Robert Stephenson Smyth Baden-Powell, Baron
d. 1948 Schwitters, Kurt (Hermann Edward Karl Julius)
d. 1948 Tauber, Richard
d. 1950 Schumpeter, Joseph Alois
d. 1952 Maury, Antonia Caetana De Paiua Pereira
d. 1956 Pickard, Greenleaf Whittier
d. 1960 Haynes, George Edmund
d. 1961 Rowe, Schoolboy
d. 1965 Onions, Charles Talbut
d. 1967 Heim, Jacques
d. 1968 Van Paassen, Pierre
d. 1972 Patchen, Kenneth
d. 1975 Gregson, John
d. 1975 Tucker, Richard

d. 1976 Chou En-Lai
d. 1978 Kiernan, Walter
d. 1978 Ross, Roy G
d. 1980 Mauchly, John William
d. 1981 Beard, Matthew, Jr.
d. 1981 Jagendorf, Moritz Adolf
d. 1983 McCall, Thomas Lawson
d. 1986 Fournier, Pierre
d. 1988 Eiseman, Florence
d. 1988 Pace, Frank, Jr.
d. 1990 Terry-Thomas
d. 1991 Clark, Steve
d. 1994 Blackton, Jay S
d. 1994 Buttram, Pat
d. 1996 Mitterrand, Francois (Maurice Marie)
d. 1996 Taubman, (Hyman) Howard
d. 1997 Calvin, Melvin
d. 1998 Diemer, Walter
d. 1998 Tippett, Michael Kemp, Sir

January 9
b. 1554 Gregory XV
b. 1590 Vouet, Simon
b. 1674 Keiser, Reinhard
b. 1724 Backus, Isaac
b. 1728 Warton, Thomas
b. 1781 Shaw, Lemuel
b. 1797 Wrangel, Ferdinand Petrovich, Baron
b. 1803 Memminger, Christopher Gustavus
b. 1819 Frith, William Powell
b. 1837 Chesebrough, Robert Augustus
b. 1839 Paine, John Knowles
b. 1854 Churchill, Jennie Jerome
b. 1856 Reese, Lizette Woodworth
b. 1857 Fuller, Henry Blake
b. 1859 Catt, Carrie Chapman
b. 1864 Roebuck, Alvah Curtis
b. 1870 Strauss, Joseph Baermann
b. 1873 Bialik, Chaim Nachman
b. 1876 Michels, Robert
b. 1878 Watson, John Broadus
b. 1881 Abercrombie, Lascelles
b. 1881 Papini, Giovanni
b. 1886 Brooks, Walter R(ollin)
b. 1886 Guthrie, Edwin Ray
b. 1886 Holt, Ivan Lee
b. 1886 Rosenthal, Ida Cohen

b. 1890 Capek, Karel
b. 1891 Stone, Grace Zaring
b. 1894 Markel, Lester
b. 1895 Farr, Wanda K.
b. 1897 Gautier, Felisa Rincon de
b. 1898 Fields, Gracie
b. 1900 Halliburton, Richard
b. 1901 Young, Chic
b. 1902 Bing, Rudolf (Franz Josef), Sir
b. 1902 Escriva de Balaguer, Josemarie
b. 1903 Banky, Vilma
b. 1908 Beauvoir, Simone de
b. 1908 Trefflich, Henry Herbert Frederick
b. 1909? Miller, Otto Neil
b. 1909 Wood, Evelyn
b. 1910 Hitch, Charles J(ohnston)
b. 1913 Donahue, Woolworth
b. 1913 Nixon, Richard M(ilhous)
b. 1913 Tatum, Donn B
b. 1914 Clarke, Kenny
b. 1915 Mikkelsen, Henning Dahl
b. 1916 Holland, Jerome Heartwell
b. 1917 Lom, Herbert
b. 1917 Louise, Anita
b. 1918 Chaikin, Sol Chick
b. 1922 Khorana, Har Gobind
b. 1922 Toure, Ahmed Sekou
b. 1925 Bloch, Eric
b. 1925 Lamas, Fernando
b. 1925 Van Cleef, Lee
b. 1928 Krantz, Judith
b. 1929 Friel, Brian
b. 1929 Grosbard, Ulu
b. 1929 Matheson, Scott Milne
b. 1930 Sloane, Dennis
b. 1932 Casey, Robert P
b. 1934 Starr, Bart
b. 1935 Denver, Bob
b. 1935 Graves, Earl Gilbert
b. 1937 Epstein, Joseph
b. 1941 Baez, Joan
b. 1941 Hands, Terry
b. 1941 York, Susannah
b. 1943 Moskowitz, J(ay)
b. 1944 Page, Jimmy
b. 1945 Biondi, Frank J., Jr.
b. 1945 Ter-Petrosyan, Levon
b. 1950 Johansen, David
b. 1950 Stein, James R
b. 1951 Gayle, Crystal
b. 1958 Agca, Mehmet Ali
b. 1958 McClanahan, Rob

b. 1965 Bogues, Mugsy
d. 1324 Polo, Marco
d. 1868 Hopkins, John Henry
d. 1872 Halleck, Henry Wager
d. 1873 Napoleon III
d. 1876 Howe, Samuel Gridley
d. 1878 Victor Emmanuel II
d. 1893 Judson, Egbert Putnam
d. 1904 Gordon, John Brown
d. 1908 Busch, Wilhelm
d. 1923 Mansfield, Katherine
d. 1927 Chamberlain, Houston Stewart
d. 1930 Bok, Edward William
d. 1936 Gilbert, John
d. 1938 Gruelle, Johnny
d. 1942 Curtis, Heber Doust
d. 1942 Rutherford, Joseph Franklin
d. 1943 Collingwood, Robin George
d. 1947 Mannheim, Karl
d. 1951 Nethersole, Olga
d. 1954 Braniff, Thomas Elmer
d. 1961 Balch, Emily G
d. 1964 Halide Edip Adivar
d. 1966 Foerster, Friedrich Wilhelm
d. 1967 Frank, Waldo
d. 1971 Flick, Elmer Harrison
d. 1972 Shawn, Ted
d. 1976 Granger, Lester
d. 1976 Taylor, Phoebe Atwood
d. 1979 Merritt, Hiram Houston
d. 1979 Nervi, Pier Luigi
d. 1981 MacTaggart, William, Sir
d. 1982 Lynde, Paul Edward
d. 1982 Musso, Vido
d. 1982 Schilt, Jan
d. 1984 Gibberd, Frederick, Sir
d. 1984 Ward, Deighton Harcourt Lisle, Sir
d. 1985 Mayer, Robert, Sir
d. 1986 Chase, Lucia
d. 1986 Powolny, Frank
d. 1987 Lake, Arthur
d. 1989 Terry, Bill
d. 1990 Chandler, Spud
d. 1993 Gonzalez, Xavier
d. 1995 Cook, Peter
d. 1995 Souphanouvong, Prince
d. 1997 White, Jesse
d. 1998 Fukui, Kenichi

d. 2000 Cony, Edward
Roger
January 10
b. 1638 Steno, Nicolaus
b. 1747 Breguet,
Abraham Louis
b. 1769 Ney, Michel de
la Moskova, Prince
b. 1804 Ames, Oakes
b. 1814 DeVere, Aubrey
Thomas
b. 1820 Drew, Louisa
Lane
b. 1834 Acton, John
Emerich Edward
Dalberg-Acton, Baron
b. 1835 Wright, Harry
b. 1841 Melville,
George Wallace
b. 1843 James, Frank
b. 1847 Schiff, Jacob
Henry
b. 1850 Root, John
Wellborn
b. 1859 U'Ren, William
Simon
b. 1860 Roberts,
Charles George
Douglas, Sir
b. 1873 Christy,
Howard Chandler
b. 1874 Mathiez, Albert
b. 1877 Cottrell,
Frederick Gardner
b. 1880 Azana y Diaz,
Manuel
b. 1880 Bayes, Nora
b. 1880 Grock
b. 1882 Sills, Milton
b. 1883 Bushman,
Francis X(avier)
b. 1883 Tolstoy, Alexey
Nikolaevich
b. 1885 Gifford, Walter
Sherman
b. 1887 Jeffers, (John)
Robinson
b. 1889 Held, John, Jr.
b. 1892 Malone, Dumas
b. 1895 Davis, Meyer
b. 1896 Lockridge,
Frances Louise
b. 1898 Blodgett,
Katherine Burr
b. 1898 Hay, George W
b. 1902 Minsky, Morton
b. 1903 Hepworth,
Barbara, Dame
b. 1903 Roos, Frank
John, Jr.
b. 1904 Bolger,
Ray(mond Wallace)
b. 1904 Burck, Jacob
b. 1908 Henreid, Paul
b. 1908 Lee, Bernard
b. 1910 Allal al-Fassi,
Mohamed
b. 1910 Martinon, Jean
b. 1910 Ulanova, Galina
b. 1911 Kirkpatrick,
Ralph Leonard
b. 1913 Husak, Gustav
b. 1913 Shehu, Mehmet
b. 1915 Dixon, Dean
b. 1916 Bergstrom,
Sune

b. 1916 Hamilton, Bob
b. 1918 Chung, Arthur
b. 1918 McGraw,
Harold Whittlesey, Jr.
b. 1924 Chillida, Eduard
b. 1924 Roach,
Max(well Lemuel)
b. 1927 MacKenzie,
Gisele
b. 1927 Ray, Johnnie
b. 1928 Brooks, Donald
Marc
b. 1928 Levine, Philip
b. 1929 Charlip, Remy
b. 1930 Disney, Roy
E(dward)
b. 1931 Barnes, Peter
b. 1931 Galella, Ron
b. 1931 Sanders,
Marlene
b. 1934 Kravchuk,
Leonid Makarovich
b. 1935 Hawkins,
Ronnie
b. 1935 Milnes, Sherrill
Eustace
b. 1936 Crane, Daniel B
b. 1936 Wilson, Robert
Woodrow
b. 1937 Walinsky,
Adam
b. 1938 Mahovlich,
Frank
b. 1938 McCovey,
Willie Lee
b. 1939 Horowitz,
David Joel
b. 1939 Mineo,
Sal(vatore)
b. 1939 Toomey, Bill
b. 1941 Caputo, Philip
Joseph
b. 1943 Annaud, Jean-
Jacques
b. 1943 Croce, Jim
b. 1944 Cox, Geraldine
V(ang)
b. 1944 Sinatra, Frank,
Jr.
b. 1945 Stewart,
Rod(erick David)
b. 1946 O'Steen, Van
b. 1947 Morris, James
Peppler
b. 1948 Fagen, Donald
b. 1949 Foreman,
George
b. 1952 Benatar, Pat
b. 1961 Salerno-
Sonnenberg, Nadja
b. 1963 Leveille,
Norm(and)
d. 1645 Laud, William
d. 1778 Linnaeus,
Carolus
d. 1785 Stiegel, Henry
William
d. 1833 Legendre,
Adrien Marie
d. 1855 Mitford, Mary
Russell
d. 1862 Colt, Samuel
d. 1863 Beecher, Lyman
d. 1878 Stokes, William
d. 1880 Leslie, Frank

d. 1883 Mudd, Samuel
Alexander
d. 1887 Roach, John
d. 1890 Dollinger,
J(ohannes) J(osef)
I(gnaz) von
d. 1895 Godard,
Benjamin Louis Paul
d. 1904 Gerome, Jean
Leon
d. 1906 Harper, William
Rainey
d. 1908 Spreckels,
Claus
d. 1917 Cody, Buffalo
Bill
d. 1937 Eddy, Clarence
d. 1941 Lavery, John,
Sir
d. 1941 Penner, Joe
d. 1946 Cullen, Countee
(Porter)
d. 1946 VonTilzer,
Harry
d. 1949 Ahearn, Daniel
F.
d. 1950 Poole, Ernest
d. 1951 Lewis, Sinclair
d. 1957 Mistral,
Gabriela
d. 1960 Laviolette, Jack
d. 1961 Hammett,
Dashiell
d. 1967 Burchfield,
Charles Ephraim
d. 1968 Reuther, Roy
d. 1969 Brownlee, John
d. 1969 Lamburn,
Richmal Crompton
d. 1970 Olson, Charles
John
d. 1971 Cacers, Ernest
d. 1971 Chanel, Coco
d. 1972 Gulbenkian,
Nubar Sarkis
d. 1973 Edwards, Turk
d. 1975 Chamberlain,
Samuel
d. 1976 Howlin' Wolf
d. 1978 Braden, Spruille
d. 1978 Gillis, Don
d. 1980 Meany, George
d. 1981 Boone, Richard
d. 1981 Brodie, Fawn
McKay
d. 1984 Souvanna,
Phouma
d. 1986 Kraft, Joseph
d. 1986 Seifert, Jaroslav
d. 1989 Voorhees,
Donald
d. 1993 Adams, Diana
d. 1993 Curtis, Thomas
B(radford)
d. 1993 Gulick, Luther
(Halsey)
d. 1993 Wallace, Phyllis
A(nn)
d. 1994 Aldridge,
Michael
d. 1994 Feeney, Chub
d. 1996 Crozier, Roger
Allan
d. 1997 Huxley, Elspeth
Josceline Grant

d. 1997 Leonard,
Sheldon
d. 1997 Todd,
Alexander (Robertus),
Sir
January 11
b. 346? Thedosius I
b. 938 Scargill, Arthur
b. 1503 Parmigano
b. 1755 Hamilton,
Alexander
b. 1759 Lunardi,
Vincenzo
b. 1801 Kirkland,
Caroline Matilda
Stansbury
b. 1807 Cornell, Ezra
b. 1814 Paget, James,
Sir
b. 1815 MacDonald,
John Alexander
b. 1825 Taylor, Bayard
b. 1836 Wyant,
Alexander Helwig
b. 1839 Hostos (y
Bonilla), Eugenio
Maria de
b. 1839 Simmons,
Franklin
b. 1841 Gierke, Otto
von
b. 1842 James, William
b. 1850 Arthur, Joseph
Charles
b. 1856 Sinding,
Christian
b. 1858 Selfridge, Harry
Gordon
b. 1859 Curzon of
Kedleston, George
Nathaniel Curzon,
Marquis
b. 1865 Dixon, Thomas
b. 1867 Titchener,
Edward Bradford
b. 1870 Rice, Alice
Caldwell Hegan
b. 1871 Eddy,
Sherwood
b. 1872 Pierce, George
Washington
b. 1873 Morrow,
Dwight Whitney
b. 1875 Gliere,
Reinhold Moritsevich
b. 1876 Flick, Elmer
Harrison
b. 1884 Fitch, Aubrey
b. 1885 Paul, Alice
b. 1886 Zucco, George
b. 1888 Conklin,
Chester
b. 1889 Bridges, Calvin
Blackman
b. 1890 Blue, Monte
b. 1890 Carey, Max
George
b. 1893 Pasero,
Tancredi
b. 1894 Ballinger,
Margaret
b. 1895 Hammond,
Laurens
b. 1896 Driscoll, Paddy
b. 1896 Stephenson,
William

b. 1897 DeVoto,
Bernard Augustine
b. 1897 Morinigo,
Higinio
b. 1897 Thuilier,
Raymond
b. 1899 Le Gallienne,
Eva
b. 1901 Lloyd-Jones,
Esther McDonald
b. 1902 Lahey, Edwin
A(loysius)
b. 1903 Paton, Alan
Stewart
b. 1905 Kluckhohn,
Clyde
b. 1905 Kluckhorn,
Clyde Kay Maben
b. 1905 Lee, Manfred
B(ennington)
b. 1907 Mendes-France,
Pierre
b. 1909 Stander, Lionel
(Jay)
b. 1910 Bratteli, Trygve
Martin
b. 1910 Solomon, Izler
b. 1911? Suzuki, Zenko
b. 1912 Lewis, Roger
b. 1912 Rowe,
Schoolboy
b. 1914 Jeakins,
Dorothy
b. 1917 Robarts, John
Parmenter
b. 1919 McCurdy, Ed
b. 1921 Kreps, Juanita
Morris
b. 1923 Ashley, Thomas
William Ludlow
b. 1923 Shelby, Carroll
(Hall)
b. 1924 Guillemin,
Roger Charles Louis
b. 1926 Tinker, Grant
Almerin
b. 1928 Wolper, David
Lloyd
b. 1930 Stacey, Thomas
Charles Gerard
b. 1930 Taylor,
Rod(ney)
b. 1931 Rodgers, Mary
b. 1934 Chretien, Jean
(Joseph-Jacques)
b. 1934 Exner, Judith
Campbell
b. 1934 Rafshoon,
Gerald Monroe
b. 1935 Mears, Walter
Robert
b. 1936 Hesse, Eva
b. 1939 Posner, Richard
Allen
b. 1942 Clemons,
Clarence
b. 1946 Hale, Janet
Campbell
b. 1946 Judd, Naomi
(Diana)
b. 1947 Calder-
Marshall, Anna Lucia
b. 1948 Jackson,
Madeline Manning
b. 1952 Crenshaw, Ben
Daniel

b. 1952 Ritenour, Lee
b. 1957 Dawkins,
Darryl
b. 1963 Caulkins, Tracy
b. 1971 Blige, Mary
J(ane)
b. 1988 L'Esperance
Quintuplets
d. 1494 Ghirlandaio,
Domenico
d. 1753 Sloane, Hans,
Sir
d. 1788 Grasse,
Francois Joseph Paul
de, Count
d. 1797 Lee, Francis
Lightfoot
d. 1801 Cimarosa,
Domenico
d. 1817 Dwight,
Timothy
d. 1836 Molson, John
d. 1837 Field, John
d. 1837 Gerard,
Francois
d. 1843 Key, Francis
Scott
d. 1874 Borden, Gail
d. 1882 Schwann,
Theodor
d. 1893 Butler,
Benjamin Franklin
d. 1896 Deus, Joao de
d. 1901 Fee, John
Gregg
d. 1904 Pleasant, Mary
Ellen
d. 1909 Wharton,
Joseph
d. 1928 Hardy, Thomas
d. 1931 Straus, Nathan
d. 1935 Sembrich,
Marcella
d. 1940 Mellor, Walter
d. 1941 Bridge, Frank
d. 1941 Lasker,
Emanuel
d. 1942 Nast, Conde
d. 1943 Guiterman,
Arthur
d. 1943 Justo, Agustin
Pedro
d. 1944 Christie, John
Walter
d. 1944 Ciano (di
Cortellazzo),
Galeazzo
d. 1944 King, Charles
d. 1947 Tanguay, Eva
d. 1949 Doubleday,
Nelson
d. 1949 Friesz, Othon
d. 1952 Lattre de
Tassigny, Jean de
(Marie Gabriel) de
d. 1954 Straus, Oskar
d. 1955 Graziani,
Rodolfo
d. 1962 Adler, Elmer
d. 1965 Pipp, Wally
d. 1966 Giacometti,
Alberto
d. 1966 Kolehmainen,
Hannes
d. 1966 Shastri, Lal
Badahur

d. 1968 Stabile,
Mariano
d. 1970 March, Hal
d. 1972 Gardiner,
Herb(ert Martin)
d. 1975 Lorenz, Max
d. 1976 Schoonmaker,
Frank Musselman
d. 1978 Leibowitz,
Samuel Simon
d. 1979 Soo, Jack
d. 1980 Pym, Barbara
Mary Crampton
d. 1981 MacDonald,
Malcolm John
d. 1982 Horikoshi, Jiro
d. 1983 Podgorny,
Nikolai Viktorovich
d. 1984 LaRue, Jack
d. 1984 Licavoli, Peter
Joseph, Sr.
d. 1985 Buzzell, Eddie
d. 1988 Boyington,
Pappy
d. 1988 Kennon, Robert
Floyd
d. 1988 Rabi, Isidor
Isaac
d. 1988 Williams, John
James
d. 1990 McCoy, Clyde
d. 1991 Anderson, Carl
David
d. 1997 Eklund, John
M(anly)
d. 1998 Tennstedt,
Klaus
d. 1999 Mitchison,
Naomi Margaret
(Haldane)
d. 1999 Moore, Brian
d. 2000 Lemon, Bob

January 12
b. 1580 Helmont, Jan
Baptista van
b. 1588 Winthrop, John
b. 1628 Perrault,
Charles
b. 1729 Burke, Edmund
b. 1729 Spallanzani,
Lazzaro
b. 1737 Hancock, John
b. 1746 Pestalozzi,
Johann Heinrich
b. 1810 Ferdinand, II
b. 1833 Duhring, Eugen
Karl
b. 1834 Marty, Martin
b. 1837 Jensen, Adolph
b. 1841 Henry, Edward
Lamson
b. 1852 Joffre, Joseph
Jacques Cesaire
b. 1853 Ricci-Curbastro,
Gregorio
b. 1854 Marquis, Albert
Nelson
b. 1856 Sargent, John
Singer
b. 1861 Baldwin, James
Mark
b. 1864 Russell, Annie
b. 1864 Schoen-Rene,
Anna
b. 1870 Richman,
Charles

b. 1876 London, Jack
b. 1876 Wolf-Ferrari,
Ermanno
b. 1878 Kahles, Charles
William
b. 1878 Molnar, Ferenc
b. 1879 Harroun, Ray
b. 1884 Horst, Louis
b. 1885 Fuess, Claude
Moore
b. 1887 Helburn,
Theresa
b. 1890 Johnson,
Mordecai Wyatt
b. 1893 Goering,
Hermann Wilhelm
b. 1893 Rosenberg,
Alfred
b. 1894 Carpentier,
Georges
b. 1896 Wechsler,
David
b. 1898 Watts, Richard,
Jr.
b. 1899 Crisler, Fritz
b. 1899 Muller, Paul
Hermann
b. 1901 Johnson, Arno
Hollock
b. 1901 Jooss, Kurt
b. 1902 Lewis, Joe E
b. 1903 Kurchatov, Igor
Vasilyevich
b. 1907 Ritter, Tex
b. 1908 Delannoy, Jean
b. 1908 Hurd, Clement
b. 1908 Limon, Jose
Arcadio
b. 1908 Lowinsky,
Edward Elias
b. 1908 Ludwig,
Leopold
b. 1910 Kelly, Patsy
b. 1911 Almond,
Gabriel Abraham
b. 1911 Bjelke-Petersen,
Johannes
b. 1912 Rainer, Luise
b. 1912 Young,
Trummy
b. 1914 Gurney, Edward
John
b. 1914 McMurrin,
Sterling M(oss)
b. 1915 Agronsky,
Martin Zama
b. 1915 Schultes,
Richard Evans
b. 1916 Botha, Pieter
Willem
b. 1916 Wehrwein,
Austin Carl
b. 1918 Sullivan, Walter
b. 1920 Farmer, James
b. 1920 Reid, William
Ronald
b. 1920 Uppman,
Theodor
b. 1923 Hayes, Ira
Hamilton
b. 1926 Feldman,
Morton
b. 1926 Price, Ray
b. 1929 MacIntyre,
Alasdair Chalmers
b. 1930 Horton, Tim

b. 1930 Makihara, (Ben)
   Minoru
b. 1930 Yarbrough,
   Glenn
b. 1935 Kreskin
b. 1936 Brannigan, Bill
b. 1939 Golden,
   William Lee
b. 1941 Howells, Anne
   Elizabeth
b. 1942 Dohrn,
   Bernadine Rae
b. 1947 Dempsey, Tom
b. 1948 Andrews,
   Anthony Corin
   Gerald
b. 1950 Jones, Randy
b. 1950 Lee, Sheila
   Jackson
b. 1951 Alley, Kirstie
b. 1951 Limbaugh,
   Rush Hudson, III
b. 1951 Madlock, Bill
b. 1951 Pearson, Drew
b. 1952 Mosley, Walter
b. 1952 Van Shelton,
   Ricky
b. 1954 Stern, Howard
   (Allan)
b. 1960 Wilkins,
   Dominique
b. 1965 Doyle, Jill
d. 1519 Balboa, Vasco
   Nunez de
d. 1519 Maximilian I
d. 1572 Sa, Mem de
d. 1628 Ribalta,
   Francisco
d. 1665 Fermat, Pierre
   de
d. 1674 Carissimi,
   Giacomo
d. 1829 Schlegel,
   Friedrich von
d. 1838 Humphreys,
   Joshua
d. 1880 Arthur, Ellen
   (Lewis) Herndon
d. 1892? Spokane Garry
d. 1897 Pitman, Isaac
d. 1899 Walker, Hiram
d. 1927 Daly, Arnold
d. 1932 King, Grace
   Elizabeth
d. 1935 Daniels, Frank
d. 1947 Eigenmann,
   Rosa Smith
d. 1956 Langford, Sam
d. 1958 Willard, Frank
   Henry
d. 1960 Shute, Nevil
d. 1965 Hansberry,
   Lorraine
d. 1967 Holt, Ivan Lee
d. 1967 Smith, Holland
   McTeire
d. 1972 Colum, Padraic
d. 1976 Christie, Agatha
   Mary Clarissa Miller,
   Dame
d. 1977 Clouzot, Henri-
   George
d. 1978 Metcalf, Lee
d. 1978 Sheekman,
   Arthur
d. 1979 Smith, Pete

d. 1980 Ronne, Finn
d. 1981 Bondi, Beulah
d. 1981 Whitehead,
   Don(ald Ford)
d. 1989 Little, Royal
d. 1990 Clark, Joseph
   Sill
d. 1990 Peter, Laurence
   Johnston
d. 1991 Luke, Keye
d. 1992 Morey, Walt(er
   Nelson)
d. 1995 Price, George
d. 1997 Huggins,
   Charles B(renton)
d. 1999 Cherne, Leo
d. 1999 Whyte, William
   H(ollingsworth)

January 13
b. 1596 Goyen, Jan
   Josephszoon van
b. 1784 Woodworth,
   Samuel
b. 1804 Gavarni, Paul
b. 1808 Chase, Salmon
   Portland
b. 1832 Alger, Horatio
b. 1843 Ferrier, David,
   Sir
b. 1850 Ray, Charlotte
   E.
b. 1858 Minkowski,
   Oskar
b. 1864 Wien, Wilhelm
   Carl Werner Otto
   Fritz Franz
b. 1867 Townsend,
   Francis Everett
b. 1878 Reid Dick,
   William, Sir
b. 1879 Harrison, Ross
   Granville
b. 1881 Lewis,
   Essington
b. 1884 Hathaway,
   Sibyl Collings
b. 1884 Tucker, Sophie
b. 1885 Fuller, Alfred
   Carl
b. 1886 Druzhinin,
   Nicolai Mikhailovich
b. 1886 Ross, Art(hur
   Howie)
b. 1890 Davis, Elmer
   Holmes
b. 1898 Tagliabue,
   Carlo
b. 1899 DeRochemont,
   Louis
b. 1900 Straus, Jack
   Isidor
b. 1901 Guthrie,
   A(lfred) B(ertram), Jr.
b. 1902 Drummond,
   Roscoe
b. 1903 Francis, Kay
b. 1904 Addinsell,
   Richard
b. 1905 Messel, Oliver
b. 1908 Wheeler, Earle
   G
b. 1911 Mecom, John
   Whitfield
b. 1913 Millner, Wayne
   E

b. 1914 Cory, John
   Mackenzie
b. 1915 Stewart, Potter
b. 1919 Archerd, Army
b. 1919 Stack, Robert
   Langford
b. 1921 Franey, Pierre
b. 1924 Heckert,
   Richard Edwin
b. 1924 Petit, Roland
b. 1925 Verdon, Gwen
b. 1926 Heilbrun,
   Carolyn Gold
b. 1927 Adams,
   Brock(man)
b. 1927 Brenner,
   Sydney
b. 1927 Murphy,
   Rosemary
b. 1927 Pope, Generoso
b. 1929 Pass, Joe
b. 1930 Lortz, Richard
b. 1931 Hendry, Ian
b. 1931 Reilly, Charles
   Nelson
b. 1933 Gallo, Frank
b. 1933 Gola, Tom
b. 1933 Goulart,
   Ron(ald Joseph)
b. 1936 Madigan,
   Edward R.
b. 1938 Nachman,
   Gerald Weil
b. 1940 White, Edmund
b. 1943 Church, Sandra
b. 1949 Tartikoff,
   Brandon
b. 1950 Forsch, Bob
b. 1952 Oliver,
   Stephanie Stokes
b. 1955 McInerney, Jay
b. 1957 O'Meara, Mark
b. 1957 Snow, Don
b. 1959 von Lipsey,
   Roderick K.
b. 1961 Louis-Dreyfus,
   Julia
b. 1962 Mitchell, Kevin
   (Darrell)
b. 1972 Shcherbo,
   Vitaly
d. 1599 Spenser,
   Edmund
d. 1691 Fox, George
d. 1864 Foster, Stephen
   Collins
d. 1867 Ingres, Jean
   Auguste Dominique
d. 1874 Baltard, Victor
d. 1885 Colfax,
   Schuyler
d. 1906 Popov,
   Aleksandr
   Stepanovich
d. 1917 Niemann,
   Albert
d. 1927 Bridgman,
   Frederic Arthur
d. 1929 Earp, Wyatt
   Berry Stapp
d. 1931 Joffre, Joseph
   Jacques Cesaire
d. 1937 Johnson, Martin
   Elmer
d. 1941 Ellis, Carleton

d. 1941 Joyce, James
   Augustus Aloysius
d. 1943 Taeuber-Arp,
   Sophie
d. 1944 Collier,
   William, Sr.
d. 1945 Deland,
   Margaret Wade
d. 1953 Marsh, Edward
   Howard, Sir
d. 1955 Dinneen, Bill
d. 1955 Lea, Fanny
   Heaslip
d. 1956 Feininger,
   Lyonel
d. 1957 Coppard,
   A(lfred) E(dgar)
d. 1958 Lasky, Jesse
   L(ouis)
d. 1958 Purviance, Edna
d. 1961 Ring, Blanche
d. 1961 Robinson,
   Henry Morton
d. 1962 Kovacs, Ernie
d. 1974 Jobin, Raoul
d. 1976 Leighton,
   Margaret
d. 1978 Humphrey,
   Hubert Horatio, Jr.
d. 1978 McCarthy, Joe
d. 1979 Buitoni,
   Giovanni
d. 1979 Hathaway,
   Donny
d. 1979 Lawrence,
   Marjorie Florence
d. 1980 Jahoda, Gloria
   (Adelaide Love)
d. 1980 Kostelanetz,
   Andre
d. 1982 Camus, Marcel
d. 1984 Atkinson,
   Brooks
d. 1984 Shanks,
   Michael
d. 1985 Holland, Jerome
   Heartwell
d. 1986 Garcia, Mike
d. 1987 Kuekes, Edward
   Daniel
d. 1988 Chiang Ching-
   Kuo
d. 1991 Rosenman,
   Dorothy
d. 1992 Dodington,
   Sven H(enry
   Marriott)
d. 1993 Pleven, Rene
   Jean
d. 1994 Alphand, Herve
d. 1995 Stibitz, George
   R.

January 14
b. 770? Constantine VI
b. 1730 Whipple,
   William
b. 1741 Arnold,
   Benedict
b. 1806 Maury,
   Matthew Fontaine
b. 1821 Mosenthal,
   Salomon Hermann
   von
b. 1836 Fantin-Latour,
   (Ignace) Henri
b. 1841 Corson, Juliet

b. 1841 Morisot, Berthe
b. 1850 DeReszke, Jean
b. 1850 Loti, Pierre
b. 1858 Solomon,
Hannah Greenebaum
b. 1861 Wesson, David
b. 1863 Outcault,
Richard Felton
b. 1866 MacCameron,
Robert L
b. 1866 Young, Art(hur
Henry)
b. 1871 Howe, Louis
McHenry
b. 1871 Warburg, Felix
Moritz
b. 1874 Burgess,
Thornton Waldo
b. 1875 Schweitzer,
Albert
b. 1880 Beach, Joseph
Warren
b. 1882 Van Loon,
Hendrik Willem
b. 1884 Wroth,
Lawrence
Counselman
b. 1886 Lofting, Hugh
b. 1890 Harger, Rolla
b. 1890 Holmes, Arthur
b. 1892 Niemoller,
Martin
b. 1892 Roach, Hal
b. 1896 Dos Passos,
John (Roderigo)
b. 1901 Daniels, Bebe
b. 1902 Kappel,
Frederick R(ussell)
b. 1902 Tarski, Alfred
b. 1904 Beaton, Cecil
(Walter Hardy), Sir
b. 1904 Siebert, Babe
b. 1905 Bavier, Frances
b. 1905 Fukuda, Takeo
b. 1905 Hahn, Emily
b. 1906 Bendix,
William
b. 1909 Losey, Joseph
Walton
b. 1912 Olsen, Tillie
b. 1914 Randall, Dudley
b. 1914 Russell, Harold
b. 1917 Butterfield,
Billy
b. 1919 Andreotti,
Giulio
b. 1919 Rooney, Andy
b. 1920 Herman,
George Edward
b. 1923 Korinetz, Yuri
b. 1925 Mishima, Yukio
b. 1926 Tryon, Thomas
b. 1928 Faircloth, Lauch
b. 1928 Mayer, Martin
Prager
b. 1929 Quilico, Louis
b. 1932 Andersson,
Harriet
b. 1933 Brakhage, Stan
b. 1934 Harris, Alice
b. 1938 Hosokawa,
Morihiro
b. 1940 Bond, Julian
b. 1940 Castle, John
b. 1940 Nunn, Trevor
Robert

b. 1941 Dunaway, Faye
b. 1941 Kucan, Milan
b. 1943 Gantt, Harvey
Bernard
b. 1944 Totenberg, Nina
b. 1945 Gortner, Marjoe
(Hugh Ross)
b. 1948 Weathers, Carl
b. 1949 Kasdan,
Lawrence Edward
b. 1952 Dowd, Maureen
(Brigid)
b. 1953 Douglas, Denzil
b. 1956 Heppner, Ben
b. 1957 Min, Anchee
b. 1968 LL Cool J
b. 1969 Bateman, Jason
d. 347BC Plato
d. 1676 Cavalli,
Francesco
d. 1676 Cavalli, Pietro
Francesco
d. 1742 Halley, Edmund
d. 1753 Berkeley,
George
d. 1817 Monsigny,
Pierre-Alexandre
d. 1831 Mackenzie,
Henry
d. 1839 Jarvis, John
Wesley
d. 1882 O'Sullivan,
Timothy H
d. 1887 Foster, Abigail
Kelley
d. 1890 Napier, Robert
Cornelis
d. 1892 Bowditch,
Henry Ingersoll
d. 1892 Davis,
Alexander Jackson
d. 1892 Manning, Henry
Edward
d. 1898 Carroll, Lewis
d. 1905 Abbe, Ernst
d. 1908 Drachmann,
Holger Henrik
Herholdt
d. 1914 Wurlitzer,
Rudolph
d. 1920 Dodge, John
Francis
d. 1925 Furniss, Harry
d. 1929 Walker, Henry
Oliver
d. 1929 Widal, Fernand
Isidore
d. 1940 Benediktsson,
Einar
d. 1942 Fisher, Fred
d. 1943 Richards, Laura
Elizabeth Howe
d. 1947 Hewitt, Bill
d. 1949 Howard, Willie
d. 1949 Sullivan, Harry
Stack
d. 1954 Carney, Don
d. 1955 Booth, Hubert
Cecil
d. 1956 Kaye-Smith,
Sheila
d. 1957 Bogart,
Humphrey de Forest
d. 1959 Cole, George
Douglas Howard

d. 1965 MacDonald,
Jeanette
d. 1966 Moran, Paddy
d. 1969 Sedran, Barney
d. 1970 Murphy, Johnny
(John Joseph)
d. 1972 Frederick IX
d. 1975 Traikov, Georgi
d. 1977 Eden, Anthony
d. 1977 Finch, Peter
d. 1978 Abrahams,
Harold
d. 1978 Godel, Kurt
d. 1978 Heger, Robert
d. 1980 Ardrey, Robert
d. 1980 Brown, Rachel
Fuller
d. 1981 Lilienthal,
David Eli
d. 1984 Haddad, Saad
d. 1984 Kroc,
Ray(mond) Albert
d. 1986 Reed, Donna
d. 1987 Sirk, Douglas
d. 1988 Malenkov,
Georgi
Maximilianovich
d. 1990 Edwards, India
Moffett
d. 1990 Jackson,
Gordon Cameron
d. 1994 Ralston, Esther
d. 1995 Root, Oren
d. 1997 Irsay, Robert
d. 1999 Grotowski,
Jerzy

January 15
b. 1622 Moliere
b. 1716 Livingston,
Philip
b. 1763 Talma, Francois
Joseph
b. 1791 Grillparzer,
Franz
b. 1809 Proudhon,
Pierre Joseph
b. 1810 Foster, Abigail
Kelley
b. 1823? Brady,
Mathew B
b. 1824 Duplessis,
Marie
b. 1825 Strakosch,
Maurice
b. 1831 Niemann,
Albert
b. 1841 Stanley,
Frederick Arthur, Earl
of Derby
b. 1842 Breuer, Josef
b. 1842 MacKillop,
Mary
b. 1844 Younger, Cole
b. 1845 Vogl, Heinrich
b. 1850 Younger, Jim
b. 1858 Segantini,
Giovanni
b. 1859 Britton,
Nathaniel, Lord
b. 1861 Bullard, Robert
Lee
b. 1862 Fuller, Loie
b. 1864 Johnston,
Frances Benjamin
b. 1866 Soderblom,
Nathan

b. 1870 DuPont, Pierre
Samuel
b. 1872 Davis, John
Stalge
b. 1877 Terman, Lewis
Madison
b. 1885 Burr, Henry
b. 1885? DeLaRoche,
Mazo
b. 1886 Howe, Clarence
Decatur
b. 1886 Newell, Edward
Theodore
b. 1890 Hayden, Palmer
b. 1891 Mandelstam,
Osip Emilyevich
b. 1891? Mandelstam,
Osip Emilyevich
b. 1893 Novello, Ivor
b. 1895 Virtanen,
Artturi Llmari
b. 1897 Barr,
Stringfellow
b. 1898 Fox, Uffa
b. 1899 Ace, Goodman
b. 1899 Whitaker,
Rogers E(rnest)
M(alcolm)
b. 1900 Kuhn, Irene
b. 1902 Saud (Ibn
Abdul Aziz al Saud)
b. 1906 Onassis,
Aristotle Socrates
b. 1907 Nitze, Paul
Henry
b. 1908 Teller, Edward
b. 1909 Krupa, Gene
b. 1909 Siegmeister,
Elie
b. 1911 Feuer, Cy
b. 1912 Debre, Michel
(Jean Pierre)
b. 1913 Bridges, Lloyd
b. 1914 Trevor-Roper,
Hugh Redwald
b. 1915 Borg, Veda
Ann
b. 1915 Lomax, Alan
b. 1918 Byrd, Robert
C(arlyle)
b. 1918 Figueiredo,
Joao Baptista de
Oliveira
b. 1918 Nasser, Gamal
Abdel
b. 1920 Davies, Bob
b. 1920 O'Connor, John
Joseph, Cardinal
b. 1921 Barker, Cliff
b. 1922 Marcinkus, Paul
Casimir
b. 1923 Lee, Teng-Hui
b. 1923 Lee Teng-hui
b. 1925 Slenczynska,
Ruth
b. 1926 Berry, Chuck
b. 1926 MacLeish,
Rod(erick)
b. 1927 Badura-Skoda,
Paul
b. 1929 King, Martin
Luther, Jr.
b. 1929 Queen Ida
b. 1931 Hoving,
Thomas Pearsall Field

b. 1933 Gaines, Ernest
J(ames)
b. 1935 Goodman,
Martin Wise
b. 1935 Silverberg,
Robert
b. 1936 Conroy, Frank
b. 1937 O'Brien,
Margaret
b. 1941 Beefheart,
Captain
b. 1941 Captain
Beefheart
b. 1941 Farmer, Forest
Jackson
b. 1942 Lucas, Phil
b. 1943 Moody, John
b. 1946 Tennant,
Veronica
b. 1949 Van Zant,
Ronnie
b. 1951 Charo
b. 1953 White, Randy
Lee
b. 1957 Van Peebles,
Mario
b. 1968 Lowe, Chad
d. 1597 Herrera, Juan
de
d. 1783 Alexander,
William
d. 1815 Hamilton,
Emma, Lady
d. 1865 Everett, Edward
d. 1876 Johnson, Eliza
(McCardle)
d. 1891 Mason, Biddy
d. 1891 Root, John
Wellborn
d. 1892 Rogers,
Randolph
d. 1893 Kemble, Fanny
d. 1893 Smith, Horace
d. 1896 Brady, Mathew
B
d. 1902 Hyatt, Alpheus
d. 1909 Reyer, (Louis)
Ernest (Etienne)
d. 1915 Farmer, Fannie
Merritt
d. 1917 De Morgan,
William Frend
d. 1919 Liebknecht,
Karl
d. 1919 Luxemburg,
Rosa
d. 1948 Daniels,
Josephus
d. 1950 Arnold, Henry
Harley
d. 1951 Ironside, Henry
Allan
d. 1951 Swinton, Ernest
Dunlop, Sir
d. 1953 Knote, Heinrich
d. 1955 Tanguy, Yves
d. 1960 Smart, Jack
Scott
d. 1964 Teagarden, Jack
d. 1966 Balewa,
Abubakar Tafawa, Sir
d. 1968 Masterton, Bill
d. 1970 Fischer, Louis
d. 1970 Piper, William
Thomas
d. 1971 Dall, John

d. 1971 Shambaugh,
Jessie Field
d. 1972 Ashford, Daisy
d. 1980 Fogarty, Anne
d. 1981 Celler, Emanuel
d. 1982 Jarman, John
d. 1982 Sender, Ramon
Jose
d. 1982 Smith, Red
d. 1983 Lansky, Meyer
d. 1983 Lauder, Joseph
H
d. 1983 Strudwick,
Shepperd
d. 1983 Weaver,
Doodles
d. 1986 Crowley, Jim
d. 1987 Bolger,
Ray(mond Wallace)
d. 1987 Young, Philip
d. 1988 MacBride, Sean
d. 1991 Rankin, K(arl)
L(ott)
d. 1993 Cahn, Sammy
d. 1993 Iba, Hank
d. 1995 Maxwell, Vera
(Huppe)
d. 1995 Schlink,
Frederick John
d. 1996 Baxter, Les
d. 1996 Moshoeshoe II
d. 1998 Van Horne,
Harriet
d. 1998 Wells, Junior

January 16
b. 1675 Saint-Simon,
Duc de
b. 1725 Piccinni, Nicola
b. 1741 Piozzi, Hester
Lynch Salisbury
b. 1749 Alfieri, Vittorio
b. 1815 Halleck, Henry
Wager
b. 1838 Brentano, Franz
Clemens
b. 1853 Forbes-
Robertson, Johnston,
Sir
b. 1853 Hamilton, Ian
Standish Monteith,
Sir
b. 1864 Bacon, Frank
b. 1872 Craig, Gordon
b. 1873 Collins, Jimmy
b. 1874 Service, Robert
William
b. 1878 Carey, Harry
b. 1882 Wilson,
Margaret
b. 1884 Decker, Alonzo
G
b. 1885 Chou Tso-Jen
b. 1890 Ackerman, Carl
William
b. 1893 Bordoni, Irene
b. 1894 Chamberlin, B
Guy
b. 1894 Mills, Irving
b. 1895 Weyerhaeuser,
Frederick Edward
b. 1901 Batista y
Zaldivar, Fulgencio
b. 1901 Jackson, Laura
Riding
b. 1901 Matthews,
T(homas) S(tanley)

b. 1901 Riding, Laura
b. 1906 Wynyard, Diana
b. 1907 Knox,
Alexander
b. 1909 Greenberg,
Clement
b. 1909 Merman, Ethel
b. 1911 Dean, Dizzy
b. 1911 Frei, Eduardo
b. 1912 Dennis, Nigel
Forbes
b. 1914 Wagner, Roger
Frances
b. 1916 Rothschild,
Edmund Leopold de
b. 1917 Hartley, Fred
Lloyd
b. 1918 Silliphant,
Stirling Dale
b. 1919 Cochran, Roy
b. 1920 Reid, Elliott
b. 1923 Hecht, Anthony
Evan
b. 1925 Schwartz,
Felice N(ierenberg)
b. 1927 Jurado, Katy
b. 1928 Kennedy,
William (Joseph)
b. 1928 Kitt, Eartha
Mae
b. 1928 Lorengar, Pilar
b. 1929 Lowenstein,
Allard Kenneth
b. 1929 Scavullo,
Francesco
b. 1930 Podhoretz,
Norman
b. 1931 Rau, Johannes
b. 1932 Berry, Jim
b. 1932 Cox, Jean
b. 1932 Fossey, Dian
b. 1933 Sontag, Susan
b. 1934 Brennan,
Edward A.
b. 1934 Horne, Marilyn
Berneice
b. 1935 Foyt, A(nthony)
J(oseph Jr.)
b. 1936 White, Michael
Simon
b. 1938 Lipsyte, Robert
Mitchell Michael
b. 1943 Harris,
Marcelite Jordan
b. 1944 Milsap, Ronnie
b. 1944 Stafford, Jim
b. 1948 Carpenter, John
Howard
b. 1950 Allen, Debbie
b. 1954 Thompson,
Starley
b. 1959 Sade
b. 1974 Moss, Kate
d. 1794 Gibbon, Edward
d. 1865 Proudhon,
Pierre Joseph
d. 1878 Bowles,
Samuel, II
d. 1885 About,
Edmond-Francois-
Valentin
d. 1886 Ponchielli,
Amilcare
d. 1887 Hazen, William
Babcock
d. 1891 Delibes, Leo

d. 1901 Barbier, Jules
d. 1901 Bocklin, Arnold
d. 1901 Revels, Hiram
Rhodes
d. 1906 Field, Marshall
d. 1915 Williams, Gus
d. 1916 Huerta,
Victoriano
d. 1917 Dewey, George
d. 1920 DeKoven,
(Henry Louis)
Reginald
d. 1935 Barker, Fred
d. 1935 Barker, Ma
d. 1936 Barnack, Oskar
d. 1936 Fish, Albert
d. 1936 Russell, Annie
d. 1938 Pickering,
William Henry
d. 1942 Lombard,
Carole
d. 1945 Patten, Gilbert
d. 1957 Toscanini,
Arturo
d. 1962 Mestrovic, Ivan
d. 1962 Tawney,
Richard Henry
d. 1962 Toffenetti,
Dario Louis
d. 1966 Hodges,
Courtney
d. 1968 Infeld, Leopold
d. 1968 Jones, Bob
d. 1969 Smith, Courtney
Craig
d. 1970 Breger, Dave
d. 1972 Seville, David
d. 1974 Lovejoy,
Clarence Earle
d. 1981 Lee, Bernard
d. 1985 Fitzgerald,
Robert Stuart
d. 1985 Orkin, Ruth
d. 1986 Armstrong,
Herbert W
d. 1987 Brenan, Gerald
d. 1987 Wilson, Earl
d. 1988 Artukovic,
Andrija
d. 1991 Cloud, Preston
(Ercelle)
d. 1994 Stowe, Leland
d. 1995 McCoy, Charles
B(relsford)
d. 1996 Davenport,
Marcia
d. 2000 Wilson, Robert
R(athbun)

January 17
b. 1600 Calderon de la
Barca, Pedro
b. 1612 Fairfax, Thomas
b. 1620 Bourgeoys,
Marguerite
b. 1624 Guarini,
Guarino
b. 1706 Franklin,
Benjamin
b. 1734 Gossec,
Francois Joseph
b. 1759 Cuffe, Paul
b. 1761 Hall, James, Sir
b. 1771 Brown, Charles
Brockden
b. 1781 Hare, Robert

b. 1796 Fairbanks, Thaddeus
b. 1800 Cushing, Caleb
b. 1814 Wood, Henry, Mrs.
b. 1820 Bronte, Anne
b. 1822 Fuller, George
b. 1824 Harvey, Hayward Augustus
b. 1829 Booth, Catherine Mumford
b. 1834 Weismann, August Friedrich Leopold
b. 1837 Browning, Oscar
b. 1849 Carriere, Eugene
b. 1851 Frost, Arthur Burdett
b. 1853 Belmont, Alva Erskine Smith Vanderbilt
b. 1857 Kienzl, Wilhelm
b. 1860 Chekhov, Anton Pavlovich
b. 1860 Hyde, Douglas
b. 1863 Stanislavsky, Konstantin Sergeyevich
b. 1867 Laemmle, Carl, Sr.
b. 1871 Beatty, David Beatty, Earl
b. 1876 Hague, Frank
b. 1883 Mackenzie, Compton
b. 1884 Beery, Noah
b. 1884 Sennett, Mack
b. 1885 Kern, Jerome David
b. 1886 Firbank, Ronald
b. 1886 Martin, Glenn Luther
b. 1886 Rugg, Harold
b. 1892 Bennett, Harry Herbert
b. 1892 Gulick, Luther (Halsey)
b. 1893 Scott, Evelyn
b. 1896 Davis, Loyal
b. 1899 Capone, Al(phonse)
b. 1899 Harris, Abram Lincoln, Jr.
b. 1899 Hutchins, Robert Maynard
b. 1899 Shute, Nevil
b. 1900 Rosenman, Dorothy
b. 1900 Sperti, George Speri
b. 1901 Asther, Nils
b. 1901 Dutra, Olin
b. 1903 Hull, Warren
b. 1905 Salam, Saeb
b. 1907 Badings, Henk
b. 1910 Catlett, Big Sid
b. 1910 Green, Edith S(tarrett)
b. 1910 Rush, (David) Kenneth
b. 1911 McCain, John Sidney, Jr.

b. 1911 Nickerson, Albert L(indsay)
b. 1912 Landis, Frederick
b. 1913 Musso, Vido
b. 1914 Stafford, William Edgar
b. 1915 Angott, Sammy
b. 1915 Smith, Mayo
b. 1918 Barr, Joseph W(alker)
b. 1918 Joseph, Keith (Sinjohn)
b. 1920 Kaye, Nora
b. 1922 Echeverria Alvarez, Louis
b. 1922 Katzenbach, Nicholas de Belleville
b. 1922 White, Betty
b. 1924 Cobb, Jewel Plummer
b. 1925 Hanson, Duane (Elwood)
b. 1926 Minow, Newton Norman
b. 1926 Shearer, Moira
b. 1927 Dooley, Thomas Anthony, III
b. 1927 Mathews, Harlan
b. 1928 Sassoon, Vidal
b. 1931 Jones, James Earl
b. 1931 Wilder, Douglas
b. 1931 Zimmer, Don(ald William)
b. 1933 Aga Khan, Sadruddin, Prince
b. 1933 North, Sheree
b. 1934 Lewis, Shari
b. 1934 Schanberg, Sydney Hillel
b. 1938 Qoboza, Percy
b. 1940 Keino, Kip
b. 1942 Ali, Muhammad
b. 1943 Preval, Rene
b. 1944 Frazier, Joe
b. 1947 Dove, Ulysses
b. 1948 Oddsson, David
b. 1948 Taylor, Mick
b. 1949 Kaufman, Andy
b. 1952 Porter, Darrell Ray
b. 1956 Caruso, David
b. 1956 Young, Paul
b. 1959 Hoffs, Susanna
b. 1962 Carrey, Jim
d. 395 Thedosius I
d. 395 Theodosius
d. 1686 Dolci, Carlo
d. 1705 Ray, John
d. 1733 Byng, George Torrington, Viscount
d. 1751 Albinoni, Tommaso
d. 1791 Pinto, Isaac
d. 1833 Rush, William
d. 1846 Inman, Henry
d. 1861 Montez, Lola
d. 1869 Dargomijsky, Alexander
d. 1874 Chang and Eng
d. 1885 Burnaby, Frederick Gustavus
d. 1889 Montalvo, Juan Maria

d. 1890 Sulzer, Salomon
d. 1891 Bancroft, George
d. 1893 Hayes, Rutherford B(irchard)
d. 1910 Crapper, Thomas
d. 1910 Nabuco de Araujo, Joaquim Aurelio
d. 1911 Galton, Francis, Sir
d. 1922 Selden, George Baldwin
d. 1929 Goldberger, Joseph
d. 1932 Gore, Charles
d. 1933 Tiffany, Louis Comfort
d. 1946 Kalisch, Paul
d. 1952 Briggs, Walter Owen
d. 1953 Jaggar, Thomas Augustus
d. 1954 Benn, Ernest John Pickstone, Sir
d. 1962 Achterberg, Gerrit
d. 1964 Allen, Arthur Augustus
d. 1964 White, T(erence) H(anbury)
d. 1964 Woodcock, Amos Walter Wright
d. 1969 Duke, Vernon
d. 1972 Hudson, Rochelle
d. 1972 Smith, Betty
d. 1972 Spectorsky, Auguste Compte
d. 1973 Walker, Ralph Thomas
d. 1975 Rojas Pinilla, Gustavo
d. 1982 Shalamov, Varlam Tikhonovich
d. 1985 Rigby, Harry
d. 1988 Qoboza, Percy
d. 1991 Manzu, Giacomo
d. 1991 Olav V
d. 1991 Walsh, Chad
d. 1992 Ventura, Charlie
d. 1994 Stephens, Helen
d. 1996 Jordan, Barbara C(harline)
d. 1996 Minnesota Fats
d. 1997 Griffith, Ernest S(tacey)
d. 1997 Tombaugh, Clyde W(illiam)

January 18
b. 1689 Montesquieu, Charles Louis de Secondat, Baron
b. 1754 Martin y Soler, Vicente
b. 1779 Roget, Peter Mark
b. 1782 Webster, Daniel
b. 1811 Laboulaye, Edouard Rose
b. 1813 Glidden, Joseph Farwell

b. 1815 De La Rue, Warren
b. 1835 Cui, Cesar Antonovich
b. 1840 Dobson, Henry Austin
b. 1841 Chabrier, Emmanuel
b. 1848 Graydon, James Weir
b. 1849 Barton, Edmund
b. 1850 Low, Seth
b. 1858 Williams, Daniel Hale
b. 1861 Kemble, Edward W(indsor)
b. 1867 Dario, Ruben
b. 1870 Nethersole, Olga
b. 1877 Zemurray, Samuel
b. 1879 Giraud, Henri Honore
b. 1880 Ehrenfest, Paul
b. 1881 Strong, Austin
b. 1882 Milne, A(lan) A(lexander)
b. 1884 Ransome, Arthur Mitchell
b. 1886 Pevsner, Antoine
b. 1888 Sopwith, Thomas O M, Sir
b. 1892 Hardy, Oliver
b. 1893 Guillen, Jorge
b. 1894 Berlin, Richard E
b. 1896 Ritola, Ville
b. 1904 Grant, Cary
b. 1904 McNickle, D'Arcy
b. 1905 Bonanno, Joseph
b. 1906 Aeschbacher, Hans
b. 1907 Ferencsik, Janos
b. 1908 Bronowski, Jacob
b. 1908 Callender, John Hancock
b. 1908 Morano, Albert Paul
b. 1910 Boulding, Kenneth E(wart)
b. 1911 Arguedas, Jose Maria
b. 1912 Sansom, William
b. 1913 Graham, Gwethalyn
b. 1913 Kaye, Danny
b. 1918 Chaney, Norman
b. 1918 Roudebush, Richard L(owell)
b. 1922 Moore, Constance
b. 1927 Lubic, Ruth Watson
b. 1930 OhEithir, Breandan
b. 1931 Lear, Evelyn
b. 1932 Schmidt, Joe
b. 1933 Boorman, John
b. 1933 Dolby, Ray M(ilton)

d. 1947 Machado (y Ruiz), Manuel
d. 1948 Sobol, Louis
d. 1952 Howard, Curly
d. 1953 Schnering, Otto
d. 1954 Greenstreet, Sydney Hughes
d. 1958 Rondon, Candido Mariano da Silva
d. 1962 Noble, Reg
d. 1965 Pate, Maurice
d. 1968 Harroun, Ray
d. 1972 Chapman, John (Arthur)
d. 1972 Rabin, Michael
d. 1975 Benton, Thomas Hart
d. 1979 Leemans, Tuffy
d. 1980 Douglas, William Orville
d. 1980 Goldman, Richard Franko
d. 1981 Evans, Clifford
d. 1982 Plumb, Charles
d. 1982 Zaturenska, Marya
d. 1983 Carson, Robert
d. 1983 Costa, Don
d. 1984 Bentley, Max(well Herbert Lloyd)
d. 1985 Voegelin, Eric (Herman Wilhelm)
d. 1990 Goldberg, Arthur Joseph
d. 1990 Gucci, Aldo
d. 1990 Rajneesh, Bhagwan Shree
d. 1992 DiDonato, Pietro
d. 1993 Lewis, Reginald F.
d. 1993 Strouse, Norman H(ulbert)
d. 1996 Gaston, Arthur George
d. 1996 Simpson, Donald C
d. 1997 Caselotti, Adriana
d. 1997 Dickey, James (Lafayette)
d. 1998 Perkins, Carl (Lee)
d. 2000 Craxi, Bettino
d. 2000 Lamarr, Hedy

January 20
b. 1562 Rinuccini, Ottavio
b. 1707 Frederick Louis
b. 1716 Charles, III
b. 1732 Lee, Richard Henry
b. 1782 Bibaud, Michel
b. 1804 Sue, Eugene Joseph Marie
b. 1806 Willis, Nathaniel Parker
b. 1814 Wilmot, David
b. 1843 Cambon, Pierre Paul
b. 1856 Blatch, Harriot Eaton Stanton
b. 1859 Lindbergh, Charles Augustus

b. 1864 Taylor, Charles Alonzo
b. 1866 Cunha, Euclides (Rodrigues Pimenta) da
b. 1866 LeGallienne, Richard
b. 1867 Guilbert, Yvette
b. 1876 Hofmann, Josef Casimir
b. 1877 Saint Denis, Ruth
b. 1877 St. Denis, Ruth
b. 1878 Currie, Finlay
b. 1883 Wrather, William Embry
b. 1884 Merritt, Abraham
b. 1889 Toffenetti, Dario Louis
b. 1890 Owsley, Frank Lawrence
b. 1894 Gray, Harold Lincoln
b. 1894 Piston, Walter
b. 1896 Burns, George
b. 1899 Tcherepnin, Alexander Nikolayevich
b. 1900 Clive, Colin
b. 1903 Ames, Leon
b. 1904 Brameld, Theodore
b. 1904 Danilova, Alexandra
b. 1906 McNeill, Robert Edward, Jr.
b. 1907 Welensky, Roy
b. 1909 Eckert, William Dole
b. 1910 Adamson, Joy Friederike Victoria Gessner
b. 1910 Johnson, Josephine Winslow
b. 1911 Hill, Abram
b. 1914 Plomley, Roy
b. 1914 Watt, Douglas Benjamin
b. 1915 Marek, Kurt W
b. 1916 Stone, Paula
b. 1918 Esquivel, Juan
b. 1919 Cooper, Lester Irving
b. 1920 Douglas, Keith Castellain
b. 1920 Fellini, Federico
b. 1920 Kelley, DeForest
b. 1920 Landau, Ely A
b. 1920 Lasky, Melvin Joseph
b. 1922 Anthony, Ray
b. 1924 Josey, E. J.
b. 1925 Bloustein, Edward J.
b. 1925 Cardenal, Ernesto
b. 1926 Neal, Patricia
b. 1928 Hebert, Lionel
b. 1930 Aldrin, Edwin E(ugene), Jr.
b. 1931 Grant, Earl
b. 1932 Carr, Martin
b. 1934 Debost, Michel H

b. 1934 Johnson, Arte
b. 1936 Feigenbaum, Edward A(lbert)
b. 1937 Howell, Bailey E
b. 1937 Provine, Dorothy Michele
b. 1939 Coverdell, Paul
b. 1940 Heiss, Carol Elizabeth
b. 1940 Jenkins, Carol Elizabeth Heiss
b. 1944 Parker, Pat
b. 1945 Butler, Robert Olen
b. 1945 Rothenberg, Susan
b. 1946 Lynch, David K
b. 1946 Williams, Samm-Art
b. 1948 Shcharansky, Anatoly Borisovich
b. 1949 Persson, Goran
b. 1949 Stanley, Paul
b. 1950 Hamad, Sheikh
b. 1950 Ousmane, Mahamane
b. 1955 Kenney, Bill
b. 1956 Maher, Bill
b. 1956 Naber, John
b. 1958 Lamas, Lorenzo
b. 1964 Guillen, Ozzie
d. 1612 Rudolf II
d. 1745 Charles VII
d. 1779 Garrick, David
d. 1811 Chalgrin, Francois
d. 1813 Wieland, Christoph Martin
d. 1830 Red Jacket
d. 1837 Soane, John, Sir
d. 1867 Willis, Nathaniel Parker
d. 1874 Kelley, Hall Jackson
d. 1875 Millet, Jean Francois
d. 1876 Dykes, John Bacchus
d. 1881 Sothern, Edward Askew
d. 1900 Blackmore, Richard Doddridge
d. 1900 Ruskin, John
d. 1901 Gramme, Zenobe Theophile
d. 1904 Mannlicher, Ferdinand
d. 1930 Cobb, Will D
d. 1936 George V
d. 1944 Cattell, James McKeen
d. 1947 Gibson, Josh(ua)
d. 1947 Volstead, Andrew J
d. 1948 Aucherlonie, Laurie
d. 1949 Sapru, Tej Bahadur
d. 1957 Connolly, James B
d. 1958 Lambert, Ward L
d. 1962 Jeffers, (John) Robinson

d. 1965 Altrock, Nick
d. 1965 Freed, Alan
d. 1968 Beatty, Alfred Chester, Sir
d. 1968 Stacton, David Derek
d. 1970 Humphrey, George Magoffin
d. 1971 Anderson, Gilbert M
d. 1972 Casadesus, Jean
d. 1973 Cabral, Amilcar Lopes
d. 1974 Blunden, Edmund Charles
d. 1975 Summersby, Kay
d. 1978 Clapper, Dit
d. 1978 Highet, Gilbert (Arthur)
d. 1982 Baxter, Frank Condie
d. 1984 Weissmuller, Johnny
d. 1988 Harper, Ken
d. 1988 Khan, Abdul Ghaffar
d. 1988 Mravinsky, Eugene
d. 1988 Rothschild, Philippe de, Baron
d. 1989 Cyrankiewicz, Josef
d. 1989 Lillie, Beatrice Gladys
d. 1990 Stanwyck, Barbara
d. 1993 Anthony, Joseph
d. 1993 Hepburn, Audrey (Edda)
d. 1993 Rothmuller, Marko A
d. 1996 Mulligan, Gerry
d. 1997 Flood, Curt(is Charles)
d. 1997 Fontaine, Marcel

January 21
b. 1337 Charles, V
b. 1721 Murray, James
b. 1738 Allen, Ethan
b. 1743 Fitch, John
b. 1779 Savigny, Friedrich Karl von
b. 1784 DeWint, Peter
b. 1813 Fremont, John Charles
b. 1815 Wells, Horace
b. 1821 Breckinridge, John Cabell
b. 1824 Jackson, Stonewall
b. 1845 Mallinckrodt, Edward
b. 1855 Browning, John Moses
b. 1867 Weygand, Maxime
b. 1878 Garrod, Heathcote William
b. 1883 Hackett, Francis
b. 1884 Baldwin, Roger Nash
b. 1885 Grant, Duncan (James Corrowr)

b. 1885 Leadbelly
b. 1885 Nobile, Umberto
b. 1887 Kohler, Wolfgang
b. 1889 Sorokin, Pitirim A(lexandrovitch)
b. 1891 Elman, Mischa
b. 1893 Barnaby, Ralph S
b. 1895 Balenciaga, Cristobal
b. 1900 Naish, J(oseph) Carrol
b. 1902 Duffy, Ben
b. 1904 Blackmur, Richard Palmer
b. 1904 Crawford, John Edmund
b. 1905 Dior, Christian
b. 1905 Wallenda, Karl
b. 1906 Johansen, Gunnar
b. 1906 Moiseyev, Igor Alexandrovich
b. 1908 Gary, Raymond
b. 1908 Stromgren, Bengt Georg Daniel
b. 1912 Bloch, Konrad Emil
b. 1915 Hewitt, Alan
b. 1915 Sefton, William
b. 1918 Janigo, Antonio
b. 1919 Falkenburg, Jinx
b. 1920 Barrow, Errol Walton
b. 1921 Clark, Barney Bailey
b. 1922 Scofield, Paul
b. 1923 Savalas, Telly
b. 1924 Hill, Benny
b. 1926 Mikva, Abner Joseph
b. 1926 Reeves, Steve
b. 1927 Butler, Robert N(eil)
b. 1928 Bignone, Reynaldo Benito Antonio
b. 1929 Hinojosa, Rolando
b. 1932 Chaney, John
b. 1933 Wrigley, William, III
b. 1938 Wolfman Jack
b. 1939 Norman, Pat
b. 1940 Nicklaus, Jack William
b. 1941 Domingo, Placido
b. 1941 Havens, Richie
b. 1942 Davis, Mac
b. 1944 Abbott, Jack
b. 1947 Eikenberry, Jill
b. 1948 Laiken, Deirdre Susan
b. 1949 Browne, Walter Shawn
b. 1950 Ocean, Billy
b. 1952 Johnson, Billy
b. 1955 Fleming, Peter
b. 1956 Benson, Robby
b. 1957 Davis, Geena
b. 1963 Olajuwon, Hakeem

d. 1609 Scaliger, Joseph Justus
d. 1793 Louis XVI
d. 1795 Wallis, Samuel
d. 1815 Claudius, Matthias
d. 1831 Arnim, Achim von (Ludwig Joachim)
d. 1851 Lortzing, Gustav Albert
d. 1870 Herzen, Aleksandr Ivanovich
d. 1872 Grillparzer, Franz
d. 1892 Adams, John Couch
d. 1901 Gray, Elisha
d. 1902 DeVere, Aubrey Thomas
d. 1914 Smith, Donald Alexander
d. 1924 Lenin, Vladimir Ilyich
d. 1926 Golgi, Camillo
d. 1928 Goethals, George Washington
d. 1931 Kahles, Charles William
d. 1932 Strachey, (Giles) Lytton
d. 1933 Moore, George Augustus
d. 1938 Melies, Georges
d. 1948 Wolf-Ferrari, Ermanno
d. 1950 Orwell, George
d. 1951 Cossart, Ernest
d. 1954 Chambers, Edmund Kerchever, Sir
d. 1955 Hahn, Archie
d. 1957 Kupka, Frank
d. 1958 Bowers, Claude Gernade
d. 1959 DeMille, Cecil B(lount)
d. 1959 Switzer, Carl
d. 1961 Cone, Russell Glenn
d. 1962 Cockrell, Ewing
d. 1964 Schildkraut, Joseph
d. 1967 Sheridan, Ann
d. 1971 Russell, Richard Brevard, Jr.
d. 1972 Lyttleton, Oliver
d. 1973 Szabolcsi, Bence
d. 1974 Strauss, Lewis Lichtenstein
d. 1975 Bosley, Harold A
d. 1978 Utley, Freda
d. 1980 Hidalgo, Elvira de
d. 1981 Douglass, Lathrop
d. 1981 Joslyn, Allyn Morgan
d. 1981 Strong, James Matthew
d. 1981 Stronge, Norman, Sir
d. 1982 Irish, Ned

d. 1984 Wilson, Jackie
d. 1987 Goodell, Charles Ellsworth
d. 1989 Furillo, Carl Anthony
d. 1990 Gervasi, Frank Henry
d. 1993 Gehringer, Charlie
d. 1993 Kelly, Bruce
d. 1995 Groza, Alex John
d. 1997 Parker, Tom, Colonel
d. 1998 Lord, Jack
d. 1999 Strasberg, Susan Elizabeth

January 22
b. 1440 Ivan III
b. 1561 Bacon, Francis, Sir
b. 1690 Lancret, Nicolas
b. 1729 Lessing, Gotthold Ephraim
b. 1758 Watson, Elkanah
b. 1775 Ampere, Andre Marie
b. 1775 Garcia, Manuel del Popolo Vincente
b. 1788 Byron, George Gordon, Baron
b. 1788 Schopenhauer, Arthur
b. 1797 Harper, John
b. 1802 Upjohn, Richard
b. 1831 Winsor, Justin
b. 1837 Moran, Thomas
b. 1845 Vidal de la Blache, Paul
b. 1848 Laffan, William Mackay
b. 1849 Powderly, Terence Vincent
b. 1849 Strindberg, August
b. 1850 Brookings, Robert Somers
b. 1853 Gore, Charles
b. 1858 Lugard, Frederick John Dealtry
b. 1858 Webb, Beatrice Potter
b. 1866 Barton, George
b. 1874 Harkness, Edward Stephen
b. 1875 Griffith, D(avid Lewelyn) W(ark)
b. 1877 Schacht, Hjalmar Horace Greeley
b. 1878 Collier, Constance
b. 1878 Fairfax, Beatrice
b. 1879 Picabia, Francis
b. 1885 Doherty, Robert Ernest
b. 1887 Olds, Irving S
b. 1889 Baumeister, Willi
b. 1890 Vinson, Frederick Moore

b. 1891 Alexander, Franz Gabriel
b. 1891 Gramsci, Antonio
b. 1892 Dassault, Marcel
b. 1893 Oursler, (Charles) Fulton
b. 1893 Veidt, Conrad
b. 1894 Morgan, Charles Langbridge
b. 1894 Ponselle, Rosa
b. 1895 Alley, Norman William
b. 1898 Barnett, Ross Robert
b. 1903 Jacobs, Al(bert T)
b. 1903 Sutton, Margaret Beebe
b. 1904 Balanchine, George
b. 1906 Cox, Gardner
b. 1906 Howard, Robert Ervin
b. 1906 Levy, Julien
b. 1907 Corrigan, Douglas
b. 1908 Keyserling, Leon Hirsch
b. 1908 Landau, Lev Davidovich
b. 1909 Sothern, Ann
b. 1909 Thant, U
b. 1911 Kreisky, Bruno
b. 1911 Powell, Gordon George
b. 1916 Durnan, Bill
b. 1916 Teichmann, Howard Miles
b. 1918 Lach, Elmer James
b. 1920 Kristol, Irving
b. 1920 Stavropoulos, George Peter
b. 1920 Volkov, Leon
b. 1920 Warfield, William Caesar
b. 1922 Moss, Howard
b. 1924 Johnson, J J
b. 1928 Bayh, Birch Evans, Jr.
b. 1930 Wildsmith, Brian
b. 1931 Rayner, Claire Berenice
b. 1932 Laurie, Piper
b. 1934 Azenberg, Emanuel
b. 1934 Bixby, Bill
b. 1934 Kerr, Graham
b. 1935 Cooke, Sam
b. 1935 DuPont, Pierre Samuel, IV
b. 1936 Ong Teng Cheong
b. 1937 Pastora (Gomez), Eden
b. 1937 Wambaugh, Joseph Aloysius, Jr.
b. 1938 Beard, Peter Hill
b. 1939 Smith, Jeff
b. 1940 Hurt, John
b. 1943 Carroll, James
b. 1944 Noble, Elaine

b. 1945 Cristofer,
Michael
b. 1945 Harris, William
b. 1945 Jackson, Isaiah
Allen
b. 1946 Savard, Serge A
b. 1948 Chavis,
Benjamin Franklin,
Jr.
b. 1949 Perry, Steve
b. 1951 Fixico, Donald
L.
b. 1953 Chung, Myung-
Whun
b. 1955 Hayes, Lester
b. 1957 Bossy, Mike
b. 1958 White, Charles
Raymond
b. 1959 Blair, Linda
Denise
b. 1960 Hutchence,
Michael
b. 1965 Lane, Diane
d. 1536 John of Leiden
d. 1552 Somerset, Duke
of
d. 1666 Shah Jahan
d. 1798 Morris, Lewis
d. 1832 Pitcher, Molly
d. 1840 Blumenbach,
Johann Friedrich
d. 1861 Velluti,
Giovanni Battista
d. 1870 Prentice,
George Denison
d. 1892 Bradley, Joseph
P
d. 1901 Victoria, Queen
d. 1919 Larsson, Carl
Olof
d. 1922 Bajer, Fredrik
d. 1922 Benedict XV
d. 1922 Bryce, James
Bryce, Viscount
d. 1925 Workman,
Fanny Bullock
d. 1927 Rhodes, James
Ford
d. 1930 Mather, Stephen
Tyng
d. 1945 Symons, Arthur
William
d. 1950 Hale, Alan
d. 1956 Greene, Ward
d. 1957 Perry, Ralph
Barton
d. 1964 Blitzstein, Marc
d. 1965 Stuhldreher,
Harry A
d. 1966 Marshall,
Herbert
d. 1967 Buckley,
Charles Anthony
d. 1968 Dargan, Olive
Tilford
d. 1968 Kahanamoku,
Duke Paoa
d. 1970 Folsom, Frank
M
d. 1971 Guggenheim,
Harry Frank
d. 1973 Johnson,
Lyndon B(aines)
d. 1974 Volkov, Leon
d. 1976 Leslie, Edgar

d. 1978 Wengenroth,
Stow
d. 1979 Stakman, Elvin
Charles
d. 1982 Farber, Edward
Rolke
d. 1982 Frei, Eduardo
d. 1983 Madden,
Donald
d. 1985 Bryant, Arthur
W M, Sir
d. 1986 Clinchy, Everett
Ross
d. 1988 Fennelly, Parker
W
d. 1990 Buehrig,
Gordon
d. 1990 Rumor,
Mariano
d. 1990 Vishniac,
Roman
d. 1991 Frye, (Herman)
Northrop
d. 1992 Antoon,
A(lfred) J(oseph)
d. 1993 Abe, Kobo
d. 1993 Pollard, Jim
d. 1994 Barrault, Jean-
Louis
d. 1994 Busby,
Matthew, Sir
d. 1994 Savalas, Telly
d. 1995 Kennedy, Rose
(Fitzgerald)
d. 1997 Panter-Downes,
Mollie
d. 1999 Batten, William
Milfred
d. 2000 Claiborne,
Craig
d. 2000 Morrison, Hobe

January 23
b. 1598 Mansart,
Francois
b. 1635 Spener, Philipp
Jakob
b. 1692 Caslon, William
b. 1730 Hewes, Joseph
b. 1783 Stendhal
b. 1818 Boutwell,
George Sewall
b. 1832 Manet, Edouard
b. 1840 Abbe, Ernst
b. 1841 Coquelin,
Benoit Constant
b. 1862 Hilbert, David
b. 1869 Croly, Herbert
David
b. 1870 Greene, Henry
Mather
b. 1871 Rasputin,
Grigori Efimovich
b. 1876 Diels, Otto Paul
Herman
b. 1880 Poole, Ernest
b. 1884 De Palma,
Ralph
b. 1884 McManus,
George
b. 1887 Wenrich, Percy
b. 1893 Carlson, Frank
b. 1893 Pangborn,
Franklin
b. 1896 Charlotte
Aldegonde E M
Wilhelmine

b. 1897 Bose, Subhas
Chandra
b. 1898 Eisenstein,
Sergei Mikhailovich
b. 1898 Gaitan, Jorge
Eliecer
b. 1898 Granick, Harry
b. 1898 Scott, Randolph
b. 1898 Utley, Freda
b. 1899 Bogart,
Humphrey de Forest
b. 1899 Denning, Alfred
Thompson
b. 1899 Kane, Joseph
Nathan
b. 1901 Wirtz, Arthur
Michael
b. 1902 Klopfer, Donald
Simon
b. 1903 Galamian, Ivan
b. 1904 Quarles,
Benjamin Arthur
b. 1904 Zukofsky, Louis
b. 1905 Zacharias,
Jerrold R(einarch)
b. 1906? Steele, Bob
b. 1907 Duryea, Dan
b. 1907 Yukawa, Hideki
b. 1910 Price, Don K.
b. 1910 Reinhardt,
Django (Jean
Baptiste)
b. 1911 Eifert, Virginia
Snider
b. 1915 Lewis, William
Arthur, Sir
b. 1916 Duncan, David
Douglas
b. 1918 Elion, Gertrude
B(ell)
b. 1919 Kovacs, Ernie
b. 1922 Golub, Leon
Albert
b. 1923 Ashenfelter,
Nip
b. 1923 Halop, Florence
b. 1923 Logan, John
b. 1924 Lautenberg,
Frank R
b. 1925 Arnold, Danny
b. 1928 Moreau, Jeanne
b. 1929 Clarkson, Ewan
b. 1929 Polanyi, John C
b. 1930 Pogue, William
R(eid)
b. 1930 Walcott, Derek
(Alton)
b. 1931 Chun Doo
Hwan
b. 1933 Rivera, Chita
b. 1935 Moses, Robert
Parris
b. 1936 Golonka,
Arlene
b. 1936 Stone, Edward
C, Jr.
b. 1937 Zylis-Gara,
Teresa
b. 1942 Bogner, Willi
b. 1943 Burton, Gary
b. 1943 Gerard, Gil
b. 1944 Hauer, Rutger
b. 1945 Harris, Michael
Wesley
b. 1946 Aleman,
Arnoldo

b. 1946 Hilbert, Stephen
C.
b. 1946 Taylor, Susan
L.
b. 1947 Carper, Thomas
Richard
b. 1948 Pointer, Anita
b. 1950 Anderson,
Richard Dean
b. 1950 Cunningham,
Bill
b. 1950 Federici, Daniel
Paul
b. 1950 Simmons,
Pat(rick)
b. 1953 Haden, Pat(rick
Capper)
b. 1953 Zander, Robin
b. 1957 Caroline,
Princess
b. 1958 Christoff, Steve
d. 1516 Ferdinand V
d. 1622 Baffin, William
d. 1744 Vico, Giovanni
Battista
d. 1750 Muratori,
Lodovico Antonio
d. 1766 Caslon, William
d. 1789 Cleland, John
d. 1795 Sullivan, John
d. 1800 Rutledge,
Edward
d. 1806 Pitt, William,
the Younger
d. 1810 Hoppner, John
d. 1828 Randolph, Mary
d. 1858 Lablache, Luigi
d. 1866 Peacock,
Thomas Love
d. 1875 Kingsley,
Charles
d. 1879 Jensen, Adolph
d. 1883 Beard, George
Miller
d. 1883 Dore, Gustave
d. 1893 Brooks, Phillips
d. 1893 Lamar, Lucius
Quintus Cincinnatus
d. 1908 MacDowell,
Edward Alexander
d. 1922 Nikisch, Arthur
d. 1924 Morrice, James
Wilson
d. 1931 Pavlova, Anna
d. 1931 Rubens, Alma
d. 1943 Rice, Cale
Young
d. 1943 Woollcott,
Alexander
Humphreys
d. 1944 Munch, Edvard
d. 1945 Moltke,
Helmuth James, Graf
von
d. 1947 Bonnard, Pierre
d. 1956 Evans, Billy
d. 1956 Korda,
Alexander, Sir
d. 1960 Suckow, Ruth
d. 1961 Lawrie, Lee
d. 1964 Horst, Louis
d. 1973 Ory, Kid
d. 1976 Robeson, Paul
Leroy
d. 1978 Damas, Leon-
Gontran

d. 1978 Kath, Terry
d. 1978 Oakie, Jack
d. 1980 Buttrick, George Arthur
d. 1980 Williams, Paul R(evere)
d. 1981 Barber, Samuel
d. 1981 Teague, Olin E
d. 1982 Sillman, Leonard
d. 1983 Bane, Frank B
d. 1985 Beard, James Andrews
d. 1986 Beuys, Joseph
d. 1986 Leser, Tina
d. 1989 Dali, Salvador
d. 1992 Bartholomew, Freddie
d. 1993 Dorsey, Thomas Andrew
d. 1994 Dubridge, L(ee) A(lvin)
d. 1994 Smith, Oliver
d. 1995 Shils, Edward Albert
d. 1996 Burden, Carter
d. 1997 Berry, Richard
d. 1998 Limann, Hilla
d. 1999 Sommer, Frederick
d. 2000 Salam, Saeb

January 24

b. 76 Hadrian
b. 1281 Aungervyle, Richard
b. 1664 Vanbrugh, John, Sir
b. 1670 Congreve, William
b. 1679 Wolff, Christian von, Baron
b. 1705 Farinelli
b. 1712 Frederick the Great
b. 1732 Beaumarchais, Pierre Augustin Caron de
b. 1733 Lincoln, Benjamin
b. 1746 Gustavus, III
b. 1749 Fox, Charles James
b. 1752 Clementi, Muzio
b. 1776 Hoffmann, E(rnst) T(heodor) A(madeus)
b. 1800 Chadwick, Edwin
b. 1811 Barnard, Henry
b. 1820 Raymond, Henry Jarvis
b. 1828 Cohn, Ferdinand Julius
b. 1832 Choate, Joseph Hodges
b. 1850 Ebbinghaus, Hermann
b. 1850 Murfree, Mary Noailles
b. 1860 Kroger, Bernard Henry
b. 1862 Wharton, Edith
b. 1865 Bartlett, Paul Wayland

b. 1867 Mayo, Katherine
b. 1870 White, William Alanson
b. 1871 Jaggar, Thomas Augustus
b. 1874 Schomburg, Arthur Alfonso
b. 1882 Babcock, Harold Delos
b. 1882 Rothstein, Arnold
b. 1883 Winwood, Estelle
b. 1885 Biddle, George
b. 1888 Baum, Vicki
b. 1888 Heinkel, Ernst Heinrich
b. 1896 King, Henry
b. 1899 Vandenberg, Hoyt Sanford
b. 1901 Romm, Mikhail
b. 1902 Kiernan, Walter
b. 1903 DeWohl, Louis
b. 1903 Gwathmey, Robert
b. 1906 Primeau, Joe
b. 1907 Couve de Murville, (Jacques) Maurice
b. 1908 Duncan-Sandys, Edwin, Lord
b. 1908 Ford, Alexander
b. 1909 Cassandre, A(dolphe) M(ouron)
b. 1909 Kagel, Sam
b. 1909 Todd, Ann
b. 1911 Mathieson, Muir
b. 1913 Dello Joio, Norman Joseph
b. 1915 Goodson, Mark
b. 1915 Motherwell, Robert Burns
b. 1916 Haas, Walter A(braham), Jr.
b. 1917 Borgnine, Ernest
b. 1918 Einem, Gottfried von
b. 1918 Roberts, Oral
b. 1920 Saddler, Donald
b. 1921 Connolly, Sybil
b. 1921 Mintz, Beatrice
b. 1923 Rama Rau, Santha
b. 1924 Hill, Herbert
b. 1925 Tallchief, Maria
b. 1927 Burns, Jerry
b. 1927 Hawkins, Paula Fickes
b. 1928 Morris, Desmond
b. 1933 Beatty, Roger
b. 1934 Goldberg, Leonard
b. 1936 Kershaw, Doug(las James)
b. 1937 Clark, Monte Dale
b. 1939 Stevens, Ray
b. 1940 Waissman, Kenneth
b. 1941 Diamond, Neil
b. 1941 Neville, Aaron
b. 1943 Tate, Sharon

b. 1946 Ontkean, Michael
b. 1947 Chinaglia, Giorgio
b. 1947 Zevon, Warren
b. 1948 Abrams, Elliott
b. 1949 Belushi, John
b. 1951 Smirnoff, Yakov
b. 1957 Eaton, Mark E
b. 1960 Kinski, Nastassja
b. 1968 Retton, Mary Lou
d. 41 Caligula
d. 1791 Falconet, Etienne Maurice
d. 1813 Clymer, George
d. 1814 Heath, William
d. 1828 Lamb, Caroline Ponsonby, Lady
d. 1848 Wells, Horace
d. 1851 Spontini, Gasparo
d. 1872 Trendelenburg, Friedrich Adolf
d. 1883 Flotow, Friedrich von, Baron
d. 1885 Delany, Martin Robinson
d. 1895 Churchill, Randolph Henry Spencer, Lord
d. 1911 Philips, David Graham
d. 1930 Felton, Rebecca Ann Latimer
d. 1930 Sammarco, Mario
d. 1938 Barlach, Ernst Heinrich
d. 1947 Timmermans, Felix
d. 1950 Montana, Bull
d. 1955 Hayes, Ira Hamilton
d. 1960 Ford, Russ(ell William)
d. 1961 Gilbert, A(lfred) C(arleton)
d. 1963 Harbach, Otto Abels
d. 1965 Churchill, Winston Leonard Spencer, Sir
d. 1966 Bhabha, Homi Jehangir
d. 1966 Foyston, Frank C
d. 1971 Wilson, William Griffith
d. 1972 Austin, Gene
d. 1972 Cowan, Jerome
d. 1973 Naish, J(oseph) Carrol
d. 1973 Weintal, Edward
d. 1975 Fine, Larry
d. 1977 Lilly, Eli
d. 1977 Shor, Toots
d. 1980 Poe, James
d. 1982 Ovando Candia, Alfredo
d. 1983 Cukor, George (Dewey)

d. 1983 Ellsberg, Edward
d. 1983 Erickson, Eric
d. 1984 Reeves, Rosser
d. 1986 Hubbard, L(afayette) Ron(ald)
d. 1986 MacRae, Gordon
d. 1987 Burcham, Lester Arthur
d. 1988 King, Charles Glen
d. 1988 Schonfield, Hugh J
d. 1989 Bundy, Ted
d. 1990 Alonso, Damaso
d. 1991 Schaefer, Jack Warner
d. 1992 Darby, Ken
d. 1993 Marshall, Thurgood
d. 1998 Edmonds, Walter D(umaux)
d. 2000 Eckart, William Joseph

January 25

b. 1467 Bude, Guillaume
b. 1615 Flinck, Govert
b. 1627 Boyle, Robert
b. 1715 Helvetius, Claude Adrien
b. 1736 Lagrange, Joseph-Louis
b. 1743 Jacobi, Friedrich Heinrich
b. 1759 Burns, Robert
b. 1783 Colgate, William
b. 1806 Maclise, Daniel
b. 1812 Page, Charles Grafton
b. 1813 Sims, James Marion
b. 1825 Pickett, George Edward
b. 1854 Shaw, Mary
b. 1860 Curtis, Charles Brent
b. 1861 Bobbs, William Conrad
b. 1863 Jones, Rufus Matthew
b. 1866 Scotti, Antonio
b. 1866 Vandervelde, Emile
b. 1870 Ratana, Taupotiki Wiremu
b. 1871 Park, Maud May Wood
b. 1874 Johnson, Hewlett
b. 1874 Maugham, W(illiam) Somerset
b. 1876 Leonard, William Ellery
b. 1878 Alexanderson, Ernst Frederik Werner
b. 1881 Ludwig, Emil
b. 1882 Woolf, Virginia
b. 1884 Kilenyi, Edward, Sr.
b. 1886 Furtwangler, Wilhelm

b. 1891 Bullitt, William Christian
b. 1895 Mills, Florence
b. 1898 Tarasova, Alla Konstantinovna
b. 1899 Spaak, Paul-Henri
b. 1900 Dobzhansky, Theodosius (Grigorievich)
b. 1901 Dunnock, Mildred
b. 1901 Wilder, Robert Ingersoll
b. 1902 Hass, H(enry) B(ohn)
b. 1906 Custin, Mildred
b. 1913 Lutoslawski, Witold
b. 1914 Flora, James (Royer)
b. 1915 Deiss, Joseph Jay
b. 1915 Maccoll, Ewan
b. 1917 Prigogine, Ilya
b. 1918 Donovan, King
b. 1918 Harwell, Ernie
b. 1919 Newman, Edwin Harold
b. 1923 Galamison, Milton Arthur
b. 1923 Rinkoff, Barbara Jean
b. 1924 Groza, Lou(is)
b. 1925 Carnesseca, Lou
b. 1926 Kedourie, Elie
b. 1926 McGuire, Dick
b. 1927 Jobim, Antonio Carlos
b. 1928 Shevardnadze, Eduard Amvrosiyevich
b. 1928 Wine, Sherwin T(heodore)
b. 1929 Golson, Benny
b. 1933 Aquino, Corazon (Cojuangco)
b. 1934 Allen, Elizabeth
b. 1935 Allen, Bob
b. 1935 Burns, Conrad Ray
b. 1935 Eanes, Antonio dos Santos Ramalho
b. 1935 Gerrard, Roy
b. 1936 Hyland, Diana
b. 1936 Jones, Dean Carroll
b. 1937 Maynard, Don(ald)
b. 1938 Vysotsky, Vladimir Semyonovich
b. 1950 Cotten, Michael
b. 1950 Johnson, Virginia (Alma Fairfax)
b. 1950 Naylor, Gloria
b. 1951 Prefontaine, Steve Roland
b. 1954 Finch, Rick
b. 1958 Manoff, Dinah
b. 1962 Chelios, Chris
d. 1366 Suso, Heinrich
d. 1640 Burton, Robert
d. 1726 Delisle, Guillaume

d. 1833 Tarleton, Banastre, Sir
d. 1852 Bellinghausen, Fabian Gottlieb von
d. 1855 Nerval, Gerard de
d. 1871 Garrett, Thomas
d. 1906 Wheeler, Joseph
d. 1908 Ouida
d. 1910 Faust, Lotta
d. 1920 Modigliani, Amedeo
d. 1921 Bonfanti, Marie
d. 1929 Underwood, Oscar Wilder
d. 1947 Capone, Al(phonse)
d. 1949 Marshall, Peter
d. 1952 Moran, Polly
d. 1953 Jacobs, Michael S
d. 1953 Pitkin, Walter Boughton
d. 1957 Tuthill, Harry J
d. 1960 Barrymore, Diana
d. 1960 Thorek, Max
d. 1967 Bastianini, Ettore
d. 1969 Castle, Irene Foote
d. 1972 Hayden, Carl Trumball
d. 1975 Kellems, Vivien
d. 1976 Henderson, Vivian Wilson
d. 1980 Harsh, George
d. 1981 Astaire, Adele
d. 1985 Clarke, Kenny
d. 1985 Smith, Paul Joseph
d. 1988 Moore, Colleen
d. 1990 Gardner, Ava
d. 1992 Riad, Mahmoud
d. 1996 Larson, Jonathan
d. 1997 Dixon, Jeane (Pinckert)
d. 1999 Shaw, Robert Lawson

January 26
b. Bible, Frances Lillian
b. 1716 Germain, George Sackville
b. 1763 Bernadotte, Jean Baptiste
b. 1781 Arnim, Achim von (Ludwig Joachim)
b. 1786 Haydon, Benjamin Robert
b. 1801 Quidor, John
b. 1826 Grant, Julia Dent
b. 1828 Sylvis, William (H.)
b. 1831 DeBary, Heinrich Anton
b. 1831 Dodge, Mary Elizabeth Mapes
b. 1832 Shiras, George, Jr.
b. 1842 Coppee, Francois Edouard Joachim

b. 1846 Keith, Benjamin Franklin
b. 1847 Clark, John Bates
b. 1848 Sierra, Justo
b. 1852 Brazza, Pierre Paul Francois Camille Savorgnan de
b. 1861 Lowden, Frank O(rren)
b. 1865 Bauer, Louis Agricola
b. 1871 Adams, Samuel Hopkins
b. 1872 Morgan, Julia
b. 1877 Dongen, Kees van
b. 1878 Gabrilowitsch, Ossip Salomonovich
b. 1880 MacArthur, Douglas
b. 1884 Andrews, Roy Chapman
b. 1884 Sapir, Edward
b. 1887 Mitscher, Marc Andrew
b. 1891 Costello, Frank
b. 1891 Penfield, Wilder Graves
b. 1893 Coleman, Bessie
b. 1893 Nighbor, Frank
b. 1898 Hickerson, John Dewey
b. 1902 Brent, Romney
b. 1904 Keys, Ancel Benjamin
b. 1904 MacBride, Sean
b. 1905 Cousins, (Sue) Margaret
b. 1905 Trapp, Maria Augusta von
b. 1907 Cotton, Henry, Sir
b. 1907 Selye, Hans
b. 1908 Esmond, Jill
b. 1908 Grappelli, Stephane
b. 1911 Kusch, P(olycarp)
b. 1912 Baird, Cora Eisenberg
b. 1912 Cannon, Howard Walter
b. 1912 Sheinwold, Alfred
b. 1913 Prince, William
b. 1913 Van Heusen, Jimmy
b. 1914 DeManio, Jack
b. 1915 Hopper, William
b. 1917 Verity, C(alvin) William, Jr.
b. 1918 Ceausescu, Nicolae
b. 1918 Farmer, Philip Jose
b. 1921 Morita, Akio
b. 1923 Jeffreys, Anne
b. 1925 Leslie, Joan
b. 1925 Newman, Paul
b. 1925 Ryan, Claude
b. 1927 Azcona Hoyo, Jose Simon
b. 1928 Vadim, Roger

b. 1929 Feiffer, Jules Ralph
b. 1929 Kronhausen, Phyllis Carmen
b. 1930 Gumbleton, Thomas J
b. 1932 Clements, George Harold
b. 1935 Uecker, Bob
b. 1936 Simitis, Costas
b. 1937 Momoh, Joseph (Saidu)
b. 1939 Garfield, Brian Wynne
b. 1940 Cadoria, Sherian Grace
b. 1940 Reilly, William Kane
b. 1942? Glenn, Scott
b. 1943 Gutierrez, Cesar Dario
b. 1943 Hite, Robert Ernest, Jr.
b. 1943 Panek, LeRoy Lad
b. 1944 Davis, Angela (Yvonne)
b. 1945 DuPre, Jacqueline
b. 1945 Jones, Thom
b. 1945 Kruger, Barbara
b. 1945 Rifkin, Jeremy
b. 1946 Hampton, Christopher James
b. 1946 Siskel, Gene
b. 1947 Dewaere, Patrick
b. 1950 Youngblood, Jack
b. 1956 Harris, Eddy L(ouis)
b. 1957 McCourt, Dale Allen
b. 1957 Van Halen, Eddie
b. 1958 Baker, Anita
b. 1958 DeGeneres, Ellen
b. 1958 Lemon, Ted
b. 1961 Gretzky, Wayne
b. 1963 Ridgeley, Andrew
d. 1823 Jenner, Edward
d. 1824 Gericault, Jean Louis Andre Theodore
d. 1839 Van Rensselaer, Stephen
d. 1850 Jeffrey, Francis Jeffrey, Lord
d. 1860 Schroder-Devrient, Wilhelmine
d. 1871 Ticknor, George
d. 1879 Fowler, Lydia Folger
d. 1884 Letcher, John
d. 1885 Gordon, Charles George
d. 1891 Otto, Nikolaus August
d. 1893 Doubleday, Abner
d. 1895 Cayley, Arthur
d. 1896 MacMillan, Alexander

d. 1932 Wrigley,
William, Jr.
d. 1933 Belmont, Alva
Erskine Smith
Vanderbilt
d. 1933 Gummere,
William Stryker
d. 1935 Ippolitov-
Ivanov, Mikhail
Mikhailovich
d. 1936 Ittner, William
Butts
d. 1938 Bonnin,
Gertrude Simmons
d. 1939 Sauveur, Albert
d. 1943 Vavilov,
Nikolai Ivanovich
d. 1945 Pendergast,
Thomas Joseph
d. 1945 Szabo, Violette
Bushell
d. 1947 Moore, Grace
d. 1948 Lomax, John
Avery
d. 1962 Luciano, Lucky
d. 1962 O'Neill, Steve
d. 1963 Olsen, Ole
d. 1967 Isaacs, Alick
d. 1973 Jones, Eli
Stanley
d. 1973 Robinson,
Edward G
d. 1974 Patzak, Julius
d. 1978 Genn, Leo
d. 1979 Rockefeller,
Nelson A(ldrich)
d. 1980 Patrick, Lynn
Howard
d. 1982 Suslov, Mikhail
Andreevich
d. 1983 Bryant, Bear
d. 1983 Reichelderfer,
Francis Wylton
d. 1984 Dart, Justin
Whitlock
d. 1985 Harlech,
William David
Ormsby-Gore, Baron
d. 1986 Lorjou, Bernard
Joseph Pierre
d. 1987 McLaren,
Norman
d. 1990 Mumford,
Lewis
d. 1991 Langan, Glenn
d. 1992 Ferrer, Jose
Vicente
d. 1993 Sauve, Jeanne
Mathilde Benoit
d. 1995 Allers, Franz
d. 1996 Brodkey,
Harold
d. 1996 Jewtraw,
Charlie
d. 1996 Lewis, Henry
(Jay)
d. 1998 Suzuki,
Shin'ichi
d. 1999 Delany, Sarah
Louise
d. 1999 Luckman,
Charles
d. 2000 Budge, Don
January 27
b. 1571 Abbas I
b. 1662 Bentley,
Richard

b. 1720 Foote, Samuel
b. 1756 Mozart,
Wolfgang Amadeus
b. 1775 Schelling,
Friedrich Wilhelm
Joseph von
b. 1780 Alvarez, Juan
b. 1808 Strauss, David
Friedrich
b. 1814 Appleton,
William Henry
b. 1814 Viollet le Duc,
Eugene Emmanuel
b. 1823 Lalo, Edouard
Victor Antoine
b. 1823 Renan, (Joseph)
Ernest
b. 1824 Israels, Josef
b. 1832 Carroll, Lewis
b. 1832 Hughes, Arthur
b. 1836? Sacher-
Masoch, Leopold von
b. 1850 Genung, John
Franklin
b. 1850 Gompers,
Samuel
b. 1859 Miliukov, Pavel
Nikolayevich
b. 1859 Wilhelm II
b. 1859 William, II
b. 1861 Modjeski,
Ralph
b. 1869 Cook, Will
Marion
b. 1872 Hand, Learned
b. 1882 Pew, J(ohn)
Howard
b. 1883 Toye, Francis
b. 1886 Downes, Olin
b. 1887 Blegen, Carl
William
b. 1888 Goldschmidt,
Victor Moritz
b. 1891 Ehrenburg, Ilya
Grigoryevich
b. 1893 Sun Yat-Sen,
Chingling Soong,
Madame
b. 1894 Pollard, Fritz
b. 1895 Rosenstock,
Joseph
b. 1895 Ruby, Harry
b. 1896 DeSylva, Buddy
b. 1899 Strong, Philip
Duffield
b. 1900 Clark, Georgia
Neese
b. 1900 Rickover,
Hyman George
b. 1901 Rooney, Art(hur
Joseph)
b. 1903 Eccles, John
C(arew), Sir
b. 1907 Compton, Joyce
b. 1908 Burtin, Will
b. 1908 Hearst, William
Randolph, Jr.
b. 1908 Page, Hot Lips
b. 1909 Eklund, Carl
Robert
b. 1910 Candela, Felix
b. 1911 Venuta, Benay
b. 1915 Brymer, Jack
b. 1918 Henderson,
Skitch

b. 1918 Heyns, Roger
W(illiam)
b. 1918 James, Elmore
b. 1919 Seville, David
b. 1920 Albert, Frank
C.
b. 1920 Box, John
b. 1921 Reed, Donna
b. 1922 Fleischmann,
Peter F(rancis)
b. 1924 Denktash, Rauf
b. 1927 Barnes, Billy
b. 1927 Dickerson,
Nancy Hanschman
b. 1927 Fulton, Richard
Harmon
b. 1927 Perry, Joe
b. 1929 Thulin, Ingrid
b. 1930 Bland, Bobby
Blue
b. 1931 Richler,
Mordecai
b. 1933 Buss, Jerry
Hatten
b. 1934 Cresson, Edith
Campion
b. 1934 Zaragosa,
Federico Mayor
b. 1935 Thomas,
D(onald) M(ichael)
b. 1936 Donahue, Troy
b. 1936 Ting, Samuel
Chao Chung
b. 1938 Cole, Kenneth
Reese
b. 1939 Lester, Julius
b. 1942 Wynn, Stephen
A.
b. 1944 Corrigan-
Maguire, Mairead
b. 1944 Maguire,
Mairead Corrigan
b. 1945 Cardinal,
Harold
b. 1945 Ghiz, Joseph A
b. 1945 Mason, Nick
b. 1952 Gottfried, Brian
b. 1953 Augustyn,
Frank Joseph
b. 1959 Collinsworth,
Cris
b. 1964 Fonda, Bridget
b. 1964 Reagon, Toshi
d. 1540 Angela Merici,
Saint
d. 1654 Andrae, Johann
Valentin
d. 1731 Cristofori,
Bartolomeo di
Francesco
d. 1788 Tryon, William
d. 1814 Fichte, Johann
Gottlieb
d. 1832 Bell, Andrew
d. 1840 Chauncey, Isaac
d. 1850 Schadow,
Gottfried
d. 1851 Audubon, John
James
d. 1855 Rossi, Gaetano
d. 1863 Robinson,
Edward
d. 1866 Gibson, John
d. 1893 Blaine, James
Gillespie

d. 1901 Verdi, Giuseppe
Fortunino Francesco
d. 1909 Coquelin,
Benoit Constant
d. 1919 Ady, Endre
d. 1919 Chadwick,
French Ensor
d. 1922 Bly, Nellie
d. 1922 Verga,
Giovanni
d. 1925 von Hugel,
Friedrich, Baron
d. 1947 Mildenburg,
Anna von
d. 1951 Mannerheim,
Carl Gustav Emil,
Baron
d. 1952 Ward, Fannie
d. 1956 Kleiber, Erich
d. 1960 Aranha,
Osvaldo
d. 1962 LeSueur, Percy
d. 1967 Chaffee, Roger
Bruce
d. 1967 Grissom, Virgil
Ivan
d. 1967 Juin, Alphonse
Pierre
d. 1967 White, Ed(ward
Higgins, III)
d. 1970 Heckel, Erich
d. 1971 Arbenz
Guzman, Jacobo
d. 1971 Campbell, E
Simms
d. 1972 Courant,
Richard
d. 1972 Jackson,
Mahalia
d. 1972 Weeks, Sinclair
d. 1974 Grivas,
Georgios Theodoros
d. 1975 Fuller, Ida
d. 1975 Sanderson, Julia
d. 1978 Homolka, Oscar
d. 1983 Bidault,
Georges
d. 1983 Bilon, Michael
Patrick
d. 1986 Borglum, James
Lincoln Delamothe
d. 1986 Palmer, Lilli
d. 1989 Sopwith,
Thomas O M, Sir
d. 1991 Long, Dale
d. 1994 Adams, Stanley
d. 1994 Akins, Claude
d. 1996 Yarborough,
Ralph W(ebster)
d. 2000 Gulda, Friedrich
January 28
b. 1457 Henry VII
b. 1611 Hevelius,
Johannes
b. 1706 Baskerville,
John
b. 1760 Carey, Mathew
b. 1780 Velluti,
Giovanni Battista
b. 1784 Aberdeen, 4th
Earl of
b. 1791 Herold,
Ferdinand
b. 1822 Mackenzie,
Alexander

b. 1833 Gordon, Charles
George
b. 1834 Baring-Gould,
Sabine
b. 1841 Nessler, Victor
E
b. 1847 Wright, George
b. 1853 Marti (y Perez),
Jose Julian
b. 1853 Soloviev,
Vladimir Sergeevich
b. 1855 Burroughs,
William Seward
b. 1858 Adams, Herbert
Samuel
b. 1858 Dubois, Eugene
b. 1861 Willard, Daniel
b. 1865 Stahlberg,
Kaarlo Juho
b. 1871 Lukeman,
Henry A
b. 1873 Colette
b. 1874 Meyerhold,
Vsevolod Emilievich
b. 1880 Boland, Mary
b. 1882 Hobart, Alice
Tisdale Nourse
b. 1884 Piccard,
Auguste
b. 1884 Piccard, Jean
Felix
b. 1887 Rubinstein,
Arthur
b. 1890 Fergusson,
Harvey
b. 1891 Doak, Bill
b. 1891 Sedran, Barney
b. 1892 Lubitsch, Ernst
b. 1893 Silver, Abba
Hillel
b. 1897 Katayev,
Valentin Petrovich
b. 1900 Neel, Alice
Hartley
b. 1900 Perkins, Milo
Randolph
b. 1901 Barthe,
Richmond
b. 1902 Barr, Alfred
Hamilton, Jr.
b. 1903 Lonsdale,
Kathleen (Yardley)
b. 1905 Fairclough,
Ellen Louks
b. 1911 Metcalf, Lee
b. 1911 Miller, Max
b. 1911 Moss, Arnold
b. 1912 Pollock,
Jackson
b. 1912 Wolfson, Louis
Elwood
b. 1922 Holley, Robert
W(illiam)
b. 1927 Teshigahara,
Hiroshi
b. 1929 Oldenburg,
Claes Thure
b. 1932 O'Brien, Parry
b. 1934 White, Bill
b. 1934 White, Bill
b. 1935 Lodge, David
(John)
b. 1935 Pryor, Nicholas
b. 1936 Alda, Alan
b. 1936 Kadare, Ismail

b. 1939 Wallace,
Cornelia Folsom
b. 1943 Howard, Susan
b. 1945 Keller, Marthe
b. 1946 Allen, Rick
b. 1946? Beck, John
b. 1946 Skolnick, Mark
H(enry)
b. 1948 Baryshnikov,
Mikhail
b. 1948 Taylor, Charles
b. 1950 Benton, Barbie
b. 1956 Schilling, Peter
b. 1957 Price, Nick
b. 1968 McLachlan,
Sarah
b. 1981 Wood, Elijah
d. 814 Charlemagne
d. 1547 Henry VIII
d. 1596 Drake, Francis,
Sir
d. 1613 Bodley,
Thomas, Sir
d. 1687 Hevelius,
Johannes
d. 1725 Peter the Great
d. 1829 Burke, William
d. 1859 Prescott,
William Hickling
d. 1865 Romani, Felice
d. 1868 Head, Edmund
Walker, Sir
d. 1876 Deak, Francis
d. 1881 Dostoyevsky,
Fyodor Mikhailovich
d. 1889 Crandall,
Prudence
d. 1903 Planquette,
Jean(-Robert)
d. 1912 Alfaro, Jose
Eloy
d. 1918 McCrae, John
d. 1926 Kohler,
Kaufmann
d. 1928 Blasco-Ibanez,
Vicente
d. 1930 Destinn, Emmy
d. 1933 Saintsbury,
George Edward
Bateman
d. 1933 Teasdale, Sara
d. 1936 Loeb, Richard
A
d. 1939 Yeats, William
Butler
d. 1947 Cohen, Morris
Raphael
d. 1953 Scullin, James
Henry
d. 1953 Tharaud,
Jerome
d. 1960 Hurston, Zora
Neale
d. 1963 Farrow, John
Villiers
d. 1963 Piccard, Jean
Felix
d. 1965 Weygand,
Maxime
d. 1966 Quill, Mike
d. 1969 Herbst,
Josephine Frey
d. 1975 Novotny,
Antonin
d. 1980 Durante, Jimmy
d. 1981 Gerber, John

d. 1981 Gribble, Harry
Wagstaff Graham
d. 1984 Dexter, Al
d. 1984 Dooley, Rae
d. 1985 Saunders, Allen
d. 1985 Smith, Dora
d. 1986 Berlin, Richard
E
d. 1986 Jarvis, Gregory
d. 1986 McAuliffe,
Christa
d. 1986 McNair, Ronald
Ervin
d. 1986 Onizuka,
Ellison
d. 1986 Resnik, Judy
d. 1986 Scobee, Dick
d. 1986 Smith, Michael
John
d. 1987 Plaza Lasso,
Galo
d. 1987 Trifa, Valerian
d. 1988 Fuchs, Klaus
d. 1989 Panchen Lama
d. 1991 Grange, Red
d. 1993 Swift, Kay
d. 1994 Douglas, Emily
Taft
d. 1994 Levitt, William
J(aird)
d. 1995 Roudebush,
Richard L(owell)
d. 1995 Tagliavini,
Ferrucio
d. 1996 Brodsky, Joseph
(Alexandrovich)
d. 1996 Hogarth, Burne
d. 1996 Siegel, Jerry
January 29
b. 1565 Meres, Francis
b. 1688 Swedenborg,
Emanuel
b. 1693 Anna Ivanovna
b. 1717 Amherst,
Jeffrey
b. 1737 Paine, Thomas
b. 1754 Cleaveland,
Moses
b. 1756 Lee, Henry
b. 1761 Gallatin, Albert
b. 1773 Mohs, Friedrich
b. 1835 Woolsey, Sarah
Chauncey
b. 1843 McKinley,
William
b. 1850 Hargrave,
Lawrence
b. 1850 Howard,
Ebenezer, Sir
b. 1860 Robertson,
William Robert, Sir
b. 1862 Delius,
Frederick
b. 1866 Rolland,
Romain
b. 1867 Blasco-Ibanez,
Vicente
b. 1870 Bordeaux,
Henry
b. 1872 Rothenstein,
William, Sir
b. 1873 Abruzzi, Luigi
Amedeo
b. 1873 Palmer,
Frederick
b. 1874 Davis, Owen

b. 1874 Rockefeller,
John D(avison), Jr.
b. 1878 Akeley, Mary
Lee Jobe
b. 1878 George, Walter
Franklin
b. 1878 Oldfield,
Barney
b. 1880 Fields, W C
b. 1881 Evans, Alice
(Catherine)
b. 1888 Chapman,
Sydney
b. 1895 Berle, Adolf
Augustus, Jr.
b. 1897 O'Meara,
Walter (Andrew)
b. 1898 Muller, Maria
b. 1901 DuMont, Allen
Balcom
b. 1905 Delmar, Vina
Croter
b. 1905 Judd, Winnie
Ruth McKinnell
b. 1905 Newman,
Barnett
b. 1907 Becker, Ralph
E(lihu)
b. 1907 Bernstein,
Sid(ney Ralph)
b. 1909 Marshal, Alan
b. 1909 Masur, Harold
Q
b. 1911 Eldridge, Roy
b. 1913 Mature, Victor
(John)
b. 1913 Schneider, Nina
b. 1914 Prudden,
Bonnie
b. 1916 Murphy,
Franklin D(avid)
b. 1918 Barber, Bernard
b. 1918 Forsythe, John
b. 1920 Allsop, Kenneth
b. 1922 Richman,
Milton
b. 1923 Burke, Jack, Jr.
b. 1923 Chayefsky,
Paddy
b. 1924 Nono, Luigi
b. 1925 Abrahams,
Doris Cole
b. 1925 Crichton,
Robert
b. 1926 Salam, Abdus
b. 1927 Abbey, Edward
b. 1929 Petri, Elio
b. 1931 Bricusse, Leslie
b. 1935 Payne, Roger S.
b. 1936 Harrison, Noel
b. 1939 Greer,
Germaine
b. 1940 Diaz, Justino
b. 1941 Morgan, Robin
b. 1942 Longet,
Claudine Georgette
b. 1943 Quinn, Pat
b. 1943 Ross, Katharine
b. 1945 Caponi, Donna
b. 1945 Selleck, Tom
b. 1951 Jillian, Ann
b. 1954 Galbreath, Tony
b. 1954 Winfrey, Oprah
Gail
b. 1958 Norton-Taylor,
Judy

b. 1960 Louganis, Greg(ory Efthimios)
b. 1965 Hasek, Dominik
d. 1647 Meres, Francis
d. 1676 Romanov, Alexis Mikhailovich
d. 1743 Fleury, Andre Hercule de
d. 1819 Charles, IV
d. 1820 George III
d. 1829 Barras, Paul Francois Jean Nicolas, Comte de
d. 1829 Pickering, Timothy
d. 1859 Thomas, Seth
d. 1888 Lear, Edward
d. 1899 Sisley, Alfred
d. 1917 Cromer, 1st Earl of
d. 1923 Vedder, Elihu
d. 1928 Haig, Douglas
d. 1930 Tappan, Eva March
d. 1934 Haber, Fritz
d. 1935 Dellenbaugh, Frederick Samuel
d. 1940 Harkness, Edward Stephen
d. 1941 Metaxas, John
d. 1944 White, William Allen
d. 1946 Hopkins, Harry Lloyd
d. 1951 Bridie, James
d. 1955 Hedtoft (-Hansen), Hans Christian
d. 1956 Mencken, H(enry) L(ouis)
d. 1962 Kreisler, Fritz
d. 1963 Frost, Robert Lee
d. 1964 Anderson, Mary
d. 1964 Ladd, Alan
d. 1968 Black, Frank J.
d. 1969 Boehm, Edward M
d. 1969 Dulles, Allen Welsh
d. 1970 Harris, Lauren
d. 1970 Liddell Hart, Basil Henry, Sir
d. 1974 Bates, H(erbert) E(rnest)
d. 1977 Prinze, Freddie
d. 1978 McCoy, Tim(othy John Fitzgerald)
d. 1979 Soby, James Thrall
d. 1981 Cole, Cozy
d. 1981 Glassco, John Stinson
d. 1982 Namgyal, Palden Thondup
d. 1983 Fury, Billy
d. 1983 Ingersoll, Stuart H
d. 1984 Goodrich, Frances
d. 1987 Impellitteri, Vincent R(ichard)
d. 1988 Killian, James Rhyne, Jr.

d. 1989 DaCosta, Morton
d. 1991 Graham, John
d. 1992 Dixon, Willie (James)
d. 1993 Hasford, Jerry Gustav
d. 1998 Alioto, Joseph L(awrence)
d. 1998 Gorman, Carl Nelson
d. 1999 Saint Cyr, Lillian

January 30
b. 570 Mohammed
b. 1628 Villers, George
b. 1720 Bellotto, Bernardo
b. 1750 Thomas, Isaiah
b. 1775 Landor, Walter Savage
b. 1785 Metcalfe, Charles Theophilus
b. 1792 Hopkins, John Henry
b. 1797 Sumner, Edwin V
b. 1801 Smet, Pierre Jean de
b. 1839 Armstrong, Samuel Chapman
b. 1841 Faure, Francois Felix
b. 1841 Townsend, George Alfred
b. 1846 Bradley, Francis Herbert
b. 1848 Mannlicher, Ferdinand
b. 1861 Loeffler, Charles Martin Tornow
b. 1862 Damrosch, Walter Johannes
b. 1866 Burgess, Gelett
b. 1873 Jensen, Johannes Vilhelm
b. 1882 Roosevelt, Franklin D(elano)
b. 1885 Towers, John Henry
b. 1891 Beech, Walter Herschel
b. 1899 Theiler, Max
b. 1900 Hunt, Martita
b. 1902 Pevsner, Nikolaus Bernhard Leon, Sir
b. 1903 Gassner, John Waldhorn
b. 1909 Alinsky, Saul David
b. 1911 Foyle, Christina Agnes Lilian
b. 1911 Sanderson, Ivan Terence
b. 1912 Tuchman, Barbara Wertheim
b. 1914 Marlowe, Hugh
b. 1914 Wayne, David
b. 1915 Ireland, John
b. 1915 Profumo, John Dennis
b. 1917 Darion, Joseph
b. 1918 Opatoshu, David

b. 1920 Anderson, Michael
b. 1920 Hightower, Rosella
b. 1923 Dropo, Walt(er)
b. 1923 Martin, Dick
b. 1924 Alexander, Lloyd Chudley
b. 1925 Malone, Dorothy
b. 1927 Palme, Olof
b. 1928 Leigh, Mitch
b. 1928 Meskill, Thomas J
b. 1928 Prince, Hal
b. 1929 Stevens, Morton
b. 1931 Crosbie, John (Carnell)
b. 1931 Hackman, Gene
b. 1931 Hazzard, Shirley
b. 1931 McKinney, Stewart Brett
b. 1933 Brautigan, Richard
b. 1933 Rukeyser, Louis (Richard)
b. 1933 Sinkford, Jeanne C(raig)
b. 1934 Grimes, Tammy Lee
b. 1934 Markus, Robert
b. 1937 Redgrave, Vanessa
b. 1937 Spassky, Boris Vasilyevich
b. 1938 Karimov, Islam Abduganievich
b. 1941 Cheney, Dick
b. 1943 Balin, Marty
b. 1943 Deane, Sandy
b. 1943 Johnson, Davey
b. 1944 Dixon, Sharon Pratt
b. 1944 Harrell, Lynn Morris
b. 1944 Kelly, Sharon Pratt
b. 1945 Dorris, Michael (Anthony)
b. 1945 Flake, Floyd H(arold)
b. 1946 Beesley, H(orace) Brent
b. 1949 King, William
b. 1951 Collins, Phil(ip)
b. 1951 Dutton, Charles S
b. 1955 Cromwell, Nolan Neil
b. 1955 Strange, Curtis
b. 1958 Butler, Brett
b. 1961 Watley, Jody
d. 1629 Maderno, Carlo
d. 1649 Charles I
d. 1652 La Tour, Georges Dumesnil de
d. 1797 Glover, John
d. 1806 Martin y Soler, Vicente
d. 1836 Ross, Betsy
d. 1838 Osceola
d. 1849 DeWint, Peter
d. 1872 Chesney, Francis Rawdon
d. 1888 Gray, Asa

d. 1888 Howitt, Mary
d. 1889 Rudolf of Hapsburg
d. 1891 Bradlaugh, Charles
d. 1891 Kalakaua, David
d. 1909 Finley, Martha
d. 1910 Woods, Granville T
d. 1916 Jacobs, Joseph
d. 1926 Doughty, Charles Montagu
d. 1926 LaMarr, Barbara
d. 1928 Fibiger, Johannes Andreas Grib
d. 1934 Doubleday, Frank Nelson
d. 1945 Haberlandt, Gottlieb
d. 1948 Gandhi, Mahatma
d. 1948 Pennock, Herb(ert Jefferis)
d. 1948 Wright, Orville
d. 1951 Porsche, Ferdinand
d. 1954 Anderson, John Murray
d. 1954 Wilson, Henry Braid
d. 1958 Heinkel, Ernst Heinrich
d. 1963 Poulenc, Francis
d. 1969 Pire, Dominique
d. 1979 Muir, Malcolm
d. 1980 Byrd, Henry
d. 1980 Dagover, Lil
d. 1980 Margolius, Sidney Senier
d. 1980 Papanin, Ivan D
d. 1980 Professor Longhair
d. 1981 Gopallawa, William
d. 1982 Holloway, Stanley
d. 1982 Hopkins, Lightnin'
d. 1982 Lynd, Helen Merrell
d. 1983 Cunningham, Alan Gordon, Sir
d. 1983 Machlup, Fritz
d. 1983 Stevens, Robert Ten Broeck
d. 1984 Coxe, George Harmon
d. 1986 Erickson, Leif
d. 1988 Groves, Wallace
d. 1988 Neddermeyer, Seth H
d. 1989 Fitzgerald, Pegeen
d. 1989 Gould, Beatrice Blackmar
d. 1991 Bardeen, John
d. 1991 McIntire, John
d. 1994 Boulle, Pierre Francois Marie-Louis
d. 1995 Durrell, Gerald (Malcolm)

d. 1999 Hall, Huntz
January 31
b. 1713 Benezet, Anthony
b. 1734 Morris, Robert
b. 1735 Crevecoeur, Michel-Guillaume Jean de
b. 1735 Crevecoeur, (Hector) St. John de
b. 1752 Morris, Gouverneur
b. 1762 Macquarie, Lachlan
b. 1788 Romani, Felice
b. 1797 Schubert, Franz Peter
b. 1798 Apess, William
b. 1806 Harper, Fletcher
b. 1830 Blaine, James Gillespie
b. 1830 Rochefort, Henri
b. 1831 Wurlitzer, Rudolph
b. 1841 Loyd, Sam(uel)
b. 1841 Stanley, Henry Morton, Sir
b. 1844 L'Hermitte, Leon Augustin
b. 1848 Straus, Nathan
b. 1851 Webb, William Seward
b. 1860 Huneker, James Gibbons
b. 1866 Shestov, Lev
b. 1868 Richards, Theodore William
b. 1872 Grey, Zane
b. 1872 Hughes, Rupert
b. 1876 Spargo, John
b. 1881 Langmuir, Irving
b. 1885 Pavlova, Anna
b. 1889 Deloria, Ella Clara
b. 1892 Cantor, Eddie
b. 1894 Jones, Isham
b. 1896 Strauss, Lewis Lichtenstein
b. 1900 Parsons, Betty Pierson
b. 1901 Fabian, Robert Honey
b. 1902 Bankhead, Tallulah Brockman
b. 1902 Myrdal, Alva Reimer
b. 1902 Steward, Julian Haynes
b. 1903 Cowles, Gardner, Jr.
b. 1905 O'Hara, John Henry
b. 1906 Sykes, Roosevelt
b. 1908 Cantwell, Robert Emmett
b. 1911 Ivan, Tommy
b. 1913 Hutson, Don(ald M)
b. 1914 Addonizio, Hugh Joseph
b. 1914 Walcott, Joe
b. 1915 Hackett, Bobby

b. 1915 Merton, Thomas
b. 1915 Moore, Garry
b. 1916 Parker, Frank
b. 1919 Robinson, Jackie
b. 1920 Udall, Stewart Lee
b. 1920 Warnke, Paul Culliton
b. 1921 Agar, John
b. 1921 Jones, Fay
b. 1921 Lanza, Mario
b. 1923 Channing, Carol
b. 1923 Dru, Joanne
b. 1923 Mailer, Norman (Kingsley)
b. 1925 Hooks, Benjamin Lawson
b. 1925 Taubman, A(dolph) Alfred
b. 1929 Mossbauer, Rudolf Ludwig
b. 1929 Simmons, Jean
b. 1931 Banks, Ernie
b. 1931 Carbine, Patricia Theresa
b. 1931 Chataway, Christopher John
b. 1934 Franciscus, James Grover
b. 1935 Oe, Kenzaburo
b. 1937 Glass, Philip
b. 1937 Pleshette, Suzanne
b. 1938 Beatrix
b. 1938 Watt, James Gaius
b. 1940? Margolin, Stuart
b. 1941 Gephardt, Richard Andrew
b. 1941 Mickelson, George Speaker
b. 1944 Walter, Jessica
b. 1946 Kath, Terry
b. 1947 Ryan, Nolan
b. 1951 Casey, H(arry) W(ayne)
b. 1955 Ruzici, Virginia
b. 1956 Lydon, John (Joseph)
b. 1957 Babashoff, Shirley
b. 1961 Cole, Lloyd
d. 1561 Menno Simonsz(con)
d. 1606 Fawkes, Guy
d. 1736 Juvara, Filippo
d. 1780 Carver, Jonathan
d. 1783 Majorano, Gaetano
d. 1788 Charles Edward Louis Philip Casimir Stuart
d. 1788 Stuart, Charles Edward Louis Philip
d. 1854 Pellico, Silvio
d. 1863 Robinson, John Beverley
d. 1866 Ruckert, Friedrich
d. 1889 Gungl, Joseph
d. 1891 Meissonier, Jean Louis Ernest

d. 1900 Queensberry, John Sholto Douglas
d. 1907 Eaton, Timothy
d. 1919 Goodwin, Nat C
d. 1922 Borglum, Solon Hannibal
d. 1923 Montezuma, Carlos
d. 1925 Cable, George Washington
d. 1933 Galsworthy, John
d. 1934 Wellman, Walter
d. 1944 Giraudoux, Jean
d. 1945 Slovik, Eddie
d. 1947 Kling, Johnny
d. 1951 Cochran, C(harles) B(lake)
d. 1954 Bates, Florence
d. 1955 Mott, John Raleigh
d. 1955 Washington, Buck
d. 1956 Milne, A(lan) A(lexander)
d. 1961 Thompson, Dorothy
d. 1965 Cooper, Kent
d. 1966 Manship, Paul
d. 1968 Pillsbury, John Sargent
d. 1970 Bell, Herbert A
d. 1972 Barlow, Howard
d. 1972 Boyce, Westray Battle
d. 1972 Mahendra, Bir Bikram Shah Dev
d. 1973 Frisch, Ragnar Anton Kittil
d. 1974 Goldwyn, Samuel
d. 1974 Morris, Glenn
d. 1974 Pryor, Roger
d. 1976 Miranda, Ernesto
d. 1976 Wells, Linton
d. 1980 Crosby, Alexander L
d. 1981 Butterfield, Roger Place
d. 1982 Calder, Peter Ritchie
d. 1982 Turnbull, Agnes Sligh
d. 1984 Bricktop
d. 1984 Cipullo, Aldo Massimo Fabrizio
d. 1986 Allegret, Yves
d. 1986 Jessup, Philip Caryl
d. 1989 Stephenson, William
d. 1992 Hein, Mel(vin John)
d. 1995 Abbott, George (Francis)

FEBRUARY

b. 1606 Davenant, William, Sir
b. 1609 Suckling, John

b. 1731 Churchill, Charles
b. 1882 Torrio, Johnny
b. 1898 Banda, Hastings Kamuzu
b. 1926 Parbo, Arvi (Hillar)
b. 1946 Dowiyogo, Bernard
b. 1960 Julien, Isaac
b. 1961 Cameron, David
b. 1965 Dell, Michael
d. 1568? Coverdale, Miles
d. 1612 Gerard, John
d. 1672 Stuyvesant, Peter
d. 1675 Dou, Gerard
d. 1766 Porpora, Niccolo
d. 1787 Mason, Charles
d. 1898 Taewon'gun, Hungson
d. 1938 King, Frederic Truby
d. 1962 Johnson, Chic
d. 1970 Wolff, Albert Louis
d. 1978 Eliot, Martha May
d. 1980 Voit, Willard Darby
d. 1982 Campagnolo, Gitullio
d. 1990 Day, Hap
d. 1992 D'Aubuisson, Roberto
d. 1994 Fisher, Avery
February 1
b. 1506 Buchanan, George
b. 1552 Coke, Edward, Sir
b. 1716 Bard, John
b. 1757 Kemble, John Philip
b. 1791 Sax, Charles Joseph
b. 1801 Cole, Thomas
b. 1805 Blanqui, Auguste
b. 1810 Remond, Charles Lennox
b. 1828 Edmunds, George Franklin
b. 1828 Guggenheim, Meyer
b. 1834 Turner, Henry McNeal
b. 1844 Hall, G(ranville) Stanley
b. 1844 Strasburger, Eduard Adolf
b. 1847 Kearney, Denis
b. 1848 Howard, Cordelia
b. 1859 Herbert, Victor
b. 1860 Miller, Henry John
b. 1871 Thaw, Harry Kendall
b. 1874 Hofmannsthal, Hugo von
b. 1878 Bailey, H(enry) C(hristopher)

b. 1878 Caraway, Hattie Wyatt
b. 1879 Chretien, Henri
b. 1880 Pratella, Francesco Balilla
b. 1882 Saint Laurent, Louis Stephen
b. 1882 St. Laurent, Louis Stephen
b. 1882 Tobias, Channing Heggie
b. 1885 Chautemps, Camille
b. 1887 Nordhoff, Charles Bernard
b. 1887 Scherman, Harry
b. 1888 Caton-Thompson, Gertrude
b. 1890 Lubin, Germaine
b. 1891 Johnson, James Price
b. 1891 Kipnis, Alexander
b. 1895 Ford, John Sean O'Feeney
b. 1895 Smythe, Conn
b. 1896 Lane, Frank C
b. 1896 Somoza, Anastasio
b. 1897 Robins, Denise Naomi
b. 1900 Busoni, Rafaello
b. 1900 Mercer, Mabel
b. 1900 Potter, Stephen
b. 1901 Gable, Clark
b. 1902 Gosho Heinosuke
b. 1902 Hughes, Langston
b. 1904 Perelman, S(idney) J(oseph)
b. 1905 Berkner, Lloyd Viel
b. 1905 Lee, Doris Emrick
b. 1905 Segre, Emilio Gino
b. 1906 Hildegarde, Loretta Sell
b. 1907 Canaday, John (Edwin John)
b. 1908 Booth, Albie
b. 1908 Pal, George
b. 1915 Matthews, Stanley, Sir
b. 1918 Spark, Muriel Sarah
b. 1919 DellaCasa, Lisa
b. 1921 Blount, Winton Malcolm
b. 1922 Tebaldi, Renata
b. 1926 Whitman, Stuart
b. 1927 Kinnell, Galway
b. 1930 Ershad, Hussain Mohammad
b. 1931 Yeltsin, Boris (Nikolayevich)
b. 1932 Hart, John Richard
b. 1932 Nott, John William Frederic, Sir
b. 1933 Anderson, Wendell Richard

b. 1933 Price, Reynolds
b. 1937 Everly, Don(ald)
b. 1938 Hemsley, Sherman
b. 1941 Shapiro, Arnold
b. 1942 Jones, Terry
b. 1943 Jamieson, Bob
b. 1944 Enzi, Michael B.
b. 1952 James, Rick
b. 1957 Adamek, Donna
b. 1965 Fenn, Sherilyn
b. 1965 Lee, Brandon
b. 1965 Stephanie, Princess
b. 1966 Akers, Michelle
b. 1968 Presley, Lisa Marie
b. 1969 Redman, Joshua
b. 1973 Van Dyken, Amy
d. 1733 Augustus II
d. 1761 Charlevoix, Pierre Francis Xavier de
d. 1818 Gazzaniga, Giuseppe
d. 1851 Shelley, Mary Wollstonecraft
d. 1873 Maury, Matthew Fontaine
d. 1875 Bennett, William Sterndale, Sir
d. 1876 Forster, John
d. 1878 Cruikshank, George
d. 1885 Thomas, Sidney Gilchrist
d. 1903 Stokes, George Gabriel, Sir
d. 1924 Prendergast, Maurice Brazil
d. 1928 Jennings, Hugh(ey Ambrose)
d. 1928 Mallinckrodt, Edward
d. 1939 Brawley, Benjamin Griffith
d. 1940 Nowlan, Phil
d. 1941 McAdoo, William Gibbs
d. 1944? Clapper, Raymond Lewis
d. 1944 Mondrian, Piet(er Cornelis)
d. 1945 Huizinga, Johan
d. 1953 Curtis, Alan (Harold Neberroth)
d. 1954 Armstrong, Edwin Howard
d. 1957 Paulus, Friedrich von
d. 1958 Davisson, Clinton Joseph
d. 1958 Jones, Ernest Alfred
d. 1959 Hoppe, Willie
d. 1966 Hopper, Hedda
d. 1966 Keaton, Buster
d. 1968 Little, Lawson
d. 1970 Dolly, Rosie
d. 1973 Brauer, Max Julius Friedrich
d. 1973 Costello, Frank

d. 1976 Heisenberg, Werner Karl
d. 1976 Richter, Hans
d. 1976 Whipple, George Hoyt
d. 1980 Bailey, Jack
d. 1981 Douglas, Donald Willis
d. 1981 Mischakoff, Mischa
d. 1986 Myrdal, Alva Reimer
d. 1988 Linen, James A(lexander), III
d. 1989 DeKooning, Elaine Marie Catherine Fried
d. 1992 Kaufman, Irving R(obert)
d. 1994 Soule, Olan
d. 1997 Caen, Herb
d. 1997 Goodman, Mitchell
d. 1997 Reynolds, Marjorie
d. 1999 Mellon, Paul

February 2
b. 1650 Gwyn, Nell
b. 1651 Phips, William, Sir
b. 1762 Crescentini, Girolamo
b. 1785 Colbran, Isabella
b. 1800 Gregg, William
b. 1802 Boussingault, Jean Baptiste
b. 1803 Johnston, Albert Sidney
b. 1811 Bacon, Delia Salter
b. 1825 Dalton, John Call
b. 1828 Meredith, George
b. 1846 Smith, Francis Marion
b. 1859 Ellis, Havelock
b. 1861 Guggenheim, Solomon Robert
b. 1864 Asquith, Emma Alice Margot
b. 1867 Saunders, Charles E, Sir
b. 1869 Child, Charles Manning
b. 1873 Neurath, Konstantin von
b. 1875 Kreisler, Fritz
b. 1877 Towne, Charles Hanson
b. 1882 Joyce, James Augustus Aloysius
b. 1883 McCulley, Johnston
b. 1883 Sakall, S Z
b. 1883 Smith, Howard Worth
b. 1885 Frunze, Mikhail Vasilievich
b. 1886 Benet, William Rose
b. 1888 Lloyd, Frank
b. 1889 Lattre de Tassigny, Jean de (Marie Gabriel) de

b. 1890 Correll, Charles J
b. 1891 Foyston, Frank C
b. 1891 Segni, Antonio
b. 1895 Halas, George Stanley
b. 1898 Brinton, Clarence Crane
b. 1899 Caudill, Rebecca
b. 1899 Rubin, Benny
b. 1900 Righter, Carroll
b. 1901 Heifetz, Jascha
b. 1901 Husch, Gerhard
b. 1901 Kahn, Louis I(sadore)
b. 1901 Kuekes, Edward Daniel
b. 1902 Morris, Newbold
b. 1904 Gruber, Frank
b. 1905 Hayward, John Davy
b. 1905 Rand, Ayn
b. 1906 Gordon, Gale
b. 1908 Ferrell, Wes(ley Cheek)
b. 1908 Rossellini, Renzo
b. 1908 Tinney, Cal(vin Lawrence)
b. 1909 Albertson, Frank
b. 1909 Randhawa, Mohinder Singh
b. 1911 Bjoerling, Jussi
b. 1912 Lane, Burton
b. 1914 Apostoli, Fred
b. 1914 Dedijer, Vladimir
b. 1915 Eban, Abba
b. 1917? Muoi, Do
b. 1919 Fogarty, Anne
b. 1923 Dickey, James (Lafayette)
b. 1923 Granville, Bonita
b. 1923 Schoendienst, Red
b. 1923 Smith, Liz
b. 1924 Stitt, Sonny
b. 1926 Giscard d'Estaing, Valery
b. 1926 Obando (y Bravo), Miguel
b. 1927 Getz, Stan
b. 1927 Kaplow, Herbert Elias
b. 1928 Stritch, Elaine
b. 1931 Agt, Andries Antonius Maria van
b. 1931 Viorst, Judith (Stahl)
b. 1932 Mandan, Robert
b. 1935 Wagner, Jane
b. 1936 LaFollette, Bronson Cutting
b. 1937 Arroyo, Martina
b. 1937 Smothers, Tommy
b. 1938 Estes, Simon Lamont
b. 1938 Katz, Jonathan Ned

b. 1942 Diller, Barry Charles
b. 1942 Hopkins, Bo
b. 1942 Nash, Graham
b. 1942 Ulmer, James
b. 1946 Konare, Alpha Oumar
b. 1947 Fawcett, Farrah Leni
b. 1948 Savitch, Jessica Beth
b. 1954 Brinkley, Christie
b. 1954 Tudor, John Thomas
b. 1959 Manley, Dexter
d. 1491 Schongauer, Martin
d. 1529 Castiglione, Baldassare, Conte
d. 1594 Palestrina, Giovanni
d. 1660 Flinck, Govert
d. 1804 Walton, George
d. 1826 Brillat-Savarin, Jean Anthelme
d. 1836 Bonaparte, Letizia
d. 1884 Matteson, Tompkins Harrison
d. 1884 Phillips, Wendell
d. 1885 Phelps, John Wolcott
d. 1900 Wittenmyer, Annie Turner
d. 1904 Whitney, William Collins
d. 1907 Mendeleev, Dmitri Ivanovich
d. 1918 Sullivan, John L(awrence)
d. 1919 Leroux, Xavier
d. 1921 Mancinelli, Luigi
d. 1922 Taylor, William Desmond
d. 1926 Sukhomlinov, Vladimir Aleksandrovich
d. 1936 Seaman, Owen, Sir
d. 1945 Goerdeler, Karl Friedrich
d. 1948 Lamont, Thomas William
d. 1956 Burns, Bob
d. 1956 Grapewin, Charley
d. 1957 Morgan, Julia
d. 1962 Budd, Ralph
d. 1963 Gaxton, William
d. 1965 Blackmur, Richard Palmer
d. 1967 Roos, Frank John, Jr.
d. 1967 Sevitzky, Fabien
d. 1968 Serafin, Tullio
d. 1969 Karloff, Boris
d. 1969 Martinelli, Giovanni
d. 1970 Russell, Bertrand Arthur William

d. 1971 Hellmann, Richard
d. 1972 Barney, Natalie Clifford
d. 1972 Landis, Jessie Royce
d. 1974 Lakatos, Imre
d. 1978 Barrie, Wendy
d. 1979 Douglas, Aaron
d. 1979 Vicious, Sid
d. 1980 Stein, William Howard
d. 1981 Addonizio, Hugh Joseph
d. 1982 Stanford, Sally
d. 1985 Meyerhoff, Joseph
d. 1987 MacLean, Alistair (Stuart)
d. 1988 Williams, G(erhard) Mennen
d. 1991 Axthelm, Pete(r Macrae)
d. 1991 Wickens, Aryness Joy
d. 1992 Parks, Bert
d. 1992 Whitehead, Edwin C(arl)
d. 1995 Pleasence, Donald
d. 1996 Kelly, Gene
d. 1997 Meisner, Sanford
d. 1997 Stamos, Theodoros
d. 1998 Stevens, Roger L(acey)

February 3
b. 540 Gregory the Great, Saint
b. 1757 Volney, (Constantin) Francois Chasseboeuf, Comte de
b. 1807 Johnston, Joseph Eggleston
b. 1809 Mendelssohn, Felix
b. 1811 Greeley, Horace
b. 1820 Kane, Elisha Kent
b. 1821 Blackwell, Elizabeth
b. 1823 Baird, Spencer Fullerton
b. 1826 Bagehot, Walter
b. 1830 Salisbury, Robert Arthur Talbot, 3rd Marquess
b. 1834 Adams, Edwin
b. 1842 Lanier, Sidney
b. 1843 Van Horne, William Cornelius, Sir
b. 1844 Lanston, Tolbert
b. 1853 Jameson, Leander Starr, Sir
b. 1853 Maxim, Hudson
b. 1859 Junkers, Hugo
b. 1869 Gatti-Casazza, Giulio
b. 1870 Haines, Robert Terrel
b. 1872 Harris, Sam Henry

b. 1872 Meiklejohn, Alexander
b. 1873 Trenchard, Hugh Montague, First Viscount
b. 1874 Stein, Gertrude
b. 1880 Price, Nancy
b. 1882 Bailey, Frederick Marshman
b. 1883 Mulford, Clarence Edward
b. 1884 Andrews, Frank M(axwell)
b. 1889 Dreyer, Carl Theodore
b. 1890 MacPhail, Larry
b. 1894 Negrin, Juan
b. 1894 Rockwell, Norman
b. 1895 Kenny, Nick
b. 1898 Aalto, Alvar Henrik Hugo
b. 1899 Trotter, Mildred
b. 1901 Floyd, Pretty Boy
b. 1901 Lehmann, Rosamond Nina
b. 1902 Armstrong, Lil(lian Hardin)
b. 1902 Pusey, Merlo John
b. 1902 Sender, Ramon Jose
b. 1904 Canham, Erwin Dain
b. 1904 Dallapiccola, Luigi
b. 1904 Makins, Roger (Mellor), Sir
b. 1906 Doherty, Brian
b. 1907 Michener, James A(lbert)
b. 1907 Morey, Walt(er Nelson)
b. 1908 Jones, Roger W(arren)
b. 1908 Miller, William Ernest
b. 1909 Cayatte, Andre
b. 1909 Weil, Simone
b. 1911 Creavy, Tom
b. 1912 Carlisle, Mary
b. 1912 Patrick, Lynn
b. 1912 Soustelle, Jacques
b. 1918 Bishop, Joey
b. 1918 Stephens, Helen
b. 1920 Heimlich, Henry Jay
b. 1920 Osterwald, Bibi
b. 1924 Gelb, Arthur
b. 1924 Stevens, Leslie
b. 1926 Berman, Shelley
b. 1926 Vogel, Hans-Jochen
b. 1926 Yates, Richard
b. 1929 Harris, Derek
b. 1930 Anger, Kenneth
b. 1930 Wojnilower, Albert Martin
b. 1931 Garner, Peggy Ann
b. 1931 Levitt, Arthur, Jr.

b. 1933 Sarbanes, Paul S(pyros)
b. 1935 Watson, Johnny "Guitar"
b. 1936 Bridges, James
b. 1938 Buono, Victor
b. 1938 Griffith, Emile Alphonse
b. 1940 Hartz, James Leroy
b. 1940 Tarkenton, Fran(cis Asbury)
b. 1941 Mann, Carol Ann
b. 1943 Bogart, Neil
b. 1943 Danner, Blythe Katharine
b. 1943 Edwards, Dennis
b. 1945 Griese, Bob
b. 1946 Wachner, Linda
b. 1947 Auster, Paul
b. 1947 Davies, Dave
b. 1948 Melanie
b. 1950 Fairchild, Morgan
b. 1952 Lynn, Fred(ric Michael)
b. 1954 Williams, Tiger
b. 1956 Jefferson, John Larry
b. 1956 Lane, Nathan
b. 1963 Berg, Matraca
d. 1399 John of Gaunt
d. 1468? Gutenberg, Johann Gensfleischzur Laden Zum
d. 1515 Manutius, Aldus
d. 1590 Pilon, Germain
d. 1679 Steen, Jan
d. 1814 Matamoros, Mariano
d. 1832 Crabbe, George
d. 1847 Duplessis, Marie
d. 1888 Maine, Henry James Sumner
d. 1889 Starr, Belle
d. 1894 Childs, George William
d. 1895 Weld, Theodore Dwight
d. 1919 Pickering, Edward Charles
d. 1924 Wilson, Woodrow
d. 1934 Cisneros, Eleanora
d. 1934 Glass, Montague (Marsden)
d. 1934 Hitchcock, Gilbert Monell
d. 1935 Junkers, Hugo
d. 1938 Palacio Valdes, Armando
d. 1942 Lillie, Gordon William
d. 1944 Bestor, Arthur Eugene
d. 1947 Mitscher, Marc Andrew
d. 1952 Ickes, Harold LeClair
d. 1956 Yerkes, Robert Mearns

d. 1957 Townsend, Willard Saxby
d. 1959 Astor, William Vincent
d. 1959 Big Bopper, The
d. 1959 Holly, Buddy
d. 1959 Valens, Ritchie
d. 1961 Wong, Anna May (Lu Tsong)
d. 1964 Lewis, Clarence Irving
d. 1966 Gannett, Lewis Stiles
d. 1969 McGill, Ralph Emerson
d. 1971 Flippen, Jay C
d. 1973 Razaf, Andy
d. 1975 Black, Eli M
d. 1975 Coolidge, William David
d. 1975 Harand, Irene
d. 1975 Kalthoum, Um
d. 1980 Heindorf, Ray
d. 1981 McNamara, Margaret Craig
d. 1982 Barr, Stringfellow
d. 1985 Oppenheimer, Frank F
d. 1988 Duncan, Robert Edward
d. 1989 Cassavetes, John
d. 1989 Vare, Glenna Collett
d. 1991 Ackerman, Harry S
d. 1991 Kulp, Nancy Jane
d. 1996 Meadows, Audrey
d. 1997 Hrabal, Bohumil
d. 1998 Wiley, W(illiam) Bradford
d. 1999 Kingsbury-Smith, Joseph
d. 1999 Service, John S(tewart)
d. 2000 Cashin, Bonnie
d. 2000 Hills, Lee

February 4
b. 1682 Bottger, Johann Friedrich
b. 1688 Marivaux, Pierre Carlet de
b. 1740 Bellman, Carl Michael
b. 1778 Candolle, Augustin Pyrame de
b. 1790 Bachman, John
b. 1792 Birney, James Gillespie
b. 1802 Hopkins, Mark
b. 1805 Ainsworth, W(illiam) H(arrison)
b. 1841 Ader, Clement
b. 1842 Brandes, Georg Morris Cohen
b. 1848 Ayer, Francis Wayland
b. 1862 Hammarskjold, Hjalmar
b. 1864 Eilshemius, Louis Michel

b. 1865? Abe, Isao
b. 1868 Markievicz, Constance Georgine, Countess
b. 1869 Haywood, William Dudley
b. 1870 Mitchell, John
b. 1871 Ebert, Friedrich
b. 1876 Cleghorn, Sarah Norcliffe
b. 1876 Dickey, Herbert Spencer
b. 1877 Pickard, Greenleaf Whittier
b. 1878 Copeau, Jacques
b. 1878 Schaefer, Germany
b. 1881 Leger, Fernand
b. 1881 Voroshilov, Kliment Efremovich
b. 1883 Pratt, Edwin John
b. 1887 Kaye-Smith, Sheila
b. 1889 Catlett, Walter
b. 1892 Betti, Ugo
b. 1893 Dart, Raymond Arthur
b. 1895 Bruce, Nigel
b. 1897 Erhard, Ludwig
b. 1898 Monroe, Marion
b. 1900 Impellitteri, Vincent R(ichard)
b. 1901 Werth, Alexander
b. 1902 Lindbergh, Charles A(ugustus)
b. 1903 Takehara Han
b. 1904 Covarrubias, Miguel
b. 1904 Kantor, Mackinlay
b. 1905 Foy, Eddie, Jr.
b. 1906 Bonhoeffer, Dietrich
b. 1906 Tombaugh, Clyde W(illiam)
b. 1907 Spivakovsky, Tossy
b. 1909 Coote, Robert
b. 1910 Ellison, Virginia Howell
b. 1912 Leinsdorf, Erich
b. 1912 Nelson, Byron
b. 1912 Richardson, Scovel
b. 1913 Parks, Rosa Lee McCauley
b. 1913 Stevenson, Janet
b. 1915 Evans, Ray
b. 1915 Talman, William
b. 1917 Yahya Khan, Agha Muhammad
b. 1918 Lupino, Ida
b. 1920 Beebe, Burdetta Faye
b. 1921 Friedan, Betty (Naomi Goldstein)
b. 1923 Bain, Conrad Stafford
b. 1923 Betancur, Belisario
b. 1925 Hoban, Russell

b. 1925 Wisdom, Norman
b. 1926 Tassell, Gustave
b. 1926 Welch, Ken
b. 1927 Cummings, Sam
b. 1929 Johnston, Neil
b. 1931 Peron, Isabel Martinez de
b. 1932 Coover, Robert (Lowell)
b. 1935 Talvela, Martti Olavi
b. 1937 Newman, David
b. 1938 Riegle, Donald Wayne, Jr.
b. 1940 Bakke, Allan Paul
b. 1940 Broadhurst, Kent
b. 1941 Chavers, Dean
b. 1943 Lee, Gary Earl
b. 1944 Davis, Andrew Frank
b. 1945 Brenner, David
b. 1947 Quayle, Dan
b. 1948 Cooper, Alice
b. 1948 Grams, Rod
b. 1949 Beck, Michael
b. 1950 Franklin, Pamela
b. 1950 Hakuta, Ken
b. 1952? Eichhorn, Lisa
b. 1952 Shipley, Jenny
b. 1959 Taylor, Lawrence Julius
b. 1961 Savard, Denis Joseph
b. 1962 Black, Clint
b. 1967 Grinkov, Sergei
b. 1973 De La Hoya, Oscar
d. 1617 Elzevir, Louis
d. 1833 O'Keeffe, John
d. 1881 Carlyle, Thomas
d. 1894 Sax, Adolphe (Antoine-Joseph)
d. 1909 Clarkson, John Gibson
d. 1923 Fischer, Carl
d. 1928 Lorentz, Hendrick Antoon
d. 1939 Sapir, Edward
d. 1942 Calder, Frank
d. 1944 Guilbert, Yvette
d. 1953 Williams, Ben Ames
d. 1959 O'Connor, Una
d. 1963 Weldon, John
d. 1964 Conroy, Frank
d. 1965 Girdler, Tom Mercer
d. 1966 Beebe, Lucius Morris
d. 1966 Grosvenor, Gilbert Hovey
d. 1968 Cassady, Neal
d. 1970 Bogan, Louise
d. 1974 Bose, Satyendranath
d. 1975 Hill, Howard
d. 1975 Jordan, Louis
d. 1977 Dresser, Davis
d. 1978 Evans, Bergen Baldwin

d. 1980 Laye, Camara
d. 1980 Summerskill, Edith Clara, Baroness
d. 1983 Ameche, Jim
d. 1983 Carpenter, Karen (Anne)
d. 1984 Kaplan, Henry Seymour
d. 1985 Blackwell, Betsy Talbot
d. 1985 Wexley, John
d. 1987 Liberace
d. 1987 Rogers, Carl Ransom
d. 1988 Miller, Otto Neil
d. 1992 Dehner, John Forkum
d. 1993 Schneider, Alexander
d. 1997 Halsey, Margaret (Frances)
d. 1998 Hillis, Margaret
d. 2000 Albert, Carl Bert
d. 2000 Kleindienst, Richard Gordon

February 5
b. 1626 Sevigne, Marie de Rabutin-Chantal, Marquise de
b. 1687 Geminiani, Francesco
b. 1703 Tennent, Gilbert
b. 1723? Witherspoon, John
b. 1725 Otis, James
b. 1779 Pike, Zebulon Montgomery
b. 1784 Hanks, Nancy
b. 1788 Peel, Robert, Sir
b. 1804 Runeberg, Johan Ludwig
b. 1808 Spitzweg, Carl
b. 1810 Bull, Ole Bornemann
b. 1837 Moody, Dwight Lyman
b. 1840 Dunlop, John Boyd
b. 1840 Maxim, Hiram Stevens, Sir
b. 1848 Huysmans, Joris Karl
b. 1848 Mancinelli, Luigi
b. 1848? Starr, Belle
b. 1855 Merriam, Clinton Hart
b. 1866 Keith, Arthur
b. 1871 Gardner, Mary Sewall
b. 1873 Elliott, Maxine
b. 1873 Heiser, Victor George
b. 1878 Citroen, Andre Gustave
b. 1882 Lattuada, Felice
b. 1888 Fraser, Bruce Austin, Sir
b. 1894 Morgan, Frederick, Sir
b. 1898 McGill, Ralph Emerson

b. 1900 Stevenson, Adlai Ewing, II
b. 1901 Sheekman, Arthur
b. 1902 Kaper, Bronislau
b. 1903 Owings, Nathaniel Alexander
b. 1903 Payson, Joan Whitney
b. 1906 Carradine, John
b. 1907 Bender, Hans
b. 1907 Simon, Norton Winfred
b. 1907 White, William S(mith)
b. 1908 Gervasi, Frank Henry
b. 1908? Hilton, Daisy
b. 1908? Hilton, Violet
b. 1914 Burroughs, William S(eward)
b. 1914 Hodgkin, Alan Lloyd, Sir
b. 1915 Hofstadter, Robert
b. 1915 Millar, Margaret (Ellis)
b. 1915 Sanderlin, George William
b. 1917 Edelmann, Otto
b. 1918 Holt, Tim
b. 1919 Buttons, Red
b. 1919 Papandreou, Andreas (George)
b. 1921 Adam, Ken
b. 1921 Pritchard, John Michael, Sir
b. 1926 Sulzberger, Arthur O(chs)
b. 1927 Davis, Martin S.
b. 1928 Greeley, Andrew Moran
b. 1928 Marty, Martin Emil
b. 1932 Kalb, Bernard
b. 1933 King, Claude
b. 1934 Aaron, Hank
b. 1934 Cherry, Don(ald Stewart)
b. 1937 Damon, Stuart
b. 1938 Guare, John
b. 1939 Quinn, Jane Bryant
b. 1941 Laird, Rick
b. 1941 Selby, David
b. 1941 Villiger, Kaspar
b. 1942 Staubach, Roger Thomas
b. 1943 Bushnell, Nolan Kay
b. 1943 Cannell, Stephen Joseph
b. 1943 Morton, Craig
b. 1944 Kooper, Al
b. 1946 Rampling, Charlotte
b. 1947 Waltrip, Darrell Lee
b. 1948 Hershey, Barbara
b. 1948 Wallechinsky, David
b. 1949 Holzer, Harold

b. 1951 Swados, Elizabeth A
b. 1956 Saar, Alison
b. 1959 Sanchez, Salvador
b. 1962 Leigh, Jennifer Jason
b. 1968 Alomar, Roberto
b. 1969 Brown, Bobby
d. 1578 Moroni, Giovanni Battista
d. 1679 Vondel, Joost van den
d. 1705 Spener, Philipp Jakob
d. 1819 Van Buren, Hannah (Hoes)
d. 1897 Radbourn, Old Hoss
d. 1903 Dawes, Henry Laurens
d. 1919 Rossetti, William Michael
d. 1919 Rozanov, Vasili Vasilyevich
d. 1933 Mizner, Addison
d. 1934 Davis, William Morris
d. 1941 Paterson, A(ndrew) B(arton)
d. 1943 Van Dyke, W(oodbridge) S(trong)
d. 1946 Arliss, George
d. 1953 Hannagan, Steve
d. 1955 Blood, Ernest
d. 1958 Brown, Lew
d. 1958 Tomlinson, Henry Major
d. 1962 Ibert, Jacques (Francois Antoine)
d. 1966 Binswanger, Ludwig
d. 1967 Bean, L(eon) L(eonwood)
d. 1968 Adams, Nick
d. 1969 Ritter, Thelma
d. 1970 York, Rudy
d. 1971 Rakosi, Matyas
d. 1972 Moore, Marianne Craig
d. 1976 Kahn, Ben
d. 1976 Livesey, Roger
d. 1976 Shutta, Ethel
d. 1981 Grasso, Ella
d. 1982 Opie, Peter Mason
d. 1984 Cooper, Chuck
d. 1986 Rosenfeld, Henry J
d. 1987 Burke, Mike
d. 1988 Hurd, Clement
d. 1989 Raposo, Joseph
d. 1991 Jagger, Dean
d. 1991 Knight, James L
d. 1993 Du Bois, William Pene
d. 1993 Jonas, Hans
d. 1993 Mankiewicz, Joseph (Leo)
d. 1993 Manso, Leo

d. 1994 Abs, Hermann J(osef)
d. 1994 Sauer, George (Henry)
d. 1995 Highsmith, Patricia
d. 1995 Holifield, Chet
d. 1995 McClure, Doug
d. 1997 Harriman, Pamela
d. 1999 Leontief, Wassily W
d. 2000 Autant-Lara, Claude
d. 2000 Elvira, Pablo

February 6
b. 1577 Cenci, Beatrice
b. 1608 Vieira, Antonio
b. 1665 Anne
b. 1756 Burr, Aaron
b. 1785 Bonaparte, Elizabeth Patterson
b. 1788 Kisfaludy, Karoly
b. 1802 Wheatstone, Charles, Sir
b. 1807 Sibley, Hiram
b. 1809 Bodmer, Karl
b. 1814 Sorin, Edward Frederick
b. 1818 Evarts, William Maxwell
b. 1818 Litolff, Henri Charles
b. 1820 Durant, Thomas Clark
b. 1832 Gordon, John Brown
b. 1833 Pereda, Jose Marie de
b. 1833 Stuart, Jeb
b. 1834 Klebs, Edwin
b. 1838 Irving, Henry, Sir
b. 1845 Straus, Isidor
b. 1852 Morgan, C(onwy) Lloyd
b. 1857 Flagg, Ernest
b. 1861 Tyrrell, George
b. 1870 Braid, James
b. 1874 Medary, Milton B
b. 1878 Pitkin, Walter Boughton
b. 1879 Friesz, Othon
b. 1887? Frings, Joseph Richard
b. 1888 Gleason, Lucille
b. 1890 Cameron, Harry
b. 1892 Murphy, William Parry
b. 1893 Pudovkin, Vsevolod
b. 1893 Zafrulla Khan, Muhammad, Sir
b. 1894 Bonelli, Richard
b. 1894 Partridge, Eric Honeywood
b. 1895 Camerini, Mario
b. 1895 Ruth, Babe
b. 1897 Cavalcanti, Alberto
b. 1899 Novarro, Ramon
b. 1901 Lyon, Ben

b. 1902 Brunis, George
b. 1902 Nizer, Louis
b. 1903 Arrau, Claudio
b. 1905 Gomulka, Wladyslaw
b. 1906 Catherall, Arthur
b. 1908 Fanfani, Amintore
b. 1908 Lansdale, Edward Geary
b. 1909 Blassingale, Wyatt Rainey
b. 1911 Gage, Harlow W
b. 1911 Reagan, Ronald (Wilson)
b. 1912 Braun, Eva
b. 1912 Scott, Adrian
b. 1913 Leakey, Mary (Douglas)
b. 1914 Towns, Forrest
b. 1916 Doggett, Bill
b. 1919 Gabor, Zsa Zsa
b. 1919 Gold, Arthur
b. 1920 Jovanovich, William Iliya
b. 1922 MacNee, Patrick
b. 1926 Gelb, Barbara Stone
b. 1926 Long, Dale
b. 1927 Burgess, Smoky
b. 1927 Haynie, Hugh
b. 1927 O'Neill, Gerard Kitchen
b. 1928 Jones, Weyman
b. 1929 Waterhouse, Keith Spencer
b. 1931 Torn, Rip
b. 1932 Truffaut, Francois
b. 1933 Fauntroy, Walter E(dward)
b. 1933 Van Doren, Mamie
b. 1934 Lindauer, Lois L
b. 1937 Breuer, Lee
b. 1939 Farrell, Mike
b. 1940 Brokaw, Tom
b. 1941 Albert, Stephen Joel
b. 1942 Brady, Sarah Jane
b. 1943 Fabian
b. 1943 Gray, C(layland) Boyden
b. 1943 Hunnicutt, Gayle
b. 1945 Marley, Bob
b. 1947 Yergin, Daniel
b. 1949 Orantes, Manuel
b. 1950 Cole, Natalie
b. 1954 Prothrow-Stith, Deborah
b. 1956 Walmsley, Jon
b. 1957 Townsend, Robert
b. 1962 Rose, Axl
b. 1963 Griffith, Mark Winston
d. 1593 Amyot, Jacques
d. 1685 Charles II

d. 1783 Brown, Lancelot
d. 1793 Goldoni, Carlo
d. 1804 Priestley, Joseph
d. 1834 Lander, Richard Lemon
d. 1838 Retief, Pieter
d. 1865 Beeton, Isabella Mary Mayson
d. 1894 Billroth, Theodore
d. 1913 Weaver, James Baird
d. 1916 Dario, Ruben
d. 1918 Klimt, Gustav
d. 1919 Dietz, Angel DeCora
d. 1923 Barnard, Edward Emerson
d. 1929 Hauk, Minnie
d. 1931 Nehru, Motilal
d. 1932 Leguia y Salcedo, Augusto Bernardino
d. 1943 Coffroth, Jimmy
d. 1945 Howell, William H(enry)
d. 1947 Fallada, Hans
d. 1950 Speck, Frank Gouldsmith
d. 1952 George VI
d. 1954 Althouse, Paul Shearer
d. 1954 Bodenheim, Maxwell
d. 1956 Chretien, Henri
d. 1957 Covarrubias, Miguel
d. 1958 Morgan, Charles Langbridge
d. 1963 Abd el-Krim el-Khatabi, Mohamed ben
d. 1964 Aguinaldo, Emilio
d. 1967 Carol, Martine
d. 1967 Morgenthau, Henry, Jr.
d. 1968 Berry, James Gomer
d. 1970 Attell, Abe B
d. 1970 Karns, Roscoe
d. 1972 Steward, Julian Haynes
d. 1972 Thompson, Llewellyn E, Jr.
d. 1976 Guaraldi, Vince(nt Anthony)
d. 1978 Cole, Charles Woolsey
d. 1981 Camerini, Mario
d. 1981 Frederika Louise
d. 1981 Montenegro, Hugh
d. 1982 Nicholson, Ben
d. 1984 Ernst, Jimmy
d. 1984 Guillen, Jorge
d. 1985 Gardiner, Muriel
d. 1986 Yamasaki, Minoru

d. 1988 Laski, Marghanita
d. 1989 Field, Ron(ald)
d. 1989 Tuchman, Barbara Wertheim
d. 1991 Luria, Salvador Edward
d. 1991 Thomas, Danny
d. 1993 Ashe, Arthur
d. 1994 Cotten, Joseph
d. 1994 Kirby, Jack
d. 1994 Simms, Hilda
d. 1994 Strasfogel, Ignace
d. 1995 Merrill, James (Ingram)
d. 1996 Madison, Guy
d. 1998 Wilson, Carl (Dean)

February 7

b. 1405 Constantine XI Palaeologus
b. 1478 More, Thomas, Sir
b. 1612 Killigrew, Thomas
b. 1688 Colden, Cadwallader
b. 1741 Fuseli, Henry
b. 1804 Deere, John
b. 1806 Hoffman, Charles Fenno
b. 1809 Paludan-Muller, Frederik
b. 1812 Dickens, Charles (John Huffam)
b. 1814 Colton, Gardner Quincy
b. 1815 Beatty, Alfred Chester, Sir
b. 1824 Huggins, William, Sir
b. 1827 Saigo, Takamori
b. 1833 Palma, Ricardo
b. 1834 Mendeleev, Dmitri Ivanovich
b. 1837 Murray, James Augustus Henry, Sir
b. 1849 Mallock, William Hurrell
b. 1859 Nevada, Emma
b. 1862 Maybeck, Bernard Ralph
b. 1863 Hope-Hawkins, Anthony, Sir
b. 1867 Wilder, Laura Elizabeth Ingalls
b. 1870 Adler, Alfred
b. 1874 Fuertes, Louis Agassiz
b. 1877 Hardy, Godfrey Harold
b. 1883 Blake, Eubie
b. 1885 Lewis, Sinclair
b. 1889 Muzio, Claudia
b. 1892 Behrens, Earl Charles
b. 1895 Van Paassen, Pierre
b. 1896 Paludan, Jacob
b. 1897 Porter, Quincy
b. 1898 Charlot, Jean
b. 1904 Dorne, Albert
b. 1904 Nugent, Edward

b. 1905 Von Euler, Ulf
b. 1906 Amrouche, Jean
b. 1912 Drysdale, George Russell
b. 1918 Sager, Ruth
b. 1919 Iwama, Kazuo
b. 1919 Mahoney, Jock
b. 1920 Bracken, Eddie
b. 1920 Brand, Oscar
b. 1920 Wang, An
b. 1923 Banks, Harvey Washington
b. 1923 Brasselle, Keefe
b. 1923 Harewood, George Henry Hubert Lascelles, Earl
b. 1924 Bryan, Dora
b. 1926 Feoktistov, Konstantin Petrovich
b. 1926 Hoest, Bill
b. 1930 Bar-Ilan, David Jacob
b. 1932 Talese, Gay
b. 1932 Worden, Alfred Merrill
b. 1934 Fenech-Adami, Eddie
b. 1934 King Curtis
b. 1935 Kohl, Herbert H.
b. 1937 Jay, Peter
b. 1938 Thomopoulos, Anthony Denis
b. 1939 Reed, John S(hepard)
b. 1943 Robbins, Carrie Fishbein
b. 1950 Abramson, Lyn
b. 1953 Quisenberry, Dan(iel Raymond)
b. 1955 Benirschke, Rolf Joachim
b. 1957 Garcia y Sanchez, Damaso Domingo
b. 1960 Spader, James
b. 1962 Brooks, Garth
b. 1962 McCrory, Milton
b. 1965 Otto, Kristin
b. 1973 Howard, Juwan (Antonio)
d. 1639 Gentileschi, Orazio
d. 1728 Iberville, Pierre Le Moyne, Sieur d'
d. 1779 Boyce, William
d. 1799 Ch'ien Lung
d. 1823 Radcliffe, Ann
d. 1854 Fitzpatrick, Thomas
d. 1873 LeFanu, Joseph Sheridan
d. 1878 Pius IX
d. 1897 Ferraris, Galileo
d. 1912 Blyden, Edward Wilmot
d. 1920 Kolchak, Aleksandr Vasilievich
d. 1936 Heggie, O P
d. 1937 Root, Elihu
d. 1938 Firestone, Harvey Samuel
d. 1942 Bilibin, Ivan Iakolevich

d. 1944 Park, Robert Ezra
d. 1948 McKenzie, Red
d. 1952 Epstein, Philip G
d. 1952 Henry, Pete
d. 1954 Nelson, Battling
d. 1959 Lajoie, Nap(oleon)
d. 1959 Malan, Daniel Francois
d. 1960 Henderson, Leon N(esbit)
d. 1960 Kurchatov, Igor Vasilyevich
d. 1968 Poling, Daniel A
d. 1974 McGraw, Donald Cushing
d. 1975 Stein, Clarence S
d. 1979 Giles, Warren Crandall
d. 1979 Mengele, Josef
d. 1980 Ballinger, Margaret
d. 1982 Robinson, M(aurice) R(ichard)
d. 1985 Jacobs, Walter L
d. 1986 Diop, Cheikh Anta
d. 1987 Dunton, Davidson
d. 1987 Saunders, Stuart T(homas)
d. 1990 Van Heusen, Jimmy
d. 1994 Lutoslawski, Witold
d. 1995 Briggs, Fred
d. 1995 Sawyer, John E(dward)
d. 1998 Falco
d. 1998 Sanders, Lawrence
d. 1999 Hussein, I, King
d. 1999 Troup, Bobby
d. 2000 Henning, Doug(las James)

February 8

b. 1559 Casaubon, Isaac
b. 1577 Burton, Robert
b. 1591 Guercino, Il
b. 1700 Bernoulli, Daniel
b. 1727 Deluc, Jean Andre
b. 1777 Courtois, Bernard
b. 1804 Lander, Richard Lemon
b. 1819 Ruskin, John
b. 1820 Sherman, William Tecumseh
b. 1825 Bates, Henry Walter
b. 1825 Robinson, Harriet Jane Hanson
b. 1827 Whitney, William Dwight
b. 1828 Verne, Jules
b. 1851 Chopin, Kate
b. 1876 Modersohn-Becker, Paula

b. 1878 Buber, Martin
b. 1879 Slye, Maud
b. 1880 Faust, Lotta
b. 1880 Marc, Franz
b. 1882 Selfridge,
Thomas Etholen
b. 1883 Schumpeter,
Joseph Alois
b. 1888 Evans, Edith
Mary Booth, Dame
b. 1890 Menjou,
Adolphe Jean
b. 1890 Recto, Claro M.
b. 1892 Ruggles,
Charles
b. 1893 Ba Maw
b. 1894 Bishop, Billy
b. 1894 Vidor, King
Wallis
b. 1895 Samuel,
Maurice
b. 1897 Husain, Zakir
b. 1897 Rubens, Alma
b. 1899 Johnson, Lonnie
b. 1900 Kredel, Fritz
b. 1901 Dabney,
Virginius
b. 1902 Connell, Alex
b. 1902 Talbot, Lyle
b. 1903 Rahman, Abdul,
Prince
b. 1906 Balsam, Artur
b. 1906 Carlson,
Chester Floyd
b. 1906 Roth, Henry
b. 1907 Cole, Charles
Woolsey
b. 1907 Middleton, Ray
b. 1908 McCormick,
Myron
b. 1909 Sherrod, Robert
(Lee)
b. 1911 Bishop,
Elizabeth
b. 1915 Jenkins, Newell
b. 1915 Lustig, Alvin
b. 1918 Field, Betty
b. 1919 Morrow, Buddy
b. 1920 Smith, Bruce P
b. 1920 Turner, Lana
b. 1921 Jakobovits,
Immanuel
b. 1922 Glanzman,
Louis S
b. 1924 Meadows,
Audrey
b. 1925 Lemmon, Jack
b. 1926? Cassady, Neal
b. 1930 Rey, Alejandro
b. 1931 Dean, James
Byron
b. 1932 Williams, John
Towner
b. 1937 Raposo, Joseph
b. 1937 Wu, Harry
b. 1938 Ameling, Elly
b. 1940 Koppel, Ted
b. 1941 Rush, Tom
b. 1942 Klein, Robert
b. 1942 Nolte, Nick
b. 1945 Clodumar,
Kinza
b. 1948 Seals, Dan
Wayland
b. 1949 Adams, Brooke

b. 1956 Johnson,
Marques Kevin
b. 1958 Miller, Barry
b. 1968 Coleman, Gary
b. 1970 Mourning,
Alonzo
d. 1587 Mary, Queen of
Scots
d. 1877 Wilkes, Charles
d. 1880 Sykes, George
d. 1884 Guyot, Arnold
Henry
d. 1887 Courtright, Jim
d. 1903 Glaisher, James
d. 1909 Mendes, Catulle
d. 1918 Renault, Louis
d. 1920 Dehmel,
Richard
d. 1921 Kropotkin,
Peter Alekseyevich,
Prince
d. 1923 Bosanquet,
Bernard
d. 1925 Lawson,
Thomas William
d. 1926 Bateson,
William
d. 1935 Evans, Charles
d. 1935 Liebermann,
Max
d. 1936 Curtis, Charles
Brent
d. 1941 Van Devanter,
Willis
d. 1943 Casey, Dan(iel
Maurice)
d. 1944 Cavalieri, Lina
d. 1949 Leoni, Franco
d. 1951 Thyssen, Fritz
d. 1956 Mack, Connie
d. 1957 Bothe, Walter
Wilhelm Georg
d. 1957 Von Neumann,
John
d. 1959 Berger, Meyer
d. 1959 Donovan,
William Joseph
d. 1960 Austin, John
Langshaw
d. 1965 Danquah,
Joseph (Kwame
Kyeretwi) B(oakye)
d. 1967 Gollancz,
Victor, Sir
d. 1972 Chinard, Gilbert
d. 1973 Coates, Robert
Myron
d. 1974 Zwicky, Fritz
d. 1975 Green, Martyn
d. 1975 Robinson,
Robert, Sir
d. 1979 Catlin, George
Edward Gordon, Sir
d. 1979 Gabor, Dennis
d. 1979 Starch, Daniel
d. 1981 Kipnis, Claude
d. 1982 Whitney, John
Hay
d. 1983 Wallenstein,
Alfred Franz
d. 1984 Aries, Philippe
d. 1985 Jaffe, Sam(uel
Anderson)
d. 1985 Lyons, William,
Sir
d. 1990 Shannon, Del

d. 1992 Williams,
Tommy
d. 1993 Janeway, Eliot
d. 1994 Scott, Raymond
d. 1996 Ellington,
Mercer
d. 1996 Ennis, Del(mer)
d. 1996 Schwartz,
Felice N(ierenberg)
d. 1998 Laxness,
Halldor (Kiljan)
d. 1998 Powell, Enoch
d. 1999 Murdoch, Iris
d. 2000 Abel, Sid(ney
Gerald)
d. 2000 Maurer, Ion
Gheorghe

February 9
b. Procope, Ernesta
Gertrude Foster
Bowman
b. 1739 Bartram,
William
b. 1748 Martin, Luther
b. 1773 Harrison,
William Henry
b. 1814 Tilden, Samuel
Jones
b. 1822 Parton, James
b. 1826 Bowles,
Samuel, II
b. 1826 Logan, John
Alexander
b. 1834 Kamehameha
IV
b. 1840 Sampson,
William T
b. 1854 Carson, Edward
Henry
b. 1865 Campbell,
Patrick, Mrs.
b. 1866 Ade, George
b. 1871 Ricketts,
Howard T
b. 1874 Lowell, Amy
b. 1883 Carter, John
Garnet
b. 1885 Berg, Alban
b. 1890 Oud, Jacobus
Johannes Pieter
b. 1891 Colman, Ronald
b. 1891 Nenni, Pietro
Sandro
b. 1892 Wood, Peggy
b. 1895 Vargas, Alberto
b. 1896 Parks, Floyd
Lavinius
b. 1897 Kingsford-
Smith, Charles
Edward, Sir
b. 1899 Donlevy, Brian
b. 1899 Langer, Walter
C
b. 1899 Miller, Max
(Carlton)
b. 1902 Harman, Fred
b. 1903 Gibbs, Frederic
A
b. 1907 Clapper, Dit
b. 1909 Angel, Heather
Grace
b. 1909 Rusk, (David)
Dean
b. 1910 Monod, Jacques
Lucien

b. 1911 Snively,
William Daniel, Jr.
b. 1911 Walker, David
Harry
b. 1912 Moorer,
Thomas H(inman)
b. 1914 Lee, Gypsy
Rose
b. 1914 Tubb, Ernest
b. 1914 Veeck, Bill
b. 1915 Miranda,
Carmen
b. 1919 Gilkey,
Langdon Brown
b. 1923 Behan, Brendan
(Francis)
b. 1923 Grayson,
Kathryn
b. 1926 FitzGerald,
Garret Michael
b. 1928 Frazetta, Frank
b. 1928 Mudd, Roger
Harrison
b. 1931 Morris, Robert
b. 1932 Richter,
Gerhard
b. 1934 Ziegler, John
Augustus, Jr.
b. 1939 Suzman, Janet
b. 1940 Bordeaux,
Lionel R.
b. 1940 Coetzee, J(ohn)
M
b. 1941 Kuehl, Sheila
James
b. 1942 King, Carole
b. 1943 Pesci, Joe
b. 1944 Walker, Alice
b. 1945 Farrow, Mia
b. 1946 Webb, James
H(enry), Jr.
b. 1947 Ely, Joe
b. 1948 Love, Susan
M(argaret)
b. 1950 Light, Judith
Ellen
b. 1951 Thomas, Dennis
b. 1953 Franks, Gary A
b. 1956 Ford, Phil
Jackson
b. 1958 Lyle, Sandy
b. 1961 Kruk, John
b. 1963 Tritt, Travis
d. 1199 Minamoto
Yoritomo
d. 1567 Darnley, Henry
Stuart, Lord
d. 1811 Maskelyne,
Nevil
d. 1865 Gilliss, James
Melville
d. 1874 Michelet, Jules
d. 1886 Hancock,
Winfield Scott
d. 1891 Jongkind, Johan
Barthold
d. 1901 Harvey,
Fred(erick Henry)
d. 1906 Dunbar, Paul
Laurence
d. 1916 Richardson,
George Taylor
d. 1921 Huneker, James
Gibbons
d. 1925 Kerr, Alexander
H

b. 1888 Persinger, Louis
b. 1889 Mills, John
b. 1890 Pasternak, Boris Leonidovich
b. 1893 Kovalev, Mikhail Aleksandrovich
b. 1897 Darden, Colgate Whitehead
b. 1898 Szilard, Leo
b. 1900 Hitchcock, Tommy
b. 1901 Hulman, Tony, Jr.
b. 1902 Jacobsen, Arne
b. 1903 MacDougall, Curtis Daniel
b. 1904 Holyoake, Keith Jacka, Sir
b. 1904 Labouisse, Henry Richardson
b. 1906 Malik, Charles Habib
b. 1906 Malik, Yakov (Alexandrovich)
b. 1906 Pu-Yi, Henry
b. 1907 Levitt, William J(aird)
b. 1908 Fuchs, Vivian (Ernest), Sir
b. 1908 White, Josh(ua Daniel)
b. 1909 Baer, Max
b. 1909 Mankiewicz, Joseph (Leo)
b. 1911 Cairncross, Alexander Kirkland, Sir
b. 1912? Faiz, Faiz Ahmad
b. 1912 Firkusny, Rudolf
b. 1912 Fuller, Roy Broadbent
b. 1913 Mosley, Leonard O(swald)
b. 1916 Kennedy, Florynce
b. 1917 DeSantis, Giuseppe
b. 1917 Sheldon, Sidney
b. 1919 Bannister, Constance Gibbs
b. 1920 Farouk I
b. 1920 Halop, Billy
b. 1920 James, Daniel, Jr.
b. 1920 Wilson, Louis Hugh
b. 1921 Bentsen, Lloyd Millard, Jr.
b. 1921 Gabor, Eva
b. 1925 Johnson, Virginia E
b. 1925 Stanley, Kim
b. 1926 Bocuse, Paul
b. 1926 Nielsen, Leslie
b. 1928 Garfinkle, Louis
b. 1928 Janis, Conrad
b. 1930 Polshek, James Stewart
b. 1931 Cooper, David (Graham)
b. 1934 Carnahan, Mel Eugene
b. 1934 Quant, Mary

b. 1934 Surtees, John
b. 1935 Vincent, Gene
b. 1936 Reynolds, Burt
b. 1938 Louise, Tina
b. 1940 Ford, Kathleen DuRoss
b. 1940 Noriega (Moreno), Manuel Antonio
b. 1941 Mendes, Sergio
b. 1947 Harris, Emily Schwartz
b. 1949 Saint James, Synthia
b. 1951 Leavitt, Mike
b. 1953 Anglim, Philip
b. 1964 Crow, Sheryl
b. 1969 Aniston, Jennifer
b. 1979 Brandy
d. 641 Heraclius
d. 1650 Descartes, Rene
d. 1686 Dugdale, William, Sir
d. 1728 Stoddard, Solomon
d. 1789 Allen, Ethan
d. 1795 Bellman, Carl Michael
d. 1799 Spallanzani, Lazzaro
d. 1828 Clinton, DeWitt
d. 1848 Cole, Thomas
d. 1868 Foucault, Jean Bernard Leon
d. 1874 Trist, Nicholas Philip
d. 1878 Welles, Gideon
d. 1879 Daumier, Honore Victorin
d. 1888 Kelly, William
d. 1910 Simmons, Zalmon G
d. 1914 Clarke, Alexander Ross
d. 1924 Loeb, Jacques
d. 1926 Bobbs, William Conrad
d. 1931 Parsons, Charles Algernon, Sir
d. 1936 Harvey, William Hope
d. 1940 Buchan, John, Sir
d. 1945 Dubin, Al
d. 1945 Igoe, Hype
d. 1949 Dube, John Langalibalele
d. 1949 Zenatello, Giovanni
d. 1950 Cuyler, Kiki
d. 1955 Munson, Ona
d. 1960 Barker, Ernest, Sir
d. 1963 Plath, Sylvia
d. 1967 Muste, A(braham) J(ohannes)
d. 1968 Lindsay, Howard
d. 1970 Bateman, Henry Mayo
d. 1973 Jensen, Johannes Hans Daniel
d. 1973 Lawrence, David

d. 1974 Nilsson, Anna Q(uerentia)
d. 1976 Cobb, Lee J
d. 1977 Ahmed, Fakhruddin Ali
d. 1978 Conant, James Bryant
d. 1978 Martinson, Harry Edmund
d. 1980 Malik, Yakov (Alexandrovich)
d. 1981 Frings, Ketti
d. 1981 Ichikawa, Fusae
d. 1982 Powell, Eleanor
d. 1983 Drewry, John Eldridge
d. 1983 Kline, Nathan Schellenberg
d. 1984 Brett, George Platt, Jr.
d. 1985 Abruzzo, Ben(jamine Lou)
d. 1985 Hathaway, Henry
d. 1986 Herbert, Frank (Patrick)
d. 1988 Mizener, Arthur Moore
d. 1989 Clarke, Thomas Ernest Bennett
d. 1989 Kimbrough, Emily
d. 1990 De Mestral, Georges
d. 1992 Danton, Ray(mond)
d. 1993 Garrett, Joy
d. 1993 Holley, Robert W(illiam)
d. 1993 Meredith, Scott
d. 1994 Booke, Sorrell
d. 1994 Conrad, William
d. 1996 Regan, Phil
d. 1997 Porter, Don

February 12
b. 1567 Campion, Thomas
b. 1637 Swammerdam, Jan
b. 1663 Mather, Cotton
b. 1746 Kosciuszko, Thaddeus
b. 1768 Francis, II
b. 1775 Adams, Louisa Catherine
b. 1785 Dulong, Pierre-Louis
b. 1791 Cooper, Peter
b. 1804 Wright, Elizur
b. 1809 Darwin, Charles Robert
b. 1809 Lincoln, Abraham
b. 1813 Dana, James Dwight
b. 1813 Lossing, Benson John
b. 1815 Forbes, Edward
b. 1819 Story, William Wetmore
b. 1838 Howland, Alfred Cornelius
b. 1850 Davis, William Morris

b. 1851 Bohm von Bawerk, Eugene
b. 1857 Atget, Eugene
b. 1868 Faversham, William Alfred
b. 1870 Burkett, Jesse Cail
b. 1870 Lloyd, Marie
b. 1874 Perret, Auguste
b. 1878 Howard, Joseph Edgar
b. 1880 Lewis, John L(lewellyn)
b. 1884 Beckmann, Max
b. 1884 Longworth, Alice Roosevelt
b. 1885 Streicher, Julius
b. 1888 Coulter, John William
b. 1891 Mathews, Mitford M
b. 1893 Bradley, Omar Nelson
b. 1893 Shannon, Fred Albert
b. 1898 Bruce, David Kirkpatrick Estes
b. 1898 Ford, Wallace
b. 1898 Harris, Roy
b. 1899 Tokatyan, Armand
b. 1900 Boothby, Robert John Graham, Lord
b. 1900 Chuikov, Vasili Ivanovitch
b. 1900 Fenton, Carroll Lane
b. 1903 Duncan, Todd
b. 1903 Hafey, Chick
b. 1904 Mack, Ted
b. 1911 Guzman, Antonio
b. 1911 O'Dalaigh, Cearbhall
b. 1912 Delderfield, Ronald Frederick
b. 1914 Beneke, Tex
b. 1915 Goodpaster, Andrew Jackson
b. 1915 Greene, Lorne
b. 1916 Alioto, Joseph L(awrence)
b. 1917 Cervi, Al
b. 1917 DiMaggio, Dom(inic Paul)
b. 1917 Scherman, Thomas Kielty
b. 1918 Schwinger, Julian (Seymour)
b. 1919 Tucker, Forrest Meredith
b. 1923 Dugan, Alan
b. 1923 Zeffirelli, Franco
b. 1925 Finney, Joan Marie McInroy
b. 1926 Garagiola, Joe
b. 1926 Mitchell, Joan
b. 1926 Van Doren, Charles Lincoln
b. 1930 Specter, Arlen
b. 1932 Lutz, Robert Anthony
b. 1934 Howard, Anthony

b. 1934 Russell, Bill
b. 1935 Manzarek, Ray
b. 1936 Baker, Joe Don
b. 1936 Fang Lizhi
b. 1938 Blume, Judy
Sussman
b. 1939 Dayan, Yael
b. 1939 Hancock, John
D
b. 1940 Brown, Hank
b. 1942 Wegman,
William George
b. 1944 Torrence, Jackie
b. 1945 Adams, Maud
b. 1945 De Young,
Cliff
b. 1948 Kurzweil,
Raymond C
b. 1949 Knight, Stan
b. 1950 Hackett, Steve
b. 1953 MacCorkindale,
Simon
b. 1955 Hall, Arsenio
b. 1955 Kerns, Joanna
d. 1538 Altdorfer,
Albrecht
d. 1554 Grey, Jane,
Lady
d. 1728 Steffani,
Agostino
d. 1763 Marivaux,
Pierre Carlet de
d. 1804 Kant, Immanuel
d. 1807 Roentgen,
David
d. 1834 Schleiermacher,
Friedrich Ernst Daniel
d. 1841 Cooper, Astley
Paston, Sir
d. 1871 Cary, Alice
d. 1878 Duff, Alexander
d. 1886 Caldecott,
Randolph
d. 1886 Seymour,
Horatio
d. 1894 Bulow, Hans
Guido von
d. 1896 Thomas,
(Charles Louis)
Ambroise
d. 1897 Martin, Homer
Dodge
d. 1903 Curry, Jabez
Lamar Monroe
d. 1915 Crosby, Fanny
d. 1916 Trowbridge,
John Townsend
d. 1929 Langtry, Lillie
d. 1933 Robertson,
William Robert, Sir
d. 1935 Escoffier,
Georges Auguste
d. 1942 Wood, Grant
d. 1947 Lewin, Kurt
d. 1947 Toler, Sidney
d. 1949 Levinsky,
Battling
d. 1951 Bajor, Gizi
d. 1955 Moore, Tom
d. 1955 Sakall, S Z
d. 1959 Antheil, George
d. 1960 Clark, Bobby
d. 1962 Darling, Jay
Norwood
d. 1965 Hammond, John
Hays, Jr.

d. 1967 Spanier,
Muggsy
d. 1971 Glueck, Nelson
d. 1971 Penney, J(ames)
C(ash)
d. 1973 Maritain,
Jacques
d. 1976 Mineo,
Sal(vatore)
d. 1978 Taylor, Sydney
Brenner
d. 1979 Renoir, Jean
d. 1980 Berger, Samuel
David
d. 1980 Rukeyser,
Muriel
d. 1981 Dixon, Jean
d. 1981 Fraser, Bruce
Austin, Sir
d. 1982 Jory, Victor
d. 1983 Blake, Eubie
d. 1984 Bainton, Roland
Herbert
d. 1984 Cortazar, Julio
d. 1985 Colasanto,
Nicholas
d. 1985 Lengyel, Emil
d. 1986 Lazare, Kaplan
d. 1986 Stone, Sidney
d. 1987 Bergman, Jules
Verne
d. 1988 Goossens, Leon
Jean
d. 1991 Wagner, Robert
Ferdinand, Jr.
d. 1993 Ellingson, Mark
d. 1995 Holman,
Nat(han)
d. 1996 Samuels, Ernest
d. 2000 Auriol,
Jacqueline Douet
d. 2000 Hawkins,
Screamin' Jay
d. 2000 Landry, Tom
d. 2000 Schulz, Charles
M(onroe)
d. 2000 Vadim, Roger

February 13
b. 1703 Dodsley, Robert
b. 1728 Hunter, John
b. 1743 Banks, Joseph
b. 1754 Talleyrand-
Perigord, Charles
Maurice de
b. 1778 Sor, Fernando
b. 1805 Field, David
Dudley
b. 1815 Stoltz, Rosine
b. 1831 Rawlins, John
A
b. 1835 Ahmad, Mirza
Ghulam Hazat
b. 1849 Churchill,
Randolph Henry
Spencer, Lord
b. 1852 Dreyer, Johan
Ludwig Emil
b. 1861 Curran, Charles
Courtney
b. 1870 Godowsky,
Leopold
b. 1870 Lincoln, Joseph
C(rosby)
b. 1873 Chaliapin,
Feodor Ivanovitch, Jr.

b. 1877 Smith, (Robert)
Sidney
b. 1879 Naidu, Sarojini
b. 1881 Farjeon,
Eleanor
b. 1885 Truman, Bess
b. 1886 Guiraldes,
Ricardo (Guillermo)
b. 1888 Papandreou,
George
b. 1891 Paul, Elliot
Harold
b. 1892 Jackson, Robert
Houghwout
b. 1892 Wood, Grant
b. 1895 Wilder, Joseph
b. 1901 Gibbon, Lewis
Grassic
b. 1901 Kuznetzov,
Vassili Vasilyevich
b. 1902 Lasswell,
Harold Dwight
b. 1903 Simenon,
Georges
b. 1904 Manone, Wingy
b. 1905 McKelway, St.
Clair
b. 1907 Goodman,
Andrew
b. 1908 Dozier, William
b. 1908 Frederick,
Pauline
b. 1908 Goode, Mal
b. 1908 Hayton, Lennie
b. 1910 Cowles, Fleur
Fenton
b. 1910 Halsey,
Margaret (Frances)
b. 1910 Shockley,
William B(radford)
b. 1911 Muir, Jean
b. 1913 Agostini, Peter
b. 1915 Aung San
b. 1915 Bettger, Lyle
b. 1918 Berg, Patty
b. 1918 Smith, Oliver
b. 1919 Edwards, Joan
b. 1919 Ford, Tennessee
Ernie
b. 1919 Robinson,
Eddie
b. 1920 Bryant,
Boudleaux
b. 1920 Farrell, Eileen
b. 1921 Warner,
Rawleigh, Jr.
b. 1921 Zao-Wou-Ki
b. 1922 Pym, Francis
Leslie
b. 1923 Abdnor, James
S
b. 1923 Bilandic,
Michael Anthony
b. 1923 Chapin,
Schuyler Garrison
b. 1923 Shafran, Daniel
b. 1923 Yeager, Chuck
b. 1924 Servan-
Schreiber, Jean-
Jacques
b. 1928 Fried, Gerald
b. 1929 Torrijos
Herrera, Omar
b. 1931 Klarsfeld, Beate
b. 1932 Bergerac,
Michel C

b. 1933 Costa-Gavras
b. 1933 Ungaro,
Emanuel Matteotti
b. 1934 Segal, George
b. 1935 Hanafi, Hassan
b. 1938 Reed, Oliver
b. 1940 Eaton, Robert
James
b. 1941 Polke, Sigmar
b. 1942 Archambault,
JoAllyn
b. 1942 Lynley, Carol
b. 1943 Pagels, Elaine
b. 1944 Bando,
Sal(vatore Leonard)
b. 1944 Channing,
Stockard
b. 1944 Springer, Jerry
b. 1944 Tork, Peter
b. 1945 Schama, Simon
b. 1947 Krzyzewski,
Mike
b. 1952 De Grassi, Alex
b. 1953 Shea, Lisa
b. 1592 Bassano, Jacopo
d. 1728 Mather, Cotton
d. 1787 Boscovich,
Ruggiero Giuseppe
d. 1818 Clark, George
Rogers
d. 1882 Garnet, Henry
Highland
d. 1882 Stephens, Uriah
d. 1883 Wagner,
Richard
d. 1888 Lamy, Jean
Baptist
d. 1891 Porter, David
Dixon
d. 1913 Major, Charles
d. 1914 Bertillon,
Alphonse
d. 1926 Holt, Henry
d. 1927 Adams, Brooks
d. 1927 Adams, Peter
Chardon Brooks
d. 1937 Griffin, Walter
Burley
d. 1938 McIntyre,
O(scar) O(dd)
d. 1945 Szold, Henrietta
d. 1946 Neilson,
William A(llan)
d. 1950 Sabatini, Rafael
d. 1951 Douglas, Lloyd
Cassel
d. 1952 Einstein, Alfred
d. 1952 Tey, Josephine
d. 1954 Allen, Frederick
Lewis
d. 1954 Perry, Bliss
d. 1958 Rouault,
Georges
d. 1963 Reynolds,
Robert Rice
d. 1965 Kilpatrick,
William H(eard)
d. 1968 Marsh, Mae
d. 1968 Pizzetti,
Ildebrando
d. 1974 Golenpaul, Dan
d. 1975 Van Dusen,
Henry Pitney
d. 1976 Pons, Lily
d. 1980 Janssen, David

d. 1980 Monroney, Mike (Aimer Stillwell)
d. 1981 Kaufman, Joseph William
d. 1982 Williams, Gluyas
d. 1985 Harris, Joseph Pratt
d. 1985 Jacobs, Al(bert T)
d. 1987 Hass, H(enry) B(ohn)
d. 1994 Judd, Walter H(enry)
d. 1994 Sherrod, Robert (Lee)
d. 1995 Burri, Alberto
d. 1996 Balsam, Martin Henry
d. 1996 Conerly, Charlie
d. 1999 Jennings, Gary

February 14

b. 1404 Alberti, Leon Battista
b. 1483 Babur
b. 1602 Cavalli, Francesco
b. 1602 Cavalli, Pietro Francesco
b. 1612 Butler, Samuel
b. 1760 Allen, Richard
b. 1768 Krylov, Ivan Andreyevich
b. 1813 Dargomijsky, Alexander
b. 1817 Douglass, Frederick
b. 1819 Sholes, Christopher Latham
b. 1823 Powell, William Henry
b. 1824 Hancock, Winfield Scott
b. 1828 About, Edmond-Francois-Valentin
b. 1847 Shaw, Anna Howard
b. 1856 Harris, Frank
b. 1859 Ferris, George Washington Gale
b. 1860 Lillie, Gordon William
b. 1864 Park, Robert Ezra
b. 1864 Zangwill, Israel
b. 1865 Anderson, Carl Thomas
b. 1869 Wilson, Charles Thomson Rees
b. 1872 Grove, Frederick Philip
b. 1874 Boon, Dickie
b. 1882 Nathan, George Jean
b. 1889 Auerbach-Levy, William
b. 1893 Smith, Dora
b. 1894 Benny, Jack
b. 1898 Zwicky, Fritz
b. 1902 Erwin, Stuart
b. 1905 Ritter, Thelma
b. 1907 Longden, Johnny

b. 1908 Scribner, Fred C(lark), Jr.
b. 1909 Moss, Carlton
b. 1910? Dragonette, Jessica
b. 1911 Kolff, Willem Johan
b. 1911 Porter, Bernard H
b. 1912 Harrington, Oliver W(endell)
b. 1913 Allen, Mel
b. 1913 Hayes, Woody
b. 1913 Hoffa, Jimmy
b. 1913 Pike, James Albert, Bishop
b. 1915 Austin, John Paul
b. 1917 Hauptman, Herbert Aaron
b. 1917 Hauptman, Herbert Aaron
b. 1921 Downs, Hugh (Malcolm)
b. 1922 Kaufman, Murray
b. 1923 Hebert, Jay
b. 1925 Lawrence, Elliot
b. 1926 Sleet, Moneta, Jr.
b. 1928 Allain, William A
b. 1928 Gimbel, Peter Robin
b. 1929 Morrow, Vic
b. 1931 Geoffrion, Bernie
b. 1932 Schroeder, William J
b. 1933 Cook, Michael
b. 1934 Henderson, Florence
b. 1935 Wright, Mickey
b. 1941 Freeman, Cliff(ord Lee)
b. 1941 Shalala, Donna Edna
b. 1941 Tsongas, Paul E(fthemios)
b. 1942 Bloomberg, Michael (R.)
b. 1944 Bernstein, Carl
b. 1944 Fireman, Paul
b. 1944 Parker, Alan William
b. 1944 Threadgill, Henry
b. 1946 Hines, Gregory Oliver
b. 1947 Gregg, Judd
b. 1950 Dent, Phil
b. 1951 Gross, Terry
b. 1956 Dravecky, Dave
b. 1957 Wahl, Ken
b. 1959 Fleming, Renee
b. 1960 Kelly, Jim
b. 1970 Moe, Tommy
b. 1972 Bledsoe, Drew
d. 1400 Richard II
d. 1571 Cellini, Benvenuto
d. 1741 Fux, Johann Joseph
d. 1779 Cook, James, Captain

d. 1780 Blackstone, William, Sir
d. 1808 Dickinson, John
d. 1831 Guerrero, Vicente
d. 1864 Dyce, William
d. 1870 Harper, Joseph Wesley
d. 1881 Wood, Fernando
d. 1884 Roosevelt, Alice Lee
d. 1885 Hotchkiss, Benjamin Berkeley
d. 1891 Sherman, William Tecumseh
d. 1925 Bausch, John Jacob
d. 1928 Hubert, Conrad
d. 1943 Hilbert, David
d. 1945 Rothenstein, William, Sir
d. 1948 Brown, Mordecai Peter Centennial
d. 1958 Pankhurst, Christabel Harriette, Dame
d. 1958 Twelvetrees, Helen
d. 1959 Dodds, Baby
d. 1959 Irwin, Wallace (Admah)
d. 1963 Shannon, Fred Albert
d. 1966 Vittorini, Elio
d. 1967 Rumann, Sig(fried)
d. 1969 Genovese, Vito
d. 1975 Huxley, Julian Sorell, Sir
d. 1975 Wodehouse, P(elham) G(renville)
d. 1978 Rattner, Abraham
d. 1979 Tunnard, Christopher
d. 1980 Gruen, Victor
d. 1982 Jackson, Hurricane
d. 1984 Mili, Gjon
d. 1985 Mathews, Mitford M
d. 1985 Spigelgass, Leonard
d. 1986 Wilder, Clinton
d. 1988 Astorga, Nora Gadea
d. 1988 Benton, Nelson
d. 1988 Cohn, Al
d. 1988 Loewe, Frederick
d. 1989 Bond, James
d. 1991 McCone, John Alex
d. 1993 Lipsky, Eleazar
d. 1993 Squires, James Radcliffe
d. 1994 Belluschi, Pietro
d. 1994 Lasch, Christopher
d. 1995 Barton, Robert B(rown) M(orison)
d. 1995 Nu, U
d. 1995 Nu Thakin

d. 1999 Ehrlichman, John D(aniel)
d. 2000 Zinn, Walter Henry

February 15

b. 1368 Sigismund
b. 1519 Menendez de Aviles, Pedro
b. 1564 Galileo
b. 1571 Praetorius, Michael
b. 1710 Louis XV
b. 1726 Clark, Abraham
b. 1748 Bentham, Jeremy
b. 1759 Wolf, Friedrich August
b. 1760 Lesueur, Jean-Francois
b. 1782 Miller, William
b. 1797 Bell, John
b. 1797 Steinway, Henry Engelhard
b. 1803 Sutter, John Augustus
b. 1809 McCormick, Cyrus Hall
b. 1811 Sarmiento, Domingo Faustino
b. 1812 Tiffany, Charles Lewis
b. 1817 Daubigny, Charles Francois
b. 1820 Anthony, Susan B(rownell)
b. 1823 Li Hung-Chang
b. 1826 Stoney, George Johnstone
b. 1829 Mitchell, Silas Weir
b. 1834 Haeckel, Ernst Heinrich Philipp August
b. 1835 Dabney, Virginius
b. 1842 Quad, M
b. 1845 Root, Elihu
b. 1858 Pickering, William Henry
b. 1861 Guillaume, Charles Edouard
b. 1861 Mackinder, Halford John, Sir
b. 1861 Whitehead, Alfred North
b. 1869 Williams, Henry Sylvester
b. 1871 Nordstrom, John
b. 1873 Euler-Chelpin, Hans Karl August Simon von
b. 1874 Shackleton, Ernest Henry, Sir
b. 1876 Everleigh, Ada
b. 1880 Davidson, J Brownlee
b. 1880 Hergesheimer, Joseph
b. 1882 Barrymore, John
b. 1883 Rohmer, Sax
b. 1884 Gilbert, A(lfred) C(arleton)
b. 1887 Bateman, Henry Mayo

b. 1890 Ley, Robert
b. 1892 Forrestal, James Vincent
b. 1893 Baxter, James Phinney, III
b. 1893 Donaldson, Walter
b. 1894 Aranha, Osvaldo
b. 1895 Thomson, Earl
b. 1897 Blaik, Red
b. 1898 Ibuse, Masuji
b. 1899 Auric, Georges
b. 1899 Josephson, Matthew
b. 1899 Keppard, Freddie
b. 1899 Sondergaard, Gale (Edith Holm)
b. 1900 Thomas, Charles Allen
b. 1901 Bracken, Brendan Rendall, Viscount
b. 1901 Humphreys, Christmas
b. 1905 Arlen, Harold
b. 1907 Romero, Cesar
b. 1910 Aitken, Max
b. 1911 Woodcock, Leonard Freel
b. 1914 Boggs, Hale
b. 1914 McCarthy, Kevin
b. 1916 Ballantine, Ian (Keith)
b. 1916 Seton-Watson, Hugh
b. 1922 Anderson, John Bayard
b. 1922 Kahn, Herman
b. 1923 Bonner, Yelena
b. 1925 Gardner, Edward George
b. 1927 Dunlop, Frank
b. 1927 Korman, Harvey Herschel
b. 1929 Hill, Graham
b. 1929 Schlesinger, James Rodney
b. 1930 Moore, Sara Jane
b. 1931 Bloom, Claire
b. 1931 Harris, LaDonna (Crawford)
b. 1931 Singer, Maxine (Frank)
b. 1933 Adolfo
b. 1935 Block, John Rusling
b. 1935 Brownmiller, Susan
b. 1935 Chaffee, Roger Bruce
b. 1942 Kim Jong Il
b. 1945 Hans Adam, II
b. 1947 Adams, John Coolidge
b. 1947 Hamer, Rusty
b. 1948 Berenson, Marisa
b. 1948 Cey, Ron(ald Charles)
b. 1948 Spiegelman, Art
b. 1949 Anderson, Ken(neth Allan)

b. 1951 Jenkins, Beverly
b. 1951 Manchester, Melissa Toni
b. 1951 Seymour, Jane
b. 1952 Jones, Bill T.
b. 1953 Adams, Tony
b. 1953 Dallmeier, Francisco
b. 1954 Groening, Matt
b. 1954 Whitfield, Lynn
b. 1958 McKegney, Tony
b. 1964 Farley, Chris
b. 1972 Jagr, Jaromir
b. 923 Tabari, Muhammad ibn Jarir al-
d. 1479 Antonello da Messina
d. 1621 Praetorius, Michael
d. 1637 Ferdinand II
d. 1683 Cooper, Anthony Ashley, 1st Earl of Shaftesbury
d. 1713 Shaftesbury, Anthony Ashley Cooper, Earl
d. 1741 Donner, Georg Raphael
d. 1781 Lessing, Gotthold Ephraim
d. 1820 Ellery, William
d. 1846 Kotzebue, Otto von
d. 1857 Glinka, Mikhail Ivanovich
d. 1865 Wiseman, Nicholas Patrick Stephen
d. 1885 Damrosch, Leopold
d. 1888 Locke, David Ross
d. 1904 Hanna, Mark
d. 1905 Wallace, Lew(is)
d. 1915 Gokhale, Gopal Krishna
d. 1918 Castle, Vernon
d. 1925 DeYoung, Michel Harry
d. 1928 Asquith, Herbert Henry
d. 1929 Stone, Melville Elijah
d. 1931 Leitzel, Lillian
d. 1941 Adler, Guido
d. 1946 Johnson, Cornelius
d. 1955 Maginnis, Charles Donagh
d. 1959 Richardson, Owen Williams, Sir
d. 1965 Cole, Nat King
d. 1967 Bullitt, William Christian
d. 1967 Duryea, J(ames) Frank
d. 1969 Russell, Pee Wee
d. 1970 Dowding, Hugh Caswell Tremenheere, Baron

d. 1972 Snow, Edgar Parks
d. 1973 Cox, Wally
d. 1973 Holt, Tim
d. 1978 Chase, Ilka
d. 1981 Bloomfield, Mike
d. 1982 Dietrich, Noah
d. 1982 Enoch, Kurt
d. 1984 Long, Avon
d. 1984 Merman, Ethel
d. 1988 Feynman, Richard Phillips
d. 1988 Meng, John Joseph
d. 1990 Parkinson, Norman
d. 1991 Englund, Richard
d. 1992 Schuman, William Howard
d. 1996 Stevenson, McLean
d. 1996 Weber, Ernst
d. 1998 Gellhorn, Martha Ellis
d. 1999 Kendall, Henry Way

February 16
b. 1497 Melanchthon, Philipp
b. 1519 Coligny, Gaspard de Chatillon
b. 1728 Shippen, Edward
b. 1740 Bodoni, Giambattista
b. 1774 Rode, Jacques Pierre Joseph
b. 1812 Wilson, Henry
b. 1821 Barth, Heinrich
b. 1822 Galton, Francis, Sir
b. 1831 Leskov, Nikolai Semyonovich
b. 1838 Adams, Henry Brooks
b. 1838 Okuma, Shigenobu
b. 1840 Watterson, Henry
b. 1843 Leland, Henry Martyn
b. 1848 DeVries, Hugo
b. 1852 Russell, Charles Taze
b. 1860 Fels, Samuel Simeon
b. 1864 Harvey, George Brinton M
b. 1866 Hamilton, Billy
b. 1866 Mannes, David
b. 1876 Trevelyan, George Macaulay
b. 1877 Gougelman, Pierre
b. 1884 Flaherty, Robert Joseph
b. 1884 Kalmar, Bert
b. 1886 Brooks, Van Wyck
b. 1888 Medina, Harold Raymond
b. 1891 Gunther, Hans F K

b. 1893 Tukhachevski, Mikhail Nikolayevich
b. 1896 Brailowsky, Alexander
b. 1898 Cornell, Katharine
b. 1900 Hackett, Albert
b. 1900 Switzer, Mary E.
b. 1901 King, Wayne
b. 1901 Morris, Chester
b. 1901 Pei, Mario Andrew
b. 1903 Bergen, Edgar John
b. 1904 Kennan, George Frost
b. 1905 Franks, Oliver (Shewell), Sir
b. 1905 Waterhouse, Ellis Kirkham, Sir
b. 1906 Menchik-Stevenson, Vera Francevna
b. 1907 Anstey, Edgar Harold McFarlane
b. 1907 Previtali, Fernando
b. 1909 Beaumont, Hugh
b. 1911 Porter, Hal
b. 1914 Wakely, Jimmy
b. 1920 Andrews, Patti
b. 1922 Evans, Geraint Llewellyn, Sir
b. 1924 MacKenzie, Warren
b. 1926 Mohieddin, Ahmed Faud
b. 1926 Schlesinger, John Richard
b. 1926 Vera-Ellen
b. 1932 Kabbah, (Alhaji) Ahmad Tejan
b. 1932 Wyler, Gretchen
b. 1935 Bedford, Brian
b. 1935 Bono, Sonny
b. 1936 Harris, Joe Frank
b. 1938 Corigliano, John (Paul)
b. 1943 Dowell, Anthony James
b. 1944 Ford, Richard
b. 1944 Mascarenhas Monteiro, Antonio
b. 1953 McDonald, Lanny
b. 1953 St. Laurent, Andre
b. 1955 Katt, William
b. 1955 McManus, Sean
b. 1956? Ingram, James
b. 1957 Burton, LeVar(dis Robert Martyn Jr.)
b. 1958 Ice-T
b. 1959 McEnroe, John Patrick, Jr.
d. 1279 Alfonso, III
d. 1624 Mariana, Juan de
d. 1687 Cotton, Charles
d. 1699 Monnoyer, Jean-Baptiste

d. 1823 Prudhon, Pierre-
Paul
d. 1823 Prud'hon, Pierre
Paul
d. 1829 Gossec,
Francois Joseph
d. 1857 Kane, Elisha
Kent
d. 1871 Locke, Richard
Adams
d. 1892 Bates, Henry
Walter
d. 1899 Faure, Francois
Felix
d. 1907 Carducci,
Giosue Alessandro
Guiseppe
d. 1911 Earle, Alice
Morse
d. 1914 DeVinne,
Theodore Low
d. 1919 Sykes, Mark,
Sir
d. 1924 Bacon, Henry
d. 1928 Foy, Eddie
d. 1932 Buisson,
Ferdinand Edouard
d. 1932 Fiske, Minnie
Maddern
d. 1936 Chapin, Roy
Dikeman
d. 1936 Robinson,
James Harvey
d. 1950 Walker, Jack
d. 1953 Kraft, James
Lewis
d. 1957 Hofmann, Josef
Casimir
d. 1957 Hore-Belisha,
Leslie, Baron
d. 1957 Townsend, John
Sealy Edward, Sir
d. 1958 Frisco, Joe
d. 1959 Mara, Tim(othy
James)
d. 1961 Vance, Dazzy
d. 1965 Breck, John
Henry
d. 1967 Burnette,
Smiley
d. 1969 Martin,
Kingsley
d. 1970 Rous, Francis
Peyton
d. 1974 Garand, John
Cantius
d. 1974 Kallen, Horace
M(eyer)
d. 1978 Harriman,
E(dward) Roland
(Noel)
d. 1979 Allbritton,
Louise
d. 1979 Gargan,
William
d. 1981 Huntington,
Henry S, Jr.
d. 1981 Richter, Karl
d. 1986 DaSilva,
Howard
d. 1988 Gordon-
Lazareff, Helene
d. 1990 Haring, Keith
d. 1992 Carter, Angela
(Olive)

d. 1993 Salant, Richard
S
d. 1996 Bowen, Roger
d. 1996 Brown, Edmund
G.
d. 1996 Clark, Eleanor
d. 1997 Wu, Chien
Shiung
February 17
b. 1590? Ribera, Jusepe
(Jose) de
b. 1653 Corelli,
Arcangelo
b. 1665 Camerarius,
Rudolf Jakob
b. 1723 Mayer, Johann
Tobias
b. 1740 Sullivan, John
b. 1766 Malthus,
Thomas Robert
b. 1774 Peale, Raphael
b. 1781 Laennec, Rene
Theophile Hyacinthe
b. 1785 Krochmal,
Nachman Kohen
b. 1796 Pacini,
Giovanni
b. 1811 A'Beckett,
Gilbert Abbott
b. 1827 Cooke, Rose
Terry
b. 1836 Becquer,
Gustavo Adolfo
Dominguez
b. 1843 Ward,
Montgomery
b. 1845 McBurney,
Charles
b. 1847 Mallinger,
Mathilde
b. 1856 Ives, Frederic
Eugene
b. 1857 McClure,
Samuel Sidney
b. 1864 Paterson,
A(ndrew) B(arton)
b. 1872 Duane, William
b. 1874 Watson,
Thomas J(ohn), Sr.
b. 1875 Brian, Donald
b. 1877 Maginot, Andre
Louis Rene
b. 1879 Fisher, Dorothy
Frances Canfield
b. 1880 Obregon,
Alvaro
b. 1881 Aldrich, Bess
Streeter
b. 1881 Breckinridge,
Mary
b. 1884 Smith, Joe
b. 1885 Guardini,
Romano
b. 1887 Bech, Joseph
b. 1888 Knox, Ronald
Arbuthnott
b. 1888 Stern, Otto
b. 1889 Hunt,
H(aroldson)
L(afayette)
b. 1890 Fisher, R(onald)
A(ylmer)
b. 1890 Lesser, Sol
b. 1892 Neyland, Robert
Reese
b. 1893 Pipp, Wally

b. 1896 Hicks, Ursula
Kathleen Webb
b. 1896 Stewart, Anita
b. 1897 Chamberlin,
William Henry
b. 1903 Hidayat, Sadiq
b. 1904 Morgenthau,
Hans Joachim
b. 1906 Plaza Lasso,
Galo
b. 1906 Spivak, Charlie
b. 1907 Wilder, Alec
b. 1908 Barber, Red
b. 1908 Cotsworth,
Staats
b. 1908 Crabbe, Buster
b. 1909 Lawrence,
Marjorie Florence
b. 1911 Hunnicutt,
Arthur
b. 1911 Tucker, Orrin
b. 1912 Norton, Andre
b. 1912 Sorensen,
Virginia
b. 1913 Leibowitz, Rene
b. 1913 Nye, Russel
Blaine
b. 1914 Kennedy,
Arthur
b. 1914 Morris, Wayne
b. 1918 Vallone,
Raf(faele)
b. 1921 Manuel, George
b. 1923 Allegro, John
Marco
b. 1923 Clausen,
A(lden) W(inship)
b. 1923 DeFranco,
Buddy
b. 1924 Truman,
Margaret
b. 1925 Holbrook, Hal
b. 1926 Hoiby, Lee
b. 1926 Kohlmeier,
Louis Martin, Jr.
b. 1928 Jones, Tom
b. 1928 Peck, Robert
Newton
b. 1929 Plante, Jacques
b. 1929 Potok, Chaim
b. 1930 Rendell, Ruth
b. 1931 Craig, Roger
Lee
b. 1933 Thomas, Craig
b. 1934 Bates, Alan
Arthur
b. 1934 Humphries,
Barry
b. 1935 Cohen, Stanley
N(orman)
b. 1936 Bartholomew,
Reginald
b. 1936 Brown, Jim
b. 1937 Mobley, Mary
Ann
b. 1938 Berry, Mary
Frances
b. 1938 Henry, Martha
b. 1939 Keeton, Kathy
b. 1941 Pitney, Gene
b. 1941 Webb,
Wellington
b. 1942 Newton, Huey
P(ercy)
b. 1943 Chappell, Tom

b. 1945 Brown, Les(lie
Calvin)
b. 1947 Buckley, Tim
b. 1947 Whiteman,
Roberta Hill
b. 1949 Coleman,
Leonard S., Jr.
b. 1949 Green, Dennis
b. 1959 Lomax, Neil
Vincent
b. 1962 Phillips, Lou
Diamond
b. 1963 Jordan, Michael
(Jeffery)
b. 1966 Robitaille, Luc
b. 1972 Armstrong,
Billie Joe
d. 1600 Bruno,
Giordano
d. 1652 Allegri,
Gregorio
d. 1673 Moliere
d. 1680 Swammerdam,
Jan
d. 1793 McGillivray,
Alexander
d. 1796 Macpherson,
James
d. 1827 Pestalozzi,
Johann Heinrich
d. 1830 Rutgers, Henry
d. 1856 Heine, Heinrich
d. 1867 Bache,
Alexander Dallas
d. 1874 Quetelet,
Lambert Adolphe
Jacques
d. 1875 Argelander,
Friedrich Wilhelm
August
d. 1876 Bushnell,
Horace
d. 1876 Cushman,
Charlotte Saunders
d. 1877 Mosenthal,
Salomon Hermann
von
d. 1890 Sholes,
Christopher Latham
d. 1901 Nevin, Ethelbert
Woodbridge
d. 1907 Olcott, Henry
Steel
d. 1909 Geronimo
d. 1913 Miller, Joaquin
d. 1919 Laurier,
Wilfrid, Sir
d. 1925 Valleria,
Alwina
d. 1932 Kelley,
Florence
d. 1934 Albert I
d. 1936 Maxim, Hiram
Percy
d. 1943 Keogan, George
d. 1961 Naldi, Nita
d. 1962 Walter, Bruno
d. 1963 Lockridge,
Frances Louise
d. 1965 Bucher, Walter
Herman
d. 1966 Hofmann, Hans
d. 1966 Sloan, Alfred
Pritchard, Jr.
d. 1967 Alegria, Ciro

b. 1821 Blair, Francis Preston, Jr.
b. 1833 Ducommun, Elie
b. 1843 Patti, Adelina Juana Maria
b. 1856 Stammler, Rudolf
b. 1859 Arrhenius, Svante August
b. 1863 Leguia y Salcedo, Augusto Bernardino
b. 1865 Hedin, Sven Anders
b. 1868 Curtis, Edward Sheriff
b. 1873 Feuillade, Louis
b. 1887 Terry, Paul H
b. 1892 Lucas, Scott Wike
b. 1893 Hardwicke, Cedric Webster, Sir
b. 1895 Calhern, Louis
b. 1895 Timoshenko, Semen Konstantinovich
b. 1902 Boyle, Kay
b. 1902 Bubbles, John
b. 1902 Matthiessen, Francis Otto
b. 1902 Peabody, Eddie
b. 1903 Slobodkin, Louis
b. 1907 Bosley, Harold A
b. 1909 Rodman, Selden
b. 1910 Wood, Louise Aletha
b. 1911 Oberon, Merle
b. 1912 Buttigieg, Anton
b. 1912 Chaplin, Saul
b. 1912 Chapman, Ceil
b. 1912 Kenton, Stan(ley Newcomb)
b. 1916 Arcaro, Eddie
b. 1916 Duong Van Minh
b. 1917 McCullers, Carson (Smith)
b. 1920 Guest, C. Z.
b. 1920 Mayer, Jean
b. 1920 Rose, George Walter
b. 1921 Treurnicht, Andries Petrus
b. 1923 Hillings, Patrick J(ohn)
b. 1924 Marvin, Lee
b. 1924 Norris, Bruce A
b. 1926 Thomas, Ross (Elmore)
b. 1930 Frankenheimer, John Michael
b. 1932 Kerwin, Joseph Peter
b. 1933 Biya, Paul
b. 1934 Brown, William Melvin, Jr.
b. 1940 Krementz, Jill
b. 1940 Robinson, Smokey
b. 1943 Elliot, Cass
b. 1945 Taulbert, Clifton Lemoure

b. 1946 Silkwood, Karen
b. 1947 Curtis, Jackie
b. 1952 Tan, Amy
b. 1955 Daniels, Jeff
b. 1955 Hemingway, Margaux
b. 1955 Hustvedt, Siri
b. 1957 Falco
b. 1957 Stewart, Dave
b. 1958 Hewitt, Martin
b. 1960 Andrew
b. 1963 Mandlikova, Hana
b. 1963 Seal
b. 1966 Bateman, Justine
d. 1653 Rossi, Luigi
d. 1837 Buchner, Georg
d. 1878 Daubigny, Charles Francois
d. 1880 Brumidi, Constantino
d. 1882 Ryerson, Adolphus Egerton
d. 1893 Carroll, Anna Ella
d. 1897 Blondin, Jean Francois Gravelet
d. 1916 Mach, Ernst
d. 1917 Funston, Frederick
d. 1927 Brandes, Georg Morris Cohen
d. 1936 Mitchell, Billy
d. 1943 Overman, Lynne
d. 1950 Walker, Edyth
d. 1951 Gide, Andre (Paul Guillaume)
d. 1952 Hamsun, Knut
d. 1957 Toren, Marta
d. 1962 Barton, James
d. 1962 Papanicolaou, George Nicholas
d. 1963 Brophy, John
d. 1969 Bonham Carter, Violet
d. 1970 Flanders, Ralph Edward
d. 1970 Munshin, Jules
d. 1972 Grierson, John
d. 1973 Sanderson, Ivan Terence
d. 1975 Dallapiccola, Luigi
d. 1976 Fishbein, Harry J
d. 1976 Sullivan, Frank
d. 1978 Christophers, S(amuel) Rickard, Sir
d. 1981 Streithorst, Tom
d. 1983 Bluhdorn, Charles G
d. 1983 Boyd, William Clouser
d. 1984 Hopkins, Claude
d. 1984 Hutton, Ina Ray
d. 1985 Cummings, Nathan
d. 1985 Gorkin, Jess
d. 1985 Julesberg, Elizabeth Rider Montgomery

d. 1985 Lopez Bravo, Gregorio
d. 1985 Sutton, Carol
d. 1986 Eastland, James Oliver
d. 1987 Greene, Hugh (Carleton), Sir
d. 1987 Hitchcock, Henry Russell
d. 1988 Bishop, Isabel
d. 1988 Char, Rene (Emile)
d. 1988 Cournand, Andre Frederic
d. 1989 Goldman, Eric Frederick
d. 1989 Gorman, Mike
d. 1990 Keppel, Francis
d. 1990 Powell, Michael Latham
d. 1993 Bazelon, David L(ionel)
d. 1995 Willingham, Calder Baynard, Jr.
d. 1996 Finley, Charles O(scar)
d. 1996 Manning, Ernest (Charles)
d. 1996 Maynor, Dorothy
d. 1997 Deng Xiaoping
d. 1997 Marshall, Lois
d. 1997 Rosten, Leo C(alvin)
d. 1999 Carlson, Curtis L.
d. 2000 Hundertwasser, Friedensreich

February 20
b. 1368 Martin, V
b. 1745 Pye, Henry
b. 1772 Chauncey, Isaac
b. 1791 Czerny, Karl
b. 1803 Nevin, John Williamson
b. 1805 Grimke, Angelina Emily
b. 1816 Rimmer, William
b. 1820 Vieuxtemps, Henri Francois Joseph
b. 1829 Jefferson, Joseph
b. 1833 Crittenton, Charles Nelson
b. 1844 Boltzmann, Ludwig
b. 1844 Slocum, Joshua
b. 1860 Howell, William H(enry)
b. 1863 Pissaro, Lucien
b. 1873 Judd, Charles Hubbard
b. 1874 Bottomley, Gordon
b. 1874 Garden, Mary
b. 1886 Freuchen, Peter
b. 1886 Kun, Bela
b. 1887 Ebert, Carl
b. 1887 Massey, Vincent
b. 1888 Bernanos, Georges
b. 1888 Rambert, Marie, Dame

b. 1889 Gomez Castro, Laureano Eleuterio
b. 1892 Rice, Sam
b. 1893 Crouse, Russel
b. 1894 Richter, Curt Paul
b. 1897 Albright, Ivan Le Lorraine
b. 1897 Albright, Malvin Marr
b. 1898 Yancey, Jimmy
b. 1899 Whitney, C(ornelius) V(anderbilt)
b. 1900 Kabotie, Fred
b. 1901 Dubos, Rene Jules
b. 1901 Naguib, Mohammed
b. 1902 Adams, Ansel Easton
b. 1904 Brownell, Herbert, Jr.
b. 1904 Kosygin, Aleksei Nikolaevich
b. 1906 Fletcher, Bramwell
b. 1908 Kingsbury-Smith, Joseph
b. 1909 Alvary, Lorenzo
b. 1911 Grahame, Margot
b. 1912 Boulle, Pierre Francois Marie-Louis
b. 1912 Humphrey, Muriel Fay Buck
b. 1913 Conner, Nadine
b. 1913 Henrich, Tommy
b. 1914 Daly, John Charles, Jr.
b. 1914 MacKellar, William
b. 1914 Slavenska, Mia
b. 1915 Harbert, Chick
b. 1916 Tripp, Paul
b. 1922 Carpenter, Leslie
b. 1923 Burnham, Forbes
b. 1924 Fraser, Donald Mackay
b. 1924 Terzi, Zehdi Labib
b. 1924 Vanderbilt, Gloria Morgan
b. 1925 Altman, Robert B
b. 1926 Matheson, Richard Burton
b. 1926 Olsen, Kenneth Harry
b. 1926 Richards, Bob
b. 1927 Cohn, Roy (Marcus)
b. 1927 Poitier, Sidney
b. 1928 Face, Roy
b. 1931 Blake, Amanda
b. 1931 Paige, Emmett, Jr.
b. 1932 Sidaris, Andy
b. 1933 Christian, Mary Blount
b. 1934 Unser, Bobby
b. 1936 Abdulkarim, Mohamed Taki

d. 1976 Briggs, Ellis O(rmsbee)
d. 1980 Lauck, Chester H
d. 1981 Houghton, Amory
d. 1982 Kaufman, Murray
d. 1984 Sholokhov, Mikhail Aleksandrovich
d. 1985 Claire, Ina
d. 1985 Hayward, Louis
d. 1985 Pritikin, Nathan
d. 1986 Pomerantz, Fred P
d. 1986 Santmyer, Helen Hooven
d. 1991 Cooper, John Sherman
d. 1991 Fetzer, John Earl
d. 1991 Fonteyn, Margot, Dame
d. 1992 Hoving, Jane Pickens
d. 1993 Kurtzman, Harvey
d. 1993 Van Doren, Dorothy Graffe
d. 1994 Lasker, Mary (Woodward)
d. 1996 Gould, Morton
d. 1997 Winsten, Archer
d. 1998 Jones, Grandpa
d. 1999 Elion, Gertrude B(ell)
d. 2000 Daniel, Clifton, Jr.

February 22
b. 1403 Charles, VII
b. 1715 Cochin, Charles Nicholas
b. 1732 Washington, George
b. 1778 Peale, Rembrandt
b. 1796 Quetelet, Lambert Adolphe Jacques
b. 1810 Chopin, Frederic Francois
b. 1817 Gade, Niels Vilhelm
b. 1819 Lowell, James Russell
b. 1824 Janssen, Pierre Jules Cesar
b. 1831 Byers, William Newton
b. 1833 Clarke, Rebecca Sophia
b. 1838 Sangster, Margaret Elizabeth
b. 1840 Bebel, August
b. 1857 Baden-Powell, Robert Stephenson Smyth Baden-Powell, Baron
b. 1857 Hertz, Heinrich Rudolph
b. 1857 Stanton, Frank Lebby
b. 1863 Andrews, Charles McLean
b. 1864 Renard, Jules

b. 1870 Reiss, Albert
b. 1873 Upton, Florence Kate
b. 1874 Klem, Bill
b. 1874 Takahama Kyoshi
b. 1876 Bonnin, Gertrude Simmons
b. 1876 Zenatello, Giovanni
b. 1877 Costello, Maurice
b. 1879 Bronsted, Johannes Nicolaus
b. 1880 Europe, James Reese
b. 1882 Gill, Eric
b. 1884 Attell, Abe B
b. 1886 Markey, Enid
b. 1887 Clark, Marguerite
b. 1887 Cody, Lew
b. 1888 Brewster, (Ralph) Owen
b. 1888 Pippin, Horace
b. 1889 Baden-Powell, Olave St. Claire, Lady
b. 1889 Collingwood, Robin George
b. 1890 Gerard, Eddie
b. 1890 Norwich, Alfred Duff Cooper, Viscount
b. 1892 Dubinsky, David
b. 1892 Millay, Edna St. Vincent
b. 1893 O'Donnell, Peadar
b. 1895 Haya de la Torre, Victor Raul
b. 1896 Brown, Nacio Herb
b. 1900 Bunuel, Luis
b. 1900 Kollsman, Paul
b. 1900 O'Faolain, Sean
b. 1900 Seferiades, Giorgos Styljanou
b. 1901 Lorant, Stefan
b. 1901 Whittaker, Charles Evans
b. 1902 Strassmann, Fritz
b. 1903 Ramsey, Frank Plumpton
b. 1903 Weede, Robert
b. 1904 Hurd, Peter
b. 1904 Sidarouss, Stephanos, Cardinal
b. 1906 Henderson, Leon N(esbit)
b. 1907 Leonard, Sheldon
b. 1907 Young, Robert (George)
b. 1908 Betancourt, Romulo
b. 1908 Kolodin, Irving
b. 1908 Mills, John, Sir
b. 1909 MacIver, Loren
b. 1914 Dulbecco, Renato
b. 1915 Lesnevich, Gus
b. 1915 Munshin, Jules
b. 1915 Seymour, Dan

b. 1917 Bowles, Jane Sydney
b. 1917 Leek, Sybil
b. 1918 Abel, Sid(ney Gerald)
b. 1918 Finley, Charles O(scar)
b. 1921 Bokassa, Jean-Bedel
b. 1923 Ogilvie, Richard Buell
b. 1925 Gorey, Edward St. John
b. 1926 Hunt, Nelson Bunker
b. 1927 Yen, Samuel
b. 1929 Duren, Ryne
b. 1929 Nixon, Marni
b. 1932 Kennedy, Edward Moore
b. 1934 Anderson, Sparky
b. 1936 Bishop, J(ohn) Michael
b. 1937 Aaron, Tommy
b. 1938 Reed, Ishmael Scott
b. 1940 Walker, Chet
b. 1943 Kaskey, Ray(mond John)
b. 1944 Demme, Jonathan
b. 1947 Jay, Karla
b. 1949 Lauda, Niki
b. 1950 Erving, Julius Winfield
b. 1950 Walters, Julie
b. 1952 Frist, Bill
b. 1954 Franklin, Robert M(ichael)
b. 1956 Alcott, Amy Strum
b. 1959 Lloyd, Lewis Kevin
b. 1959 MacLachlan, Kyle
b. 1965 La Fontaine, Pat
b. 1972 Chang, Michael
b. 1975 Barrymore, Drew
d. 1512 Vespucci, Amerigo
d. 1636 Sanctorius
d. 1680 Deshayes, Catherine
d. 1690 Le Brun, Charles
d. 1781 Taylor, George
d. 1797 Munchhausen, Hieronymus Karl Friedrich von, Baron
d. 1810 Brown, Charles Brockden
d. 1827 Peale, Charles Willson
d. 1845 Smith, Sydney
d. 1875 Corot, Jean Baptiste Camille
d. 1875 Lyell, Charles, Sir
d. 1896 Nye, Edgar Wilson
d. 1903 Wolf, Hugo
d. 1904 Stephen, Leslie, Sir

d. 1911 Harper, Frances Ellen Watkins
d. 1913 Madero, Francisco Indalecio
d. 1914 Fels, Joseph
d. 1916 Smalls, Robert
d. 1916 Wallace, Henry
d. 1921 Anderson, Elizabeth Milbank
d. 1922 Yamagata, Aritomo
d. 1923 Delcasse, Theophile
d. 1932 Gadski, Johanna
d. 1939 Machado (y Ruiz), Antonio
d. 1942 Zweig, Stefan
d. 1945 Baker, Sara Josephine
d. 1945 Tolstoy, Alexey Nikolaevich
d. 1947 Thaw, Harry Kendall
d. 1949 Herelle, Felix d'.
d. 1955 Goddard, Calvin Hooker
d. 1956 Carnegie, Hattie
d. 1960 Borduas, Paul-Emile
d. 1961 DeCuevas, Marquis
d. 1965 Frankfurter, Felix
d. 1968 Arno, Peter
d. 1968 Lucas, Scott Wike
d. 1973 Bowen, Elizabeth Dorthea Cole
d. 1973 Paxinou, Katina
d. 1973 Rockefeller, Winthrop
d. 1976 Baddeley, Angela
d. 1976 Ballard, Florence
d. 1976 Polanyi, Michael
d. 1978 Borland, Hal
d. 1978 Lawrence, Josephine
d. 1978 McGinley, Phyllis
d. 1980 Kokoschka, Oskar
d. 1981 Padover, Saul Kussiel
d. 1981 Smith, Joe
d. 1984 David
d. 1985 Espriu, Salvador
d. 1985 Scourby, Alexander
d. 1985 Zimbalist, Efrem
d. 1987 Susskind, David Howard
d. 1987 Warhol, Andy
d. 1987 Wescott, Glenway
d. 1988 Solomon
d. 1990 Lasky, Victor
d. 1992 Yeshurun, Avot
d. 1995 Flanders, Ed

d. 1997 Sarnoff, Robert W(illiam)

d. 1997 Shanker, Albert

d. 1998 Ribicoff, Abraham A(lexander)

February 23

b. 1400? Gutenberg, Johann Gensfleischzur Laden Zum

b. 1633 Pepys, Samuel

b. 1649? Blow, John

b. 1680 Bienville, Sieur de

b. 1685 Handel, George Frideric

b. 1743 Rothschild, Mayer Amschel

b. 1751 Dearborn, Henry

b. 1787 Willard, Emma Hart

b. 1820 Stampfli, Jakob

b. 1831 Meilhac, Henri

b. 1832 Vincent, John Heyl

b. 1846 Horlick, William

b. 1848 Ritz, Cesar

b. 1857 Deland, Margaret Wade

b. 1861 Wilson, Henry Braid

b. 1868 DuBois, W(illiam) E(dward) B(urghardt)

b. 1873 Liang Ch'i-ch'ao

b. 1880 Chapin, Roy Dikeman

b. 1882 Fischer, Anton Otto

b. 1882? Traven, B.

b. 1883 Fleming, Victor

b. 1883 Jaspers, Karl

b. 1884 Funk, Casimir

b. 1892 Tabouis, Genevieve

b. 1894 Schilt, Jan

b. 1899 Kastner, Erich

b. 1899 Taurog, Norman

b. 1901 Nichols, Ruth Rowland

b. 1903 Alexandrov, Grigori

b. 1904 Fisher, Terence

b. 1904 Shirer, William L(awrence)

b. 1905 Victor, Sally Josephs

b. 1908 McMahon, William

b. 1911 Allen, Walter Ernest

b. 1911 Williams, G(erhard) Mennen

b. 1915 Weingarten, Violet Brown

b. 1920 Netsch, Walter Andrew, Jr.

b. 1922 Komer, Robert William

b. 1924 Cormack, Allan MacLeod

b. 1925 Stokes, Louis

b. 1929 Howard, Elston Gene

b. 1930 Davis, Gerry

b. 1931 Wesselmann, Tom

b. 1933 Calhoun, Lee

b. 1938 Chase, Sylvia B

b. 1938 Menzel, Jiri

b. 1938 Varsi, Diane

b. 1939 Castro, George (A.)

b. 1940 Fonda, Peter

b. 1942 Madhubuti, Haki R.

b. 1943 Biletnikoff, Fred(erick)

b. 1944 Winter, Johnny

b. 1945 Boesak, Allan Aubrey

b. 1949 Garneau, Marc

b. 1951 Dibbs, Eddie

b. 1951 Jones, Too Tall

b. 1955 Jones, Howard

b. 1955 Slater, Rodney E.

b. 1963 Bonilla, Bobby

b. 1965? Guillem, Sylvie

d. 1447 Gloucester, Duke of

d. 1482 DellaRobbia, Lucia

d. 1507 Bellini, Gentile

d. 1526 Colon, Diego

d. 1792 Reynolds, Joshua, Sir

d. 1800 Warton, Joseph

d. 1815 Fulton, Robert

d. 1821 Keats, John

d. 1848 Adams, John Quincy

d. 1855 Gauss, Carl Friedrich

d. 1870 Burlingame, Anson

d. 1900 Butterfield, William

d. 1900 Dowson, Ernest Christopher

d. 1911 Quanah

d. 1930 Normand, Mabel

d. 1931 Melba, Nellie, Dame

d. 1934 Elgar, Edward William, Sir

d. 1944 Baekeland, Leo Hendrik

d. 1946 Yamashita, Tomoyuki

d. 1947 Hill, Grace Livingstone

d. 1947 Janet, Pierre Marie Felix

d. 1948 Gregg, John Robert

d. 1955 Claudel, Paul Louis Charles

d. 1959 Pales Matos, Luis

d. 1963 Russell, Ernie

d. 1965 Laurel, Stan

d. 1968 Hurst, Fannie

d. 1969 Mondlane, Eduardo Chivambo

d. 1969 Saud (Ibn Abdul Aziz al Saud)

d. 1973 Richards, Dickinson Woodruff

d. 1974 Knowland, William Fife

d. 1974 Ruby, Harry

d. 1976 Lowry, Lawrence Stephen

d. 1978 McKeen, John Elmer

d. 1979 Bennett, W(illiam) A(ndrew) C(ecil)

d. 1981 Allen, Robert Sharon

d. 1981 Cabot, John Moors

d. 1981 Fields, Shep

d. 1983 Arran, Arthur Kattendyke Strange David Archibald Gore, Earl of

d. 1983 Boult, Adrian Cedric, Sir

d. 1985 Braceland, Francis J(ames)

d. 1987 Heinz, Henry John, II

d. 1987 Lansdale, Edward Geary

d. 1990 Duarte (Fuentes), Jose Napoleon

d. 1990 Gavin, James Maurice

d. 1991 Hannah, John Alfred

d. 1992 Bolinger, Dwight Lemerton

d. 1995 Franklin, Melvin

d. 1995 Herriot, James

d. 1996 Barr, Joseph W(alker)

d. 1997 Williams, Tony

d. 1998 Oliver, Edith

d. 1998 Sullivan, William Hallisey, Jr.

d. 2000 Matthews, Stanley, Sir

February 24

b. 1443 Matthias Corvinus

b. 1500 Charles V

b. 1619 Le Brun, Charles

b. 1663 Newcomen, Thomas

b. 1722 Burgoyne, John, Sir

b. 1771 Cramer, Johann Baptist

b. 1772 Crawford, William Harris

b. 1786 Grimm, Wilhelm Karl

b. 1790 Kelley, Hall Jackson

b. 1801 Maclean, George

b. 1824 Curtis, George William

b. 1826 Hollyer, Samuel

b. 1829 Spielhagen, Friedrich von

b. 1835 Vogel, Julius

b. 1836 Homer, Winslow

b. 1841 Holland, John Philip

b. 1842 Boito, Arrigo

b. 1842 Habberton, John

b. 1844 Widor, Charles Marie Jean Albert

b. 1852 Moore, George Augustus

b. 1858 Dolmetsch, Arnold

b. 1860 Updike, Daniel Berkeley

b. 1866 Pearson, Cyril Arthur, Sir

b. 1874 Wagner, Honus

b. 1876 Moore, Victor

b. 1877 Ganz, Rudolph

b. 1877 Rider-Kelsey, Corinne

b. 1880 Hoare, Samuel John Gurney, Sir

b. 1884 Bustamante, William Alexander Clarke, Sir

b. 1885 Lytell, Bert

b. 1885 Nimitz, Chester William

b. 1887 Chase, Mary Ellen

b. 1890 Main, Marjorie

b. 1892 Fedin, Konstantin Aleksandrovich

b. 1897 Breech, Ernest Robert

b. 1897 Grede, William John

b. 1901 Parry, Albert

b. 1906 Coombs, Herbert Cole

b. 1909 Derleth, August (William)

b. 1912 Trnka, Jiri

b. 1914 Scott, Zachary

b. 1915 Ferrier, Jim

b. 1917 Long, Scott

b. 1917 Raedler, Dorothy (Florence)

b. 1921 Vigoda, Abe

b. 1923 Soyer, David

b. 1924 Arison, Ted

b. 1925 Owen, Guy, Jr.

b. 1926 Dean, John Gunther

b. 1927 Lane, Mark

b. 1928 Harrington, Michael

b. 1931 Abourezk, James George

b. 1932 Legrand, Michel Jean

b. 1932 Miller, Zell (Bryan)

b. 1932 Okamura, Arthur

b. 1932 Sandrich, Jay H

b. 1932 Vernon, John

b. 1933 Mazrui, Ali A(l'Amin)

b. 1934 Craxi, Bettino

b. 1934 Scotto, Renata

b. 1936 Cristal, Linda

b. 1936 Reventlow, Lance
b. 1937 Tiede, Tom Robert
b. 1938 Farentino, James
b. 1938 Knight, Phil
b. 1938 Knight, Philip H.
b. 1942 Lieberman, Joseph Isadore
b. 1942 Neumeier, John
b. 1942 Williamson, David
b. 1945 Bostwick, Barry
b. 1947 Fratello, Mike
b. 1947 Holmes, Rupert
b. 1947 Olmos, Edward James
b. 1951 Shaver, Helen
b. 1955 Jobs, Steven Paul
b. 1955 Prost, Alain Marie Pascal
b. 1956 Murray, Eddie Clarence
b. 1956 Zahn, Paula
b. 1963 Vernon, Mike
d. 1704 Charpentier, Marc-Antoine
d. 1714 Andros, Edmund, Sir
d. 1810 Cavendish, Henry
d. 1825 Bowdler, Thomas
d. 1828 Brown, Jacob Jennings
d. 1856 Lobachevskii, Nikolai Ivanovich
d. 1887 Eastman, Mary Henderson
d. 1888 Corcoran, William Wilson
d. 1899 Nuitter, Charles Louis
d. 1900 Hovey, Richard
d. 1902 Gardiner, Samuel Rawson
d. 1921 Habberton, John
d. 1925 Branting, Karl Hjalmar
d. 1926 Plank, Eddie
d. 1929 Keenan, Frank
d. 1929 Messager, Andre Charles Prosper
d. 1937 Standing, Guy, Sir
d. 1947 Glasscock, Jack
d. 1947 Jordan, Elizabeth Garver
d. 1948 Irwin, Will(iam Henry)
d. 1950 Bacheller, Irving Addison
d. 1951 Carey, William F
d. 1953 Rundstedt, Karl Rudolf Gerd von
d. 1957 Buck, Gene
d. 1962 Hu Shih
d. 1963 Asbury, Herbert
d. 1967 Waxman, Franz
d. 1974 Barnes-Taeuber, Irene

d. 1974 Leech, Margaret Kernochan
d. 1975 Bulganin, Nikolai Aleksandrovich
d. 1976 Smith, H(arry) Allen
d. 1977 Kamen, Milt
d. 1978 Thomas, Alma (Woodsy)
d. 1981 Fish, Robert Lloyd
d. 1982 Bruce, Virginia
d. 1982 Chao, Yuen Ren
d. 1986 Douglas, Thomas Clement
d. 1986 Morgan, Russell H(edley)
d. 1987 McArthur, Edwin Douglas
d. 1988 Douglas, James Henderson, Jr.
d. 1988 Memphis Slim
d. 1988 Salem, Mamdouh
d. 1989 Cotton, Norris
d. 1990 Conigliaro, Tony
d. 1990 Forbes, Malcolm Stevenson
d. 1990 Pertini, Sandro
d. 1990 Ray, Johnnie
d. 1991 Daly, John Charles, Jr.
d. 1991 Gobel, George Leslie
d. 1991 Pierce, Webb
d. 1994 Sablon, Jean Georges
d. 1994 Shore, Dinah
d. 1998 Youngman, Henny

February 25
b. 1510 Coronado, Francisco Vasquez de
b. 1682 Morgagni, Giovanni Battista
b. 1707 Goldoni, Carlo
b. 1746 Pinckney, Charles Cotesworth
b. 1752 Simcoe, John Graves
b. 1778 San Martin, Jose de
b. 1830 Carter, William
b. 1841 Renoir, (Pierre) Auguste
b. 1842 Flammarion, Camille
b. 1842 Lewis, Ida
b. 1842 May, Karl Friedrich
b. 1848 Harriman, Edward Henry
b. 1856 Freer, Charles Lang
b. 1856 Lamprecht, Karl
b. 1861 Bates, Mary Elizabeth
b. 1863? Bannerman, Helen
b. 1866 Croce, Benedetto
b. 1873 Caruso, Enrico

b. 1881 Foster, William Zebulon
b. 1881 Rykov, Aleksey Ivanovich
b. 1883 Alice
b. 1887 McNaughton, Andrew
b. 1888 Dulles, John Foster
b. 1888 Ferguson, Homer
b. 1890 Hess, Myra, Dame
b. 1892 Madden, Ray John
b. 1894 Hansberry, William Leo
b. 1895 Bell, Bert
b. 1896 Farrar, John Chipman
b. 1896 McClellan, John Little
b. 1898 Astbury, William
b. 1900 Harris, Jed
b. 1901 Marx, Zeppo
b. 1903 Clancy, King
b. 1904 Davis, Adelle
b. 1904 Goody, Sam
b. 1905 Carter, Katherine Jones
b. 1905 Miller, Perry Gilbert Eddy
b. 1907 Chase, Mary Coyle
b. 1908 Slaughter, Frank Gill
b. 1910 Fenwick, Millicent Hammond
b. 1912 Frobe, Gerd
b. 1913 Backus, Jim
b. 1914 Bonham, Frank
b. 1917 Burgess, Anthony
b. 1917 Raymond, James C
b. 1918 Riggs, Bobby
b. 1919 Bendick, Jeanne
b. 1919 Irvin, Monte
b. 1920 Habib, Philip Charles
b. 1920 Justice, William Wayne
b. 1920 Travis, Dempsey Jerome
b. 1923 Glazer, Nathan
b. 1925 Kirk, Lisa
b. 1925 Zipprodt, Patricia
b. 1927 Stanley, Ralph Edmond
b. 1928 Gelbart, Larry
b. 1928 Higginbotham, A(loysius) Leon, Jr.
b. 1928 Stern, Richard Gustave
b. 1929 Biryukova, Aleksandra Pavlovna
b. 1929 George, Christopher
b. 1932 Young, Faron
b. 1934 Lema, Tony
b. 1937 Courtenay, Tom
b. 1937 Sarduy, Severo
b. 1937 Schieffer, Bob
b. 1938 Baker, Diane

b. 1938 Elliott, Herb
b. 1939 Leonard, John
b. 1940 Santo, Ron(ald Edward)
b. 1941 Puttnam, David Terence
b. 1943 Harrison, George
b. 1943 Raphael, Sally Jessy
b. 1944 Grassle, Karen Gene
b. 1947? Beatts, Anne
b. 1947 Evans, Lee
b. 1950 Jordan, Neil
b. 1953 Aznar, Jose Maria
b. 1954 Brenly, Bob
b. 1957 McCreesh, Raymond
b. 1957 Wood, Stuart
b. 1966 Leoni, Tea
d. 483BC Buddha
d. 1601 Devereaux, Robert
d. 1634 Wallenstein, Albrecht Wenzel Eusebius von
d. 1723 Wren, Christopher, Sir
d. 1756 Haywood, Eliza
d. 1796 Seabury, Samuel
d. 1799 Dawes, William
d. 1852 Moore, Thomas
d. 1864 Harrison, Anna (Tuthill Symmes)
d. 1865 Ludwig, Otto
d. 1874 Bachman, John
d. 1878 Harris, Townsend
d. 1894 Mackaye, James Morrison Steele
d. 1899 Reuter, Paul Julius Von
d. 1910 Whittredge, Thomas Worthington
d. 1911 Parker, Quanah
d. 1911 Spielhagen, Friedrich von
d. 1914 Tenniel, John, Sir
d. 1922 Landru, Henri Desire
d. 1925 McCormick, Joseph Medill
d. 1932 Mathiez, Albert
d. 1934 McGraw, John Joseph
d. 1944 Boyd, James
d. 1944 McNary, Charles Linza
d. 1950 Minot, George Richards
d. 1954 Perret, Auguste
d. 1957 Moran, Bugs
d. 1963 Herskovits, Melville Jean
d. 1964 Archipenko, Alexander Porfirievich
d. 1964 Burke, Johnny
d. 1964 Metalious, Grace de Repentigny
d. 1966 Norris, James D
d. 1970 Rothko, Mark

d. 1971 Svedberg, Theodor H E
d. 1974 Aldrich, Winthrop Williams
d. 1975 Muhammad, Elijah
d. 1976 Crosthwait, David Nelson, Jr.
d. 1977 McCulloch, Robert P
d. 1978 James, Daniel, Jr.
d. 1979 Focke, Heinrich Karl Johann
d. 1980 Hayden, Robert Earl
d. 1983 Cowles, John, Sr.
d. 1983 Williams, Tennessee
d. 1984 West, Jessamyn
d. 1985 Weatherwax, Rudd B
d. 1986 Lowe, Edwin S
d. 1987 Coco, James Emil
d. 1987 Nixon, E(dgar) D(aniel)
d. 1993 Constantine, Eddie
d. 1994 Walcott, Joe
d. 1995 Clayton, Jack
d. 1996 Ngor, Haing S
d. 1997 Sinyavsky, Andrei D(onatovich)
d. 1999 Seaborg, Glenn T(heodore)

February 26
b. Bernhardt, Melvin
b. 1564 Marlowe, Christopher
b. 1621 Cooper, Anthony Ashley, 1st Earl of Shaftesbury
b. 1671 Shaftesbury, Anthony Ashley Cooper, Earl
b. 1786 Arago, Dominque Francois Jean
b. 1802 Hugo, Victor Marie
b. 1808 Daumier, Honore Victorin
b. 1817 Wallace, Horace Binney
b. 1832 Nicolay, John George
b. 1836 Vedder, Elihu
b. 1841 Cromer, 1st Earl of
b. 1844 Lurton, Horace Harmon
b. 1846 Cody, Buffalo Bill
b. 1849 McDowell, Katharine Sherwood Bonner
b. 1851 Booth, Joseph
b. 1852 Kellogg, John Harvey
b. 1857 Coue, Emile
b. 1857 Lawson, Thomas William
b. 1857 Sheldon, Charles M(onroe)

b. 1866 Dow, Herbert Henry
b. 1869 Krupskaya, Nadezhda Konstantinovna
b. 1876 Justo, Agustin Pedro
b. 1877 Dirks, Rudolph
b. 1878 Destinn, Emmy
b. 1878 Malevich, Kasimir Severinovich
b. 1879 Bridge, Frank
b. 1879 Luhan, Mabel (Ganson) Dodge
b. 1882 Kimmel, Husband Edward
b. 1887 Alexander, Grover Cleveland
b. 1890 Vought, Chance Milton
b. 1891 Baugh, Albert Croll
b. 1893 Frawley, William
b. 1893 Richards, Ivor Armstrong
b. 1894 Harmon, Ernest N(ason)
b. 1896 Carlson, Evans Fordyce
b. 1896 Zhdanov, Andrei Alexandrovich
b. 1899 Petitpierre, Max
b. 1903 Natta, Giulio
b. 1903 Wingate, Orde Charles
b. 1906 Romano, Umberto
b. 1907 Yellow Robe, Rosebud
b. 1908 Avery, Tex
b. 1908 Groth, John August
b. 1908 LeFleming, Christopher Kaye
b. 1909 Carroll, Madeleine
b. 1910 Gorshkov, Sergei
b. 1912 Hunter, Floyd
b. 1913 Barker, George Granville
b. 1914 Alda, Robert
b. 1914 Wilson, Malcolm
b. 1916 Gleason, Jackie
b. 1917 Taft, Robert A(lphonso), Jr.
b. 1918 Bowen, Otis Ray
b. 1918 Sturgeon, Theodore Hamilton
b. 1919 Adams, Mason
b. 1920 Baunsgaard, Hilmar Tormod Ingolf
b. 1920 Greenhill, Basil
b. 1921 Hutton, Betty
b. 1922 Lawe, John Edward
b. 1922 Leighton, Margaret
b. 1924 Randall, Tony
b. 1924 Stone, Marvin Lawrence

b. 1924 Takeshita, Noboru
b. 1924 Varviso, Silvio
b. 1925 Williams, Robert F(ranklin)
b. 1928 Domino, Fats
b. 1930 Berman, Lazar
b. 1930 Janowicz, Vic(tor Felix)
b. 1931 Novak, Robert
b. 1931 Wiley, George A
b. 1932 Cash, Johnny
b. 1933 Cambridge, Godfrey
b. 1933 Goldsmith, James (Michael), Sir
b. 1943 Duke, Bill
b. 1943 Jones, Brian
b. 1945 Ryder, Mitch
b. 1948 Edgar, David
b. 1948 Lopez, Priscilla
b. 1953 Bolton, Michael
b. 1957 Mullen, Joe
b. 1962 Gruber, Kelly
d. 1154 Roger, II
d. 1525 Cuauhtemoc
d. 1723 D'Urfey, Thomas
d. 1770 Tartini, Giuseppe
d. 1802 Hopkins, Esek
d. 1813 Livingston, Robert R
d. 1823 Kemble, John Philip
d. 1834 Senefelder, Aloys
d. 1839 Ludington, Sybil
d. 1864 LaFontaine, Louis Hippolyte, Sir
d. 1878 Secchi, Pietro Angelo
d. 1903 Gatling, Richard Jordan
d. 1905 Schwob, Marcel
d. 1909 Ebbinghaus, Hermann
d. 1918 McGovern, Terry
d. 1925 Feuillade, Louis
d. 1931 Wallach, Otto
d. 1936 Scotti, Antonio
d. 1936 Takahashi, Korekiyo
d. 1942 Eberle, Mary Abastenia St. Leger
d. 1947 Webster, Ben(jamin)
d. 1950 Lauder, Harry MacLennan, Sir
d. 1954 Inge, William Ralph
d. 1956 Janis, Elsie
d. 1959 Belbenoit, Rene Lucien
d. 1961 Mohammed V
d. 1964 Orry-Kelly
d. 1965 Bassett, John D
d. 1969 Eshkol, Levi
d. 1969 Jaspers, Karl
d. 1970 Leginska
d. 1971 Fernandel
d. 1973 Wilson, Mitchell A

d. 1974 Sample, Paul Starrett
d. 1976 Weil, Joseph R
d. 1977 Vaughan, Bill
d. 1980 Arkell, Anthony John
d. 1980 Brook, Alexander
d. 1980 Shukairy, Ahmed
d. 1981 Hanson, Howard
d. 1982 Kinugasa, Teinosuke
d. 1984 Lattimore, Richmond Alexander
d. 1984 Taylor, Henry Junior
d. 1984 Wright, Louis Booker
d. 1985 Koopmans, Tjalling (Charles)
d. 1989 Eldridge, Roy
d. 1990 Deloria, Vine (Victor), Sr.
d. 1991 Scott, Ken
d. 1993 Ford, Constance
d. 1993 Knebel, Fletcher
d. 1993 Newhall, Beaumont
d. 1997 Doyle, David (Fitzgerald)
d. 1998 Schultz, Theodore W(illiam)
d. 1999 Quintero, Jose (Benjamin)

February 27
b. 280 Constantine I
b. 1735 Conway, Thomas
b. 1807 Longfellow, Henry Wadsworth
b. 1823 Franklin, William Buel
b. 1835 Garnett, Richard
b. 1848 Parry, Charles Hubert Hastings, Sir
b. 1848 Terry, Ellen Alicia, Dame
b. 1850 Huntington, Henry Edwards
b. 1850 Richards, Laura Elizabeth Howe
b. 1856 Battistini, Mattia
b. 1861 Steiner, Rudolf
b. 1863 Mead, George Herbert
b. 1866 MacNeil, Hermon Atkins
b. 1867 Fisher, Irving
b. 1869 Cowles, Henry Chandler
b. 1869 Hamilton, Alice
b. 1875 Torrence, Ridgely
b. 1877 Briggs, Walter Owen
b. 1880 Grimke, Angelina Emily Weld
b. 1882 Stevens, Emily A
b. 1882 Vasconcelos (Calderon), Jose

b. 1882 Wheeler,
Burton Kendall
b. 1886 Black, Hugo
LaFayette
b. 1888 Lehmann, Lotte
b. 1890 Staupers, Mabel
K.
b. 1891 Moore, Roy W
b. 1891 Sarnoff, David
b. 1892 Demarest,
William
b. 1893 Dobrowen, Issai
b. 1893 Linton, Ralph
b. 1894 Close, Upton
b. 1896 Radford, Arthur
William
b. 1897 Anderson,
Marian
b. 1897 Lyot, Bernard
Ferdinand
b. 1898 Smith, Gerald
Lyman Kenneth
b. 1899 Best, Charles
Herbert
b. 1899 Keith, Ian
b. 1901 Marini, Marino
b. 1902 Sarazen, Gene
b. 1902 Steinbeck, John
(Ernst)
b. 1903 Gardiner,
Reginald
b. 1904 Farrell, James
Thomas
b. 1905 Tone, Franchot
b. 1907 Bailey, Mildred
b. 1907 Traube, Shepard
b. 1910 Bennett, Joan
b. 1910 DeVries, Peter
b. 1910 Johnson,
Clarence Leonard
b. 1910 Sloane, Eric
b. 1912 Durrell,
Lawrence (George)
b. 1913 Ricoeur, Paul
b. 1913 Shaw, Irwin
b. 1914 Davis, Hal
Charles
b. 1917 Connally, John
B.
b. 1920 Melis, Jose
b. 1922 McGill,
William James
b. 1923 Gordon, Dexter
Keith
b. 1925 Dash, Samuel
b. 1925 Koch, Kenneth
Jay
b. 1925 Toyoda,
Shoichiro
b. 1926 Hubel, David
Hunter
b. 1926 Wheeler, Roger
Milton
b. 1927 Herlihy, James
Leo
b. 1927 Mitchell, Guy
b. 1930 Stone, Peter H
b. 1930 Woodward,
Joanne Gignilliat
b. 1931 Wille, Frank
b. 1932 Solomon, Neil
b. 1932 Taylor,
Elizabeth Rosemond
b. 1933 Berry,
Raymond Emmett

b. 1933 Wallop,
Malcolm
b. 1934 Momaday,
N(avarre) Scott
b. 1934 Nader, Ralph
b. 1935 Freni, Mirella
b. 1936? Johnson, Sonia
b. 1936 Mahony, Roger
Michael
b. 1936 Poli, Robert E
b. 1939 Revson, Peter
Jeffrey
b. 1939 Smith, Margaret
b. 1940 Hesseman,
Howard
b. 1941 Ashdown,
Paddy
b. 1942 Hunter-Gault,
Charlayne
b. 1943 Frann, Mary
b. 1946 King, Mary-
Claire
b. 1947 Guth, Alan
Harvey
b. 1947 Kremer, Gidon
b. 1951 Atwater, Lee
b. 1954 Falletta, JoAnn
b. 1958 Price, Deb(orah
Jane)
b. 1961 Worthy, James
Ager
b. 1962 Show, Grant
b. 1980 Clinton,
Chelsea Victoria
d. 1706 Evelyn, John
d. 1710 Duluth, Daniel
(Greysolon)
d. 1735 Arbuthnot, John
d. 1795 Marion, Francis
d. 1830 Hicks, Elias
d. 1844 Biddle,
Nicholas
d. 1854 Lamennais,
Hugues Felicite
Robert de
d. 1864 Hitchcock,
Edward
d. 1867 De Bow, James
Dunwoody Brownson
d. 1869 Lamartine,
Alphonse Marie
Louis de Prat de
d. 1887 Borodin,
Alexander Profirevich
d. 1887 Sill, Edward
Rowland
d. 1903 Hill, George
Birkbeck Norman
d. 1905 Boutwell,
George Sewall
d. 1906 Langley,
Samuel Pierpont
d. 1913 Sedgwick,
Adam
d. 1919 Edmunds,
George Franklin
d. 1929 Hadden, Briton
d. 1936 Pavlov, Ivan
Petrovich
d. 1939 Krupskaya,
Nadezhda
Konstantinovna
d. 1940 Behrens, Peter
d. 1940 Graves, William
Sidney

d. 1942 Berry, Martha
McChesney
d. 1955 Friganza, Trixie
d. 1955 Howard, Tom
d. 1956 Peters, Brandon
d. 1958 Cohn, Harry
d. 1959 Farrand, Beatrix
Jones
d. 1963 Makonnen
Endalkacaw
d. 1964 Cooper, Annie
d. 1969 Boles, John
d. 1969 Craven, Thomas
d. 1970 Bruce Lockhart,
Robert Hamilton, Sir
d. 1970 Dionne, Marie
d. 1972 Brady, Pat
d. 1972 Heiser, Victor
George
d. 1977 Carr, John
Dickson
d. 1977 Dahlberg,
Edward
d. 1979 Eberle,
Irmengarde
d. 1980 Tobias, George
d. 1984 Paton, Richard
d. 1985 Lodge, Henry
Cabot, Jr.
d. 1985 Moncreiffe, Iain
d. 1985 O'Malley, J Pat
d. 1986 Plante, Jacques
d. 1987 Holman, Bill
d. 1988 Boothroyd,
John Basil
d. 1988 DePaul, Gene
Vincent
d. 1989 Lorenz, Konrad
Zacharias
d. 1990 Johnson,
Josephine Winslow
d. 1992 Hayakawa,
S(amuel) I(chiye)
d. 1993 Gish, Lillian
(Diana)
d. 1993 Stuart, Kenneth
James
d. 1995 Cornfeld,
Bernard
d. 1996 Janowicz,
Vic(tor Felix)
d. 1997 Davis, Kingsley
d. 1997 Maples,
William R.
d. 1998 Hitchings,
George H(erbert)

February 28
b. 772 Po Chu-i
b. 1533 Montaigne,
Michel Eyquem de
b. 1675 Delisle,
Guillaume
b. 1743 Hauy, Rene Just
b. 1776 Boyer, Jean
Pierre
b. 1783 Rossetti,
Gabriele Pasquale
Giuseppe
b. 1797 Lyon, Mary
Mason
b. 1799 Dollinger,
J(ohannes) J(osef)
I(gnaz) von
b. 1804 Foote, Henry
Stuart
b. 1820 Rachel

b. 1820 Tenniel, John,
Sir
b. 1824 Blondin, Jean
Francois Gravelet
b. 1827 Lacombe,
Albert
b. 1833 Schlieffen,
Alfred, Graf von
b. 1857 Loisy, Alfred
Firmin
b. 1860 Berger, Victor
Louis
b. 1860 Kittredge,
G(eorge) L(yman)
b. 1865 Grenfell,
Wilfred Thomason,
Sir
b. 1865 Symons, Arthur
William
b. 1871 Irving, Isabel
b. 1876 Carpenter, John
Alden
b. 1877 Breuil, Henri
Abbe
b. 1882 Farrar,
Geraldine
b. 1882 Schlick,
Friedrich Albert
Moritz
b. 1887 Zorach, William
b. 1889 Dietrich, Noah
b. 1890 Malone, Joe
b. 1890 Nijinsky,
Vaslav
b. 1893 Hecht, Ben
b. 1893 Thomason, John
William, Jr.
b. 1895 Novaes (Pinto),
Guiomar
b. 1896 Hench, Philip
Showalter
b. 1901 Pauling, Linus
C(arl)
b. 1905 Jones, (Morgan)
Glyn
b. 1906 Siegel, Bugsy
b. 1907 Caniff, Milt(on
Arthur)
b. 1907 Cox, Herald
Rea
b. 1908 Brown, Dee
(Alexander)
b. 1909 LaBern, Arthur
Joseph
b. 1909 Soule, Olan
b. 1909 Spender,
Stephen (Harold)
b. 1910 Falter, John
b. 1912 Petacci, Claretta
b. 1912 Walsh, Michael
Patrick
b. 1913 Minnelli,
Vincente
b. 1915 Frings, Ketti
b. 1915 Medawar, Peter
Brian, Sir
b. 1915 Mostel, Zero
b. 1917 Malcolm,
George
b. 1918 Dinkeloo, John
Gerard
b. 1919 Urquhart, Brian
Edward
b. 1921 Diener, Theodor
Otto
b. 1921 Zaentz, Saul

b. 1918 Goulart, Joao
b. 1920 Bentley, Max(well Herbert Lloyd)
b. 1920 Caray, Harry
b. 1920 Fernandez-Muro, Jose Antonio
b. 1920 Nemerov, Howard (Stanley)
b. 1920 Swann, Michael Meredith, Sir
b. 1921 Clayton, Jack
b. 1921 Cooke, Terence James
b. 1921 Wilbur, Richard Purdy
b. 1922 Flanders, Michael
b. 1922 Gaines, William M(axwell)
b. 1922 Rabin, Yitzhak
b. 1924 Slayton, Donald Kent
b. 1925 Rosen, Al(bert Leonard)
b. 1926 Clary, Robert
b. 1926 Rozelle, Pete
b. 1926 Stanley, Allan Herbert
b. 1927 Abell, George O(gden)
b. 1927 Amara, Lucine
b. 1927 Belafonte, Harry, Jr.
b. 1927 Bork, Robert Heron
b. 1929 James, Sonny
b. 1930 Saint Jacques, Raymond
b. 1930 Zigler, Edward
b. 1931 Dini, Lamberto
b. 1934 Folon, Jean-Michel
b. 1934 Hackett, Joan
b. 1935 Conrad, Robert
b. 1942 Gerstner, Lou
b. 1942 Gerstner, Louis Vincent, Jr.
b. 1942 Guber, Peter
b. 1944 Breaux, John B.
b. 1944 Daltrey, Roger Harry
b. 1944 Napier, John
b. 1945 Benedict, Dirk
b. 1947 Thicke, Alan
b. 1949 Trafzer, Clifford Earl
b. 1950 Flores Facusse, Carlos Roberto
b. 1954 Bach, Catherine
b. 1954 Howard, Ron(ald William)
b. 1956 Daly, Timothy
b. 1961 Rozier, Mike
b. 1973 Webber, Chris
d. 1620 Campion, Thomas
d. 1633 Herbert, George
d. 1698 Redi, Francesco
d. 1766 Boylston, Zabdiel
d. 1792 Leopold, II
d. 1870 Lopez, Francisco Solano

d. 1875 Corbiere, Tristan (Edouard Joachim)
d. 1894 Poole, William Frederick
d. 1906 Pereda, Jose Marie de
d. 1911 Hoff, Jacobus Henricus van't
d. 1911 Van't Hoff, Jacobus Henricus
d. 1923 Barbosa, Ruy
d. 1932 Lindbergh, Charles Augustus
d. 1938 D'Annunzio, Gabriele
d. 1938 Harney, Benjamin Robertson
d. 1952 Azuela, Mariano
d. 1958 Balla, Giacomo
d. 1959 Booth, Albie
d. 1962 Piccard, Auguste
d. 1965 Beemer, Brace
d. 1966 Baillie, Hugh
d. 1969 Ames, Blanche
d. 1972 Babin, Victor
d. 1972 Golschmann, Vladimir
d. 1976 Martinon, Jean
d. 1977 Levy, David Mordecai
d. 1978 Scott, Paul Mark
d. 1979 Costello, Dolores
d. 1980 Ashford, Emmett Littleton
d. 1980 Cooper, Wilhelmina Behmenburg
d. 1980 Niles, John Jacob
d. 1981 Waldman, Max
d. 1982 Spivak, Charlie
d. 1984 Coogan, Jackie
d. 1985 Ethridge, Mark Foster, Jr.
d. 1985 List, Eugene
d. 1986 Archibald, Joe
d. 1986 Towle, Katherine Amelia
d. 1988 Besser, Joe
d. 1988 Woodall, Mary
d. 1990 Landis, Frederick
d. 1991 Land, Edwin Herbert
d. 1991 Liedtke, William C, Jr.
d. 1991 Smith, Kenneth Danforth
d. 1991 Sunderland, Thomas E(lbert)
d. 1993 Kutner, Luis
d. 1995 Blackwell, (Samuel) Earl, Jr.
d. 1995 Borch, Fred J.
d. 1995 Koehler, Georges J F
d. 1995 Rudolf, Max
d. 1996 Carr, William G(eorge)
d. 1999 Corio, Ann

d. 2000 DeRegniers, Beatrice Schenk

March 2

b. 1737 Heath, William
b. 1760 Desmoulins, Camille
b. 1769 Clinton, DeWitt
b. 1779 Poinsett, Joel Roberts
b. 1793 Houston, Sam(uel)
b. 1810 Leo XIII
b. 1813 Macfarren, George Alexander, Sir
b. 1819 Brannan, Samuel
b. 1824 Smetana, Bedrich
b. 1829 Allison, William Boyd
b. 1829 Schurz, Carl
b. 1836 Brown, Henry Billings
b. 1846 Roze, Marie
b. 1876 Pius XII
b. 1880 Kreuger, Ivar
b. 1886 O'Brien, Willis Harold
b. 1890 DeKruif, Paul Henry
b. 1894 Oparin, Aleksandr Ivanovich
b. 1895 Aurell, Tage
b. 1895 Frisch, Ragnar Anton Kittil
b. 1897 Schuster, Max Lincoln
b. 1900 Bee, Clair Francis
b. 1900 Weill, Kurt
b. 1902 Condon, Edward Uhler
b. 1902 Monroney, Mike (Aimer Stillwell)
b. 1904 Dreyfuss, Henry
b. 1904 Seuss, Doctor
b. 1905 Blitzstein, Marc
b. 1905 Grigson, Geoffrey Edward Harvey
b. 1909 Ott, Mel(vin Thomas)
b. 1917 Arnaz, Desi
b. 1917 Collins, Janet Faye
b. 1919 Jones, Jennifer
b. 1919 Toumanova, Tamara
b. 1920 Ritt, Martin
b. 1921 Haas, Ernst
b. 1922 Quackenbush, Bill
b. 1923 Michel, Robert H(enry)
b. 1923 Perlmutter, Nathan
b. 1923 Watson, Doc
b. 1927 Brademas, John
b. 1929 DiSabato, Giovanni
b. 1930 Cullum, John
b. 1931 Gorbachev, Mikhail (Sergeyevich)
b. 1931 Wolfe, Tom

b. 1932 Bauer, Peggy
b. 1933 Dillon, Leo
b. 1934 Cassady, Howard
b. 1934 Waxman, Al
b. 1937 Bouteflika, Abdelaziz
b. 1937 Crum, Denny
b. 1940 De Maiziere, Lothar
b. 1941 Finch, Jon
b. 1941 Satcher, David
b. 1942 Firbank, Louis
b. 1942 Irving, John
b. 1943 Brown, Elaine
b. 1943 Denneny, Michael (Leo)
b. 1943 Straub, Peter
b. 1944 Jones, Elaine R.
b. 1944 Reed, Lou
b. 1946 Garrett, Joy
b. 1949 Gallagher, Rory
b. 1950 Carpenter, Karen (Anne)
b. 1951 Thomson, Gordon
b. 1953 Feingold, Russell D.
b. 1954 Johnson, Pete
b. 1958 Curren, Kevin
b. 1962 Steinbach, Terry Lee
d. 1644 Frescobaldi, Girolamo
d. 1755 Saint-Simon, Duc de
d. 1797 Walpole, Horace
d. 1835 Francis, II
d. 1840 Olbers, Heinrich Wilhelm Matthaus
d. 1854 Rubini, Giovanni-Battista
d. 1855 Nicholas I
d. 1878 Wade, Benjamin Franklin
d. 1894 Early, Jubal Anderson
d. 1895 Morisot, Berthe
d. 1901 Dawson, George Mercer
d. 1902 Parker, Francis Wayland
d. 1907 Manns, August, Sir
d. 1908 Oliver, James
d. 1918 Bancroft, Hubert Howe
d. 1921 Clark, Champ
d. 1930 Lawrence, D(avid) H(erbert)
d. 1933 Walsh, Thomas James
d. 1938 Scripps, Robert Paine
d. 1939 Carter, Howard
d. 1942 Christian, Charlie
d. 1945 Carr, Emily
d. 1947 Marston, William Moulton
d. 1948 Brill, Abraham Arden
d. 1949 Naidu, Sarojini

d. 1957 Maybeck,
Bernard Ralph
d. 1958 Held, John, Jr.
d. 1959 Blore, Eric
d. 1962 Kiesling,
Walt(er)
d. 1967 Ruiz, Jose
Martinez
d. 1972 Dykstra, John
d. 1972 Feis, Herbert
d. 1972 Sack, Erna
d. 1975 Vionnet,
Madeleine
d. 1977 Bothwell, Jean
d. 1977 Mowrer, Edgar
Ansel
d. 1978 Begle, Edward
G(riffith)
d. 1978 Pei, Mario
Andrew
d. 1982 Dick, Philip
K(indred)
d. 1985 Kelly, John
Brenden, Jr.
d. 1986 Rudenko,
Lyudmila
d. 1987 Greenwood,
Joan
d. 1987 Scott, Randolph
d. 1988 Redding, Jay
Saunders
d. 1991 Mollenhoff,
Clark Raymond
d. 1992 Dennis, Sandy
d. 1995 Mahoney,
James P(atrick)
d. 1996 Ginsberg,
Mitchell I(rving)
d. 1998 Bodard, Lucien
(Albert)
d. 1998 Commager,
Henry Steele
d. 1999 Springfield,
Dusty
d. 2000 Wiggins,
Charles Edward

March 3
b. Williams, Darnell
b. 1583 Herbert,
Edward, 1st Baron
Herbert of Cherbury
b. 1606 Waller, Edmund
b. 1652 Otway, Thomas
b. 1756 Godwin,
William
b. 1802 Nourrit,
Adolphe
b. 1803 Decamps,
Alexandre Gabriel
b. 1818 Ingersoll,
Simon
b. 1823 Andrassy,
Gyula, Count
b. 1826 Wharton,
Joseph
b. 1831 Pullman,
George Mortimer
b. 1838 Hill, George
William
b. 1839 Tata, Jamshedji
Nusserwanji
b. 1841 Murray, John,
Sir
b. 1842 Burnaby,
Frederick Gustavus

b. 1845 Cantor, Georg
Ferdinand Ludwig
Philipp
b. 1847 Bell, Alexander
Graham
b. 1860 Ward, Monte
b. 1863 Machen, Arthur
b. 1867 Rogers, James
Gamble
b. 1868 Alain
b. 1869 Wood, Henry
Joseph, Sir
b. 1873 Green, William
b. 1877 Frick, Wilhelm
b. 1878 Lindsay, David
b. 1878 Thomas,
Edward
b. 1879 McCollum,
Elmer Verner
b. 1882 Ludikar, Pavel
b. 1884 Fox, Fontaine
Talbot, Jr.
b. 1889? Rentner,
Maurice
b. 1890 Bethune,
Norman
b. 1890 Lowe, Edmund
Dante
b. 1895 Ridgway,
Matthew Bunker
b. 1897 Poulter, Thomas
Charles
b. 1898 Artin, Emil
b. 1899 DeBernardi,
Forrest S
b. 1899 Gruenther,
Alfred Maximillian
b. 1900 Best, Edna
b. 1901 Cordier,
Andrew Wellington
b. 1902 Bishop, Isabel
b. 1902 Dandridge,
Ruby Jean
b. 1903 Adrian
b. 1906 Bigard, Albany
Barney Leon
b. 1906 Lundkvist,
Artur Nils
b. 1911 Harlow, Jean
b. 1913 Henry,
Charlotte
b. 1914 Fuller, Edmund
b. 1916 Hutton, Ina Ray
b. 1916 Whitehead,
Robert
b. 1918 Kornberg,
Arthur
b. 1918 Newman,
Arnold Abner
b. 1920 Boros, Julius
(Nicholas)
b. 1920 Doohan, James
Montgomery
b. 1920 Searle, Ronald
William Fordham
b. 1921 Barrymore,
Diana
b. 1922 Allen, Jay
Presson
b. 1924 Murayama,
Tomiichi
b. 1924 Nolte, Henry R,
Jr.
b. 1926 Merrill, James
(Ingram)

b. 1927 Freeling,
Nicolas
b. 1927 Kurelek,
William
b. 1927 McLaughlin,
John (Joseph)
b. 1930 Aki, Keiiti
b. 1930 Iliescu, Ion
b. 1933 Irvin, Robert W
b. 1933 Radziwill, Lee
Bouvier
b. 1934 Kuron, Jacek
b. 1934 McManus,
Jason Donald
b. 1934 Scala, Gia
b. 1935 Moore, Bert C
b. 1937 Driscoll, Bobby
b. 1940 Ellis, Perry
Edwin
b. 1948 Hundt, Reed
b. 1950 Marinaro,
Ed(ward Francis)
b. 1950 Styles, Re
b. 1952 Gradishar,
Randy Charles
b. 1955 Schlessinger,
David
b. 1958 Richardson,
Miranda
b. 1962 Joyner-Kersee,
Jackie
b. 1962 Walker,
Herschel
b. 1966 Tone-Loc
b. 1968 Leetch, Brian
d. 1604 Socinus,
Faustus
d. 1703 Hooke, Robert
d. 1706 Pachelbel,
Johann
d. 1743 Faneuil, Peter
d. 1791 Wesley, John
d. 1792 Adam, Robert
d. 1824 Viotti, Giovanni
Battista
d. 1854 Smithson,
Harriet Constance
d. 1855 Mills, Robert
d. 1879 Howitt, William
d. 1926 Lee, Sidney, Sir
d. 1927 Artsybashev,
Mikhail Petrovich
d. 1932 D'Albert,
Eugene
d. 1940 Muck, Karl
d. 1940 Ts'ai Yuan-p'ei
d. 1941 Babel, Isaac
Emmanuelovich
d. 1953 Jeffries, James
Jackson
d. 1955 Drexel, Mary
Katherine
d. 1955 Spence, Lewis
d. 1959 Costello, Lou
d. 1961 Wittgenstein,
Paul
d. 1963 Anderson,
Dorothy Hansine
d. 1963 Eddy,
Sherwood
d. 1966 Fields, Joseph
d. 1966 Frawley,
William
d. 1966 Pearce, Alice
d. 1969 Freyse, William

d. 1969 Schenck,
Nicholas Michael
d. 1973 Halliday,
Richard
d. 1974 Burckhardt,
Carl Jacob
d. 1977 Faulkner, Brian
d. 1978 Balopoulos,
Michael
d. 1978 Marsala, Joe
d. 1978 Rockwell, Doc
d. 1979 Creavy, Tom
d. 1982 DeWitt,
William Orville, Sr.
d. 1982 Villiers, Alan
John
d. 1983 Koestler, Arthur
d. 1983 Tarsis, Valery
Yakovlevich
d. 1985 Blanding, Sarah
Gibson
d. 1985 Shklovsky, Iosif
Samvilovitch
d. 1986 Halleck,
Charles Abraham
d. 1986 Randhawa,
Mohinder Singh
d. 1987 Kaye, Danny
d. 1987 Tucker, Rosina
d. 1988 Szeryng,
Henryk
d. 1989 Morris, Richard
Brandon
d. 1990 Gathers, Hank
d. 1990 Moore,
Charlotte E(mma)
d. 1991 Head, Howard
d. 1991 Murray, Arthur
d. 1991 Revolta, Johnny
d. 1992 Beatty, Robert
d. 1993 Montoya,
Carlos
d. 1993 Sabin, Albert
Bruce
d. 1994 Stone, Ezra
(Chaim)
d. 1995 Marker, Russell
Earl
d. 1996 Duras,
Marguerite
d. 1996 Krol, John
(Joseph), Cardinal
d. 1996 Schapiro,
Meyer
d. 1996 Talbot, Lyle
d. 1997 McConnell,
Joseph H(oward)
d. 1999 Herzberg,
Gerhard

March 4
b. 1394 Henry the
Navigator
b. 1678 Vivaldi,
Antonio (Lucio)
b. 1745 Dibdin, Charles
b. 1747 Pulaski,
Kazimierz
b. 1754 Waterhouse,
Benjamin
b. 1756 Raeburn,
Henry, Sir
b. 1781 Gratz, Rebecca
b. 1794 Couper, James
Hamilton
b. 1826 Buford, John

b. 1829 Gardiner,
Samuel Rawson
b. 1832 Colman,
Samuel
b. 1857 Kobbe, Gustav
b. 1864 Mannix, Daniel
b. 1869 Whitlock,
Brand
b. 1875 Rand, Ellen
Gertrude Emmet
b. 1877 Morgan, Garrett
Augustus
b. 1880 Pollock,
Channing
b. 1880 Walker, Stuart
Armstrong
b. 1881 Stribling,
Thomas Sigismund
b. 1881 Tolman,
Richard C(hace)
b. 1882 Titulescu,
Nicolae
b. 1885 Foyle, William
Alfred
b. 1886 Langford, Sam
b. 1886 Wilson, Edward
Arthur
b. 1887 Edgell, George
Harold
b. 1888 Rockne, Knute
Kenneth
b. 1889 White, Pearl
b. 1891 Bronfman,
Samuel
b. 1891 Vance, Dazzy
b. 1895 Gross, Milt
b. 1900 Biberman,
Herbert
b. 1901 Goren, Charles
Henry
b. 1901 Rabearivelo,
Jean Joseph
b. 1903 Boyd, William
Clouser
b. 1903 Scarne, John
b. 1904 Alikhanov,
Abram Isaakovich
b. 1904 Gamow, George
b. 1906 Davis, Phil
b. 1906 Dejong,
Meindert
b. 1906? Fisher, Avery
b. 1906 Macdonald,
Eleanor Josephine
b. 1906 Walgreen,
Charles Rudolph, Jr.
b. 1907 Targ, William
b. 1908 Kraus, Lili
b. 1909 Helmsley,
Harry B(rakmann)
b. 1910 Boothroyd,
John Basil
b. 1912 Leitner,
Ferdinand
b. 1913 Garfield, John
b. 1914 Cooper,
Mort(on Cecil)
b. 1914 Wilson, Robert
R(athbun)
b. 1916 Miller, Arjay
Ray
b. 1916 Whiffen,
Marcus
b. 1918 Andreas,
Dwayne Orville

b. 1921 Greenwood,
Joan
b. 1922 O'Driscoll,
Martha
b. 1923 King, Francis
Henry
b. 1924 O'Donnell,
Kenneth P
b. 1925 Albers, Hans
b. 1926 DeVos, Richard
Marvin
b. 1928 Sillitoe, Alan
b. 1929 Haitink,
Bernard
b. 1931 Cooper,
Kenneth Hardy
b. 1931 Rivlin, Alice
Mitchell
b. 1932 Kapuscinski,
Ryszard
b. 1932 Makeba,
Miriam
b. 1936 Clark, James
b. 1937 Gelb, Leslie
Howard
b. 1939 Carner, Joanne
Gunderson
b. 1939 McNair,
Barbara
b. 1939 Prentiss, Paula
b. 1941 Johnson, Bob
b. 1941 Stargell, Willie
b. 1944 Brown, Judie
b. 1944 Womack,
Bobby
b. 1948 Squire, Chris
b. 1953 Lenz, Kay
b. 1954 Ratushinskaya,
Irina
b. 1961 Mancini, Ray
b. 1966 Johnson, Kevin
b. 1969 Bono, Chastity
d. 1484 Casimir, Saint
d. 1815 Abington,
Fanny
d. 1825 Peale, Raphael
d. 1832 Champollion,
Jean Francois
d. 1842 Forten, James
d. 1852 Gogol, Nikolai
Vasilievich
d. 1858 Perry, Matthew
Calbraith,
Commodore
d. 1864 King, Thomas
Starr
d. 1868 Chisholm, Jesse
d. 1883 Stephens,
Alexander Hamilton
d. 1888 Alcott, Amos
Bronson
d. 1903 Shorthouse,
Joseph Henry
d. 1906 Schofield, John
McAllister
d. 1916 Marc, Franz
d. 1922 Williams, Bert
d. 1925 Moszkowski,
Moritz
d. 1925 Ward, Monte
d. 1932 Plenty Coups
d. 1937 Hocking, Silas
d. 1938 McDougall,
Walt(er)
d. 1940 Garland,
Hamlin

d. 1944 Buchalter,
Lepke
d. 1946 Waldron,
Charles D
d. 1948 Artaud, Antonin
d. 1949 Angell, James
Rowland
d. 1952 Christy,
Howard Chandler
d. 1952 Sherrington,
Charles Scott, Sir
d. 1957 Graham, Evarts
Ambrose
d. 1960 Warren,
Leonard
d. 1963 Belin, Edouard
d. 1963 Olds, Irving S
d. 1963 Williams,
William Carlos
d. 1974 Gottlieb,
Adolph
d. 1982 Eden, Dorothy
d. 1986 Greenfield,
Howard
d. 1988 Mosley, J(ohn)
Brooke
d. 1992 Almendros,
Nestor
d. 1993 Sale, Richard
Bernard
d. 1994 Candy, John
(Franklin)
d. 1995 Urban, Matt
d. 1996 Pearl, Minnie
d. 1999 Blackmun,
Harry A(ndrew)

March 5
b. 1133 Henry II
b. 1512 Mercator,
Gerhardus
b. 1575 Oughtred,
William
b. 1658 Cadillac,
Antoine de la Mothe
b. 1696 Tiepolo,
Giambattista
b. 1794 Grier, Robert
Cooper
b. 1817 Layard, Austen
Henry, Sir
b. 1824 Ives, James
Merritt
b. 1824 Larcom, Lucy
b. 1829 Henner, Jean
Jacques
b. 1830 Thomson,
Charles Wyville, Sir
b. 1832 Hayes, Isaac
Israel
b. 1836 Goodnight,
Charles
b. 1852 Gregory,
Isabella Augusta
Persse, Lady
b. 1853 Foote, Arthur
William
b. 1853 Pyle, Howard
b. 1859 Durand,
William F.
b. 1860 Thompson,
Sam(uel Luther)
b. 1870 Norris,
Frank(lin)
b. 1871 Luxemburg,
Rosa
b. 1876 Belin, Edouard

b. 1879 Beveridge,
William Henry, Lord
b. 1882 VanAlstyne,
Egbert Anson
b. 1887 Villa-Lobos,
Heitor
b. 1891 Fitzpatrick,
Daniel R
b. 1891 Johnson, Chic
b. 1893 Sands, Dorothy
b. 1894 Daniell, Henry
b. 1896 Marcus, Jacon
R(ader)
b. 1897 Herbst,
Josephine Frey
b. 1904 Rahner, Karl
b. 1907 Rosenbloom,
Carroll D
b. 1908 Harrison, Rex,
Sir
b. 1917 Kirbo, Charles
H(ughes)
b. 1918 Schmidt,
Milt(on Conrad)
b. 1918 Tobin, James
b. 1919 Boles, Paul
Darcy
b. 1920 Kelly, Leontine
Turpeau Current
b. 1922 Pasolini, Pier
Paolo
b. 1923 Irsay, Robert
b. 1924 Bernhard,
Harvey
b. 1927 Cassidy, Jack
b. 1929 Murray, Allen
Edward
b. 1930 Crandall,
Del(mar Wesley)
b. 1930 Maazel, Lorin
Varencove
b. 1931 Cobb, Jerrie
b. 1931 Tuckwell, Barry
Emmanuel
b. 1934 Sikking, James
B
b. 1936 Stockwell, Dean
b. 1938 Margulis, Lynn
b. 1938 Wainwright,
James
b. 1939 Fuller, Charles
b. 1940 Auletta, Robert
b. 1940 Eggar,
Samantha
b. 1941 Sand, Paul
b. 1942 Gonzalez
Marquez, Felipe
b. 1944 Gutman, Roy
b. 1945 Matson, Randy
b. 1946 Bleier, Rocky
b. 1946 Warren,
Michael
b. 1947 Hodges, Eddie
b. 1947 Tekulve,
Kent(on Charles)
b. 1948 Grant, Eddy
b. 1948 Silko, Leslie
Marmon
b. 1949 Gwilym, Mike
b. 1950 Fodor, Eugene
Nicholas
b. 1955 Otto, Whitney
b. 1955 Warfield,
Marsha
b. 1958 Gibb, Andy

b. 1958 Winans, Marvin L.
b. 1966 Irvin, Michael (Jerome)
d. 1534 Correggio, Antonio Allegri da
d. 1728 Nicholson, Francis
d. 1770 Attucks, Crispus
d. 1778 Arne, Thomas Augustine
d. 1809 Dunmore, 4th Earl of
d. 1815 Mesmer, Franz Anton
d. 1827 Laplace, Pierre Simon, Marquis de
d. 1849 Lyon, Mary Mason
d. 1876 Agoult, Marie Catherine Sophie d'
d. 1876 Piave, Francesco Maria
d. 1895 Leskov, Nikolai Semyonovich
d. 1923 Ayer, Francis Wayland
d. 1926 Ader, Clement
d. 1927 Remsen, Ira
d. 1930 Ladd-Franklin, Christine
d. 1940 Elliott, Maxine
d. 1941 Quidde, Ludwig
d. 1944 Jacob, Max
d. 1950 Grauman, Sid(ney Patrick)
d. 1950 Masters, Edgar Lee
d. 1953 Prokofiev, Sergei Sergeevich
d. 1953 Stalin, Joseph
d. 1957 Menzies, William Cameron
d. 1963 Cline, Patsy
d. 1965 Martin, Pepper
d. 1965 Mayer, Oscar Gottfried
d. 1965 Motley, Willard Francis
d. 1966 Akhmatova, Anna
d. 1967 Auer, Mischa
d. 1967 Mossadegh, Mohammed
d. 1969 Werth, Alexander
d. 1970 Woltman, Frederick Enos
d. 1971 Nevins, Allan
d. 1973 Crosse, Rupert
d. 1974 DeWolfe, Billy
d. 1974 Hurok, Sol(omon Isaievich)
d. 1977 Donlon, Mary Honor
d. 1979 Haworth, Leland John
d. 1980 Silverheels, Jay
d. 1981 Harburg, E(dgar) Y(ipsel)
d. 1982 Belushi, John
d. 1982 Case, Clifford Philip
d. 1982 Patton, Edward L

d. 1984 Powell, William
d. 1985 Stotz, Charles Morse
d. 1986 Nelson, George H
d. 1987 DeLiagre, Alfred
d. 1992 Walker, David Harry
d. 1997 Baker, Samm Sinclair
d. 1998 Friendly, Fred W.
d. 1999 Denning, Alfred Thompson
d. 1999 Kiley, Richard (Paul)

March 6
b. 1475 Michelangelo (Buonarroti)
b. 1483 Guicciardini, Francesco
b. 1619 Cyrano de Bergerac, Savinien de
b. 1787 Fraunhofer, Joseph von
b. 1797 Smith, Gerrit
b. 1806 Browning, Elizabeth Barrett
b. 1824 Skinner, Halcyon
b. 1831 Sheridan, Philip Henry
b. 1834 DuMaurier, George Louis P B
b. 1847 Hagen, Johann Georg
b. 1871 Harney, Benjamin Robertson
b. 1872 Bojer, Johan
b. 1873 Ferguson, Homer Lenoir
b. 1874 Berdyayev, Nikolay Aleksandrovich
b. 1881 Cournos, John
b. 1882 Kibbee, Guy
b. 1885 Lardner, Ring(gold Wilmer), Sr.
b. 1886 Baillie, John
b. 1891 Kilian, Victor
b. 1891 Tanner, Marion
b. 1892 Shaughnessy, Clark Daniel
b. 1893 Jones, Barry
b. 1897 MacArthur, John Donald
b. 1898 Conzelman, Jimmy
b. 1898 Flippen, Jay C
b. 1899 Simon, Richard Leo
b. 1900 Cigna, Gina
b. 1900 Grove, Lefty
b. 1901 Woodall, Mary
b. 1903 Nagako, Empress
b. 1905 Wills, Bob
b. 1906 Costello, Lou
b. 1907 Tyler, Parker
b. 1907 Wilson, Logan
b. 1909 Awolowo, Obafemi Awo
b. 1913 Logan, Ella

b. 1915 Hudson, Rochelle
b. 1917 Eisner, Will(iam E.)
b. 1917 Gray, Pete(r)
b. 1918 Von Eckardt, Wolf
b. 1920 Dickason, Olive Patricia
b. 1920 Price, Roger Taylor
b. 1921 Bealer, Alex W(inkler III)
b. 1921 Rudel, Julius
b. 1923 McMahon, Ed(ward Lee)
b. 1924 Caldwell, Sarah
b. 1924 Webster, William Hedgcock
b. 1925 Montgomery, Wes
b. 1926 Curtis, Ann
b. 1926 Greenspan, Alan
b. 1926 Wajda, Andrzej
b. 1927 Cooper, Gordon
b. 1927 Fairchild, John Burr
b. 1928 Garcia-Marquez, Gabriel Jose
b. 1928 Veronis, John James
b. 1929 Foley, Thomas S(tephen)
b. 1931 DeLavallade, Carmen
b. 1931 Needham, Hal
b. 1935 Whitman, Marina VonNeumann
b. 1936 Barry, Marion S(hepilov), Jr.
b. 1937 Boesky, Ivan Frederick
b. 1937 Tereshkova-Nikolaeva, Valentina
b. 1939 Bond, Christopher Samuel
b. 1939 Osborne, Adam
b. 1939 Spielberg, David
b. 1942 Murphy, Ben(jamin Edward)
b. 1942 Purim, Flora
b. 1944 Gilmour, Dave
b. 1944 Te Kanawa, Kiri, Dame
b. 1944 Wilson, Mary
b. 1945 Grundy, Hugh
b. 1947 Dee, Kiki
b. 1947 Fosbury, Dick
b. 1947 Reiner, Rob(ert)
b. 1948 Schwartz, Stephen L(awrence)
b. 1959 Arnold, Tom
b. 1966 Ashley, Maurice
b. 1972 O'Neal, Shaquille
d. 1616 Beaumont, Francis
d. 1683 Guarini, Guarino
d. 1809 Heyward, Thomas, Jr.
d. 1836 Bowie, Jim

d. 1836 Crockett, Davy
d. 1836 Travis, William Barret
d. 1838 Stevens, John
d. 1851 Shreve, Henry Miller
d. 1867 Cornelius, Peter von
d. 1867 Ward, Artemus
d. 1879 Burritt, Elihu
d. 1888 Alcott, Louisa May
d. 1897 Brewer, Ebenezer Cobham
d. 1900 Daimler, Gottlieb (Wilhelm)
d. 1910 Platt, Thomas Collier
d. 1929 Buick, David Dunbar
d. 1930 Hadley, Arthur Twining
d. 1930 Tirpitz, Alfred von
d. 1932 Sousa, John Philip
d. 1933 Cermak, Anton Joseph
d. 1935 Holmes, Oliver Wendell, Jr.
d. 1936 Morgan, C(onwy) Lloyd
d. 1939 Juch, Emma
d. 1941 Borglum, John Gutzon de la Mothe
d. 1942 Mooney, Tom
d. 1943 Collins, Jimmy
d. 1947 Mackinder, Halford John, Sir
d. 1948 Lockridge, Ross Franklin, Jr.
d. 1950 Lebrun, Albert
d. 1950 Lehr, Lew
d. 1951 Novello, Ivor
d. 1951 Vynnychenko, Volodymyr
d. 1959 Stone, Fred Andrew
d. 1964 Paul I
d. 1965 Dumont, Margaret
d. 1965 Morrison of Lambeth, Herbert Stanley Morrison, Baron
d. 1966 Westover, Russell (Channing)
d. 1967 Eddy, Nelson
d. 1967 Kodaly, Zoltan
d. 1968 Martin, Joseph William, Jr.
d. 1970 Hopper, William
d. 1971 Broadbent, Punch
d. 1971 Dart, Thurston
d. 1971 Evans, Herbert McLean
d. 1973 Buck, Pearl S(ydenstricker)
d. 1976 Rosenbloom, Maxie
d. 1978 MacLiammoir, Michael

d. 1981 Hightower,
Florence Josephine
Cole
d. 1982 Rand, Ayn
d. 1983 Berberian,
Cathy
d. 1983 Maclean,
Donald Duart
d. 1984 Niemoller,
Martin
d. 1984 Wilcoxon,
Henry
d. 1985 Sloane, Eric
d. 1985 Sour, Robert
B(andler)
d. 1986 Caesar, Adolph
d. 1986 O'Keeffe,
Georgia
d. 1987 Zorinsky,
Edward
d. 1989 Andrews, Harry
d. 1989 Barthe,
Richmond
d. 1990 Klassen, Elmer
Theodore
d. 1990 Merrill, Gary
Franklin
d. 1990 Sewell, Joe
d. 1991 Penney,
William George
d. 1992 Klineberg, Otto
d. 1992 Martin, David
Stone
d. 1992 Vieira Da Silva,
Maria Helena
d. 1993 Rothschild,
Judith
d. 1994 Mercouri,
Melina
d. 1995 Anello, John
David
d. 1995 Resnik, Muriel
d. 1997 Furgol,
Ed(ward)
d. 1997 Jagan, Cheddi
(Berret)
d. 1997 Manley,
Michael (Norman)
d. 2000 Colicos, John

March 7
b. 1707 Hopkins,
Stephen
b. 1765 Niepce, Joseph
Nicephore
b. 1785 Manzoni,
Alessandro (Antonio)
b. 1788 Becquerel,
Antoine-Cesar
b. 1792 Herschel, John
Frederick William,
Sir
b. 1802 Landseer,
Edwin Henry, Sir
b. 1813 Kamehameha
III
b. 1822 Masse, Victor
b. 1838 Roe, Edward
Payson
b. 1841 Nelson, William
Rockhill
b. 1842 Hyndman,
Henry Mayers
b. 1844 Comstock,
Anthony
b. 1845 Palmer, Daniel
David

b. 1849 Burbank, Luther
b. 1850 Clark, Champ
b. 1850 Masaryk,
Tomas Garrigue
b. 1857 Wagner-
Jaurregg, Julius, von
b. 1866 Ernst, Paul Karl
Friedrich
b. 1872 Mondrian,
Piet(er Cornelis)
b. 1875 Ravel, Maurice
Joseph
b. 1887 Parkhurst,
Helen
b. 1889 Williams, Ben
Ames
b. 1890 Danforth, Dave
b. 1893 Avery, Milton
Clark
b. 1902 Oenslager,
Donald Mitchell
b. 1909 Magnani, Anna
b. 1909 Revelle, Roger
Randall
b. 1914 DaCosta,
Morton
b. 1914 Hauge, Gabriel
b. 1914 Sann, Paul
b. 1915 Chaban-Delmas,
Jacques Pierre Michel
b. 1919 Stout, Juanita
Kidd
b. 1922 Phillip, Andy
b. 1924 Abe, Kobo
b. 1927 Broderick,
James Joseph
b. 1927 Watkins, James
(David)
b. 1928 Elegant, Robert
Sampson
b. 1929 Chouteau,
Yvonne
b. 1930 Armstrong-
Jones, Antony
Charles Robert
b. 1930 Marlowe,
Marion
b. 1932 Olter, Bailey
b. 1934 Scott, Willard
Herman, Jr.
b. 1934 Walker, Zena
b. 1935 DeVita, Vincent
Theodore, Jr.
b. 1935 Donghia,
Angelo R
b. 1938 Baltimore,
David
b. 1938 Guthrie, Janet
b. 1940 Travanti, Daniel
J(ohn)
b. 1941 Grimes, J
William
b. 1941 Malone, John
Charles Custer
b. 1941 Read, Piers
Paul
b. 1942 Eisner, Michael
Dammann
b. 1942? Messner,
Tammy Faye
b. 1943 White,
Chris(topher Taylor)
b. 1944 Fiennes
(Twisleton
Wykeham), Ranulph
b. 1945 Heard, John

b. 1946 Wolf, Peter
b. 1950 Harris, Franco
b. 1950 Richard,
J(ames) R(odney)
b. 1952 Boyd, William
b. 1952 Swann, Lynn
Curtis
b. 1960 Carter, Joe
b. 1960 Duchovny,
David
b. 1960 Lendl, Ivan
b. 1963 Dayne, Taylor
b. 1964 Ellis, Bret
Easton
b. 1964 Graves, Denyce
(Antoinette)
b. 1967 Bocca, Julio
d. 161 Antoninus Pius
d. 1274 Thomas
Aquinas, Saint
d. 1768 Bienville, Sieur
de
d. 1809 Blanchard,
Francois
d. 1883 Green, John
Richard
d. 1897 Jacobs, Harriet
Ann
d. 1902 Galvin, Pud
d. 1911 Fogazzaro,
Antonio
d. 1913 Johnson, Emily
Pauline
d. 1931 Doesburg, Theo
van
d. 1932 Briand, Aristide
d. 1935 Duane, William
d. 1935 Tabor,
Elizabeth Bonduel
McCourt Doe
d. 1937 White, William
Alanson
d. 1940 Finley, John
Huston
d. 1940 Markham,
Edwin
d. 1941 Eltinge, Julian
d. 1941 Sanborn, Pitts
d. 1942 Sarg, Tony
d. 1945 Dawson,
Bertrand Edward
d. 1950 Korzybski,
Alfred Habdank
d. 1951 Harkins,
William Draper
d. 1952 Yogananda,
Paramahansa, Swami
d. 1954 Diels, Otto Paul
Herman
d. 1954 Hays, Will
Harrison
d. 1954 Herrick, James
Bryan
d. 1957 Lewis,
Wyndham
d. 1959 Hatoyama
Ichiro
d. 1959 Pigou, Arthur
Cecil
d. 1967 Compton,
Wilson Martindale
d. 1967 Toklas, Alice
B(abette)
d. 1971 Balaban,
Barney
d. 1971 Smith, Stevie

d. 1975 Bakhtin,
Mikhail
(Mikhailovich)
d. 1975 Blue, Ben
d. 1975 Seredy, Kate
d. 1976 Patman, (John
Williams) Wright
d. 1979 Novaes (Pinto),
Guiomar
d. 1980 Patterson,
William Allan
d. 1981 Billington, Ray
Allen
d. 1981 Crowther,
Bosley
d. 1981 Kondrashin,
Kiril Petrovich
d. 1983 Black, William
d. 1983 Markevitch,
Igor
d. 1984 Rotha, Paul
d. 1985 Woodruff,
Robert Winship
d. 1988 Divine
d. 1990 Prestes, Luiz
Carlos
d. 1991 Bell, Cool Papa
d. 1993 Reid, Kate
d. 1993 Wrightson, Earl
d. 1994 Bolte, Charles
G(uy)
d. 1995 Rosten, Norman
d. 1997 Purcell, Edward
M(ills)
d. 1998 Rysanek,
Leonie
d. 1999 Kubrick,
Stanley
d. 2000 Levi, Edward
Hirsch

March 8
b. 1714 Bach, Carl
Philipp Emanuel
b. 1780 Bigge, John
Thomas
b. 1783 Van Buren,
Hannah (Hoes)
b. 1788 Hamilton,
William, Sir
b. 1799 Cameron,
Simon
b. 1822 Avery, Samuel
Putnam
b. 1822 Johnston,
Richard Malcolm
b. 1825 Barbier, Jules
b. 1830 Deus, Joao de
b. 1836 Butler, Matthew
Calbraith
b. 1839 Crafts, James
Mason
b. 1840 Emin Pasha
b. 1841 Holmes, Oliver
Wendell, Jr.
b. 1849 Winkelmann,
Hermann
b. 1858 Leoncavallo,
Ruggiero
b. 1859 Grahame,
Kenneth
b. 1865 Goudy, Frederic
William
b. 1867 Davenport,
Homer Calvin
b. 1873 Held, Anna

b. 1878 Currie, Barton Wood
b. 1879 Hahn, Otto
b. 1883 Starch, Daniel
b. 1886 Kendall, Edward C(alvin)
b. 1888 Chase, Stuart
b. 1890 Fowler, Gene
b. 1890 Humphrey, George Magoffin
b. 1890 Keogan, George
b. 1892 Hurt, Mississippi John
b. 1892 Mowrer, Edgar Ansel
b. 1893 Jaffe, Sam
b. 1900 Aiken, Howard Hathaway
b. 1902 Beavers, Louise
b. 1902 Randolph, Jennings
b. 1903 Ciano (di Cortellazzo), Galeazzo
b. 1905 Cooper, Louise Field
b. 1907 Karamanlis, Constantine
b. 1909 Trevor, Claire
b. 1911 Hovhaness, Alan
b. 1911 Mitchell, Clarence M
b. 1913 Wilson, Peter Cecil
b. 1915 Kitagawa, Joseph Mitsuo
b. 1916 McBride, Lloyd
b. 1917 Fiedler, Leslie Aaron
b. 1918 Donahue, Sam Koontz
b. 1918 Hale, Alan, Jr.
b. 1920 Batchelor, George (Keith)
b. 1920 Herlie, Eileen
b. 1920 Wallop, Douglass
b. 1922 Croft, Michael
b. 1922 Furillo, Carl Anthony
b. 1923 Charisse, Cyd
b. 1924 Caro, Anthony, Sir
b. 1927 Kania, Stanislaw
b. 1928 Segal, Lore Groszmann
b. 1929 Krainik, Ardis
b. 1930 Hurd, Douglas
b. 1931 McPhee, John (Angus)
b. 1936 Cryer, David
b. 1938 Dawkins, Pete(r M)
b. 1939 Bouton, Jim
b. 1939 Lowry, Mike
b. 1939 Seymour, Lynn
b. 1942 Allen, Richie
b. 1943 Redgrave, Lynn
b. 1944 Clark, Susan Nora Goulding
b. 1945 Dolenz, Mickey
b. 1945 Kiefer, Anselm Karl Albert
b. 1946 Meisner, Randy

b. 1946 Rowland, Pleasant
b. 1947 Sager, Carole Bayer
b. 1953 Rice, Jim
b. 1958 Numan, Gary
b. 1960 Williams, Charles Linwood
b. 1961 Murphy, Larry
b. 1964 Salt
b. 1967 Harkes, John
d. 1302 Arnolfo di Cambio
d. 1702 William III
d. 1796 Chambers, William, Sir
d. 1824 Cambaceres, Jean Jacques Regis de
d. 1839 Nourrit, Adolphe
d. 1844 Bernadotte, Jean Baptiste
d. 1869 Berlioz, Hector
d. 1874 Fillmore, Millard
d. 1887 Beecher, Henry Ward
d. 1887 Eads, James Buchanan
d. 1889 Ericsson, John
d. 1892 Allen, John
d. 1893 Fox, Margaret
d. 1893 Smith, Edmund Kirby
d. 1903 Franklin, William Buel
d. 1917 Zeppelin, Ferdinand Adolf August Heinrich von, Count
d. 1925 Ball, Edmund B
d. 1930 Taft, William (Howard)
d. 1937 Morenz, Howie
d. 1941 Anderson, Sherwood
d. 1942 Capablanca, Jose Raoul
d. 1943 Nielsen, Alice
d. 1949 U'Ren, William Simon
d. 1954 Balderston, John Lloyd
d. 1957 Schoech, Othmar
d. 1961 Beecham, Thomas, Sir
d. 1963 Webb, Walter Prescott
d. 1964 Alexander, Franz Gabriel
d. 1970 Peirce, Waldo
d. 1971 Lloyd, Harold
d. 1973 Connor, Bull
d. 1973 McKernan, Ron
d. 1975 Bech, Joseph
d. 1975 Stevens, George (Cooper)
d. 1976 Disney, Doris Miles
d. 1977 Hull, Henry
d. 1982 Shera, Jesse Hauk
d. 1983 Walton, William Turner, Sir

d. 1985 Andrews, Edward
d. 1985 Ingersoll, Ralph McAllister
d. 1988 Brubacher, John Seiler
d. 1992 Nelson, Christian
d. 1993 Eckstine, Billy
d. 1995 Horgan, Paul
d. 1995 Victor, Paul-Emile
d. 1997 Danielian, Leon
d. 1997 Sheinwold, Alfred
d. 1998 Nitschke, Ray(mond E.)
d. 1999 Cass, Peggy
d. 1999 DiMaggio, Joe
d. 1999 Wrigley, William, III

March 9
b. 1451 Vespucci, Amerigo
b. 1676 Boylston, Zabdiel
b. 1749 Mirabeau, Honore Gabriel Riquetti
b. 1753 Kleber, Jean Baptiste
b. 1758 Gall, Franz Joseph
b. 1773 Hull, Isaac
b. 1791 Levasseur, Nicolas Prosper
b. 1806 Forrest, Edwin
b. 1814 Evans, John
b. 1814 Shevchenko, Taras
b. 1815 Davis, David
b. 1820 Blatchford, Samuel
b. 1824 Stanford, Leland
b. 1838 Gumplowicz, Ludwig
b. 1856 Acheson, Edward Goodrich
b. 1856 Foy, Eddie
b. 1858 Stickley, Gustav
b. 1862 Widal, Fernand Isidore
b. 1864 Dawson, Bertrand Edward
b. 1880 McGovern, Terry
b. 1881 Bevin, Ernest
b. 1885 Karsavina, Tamara (Platonova)
b. 1886 Eichelberger, Robert Lawrence
b. 1886 Foyle, Gilbert Samuel
b. 1890 Molotov, Vyacheslav Mikhaylovich
b. 1892 Garnett, David
b. 1892 Sackville-West, Vita
b. 1892 Zita of Bourbon-Parma
b. 1893 Marston, William Moulton
b. 1895 Chase, William Curtis

b. 1898 Hodges, Luther Hartwell
b. 1902 Geer, Will
b. 1902 Gibbs, Anthony
b. 1902 Saint John, Robert
b. 1902 Stone, Edward Durell
b. 1904 Heydrich, Reinhard Tristan Eugen
b. 1905 Quennell, Peter (Courtney)
b. 1905 Renick, Marion Lewis
b. 1906 Smith, David
b. 1907 Eliade, Mircea
b. 1909 Tromp, Solco Walle
b. 1910 Barber, Samuel
b. 1910 Gault, William Campbell
b. 1912 Vaughan, Arky
b. 1913 Placzek, Adolf K(urt)
b. 1914 Clark, Fred
b. 1914 Ullman, Al(bert Conrad)
b. 1916 Brandon, Henry Oscar
b. 1917 Fascell, Dante B(runo)
b. 1918 Rockwell, George Lincoln
b. 1918 Spillane, Mickey
b. 1920 Betz, Carl
b. 1922 McKissick, Floyd Bixler
b. 1923 Buckley, James Lane
b. 1923 Courreges, Andre
b. 1924 Gold, Herbert
b. 1925 Miller, G(eorge) William
b. 1925 Orfilo, Alejandro
b. 1927 Jensen, Jackie
b. 1929 Hoyte, Hugh Desmond
b. 1930 Schippers, Thomas
b. 1931 Febres-Cordero, Leon
b. 1931 Hills, Roderick M
b. 1932 Smith, Keely
b. 1934 Demmert, William G., Jr.
b. 1934 Gagarin, Yuri Alexseyevich
b. 1934 Van Patten, Joyce
b. 1936 Brown, Kenneth H
b. 1936 Gilley, Mickey Leroy
b. 1936 Ingels, Marty
b. 1939 Bricklin, Malcolm N
b. 1940 Julia, Raul
b. 1942 Campaneris, Bert
b. 1943 Fischer, Bobby

b. 1943 Gibson, Charles Dewolf
b. 1945 Trower, Robin
b. 1945 Van Devere, Trish
b. 1946 Fuchs, Michael J(oseph)
b. 1947 Kennerly, David Hume
b. 1948 Fischl, Eric
b. 1950 North, Andy
b. 1950 Sullivan, Danny
b. 1951 Kinsley, Michael (E.)
b. 1954 Sands, Bobby
b. 1955 Bujones, Fernando
b. 1957 Lewis, Chris
b. 1960 Fiorentino, Linda
b. 1965 Bosworth, Brian Keith
b. 1971 Lewis, Emmanuel
d. 1661 Mazarin, Jules, Cardinal
d. 1851 Oersted, Hans Christian
d. 1872 Krieghoff, Cornelius
d. 1873 Knight, Charles
d. 1878 Anderssen, Adolf
d. 1888 William, I
d. 1893 Taine, Hippolyte Adolphe
d. 1895 Sacher-Masoch, Leopold von
d. 1904 Palmer, Erastus Dow
d. 1907 Dowie, John Alexander
d. 1909 Helper, Hinton Rowan
d. 1918 Wedekind, Frank
d. 1923 Waals, Johannes Diderik van der
d. 1925 Metcalf, Willard Leroy
d. 1927 Potthast, Edward Henry
d. 1928 Wanamaker, Lewis Rodman
d. 1930 Mercer, Henry Chapman
d. 1937 More, Paul Elmer
d. 1942 Bosch, Robert August
d. 1944 Brown, A Roy
d. 1947 Catt, Carrie Chapman
d. 1952 Kollontai, Alexandra Mikhailovna (Domantovich)
d. 1955 Henson, Matthew Alexander
d. 1957 Horthy de Nagybanya, Nicholas
d. 1963 Melcher, Frederic Gershon
d. 1964 DePaolis, Alessio

d. 1965 Murphy, Jimmy
d. 1969 Brackett, Charles
d. 1969 Christaller, Walter
d. 1969 Hawley, Cameron
d. 1971 Knaths, Karl
d. 1972 O'Connor, Basil
d. 1974 Sutherland, Earl Wilbur, Jr.
d. 1975 Dunninger, Joseph
d. 1977 Bolton, Frances Payne
d. 1981 Delbruck, Max
d. 1981 Judy, Steven
d. 1981 Nicolson, Marjorie Hope
d. 1981 Von Wangenheim, Chris
d. 1982 Butler of Saffron Walden, Richard Austen, Baron
d. 1983 Emerson, Faye Margaret
d. 1985 Jenner, William Ezra
d. 1986 Calmer, Ned
d. 1987 Kneip, Richard F
d. 1987 Locke, Bobby
d. 1987 Salt, Waldo
d. 1988 Galamison, Milton Arthur
d. 1988 Kiesinger, Kurt Georg
d. 1989 Mapplethorpe, Robert
d. 1992 Begin, Menachem (Wolfovitch)
d. 1993 Parkinson, C(yril) Northcote
d. 1994 Bukowski, Charles
d. 1994 Rey, Fernando
d. 1994 Spivak, Lawrence E(dmund)
d. 1995 Ballantine, Ian (Keith)
d. 1995 Bernays, Edward L.
d. 1996 Burns, George
d. 1996 Curti, Merle Eugene
d. 1996 Warne, William E(lmo)
d. 1997 Leighton, Robert B(enjamin)
d. 1997 Notorious B.I.G.
d. 1997 Wedgwood, C(icely) V(eronica)
d. 1997 Wilbur, Dwight L(ocke)
d. 1998 Farah, William F.

March 10
b. 1452 Ferdinand V
b. 1503 Ferdinand I
b. 1626 Malpighi, Marcello
b. 1629 Romanov, Alexis Mikhailovich

b. 1730 Ross, George
b. 1749 DaPonte, Lorenzo
b. 1772 Schlegel, Friedrich von
b. 1780 Trollope, Frances
b. 1787 Etty, William
b. 1788 Eichendorff, Joseph Karl Benedict Freiherr von
b. 1791 Saavedra, Angel de
b. 1810 McCloskey, John
b. 1823 Dykes, John Bacchus
b. 1833 Alarcon, Pedro Antonio de
b. 1839 Buck, Dudley
b. 1844 Sarasate, Pablo de
b. 1845 Alexander III
b. 1858 Fowler, Henry Watson
b. 1861 Johnson, Emily Pauline
b. 1861 Sifton, Clifford
b. 1867 Guimard, Hector Germain
b. 1867 Wald, Lillian D
b. 1873 Wassermann, Jakob
b. 1880 Jacobs, Michael S
b. 1880 Thorek, Max
b. 1883 Barrientos, Maria
b. 1886 Laubenthal, Rudolf
b. 1886 Waller, Fred(erick)
b. 1888 Fitzgerald, Barry
b. 1888 Mayer, Oscar Gottfried
b. 1891 Wang Shih-chieh
b. 1892 Honegger, Arthur
b. 1892 Turner, Eva, Dame
b. 1897 Hoyt, Palmer
b. 1898 Bacharach, Bert(ram Mark)
b. 1900 Billingsley, Sherman
b. 1900 Brayman, Harold
b. 1900 DeRose, Peter
b. 1901 Calderone, Frank Anthony
b. 1903 Beiderbecke, Bix
b. 1903 Luce, Clare Boothe
b. 1904 Fishback, Margaret
b. 1905 Masserman, Jules H(oman)
b. 1907 Frissell, Toni
b. 1908 Wragge, Sidney
b. 1909 Galento, Tony
b. 1911 Anderson, Warner

b. 1914 Harper, Chandler
b. 1914 Mitchell, Corinne
b. 1915 Bertoia, Harry
b. 1915 Groves, Charles Barnard, Sir
b. 1917 Hare, David
b. 1917 Merrill, John Putnam
b. 1918 Broun, Heywood Hale
b. 1920 Kent, Jack
b. 1922 Mason, Pamela Helen
b. 1923 Fitch, Val Logsdon
b. 1926 Haynes, Marques Oreole
b. 1928 Akins, Virgil B
b. 1928 Grebey, Ray
b. 1928 Ray, James Earl
b. 1928 Tennenbaum, Silvia
b. 1934 Rechy, John Francisco
b. 1938 Mix, Ron(ald J)
b. 1939 Press, Irina Natanovna
b. 1940 Norris, Chuck
b. 1940 Rabe, David William
b. 1941 Torrence, Dean
b. 1943 Limbert, John William, Jr.
b. 1945 Houghton, Katharine
b. 1946 Valvano, Jim
b. 1947 Campbell, Kim
b. 1947 Greene, Bob
b. 1947 Scholz, Tom
b. 1949 Radocy, Robert
b. 1953 Gareau, Jacqueline
b. 1955 DeBarge, Bunny
b. 1955 Hughes, Holly
b. 1956 Aurre, Laura
b. 1956 Lang, Helmut
b. 1956 Myricks, Larry
b. 1958 Howe, Steve
b. 1958 Stone, Sharon
b. 1963 Rubin, Rick
b. 1964 Edward
b. 1964 Guy, Jasmine
b. 1965 Woodson, Rod(erick Kevin)
b. 1977 Miller, Shannon (Lee)
d. 1762 Calas, Jean
d. 1819 Jacobi, Friedrich Heinrich
d. 1832 Clementi, Muzio
d. 1855 Brown, James
d. 1861 Shevchenko, Taras
d. 1864 Slade, Jack
d. 1870 Moscheles, Ignaz
d. 1872 Mazzini, Giuseppe
d. 1882 Thomson, Charles Wyville, Sir
d. 1889 Johannes, IV

d. 1895 Worth, Charles
Frederick
d. 1900 Symons,
George James
d. 1913 Tubman,
Harriet Ross
d. 1919 Barr, Amelia
Edith Huddleston
d. 1921 Upton, Francis
Robbins
d. 1925 Hayford, John
Fillmore
d. 1940 Bulgakov,
Mikhail Afanasyevich
d. 1943 Binyon,
Laurence
d. 1943 Marshall, Tully
d. 1944 Cobb, Irvin
Shrewsbury
d. 1944 Lincoln, Joseph
C(rosby)
d. 1944 Van Loon,
Hendrik Willem
d. 1948 Fitzgerald,
Zelda
d. 1948 Masaryk, Jan
Garrigue
d. 1952 McNamara,
George
d. 1953 Curtis, Charles
Gordon
d. 1959 Parks, Floyd
Lavinius
d. 1965 Lampkin, Daisy
d. 1966 O'Connor,
Frank
d. 1966 Sandoz, Mari
d. 1966 Zernike, Frits
d. 1969 Draper, Dorothy
Tuckerman
d. 1969 McCobb, Paul
Winthrop
d. 1969 Wilde, Jimmy
d. 1976 Sissman,
L(ouis) E(dward)
d. 1977 Biggs, Edward
George Power
d. 1980 Glueck,
Sheldon
d. 1980 Tarnower,
Herman
d. 1981 Oldfield,
Maurice, Sir
d. 1985 Chernenko,
Konstantin Ustinovich
d. 1985 Van Niel,
Cornelius B(ernardus)
d. 1986 Cohen, Myron
d. 1986 Milland,
Ray(mond Alton)
d. 1988 Cunningham,
Glenn Clarence
d. 1988 Gibb, Andy
d. 1988 Pham Hung
d. 1990 Singher, Martial
d. 1991 Knight,
Etheridge
d. 1991 Siegmeister,
Elie
d. 1996 Hunter, Ross
d. 1997 Drake, Stan(ley
Albert)
d. 1998 Bridges, Lloyd
d. 2000 Cooney,
Barbara

March 11
b. 1366 Anne of
Bohemia
b. 1544 Tasso, Torquato
b. 1731 Paine, Robert
Treat
b. 1781 Heinrich,
Anthony Philip
b. 1785 McLean, John
b. 1796 Wayland,
Francis
b. 1813 Lamperti,
Francesco
b. 1818 LeClear,
Thomas
b. 1818 Sainte-Clair
Deville, Henri
Etienne
b. 1822 Bertrand,
Joseph Louis Francois
b. 1822 Petipa, Marius
b. 1860 Hastings,
Thomas
b. 1876 Ruggles, Carl
b. 1885 Campbell,
Malcolm, Sir
b. 1887 Moran, Paddy
b. 1887 Walsh, Raoul
b. 1889 Widener,
George D
b. 1890 Bush, Vannevar
b. 1891 Polanyi,
Michael
b. 1892 Handy, Thomas
Troy
b. 1897 Cowell, Henry
Dixon
b. 1898 Gish, Dorothy
b. 1899 Douglas, James
Henderson, Jr.
b. 1899 Frederick IX
b. 1902 Rains, Albert
McKinley
b. 1903 Schiff, Dorothy
b. 1903 Welk, Lawrence
b. 1907 Matthews,
Jessie
b. 1907 Moltke,
Helmuth James, Graf
von
b. 1911 Mitchell,
Howard (Bundy)
b. 1916 Clemo, Jack
b. 1916 Keats, Ezra
Jack
b. 1916 Wilson, (James)
Harold, Sir
b. 1918 Gordon,
Thomas
b. 1919 Ellington,
Mercer
b. 1920 Bloembergen,
Nicolaas
b. 1920 Enright, Dennis
Joseph
b. 1922 Carroll,
Vinnette
b. 1923 Brough, Louise
Althea
b. 1926 Abernathy,
Ralph David
b. 1926 Starzl, Thomas
Earl
b. 1927 Mosbacher,
Robert Adam
b. 1928 Salmi, Albert

b. 1929 Browning,
Edmond Lee
b. 1929 Jacobsen, Hugh
Newell
b. 1930 Jutra, Claude
b. 1930 Ruttman, Troy
b. 1931 Eckert, Horst
b. 1931 Murdoch,
Rupert
b. 1931 Walters, Peter
Ingram, Sir
b. 1932 Lawson, Nigel
b. 1933 Rosen,
Benjamin M(aurice)
b. 1934 Donaldson,
Sam(uel Andrew)
b. 1936 Scalia, Antonin
b. 1938 Gorman,
Chester
b. 1945 Ellis, Dock
Phillip, Jr.
b. 1947 Stein, Mark
b. 1950 McFerrin,
Bobby
b. 1952 Adams,
Douglas Noel
b. 1952 Rhone, Sylvia
b. 1952 Richardson,
Susan
b. 1965 Jackson, Jesse,
Jr.
d. 1514 Bramante,
Donata d'Agnolo
d. 1722 Toland, John
d. 1759 Forbes, John
d. 1801 Paul, I
d. 1812
DeLoutherbourg,
Philip James
d. 1820 Mackenzie,
Alexander, Sir
d. 1820 West, Benjamin
d. 1847 Appleseed,
Johnny
d. 1851 McDuffie,
George
d. 1868 Moshweshwe
d. 1874 Sumner,
Charles
d. 1895 Cantu, Cesare
d. 1898 Rosecrans,
William Starke
d. 1930 Albee, Edward
Franklin
d. 1931 Murnau,
Friedrich W
d. 1932 Campana, Dino
d. 1936 Beatty, David
Beatty, Earl
d. 1941 Davies, Henry
Walford, Sir
d. 1949 Giraud, Henri
Honore
d. 1950 Dempster,
Arthur Jeffrey
d. 1950 Pemberton,
Brock
d. 1955 Fleming,
Alexander, Sir
d. 1955 Mayer, Oscar
Ferdinand
d. 1956 Vassilenko,
Sergei
d. 1957 Byrd, Richard
Evelyn, Admiral
d. 1957 Ornitz, Samuel

d. 1960 Andrews, Roy
Chapman
d. 1966 Fitzsimmons,
James E
d. 1967 Farrar,
Geraldine
d. 1970 Gardner, Erle
Stanley
d. 1971 Broad, C(harlie)
D(unbar)
d. 1971 Farnsworth,
Philo Taylor
d. 1971 Young,
Whitney Moore, Jr.
d. 1972 Wheat, Zack
d. 1973 Evergood,
Philip (Howard
Francis Dixon)
d. 1974 Gruenberg,
Sidonie Matsner
d. 1974 Holdren, Judd
Clifton
d. 1975 Gibbs, Anthony
d. 1979 Kilian, Victor
d. 1979 Power, Donald
Clinton
d. 1980 Taber, Gladys
Bagg
d. 1982 Gregory,
Horace Victor
d. 1986 Terry, Sonny
d. 1987 Elson, Robert
Truscott
d. 1987 Kilroy, James,
Jr.
d. 1988 Bearden,
Romare Howard
d. 1989 McCloy, John
Jay
d. 1990 Soupault,
Philippe
d. 1992 Brooks, Richard
d. 1992 Lehmann-
Haupt, Hellmut Emil
d. 1996 Edwards,
Vince(nt)
d. 1997 Weisgall, Hugo
(David)
March 12
b. 1607 Gerhardt,
Paul(us)
b. 1613 LeNotre, Andre
b. 1626 Aubrey, John
b. 1685 Berkeley,
George
b. 1710 Arne, Thomas
Augustine
b. 1767 Godoy y
Alvarez de Faria,
Manuel de
b. 1784 Buckland,
William
b. 1788 David d'Angers
b. 1790 Daniell, John
Frederic
b. 1795 Mackenzie,
William Lyon
b. 1799 Howitt, Mary
b. 1806 Pierce, Jane
(Means)
b. 1818 Worden, John
Lorimer
b. 1822 Read, Thomas
Buchanan
b. 1824 Kirchhoff,
Gustav Robert

b. 1824 Prang, Louis
b. 1825 Manns, August, Sir
b. 1831 Studebaker, Clement
b. 1832 Boycott, Charles Cunningham
b. 1832 Friedel, Charles
b. 1835 Newcomb, Simon
b. 1838 Perkin, William Henry, Sir
b. 1843 Tarde, Gabriel
b. 1858 Ochs, Adolph Simon
b. 1863 D'Annunzio, Gabriele
b. 1868 Whitechurch, Victor Lorenzo
b. 1873 White, Stewart Edward
b. 1877 Adams, Annette Abbott
b. 1880 Ataturk, Kemal
b. 1881 Tanner, Valno Alfred
b. 1888 Johnson, Hall
b. 1888 Knappertsbusch, Hans
b. 1889 Bucher, Walter Herman
b. 1889 Guedalla, Philip
b. 1894 Meyer, Joseph
b. 1899 Iturbi, Amparo
b. 1900 Rojas Pinilla, Gustavo
b. 1902 Fenton, Leslie
b. 1905 Suits, C(hauncey) G(uy)
b. 1908 Conley, Eugene
b. 1909 Vila, George Raymond
b. 1910 Stevens, Roger L(acey)
b. 1911 Diaz Ordaz, Gustavo
b. 1911? Moats, Alice-Leone
b. 1912 Brown, Les(ter Raymond)
b. 1912 Spyropoulos, Jannis
b. 1913 Mikhalkov, Sergei Vladimirovich
b. 1914 Farr, Tommy B
b. 1915 Mucha, Jiri
b. 1917 Withers, Googie
b. 1918 Gottschalk, Robert
b. 1919 Szmuness, Wolf
b. 1920 DeKooning, Elaine Marie Catherine Fried
b. 1920 Monroe, Rose Will
b. 1921 Agnelli, Giovanni
b. 1921 MacRae, Gordon
b. 1921 McCafferty, Don
b. 1921 Shapey, Ralph
b. 1922 Kerouac, Jack
b. 1922 Kirkland, Lane
b. 1923 Schirra, Wally

b. 1925 Delerue, Georges
b. 1925 Esaki, Leo
b. 1926 Holmes, John Clellon
b. 1928 Albee, Edward
b. 1930 Law, Vern(on Sanders)
b. 1931 Kelleher, Herb(ert David)
b. 1931 Thomas, Billy
b. 1932 Houbregs, Bob
b. 1932 Young, Andrew Jackson, Jr.
b. 1934 Ayala, Francisco J(ose)
b. 1936 Cohen, Daniel
b. 1936 Dobyns, Lloyd Allen, Jr.
b. 1938 Panov, Valery
b. 1938 White, Lois Jean
b. 1939 Feldon, Barbara
b. 1940 Jarreau, Al(wyn Lopez)
b. 1942 Kantner, Paul
b. 1943 Mladic, Ratko
b. 1945 Anson, Robert Sam
b. 1945 Summers, Anne Fairhurst
b. 1946 Minnelli, Liza
b. 1946 Schank, Roger C(arl)
b. 1948 Conrad, Kent
b. 1948 Mosely, Mark DeWayne
b. 1948 Taylor, James Vernon
b. 1953 Hiassen, Carl
b. 1956 Murphy, Dale Bryan
b. 1957 Allen, Leslie
b. 1957 Jackson, Marlon David
b. 1960 Vance, Courtney B.
b. 1962 Strawberry, Darryl (Eugene)
d. 604 Gregory the Great, Saint
d. 1471? Malory, Thomas, Sir
d. 1507 Borgia, Cesare
d. 1519 Borgia, Lucrezia
d. 1749 Magnasco, Alessandro Lissandrino
d. 1792 Favart, Charles Simon
d. 1845 Lee, Jason
d. 1872 Tseng Kuo-fan
d. 1888 Bergh, Henry
d. 1899 Vogel, Julius
d. 1902 Altgeld, John Peter
d. 1908 Amicis, Edmond de
d. 1914 Westinghouse, George
d. 1915 Witte, Sergey Yulyevich
d. 1924 Chardonnet, Louis Marie Hilaire Bernigaud

d. 1925 Sun Yat-Sen
d. 1926 Scripps, Edward Wyllis
d. 1927 Rothwell, Walter Henry
d. 1928 Yermolova, Maria Nikolayevna
d. 1929 Candler, Asa Griggs
d. 1932 Kreuger, Ivar
d. 1935 Pupin, Michael Idvorsky
d. 1937 Hubay, Jeno
d. 1937 Widor, Charles Marie Jean Albert
d. 1942 Bragg, William Henry, Sir
d. 1943 Vigeland, Gustav
d. 1944 Thomason, John William, Jr.
d. 1947 Churchill, Winston
d. 1950 Mann, Heinrich Ludwig
d. 1951 Bauer, Harold
d. 1955 Parker, Charlie
d. 1956 Bierut, Boleslaw
d. 1957 Hull, Josephine
d. 1963 Oxnam, G(arfield) Bromley
d. 1964 Aqqad, Abbas Mahmud al-
d. 1966 Meriwether, Lee
d. 1966 Wachter, Ed(ward)
d. 1967 Muller-Munk, Peter
d. 1971 Burns, David
d. 1973 Frisch, Frankie
d. 1980 Anson, Jay
d. 1980 Gero, Erno
d. 1981 Barnetson, William Denholm
d. 1983 Aldrich, Ki
d. 1985 Adams, Tom
d. 1985 Ormandy, Eugene
d. 1987 Hayes, Woody
d. 1987 Levinson, Richard Leighton
d. 1988 Holmes, John C.
d. 1989 Evans, Maurice
d. 1989 Gimpel, Jakob
d. 1990 Lehmann, Rosamond Nina
d. 1991 Granit, Ragnar Arthur
d. 1991 Rossi-Lemeni, Nicola
d. 1999 Menuhin, Yehudi
d. 1999 Sayao, Bidu

March 13
b. 1733 Priestley, Joseph
b. 1741 Joseph II
b. 1764 Grey, Charles
b. 1781 Schinkel, Karl Friedrich
b. 1782 Wyss, Johann Rudolf

b. 1798 Fillmore, Abigail (Powers)
b. 1813 Delmonico, Lorenzo
b. 1855 Lowell, Percival
b. 1860 Wolf, Hugo
b. 1862 Crippen, Hawley Harvey
b. 1863 Tokutomi Soho
b. 1864 Jawlensky, Alexej von
b. 1869 Menendez Pidal, Ramon
b. 1870 Glackens, William James
b. 1872 Keeler, Wee Willie
b. 1872 Villard, Oswald (Garrison)
b. 1883 Holland, Clifford Milburn
b. 1884 Walpole, Hugh Seymour, Sir
b. 1886 Baker, Frank
b. 1886 Stevens, Albert William
b. 1886 Untermeyer, Jean Starr
b. 1887 Vandegrift, Alexander Archer
b. 1890 Busch, Fritz
b. 1890 Idris I
b. 1892 Flanner, Janet
b. 1894 Braden, Spruille
b. 1898 Hathaway, Henry
b. 1899 Van Vleck, John Hasbrouck
b. 1900 Seferis, George
b. 1900 Soss, Wilma Porter
b. 1902 Fix, Paul
b. 1908 Annenberg, Walter Hubert
b. 1908 Key, Valdimer Orlando, Jr.
b. 1908 Stewart, Paul
b. 1911 Hubbard, L(afayette) Ron(ald)
b. 1912 Youskevitch, Igor
b. 1913 Casey, William Joseph
b. 1913? Kaye, Sammy
b. 1914 Bottel, Helen Alfea
b. 1914 Haggart, Bob
b. 1914 Mitchell, W(illiam) O(rmond)
b. 1914 Weiskopf, Bob
b. 1916 Boggs, Lindy
b. 1916 Roosevelt, John Aspinal
b. 1918 O'Shea, Tessie
b. 1921 Jaffee, Allan
b. 1922 Byers, Walter
b. 1923 Bolger, William Frederick
b. 1925 Vyvyan, Jennifer Brigit
b. 1926 Reina, Carlos Roberto
b. 1928 Raskin, Ellen
b. 1931 Berkowitz, Joan B.
b. 1931 Elias, Rosalind

d. 1972 Ford, Len
d. 1973 Aiken, Howard Hathaway
d. 1973 Young, Chic
d. 1975 Hayward, Susan
d. 1976 Berkeley, Busby
d. 1976 Dole, Charles Minot
d. 1977 Hamer, Fannie Lou Townsend
d. 1980 Brosio, Manilo Giovanni
d. 1980 Dennison, Robert Lee
d. 1980 Hatta, Mohammad
d. 1980 Lowenstein, Allard Kenneth
d. 1981 Perry, Eleanor Bayer
d. 1986 Cahners, Norman Lee
d. 1989 Abbey, Edward
d. 1989 Bechtel, Stephen Davison
d. 1989 Zita of Bourbon-Parma
d. 1990 Medina, Harold Raymond
d. 1991 Ashman, Howard
d. 1991 Zolotow, Maurice
d. 1995 Blair, Frank
d. 1995 Fowler, William A(lfred)
d. 1996 Berrill, Jack
d. 1997 Fuchs, Joseph (Philip)
d. 1997 Zinnemann, Fred

March 15
b. 1738 Beccaria, Cesare
b. 1767 Jackson, Andrew
b. 1779 Melbourne, William Lamb, Viscount
b. 1794 Diez, Friedrich Christian
b. 1815 Brown, William Wells
b. 1824 Chevalier, Jules
b. 1830 Heyse, Paul Johann Ludwig von
b. 1838 Fletcher, Alice Cunningham
b. 1848 Kendal, Madge, Dame
b. 1848 Reichmann, Theodor
b. 1854 Behring, Emil Adolph von
b. 1856 Hara Takashi
b. 1858 Bailey, Liberty Hyde
b. 1867 Johnson, Lionel Pigot
b. 1871 McIlwain, Charles Howard
b. 1874 Bagley, William Chandler
b. 1874 Ickes, Harold LeClair

b. 1875 Irwin, Wallace (Admah)
b. 1875 Shubert, Lee
b. 1876 Carias Andino, Tiburcio
b. 1879 Catto, Thomas Sivewright, Baron
b. 1883 Bernhard, Lucian
b. 1887 Post, Marjorie Merriweather
b. 1889 Jones, Billy
b. 1891 Ray, Charles
b. 1893 Lyttleton, Oliver
b. 1897 Scholz, Jackson Volney
b. 1900 Freyre, Gilberto (de Mello)
b. 1902 De La Torre(-Bueno), Lillian
b. 1904 Brent, George
b. 1904 O'Malley, J Pat
b. 1905? Hill, Chippie
b. 1905 Ross, Joe E
b. 1905 Webster, Margaret
b. 1907 McPartland, Jimmy
b. 1907 Osborne, John Franklin
b. 1908 Baum, Kurt
b. 1911 Allen, Ivan, Jr.
b. 1912 Hopkins, Lightnin'
b. 1913 Carey, Macdonald
b. 1913 Wasserman, Lew(is Robert)
b. 1913 Wasserman, Lew R
b. 1915 Schoenbach, Sol Israel
b. 1915 Schoenbrun, David
b. 1916 James, Harry
b. 1918 Ellmann, Richard David
b. 1918 Imlach, Punch
b. 1919 Avakian, George
b. 1919 Gregson, John
b. 1920 Thomas, E Donall
b. 1921 Daly, Maureen Patricia
b. 1922 Brinsmead, Hesba Fay
b. 1923 Cony, Edward Roger
b. 1923 Tisch, Laurence Alan
b. 1924 Sabu
b. 1926 Van Brocklin, Norm (an Mack)
b. 1931 Mitchell, James
b. 1932 Bean, Alan L
b. 1933 DeBroca, Philippe Claude Alex
b. 1933 Ginsburg, Ruth Bader
b. 1933 Taylor, Cecil Percival
b. 1935 Hirsch, Judd
b. 1935 Swaggart, Jimmy Lee

b. 1937 Friedman, Stephen
b. 1937? Greenfield, Howard
b. 1939 Chand, Lokendra Bahadur
b. 1940 Lesh, Phil
b. 1941 Love, Mike
b. 1942 Adelman, Sybil
b. 1943 Kanter, Rosabeth Moss
b. 1943 Schuman, Patricia Glass
b. 1944 Stone, Sly
b. 1945 Green, Mark J(oseph)
b. 1946 Bonds, Bobby (Lee)
b. 1947 Cooder, Ry(land Peter)
b. 1947 Pena, Federico F.
b. 1948 Bornstein, Kate
b. 1955 Snider, Dee
b. 1959 Baines, Harold Douglass
b. 1959 Okri, Ben
b. 1961 Cummings, Terry
b. 1961 Fabio
b. 1962 D'Arby, Terence Trent
b. 1964 Rockwell
d. 44BC Caesar, Julius
d. 220 Ts'ao Ts'ao
d. 1665 Endecott, John
d. 1673 Rosa, Salvator
d. 1842 Cherubini, Luigi Carlo Zenobio Salvadore Maria
d. 1889 Bissell, Melville Reuben
d. 1897 Sylvester, James Joseph
d. 1898 Bessemer, Henry, Sir
d. 1905 Guggenheim, Meyer
d. 1915 Crane, Walter
d. 1918 Stillman, James
d. 1925 Wassermann, August von
d. 1934 Black, Davidson
d. 1937 Lovecraft, H(oward) P(hillips)
d. 1941 Jawlensky, Alexej von
d. 1942 Field, Rachel Lyman
d. 1959 Hines, Duncan
d. 1959 Young, Lester Willis
d. 1962 Compton, Arthur Holly
d. 1965 Phillips, Harry Irving
d. 1966 Saperstein, Abe
d. 1968 Castelnuovo-Tedesco, Mario
d. 1975 Graham, Stephen
d. 1975 Onassis, Aristotle Socrates
d. 1975 Sheean, (James) Vincent

d. 1976 Mielziner, Jo
d. 1979 Britt, Steuart Henderson
d. 1981 Clair, Rene
d. 1982 Rickword, Edgell
d. 1983 Sert, Jose Luis
d. 1983 West, Rebecca, Dame
d. 1987 Cole, Sterling W(illiam)
d. 1987 Dutton, Red
d. 1988 Porter, William James
d. 1990 Harmon, Tom
d. 1991 Sherman, George
d. 1992 Deutsch, Helen
d. 1994 Zetterling, Mai (Elisabeth)
d. 1995 Chadwick, Florence (May)
d. 1996 Courlander, Harold
d. 1996 Gilpatric, Roswell L(eavitt)
d. 1997 Vasarely, Victor
d. 1998 Spock, Benjamin (McLane)
d. 1999 Callahan, Harry (Morey)
d. 2000 Kirby, Durward

March 16
b. 1581 Hooft, Pieter Corneliszoon
b. 1739 Clymer, George
b. 1751 Madison, James
b. 1771 Gros, Antoine Jean
b. 1774 Flinders, Matthew
b. 1787 Ohm, Georg Simon
b. 1789 Chesney, Francis Rawdon
b. 1820 Tamberlik, Enrico
b. 1822 Bonheur, Rosa
b. 1839 Sully Prudhomme
b. 1853 Kayser, Heinrich Gustav Johannes
b. 1859 Popov, Aleksandr Stepanovich
b. 1866 Chambers, Edmund Kerchever, Sir
b. 1874 Matthes, Francois-Emile
b. 1875 MacKaye, Percy Wallace
b. 1877 Pahlevi, Riza
b. 1878 Walthall, Henry B
b. 1879 Sykes, Mark, Sir
b. 1880 Stout, William Bushnell
b. 1885 Holloway, Emory
b. 1889 Janis, Elsie
b. 1892 Petrillo, James Caesar

b. 1892 Vallejo, Cesar Abraham
b. 1897 Nagel, Conrad
b. 1898 Messali Hadj
b. 1899 Millis, Walter
b. 1900 Burns, Eveline Mabel
b. 1903 Mansfield, Mike
b. 1904 Myer, Buddy
b. 1905 Woltman, Frederick Enos
b. 1906 Waner, Lloyd James
b. 1906 Youngman, Henny
b. 1908 Rossen, Robert
b. 1909 Dean, Patrick (Henry), Sir
b. 1911 Bedford, Sybille
b. 1911 La Tour du Pin, Patrice de
b. 1911 Mengele, Josef
b. 1912 Nixon, Patricia
b. 1912 Rosenthal, Jean E
b. 1914 Mayer, Oscar Gottfried, II
b. 1914 Westmoreland, William Childs
b. 1919 Lang, Eugene M
b. 1920 Addison, John
b. 1920 McKern, Leo
b. 1921 Truitt, Anne
b. 1924 Ludwig, Christa
b. 1926 Goodell, Charles Ellsworth
b. 1926 Lewis, Jerry
b. 1927 Braff, Ruby
b. 1927 Courtney, Clint(on Dawson)
b. 1927 Komarov, Vladimir Mikhaylovich
b. 1927 Moynihan, Daniel Patrick
b. 1929 Foley, Tom
b. 1930 Flanagan, Tommy (Lee)
b. 1932 Cunningham, R Walter
b. 1933 Weill, Sanford I.
b. 1934 Norrington, Roger Arthur Carver
b. 1935 Berganza, Teresa
b. 1935? Park, Tongsun
b. 1937 Armstrong, William L
b. 1939 Sobieski, Carol
b. 1941 Bertolucci, Bernardo
b. 1942 Crozier, Roger Allan
b. 1944 Hayden, Mike
b. 1946 Knight, J. Z.
b. 1947 Roche, Joyce
b. 1949 Estrada, Erik
b. 1951 Nelligan, Kate
b. 1952 Ford, Jack
b. 1954 Stacy, Hollis
b. 1954 Wilson, Nancy
b. 1955 Huppert, Isabelle

b. 1957 Samuelson, Joan
d. 37 Tiberius Julius Caesar Augustus
d. 1608 Sonjo
d. 1649 Brebeuf, Jean de
d. 1680 LaRochefoucauld, Francois, Duc de
d. 1726 Vanbrugh, John, Sir
d. 1736 Pergolesi, Giovanni Battista
d. 1838 Bowditch, Nathaniel
d. 1864 Surtees, Robert Smith
d. 1871 Barboncito
d. 1888 Carnot, Hippolyte
d. 1898 Beardsley, Aubrey Vincent
d. 1899 Medill, Joseph
d. 1903 Bean, Roy
d. 1909 Timken, Henry
d. 1914 Gobat, Charles Albert
d. 1914 Murray, John, Sir
d. 1917 Studebaker, John Mohler
d. 1930 Primo de Rivera (y Orbaneja), Miguel
d. 1932 Monro, Harold Edward
d. 1935 MacLeod, John James Rickard
d. 1937 Chamberlain, Austen, Sir
d. 1937 Hobson, Richmond Pearson
d. 1940 Barton, George
d. 1940 Lagerlof, Selma Ottiliana Lovisa
d. 1942 Zemlinsky, Alexander von
d. 1957 Brancusi, Constantin
d. 1963 Beveridge, William Henry, Lord
d. 1969 Brown, John Mason
d. 1970 Adamov, Arthur
d. 1970 Terrell, Tammi
d. 1971 Daniels, Bebe
d. 1971 Dewey, Thomas Edmund
d. 1972 Grant, Jane
d. 1972 Traynor, Pie
d. 1974 Gerber, Daniel Frank
d. 1975 Mesta, Perle Skirvin
d. 1975 Walker, T-Bone
d. 1977 Jumblatt, Kamal Fouad
d. 1979 Massine, Leonide Fedorovich
d. 1979 Monnet, Jean Omer Marie Gabriel
d. 1979 Pious, Minerva
d. 1981 Blumenthal, Monica David

d. 1983 Godfrey, Arthur Michael
d. 1985 Sessions, Roger Huntington
d. 1985 Shore, Eddie
d. 1985 Stone, Louis
d. 1993 Correia, Natalia
d. 1995 Hackett, Albert
d. 1998 Barton, Derek H(arold) R(ichard), Sir
d. 2000 Abram, Morris Berthold

March 17
b. 1473 James IV
b. 1524 Landa, Diego de
b. 1685 Nattier, Jean Marc
b. 1686 Oudry, Jean-Baptiste
b. 1754 Roland (de La Platiere), Jeanne-Marie
b. 1764 Pinkney, William
b. 1777 Taney, Roger Brooke
b. 1780 Chalmers, Thomas
b. 1781 Elliott, Ebenezer
b. 1787 Kean, Edmund
b. 1804 Bridger, James
b. 1805 Garcia, Manuel Patricio Rodriguez
b. 1811 Gutzkow, Karl Ferdinand
b. 1820 Ingelow, Jean
b. 1832 Conway, Moncure Daniel
b. 1834 Daimler, Gottlieb (Wilhelm)
b. 1843 Lawton, Henry Ware
b. 1846 Greenaway, Kate
b. 1848 Morris, Clara
b. 1849 Brush, Charles Francis
b. 1873 Bondfield, Margaret Grace
b. 1874 Wise, Stephen Samuel
b. 1877 Gardner, George
b. 1879 Grauman, Sid(ney Patrick)
b. 1881 Hess, Walter Rudolf
b. 1884 Buck, Frank
b. 1885 Chaplin, Sydney Dryden
b. 1890 Clarke, Harry
b. 1893 Garrett, Eileen Jeanette Lyttle
b. 1894 Green, Paul Eliot
b. 1896 Lynd, Helen Merrell
b. 1899 Summerfield, Arthur Ellsworth
b. 1900 Howard, Shemp
b. 1901 Catledge, Turner

b. 1901 Newman, Alfred
b. 1902 Carusi, Ugo
b. 1902 Jones, Bobby
b. 1903 Britain, Radie
b. 1903 Childs, Marquis William
b. 1904 Gross, Chaim
b. 1904 Hamilton, Patrick
b. 1906 O'Shea, Michael
b. 1907 Miki Takeo
b. 1907 Pastore, John Orlando
b. 1910 Rustin, Bayard
b. 1910 Werblin, Sonny
b. 1911 Gilbreth, Frank Bunker, Jr.
b. 1912 Stydahar, Joe
b. 1913 Karpin, Fred Leon
b. 1914 Baugh, Sammy
b. 1915 Arbib, Robert Simeon, Jr.
b. 1915 McGee, Gale William
b. 1917 Brisson, Frederick
b. 1918 Lubalin, Herbert Frederick
b. 1918 McCambridge, Mercedes
b. 1919 Cole, Nat King
b. 1919 Reiser, Pete
b. 1920 Rahman, Mujibur, Sheik
b. 1925 Addabbo, Joseph Patrick
b. 1925 Rees, Ennis (Samuel, Jr.)
b. 1927 Newell, Allen
b. 1927 Suazo Cordova, Roberto
b. 1929 Howe, Florence Rosenfeld
b. 1930 Allen, Betty (Lou)
b. 1930 Horn, Paul Joseph
b. 1930 Irwin, James Benson
b. 1933 Evers-Williams, Myrlie
b. 1933 Janifer, Laurence M(ark)
b. 1933 Lively, Penelope
b. 1933 Van Vooren, Monique
b. 1937 Smith, Lee
b. 1938 Nureyev, Rudolf (Hametovich)
b. 1940 White, Mark Wells, Jr.
b. 1942 Gacy, John Wayne, Jr.
b. 1943 Muluzi, Bakili
b. 1944 Gaston, Cito
b. 1944 Sebastian, John
b. 1948 Gibson, Bill
b. 1948 Stallings, George Augustus, Jr.
b. 1949 Duffy, Patrick
b. 1951 Russell, Kurt (Von Vogel)

b. 1954 Down, Lesley-
Anne
b. 1954 Stocker, Wally
b. 1955 Clark, Patrick
b. 1955 McKinney,
Cynthia A(nn)
b. 1959 Ainge, Danny
b. 1964 Lowe, Rob(ert
Hepler)
d. 180 Marcus Aurelius
Antoninus
d. 1406 Ibn Khaldun
d. 1584 Ivan IV
d. 1715 Burnet, Gilbert
d. 1781 Ewald,
Johannes
d. 1782 Bernoulli,
Daniel
d. 1846 Bessel,
Friedrich Wilhelm
d. 1847 Gerard, Jean
Ignace Isidore
d. 1847 Grandville
d. 1853 Doppler,
Christian Johann
d. 1862 Halevy, Jacques
Francois Fromental
Elie
d. 1871 Chambers,
Robert
d. 1885 Warner, Susan
Bogert
d. 1893 Ferry, Jules
Francois Camille
d. 1898 Bruce, Blanche
Kelso
d. 1912 Melville,
George Wallace
d. 1917 Brentano, Franz
Clemens
d. 1919 Cox, Kenyon
d. 1940 Anderson,
George Everett
d. 1941 Titulescu,
Nicolae
d. 1952 Wenrich, Percy
d. 1956 Allen, Fred
d. 1956 Joliot-Curie,
Irene
d. 1957 Magsaysay,
Ramon
d. 1959 Ehmke, Howard
Jonathan
d. 1962 Busoni,
Rafaello
d. 1965 Reynolds,
Quentin James
d. 1965 Stagg, Amos
Alonzo
d. 1968 Millis, Walter
d. 1969 Magnin, Grover
Arnold
d. 1970 Crommelynck,
Fernand
d. 1974 Kahn, Louis
I(sadore)
d. 1976 Visconti,
Luchino
d. 1979 Lauri-Volpi,
Giacoma
d. 1980 Bealer, Alex
W(inkler III)
d. 1981 Dean, Daffy
d. 1981 Gray, Nicholas
Stuart

d. 1983 Hartline,
Haldan Keffer
d. 1983 Tromp, Solco
Walle
d. 1986 Glubb, John
Bagot, Sir
d. 1987 Trafficante,
Santo, Jr.
d. 1988 Memminger,
Christopher Gustavus
d. 1989 Kerby, William
Frederick
d. 1990 Capucine
d. 1993 Hayes, Helen
d. 1993 Jacobs,
Raymond
d. 1995 Kray, Ronnie
d. 1996 Clement, Rene
d. 1998 Barker, Cliff

March 18
b. 1578 Elsheimer,
Adam
b. 1782 Calhoun, John
Caldwell
b. 1798 Lieber, Franz
b. 1798 Wheelwright,
William
b. 1800 Smithson,
Harriet Constance
b. 1813 Hebbel,
Friedrich
b. 1813 Lippincott,
Joshua Ballinger
b. 1823 Seiss, Joseph
Augustus
b. 1830 Fustel de
Coulanges, Numa
Denis
b. 1837 Cleveland,
Grover
b. 1838 Cremer,
William Randal, Sir
b. 1842 Mallarme,
Stephane
b. 1844 Rimsky-
Korsakov, Nikolai
Andreevich
b. 1851 Coghlan, Rose
b. 1858 Diesel, Rudolf
Christian Karl
b. 1860 Bryan, William
Jennings
b. 1869 Chamberlain,
Neville
b. 1875 Branch, Anna
Hempstead
b. 1877 Cayce, Edgar
b. 1881 Seibert, Oliver
L
b. 1882 Malipiero, Gian
Francesco
b. 1886 Koffka, Kurt
b. 1887 Horton, Edward
Everett
b. 1891 Banning,
Margaret Culkin
b. 1892 Cochrane,
Edward Lull
b. 1892 Coffin, Robert
Peter Tristram
b. 1893 Owen, Wilfred
b. 1897 Jenkins, Ray
Howard
b. 1900 Delaney, Jack
b. 1901 Hall, Manly
Palmer

b. 1901 Johnson,
William Henry
b. 1904 Conze, Edward
J D
b. 1905 Donat, Robert
b. 1905 Parnis, Mollie
b. 1906 Chiang Ching-
Kuo
b. 1910 Tarnower,
Herman
b. 1911 Burnette,
Smiley
b. 1912 Lawrence,
Robert
b. 1913 Amerasinghe,
Hamilton Shirley
b. 1913 Clement, Rene
b. 1913 Crawford,
William Hulfish
b. 1915 Condon,
Richard (Thomas)
b. 1918 Pett, Saul
b. 1922 Bahr, Egon
b. 1922 Lipset, Seymour
Martin
b. 1922 Shuttlesworth,
Fred Lee
b. 1923 Granatelli,
Andy
b. 1926 Graves, Peter
b. 1927 Kander, John
b. 1927 Katz, Lillian
b. 1927 Plimpton,
George Ames
b. 1928 Ramos, Fidel
V(aldez)
b. 1930 Maida, Adam
(Joseph)
b. 1932 Updike, John
(Hoyer)
b. 1933 Blackwell,
Unita
b. 1935 Welsing,
Frances Cress
b. 1936 De Klerk,
F(rederik) W(illem)
b. 1938 McDonnell,
John Finney
b. 1938 Pride, Charley
b. 1939 Burrell, Thomas
Jason
b. 1940 Medoff, Mark
Howard
b. 1941 Pickett, Wilson
b. 1944 Dobson, Kevin
b. 1946 Reagan,
Michael Edward
b. 1950 Dourif, Brad
b. 1952 Webster, Mike
b. 1956 Stenmark,
Ingemar
b. 1959 Cara, Irene
(Escalera)
b. 1960 Carbonneau,
Guy
b. 1961 Warner, Curt
b. 1962 McMurtry,
James Lawrence
b. 1963 Williams,
Vanessa
b. 1964 Blair, Bonnie
Kathleen
b. 1970 Latifah, Queen
d. 1455 Angelico, Fra
d. 1740 Diver, Jenny
d. 1745 Walpole, Robert

d. 1768 Sterne,
Laurence
d. 1871 De Morgan,
Augustus
d. 1877 Belcher,
Edward, Sir
d. 1882 Earp, Morgan
d. 1886 Zunz, Leopold
d. 1892 Van Depoele,
Charles Joseph
d. 1898 Gage, Matilda
Joslyn
d. 1899 Marsh, Othniel
Charles
d. 1907 Berthelot,
Marcellin
d. 1931 Johnson, Ban
d. 1932 Olcott,
Chauncey
d. 1933 Abruzzi, Luigi
Amedeo
d. 1936 Venizelos,
Eleutherios Kyriakos
d. 1945 Kalish, Max
d. 1947 Durant, William
Crapo
d. 1956 Bromfield,
Louis Brucker
d. 1956 Decker, Alonzo
G
d. 1962 Viereck, George
Sylvester
d. 1964 O'Callahan,
Joseph Timothy
d. 1964 Wiener, Norbert
d. 1965 Farouk I
d. 1965 Lubin,
Germaine
d. 1968 Kurnitz, Harry
d. 1971 Hayward,
Leland
d. 1973 Benton,
William
d. 1973 Melchior,
Lauritz
d. 1978 Wood, Peggy
d. 1980 Dragonette,
Jessica
d. 1980 Fromm, Erich
d. 1981 Dominick, Peter
Hoyt
d. 1982 Chuikov, Vasili
Ivanovitch
d. 1983 Marshall,
Catherine
d. 1983 Umberto II
d. 1984 Lau, Charlie
d. 1984 Mitchell,
Clarence M
d. 1986 Malamud,
Bernard
d. 1987 Baird, Bil
d. 1988 Butterfield,
Billy
d. 1989 Jeffreys, Harold
d. 1990 Harris, Robin
d. 1991 Banky, Vilma
d. 1991 Taft, Henry
Waters, II
d. 1991 Voelker, John
Donaldson
d. 1996 Elytis,
Odysseus
d. 1996 Jorda, Enrique

March 19
b. 1543 Anchieta, Jose de
b. 1593 La Tour, Georges Dumesnil de
b. 1698 Calas, Jean
b. 1725 Howe, Richard
b. 1748 Hicks, Elias
b. 1762 Cobbett, William
b. 1813 Livingstone, David
b. 1821 Burton, Richard Francis, Sir
b. 1824 Allingham, William
b. 1827 Ridge, John Rollin
b. 1836 Wallace, Henry
b. 1847 Ryder, Albert Pinkham
b. 1848 Earp, Wyatt Berry Stapp
b. 1849 Tirpitz, Alfred von
b. 1858 K'ang Yu-wei
b. 1864 Russell, Charles Marion
b. 1865 Wheeler, William Morton
b. 1871 McGinnity, Joe
b. 1871 Taylor, J(ohn) H(enry)
b. 1872 Diaghilev, Sergei (Pavlovich)
b. 1873 Reger, Max
b. 1879 Raskob, John J
b. 1881 Rogers, Edith
b. 1882 Lachaise, Gaston
b. 1883 Graham, Evarts Ambrose
b. 1883 Haworth, Walter Norman, Sir
b. 1883 Stilwell, Joseph Warren
b. 1886 Bellanca, Giuseppe Mario
b. 1888 Albers, Josef
b. 1891 Crawford, Frederick C(oolidge)
b. 1891 Guptill, Arthur Leighton
b. 1891 Monaghan, (James) Jay, (IV)
b. 1891 Warren, Earl
b. 1892 Van Fleet, James Alward
b. 1893 Velasco Ibarra, Jose Maria
b. 1894 Mabley, Moms
b. 1894 Wambsganss, Bill
b. 1900 Joliot(-Curie), (Jean) Frederic
b. 1900 Muccio, John Joseph
b. 1901 Mielziner, Jo
b. 1903 Ehrlich, Bettina Bauer
b. 1904 Sirica, John Joseph
b. 1905 Speer, Albert
b. 1906 Eichmann, Adolf
b. 1907 Smith, Kent

b. 1909 Hayward, Louis
b. 1911 Colonius, Lillian
b. 1911 Witte, Erich
b. 1912 Galland, Adolf
b. 1912 Wheeler, Hugh Callingham
b. 1914 Berwanger, J Jay
b. 1914 Morison, Patricia
b. 1914 Siles Zuazo, Hernan
b. 1916 Wallace, Irving
b. 1917 Lipatti, Dinu
b. 1918 Jennings, Paul Joseph
b. 1919 Abrahams, Peter Henry
b. 1919 Tristano, Leonard Joseph
b. 1920? Andrews, Tige
b. 1921 Turner, Donald F(rank)
b. 1923 Morgentaler, Henry
b. 1925 Scowcroft, Brent
b. 1927 Ashburn, Richie
b. 1928 Kung, Hans
b. 1928 McGoohan, Patrick (Joseph)
b. 1929 Muczynski, Robert
b. 1930 Coleman, Ornette
b. 1932 Brewer, Gay, Jr.
b. 1933 Roth, Philip (Milton)
b. 1935 Newman, Phyllis
b. 1936 Andress, Ursula
b. 1937 Henry, Clarence
b. 1937 Krenz, Egon
b. 1938 Kapp, Joe
b. 1943 Wertheimer, Linda (Cozby)
b. 1944 Johnson, Lynda Bird
b. 1944? Sirhan, Sirhan Bishara
b. 1946 Pointer, Ruth
b. 1947 Close, Glenn
b. 1948 Bass, Robert M(use)
b. 1952 Weinstein, Harvey
b. 1953 Schenkkan, Robert
b. 1955 Longmuir, Derek
b. 1955 Willis, Bruce
b. 1967 Konstantinov, Vladimir
b. 1969 Lopez, Josefina Maria
d. 1637 Pazmany, Peter
d. 1687 La Salle, Rene Robert Cavelier de
d. 1876 Chesney, Charles Cornwallis
d. 1879 Clairmont, Claire
d. 1907 Aldrich, Thomas Bailey

d. 1914 Bandelier, Adolph Francis Alphonse
d. 1928 Bayes, Nora
d. 1928 Ferrier, David, Sir
d. 1930 Balfour, Arthur James
d. 1942 Merriam, Clinton Hart
d. 1943 Ball, Frank
d. 1950 Burroughs, Edgar Rice
d. 1950 Haworth, Walter Norman, Sir
d. 1953 Bordoni, Irene
d. 1953 McFee, Henry Lee
d. 1957 Rascoe, Burton
d. 1965 Gheorghiu-Dej, Gheorghe
d. 1965 Lloyd, John Henry
d. 1973 Adams, Weston W, Sir
d. 1974 Klein, Anne
d. 1976 Cloete, Stuart
d. 1978 Baldwin, Faith
d. 1981 Cadieux, Marcel (Joseph David Romeo)
d. 1981 Lane, Frank C
d. 1986 Atwater, Edith
d. 1987 Broglie, Louis Prince De
d. 1987 Oboler, Arch
d. 1991 Mennen, Frederick
d. 1993? Adzhubei, Aleksei I(vanovich)
d. 1993 Boulding, Kenneth E(wart)
d. 1993 McWilliams, Alden S
d. 1994 Wilson, Edward Foss
d. 1996 Sullivan, Walter
d. 1997 deKooning, Willem
d. 1998 Ali, Ahmed
d. 2000 Placzek, Adolf K(urt)

March 20
b. 43BC Ovid
b. 1741 Houdon, Jean Antoine
b. 1770 Holderlin, Friedrich
b. 1796 Wakefield, Edward Gibbon
b. 1804 Dow, Neal
b. 1811 Bingham, George Caleb
b. 1811 Bonaparte, Francois Charles Joseph
b. 1823 Judson, Edward Zane Carroll
b. 1828 Ibsen, Henrik Johan
b. 1831 Burton, Isabel Arundel
b. 1833 Home, Daniel Douglas
b. 1834 Eliot, Charles William

b. 1834 Orton, Arthur
b. 1844 Dollar, Robert
b. 1856 Taylor, Frederick Winslow
b. 1863 Locke, William John
b. 1867 Myers, Jerome
b. 1882 Coty, Rene (Jules Gustave)
b. 1883 Funk, Wilfred John
b. 1883 Ridder, Bernard Herman
b. 1888 Stevenson, Coke Robert
b. 1890 Gigli, Beniamino
b. 1890 Melchior, Lauritz
b. 1891 Goulding, Edmund
b. 1892 Dixon, Mort
b. 1897 Sheed, Frank
b. 1898 Pales Matos, Luis
b. 1900 Cordiner, Ralph Jarron
b. 1901 Groves, Wallace
b. 1903 Buchanan, Edgar
b. 1904 Elsasser, Walter M, Dr.
b. 1904 Skinner, B(urrhus) F(rederic)
b. 1906 Beame, Abraham David
b. 1906 Nelson, Ozzie
b. 1907 Arnall, Ellis (Gibbs)
b. 1907 MacLennan, Hugh
b. 1908 Redgrave, Michael Scudamore, Sir
b. 1908 Stanton, Frank Nicholas
b. 1909 Forbes, Kathryn
b. 1909 Knipling, Edward Fred
b. 1911 Garcia Robles, Alfonso
b. 1914 Corey, Wendell
b. 1915 Kirchschlager, Rudolf
b. 1915 Richter, Sviatoslav Theofilovich
b. 1916 Fingesten, Peter
b. 1918 Barry, Jack
b. 1918 McPartland, Margaret Marian
b. 1920 Cleaver, William Joseph
b. 1920 Harriman, Pamela
b. 1920 Hershey, Lenore
b. 1921 M'Bow, Mahtar-Amadou
b. 1922 Goulding, Ray(mond Walter)
b. 1922 Reiner, Carl
b. 1922 Young, Margaret Ann Buckner

b. 1925 Ehrlichman, John D(aniel)
b. 1926 Rosen, Harold A.
b. 1928 Rogers, Fred McFeely
b. 1931 Linden, Hal
b. 1934 Brown, Willie
b. 1934 Malouf, David
b. 1936 Meader, Vaughn
b. 1936 Owen, Tobias Chant
b. 1936 Perry, Lee
b. 1937 Reed, Jerry
b. 1939 Mulroney, Brian
b. 1940 Mark, Mary Ellen
b. 1942 Schmidt, Benno C(harles), Jr.
b. 1943 Witt, Paul Junger
b. 1944 Neher, Erwin
b. 1945 Riley, Pat(rick James)
b. 1947 Boswell, John (Eastburn)
b. 1948 Orr, Bobby
b. 1949 Brown, Zora Kramer
b. 1950 Hurt, William
b. 1951 Miller, Nicole (Jacqueline)
b. 1951 Palmer, Carl
b. 1954 Simmer, Charlie
b. 1957 Lee, Spike
b. 1958 Hunter, Holly
b. 1961 Baker, Kathy
b. 1961 Gable, John Clark
b. 1961 Harrison, Kathryn
d. 1413 Henry IV
d. 1546 Elyot, Thomas, Sir
d. 1727 Newton, Isaac, Sir
d. 1730 Lecouvreur, Adrienne
d. 1751 Frederick Louis
d. 1799 Bard, John
d. 1809 Bateman, Mary
d. 1872 Wentworth, William Charles
d. 1889 Ritschl, Albrecht Benjamin
d. 1894 Kossuth, Lajos
d. 1903 Leland, Charles Godfrey
d. 1915 Adams, Charles Francis, Jr.
d. 1925 Curzon of Kedleston, George Nathaniel Curzon, Marquis
d. 1929 Foch, Ferdinand
d. 1931 Comstock, John Henry
d. 1936 Cunninghame-Graham, Robert Bontine
d. 1937 Vardon, Harry
d. 1942 Taylor, Charles Alonzo

d. 1943 Lowden, Frank O(rren)
d. 1945 Douglas, Alfred Bruce, Lord
d. 1946 Richardson, Henry Handel
d. 1947 Goldschmidt, Victor Moritz
d. 1956 Stout, William Bushnell
d. 1957 Chase, Edna Woolman
d. 1964 Behan, Brendan (Francis)
d. 1967 Morgan, Frederick, Sir
d. 1970 Hussey, Christopher Edward Clive
d. 1972 Maxwell, Marilyn
d. 1974 Clarke, Austin
d. 1974 Huntley, Chet
d. 1975 Schocken, Theodore
d. 1978 Brugnon, Jacques
d. 1979 Charlot, Jean Eugenie
d. 1981 Jaffee, Irving
d. 1982 Copeland, Jo
d. 1984 Coveleski, Stanley Anthony
d. 1985 Knight, George Wilson
d. 1988 Evans, Gil
d. 1992 Delerue, Georges
d. 1993 Kusch, P(olycarp)
d. 1994 Grizzard, Lewis M., Jr.
d. 1995 Kingsley, Sidney
d. 1997 Pritchett, V(ictor) S(awdon), Sir
d. 1997 Zale, Tony

March 21
b. 1274 Robert I
b. 1295? Suso, Heinrich
b. 1474? Angela Merici, Saint
b. 1685 Bach, Johann Sebastian
b. 1713 Lewis, Francis
b. 1736 Ledoux, Claude Nicolas
b. 1763 Richter, Jean Paul F
b. 1763 Richter, Johann Paul Friedrich
b. 1768 Fourier, Jean Baptiste Joseph
b. 1771 Dibdin, Thomas Pitt
b. 1806 Juarez, Benito Pablo
b. 1821 Leslie, Frank
b. 1831 Beale, Dorothea
b. 1839 Mussorgsky, Modest Petrovich
b. 1842 Rosa, Carl
b. 1856 Flipper, Henry Ossian
b. 1859 Savage, Henry Wilson

b. 1865 Fisher, Herbert Albert Laurens
b. 1866 Maury, Antonia Caetana De Paiua Pereira
b. 1867 Ziegfeld, Flo(renz)
b. 1869 Kahn, Albert
b. 1878 Amato, Pasquale
b. 1880 Hofmann, Hans
b. 1882 Anderson, Gilbert M
b. 1884 Birkhoff, George David
b. 1885 Gilmour, Billy
b. 1885 Pulitzer, Joseph, II
b. 1887 Mendelsohn, Eric
b. 1887 Van Dyke, W(oodbridge) S(trong)
b. 1888 Ball, Edward
b. 1898 Wyman, Willard Gordon
b. 1900 Leontovich, Eugenie
b. 1901 Weintal, Edward
b. 1902 House, Son
b. 1903 Hellinger, Mark
b. 1905 Konetzni, Hilde
b. 1905 McGinley, Phyllis
b. 1906 Deutsch, Helen
b. 1906 Rockefeller, John D(avison), III
b. 1907 Sweet, John Howard
b. 1910 Gallo, Julio
b. 1911 Hawkins, Walter Lincoln
b. 1912 Bull, Peter
b. 1914 Tortelier, Paul
b. 1916 Duke, Robin (Anthony Hare)
b. 1917 Barnetson, William Denholm
b. 1917 Yadin, Yigael
b. 1918 Lucey, Patrick Joseph
b. 1922 Casewit, Curtis
b. 1922 Meyer, Russ
b. 1922 Nederlander, James Morton
b. 1923 Lindsey, Mort
b. 1925 Brook, Peter Stephen Paul
b. 1925 Jones, Madison Percy, Jr.
b. 1927 Genscher, Hans-Dietrich
b. 1928 Kinnear, James Wesley
b. 1928 Thapa, Surya Bahadur
b. 1929 Andrews, Bert
b. 1929 Bergman, Jules Verne
b. 1929 Coco, James Emil
b. 1930 Fraser, John Malcolm
b. 1932 Gilbert, Walter

b. 1933 Heseltine, Michael Ray Dibdin
b. 1934 Freeman, Al(bert Cornelius), Jr.
b. 1934 Mehta, Ved (Parkash)
b. 1935 Kunzel, Erich
b. 1936 Broadbent, Ed
b. 1937 Flores, Tom
b. 1939 Davis, Tommy, Jr.
b. 1939 Spann, Otis
b. 1939 Widdoes, Kathleen Effie
b. 1942 Dorleac, Francoise
b. 1944 Sanguillen, Manny
b. 1946 Dalton, Timothy
b. 1947 Kylian, Jiri
b. 1953 Johnson, Robert
b. 1958 Oldman, Gary
b. 1960 Senna, Ayrton
b. 1962 Broderick, Matthew
d. 547 Benedict, Saint
d. 1556 Cranmer, Thomas
d. 1656 Ussher, James
d. 1729 Law, John
d. 1801 Abercromby, Ralph, Sir
d. 1805 Greuze, Jean-Baptiste
d. 1830 Wyss, Johann Rudolf
d. 1843 Southey, Robert
d. 1863 Sumner, Edwin V
d. 1864 Flandrin, Hippolyte Jean
d. 1884 Baez, Buenaventura
d. 1884 Fuller, George
d. 1890 Crook, George
d. 1896 Burton, Isabel Arundel
d. 1902 Nachbaur, Franz
d. 1904 Grace, William Russell
d. 1910 Nadar
d. 1915 Taylor, Frederick Winslow
d. 1916 Younger, Cole
d. 1928 Esposito, Joseph
d. 1933 Zangara, Joseph
d. 1934 Schreker, Franz
d. 1934 Tashman, Lilyan
d. 1936 Glazunov, Alexander Constantinovich
d. 1936 McCarthy, Justin Huntly
d. 1938 Clark, John Bates
d. 1942 Woodsworth, James Shaver
d. 1949 McClure, Samuel Sidney
d. 1955 White, Walter Francis

d. 1961 Arnold, Leslie
Philip
d. 1975 Hawtrey, Ralph
George, Sir
d. 1975 Medwick, Joe
d. 1976 Fulks, Joe
d. 1976 Sabich, Spider
d. 1978 O'Dalaigh,
Cearbhall
d. 1981 Baugh, Albert
Croll
d. 1981 Trifonov, Yuri
Valentinovich
d. 1984 Mays, Benjamin
E(lijah)
d. 1985 DeRivera, Jose
Ruiz
d. 1985 Redgrave,
Michael Scudamore,
Sir
d. 1987 Martin, Dean
Paul
d. 1987 Preston, Robert
d. 1988 Roush, Edd J
d. 1988 Steptoe, Patrick
Christopher
d. 1991 Fender, Leo
d. 1992 Ireland, John
d. 1994 Rambo, Dack
d. 1997 Awdry,
W(ilbert Vere)
d. 1998 Ulanova, Galina
d. 1999 Reedy, George
E(dward)

March 22
b. 1459 Maximilian I
b. 1599 Van Dyck,
Anthony, Sir
b. 1728 Mengs, Anton
Raphael
b. 1791 William, I
b. 1799 Argelander,
Friedrich Wilhelm
August
b. 1800 Pusey, Edward
Bouverie
b. 1813 Crawford,
Thomas
b. 1816 Kensett, John
Frederick
b. 1817 Bragg, Braxton
b. 1828 Kimball,
William Wallace
b. 1845 Tabb, John
Banister
b. 1846 Caldecott,
Randolph
b. 1863 Pattee, Fred
Lewis
b. 1868 Millikan,
Robert Andrews
b. 1869 Aguinaldo,
Emilio
b. 1879 Teschner,
Richard
b. 1880 Cooper, Kent
b. 1881 Martin du Gard,
Roger
b. 1884 Vandenberg,
Arthur Hendrick
b. 1887 Lualdi, Adriano
b. 1891 Gibbons, Tom
b. 1891 List, Emanuel
b. 1891 Marx, Chico
b. 1896 Cone, Russell
Glenn

b. 1896 Schildkraut,
Joseph
b. 1899 Page, Ruth
b. 1900 Robinson,
Claude Everett
b. 1902 Berlin, Ellin
(Mackay)
b. 1903 Baldwin,
Hanson Weightman
b. 1904 Anderson, Jack
Zuinglius
b. 1906 Laeri, J(ohn)
Howard
b. 1907 Gavin, James
Maurice
b. 1908 L'Amour, Louis
Dearborn
b. 1908 Stans, Maurice
H(ubert)
b. 1909 Roy, Gabrielle
b. 1910 Monsarrat,
Nicholas John Turney
b. 1911 Barron, Blue
b. 1912 Brambell,
Wilfrid
b. 1912 Martin, Agnes
b. 1912 Modl, Martha
b. 1913 Dederich,
Charles (Edwin)
b. 1913 Malden, Karl
b. 1913 McCall,
Thomas Lawson
b. 1914 Miller, William
E
b. 1914 Stokes, Donald
Gresham Stokes,
Baron
b. 1915 Williams, Roy
Lee
b. 1916 Kline, Nathan
Schellenberg
b. 1917 Grey, Virginia
b. 1917 Shaplen, Robert
Modell
b. 1918 Jagan, Cheddi
(Berret)
b. 1920 Klemperer,
Werner
b. 1920 Martin, Ross
b. 1921 Carter, Dorothy
Sharp
b. 1921 Gilligan, John
Joyce
b. 1921 Masina,
Giulietta
b. 1922 Stern, Stewart
b. 1923 Marceau,
Marcel
b. 1924 Fussell, Paul
b. 1924 Neuharth, Allen
Harold
b. 1928 Hammer,
Richard
b. 1928 Hirsch, E(ric)
D(onald), Jr.
b. 1928 Macauley, Ed
b. 1930 Bok, Derek
Curtis
b. 1930 Pindling,
Lynden Oscar
b. 1930 Robertson, Pat
b. 1930 Sondheim,
Stephen (Joshua)
b. 1931 Richter, Burton
b. 1931 Shatner,
William

b. 1931 Vessels, Billy
b. 1933 Bani-Sadr,
Abolhassan
b. 1933 Britt, May
b. 1933 McCarthy,
J(oseph) P(riestley)
b. 1934 Hatch, Orrin
G(rant)
b. 1936 Carey, Ron(ald
Robert)
b. 1940 Keon, Dave
b. 1940 Ward, Phillip R
b. 1943 Baker, Houston
A(lfred), Jr.
b. 1943 Benson, George
b. 1945 Frahm, Sheila
b. 1948 Lloyd Webber,
Andrew
b. 1952 Costas, Bob
b. 1954 Browner, Ross
b. 1956 Olin, Lena
b. 1957 Mills, Stephanie
b. 1958 Rice, Linda
Johnson
b. 1959 Modine,
Matthew
b. 1970 CasSelle,
Malcolm
d. 337 Constantine I
d. 1639 Carew, Thomas
d. 1687 Lully, Jean-
Baptiste
d. 1758 Edwards,
Jonathan
d. 1820 Decatur,
Stephen
d. 1832 Goethe, Johann
Wolfgang von
d. 1857 Scoresby,
William
d. 1861 Lerdo de
Tejada, Miguel
d. 1862 Levy, Uriah
Phillips
d. 1889 Matthews,
Stanley
d. 1892 Agnew, David
Hayes
d. 1896 Hughes,
Thomas
d. 1913 Sung Chiao-jen
d. 1918 Mitchell,
Margaret Julia
d. 1921 Hornung, Ernest
William
d. 1937 MacMonnies,
Fred W
d. 1950 Hopkins, Arthur
d. 1951 Mengelberg,
Willem
d. 1952 Senanayake,
Don Stephen
d. 1955 Stael, Nicolas
de
d. 1956 Sarton, George
d. 1958 McCardell,
Claire
d. 1958 Todd, Mike
d. 1960 Arber, Agnes
d. 1969 Schmitt,
Bernadotte Everly
d. 1974 Revson, Peter
Jeffrey
d. 1978 Dodd, John
Bruce, Mrs.
d. 1978 Wallenda, Karl

d. 1978 Wheelock, John
Hall
d. 1979 Lyon, Ben
d. 1981 Elliott, Jumbo
d. 1981 McCain, John
Sidney, Jr.
d. 1982 Fitzgerald,
Ed(ward)
d. 1982 Parker, Buddy
d. 1984 Webster, Paul
Francois
d. 1986 Arnow,
Harriette Louisa
Simpson
d. 1986 Bricker, John
William
d. 1986 Dinning, Mark
d. 1991 Engle, Paul
(Hamilton)
d. 1991 Rains, Albert
McKinley
d. 1994 Lantz, Walter
d. 1995 Guinan,
Matthew

March 23
b. 1430 Margaret of
Anjou
b. 1699 Bartram, John
b. 1736 Saint Clair,
Arthur
b. 1736 St. Clair, Arthur
b. 1749 Laplace, Pierre
Simon, Marquis de
b. 1769 Smith, William
b. 1818 Buell, Don
Carlos
b. 1823 Colfax,
Schuyler
b. 1854 Milner, Alfred,
Viscount
b. 1855 Giddings,
Franklin Henry
b. 1857 Farmer, Fannie
Merritt
b. 1858 Chapais,
Thomas, Sir
b. 1858 Quidde, Ludwig
b. 1865 Cawein,
Madison Julius
b. 1865 Ford, Paul
Leicester
b. 1872 Savage,
Michael Joseph
b. 1874 Leyendecker,
Joseph Christian
b. 1876 Bone,
Muirhead, Sir
b. 1878 Schreker, Franz
b. 1880 Wolheim, Louis
b. 1881 Staudinger,
Hermann
b. 1882 Noether,
(Amalie) Emmy
b. 1883 Burt, Cyril
Lodowic, Sir
b. 1884 Allen, Florence
Ellinwood
b. 1887 Gris, Juan
b. 1887 Hillman, Sidney
(Simcha)
b. 1892 Buttrick,
George Arthur
b. 1895 Rudhyar, Dane
b. 1897 Farrar, Margaret
(Petherbridge)
b. 1898 Dawn, Hazel

b. 1899 Adamic, Louis
b. 1900 Fromm, Erich
b. 1902 Dodge, Bertha
Sanford
b. 1902 Ober, Philip
(Nott)
b. 1906 Evans, Richard
Louis
b. 1907 Bovet, Daniele
b. 1910 Kurosawa,
Akira
b. 1911 Ruby, Jack
b. 1912 Cameron,
Eleanor Frances
b. 1912 VonBraun,
Wernher
b. 1913 Escobar, Sixto
b. 1917 Guarnieri,
Johnny
b. 1921 Campbell,
Donald Malcolm
b. 1921 Smyslov, Vasili
Vasil'evich
b. 1923 Weinmeister,
Arnie
b. 1926 Wright, Martha
b. 1927 Crespin, Regine
b. 1928 Phillips,
Channing Emery
b. 1929 Bannister,
Roger, Sir
b. 1933 Jenkins, Hayes
Alan
b. 1935 Slavitt, David R
b. 1937 Gallo, Robert
Charles
b. 1938 Breedlove,
Craig
b. 1938 Jackson,
Maynard Holbrook,
Jr.
b. 1944 Scott, George
Charles, Jr.
b. 1945 Grisman, David
b. 1951 Jaworski,
Ron(ald Vincent)
b. 1952 Stevenson,
Teofilo
b. 1953 Khan, Chaka
b. 1953 Velazquez,
Nydia Margarita
b. 1955 Malone, Moses
Eugene
b. 1957 Plummer,
Amanda
b. 1990 Eugenie,
Princess of York
d. 1555 Julius III, Pope
d. 1680 Fouquet,
Nicolas
d. 1819 Kotzebue,
August Friedrich
Ferdinand von
d. 1842 Stendhal
d. 1862 Nesselrode,
Karl Robert
d. 1877 Unger, Caroline
d. 1888 Waite, Morrison
Remick
d. 1890 Schenck, Robert
Cumming
d. 1902 Tisza, Kalman
d. 1907 Pobedonostsev,
Konstantin Petrovich
d. 1909 Davidson, John
d. 1931 Schmedes, Erik

d. 1939 Halliburton,
Richard
d. 1941 Rourke,
Constance Mayfield
d. 1943 Schillinger,
Joseph
d. 1946 Largo
Caballero, Francisco
d. 1946 Lewis, Gilbert
Newton
d. 1947 Rankin, Arthur
d. 1948 Berdyaev,
Nikolay
Aleksandrovich
d. 1948 Milne, George
Francis, Baron
d. 1949 Hendrick,
Burton Jesse
d. 1953 Dufy, Raoul
(Ernest Joseph)
d. 1956 Dixon, Mort
d. 1960 Adams,
Franklin P(ierce)
d. 1960 Hooper, Tom
d. 1961 Mason, Max
d. 1965 Murray, Mae
d. 1968 O'Connor,
Edwin Greene
d. 1969 Lismer, Arthur
d. 1970 Pyne, Joe
d. 1972 Balenciaga,
Cristobal
d. 1973 Maynard, Ken
d. 1974 Molyneux,
Edward H
d. 1977 Stydahar, Joe
d. 1980 Johnson, Gerald
White
d. 1980 Okun, Arthur
Melvin
d. 1981 Auchinleck,
Claude, Sir
d. 1981 Hailwood, Mike
d. 1981 Lasker, Edward
d. 1982 Feingold,
Benjamin Franklin
d. 1982 Greer, Sonny
d. 1982 Praz, Mario
d. 1983 Fitzgibbon,
Constantine
d. 1985 Harris, Patricia
Roberts
d. 1985 Sims, Zoot
d. 1987 Minsky, Morton
d. 1988 Somogi, Judith
d. 1988 Thompson,
Mickey
d. 1990 Dexter, John
d. 1991 Spofford,
Charles M(erville)
d. 1992 Hayek,
Friedrich August von
d. 1993 Crichton,
Robert
d. 1994 Colosio
Murrieta, Luis
Donaldo
d. 1994 Masina,
Giulietta
d. 1994 Swann, Donald
(Ibrahim)
d. 1995 Shulman, Irving
d. 2000 McCurdy, Ed

March 24
b. 1754 Barlow, Joel
b. 1755 King, Rufus

b. 1778 Gourlay, Robert
b. 1797 Rosmini-
Serbati, Antonio
b. 1803 Ryerson,
Adolphus Egerton
b. 1808 Malibran, Maria
Felicita
b. 1809 Flandrin,
Hippolyte Jean
b. 1820 Crosby, Fanny
b. 1826 Gage, Matilda
Joslyn
b. 1827 Wheeler,
Candace Thurber
b. 1828 Gray, Horace
b. 1834 Morris, William
b. 1834 Powell, John
Wesley
b. 1842 Krauss,
Gabrielle
b. 1850 Hocking, Silas
b. 1855 Mellon, Andrew
William
b. 1858 Adamowski,
Timothee
b. 1862 Benson, Frank
Weston
b. 1866 McAuliffe, Jack
B
b. 1872 Birch, Stephen
b. 1873 Coolidge, Dane
b. 1874 Einaudi, Luigi
b. 1874 Houdini, Harry
b. 1882 Marinuzzi,
Giuseppe (Gino)
b. 1884 Debye, Peter
Joseph William
b. 1886 Weston,
Edward
b. 1887 Arbuckle, Fatty
b. 1890 Rock, John
b. 1893 Baade,
(Wilhelm Heinrich)
Walter
b. 1893 Sisler, George
Harold
b. 1897 Kroeber,
Theodora Kracaw
b. 1897 Reich, Wilhelm
b. 1898 Alpert, George
b. 1899 Saunders, Allen
b. 1901 Iwerks, Ub(be)
b. 1902 Dewey, Thomas
Edmund
b. 1902 Scheuer, Philip
K(latz)
b. 1903 Butenandt,
Adolf Fredrick
Johann
b. 1903 Muggeridge,
Malcolm
b. 1904 Morrison, Hobe
b. 1906 MacDonald,
Dwight
b. 1907 Norstad, Lauris
b. 1908 Beam, Jacob
D(yneley)
b. 1910 Conte, Richard
b. 1911 Barbera, Joseph
Roland
b. 1911 Jorda, Enrique
b. 1912 Height, Dorothy
Irene
b. 1913 Porter, Richard
William

b. 1915 Cox, John
Rogers
b. 1917 Ehricke, Krafft
Arnold
b. 1917 Kendrew, John
Cowdery, Sir
b. 1919 Burrenchobay,
Dayendranath
b. 1919 Ferlinghetti,
Lawrence Monsanto
b. 1920 Nelson, Gene
b. 1923 Hamilton,
Murray
b. 1924 Fell, Norman
b. 1926 Fo, Dario
b. 1926 Porter, Bill
b. 1928 Brown, Vanessa
b. 1928 Janis, Byron
b. 1930 Dacko, David
b. 1930 McQueen,
Steve
b. 1936 Suzuki, David
T(akayoshi)
b. 1937 Sandiford,
Lloyd Erskine
b. 1938 Wilson, Larry
b. 1939 Nugent, Nelle
b. 1940 Mackie, Bob
b. 1942 Cammermeyer,
Margarethe
b. 1943 Alou, Jesus
Maria Rojas
b. 1946 Hall, Camilla
Christine
b. 1951 Bradley,
Pat(ricia Ellen)
b. 1954 Carradine,
Robert Reed
b. 1954 Pescow, Donna
b. 1954 Zepeda, Ofelia
b. 1955 Jarvis,
Doug(las)
b. 1956 Templeton,
Garry Lewis
b. 1967 Rinaldi, Kathy
d. 809? Harun-Al-
Rashid
d. 1575 Caro, Joseph
d. 1603 Elizabeth I
d. 1635 Callot, Jacques
d. 1771 Shirley,
William
d. 1773 Chesterfield,
Philip Dormer, Earl
d. 1794 Hebert, Jacques
Rene
d. 1818 Repton,
Humphry
d. 1849 Dobereiner,
Johann Wolfgang
d. 1861 Scranton,
George Whitfield
d. 1869 Gorham, Jabez
d. 1877 Bagehot, Walter
d. 1882 Longfellow,
Henry Wadsworth
d. 1882 Thompson,
William Tappan
d. 1901 Yonge,
Charlotte Mary
d. 1904 Arnold, Edwin
d. 1905 Verne, Jules
d. 1909 Synge, John
Millington
d. 1916 Granados,
Enrique

d. 1999 Ripken, Cal(vin
Edwin, Sr.)

March 26
b. 1516 Gesner, Konrad
von
b. 1724 Laurens, Henry
b. 1753 Rumford, Count
b. 1773 Bowditch,
Nathaniel
b. 1778 Ashley, William
Henry
b. 1817 Haupt, Herman
b. 1820 Upchurch, John
Jorden
b. 1838 Lecky, William
Edward Hartpole
b. 1850 Bellamy,
Edward
b. 1851 Bradley,
Andrew Cecil
b. 1854 Furniss, Harry
b. 1856 Massey,
William Ferguson
b. 1858 Delano, Jane
Arminda
b. 1859 Housman,
A(lfred) E(dward)
b. 1867 Woodbridge,
Frederick James
Eugene
b. 1868 Fuad, I
b. 1873 DuMaurier,
Gerald Hubert, Sir
b. 1874 Frost, Robert
Lee
b. 1874 Nast, Conde
b. 1875 Rhee, Syngman
b. 1876 Ammann,
Othmar Hermann
b. 1880 Hines, Duncan
b. 1884 Backhaus,
Wilhelm
b. 1892 Douglas, Paul
Howard
b. 1893 Conant, James
Bryant
b. 1893 Togliatti,
Palmiro
b. 1895 Carney, Robert
Bostwick
b. 1899 Ursuleac,
Viorica
b. 1904 Campbell,
Joseph
b. 1904 Fernandez,
Emilio
b. 1905 Cluytens, Andre
b. 1905 Frankl, Viktor
E(mil)
b. 1907 Lasch, Robert
b. 1908? Stangl, Franz
Paul
b. 1909 Campora,
Hector Jose
b. 1909 Rafferty, Chips
b. 1911 Austin, John
Langshaw
b. 1911 Katz, Bernard,
Sir
b. 1911 Williams,
Tennessee
b. 1916 Anfinsen,
Christian Boehmer
b. 1916 Hayden,
Sterling Relyea
Walter

b. 1916 Stokely, Alfred
Jehu
b. 1917 Thomas, Rufus
b. 1919 Martin, Strother
b. 1922 Milliken,
William Grawn
b. 1923 Elliott, Bob
b. 1925 Boulez, Pierre
b. 1926 Hinde, Thomas,
Sir
b. 1929 Sorel, Edward
b. 1930 Corso, Gregory
Nunzio
b. 1930 O'Connor,
Sandra Day
b. 1931 Nimoy, Leonard
b. 1932 Harris, James
Andrew
b. 1933 Deloria, Vine
(Victor), Jr.
b. 1934 Arkin, Alan
Wolf
b. 1934 Cappelletti, Gino
b. 1936 Jofre, Eder
b. 1937 Embry, Wayne
Richard
b. 1937 Lee, James
b. 1939 Jenifer,
Franklyn Green
b. 1940 Caan, James
b. 1942 Jong, Erica
(Mann)
b. 1943 Woodward, Bob
b. 1944 Ross, Diana
b. 1948 Tyler, Steven
b. 1949 Lawrence,
Vicki Ann
b. 1950 Pendergrass,
Teddy
b. 1950 Short, Martin
b. 1954 Sliwa, Curtis
b. 1959 Taylor, Kristin
Clark
b. 1960 Allen, Marcus
b. 1960 Grey, Jennifer
b. 1962 Blab, Uwe
Konstantine
b. 1962 Stockton, John
(Houston)
d. 1517 Isaac, Heinrich
d. 1649 Winthrop, John
d. 1797 Hutton, James
d. 1814 Guillotin,
Joseph Ignace
d. 1827 Beethoven,
Ludwig van
d. 1831 Allen, Richard
d. 1838 Ashley, William
Henry
d. 1863 Egg, Augustus
Leopold
d. 1870 Soule, Pierre
d. 1871 Fetis, Francois
Joseph
d. 1881 Lawrence,
William Beach
d. 1892 Whitman,
Walt(er)
d. 1900 Wise, Isaac
Mayer
d. 1902 Rhodes, Cecil
John
d. 1905 Barrymore,
Maurice
d. 1911 Williams,
Henry Sylvester

d. 1914 Keith, Benjamin
Franklin
d. 1916 Blow, Susan
Elizabeth
d. 1923 Bernhardt,
Sarah
d. 1925 Vezina,
Georges
d. 1931 Healy,
T(imothy) M(ichael)
d. 1932 Leland, Henry
Martyn
d. 1933 Lang, Eddie
d. 1942 Hinrichs,
Gustav
d. 1942 Wells, Carolyn
d. 1943 Lindsey,
Benjamin Barr
d. 1945 Lloyd George
of Dwyfor, David
Lloyd George Earl
d. 1949 Stevens, Albert
William
d. 1951 Micheaux,
Oscar
d. 1957 Herriot,
Edouard
d. 1957 Ophuls, Max
d. 1959 Chandler,
Raymond Thornton
d. 1960 Keith, Ian
d. 1962 Fischer, Anton
Otto
d. 1962 Savage,
Augusta Christine
d. 1968 Samstag,
Nicholas
d. 1968 Sears, Eleonora
Randolph
d. 1969 Toole, John
Kennedy
d. 1971 Anderson,
C(larence) W(illiam)
d. 1973 Coward, Noel
Pierce, Sir
d. 1973 Sisler, George
Harold
d. 1974 Condon,
Edward Uhler
d. 1976 Lin, Yutang
d. 1979 Stafford, Jean
d. 1981 Darlington,
Cyril Dean
d. 1983 Blunt, Anthony
Frederick
d. 1983 Waterfield, Bob
d. 1984 Toure, Ahmed
Sekou
d. 1984 Toure, Sekou
d. 1987 Abel, Walter
Charles
d. 1987 Jochum, Eugen
d. 1990 Halston
d. 1992 Frum, Barbara
d. 1993 Falco, Louis
d. 1994 Millar,
Margaret (Ellis)
d. 1995 Eazy-E
d. 1996 Muskie,
Edmund S(ixtus)
d. 1996 Packard, David
d. 1997 Applewhite,
Marshall Herff
d. 2000 Comfort,
Alexander

March 27
b. 1678 Juvara, Filippo
b. 1753 Bell, Andrew
b. 1797 Vigny, Alfred
Victor, Comte de
b. 1813 Currier,
Nathaniel
b. 1824 Hittorf, Johann
Wilhelm
b. 1840 Baker, George
Fisher
b. 1844 Greely,
Adolphus Washington
b. 1845 Roentgen,
Wilhelm Konrad
b. 1847 Wallach, Otto
b. 1851 Indy, Paul
(Marie Theodore
Vincent d')
b. 1854 Grassi,
Giovanni Battista
b. 1863 Royce,
Frederick Henry, Sir
b. 1865 Graves, William
Sidney
b. 1867 Walker, Edyth
b. 1868 Hill, Patty
Smith
b. 1871 Mann, Heinrich
Ludwig
b. 1875 Marquet, Albert
b. 1876? Thompson,
Mary
b. 1879 Huggins, Miller
James
b. 1879 MacSwiney,
Terence
b. 1879 Steichen,
Edward Jean
b. 1886 Kirov, Sergei
Mironovich
b. 1886 Mies van der
Rohe, Ludwig
b. 1892 Grofe, Ferde
b. 1893 Mannheim, Karl
b. 1893 Mihajlovic,
Dragoliub
b. 1896 Gribble, Harry
Wagstaff Graham
b. 1896 Lescaze,
William
b. 1897 Swanson,
Gloria May Josephine
b. 1899 Kaufman,
Joseph William
b. 1900 Scott, Arleigh
Winston, Sir
b. 1901 Barks, Carl
b. 1901 Sato, Eisaku
b. 1902 Wolfson, Erwin
Service
b. 1906 Russell, Pee
Wee
b. 1907 Chase, Lucia
b. 1908 Fleming, Joan
Margaret
b. 1910 Pierce, John
Robinson
b. 1912 Callaghan,
James
b. 1914 Denning,
Richard
b. 1914 Lanson, Snooky
b. 1914 Schulberg,
Budd Wilson

b. 1915 Lockwood, Robert, Jr.
b. 1916 Warner, Jack, Jr.
b. 1917 Vance, Cyrus Roberts
b. 1919 Amery, Julian
b. 1919 Furgol, Ed(ward)
b. 1920 Hayman, Richard
b. 1921 Markle, Fletcher
b. 1922 Agase, Alexander A.
b. 1922 Olderman, Murray
b. 1922 Olitski, Jules
b. 1923 Endo, Shusaku
b. 1923 Simpson, Louis
b. 1924 Holloman, Bobo
b. 1924 Vaughan, Sarah Lois
b. 1927 Lewis, Anthony
b. 1927 Ostin, Mo
b. 1931 Janssen, David
b. 1934 Mitchell, Arthur Adam
b. 1935 Glover, Julian
b. 1939 Yarborough, Cale
b. 1940 Pendleton, Austin
b. 1942 York, Michael
b. 1943 Curtis, Mike
b. 1944 Brown, Jesse
b. 1945 Aquash, Anna Mae Pictou
b. 1947 Sullivan, Tom
b. 1949 Steinberg, Leigh
b. 1950 Banks, Tony
b. 1950 Ewing, Maria Louise
b. 1952 Schneider, Maria
b. 1953 Gatti, Gabriele
b. 1953 Proell Moser, Annemarie
b. 1955 McCarron, Chris
b. 1958 Molinari, Susan
b. 1960 Mowry, Jess
b. 1963 Cunningham, Randall
b. 1963 Tarantino, Quentin
b. 1970 Carey, Mariah
d. 1625 James I
d. 1770 Tiepolo, Giambattista
d. 1848 Burke, John
d. 1849 Appleton, Daniel
d. 1866 Keble, John
d. 1868 Cardigan, James Thomas Brudenell, Earl of
d. 1869 Harper, James
d. 1878 Scott, George Gilbert, Sir
d. 1887 Tulane, Paul
d. 1888 Darley, Felix Octavius Carr
d. 1889 Bright, John

d. 1894 Cameron, Verney Lovett
d. 1895 Ballou, Maturin Murray
d. 1897 Adams, William Taylor
d. 1898 Syed Ahmed Khan
d. 1906 Carriere, Eugene
d. 1910 Agassiz, Alexander Emmanuel Rodolphe
d. 1912 Scott, Robert Falcon
d. 1917 Ezekiel, Moses Jacob
d. 1918 Adams, Henry Brooks
d. 1920 Colman, Samuel
d. 1923 Dewar, James, Sir
d. 1926 Harkness, Anna M Richardson
d. 1931 Bennett, Arnold
d. 1940 Savage, Michael Joseph
d. 1942 Gonzalez, Julio
d. 1945 Bendix, Vincent
d. 1962 Britton, Jack
d. 1964 Bordeaux, Henry
d. 1966 Menken, Helen
d. 1967 Heyrovsky, Jaroslav
d. 1968 Gagarin, Yuri Alexseyevich
d. 1969 Traven, B.
d. 1972 Escher, M(aurits) C(ornelis)
d. 1974 Wang Ming
d. 1975 Bliss, Arthur, Sir
d. 1977 Herberg, Will
d. 1977 Hyland, Diana
d. 1982 Adams, Harriet Stratemeyer
d. 1982 Khan, Fazlur Rahman
d. 1983 Stankiewicz, Richard Peter
d. 1984 Donohue, Jack
d. 1985 Rico, Don(ato)
d. 1986 Canfield, Cass
d. 1987 Goodrich, Lloyd
d. 1987 Provensen, Martin
d. 1988 Willeford, Charles Ray, II
d. 1989 Cowley, Malcolm
d. 1991 Ray, Aldo
d. 1992 Colby, Anita
d. 1992 MacGrath, Leueen (Emily)
d. 1992 Webb, James Edwin
d. 1993 Agostini, Peter
d. 1993 Larson, (Lewis) Arthur
d. 1993 White, Stephen
d. 1995 Gucci, Maurizio
d. 1997 Custin, Mildred
d. 1997 Dwinell, Lane

d. 1998 Porsche, Ferdinand
d. 2000 Dury, Ian

March 28
b. 1475 Bartolommeo, Fra
b. 1483 Raphael
b. 1515 Theresa, Saint
b. 1515 Theresa, St.
b. 1592 Comenius, Johann Amos
b. 1652 Sewall, Samuel
b. 1674 Byrd, William
b. 1750 Miranda, Francisco de
b. 1760 Clarkson, Thomas
b. 1787 Rich, Claudius James
b. 1793 Schoolcraft, Henry Rowe
b. 1800 Tamburini, Antonio
b. 1811 Neumann, John Nepomucene, Saint
b. 1817 DeSanctis, Francesco
b. 1818 Hampton, Wade
b. 1836 Pabst, Frederick
b. 1862 Briand, Aristide
b. 1868 Gorky, Maxim
b. 1868 Hapgood, Norman
b. 1868 Jaegers, Albert
b. 1871 Jones, William
b. 1871 Mengelberg, Willem
b. 1873 Sedgwick, Anne Douglas
b. 1877 Ray, Edward
b. 1878 Lehman, Herbert Henry
b. 1878 Spingarn, Arthur Barnett
b. 1879 Westley, Helen
b. 1884 Sikelianos, Angelos
b. 1891 Whiteman, Paul
b. 1892 Heymans, Corneille Jean Francois
b. 1893 Skouras, Spyros Panagiotes
b. 1894 Carlson, Wally
b. 1895 Herter, Christian Archibald
b. 1895 Kimball, Spencer Woolley
b. 1899 Busch, August Anheuser, Jr.
b. 1902 Ayme, Marcel
b. 1902 Lamont, Corliss
b. 1902 Robson, Flora McKenzie, Dame
b. 1903 Serkin, Rudolph
b. 1905 Berman, Pandro Samuel
b. 1905 Hague, Raoul (Heukelekian)
b. 1905 Perkins, Marlin
b. 1907 Lazar, Irving Paul
b. 1908 Crawford, Joan
b. 1909 Algren, Nelson
b. 1909 Warneke, Lon(nie)

b. 1910 O'Keefe, Dennis
b. 1912 Damas, Leon-Gontran
b. 1912 Taoka Kazuo
b. 1914 Anhalt, Edward
b. 1914 Hrabal, Bohumil
b. 1914 Lovejoy, Frank
b. 1914 Muskie, Edmund S(ixtus)
b. 1915 Knauer, Virginia Harrington Wright
b. 1917 Meloy, Francis Edward, Jr.
b. 1917 Rountree, William M(anning)
b. 1919 Doktor, Paul Karl
b. 1921 Bogarde, Dirk
b. 1923 Jones, Thad(deus Joseph)
b. 1924 Bartholomew, Freddie
b. 1928 Brzezinski, Zbigniew Kazimierz
b. 1929 Exley, Frederick (Earl)
b. 1930 Friedman, Jerome
b. 1931 Rule, Jane
b. 1933 Murkowski, Frank Hughes
b. 1934 Brown, Lester Russell
b. 1934 Ruddy, Al(bert Stotland)
b. 1936 Vargas Llosa, Mario
b. 1938 Stern, Leonard Norman
b. 1940 Banks, Russell
b. 1940 Loughery, Kevin Michael
b. 1942 Kinnock, Neil Gordon
b. 1942 Ramey, Samuel Edward
b. 1943 Ferrell, Conchata Galen
b. 1944 Barry, Rick
b. 1944 Howard, Ken(neth Joseph, Jr.)
b. 1947 Gilbert, Bruce
b. 1948 Wiest, Dianne
b. 1949 Pendleton, Moses Robert Andrew
b. 1951 Kain, Karen Alexandria
b. 1954 McEntire, Reba
b. 1963 King, Bernice Albertine
b. 1968 Lawless, Lucy
d. 1621 Rinuccini, Ottavio
d. 1760 Woffington, Margaret
d. 1814 Clodion
d. 1852 Braille, Louis
d. 1870 Thomas, George Henry
d. 1874 Hansen, Peter Andreas

d. 1881 Mussorgsky,
Modest Petrovich
d. 1886 Trench, Richard
Chenevix
d. 1898 Seidl, Anton
d. 1901 Jasper, John J
d. 1910 Brewer, David
Josiah
d. 1910 Colonne,
Edouard
d. 1917 Ryder, Albert
Pinkham
d. 1929 Bates,
Katharine Lee
d. 1938 House, Edward
Mandell
d. 1939 Goldsmith, Fred
Ernest
d. 1941 Woolf, Virginia
d. 1943 Rachmaninoff,
Sergei Vasilyevich
d. 1944 Leacock,
Stephen Butler
d. 1947 Evers, Johnny
d. 1953 Thorpe, Jim
d. 1954 Kiam, Omar
d. 1957 Morley,
Christopher
(Darlington)
d. 1958 Klein, Chuck
d. 1961 Crosley, Powel,
Jr.
d. 1962 Neyland, Robert
Reese
d. 1963 Templeton,
Alec
d. 1965 Dane, Clemence
d. 1965 Seagrave,
Gordon Stifler
d. 1968 Dreyer, Carl
Theodore
d. 1969 Eisenhower,
Dwight D(avid)
d. 1970 Gallo, Fortune
d. 1971 Fairchild,
Sherman Mills
d. 1972 Paul-Boncour,
Joseph
d. 1973 Kalatozov,
Mikhail
d. 1973 Rosenthal, Ida
Cohen
d. 1974 Fields, Dorothy
d. 1974 Rosay,
Francoise
d. 1976 Arlen, Richard
d. 1977 Szenkar, Eugen
d. 1978 Wragge, Sidney
d. 1979 Kelly, Emmett
Lee
d. 1980 Haymes, Dick
d. 1980 Soria, Dario
d. 1981 Hollowood,
Albert Bernard
d. 1981 Kovalev,
Mikhail
Aleksandrovich
d. 1982 Uris, Harold
David
d. 1984 Dragon,
Carmen
d. 1985 Chagall, Marc
d. 1986 Gilmore,
Virginia
d. 1987 Trapp, Maria
Augusta von

d. 1994 Goldman,
Albert
d. 1994 Ionesco, Eugene
d. 2000 Powell,
Anthony Dymoke
March 29
b. 1561 Sanctorius
b. 1790 Tyler, John
b. 1813 Letcher, John
b. 1815 Frere, Henry
Bartle Edward
b. 1819 Drake, Edwin
Laurentine
b. 1819 Wise, Isaac
Mayer
b. 1826 Liebknecht,
Wilhelm
b. 1831 Barr, Amelia
Edith Huddleston
b. 1853 Thomson, Elihu
b. 1859 Mayer, Oscar
Ferdinand
b. 1865 Bonsal, Stephen
b. 1867 Young, Cy
b. 1869 Hrdlicka, Ales
b. 1869 Lutyens, Edwin
Landseer, Sir
b. 1869 Neilson,
William A(llan)
b. 1875 Hoover, Lou
Henry
b. 1878 Von Tilzer,
Albert
b. 1880 Lhevinne,
Rosina L
b. 1881 Hood, Raymond
Matthewson
b. 1885 Bolton, Frances
Payne
b. 1886 Krupp von
Bohlen und Halbach,
Bertha
b. 1887 Read, Albert
Cushing
b. 1888 Casey, James E
b. 1889 Lindsay,
Howard
b. 1891 Baxter, Warner
b. 1892 Mindszenty,
Jozsef, Cardinal
b. 1895 Juenger, Ernst
b. 1896 Kleberg, Robert
Justus, Jr.
b. 1899 Beria, Lavrenti
Pavlovich
b. 1900 Elton, Charles
Sutherland
b. 1901 Montagu, Ewen
b. 1902 Walton,
William Turner, Sir
b. 1906 Allred, Rulon
Clark
b. 1906 Bausch, James
b. 1906 Biggs, Edward
George Power
b. 1906 Stevens,
Onslow
b. 1908 O'Connell,
Arthur
b. 1912 Reitsch, Hanna
b. 1913 Thomas, Ronald
Stuart
b. 1914 Foster, Phil
b. 1916 McCarthy,
Eugene Joseph

b. 1917 Holmes,
Tommy
b. 1918 Bailey, Pearl
Mae
b. 1918 Walton, Sam
Moore
b. 1919 Heckart, Eileen
b. 1920 Duerk, Alene
B(ertha)
b. 1922 Fain, Ferris
Roy
b. 1924 Mathers, Frank
b. 1925 Tunnell,
Em(len)
b. 1926 Adams, Diana
b. 1927 Vane, John
Robert, Sir
b. 1929 Meri, Lennart
b. 1930 Jugnauth,
Anerood
b. 1931 Tebbit, Norman
Beresford
b. 1936 Bennett,
Richard Rodney
b. 1936 Guest, Judith
Ann
b. 1937 Carter, Billy
b. 1941 Hansen, James
E(dward)
b. 1942 Lane, Vincent
b. 1942 Pressler, Larry
b. 1943 Glover,
Nathaniel, Jr.
b. 1943 Idle, Eric
b. 1943 Major, John
(Roy)
b. 1943 Vangelis
b. 1944 McLain, Denny
b. 1945 Frazier, Walt(er
Jr.)
b. 1951 Cort, Bud
b. 1951 Ut, Huynh
Cong
b. 1954 Quinlan, Karen
Ann
b. 1955 Campbell, Earl
Christian
b. 1955 Kay, Dianne
b. 1956 Thomas, Kurt
b. 1957 Lambert,
Christopher
b. 1963 Hammer
b. 1976 Capriati,
Jennifer
d. 1772 Swedenborg,
Emanuel
d. 1788 Wesley, Charles
d. 1792 Gustavus, III
d. 1848 Astor, John
Jacob
d. 1877 Macy,
R(owland) H(ussey)
d. 1891 Seurat, Georges
Pierre
d. 1903 Swift, Gustavus
Franklin
d. 1915 Denslow,
W(illiam) W(allace)
d. 1924 Stanford,
Charles Villiers, Sir
d. 1934 Kahn, Otto
Hermann
d. 1937 Szymanowski,
Karol Maciej
d. 1939 Machado y
Morales, Gerardo

d. 1943 Gillmore, Frank
d. 1951 Travers, Jerry
d. 1957 Cary, Joyce
d. 1958 Handy,
W(illiam)
C(hristopher)
d. 1958 Pangborn,
Clyde Edward
d. 1969 Wyman,
Willard Gordon
d. 1970 Brittain, Vera
Mary
d. 1970 Strong, Anna
Louise
d. 1972 Rank, J(oseph)
Arthur
d. 1972 Sayre, Francis
Bowes
d. 1973 Cooper,
Melville
d. 1975 Hibbs, Ben
d. 1978 Papashvily,
George
d. 1979 Delaney,
Beauford
d. 1980 Watt, George
Willard
d. 1981 Tieri, Frank
d. 1981 Williams, Eric
Eustace
d. 1982 Bloch,
Raymond A
d. 1982 Deutsch, Helene
R(osenbach)
d. 1982 Giauque,
William Francis
d. 1982 Hallstein,
Walter
d. 1982 Orff, Carl
d. 1982 Twining,
Nathan F(arragut)
d. 1983 Barrows,
Marjorie (Ruth)
d. 1983 Model, Lisette
d. 1985 Terry, Luther
Leonidas
d. 1986 Ritz, Harry
d. 1988 Kluszewski,
Ted
d. 1991 Atwater, Lee
d. 1992 Henreid, Paul
d. 1992 Sammartino,
Peter
d. 1993 Tajo, Italo
d. 1996 Ford, Anne
McDonnell
d. 1997 Sager, Ruth
d. 1998 Freij, Elias
d. 1998 Hicks, David
(Nightingale)
d. 1999 Williams, Joe
March 30
b. 1135 Maimonides,
Moses
b. 1432 Mehmed the
Conqueror
b. 1727 Traetta,
Tommaso
b. 1735 McKean,
Thomas
b. 1746 Goya y
Lucientes, Francisco
Jose de
b. 1793 Rosas, Juan
Manuel de
b. 1804 Sulzer, Salomon

b. 1820 Sewell, Anna
b. 1840 Booth, Charles
b. 1842 Fiske, John
b. 1844 Verlaine, Paul (Marie)
b. 1853 Van Gogh, Vincent Willem
b. 1858 Hopper, De Wolfe
b. 1863 Caillaux, Joseph Marie Auguste
b. 1872 Vassilenko, Sergei
b. 1876 Beers, Clifford Whittingham
b. 1876 Tikhomirov, Vasily Dmitrievich
b. 1880 O'Casey, Sean
b. 1880 Short, Walter Campbell
b. 1882 Klein, Melanie
b. 1883 Davidson, Jo
b. 1886 Cornford, Frances Crofts Darwin
b. 1888 Nilsson, Anna Q(uerentia)
b. 1892 Odlum, Floyd Bostwick
b. 1892 Panofsky, Erwin
b. 1894 Bainton, Roland Herbert
b. 1895 Giono, Jean
b. 1896 Raphaelson, Samson
b. 1902 Heath, Ted
b. 1913 Helms, Richard McGarrah
b. 1913 Laine, Frankie
b. 1918 Evans, Bob
b. 1919 Bundy, McGeorge
b. 1920 Bey, Turhan
b. 1926 Chaplin, Sydney
b. 1929 Dysart, Richard (Allan)
b. 1930 Astin, John Allen
b. 1930 Jones, Robert C
b. 1930 Marshall, Peter
b. 1934 Curran, Charles E(dward)
b. 1937 Beatty, Warren
b. 1940 Lucas, Jerry Ray
b. 1941 Smith, Robert C
b. 1943 Etchison, Dennis
b. 1945 Clapton, Eric
b. 1945 Miller, Bob
b. 1948 Mangrum, Jim Dandy
b. 1948 Sims, Naomi
b. 1949 Magliozzi, Ray
b. 1952 Byrd, Robert
b. 1955 Lomawaima, K(imberly) Tsianina
b. 1957 Reiser, Paul
b. 1964 Chapman, Tracy
b. 1968 Dion, Celine
d. 1450 Sejong

d. 1707 Vauban, Sebastien LePrestre de
d. 1764 Locatelli, Pietro Antonio
d. 1783 Hunter, William
d. 1837 Constable, John
d. 1840 Brummell, Beau
d. 1842 Vigee-Lebrun, Marie-Louise-Elisabeth
d. 1853 Fillmore, Abigail (Powers)
d. 1861 Shaw, Lemuel
d. 1863 Bravais, Auguste
d. 1876 Balard, Antoine-Jerome
d. 1877 Cournot, Antoine Augustin
d. 1882 Griffiths, John Willis
d. 1912 May, Karl Friedrich
d. 1914 Poynting, John Henry
d. 1925 Steiner, Rudolf
d. 1936 Fuller-Maitland, John Alexander
d. 1936 Supervia, Conchita
d. 1949 Bergius, Friedrich Karl Rudolph
d. 1950 Blum, Leon
d. 1955 Pulitzer, Joseph, II
d. 1956 Bentley, Edmund Clerihew
d. 1964 Larsen, Nella
d. 1965 Hench, Philip Showalter
d. 1966 Morris, Newbold
d. 1966 Parrish, Maxfield
d. 1967 Toomer, Jean
d. 1968 Driscoll, Bobby
d. 1968 Scholl, William M
d. 1970 McCormick, Cyrus Hall
d. 1972 Heatter, Gabriel
d. 1974 Cottam, Clarence
d. 1979 Velasco Ibarra, Jose Maria
d. 1980 Mantovani, Annunzio
d. 1980 Thang, Ton Duc
d. 1981 Edwards, Sherman
d. 1981 Wallace, DeWitt
d. 1982 McHale, Tom
d. 1982 Richardson, Scovel
d. 1982 Thomas, Charles Allen
d. 1983 Peterson, Lorraine Collett
d. 1984 Barzini, Luigi Giorgio, Jr.
d. 1984 Rahner, Karl

d. 1985 Gerasimov, Innokentii Petrovich
d. 1985 Peary, Harold
d. 1985 Spanel, Abram N
d. 1986 Cagney, James
d. 1987 Murchison, Clint(on Williams, Jr.)
d. 1988 Faure, Edgar Jean
d. 1988 Holmes, John Clellon
d. 1990 Bridges, Harry Renton
d. 1990 Hirschfelder, Joseph Oakland
d. 1992 Park, Thomas
d. 1993 Diebenkorn, Richard C.
d. 1995 Callender, John Hancock
d. 2000 Kirchschlager, Rudolf

March 31
b. 1499 Pius, IV, Pope
b. 1596 Descartes, Rene
b. 1621 Marvell, Andrew
b. 1684 Durante, Francesco
b. 1732 Haydn, Joseph
b. 1809 FitzGerald, Edward
b. 1809 Gogol, Nikolai Vasilievich
b. 1811 Bunsen, Robert Wilhelm Eberhard
b. 1823 Chesnut, Mary Boykin (Miller)
b. 1824 Hunt, William Morris
b. 1831 Couper, Archibald Scott
b. 1835 LaFarge, John
b. 1844 Lang, Andrew
b. 1848 Astor, William Waldorf Astor, Viscount
b. 1870 Cox, James Middleton, Sr.
b. 1870 Ryan, Tommy
b. 1872 Griffith, Arthur
b. 1878 Johnson, Jack
b. 1880 Birley, Oswald Hornby Joseph, Sir
b. 1882 Chukovsky, Korney Ivanovich
b. 1888 Rockwell, Willard F
b. 1890 Bragg, William Lawrence, Sir
b. 1890 Wright, Lloyd
b. 1893 Krauss, Clemens
b. 1894 Ilyushin, Sergei Vladimirovich
b. 1895 Fisher, Vardis
b. 1895 McCloy, John Jay
b. 1896 Nolan, Jeannette Covert
b. 1899 White, Antonia
b. 1900 Henry William Frederick Albert

b. 1905 Stevenson, Robert
b. 1906 Tomonaga Shinichiro
b. 1907 Quillan, Eddie
b. 1908 Kitchell, Iva
b. 1908 Norvo, Red
b. 1911 Golden, William
b. 1911 Hamer, Robert
b. 1911 Kingman, Dong Moy Shu
b. 1911 Liebow, Averill A(braham)
b. 1912 Lederer, William Julius
b. 1912 Lee, Robert E(mmet)
b. 1914 Paz, Octavio
b. 1915 Morgan, Henry
b. 1916 Mayer, Norman D
b. 1916 Oldenbourg, Zoe
b. 1916 Wood, John Howland, Jr.
b. 1918 Bolt, Tommy
b. 1922 Kiley, Richard (Paul)
b. 1922 May, John L.
b. 1925 Buscaglia, Leo
b. 1926 Alfonsin Foulkes, Raul Ricardo
b. 1926 Fowles, John (Robert)
b. 1927 Becker, Stephen David
b. 1927 Chavez, Cesar (Estrada)
b. 1927 Daniels, William
b. 1928 Costigan, James
b. 1928 Frizzell, Lefty
b. 1928 Howe, Gordie
b. 1929 Claiborne, Liz
b. 1932 Jakes, John (William)
b. 1932 McCann, Elizabeth Ireland
b. 1932 Oshima, Nagisa
b. 1934 Hutton, Jim
b. 1934 Rubbia, Carlo
b. 1935 Alpert, Herb
b. 1935 Chamberlain, Richard
b. 1935 Rossner, Judith
b. 1936 German, Bruce W
b. 1936 Piercy, Marge
b. 1936 Williams, Walter Edward
b. 1937 Stoddard, Brandon
b. 1938 Steel, David Martin Scott
b. 1939 Horovitz, Israel Arthur
b. 1939 Schlondorff, Volker
b. 1940 Frank, Barney
b. 1940 Leahy, Patrick Joseph
b. 1943 Walken, Christopher
b. 1945 Kaplan, Gabe

b. 1947 Gaviria Trujillo,
Cesar Augusto
b. 1948 Gore, Albert, Jr.
b. 1948 Perlman, Rhea
b. 1948 Ralphs, Mick
b. 1954 Brock, Tony
b. 1958 Rogers, John
W., Jr.
b. 1959 Young, Angus
b. 1961 Brown, Ron(ald
James)
b. 1965 Barrasso, Tom
d. 1547 Francis I
d. 1621 Philip, III
d. 1631 Donne, John
d. 1816 Asbury, Francis
d. 1816 Ducis, Jean
Francois
d. 1850 Calhoun, John
Caldwell
d. 1850 Giusti,
Giuseppe
d. 1855 Bronte,
Charlotte
d. 1903 Butterick,
Ebenezer
d. 1913 Morgan, J(ohn)
P(ierpont)
d. 1917 Behring, Emil
Adolph von
d. 1927 K'ang Yu-wei
d. 1931 Rockne, Knute
Kenneth
d. 1943 Miliukov, Pavel
Nikolayevich
d. 1945 Fischer, Hans
d. 1945 Hawes, Harriet
Ann Boyd
d. 1951 Forbes, Ralph
d. 1956 De Palma,
Ralph
d. 1957 Lockhart, Gene
d. 1961 Faber, Geoffrey
Cust, Sir
d. 1970 Price, Nancy
d. 1970 Timoshenko,
Semen
Konstantinovich
d. 1976 Strand, Paul
d. 1976 Streeter,
Edward
d. 1978 Best, Charles
Herbert
d. 1980 Boussac,
Marcel
d. 1980 Owens, Jesse
d. 1981 Bagnold, Enid
d. 1983 Stead, Christina
(Ellen)
d. 1985 Deckers,
Jeanine
d. 1986 Aldrich,
Richard Stoddard
d. 1986 Paris, Jerry
d. 1988 McMahon,
William
d. 1993 Lee, Brandon
d. 1993 Parish, Mitchell
d. 1995 Selena
d. 1997 Anderson,
Eugenie M(oore)
d. 1997 Spitzer, Lyman,
Jr.
d. 1998 Abzug, Bella
(Savitsky)

APRIL

b. 1645 Mansart, Jules
Hardouin
b. 1673 Nicolini
b. 1690 Beissel, Johann
Conrad
b. 1722 Warton, Joseph
b. 1793 Addison,
Thomas
b. 1875 Tobin, Daniel
Joseph
b. 1890 Zimbalist,
Efrem
b. 1921 Daubeny, Peter
Lauderdale, Sir
b. 1925 Shagari, Alhaji
Shehu Usman Aliyu
b. 1940 Campbell,
Maria
b. 1940 Holland,
Robert, Jr.
b. 1951 Hun Sen
b. 1963 Hu Na
d. 1364 John, II
d. 1377 Machaut,
Guillaume de
d. 1541 Rojas, Fernando
de
d. 1616 Garcilaso de la
Vega, Inca
d. 1618 Powhatan
d. 1839 Apess, William
d. 1870 Urquiza, Justo
Jose
d. 1899 Thayer, Eli
d. 1914 Lurton, Horace
Harmon
d. 1939 Park, William
Hallock
d. 1943 Schlemmer,
Oskar
d. 1973 Graf, Herbert
d. 1980 Henry,
Charlotte
d. 1981? Wang Shih-
chieh
d. 1982 Boykin, Otis
Frank

April 1
b. 1578 Harvey,
William
b. 1697 Prevost
d'Exiles, Antoine
Francois, Abbe
b. 1753 Maistre, Joseph
de
b. 1755 Brillat-Savarin,
Jean Anthelme
b. 1811 McCosh, James
b. 1815 Bismarck, Otto
Edward Leopold von
b. 1823 Buckner, Simon
Bolivar
b. 1826 Sothern,
Edward Askew
b. 1834 Fisk, Jim
b. 1837 Isaacs, Jorge
b. 1852 Abbey, Edwin
Austin
b. 1858 King, Frederic
Truby
b. 1858 Repplier, Agnes
b. 1865 Zsigmondy,
Richard Adolf

b. 1866 Breckinridge,
Sophonisba Preston
b. 1866 Busoni,
Ferruccio Benvenuto
b. 1867 Roper, Daniel
C(alhoun)
b. 1868 Rostand,
Edmond Alexis
b. 1872 Kollontai,
Alexandra
Mikhailovna
(Domantovich)
b. 1873 Rachmaninoff,
Sergei Vasilyevich
b. 1874 Barnes, Ernest
William
b. 1883 Chaney, Lon
b. 1885 Beery, Wallace
Fitzgerald
b. 1885 Churchill,
Clementine Ogilvy
(Hozier) Spencer,
Baroness
b. 1885 Lilly, Eli
b. 1887 Bloomfield,
Leonard
b. 1887? Taylor,
Laurette
b. 1888 Batchelor,
Clarence Daniel
b. 1892 Shippen,
Katherine Binney
b. 1892 Zanelli, Renato
b. 1893 Courtneidge,
Cicely, Dame
b. 1893 Wells, Linton
b. 1895 Hunter, Alberta
b. 1897 Derricotte,
Juliette Aline
b. 1899 Naldi, Nita
b. 1900 Benton,
William
b. 1901 Chambers,
Whittaker
b. 1901 Farrell, Johnny
b. 1902 Felton, Harold
W
b. 1905 Eyskens,
Gaston, Viscount
b. 1905 Hale, Clara
(McBride)
b. 1905 Hasluck, Paul
Meernaa, Sir
b. 1905 Moore, George
Stevens
b. 1906 Yakovlev,
Aleksandr
Sergeyevich
b. 1908 Maslow,
Abraham Harold
b. 1909 Duchin, Eddy
b. 1910 Carney, Harry
Howell
b. 1910 Lidz, Theodore
b. 1915 Conreid, Hans
b. 1915 Hemingway,
Leicester
b. 1917 Baker, Bonnie
b. 1917 Janney, Leon
b. 1918 Klein, Herbert
George
b. 1919 Murray, Joseph
b. 1920 Lund, Art(hur
Earl, Jr.)
b. 1920 Mifune, Toshiro

b. 1921 Reardon,
Ken(neth Joseph)
b. 1924 Byrne, Brendan
Thomas
b. 1927? Jump, Gordon
b. 1927 Shekhar,
Chandra
b. 1928 Grizzard,
George
b. 1928 Powell, Jane
b. 1929 Kundera, Milan
b. 1929 Schembechler,
Bo
b. 1931 Hochhuth, Rolf
b. 1932 Reynolds,
Debbie (Marie
Frances)
b. 1934 Brown, Jim Ed
b. 1934 Posner,
Vladimir
b. 1935 McDonald,
Larry
b. 1936 Kovac, Michael
b. 1936 Perranoski,
Ron(ald Peter)
b. 1937 Tekere, Edgar
Zivanai
b. 1938 MacGraw, Ali
b. 1939 Niekro, Phil(ip
Henry)
b. 1940 Jahn, Helmut
b. 1940 Maathai,
Wangari (Muta)
b. 1942 Delany, Samuel
R.
b. 1944 Staub, Rusty
b. 1946 Lane, Ronnie
b. 1947 Eisenhower,
David
b. 1955 Pohl, Dan(ny
Joe)
b. 1965 Jackson, Mark
b. 1972 Hughes, Albert
b. 1972 Hughes, Allen
d. 1204 Eleanor of
Aquitaine
d. 1865 Pasta, Giuditta
Negri
d. 1866 Harding,
Chester
d. 1872 Maurice,
Frederick Denison
d. 1878 Lohman, Ann
Trow
d. 1898 Orton, Arthur
d. 1911 Knapp, Seaman
Asahel
d. 1914 Waddell, Rube
d. 1916 Angell, James
Burrill
d. 1917 Joplin, Scott
d. 1926 Adler, Jacob
Pavlovitch
d. 1930 Wagner,
Cosima Liszt
d. 1933 Chelmsford,
Frederic John Napier
Thesiger, 1st
Viscount Chelmsford
d. 1936 Coolidge,
Charles Allerton
d. 1940 Hobson, John
Atkinson
d. 1946 Beery, Noah
d. 1947 George II

d. 1950 Drew, Charles Richard
d. 1950 Matthiessen, Francis Otto
d. 1952 Molnar, Ferenc
d. 1955 McCormick, Robert Rutherford
d. 1955 Towers, John Henry
d. 1962 Ghelderode, Michel de
d. 1965 Rubinstein, Helena
d. 1970 Warburg, Otto Heinrich
d. 1971 Lonsdale, Kathleen (Yardley)
d. 1974 Boyle, Harold Vincent
d. 1976 Blair, David
d. 1976 Ernst, Max
d. 1981 Alley, Norman William
d. 1984 Gaye, Marvin (Pentz)
d. 1984 Goudge, Elizabeth
d. 1985 Wallop, Douglass
d. 1986 Bruhn, Erik Belton Evers
d. 1986 Ciardi, John Anthony
d. 1987 Cochet, Henri
d. 1988 Jordan, Jim
d. 1991 Chaikin, Sol Chick
d. 1991 Graham, Martha
d. 1993 Juan Carlos, Count of Barcelona
d. 1993 Kulwicki, Alan
d. 1993 Zuckerman, Solly, Lord
d. 1995 Warner, Jack, Jr.
d. 1997 Gabor, Jolie
d. 1999 Carroll, Gladys Hasty

April 2
b. 742 Charlemagne
b. 1749 Ramsay, David
b. 1796 Pickering, William
b. 1805 Andersen, Hans Christian
b. 1806 Antonelli, Giacomo
b. 1812 Forster, John
b. 1814 Bigelow, Erastus Brigham
b. 1817 Palmer, Erastus Dow
b. 1827 Hunt, Holman
b. 1834 Bartholdi, Auguste
b. 1840 Zola, Emile (Edouard Charles)
b. 1847 Steel, Flora Annie Webster
b. 1850 Laughlin, James Laurence
b. 1851 Walker, Emery, Sir
b. 1862 Butler, Nicholas Murray

b. 1869 Berryman, Clifford Kennedy
b. 1870 Jennings, Hugh(ey Ambrose)
b. 1875 Chrysler, Walter Percy
b. 1883 Radin, Paul
b. 1884 Courboin, Charles
b. 1884 Hoagland, Dennis Robert
b. 1888 Ahearn, Daniel F.
b. 1889 Cardus, Neville, Sir
b. 1891 Buchanan, Jack
b. 1891 Ernst, Max
b. 1891 Howes, Frank Stewart
b. 1902 Peugeot, Rodolphe
b. 1903 Chevrier, Lionel
b. 1903 Hubbard, Orville Liscum
b. 1905 Adler, Kurt Herbert
b. 1905 Lifar, Serge
b. 1907 Appling, Luke
b. 1907 Selznick, Irene Mayer
b. 1908 Ebsen, Buddy
b. 1909 Marsala, Marty
b. 1909 Zondervan, Peter
b. 1910 Herber, Arnie
b. 1912 Mills, Herbert
b. 1913 Blofeld, John
b. 1914 Guinness, Alec, Sir
b. 1920 Webb, Jack Randolph
b. 1923 Schiess, Betty Bone
b. 1924 Avila, Bobby
b. 1925 Fraser, George MacDonald
b. 1925 Owen, Lewis James
b. 1925 Shulman, Morton
b. 1925 Stautner, Ernie
b. 1926 Brabham, Jack
b. 1926 Duffy, James Edson
b. 1927 Basilio, Carmen
b. 1927 Callaway, Howard Hollis
b. 1927 Tynan, Kenneth Peacock
b. 1928 Bernardin, Joseph L(ouis), Cardinal
b. 1928 Gam, Rita Elenore
b. 1933 Konrad, Gyorgy
b. 1935 Geyer, Georgie Anne
b. 1936 Giovenco, John Vincent
b. 1936 Owens, Rochelle
b. 1939 Gaye, Marvin (Pentz)
b. 1939 Lake, Anthony
b. 1941 Demento, Dr.

b. 1941 Ndungane, Winston N(jongonkulu)
b. 1941 Russell, Leon
b. 1943 Coryell, Larry
b. 1945 Hunt, Linda
b. 1945 Sutton, Don(ald Howard)
b. 1947 Harris, Emmylou
b. 1947 Paglia, Camille
b. 1954 Palillo, Ron
b. 1955 Carvey, Dana
b. 1959 Goodell, Brian Stuart
b. 1960 Christie, Linford
d. 1657 Ferdinand, III
d. 1709 Gaulli, Giovanni Battista
d. 1787 Gage, Thomas
d. 1791 Mirabeau, Honore Gabriel Riquetti
d. 1865 Cobden, Richard
d. 1865 Hill, Ambrose Powell
d. 1872 Morse, Samuel Finley Breese
d. 1880 Wieniawski, Henri
d. 1885 Barrios, Justo Rufino
d. 1896 Robinson, Theodore
d. 1898 Brann, William Cowper
d. 1900 Church, Frederick Edwin
d. 1914 Heyse, Paul Johann Ludwig von
d. 1922 Rorschach, Hermann
d. 1923 Jefferson, Thomas
d. 1928 Richards, Theodore William
d. 1932 Coghlan, Rose
d. 1935 Moten, Bennie
d. 1952 Lyot, Bernard Ferdinand
d. 1954 Heffelfinger, Pudge
d. 1954 O'Sheel, Shaemas
d. 1954 Vandenberg, Hoyt Sanford
d. 1956 Pisis, Filippo Tibertelli de
d. 1957 Sparks, Ned
d. 1961 Riegger, Wallingford
d. 1966 Forester, Cecil Scott
d. 1967 Gassner, John Waldhorn
d. 1968 Landau, Lev Davidovich
d. 1972 Hodges, Gil(bert Raymond)
d. 1974 Pompidou, Georges Jean Raymond
d. 1975 Cannon, Poppy
d. 1978 Noble, Ray

d. 1979 Rosenbloom, Carroll D
d. 1980 Reed, Stanley Forman
d. 1982 Bird, Junius Bouton
d. 1982 Coslow, Sam
d. 1982 McCall, Dorothy Lawson
d. 1984 Commager, Steele
d. 1985 Fernald, John Bailey
d. 1985 Tebelak, John Michael
d. 1987 Davis, Tommy
d. 1987 Rich, Buddy
d. 1988 Thomson, Vernon Wallace
d. 1993 Leontovich, Eugenie
d. 1994 Furness, Betty
d. 1995 Alfven, Hannes Olof Gosta
d. 1997 Tanaka, Tomoyuki

April 3
b. 1367 Henry IV
b. 1593 Herbert, George
b. 1751 Lemoyne, Jean-Baptiste
b. 1778 Bretonneau, Pierre Fidele
b. 1783 Irving, Washington
b. 1791 Lister, Anne
b. 1793 Lardner, Dionysius
b. 1798 Wilkes, Charles
b. 1822 Hale, Edward Everett
b. 1823 Tweed, Boss
b. 1837 Burroughs, John
b. 1838 Gambetta, Leon
b. 1861 DeKoven, (Henry Louis) Reginald
b. 1863 van de Velde, Henry
b. 1866 Hertzog, James Barry Munnik
b. 1876 Anglin, Margaret Mary
b. 1881 De Gasperi, Alcide
b. 1885 Dwan, Allan
b. 1885 Fisher, Bud
b. 1886 Gumilev, Nikolai
b. 1888 Webb, Walter Prescott
b. 1893 Howard, Leslie
b. 1894 Wilson, Dooley
b. 1895 Castelnuovo-Tedesco, Mario
b. 1895 Confrey, Zez
b. 1895 Mischakoff, Mischa
b. 1895 Strang, Ruth May
b. 1896 Traglia, Luigi, Cardinal
b. 1897 Aadlberg, John O.
b. 1898 Esau, Katherine

b. 1898 Ghelderode,
Michel de
b. 1898 Jessel, George
Albert
b. 1898 Luce, Henry
Robinson
b. 1900 Brownell,
Samuel Miller
b. 1900 Chamoun,
Camille N(imer)
b. 1901 Hare, Raymond
A(rthur)
b. 1902 Gehlen,
Reinhard
b. 1903 Bailey, Ace
b. 1904 Wright, Russel
b. 1905 Halliday,
Richard
b. 1911 DiDonato,
Pietro
b. 1911 Walsh, Stella
b. 1912 Eden, Dorothy
b. 1915 Cody, Iron
Eyes
b. 1916 Caen, Herb
b. 1917 Clements,
William Perry, Jr.
b. 1918 Ehrling, Sixten
b. 1919 Edwards,
Sherman
b. 1921? Demjanjuk,
John
b. 1921 Landers, Harry
b. 1923 Sterling, Jan
b. 1923 Wortman,
Sterling
b. 1924 Brando,
Marlon, Jr.
b. 1924 Day, Doris
b. 1925 Benn, Tony
b. 1926 Grissom, Virgil
Ivan
b. 1928 Gibson,
Don(ald)
b. 1929 Khan, Fazlur
Rahman
b. 1929 Umeki, Miyoshi
b. 1930 Chiles, Lawton
Mainor, Jr.
b. 1930 Frankel, Max
b. 1930 Kohl, Helmut
(Michael)
b. 1932 Stevens,
George, Jr.
b. 1934 Goodall, Jane
b. 1934 Mayhew,
Richard
b. 1934 Parker, Jim
b. 1935 Kushner,
Harold S(amuel)
b. 1937 Perret, Gene
b. 1937 Spuzich, Sandra
Ann
b. 1941 Berry, Jan
b. 1941 Ford, Charlotte
b. 1942 Haas, Robert
D(ouglas)
b. 1942 Mason, Marsha
b. 1942 Newton, Wayne
b. 1944 Orlando, Tony
b. 1945 Knight, John
Shively, III
b. 1945 Parent, Bernie
b. 1946 Suchocka,
Hanna

b. 1947 Namaliu,
Rabbie Langanai
b. 1948 Salinas de
Gortari, Carlos
b. 1949 Alzado, Lyle
Martin
b. 1949 Thompson,
Richard
b. 1950 West, Riff
b. 1953 Francis,
Russ(ell Ross)
b. 1958 Baldwin, Alec
b. 1959 Pierce, David
Hyde
b. 1961 Murphy, Eddie
d. 1680 Sivaji
d. 1682 Murillo,
Bartolome Esteban
d. 1826 Heber, Reginald
d. 1882 James, Jesse
Woodson
d. 1897 Brahms,
Johannes
d. 1901 Carte, Richard
d'Oyly
d. 1915 Peretz, Isaac
Loeb
d. 1918 Tillman,
Benjamin Ryan
d. 1921 Cary, Anne
Louise
d. 1925 DeReszke, Jean
d. 1935 Lukeman,
Henry A
d. 1936 Hauptmann,
Bruno Richard
d. 1943 Veidt, Conrad
d. 1946 Dixon, Thomas
d. 1950 Weill, Kurt
d. 1950 Woodson,
Carter Godwin
d. 1955 Hofer, Karl
d. 1957 Westwick,
Harry
d. 1964 Holmes, John
Haynes
d. 1966 Crouse, Russel
d. 1971 Kappel,
Gertrude
d. 1971 Lee, Manfred
B(ennington)
d. 1971 Valachi, Joe
d. 1972 Grofe, Ferde
d. 1975 Soglow, Otto
d. 1975 Ure, Mary
d. 1980 Bullard, Edward
Crisp, Sir
d. 1981 Kanner, Leo
d. 1981 Trippe, Juan
Terry
d. 1982 Oates, Warren
d. 1986 Kirstein,
George G
d. 1986 Pears, Peter, Sir
d. 1988 Caniff, Milt(on
Arthur)
d. 1990 Carlson,
Edward Elmer
d. 1990 Vaughan, Sarah
Lois
d. 1991 Goren, Charles
Henry
d. 1991 Greene, Graham
(Henry)
d. 1992 Bohrod, Aaron

d. 1993 Goodman,
Andrew
d. 1993 Lee, Pinky
d. 1993 Plage, Dieter
d. 1996 Brown, Ron(ald
Harmon)
d. 1997 Wyeth,
Henriette (Zirngiebel)
d. 1999 Bart, Lionel

April 4
b. 186 Caracalla,
Marcus Aurelius
Antonius
b. 1527 Ortelius,
Abraham
b. 1578 Philip, III
b. 1648 Gibbons,
Grinling
b. 1688 Delisle, Joseph-
Nicolas
b. 1752 Zingarelli,
Nicola Antonio
b. 1758 Hoppner, John
b. 1758 Prudhon, Pierre-
Paul
b. 1758 Prud'hon, Pierre
Paul
b. 1780 Hicks, Edward
b. 1792 Stevens,
Thaddeus
b. 1793 Delavigne, Jean
Francois Casimir
b. 1802 Dix, Dorothea
Lynde
b. 1809 Peirce,
Benjamin
b. 1810 Clarke, James
Freeman
b. 1821 Yale, Linus
b. 1823 Siemens,
William, Sir
b. 1826 Gramme,
Zenobe Theophile
b. 1828 Oliphant,
Margaret
b. 1835 Jackson, John
Hughlings
b. 1843 Jackson,
William Henry
b. 1843 Richter, Hans
b. 1846 Lautreamont,
Comte de
b. 1846 Pictet, Raoul-
Pierre
b. 1858 Gourmont,
Remy (-Marie-
Charles) de
b. 1873 Faure, Elie
b. 1875 Liggett, Louis
Kroh
b. 1875 Monteux, Pierre
b. 1876 Vlaminck,
Maurice de
b. 1880 Flint, William
Russell, Sir
b. 1884 Yamamoto,
Isoroku
b. 1886 Mott, Frank
Luther
b. 1888 Speaker,
Tris(tram E)
b. 1895 Boylston, Helen
Dore
b. 1895 Murray, Arthur
b. 1896 Sherwood,
Robert Emmet

b. 1896 Tzara, Tristan
b. 1898 Tracy, Lee
b. 1899 Belbenoit, Rene
Lucien
b. 1899 Hannagan,
Steve
b. 1903 Nabokov,
Nicolas
b. 1904 Afinogenov,
Aleksandr
Nikolaevich
b. 1905 Manero, Tony
b. 1906 Benaderet, Bea
b. 1906 Reynolds,
R(ichard) J(oshua), Jr.
b. 1906 Swayze, John
Cameron, Sr.
b. 1907 Pusey, Nathan
Marsh
b. 1908? Tudor, Antony
b. 1912 Chorell,
Walentin
b. 1913 Langford,
Frances
b. 1913 Leger, Jules
b. 1913 Weidman,
Jerome
b. 1914 Duras,
Marguerite
b. 1914 Kopal, Zdenek
b. 1914 Lane, Rosemary
b. 1915 Ahlin, Lars
b. 1915 Waters, Muddy
b. 1916 Owen, Mickey
b. 1918 Ashbrook,
Joseph
b. 1922 Bernstein,
Elmer
b. 1922 Manchester,
William Raymond
b. 1924 Hodges,
Gil(bert Raymond)
b. 1928 Angelou, Maya
b. 1931 Inman, Bobby
Ray
b. 1932 Davis, Clive
Jay
b. 1932 Lugar, Richard
Green
b. 1932 Tarkovsky,
Andrei (Arsenyich)
b. 1938 Giamatti,
A(ngelo) Bartlett
b. 1938 Parks, Michael
b. 1939 Bridges, Bill
b. 1939 Masekela, Hugh
Ramapolo
b. 1940 Bijan
b. 1940 Hailwood, Mike
b. 1942 Kelley, Kitty
b. 1944 Faisal ibn
Musaed
b. 1944 Nelson, Craig T
b. 1948 Parsons,
Richard Dean
b. 1950 Lahti, Christine
b. 1951 Hannah, John
Allen
b. 1963 Green, Benny
b. 1963 Hawerchuk,
Dale
b. 1965 Downey,
Robert, Jr.
b. 1965 Downey,
Robert, Jr.
b. 1966 McKeon, Nancy

d. 397 Ambrose, Saint
d. 1284 Alfonso, X
d. 1617 Napier, John
d. 1774 Goldsmith, Oliver
d. 1804 Necker, Jacques
d. 1807 Lalande, Joseph Jerome Lefrancais de
d. 1831 Thomas, Isaiah
d. 1841 Harrison, William Henry
d. 1861 McLean, John
d. 1879 Bonaparte, Elizabeth Patterson
d. 1879 Dove, Heinrich Wilhelm
d. 1883 Cooper, Peter
d. 1889 Mahan, Asa
d. 1889 Remington, Eliphalet
d. 1900 Bidwell, John
d. 1900 Van Camp, Gilbert C
d. 1912 Funk, Isaac Kauffman
d. 1914 Weyerhaeuser, Frederick
d. 1918 Cohen, Hermann
d. 1919 Crookes, William, Sir
d. 1919 Stefanik, Milan Rastislav
d. 1929 Benz, Karl Friedrich
d. 1932 Ostwald, Friedrich Wilhelm
d. 1933 Custer, Elizabeth Bacon
d. 1943 Laparra, Raoul
d. 1949 Kent, Arthur Atwater
d. 1953 Carol II
d. 1958 Stompanato, Johnny
d. 1959 Cleghorn, Sarah Norcliffe
d. 1961 Sachse, Leopold
d. 1963 Robards, Jason
d. 1967 Chamberlin, B Guy
d. 1968 King, Martin Luther, Jr.
d. 1969 Gallegos, Romulo
d. 1969 Welch, Herbert
d. 1972 Powell, Adam Clayton, Jr.
d. 1972 Wolpe, Stefan
d. 1979 Bhutto, Zulfikar Ali
d. 1979 Buchanan, Edgar
d. 1981 Jensen, Alfred Julio
d. 1983 Rapp, Danny
d. 1983 Swanson, Gloria May Josephine
d. 1984 Merrill, John Putnam
d. 1990 Smith, Cyrus Rowlett
d. 1991 Frisch, Max
d. 1991 Heinz, John
d. 1992 Reshevsky, Samuel

d. 1993 Butts, Alfred M(osher)
d. 1993 Shirley, Anne
d. 1994 Simms, Ginny
d. 1995 Lane, Priscilla
d. 1995 Sinclair, Jo
d. 1996 Stokes, Carl B(urton)
d. 1997 Appley, Lawrence A(sa)
d. 1998 Pilatus, Rob(ert)
d. 1999 Lortel, Lucille
d. 1999 Wynn, Early

April 5
b. 1588 Hobbes, Thomas
b. 1648 Franceschini, Marcantonio
b. 1649 Yale, Elihu
b. 1692 Lecouvreur, Adrienne
b. 1725 Casanova (de Seingalt), Giovanni Giacomo
b. 1726? Harrison, Benjamin
b. 1732 Fragonard, Jean-Honore
b. 1732 Rittenhouse, David
b. 1761 Ludington, Sybil
b. 1784 Spohr, Louis Ludwig
b. 1798 Chickering, Jonas
b. 1804 Schleiden, Matthias Jakob
b. 1816 Miller, Samuel Freeman
b. 1820 Nadar
b. 1824 Dobell, Sydney Thompson
b. 1825 Holmes, Mary Jane Hawes
b. 1827 Lister, Joseph
b. 1832 Ferry, Jules Francois Camille
b. 1834 Stockton, Frank
b. 1837 Swinburne, Algernon Charles
b. 1838 Hyatt, Alpheus
b. 1839 Smalls, Robert
b. 1856 Washington, Booker T(aliafero)
b. 1858 Burpee, W(ashington) Atlee
b. 1865 Filene, Lincoln
b. 1869 Roussel, Albert
b. 1871 Warner, Pop
b. 1874 Jones, Jesse Holman
b. 1875 Mistinguett
b. 1876 Dinneen, Bill
b. 1882 Hall, Joe
b. 1882 Sung Chiao-jen
b. 1883 Speicher, Eugene Edward
b. 1893 Burpee, David
b. 1893 DePaolis, Alessio
b. 1894 Bell, Lawrence Dale
b. 1898 Dehnert, Henry
b. 1899 Anderson, Elda Emma

b. 1899 Blalock, Alfred
b. 1900 Bayer, Herbert
b. 1900 Tracy, Spencer Bonaventure
b. 1901 Alexander, Hattie Elizabeth
b. 1901 Bowles, Chester Bliss
b. 1901 Douglas, Melvyn
b. 1901 Johnson, Raynor Carey
b. 1901 Julian, Doggie
b. 1904 Eberhart, Richard (Ghormley)
b. 1908 Carey, Ernestine Moller Gilbreth
b. 1908 Davis, Bette
b. 1908 Hemingway, Mary Welsh
b. 1908 Karajan, Herbert von
b. 1908 Ram, Jagjivan
b. 1911 Revolta, Johnny
b. 1913 Clave, Antoni
b. 1916 Peck, Gregory
b. 1917 Bloch, Robert Albert
b. 1920 Hailey, Arthur
b. 1921 Lewis, Robert Q
b. 1922 Chatichai Choonhavan
b. 1922 Storm, Gale
b. 1923 Nguyen Van Thieu
b. 1923 Rothstein, Ruth
b. 1924 Chew, Peter
b. 1926 Corman, Roger William
b. 1929 Claus, Hugo
b. 1929 Giaever, Ivar
b. 1930 Cheshire, Maxine
b. 1930 Costa, Mary
b. 1934 Gorshin, Frank John
b. 1934 Herzog, Roman
b. 1937 Carter, Ron
b. 1937 Lelyveld, Joseph Salem
b. 1937 Powell, Colin (Luther)
b. 1938 Massey, Walter E(ugene)
b. 1941 Burdon, Eric
b. 1941 Moriarty, Michael
b. 1942 Greenaway, Peter
b. 1943 Gail, Max(well Trowbridge, Jr.)
b. 1949 Borders, James
b. 1949 Resnik, Judy
b. 1950 Faltskog, Agnetha
b. 1952 Mayer, Sandy
b. 1958 Kriek, Johann
b. 1621 Carver, John
b. 1684 Van Cortlandt, Oloff Stevenszen
d. 1723 Fischer von Erlach, Johann Bernhard
b. 1765 Young, Edward

d. 1794 Danton, Georges Jacques
d. 1794 Desmoulins, Camille
d. 1833 Niepce, Joseph Nicephore
d. 1882 Le Play, Guillaume Frederic
d. 1882 Pierce, John Davis
d. 1900 Bertrand, Joseph Louis Francois
d. 1906 Johnson, Eastman
d. 1906 Johnson, Jonathan Eastman
d. 1919 Hall, Joe
d. 1921 Mifflin, George Harrison
d. 1923 Mallock, William Hurrell
d. 1928 Depew, Chauncey Mitchell
d. 1933 Biggers, Earl Derr
d. 1944 Winter, Alice Vivian Ames
d. 1946 Youmans, Vincent
d. 1954 DuPont, Pierre Samuel
d. 1961 Canby, Henry Seidel
d. 1963 Oud, Jacobus Johannes Pieter
d. 1964 MacArthur, Douglas
d. 1966 Gill, Amory Tingle
d. 1967 Elman, Mischa
d. 1967 Muller, Hermann Joseph
d. 1970 Sturtevant, Alfred Henry
d. 1971 Mowrer, Paul Scott
d. 1972 Donahue, Woolworth
d. 1972 Donlevy, Brian
d. 1973 Tarasova, Alla Konstantinovna
d. 1974 Crossman, Richard Howard Stafford
d. 1974 Vyvyan, Jennifer Brigit
d. 1975 Chiang Kai-Shek
d. 1976 Davis, Meyer
d. 1976 Hughes, Howard Robard
d. 1976 Penfield, Wilder Graves
d. 1977 Prio Socarras, Carlos
d. 1978 Tagliabue, Carlo
d. 1980 McCarty, Mary
d. 1981 Ethridge, Mark Foster
d. 1981 Hite, Robert Ernest, Jr.
d. 1982 Fortas, Abe
d. 1982 Lawrenson, Helen Brown

d. 1984 Harris, Arthur
Travers, Sir
d. 1987 Jonathan,
Leabua, Chief
d. 1991 Tower, John
Goodwin
d. 1992 Walton, Sam
Moore
d. 1993 Lee, Robert
E(mmet)
d. 1995 Pineau,
Christian (Paul
Francis)
d. 1997 Ginsberg, Allen
d. 1997 Heckscher,
August

April 6
b. 1627 Sivaji
b. 1732 Mutis, Jose
Celestino
b. 1745 Dawes, William
b. 1773 Mill, James
b. 1812 Herzen,
Aleksandr Ivanovich
b. 1823 Medill, Joseph
b. 1826 Moreau,
Gustave
b. 1839 Przhevalsky,
Nikolai Mikhailovich
b. 1852 Cole, Timothy
b. 1860 Lalique, Rene
b. 1866 Cassidy, Butch
b. 1866 Steffens,
Lincoln
b. 1869 Raemaekers,
Louis
b. 1870 Straus, Oskar
b. 1878 Eberle, Mary
Abastenia St. Leger
b. 1879 Prouty, Jed
b. 1882 Schneiderman,
Rose
b. 1884 Huston, Walter
b. 1888 Richter, Hans
b. 1890 Danjon, Andre
Louis
b. 1890 Fokker,
Anthony Herman
Gerard
b. 1890 Tydings,
Millard Evelyn
b. 1892 Douglas,
Donald Willis
b. 1892 Thomas, Lowell
Jackson
b. 1895 Craig, Cleo F
b. 1895 Robin, Leo
b. 1897 Coates, Robert
Myron
b. 1903 Cochrane,
Mickey
b. 1903 Edgerton,
Harold Eugene
b. 1903 Jackson,
Charles Reginald
b. 1904 Kiesinger, Kurt
Georg
b. 1905 Cardozo, W.
Warrick
b. 1907 Day, Chon
b. 1908 Lombardi, Ernie
b. 1910 Teague, Olin E
b. 1911 Lynen, Feodor
Felix Konrad
b. 1913 Ruchlis,
Hy(man)

b. 1917 Macy, John
Williams, Jr.
b. 1918 Ovando Candia,
Alfredo
b. 1920 Fischer,
Edmond
b. 1921 Thompson,
Moose
b. 1922 Donegan,
Dorothy
b. 1924 Benzell, Mimi
b. 1924 King, Bruce
b. 1924 Mita,
Katsushige
b. 1926 Butterfield,
Alexander Porter
b. 1926 Paisley, Ian
Richard Kyle
b. 1927 Mulligan, Gerry
b. 1928 Watson, James
Dewey
b. 1929 Previn, Andre
b. 1930 Bristow, Lonnie
b. 1930 Lansing, Joi
b. 1931 Dixon, Ivan
b. 1933 Snyder, Richard
Elliot
b. 1936 Thinnes, Roy
b. 1937 Haggard, Merle
Ronald
b. 1937 Williams, Billy
Dee
b. 1938 Smith, Jack
b. 1939 Sculley, John
b. 1942 Levinson, Barry
(Michael)
b. 1944? Dumurcq,
Charles
b. 1944 Huarte, John G
b. 1944 Phillips,
Michelle Gillam
b. 1947 Ratzenberger,
John Dezso
b. 1948 Fisher, Mary
b. 1951 Blyleven, Bert
b. 1952 Larocque,
Bunny
b. 1953 Henner, Marilu
b. 1953 Lynn, Janet
b. 1956 Darden,
Christopher A.
b. 1965 Sharpe, Sterling
b. 1972 Hervey, Jason
d. 1199 Richard I
d. 1490 Matthias
Corvinus
d. 1520 Raphael
d. 1528 Durer, Albrecht
d. 1590 Walsingham,
Francis, Sir
d. 1614 Greco, El
d. 1637 Jonson,
Ben(jamin)
d. 1641 Domenichino, Il
d. 1684? Heem, Jan
Davidsz(oon) de
d. 1779 Traetta,
Tommaso
d. 1829 Abel, Niels
Henrik
d. 1838 Andrada e
Silva, Jose Bonifacio
de
d. 1862 Johnston, Albert
Sidney

d. 1864 Kirkland,
Caroline Matilda
Stansbury
d. 1886 Forster, William
Edward
d. 1907 Drummond,
William Henry
d. 1912 Pascoli,
Giovanni
d. 1923 Fletcher, Alice
Cunningham
d. 1923 Herbert, George
Edward Stanhope
Molyneux
d. 1935 Robinson,
Edwin Arlington
d. 1936 Breese, Edmund
d. 1936 Lavigne, Kid
d. 1941 Burr, Henry
d. 1944 O'Neill, Rose
Cecil
d. 1951 Cuong De
d. 1961 Bordet, Jules
Jean Baptiste Vincent
d. 1963 Struve, Otto
d. 1966 Brunner, Emil
d. 1967 Connor,
William Neil, Sir
d. 1970 Sheppard,
Sam(uel)
d. 1970 Tenggren,
Gustaf Adolf
d. 1971 Stravinsky, Igor
Fedorovich
d. 1972 Lubke, Heinrich
d. 1974 Jackson,
A(lexander) Y(oung)
d. 1976 Thompson,
Ruth Plumly
d. 1978 Kelly, Stephen
Eugene
d. 1978 Nabokov,
Nicolas
d. 1984 Peers, William
Raymond
d. 1992 Asimov, Isaac
d. 1992 Mark, Herman
Francis
d. 1992 Picon, Molly
d. 1994 Habyarimana,
Juvenal
d. 1994 Ntaryamira,
Cyprien
d. 1995 Harris, Derek
d. 1996 Garson, Greer
d. 1996 McMurrin,
Sterling M(oss)
d. 1997 Cooke, Jack
Kent
d. 1998 Lasch, Robert
d. 1998 Williams,
Wendy O(rlean)
d. 1998 Wynette,
Tammy
d. 1999 Norvo, Red
d. 2000 Bourguiba,
Habib Ben Ali

April 7
b. 1613 Dou, Gerard
b. 1640? Hennepin,
Louis
b. 1726 Burney, Charles
b. 1770 Wordsworth,
William

b. 1772 Fourier,
Francois Marie
Charles
b. 1775 Lowell, Francis
Cabot
b. 1780 Channing,
William Ellery
b. 1781 Chantrey,
Francis Legatt, Sir
b. 1786 King, William
Rufus de Vane
b. 1792 Drexel, Francis
Martin
b. 1794 Rubini,
Giovanni-Battista
b. 1809 Glaisher, James
b. 1846 Tosti, Francesco
Paolo
b. 1847 Jacobsen, Jens
Peter
b. 1856 Fuller-Maitland,
John Alexander
b. 1859 Camp, Walter
Chauncey
b. 1859 Loeb, Jacques
b. 1860 Kellogg, Will
Keith
b. 1863 Green, Thomas
Hill
b. 1864 Hassan,
Muhammad Abdille
b. 1869 Fairchild, David
Grandison
b. 1872 Trotter, Monroe
b. 1873 McGraw, John
Joseph
b. 1882 Schleicher, Kurt
von
b. 1883 Severini, Gino
b. 1884 Dodd, Charles
Harold
b. 1884 Malinowski,
Bronislaw Kasper
b. 1890 Douglas,
Marjory (Stoneman)
b. 1891 Eliot, Martha
May
b. 1891 Low, David
Alexander Cecil, Sir
b. 1893 Armstrong,
Hamilton Fish
b. 1893 Castle, Irene
Foote
b. 1893 Dulles, Allen
Welsh
b. 1894 Brenan, Gerald
b. 1895 Flannagan, John
Bernard
b. 1895 Wheeler, Bert
b. 1896 Fairchild,
Sherman Mills
b. 1896 Leonard, Benny
b. 1897 Winchell,
Walter
b. 1899 Casadesus,
Robert
b. 1899 Mistral,
Gabriela
b. 1901 Paton, Richard
b. 1907 Gordon-Walker
of Leyton, Patrick
Chrestien Gordon-
Walker, Baron
b. 1907 Liebman,
Joshua Loth
b. 1907 Shimkin, Leon

d. 1981 Bradley, Omar Nelson

d. 1981 Russell, Edward Frederick Langley, Baron of Liverpool

d. 1984 Kapitsa, Pyotr Leonidovich

d. 1985 Coots, J Fred

d. 1988 Gianninoto, Frank Anthony

d. 1990 Greenaway, Emerson

d. 1990 White, Ryan

d. 1992 Bovet, Daniele

d. 1992 Cherberg, John A(ndrew)

d. 1993 Anderson, Marian

d. 1993 Soloveitchik, Joseph Baer

d. 1994 Cobain, Kurt

d. 1996 Johnson, Ben

d. 1997 Nyro, Laura

d. 2000 Trevor, Claire

April 9

b. 1649 Monmouth, James Scott, Duke

b. 1757 Boguslawski, Wojciech

b. 1758 Ames, Fisher

b. 1765 Narino, Antonio

b. 1770 Seebeck, Thomas Johann

b. 1798 Pasta, Giuditta Negri

b. 1806 Brunel, Isambard Kingdom

b. 1821 Baudelaire, Charles Pierre

b. 1830 Muybridge, Eadweard

b. 1835 Leopold II

b. 1855 Osgood, Herbert Levi

b. 1863 Kitson, Henry Hudson

b. 1865 Ludendorff, Erich Friedrich Wilhelm

b. 1865 Steinmetz, Charles Proteus

b. 1872 Blum, Leon

b. 1875 Futrelle, Jacques

b. 1879 Meighan, Thomas

b. 1883 King, Frank

b. 1887 Adair, Frank E(arl)

b. 1888 Hurok, Sol(omon Isaievich)

b. 1891 Szenkar, Eugen

b. 1893 Burchfield, Charles Ephraim

b. 1893 Fineman, Irving

b. 1893 Gollancz, Victor, Sir

b. 1894 Manville, Tommy

b. 1897 Gambling, John Bradley

b. 1898 Lambeau, Curly

b. 1898 Patzak, Julius

b. 1898 Robeson, Paul Leroy

b. 1899 McDonnell, James Smith

b. 1900 Jenkins, Allen

b. 1901 Kotsching, Walter Maria

b. 1902 Cecil, Edward Christian David Gascoyne

b. 1903 Bond, Ward

b. 1903 Pincus, Gregory

b. 1905 Fulbright, J(ames) William

b. 1906 Dorati, Antal

b. 1906? Faisal (Ibn Abdul-Aziz al Saud)

b. 1906 Gaitskell, Hugh (Todd Naylor)

b. 1907 Goodfellow, Ebbie

b. 1908 Allan, Elizabeth

b. 1908 Krumgold, Joseph (Quincy)

b. 1908 Vasarely, Victor

b. 1908 Wilcox, Francis (Orlando)

b. 1909 Helpmann, Robert Murray, Sir

b. 1910 Ribicoff, Abraham A(lexander)

b. 1912 Borglum, James Lincoln Delamothe

b. 1915 Wibberley, Leonard Patrick O'Connor

b. 1916 Leonard, Bill

b. 1917 Hewes, Henry

b. 1918 Utzon, Jorn

b. 1919 Eckert, John Presper, Jr.

b. 1919 Moncreiffe, Iain

b. 1923 Levy, Leonard Williams

b. 1925 Goodman, Linda

b. 1926 Hefner, Hugh Marston

b. 1928 Arizin, Paul Joseph

b. 1928 Lehrer, Tom

b. 1929 Learned, Michael

b. 1929 Lichtenstein, Harvey

b. 1929 Marshall, Paule

b. 1931 Hatfield, Richard

b. 1932 Krassner, Paul

b. 1932 Perkins, Carl (Lee)

b. 1933 Belmondo, Jean-Paul

b. 1935 Schreiber, Avery

b. 1939 Rogers, Lynn L(eroy)

b. 1942 DeWilde, Brandon

b. 1942 Fedoroff, Nina V(sevolod)

b. 1954 Quaid, Dennis William

b. 1957 Ballesteros, Seve(riano)

b. 1957 Macy, Kyle Robert

b. 1965 Porizkova, Paulina

b. 1971 Villeneuve, Jacques

b. 1979 Pulliam, Keisha Knight

d. 1483 Edward IV

d. 1588 Veronese, Paolo

d. 1626 Bacon, Francis, Sir

d. 1754 Wolff, Christian von, Baron

d. 1778 Hesselius, John

d. 1841 Ladd, William

d. 1852 Payne, John Howard

d. 1872 Corning, Erastus

d. 1882 Rossetti, Dante Gabriel

d. 1889 Chevreul, Michel Eugene

d. 1899 Field, Stephen Johnson

d. 1905 Woolsey, Sarah Chauncey

d. 1909 Crawford, Francis Marion

d. 1909 Modjeska, Helena

d. 1917 Thomas, Edward

d. 1922 Manson, Patrick, Sir

d. 1926 Miller, Henry John

d. 1936 Tonnies, Ferdinand

d. 1937 Paine, Albert Bigelow

d. 1940 Campbell, Patrick, Mrs.

d. 1941 Witmark, Isidore

d. 1945 Bonhoeffer, Dietrich

d. 1945 Canaris, Wilhelm

d. 1948 Gaitan, Jorge Eliecer

d. 1951 Bjerknes, Vilhelm (Frimann Koren)

d. 1951 Hidayat, Sadiq

d. 1952 Tharaud, Jean

d. 1956 Little, Little Jack

d. 1959 Wright, Frank Lloyd

d. 1961 Zog I

d. 1962 Lamb, Harold Albert

d. 1963 Jones, Joe

d. 1964 Brendel, El(mer)

d. 1965 Minton, Sherman

d. 1970 Wright, Cobina

d. 1971 Harridge, Will(iam)

d. 1972 Byrnes, James Francis

d. 1976 Ochs, Phil(ip David)

d. 1977 Grant, Bruce

d. 1979 Cotsworth, Staats

d. 1981 Scott, Austin Wakeman

d. 1982 Barrios, Francisco Javier

d. 1982 Pelletier, Wilfrid

d. 1984 Blackwell, Basil Henry, Sir

d. 1988 Benton, Brook

d. 1988 DuPont, Pierre Samuel, III

d. 1988 Prater, Dave

d. 1990 Faulk, John Henry

d. 1991 Rich, Louise Dickinson

d. 1991 Towns, Forrest

d. 1992 Ginsburg, Charles P

d. 1992 McGee, Gale William

d. 1995 Chamberlain, John Rensselaer

d. 1996 Condon, Richard (Thomas)

d. 1996 Rouse, James W(ilson)

d. 2000 Komer, Robert William

April 10

b. 1512 James V

b. 1583 Grotius, Hugo

b. 1755 Hahnemann, Samuel

b. 1778 Hazlitt, William

b. 1794 Perry, Matthew Calbraith, Commodore

b. 1794 Robinson, Edward

b. 1810 Day, Benjamin Henry

b. 1827 Wallace, Lew(is)

b. 1829 Booth, William

b. 1835 Villard, Henry

b. 1847 Pulitzer, Joseph

b. 1850 Davenport, Fanny Lily Gypsy

b. 1857 Levy-Bruhl, Lucien

b. 1862 Cross, Wilbur Lucius

b. 1863 Heroult, Paul Louis Toussaint

b. 1864 D'Albert, Eugene

b. 1865 Miner, Jack

b. 1867 Russell, George William

b. 1867 Sandow, Eugene

b. 1868 Arliss, George

b. 1872 Hirshfield, Morris

b. 1879 Hertz, John Daniel

b. 1881 Little, Edward Herman

b. 1882 Perkins, Frances

b. 1885 Gimbel, Bernard Feustman

b. 1885 Spaeth, Sigmund Gottfried

b. 1887 Houssay, Bernardo Alberto
b. 1889 Murray, Mae
b. 1891 McCoy, Tim(othy John Fitzgerald)
b. 1892 DeSabata, Victor
b. 1893 Mompou, Federico
b. 1894 Nicholson, Ben
b. 1895 Russell, Edward Frederick Langley, Baron of Liverpool
b. 1897 Youngs, Ross Middlebrook
b. 1898 Gregory, Horace Victor
b. 1900 Beckman, Arnold (Orville)
b. 1901 Kavan, Anna
b. 1903 Graf, Herbert
b. 1905 Fletcher, Joseph Francis (III)
b. 1906 Darvas, Lili
b. 1906 Gates, Thomas Sovereign, Jr.
b. 1907 Murphy, Charles
b. 1908 Feather, Victor
b. 1909 Cannon, Jimmy
b. 1910 Wauneka, Annie Dodge
b. 1911 Schumann, Maurice
b. 1912 Hinkle, W Clarke
b. 1912 Hofheinz, Roy Mark
b. 1913 Heym, Stefan
b. 1915 DeButts, John Dulany
b. 1915 Morgan, Harry
b. 1917 Woodward, Robert Burns
b. 1921 Connors, Chuck
b. 1921 Risling, David
b. 1921 Wooley, Sheb
b. 1922 Simonetta
b. 1923 Old Coyote, Barney
b. 1923 Popovi Da
b. 1924 Noland, Kenneth Clifton
b. 1926 Nossiter, Bernard Daniel
b. 1927 Brandon, Brumsic, Jr.
b. 1927 Nirenberg, Marshall Warren
b. 1927? Samples, Junior
b. 1929 VonSydow, Max Carl Adolf
b. 1930 Blanton, (Leonard) Ray
b. 1930 Huerta, Dolores (Fernandez)
b. 1931 Dozier, James Lee
b. 1931 Lary, Frank Strong
b. 1932 Rhodes, Hari
b. 1932 Sharif, Omar
b. 1934 Halberstam, David

b. 1935 Patterson, P(ercival Noel) J(ames)
b. 1936 Madden, John
b. 1938 Meredith, Don
b. 1939 Oliver, Daniel
b. 1941 Gleason, John James
b. 1941 Theroux, Paul Edward
b. 1942 Evans, Joni
b. 1948 Blount, Mel(vin Cornell)
b. 1949 Fay, Michael, Sir
b. 1950 Griffey, Ken
b. 1951 Roth, Mark Stephan
b. 1951 Seagal, Steven
b. 1958 Bronfman, Yefim
d. 1585 Gregory XIII
d. 1644 Brewster, William
d. 1739 Turpin, Dick
d. 1806 Gates, Horatio
d. 1813 Lagrange, Joseph-Louis
d. 1858 Benton, Thomas Hart
d. 1861 Tucker, George
d. 1876 Stewart, Alexander Turney
d. 1899 Tabor, Horace Austin Warner
d. 1909 Swinburne, Algernon Charles
d. 1911 Loyd, Sam(uel)
d. 1915 Bitter, Karl Theodore Francis
d. 1919 Zapata, Emiliano
d. 1931 Gibran, Kahlil
d. 1933 Vandyke, Henry Jackson, Jr.
d. 1944 Day, Joseph Paul
d. 1945 Becker, Carl Lotus
d. 1947 Flagg, Ernest
d. 1954 Lumiere, Auguste Marie Louis
d. 1955 Hughan, Jessie Wallace
d. 1955 Teilhard de Chardin, Pierre
d. 1960 Benjamin, Arthur
d. 1965 Darnell, Linda (Monetta Eloyse)
d. 1966 Waugh, Evelyn Arthur St. John
d. 1969 Bentley, Alvin Morell
d. 1970 Piastro, Michel
d. 1974 Collinge, Patricia
d. 1975 Evans, Walker
d. 1975 Main, Marjorie
d. 1976 Ortega, Santos
d. 1978 Nebel, Long John
d. 1980 Medford, Kay
d. 1980 White, Antonia
d. 1981 Ryan, Sylvester James

d. 1981 Thurman, Howard
d. 1983 Burton, Phillip
d. 1983 Wechsberg, Joseph
d. 1984 Middleton, Ray
d. 1985 Donghia, Angelo R
d. 1986 Addabbo, Joseph Patrick
d. 1986 Creed, Linda
d. 1986 Crosby, James Morris
d. 1987 Dassler, Horst
d. 1991 Schafer, Natalie
d. 1992 Kinison, Sam
d. 1992 Mitchell, Peter Dennis
d. 1993 Hani, Chris
d. 1995 Desai, Morarji (Ranchhodji)
d. 1997 Schwarzschild, Martin
d. 2000 Fitch, James Marston
d. 2000 Linville, Larry Lavon

April 11
b. Taylor, Meshach
b. 1492 Marguerite d'Angouleme
b. 1755 Parkinson, James
b. 1770 Canning, George
b. 1794 Everett, Edward
b. 1806 Le Play, Guillaume Frederic
b. 1819 Halle, Charles, Sir
b. 1821 Bergmann, Carl
b. 1825 Lassalle, Ferdinand
b. 1857 Davidson, John
b. 1859 Crowder, Enoch Herbert
b. 1862 Campbell, William Wallace
b. 1862 Freeman, R(ichard) Austin
b. 1862 Hughes, Charles Evans
b. 1865 Ovington, Mary White
b. 1869 Vigeland, Gustav
b. 1893 Acheson, Dean Gooderham
b. 1895 Murchison, Clint(on Williams, Sr.)
b. 1898 Holtz, Lou
b. 1899 Julian, Percy Lavon
b. 1901 Olivetti, Adriano
b. 1901 Wescott, Glenway
b. 1902 Reynolds, Quentin James
b. 1903 Gaither, Jake
b. 1905 Jozsef, Attila
b. 1905 Root, Lynn
b. 1908 Ancerl, Karel
b. 1908 Rosten, Leo C(alvin)

b. 1910 Clapp, Margaret Antoinette
b. 1910 Spinola, Antonio (Sebastiao Ribeiro) de
b. 1911 Saudek, Robert
b. 1912 George, Graham Elias
b. 1913 Cassini, Oleg Loiewski
b. 1914 Bernstein, Dorothy Lewis
b. 1914 McLaren, Norman
b. 1916 Fortmann, Danny
b. 1916 Ginastera, Alberto Evaristo
b. 1917 Sobell, Morton
b. 1919 Carey, Hugh Leo
b. 1920 Colombo, Emilio
b. 1920 O'Donnell, Peter
b. 1923 Rubin, Theodore Isaac
b. 1928 Kennedy, Ethel Skakel
b. 1930 Brady, Nicholas Frederick
b. 1932 Grey, Joel
b. 1933 Brown, Tony
b. 1934 Strand, Mark
b. 1938 Deaver, Michael Keith
b. 1939 Lasser, Louise
b. 1941 Goodman, Ellen Holtz
b. 1941 Platt, Lewis E
b. 1945 Koplovitz, Kay Smith
b. 1946 Nuridsany, Claude
b. 1949 Allison, Dorothy E.
b. 1950 Irwin, Bill
b. 1953 Wiles, Andrew J.
b. 1954 Difford, Chris
b. 1955 Richardson, Micheal Ray
b. 1956 Mayer, Gene
b. 1964 Saberhagen, Bret (William)
b. 1966 Reese, Mason
b. 1966 Stansfield, Lisa
d. 1834 Macarthur, John
d. 1839 Galt, John
d. 1842 England, John
d. 1884 Reade, Charles
d. 1890 Merrick, Joseph Carey
d. 1901 Hallstrom, Ivar
d. 1902 Hampton, Wade
d. 1906 Bailey, James Anthony
d. 1911 Harjo, Chitto
d. 1916 Davis, Richard Harding
d. 1918 Wagner, Otto
d. 1926 Burbank, Luther
d. 1932 Bradford, Gamaliel
d. 1934 DuMaurier, Gerald Hubert, Sir

d. 1935 Green, Anna Katharine
d. 1939 Van Dine, S S
d. 1943 Roper, Daniel C(alhoun)
d. 1947 Nordhoff, Charles Bernard
d. 1949 Booth, George Gough
d. 1953 Nichols, Kid
d. 1957 Crofts, Freeman Willis
d. 1962 Curtiz, Michael
d. 1964 Bok, Hannes Vajn
d. 1969 DuPont, Henry Francis
d. 1970 O'Donnell, Cathy
d. 1970 O'Hara, John Henry
d. 1973 Barker, Lex
d. 1975 Crerar, Thomas Alexander
d. 1981 Gordon, Caroline
d. 1981 Hagerty, James Campbell
d. 1981 Moore, Harry Thornton
d. 1983 DelRio, Dolores
d. 1985 Ertz, Susan
d. 1985 Hoxha, Enver
d. 1986 Goldstein, Israel
d. 1986 Karpin, Fred Leon
d. 1987 Caldwell, Erskine Preston
d. 1987 Levi, Primo
d. 1988 Cory, John Mackenzie
d. 1988 Donnell, Jeff
d. 1988 Lasky, Jesse Louis, Jr.
d. 1988 Shinichiro Imaoka
d. 1990 Ballard, Harold
d. 1992 Merriam, Eve
d. 1992 Obregon, Alejandro
d. 1995 Glennan, T(homas) Keith
d. 1996 Dubroff, Jessica
d. 1997 Dorris, Michael (Anthony)
d. 1999 Armstrong, William H(oward)

April 12
b. 1539 Garcilaso de la Vega, Inca
b. 1577 Christian IV
b. 1710 Carver, Jonathan
b. 1710 Majorano, Gaetano
b. 1716 Giardini, Felice di
b. 1724 Hall, Lyman
b. 1777 Clay, Henry
b. 1778 Strachan, John
b. 1792 Durham, 1st Earl of
b. 1823 Ostrovsky, Aleksandr Nikolaevich

b. 1831 Dodge, Grenville Mellen
b. 1840 Haberl, Franz Xaver
b. 1857 Underwood, John Thomas
b. 1871 Metaxas, John
b. 1873 Duncan, Augustin
b. 1874 Bankhead, William Brockman
b. 1875 Polacco, Giorgio
b. 1879 Melcher, Frederic Gershon
b. 1880 Joss, Addie
b. 1883 Cunningham, Imogen
b. 1883 Lewis, Clarence Irving
b. 1884 Meyerhof, Otto Fritz
b. 1885 Delaunay, Robert
b. 1885 Kuykendall, Ralph Simpson
b. 1891 Anderson, C(larence) W(illiam)
b. 1892 Dodds, Johnny
b. 1894 Gold, Michael
b. 1899 Taber, Gladys Bagg
b. 1899 Thompson, Randall
b. 1900 Lapchick, Joe
b. 1900 Leighton, Clare Veronica Hope
b. 1903 Tinbergen, Jan
b. 1904 Cockburn, Claud
b. 1904 Pons, Lily
b. 1905 Magnuson, Warren Grant
b. 1907 Gramatky, Hardie
b. 1908 Lleras Restrepo, Carlos
b. 1913 Hampton, Lionel Leo
b. 1916 Cleary, Beverly (Atlee Bunn)
b. 1917 Bijedic, Dzemal
b. 1917 Tree, Marietta Endicott Peabody
b. 1918 Forrest, Helen
b. 1920 Fizdale, Robert
b. 1922 Tiny Tim
b. 1923 Engle, Eloise Katherine
b. 1923? Miller, Ann
b. 1924 Barre, Raymond
b. 1926 Withers, Jane
b. 1927 Sargent, Alvin
b. 1927 Shanks, Michael
b. 1928 Kruger, Hardy
b. 1930 Antonelli, John(ny August)
b. 1930 Landy, John
b. 1932 Gelber, Jack
b. 1932 Rosen, Moishe Martin
b. 1933 Caballe, Montserrat Folch
b. 1933 Lau, Charlie

b. 1936 Simmonds, Kennedy Alphonse
b. 1937 Banks, Dennis J.
b. 1939 Ayckbourn, Alan
b. 1940 Hancock, Herbie
b. 1942 McDonald, Gabrielle (Anne) Kirk
b. 1943 Ludlam, Charles
b. 1944 Garrett, Mike
b. 1946 O'Neill, Ed
b. 1947 Letterman, David
b. 1949 Turow, Scott
b. 1950 Carter, Chip
b. 1950 Cassidy, David Bruce
b. 1950 Werner, Tom
b. 1952 Arguello, Alexis
b. 1952 Soto, Gary
b. 1952 Wiley, Ralph
b. 1956 Garcia, Andy
b. 1957 Gill, Vince(nt Grant)
b. 1957 Janowitz, Tama
b. 1965 Zayak, Elaine
b. 1971 Doherty, Shannen
b. 1979 Danes, Claire
d. 1684 Amati, Nicolo
d. 1704 Bossuet, Jacques Benigne
d. 1748 Kent, William
d. 1782 Metastasio, Pietro
d. 1814 Burney, Charles
d. 1824 Taylor, Jane
d. 1850 Judson, Adoniram
d. 1878 Tweed, Boss
d. 1886 Fairbanks, Thaddeus
d. 1897 Cope, Edward Drinker
d. 1902 Talmadge, Thomas de Witt
d. 1910 Sumner, William Graham
d. 1912 Barton, Clara Harlowe
d. 1922 Shrady, Henry M
d. 1928 Smith, Madeline Hamilton
d. 1929 Steel, Flora Annie Webster
d. 1932 Bauer, Louis Agricola
d. 1933 Ames, Adelbert
d. 1933 Nuttall, Zelia Maria Magdalena
d. 1945 Roosevelt, Franklin D(elano)
d. 1959 Gleason, James
d. 1962 Pevsner, Antoine
d. 1966 Allard, Sydney
d. 1970 Thorborg, Kerstin
d. 1971 Tamm, Igor Evgenevich
d. 1972 Marek, Kurt W

d. 1973 Freed, Arthur
d. 1973 Senanayake, Dudley Shelton
d. 1974 Krock, Arthur Bernard
d. 1976 Ford, Paul
d. 1976 Miller, William Ernest
d. 1976 Wolfgang, Myra K
d. 1977 Wrigley, Philip Knight
d. 1980 Tolbert, William Richard, Jr.
d. 1981 Guyer, Tennyson
d. 1981 Louis, Joe
d. 1986 Katayev, Valentin Petrovich
d. 1988 Paton, Alan Stewart
d. 1989 Hoffman, Abbie
d. 1989 Mills, Herbert
d. 1989 Robinson, Sugar Ray
d. 1991 Schuyler, James Marcus
d. 1997 Wald, George

April 13
b. 1519 Catherine de Medici
b. 1593 Strafford, 1st Earl of
b. 1721 Hanson, John
b. 1732 North, Frederick North, Baron
b. 1743 Jefferson, Thomas
b. 1748 Bramah, Joseph
b. 1771 Trevithick, Richard
b. 1795 Harper, James
b. 1801 Carnot, Hippolyte
b. 1810 David, Felicien Cesar
b. 1816 Bennett, William Sterndale, Sir
b. 1825 McGee, Thomas D'Arcy
b. 1832 Montalvo, Juan Maria
b. 1852 Woolworth, Frank Winfield
b. 1854 Drummond, William Henry
b. 1854 Ely, Richard Theodore
b. 1859 Allen, Henry Tureman
b. 1860 Ensor, James Sydney, Baron
b. 1864 Marshall, Tully
b. 1866 Davenport, Charles Benedict
b. 1873 Davis, John Williams
b. 1880 Leginska
b. 1881 Binswanger, Ludwig
b. 1885 Lukacs, Gyorgy
b. 1886 Howard, Willie
b. 1888 Hammond, John Hays, Jr.

b. 1891 Larsen, Nella
b. 1892 Harris, Arthur Travers, Sir
b. 1892 Watson-Watt, Robert Alexander, Sir
b. 1896 Eaker, Ira Clarence
b. 1897 Braestrup, Carl Bjorn
b. 1899 Butts, Alfred M(osher)
b. 1901 Dennison, Robert Lee
b. 1901 Lacan, Jacques (Marie Emile)
b. 1902 Henry, Marguerite
b. 1902 Rothschild, Philippe de, Baron
b. 1905 Agle, Nan Hayden
b. 1905 Padover, Saul Kussiel
b. 1906 Beckett, Samuel (Barclay)
b. 1906 Freeman, Bud
b. 1907 Stassen, Harold Edward
b. 1908 Bresler, Jerry
b. 1909 Welty, Eudora
b. 1913 Albritton, David
b. 1913 Hingson, Robert A(ndrew)
b. 1913 Whittingham, Charlie
b. 1915 DeJong, Petrus
b. 1917 Anderson, Robert Orville
b. 1919 Keel, Howard
b. 1919 O'Hair, Madalyn Murray
b. 1921 Griese, Arnold
b. 1921 Thyssen-Bornemisza de Kaszan, Hans Heinrich, Baron
b. 1922 Braine, John Gerard
b. 1924 Biggers, John (Thomas)
b. 1924 Donen, Stanley
b. 1925 Irving, Jules
b. 1929 McEwen, Terence Alexander
b. 1929 Old Person, Earl
b. 1930 Dillman, Bradford
b. 1931 Gurney, Dan
b. 1932 Letelier, Orlando
b. 1933 Campbell, Ben Nighthorse
b. 1935 Waggoner, Lyle
b. 1937 Fox, Edward
b. 1937 Wilson, Lanford
b. 1938 Rotimi, Ola
b. 1939 Collins, Barbara-Rose
b. 1939 Heaney, Seamus (Justin)
b. 1941 Brown, Michael Stuart
b. 1941 Price, Margaret Berenice
b. 1942 Conti, Bill

b. 1942 Parkhurst, Michael Hus
b. 1943 Kidd, William
b. 1944 Casady, Jack
b. 1945 Dow, Tony
b. 1946 Green, Al(bert Leornes)
b. 1947 Batts, Deborah A.
b. 1950 Perlman, Ron
b. 1951 Bryson, Peabo
b. 1951 Weinberg, Max M
b. 1963 Kasparov, Garry Kimovich
b. 1970 Schroder, Rick
d. 1695 LaFontaine, Jean de
d. 1827 Clapperton, Hugh
d. 1868 Tewodros II
d. 1869 Rogers, Isaiah
d. 1874 Bogardus, James
d. 1886 Noyes, John Humphrey
d. 1890 Randall, Samuel J
d. 1894 Field, David Dudley
d. 1894 Spitta, Philipp
d. 1906 Garnett, Richard
d. 1911 Keith, William
d. 1915 Nelson, William Rockhill
d. 1917 Brady, Diamond Jim
d. 1918 Kornilov, Lavr Georgyevich
d. 1925 Haynes, Elwood
d. 1936 Thurston, Howard
d. 1938 Grey Owl
d. 1941 Cannon, Annie Jump
d. 1945 Cassirer, Ernst
d. 1959 Beinum, Eduard van
d. 1964 Harlan, Veit
d. 1966 Carra, Carlo
d. 1966 Duhamel, Georges
d. 1966 Luckner, Felix von, Count
d. 1966 Nighbor, Frank
d. 1970 Henry, William M
d. 1970 Johnson, William Henry
d. 1970 Smith, Merriman
d. 1973 Courboin, Charles
d. 1975 Bolton, Isabel
d. 1975 Parks, Larry
d. 1975 Tombalbaye, Nagarta Francois
d. 1981 Thomas, Gwyn
d. 1983 Humphreys, Christmas
d. 1983 May, Morton David
d. 1984 Kirkpatrick, Ralph Leonard

d. 1987 Nyiregyhazi, Ervin
d. 1987 Taylor, Kent
d. 1993 Stegner, Wallace (Earle)
d. 1995 Rowen, Hobart
d. 1996 Brown, George Mackay
d. 1997 McCord, David (Thompson Watson)
d. 1998 MacGregor, Ian Kinloch, Sir

April 14
b. 1629 Huygens, Christian
b. 1796 Bonneville, Benjamin Louie Eulalie de
b. 1802 Bushnell, Horace
b. 1810 Morrill, Justin Smith
b. 1811 Fisher, Clara
b. 1813 Morgan, Junius Spencer
b. 1820 Ballou, Maturin Murray
b. 1840 Gardner, Isabella Stewart
b. 1842 Chaffee, Adna Romanza
b. 1857 Kelley, Edgar Stillman
b. 1862 Stolypin, Piotr Arkadevich
b. 1866 Sullivan, Anne
b. 1868 Behrens, Peter
b. 1869 Van Heusen, John
b. 1879 Cabell, James Branch
b. 1885 Janney, Russell Dixon
b. 1885 Ochs, Adolph Shelby, II
b. 1886 McFee, Henry Lee
b. 1886 Tolman, Edward Chace
b. 1887 Foerster, Norman
b. 1889 Toynbee, Arnold Joseph
b. 1892 Childe, Vere Gordon
b. 1897 McCoy, Horace
b. 1897 Windsor, Claire
b. 1899 Romulo, Carlos Pena
b. 1900 Baccaloni, Salvatore
b. 1901 Stulberg, Louis
b. 1902 Loeffler, Ken(neth D)
b. 1902 Mantha, Sylvio
b. 1904 Gielgud, (Arthur) John, Sir
b. 1907 Duvalier, Francois
b. 1914 Salant, Richard S
b. 1916 Buckley, Emerson
b. 1917 Hobson, Valerie Babette
b. 1917 Luboff, Norman

b. 1917 Miller, Marvin Julian
b. 1918 Healy, Mary
b. 1920 Saint Clair, James Draper
b. 1922 Fradon, Dana
b. 1922 Khan, Ali Akbar
b. 1923 DeVicenzo, Roberto
b. 1923 Holt, John Caldwell
b. 1924 Rogers, Shorty
b. 1924 Warnock, (Helen) Mary (Wilson)
b. 1925 Ammons, Jug
b. 1925 Muzorewa, Abel Tendekai
b. 1925 Steiger, Rod
b. 1925 Traub, Marvin Stuart
b. 1926 Calvo Sotelo (y Bustelo), Leopoldo
b. 1929 Chadli, Bendjedid
b. 1930 Robinson, Jay
b. 1932 Bennett, William
b. 1932 Perkins, Anthony
b. 1935 Lynn, Loretta
b. 1935 VonDaeniken, Erich
b. 1936 Nichols, Bobby
b. 1936 Scheer, Robert
b. 1936 Serpico, Frank
b. 1938 Scott, Gloria Dean Randle
b. 1940 Christie, Julie
b. 1941 Rose, Pete(r Edward)
b. 1941 Tomseth, Victor Lloyd
b. 1945 Blackmore, Ritchie
b. 1946 Monteleone, Thomas F(rancis)
b. 1948 Martin, Valerie
b. 1949? Shea, John
b. 1950 Collins, Francis S(ellers)
b. 1954 Sterling, Bruce
b. 1958 Millo, Aprile
b. 1963 Cooper, Cynthia
b. 1966 Justice, David
b. 1966 Justice, David (Christopher)
b. 1966 Maddux, Greg(ory Alan)
b. 1968 Hall, Anthony Thomas Charles
d. 1314 Clement, V
d. 1471 Warwick and of Salisbury, Earl of
d. 1685 Otway, Thomas
d. 1759 Handel, George Frideric
d. 1768 Cuvillies, Francois
d. 1865 Carrera, Jose Rafael
d. 1885 King, Richard
d. 1890 Morgan, Junius Spencer

d. 1894 Vance, Zebulon Baird
d. 1895 Dana, James Dwight
d. 1909 Butler, Matthew Calbraith
d. 1911 Joss, Addie
d. 1913 Hagenbeck, Carl
d. 1917 Zamenhof, Ludwik Lazar
d. 1922 Anson, Cap
d. 1924 Sullivan, Louis Henri
d. 1932 Burns, William John
d. 1935 Noether, (Amalie) Emmy
d. 1948 Roxas, Manuel
d. 1951 Bevin, Ernest
d. 1964 Carson, Rachel (Louise)
d. 1965 Ehrenfest-Afanaseva, Tatiana
d. 1965 Hickock, Richard Eugene
d. 1965 Smith, Perry Edward
d. 1974 Whalen, Michael
d. 1975 Baker, Josephine (Carson)
d. 1975 Booth, Charles Brandon
d. 1975 Flanders, Michael
d. 1975 March, Fredric
d. 1975 Tolson, Clyde Anderson
d. 1976 Hastie, William Henry
d. 1976 Ospina Perez, Mariano
d. 1978 Leavis, F(rank) R(aymond)
d. 1981 Galamian, Ivan
d. 1981 Mayer, Arthur Loeb
d. 1981 Vanderbilt, William Henry
d. 1982 Handy, Thomas Troy
d. 1983 Pearlroth, Norbert
d. 1986 Beauvoir, Simone de
d. 1991 Pacciardi, Randolfo
d. 1992 Hazelton, Nika
d. 1992 Price, Sammy
d. 1995 Ives, Burl (Icle Ivanhoe)
d. 1995 Moses, Gilbert, III
d. 1998 Stans, Maurice H(ubert)
d. 1999 Corby, Ellen
d. 1999 Newley, Anthony (George)

April 15
b. 1452 Leonardo da Vinci
b. 1469 Nanak
b. 1489 Sinan, Kodja Mimar

b. 1688 Fasch, Johann Friedrich
b. 1707 Euler, Leonhard
b. 1710 Camargo, Marie Anne de Cupis de
b. 1741 Peale, Charles Willson
b. 1772 Geoffroy Saint-Hilaire, Etienne
b. 1786 Channing, Walter
b. 1793 Struve, Friedrich Georg Wilhelm von
b. 1797 Thiers, Adolphe
b. 1800 Ross, James Clark, Sir
b. 1810 Montalembert, Comte de
b. 1812 Rousseau, (Pierre Etienne) Theodore
b. 1814 Motley, John Lothrop
b. 1817 Jowett, Benjamin
b. 1821 Brown, Joseph Emerson
b. 1832 Busch, Wilhelm
b. 1843 James, Henry, (Jr.)
b. 1856 Daniels, Frank
b. 1856 Hubert, Conrad
b. 1858 Durkheim, Emile
b. 1861 Carman, Bliss
b. 1874 Shull, George Harrison
b. 1874 Stark, Johannes
b. 1875 Jeffries, James Jackson
b. 1880 Wertheimer, Max
b. 1881 Bennett, Hugh Hammond
b. 1883 Bruce of Melbourne, 1st Viscount
b. 1884 Lloyd, John Henry
b. 1886 Ozenfant, Amedee
b. 1887 Bonham Carter, Violet
b. 1888 Bates, Florence
b. 1889 Benton, Thomas Hart
b. 1889 Holmes, Hap
b. 1889 Randolph, Asa Philip
b. 1890 DeBeck, Billy
b. 1891 Reid, Wallace Eugene
b. 1892 Ten Boom, Corrie
b. 1893 Paul, Prince
b. 1894? Smith, Bessie
b. 1896 Bean, Louis H(yman)
b. 1896 Chinn, May (Edward)
b. 1897 Jordan, Marian Driscoll
b. 1900 Taubes, Frederic
b. 1901 Davis, Joe

b. 1901 Pleven, Rene Jean
b. 1907 Tinbergen, Nikolaas
b. 1912 Kim Il Sung
b. 1914 Manso, Leo
b. 1915 Washington, Walter Edward
b. 1916 Bloomingdale, Alfred S
b. 1919 Catlett, Elizabeth
b. 1920 Simms, Hilda
b. 1920 Szasz, Thomas Stephen
b. 1920 Weizsacker, Richard Freiherr von
b. 1922 Washington, Harold
b. 1923 Aziz, Philip John Andrew Ferris
b. 1923 DePugh, Robert Bolivar
b. 1923 Lembeck, Harvey
b. 1924? Hazan, Marcella Maddalena
b. 1924 Marriner, Neville
b. 1926 Huddleston, Walter Darlington
b. 1927 Carritt, David Graham
b. 1927 Goldman, Albert
b. 1929 Cadbury, George Adrian Hayhurst, Sir
b. 1930 Finnbogadottir, Vigdis
b. 1931 Gearhart, Sally (Miller)
b. 1933 Clark, Roy Linwood
b. 1933 Montgomery, Elizabeth
b. 1938 Cardinale, Claudia
b. 1939 Paz Zamora, Jaime
b. 1940 Archer, Jeffrey Howard
b. 1940 Davis, Willie
b. 1942 Clarke, Allan
b. 1944 Edmunds, Dave
b. 1948 Bloodworth-Thomason, Linda Joyce
b. 1951 Evans, Heloise Cruse
b. 1951 Heloise
b. 1957 Ashford, Evelyn
b. 1959 Thompson, Emma
d. 1632 Baltimore, George Calvert, Baron
d. 1719 Maintenon, Francoise d'Aubigne, Marquise de
d. 1757 Carriera, Rosalba Giovanna
d. 1764 Pompadour, Jeanne Antoinette Poisson

d. 1765 Lomonosov, Mikhail Vasilyevich
d. 1800 Shippen, Edward
d. 1819 Evans, Oliver
d. 1844 Bulfinch, Charles
d. 1850 Tussaud, Marie Gresholtz, Madame
d. 1865 Lincoln, Abraham
d. 1870 Willard, Emma Hart
d. 1888 Arnold, Matthew
d. 1889 Damien, Father
d. 1898 Purvis, Robert
d. 1912 Futrelle, Jacques
d. 1912 Straus, Isidor
d. 1914 Townsend, George Alfred
d. 1919 Delano, Jane Arminda
d. 1925 Sargent, John Singer
d. 1927 LeRoux, Gaston
d. 1942 Johnson, Hugh Samuel
d. 1942 Musil, Robert Edler Von
d. 1944 Gentile, Giovanni
d. 1947 Hoess, Rudolf Franz
d. 1948 Rockefeller, Abby Aldrich
d. 1949 Beery, Wallace Fitzgerald
d. 1952 Chernov, Viktor Mikhailovich
d. 1956 Nolde, Emil
d. 1958 Taylor, Estelle
d. 1971 Brodovitch, Alexey
d. 1971 Reeves, Dan(iel F)
d. 1971 Stanley, Wendell Meredith
d. 1972 Crowley, Leo Thomas
d. 1972 Knight, Frank Hyneman
d. 1975 Conte, Richard
d. 1976 Elazar, David
d. 1976 Smith, Gerald Lyman Kenneth
d. 1979 Caniglia, Maria
d. 1980 Bailey, Raymond
d. 1980 Sartre, Jean-Paul
d. 1982 Montor, Henry
d. 1983 Ten Boom, Corrie
d. 1984 Empson, William, Sir
d. 1986 Genet, Jean
d. 1988 Egorov, Youri
d. 1989 Attwood, William Hollingsworth
d. 1989 Hu Yaobang
d. 1990 Garbo, Greta
d. 1990 Matsunaga, Spark Masayuki

d. 1993 Charteris, Leslie
d. 1993 Westall, Robert
   Atkinson
d. 1994 Curry, John
   (Anthony)
d. 1996 Niarchos,
   Stavros (Spyros)
d. 1998 Pol Pot
d. 2000 Gorey, Edward
   St. John
d. 2000 Morton, Arthur

April 16
b. 1660 Sloane, Hans,
   Sir
b. 1728 Black, Joseph
b. 1747 Baranov,
   Aleksandr
   Andreievich
b. 1755 Vigee-Lebrun,
   Marie-Louise-
   Elisabeth
b. 1786 Franklin, John,
   Sir
b. 1844 France, Anatole
b. 1850 Adams, Herbert
   Baxter
b. 1850 Thomas, Sidney
   Gilchrist
b. 1854 Coxey, Jacob
   Sechler
b. 1857 Pritchett, Henry
   S
b. 1865 Hill, Grace
   Livingstone
b. 1867 Wright, Wilbur
b. 1871 Stephenson,
   Henry
b. 1871 Synge, John
   Millington
b. 1877 Turner, Thomas
   Wyatt
b. 1881 Halifax, Edward
   Frederick Lindley
   Wood
b. 1886 Thalmann,
   Ernst
b. 1889 Chaplin, Charlie
b. 1892 Jones, Howard
   Mumford
b. 1896 Semenov,
   Nikolai Nikolaevich
b. 1897 Cross, Milton
   John
b. 1897 Glubb, John
   Bagot, Sir
b. 1898 Dykstra, John
b. 1899 Neyman, Jerzy
b. 1900 Adler, Polly
b. 1901 Akimov,
   Nikolay Pavlovich
b. 1903 Pillsbury, Philip
   Winston
b. 1903 Waner, Paul
   Glee
b. 1904 Case, Clifford
   Philip
b. 1904 D'Orsay, Fifi
b. 1906 Gimpel, Jakob
b. 1909 McCoy, Charles
   B(relsford)
b. 1911 Roueche,
   Berton
b. 1912 Williams, Garth
   Montgomery
b. 1913 Tremayne, Les
b. 1914 Hodiak, John

b. 1914 Jensen, Oliver
   Ormerod
b. 1916 Keppel, Francis
b. 1917 Salomon,
   Charlotte
b. 1918 Milligan, Spike
b. 1919 Cunningham,
   Merce
b. 1920 Nelson, Barry
b. 1921 Mollenhoff,
   Clark Raymond
b. 1921 Ustinov, Peter
   Alexander
b. 1922 Amis, Kingsley
   (William)
b. 1922 Tindemans,
   Leo(nard)
b. 1923 Moore, Arch
   Alfred, Jr.
b. 1924 Mancini, Henry
b. 1927 Ratzinger,
   Joseph Alois,
   Cardinal
b. 1928 Lane, Dick
b. 1928 Sylbert, Richard
b. 1929 Adams, Edie
b. 1929 Hamilton, Roy
b. 1930 Mann, Herbie
b. 1933 Pappas, Ike
b. 1933 Wallis, Shani
b. 1934 Stigwood,
   Robert Colin
b. 1935 Vinton, Bobby
b. 1939 Springfield,
   Dusty
b. 1940 Margrethe II
b. 1942 Lonborg, Jim
b. 1944 Davies, Dennis
   Russell
b. 1947 Abdul-Jabbar,
   Kareem
b. 1947 Rafferty, Gerry
b. 1948 Tate, Eleanora
   E(laine)
b. 1949 Spooner, Bill
b. 1951 Bentley, John
b. 1952 Westbrook,
   Peter (J.)
b. 1955 Barkin, Ellen
b. 1964 Pirner, Dave
b. 1965 Lawrence,
   Martin
b. 1971 Selena
d. 1446 Brunelleschi,
   Filippo
d. 1687 Villers, George
d. 1689 Behn, Aphra
d. 1788 Buffon,
   Georges Louis
   Leclerc
d. 1813 Kutuzov,
   Mikhail Ilarionovich
d. 1825 Fuseli, Henry
d. 1828 Goya y
   Lucientes, Francisco
   Jose de
d. 1858 Cramer, Johann
   Baptist
d. 1859 Tocqueville,
   Alexis, Comte de
d. 1864 Blanchard,
   Thomas
d. 1879 Bernadette of
   Lourdes, Saint
d. 1900 Adler, Dankmar

d. 1901 Rowland, Henry
   Augustus
d. 1914 Hill, George
   William
d. 1915 Aldrich, Nelson
   Wilmarth
d. 1916 Peck, George
   Wilbur
d. 1920 Vail, Theodore
   Newton
d. 1928 Statler,
   Ellsworth Milton
d. 1930 Mariategui, Jose
   Carlos
d. 1932 Geddes, Patrick,
   Sir
d. 1941 Bernard, Emile
d. 1941 Danforth,
   William
d. 1956 Chaplin,
   Sydney Dryden
d. 1957 Torrio, Johnny
d. 1958 Black, Walter J
d. 1958 Franklin,
   Rosalind Elsie
d. 1962 Amrouche, Jean
d. 1966 Gowers, Ernest
   Arthur, Sir
d. 1968 Bainter, Fay
   Okell
d. 1968 Ferber, Edna
d. 1970 Neutra, Richard
   Joseph
d. 1971 Eckert, William
   Dole
d. 1972 Kawabata,
   Yasunari
d. 1976 Lackey,
   Kenneth
d. 1978 Clay, Lucius du
   Bignon
d. 1978 Lindner,
   Richard
d. 1978 Tsiranana,
   Philibert
d. 1978 Whitehead,
   (Walter) Edward
d. 1981 Debus, Sigurd
   Friedrich
d. 1987 Curtis,
   Charlotte Murray
d. 1988 Reardon, John
d. 1989 Conlan, Jocko
d. 1991 Lean, David,
   Sir
d. 1992 Russell, Andy
d. 1993 Velez,
   Clemente Soto
d. 1994 Ellison, Ralph
   (Waldo)
d. 1995 Brando,
   Cheyenne
d. 1998 Calderon,
   Alberto P(edro)
d. 2000 Chayes, Abram
   J(oseph)

April 17
b. 1622 Vaughan, Henry
b. 1741 Chase, Samuel
b. 1806 Simms, William
   Gilmore
b. 1820 Cartwright,
   Alexander Joy, Jr.
b. 1837 Morgan, J(ohn)
   P(ierpont)

b. 1842 Parkhurst,
   Charles Henry
b. 1849 Day, William
   Rufus
b. 1851 Anson, Cap
b. 1859 Van Devanter,
   Willis
b. 1863 Love, Augustus
   Edward Hough
b. 1866 Starling, Ernest
   Henry
b. 1870 Baker, Ray
   Stannard
b. 1874 Mackay,
   Clarence Hungerford
b. 1879 Howell, Albert
   S
b. 1880 Woolley,
   Charles Leonard, Sir
b. 1881 Leiper, Robert
   Thomson
b. 1882 MacIver, Robert
   Morrison
b. 1882 Schnabel, Artur
b. 1885 Blixen, Karen
   Christentze, Baroness
b. 1888 Teyte, Maggie,
   Dame
b. 1889 Boussac,
   Marcel
b. 1893 Grant, Bruce
b. 1894 Khrushchev,
   Nikita Sergeyevich
b. 1897 Wilder,
   Thornton (Niven)
b. 1901 Prebisch, Raul
b. 1903 Piatigorsky,
   Gregor
b. 1904 Chodorov,
   Edward
b. 1905 Lake, Arthur
b. 1911 Elisofon, Eliot
b. 1911 Hayes, Alfred
b. 1911 Seaton, George
b. 1915 Foss, Joe
b. 1915 Harkness,
   Rebekah West
b. 1916 Bandaranaike,
   Sirimavo Ratwatte
   Dias
b. 1916? Eggerth, Marta
b. 1917 Campos,
   Roberto de Oliveira
b. 1918 Holden,
   William
b. 1918 Shirley, Anne
b. 1923 Anderson,
   Lindsay (Gordon)
b. 1923 McCallister,
   Lon
b. 1923 Reasoner, Harry
b. 1924 Gallant, Roy
   Arthur
b. 1924 Simmons,
   Althea T L
b. 1925 Wood, Robert
   Dennis
b. 1934 Kirshner, Don
b. 1935 Lundy, Lamar
b. 1937 Piech,
   Ferdinand
b. 1940 Jerusalem,
   Siegfried
b. 1940 Williams,
   Tommy
b. 1941 Fury, Billy

b. 1943 Holmes, Anna Marie
b. 1945 O'Neil, Roger
b. 1946 Koehler, Georges J F
b. 1948 Hammer, Jan
b. 1951 Hussey, Olivia
b. 1955 Moure, Erin
b. 1955 Runnels, Tom
b. 1956? Sembello, Michael
b. 1961 Esiason, Boomer
b. 1967 Phair, Liz
d. 1680 Tekakwitha, Kateri, Saint
b. 1695 Juana Ines de la Cruz, Sor
d. 1696 Sevigne, Marie de Rabutin-Chantal, Marquise de
d. 1711 Joseph I
d. 1790 Franklin, Benjamin
b. 1804 Jefferson, Mary
d. 1876 Brownson, Orestes Augustus
d. 1892 Mackenzie, Alexander
d. 1893 Larcom, Lucy
d. 1895 Isaacs, Jorge
d. 1929 Sifton, Clifford
d. 1941 Driesch, Hans Adolf Eduard
d. 1942 Hertz, Alfred
d. 1942 Perrin, Jean Baptiste
d. 1960 Cochran, Eddie
d. 1961 Anderson, Elda Emma
d. 1962 Fazenda, Louise
d. 1967 Allen, Red
d. 1967 Bailey, Frederick Marshman
d. 1971 Lombardo, Carmen
d. 1973 Kertesz, Istvan
d. 1974 Seeley, Blossom
d. 1975 McGee, Frank
d. 1975 Radhakrishnan, Sarvepalli
d. 1976 Dam, (Carl Peter) Henrik
d. 1976 Nicoll, (John Ramsay) Allardyce
d. 1980 Sjoberg, Alf
d. 1983 Leonard, Dutch
d. 1984 Clark, Mark Wayne
d. 1985 Brady, Scott
d. 1985 Bunting, Basil
d. 1986 Head, Bessie Emery
d. 1986 Kilburn, Peter
d. 1987 Shawn, Dick
d. 1987 Smith, Willi Donnell
d. 1988 Freeman, Paul Lamar
d. 1988 Frissell, Toni
d. 1988 Nevelson, Louise Berliawsky
d. 1990 Abernathy, Ralph David
d. 1991 Yellen, Jack

d. 1992 Stern, Arthur Cecil
d. 1993 Fleischmann, Peter F(rancis)
d. 1993 Ozal, Turgut
d. 1994 Sperry, Roger W(olcott)
d. 1997 Herzog, Chaim
d. 1997 Rockefeller, Mary French
d. 1998 McCartney, Linda

April 18
b. 1480 Borgia, Lucrezia
b. 1545 Yi Sunsin
b. 1580 Middleton, Thomas
b. 1732 Colman, George
b. 1817 Lewes, George Henry
b. 1819 Cespedes, Carlos Manuel de
b. 1819 Suppe, Franz von
b. 1857 Darrow, Clarence Seward
b. 1863 Berchtold, Leopold von
b. 1864 Davis, Richard Harding
b. 1880 Crawford, Sam(uel Earl)
b. 1880 Crisp, Donald
b. 1881 Weber, Max
b. 1882 Stokowski, Leopold (Anton Stanislaw Boleslawawicz)
b. 1888 Chavez, Dennis
b. 1888 Leider, Frida
b. 1888 Lunn, Arnold Henry Moore, Sir
b. 1892 Bierut, Boleslaw
b. 1892 Houdry, Eugene Jules
b. 1895 Pagnol, Marcel Paul
b. 1899 Dole, Charles Minot
b. 1902 Owens, Harry
b. 1902 Pella, Giuseppe
b. 1902 Schneerson, Menachem M(endel)
b. 1904 Markham, Pigmeat
b. 1905 Hitchings, George H(erbert)
b. 1907 Lampman, Evelyn Sibley
b. 1907 Roa (y Garcia), Raul
b. 1907 Rozsa, Miklos
b. 1911 Goldhaber, Maurice
b. 1911 Hartford, Huntington
b. 1912 Barrie, Wendy
b. 1916 Kolchin, Ellis Robert
b. 1917 Frederika Louise
b. 1918 Bazin, Andre
b. 1918 Hillegass, Clifton Keith

b. 1918 Hillegrass, C(lifton) K(eith)
b. 1922 Hale, Barbara
b. 1924 Hyde, Henry J(ohn)
b. 1927 Mazowiecki, Tadeusz
b. 1930 Revill, Clive Selsby
b. 1934 Drury, James
b. 1934 Shirley, George Irving
b. 1937 Hooks, Robert
b. 1938 Glasser, Ira
b. 1940 Garvey, Ed(ward Robert)
b. 1940 Goldstein, Joseph Leonard
b. 1942 Rindt, Jochen
b. 1946 Hunter, Catfish
b. 1946 Mills, Hayley
b. 1947 Woods, James
b. 1948 Archibald, Nate
b. 1948? Stephenson, Skip
b. 1956 James, John
b. 1956 Roberts, Eric
b. 1959 Faludi, Susan
b. 1962 Marshall, Wilbur Buddyhia
b. 1963 O'Brien, Conan
d. 1504 Lippi, Filippino
d. 1743 Blair, James
d. 1802 Darwin, Erasmus
d. 1825 Cabot, George
d. 1845 Saussure, Nicolas Thoedore de
d. 1853 King, William Rufus de Vane
d. 1873 Liebig, Justus von
d. 1888 Conkling, Roscoe
d. 1898 Moreau, Gustave
d. 1906 Huntington, Daniel
d. 1913 Ward, Lester Frank
d. 1925 Ebbets, Charles Hercules
d. 1936 Howe, Louis McHenry
d. 1936 Respighi, Ottorino
d. 1940 Beer, Thomas
d. 1940 Fisher, Herbert Albert Laurens
d. 1940 McCoy, Charles
d. 1942 Whitney, Gertrude Vanderbilt
d. 1943 Adamowski, Timothee
d. 1943 Yamamoto, Isoroku
d. 1944 Chaminade, Cecile
d. 1945 Fleming, John Ambrose, Sir
d. 1945 Pyle, Ernie
d. 1947 Leonard, Benny
d. 1949 Bloomfield, Leonard
d. 1951 Bates, Daisy Mae

d. 1951 Vandenberg, Arthur Hendrick
d. 1955 Einstein, Albert
d. 1958 Arkell, William Joscelyn
d. 1958 Gamelin, Maurice Gustave
d. 1960 Ruml, Beardsley
d. 1964 Hecht, Ben
d. 1971 Luboshutz, Pierre
d. 1973 Smith, William
d. 1974 Pagnol, Marcel Paul
d. 1982 Harnwell, Gaylord Probasco
d. 1982 Harrar, J(acob) George
d. 1984 Cole, Kenneth Stewart
d. 1984 Mahin, John Lee
d. 1985 Caton-Thompson, Gertrude
d. 1986 Bauer, Eddie
d. 1986 Dassault, Marcel
d. 1987 Baker, Carlos Heard
d. 1988 Delaplane, Stanton Hill
d. 1988 Olson, James E(lias)
d. 1991 Walters, Bucky
d. 1993 Wayne, Bernie
d. 1995 Frondizi, Arturo
d. 1996 Davies, Ronald N(orwood)
d. 1998 Sanford, Terry

April 19
b. 359 Gratian
b. 1721 Sherman, Roger
b. 1772 Ricardo, David
b. 1795 Ehrenberg, Christian Gottfried
b. 1801 Fechner, Gustav Theodor
b. 1831 Echegaray y Eizaguirre, Jose
b. 1832 Garfield, Lucretia (Rudolph)
b. 1836 Juilliard, Augustus D
b. 1858 Robson, May
b. 1868 Schillings, Max von
b. 1872 Salomon, Alice
b. 1877 Evinrude, Ole
b. 1877 Whitney, Gertrude Vanderbilt
b. 1883 Vargas, Getulio Dornelles
b. 1886? Bandeira, Manuel
b. 1891 Bacchelli, Riccardo
b. 1891 Kennedy, Madge
b. 1891 Rosay, Francoise
b. 1891 Wilcox, Herbert
b. 1892 Tailleferre, Germaine
b. 1894 Dudley, George S

b. 1897 Segal, Vivienne
b. 1897 Swift, Kay
b. 1899 Coghill, Nevill
Henry Kendall
Aylmer
b. 1899 Douglas, Emily
Taft
b. 1900 Hughes,
Richard Arthur
Warren
b. 1900 Michener,
Roland
b. 1900 O'Brien,
George
b. 1900 Talmadge,
Constance
b. 1901 Summerskill,
Edith Clara, Baroness
b. 1902 Latham, Jean
Lee
b. 1903 Ness, Eliot
b. 1904 Pough, Richard
Hooper
b. 1908 Keilberth,
Joseph
b. 1910 Walters, Bucky
b. 1911 Williams,
Ursula Moray
b. 1912 Seaborg, Glenn
T(heodore)
b. 1913 Carpenter,
Ken(neth)
b. 1915 Kennedy,
Joseph Patrick, Jr.
b. 1916 Carnegie, Mary
Elizabeth Lancaster
b. 1916 Moos, Malcolm
Charles
b. 1918 Capa, Cornell
b. 1920 Fontaine, Frank
b. 1920 Mandel, Marvin
b. 1921 Navon, Yitzhak
b. 1926 Adams, Don
b. 1927 Kenneth
b. 1928 Garwin,
Richard Lawrence
b. 1928 Korner, Alexis
b. 1930 O'Brian, Hugh
b. 1931 Knight,
Etheridge
b. 1932 Botero,
Fernando
b. 1932 Mansfield,
Jayne
b. 1933 Sargent, Dick
b. 1935 Moore, Dudley
Stuart John
b. 1936 Martens,
Wilfried
b. 1937 Donahue, Elinor
b. 1937 Estrada, Joseph
(Marcelo Ejercito)
b. 1942 Price, Alan
b. 1947 Perahia, Murray
b. 1949 Picasso, Paloma
b. 1950 Guinier, Lani
b. 1954 Francis, Trevor
b. 1956 Barker, Sue
b. 1956 Carlyle, Randy
b. 1960 Viola, Frank
John, Jr.
b. 1962 Unser, Al, Jr.
b. 1966 Knight, Suge
b. 1968 Judd, Ashley
d. 1560 Melanchthon,
Philipp

d. 1627 Beaumont,
John, Sir
d. 1689 Christina
d. 1813 Rush, Benjamin
d. 1824 Byron, George
Gordon, Baron
d. 1881 Disraeli,
Benjamin
d. 1882 Darwin, Charles
Robert
d. 1889 De La Rue,
Warren
d. 1893 Symonds, John
Addington
d. 1904 Isabella II
d. 1906 Curie, Pierre
d. 1914 Peirce, Charles
Sanders
d. 1918 Rosenberg,
Issac
d. 1920 Mallinger,
Mathilde
d. 1932 Cheyne,
William Watson, Sir
d. 1937 Parker, George
Safford
d. 1937 Wheeler,
William Morton
d. 1944 Hitchcock,
Tommy
d. 1944 Noone, Jimmie
d. 1947 Bidwell,
Charles W
d. 1949 Wise, Stephen
Samuel
d. 1960 Green, Wilf(red
Thomas)
d. 1963 Griswold,
Alfred Whitney
d. 1966 Tanner, Valno
Alfred
d. 1967 Adenauer,
Konrad
d. 1968 Bridges,
Tommy
d. 1971 Thomson, Earl
d. 1972 Burke, Billy
d. 1973 Kelsen, Hans
d. 1974 Ayub Khan,
Mohammad
d. 1975 Julian, Percy
Lavon
d. 1975 Schioetz, Aksel
d. 1978 Koch, John
d. 1979 Morton, Rogers
Clark Ballard
d. 1983 Andrzejewski,
Jerzy
d. 1986 Childress, Alvin
d. 1987 Brannum, Hugh
d. 1987 Taylor,
Maxwell Davenport
d. 1989 DuMaurier,
Daphne
d. 1993 Koresh, David
d. 1993 Mickelson,
George Speaker
d. 1993 Sellinger,
Joseph A
d. 1995 Grace, J(oseph)
Peter, Jr.
d. 1995 Hardy, Porter,
Jr.
d. 1998 Paz, Octavio

April 20
b. 121 Marcus Aurelius
Antoninus
b. 1492 Aretino, Pietro
b. 1494 Agricola,
Georgius
b. 1718 Brainerd, David
b. 1735 Henderson,
Richard
b. 1745 Pinel, Philippe
b. 1793 Laing, David
b. 1798 Logan, William
Edmond
b. 1808 Napoleon III
b. 1826 Craik, Dinah
Maria Mulock
b. 1850 French, Daniel
Chester
b. 1851 Acevedo Diaz,
Eduardo
b. 1860 Curtis, Charles
Gordon
b. 1869 Chase, Mary
Agnes
b. 1879 Poiret, Paul
b. 1882 Smith, Holland
McTeire
b. 1883 Sloane, John
b. 1887 Lazzari,
Virgilio
b. 1889 Hitler, Adolf
b. 1889 Kohler, Fred,
Sir
b. 1890 Duplessis,
Maurice le Noblet
b. 1892 Bancroft, Dave
b. 1893 Lloyd, Harold
b. 1893 Miro, Joan
b. 1893 Ratoff, Gregory
b. 1898 Firestone,
Harvey Samuel, Jr.
b. 1899 Larsen, Roy
Edward
b. 1900 Norell, Norman
b. 1902 Wolfit, Donald,
Sir
b. 1904 Cabot, Bruce
b. 1905 Hochoy,
Solomon, Sir
b. 1905 Marcus, Stanley
b. 1907 Soyer, Isaac
b. 1910 Wagner, Robert
Ferdinand, Jr.
b. 1911 Kukrit Pramoj,
Momrajawong (M.R.)
b. 1912 Chipperfield,
Joseph Eugene
b. 1916 Lowery, Robert
O
b. 1918 Siegbahn, Kai
Manne Boerje
b. 1920 Stevens, John
Paul
b. 1923 Puente, Tito
b. 1924 Foch, Nina
b. 1926 Verdugo, Elena
b. 1927 Hill, Phil(ip
Toll)
b. 1927 Muller, Karl
Alex(ander)
b. 1931 Hamilton, Lee
Herbert
b. 1936 Roberts, Pat
b. 1937 Takei, George
b. 1938 Cuthbert, Betty

b. 1939 Brundtland, Gro
Harlem
b. 1941 Cook, Blanche
Wiesen
b. 1941 O'Neal, Ryan
b. 1943 Gardiner, John
Eliot
b. 1945 Spurrier,
Steve(n Orr)
b. 1946 Chia, Sandro
b. 1947 Tobias, Andrew
Previn
b. 1948 Potts, Nadia
b. 1949 Cranston, Toller
b. 1949 Lange, Jessica
b. 1949 Quill, Timothy
E.
b. 1950 Cartwright,
Veronica
b. 1950 Lebed,
Alexander
b. 1951 Vandross,
Luther
b. 1959 Howard, Clint
b. 1961 Mattingly,
Don(ald Arthur)
b. 1964 Sumners,
Rosalyn
d. Tsedenbal,
Yumzahgin
d. 835 Kukai
d. 1707 Denner, Johann
Christoph
d. 1736 Eugene of
Savoy
d. 1768 Canaletto,
Antonio
d. 1769 Pontiac
d. 1812 Clinton, George
d. 1821 Achard, Franz
Karl
d. 1856 Stevens, Robert
Livingston
d. 1867 Bozeman, John
M
d. 1883 Manet, Edouard
d. 1899 Friedel, Charles
d. 1902 Stockton, Frank
d. 1903 Du Chaillu,
Paul Belloni
d. 1908 Chadwick,
Henry
d. 1912 Stoker, Bram
d. 1918 Braun, Karl
Ferdinand
d. 1930 Smith, Alex
d. 1932 Peano,
Giuseppe
d. 1933 Kilgour, Joseph
d. 1947 Christian X
d. 1947 Patino, Simon
Iturri
d. 1950 Deeping,
(George) Warwick
d. 1962 Whalen, Grover
(Michael) A(loysius)
d. 1968 Dirks, Rudolph
d. 1973 Armstrong,
Robert
d. 1974 Greer, Howard
d. 1975 Clark, Sydney
d. 1976 Sansom,
William
d. 1979 Dehnert, Henry
d. 1979 Donald, Peter

d. 1980 Kautner, Helmut
d. 1980 Konetzni, Hilde
d. 1981 Denny-Brown, Derek Ernest
d. 1982 MacLeish, Archibald
d. 1984 Burnford, Sheila
d. 1985 Dutton, Ralph Stawell
d. 1986 Miller, Carl S
d. 1987 Tudor, Antony
d. 1991 Nsubuga, Emmanuel, Cardinal
d. 1991 O'Faolain, Sean
d. 1991 Siegel, Don
d. 1992 Hill, Benny
d. 1992 Lennon, Jimmy, Sr.
d. 1993 Brandon, Henry Oscar
d. 1993 Cantinflas
d. 1995 Djilas, Milovan
d. 1996 Milne, Christopher Robin
d. 1997 Louis, Jean
d. 1998 Huddleston, Trevor
d. 1999 Whittingham, Charlie

April 21
b. 1555 Carracci, Lodovico
b. 1619 Riebeeck, Jan Anthonisz van
b. 1671 Law, John
b. 1775 Anderson, Alexander
b. 1782 Froebel, Friedrich Wilhelm August
b. 1783 Heber, Reginald
b. 1794 Ashmun, Jehudi
b. 1816 Bronte, Charlotte
b. 1818 Billings, Josh
b. 1828 Taine, Hippolyte Adolphe
b. 1836 Sonzogno, Edoardo
b. 1837 Bajer, Fredrik
b. 1864 Weber, Max
b. 1870 Porter, Edwin
b. 1871 Blech, Leo
b. 1872 Bitzer, George William
b. 1882 Bridgman, Percy Williams
b. 1884 Frankau, Gilbert
b. 1884 Liebling, Estelle
b. 1887 McCarthy, Joe
b. 1889 Harrison, G(eorge) Donald
b. 1889 Karrar, Paul
b. 1889 Prado Ugarteche, Manuel
b. 1891 Harkness, Georgia (Elma)
b. 1893 Christaller, Walter
b. 1898 Owen, Steve
b. 1899 Day, James Wentworth
b. 1899 Fritzsche, Hans

b. 1903 Hedtoft (-Hansen), Hans Christian
b. 1904 Helion, Jean
b. 1904 Mallory, L(ester) D(ewitt)
b. 1905 Brown, Edmund G.
b. 1907 Baker, Dorothy Dodds
b. 1909 Coker, Elizabeth Boatwright
b. 1909 May, Rollo (Reece)
b. 1911 Warren, Leonard
b. 1912 Camus, Marcel
b. 1913 Li, C(hoh) H(ao)
b. 1913 Parkinson, Norman
b. 1914 Gaines, Lee
b. 1914 Lachs, Manfred
b. 1914 Panama, Norman
b. 1916 Quinn, Anthony Rudolph Oaxaca
b. 1917 Lambert, J(ack) W(alter)
b. 1919 Cornell, Don
b. 1923 Mortimer, John Clifford
b. 1926 Elizabeth II
b. 1926 Leigh, Carolyn
b. 1927 Brustein, Robert Sanford
b. 1930 Mangano, Silvana
b. 1930 Tyson, Don
b. 1932 May, Elaine
b. 1932 Melnick, Daniel
b. 1934 Bailar, Benjamin Franklin
b. 1935 Grodin, Charles
b. 1935 Kean, Thomas Howard
b. 1939 McCabe, John
b. 1941 Boren, David (Lyle)
b. 1942 Burford, Anne McGill Gorsuch
b. 1947 Pop, Iggy
b. 1949 LuPone, Patti Ann
b. 1951 Danza, Tony
b. 1952 Early, Gerald
b. 1958 MacDowell, Andie
b. 1960 Goulet, Michel
d. 1109 Anselm, Saint
d. 1142 Abelard, Pierre
d. 1509 Henry VII
d. 1582 Toledo, Fernando Alvarez de
d. 1722 Beverley, Robert
d. 1792 Tiradentes
d. 1793 Michell, John
d. 1879 Dix, John Adams
d. 1889 Lerdo de Tejada, Sebastian
d. 1900 Vogl, Heinrich
d. 1910 Twain, Mark
d. 1914 Crockett, S(amuel) R(utherford)

d. 1915 Hugo, Adele
d. 1916 Surratt, John Harrison
d. 1918 Richthofen, Manfred von, Baron
d. 1924 Corelli, Marie
d. 1930 Bridges, Robert Seymour
d. 1932 Pickett, Bill
d. 1938 Iqbal, Mahomed, Sir
d. 1942 Stickley, Gustav
d. 1946 Keynes, John Maynard, Baron
d. 1952 Banks, Leslie
d. 1952 Cripps, Stafford, Sir
d. 1956 MacArthur, Charles
d. 1961 Melton, James
d. 1962 Page, Frederick Handley, Sir
d. 1963 Robertson, Dennis Holme
d. 1965 Appleton, Edward Victor, Sir
d. 1967 Danjon, Andre Louis
d. 1969 Iturbi, Amparo
d. 1971 Duvalier, Francois
d. 1971 Eliot, George Fielding
d. 1971 Lowe, Edmund Dante
d. 1971 Parker, Cecil
d. 1975 Westrup, J(ack) A(llan), Sir
d. 1977 Marx, Gummo
d. 1978 Craig, Cleo F
d. 1978 Turner, Thomas Wyatt
d. 1980 Oparin, Aleksandr Ivanovich
d. 1980 Paasio, Rafael
d. 1980 Page, Joe
d. 1981 Sauter, Eddie
d. 1983 Slezak, Walter
d. 1984 Mercer, Mabel
d. 1985 Gernreich, Rudi
d. 1985 Hewitt, Foster
d. 1985 Mills, Irving
d. 1987 Green, Edith S(tarrett)
d. 1988 Diamond, I(sidore) A L
d. 1988 Rudensky, Morris
d. 1989 Kirkwood, James
d. 1990 Erte
d. 1990 Lausche, Frank John
d. 1993 Mitchell, Corinne
d. 1995 O'Shea, Tessie
d. 1996 Snyder, Jimmy the Greek
d. 1997 Macapagal, Diosdado P(angan)
d. 1997 Rodriguez, Andres
d. 1998 Hayes, Peter Lind
d. 1999 Rogers, Buddy

d. 1999 Tilberis, Elizabeth
d. 2000 Moore, George Stevens

April 22
b. 1451 Isabella I
b. 1707 Fielding, Henry
b. 1711 Wheelock, Eleazar
b. 1722 Smart, Christopher
b. 1724 Kant, Immanuel
b. 1766 Stael-Holstein, Anne Louise Germaine Necker, Baroness de
b. 1792 Levy, Uriah Phillips
b. 1799 Poiseuille, Jean Louis Marie
b. 1812 Dalhousie, James Andrew Broun Ramsay, Marquess of
b. 1832 Morton, Julius Sterling
b. 1838 Yamagata, Aritomo
b. 1840 Redon, Odilon
b. 1854 La Fontaine, Henri Marie
b. 1860 Rehan, Ada
b. 1864 May, Phil(ip William)
b. 1866 Seeckt, Hans von
b. 1870 Lenin, Vladimir Ilyich
b. 1873 Glasgow, Ellen Anderson Gholson
b. 1876 Barany, Robert
b. 1876 Rolvaag, Ole Edvart
b. 1878 Gordon, Kitty
b. 1881 Kerensky, Alexander Fedorovitch
b. 1882 Brawley, Benjamin Griffith
b. 1882 Dowding, Hugh Caswell Tremenheere, Baron
b. 1884 Enskog, David
b. 1884 Rank, Otto
b. 1887 Hall, James Norman
b. 1887 Wiese, Kurt
b. 1891 Gilpin, Laura
b. 1891 Jeffreys, Harold
b. 1891 Sacco, Nicola
b. 1896 Ethridge, Mark Foster
b. 1899 Green, Martyn
b. 1901 Maxwell, Vera (Huppe)
b. 1902 Angoff, Charles
b. 1902 Tyler, Ralph W(infred)
b. 1902 Vandercook, John Womack
b. 1904 Appley, Lawrence A(sa)
b. 1904 Oppenheimer, J(ulius) Robert
b. 1905 Choquette, Robert Guy

d. 1924 Duse, Eleanora
d. 1924 Goodhue,
  Bertram G(rosvenor)
d. 1926 Pennell, Joseph
  Stanley
d. 1933 Keefe,
  Tim(othy John)
d. 1941 Fields, Stanley
d. 1941 Russell, Charles
  Edward
d. 1947 Lawes, Lewis
  Edward
d. 1951 Dawes, Charles
  Gates
d. 1952 Schumann,
  Elisabeth
d. 1953 DeRose, Peter
d. 1955 Busse, Henry
d. 1959 Guthrie, Edwin
  Ray
d. 1964 Polanyi, Karl
d. 1970 Shriner, Herb
d. 1971 Jameson, House
d. 1980 Hecht, George
  Joseph
d. 1981 Maury, Reuben
d. 1982 Townsend,
  William Cameron
d. 1982 Walsh, Michael
  Patrick
d. 1983 Crabbe, Buster
d. 1983 La Follette,
  Suzanne
d. 1983 Royle, Selena
d. 1985 Ervin, Sam(uel
  James Jr.)
d. 1985 Hughes, Sarah
  Tilghman
d. 1985 Smith, Kent
d. 1986 Arlen, Harold
d. 1986 Collett, Alec
d. 1986 Preminger, Otto
  Ludwig
d. 1987 Jutra, Claude
d. 1988 Ramsey, Arthur
  Michael, Lord
d. 1988 Rich, Irene
d. 1990 Goddard,
  Paulette
d. 1992 Ray, Satyajit
d. 1993 Chavez, Cesar
  (Estrada)
d. 1995 Cosell, Howard
d. 1995 Gerstacker, Carl
  A(llan)
d. 1995 Stennis, John
  C(ornelius)
d. 1996 Travers,
  P(amela) L(yndon)
d. 1998 Aurre, Laura
d. 1998 Karamanlis,
  Constantine
d. 1998 Ray, James Earl

April 24
b. 216? Mani
b. 1575 Boehme, Jakob
b. 1581 Vincent de
  Paul, Saint
b. 1743 Cartwright,
  Edmund
b. 1750 Trumbull, John
b. 1766 Thomas, Robert
  B
b. 1815 Trollope,
  Anthony

b. 1828 Nuitter, Charles
  Louis
b. 1837 Polk, Leonidas
  Lafayette
b. 1842 Schindler,
  Solomon
b. 1845 Spitteler, Karl
  Friedrich Georg
b. 1846 Clarke, Marcus
  (Andrew Hislop)
b. 1849 Gallieni,
  Joseph-Simon
b. 1851 Earp, Morgan
b. 1853 Bertillon,
  Alphonse
b. 1856 Petain, Henri
  Philippe
b. 1862 Benson, Arthur
  Christopher
b. 1870 Quinn, John
b. 1872 Ring, Blanche
b. 1874 Pope, John
  Russell
b. 1876 Raeder, Erich
b. 1876 Tallmadge,
  Thomas Eddy
b. 1882 Maude, Cyril
b. 1882 Sarg, Tony
b. 1889 Cripps,
  Stafford, Sir
b. 1889 Popova, Liubov
  Sergeevna
b. 1892 Hulbert, Jack
b. 1894 Ehmke, Howard
  Jonathan
b. 1900 Goudge,
  Elizabeth
b. 1902? Tamiris, Helen
b. 1903 Michalske,
  Mike
b. 1904 Davidson,
  Garrison H(olt)
b. 1904 deKooning,
  Willem
b. 1905 Warren, Robert
  Penn
b. 1908 Oppen, George
b. 1909 Grzimek,
  Bernhard
b. 1910 Joseph, Richard
b. 1911 Leonard, Jack E
b. 1911 Schiller, Karl
  (August Fritz)
b. 1912 Kane, Robert
  Joseph
b. 1912 Wunder,
  George S
b. 1914 Bingham,
  Jonathan Brewster
b. 1914 Castle, William
b. 1914 Conniff, Frank
b. 1915 Goyen, William
b. 1916 Kauffmann,
  Stanley Jules
b. 1918 Kaplan, Henry
  Seymour
b. 1919 Clerides,
  Glafcos (John)
b. 1924 Bevan, Brian
b. 1926 Falldin,
  Thorbjorn Nils Olof
b. 1930 Tahse, Martin
b. 1931 Riley, Bridget
b. 1932 Rockefeller,
  Rodman C

b. 1932 Young, John
  Alan
b. 1933 Eagleson, Alan
b. 1934 MacLaine,
  Shirley
b. 1935 Keith, Louis
  Gerald
b. 1936 Crombie, David
  Edward
b. 1936 Ireland, Jill
b. 1936 Logan, Daniel
b. 1937 Henderson, Joe
b. 1938 Dale, Carroll W
b. 1941 Williams, John
b. 1942 Daley, Richard
  Michael
b. 1942 Streisand,
  Barbra (Joan)
b. 1943 Sterban,
  Richard
b. 1944 Agron, Salvador
b. 1952 Gaultier, Jean-
  Paul
b. 1953 Bogosian, Eric
b. 1954 Abu-Jamal,
  Mumia
b. 1955 Vohor,
  (Rialuth) Serge
d. 1572 Ramus, Petrus
d. 1677 Parker, Thomas
d. 1779 Wheelock,
  Eleazar
d. 1791 Harrison,
  Benjamin
d. 1803 Tandy, James
  Napper
d. 1821 Frank, Johann
  Peter
d. 1846 Crescentini,
  Girolamo
d. 1854 Rossetti,
  Gabriele Pasquale
  Giuseppe
d. 1881 Fields, James
  Thomas
d. 1884 Taglioni, Maria
d. 1891 Moltke,
  Helmuth Karl
  Bernhard von
d. 1907 Kearney, Denis
d. 1907 Packer, Alfred
  G
d. 1924 Hall,
  G(ranville) Stanley
d. 1933 Adler, Felix
d. 1936 Dunne, Finley
  Peter
d. 1938 Barnard,
  George Grey
d. 1940 Jacobs, Joe B
d. 1941 Brush, George
d. 1942 Blackburn, Jack
d. 1942 Montgomery,
  Lucy Maud
d. 1947 Cather, Willa
  (Sibert)
d. 1956 Stephenson,
  Henry
d. 1960 Laue, Max
  Theodor Felix von
d. 1962 Hackett, Francis
d. 1964 Domagk,
  Gerhard
d. 1965 Dresser, Louise
d. 1965 Madden, Owen
  Victor

d. 1967 Komarov,
  Vladimir
  Mikhaylovich
d. 1970 Spann, Otis
d. 1971 Hayton, Lennie
d. 1971 Soong, T V
d. 1973 Armstrong,
  Hamilton Fish
d. 1974 Abbott, Bud
d. 1974 Jonas, Franz
d. 1976 Tobey, Mark
d. 1978 Nestingen, Ivan
  Arnold
d. 1980 Finletter,
  Thomas Knight
d. 1980 Semenenko,
  Serge
d. 1982 Ashbrook, John
  Milan
d. 1982 Ritola, Ville
d. 1985 Weinberg,
  Chester
d. 1986 Simpson, Wallis
  (Bessie Wallis
  Warfield)
d. 1988 Jordan, Fred
d. 1991 Dozier, William
d. 1993 Tambo, Oliver
d. 1993 Thao, Tran Duc
d. 1995 Harp, Holly
d. 1995 Rainey, Melanie
d. 1998 Stevens, Leslie

April 25
b. 1215 Louis IX
b. 1284 Edward II
b. 1599 Cromwell,
  Oliver
b. 1694 Burlington,
  Richard Boyle, Earl
b. 1769 Brunel, Marc
  Isambard, Sir
b. 1792 Keble, John
b. 1806 Duff, Alexander
b. 1825 Lerdo de
  Tejada, Sebastian
b. 1826 Deering,
  William
b. 1841 Lucca, Pauline
b. 1852 Cannon, James
  W
b. 1853 Stevens, John
  Frank
b. 1856 Hadley, Arthur
  Twining
b. 1861 Seligman,
  Edwin Robert
  Anderson
b. 1862 Grey of
  Fallodon, Edward,
  Viscount
b. 1873 DeLaMare,
  Walter
b. 1873 Garis, Howard
  Roger
b. 1873 Herelle, Felix
  d'
b. 1874 Marconi,
  Guglielmo
b. 1875 Nougues, Jean
b. 1880 Mellor, Walter
b. 1882 McLeod,
  Fred(erick)
b. 1883 Ford, Russ(ell
  William)
b. 1891 Richardson, Sid
b. 1897 Pratt, Fletcher

b. 1900? Halpert, Edith
Gregor
b. 1900 Pauli, Wolfgang
Ernst
b. 1906 Brennan,
William Joseph, Jr.
b. 1907 Matter, Herbert
b. 1907 Zinnemann,
Fred
b. 1908 Murrow,
Edward R
b. 1909 Pereira, William
Leonard
b. 1910 Hirsch, Joseph
b. 1912 Blitch, Iris
F(aircloth)
b. 1914 Lockridge, Ross
Franklin, Jr.
b. 1914 Mauriac,
Claude
b. 1914 Perez Jimenez,
Marcos
b. 1915 Tajo, Italo
b. 1916 Barber, Jerry
b. 1917 Fitzgerald, Ella
b. 1918 Varnay, Astrid
b. 1921 Appel, Karel
Christian
b. 1923 Healy, Timothy
S(tafford)
b. 1923 King, Albert
b. 1923 Miller, Arnold
Ray
b. 1925 Sohappy,
David, Sr.
b. 1925 Stacton, David
Derek
b. 1928 Clements,
Vassar
b. 1928 Hayden,
Melissa
b. 1929 Twombly, Cy
b. 1930 Mazursky, Paul
b. 1932 Lemon,
Meadowlark
b. 1933 Lukas, J(ay)
Anthony
b. 1936 Arron, Henck
Alphonsus Eugene
b. 1939 Lichfield,
Patrick
b. 1940 Pacino,
Al(fredo James)
b. 1941 Tavernier,
Bertrand
b. 1942 Kyl, Jon
b. 1942 O'Sullivan,
John
b. 1945 Ulvaeus, Bjorn
b. 1946 Shire, Talia
Rose Coppola
b. 1946 Zhirinovsky,
Vladimir
b. 1947 Cruyff, Johan
b. 1950 Fulani, Lenora
b. 1950 Humphrey,
Bobbi
b. 1950 Nussbaum,
Karen
b. 1952 Tretiak,
Vladislav
b. 1959 Terry, Randall
A.
b. 1960 Schlicter,
Art(hur E)

b. 1976 Duncan,
Tim(othy Theodore)
d. 1472 Alberti, Leon
Battista
d. 1482 Margaret of
Anjou
d. 1595 Tasso, Torquato
d. 1690 Teniers, David,
the Younger
d. 1744 Celsius, Anders
d. 1800 Cowper,
William
d. 1814 Dibdin, Charles
d. 1820 Volney,
(Constantin) Francois
Chasseboeuf, Comte
de
d. 1853 Beaumont,
William
d. 1870 Maclise, Daniel
d. 1878 Sewell, Anna
d. 1890 Crowfoot
d. 1892 Bradford,
William
d. 1905 Paine, John
Knowles
d. 1919 Juilliard,
Augustus D
d. 1928 Bennett, Floyd
d. 1928 Curel, Francois
de
d. 1928 Wrangel, Pietr
Nikolayevich
d. 1936 Fuad, I
d. 1938 Stammler,
Rudolf
d. 1943 Nemirovich-
Danchenko, Vladimir
I
d. 1944 Herriman,
George
d. 1945 Bragg, Mabel
Caroline
d. 1945 Weatherford,
Teddy
d. 1954 Hergesheimer,
Joseph
d. 1955 Collier,
Constance
d. 1955 Merriam, Frank
Finley
d. 1958 Hickman,
Herman Michael, Jr.
d. 1959 Mannes, David
d. 1960 Amanollah
Khan
d. 1960 Emerson, Hope
d. 1968 Davidson,
Donald Grady
d. 1970 Louise, Anita
d. 1972 Sanders, George
d. 1973 Shihab, Fu'ad
d. 1975 Duclos, Jacques
d. 1976 Brailowsky,
Alexander
d. 1976 Reed, Carol, Sir
d. 1982 Burnett,
W(illiam) R(iley)
d. 1982 Butterfield,
Lyman Henry
d. 1982 Cody, John
Patrick
d. 1982 Johnson, Celia,
Dame
d. 1982 Wilson,
Don(ald Harlow)

d. 1983 Glenn, Carroll
d. 1984 Kennedy, David
Anthony
d. 1985 Haydn, Richard
d. 1985 Matheson,
Murray
d. 1988 Matthews,
Burnita S(helton)
d. 1988 Simak, Clifford
Donald
d. 1989 Coulouris,
George
d. 1990 Gordon, Dexter
Keith
d. 1995 Fleming, Art
d. 1995 Rogers, Ginger
d. 1996 Bass, Saul
d. 1997 May, Brian
d. 1997 Paulsen, Pat
d. 1998 Morris, Wright
Marion
d. 1999 Hruska, Roman
L(ee)
d. 1999 Killanin,
Michael Morris, Lord

April 26
b. 1573 Marie de
Medicis
b. 1660 Defoe, Daniel
b. 1710 Reid, Thomas
b. 1711 Hume, David
b. 1718 Hopkins, Esek
b. 1761 Hamilton,
Emma, Lady
b. 1785 Audubon, John
James
b. 1798 Beckwourth,
James Pierson
b. 1798 Delacroix,
(Ferdinand Victor)
Eugene
b. 1812 Flotow,
Friedrich von, Baron
b. 1812 Krupp, Alfred
b. 1820 Cary, Alice
b. 1828 Finley, Martha
b. 1829 Billroth,
Theodore
b. 1834 Ward, Artemus
b. 1856 Morgenthau,
Henry
b. 1868 Harmsworth,
Harold Sidney
b. 1868 Rothermere,
Harold Sidney
Harmsworth
b. 1877 Taylor, William
Desmond
b. 1879 Richardson,
Owen Williams, Sir
b. 1880 Fokine, Michel
b. 1884 Norena, Eide
b. 1886 Dawson,
William L(evi)
b. 1886 Rainey,
Gertrude
b. 1888 Risdon,
Elizabeth
b. 1889 Wittgenstein,
Ludwig
b. 1890 Kennedy, Edgar
b. 1891 Hoffman, Paul
Gray
b. 1893 Loos, Anita
b. 1894 Austral,
Florence Wilson

b. 1894 Hess, Rudolf
b. 1895 Lengyel, Emil
b. 1896 Stein, Jules
Caesar
b. 1896 Udet, Ernst
b. 1897 Canfield, Cass
b. 1898 Aleixandre,
Vicente
b. 1898 Grierson, John
b. 1900 Fuchs, Joseph
(Philip)
b. 1900 Richter, Charles
Francis
b. 1900 Sirk, Douglas
b. 1900 Wilson, Hack
b. 1902 Daniels,
Jonathan Worth
b. 1905 Vigo, Jean
b. 1906 Joyce, William
b. 1908 Bugas, John
Stephen
b. 1908 Tough, Dave
b. 1908 Wilhelm, Gale
b. 1909 Connor,
William Neil, Sir
b. 1910 Tanaka,
Tomoyuki
b. 1911 Raskin,
A(braham) H(enry)
b. 1913 Burcham,
Lester Arthur
b. 1914 Malamud,
Bernard
b. 1914 Rouse, James
W(ilson)
b. 1915 Kubly, Herbert
(Oswald)
b. 1916 West, Morris
L(anglo)
b. 1917 Maglie,
Sal(vatore Anthony)
b. 1917 Pei, I(eoh)
M(ing)
b. 1920 Walsh, William
B(ertalan)
b. 1921 Costello, Robert
E
b. 1921 Giuffre, James
Peter
b. 1922 Kellin, Mike
b. 1922 Sauve, Jeanne
Mathilde Benoit
b. 1924 Nype, Russell
b. 1926 Linn, Bambi
b. 1927 Gallatin, Harry
J
b. 1930 Friedman,
Bruce Jay
b. 1931 Almond, Paul
b. 1933 Burnett, Carol
b. 1933 Penzias, Arno
Allan
b. 1934 McCloskey,
John Michael
b. 1938 Eddy, Duane
b. 1940 Cruikshank,
Margaret
b. 1941 Schroeder,
Barbet
b. 1942 Rydell, Bobby
b. 1943 Wright, Gary
b. 1944 Black, Cathleen
Prunty
b. 1946 Jaffe, Harold W
b. 1949 Schaufuss, Peter
b. 1955 Scott, Mike

d. 499 Wei Hsiao-Wen-ti
d. 1699 Racine, Jean Baptiste
d. 1731 Defoe, Daniel
d. 1865 Booth, John Wilkes
d. 1865 Sax, Charles Joseph
d. 1910 Bjornson, Bjornstjerne Martinius
d. 1915 Bunny, John
d. 1920 Ramanujan Aiyangar, Srinivasa
d. 1931 Mead, George Herbert
d. 1940 Bosch, Carl
d. 1946 Keyserling, Hermann Alexander Graf Von
d. 1947 McLean, Evalyn Walsh
d. 1948 Ross, Donald James
d. 1951 Carpenter, John Alden
d. 1956 Arnold, Edward
d. 1957 Strong, Philip Duffield
d. 1964 Pratt, Edwin John
d. 1967 Charoux, Siegfried
d. 1969 Rinehart, Stanley Marshall, Jr.
d. 1970 Lee, Gypsy Rose
d. 1972 Summerfield, Arthur Ellsworth
d. 1973 Ryan, Irene Noblette
d. 1976 Grechko, Andrei Antonovick
d. 1980 Courtneidge, Cicely, Dame
d. 1981 Davis, Jim
d. 1981 Evans, Madge
d. 1983 Buckmaster, Henrietta
d. 1984 Basie, Count
d. 1984 McAvoy, May
d. 1984 Roney, William Chapoton, Jr.
d. 1985 Maltz, Albert
d. 1986 Crawford, Broderick
d. 1986 Gmeiner, Hermann
d. 1986 Love, Bessie
d. 1988 Patterson, Frederick Douglass
d. 1988 Rempp, Adolph
d. 1988 Ross, Lanny
d. 1989 Ball, Lucille (Desiree)
d. 1991 Coppola, Carmine
d. 1991 Guthrie, A(lfred) B(ertram), Jr.
d. 1993 Henkle, Henrietta
d. 1995 Friedrich, Otto
d. 1995 Knox, Alexander
d. 1995 Lamont, Corliss

d. 1996 Silliphant, Stirling Dale
d. 1997 Beal, John
d. 1997 Faye, Joey
d. 1998 Paul, Gabe
d. 2000 Merrick, David

April 27
b. 1496 Suleiman I
b. 1654 Blount, Charles
b. 1759 Godwin, Mary Wollstonecraft
b. 1791 Morse, Samuel Finley Breese
b. 1798 Clairmont, Claire
b. 1820 Spencer, Herbert
b. 1822 Grant, Ulysses Simpson
b. 1822 Olmsted, Frederick Law
b. 1840 Whymper, Edward
b. 1845 Freshfield, Douglas William
b. 1846 Van Depoele, Charles Joseph
b. 1851 Earle, Alice Morse
b. 1855 Duke, Benjamin Newton
b. 1860 Copeland, Charles Townsend
b. 1874 Baring, Maurice
b. 1876 Farrere, Claude
b. 1882 Fauset, Jessie Redmon
b. 1892 Levy, David Mordecai
b. 1893 Geddes, Norman Bel
b. 1894 Slonimsky, Nicolas
b. 1896 Carothers, Wallace Hume
b. 1896 Hornsby, Rogers
b. 1898 Bemelmans, Ludwig
b. 1899 Diegel, Leo
b. 1900 Lantz, Walter
b. 1904 Burns, Arthur Frank
b. 1904 Day-Lewis, Cecil
b. 1906 Maeght, Aime
b. 1909 Matlock, Matty
b. 1910 Fischer, John
b. 1913 Abelson, Philip Hauge
b. 1913 Adler, Irving
b. 1914 Cole, Jack
b. 1916 Slaughter, Enos Bradsher
b. 1918 Scali, John (Alfred)
b. 1920 Morgan, Edwin George
b. 1922 Klugman, Jack
b. 1925 Baron, Samuel
b. 1926 LaHaye, Tim
b. 1926 Paterson, Basil Alexander
b. 1927 King, Coretta Scott

b. 1931 Oistrakh, Igor Davidovich
b. 1932 Botha, Roelof Frederik
b. 1932 Knox, Chuck
b. 1934 Aimee, Anouk
b. 1937 Dennis, Sandy
b. 1937 Jones, Phil(ip Howard)
b. 1938 Anthony, Earl Roderick
b. 1939 Carne, Judy
b. 1939 Vieira, Joao (Bernardo)
b. 1941 Blegen, Judith Eyer
b. 1945 Wilson, August
b. 1947 Magnuson, Keith Arlen
b. 1950 Simmons, Calvin
b. 1951 Falkenberg, Nanette
b. 1951 Frehley, Ace
b. 1952 Gervin, George
b. 1959 Easton, Sheena
d. 1521 Magellan, Ferdinand
d. 1656 Goyen, Jan Josephszoon van
d. 1702 Bart, Jean
d. 1710 Betterton, Thomas
d. 1794 Bruce, James
d. 1797 Babeuf, Francois-Noel
d. 1813 Pike, Zebulon Montgomery
d. 1854 Pickering, William
d. 1882 Emerson, Ralph Waldo
d. 1886 Richardson, Henry Hobson
d. 1889 Barnard, Frederick Augustus Porter
d. 1896 Parkes, Henry, Sir
d. 1902 Morton, Julius Sterling
d. 1915 Scriabin, Alexander Nicholaevich
d. 1927 Beveridge, Albert Jeremiah
d. 1932 Crane, Hart
d. 1937 Gramsci, Antonio
d. 1937 Schutzendorf, Gustav
d. 1938 Husserl, Edmund
d. 1948 Knudsen, William Signius
d. 1950 Cavanaugh, Hobart
d. 1954 Ralf, Torsten
d. 1959 Ogburn, W(illiam) F(ielding)
d. 1961 DelRuth, Roy
d. 1965 Murrow, Edward R
d. 1969 Barrientos Ortuno, Rene

d. 1972 Budenz, Louis Francis
d. 1972 Nkrumah, Kwame
d. 1975 Marsala, Marty
d. 1981 Battles, Cliff(ord Franklin)
d. 1981 Roosevelt, John Aspinal
d. 1982 Tully, Tom
d. 1983 Catledge, Turner
d. 1986 Hynek, J(oseph) Allen
d. 1988 Johnson, Wallace Edward
d. 1988 Wieghorst, Olaf
d. 1989 Matsushita, Konosuke
d. 1990 Spewack, Bella Cohen
d. 1992 O'Neill, Gerard Kitchen
d. 1994 Preston, John
d. 1995 Bennett, John C(oleman)
d. 1995 Wright, Jerauld
d. 1995 Wright, Peter (Maurice)
d. 1996 Colby, William E(gan)
d. 1998 Castaneda, Carlos
d. 1998 Linh, Nguyen Van
d. 1999 Hirt, Al(ois Maxwell)

April 28
b. 1442 Edward IV
b. 1630 Cotton, Charles
b. 1753 Achard, Franz Karl
b. 1758 Monroe, James
b. 1774 Baily, Francis
b. 1795 Sturt, Charles
b. 1801 Cooper, Anthony Ashley, 7th Earl of Shaftesbury
b. 1817 Curtin, Andrew Gregg
b. 1831 Tait, Peter Guthrie
b. 1840 Cox, Palmer
b. 1869 Goodhue, Bertram G(rosvenor)
b. 1871 Homer, Louise
b. 1872 Esposito, Joseph
b. 1873 Bauer, Harold
b. 1874 Toler, Sidney
b. 1878 Barrymore, Lionel Blythe
b. 1889 Salazar, Antonio de Oliveira
b. 1892 Niles, John Jacob
b. 1896 Dunninger, Joseph
b. 1898 Soutar, William
b. 1900 Gielgud, Val Henry
b. 1900 Oort, Jan Hendrik
b. 1900 Thorez, Maurice
b. 1903 Fitts, Dudley

d. 1988 Larsen,
Emmanuel
d. 1991 Sperti, George
Speri
d. 1992 Clarke, Mae
d. 1993 Gordon,
Michael
d. 1994 Kirk, Russell
(Amos)
d. 1997 Royko, Mike
d. 1999 Stader, Maria

April 30
b. 1623 Laval, Francois
Xavier de
b. 1770 Thompson,
David
b. 1777 Gauss, Carl
Friedrich
b. 1796 Cremieux,
Isaac-Adolphe
b. 1822 Goodwin,
Hannibal Williston
b. 1823 Bradford,
William
b. 1823 Houghton,
Henry Oscar
b. 1839 Peixoto,
Floriano
b. 1857 Bleuler, Eugen
b. 1858 Harrison, Mary
Scott Lord Dimmick
b. 1870 Lehar, Franz
b. 1871 Yost, Fielding
Harris
b. 1877 Toklas, Alice
B(abette)
b. 1879 Resor, Stanley
Burnett
b. 1883 Hasek, Jaroslav
b. 1885 Sayre, Francis
Bowes
b. 1888 Ransom, John
Crowe
b. 1891? Walsh, James
Edward
b. 1892 Clapper,
Raymond Lewis
b. 1893 Ribbentrop,
Joachim von
b. 1894 Bartlett, Vernon
b. 1894 Evatt, Herbert
Vere
b. 1896 Davis, Gary,
Reverend
b. 1898 Towle,
Katherine Amelia
b. 1898 Vanderbilt,
Cornelius, Jr.
b. 1899 Wieghorst, Olaf
b. 1901 Kuznets, Simon
Smith
b. 1902 Schultz,
Theodore W(illiam)
b. 1903 Lewis, Fulton,
Jr.
b. 1904 Logan, Harlan
(De Braun)
b. 1909 Juliana
b. 1912 Arden, Eve
b. 1914 Royster,
Vermont
C(onnecticut)
b. 1915 Henderson,
Bruce
b. 1916 Shannon,
Claude Elwood

b. 1916 Shaw, Robert
Lawson
b. 1917 Wain, Bea
b. 1920 Cosgrave, Liam
b. 1924 Harnick,
Sheldon Mayer
b. 1925 Calvet, Corinne
b. 1925 Leachman,
Cloris
b. 1927 Horton, Johnny
b. 1930 Guattari, Felix
b. 1930 Sarney, Jose
b. 1931 Clay, William
Lacy
b. 1933 Nelson, Willie
b. 1933 Vendler, Helen
Hennessy
b. 1939 Kleban, Edward
Lawrence
b. 1939 Ortiz, Alfonso
b. 1939 Zwilich, Ellen
Taaffe
b. 1940 Young, Burt
b. 1943 Chiluba,
Frederick Jacob Titus
b. 1943 Douglas,
Cathleen Curran
Heffernan
b. 1943 Vee, Bobby
b. 1944 Clayburgh, Jill
b. 1945 Dillard, Annie
Doak
b. 1945 Smith, Michael
John
b. 1946 Carl Gustaf
XVI
b. 1946 Schollander,
Don(ald Arthur)
b. 1948 King, Perry
b. 1949 Guterres,
Antonio Manuel de
Oliveira
b. 1951 Lucas, Craig
b. 1961 Thomas, Isiah
d. 1524 Bayard, Pierre
du Terrail
d. 1755 Oudry, Jean-
Baptiste
d. 1775 Harrison, Peter
d. 1792 Sandwich, John
Montagu
d. 1859 Aksakov, Sergei
Timofeyevich
d. 1865 Becknell,
William
d. 1879 Hale, Sarah
Josepha Buell
d. 1889 Rosa, Carl
d. 1891 Leidy, Joseph
d. 1895 Freytag, Gustav
d. 1900 Jones, Casey
d. 1918 Princip, Gavrilo
d. 1926 Coleman,
Bessie
d. 1934 Welch, William
Henry
d. 1936 Housman,
A(lfred) E(dward)
d. 1941 Porter, Edwin
d. 1942 Arthur, Joseph
Charles
d. 1943 Webb, Beatrice
Potter
d. 1944 Poiret, Paul
d. 1945 Braun, Eva
d. 1945 Hitler, Adolf

d. 1946 Hepbron,
George
d. 1947 Wright,
Almroth Edward, Sir
d. 1956 Barkley, Alben
William
d. 1959 Nagai, Sokichi
d. 1960 Polacco,
Giorgio
d. 1961 Fauset, Jessie
Redmon
d. 1966 Farina, Richard
d. 1970 Johnson, Hall
d. 1970 Stevens, Inger
d. 1971 Roper, Elmo
Burns, Jr.
d. 1972 Scala, Gia
d. 1974 Moorehead,
Agnes
d. 1977 Lewis, (Myrtle)
Tillie
d. 1980 Kronenberger,
Louis
d. 1980 Munoz Marin,
Luis
d. 1981 Anderson, Cat
d. 1981 Bordes,
Francois
d. 1982 Bangs, Lester
d. 1983 Balanchine,
George
d. 1983 Waters, Muddy
d. 1985 Aitken, Max
d. 1985 Sommers, Ben
d. 1986 Stevenson,
Robert
d. 1988 McCracken,
James (Eugene)
d. 1988 Righter, Carroll
d. 1989 Leone, Sergio
d. 1994 Scarry, Richard
(McClure)
d. 1994 White, William
S(mith)
d. 1995 Duke, Angier
Biddle
d. 1995 Haire, Bill
Martin
d. 1996 Opatoshu,
David
d. 1997 Picard, Henry
d. 2000 Jones, Jonah

MAY

b. 1527? Guerrero,
Francisco
b. 1740 Pacchierotti,
Gasparo
b. 1807 Abd el-Kadir
b. 1808? Chisholm,
Caroline
b. 1820 Surratt, Mary
Eugenia Jenkins
b. 1880 Anderson,
Willie
b. 1893 Pearlroth,
Norbert
b. 1895 Chevallier,
Gabriel
b. 1922 Kiwanuka,
Benedicto Kagima
Mugumba
b. 1925 Ghorbal, Ashraf
A

b. 1937 Nidal, Abu
b. 1940 Niyazov,
Saparmurad
Atayevich
b. 1946 Altea,
Rosemary
d. 1500 Dias de Novais,
Bartolomeu
d. 1607 Dyer, Edward,
Sir
d. 1650 Charnisay,
Charles de Menou,
Seigneur d'Aulnay
d. 1700 Jolliet, Louis
d. 1927 Nungesser,
Charles Eugene Jules
Marie
d. 1933 Whitechurch,
Victor Lorenzo
d. 1944 Smyth, Ethel,
Dame
d. 1973 Ewing, Alfred
Cyril
d. 1983 Kaper,
Bronislau

May 1
b. 1672 Addison, Joseph
b. 1764 Latrobe,
Benjamin Henry
b. 1769 Wellington,
Arthur Wellesley,
Duke
b. 1796 Booth, Junius
Brutus
b. 1825 Inness, George
b. 1827 Breton, Jules
Adolphe
b. 1830 Jones, Mary
Harris
b. 1839 Chardonnet,
Louis Marie Hilaire
Bernigaud
b. 1845 Mifflin, George
Harrison
b. 1847 Lloyd, Henry
Demarest
b. 1848 Rhodes, James
Ford
b. 1852 Patten, Simon
Nelson
b. 1852 Ramon y Cajal,
Santiago
b. 1862 Prevost, Marcel
b. 1864 Jarvis, Anna
b. 1874 Brooks,
Romaine
b. 1876 Swanson, Carl
A
b. 1880 Lasker, Albert
D(avis)
b. 1881 Teilhard de
Chardin, Pierre
b. 1884 Quimby, Harriet
b. 1887 Cunningham,
Alan Gordon, Sir
b. 1887 Wortman,
Denys
b. 1892 Barlow,
Howard
b. 1895 Sowerby, Leo
b. 1896 Clark, Mark
Wayne
b. 1896 Collins, Joseph
Lawton, General
b. 1897 Cabot, Thomas
D(udley)

b. 1900 Caples, John
b. 1900 Silone, Ignazio
b. 1901 Brown, Sterling (Allen)
b. 1901 Gill, Amory Tingle
b. 1904 Valentina
b. 1905 Cagle, Red
b. 1905 Zorbaugh, Geraldine B(one)
b. 1906 Hobart, Rose
b. 1907 Roszak, Theodore
b. 1907 Smith, Kate
b. 1908 Kline, Morris
b. 1909 Melachrino, George Miltiades
b. 1910 Battles, Cliff(ord Franklin)
b. 1910 Hynek, J(oseph) Allen
b. 1910 Rockefeller, Mary French
b. 1912 Rockefeller, Winthrop
b. 1913 Russell, Elizabeth Shull
b. 1913 Susskind, Walter
b. 1916 Ford, Glenn
b. 1917 Beradino, John
b. 1917 Darrieux, Danielle
b. 1918 Paar, Jack
b. 1919 O'Herlihy, Dan
b. 1922 Goodman, Julian B
b. 1922 Mosel, Tad
b. 1923 Heller, Joseph
b. 1924 Granville, Evelyn Boyd
b. 1924 Kayibanda, Gregoire
b. 1925 Southern, Terry
b. 1925 Bednarik, Chuck
b. 1925 Blair, Clay, Jr.
b. 1925 Carpenter, Scott
b. 1927 Bertini, Gary
b. 1927 Cordtz, Dan
b. 1927 Person, Waverly
b. 1927 Zafy, Albert
b. 1929 Weaver, Thomas
b. 1930 Hirsch, John Stephen
b. 1930 Matson, Ollie
b. 1933 Camdessus, Michel (Jean)
b. 1934 Cardenas Solorzano, Cuauhtemoc
b. 1934 Horn, Shirley
b. 1939 Beard, Frank
b. 1939 Collins, Judy
b. 1939 Robinson, Max C
b. 1940 Alcala, Jose (Ramon)
b. 1940 Cooper, Wilhelmina Behmenburg
b. 1940? Foxman, Abraham H

b. 1940 Mason, Bobbie Ann
b. 1940 Peretti, Elsa
b. 1945 Coolidge, Rita
b. 1947 Davis, Barbara
b. 1950 Foster, David
b. 1954 Parker, Ray, Jr.
b. 1960 Cauthen, Steve
b. 1966 McGraw, Tim
b. 1555 Marcellus II, Pope
d. 1572 Pius, V, Pope
d. 1700 Dryden, John
d. 1873 Livingstone, David
d. 1889 Weir, Robert W
d. 1890 Brisbane, Albert
d. 1892 Lamperti, Francesco
d. 1901 Waterman, Lewis Edson
d. 1903 Arditi, Luigi
d. 1904 Dvorak, Anton
d. 1904 His, Wilhelm
d. 1917 Rodo, Jose Enrique
d. 1918 Gilbert, Grove Karl
d. 1922 Cheney, John Vance
d. 1928 Howard, Ebenezer, Sir
d. 1928 Xiang Jingyu
d. 1940 Brooke, L Leslie
d. 1945 Goebbels, Joseph
d. 1952 Coulter, Ernest Kent
d. 1953 Shinn, Everett
d. 1957 Mitchell, Grant
d. 1965 Jones, Spike
d. 1968 Adams, Jack
d. 1968 Nicolson, Harold George, Sir
d. 1969 Logan, Ella
d. 1969 Rosenthal, Jean E
d. 1970 Celan, Paul
d. 1971 Farrell, Glenda
d. 1978 Khachaturian, Aram
d. 1978 Warner, Sylvia Townsend
d. 1981 Gosho Heinosuke
d. 1981 Sneider, Vernon John
d. 1982 Fitzgerald, Albert J
d. 1982 Primrose, William
d. 1984 Barrett, John L
d. 1984 Jenkins, Gordon
d. 1985 Crossley, Archibald Maddock
d. 1985 Robins, Denise Naomi
d. 1986 D'Aulaire, Edgar Parin
d. 1988 Darrell, R(obert) D(onaldson)
d. 1988 Lexcen, Ben
d. 1989 Janigo, Antonio
d. 1993 Beregovoy, Pierre (Eugene)

d. 1993 Knowles, Warren Perley
d. 1993 Premadasa, Ranasinghe
d. 1994 Senna, Ayrton
d. 1996 Brownell, Herbert, Jr.
d. 1996 Kennedy, David M(atthew)
d. 1997 Widerberg, Bo
d. 1998 Bettmann, Otto L(udwig)
d. 1998 Cleaver, Eldridge
d. 2000 Mahoney, David Joseph, Jr.
d. 2000 Reeves, Steve
d. 2000 Stone, Marvin Lawrence

May 2
b. 1660 Scarlatti, Alessandro
b. 1729 Catherine the Great
b. 1750 Andre, John
b. 1764 Gentz, Friedrich Von
b. 1772 Novalis
b. 1779 Galt, John
b. 1810 Brewer, Ebenezer Cobham
b. 1816 Egg, Augustus Leopold
b. 1833 Heenan, John Carmel
b. 1838 Tourgee, Albion Winegar
b. 1844 McCoy, Elijah
b. 1851 Taylor, Graham
b. 1856 Rozanov, Vasili Vasilyevich
b. 1858 Somerville, Edith Anna OEnone
b. 1859 Jerome, Jerome Klapka
b. 1860 Bayliss, William Maddock, Sir
b. 1860 Herzl, Theodor
b. 1865 Fitch, (William) Clyde
b. 1866 Lazear, Jesse William
b. 1867 Reymont, Wladyslaw Stanislaw
b. 1868 Wood, Robert Williams
b. 1869 Power, Tyrone
b. 1871 Duffy, Francis Patrick
b. 1879 Byrnes, James Francis
b. 1887 Castle, Vernon
b. 1887 Collins, Eddie
b. 1887 Griffis, Stanton
b. 1892 Richthofen, Manfred von, Baron
b. 1895 Bacon, Peggy
b. 1895 Hart, Lorenz
b. 1895 Holman, Eugene
b. 1896 Van Doren, Dorothy Graffe
b. 1897 Coots, J Fred
b. 1902 Aherne, Brian de Lacy

b. 1903 Spock, Benjamin (McLane)
b. 1904 Crosby, Bing
b. 1904 Haury, Emil W
b. 1905 Armstrong, Charlotte
b. 1906 Halsman, Philippe
b. 1908 Bakewell, William
b. 1908 O'Brien-Moore, Erin
b. 1912 Springer, Axel Caesar
b. 1914 Woss, Kurt
b. 1920 Hutt, William Ian Dewitt
b. 1921 Gottlieb, Morton Edgar
b. 1921 Ray, Satyajit
b. 1922 Rosenthal, Abraham Michael
b. 1923 Hillery, Patrick John
b. 1924 Bikel, Theodore Meir
b. 1925 Browne, Roscoe Lee
b. 1925 Neville, John
b. 1927 Unger, Irwin
b. 1928 Falls, Joe
b. 1929 Balladur, Edouard
b. 1930 Slade, Bernard
b. 1935 Faisal II
b. 1935 Wray, Link
b. 1936 Rabin, Michael
b. 1938 Moshoeshoe II
b. 1939 Shreve, Susan Richards
b. 1940 Esquivel, Manuel
b. 1940 Leghari, Sardar Farooq Ahmed Khan
b. 1941 Wijdenbosch, Jules Albert
b. 1946 Gore, Lesley
b. 1946 Henrit, Robert
b. 1947 Oglesby, Zena, (Jr.)
b. 1948 Ben-Shalom, Miriam
b. 1948 Gatlin, Larry Wayne
b. 1950 Jagger, Bianca Teresa
b. 1952 Baranski, Christine
b. 1953 Wilkes, Jamaal
b. 1954? Bofill, Angela
b. 1962 Bon Jovi, Jon
d. 1519 Leonardo da Vinci
d. 1685 Ostade, Adriaen van
d. 1821 Piozzi, Hester Lynch Salisbury
d. 1844 Beckford, William
d. 1857 Musset, Alfred de
d. 1864 Meyerbeer, Giacomo
d. 1892 Hofmann, August Wilhelm von

d. 1912 Davenport, Homer Calvin
d. 1927 Starling, Ernest Henry
d. 1929 Dorgan, Thomas Aloysius
d. 1931 Baker, George Fisher
d. 1934 Procter, William Cooper
d. 1944 Leonard, William Ellery
d. 1945 Bormann, Martin Ludwig
d. 1945 Work, Monroe (Nathan)
d. 1955 Vollmer, Lula
d. 1957 McCarthy, Joe
d. 1960 Chessman, Caryl Whittier
d. 1963 Brooks, Van Wyck
d. 1964 Astor, Nancy Witcher Langhorne
d. 1969 Papen, Franz von
d. 1971 Dozier, Edward P.
d. 1972 Hoover, J(ohn) Edgar
d. 1976 Bankhead, Dan(iel Robert)
d. 1977 Cole, Edward Nicholas
d. 1979 Natta, Giulio
d. 1980 Pal, George
d. 1981 Osborne, John Franklin
d. 1981 Wechsler, David
d. 1982 Bochner, Salomon
d. 1982 Marlowe, Hugh
d. 1983 Pridi Phanomyong
d. 1983 Van Brocklin, Norm (an Mack)
d. 1984 Barry, Jack
d. 1984 Clampett, Bob
d. 1985 Bedells, Phyllis
d. 1985 Clinton, Larry
d. 1985 Eisenhower, Milton Stover
d. 1992 Mills, Wilbur Daigh
d. 1992 Wallmann, Margherita
d. 1993 Gallo, Julio
d. 1993 Weng, Will
d. 1995 Hordern, Michael
d. 1997 Eccles, John C(arew), Sir
d. 1997 Freire, P(aulo)
d. 1997 Moore, Audley
d. 1998 Norman, Maidie (Ruth)
d. 1999 Reed, Oliver

May 3
b. 1469 Machiavelli, Niccolo
b. 1748 Sieyes, Emmanuel Joseph
b. 1761 Kotzebue, August Friedrich Ferdinand von

b. 1816 Meigs, Montgomery Cunningham
b. 1844 Carte, Richard d'Oyly
b. 1849 Bulow, Bernhard H M
b. 1849 Riis, Jacob August
b. 1853 Howe, Edgar Watson
b. 1856 Alvary, Max
b. 1859 Adams, Andy
b. 1860 Eeden, Fredrik Willem van
b. 1860 Haldane, John Scott
b. 1871 Dietz, Angel DeCora
b. 1874 Coty, Francois Marie Joseph Spoturno
b. 1879 Pollack, Egon
b. 1882 Dale, Chester
b. 1886 DuPre, Marcel
b. 1890 Fairless, Benjamin F
b. 1891 Rixey, Eppa Jephtha
b. 1892 Bondi, Beulah
b. 1892 Thomson, George Paget, Sir
b. 1895 Mark, Herman Francis
b. 1896 Menon, (Vengalil Krishnan) Krishna
b. 1896 Smith, Dodie
b. 1897 Krishna Menon, V(engalil) K(rishnan)
b. 1898 Clark, Septima
b. 1898 Meir, Golda
b. 1899 MacMahon, Aline Laveen
b. 1900 Frank, Hans
b. 1900 LaRue, Jack
b. 1900 Winwar, Frances
b. 1902 Barbanell, Maurice
b. 1902 Kastler, Alfred
b. 1902 Slezak, Walter
b. 1904 Brandt, Bill
b. 1904 DeErdely, Francis
b. 1906 Astor, Mary
b. 1906 Roosevelt, Anna Eleanor
b. 1907 Lee, Canada
b. 1907 Wilson, Earl
b. 1910 Corwin, Norman
b. 1910 Massey, D Curtis
b. 1911 Lawson, Yank
b. 1911 Margolius, Sidney Senier
b. 1912 Bay, Howard
b. 1912 Fox, Virgil Keel
b. 1912 Sarton, May
b. 1913 Blackwell, (Samuel) Earl, Jr.
b. 1913 Inge, William Motter
b. 1913 Kohut, Heinz

b. 1915 Comden, Betty
b. 1915 Lippold, Richard
b. 1916 Gonzalez, Henry Barbosa
b. 1916 Mathieu, Noel Jean
b. 1917 Gligorov, Kiro
b. 1918 Simoneau, Leopold
b. 1919 Seeger, Pete(r)
b. 1920 Bankhead, Dan(iel Robert)
b. 1920 Lewis, John Aaron
b. 1920 Schaffner, Franklin James
b. 1921 Robinson, Sugar Ray
b. 1922 Svetlova, Marina
b. 1924 Roderick, David Milton
b. 1926 Davis, Ann Bradford
b. 1926 O'Horgan, Tom
b. 1927 Lazarus, Mell
b. 1928 Brown, James
b. 1928 Eckstein, George
b. 1931 Layton, Joe
b. 1933 Weinberg, Steven
b. 1934 Cooper, Henry B
b. 1936 Humperdinck, Engelbert
b. 1937 Valli, Frankie
b. 1940 Fagan, Garth
b. 1941 Malloy, Edward Aloysius
b. 1942 Caslavska, Vera
b. 1943? Snepp, Frank Warren, III
b. 1946 Gumbel, Greg(ory)
b. 1946 Lopes, Davey
b. 1947 Henning, Doug(las James)
b. 1949 Wyden, Ron
b. 1950 Hopkin, Mary
b. 1951 Cross, Christopher
b. 1951 Lane, Stewart F
b. 1960 Lanier, Jaron (Zepel)
b. 1964 Hextall, Ron(ald Jeffrey)
d. 1481 Mehmed the Conqueror
d. 1763 Psalmanazar, George
d. 1784 Benezet, Anthony
d. 1839 Paer, Ferdinando
d. 1845 Hood, Thomas
d. 1856 Adam, Adolphe Charles
d. 1861 Heinrich, Anthony Philip
d. 1910 Ricketts, Howard T
d. 1914 Sickles, Daniel Edgar

d. 1916 MacDonagh, Thomas
d. 1916 Pearse, Padraic
d. 1926 Straus, Oscar Solomon
d. 1927 Ball, Ernest
d. 1932 Fort, Charles Hoy
d. 1935 Breitenstein, Ted
d. 1935 Manners, Charles
d. 1935 Smith, Jessie Wilcox
d. 1936 Michels, Robert
d. 1940 Flipper, Henry Ossian
d. 1943 Andrews, Frank M(axwell)
d. 1949 Fortuny
d. 1954 Hooton, Earnest Albert
d. 1958 Cornelius, Henry
d. 1961 Boon, Dickie
d. 1961 Merleau-Ponty, Maurice
d. 1968 Hickok, Lorena A
d. 1969 Husain, Zakir
d. 1972 Cabot, Bruce
d. 1974 Clapp, Margaret Antoinette
d. 1976 Nevers, Ernie
d. 1978 Downs, William Randall, Jr.
d. 1979 Angoff, Charles
d. 1979 O'Brien-Moore, Erin
d. 1980 Elliott, George Paul
d. 1982 Dantine, Helmut
d. 1982 Frazier, Brenda Diana Dudd
d. 1983 Skolsky, Sidney
d. 1984 Schneider, Alan
d. 1986 Alda, Robert
d. 1988 Hansen, Julia Butler
d. 1989 Jorgensen, Christine
d. 1989 Loveless, Herschel C(ellel)
d. 1991 Kosinski, Jerzy (Nikodem)
d. 1992 Murphy, George Lloyd
d. 1996 Weston, Jack
d. 1998 MacIver, Loren
d. 1998 Raymond, Gene
d. 2000 O'Connor, John Joseph, Cardinal

May 4
b. 1654 K'ang-hsi
b. 1655 Cristofori, Bartolomeo di Francesco
b. 1769 Lawrence, Thomas, Sir
b. 1770 Gerard, Francois
b. 1776 Herbart, Johann Friedrich
b. 1796 Mann, Horace

b. 1796 Prescott, William Hickling
b. 1806 Cooke, William Fothergil, Sir
b. 1820 Tyler, Julia Gardiner
b. 1825 Huxley, Thomas Henry
b. 1826 Church, Frederick Edwin
b. 1827 Speke, John Hanning
b. 1830 Mapleson, James Henry
b. 1851 Dewing, Thomas Wilmer
b. 1860 Reznicek, Emil von
b. 1864 Hovey, Richard
b. 1866 Corey, William Ellis
b. 1872 Palmer, Alexander Mitchell
b. 1872 Wright, Harold Bell
b. 1874 Conrad, Frank
b. 1884 Collier, John
b. 1889 Spellman, Francis Joseph
b. 1890 Carmichael, Franklin
b. 1890 Rosenfeld, Paul
b. 1896 Baxter, Frank Condie
b. 1896 Ochsner, Alton
b. 1902 Dexter, Al
b. 1902 Stone, W Clement
b. 1903 Adler, Luther
b. 1903 Layden, Elmer Francis
b. 1904 Saito, Yoshishige
b. 1907 Kirstein, Lincoln (Edward)
b. 1909 DaSilva, Howard
b. 1914 Muller, Hilgard
b. 1914 Smith, Gerard C(oad)
b. 1918 Tanaka, Kakuei
b. 1919 Heloise
b. 1920 Schreiber, Hermann Otto Ludwig
b. 1922 Hambleton, Hugh George
b. 1925 Herrera Campins, Luis
b. 1928 Ferguson, Maynard
b. 1928 Mubarak, (Mohammed) Hosni
b. 1928 Rawl, Lawrence G
b. 1928 Rawls, Betsy
b. 1929 Hepburn, Audrey (Edda)
b. 1929 Lamb, Sydney MacDonald
b. 1930 Peters, Roberta
b. 1931 Kahng, Dawon
b. 1935 Howard, Jane Temple
b. 1936 Cordobes, El

b. 1937 Edwards, Melvin
b. 1939 Abrams, George H. J.
b. 1939 Jackson, Mannie (L.)
b. 1939 Oz, Amos
b. 1940 Cook, Robin
b. 1941 Will, George F(rederick)
b. 1942 Ashford, Nickolas
b. 1943 Rice, Norm(an Blann)
b. 1946 Watson, John
b. 1951 Jackson, Jackie
b. 1955 Zadora, Pia
b. 1956 Guterson, David
b. 1957 Kreiner, Kathy
b. 1958 Haring, Keith
b. 1958 Tway, Bob
b. 1959 Travis, Randy
b. 1961 McDonough, Mary Elizabeth
d. 1873 McGuffey, William Holmes
d. 1875 Kicking Bird
d. 1882 Wood, James Rushmore
d. 1885 McDowell, Irvin
d. 1891 Pratt, Charles
d. 1902 Palmer, Potter
d. 1903 Williams, Edward Porter
d. 1912 Stevens, Nettie Maria
d. 1924 Nesbit, Edith
d. 1925 Grassi, Giovanni Battista
d. 1938 Ossietzky, Carl von
d. 1950 Benet, William Rose
d. 1953 Bellison, Simeon
d. 1953 Wagner, Robert F(erdinand)
d. 1955 Breguet, Louis Charles
d. 1955 Enesco, Georges
d. 1961 Stewart, Anita
d. 1965 Brokenshire, Norman
d. 1966 Ozenfant, Amedee
d. 1969 Sitwell, Osbert, Sir
d. 1972 Kendall, Edward C(alvin)
d. 1972 Samuel, Maurice
d. 1973 Bowles, Jane Sydney
d. 1974 Ewing, William Maurice
d. 1975 Howard, Moe
d. 1977 Bissell, Richard Pike
d. 1980 Cherrington, Ben Mark
d. 1980 Tito
d. 1981 Green, Paul Eliot

d. 1981 McNeill, Robert Edward, Jr.
d. 1982 O'Brien, Leo W
d. 1984 Boles, Paul Darcy
d. 1984 Dors, Diana
d. 1986 Richards, Paul Rapier
d. 1988 Hayter, Stanley William
d. 1988 Zambelli, Joseph
d. 1990 Dawson, William Levi
d. 1991 Delacorte, George Thomas, Jr.
d. 1991 Gross, Chaim
d. 1992 Paine, Thomas Otten
d. 1992 Parry, Albert
d. 1992 Salk, Lee
d. 1995 Harris, Thomas Anthony
d. 1996 Montana, Patsy

May 5

b. 1210 Alfonso, III
b. 1747 Leopold, II
b. 1773 Tieck, (Johann) Ludwig
b. 1809 Barnard, Frederick Augustus Porter
b. 1811 Draper, John William
b. 1813 Kierkegaard, Soren Aabye
b. 1818 Marx, Karl Heinrich
b. 1819 Moniuszko, Stanislaus
b. 1820 Soloviev, Sergei Mikhailovich
b. 1820 Wright, Horatio Gouverneur
b. 1826 Eugenie
b. 1830 Stetson, John Batterson
b. 1832 Bancroft, Hubert Howe
b. 1833 Richthofen, Ferdinand Paul Wilhelm
b. 1846 Sienkiewicz, Henryk Adam Aleksander Pius
b. 1852 von Hugel, Friedrich, Baron
b. 1856 Denslow, W(illiam) W(allace)
b. 1857 Zetkin, Clara
b. 1861 Hewitt, Peter Cooper
b. 1867 Bly, Nellie
b. 1869 Pfitzner, Hans
b. 1882 Mawson, Douglas, Sir
b. 1882 Pankhurst, Sylvia
b. 1883 Wavell, Archibald Percival Wavell, Earl
b. 1884 Bender, Chief
b. 1890 Morley, Christopher (Darlington)
b. 1892 Bloch, Bertram

b. 1892 Garrod, Dorothy Annie Elizabeth
b. 1897 Burke, Kenneth
b. 1899 Gosden, Freeman Fisher
b. 1900 Schmidt-Isserstedt, Hans
b. 1901 Blind Willie McTell
b. 1903 Beard, James Andrews
b. 1903 Stanford, Sally
b. 1904 Becker, B Jay
b. 1905 Caniglia, Maria
b. 1905 Ruffing, Red
b. 1905 Skolsky, Sidney
b. 1909 Baker, Carlos Heard
b. 1910 Burton, Glenn W(illard)
b. 1910 Lionni, Leo
b. 1911 Loveless, Herschel C(ellel)
b. 1912 Dolbier, Maurice (Wyman)
b. 1914 Power, Tyrone, Jr.
b. 1915 Faye, Alice
b. 1915 Rovere, Richard Halworth
b. 1917 Sawyer, John E(dward)
b. 1919 Papadopoulos, George
b. 1921 Schawlow, Arthur L(eonard)
b. 1924 Torre-Nilsson, Leopoldo
b. 1925 Ryan, Leo Joseph
b. 1927 Carroll, Pat(ricia Ann Angela Bridgit)
b. 1930 Ward, Douglas Turner
b. 1931 East, John Porter
b. 1932 Hutchins, Will
b. 1934 Sweeney, John J(oseph)
b. 1935 Pivot, Bernard
b. 1936 DiSant'Angelo, Giorgio
b. 1937 Obasanjo, Olusegun
b. 1938 Wagner, Barbara
b. 1939 Jones, James Robert
b. 1940 Oh, Sadaharu
b. 1940 Rudd, Paul Ryan
b. 1941 Baker, Terry Wayne
b. 1942 Wynette, Tammy
b. 1943 Palin, Michael
b. 1943 Volner, Jill Wine
b. 1944 Leaud, Jean-Pierre
b. 1944 Rees, Roger
b. 1958 Bening, Annette
b. 1961 Clooney, George

b. 1973 Yothers, Tina
d. 1600 Nicot, Jean
d. 1819 Kamehameha I
d. 1821 Napoleon I
d. 1837 Zingarelli,
  Nicola Antonio
d. 1868 Page, Charles
  Grafton
d. 1887 Grant, James
d. 1889 Brannan,
  Samuel
d. 1890 Naudin, Emilio
d. 1902 Harte, (Francis)
  Bret
d. 1915 Schindler,
  Solomon
d. 1918 Vidal de la
  Blache, Paul
d. 1921 Friese-Greene,
  William Edward
d. 1945 Lalique, Rene
d. 1951 Flynn, John
d. 1954 Reed, Austin
  Leonard
d. 1958 Cabell, James
  Branch
d. 1959 McIntyre, Hal
d. 1959 Saavdedra,
  Lamas Carlos
d. 1968 Dekker, Albert
d. 1969 Cicotte, Eddie
d. 1972 Davis, Gary,
  Reverend
d. 1972 Youlou, Fulbert
d. 1975 Keating,
  Kenneth B
d. 1975 Ridder, Bernard
  Herman
d. 1981 Sands, Bobby
d. 1982 Tjader, Cal(len
  Radcliffe, Jr.)
d. 1983 Buttigieg,
  Anton
d. 1983 Dutra, Olin
d. 1984 Gobbi, Tito
d. 1985 Bailey, Donald
  Coleman, Sir
d. 1985 Brown, Carter
d. 1986 Cook, Bill
d. 1987 Stanford-Tuck,
  Robert Roland
d. 1988 Rose, George
  Walter
d. 1993 Howe, Irving
d. 1994 Layton, Joe
d. 1995 Botvinnik,
  Mikhail
  (Moisseyevich)
d. 1997 Kempton,
  (James) Murray
May 6
b. 1501 Marcellus II,
  Pope
b. 1758 Robespierre,
  Maximilien Francois
  de
b. 1775 Sherwood,
  Mary Martha
b. 1812 Delany, Martin
  Robinson
b. 1830 Jacobi,
  Abraham
b. 1843 Gilbert, Grove
  Karl
b. 1849 Eaton, Wyatt

b. 1853 Knox, Philander
  Chase
b. 1856 Freud, Sigmund
b. 1856 Peary, Robert
  Edwin
b. 1859 Drago, Luis
  Maria
b. 1860 Sherman, Frank
  Dempster
b. 1861 Nehru, Motilal
b. 1861 Tagore,
  Rabindranath, Sir
b. 1862 Underwood,
  Oscar Wilder
b. 1865 Christie, John
  Walter
b. 1868 LeRoux, Gaston
b. 1870 Giannini,
  A(madeo) P(eter)
b. 1870 McCutcheon,
  John Tinney
b. 1871 Grignard,
  Francois Auguste
  Victor
b. 1872 Bowie, William
b. 1872 Sitter, Willem
  de
b. 1875 Leahy, William
  Daniel
b. 1880 Ironside,
  William Edmund
b. 1880 Kirchner, Ernst
  Ludwig
b. 1881 Martinez Sierra,
  Gregorio
b. 1886 Karfiol, Bernard
b. 1888 Celler, Emanuel
b. 1888 Stover, Russell
b. 1894 Cobham, Alan
  John, Sir
b. 1895 Valentino,
  Rudolph
b. 1897 Purtell, William
  Arthur
b. 1898 Gerber, Daniel
  Frank
b. 1900 Mattingley,
  Garrett
b. 1902 Ophuls, Max
b. 1903 Banks, William
  (Venoid)
b. 1903 Golden, Harry
  Lewis
b. 1904 Mallowan, Max
  Edgar Lucien, Sir
b. 1905 Irish, Ned
b. 1905 Martinson,
  Harry Edmund
b. 1905 Shor, Toots
b. 1906 Lattimore,
  Richmond Alexander
b. 1907 Ewbank, Weeb
b. 1908 Hale, Nancy
b. 1909 Christensen,
  Lew Farr
b. 1911 Ballantrae, Lord
b. 1913 Cavallaro,
  Carmen
b. 1913 Granger,
  Stewart
b. 1914 Jarrell, Randall
b. 1915 Perle, George
b. 1915 Welles, Orson
b. 1915 White,
  Theodore Harold

b. 1917 Stewart, Black
  Jack
b. 1920 Hunter, Ross
b. 1921 Wakefield, Dick
b. 1926 Piazza,
  Marguerite
b. 1930 Rykiel, Sonia
b. 1931 Mays, Willie
b. 1934 Shelby, Richard
  C.
b. 1937 Terris, Susan
b. 1939 Levin, Gerald
b. 1941 Brant, Beth
b. 1941 Dimitrova,
  Ghena
b. 1942 Dorfman, Ariel
b. 1942 Maestro, Giulio
b. 1942 Stilwell,
  Richard Dale
b. 1943 Baader,
  Andreas
b. 1945 Seger, Bob
b. 1949 Broumas, Olga
b. 1950 Bond, Victoria
b. 1950 Hyatt, Joel
b. 1951? Doe, Samuel
  Kanyon
b. 1953 Blair, Tony
b. 1963 Ferri,
  Alessandra Maria
d. 1502 Tyrrell, James,
  Sir
d. 1638 Jansen, Cornelis
  Otto
d. 1708 Laval, Francois
  Xavier de
d. 1760 Zinzendorf,
  Nikolaus Ludwig
  von, Count
d. 1802 Lowell, John
d. 1826 Levasseur,
  Rosalie
d. 1840 Gallitzin,
  Demetrius Augustine
d. 1856 Hamilton,
  William, Sir
d. 1859 Humboldt,
  Alexander, Freiherr
  von
d. 1859 Humboldt,
  Friedrich Heinrich
  Alexander von
d. 1862 Thoreau, Henry
  David
d. 1870 Simpson, James
  Young, Sir
d. 1873 Paez, Jose
  Antonio
d. 1877 Runeberg,
  Johan Ludwig
d. 1884 Gross, Samuel
  Daniel
d. 1902 Sampson,
  William T
d. 1910 Edward VII
d. 1917 Stuart, Ruth
  McEnery
d. 1919 Baum, L(yman)
  Frank
d. 1921 Fried, Alfred
  Hermann
d. 1927 Maxim, Hudson
d. 1930 Gilpin, Charles
  Sidney
d. 1943 Haines, Robert
  Terrel

d. 1947 Homer, Louise
d. 1949 Maeterlinck,
  Maurice
d. 1950 Pattee, Fred
  Lewis
d. 1950 Smedley, Agnes
d. 1952 Birley, Oswald
  Hornby Joseph, Sir
d. 1952 Montessori,
  Maria
d. 1954 Forbes, Bertie
d. 1961 Blaga, Lucien
d. 1962 Grant, Gordon
d. 1962 Woolley, Monty
d. 1963 Weems, Ted
d. 1967 Hilberseimer,
  Ludwig Karl
d. 1973 MacMillan,
  Ernest Campbell, Sir
d. 1974 Crean, Robert
d. 1975 Mindszenty,
  Jozsef, Cardinal
d. 1979 Ager, Milton
d. 1980 Bombal, Maria
  Luisa
d. 1981 Fitzsimmons,
  Frank Edward
d. 1982 Littlejohn,
  Robert McGowan
d. 1983 Keats, Ezra
  Jack
d. 1983 Masters, John
d. 1983 Winding, Kai
  Chresten
d. 1985 Desjardins, Pete
d. 1985 Higbe, Kirby
d. 1987 Casey, William
  Joseph
d. 1987 Damon,
  Cathryn
d. 1988 Caliguiri,
  Richard
d. 1988 Popper, Hans
d. 1989 Blaik, Red
d. 1990 Farrell, Charles
d. 1991 Hyde-White,
  Wilfrid
d. 1992 Dietrich,
  Marlene
d. 1993 Todd, Ann
d. 1994 Chute,
  Marchette (Gaylord)
d. 1996 Suenens, Leon
  Joseph, Cardinal
d. 1998 Chatichai
  Choonhavan
d. 1998 Connolly, Sybil
May 7
b. 1397 Sejong
b. 1643 Van Cortlandt,
  Stephanus
b. 1774 Bainbridge,
  William
b. 1812 Browning,
  Robert
b. 1833 Brahms,
  Johannes
b. 1836 Cannon, Joseph
  Gurney
b. 1840 Tchaikovsky,
  Peter Ilyich
b. 1845 Mahoney, Mary
  Eliza
b. 1847 Rosebery,
  Archibald Philip
  Primrose, Earl

b. 1850 Seidl, Anton
b. 1851 Harnack, Adolf von
b. 1870 Loew, Marcus
b. 1878 Heruy Walda-Sellase
b. 1883 Berry, James Gomer
b. 1885 Hayes, Gabby
b. 1892 MacLeish, Archibald
b. 1893 Atwood, Francis Clarke
b. 1893 Selke, Frank J, Sr.
b. 1897 Jacobs, Joe B
b. 1901 Coggeshall, L(owell) T(helwell)
b. 1901 Cooper, Gary
b. 1903 Zabolotskii, Nikolai Alekseevich
b. 1904 Lewton, Val Ivan
b. 1904 Walker, Harold Blake
b. 1905 Stoll, George E
b. 1906 Corle, Edwin
b. 1909 Land, Edwin Herbert
b. 1913 Glazer, David
b. 1913 Powers, Anne
b. 1915 Elliot, Win
b. 1917 Rafferty, Max(well Lewis, Jr.)
b. 1919 Peron, Eva Duarte
b. 1920 Post, Elizabeth Lindley
b. 1921 Davies, Rodger Paul
b. 1921 Rebuffat, Gaston Louis Simon
b. 1922 McGavin, Darren
b. 1923 Baxter, Anne
b. 1923 Roche, John P
b. 1925 Kirk, Ruth Kratz
b. 1927 Jhabvala, Ruth Prawer
b. 1927 Soderstrom, Elisabeth Anna
b. 1928 Mitchelson, Marvin M(orris)
b. 1928 Williams, Dick
b. 1930 Fields, Totie
b. 1931 Brewer, Teresa
b. 1931 Phelan, John Joseph
b. 1932 Domenici, Pete V(ichi)
b. 1932 Hogrogian, Nonny
b. 1932 Kingsley, Pat(ricia)
b. 1933 Unitas, Johnny
b. 1936 O'Reilly, Anthony John Francis
b. 1938 O'Connor, Kevin
b. 1938 Thurow, Lester C
b. 1939 Altman, Sidney
b. 1939 Clark, Joe
b. 1939 Lubbers, Ruud
b. 1939 Ruffin, Jimmy

b. 1940 Carter, Angela (Olive)
b. 1948 Rose, Wendy
b. 1950 Ian, Janis
b. 1950 Prince, Prairie
b. 1951 Hegyes, Robert
b. 1951 Roehm, Carolyne Jane Smith
b. 1954 Heckerling, Amy
b. 1617 Thou, Jacques Auguste de
d. 1795 Fouquier-Tinville, Antoine Quentin
d. 1800 Piccinni, Nicola
d. 1806 Morris, Robert
d. 1811 Cumberland, Richard
d. 1825 Salieri, Antonio
d. 1827 Volta, Alessandro Giuseppe Antonio Anastasio
d. 1840 Friedrich, Caspar David
d. 1873 Chase, Salmon Portland
d. 1879 Decoster, Charles Theodore Henri
d. 1880 Caxias, Duque de
d. 1887 Cousins, Samuel
d. 1890 Nasmyth, James
d. 1896 Mudgett, Herman Webster
d. 1915 Frohman, Charles
d. 1915 Hubbard, Elbert Green
d. 1932 Crowder, Enoch Herbert
d. 1941 Frazer, James George, Sir
d. 1942 Weingartner, Felix
d. 1950 Hill, Chippie
d. 1951 Baxter, Warner
d. 1956 Hoffmann, Josef
d. 1957 Ness, Eliot
d. 1959 Hoare, Samuel John Gurney, Sir
d. 1961 Bell, James Ford
d. 1961 Snow, Carmel White
d. 1962 Currie, Barton Wood
d. 1963 Von Karman, Theodore
d. 1965 Sheeler, Charles
d. 1966 Gifford, Walter Sherman
d. 1967 Evelyn, Judith
d. 1968 Wallace, Lurleen Burns
d. 1975 Baker, George
d. 1976 Uttley, Alice Jane Taylor
d. 1977 Erhard, Ludwig
d. 1985 Addams, Dawn
d. 1986 Forsythe, Albert E

d. 1986 Lovett, Robert A(bercrombie)
d. 1987 Blakely, Colin (George Edward)
d. 1987 McKinney, Stewart Brett
d. 1988 Van Westerborg, Edward
d. 1991 Sohappy, David, Sr.
d. 1994 Greenberg, Clement
d. 1995 McKinley, Ray
d. 1996 McNeill, Don(ald Thomas)
d. 1998 Cormack, Allan MacLeod
d. 1998 Rabbitt, Eddie
d. 1999 Hess, Leon
d. 2000 Fairbanks, Douglas, Jr.

May 8
b. 1521 Canisius, Peter
b. 1639 Gaulli, Giovanni Battista
b. 1668 Lesage, Alain-Rene
b. 1737 Gibbon, Edward
b. 1740 Paisiello, Giovanni
b. 1753 Hidalgo y Costilla, Miguel
b. 1786 Vianney, Jean (Marie) Baptiste
b. 1788 Clapperton, Hugh
b. 1818 Tilley, Samuel Leonard, Sir
b. 1821 A.L.O.E.
b. 1821 Vanderbilt, William Henry
b. 1824 Walker, William
b. 1828 Dunant, Jean Henri
b. 1829 Gottschalk, Louis Moreau
b. 1839 Beard, George Miller
b. 1843 Boyd, Belle
b. 1846 Galle, Emile
b. 1846 Hammerstein, Oscar
b. 1855 Gates, John Warne
b. 1858 Brouthers, Dan
b. 1869 Angell, James Rowland
b. 1878 Aitken, Robert
b. 1884 Truman, Harry S
b. 1885 Costain, Thomas Bertram
b. 1891 Gardiner, Herb(ert Martin)
b. 1893 Ku Chieh-kang
b. 1893 Ouimet, Francis de Sales
b. 1893 Roush, Edd J
b. 1895 Sheen, Fulton John, Bishop
b. 1895 Wilson, Edmund
b. 1897 Hillenkoetter, Roscoe H(enry)

b. 1898 Stepinac, Alojzije
b. 1899 Hayek, Friedrich August von
b. 1899 Heim, Jacques
b. 1902 Lwoff, Andre Michel
b. 1903 Fernandel
b. 1905 Nichols, Red
b. 1906 Rossellini, Roberto
b. 1908 Graham, John
b. 1909 Fitch, James Marston
b. 1910 Williams, Mary Lou
b. 1911 Flesch, Rudolf (Franz)
b. 1911 Johnson, Robert
b. 1912 Lev, Ray
b. 1913 Clampett, Bob
b. 1913 Dole, Vincent P(aul)
b. 1914 Gary, Romain
b. 1919 Barker, Lex
b. 1920 Bass, Saul
b. 1920 Wilson, Sloan
b. 1923 Cairns, John, Jr.
b. 1925 Mwinyi, Ali Hassan
b. 1926 Attenborough, David Frederick
b. 1926 Rickles, Don
b. 1928 Sorensen, Ted
b. 1929 Allen, Ethel D.
b. 1930 Atkins, Doug(las L)
b. 1930 Harper, Heather Mary
b. 1930 Scaasi, Arnold
b. 1930 Snyder, Gary Sherman
b. 1931 Scaasi, Arnold
b. 1932 Liston, Sonny
b. 1933 El-Sayed, Mostafa Amr
b. 1935 Jens, Salome
b. 1936 Thompson, James Robert
b. 1937 Cuellar, Mike
b. 1937 DeConcini, Dennis Webster
b. 1937 Pynchon, Thomas
b. 1940 Benchley, Peter Bradford
b. 1940 Nelson, Rick
b. 1941 Burr, Donald Calvin
b. 1942 Cordero, Angel Tomas
b. 1942 Lamont, Norman
b. 1943 Tennille, Toni
b. 1945 Jarrett, Keith
b. 1948? Bolan, Marc
b. 1951 Bailey, Philip
b. 1952 Henley, Beth
b. 1954 Keith, David Lemuel
b. 1954 Little, Joan
b. 1954 Talbot, John Michael
b. 1955 Van Halen, Alex
b. 1959 Lott, Ronnie

b. 1964 Gilbert, Melissa
d. 1655 Winslow,
Edward
d. 1782 Pombal,
Marques de
d. 1794 Lavoisier,
Antoine Laurent
d. 1815 Ramsay, David
d. 1822 Stark, John
d. 1842 Dumont
d'Urville, Jules
Sebastian Cesar
d. 1864 Wadsworth,
James Samuel
d. 1873 Ames, Oakes
d. 1873 Mill, John
Stuart
d. 1880 Flaubert,
Gustave
d. 1880 Very, Jones
d. 1884 Benjamin,
Judah Philip
d. 1891 Blavatsky,
Helena Petrovna
d. 1902 Ford, Paul
Leicester
d. 1903 Gauguin, Paul
d. 1904 Muybridge,
Eadweard
d. 1908 Halevy,
Ludovic
d. 1915 Turner, Henry
McNeal
d. 1924 Lyons, Sophie
Levy
d. 1936 Spengler,
Oswald
d. 1939 Cabot, Richard
C
d. 1946 Arguedas,
Alcides
d. 1947 Selfridge, Harry
Gordon
d. 1948 Gordon, Vera
d. 1949 Luden, William
H
d. 1951 Diegel, Leo
d. 1952 Fox, William
d. 1952 Kirby, Rollin
d. 1952 Robins,
Elizabeth
d. 1954 Edwards, Alan
d. 1955 Park, Maud
May Wood
d. 1957 Davidson, J
Brownlee
d. 1958 Geddes,
Norman Bel
d. 1960 Dudley, George
S
d. 1964 Nomura,
Kichisaburo
d. 1967 Andrews,
LaVerne
d. 1967 Rice, Elmer
d. 1968 Collier, John
d. 1968 Wood, Craig
Ralph
d. 1973 Vandegrift,
Alexander Archer
d. 1974 May, Mortimer
d. 1975 Brundage,
Avery
d. 1975 Slobodkin,
Louis

d. 1976 McLeod,
Fred(erick)
d. 1976 Skaggs,
M(arion) B
d. 1978 Grant, Duncan
(James Corrowr)
d. 1978 Rubicam,
Raymond
d. 1979 Parsons, Talcott
d. 1981 Andrew, Prince
of Russia
d. 1981 Lindsay,
Margaret
d. 1982 Bogart, Neil
d. 1982 Villeneuve,
Gilles
d. 1984 Matter, Herbert
d. 1984 Wallace, Lila
Bell Acheson
d. 1985 O'Brien,
Edmond
d. 1985 Sturgeon,
Theodore Hamilton
d. 1988 Heinlein,
Robert Anson
d. 1988 Pollock, Charles
d. 1991 Serkin, Rudolph
d. 1993 Nikolais, Alwin
d. 1994 Carlson,
William S(amuel)
d. 1994 Peppard,
George
d. 1996 Chermayeff,
Serge (Ivan)
d. 1996 Dominguin,
Luis Miguel
d. 1996 Williams, Garth
Montgomery
d. 1998 Randolph,
Jennings
d. 1998 Rebozo, Bebe
d. 1999 Bogarde, Dirk

May 9
b. 1773 Sismondi, Jean
Charles Leonard
Simonde de
b. 1775 Brown, Jacob
Jennings
b. 1800 Brown, John
b. 1801 Cousins,
Samuel
b. 1813 Matteson,
Tompkins Harrison
b. 1815 Blythe, David
Gilmour
b. 1828 Cramp, Charles
Henry
b. 1857 Kidman, Sidney
b. 1860 Barrie, James
Matthew, Sir
b. 1865 Jordan,
Elizabeth Garver
b. 1866 Gokhale, Gopal
Krishna
b. 1870 Vardon, Harry
b. 1873 Cermak, Anton
Joseph
b. 1874 Baylis, Lilian
Mary
b. 1874 Carter, Howard
b. 1877 Tharaud, Jean
b. 1878 Gallo, Fortune
b. 1882 Kaiser, Henry
John
b. 1883 Ortega y
Gasset, Jose

b. 1886 Biddle, Francis
Beverley
b. 1893 Barclay,
McClelland
b. 1895 Barthelmess,
Richard
b. 1895 Blaga, Lucien
b. 1896 Clarke, Austin
b. 1897 Fisher, Rudolph
b. 1904 Bateson,
Gregory
b. 1904 Wilson,
Dorothy Clarke
b. 1906 Estes, Eleanor
Ruth Rosenfeld
b. 1907 Kuhlman,
Kathryn
b. 1908 Newhall, Nancy
Wynne
b. 1908 Sillman,
Leonard
b. 1909 Bunshaft,
Gordon
b. 1909 Hagerty, James
Campbell
b. 1910 Woodhouse,
Barbara Blackburn
b. 1910 Young, Philip
b. 1911 Simeone, Harry
b. 1912 Armendariz,
Pedro
b. 1914 Giulini, Carlo
Maria
b. 1914 Kheel,
Theodore Woodrow
b. 1914 Salter, Andrew
b. 1914 Snow, Hank
b. 1916 Du Bois,
William Pene
b. 1918 Feld, Irvin
b. 1918 Freeman,
Orville Lothrop
b. 1918 Wallace, Mike
b. 1920 Adams, Richard
b. 1921 Berrigan,
Daniel J
b. 1921 Van Duyn,
Mona
b. 1925 Neville, Kris
Ottman
b. 1927 Eigen, Manfred
b. 1928 Gonzalez,
Pancho
b. 1928 Scott, Barbara
Ann
b. 1929 Franklin, Hardy
R.
b. 1931 Brand, Vance
DeVoe
b. 1934 Bennett, Alan
b. 1936 Drinkwater,
Terry
b. 1936 Finney, Albert
b. 1936 Jackson, Glenda
b. 1937 Dalrymple, G.
Brent
b. 1937 Moneo, Jose
Rafael
b. 1937 Prater, Dave
b. 1938 Simic, Charles
b. 1939 Boston, Ralph
b. 1940 Brooks, James
L.
b. 1942 Ashcroft, John
David

b. 1942 Gergen, David
(Richmond)
b. 1942 Roe, Tommy
b. 1944 Furay, Richie
b. 1944 Portzamparc,
Christian de
b. 1946 Bergen,
Candice
b. 1947 Natori, Josie
b. 1948 Mahaffey, John
b. 1948 Murphy, Calvin
Jerome
b. 1949 Joel, Billy
b. 1949 Kurzban, Ira
Jay
b. 1950 Beroff, Michel
b. 1950 Graham, Jorie
b. 1951 Harjo, Joy
b. 1954 Palligrosi, Tony
b. 1955 Meles Zenawi
b. 1955 Otter, Anne
Sofie von
b. 1960 Gwynn, Tony
b. 1960 Nanula, Richard
D.
b. 1965 Yzerman, Steve
d. 1657 Bradford,
William
d. 1707 Buxtehude,
Dietrich
d. 1791 Hopkinson,
Francis
d. 1805 Schiller,
Friedrich von
d. 1810 Lincoln,
Benjamin
d. 1850 Gay-Lussac,
Joseph-Louis
d. 1860 Goodrich,
Samuel Griswold
d. 1860 James, G(eorge)
P(ayne) R(ainsford)
d. 1864 Sedgwick, John
d. 1867 Champollin-
Figeac, Jacques-
Joseph
d. 1911 Higginson,
Thomas Wentworth
Storrow
d. 1914 Heroult, Paul
Louis Toussaint
d. 1914 Post, Charles
William
d. 1919 Henry, Edward
Lamson
d. 1920 Vincent, John
Heyl
d. 1931 Michelson,
Albert Abraham
d. 1934 Morton, Joy
d. 1942 McNamee,
Graham
d. 1948 Allen, Viola
Emily
d. 1952 Lee, Canada
d. 1957 Pinza, Ezio
d. 1958 Davies, Joseph
Edward
d. 1958 Goodwin, Bill
d. 1963 Kuykendall,
Ralph Simpson
d. 1968 Currie, Finlay
d. 1968 Dillon, George
d. 1968 Gray, Harold
Lincoln

d. 1968 Hay, George
Dewey
d. 1968 Lorne, Marion
d. 1970 Nelson, Erik
Henning
d. 1973 Brannigan,
Owen
d. 1973 Leonard, Jack E
d. 1976 Kerner, Otto
d. 1976 Meinhof, Ulrike
Marie
d. 1977 Jones, James
d. 1978 Moro, Aldo
d. 1979 Eaton, Cyrus
Stephen
d. 1981 Algren, Nelson
d. 1981 Lincoln,
Victoria Endicott
d. 1983 Rosenberg,
Anna Marie
d. 1986 Bernardi,
Hershel
d. 1986 Tenzing Norgay
d. 1987 Awolowo,
Obafemi Awo
d. 1989 Whitley, Keith
d. 1990 Frederick,
Pauline
d. 1990 Nono, Luigi
d. 1993 Gilliatt,
Penelope (Ann
Douglas Conner)
d. 1998 Faye, Alice
d. 1999 Silverstein,
Shel(by)

May 10
b. Bell, Darryl
b. 1451 James III
b. 1746 Monge,
Gaspard
b. 1755 Gray, Robert
b. 1760 Rouget de
Lisle, Claude Joseph
b. 1770 Davout, Louis
Nicholas
b. 1778 Ladd, William
b. 1788 Fresnel,
Augustin-Jean
b. 1789 Sparks, Jared
b. 1793 Baylor, Robert
Emmet Bledsoe
b. 1801 Tulane, Paul
b. 1810 Shields, James
b. 1813 Blair,
Montgomery
b. 1823 Sherman, John
b. 1832 Grace, William
Russell
b. 1837 Pinchback,
P(inckney) B(enton)
S(tewart)
b. 1838 Booth, John
Wilkes
b. 1838 Bryce, James
Bryce, Viscount
b. 1841 Bennett, James
Gordon, Jr.
b. 1843 Kohler,
Kaufmann
b. 1843 Perez Galdos,
Benito
b. 1843 Williams,
Edward Porter
b. 1850 Lipton, Thomas
Johnstone, Sir

b. 1868 Barrow,
Ed(ward Grant)
b. 1868 Hart, George
Overbury
b. 1872 Mauss, Marcel
b. 1878 Stresemann,
Gustav
b. 1881 Knox,
E(dmund) G(eorge)
V(alpy)
b. 1886 Ahearn, Frank
b. 1886 Barth, Karl
b. 1886 Stapledon, Olaf
b. 1888 Steiner, Max
b. 1890 Brown,
Clarence
b. 1893 Rau,
Dhanvanthi Rama,
Lady
b. 1897 Allen of
Hurtwood, Lady
b. 1897 Gerhardsen,
Einar Henry
b. 1897 Lowenfels,
Walter
b. 1898 Durant, Ariel
b. 1899 Astaire, Fred
b. 1899 Tiomkin,
Dimitri
b. 1900 Payne-
Gaposchkin, Cecilia
(Helena)
b. 1902 Selznick, David
O(liver)
b. 1903 Jonas, Hans
b. 1905 Kaufman, Louis
b. 1907 Hunt, Pee Wee
b. 1908 Albert, Carl
Bert
b. 1908 Barraclough,
Geoffrey
b. 1909 Carter, Mother
Maybelle
b. 1910 Berne, Eric
Lennard
b. 1910 Demaret,
Jimmy
b. 1912 Viscardi,
Henry, Jr.
b. 1913 Gemmell, Alan
b. 1914 Walsh, Chad
b. 1915 Dickens,
Monica Enid
b. 1916 Babbitt, Milton
Byron
b. 1918 Brazelton,
T(homas) Berry
b. 1918 Margo
b. 1919 Bell, Daniel
b. 1919 Grasso, Ella
b. 1921 Walker, Nancy
b. 1923 Parseghian, Ara
(Raoul)
b. 1925 Bechtel,
Stephen Davison, Jr.
b. 1929 Newman, Peter
Charles
b. 1932 Miles, Tichi
Wilkerson
b. 1935 Owens, Gary
b. 1937 Kopit, Arthur
Lee
b. 1937 Press, Tamara
b. 1938 Shostakovich,
Maxim

b. 1939 Darnton, Robert
Choate
b. 1940 Dyer, Wayne
Walter
b. 1941 Aretsky, Ken
b. 1941 Rapp, Danny
b. 1943 Darman,
Richard G(ordon)
b. 1943 Donovan
b. 1943 Jamison, Judith
b. 1944 Abrahams, Jim
b. 1944 Barboza,
Anthony
b. 1945 Greenberg,
Stanley B
b. 1946? Blacque,
Taurean
b. 1946 Mason, Dave
b. 1946 Pisier, Marie-
France
b. 1948 Galdikas, Birute
M(arija) F(ilomena)
b. 1952 Strait, George
b. 1955 Chapman, Mark
David
b. 1956 Paeniu,
Bikenibeu
b. 1957 Mahre, Phil(lip)
b. 1957 Mahre, Steve(n
Irving)
b. 1957 Vicious, Sid
b. 1958 Boucher,
Gaetan
b. 1958 Ochoa, Ellen
b. 1958 Santorum, Rick
b. 1960 Bono
d. 1521 Brant, Sebastian
d. 1696 LaBruyere, Jean
de
d. 1774 Louis XV
d. 1798 Vancouver,
George
d. 1807 Rochambeau,
Jean Baptiste
Donatien de Vimeur,
Comte
d. 1818 Revere, Paul
d. 1829 Young, Thomas
d. 1849 Hokusai,
Katsushika
d. 1860 Parker,
Theodore
d. 1863 Jackson,
Stonewall
d. 1897 Bonifacio,
Andres
d. 1904 Stanley, Henry
Morton, Sir
d. 1910 Cannizzaro,
Stanislao
d. 1914 Nordica, Lillian
d. 1914 Schuch, Ernst
von
d. 1915 Lamprecht, Karl
d. 1918 Grass, John
d. 1920 Howells,
William Dean
d. 1925 Massey,
William Ferguson
d. 1926 Parker, Alton
Brooks
d. 1930 Stratemeyer,
Edward L
d. 1933 Kurz, Selma
d. 1935 Witherspoon,
Herbert

d. 1942 Weber, Joseph
M
d. 1943 Anielewicz,
Mordecai
d. 1944 Michael, Moina
Belle
d. 1950 Greene, Belle
da Costa
d. 1952 Hull, Clark
Leonard
d. 1955 Burns, Tommy
d. 1956 Mulford,
Clarence Edward
d. 1956 Prouty, Jed
d. 1957 Malone, Annie
Minerva Turnbo Pope
d. 1958 Connell, Alex
d. 1960 Schwartz,
Maurice
d. 1963 Lipscomb,
Eugene
d. 1964 Haney, Carol
d. 1964 Lebrun, Rico
d. 1965 Wallace-
Johnson, Isaac
Theophilus Akunna
d. 1968 Bloomingdale,
Samuel
d. 1970 Reuther, Walter
Philip
d. 1973 Green, Abel
d. 1977 Allred, Rulon
Clark
d. 1977 Crawford, Joan
d. 1979 Frankel, Charles
d. 1982 Sloane, Dennis
d. 1982 Weiss, Peter
Ulrich
d. 1988 Laing, Hugh
d. 1988 Ogilvie,
Richard Buell
d. 1989 Green, Richard
R(eginald)
d. 1990 Percy, Walker
d. 1992 Lund, John
d. 1992 Syms, Sylvia
d. 1992 Thorp, Willard
Long
d. 1993 del Ray, Lester
(Ramon Alvarez)
d. 1993 Zondervan,
Peter
d. 1994 Brooks, Cleanth
d. 1994 Gacy, John
Wayne, Jr.

May 11
b. 483 Justinian I
b. 1720 Munchhausen,
Hieronymus Karl
Friedrich von, Baron
b. 1751 Earle, Ralph
b. 1752 Blumenbach,
Johann Friedrich
b. 1766 D'Israeli, Isaac
b. 1801 Labrouste,
Pierre Francois Henri
b. 1811 Chang and Eng
b. 1811 LeVerrier,
Urbain Jean Joseph
b. 1811 Scranton,
George Whitfield
b. 1824 Gerome, Jean
Leon
b. 1827 Carpeaux, Jean
Baptiste

b. 1852 Fairbanks, Charles Warren
b. 1854 Mergenthaler, Ottmar
b. 1854 Small, Albion W(oodbury)
b. 1871 Fortuny
b. 1871 Schlesinger, Frank
b. 1880 Haynes, George Edmund
b. 1881 Von Karman, Theodore
b. 1884 Gluck, Alma
b. 1885 Oliver, Joe
b. 1888 Berlin, Irving
b. 1889 Nash, Paul
b. 1891 Morgenthau, Henry, Jr.
b. 1892 Rutherford, Margaret
b. 1893 Gag, Wanda
b. 1893 Graham, Martha
b. 1894 Bunker, Ellsworth
b. 1895 Brugnon, Jacques
b. 1895 Still, William Grant
b. 1896 Pisis, Filippo Tibertelli de
b. 1897 Gross, Robert Ellsworth
b. 1898 Billings, John Shaw
b. 1899 Ewing, Alfred Cyril
b. 1900 Cotton, Norris
b. 1900 Sandoz, Mari
b. 1902 Sayao, Bidu
b. 1903 Gehringer, Charlie
b. 1904 Dali, Salvador
b. 1906 Higginbotham, Jack
b. 1907 Taylor, Kent
b. 1908 Morris, Ernest Brougham
b. 1910 Cochran, Jacqueline
b. 1911 Silvers, Phil
b. 1912 Brooks, Foster Murrell
b. 1914 Severn, William Irving
b. 1914 Weaver, Doodles
b. 1915 Philbrick, Herbert Arthur
b. 1916 Cela (Trulock), Camilo Jose
b. 1918 Burnford, Sheila
b. 1918 Feynman, Richard Phillips
b. 1919 Hayes, John Michael
b. 1920 Pyle, Denver
b. 1921 Hamm-Brucher, Hildegard
b. 1922 Chylak, Nestor
b. 1924 Garment, Leonard
b. 1924 Hewish, Antony
b. 1927 Sahl, Mort (Lyon)

b. 1928 Agam, Yaacov
b. 1930 Dijkstra, Edsger W(ybe)
b. 1930 Elkin, Stanley (Lawrence)
b. 1932 Valentino
b. 1933 Farrakhan, Louis
b. 1934 Jeffords, James Merrill
b. 1934 Twyman, Jack
b. 1935 McClure, Doug
b. 1938 Bley, Carla
b. 1939 Pappas, Milt(on Steven)
b. 1941 Charney, Nicolas Herman
b. 1943 Greene, Nancy Catherine
b. 1945 Adams, Floyd, Jr.
b. 1946 Jarvik, Robert Koffler
b. 1947? Popcorn, Faith
b. 1947 Vonnegut, Mark
b. 1949 Martin, Jerry Lindsey
b. 1950 Quaid, Randy
b. 1953 Gaines, Boyd
b. 1959 Quinn, Martha
b. 1963 Richardson, Natasha
b. 1970 Ford, Harold E(ugene), Jr.
d. 1610 Ricci, Matteo
d. 1686 Guericke, Otto Von
d. 1708 Mansart, Jules Hardouin
d. 1778 Pitt, William, the Elder
d. 1779 Hart, John
d. 1831 Trumbull, John
d. 1839 Cooper, Thomas
d. 1849 Nicolai, Carl Otto Ehrenfried
d. 1849 Recamier, Julie, Madame
d. 1871 Herschel, John Frederick William, Sir
d. 1872 Read, Thomas Buchanan
d. 1893 Armstrong, Samuel Chapman
d. 1896 Bunner, Henry Cuyler
d. 1916 Reger, Max
d. 1927 Colvin, Sidney, Sir
d. 1927 Gris, Juan
d. 1931 Cole, Timothy
d. 1934 Corey, William Ellis
d. 1935 Thompson, Edward Herbert
d. 1936 Palmer, Alexander Mitchell
d. 1944 Bamberger, Louis
d. 1945 Commons, John Rogers
d. 1947 Goudy, Frederic William

d. 1953 Tomlin, Bradley Walker
d. 1954 Ives, Charles Edward
d. 1954 Lasser, Jacob Kay
d. 1954 Stover, Russell
d. 1956 Adams, Walter Sydney
d. 1958 Lelong, Lucien
d. 1960 Rockefeller, John D(avison), Jr.
d. 1962 Speicher, Eugene Edward
d. 1963 Gasser, Herbert Spencer
d. 1969 Fleischmann, Raoul H(erbert)
d. 1970 Hodges, Johnny
d. 1972 Trendle, George Washington
d. 1976 Aalto, Alvar Henrik Hugo
d. 1976 Kempe, Rudolf
d. 1978 Khaikin, Boris
d. 1979 Flatt, Lester Raymond
d. 1979 Hutton, Barbara Woolworth
d. 1981 Fuller, Hoyt William
d. 1981 Hassel, Odd
d. 1981 Marley, Bob
d. 1981 Whitaker, Rogers E(rnest) M(alcolm)
d. 1982 Burck, Jacob
d. 1985 Gould, Chester
d. 1986 Pollard, Fritz
d. 1987 Angleton, James J(esus)
d. 1988 Daugherty, Carroll Roop
d. 1988 Foster, Tabatha
d. 1988 Philby, Kim
d. 1992 Henle, Guy
d. 1992 MacDonald, Elizabeth G.
d. 1993 Gentry, Minnie Lee
d. 1993 Wiener, Leigh Auston
d. 1996 Azikiwe, Nnamdi
d. 1999 Fifield, Elaine
d. 2000 Aardema, Verna Norberg

May 12
b. 1670 Augustus II
b. 1784 Knowles, James Sheridan
b. 1802 Lacordaire, Jean Baptiste Henri
b. 1803 Liebig, Justus von
b. 1804 Baldwin, Robert
b. 1809 Giusti, Giuseppe
b. 1812 Lear, Edward
b. 1828 Rossetti, Dante Gabriel
b. 1829 Childs, George William
b. 1842 Massenet, Jules Emile Frederic

b. 1845 Faure, Gabriel Urbain
b. 1850 Lodge, Henry Cabot
b. 1855 Isham, Samuel
b. 1857 Dunning, William Archibald
b. 1859 Nordica, Lillian
b. 1868 Shean, Al
b. 1872 Rathbone, Eleanor
b. 1873 MacDonald, J(ames) E(dward) H(ervey)
b. 1880 Ellsworth, Lincoln
b. 1885 Sironi, Mario
b. 1888 Reik, Theodor
b. 1888 Stabile, Mariano
b. 1893 Black, Walter J
b. 1895 Giauque, William Francis
b. 1895 Olsen, Harold G
b. 1895 Slotta, Karl Heinrich
b. 1900 Macy, George
b. 1900 McAfee, Mildred H(elen)
b. 1901 Hinton, Christopher, Sir
b. 1902 Wylie, Philip Gordon
b. 1903 Hyde-White, Wilfrid
b. 1906 Ewing, William Maurice
b. 1906 Jones, Gorilla
b. 1907 Charteris, Leslie
b. 1907 Hepburn, Katharine (Houghton)
b. 1910 Hodgkin, Dorothy Mary Crowfoot
b. 1910 Jenkins, Gordon
b. 1914 Smith, Howard K(ingsbury)
b. 1915 Engel, Lyle Kenyon
b. 1916 Murray, Albert L(ee)
b. 1916 Simionato, Guilietta
b. 1917 Kay, Mary
b. 1918 Ash, Mary Kay
b. 1918 Rosenberg, Julius
b. 1919 Townsend, Lynn Alfred
b. 1920 Murphy, Patrick Vincent
b. 1921 Beuys, Joseph
b. 1921 Mowat, Farley McGill
b. 1924 Alegria, Claribel
b. 1924 Mecham, Evan
b. 1925 Berra, Yogi
b. 1925 Pierson, Frank R(omer)
b. 1925 Simon, John Ivan
b. 1926 Coleman, James S(amuel)

b. 1927 Crosby, James
Morris
b. 1928 Lujan, Manuel,
Jr.
b. 1929 Bacharach, Burt
b. 1929 Nujoma,
Samuel Shafiihuma
b. 1930 Kunene, Mazisi
(Raymond)
b. 1932 Baby Leroy
b. 1932 Mitchell, David
b. 1935 Alou, Felipe
Rojas
b. 1935 Bucyk, John
Paul
b. 1936 Endara
(Galimany),
Guillermo
b. 1936 Snyder, Tom
b. 1936 Stella, Frank
Philip
b. 1937 Carlin, George
Dennis
b. 1937 Studds, Gerry
E(astman)
b. 1938 Amalrik, Andrei
Alekseyevich
b. 1939 Ziegler, Ron(ald
Louis)
b. 1940 Nestle, Joan
b. 1940 Perkins, Millie
b. 1942 Dury, Ian
b. 1942 Hampshire,
Susan
b. 1944 Patten,
Chris(topher Francis)
b. 1948 Crouse, Lindsay
Ann
b. 1948 Winwood,
Steve
b. 1950 Squier, Billy
b. 1951? Boxleitner,
Bruce
b. 1954 Borden, Barry
b. 1956 Federko, Bernie
b. 1957 Whitaker,
Lou(is Rodman)
b. 1959 Christian, Dave
b. 1962 Estevez, Emilio
b. 1966 Baldwin,
Stephen
b. 1969 Fields, Kim
b. 1973 Astin,
Mackenzie Alexander
d. 1634 Chapman,
George
d. 1641 Strafford, 1st
Earl of
d. 1799 Revillagigedo,
Conde de
d. 1814 Paine, Robert
Treat
d. 1850 Osgood,
Frances Sargent
Locke
d. 1860 Barry, Charles,
Sir
d. 1864 Stuart, Jeb
d. 1871 Auber, Daniel
Francois Esprit
d. 1871 Payen, Anselme
d. 1878 Beecher,
Catharine (Esther)
d. 1884 Smetana,
Bedrich

d. 1887 Boussingault,
Jean Baptiste
d. 1903 Stoddard,
Richard Henry
d. 1907 Huysmans, Joris
Karl
d. 1910 Huggins,
William, Sir
d. 1925 Lowell, Amy
d. 1935 Pilsudski, Jozef
d. 1936 Emerson, Peter
Henry
d. 1942 Ditmars,
Raymond Lee
d. 1943 Stoessel, Albert
d. 1944 Faust, Frederick
Schiller
d. 1944 Quiller-Couch,
Arthur Thomas, Sir
d. 1951 DePriest, Oscar
Stanton
d. 1956 Calhern, Louis
d. 1957 VonStroheim,
Erich
d. 1962 Rivers, Thomas
Milton
d. 1965 Frankfurter,
Alfred Moritz
d. 1966 Howard, Guy
Wesley
d. 1967 Masefield, John
d. 1970 Anders,
Wladyslaw
d. 1970 Sachs, Nelly
(Leonie)
d. 1971 Manush, Heinie
d. 1973 Marion, Frances
d. 1975 Allen, Larry
d. 1978 Zukofsky, Louis
d. 1980 Jones, Howard
Mumford
d. 1980 Roth, Lillian
d. 1980 Sherrill, Henry
Knox
d. 1981 Hughes, Francis
d. 1981 Sheares,
Benjamin Henry
d. 1984 Angell, Robert
Cooley
d. 1985 Dubuffet, Jean
d. 1985 Miles,
Josephine
d. 1986 Bergner,
Elisabeth
d. 1988 Osborn, Paul
d. 1992 Reed, Robert
d. 1994 Erikson, Erik
H(omburger)
d. 1999 Steinberg, Saul
d. 2000 Kingman, Dong
Moy Shu

May 13
b. 1699 Pombal,
Marques de
b. 1717 Maria Theresa
b. 1729 Stiegel, Henry
William
b. 1730 Rockingham,
2nd Marquess of
b. 1742 Cutler,
Manasseh
b. 1753 Carnot, Lazare
b. 1792 Pius IX
b. 1804 Manin, Daniele
b. 1823 McArthur, John

b. 1830 Vance, Zebulon
Baird
b. 1837 Brinton, Daniel
Garrison
b. 1840 Daudet, Leon
b. 1856 Emerson, Peter
Henry
b. 1857 Ross, Ronald,
Sir
b. 1867 Brangwyn,
Frank, Sir
b. 1869 Danforth,
William
b. 1876 Laparra, Raoul
b. 1882 Braque,
Georges
b. 1883 Papanicolaou,
George Nicholas
b. 1893 Kelly,
Shipwreck
b. 1898 Dye, Babe
b. 1904 Birney, Earle
b. 1905 Ahmed,
Fakhruddin Ali
b. 1906 McConnell,
Joseph H(oward)
b. 1907 DuMaurier,
Daphne
b. 1909 Darby, Ken
b. 1911 Sullivan,
Maxine
b. 1912 Evans, Gil
b. 1913 Reddy,
N(eelam) Sanjeeva
b. 1913 Tolbert,
William Richard, Jr.
b. 1914 Louis, Joe
b. 1915 Howe, Oscar
b. 1919 Kelly, Stephen
Eugene
b. 1920 Mara, Ratu Sir
Kamisese
b. 1924 Mann,
Theodore
b. 1926 Arthur, Beatrice
b. 1927 Barnes, Clive
Alexander
b. 1927 Castro, Raul
b. 1927 Hellerman, Fred
b. 1927 Rhodes, Dusty
b. 1927 Ross, Herbert
David
b. 1929 Galvin, John
Rogers
b. 1930 Gravel, Mike
b. 1933 Roseboro,
Johnny
b. 1934 Bell, Ralph S.
b. 1935 Benetton,
Luciano
b. 1936 Lampert, Zohra
b. 1937 Carrier, Roch
b. 1937 Somogi, Judith
b. 1938 Amato,
Giuliano
b. 1939 Keitel, Harvey
b. 1940 Chatwin, Bruce
b. 1941 Berger, Senta
b. 1941 Field, Marshall,
V
b. 1941 Valens, Ritchie
b. 1942 Boudin, Kathy
b. 1942 Dzhanibekov,
Vladimir
Alexandrovich
b. 1943 Wells, Mary

b. 1947 Baxter, Charles
(Morley)
b. 1947 Donaldson,
Stephen Reeder
b. 1947 Watts, Pete
b. 1950 Gabriel, Peter
b. 1950 Marable,
Manning
b. 1950 Wonder, Stevie
b. 1951 Kessler, David
Aaron
b. 1961 Rodman,
Dennis (Keith)
b. 1965 Rijo, Jose
Antonio Abreu
b. 1966 Rucker, Darius
d. 1619 Oldenbarnevelt,
Johan van
d. 1832 Cuvier,
Georges, Baron
d. 1835 Nash, John
d. 1878 Henry, Joseph
d. 1884 McCormick,
Cyrus Hall
d. 1885 Ewing, Julianna
Horatia (Gatty)
d. 1900 Levi, Hermann
d. 1903 Mabini,
Apolinario
d. 1904 Tarde, Gabriel
d. 1916 Aleichem,
Sholom
d. 1916 Kellogg, Clara
Louise
d. 1925 Milner, Alfred,
Viscount
d. 1931 Ysaye, Eugene
d. 1933 Ernst, Paul Karl
Friedrich
d. 1937 Wise, Thomas J
d. 1941 Sombart,
Werner
d. 1947 Gleason, Lucille
d. 1953 Jadlowker,
Hermann
d. 1957 Murry, John
Middleton
d. 1961 Cooper, Gary
d. 1962 Calkins, Dick
d. 1962 Dean, Henry
Trendley
d. 1962 Kline, Franz
Joseph
d. 1964 Basso,
Hamilton
d. 1964 Wynyard, Diana
d. 1971 O'Hanlon,
Virginia
d. 1972 Blocker, Dan
d. 1974 Shute, Denny
d. 1975 Wills, Bob
d. 1985 Behrens, Earl
Charles
d. 1985 Diamond,
Selma
d. 1985 Joy, Leatrice
d. 1986 Bohlem, Arndt
von
d. 1986 Hearst, David
W(hitmire)
d. 1986 O'Donnell,
Peadar
d. 1987 Ellmann,
Richard David
d. 1988 Gorshkov,
Sergei

d. 1991 Brinig, Myron
d. 1992 Kahng, Dawon
d. 1993 Garcia Vargas,
Joaquin
d. 1999 Greenfield, Meg
d. 1999 Sarazen, Gene
May 14
b. 1316 Charles, IV
b. 1666 Victor
Amadeus, II
b. 1686 Fahrenheit,
Gabriel Daniel
b. 1727 Gainsborough,
Thomas
b. 1752 Dwight,
Timothy
b. 1771 Owen, Robert
b. 1771 Wedgwood,
Thomas
b. 1842 Sullivan, Arthur
Seymour, Sir
b. 1843 Walker, Henry
Oliver
b. 1852 Parker, Alton
Brooks
b. 1853 Caine, Hall
b. 1860 Mudgett,
Herman Webster
b. 1867 Eisner, Kurt
b. 1867 Gillmore, Frank
b. 1868 Hirschfeld,
Magnus
b. 1870 Rogers, Bruce
b. 1873 Tcherepnin,
Nicholas
b. 1880 Forbes, Bertie
b. 1881 Fulton, Maude
b. 1881 Walsh, Ed(ward
Augustine)
b. 1883 Eltinge, Julian
b. 1884 Dornier, Claude
b. 1885 Klemperer, Otto
b. 1888 Alexander,
Archie Alphonso
b. 1894 Folsom, Frank
M
b. 1895 Lehr, Lew
b. 1897 Bechet, Sidney
b. 1897 Ye Jianying
b. 1898 Singleton, Zutty
b. 1899 Combs, Earle
Bryan
b. 1900 Borland, Hal
b. 1900 Finch, Robert
Duer Clayton
b. 1902 Chidsey,
Donald Barr
b. 1902 Dunbar, Helen
Flanders
b. 1905 O'Callahan,
Joseph Timothy
b. 1907 Ayub Khan,
Mohammad
b. 1907 Enrique
Tarancon, Vicente,
Cardinal
b. 1910 Pully, B S
b. 1911 Curtis, Thomas
B(radford)
b. 1913 Doxiadis,
Constantinos
Apostolos
b. 1913 Terry, Walter
b. 1916 Harper, Marion,
Jr.

b. 1922 Clark, Robert
Edward
b. 1922 Deacon,
Richard
b. 1922 Tudjman,
Franjo
b. 1924 Babb, Howard
Selden
b. 1925 Munsel, Patrice
Beverly
b. 1929 Thompson,
George Selden
b. 1929 Worsley, Gump
b. 1932 Estes, Richard
b. 1932 Richards,
Richard
b. 1934 Phillips, Sian
b. 1936 Darin, Bobby
b. 1936 Neuhaus,
Richard John
b. 1937 Howser, Dick
b. 1942 Dorgan, Byron
Leslie
b. 1942 Perez, Tony
b. 1943 Bruce, Jack
b. 1943 Leon, Tania
(Justina)
b. 1943 Urtain, Jose
Manuel Ibar
b. 1944 Annis,
Francesca
b. 1944 Lucas, George
b. 1945 Cornish, Gene
b. 1949 Laurel, Alicia
Bay
b. 1951 Hubley, Season
b. 1951 Zemeckis,
Robert
b. 1952 Byrne, David
b. 1959 Vaive, Rick
Claude
b. 1961 Roth, Tim
d. 1610 Henry, IV
d. 1643 Louis, XIII
d. 1734 Stahl, Georg
Ernst
d. 1818 Lewis, Matthew
Gregory
d. 1852 Adams, Louisa
Catherine
d. 1878 Okubo,
Toshimichi
d. 1897 Maretzek, Max
d. 1906 Schurz, Carl
d. 1912 Strindberg,
August
d. 1917 Choate, Joseph
Hodges
d. 1918 Bennett, James
Gordon, Jr.
d. 1919 Heinz, Henry
John
d. 1925 Haggard, Henry
Rider, Sir
d. 1931 Belasco, David
d. 1935 Frost, Edwin
Brant
d. 1935 Hirschfeld,
Magnus
d. 1936 Allenby,
Edmund Henry
Hynman
d. 1937 Haskins,
Charles Homer
d. 1940 Goldman,
Emma

d. 1943 La Fontaine,
Henri Marie
d. 1953 Kuniyoshi,
Yasuo
d. 1958 Dole, James
d. 1959 Bechet, Sidney
d. 1965 Perkins, Frances
d. 1967 Gold, Michael
d. 1970 Burke, Billie
d. 1970 Dobell, William
d. 1975 Alexanderson,
Ernst Frederik
Werner
d. 1977 Hutchins,
Robert Maynard
d. 1977 Victor, Sally
Josephs
d. 1978 Kipnis,
Alexander
d. 1978 Lear, William
Powell
d. 1978 Menzies, Robert
Gordon, Sir
d. 1979 Rhys, Jean
d. 1979 Scherman,
Thomas Kielty
d. 1980 Ebert, Carl
d. 1980 Griffith, Hugh
Emrys
d. 1980 Robinson,
Francis Arthur
d. 1982 Beaumont,
Hugh
d. 1982 Rossellini,
Renzo
d. 1983 Aleman, Miguel
d. 1987 Hayworth, Rita
d. 1987 Lynch, J(ohn)
Joseph
d. 1988 Drees, Willem
d. 1988 Guyer, David
Leigh
d. 1989 Moats, Alice-
Leone
d. 1991 Chiang, Ching
d. 1992 Alzado, Lyle
Martin
d. 1993 Hearst, William
Randolph, Jr.
d. 1994 Albritton, David
d. 1994 Claytor,
W(illiam) Graham, Jr.
d. 1994 Smith, Hazel
Brannon
d. 1995 Anfinsen,
Christian Boehmer
d. 1996 Gurney, Edward
John
d. 1997 Blackstone,
Harry, Jr.
d. 1997 Lee, Laurie
d. 1998 Douglas,
Marjory (Stoneman)
d. 1998 Sinatra, Frank
d. 2000 Rockefeller,
Rodman C
d. 2000 Shapiro, Karl
Jay
May 15
b. 1567 Monteverdi,
Claudio
b. 1633 Vauban,
Sebastien LePrestre
de
b. 1773 Metternich-
Winneburg, Clemens

b. 1788 Gadsden, James
b. 1801 Lartet, Edouard
Armand Isidore
Hippolyte
b. 1803 Lytton, Edward
George Earle Lytton
Bulwer-Lytton, 1st
Baron Lytton
b. 1808 Balfe, Michael
William
b. 1819 Crittendon,
Thomas Leonidas
b. 1820 Nightingale,
Florence
b. 1845 Metchnikoff,
Elie
b. 1852 Goldsmith, Fred
Ernest
b. 1855 Bamberger,
Louis
b. 1856 Baum, L(yman)
Frank
b. 1857 Fleming,
Williamina Paton
Stevens
b. 1859 Curie, Pierre
b. 1860 Wilson, Ellen
Axson
b. 1862 Schnitzler,
Arthur
b. 1863 Johnston, Annie
Fellows
b. 1875 Hewitt, William
Archibald
b. 1885 Daubert, Jake
b. 1886 Lambert,
Gerard Barnes
b. 1887 Muir, Edwin
b. 1890 McNaughton,
F(oye) F(isk)
b. 1891 Bulgakov,
Mikhail Afanasyevich
b. 1892 Wilde, Jimmy
b. 1892 Wills, Harry
b. 1893 Ichikawa, Fusae
b. 1894 Porter,
Katherine Anne
b. 1898 Arletty
b. 1898? Skulnik,
Menasha
b. 1900 Gordon, John F
b. 1901 Anderson,
Dorothy Hansine
b. 1901 Spanel, Abram
N
b. 1902 Daley, Richard
Joseph
b. 1903 MacTaggart,
William, Sir
b. 1904 Fadiman,
Clifton (Paul)
b. 1905 Cotten, Joseph
b. 1907 Appel, James
Ziegler
b. 1907 Dodd, Thomas
Joseph
b. 1909 Mason, James
Neville
b. 1910 Cummings,
Constance
b. 1911 Frisch, Max
b. 1912 Berger, Arthur
b. 1914 Broda, Turk
b. 1914 Tenzing Norgay
b. 1915 Monicelli,
Mario

b. 1915 Samuelson, Paul Anthony
b. 1916 Singh, Giani Zail
b. 1917 Barnes, Wade
b. 1918 Arnold, Eddy
b. 1918 Wiseman, Joseph
b. 1919 Charles, Mary Eugenia
b. 1920 Audiard, Michel
b. 1923 Avedon, Richard
b. 1923 Poussaint, Alvin F.
b. 1925 Bolin, Bert (Richard Johannes)
b. 1926 Shaffer, Anthony
b. 1926 Shaffer, Peter Levin
b. 1930 Johns, Jasper, (Jr.)
b. 1931 Califano, Joseph Anthony, Jr.
b. 1931 Venturi, Ken(neth)
b. 1932 Chavalit Yongchaiyudh
b. 1932 Gibson, Kenneth Allen
b. 1934 Bedie, Henri Konan
b. 1935 Bragg, Don(ald)
b. 1936 Alberghetti, Anna Maria
b. 1936 Zindel, Paul
b. 1937 Albright, Madeleine K(orbel)
b. 1937 Lopez, Trini(dad, III)
b. 1939 Hammer, Barbara J.
b. 1940 Ailes, Roger Eugene
b. 1940 Nelson, Don(ald Arvid)
b. 1942 Hilliard, David
b. 1942 Kazan, Lainie
b. 1943 Brosten, Harve
b. 1943 Cronenberg, David
b. 1947 Boyd, T(heophilus) B(artholomew), III
b. 1948 Eno, Brian
b. 1950 Berkowitz, Bob
b. 1951 Palminteri, Chazz
b. 1953 Brett, George (Howard)
b. 1953 Oldfield, Mike
b. 1955 Horsley, Lee
b. 1967 Smoltz, John
b. 1969 Smith, Emmitt
b. 1970 Howard, Desmond
d. 1164 Heloise
d. 1174 Nureddin
d. 1773 Butler, Alban
d. 1833 Kean, Edmund
d. 1847 O'Connell, Daniel
d. 1858 Hare, Robert
d. 1865 Blythe, David Gilmour

d. 1869 Dyce, Alexander
d. 1879 Stampfli, Jakob
d. 1883 Gorgas, Josiah
d. 1883 Henson, Josiah
d. 1886 Dickinson, Emily (Elizabeth)
d. 1898 Remenyi, Eduard
d. 1899 Sarcey, Francisque
d. 1903 Sanderson, Sybil
d. 1922 Spy
d. 1924 D'Estournelles, Paul Henri Benjamin Balleut de Constant, Baron
d. 1925 Miles, Nelson Appleton
d. 1930 Locke, William John
d. 1932 Inukai, Tsuyoshi
d. 1933 Torrence, Ernest
d. 1935 Malevich, Kasimir Severinovich
d. 1944 Seibert, Oliver L
d. 1948 Flanagan, Edward Joseph, Father
d. 1948 West, James Edward
d. 1949 Antin, Mary
d. 1952 Montemezzi, Italo
d. 1954 Campbell, William Edward March
d. 1954 Guderian, Heinz Wilhelm
d. 1956 Rollini, Adrian
d. 1960 Petersham, Miska
d. 1961 Gorman, Tommy
d. 1966 Forbes, Kathryn
d. 1967 Hopper, Edward
d. 1968 Austral, Florence Wilson
d. 1968 Kimmel, Husband Edward
d. 1969 Malone, Joe
d. 1970 Shaughnessy, Clark Daniel
d. 1971 Goslin, Goose
d. 1971 Guthrie, Tyrone, Sir
d. 1971 Maxon, Lou Russell
d. 1976 Morison, Samuel Eliot
d. 1977 Wilcox, Herbert
d. 1983 Gucci, Rodolfo
d. 1983 VanDerZee, James
d. 1986 White, Theodore Harold
d. 1987 Baur, John I(reland) H(owe)
d. 1988 Duggan, Andrew
d. 1988 Shaplen, Robert Modell

d. 1989 Green, Johnny
d. 1989 Primeau, Joe
d. 1992 Funston, George Keith
d. 1992 Marcelo, (Edward) Jovy
d. 1995 Flores, Lola
d. 1995 Porter, Eric Richard
d. 1998 Hawkes, John

May 16
b. 1788 Ruckert, Friedrich
b. 1799 Emmons, Ebenezer
b. 1801 Seward, William Henry
b. 1804 Peabody, Elizabeth Palmer
b. 1824 Morton, Levi Parsons
b. 1824 Smith, Edmund Kirby
b. 1827 Colman, Norman Jay
b. 1832 Armour, Philip Danforth
b. 1844 Hare, John, Sir
b. 1844 Reinhart, Charles S
b. 1872 Holmes, Taylor
b. 1876 West, James Edward
b. 1877 McCormick, Joseph Medill
b. 1881 McCormick, Anne (Elizabeth) O'Hare
b. 1882 Hayes, Carlton Joseph Huntley
b. 1882 Reid, Ogden Mills
b. 1885 Pool, David de Sola
b. 1886 Freeman, Douglas S
b. 1887 Montana, Bull
b. 1888 Sarett, Lew R
b. 1892 Perkins, Osgood
b. 1892 Tauber, Richard
b. 1894 Yust, Walter
b. 1896 Sullavan, Margaret
b. 1898 Mizoguchi, Kenji
b. 1901 Justus, Roy Braxton
b. 1901? Zevin, B(enjamin) D(avid)
b. 1902 Kiepura, Jan Wiktor
b. 1904 Peterson, Virgilia
b. 1905 Bates, H(erbert) E(rnest)
b. 1905 Fonda, Henry Jaynes
b. 1905 Lichty, George
b. 1906 Rey, Margret (Elizabeth)
b. 1909 Luckman, Charles
b. 1909 Ward, Deighton Harcourt Lisle, Sir
b. 1912 Terkel, Studs (Louis)

b. 1913 Herman, Woody
b. 1915 Hosmer, Craig
b. 1918 Rulfo, Juan
b. 1919 Liberace
b. 1922 Carol, Martine
b. 1924 Jawara, Alhaji Dawda Kairaba, Sir
b. 1924 Mankiewicz, Frank Fabian
b. 1925 Pierpoint, Robert Charles
b. 1926 Sinatra, Barbara Marx Spencer
b. 1927 Graves, John Earl
b. 1928 Martin, Billy
b. 1929 Conyers, John, Jr.
b. 1929 Rich, Adrienne (Cecile)
b. 1930 Carter, Betty
b. 1930 Gulda, Friedrich
b. 1931 Weicker, Lowell Palmer, Jr.
b. 1934 Kerr, Roy Patrick
b. 1936 DeMontebello, Guy-Philippe
b. 1937 Hunt, James Baxter, Jr.
b. 1943 Adams, Hank
b. 1943 Coats, Dan(iel R)
b. 1944 Cobham, Billy
b. 1947 Edwards, Bob
b. 1948 Langer, Jim
b. 1948 Legg, Adrian
b. 1950? Bednorz, J(ohannes) Georg
b. 1953 Brosnan, Pierce
b. 1955 Bronfman, Edgar Miles, Jr.
b. 1955 Korbut, Olga
b. 1956 Morris, Jack
b. 1957 Cousineau, Tom
b. 1960 Noah, Yannick Simon Camille
b. 1966 Jackson, La Toya
b. 1966 Thomas, Thurman Lee
b. 1970 Sabatini, Gabriela
b. 1973 Spelling, Tori
d. 1620 Adams, William
d. 1669 Cortona, Pietro da
d. 1691 Leisler, Jacob
d. 1703 Perrault, Charles
d. 1777 Gwinnett, Button
d. 1830 Fourier, Jean Baptiste Joseph
d. 1835 Hemans, Felicia Dorothea Browne
d. 1862 Wakefield, Edward Gibbon
d. 1919 Schaefer, Germany
d. 1920 Morton, Levi Parsons
d. 1927 Bernard, Sam
d. 1928 Gosse, Edmund William, Sir

d. 1932 Dollar, Robert
d. 1938 Strauss, Joseph Baermann
d. 1942 Gest, Morris
d. 1942 Malinowski, Bronislaw Kasper
d. 1944 Ade, George
d. 1946 Tarkington, Booth
d. 1947 Hopkins, Frederick Gowland, Sir
d. 1952 Johnston, Frances Benjamin
d. 1953 Reinhardt, Django (Jean Baptiste)
d. 1954 Krauss, Clemens
d. 1955 Agee, James Rufus
d. 1957 Irvin, Dick
d. 1959 Cook, Joe
d. 1965 Breckinridge, Mary
d. 1971 Stanley, Barney
d. 1978 Steinberg, William
d. 1979 Randolph, Asa Philip
d. 1984 Kaufman, Andy
d. 1984 Shaw, Irwin
d. 1985 Hamilton, Margaret Brainard
d. 1985 King, Wayne
d. 1988 Ortiz, Peter J(ulien)
d. 1988 Wood, Louise Aletha
d. 1990 Davis, Sammy, Jr.
d. 1990 Henson, Jim
d. 1997 Baron, Samuel
d. 1997 DeSantis, Giuseppe

May 17
b. 1741 Penn, John
b. 1749 Jenner, Edward
b. 1805 Surtees, Robert Smith
b. 1836 Lockyer, Joseph Norman, Sir
b. 1836 Steinitz, Wilhelm
b. 1855 Healy, T(imothy) M(ichael)
b. 1860 Wheeler, Schuyler Skaats
b. 1865 Bennett, John
b. 1866 Satie, Erik
b. 1868 Dodge, Horace Elgin
b. 1873 Richardson, Dorothy Miller
b. 1875 Spingarn, Joel Elias
b. 1882 Lehman, Adele Lewisohn
b. 1885 Stakman, Elvin Charles
b. 1886 Alfonso XIII
b. 1889 Mackay, John Alexander
b. 1889 Reyes, Alfonso
b. 1890 James, Philip
b. 1893 Shields, Larry

b. 1895 Davis, James Curran
b. 1895 Derby, Jane
b. 1895 Hauser, Gayelord
b. 1896 Donnelly, Ruth
b. 1897 Hassel, Odd
b. 1900 Khomeini, Ruhollah Musavi, Ayatollah
b. 1901 Egk, Werner
b. 1901 Lorenz, Max
b. 1901 Schonfield, Hugh J
b. 1902 Cleva, Fausto
b. 1903 Bell, Cool Papa
b. 1903 Norton, Elliot
b. 1904 Gabin, Jean
b. 1904 Williams, John James
b. 1905 Patrick, John
b. 1906 McIntire, Carl
b. 1906 Milanov, Zinka Kunc
b. 1907 McMahon, Horace
b. 1908 Prokosch, Frederic
b. 1908 Schorer, Mark
b. 1911 Kerr, Clark
b. 1911 O'Sullivan, Maureen
b. 1911 Rosenfeld, Henry J
b. 1912 Cox, Archibald
b. 1913 Parker, Ace
b. 1914 Alsop, Stewart Johonnot Oliver
b. 1914 Ongania, Juan Carlos
b. 1916 Maugham, Robin
b. 1917 Creach, Papa
b. 1917 Lescoulie, Jack
b. 1918 Hunt, Jack Reed
b. 1918 Nilsson, Birgit
b. 1919 Cassill, R(onald) V(erlin)
b. 1919 DeBartolo, Edward J(ohn), Sr.
b. 1919 Miller, Merle
b. 1919 Sutton, Horace (Ashley)
b. 1920 Van Horne, Harriet
b. 1921 Brain, Dennis
b. 1921 Winship, Elizabeth
b. 1923 Mahoney, David Joseph, Jr.
b. 1923 Mennin, Peter
b. 1925 Luckenbach, Edgar Frederick, Jr.
b. 1929 Greenfield, Eloise
b. 1934 Morrall, Earl E
b. 1935 Potter, Dennis (Christopher George)
b. 1936 Hopper, Dennis
b. 1937 O'Leary, Hazel R(eid)
b. 1938 Bortoluzzi, Paolo
b. 1939 Purdy, Susan Gold

b. 1941 Nelson, Ben
b. 1942 Taj Mahal
b. 1944 Winchester, Jesse (James Ridout)
b. 1950 Lacroix, Christian
b. 1950 Soltysik, Patricia Michelle
b. 1954? Sullivan, Kathleen
b. 1955 Paxton, Bill
b. 1955 Winger, Debra
b. 1956 Leonard, Sugar Ray
b. 1956 Saget, Bob
b. 1965 Reznor, Trent
b. 1966 Manning, Danny
d. 1510 Botticelli, Sandro
d. 1729 Clarke, Samuel
d. 1740 Cavalier, Jean
d. 1767 Wolcott, Roger
d. 1800 Suvorov, Aleksandr V
d. 1829 Jay, John
d. 1831 Rochester, Nathaniel
d. 1838 Talleyrand-Perigord, Charles Maurice de
d. 1839 Alison, Archibald
d. 1875 Breckinridge, John Cabell
d. 1883 Pinkham, Lydia Estes
d. 1886 Deere, John
d. 1919 Zelaya, Jose Santos
d. 1924 Cummings, Candy
d. 1929 Lehmann, Lilli
d. 1930 Croly, Herbert David
d. 1934 Gilbert, Cass
d. 1935 Dukas, Paul Abraham
d. 1948 Samaroff, Olga
d. 1962 Frazier, Edward Franklin
d. 1964 Owen, Steve
d. 1969 Baer, Bugs
d. 1969 Olczewska, Maria
d. 1970 Balchin, Nigel Marlin
d. 1977 Keita, Modibo
d. 1977 Mueller, Erwin Wilhelm
d. 1978 Lloyd, Selwyn
d. 1981 Piccard, Jeannette Ridlon
d. 1982 Walker, Dixie
d. 1984 Sinclair, Gordon
d. 1985 Burrows, Abe
d. 1987 Myrdal, Karl Gunnar
d. 1992 Hurrell, George
d. 1992 Welk, Lawrence
d. 1995 Blake, Toe
d. 1996 Smith, Ethel
d. 1996 Watson, Johnny "Guitar"
d. 1999 Jones, Henry

d. 2000 Coggan, Frederick Donald, Baron

May 18
b. 1692 Butler, Joseph
b. 1711 Boscovich, Ruggiero Giuseppe
b. 1810 Piave, Francesco Maria
b. 1815 Francis, James Bicheno
b. 1830 Goldmark, Karl
b. 1846 Faberge, Peter Carl
b. 1851 Peretz, Isaac Loeb
b. 1862 Daniels, Josephus
b. 1863 Heinemann, William
b. 1868 Nicholas II
b. 1872 Russell, Bertrand Arthur William
b. 1873 Silverman, Sime
b. 1874 Tharaud, Jerome
b. 1883 Gropius, Walter Adolf
b. 1885 Dutra, Eurico Gaspar
b. 1886 Thorarensen, Jakob
b. 1889 Midgeley, Thomas
b. 1891 Carnap, Rudolf
b. 1892 Pinza, Ezio
b. 1894 Sandino, Augusto C(esar Calderon)
b. 1897 Capra, Frank
b. 1897 LaFollete, Philip Fox
b. 1897 Swerling, Jo
b. 1900 Keating, Kenneth B
b. 1901 DuVigneaud, Vincent
b. 1901 Sauguet, Henri
b. 1901 Stratton, Julius A(dams)
b. 1902 Bein, Albert
b. 1902 Willson, Meredith
b. 1904 Javits, Jacob Koppel
b. 1907 Curzon, Clifford Michael, Sir
b. 1907 Dohanos, Stevan
b. 1908 Tucker, Tommy
b. 1909 Gidal, Tim
b. 1910 Taylor, Phoebe Atwood
b. 1911 Gurie, Sigrid
b. 1911 Turner, Joe
b. 1912 Brooks, Richard
b. 1912 Como, Perry
b. 1912 Crosby, John Campbell
b. 1913 Trenet, Charles
b. 1914 Balmain, Pierre Alexandre
b. 1917 Donald, James
b. 1918 Christoff, Boris

b. 1919 Fonteyn, Margot, Dame
b. 1919 Wurf, Jerry
b. 1920 John Paul II
b. 1920 Storr, (Charles) Anthony
b. 1921 Dennis, Patrick
b. 1922 Macy, Bill
b. 1922 Winding, Kai Chresten
b. 1924 Edmonson, Munro Sterling
b. 1924 Justice, Choo Choo
b. 1924 Whitaker, Jack
b. 1930 Roberts, Pernell
b. 1930 Rudman, Warren Bruce
b. 1930 Seed, Jenny
b. 1931 Morse, Robert Alan
b. 1933 Gowda, H(aradanahalli) D(odde) Deve
b. 1934 Hickman, Dwayne B
b. 1937 Barth, Roland Sawyer
b. 1937 Robinson, Brooks Calbert, Jr.
b. 1937 Santer, Jacques
b. 1945 Quarry, Jerry
b. 1946 Jackson, Reggie
b. 1947 Bruton, John (Gerard)
b. 1948 Bonsall, Joe
b. 1949 Wakeman, Rick
b. 1950 Milburn, Rodney, Jr.
b. 1951 Champagne, Duane (Willard)
b. 1951 Gregg, Eric
b. 1951 Sundburg, Jim
b. 1957 Wood, Sharon
b. 1960 Kurri, Jarri
d. 1525 Pomponazzi, Pietro
d. 1675 Marquette, Jacques, Pere
d. 1713 Brattle, Thomas
d. 1795 Rogers, Robert
d. 1799 Beaumarchais, Pierre Augustin Caron de
d. 1909 Meredith, George
d. 1910 Viardot-Garcia, Pauline
d. 1911 Mahler, Gustav
d. 1912 Strasburger, Eduard Adolf
d. 1917 Maskelyne, John Nevil
d. 1917 Pratt, Bela Lyon
d. 1922 Laveran, Charles Louis Alphonse
d. 1922 Raleigh, Walter Alexander, Sir
d. 1928 Haywood, William Dudley
d. 1929 Shaw, Mary
d. 1940 Bunau-Varilla, Philippe Jean
d. 1941 Ternina, Milka

d. 1949 Adams, James Truslow
d. 1951 Coxey, Jacob Sechler
d. 1954 Waller, Fred(erick)
d. 1955 Bethune, Mary McLeod
d. 1955 Pratella, Francesco Balilla
d. 1957 Rogers, Bruce
d. 1958 Davis, Elmer Holmes
d. 1960 Wurdemann, Audrey May
d. 1963 Davis, Ernie
d. 1967 Clyde, Andy
d. 1969 Fitzpatrick, Daniel R
d. 1973 Coste, Dieudonne
d. 1973 Rankin, Jeannette
d. 1974 Topping, Dan(iel Reid)
d. 1975 Anderson, Leroy
d. 1981 Rausch, James Stevens
d. 1981 Saroyan, William
d. 1983 Fielding, Temple Hornaday
d. 1986 Bubbles, John
d. 1986 Wilson, John Johnston
d. 1987 Cohen, Wilbur Joseph
d. 1988 Butler, Daws
d. 1990 Ireland, Jill
d. 1995 Cook, Elisha, Jr.
d. 1995 Godunov, Alexander
d. 1995 Harris, Robert
d. 1995 LePoer Trench, Brinsley
d. 1995 Montgomery, Elizabeth
d. 1995 Stone, Michael Patrick William
d. 1997 Saidenberg, Daniel
d. 2000 Lederer, Francis

May 19
b. 1593 Jordaens, Jacob
b. 1611 Innocent XI, Pope
b. 1762 Fichte, Johann Gottlieb
b. 1795 Hopkins, Johns
b. 1800 Brown, James
b. 1857 Abel, John Jacob
b. 1859 Melba, Nellie, Dame
b. 1860 Orlando, Vittorio Emanuele
b. 1864 Akeley, Carl Ethan
b. 1868 Hayford, John Fillmore
b. 1871 Daly, Reginald Aldworth
b. 1877 Girdler, Tom Mercer

b. 1879 Astor, Nancy Witcher Langhorne
b. 1879 Bestor, Arthur Eugene
b. 1886 Schmitt, Bernadotte Everly
b. 1887 Travers, Jerry
b. 1888 Simpson, William Hood
b. 1890 Ho Chi Minh
b. 1890 Maxwell, Steamer
b. 1892 Foster, Pops
b. 1893 VonSchmidt, Harold
b. 1894 Busse, Henry
b. 1896 Alessandri, Jorge
b. 1896 Balcon, Michael Elias, Sir
b. 1896 Thorborg, Kerstin
b. 1901 Chandler, Dorothy (Buffum)
b. 1903 Chiang, Yee
b. 1903 Samuels, Ernest
b. 1904 Bushell, Anthony
b. 1904 Creighton, Thomas H(awk)
b. 1905 Copeland, Lammot du Pont
b. 1914 Perutz, M(ax) F(erdinand)
b. 1916 Bloom, Murray Teigh
b. 1916 Jack, Homer A(lexander)
b. 1918 Pais, Abraham
b. 1923 Arbatov, Georgi
b. 1924 Wilson, Sandy
b. 1925 Malcolm X
b. 1925 Pol Pot
b. 1926 Andrews, Mark N
b. 1928 Chapman, (Anthony) Colin (Bruce)
b. 1928 McDougald, Gil(bert James)
b. 1928 Schayes, Dolph
b. 1929 Cox, Harvey Gallagher, Jr.
b. 1930 Hansberry, Lorraine
b. 1932 Erdman, Paul E(mil)
b. 1933 Feelings, Tom
b. 1933 Poniatowska, Elena
b. 1934 Fitch, Bill
b. 1934 Lehrer, Jim
b. 1935 Hartman, David Downs
b. 1936 Jenrette, John Wilson, Jr.
b. 1939 Fox, James
b. 1939 Kwan, Nancy Kashen
b. 1939 Scobee, Dick
b. 1939 Young, Stephen
b. 1940 Lorenzo, Frank
b. 1941 Brody, Jane Ellen
b. 1941 Ephron, Nora

b. 1945 Townshend, Peter Dennis Blandford
b. 1946 Rudd, Phil(lip)
b. 1946 Waihee, John David, III
b. 1947 Brady, Paul Joseph
b. 1947 Helfgott, David
b. 1949 Manning, Archie
b. 1950 Caddell, Pat(rick Hayward)
b. 1952 Jones, Grace
b. 1956 Ford, Steven Meigs
b. 1957 Laimbeer, Bill
b. 1959 Simpson, Nicole Brown
b. 1976 Garnett, Kevin
d. 804 Alcuin
d. 988 Dunstan, St.
d. 1296 Celestine V, Saint
d. 1536 Boleyn, Anne
d. 1645 Van Diemen, Anthony Meuza
d. 1683 Killigrew, Thomas
d. 1795 Bartlett, Josiah
d. 1795 Boswell, James
d. 1825 Saint-Simon, Claude-Henri de Rouvroy
d. 1846 Thomas, Robert B
d. 1864 Hawthorne, Nathaniel
d. 1895 Marti (y Perez), Jose Julian
d. 1896 Field, Kate
d. 1898 Gladstone, William Ewart
d. 1901 Pretorius, Marthinus Wessel
d. 1904 Tata, Jamshedji Nusserwanji
d. 1917 Lockwood, Belva Ann Bennett
d. 1918 Hodler, Ferdinand
d. 1921 White, Edward Douglass
d. 1935 Lawrence, T(homas) E(dward)
d. 1941 Ridge, Lola
d. 1949 Heggen, Thomas Orls, Jr.
d. 1958 Colman, Ronald
d. 1961 George, Grace
d. 1961 Howard, Joseph Edgar
d. 1963 Matzenauer, Margaret
d. 1965 Dabrowska, Maria Szumska
d. 1968 Dehn, Adolf Arthur
d. 1969 Hawkins, Bean
d. 1969 Hawkins, Coleman
d. 1970 Branner, Martin Michael
d. 1970 Schalk, Ray(mond William)

d. 1971 Nash, Ogden
Frederick
d. 1974 Allal al-Fassi,
Mohamed
d. 1981 O'Connell,
Arthur
d. 1984 Betjeman, John,
Sir
d. 1985 Lander, Toni
d. 1985 Martin, John
d. 1987 Sheldon, Alice
Hastings Bradley
d. 1989 Muccio, John
Joseph
d. 1991 Rice, Gregory
d. 1993 Burdett,
Winston M.
d. 1994 Morgan, Henry
d. 1994 Onassis,
Jacqueline (Lee
Bouvier Kennedy)
d. 1996 Beradino, John
d. 1997 Ruttman, Troy
d. 1998 Donegan,
Dorothy

May 20
b. 1364 Percy, Henry,
Sir
b. 1743 Toussaint
l'Ouverture, Pierre
Dominique
b. 1750 Girard, Stephen
b. 1764 Schadow,
Gottfried
b. 1768 Madison, Dolly
(Payne Todd)
b. 1780 Rivadavia,
Bernardino
b. 1799 Balzac, Honore
de
b. 1806 Mill, John
Stuart
b. 1808 Rice, Thomas
Dartmouth
b. 1818 Fargo, William
George
b. 1822 Passy, Frederic
b. 1825 Blackwell,
Antoinette Louisa
Brown
b. 1826 Palmer, Potter
b. 1851 Berliner, Emile
b. 1851 Lathrop, Rose
Hawthorne
b. 1857 Rice, Joseph
Mayer
b. 1860 Buchner,
Eduard
b. 1861 Smith,
Christopher
Columbus
b. 1877 MacCarthy,
Desmond Charles
Otto, Sir
b. 1880 Fields, Stanley
b. 1880 Theodorescu,
Ion N
b. 1882 Undset, Sigrid
b. 1883 Faisal, I
b. 1890 Nevins, Allan
b. 1891 Browder, Earl
Russell
b. 1892 Anslinger,
Harry Jacob
b. 1892 Russell, Sydney
Gordon, Sir

b. 1894 Saint Johns,
Adela Rogers
b. 1899 Harlan, John
Marshall, II
b. 1899 Taylor, Estelle
b. 1901 Euwe, Max
b. 1901 Fleeson, Doris
b. 1904 Allingham,
Margery
b. 1905 Achterberg,
Gerrit
b. 1907 Mydans, Carl
M
b. 1908 Stewart, James
(Maitland)
b. 1908 Whitehead,
(Walter) Edward
b. 1909 Kunz, Erich
b. 1912 Drachler,
Norman
b. 1912 Sellars, Wilfred
b. 1913 Hewlett,
William
b. 1915 Dayan, Moshe
b. 1916 Chadwick,
William Owen
b. 1917 Lawson, Donald
Elmer
b. 1918 Harlech,
William David
Ormsby-Gore, Baron
b. 1919 Gobel, George
Leslie
b. 1920 Menuhin,
Hephzibah
b. 1920 Smith, Owen
Guinn
b. 1921 Kume, Yutaka
b. 1921 Newhouser, Hal
b. 1922 Johnson, James
Ralph
b. 1923 Fellows, Edith
b. 1923 Selvon, Samuel
Dickson
b. 1926 Hurst, George
b. 1926 Jorgensen,
Christine
b. 1927 Grant, Bud
b. 1928 Hedison, David
b. 1930 McEachin,
James Elton
b. 1931 Boyer, Ken(ton
Lloyd)
b. 1931 Vassiliou,
George (Vassos)
b. 1935 Bessell, Ted
b. 1936 Zerbe, Anthony
b. 1937 Iveagh, Arthur
Francis Benjamin
Guinness, Lord
b. 1940 Mikita,
Stan(ley)
b. 1940 Schell, Orville
H(ickock), 3rd.
b. 1941 Goh Chok Tong
b. 1941 Liberia-Peters,
Maria Philomena
b. 1942 Morrison, Keith
(Anthony)
b. 1943 Kabua, Imata
b. 1944 Cocker, Joe
b. 1946 Cher
b. 1946 Murcer, Bobby
Ray
b. 1948 McKernan,
John Rettie, Jr.

b. 1949 Thomas, Dave
b. 1950 Jingsheng, Wei
b. 1954 Aho, Esko
(Tapani)
b. 1954 Henderson,
Jimmy
b. 1958 Reagan, Ronald
Prescott
b. 1959 Pinchot,
Bronson Alcott
b. 1966 Cohn, Mindy
b. 1970 Brandon,
(Thomas) Terrell
d. 1444 Bernardine of
Siena, Saint
d. 1506 Columbus,
Christopher
d. 1690 Eliot, John
d. 1834 Lafayette,
Marie Joseph Paul,
Marquis
d. 1847 Lamb, Mary
Ann
d. 1864 Clare, John
d. 1880 Foote, Henry
Stuart
d. 1896 Schumann,
Clara Josephine
Wieck
d. 1913 Flagler, Henry
Morrison
d. 1935 Loeffler,
Charles Martin
Tornow
d. 1939 Carr, Joe
d. 1940 Heidenstam,
Carl Gustaf Verner
von
d. 1942 Guimard,
Hector Germain
d. 1944 Rose, Vincent
d. 1947 Lenard, Philipp
Edward Anton
d. 1950 Fletcher, John
Gould
d. 1956 Beerbohm, Max
d. 1956 Macy, George
d. 1957 Murray, Gilbert
d. 1960 Witte, Edwin
Emil
d. 1967 Parker, Daniel
Francis
d. 1968 Lev, Ray
d. 1971 Dihigo, Martin
d. 1974 Dunn, Alan
d. 1975 Hepworth,
Barbara, Dame
d. 1977 Hershey, Lewis
Blaine
d. 1981 Vaughan, Harry
Hawkins
d. 1982 Stern, Max
d. 1982 Tuve, Merle
Antony
d. 1983 Bee, Clair
Francis
d. 1983 Claude, Albert
d. 1984 Bull, Peter
d. 1985 Wierwille,
Victor Paul
d. 1986 Taussig, Helen
Brooke
d. 1986 Wood, Robert
Dennis
d. 1988 Lewis, Tom

d. 1989 Hicks, John
Richard, Sir
d. 1989 Magnuson,
Warren Grant
d. 1989 Radner, Gilda
d. 1990 Seibert, Earl
Walter
d. 1994 Shannon, James
A(ugustine)
d. 1995 Kay, Ulysses
Simpson
d. 1997 Barco Vargas,
Virgilio
d. 1998 Mankowitz,
Wolf
d. 1999 Alfred, William
d. 2000 Drachler,
Norman
d. 2000 Rampal, Jean-
Pierre
d. 2000 Valletti, Cesare

May 21
b. 427BC Plato
b. 1471 Durer, Albrecht
b. 1688 Pope,
Alexander
b. 1759 Fouche, Joseph
b. 1775 Bonaparte,
Lucien
b. 1780 Fry, Elizabeth
Gurney
b. 1796 Johnson,
Reverdy
b. 1817 Lotze, Rudolf
Hermann
b. 1827 Pobedonostsev,
Konstantin Petrovich
b. 1843 Gobat, Charles
Albert
b. 1843 Renault, Louis
b. 1844 Rousseau, Henri
b. 1849 Stuart, Ruth
McEnery
b. 1854 Peto, John
Frederick
b. 1856 Batlle y
Ordonez, Jose
b. 1856 Dodge, Grace
Hoadley
b. 1867 Densmore,
Frances
b. 1868 Cabot, Richard
C
b. 1873 Bennett,
Richard
b. 1873 Berger, Hans
b. 1878 Curtiss, Glenn
Hammond
b. 1878 Desmond,
William
b. 1880 Arghezi, Tudor
b. 1881 Gardner, Jimmy
b. 1887 Gladstone,
James
b. 1894 MacKay,
Mickey
b. 1895 Cardenas,
Lazaro
b. 1897 McGraw,
Donald Cushing
b. 1898 Hammer,
Armand
b. 1901 Drewry, Guy
Carleton
b. 1901 Heidt, Horace
Murray

b. 1901 Nolan, Thomas Brennan
b. 1902 Averill, Earl
b. 1902 Litvak, Anatole
b. 1903 Aramburu, Pedro Eugenio
b. 1904 Montgomery, Robert Henry
b. 1904 Waller, Fats
b. 1906 Buddhadasa Bhikkhu
b. 1906 Gerasimov, Sergei Appolinarievich
b. 1906 Lane, Lola
b. 1907 Ivanov, Konstantin Konstantinovich
b. 1908 McSpaden, Byron
b. 1909 Hummel, Berta
b. 1909 Rothschild, Guy Edouard Alphonse Paul de, Baron
b. 1911 Haviland, Virginia
b. 1911 Hurkos, Peter
b. 1912 Schwarzschild, Martin
b. 1912 Soria, Dario
b. 1912 Stratton, Monty Franklin Pierce
b. 1913 Bachauer, Gina
b. 1913 Shulman, Irving
b. 1916 Robbins, Harold
b. 1917 Burr, Raymond (William Stacy)
b. 1917 Day, Dennis
b. 1917 Yunich, David Lawrence
b. 1920 Bachrach, Howard L.
b. 1920 Steel, Anthony
b. 1921 Benelli, Giovanni, Cardinal
b. 1921 Sakharov, Andrei Dmitrievich
b. 1922 Covey, Cyclone
b. 1925 Cass, Peggy
b. 1925 Kameny, Frank(lin Edward)
b. 1926 Creeley, Robert (White)
b. 1926 Jason, Rick
b. 1926 Robinson, Forbes
b. 1926 Toren, Marta
b. 1931 Frank, Anthony Melchior
b. 1932 Wakefield, Dan
b. 1934 Samuelsson, Bengt Ingemar
b. 1935 Faust, Gerry
b. 1938 Marlowe, Derek
b. 1939 Groh, David Lawrence
b. 1939 Holliger, Heinz
b. 1941 Cox, Bobby
b. 1944 Dailey, Janet
b. 1944 Deitch, Kim
b. 1944 Robinson, Mary
b. 1946 Hatch, Richard Lawrence
b. 1948 Sayer, Leo
b. 1949 Suarez, Xavier Louis

b. 1952 T, Mr.
b. 1955 Plotkin, Mark J.
b. 1956? Reinhold, Judge
b. 1960 Hrbek, Kent Alan
b. 1968 Buckmire, Ron
b. 1972 McBride, Christian
d. 1086 Wang An-shih
d. 1471 Henry VI
d. 1542 DeSoto, Hernando
d. 1639 Campanella, Tommaso
d. 1647 Hooft, Pieter Corneliszoon
d. 1771 Smart, Christopher
d. 1790 Warton, Thomas
d. 1873 Cartier, Georges Etienne, Sir
d. 1881 Scott, Thomas Alexander
d. 1895 Suppe, Franz von
d. 1902 Godkin, E(dwin) L(awrence)
d. 1905 Tourgee, Albion Winegar
d. 1911 Fleming, Williamina Paton Stevens
d. 1920 Carranza, Venustiano
d. 1920 Porter, Eleanor H
d. 1926 Firbank, Ronald
d. 1929 Rosebery, Archibald Philip Primrose, Earl
d. 1935 Addams, Jane
d. 1935 DeVries, Hugo
d. 1940 MacKay, Mickey
d. 1945 Adams, Herbert Samuel
d. 1949 Mann, Klaus
d. 1951 McIntyre, John Thomas
d. 1952 Garfield, John
d. 1955 Phillips, Lena Madesin
d. 1964 Franck, James
d. 1965 DeHavilland, Geoffrey, Sir
d. 1969 Leiper, Robert Thomson
d. 1971 King, Dennis
d. 1973 Konev, Ivan Stepanovich
d. 1973 Monroe, Vaughn
d. 1976 Geller, Bruce
d. 1976 Leon, Henry Cecil
d. 1980 Boyd, Julian Parks
d. 1980 Kaminska, Ida
d. 1981 McCreesh, Raymond
d. 1981 Mearns, David Chambers
d. 1981 O'Hara, Patrick

d. 1981 Yost, Charles Woodruff
d. 1983 Clark, Kenneth MacKenzie, Sir
d. 1983 Hoffer, Eric
d. 1987 Rey, Alejandro
d. 1988 Fitzgerald, John Dennis
d. 1988 Grandi, Dino
d. 1991 Dante, Nicholas
d. 1991 Gandhi, Rajiv Ratna
d. 1995 Aspin, Les
d. 1995 Parker, Albert
d. 1999 Brown, Vanessa
d. 2000 Cartland, Barbara Hamilton
d. 2000 Gielgud, (Arthur) John, Sir
d. 2000 Mielke, Erich

May 22
b. 1622 Frontenac, Louis de Buade de
b. 1755 Coxe, Tench
b. 1772 Roy, Ram Mohun
b. 1783 Sturgeon, William
b. 1808 Nerval, Gerard de
b. 1813 Wagner, Richard
b. 1820 Whittredge, Thomas Worthington
b. 1826 Langdell, Christopher Columbus
b. 1828 Grafe, Albrecht Friedrich Wilhelm Ernst von
b. 1841 Mendes, Catulle
b. 1844 Cassatt, Mary Stevenson
b. 1846 Hay, Oliver Perry
b. 1854 Schurman, Jacob Gould
b. 1859 Doyle, Arthur Conan, Sir
b. 1860 Einthoven, Willem
b. 1874 Malan, Daniel Francois
b. 1880 Phillips, Tommy
b. 1891 Sproul, Robert Gordon
b. 1894 Davis, Clyde Brion
b. 1895 Krishnamurti, Jiddu
b. 1900 Tolson, Clyde Anderson
b. 1902 Breuer, Marcel Lajos
b. 1903 Bonsal, Philip Wilson
b. 1903 Simmons, Al(oysius Harry)
b. 1904 Greene, Balcomb
b. 1906 Howe, Mark De Wolfe
b. 1906 Ritz, Harry
b. 1907 Olivier, Laurence Kerr, Sir

b. 1908 Smith, Horton
b. 1912 Brown, Herbert Charles
b. 1912 Dodington, Sven H(enry Marriott)
b. 1914 Hartt, Frederick
b. 1914 Packard, Vance (Oakley)
b. 1914 Sun Ra
b. 1915 Baker, George
b. 1919 Boeynants, Paul Vanden
b. 1920 Gold, Thomas
b. 1921 Alexander, Donald Crichton
b. 1922 Crist, Judith Klein
b. 1923 Lobel, Arnold Stark
b. 1923 Namgyal, Palden Thondup
b. 1924 Aznavour, Charles
b. 1925 King, James Ambros
b. 1925 Tinguely, Jean
b. 1927 Constantine, Michael
b. 1927 Martin, Quinn
b. 1928 Pickens, T(homas) Boone, Jr.
b. 1930 Lefall, LaSalle Doheny, Jr.
b. 1930 Marisol (Escobar)
b. 1930 Milk, Harvey
b. 1934 Nero, Peter
b. 1934 Wills, Garry
b. 1936 Peck, M Scott
b. 1938 Benjamin, Richard
b. 1938 Converse, Frank
b. 1938 Strasberg, Susan Elizabeth
b. 1940 Sarrazin, Michael
b. 1940 Shaw, Bernard
b. 1941 Winfield, Paul Edward
b. 1942 Kaczynski, Theodore (John)
b. 1942 Parkins, Barbara
b. 1943 John, Tommy
b. 1943 Williams, Betty Smith
b. 1943 Williams, Elizabeth Betty Smyth
b. 1946 Best, George
b. 1950 Taupin, Bernie
b. 1970 Campbell, Naomi
d. 1540 Guicciardini, Francesco
d. 1802 Washington, Martha (Dandridge Custis)
d. 1826 Karamzin, Nikolai Mikhailovich
d. 1849 Edgeworth, Maria
d. 1859 Ferdinand, II
d. 1868 Plucker, Julius

d. 1885 Hugo, Victor Marie
d. 1898 Bellamy, Edward
d. 1903 Reichmann, Theodor
d. 1910 Renard, Jules
d. 1911 Miller, Elizabeth Smith
d. 1923 Lopez-Portillo y Rojas, Jose
d. 1932? Gregory, Isabella Augusta Persse, Lady
d. 1934 Wesson, David
d. 1938 Glackens, William James
d. 1939 Toller, Ernst
d. 1943 Taft, Helen Herron
d. 1948 McKay, Claude
d. 1949 Forrestal, James Vincent
d. 1949 Pfitzner, Hans
d. 1954 Bender, Chief
d. 1955 Gallagher, Richard
d. 1965 Cooke, Samuel
d. 1967 Hughes, Langston
d. 1970 Krutch, Joseph Wood
d. 1972 Day-Lewis, Cecil
d. 1972 Rutherford, Margaret
d. 1975 Grove, Lefty
d. 1976 Bonavena, Oscar
d. 1976 Fitch, Aubrey
d. 1979 Jooss, Kurt
d. 1982 Sunay, Cevdet
d. 1984 Zaharias, George
d. 1986 Gabel, Martin
d. 1988 Almirante, Giorgio
d. 1989 Sears, Robert Richardson
d. 1990 Graziano, Rocky
d. 1992 David, Elizabeth
d. 1997 Davis, Lorenzo
d. 1997 Hershey, Alfred D(ay)
d. 1998 Derek, John

May 23
b. Fickett, Mary
b. 1707 Linnaeus, Carolus
b. 1718 Hunter, William
b. 1734 Mesmer, Franz Anton
b. 1753 Viotti, Giovanni Battista
b. 1790 Dumont d'Urville, Jules Sebastian Cesar
b. 1795 Barry, Charles, Sir
b. 1799 Hood, Thomas
b. 1810 Fuller, Margaret
b. 1820 Eads, James Buchanan

b. 1821 White, Richard Grant
b. 1824 Burnside, Ambrose Everett
b. 1840 Appleby, John Francis
b. 1844 Abdu'l-Baha
b. 1846 Mansfield, Arabella
b. 1848 Lilienthal, Otto
b. 1852 Chirol, Valentine, Sir
b. 1873 Baeck, Leo
b. 1875 Sloan, Alfred Pritchard, Jr.
b. 1883 Fairbanks, Douglas
b. 1886 Gleason, James
b. 1888 Wheat, Zack
b. 1889 Niekisch, Ernest
b. 1890 Marshall, Herbert
b. 1890 Robertson, Dennis Holme
b. 1891 Lagerkvist, Par Fabian
b. 1893 Bodenheim, Maxwell
b. 1898 Grivas, Georgios Theodoros
b. 1898 McHugh, Frank
b. 1903 O'Dell, Scott
b. 1905 Fleming, Donald M(ethuen)
b. 1906 Holman, Libby
b. 1908 Abramovitz, Max
b. 1908 Bardeen, John
b. 1910 Brown, Margaret Wise
b. 1910 Crothers, Scatman
b. 1910 Shaw, Artie
b. 1912 Francaix, Jean
b. 1912 Goring, Marius
b. 1912 Payne, John
b. 1914 Ward, Barbara Mary
b. 1917 Squires, James Radcliffe
b. 1918 Bate, Walter Jackson
b. 1919 Garrett, Betty
b. 1919 Kline, Franz Joseph
b. 1921 Blish, James Benjamin
b. 1921 Chukrai, Grigori
b. 1921 De Larrocha, Alicia
b. 1921 O'Connell, Helen
b. 1922 Conwell, Esther Marly
b. 1923 Larrocha, Alicia de
b. 1925 Lederberg, Joshua
b. 1926 Hernandez, Aileen Clark
b. 1928 Clooney, Rosemary
b. 1928 Davenport, Nigel

b. 1929 Chomsky, Marvin
b. 1929? Jacobsson, Ulla
b. 1930 Anuszkiewicz, Richard Joseph
b. 1930 Kelman, Charles David
b. 1931 Barrie, Barbara
b. 1933 Browning, John
b. 1933 Collins, Joan Henrietta
b. 1934 Moog, Robert A
b. 1935 Hodel, Donald P(aul)
b. 1936 Van Itallie, Jean-Claude
b. 1941 Davis, Rennie
b. 1941 Puryear, Martin
b. 1944 Newcombe, John
b. 1944 Schwary, Ronald L
b. 1946 Graham, David
b. 1949 Garcia Perez, Alan
b. 1950 Barr, William Pelham
b. 1951 Barad, Jill E(likann)
b. 1951 Karpov, Anatoly Yevgenyevich
b. 1952 Hagler, Marvelous Marvin
b. 1958 Carey, Drew
b. 1962 Duffy, Karen
b. 1973 Maxwell
d. 1498 Savonarola, Girolamo
d. 1701 Kidd, William, Captain
d. 1754? Wood, John the Elder
d. 1783 Otis, James
d. 1825 Weems, Mason Locke
d. 1836 Livingston, Edward
d. 1857 Cauchy, Augustin Louis
d. 1868 Carson, Kit
d. 1870 Lemon, Mark
d. 1873 Smet, Pierre Jean de
d. 1886 Ranke, Leopold von
d. 1900 Carpenter, Francis Bicknell
d. 1905 Livermore, Mary Ashton Rice
d. 1906 Ibsen, Henrik Johan
d. 1908 Coppee, Francois Edouard Joachim
d. 1923 Bradley, Henry
d. 1927 Huntington, Henry Edwards
d. 1934 Barrow, Clyde
d. 1934 Parker, Bonnie
d. 1937 Rockefeller, John D(avison)
d. 1941 Austin, Herbert

d. 1943 Aberhart, William
d. 1945 Himmler, Heinrich
d. 1947 Dupree, Minnie
d. 1949 Hansen, William Webster
d. 1960 Claude, Georges
d. 1961 Davis, Joan
d. 1963 Howard, Eddy
d. 1964 Henry, George William
d. 1965 Smith, David
d. 1966 Guggenheimer, Minnie
d. 1967 Niekisch, Ernest
d. 1967 Wilson, Lyle Campbell
d. 1969 McHugh, Jimmy
d. 1973 Allsop, Kenneth
d. 1975 Mabley, Moms
d. 1978 Colombo, Joseph Anthony
d. 1986 Hayden, Sterling Relyea Walter
d. 1988 Schoenbrun, David
d. 1991 Kempff, (Wilhelm) Walter Friedrich
d. 1991 Markle, Fletcher
d. 1992 Falcone, Giovanni
d. 1994 Pass, Joe

May 24
b. 1544 Gilbert, William
b. 1616 Maitland, John
b. 1693 Donner, Georg Raphael
b. 1743 Marat, Jean Paul
b. 1793 Hitchcock, Edward
b. 1816 Leutze, Emanuel
b. 1819 Victoria, Queen
b. 1843 Blaikie, William
b. 1849 Munroe, Charles Edward
b. 1850 Grady, Henry Woodfin
b. 1852 Cunninghame-Graham, Robert Bontine
b. 1854 Mansfield, Richard
b. 1863 Barnard, George Grey
b. 1870 Cardozo, Benjamin Nathan
b. 1870 Smuts, Jan Christian
b. 1878 Fosdick, Harry Emerson
b. 1878 Gilbreth, Lillian Moller
b. 1882 Oppenheim, James
b. 1883 Maxwell, Elsa
b. 1884 Hull, Clark Leonard

b. 1884 Odum, Howard
  Washington
b. 1886 Paray, Paul
b. 1887 Wolff, Mary
  Evaline
b. 1891 Albright,
  William Foxwell
b. 1892 Lewis,
  Elizabeth Foreman
b. 1895 Newhouse,
  Samuel Irving
b. 1898 Taussig, Helen
  Brooke
b. 1899 Lenglen,
  Suzanne
b. 1899 Michaux, Henri
b. 1899 Thorp, Willard
  Long
b. 1901 Conacher,
  Lionel Pretoria
b. 1901 Haley, William
  John, Sir
b. 1902 Chapman,
  Gilbert Whipple
b. 1905 Dihigo, Martin
b. 1905 McCardell,
  Claire
b. 1905 Sholokhov,
  Mikhail
  Aleksandrovich
b. 1906 Vishnevsky,
  Alexandr
  Alekandrovich
b. 1907 Jones, Gwynn
b. 1909 Barrow, Clyde
b. 1909 Blaiberg, Philip
b. 1909 Mills, Wilbur
  Daigh
b. 1911 Ne Win, U
b. 1912 Anthony,
  Joseph
b. 1913 Chaudhuri,
  Haridas
b. 1914 Donovan,
  Hedley Williams
b. 1914 Palmer, Lilli
b. 1918 Brennan, Peter
  J(oseph)
b. 1918 Young,
  Coleman A(lexander)
b. 1920 Kalmanoff,
  Martin
b. 1920 Valdengo,
  Giuseppe
b. 1922 McKenna,
  Siobhan
b. 1925 Epstein, Alvin
b. 1925 Zetterling, Mai
  (Elisabeth)
b. 1927 Kelly, John
  Brenden, Jr.
b. 1928 Caras, Roger
  Andrew
b. 1928 Trevor, William
b. 1930 Meselson,
  Matthew Stanley
b. 1932 Malbin, Elaine
b. 1932 Wesker, Arnold
b. 1934 Byrne, Jane
  Margaret Burke
b. 1935 Mora, Jim
b. 1938 Chong, Tommy
b. 1940 Brodsky, Joseph
  (Alexandrovich)

b. 1940 Futrell, Mary
  Alice Franklin
  Hatwood
b. 1941 Dylan, Bob
b. 1943 Burghoff, Gary
b. 1944 Oz, Frank
b. 1945 Presley,
  Priscilla Ann
  Beaulieu
b. 1946 Roosevelt,
  Anna C(urtenius)
b. 1946 Szewinska,
  Irena Kirszenstein
b. 1949 Wintle, Justin
  Beecham
b. 1955 Cash, Roseanne
b. 1959 Lindbergh,
  Pelle (Per-Eric)
b. 1963 Dumars, Joe, III
d. 1089 Lanfranc
d. 1543 Copernicus,
  Nicolaus
d. 1627 Gongora y
  Argote, Luis de
d. 1724 Harley, Robert,
  1st Earl of Oxford
  and Earl Mortimer
d. 1792 Rodney, George
  Brydges, Baron
d. 1831 Peale, James
d. 1833 Randolph, John
d. 1876 Kingsley, Henry
d. 1879 Garrison,
  William Lloyd
d. 1889 Bridgman,
  Laura Dewey
d. 1895 McCulloch,
  Hugh
d. 1924 Lindbergh,
  Charles Augustus
d. 1932 McMaster, John
  Bach
d. 1934 Whitlock,
  Brand
d. 1936 Muzio, Claudia
d. 1944 Wright, Harold
  Bell
d. 1950 Wavell,
  Archibald Percival
  Wavell, Earl
d. 1952 Oursler,
  (Charles) Fulton
d. 1956 Kibbee, Guy
d. 1959 Dulles, John
  Foster
d. 1960 Yen Hsi-shan
d. 1963 James, Elmore
d. 1964 Hazeltine,
  (Louis) Alan
d. 1966 Barnes, Jim
d. 1969 Green, Mitzi
d. 1970 Davison, Frank
  Dalby
d. 1971 Dodd, Thomas
  Joseph
d. 1974 Atwood, Angela
d. 1974 DeFreeze,
  Donald David
d. 1974 Ellington, Duke
d. 1974 Perry, Nancy
  Ling
d. 1974 Soltysik,
  Patricia Michelle
d. 1974 Wolfe, Willie
d. 1975 Lincoln, George
  A

d. 1980 Gaunt, William
d. 1981 Jessel, George
  Albert
d. 1981 Lubalin,
  Herbert Frederick
d. 1981 Roldos
  Aguilera, Jamie
d. 1986 Canutt, Yakima
d. 1986 Rubloff, Arthur
d. 1987 Gingold,
  Hermione Ferdinanda
d. 1989 McNellis,
  Maggi
d. 1992 Stevens,
  Edmund William
d. 1994 Wain, John
  Barrington
d. 1995 Wilson, (James)
  Harold, Sir
d. 1996 Druckman,
  Jacob (Raphael)
d. 1996 Mitchell, Joseph
d. 1997 Mulhare,
  Edward

May 25
b. 1616 Dolci, Carlo
b. 1803 Emerson, Ralph
  Waldo
b. 1825 Wesson, Daniel
  Baird
b. 1847 Dowie, John
  Alexander
b. 1849 Bethune,
  Thomas Greene
b. 1855 Pinero, Arthur
  Wing, Sir
b, 1860 Cattell, James
  McKeen
b. 1865 Mott, John
  Raleigh
b. 1865 Zeeman, Pieter
b. 1866 Schultze, Carl
  Emil
b. 1878 Robinson, Bill
b. 1879 Beaverbrook,
  William Maxwell
  Aitken, Baron
b. 1881 Bartok, Bela
b. 1884 Duranty, Walter
b. 1886 Murray, Philip
b. 1887 Pio da
  Pietrelcina, Francesco
  Forgione, Father
b. 1889 Sikorsky, Igor
  Ivanovich
b. 1891 Winterich, John
  Tracy
b. 1892 Tito
b. 1898 Cerf, Bennett
  Alfred
b. 1898 Tunney, Gene
b. 1899 Artzybasheff,
  Boris Mikhailovich
b. 1903 Nu Thakin
b. 1905 Harsch, Joseph
  Close
b. 1905 Livingston,
  M(ilton) Stanley
b. 1905 Wesley,
  Dorothy Porter
b. 1906 Greenaway,
  Emerson
b. 1907 Nu, U
b. 1908 Roethke,
  Theodore (Huebner)
b. 1911 Barnet, Will

b. 1913 Grace, J(oseph)
  Peter, Jr.
b. 1913 Maclean,
  Donald Duart
b. 1916 Simms, Ginny
b. 1917 Cochran, Steve
b. 1917 Cooper, Joseph
  D
b. 1917 Hesburgh,
  Theodore Martin
b. 1918 Akins, Claude
b. 1921 David, Hal
b. 1921 Steinberger,
  Jack
b. 1922 Berlinguer,
  Enrico
b. 1923 Weitz, John
b. 1925 Crain, Jeanne
b. 1926 Davis, Miles
  Dewey, III
b. 1926 Kallen, Kitty
b. 1926 Sharman, Bill
b. 1927 Ludlum, Robert
b. 1928 Lawrence, Mary
  Wells
b. 1929 Ruder, David
  Sturtevant
b. 1929 Sills, Beverly
b. 1932 Bowen, Roger
b. 1932 Dunne, John
  Gregory
b. 1932 Jones, KC
b. 1933 Panday, Basdeo
b. 1934 Nessen, Ron(ald
  Harold)
b. 1934 Samrin, Heng
b. 1936 Hall, Tom T
b. 1936 Lewis, David
  Levering
b. 1938 Carver,
  Raymond Clevie, Jr.
b. 1938 Thomas, Joyce
  Carol
b. 1939 Carter, Dixie
b. 1939 McKellen, Ian
  (Murray), Sir
b. 1943 Uggams, Leslie
  (Marian Crayne)
b. 1946 Ginsburg,
  Douglas Howard
b. 1946 Hayes, James
  C.
b. 1946 Salhany, Lucie
b. 1947 Colter, Jessie
b. 1947 Valentine,
  Karen
b. 1949 Kincaid,
  Jamaica
b. 1952 Smith, Gordon
  H.
b. 1955 Sellecca,
  Connie
b. 1956 Lynch, Kevin
b. 1965 Jammeh, Yahya
  A(bdulaziz) J(emus)
  J.
b. 1969 Heche, Ann
d. 1085 Gregory, VII
d. 1681 Calderon de la
  Barca, Pedro
d. 1693 La Fayette,
  Comtesse de
d. 1805 Paley, William
d. 1812 Malone,
  Edmund
d. 1867 Castilla, Ramon

d. 1883 Laboulaye, Edouard Rose
d. 1899 Bonheur, Rosa
d. 1917 DeReszke, Edouard
d. 1919 Walker, C. J., Madame
d. 1919 Walker, Sarah Breedlove McWilliams
d. 1924 Popova, Liubov Sergeevna
d. 1934 Holst, Gustav Theodore
d. 1937 Tanner, Henry Ossawa
d. 1939 Duveen, Joseph, Sir
d. 1939 Dyson, Frank Watson, Sir
d. 1942 Feuermann, Emanuel
d. 1946 Hill, Patty Smith
d. 1946 Rhys, Ernest Percival
d. 1954 Capa, Robert
d. 1963 Dryfoos, Orvil Eugene
d. 1965 Grew, Joseph Clark
d. 1971 Conniff, Frank
d. 1974 Crisp, Donald
d. 1979 Spenkelink, John Arthur
d. 1981 Ponselle, Rosa
d. 1983 Idris I
d. 1985 Hecht, Harold
d. 1985 Nathan, Robert
d. 1987 Harrison, William Kelly, Jr.
d. 1988 Hamilton, Hamish
d. 1988 Shimkin, Leon
d. 1990 Tayback, Vic
d. 1991 Johansen, Gunnar
d. 1992 Thompson, Marshall
d. 1993 Coxe, Louis Osborne
d. 1993 Seymour, Dan
d. 1997 Hebert, Jay
d. 1999 Brooke, Hillary

May 26
b. 673 Bede the Venerable, Saint
b. 1478 Clement VII
b. 1623 Petty, William, Sir
b. 1650 Marlborough, John Churchill, Duke
b. 1667 De Moivre, Abraham
b. 1689 Montagu, Mary Wortley, Lady
b. 1700 Zinzendorf, Nikolaus Ludwig von, Count
b. 1764 Livingston, Edward
b. 1822 Goncourt, Edmond Louis Antoine Huot de
b. 1833 Godwin, Edward William

b. 1837 Roebling, Washington Augustus
b. 1850 Lopez-Portillo y Rojas, Jose
b. 1853 Hardin, John Wesley
b. 1865 Chambers, Robert W
b. 1867 Mary
b. 1872 Urban, Joseph Maria
b. 1876 Root, Jack
b. 1876 Yerkes, Robert Mearns
b. 1877 Araki Sadao
b. 1884 Winninger, Charles
b. 1885 DeCuevas, Marquis
b. 1886 Jolson, Al
b. 1887 Bacon, Leonard
b. 1890 Croft, Arthur C
b. 1893 Goossens, Eugene, Sir
b. 1894 Lukas, Paul
b. 1895 Baron, Salo Wittmayer
b. 1895 Henderson, Leon
b. 1895 Hull, John Edwin
b. 1895 Lange, Dorothea Nutzhorn
b. 1896 Munson, Gorham B(ert)
b. 1897 Talmadge, Norma
b. 1899 Douglas, Aaron
b. 1904 O'Konski, Alvin E(dward)
b. 1905 Guffey, Burnett
b. 1905 Uris, Harold David
b. 1907 Wayne, John
b. 1908 Morley, Robert
b. 1909 Anderson, Eugenie M(oore)
b. 1909 Busby, Matthew, Sir
b. 1909 Gucci, Aldo
b. 1910 Lopez Mateos, Adolfo
b. 1910 Rockefeller, Laurance Spelman
b. 1911 Alexander, Ben
b. 1912 Ephron, Henry
b. 1912 Kadar, Janos
b. 1913 Cushing, Peter
b. 1914 Baker, Shorty
b. 1914 Elman, Ziggy
b. 1916 Hardin, Louis Thomas
b. 1917 Singer, Jane Sherrod
b. 1919 Silverheels, Jay
b. 1920 Lee, Peggy
b. 1923 Arness, James
b. 1926 McCowen, Alec
b. 1927 Bergerac, Jacques
b. 1928 Kevorkian, Jack
b. 1931 Delblanc, Sven
b. 1931 Frey, Jim
b. 1932 Altobelli, Joe
b. 1937 Murphy, Jack R

b. 1938 Bolcom, William Elden
b. 1939 Musburger, Brent Woody
b. 1939 Stratas, Teresa
b. 1940 Bikoff, James L
b. 1943 Helm, Levon
b. 1944 Allen, Verden
b. 1947 Evans, Darrell Wayne
b. 1948 Nicks, Stevie
b. 1949 Grier, Pam(ela Suzette)
b. 1949 Thomas, Philip Michael
b. 1949 Williams, Hank, Jr.
b. 1951 Ride, Sally K
b. 1952 McMillen, Thomas
b. 1953 LeBoutillier, John
b. 1954? Devine, Michael
b. 1955 Walker, Wesley Darcel
b. 1962 Francis, Genie
b. 1964 Kravitz, Lenny
b. 1966 Bonham Carter, Helena
d. 604 Augustine of Canterbury, Saint
d. 1595 Neri, Philip
d. 1703 Pepys, Samuel
d. 1786 Scheele, Karl Wilhelm
d. 1848 Belinsky, Vissarion Grigoryevich
d. 1876 Palacky, Frantisek
d. 1883 Abd el-Kadir
d. 1888 Sobrero, Ascanio
d. 1903 LaFlesche Tibbles, Susette
d. 1907 Keckley, Elizabeth Hobbs
d. 1907 McKinley, Ida Saxton
d. 1908 Ahmad, Mirza Ghulam Hazat
d. 1914 Riis, Jacob August
d. 1933 Rodgers, Jimmie
d. 1936 Black, Winifred Sweet
d. 1938 Abel, John Jacob
d. 1939 Mayo, Charles Horace
d. 1942 Brinkley, John Romulus
d. 1943 Ford, Edsel Bryant
d. 1946 Patterson, Joseph Medill
d. 1951 Ellsworth, Lincoln
d. 1953 Spalding, Albert
d. 1954 Conacher, Lionel Pretoria
d. 1956 Simmons, Al(oysius Harry)
d. 1957 Lawson, Robert

d. 1959 Walsh, Ed(ward Augustine)
d. 1962 Gibson, Wilfred Wilson
d. 1973 Higginbotham, Jack
d. 1973 Lipchitz, Jacques
d. 1974 Alsop, Stewart Johonnot Oliver
d. 1974 Gordon, Kitty
d. 1976 Heidegger, Martin
d. 1978 Icaza (Coronel), Jorge
d. 1978 Karsavina, Tamara (Platonova)
d. 1979 Brent, George
d. 1981 Wortman, Sterling
d. 1982 Larsen-Todsen, Nanny
d. 1984 Tucker, Mary Bradham
d. 1986 Bowles, Chester Bliss
d. 1989 Keogh, Eugene James
d. 1991 Eyen, Tom
d. 1993 Priestly, Jack
d. 1994 Ball, George W(ildman)
d. 1995 Freleng, Friz
d. 1997 Cunningham, William T(homas)
d. 1999 Sacher, Paul
d. 2000 Taylor, Samuel (Albert)

May 27
b. 1265 Dante Alighieri
b. 1332 Ibn Khaldun
b. 1794 Vanderbilt, Cornelius
b. 1799 Halevy, Jacques Francois Fromental Elie
b. 1815 Parkes, Henry, Sir
b. 1818 Bloomer, Amelia Jenks
b. 1819 Howe, Julia Ward
b. 1835 Adams, Charles Francis, Jr.
b. 1836 Gould, Jay
b. 1837 Hickok, Wild Bill
b. 1863 Schalk, Franz
b. 1867 Bennett, Arnold
b. 1871 Rouault, Georges
b. 1878 Duncan, Isadora
b. 1880 DuPont, Henry Francis
b. 1880 Grew, Joseph Clark
b. 1884 Brod, Max
b. 1890 Harsh, Vivian Gordon
b. 1892 Crosthwait, David Nelson, Jr.
b. 1894 Celine, Louis-Ferdinand
b. 1894 Destouches, Louis-Ferdinand

b. 1894 Hammett, Dashiell
b. 1897 Cockcroft, John Douglas, Sir
b. 1901 Godowsky, Leopold, Jr.
b. 1902 Marshall, Peter
b. 1903 Kiesling, Walt(er)
b. 1905 Corbett, Young, III
b. 1907 Carson, Rachel (Louise)
b. 1908 Rome, Harold J(acob)
b. 1909 Hansen, William Webster
b. 1911 Hirschfelder, Joseph Oakland
b. 1911 Humphrey, Hubert Horatio, Jr.
b. 1911 Kollek, Teddy
b. 1911 Price, Vincent
b. 1912 Cheever, John
b. 1912 Snead, Sam(uel Jackson)
b. 1915 Wouk, Herman
b. 1918 Nakasone, Yasuhiro
b. 1918 Sheehan, Joseph Green
b. 1921 Chessman, Caryl Whittier
b. 1922 Lee, Christopher Frank Carandini
b. 1923 Kissinger, Henry Alfred
b. 1923 Redstone, Sumner (Murray)
b. 1924 Lusinchi, Jaime
b. 1925 Hillerman, Tony
b. 1928 Musgrave, Thea
b. 1930 Barth, John (Simmons)
b. 1930 Sessions, William Steele
b. 1931 Price, Kenny
b. 1934 Ellison, Harlan Jay
b. 1934 Hess, Richard
b. 1934 Thomas, Franklin Augustine
b. 1935 Lewis, Ramsey Emanuel, Jr.
b. 1935 Meriwether, Lee
b. 1936 Edwards, Helen T(hom)
b. 1936 Gossett, Louis, Jr.
b. 1936 Green, Richard R(eginald)
b. 1939 Sigmund, Barbara Boggs
b. 1939 Williams, Don
b. 1940 Morris, Edmund
b. 1941 Carr, Allan
b. 1941 Ortiz, Simon
b. 1943 Weitz, Bruce Peter
b. 1944 Dodd, Christopher John
b. 1950 Bridgewater, Dee Dee

b. 1954 Thompson, Tazewell (Alfred)
b. 1958 Williams, Wayne Bertram
b. 1963 Dean, Laura
b. 1965 Bridges, Todd
b. 1965 Cash, Pat(rick)
b. 1968 Thomas, Frank
d. 1508 Sforza, Ludovico
d. 1525 Muntzer, Thomas
d. 1564 Calvin, John
d. 1610 Ravaillac, Francois
d. 1676 Gerhardt, Paul(us)
d. 1705 Wigglesworth, Michael
d. 1831 Smith, Jedediah Strong
d. 1840 Paganini, Niccolo
d. 1864 Giddings, Joshua Reed
d. 1867 Bulfinch, Thomas
d. 1908 Posey, Alexander Lawrence
d. 1914 Swan, Joseph Wilson, Sir
d. 1916 Gallieni, Joseph-Simon
d. 1924 Herbert, Victor
d. 1930 Ferrer, Gabriel (Francisco Victor) Miro
d. 1937 Ives, Frederic Eugene
d. 1942 Ch'en Tu-hsiu
d. 1944 Eboue, Adolphe Felix Sylvestre
d. 1947 Carlson, Evans Fordyce
d. 1949 Ripley, Robert Leroy
d. 1953 Burkett, Jesse Cail
d. 1955 Ascari, Alberto
d. 1960 Flagg, James Montgomery
d. 1963 Ribeiro, Aquilino Gomez
d. 1964 Collins, Ted
d. 1964 Nehru, Jawaharlal
d. 1967 Edinger, Tilly
d. 1969 Hunter, Jeffrey
d. 1970 Gimbel, Richard
d. 1971 Rafferty, Chips
d. 1974 Biossat, Bruce
d. 1974 Wiese, Kurt
d. 1976 McDevitt, Ruth
d. 1976 Teyte, Maggie, Dame
d. 1977 Bliven, Bruce
d. 1981 Wheeler, Roger Milton
d. 1982 McCabe, Thomas Bayard
d. 1986 Wrightsman, Charles Bierer
d. 1987 Eurich, Alvin C(hristian)

d. 1987 Northrop, John Howard
d. 1988 Friebus, Florida
d. 1988 Oliver, Sy
d. 1988 Ruska, Ernst
d. 1991 Dodd, Ed(ward) Benton
d. 1999 Adams, Alice
d. 2000 Richard, Maurice

May 28
b. 1660 George I
b. 1738 Guillotin, Joseph Ignace
b. 1759 Pitt, William, the Younger
b. 1779 Moore, Thomas
b. 1807 Agassiz, Louis
b. 1818 Beauregard, Pierre Gustav Toutant de
b. 1826 Brown, Benjamin Gratz
b. 1837 Pastor, Tony
b. 1850 Maitland, Frederic William
b. 1853 Larsson, Carl Olof
b. 1857 Hilliard, Robert Cochran
b. 1859 Janet, Pierre Marie Felix
b. 1871 Daly, Thomas Augustine
b. 1874 Cockrell, Ewing
b. 1877 Deeping, (George) Warwick
b. 1881 Bea, Augustinus
b. 1882 Hopwood, Avery
b. 1883 Zandonai, Riccardo
b. 1884 Benes, Eduard
b. 1886 Mayer, Arthur Loeb
b. 1888 Lambert, Piggy
b. 1888 Lambert, Ward L
b. 1888 Thorpe, Jim
b. 1896 Giles, Warren Crandall
b. 1897 Bolitho, Henry Hector
b. 1900 Abel, Taffy
b. 1900 Ladnier, Tommy
b. 1900 Little, Little Jack
b. 1905 Grucci, Felix
b. 1905 Kuter, Laurence S(herman)
b. 1906 Hills, Lee
b. 1906 Regan, Phil
b. 1907 Gilmore, Eddy Lanier King
b. 1908 Fleming, Ian Lancaster
b. 1909 Horner, Red
b. 1910 Kempson, Rachel
b. 1910 Takhtadzhian, Armen Leonovich
b. 1910 Walker, T-Bone
b. 1911 Churchill, Randolph Frederick Edward Spencer

b. 1912 White, Patrick Victor Martindale
b. 1915 McKay, Scott
b. 1916 Percy, Walker
b. 1917 Commoner, Barry
b. 1918 Birch, John
b. 1918 Wayne, Johnny
b. 1919 Swenson, May
b. 1922 Craveirinha, Jose
b. 1923 Ligeti, Gyorgy (Sandor)
b. 1925 Ecevit, Bulent
b. 1925 Fischer-Dieskau, Dietrich
b. 1925 Vickers, Martha
b. 1927 Levy, Allan
b. 1928 Stein, Horst
b. 1930 Drake, Frank Donald
b. 1930 Seaga, Edward Phillip George
b. 1931 Baker, Carroll
b. 1931 Birmingham, Stephen
b. 1931 Winkler, Irwin
b. 1933 Karlen, John
b. 1934 Dionne, Emilie
b. 1934 Dionne, Marie
b. 1934 Dionne Sisters
b. 1935 Brooks, Ronald E.
b. 1935 Rogers, Darryl D
b. 1936 Chappell, Fred (Davis)
b. 1936 Shabazz, Betty
b. 1938 West, Jerry
b. 1940 Binchy, Maeve
b. 1941 Howland, Beth
b. 1942 Prusiner, Stanley (Ben)
b. 1944 Giuliani, Rudolph William
b. 1944 Knight, Gladys Maria
b. 1945 Fogerty, John
b. 1945 Vera, Billy
b. 1947 Johnston, Lynn Beverley
b. 1947 Locke, Sondra
b. 1954 Egorov, Youri
b. 1955 Howe, Mark Steven
b. 1957 Gibson, Kirk Harold
b. 1962? Gift, Roland
d. 1787 Mozart, Leopold
d. 1793 Busching, Anton Friedrich
d. 1805 Boccherini, Luigi
d. 1843 Webster, Noah
d. 1849 Bronte, Anne
d. 1878 Russell, John, Lord
d. 1886 Bartlett, John Russell
d. 1886 Ostrovsky, Aleksandr Nikolaevich
d. 1890 Nessler, Victor E

d. 1900 Grove, George, Sir
d. 1910 Balakirev, Mili Alekseyevich
d. 1910 Koch, Robert
d. 1933 Loeb, James Morris
d. 1937 Adler, Alfred
d. 1940 Connolly, Walter
d. 1946 Glass, Carter
d. 1960 Zucco, George
d. 1968 Dongen, Kees van
d. 1971 Murphy, Audie
d. 1972 Edward VIII
d. 1972 Irvin, Rea
d. 1973 Schmidt-Isserstedt, Hans
d. 1975 Charles, Ezzard
d. 1977 Ba Maw
d. 1977 Cortez, Ricardo
d. 1979 Abercrombie, Michael
d. 1979 Little, Lou(is)
d. 1981 Williams, Mary Lou
d. 1981 Wyszynski, Stefan
d. 1983 Corning, Erastus, III
d. 1986 Aranason, H Harvard
d. 1986 Maclaughlin, Don
d. 1986 Tuttle, Lurene
d. 1987 Ludlam, Charles
d. 1993 Jones, Roger W(arren)
d. 1994 Boros, Julius (Nicholas)
d. 1994 Flood, Daniel J(ohn)
d. 1994 Kahn, E(ly) J(acques), Jr.
d. 1994 Praeger, Frederick A(mos)
d. 1995 Kronstam, Henning
d. 1995 Muir, Jean
d. 1995 Welsh, Matthew E(mpson)
d. 1997 Sengstacke, John H(erman Henry)
d. 1998 Hartman, Phil
d. 2000 Fryer, Robert

May 29
b. 1630 Charles II
b. 1736 Henry, Patrick
b. 1826 Butterick, Ebenezer
b. 1828 Massey, Gerald
b. 1851 Bourgeois, Leon-Victor Auguste
b. 1855 Bruce, David, Sir
b. 1860 Albeniz, Isaac Manuel Francisco
b. 1874 Chesterton, G(ilbert) K(eith)
b. 1880 Spengler, Oswald
b. 1883 Dafoe, Allan Roy

b. 1886 Khodasevich, Vladislav
b. 1887 Thurstone, Louis Leon
b. 1889 Blackwell, Basil Henry, Sir
b. 1892 Faust, Frederick Schiller
b. 1894 VonSternberg, Josef
b. 1895 Grant, Jane
b. 1896 Youngdahl, Luther Wallace
b. 1897 Korngold, Erich Wolfgang
b. 1898 Lillie, Beatrice Gladys
b. 1898 Rothermere, Esmond Cecil Harmsworth, Viscount
b. 1903 Hope, Bob
b. 1904 Toland, Gregg
b. 1906 White, T(erence) H(anbury)
b. 1907 Molson, Hartland de Montarville
b. 1912 Johnson, Pamela Hansford
b. 1912 Schweitzer, Pierre-Paul
b. 1912 Wu, Chien Shiung
b. 1913 Zale, Tony
b. 1914 Keach, Stacy, Sr.
b. 1915 Buketoff, Igor
b. 1915 Munchinger, Karl
b. 1917 Kennedy, John F(itzgerald)
b. 1918 Corona, Bert
b. 1918 Shriner, Herb
b. 1922 Xenakis, Iannis
b. 1927 Toms, Carl
b. 1928 Rohatyn, Felix George
b. 1928 Sinner, George Albert
b. 1931 Gordon, Ellen Rubin
b. 1932 Ehrlich, Paul
b. 1932 Guerin, Richard V
b. 1934 Marino, Eugene Antonio
b. 1934 Vander Zalm, William
b. 1935 Brink, Andre Philippus
b. 1937 Tung Chee-hwa
b. 1938 Vincent, Fay
b. 1939 Unser, Al, Sr.
b. 1944 Berger, Helmut
b. 1944 Bishop, Maurice Rupert
b. 1947 Geary, Anthony
b. 1948 Raimondi, John
b. 1950 Dixon, Melvin
b. 1951 Hamer, Dean H.
b. 1952 Cooney, Rory
b. 1953 Elfman, Danny
b. 1955 Hinckley, John Warnock, Jr.

b. 1961 Etheridge, Melissa
b. 1962 Davis, Eric Keith
b. 1963 Whelchel, Lisa
d. 1453 Constantine XI Palaeologus
d. 1790 Putnam, Israel
d. 1814 Josephine
d. 1829 Davy, Humphrey, Sir
d. 1838 Milder-Hauptmann, Pauline Anna
d. 1866 Scott, Winfield
d. 1876 Diez, Friedrich Christian
d. 1877 Harper, Fletcher
d. 1877 Motley, John Lothrop
d. 1880 Feuerbach, Paul Johann Anselm von
d. 1884 Frere, Henry Bartle Edward
d. 1892 Baha'u'llah
d. 1911 Gilbert, William S(chwenck), Sir
d. 1914 Irving, Laurence Sidney
d. 1916 Hill, James Jerome
d. 1921 Thayer, Abbott Handerson
d. 1924 Cambon, Pierre Paul
d. 1935 Suk, Josef
d. 1940 Anderson, Mary Antoinette
d. 1942 Barrymore, John
d. 1948 Whitty, May, Dame
d. 1950 Stoopnagle, Lemuel Q, Colonel
d. 1951 Brice, Fanny
d. 1951 Foerster, Josef Bohuslav
d. 1953 Dean, Man Mountain
d. 1953 Russell, Morgan
d. 1954 McCormick, Anne (Elizabeth) O'Hare
d. 1957 Whale, James
d. 1958 Jimenez, Juan Ramon
d. 1960 Pasternak, Boris Leonidovich
d. 1961 Gesell, Arnold
d. 1967 Pabst, Georg Wilhelm
d. 1970 Gunther, John
d. 1970 Hesse, Eva
d. 1972 Bernhard, Lucian
d. 1974 Ochs, Adolph Shelby, II
d. 1979 Pickford, Mary
d. 1979 Wood, John Howland, Jr.
d. 1980 Jaabari, Mohammed Ali, Sheik
d. 1981 Sun Yat-Sen, Chingling Soong, Madame

d. 1982 Schneider, Romy
d. 1984 Motley, Arthur Harrison
d. 1985 Plomley, Roy
d. 1986 Martin, John C
d. 1988 Stevens, Siaka Probyn
d. 1989 Homans, George Caspar
d. 1991 Browne, Coral Edith
d. 1993 Bernstein, Sid(ney Ralph)
d. 1993 Conn, Billy
d. 1994 Honecker, Erich
d. 1994 Murphy, W(illiam) B(everly)
d. 1995 Smith, Margaret (Madeline) Chase
d. 1996 Toumanova, Tamara
d. 1997 Buckley, Jeff
d. 1997 Fenneman, George
d. 1998 Goldwater, Barry M(orris)

May 30
b. 1201 Thibaut, IV
b. 1672 Peter the Great
b. 1794 Moscheles, Ignaz
b. 1810 Stephens, Ann Sophia
b. 1811 Belinsky, Vissarion Grigoryevich
b. 1814 Bakunin, Mikhail Aleksandrovich
b. 1835 Austin, Alfred
b. 1857 Peabody, Endicott
b. 1867 Davis, Arthur Vining
b. 1868 Dillingham, Charles Bancroft
b. 1874 Peabody, Josephine Preston
b. 1875 Gentile, Giovanni
b. 1879 Bell, Vanessa
b. 1882 Lewisohn, Ludwig
b. 1886 Bourne, Randolph Silliman
b. 1886 Eustis, Dorothy Leib Harrison Wood
b. 1887 Archipenko, Alexander Porfirievich
b. 1888 Farley, James A(loysius)
b. 1890 Langer, Lawrence
b. 1891 Bernie, Ben
b. 1892 Amorsolo, Fernando
b. 1893 Raisa, Rosa
b. 1896 Hawks, Howard Winchester
b. 1898 Farrington, Elizabeth Pruett (Mary)
b. 1899 Thalberg, Irving Grant

b. 1900 Villanueva, Carlos Raul
b. 1901 Felsenstein, Walter
b. 1901 Skinner, Cornelia Otis
b. 1901 Trumbauer, Frank(ie)
b. 1902 Fetchit, Stepin
b. 1903 Baldwin, Billy
b. 1903 Conklin, Gladys Plemon
b. 1903 Cullen, Countee (Porter)
b. 1904 Zuckerman, Solly, Lord
b. 1908 Alfven, Hannes Olof Gosta
b. 1908 Blanc, Mel(vin Jerome)
b. 1909 Frank, Jerome David
b. 1909 Goodman, Benny
b. 1909 Gray, Gordon
b. 1910 Metcalfe, Ralph H
b. 1912 Axelrod, Julius
b. 1912 Griffith, Hugh Emrys
b. 1912 Stein, Joseph
b. 1912 Symons, Julian (Gustave)
b. 1913 Erwin, Pee Wee
b. 1915 Blair, Frank
b. 1915 Kelley, Larry
b. 1915 Lang, Daniel
b. 1915 Manulis, Martin
b. 1915 Wiesner, Jerome B(ert)
b. 1919 Barrientos Ortuno, Rene
b. 1920 London, George
b. 1922 Coit, Margaret Louise
b. 1923 Lydon, James
b. 1924 Powell, Maxine
b. 1927 Walker, Clint
b. 1928 Varda, Agnes
b. 1930 Janklow, Morton Lloyd
b. 1933 Perryman, Jill
b. 1934 Leonov, Alexei Arkhipovich
b. 1936 Dullea, Keir
b. 1939 Pollard, Michael J
b. 1940 Sayers, Gale Eugene
b. 1941 Calasso, Robert
b. 1944 MacRae, Meredith
b. 1946 Lightner, Candy
b. 1964 Wynonna
b. 1965 McBride, Bryant
d. 1431 Joan of Arc, Saint
d. 1531 Pedrarias
d. 1593 Marlowe, Christopher
d. 1640 Rubens, Peter Paul, Sir
d. 1670 Davenport, John
d. 1744 Pope, Alexander

d. 1770 Boucher, Francois
d. 1778 Voltaire
d. 1885 Jacobsen, Jens Peter
d. 1892 Rutherfurd, Lewis Morris
d. 1911 Bradley, Milton
d. 1912 Wright, Wilbur
d. 1916 Mosby, John Singleton
d. 1918 Plekhanov, Georgi Valentinovich
d. 1930 Nansen, Fridtjof
d. 1934 Togo, Heihachiro
d. 1936 Chaney, Norman
d. 1952 Lasker, Albert D(avis)
d. 1953 Wilson, Dooley
d. 1961 Trujillo (Molina), Rafael Leonidas
d. 1964 Szilard, Leo
d. 1967 Rains, Claude
d. 1969 Briscoe, Robert
d. 1971 DuPre, Marcel
d. 1972 Bates, Ted
d. 1975 Prefontaine, Steve Roland
d. 1976 Carey, Max George
d. 1976 Fuchida, Mitsuo
d. 1976 Ghezzi, Vic(tor)
d. 1977 Desmond, Paul Breitenfeld
d. 1979 Martin, Fletcher
d. 1983 Grubert, Carl Alfred
d. 1983 Gruenther, Alfred Maximillian
d. 1983 Guffey, Burnett
d. 1985 Jennings, Talbot
d. 1986 Ellis, Perry Edwin
d. 1986 Klopfer, Donald Simon
d. 1987 Carlson, Frank
d. 1987 Murphy, Turk
d. 1988 Raines, Ella
d. 1988 Volpi, Alfredo
d. 1989 Milanov, Zinka Kunc
d. 1989 Pepper, Claude Denson
d. 1992 Carstens, Karl Walter
d. 1993 Sun Ra
d. 1994 Benson, Ezra Taft
d. 1994 Onetti, Juan Carlos
d. 2000 Beneke, Tex
d. 2000 Casey, Robert P
d. 2000 Thomas, Bill

May 31
b. 1469 Manuel I
b. 1744 Edgeworth, Richard Lovell
b. 1750 Hardenberg, Karl August von
b. 1810 Seymour, Horatio
b. 1818 Andrew, John Albion

b. 1819 Whitman, Walt(er)
b. 1834 Burns, Anthony
b. 1838 Sidgwick, Henry
b. 1841 Rockefeller, William
b. 1857 Pius XI
b. 1866 Rebikov, Vladimir Ivanovich
b. 1871 Rusie, Amos Wilson
b. 1872 Abbot, C(harles) G(reeley)
b. 1872 Robinson, W Heath
b. 1883 Alda, Frances
b. 1884 Bottome, Phyllis
b. 1887 Leger, Alexis St. Leger
b. 1888 Holt, Jack
b. 1890 Townsend, William H(enry)
b. 1893 Coatsworth, Elizabeth Jane
b. 1894 Allen, Fred
b. 1895 Stewart, George Rippey
b. 1898 Peale, Norman Vincent
b. 1899 Leonov, Leonid Maximovich
b. 1903 Russell, Honey
b. 1905 Schneider, Herman
b. 1905 Thompson, Tiny
b. 1907 Alphand, Herve
b. 1908 Ameche, Don
b. 1908 Coates, Edith
b. 1909 Coulter, Art(hur Edmund)
b. 1909 Schmitt, Gladys
b. 1911 Allais, Maurice
b. 1912 Deller, Alfred George
b. 1912 Jackson, Henry Martin
b. 1914 Valtman, Edmund Siegfried
b. 1914 Williams, Jay
b. 1918 Quarterman, Lloyd Albert
b. 1919 Hartke, Vance
b. 1920 Williams, Edward Bennett
b. 1921 Valli, Alida
b. 1922 Elliott, Denholm Mitchell
b. 1923 Kelly, Ellsworth
b. 1923 Rainier III, Prince
b. 1924 Harris, Patricia Roberts
b. 1925 Beck, Julian
b. 1926 Kemeny, John G(eorge)
b. 1928 Lateiner, Jacob
b. 1930 Eastwood, Clint
b. 1931 Jones, Reverend Jim
b. 1931 Rossi, Aldo
b. 1931 Schrieffer, John Robert
b. 1932 Briggs, Fred

b. 1933 Sedelmaier, Joe
b. 1933 Verrett, Shirley Carter
b. 1935 Bolger, Jim
b. 1938 Yarrow, Peter
b. 1939 Waite, Terry
b. 1941 Paycheck, Johnny
b. 1943 Gless, Sharon
b. 1943 Namath, Joe
b. 1946 Fassbinder, Rainer Werner
b. 1948 Molina, Gloria
b. 1949 Bonham, John Henry
b. 1950 Berenger, Tom
b. 1950 Harrison, Gregory
b. 1952 Leary, Kathryn D.
b. 1957 Craig, Jim
b. 1963 Orban, Viktor
b. 1965 Shields, Brooke
b. 1967 Lofton, Kenny
d. 1594 Tintoretto
d. 1740 Frederick William I
d. 1799 Lemonnier, Pierre Charles
d. 1809 Haydn, Joseph
d. 1832 Galois, Evariste
d. 1837 Grimaldi, Joseph
d. 1847 Chalmers, Thomas
d. 1906 Davitt, Michael
d. 1908 Frechette, Louis-Honore
d. 1910 Blackwell, Elizabeth
d. 1934 Cody, Lew
d. 1953 Mildmay, Audrey
d. 1953 Tatlin, Vladimir Yevgrapovich
d. 1960 Funk, Walther
d. 1962 Eichmann, Adolf
d. 1963 Hamilton, Edith
d. 1967 Strayhorn, Billy
d. 1970 Sawchuk, Terry
d. 1970 Sheridan, Clare Consuelo
d. 1974 Davis, Adelle
d. 1976 Mitchell, Martha Elizabeth Beall
d. 1976 Monod, Jacques Lucien
d. 1977 Castle, William
d. 1977 Grauer, Ben(jamin Franklin)
d. 1978 Liebow, Averill A(braham)
d. 1978 Purtell, William Arthur
d. 1978 Wright, Lloyd
d. 1981 Pella, Giuseppe
d. 1981 Ward, Barbara Mary
d. 1981 Zia(ur) Rahman
d. 1983 Dempsey, Jack
d. 1985 Rebuffat, Gaston Louis Simon
d. 1986 Rainwater, James

d. 1989 Drinkwater,
Terry
d. 1989 Lattimore,
Owen
d. 1990 Downey,
Fairfax Davis
d. 1991 Wilson, Angus
d. 1992 Kane, Robert
Joseph
d. 1993 Tatum, Donn B
d. 1995 Elkin, Stanley
(Lawrence)
d. 1996 Leary, Timothy
(Francis)
d. 1997 Lafontant-
Mankarious, Jewel
(Stradford)
d. 1997 Monroe, Rose
Will
d. 1999 Pierce, Charles
d. 2000 Puente, Tito

JUNE

b. 1594 Poussin,
Nicolas
b. 1652? Dampier,
William
b. 1683 Young, Edward
b. 1829 Geronimo
b. 1854 Love, Nat
b. 1855 Kelly, Ned
b. 1879 Crofts, Freeman
Willis
b. 1892 Madden, Owen
Victor
b. 1898 Ferragamo,
Salvatore
b. 1898? Goetz, Delia
b. 1920 Adhikary, Man
Mohan
b. 1949 Rubin, Gayle
b. 1956 Hockenberry,
John (Charles)
b. 1957 Adams, Scott
d. 133 Gracchus,
Tiberius Sempronius
d. 1037 Avicenna
d. 1592 Cavendish,
Thomas
d. 1633 Brule, Etienne
d. 1637 Lucaris, Cyril
d. 1638 Minuit, Peter
d. 1697 Aubrey, John
d. 1848 Keokuk
d. 1954 Turing, Alan
(Mathison)
d. 1960 Pauker, Ana
d. 1977 VonBraun,
Wernher
d. 1988 Mendez,
Aparicio
d. 1995 Burke, Glenn
d. 1996 Hemingway,
Margaux

June 1
b. 1637 Marquette,
Jacques, Pere
b. 1771 Paer,
Ferdinando
b. 1780 Clausewitz,
Karl (Philipp
Gottlieb) von
b. 1796 Carnot, Nicolas
Leonard Sadi

b. 1801 Young,
Brigham
b. 1804 Glinka, Mikhail
Ivanovich
b. 1807 Floyd, John
Buchanan
b. 1809 Hoffmann,
Heinrich
b. 1816 Monk, Maria
b. 1831 Hood, John
Bell
b. 1833 Harlan, John
Marshall, I
b. 1849 Stanley, Francis
Edgar
b. 1849 Stanley, Freelan
O
b. 1855 Angle, Edward
Hartley
b. 1862 Patino, Simon
Iturri
b. 1869 Breitenstein,
Ted
b. 1878 Masefield, John
b. 1880 Lahey, Frank
Howard
b. 1881 Matzenauer,
Margaret
b. 1882 Drinkwater,
John
b. 1887 Brook, Clive
b. 1889 Daugherty,
James Henry
b. 1891 Onegin, Sigrid
b. 1892 Amanollah
Khan
b. 1893 Stanley, Barney
b. 1895 Dulles, Eleanor
Lansing
b. 1898 Picon, Molly
b. 1899 Janssen, Werner
b. 1901 Carr, William
G(eorge)
b. 1901 Day, Hap
b. 1901 Denny-Brown,
Derek Ernest
b. 1901 Sukarno,
Achmed
b. 1901 Van Druten,
John William
b. 1902 Lindtberg,
Leopold
b. 1903 Hardy, Porter,
Jr.
b. 1905 Newton, Robert
b. 1907 Hecht, Harold
b. 1907 Whittle, Frank,
Sir
b. 1909 Rowe, James
Henry, Jr.
b. 1910 Heatherton,
Ray(mond Joseph)
b. 1916 Aldrich, Ki
b. 1917 McNellis,
Maggi
b. 1918 Astor, Gavin
b. 1919 Whitehead,
Edwin C(arl)
b. 1921 Riddle, Nelson
b. 1922 Caulfield, Joan
b. 1922 Spencer,
William
b. 1924 Coffin, William
Sloan, Jr.
b. 1926 Burton, Phillip
b. 1926 Griffith, Andy

b. 1926 Monroe,
Marilyn
b. 1926 Schweiker,
Richard Schultz
b. 1928 Dobrovolsky,
Georgi Timofeyevich
b. 1929 Billington,
James H(adley)
b. 1930 Corley, Pat
b. 1930 Woodward,
Edward
b. 1932 Lasch,
Christopher
b. 1933 Ameche, Alan
Dante
b. 1934 Boone, Pat
b. 1935 Ike, Reverend
b. 1937 Freeman,
Morgan
b. 1937 McCullough,
Colleen
b. 1939 Dodson,
Howard, Jr.
b. 1939 Little, Cleavon
Jake
b. 1940 Auberjonois,
Rene Murat
b. 1941 Chance, Dean
b. 1941 DeWaart, Edo
b. 1942 Frohnmayer,
John Edward
b. 1942 Nagler, Eric
b. 1943 Goode, Richard
Stephen
b. 1944 Powell, Robert
b. 1945 Oldfield, Brian
b. 1945 VonStade,
Frederica
b. 1947 Wood, Ron(ald)
b. 1948 Sneva, Tom
b. 1949 Boothe, Powers
b. 1953 Berkowitz,
David
b. 1956 Hartman, Lisa
b. 1961 Coffey, Paul
(Douglas)
b. 1966 Tyson, Mike
b. 1970 Lalas, Alexi
b. 1974 Morissette,
Alanis
d. 1813 Lawrence,
James
d. 1815 Gillray, James
d. 1822 Hauy, Rene Just
d. 1823 Davout, Louis
Nicholas
d. 1826 Oberlin, Johann
Friedrich
d. 1832 Sumter, Thomas
d. 1841 Wilkie, David,
Sir
d. 1854 Judson, Emily
Chubbock
d. 1868 Buchanan,
James
d. 1872 Bennett, James
Gordon
d. 1873 Howe, Joseph
d. 1879 Shields, James
d. 1898 Keene, Thomas
Wallace
d. 1910 Haden, Francis
Seymour, Sir
d. 1912 Burnham,
Daniel H(udson)

d. 1925 Marshall,
Thomas Riley
d. 1927 Borden, Lizzie
Andrew
d. 1927 Bury, John
Bagnell
d. 1940 Loisy, Alfred
Firmin
d. 1940 Woodbridge,
Frederick James
Eugene
d. 1941 Berger, Hans
d. 1941 Dolly, Jenny
d. 1941 Walpole, Hugh
Seymour, Sir
d. 1946 Antonescu, Ion
d. 1946 Slezak, Leo
d. 1947 Enskog, David
d. 1951 Altamira Y
Crevea, Rafael
d. 1952 Dewey, John
d. 1956 Jones, Jesse
Holman
d. 1959 Rohmer, Sax
d. 1960 Patrick, Lester
B
d. 1963 Gougelman,
Pierre
d. 1965 Funk, Wilfred
John
d. 1965 Lambeau, Curly
d. 1967 Rudkin,
Margaret Fogarty
d. 1968 Bynner, Harold
Witter
d. 1968 Keller, Helen
Adams
d. 1969 LeTourneau,
Robert Gilmour
d. 1969 Tannenbaum,
Frank
d. 1970 Ungaretti,
Giuseppe
d. 1971 Niebuhr,
Reinhold
d. 1973 Firestone,
Harvey Samuel, Jr.
d. 1973 Greaza, Walter
N
d. 1973 Kornman, Mary
d. 1973 Parkhurst,
Helen
d. 1979 Forssmann,
Werner Theodor Otto
d. 1979 Mulhall, Jack
d. 1979 Partridge, Eric
Honeywood
d. 1980 Marquard, Rube
d. 1980 Nielsen, Arthur
Charles
d. 1981 Vinson, Carl
d. 1982 Mikkelsen,
Henning Dahl
d. 1985 Greene, Richard
d. 1985 Price, Gwilym
Alexander
d. 1987 Barrow, Errol
Walton
d. 1987 Karami, Rashid
Abdul Hamid
d. 1988 Hurkos, Peter
d. 1989 Lichine, Alexis
d. 1991 Ruffin, David
d. 1996 Reddy,
N(eelam) Sanjeeva

d. 1997 Eastlake,
William (Derry)
d. 1998 Stickney,
Dorothy
d. 1999 Cockerell,
Christopher (Sydney),
Sir

June 2

b. 1732 Washington,
Martha (Dandridge
Custis)
b. 1740 Sade, Marquis
(Donatien Alphonse
Francoise) de
b. 1743 Cagliostro,
Alessandro, Conte di
b. 1773 Randolph, John
b. 1800 Trist, Nicholas
Philip
b. 1816 Aguilar, Grace
b. 1834 Stolz, Teresa
b. 1835 Pius X
b. 1840 Hardy, Thomas
b. 1845 MacArthur,
Arthur
b. 1857 Elgar, Edward
William, Sir
b. 1857 Gjellerup, Karl
Adolf
b. 1861 Taft, Helen
Herron
b. 1863 Weingartner,
Felix
b. 1864 Robinson,
Wilbert
b. 1864 Webster,
Ben(jamin)
b. 1868 Hope, John
b. 1869 Foerster,
Friedrich Wilhelm
b. 1875 Mott, Charles
Stewart
b. 1880 Gowers, Ernest
Arthur, Sir
b. 1886 Whalen, Grover
(Michael) A(loysius)
b. 1890 Hopper, Hedda
b. 1891 Arnold,
Thurman Wesley
b. 1893 Martin, John
b. 1896 Gulbenkian,
Nubar Sarkis
b. 1897 Mueller,
Reuben Herbert
b. 1899 Teale, Edwin
Way
b. 1901 Andrews, Bert
b. 1902 Davis,
Frederick C(lyde)
b. 1904 Weissmuller,
Johnny
b. 1907 Lehmann, John
Frederick
b. 1907 West, Dorothy
b. 1908 Grauer,
Ben(jamin Franklin)
b. 1912 Berelson,
Bernard (Reuben)
b. 1913 Pym, Barbara
Mary Crampton
b. 1915 del Ray, Lester
(Ramon Alvarez)
b. 1920 Schramm,
Tex(as Edward)
b. 1920 Waldman, Max

b. 1921? Speight,
Johnny
b. 1922 Sifford, Charlie
b. 1924 DeMott,
Benjamin Haile
b. 1926 O'Shea, Milo
b. 1929 Barris, Chuck
b. 1930 Conrad,
Charles, Jr.
b. 1932 Gayle, Addison,
Jr.
b. 1937 Grooms, Red
b. 1937 Kellerman,
Sally Claire
b. 1937 Paul, Bob
b. 1938 Brownlow,
Kevin
b. 1939 Collier, Peter
b. 1939 Hamilton,
William
b. 1940 Constantine XII
b. 1941 Keach, Stacy,
Jr.
b. 1941 Nanne, Lou(is
Vincent)
b. 1941 Watts, Charlie
b. 1944? Haid, Charles
b. 1944 Hamlisch,
Marvin Frederick
b. 1944 Yepremian,
Garo
b. 1945 Long, Richard
b. 1947 Page, Clarence
b. 1947 Rudd, Mark
b. 1948 Innaurato,
Albert
b. 1948 Mathers, Jerry
b. 1949 Vogelstein, Bert
b. 1950 Gleason, Joanna
b. 1951 Chenault,
Kenneth I
b. 1951 Robinson, Larry
b. 1953 Canova, Diana
b. 1953 Stadler, Craig
Robert
b. 1953 West, Cornel
b. 1956 Guerrero, Pedro
b. 1966 Astley, Rick
b. 1971 Wyle, Noah
d. 1701 Scudery,
Madeleine de
d. 1832 Garcia, Manuel
del Popolo Vincente
d. 1841 Appert, Nicolas
d. 1853 Alaman, Lucas
d. 1882 Garibaldi,
Giuseppe
d. 1894 Dabney,
Virginius
d. 1900 Samory Toure
d. 1910 Petipa, Marius
d. 1913 Austin, Alfred
d. 1928 Fortune,
Timothy Thomas
d. 1928 Nordenskold,
Nils Otto Gustaf
d. 1930 Bolitho,
William
d. 1941 Gehrig, Lou
d. 1942 Berigan, Bunny
d. 1943 Dafoe, Allan
Roy
d. 1943 Howard, Leslie
d. 1943 Kinnick, Nile
d. 1943 Stevens, John
Frank

d. 1951 Alain
d. 1951 Erskine, John
d. 1956 Hersholt, Jean
d. 1961 DeWohl, Louis
d. 1961 Kaufman,
George S(imon)
d. 1962 Sackville-West,
Vita
d. 1967 Upjohn,
Lawrence Northcote
d. 1969 Gorcey, Leo
d. 1970 McLaren, Bruce
Leslie
d. 1974 Lunn, Arnold
Henry Moore, Sir
d. 1977 Boyd, Stephen
d. 1979 Hutton, Jim
d. 1984 Bell, Arthur
(Irving)
d. 1985 Brown, George
Alfred
d. 1987 Kaye, Sammy
d. 1987 Sampson, Will,
Jr.
d. 1987 Segovia, Andres
d. 1988 Hildreth,
Horace A(ugusta)
d. 1989 Prokosch,
Frederic
d. 1990 Harrison, Rex,
Sir
d. 1990 Mellinger,
Frederick
d. 1993 Mize, Johnny
d. 1993 Simon, Norton
Winfred
d. 1995 Rosenfeld,
Harry N(athan)
d. 1996 Garfield, Leon
d. 1996 Lorengar, Pilar
d. 1996 Lowe, Jack
(Warren)
d. 1997 Cheatham,
Adolphus
d. 1997 Jacobs, Helen
(Hull)

June 3

b. 39 Lucan
b. 1656 Tournefort,
Joseph Pitton de
b. 1726 Hutton, James
b. 1726 Otterbein,
Philip William
b. 1761 Shrapnel, Henry
b. 1770 Belgrano,
Manuel
b. 1780 Hone, William
b. 1804 Cobden,
Richard
b. 1808 Davis, Jefferson
b. 1811 James, Henry,
Sr.
b. 1818 Faidherbe,
Louis Leon Cesar
b. 1819 Ball, Thomas
b. 1819 Jongkind, Johan
Barthold
b. 1844 Hobart, Garret
Augustus
b. 1844 Liliencron,
Detlev von
b. 1851 Baker,
Theodore
b. 1852 Robinson,
Theodore

b. 1853 Petrie, (William
Matthew) Flinders,
Sir
b. 1864 Olds, Ranson
E(li)
b. 1865 George V
b. 1868 Agramonte y
Simoni, Aristides
b. 1873 Loewi, Otto
b. 1873 Smith, Alfred
b. 1877 Dufy, Raoul
(Ernest Joseph)
b. 1878 Henderson,
Lawrence Joseph
b. 1887 Hayes, Roland
b. 1894 Szyk, Arthur
b. 1895 Hillyer, Robert
b. 1899 Von Bekesy,
Georg
b. 1900 Edwards, Alan
b. 1900 Green, Abel
b. 1900 Mundt, Karl
Earl
b. 1900 Sinclair,
Gordon
b. 1901 Evans, Maurice
b. 1903 Hitchcock,
Henry Russell
b. 1904 Drew, Charles
Richard
b. 1904 Peerce, Jan
b. 1905 Goddard,
Paulette
b. 1905 Stone, Dorothy
b. 1906 Baker,
Josephine (Carson)
b. 1907 Rotha, Paul
b. 1909 Lay, Herman
Warden
b. 1910 Hollowood,
Albert Bernard
b. 1912 Home, William
Douglas
b. 1913 Cope, Jack
b. 1913 Corby, Ellen
b. 1915 Gorcey, Leo
b. 1917 Saint Cyr,
Lillian
b. 1918 Drucker, Daniel
Charles
b. 1919 Koontz,
Elizabeth Duncan
b. 1922 Resnais, Alain
b. 1924 Van Andel, Jay
b. 1924 Wiesel, Torsten
Nils
b. 1925 Curtis, Tony
b. 1926 Dewhurst,
Colleen
b. 1926 Ginsberg, Allen
b. 1927 Randolph,
Boots
b. 1928 Judd, Donald
(Clarence)
b. 1928 Simons,
Howard
b. 1929 Arber, Werner
b. 1929 Williams, Billy
b. 1930 Bradley, Marion
Zimmer
b. 1931 Harvey,
Anthony (Kesteven)
b. 1931 Lance,
(Thomas) Bert(ram)
b. 1934 Polhill, Robert

b. 1936 McMurtry, Larry Jeff
b. 1939 Woodiwiss, Kathleen (Erin)
b. 1942 Mayfield, Curtis (Lee)
b. 1943 Cunningham, Billy
b. 1944 Clarke, Martha
b. 1945 Irwin, Hale S
b. 1946 Hunter, Ian
b. 1950 Quatro, Suzi
b. 1951 Williams, Deniece
b. 1954 Hill, Dan
b. 1954 Matola, Sharon Rose
b. 1958 Valentine, Scott
b. 1961 Hart, Charles
d. 1548 Zumarraga, Juan de
d. 1657 Harvey, William
d. 1780 Hutchinson, Thomas
d. 1861 Douglas, Stephen Arnold
d. 1875 Bizet, Georges (Alexandre Cesar Leopold)
d. 1879 Rothschild, Lionel Nathan Rothschild, Baron
d. 1882 Thomson, James
d. 1887 Carrier-Belleuse, Albert Ernest
d. 1891 Lossing, Benson John
d. 1898 Plimsoll, Samuel
d. 1899 Strauss, Johann, Jr.
d. 1922 Terhune, Mary Virginia
d. 1924 Kafka, Franz
d. 1946 Kalinin, Mikhail (Ivanovich)
d. 1949 Giannini, A(madeo) P(eter)
d. 1953 Price, Florence Beatrice Smith
d. 1955 Graham, Barbara
d. 1963 John, XXIII
d. 1964 Sillanpaa, Frans E
d. 1965 Janssen, Herbert
d. 1967 Cluytens, Andre
d. 1967 Ransome, Arthur Mitchell
d. 1967 Tedder, Arthur William Tedder, Baron
d. 1968 Rand, James Henry
d. 1969 Warburg, James Paul
d. 1970 Mellon, Richard King
d. 1970 Sawyer, Ruth
d. 1974 Messali Hadj
d. 1975 Gleason, Ralph Joseph
d. 1975 Laver, James

d. 1975 Nelson, Ozzie
d. 1975 Sato, Eisaku
d. 1977 Hill, Archibald Vivian
d. 1977 Rossellini, Roberto
d. 1981 Coon, Carleton Stevens
d. 1982 VonSchmidt, Harold
d. 1984 Wilson, Peter Cecil
d. 1986 Goldie, Grace Wyndham
d. 1986 Neagle, Anna, Dame
d. 1989 Browne, Dik
d. 1989 Khomeini, Ruhollah Musavi, Ayatollah
d. 1990 Noyce, Robert Norton
d. 1991 Le Gallienne, Eva
d. 1992 Gaines, William M(axwell)
d. 1992 Morley, Robert
d. 1994 Everson, William Oliver
d. 1995 Eckert, John Presper, Jr.
d. 1995 Waters, Frank (Joseph)
d. 1996 Goodall, John Strickland
d. 1997 James, Dennis
d. 2000 Baskin, Leonard
d. 2000 Simon, William E(dward)

June 4
b. 1694 Quesnay, Francois
b. 1738 George III
b. 1756 Chaptal, Jean Antoine, Comte de Chanteloup
b. 1862 Fitzsimmons, Bob
b. 1862 Jewett, Henry
b. 1867 Mannerheim, Carl Gustav Emil, Baron
b. 1877 Wieland, Heinrich Otto
b. 1878 Buchman, Frank Nathan Daniel
b. 1879 Lubbock, Percy
b. 1879 Nazimova, Alla
b. 1894 Pascal, Gabriel
b. 1895 Grandi, Dino
b. 1895 Waln, Nora
b. 1898 Crosby, Harry
b. 1898 Wright, Jerauld
b. 1900 Glueck, Nelson
b. 1902 Drewry, John Eldridge
b. 1903 McKeen, John Elmer
b. 1903 Mravinsky, Eugene
b. 1904 Bessie, Alvah
b. 1904 Potok, Anna Maximilian Apfelbaum
b. 1905 Power, Eugene Barnum

b. 1906 Whorf, Richard
b. 1908 Barbour, Walworth
b. 1909 Batten, William Milfred
b. 1910 Cockerell, Christopher (Sydney), Sir
b. 1911 Carlson, Edward Elmer
b. 1911 Russell, Rosalind
b. 1915 Keita, Modibo
b. 1916 Nelson, Gaylord Anton
b. 1917 Collingwood, Charles Cummings
b. 1917 Metzenbaum, Howard M(orton)
b. 1918 De Cuir, John
b. 1919 Merrill, Robert
b. 1920 Barbieri, Fedora
b. 1920 Obregon, Alejandro
b. 1920 Train, Russell Errol
b. 1921 Wanzer, Bobby
b. 1922 Barry, Gene
b. 1922 Gravely, Samuel Lee, Jr.
b. 1924 Alesana, Tofilau Eti
b. 1925 Dumas, Jean Baptiste Andre
b. 1925 Weaver, Dennis
b. 1926 Malina, Judith
b. 1930 King, Morganna
b. 1932 Barrymore, John Blythe Drew, Jr.
b. 1932 McNamara, John Francis
b. 1932 Wolfe, Digby
b. 1933 al-Khalifa, Sheikh Isa Bin Sulman
b. 1936 Dern, Bruce MacLeish
b. 1937 Fender, Freddy
b. 1937 Fulghum, Robert
b. 1937 Zuckerman, Mortimer Benjamin
b. 1940 Sherwood, Frances
b. 1943 Haynie, Sandra
b. 1945 Waller, Gordon
b. 1946 Gregory, Bettina Louise
b. 1947 Klima, Viktor
b. 1948 Post, Sandra
b. 1950 Golacinski, Alan Bruce
b. 1951? Stevenson, Parker
b. 1952 Weaver, Mike
b. 1955 Verdi-Fletcher, Mary (Regina)
b. 1958 Velez, Eddie
b. 1961 DeBarge, El(dra)
b. 1963 McDaniel, Xavier Maurice
b. 1964 Kistler, Darci Anna
b. 1965 Jaeger, Andrea
b. 1966 Bartoli, Cecilia

d. 1135 Hui-Tsung
d. 1792 Burgoyne, John, Sir
d. 1798 Casanova (de Seingalt), Giovanni Giacomo
d. 1829 Dearborn, Henry
d. 1830 Sucre, Antonio J de
d. 1849 Blessington, Marguerite Gardiner, Countess
d. 1872 Moniuszko, Stanislaus
d. 1875 Morike, Eduard Friedrich
d. 1887 Wheeler, William Alrnon
d. 1912 Sangster, Margaret Elizabeth
d. 1913 Davison, Emily Wilding
d. 1918 Fairbanks, Charles Warren
d. 1925 Louys, Pierre
d. 1928 Chang Tso-Lin
d. 1933 Ahmed Hasim
d. 1939 Ladnier, Tommy
d. 1941 Wilhelm II
d. 1941 William, II
d. 1942 Heydrich, Reinhard Tristan Eugen
d. 1943 Roosevelt, Kermit
d. 1951 Koussevitzky, Serge Alexandrovich
d. 1962 Beebe, William
d. 1962 McCarthy, Clem
d. 1964 Warwick, Robert
d. 1966 Knopf, Blanche Wolf
d. 1967 Berkner, Lloyd Viel
d. 1968 Gish, Dorothy
d. 1970 McCracken, Branch
d. 1970 Schacht, Hjalmar Horace Greeley
d. 1970 Skulnik, Menasha
d. 1971 Lewis, Joe E
d. 1971 Lukacs, Gyorgy
d. 1973 Bontemps, Arna Wendell
d. 1975 Leider, Frida
d. 1983 Tors, Ivan
d. 1985 North, John Ringling
d. 1987 Bernard, Bruno
d. 1989 Parker, Pat
d. 1990 Gilford, Jack
d. 1994 Thorneycroft, (George Edward) Peter
d. 1997 Esau, Katherine

June 5
b. 1718 Chippendale, Thomas
b. 1723 Smith, Adam

b. 1956 Borg, Bjorn
Rune
b. 1956 Chan, June
d. 53BC Crassus,
Marcus Licinius
Dives
d. 1762 Anson, George
d. 1799 Henry, Patrick
d. 1818 Dabrowski, Jan
Henryk
d. 1832 Bentham,
Jeremy
d. 1837 Portales, Diego
(Jose Victor)
d. 1861 Cavour,
Camillo Benso, Conte
di
d. 1865 Quantrill,
William Clarke
d. 1870 Wrangel,
Ferdinand Petrovich,
Baron
d. 1881 Vieuxtemps,
Henri Francois Joseph
d. 1886 Nevin, John
Williamson
d. 1891 MacDonald,
John Alexander
d. 1911 Harrigan,
Edward
d. 1913 Cramp, Charles
Henry
d. 1916 Yuan, Shih-Kai
d. 1921 Feydeau,
Georges
d. 1922 Russell, Lillian
d. 1925 Denison,
George Taylor
d. 1927 Hilliard, Robert
Cochran
d. 1935 Byng, Julian
Hedworth George,
Viscount
d. 1939 Fawcett, George
d. 1941 Chevrolet,
Louis Joseph
d. 1942 Reisner, George
Andrew
d. 1945 Lindsay, David
d. 1946 Hauptmann,
Gerhart Johann
Robert
d. 1947 Agate, James
Evershed
d. 1948 Lumiere, Louis
Jean
d. 1950 Horlick,
Alexander James
d. 1956 Bingham,
Hiram
d. 1961 Jung, Carl
Gustav
d. 1962 Profaci, Joe
d. 1966 Wycherley,
Margaret
d. 1968 Churchill,
Randolph Frederick
Edward Spencer
d. 1968 Fry, Franklin
Clark
d. 1968 Kennedy,
Robert Francis
d. 1969 Dempsey, Miles
Christopher, Sir
d. 1970 Cates, Clifton
Bledsoe

d. 1970 Johnson, Lonnie
d. 1974 Yurka, Blanche
d. 1975 Blyden, Larry
d. 1975 Hansen, Alvin
Harvey
d. 1976 Getty, J(ean)
Paul
d. 1976 Rethberg,
Elizabeth
d. 1977 Musial, Joe
d. 1979 Haley, Jack
d. 1981 Humphrey,
Elliott S
d. 1982 Rexroth,
Kenneth
d. 1982 Szmuness, Wolf
d. 1983 Casey, James E
d. 1985 Cooper, Lester
Irving
d. 1985 Hough, Henry
Beetle
d. 1986 Carmichael,
John P
d. 1990 Lund, Art(hur
Earl, Jr.)
d. 1991 Getz, Stan
d. 1992 Goodman,
Martin
d. 1993 Bridges, James
d. 1994 Downs, Johnny
d. 1994 Sullivan, Barry
d. 1996 Plotkin, Jerry
d. 1996 Snell, George
D(avis)
d. 1997 Gabor, Magda
d. 1999 Stanky, Eddie
d. 2000 Kelly, Thomas

June 7

b. 1502 Gregory XIII
b. 1770 Liverpool, 2nd
Earl of
b. 1778 Brummell, Beau
b. 1811 Simpson, James
Young, Sir
b. 1825 Blackmore,
Richard Doddridge
b. 1835 Hill, George
Birkbeck Norman
b. 1840 Carlota
b. 1843 Blow, Susan
Elizabeth
b. 1845 Auer, Leopold
b. 1845 Goucher, John
Franklin
b. 1848 Gauguin, Paul
b. 1862 Lenard, Philipp
Edward Anton
b. 1866 Hornung, Ernest
William
b. 1868 Mackintosh,
Charles Rennie
b. 1868 Townsend, John
Sealy Edward, Sir
b. 1873 Ronald,
Landon, Sir
b. 1873 Weidenreich,
Franz
b. 1875 Grant, Gordon
b. 1876 Cantacuzene,
Princess
b. 1876 Nielsen, Alice
b. 1879 Rasmussen,
Knud Johan Victor
b. 1880 McGimsie,
Billy

b. 1890 Lashley, Karl
Spencer
b. 1892 Ponselle,
Carmela
b. 1893 Feis, Herbert
b. 1894 DeSeversky,
Alexander Procofieff
b. 1896 Kellems, Vivien
b. 1896 Mulliken,
Robert Sanderson
b. 1896 Nagy, Imre
b. 1897 Szell, George
b. 1899 Bowen,
Elizabeth Dorthea
Cole
b. 1904 Deutsch, Harold
C(harles)
b. 1906 Dane, Maxwell
b. 1906 Gray, Glen
b. 1907 Chalk, O(scar)
Roy
b. 1907 Clarke, Thomas
Ernest Bennett
b. 1908 Goldovsky,
Boris
b. 1908 Goodall, John
Strickland
b. 1909 Rodino, Peter
Wallace, Jr.
b. 1909 Tandy, Jessica
b. 1909 Walker, A
Maceo, Sr.
b. 1910 Annigoni,
Pietro
b. 1913 Nash, N
Richard
b. 1916 Darcy, Tom
b. 1917 Brooks,
Gwendolyn Elizabeth
b. 1917 Cooke, David
Coxe
b. 1919 Scherer,
Ray(mond Lewis)
b. 1920 Marchais,
Georges (Rene Louis)
b. 1922 Graziano,
Rocky
b. 1924 Gray, Dolores
b. 1928 Ivory, James
b. 1928 Strouse, Charles
b. 1929 Turner, John
Napier
b. 1931 Driskell, David
C(lyde)
b. 1931 McKenna,
Virginia
b. 1933 Score, Herb(ert
Jude)
b. 1934 Blatchford,
Joseph Hoffer
b. 1934 Entremont,
Phillippe
b. 1934 Stewart, Wynn
b. 1937 Bernstein, Jay
b. 1937 Jarvi, Neemi
b. 1940 Jones, Tom
b. 1941 Laredo, Jaime
b. 1943 Giovanni, Nikki
b. 1943 Osmond, Ken
b. 1945 Tannen,
Deborah Frances
b. 1946 Kreutzmann,
Bill
b. 1947 Munson,
Thurman Lee
b. 1952 Neeson, Liam

b. 1955 Scarbury, Joey
b. 1958 Artist Formerly
Known as Prince,
The
d. 549 Liang Wu-ti
d. 1329 Robert I
d. 1358 Ashikaga,
Takauji
d. 1394 Anne of
Bohemia
d. 1667 Keyser, Thomas
De
d. 1740 Spotswood,
Alexander
d. 1821 Guemes, Martin
d. 1826 Fraunhofer,
Joseph von
d. 1843 Holderlin,
Friedrich
d. 1859 Cox, David
d. 1863 Gruber, Franz-
Xaver
d. 1866 Seattle
d. 1884 Hoffman,
Charles Fenno
d. 1886 Hoe, Richard
March
d. 1893 Booth, Edwin
Thomas
d. 1894 Whitney,
William Dwight
d. 1896 Eaton, Wyatt
d. 1899 Daly, Augustin
d. 1910 Smith, Goldwin
d. 1914 Watts-Dunton,
Theodore
d. 1932 Keen, William
Williams
d. 1933 Curtis, Cyrus
Hermann Kotszchmar
d. 1937 Harlow, Jean
d. 1954 Maverick,
Maury
d. 1956 Benda, Julien
d. 1961 Barnard,
Chester Irving
d. 1963 Pitts, Zasu
d. 1964 Lewis, Meade
Anderson Lux
d. 1965 Burgess,
Thornton Waldo
d. 1965 Holliday, Judy
d. 1966 Arp, Hans
d. 1967 Parker, Dorothy
Rothschild
d. 1968 Duryea, Dan
d. 1970 Forster,
E(dward) M(organ)
d. 1971 Burnett, Leo
d. 1971 Rodale, Jerome
Irving
d. 1975 Brent, Evelyn
d. 1976 Hackett, Bobby
d. 1978 Darken,
Lawrence Stamper
d. 1978 Gordon, Joe
d. 1978 Norrish, Ronald
George Wreyford
d. 1980 Bonelli, Richard
d. 1980 Guston, Philip
d. 1980 Miller, Henry
(Valentine)
d. 1980 Spychalski,
Marian
d. 1981 Gorman,
Chester

b. 1930 Abruzzo, Ben(jamine Lou)
b. 1930 Kalb, Marvin Leonard
b. 1932 Wilson, Jackie
b. 1934 Mason, Jackie
b. 1934 Welch, Larry Dean
b. 1936 Manatt, Charles Taylor
b. 1938 Wuorinen, Charles (Peter)
b. 1939 Cotrubas, Ileana
b. 1939 Vitale, Dick
b. 1943 Saatchi, Charles
b. 1946 Adelman, Kenneth Lee
b. 1946 Kelman, James
b. 1948? Rosen, Nathaniel
b. 1951 Parker, Dave
b. 1956 Cornwell, Patricia (Daniels)
b. 1957 Jakes, Thomas T.D.
b. 1961 Fox, Michael J.
b. 1963 Depp, Johnny
b. 1964 Tisdale, Wayman Lawrence
d. 68 Nero
d. 1597 Anchieta, Jose de
d. 1786 McDougall, Alexander
d. 1825 Borghese, Maria Paolina
d. 1826 Morse, Jedidiah
d. 1832 Gentz, Friedrich Von
d. 1834 Carey, William
d. 1870 Dickens, Charles (John Huffam)
d. 1874 Cochise
d. 1897 Clark, Alvin Graham
d. 1901 Besant, Walter, Sir
d. 1901 Moran, Edward
d. 1911 Nation, Carry A(melia Moore)
d. 1920 Griffith, Samuel Walker
d. 1921 Drago, Luis Maria
d. 1925 Hanes, Pleasant H
d. 1926 Dole, Sanford Ballard
d. 1929 Lawrence, Margaret
d. 1944 Douglas, Keith Castellain
d. 1948 Liebman, Joshua Loth
d. 1949 Cebotari, Maria
d. 1953 Betti, Ugo
d. 1954 Locke, Alain Leroy
d. 1957 Blanding, Don
d. 1958 Donat, Robert
d. 1958 Hackett, Raymond
d. 1959 Windaus, Adolf Otto Reinhold

d. 1961 Chambers, Whittaker
d. 1961 Guerin, Camille
d. 1962 Adler, Polly
d. 1964 Beaverbrook, William Maxwell Aitken, Baron
d. 1964 Gruenberg, Louis
d. 1973 Creasey, John
d. 1974 Asturias, Miguel Angel
d. 1974 Cornell, Katharine
d. 1974 Henry William Frederick Albert
d. 1976 Farley, James A(loysius)
d. 1976 Thorndike, Sybil, Dame
d. 1978 Murphy, Robert Daniel
d. 1981 Darden, Colgate Whitehead
d. 1981 Hayden, Russell
d. 1981 Ludden, Allen Ellsworth
d. 1983 Mackay, John Alexander
d. 1984 Hardin, Helen
d. 1986 Richman, Milton
d. 1989 Beadle, George Wells
d. 1991 Arrau, Claudio
d. 1991 Loloma, Charles
d. 1993 Smith, Alexis
d. 1994 Tinbergen, Jan
d. 1995 Versalles, Zoilo Casanova
d. 2000 Lawrence, Jacob Armstead
d. 2000 Segal, George

June 10
b. Suzy
b. 819 Courbet, (Jean Desire) Gustave
b. 1710 Short, James
b. 1746 Fouquier-Tinville, Antoine Quentin
b. 1803 Darcy, Henri Philibert Gaspard
b. 1819 Courbet, Gustave
b. 1832 Otto, Nikolaus August
b. 1833 Cushman, Pauline
b. 1835 Felton, Rebecca Ann Latimer
b. 1844 Hagenbeck, Carl
b. 1854 Curel, Francois de
b. 1857 Potthast, Edward Henry
b. 1862 Carter, Caroline Louise Dudley
b. 1862 Carter, Leslie, Mrs.
b. 1863 Couperius, Louis (Marie Anne)
b. 1865 Cook, Frederick Albert

b. 1867 Meier-Graefe, Julius
b. 1880 Derain, Andre
b. 1881 Gruenberg, Sidonie Matsner
b. 1886 Hayakawa, Sessue (Kintaro)
b. 1887 Byrd, Harry Flood
b. 1891 Dubin, Al
b. 1891 Levinsky, Battling
b. 1895 McDaniel, Hattie
b. 1897 Jagel, Frederick
b. 1898 Brokenshire, Norman
b. 1901 Loewe, Frederick
b. 1906 Crosby, Alexander L
b. 1907 Porter, Fairfield
b. 1910 Haydon, Julie
b. 1910 Howlin' Wolf
b. 1911 Rattigan, Terence Mervyn, Sir
b. 1912 Lesage, Jean
b. 1913 Cohen, Wilbur Joseph
b. 1913 Khrennikov, Tikhon Nikolaevich
b. 1918 Morse, Barry
b. 1921 Philip, Prince
b. 1922 Garland, Judy
b. 1922 Mofford, Rose
b. 1923 Maxwell, Robert Ian Charles
b. 1925 Costa, Don
b. 1925 Hentoff, Nat(han Irving)
b. 1926 Haver, June
b. 1926 Jeffries, Lionel Charles
b. 1926 Low, George M(ichael)
b. 1928 Sendak, Maurice Bernard
b. 1929 McDivitt, Jim
b. 1929 Wilson, Edward Osborne
b. 1930 Mirabella, Grace
b. 1932 Johnston, J. Bennett, Jr.
b. 1933 Bailey, F(rancis) Lee
b. 1933 Fairbanks, Chuck
b. 1936 Chesney, Marion
b. 1936 Freemantle, Brian Harry
b. 1937 Foreman, Richard
b. 1937 Howe, Susan
b. 1938 Skinner, Sam
b. 1938 Skinner, Samuel K(nox)
b. 1951 Fouts, Dan(iel Francis)
b. 1953 Barrios, Francisco Javier
b. 1953 Ramirez, Raul
b. 1955? Stevens, Andrew
b. 1963 Shue, Elizabeth

b. 1965 Evangelista, Linda
b. 1965 Hurley, Elizabeth
b. 1966 McKeon, Doug
b. 1982 Lipinski, Tara
d. 1552 Barclay, Alexander
d. 1836 Ampere, Andre Marie
d. 1858 Brown, Robert
d. 1865 Sigourney, Lydia Howard
d. 1899 Chausson, Ernest
d. 1906 Jacobi, Mary Corinna Putnam
d. 1906 Seddon, Richard John
d. 1909 Hale, Edward Everett
d. 1918 Boito, Arrigo
d. 1923 Loti, Pierre
d. 1926 Gaudi y Cornet, Antonio
d. 1927 Woodhull, Victoria Claflin
d. 1930 Harnack, Adolf von
d. 1930 Sperry, Elmer Ambrose
d. 1934 Delius, Frederick
d. 1937 Borden, Robert Laird, Sir
d. 1938 Schomburg, Arthur Alfonso
d. 1940 Garvey, Marcus Moziah
d. 1942 Lupino, Stanley
d. 1946 Johnson, Jack
d. 1949 McCutcheon, John Tinney
d. 1949 Undset, Sigrid
d. 1955 Abbott, Margaret I.
d. 1956 Pratt, Fletcher
d. 1958 Grimke, Angelina Emily Weld
d. 1963 Root, Jack
d. 1966 Treece, Henry
d. 1967 Tracy, Spencer Bonaventure
d. 1968 Gueye, Lamine
d. 1970 Grant, Earl
d. 1971 Rennie, Michael
d. 1973 Inge, William Motter
d. 1973 Kredel, Fritz
d. 1975 Hull, John Edwin
d. 1976 Zukor, Adolph
d. 1979 Croft-Cooke, Rupert
d. 1979 Taylor, Cyclone
d. 1980 Sullivan, A(loysius) M(ichael)
d. 1982 Dali, Gala
d. 1982? Fassbinder, Rainer Werner
d. 1983 Reisenberg, Nadia
d. 1985 Armstrong, Jack Lawrence
d. 1986 Miller, Merle

b. 1929 Frank, Anne
b. 1930 Harris, Barbara
　Clementine
b. 1932 Jaffe, Rona
b. 1932 Nabors, Jim
b. 1934 Giago, Tim
b. 1937 Claybrook, Joan
　B
b. 1941 Corea, Chick
b. 1941 Hobson, Geary
b. 1943 Albert, Marv(in
　Philip)
b. 1952 Abraham,
　Spencer
b. 1952 Knussen, Oliver
b. 1953 Farmer, Gary
　Dale
b. 1957 Busfield,
　Timothy
b. 1959? Harrison,
　Jenilee
b. 1960 Calcavecchia,
　Mark
b. 1965 Torrence,
　Gwen(dolyn Lenna)
d. 1727 George I
d. 1759 Collins,
　William
d. 1768 Delisle, Joseph-
　Nicolas
d. 1778 Livingston,
　Philip
d. 1789 Liotard, Jean-
　Etienne
d. 1842 Arnold, Thomas
d. 1870 Smith, Sophia
d. 1878 Bonneville,
　Benjamin Louie
　Eulalie de
d. 1878 Bryant, William
　Cullen
d. 1900 Hale, Lucretia
　Peabody
d. 1912 Passy, Frederic
d. 1914 Isham, Samuel
d. 1922 Kapp,
　Wolfgang
d. 1923 Stambuliski,
　Aleksandr
d. 1936 Howard, Robert
　Ervin
d. 1936 James,
　Montague Rhodes
d. 1957 Dorsey, Jimmy
d. 1957 Joyce, Peggy
　Hopkins
d. 1960 Tokatyan,
　Armand
d. 1962 Ireland, John
　Nicholson
d. 1963 Cunningham,
　Andrew Browne,
　Viscount
d. 1963 Evers, Medgar
　Wiley
d. 1966 Hocking,
　William Ernest
d. 1966 Scherchen,
　Hermann
d. 1968 Read, Herbert,
　Sir
d. 1972 Alinsky, Saul
　David
d. 1972 Wilson,
　Edmund
d. 1975 Kober, Arthur

d. 1978 Cushman,
　Austin Thomas
d. 1978 Guo Moruo
d. 1978 Kuo Mo-jo
d. 1980 Butlin, William
　Heygate Edmund, Sir
d. 1980 Stone, Milburn
d. 1982 Frisch, Karl
　von
d. 1982 Rambert, Marie,
　Dame
d. 1983 Shearer, Norma
d. 1984 Ferencsik, Janos
d. 1988 DeLeeuw,
　Adele Louise
d. 1994 Schneerson,
　Menachem M(endel)
d. 1998 Buscaglia, Leo
d. 1999 Powers, James
　Farl

June 13
b. 823 Charles II
b. 1752 Burney, Fanny
b. 1763 Andrada e
　Silva, Jose Bonifacio
　de
b. 1784 McCoy, Isaac
b. 1786 Scott, Winfield
b. 1790 Paez, Jose
　Antonio
b. 1795 Arnold, Thomas
b. 1843 Neuendorff,
　Adolf
b. 1854 Parsons,
　Charles Algernon, Sir
b. 1865 Yeats, William
　Butler
b. 1870 Bordet, Jules
　Jean Baptiste Vincent
b. 1874 Bowes, Major
b. 1875 Ferguson,
　Miriam Amanda
b. 1876 Franklin, Irene
b. 1879 Wood, Robert
　Elkington
b. 1880 Rose, Vincent
b. 1880 Stella, Joseph
b. 1881 Weber, Lois
b. 1884 Crohn, Burrill
　Bernard
b. 1884 Gilson, Etienne
　Henry
b. 1885 Igoe, Hype
b. 1885 Schumann,
　Elisabeth
b. 1887 Frank, Bruno
b. 1889 Henry, George
　William
b. 1892 Rathbone, Basil
b. 1893 Sayers, Dorothy
　Leigh
b. 1894 Kanner, Leo
b. 1894 Lartique,
　Jacques-Henri Charles
　Auguste
b. 1894 Van Doren,
　Mark
b. 1895 Wrightsman,
　Charles Bierer
b. 1896 Crown, Henry
b. 1897 Nurmi, Paavo
　Johannes
b. 1898 O'Neil, James
　F(rancis)

b. 1899 Chavez (y
　Ramirez), Carlos
　Antonio de Pauda
b. 1900 Hunter, Ian
b. 1901 Erlander, Tage
　Fritiof
b. 1903 Bennett,
　Willard Harrison
b. 1903 Grange, Red
b. 1905 Cheatham,
　Adolphus
b. 1905 Colbert, Lester
　L(um)
b. 1908 Abbott,
　L(enwood) B(allard)
b. 1908 Vieira Da Silva,
　Maria Helena
b. 1910 Christ-Janer,
　Albert
b. 1911 Agyeman,
　Jaramogi Abebe
b. 1911 Alvarez, Luis
　W(alter)
b. 1911 Hays, Wayne
　Levere
b. 1911 Mueller, Erwin
　Wilhelm
b. 1911 Root, Oren
b. 1912 Taylor, Samuel
　(Albert)
b. 1913 Edwards, Ralph
　Livingstone
b. 1913 Martin, David
　Stone
b. 1914 Franklin,
　Frederic
b. 1915 Budge, Don
b. 1916 Conway, Shirl
b. 1918 Joanis, John W
b. 1920 Evans, Clifford
b. 1920 Johnson, Ben
b. 1923 Mazzola,
　Anthony T
b. 1926 Lynde, Paul
　Edward
b. 1927 Ableman, Paul
b. 1934 Means,
　Marianne Hansen
b. 1935 Christo
b. 1936 Raven, Peter
　H(amilton)
b. 1939 Froines, John
　Radford
b. 1942 Abubakar,
　Abdulsalam (Alhaji)
b. 1943 McDowell,
　Malcolm
b. 1945 Watkins, Levi,
　Jr.
b. 1946 Deuba, Sher
　Bahadur
b. 1951 Thomas,
　Richard Earl
b. 1953 Allen, Tim
b. 1955 Sears-Collins,
　Leah J.
b. 1962 Sheedy, Ally
b. 1986 Olsen, Ashley
　Fuller
b. 1986 Olsen, Mary
　Kate
d. 323BC Alexander the
　Great
d. 1231 Anthony of ,
　Padua, Saint

d. 1817 Edgeworth,
　Richard Lovell
d. 1838 Chavis, John
d. 1871 Houdin, Jean
　Eugene Robert
d. 1886 Ludwig II
d. 1908 Bethune,
　Thomas Greene
d. 1930 Segrave, Henry
　O'Neal de Hane, Sir
d. 1931 Kitasato
　Shibasaburo
d. 1934 Gardiner,
　Chuck
d. 1938 Guillaume,
　Charles Edouard
d. 1939 Barker, Doc
d. 1946 Bowes, Major
d. 1946 Guerin, Jules
d. 1947 Marquet, Albert
d. 1951 Chifley, Joseph
　Benedict
d. 1952 Eames, Emma
　Hayden
d. 1953 Freeman,
　Douglas S
d. 1961 Jones, Benjamin
　Allyn
d. 1962 Goossens,
　Eugene, Sir
d. 1965 Buber, Martin
d. 1969 Hunt, Martita
d. 1972 McPhatter,
　Clyde
d. 1972 Von Bekesy,
　Georg
d. 1973 Cott, Ted
d. 1974 Secunda,
　Sholom
d. 1976 Anda, Geza
d. 1976 Bolles, Don F
d. 1977 Clark, Tom
d. 1979 Hood, Darla
　Jean
d. 1979 Kuznetsov,
　Anatoli Vasilievich
d. 1980 Lampman,
　Evelyn Sibley
d. 1982 Griffin, Marvin
d. 1982 Khalid Ibn
　Abdul Azia Al-Saud
d. 1982 Rafferty,
　Max(well Lewis, Jr.)
d. 1984 Owings,
　Nathaniel Alexander
d. 1986 Goodman,
　Benny
d. 1986 Greeley, Dana
　McLean
d. 1987 Caspary, Vera
d. 1987 Page, Geraldine
d. 1989 Allison,
　Fran(ces)
d. 1989 Simons,
　Howard
d. 1990 O'Neill,
　Terence Marne
d. 1993 Slayton, Donald
　Kent
d. 1994 Goldman,
　Ronald Lyle
d. 1994 Simpson,
　Nicole Brown
d. 1994 Youskevitch,
　Igor
d. 1998 Costa, Lucio

d. 1998 Smythe,
Reg(inald)

June 14
b. 1671 Albinoni,
Tommaso
b. 1716 Harrison, Peter
b. 1730 Sacchini,
Antonio
b. 1736 Coulomb,
Charles Augustin de
b. 1798 Palacky,
Frantisek
b. 1805 Anderson,
Robert
b. 1811 Stowe, Harriet
(Elizabeth) Beecher
b. 1812 Wood,
Fernando
b. 1820 Bartlett, John
b. 1832 Mitchell,
Margaret Julia
b. 1845 Maceo, Antonio
b. 1848 Bosanquet,
Bernard
b. 1850 Kitchener,
Horatio Herbert
b. 1855 LaFollette,
Robert Marion
b. 1884 McCormack,
John
b. 1889 Lincoln, Elmo
b. 1892 Reed, Peter
Hugh
b. 1895 Adams, Jack
b. 1895 Edwards, Cliff
b. 1895 Finkelstein,
Louis, Dr.
b. 1895 Mariategui, Jose
Carlos
b. 1902 Eurich, Alvin
C(hristian)
b. 1903 Rich, Louise
Dickinson
b. 1904 Bourke-White,
Margaret
b. 1906 Lamb, Gil
b. 1907 Char, Rene
(Emile)
b. 1907 Hansen, Julia
Butler
b. 1908 Trotter, John
Scott
b. 1909 Ives, Burl (Icle
Ivanhoe)
b. 1910 Kempe, Rudolf
b. 1912 Hammond,
E(dward) Cuyler
b. 1914 Peers, William
Raymond
b. 1917 Monash, Paul
b. 1917 Rootes, William
Edward Rootes,
Baron
b. 1918 Aluko, Timothy
Mofolorunso
b. 1918 McGuire,
Dorothy Hackett
b. 1918 Walker, LeRoy
Tashreau
b. 1919 Wanamaker,
Sam
b. 1922 Roche, Kevin
b. 1924 Black, James
Whyte, Sir
b. 1924 Erickson,
Arthur Charles

b. 1925 Salinger, Pierre
Emil George
b. 1926 Newcombe,
Don(ald)
b. 1928 Guevara, Che
b. 1928 Udry, Janice
May
b. 1929 Coleman, Cy
b. 1931 Gibbs, Marla
Bradley
b. 1933 Kosinski, Jerzy
(Nikodem)
b. 1934 Lehmann-
Haupt, Christopher
Charles Herbert
b. 1935 Evans, Jerry
b. 1938 Bluitt, Juliann
S.
b. 1939 Andrews,
Michael Alford
b. 1941 Wideman, John
Edgar
b. 1942 Bush, Melinda
b. 1942 Walker, Junior
b. 1944? Colwin, Laurie
b. 1945 Argent,
Rod(ney Terence)
b. 1946 Ingersoll, Ralph
McAllister, II
b. 1946 McLarty,
Thomas F, III
b. 1947 Harwood,
Vanessa Clare
b. 1952 Mekka, Eddie
b. 1957 Simpson, Mona
Elizabeth
b. 1958 Heiden, Eric
Arthur
b. 1961 Boy George
b. 1969 Graf, Steffi
d. 1205 Dandolo, Enrico
d. 1594 Lassus,
Orlandus de
d. 1768 Short, James
d. 1800 Kleber, Jean
Baptiste
d. 1801 Arnold,
Benedict
d. 1825 L'Enfant, Pierre
Charles
d. 1837 Leopardi,
Giacomo
d. 1842 Atkinson,
Henry
d. 1864 Santana, Pedro
d. 1883 FitzGerald,
Edward
d. 1886 Mould, Jacob
Wrey
d. 1886 Van Nostrand,
David
d. 1905 Tippu Tib
d. 1908 Stanley,
Frederick Arthur, Earl
of Derby
d. 1909 Prang, Louis
d. 1914 Stevenson,
Adlai Ewing
d. 1920 Weber, Max
d. 1924 Gilbreth, Frank
Bunker
d. 1926 Cassatt, Mary
Stevenson
d. 1927 Jerome, Jerome
Klapka

d. 1928 Pankhurst,
Emmeline Goulden
d. 1929 Keith, Minor
Cooper
d. 1933 Pollack, Egon
d. 1936 Chesterton,
G(ilbert) K(eith)
d. 1936 Gorky, Maxim
d. 1938 Campbell,
William Wallace
d. 1939 Khodasevich,
Vladislav
d. 1939 Pulitzer, Ralph
d. 1946 Baird, John
Logie
d. 1946 Butterworth,
Charles
d. 1946 Ubico y
Castaneda, Jorge
d. 1948 Atherton,
Gertrude Franklin
d. 1952 Kirby, John
d. 1956 Harrison,
G(eorge) Donald
d. 1965 Kaltenborn,
H(ans) V(on)
d. 1968 Quasimodo,
Salvatore
d. 1971 Garcia, Carlos
Polestico
d. 1974 Perkoff, Stuart
Z.
d. 1977 Reed, Alan
d. 1978 Fabian, Robert
Honey
d. 1978 Matlock, Matty
d. 1978 Poulter, Thomas
Charles
d. 1979 Shumlin,
Herman Elliott
d. 1984 Pillsbury, Philip
Winston
d. 1985 Johnson, Walter
d. 1986 Borges, Jorge
Luis
d. 1986 Lerner, Alan
Jay
d. 1986 Perkins, Marlin
d. 1988 Farrell, Johnny
d. 1989 Johnson, Judy
d. 1991 Ashcroft,
Peggy, Dame
d. 1991 Miles, Bernard,
Sir
d. 1993 Pett, Saul
d. 1994 Mancini, Henry
d. 1995 Gallagher, Rory
d. 1995 Zelazny, Roger
d. 1997 Jaeckel, Richard
(Hanley)
d. 2000 Jones, Robert
Trent

June 15
b. 1330 Edward the
Black Prince
b. 1542 Grenville,
Richard, Sir
b. 1645 Godolphin,
Sidney
b. 1646 La Fosse,
Charles de
b. 1767 Jackson, Rachel
(Donelson Robards)
b. 1773 Benjamin,
Asher
b. 1789 Henson, Josiah

b. 1815 Browne, Phiz
b. 1835? Menken, Adah
Isaacs
b. 1843 Grieg, Edvard
Hagerup
b. 1856 Channing,
Edward Perkins
b. 1861 Schumann-
Heink, Ernestine
Rossler
b. 1869 Witmark,
Isidore
b. 1872 Gadski, Johanna
b. 1878 Abbott,
Margaret I.
b. 1880 Nagano, Osami
b. 1881 McFee, William
b. 1882 Antonescu, Ion
b. 1884 Langdon, Harry
b. 1887 Hoffman,
Malvina
b. 1888 D'Arcy, Martin
Cyril
b. 1893 Weeks, Sinclair
b. 1894 Bennett, Robert
Russell
b. 1895 Herrick, Elinore
Morehouse
b. 1896 Jacobs, Walter
L
b. 1900 Feingold,
Benjamin Franklin
b. 1900 Luening, Otto
b. 1902 Erikson, Erik
H(omburger)
b. 1902 Rudolf, Max
b. 1905 Justice, James
Robertson
b. 1906 Taeuber,
Conrad F.
b. 1908 Anderson,
Vernon Ellsworth
b. 1908 Giancana, Sam
b. 1910 Rose, David
b. 1911 Awdry,
W(ilbert Vere)
b. 1913 Huddleston,
Trevor
b. 1914 Andropov, Yuri
Vladimirovich
b. 1914 Steinberg, Saul
b. 1915 Weller, Thomas
Huckle
b. 1916 Field, Marshall,
IV
b. 1916 Simon, Herbert
Alexander
b. 1917 Payne, Leon
b. 1918 Tombalbaye,
Nagarta Francois
b. 1920 Clampitt, Amy
b. 1921 Garner, Erroll
b. 1922 Udall, Morris
K(ing)
b. 1923 Benarde,
Melvin Albert
b. 1924 Weizman, Ezer
b. 1926 Fox, Carol
b. 1927 Hinderas,
Natalie Leota
Henderson
b. 1929 Mansouri, Lotfi
b. 1930 Pronovost,
Marcel
b. 1932 Cuomo, Mario
Matthew

b. 1932 Roberts, Gene
b. 1937 Jennings,
  Waylon
b. 1938 Williams, Billy
  Leo
b. 1939 Connerly, Ward
b. 1941 Nilsson
b. 1943 Halliday,
  Johnny
b. 1943 Kissling,
  Frances
b. 1945 Pagett, Nicola
b. 1945 Sawyer, Amos
b. 1949 Baker, Dusty
b. 1949 Varney, Jim
b. 1951? Amsterdam,
  Jane
b. 1953 Kunjufu,
  Jawanza
b. 1953 Purcell, Lee
b. 1954 Belushi, Jim
b. 1954 Gibbs, Terri
b. 1955 Metcalf, Laurie
b. 1956 Parrish, Lance
  Michael
b. 1957 Butler, Brett
b. 1958 Boggs, Wade
  (Anthony)
b. 1963 Hunt, Helen
b. 1964 Cox, Courteney
b. 1969 Ice Cube
b. 1973 Harris, Neil
  Patrick
d. 1467 Philip the Good
d. 1844 Campbell,
  Thomas
d. 1849 Polk, James
  Knox
d. 1888 Frederick III
d. 1889 Eminescu,
  Mihail
d. 1907 Jenney, William
  LeBaron
d. 1929 Brush, Charles
  Francis
d. 1934 Britton,
  Nathaniel, Lord
d. 1938 Kirchner, Ernst
  Ludwig
d. 1941 Underhill,
  Evelyn
d. 1945 Rives, Amelie
  Louise
d. 1952 Gallatin, Albert
  Eugene
d. 1961 Torroja (y
  Miret), Eduardo
d. 1962 Cortot, Alfred-
  Denis
d. 1965 Cochran, Steve
d. 1965 Norden, Carl
  Lukas
d. 1968 Crawford,
  Sam(uel Earl)
d. 1968 Montgomery,
  Wes
d. 1970 MacIver, Robert
  Morrison
d. 1970 Powdermaker,
  Hortense
d. 1976 Dykes, Jimmy
d. 1977 Knorr, Nathan
  Homer
d. 1981 Dinkeloo, John
  Gerard

d. 1981 Rinehart,
  Frederick Roberts
d. 1981 Toynbee, Philip
d. 1982 Pepper, Art(hur
  Edward)
d. 1984 Tully, Grace
  George
d. 1984 Willson,
  Meredith
d. 1985 Kamp, Irene
  Kittle
d. 1987 Heller, Walter
  Wolfgang
d. 1989 French, Victor
d. 1991 Chandler,
  Happy
d. 1992 Lopat, Ed(mund
  Walter)
d. 1993 Connally, John
  B.
d. 1993 Hunt, James
d. 1993 Vera
d. 1996 Fitzgerald, Ella

June 16
b. 1583 Oxenstierna,
  Axel Gustafsson
b. 1773 Young, Thomas
b. 1801 Plucker, Julius
b. 1836 Merritt, Wesley
b. 1874 Meighen,
  Arthur
b. 1878 Torrence,
  Ernest
b. 1885 Howard, Tom
b. 1887 Lauro, Achille
b. 1888 Clark, Bobby
b. 1889 Doubleday,
  Nelson
b. 1889 Hamlin, Talbot
  Faulkner
b. 1890 Laurel, Stan
b. 1892 Grossinger,
  Jennie
b. 1892 Rubicam,
  Raymond
b. 1895 Pitz, Henry
  Clarence
b. 1897 Wittig, Georg
  Friedrich Karl
b. 1902 McClintock,
  Barbara
b. 1902 Simpson,
  George Gaylord
b. 1906 Munson, Ona
b. 1907 Pilkington,
  Francis Meredyth
b. 1908 Sarit Thanarat
b. 1909 Beilenson, Edna
  Rudolph
b. 1910 Albertson, Jack
b. 1910 Massey, Ilona
b. 1910 Velasco
  Alvarado, Juan
b. 1912 Powell, Enoch
b. 1915 Rumor,
  Mariano
b. 1916 Luisetti, Hank
b. 1917 Graham,
  Katharine Meyer
b. 1917 Penn, Irving
b. 1918 Elliott, George
  Paul
b. 1920 Griffin, John
  Howard
b. 1923 Colombo,
  Joseph Anthony

b. 1924 Shah, Indries
b. 1926? Rios Montt,
  Jose Efrain
b. 1927 Johnson,
  George E(llis)
b. 1928 Comissiona,
  Sergiu
b. 1930 Zsigmond,
  Vilmos
b. 1931 Spong, John
b. 1935 Dine, Jim
b. 1936 Karlin,
  Frederick James
b. 1937 Busch, August
  Adolphus, III
b. 1937 Segal, Erich
  Wolf
b. 1938 Oates, Joyce
  Carol
b. 1940 Craddock,
  Crash
b. 1940 Goldschmidt,
  Neil Edward
b. 1943 Arenas,
  Reinaldo
b. 1945 Matthews, Ian
b. 1946 Sanderson,
  Derek Michael
b. 1946 Van Ark, Joan
b. 1946 Williams,
  Simon
b. 1949 Madison,
  Joseph E(dward)
b. 1951 Duran, Roberto
b. 1952 Hadley, Jerry
b. 1952 LeFlore,
  Ron(ald)
b. 1952 Vannelli, Gino
b. 1954 Nano, Fatos
b. 1955 Rollins, Wayne
  Monte
b. 1958 Griffith, Darrell
  Steven
b. 1962 Joyner, Wally
b. 1966 Jackson, Janet
  Damita
b. 1970 Jones, Cobi
b. 1971 Shakur, Tupac
d. 1464 Weyden, Rogier
  van der
d. 1722 Marlborough,
  John Churchill, Duke
d. 1752 Butler, Joseph
d. 1778 Ekhof, Konrad
d. 1779 Bernard,
  Francis, Sir
d. 1804 Hiller, Johann
  Adam
d. 1855 Gorrie, John
d. 1869 Sturt, Charles
d. 1878 Long, Crawford
  Williamson
d. 1909 Albeniz, Isaac
  Manuel Francisco
d. 1925 Das, Chitta
  Ranjan
d. 1929 Parrington,
  Vernon L(ouis)
d. 1932 Eeden, Fredrik
  Willem van
d. 1934 Skelly, Hal
d. 1939 Webb, Chick
d. 1940 Heyward,
  (Edwin) DuBose
d. 1941 Franklin, Irene
d. 1943 Onegin, Sigrid

d. 1944 Bloch, Marc
d. 1947 Huberman,
  Bronislaw
d. 1948 Jones, Rufus
  Matthew
d. 1952 Geiger, Theodor
  Julius
d. 1953 Bondfield,
  Margaret Grace
d. 1959 Reeves, George
d. 1966 Eifert, Virginia
  Snider
d. 1967 Denny,
  Reginald Leigh
d. 1969 Alexander of
  Tunis
d. 1970 Chapman,
  Sydney
d. 1970 Piccolo, Brian
d. 1971 Reith, John
  Charles Walsham
d. 1975 Courtney,
  Clint(on Dawson)
d. 1976 Meloy, Francis
  Edward, Jr.
d. 1978 Bernstein,
  Felicia Montealegre
d. 1979 Johnson, Ching
d. 1979 Ray, Nicholas
d. 1980 Nolan, Bob
d. 1981 Knight, John
  Shivley
d. 1982 Honeyman-
  Scott, James
d. 1982 Kibbee, Robert
  Joseph
d. 1983 Lee, Doris
  Emrick
d. 1986 Norwich, Diana
  (Manners) Cooper,
  Viscountess
d. 1988 Pinero, Miguel
d. 1990 Turner, Eva,
  Dame
d. 1991 Lewis, William
  Arthur, Sir
d. 1994 Murphy,
  Franklin D(avid)
d. 1994 Saltzman,
  Charles E(skridge)
d. 1996 Allen, Mel
d. 2000 Nagako,
  Empress

June 17
b. 1239 Edward I
b. 1604 John Maurice
  of Nassau
b. 1682 Charles XII
b. 1742 Hooper,
  William
b. 1743 Lowell, John
b. 1751 Humphreys,
  Joshua
b. 1800 Parsons,
  William
b. 1800 Rosse, William
  Parsons, 3rd Earl of
b. 1818 Gounod,
  Charles Francois
b. 1832 Crookes,
  William, Sir
b. 1848 Maurel, Victor
b. 1860 Frohman,
  Charles
b. 1865 LaFlesche
  Picotte, Susan

b. 1867 Gregg, John Robert
b. 1867 Lawson, Henry (Archibald Hertzberg)
b. 1871 Johnson, James Weldon
b. 1873 Bloomingdale, Samuel
b. 1875 Mitchell, Grant
b. 1876 Crerar, Thomas Alexander
b. 1877 Cady, (Walter) Harrison
b. 1880 Van Vechten, Carl
b. 1881 Burns, Tommy
b. 1882 Herne, Chrystal Katharine
b. 1882 Stravinsky, Igor Fedorovich
b. 1883 Gordon, C Henry
b. 1888 Guderian, Heinz Wilhelm
b. 1893 Helck, Peter
b. 1894 Bache, Harold Leopold
b. 1896 Lupino, Stanley
b. 1898 Escher, M(aurits) C(ornelis)
b. 1899 Fazenda, Louise
b. 1900 Bormann, Martin Ludwig
b. 1900 White, William Lindsay
b. 1902 Fain, Sammy
b. 1904 Bellamy, Ralph
b. 1907 Britt, Steuart Henderson
b. 1907 Eames, Charles
b. 1907 Murphy, W(illiam) B(everly)
b. 1910 Foley, Red
b. 1911 Stigler, George Joseph
b. 1912 Gillis, Don
b. 1914 Hersey, John (Richard)
b. 1915 Cadieux, Marcel (Joseph David Romeo)
b. 1915 Goldman, Eric Frederick
b. 1916 Atkinson, Ted
b. 1917 Martin, Dean
b. 1919 Brewster, Kingman, Jr.
b. 1919 DePaul, Gene Vincent
b. 1920 Jacob, Francois
b. 1920 Reid, Beryl
b. 1921 Anderson, William Robert
b. 1921 Scott, Tony
b. 1922 Herrera Lane, Felipe
b. 1923 Bevilacqua, Anthony Joseph, Cardinal
b. 1923 Hirsch, Crazylegs
b. 1929 Petrosian, Tigran Vartanovich
b. 1931 Baldessari, John
b. 1931 Ing, Dean

b. 1932 Murtha, John Patrick
b. 1933 Hunt, Guy
b. 1936 Cattani, Richard J.
b. 1936 Loach, Ken(neth)
b. 1937 Lupus, Peter
b. 1937 Maynard, Robert Clyve
b. 1940 Bell, Bobby
b. 1941 Hensley, William L.
b. 1943 Gingrich, Newt(on Leroy)
b. 1945 Kennedy, Paul (Michael)
b. 1945 Livingstone, Ken
b. 1946 Manilow, Barry
b. 1947 Chavez, Linda
b. 1951 Piscopo, Joe
b. 1951 Starhawk
b. 1965 Jansen, Dan
b. 1980 Williams, Venus (Ebone Starr)
d. 1696 Sobieski, John, III
d. 1719 Addison, Joseph
d. 1775 Warren, Joseph
d. 1839 Bentinck, William Henry Cavendish, Lord
d. 1851 Russwurm, John Brown
d. 1854 Holbrook, Josiah
d. 1854 Sontag, Henriette
d. 1862 Canning, Charles John, Earl
d. 1866 Cass, Lewis
d. 1871 Vallandigham, Clement Laird
d. 1887 Hopkins, Mark
d. 1898 Burne-Jones, Edward Coley, Sir
d. 1905 Gomez, Maximo
d. 1920 Hyslop, James Hervey
d. 1925 Benson, Arthur Christopher
d. 1936 Walthall, Henry B
d. 1940 Harden, Arthur, Sir
d. 1947 Perkins, Maxwell Evarts
d. 1947 Perkins, William Maxwell Evarts
d. 1948 Carroll, Earl
d. 1955 Golden, John
d. 1955 Holme, Constance
d. 1957 Richardson, Dorothy Miller
d. 1958 Nagy, Imre
d. 1958 Pound, Louise
d. 1961 Chandler, Jeff
d. 1963 Alanbrooke, Alan Francis Brooke, 1st Viscount
d. 1963 Powys, John Cowper

d. 1975 Baxter, James Phinney, III
d. 1976 Odlum, Floyd Bostwick
d. 1979 Saltonstall, Leverett
d. 1981 Sharp, Zerna A
d. 1982 Harkness, Rebekah West
d. 1983 Mennin, Peter
d. 1983 Seifert, Elizabeth
d. 1984 Hegan, Jim
d. 1984 Rowe, James Henry, Jr.
d. 1986 Reed, Dean
d. 1986 Smith, Kate
d. 1987 Howser, Dick
d. 1987 Schell, Orville H, Jr.
d. 1989 Gardner, Hy
d. 1989 Matuszak, John (Daniel)
d. 1992 Exley, Frederick (Earl)
d. 1992 Hamilton, Grace Towns
d. 1995 Sterling, Claire
d. 1996 Kuhn, Thomas Samuel
d. 1998 Carberry, John J(oseph)

June 18
b. 1769 Castlereagh, Robert Stewart, Viscount
b. 1790 Eaton, John Henry
b. 1803 Weir, Robert W
b. 1811 Osgood, Frances Sargent Locke
b. 1812 Goncharov, Ivan Aleksandrovich
b. 1841 Ward, Lester Frank
b. 1845 Colvin, Sidney, Sir
b. 1845 Laveran, Charles Louis Alphonse
b. 1850 Curtis, Cyrus Hermann Kotszchmar
b. 1854 Scripps, Edward Wyllis
b. 1857 Folger, Henry Clay
b. 1864 Casey, Edward Pearce
b. 1868 Horthy de Nagybanya, Nicholas
b. 1869 Wells, Carolyn
b. 1871 Andreyev, Leonid Nikolayevich
b. 1871 Breese, Edmund
b. 1877 Flagg, James Montgomery
b. 1882 Dimitrov, Georgi Mikhailovich
b. 1884 Daladier, Edouard
b. 1884 Reynolds, Robert Rice
b. 1886 Mallory, George Leigh

b. 1888 Burger, Carl Victor
b. 1890 Schwartz, Maurice
b. 1891 Conrad, Con
b. 1896 Barry, Philip
b. 1896 Goldstein, Israel
b. 1896 Sweet, Blanche
b. 1904 Buehrig, Gordon
b. 1904 Hafstad, Lawrence R(andolph)
b. 1904 Luke, Keye
b. 1905 Power, Thomas S(arsfield)
b. 1906 Kyser, Kay (James King Kern)
b. 1907? MacDonald, Jeanette
b. 1907 Shalamov, Varlam Tikhonovich
b. 1908 Collyer, Bud
b. 1909 Gerard, Dave
b. 1910 Foran, Dick John Nicholas
b. 1910 Long, Avon
b. 1910 Marshall, E(dda) G(unnar)
b. 1910 McKinley, Ray
b. 1910 Tourel, Jennie
b. 1912 Morris, Glenn
b. 1913 Cahn, Sammy
b. 1913 Mondavi, Robert Gerald
b. 1913 Porter, Sylvia Field
b. 1914 Allen, Jack
b. 1915 Adair, Red
b. 1915 DeFrank, Vincent
b. 1916 Turbay Ayala, Julio Cesar
b. 1917 Boone, Richard
b. 1918 Karle, Jerome
b. 1918 Modigliani, Franco
b. 1920 Carmichael, Ian
b. 1921 Bertelli, Angelo B.
b. 1922 Keene, Donald Lawrence
b. 1924 Mikan, George Lawrence, Jr.
b. 1926 Bartok, Eva
b. 1926 Wicker, Tom
b. 1929 Habermas, Juergen
b. 1931 Cardoso, Fernando Henrique
b. 1932 Herschbach, Dudley Robert
b. 1932 Hill, Geoffrey
b. 1935 Michaels, Al
b. 1935 Mirkin, Gabe
b. 1937 Godwin, Gail
b. 1937 Rockefeller, John D(avison), IV
b. 1939 Brock, Lou(is Clark)
b. 1939 Slotnick, Barry Ivan
b. 1942 Ebert, Roger (Joseph)
b. 1942 Mbeki, Thabo Mvuyelwa

b. 1942 McCartney,
Paul
b. 1947 McCashin,
Constance Broman
b. 1948 Drake, Nick
b. 1949 Hearst, William
Randolph, III
b. 1949 VanAllsburg,
Chris
b. 1952 Gazda, Ricky
b. 1952 Kane, Carol
b. 1952 Rossellini,
Isabella
b. 1953 Smith, Jerome
b. 1963 Smith, Bruce
(Bernard)
d. 741 Leo, III
d. 1408 Yi Sng-gye
d. 1794 Murray, James
d. 1835 Cobbett,
William
d. 1849 Bugeaud de la
Piconnerie, Thomas
Robert
d. 1865 Ruffin, Edmund
d. 1869 Raymond,
Henry Jarvis
d. 1871 Grote, George
d. 1880 Sutter, John
Augustus
d. 1884 Alberdi, Juan
Bautista
d. 1897 Corson, Juliet
d. 1902 Butler, Samuel
d. 1905 Cleve, Per
Teodor
d. 1922 Kapteyn,
Jacobus Cornelis
d. 1924 Acevedo Diaz,
Eduardo
d. 1925 LaFollette,
Robert Marion
d. 1928 Amundsen,
Roald Engelbregt
d. 1942 Pryor, Arthur
W
d. 1945 Bascom,
Florence
d. 1945 Buckner, Simon
Bolivar, Jr.
d. 1948 Roebuck, Alvah
Curtis
d. 1953 Fonck, Rene
d. 1957 Williams,
J(ames) R(obert)
d. 1959 Barrymore,
Ethel Mae Blythe
d. 1960 Norris,
Kathleen Thompson
d. 1961 Gaedel, Eddie
d. 1962 Sargent, George
d. 1963 Armendariz,
Pedro
d. 1964 Morandi,
Giorgio
d. 1965 Melachrino,
George Miltiades
d. 1968 Baker, Dorothy
Dodds
d. 1971 Gomez, Thomas
d. 1971 Holman, Libby
d. 1971 Karrar, Paul
d. 1973 Bonnet,
Georges Etienne
d. 1973 Mahler, Fritz

d. 1974 Kelly, George
Edward
d. 1974 Zhukov, Georgi
Konstantinovich
d. 1975 Faisal ibn
Musaed
d. 1978 Alvarez, Walter
Clement
d. 1980 Fisher, Terence
d. 1981 Johnson,
Pamela Hansford
d. 1981 Katona, George
d. 1982 Barnes, Djuna
d. 1982 Cheever, John
d. 1982 Hicks, Granville
d. 1982 Hillenkoetter,
Roscoe H(enry)
d. 1982 Jurgens, Curt
d. 1983 Lewis, Robert
Alvin
d. 1985 Xuan Thuy
d. 1986 Smith, Frances
Scott Fitzgerald
Lanahan
d. 1989 Stone, I(sidor)
F(einstein)
d. 1991 Caulfield, Joan
d. 1992 Allen, Peter
Woolnough
d. 1992 Iveagh, Arthur
Francis Benjamin
Guinness, Lord
d. 2000 Marchand,
Nancy

June 19
b. 1566 James I
b. 1623 Pascal, Blaise
b. 1764 Artigas, Jose
Gervasio
b. 1782 Lamennais,
Hugues Felicite
Robert de
b. 1790 Gibson, John
b. 1801 Flores, Juan
Jose
b. 1826 Brace, Charles
Loring
b. 1854 Catalani,
Alfredo
b. 1856 Hubbard, Elbert
Green
b. 1861 Haig, Douglas
b. 1861 Rizal, Jose
b. 1863 Brady, William
Aloysius
b. 1865 Whitty, May,
Dame
b. 1869 Addison,
Christopher, Viscount
b. 1872 Farrand, Beatrix
Jones
b. 1877 Coburn, Charles
Douville
b. 1880 Dwiggins,
William Addison
b. 1881 Walker, Jimmy
b. 1882 Stein, Clarence
S
b. 1887 Yurka, Blanche
b. 1888 Johnston, Frank
H
b. 1890 Eberstadt,
Ferdinand
b. 1894 Cicotte, Eddie

b. 1896 Simpson, Wallis
(Bessie Wallis
Warfield)
b. 1897 Hinshelwood,
Cyril Norman, Sir
b. 1897 Howard, Moe
b. 1898 Seifert,
Elizabeth
b. 1898 Tharp, Louise
Hall
b. 1899 Mellon, Richard
King
b. 1900 Hobson, Laura
Zametkin
b. 1902 Lombardo, Guy
Albert
b. 1903 Gehrig, Lou
b. 1905 Voskovec,
George
b. 1906 Chain, Ernest
Boris, Sir
b. 1908 Burdick,
Quentin Northrop
b. 1908 Natwick,
Mildred
b. 1910 Flory, Paul
John
b. 1910 Fortas, Abe
b. 1911 Senanayake,
Dudley Shelton
b. 1912 Gabel, Martin
b. 1914 Cranston, Alan
MacGregor
b. 1917 Buttram, Pat
b. 1918 Abram, Morris
Berthold
b. 1919 Kael, Pauline
b. 1919 Reisman, Simon
b. 1920 Jourdan, Louis
b. 1921 Heflin, Howell
Thomas
b. 1921 Wrightson,
Patricia
b. 1922 Bohr, Aage
Niels
b. 1923 Rodriguez,
Andres
b. 1924 Nomelleni, Leo
Joseph
b. 1925 Nzo, Alfred
(Baphethuxolo)
b. 1928 Marchand,
Nancy
b. 1931 Lander, Toni
b. 1932 Pavan, Marisa
b. 1933 Angeli, Pier
b. 1933 Patsayev,
Viktor Ivanovich
b. 1935 Borja Cevallos,
Rodrigo
b. 1935 Taylor, John
Russell
b. 1936 DeVito, Tommy
b. 1936 Rowlands, Gena
(Catherine)
b. 1938 Gwathmey,
Charles
b. 1941 Klaus, Vaclav
b. 1942 Kasten, Robert
Walter, Jr.
b. 1945 Wolff, Tobias
(Jonathan Ansell)
b. 1947 Rushdie,
Salman Ahmed
b. 1948 Rashad,
Phylicia

b. 1950 Shuster, Rosie
b. 1951 Wilson, Ann
b. 1954 Turner,
Kathleen
b. 1956 Stone, Doug
b. 1959 DeBarge, Mark
b. 1963 Abdul, Paula
(Julie)
d. 1747 Nadir Shah
d. 1786 Greene,
Nathanael
d. 1794 Lee, Richard
Henry
d. 1811 Chase, Samuel
d. 1823 Combe,
William
d. 1844 Geoffroy Saint-
Hilaire, Etienne
d. 1861 Sotheby,
Samuel Leigh
d. 1867 Maximilian
d. 1914 Thomas,
Brandon
d. 1915 Taneyev,
Sergey Ivanovich
d. 1932 Plaatje,
Sol(omon)
T(shekisho)
d. 1937 Barrie, James
Matthew, Sir
d. 1939 Abbott, Grace
d. 1940 Myers, Jerome
d. 1951 Sikelianos,
Angelos
d. 1952 Schlusnus,
Heinrich
d. 1953 Rosenberg,
Ethel Greenglass
d. 1953 Rosenberg,
Julius
d. 1956 Watson,
Thomas J(ohn), Sr.
d. 1962 Borzage, Frank
d. 1966 Wynn, Ed
d. 1971 Wood, Gar(field
A)
d. 1975 Giancana, Sam
d. 1975 Wieman, Henry
Nelson
d. 1977 Brooks,
Geraldine
d. 1982 Lockridge,
Richard
d. 1984 Krasner, Lee
d. 1985 Boulting, John
d. 1985 LeFleming,
Christopher Kaye
d. 1985 Phillips,
Marjorie Acker
d. 1986 Bias, Len
d. 1986 Coluche
d. 1987 DeAngeli,
Marguerite Lofft
d. 1991 Arthur, Jean
d. 1993 Golding,
William (Gerald), Sir
d. 1993 Parsons, James
d. 1995 Townsend,
Peter Wooldridge
d. 1996 Schine,
G(erard) David
d. 2000 Takeshita,
Noboru

June 20
b. 1615 Rosa, Salvator
b. 1658 Brattle, Thomas

b. 1674 Rowe, Nicholas
b. 1700 Faneuil, Peter
b. 1760 Wellesley, Richard Colley, 1st Marquess Wellesley
b. 1771 Selkirk, 5th Earl of
b. 1819 Offenbach, Jacques
b. 1824 Street, George Edmund
b. 1832 Bristow, Benjamin Helm
b. 1837 Brewer, David Josiah
b. 1858 Chesnutt, Charles Waddell
b. 1860 Winton, Alexander
b. 1876 Ditmars, Raymond Lee
b. 1878 Morgan, Arthur
b. 1891 Costello, John Aloysius
b. 1892 Jung, Leo
b. 1894 Delacorte, George Thomas, Jr.
b. 1894 Hall, Lloyd Augustus
b. 1895 Price, Gwilym Alexander
b. 1896 Pelletier, Wilfrid
b. 1897 Keyhoe, Donald E(dward)
b. 1899 Traubel, Helen
b. 1900 Levi, Julian Edwin
b. 1903 Croft-Cooke, Rupert
b. 1903 Vare, Glenna Collett
b. 1905 Hellman, Lillian
b. 1906 Burnshaw, Stanley
b. 1906 Jones, Robert Trent
b. 1907 Driftwood, Jimmy
b. 1908 Barr, Murray Llewellyn
b. 1909 Flynn, Errol
b. 1909 Harrison, Joan (Mary)
b. 1911 Patrick, Gail
b. 1912 Linen, James A(lexander), III
b. 1913 Juan Carlos, Count of Barcelona
b. 1913 Torrance, Jack
b. 1915 Young, Terence
b. 1920 Mondlane, Eduardo Chivambo
b. 1920 Tutuola, Amos
b. 1921 Segura, Pancho
b. 1923 Gay, Peter Jack
b. 1924 Atkins, Chet
b. 1924 Murphy, Audie
b. 1928 Le Pen, Jean-Marie
b. 1929 Bronfman, Edgar Miles
b. 1930 Craig, Wendy
b. 1931 Dukakis, Olympia
b. 1932 Baird, Bill

b. 1933 Aiello, Danny Louis, Jr.
b. 1933 Landau, Martin
b. 1934 Podesta, Rossana
b. 1935 Dawson, Len
b. 1941 Frears, Stephen Arthur
b. 1942 Wilson, Brian Douglas
b. 1944 Hebard, Caroline
b. 1945 Murray, Anne
b. 1946 Vila, Bob
b. 1946 Watts, Andre
b. 1948 Sinatra, Christina
b. 1949 Richie, Lionel (Brockman)
b. 1950 Longmuir, Alan
b. 1951 Muldoon, Paul
b. 1952 Goodman, John
b. 1952 Seth, Vikram
b. 1953 Lauper, Cyndi
b. 1955 Anthony, Michael
b. 1959 Ogrodnick, John Alexander
b. 1967 Kidman, Nicole
b. 1969 Washington, MaliVai
d. 840 Louis I
d. 1597 Barents, Willem
d. 1778 Laclede, Pierre
d. 1787 Abel, Karl Friedrich
d. 1820 Belgrano, Manuel
d. 1836 Rouget de Lisle, Claude Joseph
d. 1836 Sieyes, Emmanuel Joseph
d. 1837 William, IV
d. 1870 Goncourt, Jules Alfred Huot de
d. 1876 Santa Anna, Antonio Lopez de
d. 1898 Tamayo y Baus, Manuel
d. 1904 Seiss, Joseph Augustus
d. 1917 Crafts, James Mason
d. 1925 Breuer, Josef
d. 1928 Mead, William Rutherford
d. 1933 Zetkin, Clara
d. 1940 Chase, Charley
d. 1940 Nevada, Emma
d. 1940 Reiss, Albert
d. 1945 Frank, Bruno
d. 1947 Siegel, Bugsy
d. 1956 Tikhomirov, Vasily Dmitrievich
d. 1958 Adler, Kurt
d. 1958 Alder, Kurt
d. 1958 Swope, Herbert Bayard
d. 1960 Kelly, John Brenden
d. 1965 Baruch, Bernard Mannes
d. 1966 Lemaitre, Georges
d. 1969 Beall, Lester Thomas

d. 1969 Murchison, Clint(on Williams, Sr.)
d. 1971 Ullman, James Ramsey
d. 1972 Johnson, Howard Deering
d. 1975 Chaudhuri, Haridas
d. 1977 Cone, Fairfax Mastick
d. 1981 Erwin, Pee Wee
d. 1984 Winwood, Estelle
d. 1987 Ali, Salim A
d. 1988 Leach, Will
d. 1990 Balin, Ina
d. 1993 Thuilier, Raymond
d. 1995 Gould, Laurence M(cKinley)
d. 1996 Krick, Irving P(arkhurst)
d. 1997 Helms, Bobby
d. 1997 Payton, Lawrence
d. 1999 Fadiman, Clifton (Paul)

June 21
b. 1002 Leo, IX, St.
b. 1639 Mather, Increase
b. 1774 Tompkins, Daniel D
b. 1783 Alston, Theodosia Burr
b. 1792 Baur, Ferdinand Christian
b. 1805 Jackson, Charles Thomas
b. 1813 Aytoun, William Edmonstoune
b. 1818 Wallace, Richard, Sir
b. 1832 Rainey, Joseph Hayne
b. 1845 Griffith, Samuel Walker
b. 1850 Beard, Dan(iel Carter)
b. 1850 Cecchetti, Enrico
b. 1855 Chausson, Ernest
b. 1859 Tanner, Henry Ossawa
b. 1863 Sauveur, Albert
b. 1873 Tomlinson, Henry Major
b. 1876 Keesom, Willem Hendrik
b. 1880 Gesell, Arnold
b. 1882 Kent, Rockwell
b. 1884 Auchinleck, Claude, Sir
b. 1887 Ismay, Hastings Lionel, Baron
b. 1888 Upson, Ralph Hazlett
b. 1891 Nervi, Pier Luigi
b. 1891 Scherchen, Hermann
b. 1892 Niebuhr, Reinhold

b. 1892 Rosenberg, Hilding
b. 1895 Snyder, John Wesley
b. 1896 Stickney, Dorothy
b. 1898 Peattie, Donald Culross
b. 1899 Gard, Wayne
b. 1902 Kesselring, Joseph Otto
b. 1902 Morenz, Howie
b. 1903 Hirschfeld, Al(bert)
b. 1903 Sjoberg, Alf
b. 1905 Sartre, Jean-Paul
b. 1906 Elson, Robert Truscott
b. 1906 Elting, Mary Letha
b. 1907 Prestopino, Gregorio
b. 1907 Shea, William Alfred
b. 1912 McCarthy, Mary Therese
b. 1913 Mosconi, Willie
b. 1914 Vickrey, William
b. 1916 Friedman, Herbert
b. 1916 O'Connor, Buddy
b. 1918 Lopat, Ed(mund Walter)
b. 1918 Roosa, Robert V(incent)
b. 1919 Soleri, Paolo
b. 1920 Martin, James Slattin, Jr.
b. 1921 Emanuel, James A
b. 1921 Russell, Jane
b. 1922 Holliday, Judy
b. 1924 Bleiberg, Robert Marvin
b. 1925 Stapleton, Maureen
b. 1926 Anders, Edward
b. 1926 Ubell, Earl
b. 1927 Stokes, Carl B(urton)
b. 1928 Raskin, Judith
b. 1930 Kaufman, Gerald Bernard
b. 1930 McCormack, Mike
b. 1931 Grossman, Lawrence K(ugelmass)
b. 1931 Heckler, Margaret Mary
b. 1932 Schifrin, Lalo Claudio
b. 1932 Strong, James Matthew
b. 1933 Kopell, Bernie
b. 1935 Markham, Monte
b. 1935 Sagan, Francoise
b. 1938 Ely, Ron
b. 1940 Cooke, Hope
b. 1940 Flaherty, Joe

b. 1940 Hartley,
Mariette
b. 1941 Foat, Ginny
b. 1941 Simmons,
Adele Smith
b. 1942 Reynolds,
William Bradford
b. 1942 West, Togo D.,
Jr.
b. 1943 McKinnon,
Isaiah
b. 1943 Serban, Andrei
George
b. 1944 Davies,
Ray(mond Douglas)
b. 1946 Merrill, Steve
b. 1946 Saatchi,
Maurice
b. 1947 Baxter,
Meredith
b. 1947 Gross, Michael
b. 1948 McEwan, Ian
(Russell)
b. 1949 Urquhart, Jane
b. 1951 Lofgren, Nils
b. 1953 Bhutto, Benazir
b. 1956 Sutcliffe, Rick
b. 1957 Breathed, Berke
b. 1959 Chambers, Tom
b. 1964? Davis, Sammi
b. 1973 Lewis, Juliette
b. 1982 William of
Wales
d. 1377 Edward III
d. 1529 Skelton, John
d. 1631 Smith, John
d. 1652 Jones, Inigo
d. 1788 Hamann,
Johann Georg
d. 1846 McCoy, Isaac
d. 1852 Froebel,
Friedrich Wilhelm
August
d. 1874 Angstrom,
Anders Jonas
d. 1877 Palmer,
Nathaniel Brown
d. 1886 Home, Daniel
Douglas
d. 1893 Stanford,
Leland
d. 1908 Rimsky-
Korsakov, Nikolai
Andreevich
d. 1914 Suttner, Bertha
Felicie Sophie Kinsky
von
d. 1926 Roze, Marie
d. 1929 Hobhouse,
Leonard Trelawny
d. 1932 Winton,
Alexander
d. 1934 Smith, Thorne
d. 1935 Roller, Alfred
d. 1940 Thompson,
John Taliaferro
d. 1940 Vuillard, (Jean)
Edouard
d. 1948 Brown, Alice
d. 1948 Matthes,
Francois-Emile
d. 1951 Perrine, Charles
Dillon
d. 1957 Farrere, Claude
d. 1957 Stark, Johannes

d. 1958 Ghormley,
Robert Lee
d. 1967 List, Emanuel
d. 1968 Saint Denis,
Ruth
d. 1969 Connolly,
Maureen
d. 1970 Lucas, Jim
Griffing
d. 1970 Sukarno,
Achmed
d. 1971 Rose, Carl
d. 1973 Leahy, Frank
d. 1975 Oenslager,
Donald Mitchell
d. 1978 Youngdahl,
Luther Wallace
d. 1981 Taubes,
Frederic
d. 1983 Dodson, Owen
(Vincent)
d. 1985 Boiardi, Hector
d. 1985 Erlander, Tage
Fritiof
d. 1987 Bloch, Bertram
d. 1987 Chasins, Abram
d. 1992 Li Xiannian
d. 1994 Mallory,
L(ester) D(ewitt)
d. 1995 Jones, Tristan
d. 1998 Campanis, Al
d. 2000 Hovhaness,
Alan

June 22
b. 1653 Fleury, Andre
Hercule de
b. 1748 Day, Thomas
b. 1757 Vancouver,
George
b. 1763 Mehul, Etienne
Nicolas
b. 1767 Humboldt,
Wilhelm Freiherr von
b. 1805 Mazzini,
Giuseppe
b. 1807 Hildreth,
Richard
b. 1837 Morphy, Paul
Charles
b. 1844 Lothrop, Harriet
Mulford Stone
b. 1845 Seddon,
Richard John
b. 1846 Hawthorne,
Julian
b. 1856 Haggard, Henry
Rider, Sir
b. 1859 Damrosch,
Frank Heino
b. 1871 McDougall,
William
b. 1871 Raine, William
MacLeod
b. 1877 Vionnet,
Madeleine
b. 1882 Bercovici,
Konrad
b. 1882 Scholl, William
M
b. 1887 Huxley, Julian
Sorell, Sir
b. 1888 Namier, Lewis
Bernstein
b. 1888 Seeger, Alan
b. 1894 Eliot, George
Fielding

b. 1894 Luboshutz,
Pierre
b. 1898 Remarque,
Erich Maria
b. 1902 Burns, David
b. 1903 Hubbell, Carl
Owen
b. 1903 Sturtzel, Jane
Levington
b. 1904 Wallmann,
Margherita
b. 1906 Highet, Gilbert
(Arthur)
b. 1906 Wilder, Billy
(Samuel)
b. 1907 Lindbergh,
Anne Spencer
Morrow
b. 1908 Livingstone,
Mary
b. 1909 Adler, Buddy
b. 1909 Todd, Mike
b. 1910 Dunham,
Katherine
b. 1910 Hunt, John,
Baron
b. 1910 Pears, Peter, Sir
b. 1914 Lucas, Jim
Griffing
b. 1915 Warmerdam,
Dutch
b. 1917 O'Brien, Davey
b. 1921 Champion,
Gower
b. 1921 Papp, Joseph
b. 1922 Blass, Bill
b. 1924 Barber, Jesse
B., Jr.
b. 1928 Hermannsson,
Steingrimur
b. 1928 Waite, Ralph
b. 1930 Bonatti, Walter
b. 1930 Lindbergh,
Charles Augustus
b. 1931 Lipton, Martin
b. 1933 Feinstein,
Dianne
b. 1934 Jordan, Don
b. 1936 Kristofferson,
Kris
b. 1941 Bradley,
Ed(ward R.)
b. 1942 Deodato
b. 1943 Hume, Brit
b. 1943 Malcolm,
Andrew H(ogarth)
b. 1944 Asher, Peter
b. 1944 Brandauer,
Klaus Maria
b. 1947 Butler, Octavia
E(stelle)
b. 1947 Rawlings, Jerry
John
b. 1948 Rundgren, Todd
b. 1949 Streep, Meryl
b. 1949 Wagner,
Lindsay J
b. 1954 Prinze, Freddie
b. 1962 Drexler, Clyde
d. 1527 Machiavelli,
Niccolo
d. 1535 Fisher, John
d. 1839 Boudinot, Elias
d. 1846 Haydon,
Benjamin Robert

d. 1864 McPherson,
James Birdseye
d. 1865 Saavedra, Angel
de
d. 1874 Staunton,
Howard
d. 1875 Logan, William
Edmond
d. 1885 Mahdi,
Mohammed Ahmed
d. 1896 Bristow,
Benjamin Helm
d. 1896 Harris,
Augustus, Sir
d. 1906 Schaudinn, Fritz
Richard
d. 1928 Frost, Arthur
Burdett
d. 1936 Schlick,
Friedrich Albert
Moritz
d. 1937 Rabearivelo,
Jean Joseph
d. 1950 Cowl, Jane
d. 1952 Lipman, Clara
d. 1954 Compton, Karl
Taylor
d. 1956 DeLaMare,
Walter
d. 1962 Shaaban Robert
d. 1965 Auslander,
Joseph
d. 1965 Selznick, David
O(liver)
d. 1968 Beckman,
Johnny
d. 1969 Garland, Judy
d. 1974 Milhaud, Darius
d. 1975 Wahloo, Per
d. 1978 Krag, Jens Otto
d. 1981 Frankenstein,
Alfred Victor
d. 1981 Harris, William
Bliss
d. 1981 Lane, Lola
d. 1981 Linder, Harold
Francis
d. 1983 Hinton,
Christopher, Sir
d. 1987 Astaire, Fred
d. 1987 Nix, Robert
N(elson) C(ornelius),
Sr.
d. 1988 Day, Dennis
d. 1988 Franken, Rose
d. 1988 Matlovich,
Leonard P., Jr.
d. 1988 Mitchell,
Howard (Bundy)
d. 1990 Frank, Ilya
Mikaylovich
d. 1991 O'Connor,
Kevin
d. 1992 Fisher, M(ary)
F(rances) K(ennedy)
d. 1993 Nixon, Patricia
d. 1993 Troy, Hannah
d. 1994 Stratton, Julius
A(dams)
d. 1996 Bell, T(errel)
H(oward)
d. 1998 O'Sullivan,
Maureen

June 23
b. 1625 Fell, John

b. 1668 Vico, Giovanni
Battista
b. 1685 Bernacchi,
Antonio Maria
b. 1803 Lee, Jason
b. 1810 Elssler, Fanny
b. 1822 Darley, Felix
Octavius Carr
b. 1839 Mueller,
Christian F
b. 1851 Eddy, Clarence
b. 1875 Milles, Carl
Wilhelm Emil
b. 1876 Cobb, Irvin
Shrewsbury
b. 1883 Taylor, Cyclone
b. 1889 Bishop,
Katharine Scott
b. 1890 Buckley,
Charles Anthony
b. 1892 Butler, Paul
b. 1893 Davison, Frank
Dalby
b. 1894 Edward VIII
b. 1894 Kinsey, Alfred
Charles
b. 1894 Weiss, George
Martin
b. 1895 Noble, Reg
b. 1896 Ferril, Thomas
Hornsby
b. 1900 Noyes, Blanche
Wilcox
b. 1900 Steelman, John
Roy
b. 1903 Darling, Frank
Fraser, Sir
b. 1904 Coon, Carleton
Stevens
b. 1907 Meade, James
Edward
b. 1909 Li Xiannian
b. 1909 Parks, Sam(uel)
McLaughlin)
b. 1910 Anouilh, Jean
Marie Lucien Pierre
b. 1910 Little, Lawson
b. 1910 Morgan,
Edward P
b. 1911 Ogilvy, David
Mackenzie
b. 1912 Turing, Alan
(Mathison)
b. 1913 Humes, Helen
b. 1913 Rogers, William
Pierce
b. 1915 Price, Dennis
b. 1916 Worth, Irene
b. 1919 Gmeiner,
Hermann
b. 1924 Premadasa,
Ranasinghe
b. 1925 Blyden, Larry
b. 1925 Chennault,
Anna Chan
b. 1925 Modell, Art(hur
B)
b. 1927 Fosse, Bob
b. 1929 Carter, June
b. 1929 Lapidus, Ted
b. 1930 Dinitz, Simcha
b. 1930 Eisele, Donn
Fulton
b. 1934 Torrey, Bill
b. 1935 Ferre, Maurice
Antonio

b. 1936 Bach, Richard
David
b. 1940 Faith, Adam
b. 1940 Rudolph,
Wilma (Glodean)
b. 1940 Trask, Diana
b. 1943 Levine, James
Lawrence
b. 1946 Shackelford,
Ted
b. 1947 Brown, Bryan
b. 1948 Echo-Hawk,
Walter R.
b. 1948 Thomas,
Clarence
b. 1948 Youngblood,
Johnny Ray
b. 1957 McDormand,
Frances
b. 1959 Gustafson,
Karin
b. 1960 Deshaies, Jim
d. 1611? Hudson, Henry
d. 1822 Vesey,
Denmark
d. 1832 Hall, James, Sir
d. 1836 Mill, James
d. 1865 DuPont, Samuel
Francis
d. 1868 Vassar,
Matthew
d. 1878 Back, George,
Sir
d. 1881 Schleiden,
Matthias Jakob
d. 1891 Weber,
Wilhelm Eduard
d. 1895 Renwick,
James, Jr.
d. 1907 Stuart, Hod
d. 1945 Lake, Simon
d. 1946 Hart, William
Surrey
d. 1950 Fels, Samuel
Simeon
d. 1953 Gleizes, Albert
L
d. 1956 Gliere,
Reinhold Moritsevich
d. 1965 Boland, Mary
d. 1970 Turner, Roscoe
Wilson
d. 1973 Holden, Fay
d. 1975 Priest, Ivy
(Maude) Baker
d. 1976 Warneke,
Lon(nie)
d. 1980 Gandhi, Sanjay
d. 1980 Still, Clyfford
d. 1983 Cervantes,
Alfonso Juan
d. 1985 Kotsching,
Walter Maria
d. 1985 McIlhenny,
Walter S
d. 1989 Aflaq, Michel
d. 1989 Manning,
Timothy, Cardinal
d. 1993 Kopal, Zdenek
d. 1995 Grimsby, Roger
d. 1995 Salk, Jonas
E(dward)
d. 1996 Papandreou,
Andreas (George)
d. 1997 Shabazz, Betty

June 24
b. 1450 Cabot, John
b. 1542 John of the
Cross, Saint
b. 1747 O'Keeffe, John
b. 1750 Dolomieu,
Deodat Guy Gratet de
b. 1753 Hull, William
b. 1763 Josephine
b. 1771 DuPont,
Eleuthere Irenee
b. 1788 Blanchard,
Thomas
b. 1813 Beecher, Henry
Ward
b. 1831 Davis, Rebecca
Blaine Harding
b. 1838 Schmoller,
Gustav Friedrich von
b. 1839 Swift, Gustavus
Franklin
b. 1842 Bierce,
Ambrose Gwinett
b. 1848 Adams, Brooks
b. 1848 Adams, Peter
Chardon Brooks
b. 1850 Gummere,
William Stryker
b. 1852 Adler, Victor
b. 1856 Mercer, Henry
Chapman
b. 1872 Crowninshield,
Francis Welch
b. 1881 Randall, James
Garfield
b. 1881 Tietjen, Heinz
b. 1883 Hess, Victor
Francis
b. 1885 Tairov,
Aleksandr
Yakovlevich
b. 1887 Watson, Mark
Skinner
b. 1888 Rietveld, Gerrit
Thomas
b. 1892 Daringer, Helen
Fern
b. 1893 Disney, Roy
O(liver)
b. 1895 Dempsey, Jack
b. 1897 Ludwig, Daniel
Keith
b. 1899 George, Dan,
Chief
b. 1900 Austin, Gene
b. 1901 Partch, Harry
b. 1901 Penney,
William George
b. 1904 Harris, Phil
b. 1905 Whistler, Rex
b. 1906 Fournier, Pierre
b. 1907 Schlumberger,
Jean
b. 1909 Cavanna, Betty
b. 1909 Katims, Milton
b. 1910 Kaufman,
Irving R(obert)
b. 1911 Fangio, Juan
Manuel
b. 1911 Sabato, Ernesto
b. 1912 Cousins,
Norman
b. 1914 Peterson, Edith
R.
b. 1915 Hoyle, Fred, Sir

b. 1916 Ciardi, John
Anthony
b. 1919 Molinaro, Al
b. 1920 Ernst, Jimmy
b. 1923 Carter, Jack
b. 1923 Romiti, Cesare
b. 1927 Edwards, James
Burrows
b. 1928 Foust, Larry
b. 1928 Selzer, Richard
(Alan)
b. 1930 Chabrol, Claude
b. 1931 Casper, Billy
b. 1933 Jones, Sam(uel)
b. 1935 Hamill, Pete
b. 1936 Predock,
Antoine Samuel
b. 1939 Garrett, Henry
Lawrence, III
b. 1941 Kristeva, Julia
b. 1941 Whitman,
Charles Joseph
b. 1942 Fleetwood,
Mick
b. 1942 Frei Ruiz-Tagle,
Eduardo
b. 1942 Lee, Michele
b. 1944 Beck, Jeff
b. 1944 Wood, Chris
b. 1945 Blunstone,
Colin
b. 1945 Pataki, George
E(lmer)
b. 1945 Stove, Betty
b. 1946 Onizuka,
Ellison
b. 1946 Reich, Robert
B(ernard)
b. 1948 Calderon Sol,
Armando
b. 1949 Allen, Nancy
b. 1958 Chen, T.C.
b. 1961 Reed, Ralph
b. 1964 Suter, Gary
b. 1967 Stringfield,
Sherry
d. 79 Vespasian
d. 1398 Hung-Wu
d. 1637 Peiresc,
Nicholas-Claude
Fabri de
d. 1643 Hampden, John
d. 1729 Taylor, Edward
d. 1803 Thornton,
Matthew
d. 1817 McKean,
Thomas
d. 1860 Bonaparte,
Jerome
d. 1875 Labrouste,
Pierre Francois Henri
d. 1877 Owen, Robert
Dale
d. 1892 Ford, Bob
d. 1894 Healy, George
Peter Alexander
d. 1908 Cleveland,
Grover
d. 1909 Jewett, Sarah
Orne
d. 1922 Rathenau,
Walter
d. 1922 Rockefeller,
William
d. 1928 Blinn, Holbrook
d. 1929 Hern, Riley

d. 1930 Jewett, Henry
d. 1933 Jones, Matilda
Sissieretta Joyner
d. 1934 Rice, Joseph
Mayer
d. 1946 Hare, James
Henry
d. 1957 Bowes, Walter
d. 1957 Kupka, Frank
d. 1959 Starkweather,
Charles
d. 1964 Davis, Stuart
d. 1966 Whitman,
Charles Joseph
d. 1968 Alexander,
Hattie Elizabeth
d. 1969 King, Frank
d. 1969 Ley, Willy
d. 1969 Pegler,
Westbrook
d. 1972 Delderfield,
Ronald Frederick
d. 1976 Cunningham,
Imogen
d. 1976 White, Minor
d. 1978 Babb, Howard
Selden
d. 1980 Burpee, David
d. 1980 Kaufman, Boris
d. 1981 Albrand,
Martha
d. 1981 Ball, Edward
d. 1981 Butler, Paul
d. 1983 Miller, William
E
d. 1983 Taft, Charles
Phelps
d. 1984 Campbell,
Clarence Sutherland
d. 1987 Gleason, Jackie
d. 1991 Tamayo, Rufino
d. 1992 Nossiter,
Bernard Daniel
d. 1997 Keith, Brian
d. 1998 O'Dwyer, Paul

June 25
b. 1788 Pellico, Silvio
b. 1831 Miller, Olive
Thorne
b. 1834 Potter, Henry
Codman
b. 1842 Alfaro, Jose
Eloy
b. 1852 Gaudi y Cornet,
Antonio
b. 1860 Charpentier,
Gustave
b. 1864 Nernst, Walther
Hermann
b. 1865 Henri, Robert
b. 1870 Childers,
Erskine
b. 1874 O'Neill, Rose
Cecil
b. 1875 Benn, Ernest
John Pickstone, Sir
b. 1886 Arnold, Henry
Harley
b. 1886 McIntyre,
James Francis
Aloysius, Cardinal
b. 1887 Abbott, George
(Francis)
b. 1893 Greenwood,
Charlotte

b. 1894 Oberth,
Hermann Julius
b. 1894 Sturtzel,
Howard Allison
b. 1898 Ascoli, Max
b. 1898 Ross, Roy G
b. 1900 Chapman, John
(Arthur)
b. 1900 Mountbatten of
Burma, Louis
Mountbatten, Earl
b. 1902 Rubloff, Arthur
b. 1903 Orwell, George
b. 1903 Revere, Anne
b. 1903 Tracy, Arthur
b. 1904 Muller-Munk,
Peter
b. 1906 Livesey, Roger
b. 1907 Jensen,
Johannes Hans Daniel
b. 1907 Six, Robert
Forman
b. 1908 Quine,
W(illard) V(an
Orman)
b. 1909 Fuchs, Daniel
b. 1911 Stein, William
Howard
b. 1912 Cahill, William
T(homas)
b. 1912 Shapp, Milton
J(errold)
b. 1913 Cesaire, Aime
Fernand
b. 1915 Hayes, Peter
Lind
b. 1916 Saxbe, William
Bart
b. 1916 Toynbee, Philip
b. 1920 Harkless, Necia
Desiree
b. 1921 Franca, Celia
b. 1923 Francis,
Sam(uel Lewis)
b. 1923 Gilman,
Dorothy
b. 1923 Mosley,
Nicholas
b. 1924 Lumet, Sidney
b. 1925 Briley, John
Richard
b. 1925 Chenier, Clifton
b. 1925 Lockhart, June
b. 1925 Venturi, Robert
b. 1927 Freedman,
Gerald
b. 1928 Culliford, Peyo
b. 1929 Carle, Eric
b. 1929 Eisner, Thomas
b. 1931 Singh,
V(ishwanath) P(ratap)
b. 1933 Meredith, James
Howard
b. 1933 Siza, Alvaro
(Joaquim Melo)
b. 1935 Kramer, Larry
b. 1936 Habibie,
B(acharuddin) J(usuf)
b. 1937 Morgan,
Marabel
b. 1941 Arcand, Denys
b. 1942 Miller, James
Clifford, III
b. 1942 Reed, Willis, Jr.
b. 1942 Tremblay,
Michel

b. 1944 Goldberg, Gary
David
b. 1945 Kilpatrick,
Carolyn Cheeks
b. 1945 Simon, Carly
b. 1946 Lanier, Allen
b. 1948 Walker, Jimmie
b. 1949 George, Phyllis
b. 1963 Gilmour, Doug
b. 1963 Michael,
George
b. 1966 Mutombo,
Dikembe
d. 1634 Marston, John
d. 1767 Telemann,
Georg Philipp
d. 1822 Hoffmann,
E(rnst) T(heodor)
A(madeus)
d. 1830 George IV
d. 1830 McDowell,
Ephraim
d. 1842 Sismondi, Jean
Charles Leonard
Simonde de
d. 1876 Cummins,
George David
d. 1876 Custer, George
Armstrong
d. 1879 Cooke, William
Fothergil, Sir
d. 1889 Hayes, Lucy
Webb
d. 1896 Tilley, Samuel
Leonard, Sir
d. 1896 Trumbull,
Lyman
d. 1897 Oliphant,
Margaret
d. 1898 Cohn,
Ferdinand Julius
d. 1906 White, Stanford
d. 1912 Alma-Tadema,
Lawrence, Sir
d. 1916 Eakins, Thomas
d. 1918 Beckley, Jake
d. 1924 Darragh, Jack
d. 1931 Saunders,
William Laurence
d. 1937 Clive, Colin
d. 1947 Shaw, Albert
d. 1952 Ross,
Alex(ander)
d. 1956 Arlen, Michael
d. 1956 King, Ernest
Joseph
d. 1960 Baade,
(Wilhelm Heinrich)
Walter
d. 1961 Ferguson,
Miriam Amanda
d. 1964 Rietveld, Gerrit
Thomas
d. 1966 Jackson, Busher
d. 1969 Dix, Otto
d. 1971 Boyd-Orr, John,
Baron
d. 1971 Orr, John Boyd,
1st Baron of Brechin
d. 1972 Fleischer,
Nat(haniel Stanley)
d. 1972 McKenney,
Ruth
d. 1975 Cowdry,
Edmund Vincent
d. 1976 Mercer, Johnny

d. 1977 Kaufman, Sue
d. 1979 Halsman,
Philippe
d. 1979 Hoyt, Palmer
d. 1980 Grattan, Clinton
Hartley
d. 1983 Ginastera,
Alberto Evaristo
d. 1983 Monroe, Marion
d. 1984 Foucault,
Michel
d. 1988 Axis Sally
d. 1989 Hassenfeld,
Stephen David
d. 1990 Carney, Robert
Bostwick
d. 1990 Glanville-Hicks,
Peggy
d. 1991 Tomes, Margot
d. 1992 Stirling, James
d. 1993 John, John
P(ico)
d. 1995 Burger, Warren
E(arl)
d. 1995 Walton, Ernest
Thomas Sinton
d. 1997 Cousteau,
Jacques (Yves)

June 26
b. 1741 Langdon, John
b. 1742 Middleton,
Arthur
b. 1763 Morland,
George
b. 1793 Portales, Diego
(Jose Victor)
b. 1812 Palmer, Frances
Flora Bond
b. 1817 Bronte, Patrick
Branwell
b. 1819 Doubleday,
Abner
b. 1824 Kelvin, William
Thomson, Baron
b. 1838 Chatterji,
Bankimchandra
b. 1854 Borden, Robert
Laird, Sir
b. 1865 Berenson,
Bernard
b. 1865 Scheidemann,
Philipp
b. 1866 Herbert, George
Edward Stanhope
Molyneux
b. 1875 Stracciari,
Riccardo
b. 1881 Shambaugh,
Jessie Field
b. 1885 Hempel, Frieda
b. 1891 Cohen, Octavus
Roy
b. 1891 Howard, Sidney
Coe
b. 1892 Buck, Pearl
S(ydenstricker)
b. 1893 Broonzy, Big
Bill
b. 1894 Eagels, Jeanne
b. 1894 Kapitsa, Pyotr
Leonidovich
b. 1894 Lovejoy,
Clarence Earle
b. 1895 Hainsworth,
George

d. 1944 Menchik-Stevenson, Vera Francevna
d. 1944 Moffatt, James
d. 1946 Gag, Wanda
d. 1951 Warfield, David
d. 1952 Lincoln, Elmo
d. 1953 Lahey, Frank Howard
d. 1957 Lowry, Malcolm
d. 1960 Pollitt, Harry
d. 1964 Gilbert, Alfred Carlton, Jr.
d. 1966 Waley, Arthur David
d. 1973 Browder, Earl Russell
d. 1973 Truex, Ernest
d. 1975 Stolz, Robert
d. 1979 Bernstein, Theodore Menline
d. 1980 Bigard, Albany Barney Leon
d. 1980 Dornberger, Walter Robert
d. 1980 McWilliams, Carey
d. 1983 Anderson, Max(ie Leroy)
d. 1984 Jacoby, Oswald
d. 1985 Sarkis, Elias
d. 1986 Erteszek, Jan
d. 1986 Laeri, J(ohn) Howard
d. 1986 Rogers, Don(ald Lavert)
d. 1987 Flynt, Althea Sue
d. 1988 Adams, Leonie Fuller
d. 1988 Groth, John August
d. 1989 Ayer, Alfred Jules, Sir
d. 1992 Jones, Allan
d. 1995 Kurtz, Efrem
d. 1995 Schottland, Charles I(rwin)
d. 1996 Adair, Peter
d. 1996 Howard, Jane Temple
d. 1999 Motley, Marion
d. 1999 Papadopoulos, George
d. 2000 Kelley, Larry

June 28
b. 1476 Paul, IV
b. 1491 Henry VIII
b. 1703 Wesley, John
b. 1712 Rousseau, Jean Jacques
b. 1795 Hitchcock, Lambert
b. 1809 Borel d'Hauterive, Petrus
b. 1819 Harpignies, Henri
b. 1821 Maretzek, Max
b. 1831 Joachim, Joseph
b. 1844 Hopkins, Gerard Manley
b. 1858 Skinner, Otis
b. 1867 Pirandello, Luigi
b. 1873 Carrel, Alexis

b. 1874 Speaks, Oley
b. 1883 Laval, Pierre
b. 1883 Moran, Polly
b. 1887 Dell, Floyd
b. 1889 Aqqad, Abbas Mahmud al-
b. 1889 Dodds, Harold Willis
b. 1891 Spaatz, Carl Andrew
b. 1892 Campbell, Clifford, Sir
b. 1892 Gordon, Max
b. 1894? Forbes, Esther
b. 1894 Nicoll, (John Ramsay) Allardyce
b. 1897 Dana, Viola
b. 1899 Meland, Bernard Eugene
b. 1901 Bruce, Ailsa Mellon
b. 1902 Dillinger, John Herbert
b. 1902 Smith, Joe
b. 1904 Rollini, Adrian
b. 1905 Binns, Joseph Patterson
b. 1905 Montagu, (Montague Francis) Ashley
b. 1906 Mayer, Maria Goeppert
b. 1907 Bull, Odd
b. 1907 Victor, Paul-Emile
b. 1909 Ambler, Eric
b. 1912 Celibidache, Sergiu
b. 1912 Coons, Albert Hewett
b. 1914 Arieti, Silvano
b. 1914 Flatt, Lester Raymond
b. 1914 Seymour, Dan
b. 1914 Trifa, Valerian
b. 1920 Hotchner, Aaron Edward
b. 1921 Rao, P V Narasimha
b. 1924 Dolci, Danilo
b. 1925 Klebe, Giselher
b. 1926 Booth, George
b. 1926 Brooks, Mel
b. 1927 Levy, Raymond
b. 1928 Evans, Harold Matthew
b. 1932 Morita, Pat
b. 1934 Levin, Carl Milton
b. 1936 Magliozzi, Tom
b. 1936 Owens, Major (Robert)
b. 1937 Luciano, Ron(ald Michael)
b. 1938 Panetta, Leon E(dward)
b. 1942 Hani, Chris
b. 1942 Kopay, David
b. 1943 Johanson, Donald Carl
b. 1943 Klitzing, Klaus von
b. 1943 Laguna, Ismael
b. 1943 Von Klitzing, Klaus
b. 1946 Davison, Bruce

b. 1946 Martyn, John
b. 1946 Radner, Gilda
b. 1947 Helprin, Mark
b. 1947 Tyson, Laura D'Andrea
b. 1948 Bates, Kathy
b. 1948 Maravich, Pete(r Press)
b. 1949 Baylor, Don(ald Edward)
b. 1949 Otte, Ruth
b. 1954 Krige, Alice
b. 1955 Hampson, Thomas
b. 1959 Balukas, Jean
b. 1959 Fraser, Brad
b. 1960 Elway, John (Albert)
b. 1961 Schroeder, Jay Brian
b. 1966 Cusack, John
b. 1969 Brisebois, Danielle
d. 1598 Ortelius, Abraham
d. 1813 Scharnhorst, Gerhard Johann David von
d. 1830 Walker, David
d. 1836 Madison, James
d. 1855 Raglan, Fitzroy James Henry Somerset, Baron
d. 1889 Mitchell, Maria
d. 1904 Emmett, Daniel Decatur
d. 1914 Francis Ferdinand
d. 1914 Franz Ferdinand
d. 1923 Biggs, Hermann Michael
d. 1929 Carpenter, Edward
d. 1936 Berkman, Alexander
d. 1940 Balbo, Italo
d. 1941 Carle, Richard
d. 1946 Perry, Antoinette
d. 1955 Ljungberg, Gota
d. 1958 Noyes, Alfred
d. 1959 Shaver, Dorothy
d. 1962 Cochrane, Mickey
d. 1963 Baker, Frank
d. 1965 Nichols, Red
d. 1971 Binns, Archie Fred
d. 1971 Stangl, Franz Paul
d. 1974 Bush, Vannevar
d. 1975 Doxiadis, Constantinos Apostolos
d. 1975 Serling, Rod
d. 1975 Stevenson, Coke Robert
d. 1976 Baker, Stanley, Sir
d. 1978 DuPont, Clifford Walter
d. 1979 Cousteau, Philippe
d. 1979 Dessau, Paul
d. 1979 Schulberg, Stuart

d. 1980 Douglas, Helen Mary Gahagan
d. 1980 Iturbi, Jose
d. 1981 Beheshti, Mohammad, Ayatollah
d. 1981 Fox, Terry
d. 1982 Mills, Harry
d. 1984 Astor, Gavin
d. 1984 Yadin, Yigael
d. 1985 Ward, Lynd
d. 1987 Lay, James Selden, Jr.
d. 1989 Ivens, Joris
d. 1992 Tal, Mikhail Nekhemyevich
d. 1993 Christoff, Boris
d. 1993 Cohn, Zanvil (Alexander)
d. 1994 Washington, Fredi
d. 1995 Bonsal, Philip Wilson
d. 1996 Terra, Daniel J(ames)
d. 2000 Weinmesiter, Arnie

June 29
b. 1577 Rubens, Peter Paul, Sir
b. 1628 Molinos, Miguel de
b. 1721 Kalb, Johann de
b. 1798 Haring, Georg Wilhelm Heinrich
b. 1798 Leopardi, Giacomo
b. 1830 Ward, J(ohn) Q(uincy) A(dams)
b. 1835 Thaxter, Celia
b. 1852 McMaster, John Bach
b. 1858 Goethals, George Washington
b. 1861 Mayo, William James
b. 1863 Robinson, James Harvey
b. 1865 Borah, William Edgar
b. 1868 Hale, George Ellery
b. 1874 Tetrazzini, Luisa
b. 1880 Beck, Ludwig August Theoder
b. 1886 Cheney, Sheldon Warren
b. 1886 Ogburn, W(illiam) F(ielding)
b. 1886 Schuman, Robert
b. 1886 VanDerZee, James
b. 1890 MacFarlane, Willie
b. 1900 Saint-Exupery, Antoine (Jean Baptiste Marie Roger) de
b. 1901 Eddy, Nelson
b. 1901 Inescort, Frieda
b. 1903 Voelker, John Donaldson
b. 1905 Gardner, Ed(ward Francis)

d. 1992 Ruchlis,
Hy(man)
d. 1994 Roberts, Dennis
J(oseph)
d. 1995 Gordon, Gale
d. 1995 Hyman, Phyllis
d. 1996 Mazia, Daniel

JULY

b. 1624 Fox, George
b. 1660 Prandtauer,
Jakob
b. 1712 Bernard,
Francis, Sir
b. 1743 Paley, William
b. 1756 Rowlandson,
Thomas
b. 1877 Scholes, Percy
Alfred
b. 1910 Allard, Sydney
b. 1920 Ginsburg,
Charles P
b. 1934 Fletcher, Louise
d. 1141 Ha-Levi, Judah
d. 1368 Guy de
Chauliac
d. 1538 Almagro, Diego
de
d. 1752 Washington,
Lawrence
d. 1901 Kerr, Orpheus
C
d. 1913 Hemon, Louis
d. 1935 Meier-Graefe,
Julius
d. 1947 Lembede,
Anton
d. 1989 Higgins,
William R

July 1
b. 1646 Leibniz,
Gottfried Wilhelm
von
b. 1725 Rochambeau,
Jean Baptiste
Donatien de Vimeur,
Comte
b. 1730 Sears, Isaac
b. 1802 Welles, Gideon
b. 1818 Gorgas, Josiah
b. 1818 Semmelweis,
Ignaz Philipp
b. 1828 Chernyshevsky,
Nikolai Gavrilovich
b. 1844 Cameron,
Verney Lovett
b. 1857 Connor, Roger
b. 1858 Metcalf,
Willard Leroy
b. 1858 Stephens, Alice
Barber
b. 1861 Clarkson, John
Gibson
b. 1864 Russell, James
Earl
b. 1872 Bleriot, Louis
b. 1873 Guy-Blache,
Alice
b. 1877 Davis,
Benjamin Oliver, Sr.
b. 1879 Jouhaux, Leon
b. 1882 Glaspell, Susan
Keating
b. 1890 Morgan, Frank

b. 1892 Cain, James
M(allahan)
b. 1892 Lurcat, Jean
Marie
b. 1893 Parker, Daniel
Francis
b. 1893 White, Walter
Francis
b. 1897 Barry, Tom
b. 1897 Bickerman,
Elias Joseph
b. 1898 Lyons, Eugene
b. 1899 Laughton,
Charles
b. 1899 Tsatsos,
Constantinos
b. 1900 Dorsey, Thomas
Andrew
b. 1901 Phillips, Irna
b. 1902 Cohen, Myron
b. 1902 Sert, Jose Luis
b. 1902 Wyler, William
b. 1903 Emerson,
Gladys Anderson
b. 1904 Calderone,
Mary Steichen
b. 1906 Calder, Peter
Ritchie
b. 1907 Bolotowsky,
Ilya
b. 1907 Stern, Bill
b. 1908 Ali, Ahmed
b. 1908? Lauder, Estee
b. 1909 Evans, Madge
b. 1909 Onetti, Juan
Carlos
b. 1910 Piret, Edgar L
b. 1911 Rey, Alvino
b. 1912 Brower, David
Ross
b. 1912 Matheson,
Murray
b. 1913 Sinclair, Jo
b. 1914 Linh, Nguyen
Van
b. 1915 Dixon, Willie
(James)
b. 1915 Stafford, Jean
b. 1916 DeHavilland,
Olivia Mary
b. 1916 Shklovsky, Iosif
Samvilovitch
b. 1916 Stanford-Tuck,
Robert Roland
b. 1921 Khama, Seretse
M., Sir
b. 1925 Granger, Farley
b. 1926 Hahn, Carl
Horst
b. 1926 Henze, Hans
Werner
b. 1928 Denoff, Sam
b. 1929 Edelman,
Gerald Maurice
b. 1930 Menem, Carlos
Saul
b. 1931 Caron, Leslie
Clare Margaret
b. 1931 Kountche,
Seyni
b. 1932 Duffey, Joseph
Daniel
b. 1933 Young, Jean
Childs
b. 1934 Farr, Jamie

b. 1934 Langman,
Claude Berel
b. 1934 Marsh, Jean
b. 1934 Pollack, Sydney
b. 1936 Amos, Wally
b. 1940 Jones, Charles
A, Jr.
b. 1941 Gilbert,
Rod(rigue Gabriel)
b. 1941 Gilman, Alfred
G
b. 1941 Quinn, Sally
b. 1941 Tharp, Twyla
b. 1942 Black, Karen
b. 1942 Bujold,
Genevieve
b. 1942 Crouch, Andrae
Edward
b. 1945 Harry, Deborah
(Ann)
b. 1948 Robinson, Tom
b. 1951 Anderson,
Daryl
b. 1952 Aykroyd,
Dan(iel Edward)
b. 1952 Shutt, Steve
b. 1954 Hanauer, Chip
b. 1956 Whitley, Keith
b. 1957 Patterson, Lorna
b. 1958 Lieberman,
Nancy
b. 1960 King, Evelyn
b. 1961 Diana, Princess
of Wales
b. 1961 Lewis, Carl
b. 1967 Lee, Pamela
b. 1977 Tyler, Liv
d. 1483? Edward V
d. 1614 Casaubon, Isaac
d. 1782 Rockingham,
2nd Marquess of
d. 1784 Bach, Wilhelm
Friedemann
d. 1824 Macquarie,
Lachlan
d. 1839 Mahmud, II
d. 1855 Rosmini-
Serbati, Antonio
d. 1860 Goodyear,
Charles
d. 1876 Bakunin,
Mikhail
Aleksandrovich
d. 1881 Lotze, Rudolf
Hermann
d. 1881 Sainte-Clair
Deville, Henri
Etienne
d. 1884 Pinkerton, Allan
d. 1896 Stowe, Harriet
(Elizabeth) Beecher
d. 1905 Hay, John
Milton
d. 1906 Garcia, Manuel
Patricio Rodriguez
d. 1912 Quimby, Harriet
d. 1925 Satie, Erik
d. 1928 Hopwood,
Avery
d. 1940 Turpin, Ben
d. 1942 Daudet, Leon
d. 1949 Johnston, Frank
H
d. 1950 Jaques-
Dalcroze, Emile
d. 1950 Saarinen, Eliel

d. 1952 Rosenbach,
Abraham Simon Wolf
d. 1958 Laban, Rudolf
von
d. 1963 Chautemps,
Camille
d. 1964 Monteux, Pierre
d. 1964 Pound, Roscoe
d. 1965 Ruark, Robert
Chester
d. 1965 Thornhill,
Claude
d. 1971 Bragg, William
Lawrence, Sir
d. 1971 Constantine,
Learie Nicholas
Constantine, Baron
d. 1973 Hammond,
Laurens
d. 1974 Peron, Juan
d. 1980 Snow, C(harles)
P(ercy), Sir
d. 1981 Breuer, Marcel
Lajos
d. 1981 Daniel, Dan(iel)
d. 1981 Voskovec,
George
d. 1983 Copeland,
Lammot du Pont
d. 1983 Fuller, Richard
Buckminster
d. 1983 Hoffman, Julius
Jennings
d. 1985 Murray, Pauli
d. 1985 Sterling, John
Ewart Wallace
d. 1986 Wells, Edward
d. 1991 Landon,
Michael
d. 1992 Meredith,
Sidney
d. 1995 Smith, Robert
Weston
d. 1995 Wolfman Jack
d. 1996 Cahill, William
T(homas)
d. 1996 Tesich, Steve
d. 1997 Mitchum,
Robert
d. 1999 Dmytryk,
Edward
d. 1999 Mars, Forrest
d. 1999 Mitchell, Guy
d. 1999 Nkomo, Joshua
(Mqabuko Nyongolo)
d. 1999 Polhill, Robert
d. 1999 Sidney, Sylvia
d. 2000 Matthau, Walter
d. 2000 Scherer,
Ray(mond Lewis)

July 2
b. 1489 Cranmer,
Thomas
b. 1714 Gluck,
Christoph
b. 1724 Klopstock,
Friedrich Gottlieb
b. 1810 Toombs, Robert
Augustus
b. 1821 Tupper, Charles
b. 1836 Schnorr,
Ludwig von
Carolsfeld
b. 1855 Barron,
Clarence Walker

d. 1937 Schick, Jacob
d. 1941 Harris, Sam
  Henry
d. 1951 Casey, Hugh
  Thomas
d. 1954 Marsh,
  Reginald
d. 1957 Luque, Dolf
d. 1959 Bojer, Johan
d. 1963 Bouche, Rene
  Robert
d. 1966 Taylor, (Joseph)
  Deems
d. 1969 Jones, Brian
d. 1970 Keyes, Frances
  Parkinson
d. 1970 Newman,
  Barnett
d. 1971 Morrison, Jim
d. 1973 Ancerl, Karel
d. 1976 Netanyahu,
  Yonatan
d. 1978 Breech, Ernest
  Robert
d. 1978 Daly, James
d. 1979 Van Slyke,
  Helen Lenore Vogt
d. 1981 Berman, Emile
  Zola
d. 1981 Martin, Ross
d. 1985 Kalem,
  T(heodore) E(ustace)
d. 1986 Bingham,
  Jonathan Brewster
d. 1986 Vallee, Rudy
d. 1988 Dell, Gabriel
d. 1993 DeRita, Joe
d. 1993 Drysdale,
  Don(ald Scott)
d. 1994 George, Zelma
  W(atson)
d. 1994 Hoad, Lew(is
  A.)
d. 1995 Gonzalez,
  Pancho
d. 2000 Hejduk, John

July 4
b. 1753 Blanchard,
  Francois
b. 1790 Everest,
  George, Sir
b. 1804 Hawthorne,
  Nathaniel
b. 1807 Garibaldi,
  Giuseppe
b. 1812 Jasper, John J
b. 1816 Walker, Hiram
b. 1819 Squibb, Edward
  Robinson
b. 1826 Foster, Stephen
  Collins
b. 1842 Cohen,
  Hermann
b. 1845 Barnardo,
  Thomas John
b. 1845 Lewis, Edmonia
b. 1847 Bailey, James
  Anthony
b. 1859 Welch, Mickey
b. 1860? Pennell,
  Joseph Stanley
b. 1862 Klimt, Gustav
b. 1863 Juch, Emma
b. 1867 Mather, Stephen
  Tyng
b. 1870 Moffatt, James

b. 1872 Coolidge,
  Calvin
b. 1876 Farnum,
  William
b. 1876 Loeb, Sophia
  Irene Simon
b. 1877 Tozzer, Alfred
  Marston
b. 1878 Cohan, George
  M(ichael)
b. 1880 Rooney, Pat
b. 1883 Goldberg, Rube
b. 1884 Trendle, George
  Washington
b. 1885 Mayer, L(ouis)
  B(urt)
b. 1888 Armetta, Henry
b. 1889 Chotzinoff,
  Samuel
b. 1892 Gaston, Arthur
  George
b. 1894 Carlson, Doc
b. 1895 Caesar, Irving
b. 1899 Warren, Austin
b. 1900 Armstrong,
  Louis
b. 1900 Baddeley,
  Angela
b. 1900 Lawrence,
  Gertrude
b. 1902 Dwyer,
  Florence Price
b. 1902 Lansky, Meyer
b. 1902 Murphy,
  George Lloyd
b. 1903 Saperstein, Abe
b. 1903 Trohan, Walter
b. 1904 Keane, Mary
  Nesta
b. 1905 Trilling, Lionel
b. 1906 Schaefer,
  Vincent Joseph
b. 1907 Taubman,
  (Hyman) Howard
b. 1908 Pennell, Joseph
  Stanley
b. 1910 Hayes, Alfred
b. 1910 Larson, (Lewis)
  Arthur
b. 1910 Templeton,
  Alec
b. 1911 Miller,
  Mitch(ell William)
b. 1911 Moninari-
  Pradelli, Francesco
b. 1912 Dunton,
  Davidson
b. 1912 Graham,
  Virginia
b. 1916 Tokyo Rose
b. 1916 Toon, Malcolm
b. 1918 Landers, Ann
b. 1918 Tupou, IV
b. 1918 Van Buren,
  Abigail
b. 1919 Willis, Mary
b. 1920 Garraty, John
  Arthur
b. 1920 Helmsley,
  Leona Mindy
  Rosenthal
b. 1921 Debreu, Gerard
b. 1922 Keith, Damon
  (Jerome)
b. 1924 Saint, Eva
  Marie

b. 1927 Simon, Neil
b. 1928 Berberian,
  Cathy
b. 1928 Boyd, Stephen
b. 1928 Lollobrigida,
  Gina
b. 1929 Davis, Al(len)
b. 1930 Angelos, Peter
b. 1930 Steinbrenner,
  George Michael, III
b. 1934 Welland, Colin
b. 1938 Withers, Bill
b. 1941 Phelps, Digger
b. 1942 Lanier, Hal
b. 1943 Rivera, Geraldo
b. 1946 Kovic, Ron
b. 1948 Arnoux, Rene
  Alexandre
b. 1948 Culvahouse,
  Art(hur Boggess, Jr.)
b. 1948 Dale, Clamma
  Churita
b. 1955 Waite, John
b. 1962 Shriver,
  Pam(ela Howard)
b. 1977 Victoria Ingrid
  Alice Desiree
d. 1623 Byrd, William
d. 1627 Middleton,
  Thomas
d. 1761 Richardson,
  Samuel
d. 1808 Ames, Fisher
d. 1826 Adams, John
d. 1826 Jefferson,
  Thomas
d. 1831 Monroe, James
d. 1848 Chateaubriand,
  Francois Rene de
d. 1857 Marcy, William
  Learned
d. 1880 Ripley, George
d. 1886 Poundmaker
d. 1888 Storm, (Hans)
  Theodor (Woldsen)
d. 1891 Hamlin,
  Hannibal
d. 1896 Del Pilar,
  Marcelo Hilario
d. 1901 Fiske, John
d. 1901 Tait, Peter
  Guthrie
d. 1910 Schiaparelli,
  Giovanni
d. 1916 Seeger, Alan
d. 1931 Husein ibn Ali
d. 1934 Bialik, Chaim
  Nachman
d. 1934 Curie, Marie
d. 1938 Lenglen,
  Suzanne
d. 1942 Boule,
  Marcellin
d. 1948 Teschner,
  Richard
d. 1961 Celine, Louis-
  Ferdinand
d. 1961 Destouches,
  Louis-Ferdinand
d. 1962 Christie, John
d. 1963 Foyle, William
  Alfred
d. 1965 Bennett,
  Constance Campbell
d. 1965 Sackville-West,
  Edward Charles

d. 1970 Vanderbilt,
  Harold Stirling
d. 1971 Bowra,
  Maurice, Sir
d. 1971 Derleth, August
  (William)
d. 1974 Heyer,
  Georgette
d. 1974 Husayni, Al-
  Hajj Amin al-
d. 1974 Husseini, Haj
  Amin
d. 1975 Beatty, Morgan
d. 1979 Kroeber,
  Theodora Kracaw
d. 1980 Bateson,
  Gregory
d. 1981 Langer, Walter
  C
d. 1982 Guzman,
  Antonio
d. 1982 Sullivan, Daniel
  P
d. 1984 Hathaway,
  Starke R
d. 1985 DeQuay, Jan E
d. 1985 Visser T Hooft,
  Willem Adolf
d. 1985 Weiland,
  Cooney
d. 1986 Mack, Peter
d. 1987 Stromgren,
  Bengt Georg Daniel
d. 1991 Raushenbush,
  Stephen
d. 1992 Newman, Joe
  Dwight
d. 1992 Piazzola, Astor
d. 1994 Smith, Gerard
  C(oad)
d. 1995 Gabor, Eva
d. 1997 Kuralt, Charles
  (Bishop)
d. 1999 Graham, Ronny

July 5
b. 1709 Silhouette,
  Etienne de
b. 1755 Siddons, Sarah
  Kemble
b. 1756 Rush, William
b. 1781 Raffles, Thomas
  Stamford, Sir
b. 1794 Graham,
  Sylvester
b. 1801 Farragut, David
  Glasgow
b. 1803 Borrow, George
  Henry
b. 1810 Barnum,
  P(hineas) T(aylor)
b. 1811 Applegate,
  Jesse
b. 1831 Shaw, Richard
  Norman
b. 1841 Whitney,
  William Collins
b. 1853 Rhodes, Cecil
  John
b. 1872 Herriot,
  Edouard
b. 1878 Everleigh,
  Minna
b. 1878 Gilman,
  Lawrence
b. 1878 Holbrooke,
  Josef

d. 1533 Ariosto, Ludovico
d. 1535 More, Thomas, Sir
d. 1553 Edward VI
d. 1759 Pepperell, William, Sir
d. 1802 Morgan, Daniel
d. 1813 Sharp, Granville
d. 1817 Savage, Edward
d. 1835 Marshall, John
d. 1851 Davenport, Thomas
d. 1871 Castro Alves, Antonio de
d. 1893 Maupassant, Guy de
d. 1897 Meilhac, Henri
d. 1906 Langdell, Christopher Columbus
d. 1914 Agustini, Delmira
d. 1915 Hargrave, Lawrence
d. 1916 Redon, Odilon
d. 1918 Mitchel, John Purroy
d. 1929 Eberle, Edward Walter
d. 1931 Acheson, Edward Goodrich
d. 1932 Grahame, Kenneth
d. 1942 Willard, Daniel
d. 1944 Nagumo, Chuichi
d. 1946 Lanvin, Jeanne
d. 1946 Pippin, Horace
d. 1951 Hall, James Norman
d. 1953 Ruffo, Titta
d. 1954 Pascal, Gabriel
d. 1959 Grosz, George Ehrenfried
d. 1960 Bevan, Aneurin
d. 1962 Faulkner, William
d. 1966 Jones, Sam(uel Pond)
d. 1969 Swarthout, Gladys
d. 1971 Armstrong, Louis
d. 1972 Athenagoras I
d. 1972 DeWilde, Brandon
d. 1973 Brown, Joe E(van)
d. 1973 Klemperer, Otto
d. 1978 Paley, Barbara Cushing
d. 1979 McCoy, Van
d. 1980 Patrick, Gail
d. 1981 Villa, Luz Corral de
d. 1982 Roa (y Garcia), Raul
d. 1986 Ram, Jagjivan
d. 1989 Kadar, Janos
d. 1991 Dallis, Nicholas Peter
d. 1993 Beech, Olive Ann (Mellor)
d. 1997 Chandler, Dorothy (Buffum)

d. 1998 Knudsen, Semon E(mil)
d. 1998 Rogers, Roy
d. 1999 Williams, Sherley Anne

July 7
b. 1586 Hooker, Thomas
b. 1752 Jacquard, Joseph Marie
b. 1811 Meiggs, Henry
b. 1843 Golgi, Camillo
b. 1860 Cahan, Abraham
b. 1860 Mahler, Gustav
b. 1861 Stevens, Nettie Maria
b. 1863 Noyes, Frank B(rett)
b. 1867 Douglass, Andrew Ellicott
b. 1868 Gilbreth, Frank Bunker
b. 1869 Atterbury, Grosvenor
b. 1871 Carle, Richard
b. 1883 Adams, Frank Ramsay
b. 1884 Feuchtwanger, Lion
b. 1885 Bloch, Ernst
b. 1887 Chagall, Marc
b. 1891 Abercrombie, James Smither
b. 1891 Ross, David
b. 1895 Hoffman, Julius Jennings
b. 1899 Cukor, George (Dewey)
b. 1901 DeSica, Vittorio
b. 1906 Paige, Satchel
b. 1907 Heinlein, Robert Anson
b. 1908 Arnow, Harriette Louisa Simpson
b. 1909 Apgar, Virginia
b. 1909 Herman, Billy
b. 1910 Tunnard, Christopher
b. 1911 Menotti, Gian Carlo
b. 1914 Mayehoff, Eddie
b. 1915 Dominick, Peter Hoyt
b. 1915 Ford, Ruth Elizabeth
b. 1915 Walker, Margaret (Abigail)
b. 1916 Robbie, Joe
b. 1917 O'Brien, Larry
b. 1918 Paulucci, Jeno Francisco
b. 1919 Kunstler, William M(oses)
b. 1920 Coleman, William T, Jr.
b. 1920 Hechinger, Fred Michael
b. 1921 Charles, Ezzard
b. 1921 Wilder, Clinton
b. 1922 Cardin, Pierre
b. 1923 Ciulei, Liviu
b. 1924 Ford, Mary

b. 1926 Rushmore, Robert (William)
b. 1927 Casadesus, Jean
b. 1927 Dixon, Alan John
b. 1927 Severinsen, Doc
b. 1928 Edwards, Vince(nt)
b. 1930 Jamal, Ahmad
b. 1933 McCullough, David Gaub
b. 1939 Obraztsova, Elena
b. 1940 Armey, Richard K(eith)
b. 1940 Starr, Ringo
b. 1944 Jacklin, Tony
b. 1944 Steward, Emanuel
b. 1944 Wilmut, Ian
b. 1945 Rodford, Jim
b. 1946 Spano, Joe
b. 1948 Dalto, Jorge
b. 1949 Duvall, Shelley
b. 1954 O'Neill, Cherry Boone
b. 1955 Barker, Len
b. 1959 Hahn, Jessica
b. 1960 Sampson, Ralph Lee
b. 1968 Knoblauch, Chuck
b. 1969 Sakic, Joe
b. 1972 Leslie, Lisa
d. 1253 Thibaut, IV
d. 1307 Edward I
d. 1531 Riemenschneider, Tilman
d. 1573 Vignola, Giacomo da
d. 1816 Sheridan, Richard Brinsley
d. 1854 Ohm, Georg Simon
d. 1865 Surratt, Mary Eugenia Jenkins
d. 1879 Bingham, George Caleb
d. 1893 Blatchford, Samuel
d. 1901 Lorillard, Pierre
d. 1901 Spyri, Johanna Heuser
d. 1930 Doyle, Arthur Conan, Sir
d. 1936 Chicherin, Georgi Vasilyevich
d. 1939 White, Deacon
d. 1944 Mandel, Georges
d. 1949 Johnson, Bunk
d. 1950 Navarro, Fats
d. 1958 Rentner, Maurice
d. 1959 Newman, Ernest
d. 1959 Yarnell, Harry Ervin
d. 1960 Bennett, Hugh Hammond
d. 1960 Collins, Lee
d. 1963 Kearns, Jack
d. 1965 Gildersleeve, Virginia Crocheron
d. 1965 Sharett, Moshe

d. 1967 Leigh, Vivien
d. 1968 Keilberth, Joseph
d. 1968 Queeny, Edgar Monsanto
d. 1968 Sowerby, Leo
d. 1970 Lane, Allen, Sir
d. 1970 Rambeau, Marjorie
d. 1971 Iwerks, Ub(be)
d. 1973 Lake, Veronica
d. 1974 Newhall, Nancy Wynne
d. 1974 Vanderbilt, Cornelius, Jr.
d. 1975 Bjerknes, Jacob
d. 1976 Foster, Norman
d. 1976 Heinemann, Gustav Walter
d. 1976 Lowenfels, Walter
d. 1977 Crane, Roy(ston Campbell)
d. 1978 Baker, Rachel
d. 1978 Trefflich, Henry Herbert Frederick
d. 1979 Landolfi, Tommaso
d. 1980 Gardiner, Reginald
d. 1980 Schary, Dore
d. 1981 Brasselle, Keefe
d. 1981 Gardner, Isabella
d. 1982 Loughran, Tommy
d. 1983 Amfiteatrof, Daniele
d. 1983 Kahn, Herman
d. 1983 Morgan, Vicki
d. 1984 Oppen, George
d. 1984 Robson, Flora McKenzie, Dame
d. 1985 Scarne, John
d. 1987 Halstead, William S
d. 1987 Teichmann, Howard Miles
d. 1990 Cullen, Bill
d. 1992 Frank, Clinton Edward
d. 1998 Abiola, Moshood

July 8
b. 1621 LaFontaine, Jean de
b. 1790 Halleck, Fritz-Greene
b. 1805 Gross, Samuel Daniel
b. 1819 McClintock, Francis Leopold, Sir
b. 1826 Chrysander, Karl Franz Friedrich
b. 1836 Chamberlain, Joseph
b. 1838 Zeppelin, Ferdinand Adolf August Heinrich von, Count
b. 1839 Rockefeller, John D(avison)
b. 1844 Lincoln, Mary Johnson Bailey
b. 1850 Lanman, Charles Rockwell

b. 1851 Evans, Arthur John, Sir
b. 1857 Binet, Alfred
b. 1862 Bloor, Mother
b. 1867 Kollwitz, Kathe Schmidt
b. 1869 Moody, William Vaughn
b. 1872 VonTilzer, Harry
b. 1882 Grainger, Percy Aldridge
b. 1885 Brinkley, John Romulus
b. 1889 Pallette, Eugene
b. 1890 MacDonald-Wright, Stanton
b. 1892 Aldington, Richard (Edward Godfree)
b. 1895 Rattner, Abraham
b. 1895 Tamm, Igor Evgenevich
b. 1896 Janis, Sidney
b. 1898 Gero, Erno
b. 1898 Waugh, Alec
b. 1899 Lilienthal, David Eli
b. 1900 Antheil, George
b. 1906 Johnson, Philip Cortelyou
b. 1907 Rankin, J(ames) Lee
b. 1907 Romney, George (Wilcken)
b. 1908 Jordan, Louis
b. 1908 Rockefeller, Nelson A(ldrich)
b. 1911 Ball, John Dudley, Jr.
b. 1912 McCarthy, Frank
b. 1913 Kerr, Walter F(rancis)
b. 1914 Eckstine, Billy
b. 1914 Sellinger, Frank
b. 1917 Brown, Pamela
b. 1917 Emerson, Faye Margaret
b. 1917 Langan, Glenn
b. 1917 Powers, James Farl
b. 1919 Scheel, Walter
b. 1923 Dillard, Harrison
b. 1925 Brathwaite, Nicholas A(lexander)
b. 1926 Dingell, John David, Jr.
b. 1926 Kubler-Ross, Elisabeth
b. 1929 Grau, Shirley Ann
b. 1931 Arledge, Roone Pinckney, Jr.
b. 1931 Ballard, Louis W.
b. 1932 Vale, Jerry
b. 1933 Feldman, Marty
b. 1934 DiPrete, Edward Daniel
b. 1935 Crow, John David
b. 1935 Lawrence, Steve

b. 1937 Loden, Barbara Ann
b. 1940 Baliles, Gerald L
b. 1941 Kidwell, Clara Sue
b. 1942 Gramm, (William) Phil(ip)
b. 1946 Fuller, Kathryn S(cott)
b. 1946 Gregory, Cynthia Kathleen
b. 1948 Darby, Kim
b. 1948 Raffi
b. 1951 Huston, Anjelica
b. 1952 Lambert, Jack
b. 1952 Williamson, Marianne
b. 1953 Quindlen, Anna
b. 1958 Bacon, Kevin
b. 1961 Keith, Toby
b. 1962 Osborne, Joan
b. 1965 Walton, Jerome O'Terrell
d. 1583 Mendes Pinto, Fernao
d. 1623 Gregory XV
d. 1721 Yale, Elihu
d. 1822 Shelley, Percy Bysshe
d. 1823 Raeburn, Henry, Sir
d. 1839 Sor, Fernando
d. 1855 Parry, William Edward, Sir
d. 1875 Blair, Francis Preston, Jr.
d. 1875 Cairnes, John Elliott
d. 1882 Browne, Phiz
d. 1917 Thomson, Tom
d. 1919 Fox, John W, Jr.
d. 1933 Hope-Hawkins, Anthony, Sir
d. 1936 Meighan, Thomas
d. 1939 Ellis, Havelock
d. 1949 Knerr, H(arold) H
d. 1954 Gardner, George
d. 1956 Papini, Giovanni
d. 1957 Coolidge, Grace (Anne Goodhue)
d. 1965 Stribling, Thomas Sigismund
d. 1969 Rolfe, Red
d. 1969 Sebring, Jay
d. 1971 Dunhill, Alfred Henry
d. 1979 Tomonaga Shinichiro
d. 1979 Woodward, Robert Burns
d. 1981 McDonnell, Joe
d. 1981 Smith, Loring
d. 1981 Soyer, Isaac
d. 1984 Brassai
d. 1985 Cowles, Gardner, Jr.
d. 1985 Foster, Phil
d. 1985 Hampson, Frank

d. 1985 Kuznets, Simon Smith
d. 1986 Morgana, Nina
d. 1986 Rickover, Hyman George
d. 1987 Chevrier, Lionel
d. 1987 O'Konski, Alvin E(dward)
d. 1987 Vila, George Raymond
d. 1994 Kim Il Sung
d. 1994 Lee, Robert E(dwin)
d. 1994 Sargent, Dick
d. 1996 Albrecht, Duke
d. 1996 Amsterdam, Birdie
d. 1998 Calloway, (David) Wayne

July 9
b. 1562 Gentileschi, Orazio
b. 1578 Ferdinand II
b. 1764 Radcliffe, Ann
b. 1766 Perkins, Jacob
b. 1775 Lewis, Matthew Gregory
b. 1811 Parton, Sara Payson Willis
b. 1819 Howe, Elias
b. 1828 Spreckels, Claus
b. 1831 His, Wilhelm
b. 1835 Estrada Palma, Tomas
b. 1845 Darwin, George Howard, Sir
b. 1856 Guggenheim, Daniel
b. 1858 Boas, Franz
b. 1878 Kaltenborn, H(ans) V(on)
b. 1879 Respighi, Ottorino
b. 1887 Chapin, James Ormsbee
b. 1887 Morison, Samuel Eliot
b. 1888 Bairnsfather, Bruce
b. 1888 Marks, Simon
b. 1889 Dandurand, Leo
b. 1894 Spencer, Percy Le Baron
b. 1894 Thompson, Dorothy
b. 1897 Cassou, Jean
b. 1897 Lyons, Enid Muriel
b. 1897 Wedemeyer, Albert Coady
b. 1900 Schaefer, Rudolph Jay
b. 1901 Cartland, Barbara Hamilton
b. 1905 Campbell, Clarence Sutherland
b. 1907 Klutznick, Philip M.
b. 1908 Brown, Paul
b. 1908 White, Minor
b. 1911 Peake, Mervyn Laurence
b. 1914 Carlson, Curtis L.

b. 1915 Diamond, David
b. 1916 Heath, Edward Richard George
b. 1917 Youlou, Fulbert
b. 1919 Van Slyke, Helen Lenore Vogt
b. 1921 Jones, David Charles
b. 1922 Pollard, Jim
b. 1924 Pennario, Leonard
b. 1926 Dale, Alan
b. 1926 Krim, Mathilde Galland
b. 1926 Mottelson, Benjamin Roy
b. 1927 Ames, Ed(mund Dantes)
b. 1927 Diop, David
b. 1927 Kelly, Red
b. 1928 Hall, Donald Joyce
b. 1929 Hassan II
b. 1929 Hazelwood, Lee
b. 1930 Iness, Sim
b. 1932 Rumsfeld, Donald (Harold)
b. 1933 Sacks, Oliver Wolf
b. 1933 Smith, Hedrick Laurence
b. 1934 Graves, Michael
b. 1936 Hampton, James
b. 1936 Jordan, June
b. 1937 Hockney, David
b. 1938 Dennehy, Brian
b. 1941 Aroldingen, Karin von
b. 1943 Edmiston, Mark Morton
b. 1945 Koontz, Dean R(ay)
b. 1947 Simpson, O(renthal) J(ames)
b. 1951 Brown, Larry
b. 1953 Tesh, John
b. 1954 Sledge, Debbie
b. 1955 Dillon, Mia
b. 1955 Smits, Jimmy
b. 1955 Wilson, Willie James
b. 1956 Hanks, Tom
b. 1957 McGillis, Kelly
b. 1965 Love, Courtney
b. 1976 Savage, Fred
d. 1228 Langton, Stephen
d. 1677 Berkeley, William, Sir
d. 1746 Philip, V
d. 1747 Bononcini, Giovanni Battista
d. 1766 Mayhew, Jonathan
d. 1797 Burke, Edmund
d. 1828 Stuart, Gilbert Charles
d. 1843 Allston, Washington
d. 1850 Boyer, Jean Pierre
d. 1850 Taylor, Zachary
d. 1856 Avogadro, Amedeo

d. 1887 Merriam, Charles
d. 1923 Day, William Rufus
d. 1926 Lathrop, Rose Hawthorne
d. 1927 Drew, John
d. 1932 Gillette, King Camp
d. 1936 Wright, Henry
d. 1938 Cardozo, Benjamin Nathan
d. 1943 Beers, Clifford Whittingham
d. 1951 Heilmann, Harry Edwin
d. 1951 VanAlstyne, Egbert Anson
d. 1961 Marshal, Alan
d. 1968 Cadogan, Alexander George Montague, Sir
d. 1968 Fisher, Vardis
d. 1974 Brittain, Harry Ernest, Sir
d. 1974 Warren, Earl
d. 1976 Gingrich, Arnold
d. 1976 Yawkey, Thomas Austin
d. 1977 Eiseley, Loren Corey
d. 1977 Paul, Alice
d. 1979 Skinner, Cornelia Otis
d. 1979 Wilding, Michael
d. 1981 Levin, Meyer
d. 1982 Manone, Wingy
d. 1984 Hurd, Peter
d. 1984 Thompson, Randall
d. 1985 Charlotte Aldegonde E M Wilhelmine
d. 1988 Presser, Jackie
d. 1988 Woodhouse, Barbara Blackburn
d. 1990 Duff, Howard
d. 1991 Franciscus, James Grover
d. 1992 Sevareid, Eric
d. 1996 Belli, Melvin M(ouron)
d. 1998 Flora, James (Royer)
d. 1999 Farmer, James

July 10
b. 1509 Calvin, John
b. 1515 Toledo, Fernando Alvarez de
b. 1640 Behn, Aphra
b. 1723 Blackstone, William, Sir
b. 1792 Dallas, George Mifflin
b. 1792 Marryat, Frederick
b. 1802 Chambers, Robert
b. 1824 King, Richard
b. 1831 Pissarro, Camille Jacob
b. 1832 Arnold, Edwin
b. 1832 Clark, Alvin Graham

b. 1834 Whistler, James Abbott McNeill
b. 1835 Wieniawski, Henri
b. 1838 Allen, Joel Asaph
b. 1839 Busch, Adolphus
b. 1844 Materna, Amalia
b. 1852 Chalmers, William James
b. 1856 Tesla, Nikola
b. 1861 Paine, Albert Bigelow
b. 1867 Dunne, Finley Peter
b. 1871 Proust, Marcel
b. 1875 Bentley, Edmund Clerihew
b. 1875 Bethune, Mary McLeod
b. 1878 Partridge, Bellamy
b. 1881 Richberg, Donald R(andall)
b. 1882 Hogg, Ima
b. 1883 Flick, Friedrich
b. 1884 Wood, Samuel Grosvenor
b. 1885 O'Hara, Mary
b. 1888 Chirico, Giorgio de
b. 1888 McNamee, Graham
b. 1889 Sissle, Noble
b. 1891 Quimby, Edith H.
b. 1891 Tugwell, Rexford Guy
b. 1894? McHugh, Jimmy
b. 1895 Goldmann, Nahum
b. 1895 Orff, Carl
b. 1896 Summerville, Slim
b. 1897 Brosio, Manlio Giovanni
b. 1897 Gilbert, John
b. 1897 Goodrich, Lloyd
b. 1898 Malott, Deane W(aldo)
b. 1899 Conkle, Ellsworth Prouty
b. 1900 Cole, Kenneth Stewart
b. 1900 Parish, Mitchell
b. 1902 Adler, Kurt
b. 1902 Alder, Kurt
b. 1902 Guillen (y Batista), Nicolas (Cristobal)
b. 1903 Stoneham, Horace
b. 1905 Anderson, Ivie
b. 1905 Gomez, Thomas
b. 1906 Icaza (Coronel), Jorge
b. 1907 Stignani, Ebe
b. 1908 Heinz, Henry John, II
b. 1910 Bunting, Mary Ingraham

b. 1910 Nguyen Huu Tho
b. 1913 Welitsch, Ljuba
b. 1914 Shuster, Joe
b. 1915 Bellow, Saul
b. 1915 Connolly, Mike
b. 1916 Provensen, Martin
b. 1919 Gabor, Magda
b. 1920 Brinkley, David (McClure)
b. 1920 Chamberlain, Owen
b. 1920 Lowe, Edward
b. 1920 Shriver, Eunice Mary Kennedy
b. 1921 Donnell, Jeff
b. 1921 LaMotta, Jake
b. 1923 Hamner, Earl Henry, Jr.
b. 1923 Kerr, Jean
b. 1926 Banzer-Suarez, Hugo
b. 1926 Gwynne, Fred
b. 1927 Dinkins, David Norman
b. 1928 Buffet, Bernard
b. 1931 Adams, Nick
b. 1931 Munro, Alice
b. 1933 De Gaetani, Jan
b. 1933 Hatcher, Richard Gordon
b. 1933 Herman, Jerry
b. 1936 Boyer, Herbert Wayne
b. 1937 Cho, Alfred Y(i)
b. 1942 Millar, Jeff(rey) Lynn
b. 1943 Ashe, Arthur
b. 1945 Glass, Ron
b. 1945 Wade, Virginia
b. 1947 Guthrie, Arlo Davy
b. 1947 Schmiechen, Richard Kurt
b. 1949 Smalley, David Bruce
b. 1958 Fleck, Bela
b. 1960 Craig, Roger Timothy
b. 1960 Ellington, E. David
b. 1962 Hawkins, Steven (Wayne)
d. 138 Hadrian
d. 1099 Cid, El
d. 1686 Fell, John
d. 1806 Stubbs, George
d. 1826 Martin, Luther
d. 1863 Moore, Clement Clarke
d. 1884 Morphy, Paul Charles
d. 1889 Tyler, Julia Gardiner
d. 1914 Jacobi, Abraham
d. 1933 Arnold, Harold De Forest
d. 1933 Urban, Joseph Maria
d. 1940 Tovey, Donald Francis, Sir
d. 1941 Morton, Jelly Roll

d. 1943 Schlesinger, Frank
d. 1944 Pissaro, Lucien
d. 1946 Hillman, Sidney (Simcha)
d. 1947 Rider-Kelsey, Corinne
d. 1953 Homer, Sidney
d. 1957 Asch, Sholem
d. 1965 Audiberti, Jacques
d. 1966 Hoffman, Malvina
d. 1968 Fitts, Dudley
d. 1970 Benediktsson, Bjarni
d. 1971 Bronfman, Samuel
d. 1972 Madeira, Jean
d. 1972 Weede, Robert
d. 1973 Brown, Dean
d. 1973 Warburg, Frederick Marcus
d. 1978 Davis, Joe
d. 1978 Rockefeller, John D(avison), III
d. 1979 Fiedler, Arthur
d. 1980 Krumgold, Joseph (Quincy)
d. 1982 Jeritza, Maria
d. 1983 Castagna, Bruna
d. 1983 Egk, Werner
d. 1985 Muller, Hilgard
d. 1986 Le Duan
d. 1986 Vlasic, Joseph
d. 1987 Dana, Viola
d. 1987 Hammond, John Henry, Jr.
d. 1989 Blanc, Mel(vin Jerome)
d. 1989 Tucker, Tommy
d. 1993 Ibuse, Masuji
d. 1995 Flatt, Ernie
d. 1995 Logan, Onnie Lee
d. 1995 Price, Don K.
d. 1996 Manoogian, Alex

July 11
b. 1558 Greene, Robert
b. 1561 Gongora y Argote, Luis de
b. 1603 Digby, Kenelm, Sir
b. 1697 Anville, Jean Baptiste Bourguignon d'
b. 1723 Marmontel, Jean Francois
b. 1732 Lalande, Joseph Jerome Lefrancais de
b. 1754 Bowdler, Thomas
b. 1767 Adams, John Quincy
b. 1780 Flint, Timothy
b. 1807 Tichatschek, Joseph
b. 1808 Reed, Henry Hope
b. 1811 Grove, William Robert, Sir
b. 1818 Forster, William Edward
b. 1819 Warner, Susan Bogert

d. 1931 Soderblom,
Nathan
d. 1934 Evinrude, Ole
d. 1935 Dreyfus, Alfred
d. 1943 Loftus, Cissie
d. 1944 Roosevelt,
Theodore, Jr.
d. 1946 Baker, Ray
Stannard
d. 1949 Hyde, Douglas
d. 1950 Mendl, Lady
Elsie de Wolfe
d. 1953 Rawlinson,
Herbert
d. 1960 Adler, Buddy
d. 1961 DeLaRoche,
Mazo
d. 1963 Grant, Harry
Johnston
d. 1966 Suzuki, Daisetz
Teitaro
d. 1973 Chaney, Lon,
Jr.
d. 1975 Chapin, James
Ormsbee
d. 1976 Howe, James
Wong
d. 1976 Mack, Ted
d. 1978 Rothermere,
Esmond Cecil
Harmsworth,
Viscount
d. 1978 Williams, Jay
d. 1979 Riperton,
Minnie
d. 1981 Little, Edward
Herman
d. 1982 More, Kenneth
Gilbert
d. 1983 Wood, Chris
d. 1985 Miller, Arnold
Ray
d. 1987 Gimbel, Peter
Robin
d. 1987 Perlmutter,
Nathan
d. 1988 Logan, Josh(ua
Lockwood)
d. 1989 Hook, Sidney
d. 1992 Miller, Caroline
d. 1996 Chancellor,
John (William)
d. 1996 Einem,
Gottfried von
d. 1998 Driftwood,
Jimmy

July 13
b. 1527 Dee, John
b. 1608 Ferdinand, III
b. 1793 Clare, John
b. 1811 Scott, George
Gilbert, Sir
b. 1821 Forrest, Nathan
Bedford
b. 1826 Cannizzaro,
Stanislao
b. 1841 Wagner, Otto
b. 1853 Bonvalot, Pierre
Gabriel Edouard
b. 1859 Webb, Sidney
James
b. 1863 Murray,
Margaret Alice
b. 1878 Sterne, Maurice
b. 1879 Freyssinet,
Eugene

b. 1886 Flanagan,
Edward Joseph,
Father
b. 1889 Coveleski,
Stanley Anthony
b. 1892 Broadbent,
Punch
b. 1894 Babel, Isaac
Emmanuelovich
b. 1895 Blackmer,
Sidney Alderman
b. 1901 Benjamin,
Curtis G
b. 1901 Lewis, (Myrtle)
Tillie
b. 1901 Walker, Mickey
b. 1902 Endacott, Paul
b. 1902 Lord, Phillips H
b. 1903 Clark, Kenneth
MacKenzie, Sir
b. 1903 Portman, Eric
b. 1905 Crowther,
Bosley
b. 1906 Sosnik, Harry
b. 1908 Todd, Garfield
b. 1913 Garroway, Dave
b. 1917 Hill, Morton
A(nthony)
b. 1918 Ascari, Alberto
b. 1918 Brown, Marcia
b. 1921 Scribner,
Charles, Jr.
b. 1922 Harlan, Louis R
b. 1922 Jorgensen,
Anker Henrik
b. 1924 Bergonzi, Carlo
b. 1927 Veil, Simone
Annie Jacob
b. 1928 Bond, Sudie
b. 1928 Crane, Bob
b. 1929 Johnston, Basil
H.
b. 1932 Commager,
Steele
b. 1933 Bourassa, (Jean)
Robert
b. 1933 Storey, David
Malcolm
b. 1934 Soyinka, Wole
b. 1935 Kemp, Jack
b. 1936 Stern, Sandor
b. 1937 Coody, Charles
b. 1938 Widnall, Sheila
E.
b. 1940 Prudhomme,
Paul
b. 1940 Stewart, Patrick
b. 1941 Antonini,
Joseph
b. 1942 Ford, Harrison
b. 1942 Forster, Robert
b. 1942 McGuinn,
Roger
b. 1944 JEB
b. 1944 Rubik, Erno
b. 1946 Marin, Richard
b. 1951 Lanting, Frans
b. 1954 Mendoza, Mark
b. 1954 Thompson,
David O'Neil
b. 1957 Crowe,
Cameron
b. 1963 Carpenter,
Bobby
b. 1963 Webb, Spud
b. 1967 Peck, Dale

d. 1105 Rashi
d. 1380 Du Guesclin,
Bertrand
d. 1712 Cromwell,
Richard
d. 1755 Braddock,
Edward
d. 1762 Bradley, James
d. 1785 Hopkins,
Stephen
d. 1793 Marat, Jean
Paul
d. 1881 Pemberton,
John Clifford
d. 1890 Fremont, John
Charles
d. 1896 Kekule,
Friedrich August
d. 1901 Jackson, Peter
B
d. 1921 Lippmann,
Gabriel Jonas
d. 1924 Marshall,
Alfred
d. 1932 Stephens, Alice
Barber
d. 1937 Dalton, Emmett
d. 1945 Nazimova, Alla
d. 1946 Stieglitz, Alfred
d. 1947 Lunceford,
Jimmy
d. 1949 Kuhn, Walt
d. 1951 Schoenberg,
Arnold
d. 1954 Clark, Bennett
Champ
d. 1954 Kahlo, Frida
d. 1954 Rice, Grantland
d. 1955 Ellis, Ruth
d. 1962 Wald, Jerry
d. 1965 Gomez Castro,
Laureano Eleuterio
d. 1967 Andrus, Ethel
Percy
d. 1970 Groves, Leslie
Richard
d. 1972 Saarinen, Aline
Bernstein
d. 1974 Blackett,
Patrick Maynard
Stuart
d. 1975 Hay, George W
d. 1979 Chapman, Ceil
d. 1979 Griffith,
Corinne
d. 1980 Khama, Seretse
M., Sir
d. 1981 Hurson, Martin
d. 1983 Roy, Gabrielle
d. 1992 Ironside,
Christopher
d. 1993 Wojciechowicz,
Alex(ander)
d. 1996 Berman, Pandro
Samuel
d. 1997 Danilova,
Alexandra

July 14
b. Mottola, Tommy
b. 1454 Poliziano,
Angelo
b. 1602 Mazarin, Jules,
Cardinal
b. 1794 Lockhart, John
Gibson

b. 1800 Dumas, Jean
Baptiste Andre
b. 1801 Muller,
Johannes Peter
b. 1816 Gobineau,
Joseph Arthur, Comte
de
b. 1818 Lyon, Nathaniel
b. 1837 Douglas,
Amanda Minnie
b. 1858 Pankhurst,
Emmeline Goulden
b. 1860 Wister, Owen
b. 1862 Bascom,
Florence
b. 1865 Capper, Arthur
b. 1866 Frost, Edwin
Brant
b. 1868 Bell, Gertrude
Margaret
b. 1868 Landsteiner,
Karl
b. 1880 Meek, Donald
b. 1884 Cecchi, Emilio
b. 1887 Mowrer, Paul
Scott
b. 1890 Zadkine, Ossip
b. 1894 Dixon, Jean
b. 1895 Leavis, F(rank)
R(aymond)
b. 1897 Phibun
Songkhram, Luang
b. 1898 Brook,
Alexander
b. 1898 Chandler,
Happy
b. 1898 Watson, Moose
b. 1899 Breit, Gregory
b. 1899 Hill, Billy
b. 1900 Allen, Robert
Sharon
b. 1901 Tobias, George
b. 1902 Haenigsen,
Harry William
b. 1903 Clark, Thomas
Dionysius
b. 1903 Murray, Ken
b. 1903 Prio Socarras,
Carlos
b. 1903 Stone, Irving
b. 1904 Griswold,
Erwin N(athaniel)
b. 1904 Reisenberg,
Nadia
b. 1904 Singer, Isaac
Bashevis
b. 1908 Murphy, Johnny
(John Joseph)
b. 1908 Raphael, Chaim
b. 1910? Annabella
b. 1910 Hanna, William
Denby
b. 1911 Terry-Thomas
b. 1912 Frye, (Herman)
Northrop
b. 1912 Guthrie, Woody
b. 1912 Motley, Willard
Francis
b. 1913 Ford, Gerald
R(udolph)
b. 1915 Lawrence,
Jerome
b. 1916 Ginzburg,
Natalia
b. 1916 Harmon, Claude

b. 1917 Eastlake, William (Derry)
b. 1917 Edwards, Douglas
b. 1918 Bergman, Ingmar (Ernst)
b. 1918 Forrester, Jay Wright
b. 1918 Laurents, Arthur
b. 1919 Attwood, William Hollingsworth
b. 1921 Garfield, Leon
b. 1921 Wilkinson, Geoffrey
b. 1923 Lear, Frances
b. 1923 Robertson, Dale
b. 1923 Steele, Willie
b. 1926 Jones, Wallace
b. 1927 Chancellor, John (William)
b. 1927 Parish, Peggy
b. 1928 Olaf, Pierre
b. 1928 Olson, Nancy
b. 1930 Bergen, Polly
b. 1930 Simons, Elwyn L(aVerne)
b. 1931 Stephens, Robert, Sir
b. 1932 Grier, Rosey
b. 1934 Elder, Lee
b. 1936 Gordon, David
b. 1938 Rubin, Jerry
b. 1938 Safdie, Moshe
b. 1940 Howatch, Susan
b. 1941 Karenga, Maulana
b. 1947 Ramgoolam, Navin
d. 1223 Philip II
d. 1742 Bentley, Richard
d. 1779 Ross, George
d. 1792 Occom, Samson
d. 1816 Miranda, Francisco de
d. 1817 Stael-Holstein, Anne Louise Germaine Necker, Baroness de
d. 1824 Kamehameha II
d. 1827 Fresnel, Augustin-Jean
d. 1834 Genet, Edmond Charles Edouard
d. 1859 Borel d'Hauterive, Petrus
d. 1881 Billy the Kid
d. 1882 Ringo, John(ny)
d. 1887 Krupp, Alfred
d. 1895 Ulrichs, Karl Heinrich
d. 1904 Kruger, Paul
d. 1907 Perkin, William Henry, Sir
d. 1918 Roosevelt, Quentin
d. 1925 Villa, Pancho
d. 1934 Hawthorne, Julian
d. 1936 Mukerji, Dham Gopal
d. 1939 Mucha, Alphonse Marie
d. 1943 Bledsoe, Jules

d. 1950 Ngata, Apirana Turupa
d. 1954 Benavente y Martinez, Jacinto
d. 1958 Faisal II
d. 1958 Nuri al-Sa'id
d. 1959 Grock
d. 1963 Janney, Russell Dixon
d. 1965 Stevenson, Adlai Ewing, II
d. 1967 Arghezi, Tudor
d. 1967 Theodorescu, Ion N
d. 1970 Foster, Preston
d. 1970 Laidler, Harry Wellington
d. 1974 Hathaway, Sibyl Collings
d. 1974 Spaatz, Carl Andrew
d. 1975 Singleton, Zutty
d. 1978 Messel, Oliver
d. 1982 Jensen, Jackie
d. 1984 Delmar, Kenny
d. 1984 Schacht, Al(exander)
d. 1984 Tidyman, Ernest
d. 1986 Loewy, Raymond Fernand
d. 1987 Holt, Fritz
d. 1987 Morton, Nelle Katherine
d. 1988 Monroe, Phil
d. 1998 McDonald, Richard
d. 1999 Steelman, John Roy
d. 2000 MacRae, Meredith

July 15
b. 1573 Jones, Inigo
b. 1607 Rembrandt (Harmenszoon van Rijn)
b. 1631 Cumberland, Richard
b. 1779 Moore, Clement Clarke
b. 1796 Bulfinch, Thomas
b. 1808 Manning, Henry Edward
b. 1813 Healy, George Peter Alexander
b. 1833 Platt, Thomas Collier
b. 1850 Cabrini, Frances Xavier, Saint
b. 1864 Tempest, Marie
b. 1865 Northcliffe, Alfred Charles William Harmsworth, Viscount
b. 1867 Charcot, Jean Baptiste Etienne Auguste
b. 1867 Walker, Maggie Lena
b. 1872 Hertz, Alfred
b. 1872 Rodo, Jose Enrique
b. 1875 Morganweck, Frank

b. 1879 Arguedas, Alcides
b. 1884 Myers, Garry Cleveland
b. 1889 Rambeau, Marjorie
b. 1893 Dieterle, William
b. 1900 Francis, Thomas, Jr.
b. 1902 Hackett, Raymond
b. 1903 Edmonds, Walter D(umaux)
b. 1903 Kamaraj, Kumaraswami
b. 1905 Fields, Dorothy
b. 1906 Armour, Richard Willard
b. 1913 Innes, Hammond
b. 1917 Conquest, Robert
b. 1918 Boehm, Eric Hartzell
b. 1919 Murdoch, Iris
b. 1921 Reiss, Stuart
b. 1922 Lederman, Leon Max
b. 1923 Jackson, Cordell
b. 1924 Denton, Jeremiah Andrew, Jr.
b. 1925 Carey, Phil(ip)
b. 1926 Chraibi, Driss
b. 1926 Galtieri, Leopoldo Fortunato
b. 1927 Jellicoe, Ann
b. 1928 Benko, Paul Charles
b. 1930 Derrida, Jacques
b. 1931 Asencio, Diego Cortes
b. 1933 Bream, Julian Alexander
b. 1935 Karras, Alex(ander G)
b. 1935 Kercheval, Ken
b. 1935 Prescott, Peter Sherwin
b. 1936 Penner, Rudolph Gerhard
b. 1936 Voinovich, George V(ictor)
b. 1939 Cavaco Silva, Anibal Antonio
b. 1939 Wayne, Patrick
b. 1942 Malone, Vivian
b. 1943 Bell Burnell, Jocelyn
b. 1944 Vincent, Jan-Michael
b. 1946 Bolkiah, Muda Hassanal, Sir
b. 1946 Ronstadt, Linda
b. 1948 Diaz, Henry F(rank)
b. 1949 Bildt, Carl
b. 1950 Huffington, Arianna
b. 1952 Ros-Lehtinen, Ileana
b. 1952 Stallworth, John(ny Lee)

b. 1953 Aristide, Jean-Bertrand
b. 1960 Aames, Willie
b. 1960 Alexis, Kim
b. 1961 Whitaker, Forest
d. 1274 Bonaventure, Saint
d. 1291 Rudolf, I
d. 1609 Carracci, Annibale
d. 1782 Farinelli
d. 1828 Houdon, Jean Antoine
d. 1833 Unanue, Jose Hipolito
d. 1857 Czerny, Karl
d. 1859 Choate, Rufus
d. 1868 Morton, William Thomas Green
d. 1883 Tom Thumb, General
d. 1887 Andrews, Jane
d. 1909 Tyrrell, George
d. 1912 Hudson, Joseph Lowthian
d. 1919 Fischer, Emil Herman
d. 1924 Coryell, John Russell
d. 1927 Markievicz, Constance Georgine, Countess
d. 1929 Hofmannsthal, Hugo von
d. 1930 Auer, Leopold
d. 1930 Barry, Leonora Marie Kearney
d. 1933 Babbitt, Irving
d. 1933 Keppard, Freddie
d. 1939 Bleuler, Eugen
d. 1947 Donaldson, Walter
d. 1948? Chapais, Thomas, Sir
d. 1948 Pershing, John J(oseph)
d. 1951 Ovington, Mary White
d. 1953 Christie, John Reginald Halliday
d. 1957 Cox, James Middleton, Sr.
d. 1959 Bloch, Ernest
d. 1960 Tibbett, Lawrence Mervil
d. 1962 Maison, Rene
d. 1965 Shotwell, James Thomson
d. 1970 Berne, Eric Lennard
d. 1975 Craig, May
d. 1975 Weidman, Charles Edward, Jr.
d. 1976 Gallico, Paul William
d. 1977 Fedin, Konstantin Aleksandrovich
d. 1979 Diaz Ordaz, Gustavo
d. 1983 Foy, Eddie, Jr.
d. 1986 Halop, Florence
d. 1986 Haughton, Billy

d. 1987 Bass, Alfie
d. 1987 Gaines, Lee
d. 1988 Estes, Eleanor Ruth Rosenfeld
d. 1988 Lubin, Charles W
d. 1989 Bradley, Will
d. 1990 Lockwood, Margaret Mary
d. 1991 Convy, Bert
d. 1991 Revelle, Roger Randall
d. 1992 DeRoburt, Hammer, Sir
d. 1993 Brian, David
d. 1997 Versace, Gianni
d. 2000 Pastore, John Orlando

July 16
b. 1194 Clare of Assisi, Saint
b. 1486 Sarto, Andrea del
b. 1723 Reynolds, Joshua, Sir
b. 1754 Spode, Josiah
b. 1796 Corot, Jean Baptiste Camille
b. 1821 Eddy, Mary Baker Morse
b. 1845 Vail, Theodore Newton
b. 1858 Ysaye, Eugene
b. 1862 Wells-Barnett, Ida Bell
b. 1872 Amundsen, Roald Engelbregt
b. 1874 Goldberger, Joseph
b. 1876 Dent, Edward Joseph
b. 1877 Schick, Bela
b. 1880 Norris, Kathleen Thompson
b. 1882 Hearst, Millicent Veronica Willson
b. 1883 Sheeler, Charles
b. 1887 Gibbons, Floyd Phillips
b. 1888 Jackson, Joe
b. 1888 Kilbride, Percy
b. 1888 Zernike, Frits
b. 1890 Ed, Carl Frank Ludwig
b. 1892 Seeley, Blossom
b. 1894 Toledano, Vicente Lombardo
b. 1896 Lie, Trygve Halvdan
b. 1901 Mahler, Fritz
b. 1903 Lombardo, Carmen
b. 1906 Barnes, Lee
b. 1906 Sherman, Vincent
b. 1907 Calmer, Ned
b. 1907 Redenbacher, Orville
b. 1907 Stanwyck, Barbara
b. 1909 Saunders, Stuart T(homas)
b. 1911 Rogers, Ginger
b. 1911 Tufts, Sonny

b. 1915 Hughes, Barnard
b. 1920 Lopez Portillo (y Pacheco), Jose
b. 1921 Rogers, Bernard William
b. 1923 Laroche, Guy
b. 1924 Myerson, Bess
b. 1925 Braly, Malcolm
b. 1925 Shapiro, Stanley
b. 1925 Tjader, Cal(len Radcliffe, Jr.)
b. 1926 Carson, Mindy
b. 1927 Llewellyn, James Bruce
b. 1928 Brookner, Anita
b. 1928 Davidovich, Bella
b. 1928 Wilde, Patricia
b. 1930 Giardello, Joey
b. 1932 Protopopov, Oleg Alekseevich
b. 1932 Thornburgh, Dick
b. 1934 Ortega, Katherine Davalos
b. 1934 Payne, Donald M
b. 1937 Bryan, Richard H.
b. 1938 Vitale, Milly
b. 1939 Perry, Ruth (Sando)
b. 1939 Redgrave, Corin
b. 1942 Court, Margaret
b. 1943 Johnson, Jimmy
b. 1947 Boggs, Tom
b. 1947 Herman, Alexis M.
b. 1947 Hogan, Linda
b. 1947 Shakur, Assata
b. 1948 Blades, Ruben, Jr.
b. 1948 Zukerman, Pinchas
b. 1952 Copeland, Stewart
b. 1953 Ornish, Dean
b. 1963 Cates, Phoebe
b. 1964 Indurain, Miguel
b. 1965 Lemieux, Claude
b. 1968 Sanders, Barry
b. 1971 Feldman, Corey
d. 1216 Innocent, III, Pope
d. 1557 Anne of Cleves
d. 1857 Beranger, Pierre-Jean de
d. 1865 Jumel, Eliza
d. 1882 Lincoln, Mary Todd
d. 1886 Judson, Edward Zane Carroll
d. 1890 Keller, Gottfried
d. 1896 Goncourt, Edmond Louis Antoine Huot de
d. 1915 White, Ellen Gould Harmon
d. 1916 Metchnikoff, Elie
d. 1918 Alexandra Feodorovna

d. 1918 Carter, William
d. 1918 Nicholas II
d. 1918 Romanov, Anastasia
d. 1923 Couperius, Louis (Marie Anne)
d. 1938 Insull, Samuel
d. 1953 Belloc, Hilaire
d. 1954 Muratore, Lucien
d. 1960 Kesselring, Albert
d. 1960 Marquand, John Phillips
d. 1965 Artzybasheff, Boris Mikhailovich
d. 1970 Anthony, John J(ason)
d. 1970 Aramburu, Pedro Eugenio
d. 1979 Deller, Alfred George
d. 1979 Douglas, Robert L
d. 1979 McIntyre, James Francis Aloysius, Cardinal
d. 1980 Brackman, Robert
d. 1981 Chapin, Harry Foster
d. 1982 Dewaere, Patrick
d. 1982 Gross, Courtlandt Sherrington
d. 1982 Swart, Charles Robberts
d. 1983 Micombero, Michel
d. 1983 Raphaelson, Samson
d. 1985 Arends, Leslie Cornelius
d. 1985 Boll, Heinrich (Theodor)
d. 1985 Hicks, Ursula Kathleen Webb
d. 1986 Boothby, Robert John Graham, Lord
d. 1986 Rubin, Benny
d. 1986 Zacharias, Jerrold R(einarch)
d. 1989 Dempsey, John Noel
d. 1989 Karajan, Herbert von
d. 1991 Dejong, Meindert
d. 1991 Motherwell, Robert Burns
d. 1991 Rizzo, Frank Lazzaro
d. 1992 Buchanan, Buck
d. 1994 Schwinger, Julian (Seymour)
d. 1995 Sarton, May
d. 1995 Spender, Stephen (Harold)
d. 1998 Clarke, John Henrik
d. 1999 Kennedy, John F(itzgerald), Jr.

July 17
b. 1674 Watts, Isaac

b. 1744 Gerry, Elbridge
b. 1745 Pickering, Timothy
b. 1763 Astor, John Jacob
b. 1797 Delaroche, Hippolyte
b. 1830 Remenyi, Eduard
b. 1843 Roca, Julio Argentino
b. 1859 Rhys, Ernest Percival
b. 1859 Rivera, Luis Munoz
b. 1871 Feininger, Lyonel
b. 1871 Litvinov, Maxim
b. 1875 Tovey, Donald Francis, Sir
b. 1883 Lazare, Kaplan
b. 1883 Stiller, Mauritz
b. 1887 Conway, Jack
b. 1888 Agnon, S(hmuel) Y(osef)
b. 1889 Gardner, Erle Stanley
b. 1890 France, Harry Clinton
b. 1891 Budenz, Louis Francis
b. 1894 Lemaitre, Georges
b. 1895 Kelly, Machine Gun
b. 1896 Andresen, Ivar
b. 1896 Green, Wilf(red Thomas)
b. 1897 Banks, Monty
b. 1898 Abbott, Berenice
b. 1899 Cagney, James
b. 1902 Stead, Christina (Ellen)
b. 1905 Gargan, William
b. 1909 Amies, Hardy
b. 1909 Strasfogel, Ignace
b. 1912 Belaunde-Terry, Fernando
b. 1912 Linkletter, Art(hur Gordon)
b. 1913 Goldberg, Bertrand
b. 1913 Wilson, Mitchell A
b. 1915 Jarman, John
b. 1915 Rothstein, Arthur
b. 1916 Steber, Eleanor
b. 1917 Boudreau, Lou(is)
b. 1917 Diller, Phyllis
b. 1918 Manning, Irene
b. 1919 Cottrell, Alan Howard, Sir
b. 1920 Bell, Arthur Donald
b. 1920 Monroe, Bill
b. 1920 Samaranch, Juan Antonio
b. 1921 Isaacs, Alick
b. 1922 Davie, Donald Alfred

b. 1923 Purdy, James
b. 1928 Dyer, Charles (Raymond)
b. 1928 Guaraldi, Vince(nt Anthony)
b. 1928 Morello, Joseph A
b. 1932 Riney, Hal (Patrick)
b. 1934 Sutherland, Donald
b. 1935 Carroll, Diahann
b. 1935 Civiletti, Benjamin Richard
b. 1935 Schickele, Peter
b. 1941 Bracey, John H(enry Jr.)
b. 1941 Oswald, Marina Nikolaevna
b. 1942 Davis, Spencer
b. 1942 Garnett, Gale
b. 1942 Hawkins, Connie
b. 1942 Williams, William T(homas)
b. 1951 Arnaz, Lucie Desiree
b. 1952 Hasselhoff, David
b. 1952 Larson, Nicolette
b. 1952 Snow, Phoebe Laub
b. 1955 Lansky, Aaron
b. 1956 Trottier, Bryan John
b. 1960 Upshaw, Dawn
b. 1963 Thigpen, Bobby
b. 1967 Ashton, Susan
d. 924 Edward the Elder
d. 1726 Cadogan, William, Earl
d. 1790 Smith, Adam
d. 1793 Corday d'Armount, Charlotte
d. 1845 Grey, Charles
d. 1871 Tausig, Karl
d. 1881 Bridger, James
d. 1887 Dix, Dorothea Lynde
d. 1894 Leconte de Lisle, Charles Marie Rene
d. 1901 Butterford, Daniel
d. 1903 Whistler, James Abbott McNeill
d. 1912 Poincare, Jules Henri
d. 1924 Gardner, Isabella Stewart
d. 1928 Giolitti, Giovanni
d. 1928 Obregon, Alvaro
d. 1935 Russell, George William
d. 1937 Pierne, Gabriel
d. 1946 Mihajlovic, Dragoliub
d. 1947 Wallenberg, Raoul Gustav
d. 1949 Murphy, Frank
d. 1950 Booth, Evangeline Cory

d. 1953 Adams, Maude
d. 1954 Kelly, Machine Gun
d. 1959 Holiday, Billie
d. 1959 Munnings, Alfred James, Sir
d. 1959 Tsankov, Aleksandur
d. 1961 Cobb, Ty(rus Raymond)
d. 1961 Reulbach, Ed(ward Marvin)
d. 1967 Coltrane, Trane
d. 1969 Lahey, Edwin A(loysius)
d. 1971 Edwards, Cliff
d. 1971 Nye, Gerald Prentice
d. 1974 Dean, Dizzy
d. 1975 Omlie, Phoebe Jane Fairgrave
d. 1976 Weingarten, Violet Brown
d. 1977 Malcuzynski, Witold
d. 1980 Barry, Donald
d. 1980 Roskolenko, Harry
d. 1981 Barbanell, Maurice
d. 1984 Low, George M(ichael)
d. 1984 Sykes, Roosevelt
d. 1985 Langer, Suzanne K
d. 1985 Margo
d. 1985 Stewart, Wynn
d. 1987 Slotta, Karl Heinrich
d. 1991 Parr, A(lbert) E(ide)
d. 1991 Perry, Harold R
d. 1995 Fangio, Juan Manuel
d. 1995 Guardino, Harry
d. 1997 Liman, Arthur L(awrence)
d. 1997 Weaver, Robert C(lifton)
d. 1999 Zipprodt, Patricia

July 18
b. 1552 Rudolf II
b. 1635 Hooke, Robert
b. 1656 Fischer von Erlach, Johann Bernhard
b. 1670 Bononcini, Giovanni Battista
b. 1720 White, Gilbert
b. 1811 Thackeray, William Makepeace
b. 1821 Viardot-Garcia, Pauline
b. 1843 Earp, Virgil W
b. 1845 Corbiere, Tristan (Edouard Joachim)
b. 1853 Lorentz, Hendrick Antoon
b. 1864 Huch, Ricarda (Octavia)
b. 1865 Housman, Laurence

b. 1870 Kornilov, Lavr Georgyevich
b. 1871 Balla, Giacomo
b. 1882 Hagedorn, Hermann
b. 1883 Chiang K'ang-Hu
b. 1886 Buckner, Simon Bolivar, Jr.
b. 1887 Quisling, Vidkun Abraham
b. 1888 Cowdry, Edmund Vincent
b. 1890 Evans, Chick
b. 1890 Wilson, Charles Erwin
b. 1891 Lockhart, Gene
b. 1891 McNutt, Paul Vories
b. 1894 Dix, Richard
b. 1896 O'Boyle, Patrick Aloysius, Cardinal
b. 1897 Spottswood, Stephen Gill
b. 1900 Marshall, S(amuel) L(yman) A(twood)
b. 1900 Sarraute, Nathalie
b. 1902 West, Jessamyn
b. 1903 Gruen, Victor
b. 1903 Wills, Chill
b. 1906 Hayakawa, S(amuel) I(chiye)
b. 1906 Odets, Clifford
b. 1909 Gromyko, Andrei Andreevich
b. 1909 Wright, John Joseph
b. 1910 Baker, Elbert Hall, II
b. 1910 Velez, Lupe
b. 1911 Cronyn, Hume
b. 1912 Levin, Harry Tuchman
b. 1912 Nelson, Harriet
b. 1912 Roy, Mike
b. 1913 Rolvaag, Karl Fritjof
b. 1913 Skelton, Red
b. 1916 Armitage, Kenneth
b. 1916 Gray, Louis Patrick
b. 1918 Mandela, Nelson (Rolihlahla)
b. 1920 Redhead, Hugh McCulloch
b. 1921 Glenn, John Herschel, Jr.
b. 1922 Chayes, Abram J(oseph)
b. 1926 Jennings, Elizabeth Joan
b. 1926 Laurence, Margaret
b. 1927 Masur, Kurt
b. 1929 Button, Dick
b. 1929 Hawkins, Screamin' Jay
b. 1933 Evtushenko, Evgeniy Alexandrovich
b. 1933 Yevtushenko, Yevgeny

b. 1934 Bond, Edward
b. 1935 Albright, Tenley Emma
b. 1937 Hoffmann, Roald
b. 1939 Auger, Brian
b. 1939 Dion
b. 1939 Thompson, Hunter S(tockton)
b. 1940 Brolin, James
b. 1940 Faderman, Lillian
b. 1940 Torre, Joe
b. 1941 Masekela, Barbara
b. 1941 Reeves, Martha
b. 1943 Peete, Calvin
b. 1947 Forbes, Malcolm Stevenson, Jr.
b. 1948 Fehr, Donald Martin
b. 1948 Michel, Hartmut
b. 1949 Bryson, Wally Carter
b. 1950 Branson, Richard
b. 1954 Norwich, William
b. 1954 Skaggs, Ricky
b. 1957 Faldo, Nick
b. 1959 Landers, Audrey
b. 1961 McGovern, Elizabeth
b. 1966 O'Brien, Dan
b. 1971 Hardaway, Anfernee (Deon)
d. 1100 Godfrey of Bouillon
d. 1488 Cadamosto, Alvise Luigi da
d. 1610 Caravaggio, Michelangelo da
d. 1721 Watteau, Jean Antoine
d. 1753 Neumann, Balthasar
d. 1792 Jones, John Paul
d. 1800 Rutledge, John
d. 1817 Austen, Jane
d. 1838 Dulong, Pierre-Louis
d. 1863 Shaw, Robert Gould
d. 1868 Leutze, Emanuel
d. 1872 Juarez, Benito Pablo
d. 1892 Cooke, Rose Terry
d. 1899 Alger, Horatio
d. 1916 Immelmann, Max
d. 1918 Douglas, Amanda Minnie
d. 1931 Minkowski, Oskar
d. 1938 Marie Alexandra Victoria
d. 1943 Barclay, McClelland
d. 1944 Rommel, Erwin Johannes Eugin

d. 1944 Whistler, Rex
d. 1946 Judd, Charles
  Hubbard
d. 1949 Novak,
  Vitezslav
d. 1950 Van Doren,
  Carl Clinton
d. 1958 DuBois, Guy
  Pene
d. 1962 Houdry, Eugene
  Jules
d. 1966 Heiden, Konrad
d. 1967 Castello
  Branco, Humberto
d. 1968 Heymans,
  Corneille Jean
  Francois
d. 1969 Armstrong,
  Charlotte
d. 1972 Fosdick,
  Raymond Blaine
d. 1972 Gentele, Goeran
d. 1973 Hawkins, Jack
d. 1975 Sauer, Carl
  Ortwin
d. 1982 Jakobson,
  Roman
d. 1983 Lichty, George
d. 1985 Hoffman,
  Robert C
d. 1985 Segal, Henry
d. 1987 Freyre, Gilberto
  (de Mello)
d. 1987 Kaplan, Jacob
  Merrill
d. 1990 Menninger,
  Karl Augustus
d. 1990 Wayne, Johnny
d. 1992 Ising, Rudolf C
d. 1992 Lawrence,
  Lawrence Shubert, Jr.
d. 1992 Parnis, Mollie
d. 1997 Goldsmith,
  James (Michael), Sir

July 19
b. 1636 Monnoyer,
  Jean-Baptiste
b. 1698 Bodmer, Johann
  Jakob
b. 1802 Davenport,
  Thomas
b. 1806 Bache,
  Alexander Dallas
b. 1814 Colt, Samuel
b. 1817 Bickerdyke,
  Mary Ann Ball
b. 1819 Keller,
  Gottfried
b. 1834 Degas, (Hilaire
  Germain) Edgar
b. 1835 Barrios, Justo
  Rufino
b. 1846 Pickering,
  Edward Charles
b. 1847 Williams, Gus
b. 1849 Aulard,
  Francois Victor
  Alphonse
b. 1860 Borden, Lizzie
  Andrew
b. 1865 Mayo, Charles
  Horace
b. 1868 Nitti, Francesco
  Saverio
b. 1876 Smith, Joseph
  Fielding

b. 1879 Laviolette, Jack
b. 1879 Mitchel, John
  Purroy
b. 1883 Fleischer, Max
b. 1885 Muir, Malcolm
b. 1892 Irvin, Dick
b. 1893 Mayakovsky,
  Vladimir
b. 1896 Breeskin,
  Adelyn Dohme
b. 1896 Cronin,
  A(rchibald) J(oseph)
b. 1898 Marcuse,
  Herbert
b. 1900 Rosenberg,
  Anna Marie
b. 1901 Beals, Ralph
  Leon
b. 1901 Damita, Lily
b. 1903 Haskell, Arnold
  Lionel
b. 1905 Kentner, Louis
  Philip
b. 1905 Neel, (Louis)
  Boyd
b. 1905 Snow, Edgar
  Parks
b. 1913 Teagarden,
  Charles
b. 1916 Cavarretta,
  Phil(ip Joseph)
b. 1916 Merriam, Eve
b. 1917 Scranton,
  William Warren
b. 1920 Gould, Gordon
b. 1920 Medina, Patricia
b. 1921 O'Hearn,
  Robert Raymond
b. 1921 Yalow, Rosalyn
  Sussman
b. 1922 McGovern,
  George Stanley
b. 1923 Hannum,
  Alex(ander Murray)
b. 1923 Hansen, Joseph
b. 1923 Rusher, William
  Allen
b. 1924 Hathaway,
  Stanley Knapp
b. 1924 Hingle, Pat
b. 1925 Evers, Medgar
  Wiley
b. 1926 Gallagher,
  Helen
b. 1927 Myrdal, Jan
b. 1929 Hejduk, John
b. 1930 Callahan,
  Daniel John
b. 1935 Agee, Philip
b. 1937 Jordan, Richard
b. 1941 Bessmertnova,
  Natalya (Igorevna)
b. 1941 Carr, Vikki
b. 1943 Cole, Dennis
b. 1943 Smith, Jerry
b. 1944 Turnbull,
  Walter (J.)
b. 1945 Wexler, Nancy
  Sabin
b. 1946 Nastase, Ilie
b. 1947 Leadon, Bernie
b. 1947 May, Brian
b. 1958 Olson, Billy
  Richard
b. 1959 Treas, Terri
b. 1960 Egoyan, Atom

b. 1962 Edwards,
  Anthony
b. 1964 Edwards,
  Teresa
b. 1968 Butler, LeRoy
d. 1374 Petrarch,
  Francesco
d. 1647 Hooker,
  Thomas
d. 1814 Flinders,
  Matthew
d. 1824 Iturbide,
  Augustin de
d. 1850 Fuller, Margaret
d. 1858 Porter, William
  Trotter
d. 1868 Beach, Moses
  Yale
d. 1884 Sloan, Samuel
d. 1888 Roe, Edward
  Payson
d. 1892 Cook, Thomas
d. 1897 Boycott,
  Charles Cunningham
d. 1902 Acton, John
  Emerich Edward
  Dalberg-Acton, Baron
d. 1922 Goucher, John
  Franklin
d. 1923 Holabird,
  William
d. 1935 Sedgwick, Anne
  Douglas
d. 1941 Nutting,
  Wallace
d. 1944 Cook, Will
  Marion
d. 1947 Aung San
d. 1957 Malaparte,
  Curzio
d. 1962 Davis, Clyde
  Brion
d. 1965 Gitlow,
  Benjamin
d. 1965 Rhee, Syngman
d. 1966 Akeley, Mary
  Lee Jobe
d. 1967 Shepard, Odell
d. 1969 Kopechne,
  Mary Jo
d. 1971 Myers, Garry
  Cleveland
d. 1972 Benson, Sally
d. 1972 Roswaenge,
  Helge
d. 1974 Flynn, Joe
d. 1975 Frizzell, Lefty
d. 1980 Morgenthau,
  Hans Joachim
d. 1985 Canaday, John
  (Edwin John)
d. 1985 Montagu, Ewen
d. 1987 Rau,
  Dhanvanthi Rama,
  Lady
d. 1989 Dennis, Nigel
  Forbes
d. 1990 Quillan, Eddie
d. 1992 Newell, Allen
d. 1994 Firkusny,
  Rudolf
d. 1994 Turner, Donald
  F(rank)
d. 1996 Jenco,
  Lawrence M

d. 1997 Hines, John
  E(lbridge)
July 20
b. 1304 Petrarch,
  Francesco
b. 1661 Iberville, Pierre
  Le Moyne, Sieur d'
b. 1766 Elgin, Thomas
  Bruce
b. 1785 Mahmud, II
b. 1804 Owen, Richard,
  Sir
b. 1810 Regnault, Henri
  Victor
b. 1811 Elgin, James
  Bruce
b. 1820 De Bow, James
  Dunwoody Brownson
b. 1820 Keene, Laura
b. 1835 Giles, Ernest
b. 1838 Daly, Augustin
b. 1844 Queensberry,
  John Sholto Douglas
b. 1847 Liebermann,
  Max
b. 1864 Karlfeldt, Erik
  Axel
b. 1869 Thurston,
  Howard
b. 1880 Keyserling,
  Hermann Alexander
  Graf Von
b. 1888 McMurtrie,
  Douglas C
b. 1889 Reith, John
  Charles Walsham
b. 1890 Felton, Verna
b. 1890 George II
b. 1890 Morandi,
  Giorgio
b. 1891 Allyn, Stanley
  Charles
b. 1892 Bara, Theda
b. 1895 Corum, Martene
  Windsor
b. 1895 Moholy-Nagy,
  Laszlo
b. 1897 Reichstein,
  Tadeus
b. 1900 Arnold, Oren
b. 1901 Manush, Heinie
b. 1904 Hammon,
  William McDowell
b. 1907 Lincoln, George
  A
b. 1907 Simpson,
  Cedric Keith
b. 1909 Miller, William
  Mosley
b. 1910 Wedgwood,
  C(icely) V(eronica)
b. 1914 Uhde, Hermann
b. 1919 Collins, John
  F(rederick)
b. 1919 Ford, Benson
b. 1919 Hillary,
  Edmund Percival, Sir
b. 1919 Stevens, K T
b. 1920 Richardson,
  Elliot L(ee)
b. 1924 Albright, Lola
  Jean
b. 1924 Berger, Thomas
  Louis
b. 1924 Sarkis, Elias

b. 1925 Delors, Jacques
Lucien Jean
b. 1925 Fanon, Frantz
(Omar)
b. 1929 Ilitch, Mike
b. 1930 Daly, Chuck
b. 1932 Banham Silpa-
archa
b. 1932 Paik, Nam June
b. 1933 Doubleday,
Nelson
b. 1934 Howes, Sally
Ann
b. 1936 Mikulski,
Barbara Ann
b. 1938 Rigg, Diana
b. 1939 Chicago, Judy
b. 1939 Wood, Natalie
b. 1940 Oliva, Tony
b. 1942 Stanley, Mickey
b. 1944 Sheppard, T G
b. 1945 Craig, Larry
Edwin
b. 1946 Carnes, Kim
b. 1947 Binnig, Gerd
b. 1947 Santana, Carlos
b. 1950 Achtenberg,
Roberta
b. 1953 Friedman,
Thomas L(oren)
b. 1954 Bosley,
Freeman (Robertson),
Jr.
b. 1954 French, Jay Jay
b. 1956 Jausovec, Mima
b. 1957 Colmenares,
Margarita (H.)
b. 1960 Witt, Mike
b. 1964 Cornell, Chris
b. 1968 Carson, Jimmy
d. 1752 Pepusch,
Johann Christoph
d. 1866 Riemann, Georg
Friedrich
d. 1870 Grafe, Albrecht
Friedrich Wilhelm
Ernst von
d. 1883 Iwakura,
Tomomi
d. 1890 Wallace,
Richard, Sir
d. 1891 Alarcon, Pedro
Antonio de
d. 1897 Ingelow, Jean
d. 1902 Mackay, John
William
d. 1903 Leo XIII
d. 1912 Lang, Andrew
d. 1923 Villa, Pancho
d. 1926 Dzerzhinsky,
Felix Edmundovich
d. 1937 Marconi,
Guglielmo
d. 1940 Maytag, Elmer
Henry
d. 1941 Fields, Lew
Maurice
d. 1942 Nampeyo
d. 1944 Beck, Ludwig
August Theoder
d. 1944 Stauffenberg,
Claus (Schenk Graf)
Von
d. 1945 Valery, Paul
Ambroise

d. 1951 Abdullah Ibn
Hussein
d. 1953 Struther, Jan
d. 1958 Pangborn,
Franklin
d. 1959 Leahy, William
Daniel
d. 1968 Hammond,
Bray
d. 1969 Hamilton, Roy
d. 1970 Chace, Marian
d. 1970 Eiermann, Egon
d. 1970 MacLeod, Iain
Norman
d. 1972 Flick, Friedrich
d. 1973 Lee, Bruce
d. 1973 Smithson,
Robert (Irving)
d. 1974 Jenkins, Allen
d. 1978 Brace, Gerald
Warner
d. 1981 Kardiner,
Abram
d. 1983 Reynolds, Frank
d. 1984 Fixx, James
Fuller
d. 1985 Alexander, Leo
d. 1985 Johnson, Arno
Hollock
d. 1987 Arbib, Robert
Simeon, Jr.
d. 1987 Egan, Richard
d. 1988 Galbreath, John
Wilmer
d. 1991 Robinson, Earl
Hawley
d. 1992 Henderson,
Bruce
d. 1993 Corbett, Young,
III
d. 1994 Hillings, Patrick
J(ohn)
d. 1998 Spivakovsky,
Tossy

July 21
b. 1165 Philip II
b. 1515 Neri, Philip
b. 1620 Picard, Jean
b. 1664 Prior, Matthew
b. 1730 Adam, James
b. 1816 Reuter, Paul
Julius Von
b. 1817 Gilbert, John,
Sir
b. 1824 Matthews,
Stanley
b. 1826 Loomis,
Mahion
b. 1838 Muir, John
b. 1851 Bass, Sam
b. 1856 Bethune, Louise
Blanchard
b. 1858 Corinth, Lovis
b. 1860 Olcott,
Chauncey
b. 1863 Smith, C
Aubrey
b. 1864 Cleveland,
Frances Folsom
b. 1871 Ferrero,
Guglielmo
b. 1873 Witherspoon,
Herbert
b. 1880 Stefanik, Milan
Rastislav
b. 1881 Evers, Johnny

b. 1885 Keyes, Frances
Parkinson
b. 1891 Ripley, Elmer
Horton
b. 1893 Fallada, Hans
b. 1894 Ulric, Lenore
b. 1895 Barnes, Leonard
John
b. 1895 Maynard, Ken
b. 1896 Hickenlooper,
Bourke B
b. 1899 Crane, Hart
b. 1899 Hemingway,
Ernest (Miller)
b. 1905 Joslyn, Allyn
Morgan
b. 1905 Kennedy, David
M(atthew)
b. 1905 Trilling, Diana
(Rubin)
b. 1908 Jenner, William
Ezra
b. 1911 McLuhan,
(Herbert) Marshall
b. 1911 Polk, Ralph
Lane
b. 1914 Aries, Philippe
b. 1920 Sithole,
Ndabaningi
b. 1920 Stern, Isaac
b. 1923 Marcus,
Rudolph A
b. 1923 Wise, William
H
b. 1924 Knotts, Don
b. 1924 Starr, Kay
b. 1924 Stone, Chuck
b. 1924 Williams, Lynn
Russell
b. 1926 Burke, Paul
b. 1926 Jewison,
Norman
b. 1926 Premice,
Josephine
b. 1926 Reisz, Karel
b. 1928 Keane, John
Brendon
b. 1930 Littler, Gene
b. 1933 Gardner, John
Champlin, Jr.
b. 1934 Miller, Jonathan
(Wolfe)
b. 1934 Towns,
Edolphus
b. 1937 Frederickson, H
Gray
b. 1938 Allaire, Paul
Arthur
b. 1938 Aspin, Les
b. 1938 Kuerti, Anton
b. 1938 Reno, Janet
b. 1943 Herrmann,
Edward
b. 1944 Emecheta,
Buchi
b. 1944 Wellstone, Paul
David
b. 1945 Lawson, Leigh
b. 1946 Starr, Kenneth
b. 1948 Richards,
Michael
b. 1948 Stevens, Cat
b. 1949 Byrd, Donald
b. 1949 Hrabosky,
Al(an Thomas)
b. 1951 Williams, Robin

b. 1954 McKee, Lonette
b. 1957 Lovitz, Jon
b. 1960 Mulhern, Matt
b. 1976 Nall, Anita
b. 1403 Percy, Henry,
Sir
d. 1564 Sousa, Martim
Afonso de
d. 1796 Burns, Robert
d. 1865 Schnorr,
Ludwig von
Carolsfeld
d. 1878 Bass, Sam
d. 1899 Ingersoll,
Robert Green
d. 1908 Potter, Henry
Codman
d. 1926 Roebling,
Washington Augustus
d. 1928 Terry, Ellen
Alicia, Dame
d. 1932 Bazin, Rene
d. 1938 Kroger, Bernard
Henry
d. 1938 Wister, Owen
d. 1946 Rosenfeld, Paul
d. 1948 Gorky, Arshile
d. 1954 Carter, John
Garnet
d. 1957 Roberts,
Kenneth Lewis
d. 1960 Hoffman, Al
d. 1962 Trevelyan,
George Macaulay
d. 1965 Conover, Harry
d. 1967 Foxx, Jimmie
d. 1967 Luthuli, Albert
John Mvumbi
d. 1967 Rathbone, Basil
d. 1968 St. Denis, Ruth
d. 1979 Tugwell,
Rexford Guy
d. 1981 Fox, Carol
d. 1981 Liebman, Max
d. 1982 Barbour,
Walworth
d. 1982 Garroway, Dave
d. 1983 Wirtz, Arthur
Michael
d. 1984 Farrington,
Elizabeth Pruett
(Mary)
d. 1985 Bessie, Alvah
d. 1985 Simpson,
Cedric Keith
d. 1990 Shapiro, Stanley
d. 1991 Wilson, Allan C
d. 1991 Wilson,
Theodore Roosevelt
d. 1994 Carusi, Ugo
d. 1994 Scott, Hugh
(Doggett), Jr.
d. 1996 Cassidy,
Claudia
d. 1996 Edelman, Herb
d. 1997 Root, Lynn
d. 1998 Shepard, Alan
B(artlett), Jr.
d. 1998 Young, Robert
(George)
d. 1999 Ogilvy, David
Mackenzie
July 22
b. 1708 Ames,
Nathaniel

b. 1713 Soufflot, Jacques Germain
b. 1763 Geddes, James
b. 1784 Bessel, Friedrich Wilhelm
b. 1822 Arditi, Luigi
b. 1822 Mendel, Gregor Johann
b. 1844 Spooner, William Archibald
b. 1849 Lazarus, Emma
b. 1859 Glasscock, Jack
b. 1860 Corvo, Baron
b. 1864 Mabini, Apolinario
b. 1872 Pendergast, Thomas Joseph
b. 1876 Rosenbach, Abraham Simon Wolf
b. 1876 Ufer, Walter
b. 1878 Ball, Ernest
b. 1881 Bianco, Margery Williams
b. 1882 Hopper, Edward
b. 1884 Adler, Elmer
b. 1884 Alvarez, Walter Clement
b. 1884 Shepard, Odell
b. 1887 Hertz, Gustav Ludwig
b. 1888 Waksman, Selman Abraham
b. 1889 Fishbein, Morris
b. 1890 Kennedy, Rose (Fitzgerald)
b. 1891 Culbertson, Ely
b. 1893 Haines, Jesse Joseph
b. 1894 Totheroh, Dan
b. 1895 Rosbaud, Hans
b. 1896 Whale, James
b. 1898 Benet, Stephen Vincent
b. 1898 Calder, Alexander
b. 1898 Roy, Ross
b. 1899 Sobhuza II
b. 1900 Braceland, Francis J(ames)
b. 1900 Dahlberg, Edward
b. 1901 Weidman, Charles Edward, Jr.
b. 1902 Bennett, John C(oleman)
b. 1902 Bitter, Francis
b. 1908 Vanderbilt, Amy
b. 1910 Moorehead, Alan
b. 1910 Stevens, Edmund William
b. 1913 Albanese, Licia
b. 1913 Thornton, Charles Bates
b. 1914 Farber, Edward Rolke
b. 1916 Cerdan, Marcel B
b. 1917 McGarity, Lou
b. 1921 Roth, William Victor, Jr.
b. 1922 Robards, Jason, Jr.

b. 1923 Armstrong, Charles B
b. 1923 Dole, Robert Joseph
b. 1924 Whiting, Margaret
b. 1926 Forbes, Bryan
b. 1928 Bean, Orson
b. 1928 Bergland, Bob
b. 1929 Merchant, Vivien
b. 1932 DeLaRenta, Oscar
b. 1932 Terry, Megan
b. 1933 Trotman, Alexander J.
b. 1935 Dale, Grover
b. 1936 DellaFemina, Jerry
b. 1936 Robbins, Tom
b. 1939 Flynn, Ray
b. 1939 Flynn, Raymond (Leo)
b. 1940 Stamp, Terence
b. 1940 Trebek, Alex
b. 1941 Berning, Susie Maxwell
b. 1941 Bode, Vaughn
b. 1941 Clinton, George
b. 1941 Turcotte, Ron
b. 1943 Hutchison, Kay Bailey
b. 1944 Lyle, Sparky
b. 1945 Sherman, Bobby
b. 1946 Edgar, Jim
b. 1946 Schrader, Paul Joseph
b. 1947 Brooks, Albert (Lawrence Einstein)
b. 1947 Glover, Danny
b. 1947 Henley, Don
b. 1949 Viren, Lasse
b. 1954 DiMeola, Al
b. 1955 Dafoe, Willem
b. 1957 Stieb, Dave
b. 1962 Robertson, Alvin
b. 1966 Brown, Tim
d. 1461 Charles, VII
d. 1802 Bichat, Marie Francois Xavier
d. 1823 Bartram, William
d. 1832 Bonaparte, Francois Charles Joseph
d. 1869 Roebling, John Augustus
d. 1883 McDowell, Katharine Sherwood Bonner
d. 1883 Ord, Edward Otho Cresap
d. 1903 Clay, Cassius Marcellus
d. 1908 Cremer, William Randal, Sir
d. 1909 Liliencron, Detlev von
d. 1915 Fleming, Sandford
d. 1916 Riley, James Whitcomb
d. 1918 Gonzalez Prada, Manuel

d. 1920 Vanderbilt, William Kissam
d. 1922 Takamine, Jokichi
d. 1925 Jaegers, Albert
d. 1932 Fessenden, Reginald Aubrey
d. 1932 Ziegfeld, Flo(renz)
d. 1933 Walker, Emery, Sir
d. 1934 Dillinger, John Herbert
d. 1950 King, William Lyon Mackenzie
d. 1958 Holmes, Burton
d. 1967 Sandburg, Carl (August)
d. 1971 Fiorito, Ted
d. 1974 Darvas, Lili
d. 1974 Morse, Wayne Lyman
d. 1975 Tunnell, Em(len)
d. 1976 Goldfinger, Nathaniel
d. 1976 Wheeler, Mortimer
d. 1979 Galento, Tony
d. 1982 Stitt, Sonny
d. 1982 Waner, Lloyd James
d. 1984 Losey, Joseph Walton
d. 1987 Hinderas, Natalie Leota Henderson
d. 1987 Lescoulie, Jack
d. 1987 McMahon, Don(ald John)
d. 1988 Lucioni, Luigi
d. 1989 Talvela, Martti Olavi
d. 1989 Thompson, Frank, Jr.
d. 1990 Puig, Manuel
d. 1991 McLaren, Wayne
d. 1996 Royster, Vermont C(onnecticut)
d. 1998 Prey, Hermann
d. 1999 Targ, William

July 23
b. 1746? Galvez, Bernardo de
b. 1801 Walker, Robert James
b. 1816 Cushman, Charlotte Saunders
b. 1823 Patmore, Coventry Kersey Dighton
b. 1834 Gibbons, James, Cardinal
b. 1838 Colonne, Edouard
b. 1857 Shaw, Albert
b. 1863 Kress, Samuel Henry
b. 1871 Verrill, Alpheus Hyatt
b. 1874 Fitzsimmons, James E
b. 1877 Glass, Montague (Marsden)

b. 1881 Gallatin, Albert Eugene
b. 1883 Alanbrooke, Alan Francis Brooke, 1st Viscount
b. 1884 Krauss, Werner
b. 1884 Warner, Albert
b. 1886 Brown, Arthur Whitten, Sir
b. 1886 Madariaga (y Rojo), Salvador de
b. 1888 Chandler, Raymond Thornton
b. 1888 Williams, Gluyas
b. 1889 Bonnet, Georges Etienne
b. 1891 Cohn, Harry
b. 1891 Wright, Louis Tompkins
b. 1892 Haile Selassie, I
b. 1893 Menninger, Karl Augustus
b. 1894 Stronge, Norman, Sir
b. 1895 Poulson, Norris
b. 1895 Pringle, Aileen
b. 1895 Vidor, Florence
b. 1897 Cloete, Stuart
b. 1898 Dutton, Red
b. 1899 Heinemann, Gustav Walter
b. 1901 Hibbs, Ben
b. 1902 Cowles, William Hutchinson, Jr.
b. 1902 Schneirla, Theodore Christian
b. 1906 Prelog, Vladimir
b. 1907 Cunningham, Harry Blair
b. 1907 Huxley, Elspeth Josceline Grant
b. 1908 Vittorini, Elio
b. 1912 Miller, Carl S
b. 1913 Browne, Coral Edith
b. 1913 Foot, Michael
b. 1914 Foreman, Carl
b. 1915 Sardi, Vincent, Jr.
b. 1917 Arriola, Gus
b. 1917 Deming, Barbara
b. 1917 Kreuger, Kurt
b. 1918 Reese, Pee Wee
b. 1925 DeHaven, Gloria
b. 1925 Masire, Quett (Ketumile Jonny)
b. 1928 Fleisher, Leon
b. 1928 Selby, Hubert, Jr.
b. 1930 Freed, James I(ngo)
b. 1930 Landrieu, Moon
b. 1931 Isozaki, Arata
b. 1931 Isozaki, Arata
b. 1931 Troell, Jan
b. 1933 Convy, Bert
b. 1933 Rogers, Richard
b. 1936 Drysdale, Don(ald Scott)
b. 1936 Kennedy, Anthony McLeod

b. 1939 Gage, Nicholas
b. 1940 Goldin, Daniel S
b. 1940 Imus, Don
b. 1945 Danelli, Dino
b. 1947 Christian, Spencer
b. 1947 Essex, David
b. 1947 Manetti, Larry
b. 1948 Dell'Olio, Louis
b. 1957 Cornell, Lydia
b. 1961 Harrelson, Woody
b. 1962 LaSalle, Eriq
b. 1971 Krauss, Alison (Maria)
d. 1562 Berlichingen, Gotz von
d. 1757 Scarlatti, Domenico Girolamo
d. 1764 Tennent, Gilbert
d. 1793 Sherman, Roger
d. 1829 Boguslawski, Wojciech
d. 1845 Sublette, William L
d. 1853 Pretorius, Andries
d. 1875 Singer, Isaac Merrit
d. 1883 Dugdale, Richard Louis
d. 1885 Grant, Ulysses Simpson
d. 1904 Simon, John, Sir
d. 1905 Henner, Jean Jacques
d. 1914 Grimke, Charlotte Lottie Forten
d. 1916 Ramsay, William, Sir
d. 1930 Curtiss, Glenn Hammond
d. 1933 Schillings, Max von
d. 1941 Kittredge, G(eorge) L(yman)
d. 1948 Griffith, D(avid Lewelyn) W(ark)
d. 1951 Flaherty, Robert Joseph
d. 1951 Petain, Henri Philippe
d. 1955 Hull, Cordell
d. 1957 Sterne, Maurice
d. 1962 Moore, Victor
d. 1966 Clift, Montgomery
d. 1968 Dale, Henry Hallett
d. 1969 Dell, Floyd
d. 1969 Flanagan, Hallie Mae Ferguson
d. 1971 Heflin, Van Emmett Evan
d. 1971 Tubman, William Vacanarat Shadrach
d. 1973 Rickenbacker, Eddie
d. 1980 Manning, Olivia
d. 1981 Owen, Guy, Jr.
d. 1982 Morrow, Vic

d. 1982 Parsons, Betty Pierson
d. 1983 Auric, Georges
d. 1983 Traube, Shepard
d. 1985 Kyser, Kay (James King Kern)
d. 1985 Shaughnessy, Mickey
d. 1987 Bryant, Hugh
d. 1987 Gibbs, Erna Leonhardt
d. 1989 Barthelme, Donald
d. 1989 Harmon, Claude
d. 1993 Jordan, James
d. 1996 Mitford, Jessica
d. 1996 Muir, Jean
d. 1999 Hassan II

July 24
b. 1618 Cowley, Abraham
b. 1686 Marcello, Benedetto
b. 1725 Newton, John
b. 1783 Bolivar, Simon
b. 1796 Clayton, John Middleton
b. 1798 Dix, John Adams
b. 1802 Dumas, Alexandre Dumas Davy de la Pailleterie
b. 1803 Adam, Adolphe Charles
b. 1803 Davis, Alexander Jackson
b. 1826 Lopez, Francisco Solano
b. 1843 Abney, William de Wiveleslie, Sir
b. 1853 Gillette, William Hooker
b. 1854 Takahashi, Korekiyo
b. 1856 Picard, Charles Emile
b. 1857 Pontoppidan, Henrik
b. 1858 Kapp, Wolfgang
b. 1860 Mucha, Alphonse Marie
b. 1861 Renaud, Maurice
b. 1864 McCarthy, Tommy
b. 1864 Wedekind, Frank
b. 1867 Benson, Edward Frederic
b. 1876 Webster, Jean
b. 1878 Dunsany, Edward J M Plunkett, Baron
b. 1880 Bloch, Ernest
b. 1882 Thorndike, Lynn
b. 1886 Tanizaki Jun'ichiro
b. 1892 Jones, Thomas Hudson
b. 1893 Johnson, Charles Spurgeon
b. 1898 Earhart, Amelia (Mary)

b. 1899 Loeb, Gerald Martin
b. 1900 Fitzgerald, Zelda
b. 1904 Killian, James Rhyne, Jr.
b. 1904 Morris, Richard Brandon
b. 1908? Williams, Cootie
b. 1909 Curtis, Alan (Harold Neberroth)
b. 1910 Horner, Harry
b. 1910 Vera
b. 1911 Martinson, Joseph Bertram
b. 1911 Widgery, John Passmore, Baron
b. 1913 Byroade, Henry A(lfred)
b. 1913 Chance, Britton
b. 1913 Davis, Burke
b. 1914 Clark, Kenneth Bancroft
b. 1914 Mirvish, Edwin
b. 1914 Silvera, Frank
b. 1916 Eberle, Bob
b. 1916 MacDonald, John Dann
b. 1917 Brickman, Morrie
b. 1918 Ricci, Ruggiero
b. 1920 Abzug, Bella (Savitsky)
b. 1920 Cohen, Alexander H
b. 1920 Ter-Arutunian, Rouben
b. 1921 DiStefano, Giuseppe
b. 1921 Taylor, Billy
b. 1922 Mathias, Charles McCurdy, Jr.
b. 1923 Weaver, William
b. 1925 Addison, Adele
b. 1927 Howard, James John
b. 1927 Katz, Alex
b. 1929 Yates, Peter
b. 1934 Ruckelshaus, William Doyle
b. 1935 Oliphant, Patrick Bruce
b. 1936 Buzzi, Ruth Ann
b. 1937 Young, George
b. 1939 Bellamy, Walt(er Jones)
b. 1940 Campbell, Carroll Ashmore, Jr.
b. 1940 Moss, Cynthia Jane
b. 1942 Sarandon, Chris
b. 1947 Hays, Robert
b. 1947 Serkin, Peter A(dolf)
b. 1948 Racicot, Marc F
b. 1949 Trumka, Richard Louis
b. 1951 Carter, Lynda Jean
b. 1953 Grogan, Steve(n James)
b. 1957 O'Callahan, Jack

b. 1957 Tillis, Pam
b. 1958 Carroll, Joe Barry
b. 1963 Krone, Julie
b. 1963 Malone, Karl
b. 1964 Bonds, Barry (Lamar)
b. 1968 Leighton, Laura
b. 1970 Lopez, Jennifer
d. 1115 Matilda of Tuscany
d. 1739 Marcello, Benedetto
d. 1862 Van Buren, Martin
d. 1865 Cotman, John Sell
d. 1894 Ingersoll, Simon
d. 1922 Patten, Simon Nelson
d. 1924 Cox, Palmer
d. 1927 Akutagawa Ryunosuke
d. 1948 Patterson, Eleanor Medill
d. 1952 Copeland, Charles Townsend
d. 1954 Terrell, Mary Church
d. 1957 Guitry, Sacha
d. 1964 Roberts, Edward Glenn
d. 1966 Lema, Tony
d. 1973 Saint Laurent, Louis Stephen
d. 1974 Carpenter, Leslie
d. 1974 Chadwick, James, Sir
d. 1974 Kastner, Erich
d. 1974 Tyler, Parker
d. 1980 Sellers, Peter
d. 1981 Hauge, Gabriel
d. 1982 Lawler, Richard Harold
d. 1982 Markey, Lucille (Parker) Wright
d. 1984 Hextall, Bryan Aldwyn
d. 1985 Winwar, Frances
d. 1986 Breeskin, Adelyn Dohme
d. 1986 Lipmann, Fritz Albert
d. 1991 Singer, Isaac Bashevis
d. 1992 Ilizarov, Gavril A
d. 1993 Harris, MacDonald
d. 1996 Christine, Virginia
d. 1997 Brennan, William Joseph, Jr.
d. 1997 Parker, Frank

July 25
b. Welch, Mitzie
b. 1394 James I
b. 1654 Steffani, Agostino
b. 1750 Knox, Henry
b. 1775 Harrison, Anna (Tuthill Symmes)

b. 1799 Little, Charles
Coffin
b. 1803 Maverick,
Samuel Augustus
b. 1820 Doulton, Henry,
Sir
b. 1830 Bausch, John
Jacob
b. 1839 Garnier, Francis
b. 1840 Wright, Carroll
Davidson
b. 1844 Eakins, Thomas
b. 1848 Balfour, Arthur
James
b. 1853 Belasco, David
b. 1857 Sprague, Frank
Julian
b. 1870 Journet, Marcel
b. 1870 Parrish,
Maxfield
b. 1870? Skipworth,
Alison
b. 1880 Cohen, Morris
Raphael
b. 1884 Black,
Davidson
b. 1893 Confalonieri,
Carlo, Cardinal
b. 1894 Brennan, Walter
Andrew
b. 1895 Princip, Gavrilo
b. 1896 Gale, Richard
Nelson, Sir
b. 1898 Printemps,
Yvonne
b. 1899 Dumke, Ralph
b. 1901 Wilson, John
Johnston
b. 1902 Hoffer, Eric
b. 1902 Lee, Lila
b. 1905 Canetti, Elias
b. 1906 Hodges, Johnny
b. 1906 Wengenroth,
Stow
b. 1907 Gilford, Jack
b. 1908? Peary, Harold
b. 1911 Krauss, Ruth
Ida
b. 1914 Strode, Woody
b. 1918 Amen, Irving
b. 1920 Franklin,
Rosalind Elsie
b. 1923 Getty, Estelle
b. 1924 Church, Frank
b. 1925 Newquist, Roy
b. 1925 Paris, Jerry
b. 1927 Dancer, Stanley
b. 1927 Decter, Midge
b. 1929 Farb, Peter
b. 1931 Forrester,
Maureen
b. 1934 Calvo, Paul
McDonald
b. 1935 Bullins, Ed
b. 1935 Harris, Barbara
b. 1935 Khashoggi,
Adnan
b. 1935 Robinson, John
Alexander
b. 1937 Carmines,
Al(vin Allison Jr.)
b. 1940 Pennel, John
(Thomas)
b. 1941 Thurmond, Nate
b. 1941 Till, Emmett
(Louis)

b. 1942 Rader, Dotson
b. 1943 Margolin, Janet
b. 1943 McElligott,
Thomas J
b. 1948 Goodman,
Steve(n Benjamin)
b. 1954 Payton, Walter
b. 1955 Iman
b. 1957 Billingsley, Ray
b. 1962 Drabek,
Doug(las Dean)
b. 1967 LeBlanc, Matt
b. 1978 Brown, Louise
Joy
d. 1471 Thomas a
Kempis
d. 1564 Ferdinand I
d. 1685 Monmouth,
James Scott, Duke
d. 1794 Chenier, Marie-
Andre de
d. 1834 Coleridge,
Samuel Taylor
d. 1841 Rogers, Mary
Cecilia
d. 1843 Macintosh,
Charles
d. 1846 Bonaparte,
Louis
d. 1881 Clifford, Nathan
d. 1897 Packard,
Elizabeth Parsons
Ware
d. 1916 Tompkins, Sally
Louisa
d. 1918 Rauschenbusch,
Walter
d. 1925 L'Hermitte,
Leon Augustin
d. 1930 Vought, Chance
Milton
d. 1934 Coty, Francois
Marie Joseph
Spoturno
d. 1934 Dollfuss,
Engelbert
d. 1936 Wellcome,
Henry Solomon, Sir
d. 1937 Saunders,
Charles E, Sir
d. 1945 Craig, Malin
d. 1951 Leyendecker,
Joseph Christian
d. 1954 Raine, William
MacLeod
d. 1958 Warner, Harry
Morris
d. 1960 Defauw, Desire
d. 1964 Townsend,
William H(enry)
d. 1964 Wolff, Mary
Evaline
d. 1966 O'Hara, Frank
d. 1969 Gombrowicz,
Witold
d. 1969 Moore, Douglas
Stuart
d. 1972 Reventlow,
Lance
d. 1980 Vysotsky,
Vladimir
Semyonovich
d. 1981 Widgery, John
Passmore, Baron
d. 1982 Foster, Hal
d. 1982 Okada, Kenzo

d. 1983 Balderston,
William
d. 1984 Thornton,
Willie Mae
d. 1986 Lyons, Ted
d. 1986 Minnelli,
Vincente
d. 1987 Baldrige,
Malcolm
d. 1987 Draper, Charles
Stark
d. 1989 Rubell, Steve
d. 1991 Kaganovich,
Lazar M(oiseevich)
d. 1991 Knight, Arthur
d. 1991 Love, George
Hutchinson
d. 1992 Arletty
d. 1992 Drake, Alfred
d. 1993 Schaefer,
Vincent Joseph
d. 1995 Rich, Charlie
d. 1997 Hogan, Ben
d. 1999 Agronsky,
Martin Zama

July 26
b. 1580 Claver, Peter
b. 1678 Joseph I
b. 1728 Gates, Horatio
b. 1739 Clinton, George
b. 1782 Field, John
b. 1791 Robinson, John
Beverley
b. 1796 Catlin, George
b. 1805 Brumidi,
Constantino
b. 1829 Beernaert,
Auguste Marie
Francois
b. 1831 Florence,
William Jermyn
b. 1842 Marshall,
Alfred
b. 1850 Henry, Edward
Richard, Sir
b. 1855 Tonnies,
Ferdinand
b. 1856 Harper, William
Rainey
b. 1856 Shaw, George
Bernard
b. 1858 Boole, Ella
Alexander
b. 1858 House, Edward
Mandell
b. 1859 Bunau-Varilla,
Philippe Jean
b. 1866 Cilea,
Francesco
b. 1866 McCutcheon,
George Barr
b. 1874 Koussevitzky,
Serge Alexandrovich
b. 1875 Jung, Carl
Gustav
b. 1875 Machado (y
Ruiz), Antonio
b. 1876 Schelling,
Ernest Henry
b. 1880 Lincoln,
G(eorge) Gould
b. 1885 Maurois, Andre
b. 1886 Jannings, Emil
b. 1892 Jones, Sam(uel
Pond)
b. 1892 Leonard, Dutch

b. 1893 Grosz, George
Ehrenfried
b. 1894 Huxley, Aldous
(Leonard)
b. 1895 Graves, Robert
von Ranke
b. 1897 Butterworth,
Charles
b. 1897 Gallico, Paul
William
b. 1898 Gimbel,
Richard
b. 1899 Walker, Danton
MacIntyre
b. 1900 Mortimer,
Charles Greenough
b. 1903 Kefauver, Estes
b. 1903 Voorhees,
Donald
b. 1904 Link, Edwin
Albert
b. 1904 Roark, Garland
b. 1904 Westrup, J(ack)
A(llan), Sir
b. 1906 Allen, Gracie
Ethel Cecil Rosaline
b. 1908 Allende
Gossens, Salvador
b. 1909 Thorneycroft,
(George Edward)
Peter
b. 1912 Vance, Vivian
b. 1914 Hawkins,
Erskine (Ramsey)
b. 1918 Thompson,
Frank, Jr.
b. 1919 Gilmore,
Virginia
b. 1919 Lovelock,
James
b. 1920 Waterfield, Bob
b. 1921 Wittop, Freddy
b. 1922 Edwards, Blake
b. 1922 Lord, Marjorie
b. 1923 Wilhelm, Hoyt
b. 1928 Cossiga,
Francesco
b. 1928 Kubrick,
Stanley
b. 1928 Lougheed, Peter
b. 1929 Lalonde, Marc
b. 1929? Shepherd, Jean
Parker
b. 1929 Weissenberg,
Alexis Sigismund
b. 1931 Gorman,
R(udolph) C(arl)
b. 1939 Howard, John
(Winston)
b. 1939 Lilly, Bob
b. 1940 Kopechne,
Mary Jo
b. 1942 Gray, Dobie
b. 1942 Meciar,
Vladimir
b. 1943 Crane, Cheryl
b. 1943 Jagger, Mick
b. 1945? Martin, Kiel
b. 1946 Mirren, Helen
b. 1950 George, Susan
b. 1951 Martin, Rick
b. 1954 Gerulaitis, Vitas
b. 1956 Hamill, Dorothy
Stuart
b. 1959 Spacey, Kevin

b. 1909 Lowry, Malcolm
b. 1910 Goodwin, Bill
b. 1912 Wilding, Michael
b. 1913 Ryder, James Arthur
b. 1914 Dragon, Carmen
b. 1915 Townes, Charles Hard
b. 1916 Brown, David
b. 1916 Cregar, Laird
b. 1922 Piccard, Jacques Ernest Jean
b. 1925 Blumberg, Baruch Samuel
b. 1927 Ashbery, John (Lawrence)
b. 1929 Onassis, Jacqueline (Lee Bouvier Kennedy)
b. 1931 Hickman, Darryl
b. 1934 D'Amboise, Jacques
b. 1936 Chuan Leekpai
b. 1937 Duchin, Peter Oelrichs
b. 1938 Fujimori, Alberto
b. 1938 Hughes, Robert Studley Forrest
b. 1939 Horner, Matina Souretis
b. 1940 Grahn, Judy
b. 1941 Higgins, Colin
b. 1941 Muti, Riccardo
b. 1943 Bradley, Bill
b. 1944 Bloomfield, Mike
b. 1945 Davis, Jim
b. 1945 Wright, Rick
b. 1946 Kelsey, Linda
b. 1947 Ebersol, Dick
b. 1948 Engel, Georgia Bright
b. 1948 Struthers, Sally Anne
b. 1949 Blue, Vida Rochelle
b. 1958 Fox, Terry
b. 1958 Schulman, Sarah (Miriam)
d. 1540 Cromwell, Thomas
d. 1655 Cyrano de Bergerac, Savinien de
d. 1667 Cowley, Abraham
d. 1746 Zenger, John Peter
d. 1750 Bach, Johann Sebastian
d. 1794 Couthon, Georges
d. 1794 Robespierre, Maximilien Francois de
d. 1794 Saint-Just, Louis Antoine Leon de
d. 1802 Sarti, Giuseppe
d. 1808 Selim, III
d. 1818 Monge, Gaspard

d. 1823 Cutler, Manasseh
d. 1836 Rothschild, Nathan Meyer
d. 1840 Durham, 1st Earl of
d. 1842 Brentano, Clemens Maria
d. 1844 Bonaparte, Joseph
d. 1849 Charles Albert
d. 1852 Downing, Andrew Jackson
d. 1868 Smith, Seba
d. 1885 Montefiore, Moses Haim, Sir
d. 1903 Stoltz, Rosine
d. 1918 Treptow, Martin A
d. 1930 Gullstrand, Allvar
d. 1934 Dressler, Marie
d. 1939 Mayo, William James
d. 1939 Mercer, Beryl
d. 1942 Petrie, (William Matthew) Flinders, Sir
d. 1945 Asquith, Emma Alice Margot
d. 1952 McMahon, Brien
d. 1957 Abbott, Edith
d. 1967 Julian, Doggie
d. 1968 Hahn, Otto
d. 1969 Grau San Martin, Ramon
d. 1969 Loesser, Frank Henry
d. 1970 Barbirolli, John, Sir
d. 1970 Caston, Saul
d. 1972 Cwiklinska, Mieczyslawa
d. 1972 Traubel, Helen
d. 1973 Chase, Mary Ellen
d. 1974 McCafferty, Don
d. 1976 Feather, Victor
d. 1979 Irving, Jules
d. 1979 Miller, Don
d. 1979 Seaton, George
d. 1981 Bloom, Harry
d. 1981 O'Neil, James F(rancis)
d. 1981 Pauley, Edwin Wendell
d. 1982 Lucas, Nick
d. 1983 Crosby, Elizabeth Caroline
d. 1985 Audiard, Michel
d. 1986 Alcott, John
d. 1987 Burnham, James
d. 1987 Fredericks, Carlton
d. 1990 Esmond, Jill
d. 1994 Turnbull, Collin M(acmillan)
d. 1996 Peterson, Roger Tory

July 29

b. 1794 Corwin, Thomas
b. 1796 Hunt, Walter

b. 1797 Drew, Daniel
b. 1805 Powers, Hiram
b. 1805 Tocqueville, Alexis, Comte de
b. 1820 Vallandigham, Clement Laird
b. 1824 Johnson, Eastman
b. 1825 Pendleton, George Hunt
b. 1828 Pillsbury, John Sargent
b. 1832 Cesnola, Luigi Palma di
b. 1861 Roosevelt, Alice Lee
b. 1869 Tarkington, Booth
b. 1870 Dixon, George
b. 1874 Woodsworth, James Shaver
b. 1876 Ouspenskaya, Maria
b. 1877 Beebe, William
b. 1878 Marquis, Don Robert Perry
b. 1883 Mussolini, Benito Amilcare Andrea
b. 1884 Tietjens, Eunice
b. 1887 Mara, Tim(othy James)
b. 1887 Romberg, Sigmund
b. 1889 Reuter, Ernst
b. 1890 Zuckerman, Ben
b. 1892 Powell, William
b. 1896 Catlin, George Edward Gordon, Sir
b. 1896 Menzies, William Cameron
b. 1897 Shaver, Dorothy
b. 1898 Arkell, Anthony John
b. 1898 Rabi, Isidor Isaac
b. 1900 Johnson, Eyvind Olof Verner
b. 1900 Lattimore, Owen
b. 1900 Redman, Don
b. 1901 Bridges, Harry Renton
b. 1904 Tata, J(ehangir) R(atanji) D(adbhoy)
b. 1905 Hammarskjold, Dag (Hjalmar Agne Carl)
b. 1905 Kunitz, Stanley Jasspon
b. 1905 Todd, Thelma
b. 1906 Roebling, Mary G(indhart)
b. 1907 Belli, Melvin M(ouron)
b. 1907 Butterfield, Roger Place
b. 1908 Kaiser, Edgar Fosburgh
b. 1909 Baker, Samm Sinclair
b. 1909 Crosby, Sumner McKnight
b. 1909 Himes, Chester Bomar

b. 1911 Furcolo, (John) Foster
b. 1911 Iakovos, Demetrios A Coucouzis, Archbishop
b. 1912 Corey, Irwin
b. 1913 Grimond, Jo(seph)
b. 1914 Bich, Marcel
b. 1916 Christian, Charlie
b. 1918 O'Connor, Edwin Greene
b. 1921 Marker, Chris
b. 1922 Popa, Vasko
b. 1923 Egan, Richard
b. 1924 Bochner, Lloyd
b. 1924 Ethridge, Mark Foster, Jr.
b. 1924 Horton, Robert
b. 1925 Lindsay, Ted
b. 1925 Theodorakis, Mikis
b. 1926 Carter, Don(ald James)
b. 1930 Perkoff, Stuart Z.
b. 1930 Taylor, Paul
b. 1932 Kassebaum, Nancy Landon
b. 1933 Reuben, David Robert
b. 1934 Fuller, Robert
b. 1936 Dole, Elizabeth Hanford
b. 1937 Hashimoto, Ryutaro
b. 1938 Jennings, Peter (Charles)
b. 1941 Stofflet, Ty(rone Earl)
b. 1941 Warner, David
b. 1943 Jacobson, Michael Faraday
b. 1947 Forsyth, Bill
b. 1949 Quayle, Marilyn Tucker
b. 1950 Holzer, Jenny
b. 1953 Burns, Ken(neth Lauren)
b. 1953 Lee, Geddy
b. 1954 Adams, Alvan Leigh
b. 1956 Spinks, Michael
b. 1968 Rippy, Rodney Allen
d. 1095 Laszlo, I
d. 1573 Caius, John
d. 1833 Wilberforce, William
d. 1856 Schumann, Robert Alexander
d. 1881 Fitzhugh, George
d. 1890 Van Gogh, Vincent Willem
d. 1913 Asser, Tobias Michael Carel
d. 1929 Fuller, Henry Blake
d. 1934 Pitre, Didier
d. 1941 Leonard, Eddie
d. 1945 Mqhayi, S(amuel) E(dward) K(rune Loliwe)

d. 1955 Reynolds, Richard S
d. 1960 Kluckhohn, Clyde
d. 1960 Kluckhorn, Clyde Kay Maben
d. 1960 Simon, Richard Leo
d. 1962 Fisher, R(onald) A(ylmer)
d. 1965 Graves, Alvin Cushman
d. 1973 Charriere, Henri
d. 1974 Elliot, Cass
d. 1976 Cohen, Mickey
d. 1978 Nobile, Umberto
d. 1979 Marcuse, Herbert
d. 1979 Todman, Bill
d. 1981 Moses, Robert
d. 1981 Walsh, James Edward
d. 1982 Gale, Richard Nelson, Sir
d. 1982 Zworykin, Vladimir K(osma)
d. 1983 Bunuel, Luis
d. 1983 Crohn, Burrill Bernard
d. 1983 Massey, Raymond Hart
d. 1983 Niven, David
d. 1984 Waring, Fred Malcolm
d. 1986 Cooper, David (Graham)
d. 1988 Berlin, Ellin (Mackay)
d. 1989 Leonidoff, Leon
d. 1990 Kreisky, Bruno
d. 1992 Larocque, Bunny
d. 1995 Elgart, Les
d. 1998 Robbins, Jerome

July 30
b. 1511 Vasari, Giorgio
b. 1763 Rogers, Samuel
b. 1818 Bronte, Emily Jane
b. 1822 Adams, William Taylor
b. 1830 Hugo, Adele
b. 1831 Blavatsky, Helena Petrovna
b. 1857 Veblen, Thorstein Bunde
b. 1863 Ford, Henry
b. 1867 Beck, Martin
b. 1880 McCormick, Robert Rutherford
b. 1887 Meinesz, Felix Andries Vening
b. 1888 Jaeger, Werner Wilhelm
b. 1889 Haldeman-Julius, Emanuel
b. 1889 Wellesley, Dorothy Violet
b. 1889 Zworykin, Vladimir K(osma)
b. 1890 Stengel, Casey
b. 1894 Knopf, Blanche Wolf

b. 1898 Moore, Henry Spencer
b. 1899 Binns, Archie Fred
b. 1899 Moore, Gerald
b. 1905 Ballard, Harold
b. 1905 Ellis, John Tracy
b. 1908 Suhl, Yuri
b. 1909 Parkinson, C(yril) Northcote
b. 1912 McLaughlin, Leo (Plowden)
b. 1914 Killanin, Michael Morris, Lord
b. 1920 Tharp, Marie
b. 1921 Johannesen, Grant
b. 1922 Bloch, Henry W(ollman)
b. 1924 Gallen, Hugh J
b. 1924 Gass, William Howard
b. 1926 Bookspan, Martin
b. 1927 Johnson, Richard
b. 1929 Krofft, Sid
b. 1933 Byrnes, Edd
b. 1934 Selig, Bud
b. 1936 Guy, Buddy
b. 1939 Bogdanovich, Peter
b. 1939 Smeal, Eleanor Marie Cutri
b. 1940 Gourdine, Simon (Peter)
b. 1940 Schroeder, Patricia Scott
b. 1941 Anka, Paul
b. 1944 Rader, Doug(las Lee)
b. 1945 Sanborn, David
b. 1946? Zumwalt, Elmo Russell, III
b. 1947 Atherton, William
b. 1947 Schwarzenegger, Arnold Alois
b. 1948 Burnley, James H, IV
b. 1954 Olin, Ken
b. 1955 Kenty, Hilmer
b. 1956 Burke, Delta
b. 1956 Hill, Anita Faye
b. 1956 Larson, Reed David
b. 1957 Cartwright, Bill
b. 1958 Bush, Kate
b. 1958 Thompson, Daley
b. 1961 Fishburne, Laurence
b. 1963 Kudrow, Lisa
b. 1964 Fox, Vivica A.
d. 1718 Penn, William
d. 1771 Gray, Thomas
d. 1784 Diderot, Denis
d. 1811 Hidalgo y Costilla, Miguel
d. 1832 Chaptal, Jean Antoine, Comte de Chanteloup
d. 1849 Perkins, Jacob

d. 1875 Pickett, George Edward
d. 1894 Pater, Walter (Horatio)
d. 1898 Bismarck, Otto Edward Leopold von
d. 1901 Adams, Herbert Baxter
d. 1912 Mutsuhito
d. 1918 Kilmer, Joyce
d. 1930 Schildkraut, Rudolph
d. 1941 Welch, Mickey
d. 1942 Blanton, Jimmy
d. 1944 Bausch, Edward
d. 1948 Breckinridge, Sophonisba Preston
d. 1955 Pogany, Willy
d. 1962 McCormick, Myron
d. 1963 Hurley, Patrick Jay
d. 1964 Engle, Clair
d. 1964 Landis, James McCauley
d. 1965 Tanizaki Jun'ichiro
d. 1966 Craig, Gordon
d. 1970 Lomax, Louis
d. 1970 Perlea, Jonel
d. 1970 Szell, George
d. 1975 Blish, James Benjamin
d. 1975? Hoffa, Jimmy
d. 1976 Bultmann, Rudolf
d. 1977 Holloway, Emory
d. 1981 Taoka Kazuo
d. 1983 Dietz, Howard M
d. 1983 Fontanne, Lynn
d. 1983 Plimpton, Francis Taylor Pearson
d. 1984 Renault, Gilbert (Leon Etienne Theodore)
d. 1985 Robinson, Julia (Bowman)
d. 1986 Dalton, John Nichols
d. 1991 Ball, William
d. 1992 Marshall, Brenda
d. 1992 Shuster, Joe
d. 1996 Colbert, Claudette
d. 1996 Cousins, (Sue) Margaret
d. 1998 Smith, Bob

July 31
b. 1396 Philip the Good
b. 1527 Maximilian II
b. 1689 Richardson, Samuel
b. 1763 Kent, James
b. 1800 Wohler, Friedrich
b. 1803 Ericsson, John
b. 1816 Thomas, George Henry
b. 1820 Garrett, John Work
b. 1822 Hewitt, Abram Stevens

b. 1835 Du Chaillu, Paul Belloni
b. 1837 Quantrill, William Clarke
b. 1843 Rossegger, Peter
b. 1848 Planquette, Jean(-Robert)
b. 1859 Smith, Theobald
b. 1860 Walcott, Mary Morris Vaux
b. 1867 Kresge, Sebastian Spering
b. 1869 Brasher, Rex
b. 1882 Ives, Herbert Eugene
b. 1883 Heckel, Erich
b. 1884 Goerdeler, Karl Friedrich
b. 1892 Armstrong, Herbert W
b. 1899 Stevens, Robert Ten Broeck
b. 1900 Roper, Elmo Burns, Jr.
b. 1901 Dubuffet, Jean
b. 1901 Slansky, Rudolf Salzmann
b. 1904 Carberry, John J(oseph)
b. 1904 Daley, Arthur (John)
b. 1904 Dresser, Davis
b. 1908 Hagen, John Peter
b. 1911 Liberace, George J
b. 1912 Friedman, Milton
b. 1912 Kupcinet, Irv
b. 1913 Hextall, Bryan Aldwyn
b. 1914 Head, Howard
b. 1915 Aptheker, Herbert
b. 1916 Todman, Bill
b. 1918 Rowen, Hobart
b. 1919 Conley, Renie
b. 1919 Gowdy, Curt(is)
b. 1919 Levi, Primo
b. 1919 Morgenthau, Robert Morris
b. 1921 Young, Whitney Moore, Jr.
b. 1922 Axelson, Kenneth Strong
b. 1922 Bauer, Hank
b. 1923 Ertegun, Ahmet (Munir)
b. 1927 Nichols, Peter
b. 1929 Murray, Don(ald Patrick)
b. 1930 Popham, William James
b. 1931 Ramsey, Frank Vernon, Jr.
b. 1931 Van Wachem, Lodewijk Christiaan
b. 1932 Gittings, Barbara
b. 1934 De Vorzon, Barry
b. 1934 Jones, Shirley
b. 1939 Nuyen, France

b. 1943 Bennett, William John
b. 1944 Chaplin, Geraldine
b. 1944 Flannery, Susan
b. 1944 Lansing, Sherry Lee
b. 1945 Weld, William F(loyd)
b. 1946 Welch, Bob
b. 1948 Loulan, JoAnn
b. 1948 Redig, Patrick
b. 1951 Goolagong, Evonne
b. 1956 Patrick, Deval Laurdine
b. 1959 Jordan, Stanley
b. 1962 Murray, Troy
b. 1962 Snipes, Wesley
b. 1966 Cain, Dean
b. 1968 Ware, Andre
d. 1556 Ignatius of Loyola, Saint
d. 1564 Velasco, Luis de
d. 1653 Dudley, Thomas
d. 1806 Lunardi, Vincenzo
d. 1840 Krochmal, Nachman Kohen
d. 1854 Wilson, Samuel
d. 1867 Sedgwick, Catherine Maria
d. 1871 Cary, Phoebe
d. 1875 Johnson, Andrew
d. 1886 Liszt, Franz (Ferencz)
d. 1896 Hunt, Richard Morris
d. 1899 Brinton, Daniel Garrison
d. 1910 Carlisle, John Griffin
d. 1914 Jaures, Jean Leon
d. 1918 Stanley, Francis Edgar
d. 1922 Murfree, Mary Noailles
d. 1937 Hires, Charles E
d. 1944 Lehand, Missy
d. 1944 Saint-Exupery, Antoine (Jean Baptiste Marie Roger) de
d. 1951 Haldeman-Julius, Emanuel
d. 1953 Taft, Robert A(lphonso)
d. 1957 Tchelitchew, Pavel
d. 1964 Mendenhall, Dorothy Reed
d. 1964 Reeves, Jim
d. 1967 Kennedy, Margaret
d. 1970 Conzelman, Jimmy
d. 1972 Spaak, Paul-Henri
d. 1978 Light, Enoch Henry

d. 1978 Widdemer, Margaret
d. 1981 Boni, Albert
d. 1981 Torrijos Herrera, Omar
d. 1982 Atwood, Francis Clarke
d. 1982 Chenoweth, Dean
d. 1984 Stern, Philip Van Doren
d. 1985 Blake, Eugene Carson
d. 1985 Blum, Stella
d. 1986 Ellin, Stanley
d. 1986 Wilson, Teddy
d. 1987 Levine, Joseph Edward
d. 1989 Harrington, Michael
d. 1993 Baudouin, I, King
d. 1995 Morgan, Thomas E(llsworth)
d. 1997 Bao Dai

AUGUST

b. 1599 Blake, Robert
b. 1613 Taylor, Jeremy
b. 1635 Betterton, Thomas
b. 1652 Wise, John
b. 1685 Taylor, Brook
b. 1824 Johnson, Jonathan Eastman
b. 1901 Boyce, Westray Battle
b. 1934? Sadat, Jehan Raouf
b. 1937 Crowe, J D
b. 1974 Fisher, Amy
d. 634 Abu Bakr
d. 1498 Pacher, Michael
d. 1528 Grunewald, Matthias
d. 1574 Eustachio, Bartolomeo
d. 1643 Hutchinson, Anne
d. 1682 Maitland, John
d. 1693 Blount, Charles
d. 1784 Serra, Junipero
d. 1844 Ram Camul Sen
d. 1950 Pavese, Cesare
d. 1960 Diop, David
d. 1974 Mantha, Sylvio
d. 1984 Chukarin, Viktor Ivanovich
d. 1990 de Andrade, Mario
d. 1993 Sarduy, Severo
August 1
b. 10BC Claudius I
b. 1744 Lamarck, Jean Baptiste Pierre
b. 1770 Clark, William
b. 1778 Jefferson, Mary
b. 1779 Key, Francis Scott
b. 1791 Ticknor, George
b. 1815 Dana, Richard Henry, Jr.
b. 1818 Mitchell, Maria

b. 1819 Melville, Herman
b. 1822 Grant, James
b. 1843 Lincoln, Robert Todd
b. 1848 Gailhard, Pierre
b. 1849 Dawson, George Mercer
b. 1862 James, Montague Rhodes
b. 1864 Smith, Ellison DuRant
b. 1869 Hillquit, Morris
b. 1873 Hocking, William Ernest
b. 1874 Spaulding, Charles Clinton
b. 1878 Tanguay, Eva
b. 1881 Macaulay, (Emilie) Rose, Dame
b. 1885 Hevesy, George Charles von
b. 1886 McLean, Evalyn Walsh
b. 1888 Whitney, Richard
b. 1891 Streeter, Edward
b. 1894 Mays, Benjamin E(lijah)
b. 1898 Stotz, Charles Morse
b. 1898 Ziff, William Bernard
b. 1899 Dean, William Frishe
b. 1899 Steinberg, William
b. 1901 Villa, Pancho
b. 1902 Latzo, Pete
b. 1903 Horgan, Paul
b. 1912 Jones, Henry
b. 1914 Mangrum, Lloyd
b. 1920? Cole, Maria
b. 1921 Kramer, Jack
b. 1922 Hill, Arthur
b. 1922 McColough, C(harles Peter)
b. 1923 Brown, Carter
b. 1923 Sando, Joe
b. 1924 Medicine, Beatrice A.
b. 1927 Smale, John Gray
b. 1929 Stewart, Michael
b. 1930 Bart, Lionel
b. 1930 Eagleburger, Lawrence S.
b. 1930 Grosz, Karoly
b. 1930 Holder, Geoffrey
b. 1931 Connolly, Harold
b. 1931 Wilson, Tom
b. 1932 Kahane, Meir David
b. 1933 DeLuise, Dom
b. 1933 Love, Iris Cornelia
b. 1936 Saint Laurent, Yves Mathieu
b. 1937 D'Amato, Alfonse Marcello
b. 1937 Plotnik, Arthur

b. 1939 Waller, Robert James
b. 1941 Brown, Ron(ald Harmon)
b. 1942 Garcia, Jerry
b. 1942 Giannini, Giancarlo
b. 1944 Berisha, Sali
b. 1947 Anderson, Rich
b. 1948 Branch, Cliff(ord)
b. 1951 Carroll, Jim
b. 1952 Berbick, Trevor
b. 1952 Lemon, Ralph
b. 1953 Cray, Robert
b. 1957 Peeters, Pete(r)
b. 1958 Vandeweghe, Kiki
b. 1959 Elliott, Joe
b. 1963 Coolio
b. 1973 Bledsoe, Tempestt Kenieth
d. 870 Bukhari, Muhammad ibn Ismail al-
d. 1252 John of Piano Carpini
d. 1464 Medici, Cosimo de
d. 1714 Anne
d. 1743 Savage, Richard
d. 1863 Gourlay, Robert
d. 1866 Ross, John
d. 1896 Grove, William Robert, Sir
d. 1903 Calamity Jane
d. 1911 Abbey, Edwin Austin
d. 1919 Hammerstein, Oscar
d. 1926 Zangwill, Israel
d. 1944 Quezon (y Molina), Manuel Luis
d. 1949 Moran, George
d. 1952 Higgins, Andrew J
d. 1952 Spaulding, Charles Clinton
d. 1961 Redman, Ben Ray
d. 1963 Roethke, Theodore (Huebner)
d. 1964 Abel, Taffy
d. 1965 Howard, Eugene
d. 1965 Lynch, Joe
d. 1966 Gowdy, Hank
d. 1966 Powell, Earl
d. 1966 Smith, Tommy
d. 1967 Kuhn, Richard
d. 1970 Farmer, Frances
d. 1970 Fleeson, Doris
d. 1971 McDermott, Johnny
d. 1973 Malipiero, Gian Francesco
d. 1973 Ulbricht, Walter
d. 1977 Powers, Francis Gary
d. 1980 Martin, Strother
d. 1981 Chayefsky, Paddy
d. 1981 Lynch, Kevin
d. 1983 Carter, Ernestine Marie
d. 1985 Walker, Joseph

d. 1986 Confalonieri, Carlo, Cardinal
d. 1987 Negri, Pola
d. 1987 Thibault, Conrad
d. 1988 Dearden, John Francis, Cardinal
d. 1988 Eldridge, Florence
d. 1989 Hirsch, John Stephen
d. 1993 Kauffman, Ewing Marion
d. 1993 Manessier, Alfred
d. 1994 Cushing, Peter
d. 1996 Reichstein, Tadeus
d. 1997 Richter, Sviatoslav Theofilovich
d. 1998 Bartok, Eva

August 2
b. 1754 L'Enfant, Pierre Charles
b. 1802 Wiseman, Nicholas Patrick Stephen
b. 1820 Tyndall, John
b. 1832 Olcott, Henry Steel
b. 1835 Gray, Elisha
b. 1835 Tyler, Moses Coit
b. 1854 Crawford, Francis Marion
b. 1862 Scott, Duncan Campbell
b. 1865 Babbitt, Irving
b. 1865 Merezhkovsky, Dmitry Sergeyevich
b. 1867 Dowson, Ernest Christopher
b. 1871 Sloan, John F
b. 1880 Dove, Arthur Garfield
b. 1883 Black, Samuel Duncan
b. 1884 Gallegos, Romulo
b. 1884 Larsen-Todsen, Nanny
b. 1886 Sodero, Cesare
b. 1889 Lawrence, Margaret
b. 1891 Bliss, Arthur, Sir
b. 1892 Kieran, John Francis
b. 1892 Warner, Jack Leonard
b. 1893 Burns, Bob
b. 1894 Pegler, Westbrook
b. 1896 Hughes, Sarah Tilghman
b. 1897 Soupault, Philippe
b. 1899 Fry, E Maxwell
b. 1899 Szabolcsi, Bence
b. 1899 Wilson, Lyle Campbell
b. 1900 Holling, Holling C(lancy)

b. 1900 Morgan, Helen Riggins
b. 1905 Loy, Myrna
b. 1908 Moore, Harry Thornton
b. 1912 Dvorak, Ann
b. 1914 Crocker, Fay
b. 1914 Merrill, Gary Franklin
b. 1918 Straight, Beatrice Whitney
b. 1920 Coleman, Lonnie William
b. 1922 Laxalt, Paul
b. 1924 Baldwin, James (Arthur)
b. 1924 O'Connor, Carroll
b. 1925 Dexter, John
b. 1925 Videla, Jorge Rafael
b. 1925 Whicker, Alan Donald
b. 1926 Bloomingdale, Betsy
b. 1932 Ben-Elissar, Eliahu
b. 1932 Boivin, Leo Joseph
b. 1932 Hunt, Lamar
b. 1932 O'Toole, Peter
b. 1934 Bykovsky, Valery Fyodorovich
b. 1937 Cannon, Billy
b. 1939 Craven, Wes
b. 1940 Rosenberg, Steven A
b. 1942? Falco, Louis
b. 1944 Cassidy, Joanna
b. 1944 Healy, Bernadine
b. 1945 McCabe, Jewell Jackson
b. 1948 Rae, Bob
b. 1949 Fallows, James (Mackenzie)
b. 1951 Gold, Andrew
b. 1955 Carr, Caleb
b. 1960 Fratianne, Linda
b. 1967 Krickstein, Aaron
b. 1968 Harris, Monica
d. 1100 William II
d. 1424 Yung-lo
d. 1780 Condillac, Etienne Bonnot de
d. 1788 Gainsborough, Thomas
d. 1799 Montgolfier, Jacques Etienne
d. 1811 Williams, William
d. 1823 Carnot, Lazare
d. 1859 Mann, Horace
d. 1876 Hickok, Wild Bill
d. 1877 Douglas, James, Sir
d. 1881 Clarke, Marcus (Andrew Hislop)
d. 1887 Rainey, Joseph Hayne
d. 1891 Williams, George Washington
d. 1911 Mansfield, Arabella

d. 1921 Caruso, Enrico
d. 1922 Bell, Alexander Graham
d. 1923 Harding, Warren G(amaliel)
d. 1924 Lothrop, Harriet Mulford Stone
d. 1934 Hindenburg, Paul Ludwig Hans Anton von Beneckendorff und
d. 1936 Andrews, Mary Raymond Shipman
d. 1936 Bleriot, Louis
d. 1936 Ufer, Walter
d. 1945 Mascagni, Pietro
d. 1945 Reznicek, Emil von
d. 1955 Stevens, Wallace
d. 1958 Scholes, Percy Alfred
d. 1963 LaFarge, Oliver
d. 1967 Stace, W(alter) T(erence)
d. 1970 Desses, Jean
d. 1972 Ganz, Rudolph
d. 1972 Goodman, Paul
d. 1973 Melville, Jean-Pierre
d. 1975 Mathieson, Muir
d. 1976 Lang, Fritz
d. 1976 Rathbone, Monroe Jackson
d. 1977 Lunt, Alfred
d. 1977 Makarios III, Archbishop
d. 1978 Bobst, Elmer Holmes
d. 1978 Chavez (y Ramirez), Carlos Antonio de Pauda
d. 1978 Fields, Totie
d. 1979 Haya de la Torre, Victor Raul
d. 1979 Munson, Thurman Lee
d. 1980 Stewart, Donald Ogden
d. 1981 Doherty, Kieran
d. 1982 Nesbitt, Cathleen Mary
d. 1984 Deming, Barbara
d. 1985 Estridge, Philip D
d. 1985 Faylen, Frank
d. 1986 Cohn, Roy (Marcus)
d. 1988 Carver, Raymond Clevie, Jr.
d. 1990 Maclean, Norman (Fitzroy)
d. 1992 Nolan, Thomas Brennan
d. 1995 Reddick, L(awrence) D(unbar)
d. 1996 Debre, Michel (Jean Pierre)
d. 1997 Burroughs, William S(eward)
d. 1997 Fela
d. 1997 Kuti, Fela Anikulapo

d. 1998 Lewis, Shari
d. 1999 Morris, Willie

August 3
b. 1729 Caswell, Richard
b. 1803 Paxton, Joseph, Sir
b. 1808 Fish, Hamilton
b. 1811 Otis, Elisha Graves
b. 1821 Stephens, Uriah
b. 1832 Blyden, Edward Wilmot
b. 1841 Ewing, Julianna Horatia (Gatty)
b. 1851 Fitzgerald, George Francis
b. 1855 Bunner, Henry Cuyler
b. 1856 Deakin, Alfred
b. 1867 Baldwin, Stanley
b. 1871 Parrington, Vernon L(ouis)
b. 1872 Haakon VII
b. 1873 Posey, Alexander Lawrence
b. 1884 Gruenberg, Louis
b. 1886 Westover, Russell (Channing)
b. 1887 Brooke, Rupert Chawner
b. 1894 Heilmann, Harry Edwin
b. 1900 Kekkonen, Urho Kaleva
b. 1900 Pyle, Ernie
b. 1900 Scopes, John Thomas
b. 1900 Sprague, R(obert) C(hapman)
b. 1901 Stennis, John C(ornelius)
b. 1901 Wyszynski, Stefan
b. 1902 Bloch, Raymond A
b. 1902 DeWitt, William Orville, Sr.
b. 1903 Bourguiba, Habib Ben Ali
b. 1903 Hopkins, Claude
b. 1904 Halper, Albert
b. 1904 Simak, Clifford Donald
b. 1905 DelRio, Dolores
b. 1905 Kuhn, Maggie
b. 1906 Trauner, Alexander
b. 1907 Staggers, Harley O(rrin)
b. 1908 Geisel, Ernesto
b. 1909 Clark, Walter van Tilburg
b. 1909 Jones, Edward Vason
b. 1915 Peterson, Helen White
b. 1918 Burns, James MacGregor
b. 1918 Elgart, Les
b. 1919 Wriston, Walter Bigelow
b. 1920 Hegan, Jim

b. 1920 James, P(hyllis) D(orothy)
b. 1921 Adler, Richard
b. 1921 Carruth, Hayden
b. 1921 Maxwell, Marilyn
b. 1922 Eisenhower, John Sheldon Doud
b. 1923 Hagen, Jean
b. 1923 Klein, Anne
b. 1924 Campeau, Robert Joseph
b. 1924 Uris, Leon Marcus
b. 1925 Hargis, Billy James
b. 1925 Touraine, Alain (Louis)
b. 1926 Bennett, Tony
b. 1926 Murphy, John Michael
b. 1927 Scott, Gordon
b. 1927 Silverstein, Elliot
b. 1930 Popov, Oleg Konstantinovich
b. 1931 Cord, Alex
b. 1933 Martinelli, Elsa
b. 1934 Savimbi, Jonas Malheiro
b. 1935 Lamm, Richard Douglas
b. 1937 Habyarimana, Juvenal
b. 1937 Wakoski, Diane
b. 1939 Krogh, Egil, Jr.
b. 1940 Alworth, Lance Dwight
b. 1940 Sheen, Martin
b. 1950 Landis, John David
b. 1950 Samper Pizano, Ernesto
b. 1951 Dionne, Marcel Elphege
b. 1952 North, Jay
d. 1460 James II
d. 1677 Borromini, Francesco
d. 1721 Gibbons, Grinling
d. 1792 Arkwright, Richard, Sir
d. 1797 Amherst, Jeffrey
d. 1857 Sue, Eugene Joseph Marie
d. 1881 Fargo, William George
d. 1888 Goodrich, Benjamin Franklin
d. 1891 Comstock, Elizabeth L
d. 1894 Inness, George
d. 1898 Gardner, Jean Louis Charles
d. 1898 Garnier, Jean Louis Charles
d. 1907 Saint Gaudens, Augustus
d. 1916 Casement, Roger David
d. 1924 Conrad, Joseph
d. 1927 Titchener, Edward Bradford

d. 1929 Berliner, Emile
d. 1929 Veblen, Thorstein Bunde
d. 1932 Brouthers, Dan
d. 1940 Jabotinsky, Vladimir Evgenevich
d. 1942 Ferrero, Guglielmo
d. 1942 Willstater, Richard Martin
d. 1948 Pollard, Albert Frederick
d. 1948 Ryan, Tommy
d. 1954 Aldrich, Bess Streeter
d. 1954 Colette
d. 1962 Cromwell, Dean Bartlett
d. 1963 Scott, Evelyn
d. 1964 O'Connor, Flannery
d. 1966 Bruce, Lenny
d. 1968 Rokossovsky, Konstantin Konstantinovich
d. 1969 Hyman, Libbie Henrietta
d. 1971 Sloane, John
d. 1973 Condon, Eddie
d. 1976 Warner, Roger Sherman, Jr.
d. 1979 Ohlin, Bertil Gotthard
d. 1979 Ottaviani, Alfredo, Cardinal
d. 1982 Carritt, David Graham
d. 1983 Jones, Carolyn
d. 1984 Perkins, Carl Dewey
d. 1986 Markham, Beryl
d. 1987 Moorhead, William Singer
d. 1989 Brico, Antonia
d. 1989 Mellon, William Larimer, Jr.
d. 1991 Drewry, Guy Carleton
d. 1992 Costa Mendez, Nicanor
d. 1993 Donald, James
d. 1993 Maleska, Eugene T.
d. 1995 Lupino, Ida
d. 1996 Thompson, Mary
d. 1998 Schnittke, Alfred

August 4

b. 1540 Scaliger, Joseph Justus
b. 1792 Irving, Edward
b. 1792 Shelley, Percy Bysshe
b. 1805 Hamilton, William Rowan, Sir
b. 1810 Purvis, Robert
b. 1816 Sage, Russell
b. 1823 Morton, Oliver Hazard Perry Throck
b. 1841 Hudson, William Henry
b. 1853 Twachtman, John Henry
b. 1859 Hamsun, Knut

b. 1863 McAdie, Alexander George
b. 1867 Beckley, Jake
b. 1870 Lauder, Harry MacLennan, Sir
b. 1873 Paul-Boncour, Joseph
b. 1875 Montemezzi, Italo
b. 1877 Thomson, Tom
b. 1890 Luque, Dolf
b. 1892 Swigert, Ernest Goodnough
b. 1895 Anthony, Edward
b. 1897 Lyman, Abe
b. 1898 O'Connell, Hugh
b. 1900 Elizabeth, Queen Mother
b. 1900 Illia, Arturo Umberto
b. 1904 Hobson, Harold
b. 1908 Kane, Helen
b. 1908 Lancaster, Osbert, Sir
b. 1909 Cunningham, Glenn Clarence
b. 1910 Birnie, William Alfred Hart
b. 1910 Schuman, William Howard
b. 1912 Wallenberg, Raoul Gustav
b. 1913 Addy, Wesley
b. 1913 Hayden, Robert Earl
b. 1914 Colville, Neil McNeil
b. 1915 Martin, John Bartlow
b. 1918 Iceberg Slim
b. 1920 Thomas, Helen A.
b. 1921 Ellis, Herb
b. 1921 Richard, Maurice
b. 1922 Aponte-Martinez, Luis, Cardinal
b. 1926 Goscinny, Rene
b. 1934 Green, Dallas
b. 1938 Coburn, D(onald) L(ee)
b. 1938 Jones, Hayes
b. 1942 Lange, David Russell
b. 1942 Michelman, Kate
b. 1944 Belzer, Richard
b. 1947 Derringer, Rick
b. 1947 Ingraham, Hubert
b. 1949 Riggins, John
b. 1952 Tabori, Kristoffer
b. 1953 Brand, Jack
b. 1958 Decker Slaney, Mary
b. 1962 Clemens, (William) Roger
b. 1971 Gordon, Jeff
d. 1265 Montfort, Simon de

d. 1639 Alarcon y Mendoza, Juan Ruiz de
d. 1741 Hamilton, Andrew
d. 1821 Floyd, William
d. 1834 Johnson, William
d. 1852 D'Orsay, Alfred Guillaume, Count
d. 1859 Vianney, Jean (Marie) Baptiste
d. 1865 Aytoun, William Edmonstoune
d. 1875 Andersen, Hans Christian
d. 1886 Tilden, Samuel Jones
d. 1893 Bolton, Sarah Tittle Barrett
d. 1908 Allison, William Boyd
d. 1908 Howard, Bronson Crocker
d. 1922 Enver Pasha
d. 1927 Atget, Eugene
d. 1929 Welsbach, Carl Auer von, Baron
d. 1930 Wagner, Siegfried (Helferich)
d. 1931 Williams, Daniel Hale
d. 1932 Oppenheim, James
d. 1938 White, Pearl
d. 1950 Coveleski, Harry Frank
d. 1957 George, Walter Franklin
d. 1976 Thomson, Roy Herbert
d. 1977 Adrian, Edgar Douglas, Baron
d. 1978 Fontaine, Frank
d. 1980 Ashbrook, Joseph
d. 1981 Douglas, Melvyn
d. 1982 De Rochemont, Richard Guertis
d. 1987 Price, Kenny
d. 1987 Unruh, Jesse Marvin
d. 1991 Burch, Dean
d. 1996 Kubelik, Rafael (Jeronym)
d. 1997 Calment, Jean
d. 1999 Mature, Victor (John)
d. 1999 Toms, Carl

August 5

b. 1604 Eliot, John
b. 1623 Cesti, Pietro
b. 1694 Leo, Leonardo
b. 1749 Lynch, Thomas, Jr.
b. 1802 Abel, Niels Henrik
b. 1802 Collins, Edward Knight
b. 1809 Kinglake, Alexander William
b. 1811 Thomas, (Charles Louis) Ambroise

b. 1815 Eyre, Edward John
b. 1819 Bidwell, John
b. 1819 Tait, Arthur Fitzwilliam
b. 1827 Fonseca, Manuel Deodoro da
b. 1839 Pater, Walter (Horatio)
b. 1844 Repin, Ilya Yefimovich
b. 1848 Taylor, Susie Baker King
b. 1850 Maupassant, Guy de
b. 1855 Dines, William Henry
b. 1862 Merrick, Joseph Carey
b. 1874 Mitchell, Wesley Clair
b. 1875 Briggs, Clare A
b. 1875 Craig, Malin
b. 1876 Beard, Mary Ritter
b. 1880 Sawyer, Ruth
b. 1881 Reynolds, Richard S
b. 1882 Johnson, Hugh Samuel
b. 1886 Barton, Bruce
b. 1887 Owen, (John) Reginald
b. 1889 Aiken, Conrad Potter
b. 1890 Gabo, Naum
b. 1890 Kleiber, Erich
b. 1890 Petersham, Maud
b. 1895 Flowers, Tiger
b. 1902 Liebman, Max
b. 1903 Autant-Lara, Claude
b. 1905 Leontief, Wassily W
b. 1906 Huston, John
b. 1908 Holt, Harold Edward
b. 1908 Rothschild, Miriam Louisa
b. 1911 Taylor, Robert
b. 1914 Brian, David
b. 1914 Colby, Anita
b. 1915 Lisagor, Peter Irvin
b. 1916 Chubak, Sadeq-i
b. 1916 Viereck, Peter Robert Edwin
b. 1917 Reedy, George E(dward)
b. 1918 Drake, Tom
b. 1920 Diamond, Selma
b. 1922 Ginott, Haim
b. 1923 Kleindienst, Richard Gordon
b. 1926 Jolas, Betsy
b. 1926 Omarr, Sydney
b. 1926 Wahloo, Per
b. 1928 Maglich, Bogdan C
b. 1929 Alvarez, Alfred
b. 1930 Armstrong, Neil Alden
b. 1933 Weldon, Joan

b. 1934 Berry, Wendell
b. 1934 King, Cammie
b. 1935 Saxon, John
b. 1936 Dancy, John Albert
b. 1937 Brooks, Herb(ert Paul)
b. 1937 Pinto da Costa, Manuel
b. 1938 Cone, James H
b. 1939 Irene
b. 1940 Gabriel, Roman, Jr.
b. 1943 Smith, Sammi
b. 1946 Anderson, Loni
b. 1946 Beban, Gary Joseph
b. 1946 Jackson, Shirley Ann
b. 1946 Slezak, Erika
b. 1950 Mittermaier, Rosi
b. 1953 Sang, Samantha
b. 1954 Ojeda, Eddie
b. 1959 Stastny, Anton
b. 1962 Ewing, Patrick Aloysius
b. 1966 Silverman, Jonathan
d. 1572 Luria, Isaac ben Solomon
d. 1729 Newcomen, Thomas
d. 1754 Gibbs, James
d. 1792 North, Frederick North, Baron
d. 1799 Howe, Richard
d. 1881 Spotted Tail
d. 1888 Sheridan, Philip Henry
d. 1895 Engels, Friedrich
d. 1922 McCarthy, Tommy
d. 1923 Wheeler, Candace Thurber
d. 1929 Fawcett, Millicent Garrett, Dame
d. 1930 Alden, Isabella Macdonald
d. 1936 Brownscombe, Jennie Augusta
d. 1938 Oland, Warner
d. 1940 Cook, Frederick Albert
d. 1948 Walker, Cyril
d. 1953 Clark, Barrett H
d. 1955 Miranda, Carmen
d. 1957 Wieland, Heinrich Otto
d. 1958 Holbrooke, Josef
d. 1959 Guest, Edgar A(lbert)
d. 1960 Meighen, Arthur
d. 1962 Monroe, Marilyn
d. 1964 Ross, Art(hur Howie)
d. 1972 Mezzrow, Mezz
d. 1978 Clark, Dutch

d. 1978 Haines, Jesse Joseph
d. 1979 Potofsky, Jacob Samuel
d. 1981 Neyman, Jerzy
d. 1983 Bok, Bart J(an)
d. 1983 Canova, Judy
d. 1984 Burton, Richard
d. 1986 Lundberg, Daniel
d. 1988 Higgins, Colin
d. 1988 Meeker, Ralph
d. 1991 Brown, Paul
d. 1991 Hess, Richard
d. 1991 Honda, Soichiro
d. 1992 Muldoon, Robert David, Sir
d. 1993 Jack, Homer A(lexander)
d. 1994 Bean, Louis H(yman)
d. 1996 Marcus, Frank
d. 1997 Gerrard, Roy
d. 1997 Kelley, Clarence Marion
d. 1998 Zhivkov, Todor Khristov

August 6
b. 1651 Fenelon, Francois de Salignac
b. 1697 Charles VII
b. 1775 O'Connell, Daniel
b. 1789 List, Georg Friedrich
b. 1809 Tennyson, Alfred, Lord
b. 1818 Anderssen, Adolf
b. 1820 Smith, Donald Alexander
b. 1828 Still, Andrew Taylor
b. 1830 Carpenter, Francis Bicknell
b. 1838 Symons, George James
b. 1840 Bandelier, Adolph Francis Alphonse
b. 1845 Fillmore, Myrtle Page
b. 1866 Schmedes, Erik
b. 1867 Loeb, James Morris
b. 1868 Claudel, Paul Louis Charles
b. 1874 Lefebvre, Georges
b. 1874 Shotwell, James Thomson
b. 1880 Carrillo, Leo
b. 1881 Fleming, Alexander, Sir
b. 1881 Parsons, Louella Oettinger
b. 1883 Bolton, Isabel
b. 1883 Nearing, Scott
b. 1888 Schlusnus, Heinrich
b. 1889 Kenney, George Churchill
b. 1889 Murry, John Middleton
b. 1890 Johnson, Gerald White

b. 1891 Slim, William Joseph
b. 1892 Gibson, Hoot
b. 1892 Suckow, Ruth
b. 1893 McClintic, Guthrie
b. 1893 Patman, (John Williams) Wright
b. 1895 Reichelderfer, Francis Wylton
b. 1900 Hillcourt, William
b. 1902 Heyer, Georgette
b. 1902 Schultz, Dutch
b. 1903 Morse, Philip McCord
b. 1904 Desses, Jean
b. 1904 Iba, Hank
b. 1904 Renault, Gilbert (Leon Etienne Theodore)
b. 1905 Allers, Franz
b. 1905 Klose, Margarete
b. 1906 Sterling, John Ewart Wallace
b. 1906 Strong, Ken(neth E)
b. 1908 Jacobs, Helen (Hull)
b. 1908 Keener, Jefferson Ward
b. 1908 Lee, Will
b. 1909 Craig, George N(orth)
b. 1909 Schnabel, Karl Ulrich
b. 1910 Crichton, Charles
b. 1911 Ball, Lucille (Desiree)
b. 1916 Burke, Mike
b. 1916 Cooney, Barbara
b. 1916 Gerstacker, Carl A(llan)
b. 1916 Hofstadter, Richard
b. 1917 Mitchum, Robert
b. 1917 Tyne, George
b. 1918 Granz, Norman
b. 1919 Betz, Pauline
b. 1921 Raines, Ella
b. 1922 Cardus, David
b. 1922 Laingen, (Lowell) Bruce
b. 1922 Laker, Freddie, Sir
b. 1922 Lomax, Louis
b. 1922 Walker, Daniel
b. 1924 Jenkins, Ella (Louise)
b. 1926 Finlay, Frank
b. 1926 Presser, Jackie
b. 1927 Warhol, Andy
b. 1930 Duberman, Martin
b. 1930 Lincoln, Abbey
b. 1932 Carriere, Jean-Claude
b. 1932 Ford, Doug
b. 1932 Hodgkin, Howard

b. 1935 Benjamin, Adam, Jr.
b. 1938 Bonerz, Peter
b. 1943 Anderson, Michael, Jr.
b. 1945 Messersmith, Andy
b. 1946 Lynch, Benny
b. 1951 Harewood, Dorian
b. 1957 Horner, Bob
b. 1958 DeBarge, Randy
b. 1965 Robinson, David (Maurice)
d. 1623 Hathaway, Anne
d. 1657 Chmielnicki, Bogdan
d. 1660 Velazquez, Diego Rodriguez de Silva
d. 1846 Dew, Thomas Roderick
d. 1875 Moreno, Gabriel Garcia
d. 1891 Litolff, Henri Charles
d. 1893 Schirmer, Gustave
d. 1904 Hanslick, Eduard
d. 1914 Wilson, Ellen Axson
d. 1925 Banerjee, Surendranath
d. 1925 Ricci-Curbastro, Gregorio
d. 1945 Bong, Richard Ira
d. 1945 Johnson, Hiram Warren
d. 1946 Lazzeri, Tony
d. 1954 Dionne, Emilie
d. 1954 Fairchild, David Grandison
d. 1955 Beecher, Janet
d. 1959 Sturges, Preston
d. 1960 Kemp, Harry (Hibbard)
d. 1964 Hardwicke, Cedric Webster, Sir
d. 1965 Carroll, Nancy
d. 1965 Sloane, Everett
d. 1967 Kiplinger, W(illard) M(onroe)
d. 1967 Weinberger, Jaromir
d. 1969 Adorno, Theodor Wiesengrund
d. 1971 Cleva, Fausto
d. 1973 Batista y Zaldivar, Fulgencio
d. 1974 Ammons, Jug
d. 1974 Rounseville, Robert Field
d. 1975 Daubeny, Peter Lauderdale, Sir
d. 1976 Chu Te
d. 1976 Piatigorsky, Gregor
d. 1977 Bustamante, William Alexander Clarke, Sir
d. 1978 Paul VI

d. 1978 Stone, Edward Durell
d. 1979 Kasznar, Kurt
d. 1979 Lynen, Feodor Felix Konrad
d. 1980 Marini, Marino
d. 1981 Bliss, Ray C(harles)
d. 1981 Price, Byron
d. 1982 Clarke, Gilmore David
d. 1985 Burnham, Forbes
d. 1986 Fernandez, Emilio
d. 1986 Schroeder, William J
d. 1987 Eaker, Ira Clarence
d. 1989 Beuve-Mery, Hubert
d. 1990 Bunshaft, Gordon
d. 1991 Michener, Roland
d. 1991 Reasoner, Harry
d. 1996 Ruppe, Loret Miller
d. 1996 Siles Zuazo, Hernan
d. 1999 Murray, Kathryn (Hazel)

August 7
b. 1533 Ercilla y Zuniga, Alonso de
b. 1586 Andrae, Johann Valentin
b. 1726 Bowdoin, James
b. 1742 Greene, Nathanael
b. 1839 Dryden, John Fairfield
b. 1860 Moses, Grandma
b. 1867 Nolde, Emil
b. 1868 Bantock, Granville, Sir
b. 1873 Peguy, Charles Pierre
b. 1876 Mata Hari
b. 1881 Darlan, Jean Louis Xavier Francois
b. 1886 Burke, Billie
b. 1886 Hazeltine, (Louis) Alan
b. 1887 McKechnie, Bill
b. 1890 Flynn, Elizabeth Gurley
b. 1896 Bergen, John Joseph
b. 1901 Heiden, Konrad
b. 1903 Leakey, Louis Seymour Bazett
b. 1904 Bunche, Ralph Johnson
b. 1907 Dart, Justin Whitlock
b. 1911 Ray, Nicholas
b. 1912 Dorman, Maurice Henry, Sir
b. 1919 Borg, Kim
b. 1921 Covington, Warren
b. 1925 Bryant, Felice

b. 1925 Swaminathan, M(onkombu) S(ambisivan)
b. 1925 Weber, Carl
b. 1926 Freberg, Stan
b. 1926? Kaufman, Sue
b. 1927 Busbee, George Dekle
b. 1927 Edwards, Edwin Washington
b. 1927 Switzer, Carl
b. 1928 Byars, Betsy
b. 1928 Randi, James
b. 1929 Larsen, Don(ald James)
b. 1929 Stapleton, Ruth Carter
b. 1934 Levinson, Richard Leighton
b. 1935 Deer, Ada E(lizabeth)
b. 1936 Kirk, Rahsaan Roland
b. 1937 Maples, William R.
b. 1937 Stern, Carl Leonard
b. 1938 Caldicott, Helen Broinowski
b. 1939 Kantor, Mickey
b. 1940 Dehaene, Jean-Luc
b. 1941 Wolf, Stephen M
b. 1942 Comer, Anjanette
b. 1942 Keillor, Garrison
b. 1942 Thomas, B(illy) J(oe)
b. 1943 Cantrell, Lana
b. 1943 Wattleton, Faye
b. 1945 Page, Alan Cedric
b. 1949 Novi, Carlo
b. 1950 Crowell, Rodney
b. 1950 Keyes, Alan L(ee)
b. 1950 Wottle, Dave
b. 1954 Kemp, Steve(n F)
b. 1958 Salazar, Alberto
b. 1963 Kennedy, Patrick Bouvier
b. 1963 Roberts, Marcus
d. 1547 Cajetan, St.
d. 1657 Blake, Robert
d. 1817 DuPont de Nemours, Pierre Samuel
d. 1834 Jacquard, Joseph Marie
d. 1847 Rapp, George
d. 1848 Berzelius, Jons Jacob, Baron
d. 1893 Catalani, Alfredo
d. 1898 Ebers, Georg Moritz
d. 1898 Hall, James
d. 1900 Liebknecht, Wilhelm
d. 1911 Allen, Elizabeth Ann Chase Akers

d. 1912 Hartmann, Franz
d. 1921 Blok, Aleksandr Aleksandrovich
d. 1927 Wood, Leonard
d. 1929 Berger, Victor Louis
d. 1929 Medary, Milton B
d. 1931 Beiderbecke, Bix
d. 1937 Gerard, Eddie
d. 1938 Stanislavsky, Konstantin Sergeyevich
d. 1941 Tagore, Rabindranath, Sir
d. 1956 LaTouche, John
d. 1957 Hardy, Oliver
d. 1958 Lashley, Karl Spencer
d. 1958 Lewis, Elizabeth Foreman
d. 1960 Ferragamo, Salvatore
d. 1960 Firpo, Luis Angel
d. 1961 Buchman, Frank Nathan Daniel
d. 1961 Robinson, Claude Everett
d. 1965 Derby, Jane
d. 1965 Marshall, Jack
d. 1969 Morgan, Russ
d. 1971 Evans, Orrin C
d. 1972 Lansing, Joi
d. 1973 Tunis, Edwin Burdett
d. 1974 Apgar, Virginia
d. 1979 Monsarrat, Nicholas John Turney
d. 1981 Arieti, Silvano
d. 1983 Lyttle, Hulda Margaret
d. 1984 Phillips, Esther
d. 1987 Chamoun, Camille N(imer)
d. 1987 Holt, A(ndrew) D(avid, Jr.)
d. 1987 Kishi, Nobusuke
d. 1989 Leland, Mickey
d. 1990 Soustelle, Jacques
d. 1991 Goody, Sam
d. 1994 Nickerson, Albert L(indsay)
d. 1995 Begelman, David
d. 1995 Brophy, Brigid Antonia
d. 1996 Kubly, Herbert (Oswald)

August 8
b. Bellisario, Donald P
b. 1646 Kneller, Godfrey, Sir
b. 1694 Hutcheson, Francis
b. 1705 Hartley, David
b. 1763 Bulfinch, Charles
b. 1779 Silliman, Benjamin
b. 1799 Palmer, Nathaniel Brown

b. 1819 Dana, Charles Anderson
b. 1822 Stoneman, George
b. 1825 Mould, Jacob Wrey
b. 1839 Miles, Nelson Appleton
b. 1846 Jones, Samuel Milton
b. 1857 McIntyre, James
b. 1857 Osborn, Henry Fairfield
b. 1861 Bateson, William
b. 1861 Chaminade, Cecile
b. 1863 Bailey, Florence Augusta Merriam
b. 1866 Henson, Matthew Alexander
b. 1875 Hamilton, Charles Harold St. John
b. 1879 Smith, Robert H
b. 1879? Zapata, Emiliano
b. 1882 Samaroff, Olga
b. 1884 Teasdale, Sara
b. 1886 Buck, Gene
b. 1886 Yon, Pietro Alessandro
b. 1890 Lord, Pauline
b. 1896 Rawlings, Marjorie Kinnan
b. 1899 Markert, Russell
b. 1900 Young, Victor
b. 1901 Berberova, Nina Nikolaevna
b. 1901 Lawrence, Ernest Orlando
b. 1902 Dirac, Paul Adrien Maurice
b. 1905? Martini, Nino
b. 1905 Smith, Carleton Sprague
b. 1906 Thon, William
b. 1907 Carter, Benny
b. 1907 Stuart, Jesse Hilton
b. 1908 Goldberg, Arthur Joseph
b. 1908 Morton, Arthur
b. 1909 Butterfield, Lyman Henry
b. 1909 Service, John S(tewart)
b. 1910 Sidney, Sylvia
b. 1913 Stafford, Robert Theodore
b. 1915 Elliott, Jumbo
b. 1919 DeLaurentiis, Dino
b. 1922 Calhoun, Rory
b. 1922 Gernreich, Rudi
b. 1922 Himmelfarb, Gertrude
b. 1923 Williams, Esther
b. 1925 Izetbegovic, Alija
b. 1926 Anderson, Richard Norman

b. 1926 Pierce, Webb
b. 1927 Gadsby, Bill
b. 1929? Biggs, Ronald Arthur
b. 1930 Mondale, Joan Adams
b. 1930 Talbot, Nita
b. 1930 Tarkanian, Jerry
b. 1931 Penrose, Roger
b. 1932 Culver, John Chester
b. 1932 Montagnier, Luc
b. 1932 Tillis, Mel(vin)
b. 1933 Tex, Joe
b. 1936 Bowden, Don
b. 1936 Howard, Frank Oliver
b. 1937 Hoffman, Dustin (Lee)
b. 1938 Pinson, Vada Edward
b. 1938 Stevens, Connie
b. 1939 Kuchma, Leonid Danylovich
b. 1942 Blanchard, Jim
b. 1942 Ramo, Roberta Cooper
b. 1944 Weir, Peter
b. 1945 Bowles, Erskine B.
b. 1947 Dryden, Ken(neth Wayne)
b. 1947 Wilcox, Larry Dee
b. 1948 Erasmus, Georges Henry
b. 1949 Carradine, Keith Ian
b. 1951 Shilts, Randy (Martin)
b. 1953 Most, Donny
b. 1954 Mansell, Nigel
b. 1958 Norville, Deborah (Anne)
b. 1963 Lewis, Carol
b. 1988 Beatrice, Princess of York
d. 117 Trajan
d. 1553 Fracastoro, Gerolamo
d. 1796 Maulbertsch, Franz Anton
d. 1824 Wolf, Friedrich August
d. 1827 Canning, George
d. 1856 Vestris, Lucia Elizabeth, Madame
d. 1898 Boudin, Eugene Louis
d. 1900 Cox, Jacob Dolson
d. 1902 Tissot, James Joseph Jacques
d. 1902 Twachtman, John Henry
d. 1908 Olbrich, Joseph Maria
d. 1909 MacKillop, Mary
d. 1919 Haeckel, Ernst Heinrich Philipp August
d. 1921 Ladd, George Trumbull

d. 1922 Gould, George Milbry
d. 1934 Robinson, Wilbert
d. 1936 Mourning Dove
d. 1938 Dufresne, Charles
d. 1940 Bonci, Alessandro
d. 1940 Coolidge, Dane
d. 1940 Dodds, Johnny
d. 1942 Genthe, Arnold
d. 1946 Barrientos, Maria
d. 1947 Denikin, Anton Ivanovich
d. 1948 Door, Rheta Childe
d. 1952 Weinman, Adolph A
d. 1955 Hartman, Grace
d. 1958 Bracken, Brendan Rendall, Viscount
d. 1959 Hinton, William Augustus
d. 1960 Walker, Danton MacIntyre
d. 1965 Jackson, Shirley (Hardie)
d. 1969 Hyland, Harry
d. 1970 Goodman, Johnny
d. 1973 Wiley, George A
d. 1975 Adderley, Cannonball
d. 1978 Bakeless, John Edwin
d. 1979 McDonald, David John
d. 1980 Mercer, David
d. 1980 Yahya Khan, Agha Muhammad
d. 1981 McIlwee, Thomas
d. 1982 Braestrup, Carl Bjorn
d. 1983 Harger, Rolla
d. 1984 Khrushchev, Nina Petrovna
d. 1984 Raskin, Ellen
d. 1985 Brooks, Louise
d. 1986 Druzhinin, Nicolai Mikhailovich
d. 1988 Ameche, Alan Dante
d. 1988 Kid Chocolate
d. 1991 Irwin, James Benson
d. 1991 Levine, Herbert
d. 1992 Bakhtiar, Shahpur
d. 1992 Gertz, Alison L.
d. 1994 Leonov, Leonid Maximovich
d. 1996 Mott, Nevill Francis, Sir
d. 1996 Whittle, Frank, Sir
d. 1997 Rudolph, Paul Marvin

August 9
b. 1387 Henry V
b. 1593 Walton, Izaak
b. 1631 Dryden, John

b. 1733 Clinton, James
b. 1762 Randolph, Mary
b. 1788 Judson, Adoniram
b. 1799 James, G(eorge) P(ayne) R(ainsford)
b. 1808 Bowditch, Henry Ingersoll
b. 1809 Travis, William Barret
b. 1812 Judson, Egbert Putnam
b. 1819 Morton, William Thomas Green
b. 1836 Gamble, James Norris
b. 1869 Malone, Annie Minerva Turnbo Pope
b. 1877 Young, Mahonri Mackintosh
b. 1882 Guion, Connie Myers
b. 1883 Lampkin, Daisy
b. 1893 Bedells, Phyllis
b. 1894 Starkie, Walter Fitzwilliam
b. 1896 Massine, Leonide Fedorovich
b. 1896 Piaget, Jean
b. 1896 Sullivan, A(loysius) M(ichael)
b. 1897 Galbreath, John Wilmer
b. 1898 Hays, Brooks
b. 1899 Kelly, Paul
b. 1899 Pendleton, Nat
b. 1900 Tully, Grace George
b. 1901 Casadesus, Gaby (Lhote)
b. 1901 Farrell, Charles
b. 1902 Francescatti, Zino Rene
b. 1902 Solomon
b. 1904 Adams, Weston W, Sir
b. 1904 Shannon, James A(ugustine)
b. 1905 Gaud, William Steen, Jr.
b. 1905 Genn, Leo
b. 1905 Nix, Robert N(elson) C(ornelius), Sr.
b. 1906 Travers, P(amela) L(yndon)
b. 1906 Wallace, Ed(ward Tatum)
b. 1908 Landolfi, Tommaso
b. 1909 Baur, John I(reland) H(owe)
b. 1910 Tobin, Richard L(ardner)
b. 1911 Fowler, William A(lfred)
b. 1913 Talmadge, Herman Eugene
b. 1918 Aldrich, Robert
b. 1918 Cooper, Giles (Stannus)
b. 1919 Den Uyl, Joop
b. 1919 Houk, Ralph George

b. 1920 Hoskins, Allen Clayton
b. 1921 Exon, (John) James, (Jr.)
b. 1922 Larkin, Philip Arthur
b. 1924 Quaison-Sackey, Alex(ander)
b. 1927 Keyes, Daniel
b. 1927 Minsky, Marvin Lee
b. 1927 Shaw, Robert
b. 1928 Cousy, Bob
b. 1928 Johnson, Harold
b. 1930 Parizeau, Jacques
b. 1931 Jackson, Hurricane
b. 1932 Halberstam, Michael Joseph
b. 1933 Kohan, Buz
b. 1938 Laver, Rod(ney George)
b. 1939 Prodi, Romano
b. 1940 Saint John, Jill
b. 1941? Bandy, Way
b. 1942 DeJohnette, Jack
b. 1942 Steinberg, David
b. 1944 Elliott, Sam
b. 1945 Norton, Ken(neth Howard)
b. 1946 Kiick, Jim
b. 1948 Daley, William M.
b. 1952 Cappelletti, John Raymond
b. 1952 Morgan, Vicki
b. 1955 Ovett, Steve
b. 1955 Williams, Doug(las Lee)
b. 1957 Griffith, Melanie
b. 1958 Bearse, Amanda
b. 1963 Houston, Whitney
b. 1964 Hull, Brett (A.)
b. 1967 Sanders, Deion (Luwynn)
b. 1968 Anderson, Gillian
d. 1516 Bosch, Hieronymous
d. 1848 Marryat, Frederick
d. 1869 Little, Charles Coffin
d. 1871 Marmol, Jose
d. 1884 Elliott, Robert Brown
d. 1892 Denver, James William
d. 1898 Colton, Gardner Quincy
d. 1904 Ratzel, Friedrich
d. 1911 Gates, John Warne
d. 1916 Braun, Lily von Kretschman
d. 1919 Blakelock, Ralph Albert
d. 1919 Leoncavallo, Ruggiero

d. 1936 Steffens, Lincoln
d. 1943 Soutine, Chaim
d. 1949 Davenport, Harry George Bryant
d. 1949 Thorndike, Edward L(ee)
d. 1952 Farnol, Jeffery
d. 1954 Marcantonio, Vito Anthony
d. 1958 Durand, William F.
d. 1961 Smith, Walter Bedell
d. 1962 Hesse, Hermann
d. 1963 Kennedy, Patrick Bouvier
d. 1965 Freeman, Joseph
d. 1967 Orton, Joe
d. 1967 Walbrook, Anton
d. 1968 Stiedry, Fritz
d. 1969 Marshall, George Preston
d. 1969 Powell, Cecil Frank
d. 1969 Stratemeyer, George E, General
d. 1969 Tate, Sharon
d. 1973 Behrman, S(amuel) N(athaniel)
d. 1973 Moberg, Vihelm
d. 1973 Roxon, Lillian
d. 1974 Luckenbach, Edgar Frederick, Jr.
d. 1975 Shostakovich, Dmitri Dmitryevich
d. 1975 Shostakovich, Maxim
d. 1976 Schmidt-Rottluf, Karl
d. 1976 Scott, Arleigh Winston, Sir
d. 1977 Kenney, George Churchill
d. 1978 Cozzens, James Gould
d. 1979 O'Malley, Walter Francis
d. 1979 Zuckerman, Ben
d. 1980 Cochran, Jacqueline
d. 1980 Nugent, Elliott
d. 1981 Feldman, Alvin Lindbergh
d. 1981 Lawrence, Robert
d. 1984 Deacon, Richard
d. 1984 Tevis, Walter
d. 1987 Keyserling, Leon Hirsch
d. 1988 Fidler, Jimmie
d. 1995 Garcia, Jerry
d. 1995 Katz, Milton
d. 1996 King, John W(illiam)

August 10
b. 1645 Kino, Eusebio Francisco
b. 1729 Howe, William, Viscount

b. 1753 Randolph, Edmund Jennings
b. 1782 Napier, Charles James, Sir
b. 1783 Guerrero, Vicente
b. 1790 McDuffie, George
b. 1794 Zunz, Leopold
b. 1798 LaFever Minard
b. 1810 Cavour, Camillo Benso, Conte di
b. 1813 Fry, William Henry
b. 1814 Pemberton, John Clifford
b. 1814 Yancey, William Lowndes
b. 1821 Cooke, Jay
b. 1823 Keene, Charles Samuel
b. 1830 Okubo, Toshimichi
b. 1848 Harnett, William Michael
b. 1848 Scott, Austin
b. 1856 Doheny, Edward Lawrence
b. 1858 Cooper, Annie
b. 1861 Wright, Almroth Edward, Sir
b. 1865 Glazunov, Alexander Constantinovich
b. 1865 Morrice, James Wilson
b. 1868 Eckener, Hugo
b. 1869 Binyon, Laurence
b. 1874 Hoover, Herbert C(lark)
b. 1877 Marshall, Frank James
b. 1881 Bynner, Harold Witter
b. 1887 Herbert, Hugh
b. 1887 Thompson, Oscar
b. 1887 Warner, Sam(uel Louis)
b. 1890 Hart, Frances Noyes
b. 1891 Donovan, Arthur
b. 1893 Moore, Douglas Stuart
b. 1895 Richman, Harry
b. 1895 Vertes, Marcel
b. 1896 Sobol, Louis
b. 1897 Nakian, Reuben
b. 1898 Haley, Jack
b. 1900 Levine, Philip
b. 1900 Porritt, Arthur Espie, Sir
b. 1900 Shearer, Norma
b. 1902 Siodmark, Curt
b. 1902 Tiselius, Arne Wilhelm Kaurin
b. 1908 Thornhill, Claude
b. 1909 Crockett, George (William), Jr.
b. 1909 Fender, Leo
b. 1909 Hughes, Richard J(oseph)

b. 1910 Mohammed V
b. 1911 Chodorov, Jerome
b. 1911 Elkin, Benjamin
b. 1912 Amado, Jorge
b. 1913 Paul, Wolfgang
b. 1914 Corey, Jeff
b. 1914 Malcuzynski, Witold
b. 1916 Beery, Noah, Jr.
b. 1917 Tomes, Margot
b. 1918 Cobb, Arnett Cleophus
b. 1920 Holzman, Red
b. 1922 von Mehren, Robert Brandt
b. 1923 Fleming, Rhonda
b. 1924 Hyer, Martha
b. 1926 Ward, Benjamin
b. 1928 Dean, Jimmy
b. 1928 Fisher, Eddie
b. 1929 Vagelos, P Roy
b. 1930 Goodman, George Jerome Waldo
b. 1930 Unsworth, Barry (Foster)
b. 1931 Perry, Carrie Saxon
b. 1933 Colavito, Rocky
b. 1938 Muldaur, Diana Charlton
b. 1940 Hatfield, Bobby
b. 1942 Johnson, Betsey Lee
b. 1947 Anderson, Ian
b. 1948 Austin, Patti
b. 1950 Buse, Don(ald R)
b. 1956 Fromholtz, Dianne
b. 1960 Arquette, Rosanna
b. 1960 Banderas, Antonio
b. 1964 Cherry, Neneh
b. 1967 Bowe, Riddick (Lamont)
d. 1815 Handsome Lake
d. 1817 Lowell, Francis Cabot
d. 1838 Rodgers, John
d. 1861 Lyon, Nathaniel
d. 1867 Aldridge, Ira Frederick
d. 1868 Menken, Adah Isaacs
d. 1876 Lane, Edward William
d. 1881 Burton, John Hill, Sir
d. 1896 Lilienthal, Otto
d. 1906 Clarke, Rebecca Sophia
d. 1910 Gans, Joe
d. 1920 O'Neill, James
d. 1934 Kane, John
d. 1941 Howard, Cordelia
d. 1945 Goddard, Robert Hutchings
d. 1951 Bloor, Mother
d. 1953 Burns, John Horne
d. 1960 Lloyd, Frank

d. 1961 Peterkin, Julia
Mood
d. 1962 Husing, Ted
d. 1963 Kefauver, Estes
d. 1964 Fox, Fontaine
Talbot, Jr.
d. 1966 Dressen, Chuck
d. 1970 Lapchick, Joe
d. 1974 Massey, Ilona
d. 1979 Foran, Dick
John Nicholas
d. 1979 Wright, John
Joseph
d. 1981 Fisk, James
Brown
d. 1984 Partch, Virgil
Franklin, II
d. 1985 Baker, Kenny
d. 1986 Engel, Lyle
Kenyon
d. 1987 Abel, I(orwith)
W(ilbur)
d. 1987 O'Boyle,
Patrick Aloysius,
Cardinal
d. 1988 Arias Madrid,
Arnulfo
d. 1988 Saint Johns,
Adela Rogers
d. 1994 Sumner, Jessie
d. 1997 Jordy, William
H(enry)
d. 1997 Moss, Carlton
d. 1999 Darrow,
Whitney, Jr.

August 11
b. 1743 Roentgen,
David
b. 1778 Jahn, Friedrich
Ludwig
b. 1807 Atchison, David
R
b. 1811 Benjamin,
Judah Philip
b. 1819 Heade, Martin
Johnson
b. 1823 Yonge,
Charlotte Mary
b. 1833 Ingersoll,
Robert Green
b. 1842 Elliott, Robert
Brown
b. 1847 Tillman,
Benjamin Ryan
b. 1858 Eijkman,
Christiaan
b. 1860 Melchers, Gari
b. 1861 Herrick, James
Bryan
b. 1862 Bond, Carrie
Jacobs
b. 1865 Pinchot, Gifford
b. 1867 Bosworth,
Hobart van Zandt
b. 1867 Weber, Joseph
M
b. 1872 Fuller, Solomon
Carter, Jr.
b. 1879 Lawrence,
Frieda
b. 1882 Graziani,
Rodolfo
b. 1882 Kallen, Horace
M(eyer)
b. 1891 Broderick,
Helen

b. 1892 Anders,
Wladyslaw
b. 1892 MacDiarmid,
Hugh
b. 1897 Blyton, Enid
Mary
b. 1897 Bogan, Louise
b. 1899 Hirshhorn,
Joseph Herman
b. 1900 Brogan, Denis
William, Sir
b. 1900 Dunn, Alan
b. 1900 Mayes, Herbert
Raymond
b. 1902 Nolan, Lloyd
b. 1902 Shoemaker,
Vaughn Richard
b. 1903 Seagram,
Joseph Edward
Frowde
b. 1904 Woolley,
Catherine
b. 1905 Chargaff, Erwin
b. 1907 Newsom, Bobo
b. 1908 Abel, I(orwith)
W(ilbur)
b. 1910 Homans,
George Caspar
b. 1911 Kittikachorn,
Thanom
b. 1911 McCormick,
Robert K
b. 1912 Harvey, Frank
Laird
b. 1912 Parker, Jean
b. 1913 Crane, Nathalia
Clara Ruth
b. 1913 Oliver, Edith
b. 1913 Wilson, Angus
b. 1916 Harlow, Bryce
Nathaniel
b. 1916 Wind, Herbert
Warren
b. 1917 Browne, Dik
b. 1920 Masselos,
William
b. 1920 Rayner, Chuck
b. 1921 Graff, Henry
Franklin
b. 1921 Haley, Alex
(Murray Palmer)
b. 1922 Gallant, Mavis
b. 1922 Stuart, Lyle
b. 1925 Douglas, Mike
b. 1925 Rowan, Carl
Thomas
b. 1926 Klug, Aaron,
Sir
b. 1926 Von Bulow,
Claus
b. 1927 Dahl, Arlene
b. 1927 Leppard,
Raymond John
b. 1927 Rubin, William
Stanley
b. 1929 Bustamante,
John H
b. 1930 O'Neill,
William Atchison
b. 1932 Arrabal (Teran),
Fernando
b. 1932 Eisenman, Peter
b. 1933 Berger, Terry
b. 1933 Falwell, Jerry L
b. 1933 Grotowski,
Jerzy

b. 1933 Yetnikoff,
Walter
b. 1937 Massey, Anna
b. 1937
Theodoracopulos,
Taki
b. 1938 Kent, Allegra
b. 1941 Holtzman,
Elizabeth
b. 1943 Gamble, Kenny
b. 1944 Coles, Joanna
b. 1944 Smith,
Frederick Wallace
b. 1945 Echohawk, John
E.
b. 1946 Savant, Marilyn
vos
b. 1949 Carmen, Eric
b. 1949 Charleson, Ian
b. 1949 Hutchinson,
Tim
b. 1953 Hogan, Hulk
b. 1954 Jackson, Joe
b. 1957 Hwang, David
Henry
d. 1253 Clare of Assisi,
Saint
d. 1464 Nicholas of
Cusa
d. 1486 William of
Waynflete
d. 1494 Memling, Hans
d. 1778 Toplady,
Augustus Montague
d. 1813 Pye, Henry
d. 1841 Herbart, Johann
Friedrich
d. 1868 Stevens,
Thaddeus
d. 1872 Mason, Lowell
d. 1875 Graham,
William Alexander
d. 1881 Fillmore,
Caroline Carmichael
McIntosh
d. 1890 Brace, Charles
Loring
d. 1890 Newman, John
Henry, Cardinal
d. 1901 Crispi,
Francesco
d. 1903 Hayford,
J(oseph)
E(phraim)Casely
d. 1903 Hostos (y
Bonilla), Eugenio
Maria de
d. 1914 Plancon, Pol-
Henri
d. 1919 Carnegie,
Andrew
d. 1930 Angle, Edward
Hartley
d. 1937 Wharton, Edith
d. 1955 Seiberling,
Frank Augustus
d. 1955 Wood, Robert
Williams
d. 1956 Lawrence,
Frieda
d. 1956 Pollock,
Jackson
d. 1962 Cardozo, W.
Warrick
d. 1963 Seymour,
Charles

d. 1964 Mannes,
Leopold Damrosch
d. 1965 Lehman, Adele
Lewisohn
d. 1972 Theiler, Max
d. 1973 Castle, Peggie
d. 1975 McAuliffe,
Anthony Clement
d. 1976 May, Robert
Lewis
d. 1977 Schorer, Mark
d. 1980 Robert, Paul
d. 1982 Drake, Tom
d. 1983 Wigg, George
(Edward Cecil)
d. 1984 Knopf, Alfred
Abraham
d. 1986 Jarvis, Howard
Arnold
d. 1986 McKinley,
Chuck
d. 1987 Peller, Clara
d. 1988 Ramsey, Anne
d. 1995 Harris, Phil

August 12
b. 1720 Ekhof, Konrad
b. 1753 Bewick,
Thomas
b. 1762 George IV
b. 1774 Southey, Robert
b. 1781 Mills, Robert
b. 1849 Thayer, Abbott
Handerson
b. 1852 McGivney,
Michael Joseph
b. 1854 Thomas, Edith
Matilda
b. 1856 Brady,
Diamond Jim
b. 1859 Bates,
Katharine Lee
b. 1862 Rosenwald,
Julius
b. 1866 Benavente y
Martinez, Jacinto
b. 1867 Hamilton, Edith
b. 1868 Chelmsford,
Frederic John Napier
Thesiger, 1st
Viscount Chelmsford
b. 1875 Panizza, Ettore
b. 1876 Rinehart, Mary
Roberts
b. 1880 Hall, Radclyffe
b. 1880 Mathewson,
Christy
b. 1881 DeMille, Cecil
B(lount)
b. 1882 Bellows,
George Wesley
b. 1882 Bendix, Vincent
b. 1884 Swinnerton,
Frank Arthur
b. 1885 Frederick,
Pauline
b. 1887 Schroedinger,
Erwin
b. 1888 Lorne, Marion
b. 1889 Sharp, Zerna A
b. 1891 McDermott,
Johnny
b. 1892 Olczewska,
Maria
b. 1892 Rea, Gardner
b. 1892 Schalk,
Ray(mond William)

b. 1895 Lawler, Richard
Harold
b. 1897 Struve, Otto
b. 1899 DeLeeuw,
Adele Louise
b. 1902 Hatta,
Mohammad
b. 1903 Homolka, Oscar
b. 1905 Ferrell, Rick
b. 1905 Isbell, Marion
William
b. 1907 Bentley, Gladys
b. 1907? Besser, Joe
b. 1907 Sheares,
Benjamin Henry
b. 1910 Ishak, Yusof
bin
b. 1910 Sutermeister,
Heinrich
b. 1911 Cantinflas
b. 1911 Downes,
Edward Olin
Davenport
b. 1912 Fuller, Samuel
b. 1912 Sullivan, Barry
b. 1912 Timmerman,
George Bell, Jr.
b. 1915 Wojciechowicz,
Alex(ander)
b. 1916 Nelson, Ralph
b. 1919 Kidd, Michael
b. 1921 Monty, Gloria
b. 1921 Reynolds,
Marjorie
b. 1922 Jakes, Milos
b. 1923 Gannett, Ruth
b. 1924 Zia-ul-Haq,
Mohammad
b. 1925 Bumpers, Dale
Leon
b. 1925 McWhirter,
A(lan) Ross
b. 1925 McWhirter,
Norris Dewar
b. 1926 Derek, John
b. 1927 Rostropovich,
Mstislav
Leopoldovich
b. 1927 Wagoner, Porter
b. 1929 Owens, Buck
b. 1930 Borge Martinez,
Tomas
b. 1930 Soros, George
b. 1931 Goldman,
William
b. 1933 Jones, Parnelli
b. 1936 Haacke, Hans
Christoph
b. 1936 Kolingba,
Andre-Dieudonne
b. 1936 Poindexter,
John Marlan
b. 1937 Myers, Walter
Dean
b. 1938 Marshall, Alan
Peter
b. 1939 Gabor, Mark
b. 1939 Hamilton,
George, IV
b. 1941 Ducharme,
Rejean
b. 1941 Feulner, Edwin
John, Jr.
b. 1945 Symington, J
Fife, III

b. 1949 Collor de
Mello, Fernando
Affonso
b. 1949 Knopfler, Mark
b. 1949 Ridgeway, Rick
b. 1950 Kleinfield,
Sonny
b. 1950 McGinnis,
George
b. 1954 Metheny,
Pat(rick Bruce)
b. 1971 Sampras,
Pete(r)
d. 1546 Vitoria,
Francisco de
d. 1612 Gabrieli,
Giovanni
d. 1633 Peri, Jacopo
d. 1689 Innocent XI,
Pope
d. 1715 Tate, Nahum
d. 1822 Castlereagh,
Robert Stewart,
Viscount
d. 1827 Blake, William
d. 1848 Stephenson,
George
d. 1849 Gallatin, Albert
d. 1865 Hooker,
William Jackson, Sir
d. 1885 Jackson, Helen
Maria Hunt Fiske
d. 1891 Lowell, James
Russell
d. 1900 Keeler, James
Edward
d. 1900 Steinitz,
Wilhelm
d. 1901 Nordenskiold,
Nils Adolph Erik,
Baron
d. 1911 Israels, Josef
d. 1914 Holland, John
Philip
d. 1918 Held, Anna
d. 1922 Griffith, Arthur
d. 1928 Janacek, Leos
d. 1934 Berlage,
Hendrik Petrus
d. 1942 Amato,
Pasquale
d. 1944 Kennedy,
Joseph Patrick, Jr.
d. 1949 Shean, Al
d. 1955 Mann, Thomas
d. 1962 Holman,
Eugene
d. 1964 Fleming, Ian
Lancaster
d. 1966 Meinesz, Felix
Andries Vening
d. 1967 Forbes, Esther
d. 1971 Cowles,
William Hutchinson,
Jr.
d. 1973 Hess, Walter
Rudolf
d. 1973 Ziegler, Karl
d. 1975 Sapir, Pinchas
d. 1977 Lawson, John
Howard
d. 1979 Chain, Ernest
Boris, Sir
d. 1979 Karpis, Alvin
d. 1982 Charnley, John,
Sir

d. 1982 Fonda, Henry
Jaynes
d. 1982 Sanchez,
Salvador
d. 1988 Basquiat, Jean-
Michel
d. 1989 Shockley,
William B(radford)
d. 1992 Cage, John
d. 1995 Mantle, Mickey
(Charles)
d. 1996 Ambartsumyan,
Viktor Amazaspovich
d. 1999 Drapeau, Jean

August 13
b. 1422 Caxton,
William
b. 1655 Denner, Johann
Christoph
b. 1743 Lavoisier,
Antoine Laurent
b. 1755 Unanue, Jose
Hipolito
b. 1756 Gillray, James
b. 1814 Angstrom,
Anders Jonas
b. 1815 Phelps,
Elizabeth Stuart Ward
b. 1818 Stone, Lucy
b. 1819 Stokes, George
Gabriel, Sir
b. 1820 Grove, George,
Sir
b. 1823 Smith, Goldwin
b. 1849 Barry, Leonora
Marie Kearney
b. 1851 Adler, Felix
b. 1860 Oakley, Annie
b. 1863 Thomas,
W(illiam) I(saac)
b. 1865 Eames, Emma
Hayden
b. 1866 Agnelli,
Giovanni
b. 1867 Luks, George
Benjamin
b. 1870 Levy, Florence
b. 1871 Liebknecht,
Karl
b. 1872 Willstater,
Richard Martin
b. 1879 Ireland, John
Nicholson
b. 1882 Mercer, Beryl
b. 1884 Powys,
Llewelyn
b. 1888 Baird, John
Logie
b. 1895 Lahr, Bert
b. 1897 Bronk, Detlev
Wulf
b. 1898 Borotra, Jean
Robert
b. 1898 Toomey, Regis
b. 1899 Hitchcock,
Alfred Joseph, Sir
b. 1902 Wankel, Felix
b. 1904 Rogers, Buddy
b. 1904 Waldock,
Humphrey Meredith,
Sir
b. 1907 Spence, Basil
Urwin, Sir
b. 1908 Ennis, Skinnay
b. 1908 Raymond, Gene
b. 1909 Beal, John

b. 1910 Said bin Taimur
b. 1910 Spectorsky,
Auguste Compte
b. 1911 Bernbach,
William
b. 1911 Parsons, James
b. 1912 Hogan, Ben
b. 1912 Luria, Salvador
Edward
b. 1912 Wyatt, Jane
b. 1913 Kasznar, Kurt
b. 1913 Makarios III,
Archbishop
b. 1913 Newell, Pete
b. 1917 McNeil,
Claudia Mae
b. 1918 Sanger,
Frederick
b. 1919 Humbard, Rex
b. 1919 Shearing,
George Albert
b. 1921 Brand, Neville
b. 1927 Castro (Ruz),
Fidel
b. 1929 Harrington, Pat
b. 1930 Culp, Robert
b. 1930 Ho, Don
b. 1933 Elders, Joycelyn
b. 1935 Grant, Mudcat
b. 1937 Weathers,
Felicia
b. 1941? Fleming, Erin
b. 1943 Pascal-Trouillot,
Ertha
b. 1943 Walley,
Deborah
b. 1947 McDougall,
Gay J.
b. 1948 Battle, Kathleen
Deanne
b. 1949 Clarke, Bobby
b. 1949 Petit, Philippe
b. 1951 Fogelberg,
Dan(iel Grayling)
b. 1951 White, Michael
R(eed)
b. 1960 Simpson, Lorna
b. 1967 Cummings,
Quinn
d. 1523 David, Gerard
d. 1608 Giovanni da
Bologna
d. 1667 Taylor, Jeremy
d. 1755 Durante,
Francesco
d. 1826 Laennec, Rene
Theophile Hyacinthe
d. 1841 Romberg,
Bernhard
d. 1863 Delacroix,
(Ferdinand Victor)
Eugene
d. 1865 Lane, Fitz Hugh
d. 1865 Semmelweis,
Ignaz Philipp
d. 1878 Duyckinck,
Evert Augustus
d. 1881 Trelawny,
Edward John
d. 1887 Pasdeloup, Jules
Etienne
d. 1896 Millais, John
Everett, Sir
d. 1900 Huntington,
Collis Potter

d. 1900 Soloviev, Vladimir Sergeevich
d. 1910 Nightingale, Florence
d. 1912 Massenet, Jules Emile Frederic
d. 1913 Bebel, August
d. 1917 Buchner, Eduard
d. 1918 Gulick, Luther (Halsey)
d. 1927 Curwood, James Oliver
d. 1934 Austin, Mary Hunter
d. 1941 Blackton, James Stuart
d. 1942 Schurman, Jacob Gould
d. 1946 Wells, H(erbert) G(eorge)
d. 1952 Sullivan, Mark
d. 1955 Easton, Florence Gertrude
d. 1955 Horder, Thomas Jeeves
d. 1957 Beach, Joseph Warren
d. 1957 Stormer, Fredrik (Carl Mulertz)
d. 1961 Sironi, Mario
d. 1962 Luhan, Mabel (Ganson) Dodge
d. 1967 Darwell, Jane
d. 1968 Upson, Ralph Hazlett
d. 1971 Bentley, Walter Owen
d. 1972 Weiss, George Martin
d. 1979 Berndt, Walter
d. 1982 Coleman, Lonnie William
d. 1982 Ross, Joe E
d. 1982 Tex, Joe
d. 1982 Walters, Charles
d. 1984 Petrosian, Tigran Vartanovich
d. 1985 Marriott, John Willard
d. 1986 Bandy, Way
d. 1988 Williams, Edward Bennett
d. 1988 Zumwalt, Elmo Russell, III
d. 1989 Brooks, Ronald E.
d. 1991 Roosevelt, James
d. 1994 Canetti, Elias
d. 1994 Preus, Jacob A(all) O(ttesen)
d. 1994 Worner, Manfred
d. 1996 Spinola, Antonio (Sebastiao Ribeiro) de
d. 1998 Green, Julian (Hartridge)

August 14
b. 1734 Sumter, Thomas
b. 1740 Pius, VII
b. 1777 Oersted, Hans Christian

b. 1836 Besant, Walter, Sir
b. 1840 Krafft-Ebing, Richard von
b. 1849 Godard, Benjamin Louis Paul
b. 1860 Seton, Ernest Thompson
b. 1863 Thayer, Ernest L
b. 1865 Merejkowski, Dmitri Sergeyevich
b. 1867 Galsworthy, John
b. 1883 Just, Ernest Everett
b. 1886 Dempster, Arthur Jeffrey
b. 1889 Woolsey, Robert
b. 1891 Oxnam, G(arfield) Bromley
b. 1893 Leibowitz, Samuel Simon
b. 1893 Williams, Roger J
b. 1894 Bricktop
b. 1898 Bullard, Dexter Means
b. 1899 Burnett, Whit
b. 1900 Bauer, Helen
b. 1901 Konwitschny, Franz
b. 1901 Pitman, James
b. 1903 North, John Ringling
b. 1904 Singher, Martial
b. 1906 Horst, Horst P(aul)
b. 1907 Adams, Stanley
b. 1907 Dichter, Ernest
b. 1907 Topolski, Feliks
b. 1912 Abercrombie, Michael
b. 1912 Oppenheimer, Frank F
b. 1913 Dean, Daffy
b. 1913 Tagliavini, Ferrucio
b. 1915 Santamaria, Bartholomew Augustine
b. 1916 Mara, Wellington T
b. 1918 Provensen, Alice Rose Twitchell
b. 1920 Persoff, Nehemiah
b. 1921 Bartlett, Charles Leffingwell
b. 1921 Strehler, Giorgio
b. 1921 Wright, Cobina
b. 1922 Messick, Hank
b. 1925 Baker, Russell Wayne
b. 1926 Adams, Alice
b. 1926 Ghostley, Alice
b. 1926 Greco, Buddy
b. 1928 Wertmuller, Lina von Eigg
b. 1930 Weaver, Earl Sidney
b. 1931 Raphael, Frederic Michael

b. 1932 Meehan, Thomas Edward
b. 1935 Brodie, John Riley
b. 1937 Lord, Winston
b. 1938 Sudarkasa, Niara
b. 1940 Crofts, Dash
b. 1940 Laffer, Arthur Betz
b. 1940 Royo, Aristides
b. 1941 Cheney, Lynne V
b. 1941 Crosby, David (Van Cortlandt)
b. 1941 Eyen, Tom
b. 1942 Asante, Molefi Kete
b. 1943 Snyder, Mitch
b. 1944 Smith, Robyn Caroline
b. 1945 Benet, Brenda
b. 1945 Martin, Steve
b. 1945 Wenders, Wim
b. 1946 Graham, Larry
b. 1946 Saint James, Susan
b. 1947 Steel, Danielle Fernande
b. 1950 Larson, Gary
b. 1952 Meyer, Debbie
b. 1953 Claiborne, Loretta (Lynn)
b. 1954 Fidrych, Mark Steven
b. 1957 Jackee
b. 1959 Johnson, Earvin, Jr.
b. 1968 Berry, Halle
d. 1794 Colman, George
d. 1856 Buckland, William
d. 1858 Combe, George
d. 1863 Clyde, Colin Campbell, Baron
d. 1870 Farragut, David Glasgow
d. 1887 Jeffries, Richard
d. 1888 Crocker, Charles
d. 1890 McGivney, Michael Joseph
d. 1891 Polk, Sarah Childress
d. 1897 George, James Zachariah
d. 1904 Avery, Samuel Putnam
d. 1922 Northcliffe, Alfred Charles William Harmsworth, Viscount
d. 1930 Mayakovsky, Vladimir
d. 1934 Hood, Raymond Matthewson
d. 1937 McNeile, Herman Cyril
d. 1938 Ronald, Landon, Sir
d. 1941 Kolbe, Maximilian Maria, Saint
d. 1941 Sabatier, Paul
d. 1943 Kelley, Joe

d. 1951 Hearst, William Randolph
d. 1953 Schorr, Friedrich
d. 1954 Eckener, Hugo
d. 1955 Kimball, Fiske
d. 1956 Brecht, Bertolt (Eugen Friedrich)
d. 1956 Neurath, Konstantin von
d. 1958 Beard, Mary Ritter
d. 1958 Broonzy, Big Bill
d. 1958 Joliot(-Curie), (Jean) Frederic
d. 1960 Clarke, Fred Clifford
d. 1961 Breuil, Henri Abbe
d. 1963 Odets, Clifford
d. 1964 Burnette, Johnny
d. 1966 Kreymborg, Alfred
d. 1967 Prado Ugarteche, Manuel
d. 1969 Gurie, Sigrid
d. 1969 Woolf, Leonard Sidney
d. 1971 Heard, Gerald
d. 1971 King Curtis
d. 1972 Levant, Oscar
d. 1972 Romains, Jules
d. 1980 Snider, Paul
d. 1980 Stratten, Dorothy
d. 1981 Bohm, Karl
d. 1981 Curran, Joseph Edwin
d. 1982 Magee, Patrick
d. 1982 Morton, Thruston Ballard
d. 1984 Priestley, (J)ohn (B)oynton
d. 1985 Hayes, Alfred
d. 1985 Sondergaard, Gale (Edith Holm)
d. 1986 Haider, Michael Lawrence
d. 1987 Persichetti, Vincent
d. 1988 Ferrari, Enzo
d. 1988 Sweet, John Howard
d. 1990 Crown, Henry
d. 1990 Donovan, Hedley Williams
d. 1991 Elias, Taslim Olawale
d. 1991 Kiker, Douglas
d. 1991 Suits, C(hauncey) G(uy)
d. 1992 Jordan, Joseph
d. 1992 Sirica, John Joseph
d. 1994 Childress, Alice
d. 1994 Harrison, Joan (Mary)
d. 1996 Celibidache, Sergiu
d. 1999 Kirkland, Lane
d. 1999 Klutznick, Philip M.
d. 1999 Reese, Pee Wee

August 15
b. 1195 Anthony of Padua, Saint
b. 1432 Pulci, Luigi
b. 1688 Frederick William I
b. 1740 Claudius, Matthias
b. 1769 Napoleon I
b. 1771 Scott, Walter, Sir
b. 1785 DeQuincey, Thomas
b. 1803 Douglas, James, Sir
b. 1807 Grevy, Francois Paul Jules
b. 1818 Mason, Biddy
b. 1822 Maine, Henry James Sumner
b. 1824 Chisum, John Simpson
b. 1824 Leland, Charles Godfrey
b. 1845 Crane, Walter
b. 1848 Pareto, Vilfredo
b. 1855 Page, Walter Hines
b. 1856 Hardie, James Keir
b. 1858 Calve, Emma
b. 1859 Comiskey, Charlie
b. 1860 Harding, Florence Kling (De Wolfe)
b. 1866 Work, Monroe (Nathan)
b. 1869 Michael, Moina Belle
b. 1875 Bartlett, Robert Abram
b. 1875 Coleridge-Taylor, Samuel
b. 1879 Barrymore, Ethel Mae Blythe
b. 1880 Shubert, Jacob J
b. 1883 Mestrovic, Ivan
b. 1885 Burton, Montague Maurice, Sir
b. 1886 Yeats-Brown, F(rancis Charles Claypon)
b. 1887 Campbell, Walter Stanley
b. 1887 Ferber, Edna
b. 1888 Lawrence, T(homas) E(dward)
b. 1888 Spalding, Albert
b. 1889 Crowley, Leo Thomas
b. 1890 Ibert, Jacques (Francois Antoine)
b. 1890 Jellinek, Elvin Morton
b. 1892 Broglie, Louis Prince De
b. 1893 Curtice, Harlow Herbert
b. 1896 Cori, Gerty Theresa (Radnitz)
b. 1896 Glueck, Sheldon
b. 1898 Carter, Lillian

b. 1900 Parr, A(lbert) E(ide)
b. 1900 Tworkov, Jack
b. 1901 Arias Madrid, Arnulfo
b. 1904 Baird, Bil
b. 1904 Sammartino, Peter
b. 1907 Trotta, Maurice S
b. 1908 Kerner, Otto
b. 1909 Winterhalter, Hugo
b. 1910 Kuchel, Thomas H(enry)
b. 1912 Child, Julia McWilliams
b. 1912 Hiller, Wendy, Dame
b. 1914 Rand, Paul
b. 1915 Hasso, Signe Eleonora Cecilia
b. 1915 Turkle, Brinton Cassaday
b. 1917 Romero y Galdamez, Oscar Arnulfo
b. 1919 Arundel, Honor Morfydd
b. 1919 Goheen, Robert Francis
b. 1919 Kiely, Benedict
b. 1920 Hall, Huntz
b. 1921 Banner, Bob
b. 1921 Zabach, Florian
b. 1922 Baskin, Leonard
b. 1922 Foss, Lukas
b. 1924 Bolt, Robert (Oxton)
b. 1924 Schlafly, Phyllis Stewart
b. 1925 Connors, Mike
b. 1925 Khaleda Zia
b. 1925 Peterson, Oscar Emanuel
b. 1925 Rose-Marie
b. 1926 Silber, John Robert
b. 1927 Cranko, John
b. 1928 Roeg, Nicholas (Jack)
b. 1930 Mboya, Tom
b. 1931 Rule, Janice
b. 1935 Dale, Jim
b. 1935 Dalton, Abby
b. 1935 Jordan, Vernon Eulion, Jr.
b. 1938 Breyer, Stephen Gerald
b. 1938 Waters, Maxine
b. 1941 Worrill, Conrad (W.)
b. 1944 Ellerbee, Linda
b. 1944 Ferre, Gianfranco
b. 1945 Upshaw, Gene
b. 1946 Webb, Jim
b. 1946 Whitmire, Kathy
b. 1947 Costello, Chris
b. 1950 Anne
b. 1950 Harper, Tess
b. 1950 Kelly, Tom
b. 1950 Serrano, Andres
b. 1958 Cowley, Joe
d. 797? Constantine VI

d. 803 Irene of Athens
d. 1057 Macbeth
d. 1118 Alexius Comnenus
d. 1464 Pius, II
d. 1907 Joachim, Joseph
d. 1909 Cunha, Euclides (Rodrigues Pimenta) da
d. 1922 Dunning, William Archibald
d. 1927 Gary, Elbert Henry
d. 1935 Post, Wiley
d. 1935 Rogers, Will(iam Penn Adair)
d. 1935 Signac, Paul
d. 1936 Lytton, Henry Alfred, Sir
d. 1945 Lowes, John Livingston
d. 1951 Schnabel, Artur
d. 1958 Dean, Gordon Evans
d. 1962 Bain, Dan
d. 1966 Kiepura, Jan Wiktor
d. 1967 Magritte, Rene Francois Ghislain
d. 1968 Kilenyi, Edward, Sr.
d. 1969 Munson, Gorham B(ert)
d. 1970 Winterich, John Tracy
d. 1971 Lukas, Paul
d. 1973 Tregaskis, Richard William
d. 1974 Braun, Otto
d. 1975 Edwards, Willard Eldridge
d. 1975 Rahman, Mujibur, Sheik
d. 1980 Simpson, William Hood
d. 1981 Barr, Alfred Hamilton, Jr.
d. 1981 Brink, Carol Ryrie
d. 1981 Meek, Samuel Williams
d. 1981 Waldock, Humphrey Meredith, Sir
d. 1982 Bushmiller, Ernie
d. 1982 Mumford, Lawrence Quincy
d. 1982 Taishoff, Sol Joseph
d. 1982 Theorell, (Axel) Hugh Teodor
d. 1983 Cohen, Benjamin Victor
d. 1983 Kilgore, Al
d. 1986 Sargeant, Winthrop
d. 1988 Bingham, Barry
d. 1991 Tree, Marietta Endicott Peabody
d. 1991 Zampa, Luigi
d. 1992 Peterson, Edith R.
d. 1993 Kempner, Robert M(aximilian) W(asilii)

d. 1995 Swayze, John Cameron, Sr.
d. 1996 McLaughlin, Leo (Plowden)
d. 1997 Heatherton, Ray(mond Joseph)

August 16
b. 1645 LaBruyere, Jean de
b. 1782 Cotman, John Sell
b. 1789 Kendall, Amos
b. 1795 Marschner, Heinrich August
b. 1817 Davis, Henry Winter
b. 1821 Cayley, Arthur
b. 1831 Timken, Henry
b. 1832 Wundt, Wilhelm Max
b. 1845 Lippmann, Gabriel Jonas
b. 1848 Holland, William Jacob
b. 1848 Sukhomlinov, Vladimir Aleksandrovich
b. 1851 Harvey, William Hope
b. 1860 Laforgue, Jules
b. 1861 Roosevelt, Edith Kermit (Carow)
b. 1862 Stagg, Amos Alonzo
b. 1863 Pierne, Gabriel
b. 1868 Macfadden, Bernarr Adolphus
b. 1876 Bilibin, Ivan Iakolevich
b. 1879 Bell, James Ford
b. 1884 Gernsback, Hugo
b. 1892 Braslau, Sophie
b. 1892 Foster, Hal
b. 1892 Messmer, Otto
b. 1894 Meany, George
b. 1898 Rodale, Jerome Irving
b. 1902 Thurman, Wallace (Henry)
b. 1904 Hruska, Roman L(ee)
b. 1904 Stanley, Wendell Meredith
b. 1906 Franz Joseph II
b. 1907 Clarke, Mae
b. 1908 Maxwell, William
b. 1909 Chute, Marchette (Gaylord)
b. 1909 Koch, John
b. 1911 Schumacher, E(rnst) F(riedrich)
b. 1912 Price, H(enry) Ryan
b. 1913 Begin, Menachem (Wolfovitch)
b. 1913 Hawkins, Osie Penman, Jr.
b. 1914 DeRegniers, Beatrice Schenk
b. 1915 Hibbler, Al
b. 1917 Christopher, Matt(hew F.)

b. 1920 Bukowski, Charles
b. 1921 O'Brian, Jack
b. 1922 Alfred, William
b. 1923 Peres, Shimon
b. 1926 Wexler, Norman
b. 1927 Parker, Fess
b. 1927 Strawser, Neil Edward
b. 1928 Blyth, Ann Marie
b. 1929 Evans, Bill
b. 1929 Kenny, Maurice (Francis)
b. 1930 Gifford, Frank
b. 1931 Nettleton, Lois June
b. 1932 Gorme, Eydie
b. 1932 VonFurstenberg, Betsy
b. 1933 Roosa, Stuart Allen
b. 1935 Newmar, Julie
b. 1938 Masterton, Bill
b. 1938 Rodgers, Bob
b. 1939 Shelley, Carole Augusta
b. 1940 Beresford, Bruce
b. 1940 Dobkin, Alix
b. 1943 Altman, Dennis
b. 1945 Farrell, Suzanne
b. 1946 Warren, Lesley Ann
b. 1947 Moseley-Braun, Carol
b. 1949 Swift, Graham (Colin)
b. 1953 Gifford, Kathie Lee
b. 1953 Taylor, J T
b. 1954 Cameron, James
b. 1955 Gayle, Helene Doris
b. 1958 Bassett, Angela
b. 1958 Clerc, Jose-Luis
b. 1958 Madonna
b. 1960 Hutton, Timothy James
b. 1961 Okoye, Christian
b. 1964 Arias, Jimmy
b. 1977 Mingxia, Fu
d. 1641 Heywood, Thomas
d. 1777 Herkimer, Nicholas
d. 1825 Pinckney, Charles Cotesworth
d. 1840 Flint, Timothy
d. 1854 Phyfe, Duncan
d. 1875 Finney, Charles Grandison
d. 1876 Bergmann, Carl
d. 1882 Hill, Benjamin Harvey
d. 1886 Ramakrishna, Sri
d. 1893 Charcot, Jean Martin
d. 1899 Bunsen, Robert Wilhelm Eberhard
d. 1916 Boccioni, Umberto

d. 1920 Lockyer, Joseph Norman, Sir
d. 1921 Peter, I
d. 1922 Scott, Austin
d. 1931 Walker, A'lelia
d. 1936 Deledda, Grazia
d. 1941 Ripley, William Zebina
d. 1948 Ruth, Babe
d. 1949 Mitchell, Margaret
d. 1951 Jouvet, Louis
d. 1952 Karfiol, Bernard
d. 1957 Langmuir, Irving
d. 1958 Gibbs, Woolcott
d. 1958 Jackson, Chevalier
d. 1959 Halsey, William Frederick, Jr.
d. 1959 Landowska, Wanda Louise
d. 1962 Martin, Mungo
d. 1971 Anthony, Edward
d. 1971 Skouras, Spyros Panagiotes
d. 1973 Borg, Veda Ann
d. 1973 Waksman, Selman Abraham
d. 1974 Mundt, Karl Earl
d. 1975 Villanueva, Carlos Raul
d. 1977 Presley, Elvis Aaron
d. 1979 Diefenbaker, John George
d. 1980 Longley, James Bernard
d. 1983 Averill, Earl
d. 1983 Roy, Ross
d. 1986 Price, H(enry) Ryan
d. 1987 Lubell, Samuel
d. 1987 Wesley, Charles Harris
d. 1989 Blake, Amanda
d. 1993 Beam, Jacob D(yneley)
d. 1993 Granger, Stewart
d. 1993 Philbrick, Herbert Arthur
d. 1993 Sharaff, Irene
d. 1994 Gęldzahler, Henry
d. 1995 Hobby, Oveta Culp
d. 1995 McCarthy, J(oseph) P(riestley)
d. 1998 Fowlie, Wallace
d. 1998 Murray, Jim
d. 1998 West, Dorothy

August 17
b. 1601? Fermat, Pierre de
b. 1624 Sobieski, John, III
b. 1699 Jussieu, Bernard de
b. 1761 Carey, William
b. 1779 Ritter, Karl
b. 1784 Feijo, Diogo Antonio

b. 1786 Crockett, Davy
b. 1795 Drake, Joseph Rodman
b. 1800 Rogers, Isaiah
b. 1837? Grimke, Charlotte Lottie Forten
b. 1840 Blunt, Wilfrid Scawen
b. 1844 Menelik II
b. 1849 Grimke, Archibald H(enry)
b. 1864 Cooley, Charles Horton
b. 1864 Eberle, Edward Walter
b. 1866 Marlowe, Julia
b. 1868 Porter, Gene Stratton
b. 1870 Hobson, Richmond Pearson
b. 1876 Perth, 16th Earl of
b. 1878 Gogarty, Oliver St. John
b. 1882 Kearns, Jack
b. 1885 Fleischmann, Raoul H(erbert)
b. 1887 Garvey, Marcus Moziah
b. 1888 Woolley, Monty
b. 1890 Hopkins, Harry Lloyd
b. 1891 Kardiner, Abram
b. 1893 West, Mae
b. 1896 Groves, Leslie Richard
b. 1896 Larkin, Oliver Waterman
b. 1899 Lewis, Janet
b. 1900 Howe, Quincy
b. 1901 MacDonald, Malcolm John
b. 1902 Aldrich, Richard Stoddard
b. 1903 Chasins, Abram
b. 1904 Harding, Ann
b. 1904 Whitney, John Hay
b. 1906 Bishop, Hazel
b. 1906 Caetano, Marcello
b. 1907 Peyrefitte, Roger
b. 1909 Clinton, Larry
b. 1909 McNally, Andrew, III
b. 1911 Botvinnik, Mikhail (Moisseyevich)
b. 1911 Rosenfeld, Harry N(athan)
b. 1913 York, Rudy
b. 1914 Downs, William Randall, Jr.
b. 1914 Roosevelt, Franklin Delano, Jr.
b. 1916 Toledano, Ralph de
b. 1918 Ankers, Evelyn
b. 1918 Brown, George Scratchley
b. 1918 Howe, Harold, II

b. 1921 O'Hara, Maureen
b. 1923 Rivers, Larry
b. 1924 Connell, Evan Shelby, Jr.
b. 1925 Hawkes, John
b. 1926 Jiang Zemin
b. 1927 Cornfeld, Bernard
b. 1928 Rossant, James Stephane
b. 1929 Powers, Francis Gary
b. 1930 Bennett, Harve
b. 1930 Hughes, Ted
b. 1930 Warren, Gerald Lee
b. 1932 Kerr, Red
b. 1932 Naipaul, V(idiahar) S(urajprasad)
b. 1935? Dinning, Mark
b. 1935 Tsegaye, Gabre-Medhin
b. 1939 Sanders, Ed
b. 1941 Babangida, Ibrahim Badamasi
b. 1941 Powell, Boog
b. 1942 Bereano, Nancy K(irp)
b. 1943 DeNiro, Robert
b. 1944 Drexler, Millard S
b. 1946 Manning, Patrick (Augustus Mervyn)
b. 1947 Talley, Gary
b. 1952 Piquet, Nelson
b. 1952 Vilas, Guillermo
b. 1954 Pastrana, Andres
b. 1958 Carlisle, Belinda
b. 1960 Penn, Sean
b. 1969 Wahlberg, Donnie
b. 1970 Courier, Jim
d. 1676 Grimmelshausen, Hans Jakob Christoffel von
d. 1785 Trumbull, Jonathan
d. 1786 Frederick II
d. 1786 Frederick the Great
d. 1804 Heck, Barbara Ruckle
d. 1809 Boulton, Matthew
d. 1838 DaPonte, Lorenzo
d. 1850 San Martin, Jose de
d. 1878 Upjohn, Richard
d. 1880 Bull, Ole Bornemann
d. 1911 Reed, Myrtle
d. 1938 Lewisohn, Adolph
d. 1945 Marinuzzi, Giuseppe (Gino)
d. 1946 Pollock, Channing

d. 1950 Black Elk
d. 1954 Sarett, Lew R
d. 1955 Leger, Fernand
d. 1958 Brooks, Walter
R(ollin)
d. 1960 Harsh, Vivian
Gordon
d. 1963 Barthelmess,
Richard
d. 1963 Gardner,
Ed(ward Francis)
d. 1966 Spargo, John
d. 1969 Blaiberg, Philip
d. 1969 Stern, Otto
d. 1971 McMahon,
Horace
d. 1973 Aiken, Conrad
Potter
d. 1973 Radford, Arthur
William
d. 1979 Vance, Vivian
d. 1981 Keylor, Arthur
W
d. 1983 Gershwin, Ira
d. 1985 Eden, Nicholas
d. 1987 Andrews,
Wayne
d. 1987 Brown,
Clarence
d. 1987 Drummond de
Andrade, Carlos
d. 1987 Hess, Rudolf
d. 1988 Roosevelt,
Franklin Delano, Jr.
d. 1988 Zia-ul-Haq,
Mohammad
d. 1990 Bailey, Pearl
Mae
d. 1993 Maynard,
Robert Clyve

August 18
b. 1587 Dare, Virginia
b. 1750 Salieri, Antonio
b. 1774 Lewis,
Meriwether
b. 1792 Russell, John,
Lord
b. 1803 Clifford, Nathan
b. 1807 Adams, Charles
Francis, Sr.
b. 1810 Troyon,
Constant
b. 1830 Francis Joseph,
(I)
b. 1830 Franz Joseph I
b. 1834 Field, Marshall
b. 1838 Neumann,
Angelo
b. 1846 Evans, Robley
Dunglison
b. 1854 Hyslop, James
Hervey
b. 1873 Harbach, Otto
Abels
b. 1875? Slezak, Leo
b. 1879 Edwards, Gus
b. 1880 Cleland,
Thomas Maitland
b. 1888 Williams,
J(ames) R(obert)
b. 1890 Clark, Sydney
b. 1890 Funk, Walther
b. 1890 Podoloff,
Maurice
b. 1893 Davidson,
Donald Grady

b. 1893 Grimes,
Burleigh Arland
b. 1893 MacMillan,
Ernest Campbell, Sir
b. 1896 Pickford, Jack
b. 1896 Warburg, James
Paul
b. 1897 Mowbray, Alan
b. 1897 Rinehart,
Stanley Marshall, Jr.
b. 1899 Belluschi,
Pietro
b. 1900 O'Keefe,
Walter
b. 1900 Pandit, Vijaya
Lakshmi (Nehru)
b. 1901 Keller, Arthur
C
b. 1904 Cole, Sterling
W(illiam)
b. 1904 Factor, Max, Jr.
b. 1905 Lewis, Boyd de
Wolf
b. 1907 Bolinger,
Dwight Lemerton
b. 1907 Light, Enoch
Henry
b. 1908 Faure, Edgar
Jean
b. 1909 Carne, Marcel
Albert
b. 1913 Cornelius,
Henry
b. 1916 Lympany,
Moura
b. 1917 Weinberger,
Caspar Willard
b. 1918 Shelepin,
Aleksandr
(Nikolaevich)
b. 1919 Hickel, Wally
b. 1922 Robbe-Grillet,
Alain
b. 1922 Winters,
Shelley
b. 1925 Aldiss, Brian
Wilson
b. 1927 Carter,
Rosalynn
b. 1928 Schott, Marge
b. 1929 Kuznetsov,
Anatoli Vasilievich
b. 1929 Sadik, Nafis
b. 1931 Chwast,
Seymour
b. 1931 Kassorla, Irene
Chamie
b. 1933 Polanski,
Roman
b. 1934 Bugliosi,
Vincent T
b. 1934 Clemente,
Roberto Walker
b. 1934 Levitin, Sonia
b. 1935 Fisher, Gail
b. 1935 Johnson, Rafer
Lewis
b. 1937 Redford, Robert
b. 1939 Bee, Molly
b. 1941 Jones,
Christopher
b. 1943 Mull, Martin
b. 1944 Moffett,
Anthony Toby
b. 1950 Ingrassia, Paul

b. 1951 Pruitt, Greg(ory
Donald)
b. 1952 Boosler, Elayne
b. 1952 Carter, Jeff
b. 1952 Swayze, Patrick
b. 1954 Green, Rickey
Anthony
b. 1958 Stowe,
Madeleine
b. 1969 Slater, Christian
b. 1970 Warner,
Malcolm-Jamal
d. 472 Ricimer
d. 1227 Genghis Khan
d. 1503 Alexander VI
d. 1559 Paul, IV
d. 1642 Reni, Guido
d. 1678 Marvell,
Andrew
d. 1697 Vieira, Antonio
d. 1800 Chongjo
d. 1850 Balzac, Honore
de
d. 1852 Taylor,
Margaret (Smith)
d. 1855 Lawrence,
Abbott
d. 1862 Fraser, Simon
d. 1870 Kennedy, John
Pendleton
d. 1887 Fowler, Orson
Squire
d. 1922 Hudson,
William Henry
d. 1922 Lavisse, Ernest
d. 1937 McIntyre,
James
d. 1940 Chrysler,
Walter Percy
d. 1944 Thalmann,
Ernst
d. 1948 Grove,
Frederick Philip
d. 1953 Flynn, Edward
Joseph
d. 1959 Helburn,
Theresa
d. 1961 Hand, Learned
d. 1961 MacFarlane,
Willie
d. 1965 LaFollete,
Philip Fox
d. 1968 Sande, Earl
d. 1968 Walter, Cyril
d. 1969 Mies van der
Rohe, Ludwig
d. 1978 Fischer, John
d. 1981 Bennett, Robert
Russell
d. 1981 Loos, Anita
d. 1982 Bayne, Beverly
Pearl
d. 1983 Pevsner,
Nikolaus Bernhard
Leon, Sir
d. 1988 Ashton,
Frederick William,
Sir
d. 1990 Skinner,
B(urrhus) F(rederic)
d. 1991 Shoemaker,
Vaughn Richard
d. 1997 Westwood, Jean
Miles
d. 1998 Khambatta,
Persis

August 19
b. 1398 Santillana, Inigo
Lopez de Mendoza
b. 1560 Crichton, James
b. 1580 Vernier, Pierre
b. 1621 Eeckhout,
Gerbrand van den
b. 1646 Flamsteed, John
b. 1686 Porpora,
Niccolo
b. 1746 Du Barry,
Marie Jeanne Gomard
de Vaubernier,
Comtesse
b. 1751 Prescott,
Samuel
b. 1780 Beranger,
Pierre-Jean de
b. 1785 Thomas, Seth
b. 1793 Goodrich,
Samuel Griswold
b. 1808 Nasmyth, James
b. 1814 Pleasant, Mary
Ellen
b. 1829 Moran, Edward
b. 1835 Bland, Richard
Parks
b. 1843 Doughty,
Charles Montagu
b. 1849 Nabuco de
Araujo, Joaquim
Aurelio
b. 1851 Hires, Charles
E
b. 1856 Frederic, Harold
b. 1858 Nesbit, Edith
b. 1860 Kane, John
b. 1865 Berdichevsky,
Micah Joseph
b. 1870 Baruch, Bernard
Mannes
b. 1871 Wright, Orville
b. 1873 Stone, Fred
Andrew
b. 1877 Connally, Tom
b. 1878 Quezon (y
Molina), Manuel Luis
b. 1881 Enesco,
Georges
b. 1882 Chanel, Coco
b. 1884 Wieman, Henry
Nelson
b. 1885 Ferguson, Elsie
b. 1886 Heger, Robert
b. 1889 Waley, Arthur
David
b. 1892 Lunt, Alfred
b. 1897 Vishniac,
Roman
b. 1899 Baclanova,
Olga
b. 1899 Tomlin, Bradley
Walker
b. 1900 Ryle, Gilbert
b. 1902 Moore, Colleen
b. 1902 Nash, Ogden
Frederick
b. 1903 Barton, Robert
B(rown) M(orison)
b. 1903 Cozzens, James
Gould
b. 1903 Dauphin,
Claude Le Grand
Maria Eugene
b. 1906 Farnsworth,
Philo Taylor

b. 1907 Morton,
Thruston Ballard
b. 1907 Singh, (Sardar)
Swaran
b. 1908 Knowles,
Warren Perley
b. 1909 Andrzejewski,
Jerzy
b. 1913 Mills, Harry
b. 1915 Lardner,
Ring(gold Wilmer),
Jr.
b. 1916 Wilson, Marie
(Katherine Elizabeth)
b. 1919 Forbes,
Malcolm Stevenson
b. 1920 Kibbee, Robert
Joseph
b. 1921 Roddenberry,
Gene
b. 1924 Marshall,
William
b. 1926 Rock, Arthur
b. 1928 Levin, Bernard
b. 1928 Stewart,
Thomas
b. 1930 McCourt, Frank
b. 1931 Shoemaker,
Willie
b. 1932 Cohen, Joan
Lebold
b. 1934 Bell, Gordon
(Bennett)
b. 1934 Durenberger,
David Ferdinand
b. 1934 Richards, Rene
b. 1935 Richardson,
Bobby
b. 1936 Oerter, Al(fred
A)
b. 1938 Cobb, Vicki
b. 1938 Goode, Wilson
b. 1938 Graham, Robert
b. 1939 Baker, Alan
b. 1940 Baker, Ginger
b. 1940 Nash, Johnny
b. 1942 Monk, Allan
James
b. 1942 Thompson, Fred
b. 1943 Violet, Arlene
b. 1946 Bolden, Charles
F(rank), Jr.
b. 1946 Clinton, Bill
b. 1946 Steel, Dawn
b. 1947 Schwarz,
Gerard
b. 1948 Gore, Tipper
b. 1948 McRaney,
Gerald
b. 1953 Matalin, Mary
(Joe)
b. 1960 Darling,
Ron(ald Maurice), Jr.
b. 1960 Hebert, Bobby
Joseph
b. 1963 Stamos, John
b. 1967 Dillon, Kevin
b. 1967 Soren, Tabitha
b. 1969 Perry, Matthew
d. 14 Augustus
d. 1419 Wenceslaus
d. 1457 Castagno,
Andrea del
d. 1493 Frederick, III
d. 1580 Palladio,
Andrea

d. 1662 Pascal, Blaise
d. 1780 Kalb, Johann de
d. 1819 Watt, James
d. 1823 Bloomfield,
Robert
d. 1838 Geddes, James
d. 1856 Gerhardt,
Charles Frederic
d. 1887 Baird, Spencer
Fullerton
d. 1895 Hardin, John
Wesley
d. 1896 Whitney, Josiah
Dwight
d. 1923 Pareto, Vilfredo
d. 1925 Lawson, Victor
Fremont
d. 1929 Diaghilev,
Sergei (Pavlovich)
d. 1931 Agramonte y
Simoni, Aristides
d. 1936 Garcia Lorca,
Federico
d. 1938 Frederick,
Pauline
d. 1944 Wood, Henry
Joseph, Sir
d. 1945 Bose, Subhas
Chandra
d. 1950 Giorgi,
Giovanni
d. 1951 Bomberg, Dave
d. 1954 De Gasperi,
Alcide
d. 1955 Sumner, James
Batcheller
d. 1959 Blind Willie
McTell
d. 1959 Epstein, Jacob,
Sir
d. 1960 Cornford,
Frances Crofts
Darwin
d. 1960 Namier, Lewis
Bernstein
d. 1967 Gernsback,
Hugo
d. 1968 Gamow, George
d. 1971 Melford, Austin
d. 1974 Davies, Rodger
Paul
d. 1975 Hogg, Ima
d. 1976 Sim, Alastair
d. 1977 Marx, Groucho
d. 1977 Powers, John
Robert
d. 1978 Mallowan, Max
Edgar Lucien, Sir
d. 1981 Matthews,
Jessie
d. 1982 Crisler, Fritz
d. 1982 Davis, Loyal
d. 1985 Henderson,
Robert W
d. 1986 Baddeley,
Hermione Clinton
d. 1986 Tucker,
Lorenzo
d. 1987 Rorke, Hayden
d. 1990 Strout, Richard
Lee
d. 1991 Maltby, Richard
E
d. 1993 Blitch, Iris
F(aircloth)

d. 1993 Kerst, Donald
W(illiam)
d. 1994 Pauling, Linus
C(arl)
d. 1995 Arnold, Danny
August 20
b. Horton, Peter
William
b. 1561 Peri, Jacopo
b. 1745 Asbury, Francis
b. 1775 Tucker, George
b. 1778 O'Higgins,
Bernardo
b. 1785 Perry, Oliver
Hazard, Admiral
b. 1795 Stockton,
Robert Field
b. 1827 Decoster,
Charles Theodore
Henri
b. 1833 Harrison,
Benjamin
b. 1843 Nilsson,
Christine
b. 1846 Mead, William
Rutherford
b. 1860 Poincare,
Raymond
b. 1869 Anderson,
George Everett
b. 1875 Tchernichowski,
Saul Gutmanovich
b. 1879 Budd, Ralph
b. 1881 Guest, Edgar
A(lbert)
b. 1884 Bultmann,
Rudolf
b. 1885 Campana, Dino
b. 1886 Tillich, Paul
Johannes
b. 1888 Thang, Ton
Duc
b. 1890 Lovecraft,
H(oward) P(hillips)
b. 1892 Aiken, George
David
b. 1896? Gersten, Berta
b. 1898 Infeld, Leopold
b. 1898 Moberg,
Vihelm
b. 1899 Bochner,
Salomon
b. 1901 Quasimodo,
Salvatore
b. 1905 Naruse, Mikio
b. 1905 Schoonmaker,
Frank Musselman
b. 1905 Teagarden, Jack
b. 1906 Tuttle, Lurene
b. 1907 Reed, Alan
b. 1908 Davis, Kingsley
b. 1908 Lopez, Al(fonso
Ramon)
b. 1910 Saarinen, Eero
b. 1913 Sperry, Roger
W(olcott)
b. 1916 Goldfinger,
Nathaniel
b. 1917 Sanford, Terry
b. 1920 Kovel, Ralph
Mallory
b. 1921 Susann,
Jacqueline
b. 1922 Resnik, Regina
b. 1923 Granville,
Joseph E(nsign)

b. 1923 Shattuck, Roger
Whitney
b. 1924 Reeves, Jim
b. 1926 Vickrey, Robert
(Remsen)
b. 1931 King, Don(ald)
b. 1932 Aksyonov,
Vassily Pavlovich
b. 1933 Alexander, Sue
b. 1933 Mitchell,
George John
b. 1935 Yokich,
Stephen P.
b. 1936 Fracci, Carla
b. 1941 Gray, William
H, III
b. 1941 Pfeiffer,
Eckhard
b. 1942 Hayes, Isaac
b. 1942 Moses, Gilbert,
III
b. 1944 Gandhi, Rajiv
Ratna
b. 1944 Nettles, Graig
b. 1946 Chung, Connie
b. 1946 Fabius, Laurent
b. 1947 Pankow, James
b. 1948 Plant, Robert
Anthony
b. 1948 Watkins, Perry
b. 1951 Lynott, Phil(ip)
b. 1956 Allen, Joan
b. 1957 Donaldson,
Simon (Kirwan)
b. 1957 Nicholas, Cindy
d. 1153 Bernard of
Clairvaux, Saint
d. 1384 Groote, Gerhard
d. 1648 Herbert,
Edward, 1st Baron
Herbert of Cherbury
d. 1672 Witt, Johan de
d. 1823 Pius, VII
d. 1854 Schelling,
Friedrich Wilhelm
Joseph von
d. 1858 Oshkosh
d. 1876 Palmer, Frances
Flora Bond
d. 1879 Rimmer,
William
d. 1886 Stephens, Ann
Sophia
d. 1887 Laforgue, Jules
d. 1895 Min
d. 1912 Booth, William
d. 1914 Pius X
d. 1915 Ehrlich, Paul
Ralph
d. 1915 Finlay, Carlos
Juan
d. 1917 Baeyer, Adolf
Johann Friedrich
Wilhelm, von
d. 1928 Harvey, George
Brinton M
d. 1946 Ragland, Rags
d. 1946 Yost, Fielding
Harris
d. 1953 Morrison,
Cameron
d. 1957 Evans, Edward
Ratcliffe Garth
Russell
d. 1961 Bridgman,
Percy Williams

d. 1968 Schneirla,
Theodore Christian
d. 1972 Stark, Harold
Raynsford
d. 1981 Cleaver,
William Joseph
d. 1981 Devine,
Michael
d. 1982 Bloomingdale,
Alfred S
d. 1986 Jones,
Thad(deus Joseph)
d. 1986 Warren, Austin
d. 1988 Robinson, Joan
Mary Gale Thomas
d. 1989 Adamson,
George
d. 1991 Staggers,
Harley O(rrin)
d. 1992 Hawkins,
Walter Lincoln
d. 1992 Liss, Alan R
d. 1992 Wilson, Hazel
Hutchins

August 21
b. 1567 Francis of
Sales, St.
b. 1725 Greuze, Jean-
Baptiste
b. 1754 Tarleton,
Banastre, Sir
b. 1765 William, IV
b. 1789 Cauchy,
Augustin Louis
b. 1789 Garrett, Thomas
b. 1796 Durand, Asher
Brown
b. 1798 Michelet, Jules
b. 1811 Kelly, William
b. 1816 Gerhardt,
Charles Frederic
b. 1853 Wellcome,
Henry Solomon, Sir
b. 1854 Munsey, Frank
Andrew
b. 1858 Rudolf of
Hapsburg
b. 1872 Beardsley,
Aubrey Vincent
b. 1887? Snow, Carmel
White
b. 1890 Henry, William
M
b. 1890 Liston, Emil
b. 1896 Bradford, Roark
Whitney Wickliffe
b. 1897 Green,
Constance Windsor
McLaughlin
b. 1901 Rogell, Albert S
b. 1902 Kennon, Robert
Floyd
b. 1902 Tully, Tom
b. 1904 Basie, Count
b. 1906 Freleng, Friz
b. 1908 Kaye, Mary
Margaret Mollie
b. 1909 Dillon,
(Clarence) Douglas
b. 1912 Blake, Toe
b. 1912 Donovan,
Robert John
b. 1912 Fish, Robert
Lloyd
b. 1913 Boehm, Edward
M

b. 1913 Churchill,
Diana Josephine
b. 1913 Faulk, John
Henry
b. 1913 Johnson,
Cornelius
b. 1916 Gagne, Robert
Mills
b. 1920 Milne,
Christopher Robin
b. 1921 Hunthausen,
Raymond Gerhardt
b. 1924 Janov, Arthur
b. 1924 Schenkel,
Chris(topher Eugene)
b. 1925 Weston, Jack
b. 1927 Marcum, John
Arthur
b. 1928 de Andrade,
Mario
b. 1928 Farmer, Art(hur
Stewart)
b. 1929 Badillo,
Herman
b. 1929 Cox, Richard
Joseph
b. 1929 Kennedy, X J
b. 1930 Margaret
b. 1930 Perry, Frank
b. 1932 Van Peebles,
Melvin
b. 1933 Baker, Janet
Abbott, Dame
b. 1936 Chamberlain,
Wilt(on Norman)
b. 1936 Gardner, Booth
b. 1937 Stone, Robert
Anthony
b. 1938 Cowper, Steve
Cambreleng
b. 1938 Rogers, Kenny
b. 1939 Burton, James
b. 1939 Mogae, Festus
Gontebanye
b. 1939 Williams,
Clarence, III
b. 1943 Schell,
Johnathan Edward
b. 1944 DeShannon,
Jackie
b. 1945 Lanier, Willie E
b. 1945 McCormack,
Patty
b. 1946? Bazell, Robert
Joseph
b. 1950 Bremer, Arthur
Herman
b. 1954 Griffin, Archie
Mason
b. 1956 Cattrall, Kim
b. 1957 Sledge, Kim
b. 1958 Case, Steve
b. 1959 Kaplan, John
b. 1959 McMahon, Jim
b. 1962 Weber, Pete(r)
d. 487 Apollinaris
Sidonius, Gaius
Sollius
d. 1245 Alexander of
Hales
d. 1649 Crashaw,
Richard
d. 1762 Montagu, Mary
Wortley, Lady
d. 1798 Wilson, James
d. 1824 Taylor, John

d. 1867 Alvarez, Juan
d. 1905 Dodge, Mary
Elizabeth Mapes
d. 1937 Halevy, Elie
d. 1940 Thayer, Ernest
L
d. 1940 Trotsky, Leon
d. 1943 Phelps, William
Lyon
d. 1943 Pontoppidan,
Henrik
d. 1947 Bilbo, Theodore
Gilmore
d. 1947 Bugatti, Ettore
Arco Isidoro
d. 1951 Lambert,
Constant
d. 1952 Schumacher,
Kurt
d. 1953 Andrews, Bert
d. 1953 Smith, Alfred
d. 1957 Stewart,
Nels(on Robert)
d. 1957 Sverdrup,
H(arald) U(lrik)
d. 1958 Schumann,
Walter
d. 1959 Dunbar, Helen
Flanders
d. 1964 Togliatti,
Palmiro
d. 1966 Lewis, Fulton,
Jr.
d. 1971 Jackson, George
d. 1974 Pusser, Buford
d. 1978 Diederichs,
Nicholaas
d. 1978 Eames, Charles
d. 1978 Lord, Mary
Pillsbury
d. 1981 Popov, Dusko
d. 1982 Simmons,
Calvin
d. 1982 Sobhuza II
d. 1983 Aquino,
Benigno Simeon, Jr.
d. 1986 Chase, William
Curtis
d. 1988 Eames, Ray
d. 1989 Bolger, William
Frederick
d. 1991 Hildesheimer,
Wolfgang
d. 1991 Miller, Paul
d. 1991 Wilson, Richard
d. 1993 Troyanos,
Tatiana
d. 1995 Chandrasekhar,
Subrahmanyan
d. 1998 Stout, Juanita
Kidd

August 22
b. 1733 Ducis, Jean
Francois
b. 1809 Brisbane, Albert
b. 1809 Burton, John
Hill, Sir
b. 1817 Judson, Emily
Chubbock
b. 1834 Langley,
Samuel Pierpont
b. 1836 Willard,
Archibald MacNeal
b. 1844 DeLong,
George Washington

b. 1847 Mackenzie,
Alexander Campbell,
Sir
b. 1848 Stone, Melville
Elijah
b. 1851 Frohman,
Daniel
b. 1862 Debussy,
Claude Achille
b. 1866 Graham, Ernest
Robert
b. 1867 Powell, Maud
b. 1877
Coomaraswamy,
Ananda Kentish
b. 1880 Herriman,
George
b. 1887 Sanderson, Julia
b. 1891 Lipchitz,
Jacques
b. 1893 Holbrook,
Stewart Hall
b. 1893 Kellaway, Cecil
b. 1893 Parker, Dorothy
Rothschild
b. 1896 Gould,
Laurence M(cKinley)
b. 1897 Lucas, Nick
b. 1900 Bergner,
Elisabeth
b. 1900 Halleck,
Charles Abraham
b. 1900 Motley, Arthur
Harrison
b. 1901 Caston, Saul
b. 1901 Stouffer,
Vernon B
b. 1902 Riefenstahl,
Leni
b. 1903 Hathaway,
Starke R
b. 1903 Wellek, Rene
b. 1904 Deng Xiaoping
b. 1908 Cartier-Bresson,
Henri
b. 1909 Darrow,
Whitney, Jr.
b. 1909 Epstein, Julius
b. 1909 Epstein, Philip
G
b. 1909 Hein, Mel(vin
John)
b. 1909 Vronsky, Vitya
b. 1912 Peel, Ronald
Francis (Edward
Waite)
b. 1915 Dellinger,
David T
b. 1915 Hillier, James
b. 1915 McNamara,
Margaret Craig
b. 1917 Hooker, John
Lee
b. 1918 McGrory, Mary
b. 1919 Bauer, Erwin
Adam
b. 1920 Bradbury, Ray
Douglas
b. 1920 Cooley, Denton
Arthur
b. 1921 Corn, Ira
George, Jr.
b. 1922 Presle,
Micheline
b. 1926 Blackman,
Honor

b. 1928 Marshall, Ray
b. 1930 Kirkwood, James
b. 1932 Aldredge, Theoni (Athanasiou) V(achliotis)
b. 1932 Carr, Gerald Paul
b. 1934 Sands, Diana Patricia
b. 1934 Schwarzkopf, H Norman
b. 1935 Dean, Morton
b. 1935 Proulx, E(dna) Annie
b. 1936 Moritz, Charles Worthington
b. 1937 Kohl, Herbert R
b. 1939 Milano, Fred
b. 1939 Yastrzemski, Carl Michael
b. 1940 Harper, Valerie
b. 1940 McCartney, Bill
b. 1941 Parcells, Bill
b. 1942 Lennon, Kathy
b. 1944 Lawrence-Lightfoot, Sara
b. 1945 Chase, David
b. 1945 Kroft, Steve
b. 1948 Williams, Cindy
b. 1949 Nyad, Diana
b. 1956 Molitor, Paul Leo
b. 1957 Dunn, Holly
b. 1963 DeBarge, James
b. 1964 Amos, Tori
d. 408 Stilicho, Flavius
d. 1485 Richard III
d. 1532 Warham, William
d. 1540 Bude, Guillaume
d. 1553 Northumberland, Duke of
d. 1599 Marenzio, Luca
d. 1806 Fragonard, Jean-Honore
d. 1818 Hastings, Warren
d. 1828 Gall, Franz Joseph
d. 1839 Lundy, Benjamin
d. 1860 Decamps, Alexandre Gabriel
d. 1874 Dobell, Sydney Thompson
d. 1903 May, Phil(ip William)
d. 1903 Salisbury, Robert Arthur Talbot, 3rd Marquess
d. 1904 Chopin, Kate
d. 1915 Castlemon, Harry
d. 1920 Zorn, Anders Leonard
d. 1922 Collins, Michael
d. 1922 Scalchi, Sofia
d. 1926 Eliot, Charles William
d. 1927 Fuertes, Louis Agassiz
d. 1939 Goldin, Horace

d. 1940 Lodge, Oliver Joseph, Sir
d. 1940 Walcott, Mary Morris Vaux
d. 1941 Chaffee, Adna Romanza
d. 1942 Fokine, Michel
d. 1942 Miller, Alice Duer
d. 1945 Maraghi, Mustafa al-
d. 1955 Downes, Olin
d. 1957 Dent, Edward Joseph
d. 1958 Martin du Gard, Roger
d. 1960 Hammerstein, Oscar, II
d. 1960 Steinman, David Barnard
d. 1963 Morris, William Richard
d. 1963 Nuffield, William Richard Morris
d. 1967 Pincus, Gregory
d. 1973 MacDonald-Wright, Stanton
d. 1974 Bronowski, Jacob
d. 1974 Wilder, Robert Ingersoll
d. 1976 Bachauer, Gina
d. 1976 Kubitschek (de Oliveira), Juscelino
d. 1978 Kenyatta, Jomo
d. 1978 Silone, Ignazio
d. 1979 Farrell, James Thomas
d. 1980 McDonnell, James Smith
d. 1980 Stewart, George Rippey
d. 1982 Jacobsson, Ulla
d. 1987 Lash, Joseph P
d. 1989 Newton, Huey P(ercy)
d. 1989 Vreeland, Diana (Dalziel)
d. 1989 Yakovlev, Aleksandr Sergeyevich
d. 1991 Dewhurst, Colleen
d. 1994 Houser, Allan

August 23
b. 1213 Chia Ssu-tao
b. 1754 Louis XVI
b. 1761 Morse, Jedidiah
b. 1768 Cooper, Astley Paston, Sir
b. 1769 Cuvier, Georges, Baron
b. 1773 Fries, Jakob Friedrich
b. 1811 Bravais, Auguste
b. 1833 Burne-Jones, Edward Coley, Sir
b. 1849 Henley, William Ernest
b. 1854 Moszkowski, Moritz
b. 1863 Rives, Amelie Louise

b. 1864 Venizelos, Eleutherios Kyriakos
b. 1867 Schwob, Marcel
b. 1869 Masters, Edgar Lee
b. 1883 Wainwright, Jonathan Mayhew
b. 1884 Cuppy, Will(iam Jacob)
b. 1884 Mills, Ogden Livingston
b. 1885 Tizard, Henry Thomas, Sir
b. 1887 Hansen, Alvin Harvey
b. 1889 Faber, Geoffrey Cust, Sir
b. 1890 Guggenheim, Harry Frank
b. 1894 Secunda, Sholom
b. 1898 Claude, Albert
b. 1898 Papashvily, George
b. 1900 Krenek, Ernst
b. 1901 Bush, Guy Terrell
b. 1901 Cooper, John Sherman
b. 1903 Millikan, Clark Blanchard
b. 1903 Semenenko, Serge
b. 1904 Primrose, William
b. 1905 Bushmiller, Ernie
b. 1905 Lambert, Constant
b. 1906 Ragland, Rags
b. 1908 Adamov, Arthur
b. 1910 Cromley, Raymond Avolon
b. 1912 Kelly, Gene
b. 1912 Knutson, Coya
b. 1913 Crosby, Bob
b. 1917 Williams, Tex
b. 1921 Arrow, Kenneth Joseph
b. 1921 Brown, Charles Lee
b. 1922 Dumas, Roland
b. 1922 Kell, George (Clyde)
b. 1924 Solow, Robert Merton
b. 1926 Geertz, Clifford James
b. 1927 Berger, Melvin H
b. 1927 Boumedienne, Houari
b. 1927 Kaprow, Allan
b. 1927 Solal, Martial
b. 1928 Seldes, Marian
b. 1929 Thomson, Peter William
b. 1930 Miles, Vera
b. 1930 Rocard, Michel Louis Leon
b. 1931 Smith, Hamilton Othanel
b. 1932 Johnson, Howard Brennan
b. 1932 Russell, Mark
b. 1933 Fraser, Ian

b. 1933 Wilson, Pete Barton
b. 1934 Eden, Barbara
b. 1934 Jurgenson, Sonny
b. 1935 Berger, Marilyn
b. 1940 Bill, Tony
b. 1940 Sanders, Richard Kinard
b. 1942 Barnett, Steve
b. 1942 McBride, Patricia
b. 1944 D'Aubuisson, Roberto
b. 1944 Novello, Antonia Coello
b. 1946 Moon, Keith
b. 1947 O'Hara, Jill
b. 1947 Whittle, Christopher
b. 1948 Blomberg, Ron(ald Mark)
b. 1949 Springfield, Rick
b. 1950 Long, Shelley
b. 1951 Noor, Queen
b. 1953 Williams, Randy
b. 1954 Busch, Charles
b. 1957 Boddicker, Mike
b. 1959 Ricci, Nino
b. 1970 Phoenix, River
b. 1978 Bryant, Kobe
d. 1723 Mather, Increase
d. 1806 Coulomb, Charles Augustin de
d. 1813 Wilson, Alexander
d. 1819 Perry, Oliver Hazard, Admiral
d. 1831 Gneisenau, August Neithardt von
d. 1849 Hicks, Edward
d. 1863 Bartlett, John Sherren
d. 1892 Fonseca, Manuel Deodoro da
d. 1902 Stolz, Teresa
d. 1926 Valentino, Rudolph
d. 1927 Sacco, Nicola
d. 1927 Vanzetti, Bartolomeo
d. 1927 Zaghlul Pasha, Saad
d. 1933 Cahill, Marie
d. 1933 Loos, Adolf
d. 1936 Adam, Juliette Lamber
d. 1937 Roussel, Albert
d. 1939 Howard, Sidney Coe
d. 1959 Catto, Thomas Sivewright, Baron
d. 1959 Thayer, Tiffany Ellsworth
d. 1962 Gibson, Hoot
d. 1963 Bottome, Phyllis
d. 1963 Gray, Glen
d. 1966 Bushman, Francis X(avier)
d. 1968 Stromberg, Hunt

d. 1977 Cabot, Sebastian
d. 1977 Gabo, Naum
d. 1982 Cavalcanti, Alberto
d. 1982 Moore, Stanford
d. 1987 Sidarouss, Stephanos, Cardinal
d. 1989 Laing, R(onald) D(avid)
d. 1990 Rose, David
d. 1991 Adams, Eva Bertrand
d. 1991 Seibert, Florence B(arbara)
d. 1991 Trotter, Mildred
d. 1995 Eisenstaedt, Alfred
d. 1995 Simpson, Adele (Smithline)
d. 1997 Gairy, Eric Matthew, Sir
d. 1997 Kendrew, John Cowdery, Sir
d. 1999 Wexler, Norman

August 24
b. 1724 Stubbs, George
b. 1750 Bonaparte, Letizia
b. 1759 Wilberforce, William
b. 1784 Worcester, Joseph Emerson
b. 1787 Weddell, James
b. 1795 Wallack, James William
b. 1810 Parker, Theodore
b. 1839 Napravnik, Eduard
b. 1847 McKim, Charles Follen
b. 1849 Comstock, John Henry
b. 1852 O'Rourke, Jim
b. 1856 Mottl, Felix
b. 1872 Beerbohm, Max
b. 1875 Craven, Frank
b. 1880 Bowie, Russell
b. 1882 Pogany, Willy
b. 1884 Melford, Austin
b. 1886 Gibbs, William Francis
b. 1887 Hooper, Harry Bartholomew
b. 1888 Jagendorf, Moritz Adolf
b. 1889 Gowdy, Hank
b. 1890 Kahanamoku, Duke Paoa
b. 1890 Kendrick, Pearl Luella
b. 1894 Rhys, Jean
b. 1895 Cushing, Richard James, Cardinal
b. 1896 Baker, Phil
b. 1897 Rose, Fred
b. 1898 Cowley, Malcolm
b. 1898 Duffy, Clinton Truman
b. 1899 Borges, Jorge Luis

b. 1900 Chervenkov, Vulko
b. 1900 Fidler, Jimmie
b. 1900 Foster, Preston
b. 1902 Brandel, Fernand Paul
b. 1902 Braudel, Fernand (Paul)
b. 1903 Sutherland, Graham Vivian
b. 1904 Castroviejo, Ramon
b. 1904 Mendez, Aparicio
b. 1904 Thompson, Llewellyn E, Jr.
b. 1905 Stevens, Siaka Probyn
b. 1906 Kaufman, Boris
b. 1911 Lay, James Selden, Jr.
b. 1912 Kirby, Durward
b. 1913 Knowles, Malcolm Shepherd
b. 1913 Wilkinson, J(ohn) Burke
b. 1915 Sheldon, Alice Hastings Bradley
b. 1917 Causley, Charles Stanley
b. 1917 James, Dennis
b. 1920 Colville, Alex
b. 1922 Levesque, Rene
b. 1922 Zinn, Howard
b. 1923 Cater, Douglass
b. 1923 Jensen, Arthur Robert
b. 1924 Ahidjo, Ahmadou
b. 1924 Ikle, Fred Charles
b. 1924 Teicher, Louis
b. 1924 Witcover, Walt
b. 1925 Hufstedler, Shirley (Ann) M(ount)
b. 1927 Shannon, William Vincent
b. 1928 Brooks, Angie Elizabeth
b. 1929 Arafat, Yasir
b. 1934 Baker, Kenny
b. 1934 Myers, Norman
b. 1936 Byatt, A S
b. 1936 Spikes, Dolores
b. 1937 Abiola, Moshood
b. 1938 Williams, Mason
b. 1940 Grafton, Sue
b. 1942 Cleland, Max
b. 1942 Uhlenbeck, Karen (Keskulla)
b. 1944 Capaldi, Jim
b. 1944 Jarvis, Gregory
b. 1948 Jarre, Jean-Michel
b. 1949 Smith, Barbara
b. 1951 Randisi, Robert Joseph
b. 1955 Guyton, Tyree
b. 1956 Cooney, Gerry
b. 1958 Guttenberg, Steve
b. 1960 Ripken, Cal(vin Edwin, Jr.)

b. 1962 Louis, Errol T.
b. 1964 Wilander, Mats
b. 1965 Matlin, Marlee
b. 1965 Miller, Reggie
b. 1971 Schiffer, Claudia
d. 79 Pliny the Elder
d. 1313 Henry, VII
d. 1540 Parmigano
d. 1572 Coligny, Gaspard de Chatillon
d. 1679 Gondi, Cardinal
d. 1680 Blood, Thomas
d. 1795 Philidor, Francois Andre Danican
d. 1814 Rumford, Count
d. 1841 Hook, Theodore Edward
d. 1888 Clausius, Rudolf Julius Emmanuel
d. 1918 Bates, Arlo
d. 1923 Wiggin, Kate Douglas
d. 1943 Weil, Simone
d. 1949 Dunne, John William
d. 1950 Alessandri Palma, Arturo
d. 1954 Vargas, Getulio Dornelles
d. 1956 Mizoguchi, Kenji
d. 1957 Knox, Ronald Arbuthnott
d. 1958 Blech, Leo
d. 1960 Stouffer, Samuel A.
d. 1963 Smith, Hooley
d. 1967 Kaiser, Henry John
d. 1971 Blegen, Carl William
d. 1971 Fergusson, Harvey
d. 1974 DeSeversky, Alexander Procofieff
d. 1975 Revson, Charles Haskell
d. 1978 Prima, Louis
d. 1979 Reitsch, Hanna
d. 1981 Dean, William Frishe
d. 1982 Iwama, Kazuo
d. 1983 Nearing, Scott
d. 1985 Banks, William (Venoid)
d. 1985 Creston, Paul
d. 1985 Ryskind, Morrie
d. 1987 Keeler, William Wayne
d. 1987 Rustin, Bayard
d. 1989 Topolski, Feliks
d. 1990 Masursky, Harold
d. 1994 Becker, Ralph E(lihu)
d. 1995 Crosby, Gary
d. 1998 Diggs, Charles C(oles), Jr.
d. 1998 Marshall, E(dda) G(unnar)

August 25
b. 1530 Ivan IV

b. 1744 Herder, Johann Gottfried von
b. 1767 Saint-Just, Louis Antoine Leon de
b. 1803 Caxias, Duque de
b. 1819 Pinkerton, Allan
b. 1836 Harte, (Francis) Bret
b. 1841 Kocher, Emil Theodor
b. 1845 Ludwig II
b. 1850 Nye, Edgar Wilson
b. 1861 Fawcett, George
b. 1862 Procter, William Cooper
b. 1873 Bates, Blanche Lyon
b. 1880 Cowen, Joshua Lionel
b. 1884 Auriol, Vincent
b. 1886 Stolz, Robert
b. 1889 Frank, Waldo
b. 1893 Dean, Henry Trendley
b. 1898 Dutton, Ralph Stawell
b. 1900 Kober, Arthur
b. 1900 Krebs, Hans Adolf, Sir
b. 1901 Engstrom, Elmer William
b. 1902 Wolpe, Stefan
b. 1905 Bow, Clara Gordon
b. 1906 Panter-Downes, Mollie
b. 1908 Heindorf, Ray
b. 1909 Keeler, Ruby
b. 1912 Honecker, Erich
b. 1912 Key, Ted
b. 1913 Kelly, Walt(er Crawford)
b. 1913 Rostow, Eugene Victor
b. 1915 Trampler, Walter
b. 1916 Johnson, Van
b. 1916 Robbins, Fredrick Chapman
b. 1917 DeFore, Don
b. 1917 Ferrer, Mel(chor Gaston)
b. 1918 Bernstein, Leonard
b. 1918 Greene, Richard
b. 1919 Urban, Matt
b. 1919 Wallace, George C(orley)
b. 1921 Moore, Brian
b. 1921 Oduber (Quiros), Daniel
b. 1924 Hall, Monty
b. 1927 Gibson, Althea
b. 1928 Epstein, Jason
b. 1930 Connery, Sean
b. 1931 Andrus, Cecil D(ale)
b. 1932 Goldberg, Bernard
b. 1933 Philbin, Regis (Francis Xavier)
b. 1933 Shorter, Wayne
b. 1933 Skerritt, Tom

b. 1938 Forsyth, Frederick
b. 1939 Canary, David
b. 1941 Bolt, Carol
b. 1941 Burden, Carter
b. 1943 Eldredge, Niles
b. 1944 Black, Conrad Moffat
b. 1944 Demers, Jacques
b. 1944 Martino, Pat
b. 1944 Williams, Sherley Anne
b. 1946 Fingers, Rollie
b. 1947? Archer, Anne
b. 1947 Castillo, Edward (Daniel)
b. 1949 Amis, Martin (Louis)
b. 1949 Simmons, Gene
b. 1949 Watson, Elizabeth
b. 1950? Savage, John
b. 1953 English, Doug
b. 1953 Tito, Teburoro
b. 1954 Costello, Elvis
b. 1955 Bell, Earl
b. 1961 Cyrus, Billy Ray
b. 1962 Nasrin, Taslima
b. 1964 Underwood, Blair
b. 1966 Belle, Albert
d. 383 Gratian
d. 1270 Louis IX
d. 1554 Norfolk, 3d Duke of
d. 1688 Morgan, Henry, Sir
d. 1770 Chatterton, Thomas
d. 1774 Jommelli, Niccolo
d. 1776 Hume, David
d. 1797 Chittenden, Thomas
d. 1818 Billington, Elizabeth
d. 1822 Herschel, William Frederick, Sir
d. 1835 Rutledge, Ann
d. 1867 Faraday, Michael
d. 1868 Elliott, Charles Loring
d. 1895 Houghton, Henry Oscar
d. 1900 Nietzsche, Friedrich Wilhelm
d. 1904 Fantin-Latour, (Ignace) Henri
d. 1907 Coleridge, Mary Elizabeth
d. 1908 Becquerel, Antoine Henri
d. 1921 Gumilev, Nikolai
d. 1921 Hewitt, Peter Cooper
d. 1925 Goldie, George Dashwood Taubman
d. 1926 Moran, Thomas
d. 1936 Zinoviev, Grigori Evseevich
d. 1939 Siebert, Babe

d. 1940 Michelin, Edouard
d. 1942 George Edward Alexander Edmund
d. 1945 Birch, John
d. 1948 Bottomley, Gordon
d. 1956 Kinsey, Alfred Charles
d. 1956 Pierce, George Washington
d. 1966 Sayyid Qutb
d. 1966 Tamiris, Helen
d. 1967 Bruce of Melbourne, 1st Viscount
d. 1967 Muni, Paul
d. 1967 Rockwell, George Lincoln
d. 1969 Bruce, Ailsa Mellon
d. 1971 Lewis, Ted
d. 1973 Corcos, Lucille
d. 1975 Billings, John Shaw
d. 1975 Dunning, John Ray
d. 1976 Johnson, Eyvind Olof Verner
d. 1977 Arvey, Jacob Meyer
d. 1979 Kenton, Stan(ley Newcomb)
d. 1980 Champion, Gower
d. 1981 Hulme, Kathryn Cavarly
d. 1983 Keller, Arthur C
d. 1984 Capote, Truman
d. 1984 Hoyt, Waite Charles
d. 1984 Varipapa, Andy
d. 1985 Smith, Samantha
d. 1986 Livingston, M(ilton) Stanley
d. 1988 Daniel, Price
d. 1988 Rooney, Art(hur Joseph)
d. 1990 Callaghan, Morley Edward
d. 1991 Busch, Niven
d. 1992 O'Neal, Frederick
d. 1993 Biehl, Amy
d. 1993 Elson, Edward L(ee) R(oy)
d. 1998 Powell, Lewis F(ranklin), Jr.

August 26
b. 1676 Walpole, Robert
b. 1740 Montgolfier, Joseph Michel
b. 1745 Mackenzie, Henry
b. 1819 Albert, Prince
b. 1827 Wittenmyer, Annie Turner
b. 1833 Fawcett, Henry
b. 1850 Richet, Charles Robert
b. 1873 DeForest, Lee
b. 1874 Gale, Zona
b. 1875 Buchan, John, Sir

b. 1876 Couzens, James Joseph, Jr.
b. 1880 Apollinaire, Guillaume
b. 1880 Moeller, Philip
b. 1881 Irvin, Rea
b. 1882 Franck, James
b. 1884 Biggers, Earl Derr
b. 1885 Romains, Jules
b. 1886 Hunsaker, Jerome Clarke
b. 1886 McNamara, George
b. 1890 Clark, Barrett H
b. 1895 Long, Earl Kemp
b. 1897 Roland, Ruth
b. 1898 Guggenheim, Peggy
b. 1899 Tamayo, Rufino
b. 1900 Woodruff, Hale (Aspacio)
b. 1901 DeQuay, Jan E
b. 1901 Genaro, Frankie
b. 1901 Taylor, Maxwell Davenport
b. 1903 Dalrymple, Ian (Murray)
b. 1903 Miller, Caroline
b. 1903 Rushing, Jimmy
b. 1904 Isherwood, Christopher (William)
b. 1906 Bloom, Mickey
b. 1906 Sabin, Albert Bruce
b. 1910 Wells, Edward
b. 1911 Lanin, Lester
b. 1914 Cortazar, Julio
b. 1915 Davis, Jim
b. 1915 Murphy, Arthur Richard, Jr.
b. 1916 Hill, Virginia
b. 1917 Smith, William French
b. 1919 Graham, Ronny
b. 1920 Parker, Brant (Julian)
b. 1920 Prem Tinsulanonda
b. 1921 Begelman, David
b. 1921 Bradlee, Ben(jamin Crowninshield)
b. 1922 Levine, Irving R(askin)
b. 1925 Clayton, Jan(e Byral)
b. 1926 Gibbs, Georgia
b. 1932 Engle, Joe Henry
b. 1933 Chartoff, Robert
b. 1933 Wattenberg, Ben J
b. 1934 Heinsohn, Tommy
b. 1934 Leach, Will
b. 1935 Ferraro, Geraldine Anne
b. 1941 Ehrenreich, Barbara
b. 1941 Tuttle, Merlin Devere
b. 1948 Simpson, Valerie

b. 1951 Torricelli, Robert G.
b. 1951 Witten, Edward
b. 1952 Rush, Billy
b. 1952 Shortz, Will(iam Frederic)
b. 1960 Marsalis, Branford
b. 1965 Burke, Christopher
b. 1980 Culkin, Macaulay
d. 1723 Leeuwenhoek, Antonie van
d. 1744 Byrd, William
d. 1785 Germain, George Sackville
d. 1795 Cagliostro, Alessandro, Conte di
d. 1850 Louis Phillippe
d. 1863 Floyd, John Buchanan
d. 1871 Scribner, Charles
d. 1894 Thaxter, Celia
d. 1908 Pastor, Tony
d. 1909 Fenn, George Manville
d. 1910 James, William
d. 1921 Erzberger, Matthias
d. 1930 Chaney, Lon
d. 1931 Harris, Frank
d. 1935 Willys, John North
d. 1937 Mellon, Andrew William
d. 1945 Werfel, Franz
d. 1950 Olds, Ranson E(li)
d. 1957 Tyrrell, Joseph Burr
d. 1958 Vaughan Williams, Ralph
d. 1961 Russell, Gail
d. 1962 Chase, Richard Volney
d. 1962 Stefansson, Vihjalmur
d. 1968 Francis, Kay
d. 1972 Chichester, Francis Charles, Sir
d. 1974 Lindbergh, Charles A(ugustus)
d. 1976 Anderson, Warner
d. 1976 Lehmann, Lotte
d. 1977 Rey, Hans Augustus
d. 1978 Boyer, Charles
d. 1979 Waltari, Mika
d. 1980 Korjus, Miliza
d. 1981 Baldwin, Roger Nash
d. 1983 Kellin, Mike
d. 1985 Wakefield, Dick
d. 1986 Knight, Ted
d. 1987 Wittig, Georg Friedrich Karl
d. 1988 DeLue, Donald Harcourt
d. 1989 Stone, Irving
d. 1990 Hagen, John Peter
d. 1993 Rockin' Dopsie

d. 1995 Wood, Evelyn
d. 1996 Lanusse,
Alejandro Agustin
August 27
b. 551BC Confucius
b. 1545 Farnese,
Alessandro
b. 1637 Calvert, Charles
b. 1730 Hamann,
Johann Georg
b. 1770 Hegel, Georg
Wilhelm Friedrich
b. 1777 Campbell,
Thomas
b. 1796 Smith, Sophia
b. 1797 James, Edwin
b. 1809 Hamlin,
Hannibal
b. 1825 Baikie, William
Balfour
b. 1858 Peano,
Giuseppe
b. 1863 Hepbron,
George
b. 1865 Breasted, James
Henry
b. 1865 Dawes, Charles
Gates
b. 1867 Giordano,
Umberto
b. 1869 Haushofer, Karl
Ernst
b. 1871 Dreiser,
Theodore
b. 1872 Anderson, Mary
b. 1874 Bosch, Carl
b. 1877 Douglas, Lloyd
Cassel
b. 1877 Rolls, Charles
Stewart
b. 1878 Wrangel, Pietr
Nikolayevich
b. 1882 Goldwyn,
Samuel
b. 1884 Arbuthnot, May
Hill
b. 1885 Pabst, Georg
Wilhelm
b. 1890 Flanagan, Hallie
Mae Ferguson
b. 1890 Ray, Man
b. 1893 Henderson,
Arthur
b. 1899 Forester, Cecil
Scott
b. 1899 Torroja (y
Miret), Eduardo
b. 1901 Pryor, Roger
b. 1901 Ritz, Al
b. 1902 Christensen,
William
b. 1904 Lofts, Norah
Robinson
b. 1905 Ward, Mary
Jane
b. 1906 Gein, Ed
b. 1908 Bradman,
Donald George
b. 1908 Johnson,
Lyndon B(aines)
b. 1908 Leahy, Frank
b. 1909 George, Don
b. 1909 Sexton, Leo
b. 1909 Yates, Sidney
R(ichard)

b. 1909 Young, Lester
Willis
b. 1910 Teresa, Mother
b. 1912 Dorsey, Bob
Rawls
b. 1913 Kamen, Martin
David
b. 1915 Heller, Walter
Wolfgang
b. 1915 Ramsey,
Norman
b. 1916 Raye, Martha
b. 1916 Stein, Herbert
b. 1918 Lowrey,
Peanuts
b. 1928 Buthelezi,
Gatsha Mangosuthu
b. 1929 Cervantes,
Alfonso Juan
b. 1929 Levin, Ira
b. 1931 Ghose, Sri
Chinmoy Kumar
b. 1932 Fraser, Antonia
Pakenham, Lady
b. 1935 Holroyd,
Michael De Courcy
Fraser
b. 1935 Yablans, Frank
b. 1937 Sands, Tommy
b. 1939 Least Heat
Moon, William
b. 1942 Dragon, Daryl
b. 1942 Peckford, Brian
b. 1943 Axthelm, Pete(r
Macrae)
b. 1943 Kerrey, Bob
b. 1943 Weld, Tuesday
b. 1944 Bogert, Tim
b. 1947 Bach, Barbara
b. 1947 Reems, Harry
b. 1951 Bell, Buddy
b. 1951 Kavanaugh,
Kevin
b. 1954 Lloyd, John
b. 1957 Langer,
Bernhard
b. 1961 Adams,
Yolanda
b. 1985 Nechita,
Alexandra
d. 1521 DesPres,
Josquin
d. 1576 Titian
d. 1590 Sixtus, V
d. 1635 Lope de Vega
d. 1664 Zurbaran,
Francisco
d. 1681 Nikon, Nikita
Minov
d. 1748 Thomson,
James
d. 1865 Haliburton,
Thomas Chandler
d. 1876 Fromentin,
Eugene
d. 1879 Hill, Rowland,
Sir
d. 1880 Ouray
d. 1914 Bohm von
Bawerk, Eugene
d. 1919 Botha, Louis
d. 1923 Ayrton, Hertha
d. 1924 Bayliss,
William Maddock,
Sir

d. 1931 Smith, Francis
Marion
d. 1935 Hassam, Childe
d. 1937 Pope, John
Russell
d. 1948 Hughes, Charles
Evans
d. 1948 Speaks, Oley
d. 1950 DeLuca,
Giuseppe
d. 1957 Filene, Lincoln
d. 1958 Lawrence,
Ernest Orlando
d. 1963 DuBois,
W(illiam) E(dward)
B(urghardt)
d. 1964 Allen, Gracie
Ethel Cecil Rosaline
d. 1965 LeCorbusier
d. 1967 Epstein, Brian
d. 1968 Marina
d. 1969 Compton-
Burnett, Ivy, Dame
d. 1969 Mann, Erika
d. 1971 Armstrong,
Lil(lian Hardin)
d. 1971 Bourke-White,
Margaret
d. 1971 Cerf, Bennett
Alfred
d. 1971 Turnesa, Jim
d. 1975 Haile Selassie, I
d. 1975 Stillman, Irwin
Maxwell
d. 1979 Mountbatten of
Burma, Louis
Mountbatten, Earl
d. 1980 Avery, Tex
d. 1980 Kenney,
Douglas C
d. 1980 Levenson,
Sam(uel)
d. 1981 Edwards, Joan
d. 1987 Smalls, Charlie
d. 1989 Gould, Charles
Bruce
d. 1990 Saint Jacques,
Raymond
d. 1990 Vaughan, Stevie
Ray
d. 1992 Ludwig, Daniel
Keith
d. 1993 Foster, Vincent
d. 1995 Von Eckardt,
Wolf
d. 1996 Morris, Greg
d. 1997 Blane, Sally
d. 1997 Tartikoff,
Brandon
August 28
b. 1476 Kano,
Motonobu
b. 1728 Stark, John
b. 1749 Goethe, Johann
Wolfgang von
b. 1774 Seton, Elizabeth
Ann Bayley, Saint
b. 1801 Cournot,
Antoine Augustin
b. 1813 Very, Jones
b. 1814 LeFanu, Joseph
Sheridan
b. 1823 Oliver, James
b. 1825 Ulrichs, Karl
Heinrich

b. 1831 Hayes, Lucy
Webb
b. 1841 Weir, John
F(erguson)
b. 1873 Saarinen, Eliel
b. 1879 Whipple,
George Hoyt
b. 1884 Fraser, Peter
b. 1886 Higgins,
Andrew J
b. 1891 Chekhov,
Michael
b. 1893 Arnold, Leslie
Philip
b. 1894 Bohm, Karl
b. 1896 O'Flaherty,
Liam
b. 1899 Boyer, Charles
b. 1899 Grimm, Charlie
b. 1899 Howe, James
Wong
b. 1901 Lang, Paul
Henry
b. 1903 Bettelheim,
Bruno
b. 1903 Wagner-
Regeny, Rudolf
b. 1904 Duvoisin, Roger
Antoine
b. 1905 Levene, Sam
b. 1906 Betjeman, John,
Sir
b. 1907 Hart-Davis,
Rupert
b. 1908 Peterson, Roger
Tory
b. 1910 Graves, Morris
Cole
b. 1910 Koopmans,
Tjalling (Charles)
b. 1911 Luns, Joseph
Marie Antoine Hubert
b. 1913 Cudlipp, Hugh
b. 1913 Davies,
(William) Robertson
b. 1913 Irving, Robert
Augustine
b. 1913 Tucker, Richard
b. 1916 Mills, C(harles)
Wright
b. 1917 Kirby, Jack
b. 1918 Lanusse,
Alejandro Agustin
b. 1919 Hounsfield,
Godfrey Newbold, Sir
b. 1921 Kulp, Nancy
Jane
b. 1922 Oakland, Simon
b. 1924 Ryan, Peggy
b. 1925 Davis, Marvin
b. 1925 O'Connor,
Donald
b. 1925 Trifonov, Yuri
Valentinovich
b. 1928 Stockhausen,
Karlheinz
b. 1929 Roker, Roxie
b. 1929 Wiener, Leigh
Auston
b. 1930 Gazzara, Ben
b. 1930 Rothwax,
Harold
b. 1931 Shirley-Quirk,
John Stanton
b. 1932 Bathgate, Andy
b. 1933 Seal, Elizabeth

b. 1939 Fahrenkopf, Frank Joseph, Jr.
b. 1939 Mackin, Catherine Patricia
b. 1940 Cohen, William S(ebastian)
b. 1941 Plishka, Paul Peter
b. 1942 Santos, Jose Eduardo dos
b. 1943 LeVay, Simon
b. 1943 Piniella, Lou(is Victor)
b. 1946 Soul, David
b. 1948 Seraphine, Danny
b. 1950 Guidry, Ron(ald Ames)
b. 1951 Williams, Patricia J(oyce)
b. 1952 Dove, Rita (Frances)
b. 1958 Hamilton, Scott
b. 1958 Henry, Lenny
b. 1960 Samms, Emma
b. 1965 Boykin, Keith (O.)
b. 1969 Priestly, Jason
b. 1971 Evans, Janet
b. 1982 Rimes, LeAnn
d. 430 Augustine, Saint
d. 1572 Goudimel, Claude
d. 1645 Grotius, Hugo
d. 1654 Oxenstierna, Axel Gustafsson
d. 1757 Hartley, David
d. 1818 DuSable, Jean Baptiste
d. 1839 Smith, William
d. 1859 Hunt, Leigh
d. 1861 Mackenzie, William Lyon
d. 1863 Mitscherlich, Eilhardt
d. 1864 Lassalle, Ferdinand
d. 1880 Jackson, Charles Thomas
d. 1893 Harvey, Hayward Augustus
d. 1900 Sidgwick, Henry
d. 1903 Olmsted, Frederick Law
d. 1916 Harpignies, Henri
d. 1932 Nougues, Jean
d. 1937 Opper, Frederick Burr
d. 1939 Pritchett, Henry S
d. 1940 Bowie, William
d. 1943 Ray, Edward
d. 1951 Walker, Robert
d. 1954 Burt, Maxwell Struthers
d. 1955 Till, Emmett (Louis)
d. 1957 Randolph, Georgiana Ann
d. 1957 Rice, Craig
d. 1959 Lefebvre, Georges
d. 1959 Martinu, Bohuslav

d. 1967 Smith, Bruce P
d. 1968 Henderson, Arthur
d. 1968 Mein, John Gordon
d. 1971 Leopold, Nathan Freudenthal
d. 1971 McGarity, Lou
d. 1972 Gold, Harry
d. 1972 Leibowitz, Rene
d. 1978 Busia, Kofi A(brefa)
d. 1978 Catton, Bruce
d. 1978 Mason, F(rancis) van Wyck
d. 1978 Shaw, Robert
d. 1983 Clayton, Jan(e Byral)
d. 1984 Naguib, Mohammed
d. 1985 Gordon, Ruth
d. 1987 Huston, John
d. 1988 Dawn, Hazel
d. 1988 Shulman, Max
d. 1989 Alsop, Joseph Wright, Jr.
d. 1993 Stafford, William Edgar
d. 1995 Smith, (Charles) Page

August 29
b. 1619 Colbert, Jean-Baptiste
b. 1632 Locke, John
b. 1755 Dabrowski, Jan Henryk
b. 1779 Berzelius, Jons Jacob, Baron
b. 1780 Ingres, Jean Auguste Dominique
b. 1780 Laffite, Jean
b. 1792 Finney, Charles Grandison
b. 1805 Brownlow, William Gannaway
b. 1805 Maurice, Frederick Denison
b. 1809 Holmes, Oliver Wendell, Sr.
b. 1810 Alberdi, Juan Bautista
b. 1811 Bergh, Henry
b. 1815 Carroll, Anna Ella
b. 1817 Leech, John
b. 1844 Carpenter, Edward
b. 1854 Jacobs, Joseph
b. 1862 Fisher, Andrew
b. 1862 Maeterlinck, Maurice
b. 1864 Dalton, Charles
b. 1871 Lebrun, Albert
b. 1874 Machado (y Ruiz), Manuel
b. 1876 Kettering, Charles Franklin
b. 1876 Muratore, Lucien
b. 1892 Norwich, Diana (Manners) Cooper, Viscountess
b. 1895 Dial, Morris Grant
b. 1897 Roswaenge, Helge

b. 1897 Singmaster, Elsie
b. 1898 Sturges, Preston
b. 1899 Lemnitzer, Lyman Louis
b. 1899 Streibert, Theodore Cuyler
b. 1900 Dollard, John
b. 1900 Kazee, Buell Hilton
b. 1901 Joliat, Aurel
b. 1904 Forssmann, Werner Theodor Otto
b. 1906 Gerold, Karl
b. 1907 Wechsberg, Joseph
b. 1909 Macready, George
b. 1909 Rennie, Michael
b. 1911 Charnley, John, Sir
b. 1911 Conover, Harry
b. 1913 Fine, Sylvia
b. 1915 Bergman, Ingrid
b. 1915 Pritikin, Nathan
b. 1916 Montgomery, George
b. 1920 Boykin, Otis Frank
b. 1920 Parker, Charlie
b. 1921 Wendell Oliver, Scott, Sr.
b. 1923 Attenborough, Richard Samuel, Sir
b. 1923 Gershon, Karen
b. 1924 Mayer, Dick
b. 1924 Washington, Dinah
b. 1926 Lewenthal, Raymond
b. 1929 Gunn, Thom(son William)
b. 1929 Kertesz, Istvan
b. 1932 Valeriani, Richard Gerard
b. 1933? Sanford, Isabel Gwendolyn
b. 1934 Pryor, David Hampton
b. 1936 McCain, John Sidney, III
b. 1937 Florio, James Joseph
b. 1938 Gould, Elliott
b. 1938 Rubin, Robert E.
b. 1939 Carruthers, Garrey E
b. 1939 Chan, Julius
b. 1939 Friedkin, William
b. 1939 Thornell, Jack Randolph
b. 1940 Brady, James Scott
b. 1941 Days, Drew S(aunders), III
b. 1941 Leach, Robin
b. 1941 Milosevic, Slobodan
b. 1942 Morrison, Sterling
b. 1944 Holland, Endesha Ida Mae
b. 1945 Tyus, Wyomia

b. 1946 Bagaza, Jean-Baptiste
b. 1946 Beamon, Bob
b. 1947 Grandin, Temple
b. 1947 Hunt, James
b. 1947 Lutz, Bob
b. 1953 Downey, Rick
b. 1956 Morris, Mark
b. 1958 Jackson, Michael Joseph
b. 1962 DeMornay, Rebecca
b. 1968 Me'Shell Ndegeocello
d. 886 Basil, I
d. 1300 Cavalcanti, Guido
d. 1499 Baldovinetti, Alesso
d. 1533 Atahualpa
d. 1625 Fletcher, John
d. 1657 Lilburne, John
d. 1769 Hoyle, Edmond
d. 1780 Soufflot, Jacques Germain
d. 1803 Galloway, Joseph
d. 1853 Napier, Charles James, Sir
d. 1868 Schonbein, Christian Friedrich
d. 1869 Gratz, Rebecca
d. 1876 David, Felicien Cesar
d. 1877 Young, Brigham
d. 1914 Samsonov, Aleksandr Vasilievich
d. 1917 Hartford, George Huntington
d. 1921 Allen, Joel Asaph
d. 1935 Magonigle, Harold Van Buren
d. 1946 Curry, John Steuart
d. 1947 Manolete
d. 1960 Baum, Vicki
d. 1965 Waner, Paul Glee
d. 1966 Cournos, John
d. 1967 Darrow, Charles Brace
d. 1970 Sockman, Ralph W
d. 1973 Dunn, Michael
d. 1974 Griffis, Stanton
d. 1977 Hagen, Jean
d. 1979 Newhouse, Samuel Irving
d. 1981 Thomas, Lowell Jackson
d. 1982 Bergman, Ingrid
d. 1982 Engel, Lehman
d. 1982 Goldmann, Nahum
d. 1983 Goyen, William
d. 1983 Oakland, Simon
d. 1985 Ankers, Evelyn
d. 1985 Stein, Aaron Marc
d. 1987 Marvin, Lee
d. 1987 Murphy, Arthur Richard, Jr.

d. 1987 Schlumberger, Jean
d. 1989 DiSant'Angelo, Giorgio
d. 1989 Scott, Peter Markham, Sir
d. 1990 Hall, Manly Palmer
d. 1992 Guattari, Felix
d. 1992 Norton, Mary
d. 1995 Burke, Selma (Hortense)
d. 1995 Perry, Frank

August 30
b. 1494 Correggio, Antonio Allegri da
b. 1569 Jahangir
b. 1748 David, Jacques Louis
b. 1779 Bellinghausen, Fabian Gottlieb von
b. 1785 Lin Tse-hsu
b. 1794 Kearny, Stephen Watts
b. 1797 Shelley, Mary Wollstonecraft
b. 1837 Arthur, Ellen (Lewis) Herndon
b. 1844 Ratzel, Friedrich
b. 1850 Del Pilar, Marcelo Hilario
b. 1852 Hoff, Jacobus Henricus van 't
b. 1852 Van't Hoff, Jacobus Henricus
b. 1852 Weir, Julian Alden
b. 1871 Rutherford, Ernest, Baron
b. 1879 Scheff, Fritzi
b. 1884 Svedberg, Theodor H E
b. 1893 Long, Huey Pierce
b. 1896 Massey, Raymond Hart
b. 1899 Cuyler, Kiki
b. 1900 Fry, Franklin Clark
b. 1900 Rankin, Arthur
b. 1901 Gunther, John
b. 1901 Wilkins, Roy
b. 1904 Bohlen, Charles Eustis
b. 1907 Booth, Shirley
b. 1907 Keogh, Eugene James
b. 1907 Mauchly, John William
b. 1908 Brown, Frank Arthur, Jr.
b. 1908 Fini, Leonor
b. 1908 MacMurray, Fred(erick Martin)
b. 1909 Burton, Virginia Lee
b. 1910 Fisk, James Brown
b. 1912 Blondell, Joan
b. 1912 Purcell, Edward M(ills)
b. 1913 Stone, John Richard Nicholas, Sir
b. 1914 Bishop, Julie
b. 1917 Gates, Pop

b. 1918 Bentley, Alvin Morell
b. 1918 Williams, Ted
b. 1919 Wagner, Wolfgang
b. 1919 Wells, Kitty
b. 1921 Dundee, Angelo Mirena, Jr.
b. 1925 Brunhoff, Laurent de
b. 1926 Gates, Daryl F
b. 1927 Beene, Geoffrey
b. 1930 Buffett, Warren Edward
b. 1930 Clayton, Xernona
b. 1931 Swigert, Jack
b. 1933 Getty, Donald
b. 1934 Craig, Helen
b. 1935 Earle, Sylvia Alice
b. 1935 Phillips, John
b. 1937 McLaren, Bruce Leslie
b. 1938 Collins, Gary
b. 1941 Ashley, Elizabeth
b. 1943 Crumb, R(obert)
b. 1943 Killy, Jean-Claude
b. 1944 McGraw, Tug
b. 1947 Gilles, D(onald) B(ruce)
b. 1947 Lipton, Peggy
b. 1951 Bottoms, Timothy
b. 1952 Fibak, Wojtek
b. 1953 Harris, Robin
b. 1953 Parish, Robert L
b. 1954 Lukashenka, Alyaksandr Hrihoryevich
d. 30BC Cleopatra VII
d. 1483 Louis XI
d. 1826 Douvillier, Suzanne Theodore Vaillande
d. 1844 Baily, Francis
d. 1856 A'Beckett, Gilbert Abbott
d. 1879 Hood, John Bell
d. 1879 Jackson, John Adams
d. 1896 Reinhart, Charles S
d. 1907 Mansfield, Richard
d. 1908 Stewart, Alexander Peter
d. 1928 Wien, Wilhelm Carl Werner Otto Fritz Franz
d. 1930 Allen, Henry Tureman
d. 1934 Dillingham, Charles Bancroft
d. 1938 Factor, Max
d. 1940 Thomson, Joseph John, Sir
d. 1943 Merritt, Abraham
d. 1948 Salomon, Alice
d. 1949 Kindler, Hans

d. 1952 Vaughan, Arky
d. 1953 Merola, Gaetano
d. 1961 Coburn, Charles Douville
d. 1967 Reinhardt, Ad(olph Frederick)
d. 1968 Talman, William
d. 1975 DeValera, Eamon
d. 1978 Lazarsfeld, Paul F(elix)
d. 1981 Rajai, Mohammed Ali
d. 1981 Vera-Ellen
d. 1982 Loring, Eugene
d. 1984 Aadlberg, John O.
d. 1984 Gemayel, Pierre, Sheikh
d. 1985 Caldwell, Taylor
d. 1986 Kutschmann, Walter
d. 1987 McCree, Wade Hampton, Jr.
d. 1988 Frey-Wyssling, Albert F
d. 1989 Schiff, Dorothy
d. 1991 Tinguely, Jean
d. 1993 Jordan, Richard
d. 1994 Anderson, Lindsay (Gordon)

August 31
b. 12 Caligula
b. 1739 Eberhard, Johann August
b. 1740 Oberlin, Johann Friedrich
b. 1786 Chevreul, Michel Eugene
b. 1797 Castilla, Ramon
b. 1801 Soule, Pierre
b. 1805 Sotheby, Samuel Leigh
b. 1811 Gautier, Theophile
b. 1812 Thompson, William Tappan
b. 1820 Creighton, Edward
b. 1821 Helmholtz, Hermann Ludwig Ferdinand von
b. 1834 Ponchielli, Amilcare
b. 1839 Denison, George Taylor
b. 1840 Verga, Giovanni
b. 1842 Jacobi, Mary Corinna Putnam
b. 1870 Montessori, Maria
b. 1874 Pierce, Edward Allen
b. 1874 Thorndike, Edward L(ee)
b. 1875 Plank, Eddie
b. 1879 Yoshihito
b. 1880 Wilhelmina
b. 1884 Cates, Clifton Bledsoe
b. 1884 Sarton, George

b. 1884 Scott, Austin Wakeman
b. 1885 Heyward, (Edwin) DuBose
b. 1885 Ohrbach, Nathan M
b. 1887 Paneth, Friedrich Adolf
b. 1893 Laskin, Lily
b. 1897 March, Fredric
b. 1899 Riggs, Lynn
b. 1903 Godfrey, Arthur Michael
b. 1905 Meisner, Sanford
b. 1905 Schary, Dore
b. 1907 Hawkins, Gus
b. 1907 Magsaysay, Ramon
b. 1907 Shawn, William
b. 1908 Saroyan, William
b. 1908 Sears, Robert Richardson
b. 1910 Baker, Charlotte
b. 1912 Vinay, Ramon
b. 1913 Lovell, Bernard, Sir
b. 1914 Basehart, Richard
b. 1916 Schorr, Daniel Louis
b. 1917 Jordy, William H(enry)
b. 1918 Lerner, Alan Jay
b. 1921 Feeney, Chub
b. 1921 Pike, Otis Grey
b. 1924 Hackett, Buddy
b. 1925 Schwinden, Ted
b. 1928 Coburn, James
b. 1928 Sin, Jaime L(achica)
b. 1930 Donovan, Raymond James
b. 1931 Beliveau, Jean (Marc A)
b. 1933 Wagner, Robin
b. 1935 Cleaver, Eldridge
b. 1935 Robinson, Frank
b. 1936 Collins, Marva Deloise Nettles
b. 1937 Berlinger, Warren
b. 1938 Little, Robert Langdon
b. 1939 Stevens, Eileen
b. 1939 Winter, Paul Theodore
b. 1942 Aoki, Isao
b. 1945 Morrison, Van
b. 1945 Perlman, Itzhak
b. 1945 Shavers, Ernie
b. 1949 Gere, Richard
b. 1954 Kocharyan, Robert
b. 1955 Moses, Edwin Corley
b. 1957 Tilbrook, Glenn
b. 1968 Nomo, Hideo
b. 1971 Gibson, Deborah (Ann)
b. 1973 Gooch, George Peabody

d. 1971 Romanoff, Mike
d. 1972 Duffy, Ben
d. 1973 Watkins, Arthur V(ivian)
d. 1977 Waters, Ethel
d. 1980 Donovan, Arthur
d. 1980 Evans, Bill
d. 1981 Harding, Ann
d. 1981 Speer, Albert
d. 1982 Curzon, Clifford Michael, Sir
d. 1982 Gomulka, Wladyslaw
d. 1983 Herzog, Arthur, Jr.
d. 1983 Jackson, Henry Martin
d. 1983 McDonald, Larry
d. 1985 Lewis, Saunders
d. 1985 Pitman, James
d. 1985 Zafrulla Khan, Muhammad, Sir
d. 1986 Alessandri, Jorge
d. 1986 Hamilton, Murray
d. 1988 Alvarez, Luis W(alter)
d. 1989 Giamatti, A(ngelo) Bartlett
d. 1992 Carnovsky, Morris
d. 1993 Coker, Elizabeth Boatwright
d. 1996 Welitsch, Ljuba
d. 1998 Middlecoff, Cary

September 2
b. 1766 Forten, James
b. 1778 Bonaparte, Louis
b. 1805 Echeverria, Jose Esteban (Antonino)
b. 1820 Hale, Lucretia Peabody
b. 1837 Chang Chih-tung
b. 1838 Liliuokalani, Queen
b. 1839 George, Henry, Sr.
b. 1841 Ito, Hirobumi
b. 1850 Field, Eugene
b. 1850 Spalding, Albert Goodwill
b. 1852 Bourget, Paul (Charles Joseph)
b. 1853 Ostwald, Friedrich Wilhelm
b. 1861 Crosman, Henrietta
b. 1864 Ruef, Abraham
b. 1866 Johnson, Hiram Warren
b. 1869 Maxim, Hiram Percy
b. 1877 Soddy, Frederick
b. 1887 Bruce Lockhart, Robert Hamilton, Sir
b. 1888 Schorr, Friedrich
b. 1892 Szigeti, Joseph

b. 1898 Archibald, Joe
b. 1899 Maury, Reuben
b. 1901 Rupp, Adolph Frederick
b. 1902 Dalrymple, Jean
b. 1902 Illingworth, Leslie Gilbert
b. 1902 Taylor, Henry Junior
b. 1904 Svanholm, Set
b. 1904 Trevino, Elizabeth Borton de
b. 1905 Warne, William E(lmo)
b. 1911 Harrah, Bill
b. 1912 Daiches, David
b. 1912 Xuan Thuy
b. 1914 Bearden, Romare Howard
b. 1914 Brown, George Alfred
b. 1917 Almeida, Laurindo
b. 1917 Amory, Cleveland
b. 1918 Drury, Allen (Stuart)
b. 1918 Fenelon, Fania
b. 1918 Mitchell, Martha Elizabeth Beall
b. 1921 Williams, O(swald) S.
b. 1923 Champion, Marge Celeste
b. 1924 Moi, Daniel arap
b. 1928 Stuart, Mel
b. 1931 Simpson, Alan Kooi
b. 1933 Kerekou, Mathieu Ahmed
b. 1936 Werner, Helmut (Eberhard)
b. 1937 Ueberroth, Peter Victor
b. 1938 Markle, C(larke) Wilson, Jr.
b. 1938 Mengers, Sue
b. 1940 Debray, Regis
b. 1941 Thompson, John
b. 1942 Chaudhry, Mahendra
b. 1943 Sather, Glen Cameron
b. 1943 Simon, Joe
b. 1946 Avalos, Luis
b. 1948 Bradshaw, Terry Paxton
b. 1948 McAuliffe, Christa
b. 1951 Harmon, Mark
b. 1952 Connors, Jimmy
b. 1953 Danelo, Joe
b. 1955 Gordon, Pamela (Felicity)
b. 1955 Purl, Linda
b. 1960 Dickerson, Eric Demetric
b. 1961 Lang, K(atherine) D(awn)
b. 1972 Mohajer, Dineh
d. 1652 Ribera, Jusepe (Jose) de
d. 1765 Bouquet, Henry

d. 1793 Brown, William Hill
d. 1845 Rivadavia, Bernardino
d. 1859 Bacon, Delia Salter
d. 1865 Hamilton, William Rowan, Sir
d. 1870 Maverick, Samuel Augustus
d. 1910 Rousseau, Henri
d. 1921 Dobson, Henry Austin
d. 1922 Lawson, Henry (Archibald Hertzberg)
d. 1924 Shiras, George, Jr.
d. 1931 Schalk, Franz
d. 1934 Columbo, Russ
d. 1935 Bradley, Andrew Cecil
d. 1940 Gatti-Casazza, Giulio
d. 1943 Hartley, Marsden
d. 1953 Wainwright, Jonathan Mayhew
d. 1957 Freuchen, Peter
d. 1958 Palmer, Frederick
d. 1962 Blair, William Richards
d. 1966 Roberts, Gordon
d. 1967 Ouimet, Francis de Sales
d. 1969 Pike, James Albert, Bishop
d. 1973 Tolkien, J(ohn) R(onald) R(euel)
d. 1974 Soyer, Moses
d. 1981 Lyons, Enid Muriel
d. 1982 Schaefer, Rudolph Jay
d. 1985 Burns, Eveline Mabel
d. 1991 Garcia Robles, Alfonso
d. 1991 Jackson, Laura Riding
d. 1991 Riding, Laura
d. 1992 Harbert, Chick
d. 1992 Jaroszewicz, Piotr
d. 1992 McClintock, Barbara
d. 1994 McAfee, Mildred H(elen)
d. 1994 TallMountain, Mary
d. 1996 Kirbo, Charles H(ughes)
d. 1996 Luening, Otto
d. 1996 Morrison, Sterling
d. 1997 Bing, Rudolf (Franz Josef), Sir
d. 1997 Frankl, Viktor E(mil)
d. 1998 Drury, Allen (Stuart)

September 3
b. 1693 Locatelli, Pietro Antonio
b. 1724 Carleton, Guy

b. 1728 Boulton, Matthew
b. 1735 Bach, Johann Christian
b. 1803 Crandall, Prudence
b. 1810 Kane, Paul
b. 1811 Noyes, John Humphrey
b. 1814 Sylvester, James Joseph
b. 1820 Hearst, George
b. 1849 Jewett, Sarah Orne
b. 1856 Sullivan, Louis Henri
b. 1859 Jaures, Jean Leon
b. 1859 Pregl, Fritz
b. 1860 Filene, Edward Albert
b. 1871 Kupka, Frank
b. 1874 Stormer, Fredrik (Carl Mulertz)
b. 1875 Porsche, Ferdinand
b. 1883 Arnold, Harold De Forest
b. 1888 Rivers, Thomas Milton
b. 1891 Delany, Annie Elizabeth
b. 1894 Niebuhr, Helmut Richard
b. 1895 Houston, Charles Hamilton
b. 1898 Parker, Cecil
b. 1899 Benson, Ezra Taft
b. 1899 Burnet, F(rank) MacFarlane, Sir
b. 1900 Beinum, Eduard van
b. 1900 Benson, Sally
b. 1903 Bolz, Lothar
b. 1905 Anderson, Carl David
b. 1906 Powell, Lawrence Clark
b. 1907 Eiseley, Loren Corey
b. 1907 Mizener, Arthur Moore
b. 1909 Bazelon, David L(ionel)
b. 1910 Maynor, Dorothy
b. 1912 Fisher, James Maxwell McConnell
b. 1913 Ladd, Alan
b. 1914 Ray, Dixy Lee
b. 1915 Carlisle, Kitty
b. 1916 Bentley, Doug(las Wagner)
b. 1916 Knight, Arthur
b. 1916 Memphis Slim
b. 1916 Stanky, Eddie
b. 1920 Higgins, Marguerite
b. 1921 Bellmon, Henry Louis
b. 1921 Dart, Thurston
b. 1921 Orkin, Ruth
b. 1923 Walker, Mort

b. 1925 Thompson,
Hank
b. 1926 Flemming, Bill
b. 1926 Jackson, Anne
b. 1926 Lurie, Alison
b. 1926 Papas, Irene
b. 1927 Sidey, Hugh
Swanson
b. 1928 Thorn, Gaston
b. 1931 DeSalvo, Albert
b. 1931 Motta, Dick
b. 1934 King, Freddy
b. 1935? Brennan,
Eileen Regina
b. 1938 Churchill, Caryl
b. 1939 Nicholas,
Nicholas John, Jr.
b. 1940 Galeano,
Eduardo (Hughes)
b. 1942 Jardine, Al(lan)
b. 1943 McCoo,
Marilyn
b. 1943 Perrine, Valerie
b. 1957 Ancier, Garth
b. 1965 Santiago,
Benito
b. 1965 Sheen, Charlie
d. 1588 Tarlton, Richard
d. 1592 Greene, Robert
d. 1634 Coke, Edward,
Sir
d. 1658 Cromwell,
Oliver
d. 1815 Murray, John
d. 1820 Latrobe,
Benjamin Henry
d. 1857 McLoughlin,
John
d. 1877 Thiers, Adolphe
d. 1881 Delmonico,
Lorenzo
d. 1883 Turgenev, Ivan
Sergeevich
d. 1924 Wagnalls,
Adam Willis
d. 1939 Westermarck,
Edward Alexander
d. 1942 James, Will(iam
Roderick)
d. 1943 Moisseiff, Leon
Solomon
d. 1943 Pallette, Eugene
d. 1944 Norris, George
William
d. 1946 Rosenthal,
Moriz
d. 1948 Benes, Eduard
d. 1949 Short, Walter
Campbell
d. 1961 Gross, Robert
Ellsworth
d. 1962 Cummings,
E(dward) E(stlin)
d. 1963 MacNeice,
Louis
d. 1964 Hayes, Carlton
Joseph Huntley
d. 1964 Holbrook,
Stewart Hall
d. 1967 Dunn, James
Howard
d. 1969 Ho Chi Minh
d. 1970 Lombardi,
Vince(nt Thomas)
d. 1974 Partch, Harry

d. 1979 Capehart,
Homer Earl
d. 1980 Renaldo,
Duncan
d. 1981 Roszak,
Theodore
d. 1981 Waugh, Alec
d. 1982 Dannay,
Frederic
d. 1984 Schwartz,
Arthur
d. 1985 Jones,
Jo(nathan)
d. 1985 Marks, Johnny
d. 1987 Feldman,
Morton
d. 1987 Fry, E Maxwell
d. 1991 Capra, Frank
d. 1992 Rauh, Joseph
Louis, Jr.
d. 1994 Aubrey, James
(Thomas), Jr.

September 4
b. 518?BC Pindar
b. 973 Biruni, Abu
Rayhan al-
b. 1768 Chateaubriand,
Francois Rene de
b. 1801 D'Orsay, Alfred
Guillaume, Count
b. 1802 Whitman,
Marcus
b. 1803 Polk, Sarah
Childress
b. 1804 Walter, Thomas
Ustick
b. 1810 McKay, Donald
b. 1824 Bruckner,
Anton
b. 1824 Bruckner,
Joseph Anton
b. 1824 Cary, Phoebe
b. 1846 Burnham,
Daniel H(udson)
b. 1848 Bowker,
R(ichard) R(ogers)
b. 1862 Kerr, Alexander
H
b. 1864 Ittner, William
Butts
b. 1866 Lake, Simon
b. 1876 Kirby, Rollin
b. 1882 Knerr, H(arold)
H
b. 1892 Milhaud, Darius
b. 1892 Smith, Pete
b. 1895 Xiang Jingyu
b. 1896 Artaud, Antonin
b. 1898 Ayres, Agnes
b. 1898 Rankin, K(arl)
L(ott)
b. 1899 Kaminska, Ida
b. 1900 Love, George
Hutchinson
b. 1901 Lyons, William,
Sir
b. 1901 Osborn, Paul
b. 1904 Carr, Sabin
b. 1904 Christian-
Jacque
b. 1904 Gombrowicz,
Witold
b. 1905 Lewis, Meade
Anderson Lux
b. 1905 Renault, Mary
b. 1906 Delbruck, Max

b. 1907 Griffin, Marvin
b. 1908 Dmytryk,
Edward
b. 1908 Wright, Richard
(Nathaniel)
b. 1910 Celebrezze,
Anthony J(oseph)
b. 1912 Hoff, Sydney
b. 1912 Liberman,
Alexander
(Semeonovitch)
b. 1913 Cohen, Mickey
b. 1913 Moore, Stanford
b. 1913 Savitt, Jan
b. 1913 Tange, Kenzo
b. 1914 Hutson, Jean
Blackwell
b. 1916 Lowndes,
Robert A(ugustine)
W(ard)
b. 1917 Ford, Henry, II
b. 1918 Harvey, Paul
b. 1919 Morris, Howard
b. 1920 Claiborne,
Craig
b. 1924 Aiken, Joan
Delano
b. 1924 Kraft, Joseph
b. 1925 Hrawi, Elias
b. 1926 Illich, Ivan
b. 1926 Keough, Donald
Raymond
b. 1926 Olmstead, Bert
b. 1926 Petersen,
Donald Eugene
b. 1927 McCarthy, John
b. 1928 Rausch, James
Stevens
b. 1928 York, Dick
b. 1929 Eagleton,
Thomas Francis
b. 1931 Gaynor, Mitzi
b. 1933 Castellano,
Richard
b. 1934 Sawyer,
Eugene, Jr.
b. 1937 Fraser, Dawn
b. 1940 Tribble, Isreal,
Jr.
b. 1941 Harrelson,
Ken(neth Smith)
b. 1944 Salt, Jennifer
b. 1945 Edelin, Ramona
Hoage
b. 1949 Watson, Tom
b. 1950 LaPread,
Ronald
b. 1950 White, Frank,
Jr.
b. 1951 Ivey, Judith
b. 1951 Reese, Don(ald
Francis)
b. 1952 Romero
Barcelo, Carlos
Antonio
b. 1955 Schiavo, Mary
(Fackler)
b. 1956 Gould, Shane
b. 1963 Vanbiesbrouck,
John
b. 1964 Reeves, Keanu
b. 1965 Boyd, John W.,
Jr.
b. 1968 Piazza, Mike
d. 1588 Leicester, Earl
of

d. 1821 Carrera, Jose
Miguel
d. 1846 Jouy, Victor
(Joseph-Etienne) de
d. 1849 Monk, Maria
d. 1851 Woodbury, Levi
d. 1864 Long, Stephen
H
d. 1902 Eggleston,
Edward
d. 1904 Heade, Martin
Johnson
d. 1907 Grieg, Edvard
Hagerup
d. 1909 Fitch, (William)
Clyde
d. 1913 Brown, Henry
Billings
d. 1932 Bern, Paul
d. 1938 Hayes, Patrick
Joseph, Cardinal
d. 1944 Bianco,
Margery Williams
d. 1951 Adamic, Louis
d. 1952 Sforza, Carlo
d. 1963 Schuman,
Robert
d. 1965 Schweitzer,
Albert
d. 1971 Gladstone,
James
d. 1971 Hickenlooper,
Bourke B
d. 1973 Behn, Harry
d. 1974 Abrams,
Creighton Williams
d. 1974 Achard, Marcel
d. 1977 Schumacher,
E(rnst) F(riedrich)
d. 1982 Tworkov, Jack
d. 1984 Kane, Harnett
T(homas)
d. 1985 McCormick,
Robert K
d. 1985 O'Brien,
George
d. 1986 Greenberg,
Hank
d. 1987 Marquand,
Richard
d. 1989 Simenon,
Georges
d. 1990 Dunne, Irene
Marie
d. 1990 Whitman,
Alden
d. 1991 Barnet, Charlie
d. 1991 Tryon, Thomas
d. 1991 West, Dottie
d. 1992 Gillenson,
Lewis W
d. 1993 Villechaize,
Herve Jean Pierre
d. 1995 Henry, David
D(odds)
d. 1995 Kunstler,
William M(oses)
d. 1997 Eysenck, Hans
J(urgen)

September 5
b. 1568 Campanella,
Tommaso
b. 1733 Wieland,
Christoph Martin
b. 1745 Kutuzov,
Mikhail Ilarionovich

b. 1774 Friedrich, Caspar David
b. 1791 Meyerbeer, Giacomo
b. 1804 Graham, William Alexander
b. 1807 Trench, Richard Chenevix
b. 1825 Mills, Darius Ogden
b. 1833 Hartford, George Huntington
b. 1835 Carlisle, John Griffin
b. 1847 James, Jesse Woodson
b. 1856 Watson, Thomas Edward
b. 1861 Raleigh, Walter Alexander, Sir
b. 1867 Beach, H H A, Mrs.
b. 1875 Lajoie, Nap(oleon)
b. 1879 Jewett, Frank Baldwin
b. 1879 Rogers, Will(iam Penn Adair)
b. 1883 Petri, Angelo
b. 1885 Defauw, Desire
b. 1885 Wylie, Elinor Hoyt
b. 1891 Molyneux, Edward H
b. 1891 Roberts, Gordon
b. 1893 Rosenberg, Jakob
b. 1893 Sokolsky, George E
b. 1896 VonDoderer, Heimito
b. 1897 Carnovsky, Morris
b. 1897 Nielsen, Arthur Charles
b. 1898 Carlson, William Hugh
b. 1901 Bailey, Donald Coleman, Sir
b. 1901 Eldridge, Florence
b. 1902 Zanuck, Darryl Francis
b. 1904 Basso, Hamilton
b. 1905 Koestler, Arthur
b. 1907 Blough, Glenn Orlando
b. 1907 Douglass, Lathrop
b. 1912 Cage, John
b. 1913 Andrews, Wayne
b. 1914 Parra, Nicanor
b. 1916 Shuster, Frank
b. 1916 Yerby, Frank (Garvin)
b. 1921 Valenti, Jack Joseph
b. 1925 Kaplan, Justin
b. 1927 Volcker, Paul Adolph
b. 1929 Nikolayev, Andriyan Grigoryevich

b. 1929 Schultz, Richard D(ale)
b. 1935 Erhard, Werner
b. 1935 Just, Ward
b. 1935 Lawrence, Carol
b. 1936 Danforth, John Claggett
b. 1936 Hastings, Alcee L
b. 1936 Kennedy, Joan Bennett
b. 1936 Kozol, Jonathan
b. 1936 Mazeroski, Bill
b. 1937 Neal, Larry
b. 1938 Ferguson, John Bowie
b. 1939 Devane, William
b. 1939 Stewart, John
b. 1939 Tonegawa, Susumu
b. 1940 Welch, Raquel
b. 1941 Boudjedra, Rachid
b. 1942 Herzog, Werner
b. 1945 Stewart, Al
b. 1946 Miles, Buddy
b. 1947 Wainwright, Loudon, III
b. 1950 Guisewite, Cathy Lee
b. 1956 Denton, Steve
b. 1960 Gault, Willie James
b. 1965 Nolan, Christopher
b. 1969 Zappa, Dweezil
d. 1566 Suleiman I
d. 1846 Metcalfe, Charles Theophilus
d. 1857 Comte, Auguste
d. 1857 Duff, Mary Ann Dyke
d. 1877 Crazy Horse
d. 1885 Tso Tsung-t'ang
d. 1894 Stoneman, George
d. 1898 Edmonds, Emma E
d. 1905 Virchow, Rudolf
d. 1906 Boltzmann, Ludwig
d. 1910 Haberl, Franz Xaver
d. 1912 MacArthur, Arthur
d. 1914 Peguy, Charles Pierre
d. 1927 Loew, Marcus
d. 1930 Hagen, Johann Georg
d. 1932 LaFlesche, Francis
d. 1933 Journet, Marcel
d. 1937 Bergey, David Hendricks
d. 1943 Hrdlicka, Ales
d. 1948 Tolman, Richard C(hace)
d. 1949 Hoagland, Dennis Robert
d. 1949 Minsky, Abraham Bennett

d. 1952 Robinson, Boardman
d. 1957 Parrish, Anne
d. 1960 Long, Earl Kemp
d. 1964 Flynn, Elizabeth Gurley
d. 1965 Sullivan, C(harles) Gardner
d. 1966 Cecchi, Emilio
d. 1967 DeJong, David Cornel
d. 1969 Ayres, Mitchell
d. 1969 White, Josh(ua Daniel)
d. 1970 Rindt, Jochen
d. 1971 Trafton, George
d. 1972 Berger, David
d. 1972 Friedman, Ze'ev
d. 1972 Gutfreund, Yosef
d. 1972 Halfin, Eliezer
d. 1972 Romano, Joseph
d. 1972 Shapira, Amitzur
d. 1972 Shorr, Kehat
d. 1972 Slavin, Mark
d. 1972 Spitzer, Andre
d. 1972 Springer, Ya'acov
d. 1972 Weinberg, Moshe
d. 1974 Swinnerton, James Guilford
d. 1975 Evans, Alice (Catherine)
d. 1977 Batchelor, Clarence Daniel
d. 1977 Foley, Martha
d. 1979 Bolton, Guy Reginald
d. 1980 Loden, Barbara Ann
d. 1981 Maeght, Aime
d. 1982 Bader, Douglas Robert Steuart, Sir
d. 1982 Sebelius, Keith George
d. 1985 Morse, Philip McCord
d. 1987 Martin, Quinn
d. 1988 Frobe, Gerd
d. 1992 Herman, Billy
d. 1992 Leiber, Fritz (Reuter), Jr.
d. 1997 Edel, Leon
d. 1997 Solti, Georg, Sir
d. 1997 Teresa, Mother
d. 1999 Funt, Allen

September 6
b. 1711 Muhlenberg, Heinrich Melchior
b. 1729 Mendelssohn, Moses
b. 1757 Lafayette, Marie Joseph Paul, Marquis
b. 1766 Dalton, John
b. 1795 Wright, Frances
b. 1800 Beecher, Catharine (Esther)
b. 1805 Greenough, Horatio

b. 1811 Gilliss, James Melville
b. 1814 Cartier, Georges Etienne, Sir
b. 1817 Galt, Alexander Tilloch
b. 1819 Rosecrans, William Starke
b. 1857 Nuttall, Zelia Maria Magdalena
b. 1860 Addams, Jane
b. 1868 Bolden, Buddy
b. 1869 Davies, Henry Walford, Sir
b. 1869 Salten, Felix
b. 1870 Halevy, Elie
b. 1873 Coffin, Howard Earle
b. 1875 Fuller, Ida
b. 1875 Train, Arthur Cheney
b. 1876 MacLeod, John James Rickard
b. 1876 Robinson, Boardman
b. 1878 Canby, Henry Seidel
b. 1882 Marks, Charles
b. 1885 Kruger, Otto
b. 1888 Faber, Red
b. 1888 Kennedy, Joseph Patrick, Sr.
b. 1890 Chennault, Claire Lee
b. 1890? Weldon, John
b. 1891 Thomas, John Charles
b. 1892 Appleton, Edward Victor, Sir
b. 1893 Bricker, John William
b. 1895 Dornberger, Walter Robert
b. 1896 Praz, Mario
b. 1899 Rose, Billy
b. 1900 Bennett, W(illiam) A(ndrew) C(ecil)
b. 1900 Green, Julian (Hartridge)
b. 1900 Harand, Irene
b. 1901 Jonsson, John Erik
b. 1901 Weber, Ernst
b. 1902 Beatty, Morgan
b. 1903 Sananikone, Phoui
b. 1904 Rosenbloom, Maxie
b. 1906 Leloir, Luis Federico
b. 1908 Essen, Louis
b. 1908 Lavalle, Paul
b. 1908 Ziolkowski, Korczak
b. 1909 Gordon, Michael
b. 1911 Lipsky, Eleazar
b. 1912 DiMaggio, Vince(nt Paul)
b. 1915 Strauss, Franz Josef
b. 1917 Smith, (Charles) Page
b. 1921 Laforet (Diaz), Carmen

b. 1923 Peter II
b. 1924 Melcher, John
b. 1928 Pirsig, Robert M(aynard)
b. 1928 Svetlanov, Evgeni Fyodorovich
b. 1929 Finsterwald, Dow
b. 1937 Worley, Jo Anne
b. 1938 Tower, Joan Peabody
b. 1939 Coe, David Allan
b. 1939 Mark, Norman (Barry)
b. 1944 Kurtz, Swoosie
b. 1946 Boone, Ron(ald Bruce)
b. 1947 Curtin, Jane (Therese)
b. 1948 Smith, Claydes
b. 1958 Foxworthy, Jeff
d. 1683 Colbert, Jean-Baptiste
d. 1782 Jefferson, Martha (Wayles Skelton)
d. 1869 Rawlins, John A
d. 1893 Fish, Hamilton
d. 1923 Dutton, E(dward) P(ayson)
d. 1932 Parker, Gilbert, Sir
d. 1937 Hadley, Henry Kimball
d. 1944 Tietjens, Eunice
d. 1950 Stapledon, Olaf
d. 1952 Lawrence, Gertrude
d. 1956 Raymond, Alex(ander Gillespie)
d. 1957 Salvemini, Gaetano
d. 1959 Gwenn, Edmund
d. 1959 Kendall, Kay
d. 1960 Savo, Jimmy
d. 1966 Menninger, William C
d. 1966 Sanger, Margaret
d. 1966 Verwoerd, Hendrik F
d. 1967 Gibbs, William Francis
d. 1968 Akimov, Nikolay Pavlovich
d. 1968 Sexton, Leo
d. 1971 Hawes, Elizabeth
d. 1974 Baclanova, Olga
d. 1974 Kruger, Otto
d. 1975 Croft, Arthur C
d. 1977 Wummer, John
d. 1981 Brown, Christy
d. 1983 Hazam, Lou(is J)
d. 1984 Feld, Irvin
d. 1984 Tubb, Ernest
d. 1985 Desmond, Johnny
d. 1985 Porter, Rodney Robert

d. 1986 Sweet, Blanche
d. 1987 Chute, Beatrice Joy
d. 1987 Haley, William John, Sir
d. 1990 Fogerty, John
d. 1992 Ephron, Henry
d. 1994 Clavell, James (Edmund Du Maresq)
d. 1998 Kurosawa, Akira

September 7
b. 1533 Elizabeth I
b. 1707 Buffon, Georges Louis Leclerc
b. 1726 Philidor, Francois Andre Danican
b. 1814 Butterfield, William
b. 1819 Hendricks, Thomas Andrews
b. 1829 Kekule, Friedrich August
b. 1831 Sardou, Victorien
b. 1836 Campbell-Bannerman, Henry, Sir
b. 1840 Crowell, Luther Childs
b. 1855 Friese-Greene, William Edward
b. 1867 Morgan, J(ohn) P(ierpont), Jr.
b. 1870 Kuprin, Aleksandr Ivanovich
b. 1873 Becker, Carl Lotus
b. 1876 Darwin, Bernard Richard Meirion
b. 1877 Stone, George Robert
b. 1887 Sitwell, Edith, Dame
b. 1890 Komroff, Manuel
b. 1893 Hore-Belisha, Leslie, Baron
b. 1893 Karns, Roscoe
b. 1895 Harrison, William Kelly, Jr.
b. 1895 Horrocks, Brian Gwynne, Sir
b. 1898 Robinson, Henry Morton
b. 1900 Caldwell, Taylor
b. 1903 Landon, Margaret (Dorothea Mortenson)
b. 1904 Colby, Carroll Burleigh
b. 1905 Priest, Ivy (Maude) Baker
b. 1905 Sommer, Frederick
b. 1907 Neddermeyer, Seth H
b. 1908 DeBakey, Michael Ellis
b. 1908 Kaminsky, Max
b. 1909 Kazan, Elia

b. 1910 Stahl, Ben(jamin Albert)
b. 1911 Haughton, Daniel Jeremiah
b. 1911 Zhivkov, Todor Khristov
b. 1912 Packard, David
b. 1913 Crowe, Colin Tradescant, Sir
b. 1913 Quayle, (John) Anthony, Sir
b. 1914 Van Allen, James Alfred
b. 1915 Gardner, Isabella
b. 1917 Cornforth, John Warcup, Sir
b. 1918 Swearingen, John Eldred
b. 1921 Ferrante, Arthur
b. 1921 Harris, MacDonald
b. 1923 Lawford, Peter
b. 1923 Suggs, Louise
b. 1924 Aitken, Hugh
b. 1924 Inouye, Daniel Ken
b. 1925? Ashley, Laura Mountney
b. 1925 Jastrow, Robert
b. 1928 McGuire, Al
b. 1929 Neal, James Foster
b. 1930 Baudouin, I, King
b. 1930 Rollins, Sonny
b. 1932 Bradbury, Malcolm Stanley
b. 1934 Cardona, Manuel
b. 1935 Diouf, Abdou
b. 1936 Holly, Buddy
b. 1937 Law, John Phillip
b. 1942 Roundtree, Richard
b. 1945 Lemaire, Jacques Gerald
b. 1946 Rudi, Joe
b. 1947 Tilberis, Elizabeth
b. 1948 Blakely, Susan
b. 1948 Brockington, John Stanley
b. 1949 Gaynor, Gloria
b. 1950 Bradley, David Henry, Jr.
b. 1950 Noonan, Peggy
b. 1951? Hynde, Chrissie
b. 1951 Jones, Bert(ram Hays)
b. 1951 Kavner, Julie Deborah
b. 1955 Bernsen, Corbin
b. 1956 Feinstein, Michael Jay
b. 1963 Eazy-E
d. 1799 Ingenhousz, Jan
d. 1866 Baldwin, Matthias William
d. 1872 Thayer, Sylvanus, General
d. 1881 Lanier, Sidney
d. 1891 Graetz, Heinrich Hirsch

d. 1892 Whittier, John Greenleaf
d. 1907 Lee-Hamilton, Eugene Jacob
d. 1907 Sully Prudhomme
d. 1909 Lassale, Jean
d. 1910 Blackwell, Emily
d. 1910 Hunt, Holman
d. 1922 Cobden-Sanderson, Thomas James
d. 1922 Halsted, William Stewart
d. 1933 Grey of Fallodon, Edward, Viscount
d. 1936 Le Chatelier, Henry-Louis
d. 1941 Roosevelt, Sara Delano
d. 1949 Orozco, Jose Clemente
d. 1951 Montez, Maria
d. 1954 Fisher, Bud
d. 1954 Warner, Pop
d. 1955 Bernstein, Alice Frankau
d. 1956 Fry, Charles Burgess
d. 1957 Helland-Hansen, Bjorn
d. 1959 Duplessis, Maurice le Noblet
d. 1960 Pieck, Wilhelm
d. 1962 Blixen, Karen Christentze, Baroness
d. 1962 Louis, Morris
d. 1964 Brown, Walter Augustine
d. 1968 Brinton, Clarence Crane
d. 1969 Dirksen, Everett McKinley
d. 1970 MacMillan, Donald Baxter
d. 1970 Spencer, Percy Le Baron
d. 1971 Byington, Spring
d. 1973 Holling, Holling C(lancy)
d. 1978 Moon, Keith
d. 1979 Richards, Ivor Armstrong
d. 1981 Link, Edwin Albert
d. 1982 Benjamin, Adam, Jr.
d. 1982 Boyer, Ken(ton Lloyd)
d. 1984 Cronin, Joe
d. 1984 O'Flaherty, Liam
d. 1985 Polya, George
d. 1985 Waterhouse, Ellis Kirkham, Sir
d. 1987 Jennings, Paul Joseph
d. 1990 Taylor, A(lan) J(ohn) P(ercivale)
d. 1991 Crosby, John Campbell
d. 1991 McMillan, Edwin Mattison

d. 1996 Flemming,
Arthur S(herwood)
d. 1997 Crockett,
George (William), Jr.
d. 1997 Mobutu Sese
Seko
September 8
b. 1157 Richard I
b. 1380 Bernardine of
Siena, Saint
b. 1474 Ariosto,
Ludovico
b. 1573 Caravaggio,
Michelangelo da
b. 1621 Conde, Prince
de
b. 1643 Burnet, Gilbert
b. 1778 Brentano,
Clemens Maria
b. 1804 Morike, Eduard
Friedrich
b. 1828 Sage, Margaret
Olivia
b. 1830 Mistral,
Frederic
b. 1837 Miller, Joaquin
b. 1841 Dvorak, Anton
b. 1844 Guiteau,
Charles Julius
b. 1863 Jacobs,
W(illiam) W(ymark)
b. 1864 Hobhouse,
Leonard Trelawny
b. 1873 McKay, David
O
b. 1873 Salvemini,
Gaetano
b. 1876 Thomas, Elmer
b. 1886 Sassoon,
Siegfried
b. 1887 Devers, Jacob
Loucks
b. 1889 Taft, Robert
A(lphonso)
b. 1896 Dietz, Howard
M
b. 1897 Rodgers,
Jimmie
b. 1900 Pepper, Claude
Denson
b. 1901 McAvoy, May
b. 1901 Verwoerd,
Hendrik F
b. 1902 Kaplan, Joseph
b. 1904 Cousins, Frank
b. 1905 Elder, Ruth
b. 1905 Glennan,
T(homas) Keith
b. 1905 Quill, Mike
b. 1905 Wilcoxon,
Henry
b. 1906 Prescott, Orville
b. 1907 Leonard, Buck
b. 1908 Briggs, Austin
Eugene
b. 1910 Barrault, Jean-
Louis
b. 1911 Gibbons, Euell
b. 1912 Cherne, Leo
b. 1914 Albrand,
Martha
b. 1914 Brooke, Hillary
b. 1914 Dimitrios I,
Patriarch
b. 1915 Daugherty,
Duffy

b. 1918 Barton, Derek
H(arold) R(ichard),
Sir
b. 1919 Bowker, Albert
Hosmer
b. 1921 Secombe, Harry
b. 1922 Caesar, Sid
b. 1922 Larouche,
Lyndon Hermyle, Jr.
b. 1922 Pierce, Samuel
Riley, Jr.
b. 1924 Ford, Wendell
Hampton
b. 1924 Metalious,
Grace de Repentigny
b. 1925 Darcel, Denise
b. 1925 Sellers, Peter
b. 1927 Altizer, Thomas
J(onathan) J(ackson)
b. 1929 Dohnanyi,
Christoph von
b. 1930 Ky, Nguyen
Cao
b. 1931 Washam,
Wisner McCamey
b. 1932 Cline, Patsy
b. 1933 Frayn, Michael
b. 1934 Davies, Peter
Maxwell
b. 1937 Frum, Barbara
b. 1937 Lisi, Virna
b. 1937 Wexner, Leslie
b. 1938 Nunn, Sam(uel
Augustus, Jr.)
b. 1941 Connelly,
Christopher
b. 1941 Sanders,
Bernard
b. 1945 Barney,
Lem(uel Jackson)
b. 1945 Vachon, Rogie
b. 1946 Forsch,
Ken(neth Roth)
b. 1946 McKernan, Ron
b. 1946 Mercury,
Freddie
b. 1947 Beattie, Ann
b. 1947 Lavelle, Rita
Marie
b. 1950 Richard,
Zachary
b. 1960 Casiraghi,
Stefano
b. 1966 Robinson,
Patrick
b. 1972 Thomas, Henry
b. 1975 Tate, Larenz
b. 1981 Thomas,
Jonathan Taylor
d. 1613 Gesualdo, Carlo
d. 1645 Quevado y
Villegas, Francisco
Gomez de
d. 1654 Claver, Peter
d. 1784 Lee, Ann
d. 1853 Ozanam,
(Antoine) Frederic
d. 1869 Fessenden,
William Pitt
d. 1879 Hunt, William
Morris
d. 1894 Helmholtz,
Hermann Ludwig
Ferdinand von
d. 1933 Chesebrough,
Robert Augustus

d. 1933 Faisal, I
d. 1933 Parkhurst,
Charles Henry
d. 1935 Doheny,
Edward Lawrence
d. 1937 Branch, Anna
Hempstead
d. 1939 Gilman,
Lawrence
d. 1945 Cret, Paul
P(hilippe)
d. 1946 Eustis, Dorothy
Leib Harrison Wood
d. 1948 Mofolo,
Thomas (Mokopu)
d. 1949 Strauss, Richard
Georg
d. 1951 Hewitt, William
Archibald
d. 1951 Sloan, John F
d. 1953 Vinson,
Frederick Moore
d. 1960 Pettiford, Oscar
d. 1964 Singer, Burns
James Hyman
d. 1965 Cowen, Joshua
Lionel
d. 1965 Dandridge,
Dorothy
d. 1969 Collyer, Bud
d. 1969 David-Neel,
Alexandra
d. 1969 Varley,
F(rederick)
H(orseman)
d. 1974 Windgassen,
Wolfgang Friedrich
Hermann
d. 1977 Mostel, Zero
d. 1978 Torre-Nilsson,
Leopoldo
d. 1980 Libby, Willard
Frank
d. 1981 Wilkins, Roy
d. 1981 Yukawa, Hideki
d. 1982 Abdullah,
Mohammad, Sheik
d. 1983 Abboud, (El
Ferik) Ibrahim
d. 1985 Enders, John
Franklin
d. 1991 Davis, Brad
d. 1991 North, Alex
d. 1992 Barrett, William
Christopher
d. 1992 Burdick,
Quentin Northrop
d. 1995 Ode, Robert C
d. 1996 Burns, John
L(awrence)
d. 1999 Hardin, Louis
Thomas
d. 1999 Stein, Herbert
September 9
b. 1585 Richelieu,
Armand Jean du
Plessis, Cardinal
b. 1711 Hutchinson,
Thomas
b. 1721 Pendleton,
Edmund
b. 1737 Galvani, Luigi
b. 1754 Bligh, William,
Captain
b. 1816 Fee, John
Gregg

b. 1823 Leidy, Joseph
b. 1825 Lea, Henry
Charles
b. 1828 Tolstoy, Leo
Nikolayevich
b. 1834 Shorthouse,
Joseph Henry
b. 1842 Coues, Elliott
b. 1850 Lawson, Victor
Fremont
b. 1852 Poynting, John
Henry
b. 1855 Chamberlain,
Houston Stewart
b. 1857 Hervieu, Paul-
Ernest
b. 1868 Austin, Mary
Hunter
b. 1870 Pears, Charles
b. 1873 Reinhardt, Max
b. 1877 Agate, James
Evershed
b. 1877 Chance, Frank
Leroy
b. 1878 Crapsey,
Adelaide
b. 1878 Osmena,
Sergio, Jr.
b. 1882 McCarthy,
Clem
b. 1885 Sheridan, Clare
Consuelo
b. 1886 Wheelock, John
Hall
b. 1887 Landon, Alf(red
Mossman)
b. 1887 Walburn,
Raymond
b. 1890 Eccles,
Marriner Stoddard
b. 1890 Lewin, Kurt
b. 1890 Sanders,
Colonel
b. 1891 Marks, Percy
b. 1894 Freed, Arthur
b. 1898 Bridges, Styles
b. 1898 Frisch, Frankie
b. 1898 Nichols,
Beverley
b. 1899 Brassai
b. 1899 Hamilton, Neil
b. 1899 Hoyt, Waite
Charles
b. 1899 Smith, Cyrus
Rowlett
b. 1900 Hilton, James
b. 1901 Hicks, Granville
b. 1903 Whitney,
Phyllis Ayame
b. 1905 Levine, Joseph
Edward
b. 1907 Edel, Leon
b. 1908 Lorjou, Bernard
Joseph Pierre
b. 1908 Pavese, Cesare
b. 1908 Tomlin, Pinky
b. 1911 Goodman, Paul
b. 1911 Gorton, John
Grey, Sir
b. 1917 Robbins, Frank
b. 1918 Scalfaro, Oscar
Luigi
b. 1919 Snyder, Jimmy
the Greek
b. 1920 Aldridge,
Michael

b. 1921 Prather, Richard Scott
b. 1922 Dehmelt, Hans Georg
b. 1923 Gajdusek, D(aniel) Carleton
b. 1924 Greer, Jane
b. 1925 Poirier, Richard
b. 1925 Robertson, Cliff
b. 1926 Duncan, Charles William, Jr.
b. 1927 Jones, Elvin
b. 1928 Adderley, Cannonball
b. 1928 LeWitt, Sol
b. 1930 Morefield, Richard H
b. 1931 Tyzack, Margaret Maud
b. 1932 Miles, Sylvia
b. 1934 Chandler, Don(ald G)
b. 1934 Sanchez, Sonia (Benita)
b. 1935 Topol, Chaim
b. 1940 Smith, Dennis
b. 1941 Redding, Otis
b. 1944 Rodin, Judith
b. 1946 Preston, Billy
b. 1949 Curry, John (Anthony)
b. 1949 Theismann, Joe
b. 1951 Keaton, Michael
b. 1951 Wopat, Tom
b. 1952 Cartwright, Angela
b. 1954 Davis, Walter Paul
b. 1960 Grant, Hugh
b. 1962 McNichol, Kristy
b. 1965 Majerle, Dan
b. 1966 Sandler, Adam
b. 1969 Pepa
d. 1513 James IV
d. 1583 Gilbert, Humphrey, Sir
d. 1806 Paterson, William
d. 1815 Copley, John Singleton
d. 1817 Cuffe, Paul
d. 1834 Weddell, James
d. 1841 Candolle, Augustin Pyrame de
d. 1871 Watie, Stand
d. 1888 Savage, John
d. 1898 Mallarme, Stephane
d. 1901 Toulouse-Lautrec (Monfa), (Henri Marie Raymond de)
d. 1909 Harriman, Edward Henry
d. 1915 Spalding, Albert Goodwill
d. 1919 Mitchell, John
d. 1929 Quinn, Edmond T
d. 1933 Hart, George Overbury
d. 1934 Fry, Roger Eliot

d. 1939 Smith, Christopher Columbus
d. 1943 Andrews, Charles McLean
d. 1947 Coomaraswamy, Ananda Kentish
d. 1956 Hughes, Rupert
d. 1960 Bjoerling, Jussi
d. 1962 Rooney, Pat
d. 1963 Fuess, Claude Moore
d. 1965 Staudinger, Hermann
d. 1975 McGiver, John
d. 1976 Mao Zedong
d. 1977 O'Donnell, Kenneth P
d. 1978 MacDiarmid, Hugh
d. 1978 Warner, Jack Leonard
d. 1979 Larsen, Roy Edward
d. 1980 Clurman, Harold Edgar
d. 1980 Griffin, John Howard
d. 1981 Lacan, Jacques (Marie Emile)
d. 1985 Flory, Paul John
d. 1985 McNair, Malcolm Perrine
d. 1987 Fingesten, Peter
d. 1990 Doe, Samuel Kanyon
d. 1991 Mason, Belinda
d. 1995 Douglas-Home, Alexander Frederick, Sir
d. 1996 Monroe, Bill
d. 1997 Ashburn, Richie
d. 1997 Meredith, Burgess
d. 1999 Hunter, Catfish
d. 1999 Roman, Ruth

September 10
b. 1487 Julius III, Pope
b. 1624 Sydenham, Thomas
b. 1714 Jommelli, Niccolo
b. 1736 Braxton, Carter
b. 1753 Soane, John, Sir
b. 1771 Park, Mungo
b. 1787 Crittenden, John Jordan
b. 1828 Simmons, Zalmon G
b. 1836 Wheeler, Joseph
b. 1839 Funk, Isaac Kauffman
b. 1839 Peirce, Charles Sanders
b. 1857 Keeler, James Edward
b. 1870 Danforth, William H
b. 1873 Onions, Charles Talbut
b. 1874 Sullivan, Mark
b. 1885 Van Doren, Carl Clinton

b. 1887 Gronchi, Giovanni
b. 1888 Fleming, Ian
b. 1890 Schiaparelli
b. 1890 Werfel, Franz
b. 1890 Wheeler, Mortimer
b. 1891 Burckhardt, Carl Jacob
b. 1892 Compton, Arthur Holly
b. 1895 Herskovits, Melville Jean
b. 1895 Kelly, George Lange
b. 1896 Ryan, Sylvester James
b. 1898 Astaire, Adele
b. 1900 Stern, Philip Van Doren
b. 1902 Crowley, Jim
b. 1903 Connolly, Cyril Vernon
b. 1904 Arevalo, Juan Jose
b. 1906 Lyons, Leonard
b. 1907 Landrum, Phil(lip) M(itchell)
b. 1907 Wray, Fay
b. 1908 Adams, Eva Bertrand
b. 1909 Bacon, Selden D(askam)
b. 1909 Brioni, Gaetano Savini, Marquis
b. 1909 Scott, Raymond
b. 1910 Reeves, Rosser
b. 1911 Grubert, Carl Alfred
b. 1912 Everson, William Oliver
b. 1913 Mein, John Gordon
b. 1914 O'Neill, Terence Marne
b. 1914 Wise, Robert
b. 1915 O'Brien, Edmond
b. 1916? McCarten, John
b. 1916 Sebelius, Keith George
b. 1917 Gentele, Goeran
b. 1919 Leighton, Robert B(enjamin)
b. 1924 Kluszewski, Ted
b. 1925 Dennison, George
b. 1926 Fuller, Hoyt William
b. 1928 Sumac, Yma
b. 1929 Leonetti, Tommy
b. 1929 Palmer, Arnold Daniel
b. 1932 Goldman, Bo
b. 1933 Khrunov, Evgeny Vasilievich
b. 1934? Anderson, Max(ie Leroy)
b. 1934 Kuralt, Charles (Bishop)
b. 1934 Maris, Roger (Eugene)

b. 1936 Lovesey, Peter Harmer
b. 1938 Lagerfeld, Karl
b. 1939 Mullavey, Greg
b. 1940 Ayers, Roy
b. 1940 Buchanan, Buck
b. 1941 Gould, Stephen Jay
b. 1941 Hogwood, Christopher
b. 1942 Darden, Christine (Mann)
b. 1944 Entwistle, John Alec
b. 1944 Fontaine, Philip
b. 1945 Feliciano, Jose
b. 1946 Hines, Jim
b. 1947 Nelson, Larry Gene
b. 1948 Geeson, Judy
b. 1948 Lanier, Bob
b. 1948 Trudeau, Margaret Joan Sinclair
b. 1951 Rogers, Bill
b. 1953 Irving, Amy
b. 1955 Kudelka, James
b. 1957 Burton, Kate
b. 1958 Columbus, Chris
b. 1960 Bechdel, Alison
b. 1963 Johnson, Randy
b. 1966 Nieuwendyk, Joe
b. 1968 Kane, Big Daddy
d. 1544 Marot, Clement
d. 1797 Godwin, Mary Wollstonecraft
d. 1827 Foscolo, (Niccolo) Ugo
d. 1842 Hobson, William
d. 1842 Tyler, Letitia Christian
d. 1845 Story, Joseph
d. 1851 Gallaudet, Thomas Hopkins
d. 1862 Lopez, Carlos Antonio
d. 1869 Bell, John
d. 1884 Bentham, George
d. 1922 Blunt, Wilfrid Scawen
d. 1935 Long, Huey Pierce
d. 1954 Derain, Andre
d. 1955 Goodfellow, Ebbie
d. 1960 Rogers, Edith
d. 1961 Carrillo, Leo
d. 1965 Divine, Father Major Jealous
d. 1965 Jordan, Bobby
d. 1970 Denneny, Cy(ril)
d. 1971 Angeli, Pier
d. 1971 Darvi, Bella
d. 1972 Gersten, Berta
d. 1975 Sproul, Robert Gordon
d. 1975 Thomson, George Paget, Sir
d. 1976 Johnson, Mordecai Wyatt

d. 1976 Trumbo, Dalton
d. 1979 Neto, Agostinho
d. 1980 Kirkus, Virginia
d. 1982 DeCreeft, Jose
d. 1983 Bloch, Felix
d. 1983 Lofts, Norah Robinson
d. 1983 Vorster, Balthazar Johannes
d. 1984 Hunsaker, Jerome Clarke
d. 1985 Overstreet, Bonaro Wilkinson
d. 1993 O'Connell, Helen
d. 1993 Schifter, Peter Mark
d. 1994 Clampitt, Amy
d. 1995 Tobin, Richard L(ardner)
d. 1996 Dru, Joanne
d. 1999 Kraus, Alfredo

September 11
b. 1524 Ronsard, Pierre de
b. 1611 Turenne, Henri de La Tour Auvergne, Viscount
b. 1700 Thomson, James
b. 1724 Basedow, Johann Bernhard
b. 1809 Price, Sterling
b. 1816 Zeiss, Carl
b. 1821 Beadle, Erastus Flavel
b. 1825 Hanslick, Eduard
b. 1829 Hill, Thomas
b. 1833 Hatch, William Henry
b. 1836 Ludlow, Fitz Hugh
b. 1854 Holabird, William
b. 1862 Byng, Julian Hedworth George, Viscount
b. 1862 Henry, O
b. 1877 Dzerzhinsky, Felix Edmundovich
b. 1877 Jeans, James Hopwood, Sir
b. 1883 Miller, Olive Beaupre
b. 1885 Lawrence, D(avid) H(erbert)
b. 1894 Dovzhenko, Alexander
b. 1895 Bhave, Acharya Vinoba
b. 1895 Stillman, Irwin Maxwell
b. 1896 Hoopes, Darlington
b. 1896 Kerr, Robert Samuel
b. 1901 Bates, Ted
b. 1901 Sebrell, W(illiam) H(enry), Jr.
b. 1903 Adorno, Theodor Wiesengrund
b. 1909 Seymour, Anne Eckert
b. 1910 Schroder, Gerhard

b. 1913 Bryant, Bear
b. 1913 Lamarr, Hedy
b. 1917 Forsythe, Henderson
b. 1917 Marcos, Ferdinand Edralin
b. 1917 Mitford, Jessica
b. 1918 Martin, Robert Bernard
b. 1920 Bouchard, Butch
b. 1921 Jobert, Michel
b. 1923 Drake, Betsy
b. 1923 Evers, James Charles
b. 1923 Kotzky, Alex Sylvester
b. 1923 Schultz, Harry D
b. 1924 Akaka, Daniel Kahikina
b. 1924 Landry, Tom
b. 1925 Bergman, Alan
b. 1926 Richardson, Lee
b. 1927 Nipon, Albert
b. 1927 Schine, G(erard) David
b. 1928 Askew, Reubin O'Donovan
b. 1928 Holliman, Earl
b. 1928 Kienzle, William X(avier)
b. 1929 Broder, David S
b. 1931? Damon, Cathryn
b. 1931 Moffett, Ken(neth Elwood)
b. 1932 Packwood, Bob
b. 1935 Part, Arvo
b. 1935 Titov, Gherman Stepanovich
b. 1937 Crippen, Robert Laurel
b. 1940 DePalma, Brian Russell
b. 1940 Rhodes, Zandra
b. 1943 Falana, Lola
b. 1943 Hart, Mickey
b. 1945 Kottke, Leo
b. 1948 Gomez, Jewelle
b. 1949 Liquori, Marty
b. 1952 Saporta, Vicki
b. 1956 Camp, Kimberly
b. 1961 Washington, Patrice Clarke
b. 1965 Moby
b. 1967 Connick, Harry, Jr.
d. 1599 Cenci, Beatrice
d. 1677 Harrington, James
d. 1721 Camerarius, Rudolf Jakob
d. 1808 Mutis, Jose Celestino
d. 1823 Ricardo, David
d. 1851 Graham, Sylvester
d. 1878 Satanta
d. 1888 Sarmiento, Domingo Faustino
d. 1915 Van Horne, William Cornelius, Sir

d. 1917 Guynemer, Georges Marie
d. 1918 Osgood, Herbert Levi
d. 1931 Omar al-Mukhtar
d. 1940 Waugh, Frederick Judd
d. 1947 Bullard, Robert Lee
d. 1948 Jinnah, Mohammed Ali
d. 1949 Rabaud, Henri
d. 1950 Smuts, Jan Christian
d. 1953 Stone, Lewis
d. 1956 Bishop, Billy
d. 1957 Watson, Moose
d. 1958 Service, Robert William
d. 1959 Dinwiddie, John Ekin
d. 1959 Douglas, Paul
d. 1963 Low, David Alexander Cecil, Sir
d. 1968 Armour, Tommy
d. 1969 Payne, Leon
d. 1970 Morris, Chester
d. 1971 Blotta, Anthony
d. 1971 Khrushchev, Nikita Sergeyevich
d. 1972 Fleischer, Max
d. 1973 Allende Gossens, Salvador
d. 1973 Evans-Pritchard, Edward Evan
d. 1974 Lenski, Lois
d. 1976 Carmer, Carl Lamson
d. 1980 Sands, Dorothy
d. 1981 McHugh, Frank
d. 1982 Ryan, T(ubal) Claude
d. 1983 Heaton, Leonard
d. 1983 Wechsler, James Arthur
d. 1987 Greene, Lorne
d. 1987 Tosh, Peter
d. 1988 Alpert, George
d. 1992 Crile, George Washington, Jr.
d. 1993 Butler, John
d. 1993 Leinsdorf, Erich
d. 1994 Tandy, Jessica
d. 1995 Heyns, Roger W(illiam)
d. 1995 Hitch, Charles J(ohnston)
d. 1996 Malott, Deane W(aldo)
d. 1998 Clark, Dane
d. 1999 Taeuber, Conrad F.

September 12
b. 1494 Francis I
b. 1575? Hudson, Henry
b. 1605 Dugdale, William, Sir
b. 1652 Tate, Nahum
b. 1788 Campbell, Alexander
b. 1806 Foote, Andrew Hull
b. 1811 Hall, James

b. 1812 Hoe, Richard March
b. 1818 Gatling, Richard Jordan
b. 1829 Warner, Charles Dudley
b. 1852 Asquith, Herbert Henry
b. 1855 Sharp, William
b. 1859 Kelley, Florence
b. 1880 Mencken, H(enry) L(ouis)
b. 1886 Ryden, Ernest Edwin
b. 1888 Chevalier, Maurice Auguste
b. 1891 Sulzberger, Arthur Hays
b. 1892 Knopf, Alfred Abraham
b. 1893 Hershey, Lewis Blaine
b. 1894 Gilbert, Billy
b. 1897 Gibson, Walter B(rown)
b. 1897 Joliot-Curie, Irene
b. 1898 Shahn, Ben(jamin)
b. 1901 Blue, Ben
b. 1902 Hamilton, Margaret Brainard
b. 1902 Kubitschek (de Oliveira), Juscelino
b. 1902 Zaturenska, Marya
b. 1905 DeMille, Agnes (George)
b. 1907 MacNeice, Louis
b. 1907 McMillan, Edwin Mattison
b. 1909 Chandler, Spud
b. 1909 Howard, Eddy
b. 1909 Kintner, Robert Edmonds
b. 1910 Engel, Lehman
b. 1910 Fields, Shep
b. 1912 Fath, Jacques
b. 1913 Owens, Jesse
b. 1913 Toyoda, Eiji
b. 1915 Daniels, Billy
b. 1915 Kronhausen, Eberhard Wilhelm
b. 1916 Anderson, Cat
b. 1917 Han Suyin
b. 1920 Dailey, Irene
b. 1921 McGee, Frank
b. 1924 Cabral, Amilcar Lopes
b. 1924 Morse, Ella Mae
b. 1925 Moore, Dick(ie)
b. 1928 Irwin, Robert
b. 1931 Holm, Ian
b. 1931 Jones, George (Glenn)
b. 1931 Rogers, Adrian Pierce
b. 1933 Throneberry, Marv(in Eugene)
b. 1934 Davis, Glenn
b. 1934 Gebel-Williams, Gunther

Stanislaw
Boleslawawicz)
d. 1980 Abu Salma
d. 1981 Breit, Gregory
d. 1981 Humes, Helen
d. 1981 Loeb, William
d. 1982 Eldjarn,
Kristjan
d. 1982 Hemingway,
Leicester
d. 1982 Ober, Philip
(Nott)
d. 1982 Wallenberg,
Marcus
d. 1985 Rudhyar, Dane
d. 1987 Leroy, Mervyn
d. 1990 Mannes, Marya
d. 1990 Simmons,
Althea T L
d. 1990 Stratton,
Samuel S(tuddiford)
d. 1991 Irving, Robert
Augustine
d. 1991 Pasternak, Joe
d. 1992 Jacobs, Lou
d. 1993 De La Torre(-
Bueno), Lillian
d. 1996 Shakur, Tupac
d. 1998 Lumley, Harry
d. 1998 Wallace,
George C(orley)

September 14
b. 1486 Agrippa,
Heinrich Cornelius
b. 1547 Oldenbarnevelt,
Johan van
b. 1728 Warren, Mercy
Otis
b. 1739 DuPont de
Nemours, Pierre
Samuel
b. 1742 Wilson, James
b. 1760 Cherubini,
Luigi Carlo Zenobio
Salvadore Maria
b. 1769 Humboldt,
Alexander, Freiherr
von
b. 1769 Humboldt,
Friedrich Heinrich
Alexander von
b. 1774 Bentinck,
William Henry
Cavendish, Lord
b. 1775 Hobart, John
Henry
b. 1802 Buckstone, John
Baldwin
b. 1816 Wood, James
Rushmore
b. 1817 Storm, (Hans)
Theodor (Woldsen)
b. 1818 Congreve,
Richard
b. 1823 Hill, Benjamin
Harvey
b. 1846 Selden, George
Baldwin
b. 1849 Pavlov, Ivan
Petrovich
b. 1858 Hubay, Jeno
b. 1860 Garland,
Hamlin
b. 1864 Cecil, Edgar
Algernon Robert

b. 1867 Gibson, Charles
Dana
b. 1869 Nichols, Kid
b. 1873 Irwin, Will(iam
Henry)
b. 1878 Carey, William
F
b. 1880 Wilkins, Ernest
Hatch
b. 1883 Sanger,
Margaret
b. 1884 Pile, Frederick
Alfred
b. 1885 Gui, Vittorio
b. 1885 Hilberseimer,
Ludwig Karl
b. 1886 Masaryk, Jan
Garrigue
b. 1887 Compton, Karl
Taylor
b. 1887 Ketchel, Stanley
b. 1895 Lovett, Robert
A(bercrombie)
b. 1896 Powers, John
Robert
b. 1896 Sample, Paul
Starrett
b. 1897 Rudkin,
Margaret Fogarty
b. 1899 Chandler,
Norman
b. 1899 Wallis, Hal
Brent
b. 1902 Mullin, Willard
b. 1904 Germi, Pietro
b. 1907 Brown, Cecil B
b. 1907 Wexley, John
b. 1908 Gaddis, Thomas
(Eugene)
b. 1909 Eklund, John
M(anly)
b. 1909 Scott, Peter
Markham, Sir
b. 1910 Hawkins, Jack
b. 1910 Liebermann,
Rolf
b. 1913 Arbenz
Guzman, Jacobo
b. 1914 Armstrong,
William H(oward)
b. 1914 Moore, Clayton
b. 1916 Bentley, Eric
b. 1917 Harris, Sydney
J(ustin)
b. 1920 Calderon,
Alberto P(edro)
b. 1920 Klein,
Lawrence Robert
b. 1920 Medford, Kay
b. 1921 Motley,
Constance Baker
b. 1921 Rudd, Hughes
Day
b. 1923 Rollins, Kenny
b. 1923 Rubin, Vitalii
b. 1926 Butor, Michel
b. 1927 Caidin, Martin
b. 1927 Szoka, Edmund
Casimir, Cardinal
b. 1928 Shanker, Albert
b. 1929 Clark, Richard
Clarence
b. 1929 Collins, Larry
b. 1930 Bloom, Allan
David
b. 1931 Klima, Ivan

b. 1933 Caldwell, Zoe
b. 1933 Presnell, Harve
b. 1934 Millett, Kate
b. 1936 Koenig, Walter
b. 1936 Samaras, Lucas
b. 1938 Stanford, John
(Henry)
b. 1938 Williamson,
Nicol
b. 1940 Brown, Larry
b. 1942 Floyd,
Raymond Loran
b. 1942 Lehman, John
Francis, Jr.
b. 1944 Heatherton,
Joey
b. 1946 Russell-
McCloud, Patricia
(A.)
b. 1948 Natividad, Irene
b. 1948 Rabuka,
Sitiveni
(Ligamamada)
b. 1959 Berry, John
b. 1959 Crosby, Mary
Frances
d. 258 Cyprianus,
Thascius Caecilianus
d. 407 Chrysostom,
John, Saint
d. 775 Constantine V
d. 1321 Dante Alighieri
d. 1510 Catherine of
Genoa, Saint
d. 1637 Vernier, Pierre
d. 1638 Harvard, John
d. 1743 Lancret, Nicolas
d. 1759 Montcalm,
Louis Joseph de
d. 1788 Penn, John
d. 1836 Burr, Aaron
d. 1851 Cooper, James
Fenimore
d. 1852 Wellington,
Arthur Wellesley,
Duke
d. 1876 Rhett, Robert
Barnwell
d. 1882 Pusey, Edward
Bouverie
d. 1895 Riley, Charles
Valentine
d. 1898 Burroughs,
William Seward
d. 1901 McKinley,
William
d. 1905 Brazza, Pierre
Paul Francois Camille
Savorgnan de
d. 1905 Rain-in-the-
Face
d. 1909 McKim,
Charles Follen
d. 1911 Stolypin, Piotr
Arkadevich
d. 1916 Duhem, Pierre
Maurice Marie
d. 1916 Royce, Josiah
d. 1924 Chance, Frank
Leroy
d. 1926 Dreyer, Johan
Ludwig Emil
d. 1927 Duncan, Isadora
d. 1935 Kendal, Madge,
Dame

d. 1936 Gabrilowitsch,
Ossip Salomonovich
d. 1936 Thalberg, Irving
Grant
d. 1937 Masaryk,
Tomas Garrigue
d. 1941 Cubberley,
Ellwood Patterson
d. 1947 LeGallienne,
Richard
d. 1951 Busch, Fritz
d. 1959 Morris, Wayne
d. 1966 Berg, Gertrude
d. 1970 Carnap, Rudolf
d. 1972 Boyd, Louise
Arner
d. 1976 Paul, Prince
d. 1982 Gardner, John
Champlin, Jr.
d. 1982 Gemayel,
Bashir
d. 1982 Kelly, Grace
Patricia
d. 1983 Albright,
Malvin Marr
d. 1984 Gaynor, Janet
d. 1985 Beck, Julian
d. 1985 Holt, John
Caldwell
d. 1989 Valentina
d. 1991 Lynes, Joseph
Russell, Jr.
d. 1992 Weiss, Ted
d. 1996 Prowse, Juliet
d. 1998 McEwen,
Terence Alexander
d. 1999 Crichton,
Charles

September 15
b. 1613
LaRochefoucauld,
Francois, Duc de
b. 1649 Oates, Titus
b. 1736 Bailly, Jean
Sylvain
b. 1789 Cooper, James
Fenimore
b. 1819 Pasdeloup, Jules
Etienne
b. 1825 Iwakura,
Tomomi
b. 1829 Tamayo y Baus,
Manuel
b. 1830 Diaz, Porfirio
b. 1834 Treitschke,
Heinrich Gotthard
von
b. 1852 Bouchet,
Edward Alexander
b. 1857 Taft, William
(Howard)
b. 1863 Parker, Horatio
William
b. 1870 Bragg, Mabel
Caroline
b. 1876 Altrock, Nick
b. 1876 Gannett, Frank
Ernest
b. 1876 Walter, Bruno
b. 1879 Lyons, Joseph
Aloysius
b. 1881 Bugatti, Ettore
Arco Isidoro
b. 1881 Grant, Harry
Johnston

b. 1955 Yount, Robin (R.)
b. 1956 Copperfield, David
b. 1958 Hershiser, Orel Leonard, IV
b. 1959 Raines, Tim(othy)
b. 1963 Marx, Richard
b. 1966 Young, Kevin
d. 1380 Charles, V
d. 1672 Bradstreet, Anne
d. 1701 James II
d. 1726 Prandtauer, Jakob
d. 1736 Fahrenheit, Gabriel Daniel
d. 1824 Louis, XVIII
d. 1839 Carey, Mathew
d. 1841 Dibdin, Thomas Pitt
d. 1847 Aguilar, Grace
d. 1869 Graham, Thomas
d. 1877 Coffin, Levi
d. 1903 Crowell, Luther Childs
d. 1911 Whymper, Edward
d. 1916 McGee, Frank
d. 1932 Ross, Ronald, Sir
d. 1936 Charcot, Jean Baptiste Etienne Auguste
d. 1945 McCormack, John
d. 1948 Everleigh, Minna
d. 1951 Klem, Bill
d. 1953 Corey, Lewis
d. 1956 Lugosi, Bela
d. 1956 Ray, Shorty
d. 1957 Ch'i Pai-Shih
d. 1964 Meiklejohn, Alexander
d. 1970 Garrett, Eileen Jeanette Lyttle
d. 1973 Licavoli, Thomas
d. 1974 Allen, Forrest Claire
d. 1977 Bolan, Marc
d. 1977 Callas, Maria
d. 1977 Sheldon, William Herbert
d. 1980 Piaget, Jean
d. 1984 Reard, Louis
d. 1987 Moss, Howard
d. 1987 Soames, Christopher
d. 1992 Fenwick, Millicent Hammond
d. 1994 Gautier, Felisa Rincon de
d. 1994 Young, Jean Childs
d. 1996 Bundy, McGeorge
d. 1996 Nelson, Gene
d. 1997 Jepson, Helen

September 17
b. 1580 Quevado y Villegas, Francisco Gomez de

b. 1677 Hales, Stephen
b. 1721 Hopkins, Samuel
b. 1730 Steuben, Friedrich Wilhelm Ludolf Gerhard Augustin, Baron
b. 1743 Condorcet, Marie-Jean-Antoine
b. 1792 Smith, Seba
b. 1795 Mercadante, Saverio
b. 1801 Lane, Edward William
b. 1819 Pretorius, Marthinus Wessel
b. 1825 Lamar, Lucius Quintus Cincinnatus
b. 1826 Riemann, Georg Friedrich
b. 1854 Buick, David Dunbar
b. 1854? Ellsler, Effie
b. 1857 Tsiolkovsky, Konstantin Eduardovich
b. 1858 Vonnoh, Robert William
b. 1869 Lange, Christian Louis
b. 1869 Turpin, Ben
b. 1879 Foster, Rube
b. 1880 Russell, Blair
b. 1883 Williams, William Carlos
b. 1884 Griffes, Charles Tomlinson
b. 1890 Heatter, Gabriel
b. 1894 McKinney, Bill
b. 1900 Marriott, John Willard
b. 1900 Ostenso, Martha
b. 1901 Chichester, Francis Charles, Sir
b. 1902 Ralston, Esther
b. 1905 Colonna, Jerry
b. 1905 Costello, Dolores
b. 1906 Ashton, Frederick William, Sir
b. 1906 Jayewardene, J(unius) R(ichard)
b. 1907 Burger, Warren E(arl)
b. 1907 Vinson, Helen
b. 1908 Creasey, John
b. 1909 Cole, Edward Nicholas
b. 1909 Enright, Elizabeth
b. 1909 Hightower, John Marmann
b. 1916 Stewart, Mary (Florence Elinor)
b. 1916 Tsedenbal, Yumzhagin
b. 1917 Lawrence, Jacob Armstead
b. 1918 Herzog, Chaim
b. 1921 Barco Vargas, Virgilio
b. 1922 Bourjaily, Vance
b. 1922 Neto, Agostinho

b. 1927 Blanda, George Frederick
b. 1927 Weiss, Ted
b. 1928 McDowall, Roddy
b. 1929 Crowley, Pat
b. 1929 Moss, Stirling Crauford
b. 1930 Mitchell, Edgar Dean
b. 1930 Stafford, Thomas P(atten)
b. 1931 Bancroft, Anne
b. 1932 Parker, Robert B(rown)
b. 1933 Grassley, Charles Ernest
b. 1933 Loudon, Dorothy
b. 1934 Connolly, Maureen
b. 1935 Kesey, Ken
b. 1937 Cepeda, Orlando Manuel
b. 1938 Yarbrough, Lee Roy
b. 1939 Fey, Thomas Hossler
b. 1939 Souter, David Hackett
b. 1941 Matsui, Robert T(akeo)
b. 1941 Segretti, Donald H
b. 1944 Messner, Reinhold
b. 1945 Jackson, Phil(ip D.)
b. 1947 MacNelly, Jeff(rey Kenneth)
b. 1948 Ritter, John(athan Southworth)
b. 1950 Waybill, Fee
b. 1951 Elvira
b. 1952 Solomon, Harold Charles
b. 1955 Simpson, Scott
b. 1958 Jahan, Marine
b. 1960 Carter, Anthony Calvin
b. 1962 Rogers, Don(ald Lavert)
b. 1967 Yoba, Malik
d. 1179 Hildegard of Bingen, Saint
d. 1574 Menendez de Aviles, Pedro
d. 1621 Bellarmine, Robert, Saint
d. 1762 Geminiani, Francesco
d. 1771 Smollett, Tobias George
d. 1823 Breguet, Abraham Louis
d. 1858 Scott, Dred
d. 1863 Vigny, Alfred Victor, Comte de
d. 1864 Landor, Walter Savage
d. 1877 Talbot, William Henry Fox
d. 1879 Viollet le Duc, Eugene Emmanuel

d. 1886 Durand, Asher Brown
d. 1899 Pillsbury, Charles Alfred
d. 1908 Selfridge, Thomas Etholen
d. 1916 Low, Seth
d. 1942 Beaux, Cecilia
d. 1946 Jeans, James Hopwood, Sir
d. 1948 Benedict, Ruth (Fulton)
d. 1948 Bernadotte, Folke, Count
d. 1948 Ludwig, Emil
d. 1950 DeCordoba, Pedro
d. 1951 Yancey, Jimmy
d. 1952 Strong, Austin
d. 1954 Slye, Maud
d. 1958 Paneth, Friedrich Adolf
d. 1965 Hayward, John Davy
d. 1966 Wellman, Paul Iselin
d. 1966 Wunderlich, Fritz
d. 1972 Tamiroff, Akim
d. 1973 Winterhalter, Hugo
d. 1974 Dunoyer de Segonzac, Andre
d. 1975 Moscona, Nicola
d. 1980 Somoza Debayle, Anastasio
d. 1981 Kemper, James S(cott)
d. 1982 Dubinsky, David
d. 1982 Stravinsky, Vera de Bossett
d. 1983 Medeiros, Humberto, Cardinal
d. 1984 Basehart, Richard
d. 1985 Ashley, Laura Mountney
d. 1986 Barrett, William Edmund
d. 1988 Gueden, Hilde
d. 1991 Francescatti, Zino Rene
d. 1991 Tyner, Rob
d. 1992 Chaliapin, Feodor Ivanovitch, Jr.
d. 1992 Swanberg, William Andrew
d. 1992 Wagner, Roger Frances
d. 1994 Popper, Karl R(aimund), Sir
d. 1996 Agnew, Spiro T(heodore)
d. 1997 Skelton, Red
d. 1998 Elliot, Win
d. 1998 Frank, Gerold

September 18
b. 53? Trajan
b. 1596 Shirley, James
b. 1709 Johnson, Samuel
b. 1733 Read, George
b. 1752 Legendre, Adrien Marie

b. 1779 Story, Joseph
b. 1804 Forbes, Robert
Bennet
b. 1815 Strepponi,
Giuseppina
b. 1819 Foucault, Jean
Bernard Leon
b. 1827 Trowbridge,
John Townsend
b. 1843 Riley, Charles
Valentine
b. 1859 Hitchcock,
Gilbert Monell
b. 1861 Seaman, Owen,
Sir
b. 1866 Talbert, Mary
Morris Burnett
b. 1879 Fisher, Welthy
(Blakesley Honsinger)
b. 1883 Maytag, Elmer
Henry
b. 1886 Crosley, Powel,
Jr.
b. 1886? Sullivan,
C(harles) Gardner
b. 1893 Benjamin,
Arthur
b. 1893 Campbell,
William Edward
March
b. 1894 Compton, Fay
b. 1895 Diefenbaker,
John George
b. 1895 Wilder, Amos
Niven
b. 1900 Ramgoolam,
Seewoosagur, Sir
b. 1901 Clurman,
Harold Edgar
b. 1903 Washington,
Val J.
b. 1903 Wilbur, Dwight
L(ocke)
b. 1904 DeRivera, Jose
Ruiz
b. 1904 Winsten, Archer
b. 1905 Anderson,
Eddie
b. 1905 Garbo, Greta
b. 1906 Gellhorn,
Walter
b. 1908 Ambartsumyan,
Viktor Amazaspovich
b. 1908 Courlander,
Harold
b. 1909 Darken,
Lawrence Stamper
b. 1911 LePoer Trench,
Brinsley
b. 1916 Brazzi, Rossano
b. 1916 Rhodes, John
Jacob
b. 1919 Losonczi, Pal
b. 1920 Warden, Jack
b. 1923 Wilson, Bertha
b. 1924 Fichandler,
Zelda Diamond
b. 1927 Green, Paula
b. 1927 Greenspan, Bud
b. 1928 Smith, Robert
Lee
b. 1930 Kirk, Phyllis
b. 1933 Bennett, Robert
F.
b. 1933 Bowman,
Scotty

b. 1933 DiSuvero, Mark
b. 1933 Rodgers, Jimmy
F
b. 1934 Blake, Robert
b. 1940 Avalon, Frankie
b. 1940 Keohane,
Nannerl Overholser
b. 1950 Sittler, Darryl
Glen
b. 1950 Smith, Anna
Deavere
b. 1951 Carson,
Benjamin S.
b. 1951 Stingley, Darryl
b. 1954 Johnson, Dennis
Wayne
b. 1955 Sims, Billy Ray
b. 1956 Fields, Debbi
b. 1956 Stastny, Peter
b. 1959 Sandberg, Ryne
(Dee)
b. 1965 Peete, Holly
Robinson
b. 1968 Kukoc, Toni
b. 1971 Smith, Jada
Pinkett
d. 96 Domitian
d. 1721 Prior, Matthew
d. 1783 Euler, Leonhard
d. 1819 Langdon, John
d. 1830 Hazlitt, William
d. 1864 Speke, John
Hanning
d. 1879 Drew, Daniel
d. 1890 Boucicault,
Dion Lardner
d. 1891 Balmaceda
Fernandez, Jose
Manuel
d. 1892 Francis, James
Bicheno
d. 1896 Fizeau, Armand
Hippolyte Louis
d. 1903 Bain, Alexander
d. 1905 MacDonald,
George
d. 1914 Leslie, Miriam
Florence Folline
d. 1924 Bradley, Francis
Herbert
d. 1938 Trumbauer,
Horace
d. 1939 Ratana,
Taupotiki Wiremu
d. 1939 Schwab,
Charles Michael
d. 1946 White, Stewart
Edward
d. 1947 Kalmar, Bert
d. 1949 Morgan, Frank
d. 1951 Burgess, Gelett
d. 1952 Alda, Frances
d. 1961 Hammarskjold,
Dag (Hjalmar Agne
Carl)
d. 1964 Bell, Clive
d. 1964 Dobie, J(ames)
Frank
d. 1964 O'Casey, Sean
d. 1965 Field, Marshall,
IV
d. 1967 Cockcroft, John
Douglas, Sir
d. 1968 Tone, Franchot
d. 1969 Wagner-
Regeny, Rudolf

d. 1970 Hendrix, Jimi
d. 1974 Best, Edna
d. 1975 Brown, Pamela
d. 1975 Porter, Fairfield
d. 1978 Dassler, Adolf
d. 1980 Porter,
Katherine Anne
d. 1981 Doubrovska,
Felia
d. 1985 Cameron,
Roderick W
d. 1986 Kent, Corita
d. 1987 Schram, Emil
d. 1987 Thomaz,
Americo
d. 1989 Mitchell,
William Leroy
d. 1992 Jacobson, Leon
Orris
d. 1994 Gerulaitis, Vitas
d. 1995 Davie, Donald
Alfred
d. 1996 Annabella

September 19
b. 86 Antoninus Pius
b. 1721 Robertson,
William
b. 1737 Carroll, Charles
b. 1796 Coleridge,
Hartley
b. 1802 Kossuth, Lajos
b. 1806 Dyce, William
b. 1829 Schirmer,
Gustave
b. 1855 Klafsky,
Katharina
b. 1867 Rackham,
Arthur
b. 1871 Schaudinn, Fritz
Richard
b. 1879 Drum, Hugh A
b. 1879 Vance, Louis
Joseph
b. 1879 Westheimer,
Irvin Ferdinand
b. 1886 Doolittle, Hilda
b. 1886 O'Sheel,
Shaemas
b. 1887 Overman,
Lynne
b. 1888 Alexander,
James Waddell, II
b. 1889 Delany, Sarah
Louise
b. 1890? Truex, Ernest
b. 1894 Field, Rachel
Lyman
b. 1897 Knight, George
Wilson
b. 1898 Love, Bessie
b. 1898 Saragat,
Giuseppe
b. 1899 Cortez, Ricardo
b. 1901 Pasternak, Joe
b. 1902 Leon, Henry
Cecil
b. 1903 Saltzman,
Charles E(skridge)
b. 1904 Evans, Bergen
Baldwin
b. 1905 Hawley,
Cameron
b. 1905 Jaworski, Leon
b. 1906 Reifel, Ben
b. 1907 Powell, Lewis
F(ranklin), Jr.

b. 1908 Waltari, Mika
b. 1909 Porsche,
Ferdinand
b. 1910 Lasky, Jesse
Louis, Jr.
b. 1910 Lindsay,
Margaret
b. 1911 Golding,
William (Gerald), Sir
b. 1912 Daniel, Clifton,
Jr.
b. 1914 Farmer, Frances
b. 1914 Morton, Rogers
Clark Ballard
b. 1916 Tiller, Rogers
b. 1918 Kiplinger,
Austin Huntington
b. 1918 Velarde, Pablita
b. 1919 Thebom,
Blanche
b. 1920 Angell, Roger
b. 1921 Chapman,
Christian Addison
b. 1921 Conerly,
Charlie
b. 1922 Pep, Willie
b. 1922 Zatopek, Emil
b. 1926 Snider, Duke
b. 1926 Wallace,
Lurleen Burns
b. 1927 Brown, Harold
b. 1927 Ross, Steven J
b. 1930 Harris,
Rosemary Ann
b. 1931 Benton, Brook
b. 1931 Calvet, Jacques
b. 1931 Danton,
Ray(mond)
b. 1932 Royko, Mike
b. 1932 Wille, Lois Jean
b. 1933 McCallum,
David
b. 1934 Epstein, Brian
b. 1935 Massi, Nick
b. 1936 Cowans, Adger
W.
b. 1938 Eigsti, Karl
b. 1938 West, Adam
b. 1940 Medley, Bill
b. 1940 Tyson, Sylvia
Fricker
b. 1940 Williams, Paul
Hamilton
b. 1943 Morgan, Joe
(Leonard)
b. 1944 Schenk, Ard
b. 1945 Blalock, Jane
b. 1945 Bromberg,
David
b. 1945 Christian-Green,
Donna M.
b. 1945 Payne, Freda
b. 1947 Brown, Larry
b. 1947 Perry, Nancy
Ling
b. 1948 Irons, Jeremy
John
b. 1949 Twiggy
b. 1950 Lunden, Joan
(Elise)
b. 1952 Rodgers, Nile
b. 1952 Stewart, David
b. 1955 Dawkins,
Wayne J(esse)
b. 1956? Smith, Rex
b. 1958 Hooks, Kevin

b. 1967 Abbott, Jim
d. 1668 Waller,
  William, Sir
d. 1812 Rothschild,
  Mayer Amschel
d. 1841 Sydenham,
  Baron
d. 1860 Rice, Thomas
  Dartmouth
d. 1881 Garfield, James
  Abram
d. 1891 Grevy, Francois
  Paul Jules
d. 1893 Galt, Alexander
  Tilloch
d. 1896 Marty, Martin
d. 1898 Grey, George
d. 1902 Masaoka,
  Tsunenori
d. 1905 Barnardo,
  Thomas John
d. 1916 Sherman, Frank
  Dempster
d. 1927 Barker, Herman
d. 1931 Jordan, David
  Starr
d. 1933 Kemble,
  Edward W(indsor)
d. 1935 Tsiolkovsky,
  Konstantin
  Eduardovich
d. 1937 Loeb, William
d. 1946 Carr, Alexander
d. 1949 Cuppy,
  Will(iam Jacob)
d. 1950 Herne, Chrystal
  Katharine
d. 1954 Franklin, Miles
d. 1955 Milles, Carl
  Wilhelm Emil
d. 1957 Childe, Vere
  Gordon
d. 1957 Daly, Reginald
  Aldworth
d. 1965 Thomas, Elmer
d. 1967 Block, Martin
d. 1968 Carlson,
  Chester Floyd
d. 1968 Foley, Red
d. 1968 Genet, Arthur
  Samuel
d. 1969 Ingram, Rex
d. 1970 Danforth, Dave
d. 1971 Albright,
  William Foxwell
d. 1972 Casadesus,
  Robert
d. 1973 Parsons, Gram
d. 1973 Wurster,
  William
d. 1978 Gilson, Etienne
  Henry
d. 1979 Birnie, William
  Alfred Hart
d. 1979 Jones, Preston
  St. Vrain
d. 1980 Gillott, Jacky
d. 1980 Lesser, Sol
d. 1985 Calvino, Italo
d. 1985 Straus, Jack
  Isidor
d. 1987 Gerhardsen,
  Einar Henry
d. 1989 Hammon,
  William McDowell
d. 1990 Pan, Hermes

d. 1992 Evans, Geraint
  Llewellyn, Sir
d. 1994 Smith, Carleton
  Sprague
d. 1995 Redenbacher,
  Orville
d. 1997 Keeton, Kathy
September 20
b. 356BC Alexander the
  Great
b. 1754 Paul, I
b. 1778 Emmet, Robert
b. 1780 Borghese,
  Maria Paolina
b. 1791 Aksakov, Sergei
  Timofeyevich
b. 1822 Miller,
  Elizabeth Smith
b. 1833 Locke, David
  Ross
b. 1833 Moneta, Ernesto
  Teodora
b. 1842 Dewar, James,
  Sir
b. 1853 Chulalongkorn
b. 1869 Robey, George,
  Sir
b. 1872 Gamelin,
  Maurice Gustave
b. 1875 Erzberger,
  Matthias
b. 1876 Ellis, Carleton
b. 1878 Sinclair, Upton
  Beall
b. 1879 Banning,
  Kendall
b. 1879 Cromwell, Dean
  Bartlett
b. 1879 Sjostrom,
  Victor
b. 1880 Pizzetti,
  Ildebrando
b. 1884 Brightman,
  Edgar Sheffield
b. 1884 Perkins,
  Maxwell Evarts
b. 1884 Perkins,
  William Maxwell
  Evarts
b. 1885 Morton, Jelly
  Roll
b. 1886 Anderson, John
  Murray
b. 1886 Kenny, Sister
  Elizabeth
b. 1888 Petersham,
  Miska
b. 1894 Collinge,
  Patricia
b. 1897 Barea, Arturo
b. 1897 Taft, Charles
  Phelps
b. 1898 Dressen, Chuck
b. 1899 Nugent, Elliott
b. 1899 Strauss, Leo
b. 1900 Castello
  Branco, Humberto
b. 1900 DeParis, Wilbur
b. 1900 Visser T Hooft,
  Willem Adolf
b. 1901 Edson, Gus
b. 1903 Smith, Stevie
b. 1905 Bouche, Rene
  Robert
b. 1908 Bestor, Arthur
  (Eugene)

b. 1908 Manning,
  Ernest (Charles)
b. 1908 Mitscherlich,
  Alexander
b. 1914 More, Kenneth
  Gilbert
b. 1915 Lee-Smith,
  Hughie
b. 1917 Auerbach, Red
b. 1917 Rey, Fernando
b. 1920 Mitchell, Peter
  Dennis
b. 1922 Kapell, William
b. 1924 Galanos, James
b. 1924 Grant, Gogi
b. 1924 Meara, Anne
b. 1926 Bluhdorn,
  Charles G
b. 1927 Dankworth,
  John Philip William
b. 1927 Roberts, Rachel
b. 1928 Hall, Donald
  Andrew
b. 1928 Jennings, Gary
b. 1931 Palmer, Peter
b. 1934 Loren, Sophia
b. 1935 Taylor, Jim
b. 1936 Church,
  Sam(uel Morgan Jr.)
b. 1938 Gale, Eric
b. 1938 Lindstrom, Pia
b. 1941 Chihuly, Dale
  (Patrick)
b. 1943 Abacha, Sani
b. 1951 Lafleur, Guy
  Damien
b. 1952 Jeter, Michael
d. 1415 Glendower,
  Owen
d. 1586 Babington,
  Anthony
d. 1803 Emmet, Robert
d. 1852 Chase,
  Philander
d. 1860 Schopenhauer,
  Arthur
d. 1863 Grimm, Jakob
  Ludwig Karl
d. 1878 Thorpe, Thomas
  Bangs
d. 1880 McKay, Donald
d. 1894 Hoffmann,
  Heinrich
d. 1898 Fontane,
  Theodor
d. 1908 Sarasate, Pablo
  de
d. 1925 Bartlett, Paul
  Wayland
d. 1933 Besant, Annie
  Wood
d. 1946 Raimu
d. 1947 La Guardia,
  Fiorello Henry
d. 1949 Dix, Richard
d. 1951 Hartford, John
  Augustine
d. 1957 Sibelius, Jean
d. 1958 Wortman,
  Denys
d. 1960 Goodpasture,
  E(rnest) W(illiam)
d. 1965 Holmes, Arthur
d. 1971 Seferiades,
  Giorgos Styljanou
d. 1971 Seferis, George

d. 1972 Liebes, Dorothy
  Katherine Wright
d. 1972 Oakes, Richard
d. 1973 Croce, Jim
d. 1975 Bishop,
  Katharine Scott
d. 1975 Leger, Alexis
  St. Leger
d. 1975 Lopez, Vincent
d. 1976 Bloomgarden,
  Kermit
d. 1979 Svoboda,
  Ludvik
d. 1982 Hughes, Emmet
  John
d. 1984 Goodman,
  Steve(n Benjamin)
d. 1986 Rushmore,
  Robert (William)
d. 1987 Bester, Alfred
d. 1987 Stewart,
  Michael
d. 1993 Sulzberger,
  C(yrus) L(eo)
d. 1994 Styne, Jule
d. 1995 Haas, Walter
  A(braham), Jr.
d. 1996 Draper, Paul
  (Nathaniel Saltonstall)
d. 1996 Erdos, Paul
d. 1997 Christopher,
  Matt(hew F.)
d. 1998 Humphrey,
  Muriel Fay Buck
d. 1999 Gorbachev,
  Raisa (Maksimovna
  Titorenko)
September 21
b. 1415 Frederick, III
b. 1452 Savonarola,
  Girolamo
b. 1737 Hopkinson,
  Francis
b. 1756 McAdam, John
  Loudoun
b. 1788 Taylor,
  Margaret (Smith)
b. 1842 Abdul-Hamid,
  II
b. 1842 Abdulhamid II
b. 1849 Barrymore,
  Maurice
b. 1849 Gosse, Edmund
  William, Sir
b. 1853 Kamerlingh
  Onnes, Heike
b. 1855 Roosevelt, Sara
  Delano
b. 1863 Bunny, John
b. 1863 Howell, Clark
b. 1866 Nicolle, Charles
  Jules Henri
b. 1866 Wells, H(erbert)
  G(eorge)
b. 1867 Stimson, Henry
  Lewis
b. 1874 Holst, Gustav
  Theodore
b. 1876 Gonzalez, Julio
b. 1884 Andrus, Ethel
  Percy
b. 1884 Price, Irving L
b. 1884 Ray, Shorty
b. 1885 Webster,
  H(arold) T(ucker)

b. 1948 Phillips, Mark
Anthony Peter
b. 1949 Carmichael,
Harold
b. 1950 Tyler, Richard
b. 1951 Sulzberger,
Arthur O(chs), Jr.
b. 1954 Belafonte, Shari
b. 1956 Boone, Debby
b. 1957 Johnson, Mark
b. 1959 Renvall, Johan
Bengt Erik
b. 1960 Babilonia, Tai
(Reina)
b. 1960 Coleman,
Vince(nt Maurice)
b. 1960 Jett, Joan
b. 1961 Baio, Scott
Vincent
d. 1158 Otto of Freising
d. 1468 Sejo
d. 1520 Selim I
d. 1554 Coronado,
Francisco Vasquez de
d. 1566 Agricola,
Georgius
d. 1662 Biddle, John
d. 1774 Clement XIV,
Pope
d. 1776 Hale, Nathan
d. 1777 Bartram, John
d. 1828 Shaka
d. 1851 Sherwood,
Mary Martha
d. 1857 Manin, Daniele
d. 1896 Klafsky,
Katharina
d. 1905 Galli-Marie,
Marie Celestine
d. 1914 Alain-Fournier
d. 1933 Silverman,
Sime
d. 1937 Roland, Ruth
d. 1942 Cram, Ralph
Adams
d. 1945 Burke, Thomas
d. 1948 Bailey, Florence
Augusta Merriam
d. 1949 Wood, Samuel
Grosvenor
d. 1952 Stahlberg,
Kaarlo Juho
d. 1952 Webster,
H(arold) T(ucker)
d. 1955 Kress, Samuel
Henry
d. 1956 Soddy,
Frederick
d. 1957 Gogarty, Oliver
St. John
d. 1958 Rinehart, Mary
Roberts
d. 1959 Ironside,
William Edmund
d. 1960 Klein, Melanie
d. 1961 Davies, Marion
d. 1965 Ammann,
Othmar Hermann
d. 1968 Scott, Norman
d. 1969 Lopez Mateos,
Adolfo
d. 1970 Hamilton, Alice
d. 1973 Dodd, Charles
Harold
d. 1974 Brennan, Walter
Andrew

d. 1976 Strode, Hudson
d. 1981 Warren, Harry
d. 1984 Mathieu, Noel
Jean
d. 1985 Nagel, Ernest
d. 1985 Springer, Axel
Caesar
d. 1985 Tabouis,
Genevieve
d. 1987 Gross, H(arold)
R(oyce)
d. 1987 Luboff, Norman
d. 1987 Rowan, Dan
d. 1989 Berlin, Irving
d. 1993 Abravanel,
Maurice
d. 1996 Lamour,
Dorothy
d. 1999 Scott, George
C(ampbell)

September 23
b. Pena, Elizabeth
b. 484?BC Euripides
b. 63BC Augustus
b. 1745 Sevier, John
b. 1783 Cornelius, Peter
von
b. 1786 England, John
b. 1800 McGuffey,
William Holmes
b. 1819 Fizeau, Armand
Hippolyte Louis
b. 1829 Crook, George
b. 1838 Woodhull,
Victoria Claflin
b. 1852 Halsted,
William Stewart
b. 1859 Osborne,
Thomas Mott
b. 1861 Bosch, Robert
August
b. 1861 Coleridge, Mary
Elizabeth
b. 1863 Terrell, Mary
Church
b. 1865 Orczy,
Emmuska, Baroness
b. 1867 Lomax, John
Avery
b. 1869 Valadon,
Suzanne
b. 1871 Kupka, Frank
b. 1874 Barker, Ernest,
Sir
b. 1877 Kaempffert,
Waldemar (Bernhard)
b. 1880 Boyd-Orr, John,
Baron
b. 1880 Orr, John Boyd,
1st Baron of Brechin
b. 1882 Evans, Herbert
McLean
b. 1884 Chaffee, Adna
Romanza
b. 1884 Talmadge,
Eugene
b. 1889 Lippmann,
Walter
b. 1890 Paulus,
Friedrich von
b. 1894 Cohen,
Benjamin Victor
b. 1898 Pidgeon, Walter
b. 1899 Clark, Tom
b. 1899 Nevelson,
Louise Berliawsky

b. 1901 Brace, Gerald
Warner
b. 1901 Seifert, Jaroslav
b. 1902 Maurer, Ion
Gheorghe
b. 1903 Villiers, Alan
John
b. 1904 Schapiro,
Meyer
b. 1905 Hardy, Harriet
b. 1906 Tarsis, Valery
Yakovlevich
b. 1907 Moscona,
Nicola
b. 1907 Novotna,
Jarmila
b. 1910 Roosevelt,
Elliott
b. 1911 Moss, Frank
Edward
b. 1912 Bloom, Julius
b. 1915 Baker, Julius
b. 1916 Moro, Aldo
b. 1918 Sinclair, Mary
b. 1920 Rooney,
Mickey
b. 1921 Bogart, Leo
b. 1921 Nestingen, Ivan
Arnold
b. 1922 Gidal, Sonia
b. 1924 Russell, Gail
b. 1927 Breitschwerdt,
Werner
b. 1927 Daily, Thomas
V, Bishop
b. 1929 Horrigan,
Edward, Jr.
b. 1930 Blakely, Colin
(George Edward)
b. 1930 Charles, Ray
b. 1930 Weinberg,
Chester
b. 1931 Maunick,
Edouard Joseph Marc
b. 1931 Suzuki, Pat
b. 1932 Manley, Joan
Adele Daniels
b. 1933 Viguerie,
Richard A(rt)
b. 1934 Johnson,
Nicholas
b. 1935 McCann, Les
b. 1938 Schneider,
Romy
b. 1939 Sullivan, Mike
b. 1940 Peters,
C(larence) J(ames),
(Jr.)
b. 1941 Jackson, George
b. 1943 Iglesias, Julio
b. 1945 Boskin, Michael
J(ay)
b. 1945 Petersen, Paul
b. 1947 Place, Mary
Kay
b. 1949 Springsteen,
Bruce
b. 1954 Wolfe, George
C.
b. 1958 Mize, Larry
b. 1959 Alexander,
Jason
b. 1972 Dupri, Jermaine
d. 1666 Mansart,
Francois
d. 1728 Thomasius

d. 1738 Boerhaave,
Hermann
d. 1764 Dodsley, Robert
d. 1789 Deane, Silas
d. 1828 Bonington,
Richard Parkes
d. 1830 Monroe,
Elizabeth (Kortright)
d. 1835 Bellini,
Vincenzo
d. 1836 Malibran, Maria
Felicita
d. 1843 Clevenger,
Shobal Vail
d. 1850 Artigas, Jose
Gervasio
d. 1852 Vanderlyn, John
d. 1870 Merimee,
Prosper
d. 1882 Wohler,
Friedrich
d. 1885 Spitzweg, Carl
d. 1889 Collins, Wilkie
d. 1896 DuPrez, Gilbert
d. 1898 Johnston,
Richard Malcolm
d. 1902 Powell, John
Wesley
d. 1904 Galle, Emile
d. 1923 Morley, John,
Viscount
d. 1935 Hopper, De
Wolfe
d. 1937 Perkins, Osgood
d. 1939 Freud, Sigmund
d. 1943 Glyn, Elinor
Sutherland
d. 1957 Hartford,
George Ludlum
d. 1962 Hamilton,
Patrick
d. 1968 Pio da
Pietrelcina, Francesco
Forgione, Father
d. 1971 Alexander,
James Waddell, II
d. 1971 Gilbert, Billy
d. 1971 Woodward,
Ellen S.
d. 1972 Huebner,
Clarence R
d. 1973 Neruda, Pablo
d. 1974 Arquette, Cliff
d. 1981 Eckstein,
Gustav
d. 1981 George, Dan,
Chief
d. 1982 Dobozy, Imre
d. 1982 Wakely, Jimmy
d. 1987 Fosse, Bob
d. 1989 Kraushaar, Otto
d. 1991 Pao, Y(ue)
K(ong), Sir
d. 1992 Home, William
Douglas
d. 1992 Ivask, Ivar
Vidrik
d. 1992 Swarthout,
Glendon (Fred)
d. 1992 Van Fleet,
James Alward
d. 1994 Barber, Jerry
d. 1994 Bloch, Robert
Albert
d. 1994 Renaud,
Madeleine

d. 1997 Clarke, Shirley
d. 1998 Frann, Mary

September 24
b. 1501 Cardano, Geronimo
b. 1583 Wallenstein, Albrecht Wenzel Eusebius von
b. 1625 Witt, Johan de
b. 1717 Walpole, Horace
b. 1755 Marshall, John
b. 1825 Harper, Frances Ellen Watkins
b. 1837 Hanna, Mark
b. 1843 Wagnalls, Adam Willis
b. 1860 Crockett, S(amuel) R(utherford)
b. 1862 Brooke, L Leslie
b. 1864 Booth, George Gough
b. 1870 Claude, Georges
b. 1876 Cossart, Ernest
b. 1884 Inonu, Ismet
b. 1890 Ellender, Allen Joseph
b. 1890 Herbert, A(lan) P(atrick), Sir
b. 1891 Branzell, Karin
b. 1891 Friedman, William Frederick
b. 1895 Armour, Tommy
b. 1895 Cournand, Andre Frederic
b. 1896 Fitzgerald, F(rancis) Scott (Key)
b. 1897 Frazier, Edward Franklin
b. 1898 Behn, Harry
b. 1898 Florey, Howard Walter
b. 1898 Moore, Charlotte E(mma)
b. 1899 Dobell, William
b. 1899 Doriot, Georges Frederic
b. 1900 Bechtel, Stephen Davison
b. 1900 Fisher, Ham(mond Edward)
b. 1902 Coy, Harold
b. 1902 Crawford, Cheryl
b. 1905 Ochoa, Severo
b. 1907 Dunning, John Ray
b. 1907 McArthur, Edwin Douglas
b. 1910 Walker, Dixie
b. 1911 Chernenko, Konstantin Ustinovich
b. 1912 Serraillier, Ian Lucien
b. 1915 Gates, Larry
b. 1915 Montoya, Joseph Manuel
b. 1916 Alpert, Hollis
b. 1917 Bundy, William Putnam
b. 1918 Daddario, Emilio Quincy
b. 1918 Lindley, Audra

b. 1919 Ford, Anne McDonnell
b. 1920 Bong, Richard Ira
b. 1921 McKay, Jim
b. 1923 MacRae, Sheila
b. 1923 Navarro, Fats
b. 1924 Bardis, Panos Demetrios
b. 1925 Burbidge, Geoffrey
b. 1925 Guyer, David Leigh
b. 1927 Corman, Gene
b. 1927 Kraus, Alfredo
b. 1928 Brown, Kelly
b. 1930 Langner, Nola
b. 1930 Young, John Watts
b. 1931 Adams, Tom
b. 1931 Collins, Cardiss (Hortense Robertson)
b. 1931 Newley, Anthony (George)
b. 1932 Beriosova, Svetlana
b. 1932 Greenberg, Joanne
b. 1934 Carlson, Arne Helge
b. 1934 Worner, Manfred
b. 1936 Henson, Jim
b. 1937 Elvira, Pablo
b. 1937 Leland, Timothy
b. 1939 Gillott, Jacky
b. 1941 McCartney, Linda
b. 1942 Marsden, Gerry
b. 1946 Greene, Joe
b. 1948 Hartman, Phil
b. 1952 Kennedy, Joseph Patrick, II
b. 1954 Kelly, Patrick
d. 1180 Manuel, I
d. 1541 Paracelsus, Philippus Aureolus
d. 1812 Bagration, Petr Ivanovich
d. 1813 Gretry, Andre Ernest Modeste
d. 1815 Sevier, John
d. 1834 Pedro I
d. 1839 Hayne, Robert Young
d. 1877 Saigo, Takamori
d. 1892 Gilmore, Patrick Sarsfield
d. 1904 Finsen, Niels Ryberg
d. 1920 Faberge, Peter Carl
d. 1924 Estrada Cabrera, Manuel
d. 1929 Zsigmondy, Richard Adolf
d. 1930 Mueller, Otto
d. 1933 Liveright, Horace Brisbin
d. 1939 Gibbons, Floyd Phillips
d. 1939 Laemmle, Carl, Sr.
d. 1945 Argentinita

d. 1945 Geiger, Hans
d. 1948 William, Warren
d. 1961 Welles, Sumner
d. 1963 Chase, Mary Agnes
d. 1973 Neill, A(lexander) S(utherland)
d. 1974 Stone, Dorothy
d. 1975 Hunter, Ian
d. 1976 Brent, Romney
d. 1976 Douglas, Paul Howard
d. 1978 Bostock, Lyman Wesley
d. 1978 Etting, Ruth
d. 1981 Kelly, Patsy
d. 1981 Ochsner, Alton
d. 1982 Churchill, Sarah
d. 1984 Hamilton, Neil
d. 1985 Mann, Paul
d. 1986 Gard, Wayne
d. 1986 Gordy, Robert
d. 1987 Meyer, Joseph
d. 1988 Hale, Nancy
d. 1991 Seuss, Doctor
d. 1999 Exner, Judith Campbell

September 25
b. 1559 Borromini, Francesco
b. 1613 Perrault, Claude
b. 1683 Rameau, Jean-Philippe
b. 1711 Ch'ien Lung
b. 1749 Werner, Abraham Gottlob
b. 1793 Hemans, Felicia Dorothea Browne
b. 1807 Vail, Alfred Lewis
b. 1829 Rossetti, William Michael
b. 1832 Jenney, William LeBaron
b. 1843 Bissell, Melville Reuben
b. 1843 Chamberlin, Thomas Chrowder
b. 1860 Russell, Charles Edward
b. 1864 Hughes, William Morris
b. 1866 Morgan, Thomas Hunt
b. 1872 Cochran, C(harles) B(lake)
b. 1872 Sforza, Carlo
b. 1877 Calles, Plutarco Elias
b. 1889 Cole, George Douglas Howard
b. 1890 Sackheim, Maxwell Byron
b. 1894 Briscoe, Robert
b. 1895 Lawson, John Howard
b. 1896 Pertini, Sandro
b. 1897 Faulkner, William
b. 1898 Brackman, Robert
b. 1898 Judd, Walter H(enry)

b. 1899 Buck, Paul Herman
b. 1899 Landis, James McCauley
b. 1901 Bresson, Robert
b. 1901 Houser, Clarence
b. 1902 Hoffman, Al
b. 1903 Beech, Olive Ann (Mellor)
b. 1903 Rothko, Mark
b. 1905 Smith, Red
b. 1906 Figueres Ferrer, Jose
b. 1906 Shostakovich, Dmitri Dmitryevich
b. 1909 Glasspole, Florizel Augustus
b. 1911 Williams, Eric Eustace
b. 1912 Cooke, Jack Kent
b. 1914 Osborne, Leone Neal
b. 1915 Sperling, Godfrey, Jr.
b. 1918 Rizzuto, Phil(ip Francis)
b. 1921 Muldoon, Robert David, Sir
b. 1922 Bondarchuk, Sergei (Fedorovich)
b. 1923 DeRoburt, Hammer, Sir
b. 1926 Ray, Aldo
b. 1927 Davis, Colin Rex, Sir
b. 1928 Gwaltney, John Langston
b. 1929 Barker, Ronnie
b. 1929 White, Kevin Hagan
b. 1931 Cronin, James Watson
b. 1931 Walters, Barbara
b. 1932 Gould, Glenn Herbert
b. 1932 Silverstein, Shel(by)
b. 1932 Suarez Gonzales, Adolfo
b. 1933 Brown, Hubie
b. 1933 Darling, Erik
b. 1933 Tyson, Ian
b. 1934 Comer, James P(ierpont)
b. 1935 Sjowall, Maj
b. 1936 Prowse, Juliet
b. 1936 Traore, Moussa
b. 1939 Brittan, Leon
b. 1942 Bonavena, Oscar
b. 1943 Gates, Robert M(ichael)
b. 1943 Walden, Robert
b. 1944 Douglas, Michael Kirk
b. 1946 Kendal, Felicity
b. 1947 Tiegs, Cheryl
b. 1949 Williams, Anson
b. 1951 Almodovar, Pedro
b. 1951 McAdoo, Bob
b. 1952 Hamill, Mark

b. 1952 Hooks, Bell
b. 1952 Moraga, Cherrie
b. 1952 Reeve, Christopher
b. 1958 Hillis, W(illiam) Daniel, (Jr.)
b. 1961 Locklear, Heather
b. 1965 Pippen, Scottie
b. 1968 Smith, Will
d. 1534 Clement VII
d. 1617 Suarez, Francisco
d. 1680 Butler, Samuel
d. 1849 Strauss, Johann, Sr.
d. 1870 Grier, Robert Cooper
d. 1871 Papineau, Louis-Joseph
d. 1872 Cartwright, Peter
d. 1877 LeVerrier, Urbain Jean Joseph
d. 1900 Lazear, Jesse William
d. 1900 Van Lew, Elizabeth
d. 1910 Mills, Darius Ogden
d. 1915 Hervieu, Paul-Ernest
d. 1919 Freer, Charles Lang
d. 1920 Schiff, Jacob Henry
d. 1924 Crabtree, Lotta
d. 1928 Outcault, Richard Felton
d. 1929 Huggins, Miller James
d. 1933 Ehrenfest, Paul
d. 1933 Lardner, Ring(gold Wilmer), Sr.
d. 1936 Horlick, William
d. 1936 Sims, William Sowden
d. 1940 Clark, Marguerite
d. 1950 Tairov, Aleksandr Yakovlevich
d. 1958 Watson, John Broadus
d. 1959 Broderick, Helen
d. 1960 Nichols, Ruth Rowland
d. 1960 Post, Emily (Price)
d. 1961 Fay, Frank
d. 1968 Gunther, Hans F K
d. 1968 Woolrich, Cornell
d. 1969 Reed, Peter Hugh
d. 1970 Fisher, James Maxwell McConnell
d. 1970 Liebling, Estelle
d. 1970 Remarque, Erich Maria

d. 1971 Black, Hugo LaFayette
d. 1975 Considine, Bob
d. 1976 Faber, Red
d. 1980 Bonham, John Henry
d. 1980 Milestone, Lewis
d. 1982 Poulson, Norris
d. 1983 Leopold III
d. 1984 Pidgeon, Walter
d. 1985 Fishback, Margaret
d. 1987 Astor, Mary
d. 1987 Daugherty, Duffy
d. 1987 Williams, Emlyn
d. 1988 Carter, Billy
d. 1989 Hoopes, Darlington
d. 1991 Barbie, Klaus
d. 1995 Delany, Annie Elizabeth

September 26
b. 1754 Proust, Joseph Louis
b. 1774 Appleseed, Johnny
b. 1783 Taylor, Jane
b. 1791 Gericault, Jean Louis Andre Theodore
b. 1793 Hobson, William
b. 1798 Mosquera, Tomas Cipriano de
b. 1833 Bradlaugh, Charles
b. 1848 Walters, Henry
b. 1854 Bausch, Edward
b. 1859 Bacheller, Irving Addison
b. 1862 Davies, Arthur Bowen
b. 1869 McCay, Winsor
b. 1870 Christian X
b. 1874 Hine, Lewis Wickes
b. 1875 Gwenn, Edmund
b. 1876 Abbott, Edith
b. 1877 Cortot, Alfred-Denis
b. 1886? Hill, Archibald Vivian
b. 1887 Wallis, Barnes Neville, Sir
b. 1888 Dobie, J(ames) Frank
b. 1888 Eliot, T(homas) S(tearns)
b. 1889 Heidegger, Martin
b. 1891 Munch, Charles
b. 1892 Lynd, Robert Staughton
b. 1892? Tsvetayeva, Marina Ivanovna
b. 1893 Rosenstein, Nettie
b. 1895 Holden, Fay
b. 1895 Raft, George
b. 1897 Paul VI
b. 1897 Telva, Marion

b. 1898 Gershwin, George
b. 1898 Lockridge, Richard
b. 1899 Dawson, William Levi
b. 1901 Cook, Donald
b. 1902 Anastasia, Albert
b. 1907 Blunt, Anthony Frederick
b. 1908 Marlowe, Sylvia
b. 1912 Cloud, Preston (Ercelle)
b. 1914 LaLanne, Jack
b. 1915 Brimsek, Frankie
b. 1917 Rico, Don(ato)
b. 1918 Morley, Eric Douglas
b. 1919 Britton, Barbara
b. 1920 Anthony, Michael
b. 1921 Ekwensi, Cyprian Odiatu Duaka
b. 1924 Wincelberg, Shimon
b. 1925 Robbins, Marty
b. 1926 Coltrane, Trane
b. 1926 London, Julie
b. 1927 O'Neal, Patrick
b. 1928 Ray, Robert D
b. 1928? Strenger, Hermann Josef
b. 1929 Murray, Cecil (Leonard)
b. 1930 Wunderlich, Fritz
b. 1934 Mandela, Winnie
b. 1934 Mihajlov, Mihajlo
b. 1934 Morris, Greg
b. 1937 Weintraub, Jerry
b. 1938 Lukanov, Andrei
b. 1939 Douglas, Donna
b. 1942 Anzaldua, Gloria
b. 1942 McCord, Kent
b. 1945 Ferry, Bryan
b. 1946 Dworkin, Andrea
b. 1946 Whitman, Christine Todd
b. 1947 Anderson, Lynn
b. 1948? Hurt, Mary Beth Supinger
b. 1948 Newton-John, Olivia
b. 1949 Smiley, Jane (Graves)
b. 1951 Defeo, Ronald
b. 1953 Skate, Bill
b. 1955 Carter, Carlene
b. 1956 Bulatovic, Momir
b. 1957 Hamilton, Linda
b. 1959 Gedman, Rich(ard Leo, Jr.)
b. 1962 Anderson, Melissa Sue

b. 1981 Williams, Serena
d. 1600 Le Jeune, Claude
d. 1781 Lewis, Andrew
d. 1820 Boone, Daniel
d. 1826 Laing, Alexander Gordon
d. 1842 Wellesley, Richard Colley, 1st Marquess Wellesley
d. 1846 Clarkson, Thomas
d. 1848 Bronte, Patrick Branwell
d. 1854 LaFever Minard
d. 1868 Mobius, August Ferdinand
d. 1873 Wheelwright, William
d. 1884 Garrett, John Work
d. 1898 Davenport, Fanny Lily Gypsy
d. 1901 Nicolay, John George
d. 1904 Hearn, Lafcadio
d. 1908 Parsons, Frank
d. 1914 Macke, August
d. 1915 Hardie, James Keir
d. 1918 Simmel, Georg
d. 1922 Watson, Thomas Edward
d. 1932 Davenport, Eva
d. 1935 Adams, Andy
d. 1936 Monroe, Harriet
d. 1937 Filene, Edward Albert
d. 1937 Smith, Bessie
d. 1938 Taylor, Graham
d. 1941 Walter, Eugene
d. 1947 Lofting, Hugh
d. 1951 Allan, Montagu, Sir
d. 1951 Bryant, Lane
d. 1952 Parker, George Swinnerton
d. 1952 Santayana, George
d. 1957 Clark, Charles Badger
d. 1959 Bandaranaike, S(olomon) W(est) R(idgeway) D(ias)
d. 1961 Eichelberger, Robert Lawrence
d. 1961 Wilson, Charles Erwin
d. 1963 Pennell, Joseph Stanley
d. 1966 Edson, Gus
d. 1966 Kane, Helen
d. 1971 Gipson, Lawrence Henry
d. 1972 Correll, Charles J
d. 1973 Bemis, Samuel Flagg
d. 1973 Magnani, Anna
d. 1974 McCarten, John
d. 1975 Paludan, Jacob
d. 1976 Ruzicka, Leopold Stephen
d. 1977 Lombardi, Ernie
d. 1977 Shankar, Uday

d. 1978 Siegbahn, Karl
Manne Georg
d. 1979 Cromwell, John
d. 1982 Bettis, Valerie
d. 1982 Cox, Allyn
d. 1982 Kollsman, Paul
d. 1983 Stapleton, Ruth
Carter
d. 1984 Manne, Shelly
d. 1987 Anstey, Edgar
Harold McFarlane
d. 1990 Moravia,
Alberto
d. 1992 Manheim,
Ralph
d. 1993 Berberova, Nina
Nikolaevna
d. 1993 Pennel, John
(Thomas)
d. 1996 Kotzky, Alex
Sylvester
d. 1998 Carter, Betty
d. 1999 Brauer, Jerald
C(arl)

September 27
b. 1389 Medici, Cosimo
de
b. 1627 Bossuet,
Jacques Benigne
b. 1722 Adams, Samuel
b. 1724 Busching,
Anton Friedrich
b. 1772 Jefferson,
Martha
b. 1783 Iturbide,
Augustin de
b. 1792 Cruikshank,
George
b. 1803 DuPont, Samuel
Francis
b. 1827 Revels, Hiram
Rhodes
b. 1830 Hazen, William
Babcock
b. 1840 Mahan, Alfred
Thayer
b. 1840 Nast, Thomas
b. 1842 Sherwin, Henry
Alden
b. 1855 Morton, Joy
b. 1862 Botha, Louis
b. 1864 Dharmapala,
Anagarika
b. 1873 Chatfield,
Alfred E Montacute,
Baron
b. 1874 Reed, Myrtle
b. 1875 Deledda, Grazia
b. 1877 Dole, James
b. 1879 Scott, Cyril
(Meir)
b. 1884 Zirato, Bruno
b. 1885 Blackstone,
Harry
b. 1885 Smith, Tommy
b. 1886 Moley,
Raymond Charles
b. 1888 Dean, Basil
b. 1895 Arends, Leslie
Cornelius
b. 1896 Ervin, Sam(uel
James Jr.)
b. 1898 Youmans,
Vincent
b. 1899 Eiseman,
Florence

b. 1900 Paddleford,
Clementine Haskin
b. 1906 Empson,
William, Sir
b. 1908 Chappell,
William
b. 1909 Hauser, Philip
M(orris)
b. 1913 Ellis, Albert
(Isaac)
b. 1914 Marshall,
Catherine
b. 1916 Fischetti, John
b. 1916 Stratton,
Samuel S(tuddiford)
b. 1917 Auchincloss,
Louis
b. 1918 Ryle, Martin,
Sir
b. 1919 Percy, Charles
Harting
b. 1920 Conrad,
William
b. 1920 Stommel, Henry
Melson
b. 1922 Jancso, Miklos
b. 1922 Newman, Joe
Dwight
b. 1922 Penn, Arthur
Hiller
b. 1924 Powell, Earl
b. 1925 Edwards,
Robert Geoffrey
b. 1926 Meadows,
Jayne Cotter
b. 1927 Gellis, Roberta
Leah Jacobs
b. 1928 Neufeld,
Elizabeth F(ondal)
b. 1929 Harris, Leonard
b. 1929 Thompson,
Sada Carolyn
b. 1930 Kipnis, Igor
b. 1933 Nolan, Kathy
b. 1934 Brimley,
Wilford
b. 1934 Howar, Barbara
b. 1934 Jarman, Claude,
Jr.
b. 1934 Schaap, Dick
b. 1936 Cornelius, Don
b. 1938 Farmer,
Don(ald Edwin)
b. 1939 Whitworth,
Kathy
b. 1941 Richie, Leroy
C.
b. 1941 Schopf, J(ames)
William
b. 1942 Dith Pran
b. 1942 Weller, Michael
b. 1943 Bachman,
Randy
b. 1945 Dichter, Mischa
b. 1948? Meat Loaf
b. 1949? Martinez,
A(dolpe)
b. 1949 Schmidt, Mike
b. 1953 Abbott, Diane
(Julie)
b. 1953 Watts, Heather
b. 1954 Barrow, Keith
E
b. 1956 Handford,
Martin

b. 1958 Cassidy, Shaun
Paul
d. 1660 Vincent de
Paul, Saint
d. 1730 Eusden,
Laurence
d. 1805 Moultrie,
William
d. 1833 Roy, Ram
Mohun
d. 1838 Courtois,
Bernard
d. 1854 Ogden, Peter
Skene
d. 1854 Reed, Henry
Hope
d. 1870 Comstock,
Henry Tompkins
Paige
d. 1876 Bragg, Braxton
d. 1886 Cooke, John
Esten
d. 1891 Goncharov,
Ivan Aleksandrovich
d. 1915 Gourmont,
Remy (-Marie-
Charles) de
d. 1917 Degas, (Hilaire
Germain) Edgar
d. 1919 Patti, Adelina
Juana Maria
d. 1921 Humperdinck,
Engelbert
d. 1940 Wagner-
Jaurregg, Julius, von
d. 1944 McPherson,
Aimee Semple
d. 1949 Adler, David
d. 1950 Knox, Rose
Markward
d. 1950 Woodward,
William E
d. 1953 Fritzsche, Hans
d. 1956 Zaharias, Babe
Didrikson
d. 1960 Pankhurst,
Sylvia
d. 1961 Doolittle, Hilda
d. 1962 Skidmore,
Louis
d. 1963 Christiansen,
Arthur
d. 1964 Waln, Nora
d. 1965 Bow, Clara
Gordon
d. 1975 Lang, John
Thomas
d. 1976 Fishbein,
Morris
d. 1977 Winslow, Ola
Elizabeth
d. 1978 Johnston, Neil
d. 1979 Fields, Gracie
d. 1979 Hunnicutt,
Arthur
d. 1980 Gelb, Lawrence
d. 1981 Montgomery,
Robert Henry
d. 1982 Armour,
Norman
d. 1982 Bowen, Billy
d. 1982 Romano,
Umberto
d. 1983 Shear, Murray
Jacob

d. 1984 Bunker,
Ellsworth
d. 1985 Kertesz, Andre
d. 1985 Nolan, Lloyd
d. 1988 Shannon,
William Vincent
d. 1990 O'Brien, Larry
d. 1991 Fuller, Roy
Broadbent
d. 1991 Sprague,
R(obert) C(hapman)
d. 1993 Doolittle, James
H(arold)
d. 1994 Lleras Restrepo,
Carlos
d. 1996 Najib Ahmadzi
d. 1997 Trampler,
Walter
d. 1998 Walker, Doak

September 28
b. 1547 Aleman, Mateo
b. 1778 Douvillier,
Suzanne Theodore
Vaillande
b. 1785 Walker, David
b. 1789 Bright, Richard
b. 1803 Merimee,
Prosper
b. 1807 Guyot, Arnold
Henry
b. 1834 Lamoureux,
Charles
b. 1839 Willard,
Frances Elizabeth
Caroline
b. 1840 Peck, George
Wilbur
b. 1841 Clemenceau,
Georges Eugene
Benjamin
b. 1852 Moissan,
Ferdinand Frederick
Henri
b. 1854 Sedgwick,
Adam
b. 1855 Brush, George
b. 1856 Thompson,
Edward Herbert
b. 1856 Wiggin, Kate
Douglas
b. 1863 MacMonnies,
Fred W
b. 1866 Tschirky, Oscar
b. 1871 Badoglio, Pietro
b. 1880 Flanders, Ralph
Edward
b. 1881 DeCordoba,
Pedro
b. 1881 Sears, Eleonora
Randolph
b. 1887 Brundage,
Avery
b. 1888 McNeile,
Herman Cyril
b. 1892 Rice, Elmer
b. 1893 Field, Marshall,
III
b. 1895 Harrison,
Wallace Kirkman
b. 1895 Petrie, Charles
Alexander, Sir
b. 1897 Fraenkel,
Heinrich
b. 1898 Carter, Boake
b. 1901 Paley, William
Samuel

b. 1902 Okada, Kenzo
b. 1902 Sullivan,
Ed(ward Vincent)
b. 1903 Billington, Ray
Allen
b. 1903 Hansell,
Haywood Shepherd,
Jr.
b. 1905 Rivers, L(ucius)
Mendel
b. 1905 Schmeling,
Max(imilian)
b. 1906 Miller, Paul
b. 1907 Edwards, Turk
b. 1908 Frondizi, Arturo
b. 1909 Capp, Al
b. 1910 Macapagal,
Diosdado P(angan)
b. 1911 Howe, Syd(ney
Harris)
b. 1911 Vines,
Ellsworth
b. 1913 Marble, Alice
b. 1913 Peters, Ellis
b. 1915 Rosenberg,
Ethel Greenglass
b. 1916 Finch, Peter
b. 1917 Davison,
Frederic Ellis
b. 1917 Somes, Michael
(George)
b. 1919 Harmon, Tom
b. 1920 Davie, Alan
b. 1922 Sedney, Jules
b. 1923 Windom,
William
b. 1924 Mastroianni,
Marcello
b. 1925 Cray, Seymour
R.
b. 1925 Stang, Arnold
b. 1926 Bressani,
Ricardo
b. 1928 Silver, Horace
Ward Martin Tavares
b. 1933 Kunin,
Madeleine May
b. 1934 Bardot, Brigitte
b. 1935 Crampton,
Bruce Sidney
b. 1935 Sears, Heather
b. 1937 Dickinson,
Brian
b. 1937 Schul, Bob
b. 1938 King, Ben E.
b. 1939 Luedtke, Kurt
(Mamre)
b. 1942 Taylor, Charley
b. 1946 Vermeij, Geerat
J(acobus)
b. 1947 Hasina Wajed
b. 1950 Hofsiss, Jack
Bernard
b. 1950 Sayles, John
b. 1950 Tosovsky, Josef
b. 1952 Kristel, Sylvia
b. 1954 Largent, Steve
M
b. 1959 Worrell, Todd
Roland
b. 1962 Fuhr, Grant
Scott
b. 1964 Garofalo,
Janeane
b. 1968? Zappa, Moon
Unit

b. 1973 Paltrow,
Gwyneth
d. 1494 Poliziano,
Angelo
d. 1582 Buchanan,
George
d. 1776 Colden,
Cadwallader
d. 1789 Day, Thomas
d. 1839 Dunlap,
William
d. 1859 Ritter, Karl
d. 1891 Melville,
Herman
d. 1895 Pasteur, Louis
d. 1898 Bayard, Thomas
Francis
d. 1899 Segantini,
Giovanni
d. 1914 Sears, Richard
Warren
d. 1917 Hulme, Thomas
Ernest
d. 1927 Einthoven,
Willem
d. 1930 Guggenheim,
Daniel
d. 1938 Conrad, Con
d. 1938 Duryea, Charles
Edgar
d. 1948 Toland, Gregg
d. 1953 Hubble, Edwin
Powell
d. 1954 Lytell, Bert
d. 1954 Shull, George
Harrison
d. 1956 Boeing,
William Edward
d. 1956 Hodge,
Frederick Webb
d. 1963 Raisa, Rosa
d. 1964 Brown, Nacio
Herb
d. 1964 Marx, Harpo
d. 1966 Breton, Andre
d. 1966 Smith, Lillian
d. 1970 Dos Passos,
John (Roderigo)
d. 1970 Nasser, Gamal
Abdel
d. 1973 Auden,
W(ystan) H(ugh)
d. 1974 Howes, Frank
Stewart
d. 1976 Folsom, Marion
Bayard
d. 1978 John Paul I
d. 1981 Betancourt,
Romulo
d. 1981 Hinton, Walter
d. 1985 Abbott,
L(enwood) B(allard)
d. 1986 Helpmann,
Robert Murray, Sir
d. 1986 Semenov,
Nikolai Nikolaevich
d. 1987 Madden, Ray
John
d. 1989 Marcos,
Ferdinand Edralin
d. 1991 Davis, Miles
Dewey, III
d. 1993 DeVries, Peter

September 29
b. 1511 Servetus,
Michael

b. 1518 Tintoretto
b. 1547 Cervantes
(Saavedra), Miguel
(de)
b. 1640 Coysevox,
Antoine
b. 1703 Boucher,
Francois
b. 1725 Clive, Robert
b. 1758 Nelson, Horatio
Nelson, Viscount
b. 1759 Beckford,
William
b. 1803 Sturm, Charles
Francois
b. 1810 Gaskell,
Elizabeth Cleghorn
b. 1826 Chesney,
Charles Cornwallis
b. 1831 Schofield, John
McAllister
b. 1838 Richardson,
Henry Hobson
b. 1849 Schwatka,
Frederik
b. 1858 Mugnone,
Leopoldo
b. 1859 Biggs, Hermann
Michael
b. 1864 Unamuno (y
Jugo), Miguel de
b. 1866 Hayford,
J(oseph)
E(phraim)Casely
b. 1871 Machado y
Morales, Gerardo
b. 1872 Murchison,
Kenneth MacKenzie
b. 1881 von Mises,
Ludwig (Edler)
b. 1891 James, Marquis
b. 1891 Sevitzky,
Fabien
b. 1895 Rhine, J(oseph)
B(anks)
b. 1895 Turner, Roscoe
Wilson
b. 1897 Agar, Herbert
Sebastian
b. 1897 Queeny, Edgar
Monsanto
b. 1898 Lysenko,
Trofim Denisovich
b. 1899 Butlin, William
Heygate Edmund, Sir
b. 1900 Gabor, Jolie
b. 1901 Fermi, Enrico
b. 1903 Aleman, Miguel
b. 1903 Garson, Greer
b. 1903 Harnwell,
Gaylord Probasco
b. 1903 Neher, Fred
b. 1904 Eiermann, Egon
b. 1905 La Barba, Fidel
b. 1907 Autry, Gene
b. 1910 Boyd, Bill
b. 1910 Bruce, Virginia
b. 1910 Frankovich,
Mike J
b. 1912 Antonioni,
Michelangelo
b. 1913 Dixon, Paul
Rand
b. 1913 Kramer, Stanley
E

b. 1914 Condit, Carl
Wilbur
b. 1915 Handlin, Oscar
b. 1915 Marshall,
Brenda
b. 1916 Buero Vallejo,
Antonio
b. 1916 Howard, Trevor
Wallace
b. 1917 Luce, Charles
(Franklin)
b. 1920 Butler, John
b. 1922 Scott, Lizabeth
b. 1923 Phillips, Bum
b. 1925 Forrest, Steve
b. 1925 Mac Cready,
Paul Beattie
b. 1925 Tower, John
Goodwin
b. 1927 McCloskey,
Paul Norton, Jr.
b. 1927 Mertz, Barbara
Louise Gross
b. 1929 Newhart, Bob
b. 1930 Bonynge,
Richard
b. 1931 Ekberg, Anita
b. 1932 Benton, Robert
Douglass
b. 1932 Pfeiffer, Jane
Cahill
b. 1933 Machel, Samora
Moises
b. 1938 Berlusconi,
Silvio
b. 1938 Kok, Wim
b. 1939 Linville, Larry
Lavon
b. 1940 Lewis, Jerry
Lee
b. 1942 Kahn, Madeline
(Gail)
b. 1942 McShane, Ian
b. 1942 Ponty, Jean-Luc
b. 1942 Tesich, Steve
b. 1943 Walesa, Lech
b. 1944 Gibson,
Michael
b. 1948 Gumbel, Bryant
(Charles)
b. 1956 Coe, Sebastian
Newbold
b. 1960 Deer, Rob(ert
George)
d. 48BC Pompey the
Great
d. 1531 Sarto, Andrea
del
d. 1674 Eeckhout,
Gerbrand van den
d. 1825 Shays, Daniel
d. 1833 Ferdinand, VII
d. 1839 Mohs, Friedrich
d. 1867 Price, Sterling
d. 1877 Meiggs, Henry
d. 1889 Faidherbe,
Louis Leon Cesar
d. 1902 Zola, Emile
(Edouard Charles)
d. 1910 Davis, Rebecca
Blaine Harding
d. 1910 Homer,
Winslow
d. 1913 Diesel, Rudolf
Christian Karl

b. 1759 Weems, Mason Locke
b. 1759 Wood, Sarah Sayward Barrell Keating
b. 1781 Lawrence, James
b. 1799 Choate, Rufus
b. 1799 Russwurm, John Brown
b. 1804 Stokes, William
b. 1826 Hotchkiss, Benjamin Berkeley
b. 1832 Harrison, Caroline (Lavinia Scott)
b. 1838 Field, Kate
b. 1847 Besant, Annie Wood
b. 1849 DeYoung, Michel Harry
b. 1865 Dukas, Paul Abraham
b. 1868 Ozaki, Koyo
b. 1881 Boeing, William Edward
b. 1885 Untermeyer, Louis
b. 1889 Sockman, Ralph W
b. 1890 Holloway, Stanley
b. 1890 Joyce, Alice
b. 1891 McLean, Robert
b. 1893 Baldwin, Faith
b. 1895 Liaquat Ali, Khan
b. 1896 Healy, Ted
b. 1899 Patterson, William Allan
b. 1903 Coulouris, George
b. 1904 Frisch, O(tto) R(obert)
b. 1904 Haider, Michael Lawrence
b. 1904 Horowitz, Vladimir
b. 1907 Fong, Hiram Leong
b. 1907 Lawrenson, Helen Brown
b. 1909 Sloane, Everett
b. 1909 Yorty, Sam(uel William)
b. 1910 Parker, Bonnie
b. 1911 Boland, Edward P(atrick)
b. 1911 Hickman, Herman Michael, Jr.
b. 1911 Knebel, Fletcher
b. 1914 Boorstin, Daniel J(oseph)
b. 1915 Bruner, Jerome Seymour
b. 1917 Whyte, William H(ollingsworth)
b. 1920 Matthau, Walter
b. 1921 Hillis, Margaret
b. 1921 Whitmore, James Allen
b. 1924 Carter, Jimmy
b. 1924 Rehnquist, William Hubbs

b. 1925 Biebuyck, Daniel Prosper
b. 1926 Morath, Max Edward
b. 1926 Williams, Roger
b. 1927 Bosley, Tom
b. 1928 Harvey, Laurence
b. 1928 Peppard, George
b. 1930 Harris, Richard, Sir
b. 1932 Collins, Albert
b. 1935 Andrews, Julie
b. 1935 Hermann, Jane Pomerance
b. 1936 Villella, Edward Joseph
b. 1937 Poons, Lawrence
b. 1938 Gillette, Paul
b. 1938 McFadden, Mary Josephine
b. 1938 Stevens, Stella
b. 1939 Archer, George
b. 1939 Carruthers, George Robert, Dr.
b. 1940 Corben, Richard Vance
b. 1943 Williams, Willie Lawrence
b. 1945 Carew, Rod(ney Cline)
b. 1945 Hathaway, Donny
b. 1946 O'Brien, Tim
b. 1947 Collins, Stephen
b. 1952 James, Juanita (T.)
b. 1953 Waitz, Grete
b. 1959 Ndour, Youssou
b. 1962 Morales, Esai
b. 1963 McGwire, Mark (David)
d. 1499 Ficino, Marsilio
d. 1684 Corneille, Pierre
d. 1708 Blow, John
d. 1854 Royall, Anne Newport
d. 1863 Emmons, Ebenezer
d. 1864 Flores, Juan Jose
d. 1873 Landseer, Edwin Henry, Sir
d. 1885 Cooper, Anthony Ashley, 7th Earl of Shaftesbury
d. 1893 Jowett, Benjamin
d. 1926 Finck, Henry Theophilus
d. 1929 Bourdelle, Emile-Antoine
d. 1935 Nieman, Lucius William
d. 1945 Cannon, Walter Bradford
d. 1947 Martinez Sierra, Gregorio
d. 1947 Rogers, James Gamble
d. 1949 Villard, Oswald (Garrison)
d. 1953 Cohn, Edwin Joseph

d. 1953 Marin, John
d. 1953 Munn, Frank
d. 1956 Von Tilzer, Albert
d. 1957 Candler, Charles Howard
d. 1961 Cook, Donald
d. 1961 Reid Dick, William, Sir
d. 1962 Bemelmans, Ludwig
d. 1963 Nordstrom, John
d. 1964 Toch, Ernst
d. 1968 Duchamp, Marcel
d. 1968 Guardini, Romano
d. 1969 Francis, Thomas, Jr.
d. 1972 Leakey, Louis Seymour Bazett
d. 1975 MacPhail, Larry
d. 1979 Arzner, Dorothy
d. 1979 Harris, Roy
d. 1980 Jones, Edward Vason
d. 1982 Bernbach, William
d. 1984 Alston, Walter Emmons
d. 1985 White, E(lwyn) B(rooks)
d. 1988 Sitwell, Sacheverell, Sir
d. 1990 LeMay, Curtis Emerson
d. 1999 Arison, Ted

October 2
b. 1452 Richard III
b. 1538 Borromeo, Charles, Saint
b. 1755 Adams, Hannah
b. 1790 Ross, John
b. 1800 Turner, Nat
b. 1821 Stewart, Alexander Peter
b. 1830 Pratt, Charles
b. 1831 Godkin, E(dwin) L(awrence)
b. 1832 Tylor, Edward Bennett, Sir
b. 1839 Thoma, Hans
b. 1847 Hindenburg, Paul Ludwig Hans Anton von Beneckendorff und
b. 1851 Foch, Ferdinand
b. 1852 Ramsay, William, Sir
b. 1854 Geddes, Patrick, Sir
b. 1865 Casey, Dan(iel Maurice)
b. 1869 Gandhi, Mahatma
b. 1871 Hull, Cordell
b. 1874 Woodward, William E
b. 1877 Hayden, Carl Trumball
b. 1878 Gibson, Wilfred Wilson
b. 1879 Stevens, Wallace

b. 1885 Rohde, Ruth Bryan Owen
b. 1890 Marx, Groucho
b. 1895 Streeter, Ruth
b. 1896 Duclos, Jacques
b. 1898? Profaci, Joe
b. 1898 Wank, Roland A
b. 1900 Abbott, Bud
b. 1901 Campbell, Roy
b. 1901 Draper, Charles Stark
b. 1904 Greene, Graham (Henry)
b. 1904 Shastri, Lal Badahur
b. 1905 Seper, Franjo
b. 1906 Ley, Willy
b. 1907 Todd, Alexander (Robertus), Sir
b. 1909 Fielding, Lewis J
b. 1909 Hosking, Eric J
b. 1909 Raymond, Alex(ander Gillespie)
b. 1910 Carmichael, James Vinson
b. 1912 Knudsen, Semon E(mil)
b. 1917 DeDuve, Christian Rene Marie Joseph
b. 1919 Buchanan, James McGill
b. 1921 Crispin, Edmund
b. 1926 Farenthold, Frances T(arlton)
b. 1926 Morris, Jan
b. 1927 Clarke, Shirley
b. 1928 Felker, Clay S
b. 1928 McFarland, Spanky
b. 1928 Pannenberg, Wolfhart Ulrich
b. 1929 Gunn, Moses
b. 1932 Wills, Maury
b. 1935 Lawrence, Robert (Henry), Jr.
b. 1937 Cochran, Johnnie
b. 1939 Reed, Rex
b. 1945 McLean, Don
b. 1946 Cox, Edward Finch
b. 1948 Karan, Donna Faske
b. 1949 Leibovitz, Annie
b. 1950 Khambatta, Persis
b. 1950 Rutherford, Michael
b. 1951 Sting
b. 1957 Saint, Assotto
b. 1958 Jackson, Freddie
b. 1960 Anderson, Glenn Chris
b. 1962 Rypien, Mark
b. 1967 Muster, Thomas
b. 1971 Tiffany
d. 1780 Andre, John
d. 1782 Lee, Charles
d. 1799 Iredell, James

d. 1803 Adams, Samuel
d. 1842 Channing, William Ellery
d. 1846 Waterhouse, Benjamin
d. 1849 Mohammed Ali
d. 1853 Arago, Dominque Francois Jean
d. 1872 Lieber, Franz
d. 1892 Renan, (Joseph) Ernest
d. 1897 Andree, Salomon August
d. 1897 Dow, Neal
d. 1909 Schley, Winfield Scott
d. 1920 Bruch, Max
d. 1927 Arrhenius, Svante August
d. 1928 Barron, Clarence Walker
d. 1931 Lipton, Thomas Johnstone, Sir
d. 1931 Nielsen, Carl August
d. 1933 Stribling, Young
d. 1939 Mundelein, George William
d. 1940 Stanley, Freelan O
d. 1943 Dett, Robert Nathaniel
d. 1947 MacNeil, Hermon Atkins
d. 1950 Fitzgerald, John Francis
d. 1954 Greene, Henry Mather
d. 1956 Bancroft, George
d. 1958 Stopes, Marie Charlotte Carmichael
d. 1960 Recto, Claro M.
d. 1961 Lewis, Essington
d. 1962 Lovejoy, Frank
d. 1969 Arbuthnot, May Hill
d. 1970 Wilson, Edward Arthur
d. 1971 Laubenthal, Rudolf
d. 1973 Hartman, Paul
d. 1973 Nurmi, Paavo Johannes
d. 1974 Shukshin, Vasilii Makarovich
d. 1975 Kamaraj, Kumaraswami
d. 1981 Golden, Harry Lewis
d. 1981 La Barba, Fidel
d. 1981 Scott, Hazel Dorothy
d. 1985 Caudill, Rebecca
d. 1985 Hudson, Rock
d. 1987 Carroll, Madeleine
d. 1987 Medawar, Peter Brian, Sir
d. 1987 Piret, Edgar L

d. 1988 Issigonis, Alec Arnold Constantine, Sir
d. 1988 Pope, Generoso
d. 1990 Adler, Peter Herman
d. 1990 Holland, Leland James
d. 1991 Dimitrios I, Patriarch
d. 1991 Garrison, Lloyd K(irkham)
d. 1991 Shea, William Alfred
d. 1994 Nelson, Harriet
d. 1996 Bourassa, (Jean) Robert
d. 1996 Brennan, Peter J(oseph)
d. 1998 Autry, Gene
d. 1999 Richardson, Lee

October 3
b. 1771 Place, Francis
b. 1792 Morazan, Jose Francisco
b. 1800 Bancroft, George
b. 1802 Ripley, George
b. 1803 Gorrie, John
b. 1804 Harris, Townsend
b. 1818 MacMillan, Alexander
b. 1829 Holly, James Theodore
b. 1844 Manson, Patrick, Sir
b. 1854 Gorgas, William Crawford
b. 1856 Fortune, Timothy Thomas
b. 1856 Hare, James Henry
b. 1858 Duse, Eleanora
b. 1870 Kraus, Felix von
b. 1872 Clarke, Fred Clifford
b. 1873 Horlick, Alexander James
b. 1873 Post, Emily (Price)
b. 1877 Gildersleeve, Virginia Crocheron
b. 1879 Bigelow, Henry Bryant
b. 1880 Oland, Warner
b. 1882 Jackson, A(lexander) Y(oung)
b. 1886 Alain-Fournier
b. 1889 Ossietzky, Carl von
b. 1890 Hull, Henry
b. 1890 Obolensky, Serge
b. 1891 Gannett, Lewis Stiles
b. 1894 Sharett, Moshe
b. 1897 Aragon, Louis Marie Antoine Alfred
b. 1898 McCarey, Leo
b. 1899 Berg, Gertrude
b. 1900 Wolfe, Thomas (Clayton)
b. 1902 Costa e Silva, Arthur da

b. 1908 Burke, Johnny
b. 1910 Hines, John E(lbridge)
b. 1911 Hordern, Michael
b. 1913 Pitt, David Thomas
b. 1916 Alvarino (de Leira), Angeles
b. 1916 Herriot, James
b. 1918 Cone, Molly Lamken
b. 1923 Skrowaczewski, Stanislaw
b. 1924 Kurtzman, Harvey
b. 1925 Vidal, Gore
b. 1925 Wein, George Theodore
b. 1927 Kenojuak
b. 1928 Bruhn, Erik Belton Evers
b. 1928 Ramphal, Shridath Surendranath
b. 1929 Stern, Bert
b. 1930 Eden, Nicholas
b. 1930 Lee, Ming Cho
b. 1931 Hall, Glenn Henry
b. 1933 Thompson, Thomas
b. 1935 Duke, Charles Moss, Jr.
b. 1936 Perry, Jim
b. 1936 Reich, Steve
b. 1938 Cochran, Eddie
b. 1940 Ferris, Barbara Gillian
b. 1940 Ratelle, Jean
b. 1941 Checker, Chubby
b. 1943 Bingaman, Jeff
b. 1945 Saneyev, Viktor
b. 1946 Dotson, Bob
b. 1947 Buckingham, Lindsey
b. 1950 Hensley, Pamela Gail
b. 1951 Winfield, Dave
b. 1954 Sharpton, Al(fred), Jr.
b. 1954 Vaughan, Stevie Ray
b. 1959 Couples, Fred
b. 1959 Wagner, Jack Peter
b. 1973 Campbell, Neve
d. 1226 Francis of Assisi, Saint
d. 1282 Llewelyn ap Gruffydd
d. 1656 Standish, Miles
d. 1750 Mottley, John
d. 1838 Black Hawk
d. 1860 Peale, Rembrandt
d. 1867 Howe, Elias
d. 1873 Captain Jack
d. 1895 Wright, Harry
d. 1896 Morris, William
d. 1910 Taylor, Lucy Beaman Hobbs
d. 1911 Dilthey, Wilhelm Christian Ludwig
d. 1929 Eagels, Jeanne

d. 1929 Stresemann, Gustav
d. 1936 Heisman, John William
d. 1937 Howe, Edgar Watson
d. 1939 Templeton, Fay
d. 1941 Kienzl, Wilhelm
d. 1947 Adams, Charles Francis
d. 1951 Drum, Hugh A
d. 1953 Bax, Arnold Edward Trevor, Sir
d. 1953 Creel, George Edward
d. 1953 Sabin, Florence Rena
d. 1955 Adler, Julius Ochs
d. 1957 Duranty, Walter
d. 1965 Scott, Zachary
d. 1967 Guthrie, Woody
d. 1967 Sargent, Malcolm, Sir
d. 1969 James, Skip
d. 1970 Joplin, Janis
d. 1971 Germer, Lester Halbert
d. 1972 Schmitt, Gladys
d. 1975 Mollet, Guy
d. 1976 Smith, Howard Worth
d. 1982 Merchant, Vivien
d. 1983 Tupper, Earl Silas
d. 1985 Collingwood, Charles Cummings
d. 1986 DiMaggio, Vince(nt Paul)
d. 1987 Anouilh, Jean Marie Lucien Pierre
d. 1987 Ivogun, Maria
d. 1988 Hatem, George
d. 1988 Strauss, Franz Josef
d. 1990 Casiraghi, Stefano
d. 1990 Steber, Eleanor
d. 1991 Gayle, Addison, Jr.
d. 1991 Kaplan, Joseph
d. 1997 Rowse, A(lfred) L(eslie)
d. 1998 McDowall, Roddy
d. 1999 Morita, Akio
October 4
b. 1472 Cranach, Lucas
b. 1542 Bellarmine, Robert, Saint
b. 1570 Pazmany, Peter
b. 1626 Cromwell, Richard
b. 1720 Piranesi, Giovanni Battista
b. 1741 Malone, Edmund
b. 1787 Guizot, Francois Pierre Guillaume
b. 1809 Schenck, Robert Cumming
b. 1810 Johnson, Eliza (McCardle)

b. 1812 Persiani, Fanny
b. 1814 Millet, Jean Francois
b. 1819 Crispi, Francesco
b. 1822 Hayes, Rutherford B(irchard)
b. 1825 Wales, Salem Howe
b. 1836 Adam, Juliette Lamber
b. 1853 Palacio Valdes, Armando
b. 1858 Pupin, Michael Idvorsky
b. 1861 Rauschenbusch, Walter
b. 1861 Remington, Frederic
b. 1862 Stratemeyer, Edward L
b. 1872 Blood, Ernest
b. 1872 Zemlinsky, Alexander von
b. 1875 Daly, Arnold
b. 1877 Gerould, Gordon Hall
b. 1878 Hopkins, Arthur
b. 1879 East, Edward Murray
b. 1881 Brauchitsch, Heinrich Alfred
b. 1884 Runyon, Damon
b. 1886 Robinson, Lennox
b. 1887 Armour, Norman
b. 1890 Breen, Joseph Ignatius
b. 1890 Kelly, John Brenden
b. 1892 Dollfuss, Engelbert
b. 1892 Lawson, Robert
b. 1893 Ljungberg, Gota
b. 1895 Keaton, Buster
b. 1897 Stoopnagle, Lemuel Q, Colonel
b. 1899 Jonas, Franz
b. 1903 Lehmann-Haupt, Hellmut Emil
b. 1906 Frankfurter, Alfred Moritz
b. 1906 Kepes, Gyorgy
b. 1913 Janson, Horst Woldemar
b. 1914 Gill, Brendan
b. 1916 Sidney, George
b. 1917 Murray, Jan
b. 1918 Fukui, Kenichi
b. 1918 Kantrowitz, Adrian
b. 1921 Hills, Argentina (Schifano)
b. 1921 Morales Bermudez, Francisco
b. 1921 Poe, James
b. 1922 Baldrige, Malcolm
b. 1922 Heston, Charlton
b. 1923 Martin, Harold Eugene
b. 1925 Schindler, Alexander Moshe

b. 1927 Tucker, C(ynthia) DeLores (Nottage)
b. 1928 Forman, James
b. 1928 Toffler, Alvin
b. 1932 Davignon, Viscount
b. 1932 Farr, Felicia
b. 1934 Huff, Sam
b. 1937 Brown, Lee P(atrick)
b. 1937 Vranitzky, Franz
b. 1941 Collins, Jackie
b. 1941 Rice, Anne
b. 1941 Saunders, Lori
b. 1942 Reagon, Bernice Johnson
b. 1943 Al-Amin, Jamil Abdullah
b. 1943 Brown, H(ubert) Rap
b. 1943 Roemer, Buddy
b. 1944 LaBelle, Patti
b. 1944 LaRussa, Tony
b. 1944 Wilson, Robert M
b. 1945 Davis, Clifton
b. 1946 Hagel, Chuck
b. 1946 Sarandon, Susan
b. 1949 Adamle, Mike
b. 1949 Assante, Armand
b. 1957 Simmons, Russell
b. 1976 Silverstone, Alicia
d. 1497 Gozzoli, Benozzo
d. 1582 Theresa, Saint
d. 1669 Rembrandt (Harmenszoon van Rijn)
d. 1851 Godoy y Alvarez de Faria, Manuel de
d. 1859 Baedeker, Karl
d. 1874 Procter, Bryan Waller
d. 1879 Soloviev, Sergei Mikhailovich
d. 1880 Offenbach, Jacques
d. 1890 Booth, Catherine Mumford
d. 1902 Johnson, Lionel Pigot
d. 1904 Bartholdi, Auguste
d. 1904 Bishop, Isabella Lucy Bird
d. 1909 Chang Chih-tung
d. 1943 Ely, Richard Theodore
d. 1944 Beresford, Harry
d. 1944 Smith, Alfred Emanuel
d. 1946 Oldfield, Barney
d. 1946 Pinchot, Gifford
d. 1947 Planck, Max Karl Ernst Ludwig

d. 1948 Brown, Arthur Whitten, Sir
d. 1948 Daly, Thomas Augustine
d. 1948 Savitt, Jan
d. 1953 Lazzari, Virgilio
d. 1961 Petri, Angelo
d. 1961 Weber, Max
d. 1963 Key, Valdimer Orlando, Jr.
d. 1964 Calkins, Earnest Elmo
d. 1964 Svanholm, Set
d. 1966 Billingsley, Sherman
d. 1968 Biddle, Francis Beverley
d. 1974 Sexton, Anne Harvey
d. 1975 Payson, Joan Whitney
d. 1981 Lindstrom, Freddie
d. 1982 Bakr, Ahmad Hasan al
d. 1982 Dial, Morris Grant
d. 1982 Gould, Glenn Herbert
d. 1982 Grumman, Leroy Randle
d. 1982 Terry, Walter
d. 1985 Buckley, William F
d. 1988 Household, Geoffrey Edward West
d. 1989 Chapman, Graham
d. 1995 Lowe, Edward
d. 1996 Friedman, Stephen
d. 1999 Buffet, Bernard
d. 1999 Davis, Martin S.
d. 1999 Farmer, Art(hur Stewart)

October 5
b. 1458 Casimir, Saint
b. 1703 Edwards, Jonathan
b. 1712 Guardi, Francesco
b. 1713 Diderot, Denis
b. 1743 Gazzaniga, Giuseppe
b. 1751 Iredell, James
b. 1778 Champollin-Figeac, Jacques-Joseph
b. 1789 Scoresby, William
b. 1824 Chadwick, Henry
b. 1830 Arthur, Chester A(lan)
b. 1840 Symonds, John Addington
b. 1848 O'Connor, Thomas Power
b. 1848 Trudeau, Edward Livingston
b. 1864 Lumiere, Louis Jean

b. 1869 Morrison, Cameron
b. 1879 Erskine, John
b. 1879 Rous, Francis Peyton
b. 1882 Dresser, Louise
b. 1882 Goddard, Robert Hutchings
b. 1887 Cassin, Rene-Samuel
b. 1890 Schmid, Eduard
b. 1893 Hibberd, Andrew Stuart
b. 1895 Smith, Walter Bedell
b. 1897 DeLue, Donald Harcourt
b. 1899 Bidault, Georges
b. 1899 Wallenberg, Marcus
b. 1902 Fine, Larry
b. 1902 Kroc, Ray(mond) Albert
b. 1905 Fodor, Eugene
b. 1905 Ritz, Jimmy
b. 1906 Frankenstein, Alfred Victor
b. 1906 Jones, R(enato) William
b. 1907 Gorman, Carl Nelson
b. 1907 Louis, Jean
b. 1908 Logan, Josh(ua Lockwood)
b. 1917 Worsham, Lew(is Elmer)
b. 1918 Ludden, Allen Ellsworth
b. 1919 Pleasence, Donald
b. 1921 Tabbert, William
b. 1922 Keane, Bil
b. 1923 Berrigan, Philip Francis
b. 1923 Johns, Glynis
b. 1924 Dana, Bill
b. 1924 Donoso, Jose
b. 1924 Morton, Frederic
b. 1925 Miller, Walter Dale
b. 1925 Morgan, Robert Burren
b. 1929 Gordon, Richard Francis, Jr.
b. 1930 Popovich, Pavel Romanovich
b. 1932 Burke, Yvonne Watson Brathwaite
b. 1933 Cilento, Diane
b. 1934 Taylor, Kenneth Douglas
b. 1936 Havel, Vaclav
b. 1937 Switzer, Barry
b. 1943 Miller, Steve
b. 1949 Ackroyd, Peter
b. 1950 Conaway, Jeff
b. 1950 Jones, Edward P.
b. 1951 Allen, Karen Jane
b. 1952 Barker, Clive
b. 1954 Geldof, Bob

b. 1728 Rodney, Caesar
b. 1734 Abercromby, Ralph, Sir
b. 1745 Rutgers, Henry
b. 1747 Zane, Ebenezer
b. 1786 Papineau, Louis-Joseph
b. 1816 Hargraves, Edward Hammond
b. 1821 Still, William
b. 1833 Fox, Margaret
b. 1842 Bateman, Kate Josephine
b. 1842 Howard, Bronson Crocker
b. 1849 Riley, James Whitcomb
b. 1858 Eigenmann, Rosa Smith
b. 1859 Wise, Thomas J
b. 1879 Hill, Joe
b. 1880 Holme, Constance
b. 1885 Bohr, Niels Henrik David
b. 1888 Wallace, Henry Agard
b. 1893 Dalgleish, Alice
b. 1894 Mulhall, Jack
b. 1896 Lasser, Jacob Kay
b. 1897 Freeman, Joseph
b. 1898 Wallenstein, Alfred Franz
b. 1900 Butterfield, Herbert, Sir
b. 1900 Himmler, Heinrich
b. 1901 Boucher, Frank
b. 1901 Souvanna, Phouma
b. 1904 Klein, Chuck
b. 1905 Devine, Andy
b. 1906 Webb, James Edwin
b. 1907 MacInnes, Helen
b. 1908 Wilson, Sunnie
b. 1909 Corning, Erastus, III
b. 1909 Genet, Arthur Samuel
b. 1911 Jones, Jo(nathan)
b. 1911 Monroe, Vaughn
b. 1912 Benn, Anthony
b. 1912 Waddles, Charleszetta, Mother
b. 1913 Janeway, Elizabeth Hall
b. 1914 Churchill, Sarah
b. 1914 Drake, Alfred
b. 1914 Golub, William Weldon
b. 1914 Keiser, Herman
b. 1916 Burns, John Horne
b. 1916 Rostow, Walt Whitman
b. 1917 Allyson, June
b. 1917 Dantine, Helmut
b. 1917 Smythe, Reg(inald)

b. 1919 Cowen, Zelman, Sir
b. 1919 Dell, Gabriel
b. 1923 Riopelle, Jean-Paul
b. 1926 Groza, Alex John
b. 1926 Lynn, Diana
b. 1927 Laing, R(onald) D(avid)
b. 1929 Westall, Robert Atkinson
b. 1930 Dubinin, Yuri Vladimirovich
b. 1931 Stewart, Ellen
b. 1931 Tutu, Desmond (Mpilo)
b. 1934 Baraka, Amiri
b. 1934 Meinhof, Ulrike Marie
b. 1935 Keneally, Thomas (Michael)
b. 1936 Dutoit, Charles
b. 1943 North, Oliver Laurence, Jr.
b. 1946 MacKinnon, Catharine A(lice)
b. 1946 Soren, David
b. 1948 Ackerman, Diane
b. 1951 Mellencamp, John
b. 1952 Turischeva, Ludmila
b. 1953 Norris, Christopher
b. 1954 Dawson, Andre (Nolan)
b. 1954 Eckersley, Dennis
b. 1955 Ma, Yo-Yo
b. 1961 Landers, Judy
d. 1488 Verrocchio, Andrea del
d. 1772 Woolman, John
d. 1786 Muhlenberg, Heinrich Melchior
d. 1792 Mason, George
d. 1796 Reid, Thomas
d. 1845 Colbran, Isabella
d. 1849 Poe, Edgar Allan
d. 1866 Stockton, Robert Field
d. 1878 Mosquera, Tomas Cipriano de
d. 1894 Curtin, Andrew Gregg
d. 1894 Holmes, Oliver Wendell, Sr.
d. 1895 Story, William Wetmore
d. 1911 Jackson, John Hughlings
d. 1913 Altman, Benjamin
d. 1918 Parry, Charles Hubert Hastings, Sir
d. 1919 Alden, Henry M
d. 1919 Deakin, Alfred
d. 1922 Lloyd, Marie
d. 1925 Mathewson, Christy

d. 1931 French, Daniel Chester
d. 1933 Hillquit, Morris
d. 1939 Cushing, Harvey Williams
d. 1943 Hall, Radclyffe
d. 1950 Carrier, Willis Haviland
d. 1955 Hempel, Frieda
d. 1956 Birdseye, Clarence Frank
d. 1956 Hamlin, Talbot Faulkner
d. 1959 Lanza, Mario
d. 1963 Hadamard, Jacques Salomon
d. 1967 Angell, Norman
d. 1973 Price, Dennis
d. 1976 Lyons, Leonard
d. 1979 Lewis, Wilmarth Sheldon
d. 1980 Russell, Sydney Gordon, Sir
d. 1983 Abell, George O(gden)
d. 1983 Howe, Oscar
d. 1986 Crawford, Cheryl
d. 1986 Jacuzzi, Candido
d. 1986 Kressy, Edmund
d. 1987 Flavin, Joseph B(ernard)
d. 1988 Daniels, Billy
d. 1991 Durocher, Leo Ernest
d. 1991 Ginzburg, Natalia
d. 1991 Goerlich, John
d. 1992 Bloom, Allan David
d. 1992 Kitagawa, Joseph Mitsuo
d. 1993 DeMille, Agnes (George)
d. 1996 Salter, Andrew

October 8
b. 1553 Thou, Jacques Auguste de
b. 1585 Schutz, Heinrich
b. 1609 Clarke, John
b. 1720 Mayhew, Jonathan
b. 1749 Levasseur, Rosalie
b. 1765 Otis, Harrison Gray
b. 1827 Sarcey, Francisque
b. 1833 Stedman, Edmund Clarence
b. 1838 Hay, John Milton
b. 1846 Gary, Elbert Henry
b. 1850 Le Chatelier, Henry-Louis
b. 1857 Albee, Edward Franklin
b. 1861 Van Zandt, Marie
b. 1869 Duryea, J(ames) Frank

b. 1872 Powys, John Cowper
b. 1873 Hertzsprung, Ejnar
b. 1873 Jarry, Alfred
b. 1878 Munnings, Alfred James, Sir
b. 1883 Warburg, Otto Heinrich
b. 1884 Agus Salim, Hadji
b. 1890 Hoffenstein, Samuel Goodman
b. 1890 Rickenbacker, Eddie
b. 1892 Smith, Lowell Herbert
b. 1895 Peron, Juan
b. 1895 Zog I
b. 1896 Duvivier, Julien
b. 1897 Cisler, Walker (Lee)
b. 1897 Mamoulian, Rouben (Zachary)
b. 1897 Stoodard, George Dinsmore
b. 1897 Throckmorton, Cleon
b. 1900 Chermayeff, Serge (Ivan)
b. 1902 Currie, Lauchlin (Bernard)
b. 1904 Taishoff, Sol Joseph
b. 1905 Levin, Meyer
b. 1908 Maltz, Albert
b. 1909 Hewitt, Bill
b. 1909 Jaroszewicz, Piotr
b. 1910 Hall, Gus
b. 1912 Gardner, John William
b. 1913 Fielding, Temple Hornaday
b. 1913 Gilruth, Robert Rowe
b. 1913 Schumann, Walter
b. 1914 Schocken, Theodore
b. 1915 Vaughan, Bill
b. 1916 Matsunaga, Spark Masayuki
b. 1917 Conn, Billy
b. 1917 Lord, Walter
b. 1917 Porter, Rodney Robert
b. 1919 Miyazawa, Kiichi
b. 1919 Ramsbotham, Peter, Sir
b. 1920 Herbert, Frank (Patrick)
b. 1922 Barnard, Christiaan Neethling
b. 1925 Dalis, Irene
b. 1925 Magana, Alvaro (Alfredo)
b. 1925 Sinyavsky, Andrei D(onatovich)
b. 1927 Milstein, Cesar
b. 1929 Stahl, Franklin William
b. 1930 Ringgold, Faith
b. 1930 Takemitsu, Toru

b. 1931 Kerr, Malcolm (Hooper)
b. 1933 Korda, Michael Vincent
b. 1934 Brown, John Carter
b. 1936 Andrews, James Frederick
b. 1936 Barrett, Rona
b. 1937 Clodagh
b. 1939 Hogan, Paul
b. 1941 Jackson, Jesse Louis
b. 1941 Stevens, Shane
b. 1942 Tomasson, Helgi
b. 1943 Chase, Chevy
b. 1943 Stine, R. L.
b. 1944 Browles, William Dodson, Jr.
b. 1946 Kucinich, Dennis John
b. 1948 Purcell, Sarah
b. 1949 Weaver, Sigourney
b. 1950 Bell, Kool
b. 1952 Adams, Cliff
b. 1952 Bell, John Kim
b. 1956 Zimbalist, Stephanie
b. 1965 Biondi, Matt
d. 1354 Rienzi, Cola di
d. 1754 Fielding, Henry
d. 1793 Hancock, John
d. 1803 Alfieri, Vittorio
d. 1820 Christophe, Henri
d. 1834 Boieldieu, Francois Adrien
d. 1837 Fourier, Francois Marie Charles
d. 1869 Pierce, Franklin
d. 1895 Mahone, William
d. 1896 DuMaurier, George Louis P B
d. 1911 Binet, Alfred
d. 1914 Crapsey, Adelaide
d. 1927 Guiraldes, Ricardo (Guillermo)
d. 1931 Monash, John
d. 1941 Kahn, Gus
d. 1942 Ellsler, Effie
d. 1944 Willkie, Wendell Lewis
d. 1945 Salten, Felix
d. 1949 Somerville, Edith Anna OEnone
d. 1952 Wright, Louis Tompkins
d. 1953 Bruce, Nigel
d. 1953 Ferrier, Kathleen
d. 1961 Hertz, John Daniel
d. 1963 Adams, Frank Ramsay
d. 1965 Costain, Thomas Bertram
d. 1967 Attlee, Clement Richard Attlee, Earl
d. 1967 Guevara, Che
d. 1967 Manville, Tommy

d. 1974 Carney, Harry Howell
d. 1974 Hoffman, Paul Gray
d. 1975 Felsenstein, Walter
d. 1978 Gilliam, Jim
d. 1979 Narayan, Jayaprakash
d. 1979 Sampson, Edith Spurlock
d. 1980 Dollard, John
d. 1980 Kendrick, Pearl Luella
d. 1981 Kohut, Heinz
d. 1982 Freud, Anna
d. 1982 Lamas, Fernando
d. 1982 Noel-Baker, Philip John
d. 1983 Hackett, Joan
d. 1984 Brisson, Frederick
d. 1985 Bacchelli, Riccardo
d. 1985 Blough, Roger Miles
d. 1985 Welchman, Gordon
d. 1987 Dennison, George
d. 1987 Johnson, Eleanor M
d. 1987 Tsatsos, Constantinos
d. 1991 Humphry, Ann Wickett
d. 1992 Brandt, Willy
d. 1995 Keene, Christopher
d. 1996 Eberhart, Mignon Good
d. 1996 Prince, William
d. 1997 Goldberg, Bertrand

October 9

b. 1782 Cass, Lewis
b. 1822 Sykes, George
b. 1830 Hosmer, Harriet Goodhue
b. 1832 Allen, Elizabeth Ann Chase Akers
b. 1835 Saint-Saens, (Charles) Camille
b. 1837 Parker, Francis Wayland
b. 1839 Schley, Winfield Scott
b. 1846 Drachmann, Holger Henrik Herholdt
b. 1848 Duveneck, Frank
b. 1852 Fischer, Emil Herman
b. 1859 Dreyfus, Alfred
b. 1860 Wood, Leonard
b. 1863 Bok, Edward William
b. 1863 Bradford, Gamaliel
b. 1866 Loeb, William
b. 1873 Flesch, Karl
b. 1873 Walgreen, Charles Rudolph

b. 1876 Warwick, Robert
b. 1879 Laue, Max Theodor Felix von
b. 1884 Deutsch, Helene R(osenbach)
b. 1884 Johnson, Martin Elmer
b. 1888 Bukharin, Nikolai Ivanovich
b. 1889 Marquard, Rube
b. 1890 McPherson, Aimee Semple
b. 1891 Schnering, Otto
b. 1894 Bullard, Eugene
b. 1894 McFarland, Ernest William
b. 1896 Cook, Bill
b. 1898 Sewell, Joe
b. 1899 Catton, Bruce
b. 1900 Sim, Alastair
b. 1901 Jemison, Alice Mae
b. 1902 Hannah, John Alfred
b. 1903 O'Malley, Walter Francis
b. 1905 Saint John, Howard
b. 1905 Ward, Paul W
b. 1906 Senghor, Leopold Sedar
b. 1908 Folsom, James E(lisha)
b. 1908 Tati, Jacques
b. 1909 Beatty, Robert
b. 1909 Coggan, Frederick Donald, Baron
b. 1910 Graham, Wallace H(arry)
b. 1910 Robert, Paul
b. 1911 Morgan, Russell H(edley)
b. 1911 Rosenthal, Joe
b. 1915 Andrews, Edward
b. 1915 Crockett, James Underwood
b. 1916 Perry, Harold R
b. 1918 Burkemo, Walter
b. 1918 Hunt, E(verette) Howard
b. 1919 Plain, Belva
b. 1919 Seefried, Irmgard Maria Theresia
b. 1921 Nader, George
b. 1923 Sinden, Donald (Alfred)
b. 1925 Finch, Robert H(utchison)
b. 1926 Russell, Franklin Alexander
b. 1928 Solotaroff, Theodore
b. 1929 Morial, Ernest Nathan
b. 1930 Rounds, David
b. 1932 Plowden, David
b. 1933 Gottfried, Martin
b. 1934 Conway, Jill Kathryn Ker

b. 1935 McCullin, Donald
b. 1938 Myers, Russell
b. 1940 Humphrey, Gordon John
b. 1940 Lennon, John Winston
b. 1940 Pepitone, Joe
b. 1941 Lamb, Brian (P.)
b. 1941 Lott, Trent
b. 1944 Tosh, Peter
b. 1948 Browne, Jackson
b. 1948 Osbourne, Jeffrey
b. 1949 Messing, Shep
b. 1955 Bakula, Scott
b. 1958 Singletary, Mike
b. 1971 Kissin, Evgeny
d. 1253 Grosseteste, Robert
d. 1469 Lippi, Filippo, Fra
d. 1688 Perrault, Claude
d. 1718 Cumberland, Richard
d. 1747 Brainerd, David
d. 1806 Banneker, Benjamin
d. 1826 Kelly, Michael
d. 1841 Schinkel, Karl Friedrich
d. 1887 Strakosch, Maurice
d. 1906 Glidden, Joseph Farwell
d. 1920 Kronold, Selma
d. 1924 Daubert, Jake
d. 1934 Alexander of Yugoslavia
d. 1940 Grenfell, Wilfred Thomason, Sir
d. 1940 Mayo, Katherine
d. 1941 Morgan, Helen Riggins
d. 1943 Zeeman, Pieter
d. 1949 Swanson, Carl A
d. 1950 Hainsworth, George
d. 1952 Murray, Philip
d. 1954 Jackson, Robert Houghwout
d. 1955 Joyce, Alice
d. 1955 Rogers, Mary Joseph(ine)
d. 1958 Pius XII
d. 1959 Tizard, Henry Thomas, Sir
d. 1967 Allport, Gordon William
d. 1967 Hinshelwood, Cyril Norman, Sir
d. 1967 Maurois, Andre
d. 1970 Ackerman, Carl William
d. 1970 Giono, Jean
d. 1970 Lonsdale, Gordon Arnold
d. 1972 Bancroft, Dave
d. 1972 Hopkins, Miriam

d. 1972 Magee, Harry L
d. 1973 Marcel, Gabriel
Honore
d. 1974 Schindler,
Oskar
d. 1977 Elder, Ruth
d. 1978 Brel, Jacques
d. 1984 Christensen,
Lew Farr
d. 1985 Snyder, John
Wesley
d. 1987 Becker, B Jay
d. 1987 Converse,
Frederick J
d. 1987 Luce, Clare
Boothe
d. 1987 Murphy,
William Parry
d. 1988 Chodorov,
Edward
d. 1988 Wankel, Felix
d. 1991 Lilly, Doris
d. 1992 Cooper, Louise
Field
d. 1992 Maddow, Ben
d. 1993 Smith, Austin
E(dward)
d. 1995 Scali, John
(Alfred)
d. 1996 Hingson, Robert
A(ndrew)
d. 1996 Kerr, Walter
F(rancis)
d. 1999 Cabral de Melo
Neto, Joao
d. 1999 Jackson,
Milt(on)
d. 1999 West, Morris
L(anglo)

October 10
b. 1560 Arminius,
Jacobus
b. 1684 Watteau, Jean
Antoine
b. 1731 Cavendish,
Henry
b. 1738 West, Benjamin
b. 1813 Verdi, Giuseppe
Fortunino Francesco
b. 1816 Simon, John,
Sir
b. 1819 Monck, Charles
Stanley, Sir
b. 1825 Kruger, Paul
b. 1828 Randall, Samuel
J
b. 1830 Isabella II
b. 1833 Studebaker,
John Mohler
b. 1837 Shaw, Robert
Gould
b. 1845 Saintsbury,
George Edward
Bateman
b. 1860 Reading, 1st
Marquess of
b. 1861 Nansen, Fridtjof
b. 1873 Lovejoy, Arthur
Oncken (Schauffler)
b. 1877 Morris, William
Richard
b. 1877 Nuffield,
William Richard
Morris
b. 1882 Traphagen,
Ethel Leigh

b. 1885 Britton, Jack
b. 1889 Roosevelt,
Kermit
b. 1892 Andric, Ivo
b. 1892 Dickson, Earle
Ensign
b. 1895 Lin, Yutang
b. 1896 Germer, Lester
Halbert
b. 1897 Muhammad,
Elijah
b. 1900 Hayes, Helen
b. 1901 Giacometti,
Alberto
b. 1901 Patterson,
Frederick Douglass
b. 1902 Davis,
(William) Allison
b. 1903 Duke, Vernon
b. 1906 Creston, Paul
b. 1906 Narayan,
R(asipuram)
K(rishnaswami)
b. 1908 Chang, M(in)
C(heuh), Dr.
b. 1908 Green, Johnny
b. 1909 Friebus, Florida
b. 1910 Daniel, Price
b. 1913 Downs, Johnny
b. 1913 Pressman,
David
b. 1913 Simon, Claude
Eugene Henri
b. 1916 Gascoyne,
David Emery
b. 1918 Allon, Yigal
b. 1918 King, John
W(illiam)
b. 1920 Sinkwich, Frank
b. 1922 Holladay,
Wilhelmina Cole
b. 1924 Clavell, James
(Edmund Du Maresq)
b. 1924 Wood, Edward
D., Jr.
b. 1926 Brown, Oscar,
Jr.
b. 1929 Boutte, Alvin J
b. 1930 Pinter, Harold
b. 1930 Stevenson,
Adlai Ewing, III
b. 1933 Massey, Daniel
(Raymond)
b. 1933 Sebring, Jay
b. 1941 Nena, Jacob
b. 1941 Saro-Wiwa,
Ken
b. 1941 Tribe, Laurence
Henry
b. 1942 Marshall, James
Edward
b. 1946 Mahovlich,
Pete(r Joseph)
b. 1946 Prine, John
b. 1946 Tenace, Gene
b. 1946 Vereen,
Ben(jamin Augustus)
b. 1952 Nystrom, Bob
b. 1953 Williams, Gus
b. 1955 Roth, David
Lee
b. 1958 Tucker, Tanya
(Denise)
b. 1969 Favre, Brett
(Lorenzo)

d. 1531 Zwingli,
Huldreich
d. 1538 Nanak
d. 1720 Coysevox,
Antoine
d. 1797 Braxton, Carter
d. 1836 Jefferson,
Martha
d. 1857 Crawford,
Thomas
d. 1872 Parton, Sara
Payson Willis
d. 1872 Seward,
William Henry
d. 1885 McCloskey,
John
d. 1894 Allen, Macon B
d. 1898 Puvis de
Chavannes, Pierre
Cecile
d. 1913 Busch,
Adolphus
d. 1919 Genung, John
Franklin
d. 1921 Gierke, Otto
von
d. 1925 Duke, James
Buchanan
d. 1930 Engler, Adolph
Gustav Heinrich
d. 1944 Gottschalk,
Ferdinand
d. 1948 Eaton, Mary
d. 1955 Stracciari,
Riccardo
d. 1959 Ed, Carl Frank
Ludwig
d. 1962 Allen, Vivian
Beaumont
d. 1962 Boswell,
Connee
d. 1964 Cantor, Eddie
d. 1965 Uhde, Hermann
d. 1967 Keaney, Frank
d. 1967 Read, Albert
Cushing
d. 1970 Daladier,
Edouard
d. 1970 Rapacki, Adam
d. 1971 Burt, Cyril
Lodowic, Sir
d. 1971 Saerchinger,
Cesar Victor Charles
d. 1976 Wallace,
Ed(ward Tatum)
d. 1978 Metcalfe, Ralph
H
d. 1979 Paray, Paul
d. 1980 Cheney,
Sheldon Warren
d. 1980 Thomas, Billy
d. 1983 Debus, Kurt
Heinrich
d. 1983 Richardson,
Ralph David, Sir
d. 1984 Gaddis, Thomas
(Eugene)
d. 1985 Brynner, Yul
d. 1985 Welles, Orson
d. 1986 Soss, Wilma
Porter
d. 1988 Flowers,
Wayland Parrott, Jr.
d. 1990 Selznick, Irene
Mayer
d. 1994 Raphael, Chaim

d. 1995 Finch, Robert
H(utchison)
d. 1996 Knutson, Coya
d. 1997 Malcolm,
George
d. 1998 Cates, Joseph
d. 1998 Clifford, Clark
M(cAdams)

October 11
b. 1675 Clarke, Samuel
b. 1738 Phillip, Arthur
b. 1758 Olbers,
Heinrich Wilhelm
Matthaus
b. 1809 Fowler, Orson
Squire
b. 1835 Thomas,
Theodore
b. 1844 Heinz, Henry
John
b. 1860 Litvinne, Felia
b. 1863 Leroux, Xavier
b. 1871 Hawes, Harriet
Ann Boyd
b. 1872 Stone, Harlan
Fiske
b. 1878 Hofer, Karl
b. 1881 Kelsen, Hans
b. 1881 Richardson,
Lewis Fry
b. 1881 Young, Stark
b. 1882 Dett, Robert
Nathaniel
b. 1883 Stiedry, Fritz
b. 1884 Bergius,
Friedrich Karl
Rudolph
b. 1884 Roosevelt,
Eleanor
b. 1884 Rumann,
Sig(fried)
b. 1885 Mauriac,
Francois
b. 1885 Sherman,
Lowell
b. 1887 Hoppe, Willie
b. 1889 Lelong, Lucien
b. 1891 Ault, George
Christian
b. 1891 Dickinson,
Edwin W
b. 1894 Lubke, Heinrich
b. 1894 Stoessel, Albert
b. 1896 Firpo, Luis
Angel
b. 1896 Jakobson,
Roman
b. 1896 Marshall,
George Preston
b. 1897 Auslander,
Joseph
b. 1897 Twining,
Nathan F(arragut)
b. 1899 Ewen, Frederic
b. 1900 Hartmann,
Rudolph
b. 1900 Hubbard, Cal
b. 1902 Ilg, Frances
Lillian
b. 1902 Narayan,
Jayaprakash
b. 1902 Tully, Alice
b. 1903 Weatherford,
Teddy
b. 1905 Alexander, Leo
b. 1906 Clark, Dutch

d. 1905 Lowell, Josephine Shaw
d. 1907 Massey, Gerald
d. 1912 Taylor, Susie Baker King
d. 1915 Cavell, Edith Louisa
d. 1918 Gailhard, Pierre
d. 1921 Knox, Philander Chase
d. 1924 France, Anatole
d. 1936 Blashfield, Edwin Howland
d. 1936 Litvinne, Felia
d. 1940 Mix, Tom
d. 1943 Wertheimer, Max
d. 1946 Stilwell, Joseph Warren
d. 1947 Hamilton, Ian Standish Monteith, Sir
d. 1951 Errol, Leon
d. 1953 Hammarskjold, Hjalmar
d. 1953 Mitchell, Millard
d. 1955 Macfadden, Bernarr Adolphus
d. 1963 Cocteau, Jean
d. 1965 Muller, Paul Hermann
d. 1969 Henie, Sonja
d. 1970 Denny, Ludwell
d. 1971 Acheson, Dean Gooderham
d. 1971 Crawford, John Edmund
d. 1971 Vincent, Gene
d. 1974 Krips, Josef
d. 1974 Nolan, Jeannette Covert
d. 1981 Mecom, John Whitfield
d. 1985 Olson, Johnny
d. 1987 Koruturk, Fahri S
d. 1987 Landon, Alf(red Mossman)
d. 1987 Nash, Philleo
d. 1988 Murray, Ken
d. 1989 Franco
d. 1989 Ward, Jay
d. 1990 Brownell, Samuel Miller
d. 1991 MacMahon, Aline Laveen
d. 1991 Toomey, Regis
d. 1993 Ames, Leon
d. 1993 Hafstad, Lawrence R(andolph)
d. 1997 Denver, John
d. 1999 Chamberlain, Wilt(on Norman)

October 13
b. 467 Wei Hsiao-Wen-ti
b. 1750 Pitcher, Molly
b. 1797 Motherwell, William
b. 1825 Worth, Charles Frederick
b. 1833 Lorillard, Pierre
b. 1853 Langtry, Lillie
b. 1860 Allan, Montagu, Sir

b. 1862 Commons, John Rogers
b. 1867 Ripley, William Zebina
b. 1873 McCoy, Charles
b. 1876 Waddell, Rube
b. 1877 Bilbo, Theodore Gilmore
b. 1885 Hershfield, Harry
b. 1894 Corey, Lewis
b. 1895 Schumacher, Kurt
b. 1897 Rich, Irene
b. 1901 Sampson, Edith Spurlock
b. 1901 Shirley-Smith, Hubert
b. 1902 Bontemps, Arna Wendell
b. 1906 Morgan, Thomas E(llsworth)
b. 1906 Redding, Jay Saunders
b. 1907 Allegret, Yves
b. 1909 Herblock
b. 1910 Gann, Ernest Kellogg
b. 1910 McCrary, Tex
b. 1910 Tatum, Art(hur)
b. 1912 Weisgall, Hugo (David)
b. 1915 Wilde, Cornel
b. 1917? Stark, Ray
b. 1917 Tillstrom, Burr
b. 1918 Walker, Robert
b. 1920 Day, Laraine
b. 1920 Hague, Albert
b. 1921 Montand, Yves
b. 1921 Thomas, Bill
b. 1924 Gibbs, Terry
b. 1924 Russell, Nipsey
b. 1925 Bruce, Lenny
b. 1925 Gilroy, Frank Daniel
b. 1925 Thatcher, Margaret (Hilda Roberts)
b. 1926 Herbert, John
b. 1926 Lamb, Lawrence Edward
b. 1927 Ozal, Turgut
b. 1930 Geller, Bruce
b. 1931 Dennis, Jack B(onnell)
b. 1931 Mathews, Eddie
b. 1934 Davis, Tommy
b. 1936 Gorman, Cliff
b. 1938 Caesar, Shirley
b. 1938 Ceasar, Shirley
b. 1938 McHenry, Donald Franchot
b. 1938 Smuin, Michael
b. 1939 Colbert, Virgis William
b. 1941 Simon, Paul
b. 1942 Jones, Jerry
b. 1942 Tiffin, Pamela Kimberley
b. 1944 Lamm, Robert
b. 1946 Dalton, Lacy J
b. 1946 Wilson, Demond
b. 1949 Hagar, Sammy
b. 1950 Katzen, Mollie

b. 1950 Shanley, John Patrick
b. 1951 Garzarelli, Elaine Marie
b. 1952 Johnson, Beverly
b. 1953 Day, Pat
b. 1956 Hannah, Marc (Regis)
b. 1958 Berliner, Ron
b. 1959 Osmond, Marie
b. 1962 Rice, Jerry (Lee)
b. 1969 Kerrigan, Nancy
d. 54 Claudius I
d. 1799 Paca, William
d. 1812 Brock, Isaac, Sir
d. 1815 Murat, Joachim
d. 1822 Canova, Antonio
d. 1867 Parsons, William
d. 1869 Sainte-Beuve, Charles Augustin
d. 1879 Carey, Henry Charles
d. 1882 Gobineau, Joseph Arthur, Comte de
d. 1886 Loomis, Mahion
d. 1890 Belknap, William Worth
d. 1890 Miller, Samuel Freeman
d. 1905 Irving, Henry, Sir
d. 1908 Gilman, Daniel Coit
d. 1929 Bentley, Charles Edwin
d. 1934 Baker, Theodore
d. 1938 Segar, Elzie Crisler
d. 1939 Sterling, Ford
d. 1945 Hershey, Milton Snavely
d. 1946 Bannerman, Helen
d. 1947 Webb, Sidney James
d. 1955 Avila Camacho, Manuel
d. 1956 Davis, Owen
d. 1961 Deren, Maya
d. 1966 Webb, Clifton
d. 1968 Bandeira, Manuel
d. 1968 Benaderet, Bea
d. 1968 Unwin, Stanley, Sir
d. 1969 Crittenden, Christopher
d. 1973 Briggs, Austin Eugene
d. 1974 Kleberg, Robert Justus, Jr.
d. 1974 Rice, Sam
d. 1974 Rubin, Reuven
d. 1974 Sullivan, Ed(ward Vincent)
d. 1977 Condon, Jackie
d. 1981 Asther, Nils

d. 1981 Horan, James David
d. 1984 Kelly, George Lange
d. 1984 Neel, Alice Hartley
d. 1986 Angel, Heather Grace
d. 1987 Brattain, Walter Houser
d. 1987 Monroe, Lucy
d. 1990 Edwards, Douglas
d. 1990 Le Duc Tho
d. 1992 Marshall, James Edward
d. 1992 Rudd, Hughes Day
d. 1993 Hardy, Harriet
d. 1995 Roth, Henry
d. 1996 Reid, Beryl
d. 1997 Compton, Joyce

October 14
b. 1427 Baldovinetti, Alesso
b. 1542 Akbar
b. 1618 Lely, Peter, Sir
b. 1633? James II
b. 1644 Penn, William
b. 1734 Lee, Francis Lightfoot
b. 1767 Saussure, Nicolas Thoedore de
b. 1784 Ferdinand, VII
b. 1814 Lamy, Jean Baptist
b. 1816 Huntington, Daniel
b. 1847 O'Neill, James
b. 1857 Haynes, Elwood
b. 1857 Lamar, Joseph Rucker
b. 1863 Black, Winifred Sweet
b. 1867 Masaoka, Tsunenori
b. 1869 Duveen, Joseph, Sir
b. 1872 Hess, Sol
b. 1873 Ewry, Ray C
b. 1876 Ironside, Henry Allan
b. 1879 Franklin, Miles
b. 1880 Bely, Andrey
b. 1882 DeValera, Eamon
b. 1888 Mansfield, Katherine
b. 1888 Turnbull, Agnes Sligh
b. 1890 Conroy, Frank
b. 1890 Eisenhower, Dwight D(avid)
b. 1891 Gray, James, Sir
b. 1892 Welles, Sumner
b. 1893 Gish, Lillian (Diana)
b. 1893 Lenski, Lois
b. 1894 Cummings, E(dward) E(stlin)
b. 1894 Pate, Maurice
b. 1895 Baldwin, Horace
b. 1896 Cummings, Nathan

d. 1910 Ketchel, Stanley
d. 1917 Mata Hari
d. 1923 Talbert, Mary
Morris Burnett
d. 1930 Dow, Herbert
Henry
d. 1934 Poincare,
Raymond
d. 1942 Tempest, Marie
d. 1943 Soutar, William
d. 1945 Laval, Pierre
d. 1946 Goering,
Hermann Wilhelm
d. 1958 Norton, Jack
d. 1960 Young, Clara
Kimball
d. 1963 Kirk, Alan
Goodrich
d. 1963 Smith, Horton
d. 1964 Porter, Cole
d. 1968 Burton, Virginia
Lee
d. 1969 LaRocque, Rod
d. 1976 Gambino, Carlo
d. 1978 Smith,
W(illiam) Eugene
d. 1979 Devers, Jacob
Loucks
d. 1980 Farago, Ladislas
d. 1980 O'Hara, Mary
d. 1983 O'Brien, Pat
d. 1985 Browning,
Alice Crolley
d. 1985 Zaslofsky, Max
d. 1986 Smith, Jerry
d. 1988 Ball, John
Dudley, Jr.
d. 1989 O'Dell, Scott
d. 1992 Franks, Oliver
(Shewell), Sir
d. 1995 Peters, Ellis
d. 1995 Walker, John
d. 1996 Franey, Pierre
d. 1998 Smith, Iain
Crichton

October 16
b. Corbin, Barry
b. 1430 James II
b. 1620 Puget, Pierre
b. 1708 Haller, Albrecht
von
b. 1735 Morgan, John
b. 1758 Webster, Noah
b. 1797 Cardigan, James
Thomas Brudenell,
Earl of
b. 1806 Fessenden,
William Pitt
b. 1815 Lubbock,
Francis Richard
b. 1827 Bocklin, Arnold
b. 1835 Shafter,
William Rufus
b. 1845 Hanes, Pleasant
H
b. 1847 Mueller, Otto
b. 1849 Williams,
George Washington
b. 1856 Wilde, Oscar
(Fingal O'Flahertie
Wills)
b. 1861 Bury, John
Bagnell
b. 1863 Chamberlain,
Austen, Sir

b. 1877 Helland-
Hansen, Bjorn
b. 1877 Lawrie, Lee
b. 1881 Harridge,
Will(iam)
b. 1882 Buttenheim,
Edgar Joseph
b. 1886 Ben-Gurion,
David
b. 1888 O'Neill, Eugene
Gladstone
b. 1890 Collins,
Michael
b. 1890 Strand, Paul
b. 1893 Carmer, Carl
Lamson
b. 1893 Carol II
b. 1898 Dean, Arthur
H(obson)
b. 1898 Douglas,
William Orville
b. 1900 Ardizzone,
Edward Jeffrey Irving
b. 1900 Goslin, Goose
b. 1903 Washington,
Buck
b. 1906 Brooks, Cleanth
b. 1908 Ardrey, Robert
b. 1908 Hoxha, Enver
b. 1912 Hansen,
Clifford Peter
b. 1912 Norman, Maidie
(Ruth)
b. 1912 Siegel, Don
b. 1915 Holdren, Judd
Clifton
b. 1916 Winsor,
Kathleen
b. 1918 Althusser, Louis
b. 1919 Pearce, Alice
b. 1922 Sullivan, Leon
H
b. 1923 Darnell, Linda
(Monetta Eloyse)
b. 1923 Hicks, Louise
Day
b. 1923 Kaempfert, Bert
b. 1923 Ponnamperuma,
Cyril (Andrew)
b. 1925 Evans, Daniel
Jackson
b. 1925 Lansbury,
Angela Brigid
b. 1927? Conrad,
Michael
b. 1927 Grass, Gunter
(Wilhelm)
b. 1928 Daly, Mary
b. 1928 Flavin, Joseph
B(ernard)
b. 1929 VonHoffman,
Nicholas
b. 1931 Colson, Chuck
b. 1932 Lewis, Henry
(Jay)
b. 1937 Anthony, Tony
b. 1940 DeBusschere,
Dave
b. 1942 Bruchac,
Joseph, III
b. 1944 Durcan, Paul
b. 1945 Monette, Paul
b. 1946 Somers,
Suzanne
b. 1949 Weir, Bob

b. 1951 Wheat, Alan
(Dupree)
b. 1954 Carcaterra,
Lorenzo
b. 1956 Belote, Melissa
b. 1956? Doherty,
Kieran
b. 1958 Robbins,
Tim(othy Francis)
b. 1962 Bol, Manute
d. 1523 Signorelli, Luca
d. 1553 Cranach, Lucas
d. 1555 Latimer, Hugh
d. 1621 Sweelinck, Jan
Pieterszoon
d. 1628 Malherbe,
Francois de
d. 1793 Hunter, John
d. 1793 Marie
Antoinette
d. 1802 Strutt, Joseph
d. 1841 Barbaja,
Domenico
d. 1852 Ballivian, Jose
d. 1891 Winnemucca,
Sarah
d. 1928 Thompson,
J(ames) Walter
d. 1933 Renaud,
Maurice
d. 1937 Brunhoff, Jean
de
d. 1946 Bantock,
Granville, Sir
d. 1946 Frank, Hans
d. 1946 Frick, Wilhelm
d. 1946 Jodl, Alfred
d. 1946 Keitel, Wilhelm
d. 1946 Ribbentrop,
Joachim von
d. 1946 Rosenberg,
Alfred
d. 1946 Seyss-Inquart,
Artur von
d. 1946 Streicher, Julius
d. 1951 Liaquat Ali,
Khan
d. 1954 Crump, Edward
Hull
d. 1958 Redfield, Robert
d. 1959 Marshall,
George Catlett
d. 1960 Quinn, Arthur
Hobson
d. 1966 Wagner,
Wieland Adolf
Gottfried
d. 1971 Switzer, Mary
E.
d. 1972 Carroll, Leo G
d. 1972 Hatathli, Ned
d. 1973 Krupa, Gene
d. 1975 Gui, Vittorio
d. 1978 Rockwell,
Willard F
d. 1981 Dayan, Moshe
d. 1982 DelMonaco,
Mario
d. 1982 Selye, Hans
d. 1983 Liberace,
George J
d. 1987 Hoffner,
Joseph, Cardinal
d. 1987 Suesse, Dana
Nadine
d. 1989 Wilde, Cornel

d. 1990 Autori, Franco
d. 1990 Blakey, Art
d. 1990 Bolet, Jorge
d. 1991 Hennard,
George, Jr.
d. 1992 Ellis, John
Tracy
d. 1993 Bortoluzzi,
Paolo
d. 1997 Lindley, Audra
d. 1999 Morse, Ella
Mae
d. 1999 Shepherd, Jean
Parker

October 17
b. 1727 Wilkes, John
b. 1729 Monsigny,
Pierre-Alexandre
b. 1760 Saint-Simon,
Claude-Henri de
Rouvroy
b. 1781 Johnson,
Richard Mentor
b. 1803 Deak, Francis
b. 1810 Mario,
Giovanni Matteo
b. 1813 Buchner, Georg
b. 1817 Syed Ahmed
Khan
b. 1818 Van Lew,
Elizabeth
b. 1821 Gardner,
Alexander
b. 1846 Hudson, Joseph
Lowthian
b. 1848 Cummings,
Candy
b. 1851 Ryan, Thomas
Fortune
b. 1859 Hassam, Childe
b. 1864 Glyn, Elinor
Sutherland
b. 1864 Lansing, Robert
b. 1867 Magonigle,
Harold Van Buren
b. 1881 Chinard, Gilbert
b. 1883 Neill,
A(lexander)
S(utherland)
b. 1886 Goodpasture,
E(rnest) W(illiam)
b. 1891 Banting,
Frederick Grant, Sir
b. 1893 Byington,
Spring
b. 1895 Humphrey,
Doris
b. 1895 Ydigoras
Fuentes Miguel
b. 1898 Suzuki,
Shin'ichi
b. 1899 Kempner,
Robert M(aximilian)
W(asilii)
b. 1901 Arthur, Jean
b. 1901 Collins, Lee
b. 1903 Birdwell,
Russell Juarez
b. 1903 Grechko,
Andrei Antonovick
b. 1903 Ryan, Irene
Noblette
b. 1903 West, Nathanael
b. 1906 Cassidy, Harold
Gomes

b. 1908 Johnson, U(ral) Alexis
b. 1909 Cole, Cozy
b. 1910 Cherberg, John A(ndrew)
b. 1912 John Paul I
b. 1914 Siegel, Jerry
b. 1915 Miller, Arthur
b. 1916 Marley, John
b. 1916 Partch, Virgil Franklin, II
b. 1917 Kahn, Alfred Edward
b. 1917 Monk, Thelonious Sphere, Jr.
b. 1918 Hayworth, Rita
b. 1919 Zhao Ziyang
b. 1920 Abel, Elie
b. 1920 Clift, Montgomery
b. 1920 Kilbracken, John Raymond Godley, Baron
b. 1921 Brown, George Mackay
b. 1922 Juneau, Pierre
b. 1924 Coryell, Don(ald David)
b. 1926 Adams, Julie
b. 1926 Garland, Beverly
b. 1926 Henize, Karl G(ordon)
b. 1927 Bailey, Martin Jean
b. 1927 Boolootian, Richard Andrew
b. 1927 Poston, Tom
b. 1928 Bennett, Lerone, Jr.
b. 1928 Gilliam, Jim
b. 1930 Breslin, Jimmy
b. 1933 Anders, William Alison
b. 1938 Knievel, Evel
b. 1942 Seals, Jim
b. 1945 Cutler, Dave
b. 1946 Mackintosh, Cameron
b. 1946 Michnik, Adam
b. 1946 Seagren, Bob
b. 1947? McKean, Michael
b. 1948 Kidder, Margot
b. 1948 Wendt, George (Robert)
b. 1949 Arthur, Owen
b. 1950 Rollins, Howard Ellsworth, Jr.
b. 1951 Hickman, Fred(erick Douglass)
b. 1955 Bottoms, Sam
b. 1955 Driver, David E.
b. 1956 Jemison, Mae C(arol)
b. 1956 Morrow, Ken(neth)
b. 1957 Van Patten, Vince(nt)
b. 1958 Jackson, Alan Eugene
b. 1959 Flores, Francisco
b. 1962 Judge, Mike

d. 1586 Sidney, Philip, Sir
d. 1705 Lenclos, Ninon de
d. 1740 Anna Ivanovna
d. 1780 Bellotto, Bernardo
d. 1806 Dessalines, Jean Jacques
d. 1836 Colman, George
d. 1837 Hummel, Johann Nepomuk
d. 1849 Chopin, Frederic Francois
d. 1868 Secord, Laura Ingersoll
d. 1887 Kirchhoff, Gustav Robert
d. 1891 Parton, James
d. 1893 Gounod, Charles Francois
d. 1896 Abbey, Henry Eugene
d. 1897 Dana, Charles Anderson
d. 1910 Howe, Julia Ward
d. 1910 Moody, William Vaughn
d. 1918 Duchamp-Villon, Raymond
d. 1922 Upton, Florence Kate
d. 1937 Ismay, Joseph Bruce
d. 1947 Huntington, Ellsworth
d. 1948 Cortissoz, Royal
d. 1960 Boucher, Buck
d. 1967 Pu-Yi, Henry
d. 1971 Popovi Da
d. 1972 Broda, Turk
d. 1973 Balchen, Bernt
d. 1977 Balcon, Michael Elias, Sir
d. 1977 Chiang, Yee
d. 1977 Hubbard, Cal
d. 1978 Dailey, Dan
d. 1978 Gronchi, Giovanni
d. 1979 Perelman, S(idney) J(oseph)
d. 1981 Guion, David Wendel Fentress
d. 1982 Riddleberger, James Williams
d. 1982 Rothschild, Alain de, Baron
d. 1983 Aron, Raymond Claude Ferdinand
d. 1984 Garner, Peggy Ann
d. 1984 Hunter, Alberta
d. 1984 Michaux, Henri
d. 1984 Thill, Georges
d. 1985 Rosenstock, Joseph
d. 1987 Dandridge, Ruby Jean
d. 1989 Farley, Walter Lorimer
d. 1991 Ford, Tennessee Ernie
d. 1992 Ter-Arutunian, Rouben

October 18
b. 1595 Winslow, Edward
b. 1631 Wigglesworth, Michael
b. 1632 Giordano, Luca
b. 1663 Eugene of Savoy
b. 1697 Canaletto, Antonio
b. 1706 Galuppi, Baldassare
b. 1714 Woffington, Margaret
b. 1740 Boswell, James
b. 1741 Laclos, Pierre (Ambroise Francois) Choderlos de
b. 1753 Cambaceres, Jean Jacques Regis de
b. 1777 Kleist, Heinrich von
b. 1785 Peacock, Thomas Love
b. 1787 Stevens, Robert Livingston
b. 1792 Alaman, Lucas
b. 1799 Schonbein, Christian Friedrich
b. 1801 Urquiza, Justo Jose
b. 1804 Mongkut
b. 1818 Ord, Edward Otho Cresap
b. 1818 Wen-hsiang
b. 1831 Frederick III
b. 1831 Jackson, Helen Maria Hunt Fiske
b. 1839 Reed, Thomas Brackett
b. 1844 Wiley, Harvey Washington
b. 1854 Andree, Salomon August
b. 1859 Bergson, Henri Louis
b. 1870 Suzuki, Daisetz Teitaro
b. 1875 Leonard, Eddie
b. 1875 Yarnell, Harry Ervin
b. 1876 Adams, Charles Francis
b. 1878 Adams, James Truslow
b. 1878 Artsybashev, Mikhail Petrovich
b. 1880 Jabotinsky, Vladimir Evgenevich
b. 1882 Burt, Maxwell Struthers
b. 1888 Waymack, W(illiam) W(esley)
b. 1892 Carroll, Leo G
b. 1895 DelRuth, Roy
b. 1896 Davis, Harold Lenoir
b. 1896 Holman, Nat(han)
b. 1900 Lenya, Lotte
b. 1902 Hopkins, Miriam
b. 1904 Liebling, Abbot Joseph
b. 1905? Houphouet-Boigny, Felix

b. 1906 Kingsley, Sidney
b. 1911 Mahesh Yogi, Maharishi
b. 1912 Tsiranana, Philibert
b. 1914 Salt, Waldo
b. 1915 Mosley, J(ohn) Brooke
b. 1915 Yung, Victor Sen
b. 1918 Mitsotakis, Constantine
b. 1918 Troup, Bobby
b. 1919 O'Day, Anita
b. 1919 Trudeau, Pierre Elliott
b. 1921 Helms, Jesse Alexander, Jr.
b. 1922 Stankiewicz, Richard Peter
b. 1925 Alia, Ramiz
b. 1925 Mercouri, Melina
b. 1926 Kinski, Klaus
b. 1927 Fanning, Katherine Woodruff
b. 1927 Scott, George C(ampbell)
b. 1929 Chamorro, Violeta Barrios de
b. 1929 Elkins, Hillard
b. 1930 Carlucci, Frank Charles, III
b. 1932 Landsbergis, Vytautas
b. 1933 Gregg, Forrest
b. 1934 Stevens, Inger
b. 1934 Wilson, Allan C
b. 1935 Boyle, Peter
b. 1937 Dowler, Boyd H
b. 1939 Cotti, Flavio
b. 1939 Ditka, Mike
b. 1939 Oswald, Lee Harvey
b. 1942 Horton, Willie
b. 1944 Kurtz, Katherine
b. 1947 Morton, Joe
b. 1947 Nyro, Laura
b. 1948 Shange, Ntozake
b. 1950 Wasserstein, Wendy
b. 1951 Dawber, Pam
b. 1951 McMillan, Terry
b. 1954 Weinstein, Bob
b. 1956 Navratilova, Martina
b. 1958 Hearns, Thomas
b. 1960 Van Damme, Jean-Claude
b. 1961 Marsalis, Wynton
b. 1961 Moran, Erin
b. 1989 Brubacher, John Seiler
d. 31 Sejanus, Lucius Aelius
d. 1179 Chong Chung-bu
d. 1417 Gregory, XII
d. 1678 Jordaens, Jacob

d. 1817 Mehul, Etienne Nicolas
d. 1865 Palmerston, Henry John Temple, Viscount
d. 1871 Babbage, Charles
d. 1878 Laing, David
d. 1893 Stone, Lucy
d. 1897 Worden, John Lorimer
d. 1901 Pillsbury, John Sargent
d. 1931 Edison, Thomas Alva
d. 1934 Ramon y Cajal, Santiago
d. 1935 Lachaise, Gaston
d. 1944 Fleischmann, Gisi
d. 1945 Weyerhaeuser, Frederick Edward
d. 1948 Brauchitsch, Heinrich Alfred
d. 1955 Ortega y Gasset, Jose
d. 1956 Atterbury, Grosvenor
d. 1961 Darwin, Bernard Richard Meirion
d. 1966 Arden, Elizabeth
d. 1966 Kresge, Sebastian Spering
d. 1968 Tracy, Lee
d. 1973 Anderson, Margaret (Carolyn)
d. 1973 Kelly, Walt(er Crawford)
d. 1977 Baader, Andreas
d. 1978 Mercader, Ramon
d. 1980 Teale, Edwin Way
d. 1981 Muncey, Bill
d. 1981 Rubin, Vitalii
d. 1982 Mendes-France, Pierre
d. 1982 Robarts, John Parmenter
d. 1982 Truman, Bess
d. 1984 Hexum, Jon-Erik
d. 1985 Kent, Jack
d. 1987 Brameld, Theodore
d. 1987 Levine, Philip
d. 1992 Gibbs, Frederic A
d. 1992 Lipman, Howard W
d. 1994 Cisler, Walker (Lee)
d. 1997 Dickerson, Nancy Hanschman
d. 1997 Goizueta, Roberto C(rispulo)

October 19
b. 1433 Ficino, Marsilio
b. 1605 Browne, Thomas
b. 1720 Woolman, John

b. 1748 Jefferson, Martha (Wayles Skelton)
b. 1784 Hunt, Leigh
b. 1784 McLoughlin, John
b. 1810 Clay, Cassius Marcellus
b. 1831 Hunter, Thomas
b. 1861 Burns, William John
b. 1862 Lumiere, Auguste Marie Louis
b. 1863 Finley, John Huston
b. 1868 Landes, Bertha Ethel
b. 1871 Cannon, Walter Bradford
b. 1876 Brown, Mordecai Peter Centennial
b. 1878 Sanborn, Pitts
b. 1882 Boccioni, Umberto
b. 1885 Merrill, Charles Edward
b. 1889 Hurst, Fannie
b. 1889 Satherly, Arthur Edward
b. 1895 Mumford, Lewis
b. 1899 Asturias, Miguel Angel
b. 1899 Bauer, Eddie
b. 1900 Worters, Roy
b. 1901 Burke, Arleigh A(lbert)
b. 1902 Grattan, Clinton Hartley
b. 1903 Giannini, Vittorio
b. 1908 Allen, Larry
b. 1909 Mott, William Penn, Jr.
b. 1910 Chandrasekhar, Subrahmanyan
b. 1912 Ghezzi, Vic(tor)
b. 1913 Jennings, Robert Yewdall
b. 1916 Blum, Stella
b. 1916 Dausset, Jean (Baptiste Gabriel Joachim)
b. 1916 Gilels, Emil Grigoyevich
b. 1918 Kirk, Russell (Amos)
b. 1918 Strauss, Robert Schwarz
b. 1921 Kalmbach, Herbert Warren
b. 1921 Power, Jules
b. 1922 Anderson, Jack Northman
b. 1924 Strougal, Lubomir
b. 1926 Wallant, Edward Lewis
b. 1927 Alechinsky, Pierre
b. 1927 Tallchief, Marjorie
b. 1931 LeCarre, John
b. 1932 Reed, Robert
b. 1934 Gowon, Yakubu

b. 1935 Haynes, Lloyd
b. 1936 Bevel, James Luther
b. 1936 Cole, Johnnetta Betsch
b. 1937 Bell, Marilyn
b. 1937 Max, Peter
b. 1941 Ward, Simon
b. 1945 Ireland, Patricia
b. 1945 Lithgow, John (Arthur)
b. 1945 Riley, Jeannie C
b. 1946 Divine
b. 1960 Davis, Mark William
b. 1960 Holliday, Jennifer Yvette
b. 1962 Holyfield, Evander
b. 1967 Carter, Amy Lynn
d. 1587 Medici, Francesco de
d. 1609 Arminius, Jacobus
d. 1745 Swift, Jonathan
d. 1749 Ged, William
d. 1790 Hall, Lyman
d. 1814 Warren, Mercy Otis
d. 1826 Talma, Francois Joseph
d. 1848 Guthrie, Samuel
d. 1856 Said, Seyyid
d. 1856 Said ibn Sultan
d. 1875 Wheatstone, Charles, Sir
d. 1897 Pullman, George Mortimer
d. 1898 Frederic, Harold
d. 1899 Appleton, William Henry
d. 1902 Younger, Jim
d. 1909 Lombroso, Cesare
d. 1914 Roca, Julio Argentino
d. 1915 McCoy, Joseph Geiting
d. 1920 Reed, John Silas
d. 1937 Rutherford, Ernest, Baron
d. 1945 Calles, Plutarco Elias
d. 1945 Wyeth, N(ewell) C(onvers)
d. 1950 Doherty, Robert Ernest
d. 1950 Millay, Edna St. Vincent
d. 1952 Curtis, Edward Sheriff
d. 1954 Duffy, Hugh
d. 1955 Hodiak, John
d. 1956 Jones, Isham
d. 1961 Gunnison, Foster
d. 1961 Jaeger, Werner Wilhelm
d. 1961 Osmena, Sergio, Jr.
d. 1970 Cardenas, Lazaro
d. 1972 Drinker, Philip

d. 1972 Said bin Taimur
d. 1975 Lord, Phillips H
d. 1976 Ford, Eleanor Clay
d. 1978 Young, Gig
d. 1980 Andrews, James Frederick
d. 1983 Bishop, Maurice Rupert
d. 1986 Henderson, Leon
d. 1986 Lebowsky, Stanley Richard
d. 1986 Machel, Samora Moises
d. 1987 DuPre, Jacqueline
d. 1987 Stahl, Ben(jamin Albert)
d. 1988 House, Son
d. 1990 Hartley, Fred Lloyd
d. 1990 Worsham, Lew(is Elmer)
d. 1992 Golub, William Weldon
d. 1992 Kelly, Petra (Karin)
d. 1994 Raye, Martha
d. 1997 McGill, William James

October 20
b. 1602 Guericke, Otto Von
b. 1632 Wren, Christopher, Sir
b. 1674 Logan, James
b. 1784 Palmerston, Henry John Temple, Viscount
b. 1785 Drake, Daniel
b. 1792 Clyde, Colin Campbell, Baron
b. 1812 Flint, Austin
b. 1822 Hughes, Thomas
b. 1825 Sickles, Daniel Edgar
b. 1826 George, James Zachariah
b. 1854 Rimbaud, (Jean Nicolas) Arthur
b. 1859 Dewey, John
b. 1873 Kellor, Frances (Alice)
b. 1873 McClung, Nellie Letitia Mooney
b. 1874 Ives, Charles Edward
b. 1882 Lugosi, Bela
b. 1884 Senanayake, Don Stephen
b. 1889 Dumont, Margaret
b. 1890 Minton, Sherman
b. 1891 Bemis, Samuel Flagg
b. 1891 Kenyatta, Jomo
b. 1893 Chase, Charley
b. 1895 Ingram, Rex
b. 1895 Ryskind, Morrie
b. 1895 Wurster, William
b. 1897 Deutsch, Adolph

b. 1899 Brent, Evelyn
b. 1900 Morse, Wayne Lyman
b. 1904 Douglas, Thomas Clement
b. 1904 Neagle, Anna, Dame
b. 1905 Dannay, Frederic
b. 1906 Johnson, Crockett
b. 1908 Francis, Arlene
b. 1913 Jones, Grandpa
b. 1914 Davies, Leslie Purnell
b. 1915 Ginsberg, Mitchell I(rving)
b. 1917 Melville, Jean-Pierre
b. 1918 Ash, Roy Lawrence
b. 1919 Mathison, Richard Randolph
b. 1920 Jagan, Janet
b. 1923 Craft, Robert
b. 1925 Buchwald, Art(hur)
b. 1927 Kaufman, Henry
b. 1928 Brothers, Joyce Diane Bauer
b. 1930 Kountz, Samuel L(ee)
b. 1931 Caliguiri, Richard
b. 1931 Mantle, Mickey (Charles)
b. 1932 Brown, Roosevelt
b. 1932 Christopher, William
b. 1932 McClure, Michael Thomas
b. 1934 Dunn, Michael
b. 1935 Buatta, Mario
b. 1935 Orbach, Jerry
b. 1936 Horse Capture, George, Sr.
b. 1936 Seale, Bobby G
b. 1938 Goldston, Nathaniel R, III
b. 1938 Marichal, Juan Antonio Sanchez
b. 1939 Slick, Grace Wing
b. 1942 Nuesslein-Volhard, Christiane
b. 1946 Grizzard, Lewis M., Jr.
b. 1949 Collett, Wayne
b. 1950 Curtis, Isaac Fisher
b. 1950 Rhodes, Ray
b. 1952 Petty, Tom
b. 1953 Hernandez, Keith
b. 1954 Selmon, Lee Roy
b. 1958 Pogorelich, Ivo
b. 1969 Gonzales, Juan (Alberto)
b. 1970 Cameron, Kirk
d. 1524 Linacre, Thomas
d. 1570 Barros, Joao de
d. 1794 Adam, James

d. 1821 Azara, Felix de
d. 1870 Balfe, Michael William
d. 1889 Babbitt, Benjamin Talbot
d. 1890 Burton, Richard Francis, Sir
d. 1893 Schaff, Philip
d. 1894 Froude, James Anthony
d. 1900 Warner, Charles Dudley
d. 1906 Ewing, Buck
d. 1909 Lea, Henry Charles
d. 1913 Palmer, Daniel David
d. 1926 Debs, Eugene Victor
d. 1926 Osborne, Thomas Mott
d. 1929 Batlle y Ordonez, Jose
d. 1935 Greely, Adolphus Washington
d. 1935 Henderson, Arthur
d. 1935 Smith, (Robert) Sidney
d. 1936 Sullivan, Anne
d. 1937 Warburg, Felix Moritz
d. 1942 Robson, May
d. 1942 Stock, Frederick A
d. 1943 Bernie, Ben
d. 1949 Copeau, Jacques
d. 1950 Stimson, Henry Lewis
d. 1952 Rostovtzeff, Michael Ivanovich
d. 1953 Cameron, Harry
d. 1955 Gulbenkian, Calouste S
d. 1956 Bell, Lawrence Dale
d. 1957 Buchanan, Jack
d. 1959 Krauss, Werner
d. 1962 Douglass, Andrew Ellicott
d. 1964 Hoover, Herbert C(lark)
d. 1966 Byrd, Harry Flood
d. 1967 Yoshida, Shigeru
d. 1970 Lewis, Ted
d. 1972 Shapley, Harlow T
d. 1973 Chandler, Norman
d. 1974 Tabbert, William
d. 1977 Gaines, Steve
d. 1977 Van Zant, Ronnie
d. 1981 Chase, Mary Coyle
d. 1982 Ziolkowski, Korczak
d. 1983 Theriault, Yves
d. 1983 Travis, Merle Robert
d. 1984 Cori, Carl Ferdinand

d. 1984 Dirac, Paul Adrien Maurice
d. 1987 Kolmogorov, Andrey Nikolayevich
d. 1988 Isbell, Marion William
d. 1989 Quayle, (John) Anthony, Sir
d. 1990 McCrea, Joel
d. 1991 Massey, D Curtis
d. 1993 Dolbier, Maurice (Wyman)
d. 1994 Lancaster, Burt(on Stephen)
d. 1996 Lee, J(oseph) Bracken
d. 1999 Sarraute, Nathalie

October 21
b. 1328 Hung-Wu
b. 1581 Domenichino, Il
b. 1651 Bart, Jean
b. 1660 Stahl, Georg Ernst
b. 1672 Muratori, Lodovico Antonio
b. 1762 Colman, George
b. 1772 Coleridge, Samuel Taylor
b. 1785 Shreve, Henry Miller
b. 1788 Combe, George
b. 1790 Lamartine, Alphonse Marie Louis de Prat de
b. 1808 Smith, Samuel Francis
b. 1813 Fillmore, Caroline Carmichael McIntosh
b. 1833 Nobel, Alfred Bernhard
b. 1845 Carleton, Will
b. 1846 Amicis, Edmond de
b. 1855 Ball, Edmund B
b. 1868 Swinton, Ernest Dunlop, Sir
b. 1869 Dodd, William Edward
b. 1870 Douglas, Alfred Bruce, Lord
b. 1876 Darling, Jay Norwood
b. 1877 Avery, Oswald T
b. 1883 Russell, Ernie
b. 1884 Beecher, Janet
b. 1885 Wellesz, Egon
b. 1891 Burnett, Leo
b. 1891 Knaths, Karl
b. 1891 Shawn, Ted
b. 1892 Boni, Albert
b. 1892 Lopokova, Lydia Vasilievna
b. 1894 Purviance, Edna
b. 1898 Walker, Stanley
b. 1899 Hussey, Christopher Edward Clive
b. 1901 Clark, Joseph Sill
b. 1901 von Rad, Gerhard

b. 1904 Kavanagh, Patrick
b. 1905 Henry, David D(odds)
b. 1908 Ferguson, Howard
b. 1908 Schneider, Alexander
b. 1911 Graves, Peter
b. 1912 Solti, Georg, Sir
b. 1914 Gardner, Martin
b. 1917 Gillespie, Dizzy
b. 1920 Eckart, William Joseph
b. 1921 Arnold, Malcolm, Sir
b. 1921 Runcie, Robert Alexander Kennedy
b. 1924 Wilson, Julie
b. 1926 Rosburg, Bob
b. 1927 Blucker, Robert Olof
b. 1927 Jordan, Charles Morrell
b. 1928 Ford, Whitey
b. 1928 Mikkelsen, Vern
b. 1929 Cruz, Celia
b. 1929 LeGuin, Ursula K(roeber)
b. 1931 Royer, William Blackburn, Jr.
b. 1933 Brown, Georgia
b. 1936 Gray, Simon James Holliday
b. 1940 FitzGerald, Frances
b. 1942 Bishop, Elvin
b. 1943 Piccolo, Brian
b. 1945 Mikhalkov, Nikita
b. 1946 Loughname, Lee
b. 1949 Keenan, Mike
b. 1949 Netanyahu, Benjamin
b. 1955 Faulkner, Eric
b. 1956 Fisher, Carrie Frances
b. 1959 Bell, George Antonio
d. 1422 Charles, VI
d. 1556 Aretino, Pietro
d. 1687 Waller, Edmund
d. 1777 Foote, Samuel
d. 1805 Nelson, Horatio Nelson, Viscount
d. 1886 Hernandez, Jose
d. 1907 Chevalier, Jules
d. 1908 Norton, Charles Eliot
d. 1931 Schnitzler, Arthur
d. 1944 Brinkley, Nell
d. 1945 Armetta, Henry
d. 1956 Owsley, Frank Lawrence
d. 1965 McDonald, Marie
d. 1967 Hertzsprung, Ejnar
d. 1969 Kerouac, Jack
d. 1970 Rojankovsky, Feodor Stepanovich

d. 1970 Scopes, John Thomas
d. 1971 Bronson, Betty
d. 1973 Cobham, Alan John, Sir
d. 1974 Goines, Donald
d. 1979 Sugiura, Kanematsu
d. 1980 Chervenkov, Vulko
d. 1981 Dixon, Robert Ellington
d. 1984 Truffaut, Francois
d. 1985 White, Dan(iel James)
d. 1987 Ho, Ying-Chin
d. 1990 Carvel, Thomas A
d. 1992 Garrison, Jim C.
d. 1993 Herlihy, James Leo
d. 1993 Ndadaye, Melchior
d. 1994 Wiesner, Jerome B(ert)
d. 1995 Andrews, Maxene
d. 1995 Goodman, Linda
d. 1995 Graves, Nancy (Stevenson)
d. 1995 Pinson, Vada Edward
d. 1997 Camilli, Dolph
d. 1998 Cairncross, Alexander Kirkland, Sir

October 22
b. 1688 Nadir Shah
b. 1759 Cooper, Thomas
b. 1811 Liszt, Franz (Ferencz)
b. 1812 Clevenger, Shobal Vail
b. 1818 Leconte de Lisle, Charles Marie Rene
b. 1821 Huntington, Collis Potter
b. 1832 Damrosch, Leopold
b. 1834 Duniway, Abigail Jane Scott
b. 1842 Cary, Anne Louise
b. 1842 Giolitti, Giovanni
b. 1843 Babcock, Stephen Moulton
b. 1844 Bernhardt, Sarah
b. 1859 Muck, Karl
b. 1865 Hitchcock, Raymond
b. 1870 Bunin, Ivan Alekseevich
b. 1880 Carr, Joe
b. 1881 Davisson, Clinton Joseph
b. 1882 Dulac, Edmund
b. 1882 Guggenheimer, Minnie

b. 1882 Wyeth, N(ewell) C(onvers)
b. 1884 Hill, George Washington
b. 1885 Martinelli, Giovanni
b. 1886 Bartlett, F(rederic) C(harles)
b. 1887 Reed, John Silas
b. 1889 Balderston, John Lloyd
b. 1890 Welch, Joseph Nye
b. 1891 Chadwick, James, Sir
b. 1892 Rascoe, Burton
b. 1895 Beckman, Johnny
b. 1898 Alonso, Damaso
b. 1898 Rickword, Edgell
b. 1899 Morris, William, Jr.
b. 1900 Stettinius, Edward R, Jr.
b. 1902 Spedding, Frank Harold
b. 1903 Beadle, George Wells
b. 1903 Howard, Curly
b. 1905 Bennett, Constance Campbell
b. 1907 Foxx, Jimmie
b. 1907 Wyeth, Henriette (Zirngiebel)
b. 1908 Sutton, John
b. 1912 Callahan, Harry (Morey)
b. 1913 Bao Dai
b. 1913 Capa, Robert
b. 1917 Fontaine, Joan
b. 1919 Janowitz, Morris
b. 1919 Lessing, Doris May
b. 1920 Green, Mitzi
b. 1920 Leary, Timothy (Francis)
b. 1921 Brassens, Georges
b. 1922 Chafee, John H(ubbard)
b. 1923 Pihos, Pete(r L)
b. 1924 Levine, Albert Norman
b. 1925 Martin, Slater
b. 1925 Previn, Dory Langdon
b. 1925 Rauschenberg, Robert
b. 1931 Hanley, William
b. 1934 Vizenor, Gerald
b. 1937 Ladd, Alan Walbridge, Jr.
b. 1938 Gillett, George Nield, Jr.
b. 1938 Jacobi, Derek George
b. 1938 Lloyd, Christopher
b. 1939 Chissano, Joaquim Alberto
b. 1939 Roberts, Tony

b. 1941 Wood, Wilbur Forrester
b. 1942 Funicello, Annette
b. 1943 Deneuve, Catherine
b. 1946 Brigati, Eddie
b. 1947 Barbour, Haley (Reeves)
b. 1949 Goring, Butch
b. 1952 Davis, Patti
b. 1952 Goldblum, Jeff
b. 1955 Anderson, Bonnie Marie
b. 1963 Boitano, Brian
b. 1965 Harding, John Wesley
d. 1565 Grolier, Jean
d. 1775 Randolph, Peyton
d. 1806 Sheraton, Thomas
d. 1853 Lavalleja, Juan Antonio
d. 1859 Spohr, Louis Ludwig
d. 1871 Murchison, Roderick Impey
d. 1880 Child, Lydia Maria Francis
d. 1897 Winsor, Justin
d. 1900 Sherman, John
d. 1903 Lecky, William Edward Hartpole
d. 1906 Cezanne, Paul
d. 1917 Fitzsimmons, Bob
d. 1922 Abbott, Lyman
d. 1923 Maurel, Victor
d. 1926 Greb, Harry
d. 1927 Youngs, Ross Middlebrook
d. 1928 Fisher, Andrew
d. 1929 Chirol, Valentine, Sir
d. 1929 Hastings, Thomas
d. 1934 Floyd, Pretty Boy
d. 1935 Carson, Edward Henry
d. 1936 Couzens, James Joseph, Jr.
d. 1937 Damrosch, Frank Heino
d. 1938 Irwin, May
d. 1944 Bennett, Richard
d. 1954 Kauffer, Edward McKnight
d. 1954 McManus, George
d. 1961 Schenck, Joseph M
d. 1962 Marcoux, Vanni
d. 1963 Jellinek, Elvin Morton
d. 1965 Tillich, Paul Johannes
d. 1966 Johnson, Hewlett
d. 1973 Casals, Pablo (Pau Carlos Salvador)
d. 1975 Toynbee, Arnold Joseph

d. 1978 Mikoyan, Anastas Ivanovich
d. 1979 Boulanger, Nadia Juliette
d. 1982 Jessup, Richard
d. 1983 Barrow, Keith E
d. 1986 Szent-Gyorgyi, Albert (von Nagyrapolt)
d. 1986 Ye Jianying
d. 1988 Armstrong, Henry
d. 1989 Hayes, Alfred
d. 1989 Maccoll, Ewan
d. 1990 Sinkwich, Frank
d. 1992 Barber, Red
d. 1992 Little, Cleavon Jake
d. 1994 May, Rollo (Reece)
d. 1995 Amis, Kingsley (William)
d. 1995 Boswell, Charles Albert
d. 1997 Rothwax, Harold
d. 1998 Ambler, Eric

October 23
b. 1695 Cuvillies, Francois
b. 1698 Gabriel, Ange-Jacques
b. 1740 Dalzel, Archibald
b. 1773 Jeffrey, Francis Jeffrey, Lord
b. 1800 Lawrence, William Beach
b. 1801 Lortzing, Gustav Albert
b. 1805 Bartlett, John Russell
b. 1817 Denver, James William
b. 1817 Larousse, Pierre Athanase
b. 1823 Naudin, Emilio
b. 1835 Stevenson, Adlai Ewing
b. 1844 Bridges, Robert Seymour
b. 1844 Riel, Louis David, Jr.
b. 1849 Saionji, Kimmochi
b. 1861 Converse, Marquis M
b. 1869 Heisman, John William
b. 1873 Coolidge, William David
b. 1875 Lewis, Gilbert Newton
b. 1876 Cret, Paul P(hilippe)
b. 1881 O'Connor, Una
b. 1885 Harris, Lauren
b. 1889 Saerchinger, Cesar Victor Charles
b. 1890 Baillie, Hugh
b. 1890 Littlejohn, Robert McGowan
b. 1893 Marx, Gummo
b. 1895 Anderson, Clint(on Presba)

b. 1895 Maverick, Maury
b. 1899 Balchen, Bernt
b. 1899 Kimbrough, Emily
b. 1899 Tashman, Lilyan
b. 1904 Lincoln, Victoria Endicott
b. 1905 Bloch, Felix
b. 1906 Ederle, Gertrude Caroline
b. 1906 Monroe, Lucy
b. 1908 Frank, Ilya Mikaylovich
b. 1908 Oistrakh, David Fyodorovich
b. 1910 Fredericks, Carlton
b. 1910 Rorke, Hayden
b. 1913 Gorkin, Jess
b. 1914 Drillon, Gordie
b. 1914 Kinard, Frank M
b. 1916 Whittemore, Arthur Austin
b. 1918 Daly, James
b. 1918 Rudolph, Paul Marvin
b. 1920 Montana, Bob
b. 1920 Rizzo, Frank Lazzaro
b. 1922 Gray, Coleen
b. 1922 Gray, Nicholas Stuart
b. 1923 Mardian, Robert Charles
b. 1923 Rorem, Ned
b. 1925 Carson, Johnny
b. 1927 Kienholz, Edward
b. 1927 Kolakowski, Leszek
b. 1927 Lamantia, Philip
b. 1928 Woodwell, George M(asters)
b. 1929 Darvi, Bella
b. 1931 Bunning, Jim
b. 1931 Clark, William P(atrick Jr.)
b. 1931 Davis, Margaret B(ryan)
b. 1931 Dors, Diana
b. 1932? Barfield, Velma
b. 1932 Zimmerman, Paul L
b. 1934 Rodriguez, Chi-Chi
b. 1938 Heinz, John
b. 1940 Pele
b. 1942 Crichton, Michael
b. 1942 Roddick, Anita Lucia Perella
b. 1944 Leavell, Dorothy R.
b. 1954 Lee, Ang
b. 1956 Yoakam, Dwight
b. 1958 Dyson, Michael Eric
b. 1959 Yankovic, Weird Al

b. 1962 Flutie, Doug(las Richard)
b. 1966 Zanardi, Alex
d. 1872 Gautier, Theophile
d. 1893 Crittendon, Thomas Leonidas
d. 1910 Chulalongkorn
d. 1913 Klebs, Edwin
d. 1927 Dickman, Joseph Theodore
d. 1928 Aulard, Francois Victor Alphonse
d. 1928 McCutcheon, George Barr
d. 1935 Demuth, Charles
d. 1939 Grey, Zane
d. 1943 Antoine, Andre
d. 1944 Barkla, Charles Glover
d. 1946 Seton, Ernest Thompson
d. 1950 Jolson, Al
d. 1952 Peters, Susan
d. 1953 Bone, Muirhead, Sir
d. 1957 Lyman, Abe
d. 1959 Golden, William
d. 1962 Telva, Marion
d. 1964 Mott, Frank Luther
d. 1965 Throckmorton, Cleon
d. 1968 Cassidy, Marshall
d. 1977 Markel, Lester
d. 1978 Carter, Mother Maybelle
d. 1983 Savitch, Jessica Beth
d. 1984 Petrillo, James Caesar
d. 1984 Werner, Oskar
d. 1984 Whittemore, Arthur Austin
d. 1989 Barrett, Edward Ware
d. 1992 Masselos, William
d. 1994 Leonard, Bill
d. 1995 Pendleton, Don
d. 1996 Trilling, Diana (Rubin)
d. 1998 Judd, Winnie Ruth McKinnell

October 24
b. 51 Domitian
b. 1618 Aurangzeb
b. 1632 Leeuwenhoek, Antonie van
b. 1710 Butler, Alban
b. 1784 Montefiore, Moses Haim, Sir
b. 1788 Hale, Sarah Josepha Buell
b. 1804 Weber, Wilhelm Eduard
b. 1808 Sartain, John
b. 1820 Fromentin, Eugene
b. 1830 Lockwood, Belva Ann Bennett

b. 1855 Sherman, James Schoolcraft
b. 1864 Leoni, Franco
b. 1868 David-Neel, Alexandra
b. 1871 Shrady, Henry M
b. 1873 Bode, Boyd Henry
b. 1877 Hutton, Bouse
b. 1879 Weston, Edward F
b. 1882 Thorndike, Sybil, Dame
b. 1886 Agustini, Delmira
b. 1890 Mainbocher
b. 1891 Trujillo (Molina), Rafael Leonidas
b. 1894 Lewis, Ted
b. 1896 Gray, Gilda
b. 1899 Abbas, Ferhat
b. 1901 Eichenberg, Fritz
b. 1903 Purvis, Melvin
b. 1904 Hart, Moss
b. 1906 Gelfond, Aleksandr Osipovich
b. 1911 Kelley, Clarence Marion
b. 1911 Terry, Sonny
b. 1912 Gellhorn, Peter
b. 1912 Lundberg, Daniel
b. 1915 Gobbi, Tito
b. 1915 Laski, Marghanita
b. 1921 Jurinac, Sena
b. 1923 Levertov, Denise
b. 1925 Berio, Luciano
b. 1926 Tittle, Y(elberton) A(braham)
b. 1927 Becaud, Gilbert (Francois Silly)
b. 1929 Brosnan, Jim
b. 1929 Crumb, George Henry
b. 1930 Big Bopper, The
b. 1932 Covey, Stephen R.
b. 1932 Dorfman, Dan
b. 1932 Lattner, Johnny
b. 1933 Bray, Charles William, III
b. 1933 Kray, Reggie
b. 1933 Kray, Ronnie
b. 1934 Walton, Tony
b. 1936 Hernandez-Colon, Rafael
b. 1936 Nelson, David
b. 1938 Watson, Jack Hearn, Jr.
b. 1939 Allen, Paula Gunn
b. 1940 Abraham, F(ahrid) Murray
b. 1941 Woo, Merle
b. 1941 Wyman, Bill
b. 1943 Powell, Earl A, III
b. 1945 Dunn, Katherine (Karen)

b. 1945 Ward, David S
b. 1947 Kline, Kevin Delaney
b. 1948 Griffin, Dale
b. 1948 Mfume, Kweisi
b. 1949 White, Stan(ley Ray)
b. 1955 Studer, Cheryl
b. 1956 Gerstler, Amy
b. 1962 Wong, B D
d. 42BC Brutus, Marcus Junius
d. 1537 Seymour, Jane
d. 1601 Brahe, Tycho
d. 1838 Lancaster, Joseph
d. 1842 O'Higgins, Bernardo
d. 1852 Webster, Daniel
d. 1911 Lewis, Ida
d. 1920 MacSwiney, Terence
d. 1926 Russell, Charles Marion
d. 1928 Davies, Arthur Bowen
d. 1935 Pirenne, Jean Henri Otto Lucien Marie
d. 1935 Schultz, Dutch
d. 1944 Renault, Louis
d. 1945 Carmichael, Franklin
d. 1945 Quisling, Vidkun Abraham
d. 1946 Kline, Otis Adelbert
d. 1947 Digges, Dudley
d. 1948 Lehar, Franz
d. 1957 Dior, Christian
d. 1958 Moore, George Edward
d. 1970 Hofstadter, Richard
d. 1971 Ruggles, Carl
d. 1972 Robinson, Jackie
d. 1972 Votipka, Thelma
d. 1972 Windsor, Claire
d. 1974 Oistrakh, David Fyodorovich
d. 1979 Belmont, Eleanor Robson
d. 1980 D'Aulaire, Ingri Mortenson
d. 1981 Head, Edith
d. 1981 Holm, John Cecil
d. 1986 Doisy, Edward Adelbert, Sr.
d. 1987 Alajalov, Constantin
d. 1988 Fuller, S(amuel) B.
d. 1991 Roddenberry, Gene
d. 1992 Colwin, Laurie
d. 1992 Miller, Max
d. 1992 Moore, William
d. 1993 Barnhart, Clarence L(ewis)
d. 1993 Grimond, Jo(seph)
d. 1994 Julia, Raul

d. 1994 Shelepin,
Aleksandr
(Nikolaevich)
d. 1996 Hughes, Harold
E(verett)
d. 1998 Calderone,
Mary Steichen
d. 1999 Chafee, John
H(ubbard)
October 25
b. 1767 Constant de
Rebeque, (Henri)
Benjamin
b. 1795 Kennedy, John
Pendleton
b. 1800 Macaulay,
Thomas Babington
Macaulay, Baron
b. 1802 Bonington,
Richard Parkes
b. 1806 Stirner, Max
b. 1811 Galois, Evariste
b. 1814 Carrera, Jose
Rafael
b. 1825 Strauss, Johann,
Jr.
b. 1837 Harkness, Anna
M Richardson
b. 1838 Bizet, Georges
(Alexandre Cesar
Leopold)
b. 1864 Dodge, John
Francis
b. 1864 Gretchaninov,
Aleksandr
Tikhonovich
b. 1866 Patten, Gilbert
b. 1873 Willys, John
North
b. 1874 Dawson,
Geoffrey
b. 1877 Russell, Henry
Norris
b. 1881 Picasso, Pablo
Ruiz y
b. 1884 Easton,
Florence Gertrude
b. 1886 Polanyi, Karl
b. 1888 Byrd, Richard
Evelyn, Admiral
b. 1888 Crosby,
Elizabeth Caroline
b. 1889 Gance, Abel
b. 1889 Wood, Joe
b. 1890 Bennett, Floyd
b. 1891 Coughlin,
Charles Edward,
Father
b. 1892 Dolly, Jenny
b. 1892 Dolly, Rosie
b. 1894 Phillips,
Marjorie Acker
b. 1895 Eshkol, Levi
b. 1899 MacLiammoir,
Michael
b. 1902 Commager,
Henry Steele
b. 1902 Lang, Eddie
b. 1904 Gorky, Arshile
b. 1904 Shute, Denny
b. 1909 Draper, Paul
(Nathaniel Saltonstall)
b. 1909 Nash, Philleo
b. 1910 Higinbotham,
William A(lfred)
b. 1910 Lichine, David

b. 1911 Jackson,
Mahalia
b. 1912 Pearl, Minnie
b. 1913 Barbie, Klaus
b. 1913 Fletcher, Grant
b. 1914 Berryman, John
b. 1915 Cox, Constance
b. 1917 MacPhail, Lee
b. 1921 Michael V
b. 1923 Thomson,
Bobby
b. 1924 Brown, Bobby
b. 1924 Elliott, Osborn
b. 1926 Butcher,
Willard C(arlisle)
b. 1926 McGuire, Biff
b. 1926 Vishnevskaya,
Galina (Pavlovna)
b. 1927 Cook, Barbara
b. 1927 Shagan, Steve
b. 1928 Franciosa,
Anthony
b. 1928? Ross, Marion
b. 1930 Brodkey,
Harold
b. 1930 Gray, Hanna
(Holborn)
b. 1931 Girardot, Annie
b. 1933 Haley, Jack, Jr.
b. 1935 Schweickart,
Russell L
b. 1936 Gilbert, Martin
John
b. 1938 Gartner,
Michael Gay
b. 1940 Knight, Bobby
b. 1941 Reddy, Helen
b. 1941 Tyler, Anne
b. 1943 Smalls, Charlie
b. 1944 Anderson, Jon
b. 1944 Carville, James
b. 1945 Borysenko,
Joan
b. 1948 Cowens, Dave
b. 1948 Issel, Dan(iel
Paul)
b. 1951 Stemrick,
Greg(ory Earl, Sr.)
b. 1951 Wilson,
Ransom
b. 1954 Eruzione, Mike
b. 1958 Ender, Kornelia
b. 1963 Nelson, Tracy
b. 1966 Clark, Wendel
b. 1971 Midori
d. 1154 Stephen
d. 1180 John of
Salisbury
d. 1400 Chaucer,
Geoffrey
d. 1647 Torricelli,
Evangelista
d. 1760 George II
d. 1806 Knox, Henry
d. 1861 Savigny,
Friedrich Karl von
d. 1877 Adams, Edwin
d. 1892 Harrison,
Caroline (Lavinia
Scott)
d. 1895 Halle, Charles,
Sir
d. 1897 Sartain, John
d. 1900 Squibb, Edward
Robinson

d. 1902 Norris,
Frank(lin)
d. 1916 Chase, William
Merritt
d. 1921 Masterson, Bat
d. 1924 Gokalp,
Mehmet Ziya
d. 1934 Sprague, Frank
Julian
d. 1938 Kuprin,
Aleksandr Ivanovich
d. 1941 Delaunay,
Robert
d. 1943 Hart, Frances
Noyes
d. 1945 Ley, Robert
d. 1947 Ziegler, Edward
d. 1957 Anastasia,
Albert
d. 1957 Dunsany,
Edward J M Plunkett,
Baron
d. 1959 Cline,
Genevieve Rose
d. 1960 Ferguson, Harry
George
d. 1965 Knappertsbusch,
Hans
d. 1971 Terry, Paul H
d. 1971 Wylie, Philip
Gordon
d. 1972 Norell, Norman
d. 1974 Furtseva,
Ekaterina Alexeyevna
d. 1974 Kroll, Leon
d. 1979 Darling, Frank
Fraser, Sir
d. 1980 Dodds, Harold
Willis
d. 1980 Fox, Virgil
Keel
d. 1981 Durant, Ariel
d. 1981 Reiser, Pete
d. 1983 Epperson, Frank
W
d. 1984 Brautigan,
Richard
d. 1985 Downey,
Morton
d. 1985 Slotnick, Daniel
Leonid
d. 1986 Tucker, Forrest
Meredith
d. 1987 Brown, Cecil B
d. 1989 Harper, Marion,
Jr.
d. 1989 McCarthy,
Mary Therese
d. 1991 Graham, Bill
d. 1992 Klein, Marty
d. 1992 Miller, Roger
Dean
d. 1993 Price, Vincent
d. 1994 Natwick,
Mildred
d. 1994 Roebling, Mary
G(indhart)
d. 1995 Lindfors,
Viveca
d. 1995 Riggs, Bobby
October 26
b. 1685 Scarlatti,
Domenico Girolamo
b. 1757 Stein, Heinrich
Friedrich Karl vom
und zum, Baron

b. 1786 Deringer, Henry
b. 1800 Moltke,
Helmuth Karl
Bernhard von
b. 1803 Hansom, Joseph
Aloysius
b. 1840 Keene, Thomas
Wallace
b. 1842 Vereshchagin,
Vasily Vasilyevich
b. 1845 Harrigan,
Edward
b. 1846 Claflin,
Tennessee Celeste
b. 1846 Scott, Charles
Prestwich
b. 1854 Post, Charles
William
b. 1861 Sears, Richard
Dudley
b. 1863 Statler,
Ellsworth Milton
b. 1874 Rockefeller,
Abby Aldrich
b. 1876 Loftus, Cissie
b. 1877 Mason, Max
b. 1886 Starrett, Vincent
b. 1890 Eckstein,
Gustav
b. 1891 Schlink,
Frederick John
b. 1894 Knight, John
Shivley
b. 1897 Lemnitz, Tiana
b. 1898 Oliver, Harry
b. 1899 Johnson, Judy
b. 1900 Abboud, (El
Ferik) Ibrahim
b. 1901 Evergood,
Philip (Howard
Francis Dixon)
b. 1902 Markham, Beryl
b. 1904 Osborn, Robert
C(hesley)
b. 1906 Carnera, Primo
b. 1907 Pastor, Tony
b. 1908 Gorin, Igor
b. 1909 Lewis, Allen
Montgomery, Sir
b. 1910 Krol, John
(Joseph), Cardinal
b. 1911 Chern, Shiing-
shen
b. 1911 Gillman, Sidney
b. 1913 Barnet, Charlie
b. 1913 Scanlon, Hugh
Parr
b. 1914 Coogan, Jackie
b. 1914 Masters, John
b. 1916 Mitterrand,
Francois (Maurice
Marie)
b. 1917 Biaggi, Mario
b. 1919 Bourgholtzer,
Frank
b. 1919 Brooke, Edward
William, III
b. 1919 Gronouski, John
A(ustin)
b. 1919 Pahlevi,
Mohammed Riza
b. 1921 Fulks, Joe
b. 1925 DeMoss, Arthur
S
b. 1926 Jaeckel, Richard
(Hanley)

b. 1759 Danton, Georges Jacques
b. 1798 Coffin, Levi
b. 1801 Inman, Henry
b. 1803 Unger, Caroline
b. 1808 Smith, Horace
b. 1844 Ezekiel, Moses Jacob
b. 1846 Escoffier, Georges Auguste
b. 1847 Thompson, J(ames) Walter
b. 1867 Driesch, Hans Adolf Eduard
b. 1868 Connolly, James B
b. 1875 Grosvenor, Gilbert Hovey
b. 1880 Evans, Edward Ratcliffe Garth Russell
b. 1892 Johnson, Dink
b. 1893 Ingold, Christopher Kelk, Sir
b. 1894 Murphy, Robert Daniel
b. 1894 Pangborn, Clyde Edward
b. 1894 Wolff, Fritz
b. 1895 Boles, John
b. 1895 Chamberlain, Samuel
b. 1896 Hanson, Howard
b. 1897 Speidel, Hans
b. 1902 Lanchester, Elsa
b. 1903 Chamberlain, John Rensselaer
b. 1903 Waugh, Evelyn Arthur St. John
b. 1904 Dangerfield, George Bubb
b. 1907 Head, Edith
b. 1908 Oppenheimer, Harry Frederick
b. 1909 Bacon, Francis
b. 1909 Gingold, Josef
b. 1910 Kamp, Irene Kittle
b. 1914 Salk, Jonas E(dward)
b. 1914 Synge, Richard Laurence Millington
b. 1915 Soo, Jack
b. 1916 Harris, Willard Palmer
b. 1917 Page, Joe
b. 1920 Robitscher, Jonas Bondi, Jr.
b. 1920 Swados, Harvey
b. 1922? Glenn, Carroll
b. 1926 Kuhn, Bowie Kent
b. 1927 Laine, Cleo
b. 1929 Ginzburg, Ralph
b. 1929 Goodman, Dody
b. 1929 Hollander, John
b. 1929 Plowright, Joan Anne
b. 1930 Fifield, Elaine
b. 1930 Morton, Bruce Alexander
b. 1932 Kyprianou, Spyros Achilles

b. 1933 Parker, Suzy
b. 1934 Beatty, Jim
b. 1936 Antes, Horst
b. 1936 Daniels, Charlie
b. 1937 Wilkens, Lenny
b. 1938 Perry, Anne
b. 1939 Alexander, Jane
b. 1941 Hightower, Dennis F(owler)
b. 1944 Coluche
b. 1944 Franz, Dennis
b. 1945 Brett, Simon Anthony Lee
b. 1948 Hopkins, Telma Louise
b. 1949 Jenner, Bruce
b. 1952 Potts, Annie
b. 1952 Tcherkassky, Marianna Alexsavena
b. 1956 Story, Liz
b. 1967 Roberts, Julia
b. 1969 Harper, Ben
b. 1972 Davis, Terrell
d. 901? Alfred the Great
d. 1704 Locke, John
d. 1721 Rogers, John
d. 1730 Rottmayr, Johann Michael
d. 1786 Sears, Isaac
d. 1792 Smeaton, John
d. 1818 Adams, Abigail (Smith)
d. 1821 Pacchierotti, Gasparo
d. 1848 Otis, Harrison Gray
d. 1861 James, Edwin
d. 1873 Heenan, John Carmel
d. 1874 Rinehart, William H
d. 1899 Mergenthaler, Ottmar
d. 1916 Abbe, Cleveland
d. 1918 Bouchet, Edward Alexander
d. 1925 Leggett, William
d. 1929 Bulow, Bernhard H M
d. 1933 Sothern, Edward Hugh
d. 1938 Kohler, Fred, Sir
d. 1939 Brady, Alice
d. 1944 White, Helen Magill
d. 1948 Dickey, Herbert Spencer
d. 1951 Christians, Mady
d. 1952 Hughes, William Morris
d. 1954 Gorman, Herbert Sherman
d. 1959 Bauersfeld, Walther
d. 1961 Stuart, Bruce
d. 1963 Connally, Tom
d. 1968 McGimsie, Billy
d. 1968 Meitner, Lise
d. 1969 Chukovsky, Korney Ivanovich

d. 1971 Foyle, Gilbert Samuel
d. 1973 Taha Hussein
d. 1974 Jones, David
d. 1975 La Tour du Pin, Patrice de
d. 1980 Janney, Leon
d. 1983 Messmer, Otto
d. 1986 Arthur, Robert
d. 1986 Braine, John Gerard
d. 1987 Masson, Andre (Aime Rene)
d. 1988 Annigoni, Pietro
d. 1991 Fine, Sylvia
d. 1991 Fletcher, Joseph Francis (III)
d. 1993 Duke, Doris
d. 1996 Amsterdam, Morey
d. 1998 Goldman, James
d. 1998 Hughes, Ted
d. 1999 Alberti, Rafael

October 29

b. 1507 Alba, Duke of
b. 1682 Charlevoix, Pierre Francis Xavier de
b. 1745 Lee, Thomas Sim
b. 1811 Blanc, Louis
b. 1815 Emmett, Daniel Decatur
b. 1828 Bayard, Thomas Francis
b. 1831 Marsh, Othniel Charles
b. 1859 Ebbets, Charles Hercules
b. 1873 Kelly, Walter C
b. 1875 Marie Alexandra Victoria
b. 1879 Papen, Franz von
b. 1882 Giraudoux, Jean
b. 1882 Martinez, Maximiliano Hernandez
b. 1883 Woodcock, Amos Walter Wright
b. 1885 Kidder, Alfred Vincent
b. 1890 Ottaviani, Alfredo, Cardinal
b. 1891 Brice, Fanny
b. 1895 Pearl, Jack
b. 1897 Goebbels, Joseph
b. 1898 Emerson, Hope
b. 1901 Amfiteatrof, Daniele
b. 1901 Tamiroff, Akim
b. 1904 Westmore, Perc(ival)
b. 1905 Green, Henry
b. 1906 Schottland, Charles I(rwin)
b. 1908 Ames, Louise (Bates)
b. 1910 Ayer, Alfred Jules, Sir
b. 1916 Keogh, James
b. 1920 Benacerraf, Baruj

b. 1921 Mauldin, Bill
b. 1922 Hefti, Neal Paul
b. 1923 Djerassi, Carl
b. 1925 Brooks, Geraldine
b. 1925 Dunne, Dominick
b. 1925 Siegel, Larry
b. 1925 Sims, Zoot
b. 1926 Vickers, Jon
b. 1927 Sedgman, Frank
b. 1932 Kitaj, R(onald) B(rooks)
b. 1936 Jayston, Michael
b. 1937 Heth, Charlotte
b. 1940 Mack, Connie
b. 1941 Crocker, Chester Arthur
b. 1945 Moore, Melba
b. 1945 Simpson, Donald C
b. 1946 Green, Peter
b. 1947 Dreyfuss, Richard (Stephan)
b. 1948 Reynolds, Ricky
b. 1949 Jackson, Kate
b. 1951 Barfield, Jesse Lee
b. 1951 Boone, Mary
b. 1951 Kempthorne, Dirk Arthur
b. 1953 Potvin, Denis Charles
b. 1959 Parsons, David
b. 1961 Crosby, Nathaniel
b. 1961 Jackson, Randy
b. 1971 Ryder, Winona
d. 1099 Urban II
d. 1216 John, King of England
d. 1618 Raleigh, Walter, Sir
d. 1666 Shirley, James
d. 1783 Alembert, Jean le Rond d'
d. 1804 Morland, George
d. 1864 Leech, John
d. 1877 Forrest, Nathan Bedford
d. 1885 McClellan, George Brinton
d. 1889 Chernyshevsky, Nikolai Gavrilovich
d. 1891 Hargraves, Edward Hammond
d. 1892 Harnett, William Michael
d. 1897 George, Henry, Sr.
d. 1901 Czolgosz, Leon F
d. 1911 Pulitzer, Joseph
d. 1924 Burnett, Frances Eliza Hodgson
d. 1926 Webb, William Seward
d. 1930 Repin, Ilya Yefimovich
d. 1933 Calmette, Albert Leon Charles
d. 1933 Luks, George Benjamin

d. 1947 Brach, Emil J
d. 1947 Cleveland, Frances Folsom
d. 1948 Mitchell, Wesley Clair
d. 1949 Gurdjieff, George Ivanovitch
d. 1951 Aitkin, Robert Grant
d. 1953 Kapell, William
d. 1953 Olsen, Harold G
d. 1956 Coffin, Robert Peter Tristram
d. 1957 Mayer, L(ouis) B(urt)
d. 1958 Akins, Zoe
d. 1960 Andersson, Johan Gunnar
d. 1961 McClintic, Guthrie
d. 1962 Resor, Stanley Burnett
d. 1963 Menjou, Adolphe Jean
d. 1965 McKechnie, Bill
d. 1967 Duvivier, Julien
d. 1969 Douglas, Sholto
d. 1971 Allman, Duane
d. 1971 Tiselius, Arne Wilhelm Kaurin
d. 1975 Trotter, John Scott
d. 1982 Hall, Joyce Clyde
d. 1982 Thompson, Thomas
d. 1984 Bloom, Ursula
d. 1985 Allen, William McPherson
d. 1985 Douglas-Home, Charles
d. 1986 Schwarzhaupt, Elisabeth
d. 1987 ElMallakh, Kamal
d. 1987 Herman, Woody
d. 1990 Smith, William French
d. 1992 MacMillan, Kenneth, Sir
d. 1994 Primus, Pearl
d. 1995 Southern, Terry
d. 1996 Day, J(ames) Edward
d. 1997 Coombs, Herbert Cole

October 30
b. 1513 Amyot, Jacques
b. 1632 Vermeer, Jan
b. 1698 Troger, Paul
b. 1735 Adams, John
b. 1741 Kauffmann, Angelica
b. 1751 Sheridan, Richard Brinsley
b. 1762 Chenier, Marie-Andre de
b. 1807 Wadsworth, James Samuel
b. 1815 Comstock, Elizabeth L
b. 1815 Downing, Andrew Jackson

b. 1816 Dawes, Henry Laurens
b. 1820 Dawson, John William, Sir
b. 1829 Conkling, Roscoe
b. 1829 Rogers, John
b. 1835 Patti, Carlotta
b. 1839 Sisley, Alfred
b. 1840 Sumner, William Graham
b. 1857 Atherton, Gertrude Franklin
b. 1861 Bourdelle, Emile-Antoine
b. 1867 Bonnard, Pierre
b. 1871 Valery, Paul Ambroise
b. 1873 Madero, Francisco Indalecio
b. 1877 Rombauer, Irma von Starkloff
b. 1882 Halsey, William Frederick, Jr.
b. 1883 Jones, Bob
b. 1884 Lea, Fanny Heaslip
b. 1885 Pound, Ezra Loomis
b. 1886 Akins, Zoe
b. 1888 Kirk, Alan Goodrich
b. 1891 Goddard, Calvin Hooker
b. 1894 Atlas, Charles
b. 1894 Heseltine, Philip Arnold
b. 1895 Domagk, Gerhard
b. 1895 Richards, Dickinson Woodruff
b. 1896 Dooley, Rae
b. 1896 Gordon, Ruth
b. 1898 Terry, Bill
b. 1900 Granit, Ragnar Arthur
b. 1902 Overstreet, Bonaro Wilkinson
b. 1904 Foster, Joseph C
b. 1904 McElroy, Neil Hosler
b. 1904 Still, Clyfford
b. 1906 Smith, Paul Joseph
b. 1907 Leventhal, Albert Rice
b. 1907 Tax, Sol
b. 1908 Ustinov, Dmitri Fedorovich
b. 1909 Bassett, Ben
b. 1909 Bhabha, Homi Jehangir
b. 1912 Haynsworth, Clement Furman, Jr.
b. 1912 Parks, Gordon Alexander Buchanan
b. 1914 Jonathan, Joseph Leabua
b. 1914 Laughlin, James, IV
b. 1914 Mohammed Zahir Shah
b. 1914 Montana, Patsy
b. 1915 Carnevale, Ben

b. 1915 Friendly, Fred W.
b. 1915 Hussey, Ruth Carol
b. 1917 Dobozy, Imre
b. 1917 Ogarkov, Nikolai
b. 1922 Costa Mendez, Nicanor
b. 1923 Bernardi, Hershel
b. 1928 Nathans, Daniel
b. 1928 Wigle, Ernest Douglas
b. 1930 Almendros, Nestor
b. 1930 Pullein-Thompson, Diana
b. 1931 Araskog, Rand Vincent
b. 1932 Malle, Louis
b. 1933 Muhammad, Wallace D
b. 1936 Caro, Robert A
b. 1936 Vermeil, Dick
b. 1937 Gautier, Dick
b. 1937 LeLouch, Claude
b. 1940 Fox, Charles
b. 1941 Hill, Bonnie Guiton
b. 1941 Woiwode, Larry
b. 1945 Winkler, Henry Franklin
b. 1947 Schmidt, Tim(othy B)
b. 1951 Hamlin, Harry Robinson
b. 1957? Mintz, Shlomo
b. 1958 Delaney, Joe Alton
b. 1960 Maradona, Diego
b. 1970 Long, Nia
d. 1466 Fust, Johann
d. 1676 Koprulu, Ahmed
d. 1787 Galiani, Ferdinando
d. 1823 Cartwright, Edmund
d. 1867 Andrew, John Albion
d. 1881 DeLong, George Washington
d. 1887 Walter, Thomas Ustick
d. 1893 Bodmer, Karl
d. 1903 Ozaki, Koyo
d. 1910 Dunant, Jean Henri
d. 1912 Sherman, James Schoolcraft
d. 1915 Tupper, Charles
d. 1923 Law, Andrew Bonar
d. 1928 Lansing, Robert
d. 1928 Sonneck, Oscar George Theodore
d. 1936 Taft, Lorado
d. 1937 Kraus, Felix von
d. 1940 Asplund, Erik Gunnar
d. 1950 Costello, Maurice

d. 1954 Shaw, Wilbur
d. 1956 Baroja (y Nessi), Pio
d. 1958 Macaulay, (Emilie) Rose, Dame
d. 1961 Einaudi, Luigi
d. 1968 Kelton, Pert
d. 1968 Lane, Rose Wilder
d. 1968 Richter, Conrad Michael
d. 1969 Foster, Pops
d. 1970 Martinson, Joseph Bertram
d. 1975 Hertz, Gustav Ludwig
d. 1975 Kellerman, Annette
d. 1979 Mussolini, Rachele Guidi
d. 1979 Wallis, Barnes Neville, Sir
d. 1981 Brassens, Georges
d. 1983 Carter, Lillian
d. 1984 Engstrom, Elmer William
d. 1985 Grant, Kirby
d. 1985 Tanner, Marion
d. 1987 Mayes, Herbert Raymond
d. 1991 Kolchin, Ellis Robert
d. 1992 Mitchell, Joan
d. 1994 Singh, (Sardar) Swaran
d. 1995 Morini, Erica
d. 1996 Dulles, Eleanor Lansing
d. 1997 Fuller, Samuel
d. 1998 Celebrezze, Anthony J(oseph)

October 31
b. 1620 Evelyn, John
b. 1694 Yngjo
b. 1705 Clement XIV, Pope
b. 1740 DeLoutherbourg, Philip James
b. 1740 Paca, William
b. 1795 Keats, John
b. 1817 Graetz, Heinrich Hirsch
b. 1821 Virchow, Rudolf
b. 1825 Lavigerie, Charles Martel Allemand
b. 1828 Hunt, Richard Morris
b. 1828 Swan, Joseph Wilson, Sir
b. 1831 Butterford, Daniel
b. 1835 Ames, Adelbert
b. 1835 Baeyer, Adolf Johann Friedrich Wilhelm, von
b. 1847 Ferraris, Galileo
b. 1852 Freeman, Mary E Wilkins
b. 1853 Zelaya, Jose Santos
b. 1860 Low, Juliette Gordon

b. 1860 Volstead, Andrew J
b. 1863 McAdoo, William Gibbs
b. 1864 Benediktsson, Einar
b. 1864 Lang, William Cosmo Gordon, Baron
b. 1867 Delahanty, Ed(ward James)
b. 1867 Philips, David Graham
b. 1876 Barney, Natalie Clifford
b. 1880 Peterkin, Julia Mood
b. 1883 Allgood, Sara
b. 1885 Laurencin, Marie
b. 1886 Chiang Kai-Shek
b. 1888 Wilkins, George Hubert, Sir
b. 1893 Strode, Hudson
b. 1894 King, Charles
b. 1895 Liddell Hart, Basil Henry, Sir
b. 1896 Chace, Marian
b. 1896 Waters, Ethel
b. 1897 Henry, Pete
b. 1899 Mandelstam, Nadezhda Yakovlevna
b. 1902 Drummond de Andrade, Carlos
b. 1902 Franz, Eduard
b. 1902 Shaw, Wilbur
b. 1904? Taylor, Sydney Brenner
b. 1905 Sour, Robert B(andler)
b. 1912 Evans, Dale
b. 1915 Wechsler, James Arthur
b. 1916 Barnett, Marvin Robert
b. 1917 McNeill, William Hardy
b. 1918 Bell, Griffin Boyette
b. 1919 Sisco, Joseph John
b. 1920 Danielian, Leon
b. 1920 Francis, Dick
b. 1920 Newton, Helmut
b. 1922 Geddes, Barbara Bel
b. 1922 Jacquet, Illinois (Robert Russell)
b. 1922 Sihanouk, Norodom
b. 1923 Waldron, Hicks Benjamin
b. 1927 Kahn, Roger
b. 1928 Romer, Roy R
b. 1928 Sarris, Andrew George
b. 1930 Collins, Mike
b. 1931 Grant, Lee
b. 1931 Rather, Dan(iel Irvin)
b. 1934 Beaton, Norman
b. 1934 Humes, James Calhoun

b. 1936 Wexler, Peter John
b. 1937 Landon, Michael
b. 1937 Paxton, Tom
b. 1937 Pender, Mel(vin)
b. 1939 Dillon, Melinda
b. 1942 McNally, Dave
b. 1942 Stiers, David Ogden
b. 1945 Keefe, Barrie Colin
b. 1947 Ballard, Russ(ell)
b. 1947 Shorter, Frank C
b. 1948 Hall, Deidre
b. 1950 Candy, John (Franklin)
b. 1950 Goodfriend, Lynda
b. 1950 Pauley, Jane
b. 1953 Clegg, Johnny
b. 1953 Lucas, John
b. 1955 Roberts, Xavier
b. 1959 Nasland, Mats
b. 1960 Pahlevi, Riza Cyrus
b. 1963 McGriff, Fred(erick Stanley)
b. 1965 Annabella
b. 1965 Schneider, Rob
b. 1967 Vanilla Ice
d. 1517 Bartolommeo, Fra
d. 1732 Victor Amadeus, II
d. 1744 Leo, Leonardo
d. 1751 Logan, James
d. 1769 Mabuchi, Kamo
d. 1834 DuPont, Eleuthere Irenee
d. 1848 Kearny, Stephen Watts
d. 1867 Rosse, William Parsons, 3rd Earl of
d. 1879 Abbott, Jacob
d. 1879 Buckstone, John Baldwin
d. 1879 Hooker, Joseph
d. 1887 Macfarren, George Alexander, Sir
d. 1893 Sorin, Edward Frederick
d. 1916 Russell, Charles Taze
d. 1918 Schiele, Egon
d. 1919 Wilcox, Ella Wheeler
d. 1925 Frunze, Mikhail Vasilievich
d. 1926 Houdini, Harry
d. 1927 Long, John Luther
d. 1937 Faure, Elie
d. 1938 Woolsey, Robert
d. 1939 Rank, Otto
d. 1940 Pulford, Harvey
d. 1941 Berry, Chu
d. 1943 Reinhardt, Max
d. 1944 Crosman, Henrietta
d. 1948 Landi, Elissa

d. 1949 Stettinius, Edward R, Jr.
d. 1950 Boettiger, John
d. 1954 Baillie, D(onald) M(acpherson)
d. 1956 Badoglio, Pietro
d. 1960 Avery, Sewell
d. 1960 Davis, Harold Lenoir
d. 1961 John, Augustus Edwin
d. 1961 Vertes, Marcel
d. 1963 Daniell, Henry
d. 1964 Toye, Francis
d. 1968 Novarro, Ramon
d. 1969 Pastor, Tony
d. 1970 Allyn, Stanley Charles
d. 1971 von Rad, Gerhard
d. 1972 Durnan, Bill
d. 1973 White, Paul Dudley
d. 1974 Myer, Buddy
d. 1976 Wilder, Joseph
d. 1977 Colby, Carroll Burleigh
d. 1977 Smith, Chard Powers
d. 1981 Scherr, Max
d. 1983 Halas, George Stanley
d. 1983 Rashidov, Sharaf Rashidovich
d. 1984 Gandhi, Indira Priyadarshini Nehru
d. 1986 Mulliken, Robert Sanderson
d. 1987 Campbell, Joseph
d. 1988 Houseman, John
d. 1990 Price, Roger Taylor
d. 1991 Hartt, Frederick
d. 1991 Papp, Joseph
d. 1993 Fellini, Federico
d. 1993 Phoenix, River
d. 1995 Bush, Alan (Dudley)
d. 1995 Campbell, James
d. 1996 Ames, Louise (Bates)
d. 1996 Carne, Marcel Albert
d. 1999 Jakobovits, Immanuel

NOVEMBER

b. 1296 Palamas, Gregory, Saint
b. 1648 Juana Ines de la Cruz, Sor
b. 1774 Bell, Charles
b. 1806 Merriam, Charles
b. 1840 Galli-Marie, Marie Celestine
b. 1869 Rutherford, Joseph Franklin
b. 1886 Burke, Thomas

b. 1892 Guo Moruo
b. 1900 Axis Sally
b. 1931 Lissouba, Pascal
b. 1936 Bishara, Abdullah Yaccoub
b. 1939 Flowers, Wayland Parrott, Jr.
b. 1942 Honwana, Luis Bernardo
b. 1949 Ackerman, Will
b. 1954 Fenley, Molissa
b. 1955 Nye, Bill
d. 1484 Pulci, Luigi
d. 1528 Verrazano, Giovanni da
d. 1546 Orellana, Francisco de
d. 1595 Mendana de Neyra, Alvaro de
d. 1691 Cuyp, Aelbert Jacobsz(oon)
d. 1779 Chippendale, Thomas
d. 1792 Guadagni, Gaetano
d. 1792 Hearne, Samuel
d. 1813 Colter, John
d. 1848 Ibrahim Pasha
d. 1930 Wegener, Alfred Lothar
d. 1966 Chou Tso-Jen
d. 1983 Hibberd, Andrew Stuart
d. 1989 Baron, Salo Wittmayer
d. 1989 Hughes, George
d. 1994 Feld, Fritz
d. 1998 Abdulkarim, Mohamed Taki

November 1
b. 1500 Cellini, Benvenuto
b. 1596 Cortona, Pietro da
b. 1636 Boileau(-Despreaux), Nicolas
b. 1757 Canova, Antonio
b. 1757 Rapp, George
b. 1764 Van Rensselaer, Stephen
b. 1815 Long, Crawford Williamson
b. 1818 Renwick, James, Jr.
b. 1835 Jevons, William Stanley
b. 1849 Chase, William Merritt
b. 1855 Adler, Guido
b. 1856 Saunders, William Laurence
b. 1858 Tyrrell, Joseph Burr
b. 1859 Hunt, George Wylie Paul
b. 1860 Penrose, Boies
b. 1863 Parker, George Safford
b. 1871 Crane, Stephen
b. 1878 Cisneros, Eleanora
b. 1878 Saavdedra, Lamas Carlos
b. 1879 Barnack, Oskar

b. 1880 Asch, Sholem
b. 1880 Rice, Grantland
b. 1880 Wegener, Alfred Lothar
b. 1885 Cherrington, Ben Mark
b. 1887 Lowry, Lawrence Stephen
b. 1889 Noel-Baker, Philip John
b. 1890 Barton, James
b. 1892 Alekhine, Alexander
b. 1894 Smith, Chard Powers
b. 1895 Hecht, George Joseph
b. 1895 Jones, David
b. 1896 Blunden, Edmund Charles
b. 1897 Mitchison, Naomi Margaret (Haldane)
b. 1898 Wallace, Sippie
b. 1902 Grieg, Nordahl Brun
b. 1904 LaPlante, Laura
b. 1905 Borduas, Paul-Emile
b. 1905 Gemayel, Pierre, Sheikh
b. 1907 Cuneo, Terence Tenison
b. 1908 Wolfert, Ira
b. 1909 Arthur, Robert
b. 1911 Jones, Jenkin Lloyd
b. 1911 Kerst, Donald W(illiam)
b. 1911 Troyat, Henri
b. 1916 Mack, Peter
b. 1917 Burroughs, Margaret Taylor
b. 1919 Bondi, Hermann, Sir
b. 1920 Kilpatrick, James J(ackson), Jr.
b. 1922 Irving, George Steven
b. 1923 Angeles, Victoria de los
b. 1923 Dickson, Gordon Rupert
b. 1926 Knight, Hilary
b. 1926 Palmer, Betsy
b. 1927 Ophuls, Marcel
b. 1930 Gurney, A(lbert) R(amsdell), Jr.
b. 1932 Arbour, Al(ger Joseph)
b. 1932 Arinze, Francis Cardinal
b. 1934 Jensen, Mike
b. 1935 Player, Gary Jim
b. 1935 Said, Edward W
b. 1937 Anderson, Bill
b. 1939 Bosson, Barbara
b. 1939 Kouchner, Bernard
b. 1940 Sloan, Hugh W
b. 1941 Foxworth, Robert

b. 1941 Payton-Wright, Pamela
b. 1942 Flynt, Larry (Claxton)
b. 1944 Emerson, Keith
b. 1946 Muren, Dennis
b. 1947 Hendricks, Ted
b. 1951 Bell, Ronald
b. 1957 Lovett, Lyle
b. 1960 Valenzuela, Fernando
b. 1962 Kiedis, Anthony
b. 1963 Allen, Rick
b. 1972 McCarthy, Jenny
d. 1642 Nicolet, Jean
d. 1678 Coddington, William
d. 1700 Charles, II
d. 1778 Piranesi, Giovanni Battista
d. 1835 Motherwell, William
d. 1867 Strachan, John
d. 1877 Morton, Oliver Hazard Perry Throck
d. 1879 Chandler, Zachariah
d. 1888 Przhevalsky, Nikolai Mikhailovich
d. 1894 Alexander III
d. 1903 Mommsen, Theodor
d. 1907 Jarry, Alfred
d. 1912 Lea, Homer
d. 1918 Ritz, Cesar
d. 1922 Page, Thomas Nelson
d. 1927 Mills, Florence
d. 1938 Jammes, Francis
d. 1943 McAdie, Alexander George
d. 1949 Hokinson, Helen
d. 1950 Torresola, Griselio
d. 1952 Lee, Dixie
d. 1955 Carnegie, Dale
d. 1961 McCracken, Joan
d. 1963 Maxwell, Elsa
d. 1964 Carlson, Doc
d. 1967 Tietjen, Heinz
d. 1968 Papandreou, George
d. 1970 Lynd, Robert Staughton
d. 1971 Evans, Richard Louis
d. 1971 Romm, Mikhail
d. 1972 Pound, Ezra Loomis
d. 1973 Bowen, Catherine Drinker
d. 1975 James, Philip
d. 1977 Hobbs, Leonard Sinclair
d. 1979 Eisenhower, Mamie (Geneva) Doud
d. 1981 DeGraff, Robert F(air)
d. 1982 Broderick, James Joseph

d. 1982 Vidor, King Wallis
d. 1984 Krasna, Norman
d. 1985 Silvers, Phil
d. 1986 Moczar, Mieczyslaw
d. 1986 Wallace, Sippie
d. 1987 Levesque, Rene
d. 1988 Kraus, Hans Peter
d. 1992 Rowley, James Joseph
d. 1993 Ochoa, Severo
d. 1994 Beery, Noah, Jr.
d. 1995 Thompson, Bradbury James
d. 1996 Jayewardene, J(unius) R(ichard)
d. 1999 Payton, Walter

November 2
b. 1470 Edward V
b. 1699 Chardin, Jean Baptiste Simeon
b. 1734 Boone, Daniel
b. 1739 Ditters, Karl
b. 1755 Marie Antoinette
b. 1795 Polk, James Knox
b. 1797 Power, Tyrone William Grattan
b. 1815 Boole, George
b. 1865 Harding, Warren G(amaliel)
b. 1866 Door, Rheta Childe
b. 1877 Aga Khan III
b. 1880 Hooker, Brian
b. 1880 Merivale, Philip
b. 1883 Ames, Jessie Daniel
b. 1883 Flavin, Martin Archer
b. 1885 Aldrich, Winthrop Williams
b. 1885 Shapley, Harlow T
b. 1886 Giesler, Jerry
b. 1887 Wolfson, Harry Austryn
b. 1893 Brady, Alice
b. 1897 Bjerknes, Jacob
b. 1897 King, Dennis
b. 1897 Russell, Richard Brevard, Jr.
b. 1899 Klineberg, Otto
b. 1901 Ford, Paul
b. 1902 Jochum, Eugen
b. 1902 Wells, James Lesesne
b. 1903 Berman, Emile Zola
b. 1903 Jackson, Travis Calvin
b. 1905 Clark, Colin Grant
b. 1905 Dunn, James Howard
b. 1905 Keyserlingk, Robert Wendelin Henry
b. 1906 Visconti, Luchino
b. 1909 Berigan, Bunny
b. 1911 Elytis, Odysseus

b. 1912 Conklin, Peggy
b. 1913 Lancaster, Burt(on Stephen)
b. 1914 Guerard, Albert Joseph
b. 1914 Vander Meer, Johnny
b. 1917 Rutherford, Ann
b. 1917 Wasserman, Dale
b. 1918 Adams, John Hanly
b. 1921 Mosienko, Bill
b. 1921 Schaefer, William Donald
b. 1922 Conable, Barber B., Jr.
b. 1928 Cobbs, Price M(ashaw)
b. 1928 Hart, Leon J
b. 1928 Johnson, Paul (Bede)
b. 1929 Bose, Amar Gopal
b. 1929 Taylor, Richard Edward
b. 1932 Mazzoli, Romano L
b. 1932 Namphy, Henri
b. 1932 Schwartz, Melvin
b. 1934 Rosewall, Ken(neth R)
b. 1936 Ruether, Rosemary Radford
b. 1938 Buchanan, Patrick Joseph
b. 1939 Serra, Richard Anthony
b. 1940 Bakken, Jim
b. 1941 Black, David (Jay)
b. 1941 Stockton, Dave
b. 1942 Hite, Shere
b. 1944 Chereau, Patrice
b. 1945 Souther, J(ohn) D(avid)
b. 1946 Carter, Mandy
b. 1946 Sinopoli, Giuseppe
b. 1958 McGee, Willie Dean
b. 1960 Aouita, Said
d. 1600 Hooker, Richard
d. 1863 Judah, Theodore Dehone
d. 1879 Einhorn, David
d. 1887 Lind, Jenny
d. 1892 Schwatka, Frederik
d. 1909 Frith, William Powell
d. 1920 Guiney, Louise Imogene
d. 1926 Oakley, Annie
d. 1930 Hay, Oliver Perry
d. 1944 Midgeley, Thomas
d. 1950 Shaw, George Bernard
d. 1957 Young, Mahonri Mackintosh
d. 1960 Mitropoulos, Dimitri

d. 1961 Thurber, James
Grover
d. 1962 Lattuada, Felice
d. 1965 Evatt, Herbert
Vere
d. 1966 Araki Sadao
d. 1966 Debye, Peter
Joseph William
d. 1966 Hurt,
Mississippi John
d. 1969 Friedman,
William Frederick
d. 1970 Cushing,
Richard James,
Cardinal
d. 1971 Vickers, Martha
d. 1973 Neale, Greasy
d. 1975 Pasolini, Pier
Paolo
d. 1976 Starkie, Walter
Fitzwilliam
d. 1978 Gordon, Max
d. 1980 Sutton, Willie
d. 1982 Roloff, Lester
d. 1984 Barfield, Velma
d. 1990 Porter, Eliot
Furness
d. 1991 Allen, Irwin
d. 1992 Deutsch, Karl
Wolfgang
d. 1992 Roach, Hal
d. 1994 Taylor, Peter
(Hillsman)
d. 1997 Rothschild,
Edmund Leopold de

November 3
b. 1560 Carracci,
Annibale
b. 1718 Sandwich, John
Montagu
b. 1782 Warrington,
Lewis
b. 1793 Austin, Stephen
Fuller
b. 1794 Bryant, William
Cullen
b. 1798 Mason, James
Murray
b. 1801 Baedeker, Karl
b. 1801 Bellini,
Vincenzo
b. 1816 Early, Jubal
Anderson
b. 1830 Cooke, John
Esten
b. 1831 Donnelly,
Ignatius
b. 1834 Fleischmann,
Charles Louis
b. 1841 Alden, Isabella
Macdonald
b. 1845 White, Edward
Douglass
b. 1852 Mutsuhito
b. 1854 Takamine,
Jokichi
b. 1858 Wellman,
Walter
b. 1862 George, Henry,
Jr.
b. 1877 Ibanez del
Campo, Carlos
b. 1879 Stefansson,
Vihjalmur
b. 1880 Sterling, Ford

b. 1884 Martin, Joseph
William, Jr.
b. 1887 Fleischer,
Nat(haniel Stanley)
b. 1892 Chao, Yuen
Ren
b. 1895 Arvey, Jacob
Meyer
b. 1896 Tenggren,
Gustaf Adolf
b. 1901 Leopold III
b. 1901 Malraux, Andre
Georges
b. 1903 Boyd, Julian
Parks
b. 1903 Evans, Walker
b. 1904 Lee, Jennie
b. 1905 Ball, Joseph
H(urst)
b. 1905 Jones, Lois
Mailou
b. 1907 Crile, George
Washington, Jr.
b. 1907 Haydn, Hiram
Collins
b. 1908 Leone,
Giovanni
b. 1908 Nagurski,
Bronko
b. 1909 Reston, James
(Barrett)
b. 1911 Lubell, Samuel
b. 1911 Ussachevsky,
Vladimir Alexis
b. 1912 Donohue, Jack
b. 1912 Stroessner,
Alfredo
b. 1913 Chapman,
Leonard F., Jr.
b. 1914 Shamir, Yitzhak
b. 1917 O'Brien, Conor
Cruise
b. 1918 Boullioun,
E(rnest) H(erman Jr.)
b. 1918 Feller, Bob
b. 1918 Long, Russell
Billiu
b. 1919 Freed, Bert
b. 1921? Bronson,
Charles
b. 1926 Adamkus,
Valdas (V.)
b. 1927 Nordli, Odvar
b. 1930 Crane, Philip
Miller
b. 1931 Lewis, Drew
b. 1931 Vitti, Monica
b. 1932 Reynolds,
Albert
b. 1933 Barry, John
b. 1933 Berry, Ken
b. 1933 Dukakis,
Michael Stanley
b. 1933 Sullivan, Louis
W(ade)
b. 1935 Brett, Jeremy
b. 1936 Emerson, Roy
b. 1937 Wayne, Paula
b. 1938 Lord, Bette Bao
b. 1939 McNally,
Terrence
b. 1942 Smith, Martin
Cruz
b. 1943 Corinne, Tee A.
b. 1944? Collin, Frank
b. 1947 Stevens, Shadoe

b. 1948 Lulu
b. 1948 Shales, Tom
b. 1949? Epps, Jack, Jr.
b. 1949 Evans, Mike
b. 1949 Holmes, Larry
b. 1949 Wintour, Anna
b. 1952 Ho, David D.
b. 1952 Roseanne
b. 1953 Banks, Jeffrey
(Laurence)
b. 1953 Miller, Dennis
b. 1954 Adam Ant
b. 1955 Simms, Phil(ip)
b. 1956 Welch, Bob
b. 1957 Johnson, Steve
b. 1959 Hartley, Hal
d. 1584 Borromeo,
Charles, Saint
d. 1867 Persiani, Fanny
d. 1876 Maywood,
Augusta
d. 1891 Bonaparte,
Louis Lucien
d. 1911 Colman,
Norman Jay
d. 1917 Bloy, Leon
Marie
d. 1937 Ames,
Winthrop
d. 1940 Hine, Lewis
Wickes
d. 1944 Miner, Jack
d. 1949 Desmond,
William
d. 1949 Guggenheim,
Solomon Robert
d. 1954 Matisse, Henri
Emile Benoit
d. 1956 Metzinger, Jean
d. 1957 Reich, Wilhelm
d. 1957 Tokutomi Soho
d. 1960 Wallace, Bobby
d. 1962 Curtice, Harlow
Herbert
d. 1963 Ngo-Dinh-Diem
d. 1965 Hansberry,
William Leo
d. 1972 Richman, Harry
d. 1973 Neihardt, John
Gneisenau
d. 1976 Dixon, Dean
d. 1977 Kurelek,
William
d. 1977 Vidor, Florence
d. 1981 Westermann,
H(orace) C(lifford)
d. 1986 Hammond,
E(dward) Cuyler
d. 1990 Martin, Mary
d. 1992 Holm, Hanya
d. 1995 Rountree,
William M(anning)
d. 1996 Bokassa, Jean-
Bedel
d. 1997 Bleiberg,
Robert Marvin
d. 1998 O'Driscoll,
Martha
d. 1999 Bannen, Ian

November 4
b. 1575 Reni, Guido
b. 1650 William III
b. 1740 Toplady,
Augustus Montague
b. 1790 Lipinski, Carl

b. 1792 Lopez, Carlos
Antonio
b. 1806 Fitzhugh,
George
b. 1809 Curtis,
Benjamin Robbins
b. 1810 Allen, John
b. 1816 Alcorn, James
Lusk
b. 1816 Field, Stephen
Johnson
b. 1841 Goodrich,
Benjamin Franklin
b. 1841 Tausig, Karl
b. 1842 Cushing,
William Barker
b. 1858 Benson, Frank
Robert, Sir
b. 1862 Phillpotts, Eden
b. 1865 Jackson,
Chevalier
b. 1873 Moore, George
Edward
b. 1874 Avery, Sewell
b. 1874 Wallace, Bobby
b. 1876 Fraser, James
Earle
b. 1878 Schwartz, Jean
b. 1881 Tucker, Rosina
b. 1884 Douglas, Robert
L
b. 1884 Ferguson, Harry
George
b. 1885 Covici, Pascal
b. 1888 O'Brien, John J
b. 1889 Husayn, Taha
b. 1893 Coste,
Dieudonne
b. 1896 Garcia, Carlos
Polestico
b. 1897 Van Niel,
Cornelius B(ernardus)
b. 1899 Berman,
Eugene
b. 1900 Lucioni, Luigi
b. 1901 Morrison,
Theodore
b. 1904 Delano, Isaac O
b. 1904 Holm, John
Cecil
b. 1906 Considine, Bob
b. 1906 Herberg, Will
b. 1906 North, Sterling
b. 1906 Stevens,
S(tanley) S(mith)
b. 1906 Strouse,
Norman H(ulbert)
b. 1907 Douglas, Paul
b. 1909 Alegria, Ciro
b. 1909 Graves, Alvin
Cushman
b. 1911 Lee, Dixie
b. 1911 Medwick, Joe
b. 1912 Trigere, Pauline
b. 1913 Young, Gig
b. 1914 Cowan, Peter
Wilkinshaw
b. 1915 Feifel, Herman
b. 1916 Cronkite,
Walter Leland, Jr.
b. 1916 Handler, Ruth
b. 1918 Carney, Art
b. 1918 Mitchell,
Cameron
b. 1919 Balsam, Martin
Henry

b. 1919 Broyhill, Joel
Thomas
b. 1924 Anson, Jay
b. 1924 Meeker, Howie
b. 1930 Groat, Dick
b. 1930 Reid, Kate
b. 1930 Roberts, Doris
b. 1931 Hood, Darla
Jean
b. 1931 Law, Bernard
Francis, Cardinal
b. 1932 Klestil, Thomas
b. 1932 Pitlik, Noam
b. 1933 Grier, Barbara
b. 1933 McDaniel,
Mildred
b. 1933 Ojukwu,
Chukwuemeka
Odumegwu
b. 1936 Ratsiraka,
Didier
b. 1937 Wilson,
Michael (Holcombe)
b. 1939 Swit, Loretta
b. 1940 McClinton,
Delbert
b. 1943 Graebner, Clark
b. 1944 Niekro, Joe
b. 1946 Mapplethorpe,
Robert
b. 1954 Yanni
b. 1962 Macchio, Ralph
George, Jr.
b. 1963 McArdle,
Andrea
b. 1969 McConaughey,
Matthew (David)
d. 1764 Churchill,
Charles
d. 1781 Bordoni,
Faustina
d. 1847 Mendelssohn,
Felix
d. 1859 Delaroche,
Hippolyte
d. 1869 Peabody,
George
d. 1873 Keene, Laura
d. 1895 Field, Eugene
d. 1906 Sage, Russell
d. 1908 Estrada Palma,
Tomas
d. 1918 Owen, Wilfred
d. 1918 Sage, Margaret
Olivia
d. 1918 White, Andrew
Dickson
d. 1921 Hara, Kei
d. 1921 Hara Takashi
d. 1924 Faure, Gabriel
Urbain
d. 1931 Bolden, Buddy
d. 1940 Azana y Diaz,
Manuel
d. 1941 Afinogenov,
Aleksandr
Nikolaevich
d. 1944 Dill, John
Greer, Sir
d. 1945 Ritchey, George
Willis
d. 1945 Smith, Lowell
Herbert
d. 1948 Anderson, Carl
Thomas

d. 1950 Alexander,
Grover Cleveland
d. 1950 Fulton, Maude
d. 1952 Frankau, Gilbert
d. 1954 Agus Salim,
Hadji
d. 1955 Young, Cy
d. 1956 Tatum, Art(hur)
d. 1962 Eklund, Carl
Robert
d. 1965 Chapelle,
Dickey
d. 1969 Jones, Thomas
Hudson
d. 1970 Peter II
d. 1971 Pennington,
Ann
d. 1973 Ginott, Haim
d. 1980 Langley, Noel
d. 1982 Dunne,
Dominique
d. 1985 Groppi, James
E
d. 1985 Hill, Morton
A(nthony)
d. 1987 Soyer, Raphael
d. 1993 Landau, Ely A
d. 1994 Francis,
Sam(uel Lewis)
d. 1995 Egan, Eddie
d. 1995 Rabin, Yitzhak
d. 1999 Bates, Daisy
Lee Gatson

November 5
b. 430 Apollinaris
Sidonius, Gaius
Sollius
b. 1494 Sachs, Hans
b. 1753 Glover, John
b. 1778 Ritchie, Thomas
b. 1779 Allston,
Washington
b. 1787 Richardson,
John, Sir
b. 1818 Butler,
Benjamin Franklin
b. 1825 Jackson, John
Adams
b. 1834 Leonowens,
Anna Harriette
Crawford
b. 1849 Barbosa, Ruy
b. 1850 Wilcox, Ella
Wheeler
b. 1854 Sabatier, Paul
b. 1855 Debs, Eugene
Victor
b. 1855 Teisserenc de
Bort, Leon-Philippe
b. 1857 Tarbell, Ida
Minerva
b. 1866 Milne, George
Francis, Baron
b. 1867 Reisner, George
Andrew
b. 1870 Das, Chitta
Ranjan
b. 1871 Whitehill,
Clarence Eugene
b. 1876 Duchamp-
Villon, Raymond
b. 1877 Mead, George
Houk
b. 1879 Hays, Will
Harrison

b. 1885 Durant,
Will(iam James)
b. 1887 Baillie,
D(onald)
M(acpherson)
b. 1887 Wittgenstein,
Paul
b. 1891 Neale, Greasy
b. 1892 Haldane, J(ohn)
B(urdon) S(anderson)
b. 1893 Loewy,
Raymond Fernand
b. 1894 Ruml,
Beardsley
b. 1895? Garber, Jan
b. 1895 Gieseking,
Walter Wilhelm
b. 1895 MacArthur,
Charles
b. 1900 Dies, Martin, Jr.
b. 1901 Moten, Etta
b. 1902 Schafer, Natalie
b. 1904 Weiland,
Cooney
b. 1905 Bangor, Edward
Henry Harold Ward,
Viscount
b. 1905 Mantovani,
Annunzio
b. 1905 McCrea, Joel
b. 1905 Thomson,
Vernon Wallace
b. 1907 Browning,
Alice Crolley
b. 1911 Rogers, Roy
b. 1911 Stader, Maria
b. 1913 Leigh, Vivien
b. 1913 McGiver, John
b. 1914 Nsubuga,
Emmanuel, Cardinal
b. 1915 Biller, Moe
b. 1917 Auriol,
Jacqueline Douet
b. 1919 Floren, Myron
b. 1923 Sheppard,
Sam(uel)
b. 1926 Berger, John
b. 1927 Abernethy,
Robert Gordon
b. 1930 Irving, Clifford
Michael
b. 1930 Kennedy,
Moorehead Cowell,
Jr.
b. 1931 Pickering,
Thomas (Reeve)
b. 1931 Turner, Ike
b. 1932 Jacobs, Sally
b. 1932 Liman, Arthur
L(awrence)
b. 1933 Edelman, Herb
b. 1933 Fornos, Werner
H(orst)
b. 1933 Madden,
Donald
b. 1934 Magruder, Jeb
Stuart
b. 1937 Wolff, Geoffrey
(Ansell)
b. 1940 Roldos
Aguilera, Jamie
b. 1941 Garfunkel,
Art(hur)
b. 1941 Sommer, Elke
b. 1943 Shepard, Sam

b. 1944 Rand,
A(ddison) Barry
b. 1946 Parsons, Gram
b. 1947 Noone, Peter
b. 1948 Levy, Bernard-
Henri
b. 1952 Walton, Bill
b. 1957 Hexum, Jon-
Erik
b. 1957 Winslow,
Kellen Boswell
b. 1959 Adams, Bryan
Guy
b. 1963 O'Neal, Tatum
d. 1459 Fastolf, John,
Sir
d. 1559 Kano,
Motonobu
d. 1803 Laclos, Pierre
(Ambroise Francois)
Choderlos de
d. 1807 Kauffmann,
Angelica
d. 1872 Sully, Thomas
d. 1874 Creighton,
Edward
d. 1879 Maxwell, James
Clerk
d. 1921 Blackwell,
Antoinette Louisa
Brown
d. 1930 Eijkman,
Christiaan
d. 1931 Rolvaag, Ole
Edvart
d. 1933 Guinan, Texas
d. 1937 McAuliffe, Jack
B
d. 1938 Dewing,
Thomas Wilmer
d. 1942 Cohan, George
M(ichael)
d. 1944 Carrel, Alexis
d. 1946 Stella, Joseph
d. 1954 Page, Hot Lips
d. 1955 Utrillo, Maurice
d. 1960 Bond, Ward
d. 1960 Horton, Johnny
d. 1960 Sennett, Mack
d. 1960 Waymack,
W(illiam) W(esley)
d. 1961 Tobias,
Channing Heggie
d. 1962 Garis, Howard
Roger
d. 1967 Kesselring,
Joseph Otto
d. 1972 Owen, (John)
Reginald
d. 1973 Romer, Alfred
Sherwood
d. 1975 Tatum, Edward
Lawrie
d. 1975 Trilling, Lionel
d. 1977 Garst, Roswell
d. 1977 Goscinny, Rene
d. 1977 Lombardo, Guy
Albert
d. 1979 Capp, Al
d. 1980 Lortz, Richard
d. 1980 Marshall,
Laurence
d. 1982 Tati, Jacques
d. 1983 Benjamin,
Curtis G

d. 1985 Kimball,
Spencer Woolley
d. 1986 Lorillard, Louis
Livingston
d. 1986 Nunn, Bobby
d. 1987 Andrews,
Eamonn
d. 1988 Freeman,
Cynthia
d. 1989 Horowitz,
Vladimir
d. 1989 Sadler, Barry
d. 1990 Kahane, Meir
David
d. 1991 MacMurray,
Fred(erick Martin)
d. 1991 Maxwell,
Robert Ian Charles
d. 1994 Dean, Patrick
(Henry), Sir
d. 1995 Hemphill, Essex
d. 1997 Berlin, Isaiah,
Sir
November 6
b. 1558 Kyd, Thomas
b. 1661 Charles, II
b. 1671 Cibber, Colley
b. 1771 Senefelder,
Aloys
b. 1796 Back, George,
Sir
b. 1814 Sax, Adolphe
(Antoine-Joseph)
b. 1825 Gardner, Jean
Louis Charles
b. 1825 Garnier, Jean
Louis Charles
b. 1833 Lie, Jonas
Laurite Idemil
b. 1836 Lombroso,
Cesare
b. 1841 Aldrich, Nelson
Wilmarth
b. 1847 Meggendorfer,
Lothar
b. 1848 Jeffries, Richard
b. 1851 Dow, Charles
Henry
b. 1854 Sousa, John
Philip
b. 1855 Kalisch, Paul
b. 1861 Naismith, James
A
b. 1875 Dixon, Roland
Burrage
b. 1877 Dillon, William
A
b. 1880 Musil, Robert
Edler Von
b. 1882 Ince, Thomas
H(arper)
b. 1882 Wallerstein,
Lothar
b. 1883 Brophy, John
b. 1886 Kahn, Gus
b. 1887 Johnson, Walter
Perry
b. 1890 Quirino, Elpidio
b. 1890 Sherrill, Henry
Knox
b. 1891 Buitoni,
Giovanni
b. 1892 Alcock, John
William, Sir
b. 1892 Olsen, Ole

b. 1892 Ross, Harold
Wallace
b. 1893 Ford, Edsel
Bryant
b. 1901 Hall, Juanita
b. 1901 Katona, George
b. 1904 Gilpatric,
Roswell L(eavitt)
b. 1906 Charriere, Henri
b. 1906 Lederer, Francis
b. 1906 Norris, James D
b. 1907 Yost, Charles
Woodruff
b. 1908 Canzoneri,
Tony
b. 1908 Klassen, Elmer
Theodore
b. 1911 Bosustow,
Stephen
b. 1912 Brasch,
Rudolph
b. 1912 Cakobau, Ratu
George, Sir
b. 1914 Gerson, Noel
Bertram
b. 1915 Oldfield,
Maurice, Sir
b. 1916 Bushkin, Joe
b. 1916 Conniff, Ray
b. 1917 Rashidov,
Sharaf Rashidovich
b. 1918 Scott, Ken
b. 1919? Harris,
Jonathan
b. 1920 Rossi-Lemeni,
Nicola
b. 1921 Jones, James
b. 1923 Griffin, Bob
b. 1930 Bell, Derrick
Albert, Jr.
b. 1930 McCormach,
Mark Hume
b. 1931 Nichols, Mike
b. 1932 Castle, Wendell
Keith
b. 1933 Krea, Henri
b. 1938 Pike, Jim
b. 1939 Bell, Arthur
(Irving)
b. 1941 Clark, Guy
b. 1941 Stoddard,
Alexandra
b. 1942 Shrimpton, Jean
Rosemary
b. 1946 DeBartolo,
Edward J, Jr.
b. 1946 Field, Sally
Margaret
b. 1946 Penner, Fred
b. 1948 Frey, Glenn
b. 1948 McPhail,
Sharon
b. 1949 Davis, Brad
b. 1950 Thompson,
Ernest
b. 1953 Flynt, Althea
Sue
b. 1955 Shriver, Maria
(Owings)
b. 1960 Kerwin, Lance
b. 1964 Keough, Danny
b. 1970 Hawke, Ethan
d. 1632 Gustavus
Adophus
d. 1672 Schutz,
Heinrich

d. 1790 Bowdoin, James
d. 1796 Catherine the
Great
d. 1816 Morris,
Gouverneur
d. 1822 Berthollet,
Claude Louis, Comte
d. 1822 Hardenberg,
Karl August von
d. 1842 Hone, William
d. 1872 Meade, George
Gordon
d. 1873 Hardee,
William Joseph
d. 1876 Antonelli,
Giacomo
d. 1884 Brown, William
Wells
d. 1884 Fawcett, Henry
d. 1893 Tchaikovsky,
Peter Ilyich
d. 1901 Greenaway,
Kate
d. 1905 Lemoyne,
W(illiam) J
d. 1914 Weismann,
August Friedrich
Leopold
d. 1917 Kendal,
William Hunter
d. 1922 Bulkeley,
Morgan G
d. 1928 Rothstein,
Arnold
d. 1931 Chesbro, Jack
d. 1935 Osborn, Henry
Fairfield
d. 1935 Sunday, Billy
d. 1937 Forbes-
Robertson, Johnston,
Sir
d. 1941 Leblanc,
Maurice
d. 1946 Hummel, Berta
d. 1950 Tschirky, Oscar
d. 1956 Kelly, Paul
d. 1960 Raeder, Erich
d. 1963 Mannix, Daniel
d. 1964 Euler-Chelpin,
Hans Karl August
Simon von
d. 1965 Varese, Edgar
d. 1968 Munch, Charles
d. 1969 Wood, Robert
Elkington
d. 1973 Biddle, George
d. 1974 Farrar, John
Chipman
d. 1975 Hanfstaengl,
Ernst Franz Sedgwick
d. 1976 Dennis, Patrick
d. 1978 Bertoia, Harry
d. 1979 Evans, Chick
d. 1980 Coghill, Nevill
Henry Kendall
Aylmer
d. 1981 Daniels,
Jonathan Worth
d. 1982 Swinnerton,
Frank Arthur
d. 1983 McBride, Lloyd
d. 1986 Kraus, Lili
d. 1987 Barnett, Ross
Robert
d. 1987 Logan, John

d. 1987 Pahlmann,
William Carroll
d. 1991 Tierney, Gene
d. 1994 Masserman,
Jules H(oman)
d. 1995 Hechinger, Fred
Michael
d. 1997 Parks, Lillian
(Adele) Rogers
d. 1999 Higgins, George
V.
d. 1999 Messick, Hank
November 7
b. 1417 Sejo
b. 1598 Zurbaran,
Francisco
b. 1731 Rogers, Robert
b. 1801 Saint Georges,
Jules
b. 1805 Brassey,
Thomas
b. 1818 Du Bois-
Reymond, Emil
b. 1832 White, Andrew
Dickson
b. 1839 Levi, Hermann
b. 1847 Crabtree, Lotta
b. 1855 Hall, Edwin
Herbert
b. 1862 Welch, Herbert
b. 1864 Hartford,
George Ludlum
b. 1867 Curie, Marie
b. 1874 Blair, William
Richards
b. 1876 Shinn, Everett
b. 1878 Meitner, Lise
b. 1884 Patterson,
Eleanor Medill
b. 1885 Crawford,
Rusty
b. 1885 Knight, Frank
Hyneman
b. 1886 Barnard,
Chester Irving
b. 1888 Raman,
Chandrasekhara
Venkata, Sir
b. 1890 Spitalny, Phil
b. 1891 Howard, Guy
Wesley
b. 1893 Joy, Leatrice
b. 1893 Leech, Margaret
Kernochan
b. 1894 Blanding, Don
b. 1897 Sperry,
Armstrong W
b. 1899 Shear, Murray
Jacob
b. 1900 Kurtz, Efrem
b. 1902 Dodd, Ed(ward)
Benton
b. 1903 Jagger, Dean
b. 1903 Lorenz, Konrad
Zacharias
b. 1906 Blake, Eugene
Carson
b. 1909 Krasna, Norman
b. 1913 Camus, Albert
b. 1914 Lafferty,
Raphael Aloysius
b. 1915 Morrison, Philip
b. 1917 Cobb, Joe
b. 1918 Graham, Billy
b. 1920 Kampelman,
Max M

b. 1922 Hirt, Al(ois Maxwell)
b. 1924 Mankowitz, Wolf
b. 1927 Martino, Al
b. 1929 Abdul, Raoul
b. 1929 Sutherland, Joan, Dame
b. 1930 Bell, Greg
b. 1936 Attles, Al(vin A)
b. 1936 Jones, Gwyneth
b. 1936 McLaughlin, Audrey
b. 1937 Travers, Mary
b. 1938 Kaat, Jim
b. 1938 Newman, Barry Foster
b. 1939 Egan, John Leopold, Sir
b. 1942 Peters, Tom
b. 1942 Rivers, Johnny
b. 1943 Mitchell, Joni
b. 1946 Chrystos
b. 1947 Bryant, Wayne R(ichard)
b. 1950 Canady, Alexa I(rene)
b. 1951 Gilder, Nick
b. 1964 McKerrow, Amanda
d. 1627 Jahangir
d. 1723 Kneller, Godfrey, Sir
d. 1766 Nattier, Jean Marc
d. 1817 Deluc, Jean Andre
d. 1837 Lovejoy, Elijah Parish
d. 1886 Thurber, Charles
d. 1898 Alvary, Max
d. 1901 Li Hung-Chang
d. 1913 McBurney, Charles
d. 1913 Wallace, Alfred Russell
d. 1922 Thompson, Sam(uel Luther)
d. 1924 Thoma, Hans
d. 1928 Battistini, Mattia
d. 1931 Derricotte, Juliette Aline
d. 1936 Sale, Charles Partlow
d. 1940 Gardner, Jimmy
d. 1944 Dawson, Geoffrey
d. 1944 Senesh, Hannah
d. 1945 Edwards, Gus
d. 1957 Worters, Roy
d. 1959 McLaglen, Victor
d. 1962 Roosevelt, Eleanor
d. 1967 Garner, John Nance
d. 1968 Gelfond, Aleksandr Osipovich
d. 1969 Arnold, Thurman Wesley
d. 1970 Peabody, Eddie
d. 1978 Tunney, Gene

d. 1980 McQueen, Steve
d. 1981 Durant, Will(iam James)
d. 1983 Friendly, Alfred
d. 1983 Tailleferre, Germaine
d. 1986 Hewitt, Alan
d. 1987 Holland, Charles
d. 1988 Hoest, Bill
d. 1988 Janowitz, Morris
d. 1990 Durrell, Lawrence (George)
d. 1990 MacLennan, Hugh
d. 1990 Wilson, Logan
d. 1992 Dubcek, Alexander
d. 1992 Yates, Richard
d. 1995 Patrick, John
d. 1995 White, Slappy
d. 1997 Harshaw, Margaret
November 8
b. 1656 Halley, Edmund
b. 1732 Dickinson, John
b. 1801 Owen, Robert Dale
b. 1827 Cremazie, Octave
b. 1830 Howard, Oliver Otis
b. 1831 Lytton, Edward Robert Bulwer-Lytton, Earl
b. 1836 Bradley, Milton
b. 1847 Stoker, Bram
b. 1848 Frege, (Friedrich Ludwig) Gottlob
b. 1848 Gould, George Milbry
b. 1866 Austin, Herbert
b. 1869 Hartmann, Sadakichi
b. 1879 Trotsky, Leon
b. 1881 Speck, Frank Gouldsmith
b. 1883 Bax, Arnold Edward Trevor, Sir
b. 1883 Demuth, Charles
b. 1884 Rorschach, Hermann
b. 1885 Yamashita, Tomoyuki
b. 1890 Willis, Paul S
b. 1896 Harris, Bucky
b. 1896 Hough, Henry Beetle
b. 1897 Day, Dorothy
b. 1900 Frey-Wyssling, Albert F
b. 1900 Gleason, Thomas W(illiam)
b. 1900 Mitchell, Margaret
b. 1901 Gheorghiu-Dej, Gheorghe
b. 1902 Smith, A(rthur) J(ames) M(arshall)
b. 1908 Fowlie, Wallace
b. 1910 Kane, Harnett T(homas)

b. 1910 Voit, Willard Darby
b. 1912 Dryfoos, Orvil Eugene
b. 1912 Ronan, William John
b. 1913 Ambers, Lou
b. 1913 Strauss, Robert
b. 1916 Havoc, June
b. 1916 Weiss, Peter Ulrich
b. 1918 Kirby, Robert E(mory)
b. 1918 Zapf, Hermann
b. 1920? Rolle, Esther
b. 1921 Mirisch, Walter Mortimer
b. 1921 Saks, Gene
b. 1924 Bower, Johnny
b. 1925 Flynn, Joe
b. 1927 Newhouse, S(amuel) I(rving), Jr.
b. 1927 Page, Patti
b. 1929 Bowden, Bobby
b. 1930 Malavasi, Ray(mondo Guiseppi Giovanni Baptiste)
b. 1931 Safer, Morley
b. 1932 Aganbegyan, Abel Gezevich
b. 1932 Audran, Stephane
b. 1932 Bova, Ben(jamin William)
b. 1935 Delon, Alain
b. 1936 Gibson, Edward George
b. 1947 Allman, Gregg
b. 1947 Magaziner, Ira C(harles)
b. 1948 Riperton, Minnie
b. 1949 Berger, Al
b. 1949 Mittermeier, Russell A
b. 1949 Raitt, Bonnie
b. 1951 Hart, Mary
b. 1952 Denny, John Allen
b. 1952 Hefner, Christie
b. 1953 Woodard, Alfre
b. 1954 Ishiguro, Kazuo
b. 1954 Jones, Rickie Lee
b. 1961 Garrett, Leif
b. 1969 Zal, Roxana
d. 1308 Duns Scotus, John
d. 1599 Guerrero, Francisco
d. 1633 Xu Guangqi
d. 1674 Milton, John
d. 1793 Roland (de La Platiere), Jeanne-Marie
d. 1803 Christie, James
d. 1828 Bewick, Thomas
d. 1856 Cabet, Etienne
d. 1860 Fellows, Charles, Sir
d. 1871 Hall, Charles Francis
d. 1880 Drake, Edwin Laurentine
d. 1887 Holliday, Doc

d. 1890 Franck, Cesar Auguste
d. 1893 Parkman, Francis
d. 1894 Kelly, King
d. 1901 Bickerdyke, Mary Ann Ball
d. 1905 Richards, William Trost
d. 1908 Sardou, Victorien
d. 1917 Appleby, John Francis
d. 1928 Stiller, Mauritz
d. 1934 Baldwin, James Mark
d. 1935 Kingsford-Smith, Charles Edward, Sir
d. 1948 Taggard, Genevieve
d. 1953 Bunin, Ivan Alekseevich
d. 1954 Odum, Howard Washington
d. 1956 Field, Marshall, III
d. 1962 O'Brien, Willis Harold
d. 1965 Kilgallen, Dorothy
d. 1966 Baker, Shorty
d. 1969 Slipher, Vesto Melvin
d. 1974 Hunter, Ivory Joe
d. 1976 Cramm, Gottfried von, Baron
d. 1977 Harris, Bucky
d. 1978 Fischetti, John
d. 1978 Rockwell, Norman
d. 1979 Ardizzone, Edward Jeffrey Irving
d. 1982 Politz, Alfred
d. 1983 Kaplan, Mordecai
d. 1986 Molotov, Vyacheslav Mikhaylovich
d. 1986 Suhl, Yuri
d. 1988 Brewster, Kingman, Jr.
d. 1990 Seton, Anya Chase
d. 1992 Kelly, Jack
d. 1998 Godden, Rumer
d. 1998 Hunt, John, Baron
d. 1998 Marais, Jean
November 9
b. 1731 Banneker, Benjamin
b. 1799 Mahan, Asa
b. 1801 Borden, Gail
b. 1802 Lovejoy, Elijah Parish
b. 1809 Bledsoe, Albert Taylor
b. 1818 Turgenev, Ivan Sergeevich
b. 1825 Hill, Ambrose Powell
b. 1833 Tompkins, Sally Louisa
b. 1841 Edward VII

b. 1853 White, Stanford
b. 1859 Ippolitov-
Ivanov, Mikhail
Mikhailovich
b. 1861 Bache, Jules
Sermon
b. 1865 Funston,
Frederick
b. 1869 Dressler, Marie
b. 1871 Sabin, Florence
Rena
b. 1873 Thyssen, Fritz
b. 1877 Iqbal,
Mahomed, Sir
b. 1879 Holmes, John
Haynes
b. 1881 Kalmus,
Herbert Thomas
b. 1883 Oliver, Edna
May
b. 1886 Wynn, Ed
b. 1888 Monnet, Jean
Omer Marie Gabriel
b. 1889 Rains, Claude
b. 1891 Geiger, Theodor
Julius
b. 1895 Hay, George
Dewey
b. 1897 Norrish, Ronald
George Wreyford
b. 1899 Mezzrow, Mezz
b. 1902 Asquith,
Anthony
b. 1906 Spanier,
Muggsy
b. 1908 Kilgore,
Bernard
b. 1912 Fedorenko,
Nikolai Trofimovich
b. 1912 Thompson, Kay
b. 1915 Shriver,
(Robert) Sargent
b. 1918 Agnew, Spiro
T(heodore)
b. 1918 Chadwick,
Florence (May)
b. 1921 Chukarin,
Viktor Ivanovich
b. 1921 Drake, Stan(ley
Albert)
b. 1921 Hines, Jerome
b. 1921 Paine, Thomas
Otten
b. 1922? Dandridge,
Dorothy
b. 1922 Lakatos, Imre
b. 1923 Coachman,
Alice
b. 1923 Schuyler, James
Marcus
b. 1924 Frank, Robert
b. 1926 Leonard, Hugh
b. 1928 Duke, Wayne
b. 1928 Sexton, Anne
Harvey
b. 1931 Herzog, Whitey
b. 1931 Lipscomb,
Eugene
b. 1932 Christy, Marian
b. 1934 Carlsson, Ingvar
Gosta
b. 1934 Sagan, Carl
(Edward)
b. 1935 Gibson, Bob
b. 1936 Graham, Bob
b. 1941 Gossett, Bruce

b. 1942 Weiskopf, Tom
b. 1948 Bouchard, Joe
b. 1952 Ferrigno, Lou
b. 1958 Higuera, Teddy
d. 1802 Girtin, Thomas
d. 1819 Lee, Thomas
Sim
d. 1856 Clayton, John
Middleton
d. 1876 Tamburini,
Antonio
d. 1906 Beale, Dorothea
d. 1911 Pyle, Howard
d. 1924 Lodge, Henry
Cabot
d. 1926 Coffin, Charles
Albert
d. 1930 Bliss, Tasker
Howard
d. 1931 Lewis, Isaac
Newton
d. 1937 MacDonald,
James Ramsay
d. 1938 East, Edward
Murray
d. 1940 Chamberlain,
Neville
d. 1942 Curran, Charles
Courtney
d. 1942 Oliver, Edna
May
d. 1944 Marshall, Frank
James
d. 1948 Kennedy, Edgar
d. 1951 Romberg,
Sigmund
d. 1952 Weizmann,
Chaim
d. 1953 Ibn Saud
d. 1953 Thomas, Dylan
Marlais
d. 1958 Fisher, Dorothy
Frances Canfield
d. 1960 Mountain Wolf
Woman
d. 1964 Cleland,
Thomas Maitland
d. 1967 Bickford,
Charles Ambrose
d. 1968 Corey, Wendell
d. 1970 Dawson,
William L(evi)
d. 1970 DeGaulle,
Charles Andre Joseph
Marie
d. 1972 Berwind,
Charles G
d. 1972 James, Art
d. 1974 Wellesz, Egon
d. 1976 Halop, Billy
d. 1976 Lhevinne,
Rosina L
d. 1980 Yung, Victor
Sen
d. 1985 Rose, Helen
Bronberg
d. 1987? Bernstein,
Allan
d. 1988 Hinkle, W
Clarke
d. 1988 Mitchell, John
Newton
d. 1991 Montand, Yves
d. 1992 Hillcourt,
William

d. 1994 O'Donoghue,
Michael
d. 1996 Makins, Roger
(Mellor), Sir

November 10
b. 1483 Luther, Martin
b. 1493 Paracelsus,
Philippus Aureolus
b. 1620 Lenclos, Ninon
de
b. 1668 Couperin,
Francois
b. 1683 George II
b. 1697 Hogarth,
William
b. 1728 Goldsmith,
Oliver
b. 1728 Herkimer,
Nicholas
b. 1735 Sharp, Granville
b. 1759 Schiller,
Friedrich von
b. 1791 Hayne, Robert
Young
b. 1802 Howe, Samuel
Gridley
b. 1809 Einhorn, David
b. 1812 Tso Tsung-
t'ang
b. 1827 Terry, Alfred
Howe
b. 1828 Wang T'ao
b. 1834 Hernandez, Jose
b. 1844 Thompson,
John S(parrow)
D(avid), Sir
b. 1847 Bridgman,
Frederic Arthur
b. 1848 Banerjee,
Surendranath
b. 1852 Vandyke, Henry
Jackson, Jr.
b. 1855 Darracq,
Alexandre
b. 1856 Todd, Mabel
Loomis
b. 1870 Rostovtzeff,
Michael Ivanovich
b. 1871 Churchill,
Winston
b. 1872 Moisseiff, Leon
Solomon
b. 1873 Rabaud, Henri
b. 1874 MacMillan,
Donald Baxter
b. 1878 Ubico y
Castaneda, Jorge
b. 1879 Lindsay, Vachel
b. 1879 Pearse, Padraic
b. 1880 Epstein, Jacob,
Sir
b. 1882 Dewey, Charles
Schuveldt
b. 1883 Ficke, Arthur
Davidson
b. 1886 Stavisky, Serge
Alexandre
b. 1887 Zweig, Arnold
b. 1888 Tupolev, Andrei
Nikolaevich
b. 1889 Hinton, Walter
b. 1893 Marquand, John
Phillips
b. 1894 Normand,
Mabel

b. 1895 Northrop, John
Knudsen
b. 1896 Dykes, Jimmy
b. 1899 Seredy, Kate
b. 1899 Stowe, Leland
b. 1904 Geray, Steven
b. 1906 Model, Lisette
b. 1907 Bates, Peg Leg
b. 1907 Froman, Jane
b. 1907 Lawrence,
Mildred Elwood
b. 1909 Marks, Johnny
b. 1911 Andrews, Harry
b. 1912 Tebbetts, Birdie
b. 1913 Shapiro, Karl
Jay
b. 1916 May, Billy
b. 1918 Fischer, Ernst
Otto
b. 1919 Fenneman,
George
b. 1919 Tshombe,
Moise
b. 1925 Burton, Richard
b. 1929 Bergman,
Marilyn Keith
b. 1930 Pendleton,
Clarence McLane, Jr.
b. 1930 Watt, Richard
Martin
b. 1933 Bessmertnykh,
Aleksandr
Aleksandrovich
b. 1933 Evans, Ronald
Ellwin
b. 1934 Cash, Norm(an
Dalton)
b. 1935 Scheider, Roy
Richard
b. 1935 Scott, Pippa
b. 1938 Schultz,
Michael A.
b. 1940 Means, Russell
C(harles)
b. 1944 Akayev, Askar
Akayevich
b. 1944 Neely, Mark E.,
Jr.
b. 1944 Rice, Tim(othy
Miles Bindon)
b. 1946 Stockman,
David Allen
b. 1947 Gemayel,
Bashir
b. 1947 Sneed, Paula
A(nn)
b. 1948 Lake, Greg(ory)
b. 1949 Fargo, Donna
b. 1949 Reinking, Ann
H
b. 1955 Clark, Jack
Anthony
b. 1956 Sinbad
b. 1959 Phillips,
MacKenzie
b. 1963 Powell, Mike
d. 461 Leo, I, St.
d. 1549 Paul III
d. 1556 Chancellor,
Richard
d. 1624 Southampton,
Henry Wriothesley,
Earl
d. 1763 Dupleix, Joseph
Francois
d. 1779 Hewes, Joseph

b. 1840 Rodin, Auguste
b. 1842 Rayleigh, John William Strutt, Baron
b. 1866 Collier, William, Sr.
b. 1866 Sun Yat-Sen
b. 1874 Williams, Bert
b. 1877 Austin, Warren R(obinson)
b. 1880 Stark, Harold Raynsford
b. 1886 Travers, Ben
b. 1888 Parrish, Anne
b. 1889 Wallace, DeWitt
b. 1891 Nicholson, Seth Barnes
b. 1891 Whiting, Richard Armstrong
b. 1896 Ali, Salim A
b. 1901 Adams, James Luther
b. 1903 Oakie, Jack
b. 1906 Dillon, George
b. 1906 Saidenberg, Daniel
b. 1908 Blackmun, Harry A(ndrew)
b. 1911 Clayton, Buck
b. 1914 Schillebeeckx, Edward (Cornelis Florentius Alfons)
b. 1915 Barthes, Roland (Gerard)
b. 1917 Coors, Joseph
b. 1918 Stafford, Jo
b. 1919 Lefever, Ernest Warren
b. 1920 Quine, Richard
b. 1922 Hunter, Kim
b. 1926 Rysanek, Leonie
b. 1927 Secunda, Arthur
b. 1928 Baker, Bobby
b. 1928 Muncey, Bill
b. 1928 Sharmat, Marjorie Weinman
b. 1929 Kelly, Grace Patricia
b. 1931 Slotnick, Daniel Leonid
b. 1932 Forman, James Douglas
b. 1935 Briand, Rena
b. 1937 Balin, Ina
b. 1937 Fisher, Jules Edward
b. 1937 Truly, Richard H
b. 1938 Lewis, Delano (Eugene)
b. 1938 Mkapa, Benjamin William
b. 1943 Hyland, Brian
b. 1943 Shawn, Wallace
b. 1943 Williams, Gregory (Howard)
b. 1944 Houston, Ken(neth Ray)
b. 1944 Jones, Booker T
b. 1945 Powers, Stefanie
b. 1945 Young, Neil
b. 1947 Roeser, Donald
b. 1949 Reed, Jack

b. 1952 Bartkowski, Steve(n Joseph)
b. 1952 Hayes, Robert Michael
b. 1961 Comaneci, Nadia
b. 1966 Schwimmer, David
b. 1967 Moorer, Michael
b. 1976 Campbell, Tevin
d. 1035 Canute
d. 1595 Hawkins, John, Sir
d. 1671 Fairfax, Thomas
d. 1793 Bailly, Jean Sylvain
d. 1813 Crevecoeur, Michel-Guillaume Jean de
d. 1854 Kemble, Charles
d. 1865 Gaskell, Elizabeth Cleghorn
d. 1869 Kendall, Amos
d. 1898 Fisher, Clara
d. 1900 Daly, Marcus
d. 1900 Villard, Henry
d. 1906 Shafter, William Rufus
d. 1908 Brooks, William Keith
d. 1926 Cannon, Joseph Gurney
d. 1933 Bowker, R(ichard) R(ogers)
d. 1937 Carter, Leslie, Mrs.
d. 1938 Mackay, Clarence Hungerford
d. 1939 Bethune, Norman
d. 1944 Birkhoff, George David
d. 1944 Kelley, Edgar Stillman
d. 1947 Moore, John Bassett
d. 1947 Orczy, Emmuska, Baroness
d. 1948 Giordano, Umberto
d. 1950 Marlowe, Julia
d. 1958 Curley, James Michael
d. 1963 Hodge, John Reed
d. 1965 Spaeth, Sigmund Gottfried
d. 1966 Porter, Quincy
d. 1969 Scherman, Harry
d. 1972 Friml, Rudolf
d. 1975 Morgan, Arthur
d. 1975 Ross, David
d. 1976 Piston, Walter
d. 1984 Burman, Ben Lucien
d. 1984 Himes, Chester Bomar
d. 1985 Lindbergh, Pelle (Per-Eric)
d. 1987 Lewis, Roger
d. 1988 Boswell, Vet

d. 1988 Lemnitzer, Lyman Louis
d. 1989 Apithy, Sourou Migan
d. 1989 Ibarruri, Dolores Gomez
d. 1990 Arden, Eve
d. 1990 Greene, Balcomb
d. 1992 Mayehoff, Eddie
d. 1993 Haldeman, H(arry) R(obbins)
d. 1994 Rudolph, Wilma (Glodean)
d. 1994 Stewart, J(ohn) I(nnes) M(ackintosh)
d. 1995 Mann, Jack
d. 1995 Stephens, Robert, Sir
d. 1997 Laughlin, James, IV
d. 1999 Casadesus, Gaby (Lhote)
d. 1999 Vanderbilt, Alfred G(wynne)

November 13
b. 354 Augustine, Saint
b. 1312 Edward III
b. 1486 Eck, Johann Maier von
b. 1572 Lucaris, Cyril
b. 1710 Favart, Charles Simon
b. 1785 Lamb, Caroline Ponsonby, Lady
b. 1792 Trelawny, Edward John
b. 1809 Dahlgren, John Adolphus Bernard
b. 1813 Phelps, John Wolcott
b. 1814 Hooker, Joseph
b. 1831 Maxwell, James Clerk
b. 1833 Booth, Edwin Thomas
b. 1850 Evans, Charles
b. 1850 Stevenson, Robert Louis (Balfour)
b. 1853 Drew, John
b. 1854 Chadwick, George Whitefield
b. 1856 Brandeis, Louis Dembitz
b. 1866 Flexner, Abraham
b. 1872 Hupp, Louis Gorham
b. 1875 Kling, Johnny
b. 1875 Swinnerton, James Guilford
b. 1882 Bartlett, Francis Alonzo
b. 1886 Wigman, Mary
b. 1890 Richter, Conrad Michael
b. 1893 Beals, Carleton
b. 1893 Doisy, Edward Adelbert, Sr.
b. 1893 Rubin, Reuven
b. 1894 Moten, Bennie
b. 1896 Beard, Myron Gould

b. 1896 Kishi, Nobusuke
b. 1897 Edinger, Tilly
b. 1898 Bennett, Wallace F(oster)
b. 1900 Allison, Samuel King
b. 1900 King, Alexander
b. 1900 Miner, Worthington C
b. 1901 Sackville-West, Edward Charles
b. 1904 Caspary, Vera
b. 1904 Terris, Norma
b. 1906 Baddeley, Hermione Clinton
b. 1907 Buzzell, Eddie
b. 1908 Thibault, Conrad
b. 1908 Woodward, C(omer) Vann
b. 1910 Huie, William Bradford
b. 1911 O'Neil, Buck
b. 1913 Nol, Lon
b. 1913 Scourby, Alexander
b. 1914 Gibson, William
b. 1915 Benchley, Nathaniel Goddard
b. 1916 Ashford, Emmett Littleton
b. 1916 Elam, Jack
b. 1917 LaTouche, John
b. 1917 Sterling, Robert
b. 1920 Saxon, Charles David
b. 1922 Werner, Oskar
b. 1923 Christian, Linda
b. 1930 Harris, Fred Roy
b. 1932 Connolly, Olga Fikotova
b. 1932 Mulligan, Richard
b. 1933 Corri, Adrienne
b. 1934 Arnett, Peter Gregg
b. 1934 Densen-Gerber, Judianne
b. 1934 Marshall, Garry Kent
b. 1935 Carey, George Leonard, Archbishop
b. 1938 Seberg, Jean
b. 1939 Higgins, George V.
b. 1941 Rambo, Dack
b. 1941 Stottlemyre, Mel(vin Leon)
b. 1947 Lovins, Amory B(loch)
b. 1947 Mantegna, Joe
b. 1949 Goldberg, Whoopi
b. 1949 Steen, Roger
b. 1950 Perreault, Gilbert
b. 1953 Tickner, Charlie
b. 1954 McNealy, Scott (G.)
b. 1963 Testaverde, Vinny

d. 1460 Henry the Navigator
d. 1619 Carracci, Lodovico
d. 1687 Gwyn, Nell
d. 1849 Etty, William
d. 1849 Manning, Maria
d. 1861 Clough, Arthur Hugh
d. 1864 Hammond, James Henry
d. 1868 Rossini, Gioacchino Antonio
d. 1883 Sims, James Marion
d. 1897 Giles, Ernest
d. 1903 Pissarro, Camille Jacob
d. 1907 Thompson, Francis Joseph
d. 1916 Lowell, Percival
d. 1916 Saki
d. 1937 Carter, Caroline Louise Dudley
d. 1939 Weber, Lois
d. 1942 Crews, Laura Hope
d. 1942 Schoen-Rene, Anna
d. 1943 Denis, Maurice
d. 1948 Bradford, Roark Whitney Wickliffe
d. 1949 Wallerstein, Lothar
d. 1951 Medtner, Nicholas
d. 1952 Brown, Margaret Wise
d. 1952 Egan, Raymond B
d. 1953 Ives, Herbert Eugene
d. 1954 Fath, Jacques
d. 1955 DeVoto, Bernard Augustine
d. 1960 Close, Upton
d. 1961 Biddle, Anthony Joseph
d. 1963 Murray, Margaret Alice
d. 1967 Paddleford, Clementine Haskin
d. 1969? Liu Shao-Ch'i
d. 1971 Bleeker, Sonia
d. 1972 Webster, Margaret
d. 1973 Lee, Lila
d. 1974 DeSica, Vittorio
d. 1974 Silkwood, Karen
d. 1975 Sherriff, Robert Cedric
d. 1976 Benedict, Clint(on Stephen)
d. 1979 Harmon, Ernest N(ason)
d. 1982 Deutsch, Babette
d. 1982 Kim, Duk Koo
d. 1983 Samples, Junior
d. 1985 Pereira, William Leonard
d. 1988 Dorati, Antal
d. 1988 Miki Takeo
d. 1989 Franz Joseph II

d. 1991 Baldwin, Hanson Weightman
d. 1996 Doggett, Bill
d. 1998 Hobson, Valerie Babette
d. 1998 Holzman, Red
d. 1999 Mills, Donald

November 14
b. Yarmon, Betty
b. 1567 Maurice of Nassau
b. 1663 Hildebrandt, Johann Lucas von
b. 1719 Mozart, Leopold
b. 1765 Fulton, Robert
b. 1774 Spontini, Gasparo
b. 1778 Hummel, Johann Nepomuk
b. 1797 Lyell, Charles, Sir
b. 1819 Rodgers, Christopher Raymond Perry
b. 1820 Burlingame, Anson
b. 1828 McPherson, James Birdseye
b. 1829 Feuerbach, Paul Johann Anselm von
b. 1838 Richards, William Trost
b. 1840 Monet, Claude-Oscar
b. 1854 Parsons, Frank
b. 1861 Turner, Frederick Jackson
b. 1863 Baekeland, Leo Hendrik
b. 1871 Coulter, Ernest Kent
b. 1871 Russell, Henry
b. 1881 Schenck, Nicholas Michael
b. 1885 Delaunay-Terk, Sonia
b. 1885 Rourke, Constance Mayfield
b. 1889 Nehru, Jawaharlal
b. 1889 Taha Hussein
b. 1890 Egan, Raymond B
b. 1895 Lausche, Frank John
b. 1895 Lewis, Wilmarth Sheldon
b. 1896 Eisenhower, Mamie (Geneva) Doud
b. 1897 Curry, John Steuart
b. 1897 Ricca, Paul
b. 1900 Copland, Aaron
b. 1902 Downey, Morton
b. 1904 Lord, Mary Pillsbury
b. 1904 Mannes, Marya
b. 1904 Ramsey, Arthur Michael, Lord
b. 1906 Brooks, Louise
b. 1906 Dwinell, Lane
b. 1907 Lindgren, Astrid

b. 1907 Steig, William
b. 1908 McCarthy, Joe
b. 1908 Salisbury, Harrison Evans
b. 1910 Arnon, Daniel I(srael)
b. 1910 DeCamp, Rosemary
b. 1912 Hutton, Barbara Woolworth
b. 1913 Smathers, George Armistead
b. 1914 Crozier, Eric John
b. 1915? Trafficante, Santo, Jr.
b. 1917 Field, Virginia (Margaret Cynthia St. John)
b. 1918 Madeira, Jean
b. 1919 Desmond, Johnny
b. 1919 Lake, Veronica
b. 1921 Keith, Brian
b. 1922 Boutros-Ghali, Boutros
b. 1925 Medvedev, Zhores Aleksandrovich
b. 1929 Piersall, Jimmy
b. 1929 Stevenson, McLean
b. 1930 Berge, Pierre (Vital Georges)
b. 1930 Ketelsen, James Lee
b. 1930 White, Ed(ward Higgins, III)
b. 1933 Haise, Fred W(allace, Jr.)
b. 1934 De Benedetti, Carlo
b. 1935 Hussein, I, King
b. 1942 Watson, Bryan Joseph
b. 1943 Callejas Romero, Rafael Leonardo
b. 1947 O'Rourke, P J
b. 1948 Charles, Prince of Wales
b. 1951 Bishop, Stephen
b. 1952 Sharkey, Ray
b. 1954 Rice, Condoleezza
b. 1955 Hernandez, Willie (Guillermo Villaneuva)
b. 1959 Stevenson, Bryan (Allen)
d. 565 Justinian I
d. 1716 Leibniz, Gottfried Wilhelm von
d. 1825 Richter, Jean Paul F
d. 1825 Richter, Johann Paul Friedrich
d. 1831 Hegel, Georg Wilhelm Friedrich
d. 1832 Carroll, Charles
d. 1841 Elgin, Thomas Bruce

d. 1852 Pugin, A(ugustus) W(elby) N(orthmore)
d. 1869 Butterfield, John
d. 1901 Mapleson, James Henry
d. 1908 Kuang-hsu
d. 1908 Tz'u Hsi
d. 1910 LaFarge, John
d. 1914 Chaffee, Adna Romanza
d. 1914 Roberts, Frederick Sleigh
d. 1915 Washington, Booker T(aliafero)
d. 1916 George, Henry, Jr.
d. 1929 McGinnity, Joe
d. 1936 Howell, Clark
d. 1938 Gram, Hans Christian Joachim
d. 1944 Dallin, Cyrus Edwin
d. 1946 Falla, Manuel de
d. 1951 Benson, Frank Weston
d. 1954 Verrill, Alpheus Hyatt
d. 1955 Ayres, Ruby Mildred
d. 1955 Sherwood, Robert Emmet
d. 1955 Tobin, Daniel Joseph
d. 1956 Negrin, Juan
d. 1959 Cochrane, Edward Lull
d. 1960 Catlett, Walter
d. 1965 DeMarco, Tony
d. 1967 Kilgore, Bernard
d. 1968 Menendez Pidal, Ramon
d. 1972 Dies, Martin, Jr.
d. 1973 Schiaparelli
d. 1974 Brown, Johnny Mack
d. 1975 Anslinger, Harry Jacob
d. 1976 Pile, Frederick Alfred
d. 1977 Bhaktivedanta, A(bhay) C(haranaravinda)
d. 1979 Harris, Jed
d. 1980 Haskell, Arnold Lionel
d. 1983 Sheehan, Joseph Green
d. 1985 Koo, V(i) K(yuin) Wellington
d. 1988 Hansell, Haywood Shepherd, Jr.
d. 1989 Davison, Wild Bill
d. 1990 Muggeridge, Malcolm
d. 1993 Millett, John D(avid)
d. 1995 Finney, Jack
d. 1995 Marcus, Jacon R(ader)

d. 1995 Rifkind, Simon
H(irsch)
d. 1996 Bernardin,
Joseph L(ouis),
Cardinal
d. 1997 Arcaro, Eddie
d. 1997 Lorant, Stefan
November 15
b. 1607 Scudery,
Madeleine de
b. 1731 Cowper,
William
b. 1738 Herschel,
William Frederick,
Sir
b. 1741 Lavater, Johann
Casper
b. 1784 Bonaparte,
Jerome
b. 1787 Cunard,
Samuel, Sir
b. 1787 Leslie, Eliza
b. 1797 Weed, Thurlow
b. 1803 Abbott, Jacob
b. 1807 Petrov, Ossip
b. 1861 Haley, Margaret
A(ngela)
b. 1862 Hauptmann,
Gerhart Johann
Robert
b. 1869 Mew, Charlotte
Mary
b. 1873 Baker, Sara
Josephine
b. 1874 Krogh, Schack
August Steenberg
b. 1875 Kurz, Selma
b. 1879 Cape, Herbert
Jonathan
b. 1879 Stone, Lewis
b. 1881 Adams,
Franklin P(ierce)
b. 1882 Frankfurter,
Felix
b. 1883 Rawlinson,
Herbert
b. 1885 Page, Frederick
Handley, Sir
b. 1887 Moore,
Marianne Craig
b. 1887 O'Keeffe,
Georgia
b. 1888 Sverdrup,
H(arald) U(lrik)
b. 1890 Lamburn,
Richmal Crompton
b. 1890 Nygren, Anders
T(heodor) S(amuel)
b. 1890 Ornitz, Samuel
b. 1891 Astor, William
Vincent
b. 1891 Harriman,
W(illiam) Averell
b. 1891 Rommel, Erwin
Johannes Eugin
b. 1897 Bevan, Aneurin
b. 1897 McCord, David
(Thompson Watson)
b. 1897 Sitwell,
Sacheverell, Sir
b. 1899 Johnson,
Herbert Fisk
b. 1900 Hamilton,
Hamish
b. 1902 Losch, Tilly

b. 1906 LeMay, Curtis
Emerson
b. 1906 Niwano,
Nikkyo
b. 1906 Stein, Aaron
Marc
b. 1907 Stauffenberg,
Claus (Schenk Graf)
Von
b. 1909 Manning,
Timothy, Cardinal
b. 1910 Greene, Hugh
(Carleton), Sir
b. 1912 Baez, Albert V.
b. 1913 Cameron,
Roderick W
b. 1914 Bolet, Jorge
b. 1916 Barrow, Ruth
Nita, Dame
b. 1916 Davis, Edward
Michael
b. 1917 Begay, Harrison
b. 1919 Bruce, Carol
b. 1919 Wapner, Joseph
A
b. 1920 Bufalino,
Gesualdo
b. 1920 Thiebaud,
(Morton) Wayne
b. 1923 Schapiro,
Miriam
b. 1925 Baker, Howard
Henry, Jr.
b. 1928 Brady, James
Winston
b. 1929 Asner,
Ed(ward)
b. 1930 Ballard, J(ames)
G(raham)
b. 1931 Kerr, John
b. 1932 Clark, Petula
b. 1933 Burns, Jack
b. 1933 McPhatter,
Clyde
b. 1934 Barnes, Joanna
b. 1935 Coleman, John
b. 1935 White, Neva
b. 1940 Waterston,
Sam(uel Atkinson)
b. 1941 Pinkwater,
Daniel Manus
b. 1942 Barenboim,
Daniel
b. 1944 Kotto, Yaphet
Frederick
b. 1945 Lyngstad-
Fredriksson, Annifrid
b. 1946 Lennon, Janet
b. 1947 Richardson, Bill
b. 1950 Wilkins, Mac
b. 1953? D'Angelo,
Beverly
b. 1953 Widdoes, James
b. 1954 Kwasniewski,
Aleksander
d. 1280 Albert the Great
d. 1630 Kepler,
Johannes
d. 1670 Comenius,
Johann Amos
d. 1787 Gluck,
Christoph
d. 1794 Witherspoon,
John
d. 1802 Romney,
George

d. 1817 Kosciuszko,
Thaddeus
d. 1832 Say, Jean
Baptiste
d. 1897 Langston, John
Mercer
d. 1897 Strepponi,
Giuseppina
d. 1907 Conway,
Moncure Daniel
d. 1915 Trudeau,
Edward Livingston
d. 1916 Rivera, Luis
Munoz
d. 1916 Sienkiewicz,
Henryk Adam
Aleksander Pius
d. 1917 Durkheim,
Emile
d. 1919 Werner, Alfred
d. 1928 Chamberlin,
Thomas Chrowder
d. 1932 Brookings,
Robert Somers
d. 1932 Chesnutt,
Charles Waddell
d. 1944 Flesch, Karl
d. 1945 Chapman,
Frank Michler
d. 1947 Levy, Florence
d. 1954 Barrymore,
Lionel Blythe
d. 1958 Adams, Samuel
Hopkins
d. 1958 Power, Tyrone,
Jr.
d. 1959 Wilson, Charles
Thomson Rees
d. 1961 Ferguson, Elsie
d. 1962 Irene
d. 1963 Reiner, Fritz
d. 1965 Kalmus, Natalie
Mabelle Dunfee
d. 1967 Chatfield,
Alfred E Montacute,
Baron
d. 1967 McCollum,
Elmer Verner
d. 1967 Zorach, William
d. 1969 Aldecoa,
Ignacio
d. 1971 Abel, Rudolf
Ivanovich
d. 1973 Russell, Honey
d. 1976 Gabin, Jean
d. 1977 Addinsell,
Richard
d. 1978 Mead, Margaret
d. 1980 Fleming, Joan
Margaret
d. 1981 Markey, Enid
d. 1982 Bhave, Acharya
Vinoba
d. 1983 Grimm, Charlie
d. 1986 Croft, Michael
d. 1989 Terris, Norma
d. 1991 Richardson,
Tony
d. 1994 Speare,
Elizabeth George
d. 1996 Hiss, Alger
d. 1997 Chaplin, Saul
d. 1998 Carmichael,
Stokely
d. 1998 Dalrymple, Jean

November 16
b. 42BC Tiberius Julius
Caesar Augustus
b. 1717 Alembert, Jean
le Rond d'
b. 1766 Kreutzer,
Rodolphe
b. 1811 Bright, John
b. 1827 Norton, Charles
Eliot
b. 1835 Beltrami,
Eugenio
b. 1836 Kalakaua,
David
b. 1839 De Morgan,
William Frend
b. 1839 Frechette,
Louis-Honore
b. 1851 Hauk, Minnie
b. 1867 Daudet, Leon
b. 1873 Handy,
W(illiam)
C(hristopher)
b. 1886 Krock, Arthur
Bernard
b. 1889 Kaufman,
George S(imon)
b. 1890 Seldes, George
(Henry)
b. 1894 Potofsky, Jacob
Samuel
b. 1895 Arlen, Michael
b. 1895 Hindemith, Paul
b. 1895 Mathews, John
Joseph
b. 1896 Jordan, Jim
b. 1896 Mosley, Oswald
Ernald, Sir
b. 1896 Tibbett,
Lawrence Mervil
b. 1899 McBride, Mary
Margaret
b. 1900 Barrett, William
Edmund
b. 1901 Nagel, Ernest
b. 1904 Azikiwe,
Nnamdi
b. 1905 Condon, Eddie
b. 1906 Dowling,
Dan(iel Blair)
b. 1907 Meredith,
Burgess
b. 1908 Burns, John
L(awrence)
b. 1912 Bennett, Robert
LaFollette
b. 1912 Tebbel, John
William
b. 1914 Dunham, Sonny
b. 1915 Fritz, Jean
Guttery
b. 1916 Butler, Daws
b. 1919 Dobrynin,
Anatoly Fedorovich
b. 1920 Viertel, Peter
b. 1922 Amdahl, Gene
M(yron)
b. 1926 Cohn, Zanvil
(Alexander)
b. 1927 Butler, Robert
b. 1928 Gulager, Clu
b. 1930 Achebe, Chinua
b. 1930 Groppi, James
E
b. 1931 Gibson, Bob
b. 1932 Kelly, Thomas

b. 1935 Drew, Elizabeth Brenner
b. 1935 Rene, (France) Albert
b. 1936 Callender, Clive O(rville)
b. 1938 Nozick, Robert
b. 1938 Stockwell, Guy
b. 1940 Bloch, Ivan Sol
b. 1941 McLaughlin, Ann Dore
b. 1942 McKechnie, Donna
b. 1943 DeFreeze, Donald David
b. 1944 Pettet, Joanna
b. 1945 Van Hamel, Martine
b. 1946 Smith, Barbara
b. 1946 White, Jo Jo
b. 1947 Giddings, Paula (Jane)
b. 1950 Martin, Harvey Banks
b. 1951 Long, Irene D.
b. 1951 Vogel, Paula (Anne)
b. 1958 Guerrero, Roberto
b. 1958 Shabazz, Attallah
b. 1959 Pavin, Corey
b. 1963 Garrison, Zina
b. 1964 Gooden, Dwight Eugene
b. 1967 Bonet, Lisa
b. 1977 Baiul, Oksana
d. 1272 Henry III
b. 1603 Charron, Pierre
d. 1724 Sheppard, Jack
d. 1806 Cleaveland, Moses
d. 1812 Walter, John, I
d. 1813 Franklin, William
d. 1831 Clausewitz, Karl (Philipp Gottlieb) von
d. 1885 Riel, Louis David, Jr.
d. 1894 McCosh, James
d. 1895 Smith, Samuel Francis
d. 1902 Henty, George Alfred
d. 1909 Crittenton, Charles Nelson
d. 1927 Flowers, Tiger
d. 1928 Cecchetti, Enrico
d. 1936 Schumann-Heink, Ernestine Rossler
d. 1940 Beck, Martin
d. 1947 Carter, Boake
d. 1948 Cottrell, Frederick Gardner
d. 1950 Smith, Robert H
d. 1960 Gable, Clark
d. 1961 Rayburn, Sam(uel Taliaferro)
d. 1964 Peattie, Donald Culross
d. 1965 Cosgrave, William Thomas

d. 1965 DuMont, Allen Balcom
d. 1965 King, Alexander
d. 1968 Toledano, Vicente Lombardo
d. 1969 Fenton, Carroll Lane
d. 1972 Hurley, Jack B
d. 1973 Watts, Alan Wilson
d. 1980 Aronson, Boris
d. 1981 Holden, William
d. 1982 Crosby, Sumner McKnight
d. 1984 Rose, Leonard
d. 1985 Sparkman, John Jackson
d. 1986 McKenna, Siobhan
d. 1988 Lee, Jennie
d. 1992 Booth, Shirley
d. 1995 Horvath, Leslie
d. 1996 Quarles, Benjamin Arthur
d. 1997 Marchais, Georges (Rene Louis)
d. 1999 Nathans, Daniel

November 17
b. 8 Vespasian
b. 331 Julian
b. 1019 Ssu-ma kuang
b. 1503 Bronzino, Il
b. 1503 Bronzino, Agnolo
b. 1587 Vondel, Joost van den
b. 1749 Appert, Nicolas
b. 1790 Mobius, August Ferdinand
b. 1793 Eastlake, Charles Lock, Sir
b. 1794 Grote, George
b. 1799 Peale, Titian Ramsay
b. 1807 Hammond, James Henry
b. 1815 Farnham, Eliza Wood Burhans
b. 1854 Lyautey, Louis Hubert Gonzalve
b. 1861 Lampman, Archibald
b. 1861 Nutting, Wallace
b. 1876 Lea, Homer
b. 1878 Abbott, Grace
b. 1879 Heggie, O P
b. 1886 Stace, W(alter) T(erence)
b. 1887 Montgomery of Alamein, Bernard Law Montgomery, Viscount
b. 1893 Christison, (Alexander Frank) Philip
b. 1895 Bakhtin, Mikhail (Mikhailovich)
b. 1897 Fay, Frank
b. 1901 Hallstein, Walter
b. 1901 Strasberg, Lee

b. 1902 Spofford, Charles M(erville)
b. 1902 Wigner, Eugene P(aul)
b. 1903? Walters, Charles
b. 1904 Bernstein, Theodore Menline
b. 1904 Diederichs, Nicholaas
b. 1904 Hastie, William Henry
b. 1904 Noguchi, Isamu
b. 1905 Auer, Mischa
b. 1906 Bronson, Betty
b. 1906 Honda, Soichiro
b. 1907 Wimsatt, William Kurtz, Jr.
b. 1908 Park, Thomas
b. 1910 Wiley, W(illiam) Bradford
b. 1912 Ackerman, Harry S
b. 1912 Burgess, John Lawrie, Sir
b. 1912 Rebozo, Bebe
b. 1916 Silk, George
b. 1917 Orr, Robert Dunkerson
b. 1919 Kay, Hershy
b. 1922 Cohen, Stanley
b. 1922 Schulberg, Stuart
b. 1923 Garcia, Mike
b. 1924 Heath, Catherine
b. 1924 Pereira, Aristides
b. 1925 Hudson, Rock
b. 1925 Mackerras, Charles
b. 1928 Arman
b. 1928 Kabua, Amata
b. 1930 Amram, David Werner, III
b. 1930 Cook-Lynn, Elizabeth
b. 1930 Mathias, Bob
b. 1934 Inhofe, James M.
b. 1937 Cook, Peter
b. 1938 Lightfoot, Gordon Meredith
b. 1938 Vinton, Will
b. 1939 Waugh, Auberon
b. 1942 Gaudio, Bob
b. 1942 Scorsese, Martin
b. 1943 Hutton, Lauren
b. 1944 DeVito, Danny
b. 1944 Michaels, Lorne
b. 1944 Seaver, Tom
b. 1945 Hayes, Elvin Ernest
b. 1946 Branstad, Terry Edward
b. 1947 Vollbracht, Michaele J
b. 1948 Agyeman-Rawlings, Nana Konadu
b. 1948 Dean, Howard
b. 1950 Matthes, Roland
b. 1951 Martin, Dean Paul

b. 1952 Ramaphosa, Cyril
b. 1955 King, Yolanda Denise
b. 1961 VanKamp, Merete
d. 594 Gregory of Tours, St.
d. 1311 Gertrude the Great, Saint
d. 1558 Mary I
d. 1624 Boehme, Jakob
d. 1747 Lesage, Alain-Rene
d. 1813 Otterbein, Philip William
d. 1818 Charlotte Sophia
d. 1856 Eaton, John Henry
d. 1858 Owen, Robert
d. 1907 McClintock, Francis Leopold, Sir
d. 1917 Rodin, Auguste
d. 1926 Akeley, Carl Ethan
d. 1929 Hollerith, Herman
d. 1941 Udet, Ernst
d. 1944 Peabody, Endicott
d. 1944 Smith, Ellison DuRant
d. 1946 Horne, Herman Harrell
d. 1947 Huch, Ricarda (Octavia)
d. 1955 Johnson, James Price
d. 1958 Cooper, Mort(on Cecil)
d. 1959 Villa-Lobos, Heitor
d. 1961 Kauff, Benny
d. 1962 Ahearn, Frank
d. 1962 Davis, Arthur Vining
d. 1965 Blackstone, Harry
d. 1968 Peake, Mervyn Laurence
d. 1971 Cooper, Gladys, Dame
d. 1973 Mangrum, Lloyd
d. 1974 Childers, Erskine Hamilton
d. 1975 Bronk, Detlev Wulf
d. 1976 Bhashani, Maulana Abdul Hamid Khan
d. 1978 Dauphin, Claude Le Grand Maria Eugene
d. 1981 Eberle, Bob
d. 1981 Lang, Daniel
d. 1982 Donnelly, Ruth
d. 1985 Chase, Stuart
d. 1985 Nol, Lon
d. 1985 Ritz, Jimmy
d. 1986 Besse, Georges Noel
d. 1987 Wicker, Ireene Seaton

d. 1988 Graham,
Sheilah
d. 1990 Hofstadter,
Robert
d. 1992 Block, Joseph
L(eopold)
d. 1992 Lorde, Audre
(Geraldine)
d. 1995 Gordone,
Charles Edward
d. 1998 Ewbank, Weeb
d. 1998 Rolle, Esther

November 18
b. 1647 Bayle, Pierre
b. 1743 Ewald,
Johannes
b. 1785 Wilkie, David,
Sir
b. 1786 Weber, Carl
Maria von
b. 1787 Daguerre, Louis
Jacques Mande
b. 1801 Butterfield,
John
b. 1810 Gray, Asa
b. 1826 Newberry, John
Stoughton
b. 1832 Nordenskiold,
Nils Adolph Erik,
Baron
b. 1836 Gilbert, William
S(chwenck), Sir
b. 1836 Gomez,
Maximo
b. 1857 Knox, Rose
Markward
b. 1860 Paderewski,
Ignace Jan
b. 1862 Sunday, Billy
b. 1866 Guerin, Jules
b. 1868 Dehmel,
Richard
b. 1870 Dix, Dorothy
b. 1871 Bonstelle, Jessie
b. 1872 Marsh, Edward
Howard, Sir
b. 1874 Day, Clarence
Shepard, Jr.
b. 1877 Mayr, Richard
b. 1877 Pigou, Arthur
Cecil
b. 1881 LeSueur, Percy
b. 1882 Galli-Curci,
Amelita
b. 1882 Maritain,
Jacques
b. 1883 Vinson, Carl
b. 1884 Lewis,
Wyndham
b. 1885 Allen, Forrest
Claire
b. 1886 Kemper, James
S(cott)
b. 1886 Rand, James
Henry
b. 1886 Wilson, Charles
Edward
b. 1888 Marion, Frances
b. 1891 Ponti,
Gio(vanni)
b. 1894 Denny, Ludwell
b. 1895 Smith, Loring
b. 1897 Blackett,
Patrick Maynard
Stuart
b. 1898 Ivens, Joris

b. 1899 Ormandy,
Eugene
b. 1900 Alajalov,
Constantin
b. 1900 Kistiakowsky,
George Bogdan
b. 1900 Thurman,
Howard
b. 1901 Gallup, George
Horace
b. 1901 Wood, Craig
Ralph
b. 1905 Carlson,
William S(amuel)
b. 1906 Mann, Klaus
b. 1906 Wald, George
b. 1907 Dreyfus, Pierre
b. 1909 Mercer, Johnny
b. 1911 McKenney,
Ruth
b. 1912 Martin, Louis
E.
b. 1912 Zablocki,
Clement John
b. 1917 DePinies, Jaime
b. 1920 Khalil, Mustafa
b. 1923 Gregor, Arthur
b. 1923 Shepard, Alan
B(artlett), Jr.
b. 1923 Stevens, Ted
b. 1925 Mauch, Gene
William
b. 1926 Collins,
Dorothy
b. 1928 Laurel,
Salvador H(idalgo)
b. 1931 Goizueta,
Roberto C(rispulo)
b. 1936 Ballard, Hank
b. 1936 Cherry, Don
b. 1938 Cipullo, Aldo
Massimo Fabrizio
b. 1938 Schranz, Karl
b. 1939 Atwood,
Margaret (Eleanor)
b. 1939 Vaccaro,
Brenda
b. 1940 Qaboos Bin Al
Sai'id
b. 1940 Quabus bin
Saud
b. 1941 Hemmings,
David Leslie Edward
b. 1941 Pocklington,
Peter H
b. 1942 Evans, Linda
b. 1944 Sullivan, Susan
b. 1945 Mankiller,
Wilma P(earl)
b. 1946 Begiebing,
Robert J.
b. 1948 Tatum, Jack
b. 1950 Parker, Graham
b. 1950 Parker, Jameson
b. 1952 Lindo, Delroy
b. 1954 Williams,
Charles
b. 1956 Moon, Warren
(Harold)
b. 1957 Watts, J(ulius)
C(aesar), (Jr.)
b. 1960 Wilde, Kim
b. 1963 Bias, Len
b. 1968 Sheffield, Gary
(Antonian)
b. 1969 Ismail, Raghib

d. 1804 Schuyler, Philip
John
d. 1827 Hauff, Wilhelm
d. 1847 Dibdin, Thomas
Frognall
d. 1854 Forbes, Edward
d. 1883 Siemens,
William, Sir
d. 1886 Arthur, Chester
A(lan)
d. 1887 Fechner, Gustav
Theodor
d. 1889 Allingham,
William
d. 1897 Doulton, Henry,
Sir
d. 1921 Berdichevsky,
Micah Joseph
d. 1922 Proust, Marcel
d. 1926 Sterling, George
d. 1929 O'Connor,
Thomas Power
d. 1935 Bulova, Joseph
d. 1940 Gill, Eric
d. 1941 Nernst, Walther
Hermann
d. 1946 Meek, Donald
d. 1946 Walker, Jimmy
d. 1949 Jewett, Frank
Baldwin
d. 1952 Eluard, Paul
d. 1962 Bax, Clifford
d. 1962 Bohr, Niels
Henrik David
d. 1962 Chavez, Dennis
d. 1965 Wallace, Henry
Agard
d. 1968 Wanger, Walter
d. 1969 Heath, Ted
d. 1969 Kennedy,
Joseph Patrick, Sr.
d. 1974 Brook, Clive
d. 1976 Jerger, Alfred
d. 1976 Ray, Man
d. 1976 Spence, Basil
Urwin, Sir
d. 1977 O'Brien, Davey
d. 1977 Schuschnigg,
Kurt von
d. 1978 Jones, Reverend
Jim
d. 1978 Tristano,
Leonard Joseph
d. 1980 Smythe, Conn
d. 1981 Wertham,
Fredric
d. 1982 McGivern,
William Peter
d. 1983 Albright, Ivan
Le Lorraine
d. 1987 Anquetil,
Jacques
d. 1988 Parish, Peggy
d. 1989 Buckley,
Emerson
d. 1990 Harris, Harwell
Hamilton
d. 1991 Husak, Gustav
d. 1992 Kirsten,
Dorothy
d. 1994 Calloway, Cab
d. 1994 Somes, Michael
(George)
d. 1999 Bowles, Paul
(Frederick)

d. 1999 Horst, Horst
P(aul)

November 19
b. 1566 Devereaux,
Robert
b. 1600 Charles I
b. 1711 Lomonosov,
Mikhail Vasilyevich
b. 1752 Clark, George
Rogers
b. 1799 Caillie, Rene
Auguste
b. 1805 Lesseps,
Ferdinand Marie de
b. 1831 Garfield, James
Abram
b. 1833 Dilthey,
Wilhelm Christian
Ludwig
b. 1835 Lee, Fitzhugh
b. 1875 Bingham,
Hiram
b. 1876 Ehrenfest-
Afanaseva, Tatiana
b. 1885 Crommelynck,
Fernand
b. 1887 Sumner, James
Batcheller
b. 1888 Capablanca,
Jose Raoul
b. 1891 Webb, Clifton
b. 1894 Thomaz,
Americo
b. 1895 Marsh, Mae
b. 1897 Garrison, Lloyd
K(irkham)
b. 1897 Roosevelt,
Quentin
b. 1898 Sheldon,
William Herbert
b. 1899 Tate, Allen
(John Orley)
b. 1900 Walbrook,
Anton
b. 1901 Kraushaar, Otto
b. 1904 Leopold,
Nathan Freudenthal
b. 1905 Dorsey, Tommy
b. 1905 Kashdan, Isaac
b. 1906 Carroll, Nancy
b. 1907 Schaefer, Jack
Warner
b. 1908 Coca, Imogene
Fernandez y
b. 1909 Drucker, Peter
Ferdinand
b. 1912 Palade, George
Emil
b. 1915 Halaby, Najeeb
E(lias)
b. 1915 Sutherland, Earl
Wilbur, Jr.
b. 1917 Gandhi, Indira
Priyadarshini Nehru
b. 1919 Pontecorvo,
Gillo
b. 1919 Young, Alan
(Angus)
b. 1921 Anda, Geza
b. 1921 Campanella,
Roy
b. 1922 Harris, Mark
b. 1924 Mutesa II
b. 1926 Kirkpatrick,
Jeane Duane Jordan
b. 1933 King, Larry

b. 1935 Robertson, James D, III
b. 1935 Welch, John Francis, Jr.
b. 1936 Cavett, Dick
b. 1937 Leach, Penelope
b. 1938 Turner, Ted
b. 1939 Constantinescu, Emil
b. 1939 Harkin, Thomas R(ichard)
b. 1939 Utley, (Clifton) Garrick
b. 1941 Haggerty, Dan
b. 1941 Johnson, Cletus Merlin
b. 1941 Thompson, Tommy George
b. 1942 Klein, Calvin
b. 1942 Olds, Sharon
b. 1947 Boone, Bob
b. 1949 Rashad, Ahmad
b. 1950 Moffatt, Katy
b. 1951 Jojola, Ted
b. 1953 Todd, Richard
b. 1954 Quinlan, Kathleen
b. 1956 Collins, Eileen
b. 1958 McGinnis, Scott
b. 1961 Ryan, Meg
b. 1962 Foster, Jodie
b. 1966 Devers, Gail
b. 1973 Glover, Savion
b. 1977 Strug, Kerri
b. 1665 Poussin, Nicolas
d. 1806 Ledoux, Claude Nicolas
d. 1828 Schubert, Franz Peter
d. 1850 Johnson, Richard Mentor
d. 1867 Halleck, Fritz-Greene
d. 1868 Mount, William Sidney
d. 1873 Mallory, Stephen R
d. 1887 Lazarus, Emma
d. 1891 Florence, William Jermyn
d. 1895 Vaux, Calvert
d. 1898 Buell, Don Carlos
d. 1909 Laffan, William Mackay
d. 1909 Tabb, John Banister
d. 1915 Hill, Joe
d. 1922 Bacon, Frank
d. 1924 Ince, Thomas H(arper)
d. 1949 Ensor, James Sydney, Baron
d. 1955 James, Marquis
d. 1956 Sullivan, Francis Loftus
d. 1959 Tolman, Edward Chace
d. 1960 Cooper, Emil
d. 1960 Gibbons, Tom
d. 1966 Connolly, Mike
d. 1967 Funk, Casimir
d. 1968 Norena, Eide
d. 1969 Sardi, Vincent, Sr.

d. 1971 Stern, Bill
d. 1972 Ohrbach, Nathan M
d. 1974 Brunis, George
d. 1975 Vishnevsky, Alexandr Alekandrovich
d. 1978 Ryan, Leo Joseph
d. 1983 Kitchell, Iva
d. 1983 Leigh, Carolyn
d. 1984 Aiken, George David
d. 1985 Fetchit, Stepin
d. 1985 Joanis, John W
d. 1988 Hubbell, Carl Owen
d. 1988 Onassis, Christina
d. 1990 Landrum, Phil(lip) M(itchell)
d. 1992 Varsi, Diane
d. 1993 Burke, Kenneth
d. 1994 Symons, Julian (Gustave)
d. 1998 McCarthy, William J.
d. 1998 Pakula, Alan J(ay)
d. 1999 Liberman, Alexander (Semeonovitch)

November 20
b. 1733 Schuyler, Philip John
b. 1752 Chatterton, Thomas
b. 1837 Waterman, Lewis Edson
b. 1841 Laurier, Wilfrid, Sir
b. 1851 Coulter, John Merle
b. 1855 Royce, Josiah
b. 1858 Lagerlof, Selma Ottiliana Lovisa
b. 1862 Westermarck, Edward Alexander
b. 1866 Landis Kenesaw, Mountain, Judge
b. 1867 Hayes, Patrick Joseph, Cardinal
b. 1869 Griffith, Clark Calvin
b. 1871 Guiterman, Arthur
b. 1871 Kilpatrick, William H(eard)
b. 1873 Mason, Daniel Gregory
b. 1874 Curley, James Michael
b. 1875 Kalinin, Mikhail (Ivanovich)
b. 1878? Bowers, Claude Gernade
b. 1878 Gilpin, Charles Sidney
b. 1884 Thomas, Norman Mattoon
b. 1885 Kesselring, Albert
b. 1886 Frisch, Karl von

b. 1886 Hammond, Bray
b. 1887 Hooton, Earnest Albert
b. 1889 Hubble, Edwin Powell
b. 1890 Armstrong, Robert
b. 1891 Denny, Reginald Leigh
b. 1891 Murphy, Jimmy
b. 1894 Humphries, Rolfe
b. 1900 Burch, Billy
b. 1900 Gould, Chester
b. 1903 Onsager, Lars
b. 1907 Clouzot, Henri-George
b. 1908 Cooke, (Alfred) Alistair
b. 1909 Bible, Alan
b. 1910 Murray, Pauli
b. 1911 Hanfmann, George Maxim Anossov
b. 1914 Pucci, Emilio Marchese di Barsento
b. 1915 Hu Yaobang
b. 1916 Canova, Judy
b. 1917 Locke, Bobby
b. 1918 Kent, Corita
b. 1919 Gray, Dulcie
b. 1919 Keyes, Evelyn Louise
b. 1920 Thaxter, Phyllis
b. 1921 Garrison, Jim C.
b. 1923 Gordimer, Nadine
b. 1923 Sprinkel, Beryl Wayne
b. 1924 Allison, Fran(ces)
b. 1924 Mandelbrot, Benoit B.
b. 1925 Kennedy, Robert Francis
b. 1925 Plisetskaya, Maya Mikhailovna
b. 1926 Ballard, Kaye
b. 1926 Luz, Arturo Rogerio
b. 1927 Parsons, Estelle
b. 1928 Cover, Franklin
b. 1929 Denenberg, Herbert Sidney
b. 1929 January, Don(ald)
b. 1932 Dawson, Richard
b. 1934 Apple, R(aymond) W(alter), Jr.
b. 1934 Peter, Valentine J
b. 1936 DeLillo, Don
b. 1937 Laredo, Ruth
b. 1938 Smothers, Dick
b. 1940 Butala, Tony
b. 1940 Einstein, Bob
b. 1942 Biden, Joe
b. 1942 Greenbaum, Norman
b. 1942 Monk, Meredith Jane

b. 1945 Hamel, Veronica
b. 1945 Johnstone, Jay
b. 1946 Allman, Duane
b. 1946 Cook, Greg(ory Lynn)
b. 1946 Woodruff, Judy Carline
b. 1947 Walsh, Joe
b. 1948 Hendricks, Barbara
b. 1951 Walters, David
b. 1956 Derek, Bo
b. 1956 Gastineau, Mark
b. 1959 Dunne, Dominique
b. 1959 Young, Sean
b. 1976 Dawes, Dominique (Margaux)
d. 1591 Hatton, Christopher, Sir
d. 1679 John Maurice of Nassau
d. 1692 Shadwell, Thomas
d. 1806 Backus, Isaac
d. 1813 Bodoni, Giambattista
d. 1863 Elgin, James Bruce
d. 1888 Currier, Nathaniel
d. 1894 Rubinstein, Anton Gregorovitch
d. 1899 Dawson, John William, Sir
d. 1903 Horn, Tom
d. 1904 Cesnola, Luigi Palma di
d. 1907 Modersohn-Becker, Paula
d. 1910 Tolstoy, Leo Nikolayevich
d. 1915 Schechter, Solomon
d. 1925 Alexandra Caroline Mary Charlotte
d. 1925 Morris, Clara
d. 1933 Birrell, Augustine
d. 1934 Sitter, Willem de
d. 1935 Jellicoe, John Rushworth
d. 1938 Hall, Edwin Herbert
d. 1940 Blatch, Harriot Eaton Stanton
d. 1945 Aston, Francis William
d. 1950 Cilea, Francesco
d. 1952 Croce, Benedetto
d. 1954 Cessna, Clyde Vernon
d. 1957 Swope, Gerard
d. 1960 Rollins, Carl Purington
d. 1964 Howard, Roy Wilson
d. 1965 Anthony, Katharine Susan

d. 1972 Grossinger, Jennie
d. 1973 Sherman, Allan
d. 1975 Franco, Francisco
d. 1976 Auchincloss, Hugh D
d. 1976 D'Arcy, Martin Cyril
d. 1976 Lysenko, Trofim Denisovich
d. 1976 Millner, Wayne E
d. 1978 Chirico, Giorgio de
d. 1981 Sheed, Frank
d. 1982 Mackin, Catherine Patricia
d. 1983 Loo, Richard
d. 1984 Bratteli, Trygve Martin
d. 1984 Faiz, Faiz Ahmad
d. 1988 Gerson, Noel Bertram
d. 1989 Bari, Lynn
d. 1990 Cobb, William Montague
d. 1995 Grinkov, Sergei
d. 1999 Fanfani, Amintore

November 21
b. 1694 Voltaire
b. 1729 Bartlett, Josiah
b. 1768 Schleiermacher, Friedrich Ernst Daniel
b. 1785 Beaumont, William
b. 1787 Procter, Bryan Waller
b. 1818 Morgan, Lewis Henry
b. 1834 Green, Hetty
b. 1834 Weyerhaeuser, Frederick
b. 1839 Keith, William
b. 1842 Packer, Alfred G
b. 1851 Spy
b. 1854 Benedict XV
b. 1857 Estrada Cabrera, Manuel
b. 1863 Quiller-Couch, Arthur Thomas, Sir
b. 1870 Berkman, Alexander
b. 1886 Nicolson, Harold George, Sir
b. 1891 Ellsberg, Edward
b. 1891 Sturtevant, Alfred Henry
b. 1895 Gerhardi, William Alexander
b. 1898 Magritte, Rene Francois Ghislain
b. 1899 Borgmann, Benny
b. 1902 Omlie, Phoebe Jane Fairgrave
b. 1902 Suslov, Mikhail Andreevich
b. 1903 Hewitt, Foster
b. 1904 Gross, Courtlandt Sherrington

b. 1904 Hawkins, Bean
b. 1904 Hawkins, Coleman
b. 1905 Fernald, John Bailey
b. 1905 Lindstrom, Freddie
b. 1905 Wyatt, Wilson W(atkins)
b. 1907 Bishop, Jim
b. 1907 Bohrod, Aaron
b. 1908 Politi, Leo
b. 1908 Richards, Paul Rapier
b. 1908 Speare, Elizabeth George
b. 1908 Young, Marian
b. 1912 Joyce, Eileen
b. 1912 Powell, Eleanor
b. 1913 Boulting, John
b. 1913 Boulting, Roy
b. 1913 Unkelbach, Kurt
b. 1914 Grant, Michael
b. 1914 Kassem, Abdul Karim (el)
b. 1916 Luckman, Sid(ney)
b. 1917 Chung, Il-Kwon
b. 1920 Meeker, Ralph
b. 1920 Musial, Stan(ley Frank)
b. 1924? Blaine, Vivian
b. 1924 Planinc, Milka
b. 1925 Garrett, Lila
b. 1926 Baum, William Wakefield, Cardinal
b. 1927 Campanella, Joseph Mario
b. 1928 Cook, Samuel DuBois
b. 1929 French, Marilyn
b. 1932 Ringo, Jim
b. 1933 Bainbridge, Beryl
b. 1934 Pawley, Howard Russell
b. 1934 Tawley, Howard
b. 1936 DePreist, James Anderson
b. 1936 Ginzburg, Aleksandr Ilich
b. 1937 Howe, Tina
b. 1938 Thomas, Marlo
b. 1940 Makarova, Natalia
b. 1941 Hough, John
b. 1941 Mills, Juliet
b. 1943 Laffite, Jacques Henry Sabin
b. 1943 Mahan, Larry
b. 1944 Carsey, Marcy
b. 1944 Durbin, Richard J.
b. 1944 Monroe, Earl
b. 1945 Hawn, Goldie (Jean)
b. 1949 Rubin, Barbara Jo
b. 1949 Siegel, Morris J
b. 1950 Taylor, Livingston
b. 1952 Luft, Lorna
b. 1953 Brown, Tina

b. 1955 Maxwell, Cedric Bryan
b. 1956 Fattah, Chaka
b. 1956 Simionescu, Mariana
b. 1961 Hemingway, Mariel
b. 1963 Sheridan, Nicollette
b. 1964 Vincent, Marjorie Judith
b. 1965 Bjork
b. 1966 Aikman, Troy (Kenneth)
b. 1969 Griffey, Ken, Jr.
d. 479BC Confucius
d. 1579 Gresham, Thomas, Sir
d. 1682 Lorrain, Claude
d. 1695 Purcell, Henry
d. 1811 Kleist, Heinrich von
d. 1830 Kisfaludy, Karoly
d. 1835 Hogg, James
d. 1844 Krylov, Ivan Andreyevich
d. 1861 Lacordaire, Jean Baptiste Henri
d. 1880 Cockburn, Alexander James Edmund, Sir
d. 1885 Wright, Elizur
d. 1886 Adams, Charles Francis, Sr.
d. 1899 Hobart, Garret Augustus
d. 1904 Bloomingdale, Joseph Bernard
d. 1916 Francis Joseph, (I)
d. 1916 Franz Joseph I
d. 1924 Harding, Florence Kling (De Wolfe)
d. 1928 Sudermann, Hermann
d. 1937 Coffin, Howard Earle
d. 1938 Godowsky, Leopold
d. 1942 Berchtold, Leopold von
d. 1942 Hertzog, James Barry Munnik
d. 1944 Caillaux, Joseph Marie Auguste
d. 1944 Hartmann, Sadakichi
d. 1945 Benchley, Robert Charles
d. 1945 Glasgow, Ellen Anderson Gholson
d. 1945 Patch, Alexander M(c Carrell)
d. 1952 Conklin, Edwin Grant
d. 1952 Green, William
d. 1952 Upshaw, William David
d. 1956 Burchenal, Elizabeth
d. 1958 Ott, Mel(vin Thomas)

d. 1959 Baer, Max
d. 1963 Bartlett, Francis Alonzo
d. 1963 Stroud, Robert Franklin
d. 1969 Mutesa II
d. 1970 Lalonde, Newsy
d. 1970 Raman, Chandrasekhara Venkata, Sir
d. 1970 Yezierska, Anzia
d. 1974 Gambling, John Bradley
d. 1974 Martin, Frank
d. 1980 Smith, A(rthur) J(ames) M(arshall)
d. 1981 Bolotowsky, Ilya
d. 1981 Von Zell, Harry
d. 1982 Hofheinz, Roy Mark
d. 1982 Patrick, Lee
d. 1983 Davis, (William) Allison
d. 1984 Husch, Gerhard
d. 1986 Bay, Howard
d. 1986 Colonna, Jerry
d. 1987 Folsom, James E(lisha)
d. 1988 Lewenthal, Raymond
d. 1991 Dichter, Ernest
d. 1991 Lloyd-Jones, Esther McDonald
d. 1991 Werblin, Sonny
d. 1992 Gazzelloni, Severino
d. 1993 Bixby, Bill
d. 1994 Kuchel, Thomas H(enry)
d. 1995 Jeakins, Dorothy
d. 1996 Salam, Abdus
d. 1997 Geneen, Harold S(ydney)
d. 1997 Kirk, Grayson Louis
d. 1999 Crisp, Quentin
November 22
b. 1428 Warwick and of Salisbury, Earl of
b. 1643 La Salle, Rene Robert Cavelier de
b. 1698 Vaudreuil-Cavagnal, Marquis de
b. 1710 Bach, Wilhelm Friedemann
b. 1725 Gunther, Ignaz
b. 1735 Stewart, Dugald
b. 1767 Hofer, Andreas
b. 1808 Cook, Thomas
b. 1808 Rothschild, Lionel Nathan Rothschild, Baron
b. 1819 Eliot, George
b. 1838 Hartmann, Franz
b. 1852 D'Estournelles, Paul Henri Benjamin Balleut de Constant, Baron
b. 1857 Gissing, George Robert
b. 1861 Dallin, Cyrus Edwin

b. 1863 Ch'i Pai-Shih
b. 1868 Garner, John Nance
b. 1869 Gide, Andre (Paul Guillaume)
b. 1874 Horne, Herman Harrell
b. 1877 Ady, Endre
b. 1879 Hawtrey, Ralph George, Sir
b. 1889 Beer, Thomas
b. 1889 Draper, Dorothy Tuckerman
b. 1890 DeGaulle, Charles Andre Joseph Marie
b. 1890 Pollitt, Harry
b. 1891 Bernays, Edward L.
b. 1893 Dundee, Johnny
b. 1893 Kaganovich, Lazar M(oiseevich)
b. 1894 Bayne, Beverly Pearl
b. 1895 Dehn, Adolf Arthur
b. 1895 Enoch, Kurt
b. 1896 Mays, David John
b. 1898 Blanding, Sarah Gibson
b. 1899 Berndt, Walter
b. 1899 Carmichael, Hoagy
b. 1900 Pantaleoni, Helenka (Tradeusa Adamowski)
b. 1900 Post, Wiley
b. 1901 Crane, Roy(ston Campbell)
b. 1902 Adonis, Joe
b. 1902 Feuermann, Emanuel
b. 1902 McDonald, David John
b. 1904 Neel, Louis Eugene Felix
b. 1905 Burnham, James
b. 1906 Patrick, Lee
b. 1910 Smith, Ethel
b. 1911 Cacers, Ernest
b. 1912 Duke, Doris
b. 1912 Guldahl, Ralph
b. 1913 Berlitz, Charles L Frambach
b. 1913 Britten, (Edward) Benjamin
b. 1914 Townsend, Peter Wooldridge
b. 1915 White, Stephen
b. 1916 Ross, Percy Nathan
b. 1917 Huxley, Andrew Fielding, Sir
b. 1918 Pell, Claiborne DeBorda
b. 1918 Walston, Ray
b. 1921 Atherton, Alfred LeRoy, Jr.
b. 1921 Dangerfield, Rodney
b. 1923 Hiller, Arthur
b. 1923 Westwood, Jean Miles
b. 1924 Page, Geraldine

b. 1925 Schuller, Gunther
b. 1926 Burdette, Lew
b. 1929 Lynd, Staughton (Craig)
b. 1930 Garriott, Owen
b. 1930 Hall, Peter Reginald Frederick, Sir
b. 1932 Vaughn, Robert
b. 1935 Callan, Michael
b. 1935 Protopopov, Ludmilla Evgenievna Belousova
b. 1937 Idei, Nobuyuki
b. 1938 Lee, Henry C.
b. 1940 Gilliam, Terry (Vance)
b. 1941 Conti, Tom
b. 1941 Dante, Nicholas
b. 1941 Laperriere, Jacques
b. 1941 Price, Hugh B.
b. 1942 Bluford, Guy
b. 1942 Edwards, Harry, Jr.
b. 1943 Courneyor, Yvan Serge
b. 1943 King, Billie Jean
b. 1947 Buckard, Alfredo Cristiani
b. 1947 Cristiani, Alfredo
b. 1947 Reynolds, Jack
b. 1950 Bostock, Lyman Wesley
b. 1950 Luzinski, Greg(ory Michael)
b. 1958 Curtis, Jamie Lee
b. 1962 Fields, Cleo
b. 1967 Becker, Boris
d. 1594 Frobisher, Martin
d. 1718 Blackbeard
d. 1774 Clive, Robert
d. 1783 Hanson, John
d. 1882 Weed, Thurlow
d. 1886 Chesnut, Mary Boykin (Miller)
d. 1896 Ferris, George Washington Gale
d. 1900 Sullivan, Arthur Seymour, Sir
d. 1902 Reed, Walter
d. 1907 Hall, Asaph
d. 1916 London, Jack
d. 1921 Hyndman, Henry Mayers
d. 1921 Nilsson, Christine
d. 1932 Atkinson, William Walker
d. 1936 Graham, Ernest Robert
d. 1938 Shestov, Lev
d. 1941 Koffka, Kurt
d. 1943 Hart, Lorenz
d. 1943 Yon, Pietro Alessandro
d. 1944 Eddington, Arthur Stanley, Sir
d. 1953 Shields, Larry
d. 1954 Vyshinsky, Andrei Yanuarievich

d. 1955 Howard, Shemp
d. 1959 Mallory, Molla
d. 1962 Coty, Rene (Jules Gustave)
d. 1963 Huxley, Aldous (Leonard)
d. 1963 Kennedy, John F(itzgerald)
d. 1963 Lewis, C(live) S(taples)
d. 1971 Confrey, Zez
d. 1971 Wilson, Joseph Chamberlain
d. 1972 Loper, Don
d. 1976 Davies, Rupert
d. 1977 Traglia, Luigi, Cardinal
d. 1980 Leger, Jules
d. 1980 McCormack, John William
d. 1980 West, Mae
d. 1981 Krebs, Hans Adolf, Sir
d. 1981 Lightner, Theodore
d. 1982 Batten, Jean Gardner
d. 1982 Turkus, Burton B
d. 1983 Conrad, Michael
d. 1983 Wibberley, Leonard Patrick O'Connor
d. 1986 Crothers, Scatman
d. 1988 Barragan, Luis
d. 1988 Dart, Raymond Arthur
d. 1989 Arias, Roberto Emilio
d. 1989 Beck, C(harles) C(larence)
d. 1992 Holloway, Sterling Price
d. 1993 Stern, James
d. 1996 Blanton, (Leonard) Ray
d. 1998 Hampton, Henry

November 23
b. 1221 Alfonso, X
b. 1632 Mabillon, Jean
b. 1715 Lemonnier, Pierre Charles
b. 1743 LaTour D'Auvergne, Theophile de
b. 1749 Rutledge, Edward
b. 1803 Weld, Theodore Dwight
b. 1804 Pierce, Franklin
b. 1816 Duyckinck, Evert Augustus
b. 1819 Whitney, Josiah Dwight
b. 1834 Thomson, James
b. 1837 Waals, Johannes Diderik van der
b. 1841 Croker, Boss
b. 1846 Schuch, Ernst von
b. 1859 Billy the Kid

b. 1860 Branting, Karl Hjalmar
b. 1862 Parker, Gilbert, Sir
b. 1872 Ward, Fannie
b. 1873 Ross, Donald James
b. 1876 Dufresne, Charles
b. 1876 Falla, Manuel de
b. 1878 King, Ernest Joseph
b. 1881 Enver Pasha
b. 1882 Reid, Helen Rogers
b. 1883 Orozco, Jose Clemente
b. 1884 Bolton, Guy Reginald
b. 1887 Karloff, Boris
b. 1889 Patch, Alexander M(c Carrell)
b. 1891 Rodchenko, Alexander Mikhailovich
b. 1892 Erte
b. 1893 Marx, Harpo
b. 1893 Schram, Emil
b. 1894 Folsom, Marion Bayard
b. 1896 Gottwald, Klement
b. 1897 Etting, Ruth
b. 1897 Smith, William
b. 1898 Brown, Rachel Fuller
b. 1898 Malinovsky, Rodion Yakovlevich
b. 1901 Gardiner, Muriel
b. 1902 Jory, Victor
b. 1907 Swanberg, William Andrew
b. 1913 Zolotow, Maurice
b. 1915 Dehner, John Forkum
b. 1920 Celan, Paul
b. 1923 Haughton, Billy
b. 1926 Duarte (Fuentes), Jose Napoleon
b. 1926 Hunter, Jeffrey
b. 1927 Chandler, Otis
b. 1928 Bock, Jerry
b. 1928 Yardley, George Harry
b. 1930 Brock, Bill
b. 1930 Kazmaier, Richard W, Jr.
b. 1931 Keen, Sam
b. 1932 Toye, Clive Roy
b. 1933 Penderecki, Krzysztof
b. 1934 Colwell, Rita R(ossi)
b. 1934 Hoad, Lew(is A.)
b. 1935 Volkov, Vladislav Nikolayevich
b. 1937 Kroll, Alexander S

b. 1940 Tiant, Luis Clemente
b. 1941 Nero, Franco
b. 1945 Anspach, Susan
b. 1947 Landesberg, Steve
b. 1950 Schumer, Charles E(llis)
b. 1954 Hornsby, Bruce
b. 1955 Landrieu, Mary L.
b. 1959 Caulfield, Maxwell
b. 1960 Roberts, Robin
d. 615 Columban, Saint
d. 1572 Bronzino, Il
d. 1572 Bronzino, Agnolo
d. 1585 Tallis, Thomas
d. 1616 Hakluyt, Richard
d. 1763 Prevost d'Exiles, Antoine Francois, Abbe
d. 1814 Gerry, Elbridge
d. 1817 Clairborne, William Charles Coles
d. 1864 Struve, Friedrich Georg Wilhelm von
d. 1866 Gavarni, Paul
d. 1903 Ayer, Harriet Hubbard
d. 1907 Peto, John Frederick
d. 1910 Chanute, Octave
d. 1910 Crippen, Hawley Harvey
d. 1916 Booth, Charles
d. 1916 Napravnik, Eduard
d. 1928 Ryan, Thomas Fortune
d. 1932 Pitt, Percy
d. 1934 Budge, Ernest Alfred Thompson Wallis, Sir
d. 1934 Pinero, Arthur Wing, Sir
d. 1937 Bose, Jagadis Chandra, Sir
d. 1939 Bodanzky, Artur
d. 1940 Jones, Billy
d. 1943 Ray, Charles
d. 1943 Ullstein, Hermann
d. 1946 Dove, Arthur Garfield
d. 1948 Wilson, Hack
d. 1958 McCulley, Johnston
d. 1958 Moeller, Philip
d. 1964 Buttenheim, Edgar Joseph
d. 1968 Bea, Augustinus
d. 1969 Lewis, Dominic Bevan Wyndham
d. 1970 Ishak, Yusof bin
d. 1972 Wilson, Marie (Katherine Elizabeth)
d. 1973 Talmadge, Constance

d. 1973 Tourel, Jennie
d. 1974 Hayakawa, Sessue (Kintaro)
d. 1974 Ryan, Cornelius John
d. 1976 Malraux, Andre Georges
d. 1976 Price, Irving L
d. 1979 Oberon, Merle
d. 1979 Rovere, Richard Halworth
d. 1980 Binns, Joseph Patterson
d. 1980 Pennington, John Selman
d. 1983 Putch, William Henry
d. 1986 Huie, William Bradford
d. 1989 Janis, Sidney
d. 1990 Dahl, Roald
d. 1991 Kinski, Klaus
d. 1992 Acuff, Roy (Claxton)
d. 1994 Hawkins, Erick
d. 1995 Collins, John F(rederick)
d. 1995 Malle, Louis
d. 1995 Walker, Junior
d. 1996 Shah, Indries
d. 1997 Hutchence, Michael
d. 1997 Mas Canosa, Jorge
d. 1999 Little, Robert Langdon

November 24
b. 1632 Spinoza, Baruch (Benedictus de)
b. 1713 Sterne, Laurence
b. 1784 Taylor, Zachary
b. 1818 Agnew, David Hayes
b. 1821 Buckle, Henry Thomas
b. 1826 Collodi, Carlo
b. 1828 Sala, George Augustus
b. 1848 Lehmann, Lilli
b. 1849 Burnett, Frances Eliza Hodgson
b. 1853 Masterson, Bat
b. 1857 Ball, Frank
b. 1859 Gilbert, Cass
b. 1863 Conklin, Edwin Grant
b. 1864 Toulouse-Lautrec (Monfa), (Henri Marie Raymond de)
b. 1868 Joplin, Scott
b. 1876 Griffin, Walter Burley
b. 1877 Barkley, Alben William
b. 1883 Hooper, Tom
b. 1885 Strong, Anna Louise
b. 1886 Anderson, Margaret (Carolyn)
b. 1888 Carnegie, Dale
b. 1888 Huebner, Clarence R
b. 1889 Nesbitt, Cathleen Mary

b. 1889 Shazar, Zalman
b. 1890 Stratemeyer, George E, General
b. 1891 Ospina Perez, Mariano
b. 1895 Maison, Rene
b. 1896 Griffith, Corinne
b. 1897 Luciano, Lucky
b. 1899 Morehouse, Ward
b. 1902 Vanderbilt, William Henry
b. 1903 Popper, Hans
b. 1904 Powell, Dick
b. 1904 Rogell, Billy
b. 1905 Wicker, Ireene Seaton
b. 1907 Maclaughlin, Don
b. 1907 Ullman, James Ramsey
b. 1908 Kemelman, Harry
b. 1909 Gerstenberg, Richard Charles
b. 1910 Fitzgerald, Pegeen
b. 1911 Grant, Kirby
b. 1912 Kanin, Garson
b. 1912 Wilson, Teddy
b. 1914 Chadwick, Lynn Russell
b. 1914 DiMaggio, Joe
b. 1914 Fitzgerald, Geraldine
b. 1916 Ackerman, Forest J
b. 1917 Duff, Howard
b. 1918 Sandburg, Helga
b. 1920 Zumwalt, Elmo R(ussell), Jr.
b. 1921 Lindsay, John Vliet
b. 1923 Meredith, Scott
b. 1925 Buckley, William Frank, Jr.
b. 1925 Cohn, Al
b. 1925 Meer, Simon van der
b. 1925 Van der Meer, Simon
b. 1926 Lee, Tsung-Dao
b. 1927 Diemer, Emma Lou
b. 1929 Johnson, John Henry
b. 1929 Moscone, George Richard
b. 1930 Friend, Bob
b. 1930 Wolsky, Albert
b. 1934 Charnin, Martin
b. 1934 Schnittke, Alfred
b. 1935 Dellums, Ronald Vernie
b. 1938 Robertson, Oscar Palmer
b. 1938 Starkweather, Charles
b. 1939 Northrup, Jim
b. 1940 Tagliabue, Paul John
b. 1941? Best, Peter

b. 1942 Fitzwater, Marlin
b. 1942 Thomas, Craig D
b. 1943 Williamson, Robin
b. 1944 Dreifus, Claudia
b. 1944 Glickman, Daniel R.
b. 1946 Bundy, Ted
b. 1950 Livingston, Stanley
d. 62? Persius
d. 1072 Alp Arslan
d. 1572 Knox, John
d. 1694 Talon, Jean
d. 1725 Scarlatti, Alessandro
d. 1801 Earle, Ralph
d. 1807 Brant, Joseph
d. 1848 Melbourne, William Lamb, Viscount
d. 1864 Silliman, Benjamin
d. 1870 Lautreamont, Comte de
d. 1889 Pendleton, George Hunt
d. 1890 Belmont, August
d. 1891 Lytton, Edward Robert Bulwer-Lytton, Earl
d. 1911 Dryden, John Fairfield
d. 1916 Maxim, Hiram Stevens, Sir
d. 1922 Childers, Erskine
d. 1929 Clemenceau, Georges Eugene Benjamin
d. 1940 Saionji, Kimmochi
d. 1946 Moholy-Nagy, Laszlo
d. 1948 Jarvis, Anna
d. 1958 Cecil, Edgar Algernon Robert
d. 1961 Chatterton, Ruth
d. 1961 Wenner-Gren, Axel (Lenard)
d. 1963 Ostenso, Martha
d. 1963 Oswald, Lee Harvey
d. 1964 O'Dwyer, William
d. 1964 Schauffler, Robert Haven
d. 1965 Graham, Gwethalyn
d. 1972 Bentley, Doug(las Wagner)
d. 1972 Smallens, Alexander
d. 1974 Drake, Nick
d. 1976 Ward, Paul W
d. 1977 Smith, Mayo
d. 1980 Agar, Herbert Sebastian
d. 1980 Raft, George
d. 1981 Thornton, Charles Bates
d. 1985 Turner, Joe

d. 1987 Benoit, Jehane
d. 1988 Seefried, Irmgard Maria Theresia
d. 1990 Smith, Dodie
d. 1991 Furst, Anton
d. 1991 Mercury, Freddie
d. 1993 Collins, Albert
d. 1993 Gres, Alix
d. 1994 Shapp, Milton J(errold)

November 25
b. 1562 Lope de Vega
b. 1712 Epee, Charles-Michel
b. 1729 Suvorov, Aleksandr V
b. 1752 Reichardt, Johann Friedrich
b. 1760 Babeuf, Francois-Noel
b. 1775 Kemble, Charles
b. 1778 Lancaster, Joseph
b. 1793 Havell, Robert, Jr.
b. 1816 Rutherfurd, Lewis Morris
b. 1817 Bigelow, John
b. 1835 Carnegie, Andrew
b. 1842 Visscher, William Lightfoot
b. 1844 Benz, Karl Friedrich
b. 1846 Nation, Carry A(melia Moore)
b. 1856 Taneyev, Sergey Ivanovich
b. 1860 Perry, Bliss
b. 1862 Nevin, Ethelbert Woodbridge
b. 1869 Lindsey, Benjamin Barr
b. 1870 Denis, Maurice
b. 1871 Ames, Winthrop
b. 1874 Gans, Joe
b. 1874 Spence, Lewis
b. 1877 Granville-Barker, Harley
b. 1878 Kaiser, Georg
b. 1880 Flynn, John
b. 1880 Woolf, Leonard Sidney
b. 1881 John, XXIII
b. 1881 John XXIII
b. 1884 Cadogan, Alexander George Montague, Sir
b. 1887 Vavilov, Nikolai Ivanovich
b. 1890 Rosenberg, Issac
b. 1893 Krutch, Joseph Wood
b. 1894 Stallings, Laurence
b. 1895 Kempff, (Wilhelm) Walter Friedrich
b. 1895 Mikoyan, Anastas Ivanovich

b. 1895 Santmyer, Helen Hooven
b. 1895 Svoboda, Ludvik
b. 1896 Thomson, Virgil Garnett
b. 1899 Burnett, W(illiam) R(iley)
b. 1900 Douglas, Helen Mary Gahagan
b. 1900 Hoess, Rudolf Franz
b. 1900 Schwartz, Arthur
b. 1902 Lapidus, Morris
b. 1902 Shore, Eddie
b. 1904 Landis, Jessie Royce
b. 1906 Jepson, Helen
b. 1911 Hogarth, Burne
b. 1912 Nikolais, Alwin
b. 1912 Sengstacke, John H(erman Henry)
b. 1912 Smith, Austin E(dward)
b. 1913 Thomas, Lewis
b. 1915 Pinochet Ugarte, Augusto
b. 1917 Chestnut, Harold
b. 1918 Opie, Peter Mason
b. 1919 Brodie, Steve
b. 1920 Montalban, Ricardo
b. 1922 Duggan, Maurice Noel
b. 1922 McCloskey, Robert James
b. 1923 Koivisto, Mauno Henrik
b. 1923 Wall, Art(hur Jonathan), Jr.
b. 1924 Desmond, Paul Breitenfeld
b. 1924 Markovic, Ante
b. 1924 Turnbull, Collin M(acmillan)
b. 1926 Drexler, Rosalyn
b. 1926 Schisgal, Murray Joseph
b. 1933 Crosby, Kathryn
b. 1933 Moore, Lenny
b. 1935 Berner, Robert A(rbuckle)
b. 1936 Brown, Trisha
b. 1937 Joseph, Stephen (Carl)
b. 1939 Delaney, Shelagh
b. 1939 Feldstein, Martin Stuart
b. 1940 Gibbs, Joe Jackson
b. 1943 Mortier, Gerard
b. 1945 Hagegard, Hakan
b. 1947 Larroquette, John (Bernard)
b. 1948 Niezabitowska, Malgorzata
b. 1951 Dent, Bucky
b. 1960 Grant, Amy

b. 1960 Kennedy, John F(itzgerald), Jr.
b. 1963 Kosar, Bernie, Jr.
b. 1966 Lattisaw, Stacy
d. 1456 Coeur, Jacques
d. 1560 Doria, Andrea
d. 1700 Van Cortlandt, Stephanus
d. 1748 Watts, Isaac
d. 1830 Rode, Jacques Pierre Joseph
d. 1841 Chantrey, Francis Legatt, Sir
d. 1854 Lockhart, John Gibson
d. 1857 Birney, James Gillespie
d. 1885 Hendricks, Thomas Andrews
d. 1928 Lummis, Charles Fletcher
d. 1937 Baylis, Lilian Mary
d. 1944 Landis Kenesaw, Mountain, Judge
d. 1946 Morgenthau, Henry
d. 1949 Robinson, Bill
d. 1950 Jensen, Johannes Vilhelm
d. 1954 Coffin, Henry Sloane
d. 1956 Dovzhenko, Alexander
d. 1957 Kyne, Peter Bernard
d. 1957 Rivera, Diego
d. 1958 Kettering, Charles Franklin
d. 1962 Walker, Stanley
d. 1967 Zadkine, Ossip
d. 1968 Sinclair, Upton Beall
d. 1968 Siple, Paul Allman
d. 1970 Madison, Helene
d. 1970 Mishima, Yukio
d. 1972 Coanda, Henri Marie
d. 1973 Harvey, Laurence
d. 1974 Lane, Rosemary
d. 1974 Thant, U
d. 1977 Carlson, Richard
d. 1979 Abrams, Harry Nathan
d. 1981 Albertson, Jack
d. 1982 Coote, Robert
d. 1982 Gray, Gordon
d. 1983 Baldwin, Billy
d. 1983 Dolin, Anton, Sir
d. 1984 Goldman, Sylvan N
d. 1985 Grigson, Geoffrey Edward Harvey
d. 1985 Podoloff, Maurice
d. 1985 Pusey, Merlo John

d. 1987 Washington, Harold
d. 1989 Cakobau, Ratu George, Sir
d. 1989 Diop, Birago
d. 1993 Burgess, Anthony
d. 1997 Banda, Hastings Kamuzu
d. 1998 Wilson, Flip

November 26
b. 1552 Sonjo
b. 1607 Harvard, John
b. 1726 Wolcott, Oliver, Sr.
b. 1761 Savage, Edward
b. 1792 Grimke, Sarah Moore
b. 1807 Mount, William Sidney
b. 1811 Tseng Kuo-fan
b. 1827 White, Ellen Gould Harmon
b. 1830 Tabor, Horace Austin Warner
b. 1832 Walker, Mary Edwards
b. 1857 Plekhanov, Georgi Valentinovich
b. 1858 Drexel, Mary Katherine
b. 1861 Fall, Albert Bacon
b. 1866 Duffy, Hugh
b. 1870 Knote, Heinrich
b. 1871 McIntyre, John Thomas
b. 1876 Carrier, Willis Haviland
b. 1889 Phillips, Harry Irving
b. 1891? Nichols, Anne
b. 1892 Brackett, Charles
b. 1892 Guyon, Joe
b. 1893 Vaughan, Harry Hawkins
b. 1894 Papanin, Ivan D
b. 1894 Wiener, Norbert
b. 1895 Wilson, William Griffith
b. 1897 Odria Amoretti, Manuel Apolinario
b. 1898 Ziegler, Karl
b. 1899 Hauptmann, Bruno Richard
b. 1901 Grosvenor, Melville Bell
b. 1904 Flood, Daniel J(ohn)
b. 1905 Williams, Emlyn
b. 1907 Dee, Frances
b. 1907 Patrick, Ruth
b. 1908 Forte, Charles, Sir
b. 1908 Spigelgass, Leonard
b. 1909 Gomez, Lefty
b. 1909 Ionesco, Eugene
b. 1910 Cusack, Cyril
b. 1910 Kahane, Melanie
b. 1911 Reshevsky, Samuel
b. 1912 Sevareid, Eric

b. 1915 Wild, Earl
b. 1917 Jergens, Adele
b. 1918 Aylwin
   (Azocar), Patricio
b. 1919 Pohl, Frederik
b. 1921 Gilot, Francoise
b. 1922 Schulz, Charles
   M(onroe)
b. 1924 Hoffman, Irwin
b. 1924 Segal, George
b. 1925 Hunt, Lois
b. 1925 Istomin, Eugene
   George
b. 1926 Butler, Michael
b. 1926 Lebowsky,
   Stanley Richard
b. 1929 Saint John,
   Betta
b. 1931 Perez Esquivel,
   Adolfo
b. 1933 Goulet, Robert
   Gerard
b. 1933 Pozsgay, Imre
b. 1935 Pringle,
   Laurence
b. 1937 Yegorov, Boris
   (Borisovitch)
b. 1938 Goldsmith,
   Judith Ann Becker
b. 1938 Little, Rich(ard
   Caruthers)
b. 1939 Turner, Tina
b. 1940 Kantrowitz,
   Arnie
b. 1941 Torborg,
   Jeff(rey Allen)
b. 1942 Cole, Olivia
b. 1942 Hauptman,
   William
b. 1943 Paltrow, Bruce
b. 1943 Stenerud, Jan
b. 1946 Hill, Norbert S.,
   Jr.
b. 1946 McVie, John
b. 1946 Shell, Art
b. 1947 Hebner, Richie
b. 1948 Blackburn,
   Elizabeth Helen
b. 1948 Sargent, Ben
b. 1952 Turnbull,
   Wendy
b. 1969 Kemp, Shawn
d. 1504 Isabella I
d. 1686 Steno, Nicolaus
d. 1801 Dolomieu,
   Deodat Guy Gratet de
d. 1807 Ellsworth,
   Oliver
d. 1836 McAdam, John
   Loudoun
d. 1857 Eichendorff,
   Joseph Karl Benedict
   Freiherr von
d. 1868 Black Kettle
d. 1882 LeClear,
   Thomas
d. 1883 Truth,
   Sojourner
d. 1892 Lavigerie,
   Charles Martel
   Allemand
d. 1896 Patmore,
   Coventry Kersey
   Dighton
d. 1915 Burpee,
   W(ashington) Atlee

d. 1917 Jameson,
   Leander Starr, Sir
d. 1926 Browning, John
   Moses
d. 1930 Sverdrup, Otto
d. 1932 MacDonald,
   J(ames) E(dward)
   H(ervey)
d. 1940 Andresen, Ivar
d. 1940 Harmsworth,
   Harold Sidney
d. 1943 Roberts,
   Charles George
   Douglas, Sir
d. 1954 Doak, Bill
d. 1954 Jones, Robert
   Edmond
d. 1956 Dorsey, Tommy
d. 1961 Bridges, Styles
d. 1963 Galli-Curci,
   Amelita
d. 1967 Warner, Albert
d. 1968 Zweig, Arnold
d. 1970 Davis,
   Benjamin Oliver, Sr.
d. 1971 Adonis, Joe
d. 1971 Young, Andrew
d. 1973 Haines, William
d. 1973 Whittaker,
   Charles Evans
d. 1974 Connolly, Cyril
   Vernon
d. 1976 Pitz, Henry
   Clarence
d. 1980 Roberts, Rachel
d. 1981 Euwe, Max
d. 1982 Harman, Hugh
d. 1984 Corena,
   Fernando
d. 1984 Lonergan,
   Bernard J F
d. 1987 Duncan-Sandys,
   Edwin, Lord
d. 1991 Andrews,
   Raymond
d. 1991 Heinemann,
   Edward H
d. 1991 Johnson, Bob
d. 1996 Rand, Paul
d. 1997 Henry,
   Marguerite
d. 1999 Haynie, Hugh
d. 1999 Montagu,
   (Montague Francis)
   Ashley

November 27
b. 1635 Maintenon,
   Francoise d'Aubigne,
   Marquise de
b. 1701 Celsius, Anders
b. 1746 Livingston,
   Robert R
b. 1798 Pretorius,
   Andries
b. 1809 Kemble, Fanny
b. 1843 Vanderbilt,
   Cornelius
b. 1848 Rowland, Henry
   Augustus
b. 1857 Sherrington,
   Charles Scott, Sir
b. 1870 Paasikivi, Juho
   Kusti
b. 1871 Giorgi,
   Giovanni

b. 1873 Christophers,
   S(amuel) Rickard, Sir
b. 1874 Beard, Charles
   Austin
b. 1874 Walter, Eugene
b. 1874 Weizmann,
   Chaim
b. 1875 Parsons, Elsie
   Clews
b. 1877 Anthony,
   Katharine Susan
b. 1878 Orpen, William
   Newneham, Sir
b. 1884 DeCreeft, Jose
b. 1889 Hatch, Carl A
b. 1891 Salinas (y
   Serrano), Pedro
b. 1894 Matsushita,
   Konosuke
b. 1897 Genovese, Vito
b. 1899 Abramson,
   Harold A(lexander)
b. 1900 Barzin, Leon
   Eugene
b. 1901 Husing, Ted
b. 1904 McNally, John
   Victor
b. 1906 Morton, Digby
b. 1906 Scheffer, Victor
   B(lanchard)
b. 1907 DeCamp,   •
   L(yon) Sprague
b. 1908 Howells,
   William White
b. 1909 Agee, James
   Rufus
b. 1912 Merrick, David
b. 1914 Begle, Edward
   G(riffith)
b. 1915 Adonias
   (Aguiar) Filho
b. 1915 Alessandro,
   Victor Nicholas
b. 1917 Smith, Bob
b. 1918 Beard, Dita
   Davis
b. 1921 Dubcek,
   Alexander
b. 1925 Boley, Forrest
   Irving
b. 1926 Thompson,
   Marshall
b. 1927 Rowling,
   Wallace Edward
b. 1927 Simon, William
   E(dward)
b. 1932 Aquino,
   Benigno Simeon, Jr.
b. 1934 Jenco,
   Lawrence M
b. 1937 Sheehy, Gail
   Henion
b. 1939 Giusti, Dave
b. 1940 Lee, Bruce
b. 1941 Rabbitt, Eddie
b. 1942 Carr, Henry
b. 1942 Hacker, Marilyn
b. 1942 Hendrix, Jimi
b. 1943 Sander, Jil
b. 1944 Leland, Mickey
b. 1952 Copps, Sheila
   Maureen
b. 1953 Grebenshikov,
   Boris
b. 1957 Kennedy,
   Caroline Bouvier

b. 1960 Nelson, Judd
b. 1964 Givens, Robin
b. 1976 White, Jaleel
d. 8BC Horace
d. 511 Clovis I
d. 1474 Dufay,
   Guillaume
d. 1570 Sansovino,
   Jacopo
d. 1628 Buckingham,
   1st Duke of
d. 1754 De Moivre,
   Abraham
d. 1852 Lovelace, Ada
   Byron
d. 1863 Davis, Sam(uel)
d. 1884 Elssler, Fanny
d. 1895 Dumas,
   Alexandre
d. 1901 Studebaker,
   Clement
d. 1922 Meynell, Alice
   Christina Gertrude
d. 1931 Bruce, David,
   Sir
d. 1934 Nelson, Baby
   Face
d. 1936 Zaharoff, Basil,
   Sir
d. 1948 Delaney, Jack
d. 1950 Braid, James
d. 1953 O'Neill, Eugene
   Gladstone
d. 1953 Powys,
   Theodore Francis
d. 1955 Honegger,
   Arthur
d. 1956 Kaempffert,
   Waldemar (Bernhard)
d. 1958 Rodzinski,
   Artur
d. 1959 Philipe, Gerard
d. 1960 Richberg,
   Donald R(andall)
d. 1971 Guyon, Joe
d. 1971 Pew, J(ohn)
   Howard
d. 1975 McWhirter,
   A(lan) Ross
d. 1976 Alessandro,
   Victor Nicholas
d. 1977 McClellan, John
   Little
d. 1978 Milk, Harvey
d. 1978 Moscone,
   George Richard
d. 1979 Cavanagh,
   Jerome Patrick
d. 1981 Lenya, Lotte
d. 1982 Gordon, Steve
d. 1983 Furman, Roger
d. 1984 Duke, Robin
   (Anthony Hare)
d. 1986 Fielding,
   Gabriel
d. 1986 Hemingway,
   Mary Welsh
d. 1987 Herman, Babe
d. 1988 Carradine, John
d. 1988 Morrison,
   Theodore
d. 1989 Hoving, Walter
d. 1991 Heath,
   Catherine
d. 1992 Nolan, Sidney,
   Sir

d. 1997 Knowles,
Malcolm Shepherd
d. 1997 Leonard, Buck
November 28
b. 1628 Bunyan, John
b. 1632 Lully, Jean-
Baptiste
b. 1681 Cavalier, Jean
b. 1729 Estaing, Charles
Henri Hector, Comte
d'
b. 1757 Blake, William
b. 1792 Cousin, Victor
b. 1805 Stephens, John
Lloyd
b. 1820 Engels,
Friedrich
b. 1829 Rubinstein,
Anton Gregorovitch
b. 1831 Mackay, John
William
b. 1832 Stephen, Leslie,
Sir
b. 1836 Martin, Homer
Dodge
b. 1853 White, Helen
Magill
b. 1854 Haberlandt,
Gottlieb
b. 1865 Winter, Alice
Vivian Ames
b. 1866 Bacon, Henry
b. 1866 Warfield, David
b. 1873 Ginzberg, Louis
b. 1880 Blok, Aleksandr
Aleksandrovich
b. 1881 Zweig, Stefan
b. 1887 Rohm, Ernst
b. 1888 Walker, Jack
b. 1889 Walker, Ralph
Thomas
b. 1893 Downey,
Fairfax Davis
b. 1894 Atkinson,
Brooks
b. 1894 Taggard,
Genevieve
b. 1895 Iturbi, Jose
b. 1896 Black, Frank J.
b. 1896 Griffith, Ernest
S(tacey)
b. 1900 Wigg, George
(Edward Cecil)
b. 1901 Havighurst,
Walter Edwin
b. 1901 Mountbatten,
Edwina
b. 1902 Leclerc,
Jacques-Philippe
b. 1904 Cherenkov,
Pavel Alekseyevich
b. 1904 Eastland, James
Oliver
b. 1904 Mili, Gjon
b. 1904 Mitford, Nancy
Freeman
b. 1907 Moravia,
Alberto
b. 1907 Picard, Henry
b. 1908 Levi-Strauss,
Claude Gustave
b. 1909 Bampton, Rose
Elizabeth
b. 1909 Bleeker, Sonia
b. 1912 Louis, Morris

b. 1914 Dodson, Owen
(Vincent)
b. 1915 Simonov,
Konstantin (Kirill)
Mikhailovich
b. 1916 Theriault, Yves
b. 1916 Tregaskis,
Richard William
b. 1924 Brutus, Dennis
Vincent
b. 1925 Grahame,
Gloria
b. 1926 Kops, Bernard
b. 1928 Costanza,
Midge
b. 1928 Okun, Arthur
Melvin
b. 1929 Gordy, Berry,
Jr.
b. 1931 Ungerer, Tomi
b. 1933 Lange, Hope
Elise Ross
b. 1935 Stow, (Julian)
Randolph
b. 1936 Gilligan, Carol
b. 1936 Hart, Gary
Warren
b. 1942 Warfield, Paul
Dryden
b. 1943 Newman,
Randy
b. 1944 Brown, Rita
Mae
b. 1947 Hasford, Jerry
Gustav
b. 1948 Lightman, Alan
(Paige)
b. 1949 Godunov,
Alexander
b. 1949 Shaffer, Paul
b. 1950 Harris, Ed
b. 1953 Mbuende, Kaire
(Munionganda)
b. 1958 Righetti, Dave
b. 1960 Galliano, John
b. 1963 Weiss, Walt(er
William, Jr.)
d. 1680 Bernini,
Giovanni Lorenzo
d. 1694 Basho
d. 1695 Wood, Anthony
d. 1698 Frontenac,
Louis de Buade de
d. 1708 Tournefort,
Joseph Pitton de
d. 1721 Cartouche,
Louis Dominique
d. 1785 Whipple,
William
d. 1794 Beccaria,
Cesare
d. 1794 Steuben,
Friedrich Wilhelm
Ludolf Gerhard
Augustin, Baron
d. 1859 Irving,
Washington
d. 1876 Baer, Karl Ernst
von
d. 1878 Lewes, George
Henry
d. 1900 Skinner,
Halcyon
d. 1914 Hittorf, Johann
Wilhelm
d. 1921 Abdu'l-Baha

d. 1932 Van Rooy,
Anton
d. 1933 Laughlin, James
Laurence
d. 1938 McDougall,
William
d. 1939 Naismith, James
A
d. 1945 Davis, Dwight
Filley
d. 1945 Fairfax,
Beatrice
d. 1947 Leclerc,
Jacques-Philippe
d. 1954 Fermi, Enrico
d. 1959 DeErdely,
Francis
d. 1960 Wright, Richard
(Nathaniel)
d. 1962 Wilhelmina
d. 1963 Silver, Abba
Hillel
d. 1963 Wrather,
William Embry
d. 1966 Giannini,
Vittorio
d. 1968 Blyton, Enid
Mary
d. 1969 Arguedas, Jose
Maria
d. 1972 Carmichael,
James Vinson
d. 1972 Zirato, Bruno
d. 1975 Cartier, Claude
d. 1975 Verissimo,
Erico Lopes
d. 1976 Russell,
Rosalind
d. 1979 Classen, Willie
d. 1979 Seagram,
Joseph Edward
Frowde
d. 1980 Ballantrae, Lord
d. 1980 Van Vleck,
John Hasbrouck
d. 1981 Gimbel, Sophie
Haas
d. 1984 Bell, Ricky
Lynn
d. 1984 Speidel, Hans
d. 1985 Brandel,
Fernand Paul
d. 1985 Gerasimov,
Sergei
Appolinarievich
d. 1985 McNally, John
Victor
d. 1987 Li, C(hoh)
H(ao)
d. 1993 Moore, Garry
d. 1994 Dahmer, Jeffrey
L
d. 1994 Enrique
Tarancon, Vicente,
Cardinal
d. 1994 Rubin, Jerry
d. 1994 Serraillier, Ian
Lucien
d. 1996 McCloskey,
Robert James
d. 1998 Fascell, Dante
B(runo)
November 29
b. 1627 Ray, John
b. 1781 Bello y Lopez,
Andres

b. 1797 Donizetti,
Gaetano
b. 1799 Alcott, Amos
Bronson
b. 1802 Hauff, Wilhelm
b. 1811 Phillips,
Wendell
b. 1816 Waite, Morrison
Remick
b. 1825 Charcot, Jean
Martin
b. 1832 Alcott, Louisa
May
b. 1835 Tz'u Hsi
b. 1849 Fleming, John
Ambrose, Sir
b. 1850 Scalchi, Sofia
b. 1870 Friganza, Trixie
b. 1872 Mildenburg,
Anna von
b. 1874 Egas Moniz,
Antonio C A F
b. 1876 Davies, Joseph
Edward
b. 1876 Ross, Nellie
Taylor
b. 1883 Hunter, Dard
b. 1895 Berkeley,
Busby
b. 1895 Canutt, Yakima
b. 1895 Rocca,
Lodovico
b. 1895 Tubman,
William Vacanarat
Shadrach
b. 1898 LaRocque, Rod
b. 1898 Lewis, C(live)
S(taples)
b. 1899 Artukovic,
Andrija
b. 1902 Levi, Carlo
b. 1902 Loughran,
Tommy
b. 1903 Autori, Franco
b. 1903 Rooney, John
(James)
b. 1905 Lefebvre,
Marcel Francois
b. 1907 Katz, Milton
b. 1908 Debus, Kurt
Heinrich
b. 1908 Powell, Adam
Clayton, Jr.
b. 1913 Guyer,
Tennyson
b. 1914 Du Bois, Raoul
Pene
b. 1914 McIntyre, Hal
b. 1915 Schonberg,
Harold C
b. 1915 Strayhorn, Billy
b. 1917 Travis, Merle
Robert
b. 1918 L'Engle,
Madeleine
b. 1919 Kermode,
(John) Frank
b. 1919 Primus, Pearl
b. 1920 Ligachev,
Yegor (Kuzmich)
b. 1922 Gibran, Kahlil
George
b. 1922 Minoso, Minnie
b. 1923 Reynolds, Frank
b. 1924 Freilicher, Jane
b. 1926 Dagmar

b. 1927 Scully, Vin(cent Edward)
b. 1928 Crosse, Rupert
b. 1928 Simon, Paul M(artin)
b. 1932 Chirac, Jacques (Rene)
b. 1932 Gary, John
b. 1932 Ladd, Diane
b. 1933 Mayall, John Brumwell
b. 1933 Rosenquist, James Albert
b. 1934 Morris, Willie
b. 1935 Pozzi, Lucio
b. 1936 Lee, Yuan Tseh
b. 1939 Gilder, George
b. 1939 McAuliffe, Dick
b. 1940 Mangione, Chuck
b. 1941 Freehan, Bill
b. 1942 Grillo, John
b. 1943 Bing, Dave
b. 1943 Galati, Frank
b. 1944 Cavaliere, Felix
b. 1946 Chaffee, Suzy
b. 1947 Kelly, Petra (Karin)
b. 1949 Shandling, Garry
b. 1955 Mandel, Howie
b. 1956 Baker, Bill
b. 1956 Cary, Lorene
b. 1957 Napolitano, Janet
b. 1959 Broten, Neal LaMoy
b. 1960 Moriarty, Cathy
b. 1963 Auguste, Rose-Anne
d. 1314 Philip, IV
d. 1378 Charles, IV
d. 1516 Bellini, Giovanni
d. 1530 Wolsey, Thomas, Cardinal
d. 1594 Ercilla y Zuniga, Alonso de
d. 1643 Monteverdi, Claudio
d. 1780 Maria Theresa
d. 1825 Hull, William
d. 1847 Whitman, Marcus
d. 1869 Grisi, Giulia
d. 1872 Greeley, Horace
d. 1878 Godey, Louis Antoine
d. 1892 Wyant, Alexander Helwig
d. 1894 Monck, Charles Stanley, Sir
d. 1924 Puccini, Giacomo
d. 1927 Savage, Henry Wilson
d. 1939 Scheidemann, Philipp
d. 1941 Papi, Genarro
d. 1943 Landes, Bertha Ethel
d. 1950 Beech, Walter Herschel
d. 1952 Capone, Teresa

d. 1953 Barnes, Ernest William
d. 1953 Gross, Milt
d. 1954 Johnson, Dink
d. 1954 Robey, George, Sir
d. 1957 Korngold, Erich Wolfgang
d. 1967 Panizza, Ettore
d. 1970 Ricci, Nina
d. 1971 Petersham, Maud
d. 1973 Apostoli, Fred
d. 1974 Braddock, Jim
d. 1974 Hunt, H(aroldson) L(afayette)
d. 1976 Cambridge, Godfrey
d. 1976 Lowry, Judith Ives
d. 1980 Day, Dorothy
d. 1981 Wood, Natalie
d. 1983 George, Christopher
d. 1984 Crankshaw, Edward
d. 1985 Keough, William Francis, Jr.
d. 1986 Grant, Cary
d. 1987 Pyle, Howard
d. 1988 Keyhoe, Donald E(dward)
d. 1989 Staupers, Mabel K.
d. 1991 Bellamy, Ralph
d. 1991 Finkelstein, Louis, Dr.
d. 1991 Yerby, Frank (Garvin)
d. 1992 Pucci, Emilio Marchese di Barsento
d. 1993 Tata, J(ehangir) R(atanji) D(adbhoy)
d. 1994 Griswold, Erwin N(athaniel)
d. 1994 Timmerman, George Bell, Jr.
d. 1997 Young, Coleman A(lexander)
d. 1999 Arciniegas, German
d. 1999 Rayburn, Gene

November 30
b. 538 Gregory of Tours, St.
b. 1466 Doria, Andrea
b. 1508 Palladio, Andrea
b. 1554 Sidney, Philip, Sir
b. 1667 Swift, Jonathan
b. 1670 Toland, John
b. 1729 Seabury, Samuel
b. 1802 Trendelenburg, Friedrich Adolf
b. 1803 Doppler, Christian Johann
b. 1805 Ballivian, Jose
b. 1809 Lemon, Mark
b. 1810 Winchester, Oliver Fisher
b. 1817 Mommsen, Theodor

b. 1819 Field, Cyrus West
b. 1835 Twain, Mark
b. 1858 Bose, Jagadis Chandra, Sir
b. 1858 Coolidge, Charles Allerton
b. 1863 Bonifacio, Andres
b. 1868 Newman, Ernest
b. 1869 Dalen, Nils Gustaf
b. 1872 McCrae, John
b. 1874 Churchill, Winston Leonard Spencer, Sir
b. 1874 Montgomery, Lucy Maud
b. 1880 Tawney, Richard Henry
b. 1884 Poling, Daniel A
b. 1886 Struss, Karl
b. 1888 LeTourneau, Robert Gilmour
b. 1889 Adrian, Edgar Douglas, Baron
b. 1894 Stewart, Donald Ogden
b. 1898 Lyman, Link
b. 1898 Lynch, Joe
b. 1900 Household, Geoffrey Edward West
b. 1900 Lasker, Mary (Woodward)
b. 1903 Gres, Alix
b. 1906 Carr, John Dickson
b. 1907 Barzun, Jacques Martin
b. 1911 Schriner, Sweeney
b. 1915 Duke, Angier Biddle
b. 1915 Taube, Henry
b. 1919 Wright, Jane Cooke
b. 1920 Mayo, Virginia
b. 1923 Gowans, Alan
b. 1923 Zimbalist, Efrem, Jr.
b. 1924 Chisholm, Shirley Anita St. Hill
b. 1924 Sherman, Allan
b. 1926 Schally, Andrew Victor
b. 1927 Crenna, Richard
b. 1927 Guillaume, Robert
b. 1928 Doi, Takako
b. 1928 Hall, Joe Beasman
b. 1928 Hecht, Chic
b. 1928 Scott, Norman
b. 1929 Clark, Dick
b. 1929 Cooney, Joan Ganz
b. 1929 Wyman, Thomas Hunt
b. 1930 Liddy, G(eorge) Gordon
b. 1931 Walsh, Bill
b. 1933 Proctor, Barbara Gardner

b. 1935 Sachs, Samuel, II
b. 1936 Hoffman, Abbie
b. 1937 Chaudhari, Praveen
b. 1937 Threlkeld, Richard D
b. 1939 Keyworth, George Albert
b. 1940 Phillips, Kevin (Price)
b. 1943 Malick, Terence
b. 1945 Hair, Jay D(ee)
b. 1945 Lupu, Radu
b. 1947 Mamet, David Alan
b. 1950 Westphal, Paul Douglas
b. 1952 Patinkin, Mandy
b. 1953 Espy, Mike
b. 1954 Pointer, June
b. 1955 Idol, Billy
b. 1956? Goodman, Robert O, Jr.
b. 1957 McIlwee, Thomas
b. 1959 Hanika, Sylvia
b. 1962 Jackson, Bo
b. 1965 Stiller, Ben
b. 406BC Euripides
d. 70? Andrew, Saint
d. 1654 Selden, John
d. 1694 Malpighi, Marcello
d. 1718 Charles XII
d. 1750 Saxe, Maurice
d. 1786 Galvez, Bernardo de
d. 1846 List, Georg Friedrich
d. 1852 Booth, Junius Brutus
d. 1852 Phelps, Elizabeth Stuart Ward
d. 1862 Knowles, James Sheridan
d. 1863 Kamehameha IV
d. 1894 Brown, Joseph Emerson
d. 1896 Steinway, Henry Engelhard
d. 1900 Wilde, Oscar (Fingal O'Flahertie Wills)
d. 1901 Eyre, Edward John
d. 1930 Jones, Mary Harris
d. 1931 Walters, Henry
d. 1932 Melchers, Gari
d. 1933 Currie, Arthur William
d. 1938 Kun, Bela
d. 1942 Jones, Buck
d. 1944 Fall, Albert Bacon
d. 1945 Ficke, Arthur Davidson
d. 1947 Lubitsch, Ernst
d. 1952 Kenny, Sister Elizabeth
d. 1953 Picabia, Francis
d. 1954 Furtwangler, Wilhelm

d. 1956 Schwartz, Jean
d. 1957 Gigli, Beniamino
d. 1961 Zemurray, Samuel
d. 1963 Baker, Phil
d. 1963 Hatlo, Jimmy
d. 1964 Redman, Don
d. 1967 Kavanagh, Patrick
d. 1972 Mackenzie, Compton
d. 1972 McElroy, Neil Hosler
d. 1973 Yarnell, Bruce
d. 1975 Hill, Graham
d. 1977 Rattigan, Terence Mervyn, Sir
d. 1979 Gilpin, Laura
d. 1979 Grenfell, Joyce Irene
d. 1979 Kuter, Laurence S(herman)
d. 1979 Marx, Zeppo
d. 1981 Gielgud, Val Henry
d. 1982 Merrill, Henry Tindall
d. 1983 Llewellyn, Richard
d. 1986 Swigert, Ernest Goodnough
d. 1987 Baldwin, James (Arthur)
d. 1987 Dean, Arthur H(obson)
d. 1989 Ahidjo, Ahmadou
d. 1990 Cousins, Norman
d. 1990 Eichenberg, Fritz
d. 1992 Blume, Peter
d. 1994 Stander, Lionel (Jay)
d. 1996 Tiny Tim
d. 1998 Lewis, Janet

DECEMBER

b. 1594 Cuyp, Jacob Gerritsz(oon)
b. 1639 Racine, Jean Baptiste
b. 1723 Holbach, Baron d'
b. 1841 Edmonds, Emma E
b. 1844 Coffin, Charles Albert
b. 1849 Schechter, Solomon
b. 1873 Mantle, (Robert) Burns
b. 1875 Wallace, Edgar
b. 1877 Nomura, Kichisaburo
b. 1895 Danquah, Joseph (Kwame Kyeretwi) B(oakye)
b. 1898 Gidlow, Elsa
b. 1899 Ulreich, Nura Woodson
b. 1915 Piaf, Edith

b. 1932 Diggs-Taylor, Anna
b. 1947 De Lucia, Paco
b. 1948 Bangs, Lester
b. 1951 Tolliver, William (Mack)
b. 1962 Turner, Janine
b. 1965 Witt, Katarina
d. 1556 Pontormo, Jacopo da
d. 1556 Udall, Nicholas
d. 1608 Dee, John
d. 1610 Elsheimer, Adam
d. 1635 Mason, John
d. 1879 Stewart, Maria W. Miller
d. 1923 Barres, (Auguste) Maurice
d. 1943 Miller, Dorie
d. 1950 Burch, Billy
d. 1972 Bond, Horace Mann
d. 1973 O'Shea, Michael
d. 1977 McNickle, D'Arcy
d. 1978 Dent, Alan Holmes
d. 1978 Winston, Harry
d. 1988 Rees, Lloyd Frederic
d. 1988 Richards, Richard
d. 1996 Kabua, Amata

December 1
b. 1580 Peiresc, Nicholas-Claude Fabri de
b. 1716 Falconet, Etienne Maurice
b. 1729 Sarti, Giuseppe
b. 1765 Brown, William Hill
b. 1766 Karamzin, Nikolai Mikhailovich
b. 1784 Castil-Blaze, Francois-Joseph
b. 1810 Gungl, Joseph
b. 1823 Reyer, (Louis) Ernest (Etienne)
b. 1826 Mahone, William
b. 1833 Andrews, Jane
b. 1844 Alexandra Caroline Mary Charlotte
b. 1847 Ladd-Franklin, Christine
b. 1847 Moore, Julia A Davis
b. 1854 Vinogradoff, Paul Gavrilovitch
b. 1863 Herford, Oliver
b. 1869 Sterling, George
b. 1872 Swope, Gerard
b. 1873 Chernov, Viktor Mikhailovich
b. 1875 Mqhayi, S(amuel) E(dward) K(rune Loliwe)
b. 1876 Creel, George Edward
b. 1877 Beach, Rex Ellingwood
b. 1879 Bryant, Lane

b. 1884 Schmidt-Rottluf, Karl
b. 1885 Hunt, Frazier
b. 1886 Stout, Rex Todhunter
b. 1893 Toller, Ernst
b. 1896 Henderson, Ray
b. 1896 Shutta, Ethel
b. 1897 Ritchard, Cyril
b. 1899 Briggs, Ellis O(rmsbee)
b. 1899 Welch, Robert Henry Winborne, Jr.
b. 1901 Moore, Grace
b. 1902 Crittenden, Christopher
b. 1904 Boyle, Tony
b. 1906 Sommers, Ben
b. 1910 Markova, Alicia, Dame
b. 1911 Alston, Walter Emmons
b. 1912 Yamasaki, Minoru
b. 1913 Martin, Mary
b. 1915 Johnston, Johnny
b. 1916 Stoutenburg, Adrien Pearl
b. 1917 Marion, Marty
b. 1919 Chambers, Anne Cox
b. 1919 Gilbert, Alfred Carlton, Jr.
b. 1920 Rohmer, Eric
b. 1923 Turner, Stansfield
b. 1926 McLerie, Allyn Ann
b. 1926 Rakowski, Mieczyslaw Franciszek
b. 1927 Beard, Ralph Milton
b. 1927 Mann, Abby
b. 1928 Michell, Keith
b. 1929 Doyle, David (Fitzgerald)
b. 1929 Shawn, Dick
b. 1931 Sovern, Michael I(ra)
b. 1933 Verdy, Violette
b. 1933 Wolfensohn, James David
b. 1935 Allen, Woody
b. 1935 Goody, Joan
b. 1936 Rawls, Lou(is Allen)
b. 1939? Lennon, Dianne
b. 1939 Trevino, Lee Buck
b. 1940 Pryor, Richard (Franklin Lennox Thomas)
b. 1942 Kalikow, Peter Stephen
b. 1944 Bloom, Eric
b. 1945 Densmore, John
b. 1945 Midler, Bette
b. 1946 O'Sullivan, Gilbert
b. 1947 Shanley, Kathryn W.
b. 1949 Brett, Jan Churchill

b. 1949 Foster, George Arthur
b. 1949 Schmoke, Kurt L(idell)
b. 1951 Pastorius, Jaco
b. 1951 Williams, Treat
b. 1957 Bissell, Patrick
b. 1958? Tilton, Charlene
b. 1960 Alt, Carol
d. 1135 Henry I
d. 1455 Ghiberti, Lorenzo
d. 1521 Leo, X
d. 1701 Clarke, Jeremiah
d. 1797 Wolcott, Oliver, Sr.
d. 1825 Alexander I
d. 1849 Elliott, Ebenezer
d. 1866 Everest, George, Sir
d. 1914 Mahan, Alfred Thayer
d. 1920 Rebikov, Vladimir Ivanovich
d. 1934 Kirov, Sergei Mironovich
d. 1935 Mayr, Richard
d. 1940 Richman, Charles
d. 1947 Crowley, Aleister (Edward Alexander)
d. 1947 Hardy, Godfrey Harold
d. 1948 Noyes, Frank B(rett)
d. 1952 Orlando, Vittorio Emanuele
d. 1954 Rose, Fred
d. 1958 Wilkins, George Hubert, Sir
d. 1964 Haldane, J(ohn) B(urdon) S(anderson)
d. 1970 Pool, David de Sola
d. 1971 Spingarn, Arthur Barnett
d. 1972 Segni, Antonio
d. 1973 Ben-Gurion, David
d. 1974 Lincoln, G(eorge) Gould
d. 1974 Spottswood, Stephen Gill
d. 1975 Fox, Nellie
d. 1975 Kenny, Nick
d. 1975 Mayer, Edward Newton, Jr.
d. 1975 Roosevelt, Anna Eleanor
d. 1980 Coulter, John William
d. 1980 Irvin, Robert W
d. 1986 Heidt, Horace Murray
d. 1986 Layne, Bobby
d. 1986 McCarthy, Frank
d. 1987 Imlach, Punch
d. 1989 Ailey, Alvin
d. 1990 Markert, Russell

d. 1990 Pandit, Vijaya Lakshmi (Nehru)
d. 1991 Stigler, George Joseph
d. 1995 Chalk, O(scar) Roy
d. 1996 Karmal, Babrak
d. 1997 Grappelli, Stephane
d. 1999 Byrd, Charlie
d. 1999 Gates, Pop

December 2
b. 1694 Shirley, William
b. 1728 Galiani, Ferdinando
b. 1736 Montgomery, Richard
b. 1760 Breckinridge, John
b. 1792 Lobachevskii, Nikolai Ivanovich
b. 1817 Marmol, Jose
b. 1825 Pedro II
b. 1840 Cobden-Sanderson, Thomas James
b. 1859 Seurat, Georges Pierre
b. 1863 Ringling, Charles
b. 1866 Burleigh, Harry Thacker
b. 1868 Jammes, Francis
b. 1878 Candler, Charles Howard
b. 1883 Kazantzakis, Nikos
b. 1884 Draper, Ruth
b. 1885 Minot, George Richards
b. 1889 Althouse, Paul Shearer
b. 1891 Dix, Otto
b. 1891 Merida, Carlos
b. 1891 Wesley, Charles Harris
b. 1893 Gaxton, William
b. 1895 William, Warren
b. 1896 Zhukov, Georgi Konstantinovich
b. 1897 Alley, Rewi
b. 1897 Bagramian, Ivan Christofovorich
b. 1897 Hoving, Walter
b. 1899 Adler, Peter Herman
b. 1899 Barbirolli, John, Sir
b. 1899 Benary-Isbert, Margot
b. 1899 Cobb, John Rhodes
b. 1902 Bernhard, Arnold
b. 1902 Hildreth, Horace A(ugusta)
b. 1904 Woods, Donald
b. 1906 Goldmark, Peter Carl
b. 1906 Harrar, J(acob) George
b. 1908 Gardner, Hy

b. 1909 Lash, Joseph P
b. 1910 Lynes, Joseph Russell, Jr.
b. 1910 Paige, Robert (John Arthur)
b. 1912 Sukman, Harry
b. 1914 Sauter, Eddie
b. 1915 Gentry, Minnie Lee
b. 1915 Green, Adolf
b. 1915 Hearst, Randolph Apperson
b. 1916 Bentley, John
b. 1916 Hearst, David W(hitmire)
b. 1916 Ventura, Charlie
b. 1916 Williams, Carroll Milton
b. 1917 Stone, Ezra (Chaim)
b. 1917 Syms, Sylvia
b. 1918 DeLugg, Milton
b. 1921 Karle, Isabella (L.)
b. 1922 Diggs, Charles C(oles), Jr.
b. 1923 Riklis, Meshulam
b. 1924 Haig, Alexander Meigs, Jr.
b. 1925 Harris, Julie
b. 1928 Demus, Joreg
b. 1929 Phillips, Harvey Gene
b. 1930 Becker, Gary S(tanley)
b. 1930 Silkin, Jon
b. 1931 Calder, Nigel David Ritchie
b. 1931 Meese, Edwin, III
b. 1934 Bok, Sissela
b. 1935 Sample, Bill
b. 1937 Dumas, Charles
b. 1937 Zah, Peterson
b. 1938 Valerio, James Robert
b. 1939 Reid, Harry
b. 1940 Brown, Willie
b. 1940 Chapin, Dwight Lee
b. 1941 Chu, Paul C W
b. 1943 Allard, Wayne
b. 1945 Watson, Charles
b. 1946 Versace, Gianni
b. 1947 Scharping, Rudolf
b. 1948 Boyle, T. Coraghessan
b. 1949 Crosby, Cathy Lee
b. 1950 Ashley, Merrill
b. 1952 McDonald, Michael
b. 1952 Roberts, Steven K
b. 1955 Christopher, Dennis
b. 1958 Gardner, Randy
b. 1960 Moore, Julianne
b. 1960 Savage, Rick
b. 1973 Seles, Monica
d. 1594 Mercator, Gerhardus
d. 1694 Puget, Pierre

d. 1723 Orleans, Philippe II d'
d. 1812? Sacagawea
d. 1814 Sade, Marquis (Donatien Alphonse Francoise) de
d. 1859 Brown, John
d. 1860 Baur, Ferdinand Christian
d. 1863 Pierce, Jane (Means)
d. 1892 Gould, Jay
d. 1893 A.L.O.E.
d. 1893 Cushman, Pauline
d. 1894 Thompson, John S(parrow) D(avid), Sir
d. 1918 Rostand, Edmond Alexis
d. 1919 Frick, Henry Clay
d. 1921 Lincoln, Mary Johnson Bailey
d. 1931 Indy, Paul (Marie Theodore Vincent d')
d. 1933 Breasted, James Henry
d. 1935 Thomas, Martha Carey
d. 1937 Smith, Joe
d. 1939 Powys, Llewelyn
d. 1940 Revel, Bernard
d. 1941 Merezhkovsky, Dmitry Sergeyevich
d. 1943 Dashwood, Elizabeth Monica
d. 1943 Grieg, Nordahl Brun
d. 1944 Lhevinne, Josef
d. 1944 Marinetti, Filippo Tommaso Emilio
d. 1949 Ammons, Albert C
d. 1950 Lipatti, Dinu
d. 1963 Sabu
d. 1964 York, Sergeant
d. 1966 Cooper, Giles (Stannus)
d. 1967 Spellman, Francis Joseph
d. 1969 Potter, Stephen
d. 1969 Voroshilov, Kliment Efremovich
d. 1972 Limon, Jose Arcadio
d. 1973 Haydn, Hiram Collins
d. 1975 Maserati, Ernesto
d. 1978 Dickinson, Edwin W
d. 1980 Gary, Romain
d. 1980 Gordon-Walker of Leyton, Patrick Chrestien Gordon-Walker, Baron
d. 1980 Mosley, Oswald Ernald, Sir
d. 1981 Harrison, Wallace Kirkman
d. 1981 Kay, Hershy

d. 1981 Oliver, James A(rthur)
d. 1982 Bugas, John Stephen
d. 1982 Feldman, Marty
d. 1982 Sackheim, Maxwell Byron
d. 1983 D'Orsay, Fifi
d. 1984 Hauser, Gayelord
d. 1984 Sukman, Harry
d. 1985 Larkin, Philip Arthur
d. 1986 Arnaz, Desi
d. 1987 Eisele, Donn Fulton
d. 1987 Leloir, Luis Federico
d. 1990 Copland, Aaron
d. 1990 Cummings, Bob
d. 1995 Davies, (William) Robertson
d. 1995 Roker, Roxie
d. 1995 Telkes, Maria (de)
d. 1997 Hedges, Michael
d. 1998 Haggart, Bob
d. 1999 Adams, Joey

December 3
b. 1368 Charles, VI
b. 1478 Castiglione, Baldassare, Conte
b. 1596 Amati, Nicolo
b. 1755 Stuart, Gilbert Charles
b. 1764 Lamb, Mary Ann
b. 1766 Bloomfield, Robert
b. 1795 Hill, Rowland, Sir
b. 1807 Bailey, Gamaliel
b. 1826 McClellan, George Brinton
b. 1833 Finlay, Carlos Juan
b. 1838 Abbe, Cleveland
b. 1842 Pillsbury, Charles Alfred
b. 1842 Richards, Ellen Henrietta Swallow
b. 1845 Bradley, Henry
b. 1857 Conrad, Joseph
b. 1860 Moore, John Bassett
b. 1873 Kent, Arthur Atwater
b. 1874 Lhevinne, Josef
b. 1879 Nagai, Sokichi
b. 1883 Webern, Anton Friedrich Ernst von
b. 1884 Prasad, Rajendra
b. 1885 Lasker, Edward
b. 1886 Siegbahn, Karl Manne Georg
b. 1889 Bern, Paul
b. 1892 Adler, Julius Ochs
b. 1895 Freud, Anna
b. 1897 Gropper, William

b. 1900 Daugherty, Carroll Roop
b. 1900 Kuhn, Richard
b. 1903 Fuchida, Mitsuo
b. 1903 Holifield, Chet
b. 1903 Von Neumann, John
b. 1905 Murphy, Thomas F(rancis)
b. 1907 Boswell, Connee
b. 1907 McNeill, Don(ald Thomas)
b. 1908 Balchin, Nigel Marlin
b. 1911 Suesse, Dana Nadine
b. 1913 Lichine, Alexis
b. 1914 Parks, Larry
b. 1915 Hodgson, James Day
b. 1920 Canfield, Francis X(avier)
b. 1921 Doar, John Michael
b. 1922 Grunwald, Henry Anatole
b. 1922 Nykvist, Sven Vilhem
b. 1923 Callas, Maria
b. 1923 Fears, Tom
b. 1923 Guarrera, Frank
b. 1923 Keller, George Matthew
b. 1924 Backus, John
b. 1925 Olson, James E(lias)
b. 1927 Curtin, Phyllis Smith
b. 1927 Hall, Adrian
b. 1927 Husky, Ferlin
b. 1927 Wiggins, Charles Edward
b. 1930 Godard, Jean Luc
b. 1930 Williams, Andy
b. 1932 Morgan, Jaye P
b. 1934 Syms, Sylvia
b. 1935 Johnson, Eddie Bernice
b. 1935 Wu, Gordon (Ying Sheung)
b. 1937 Allison, Bobby
b. 1938 Martin, John
b. 1940 Swift, Elizabeth Ann
b. 1941 Mary Alice
b. 1945 Dean, Laura
b. 1947 Krenwinkel, Patricia
b. 1948 Osbourne, Ozzy
b. 1951 Juantorena, Alberto
b. 1951 Mears, Rick Ravon
b. 1952 Roland, Duane
b. 1956 Bochner, Hart
b. 1957 Jordan, Kathy
b. 1960 Hannah, Daryl
b. 1960 Ramsey, Mike
b. 1981 Filipovic, Zlata
d. 1533 Vasily III
d. 1592 Farnese, Alessandro
d. 1753 Burlington, Richard Boyle, Earl

d. 1815 Carroll, John
d. 1854 Ritchie, Thomas
d. 1888 Zeiss, Carl
d. 1894 Stevenson, Robert Louis (Balfour)
d. 1905 Bartlett, John
d. 1910 Eddy, Mary Baker Morse
d. 1910 Merritt, Wesley
d. 1920 Abney, William de Wiveleslie, Sir
d. 1926 Ringling, Charles
d. 1937 Jozsef, Attila
d. 1940 Gordon, C Henry
d. 1941 Sinding, Christian
d. 1949 Barry, Philip
d. 1949 Ouspenskaya, Maria
d. 1952 Slansky, Rudolf Salzmann
d. 1956 Rodchenko, Alexander Mikhailovich
d. 1957 Gannett, Frank Ernest
d. 1963 Bentley, Elizabeth Terrill
d. 1978 Still, William Grant
d. 1981 Knott, Walter
d. 1983 Zablocki, Clement John
d. 1993 Glaser, Elizabeth
d. 1993 Thomas, Lewis
d. 1999 Kahn, Madeline (Gail)

December 4
b. 34? Persius
b. 1584 Cotton, John
b. 1730 Moultrie, William
b. 1777 Recamier, Julie, Madame
b. 1795 Carlyle, Thomas
b. 1835 Butler, Samuel
b. 1858 Greenwood, Chester
b. 1860 Hormel, George Albert
b. 1861 Russell, Lillian
b. 1865 Cavell, Edith Louisa
b. 1865 Gulick, Luther (Halsey)
b. 1866 Kandinsky, Wassily
b. 1876 Rilke, Rainer Maria
b. 1880 Wood, Gar(field A)
b. 1881 Cadman, Charles Wakefield
b. 1882 Reulbach, Ed(ward Marvin)
b. 1883 Bellison, Simeon
b. 1885 Magnin, Grover Arnold
b. 1890 Darragh, Jack
b. 1891 Jones, Buck

b. 1892 Franco, Francisco
b. 1893 Read, Herbert, Sir
b. 1894 Soong, T V
b. 1895 Townsend, Willard Saxby
b. 1897 Redfield, Robert
b. 1903 Merrill, Frank Dow
b. 1903 Rowse, A(lfred) L(eslie)
b. 1903 Wiggins, J(ames) R(ussell)
b. 1903 Woolrich, Cornell
b. 1904 Holt, A(ndrew) D(avid, Jr.)
b. 1905 Leaf, Munro
b. 1908 Hershey, Alfred D(ay)
b. 1910 North, Alex
b. 1910 Venkataraman, Ramaswamy
b. 1911 Payne, Robert
b. 1912 Boyington, Pappy
b. 1915 Heywood, Eddie, Jr.
b. 1916 Kahn, E(ly) J(acques), Jr.
b. 1921 Durbin, Deanna
b. 1922 Philipe, Gerard
b. 1924 Portman, John Calvin, Jr.
b. 1929 McGovern, Arthur F
b. 1930 Kuenn, Harvey Edward
b. 1931 Delvecchio, Alex Peter
b. 1932 Cheek, James Edward
b. 1932 Roh Tae Woo
b. 1933 Buchholz, Horst
b. 1934 French, Victor
b. 1934 Martindale, Wink
b. 1935 Vesco, Robert Lee
b. 1936 Giorno, John
b. 1937 Baer, Max, Jr.
b. 1937 Mott, Stewart Rawlings
b. 1939 Brady, Joan
b. 1942 Hillman, Chris
b. 1944 Wilson, Dennis
b. 1948 Lyon, Southside Johnny
b. 1949 Bridges, Jeff
b. 1949 Kemp, Barry
b. 1951 Wettig, Patricia
b. 1955 Taylor, Dave
b. 1956 King, Bernard
b. 1957 Smith, Lee (Arthur)
b. 1963 Bubka, Sergei (Nazarovich)
b. 1964 Tomei, Marisa
b. 1973 Banks, Tyra
d. 1603 Vos, Martin de
d. 1642 Richelieu, Armand Jean du Plessis, Cardinal

d. 1649 Drummond of Hawthornden, William
d. 1679 Hobbes, Thomas
d. 1720 Read, Mary
d. 1732 Gay, John
d. 1798 Galvani, Luigi
d. 1828 Liverpool, 2nd Earl of
d. 1850 Sturgeon, William
d. 1893 Tyndall, John
d. 1897 Neuendorff, Adolf
d. 1902 Dow, Charles Henry
d. 1922 Peabody, Josephine Preston
d. 1931 Zorrilla de San Martin, Juan
d. 1933 George, Stefan
d. 1935 Richet, Charles Robert
d. 1939 Wu P'ei-fu
d. 1943 Olivetti, Camillo
d. 1944 Bresnaham, Roger Philip
d. 1945 Morgan, Thomas Hunt
d. 1947 Butler, Nicholas Murray
d. 1951 Salinas (y Serrano), Pedro
d. 1952 Horney, Karen Danielson
d. 1952 Norris, James, Sr.
d. 1953 Mason, Daniel Gregory
d. 1955 Lustig, Alvin
d. 1955 Martin, Glenn Luther
d. 1963 Hamer, Robert
d. 1967 Lahr, Bert
d. 1969 Hampton, Fred
d. 1973 Cordiner, Ralph Jarron
d. 1973 Fuller, Alfred Carl
d. 1975 Arendt, Hannah
d. 1976 Britten, (Edward) Benjamin
d. 1977 Eglevsky, Andre
d. 1978 Bruce, David Kirkpatrick Estes
d. 1978 Goudsmit, Samuel Abraham
d. 1980 Amerasinghe, Hamilton Shirley
d. 1980 Walsh, Stella
d. 1983 Sananikone, Phoui
d. 1984 Rock, John
d. 1986 Nakian, Reuben
d. 1987 Mamoulian, Rouben (Zachary)
d. 1989 Pritchard, John Michael, Sir
d. 1992 Derthick, L(awrence) G(ridley)
d. 1993 Landon, Margaret (Dorothea Mortenson)

d. 1993 Zappa, Frank

December 5

b. 1443 Julius II, Pope
b. 1539 Socinus, Faustus
b. 1661 Harley, Robert, 1st Earl of Oxford and Earl Mortimer
b. 1782 Van Buren, Martin
b. 1792 Santa Cruz, Andres de
b. 1802 Dew, Thomas Roderick
b. 1804 Cantu, Cesare
b. 1811 Van Nostrand, David
b. 1822 Agassiz, Elizabeth Cabot Cary
b. 1830 Rossetti, Christina Georgina
b. 1839 Custer, George Armstrong
b. 1841 Daly, Marcus
b. 1856 Brown, Alice
b. 1859 Jellicoe, John Rushworth
b. 1859 Lee, Sidney, Sir
b. 1862 Atkinson, William Walker
b. 1867 Pilsudski, Jozef
b. 1870 Novak, Vitezslav
b. 1870 Pickett, Bill
b. 1875 Currie, Arthur William
b. 1879 Cessna, Clyde Vernon
b. 1880 Hern, Riley
b. 1886 Lane, Rose Wilder
b. 1886 Spry, Constance
b. 1887 Daryush, Elizabeth Bridges
b. 1890 Bomberg, Dave
b. 1890 Lang, Fritz
b. 1894 Swart, Charles Robberts
b. 1894 Wrigley, Philip Knight
b. 1896 Cori, Carl Ferdinand
b. 1897 Johnson, Nunnally
b. 1897 Scholem, Gershom Gerhard
b. 1899 Conroy, Jack
b. 1899 Sheean, (James) Vincent
b. 1899 Williamson, Sonny Boy
b. 1901 Disney, Walt(er Elias)
b. 1901 Heisenberg, Werner Karl
b. 1902 Thurmond, Strom
b. 1903 Gingrich, Arnold
b. 1903 Powell, Cecil Frank
b. 1905 Abdullah, Mohammad, Sheik
b. 1905 Magnante, Charles

b. 1906 Preminger, Otto Ludwig
b. 1907 Lin, Piao (Yu-Yung)
b. 1911 Manessier, Alfred
b. 1914 Magyar, Gabriel
b. 1917 Resor, Stanley Rogers
b. 1922 Robertson, Don
b. 1924 Sobukwe, Robert Mangaliso
b. 1925 Nizami, Khaliq Ahmad
b. 1925 Somoza Debayle, Anastasio
b. 1925 Williams, John A(lfred)
b. 1927 Bhumibol, Adulyadej
b. 1930 Estevez (de Galvez), Luis
b. 1930 Kert, Larry
b. 1931 Cleveland, James
b. 1932 Glashow, Sheldon Lee
b. 1933 Hackney, (Francis) Sheldon
b. 1934 Didion, Joan
b. 1935 Donahue, Phil
b. 1935 Trillin, Calvin Marshall
b. 1936 Mitchell, Chad
b. 1936 Nkosi, Lewis
b. 1938 Cale, J J
b. 1939 Berendt, John
b. 1939 Bofill, Ricardo
b. 1942 Cale, John
b. 1945 Kemmis, Daniel (Orra)
b. 1946 Carreras, Jose
b. 1947 Messina, Jim
b. 1947 Plunkett, Jim
b. 1949 Wadkins, Lanny
b. 1951 Brittany, Morgan
b. 1953 Lane, Charles
b. 1954? Kureishi, Hanif
b. 1957 Monk, Art
b. 1963 Hamilton, Carrie
d. 1654 Sarasin, Jean Francois
d. 1749 la Verendrye, Sieur de
d. 1758 Fasch, Johann Friedrich
d. 1784 Wheatley, Phillis
d. 1791 Mozart, Wolfgang Amadeus
d. 1870 Dumas, Alexandre Dumas Davy de la Pailleterie
d. 1891 Pedro II
d. 1916 Richter, Hans
d. 1923 Phillips, Tommy
d. 1925 Reymont, Wladyslaw Stanislaw
d. 1926 Monet, Claude-Oscar
d. 1931 Lindsay, Vachel
d. 1940 Kubelik, Jan

d. 1945 Lang, William Cosmo Gordon, Baron
d. 1947 Thomas, W(illiam) I(saac)
d. 1951 Jackson, Joe
d. 1960 Teague, Walter Dorwin
d. 1962 Wallant, Edward Lewis
d. 1963 Lehman, Herbert Henry
d. 1965 Erlanger, Joseph
d. 1967 Kavan, Anna
d. 1968 Clark, Fred
d. 1969 Dornier, Claude
d. 1973 Cannon, Jimmy
d. 1973 Watson-Watt, Robert Alexander, Sir
d. 1974 Germi, Pietro
d. 1974 Whitney, Richard
d. 1974 Wightman, Hazel Virginia Hotchkiss
d. 1975 Green, Constance Windsor McLaughlin
d. 1977 Gaud, William Steen, Jr.
d. 1977 Kirk, Rahsaan Roland
d. 1978 Brown, George Scratchley
d. 1979 Delaunay-Terk, Sonia
d. 1980 Halberstam, Michael Joseph
d. 1980 McLean, Robert
d. 1983 Aldrich, Robert
d. 1983 Brown, Charlie
d. 1983 Morton, Digby
d. 1989 Payne, John
d. 1989 Thompson, George Selden
d. 1991 Speck, Richard Franklin
d. 1991 Welensky, Roy
d. 1992 Haury, Emil W
d. 1994 Horner, Harry
d. 1994 Zim, Herbert S(pencer)
d. 1995 Washington, Thomas L.
d. 1998 Bishop, Hazel
d. 1998 Gore, Albert Arnold

December 6

b. 1421 Henry VI
b. 1608 Monck, George, 1st Duke of Albemarle
b. 1637 Andros, Edmund, Sir
b. 1778 Gay-Lussac, Joseph-Louis
b. 1794 Lablache, Luigi
b. 1803 Moodie, Susanna
b. 1804 Schroder-Devrient, Wilhelmine
b. 1805 Houdin, Jean Eugene Robert
b. 1806 DuPrez, Gilbert

b. 1810 Napier, Robert Cornelis
b. 1833 Mosby, John Singleton
b. 1859 Sothern, Edward Hugh
b. 1863 Hall, Charles Martin
b. 1867 Bitter, Karl Theodore Francis
b. 1869 Lavigne, Kid
b. 1869 Nordenskold, Nils Otto Gustaf
b. 1870 Hart, William Surrey
b. 1875 Underhill, Evelyn
b. 1876 Duesenberg, Frederick S
b. 1878 Braithwaite, William Stanley Beaumont
b. 1878 Pillsbury, John Sargent
b. 1883 Braniff, Thomas Elmer
b. 1884 Kroll, Leon
b. 1886 Kilmer, Joyce
b. 1887 Fontanne, Lynn
b. 1888 Hyman, Libbie Henrietta
b. 1889 Lipman, Clara
b. 1889 Woodruff, Robert Winship
b. 1892 Lawless, Theodore K(enneth)
b. 1892 Sitwell, Osbert, Sir
b. 1893 Little, Lou(is)
b. 1893 Warner, Sylvia Townsend
b. 1894 Lynch, J(ohn) Joseph
b. 1896 Gershwin, Ira
b. 1896 Trafton, George
b. 1898 Eisenstaedt, Alfred
b. 1898 Myrdal, Karl Gunnar
b. 1898 Shumlin, Herman Elliott
b. 1899 Conlan, Jocko
b. 1900 Arciniegas, German
b. 1901 Porter, Eliot Furness
b. 1904 Curie, Eve
b. 1904 Landi, Elissa
b. 1905 Braddock, Jim
b. 1905 DuPont, Clifford Walter
b. 1905 Yates, Elizabeth
b. 1906 Moorehead, Agnes
b. 1906 Spychalski, Marian
b. 1907 Ewen, David
b. 1908 Nelson, Baby Face
b. 1909 Oboler, Arch
b. 1911 Berger, Samuel David
b. 1913 Holm, Eleanor
b. 1916 Eldjarn, Kristjan

b. 1918 Hamilton, Denis, Sir
b. 1920 Brubeck, Dave
b. 1920 Dimmock, Peter
b. 1920 Porter, George, Sir
b. 1921 Graham, Otto Everett, Jr.
b. 1922 McGivern, William Peter
b. 1924 Cox, Wally
b. 1924 Foster, Susanna
b. 1927 Mink, Patsy Takemoto
b. 1929 Harnoncourt, Nikolaus
b. 1929 Tanner, Alain
b. 1930 Robustelli, Andy
b. 1933 Gorecki, Henryk (Mikolaj)
b. 1935 Crandall, Robert Lloyd
b. 1935 Epstein, Edward Jay
b. 1935 Mathews, Forrest David
b. 1940 Edlund, Richard
b. 1941 Nauman, Bruce
b. 1941 Perkins, Ray
b. 1941 Speck, Richard Franklin
b. 1942 Handke, Peter
b. 1945 Bowa, Larry
b. 1948 Nickles, Donald Lee
b. 1948 Rosberg, Keke
b. 1953 Hulce, Thomas
b. 1953 Stones, Dwight
b. 1955 Wright, Steven
b. 1957 Bedrosian, Steve
b. 1957 Cuomo, Andrew M.
b. 1971 White, Ryan
d. 345 Nicholas, Saint
d. 1185 Alfonso, I
d. 1658 Gracian y Morales, Baltasar Jeronimo
d. 1718 Rowe, Nicholas
d. 1771 Morgagni, Giovanni Battista
d. 1777? Jussieu, Bernard de
d. 1779 Chardin, Jean Baptiste Simeon
d. 1867 Pacini, Giovanni
d. 1879 Bigelow, Erastus Brigham
d. 1882 Blanc, Louis
d. 1882 Trollope, Anthony
d. 1889 Davis, Jefferson
d. 1892 Siemens, (Ernst) Werner von
d. 1902 Palmer, Alice Elvira Freeman
d. 1904 Blaikie, William
d. 1916 Tosti, Francesco Paolo
d. 1924 Porter, Gene Stratton

d. 1939 Dalmores, Charles
d. 1942 Rusie, Amos Wilson
d. 1948 Tough, Dave
d. 1949 Leadbelly
d. 1951 Bromberg, J Edward
d. 1951 Ross, Harold Wallace
d. 1951 Rothier, Leon
d. 1955 Wagner, Honus
d. 1956 Ambedkar, Bhimrao Ramji
d. 1961 Fanon, Frantz (Omar)
d. 1967 Schick, Bela
d. 1969 Horsbrugh, Florence
d. 1974 Hearst, Millicent Veronica Willson
d. 1976 Goulart, Joao
d. 1981 Corcoran, Thomas Gardiner
d. 1982 Lay, Herman Warden
d. 1985 Gibson, Walter B(rown)
d. 1985 Tillstrom, Burr
d. 1987 Lobel, Arnold Stark
d. 1988 Orbison, Roy
d. 1988 Saxon, Charles David
d. 1989 Bavier, Frances
d. 1989 Fain, Sammy
d. 1990 Rahman, Abdul, Prince
d. 1991 Goodrich, Bert
d. 1992 Bacon, Selden D(askam)
d. 1993 Ameche, Don
d. 1993 Taft, Robert A(lphonso), Jr.
d. 1995 Fizdale, Robert
d. 1995 Reston, James (Barrett)
d. 1996 Rozelle, Pete
d. 1998 Bates, Peg Leg

December 7
b. 1542 Mary, Queen of Scots
b. 1545 Darnley, Henry Stuart, Lord
b. 1598 Bernini, Giovanni Lorenzo
b. 1760 Tussaud, Marie Gresholtz, Madame
b. 1804 Swayne, Noah Haynes
b. 1808 McCulloch, Hugh
b. 1810 Schwann, Theodor
b. 1812 Linton, William James
b. 1841 Cudahy, Michael
b. 1843 Perky, Henry D
b. 1847 White, Deacon
b. 1849 Fischer, Carl
b. 1862 Adam, Paul
b. 1863 Mascagni, Pietro

b. 1863 Sears, Richard Warren
b. 1865 Sanderson, Sybil
b. 1872 Huizinga, Johan
b. 1872 Rice, Cale Young
b. 1873 Cather, Willa (Sibert)
b. 1879 Friml, Rudolf
b. 1880 Gipson, Lawrence Henry
b. 1887 Toch, Ernst
b. 1888 Broun, (Matthew) Heywood (Campbell)
b. 1888 Cary, Joyce
b. 1888 Fish, Hamilton, III
b. 1889 Marcel, Gabriel Honore
b. 1891 Bainter, Fay Okell
b. 1893 Kirkus, Virginia
b. 1894 Davis, Stuart
b. 1895 Margai, Milton Augustus Striery
b. 1896 Crossley, Archibald Maddock
b. 1898 Johnson, Ching
b. 1900 Plimpton, Francis Taylor Pearson
b. 1902 Edwards, Willard
b. 1905 Goldenson, Leonard H(arry)
b. 1905 Kuiper, Gerard Peter
b. 1905 Nash, Clarence
b. 1909 Kainen, Jacob
b. 1910 Furtseva, Ekaterina Alexeyevna
b. 1910 Goldman, Richard Franko
b. 1911 Seibert, Earl Walter
b. 1912 Cameron, Rod
b. 1912 Prima, Louis
b. 1913 Linowitz, Sol Myron
b. 1915 Wallach, Eli
b. 1918 Hatfield, Hurd
b. 1918 Maier, Henry W
b. 1923 Knight, Ted
b. 1924 Soares, Mario Alberto Nobre Lopes
b. 1925 Zaslofsky, Max
b. 1926 Kiam, Victor Kermit, II
b. 1927 Mahoney, James P(atrick)
b. 1928 Chomsky, Noam Avram
b. 1931 Cottrell, Comer J(oseph), Jr.
b. 1931 Goodwin, Richard N(aradhof)
b. 1932 Burstyn, Ellen
b. 1933 Rogers, Rosemary
b. 1936 Belinsky, Bo
b. 1936 Collins, Martha Layne Hall
b. 1937 Cochran, Thad

b. 1940 Cheevers, Gerry
b. 1940 Simpson, Carole
b. 1942 Chapin, Harry Foster
b. 1942 Johnson, Alex(ander)
b. 1942 Lewis, Reginald F.
b. 1943 Isaacs, Susan
b. 1943 Parks, Bernard C.
b. 1944 Antoon, A(lfred) J(oseph)
b. 1944 Chorzempa, Daniel Walter
b. 1947 Bench, Johnny Lee
b. 1947 Unger, Garry Douglas
b. 1948 Cleage, Pearl (Michelle)
b. 1949 Waits, Tom
b. 1952 Collins, Susan M.
b. 1956 Bird, Larry (Joe)
d. 43BC Cicero, Marcus Tullius
d. 1680 Lely, Peter, Sir
d. 1683 Sidney, Algernon
d. 1709 Hobbema, Meindert
d. 1793 Du Barry, Marie Jeanne Gomard de Vaubernier, Comtesse
d. 1815 Ney, Michel de la Moskova, Prince
d. 1817 Bligh, William, Captain
d. 1826 Flaxman, John
d. 1834 Irving, Edward
d. 1871 Levasseur, Nicolas Prosper
d. 1894 Lesseps, Ferdinand Marie de
d. 1896 Maceo, Antonio
d. 1898 Jenner, William, Sir
d. 1902 Nast, Thomas
d. 1902 Reed, Thomas Brackett
d. 1906 Ducommun, Elie
d. 1912 Darwin, George Howard, Sir
d. 1913 Ward, Montgomery
d. 1914 Cawein, Madison Julius
d. 1932 Brieux, Eugene
d. 1938 Munroe, Charles Edward
d. 1941 Fiske, Billy
d. 1942 Solomon, Hannah Greenebaum
d. 1946 Taylor, Laurette
d. 1949 Beach, Rex Ellingwood
d. 1961 Russell, Blair
d. 1962 Flagstad, Kirsten
d. 1962 Newsom, Bobo

d. 1965 Breen, Joseph
Ignatius
d. 1966 Morehouse,
Ward
d. 1967 Baird, Cora
Eisenberg
d. 1969 Portman, Eric
d. 1970 Goldberg, Rube
d. 1970 Power, Thomas
S(arsfield)
d. 1971 Pecora,
Ferdinand
d. 1973 Gorbatov,
Aleksandr
Vassil'evich
d. 1975 Knight, John
Shively, III
d. 1975 Wilder,
Thornton (Niven)
d. 1977 Goldmark, Peter
Carl
d. 1979 Gottlieb, Eddie
d. 1979 Haas, Walter
A(braham), Sr.
d. 1979 Payne-
Gaposchkin, Cecilia
(Helena)
d. 1980 Drew, Richard
G
d. 1982 Brooks, Charlie,
Jr.
d. 1982 Kistiakowsky,
George Bogdan
d. 1982 Lee, Will
d. 1984 Yarbrough, Lee
Roy
d. 1985 Graves, Robert
von Ranke
d. 1985 Stewart, Potter
d. 1986 Harris, Sydney
J(ustin)
d. 1988 Connelly,
Christopher
d. 1989 Hartung, Hans
d. 1990 Arenas,
Reinaldo
d. 1990 Bennett, Joan
d. 1991 Jaffe, Herb
d. 1992 Hughes,
Richard J(oseph)
d. 1993 Houphouet-
Boigny, Felix
d. 1994 Hickey,
Margaret A.
d. 1994 Madigan,
Edward R.
d. 1996 Donoso, Jose

December 8
b. 65BC Horace
b. 1626 Christina
b. 1730 Ingenhousz, Jan
b. 1765 Whitney, Eli
b. 1786 Charpentier,
Johann von
b. 1790 Carlile, Richard
b. 1795 Hansen, Peter
Andreas
b. 1812 Burritt, Elihu
b. 1816 Belmont,
August
b. 1828 Timrod, Henry
b. 1832 Bjornson,
Bjornstjerne
Martinius
b. 1832 Henty, George
Alfred

b. 1861 Durant, William
Crapo
b. 1861 Maillol,
Aristide
b. 1861 Melies, Georges
b. 1862 Feydeau,
Georges
b. 1865 Hadamard,
Jacques Salomon
b. 1865 Sibelius, Jean
b. 1868 Douglas,
Norman
b. 1878 Serafin, Tullio
b. 1881 Colum, Padraic
b. 1881 Gleizes, Albert
L
b. 1885 Roberts,
Kenneth Lewis
b. 1886 Rivera, Diego
b. 1888 Kimball, Fiske
b. 1889 Allen, Hervey
b. 1890 Martinu,
Bohuslav
b. 1891 Crosby, Percy
L
b. 1892? Mooney, Tom
b. 1894 Segar, Elzie
Crisler
b. 1894 Thurber, James
Grover
b. 1897 Tunis, Edwin
Burdett
b. 1898 Burchard, John
Ely
b. 1899 Qualen, John
Mandt
b. 1899 Supervia,
Conchita
b. 1900 Ingersoll, Ralph
McAllister
b. 1901 Urrutia Lleo,
Manuel
b. 1902 Jacoby, Oswald
b. 1903 George, Zelma
W(atson)
b. 1903 Shera, Jesse
Hauk
b. 1903 Simpson, Adele
(Smithline)
b. 1904 Abrams, Harry
Nathan
b. 1905 Barry, Marty
b. 1906 Llewellyn,
Richard
b. 1907 Faylen, Frank
b. 1907 Irene
b. 1908 Volpe, John
A(nthony)
b. 1913 Schwartz,
Delmore (David)
b. 1913 Thomas, Caitlin
Macnamara
b. 1914 Garrigue, Jean
b. 1917 Cantrick,
Robert
b. 1919 Robinson, Julia
(Bowman)
b. 1920 DiCamerino,
Roberta
b. 1920? Souzay,
Gerard
b. 1921 Morgan,
Terence
b. 1922 Freud, Lucian
b. 1922 Ritchie, Jean

b. 1925 Davis, Sammy,
Jr.
b. 1927 Luhmann,
Niklas
b. 1928 Caldwell, John
Charles
b. 1930 Schell,
Maximilian
b. 1933 Wilson, Flip
b. 1936 Carradine,
David
b. 1937 Berle, Peter A.
A.
b. 1937 MacArthur,
James
b. 1937 Shively, Charles
b. 1938 Krause, Bernie
b. 1939 Galway, James
b. 1941 Berenson, Red
b. 1943 Morrison, Jim
b. 1943 Tate, James
b. 1945 Banville, John
b. 1946 Rubinstein,
John Arthur
b. 1947 Cech, Thomas
Robert
b. 1947 Geller,
Margaret J(oan)
b. 1949 Gordon, Mary
Catherine
b. 1950 Baker, Rick
b. 1953 Basinger, Kim
b. 1953 Firestone, Roy
b. 1958 Rogers, George
Washington, Jr.
b. 1959 Junior, E(ster)
J(ames, III)
b. 1964 Hatcher, Teri
b. 1966 O'Connor,
Sinead
d. 1681 Ter Borch,
Gerard
d. 1691 Baxter, Richard
d. 1792 Laurens, Henry
d. 1830 Constant de
Rebeque, (Henri)
Benjamin
d. 1831 Hoban, James
d. 1853 Chickering,
Jonas
d. 1859 DeQuincey,
Thomas
d. 1864 Boole, George
d. 1870 Brassey,
Thomas
d. 1877 Bledsoe, Albert
Taylor
d. 1885 Vanderbilt,
William Henry
d. 1895 Sala, George
Augustus
d. 1903 Spencer,
Herbert
d. 1913 Simmons,
Franklin
d. 1919 Weir, Julian
Alden
d. 1939 Schelling,
Ernest Henry
d. 1941 Morganweck,
Frank
d. 1942 Kahn, Albert
d. 1944 Cregar, Laird
d. 1954 George, Gladys
d. 1958 Speaker,
Tris(tram E)

d. 1963 Sarit Thanarat
d. 1964 Crosby, Percy
L
d. 1964 Marks, Simon
d. 1967 Lawrence,
Robert (Henry), Jr.
d. 1967 Mills, John
d. 1970 Alikhanov,
Abram Isaakovich
d. 1970 Ingold,
Christopher Kelk, Sir
d. 1970 Poor, Henry
Varnum, III
d. 1971 Widener,
George D
d. 1977 Solomon,
Samuel Joseph
d. 1978 Cantwell,
Robert Emmett
d. 1978 Meir, Golda
d. 1980 Lennon, John
Winston
d. 1982 Mayer, Norman
D
d. 1982 Robbins, Marty
d. 1983 Holyoake, Keith
Jacka, Sir
d. 1983 Pickens, Slim
d. 1984 Adler, Luther
d. 1985 Wambsganss,
Bill
d. 1988 Seymour, Anne
Eckert
d. 1990 Ritt, Martin
d. 1991 Bergalis,
Kimberly
d. 1991 Clayton, Buck
d. 1992 Shawn, William
d. 1994 Jobim, Antonio
Carlos
d. 1995 Boyer, Ernest
L(eroy)
d. 1996 Rollins, Howard
Ellsworth, Jr.
d. 1997 Rugambwa,
Laurean
d. 1999 Hart-Davis,
Rupert

December 9
b. 1561 Sandys, Edwin,
Sir
b. 1594 Gustavus
Adophus
b. 1608 Milton, John
b. 1717 Winckelmann,
Johann Joachim
b. 1742 Scheele, Karl
Wilhelm
b. 1749 Berthollet,
Claude Louis, Comte
b. 1848 Harris, Joel
Chandler
b. 1864 Homer, Sidney
b. 1865 Woods, Robert
Archey
b. 1868 Haber, Fritz
b. 1871 Kelley, Joe
b. 1886 Birdseye,
Clarence Frank
b. 1889 Counts, George
S(ylvester)
b. 1889 Kolehmainen,
Hannes
b. 1893 Brett, George
Platt, Jr.

b. 1895 Ibarruri,
Dolores Gomez
b. 1897 Gingold,
Hermione Ferdinanda
b. 1897 Hurley, Jack B
b. 1898 Kelly, Emmett
Lee
b. 1899 Adams, Leonie
Fuller
b. 1900 Needham,
Joseph
b. 1902 Beebe, Lucius
Morris
b. 1902 Butler of
Saffron Walden,
Richard Austen,
Baron
b. 1904 Kronenberger,
Louis
b. 1905 Trumbo, Dalton
b. 1906 Hopper, Grace
Brewster Murray
b. 1906 Martin, Freddy
b. 1909 Fairbanks,
Douglas, Jr.
b. 1911 Cobb, Lee J
b. 1911 Crawford,
Broderick
b. 1912 O'Neill,
Thomas P(hilip), Jr.
b. 1914 Turnesa, Jim
b. 1915 Schwarzkopf,
Elisabeth
b. 1916 Douglas, Kirk
b. 1916 Hildesheimer,
Wolfgang
b. 1917 Rainwater,
James
b. 1919 DeCarava, Roy
b. 1919 Lipscomb,
William Nunn
b. 1921 Ellis, Harry
Bearse
b. 1922 Foxx, Redd
b. 1926 Dominguin,
Luis Miguel
b. 1926 Kendall, Henry
Way
b. 1928 Van Patten,
Dick Vincent
b. 1929 Cassavetes,
John
b. 1929 Hawke, Bob
b. 1930 Henry, Buck
b. 1930 Mejia Victores,
Oscar Humberto
b. 1931 Hagan,
Cliff(ord Oldham)
b. 1931 Reynolds,
William
b. 1932 Byrd, Donald
b. 1932 Hartack, Billy
b. 1933 Moody, Orville
b. 1934 Wells, Junior
b. 1935 Bell, Steve
b. 1935 Pratt,
Christopher
b. 1938 Jones, Deacon
b. 1941 Bridges, Beau
b. 1942 Butkus, Dick
b. 1942 McGinniss, Joe
b. 1943 Martin, Pit
b. 1943 Ondaatje,
Michael
b. 1943 Vance, Kenny
b. 1945 Nouri, Michael

b. 1947 Daschle,
Thomas Andrew
b. 1947 Owens, Steve E
b. 1949 Kite, Tom
b. 1950 Armatrading,
Joan
b. 1953 Free, World B
b. 1953 Malkovich,
John
b. 1954 Juncker, Jean-
Claude
b. 1957 Osmond, Donny
b. 1969 Smith, Allison
d. 1565 Pius, IV, Pope
d. 1641 Van Dyck,
Anthony, Sir
d. 1674 Clarendon,
Edward Hyde, Earl of
d. 1814 Bramah, Joseph
d. 1842 Woodworth,
Samuel
d. 1858 Baldwin, Robert
d. 1874 Cornell, Ezra
d. 1906 Maitland,
Frederic William
d. 1908 Gibbs, Oliver
Wolcott
d. 1913 Deering,
William
d. 1921 Pearson, Cyril
Arthur, Sir
d. 1930 Foster, Rube
d. 1937 Dalen, Nils
Gustaf
d. 1941 Merejkowski,
Dmitri Sergeyevich
d. 1942 Trihey, Harry
d. 1953 Dobrowen, Issai
d. 1959 Canzoneri,
Tony
d. 1963 Fagunwa,
D(aniel) O(lorunfemi)
d. 1963 Miller, Perry
Gilbert Eddy
d. 1964 Sitwell, Edith,
Dame
d. 1965 Rickey, Branch
d. 1966 Barth, Karl
d. 1967 O'Brien, John J
d. 1969 Gruber, Frank
d. 1970 Cady, (Walter)
Harrison
d. 1970 Mikoyan,
Artem Ivanovich
d. 1971 Bunche, Ralph
Johnson
d. 1972 Dieterle,
William
d. 1972 Parsons,
Louella Oettinger
d. 1973 Young, Marian
d. 1975 Wellman,
William Augustus
d. 1976 Ferrell, Wes(ley
Cheek)
d. 1976 Martini, Nino
d. 1977 Lispector,
Clarice
d. 1982 Jaworski, Leon
d. 1983 Rounds, David
d. 1984 Dietz, David
d. 1988 Peyre, Henri
Maurice
d. 1989 Bloustein,
Edward J.
d. 1990 Mazurki, Mike

d. 1994 Crawford,
Frederick C(oolidge)
d. 1995 Bambara, Toni
Cade
d. 1995 Blaine, Vivian
d. 1995 Corrigan,
Douglas
d. 1995 Gellhorn,
Walter
d. 1996 Leakey, Mary
(Douglas)
d. 1997 Geva, Tamara
d. 1998 Moore, Archie

December 10
b. 1584 Selden, John
b. 1610 Ostade, Adriaen
van
b. 1654 Rottmayr,
Johann Michael
b. 1741 Murray, John
b. 1785 Appleton,
Daniel
b. 1787 Gallaudet,
Thomas Hopkins
b. 1795 Baldwin,
Matthias William
b. 1804 Jacobi, Carl
Gustav Jacob
b. 1813 Chandler,
Zachariah
b. 1815 Lovelace, Ada
Byron
b. 1821 Nekrasov,
Nikolay Alexeyevich
b. 1822 Franck, Cesar
Auguste
b. 1824 MacDonald,
George
b. 1830 Dickinson,
Emily (Elizabeth)
b. 1837 Eggleston,
Edward
b. 1850 Brownscombe,
Jennie Augusta
b. 1850 Hinrichs,
Gustav
b. 1851 Dewey, Melvil
b. 1870 Loos, Adolf
b. 1870 Louys, Pierre
b. 1879 Norris, James,
Sr.
b. 1879 Shepard, Ernest
Howard
b. 1882 Neurath, Otto
b. 1883 Kreymborg,
Alfred
b. 1883 Vyshinsky,
Andrei Yanuarievich
b. 1886 Liveright,
Horace Brisbin
b. 1888 Reiner, Fritz
b. 1889 Collins, Ray
b. 1891 Alexander of
Tunis
b. 1891 Sachs, Nelly
(Leonie)
b. 1892? Johnson,
Eleanor M
b. 1893 Brown, Lew
b. 1897 LaFarge,
Christopher
b. 1900 Lebrun, Rico
b. 1902 Marcantonio,
Vito Anthony
b. 1903 Merkel, Una
b. 1903 Norton, Mary

b. 1903 Plomer,
William Charles
Franklyn
b. 1903 Sargeant,
Winthrop
b. 1904 Novotny,
Antonin
b. 1905 Wilhelm,
Hellmut
b. 1906 Zinn, Walter
Henry
b. 1907 Godden, Rumer
b. 1908 DeSapio,
Carmine Gerard
b. 1908 Messiaen,
Olivier (Eugene
Prosper Charles)
b. 1909 Kirstein,
George G
b. 1911 Huntley, Chet
b. 1911 Pan, Hermes
b. 1912 Hart, Philip
Aloysius
b. 1913 Gould, Morton
b. 1914 Lamour,
Dorothy
b. 1915 Murphy,
Thomas Aquinas
b. 1915 Ode, Robert C
b. 1919 Williams,
Harrison Arlington,
Jr.
b. 1920 Menard, H
William
b. 1920 Morgan, Dennis
b. 1924 Manley,
Michael (Norman)
b. 1924 Winpisinger,
William W(ayne)
b. 1925 Kizer, Carolyn
(Ashley)
b. 1925 Lispector,
Clarice
b. 1926 Rich, Lee
b. 1927 McGowan,
William George
b. 1928 Colicos, John
b. 1930 Yeutter,
Clayton Keith
b. 1934 Temin, Howard
Martin
b. 1940 Smitherman,
Geneva
b. 1941 Considine, Tim
b. 1943 Wilson,
Theodore Roosevelt
b. 1944 Rockefeller,
Sharon Percy
b. 1946 Loring, Gloria
Jean
b. 1947 Kenney,
Douglas C
b. 1951 Rodriguez,
Johnny
b. 1952 Dey, Susan
Hallock
b. 1953 Schuur, Diane
b. 1957 Arkadie, Kevin
b. 1957 Maharaj Ji,
Guru
b. 1959 Aguirre, Mark
(Anthony)
b. 1960 Branagh,
Kenneth (Charles)
d. 1198 Averroes
d. 1475 Uccello, Paolo

d. 1603 Gilbert, William
d. 1618 Caccini, Giulio
d. 1831 Seebeck,
Thomas Johann
d. 1864 Schoolcraft,
Henry Rowe
d. 1865 Leopold, I
d. 1878 Wells, Henry
d. 1896 Nobel, Alfred
Bernhard
d. 1897 Fleischmann,
Charles Louis
d. 1917 Bowell,
Mackenzie, Sir
d. 1920 Dodge, Horace
Elgin
d. 1924 Belmont,
August, Jr.
d. 1929 Crosby, Harry
d. 1929 Rosenzweig,
Franz
d. 1934 Smith,
Theobald
d. 1936 Pirandello,
Luigi
d. 1936 Tweedale,
Violet Chambers
d. 1938 Chalmers,
William James
d. 1946 Johnson, Walter
Perry
d. 1946 Runyon, Damon
d. 1951 Blackwood,
Algernon Henry
d. 1957 Elmen, Gustav
Waldemar
d. 1961 Hupp, Louis
Gorham
d. 1965 Cowell, Henry
Dixon
d. 1967 Redding, Otis
d. 1968 Merton,
Thomas
d. 1972 Van Doren,
Mark
d. 1974 Komroff,
Manuel
d. 1976 Lisagor, Peter
Irvin
d. 1977 Rupp, Adolph
Frederick
d. 1978 Wood, Edward
D., Jr.
d. 1979 Blodgett,
Katherine Burr
d. 1979 Dvorak, Ann
d. 1979 Sheen, Fulton
John, Bishop
d. 1980 Benedictos I
d. 1981 Kieran, John
Francis
d. 1981 Marlowe,
Sylvia
d. 1981 Wurf, Jerry
d. 1982 Gosden,
Freeman Fisher
d. 1984 Teagarden,
Charles
d. 1985 Grimes,
Burleigh Arland
d. 1986 Cabot, Susan
d. 1987 Heifetz, Jascha
d. 1987 Stewart, Slam
d. 1988 Castellano,
Richard

d. 1990 Hammer,
Armand
d. 1990 Stavropoulos,
George Peter
d. 1991 Abbott,
Berenice
d. 1991 Tshabalala,
Headman
d. 1993 Tully, Alice
d. 1994 Joseph, Keith
(Sinjohn)
d. 1996 Young, Faron
d. 1999 Tudjman,
Franjo

December 11
b. 1668 Zeno, Apostolo
b. 1781 Brewster,
David, Sir
b. 1803 Berlioz, Hector
b. 1810 Musset, Alfred
de
b. 1822 Cummins,
George David
b. 1830 Kamehameha V
b. 1843 Koch, Robert
b. 1854 Radbourn, Old
Hoss
b. 1863 Cannon, Annie
Jump
b. 1867 Pratt, Bela
Lyon
b. 1870 Weinman,
Adolph A
b. 1874 Kraft, James
Lewis
b. 1876 Comstock, Ada
Louise
b. 1882 Born, Max
b. 1882 La Guardia,
Fiorello Henry
b. 1886 McLaglen,
Victor
b. 1889 Knott, Walter
b. 1890 Tobey, Mark
b. 1892? Adams, Harriet
Stratemeyer
b. 1892? Bloom, Ursula
b. 1892 Larson, John
Augustus
b. 1894 Dowling, Eddie
b. 1894 Lauri-Volpi,
Giacoma
b. 1897 Van Dusen,
Henry Pitney
b. 1901 Cabot, John
Moors
b. 1901 Oakeshott,
Michael Joseph
b. 1903 Edwards,
Willard Eldridge
b. 1903 Jensen, Alfred
Julio
b. 1903 Mumford,
Lawrence Quincy
b. 1904 Davies, Ronald
N(orwood)
b. 1904 Woolsey,
Janette
b. 1905 Childers,
Erskine Hamilton
b. 1905 Lorentz, Pare
b. 1905 Roland, Gilbert
b. 1906 Diop, Birago
b. 1908 Carter, Elliott
Cook, Jr.

b. 1910 Sauer, George
(Henry)
b. 1911 Mahfouz,
Naguib
b. 1913 Marais, Jean
b. 1913 Ponti, Carlo
b. 1918 Solzhenitsyn,
Aleksandr (Isayevich)
b. 1922 Westermann,
H(orace) C(lifford)
b. 1923 Blair, Betsy
b. 1923 Turner, Morrie
b. 1924 Blanchard, Doc
b. 1924 Windsor, Marie
b. 1926 Barnet, Sylvan
M., Jr.
b. 1926 Cooper, Edward
S(awyer)
b. 1926 Thornton,
Willie Mae
b. 1929 MacMillan,
Kenneth, Sir
b. 1930 Trintignant,
Jean-Louis Xavier
b. 1931 Moreno, Rita
b. 1931 Pilote, Pierre
Paul
b. 1931 Rajneesh,
Bhagwan Shree
b. 1931 Rothenberg,
Jerome
b. 1935 Martin, James
Grubbs
b. 1938 Tyner, McCoy
Alfred
b. 1939 Hayden, Tom
b. 1939 McGuane,
Thomas Francis
b. 1940 Gates, David
b. 1941 Baucus, Max
Sieben
b. 1943 Kerry, John
F(orbes)
b. 1943 Mills, Donna
b. 1944 Lee, Brenda
b. 1945 Preston, John
b. 1946 George, Lynda
Day
b. 1949 Garr, Teri Ann
b. 1949? Martin, Jared
b. 1950 Onassis,
Christina
b. 1952 Seidelman,
Susan
b. 1953 Armstrong,
Bess
b. 1954 Jackson,
Jermaine La Jaune
b. 1962 Williams, Curtis
d. 1282 Michael, VIII
d. 1513 Pintuicchio
d. 1582 Alba, Duke of
d. 1843 Delavigne, Jean
Francois Casimir
d. 1857 Castil-Blaze,
Francois-Joseph
d. 1872 Kamehameha V
d. 1873 Beadle, William
d. 1880 Winchester,
Oliver Fisher
d. 1883 Doyle, Richard
d. 1883 Mario,
Giovanni Matteo
d. 1911 Ball, Thomas
d. 1938 Lange,
Christian Louis

d. 1939 Walgreen,
Charles Rudolph
d. 1941 Conrad, Frank
d. 1941 Picard, Charles
Emile
d. 1944 Mendes, Chico
d. 1945 Fabry, Charles
d. 1949 Berryman,
Clifford Kennedy
d. 1951 Addison,
Christopher, Viscount
d. 1953 Coates, Albert
d. 1955 Merrill, Frank
Dow
d. 1959 Bottomley, Jim
d. 1964 Cooke, Sam
d. 1964 Kilbride, Percy
d. 1967 Bigelow, Henry
Bryant
d. 1967 DeSabata,
Victor
d. 1968 Sulzberger,
Arthur Hays
d. 1972 Swados, Harvey
d. 1974 Hadley, Reed
d. 1978 DuVigneaud,
Vincent
d. 1980 Bergen, John
Joseph
d. 1980 Lesage, Jean
d. 1980 Orwell, Sonia
d. 1981 Kaiser, Edgar
Fosburgh
d. 1982 Miner,
Worthington C
d. 1984 Ehricke, Krafft
Arnold
d. 1991 Lewis, Robert
Q
d. 1991 Lundkvist,
Artur Nils
d. 1992 Gardenia,
Vincent
d. 1993 Gary, Raymond
d. 1993 Raedler,
Dorothy (Florence)
d. 1994 Rush, (David)
Kenneth
d. 1996 Hamilton,
Charles
d. 1997 Winpisinger,
William W(ayne)
December 12
b. 1648 Rogers, John
b. 1731 Darwin,
Erasmus
b. 1745 Jay, John
b. 1747 Seward, Anna
b. 1786 Marcy, William
Learned
b. 1791 Marie Louise
b. 1805 Garrison,
William Lloyd
b. 1805 Wells, Henry
b. 1821 Flaubert,
Gustave
b. 1837 Green, John
Richard
b. 1849 Vanderbilt,
William Kissam
b. 1862 Ismay, Joseph
Bruce
b. 1863 Munch, Edvard
b. 1864 Brisbane,
Arthur

b. 1947 Gonzalez Macchi, Luis
b. 1948 Nugent, Ted
b. 1953 Gainey, Bob
b. 1954 Anderson, John
b. 1959 Whitaker, Johnny
b. 1969 Fedorov, Sergei
d. 1204 Maimonides, Moses
d. 1250 Frederick II
d. 1466 Donatello
d. 1521 Manuel I
d. 1557 Tartaglia, Niccolo (Fontana)
d. 1565 Gesner, Konrad von
d. 1628 Bull, John
d. 1716 La Fosse, Charles de
d. 1784 Johnson, Samuel
d. 1823 Narino, Antonio
d. 1823 Reeve, Tapping
d. 1843 Hull, Isaac
d. 1852 Wright, Frances
d. 1861 Albert, Prince
d. 1863 Hebbel, Friedrich
d. 1881 Quidor, John
d. 1924 Gompers, Samuel
d. 1930 Pregl, Fritz
d. 1931 Le Bon, Gustave
d. 1932 Holland, William Jacob
d. 1935 Grignard, Francois Auguste Victor
d. 1945 Grese, Irma
d. 1955 Egas Moniz, Antonio C A F
d. 1960 Thomas, John Charles
d. 1961 Moses, Grandma
d. 1962 Sokolsky, George E
d. 1965 Robeson, Eslanda Cardoza Goode
d. 1969 Spruance, Raymond Ames
d. 1972 Hartley, L(eslie) P(oles)
d. 1973 Green, Henry
d. 1977 Petrie, Charles Alexander, Sir
d. 1978 Johnson, Herbert Fisk
d. 1981 Markham, Pigmeat
d. 1983 Renault, Mary
d. 1983 Schmemann, Alexander
d. 1985 Russell, Donald Joseph
d. 1986 Baker, Ella
d. 1987 Wunder, George S
d. 1990 Marble, Alice
d. 1992 Arnall, Ellis (Gibbs)
d. 1992 Irving, Kenneth Colin

d. 1992 Whitney, C(ornelius) V(anderbilt)
d. 1994 Bestor, Arthur (Eugene)
d. 1994 Hauser, Philip M(orris)
d. 1994 Pinay, Antoine
d. 1996 Alvary, Lorenzo
d. 1998 Grade, Lew, Sir

December 14
b. 1475 Leo, X
b. 1503 Nostradamus
b. 1546 Brahe, Tycho
b. 1553 Henry, IV
b. 1610 Teniers, David, the Younger
b. 1730 Bruce, James
b. 1775 Chase, Philander
b. 1780 Nesselrode, Karl Robert
b. 1794 Corning, Erastus
b. 1812 Canning, Charles John, Earl
b. 1824 Puvis de Chavannes, Pierre Cecile
b. 1829 Langston, John Mercer
b. 1847 Lassale, Jean
b. 1852 Cheyne, William Watson, Sir
b. 1866 Fry, Roger Eliot
b. 1870 Renner, Karl
b. 1882 Christie, John
b. 1884 Cowl, Jane
b. 1885 Pemberton, Brock
b. 1895 Eluard, Paul
b. 1895 George VI
b. 1896 Doolittle, James H(arold)
b. 1896 Markey, Lucille (Parker) Wright
b. 1897 Schuschnigg, Kurt von
b. 1897 Smith, Margaret (Madeline) Chase
b. 1897 Thill, Georges
b. 1898 Cowles, John, Sr.
b. 1901 Cochet, Henri
b. 1901 Michalowski, Kazimierz
b. 1901 Paul I
b. 1902 Burke, Billy
b. 1902 Feigl, Herbert
b. 1906 Soby, James Thrall
b. 1909 Tatum, Edward Lawrie
b. 1911 Jones, Spike
b. 1914 Amsterdam, Morey
b. 1914 Carstens, Karl Walter
b. 1914 Tureck, Rosalyn
b. 1915 Dailey, Dan
b. 1916 Priscilla of Boston
b. 1918 Aubrey, James (Thomas), Jr.

b. 1919 Jackson, Shirley (Hardie)
b. 1920 Cary, Frank Taylor
b. 1920 Wilt, Fred(erick Loren)
b. 1922 Basov, Nikolai Gennadievich
b. 1922 Hewitt, Don S.
b. 1922 Trippi, Charlie
b. 1923 McNair, Robert Evander
b. 1927 Feldman, Alvin Lindbergh
b. 1931 Shrontz, Frank Anderson
b. 1932 Lane, Abbe
b. 1932 Rich, Charlie
b. 1935 Remick, Lee
b. 1936 Bach, Bert Coates
b. 1938 Boff, Leonardo
b. 1938 Brand, Stewart
b. 1939 Davis, Ernie
b. 1945 Crouch, Stanley
b. 1946 Botstein, Leon
b. 1946 Duke, Patty
b. 1946 Gandhi, Sanjay
b. 1946 Ovitz, Michael S.
b. 1946 Smith, Stan(ley Roger)
b. 1947 Parkening, Christopher William
b. 1949 Buckner, Bill
b. 1949 Williams, Cliff
b. 1954 Andersen, Ib Steen
b. 1977 Hall, Bridget
d. 1124 Callistus II, Pope
d. 1542 James V
d. 1591 John of the Cross, Saint
d. 1729 Franceschini, Marcantonio
d. 1788 Charles, III
d. 1799 Washington, George
d. 1806 Breckinridge, John
d. 1860 Aberdeen, 4th Earl of
d. 1861 Marschner, Heinrich August
d. 1872 Kensett, John Frederick
d. 1902 Grant, Julia Dent
d. 1905 Haupt, Herman
d. 1920 Gipp, George
d. 1943 Kellogg, John Harvey
d. 1944 Velez, Lupe
d. 1945 Baring, Maurice
d. 1947 Baldwin, Stanley
d. 1947 Fyffe, Will
d. 1953 Rawlings, Marjorie Kinnan
d. 1956 Paasikivi, Juho Kusti
d. 1959 Spencer, Stanley, Sir
d. 1960 Ratoff, Gregory

d. 1963 Washington, Dinah
d. 1964 Bendix, William
d. 1964 Reynolds, R(ichard) J(oshua), Jr.
d. 1966 Felton, Verna
d. 1966 Whorf, Richard
d. 1968 Klose, Margarete
d. 1970 Slim, William Joseph
d. 1972 Berman, Eugene
d. 1974 Lippmann, Walter
d. 1975 Gray, James, Sir
d. 1975 Treacher, Arthur
d. 1977 Stulberg, Louis
d. 1978 Madariaga (y Rojo), Salvador de
d. 1980 Howard, Elston Gene
d. 1981 Benchley, Nathaniel Goddard
d. 1984 Aleixandre, Vicente
d. 1985 Maris, Roger (Eugene)
d. 1987 Josefsberg, Milt
d. 1988 Symington, Stuart
d. 1989 Sakharov, Andrei Dmitrievich
d. 1990 Durrenmatt, Friedrich
d. 1991 Dyer-Bennet, Richard
d. 1993 Loy, Myrna
d. 1994 Beaton, Norman
d. 1994 Faubus, Orval E(ugene)
d. 1997 Kaye, Stubby
d. 1998 Fell, Norman

December 15
b. 37 Nero
b. 1734 Romney, George
b. 1780 Dobereiner, Johann Wolfgang
b. 1793 Carey, Henry Charles
b. 1812 Levy, Joseph Moses
b. 1832 Eiffel, Alexandre Gustave
b. 1834 Young, Charles Augustus
b. 1848 Blashfield, Edwin Howland
b. 1848? Coryell, John Russell
b. 1852 Becquerel, Antoine Henri
b. 1859 Zamenhof, Ludwik Lazar
b. 1860 Finsen, Niels Ryberg
b. 1862 Duryea, Charles Edgar
b. 1870 Hoffmann, Josef
b. 1879 Laban, Rudolf von

b. 1883 Hinton, William Augustus
b. 1883 Kemp, Harry (Hibbard)
b. 1888 Anderson, Maxwell
b. 1890 Babcock, Harry
b. 1892 Getty, J(ean) Paul
b. 1892 Guion, David Wendel Fentress
b. 1893 Fruehauf, Harvey Charles
b. 1895 Razaf, Andy
b. 1896 Dempsey, Miles Christopher, Sir
b. 1899 Abrahams, Harold
b. 1902 Machlup, Fritz
b. 1904 Bloomgarden, Kermit
b. 1904 Legg, W(illiam) Dorr
b. 1904 Smith, Betty
b. 1907 Crossman, Richard Howard Stafford
b. 1907 Niemeyer, Oscar
b. 1909 Glassco, John Stinson
b. 1910 Hammond, John Henry, Jr.
b. 1911 Dallis, Nicholas Peter
b. 1913 Rukeyser, Muriel
b. 1916 Wilkins, Maurice Hugh Frederick
b. 1918 Chandler, Jeff
b. 1920 Anderson, Roy A(rnold)
b. 1922 Freed, Alan
b. 1923 Carter, Jimmy
b. 1923 Dyson, Freeman John
b. 1924 McGee, Charles
b. 1925 Pollock, Sam
b. 1928 Hundertwasser, Friedensreich
b. 1930 Sullivan, Haywood Cooper
b. 1931 O'Brien, Edna
b. 1933 Conway, Tim
b. 1933 Woods, Donald
b. 1935 Walton, Joe
b. 1936 Palmieri, Eddie
b. 1937 Goines, Donald
b. 1940 Buoniconti, Nick
b. 1942 Clark, Dave
b. 1944 Leyland, Jim
b. 1944 Mendes, Chico
b. 1946 Appice, Carmine
b. 1948 Cowings, Patricia S.
b. 1949 Johnson, Don
b. 1950 Gates, Sylvester James, Jr.
b. 1954 Cox, Alex
b. 1959 Bohay, Heidi
b. 1967 Vaughn, Mo
d. 1025 Basil, II
d. 1598 Yi Sunsin

d. 1643 Pym, John
d. 1675 Vermeer, Jan
d. 1683 Walton, Izaak
d. 1788 Bach, Carl Philipp Emanuel
d. 1796 Wayne, Anthony
d. 1831 Adams, Hannah
d. 1854 Kamehameha III
d. 1857 Cayley, George, Sir
d. 1864 Farnham, Eliza Wood Burhans
d. 1885 Toombs, Robert Augustus
d. 1890 Sitting Bull
d. 1912 Reid, Whitelaw
d. 1934 Walker, Maggie Lena
d. 1943 Waller, Fats
d. 1944? Miller, Glenn
d. 1945 Konoye, Fumimaro, Prince
d. 1947 Machen, Arthur
d. 1950 Repplier, Agnes
d. 1951 Perth, 16th Earl of
d. 1953 Barrow, Ed(ward Grant)
d. 1958 Pauli, Wolfgang Ernst
d. 1962 Laughton, Charles
d. 1965 Dorne, Albert
d. 1966 Disney, Walt(er Elias)
d. 1968 Willard, Jess
d. 1974 Branzell, Karin
d. 1974 Hershfield, Harry
d. 1974 Litvak, Anatole
d. 1977 Birdwell, Russell Juarez
d. 1978 Wills, Chill
d. 1981 Cockburn, Claud
d. 1984 Peerce, Jan
d. 1984 Spedding, Frank Harold
d. 1985 Ramgoolam, Seewoosagur, Sir
d. 1985 Romulo, Carlos Pena
d. 1986 Lifar, Serge
d. 1987 Clark, Septima
d. 1987 Haggar, Joseph M(arion)
d. 1987 Malavasi, Ray(mondo Guiseppi Giovanni Baptiste)
d. 1987 Tomlin, Pinky
d. 1989 Moss, Arnold
d. 1996 Kemelman, Harry
d. 1996 Van Der Post, Laurens (Jan), Sir
d. 1998 Meyerowitz, Jan

December 16
b. 1485 Catherine of Aragon
b. 1742 Blucher, Gebhard Leberecht von
b. 1751 Cabot, George

b. 1770 Beethoven, Ludwig van
b. 1775 Austen, Jane
b. 1775 Boieldieu, Francois Adrien
b. 1787 Mitford, Mary Russell
b. 1790 Leopold, I
b. 1792 Lawrence, Abbott
b. 1828 Clarke, Alexander Ross
b. 1830 Tisza, Kalman
b. 1833 Knapp, Seaman Asahel
b. 1843 Kendal, William Hunter
b. 1843 Lowell, Josephine Shaw
b. 1844 Villard, Helen Francis Garrison
b. 1850 Bates, Arlo
b. 1854 Fels, Joseph
b. 1857 Barnard, Edward Emerson
b. 1863 Cram, Ralph Adams
b. 1863 Fox, John W, Jr.
b. 1863 Santayana, George
b. 1869 Pollard, Albert Frederick
b. 1882 Kodaly, Zoltan
b. 1884 Bobst, Elmer Holmes
b. 1887 Bodanzky, Artur
b. 1888 Alexander of Yugoslavia
b. 1888 Juin, Alphonse Pierre
b. 1895 Ets, Marie Hall
b. 1896 Clinchy, Everett Ross
b. 1899 Coward, Noel Pierce, Sir
b. 1900 Lortel, Lucille
b. 1900 Pritchett, V(ictor) S(awdon), Sir
b. 1901 Mead, Margaret
b. 1902 Alberti, Rafael
b. 1903 Hawes, Elizabeth
b. 1907 Bliss, Ray C(harles)
b. 1911 Jacobson, Leon Orris
b. 1913 Parker, Buddy
b. 1914 Link, O(gle) Winston
b. 1915 Murphy, Turk
b. 1916 Weiss, Theodore (Russell)
b. 1917 Clarke, Arthur C(harles)
b. 1917 Kempton, (James) Murray
b. 1926 Brinegar, Claude Stout
b. 1926 McCracken, James (Eugene)
b. 1926 Robinson, A(rthur) N(apoleon) R(aymond)

b. 1928 Ames, Bruce N(athan)
b. 1928 Dick, Philip K(indred)
b. 1928 MacDonald, Peter
b. 1932 Blake, Quentin
b. 1932 Shchedrin, Rodion Konstantinovich
b. 1934 Jacob, John Edward
b. 1936 Dees, Morris S(eligman), Jr.
b. 1936 Kicknosway, Faye
b. 1937 Ruscha, Edward
b. 1938 Deford, Frank
b. 1938 Ullmann, Liv (Johanne)
b. 1939 Gayoom, Maumoon Abdul
b. 1941 Stahl, Lesley (Rene)
b. 1941 Stahl, Leslie
b. 1943 Bochco, Steven Ronald
b. 1943 Hicks, Tony
b. 1946 Andersson, Benny
b. 1946 Pinnock, Trevor David
b. 1947? Cross, Ben
b. 1947 Matthews, Vince(nt)
b. 1950 Tabai, Ieremia Tienang
b. 1951 Flanagan, Mike
b. 1952 Estrich, Susan
b. 1955 Browner, Carol M.
b. 1962 Perry, William
b. 1964 Ripken, Bill
b. 1515 Albuquerque, Affonso de
d. 1687 Petty, William, Sir
d. 1745 Hildebrandt, Johann Lucas von
d. 1774 Quesnay, Francois
d. 1783 Hasse, Johann Adolph
d. 1852 Wallace, Horace Binney
d. 1858 Bright, Richard
d. 1859 Grimm, Wilhelm Karl
d. 1861 Lipinski, Carl
d. 1863 Buford, John
d. 1871 Haring, Georg Wilhelm Heinrich
d. 1878 Gutzkow, Karl Ferdinand
d. 1890 Terry, Alfred Howe
d. 1897 Daudet, Leon
d. 1921 Saint-Saens, (Charles) Camille
d. 1922 Ben-Yehuda, Eliezer
d. 1928 Wylie, Elinor Hoyt
d. 1933 Chambers, Robert W

d. 1933 Vance, Louis
Joseph
d. 1938 Murchison,
Kenneth MacKenzie
d. 1940 Dubois, Eugene
d. 1940 Hamilton, Billy
d. 1944 Guedalla, Philip
d. 1945 Agnelli,
Giovanni
d. 1947 Sodero, Cesare
d. 1951 Dix, Dorothy
d. 1958 Corum, Martene
Windsor
d. 1962 Dale, Chester
d. 1964 Davis, Phil
d. 1965 Maugham,
W(illiam) Somerset
d. 1965 Schipa, Tito
d. 1970 Lewis, Oscar
d. 1974 Pierce, Edward
Allen
d. 1975 Kang, Sheng
d. 1977 Schippers,
Thomas
d. 1978 Buzhardt,
J(oseph) Fred, Jr.
d. 1979 Chapman,
Gilbert Whipple
d. 1980 Fisher, Welthy
(Blakesley Honsinger)
d. 1980 Sanders,
Colonel
d. 1981 Allen, Ethel D.
d. 1981 Struss, Karl
d. 1982 Chapman,
(Anthony) Colin
(Bruce)
d. 1982 Hubbard,
Orville Liscum
d. 1984 Prestopino,
Gregorio
d. 1987 Morano, Albert
Paul
d. 1988 Pratt, Babe
d. 1989 Mangano,
Silvana
d. 1989 Pringle, Aileen
d. 1989 Van Cleef, Lee
d. 1993 Moore, Charles
Willard
d. 1993 Tanaka, Kakuei
d. 1994 Logan, Harlan
(De Braun)
d. 1997 Disney, Lillian
d. 1997 Larson,
Nicolette
d. 1998 Blair, Clay, Jr.
d. 1998 Gaddis, William
(Thomas)

December 17
b. 1632 Wood, Anthony
b. 1732 Hastings,
Warren
b. 1734 Floyd, William
b. 1737 Almon, John
b. 1749 Cimarosa,
Domenico
b. 1758 Macon,
Nathaniel
b. 1760 Gannett,
Deborah Sampson
b. 1760 Sampson,
Deborah
b. 1778 Davy,
Humphrey, Sir

b. 1796 Haliburton,
Thomas Chandler
b. 1797 Henry, Joseph
b. 1807 Whittier, John
Greenleaf
b. 1824 King, Thomas
Starr
b. 1830 Goncourt, Jules
Alfred Huot de
b. 1835 Agassiz,
Alexander Emmanuel
Rodolphe
b. 1842 Lavisse, Ernest
b. 1853 Tree, Herbert
Beerbohm
b. 1866 Menocal, Mario
Garcia
b. 1873 Ford, Ford
Madox
b. 1873 Goldin, Horace
b. 1874 King, William
Lyon Mackenzie
b. 1883 Raimu
b. 1884 Peirce, Waldo
b. 1884 Uttley, Alice
Jane Taylor
b. 1891 Hu Shih
b. 1892 Cohn, Edwin
Joseph
b. 1894 Fiedler, Arthur
b. 1896 Biddle,
Anthony Joseph
b. 1900 Paxinou, Katina
b. 1902 Jameson, House
b. 1903 Caldwell,
Erskine Preston
b. 1903 Noble, Ray
b. 1904 Cadmus, Paul
b. 1904 Lonergan,
Bernard J F
b. 1905 McLarnin,
Jimmy
b. 1905 Verissimo,
Erico Lopes
b. 1906 Martin, William
McChesney, Jr.
b. 1908 Ashton-Warner,
Sylvia Constance
b. 1908 Libby, Willard
Frank
b. 1910 Oliver, Sy
b. 1911 Sale, Richard
Bernard
b. 1917 Dike, Kenneth
(Onwuka)
b. 1919 Mphahlele,
Ezekiel
b. 1923 Pelikan,
Jaroslav
b. 1927 Ivask, Ivar
Vidrik
b. 1927 Long, Richard
b. 1928 Beck, Marilyn
(Mohr)
b. 1929 Safire, William
L
b. 1930 Guccione, Bob
b. 1930 Meade, Julia
b. 1935 Costa, Victor
Charles
b. 1935 Ripken, Cal(vin
Edwin, Sr.)
b. 1936 Steele, Tommy
b. 1937 Harris, Bertha
b. 1938 Snell, Peter
George

b. 1940 Kendricks,
Eddie
b. 1940 McIntyre,
James Talmadge, Jr.
b. 1942 Butterfield, Paul
b. 1945 Cazenove,
Christopher
b. 1945 Muske, Carol
(Anne)
b. 1948 Bonfanti, Jim
Alexander
b. 1953 Livingston,
Barry
b. 1958 Poulin, Dave
b. 1962 Brown, Eddie
Lee
b. 1971 McCray, Nikki
d. 1737 Stradivari,
Antonio
d. 1830 Bolivar, Simon
d. 1847 Marie Louise
d. 1870 Mercadante,
Saverio
d. 1874 Cushing,
William Barker
d. 1881 Hayes, Isaac
Israel
d. 1881 Morgan, Lewis
Henry
d. 1899 Quaritch,
Bernard
d. 1907 Kelvin, William
Thomson, Baron
d. 1909 Leopold II
d. 1917 Anderson,
Elizabeth Garrett
d. 1919 Renoir, (Pierre)
Auguste
d. 1930 Heseltine,
Philip Arnold
d. 1935 Gomez, Juan
Vicente
d. 1935 Reese, Lizette
Woodworth
d. 1938 Tammann,
Gustav Heinrich
Johann Apollon
d. 1944 Kandinsky,
Wassily
d. 1944 McLaughlin,
Frederic
d. 1946 Garnett,
Constance
d. 1947 Bronsted,
Johannes Nicolaus
d. 1947 Spilsbury,
Bernard Henry, Sir
d. 1955 McCoy, Horace
d. 1957 Sayers, Dorothy
Leigh
d. 1959 Touhy, Roger
d. 1962 Mitchell,
Thomas
d. 1964 Hess, Victor
Francis
d. 1965 Ismay, Hastings
Lionel, Baron
d. 1967 Holt, Harold
Edward
d. 1969 Costa e Silva,
Arthur da
d. 1971 Larkin, Oliver
Waterman
d. 1973 Abbot,
C(harles) G(reeley)
d. 1975 Sissle, Noble

d. 1975 Wimsatt,
William Kurtz, Jr.
d. 1977 Marshall,
S(amuel) L(yman)
A(twood)
d. 1978 Frings, Joseph
Richard
d. 1981 Shehu, Mehmet
d. 1982 Ferguson,
Homer
d. 1982 Hoyt, Lawrence
W
d. 1982 Kogan, Leonid
Borisovich
d. 1986 DeButts, John
Dulany
d. 1987 Alfrink,
Bernard (Jan),
Cardinal
d. 1987 Yourcenar,
Marguerite
d. 1989 Wedemeyer,
Albert Coady
d. 1991 Smallwood,
Joey
d. 1992 Andrews,
(Carver) Dana
d. 1992 Craig, George
N(orth)
d. 1993 Gunn, Moses
d. 1995 Wesley,
Dorothy Porter
d. 1996 Caesar, Irving
d. 1999 Allen, Rex E.,
Sr.
d. 1999 Washington,
Grover, Jr.
d. 1999 Woodward,
C(omer) Vann

December 18
b. 1021 Wang An-shih
b. 1707 Wesley, Charles
b. 1709 Elizabeth
Petrovna
b. 1778 Grimaldi,
Joseph
b. 1792 Howitt, William
b. 1802 Prentice,
George Denison
b. 1814 Bolton, Sarah
Tittle Barrett
b. 1819 Hecker, Isaac
Thomas
b. 1835 Abbott, Lyman
b. 1856 Thomson,
Joseph John, Sir
b. 1859 Thompson,
Francis Joseph
b. 1861 MacDowell,
Edward Alexander
b. 1862 Rosenthal,
Moriz
b. 1863 Francis
Ferdinand
b. 1863 Franz Ferdinand
b. 1870 Saki
b. 1879 Klee, Paul
b. 1883 Teague, Walter
Dorwin
b. 1886 Chu Te
b. 1886 Cobb, Ty(rus
Raymond)
b. 1886 Watkins, Arthur
V(ivian)
b. 1888 Cooper, Gladys,
Dame

d. 1954 Child, Charles
Manning
d. 1957 Van Druten,
John William
d. 1968 Thomas,
Norman Mattoon
d. 1977 Ross, Nellie
Taylor
d. 1980 Campora,
Hector Jose
d. 1980 Kosygin,
Aleksei Nikolaevich
d. 1981 Frailberg,
Selma
d. 1982 MacDonald,
Dwight
d. 1983 Alexandrov,
Grigori
d. 1984 Seton-Watson,
Hugh
d. 1986 Andrews,
V(irginia) C(leo)
d. 1986 Fergusson,
Francis
d. 1989 Gibbons, Stella
(Dorothea)
d. 1991 Gann, Ernest
Kellogg
d. 1993 Bennett,
Wallace F(oster)
d. 1995 Barrow, Ruth
Nita, Dame
d. 1996 Mastroianni,
Marcello

December 20
b. Callas, Charlie
b. 1579 Fletcher, John
b. 1629? Hooch, Pieter
de
b. 1738 Clodion
b. 1805 Graham,
Thomas
b. 1824 Vaux, Calvert
b. 1833 Mudd, Samuel
Alexander
b. 1841 Buisson,
Ferdinand Edouard
b. 1849 Eminescu,
Mihail
b. 1850 Anderson,
Elizabeth Milbank
b. 1852 Kitasato
Shibasaburo
b. 1856 Blomfield,
Reginald Theodore,
Sir
b. 1865 Mendl, Lady
Elsie de Wolfe
b. 1867 Heffelfinger,
Pudge
b. 1867 Lowes, John
Livingston
b. 1868 Alessandri
Palma, Arturo
b. 1868 Firestone,
Harvey Samuel
b. 1868 Quinn, Edmond
T
b. 1869 Grapewin,
Charley
b. 1870 Cahill, Marie
b. 1871 Hadley, Henry
Kimball
b. 1875 Powys,
Theodore Francis

b. 1876 Adams, Walter
Sydney
b. 1877 Cooper, Emil
b. 1881 Rickey, Branch
b. 1884 Mennen,
William Gerhard
b. 1886 Wightman,
Hazel Virginia
Hotchkiss
b. 1890 Heyrovsky,
Jaroslav
b. 1892 May, Mortimer
b. 1894 Menzies, Robert
Gordon, Sir
b. 1895 Langer,
Suzanne K
b. 1896 Browning,
Frederick A(rthur)
M(ontague), Sir
b. 1896 Hobbs, Leonard
Sinclair
b. 1898 Dunne, Irene
Marie
b. 1898 Votipka,
Thelma
b. 1899 Ronne, Finn
b. 1899 Sparkman, John
Jackson
b. 1900 Fiorito, Ted
b. 1900 Hartnett, Gabby
b. 1902 George Edward
Alexander Edmund
b. 1902 Hook, Sidney
b. 1902 Lerner, Max
b. 1905 Dekker, Albert
b. 1906 Krick, Irving
P(arkhurst)
b. 1907 Webster, Paul
Francois
b. 1910 Conacher,
Charlie
b. 1911 Calisher,
Hortense
b. 1914 Byrd, Harry
Flood, Jr.
b. 1915 Mann, Paul
b. 1916 Smith, Courtney
Craig
b. 1918 Totter, Audrey
b. 1919 Bettis, Valerie
b. 1920 Pitrone, Jean
Maddern
b. 1920 Thomas, Gerald
b. 1922 Hill, George
Roy
b. 1924 LaMarsh, Judy
b. 1925 Mahathir Bin
Mohamad
b. 1926 Howe, Geoffrey
Richard Edward, Sir
b. 1926 Lambsdorff,
Otto
b. 1926 Levine, David
b. 1927 Burch, Dean
b. 1927 Kim Young
Sam
b. 1927 Simpson, Jim
b. 1928 Brown, Les(ter
Louis)
b. 1928 Christiansen,
Jack L
b. 1929 Panic, Milan
b. 1932 Hillerman, John
Benedict
b. 1933 Getty, Gordon
Peter

b. 1934 Gorman, Leon
Arthur
b. 1935 Wilson,
William Julius
b. 1938 Harbison, John
Harris
b. 1940 Goffstein,
Marilyn
b. 1942 Hayes, Bob
b. 1943 Barden, Don H.
b. 1946 Codrescu,
Andrei
b. 1946 Geller, Uri
b. 1947 Criss, Peter
b. 1948 Uchida,
Mitsuko
b. 1949 Cooper, Cecil
Celester
b. 1950 Dolan, Terry
b. 1950 Ferguson, Tom
R
b. 1952 Agutter, Jenny
b. 1954 Cisneros,
Sandra
b. 1956 Baker, Blanche
b. 1957 Bragg, Billy
b. 1965 Utley, Mike
d. 1722 K'ang-hsi
d. 1849 Miller, William
d. 1866 Taylor, Ann
d. 1894 Alcorn, James
Lusk
d. 1910 Neumann,
Angelo
d. 1937 Ludendorff,
Erich Friedrich
Wilhelm
d. 1948 Smith, C
Aubrey
d. 1953 Connelly, One-
Eyed
d. 1953 Ziff, William
Bernard
d. 1954 Hilton, James
d. 1956 Risdon,
Elizabeth
d. 1961 Hart, Moss
d. 1968 Brod, Max
d. 1968 Steinbeck, John
(Ernst)
d. 1970 Schuster, Max
Lincoln
d. 1971 Crawford,
Rusty
d. 1971 Disney, Roy
O(liver)
d. 1972 Hartnett, Gabby
d. 1972 Wright, John
Lloyd
d. 1973 Darin, Bobby
d. 1976 Daley, Richard
Joseph
d. 1979 Illingworth,
Leslie Gilbert
d. 1980 Kintner, Robert
Edmonds
d. 1981 Goodman,
Martin Wise
d. 1982 Rubinstein,
Arthur
d. 1983 Brandt, Bill
d. 1983 Fenelon, Fania
d. 1984 Hill, Lester
d. 1984 Ustinov, Dmitri
Fedorovich

d. 1988 Robinson, Max
C
d. 1990 Rolvaag, Karl
Fritjof
d. 1992 Ross, Steven J
d. 1993 Deming,
W(illiam) Edwards
d. 1994 Arnon, Daniel
I(srael)
d. 1994 Osborn, Robert
C(hesley)
d. 1994 Ponnamperuma,
Cyril (Andrew)
d. 1994 Rusk, (David)
Dean
d. 1994 Trueblood,
D(avid) Elton
d. 1995 Sinclair, Madge
d. 1996 Sagan, Carl
(Edward)
d. 1997 Itami, Juzo
d. 1997 Levertov,
Denise
d. 1997 Steel, Dawn
d. 1998 Hodgkin, Alan
Lloyd, Sir
d. 1999 Snow, Hank
December 21
b. 1118 A'Becket,
Thomas, Saint
b. 1401 Masaccio
b. 1773 Brown, Robert
b. 1795 Ranke, Leopold
von
b. 1800 Rhett, Robert
Barnwell
b. 1804 Disraeli,
Benjamin
b. 1829 Bridgman,
Laura Dewey
b. 1837 McCoy, Joseph
Geiting
b. 1842 Kropotkin,
Peter Alekseyevich,
Prince
b. 1849 Allen, James
Lane
b. 1860 Szold, Henrietta
b. 1870 Haskins,
Charles Homer
b. 1871 Irving,
Laurence Sidney
b. 1872 Terhune, Albert
Payson
b. 1876 Lang, John
Thomas
b. 1879 Stalin, Joseph
b. 1885 Patrick, Frank
A
b. 1886 Papi, Genarro
b. 1890 Muller,
Hermann Joseph
b. 1891 McCormack,
John William
b. 1892 Hagen, Walter
Charles
b. 1896 Rokossovsky,
Konstantin
Konstantinovich
b. 1903 Stroup, Thomas
Bradley
b. 1903 Treat, Lawrence
b. 1905 Powell,
Anthony Dymoke
b. 1908 Barzini, Luigi
Giorgio, Jr.

d. 1921 Watterson, Henry
d. 1925 Munsey, Frank Andrew
d. 1935 Braslau, Sophie
d. 1939 Rainey, Gertrude
d. 1940 West, Nathanael
d. 1941 Mugnone, Leopoldo
d. 1943 Potter, Beatrix
d. 1944 Langdon, Harry
d. 1945 Neurath, Otto
d. 1945 Train, Arthur Cheney
d. 1948 Brian, Donald
d. 1950 Damrosch, Walter Johannes
d. 1957 Zuppke, Robert Carl
d. 1959 Gray, Gilda
d. 1965 Ritz, Al
d. 1968 Swing, Raymond Gram
d. 1969 VonSternberg, Josef
d. 1972 Wallington, Jimmy
d. 1973 Phillips, Irna
d. 1974 Long, Richard
d. 1976 Wright, Russel
d. 1979 Zanuck, Darryl Francis
d. 1984 Merida, Carlos
d. 1985 Condie, Richard P
d. 1986 Macy, John Williams, Jr.
d. 1987 Bernhard, Arnold
d. 1987 Cotton, Henry, Sir
d. 1988 Kahane, Melanie
d. 1989 Beckett, Samuel (Barclay)
d. 1991 Morris, Ernest Brougham
d. 1993 Raskin, A(braham) H(enry)
d. 1995 Meade, James Edward
d. 1995 Pettit, William Thomas
d. 1998 Graham, Virginia

December 23
b. 1682 Gibbs, James
b. 1732 Arkwright, Richard, Sir
b. 1777 Alexander I
b. 1790 Champollion, Jean Francois
b. 1804 Sainte-Beuve, Charles Augustin
b. 1805 Smith, Joseph
b. 1815 Garnet, Henry Highland
b. 1828 Wesendonck, Mathilde Luckemeyer
b. 1850 Straus, Oscar Solomon
b. 1854 Huerta, Victoriano
b. 1856 Duke, James Buchanan

b. 1858 Nemirovich-Danchenko, Vladimir I
b. 1860 Monroe, Harriet
b. 1862 Pirenne, Jean Henri Otto Lucien Marie
b. 1867 Walker, C. J., Madame
b. 1867 Walker, Sarah Breedlove McWilliams
b. 1872 Marin, John
b. 1875 Waldron, Charles D
b. 1885 Sardi, Vincent, Sr.
b. 1887 Blore, Eric
b. 1887 Cromwell, John
b. 1888 Rank, J(oseph) Arthur
b. 1889 Brunner, Emil
b. 1891 Kaplan, Jacob Merrill
b. 1892 Greene, Ward
b. 1893 Douglas, Sholto
b. 1896 Tomasi di Lampedusa, Guiseppe
b. 1897 Denneny, Cy(ril)
b. 1900 Soglow, Otto
b. 1902 Maclean, Norman (Fitzroy)
b. 1903 Kalatozov, Mikhail
b. 1903 Washington, Fredi
b. 1905 Derthick, L(awrence) G(ridley)
b. 1906 Elson, Edward L(ee) R(oy)
b. 1907 Roosevelt, James
b. 1907 Ross, Barney
b. 1908 Karsh, Yousuf
b. 1911 Gregory, James
b. 1911 Jerne, Niels Kaj
b. 1914 Coe, Frederick H
b. 1918 Greco, Jose
b. 1918 Schmidt, Helmut Heinrich Waldemar
b. 1919 Heggen, Thomas Orls, Jr.
b. 1921 Johnson, Robert Willard
b. 1922 Willingham, Calder Baynard, Jr.
b. 1923 Diop, Cheikh Anta
b. 1923 Frankel, Gene
b. 1923 Masursky, Harold
b. 1923 Okun, Milton Theodore
b. 1923 Roman, Ruth
b. 1923 Stern, Leonard B
b. 1923 Stockdale, James
b. 1924 Devine, Dan(iel John)
b. 1924 Kalber, Floyd
b. 1924 Kurland, Bob

b. 1925 Beregovoy, Pierre (Eugene)
b. 1925 Guardino, Harry
b. 1926 Bly, Robert Elwood
b. 1928 Jepsen, Roger William
b. 1929 Weber, Dick
b. 1933 Akihito
b. 1933 Morgan, Frank
b. 1935 Hornung, Paul Vernon
b. 1935 Phillips, Esther
b. 1936 Stacy, James
b. 1940 Graves, Nancy (Stevenson)
b. 1940 Kauokenen, Jorma
b. 1941 Hardin, Tim
b. 1941 Hartman, Elizabeth
b. 1942 Lewis, Loida Nicolas
b. 1943 Silvia
b. 1946 Lucci, Susan
b. 1947 Rodgers, Bill
b. 1948 Ham, Jack Raphael
b. 1948 Sharif, Nawaz
b. 1949 Bender, Ariel
b. 1949 Kostov, Ivan
b. 1952 Kristol, William
b. 1954 Teacher, Brian
b. 1964 Klima, Petr
b. 1964 Vedder, Eddie
d. 1631 Drayton, Michael
d. 1652 Cotton, John
d. 1789 Epee, Charles-Michel
d. 1795 Clinton, Henry, Sir
d. 1810 Queensberry, William Douglas, Duke
d. 1824 Pushmataha
d. 1834 Malthus, Thomas Robert
d. 1872 Catlin, George
d. 1873 Grimke, Sarah Moore
d. 1875 Saint Georges, Jules
d. 1884 Chisum, John Simpson
d. 1888 Oliphant, Laurence
d. 1889 Grady, Henry Woodfin
d. 1896 Hatch, William Henry
d. 1899 Eaton, Dorman Bridgman
d. 1901 Croly, Jane Cunningham
d. 1907 Janssen, Pierre Jules Cesar
d. 1928 Coulter, John Merle
d. 1939 Fokker, Anthony Herman Gerard
d. 1942 Cagle, Red
d. 1944 Gibson, Charles Dana

d. 1946 Davis, John Staige
d. 1948 Tojo, Hideki
d. 1953 Beria, Lavrenti Pavlovich
d. 1959 Halifax, Edward Frederick Lindley Wood
d. 1966 VonDoderer, Heimito
d. 1969 Carias Andino, Tiburcio
d. 1970 Benzell, Mimi
d. 1970 Ruggles, Charles
d. 1972 Atlas, Charles
d. 1972 Heschel, Abraham Joshua
d. 1973 Kuiper, Gerard Peter
d. 1978 Buck, Paul Herman
d. 1978 DeRochemont, Louis
d. 1979 Guggenheim, Peggy
d. 1979 Kunhardt, Dorothy (Meserve)
d. 1981 Kountz, Samuel L(ee)
d. 1982 Webb, Jack Randolph
d. 1986 Husted, Marjorie Child
d. 1986 Wasson, R(obert) Gordon
d. 1991 Krenek, Ernst
d. 1992 Marshak, Robert E(ugene)
d. 1993 Currie, Lauchlin (Bernard)
d. 1993 Roosa, Robert V(incent)
d. 1995 Knowles, Patric
d. 1995 McQueen, Butterfly

December 24
b. 1167 John, King of England
b. 1491 Ignatius of Loyola, Saint
b. 1737 Deane, Silas
b. 1745 Paterson, William
b. 1745 Rush, Benjamin
b. 1754 Crabbe, George
b. 1761 Selim, III
b. 1802 Cockburn, Alexander James Edmund, Sir
b. 1809 Carson, Kit
b. 1809 Porter, William Trotter
b. 1818 Joule, James Prescott
b. 1821 Moreno, Gabriel Garcia
b. 1821 Poole, William Frederick
b. 1822 Arnold, Matthew
b. 1824 Cornelius, Peter
b. 1838 Morley, John, Viscount
b. 1848 Lyons, Sophie Levy

b. 1868 Lasker, Emanuel
b. 1873 Brittain, Harry Ernest, Sir
b. 1880 Gruelle, Johnny
b. 1880 Medtner, Nicholas
b. 1881 Jimenez, Juan Ramon
b. 1887 Jouvet, Louis
b. 1888 Curtiz, Michael
b. 1889 Craig, May
b. 1889 Sauer, Carl Ortwin
b. 1891 Rojankovsky, Feodor Stepanovich
b. 1893 Chatterton, Ruth
b. 1893 Warren, Harry
b. 1894 Guynemer, Georges Marie
b. 1895 Harriman, E(dward) Roland (Noel)
b. 1895 Robinson, M(aurice) R(ichard)
b. 1896 Powdermaker, Hortense
b. 1898 Dodds, Baby
b. 1900 Smallwood, Joey
b. 1903 Cornell, Joseph
b. 1905 Hughes, Howard Robard
b. 1906 Hoffner, Joseph, Cardinal
b. 1906 Walker, John
b. 1906 Waxman, Franz
b. 1907 Cody, John Patrick
b. 1907 Stone, I(sidor) F(einstein)
b. 1909 Rapacki, Adam
b. 1910 Ayres, Mitchell
b. 1912 Llewelyn-Davies, Richard
b. 1913 Erteszek, Jan
b. 1913 Hamilton, Charles
b. 1913 Reinhardt, Ad(olph Frederick)
b. 1914 Cushman, Robert Everton, Jr.
b. 1914 Marterie, Ralph
b. 1919 Soulages, Pierre
b. 1921 Dudley, Bill
b. 1922 Gardner, Ava
b. 1924 Haney, Carol
b. 1925 Sherrill, Robert Glenn
b. 1926 Gunn, Hartford Nelson, Jr.
b. 1927 Simon, Norma Feldstein
b. 1927 Stich-Randall, Teresa
b. 1929 Clark, Mary Higgins
b. 1930 De Patie, David H
b. 1930 Joffrey, Robert
b. 1932 Cowdrey, (Michael) Colin
b. 1935 Carlisle, Kevin
b. 1940 Fauci, Anthony Stephen

b. 1944 Curb, Mike
b. 1944 Gordy, Emory, Jr.
b. 1945 Meyer, Nicholas
b. 1946 Sessions, Jeff
b. 1954 Figueres Olsen, Jose Maria
d. 1453 Dunstable, John
d. 1524 DaGama, Vasco
d. 1799 Ditters, Karl
d. 1812 Barlow, Joel
d. 1863 Thackeray, William Makepeace
d. 1865 Eastlake, Charles Lock, Sir
d. 1869 Stanton, Edwin McMasters
d. 1873 Hopkins, Johns
d. 1881 Bacon, Leonard Woolsey
d. 1901 King, Clarence
d. 1914 Muir, John
d. 1927 Dines, William Henry
d. 1929 Hitchcock, Raymond
d. 1934 Hunt, George Wylie Paul
d. 1935 Berg, Alban
d. 1938 Capek, Karel
d. 1940 Hill, Billy
d. 1942 Darlan, Jean Louis Xavier Francois
d. 1944 Castle, Frederick W
d. 1950 Elliott, Gertrude
d. 1952 Danforth, William H
d. 1953 Linton, Ralph
d. 1957 Barea, Arturo
d. 1957 Talmadge, Norma
d. 1959 Goulding, Edmund
d. 1961 Hamilton, Charles Harold St. John
d. 1961 Hillyer, Robert
d. 1963 Tzara, Tristan
d. 1966 Peterson, Virgilia
d. 1967 Hunt, Frazier
d. 1973 Korda, Michael
d. 1975 Herrmann, Bernard
d. 1975 Losch, Tilly
d. 1977 Velasco Alvarado, Juan
d. 1980 Doenitz, Karl C
d. 1980 Neville, Kris Ottman
d. 1980 Wilder, Alec
d. 1982 Aragon, Louis Marie Antoine Alfred
d. 1984 Lawford, Peter
d. 1985 Abbas, Ferhat
d. 1987 Den Uyl, Joop
d. 1989 Morial, Ernest Nathan
d. 1990 Wendell Oliver, Scott, Sr.
d. 1991 Hudson, Walter
d. 1991 Sorensen, Virginia
d. 1992 Culliford, Peyo

d. 1992 Gleason, Thomas W(illiam)
d. 1993 Peale, Norman Vincent
d. 1994 Boswell, John (Eastburn)
d. 1994 Brazzi, Rossano
d. 1994 Haydon, Julie
d. 1994 Osborne, John (James)
d. 1996 Jenkins, Newell
d. 1997 Mifune, Toshiro
d. 1998 Apps, Syl
d. 1999 Cattani, Richard J.
d. 1999 Couve de Murville, (Jacques) Maurice
d. 1999 Figueiredo, Joao Baptista de Oliveira

December 25
b. 1642 Newton, Isaac, Sir
b. 1709 La Mettrie, Julien Offray de
b. 1717 Pius, VI
b. 1721 Collins, William
b. 1728 Hiller, Johann Adam
b. 1762 Kelly, Michael
b. 1796 Caballero, Fernan
b. 1801 Harper, Joseph Wesley
b. 1810 Langstroth, Lorenzo Lorraine
b. 1813 Roach, John
b. 1817 Van Camp, Gilbert C
b. 1821 Barton, Clara Harlowe
b. 1828 DeVinne, Theodore Low
b. 1829 Gilmore, Patrick Sarsfield
b. 1837 Gerry, Elbridge Thomas
b. 1837 Wagner, Cosima Liszt
b. 1856 Galvin, Pud
b. 1856 Thomas, Brandon
b. 1857? LaFlesche, Francis
b. 1862 Meriwether, Lee
b. 1863 Pathe, Charles
b. 1864 Maher, George Washington
b. 1865 Booth, Evangeline Cory
b. 1865 Templeton, Fay
b. 1870 Rubinstein, Helena
b. 1874 Cavalieri, Lina
b. 1876 Hughan, Jessie Wallace
b. 1876 Jinnah, Mohammed Ali
b. 1876 Windaus, Adolf Otto Reinhold
b. 1877 Trihey, Harry
b. 1878 Chevrolet, Louis Joseph

b. 1878 Schenck, Joseph M
b. 1879 George, Grace
b. 1881 Dill, John Greer, Sir
b. 1883 Utrillo, Maurice
b. 1885 Manship, Paul
b. 1885 Nesbit, Evelyn
b. 1886 Barker, Elliott
b. 1886 Ory, Kid
b. 1886 Rosenzweig, Franz
b. 1887 Hilton, Conrad Nicholson
b. 1888 Henderson, Robert W
b. 1888 Lawrence, David
b. 1888 Stravinsky, Vera de Bossett
b. 1889 Wallace, Lila Bell Acheson
b. 1892 West, Rebecca, Dame
b. 1893 Ripley, Robert Leroy
b. 1899 Power, Donald Clinton
b. 1899 Soyer, Moses
b. 1899 Soyer, Raphael
b. 1900 MacLane, Barton
b. 1903 Bromberg, J Edward
b. 1903 Cobleigh, Ira Underwood
b. 1903 Samstag, Nicholas
b. 1904 Christensen, Harold
b. 1904 Herzberg, Gerhard
b. 1904 Swarthout, Gladys
b. 1906 Barnes-Taeuber, Irene
b. 1906 Clifford, Clark M(cAdams)
b. 1906 Grade, Lew, Sir
b. 1906 Ruska, Ernst
b. 1907 Calloway, Cab
b. 1907 Cruickshank, Andrew John
b. 1908 Crisp, Quentin
b. 1908 Twelvetrees, Helen
b. 1909 Mazurki, Mike
b. 1910 Leiber, Fritz (Reuter), Jr.
b. 1911 Langley, Noel
b. 1913 Martin, Tony
b. 1913 Moczar, Mieczyslaw
b. 1914 Lewis, Oscar
b. 1914 Mabee, Carleton
b. 1915 Wilson, Richard
b. 1917 Lowe, Jack (Warren)
b. 1918 Ben Bella, Ahmed
b. 1918 Sadat, Anwar el
b. 1922 Lahbabi, Mohammed Aziz
b. 1924 Daddah, Moktar Ould

b. 1924 Serling, Rod
b. 1926 Vajpayee, Atal Behari
b. 1927 Besse, Georges Noel
b. 1927 Fox, Nellie
b. 1931 Castaneda, Carlos
b. 1931 Lewis, Byron E(ugene)
b. 1934 Martinez, Bob
b. 1935 Hoge, James Fulton, Jr.
b. 1935 Little Richard
b. 1936 Merchant, Ismail
b. 1937 Casper, Gerhard
b. 1939 James, Bob
b. 1940 Brown, Peter
b. 1945 Stabler, Ken(neth Michael)
b. 1946 Buffett, Jimmy
b. 1946 Csonka, Larry
b. 1946? Sandy, Gary
b. 1948 Mandrell, Barbara Ann
b. 1949 Pastorini, Dan(te Anthony, Jr.)
b. 1949 Spacek, Sissy
b. 1950 DiBello, Paul
b. 1950 Rote, Kyle, Jr.
b. 1954 Lennox, Annie
b. 1954 Wariner, Steve
b. 1954 Williams, Maggie
b. 1957 Persinger, Gregory A
b. 1958 Henderson, Rickey (Henley)
b. 1962 Graham, Lawrence Otis
b. 1965 Webb, Veronica
d. 1306 Jacopone da Todi
d. 1635 Champlain, Samuel de
d. 1676 Cavendish, William, Duke of Newcastle
d. 1761 Elizabeth Petrovna
d. 1820 Fouche, Joseph
d. 1822 Pinkney, William
d. 1864 Wallack, James William
d. 1865 Barth, Heinrich
d. 1868 Yale, Linus
d. 1899 Coues, Elliott
d. 1918 Miller, Olive Thorne
d. 1921 Korolenko, Vladimir Galaktionovich
d. 1926 Yoshihito
d. 1935 Bourget, Paul (Charles Joseph)
d. 1936 Brisbane, Arthur
d. 1937 Baker, Newton D(iehl)
d. 1940 Ayres, Agnes
d. 1941 Bates, Blanche Lyon
d. 1946 Fields, W C

d. 1950 Torrence, Ridgely
d. 1953 Shubert, Lee
d. 1954 Ace, Johnny
d. 1954 Bailey, Liberty Hyde
d. 1956 Dwiggins, William Addison
d. 1957 Campbell, Walter Stanley
d. 1957 Pathe, Charles
d. 1960 Garrod, Heathcote William
d. 1961 Brewster, (Ralph) Owen
d. 1961 Loewi, Otto
d. 1962 Austin, Warren R(obinson)
d. 1962 Davis, Tobe
d. 1966 Brady, St. Elmo
d. 1966 Nick the Greek
d. 1970 Wroth, Lawrence Counselman
d. 1973 Inonu, Ismet
d. 1974 Beard, Myron Gould
d. 1975 Burchard, John Ely
d. 1976 Darro, Frankie
d. 1977 Chaplin, Charlie
d. 1978 Mortimer, Charles Greenough
d. 1979 Blondell, Joan
d. 1980 Ku Chieh-kang
d. 1982 Bowling, Roger
d. 1982 Pearl, Jack
d. 1983 Miro, Joan
d. 1989 Ceausescu, Nicolae
d. 1989 Martin, Billy
d. 1992 Davidson, Garrison H(olt)
d. 1992 Dickens, Monica Enid
d. 1992 Joseph, Helen
d. 1994 Dreyfus, Pierre
d. 1994 Singh, Giani Zail
d. 1995 Levinas, Emmanuel
d. 1995 Martin, Dean
d. 1995 Slonimsky, Nicolas
d. 1997 Pyle, Denver
d. 1997 Strehler, Giorgio
d. 1998 Hatfield, Hurd

December 26
b. 1194 Frederick II
b. 1716 Gray, Thomas
b. 1738 Nelson, Thomas, Jr.
b. 1792 Babbage, Charles
b. 1819 Southworth, Emma Dorothy Eliza Nevitte
b. 1820 Boucicault, Dion Lardner
b. 1823 Cairnes, John Elliott
b. 1837 Bulkeley, Morgan G
b. 1837 Dewey, George
b. 1853 Bazin, Rene

b. 1854 Tappan, Eva March
b. 1874 Angell, Norman
b. 1874 Rothier, Leon
b. 1878 Bowman, Isaiah
b. 1885 Eboue, Adolphe Felix Sylvestre
b. 1887 Booth, Charles Brandon
b. 1891 Miller, Henry (Valentine)
b. 1893 Golschmann, Vladimir
b. 1893 Mao Zedong
b. 1894 Toomer, Jean
b. 1899 Mannes, Leopold Damrosch
b. 1901 Lipsig, Harry H(avon)
b. 1902 Lytle, Andrew Nelson
b. 1903 Lazzeri, Tony
b. 1904 Stern, James
b. 1904 Stribling, Young
b. 1905 Loeb, William
b. 1906 Cook, Elisha, Jr.
b. 1907 Gore, Albert Arnold
b. 1909 Wakeman, Frederic
b. 1914 Widmark, Richard
b. 1917 Woods, Rose Mary
b. 1920 Gendron, Maurice
b. 1920 Hughes, Emmet John
b. 1921 Allen, Steve
b. 1923 Artschwager, Richard (Ernst)
b. 1924 Davis, Glenn W
b. 1926 Brown, Earle
b. 1926 Lilly, Doris
b. 1927 King, Alan
b. 1929 Regine
b. 1930 Moffat, Donald
b. 1935 Humphries, Frederick (S.)
b. 1935 Ullman, Norm(an Victor Alexander)
b. 1936 Ross, Bobby
b. 1937? Dukakis, Kitty
b. 1937 Eyadema, Etienne Gnassingbe
b. 1938 Fakir, Abdul
b. 1938 Snyder, Solomon H(albert)
b. 1939 Martin, Lynn
b. 1940 Spector, Phil(lip Harvey)
b. 1942 Cerezo (Arevalo), Vinicio
b. 1944 Lapotaire, Jane
b. 1946 Krens, Thomas
b. 1947 Fisk, Carlton Ernest
b. 1948 Justiz, Manuel Jon
b. 1951 Scofield, John
b. 1953 Fernandez, Leonel
b. 1954 Butcher, Susan

b. 1954 Smith, Ozzie
b. 1955 Bayh, Evan
d. 1530 Babur
d. 1585 Ronsard, Pierre de
d. 1771 Helvetius, Claude Adrien
d. 1797 Wilkes, John
d. 1831 Girard, Stephen
d. 1858 Gadsden, James
d. 1869 Poiseuille, Jean Louis Marie
d. 1886 Logan, John Alexander
d. 1890 Schliemann, Heinrich
d. 1896 Du Bois-Reymond, Emil
d. 1909 Remington, Frederic
d. 1930 Hubbard, Kin
d. 1931 Dewey, Melvil
d. 1934 Fisher, Rudolph
d. 1940 Frohman, Daniel
d. 1945 Keyes, Roger John Brownlow, Baron
d. 1950 Stephens, James
d. 1952 Hedin, Sven Anders
d. 1953 Milne, David Brown
d. 1960 Bellanca, Giuseppe Mario
d. 1962 Langer, Lawrence
d. 1963 Shubert, Jacob J
d. 1965 Hess, Myra, Dame
d. 1968 Fellig, Arthur
d. 1971 O'Donnell, Emmett, Jr.
d. 1972 Truman, Harry S
d. 1973 Geray, Steven
d. 1974 Benny, Jack
d. 1976 Hart, Philip Aloysius
d. 1977 Hawks, Howard Winchester
d. 1980 Dewey, Charles Schuveldt
d. 1980 Jenkins, Ray Howard
d. 1980 Smith, Tony
d. 1984 Barraclough, Geoffrey
d. 1985 Austin, John Paul
d. 1986 Lanchester, Elsa
d. 1989 Harvey, Doug(las Norman)
d. 1990 Cruzan, Nancy
d. 1992 Kemeny, John G(eorge)
d. 1992 Rajagopalachari, Chakravarti
d. 1993 Beck, Dave
d. 1994 Schiller, Karl (August Fritz)
d. 1999 Mayfield, Curtis (Lee)

December 27

b. 1525 Palestrina, Giovanni
b. 1571 Kepler, Johannes
b. 1714 Whitefield, George
b. 1771 Johnson, William
b. 1773 Cayley, George, Sir
b. 1793 Laing, Alexander Gordon
b. 1798 Corcoran, William Wilson
b. 1814 Simon, Jules Francois
b. 1822 Pasteur, Louis
b. 1823 Bowell, Mackenzie, Sir
b. 1829 Helper, Hinton Rowan
b. 1841 Spitta, Philipp
b. 1857 Manners, Charles
b. 1860 Bergey, David Hendricks
b. 1867 Benda, Julien
b. 1879 Greenstreet, Sydney Hughes
b. 1879 Johnson, Bunk
b. 1882 Hidalgo, Elvira de
b. 1883 Eaton, Cyrus Stephen
b. 1896 Bromfield, Louis Brucker
b. 1896 Zuckmayer, Carl
b. 1897 Konev, Ivan Stepanovich
b. 1901 Dietrich, Marlene
b. 1901 Hayter, Stanley William
b. 1904 D'Aulaire, Ingri Mortenson
b. 1905 Coslow, Sam
b. 1906 Feininger, Andreas (Bernhard Lyonel)
b. 1906 Levant, Oscar
b. 1909 Holland, Charles
b. 1909 Jablonski, Henryk
b. 1910 Olson, Charles John
b. 1911 Russell, Anna
b. 1915 Masters, William Howell
b. 1921 Lipshutz, Robert Jerome
b. 1921 Rossi, Peter Henry
b. 1921 Wallerstein, Jusith S.
b. 1924 McClure, James A
b. 1925 Arens, Moshe
b. 1926 Carazo (Odio), Rodrigo
b. 1926 Salk, Lee
b. 1927 Armstrong, Anne Legendre
b. 1930 Greenfield, Meg

b. 1930 Sheed, Wilfrid John Joseph
b. 1931 Phieu, Le Kha
b. 1931 Tomlinson, Jill
b. 1933 Marr, Dave
b. 1934 Latynina, Larisa Semyonovna
b. 1935 Lanvin, Bernard
b. 1936 Trovoada, Miguel
b. 1941 Amos, John
b. 1941 Richardson, Nolan
b. 1942 Rothstein, Ron
b. 1943 Roberts, Cokie
b. 1945 Jones, Ingrid Saunders
b. 1948 Depardieu, Gerard
b. 1951 Zedillo Ponce de Leon, Ernesto
b. 1952 Bonoff, Karla
b. 1952 Feldshuh, Tovah
b. 1953 Kent, Arthur
b. 1963 Cohen, Anthony
d. 1707 Mabillon, Jean
d. 1834 Lamb, Charles
d. 1836 Austin, Stephen Fuller
d. 1914 Dodge, Grace Hoadley
d. 1914 Hall, Charles Martin
d. 1923 Owens, Michael Joseph
d. 1933 Fowler, Henry Watson
d. 1936 Seeckt, Hans von
d. 1938 Bridges, Calvin Blackman
d. 1938 Gale, Zona
d. 1938 Lawrence, Florence
d. 1938 Mandelstam, Osip Emilyevich
d. 1938 Vandervelde, Emile
d. 1944 Banning, Kendall
d. 1944 Beach, H H A, Mrs.
d. 1947 Beam, James B
d. 1950 Beckmann, Max
d. 1955 Culbertson, Ely
d. 1955 Fisher, Ham(mond Edward)
d. 1956 Marks, Percy
d. 1959 Reyes, Alfonso
d. 1961 Bercovici, Konrad
d. 1965 Kiesler, Frederick John
d. 1966 Rea, Gardner
d. 1967 Flavin, Martin Archer
d. 1967 Miller, Max (Carlton)
d. 1969 Flint, William Russell, Sir
d. 1972 Garrigue, Jean
d. 1972 Pearson, Lester B(owles)
d. 1973 DeSalvo, Albert

d. 1974 Vanderbilt, Amy
d. 1976 Mainbocher
d. 1978 Boumedienne, Houari
d. 1981 Carmichael, Hoagy
d. 1982 Swigert, Jack
d. 1983 Demarest, William
d. 1984 Zevin, B(enjamin) D(avid)
d. 1985 Fossey, Dian
d. 1986 Dangerfield, George Bubb
d. 1986 Malone, Dumas
d. 1987 Alley, Rewi
d. 1988 Ashby, Hal
d. 1989 Baum, Kurt
d. 1992 Albert, Stephen Joel
d. 1992 Boyle, Kay
d. 1993 Callen, Michael
d. 1994 Reynolds, Allie
d. 1995 Cherkassky, Shura
d. 1996 Walsh, William B(ertalan)
d. 1997 Gill, Brendan
d. 1999 Goldenson, Leonard H(arry)

December 28

b. 1789 Sedgwick, Catherine Maria
b. 1816 Packard, Elizabeth Parsons Ware
b. 1823 Scott, Thomas Alexander
b. 1835 Geikie, Archibald, Sir
b. 1850 Tamagno, Francesco
b. 1855 Zorrilla de San Martin, Juan
b. 1856 Wilson, Woodrow
b. 1859 Taussig, Frank William
b. 1869 Trumbauer, Horace
b. 1870 Hendrick, Burton Jesse
b. 1872 Baroja (y Nessi), Pio
b. 1873 Harkins, William Draper
b. 1882 Eddington, Arthur Stanley, Sir
b. 1885 Allen, Arthur Augustus
b. 1885 Tatlin, Vladimir Yevgrapovich
b. 1886 Cloud, Henry Roe
b. 1888 Branner, Martin Michael
b. 1894 Matthews, Burnita S(helton)
b. 1894 Romer, Alfred Sherwood
b. 1895 Brink, Carol Ryrie
b. 1896 Sessions, Roger Huntington
b. 1898 Franken, Rose

b. 1899 Murnau, Friedrich W
b. 1899 Poage, W(illiam) R(obert)
b. 1900 Lyons, Ted
b. 1902 Adler, Mortimer J(erome)
b. 1905 Arquette, Cliff
b. 1905 Dean, Gordon Evans
b. 1905 Hines, Fatha
b. 1906 Bridges, Tommy
b. 1908 Ayres, Lew
b. 1908 Mielke, Erich
b. 1911 Levenson, Sam(uel)
b. 1913 Jacobi, Lou
b. 1914 Bowman, Lee
b. 1917 Clarke, Ellis Emmanuel Innocent, Sir
b. 1920 Van Buren, Steve W
b. 1922 Lee, Stan
b. 1923 Duggan, Andrew
b. 1924 Obote, Milton
b. 1925 Neff, Hildegarde
b. 1927 Babiuch, Edward
b. 1929 Bieber, Owen Frederick
b. 1929 Sawchuk, Terry
b. 1931 Milner, Martin Sam
b. 1932 Haber, Joyce
b. 1932 Howell, Harry
b. 1932 Puig, Manuel
b. 1933 Brown, John Young, Jr.
b. 1933 Portis, Charles
b. 1934 Akers, John Fellows
b. 1934 Smith, Maggie Natalie
b. 1938 Yarnell, Bruce
b. 1942 Horowitz, Paul
b. 1943 Peterson, David Robert
b. 1944 Faber, Sandra M(oore)
b. 1944 Mullis, Kary B(anks)
b. 1945 Birendra Bir Bikram, Shah Dev
b. 1946 Green, Hubie
b. 1946 Johnson, Tim
b. 1946 Winter, Edgar Holand
b. 1950 Chilton, Alex
b. 1950 Tutwiler, Margaret (DeBardeleben)
b. 1952 Knight, Ray
b. 1953 Clayderman, Richard
b. 1953 Pittman, Robert W(arren)
b. 1954 Washington, Denzel, Jr.
b. 1956 Kennedy, Nigel Paul
b. 1958 Diffie, Joe

b. 1959 Walls, Everson
Collins
b. 1960 Bourque,
Ray(mond Jean)
b. 1981 Carr, Elizabeth
Jordan
d. 1446 Clement VIII
d. 1622 Francis of
Sales, St.
d. 1694 Mary, II
d. 1706 Bayle, Pierre
d. 1825 Wilkinson,
James
d. 1859 Macaulay,
Thomas Babington
Macaulay, Baron
d. 1874 Smith, Gerrit
d. 1876 Paludan-Muller,
Frederik
d. 1898 Morrill, Justin
Smith
d. 1900 Tyler, Moses
Coit
d. 1903 Gissing, George
Robert
d. 1921 Hare, John, Sir
d. 1923 Eiffel,
Alexandre Gustave
d. 1924 Spitteler, Karl
Friedrich Georg
d. 1925 Esenin, Sergei
Aleksandrovich
d. 1933 Vonnoh, Robert
William
d. 1934 Sherman,
Lowell
d. 1935 Day, Clarence
Shepard, Jr.
d. 1937 Ravel, Maurice
Joseph
d. 1941 Updike, Daniel
Berkeley
d. 1942 Blomfield,
Reginald Theodore,
Sir
d. 1943? Mandelstam,
Osip Emilyevich
d. 1945 Dreiser,
Theodore
d. 1946 Bond, Carrie
Jacobs
d. 1946 Hooker, Brian
d. 1947 Crowninshield,
Francis Welch
d. 1947 Victor
Emmanuel III
d. 1949 Allen, Hervey
d. 1949 Anderson, Ivie
d. 1951 Fairbank, Janet
Ayer
d. 1956 Bennett, John
d. 1961 Wilson, Edith
Bolling (Galt)
d. 1963 Hindemith, Paul
d. 1963 Liebling, Abbot
Joseph
d. 1964 Sterrett, Cliff
d. 1965 Thorndike,
Lynn
d. 1969 Molinos,
Miguel de
d. 1970 Rivers, L(ucius)
Mendel
d. 1971 Steiner, Max
d. 1976 King, Freddy
d. 1977 Heloise

d. 1977 Minsky, Harold
d. 1980 Levene, Sam
d. 1981 Davis, James
Curran
d. 1981 Stoodard,
George Dinsmore
d. 1983 Demaret,
Jimmy
d. 1983 Wilson, Dennis
d. 1984 Peckinpah, Sam
d. 1985 Blackburn,
Molly
d. 1986 Dolan, Terry
d. 1986 MacDonald,
John Dann
d. 1987 Kleban, Edward
Lawrence
d. 1987 Malik, Charles
Habib
d. 1988 Loder, John
d. 1990 Martin, Kiel
d. 1992 Maglie,
Sal(vatore Anthony)
d. 1992 Quaison-
Sackey, Alex(ander)
d. 1993 Shirer, William
L(awrence)
d. 1995 Dabney,
Virginius
d. 1996 Carfagno,
Edward
d. 1999 Moore, Clayton

December 29
b. 1721 Pompadour,
Jeanne Antoinette
Poisson
b. 1766 Macintosh,
Charles
b. 1800 Goodyear,
Charles
b. 1808 Johnson,
Andrew
b. 1809 Gladstone,
William Ewart
b. 1816 Ludwig, Karl
Friedrich Wilhelm
b. 1848 Cheney, John
Vance
b. 1859 Carranza,
Venustiano
b. 1874 Honeywell,
Mark Charles
b. 1876 Casals, Pablo
(Pau Carlos Salvador)
b. 1876 DeLuca,
Giuseppe
b. 1879 Mitchell, Billy
b. 1881 Willard, Jess
b. 1891 Hall, Joyce
Clyde
b. 1894 Hill, Lester
b. 1896 Siqueiros,
David A
b. 1897 Mayer, Albert
b. 1898 Bledsoe, Jules
b. 1898 Cooke, Samuel
b. 1900 Corcoran,
Thomas Gardiner
b. 1902 Stewart,
Nels(on Robert)
b. 1903 McCoy, Clyde
b. 1907 Weaver, Robert
C(lifton)
b. 1911 Fuchs, Klaus
b. 1912 Glanville-Hicks,
Peggy

b. 1913 Werner, Pierre
b. 1915 Ruark, Robert
Chester
b. 1917 Bradley, Tom
b. 1919 Murray, Jim
b. 1920 Lindfors,
Viveca
b. 1922 Gaddis, William
(Thomas)
b. 1924 Yankelovich,
Daniel
b. 1925 Merrill, Dina
b. 1927 Stanfield, Andy
b. 1932 Swenson, Inga
b. 1934 Flanders, Ed
b. 1934 Jarriel, Tom
b. 1936 Moore, Mary
Tyler
b. 1936 Nitschke,
Ray(mond E.)
b. 1938 Voight, Jon
b. 1939 Huizenga,
H(arry) Wayne
b. 1940 Hansen, Fred
Morgan
b. 1946 Faithfull,
Marianne
b. 1946 Pincay, Laffit,
Jr.
b. 1946 Trible, Paul
Seward, Jr.
b. 1947 Danson, Ted
b. 1950 Kimbro, Dennis
(Paul)
b. 1952 Kirkland,
Gelsey
b. 1953 Elliman,
Yvonne
d. 1170 A'Becket,
Thomas, Saint
d. 1605 Davis, John
d. 1689 Sydenham,
Thomas
d. 1743 Rigaud,
Hyacinthe
d. 1825 David, Jacques
Louis
d. 1890 Big Foot
d. 1890 Feuillet, Octave
d. 1894 Rossetti,
Christina Georgina
d. 1897 Linton, William
James
d. 1912 MacCameron,
Robert L
d. 1919 Osler, William,
Sir
d. 1926 Rilke, Rainer
Maria
d. 1929 Jefferson, Blind
Lemon
d. 1937 Marquis, Don
Robert Perry
d. 1940 Birch, Stephen
d. 1941 Eilshemius,
Louis Michel
d. 1943 Young, Art(hur
Henry)
d. 1946 Shirley, Ralph
d. 1952 Henderson,
Fletcher
d. 1958 Humphrey,
Doris
d. 1960 Phillpotts, Eden
d. 1967 Whiteman, Paul
d. 1970 Liston, Sonny

d. 1971 Harlan, John
Marshall, II
d. 1972 Cornell, Joseph
d. 1975 Gibbons, Euell
d. 1979 Hebert, F(elix)
Edward
d. 1980 Hardin, Tim
d. 1980 Mandelstam,
Nadezhda
Yakovlevna
d. 1980 Westheimer,
Irvin Ferdinand
d. 1981 McNaughton,
F(oye) F(isk)
d. 1982 Gallen, Hugh J
d. 1984 Robin, Leo
d. 1986 Bolz, Lothar
d. 1986 MacMillan,
Harold
d. 1986 Tarkovsky,
Andrei (Arsenyich)
d. 1987 Bissell, Patrick
d. 1989 Oberth,
Hermann Julius
d. 1992 Segal, Vivienne

December 30
b. 40 Titus
b. 1784 Long, Stephen
H
b. 1787 Kotzebue, Otto
von
b. 1819 Fontane,
Theodor
b. 1847 Altgeld, John
Peter
b. 1851 Candler, Asa
Griggs
b. 1853 Messager,
Andre Charles
Prosper
b. 1859 Foerster, Josef
Bohuslav
b. 1865 Kipling,
Rudyard
b. 1865 Shirley, Ralph
b. 1869 Leacock,
Stephen Butler
b. 1873 Smith, Alfred
Emanuel
b. 1878 Aberhart,
William
b. 1880 Einstein, Alfred
b. 1883 Patrick, Lester
B
b. 1884 Tojo, Hideki
b. 1887 Broad, C(harlie)
D(unbar)
b. 1890 Ruiz Cortines,
Adolfo
b. 1891 Pinay, Antoine
b. 1894 Bakeless, John
Edwin
b. 1895 Hartley, L(eslie)
P(oles)
b. 1895 Lopez, Vincent
b. 1899 Ingstad, Helge
Marcus
b. 1900 Barnhart,
Clarence L(ewis)
b. 1901 Delaney,
Beauford
b. 1904 Kabalevsky,
Dmitri Borisovich
b. 1906 Bruce, Louis
R., Jr.
b. 1906 Reed, Carol, Sir

b. 1907 Lovelace, William Randolph, II
b. 1910 Bowles, Paul (Frederick)
b. 1911 Friendly, Alfred
b. 1911 Nolan, Jeanette
b. 1912 Curry, Peggy Simson
b. 1913 Barrett, William Christopher
b. 1914 Parks, Bert
b. 1918 Smith, W(illiam) Eugene
b. 1919 Van Fleet, Jo
b. 1920 Lord, Jack
b. 1921 Karami, Rashid Abdul Hamid
b. 1924 Brill, Yvonne Claeys
b. 1928 Diddley, Bo
b. 1931 Davis, Skeeter
b. 1933 Silverstein, Alvin
b. 1934 Daniloff, Nicholas
b. 1935 Bongo, Albert-Bernard (Omar)
b. 1935 Koufax, Sandy
b. 1935 Tamblyn, Russ
b. 1937 Hartford, John Cowan
b. 1937 Stookey, Paul
b. 1938 Bologna, Joseph
b. 1939 Shannon, Del
b. 1940 Burrows, James
b. 1940 Cousteau, Philippe
b. 1940 Pentifallo, Kenny
b. 1941 Renfro, Mel(vin Lacy)
b. 1942 Bukovsky, Vladimir
b. 1942 Nesmith, Mike
b. 1945 Jones, Davy
b. 1946 Smith, Patti
b. 1946 Takei, Kei
b. 1947 Lynne, Jeff
b. 1949 Forsythe, William
b. 1952 Anderson, June
b. 1954 Beam, Joseph
b. 1956 Ralph, Sheryl Lee
b. 1957 Lauer, Matt
b. 1959 Ullman, Tracey
b. 1961 Johnson, Ben
b. 1975 Woods, Tiger
d. 1644 Helmont, Jan Baptista van
d. 1691 Boyle, Robert
d. 1796 Lemoyne, Jean-Baptiste
d. 1802 Lewis, Francis
d. 1865 Davis, Henry Winter
d. 1873 Baylor, Robert Emmet Bledsoe
d. 1893 Baker, Samuel White, Sir
d. 1894 Bloomer, Amelia Jenks
d. 1896 Rizal, Jose
d. 1899 Paget, James, Sir

d. 1928 York, Edward Palmer
d. 1931 Power, Tyrone
d. 1935 Reading, 1st Marquess of
d. 1943 Bosworth, Hobart van Zandt
d. 1944 Rolland, Romain
d. 1945 Hunter, Glenn
d. 1946 Cadman, Charles Wakefield
d. 1947 Whitehead, Alfred North
d. 1948 Ault, George Christian
d. 1956 Draper, Ruth
d. 1962 Lovejoy, Arthur Oncken (Schauffler)
d. 1962 Rosbaud, Hans
d. 1966 Herter, Christian Archibald
d. 1967 Burger, Carl Victor
d. 1967 Conacher, Charlie
d. 1967 Massey, Vincent
d. 1968 Lie, Trygve Halvdan
d. 1969 Trnka, Jiri
d. 1970 Ulric, Lenore
d. 1979 Rodgers, Richard
d. 1983 Vargas, Alberto
d. 1988 Noguchi, Isamu
d. 1992 Healy, Timothy S(tafford)
d. 1993 Lazar, Irving Paul
d. 1995 Kuhn, Irene
d. 1996 Ayres, Lew
d. 1996 Nance, Jack
d. 1997 Dolci, Danilo

December 31
b. Neuwirth, Bebe
b. 1320 Wycliffe, John
b. 1491 Cartier, Jacques
b. 1514 Vesalius, Andreas
b. 1668 Boerhaave, Hermann
b. 1720 Charles Edward Louis Philip Casimir Stuart
b. 1720 Stuart, Charles Edward Louis Philip
b. 1738 Cornwallis, Charles, Marquis
b. 1783 MacDonough, Thomas
b. 1805 Agoult, Marie Catherine Sophie d'
b. 1815 Meade, George Gordon
b. 1817 Fields, James Thomas
b. 1830? Smith, Alexander
b. 1831 Terhune, Mary Virginia
b. 1853 Bliss, Tasker Howard
b. 1855 Pascoli, Giovanni
b. 1857 Kelly, King

b. 1860 Thompson, John Taliaferro
b. 1864 Aitkin, Robert Grant
b. 1864 Ritchey, George Willis
b. 1866 Harding, Chester
b. 1869 Matisse, Henri Emile Benoit
b. 1870 Connolly, Tommy
b. 1878 Quiroga, Horacio
b. 1880 Marshall, George Catlett
b. 1881 Pechstein, Max
b. 1882 Jones, Benjamin Allyn
b. 1884 Arden, Elizabeth
b. 1884 Reed, Stanley Forman
b. 1884 Viereck, George Sylvester
b. 1885 Leslie, Edgar
b. 1887 Lalonde, Newsy
b. 1892 Robards, Jason
b. 1894 Negri, Pola
b. 1897 Orry-Kelly
b. 1899 Mearns, David Chambers
b. 1899 Wummer, John
b. 1900 Burke, Selma (Hortense)
b. 1904 Gardiner, Chuck
b. 1904 Milstein, Nathan
b. 1905 Mollet, Guy
b. 1905 Styne, Jule
b. 1908 Kirby, John
b. 1908 Lewyt, Alexander Milton
b. 1908 Rothmuller, Marko A
b. 1908 Wiesenthal, Simon
b. 1909 Jones, Jonah
b. 1910 Kollmar, Richard
b. 1914 Brady, Pat
b. 1916 Boller, Paul Franklin, Jr.
b. 1916 Wierwille, Victor Paul
b. 1918 Hagg, Gunder
b. 1922 Bookout, John Frank, Jr.
b. 1922 McCracken, Joan
b. 1922 Stamos, Theodoros
b. 1924 Allen, Rex E., Sr.
b. 1924 Brown, Pamela Beatrice
b. 1924 Kelley, Frank Joseph
b. 1925 Jones, Candy
b. 1926 Riley, Helen Caldwell Day
b. 1927 Hanks, Nancy
b. 1928 McElhenny, Hugh

b. 1930 Escalante, Jaime
b. 1930 Odetta
b. 1931 Baker, Gwendolyn Calvert
b. 1936 Anderson, W(illiam) French
b. 1936 Major, Clarence
b. 1937 Hopkins, Anthony (Philip), Sir
b. 1942 Summers, Andy
b. 1943 Denver, John
b. 1943 Kingsley, Ben
b. 1943 Miles, Sarah
b. 1944 Hackford, Taylor
b. 1945? Carrera, Barbara
b. 1946 Furstenberg, Diane Halfin von
b. 1947 Cummings, Burton
b. 1948? Matheson, Tim
b. 1948 Robert, Rene Paul
b. 1948 Summer, Donna
b. 1951 Goytisolo, Fermin
b. 1952 Briscoe, Connie
b. 1952 Ogletree, Charles (J.), Jr.
b. 1953 Hedges, Michael
b. 1959 Kilmer, Val
b. 1961 Coupland, Douglas
b. 1965 Gong Li
d. 1384 Wycliffe, John
d. 1646 Mogila, Peter
d. 1719 Flamsteed, John
d. 1775 Montgomery, Richard
d. 1799 Marmontel, Jean Francois
d. 1864 Dallas, George Mifflin
d. 1877 Courbet, Gustave
d. 1877 Courbet, (Jean Desire) Gustave
d. 1882 Gambetta, Leon
d. 1891 Crowther, Samuel Adjai
d. 1900 Goodwin, Hannibal Williston
d. 1916 Rasputin, Grigori Efimovich
d. 1919 Van Zandt, Marie
d. 1921 Penrose, Boies
d. 1936 Unamuno (y Jugo), Miguel de
d. 1939 Benson, Frank Robert, Sir
d. 1941 Hess, Sol
d. 1944 Nash, George Frederick
d. 1950 Renner, Karl
d. 1951 Litvinov, Maxim
d. 1955 Lewisohn, Ludwig
d. 1959 Giovannitti, Arturo
d. 1960 Howe, Clarence Decatur

d. 1966 Persinger, Louis
d. 1969 Baccaloni,
  Salvatore
d. 1969 Reik, Theodor
d. 1971 Duel, Peter
d. 1971 Henderson, Ray
d. 1972 Clemente,
  Roberto Walker
d. 1976 Hayes, Roland
d. 1980 McLuhan,
  (Herbert) Marshall

d. 1980 Walsh, Raoul
d. 1981 Adair, Frank
  E(arl)
d. 1981 Seper, Franjo
d. 1984 Ronning,
  Chester A
d. 1985 Nelson, Rick
d. 1985 Spiegel, Sam
d. 1986 Fleming,
  Donald M(ethuen)
d. 1986 Haynes, Lloyd

d. 1987? Arliss, Leslie
d. 1989 Dache, Lilly
d. 1989 Schroder,
  Gerhard
d. 1990 Allen, George
  Herbert
d. 1993 Byroade, Henry
  A(lfred)
d. 1993 Watson,
  Thomas J(ohn), Jr.
d. 1994 Strode, Woody

d. 1996 Addy, Wesley
d. 1997 Cramer, Floyd
d. 1998 Kirby, Robert
  E(mory)
d. 1999 Richardson,
  Elliot L(ee)

Geographic Index

AFGHANISTAN

Badakhstan, Afghanistan
b. Rabani, Burhanuddin

Herat, Afghanistan
b. Jami
d. Jami

Kabul, Afghanistan
b. Karmal, Babrak
b. Mohammed Zahir Shah
d. Najib Ahmadzi

Paghman, Afghanistan
b. Amanollah Khan

AFRICA

b. Hannibal
b. Vesey, Denmark

Boubangui, Africa
b. Bokassa I

Leptis Magna, Africa
b. Septimius Severus, Lucius

Zonta, Africa
d. Omar al-Mukhtar

ALBANIA

b. Cicero
d. Sabbatai Zevi

Burgayeti, Albania
b. Zog I

Gjirokaster, Albania
b. Hoxha, Enver
b. Kadare, Ismail

Kerce, Albania
b. Mili, Gjon

Shkoder, Albania
b. Alia, Ramiz

Tepeleni, Albania
b. Ali Pasha

Tirana, Albania
b. Nano, Fatos
b. Shehu, Mehmet
d. Hoxha, Enver
d. Shehu, Mehmet

Tropoje, Albania
b. Berisha, Sali

ALGERIA

b. Morceli, Noureddine
d. Abd al-Mumin
d. Leclerc, Jacques-Philippe

Ain Beida, Algeria
b. Boudjedra, Rachid

Algiers, Algeria
b. Krea, Henri
b. Schoonmaker, Thelma
b. Solal, Martial
d. Abbas, Ferhat
d. Boumedienne, Houari
d. Darlan, Jean Louis Xavier Francois
d. Egg, Augustus Leopold
d. Lavigerie, Charles Martel Allemand
d. Saint-Saens, (Charles) Camille
d. Tshombe, Moise

Beni-Saf, Algeria
b. Levy, Bernard-Henri

Birmandreis, Algeria
b. Althusser, Louis

Blida, Algeria
b. Coulomb, Jean (Marie)

Bone, Algeria
b. Juin, Alphonse Pierre

Bouteldja, Algeria
b. Chadli, Bendjedid

Clauzel, Algeria
b. Boumedienne, Houari

Constantine, Algeria
b. Ben Badis, Abd al-Hamid

Dellys, Algeria
b. Widal, Fernand Isidore

El-Biar, Algeria
b. Derrida, Jacques

Ighil Ali, Algeria
b. Amrouche, Jean

Marnia, Algeria
b. Ben Bella, Ahmed

Mondovi, Algeria
b. Camus, Albert

Mostaganem, Algeria
d. Borel d'Hauterive, Petrus

Mustapha, Algeria
d. Vieuxtemps, Henri Francois Joseph

Oran, Algeria
b. Abd el-Kadir
b. Saint Laurent, Yves Mathieu

Orleansville, Algeria
b. Robert, Paul

Sidi Bel-Abbes, Algeria
b. Cerdan, Marcel B

Taher, Algeria
b. Abbas, Ferhat

Tlemcen, Algeria
b. Messali Hadj

AMERICAN SAMOA

b. Alesana, Tofilau Eti

ANGOLA

Dande, Angola
b. Bonga, Kuenda

Galungo Alto, Angola
b. de Andrade, Mario

Icolo e Bengo, Angola
b. Neto, Agostinho

Luanda, Angola
b. Santos, Jose Eduardo dos

Munhango, Angola
b. Savimbi, Jonas Malheiro

ANTARCTICA

South Georgia, Antarctica
d. Shackleton, Ernest Henry, Sir

ANTIGUA-BARBUDA

b. Bird, Lester
b. Bird, Vere Cornwall, Sr.

Saint Johns, Antigua-Barbuda
b. Kincaid, Jamaica
d. Beatty, Morgan

ARABIA

Afshana, Arabia
b. Avicenna

Mecca, Arabia
b. Abdullah Ibn Hussein
b. Abu Bakr
b. Fatima
b. Mohammed
d. Mansur, (Abu Jafar Ibn Muhammad), Al

Medina, Arabia
b. Ayesha
d. Fatima
d. Omar I

Riyadh, Arabia
b. Faisal (Ibn Abdul-Aziz al Saud)
b. Ibn Saud
b. Khalid Ibn Abdul Azia Al-Saud

Taif, Arabia
b. Faisal, I

ARCTIC

d. Franklin, John, Sir

ARGENTINA

b. DeVicenzo, Roberto
b. Frondizi, Arturo
b. Hunt, Martita
d. Fangio, Juan Manuel
d. Piazzola, Astor
d. Quiroga, Juan Facundo
d. Thyssen, Fritz

Alta Gracia, Argentina
d. Falla, Manuel de

Anillaco, Argentina
b. Menem, Carlos Saul

Arroyo de la China, Entre Rios, Argentina
b. Urquiza, Justo Jose

Bahia Blanca, Argentina
b. Milstein, Cesar

Belgrano, Argentina
d. Tsankov, Aleksandur

Buenos Aires, Argentina
b. Aramburu, Pedro Eugenio
b. Argentinita
b. Barenboim, Daniel
b. Belgrano, Manuel
b. Bioy Casares, Adolfo
b. Bonavena, Oscar
b. Borges, Jorge Luis
b. Clerc, Jose-Luis
b. Costa Mendez, Nicanor
b. Cristal, Linda
b. Dorfman, Ariel
b. Drago, Luis Maria
b. Echeverria, Jose Esteban (Antonino)
b. Fini, Leonor
b. Firpo, Luis Angel
b. Ginastera, Alberto Evaristo
b. Guiraldes, Ricardo (Guillermo)
b. Haymes, Dick
b. Hernandez, Jose
b. Herrera, Paloma
b. Houssay, Bernardo Alberto
b. Hussey, Olivia
b. Lamas, Fernando
b. Marmol, Jose
b. Panizza, Ettore
b. Perez Esquivel, Adolfo
b. Rey, Alejandro
b. Rivadavia, Bernardino
b. Rosas, Juan Manuel de
b. Saavdedra, Lamas Carlos
b. Sabatini, Gabriela
b. Schifrin, Lalo Claudio
b. Torre-Nilsson, Leopoldo
d. Acevedo Diaz, Eduardo
d. Alcala Zamora, Niceto
d. Belgrano, Manuel
d. Bergius, Friedrich Karl Rudolph
d. Cunninghame-Graham, Robert Bontine
d. Drago, Luis Maria
d. Falconetti, Renee Maria
d. Firpo, Luis Angel
d. Frondizi, Arturo
d. Hernandez, Jose
d. Houssay, Bernardo Alberto
d. Justo, Agustin Pedro
d. Kutschmann, Walter
d. Lanusse, Alejandro Agustin
d. Leloir, Luis Federico
d. Loder, John
d. Marmol, Jose
d. Moringo, Higinio
d. Onassis, Christina
d. Ongania, Juan Carlos
d. Patino, Simon Iturri
d. Peron, Eva Duarte
d. Peron, Juan
d. Quiroga, Horacio

d. Roca, Julio Argentino
d. Saavdedra, Lamas Carlos
d. Timerman, Jacobo
d. Torre-Nilsson, Leopoldo

Caseros, Argentina
b. Galtieri, Leopoldo Fortunato

Chascomus, Argentina
b. Alfonsin Foulkes, Raul Ricardo

Concepcion del Uruguay, Argentina
b. Justo, Agustin Pedro

Cordoba, Argentina
b. Illia, Arturo Umberto
d. Illia, Arturo Umberto

Corrientes Province, Argentina
d. Goulart, Joao

General Villegas, Argentina
b. Puig, Manuel

Jorge Perez, Argentina
b. Dalto, Jorge

La Plata, Argentina
b. Favaloro, Rene Geronimo

La Rioja Province, Argentina
b. Quiroga, Juan Facundo

Lanus, Argentina
b. Maradona, Diego

Las Rioja, Argentina
b. Peron, Isabel Martinez de

Lobos, Argentina
b. Peron, Juan

Los Toldos, Argentina
b. Peron, Eva Duarte

Mar del Plata, Argentina
b. Piazzola, Astor
b. Vilas, Guillermo

Mendoza, Argentina
b. Calderon, Alberto P(edro)
b. Orfilo, Alejandro
d. Carrera, Jose Miguel

Mercedes, Argentina
b. Campora, Hector Jose
b. Videla, Jorge Rafael

Moron, Argentina
b. Bignone, Reynaldo Benito Antonio

Munro, Argentina
b. Bocca, Julio

Pinamar, Argentina
d. Castagna, Bruna

Quilmes, Argentina
b. Hudson, William Henry

Rojas, Argentina
b. Sabato, Ernesto

Rosario, Argentina
b. Guevara, Che

Salta, Argentina
b. Guemes, Martin
d. Guemes, Martin

San Juan, Argentina
b. Sarmiento, Domingo Faustino

Timote, Argentina
d. Aramburu, Pedro Eugenio

Tucuman, Argentina
b. Alberdi, Juan Bautista
b. Pelli, Cesar
b. Prebisch, Raul
b. Roca, Julio Argentino
b. Sosa, Mercedes

Villa General Mitre, Argentina
d. Perrine, Charles Dillon

Yapeyu, Argentina
b. San Martin, Jose de

ARMENIA

b. Mikoyan, Artem Ivanovich

Gyandzha, Armenia
b. Bagramian, Ivan Christofovorich

Mardin, Armenia
b. Karsh, Yousuf

Nagorno Karabakh, Armenia
b. Kocharyan, Robert

Yerevan, Armenia
d. Ambartsumyan, Viktor
   Amazaspovich

ARUBA

b. Bishop, Maurice Rupert

ASIA

d. Cyrus the Great

ASIA MINOR

b. Anaxagoras

Colophon, Asia Minor
b. Xenophanes

Ephesus, Asia Minor
b. Heraclitus of Ephesus
b. Parrhasius

Halicarnassus, Asia Minor
b. Herodotus

Ionia, Asia Minor
b. Apelles

Ipsus, Asia Minor
d. Antigonus, I

Lycia, Asia Minor
b. Nicholas, Saint

Miletus, Asia Minor
b. Anaximander
b. Anaximenes of Miletus
b. Thales

Nicaea, Asia Minor
b. Hipparchus

Perga, Asia Minor
b. Appollonius of Perga

Teos, Asia Minor
b. Anacreon

AT SEA

b. Cheyne, William Watson, Sir
d. Barclay, McClelland
d. Crane, Hart
d. Davis, John
d. Geiger, Theodor Julius
d. Gilbert, Humphrey, Sir
d. Halliburton, Richard
d. Hibbert, Eleanor Alice Burford
d. Hosmer, Craig
d. Howard, Leslie
d. Hubbard, Elbert Green
d. Kennedy, John F(itzgerald), Jr.
d. Kinnick, Nile
d. Llull, Ramon
d. Miller, Dorie
d. Said ibn Sultan

AUSTRALIA

b. Coombs, Herbert Cole
b. Namatjira, Albert
b. Rafferty, Chips
b. Scanlon, Hugh Parr
d. Barton, Edmund
d. Clarke, Marcus (Andrew Hislop)
d. Fisher, R(onald) A(ylmer)
d. Hughes, William Morris
d. Kidman, Sidney
d. Monash, John
d. Porter, Hal

Adelaide, Australia
b. Anderson, Judith, Dame
b. Bragg, William Lawrence, Sir
b. Florey, Howard Walter
b. Kidman, Sidney
b. Michell, Keith
b. Oliphant, Patrick Bruce
b. Stigwood, Robert Colin
d. Bates, Daisy Mae
d. Mawson, Douglas, Sir

Albury, Australia
b. Court, Margaret
b. Fromholtz, Dianne

Angaston, Australia
b. Heggie, O P

Atherton, Australia
b. Prokhorov, Alexander Mikhailovich

Bacchus Marsh, Victoria, Australia
b. Carey, Peter (Philip)

Balmain, Australia
b. Fraser, Dawn

Barellan, Australia
b. Goolagong, Evonne

Bathurst, New South Wales, Australia
b. Chifley, Joseph Benedict

Beveridge, Australia
b. Kelly, Ned

Boggabri, Australia
b. Lexcen, Ben

Bordertown, Australia
b. Hawke, Bob

Brisbane, Australia
b. Cilento, Diane
b. Gould, Shane
b. Kingsford-Smith, Charles Edward, Sir
b. Malouf, David
b. Turnbull, Wendy
d. Griffith, Samuel Walker

Brunswick, Victoria, Australia
b. Santamaria, Bartholomew Augustine

Burra Burra, Australia
b. Lewis, Essington

Canberra, Australia
d. Chifley, Joseph Benedict
d. Curtin, John Joseph
d. Evatt, Herbert Vere

Canterbury, Australia
b. Southall, Ivan Francis

Casterton, Australia
b. Matheson, Murray

Claremont, Australia
d. Furphy, Joseph

Cooper's Creek, Australia
d. Burke, Robert O'Hara

Cootamundra, New South Wales, Australia
b. Bradman, Donald George

Creswick, Australia
b. Curtin, John Joseph

Deans Marsh, Australia
b. Lawrence, Marjorie Florence

Deniliquin, Australia
b. Summers, Anne Fairhurst

Duck River, Australia
b. Lyons, Enid Muriel

Ealing, Australia
b. Shute, Nevil

Earlwood, Australia
b. Howard, John (Winston)

East Maitland, New South Wales, Australia
b. Evatt, Herbert Vere

Fremantle, Australia
b. Hasluck, Paul Meernaa, Sir

Geelong, Australia
b. Brownlee, John

Geraldton, Australia
b. Stow, (Julian) Randolph

Grenfell, Australia
b. Lawson, Henry (Archibald Hertzberg)

Hillston, Australia
b. Conway, Jill Kathryn Ker

Hobart, Australia
b. Blackburn, Elizabeth Helen
b. Warner, Denis Ashton
d. Rees, Lloyd Frederic

Jeparit, Australia
b. Menzies, Robert Gordon, Sir

Kalgoorlie, Australia
b. Marshall, Barry J(ames)

Kiama, Australia
b. Orry-Kelly

Kingsway, Australia
b. Emerson, Roy

Lightning Ridge, Australia
b. Hogan, Paul

Lismore, Australia
b. Wrightson, Patricia

Melbourne, Australia
b. Armstrong, Gillian (May)
b. Austral, Florence Wilson
b. Batchelor, George (Keith)
b. Bridges, Harry Renton
b. Browne, Coral Edith
b. Bruce, David, Sir
b. Bruce of Melbourne, 1st Viscount
b. Caldicott, Helen Broinowski
b. Caldwell, Zoe
b. Cash, Pat(rick)
b. Clarke, Ron
b. Cowen, Zelman, Sir
b. Davison, Frank Dalby

b. Deakin, Alfred
b. Eccles, John C(arew), Sir
b. Evans, Mark
b. Fleming, Ian
b. Fraser, John Malcolm
b. Glanville-Hicks, Peggy
b. Gorton, John Grey, Sir
b. Grainger, Percy Aldridge
b. Greer, Germaine
b. Helfgott, David
b. Humphries, Barry
b. Landy, John
b. MacKillop, Mary
b. Melba, Nellie, Dame
b. Monash, John
b. Moorehead, Alan
b. Murdoch, Rupert
b. Nolan, Sidney, Sir
b. Perryman, Jill
b. Reddy, Helen
b. Richardson, Henry Handel
b. Robson, May
b. Rudd, Phil(lip)
b. Sang, Samantha
b. Singer, Peter
b. Thomson, Peter William
b. Tuckwell, Barry Emmanuel
b. Villiers, Alan John
b. Whitlam, Edward Gough
b. Williams, John
b. Williamson, David
d. Burnet, F(rank) MacFarlane, Sir
d. Davison, Frank Dalby
d. Deakin, Alfred
d. DeRoburt, Hammer, Sir
d. Kelly, Ned
d. May, Brian
d. Menzies, Robert Gordon, Sir
d. Shute, Nevil

Merthyr Tydfil, South Wales, Australia
b. Griffith, Samuel Walker

Moliagul, Victoria, Australia
b. Flynn, John

Mont Albert, Australia
b. Sedgman, Frank

Mount Bryan, Australia
b. Wilkins, George Hubert, Sir

Mount Duneed, Victoria, Australia
b. Streeton, Arthur Ernest

Mount Gambier, Australia
b. Helpmann, Robert Murray, Sir

Mount Victoria, Australia
d. Childe, Vere Gordon

Narrambla, New South Wales, Australia
b. Paterson, A(ndrew) B(arton)

New South Wales, Australia
b. Bateman, Henry Mayo
b. Brinsmead, Hesba Fay
b. Murray, Les(lie) A(llan)

Newcastle, New South Wales, Australia
b. Dobell, William

North Sydney, Australia
d. MacKillop, Mary

Olinda, Victoria, Australia
d. Streeton, Arthur Ernest

Paddington, Australia
b. Carruthers, John(ny)

Perth, Australia
b. Cowan, Peter Wilkinshaw
b. Davis, Judy
b. Elliott, Herb
d. Fifield, Elaine

Port Philip Bay, Australia
d. Holt, Harold Edward

Queensland, Australia
b. Norman, Greg
b. Travers, P(amela) L(yndon)

Rockhampton, Australia
b. Laver, Rod(ney George)

Roma, Australia
d. Jackson, Peter B

Saint Croix, Australia
b. Jackson, Peter B

Southport, Australia
d. Kellerman, Annette

St. Kilda, Australia
b. West, Morris L(anglo)

Stanley, Tasmania, Australia
b. Lyons, Joseph Aloysius

Sunshine, Australia
b. Tyler, Richard

Sydney, Australia
b. Alexander, Samuel
b. Altman, Dennis
b. Barton, Edmund
b. Benjamin, Arthur
b. Beresford, Bruce
b. Bevan, Brian
b. Bonynge, Richard
b. Brabham, Jack
b. Browne, Walter Shawn
b. Caldwell, John Charles
b. Cantrell, Lana
b. Childe, Vere Gordon
b. Clavell, James (Edmund Du Maresq)
b. Cornforth, John Warcup, Sir
b. Courtneidge, Cicely, Dame
b. Crampton, Bruce Sidney
b. Cuthbert, Betty
b. Dent, Phil
b. Errol, Leon
b. Farrow, John Villiers
b. Ferrier, Jim
b. Fifield, Elaine
b. Hazzard, Shirley
b. Holt, Harold Edward
b. Hughes, Robert Studley Forrest
b. Hutchence, Michael
b. Jacobs, Joseph
b. Keating, Paul John

b. Kellerman, Annette
b. Keneally, Thomas (Michael)
b. Lang, John Thomas
b. Macpherson, Elle
b. Marshal, Alan
b. McKern, Leo
b. Murray, Gilbert
b. Nagle, Kel(vin David George)
b. Newcombe, John
b. Powter, Susan
b. Ritchard, Cyril
b. Rosewall, Ken(neth R)
b. Sheed, Frank
b. Shorrock, Glenn
b. Springfield, Rick
b. Stead, Christina (Ellen)
b. Stephenson, Jan Lynn
b. Sutherland, Joan, Dame
b. Taylor, Rod(ney)
b. Weir, Peter
b. Wolfensohn, James David
d. Austral, Florence Wilson
d. Brown, Carter
d. Franklin, Miles
d. Glanville-Hicks, Peggy
d. Hargrave, Lawrence
d. Hargraves, Edward Hammond
d. Helpmann, Robert Murray, Sir
d. Hutchence, Michael
d. Knight, Arthur
d. Lang, John Thomas
d. Lexcen, Ben
d. Lyons, Enid Muriel
d. Lyons, Joseph Aloysius
d. McMahon, William
d. Melba, Nellie, Dame
d. Parkes, Henry, Sir
d. Paterson, A(ndrew) B(arton)
d. Rafferty, Chips
d. Stead, Christina (Ellen)
d. West, Morris L(anglo)
d. White, Patrick Victor Martindale
d. Wright, Peter (Maurice)

Talbingo, Australia
b. Franklin, Miles

Tasmania, Australia
b. Flynn, Errol

Tenterfield, Australia
b. Allen, Peter Woolnough

Toowong, Australia
b. Dart, Raymond Arthur

Toowoomba, Australia
d. Kenny, Sister Elizabeth

Traralgon, Australia
b. Burnet, F(rank) MacFarlane, Sir

Victoria, Australia
b. Savage, Michael Joseph
b. Scullin, James Henry

Victoria Park, Australia
b. Porter, Hal

Wangi, Australia
d. Dobell, William

Warracknabeal, Australia
b. Cave, Nicholas Edward

Warrialda, Australia
b. Kenny, Sister Elizabeth

Warrnambool, Australia
b. Jewett, Henry
b. Powell, Gordon George

Wellington, Australia
b. McCullough, Colleen

Windsor, Australia
b. Graham, David

Yering, Australia
b. Furphy, Joseph

Yeronga, Queensland, Australia
b. Rees, Lloyd Frederic

Zeehan, Australia
b. Joyce, Eileen

AUSTRASIA

Aix-la-Chapelle, Austrasia
d. Charlemagne

AUSTRIA

b. Chargaff, Erwin
b. Golacinski, Alan Bruce
b. Goldberger, Joseph
b. Hummel, Lisl
b. Kronberger, Petra
b. Liebow, Averill A(braham)
b. Pacher, Michael
b. Reich, Wilhelm
b. Root, Jack
b. Tannenbaum, Frank

Abbazia, Austria
d. Billroth, Theodore

Alberschwende, Austria
b. Gmeiner, Hermann

Alpbach, Austria
d. Schroedinger, Erwin

Alpl, Austria
b. Rossegger, Peter

Altaussee, Austria
b. Brandauer, Klaus Maria
d. Wassermann, Jakob

Altenburg, Austria
d. Lorenz, Konrad Zacharias

Altmunster, Austria
b. Stangl, Franz Paul

Anif, Austria
d. Karajan, Herbert von

Ansfelden, Austria
b. Bruckner, Joseph Anton

Bad Ischl, Austria
d. Lehar, Franz
d. Straus, Oskar

Baden, Austria
b. Reinhardt, Max
d. Hanslick, Eduard

Bellagio, Austria
b. Wagner, Cosima Liszt

Bielitz, Austria
b. Kurz, Selma

Bolzano, Austria
b. Vogelweide, Walther von der

Braunau, Austria
b. Hitler, Adolf

Bregenz, Austria
b. Hagen, Johann Georg

Brody, Austria
b. Kober, Arthur

Brunn, Austria
b. Edelmann, Otto
b. Jerger, Alfred
b. Jeritza, Maria
b. Korngold, Erich Wolfgang
b. Schauffler, Robert Haven

Budzanow, Austria
b. Strasberg, Lee

Cremona, Austria
b. Beltrami, Eugenio

Czernowitz, Austria
b. Jagendorf, Moritz Adolf

Dornbirn, Austria
b. Drexel, Francis Martin

Edlach, Austria
d. Herzl, Theodor
d. Schalk, Franz

Elberfeld, Austria
b. Wesendonck, Mathilde Luckemeyer

Esslingen, Austria
b. Donner, Georg Raphael

Graz, Austria
b. Bohm, Karl
b. Ferdinand II
b. Fischer von Erlach, Johann
  Bernhard
b. Franz Ferdinand
b. Rosbaud, Hans
b. Schuch, Ernst von
b. Schwarzenegger, Arnold Alois
b. Stolz, Robert
d. Pregl, Fritz

Griffin, Austria
b. Handke, Peter

Haag, Austria
b. Bayer, Herbert

Henndorf, Austria
  b. Mayr, Richard

Hirtenfeld, Styria, Austria
  b. Fux, Johann Joseph

Hohenems, Austria
  b. Sulzer, Salomon

Innsbruck, Austria
  d. Gmeiner, Hermann
  d. Keyserling, Hermann Alexander
    Graf Von
  d. Rahner, Karl
  d. Schuschnigg, Kurt von

Jaroslau, Austria
  b. Spiegel, Sam

Judenburg, Austria
  b. Kotsching, Walter Maria

Kalusz, Austria
  b. Schuster, Max Lincoln

Kanczuga, Austria
  b. Brill, Abraham Arden

Kapfenberg, Austria
  d. Stein, Heinrich Friedrich Karl vom
    und zum, Baron

Kierling, Austria
  d. Kafka, Franz

Klagenfurt, Austria
  b. Musil, Robert Edler Von

Kleinarl, Austria
  b. Proell Moser, Annemarie

Klekotow, Austria
  b. Kanner, Leo

Kolomea, Austria
  b. Gross, Chaim

Kraljevic, Austria
  b. Steiner, Rudolf

Kramsach, Austria
  d. Bohm von Bawerk, Eugene

Krieglach, Austria
  d. Rossegger, Peter

Kufstein, Austria
  d. List, Georg Friedrich

Laibach, Austria
  b. Pregl, Fritz

Lake Wolfgang, Austria
  d. Jannings, Emil

Langenargen, Austria
  b. Maulbertsch, Franz Anton

Laufen, Austria
  b. Rottmayr, Johann Michael

Laxenberg, Austria
  b. Rudolf of Hapsburg

Leibnitz, Austria
  b. Muster, Thomas

Lemberg, Austria
  b. Ewen, David
  b. Ewen, Frederic
  b. Gimpel, Jakob
  b. Muni, Paul
  b. Sacher-Masoch, Leopold von

Linz, Austria
  b. Tauber, Richard
  b. Woss, Kurt

Lipnik, Austria
  b. Schnabel, Artur

Lvov, Austria
  d. Maywood, Augusta

Mariagru, Austria
  d. Krafft-Ebing, Richard von

Mittersill, Austria
  d. Webern, Anton Friedrich Ernst von

Moaswald, Austria
  b. Klammer, Franz

Muerzzuschlag, Austria
  d. Arrau, Claudio

Niederkappel, Austria
  b. Kirchschlager, Rudolf

Obernduernbach, Austria
  d. Einem, Gottfried von

Ostend, Austria
  b. Weddell, James

Panania, Austria
  b. Brown, Bryan

Pirnitz (Brtnice), Austria
  b. Hoffmann, Josef

Pochlarn, Austria
  b. Kokoschka, Oskar

Prague, Austria
  b. Cori, Carl Ferdinand
  b. Cori, Gerty Theresa (Radnitz)

Reichenberg, Austria
  b. Feigl, Herbert

Rodaun, Austria
  d. Hofmannsthal, Hugo von

Rohrau, Austria
  b. Haydn, Joseph

Rohrbrunn, Austria
  b. Brunner, Alois

Ruttka, Austria
  b. Hertz, John Daniel

Rymahow, Austria
  b. Rabi, Isidor Isaac

Saint Anton, Austria
  b. Schranz, Karl

Saint Georgen, Austria
  b. Materna, Amalia

Saint Leonhard, Austria
  b. Hofer, Andreas

Saint Poelten, Austria
  b. Demus, Joreg

Saint Veit, Austria
  b. Puck, Wolfgang

Salzburg, Austria
  b. Berger, Helmut
  b. Doppler, Christian Johann
  b. Karajan, Herbert von
  b. Mozart, Wolfgang Amadeus
  d. Bohm, Karl
  d. Hill, Virginia
  d. Hofhaimer, Paul
  d. Lorenz, Max
  d. Paracelsus, Philippus Aureolus
  d. Pfitzner, Hans

Sankt Polten, Austria
  d. Prandtauer, Jakob

Schonbrunn, Austria
  d. Bonaparte, Francois Charles Joseph

Spalato, Austria
  b. Suppe, Franz von

Stanislau, Austria
  b. Burns, Arthur Frank

Stanz, Austria
  b. Prandtauer, Jakob

Straubing, Austria
  b. Schikaneder, Emanuel

Tarnopal, Austria
  b. Mazurki, Mike

Tarnow, Austria
  b. Baron, Salo Wittmayer

Tirol, Austria
  b. Bemelmans, Ludwig

Traunblick, Austria
  d. Wesendonck, Mathilde Luckemeyer

Tulln, Austria
  b. Schiele, Egon

Tysmenica, Austria
  b. Roth, Henry

Unter Saint Veit, Austria
  b. Mottl, Felix

Unter-Tannowitz, Austria
  b. Renner, Karl

Valdi Sole, Austria
b. Toffenetti, Dario Louis

Vienna, Austria
b. Adler, Alfred
b. Adler, Kurt Herbert
b. Artin, Emil
b. Barany, Robert
b. Baum, Vicki
b. Berchtold, Leopold von
b. Berg, Alban
b. Berger, Senta
b. Bergner, Elisabeth
b. Bernays, Edward L.
b. Berry, Walter
b. Bettelheim, Bruno
b. Bey, Turhan
b. Bikel, Theodore Meir
b. Bing, Rudolf (Franz Josef), Sir
b. Bitter, Karl Theodore Francis
b. Bluhdorn, Charles G
b. Bodanzky, Artur
b. Boltzmann, Ludwig
b. Bondi, Hermann, Sir
b. Breuer, Josef
b. Buber, Martin
b. Carnegie, Hattie
b. Charoux, Siegfried
b. Christians, Mady
b. Cortez, Ricardo
b. Czerny, Karl
b. Dantine, Helmut
b. Dichter, Ernest
b. Ditters, Karl
b. Djerassi, Carl
b. Doktor, Paul Karl
b. Drucker, Peter Ferdinand
b. Ehrlich, Bettina Bauer
b. Elssler, Fanny
b. Falco
b. Fall, Bernard B
b. Felsenstein, Walter
b. Fleischer, Max
b. Flesch, Rudolf (Franz)
b. Francis Joseph, (I)
b. Frankfurter, Felix
b. Frankl, Viktor E(mil)
b. Franz Joseph I
b. Freud, Anna
b. Fried, Alfred Hermann
b. Frisch, Karl von
b. Frisch, O(tto) R(obert)
b. Gernreich, Rudi
b. Gies, Miep
b. Gittings, Barbara
b. Gold, Thomas
b. Graf, Herbert
b. Gregor, Arthur
b. Grillparzer, Franz
b. Grossinger, Jennie
b. Gruen, Victor
b. Gruenberg, Sidonie Matsner
b. Grunwald, Henry Anatole
b. Gueden, Hilde
b. Guiterman, Arthur
b. Gulda, Friedrich
b. Haas, Ernst
b. Harand, Irene
b. Harris, Jed
b. Hayek, Friedrich August von
b. Hofmannsthal, Hugo von
b. Homolka, Oscar
b. Hundertwasser, Friedensreich
b. Illich, Ivan
b. Jaques-Dalcroze, Emile
b. Jonas, Franz

b. Joseph I
b. Joseph II
b. Juch, Emma
b. Kasznar, Kurt
b. Kiesler, Frederick John
b. King, Alexander
b. Kleiber, Erich
b. Klein, Melanie
b. Klestil, Thomas
b. Klima, Viktor
b. Klimt, Gustav
b. Kohut, Heinz
b. Kollek, Teddy
b. Konetzni, Hilde
b. Kraus, Felix von
b. Kraus, Hans Peter
b. Krauss, Clemens
b. Krauss, Gabrielle
b. Kreisky, Bruno
b. Kreisler, Fritz
b. Krenek, Ernst
b. Krips, Josef
b. Kuerti, Anton
b. Kuhn, Richard
b. Kunz, Erich
b. Lamarr, Hedy
b. Landsteiner, Karl
b. Lang, Fritz
b. Lang, Helmut
b. Lauda, Niki
b. Lazarsfeld, Paul F(elix)
b. Leinsdorf, Erich
b. Lenya, Lotte
b. Leopold, II
b. Liebman, Max
b. Lind, Jakov
b. Lindtberg, Leopold
b. List, Emanuel
b. Loewe, Frederick
b. Lorenz, Konrad Zacharias
b. Losch, Tilly
b. Low, George M(ichael)
b. Lowie, Robert Harry
b. Lucca, Pauline
b. Mahler, Fritz
b. Maria Theresa
b. Marie Antoinette
b. Marie Louise
b. Mark, Herman Francis
b. Maximilian
b. Maximilian II
b. Meitner, Lise
b. Mildenburg, Anna von
b. Model, Lisette
b. Morini, Erica
b. Morton, Frederic
b. Neumann, Angelo
b. Neumann, Robert Gerhard
b. Neurath, Otto
b. Neutra, Richard Joseph
b. Newman, Peter Charles
b. Ohrbach, Nathan M
b. Padover, Saul Kussiel
b. Paneth, Friedrich Adolf
b. Patzak, Julius
b. Pauli, Wolfgang Ernst
b. Perutz, M(ax) F(erdinand)
b. Piech, Ferdinand
b. Placzek, Adolf K(urt)
b. Polanyi, Karl
b. Popper, Hans
b. Popper, Karl R(aimund), Sir
b. Praeger, Frederick A(mos)
b. Preminger, Otto Ludwig
b. Rainer, Luise
b. Rank, Otto

b. Reichmann, Paul
b. Reik, Theodor
b. Reznicek, Emil von
b. Rohatyn, Felix George
b. Roller, Alfred
b. Rosenstein, Nettie
b. Rudel, Julius
b. Rudolf II
b. Rysanek, Leonie
b. Schalk, Franz
b. Scheff, Fritzi
b. Schell, Maria Margarethe
b. Schell, Maximilian
b. Schildkraut, Joseph
b. Schlamme, Martha
b. Schneider, Romy
b. Schnitzler, Arthur
b. Schoenberg, Arnold
b. Schroedinger, Erwin
b. Schubert, Franz Peter
b. Segal, Lore Groszmann
b. Selye, Hans
b. Slezak, Walter
b. Steiner, Max
b. Stiedry, Fritz
b. Straus, Oskar
b. Strauss, Johann, Sr.
b. Strauss, Johann, Jr.
b. Toch, Ernst
b. Trapp, Maria Augusta von
b. Unger, Caroline
b. Urban, Joseph Maria
b. VonSternberg, Josef
b. VonStroheim, Erich
b. Vranitzky, Franz
b. Wagner, Otto
b. Walbrook, Anton
b. Wallmann, Margherita
b. Weber, Ernst
b. Webern, Anton Friedrich Ernst von
b. Wellek, Rene
b. Wellesz, Egon
b. Werner, Oskar
b. Wittgenstein, Ludwig
b. Wittgenstein, Paul
b. Wojnilower, Albert Martin
b. Zemlinsky, Alexander von
b. Zinnemann, Fred
b. Zsigmondy, Richard Adolf
b. Zweig, Stefan
d. Adler, Guido
d. Adler, Victor
d. Auden, W(ystan) H(ugh)
d. Beethoven, Ludwig van
d. Berg, Alban
d. Bononcini, Giovanni Battista
d. Brahms, Johannes
d. Breuer, Josef
d. Bruckner, Joseph Anton
d. Cebotari, Maria
d. Czerny, Karl
d. Dollfuss, Engelbert
d. Donner, Georg Raphael
d. Elssler, Fanny
d. Ferdinand I
d. Ferdinand II
d. Francis, II
d. Francis Joseph, (I)
d. Frank, Johann Peter
d. Frankl, Viktor E(mil)
d. Franz Joseph I
d. Fried, Alfred Hermann
d. Fux, Johann Joseph
d. Gentz, Friedrich Von
d. Gluck, Christoph
d. Goldmark, Karl

d. Grillparzer, Franz
d. Gruen, Victor
d. Gueden, Hilde
d. Haydn, Joseph
d. Hebbel, Friedrich
d. Hildebrandt, Johann Lucas von
d. Hoffmann, Josef
d. Hubay, Jeno
d. Jacobsson, Ulla
d. Jerger, Alfred
d. Jonas, Franz
d. Joseph I
d. Joseph II
d. Jurgens, Curt
d. Kautsky, Karl Johann
d. Kienzl, Wilhelm
d. Klimt, Gustav
d. Konetzni, Hilde
d. Krauss, Werner
d. Kreisky, Bruno
d. Kurz, Selma
d. Leopold, II
d. List, Emanuel
d. Lucca, Pauline
d. Mahler, Gustav
d. Mannlicher, Ferdinand
d. Maria Theresa
d. Materna, Amalia
d. Matthias Corvinus
d. Maulbertsch, Franz Anton
d. Mayr, Richard
d. Metastasio, Pietro
d. Metternich-Winneburg, Clemens
d. Mildenburg, Anna von
d. Mindszenty, Jozsef, Cardinal
d. Mosenthal, Salomon Hermann von
d. Mozart, Wolfgang Amadeus
d. Pabst, Georg Wilhelm
d. Paneth, Friedrich Adolf
d. Piaget, Jean
d. Renner, Karl
d. Roller, Alfred
d. Rottmayr, Johann Michael
d. Rudolf of Hapsburg
d. Rysanek, Leonie
d. Salieri, Antonio
d. Schiele, Egon
d. Schikaneder, Emanuel
d. Schlick, Friedrich Albert Moritz
d. Schmedes, Erik
d. Schnitzler, Arthur
d. Schubert, Franz Peter
d. Seefried, Irmgard Maria Theresia
d. Semmelweis, Ignaz Philipp
d. Strauss, Johann, Sr.
d. Strauss, Johann, Jr.
d. Sulzer, Salomon
d. Suppe, Franz von
d. Suttner, Bertha Felicie Sophie
    Kinsky von
d. Teschner, Richard
d. Vivaldi, Antonio (Lucio)
d. VonDoderer, Heimito
d. Wagner, Otto
d. Wagner-Jaurregg, Julius, von
d. Wechsberg, Joseph
d. Welitsch, Ljuba
d. Winkelmann, Hermann
d. Wolf, Hugo

Vigevano, Austria
b. Duse, Eleanora

Villach, Austria
d. Backhaus, Wilhelm

Vindobona, Austria
d. Marcus Aurelius Antoninus

Waizenkircen, Austria
b. Kienzl, Wilhelm

Waldstein, Austria
b. Hess, Victor Francis

Weissenbach, Austria
d. Gulda, Friedrich

Wels, Austria
b. Wagner-Jaurregg, Julius, von
d. Maximilian I

Welsberg, Austria
b. Troger, Paul

Wiener Neustadt, Austria
b. Machlup, Fritz
b. Maximilian I
b. Schreiber, Hermann Otto Ludwig

Windischgraez, Austria
b. Wolf, Hugo

Wisenberg, Austria
b. Brendel, Alfred

Witfowitz, Austria
b. Ludwig, Leopold

Woerdern, Austria
b. Waldheim, Kurt

Zara, Austria
b. Weingartner, Felix

Zell am See, Austria
d. Porsche, Ferdinand

Zloczew, Austria
b. Fellig, Arthur

AUSTRIA-HUNGARY

b. Beck, Martin
b. Dobozy, Imre
b. Erdos, Paul
b. Kopits, Steven E
b. Pascal, Gabriel
b. Telkes, Maria (de)
b. Thorek, Max

Bacsbarsod, Austria-Hungary
b. Moholy-Nagy, Laszlo

Bekes, Austria-Hungary
b. Kilenyi, Edward, Sr.

Blato, Austria-Hungary
b. Adamic, Louis

Bolgar, Austria-Hungary
b. Schick, Bela

Bosnia, Austria-Hungary
b. Princip, Gavrilo

Brasso, Austria-Hungary
b. Brassai

Bratislava, Austria-Hungary
b. Laban, Rudolf von

Brno, Austria-Hungary
b. Hrabal, Bohumil

Brunn, Austria-Hungary
b. Bohm von Bawerk, Eugene
b. Godel, Kurt

Budapest, Austria-Hungary
b. Alexander, Franz Gabriel
b. Capa, Robert
b. Curtiz, Michael
b. Darvas, Lili
b. DeErdely, Francis
b. Dolly, Jenny
b. Dolly, Rosie
b. Dorati, Antal
b. Eggerth, Marta
b. Fabri, Zoltan
b. Ferencsik, Janos
b. Gabor, Dennis
b. Gabor, Jolie
b. Gabor, Magda
b. Gero, Erno
b. Goldmark, Peter Carl
b. Hevesy, George Charles von
b. Ivogun, Maria
b. Jozsef, Attila
b. Karfiol, Bernard
b. Katona, George
b. Kertesz, Andre
b. Koestler, Arthur
b. Kraus, Lili
b. Lengyel, Emil
b. Lukas, Paul
b. Magyar, Gabriel
b. Mannheim, Karl
b. Massey, Ilona
b. Molnar, Ferenc
b. Nyiregyhazi, Ervin
b. Ormandy, Eugene
b. Penner, Joe
b. Petersham, Miska
b. Polya, George
b. Reiner, Fritz
b. Rosenberg, Anna Marie
b. Sakall, S Z
b. Schwartz, Jean
b. Seredy, Kate
b. Szabolcsi, Bence
b. Szell, George
b. Szenkar, Eugen
b. Szent-Gyorgyi, Albert (von
    Nagyrapolt)
b. Szilard, Leo
b. Teller, Edward
b. Tors, Ivan
b. Von Bekesy, Georg
b. Von Karman, Theodore
b. Von Neumann, John
b. Wank, Roland A
b. Wise, Stephen Samuel
d. Deak, Francis
d. Ferencsik, Janos
d. Tisza, Kalman

Bychory, Austria-Hungary
b. Kubelik, Rafael (Jeronym)

Dacca, Bangladesh
 d. Rahman, Mujibur, Sheik

Dinajpur, Bangladesh
 b. Khaleda Zia

Faridpur, Bangladesh
 b. Hasina Wajed

Netrokona, Bangladesh
 b. Ahmed, Shahabuddin

Rangpur, North Bengal, Bangladesh
 b. Ershad, Hussain Mohammad

BARBADOS

 b. Adams, Tom
 b. Arthur, Owen
 b. Barrow, Ruth Nita, Dame
 b. Dell, Gabriel
 b. Laing, Hugh
 b. Locke, William John
 b. Scott, Arleigh Winston, Sir
 b. Staupers, Mabel K.
 b. Ward, Deighton Harcourt Lisle, Sir
 d. Ward, Deighton Harcourt Lisle, Sir

Bellerive, Barbados
 d. Colbert, Claudette

Bridgeport, Barbados
 d. Lewis, William Arthur, Sir

Bridgetown, Barbados
 d. Adams, Tom
 d. Barrow, Errol Walton
 d. Barrow, Ruth Nita, Dame
 d. Eastman, Max Forrester
 d. Gairy, Eric Matthew, Sir
 d. Messel, Oliver

Georgetown, Barbados
 d. Scott, Arleigh Winston, Sir

Porters St. James, Barbados
 b. Sandiford, Lloyd Erskine

Saint Lucy, Barbados
 b. Barrow, Errol Walton

BAVARIA

 b. Hartmann, Franz

Anspach, Bavaria
 b. Stahl, Georg Ernst

Aschaffenburg, Bavaria
 d. Brentano, Clemens Maria

Bamberg, Bavaria
 b. Wassermann, August von

Bayreuth, Bavaria
 b. Stirner, Max

Brand, Bavaria
 b. Reger, Max

Calm, Bavaria
 b. Stautner, Ernie

Dispeck, Bavaria
 b. Einhorn, David

Essingen, Bavaria
 b. Nicolay, John George

Furth, Bavaria
 b. Wassermann, Jakob

Gunzburg, Bavaria
 b. Mengele, Josef

Hof, Bavaria
 b. Dobereiner, Johann Wolfgang

Huttendorf, Bavaria
 b. Kalb, Johann de

Ingolstadt, Bavaria
 d. Eck, Johann Maier von

Kempten, Bavaria
 b. Dornier, Claude
 d. Hartmann, Franz

Lake Starnberg, Bavaria
 d. Ludwig II

Landshut, Bavaria
 b. Feuerbach, Ludwig Andreas

Massing, Bavaria
 b. Hummel, Berta

Munich, Bavaria
 b. Haushofer, Karl Ernst
 d. Fraunhofer, Joseph von
 d. William of Ockham

Nurnberg, Bavaria
 d. Denner, Johann Christoph

Nymphenburg, Bavaria
 b. Ludwig II

Oberellenbach, Bavaria
 b. Haberl, Franz Xaver

Oberhausen, Bavaria
 d. LaTour D'Auvergne, Theophile de

Otterberg, Bavaria
 b. Straus, Nathan

Speyer, Bavaria
 b. Villard, Henry

Straubing, Bavaria
 b. Fraunhofer, Joseph von

Tegernsee, Bavaria
 d. Acton, John Emerich Edward
  Dalberg-Acton, Baron

Trostberg an der Alz, Bavaria
 b. Schonhuber, Franz Xaver

Wunsiedel, Bavaria
 b. Richter, Jean Paul F

BECHUANALAND

Kanye, Bechuanaland
 b. Masire, Quett (Ketumile Jonny)

Serowe, Bechuanaland
 b. Khama, Seretse M., Sir

BELGIAN CONGO

Kivu, Belgian Congo
 b. Ongala, Remmy

Lisala, Belgian Congo
 b. Mobutu Sese Seko

Oualua, Belgian Congo
 b. Lumumba, Patrice

Tshela, Belgian Congo
 b. Kasavubu, Joseph

BELGIUM

 b. Burnison, Chantal Simone
 d. Davidson, Scotty

Antwerp, Belgium
 b. Cluytens, Andre
 b. Courboin, Charles
 b. Grosbard, Ulu
 b. Jordaens, Jacob
 b. Mallet-Joris, Francoise
 b. Ortelius, Abraham
 b. Schillebeeckx, Edward (Cornelis
   Florentius Alfons)
 b. Schneider, Nina
 b. Teniers, David, the Younger
 b. van de Velde, Henry
 b. Van Dyck, Anthony, Sir
 d. Brouwer, Adriaen C
 d. Bull, John
 d. Cleve, Joos van
 d. Heem, Jan Davidsz(oon) de
 d. Jordaens, Jacob
 d. Mabuse, Jan de
 d. Massys, Quentin
 d. Ortelius, Abraham
 d. Rubens, Peter Paul, Sir
 d. Tyndale, William

Ath, Belgium
 b. Hennepin, Louis

Baerle, Belgium
 b. Christus, Petrus

Bruges, Belgium
 b. Brangwyn, Frank, Sir
 b. Stevin, Simon
 b. Willaert, Adrian
 d. Christus, Petrus
 d. Memling, Hans
 d. Philip the Good
 d. Smalls, Charlie

Brussels, Belgium
b. Akerman, Chantal
b. Albert, II
b. Albert I
b. Alechinsky, Pierre
b. Barzin, Leon Eugene
b. Baudouin, I, King
b. Brel, Jacques
b. Bruegel, Jan
b. Camargo, Marie Anne de Cupis de
b. Charles VII
b. Claiborne, Liz
b. Cortazar, Julio
b. Crommelynck, Fernand
b. Culliford, Peyo
b. Deutch, John
b. Furstenberg, Diane Halfin von
b. Helmont, Jan Baptista van
b. Hepburn, Audrey (Edda)
b. La Fontaine, Henri Marie
b. Leopold II
b. Leopold III
b. Levi-Strauss, Claude Gustave
b. Monro, Harold Edward
b. Orley, Bernard van
b. Perret, Auguste
b. Piccard, Jacques Ernest Jean
b. Van Damme, Jean-Claude
b. Van Hamel, Martine
b. Van Itallie, Jean-Claude
b. Van Vooren, Monique
b. Varda, Agnes
b. Vesalius, Andreas
b. Weygand, Maxime
b. Yourcenar, Marguerite
d. Bordet, Jules Jean Baptiste Vincent
d. Bortoluzzi, Paolo
d. Boulanger, Georges Ernest Jean
   Marie
d. Bruegel, Pieter, the El
d. Carlota
d. Cavell, Edith Louisa
d. Claude, Albert
d. Culliford, Peyo
d. David, Jacques Louis
d. Decoster, Charles Theodore Henri
d. Fetis, Francois Joseph
d. Franco
d. Ghelderode, Michel de
d. Jorda, Enrique
d. La Fontaine, Henri Marie
d. Leopold III
d. Magritte, Rene Francois Ghislain
d. North, John Ringling
d. Orley, Bernard van
d. Pendleton, George Hunt
d. Puccini, Giacomo
d. Quetelet, Lambert Adolphe Jacques
d. Ruysbroeck, Jan van
d. Spaak, Paul-Henri
d. Suenens, Leon Joseph, Cardinal
d. Teniers, David, the Younger
d. Vandervelde, Emile
d. Weyden, Rogier van der
d. Worner, Manfred
d. Wrangel, Pietr Nikolayevich
d. Ysaye, Eugene

Cambrai, Belgium
d. Dufay, Guillaume

Charleroi, Belgium
b. Lemaitre, Georges

Deinze, Belgium
b. Biebuyck, Daniel Prosper

Dendermonde, Belgium
b. Smet, Pierre Jean de

Dinant, Belgium
b. Pire, Dominique
b. Sax, Adolphe (Antoine-Joseph)
b. Sax, Charles Joseph

Douai, Flanders, Belgium
b. Giovanni da Bologna

Etterbeck, Belgium
b. Regine

Ghent, Belgium
b. Defauw, Desire
b. Gorr, Rita
b. Heymans, Corneille Jean Francois
b. John of Gaunt
b. Louys, Pierre
b. Maeterlinck, Maurice
b. Mortier, Gerard
b. Quetelet, Lambert Adolphe Jacques
b. Sarton, George

Hainaut, Belgium
b. Dufay, Guillaume

Ixelles, Belgium
b. Ghelderode, Michel de
b. Vandervelde, Emile

Jehay-Bodegnee, Belgium
b. Gramme, Zenobe Theophile

Knokke, Belgium
d. Heymans, Corneille Jean Francois

Laeken, Belgium
b. Carlota
d. Leopold, I
d. Leopold II

Lessines, Belgium
b. Magritte, Rene Francois Ghislain

Lichtervelde, Belgium
b. Van Depoele, Charles Joseph

Liege, Belgium
b. Corneille
b. Franck, Cesar Auguste
b. Gretry, Andre Ernest Modeste
b. Simenon, Georges
b. Ysaye, Eugene
d. Browning, John Moses
d. Castle, Frederick W
d. Schwann, Theodor

Lier, Belgium
b. Eyskens, Gaston, Viscount
b. Timmermans, Felix
d. Timmermans, Felix

Liverchies, Belgium
b. Reinhardt, Django (Jean Baptiste)

Louvain, Belgium
b. Elzevir, Louis
b. Massys, Quentin
b. Sauveur, Albert
d. Bouts, Dierick C
d. Eyskens, Gaston, Viscount

d. Lemaitre, Georges
d. Pire, Dominique

Luxembourg, Belgium
b. Claude, Albert

Mons, Belgium
b. Fetis, Francois Joseph

Montepellier, Belgium
b. Dehaene, Jean-Luc

Namur, Belgium
b. Michaux, Henri
d. Albert I

Ostend, Belgium
b. Beernaert, Auguste Marie Francois
b. Ensor, James Sydney, Baron
d. Ensor, James Sydney, Baron

Oudenaarde, Belgium
b. Brouwer, Adriaen C

Poelcapelle, Belgium
d. Guynemer, Georges Marie

Ruysbroeck, Belgium
b. Ruysbroeck, Jan van

Saint Martens-Latem, Belgium
b. Baekeland, Leo Hendrik

Schaerbeeck, Belgium
b. Spaak, Paul-Henri

Seligenstadt, Belgium
b. Memling, Hans

Sleidinge, Belgium
b. Martens, Wilfried

Soignies, Hainaut, Belgium
b. Bordet, Jules Jean Baptiste Vincent
b. Cuvillies, Francois

Tournai, Belgium
b. Weyden, Rogier van der

Traumeries, Belgium
b. Maison, Rene

Tremeloo, Belgium
b. Damien, Father

Uccle, Belgium
b. Folon, Jean-Michel

Ukkel, Belgium
d. Pirenne, Jean Henri Otto Lucien
   Marie

Vergnies, Belgium
b. Gossec, Francois Joseph

Verviers, Belgium
b. Pirenne, Jean Henri Otto Lucien
   Marie
b. Vieuxtemps, Henri Francois Joseph

Vilvoorde, Belgium
  d. Helmont, Jan Baptista van

Wavre, Belgium
  d. Deckers, Jeanine

Wondelgem, Belgium
  b. Sarton, May

Zolder, Belgium
  d. Villeneuve, Gilles

Zwijndrecht, Belgium
  b. Tindemans, Leo(nard)

BELIZE

Belize City, Belize
  b. Esquivel, Manuel
  b. Price, George

BELORUSSIA

  b. Kosciuszko, Thaddeus

BENIN

  d. Apithy, Sourou Migan

Cotenou, Benin
  b. Hounsou, Djimon

Porto Novo, Benin
  b. Apithy, Sourou Migan

Quidah, Benin
  b. Kidjo, Anjelique

BERING ISLAND

  d. Bering, Vitus Jonassen

BERMUDA

  d. Harmsworth, Harold Sidney
  d. Loeb, Jacques

Hamilton, Bermuda
  b. Gordon, Pamela (Felicity)
  d. Fessenden, Reginald Aubrey
  d. Payne, Robert
  d. Rattigan, Terence Mervyn, Sir
  d. Rothermere, Harold Sidney
    Harmsworth
  d. Stephenson, William

Southampton, Bermuda
  d. Mason, F(rancis) van Wyck

St. George's, Bermuda
  b. Tucker, George

BITHYNIA

  b. Osman I
  d. Pliny the Younger

Libyssa, Bithynia
  d. Hannibal

BOHEMIA

  b. Charles, IV
  b. Heinrich, Anthony Philip
  b. Wenceslaus

Aussig, Bohemia
  b. Mengs, Anton Raphael

Beischt, Bohemia
  b. Napravnik, Eduard

Brunn, Bohemia
  d. Mendel, Gregor Johann

Carlsbad, Bohemia
  b. Teschner, Richard
  d. Drexel, Anthony Joseph

Dux, Bohemia
  d. Casanova (de Seingalt), Giovanni
    Giacomo

Eger, Bohemia
  b. Serkin, Rudolph
  d. Wallenstein, Albrecht Wenzel
    Eusebius von

Elbe Kosteletz, Bohemia
  b. Stolz, Teresa

Hermanitz, Bohemia
  b. Wallenstein, Albrecht Wenzel
    Eusebius von

Humpolec, Bohemia
  b. Hrdlicka, Ales

Husinec, Bohemia
  b. Hus, Jan

Jablonec, Bohemia
  b. Adler, Peter Herman

Kalischt, Bohemia
  b. Mahler, Gustav

Kamenitz, Bohemia
  b. Novak, Vitezslav

Kozlany, Bohemia
  b. Benes, Eduard

Krecovic, Bohemia
  b. Suk, Josef

Leitmoritz, Bohemia
  b. Muller, Maria

Lieben, Bohemia
  b. Schumann-Heink, Ernestine Rossler

Litomischl, Bohemia
  b. Smetana, Bedrich

Maffersdorf, Bohemia
  b. Porsche, Ferdinand

Male Svatonovice, Bohemia
  b. Capek, Karel

Nalahozeves, Bohemia
  b. Dvorak, Anton

Neuhof, Bohemia
  d. Ditters, Karl

Opocno, Bohemia
  b. Kupka, Frank

Pilsen, Bohemia
  b. Trnka, Jiri

Policka, Bohemia
  b. Martinu, Bohuslav

Prachatice, Bohemia
  b. Neumann, John Nepomucene, Saint

Prague, Bohemia
  b. Anne of Bohemia
  b. Baum, Kurt
  b. Brod, Max
  b. Cermak, Anton Joseph
  b. Destinn, Emmy
  b. Deutsch, Karl Wolfgang
  b. Foerster, Josef Bohuslav
  b. Friml, Rudolf
  b. Hanslick, Eduard
  b. Hasek, Jaroslav
  b. Heyrovsky, Jaroslav
  b. Kafka, Franz
  b. Lederer, Francis
  b. Lom, Herbert
  b. Ludikar, Pavel
  b. Masaryk, Jan Garrigue
  b. Moscheles, Ignaz
  b. Mucha, Jiri
  b. Pollack, Egon
  b. Rilke, Rainer Maria
  b. Seifert, Jaroslav
  b. Senefelder, Aloys
  b. Steinitz, Wilhelm
  b. Susskind, Walter
  b. Wallerstein, Lothar
  b. Weinberger, Jaromir
  b. Werfel, Franz
  b. Wertheimer, Max
  d. Brahe, Tycho
  d. Charles, IV
  d. Dvorak, Anton

Raudnitz, Bohemia
  b. Pabst, Georg Wilhelm

Sheen, Bohemia
  d. Anne of Bohemia

Sinope, Bohemia
  b. Diogenes

Stannern, Bohemia
  b. Seyss-Inquart, Artur von

Steingrub, Bohemia
b. Wise, Isaac Mayer

Znojmo, Bohemia
d. Sigismund

BOLIVIA

d. Guevara, Che

Chulumani, Bolivia
d. Arguedas, Alcides

Coboja, Bolivia
b. Ovando Candia, Alfredo

Cochabamba, Bolivia
b. Laredo, Jaime
b. Patino, Simon Iturri
b. Paz Zamora, Jaime
d. Barrientos Ortuno, Rene

La Paz, Bolivia
b. Arguedas, Alcides
b. Ballivian, Jose
b. Escalante, Jaime
b. Santa Cruz, Andres de
b. Siles Zuazo, Hernan
d. Ovando Candia, Alfredo

Santa Cruz, Bolivia
b. Banzer-Suarez, Hugo

Tarija, Bolivia
b. Paz Estenssoro, Victor

Tunary, Bolivia
b. Barrientos Ortuno, Rene

BOTSWANA

Gaborone, Botswana
d. Khama, Seretse M., Sir

Serowe, Botswana
b. Chiepe, Gaositwe Keagakwa Tibe
b. Mogae, Festus Gontebanye
d. Head, Bessie Emery

BRAZIL

b. Castro Alves, Antonio de
b. Xuxa
d. Cruz, Oswaldo Goncalves
d. Rondon, Candido Mariano da Silva
d. Santos-Dumont, Alberto

Aimores, Brazil
b. Salgado, Sebastiao

Alagoas, Brazil
b. Fonseca, Manuel Deodoro da

Alegrete, Rio Grande do Sul, Brazil
b. Aranha, Osvaldo

Bahia, Brazil
b. Amado, Jorge

Bento Goncalves, Brazil
b. Geisel, Ernesto

Bertioga, Brazil
d. Mengele, Josef

Brasilia, Brazil
b. Piquet, Nelson
d. Halliday, Richard

Brodosque, Brazil
b. Portinari, Candido

Concordia, Brazil
b. Boff, Leonardo

Cuiaba, Mato Grosso, Brazil
b. Campos, Roberto de Oliveira
b. Dutra, Eurico Gaspar
b. Rondon, Candido Mariano da Silva

Diamantina, Brazil
b. Kubitschek (de Oliveira), Juscelino

Fortaleza, Brazil
b. Castello Branco, Humberto

Itabira, Brazil
b. Drummond de Andrade, Carlos

Itajuipe, Brazil
b. Adonias (Aguiar) Filho

Maceio, Alagoas, Brazil
b. Peixoto, Floriano

Mato Grosso, Brazil
d. Tors, Ivan

Minas Gerais, Brazil
b. Fonseca, Rubem
b. Santos-Dumont, Alberto

Niteroi, Brazil
b. Mendes, Sergio

Ouro Preto, Minas Gerais, Brazil
b. Aleijadinho, O

Paqueta, Brazil
d. Andrada e Silva, Jose Bonifacio de

Pernambuco, Brazil
b. Nabuco de Araujo, Joaquim Aurelio

Petropolis, Brazil
d. Zweig, Stefan

Pombal, Minas Gerais, Brazil
b. Tiradentes

Porto Alegre, Brazil
d. Verissimo, Erico Lopes

Recife, Brazil
b. Bandeira, Manuel
b. Cabral de Melo Neto, Joao
b. Freire, P(aulo)
b. Freyre, Gilberto (de Mello)
d. Freyre, Gilberto (de Mello)

Reritiba, Espirito Santo, Brazil
d. Anchieta, Jose de

Rio Grande do Sul, Brazil
b. Verissimo, Erico Lopes

Rio de Janeiro, Brazil
b. Cardoso, Fernando Henrique
b. Cavalcanti, Alberto
b. Collor de Mello, Fernando Affonso
b. da Silva, Benedita
b. Deodato
b. Figueiredo, Joao Baptista de
   Oliveira
b. Jobim, Antonio Carlos
b. Machado de Assis, Joaquim Maria
b. Medawar, Peter Brian, Sir
b. Nascimento, Milton
b. Niemeyer, Oscar
b. O'Neill, Jennifer
b. Pedro II
b. Purim, Flora
b. Rio Branco, Barao do
b. Sayao, Bidu
b. Villa-Lobos, Heitor
d. Ballivian, Jose
d. Bandeira, Manuel
d. Barbosa, Ruy
d. Cabral de Melo Neto, Joao
d. Caetano, Marcello
d. Caxias, Duque de
d. Costa, Lucio
d. Costa e Silva, Arthur da
d. Cunha, Euclides (Rodrigues
   Pimenta) da
d. Drummond de Andrade, Carlos
d. Dutra, Eurico Gaspar
d. Figueiredo, Joao Baptista de
   Oliveira
d. Fonseca, Manuel Deodoro da
d. Geisel, Ernesto
d. Gottschalk, Louis Moreau
d. Kubitschek (de Oliveira), Juscelino
d. Lispector, Clarice
d. Moraes, Vinicius de
d. Peixoto, Floriano
d. Portinari, Candido
d. Rio Branco, Barao do
d. Tiradentes
d. Vargas, Getulio Dornelles
d. Villa-Lobos, Heitor

Salvador, Brazil
d. Castro Alves, Antonio de
d. Vieira, Antonio

Salvador da Bahia, Brazil
d. Sa, Mem de

Santa Rita, Brazil
b. Cunha, Euclides (Rodrigues
   Pimenta) da

Santos, Brazil
b. Andrada e Silva, Jose Bonifacio de

Sao Bento, Brazil
b. Sarney, Jose

Sao Borja, Brazil
b. Goulart, Joao
b. Vargas, Getulio Dornelles

Sao Paulo, Brazil
b. Almeida, Laurindo
b. Bueno, Maria Ester Audion
b. Castaneda, Carlos
b. Cruz, Oswaldo Goncalves
b. Feijo, Diogo Antonio
b. Fittipaldi, Emerson
b. Jofre, Eder
b. Novaes (Pinto), Guiomar
b. Senna, Ayrton
d. Freire, P(aulo)
d. Novaes (Pinto), Guiomar
d. Volpi, Alfredo

Sao Salvador, Bahia, Brazil
b. Barbosa, Ruy

Taquari, Brazil
b. Costa e Silva, Arthur da

Tres Coracoes, Brazil
b. Pele

Xapuri, Brazil
b. Mendes, Chico
d. Mendes, Chico

BRITISH EAST AFRICA

b. Snow, Don

Ichaweri, British East Africa
b. Kenyatta, Jomo

Kaptagunyo, British East Africa
b. Keino, Kip

Nairobi, British East Africa
b. Leakey, Richard E(rskine Frere)
d. Hannagan, Steve

Nyeri, British East Africa
d. Baden-Powell, Robert Stephenson
Smyth Baden-Powell, Baron

Rusinga Island, British East Africa
b. Mboya, Tom

BRITISH GUIANA

b. Jagan, Cheddi (Berret)

Demerara, British Guiana
b. Chung, Arthur
b. Douglas, James, Sir

Kitty, British Guiana
b. Burnham, Forbes

New Amsterdam, British Guiana
b. Ramphal, Shridath Surendranath

Plaisance, British Guiana
b. Grant, Eddy

BRITISH INDIA

Jullunder, British India
b. Zia-ul-Haq, Mohammad

Rangpur, British India
b. Beveridge, William Henry, Lord

Sialkot, British India
b. Faiz, Faiz Ahmad

BRITISH VIRGIN ISLANDS

Virgin Gorda, British Virgin Islands
d. Moyes, Patricia

BRITISH WEST INDIES

Saint Kitts, British West Indies
b. Phillips, Caryl

BRUNEI DARUSSALAM

Bandar Seri Begawan, Brunei Darussalam
b. Bolkiah, Muda Hassanal, Sir

BUGANDA

Nabulagala, Buganda
d. Mutesa I

BULGARIA

b. Traikov, Georgi

Beglezh, Bulgaria
b. Dimitrova, Ghena

Borissova, Bulgaria
b. Welitsch, Ljuba

Gabrovo, Bulgaria
b. Christo

Kovachevtsi, Bulgaria
b. Dimitrov, Georgi Mikhailovich

Oriakhova, Bulgaria
b. Tsankov, Aleksandur

Plovdiv, Bulgaria
b. Tokatyan, Armand
b. Videnov, Zhan (Vassilev)

Pravets, Bulgaria
b. Zhivkov, Todor Khristov

Roustchouk, Bulgaria
b. Arlen, Michael

Ruschuk, Bulgaria
b. Canetti, Elias

Silven, Bulgaria
b. Kristeva, Julia

Slavovitsa, Bulgaria
b. Stambuliski, Aleksandr
d. Stambuliski, Aleksandr

Sofia, Bulgaria
b. Christoff, Boris
b. Kostov, Ivan
b. Weissenberg, Alexis Sigismund
d. Chervenkov, Vulko
d. Zhivkov, Todor Khristov

Varna, Bulgaria
b. Zwicky, Fritz

Velimgrad, Bulgaria
b. Ghiaurov, Nicolai

Zlatitsa, Bulgaria
b. Chervenkov, Vulko

BURKINA FASO

Ouagadougou, Burkina Faso
d. Sankara, Thomas

Ziniare, Burkina Faso
b. Compaore, Blaise

BURMA

b. Drake, Nick
d. Ba Maw
d. Mindon Min

Akyab, Burma
b. Saki

Assam, Burma
d. Wingate, Orde Charles

Mandalay, Burma
b. Saw Maung

Maubin, Burma
b. Ba Maw

Mergui, Burma
d. Ram Singh

Moksobo, Burma
b. Alaungpaya

Namkham, Burma
d. Seagrave, Gordon Stifler

Natmauk, Burma
b. Aung San

Pantanaw, Burma
b. Thant, U

Paungdale, Burma
b. Ne Win, U

Rangoon, Burma
b. Annabella

b. Seagrave, Gordon Stifler
b. Suu Kyi, Aung San

Wakema, Burma
b. Nu, U

BURUNDI

b. Buyoya, Pierre
b. Ndadaye, Melchior
b. Ntaryamira, Cyprien

Bujumbura, Burundi
d. Ndadaye, Melchior

Murambi, Burundi
b. Bagaza, Jean-Baptiste

BYZACIUM

Madaura, Byzacium
b. Apuleius, Lucius

BYZANTINE EMPIRE

Cappadocia, Byzantine Empire
b. Heraclius

Constantinople, Byzantine Empire
b. Constantine V
b. Palamas, Gregory, Saint
d. Heraclius

Thessalonia, Byzantine Empire
d. Palamas, Gregory, Saint

BYZANTIUM

d. Justinian I

CAMBODIA

b. Ngor, Haing S
d. Pol Pot

Kroch Chhmar, Cambodia
b. Hun Sen

Memot, Cambodia
b. Pol Pot

Phnom Penh, Cambodia
b. Rannaridh, Norodom, Prince
b. Sihanouk, Norodom

Preyveng, Cambodia
b. Nol, Lon

Siem Reap, Cambodia
b. Dith Pran

CAMEROON

b. Milla, Roger

Garoua, Cameroon
b. Ahidjo, Ahmadou

Mbalmayo, Cameroon
b. Beti, Mongo
b. Biyidi, Alexandre

Mvomeka'a, Cameroon
b. Biya, Paul

CAMPANIA

Campania, Campania
b. Lucilius, Gaius
d. Sulla, Lucius C

Liternum, Campania
d. Scipio Africanus, Publius Cornelius

Minturnae, Campania
d. Plotinus

CANADA

b. Cardinal, Harold
b. Cremazie, Octave
b. Evangelista, Linda
b. Jones, Peter
b. Kielburger, Craig
b. Myles, Alannah
b. Nolan, Bob
b. Ontkean, Michael
b. Rheaume, Manon
b. Vickrey, William
d. Brule, Etienne
d. Crerar, Thomas Alexander
d. Currie, Arthur William
d. Heavysege, Charles
d. Martin, Mungo

Chapleau, Canada
d. Hemon, Louis

Hudson Bay, Canada
d. Hudson, Henry

Lakefield, Canada
d. Traill, Catharine Parr

ALBERTA

Anzac, Alberta
b. Cardinal, Tantoo

Banff, Alberta
b. Robarts, John Parmenter

Blackfoot Crossing, Alberta
b. Crowfoot

Calgary, Alberta
b. Birney, Earle
b. Cameron, Rod
b. Gadsby, Bill
b. Goodman, Martin Wise
b. Graham, Nicholas
b. Lougheed, Peter
b. Moure, Erin
b. Rypien, Mark
b. Schriner, Sweeney

b. Taylor, Kenneth Douglas
b. Vernon, Mike
d. Aberhart, William
d. Dutton, Red
d. Manning, Ernest (Charles)
d. McGimsie, Billy
d. Thompson, Tiny

Camrose, Alberta
d. Ronning, Chester A

Cardston, Alberta
b. Wray, Fay

Consort, Alberta
b. Lang, K(atherine) D(awn)

Edmonton, Alberta
b. Bucyk, John Paul
b. Chong, Tommy
b. Colville, Neil McNeil
b. Dickson, Gordon Rupert
b. Ebbers, Bernie
b. Fraser, Brad
b. Hiller, Arthur
b. McLuhan, (Herbert) Marshall
b. Messier, Mark (Douglas)
b. Miller, Carl S
b. Peeters, Pete(r)
b. Raskin, A(braham) H(enry)
b. Unger, Garry Douglas

Fort Macleod, Alberta
b. Mitchell, Joni

Hanna, Alberta
b. McDonald, Lanny

High River, Alberta
b. Clark, Joe
b. Sather, Glen Cameron

Lacombe, Alberta
b. Michener, Roland

Lethbridge, Alberta
b. Bain, Conrad Stafford

MacLeon, Alberta
b. Cowdry, Edmund Vincent

Medicine Hat, Alberta
b. Gerussi, Bruno
b. Kent, Arthur
b. Taylor, Richard Edward

Midnapore, Alberta
d. Lacombe, Albert

Provost, Alberta
b. Ullman, Norm(an Victor Alexander)

Red Deer, Alberta
b. Cardinal, Douglas

Spruce Grove, Alberta
b. Fuhr, Grant Scott

Wainwright, Alberta
b. Seymour, Lynn

Whitford, Alberta
b. Kurelek, William

BRITISH COLUMBIA
d. MacKay, Mickey

Burnaby, British Columbia
b. Sakic, Joe

Comox, British Columbia
b. Lee, Pamela

Cranbrook, British Columbia
b. Yzerman, Steve

Fernie, British Columbia
d. Gladstone, James

Fort Ruport, British Columbia
b. Martin, Mungo

Grand Forks, British Columbia
b. Dmytryk, Edward

Kelowna, British Columbia
b. Bennett, William
d. Bennett, W(illiam) A(ndrew) C(ecil)

Mission City, British Columbia
b. Holmes, Anna Marie
b. Monk, Allan James

Murrayville, British Columbia
b. Heppner, Ben

Neskainlith, British Columbia
b. Manuel, George

New Westminster, British Columbia
b. Burr, Raymond (William Stacy)
d. Fox, Terry

North Vancouver, British Columbia
b. George, Dan, Chief

Penticton, British Columbia
b. Smith, Alexis

Port Alberni, British Columbia
b. Campbell, Kim

Sandon, British Columbia
b. Thompson, Tiny

Skidegate, British Columbia
b. Edenshaw, Charles

Vancouver, British Columbia
b. Adams, Bryan Guy
b. Anderson, Glenn Chris
b. Cerovsek, Corey
b. DeCarlo, Yvonne
b. Dodington, Sven H(enry Marriott)
b. Doohan, James Montgomery
b. Erickson, Arthur Charles
b. Ferguson, John Bowie
b. Fox, Michael J.
b. Hartley, Fred Lloyd
b. Hayakawa, S(amuel) I(chiye)
b. Holmes, David
b. Markle, C(larke) Wilson, Jr.
b. McNeill, William Hardy

b. McTaggart, David
b. Newell, Pete
b. Parkins, Barbara
b. Peter, Laurence Johnston
b. Priestly, Jason
b. Qualen, John Mandt
b. Reno, Mike
b. Stratten, Dorothy
b. Suzuki, David T(akayoshi)
b. Trudeau, Margaret Joan Sinclair
d. Burns, Tommy
d. Cameron, Harry
d. Flynn, Errol
d. George, Dan, Chief
d. Guinan, Texas
d. Harris, Lauren
d. Johnson, Emily Pauline
d. Patrick, Frank A
d. Pratt, Babe
d. Whitcroft, Fred(rick)
d. Woodsworth, James Shaver

Victoria, British Columbia
b. Bosustow, Stephen
b. Carr, Emily
b. Foster, David
b. Ireland, John
b. Patrick, Lynn
b. Reid, William Ronald
b. Tunnard, Christopher
b. Tyson, Ian
d. Cabot, Sebastian
d. Carr, Emily
d. Douglas, James, Sir
d. McClung, Nellie Letitia Mooney
d. Patrick, Lester B

White Rock, British Columbia
d. Johnson, Moose

MANITOBA
b. Harper, Elijah
b. Highway, Thomson

Arnes, Manitoba
b. Stefansson, Vihjalmur

Baldur, Manitoba
b. Johnson, Tom

Beausejour, Manitoba
b. Schreyer, Edward Richard

Brandon, Manitoba
b. Broda, Turk
b. Bronfman, Samuel
b. Ford, Russ(ell William)
b. Woods, Donald

Carman, Manitoba
b. Carson, Jack

Emerson, Manitoba
b. Sweet, John Howard

Flin Flon, Manitoba
b. Clarke, Bobby

Fort Alexander Indian Reserve, Manitoba
b. Fontaine, Philip

Fort Gary, Manitoba
b. Henning, Doug(las James)

Neepawa, Manitoba
b. Laurence, Margaret

Oak Lake, Manitoba
b. Strong, Maurice Frederick

Pilot Mound, Manitoba
b. Stewart, Black Jack

Portage La Prairie, Manitoba
d. Hextall, Bryan Aldwyn

Riverton, Manitoba
b. Leach, Reggie

Russell, Manitoba
b. Dutton, Red

Saint Boniface, Manitoba
b. Cariou, Len
b. Goring, Butch
b. Riel, Louis David, Jr.
b. Roy, Gabrielle

Selkirk, Manitoba
b. Oliver, Harry

Stony Mountain, Manitoba
b. Pratt, Babe

Swan River, Manitoba
b. Delblanc, Sven

Virden, Manitoba
b. Wallace, Lila Bell Acheson

Winnipeg, Manitoba
b. Adelman, Sybil
b. Armstrong, Jack Lawrence
b. Bachman, Randy
b. Bathgate, Andy
b. Bolt, Carol
b. Brand, Oscar
b. Cameron, Eleanor Frances
b. Coulter, Art(hur Edmund)
b. Cummings, Burton
b. Dickason, Olive Patricia
b. Dumont, Gabriel
b. Durbin, Deanna
b. Fox, Terry
b. Frederickson, Frank
b. Gardiner, Herb(ert Martin)
b. Hall, Monty
b. Hextall, Ron(ald Jeffrey)
b. Johnson, Ching
b. Johnson, F(rederick) Ross
b. Livesay, Dorothy (Kathleen)
b. MacKenzie, Gisele
b. Markle, Fletcher
b. Masterton, Bill
b. Mathers, Frank
b. Maxwell, Steamer
b. Mosienko, Bill
b. Murray, Troy
b. Penner, Fred
b. Piret, Edgar L
b. Reardon, Ken(neth Joseph)
b. Saidenberg, Daniel
b. Sawchuk, Terry
b. Steinberg, David

d. Jones, Peter

Addington, Ontario
b. Parker, Gilbert, Sir

Alliston, Ontario
b. Banting, Frederick Grant, Sir
d. Noble, Reg

Almonte, Ontario
b. Naismith, James A

Anderson, Ontario
b. Meighen, Arthur

Arva, Ontario
b. Sifton, Clifford

Augusta, Ontario
d. Heck, Barbara Ruckle

Aurora, Ontario
b. Holmes, Hap

Ayr, Ontario
b. Kilgour, Joseph

Bancroft, Ontario
b. Watson, Bryan Joseph

Belleville, Ontario
b. Bain, Dan
b. Boon, Dickie
b. Dow, Herbert Henry
b. Hull, Brett (A.)
b. Laviolette, Jack
b. Mowat, Farley McGill
d. Bowell, Mackenzie, Sir
d. Stuart, Hod

Belmont, Ontario
b. Barr, Murray Llewellyn

Berlin, Ontario
b. King, William Lyon Mackenzie
b. Seibert, Oliver L

Bondhead, Ontario
b. Osler, William, Sir

Bracebridge, Ontario
b. Bailey, Ace
b. Crozier, Roger Allan

Brampton, Ontario
b. Pawley, Howard Russell
b. Tawley, Howard

Brantford, Ontario
b. Cook, Bill
b. Costain, Thomas Bertram
b. Gretzky, Wayne
b. Harris, Lauren
b. Hartman, Phil
b. Hillier, James
b. Jarvis, Doug(las)

Callander, Ontario
b. Dionne, Emilie
b. Dionne, Marie
b. Dionne Sisters

Canoe Lake, Ontario
d. Thomson, Tom

Cardinal, Ontario
b. Crawford, Rusty

Carleton Place, Ontario
b. Brown, A Roy

Charlotteville, Ontario
b. Ryerson, Adolphus Egerton

Chatham, Ontario
b. Couzens, James Joseph, Jr.
b. Jenkins, Ferguson Arthur
b. LaMarsh, Judy
b. Tyson, Sylvia Fricker

Chatsworth, Ontario
b. McClung, Nellie Letitia Mooney

Chesley, Ontario
b. MacKay, Mickey

Chiefswood, Ontario
b. Johnson, Emily Pauline

Chippewa, Ontario
d. Secord, Laura Ingersoll

Claremont, Ontario
b. Thomson, Tom

Cobalt, Ontario
d. Drummond, William Henry

Cobourg, Ontario
b. Dressler, Marie
b. Duffy, Francis Patrick
b. Hewitt, William Archibald
b. Murray, John, Sir

Cochrane, Ontario
b. Horton, Tim

Colchester, Ontario
b. McCoy, Elijah

Collingwood, Ontario
b. Johnston, Lynn Beverley
b. Noble, Reg

Cornwall, Ontario
b. Chevrier, Lionel
b. Lalonde, Newsy

Dresden, Ontario
d. Henson, Josiah

Drummondsville, Ontario
b. Dett, Robert Nathaniel

Dutton, Ontario
b. McLaughlin, Audrey

Exeter, Ontario
b. Fleming, Donald M(ethuen)

Falconbridge, Ontario
b. McCourt, Dale Allen

Farran's Point, Ontario
b. Denneny, Cy(ril)

Fort Erie, Ontario
d. Delahanty, Ed(ward James)

Fort Perry, Ontario
b. Whitcroft, Fred(rick)

Fort William, Ontario
b. Adams, Jack
b. Delvecchio, Alex Peter

Geraldton, Ontario
b. Urquhart, Jane

Gravenhurst, Ontario
b. Bethune, Norman
d. Hainsworth, George

Grey County, Ontario
b. Diefenbaker, John George

Guelph, Ontario
b. Campbell, Neve
b. Hill, James Jerome
b. McCrae, John
b. Sparks, Ned

Hamilton, Ontario
b. Augustyn, Frank Joseph
b. Beatty, Robert
b. Cooke, Jack Kent
b. Copps, Sheila Maureen
b. Coughlin, Charles Edward, Father
b. Cranston, Toller
b. Dupuy, Diane
b. Dye, Babe
b. Fairclough, Ellen Louks
b. Howell, Harry
b. Kain, Karen Alexandria
b. Lawrence, Florence
b. Quinn, Pat
b. Short, Martin
b. Spedding, Frank Harold
d. LeSueur, Percy

Hanover, Ontario
b. Burns, Tommy

Hibbard Township, Ontario
b. Aberhart, William

Humberstone, Ontario
b. Kennedy, Ted

Ingersoll, Ontario
b. McPherson, Aimee Semple

Iona Station, Ontario
b. Galbraith, John Kenneth

Islington, Ontario
b. Dryden, Ken(neth Wayne)

Kapuskasing, Ontario
b. Cameron, James

Kenora, Ontario
b. Phillips, Tommy

Paisley, Ontario
b. Milne, David Brown
b. Stanley, Barney

Paris, Ontario
b. Apps, Syl

Parry Island Indian Reserve, Ontario
b. Johnston, Basil H.

Parry Sound, Ontario
b. Orr, Bobby

Pembroke, Ontario
b. Cameron, Harry
b. Lehman, Hughie
b. Neuhaus, Richard John
b. Nighbor, Frank
d. Nighbor, Frank

Penetanguishene, Ontario
b. Orser, Brian

Perth, Ontario
b. Smith, Billy

Peterborough, Ontario
b. Gainey, Bob
b. Hall, Manly Palmer
b. Paley, William

Pickering, Ontario
d. Lonergan, Bernard J F

Plattsville, Ontario
b. Siebert, Babe

Point Anne, Ontario
b. Hull, Bobby

Port Hope, Ontario
b. Sims, William Sowden

Prescott, Ontario
b. Boivin, Leo Joseph

Queenston, Ontario
d. Brock, Isaac, Sir

Rainy River, Ontario
b. Nagurski, Bronko

Rat Portage, Ontario
b. Hooper, Tom

Red Rock, Ontario
b. Kroker, Arthur

Renfrew, Ontario
b. Lindsay, Ted
d. Casadesus, Jean

Rice Lake, Ontario
b. Copway, George

Saint Catharines, Ontario
b. Bell, Ralph S.
b. Cheevers, Gerry
b. Eagleson, Alan
b. Froese, Bob
b. Norris, James, Sr.
b. Slade, Bernard

b. Thomas, Dave
d. Horton, Tim

Saint Joseph, Ontario
d. Siebert, Babe

Saint Marys, Ontario
b. Hern, Riley

Saint Thomas, Ontario
b. Aziz, Philip John Andrew Ferris
b. Shaver, Helen

Sand Point Reserve, Ontario
b. Morrisseau, Norval

Sarnia, Ontario
b. Clark, Susan Nora Goulding

Sault Sainte Marie, Ontario
b. Esposito, Phil(ip Anthony)
b. Esposito, Tony
b. McNamara, George
b. Nanne, Lou(is Vincent)
b. Pitre, Didier
b. Rosenthal, Abraham Michael

Scarborough, Ontario
b. Hiller, John Frederick
b. Murphy, Larry
b. Myers, Mike

Seaforth, Ontario
b. Weiland, Cooney

Silver Mountain, Ontario
b. Walker, Jack

Simcoe, Ontario
b. Kelly, Red
d. Grove, Frederick Philip

Six Nations Indian Reservation, Ontario
b. Silverheels, Jay

Skead, Ontario
b. Armstrong, George Edward

Spadina, Ontario
d. Baldwin, Robert

Springfield, Ontario
b. Williams, Lynn Russell

St. Catharines, Ontario
d. Burns, Anthony

Stevensville, Ontario
b. Kraft, James Lewis

Stouffville, Ontario
d. Brown, A Roy

Stratford, Ontario
b. Erdman, Paul E(mil)
b. Patterson, Tom
d. Reid, Kate

Strathroy, Ontario
b. Chadwick, Cassie L
b. Knox, Alexander

b. Shotwell, James Thomson

Sudbury, Ontario
b. Arbour, Al(ger Joseph)
b. Campeau, Robert Joseph
b. Carlyle, Randy
b. Giacomin, Eddie
b. Green, Wilf(red Thomas)
b. Trebek, Alex

Tara, Ontario
b. Taylor, Cyclone

Terrace Bay, Ontario
b. Simmer, Charlie

Thamesville, Ontario
b. Davies, (William) Robertson
d. Tecumseh

Thunder Bay, Ontario
b. McEwen, Terence Alexander
b. Shaffer, Paul

Timmins, Ontario
b. Kreiner, Kathy
b. Mahovlich, Frank
b. Mahovlich, Pete(r Joseph)
b. Stanley, Allan Herbert
b. Stern, Sandor

Toronto, Ontario
b. Baldwin, Robert
b. Ballard, Harold
b. Bell, Marilyn
b. Black, Davidson
b. Bochner, Hart
b. Bochner, Lloyd
b. Booth, George Gough
b. Callaghan, Morley Edward
b. Candy, John (Franklin)
b. Chuvalo, George
b. Clark, Barrett H
b. Colicos, John
b. Colville, Alex
b. Conacher, Charlie
b. Conacher, Lionel Pretoria
b. Crombie, David Edward
b. Cronenberg, David
b. DeLaRoche, Mazo
b. Dempster, Arthur Jeffrey
b. Denison, George Taylor
b. Doherty, Brian
b. Durnan, Bill
b. Dwan, Allan
b. Evans, Gil
b. Faith, Percy
b. Fowler, Mark Stapleton
b. Furie, Sidney J
b. Gehry, Frank Owen
b. Gleason, Joanna
b. Gold, Arthur
b. Gould, Glenn Herbert
b. Gowans, Alan
b. Graham, Gwethalyn
b. Hainsworth, George
b. Harris, Michael Wesley
b. Hawerchuk, Dale
b. Hayden, Melissa
b. Healey, Jeff
b. Herbert, John
b. Hewitt, Foster
b. Hill, Dan
b. Hinkle, W Clarke
b. Houston, James Archibold

b. Lonergan, Bernard J F

Caughnawaga, Quebec
d. Tekakwitha, Kateri, Saint

Chambly, Quebec
d. Cullen, Maurice Galbraith

Charlemagne, Quebec
b. Dion, Celine

Charlesbourg, Quebec
b. Boucher, Gaetan

Chicoutimi, Quebec
b. Vezina, Georges

Compton, Quebec
b. St. Laurent, Louis Stephen

Cote des Neiges, Quebec
b. Bibaud, Michel

Deschambault, Quebec
b. Arcand, Denys

Drummondville, Quebec
b. Courneyor, Yvan Serge
b. Dionne, Marcel Elphege
b. Patrick, Lester B

Granby, Quebec
b. Cox, Palmer
d. Cox, Palmer

Grand Mere, Quebec
b. McLerie, Allyn Ann

Hull, Quebec
b. Lanois, Daniel
b. Larocque, Bunny
b. Potvin, Denis Charles
d. Larocque, Bunny

Ile Perrot, Quebec
b. Lalonde, Marc

Kenogami, Quebec
b. Pilote, Pierre Paul

La Salle, Quebec
b. Lemaire, Jacques Gerald

Lac Saint Jean, Quebec
b. Ratelle, Jean

Lac-la-Tortue, Quebec
b. Pronovost, Marcel

Lachine, Quebec
b. Bellow, Saul

Levis, Quebec
b. Frechette, Louis-Honore

Marbleton, Quebec
b. Tanguay, Eva

Matapedia, Quebec
d. Hill, George Washington

Milton, Quebec
b. Fessenden, Reginald Aubrey

Montebello, Quebec
d. Papineau, Louis-Joseph

Montreal, Quebec
b. Abel, Elie
b. Aitken, Max
b. Allan, Montagu, Sir
b. Almond, Paul
b. Altman, Sidney
b. Berne, Eric Lennard
b. Black, Conrad Moffat
b. Blue, Ben
b. Bossy, Mike
b. Bouchard, Butch
b. Bourassa, Henri
b. Bourassa, (Jean) Robert
b. Bourque, Ray(mond Jean)
b. Bowie, Russell
b. Bowman, Scotty
b. Bronfman, Edgar Miles
b. Bujold, Genevieve
b. Cadieux, Marcel (Joseph David Romeo)
b. Cleghorn, Sprague
b. Cohen, Leonard Norman
b. Cox, Jacob Dolson
b. Demers, Jacques
b. Dewhurst, Colleen
b. D'Orsay, Fifi
b. Drapeau, Jean
b. Drinkwater, Charles Graham
b. Dumas, Jean Baptiste Andre
b. Dunton, Davidson
b. Fonyo, Steve
b. Forrester, Maureen
b. Forsyth, Rosemary
b. Frazier, Brenda Diana Dudd
b. Gallant, Mavis
b. Gardner, Jimmy
b. Geoffrion, Bernie
b. Gilbert, Rod(rigue Gabriel)
b. Glassco, John Stinson
b. Guston, Philip
b. Harvey, Doug(las Norman)
b. Herelle, Felix d'
b. Hyland, Harry
b. Iberville, Pierre Le Moyne, Sieur d'
b. Jackson, A(lexander) Y(oung)
b. Johnson, Moose
b. Johnson, Pierre Marc
b. Jutra, Claude
b. Karpis, Alvin
b. Keats, Duke
b. Klein, Marty
b. Krofft, Marty
b. Lemieux, Mario
b. Lesage, Jean
b. Leveille, Norm(and)
b. Levy, David H.
b. Logan, William Edmond
b. London, George
b. MacDermot, Galt
b. MacNeil, Robert Breckenridge Ware
b. Makepeace, Chris
b. Mantha, Sylvio
b. Marcus, Rudolph A
b. Martin, Rick
b. McKegney, Tony
b. Molson, Hartland de Montarville
b. Moore, Dickie
b. Morin, Paul
b. Morrice, James Wilson
b. O'Connor, Buddy

b. Papineau, Louis-Joseph
b. Parent, Bernie
b. Parizeau, Jacques
b. Pelletier, Wilfrid
b. Peterson, Oscar Emanuel
b. Pierce, Mary
b. Pollock, Sam
b. Quilico, Louis
b. Reisman, Simon
b. Richard, Henri
b. Richard, Maurice
b. Richler, Mordecai
b. Riopelle, Jean-Paul
b. Robinson, Arthur H(oward)
b. Robitaille, Luc
b. Ruddy, Al(bert Stotland)
b. Russell, Ernie
b. Ryan, Claude
b. Sahl, Mort (Lyon)
b. Savard, Serge A
b. Scaasi, Arnold
b. Scherman, Harry
b. Shapiro, Harold Tafler
b. Shatner, William
b. Shearer, Norma
b. Smith, A(rthur) J(ames) M(arshall)
b. Stewart, Nels(on Robert)
b. Torrey, Bill
b. Tourel, Jennie
b. Tremblay, Michel
b. Trihey, Harry
b. Trudeau, Pierre Elliott
b. Vannelli, Gino
b. Vincennes, Francois Marie Bissot
b. Whitehead, Robert
b. Wiseman, Joseph
b. Worsley, Gump
b. Zuckerman, Mortimer Benjamin
d. Bibaud, Michel
d. Blake, Toe
d. Bourassa, Henri
d. Bourassa, (Jean) Robert
d. Bronfman, Samuel
d. Buchan, John, Sir
d. Calder, Frank
d. Campbell, Clarence Sutherland
d. Chevrier, Lionel
d. Cleghorn, Sprague
d. Dawson, John William, Sir
d. Dionne, Marie
d. Drapeau, Jean
d. Drysdale, Don(ald Scott)
d. Duluth, Daniel (Greysolon)
d. Frechette, Louis-Honore
d. Galt, Alexander Tilloch
d. Gardner, Jimmy
d. Giddings, Joshua Reed
d. Glassco, John Stinson
d. Graham, Gwethalyn
d. Harvey, Doug(las Norman)
d. Hern, Riley
d. Howe, Clarence Decatur
d. Hyland, Harry
d. Irvin, Dick
d. Klein, Abraham Moses
d. LaFontaine, Louis Hippolyte, Sir
d. Lalonde, Newsy
d. la Verendrye, Sieur de
d. Laviolette, Jack
d. Leonowens, Anna Harriette Crawford
d. Levesque, Rene
d. Lismer, Arthur
d. MacLennan, Hugh
d. Marshall, Jack
d. McGill, James

North Battleford, Saskatchewan
b. Francis, Emile Percy

Park Valley, Saskatchewan
b. Campbell, Maria

Prince Albert, Saskatchewan
b. Bower, Johnny
b. Thomson, Earl
b. Vickers, Jon
d. Grey Owl

Prud'Homme, Saskatchewan
b. Sauve, Jeanne Mathilde Benoit

Regina, Saskatchewan
b. Berenson, Red
b. Devine, Donald
b. Gillies, Clark
b. Nielsen, Leslie
b. Pocklington, Peter H
b. Vernon, John
d. Riel, Louis David, Jr.

Rhein, Saskatchewan
b. Weinmeister, Arnie

Saskatoon, Saskatchewan
b. Howe, Gordie
b. Magnuson, Keith Arlen
b. Mahoney, James P(atrick)
d. Bentley, Doug(las Wagner)
d. Bentley, Max(well Herbert Lloyd)
d. Mahoney, James P(atrick)

Scepter, Saskatchewan
b. Olmstead, Bert

Sutherland, Saskatchewan
b. Rayner, Chuck

Val Marie, Saskatchewan
b. Trottier, Bryan John

Waldheim, Saskatchewan
b. Schultz, Dave

Weyburn, Saskatchewan
b. Mitchell, W(illiam) O(rmond)
b. Williams, Tiger

YUKON TERRITORY

Whitehorse, Yukon Territory
b. Berton, Pierre

CAPE VERDE

Boa Vista, Cape Verde
b. Pereira, Aristides

Fogo, Cape Verde
b. Sousa, Henrique Teixeira de

Mindello, Cape Verde
b. Evora, Cesaria

Sao Tiago, Cape Verde
b. Mascarenhas Monteiro, Antonio

CAPPADOCIA

Caesarea, Cappadocia
b. Basil, Saint
d. Basil, Saint

Comana, Cappadocia
d. Chrysostom, John, Saint

CENTRAL AFRICAN REPUBLIC

Bangui, Central African Republic
b. Kolingba, Andre-Dieudonne
d. Bokassa, Jean-Bedel

Boubangui, Central African Republic
b. Bokassa, Jean-Bedel

CEYLON

Botale, Ceylon
b. Senanayake, Don Stephen

Colombo, Ceylon
b. Amerasinghe, Hamilton Shirley
b. Bandaranaike, S(olomon) W(est) R(idgeway) D(ias)
b. Coomaraswamy, Ananda Kentish
b. Dharmapala, Anagarika
b. Jayewardene, J(unius) R(ichard)
b. Kumaratunga, Chandrika Bandaranaike
b. Napier, Robert Cornelis
b. Senanayake, Dudley Shelton
b. Waldock, Humphrey Meredith, Sir
d. Bandaranaike, S(olomon) W(est) R(idgeway) D(ias)
d. Senanayake, Don Stephen

Dullewa, Ceylon
b. Gopallawa, William

Kandy, Ceylon
b. Bandaranaike, Sirimavo Ratwatte Dias

Panadura, Ceylon
b. Rogers, Rosemary

Rambodde, Ceylon
b. Fisher, John Arbuthnot

CHAD

Badaya, Chad
b. Tombalbaye, Nagarta Francois

Fada, Chad
b. Deby, Idriss

Faya Largeau, Chad
b. Habre, Hissene

Fort Lamy, Chad
d. Tombalbaye, Nagarta Francois

CHILE

Araucania, Chile
b. Lautaro

Chillan, Chile
b. Arrau, Claudio
b. O'Higgins, Bernardo
b. Vinay, Ramon

Coquimbo, Chile
b. Albright, William Foxwell

Linares, Chile
b. Ibanez del Campo, Carlos

Longavi, Chile
b. Alessandri Palma, Arturo

Parral, Chile
b. Neruda, Pablo

San Fabian, Chile
b. Parra, Nicanor

Santiago, Chile
b. Alessandri, Jorge
b. Balmaceda Fernandez, Jose Manuel
b. Carrera, Jose Miguel
b. DeCuevas, Marquis
b. Donoso, Jose
b. Frei, Eduardo
b. Frei Ruiz-Tagle, Eduardo
b. Hebard, Caroline
b. Matta, Roberto Sebastian Antonio Echaurren
b. Portales, Diego (Jose Victor)
d. Alessandri, Jorge
d. Alessandri Palma, Arturo
d. Allende Gossens, Salvador
d. Bello y Lopez, Andres
d. Bombal, Maria Luisa
d. Donoso, Jose
d. Frei, Eduardo
d. Honecker, Erich
d. Neruda, Pablo
d. Prebisch, Raul
d. Zanelli, Renato

Temuco, Chile
b. Letelier, Orlando

Valparaiso, Chile
b. Allende Gossens, Salvador
b. Ankers, Evelyn
b. Herrera Lane, Felipe
b. Pinochet Ugarte, Augusto
b. Zanelli, Renato
d. Portales, Diego (Jose Victor)

Vicuna, Chile
b. Mistral, Gabriela

Vina del Mar, Chile
b. Aylwin (Azocar), Patricio
b. Bombal, Maria Luisa

CHINA

b. Chang Chih-tung
b. Ch'en Tu-hsiu
b. Chih-i

b. Ch'i-ying
b. Chu, Paul C W
b. Chuang Tzu
b. Han Kao-tsu
b. Hsuan Tsang
b. Hsun-tzu
b. Jingsheng, Wei
b. K'ang-hsi
b. Liddell, Eric
b. Li Ssu
b. Liu Pang
b. Lu Chi
b. Lucid, Shannon
b. Mingxia, Fu
b. Quin Shi Huang-Di
b. Roosevelt, Anna C(urtenius)
b. Ssu-ma Hsiang-ju
b. Sui Wen-ti
b. Sung T'ai-tsu
b. Tai-Tsung
b. Tao-hsuan
b. Tung Chung-shu
b. Wang Ch'ung
b. Wang Hung-Wen
b. Wu, Chien Shiung
b. Wu Tse-t'ien
d. Bethune, Norman
d. Chang Hsueh-ch'eng
d. Cheng Ho
d. Ch'en Tu-hsiu
d. Chiang K'ang-Hu
d. Chih-i
d. Ch'in Kuei
d. Ch'i-ying
d. Chuang Tzu
d. Chu Hsi
d. Gao Gang
d. Hsuan Tsang
d. Hsun-tzu
d. Hui-Tsung
d. Hung-Wu
d. Lin Tse-hsu
d. Liu Pang
d. Lu, Yu
d. Lu Chi
d. Mencius
d. Ni Tsan
d. Quin Shi Huang-Di
d. Ricci, Matteo
d. Shih Le
d. Sui Wen-ti
d. Tai-Tsung
d. Tao-hsuan
d. Tung Chung-shu
d. Wang Mang
d. Wu Tse-t'ien
d. Xiang Jingyu
d. Yen Fu
d. Yen Li-pen
d. Yo Fei

Anhui Province, China
b. Ming, T'ai-Tsu

Anwei, China
b. Wang Ming

Baodingfu, China
b. Lattimore, Richmond Alexander

Beijing, China
b. Chennault, Anna Chan
b. Ch'ien Lung
b. Fang Lizhi
b. Fenneman, George

b. Han Suyin
b. Pu-Yi, Henry
b. Robertson, Don
b. Tz'u Hsi
b. Yen, Samuel
b. Zao-Wou-Ki
d. Alley, Rewi
d. Chen Yi
d. Chiang, Ching
d. Ch'ien Lung
d. Ch'i Pai-Shih
d. Chou En-Lai
d. Chou Tso-Jen
d. Chu Te
d. Deng Xiaoping
d. Guo Moruo
d. Hatem, George
d. Hsiung Shih-Li
d. Hu Yaobang
d. Kang, Sheng
d. Ku Chieh-kang
d. Li Xiannian
d. Mao Zedong
d. Pu-Yi, Henry
d. Strong, Anna Louise
d. Sun Yat-Sen
d. Sun Yat-Sen, Chingling Soong, Madame
d. Tz'u Hsi
d. Ye Jianying

Canton, China
b. Hung Hsiu-ch'uan
b. Liang Ch'i-ch'ao
b. Wang Ching-wei

Ch'ai-sang, Kiangsi Province, China
b. T'ao Ch'ien

Ch'ang-an, China
b. Liu Tsung-yuan
d. T'ai-tsung, T'ang
d. Tao-an

Chekiang, China
b. Chang Hsueh-ch'eng
b. Ts'ai Yuan-p'ei

Chengdu, China
b. Li Peng
b. Service, John S(tewart)

Chengtu, China
b. Pa Chin

Chi-an, Kiangsi, China
b. Wen T'ien-hsiang

Chiang-ning, Kiangsu Province, China
b. Ch'in Kuei

Chongqing, China
b. Bodard, Lucien (Albert)

Chucheng, China
b. Chiang, Ching

Dangtu, China
d. Li Po

Fancheng, China
b. Ronning, Chester A

Fenghua, China
b. Chiang Ching-Kuo
b. Chiang Kai-Shek

Foochow, China
d. Tso Tsung-t'ang

Fukien, China
b. Lin Tse-hsu

Fukien Province, China
b. Yen Fu

Fuzhou, China
b. Beard, Myron Gould

Gongxian, China
b. Tu, Fu

Guangchou, China
b. Woo, John

Guangdong Province, China
b. Howe, James Wong
b. K'ang Yu-wei

Guangzhou, China
b. Li, C(hoh) H(ao)
b. Luke, Keye
b. Pei, I(eoh) M(ing)
d. Sears, Isaac

Guiyang, China
b. Ts'ai, Lun

Hailar, China
b. Ussachevsky, Vladimir Alexis

Hangchow, China
b. Wang Yang-ming
d. Wei Yuan

Hangzhou, China
b. Hsia Kuei

Hankou, China
b. Fritz, Jean Guttery

Hao-Chou, China
b. Hung-Wu

Harbin, China
d. Ito, Hirobumi

Hefei, China
b. Yang, Chen Ning

Henan Province, China
b. Wo-jen
b. Yuan, Shih-Kai

Heng Shan, China
b. Gao Gang

Ho-pien, China
b. Yen Hsi-shan

Hofei, China
b. Li Hung-Chang

Hopei Province, China
b. Tao-an

Hsiang-hsiang, Hunan, China
b. Tseng Kuo-fan

Hsiang-yang, China
b. Mi Fei

Hsiangyin, Hunan, China
b. Tso Tsung-t'ang

Hsin-cheng, China
b. Po Chu-i

Hsingchi-chen, Chihli (Hopei), China
b. Feng Yu-hsiang

Huang-Kang, China
b. Hsiung Shih-Li

Huangang, China
b. Lin, Piao (Yu-Yung)

Hubei Province, China
b. Li Xiannian

Huchow, Chekiang Province, China
b. Chao Meng-fu

Hunan, China
b. Wang Fu-chih
b. Zhao Ziyang

Hupei, China
d. Wei Hsiao-Wen-ti

Jiangsu, China
b. Huang Hua
b. Lee, Henry C.

Jiaxing, China
b. Chern, Shiing-shen

Jiujiang, China
b. Bowra, Maurice, Sir

Kaifeng, China
d. Liu Shao-Ch'i
d. Zhao Kuang-yin

Kiangsi, China
b. Wang An-shih

Kiangsu Province, China
b. Wang T'ao

Kuang-shan, Hunan, China
b. Ssu-ma kuang

Kuling, China
b. Peake, Mervyn Laurence

Liuyang City, China
b. Hu Yaobang

Lo-chih, China
b. Chen Yi

Lo-yang, China
b. Zhao Kuang-yin

Loshan, China
b. Kuo Mo-jo

Lushun, China
d. Vereshchagin, Vasily Vasilyevich

Manchuria, China
b. Mifune, Toshiro
d. Chang Tso-Lin

Mei-shan, China
b. Su Shih

Meixien, China
b. Ye Jianying

Mienchow, China
b. Ou-yang Hsiu

Mt. Lu, China
d. Hui-yuan

Mukden, China
b. Wen-hsiang

Nanking, China
b. Owen, Lewis James
d. Tseng Kuo-fan
d. Wang An-shih

Ningbo, China
b. Coulter, John Merle

P'ing-ch'eng, China
b. Wei Hsiao-Wen-ti

P'u-chou, China
b. Wang Wei

Peking, China
b. Lao She
d. Chang Chih-tung
d. K'ang-hsi
d. Kuo Mo-jo
d. Lao She

Qingdao, China
b. Wilhelm, Hellmut
d. K'ang Yu-wei

Qinghai, China
b. Panchen Lama

Qufu, China
d. Confucius

Shaeshan, China
b. Mao Zedong

Shandong, China
b. Chai Ling
b. Kang, Sheng
b. Mencius

Shang, China
d. Shang Yang

Shanghai, China
b. Ballard, J(ames) G(raham)
b. Dichter, Mischa
b. DiSuvero, Mark
b. Eames, Emma Hayden

b. Fischer, Edmond
b. Hu Shih
b. Koo, V(i) K(yuin) Wellington
b. Kwoh, Yik San
b. Lee, Ming Cho
b. Lee, Tsung-Dao
b. Lord, Bette Bao
b. Mabee, Carleton
b. Min, Anchee
b. Raven, Peter H(amilton)
b. Song Sisters, The
b. Soong, T V
b. Sun Yat-Sen, Chingling Soong,
  Madame
b. Tribe, Laurence Henry
b. Tung Chee-hwa
b. Tung Ch'i-ch'ang
b. Wang, An
b. Wu, Harry
b. Yard, Molly
b. Young, Terence
d. Lu Hsun
d. Sung Chiao-jen
d. Wang T'ao

Shangrao, China
b. Chiang K'ang-Hu

Shansi, China
b. Shih Le

Shantung, China
b. Wu P'ei-fu

Shanxi Province, China
b. Hua Guofeng

Shaoxing, China
b. Chou En-Lai
b. Chou Tso-Jen
b. Lu Hsun

Shaoyang, Hunan, China
b. Wei Yuan

Shawan, China
b. Guo Moruo

Shenyang, China
b. Chang Tso-Lin
b. Gong Li
b. Ozawa, Seiji

Shuzhou, China
d. Birch, John

Sichuan, China
b. Chu Te
b. Deng Xiaoping
b. Li Po

Soochow, China
b. Ku Chieh-kang

T'ai-chou, Chekiang Province, China
d. Chia Ssu-tao

T'ang-yin, Honan, China
b. Yo Fei

Ta-hsing-ch'eng, China
b. T'ai-tsung, T'ang

Taiyuan, China
b. Chang, M(in) C(heuh), Dr.

Tanzhou, China
d. Tu, Fu

Taoyuan, China
b. Sung Chiao-jen

Tianjin, China
b. Hersey, John (Richard)

Tientsin, China
d. Liang Ch'i-ch'ao

Tuo, China
b. Confucius

Wei, China
b. Shang Yang

Weifang, China
d. Liddell, Eric

Wu-hsi, China
b. Ni Tsan

Wuchang, China
b. Meadows, Audrey
b. Meadows, Jayne Cotter

Wuzhou, China
b. Tao-chi

Xi'an, China
b. Pan Ku
b. Zhang Yimou

Xiamen, China
b. Brattain, Walter Houser

Xiangtan, China
b. Ch'i Pai-Shih

Xigaze, China
d. Panchen Lama

Xingyi, China
b. Ho, Ying-Chin

Xupu, Hunan, China
b. Xiang Jingyu

Yang-ti, Honan Province, China
b. Wu Tao-tzu

Yangchow, China
d. Shih Ko-fa

Yangzhou City, China
b. Jiang Zemin

Yibin, China
b. Chang, Jung

Yu-hsi Prefecture, Fukien, China
b. Chu Hsi

Yu-mu-ch'uan, Jehol, China
d. Yung-lo

Yunnan Province, China
b. Cheng Ho

Zhangzhou, China
b. Lin, Yutang

CILICIA

Selinus, Cilicia
d. Trajan

Tarsus, Cilicia
b. Paul, Saint

COCHINCHINA

Gia Dinh, Cochinchina
b. Duras, Marguerite

COLOMBIA

b. Obregon, Alejandro
d. Reyes, Rafael

Amaga, Colombia
b. Betancur, Belisario

Antioquia, Colombia
b. Guerrero, Roberto

Aracataca, Colombia
b. Garcia-Marquez, Gabriel Jose

Bogota, Colombia
b. Arciniegas, German
b. Gomez Castro, Laureano Eleuterio
b. Lleras Camargo, Alberto
b. Lleras Restrepo, Carlos
b. Narino, Antonio
b. Pastrana, Andres
b. Samper Pizano, Ernesto
b. Turbay Ayala, Julio Cesar
d. Arciniegas, German
d. Barco Vargas, Virgilio
d. Currie, Lauchlin (Bernard)
d. Gaitan, Jorge Eliecer
d. Gomez Castro, Laureano Eleuterio
d. Lleras Camargo, Alberto
d. Lleras Restrepo, Carlos
d. Mutis, Jose Celestino
d. Ospina Perez, Mariano
d. Rojas Pinilla, Gustavo

Cali, Colombia
b. Isaacs, Jorge

Cartagena, Colombia
d. Benalcazar, Sebastian de
d. Merriam, Eve
d. Obregon, Alejandro

Caucasia, Colombia
b. Chermayeff, Serge (Ivan)

Cucuta Norte de Santander, Colombia
b. Barco Vargas, Virgilio

Envigado, Colombia
b. Escobar Gaviria, Pablo

Ibague, Colombia
d. Isaacs, Jorge

Leiva, Colombia
d. Narino, Antonio

Medellin, Colombia
b. Botero, Fernando
b. Ospina Perez, Mariano

Nieva, Colombia
b. Rivera, Jose Eustasio

Pasto, Colombia
d. Sucre, Antonio J de

Pereira, Colombia
b. Gaviria Trujillo, Cesar Augusto

Popayan, Colombia
b. Mosquera, Tomas Cipriano de
d. Mosquera, Tomas Cipriano de

Santa Marta, Colombia
d. Bolivar, Simon

Santa Rosa, Colombia
b. Reyes, Rafael

Tunja, Colombia
b. Rojas Pinilla, Gustavo

COMOROS

Grande-Comore, Comoros
b. Azali, Assoumani

Mbeni, Grande Comore, Comoros
b. Abdulkarim, Mohamed Taki

CONGO

Brazzaville, Congo
b. Youlou, Fulbert
d. Massamba-Debat, Alphonse

Edou, Congo
b. Sassou-Nguesso, Denis

Musumba, Congo
b. Tshombe, Moise

Niari, Congo
b. Lissouba, Pascal

Stanley Falls, Congo
d. Emin Pasha

COSTA RICA

b. Bernstein, Felicia Montealegre

Cartago, Costa Rica
b. Carazo (Odio), Rodrigo

Heredia, Costa Rica
b. Arias Sanchez, Oscar

Limon, Costa Rica
b. McDonald, Erroll

San Jose, Costa Rica
b. Figueres Olsen, Jose Maria
b. Oduber (Quiros), Daniel
b. Rodriguez, Miguel Angel
d. Figueres Ferrer, Jose
d. Morazan, Jose Francisco

San Ramon, Costa Rica
b. Figueres Ferrer, Jose

COTE D'IVOIRE

Assini, Cote d'Ivoire
b. Dadie, Bernard Binlin

Dadiekro, Cote d'Ivoire
b. Bedie, Henri Konan

Yamoussouko, Cote d'Ivoire
b. Houphouet-Boigny, Felix
d. Houphouet-Boigny, Felix

CRETE

Candia, Crete
b. Greco, El

Iraklion, Crete
b. Elytis, Odysseus
b. Kazantzakis, Nikos

Mournies, Crete
b. Venizelos, Eleutherios Kyriakos

Rethymon, Crete
b. Nick the Greek

CROATIA

Agram, Croatia
b. Mallinger, Mathilde

Dubrovnik, Croatia
d. Brown, Ron(ald Harmon)

Krasic, Croatia
b. Stepinac, Alojzije

Veliko-Tgrovisce, Croatia
b. Tudjman, Franjo

Vrpolje, Croatia
b. Mestrovic, Ivan

Zagreb, Croatia
d. Tudjman, Franjo

CUBA

b. Arenas, Reinaldo

b. Emerson, Peter Henry
b. Garcia, Cristina
b. Marley, Rita
b. Zamora, Pedro
d. Brooks, Maria Gowen

Bahia Honda, Cuba
b. Prio Socarras, Carlos

Banes, Cuba
b. Batista y Zaldivar, Fulgencio

Bayamo, Cuba
b. Cespedes, Carlos Manuel de
b. Estrada Palma, Tomas
d. Estrada Palma, Tomas

Camaguey, Cuba
b. Agramonte y Simoni, Aristides
b. Finlay, Carlos Juan
b. Gavilan, Kid
b. Guillen (y Batista), Nicolas
(Cristobal)
b. Perez, Tony
b. Sarduy, Severo

Cardones, Cuba
b. Adolfo

Cerro, Cuba
b. Kid Chocolate

Cienfuegos, Cuba
d. Dihigo, Martin

Delicias, Cuba
b. Stevenson, Teofilo

Dos Rios, Cuba
d. Marti (y Perez), Jose Julian

Gibara, Cuba
b. Cabrera Infante, Guillermo

Havana, Cuba
b. Acosta, Carlos
b. Alonso, Alicia
b. Anderson, Bonnie Marie
b. Avalos, Luis
b. Barker, Bernard L
b. Bolet, Jorge
b. Canseco, Jose
b. Capablanca, Jose Raoul
b. Cassidy, Harold Gomes
b. Cruz, Celia
b. Dihigo, Martin
b. Estefan, Gloria
b. Estevez (de Galvez), Luis
b. Fletcher, Alice Cunningham
b. Garcia, Andy
b. Goizueta, Roberto C(rispulo)
b. Goytisolo, Fermin
b. Justiz, Manuel Jon
b. Lateiner, Jacob
b. Leon, Tania (Justina)
b. Luque, Dolf
b. Marti (y Perez), Jose Julian
b. Melis, Jose
b. Minoso, Minnie
b. Mitchell, Millard
b. Roa (y Garcia), Raul
b. Ros-Lehtinen, Ileana
b. Salazar, Alberto
b. Sununu, John Henry

b. Tiant, Luis Clemente
d. Finlay, Carlos Juan
d. Grau San Martin, Ramon
d. Kane, Elisha Kent
d. Kid Chocolate
d. Lopez, Narciso
d. Luque, Dolf
d. Menocal, Mario Garcia
d. Mercader, Ramon
d. Ord, Edward Otho Cresap
d. Ponce de Leon, Juan
d. Roa (y Garcia), Raul

La Habana, Cuba
b. Revillagigedo, Conde de

Las Villas, Cuba
b. Suarez, Xavier Louis

Matanzas, Cuba
b. Menocal, Mario Garcia

Mayari, Cuba
b. Castro, Raul
b. Castro (Ruz), Fidel

Pinar del Rio, Cuba
b. Grau San Martin, Ramon
b. Oliva, Tony

Pueblo Nuevo, Cuba
b. Campaneris, Bert

Quemados, Cuba
d. Lazear, Jesse William

San Lorenzo, Oriente, Cuba
d. Cespedes, Carlos Manuel de

San Pedro, Havana, Cuba
d. Maceo, Antonio

Santa Clara, Cuba
b. Cuellar, Mike
b. Machado y Morales, Gerardo

Santiago, Cuba
b. Mas Canosa, Jorge

Santiago de Cuba, Cuba
b. Arnaz, Desi
b. Bustamante, John H
b. Diaz, Henry F(rank)
b. Juantorena, Alberto
b. Maceo, Antonio
b. Quirot, Ana

Santiago de Las Vegas, Cuba
b. Calvino, Italo

Vedado, Cuba
b. Versalles, Zoilo Casanova

Yaguajay, Cuba
b. Urrutia Lleo, Manuel

CYPRUS

b. Denktash, Rauf
b. Makarios III, Archbishop
b. Zeno of Citium

DANISH WEST INDIES

Saint Thomas, Danish West Indies
b. Benjamin, Judah Philip
b. Pissarro, Camille Jacob
b. Sainte-Clair Deville, Henri Etienne

DEMOCRATIC REPUBLIC OF THE CONGO

Boma, Democratic Republic of the Congo
d. Kasavubu, Joseph

Elisabethville, Democratic Republic of the Congo
d. Lumumba, Patrice

Kinshasa, Democratic Republic of the Congo
b. Mutombo, Dikembe

Shaba, Democratic Republic of the Congo
b. Kabila, Laurent Desire

Suna Bata, Democratic Republic of the Congo
b. Franco

DENMARK

b. Jantzen, Carl
b. Kristiansen, Kjeld Kirk
b. Margaret of Denmark
b. Nexo, Martin Andersen
b. Nielson, Brigitte
d. Margaret of Denmark

Aarhus, Denmark
b. Hedtoft (-Hansen), Hans Christian
b. Hillcourt, William
b. Winding, Kai Chresten

Charlottenlund, Denmark
b. Haakon VII

Copenhagen, Denmark
b. Alexandra Caroline Mary Charlotte
b. Andersen, Ib Steen
b. Bohr, Aage Niels
b. Bohr, Niels Henrik David
b. Borge, Victor
b. Braestrup, Carl Bjorn
b. Brandes, Georg Morris Cohen
b. Brisson, Frederick
b. Bruhn, Erik Belton Evers
b. Christian X
b. Dam, (Carl Peter) Henrik
b. Drachmann, Holger Henrik Herholdt
b. Dreyer, Carl Theodore
b. Dreyer, Johan Ludwig Emil
b. Esposito, Giancarlo (Giusseppi)
b. Ewald, Johannes
b. Frederick IX
b. Gade, Niels Vilhelm
b. Gram, Hans Christian Joachim
b. Hersholt, Jean
b. Jacobsen, Arne
b. Johansen, Gunnar

b. Jorgensen, Anker Henrik
b. Kierkegaard, Soren Aabye
b. Klenau, Paul von
b. Knudsen, William Signius
b. Kronstam, Henning
b. Lander, Toni
b. Margrethe II
b. Martins, Peter
b. Melchior, Lauritz
b. Nelson, Battling
b. Niebuhr, Barthold Georg
b. Paludan, Jacob
b. Roswaenge, Helge
b. Schaufuss, Peter
b. Steno, Nicolaus
b. Thorvaldsen, Albert Bertel
b. Utzon, Jorn
b. Von Bulow, Claus
d. Andersen, Hans Christian
d. Bajer, Fredrik
d. Baker, Phil
d. Bohr, Niels Henrik David
d. Christian IV
d. Christian X
d. Dam, (Carl Peter) Henrik
d. Dreyer, Carl Theodore
d. Ellington, Mercer
d. Ewald, Johannes
d. Fibiger, Johannes Andreas Grib
d. Finsen, Niels Ryberg
d. Frederick IX
d. Gade, Niels Vilhelm
d. Gram, Hans Christian Joachim
d. Jacobsen, Arne
d. Jensen, Johannes Vilhelm
d. Jones, Thad(deus Joseph)
d. Kierkegaard, Soren Aabye
d. Klenau, Paul von
d. Krogh, Schack August Steenberg
d. Kronstam, Henning
d. Leitzel, Lillian
d. Moore, Grace
d. Nielsen, Carl August
d. Oersted, Hans Christian
d. Pais, Abraham
d. Paludan, Jacob
d. Paludan-Muller, Frederik
d. Pettiford, Oscar
d. Pontoppidan, Henrik
d. Rohde, Ruth Bryan Owen
d. Scheidemann, Philipp
d. Schioetz, Aksel
d. Stromgren, Bengt Georg Daniel
d. Uhde, Hermann

Elsinore, Denmark
b. Buxtehude, Dietrich

Esbjerg, Denmark
b. Nyrup Rasmussen, Poul

Eutin, Denmark
b. Weber, Carl Maria von

Farso, Denmark
b. Jensen, Johannes Vilhelm

Fredericia, Denmark
b. Pontoppidan, Henrik

Frederiksberg, Denmark
b. Hertzsprung, Ejnar

Frederikshavn, Denmark
d. Krag, Jens Otto

Gjentofte, Denmark
b. Schmedes, Erik

Grenaa, Denmark
b. Krogh, Schack August Steenberg

Hillerod, Denmark
b. Christian IV

Hornbaek, Denmark
d. Drachmann, Holger Henrik Herholdt

Horsens, Denmark
b. Bering, Vitus Jonassen

Jutland, Denmark
b. Wieghorst, Olaf

Kalundborg, Denmark
b. Undset, Sigrid

Kerteminde, Denmark
b. Paludan-Muller, Frederik

Kolding, Denmark
b. VanKamp, Merete

Norre-Lyndelse, Denmark
b. Nielsen, Carl August

Odense, Denmark
b. Andersen, Hans Christian

Randers, Denmark
b. Krag, Jens Otto

Ribe, Denmark
b. Riis, Jacob August

Roholte, Denmark
b. Gjellerup, Karl Adolf

Roskilde, Denmark
b. Schioetz, Aksel
d. Hertzsprung, Ejnar

Rudkobing, Denmark
b. Oersted, Hans Christian

Rungsted, Denmark
b. Blixen, Karen Christentze, Baroness
d. Blixen, Karen Christentze, Baroness

Silkeborg, Denmark
b. Fibiger, Johannes Andreas Grib

Skagen, Denmark
b. Sirk, Douglas

Skane, Denmark
b. Brahe, Tycho

Skive, Denmark
b. Mikkelsen, Henning Dahl

Slagelse, Denmark
b. Baunsgaard, Hilmar Tormod Ingolf

Thisted, Denmark
b. Jacobsen, Jens Peter
d. Jacobsen, Jens Peter

b. Claudian
b. Cleopatra VII
b. Cyril of Alexandria, Saint
b. Desses, Jean
b. Ghorbal, Ashraf A
b. Hess, Rudolf
b. Magnani, Anna
b. Marinetti, Filippo Tommaso Emilio
b. Moussa, Ibrahim
b. Origen Adamantius
b. Pilou, Jeannette
b. Ptolemy
b. Salem, Mamdouh
b. Sharif, Omar
b. Ungaretti, Giuseppe
d. Abercromby, Ralph, Sir
d. Arius
d. Cavafy, C(onstantine) P(eter)
d. Cleopatra VII
d. Cyril of Alexandria, Saint
d. Maraghi, Mustafa al-
d. Mark, Saint
d. Pompey the Great
d. Victor Emmanuel III

Ankhtowe, Egypt
b. Imhotep

Assuite, Egypt
b. ElMallakh, Kamal

Aswan, Egypt
b. Aqqad, Abbas Mahmud al-

Beni Mor, Egypt
b. Nasser, Gamal Abdel

Cairo, Egypt
b. Arafat, Yasir
b. Boutros-Ghali, Boutros
b. Dolby, Thomas
b. Egoyan, Atom
b. Farouk I
b. Forester, Cecil Scott
b. Hanafi, Hassan
b. Haykal, Muhammad Husain
b. Hodgkin, Dorothy Mary Crowfoot
b. Ismail Pasha
b. Lively, Penelope
b. Mahfouz, Naguib
b. Opie, Peter Mason
b. Pagett, Nicola
b. Raffi
b. Sadat, Jehan Raouf
b. Sidarouss, Stephanos, Cardinal
b. Whicker, Alan Donald
d. Abd el-Krim el-Khatabi, Mohamed ben
d. Aqqad, Abbas Mahmud al-
d. Ballou, Maturin Murray
d. Bulow, Hans Guido von
d. Burckhardt, Johann Ludwig
d. Cramm, Gottfried von, Baron
d. Eboue, Adolphe Felix Sylvestre
d. ElMallakh, Kamal
d. Herbert, George Edward Stanhope Molyneux
d. Ibn Khaldun
d. Idris I
d. Kalthoum, Um
d. Kleber, Jean Baptiste
d. Lyot, Bernard Ferdinand
d. Maimonides, Moses
d. Martin, Kingsley
d. Mohammed Ali

d. Mohieddin, Ahmed Faud
d. Naguib, Mohammed
d. Nasser, Gamal Abdel
d. Pahlevi, Mohammed Riza
d. Reisner, George Andrew
d. Riad, Mahmoud
d. Sadat, Anwar el
d. Sidarouss, Stephanos, Cardinal
d. Taha Hussein

Daqahliya Province, Egypt
b. Abdel-Rahman, Omar

El Kalyoubleh, Egypt
b. Khalil, Mustafa

Giza, Egypt
b. Fuad, I

Ibyana, Egypt
b. Zaghlul Pasha, Saad

Kafr-El Meselha, Egypt
b. Mubarak, (Mohammed) Hosni

Lycopolis, Egypt
b. Plotinus

Maghagha, Egypt
b. Husayn, Taha
b. Taha Hussein

Memphis, Egypt
b. Anthony, Saint
d. Imhotep

Mit Abul-Kum, Egypt
b. Sadat, Anwar el

Mount Kolzim, Egypt
d. Anthony, Saint

Musha, Asyut, Egypt
b. Sayyid Qutb

Oasis, Egypt
d. Nestorius

Tamay-al-Zahirah, Egypt
b. Kalthoum, Um

Zifta, Egypt
b. El-Sayed, Mostafa Amr

EL SALVADOR

b. Zamora, Ruben

Ahuchapan, El Salvador
b. Magana, Alvaro (Alfredo)

Chalatenango, El Salvador
b. Romero, Carlos Humberto

Chalchuapa, El Salvador
d. Barrios, Justo Rufino

Ciudad Barrios, El Salvador
b. Romero y Galdamez, Oscar Arnulfo

San Salvador, El Salvador
b. Buckard, Alfredo Cristiani
b. Calderon Sol, Armando
b. Cristiani, Alfredo
b. Duarte (Fuentes), Jose Napoleon
d. D'Aubuisson, Roberto
d. Duarte (Fuentes), Jose Napoleon
d. Romero y Galdamez, Oscar Arnulfo

Santa Ana, El Salvador
b. Flores, Francisco

Santa Tecla, El Salvador
b. D'Aubuisson, Roberto

ENGLAND

b. Alden, John
b. Baffin, William
b. Bangor, Edward Henry Harold Ward, Viscount
b. Bernard, Francis, Sir
b. Berners-Lee, Tim
b. Bowes, Walter
b. Buckingham, 1st Duke of
b. Cadogan, Alexander George Montague, Sir
b. Caedmon, Saint
b. Carritt, David Graham
b. Carr-Saunders, Alexander Morris
b. Christian, Fletcher
b. Christie, James
b. Clapham, John Harold
b. Clarkson, Ewan
b. Colet, John
b. Curry, Tim
b. Daly, John
b. Emanuel, David
b. Ford, Lita
b. Fox, Samantha
b. Furst, Anton
b. Godolphin, Sidney
b. Gorman, Leroy
b. Graham, Stephen
b. Hart-Davis, Rupert
b. Hudson, Henry
b. Ironside, Christopher
b. Kaufman, Gerald Bernard
b. Kelsey, Henry
b. Leicester, Earl of
b. Little Tich
b. Lodge, David (John)
b. Lucile
b. Lyne, Adrian
b. Macarthur, John
b. MacNee, Patrick
b. Mann, Jack
b. Mason, Charles
b. McCarthy, John
b. Miles, Bernard, Sir
b. Monck, George, 1st Duke of Albemarle
b. Phillips, Mark Anthony Peter
b. Pigou, Arthur Cecil
b. Pile, Frederick Alfred
b. Pitt, William, the Elder
b. Queensberry, John Sholto Douglas
b. Read, Mary
b. Reid, Vernon
b. Robertson, Dennis Holme
b. Rockingham, 2nd Marquess of
b. Rutherford, Michael
b. Ryle, Gilbert
b. Saatchi, Charles

b. Lawson, Leigh

Austerfield, England
b. Bradford, William

Austhorpe, Yorkshire, England
b. Smeaton, John
d. Smeaton, John

Avening, England
d. Powell, Michael Latham

Axminster, England
b. Buckland, William

Aylesbury, England
d. Bernard, Francis, Sir
d. Gielgud, (Arthur) John, Sir

Ayot Saint Lawrence, England
d. Shaw, George Bernard

Badminton, England
b. Raglan, Fitzroy James Henry
Somerset, Baron

Bakewell, England
b. Oldfield, Maurice, Sir

Balham, England
b. Rutherford, Margaret

Banbury, England
b. Hodgkin, Alan Lloyd, Sir
d. Comfort, Alexander
d. Household, Geoffrey Edward West

Bannavem Taberniae, England
b. Patrick, Saint

Bardsey, England
b. Congreve, William

Barnack, England
b. Kingsley, Henry

Barnes, England
b. Meynell, Alice Christina Gertrude

Barnet, England
b. A.L.O.E.
b. Byng, Julian Hedworth George,
Viscount
b. White, Chris(topher Taylor)
d. Taylor, A(lan) J(ohn) P(ercivale)

Barnsley, England
b. Arden, John
b. Davie, Donald Alfred
b. Scargill, Arthur

Barnstaple, England
b. Gay, John

Barnt Green, England
b. Leighton, Margaret

Barton, England
b. Johnson, Paul (Bede)

Barton-on-Humber, England
d. Treece, Henry

Basingstoke, England
b. Warton, Thomas
d. Makins, Roger (Mellor), Sir

Bath, England
b. D'Arcy, Martin Cyril
b. Edgeworth, Richard Lovell
b. Hone, William
b. Humphry, Derek John
b. Parry, William Edward, Sir
b. Scott, Charles Prestwich
b. Tilberis, Elizabeth
d. Beckford, William
d. Brooke, James, Sir
d. Butler, Joseph
d. Ewing, Julianna Horatia (Gatty)
d. Grierson, John
d. Hartley, David
d. Haskell, Arnold Lionel
d. Heruy Walda-Sellase
d. Malthus, Thomas Robert
d. Phillip, Arthur
d. Saintsbury, George Edward
Bateman
d. Sickert, Walter Richard
d. Speke, John Hanning

Batley, England
b. Palmer, Robert

Battersea, England
d. Bolingbroke, Henry St. John,
Viscount

Batton, England
b. Ford, Wallace

Beaconsfield, England
b. Read, Piers Paul
d. Burke, Edmund
d. Machen, Arthur
d. Waller, Edmund

Beckenham, England
b. Blyton, Carey
b. Frampton, Peter Kenneth
d. Richardson, Dorothy Miller

Beckington, England
d. Daniel, Samuel

Bedford, England
b. Abrahams, Harold
b. Barker, Ronnie
b. Burnaby, Frederick Gustavus
b. Huddleston, Trevor
b. Lavis, Gilson

Bedfordshire, England
b. Young, Paul

Beer, England
d. Chambers, Edmund Kerchever, Sir

Bekesbourne, England
b. Hales, Stephen

Benson, England
d. Dines, William Henry

Bentley, England
b. Storr, (Charles) Anthony

Beresford Hall, England
b. Cotton, Charles

Berkeley, England
b. Jenner, Edward
d. Jenner, Edward

Berkeley Castle, England
d. Edward II

Berkhampstead, England
b. Cowper, William
b. Greene, Graham (Henry)
b. Greene, Hugh (Carleton), Sir
b. Hordern, Michael

Berkshire, England
b. Benson, Edward Frederic
b. Chambers, Edmund Kerchever, Sir
b. Dangerfield, George Bubb
b. Newbery, John
d. Masefield, John

Berkswell, England
b. Brett, Jeremy

Bermondsey Abbey, England
d. Catherine of Valois

Berry Hill, England
b. Potter, Dennis (Christopher George)

Berwick-upon-Tweed, England
d. Knox, Alexander

Beverley, England
b. Fisher, John

Bewdley, England
b. Baldwin, Stanley

Bexhill, England
b. Andrews, Michael Alford
b. Wilson, Angus
d. Baird, John Logie

Bexleyheath, England
b. Boy George
b. Bush, Kate

Bicester, England
b. Rose, George Walter

Billericay, England
b. Dury, Ian

Bingley, England
b. Hoyle, Fred, Sir

Birchington, England
d. Rossetti, Dante Gabriel

Birkdale, England
b. Taylor, A(lan) J(ohn) P(ercivale)

Birkenhead, England
b. Brooke, L Leslie
b. Jackson, Glenda

Brighton, England
b. Armour, Norman
b. Beardsley, Aubrey Vincent
b. Bridge, Frank
b. Carpenter, Edward
b. Clayton, Jack
b. Garfield, Leon
b. Garnett, Constance
b. Garnett, David
b. Gill, Eric
b. Hilton, Daisy
b. Hilton, Violet
b. Kennedy, Nigel Paul
b. Noble, Ray
b. Ovett, Steve
b. Rawlinson, Herbert
b. Simpson, Cedric Keith
b. Treacher, Arthur
d. Addison, Thomas
d. Astor, William Waldorf Astor, Viscount
d. Crowley, Aleister (Edward Alexander)
d. Hughes, Thomas
d. Leon, Henry Cecil
d. Lindsay, David
d. Maugham, Robin
d. Parker, Cecil
d. Parnell, Charles Stewart
d. Robins, Elizabeth
d. Robson, Flora McKenzie, Dame
d. Sala, George Augustus
d. Soddy, Frederick
d. Spencer, Herbert
d. Surtees, Robert Smith

Brightwell Baldwin, England
d. Hicks, David (Nightingale)

Bristol, England
b. Bedells, Phyllis
b. Blackbeard
b. Blackwell, Elizabeth
b. Blackwell, Emily
b. Bright, Richard
b. Cartwright, Veronica
b. Chatterton, Thomas
b. Coleridge, Hartley
b. Combe, William
b. Cousins, Robin
b. Dirac, Paul Adrien Maurice
b. Donald, Peter
b. Durie, Jo
b. Friese-Greene, William Edward
b. Fry, Christopher
b. Giles, Ernest
b. Godwin, Edward William
b. Grant, Cary
b. Hill, Archibald Vivian
b. Household, Geoffrey Edward West
b. Lane, Allen, Sir
b. Lawrence, Thomas, Sir
b. Long, Richard
b. Nichols, Beverley
b. Nichols, Peter
b. Plimsoll, Samuel
b. Redgrave, Michael Scudamore, Sir
b. Rosenberg, Issac
b. Satherly, Arthur Edward
b. Sisson, Charles Hubert
b. Slim, William Joseph
b. Southey, Robert
b. Stephens, Robert, Sir
b. Symonds, John Addington
b. Tricky
b. Trollope, Frances

d. Chatterton, Thomas
d. Dinwiddie, Robert
d. Roy, Ram Mohun
d. Savage, Richard
d. Scott, Peter Markham, Sir

Brixton, England
b. Biggs, Ronald Arthur
b. Morrison of Lambeth, Herbert Stanley Morrison, Baron

Brixton Prison, England
d. MacSwiney, Terence

Broad Town, England
d. Grigson, Geoffrey Edward Harvey

Broadheath, England
b. Elgar, Edward William, Sir

Broadlands, England
b. Palmerston, Henry John Temple, Viscount

Broadstairs, England
b. Bennett, Richard Rodney
b. Heath, Edward Richard George
b. Johnson, Lionel Pigot
b. Vyvyan, Jennifer Brigit
d. Monro, Harold Edward

Broadstone, England
d. Christophers, S(amuel) Rickard, Sir
d. Wallace, Alfred Russell

Broadway, England
d. Anderson, Mary Antoinette

Brockenhurst, England
d. Gilbert, Cass

Brockley, England
b. Jones, David

Brockmoor, England
b. Carder, Frederick

Bromham, England
d. Moore, Thomas

Bromhill, England
b. Shadwell, Thomas

Bromley, England
b. Chadwick, William Owen
b. Gillott, Jacky
b. Kureishi, Hanif
b. Wells, H(erbert) G(eorge)
d. Craik, Dinah Maria Mulock

Brompton, England
b. Carter, Howard
d. Hutchinson, Thomas
d. Wellesley, Richard Colley, 1st Marquess Wellesley

Bromsgrove, England
b. Hill, Geoffrey
b. Housman, Laurence
d. Austin, Herbert

Bromwich, England
b. Plant, Robert Anthony

Broseley, England
b. Baddeley, Hermione Clinton

Brozbourne, England
b. Bolton, Guy Reginald

Buckfastleigh Abbey, England
d. Sotheby, Samuel Leigh

Buckingham, England
d. Keyes, Roger John Brownlow, Baron

Buckinghamshire, England
b. Cripps, Stafford, Sir
d. Moore, Gerald
d. Woodhouse, Barbara Blackburn

Bucklers Hard, England
d. Burnford, Sheila

Buerton, England
b. Brassey, Thomas

Bulstrode, England
b. Bentinck, William Henry Cavendish, Lord

Bulwell, England
b. Cousins, Frank

Burcot, England
d. Peake, Mervyn Laurence

Burford, England
d. Barraclough, Geoffrey

Burg, England
b. Charnley, John, Sir

Burgh-on-Sands, England
d. Edward I

Burnham Thorpe, England
b. Nelson, Horatio Nelson, Viscount

Burnley, England
b. McKellen, Ian (Murray), Sir
b. O'Malley, J Pat

Burslem, England
b. Hollowood, Albert Bernard
b. Wedgwood, Josiah

Burton-on-Trent, England
b. Jackson, Joe
b. Mercer, Mabel

Burwash, England
d. Kipling, Rudyard

Bury, England
b. Dunster, Henry
b. Lamburn, Richmal Crompton

Bury Saint Edmunds, England
b. Aungervyle, Richard
b. Hall, Peter Reginald Frederick, Sir

Chesham, England
d. Bevan, Aneurin

Chesham Bois, England
b. Crispin, Edmund

Cheshire, England
b. Abercrombie, Lascelles
b. Barnes, Ernest William
b. Carroll, Lewis
b. Cartwright, Angela
b. Cotton, Henry, Sir
b. Davies, Leslie Purnell
b. Holmes, Rupert
b. Isherwood, Christopher (William)
b. Robinson, Forbes
d. Stapledon, Olaf
d. Westall, Robert Atkinson

Cheshunt, England
d. Cromwell, Richard

Chester, England
b. Best, Oswald Herbert
b. Boult, Adrian Cedric, Sir
b. Caldecott, Randolph

Chesterfield, England
b. Baden-Powell, Olave St. Claire, Lady
b. Castle, Barbara Anne Betts
b. Hurt, John
b. Robinson, Robert, Sir
b. Wright, Peter (Maurice)
d. Cousins, Frank
d. Stephenson, George

Chichester, England
b. Collins, William
b. Titchener, Edward Bradford
d. Collins, William
d. Leighton, Margaret
d. Wilding, Michael

Chilswell, England
d. Bridges, Robert Seymour

Chiltern Hills, England
d. Chesterton, G(ilbert) K(eith)

Chipping Camden, England
d. Guiney, Louise Imogene

Chipping Norton, England
b. Burbidge, Geoffrey

Chislehurst, England
b. Campbell, Malcolm, Sir
b. Mould, Jacob Wrey
b. Watts, Alan Wilson
d. Napoleon III

Chiswick, England
b. Collins, Phil(ip)
d. DeLoutherbourg, Philip James
d. Fox, Charles James

Chorley, England
b. Ambrose, David Edwin
b. Darlington, Cyril Dean
b. Haworth, Walter Norman, Sir

Chorley Wood, England
d. Kendal, Madge, Dame

Churchill, England
b. Hastings, Warren
b. Smith, William

Clacton, England
d. Booth, Catherine Mumford

Clapham, England
b. Bradley, Francis Herbert
d. Pepys, Samuel

Claremont, England
d. Louis Phillippe

Clay Hill, England
b. Grote, George

Cleethorpes, England
b. Kendal, Madge, Dame

Clevedon, England
b. Morris, Jan

Clifton, England
b. Clairmont, Claire
b. Fisher, James Maxwell McConnell
d. Piozzi, Hester Lynch Salisbury

Cliftonville-Margate, England
b. Howard, Trevor Wallace

Clive, Shropshire, England
b. Wycherley, William

Cliveden, England
d. Wright, Almroth Edward, Sir

Cockermouth, England
b. Wordsworth, William

Colchester, England
b. Brown, Pamela Beatrice
b. Cavendish, Margaret
b. Gilbert, William
b. Penrose, Roger
b. Rickword, Edgell
b. Wavell, Archibald Percival Wavell, Earl
d. Allingham, Margery

Coleford, England
b. Howitt, Mary

Coleshill, England
b. Waller, Edmund

Collingwood, England
d. Herschel, John Frederick William, Sir

Combe, England
d. Howes, Frank Stewart

Compton, England
b. Gilbert, Humphrey, Sir

Condover, England
b. Tarlton, Richard

Coningsby, England
d. Eusden, Laurence

Coniston, England
d. Campbell, Donald Malcolm
d. Collingwood, Robin George
d. Ruskin, John

Cookham-on-Thames, England
b. Spencer, Stanley, Sir

Cornwall, England
b. Budge, Ernest Alfred Thompson Wallis, Sir
b. Davy, Humphrey, Sir
b. Fleetwood, Mick
b. Grenville, Richard, Sir
d. Browning, Frederick A(rthur) M(ontague), Sir
d. Hull, Henry
d. Rowse, A(lfred) L(eslie)

Cornwall Gardens, England
b. Rattigan, Terence Mervyn, Sir

Cotherstone, England
d. Fry, E Maxwell

Cotterstock, England
b. Simcoe, John Graves

Coventry, England
b. Connolly, Cyril Vernon
b. Gibberd, Frederick, Sir
b. King, Dennis
b. Larkin, Philip Arthur
b. Martin, John C
b. Taylor, Edward
b. Terry, Ellen Alicia, Dame
b. Whitelaw, Billie
b. Whittle, Frank, Sir
d. Ashley, Laura Mountney
d. Forster, E(dward) M(organ)

Cowes, Isle of Wight, England
b. Arnold, Thomas
b. Fox, Uffa
b. Irons, Jeremy John
d. Durham, 1st Earl of
d. Fox, Uffa
d. Nash, John

Cradley, England
b. Caslon, William

Craike, England
b. Inge, William Ralph

Cranborne, England
d. Cecil, Edward Christian David Gascoyne

Cranbrook, England
b. Dobell, Sydney Thompson
d. Nicolson, Harold George, Sir
d. Sackville-West, Vita

Cranleigh, England
b. Hardy, Godfrey Harold
d. Swinnerton, Frank Arthur

Cranley, England
d. Lemon, Mark

Earlham, England
d. Fry, Elizabeth Gurney

Easington, England
b. Skelton, Robin

East Bergholt, England
b. Constable, John
d. Churchill, Randolph Frederick
Edward Spencer

East Brent, England
b. Locke, Richard Adams

East Coker, England
b. Dampier, William

East Dereham, England
b. Borrow, George Henry

East Dulwich, England
b. Blyton, Enid Mary

East Grinstead, England
d. Bouche, Rene Robert

East Heathly, England
b. Banks, Tony

East Hendred, England
d. Penney, William George

East Knoyle, England
b. Wren, Christopher, Sir

East London, England
d. Kadalie, Clements

East Molesey, England
d. Vogel, Julius

East Shefford, England
b. Bell, Clive

East Sussex, England
d. Bell, Vanessa

East Tuddingham, England
b. Vassar, Matthew

Eastbourne, England
b. Carter, Angela (Olive)
b. Farnol, Jeffery
b. Hopkins, Frederick Gowland, Sir
b. Soddy, Frederick
d. Farnol, Jeffery
d. Gielgud, Val Henry
d. Hailwood, Mike
d. Huxley, Thomas Henry
d. Mahan, Asa
d. Sherrington, Charles Scott, Sir

Easton Pierce, England
b. Aubrey, John

Eastwood, England
b. Lawrence, D(avid) H(erbert)

Eccles, England
b. Chapman, Sydney

Ecclesfield, England
b. Ewing, Julianna Horatia (Gatty)

Edenbridge, England
b. Croft-Cooke, Rupert
d. Garnett, Constance

Edgbaston, England
b. Chamberlain, Neville

Edmonton, England
d. Lamb, Charles

Elderfield, England
d. Yonge, Charlotte Mary

Elstead, England
b. Herbert, A(lan) P(atrick), Sir

Elston Hall, England
b. Darwin, Erasmus

Elstow, England
b. Bunyan, John

Eltham, England
b. Hope, Bob
b. Whistler, Rex
d. Lilburne, John

Ely, England
b. Hulbert, Jack

Endon, England
b. Hulme, Thomas Ernest

Enfield, England
b. Mackintosh, Cameron

Epsom, England
b. Clark, Petula
b. Hunt, James
b. Ormond, Julia (Karin)
b. Waterhouse, Ellis Kirkham, Sir
d. Fabian, Robert Honey
d. Rosebery, Archibald Philip
Primrose, Earl

Epworth, Lincolnshire, England
b. Wesley, Charles

Esher, England
b. Cobb, John Rhodes

Essex, England
b. Hicks, David (Nightingale)
b. Rayleigh, John William Strutt,
Baron
b. Turpin, Dick
d. Baddeley, Angela
d. Foyle, Christina Agnes Lilian
d. Oglethorpe, James Edward

Eton, England
b. Oughtred, William
b. Tovey, Donald Francis, Sir
d. James, Montague Rhodes
d. Oliphant, Margaret

Etruria, England
d. Wedgwood, Josiah

Eversley, England
d. Kingsley, Charles
d. Lowndes, Marie Adelaide Belloc

Evesham, England
b. Bender, Ariel
b. Capaldi, Jim
d. Clementi, Muzio
d. Montfort, Simon de

Exeter, England
b. Baring-Gould, Sabine
b. Bodley, Thomas, Sir
b. Chadwick, Henry
b. Cousins, Samuel
b. D'Urfey, Thomas
b. Halifax, Edward Frederick Lindley
Wood
b. Hilliard, Nicholas
b. Temple, William
d. Davie, Donald Alfred
d. Phillpotts, Eden
d. Rhys, Jean
d. Simcoe, John Graves

Exning, England
b. Day, James Wentworth

Eyam, England
b. Seward, Anna

Eye, England
d. Spence, Basil Urwin, Sir

Failsworth, England
b. Fuller, Roy Broadbent

Fairfield, England
b. Price, Alan

Fairford, England
b. Keble, John

Fallodon, England
b. Grey, Charles

Falmouth, England
d. Emerson, Peter Henry

Fareham, England
b. Cremer, William Randal, Sir

Faringdon, England
d. Barea, Arturo

Farnborough, England
b. Harriman, Pamela

Farnham, England
b. Cobbett, William
b. Pears, Peter, Sir
b. Toplady, Augustus Montague
d. Combe, George

Farnworth, England
b. Finlay, Frank

Felixstowe, England
b. Addams, Dawn
b. Hinde, Thomas, Sir
b. Mills, John, Sir

Field Place, England
b. Shelley, Percy Bysshe

Fieldhead, England
b. Priestley, Joseph

Firle, England
b. Gage, Thomas

Fishbourne, England
d. Horrocks, Brian Gwynne, Sir

Fisher's Hill, England
d. Balfour, Arthur James

Flixton, England
d. Boycott, Charles Cunningham

Fockbury, England
b. Housman, A(lfred) E(dward)

Folkestone, England
b. Coppard, A(lfred) E(dgar)
b. Gordon, Kitty
b. Harvey, William
d. Abney, William de Wiveleslie, Sir
d. Harris, Augustus, Sir

Fonthill, England
b. Beckford, William

Fontmell Magna, England
b. Gardiner, John Eliot

Footscray, England
b. Walsingham, Francis, Sir

Fordingbridge, England
d. John, Augustus Edwin

Forest Rowe, England
d. Freshfield, Douglas William

Fotheringhay Castle, England
b. Richard III
d. Mary, Queen of Scots

Fowey, England
b. Hewish, Antony
d. Quiller-Couch, Arthur Thomas, Sir

Frognal, England
d. Blomfield, Reginald Theodore, Sir

Frome, England
b. Green, Guy
d. Powell, Anthony Dymoke

Fulham, England
d. Sharp, Granville

Fulmer, England
b. York, Michael

Fulneck, England
b. Latrobe, Benjamin Henry

Furnham, England
b. Bondfield, Margaret Grace

Gainsborough, England
b. Mackinder, Halford John, Sir
b. Thorndike, Sybil, Dame

Garnant, England
b. Cale, John

Gatcomb Park, England
d. Ricardo, David

Gateshead, England
d. Bewick, Thomas

Gawcott, England
b. Scott, George Gilbert, Sir

Gayhurst, England
b. Digby, Kenelm, Sir

Gerrards Cross, England
b. More, Kenneth Gilbert
b. Robinson, Joan Mary Gale Thomas
d. Currie, Finlay
d. Reed, Austin Leonard

Gibraltar, England
b. Penney, William George

Giggleswick, England
b. Hare, John, Sir

Gillingham, England
b. Tizard, Henry Thomas, Sir

Glanton, England
b. Trevor-Roper, Hugh Redwald

Glastonbury, England
b. Aldridge, Michael
b. Dunstan, St.
b. Irving, Henry, Sir
d. Housman, Laurence

Glossop, England
d. Lowry, Lawrence Stephen

Gloucester, England
b. Brent, Margaret
b. Gwinnett, Button
b. Henley, William Ernest
b. Horlick, William
b. Hyde-White, Wilfrid
b. Mitford, Jessica
b. Tyndale, William
b. Webb, Beatrice Potter
b. Wheatstone, Charles, Sir
b. Whitefield, George

Gloucestershire, England
d. Lee, Laurie

Glyndebourne, England
b. Christie, John
d. Christie, John

Godalming, England
b. Huxley, Aldous (Leonard)
d. Terry-Thomas

Godshill, England
d. Dickens, Charles (John Huffam)

Goodmayes, England
b. Holm, Ian

Goodnestone, England
b. James, Montague Rhodes

Goole, England
b. Empson, William, Sir

Goring, England
d. Bolton, Guy Reginald
d. Dodd, Charles Harold
d. Harris, Arthur Travers, Sir

Gorton, England
b. Gorton, Samuel

Gosport, England
b. Dawson, Richard
b. Hargraves, Edward Hammond

Grace-Dieu, England
b. Beaumont, Francis
b. Beaumont, John, Sir

Grantham, England
b. Stokes, Doris
b. Thatcher, Margaret (Hilda Roberts)

Grasmere, England
d. Coleridge, Hartley
d. Richardson, John, Sir
d. Wordsworth, William

Gravesend, England
b. Arnold, Edwin
b. Barton, Derek H(arold) R(ichard),
Sir
b. Gunn, Thom(son William)
b. Wise, Thomas J
d. Freeman, R(ichard) Austin
d. Pocahontas

Great Haughton, England
d. Elliott, Ebenezer

Great Neston, England
b. Hamilton, Emma, Lady

Great Yeldham, England
d. Butler of Saffron Walden, Richard
Austen, Baron

Greeba Castle, Isle of Man, England
d. Caine, Hall

Green Hammerton, England
b. Jackson, John Hughlings

Greenbank, England
b. Bright, John
d. Bright, John

Greenheys, England
b. DeQuincey, Thomas

Greenway, England
d. Godkin, E(dwin) L(awrence)

Greenwich, England
b. Elizabeth I
b. Hargrave, Lawrence

b. Henry VIII
b. Lilburne, John
b. Mary I
b. Tallis, Thomas
b. Wallace, Edgar
d. Airy, George Biddell, Sir
d. Flamsteed, John
d. Halley, Edmund
d. Tallis, Thomas

Grove Lodge, England
d. Galsworthy, John

Guildford, England
b. Hemmings, David Leslie Edward
b. Lacey, Robert
b. Wodehouse, P(elham) G(renville)
d. Baden-Powell, Olave St. Claire, Lady
d. Belloc, Hilaire
d. Carpenter, Edward
d. Carroll, Lewis
d. Hollowood, Albert Bernard

Hackney, England
b. Benn, Ernest John Pickstone, Sir

Haggerston, England
b. Halley, Edmund

Hale, England
b. Falkner, Frank T(ardrew)

Hales, England
b. Alexander of Hales

Halifax, England
b. Blair, David
b. Portman, Eric

Halliford, England
d. Peacock, Thomas Love

Hambleden, England
b. Cardigan, James Thomas Brudenell, Earl of

Hammersmith, England
d. Cobden-Sanderson, Thomas James
d. Morris, William

Hampole, England
d. Rolle of Hampole, Richard

Hampshire, England
b. Dutton, Ralph Stawell
b. Hurley, Elizabeth
b. Udall, Nicholas
d. Alanbrooke, Alan Francis Brooke, 1st Viscount
d. Davis, Joe

Hampstead, England
b. Anderson, Gerry
b. Eggar, Samantha
b. Freshfield, Douglas William
b. Mortimer, John Clifford
b. Springfield, Dusty
d. Allingham, William
d. Bottome, Phyllis
d. Congreve, Richard
d. Cort, Henry
d. Farjeon, Eleanor

d. Frankau, Pamela
d. Hill, Rowland, Sir
d. Hyndman, Henry Mayers
d. Quaritch, Bernard
d. Shaw, Richard Norman
d. Sutherland, Graham Vivian

Hampton, England
b. May, Brian

Hampton Court, England
b. Edward VI
d. Faraday, Michael

Hampton Lucey, England
b. Wilmut, Ian

Hampton-Wick, England
b. Sherriff, Robert Cedric

Harbledown, England
b. Behn, Aphra

Harborne, England
b. Aston, Francis William
d. Cox, David

Hardwick Hall, England
d. Hobbes, Thomas

Harle-Kirk, England
b. Brown, Lancelot

Harlesden, England
b. Broad, C(harlie) D(unbar)

Harpenden, England
b. Craig, Gordon

Harrogate, England
d. Coleridge, Mary Elizabeth
d. Rennie, Michael

Harrow, England
b. Bannister, Roger, Sir
b. Gascoyne, David Emery
b. Steel, Flora Annie Webster
b. Turnbull, Collin M(acmillan)
b. Warner, Sylvia Townsend
d. Gibberd, Frederick, Sir
d. Gilbert, William S(chwenck), Sir
d. Wiggin, Kate Douglas

Hartfield, England
d. Balcon, Michael Elias, Sir
d. Milne, A(lan) A(lexander)

Hartford, England
b. Todd, Ann

Hartland, England
d. Norton, Mary

Hartlepool, England
b. Smythe, Reg(inald)
d. Smythe, Reg(inald)

Haslemere, England
b. DeHavilland, Geoffrey, Sir
b. Phillips, Robin
d. Dolmetsch, Arnold
d. Galton, Francis, Sir

d. Geikie, Archibald, Sir
d. Tennyson, Alfred, Lord

Hassocks, England
b. Hamilton, Patrick
b. Hartnell, Norman Bishop, Sir

Hastings, England
b. Grey Owl
b. Harding, John Wesley
b. Kaye-Smith, Sheila
b. Parker, Cecil
d. Blackwell, Elizabeth
d. Brassey, Thomas
d. Cartwright, Edmund
d. Furniss, Harry
d. Harold II
d. Illingworth, Leslie Gilbert
d. Morgan, C(onwy) Lloyd
d. Richardson, Henry Handel
d. Russell, Edward Frederick Langley, Baron of Liverpool

Hatfield, England
b. Blunstone, Colin
b. Cartland, Barbara Hamilton
b. Salisbury, Robert Arthur Talbot, 3rd Marquess
d. Brain, Dennis
d. Cartland, Barbara Hamilton
d. Salisbury, Robert Arthur Talbot, 3rd Marquess

Hawick, England
b. Blyth, Chay

Haworth, England
d. Bronte, Charlotte
d. Bronte, Emily Jane
d. Bronte, Patrick Branwell

Hayes, England
b. Pitt, William, the Younger

Hayling Island, England
b. Gray, Simon James Holliday

Hazelmere, England
d. Ramsay, William, Sir

Heacham, England
b. Goodall, John Strickland

Headingley, England
b. Austin, Alfred

Headley, England
d. Westrup, J(ack) A(llan), Sir

Heanor, England
b. Howitt, William

Heathfield, England
d. Watt, James

Heavitree, England
b. Hooker, Richard

Hebburn, England
b. Holmes, Arthur

Heckfield, England
d. Chamberlain, Neville

Heddington, England
d. Lewis, C(live) S(taples)

Hedon, England
b. Wigglesworth, Michael

Helensburgh, England
b. Cronin, A(rchibald) J(oseph)

Helpstone, England
b. Clare, John

Helston, England
b. Fitzsimmons, Bob
b. Page, Jimmy

Hemel Hempstead, England
b. Evans, Arthur John, Sir
d. Arran, Arthur Kattendyke Strange
David Archibald Gore, Earl of

Hendon, England
b. Shirley-Smith, Hubert
d. Fisher, James Maxwell McConnell

Hendre, England
b. Rolls, Charles Stewart

Henley, England
d. Hunt, John, Baron

Henley-on-Thames, England
d. Blish, James Benjamin
d. Cooper, Gladys, Dame
d. Frederic, Harold
d. Goudge, Elizabeth
d. Lillie, Beatrice Gladys
d. Springfield, Dusty

Hereford, England
b. Allen, Verden
b. Garrick, David
b. Honeyman-Scott, James
b. Lane, Edward William
b. Oz, Frank
b. Ralphs, Mick
b. Reid, Beryl

Herefordshire, England
b. Evans, George Henry

Hertfordshire, England
b. Beacham, Stephanie
b. Burton, Richard Francis, Sir
b. Elizabeth, Queen Mother
b. Faldo, Nick
b. Martin, Kingsley
b. Melbourne, William Lamb,
Viscount
b. Taylor, Mick
d. Kubrick, Stanley
d. Melbourne, William Lamb,
Viscount
d. Palmerston, Henry John Temple,
Viscount
d. Toms, Carl

Heversham, England
b. Bibby, Thomas Geoffrey

Hexham, England
b. Fielding, Gabriel
b. Gibson, Wilfred Wilson
d. Bunting, Basil

High Wycombe, England
b. Shrimpton, Jean Rosemary
d. Uttley, Alice Jane Taylor

Higher Bockhampton, England
b. Hardy, Thomas

Higher Walter, England
b. Ferrier, Kathleen

Highgate, England
b. Betjeman, John, Sir
b. Lear, Edward
d. Bacon, Francis, Sir

Highworth, England
b. Arkell, William Joscelyn

Hillingdon, England
b. Seymour, Jane
d. Goossens, Eugene, Sir

Hindhead, England
d. Tyndall, John

Hintlesham, England
d. Ellis, Havelock

Hinxhill, England
b. Arkell, Anthony John

Hitchin, England
b. Chapman, George

Hogsthorpe, England
b. Addison, Christopher, Viscount

Holbeach, England
b. Angell, Norman

Holborn, England
b. Taylor, Jane

Holdenby, England
b. Hatton, Christopher, Sir

Hollingbourne, England
b. Colgate, William

Hollow Park, England
d. Bell, Charles

Holmbury Saint Mary, England
d. Catto, Thomas Sivewright, Baron

Honington, England
b. Bloomfield, Robert

Hore, England
d. Bruce Lockhart, Robert Hamilton,
Sir

Horncastle, England
b. Sully, Thomas

Hornsea, England
b. Eyre, Edward John

Hornsey, England
b. Keene, Charles Samuel

Horsehay, England
b. Peters, Ellis

Horsforth, England
b. Knowles, Patric

Horsham, England
b. Innes, Hammond

Horsley, England
b. Somes, Michael (George)

Horwich, England
b. Fleming, Joan Margaret

Houghton, England
b. Walpole, Robert
d. Walpole, Robert

Hove, England
b. Best, Edna
b. Fraser, Ian
d. Arditi, Luigi
d. Compton, Fay
d. Dunhill, Alfred Henry
d. Frankau, Gilbert

Howick, England
d. Grey, Charles

Hoylake, England
b. Dempsey, Miles Christopher, Sir

Huddersfield, England
b. Harrison, G(eorge) Donald
b. Heavysege, Charles
b. Mason, James Neville
b. Wilson, (James) Harold, Sir

Hull, England
b. Carmichael, Ian
b. Courtenay, Tom
b. Duveen, Joseph, Sir
b. Gaunt, William
b. Gidlow, Elsa
b. Kendall, Kay
b. Leginska
b. Rank, J(oseph) Arthur
b. Smith, Stevie
b. Thomas, Gerald
b. Wilberforce, William

Hungerford, England
d. Strachey, (Giles) Lytton

Hunslet, England
b. Waterhouse, Keith Spencer

Huntercombe, England
d. Nuffield, William Richard Morris

Huntingdon, England
b. Cromwell, Oliver

Hurstmonceaux, England
b. Mildmay, Audrey

Hurstpierpoint, England
b. Scofield, Paul

Huyton, England
b. Harrison, Rex, Sir
b. McCabe, John

Hythe, England
d. Clark, Kenneth MacKenzie, Sir
d. Cockerell, Christopher (Sydney), Sir

Idle, England
b. Jennings, Robert Yewdall

Igatestone, England
b. Miles, Sarah

Ilchester, England
b. Bacon, Roger

Ilford, England
b. Levertov, Denise
b. Smith, Maggie Natalie

Ilkeston, England
b. Bainton, Roland Herbert

Illogan, England
b. Trevithick, Richard

Ilsington, England
b. Ford, John

Ince, England
b. Jones, Robert Trent

Inglewood, England
b. Ireland, John Nicholson

Ipsden, England
b. Reade, Charles

Ipswich, England
b. Hendry, Ian
b. Lapotaire, Jane
b. Leslie, Frank
b. Nunn, Trevor Robert
b. Pritchett, V(ictor) S(awdon), Sir
b. Wolsey, Thomas, Cardinal
d. Clarkson, Thomas

Isle of Guernsey, England
b. De La Rue, Warren
b. Jones, Barry
d. Price, Dennis

Isle of Jersey, England
b. Glyn, Elinor Sutherland
b. Haley, William John, Sir
b. Langtry, Lillie
b. Ray, Edward
b. Vardon, Harry
d. Butlin, William Heygate Edmund, Sir
d. Haley, William John, Sir

Isle of Man, England
b. Forbes, Edward
b. Goldie, George Dashwood Taubman
b. Kermode, (John) Frank

Isle of Wight, England
b. Fuchs, Vivian (Ernest), Sir
b. Hooke, Robert
b. Pollard, Albert Frederick
d. Noyes, Alfred
d. Victoria, Queen

Isleworth, England
d. Fenn, George Manville
d. Haliburton, Thomas Chandler

Islington, England
b. Pinero, Arthur Wing, Sir
b. Watts, Charlie
d. Montgomery of Alamein, Bernard
Law Montgomery, Viscount

Islip, England
d. Buckland, William
d. Ryle, Gilbert

Itteringham, England
d. Barker, George Granville

Jarrow, England
d. Bede the Venerable, Saint

Jordans, England
b. Speke, John Hanning

Jordanthorpe, England
b. Chantrey, Francis Legatt, Sir

Kedleston Hall, England
b. Curzon of Kedleston, George
Nathaniel Curzon, Marquis

Keighley, England
b. Bottomley, Gordon

Kendal, England
b. Eddington, Arthur Stanley, Sir
b. Walker, Adam
d. Romney, George
d. Schwitters, Kurt (Hermann Edward
Karl Julius)

Kenley, England
b. Cushing, Peter

Kennington Oval, England
b. Montgomery of Alamein, Bernard
Law Montgomery, Viscount

Kensington, England
b. Browne, Phiz
b. Chesterton, G(ilbert) K(eith)
b. Tree, Herbert Beerbohm
d. Anne
d. Boyce, William
d. Jellicoe, John Rushworth
d. Macaulay, Thomas Babington
Macaulay, Baron
d. Mercury, Freddie
d. Newton, Isaac, Sir

Kensington Gravel Pits, England
d. Cadogan, William, Earl

Kent, England
b. Adams, William
b. Blackwood, Algernon Henry
b. Box, John

b. Bushell, Anthony
b. Darwin, George Howard, Sir
b. Dowson, Ernest Christopher
b. Lovelace, Richard
b. Morgan, Charles Langbridge
b. Oakeshott, Michael Joseph
b. Sidney, Philip, Sir
b. Wyatt, Thomas, Sir
d. Amherst, Jeffrey
d. Boult, Adrian Cedric, Sir
d. Doughty, Charles Montagu
d. Dowding, Hugh Caswell
Tremenheere, Baron
d. Elliott, Gertrude
d. Evans, Edith Mary Booth, Dame
d. Hamilton, Charles Harold St. John
d. Lamburn, Richmal Crompton
d. Stanley, Frederick Arthur, Earl of
Derby
d. Terry, Ellen Alicia, Dame
d. Wellington, Arthur Wellesley, Duke

Kersey, England
d. Innes, Hammond

Keswick, England
d. Southey, Robert

Kew, England
d. Charlotte Sophia
d. Hooker, William Jackson, Sir

Kew Green, England
d. Hughes, Arthur

Kibworth, England
b. Knox, Ronald Arbuthnott

Kidderminster, England
b. Davis, Sammi
b. Hamer, Robert
b. Hill, Rowland, Sir

Kilburn, England
b. Hore-Belisha, Leslie, Baron
d. Drinkwater, John

Kimbolton, England
d. Catherine of Aragon

King's Cliffe, England
b. Law, William
d. Law, William

King's Lynn, England
b. Burney, Fanny
b. Coulton, George Gordon
b. Mason, John
b. Vancouver, George

King's Norton, England
b. Aherne, Brian de Lacy

Kings Bench, England
d. Smart, Christopher

Kingston, England
b. Muybridge, Eadweard
d. Dean, Patrick (Henry), Sir
d. Muybridge, Eadweard

Kingston Hill, England
b. Galsworthy, John

Lindley, England
b. Burton, Robert

Liphook, England
d. Webb, Beatrice Potter
d. Webb, Sidney James

Liskeard, England
b. Nesbitt, Cathleen Mary

Litchfield, England
b. Johnson, Samuel

Little Barford, England
b. Rowe, Nicholas

Littlehampton, England
b. Roddick, Anita Lucia Perella
d. Holloway, Stanley
d. Parry, Charles Hubert Hastings, Sir

Littleover, England
b. Harris, Derek

Liverpool, England
b. Almon, John
b. Bainbridge, Beryl
b. Banks, Leslie
b. Barker, Clive
b. Bell, Tom
b. Best, Peter
b. Booth, Charles
b. Boulding, Kenneth E(wart)
b. Catlin, George Edward Gordon, Sir
b. Cattrall, Kim
b. Christophers, S(amuel) Rickard, Sir
b. Clough, Arthur Hugh
b. Cox, Alex
b. Crane, Walter
b. Davies, Rupert
b. Draper, John William
b. Duranty, Walter
b. Elton, Charles Sutherland
b. Epstein, Brian
b. Fenton, Leslie
b. Franklin, Frederic
b. Fury, Billy
b. Gladstone, William Ewart
b. Goossens, Leon Jean
b. Gregson, John
b. Harrison, George
b. Hemans, Felicia Dorothea Browne
b. Jevons, William Stanley
b. Laver, James
b. LeGallienne, Richard
b. Lennon, John Winston
b. Lennon, Julian
b. Lowry, Malcolm
b. Madden, Owen Victor
b. Marsden, Gerry
b. Maxwell, Hamish
b. McCartney, Paul
b. Monsarrat, Nicholas John Turney
b. Morris, Robert
b. Newman, Ernest
b. O'Sullivan, John
b. Petrie, Charles Alexander, Sir
b. Porter, Rodney Robert
b. Rattle, Simon
b. Rimmer, William
b. Royden, Agnes Maude
b. Runcie, Robert Alexander Kennedy
b. Russell, Annie
b. Russell, Edward Frederick Langley,
   Baron of Liverpool

b. Scala, Gia
b. Shaffer, Anthony
b. Shaffer, Peter Levin
b. Shirley-Quirk, John Stanton
b. Smith, Geoff
b. Sothern, Edward Askew
b. Starr, Ringo
b. Stubbs, George
b. Synge, Richard Laurence Millington
b. Tait, Arthur Fitzwilliam
b. Tarleton, Banastre, Sir
b. Thomas, Brandon
b. Tushingham, Rita
b. Whitty, May, Dame
b. Youngman, Henny
d. Arnold, Matthew
d. Liverpool, 2nd Earl of
d. Nevada, Emma

Lodsworth, England
d. Ward, Barbara Mary

London, England
b. Abbott, Diane (Julie)
b. A'Becket, Thomas, Saint
b. A'Beckett, Gilbert Abbott
b. Abrams, Harry Nathan
b. Ackland, Joss
b. Ackroyd, Peter
b. Adam Ant
b. Adams, Louisa Catherine
b. Adrian, Edgar Douglas, Baron
b. Aguilar, Grace
b. Alcott, John
b. Allard, Sydney
b. Allegro, John Marco
b. Allen of Hurtwood, Lady
b. Allingham, Margery
b. Alvarez, Alfred
b. Amanpour, Christiane
b. Ambler, Eric
b. Amery, Julian
b. Amies, Hardy
b. Amis, Kingsley (William)
b. Anderson, Michael
b. Anderson, Michael, Jr.
b. Andre, John
b. Andrew
b. Andrews, Anthony Corin Gerald
b. Andros, Edmund, Sir
b. Anne
b. Annis, Francesca
b. Anthony, Evelyn
b. Apted, Michael
b. Arber, Agnes
b. Arliss, George
b. Arliss, Leslie
b. Armstrong-Jones, Antony Charles
   Robert
b. Arne, Thomas Augustine
b. Asher, Peter
b. Ashman, Matthew
b. Asquith, Anthony
b. Attenborough, David Frederick
b. Attlee, Clement Richard Attlee, Earl
b. Auger, Brian
b. Ayckbourn, Alan
b. Ayer, Alfred Jules, Sir
b. Aylward, Gladys May
b. Bacon, Francis, Sir
b. Baddeley, Angela
b. Baden-Powell, Robert Stephenson
   Smyth Baden-Powell, Baron
b. Bader, Douglas Robert Steuart, Sir
b. Bailey, H(enry) C(hristopher)
b. Baker, Alan

b. Baker, Samuel White, Sir
b. Ballantrae, Lord
b. Banks, Joseph
b. Bantock, Granville, Sir
b. Barbanell, Maurice
b. Barbirolli, John, Sir
b. Baring, Maurice
b. Barnes, Binnie
b. Barnes, Clive Alexander
b. Barnes, Leonard John
b. Barnes, Peter
b. Barrie, Mona
b. Barrie, Wendy
b. Barry, Charles, Sir
b. Bart, Lionel
b. Bass, Alfie
b. Bauer, Harold
b. Bawden, Nina Mary Mabey
b. Baylis, Lilian Mary
b. Beame, Abraham David
b. Beaton, Cecil (Walter Hardy), Sir
b. Beatrice, Princess of York
b. Beerbohm, Max
b. Beeton, Isabella Mary Mayson
b. Bell, Vanessa
b. Benedictus, David
b. Benn, Tony
b. Bentham, Jeremy
b. Bentley, Edmund Clerihew
b. Bentley, John
b. Bentley, Walter Owen
b. Beresford, Harry
b. Berger, John
b. Besant, Annie Wood
b. Betterton, Thomas
b. Bianco, Margery Williams
b. Billington, Elizabeth
b. Blackett, Patrick Maynard Stuart
b. Blackman, Honor
b. Blackstone, William, Sir
b. Blake, William
b. Bliss, Arthur, Sir
b. Blofeld, John
b. Bloom, Claire
b. Blore, Eric
b. Blunden, Edmund Charles
b. Bogarde, Dirk
b. Bolan, Marc
b. Bolingbroke, Henry St. John,
   Viscount
b. Bond, Alan
b. Bond, Edward
b. Bonham Carter, Helena
b. Bonham Carter, Violet
b. Booth, Evangeline Cory
b. Booth, Junius Brutus
b. Bowie, David
b. Boyce, William
b. Bradlaugh, Charles
b. Bragg, Billy
b. Brain, Aubrey
b. Brain, Dennis
b. Brandt, Bill
b. Bream, Julian Alexander
b. Brewer, Ebenezer Cobham
b. Bricusse, Leslie
b. Brittan, Leon
b. Brook, Clive
b. Brook, Peter Stephen Paul
b. Brookner, Anita
b. Brophy, Brigid Antonia
b. Brown, Carter
b. Brown, George Alfred
b. Brown, Georgia
b. Brown, Herbert Charles
b. Brown, Pamela

b. Gilbert, William S(chwenck), Sir
b. Gilder, Nick
b. Gilliatt, Penelope (Ann Douglas
  Conner)
b. Gingold, Hermione Ferdinanda
b. Girtin, Thomas
b. Glaisher, James
b. Glass, David Victor
b. Glover, Julian
b. Gluck
b. Godwin, Mary Wollstonecraft
b. Gollancz, Victor, Sir
b. Gompers, Samuel
b. Gonne, Maud
b. Goodall, Jane
b. Goossens, Eugene, Sir
b. Gordon, Richard
b. Gosse, Edmund William, Sir
b. Gottschalk, Ferdinand
b. Goulding, Edmund
b. Gowers, Ernest Arthur, Sir
b. Graham, Sheilah
b. Granger, Stewart
b. Grant, Hugh
b. Grant, Michael
b. Granville-Barker, Harley
b. Graves, Peter
b. Graves, Robert von Ranke
b. Gray, James, Sir
b. Gray, Thomas
b. Green, Martyn
b. Green, Peter
b. Greenaway, Kate
b. Greenaway, Peter
b. Greenwood, Joan
b. Grenfell, Joyce Irene
b. Gresham, Thomas, Sir
b. Grey of Fallodon, Edward, Viscount
b. Grimaldi, Joseph
b. Grosvenor, Gerald Cavendish
b. Grove, George, Sir
b. Groves, Charles Barnard, Sir
b. Guinness, Alec, Sir
b. Gwyn, Nell
b. Hackett, Steve
b. Haden, Francis Seymour, Sir
b. Hampden, John
b. Hampshire, Susan
b. Handford, Martin
b. Hare, James Henry
b. Harlech, William David Ormsby-
  Gore, Baron
b. Harley, Robert, 1st Earl of Oxford
  and Earl Mortimer
b. Harmsworth, Harold Sidney
b. Harris, Sydney J(ustin)
b. Harrison, Noel
b. Hart, Charles
b. Harvard, John
b. Harvey, Anthony (Kesteven)
b. Harvey, Fred(erick Henry)
b. Haskell, Arnold Lionel
b. Hawkins, Jack
b. Haydn, Richard
b. Hayes, Alfred
b. Hayter, Stanley William
b. Hayward, John Davy
b. Heard, Gerald
b. Hearne, Samuel
b. Heath, Catherine
b. Heath, Ted
b. Helmore, Tom
b. Henry of Wales
b. Herrick, Robert
b. Heseltine, Philip Arnold
b. Hess, Myra, Dame

b. Hibbert, Eleanor Alice Burford
b. Hill, Graham
b. Hinshelwood, Cyril Norman, Sir
b. Hitchcock, Alfred Joseph, Sir
b. Hitchcock, Robyn
b. Hoare, Samuel John Gurney, Sir
b. Hodgkin, Howard
b. Hogarth, William
b. Holloway, Stanley
b. Holroyd, Michael De Courcy Fraser
b. Hood, Thomas
b. Hook, Theodore Edward
b. Hope-Hawkins, Anthony, Sir
b. Hoppner, John
b. Hosking, Eric J
b. Hough, John
b. Howard, Anthony
b. Howard, Ebenezer, Sir
b. Howard, Leslie
b. Howe, Richard
b. Howe, William, Viscount
b. Howes, Sally Ann
b. Huggins, William, Sir
b. Hughes, Arthur
b. Hughes, William Morris
b. Humphreys, Christmas
b. Hunt, Holman
b. Hussey, Christopher Edward Clive
b. Huxley, Andrew Fielding, Sir
b. Huxley, Elspeth Josceline Grant
b. Huxley, Julian Sorell, Sir
b. Hyndman, Henry Mayers
b. Idol, Billy
b. Ingold, Christopher Kelk, Sir
b. Insull, Samuel
b. Ireland, Jill
b. Irving, Laurence Sidney
b. Irwin, Margaret
b. Jacobi, Derek George
b. Jacobi, Mary Corinna Putnam
b. Jacobs, Sally
b. Jacobs, W(illiam) W(ymark)
b. James, G(eorge) P(ayne) R(ainsford)
b. James II
b. Jay, Peter
b. Jean-Baptiste, Marianne
b. Jeffries, Lionel Charles
b. Jerne, Niels Kaj
b. Johnson, Pamela Hansford
b. Johnston, Henry Hamilton
b. Jones, Inigo
b. Jones, Kenny
b. Jowett, Benjamin
b. Julien, Isaac
b. Karloff, Boris
b. Kean, Edmund
b. Keats, John
b. Keefe, Barrie Colin
b. Keegan, John
b. Keene, Laura
b. Kemble, Fanny
b. Kendal, William Hunter
b. Kennedy, Margaret
b. Kerr, Graham
b. Kilbracken, John Raymond Godley,
  Baron
b. Killanin, Michael Morris, Lord
b. Killigrew, Thomas
b. Kops, Bernard
b. Korda, Michael Vincent
b. Kray, Reggie
b. Kray, Ronnie
b. Kyd, Thomas
b. LaBern, Arthur Joseph
b. Lamb, Charles
b. Lamb, Mary Ann

b. Lambert, Constant
b. Lambert, J(ack) W(alter)
b. Lancaster, Joseph
b. Lancaster, Osbert, Sir
b. Landseer, Charles
b. Landseer, Edwin Henry, Sir
b. Lansbury, Angela Brigid
b. Laski, Marghanita
b. Lawford, Peter
b. Lawrence, Gertrude
b. Lawson, Nigel
b. Leach, Penelope
b. Leach, Robin
b. Leakey, Mary (Douglas)
b. Lee, Bernard
b. Lee, Christopher Frank Carandini
b. Lee, Sidney, Sir
b. Leech, John
b. Lee-Hamilton, Eugene Jacob
b. Le Gallienne, Eva
b. Legg, Adrian
b. Lehmann, Rosamond Nina
b. Leighton, Clare Veronica Hope
b. Lemon, Mark
b. Leppard, Raymond John
b. Leverson, Ada
b. Levy, Joseph Moses
b. Lewes, George Henry
b. Lewis, Matthew Gregory
b. Lewis, Ted
b. Liddell Hart, Basil Henry, Sir
b. Lindsay, David
b. Linton, William James
b. Litolff, Henri Charles
b. Little, Little Jack
b. Littlewood, Joan
b. Litvinoff, Emanuel
b. Liverpool, 2nd Earl of
b. Livingstone, Ken
b. Lloyd, Marie
b. Lloyd Webber, Andrew
b. Loder, John
b. Lord, Shirley
b. Lovelace, Ada Byron
b. Lubbock, Percy
b. Lupino, Ida
b. Lupino, Stanley
b. Lutyens, Edwin Landseer, Sir
b. Lydon, John (Joseph)
b. Lynch, J(ohn) Joseph
b. Lyttleton, Oliver
b. Lytton, Edward George Earle
  Lytton Bulwer-Lytton, 1st Baron
  Lytton
b. Lytton, Edward Robert Bulwer-
  Lytton, Earl
b. Lytton, Henry Alfred, Sir
b. Macfarren, George Alexander, Sir
b. MacGrath, Leueen (Emily)
b. Maclean, Donald Duart
b. MacMillan, Harold
b. MacRae, Sheila
b. Maitland, Frederic William
b. Major, John (Roy)
b. Makihara, (Ben) Minoru
b. Malcolm, George
b. Mallowan, Max Edgar Lucien, Sir
b. Manners, Charles
b. Mapleson, James Henry
b. Marie Alexandra Victoria
b. Markievicz, Constance Georgine,
  Countess
b. Markova, Alicia, Dame
b. Marlowe, Derek
b. Marryat, Frederick
b. Marsh, Edward Howard, Sir

b. Stanley, Frederick Arthur, Earl of
Derby
b. Starling, Ernest Henry
b. Steel, Anthony
b. Steele, Tommy
b. Stephen, Leslie, Sir
b. Stevens, Cat
b. Stevenson, Robert
b. Stocker, Wally
b. Stokes, Donald Gresham Stokes,
Baron
b. Stokowski, Leopold (Anton
Stanislaw Boleslawawicz)
b. Stone, John Richard Nicholas, Sir
b. Strachey, (Giles) Lytton
b. Struther, Jan
b. Styne, Jule
b. Sullivan, Arthur Seymour, Sir
b. Sullivan, Francis Loftus
b. Summerskill, Edith Clara, Baroness
b. Sutherland, Graham Vivian
b. Sutherland, Keifer
b. Swift, Graham (Colin)
b. Swinburne, Algernon Charles
b. Sykes, Mark, Sir
b. Sylvester, James Joseph
b. Symons, George James
b. Symons, Julian (Gustave)
b. Syms, Sylvia
b. Tandy, Jessica
b. Taylor, Ann
b. Taylor, Elizabeth Rosemond
b. Tebbit, Norman Beresford
b. Tempest, Marie
b. Tennant, Veronica
b. Tenniel, John, Sir
b. Terry-Thomas
b. Tharoor, Shashi
b. Thomas, Caitlin Macnamara
b. Thomas, Edward
b. Thomas, Lowell Jackson, Jr.
b. Thomas, Sidney Gilchrist
b. Thompson, Daley
b. Thompson, David
b. Thompson, Emma
b. Thompson, Richard
b. Thorpe, Jeremy
b. Tilbrook, Glenn
b. Tippett, Michael Kemp, Sir
b. Tomlinson, Henry Major
b. Toulmin, Stephen Edelston
b. Townshend, Peter Dennis Blandford
b. Toynbee, Arnold Joseph
b. Traill, Catharine Parr
b. Travers, Ben
b. Trelawny, Edward John
b. Tremayne, Les
b. Trollope, Anthony
b. Trower, Robin
b. Tudor, Antony
b. Turing, Alan (Mathison)
b. Turner, Joseph Mallord William
b. Twiggy
b. Tylor, Edward Bennett, Sir
b. Underwood, John Thomas
b. Unsworth, Geoffrey
b. Unwin, Stanley, Sir
b. Ustinov, Peter Alexander
b. Utley, Freda
b. Vanbrugh, John, Sir
b. Vanderbilt, Alfred G(wynne)
b. Vandercook, John Womack
b. Van Druten, John William
b. Vaux, Calvert
b. Vestris, Lucia Elizabeth, Madame
b. Vicious, Sid

b. Victoria, Queen
b. Villers, George
b. Vogel, Julius
b. Wakeman, Rick
b. Waley, Arthur David
b. Walker, Emery, Sir
b. Wallace, Richard, Sir
b. Wallack, James William
b. Wallis, Shani
b. Walpole, Horace
b. Ward, Rachel
b. Ward, Simon
b. Watts, George Frederic
b. Waugh, Alec
b. Waugh, Evelyn Arthur St. John
b. Webb, Sidney James
b. Webster, Ben(jamin)
b. Webster, John
b. Wesker, Arnold
b. Westrup, J(ack) A(llan), Sir
b. Wheeler, Hugh Callingham
b. White, Antonia
b. White, Patrick Victor Martindale
b. Whitlock, Albert
b. Whymper, Edward
b. Wilde, Kim
b. Wilkes, John
b. William, IV
b. William of Wales
b. Williams, Darnell
b. Williams, Roger
b. Williams, Shirley
b. Wintle, Justin Beecham
b. Wintour, Anna
b. Wisdom, Norman
b. Wood, Henry Joseph, Sir
b. Wood, Ron(ald)
b. Woolf, Leonard Sidney
b. Woolf, Virginia
b. Woolley, Charles Leonard, Sir
b. Wright, Rick
b. Wycherley, Margaret
b. Wyman, Bill
b. Wynter, Dana
b. Wynyard, Diana
b. York, Susannah
b. Young, Roland
b. Young MC
b. Zangwill, Israel
d. Abbey, Edwin Austin
d. Abel, Karl Friedrich
d. Abercrombie, Lascelles
d. Aberdeen, 4th Earl of
d. Abington, Fanny
d. Abrahams, Harold
d. Adam, James
d. Adam, Robert
d. Addams, Dawn
d. Addinsell, Richard
d. Addison, Joseph
d. Adrian, Edgar Douglas, Baron
d. Agate, James Evershed
d. Aitken, Max
d. Albert, Prince
d. Aldridge, Michael
d. Alice
d. Allegro, John Marco
d. Allenby, Edmund Henry Hynman
d. Ambler, Eric
d. Amis, Kingsley (William)
d. Anders, Wladyslaw
d. Andrews, Eamonn
d. Andros, Edmund, Sir
d. Anne of Cleves
d. Anstey, Edgar Harold McFarlane
d. Arbuthnot, John

d. Ardizzone, Edward Jeffrey Irving
d. Arliss, George
d. Arliss, Leslie
d. Arne, Thomas Augustine
d. Arnold, Benedict
d. Arnold, Edwin
d. Asch, Sholem
d. Ashcroft, Peggy, Dame
d. Asquith, Anthony
d. Asquith, Emma Alice Margot
d. Attlee, Clement Richard Attlee, Earl
d. Ayer, Alfred Jules, Sir
d. Babbage, Charles
d. Babington, Anthony
d. Bach, Johann Christian
d. Back, George, Sir
d. Bader, Douglas Robert Steuart, Sir
d. Bagnold, Enid
d. Baily, Francis
d. Balchin, Nigel Marlin
d. Ballantrae, Lord
d. Baltimore, George Calvert, Baron
d. Banks, Leslie
d. Bantock, Granville, Sir
d. Barbirolli, John, Sir
d. Barnetson, William Denholm
d. Barrie, James Matthew, Sir
d. Barry, Charles, Sir
d. Bart, Lionel
d. Bartok, Eva
d. Bass, Alfie
d. Bateman, Kate Josephine
d. Bates, Henry Walter
d. Bayliss, William Maddock, Sir
d. Beatty, David Beatty, Earl
d. Beatty, Robert
d. Beaumont, Francis
d. Beaumont, John, Sir
d. Beecham, Thomas, Sir
d. Behn, Aphra
d. Belcher, Edward, Sir
d. Bell, Clive
d. Benjamin, Arthur
d. Bennett, Arnold
d. Bennett, William Sterndale, Sir
d. Benson, Frank Robert, Sir
d. Bentham, George
d. Bentham, Jeremy
d. Bentley, Edmund Clerihew
d. Bergman, Ingrid
d. Bergner, Elisabeth
d. Beriosova, Svetlana
d. Besant, Walter, Sir
d. Bessemer, Henry, Sir
d. Betterton, Thomas
d. Bevin, Ernest
d. Biddle, John
d. Bigge, John Thomas
d. Birley, Oswald Hornby Joseph, Sir
d. Birrell, Augustine
d. Blackett, Patrick Maynard Stuart
d. Blackstone, William, Sir
d. Blackwood, Algernon Henry
d. Blair, David
d. Blake, William
d. Blakely, Colin (George Edward)
d. Blavatsky, Helena Petrovna
d. Bligh, William, Captain
d. Bliss, Arthur, Sir
d. Blondin, Jean Francois Gravelet
d. Bloom, Ursula
d. Blow, John
d. Blunt, Anthony Frederick
d. Blyton, Enid Mary
d. Bodley, Thomas, Sir

d. Dyce, Alexander
d. Dyer, Edward, Sir
d. Eden, Dorothy
d. Eden, Nicholas
d. Edward IV
d. Edward the Black Prince
d. Edward V
d. Edward VI
d. Edward VII
d. Elgar, Edward William, Sir
d. Eliot, George
d. Eliot, T(homas) S(tearns)
d. Elliot, Cass
d. Ellis, Ruth
d. Empson, William, Sir
d. Engels, Friedrich
d. Epstein, Brian
d. Epstein, Jacob, Sir
d. Equiano, Olaudah
d. Everest, George, Sir
d. Eysenck, Hans J(urgen)
d. Farquhar, George
d. Fawcett, Millicent Garrett, Dame
d. Fawkes, Guy
d. Feather, Victor
d. Fellows, Charles, Sir
d. Fenollosa, Ernest Francisco
d. Fernald, John Bailey
d. Ferrier, David, Sir
d. Ferrier, Kathleen
d. Fisher, Andrew
d. Fisher, Herbert Albert Laurens
d. Fisher, John
d. Flaxman, John
d. Fleming, Alexander, Sir
d. Fleming, Ian
d. Fletcher, John
d. Flinders, Matthew
d. Flint, William Russell, Sir
d. Florey, Howard Walter
d. Florio, John
d. Forster, John
d. Forster, William Edward
d. Foscolo, (Niccolo) Ugo
d. Fowler, Henry Watson
d. Fowler, Lydia Folger
d. Fraser, Bruce Austin, Sir
d. Frederick Louis
d. Freud, Anna
d. Freud, Sigmund
d. Friese-Greene, William Edward
d. Frith, William Powell
d. Fry, Charles Burgess
d. Fry, Roger Eliot
d. Fuller, Roy Broadbent
d. Fury, Billy
d. Fuseli, Henry
d. Gabor, Dennis
d. Gainsborough, Thomas
d. Gaitskell, Hugh (Todd Naylor)
d. Garcia, Manuel Patricio Rodriguez
d. Gardner, Ava
d. Garfield, Leon
d. Garland, Judy
d. Garnett, Richard
d. Garrick, David
d. Garvey, Marcus Moziah
d. Gaunt, William
d. Gay, John
d. Gellhorn, Martha Ellis
d. Genn, Leo
d. Gentileschi, Orazio
d. George II
d. Gerard, John
d. Gerhardi, William Alexander
d. Gershon, Karen

d. Gibbon, Edward
d. Gibbons, Grinling
d. Gibbons, Stella (Dorothea)
d. Gibbs, James
d. Gieseking, Walter Wilhelm
d. Gilbert, Alfred, Sir
d. Gilbert, John, Sir
d. Gilbert, William
d. Gilliatt, Penelope (Ann Douglas Conner)
d. Gillray, James
d. Gilmore, Eddy Lanier King
d. Girtin, Thomas
d. Glyn, Elinor Sutherland
d. Godwin, Edward William
d. Godwin, Mary Wollstonecraft
d. Godwin, William
d. Goldie, George Dashwood Taubman
d. Goldie, Grace Wyndham
d. Goldin, Horace
d. Goldsmith, Oliver
d. Gollancz, Victor, Sir
d. Goodall, John Strickland
d. Gordon-Walker of Leyton, Patrick Chrestien Gordon-Walker, Baron
d. Gore, Charles
d. Gorgas, William Crawford
d. Gosse, Edmund William, Sir
d. Gottschalk, Ferdinand
d. Grade, Lew, Sir
d. Graham, Stephen
d. Graham, Thomas
d. Gray, Nicholas Stuart
d. Green, Henry
d. Greenaway, Kate
d. Greene, Hugh (Carleton), Sir
d. Greene, Robert
d. Greenwood, Joan
d. Grenfell, Joyce Irene
d. Gresham, Thomas, Sir
d. Grew, Nehemiah
d. Grey, Jane, Lady
d. Griffith, Hugh Emrys
d. Grimaldi, Joseph
d. Grote, George
d. Grove, George, Sir
d. Grove, William Robert, Sir
d. Guedalla, Philip
d. Gwyn, Nell
d. Haggard, Henry Rider, Sir
d. Haig, Douglas
d. Hakluyt, Richard
d. Hall, Radclyffe
d. Hamer, Robert
d. Hamilton, Denis, Sir
d. Hamilton, Hamish
d. Hamilton, Ian Standish Monteith, Sir
d. Handel, George Frideric
d. Hansom, Joseph Aloysius
d. Hare, John, Sir
d. Harley, Robert, 1st Earl of Oxford and Earl Mortimer
d. Harris, Robert
d. Harrison, Joan (Mary)
d. Harte, (Francis) Bret
d. Hartley, L(eslie) P(oles)
d. Harvey, Laurence
d. Harvey, William
d. Hathaway, Sibyl Collings
d. Hatton, Christopher, Sir
d. Hawkins, Jack
d. Hawtrey, Ralph George, Sir
d. Haydon, Benjamin Robert
d. Haywood, Eliza
d. Hazlitt, William

d. Head, Edmund Walker, Sir
d. Heinemann, William
d. Henderson, Arthur
d. Hendrix, Jimi
d. Henry IV
d. Henry VI
d. Henslowe, Philip
d. Hepplewhite, George
d. Herbert, A(lan) P(atrick), Sir
d. Herbert, Edward, 1st Baron Herbert of Cherbury
d. Heseltine, Philip Arnold
d. Hess, Myra, Dame
d. Heyer, Georgette
d. Heywood, Thomas
d. Hill, George Birkbeck Norman
d. Hill, Graham
d. Hilliard, Nicholas
d. Hinshelwood, Cyril Norman, Sir
d. Hinton, Christopher, Sir
d. Hoare, Samuel John Gurney, Sir
d. Hobson, John Atkinson
d. Hobson, Valerie Babette
d. Hogarth, William
d. Hogg, Ima
d. Holbein, Hans, the Younger
d. Holbrooke, Josef
d. Holmes, Arthur
d. Holst, Gustav Theodore
d. Honeyman-Scott, James
d. Hood, Thomas
d. Hook, Theodore Edward
d. Hooke, Robert
d. Hoppner, John
d. Howard, Trevor Wallace
d. Howe, Richard
d. Hoyle, Edmond
d. Hudson, William Henry
d. Huggins, William, Sir
d. Hughes, Ted
d. Hulbert, Jack
d. Humphreys, Christmas
d. Hunt, Holman
d. Hunt, James
d. Hunt, Martita
d. Hunter, John
d. Hunter, William
d. Hussey, Christopher Edward Clive
d. Huxley, Julian Sorell, Sir
d. Ingelow, Jean
d. Ingold, Christopher Kelk, Sir
d. Ironside, William Edmund
d. Isaacs, Alick
d. Ismay, Joseph Bruce
d. Iveagh, Arthur Francis Benjamin Guinness, Lord
d. Jackson, Gordon Cameron
d. Jackson, John Hughlings
d. Jacobs, W(illiam) W(ymark)
d. Jakobovits, Immanuel
d. James, Henry, (Jr.)
d. Jameson, Leander Starr, Sir
d. John of Gaunt
d. Johnson, Lionel Pigot
d. Johnson, Pamela Hansford
d. Johnson, Samuel
d. Jones, Brian
d. Jones, David
d. Jones, Ernest Alfred
d. Jones, Inigo
d. Joseph, Keith (Sinjohn)
d. Kamehameha II
d. Karsavina, Tamara (Platonova)
d. Kavan, Anna
d. Kean, Edmund
d. Keene, Charles Samuel

d. Psalmanazar, George
d. Pym, John
d. Quayle, (John) Anthony, Sir
d. Queensberry, John Sholto Douglas
d. Quennell, Peter (Courtney)
d. Radcliffe, Ann
d. Raffles, Thomas Stamford, Sir
d. Raleigh, Walter, Sir
d. Rambert, Marie, Dame
d. Raphael, Chaim
d. Rathbone, Eleanor
d. Ray, Edward
d. Reade, Charles
d. Recorde, Robert
d. Reed, Carol, Sir
d. Reid, Beryl
d. Reid, Whitelaw
d. Reid Dick, William, Sir
d. Reynolds, Joshua, Sir
d. Rhys, Ernest Percival
d. Richardson, Ralph David, Sir
d. Richardson, Samuel
d. Robertson, William Robert, Sir
d. Robins, Denise Naomi
d. Robinson, W Heath
d. Rodney, George Brydges, Baron
d. Rogers, Robert
d. Rogers, Samuel
d. Rohmer, Sax
d. Ronald, Landon, Sir
d. Ross, Ronald, Sir
d. Rossetti, Christina Georgina
d. Rossetti, Gabriele Pasquale
    Giuseppe
d. Rossetti, William Michael
d. Rothermere, Esmond Cecil
    Harmsworth, Viscount
d. Rothschild, Lionel Nathan
    Rothschild, Baron
d. Rowe, Nicholas
d. Rowlandson, Thomas
d. Ruark, Robert Chester
d. Russell, Henry
d. Said bin Taimur
d. Salem, Mamdouh
d. Sandow, Eugene
d. Sandwich, John Montagu
d. Sansom, William
d. Sargent, John Singer
d. Sargent, Malcolm, Sir
d. Savery, Thomas
d. Schneider, Alan
d. Schonfield, Hugh J
d. Scott, George Gilbert, Sir
d. Scott, Paul Mark
d. Seaman, Owen, Sir
d. Sedgwick, Adam
d. Selden, John
d. Selfridge, Harry Gordon
d. Sellers, Peter
d. Shadwell, Thomas
d. Shah, Indries
d. Sheppard, Jack
d. Sheraton, Thomas
d. Sheridan, Richard Brinsley
d. Shirley, James
d. Short, James
d. Shorthouse, Joseph Henry
d. Siddons, Sarah Kemble
d. Sidney, Algernon
d. Siemens, William, Sir
d. Sim, Alastair
d. Simon, John, Sir
d. Simpson, James Young, Sir
d. Sitwell, Edith, Dame
d. Sitwell, Sacheverell, Sir

d. Slim, William Joseph
d. Sloane, Hans, Sir
d. Smith, Donald Alexander
d. Smith, John
d. Smith, Sydney
d. Snow, C(harles) P(ercy), Sir
d. Soames, Christopher
d. Soane, John, Sir
d. Solomon
d. Somes, Michael (George)
d. Sothern, Edward Askew
d. Speer, Albert
d. Spender, Stephen (Harold)
d. Spenser, Edmund
d. Spilsbury, Bernard Henry, Sir
d. Spy
d. Stanford, Charles Villiers, Sir
d. Stanford-Tuck, Robert Roland
d. Stanley, Henry Morton, Sir
d. Staunton, Howard
d. Stephen, Leslie, Sir
d. Stephens, James
d. Stephens, Robert, Sir
d. Sterne, Laurence
d. Stevenson, Adlai Ewing, II
d. Stewart, Donald Ogden
d. Stirling, James
d. Stoker, Bram
d. Stoney, George Johnstone
d. Strafford, 1st Earl of
d. Street, George Edmund
d. Strutt, Joseph
d. Stubbs, George
d. Sullivan, Arthur Seymour, Sir
d. Summerskill, Edith Clara, Baroness
d. Supervia, Conchita
d. Swann, Donald (Ibrahim)
d. Swinburne, Algernon Charles
d. Sydenham, Thomas
d. Sylvester, James Joseph
d. Symons, George James
d. Tarlton, Richard
d. Tate, Nahum
d. Tauber, Richard
d. Tawney, Richard Henry
d. Tempest, Marie
d. Tenniel, John, Sir
d. Teyte, Maggie, Dame
d. Thackeray, William Makepeace
d. Thomas, Brandon
d. Thompson, Francis Joseph
d. Thomson, James
d. Thomson, Roy Herbert
d. Thorneycroft, (George Edward)
    Peter
d. Tidyman, Ernest
d. Tinbergen, Nikolaas
d. Tiomkin, Dimitri
d. Tippett, Michael Kemp, Sir
d. Todd, Ann
d. Toland, John
d. Tomlinson, Henry Major
d. Toplady, Augustus Montague
d. Topolski, Feliks
d. Travers, Ben
d. Travers, P(amela) L(yndon)
d. Tree, Herbert Beerbohm
d. Trench, Richard Chenevix
d. Trenchard, Hugh Montague, First
    Viscount
d. Trollope, Anthony
d. Tryon, William
d. Tubman, William Vacanarat
    Shadrach
d. Turner, Eva, Dame
d. Turner, Joseph Mallord William

d. Tussaud, Marie Gresholtz, Madame
d. Tyrrell, James, Sir
d. Udall, Nicholas
d. Underhill, Evelyn
d. Unwin, Stanley, Sir
d. Upton, Florence Kate
d. Ure, Mary
d. Vanbrugh, John, Sir
d. Van Der Post, Laurens (Jan), Sir
d. Van Dyck, Anthony, Sir
d. Vardon, Harry
d. Vaughan Williams, Ralph
d. Velde, Willem van de
d. Vestris, Lucia Elizabeth, Madame
d. Viotti, Giovanni Battista
d. von Hugel, Friedrich, Baron
d. Vyvyan, Jennifer Brigit
d. Walker, Emery, Sir
d. Wallace, William
d. Waller, William, Sir
d. Walpole, Horace
d. Walsingham, Francis, Sir
d. Watts, George Frederic
d. Watts-Dunton, Theodore
d. Wavell, Archibald Percival Wavell,
    Earl
d. Weber, Carl Maria von
d. Webster, Margaret
d. Weddell, James
d. Wedgwood, J(osiah) V(eronica)
d. Wellcome, Henry Solomon, Sir
d. Wells, H(erbert) G(eorge)
d. Wesley, Charles
d. Wesley, John
d. West, Benjamin
d. West, Rebecca, Dame
d. Wheelwright, William
d. Whistler, James Abbott McNeill
d. White, Antonia
d. Widgery, John Passmore, Baron
d. Wigg, George (Edward Cecil)
d. Wilberforce, William
d. Wilcox, Herbert
d. Wilkes, John
d. William III
d. Williams, Emlyn
d. Williams, George Washington
d. Williams, Jay
d. Wilson, (James) Harold, Sir
d. Wise, Thomas J
d. Wiseman, Nicholas Patrick Stephen
d. Woffington, Margaret
d. Wolfenden, John Frederick, Sir
d. Wolfit, Donald, Sir
d. Wood, Henry, Mrs.
d. Wood, Henry Joseph, Sir
d. Woodville, Richard Caton
d. Woolley, Charles Leonard, Sir
d. Wren, Christopher, Sir
d. Wynyard, Diana
d. Yeats-Brown, F(rancis Charles
    Claypon)
d. Zaleski, August
d. Zangwill, Israel
d. Zinnemann, Fred
d. Zuckerman, Solly, Lord

Long Ashton, England
    d. Gorges, Ferdinando, Sir

Long Benton, England
    b. Addison, Thomas
    b. Bigge, John Thomas

Longsight, Lancashire, England
    b. Chadwick, Edwin

Mirfield, England
b. Stewart, Patrick

Missenden, England
b. Austin, Herbert
d. Robinson, Robert, Sir

Mitcham, England
b. Mitchell, Peter Dennis

Mobberley, England
b. Mallory, George Leigh

Moor Park, England
d. Anson, George

Morley, England
b. Asquith, Herbert Henry
b. Bedford, Brian

Mortlake, England
d. Dee, John

Morton Village, England
b. Cook, James, Captain

Muswell Hill, England
b. Davies, Dave
b. Davies, Ray(mond Douglas)

Mytholmroyd, England
b. Hughes, Ted

Nailsworth, England
d. Dobell, Sydney Thompson

Nantwich, England
b. Beatty, David Beatty, Earl
b. Gerard, John

Nelson, England
b. Hicks, Tony

Nether Wallop, England
d. Stokowski, Leopold (Anton
Stanislaw Boleslawawicz)

Netherwood, England
b. Devereaux, Robert

Nettlebed, England
d. Johnson, Celia, Dame

New Windsor, England
d. Dors, Diana

Newark, England
b. Hounsfield, Godfrey Newbold, Sir
b. Kell, Reginald George
b. Wolfit, Donald, Sir
d. John, King of England

Newark-on-Trent, England
b. Blow, John

Newberry, England
b. Baily, Francis

Newbuildings, England
d. Blunt, Wilfrid Scawen

Newbury, England
b. Adams, Richard
b. Herbert, George Edward Stanhope
Molyneux

Newcastle-Under-Lyme, England
d. Matthews, Stanley, Sir

Newcastle-upon-Tyne, England
b. Bartlett, Neil
b. Brittain, Vera Mary
b. Catto, Thomas Sivewright, Baron
b. Forster, John
b. Hudson, Joseph Lowthian
b. Richardson, Lewis Fry
b. Shaw, Anna Howard
b. Sting
b. Surtees, Robert Smith
b. Travers, Bill
d. Brannigan, Owen

Newington, England
b. Faraday, Michael

Newington Butts, England
d. Middleton, Thomas

Newport, England
b. Goring, Marius

Newton, England
d. Vaughan, Henry

Newton-le-Willows, England
b. Astley, Rick

Norfolk, England
b. Boycott, Charles Cunningham
b. Bryant, Arthur W M, Sir
b. Cromer, 1st Earl of
b. Day, John
d. Chapman, (Anthony) Colin (Bruce)
d. Greene, Richard

Norham, England
b. Whitechurch, Victor Lorenzo

Normanston, England
b. Maurice, Frederick Denison

North Devon, England
b. Taylor, J(ohn) H(enry)

North London, England
b. Stewart, Rod(erick David)

North Shields, England
b. Young, Alan (Angus)

North Wiltshire, England
b. Jeffries, Richard

North Yorkshire, England
d. Hart-Davis, Rupert

Northampton, England
b. Arnold, Malcolm, Sir
b. Bradstreet, Anne
b. Butler, Alban
b. Carne, Judy
b. Chisholm, Caroline
b. Crick, Francis Harry Compton

b. Dudley, Thomas
d. Clare, John
d. Douglas, Sholto
d. Jerome, Jerome Klapka
d. Smith, William

Northamptonshire, England
b. Dryden, John
d. Henry William Frederick Albert

Northumbria, England
b. Bede the Venerable, Saint

Northwood, England
b. Jarman, Derek
d. Lane, Allen, Sir
d. Morgan, Frederick, Sir

Norton, England
d. Bairnsfather, Bruce

Norton Park, England
d. Woodhull, Victoria Claflin

Norwich, England
b. Bullard, Edward Crisp, Sir
b. Caius, John
b. Castle, Vernon
b. Clarke, Samuel
b. Cooper, Astley Paston, Sir
b. Cotman, John Sell
b. Crome, John
b. Gambling, John Bradley
b. George, Graham Elias
b. Greene, Robert
b. Hooker, William Jackson, Sir
b. Martineau, Harriet
b. Sedgwick, Adam
d. Ashford, Daisy
d. Christiansen, Arthur
d. Crome, John
d. Sewell, Anna

Norwood, England
b. Colvin, Sidney, Sir

Nottingham, England
b. Clarke, Kenneth Harry
b. Dean, Christopher
b. Essen, Louis
b. Fellows, Charles, Sir
b. Hogwood, Christopher
b. Jayston, Michael
b. Sillitoe, Alan
b. Torvill, Jayne

Nottinghamshire, England
b. Booth, William
b. Brewster, William
b. Butler, Samuel
b. Carver, John
b. Hawksmoor, Nicholas
b. Michell, John
d. Hargreaves, James

Nuneaton, England
b. Loach, Ken(neth)

Oakham, England
b. Oates, Titus

Oare, England
d. Bottomley, Gordon

d. Matthews, Jessie

Plaistow, England
 b. Essex, David
 b. Lane, Ronnie

Plymouth, England
 b. Bligh, William, Captain
 b. Dobson, Henry Austin
 b. Eastlake, Charles Lock, Sir
 b. Foot, Michael
 b. Francis, Trevor
 b. Greene, Richard
 b. Hawkins, John, Sir
 b. Haydon, Benjamin Robert
 b. Hodge, Frederick Webb
 b. MacCarthy, Desmond Charles Otto, Sir
 b. Moffat, Donald
 b. Sinden, Donald (Alfred)
 b. Toye, Clive Roy
 d. Buckingham, 1st Duke of
 d. Chichester, Francis Charles, Sir
 d. Crispin, Edmund
 d. Frobisher, Martin
 d. Howe, William, Viscount
 d. Singer, Burns James Hyman

Plympton, England
 b. Owen, David Anthony Llewellyn
 b. Reynolds, Joshua, Sir

Pontefract, England
 b. Pears, Charles

Poole, England
 b. LeCarre, John

Porlock Weir, England
 d. Gregson, John

Portsea, England
 b. Ayrton, Hertha

Portsmouth, England
 b. Aldington, Richard (Edward Godfree)
 b. Besant, Walter, Sir
 b. Brunel, Isambard Kingdom
 b. Callaghan, James
 b. Dickens, Charles (John Huffam)
 b. Manning, Olivia
 b. Meredith, George
 b. Sellers, Peter
 d. Napier, Charles James, Sir

Poulton-Fylde, England
 b. Summers, Andy

Prescott, England
 b. Kemble, John Philip

Preston, England
 b. Arkwright, Richard, Sir
 b. Glubb, John Bagot, Sir
 b. Park, Nick
 b. Service, Robert William
 b. Shirley, William
 b. Thompson, Francis Joseph

Prestwich, England
 d. Sturgeon, William

Pulborough, England
 d. McNeile, Herman Cyril

Purton, England
 b. Morris, Desmond
 d. Sassoon, Siegfried

Pusey, England
 b. Pusey, Edward Bouverie

Putney, England
 b. Cromwell, Thomas
 b. Gibbon, Edward
 d. Hunt, Leigh
 d. Pitt, William, the Younger

Radipole, England
 b. Cameron, Verney Lovett

Radnage, England
 d. Addison, Christopher, Viscount

Raleigh, England
 b. Head, Edmund Walker, Sir

Ramsgate, England
 b. Fry, Elizabeth Gurney
 b. Whitehead, Alfred North
 d. Dunmore, 4th Earl of
 d. Levy, Joseph Moses
 d. Montefiore, Moses Haim, Sir
 d. Pugin, A(ugustus) W(elby) N(orthmore)

Rawtenstall, England
 b. Egan, John Leopold, Sir

Reading, England
 b. Clarke, Alexander Ross
 b. Havell, Robert, Jr.
 b. Laud, William
 b. Oldfield, Mike
 b. Smith, Goldwin
 d. Dickens, Monica Enid
 d. Morley, Robert

Redditch, England
 b. Bonham, John Henry

Reigate, England
 b. Campbell, Donald Malcolm
 b. Fonteyn, Margot, Dame
 b. Hesse, Mary B(renda)
 d. Ainsworth, W(illiam) H(arrison)
 d. Clarke, Alexander Ross
 d. Ussher, James

Rendcomb, England
 b. Sanger, Frederick

Rhyddings, England
 d. Bowdler, Thomas

Ribston, England
 b. Dent, Edward Joseph

Richmond, England
 b. Cayley, Arthur
 b. Chapman, (Anthony) Colin (Bruce)
 b. Colman, Ronald
 b. Denny, Reginald Leigh
 b. Edward VIII
 b. Johnson, Celia, Dame

 b. Lester, Mark
 b. Turner, John Napier
 b. Wright, Almroth Edward, Sir
 b. Wycliffe, John
 d. Edward III
 d. Elizabeth I
 d. Henry VII
 d. Russell, John, Lord
 d. Thomson, James

Rickinghall, England
 b. Bowell, Mackenzie, Sir

Ripe, England
 d. Lowry, Malcolm

Ripley, England
 b. Clapton, Eric
 b. Wallis, Barnes Neville, Sir

Riverhead, England
 b. Amherst, Jeffrey

Rochdale, England
 b. Clegg, Johnny
 b. Fields, Gracie
 b. Meiklejohn, Alexander
 b. Stansfield, Lisa

Rochester, England
 b. Bagnold, Enid
 b. Bottome, Phyllis

Rodmell, England
 d. Woolf, Leonard Sidney

Roehampton, England
 b. Lamb, Caroline Ponsonby, Lady
 b. Parkinson, Norman

Romford, England
 b. Martin, Millicent
 d. Repton, Humphry

Romney Marshes, England
 b. Williams, Kit

Romsey, England
 b. Petty, William, Sir

Ross-on-Wye, England
 b. Griffin, Dale
 d. Potter, Dennis (Christopher George)

Rotherham, England
 b. Hobson, Harold

Rothwell, England
 b. Dale, Jim

Rottingdean, England
 d. Evans, Maurice

Rowney Abbey, England
 d. Balfe, Michael William

Rowton, England
 b. Baxter, Richard

Royal Tunbridge Wells, England
 d. Cunningham, Alan Gordon, Sir

b. Varley, F(rederick) H(orseman)
b. Wright, Harry
d. Shanks, Michael

Shefford, England
d. Bloomfield, Robert

Shelford, England
b. Davenport, Nigel

Shepperton, England
b. Boorman, John

Sherbourne, England
d. Wyatt, Thomas, Sir

Sheringham, England
d. Hamilton, Patrick

Shilstone, England
b. Savery, Thomas

Shipbourne, England
b. Smart, Christopher

Shipdham, England
b. Lofts, Norah Robinson

Shipley, England
b. Richardson, Tony

Shireborn, England
b. Bradley, James

Shirley, England
b. Powys, John Cowper
b. Powys, Theodore Francis

Shirwell, England
b. Chichester, Francis Charles, Sir

Shoreham, England
b. Sayer, Leo

Shortlands, England
b. Swann, Michael Meredith, Sir

Shrewsbury, England
b. Burney, Charles
b. Darwin, Charles Robert
b. Dyer, Charles (Raymond)
b. Hunter, Ian
b. Lyle, Sandy
d. Harlech, William David Ormsby-
  Gore, Baron
d. Percy, Henry, Sir

Shropshire, England
b. Herbert, Edward, 1st Baron Herbert
  of Cherbury
b. Langland, William
b. Wilson, Erica
d. Osborne, John (James)
d. Peters, Ellis
d. Tarleton, Banastre, Sir

Shugborough, England
b. Anson, George

Shustoke, England
b. Dugdale, William, Sir

Sidcup, England
b. Blake, Quentin
b. Jones, John Paul

Sidmouth, England
b. Cherwell, Frederick Alexander L,
  Viscount
d. Bryce, James Bryce, Viscount
d. Delderfield, Ronald Frederick
d. Fleming, John Ambrose, Sir

Skegness, England
b. Allan, Elizabeth

Skipton, England
b. MacLeod, Iain Norman

Skipton-in-Craven, England
b. Dawson, Geoffrey

Sleaford, England
b. Taupin, Bernie

Slindon, England
d. Langton, Stephen

Slinfold, England
b. Dolin, Anton, Sir

Slough, England
b. Hawtrey, Ralph George, Sir
b. Herschel, John Frederick William,
  Sir
b. McPartland, Margaret Marian
b. Ullman, Tracey
d. Alexander of Tunis
d. Clayton, Jack
d. Herschel, William Frederick, Sir
d. Kray, Ronnie

Smithfield, England
d. Tyler, Wat

Snaiton, England
b. Kingsley, Ben

Solway Moss, England
d. James V

Somersby, England
b. Tennyson, Alfred, Lord

Somerset, England
b. Berkeley, William, Sir
b. Bull, John
b. Dyer, Edward, Sir
d. Gillott, Jacky
d. MacGregor, Ian Kinloch, Sir
d. Pitman, Isaac

Sompting, England
d. Trelawny, Edward John

South Shields, England
b. Brymer, Jack
b. Hamilton, Denis, Sir
b. Henderson, Robert W
b. Jarvis, John Wesley
b. Robson, Flora McKenzie, Dame
b. Scott, Ridley
b. Seton, Ernest Thompson

Southall, England
b. Laine, Cleo

Southampton, England
b. Dibdin, Charles
b. Freemantle, Brian Harry
b. Hill, Benny
b. Jellicoe, John Rushworth
b. Jones, Howard
b. Millais, John Everett, Sir
b. Russell, Ken
b. Saintsbury, George Edward
  Bateman
b. Watts, Isaac
d. Franey, Pierre
d. O'Keeffe, John
d. Rice, Elmer
d. Rosas, Juan Manuel de
d. Shrapnel, Henry
d. Summersby, Kay
d. Ward, Artemus

Southend, England
b. Deeping, (George) Warwick

Southfields, England
b. Creasey, John

Southgate, England
b. Hunt, Leigh

Southleigh, England
b. Francis, James Bicheno

Southport, England
b. Bryan, Dora
b. Howells, Anne Elizabeth

Southsea, England
b. Chamberlain, Houston Stewart
b. Chatfield, Alfred E Montacute,
  Baron

Southwell, England
b. Allenby, Edmund Henry Hynman

Spilsby, England
b. Franklin, John, Sir
b. Henry IV

Spofforth, England
b. Eusden, Laurence

St. Albans, England
d. Matthew Paris
d. Runcie, Robert Alexander Kennedy

St. Helens, Lancashire, England
b. Seddon, Richard John

St. Ives, Cornwall, England
b. Hobhouse, Leonard Trelawny

Staffordshire, England
b. Asbury, Francis
b. Bennett, Arnold
b. DeWint, Peter
b. Dorman, Maurice Henry, Sir
b. Garnett, Richard
b. Hall, Joe
b. Mosley, Oswald Ernald, Sir
b. Treece, Henry
b. Walton, Izaak

b. Wilson, Sarah

Stainborough, England
b. Bramah, Joseph

Stainforth, England
b. Porter, George, Sir

Staleybridge, England
b. Porter, William James

Stamford, England
b. Sargent, Malcolm, Sir
b. Sherwood, Mary Martha

Stanmore, England
b. Bron, Eleanor

Stepney, England
b. Sheppard, Jack

Steventon, England
b. Austen, Jane

Steying, England
b. Dashwood, Elizabeth Monica

Stiffkey, England
d. Bailey, Frederick Marshman

Stithians, England
b. Spargo, John

Stockport, England
b. Back, George, Sir
d. Ali, Ahmed

Stockton, England
b. Sheraton, Thomas

Stockwell, England
d. Daryush, Elizabeth Bridges

Stoke, England
b. Bentham, George

Stoke Poges, England
d. Coke, Edward, Sir
d. Watts, Isaac

Stoke-on-Trent, England
b. Craik, Dinah Maria Mulock
b. Leek, Sybil
b. Matthews, Stanley, Sir
b. Slash
b. Wain, John Barrington
b. Wedgwood, Thomas

Stone, England
b. Wilson, A(ndrew) N(orman)

Stoneleigh, England
b. Parkes, Henry, Sir

Stony Stratford, England
b. Eaton, Theophilus

Storrington, England
d. Tyrrell, George

Stourbridge, England
b. Richardson, Benjamin

Stradbrooke, Suffolk, England
b. Grosseteste, Robert

Stratford-upon-Avon, England
b. Hopkins, Gerard Manley
b. Shakespeare, William
b. Trevelyan, George Macaulay
d. Corelli, Marie
d. Curry, John (Anthony)
d. Hathaway, Anne
d. Priestley, (J)ohn (B)oynton
d. Shakespeare, William

Streatham, England
b. Bax, Arnold Edward Trevor, Sir
d. Dyce, William
d. Maxim, Hiram Stevens, Sir

Streatley, England
d. Binyon, Laurence

Stroud, England
b. Lee, Laurie
d. Awdry, W(ilbert Vere)

Sturmer, England
b. Rampling, Charlotte

Sturminster, England
d. Powys, Theodore Francis

Styal, England
b. Waite, Terry

Styche, England
b. Clive, Robert

Sudbury, England
b. Gainsborough, Thomas
d. Blunden, Edmund Charles
d. Perkin, William Henry, Sir

Suffolk, England
b. Bacon, Nathaniel
b. Cavendish, Thomas
b. Doughty, Charles Montagu
b. Fiennes, Ralph
b. Lowe, Nick
b. Moodie, Susanna
b. Munnings, Alfred James, Sir
b. Winthrop, John
d. Kennedy, Joseph Patrick, Jr.
d. Neill, A(lexander) S(utherland)

Sunderland, England
b. Daiches, David
b. Stewart, David
b. Stewart, Mary (Florence Elinor)
b. Swan, Joseph Wilson, Sir

Surbiton, England
b. Heinemann, William
d. Cooper, Giles (Stannus)

Surrey, England
b. Alden, Priscilla Mullens
b. Beck, Jeff
b. Branson, Richard
b. Malthus, Thomas Robert
b. Mayle, Peter

b. Moore, George Edward
b. Tryon, William
b. William of Ockham
d. Angell, Norman
d. Cooke, William Fothergil, Sir
d. Denny, Reginald Leigh
d. Hampson, Frank
d. Lewes, George Henry
d. Panter-Downes, Mollie
d. Tedder, Arthur William Tedder, Baron

Sussex, England
b. Cobden, Richard
b. Godden, Rumer
b. Joseph, Helen
b. Sheridan, Nicollette
d. Agar, Herbert Sebastian
d. Ashton, Frederick William, Sir
d. Barnes, Ernest William
d. Douglas, Alfred Bruce, Lord
d. Fox, George
d. Godfrey, Isadore
d. Homolka, Oscar
d. MacMillan, Harold
d. McLaren, Bruce Leslie
d. Murray, James
d. Sheridan, Clare Consuelo
d. Walker, John

Sutton, England
b. Burgoyne, John, Sir
b. Cox, Constance
b. Crisp, Quentin
b. Knight, George Wilson

Sutton Courtney, England
d. Asquith, Herbert Henry

Sutton Place, England
d. Getty, J(ean) Paul

Sutton Scotney, England
d. Rank, J(oseph) Arthur

Swallowfield, England
d. Mitford, Mary Russell

Swanage, England
b. Meade, James Edward

Swanmore, England
b. Leacock, Stephen Butler

Swardeston, England
b. Cavell, Edith Louisa

Swindon, England
b. Dors, Diana
b. Wolfenden, John Frederick, Sir

Sydenham, England
d. Paxton, Joseph, Sir

Tadworth, England
d. Hope-Hawkins, Anthony, Sir
d. Newman, Ernest

Tamworth-on-Arden, England
d. Drake, Nick

Taplow, England
d. Spencer, Stanley, Sir

Tardebigg, England
b. Vane, John Robert, Sir

Taunton, England
b. Agutter, Jenny
b. Daniel, Samuel
b. Kinglake, Alexander William
b. Trenchard, Hugh Montague, First
   Viscount
d. Waugh, Evelyn Arthur St. John

Tavistock, England
b. Drake, Francis, Sir
d. Eyre, Edward John

Teddington, England
d. Blackmore, Richard Doddridge
d. Hales, Stephen
d. Hill, Benny

Temple Grafton, England
b. Hathaway, Anne

Temple Newsom, England
b. Darnley, Henry Stuart, Lord

Tenterden, England
b. Frost, David

Tetbury, England
d. Huxley, Elspeth Josceline Grant

Tewkesbury, England
b. Green, Henry

Teynham, England
d. Andrew, Prince of Russia

Thakeham, England
b. Massey, Anna

Thame, England
d. Hampden, John

Thames Ditton, England
b. DeDuve, Christian Rene Marie
   Joseph

Theobalds, England
d. James I

Thetford, England
b. Paine, Thomas

Thirsk, England
d. Herriot, James

Thorngrove, England
b. Bonaparte, Louis Lucien

Thornhill, England
d. Michell, John

Thornton, England
b. Bronte, Anne
b. Bronte, Charlotte
b. Bronte, Emily Jane
b. Bronte, Patrick Branwell
d. Coleridge-Taylor, Samuel

Thornton-le-street, England
b. Rolle of Hampole, Richard

Thorpe-le-Soken, England
d. Byng, Julian Hedworth George,
   Viscount

Thurcaston, England
b. Latimer, Hugh

Ticehurst, England
d. Dykes, John Bacchus

Tinwhistle, England
b. Westwood, Vivienne

Tisbury, England
b. Hinton, Christopher, Sir
d. Stern, James

Todmoor, England
b. Cockcroft, John Douglas, Sir

Todmorden, England
b. Emerson, Keith
b. Wilkinson, Geoffrey

Tonbridge, England
b. Andrews, Harry
b. Fowler, Henry Watson
b. Powell, Cecil Frank

Torquay, England
b. Christie, Agatha Mary Clarissa
   Miller, Dame
d. Knowles, James Sheridan
d. Lytton, Edward George Earle
   Lytton Bulwer-Lytton, 1st Baron
   Lytton
d. Maude, Cyril
d. O'Casey, Sean
d. Scoresby, William
d. Singer, Isaac Merrit

Totnes, England
b. Babbage, Charles

Tottenham, England
b. Hill, George Birkbeck Norman
d. Hone, William

Totteridge, England
b. Manning, Henry Edward

Toxteth Park, England
b. Horrocks, Jeremiah
d. Horrocks, Jeremiah

Trebetherick, England
d. Betjeman, John, Sir

Tring, England
b. Massey, Gerald

Trotton, England
b. Otway, Thomas

Trowbridge, England
b. Bullock, Alan Louis Charles
b. Pitman, Isaac
d. Crabbe, George

Trumpington, England
b. Henty, George Alfred

Truro, England
b. Foote, Samuel
b. Lander, Richard Lemon
b. Tiller, Rogers
d. Brown, George Alfred

Tunbridge Wells, England
b. Douglas, Keith Castellain
b. Guthrie, Tyrone, Sir
b. McCowen, Alec
b. McLaglen, Victor
d. Cecil, Edgar Algernon Robert
d. Goossens, Leon Jean
d. Maitland, John
d. Mantovani, Annunzio

Tunstead, England
b. Brindley, James

Turnhurst, England
d. Brindley, James

Twickenham, England
b. Tomlinson, Jill
d. Berkeley, William, Sir
d. DeLaMare, Walter
d. Fisher, Terence
d. Oliphant, Laurence
d. Pope, Alexander

Twyford, England
b. Price, Dennis

Tynemouth, England
b. Westall, Robert Atkinson

Uffington, England
b. Hughes, Thomas

Ulverston, England
b. Laurel, Stan

Upham, England
b. Young, Edward

Upminster, England
b. Johnson, Richard

Upper Holloway, England
b. Blount, Charles

Upton, England
b. Lister, Joseph

Upton-on-Severn, England
b. Mansell, Nigel

Usk, England
b. Wallace, Alfred Russell

Uxbridge, England
b. Nicholson, Ben
d. Gill, Eric

Virginia Water, England
d. Gibson, Wilfred Wilson
d. Heath, Ted
d. Uspenskii, Petr Dem'yanovich

Wakefield, England
b. Gissing, George Robert
b. Hepworth, Barbara, Dame

b. Longden, Johnny
b. McCormick, Anne (Elizabeth)
   O'Hare
b. Mercer, David
b. Storey, David Malcolm
d. Richard, Duke of York

Walker-on-Tyne, England
b. Burdon, Eric

Wallasey, England
b. Christiansen, Arthur
b. Crichton, Charles
b. Fry, E Maxwell
b. Lewis, Saunders
b. Stapledon, Olaf

Wallingford, England
d. Christie, Agatha Mary Clarissa
   Miller, Dame
d. Inge, William Ralph
d. Rotha, Paul

Wallington, England
b. Crane, Eva

Wallsend, England
b. Kennedy, Paul (Michael)

Walmer, England
b. Bridges, Robert Seymour
d. Lister, Joseph

Walsall, England
b. Jerome, Jerome Klapka

Waltham Cross, England
b. Ballard, Russ(ell)

Walthamstow, England
b. Morris, William
b. Williams, Billy

Walton-on-Thames, England
b. Andrews, Julie
b. Ertz, Susan
b. Rodney, George Brydges, Baron
b. Walton, Tony

Wandsworth, England
d. Joyce, William

Wansford, England
b. Peach, Charles William

Wantage, England
b. Alfred the Great
b. Butler, Joseph

Wardington, England
b. Marston, John

Warfield Dale, England
d. Boulting, John

Warlingham, England
d. Swan, Joseph Wilson, Sir

Warwickshire, England
b. Bentley, John
b. Congreve, Richard
b. Drayton, Michael

b. Eliot, George

Washington, England
d. Ireland, John Nicholson

Watford, England
b. Anstey, Edgar Harold McFarlane
b. Clarke, Thomas Ernest Bennett
b. Grillo, John
b. Moore, Gerald
d. Bush, Alan (Dudley)
d. Livesey, Roger

Wavertree, England
b. Birrell, Augustine

Weald, England
b. Caxton, William
b. Lyly, John

Wednesbury, England
b. Bayliss, William Maddock, Sir

Weedon, England
b. Carroll, Leo G

Welbourne, England
b. Robertson, William Robert, Sir

Wellington, England
b. Benson, Arthur Christopher
d. Tylor, Edward Bennett, Sir

Wells, England
b. Garrod, Heathcote William
b. Goudge, Elizabeth
b. Pearson, Cyril Arthur, Sir

Welwyn Garden City, England
b. Purdom, Edmund
d. Gibbon, Lewis Grassic
d. Howard, Ebenezer, Sir
d. Young, Edward

Wembley, England
b. Churchill, Diana Josephine
b. Moon, Keith

Wendover, England
b. Payne-Gaposchkin, Cecilia (Helena)

Wessex, England
b. Boniface, Saint

West Brighton, England
d. Browne, Phiz

West Bronwich, England
b. Carroll, Madeleine

West Cobham, England
b. Addison, John

West Ham, England
b. Lodge, Thomas

West Hartlepool, England
b. Mackenzie, Compton

West Horsley, England
b. Ogilvy, David Mackenzie

West Kirby, England
b. Lloyd, Selwyn

West Liss, England
d. Opie, Peter Mason

West Malvern, England
d. Roget, Peter Mark

West Milton, England
d. Allsop, Kenneth

West Sussex, England
d. Goring, Marius
d. Guinness, Alec, Sir

West Wickham, England
b. Carew, Thomas

Westbury, England
b. Bartlett, Vernon

Westcliff, England
b. Biggs, Edward George Power

Westcliff-on-Sea, England
b. Wilding, Michael

Westerham, England
b. Wolfe, James

Westhorpe, England
b. Clarke, John

Westhoughton, England
b. Shaw, Robert

Westminster, England
b. Clark, Colin Grant
b. Edward I
b. Edward V
b. Hickey, William
b. Jonson, Ben(jamin)
d. Caxton, William
d. Henry III
d. Henry VIII
d. Jonson, Ben(jamin)
d. Purcell, Henry
d. Pye, Henry
d. Skelton, John

Westmoreland, England
b. Staunton, Howard
d. Martineau, Harriet

Weston-super-Mare, England
b. Archer, Jeffrey Howard
b. Blackmore, Ritchie
b. Cleese, John Marwood
b. Greenhill, Basil
b. Love, Augustus Edward Hough
d. Booth, Joseph

Weston-under-Penyard, England
b. Whiffen, Marcus

Westport, England
b. Hobbes, Thomas

Westward, England
b. Bragg, William Henry, Sir

Weybridge, England
b. Bisset, Jacqueline Fraser
b. Davis, Colin Rex, Sir
b. Hughes, Richard Arthur Warren
d. Ayres, Ruby Mildred
d. Deeping, (George) Warwick
d. Laban, Rudolf von

Weymouth, England
b. Peacock, Thomas Love
d. Henty, George Alfred

Wheathampstead, England
b. Owen, (John) Reginald

Whitby, England
b. Bateson, William
b. Jameson, Margaret Storm
b. Scoresby, William

Whitchurch, England
b. Denning, Alfred Thompson
b. Soane, John, Sir

White Waltham, England
b. Wellesley, Dorothy Violet

Whitechapel, England
b. Mankowitz, Wolf

Whitefield, England
b. Smith, Dodie

Whitewell, England
b. Davis, Joe
b. Myers, Norman

Whitstable, England
d. Horn, Alfred Aloysius

Whittington, England
b. Sturgeon, William

Whitton, England
b. Lovesey, Peter Harmer

Wickham, England
d. Warton, Joseph

Widford, England
b. Eliot, John

Widness, England
b. Barkla, Charles Glover

Wigan, England
b. Belmont, Eleanor Robson

Willoughby, England
b. Smith, John

Wilmslow, England
d. Kopal, Zdenek

Wiltshire, England
b. Balchin, Nigel Marlin
b. Clarendon, Edward Hyde, Earl of
b. Elyot, Thomas, Sir
b. Parker, Thomas
b. Sandwich, John Montagu
d. Donald, James
d. Ingenhousz, Jan

Wimbledon, England
b. Gardiner, Reginald
b. Gore, Charles
b. Heyer, Georgette
b. Pullein-Thompson, Diana
d. Esmond, Jill

Wimborne Minster, England
b. Fripp, Robert
b. LeFleming, Christopher Kaye

Winborne, England
b. Prior, Matthew

Wincanton, England
d. Mallock, William Hurrell

Winchcomb, England
d. Parrington, Vernon L(ouis)

Winchester, England
b. Aelfric
b. Cazenove, Christopher
b. Grundy, Hugh
b. Henry III
b. Irving, Robert Augustine
b. Toye, Francis
b. Warnock, (Helen) Mary (Wilson)
d. Austen, Jane
d. Denning, Alfred Thompson
d. Irving, Robert Augustine
d. Justice, James Robertson
d. Owsley, Frank Lawrence
d. Porter, Rodney Robert
d. Sopwith, Thomas O M, Sir
d. Walton, Izaak

Windsor, England
b. Alice
b. Collier, Constance
b. Edward III
b. Fiennes (Twisleton Wykeham),
   Ranulph
b. Henry VI
b. Knight, Charles
b. Mountbatten of Burma, Louis
   Mountbatten, Earl
b. Williams, Simon
d. Bonham, John Henry
d. Charteris, Leslie
d. Deluc, Jean Andre
d. George III
d. George IV
d. Hartnell, Norman Bishop, Sir
d. Marlborough, John Churchill, Duke
d. Spry, Constance

Windsor Castle, England
d. Thompson, John S(parrow) D(avid),
   Sir

Winestead, England
b. Marvell, Andrew

Wing, England
d. Meres, Francis

Wingate, England
b. Unsworth, Barry (Foster)

Winsford, England
b. Bevin, Ernest

Wisbech, England
b. Clarkson, Thomas
b. Godwin, William

Witham, England
d. Rayleigh, John William Strutt,
   Baron
d. Sayers, Dorothy Leigh

Withyham, England
d. Germain, George Sackville
d. Wellesley, Dorothy Violet

Wittersham, England
d. Symons, Arthur William

Woburn, England
b. Paxton, Joseph, Sir

Woking, England
b. Ogilvy, Ian
d. Bentley, Walter Owen
d. Henley, William Ernest –

Wolverhampton, England
b. Chappell, William
b. Noyes, Alfred
b. Teyte, Maggie, Dame
b. Underhill, Evelyn

Wolverley, England
b. Baskerville, John

Wood Green, England
b. Swinnerton, Frank Arthur

Woodbridge, England
b. Eno, Brian

Woodbury, England
d. LeFleming, Christopher Kaye

Woodford, England
b. Crankshaw, Edward
b. Patmore, Coventry Kersey Dighton
b. Smith, Sydney
b. Street, George Edmund

Woodley, England
b. Barker, Ernest, Sir

Woodstock, England
b. Churchill, Randolph Henry Spencer,
   Lord
b. Churchill, Winston Leonard
   Spencer, Sir
b. Edward the Black Prince

Woolsthorpe, England
b. Newton, Isaac, Sir

Woolwich, England
b. Gordon, Charles George

Worcester, England
b. Brett, Simon Anthony Lee
b. Douglas, Alfred Bruce, Lord
b. Mason, Dave
b. Morris, William Richard
b. Wilding, Michael
b. Wood, Henry, Mrs.
d. Sherwood, Mary Martha

Hameenkyro, Finland
b. Sillanpaa, Frans E

Helsingfors, Finland
b. Westermarck, Edward Alexander

Helsinki, Finland
b. Anhava, Tuomas
b. Borg, Kim
b. Granit, Ragnar Arthur
b. Kurri, Jarri
b. Nordenskiold, Nils Adolph Erik,
Baron
b. Stiller, Mauritz
b. Tanner, Valno Alfred
b. Virtanen, Artturi Llmari
b. Waltari, Mika
d. Aalto, Alvar Henrik Hugo
d. Andreyev, Leonid Nikolayevich
d. Bryant, Hugh
d. Gaines, Lee
d. Kekkonen, Urho Kaleva
d. Kolehmainen, Hannes
d. Nurmi, Paavo Johannes
d. Paasikivi, Juho Kusti
d. Ritola, Ville
d. Sillanpaa, Frans E
d. Stahlberg, Kaarlo Juho
d. Tanner, Valno Alfred
d. Virtanen, Artturi Llmari
d. Waltari, Mika

Hiitola, Finland
b. Talvela, Martti Olavi

Jakobstad, Finland
b. Runeberg, Johan Ludwig

Jarvenpaa, Finland
d. Sibelius, Jean

Juva, Finland
d. Talvela, Martti Olavi

Knokkala, Finland
d. Repin, Ilya Yefimovich

Kuopio, Finland
b. Kolehmainen, Hannes

Kuortane, Finland
b. Aalto, Alvar Henrik Hugo

Kyrkslatt, Finland
b. Saarinen, Eero

Lahti, Finland
b. Nieminen, Toni

Lapinlahti, Finland
d. Westermarck, Edward Alexander

Louhissaari, Finland
b. Mannerheim, Carl Gustav Emil,
Baron

Oripaa, Finland
b. Holkeri, Harri (Hermanni)

Peraseinajoki, Finland
b. Ritola, Ville

Pielavesi, Finland
b. Kekkonen, Urho Kaleva

Rantasalmi, Finland
b. Saarinen, Eliel

Suomusselmi, Finland
b. Stahlberg, Kaarlo Juho

Tampere, Finland
b. Paasikivi, Juho Kusti

Tavastehus, Finland
b. Sibelius, Jean

Turku, Finland
b. Chorell, Walentin
b. Koivisto, Mauno Henrik
b. Nurmi, Paavo Johannes
d. Paasio, Rafael

Turtola, Finland
b. Lipponen, Paavo (T.)

Uskela, Finland
b. Paasio, Rafael

Veteli, Finland
b. Aho, Esko (Tapani)

FLANDERS

Dixmuide, Flanders
d. Clemens non Papa, Jacobus

Ghent, Flanders
b. Charles V

Renescure, Flanders
b. Comines, Philippe de

Rupelmonde, Flanders
b. Mercator, Gerhardus

Ypres, Flanders
b. Clemens non Papa, Jacobus

FRANCE

b. Bernard De Chartres
b. Boffrand, Gabriel Germain
b. Brunhoff, Jean de
b. Cartier, Pierre C
b. Charles, VII
b. Clement, V
b. Cohn-Bendit, Daniel
b. Condillac, Etienne Bonnot de
b. Dolomieu, Deodat Guy Gratet de
b. Dumont d'Urville, Jules Sebastian
Cesar
b. Garretta, Michel
b. Hansen, Georges
b. Hebert, Jacques Rene
b. Jarre, Jean-Michel
b. Kauffman, Jean-Paul
b. Lai, Francis
b. Louis, VII
b. Louis, XII
b. Louiseboulanger
b. Manasseh ben Israel

b. Michelin, Edouard
b. Normandin, Jean-Louis
b. Reard, Louis
b. Rebbot, Olivier
b. Rigaud, Hyacinthe
b. Sorel, Albert
b. Sully, Maximilien de Bethune, Duc
b. Tuck, Lily
b. Wittig, Monique
d. Baker, Hobey
d. Barres, (Auguste) Maurice
d. Ben Barka, Mehdi
d. Charles, VI
d. Charles, VII
d. Clement, Rene
d. Conde, Prince de
d. Condillac, Etienne Bonnot de
d. Crevecoeur, (Hector) St. John de
d. Diaz, Jose de la Cruz Porfirio
d. Dreyfus, Alfred
d. Gres, Alix
d. Haussmann, Georges Eugene
d. Holbach, Baron d'
d. Hulme, Thomas Ernest
d. Jean de Meun
d. Louis, VII
d. Louis, XII
d. Louis, Pierre Charles Alexandre
d. McGee, Frank
d. Peguy, Charles Pierre
d. Ramus, Petrus
d. Richardson, George Taylor
d. Richthofen, Manfred von, Baron
d. Rosenberg, Issac
d. Saint-Exupery, Antoine (Jean
Baptiste Marie Roger) de
d. Sully, Maximilien de Bethune, Duc
d. Vaudreuil-Cavagnal, Marquis de
d. Wagner, Roger Frances

Abloville, France
d. Marmontel, Jean Francois

Agen, France
b. Scaliger, Joseph Justus

Ahuille, France
b. Sorin, Edward Frederick

Aigueperse, France
b. L'Hopital, Michel de

Aisne, France
b. LaFontaine, Jean de

Aix-en-Provence, France
b. Cezanne, Paul
b. Milhaud, Darius
b. Tournefort, Joseph Pitton de
b. Ungaro, Emanuel Matteotti
d. Cezanne, Paul
d. Guilbert, Yvette
d. Peiresc, Nicholas-Claude Fabri de

Aix-la-Chapelle, France
b. Charlemagne
b. Regnault, Henri Victor

Aix-les-Bains, France
d. Miliukov, Pavel Nikolayevich
d. Rochefort, Henri

Ajaccio, Corsica, France
b. Bonaparte, Jerome

Bealieu, France
d. Bennett, James Gordon, Jr.

Beaugency, France
b. Charles, Jacques-Alexandre-Cesar

Beaugensier, France
b. Peiresc, Nicholas-Claude Fabri de

Beaumont-Hamel, France
d. Saki

Beaumont-de-Lomagne, France
b. Fermat, Pierre de

Beaumont-en-Auge, France
b. Laplace, Pierre Simon, Marquis de

Beaune, France
b. Monge, Gaspard
d. Copeau, Jacques

Beauvais, France
b. Givenchy, Hubert James Marcel
Taffin de
d. Oudry, Jean-Baptiste

Bedous, France
b. Laclede, Pierre

Beigles, France
b. Dache, Lilly

Bellac, France
b. Giraudoux, Jean

Bellay, France
b. Brillat-Savarin, Jean Anthelme

Bellebat, France
d. L'Hopital, Michel de

Belleme, France
d. Martin du Gard, Roger

Belleville, France
d. Favart, Charles Simon

Belloy Saint Leonard, France
b. Leclerc, Jacques-Philippe

Belloy en Senterre, France
d. Seeger, Alan

Bercheron, France
d. Davidson, Jo

Bernwiller, France
b. Henner, Jean Jacques

Besancon, France
b. Chardonnet, Louis Marie Hilaire
Bernigaud
b. Fourier, Francois Marie Charles
b. Goudimel, Claude
b. Hugo, Victor Marie
b. Lumiere, Auguste Marie Louis
b. Lumiere, Louis Jean
b. Proudhon, Pierre Joseph

Bessines, France
b. Valadon, Suzanne

Beziers, France
b. Faure, Edgar Jean

Biarritz, France
b. Bergerac, Jacques
b. Bergerac, Michel C
b. Carol, Martine
d. Sarasate, Pablo de

Bignon, France
b. Mirabeau, Honore Gabriel Riquetti

Blainville, France
b. Duchamp, Marcel

Blois, France
b. Aries, Philippe
b. Houdin, Jean Eugene Robert
b. Lorjou, Bernard Joseph Pierre
b. Thierry, Augustin
d. Catherine de Medici
d. Houdin, Jean Eugene Robert
d. Lorjou, Bernard Joseph Pierre

Bobigny, France
d. Brel, Jacques

Bois de Saint Remy, France
d. Alain-Fournier

Bois de Vincennes, France
d. Henry V

Bois-Colombes, France
d. Gramme, Zenobe Theophile

Bordeaux, France
b. Anouilh, Jean Marie Lucien Pierre
b. Black, Joseph
b. Bonheur, Rosa
b. Clement, Rene
b. Colonne, Edouard
b. Damita, Lily
b. Darracq, Alexandre
b. Darrieux, Danielle
b. Diaz de la Pena, Narciso Virgilio
b. Diop, David
b. Girard, Stephen
b. Lamoureux, Charles
b. Laparra, Raoul
b. Marquet, Albert
b. Mauriac, Francois
b. Mendes, Catulle
b. Montaigne, Michel Eyquem de
b. Montesquieu, Charles Louis de
Secondat, Baron
b. Nougues, Jean
b. Redon, Odilon
b. Renaud, Maurice
b. Richard II
b. Rode, Jacques Pierre Joseph
b. Sauguet, Henri
b. Thomas, Michel
d. D'Estournelles, Paul Henri
Benjamin Balleut de Constant,
Baron
d. Goya y Lucientes, Francisco Jose
de
d. Lichine, Alexis
d. Montaigne, Michel Eyquem de
d. Rode, Jacques Pierre Joseph

d. Tandy, James Napper
d. Tourgee, Albion Winegar

Bort-les-Orgues, France
b. Marmontel, Jean Francois

Bossy-Saint-Antoine, France
b. Dunoyer de Segonzac, Andre

Bougival, France
d. Bizet, Georges (Alexandre Cesar
Leopold)
d. Mistinguett
d. Turgenev, Ivan Sergeevich

Boulogne, France
d. Sainte-Clair Deville, Henri Etienne

Boulogne-Billancourt, France
b. Blier, Bertrand
b. Cresson, Edith Campion

Boulogne-sur-Mer, France
b. Coquelin, Benoit Constant
b. Sainte-Beuve, Charles Augustin
d. A'Beckett, Gilbert Abbott
d. Campbell, Thomas
d. Churchill, Charles
d. Lesage, Alain-Rene
d. San Martin, Jose de

Boulogne-sur-Seine, France
b. Calvet, Jacques
b. Mnouchkine, Ariane
d. Gris, Juan

Bourg-en-Bresse, France
b. Lalande, Joseph Jerome Lefrancais
de

Bourg-la-Reine, France
b. Galois, Evariste
d. Bloy, Leon Marie
d. Condorcet, Marie-Jean-Antoine

Bourges, France
b. Coeur, Jacques
b. Louis XI
b. Morisot, Berthe

Bresles, France
b. Levasseur, Nicolas Prosper

Brest, France
b. Hemon, Louis
b. Robbe-Grillet, Alain

Brestin, France
d. Antoine, Andre

Brittany, France
b. La Mettrie, Julien Offray de

Broglie, France
b. Fresnel, Augustin-Jean

Bromont-Lamothe, France
b. Bresson, Robert

Bruyeres, France
b. Lurcat, Jean Marie

Chatellerault, France
b. Chinard, Gilbert

Chatillon-sur-Loing, France
b. Coligny, Gaspard de Chatillon

Chatillon-sur-Marne, France
b. Urban II

Chatou, France
b. Derain, Andre
b. Mandel, Georges

Chauliac, France
b. Guy de Chauliac

Chavaniac, France
b. Lafayette, Marie Joseph Paul,
Marquis

Chaville, France
b. Schwob, Marcel
b. Soupault, Philippe

Chenevelles, France
b. Tiffeau, Jacques Emile

Cherbourg, France
b. Barthes, Roland (Gerard)
b. Grignard, Francois Auguste Victor
b. Marais, Jean
b. Nicolet, Jean
d. Roosevelt, Theodore, Jr.

Chevry Cossigny, France
b. Pathe, Charles

Chilleurs-aux-Bois, France
b. Vionnet, Madeleine

Chimay, France
d. Froissart, Jean

Chinon, France
b. Rabelais, Francois
d. Henry II

Choisy le Roi, France
d. Rouget de Lisle, Claude Joseph

Ciboure, France
b. Ravel, Maurice Joseph
d. Barrientos, Maria

Clairvaux, France
d. Bernard of Clairvaux, Saint

Clamart, France
d. Berdyayev, Nikolay Aleksandrovich
d. Carne, Marcel Albert

Clamecy, France
b. Rolland, Romain

Clermont, France
b. Pascal, Blaise
d. Apollinaris Sidonius, Gaius Sollius

Clermont-Ferrand, France
b. Besse, Georges Noel
b. Michelin, Francois

Cluny, France
b. Prudhon, Pierre-Paul

Cognac, France
b. Francis I
b. Monnet, Jean Omer Marie Gabriel

Collioure, France
d. Machado (y Ruiz), Antonio

Collonges, France
b. Bocuse, Paul

Colmar, France
b. Bartholdi, Auguste
b. Jean, Prince
d. Meyerowitz, Jan

Colombes, France
b. Guattari, Felix

Colombey les deux Eglises, France
d. DeGaulle, Charles Andre Joseph
Marie

Colombieres, France
b. Carriere, Jean-Claude

Compiegne, France
b. Lenglen, Suzanne

Conde, France
d. DesPres, Josquin

Conde sur l'Escaut, France
b. DesPres, Josquin

Conde-sur-Vire, France
b. Brebeuf, Jean de

Corbeil, France
b. Dauphin, Claude Le Grand Maria
Eugene

Cormeilles en Parisis, France
b. Daguerre, Louis Jacques Mande

Corte, Corsica, France
b. Bonaparte, Joseph

Cote d'Evrard, France
d. Alcock, John William, Sir

Coupvray, France
b. Braille, Louis

Courbevoie, France
b. Arletty
b. Celine, Louis-Ferdinand
b. Lartigue, Jacques-Henri Charles
Auguste
b. Rocard, Michel Louis Leon
d. Carpeaux, Jean Baptiste

Couterne, France
b. Helion, Jean

Craon, France
b. Volney, (Constantin) Francois
Chasseboeuf, Comte de

Cravant, France
d. Gilson, Etienne Henry

Creteil, France
b. Barzun, Jacques Martin
b. Gleizes, Albert L

Croisset, France
d. Flaubert, Gustave

Crozon, France
b. Jouvet, Louis

Cuiseaux, France
b. Vuillard, (Jean) Edouard

Cuth, France
b. Ramus, Petrus

Damery, France
b. Lecouvreur, Adrienne

Dax, France
d. Utrillo, Maurice

Deauville, France
d. Boudin, Eugene Louis
d. Ford, Ford Madox

Decazevelle, France
b. Calve, Emma

Decize, France
b. Saint-Just, Louis Antoine Leon de

Deusto, France
b. Cassou, Jean

Deville-les-Rouen, France
b. Beregovoy, Pierre (Eugene)

Dieppe, France
b. Broglie, Louis Prince De
b. Maupassant, Guy de
d. John, Gwendolyn Mary

Dierize, France
b. About, Edmond-Francois-Valentin

Dieuze, France
b. Charpentier, Gustave

Digne, France
d. David-Neel, Alexandra

Dijon, France
b. Bossuet, Jacques Benigne
b. Cabet, Etienne
b. Courtois, Bernard
b. Darcy, Henri Philibert Gaspard
b. Eiffel, Alexandre Gustave
b. Guillemin, Roger Charles Louis
b. Philip the Good
b. Rameau, Jean-Philippe
b. Rich, Claudius James
d. Giraud, Henri Honore
d. Sluter, Claus

Dinan, France
b. Du Guesclin, Bertrand

Hendaye, France
d. Loti, Pierre

Hermanville, France
b. Touraine, Alain (Louis)

Herouel, France
b. Fouquier-Tinville, Antoine Quentin

Hesdin, France
b. Prevost d'Exiles, Antoine Francois, Abbe

Honfleur, France
b. Boudin, Eugene Louis
b. Satie, Erik

Hyeres, France
d. Michelet, Jules

Ile Bourbon, France
b. Bourdonnais, Louis Charles de la

Ile d'Oleron, France
b. Berge, Pierre (Vital Georges)

Ile d'Yeu, France
d. Petain, Henri Philippe

Irancy, Yonne, France
b. Soufflot, Jacques Germain

Isenheim, France
d. Holbein, Hans, the Elder

Issoudun, France
d. Chevalier, Jules

Jarcy, France
d. Boieldieu, Francois Adrien

Jarnac, France
b. Mitterrand, Francois (Maurice Marie)

Joigny, France
b. Ayme, Marcel

Jouy, France
b. Jouy, Victor (Joseph-Etienne) de

Juan les Pins, France
d. Elliott, Maxine
d. Hopwood, Avery

Kerlouanec, France
d. Laennec, Rene Theophile Hyacinthe

L'Isle Sorgue, France
b. Char, Rene (Emile)

L'Isle-Adam, France
d. Breuil, Henri Abbe

La Badere, France
d. Caillie, Rene Auguste

La Baslide-Fortumiere, France
b. Murat, Joachim

La Baule, France
d. Vuillard, (Jean) Edouard

La Bruyere, France
b. Mathiez, Albert

La Celle-Saint-Cloud, France
b. Belloc, Hilaire

La Chanaie, France
d. Lesseps, Ferdinand Marie de

La Chapelle-d'Angillon, France
b. Alain-Fournier

La Ciotat, France
d. Francescatti, Zino Rene

La Cote-Saint-Andre, France
b. Berlioz, Hector

La Fleche, France
b. D'Estournelles, Paul Henri Benjamin Balleut de Constant, Baron
b. Picard, Jean
d. Charlevoix, Pierre Francis Xavier de

La Haye, France
b. Descartes, Rene

La Hoguette, France
b. Marchais, Georges (Rene Louis)

La Riviere, France
b. Le Play, Guillaume Frederic

La Rochelle, France
b. DeVries, David Pietersen
b. Fromentin, Eugene
b. Laroche, Guy
d. Fromentin, Eugene

La Trinite-sur-Mer, France
b. Le Pen, Jean-Marie

Lacabarede, France
b. Calas, Jean

Laferte-Milon, France
b. Racine, Jean Baptiste

Lancieux, France
d. Service, Robert William

Landrecies, France
b. Dupleix, Joseph Francois
d. Owen, Wilfred

Langres, France
b. Diderot, Denis

Languedoc, France
b. Psalmanazar, George
d. Du Guesclin, Bertrand

Lanurium, France
b. Antoninus Pius

Laon, France
b. Marquette, Jacques, Pere

d. Bodin, Jean

Laval, France
b. Jarry, Alfred
b. Pare, Ambroise
b. Rousseau, Henri

Lavandou, France
d. Gordon-Lazareff, Helene

Le Bar, France
b. Grasse, Francois Joseph Paul de, Count

Le Blanc-Mesnil, France
b. Guillem, Sylvie

Le Cannet, France
d. Anderson, Margaret (Carolyn)
d. Bonnard, Pierre

Le Cateau, France
b. Matisse, Henri Emile Benoit

Le Chesnay, France
d. Bravais, Auguste

Le Croisic, France
d. Becquerel, Antoine Henri

Le Havre, France
b. Coty, Rene (Jules Gustave)
b. Delavigne, Jean Francois Casimir
b. Dubuffet, Jean
b. Dufy, Raoul (Ernest Joseph)
b. Friesz, Othon
b. Honegger, Arthur
b. Scudery, Madeleine de
d. Coty, Rene (Jules Gustave)
d. Cremazie, Octave

Le Mans, France
b. Caillaux, Joseph Marie Auguste
b. Dolmetsch, Arnold
b. Francaix, Jean
b. Henry II

Le Pecq, France
b. Tati, Jacques

Le Pellerin, France
b. Fouche, Joseph

Le Plessis-Aux-Bois, France
b. Jahan, Marine

Le Puy, France
b. Wagner, Roger Frances

Le Verger Charry, France
d. Garnett, David

Le Vesinet, France
d. Alain

Lempdes, France
b. Lamy, Jean Baptist

Lens, France
b. Carpentier, Georges

Les Andelys, France
b. Blanchard, Francois

Les Laumets, France
b. Cadillac, Antoine de la Mothe

Lethor, France
d. Brodovitch, Alexey

Levandou, France
d. Reyer, (Louis) Ernest (Etienne)

Leyden, France
d. Scaliger, Joseph Justus

Lezigne, France
b. Chereau, Patrice

Libourne, France
b. Atget, Eugene

Lille, France
b. Adoree, Renee
b. DeGaulle, Charles Andre Joseph
    Marie
b. Duvivier, Julien
b. Faidherbe, Louis Leon Cesar
b. Lalo, Edouard Victor Antoine
b. Lefebvre, Georges
b. Monnoyer, Jean-Baptiste
b. Perrin, Jean Baptiste

Lillebonne, France
b. Ernaux, Annie

Limay, France
d. Chausson, Ernest

Limoges, France
b. Antoine, Andre
b. Bugeaud de la Piconnerie, Thomas
    Robert
b. Dumas, Roland
b. Renoir, (Pierre) Auguste

Lisieux, France
d. Nicholas of Oresme
d. Therese of Lisieux, Saint

Loches, France
b. Vigny, Alfred Victor, Comte de
d. Sforza, Ludovico

Lodeve, France
b. Auric, Georges
b. Fleury, Andre Hercule de

Loire Valley, France
d. Ogilvy, David Mackenzie

Loire-et-cher, France
d. Rochambeau, Jean Baptiste
    Donatien de Vimeur, Comte

Loiret, France
b. Becquerel, Antoine-Cesar

Lons-le-Saunier, France
b. Rouget de Lisle, Claude Joseph

Lorette, France
b. Prost, Alain Marie Pascal

Lorient, France
b. Masse, Victor
b. Simon, Jules Francois

Lorraine, France
b. Kaas, Patricia
b. Lorrain, Claude
b. Margaret of Anjou

Louey, France
b. Duclos, Jacques

Lourdes, France
b. Bernadette of Lourdes, Saint

Louveciennes, France
d. Coty, Francois Marie Joseph
    Spoturno
d. Dache, Lilly
d. Leconte de Lisle, Charles Marie
    Rene

Louvre, France
d. Louis, XIII

Lozere, France
b. Chaptal, Jean Antoine, Comte de
    Chanteloup

Lugdunum, France
b. Caracalla, Marcus Aurelius
    Antonius

Lumeville, France
b. Brandel, Fernand Paul

Lunel, France
b. Feuillade, Louis

Luneville, France
b. Braudel, Fernand (Paul)
d. La Tour, Georges Dumesnil de

Luzarches, France
b. Autant-Lara, Claude

Lyons, France
b. Ampere, Andre Marie
b. Apollinaris Sidonius, Gaius Sollius
b. Bloch, Marc
b. Borel d'Hauterive, Petrus
b. Chevallier, Gabriel
b. Cochet, Henri
b. Coysevox, Antoine
b. Cret, Paul P(hilippe)
b. Farrere, Claude
b. Flandrin, Hippolyte Jean
b. Gieseking, Walter Wilhelm
b. Grolier, Jean
b. Guimard, Hector Germain
b. Jacquard, Joseph Marie
b. Jarre, Maurice
b. Jussieu, Bernard de
b. Lassale, Jean
b. l'Orme, Philibert de
b. Martinon, Jean
b. Meissonier, Jean Louis Ernest
b. Neel, Louis Eugene Felix
b. Pivot, Bernard
b. Puvis de Chavannes, Pierre Cecile
b. Radisson, Pierre Espirit
b. Recamier, Julie, Madame

b. Saint-Exupery, Antoine (Jean
    Baptiste Marie Roger) de
b. Say, Jean Baptiste
b. Tavernier, Bertrand
b. Vianney, Jean (Marie) Baptiste
b. Widor, Charles Marie Jean Albert
d. Barbie, Klaus
d. Bonaventure, Saint
d. Delavigne, Jean Francois Casimir
d. Estienne, Henri
d. Francis of Sales, St.
d. Gerson, Jean
d. Goudimel, Claude
d. Grignard, Francois Auguste Victor
d. Herriot, Edouard
d. Lumiere, Auguste Marie Louis

Lyons-la-Foret, France
d. Henry I

Macon, France
b. Lamartine, Alphonse Marie Louis
    de Prat de

Magny Cours, France
b. Laffite, Jacques Henry Sabin

Maillane, France
b. Mistral, Frederic
d. Mistral, Frederic

Maine-et-Loire, France
d. Eleanor of Aquitaine

Maisons-Lafitte, France
b. Cocteau, Jean

Malmaison, France
d. Josephine

Malrome, France
d. Toulouse-Lautrec (Monfa), (Henri
    Marie Raymond de)

Manosque, France
b. Giono, Jean
d. Giono, Jean

Mans-en-Baroeul, France
b. Butor, Michel

Mantauban, France
d. Friedel, Charles

Mantes, France
d. Philip II

Marly, France
d. Mansart, Jules Hardouin

Marne, France
b. Louis, Pierre Charles Alexandre

Marne-la-Coquette, France
d. Le Bon, Gustave

Marseilles, France
b. Artaud, Antonin
b. Bejart, Maurice
b. Casadesus, Gaby (Lhote)
b. Crespin, Regine
b. Daumier, Honore Victorin

b. Fabry, Charles
b. Fernandel
b. Francescatti, Zino Rene
b. Jourdan, Louis
b. Maurel, Victor
b. Muratore, Lucien
b. Nuyen, France
b. Petipa, Marius
b. Petri, Angelo
b. Puget, Pierre
b. Rampal, Jean-Pierre
b. Rebuffat, Gaston Louis Simon
b. Revel, Jean Francois
b. Reyer, (Louis) Ernest (Etienne)
b. Rostand, Edmond Alexis
b. Simon, Simone
b. Thiers, Adolphe
d. Alexander of Yugoslavia
d. Ampere, Andre Marie
d. Ozanam, (Antoine) Frederic
d. Phillips, Lena Madesin
d. Puget, Pierre
d. Rimbaud, (Jean Nicolas) Arthur
d. Taglioni, Maria
d. Wolf, Friedrich August

Martigues, France
b. Maurras, Charles Marie Photius

Mas Roux, France
b. Cavalier, Jean

Massy, France
d. Appert, Nicolas

Maubeuge, France
b. Mabuse, Jan de

Mauze, France
b. Caillie, Rene Auguste

Melun, France
b. Amyot, Jacques
d. Bonheur, Rosa

Menerbes, France
d. Cameron, Roderick W

Menton, France
d. Blasco-Ibanez, Vicente
d. Erickson, Eric
d. Green, John Richard
d. LeGallienne, Richard
d. Yeats, William Butler

Mercy-le-Haut, France
b. Lebrun, Albert

Merey, France
b. Quesnay, Francois

Metz, France
b. Curel, Francois de
b. Lemnitz, Tiana
b. Pierne, Gabriel
b. Schwarz-Bart, Andre
b. Thomas, (Charles Louis) Ambroise
b. Verlaine, Paul (Marie)
d. Schuman, Robert

Meudon, France
d. Celine, Louis-Ferdinand
d. DuPre, Marcel

d. Janssen, Pierre Jules Cesar
d. Rodin, Auguste

Meun-sur-Loire, France
b. Jean de Meun

Millau, France
d. Calve, Emma

Millemont, France
b. Dufresne, Charles

Mont Cenis, France
d. Charles II

Mont-Dore, France
d. Maison, Rene

Mont-Pelerin-sur-Vevey, France
d. Ferrero, Guglielmo

Mont-Saint-Pere, France
b. L'Hermitte, Leon Augustin

Mont-sous-Vaudrey, France
b. Grevy, Francois Paul Jules
d. Grevy, Francois Paul Jules

Montagne, France
b. Alain

Montargis, France
d. Boussac, Marcel

Montauban, France
b. Bourdelle, Emile-Antoine
b. Ingres, Jean Auguste Dominique
d. Azana y Diaz, Manuel

Montaud, France
b. Massenet, Jules Emile Frederic

Montbard, France
b. Buffon, Georges Louis Leclerc

Montbeliard, France
b. Cuvier, Georges, Baron

Montbrison, France
b. Boulez, Pierre

Montbron, France
b. Aulard, Francois Victor Alphonse

Montdidier, France
b. Fernel, Jean Francois

Montigny-le-Roi, France
b. Flammarion, Camille

Montigny-sur-Avre, France
b. Laval, Francois Xavier de

Montlouis-sur-Loire, France
d. Debre, Michel (Jean Pierre)

Montlucon, France
b. Messager, Andre Charles Prosper

Montmirail, France
b. Gondi, Cardinal

Montmorency, France
d. Gretry, Andre Ernest Modeste

Montpellier, France
b. Balard, Antoine-Jerome
b. Cambaceres, Jean Jacques Regis de
b. Comte, Auguste
b. Soustelle, Jacques
d. Delaunay, Robert
d. Geddes, Patrick, Sir
d. Richier, Germaine

Montreuil-sous-Bois, France
d. Clarke, Kenny

Montrouge, France
d. Gall, Franz Joseph

Montsalvy, France
b. Boule, Marcellin
d. Boule, Marcellin

Moret, France
d. Sisley, Alfred

Morlaix, France
b. Corbiere, Tristan (Edouard Joachim)
d. Corbiere, Tristan (Edouard Joachim)
d. Serusier, Paul

Mortain, France
b. Breuil, Henri Abbe

Morvan, France
d. Charcot, Jean Martin

Mougins, France
d. Picasso, Pablo Ruiz y
d. Robert, Paul

Mouilleron-en-Pareds, France
b. Clemenceau, Georges Eugene
    Benjamin
b. Lattre de Tassigny, Jean de (Marie
    Gabriel) de

Moulins, France
b. Bidault, Georges

Mulhouse, France
b. Dreyfus, Alfred
b. Loeffler, Charles Martin Tornow
b. Roebling, John Augustus
b. Werner, Alfred

Muret, France
b. Ader, Clement

Nancy, France
b. Callot, Jacques
b. Clodion
b. Dalmores, Charles
b. Galle, Emile
b. Gerard, Jean Ignace Isidore
b. Goncourt, Edmond Louis Antoine
    Huot de
b. Grandville
b. Jacob, Francois
b. Lyautey, Louis Hubert Gonzalve
b. Poincare, Jules Henri
b. Rohmer, Eric
d. Callot, Jacques
d. Coue, Emile

d. Galle, Emile

Nanterre, France
b. Genevieve, Saint

Nantes, France
b. Briand, Aristide
b. Metzinger, Jean
b. Peret, Benjamin
b. Tissot, James Joseph Jacques
b. Verne, Jules

Navarre, France
d. Borgia, Cesare

Nemours, France
b. Petit, Philippe

Nerac, France
b. Darlan, Jean Louis Xavier Francois

Neuilly, France
b. Lanvin, Bernard
b. Maazel, Lorin Varencove
b. Morgan, Michele
d. Bullitt, William Christian
d. Duchamp, Marcel
d. Gabin, Jean
d. Gurdjieff, George Ivanovitch
d. Litvak, Anatole
d. Persiani, Fanny
d. Renaud, Madeleine
d. Reynaud, Paul
d. Stein, Gertrude

Neuilly-sur-Seine, France
b. Belmondo, Jean-Paul
b. Charcot, Jean Baptiste Etienne
  Auguste
b. Gilot, Francoise
b. Hervieu, Paul-Ernest
b. Marker, Chris
b. Martin du Gard, Roger
d. Annabella
d. Clair, Rene
d. Gautier, Theophile
d. Hawkins, Screamin' Jay
d. Passy, Frederic
d. Soustelle, Jacques
d. Truffaut, Francois

Neuville-Saint-Vaast, France
b. Hennebique, Francois

Nevers, France
d. Beregovoy, Pierre (Eugene)
d. Bernadette of Lourdes, Saint

Nice, France
b. Arman
b. Binet, Alfred
b. Bonaly, Surya
b. Calmette, Albert Leon Charles
b. Cavendish, Henry
b. Garibaldi, Giuseppe
b. Gendron, Maurice
b. Mitchell, Billy
b. Veil, Simone Annie Jacob
d. Anderson, Robert
d. Berkman, Alexander
d. Brassai
d. Brieux, Eugene
d. Brown, Margaret Wise
d. Burri, Alberto

d. Chaplin, Sydney Dryden
d. Chatwin, Bruce
d. Delcasse, Theophile
d. DeReszke, Jean
d. Dorleac, Francoise
d. Du Bois, William Pene
d. Duncan, Isadora
d. Garrett, Eileen Jeanette Lyttle
d. Gombrowicz, Witold
d. Halevy, Jacques Francois Fromental
  Elie
d. Harris, Frank
d. Hirschfeld, Magnus
d. Lartique, Jacques-Henri Charles
  Auguste
d. LeRoux, Gaston
d. Maeterlinck, Maurice
d. Matisse, Henri Emile Benoit
d. Maugham, W(illiam) Somerset
d. Paganini, Niccolo
d. Reiss, Albert
d. Reuter, Paul Julius Von
d. Tamburini, Antonio
d. Valleria, Alwina

Nimes, France
b. Cremieux, Isaac-Adolphe
b. Guizot, Francois Pierre Guillaume
b. Montcalm, Louis Joseph de
b. Nicot, Jean

Niort, France
b. Clouzot, Henri-George
b. Maintenon, Francoise d'Aubigne,
  Marquise de

Nogent-sur-Marne, France
b. Sablon, Jean Georges
d. Watteau, Jean Antoine

Nohant, France
d. Sand, George

Noisy, France
b. Delannoy, Jean

Nolay, France
b. Carnot, Lazare

Normandy, France
b. Duplessis, Marie
b. Gourmont, Remy (-Marie-Charles)
  de
b. Montfort, Simon de
b. Nicholas of Oresme
b. Sorel, Georges
d. Signoret, Simone Henrietta
  Charlotte
d. Whistler, Rex

Nouvion-en-Thierache, France
b. Lavisse, Ernest

Noyelles Godault, France
b. Thorez, Maurice

Noyon, France
b. Calvin, John

Objat, France
b. Freyssinet, Eugene

Oloron Saint Marie, France
b. Singher, Martial

Opio, France
d. Coluche
d. Popov, Dusko

Orcet, France
b. Couthon, Georges

Orleans, France
b. Jogues, Isaac
b. Peguy, Charles Pierre
d. Manessier, Alfred

Ornans, France
b. Courbet, Gustave
b. Courbet, (Jean Desire) Gustave
b. Vernier, Pierre
d. Vernier, Pierre

Orne, France
b. Mollet, Guy

Orsay, France
d. Mosley, Oswald Ernald, Sir

Oullins, France
d. Jacquard, Joseph Marie

Pallet, France
b. Abelard, Pierre

Pamiers, France
b. Delcasse, Theophile
b. Faure, Gabriel Urbain

Pamplona, France
d. Thibaut, IV

Paraclete Abbey, France
d. Heloise

Paris, France
b. Adam, Adolphe Charles
b. Adam, Paul
b. Adjani, Isabelle
b. Aga Khan, Sadruddin, Prince
b. Aimee, Anouk
b. Alembert, Jean le Rond d'
b. Allais, Maurice
b. Allegret, Yves
b. Annabella
b. Anville, Jean Baptiste Bourguignon
  d'
b. Aragon, Louis Marie Antoine
  Alfred
b. Aron, Raymond Claude Ferdinand
b. Attwood, William Hollingsworth
b. Audiard, Michel
b. Aumont, Jean-Pierre
b. Aznavour, Charles
b. Bailly, Jean Sylvain
b. Baltard, Victor
b. Balthus
b. Barbier, Jules
b. Bardot, Brigitte
b. Baruch, Andre
b. Baudelaire, Charles Pierre
b. Beaumarchais, Pierre Augustin
  Caron de
b. Beauvoir, Simone de
b. Becker, Jacques

b. Becquerel, Antoine Henri
b. Belbenoit, Rene Lucien
b. Benda, Julien
b. Beranger, Pierre-Jean de
b. Bergson, Henri Louis
b. Bernanos, Georges
b. Bernhardt, Sarah
b. Berthelot, Marcellin
b. Bertillon, Alphonse
b. Bertrand, Joseph Louis Francois
b. Beuve-Mery, Hubert
b. Biddle, Francis Beverley
b. Bizet, Georges (Alexandre Cesar Leopold)
b. Blum, Leon
b. Boccaccio, Giovanni
b. Boileau(-Despreaux), Nicolas
b. Bonaparte, Francois Charles Joseph
b. Bonneville, Benjamin Louie Eulalie de
b. Boucher, Francois
b. Bougainville, Louis-Antoine de
b. Boulanger, Nadia Juliette
b. Boulle, Andre Charles
b. Bourgeois, Leon-Victor Auguste
b. Bourgeois, Louise
b. Boussingault, Jean Baptiste
b. Breguet, Louis Charles
b. Brieux, Eugene
b. Brugnon, Jacques
b. Brunhoff, Laurent de
b. Bude, Guillaume
b. Buffet, Bernard
b. Buisson, Ferdinand Edouard
b. Bunau-Varilla, Philippe Jean
b. Calvet, Corinne
b. Cambert, Robert
b. Cambon, Pierre Paul
b. Carne, Marcel Albert
b. Carnot, Nicolas Leonard Sadi
b. Caron, Leslie Clare Margaret
b. Casadesus, Jean
b. Casadesus, Robert
b. Cassini, Oleg Loiewski
b. Catherine of Valois
b. Cauchy, Augustin Louis
b. Chaban-Delmas, Jacques Pierre Michel
b. Chabrol, Claude
b. Chalgrin, Francois
b. Chaminade, Cecile
b. Chanute, Octave
b. Chapman, Christian Addison
b. Charcot, Jean Martin
b. Chardin, Jean Baptiste Simeon
b. Charles, VI
b. Charlot, Jean
b. Charpentier, Marc-Antoine
b. Charron, Pierre
b. Chausson, Ernest
b. Chautemps, Camille
b. Chauvire, Yvette
b. Chevalier, Maurice Auguste
b. Chirac, Jacques (Rene)
b. Chretien, Henri
b. Christian-Jacque
b. Cigna, Gina
b. Citroen, Andre Gustave
b. Clair, Rene
b. Clary, Robert
b. Claude, Georges
b. Clayderman, Richard
b. Cloete, Stuart
b. Cochin, Charles Nicholas
b. Colbert, Claudette
b. Coluche

b. Conde, Prince de
b. Copeau, Jacques
b. Coppee, Francois Edouard Joachim
b. Corot, Jean Baptiste Camille
b. Coubertin, Pierre de, Baron
b. Couperin, Francois
b. Cournand, Andre Frederic
b. Cousin, Victor
b. Crowninshield, Francis Welch
b. Curie, Eve
b. Curie, Pierre
b. Cyrano de Bergerac, Savinien de
b. Daniloff, Nicholas
b. Darcel, Denise
b. Dassault, Marcel
b. Daubigny, Charles Francois
b. Daudet, Leon
b. David, Jacques Louis
b. Debost, Michel H
b. Debray, Regis
b. Debre, Michel (Jean Pierre)
b. DeBroca, Philippe Claude Alex
b. Decamps, Alexandre Gabriel
b. Degas, (Hilaire Germain) Edgar
b. DeGennes, Pierre-Gilles
b. Delaroche, Hippolyte
b. Delaunay, Robert
b. Delisle, Guillaume
b. Delisle, Joseph-Nicolas
b. Delors, Jacques Lucien Jean
b. DeMontebello, Guy-Philippe
b. Deneuve, Catherine
b. De Ribes, Jacqueline
b. Destouches, Louis-Ferdinand
b. Diesel, Rudolf Christian Karl
b. Doriot, Georges Frederic
b. Dorleac, Francoise
b. D'Orsay, Alfred Guillaume, Count
b. Drake, Betsy
b. Dugdale, Richard Louis
b. Duhamel, Georges
b. Duhem, Pierre Maurice Marie
b. Dukas, Paul Abraham
b. Dumas, Alexandre
b. DuMaurier, George Louis P B
b. DuPont, Eleuthere Irenee
b. DuPont de Nemours, Pierre Samuel
b. DuPrez, Gilbert
b. Epee, Charles-Michel
b. Estienne, Henri
b. Eugene of Savoy
b. Fabius, Laurent
b. Falconet, Etienne Maurice
b. Faure, Francois Felix
b. Favart, Charles Simon
b. Feininger, Andreas (Bernhard Lyonel)
b. Fenelon, Fania
b. Feydeau, Georges
b. Fizeau, Armand Hippolyte Louis
b. Foucault, Jean Bernard Leon
b. Fouquet, Nicolas
b. Fournier, Pierre
b. France, Anatole
b. Frizon, Maud
b. Fustel de Coulanges, Numa Denis
b. Gabin, Jean
b. Gabriel, Ange-Jacques
b. Galli-Marie, Marie Celestine
b. Gamelin, Maurice Gustave
b. Gance, Abel
b. Garamond, Claude
b. Gardner, Jean Louis Charles
b. Garnier, Jean Louis Charles
b. Gauguin, Paul
b. Gaultier, Jean-Paul

b. Gavarni, Paul
b. Genet, Jean
b. Gide, Andre (Paul Guillaume)
b. Gifford, Kathie Lee
b. Gilson, Etienne Henry
b. Girardot, Annie
b. Giraud, Henri Honore
b. Godard, Benjamin Louis Paul
b. Godard, Jean Luc
b. Goldsmith, James (Michael), Sir
b. Golschmann, Vladimir
b. Goncourt, Jules Alfred Huot de
b. Goscinny, Rene
b. Gounod, Charles Francois
b. Grappelli, Stephane
b. Green, Julian (Hartridge)
b. Gres, Alix
b. Gros, Antoine Jean
b. Guilbert, Yvette
b. Guy-Blache, Alice
b. Guynemer, Georges Marie
b. Halevy, Jacques Francois Fromental Elie
b. Halevy, Ludovic
b. Halliday, Johnny
b. Hamilton, Guy
b. Harris, Augustus, Sir
b. Haussmann, Georges Eugene
b. Heim, Jacques
b. Held, Anna
b. Helvetius, Claude Adrien
b. Herold, Ferdinand
b. Herter, Christian Archibald
b. Hugo, Adele
b. Huppert, Isabelle
b. Huysmans, Joris Karl
b. Ibert, Jacques (Francois Antoine)
b. Indy, Paul (Marie Theodore Vincent d')
b. Janet, Pierre Marie Felix
b. Janssen, Pierre Jules Cesar
b. Jeanmaire, Renee Marcelle
b. Jolas, Betsy
b. Joliot(-Curie), (Jean) Frederic
b. Joliot-Curie, Irene
b. Jouhaux, Leon
b. Kaprisky, Valerie
b. Kipnis, Claude
b. Korner, Alexis
b. Laboulaye, Edouard Rose
b. Labrouste, Pierre Francois Henri
b. LaBruyere, Jean de
b. Lacan, Jacques (Marie Emile)
b. Lachaise, Gaston
b. Lacoste, Catherine
b. Lacoste, Rene
b. La Fayette, Comtesse de
b. La Fosse, Charles de
b. Lancret, Nicolas
b. Langman, Claude Berel
b. Lapidus, Ted
b. LaRochefoucauld, Francois, Duc de
b. Laskin, Lily
b. La Tour du Pin, Patrice de
b. Laurencin, Marie
b. Laurens, Henri
b. Laveran, Charles Louis Alphonse
b. Lavoisier, Antoine Laurent
b. Layard, Austen Henry, Sir
b. Leaud, Jean-Pierre
b. Leboyer, Frederick
b. Le Brun, Charles
b. Le Chatelier, Henry-Louis
b. Legendre, Adrien Marie
b. Legrand, Michel Jean
b. Leloir, Luis Federico

b. Lelong, Lucien
b. LeLouch, Claude
b. Lemonnier, Pierre Charles
b. Lenclos, Ninon de
b. L'Enfant, Pierre Charles
b. LeNotre, Andre
b. LeRoux, Gaston
b. Lescot, Pierre
b. Le Vau, Louis
b. Levy, Raymond
b. Levy-Bruhl, Lucien
b. Loewy, Raymond Fernand
b. Loisy, Alfred Firmin
b. Longet, Claudine Georgette
b. Louis, Jean
b. Louis Phillippe
b. Lubin, Germaine
b. Lyot, Bernard Ferdinand
b. Ma, Yo-Yo
b. MacBride, Sean
b. Maginot, Andre Louis Rene
b. Malebranche, Nicolas
b. Malibran, Maria Felicita
b. Mallarme, Stephane
b. Malraux, Andre Georges
b. Manet, Edouard
b. Mansart, Francois
b. Mansart, Jules Hardouin
b. Marcel, Gabriel Honore
b. Marisol (Escobar)
b. Maritain, Jacques
b. Marivaux, Pierre Carlet de
b. Marsh, Reginald
b. Maugham, W(illiam) Somerset
b. Mauriac, Claude
b. Mayer, Jean
b. Meilhac, Henri
b. Melies, Georges
b. Melville, Jean-Pierre
b. Mendes-France, Pierre
b. Merimee, Prosper
b. Michelet, Jules
b. Mielziner, Jo
b. Moissan, Ferdinand Frederick Henri
b. Moliere
b. Monet, Claude-Oscar
b. Monod, Jacques Lucien
b. Montana, Claude
b. Monteilhet, Hubert
b. Monteux, Pierre
b. Moreau, Gustave
b. Moreau, Jeanne
b. Musset, Alfred de
b. Nadar
b. Napoleon III
b. Nattier, Jean Marc
b. Nerval, Gerard de
b. Neufeld, Elizabeth F(ondal)
b. Nin, Anais
b. Nourrit, Adolphe
b. Nuitter, Charles Louis
b. Nungesser, Charles Eugene Jules Marie
b. Nuridsany, Claude
b. Oudry, Jean-Baptiste
b. Pareto, Vilfredo
b. Pasdeloup, Jules Etienne
b. Passy, Frederic
b. Payen, Anselme
b. Perennou, Marie
b. Perrault, Charles
b. Perrault, Claude
b. Petrossian, Christian
b. Peyre, Henri Maurice
b. Piaf, Edith
b. Picabia, Francis

b. Picard, Charles Emile
b. Picasso, Paloma
b. Pilon, Germain
b. Pissaro, Lucien
b. Planquette, Jean(-Robert)
b. Poiret, Paul
b. Poiseuille, Jean Louis Marie
b. Polanski, Roman
b. Pompadour, Jeanne Antoinette Poisson
b. Poniatowska, Elena
b. Posner, Vladimir
b. Poulenc, Francis
b. Presle, Micheline
b. Prevost, Marcel
b. Proust, Marcel
b. Rabaud, Henri
b. Renault, Louis
b. Renoir, Jean
b. Richelieu, Armand Jean du Plessis, Cardinal
b. Richet, Charles Robert
b. Robert, Hubert
b. Rochefort, Henri
b. Rodin, Auguste
b. Roland (de La Platiere), Jeanne-Marie
b. Rosay, Francoise
b. Rothschild, Alain de, Baron
b. Rothschild, Guy Edouard Alphonse Paul de, Baron
b. Rothschild, Philippe de, Baron
b. Rouault, Georges
b. Rousseau, Theodore
b. Rousseau, (Pierre Etienne) Theodore
b. Roze, Marie
b. Rudhyar, Dane
b. Rykiel, Sonia
b. Sade, Marquis (Donatien Alphonse Francoise) de
b. Saint Georges, Jules
b. Saint-Saens, (Charles) Camille
b. Saint-Simon, Duc de
b. Saint-Simon, Claude-Henri de Rouvroy
b. Sand, George
b. Sanda, Dominique
b. Sardou, Victorien
b. Sartre, Jean-Paul
b. Schneider, Maria
b. Schumann, Maurice
b. Scribe, (Augustin) Eugene
b. Serusier, Paul
b. Servan-Schreiber, Jean-Jacques
b. Seurat, Georges Pierre
b. Sevigne, Marie de Rabutin-Chantal, Marquise de
b. Signac, Paul
b. Sisley, Alfred
b. Smithson, James (Louis Macie)
b. Spectorsky, Auguste Compte
b. Stael-Holstein, Anne Louise Germaine Necker, Baroness de
b. Stoltz, Rosine
b. Sue, Eugene Joseph Marie
b. Sully Prudhomme
b. Svetlova, Marina
b. Talleyrand-Perigord, Charles Maurice de
b. Talma, Francois Joseph
b. Tanguy, Yves
b. Teisserenc de Bort, Leon-Philippe
b. Thill, Georges
b. Tournier, Michel
b. Trigere, Pauline
b. Truffaut, Francois

b. Utrillo, Maurice
b. Vadim, Roger
b. Varese, Edgar
b. Viardot-Garcia, Pauline
b. Vigee-Lebrun, Marie-Louise-Elisabeth
b. Vigo, Jean
b. Villechaize, Herve Jean Pierre
b. Villon, Francois
b. Viollet le Duc, Eugene Emmanuel
b. Vitry, Philippe de
b. Vlaminck, Maurice de
b. Voltaire
b. Vouet, Simon
b. Vreeland, Diana (Dalziel)
b. Weicker, Lowell Palmer, Jr.
b. Weil, Simone
b. Wolff, Albert Louis
b. Wolff, Hugh (MacPherson)
b. Wolsky, Albert
b. Zola, Emile (Edouard Charles)
d. About, Edmond-Francois-Valentin
d. Achard, Marcel
d. Adam, Adolphe Charles
d. Adam, Paul
d. Adamov, Arthur
d. Aflaq, Michel
d. Agoult, Marie Catherine Sophie d'
d. Alberdi, Juan Bautista
d. Alembert, Jean le Rond d'
d. Alexander of Hales
d. Allegret, Yves
d. Alphand, Herve
d. Amrouche, Jean
d. Andrews, Wayne
d. Apollinaire, Guillaume
d. Arago, Dominique Francois Jean
d. Aragon, Louis Marie Antoine Alfred
d. Arletty
d. Aron, Raymond Claude Ferdinand
d. Artaud, Antonin
d. Atget, Eugene
d. Auber, Daniel Francois Esprit
d. Audiard, Michel
d. Audiberti, Jacques
d. Aulard, Francois Victor Alphonse
d. Aulnoy, Marie-Catherine Jumel de Berneville
d. Auric, Georges
d. Auriol, Jacqueline Douet
d. Auriol, Vincent
d. Ayme, Marcel
d. Babeuf, Francois-Noel
d. Bailly, Jean Sylvain
d. Baker, Josephine (Carson)
d. Bakhtiar, Shahpur
d. Balard, Antoine-Jerome
d. Baldwin, James Mark
d. Balmain, Pierre Alexandre
d. Balzac, Honore de
d. Bao Dai
d. Barbier, Jules
d. Barney, Natalie Clifford
d. Barrault, Jean-Louis
d. Barthes, Roland (Gerard)
d. Bartholdi, Auguste
d. Bartlett, Paul Wayland
d. Baudelaire, Charles Pierre
d. Bazin, Andre
d. Beach, Sylvia
d. Beauchamp, Pierre
d. Beaumarchais, Pierre Augustin Caron de
d. Beauvoir, Simone de
d. Bechet, Sidney

d. Becker, Jacques
d. Beckett, Samuel (Barclay)
d. Becquerel, Antoine-Cesar
d. Belmont, Alva Erskine Smith Vanderbilt
d. Ben-Elissar, Eliahu
d. Benjamin, Judah Philip
d. Bentinck, William Henry Cavendish, Lord
d. Beranger, Pierre-Jean de
d. Bergson, Henri Louis
d. Berlioz, Hector
d. Bernanos, Georges
d. Bernard, Claude
d. Bernard, Emile
d. Bernard De Chartres
d. Bernhardt, Sarah
d. Berthelot, Marcellin
d. Bertillon, Alphonse
d. Bertrand, Joseph Louis Francois
d. Besse, Georges Noel
d. Bichat, Marie Francois Xavier
d. Bienville, Sieur de
d. Binet, Alfred
d. Bjornson, Bjornstjerne Martinius
d. Blanchard, Francois
d. Blanco, Antonio Guzman
d. Blanqui, Auguste
d. Bleriot, Louis
d. Blessington, Marguerite Gardiner, Countess
d. Bodard, Lucien (Albert)
d. Boileau(-Despreaux), Nicolas
d. Bonaparte, Jerome
d. Bonnet, Georges Etienne
d. Bonvalot, Pierre Gabriel Edouard
d. Bordeaux, Henry
d. Borduas, Paul-Emile
d. Bossuet, Jacques Benigne
d. Boucher, Francois
d. Bougainville, Louis-Antoine de
d. Boulanger, Nadia Juliette
d. Boulle, Andre Charles
d. Boulle, Pierre Francois Marie-Louis
d. Bourget, Paul (Charles Joseph)
d. Boussingault, Jean Baptiste
d. Boyer, Jean Pierre
d. Brancusi, Constantin
d. Brandel, Fernand Paul
d. Braque, Georges
d. Breguet, Abraham Louis
d. Breguet, Louis Charles
d. Breton, Andre
d. Breton, Jules Adolphe
d. Briand, Aristide
d. Briggs, Austin Eugene
d. Brillat-Savarin, Jean Anthelme
d. Broglie, Louis Prince De
d. Brugnon, Jacques
d. Bude, Guillaume
d. Buffon, Georges Louis Leclerc
d. Bugatti, Ettore Arco Isidoro
d. Bugeaud de la Piconnerie, Thomas Robert
d. Bunau-Varilla, Philippe Jean
d. Bunin, Ivan Alekseevich
d. Caillaux, Joseph Marie Auguste
d. Callas, Maria
d. Calmette, Albert Leon Charles
d. Camargo, Marie Anne de Cupis de
d. Cambaceres, Jean Jacques Regis de
d. Cambon, Pierre Paul
d. Campanella, Tommaso
d. Camus, Marcel
d. Canot, Theodore
d. Carnot, Hippolyte

d. Carpentier, Georges
d. Carrel, Alexis
d. Carriere, Eugene
d. Casadesus, Gaby (Lhote)
d. Casadesus, Robert
d. Cassin, Rene-Samuel
d. Castil-Blaze, Francois-Joseph
d. Cavalcanti, Alberto
d. Celan, Paul
d. Celibidache, Sergiu
d. Chabrier, Emmanuel
d. Chalgrin, Francois
d. Champollion, Jean Francois
d. Chanel, Coco
d. Chaptal, Jean Antoine, Comte de Chanteloup
d. Char, Rene (Emile)
d. Chardin, Jean Baptiste Simeon
d. Chardonnet, Louis Marie Hilaire Bernigaud
d. Charles, Jacques-Alexandre-Cesar
d. Charpentier, Gustave
d. Charpentier, Marc-Antoine
d. Charron, Pierre
d. Chateaubriand, Francois Rene de
d. Chenier, Marie-Andre de
d. Cherubini, Luigi Carlo Zenobio Salvadore Maria
d. Chevalier, Maurice Auguste
d. Chevreul, Michel Eugene
d. Chopin, Frederic Francois
d. Citroen, Andre Gustave
d. Claudel, Paul Louis Charles
d. Clemenceau, Georges Eugene Benjamin
d. Clodion
d. Clouet, Francois
d. Clouet, Jean
d. Clouzot, Henri-George
d. Cluytens, Andre
d. Cochin, Charles Nicholas
d. Cocteau, Jean
d. Colbert, Jean-Baptiste
d. Colette
d. Coligny, Gaspard de Chatillon
d. Colonne, Edouard
d. Comte, Auguste
d. Constant de Rebeque, (Henri) Benjamin
d. Conway, Moncure Daniel
d. Cooper, David (Graham)
d. Coppee, Francois Edouard Joachim
d. Corday d'Armount, Charlotte
d. Corneille, Pierre
d. Corot, Jean Baptiste Camille
d. Cortazar, Julio
d. Coulomb, Charles Augustin de
d. Couperin, Francois
d. Cournot, Antoine Augustin
d. Courtois, Bernard
d. Cousteau, Jacques (Yves)
d. Couthon, Georges
d. Couve de Murville, (Jacques) Maurice
d. Coysevox, Antoine
d. Cremieux, Isaac-Adolphe
d. Curel, Francois de
d. Curie, Pierre
d. Cuvier, Georges, Baron
d. Cyrano de Bergerac, Savinien de
d. Daguerre, Louis Jacques Mande
d. Daladier, Edouard
d. Daly, Augustin
d. Danjon, Andre Louis
d. Danton, Georges Jacques
d. Darcy, Henri Philibert Gaspard

d. Dassault, Marcel
d. Dauphin, Claude Le Grand Maria Eugene
d. David d'Angers
d. Davis, Bette
d. Davout, Louis Nicholas
d. Debussy, Claude Achille
d. Degas, (Hilaire Germain) Edgar
d. Delacroix, (Ferdinand Victor) Eugene
d. Delaney, Beauford
d. Delaroche, Hippolyte
d. Delaunay-Terk, Sonia
d. Delibes, Leo
d. Delisle, Guillaume
d. Delisle, Joseph-Nicolas
d. Demy, Jacques
d. Deshayes, Catherine
d. DeSica, Vittorio
d. Desmoulins, Camille
d. Destouches, Louis-Ferdinand
d. Dew, Thomas Roderick
d. Dewaere, Patrick
d. Diana, Princess of Wales
d. Diaz, Porfirio
d. Diderot, Denis
d. Dietrich, Marlene
d. Dolin, Anton, Sir
d. Dore, Gustave
d. D'Orsay, Alfred Guillaume, Count
d. Dreyfus, Pierre
d. Du Barry, Marie Jeanne Gomard de Vaubernier, Comtesse
d. Dubuffet, Jean
d. Duclos, Jacques
d. Dukas, Paul Abraham
d. Dulong, Pierre-Louis
d. Dumas, Alexandre
d. Dumas, Jean Baptiste Andre
d. Dunoyer de Segonzac, Andre
d. Dupleix, Joseph Francois
d. Duplessis, Marie
d. Duras, Marguerite
d. Durkheim, Emile
d. Duvivier, Julien
d. Edward VIII
d. Eiffel, Alexandre Gustave
d. Elgin, Thomas Bruce
d. Enesco, Georges
d. Epee, Charles-Michel
d. Ernst, Max
d. Erte
d. Estaing, Charles Henri Hector, Comte d'
d. Etherege, George, Sir
d. Fabry, Charles
d. Faidherbe, Louis Leon Cesar
d. Falconet, Etienne Maurice
d. Farrere, Claude
d. Fath, Jacques
d. Faure, Edgar Jean
d. Faure, Elie
d. Faure, Francois Felix
d. Faure, Gabriel Urbain
d. Fenelon, Fania
d. Fernandel
d. Ferry, Jules Francois Camille
d. Feuillade, Louis
d. Feuillet, Octave
d. Filene, Edward Albert
d. Fini, Leonor
d. Fleury, Andre Hercule de
d. Foch, Ferdinand
d. Fonck, Rene
d. Fontaine, Marcel
d. Forain, Jean-Louis

d. Monsigny, Pierre-Alexandre
d. Montalembert, Comte de
d. Montalvo, Juan Maria
d. Montesquieu, Charles Louis de
   Secondat, Baron
d. Montez, Maria
d. Moreau, Gustave
d. Morisot, Berthe
d. Morrison, Jim
d. Moszkowski, Moritz
d. Muratore, Lucien
d. Musset, Alfred de
d. Nadar
d. Nattier, Jean Marc
d. Negrin, Juan
d. Nerval, Gerard de
d. Ney, Michel de la Moskova, Prince
d. Nicot, Jean
d. Nougues, Jean
d. Nuitter, Charles Louis
d. Nureyev, Rudolf (Hametovich)
d. Offenbach, Jacques
d. Onassis, Aristotle Socrates
d. Paer, Ferdinando
d. Pagnol, Marcel Paul
d. Palmer, Alice Elvira Freeman
d. Pare, Ambroise
d. Pascal, Blaise
d. Pater, Jean-Baptiste
d. Patou, Jean
d. Patti, Carlotta
d. Paul, Prince
d. Payen, Anselme
d. Pedro II
d. Peret, Benjamin
d. Perrault, Charles
d. Perrault, Claude
d. Perret, Auguste
d. Pevsner, Antoine
d. Philipe, Gerard
d. Piaf, Edith
d. Picabia, Francis
d. Picard, Charles Emile
d. Picard, Jean
d. Pickford, Jack
d. Pictet, Raoul-Pierre
d. Pilon, Germain
d. Pineau, Christian (Paul Francis)
d. Pinel, Philippe
d. Pissarro, Camille Jacob
d. Plancon, Pol-Henri
d. Planquette, Jean(-Robert)
d. Pleven, Rene Jean
d. Poincare, Jules Henri
d. Poincare, Raymond
d. Poiret, Paul
d. Poiseuille, Jean Louis Marie
d. Pollock, Charles
d. Pompidou, Georges Jean Raymond
d. Poulenc, Francis
d. Pridi Phanomyong
d. Primaticcio, Francesco
d. Primo de Rivera (y Orbaneja),
   Miguel
d. Printemps, Yvonne
d. Proudhon, Pierre Joseph
d. Proust, Marcel
d. Prudhon, Pierre-Paul
d. Puvis de Chavannes, Pierre Cecile
d. Rabaud, Henri
d. Rabelais, Francois
d. Racine, Jean Baptiste
d. Raimu
d. Rameau, Jean-Philippe
d. Rampal, Jean-Pierre
d. Ravel, Maurice Joseph

d. Ray, Man
d. Rebuffat, Gaston Louis Simon
d. Recamier, Julie, Madame
d. Redon, Odilon
d. Renan, (Joseph) Ernest
d. Renard, Jules
d. Renaud, Maurice
d. Renault, Louis
d. Ricci, Nina
d. Richelieu, Armand Jean du Plessis,
   Cardinal
d. Richer, Jean
d. Richet, Charles Robert
d. Rigaud, Hyacinthe
d. Robert, Hubert
d. Robespierre, Maximilien Francois
   de
d. Roland (de La Platiere), Jeanne-
   Marie
d. Romains, Jules
d. Rosa, Carl
d. Rosay, Francoise
d. Rosso, Il
d. Rostand, Edmond Alexis
d. Rothschild, Philippe de, Baron
d. Rouault, Georges
d. Rousseau, Henri
d. Roze, Marie
d. Rubirosa, Porfirio
d. Sacchini, Antonio
d. Sainte-Beuve, Charles Augustin
d. Saint Georges, Jules
d. Saint-Just, Louis Antoine Leon de
d. Saint-Simon, Duc de
d. Saint-Simon, Claude-Henri de
   Rouvroy
d. Sananikone, Phoui
d. Sanderson, Sybil
d. Sarcey, Francisque
d. Sardou, Victorien
d. Sarkis, Elias
d. Sarraute, Nathalie
d. Sartre, Jean-Paul
d. Satie, Erik
d. Sax, Adolphe (Antoine-Joseph)
d. Sax, Charles Joseph
d. Schiaparelli
d. Schlumberger, Jean
d. Schneider, Romy
d. Schumann, Maurice
d. Schweitzer, Pierre-Paul
d. Schwob, Marcel
d. Scribe, (Augustin) Eugene
d. Scudery, Madeleine de
d. Seberg, Jean
d. Seurat, Georges Pierre
d. Severini, Gino
d. Shestov, Lev
d. Sieyes, Emmanuel Joseph
d. Signac, Paul
d. Simon, Jules Francois
d. Simpson, Wallis (Bessie Wallis
   Warfield)
d. Sinyavsky, Andrei D(onatovich)
d. Sor, Fernando
d. Soufflot, Jacques Germain
d. Soupault, Philippe
d. Soutine, Chaim
d. Stael-Holstein, Anne Louise
   Germaine Necker, Baroness de
d. Stendhal
d. Stoltz, Rosine
d. Strakosch, Maurice
d. Sturm, Charles Francois
d. Sullivan, Harry Stack
d. Sully Prudhomme

d. Sulzberger, C(yrus) L(eo)
d. Sykes, Mark, Sir
d. Tabouis, Genevieve
d. Tailleferre, Germaine
d. Taine, Hippolyte Adolphe
d. Talleyrand-Perigord, Charles
   Maurice de
d. Talma, Francois Joseph
d. Talon, Jean
d. Tamberlik, Enrico
d. Tarde, Gabriel
d. Tarkovsky, Andrei (Arsenyich)
d. Tati, Jacques
d. Tcherepnin, Alexander Nikolayevich
d. Tcherepnin, Nicholas
d. Thao, Tran Duc
d. Tharaud, Jean
d. Thomas, (Charles Louis) Ambroise
d. Thomas, Sidney Gilchrist
d. Toklas, Alice B(abette)
d. Tournefort, Joseph Pitton de
d. Townsend, Peter Wooldridge
d. Troyon, Constant
d. Tzara, Tristan
d. Vadim, Roger
d. Valadon, Suzanne
d. Valery, Paul Ambroise
d. Vanderbilt, William Kissam
d. Vasarely, Victor
d. Vauban, Sebastien LePrestre de
d. Venizelos, Eleutherios Kyriakos
d. Verlaine, Paul (Marie)
d. Vertes, Marcel
d. Viardot-Garcia, Pauline
d. Vieira Da Silva, Maria Helena
d. Vigee-Lebrun, Marie-Louise-
   Elisabeth
d. Vigny, Alfred Victor, Comte de
d. Vigo, Jean
d. Villon, Francois
d. Vincent de Paul, Saint
d. Vionnet, Madeleine
d. Vlaminck, Maurice de
d. Volney, (Constantin) Francois
   Chasseboeuf, Comte de
d. Voltaire
d. VonStroheim, Erich
d. Vouet, Simon
d. Vynnychenko, Volodymyr
d. Wallace, Horace Binney
d. Wallace, Richard, Sir
d. Werth, Alexander
d. Weygand, Maxime
d. Wharton, Edith
d. Wheatstone, Charles, Sir
d. White, Pearl
d. Widal, Fernand Isidore
d. Widor, Charles Marie Jean Albert
d. Wilde, Oscar (Fingal O'Flahertie
   Wills)
d. Wilson, Peter Cecil
d. Wolff, Albert Louis
d. Worth, Charles Frederick
d. Wright, Richard (Nathaniel)
d. Zadkine, Ossip
d. Zola, Emile (Edouard Charles)

Passy, France
d. Bretonneau, Pierre Fidele
d. DuPrez, Gilbert
d. Gossec, Francois Joseph
d. Piccinni, Nicola
d. Rossini, Gioacchino Antonio

Pau, France
b. Bernadotte, Jean Baptiste

b. Courreges, Andre
b. Henry, IV
d. Campbell, Patrick, Mrs.
d. Selkirk, 5th Earl of

Pau-Saint Maur, France
b. Tailleferre, Germaine

Perigord, France
b. Fenelon, Francois de Salignac

Perigueux, France
b. Bloy, Leon Marie

Perpignan, France
b. Arago, Dominque Francois Jean
b. Trenet, Charles
d. Leblanc, Maurice

Perthes-les-Hurlus, France
d. Macke, August

Pezenas, Herault, France
b. Vidal de la Blache, Paul

Picardy, France
b. Lafarge, Marie

Pignerol, France
d. Fouquet, Nicolas

Plan de Grasse, France
d. Prokosch, Frederic

Plessis-les-Tours, France
d. Louis XI

Ploujean, France
d. Pierne, Gabriel

Poissy, France
b. Louis IX

Poitiers, France
b. Foucault, Michel
b. Guerin, Camille
d. Lashley, Karl Spencer

Polenc, France
b. Trintignant, Jean-Louis Xavier

Pont Chateau, France
b. Demy, Jacques

Pont-L'Abbe, France
b. Verdy, Violette

Pont-aux-Dames, France
d. Coquelin, Benoit Constant

Pouy, France
b. Vincent de Paul, Saint

Prades, France
b. Merton, Thomas

Puteaux, France
d. Bellini, Vincenzo
d. Kupka, Frank

Puys, France
d. Dumas, Alexandre Dumas Davy de
la Pailleterie

Quimper, France
b. Jacob, Max
b. Laennec, Rene Theophile Hyacinthe

Rambouillet, France
d. Francis I
d. Monnet, Jean Omer Marie Gabriel

Recey-sur-Ourse, France
b. Lacordaire, Jean Baptiste Henri

Reims, France
b. Baudrillard, Jean
b. Cauchon, Pierre
b. Colbert, Jean-Baptiste
b. Couve de Murville, (Jacques)
Maurice
b. Entremont, Phillippe
b. Forain, Jean-Louis
b. Mabillon, Jean
b. Machaut, Guillaume de
b. Rothier, Leon
d. Hore-Belisha, Leslie, Baron

Rennes, France
b. Boulanger, Georges Ernest Jean
Marie

Revel, France
b. Auriol, Vincent

Ribemont, France
b. Condorcet, Marie-Jean-Antoine

Richelieu, France
b. Chevalier, Jules

Rivesaltes, France
b. Joffre, Joseph Jacques Cesaire

Rochefort, France
b. Champlain, Samuel de
b. Loti, Pierre

Rochefort-sur-Mer, France
b. Merleau-Ponty, Maurice

Rodez, France
b. Soulages, Pierre

Roquebrune, France
d. LeCorbusier

Rosheim, France
b. Lehn, Jean-Marie

Roubaix, France
b. Delerue, Georges

Rouen, France
b. Boieldieu, Francois Adrien
b. Corneille, Pierre
b. Dulong, Pierre-Louis
b. DuPre, Marcel
b. Edward IV
b. Flaubert, Gustave
b. Gericault, Jean Louis Andre
Theodore

b. La Salle, Rene Robert Cavelier de
b. Nicolle, Charles Jules Henri
d. Anquetil, Jacques
d. Bridgman, Frederic Arthur
d. Clarendon, Edward Hyde, Earl of
d. Joan of Arc, Saint
d. William the Conqueror

Roven, France
d. Cauchon, Pierre

Royan, France
d. Roussel, Albert

Rueil-Malmaison, France
d. Feydeau, Georges

Ruget, France
b. Blanqui, Auguste

Saarlouis, France
b. Ney, Michel de la Moskova, Prince

Saint-Aignan, France
b. Paul-Boncour, Joseph

Saint-Andre, France
b. Pinel, Philippe
b. Werner, Pierre

Saint-Beat, France
b. Gallieni, Joseph-Simon

Saint-Brice, France
b. Dubos, Rene Jules

Saint-Brieuc, France
b. Dewaere, Patrick

Saint-Chamond, France
d. Pinay, Antoine

Saint-Cloud, France
b. Killy, Jean-Claude
d. Claude, Georges
d. Gounod, Charles Francois
d. Pasteur, Louis

Saint-Cyr, France
d. Maintenon, Francoise d'Aubigne,
Marquise de

Saint-Denis, France
b. Barre, Raymond
b. Eluard, Paul

Saint-Didier-de-Formans, France
d. Bloch, Marc

Saint-Die, France
b. Ferry, Jules Francois Camille

Saint-Etienne, France
b. Garnier, Francis

Saint-Foy, France
b. Faure, Elie

Saint-Georges-sur-Cher, France
b. Bretonneau, Pierre Fidele

Saint-Germain-du-Val, France
b. Delibes, Leo

Saint-Germain-en-Laye, France
b. Debussy, Claude Achille
b. Duluth, Daniel (Greysolon)
b. Frontenac, Louis de Buade de
b. Louis XIV
d. Cochet, Henri
d. Crommelynck, Fernand
d. David, Felicien Cesar
d. James II
d. Jouy, Victor (Joseph-Etienne) de
d. Mendes, Catulle
d. Thiers, Adolphe

Saint-Guirauld, France
b. Lartet, Edouard Armand Isidore
Hippolyte

Saint-Jean-de-Luz, France
d. Gissing, George Robert
d. Hornung, Ernest William
d. Lacoste, Rene

Saint-Jean-de-Maurienne, France
b. Balmain, Pierre Alexandre

Saint-Julien, France
b. Bernard, Claude

Saint-Junien, France
b. Tharaud, Jean
b. Tharaud, Jerome

Saint-Just-en-Chaussee, France
b. Hauy, Rene Just

Saint-Leger-de-Foucherest, France
b. Vauban, Sebastien LePrestre de

Saint-Leonard-de-Noblat, France
b. Gay-Lussac, Joseph-Louis

Saint-Leons, France
b. Fabre, Jean Henri

Saint-Lo, France
b. Feuillet, Octave
b. LeVerrier, Urbain Jean Joseph

Saint-Malo, France
b. Cartier, Jacques
b. Chateaubriand, Francois Rene de
b. Clive, Colin
b. Lamennais, Hugues Felicite Robert
de
d. Cartier, Jacques

Saint-Martin-Vesubie, France
d. Freyssinet, Eugene

Saint-Omer, France
b. Blondin, Jean Francois Gravelet
b. Carnot, Hippolyte
d. Butler, Alban
d. Roberts, Frederick Sleigh

Saint-Ouen, France
b. Manessier, Alfred

Saint-Paul, France
b. Leconte de Lisle, Charles Marie
Rene

Saint-Paul de Vence, France
d. Pleasence, Donald

Saint-Paul-de-Vence, France
d. Baldwin, James (Arthur)
d. Chagall, Marc
d. Lurcat, Jean Marie
d. Maeght, Aime

Saint-Pierre, France
d. Douglas, Keith Castellain

Saint-Prive, France
d. Harpignies, Henri

Saint-Quentin, France
b. Babeuf, Francois-Noel
b. Benezet, Anthony
b. Charlevoix, Pierre Francis Xavier de
b. Ozenfant, Amedee

Saint-Remy, France
b. Nostradamus

Saint-Remy-de-Provence, France
d. Daudet, Leon

Saint-Saturnin, France
b. Corday d'Armount, Charlotte

Saint-Sauveur, France
b. Colette

Saint-Tropez, France
d. Laing, R(onald) D(avid)

Sainte-Andre de Cubzac, France
b. Cousteau, Jacques (Yves)

Sainte-Foy-les-Lyon, France
b. Carrel, Alexis

Sainte-Marie Mines, France
d. Slovik, Eddie

Saintes, France
b. Guillotin, Joseph Ignace
b. Richard, Gabriel

Salon, France
d. Nostradamus

Sarcelles, France
d. Crevecoeur, Michel-Guillaume Jean
de

Sarlat, France
b. Tarde, Gabriel

Sarzeau, France
b. Lesage, Alain-Rene

Saumur, France
b. Chanel, Coco

Savenay, France
d. Delano, Jane Arminda

Savoy, France
b. Maistre, Joseph de

Saxony, France
b. Saxe, Maurice

Seceaux, France
b. Delon, Alain

Sedan, France
b. Noah, Yannick Simon Camille
b. Turenne, Henri de La Tour
Auvergne, Viscount

Seissan, France
d. Lartet, Edouard Armand Isidore
Hippolyte

Selancourt, France
b. Peugeot, Rodolphe

Senlis, France
d. Montand, Yves

Sens, France
d. Camus, Albert

Serigran, France
d. Fabre, Jean Henri

Seringes, France
d. Kilmer, Joyce

Sermano, France
b. Falconetti, Renee Maria

Serrieres, France
d. Montgolfier, Jacques Etienne

Sete, France
b. Brassens, Georges
b. Valery, Paul Ambroise
d. Brassens, Georges

Sevres, France
b. Troyon, Constant
d. Carrier-Belleuse, Albert Ernest
d. Guillaume, Charles Edouard

Seyne-sur-Mer, France
d. Dufresne, Charles

Sommieres, France
d. Durrell, Lawrence (George)

Strasbourg, France
b. Arp, Hans
b. Baulieu, Etienne-Emile
b. Dore, Gustave
b. Friedel, Charles
b. Gerhardt, Charles Frederic
b. Kleber, Jean Baptiste
b. Marceau, Marcel
b. Munch, Charles
b. Oberlin, Johann Friedrich
b. Ungerer, Tomi
d. Gerhardt, Charles Frederic

Sucy-en-Brie, France
d. Halevy, Elie

Vezelay, France
d. Rolland, Romain

Vianne, France
d. Prevost, Marcel

Vic sur Seille, France
b. La Tour, Georges Dumesnil de

Vidalon les Annonay, France
b. Montgolfier, Jacques Etienne
b. Montgolfier, Joseph Michel

Villarceaux, France
d. Tortelier, Paul

Ville-d'Avray, France
b. Gobineau, Joseph Arthur, Comte de
d. Fresnel, Augustin-Jean
d. Gambetta, Leon

Villehardouin, Champagne, France
b. Villehardouin, Geffroi de

Villemomble, France
b. Petit, Roland

Villeneuve, France
b. Claudel, Paul Louis Charles

Villeneuve-Loubet, France
b. Escoffier, Georges Auguste

Villers, France
b. Poussin, Nicolas

Villers-Cotterets, France
b. Dumas, Alexandre Dumas Davy de la Pailleterie

Vincennes, France
b. Charles, V
b. Fath, Jacques
d. Mata Hari
d. Mazarin, Jules, Cardinal

Vittel, France
d. Journet, Marcel

Vouziers, France
b. Taine, Hippolyte Adolphe

Wimereux, France
d. McCrae, John

Yvelines, France
d. Strand, Paul

FRANCONIA (WEST)

Bockelheim, Franconia (West)
b. Hildegard of Bingen, Saint

Rupertsberg, Franconia (West)
d. Hildegard of Bingen, Saint

FRENCH GUIANA

Cayenne, French Guiana
b. Damas, Leon-Gontran
b. Eboue, Adolphe Felix Sylvestre

Kouroussa, French Guiana
b. Laye, Camara

FRENCH MOROCCO

Meknes, French Morocco
b. Jobert, Michel

Rabat, French Morocco
b. Levy, David

FRENCH POLYNESIA

d. Gauguin, Paul

Bora Bora, French Polynesia
d. Victor, Paul-Emile

Papeete, Tahiti, French Polynesia
d. Hall, James Norman

FRENCH SUDAN

Medine, French Sudan
b. Gueye, Lamine

FRENCH WEST AFRICA

Douala, French West Africa
b. Bebey, Francis

FRISIA

Dokkum, Frisia
d. Boniface, Saint

FULAH EMPIRE

Sokoto, Fulah Empire
d. Clapperton, Hugh

GABON

d. Samory Toure

Franceville, Gabon
b. Bongo, Albert-Bernard (Omar)

Lambarene, Gabon
d. Schweitzer, Albert

GALICIA

Buczacz, Galicia
b. Agnon, S(hmuel) Y(osef)

GAMBIA

Barajally, Gambia
b. Jawara, Alhaji Dawda Kairaba, Sir
b. Jawara, Dauda Kairaba

Kanilai, Foni Kansala, Gambia
b. Jammeh, Yahya A(bdulaziz) J(emus) J.

GAUL

b. Vercingetorix

Lugdunum, Gaul
b. Claudius I
d. Gratian

Mantua, Gaul
b. Vergil

Paris, Gaul
d. Clovis I

Verona, Gaul
b. Catullus, Gaius Valerius

GEORGIA

Tbilisi, Georgia
b. Ambartsumyan, Viktor Amazaspovich

GERMAN DEMOCRATIC REPUBLIC

b. Hoffmann, Jan
b. Potzsch, Anett
d. Reed, Dean

Berlin, German Democratic Republic
d. Bolz, Lothar
d. Brecht, Bertolt (Eugen Friedrich)
d. Dessau, Paul
d. Felsenstein, Walter
d. Fuchs, Klaus
d. Hertz, Gustav Ludwig
d. Pieck, Wilhelm
d. Ulbricht, Walter
d. Wagner-Regeny, Rudolf
d. Zweig, Arnold

Dresden, German Democratic Republic
b. Enke, Karin
d. Nexo, Martin Andersen
d. Paulus, Friedrich von

Karl-Marx-Stadt, German Democratic Republic
b. Witt, Katarina

Koenigstein, German Democratic Republic
d. Christaller, Walter

Leipzig, German Democratic Republic
b. Otto, Kristin

Plauen, German Democratic Republic
b. Ender, Kornelia

Possneck, German Democratic Republic
b. Matthes, Roland

Rottach-Egern, German Democratic Republic
d. Patzak, Julius

GERMANY

b. Bernhard, Ruth
b. Bethmann Hollweg, Theobald von
b. Bloch, Ernst
b. Coors, Adolph
b. Dean, John Gunther
b. Dehmel, Richard
b. Deisenhofer, Johann
b. Fraenkel, Heinrich
b. Friedrich, Carl Joachim
b. Gruber, Franz-Xaver
b. Henry, III
b. Henry, V
b. Henry, VII
b. Hochhuth, Rolf
b. Jodl, Alfred
b. Nestle, Henri
b. Perls, Frederick Salomon
b. Phillips, Irna
b. Polke, Sigmar
b. Pufendorf, Samuel von
b. Ritter, Karl
b. Sack, Erna
b. Schluter, Andreas
b. Schwarzschild, Martin
b. Simpson, Nicole Brown
b. Tennenbaum, Silvia
b. Ulrichs, Karl Heinrich
b. Zenger, John Peter
d. Beck, Ludwig August Theoder
d. Bethmann Hollweg, Theobald von
d. Deterding, Henri Wilhelm August, Sir
d. Henry, III
d. Henry, IV
d. Henry, V
d. Junkers, Hugo
d. Kalisch, Paul
d. Kapp, Wolfgang
d. Levasseur, Rosalie
d. Levi, Hermann
d. Modersohn-Becker, Paula
d. Spener, Philipp Jakob
d. Szabo, Violette Bushell

Aachen, Germany
b. Lambsdorff, Otto
b. Mies van der Rohe, Ludwig
b. Saerchinger, Cesar Victor Charles

Agnetendorf, Germany
d. Hauptmann, Gerhart Johann Robert

Aichach, Germany
d. Koch, Ilse

Allenskin, Germany
b. Mendelsohn, Eric

Allersberg, Germany
b. Jahn, Helmut

Alsace, Germany
b. Leo, IX, St.

Alsace-Lorraine, Germany
b. Bloch, Raymond A

Alsenz, Germany
b. Frick, Wilhelm

Alsfeld, Germany
b. Stammler, Rudolf

Altmannstein, Germany
b. Gunther, Ignaz

Altona, Germany
b. Bulow, Bernhard H M
b. Struve, Friedrich Georg Wilhelm von

Alzey, Germany
b. Adler, Felix
b. Belmont, August

Amberg, Germany
b. Switzer, Katherine Virginia

Ammerland, Germany
d. Ratzel, Friedrich

Andermach, Germany
b. Bukowski, Charles

Anklam, Germany
b. Gadski, Johanna

Annemasse, Germany
b. Windgassen, Wolfgang Friedrich Hermann

Apenrade, Germany
b. Reuter, Ernst

Aplerbeck, Germany
b. Canaris, Wilhelm

Arbergen, Germany
b. Olbers, Heinrich Wilhelm Matthaus

Arnstadt, Germany
d. Haring, Georg Wilhelm Heinrich

Aschaffenburg, Germany
b. Kirchner, Ernst Ludwig

Aschersleben, Germany
b. Rundstedt, Karl Rudolf Gerd von

Auchsensheim, Germany
b. Egk, Werner

Aue, Germany
b. Vogl, Heinrich

Augsburg, Germany
b. Boyle, Gertrude
b. Brecht, Bertolt (Eugen Friedrich)
b. Euler-Chelpin, Hans Karl August Simon von
b. Holbein, Hans, the Elder
b. Holbein, Hans, the Younger

b. Messerschmitt, Willy
b. Mozart, Leopold
b. Olczewska, Maria
b. Troeltsch, Ernst

Aurich, Germany
b. Eucken, Rudolf Christoph

Babenhausen, Germany
b. Jochum, Eugen

Bad Godesberg, Germany
b. Barbie, Klaus

Bad Kissinger, Germany
b. Steinberger, Jack

Bad Kleinen, Germany
d. Frege, (Friedrich Ludwig) Gottlob

Bad Nauheim, Germany
d. Barnack, Oskar

Bad Soden, Germany
d. Abs, Hermann J(osef)

Bad Worishofen, Germany
b. Fassbinder, Rainer Werner

Baden, Germany
b. Wundt, Wilhelm Max

Baden-Baden, Germany
b. Hoess, Rudolf Franz
b. Mesmer, Franz Anton
d. Eiermann, Egon
d. Jensen, Adolph
d. Koch, Robert
d. Schlemmer, Oskar

Baden-Sollingen, Germany
b. Coupland, Douglas

Badenweiler, Germany
d. Chekhov, Anton Pavlovich
d. Crane, Stephen

Baldenheim, Germany
b. Nessler, Victor E

Bamberg, Germany
b. Dollinger, J(ohannes) J(osef) I(gnaz) von

Barbony, Saxony, Germany
b. Fries, Jakob Friedrich

Barenstadt, Germany
b. Kallen, Horace M(eyer)

Bautzen, Germany
b. Lotze, Rudolf Hermann

Bavaria, Germany
b. Gimbel, Adam

Bayreuth, Germany
b. Wagner, Wieland Adolf Gottfried
b. Wagner, Wolfgang
d. Chamberlain, Houston Stewart
d. Liszt, Franz (Ferencz)
d. Richter, Hans

d. Richter, Jean Paul F
d. Richter, Johann Paul Friedrich
d. Wagner, Cosima Liszt
d. Wagner, Siegfried (Helferich)

Beelitz, Germany
b. Plage, Dieter

Bergedorf, Germany
b. Hasse, Johann Adolph

Bergen-Belsen, Germany
d. Frank, Anne

Berlin, Germany
b. Achard, Franz Karl
b. Adam, Ken
b. Arnim, Achim von (Ludwig Joachim)
b. Auermann, Nadja
b. Baeyer, Adolf Johann Friedrich Wilhelm, von
b. Bernstein, Eduard
b. Blumenthal, W Michael
b. Boschwitz, Rudy
b. Brasch, Rudolph
b. Brauchitsch, Heinrich Alfred
b. Buchholz, Horst
b. Busoni, Rafaello
b. Chain, Ernest Boris, Sir
b. Cornell, Katharine
b. Dean, Patrick (Henry), Sir
b. Delbruck, Max
b. DeWohl, Louis
b. Diamand, Peter
b. Dietrich, Marlene
b. Doenitz, Karl C
b. Dohnanyi, Christoph von
b. Du Bois-Reymond, Emil
b. Duhring, Eugen Karl
b. Ebers, Georg Moritz
b. Ebert, Carl
b. Ehricke, Krafft Arnold
b. Eisner, Kurt
b. Eisner, Thomas
b. Eysenck, Hans J(urgen)
b. Faas, Horst
b. Fassbaender, Brigitte
b. Feld, Fritz
b. Fingesten, Peter
b. Fischer-Dieskau, Dietrich
b. Foerster, Friedrich Wilhelm
b. Forssmann, Werner Theodor Otto
b. Foss, Lukas
b. Frank, Anthony Melchior
b. Frederick the Great
b. Frederick William, IV
b. Frederick William I
b. Freud, Lucian
b. Furtwangler, Wilhelm
b. Gay, Peter Jack
b. Genthe, Arnold
b. Gidal, Sonia
b. Grafe, Albrecht Friedrich Wilhelm Ernst von
b. Graham, Bill
b. Gropius, Walter Adolf
b. Grosz, George Ehrenfried
b. Hague, Albert
b. Hammerstein, Oscar
b. Harlan, Veit
b. Harnoncourt, Nikolaus
b. Heyse, Paul Johann Ludwig von
b. Humboldt, Alexander, Freiherr von

b. Humboldt, Friedrich Heinrich Alexander von
b. Kalisch, Paul
b. Kipnis, Igor
b. Klarsfeld, Beate
b. Kleiber, Carlos
b. Klose, Margarete
b. Koffka, Kurt
b. Kronhausen, Eberhard Wilhelm
b. Kruger, Hardy
b. Lehmann-Haupt, Hellmut Emil
b. Leider, Frida
b. Leitner, Ferdinand
b. Levitin, Sonia
b. Lewisohn, Ludwig
b. Ley, Willy
b. Lieber, Franz
b. Liebermann, Max
b. Lortzing, Gustav Albert
b. Lovejoy, Arthur Oncken (Schauffler)
b. Lubitsch, Ernst
b. Ludwig, Christa
b. Mansfield, Richard
b. Marcuse, Herbert
b. Marek, Kurt W
b. Max, Peter
b. Me'Shell Ndegeocello
b. Meyerbeer, Giacomo
b. Mielke, Erich
b. Mueller, Erwin Wilhelm
b. Muller-Munk, Peter
b. Newton, Helmut
b. Nichols, Mike
b. Nin-Culmell, Joaquin Maria
b. Pepusch, Johann Christoph
b. Polanyi, John C
b. Politz, Alfred
b. Previn, Andre
b. Prey, Hermann
b. Rathenau, Walter
b. Reiss, Albert
b. Richter, Hans
b. Riefenstahl, Leni
b. Ritschl, Albrecht Benjamin
b. Rosenberg, Jakob
b. Sachs, Nelly (Leonie)
b. Sachse, Leopold
b. Salomon, Alice
b. Salomon, Charlotte
b. Schadow, Gottfried
b. Scherchen, Hermann
b. Schlick, Friedrich Albert Moritz
b. Schlieffen, Alfred, Graf von
b. Schmidt-Isserstedt, Hans
b. Schnabel, Karl Ulrich
b. Scholem, Gershom Gerhard
b. Simmel, Georg
b. Sommer, Elke
b. Sonnenfeldt, Helmut
b. Stresemann, Gustav
b. Tieck, (Johann) Ludwig
b. Trotta, Margarethe Von
b. Veidt, Conrad
b. Von Eckardt, Wolf
b. Walter, Bruno
b. Wegener, Alfred Lothar
b. Weitz, John
b. Wilhelm II
b. William, I
b. Windaus, Adolf Otto Reinhold
b. Wittig, Georg Friedrich Karl
b. Wolpe, Stefan
b. Zorina, Vera
b. Zuppke, Robert Carl
d. Agricola, Georgius

d. Bach, Wilhelm Friedemann
d. Barth, Heinrich
d. Baum, Herbert (M.)
d. Behrens, Peter
d. Berdichevsky, Micah Joseph
d. Bernstein, Eduard
d. Bormann, Martin Ludwig
d. Brandes, Georg Morris Cohen
d. Braun, Eva
d. Busoni, Ferruccio Benvenuto
d. Cohen, Hermann
d. Cornelius, Peter von
d. Dove, Heinrich Wilhelm
d. Du Bois-Reymond, Emil
d. Ebert, Friedrich
d. Ehrenberg, Christian Gottfried
d. Fallada, Hans
d. Fichte, Johann Gottlieb
d. Fischer, Emil Herman
d. Flanagan, Edward Joseph, Father
d. Fontane, Theodor
d. Frederick III
d. Frederick the Great
d. Gadski, Johanna
d. Geiger, Hans
d. Glinka, Mikhail Ivanovich
d. Goebbels, Joseph
d. Goerdeler, Karl Friedrich
d. Grafe, Albrecht Friedrich Wilhelm Ernst von
d. Grieg, Nordahl Brun
d. Grimm, Jakob Ludwig Karl
d. Grimm, Wilhelm Karl
d. Haberlandt, Gottlieb
d. Hegel, Georg Wilhelm Friedrich
d. Hitler, Adolf
d. Hoff, Jacobus Henricus van't
d. Hoffmann, E(rnst) T(heodor) A(madeus)
d. Hofmann, August Wilhelm von
d. Humboldt, Alexander, Freiherr von
d. Humboldt, Friedrich Heinrich Alexander von
d. Jacobi, Carl Gustav Jacob
d. Joachim, Joseph
d. Kirchhoff, Gustav Robert
d. Lehmann, Lilli
d. Lehmbruck, Wilhelm
d. Liebermann, Max
d. Liebknecht, Karl
d. Liebknecht, Wilhelm
d. Lilienthal, Otto
d. Lorengar, Pilar
d. Lortzing, Gustav Albert
d. Lotze, Rudolf Hermann
d. Luxemburg, Rosa
d. Mallinger, Mathilde
d. Mendelssohn, Moses
d. Menuhin, Yehudi
d. Mielke, Erich
d. Milder-Hauptmann, Pauline Anna
d. Mitscherlich, Eilhardt
d. Moltke, Helmuth Karl Bernhard von
d. Muller, Johannes Peter
d. Nicolai, Carl Otto Ehrenfried
d. Niemann, Albert
d. Ossietzky, Carl von
d. Pechstein, Max
d. Ranke, Leopold von
d. Rathenau, Walter
d. Reznicek, Emil von
d. Richthofen, Ferdinand Paul Wilhelm
d. Ritter, Karl
d. Sarti, Giuseppe
d. Savigny, Friedrich Karl von
d. Schadow, Gottfried

d. Schillings, Max von
d. Schinkel, Karl Friedrich
d. Schleicher, Kurt von
d. Schleiermacher, Friedrich Ernst
   Daniel
d. Schlieffen, Alfred, Graf von
d. Schreker, Franz
d. Schutzendorf, Gustav
d. Seeckt, Hans von
d. Siemens, (Ernst) Werner von
d. Sombart, Werner
d. Spielhagen, Friedrich von
d. Spitta, Philipp
d. Stirner, Max
d. Stresemann, Gustav
d. Sudermann, Hermann
d. Sukhomlinov, Vladimir
   Aleksandrovich
d. Taylor, Bayard
d. Tieck, (Johann) Ludwig
d. Treitschke, Heinrich Gotthard von
d. Trendelenburg, Friedrich Adolf
d. Van't Hoff, Jacobus Henricus
d. Virchow, Rudolf
d. Wassermann, August von
d. Wigman, Mary
d. Zunz, Leopold

Bernau, Germany
b. Thoma, Hans

Berneck, Germany
b. Christaller, Walter

Biebrich, Germany
b. Beck, Ludwig August Theoder
b. Dilthey, Wilhelm Christian Ludwig

Bielefeld, Germany
b. Gershon, Karen
b. Murnau, Friedrich W

Bingen, Germany
b. Kayser, Heinrich Gustav Johannes

Blankenburg, Germany
b. Frederika Louise
b. Kusch, P(olycarp)
b. Spengler, Oswald

Blankenese, Germany
d. Dehmel, Richard

Bliesheim, Germany
b. Zimmermann, Bernd Alois

Bochum, Germany
b. Eigen, Manfred
b. Schily, Otto

Bonn, Germany
b. Beethoven, Ludwig van
b. Ebbinghaus, Hermann
b. Hittorf, Johann Wilhelm
b. Schumacher, E(rnst) F(riedrich)
d. Clausius, Rudolf Julius Emmanuel
d. Diez, Friedrich Christian
d. Erhard, Ludwig
d. Hertz, Heinrich Rudolph
d. Kayser, Heinrich Gustav Johannes
d. Kekule, Friedrich August
d. Kelly, Petra (Karin)
d. Niebuhr, Barthold Georg
d. Plucker, Julius

d. Schumacher, Kurt
d. Strasburger, Eduard Adolf

Boppard, Germany
b. Strassmann, Fritz

Bottrop, Germany
b. Albers, Josef

Brandenburg, Germany
b. Schleicher, Kurt von
b. Schmeling, Max(imilian)

Braubach, Germany
b. Schlusnus, Heinrich

Breisach, Germany
d. Schongauer, Martin

Breitenau, Germany
b. Paulus, Friedrich von

Bremen, Germany
b. Carstens, Karl Walter
b. Quidde, Ludwig
b. Timken, Henry
b. Uhde, Hermann
b. Witte, Erich
d. Olbers, Heinrich Wilhelm Matthaus

Bremerhaven, Germany
b. Jacobs, Lou

Bremerhaven-Lebe, Germany
b. Butenandt, Adolf Fredrick Johann

Breselanz, Germany
b. Riemann, Georg Friedrich

Breslau, Germany
b. Bonhoeffer, Dietrich
b. Born, Max
b. Gellhorn, Peter
b. Haring, Georg Wilhelm Heinrich
b. Klemperer, Otto
b. Leitzel, Lillian
b. Ludwig, Emil
b. Marcus, Frank
b. Meyerowitz, Jan
b. Moszkowski, Moritz
b. Prang, Louis
b. Richthofen, Manfred von, Baron
b. Schleiermacher, Friedrich Ernst
   Daniel
b. Slotta, Karl Heinrich
b. Stein, Edith
b. Von Wangenheim, Chris
b. Wolff, Christian von, Baron

Bretten, Germany
b. Melanchthon, Philipp

Brieg, Germany
b. Masur, Kurt

Briesen, Germany
b. Nernst, Walther Hermann

Brunswick, Germany
b. Gauss, Carl Friedrich
b. Huch, Ricarda (Octavia)
b. Spohr, Louis Ludwig
b. Winkelmann, Hermann

d. Lessing, Gotthold Ephraim

Buchenwald, Germany
d. Thalmann, Ernst

Budesheim, Germany
b. George, Stefan

Buttelstedt, Germany
b. Fasch, Johann Friedrich

Buttenhausen, Wurttemberg, Germany
b. Erzberger, Matthias

Calw, Germany
b. Hesse, Hermann

Cassel, Germany
b. Mosenthal, Salomon Hermann von
d. Spohr, Louis Ludwig

Charlottenburg, Germany
b. Bedford, Sybille
d. Helmholtz, Hermann Ludwig
   Ferdinand von
d. Mommsen, Theodor
d. Zeppelin, Ferdinand Adolf August
   Heinrich von, Count

Chemnitz, Germany
b. Hahn, Carl Horst
b. Heym, Stefan
b. Kluge, John Werner
b. May, Karl Friedrich

Cleves, Germany
b. Anne of Cleves

Coburg, Germany
b. Leopold, I
b. Morgenthau, Hans Joachim
d. Schroder-Devrient, Wilhelmine

Colmar, Germany
b. Schongauer, Martin

Cologne, Germany
b. Adenauer, Konrad
b. Agrippa, Heinrich Cornelius
b. Boll, Heinrich (Theodor)
b. Bosch, Carl
b. Bruch, Max
b. Burtin, Will
b. Eichenberg, Fritz
b. Ernst, Jimmy
b. Ernst, Max
b. Etzioni, Amitai Werner
b. Fisher, Fred
b. Haacke, Hans Christoph
b. Janssen, Herbert
b. Jhabvala, Ruth Prawer
b. Klemperer, Werner
b. Michels, Robert
b. Offenbach, Jacques
b. Schurz, Carl
b. Schutzendorf, Gustav
b. Soelle, Dorothee
b. Steinberg, William
b. Stiegel, Henry William
b. Strenger, Hermann Josef
b. Voegelin, Eric (Herman Wilhelm)
b. Vondel, Joost van den
b. Werner, Helmut (Eberhard)

d. Adler, Kurt
d. Albert the Great
d. Alder, Kurt
d. Duns Scotus, John
d. Marie de Medicis
d. Nsubuga, Emmanuel, Cardinal
d. Otto, Nikolaus August

Constance, Germany
b. Wingler, Hans Maria
d. Hus, Jan

Coswig, Anhalt, Germany
b. Cohen, Hermann

Cothen, Germany
b. Abel, Karl Friedrich

Cusa, Germany
b. Nicholas of Cusa

Danzig, Germany
b. Fahrenheit, Gabriel Daniel
b. Grass, Gunter (Wilhelm)
b. Rosovsky, Henry
b. Schopenhauer, Arthur

Darmstadt, Germany
b. Kekule, Friedrich August
b. Liebig, Justus von
b. Muck, Karl
b. Schmid, Eduard
d. Flotow, Friedrich von, Baron

Delitzsch, Germany
b. Ehrenberg, Christian Gottfried

Dessau, Germany
b. Mendelssohn, Moses
b. Weill, Kurt

Deutz, Germany
b. Bebel, August

Dillenburg, Germany
b. Maurice of Nassau
b. Otterbein, Philip William

Dinklage, Germany
b. Romberg, Bernhard

Dirschau, Germany
b. Eisenstaedt, Alfred

Dobeln, Germany
b. Heckel, Erich

Donaueschingen, Germany
b. Kiefer, Anselm Karl Albert

Dornum, Germany
b. Shean, Al

Dortmund, Germany
b. Weber, Carl

Dresden, Germany
b. Augustus II
b. Bulow, Hans Guido von
b. Fritzsche, Hans
b. Hamilton, Edith
b. Kastner, Erich

b. Koch, Ilse
b. Luckner, Felix von, Count
b. Modersohn-Becker, Paula
b. Richter, Gerhard
b. Siodmark, Curt
b. Treitschke, Heinrich Gotthard von
b. Viertel, Peter
b. Zimmerman, Udo
b. Zinzendorf, Nikolaus Ludwig von, Count
d. Baker, Theodore
d. Friedrich, Caspar David
d. Kollwitz, Kathe Schmidt
d. Ludwig, Otto
d. Schlegel, Friedrich von
d. Schnorr, Ludwig von Carolsfeld
d. Schuch, Ernst von
d. Schutz, Heinrich
d. Tichatschek, Joseph
d. Werner, Abraham Gottlob

Duesseldorf, Germany
d. Szenkar, Eugen

Duisburg, Germany
d. Mercator, Gerhardus

Dulich, Germany
b. Stock, Frederick A

Duren, Germany
b. Schillings, Max von

Dusseldorf, Germany
b. Alvary, Max
b. Bierstadt, Albert
b. Cornelius, Peter von
b. Habermas, Juergen
b. Jacobi, Friedrich Heinrich
b. Kautner, Helmut
b. Laubenthal, Rudolf
b. Lorenz, Max
b. Schiffer, Claudia
b. Wenders, Wim

Ebenhausen, Germany
d. Tirpitz, Alfred von

Eberbach, Germany
b. Beissel, Johann Conrad

Ebersbach, Germany
b. Bergmann, Carl

Ebingen, Germany
b. Kiesinger, Kurt Georg

Eck, Germany
b. Eck, Johann Maier von

Edenkoben, Germany
b. Weidenreich, Franz

Edesheim, Germany
b. Holbach, Baron d'

Eger, Germany
b. Neumann, Balthasar

Egern, Germany
d. Slezak, Leo

Ehrenbrehstein, Germany
b. Brentano, Clemens Maria

Eiderstedt, Germany
b. Tonnies, Ferdinand

Einbeck, Germany
b. Muhlenberg, Heinrich Melchior

Eisenach, Germany
b. Abbe, Ernst
b. Bach, Johann Sebastian
d. Schirmer, Gustave

Eisfield, Germany
b. Ludwig, Otto

Eisleben, Germany
b. Agricola, Georgius
b. Gertrude the Great, Saint
b. Luther, Martin
d. Gertrude the Great, Saint
d. Luther, Martin

Elberfeld, Germany
b. Jaegers, Albert
b. Knappertsbusch, Hans
b. Plucker, Julius
b. Stein, Horst

Elbingerode, Germany
b. Ernst, Paul Karl Friedrich

Elmshorn, Germany
b. Stich, Michael

Emden, Germany
b. Petersen, Wolfgang

Ems, Germany
d. Parry, William Edward, Sir

Endenick, Germany
d. Schumann, Robert Alexander

Enkhausen, Germany
b. Lubke, Heinrich

Erasbach, Germany
b. Gluck, Christoph

Erfurt, Germany
b. Gehlen, Reinhard

Erlangen, Germany
b. Noether, (Amalie) Emmy
b. Ohm, Georg Simon

Ermsleben, Germany
b. Sombart, Werner

Ernshorf, Germany
b. Flick, Friedrich

Erxleben, Germany
b. Niemann, Albert

Eschershelm, Germany
b. Wohler, Friedrich

Essen, Germany
b. Baedeker, Karl
b. Freed, James I(ngo)
b. Hamm-Brucher, Hildegard
b. Krupp, Alfred
b. Krupp von Bohlen und Halbach, Bertha
b. Spethmann, Dieter
b. Thomas, Theodore
d. Krupp, Alfred

Essenrode, Germany
b. Hardenberg, Karl August von

Esslingen, Germany
b. Mayer, Johann Tobias

Eutin, Germany
b. Trendelenburg, Friedrich Adolf

Fichtel Gebirge, Germany
b. Richter, Johann Paul Friedrich

Fleinhausen, Germany
b. Streicher, Julius

Flossenberg, Germany
d. Bonhoeffer, Dietrich
d. Canaris, Wilhelm

Frankfurt, Germany
b. Blakely, Susan
b. Lawrence, Martin
b. Leisler, Jacob
b. Rothschild, Nathan Meyer
d. Grzimek, Bernhard
d. Kempner, Robert M(aximilian) W(asilii)
d. Pilatus, Rob(ert)

Frankfurt am Main, Germany
b. Adorno, Theodor Wiesengrund
b. Agoult, Marie Catherine Sophie d'
b. Charles II
b. DeBary, Heinrich Anton
b. Debus, Kurt Heinrich
b. Edinger, Tilly
b. Elsheimer, Adam
b. Erikson, Erik H(omburger)
b. Frank, Anne
b. Fromm, Erich
b. Geiger, Abraham
b. Goethe, Johann Wolfgang von
b. Hahn, Otto
b. Hertz, Alfred
b. Hoffmann, Heinrich
b. Loewi, Otto
b. Ophuls, Marcel
b. Rothschild, Mayer Amschel
b. Rudolf, Max
b. Savigny, Friedrich Karl von
b. Schiff, Jacob Henry
b. Schwarzhaupt, Elisabeth
b. Udet, Ernst
b. Weismann, August Friedrich Leopold
b. Westheimer, Ruth
d. Aguilar, Grace
d. Feuerbach, Paul Johann Anselm von
d. Hoffmann, Heinrich
d. Huch, Ricarda (Octavia)
d. Rosenzweig, Franz
d. Schleiden, Matthias Jakob
d. Schopenhauer, Arthur

d. Schumann, Clara Josephine Wieck
d. Steffani, Agostino

Frankfurt an der Oder, Germany
b. Kleist, Heinrich von

Freiburg, Germany
b. Bender, Hans
b. Gunther, Hans F K
b. Lasker, Albert D(avis)
b. Rahner, Karl
b. Warburg, Otto Heinrich
d. Hayek, Friedrich August von
d. Husserl, Edmund
d. Koehler, Georges J F
d. Spemann, Hans
d. Weismann, August Friedrich Leopold

Freudenstadt, Germany
b. Kollsman, Paul
d. Buchman, Frank Nathan Daniel

Freyburg, Germany
d. Jahn, Friedrich Ludwig

Friedenau, Germany
d. Bruch, Max

Friedrichsruh, Germany
d. Bismarck, Otto Edward Leopold von

Fuerth, Germany
b. Erhard, Ludwig
b. Kissinger, Henry Alfred
b. Kohler, Kaufmann

Fulda, Germany
b. Braun, Karl Ferdinand
b. Hutten, Ulrich von
b. Stern, Max

Fulnek, Germany
b. Konwitschny, Franz

Furstenberg an der Havel, Germany
d. Minkowski, Oskar

Garding, Germany
b. Mommsen, Theodor

Gelnhausen, Hesse, Germany
b. Grimmelshausen, Hans Jakob Christoffel von

Gera, Germany
b. Dix, Otto
b. Frankel, Max

Gernrode, Germany
b. Mohs, Friedrich

Gestungshausen, Germany
b. Krauss, Werner

Giebichenstein, Germany
d. Reichardt, Johann Friedrich

Giessen, Germany
b. Diez, Friedrich Christian
b. Dornberger, Walter Robert

b. Hofmann, August Wilhelm von
b. Levi, Hermann
b. Liebknecht, Wilhelm
b. Milner, Alfred, Viscount

Gleiwitz, Germany
b. Bolz, Lothar

Goerlitz, Germany
b. Dehmelt, Hans Georg

Goldschmieden, Germany
b. Bergius, Friedrich Karl Rudolph

Goslar, Germany
b. Henry, IV

Gotha, Germany
b. Blumenbach, Johann Friedrich
d. Ekhof, Konrad
d. Hansen, Peter Andreas

Gottingen, Germany
b. Bunsen, Robert Wilhelm Eberhard
b. Hagen, Uta Thyra
b. Vogel, Hans-Jochen
d. Andreas-Salome, Lou
d. Blumenbach, Johann Friedrich
d. Franck, James
d. Gauss, Carl Friedrich
d. Herbart, Johann Friedrich
d. Hilbert, David
d. Mayer, Johann Tobias
d. Planck, Max Karl Ernst Ludwig
d. Ritschl, Albrecht Benjamin
d. Tammann, Gustav Heinrich Johann Apollon
d. Wallach, Otto
d. Weber, Wilhelm Eduard
d. Wohler, Friedrich
d. Zsigmondy, Richard Adolf

Greifswald, Germany
b. Friedrich, Caspar David

Greiz, Germany
b. Aroldingen, Karin von

Gross-Sarchen, Germany
b. Fechner, Gustav Theodor

Gross-Tabarz, Germany
d. Alvary, Max

Grossjena, Germany
d. Klinger, Max

Grunbach, Germany
b. Heinkel, Ernst Heinrich

Guben, Germany
b. Pieck, Wilhelm

Gumund, Germany
b. Leutze, Emanuel

Gunzberg, Germany
b. Kelly, Petra (Karin)

Gustrow, Germany
d. Barlach, Ernst Heinrich

Gutersloh, Germany
b. Henze, Hans Werner

Haar, Germany
d. Mach, Ernst

Hachtel, Germany
b. Mergenthaler, Ottmar

Hademarschen, Germany
d. Storm, (Hans) Theodor (Woldsen)

Hagen, Germany
b. Halle, Charles, Sir

Hagenrode, Germany
b. Wolf, Friedrich August

Halberstadt, Germany
b. Bormann, Martin Ludwig

Halle, Germany
b. Heydrich, Reinhard Tristan Eugen
b. Kappel, Gertrude
b. Novalis
d. Cantor, Georg Ferdinand Ludwig
   Philipp
d. Ebbinghaus, Hermann
d. Eberhard, Johann August
d. Grunewald, Matthias
d. Roux, Wilhelm
d. Thomasius
d. Wolff, Christian von, Baron

Hamburg, Germany
b. Barth, Heinrich
b. Basedow, Johann Bernhard
b. Behrens, Peter
b. Brahms, Johannes
b. Casper, Gerhard
b. Dessau, Paul
b. Diels, Otto Paul Herman
b. Ekhof, Konrad
b. Enoch, Kurt
b. Franck, James
b. Hagenbeck, Carl
b. Hertz, Gustav Ludwig
b. Hertz, Heinrich Rudolph
b. Herzberg, Gerhard
b. Hesse, Eva
b. Hildesheimer, Wolfgang
b. Horney, Karen Danielson
b. Jensen, Johannes Hans Daniel
b. Kaempfert, Bert
b. Lagerfeld, Karl
b. Lewisohn, Adolph
b. Lindner, Richard
b. Mendelssohn, Felix
b. Mengers, Sue
b. Moltmann, Juergen (Dankwart)
b. Neuendorff, Adolf
b. Ossietzky, Carl von
b. Rey, Hans Augustus
b. Rey, Margret (Elizabeth)
b. Rosa, Carl
b. Rumann, Sig(fried)
b. Schleiden, Matthias Jakob
b. Schmidt, Helmut Heinrich
   Waldemar
b. Schroder-Devrient, Wilhelmine
b. Springer, Axel Caesar
b. Thalmann, Ernst
b. Trefflich, Henry Herbert Frederick
b. Warburg, Felix Moritz

b. Warburg, James Paul
b. Warburg, Paul Moritz
d. Bach, Carl Philipp Emanuel
d. Brauchitsch, Heinrich Alfred
d. Chrysander, Karl Franz Friedrich
d. Claudius, Matthias
d. Guericke, Otto Von
d. Hagenbeck, Carl
d. Keiser, Reinhard
d. Klafsky, Katharina
d. Klopstock, Friedrich Gottlieb
d. Liliencron, Detlev von
d. Romberg, Bernhard
d. Schiller, Karl (August Fritz)
d. Schnittke, Alfred
d. Telemann, Georg Philipp

Hamelin, Germany
d. Grese, Irma

Hammelburg, Germany
b. Froben, Johann

Hanau, Germany
b. Grimm, Jakob Ludwig Karl
b. Grimm, Wilhelm Karl
b. Hindemith, Paul

Hannover, Germany
b. Arendt, Hannah
b. Berliner, Emile
b. Busch, Wilhelm
b. Frederick Louis
b. Husch, Gerhard
b. Meyerhof, Otto Fritz
b. Munchhausen, Hieronymus Karl
   Friedrich von, Baron
b. Otto, Louis Karl Rudolf
b. Panofsky, Erwin
b. Schlegel, Friedrich von
b. Schwitters, Kurt (Hermann Edward
   Karl Julius)
b. Wigman, Mary
d. Leibniz, Gottfried Wilhelm von

Heidelberg, Germany
b. Astor, John Jacob
b. Browne, Jackson
b. Ebert, Friedrich
b. Gray, Hanna (Holborn)
b. Juenger, Ernst
b. Ruska, Ernst
b. Silvia
d. Bosch, Carl
d. Bunsen, Robert Wilhelm Eberhard
d. Burnham, Daniel H(udson)
d. Harnack, Adolf von
d. Kossel, Karl Martin Leonhard
   Albrecht
d. Patton, George Smith, Jr.

Heidenheim, Germany
b. Rommel, Erwin Johannes Eugin

Heilgenstadt, Germany
b. Riemenschneider, Tilman

Heinde, Germany
b. Dirks, Rudolph

Helmscherode, Germany
b. Keitel, Wilhelm

Helsa, Germany
b. Ziegler, Karl

Heppenheim, Germany
b. Antes, Horst

Herrenburg, Germany
b. Andrae, Johann Valentin

Herrligen, Germany
d. Rommel, Erwin Johannes Eugin

Hesse-Darmstadt, Germany
b. Alexandra Feodorovna

Hesse-Nasseau, Germany
b. Wagner, Robert F(erdinand)

Hildesheim, Germany
b. Krebs, Hans Adolf, Sir

Hirschberg, Germany
b. Reitsch, Hanna

Hochheim, Germany
b. Eckhart, Johannes

Hochstam-Main, Germany
b. Fischer, Hans

Hof, Germany
b. Boehm, Eric Hartzell

Hohensaliza, Germany
b. Edwards, Gus

Holstein, Germany
b. Barlach, Ernst Heinrich

Holzhausen, Germany
b. Otto, Nikolaus August

Hornberg Castle, Germany
d. Berlichingen, Gotz von

Husum, Germany
b. Storm, (Hans) Theodor (Woldsen)

Idar-Oberstein, Germany
b. Willis, Bruce

Ingolstadt, Germany
b. Hartmann, Rudolph

Iptingen, Germany
b. Rapp, George

Jagsthausen Castle, Germany
b. Berlichingen, Gotz von

Jena, Germany
b. Bernhard, Prince
b. Roux, Wilhelm
d. Abbe, Ernst
d. Dobereiner, Johann Wolfgang
d. Eucken, Rudolf Christoph
d. Haeckel, Ernst Heinrich Philipp
   August
d. Zeiss, Carl

b. Siemens, William, Sir

Liebau, Germany
b. Mueller, Otto

Lindheim, Germany
d. Sacher-Masoch, Leopold von

Lingen, Germany
b. Albers, Hans
b. Frelinghuysen, Theodorus Jacobus

Lippe, Germany
b. Duesenberg, Frederick S
b. Zunz, Leopold

Lippstadt, Germany
b. Niemoller, Martin

Lorenzkirch, Germany
b. Paul, Wolfgang

Loschwitz, Germany
d. Auer, Leopold

Louenburg, Germany
b. Sapir, Edward

Lubbenau, Germany
d. Gerhardt, Paul(us)

Lubeck, Germany
b. Brandt, Willy
b. Kneller, Godfrey, Sir
b. Mann, Heinrich Ludwig
b. Mann, Thomas
d. Buxtehude, Dietrich
d. Eulenspiegel, Till

Lubtheen, Germany
b. Chrysander, Karl Franz Friedrich

Ludwigsburg, Germany
d. Strauss, David Friedrich

Ludwigshafen, Germany
b. Dieterle, William

Ludwigshafen am Rhein, Germany
b. Kohl, Helmut (Michael)

Luneburg, Germany
b. Luhmann, Niklas
d. Himmler, Heinrich

Lynow, Germany
b. Barnack, Oskar

Magdeburg, Germany
b. Busse, Henry
b. Kaiser, Georg
b. Nuesslein-Volhard, Christiane
b. Telemann, Georg Philipp
b. Wallenda, Karl

Mainz, Germany
b. Cornelius, Peter
b. Fust, Johann
b. Gutenberg, Johann Gensfleischzur
   Laden Zum
b. Hallstein, Walter
b. Mannlicher, Ferdinand

b. Rindt, Jochen
b. Weyerhaeuser, Frederick
d. Cornelius, Peter
d. Gutenberg, Johann Gensfleischzur
   Laden Zum
d. Strassmann, Fritz

Mannheim, Germany
b. Casewit, Curtis
b. Cramer, Johann Baptist
b. Elsasser, Walter M, Dr.
b. Kahn, Otto Hermann
b. Klebe, Giselher
b. Krafft-Ebing, Richard von
b. Mayer, Robert, Sir
b. Morgenthau, Henry
b. Speer, Albert
d. Kotzebue, August Friedrich
   Ferdinand von

Marbach, Germany
b. Schiller, Friedrich von

Marburg, Germany
b. Gadamer, Hans-Georg
b. Hildebrand, Adolf von
d. Behring, Emil Adolph von

Marienberg, Germany
b. Brentano, Franz Clemens

Marienthal, Germany
d. Froebel, Friedrich Wilhelm August

Markstedt, Germany
b. Kesselring, Albert

Marktyl am Inn, Germany
b. Ratzinger, Joseph Alois, Cardinal

Mayen, Germany
b. Loeb, Jacques

Mechtshausen, Germany
d. Busch, Wilhelm

Meckenheim, Germany
d. Carstens, Karl Walter

Mecklenburg, Germany
b. Hinrichs, Gustav

Meidereich, Germany
b. Lehmbruck, Wilhelm

Melz, Germany
b. Lawrence, Frieda

Merseburg, Germany
b. Schumann, Elisabeth
b. Tennstedt, Klaus
d. Mesmer, Franz Anton

Meschede, Germany
b. Macke, August

Messelhausen, Germany
d. Lenard, Philipp Edward Anton

Messkirch, Germany
b. Heidegger, Martin

Metzingen, Germany
b. Schonbein, Christian Friedrich
b. Speidel, Hans

Minden, Germany
b. Bessel, Friedrich Wilhelm
b. Boas, Franz
b. Wiese, Kurt

Modrath, Germany
b. Stockhausen, Karlheinz

Moenchengladbach, Germany
b. Jonas, Hans

Montabour, Germany
b. Leyendecker, Joseph Christian

Moschin/Posen, Germany
b. Baum, Herbert (M.)

Muhlhausen, Germany
b. Schlumberger, Jean
b. Wyler, William
d. Muntzer, Thomas

Munich, Germany
b. Albrecht, Duke
b. Baader, Andreas
b. Badura-Skoda, Paul
b. Ben-Haim, Paul
b. Bogner, Willi
b. Buchner, Eduard
b. D'Aulaire, Edgar Parin
b. Decoster, Charles Theodore Henri
b. Einstein, Alfred
b. Feuchtwanger, Lion
b. Fischer, Anton Otto
b. Fischer, Ernst Otto
b. Geiger, Theodor Julius
b. Gidal, Tim
b. Hanfstaengl, Ernst Franz Sedgwick
b. Heiden, Konrad
b. Himmler, Heinrich
b. Huber, Robert
b. Jurgens, Curt
b. Knote, Heinrich
b. Koehler, Georges J F
b. Lynen, Feodor Felix Konrad
b. Mann, Erika
b. Mann, Klaus
b. Marc, Franz
b. Meggendorfer, Lothar
b. Mitscherlich, Alexander
b. Mossbauer, Rudolf Ludwig
b. Murphy, Rosemary
b. Orff, Carl
b. Penzias, Arno Allan
b. Rohm, Ernst
b. Schindler, Alexander Moshe
b. Schnorr, Ludwig von Carolsfeld
b. Sickert, Walter Richard
b. Spitzweg, Carl
b. Strauss, Franz Josef
b. Strauss, Richard Georg
b. Trampler, Walter
b. Viereck, George Sylvester
b. Wertham, Fredric
b. Wolff, Fritz
d. Butenandt, Adolf Fredrick Johann
d. Charles VII
d. Cicero
d. Dollinger, J(ohannes) J(osef) I(gnaz)
   von
d. Eisner, Kurt

d. Fischer, Hans
d. Gunther, Ignaz
d. Heyse, Paul Johann Ludwig von
d. Hildebrand, Adolf von
d. Husch, Gerhard
d. Jacobi, Friedrich Heinrich
d. Kastner, Erich
d. Kraus, Felix von
d. Lassus, Orlandus de
d. Liebig, Justus von
d. Ludendorff, Erich Friedrich
Wilhelm
d. Meggendorfer, Lothar
d. Messerschmitt, Willy
d. Mottl, Felix
d. Nachbaur, Franz
d. Ohm, Georg Simon
d. Prey, Hermann
d. Quidde, Ludwig
d. Roentgen, Wilhelm Konrad
d. Rohm, Ernst
d. Roswaenge, Helge
d. Senefelder, Aloys
d. Spengler, Oswald
d. Spitzweg, Carl
d. Strauss, Franz Josef
d. Van Rooy, Anton
d. Vogl, Heinrich
d. Weber, Max
d. Wedekind, Frank
d. Wien, Wilhelm Carl Werner Otto
Fritz Franz

Munster, Germany
d. Gorbachev, Raisa (Maksimovna
Titorenko)
d. Hamann, Johann Georg
d. Hardin, Louis Thomas
d. John of Leiden

Murnau, Germany
d. Loeb, James Morris

Muskau, Germany
d. Nernst, Walther Hermann

Nackenheim, Germany
b. Zuckmayer, Carl

Nassau, Germany
b. Altgeld, John Peter

Nauheim, Germany
d. Tata, Jamshedji Nusserwanji

Neisse, Germany
b. Bloch, Konrad Emil
b. Schindler, Solomon

Neu-Ruppin, Germany
b. Fontane, Theodor

Neubuckow, Germany
b. Schliemann, Heinrich

Neudeck, Germany
d. Hindenburg, Paul Ludwig Hans
Anton von Beneckendorff und

Neuende, Germany
b. Mitscherlich, Eilhardt

Neuendorf, Germany
b. Eiermann, Egon

Neuhaus, Germany
b. Peters, Carl

Neuruppin, Germany
b. Schinkel, Karl Friedrich

Neuses, Germany
b. Berger, Hans

Neuss, Germany
b. Frings, Joseph Richard
d. Ruckert, Friedrich

Neustadt, Germany
b. Howard, Eugene
b. Howard, Willie

Neustadt an der Haardt, Germany
b. Geiger, Hans

Neustrelitz, Germany
d. Humperdinck, Engelbert

Niederbreitenbach, Germany
b. Ley, Robert

Niederpoyritz, Germany
b. Kempe, Rudolf

Nolde, Germany
b. Nolde, Emil

Nordhausen, Germany
b. De Maiziere, Lothar

Nowawes, Germany
b. Weiss, Peter Ulrich

Nuremberg, Germany
b. Durer, Albrecht
b. Edmund, Saint
b. Hechinger, Fred Michael
b. Modl, Martha
b. Pachelbel, Johann
b. Sachs, Hans
b. Sigismund
b. Stoss, Veit
b. von Rad, Gerhard
b. Zapf, Hermann
d. Durer, Albrecht
d. Frank, Hans
d. Frick, Wilhelm
d. Goering, Hermann Wilhelm
d. Keitel, Wilhelm
d. Ley, Robert
d. Oberth, Hermann Julius
d. Pachelbel, Johann
d. Ribbentrop, Joachim von
d. Rosenberg, Alfred
d. Sachs, Hans
d. Seyss-Inquart, Artur von
d. Stoss, Veit
d. Streicher, Julius

Oberhausen, Germany
b. Jerusalem, Siegfried

Oberweissbach, Germany
b. Froebel, Friedrich Wilhelm August

Oberwinter, Germany
d. Galland, Adolf

Offenbach am Main, Germany
b. Hotter, Hans

Oldenburg, Germany
b. Behrens, Hildegard
b. Herbart, Johann Friedrich
b. Jaspers, Karl
b. Meinhof, Ulrike Marie

Oranienburg, Germany
b. Bothe, Walter Wilhelm Georg

Osnabruck, Germany
b. Remarque, Erich Maria

Otterberg, Germany
b. Straus, Isidor
b. Straus, Oscar Solomon

Perlberg, Germany
b. Lehmann, Lotte

Pforzheim, Germany
b. Reuchlin, Johann
b. Wieland, Heinrich Otto

Planitz, Germany
b. Frobe, Gerd

Plauen, Germany
b. Richter, Karl

Plotzensee Prison, Germany
d. Moltke, Helmuth James, Graf von

Posen, Germany
b. Palmer, Lilli

Potsdam, Germany
b. Frederick III
b. Helmholtz, Hermann Ludwig
Ferdinand von
b. Jacobi, Carl Gustav Jacob
d. Duhring, Eugen Karl
d. Frederick William, IV
d. Frederick William I

Pressburg, Germany
b. Hummel, Johann Nepomuk

Quedlinburg, Germany
b. Klopstock, Friedrich Gottlieb

Radebeul, Germany
d. May, Karl Friedrich

Radolfzell, Germany
b. Waldseemuller, Martin

Rammenau, Germany
b. Fichte, Johann Gottlieb

Rappoltsweiler, Germany
b. Spener, Philipp Jakob

Rastenburg, Germany
d. Stauffenberg, Claus (Schenk Graf)
Von

Rechenberg, Germany
d. Feuerbach, Ludwig Andreas

Regensburg, Germany
b. Altdorfer, Albrecht
d. Altdorfer, Albrecht
d. Haberl, Franz Xaver
d. Kepler, Johannes
d. Maximilian II

Reideburg, Germany
b. Genscher, Hans-Dietrich

Reinfeld, Germany
b. Claudius, Matthias

Renchen, Germany
d. Grimmelshausen, Hans Jakob
Christoffel von

Resitza, Germany
b. Meier-Graefe, Julius

Rhaunen, Germany
b. Kahn, Albert

Rheydt, Germany
b. Goebbels, Joseph

Rhondorf, Germany
d. Adenauer, Konrad

Riedbohringen, Germany
b. Bea, Augustinus

Rixdorf, Germany
b. Lawrie, Lee

Rodalben, Germany
b. Frank, Johann Peter

Ronsdorf, Germany
b. Carnap, Rudolf

Rosenau, Germany
b. Albert, Prince

Rosenheim, Germany
b. Goering, Hermann Wilhelm

Rostock, Germany
b. Albrand, Martha
b. Blucher, Gebhard Leberecht von
b. Kossel, Karl Martin Leonhard
Albrecht
b. Reichmann, Theodor
d. Grotius, Hugo

Rottluff, Germany
b. Schmidt-Rottluf, Karl

Rottweil, Germany
b. Witz, Konrad

Russelsheim, Germany
b. Fuchs, Klaus

Saarbrucken, Germany
b. Benary-Isbert, Margot
b. Ophuls, Max
b. Schroder, Gerhard

Sachrang, Germany
b. Herzog, Werner

Saint Georgen, Germany
d. Ernst, Paul Karl Friedrich

Salzburg, Germany
b. Bloch, Eric
d. Mozart, Leopold

Salzwedel, Germany
b. Meinecke, Friedrich

Samotschin, Germany
b. Toller, Ernst

Sasbach, Germany
d. Turenne, Henri de La Tour
Auvergne, Viscount

Sauersberg, Germany
d. Schonbein, Christian Friedrich

Saxony, Germany
b. Gerhardt, Paul(us)
b. Lamprecht, Karl
b. Pabst, Frederick

Schickenhof, Germany
b. Stark, Johannes

Schlesian, Germany
d. Blucher, Gebhard Leberecht von

Schmiden, Germany
b. Baur, Ferdinand Christian

Schneidemuhl, Germany
b. Goerdeler, Karl Friedrich

Schoenwald, Germany
b. Brach, Emil J

Schoneck, Germany
b. Wurlitzer, Rudolph

Schonhausen, Germany
b. Bismarck, Otto Edward Leopold
von

Schroda, Germany
b. Von Klitzing, Klaus

**Schrottinghausen, Westphalia,
Germany**
b. Baade, (Wilhelm Heinrich) Walter

Schulpforte, Germany
b. Mobius, August Ferdinand

Schwarzenburg, Germany
b. Rethberg, Elizabeth

Schweidnitz, Germany
b. Gebel-Williams, Gunther

Schweinfurt, Germany
b. Ruckert, Friedrich

Schwelm, Germany
b. Heinemann, Gustav Walter

Schwerin, Germany
d. Steno, Nicolaus

Schwiebus, Germany
b. Traven, B.

Seis, Germany
d. Dilthey, Wilhelm Christian Ludwig

Siegburg, Germany
b. Humperdinck, Engelbert

Siegen, Germany
b. Busch, Fritz

Siessen, Germany
d. Hummel, Berta

Simbach am Inn, Germany
b. Braun, Eva

Soest, Germany
b. Lely, Peter, Sir

Solingen, Germany
b. Bausch, Pina
b. Eichmann, Adolf
b. Scheel, Walter

Soran, Germany
b. Stern, Otto

Speyer, Germany
d. Rudolf, I

Stadthagen, Germany
b. Busching, Anton Friedrich

Starnberg, Germany
d. Baeyer, Adolf Johann Friedrich
Wilhelm, von
d. Wieland, Heinrich Otto

Starzeddal, Germany
b. Tillich, Paul Johannes

Stettin, Germany
b. Catherine the Great
b. Gierke, Otto von
b. Manns, August, Sir
b. Pannenberg, Wolfhart Ulrich

Strassburg, Germany
b. Baldung(-Grien), Hans
b. Bethe, Hans Albrecht
b. Brant, Sebastian
b. DeLoutherbourg, Philip James
b. Gottfried von Strassburg
b. Heger, Robert
d. Baldung(-Grien), Hans
d. Brant, Sebastian
d. DeBary, Heinrich Anton
d. Nessler, Victor E
d. Simmel, Georg

Strelno, Germany
b. Michelson, Albert Abraham

Stuttgart, Germany
b. Baumeister, Willi
b. Bernhard, Lucian
b. Breitschwerdt, Werner

Geographic Index

b. Frank, Bruno
b. Frick, Gottlob
b. Lowinsky, Edward Elias
b. Munchinger, Karl
b. Schlemmer, Oskar
b. Spemann, Hans
b. Strauss, David Friedrich
b. Weizsacker, Richard Freiherr von
b. Worner, Manfred
d. Andrae, Johann Valentin
d. Bosch, Robert August
d. Daimler, Gottlieb (Wilhelm)
d. Hallstein, Walter
d. Heinkel, Ernst Heinrich
d. Muck, Karl
d. Munchinger, Karl

Suessen, Germany
b. Bausch, John Jacob

Teuchern, Germany
b. Keiser, Reinhard

Teutendorf, Germany
b. Flotow, Friedrich von, Baron

Tiefenbronn, Germany
b. Gall, Franz Joseph

Tingleff, Germany
b. Schacht, Hjalmar Horace Greeley

Torgau, Germany
d. Walter, Johann

Treffurt, Germany
b. Bahr, Egon

Trier, Germany
b. Ambrose, Saint
b. Hoffner, Joseph, Cardinal

Tubingen, Germany
b. Blumenthal, Monica David
b. Camerarius, Rudolf Jakob
b. Hauser, Gayelord
d. Baur, Ferdinand Christian
d. Camerarius, Rudolf Jakob
d. Holderlin, Friedrich

Tutzing, Germany
d. Ebers, Georg Moritz

Uberlingen, Germany
b. Suso, Heinrich

Ulm, Germany
b. Einstein, Albert
b. Neff, Hildegarde
d. Suso, Heinrich

Unkel, Germany
d. Brandt, Willy

Upper Franconia, Germany
b. Stauffenberg, Claus (Schenk Graf) Von

Vetschau, Germany
b. Hellmann, Richard

Wandsbek, Germany
b. Bern, Paul
b. Raeder, Erich

Wannsee, Germany
d. Kleist, Heinrich von

Wasseralfingen, Germany
b. Jooss, Kurt

Wechold, Germany
b. Spitta, Philipp

Weckseldorf, Germany
b. Tichatschek, Joseph

Weil der Stadt, Germany
b. Kepler, Johannes

Weiler Giessen, Germany
b. Nachbaur, Franz

Weimar, Germany
b. Bach, Carl Philipp Emanuel
b. Bach, Wilhelm Friedemann
b. Kotzebue, August Friedrich Ferdinand von
b. Zeiss, Carl
d. Cranach, Lucas
d. Goethe, Johann Wolfgang von
d. Gungl, Joseph
d. Herder, Johann Gottfried von
d. Hummel, Johann Nepomuk
d. Nietzsche, Friedrich Wilhelm
d. Schiller, Friedrich von

Weissenberg, Germany
b. Hofmann, Hans

Weissenfels, Germany
d. Novalis

Weissenfels-an-der-Saale, Germany
b. Horst, Horst P(aul)

Wenings, Germany
b. Kaufman, Henry

Werl, Germany
b. Papen, Franz von

Wernigerode, Germany
d. Stammler, Rudolf

Wesel, Germany
b. Minuit, Peter
b. Ribbentrop, Joachim von

Wesselburen, Germany
b. Hebbel, Friedrich
b. Sander, Jil

Westerholt, Germany
b. Galland, Adolf

Westphalia, Germany
b. Jacobi, Abraham
b. VonFurstenberg, Betsy

Wiebelskirchen, Germany
b. Honecker, Erich

Wiederau, Germany
b. Zetkin, Clara

Wiefelstede, Germany
b. Bultmann, Rudolf

Wiehe, Germany
b. Ranke, Leopold von

Wiepersdorf, Brandenburg, Germany
d. Arnim, Achim von (Ludwig Joachim)

Wiesbaden, Germany
b. Daubeny, Peter Lauderdale, Sir
b. Galdikas, Birute M(arija) F(ilomena)
b. Schlondorff, Volker
b. Signoret, Simone Henrietta Charlotte
b. Villard, Oswald (Garrison)
d. Alma-Tadema, Lawrence, Sir
d. Freytag, Gustav
d. Niemoller, Martin
d. Roentgen, David

Wildhause, Germany
b. Zwingli, Huldreich

Wilflingen, Germany
d. Juenger, Ernst

Wirsitz, Germany
b. VonBraun, Wernher

Wismar, Germany
b. Frege, (Friedrich Ludwig) Gottlob

Witmarsum, Germany
b. Menno Simonsz(con)

Wittenberg, Germany
b. Weber, Wilhelm Eduard

Witzenhausen, Germany
b. Ludwig, Karl Friedrich Wilhelm

Wolfenbuttel, Germany
d. Praetorius, Michael

Wolfshagen, Germany
b. Steinway, Henry Engelhard

Worms, Germany
b. Staudinger, Hermann

Worms am Rhein, Germany
b. Holm, Hanya

Wuppertal-Barmen, Germany
b. Rau, Johannes

Wurttemberg, Germany
b. Daimler, Gottlieb (Wilhelm)
b. List, Georg Friedrich
b. Memminger, Christopher Gustavus
b. Mueller, Christian F
b. Schelling, Friedrich Wilhelm Joseph von
b. Wieland, Christoph Martin

Wurttemberg-Baden, Germany
b. Schmoller, Gustav Friedrich von

Wurzburg, Germany
b. Grunewald, Matthias
b. Heisenberg, Werner Karl
b. Lehmann, Lilli
d. Neumann, Balthasar
d. Riemenschneider, Tilman

Zehlendorf, Germany
d. Braun, Lily von Kretschman

Zerbst, Germany
d. Fasch, Johann Friedrich

Zusamaltheim, Germany
b. Deisenhofer, Johann

Zwickau, Germany
b. Pechstein, Max
b. Schocken, Theodore
b. Schumann, Robert Alexander

GERMANY (WEST)

b. Bednorz, J(ohannes) Georg
b. Tikaram, Tanita
d. Bloch, Ernst
d. Knote, Heinrich

Aachen, Germany (West)
d. Von Karman, Theodore

Anhousen, Germany (West)
b. Langer, Bernhard

Bad Brueckenau, Germany (West)
d. Anderson, Max(ie Leroy)

Bad Honnef, Germany (West)
d. Speidel, Hans

Bad Nauheim, Germany (West)
d. Kesselring, Albert

Bad Reichenhall, Germany (West)
d. Goldmann, Nahum

Baden-Baden, Germany (West)
d. Olczewska, Maria

Bayreuth, Germany (West)
d. Muller, Maria
d. Tietjen, Heinz

Beirberg, Germany (West)
d. Domagk, Gerhard

Berlin, Germany (West)
b. Audra (Ann), McDonald
b. Kinski, Nastassja
d. Benn, Gottfried
d. Blech, Leo
d. Braun, Otto
d. Grosz, George Ehrenfried
d. Hempel, Frieda
d. Hess, Rudolf
d. Hofer, Karl
d. Katona, George
d. Klose, Margarete

d. Laue, Max Theodor Felix von
d. Leider, Frida
d. Niekisch, Ernest
d. Reuter, Ernst
d. Ruska, Ernst
d. Springer, Axel Caesar
d. Stolz, Robert
d. Warburg, Otto Heinrich

Bonn, Germany (West)
d. Brauer, Max Julius Friedrich
d. Lubke, Heinrich

Braunschweig, Germany (West)
b. Brand, Jack

Bremen, Germany (West)
d. Focke, Heinrich Karl Johann

Cologne, Germany (West)
d. Frings, Joseph Richard
d. Fritzsche, Hans
d. Hoffner, Joseph, Cardinal
d. Massine, Leonide Fedorovich

Dusseldorf, Germany (West)
d. Beuys, Joseph
d. Funk, Walther
d. Stangl, Franz Paul

Eberstein, Germany (West)
d. Furtwangler, Wilhelm

Enzweihingen, Germany (West)
d. Neurath, Konstantin von

Eslingen, Germany (West)
b. Ackerman, Will

Essen, Germany (West)
d. Bohlem, Arndt von
d. Heinemann, Gustav Walter
d. Krupp von Bohlen und Halbach,
  Bertha

Frankfurt, Germany (West)
d. Gerold, Karl
d. Hindemith, Paul
d. Kiesinger, Kurt Georg
d. Mitscherlich, Alexander
d. Schindler, Oskar
d. Schlusnus, Heinrich
d. Schwarzhaupt, Elisabeth

Frankfurt am Main, Germany (West)
b. Binnig, Gerd
d. Reitsch, Hanna

Freiburg, Germany (West)
d. Gunther, Hans F K
d. Kazantzakis, Nikos
d. Staudinger, Hermann

**Freiburg im Breisgau, Germany
(West)**
d. Hevesy, George Charles von

Friedrichshafen, Germany (West)
d. Eckener, Hugo

Garmisch, Germany (West)
d. Brundage, Avery
d. Strauss, Richard Georg

Gottingen, Germany (West)
d. Born, Max
d. Hahn, Otto
d. Windaus, Adolf Otto Reinhold

Hamburg, Germany (West)
d. Debus, Sigurd Friedrich
d. Doenitz, Karl C
d. Dornberger, Walter Robert
d. Marek, Kurt W
d. Ophuls, Max
d. Schaudinn, Fritz Richard
d. Schmidt-Isserstedt, Hans

Hannover, Germany (West)
d. Rundstedt, Karl Rudolf Gerd von

Heidelberg, Germany (West)
b. Sears-Collins, Leah J.
d. Bothe, Walter Wilhelm Georg
d. Jensen, Johannes Hans Daniel
d. Kuhn, Richard
d. Wittig, Georg Friedrich Karl
d. Wunderlich, Fritz

Heidenheim, Germany (West)
d. Bauersfeld, Walther

Heilbronn, Germany (West)
d. Jooss, Kurt

Herzogenaurach, Germany (West)
d. Dassler, Adolf
d. Dassler, Horst

Hochheim, Germany (West)
d. Clark, James

Hurtgenwald, Germany (West)
d. Boll, Heinrich (Theodor)

Inning, Germany (West)
d. Egk, Werner

Kassel, Germany (West)
d. Szeryng, Henryk

Kiel, Germany (West)
d. Diels, Otto Paul Herman
d. Raeder, Erich

Kilchberg, Germany (West)
d. Foerster, Friedrich Wilhelm

Lake Starnberg, Germany (West)
d. Gehlen, Reinhard

Landstuhl, Germany (West)
b. Burton, LeVar(dis Robert Martyn
  Jr.)

Liemen, Germany (West)
b. Becker, Boris

Lindau, Germany (West)
d. Wankel, Felix

Ludwigsburg, Germany (West)
b. Michel, Hartmut

Luneberg, Germany (West)
d. Ludwig, Leopold

b. Thucydides
b. Tsatsos, Constantinos
b. Xenophon
d. Antisthenes
d. Aristides
d. Bachauer, Gina
d. Balopoulos, Michael
d. Blegen, Carl William
d. Cleva, Fausto
d. Desses, Jean
d. Doxiadis, Constantinos Apostolos
d. Elytis, Odysseus
d. Isocrates
d. Kanaris, Constantine
d. Menander
d. Metaxas, John
d. Palamas, Kostes
d. Papadopoulos, George
d. Papandreou, Andreas (George)
d. Papandreou, George
d. Paxinou, Katina
d. Pericles
d. Plato
d. Polygnotus
d. Saud (Ibn Abdul Aziz al Saud)
d. Seferiades, Giorgos Styljanou
d. Seferis, George
d. Sevitzky, Fabien
d. Sikelianos, Angelos
d. Socrates
d. Sophocles
d. Thucydides
d. Tsatsos, Constantinos

Attica, Greece
b. Demosthenes
b. Thespis

Calavria, Greece
d. Demosthenes

Cephalonia, Greece
b. Metaxas, John

Chaeronea, Greece
b. Plutarch
d. Plutarch

Chalcidice, Greece
b. Aristotle

Chalcis, Greece
d. Aristotle

Chania, Greece
b. Mitsotakis, Constantine

Chiliomondion, Greece
b. Papas, Irene

Chios, Greece
b. Papandreou, Andreas (George)
b. Theodorakis, Mikis

Cnidus, Greece
b. Eudoxus of Cnidus

Colonus, Greece
b. Sophocles

Comi, Greece
b. Papanicolaou, George Nicholas

Corfu, Greece
b. Philip, Prince
b. Somerville, Edith Anna OEnone

Corinth, Greece
d. Xenophon

Crete, Greece
b. Lucaris, Cyril

Cyrene, Greece
b. Callimachus
b. Carneades
b. Eratosthenes

Eleochorian, Greece
b. Papadopoulos, George

Island of Cos, Greece
b. Hippocrates

Kalamata, Greece
b. Yanni

Kastoria, Greece
b. Samaras, Lucas

Kavalla, Greece
b. Ibrahim Pasha

Lampsacus, Greece
d. Anaxagoras

Larissa, Greece
d. Hippocrates

Lefcohorion, Greece
b. Bardis, Panos Demetrios

Leucas Island, Greece
b. Sikelianos, Angelos

Lia, Greece
b. Gage, Nicholas

Megalopolis, Greece
b. Polybius
d. Polybius

Missolonghi, Greece
d. Byron, George Gordon, Baron

Orchomenus, Greece
d. Hesiod

Paros, Greece
b. Scopas

Patras, Greece
b. Palamas, Kostes
b. Papandreou, George
d. Andrew, Saint

Pella, Greece
d. Euripides

Pergamum, Greece
b. Galen

Piraeus, Greece
b. Paxinou, Katina

d. White, T(erence) H(anbury)

Prote, Greece
b. Karamanlis, Constantine

Psara, Greece
b. Kanaris, Constantine

Pylos, Greece
b. Spyropoulos, Jannis

Salamis, Greece
b. Euripides

Salonika, Greece
b. Abravanel, Maurice
b. Aldredge, Theoni (Athanasiou)
  V(achliotis)

Samos, Greece
b. Aristarchus of Samos
b. Epicurus
b. Pythagoras

Skourokhori, Greece
b. Skouras, Spyros Panagiotes

Skyros, Greece
d. Brooke, Rupert Chawner

Stenimochos, Greece
b. Doxiadis, Constantinos Apostolos

Syros, Greece
b. Broumas, Olga

Tatoi, Greece
d. Paul I

Thaos, Greece
b. Polygnotus

Thebes, Greece
b. Pindar

Thermopylae, Greece
d. Leonidas I

Tripolis, Greece
b. Stavropoulos, George Peter

Vassilikon, Greece
b. Athenagoras I

Volos, Greece
b. Chirico, Giorgio de
b. Vangelis
d. Heyns, Roger W(illiam)

Yianina, Greece
d. Stamos, Theodoros

Zante, Greece
b. Foscolo, (Niccolo) Ugo
d. Vesalius, Andreas

GREENLAND

b. Rasmussen, Knud Johan Victor
d. Wegener, Alfred Lothar

GRENADA

b. Brathwaite, Nicholas A(lexander)
b. Christophe, Henri

Grenville, Grenada
b. Buckmire, Ron

Saint Andrew's, Grenada
b. Gairy, Eric Matthew, Sir

Saint David's, Grenada
b. Pitt, David Thomas

Saint George's, Grenada
b. Mitchell, Keith
d. Bishop, Maurice Rupert

GUADELOUPE

b. Leger, Alexis St. Leger

GUAM

d. Mabini, Apolinario

Agana, Guam
b. Calvo, Paul McDonald
d. Canham, Erwin Dain

GUATEMALA

b. de Leon Carpio, Ramiro
b. Sarg, Tony
d. Carrera, Jose Rafael
d. Cochran, Steve

Chimel, Guatemala
b. Menchu, Rigoberta

Guatemala City, Guatemala
b. Asturias, Miguel Angel
b. Bressani, Ricardo
b. Carrera, Jose Rafael
b. Cerezo (Arevalo), Vinicio
b. Hendricks, Ted
b. Jensen, Alfred Julio
b. Mejia Victores, Oscar Humberto
b. Merida, Carlos
b. Serrano Elias, Jorge Antonio
b. Ubico y Castaneda, Jorge
d. Arevalo, Juan Jose
d. Ydigoras Fuentes Miguel

Huehuetenango, Guatemala
b. Rios Montt, Jose Efrain

Quetzaltenango, Guatemala
b. Arbenz Guzman, Jacobo
b. Estrada Cabrera, Manuel

San Marcos, Guatemala
b. Barrios, Justo Rufino

Taxisco, Guatemala
b. Arevalo, Juan Jose

GUINEA

b. Conte, Lansana
b. Dessalines, Jean Jacques

Conakry, Guinea
d. Carmichael, Stokely

Faranah, Guinea
b. Toure, Ahmed Sekou
b. Toure, Sekou

GUINEA-BISSAU

b. Cabral, Pedro Alvarez

Bissau, Guinea-Bissau
b. Vieira, Joao (Bernardo)

GUYANA

d. Beaton, Norman

Georgetown, Guyana
b. Beaton, Norman
b. Hoyte, Hugh Desmond
d. Burnham, Forbes

Jonestown, Guyana
d. Jones, Reverend Jim
d. Ryan, Leo Joseph

HAITI

b. Audubon, John James
b. Cedras, Raoul
b. Pierre, Andre
b. Preval, Rene
b. Saint, Assotto .
d. Dessalines, Jean Jacques

Cap Haitien, Haiti
b. Namphy, Henri
d. Christophe, Henri

Cape Francois, Haiti
b. Toussaint l'Ouverture, Pierre Dominique

Jeremie, Haiti
b. Auguste, Rose-Anne

Leogane, Haiti
b. Danticat, Edwidge

Petionville, Haiti
b. Pascal-Trouillot, Ertha

Port-Salut, Haiti
b. Aristide, Jean-Bertrand

Port-au-Prince, Haiti
b. Boyer, Jean Pierre
b. Charlemagne, Manno
b. Duvalier, Francois
b. Duvalier, Jean-Claude
d. Duvalier, Francois
d. Holly, James Theodore

d. Kostelanetz, Andre

HANNOVER

b. Herschel, William Frederick, Sir
b. Wedekind, Frank
d. Marschner, Heinrich August

Herrenhausen Palace, Hannover
b. George II

Osnabruck, Hannover
d. George I

HONDURAS

d. Carias Andino, Tiburcio
d. Martinez, Maximiliano Hernandez

Comayaguela, Honduras
b. Reina, Carlos Roberto

La Ceiba, Honduras
b. Azcona Hoyo, Jose Simon
b. Van Buren, Steve W

La Paz, Honduras
b. Suazo Cordova, Roberto

Tegucigalpa, Honduras
b. Callejas Romero, Rafael Leonardo
b. Carias Andino, Tiburcio
b. Flores Facusse, Carlos Roberto
b. Morazan, Jose Francisco

Trujillo, Honduras
d. Walker, William

HONG KONG

b. Anders, William Alison
b. Chan, Jackie
b. Higgins, Marguerite
b. Kwan, Nancy Kashen
b. Lee, Martin (Yongho)
b. Lorring, Joan
b. Tsang, Daniel C.
b. Tsui, Kitty
b. Wu, Gordon (Ying Sheung)
d. Lee, Bruce
d. Lin, Yutang
d. Pao, Y(ue) K(ong), Sir
d. Ts'ai Yuan-p'ei

HUNGARY

b. Antall, Jozsef, Jr.
b. Kemeny, John G(eorge)
b. Leiber, Judith
b. Papp, Laszlo
b. Stephen, I
d. Attila
d. Berchtold, Leopold von
d. Stephen, I

Balatonszarszo, Hungary
d. Jozsef, Attila

Belgrade, Hungary
d. Hunyadi, John

Bolho, Hungary
b. Losonczi, Pal

Buda, Hungary
b. Semmelweis, Ignaz Philipp

Budapest, Hungary
b. Anda, Geza
b. Bajor, Gizi
b. Biro, Val
b. Capa, Cornell
b. Cicciolina
b. Davignon, Viscount
b. Esslin, Martin Julius
b. Fleischmann, Charles Louis
b. Gabor, Eva
b. Gabor, Zsa Zsa
b. Grove, Andrew S.
b. Herzl, Theodor
b. Horn, Gyula
b. Houdini, Harry
b. Hubay, Jeno
b. Kertesz, Istvan
b. Lang, Paul Henry
b. Lorant, Stefan
b. Lukacs, Gyorgy
b. Polanyi, Michael
b. Rozsa, Miklos
b. Rubik, Erno
b. Salten, Felix
b. Schwimmer, Rosika
b. Seidl, Anton
b. Senesh, Hannah
b. Solti, Georg, Sir
b. Soros, George
b. Stader, Maria
b. Staller, Ilona
b. Starker, Janos
b. Szasz, Thomas Stephen
b. Szigeti, Joseph
b. Trauner, Alexander
b. Weiss, Ted
b. Wigner, Eugene P(aul)
d. Ady, Endre
d. Antall, Jozsef, Jr.
d. Bajor, Gizi
d. Gero, Erno
d. Kadar, Janos
d. Kodaly, Zoltan
d. Lukacs, Gyorgy
d. Nagy, Imre
d. Polanyi, Michael
d. Szabolcsi, Bence
d. Telkes, Maria (de)

Czeged, Hungary
b. Zsigmond, Vilmos

Debrecen, Hungary
b. Alvary, Lorenzo
b. Konrad, Gyorgy
b. Lakatos, Imre

Ermindszent, Hungary
b. Ady, Endre

Geszt, Hungary
b. Tisza, Kalman

Goedoelloe, Hungary
d. Grosz, Karoly

Heves, Hungary
b. Remenyi, Eduard

Idvor, Hungary
b. Pupin, Michael Idvorsky

Kecskemet, Hungary
b. Bartok, Eva

Keszthely, Hungary
b. Goldmark, Karl

Kisstee, Hungary
b. Joachim, Joseph

Kony, Hungary
b. Pozsgay, Imre

Lebenyi Szent, Hungary
b. Nikisch, Arthur

Lugos, Hungary
b. Lugosi, Bela

Mako, Hungary
b. Pulitzer, Joseph

Marosvasarhely, Hungary
b. Laszlo, Magda

Miskolc, Hungary
b. Grosz, Karoly

Monok, Hungary
b. Kossuth, Lajos

Nagyvarad, Hungary
b. Pazmany, Peter

Pest, Hungary
d. Kisfaludy, Karoly

Pozsony, Hungary
d. Pazmany, Peter

Pressburg, Hungary
b. Lenard, Philipp Edward Anton

Raab, Hungary
b. Richter, Hans

Raiding, Hungary
b. Liszt, Franz (Ferencz)

Saint Johann, Hungary
b. Klafsky, Katharina

Selyp, Hungary
b. Kepes, Gyorgy

Siofok, Hungary
b. Hirsch, John Stephen

Sojtor, Hungary
b. Deak, Francis

Sucha, Hungary
b. Wilder, Billy (Samuel)

Szeged, Hungary
b. Pogany, Willy

Szekesfehervar, Hungary
b. Orban, Viktor

Szigetvar, Hungary
d. Suleiman I

Tapolcza, Hungary
b. Kaplan, Joseph

Tarna-Ors, Hungary
b. Orczy, Emmuska, Baroness

Tete, Hungary
b. Kisfaludy, Karoly

Tulchva, Hungary
b. Fox, William

Ungarisch-Altenburg, Hungary
b. Haberlandt, Gottlieb

Vac, Hungary
b. Jancso, Miklos

Vesprem, Hungary
b. Auer, Leopold

Volosca, Hungary
d. Andrassy, Gyula, Count

Zsambek, Hungary
b. Gungl, Joseph

ICELAND

b. Ericson, Leif
b. Hermannsson, Steingrimur
d. Charcot, Jean Baptiste Etienne
   Auguste
d. Thorarensen, Jakob

Ellidhavatn, Iceland
b. Benediktsson, Einar

Herdisarvik, Iceland
d. Benediktsson, Einar

Hunavatnssysla, Iceland
b. Thorarensen, Jakob

Reykjavik, Iceland
b. Bjork
b. Finnbogadottir, Vigdis
b. Laxness, Halldor (Kiljan)
b. Oddsson, David
b. Tomasson, Helgi
d. Andrews, Frank M(axwell)
d. Laxness, Halldor (Kiljan)

Thingvalla, Iceland
d. Benediktsson, Bjarni

Tjorn, Iceland
b. Eldjarn, Kristjan

ILLYRIA

Germania, Illyria
b. Belisarius

Faizabad, Oudh, India
b. Mahal, Hazrat

Ferozepore, India
b. Rai, Lala Lajpat

Frederiksnagar, India
d. Carey, William

Gagoda, India
b. Bhave, Acharya Vinoba

Ghazipur, India
d. Cornwallis, Charles, Marquis

Giridih, India
d. Bose, Jagadis Chandra, Sir

Goa, India
d. Albuquerque, Affonso de

Gorakhpur, India
b. Yogananda, Paramahansa, Swami

Gujarat, India
b. Dayananda Saraswati, Swami
b. Patel, Vallabhbhai

Gwalior, Madahya Pradesh, India
b. Vajpayee, Atal Behari

Haradanalli, India
b. Gowda, H(aradanahalli) D(odde)
Deve

Hardwar, India
b. Maharaj Ji, Guru

Hazara, India
b. Ayub Khan, Mohammad

Hubli, India
b. Rau, Dhanvanthi Rama, Lady

Hyderabad, India
b. Husain, Zakir
b. Naidu, Sarojini

Ibrahimpatti, Uttar Pradesh, India
b. Shekhar, Chandra

Illure, India
b. Reddy, N(eelam) Sanjeeva

Jamshedpur, India
b. Durrell, Gerald (Malcolm)

Jaunpur, India
b. Sadik, Nafis

Kaladi, India
b. Sankara

Kamapukur, India
b. Ramakrishna, Sri

Kanthalpara, India
b. Chatterji, Bankimchandra

Kapilavastu, India
b. Buddha

Kartarpur, India
d. Nanak

Kedarnath, India
d. Sankara

Kozhikode, India
b. Krishna Menon, V(engalil)
K(rishnan)

Ksatriyakundagrama, India
d. Mahavira

Kucha, India
b. Kumarajiva

Kumbakonam, India
b. Swaminathan, M(onkombu)
S(ambisivan)

Kushtia, India
b. Dasgupta, S(urendra) N(ath)

Kusinagara, India
d. Buddha

Kuthwara, India
b. Rajneesh, Bhagwan Shree

Lahore, India
b. Bailey, Frederick Marshman
b. Chandrasekhar, Subrahmanyan
b. Mehta, Ved (Parkash)
b. Shah Jahan
d. Iqbal, Mahomed, Sir

Lamhi, India
b. Premchand

Landour, India
b. Birch, John

Lucknow, India
b. Richard, Cliff
d. Dasgupta, S(urendra) N(ath)
d. Griffin, Walter Burley
d. Naidu, Sarojini

Ludhiana, India
b. Chaudhari, Praveen

Madanapelle, India
b. Krishnamurti, Jiddu

Madras, India
b. Humperdinck, Engelbert
b. Lunn, Arnold Henry Moore, Sir
b. Narayan, R(asipuram)
K(rishnaswami)
b. Radhakrishnan, Sarvepalli
b. Rajagopalachari, Chakravarti
b. Raman, Chandrasekhara Venkata,
Sir
b. Rama Rau, Santha
d. Kamaraj, Kumaraswami
d. Radhakrishnan, Sarvepalli
d. Rajagopalachari, Chakravarti

Madura, India
b. De Morgan, Augustus

Mhow, Madhya Pradesh, India
b. Ambedkar, Bhimrao Ramji

Motihari, India
b. Orwell, George

Mount Aber, India
b. Phillpotts, Eden

Mughalsarai, India
b. Shastri, Lal Badahur

Murree, India
b. Bairnsfather, Bruce

Mymensingh, India
b. Bose, Jagadis Chandra, Sir

Mysore, India
d. Chandragupta Maurya

Naini Tal, India
b. Ismay, Hastings Lionel, Baron
b. Wingate, Orde Charles

Navsari, India
b. Tata, Jamshedji Nusserwanji

New Delhi, India
b. Ashdown, Paddy
b. Chopra, Deepak
b. Gandhi, Sanjay
d. Ahmed, Fakhruddin Ali
d. Gandhi, Indira Priyadarshini Nehru
d. Gandhi, Mahatma
d. Gandhi, Sanjay
d. Husain, Zakir
d. Menon, (Vengalil Krishnan) Krishna
d. Pandit, Vijaya Lakshmi (Nehru)
d. Ram, Jagjivan
d. Singh, (Sardar) Swaran

Ootacamund, India
b. Williams, Roger J

Panipat, India
b. Abbas, Khwaja Ahmad

Patna, India
d. Narayan, Jayaprakash
d. Prasad, Rajendra

Paunar, India
d. Bhave, Acharya Vinoba

Peshawar, India
b. Anand, Mulk Raj

Poona, India
b. Sivaji
d. Gokhale, Gopal Krishna

Porbandar, India
b. Gandhi, Mahatma

Pune, India
d. Rajneesh, Bhagwan Shree

Radhanagar, India
b. Roy, Ram Mohun

Rafsanjan, India
b. Rafsanjani, Hashemi

Rai Bhoi di Talvandi, India
b. Nanak

Rainkhet, India
b. Horrocks, Brian Gwynne, Sir

Raipur, India
b. Khorana, Har Gobind

Rajamadam, India
b. Venkataraman, Ramaswamy

Rajgarh, India
d. Sivaji

Rawalpindi, India
b. Sutton, John
d. Yahya Khan, Agha Muhammad

Rehutia, India
b. Merivale, Philip

Sandhwan, India
b. Singh, Giani Zail

Sarnath, India
d. Dharmapala, Anagarika

Shakpura, India
b. Ghose, Sri Chinmoy Kumar

Shivpur, India
b. Khan, Ali Akbar

Sialkot, India
b. Iqbal, Mahomed, Sir
b. Zafrulla Khan, Muhammad, Sir

Sikri, India
b. Jahangir

Simla, India
b. Kaye, Mary Margaret Mollie

Sriperumbudur, India
d. Gandhi, Rajiv Ratna

Trichinopoly, India
d. Heber, Reginald

Tungipara, India
b. Rahman, Mujibur, Sheik

Uttar Pradesh, India
b. Devi, Phoolan
b. Mahesh Yogi, Maharishi

Vaardhamana, India
b. Mahavira

Vengurla, India
b. Goheen, Robert Francis

Virudunagar, India
b. Kamaraj, Kumaraswami

Vrindavan, India
d. Bhaktivedanta, A(bhay) C(haranaravinda)

Zira, India
b. Randhawa, Mohinder Singh

INDONESIA

Jakarta, Indonesia
d. Hatta, Mohammad
d. Sukarno, Achmed

Java, Indonesia
b. Soeharto

Jogjakarta, Indonesia
d. Agus Salim, Hadji

Pare-Pare, Indonesia
b. Habibie, B(acharuddin) J(usuf)

West Java, Indonesia
d. Van Diemen, Anthony Meuza

IONIAN ISLANDS

Corfu, Ionian Islands
b. Hamilton, Ian Standish Monteith, Sir

Levkas, Ionian Islands
b. Hearn, Lafcadio

IRAN

b. Hallaj, Al-Husayn ibn Mansur al-

Ardakan, Iran
b. Khatami, Mohammad

Bushire, Iran
b. Chubak, Sadeq-i

Fathabad, Iran
d. Nadir Shah

Kashan, Iran
d. Taqi Khan Amir-e Kabir, Mirza

Khorasan, Iran
b. Khamenei, (Sayed) Ali, Hojatolislam

Luristan, Iran
d. Antiochus, III

Mazinan, Khurasan, Iran
b. Shariati, Ali

Qum, Iran
b. Sadr, Musa al-

Tabriz, Iran
b. Gregorian, Vartan

Tehran, Iran
b. Bijan
b. Mansouri, Lotfi
b. Pahlevi, Farah Diba
b. Schroeder, Barbet
d. Beheshti, Mohammad, Ayatollah
d. Ghotbzadeh, Sadegh
d. Hoveyda, Amir Abbas
d. Khomeini, Ruhollah Musavi, Ayatollah
d. Mossadegh, Mohammed
d. Rajai, Mohammed Ali

Tus, Iran
d. Ghazali, al

IRAQ

b. Kamel, Hussein

Baghdad, Iraq
b. Faisal II
b. Husseini, Faisal
b. Kedourie, Elie
b. Nuri al-Sa'id
b. Saatchi, Maurice
d. Abu Nuwas
d. Ashari, Abu al-Hasan Ali al-
d. Bakr, Ahmad Hasan al
d. Bell, Gertrude Margaret
d. Kassem, Abdul Karim (el)
d. Nidal, Abu

Basra, Iraq
b. Abu 'Ali al-Hasan ibn al-Haytham
b. Ashari, Abu al-Hasan Ali al-

Kazimayn, Iraq
b. Fadil al-Jamali, Muhammad

Mosul, Iraq
b. Aziz, Tariq Mikhayl

Najaf, Iraq
b. Fadlallah, Sayyid Muhammad Husayn

Tikrit, Iraq
b. Hussein, Saddam (Al-Tikriti)

IRELAND

b. Blood, Thomas
b. Brown, Alexander
b. Burke, Robert O'Hara
b. Colden, Cadwallader
b. Conway, Thomas
b. Craig, May
b. Cullen, Paul, Cardinal
b. Guinan, Matthew
b. Keenan, Brian
b. Thornton, Matthew
d. Burke, Mike
d. Cullen, Paul, Cardinal
d. Hyde, Douglas
d. Ivask, Ivar Vidrik

Altimore, Ireland
b. Shields, James

Annaghdown, Ireland
d. Brendan of Clonfert, Saint

Annalong, Ireland
b. Chesney, Francis Rawdon

Aran Island, Ireland
b. OhEithir, Breandan

Ardglass, Ireland
b. Hunter, Thomas

Ardmore, Ireland
d. Keane, Mary Nesta

Athlone, Ireland
b. McCormack, John
b. O'Connor, Thomas Power

Avondale, Ireland
b. Parnell, Charles Stewart

Ballaghaderin, Ireland
b. O'Doherty, Brian

Ballina, Ireland
b. Robinson, Mary

Ballintemple, Ireland
d. Boole, George

Ballintogher, Ireland
b. Day-Lewis, Cecil

Ballychrine, Tipperary, Ireland
b. Bates, Daisy Mae

Ballyjamesduff, Ireland
b. Daly, Marcus

Ballylongford, Ireland
b. Kitchener, Horatio Herbert

Ballyshannon, Ireland
b. Allingham, William
b. Gallagher, Rory

Bantry, Ireland
b. Healy, T(imothy) M(ichael)

Beal-na-Blath, Ireland
d. Collins, Michael

Beau Park, Ireland
b. Garrett, Eileen Jeanette Lyttle

Belfast, Ireland
b. Bell Burnell, Jocelyn
b. Teggart, Frederick J.

Blessington, Ireland
b. DeValois, Ninette, Dame

Bohola, Ireland
b. O'Dwyer, Paul
b. O'Dwyer, William

Bray, Ireland
b. Moyes, Patricia
b. O'Dalaigh, Cearbhall

Cahir, Ireland
b. Dempsey, John Noel

Cahirsiveen, Ireland
b. O'Connell, Daniel

Callan, Ireland
b. Cudahy, Michael
b. Hoban, James

Carlingford, Ireland
b. McGee, Thomas D'Arcy

Carlow, Ireland
b. Taylor, William Desmond

Castlebar, Ireland
b. Haughey, Charles James

Castletownshend, Ireland
d. Somerville, Edith Anna OEnone

Chapelizod, Ireland
b. Northcliffe, Alfred Charles William
Harmsworth, Viscount

Charleville, Ireland
b. Mannix, Daniel

Clogheen, Ireland
d. Sackville-West, Edward Charles

Clonakilty, Ireland
b. Collins, Michael
b. Croker, Boss
b. Harnett, William Michael

Clonmel, Ireland
b. Sterne, Laurence

Clontarf, Ireland
d. Brian Boru

Cloughjordan, Ireland
b. MacDonagh, Thomas

Coleraine, Ireland
b. Blair, William Richards

Connemara, Ireland
b. O'Toole, Peter

Coole, Ireland
d. Gregory, Isabella Augusta Persse,
Lady

County Antrim, Ireland
b. Campbell, Alexander
b. Paterson, William

County Armagh, Ireland
b. Russell, George William
b. Tennent, Gilbert

County Cavan, Ireland
b. Fitzpatrick, Thomas

County Clare, Ireland
b. Tobin, Daniel Joseph

County Cork, Ireland
b. England, John
b. Jones, Mary Harris
b. Kearney, Denis
b. Knowles, James Sheridan
b. MacLiammoir, Michael
b. Maclise, Daniel
b. MacSwiney, Terence
b. Manning, Timothy, Cardinal
b. McAuliffe, Jack B
b. Mulhare, Edward
b. O'Connor, Frank
b. O'Faolain, Sean
b. Summersby, Kay
b. Wilcox, Herbert
d. Barry, Tom
d. Bax, Arnold Edward Trevor, Sir
d. Cockburn, Claud
d. Mankowitz, Wolf

County Donegal, Ireland
b. Lewis, Andrew
b. Makemie, Francis

County Down, Ireland
b. Hutcheson, Francis

County Galway, Ireland
b. Clodagh
b. Gilmore, Patrick Sarsfield
b. Harris, Frank
b. O'Brian, Patrick
b. O'Flaherty, Liam
b. Townsend, John Sealy Edward, Sir

County Kerry, Ireland
b. West, Rebecca, Dame

County Kildare, Ireland
b. Keane, Mary Nesta
d. Brigid of Kildare

County Kilkenny, Ireland
b. Hackett, Francis
b. O'Neill, James

County Limerick, Ireland
b. Ahearn, Daniel F.
b. Harris, Richard, Sir
b. Heck, Barbara Ruckle
b. Montez, Lola
b. Rehan, Ada

County Mayo, Ireland
b. Moore, George Augustus
b. Redman, Joyce

County Meath, Ireland
b. Moore, Tom
b. Stern, James

County Meenmore, Ireland
b. O'Donnell, Peadar

County Tyrone, Ireland
b. Alexander of Tunis
b. Brady, Paul Joseph
b. Howard, Tom
b. Kiely, Benedict

Curragh Chase, Ireland
b. DeVere, Aubrey Thomas
d. DeVere, Aubrey Thomas

Dangan Castle, Ireland
b. Wellesley, Richard Colley, 1st
Marquess Wellesley

Douglas, Ireland
b. Robinson, Lennox

Dublin, Ireland
b. Adams, Tony
b. Ahern, Bertie
b. Allgood, Sara
b. Andrews, Eamonn
b. Bacon, Francis
b. Balfe, Michael William
b. Barnardo, Thomas John
b. Bartholomew, Freddie
b. Beckett, Samuel (Barclay)
b. Behan, Brendan (Francis)
b. Binchy, Maeve
b. Bono
b. Boucicault, Dion Lardner
b. Bowen, Elizabeth Dorthea Cole
b. Brambell, Wilfrid
b. Brent, George
b. Briscoe, Robert
b. Brown, Christy
b. Bruton, John (Gerard)
b. Burke, Edmund
b. Byrne, Gabriel
b. Cadogan, William, Earl
b. Carey, Mathew
b. Carson, Edward Henry
b. Castlereagh, Robert Stewart,
Viscount
b. Clarke, Austin
b. Clarke, Harry
b. Coghlan, Eamonn
b. Collinge, Patricia
b. Cooper, Giles (Stannus)
b. Cosgrave, Liam
b. Cosgrave, William Thomas
b. Costello, John Aloysius
b. Crofts, Freeman Willis
b. Cunningham, Alan Gordon, Sir
b. Cunningham, Andrew Browne,
Viscount
b. Desmond, William
b. Digges, Dudley
b. Doggett, Thomas
b. Dowland, John
b. Doyle, Jill
b. Doyle, Roddy
b. Durcan, Paul
b. Emmet, Robert
b. Field, John
b. Fitzgerald, Barry
b. FitzGerald, Garret Michael
b. Fitzgerald, George Francis
b. Fitzgerald, Geraldine
b. Geldof, Bob
b. Gogarty, Oliver St. John
b. Griffith, Arthur
b. Guerin, Veronica
b. Hamilton, William Rowan, Sir
b. Herbert, Victor
b. Hicks, Ursula Kathleen Webb
b. Hopkins, John Henry
b. Joyce, James Augustus Aloysius
b. Kelly, Michael
b. Laffan, William Mackay
b. Laird, Rick
b. Lardner, Dionysius
b. LeFanu, Joseph Sheridan
b. Leonard, Hugh
b. Lynott, Phil(ip)
b. Mackay, John William

b. Malone, Edmund
b. Moore, Thomas
b. Morton, Digby
b. Murdoch, Iris
b. O'Brien, Conor Cruise
b. O'Casey, Sean
b. O'Connor, Sinead
b. O'Keeffe, John
b. O'Reilly, Anthony John Francis
b. O'Shea, Milo
b. Pearse, Padraic
b. Pilkington, Francis Meredyth
b. Ridge, Lola
b. Roche, Kevin
b. Ryan, Cornelius John
b. Saint Gaudens, Augustus
b. Savage, John
b. Shaw, George Bernard
b. Sheridan, Richard Brinsley
b. Snow, Carmel White
b. Steele, Richard, Sir
b. Stephens, James
b. Stoker, Bram
b. Stokes, William
b. Swift, Jonathan
b. Synge, John Millington
b. Tandy, James Napper
b. Tate, Nahum
b. Todd, Richard
b. Trench, Richard Chenevix
b. Tyrrell, George
b. Ussher, James
b. Wellington, Arthur Wellesley, Duke
b. Wibberley, Leonard Patrick
O'Connor
b. Wilde, Oscar (Fingal O'Flahertie
Wills)
b. Woffington, Margaret
b. Yeats, William Butler
d. Behan, Brendan (Francis)
d. Briscoe, Robert
d. Childers, Erskine
d. Childers, Erskine Hamilton
d. Clarke, Austin
d. Connolly, Sybil
d. Cosgrave, William Thomas
d. Costello, John Aloysius
d. Craig, May
d. Davitt, Michael
d. DeValera, Eamon
d. Dunsany, Edward J M Plunkett,
Baron
d. Emmet, Robert
d. Fitzgerald, Barry
d. Fitzgerald, George Francis
d. Fitzgibbon, Constantine
d. Flynn, Edward Joseph
d. Geminiani, Francesco
d. Griffith, Arthur
d. Guerin, Veronica
d. Hamilton, William Rowan, Sir
d. Healy, T(imothy) M(ichael)
d. Hemans, Felicia Dorothea Browne
d. Hopkins, Gerard Manley
d. Kavanagh, Patrick
d. Killanin, Michael Morris, Lord
d. LeFanu, Joseph Sheridan
d. Llewellyn, Richard
d. MacBride, Sean
d. MacDonagh, Thomas
d. MacLiammoir, Michael
d. Manners, Charles
d. Markievicz, Constance Georgine,
Countess
d. McCormack, John
d. McKenna, Siobhan

d. O'Brian, Patrick
d. O'Connor, Frank
d. O'Donnell, Peadar
d. O'Faolain, Sean
d. O'Flaherty, Liam
d. OhEithir, Breandan
d. Pearse, Padraic
d. Robinson, Lennox
d. Swift, Jonathan
d. Synge, John Millington
d. Weldon, John

Dun Laoghaire, Ireland
b. Casement, Roger David

Dundalk, Ireland
b. McClintock, Francis Leopold, Sir

Dungorvan, Ireland
b. Walton, Ernest Thomas Sinton

Edgeworthstown, Ireland
d. Edgeworth, Maria
d. Edgeworth, Richard Lovell

Ennis, Ireland
b. Smithson, Harriet Constance

Enniskerry, Ireland
d. Monck, Charles Stanley, Sir

Faughart, Ireland
b. Brigid of Kildare

**Frenchpark, County Roscommon,
Ireland**
b. Hyde, Douglas

Fublin, Ireland
b. Stanford, Charles Villiers, Sir

Gweedore, Ireland
b. Enya

Hiskenstown, Ireland
b. Weldon, John

Howth, Ireland
d. Stokes, William

Inniskeen, Ireland
b. Kavanagh, Patrick

Keady, Ireland
b. Makem, Tommy

Kearney, Ireland
b. Barry, Leonora Marie Kearney

Kilkee, Ireland
b. Shackleton, Ernest Henry, Sir

Kilkeel, Ireland
b. Chesney, Charles Cornwallis

Kilkenny West, Ireland
b. Goldsmith, Oliver

Killiney, Ireland
b. Starkie, Walter Fitzwilliam

Killyleagh, Ireland
b. Sloane, Hans, Sir

Kilmacthomas, Ireland
b. Power, Tyrone William Grattan

Kilmogarny, Ireland
d. Lavery, John, Sir

Kinsdale, Ireland
d. Tourneur, Cyril

Knockbrit, Ireland
b. Blessington, Marguerite Gardiner, Countess

Langford, Ireland
b. Colum, Padraic

Leighlin Bridge, Ireland
b. Tyndall, John

Leinster, Ireland
b. Columban, Saint

Limavady, Ireland
b. Massey, William Ferguson

Liscannor, Ireland
b. Holland, John Philip

Lisdoonvarna, Ireland
b. Gardner, George

Lismore, Ireland
b. Boyle, Robert

Listowel, Ireland
b. Keane, John Brendon

Londonderry, Ireland
b. Toland, John

Louth, Ireland
b. Cairnes, John Elliott

Lurgan, Ireland
b. Logan, James

Mallow, Ireland
b. Kane, Paul

Milltown, Ireland
b. Hillery, Patrick John
b. O'Hara, Maureen

Mitchelstown, Ireland
b. Roach, John
b. Trevor, William

Mohill, Ireland
b. Drummond, William Henry

Monaghan, Ireland
b. Bury, John Bagnell

Monkstown, Ireland
d. Hatfield, Hurd
d. Parsons, William
d. Rosse, William Parsons, 3rd Earl of

Mourne, Ireland
d. Chesney, Francis Rawdon

Moyne, Ireland
b. Godkin, E(dwin) L(awrence)

Mullaghmore, Ireland
d. Mountbatten of Burma, Louis Mountbatten, Earl

Mullingar, Ireland
b. Hart, Josephine
b. Nolan, Christopher

Mulranny, Ireland
d. Chain, Ernest Boris, Sir

Navan, Ireland
b. Brosnan, Pierce

Newbliss, Ireland
d. Guthrie, Tyrone, Sir

Newbridge, Ireland
b. Lonsdale, Kathleen (Yardley)

Newton Park, Ireland
b. Lecky, William Edward Hartpole

Oakley Park, Ireland
b. Stoney, George Johnstone

Orrery, Ireland
b. Burke, William

Portadown, Ireland
b. Donlevy, Brian

Queenstown, Ireland
b. Grace, William Russell

Rathfarnham, Ireland
b. Woodhouse, Barbara Blackburn

Rockcorry, Ireland
b. Gregg, John Robert

Rooskey, Ireland
b. Reynolds, Albert

Roscommon, Ireland
b. Flanagan, Edward Joseph, Father
b. O'Sullivan, Maureen

Rosscarbery, Ireland
b. Barry, Tom

Roxborough, Ireland
b. Gregory, Isabella Augusta Persse, Lady

Saul, Ireland
d. Patrick, Saint

Skreen, Ireland
b. Stokes, George Gabriel, Sir

Sligo, Ireland
b. Churchill, May
b. Jordan, Neil

Smithtown, Ireland
b. Johnson, William, Sir

Sneem, Ireland
d. O'Dalaigh, Cearbhall

Stillorgan, Ireland
b. Orpen, William Newneham, Sir

Strabane, Tyrone County, Ireland
b. Carleton, Guy

Straide, Ireland
b. Davitt, Michael

Strokestown, Ireland
b. Lawe, John Edward

Surbiton, Ireland
d. Barnardo, Thomas John

Swords, Ireland
b. Montgomery, Richard

Tacumshane, Ireland
b. Barry, John

Templemore, Ireland
b. Monck, Charles Stanley, Sir

Thomastown, Ireland
b. Berkeley, George

Tipperary, Ireland
b. Bracken, Brendan Rendall, Viscount
b. Burke, John

Tourmakeady, Ireland
d. Shaw, Robert

Tralee, Ireland
b. Brendan of Clonfert, Saint

Tuamgraney, Ireland
b. O'Brien, Edna

Tyrconnell, Ireland
b. Columba, Saint

Waterford, Ireland
b. Hobson, William
b. O'Sullivan, Gilbert

Wexford, Ireland
b. Banville, John
b. Furniss, Harry
b. McClure, Robert (John Le Mesurier)
b. O'Herlihy, Dan

ISRAEL

d. Gluckman, Max
d. Pike, James Albert, Bishop

Afula, Israel
d. Allon, Yigal

Beersheba, Israel
d. Rubin, Vitalii

d. Sapir, Pinchas

Hadera, Israel
d. Yadin, Yigael

Haifa, Israel
b. Simmons, Gene
d. Mercer, David

Hebron, Israel
d. Jaabari, Mohammed Ali, Sheik

Jerusalem, Israel
b. Luria, Isaac ben Solomon
d. Abdullah Ibn Hussein
d. Benedictos I
d. Bernadotte, Folke, Count
d. Buber, Martin
d. Eshkol, Levi
d. Frankfurter, Alfred Moritz
d. Levin, Meyer
d. Meir, Golda
d. Montor, Henry
d. Scholem, Gershom Gerhard
d. Sharett, Moshe
d. Shazar, Zalman
d. Sukenik, Eliazer Lipa
d. Yeshurun, Avot

Mishmar HaSharon, Israel
b. Barak, Ehud

Nablus, Israel
b. Justin Martyr

Ramle, Israel
d. Eichmann, Adolf

Rehovot, Israel
d. Agnon, S(hmuel) Y(osef)
d. Weizmann, Chaim

Tel Aviv, Israel
b. Netanyahu, Benjamin
b. Zukerman, Pinchas
d. Arison, Ted
d. Begin, Menachem (Wolfovitch)
d. Ben-Gurion, David
d. Ben-Haim, Paul
d. Bickerman, Elias Joseph
d. Brod, Max
d. Dayan, Moshe
d. Elazar, David
d. Goldstein, Israel
d. Herzog, Chaim
d. Jadlowker, Hermann
d. Kertesz, Istvan
d. Rabin, Yitzhak
d. Rubin, Reuven
d. Schwartz, Maurice

ITALIAN SOMALILAND

Duca degli Abruzzi, Italian Somaliland
d. Abruzzi, Luigi Amedeo

Mogadishu, Italian Somaliland
b. Iman

ITALY

b. Ascari, Alberto
b. Blotta, Anthony
b. Campagnolo, Gitullio
b. Capone, Teresa
b. Casiraghi, Stefano
b. De Palma, Ralph
b. Gioconda, Lisa Gherardini
b. Guido d'Arezzo
b. Marius, Gaius
b. Molinari, Alberto
b. Olivetti, Camillo
b. Parmenides
b. Porta, Giambattista della
b. Rodia, Simon
b. Roger, II
b. Zangara, Joseph
d. Aesop
d. Bembo, Pietro
d. Cassiodorus, Flavius Magnus Aurelius
d. Guido d'Arezzo
d. Henry, VII
d. Roger, II
d. Rosmini-Serbati, Antonio
d. Scamozzi, Vincenzo

Acerra, Italy
b. Esposito, Joseph

Acqualagna, Italy
b. Mattei, Enrico

Acragas, Italy
b. Empedocles

Acri, Italy
b. Atlas, Charles

Adria, Italy
b. Previtali, Fernando

Agardo, Italy
d. Mohs, Friedrich

Agrigento, Sicily, Italy
b. Pirandello, Luigi

Albano Laziale, Italy
b. Traglia, Luigi, Cardinal

Albino, Italy
b. Moroni, Giovanni Battista

Albisola, Italy
b. Julius II, Pope

Ales, Sardinia, Italy
b. Gramsci, Antonio

Alessandria, Italy
b. Canot, Theodore
b. Eco, Umberto
b. Pius, V, Pope

Altamura, Italy
b. Mercadante, Saverio

Anagni, Italy
b. Boniface, VIII

Ancona, Italy
b. Belluschi, Pietro
b. Corelli, Franco
b. Lisi, Virna
d. Pius, II

Andria, Italy
b. Farinelli

Angri, Italy
b. Sommer, Frederick

Antium, Italy
b. Caligula

Anzi, Italy
b. Celebrezze, Anthony J(oseph)

Aosta, Italy
b. Anselm, Saint

Apulia, Italy
b. Sacco, Nicola
d. Bohemund, I

Aquapendente, Italy
b. Fabricius, Hieronymus ab Aquapendente

Aquila, Italy
d. Bernardine of Siena, Saint

Aquinum, Italy
b. Juvenal

Arcetri, Italy
d. Galileo

Arco, Italy
b. Segantini, Giovanni

Ardea, Italy
d. Manzu, Giacomo

Arezzo, Italy
b. Aretino, Pietro
b. Cesti, Pietro
b. Petrarch, Francesco
b. Redi, Francesco
b. Vasari, Giorgio
d. Sterling, Claire

Arolo, Italy
d. Sheean, (James) Vincent

Arona, Italy
d. Banks, Monty

Arqua, Italy
d. Petrarch, Francesco

Assisi, Italy
b. Clare of Assisi, Saint
b. Francis of Assisi, Saint
b. Lazzari, Virgilio
b. Propertius, Sextus
d. Clare of Assisi, Saint

Asti, Italy
b. Alfieri, Vittorio

Aucona, Italy
d. Adonis, Joe

Aversa, Italy
b. Cimarosa, Domenico
b. Jommelli, Niccolo

Avignon, Italy
d. Martini, Simone

Bagni di Lucca, Italy
b. Crawford, Francis Marion

Bagnoregio, Italy
b. Bonaventure, Saint

Baiae, Italy
d. Hadrian

Baige, Italy
d. Agrippina

Bari, Italy
b. Albanese, Licia
b. Castagna, Bruna
b. Piccinni, Nicola

Barletta, Italy
b. Giulini, Carlo Maria

Bassano, Italy
b. Bassano, Jacopo
b. Gobbi, Tito
d. Bassano, Jacopo

Bellagio, Italy
d. Marinetti, Filippo Tommaso Emilio

Belluno, Italy
b. John Paul I
d. Powell, Cecil Frank

Bergamo, Italy
b. Bonatti, Walter
b. Donizetti, Gaetano
b. Locatelli, Pietro Antonio
b. Manzu, Giacomo
d. Donizetti, Gaetano
d. Moroni, Giovanni Battista
d. Natta, Giulio

Biella, Italy
d. Olivetti, Camillo

Bissone, Italy
b. Borromini, Francesco

Bitonto, Italy
b. Logroscino, Nicola
b. Majorano, Gaetano
b. Traetta, Tommaso

Bobbia, Italy
d. Columban, Saint

Bogni di Lucca, Italy
d. Lee-Hamilton, Eugene Jacob

Bologna, Italy
b. Bacchelli, Riccardo
b. Bernacchi, Antonio Maria
b. Brazzi, Rossano

b. Carracci, Annibale
b. Carracci, Lodovico
b. Domenichino, Il
b. Franceschini, Marcantonio
b. Galvani, Luigi
b. Gregory XIII
b. Marconi, Guglielmo
b. Masina, Giulietta
b. Moninari-Pradelli, Francesco
b. Morandi, Giorgio
b. Pasolini, Pier Paolo
b. Primaticcio, Francesco
b. Reni, Guido
b. Respighi, Ottorino
b. Varthema, Ludovico di
b. Zanardi, Alex
d. Bernacchi, Antonio Maria
d. Carducci, Giosue Alessandro
   Guiseppe
d. Carracci, Lodovico
d. Colbran, Isabella
d. Cuzzoni, Francesca
d. Deller, Alfred George
d. Farinelli
d. Franceschini, Marcantonio
d. Galvani, Luigi
d. Grandi, Dino
d. Maserati, Ernesto
d. Morandi, Giorgio
d. Naudin, Emilio
d. Pomponazzi, Pietro
d. Reni, Guido
d. Ricci-Curbastro, Gregorio

Bondeno, Italy
d. Matilda of Tuscany

Bonito, Italy
b. Ferragamo, Salvatore

Bordighera, Italy
d. Amicis, Edmond de

Borgo San Sepolcro, Italy
b. Piero della Francesca
d. Piero della Francesca

Bracigliano, Italy
b. Romano, Umberto

Brescello, Italy
b. Panizzi, Anthony, Sir

Brescia, Italy
b. Arnold of Brescia
b. Michelangeli, Arturo Benedetti
b. Tartaglia, Niccolo (Fontana)
d. Angela Merici, Saint
d. Marcello, Benedetto

Bressanone, Italy
b. Messner, Reinhold

Brivio, Italy
b. Cantu, Cesare

Brundisium, Italy
d. Vergil

Burano, Italy
b. Galuppi, Baldassare

Busseto, Italy
d. Strepponi, Giuseppina

Cadigliano, Italy
b. Menotti, Gian Carlo

Cagliari, Sardinia, Italy
b. Mario, Giovanni Matteo
b. Pavan, Marisa

Calabria, Italy
b. Ennius, Quintus
b. Zirato, Bruno

Camerino, Italy
b. Betti, Ugo

Campania, Italy
d. Tiberius Julius Caesar Augustus

Campobasso, Italy
b. Giovannitti, Arturo

Canelli, Italy
b. Sardi, Vincent, Sr.

Canino, Italy
b. Paul III

Capo d'Istria, Italy
b. Sanctorius

Capolago, Italy
b. Maderno, Carlo

Caprera, Italy
d. Garibaldi, Giuseppe

Caprese, Italy
b. Michelangelo (Buonarroti)

Capri, Italy
d. Douglas, Norman
d. Fields, Gracie
d. Harlan, Veit
d. Lipchitz, Jacques

Capriglio a Scala, Italy
b. Paul, IV

Caravaggio, Italy
b. Caravaggio, Michelangelo da

Careggi, Italy
d. Ficino, Marsilio

Carpi, Italy
b. Berengario da Carpi, Jacopo

Carpineto, Italy
b. Leo XIII

Carrara, Italy
b. Chinaglia, Giorgio

Carrini, Sicily, Italy
b. Musso, Vido

Casale, Italy
b. Sobrero, Ascanio

Casalecchio, Italy
b. Stracciari, Riccardo

Casalmaggiore, Italy
d. Parmigano

Casarsa de Delicia, Italy
b. Jacuzzi, Candido

Casatico, Italy
b. Castiglione, Baldassare, Conte

Casene, Italy
b. Banks, Monty

Caserta, Italy
d. Ferdinand, II

Castel Gandolfo, Italy
b. Tieri, Frank
d. Lazzari, Virgilio
d. Paul VI

Castelfranco, Italy
b. Giorgione
b. Steffani, Agostino

Castellammare del Golfo, Italy
b. Bonanno, Joseph

Castellaneta, Italy
b. Valentino, Rudolph

Castellina, Italy
d. Kautner, Helmut

Castello de Manlace, Sicily, Italy
d. Sharp, William

Castelnuovo Scrivia, Italy
b. Bandello, Matteo

Castelvecchio, Italy
d. Pascoli, Giovanni

Castelvetrano, Italy
b. Gentile, Giovanni

Castiglioncello, Italy
d. Giorgi, Giovanni

Catania, Sicily, Italy
b. Bellini, Vincenzo
b. DiStefano, Giuseppe
b. Pacini, Giovanni
b. Verga, Giovanni
d. Verga, Giovanni

Catanzaro, Italy
b. Dulbecco, Renato

Cavour, Italy
d. Giolitti, Giovanni

Celano, Italy
b. Corsi, Jacopo

Celico, Calabria, Italy
b. Joachim of Fiore

Ceneda, Italy
b. DaPonte, Lorenzo

Certaldo, Italy
d. Boccaccio, Giovanni

Cesena, Italy
b. Bonci, Alessandro
b. Pius, VI
b. Pius, VII

Cesenatico, Italy
b. Hazan, Marcella Maddalena

Chianti, Italy
d. Lionni, Leo

Chiaramonte, Italy
b. Gianninoto, Frank Anthony

Chiaravalle, Italy
b. Montessori, Maria

Chieti, Italy
b. Galiani, Ferdinando

Chioggia, Italy
b. Zarlino, Gioseffo

Citta di Castello, Italy
b. Burri, Alberto

Collebaccaro, Italy
d. Battistini, Mattia

Comiso, Italy
b. Bufalino, Gesualdo

Como, Italy
b. Innocent XI, Pope
b. Krim, Mathilde Galland
b. Pliny the Elder
b. Pliny the Younger
b. Tagliabue, Carlo
b. Volta, Alessandro Giuseppe Antonio Anastasio
d. Christ-Janer, Albert
d. Lamperti, Francesco
d. Pasta, Giuditta Negri
d. Volta, Alessandro Giuseppe Antonio Anastasio

Concesio, Italy
b. Paul VI

Consentia, Italy
d. Alaric I

Correggio, Italy
b. Correggio, Antonio Allegri da
d. Correggio, Antonio Allegri da

Corsigniano, Italy
b. Pius, II

Corteno, Italy
b. Golgi, Camillo

Cortona, Italy
b. Cortona, Pietro da
b. Severini, Gino
b. Signorelli, Luca

d. Signorelli, Luca

Cosenza, Italy
b. Costello, Frank
b. Telesio, Bernardino
d. Telesio, Bernardino

Crema, Italy
b. Cavalli, Francesco
b. Cavalli, Pietro Francesco
d. Gazzaniga, Giuseppe

Cremona, Italy
b. Amati, Nicolo
b. Guarneri, Giuseppe Antonio
b. Monteverdi, Claudio
b. Stradivari, Antonio
d. Amati, Nicolo
d. Stradivari, Antonio

Crescentino, Italy
b. Arditi, Luigi
b. Cossotto, Fiorenza

Crevalcore, Italy
b. Malpighi, Marcello

Cuneo, Italy
b. Einaudi, Luigi
b. Pavese, Cesare

Desenzano, Italy
b. Angela Merici, Saint

Desio, Italy
b. Pius XI

Domenico, Italy
d. Bocklin, Arnold

Duino, Italy
d. Boltzmann, Ludwig

Emilia-Romagna, Italy
b. Prodi, Romano

Empoli, Italy
b. Busoni, Ferruccio Benvenuto

Fabriano, Italy
b. Pacchierotti, Gasparo

Faenza, Italy
b. Gigli, Romeo
b. Nenni, Pietro Sandro
b. Sarti, Giuseppe
b. Tamburini, Antonio

Fano, Italy
d. Bonaparte, Louis Lucien

Feltre, Italy
b. Feltre, Vittorino da

Ferrara, Italy
b. Antonioni, Michelangelo
b. Ascoli, Max
b. Balbo, Italo
b. Frescobaldi, Girolamo
b. Lamborghini, Ferruccio
b. Pisis, Filippo Tibertelli de
b. Roberti, Ercole

b. Savonarola, Girolamo
b. Tura, Cosme
d. Ariosto, Ludovico
d. Berengario da Carpi, Jacopo
d. Gatti-Casazza, Giulio
d. Obrecht, Jacob
d. Tura, Cosme

Figline, Italy
b. Ficino, Marsilio

Filettino, Italy
b. Graziani, Rodolfo

Fiumetto, Italy
d. Ferragamo, Salvatore

Florence, Italy
b. Agostino di Duccio
b. Animuccia, Giovanni
b. Baldovinetti, Alesso
b. Bartolommeo, Fra
b. Bechi, Gino
b. Botticelli, Sandro
b. Brunelleschi, Filippo
b. Bussotti, Sylvano
b. Calasso, Robert
b. Castelnuovo-Tedesco, Mario
b. Catherine de Medici
b. Cavalcanti, Guido
b. Cecchi, Emilio
b. Cellini, Benvenuto
b. Cherubini, Luigi Carlo Zenobio
   Salvadore Maria
b. Chia, Sandro
b. Cimabue, Giovanni
b. Clement VII
b. Colman, George
b. Dante Alighieri
b. DellaRobbia, Andrea
b. DellaRobbia, Giovanni
b. DellaRobbia, Lucia
b. DelMonaco, Mario
b. Dini, Lamberto
b. DiSant'Angelo, Giorgio
b. Dolci, Carlo
b. Donatello
b. Draper, Paul (Nathaniel Saltonstall)
b. Fallaci, Oriana
b. Francis, II
b. Ghirlandaio, Domenico
b. Gozzoli, Benozzo
b. Gucci, Aldo
b. Gucci, Maurizio
b. Guicciardini, Francesco
b. John, John P(ico)
b. Leo, X
b. Lippi, Filippo, Fra
b. Lully, Jean-Baptiste
b. Machiavelli, Niccolo
b. Marie de Medicis
b. Medici, Cosimo de
b. Medici, Lorenzo de
b. Michelozzo
b. Neri, Philip
b. Nightingale, Florence
b. Papini, Giovanni
b. Patti, Carlotta
b. Peretti, Elsa
b. Pollaiuolo, Antonio
b. Pulci, Luigi
b. Rinuccini, Ottavio
b. Rogers, Richard
b. Rosso, Il
b. Sacchini, Antonio

b. Sansovino, Jacopo
b. Sargent, John Singer
b. Sarto, Andrea del
b. Tetrazzini, Luisa
b. Uccello, Paolo
b. Verrocchio, Andrea del
b. Vespucci, Amerigo
b. Villani, Giovanni
b. von Hugel, Friedrich, Baron
b. Zeffirelli, Franco
d. Agostino di Duccio
d. Alfieri, Vittorio
d. Annigoni, Pietro
d. Arnolfo di Cambio
d. Baldovinetti, Alesso
d. Bartolommeo, Fra
d. Benelli, Giovanni, Cardinal
d. Bonaparte, Joseph
d. Borghese, Maria Paolina
d. Botticelli, Sandro
d. Bronzino, Il
d. Bronzino, Agnolo
d. Browning, Elizabeth Barrett
d. Brunelleschi, Filippo
d. Caccini, Giulio
d. Campana, Dino
d. Castagno, Andrea del
d. Cavalcanti, Guido
d. Cavalieri, Lina
d. Cellini, Benvenuto
d. Cesti, Pietro
d. Cimabue, Giovanni
d. Clairmont, Claire
d. Clough, Arthur Hugh
d. Collodi, Carlo
d. Corsi, Jacopo
d. Cristofori, Bartolomeo di Francesco
d. Dallapiccola, Luigi
d. Davies, Arthur Bowen
d. DellaRobbia, Lucia
d. Dolci, Carlo
d. Donatello
d. Gentile, Giovanni
d. Ghiberti, Lorenzo
d. Ghirlandaio, Domenico
d. Giotto di Bondone
d. Giovanni da Bologna
d. Giusti, Giuseppe
d. Gui, Vittorio
d. Hildreth, Richard
d. Hoe, Richard March
d. Isaac, Heinrich
d. Landor, Walter Savage
d. Leland, Charles Godfrey
d. Lippi, Filippino
d. Lippi, Filippo, Fra
d. Machiavelli, Niccolo
d. Medici, Cosimo de
d. Medici, Lorenzo de
d. Michelozzo
d. Papini, Giovanni
d. Parker, Theodore
d. Peri, Jacopo
d. Pico della Mirandola, Giovanni
d. Poliziano, Angelo
d. Pontormo, Jacopo da
d. Powers, Hiram
d. Pucci, Emilio Marchese di Barsento
d. Pyle, Howard
d. Rinuccini, Ottavio
d. Ruffo, Titta
d. Salvemini, Gaetano
d. Sarto, Andrea del
d. Savonarola, Girolamo
d. Scherchen, Hermann
d. Torricelli, Evangelista

d. Toye, Francis
d. Trollope, Frances
d. Uccello, Paolo
d. Unger, Caroline
d. Vasari, Giorgio
d. Villani, Giovanni

Florentino, Italy
d. Frederick II

Foggia, Italy
b. Giordano, Umberto

Fondi, Italy
b. DeSantis, Giuseppe

Fontana Liri, Italy
b. Mastroianni, Marcello

Forli, Italy
b. Morgagni, Giovanni Battista
b. Mussolini, Rachele Guidi
b. Simionato, Guilietta
d. Mussolini, Rachele Guidi

Fossannova, Italy
d. Thomas Aquinas, Saint

Fratta Polesine, Italy
b. Matteotti, Giacomo

Frattamaggiore, Italy
b. Durante, Francesco

Fusignano, Italy
b. Corelli, Arcangelo

Galdo, Italy
b. Corey, Lewis

Gela, Italy
d. Aeschylus

Genazzano, Italy
b. Martin, V

Genoa, Italy
b. Alberti, Leon Battista
b. Benedict XV
b. Bortoluzzi, Paolo
b. Cabot, John
b. Catherine of Genoa, Saint
b. Columbus, Christopher
b. Gassman, Vittorio
b. Gaulli, Giovanni Battista
b. Germi, Pietro
b. Hildebrandt, Johann Lucas von
b. Magnasco, Alessandro Lissandrino
b. Mazzini, Giuseppe
b. Montale, Eugenio
b. Paganini, Niccolo
b. Romani, Felice
b. Seal, Elizabeth
b. Taddei, Giuseppe
b. Togliatti, Palmiro
b. Yeats-Brown, F(rancis Charles
   Claypon)
d. Catherine of Genoa, Saint
d. Doria, Andrea
d. Hardenberg, Karl August von
d. Magnasco, Alessandro Lissandrino
d. O'Connell, Daniel
d. Smithson, James (Louis Macie)

d. Schiaparelli, Giovanni
d. Sironi, Mario
d. Sonzogno, Edoardo
d. Stabile, Mariano
d. Stolz, Teresa
d. Tetrazzini, Luisa
d. Ungaretti, Giuseppe
d. Varesi, Felice
d. Verdi, Giuseppe Fortunino Francesco
d. Vittorini, Elio

Modena, Italy
b. Bononcini, Giovanni Battista
b. Ferrari, Enzo
b. Freni, Mirella
b. Guarini, Guarino
b. Pavarotti, Luciano
b. Pico della Mirandola, Giovanni
d. Ferrari, Enzo

Molfetta, Italy
b. Salvemini, Gaetano

Moneglia, Italy
d. Romani, Felice

Monferrato, Italy
b. Badoglio, Pietro
d. Badoglio, Pietro

Monselice, Italy
d. Campagnolo, Gitullio

Monsummano, Italy
b. Giusti, Giuseppe

Monsummano Alto, Italy
b. Montand, Yves

Montagnana, Italy
b. Martinelli, Giovanni
d. Sitwell, Osbert, Sir

Monte Cassino, Italy
d. Benedict, Saint

Monte Nero, Italy
d. Smollett, Tobias George

Monte Sansavino, Italy
b. Sansovino, Andrea

Montecatini, Italy
d. Dior, Christian
d. Leoncavallo, Ruggiero

Montecelli, Italy
b. Bronzino, Il

Monteforte, Italy
b. Forte, Charles, Sir

Montemarano, Italy
b. Adonis, Joe

Montepulciano, Italy
b. Bellarmine, Robert, Saint
b. Marcellus II, Pope

Montepulciano, Tuscany, Italy
b. Poliziano, Angelo

Monterone, Italy
b. Velluti, Giovanni Battista

Monticelli, Italy
b. Bronzino, Agnolo

Montona Trieste, Italy
b. Andretti, Mario Gabriel

Montorio, Italy
b. Greco, Jose

Monza, Italy
d. Ascari, Alberto
d. Bacchelli, Riccardo
d. Rindt, Jochen
d. Tagliabue, Carlo

Mordano, Italy
b. Grandi, Dino

Morimondo, Italy
b. Lattuada, Felice

Morra Irpino, Italy
b. DeSanctis, Francesco

Motta di Livenza, Italy
d. Svevo, Italo

Munra Lucano, Italy
b. Stella, Joseph

Mureno, Italy
b. Piave, Francesco Maria

Naples, Italy
b. Acton, John Emerich Edward Dalberg-Acton, Baron
b. Amato, Pasquale
b. Autori, Franco
b. Bernini, Giovanni Lorenzo
b. Caniglia, Maria
b. Caruso, Enrico
b. Charles, IV
b. Cipullo, Aldo Massimo Fabrizio
b. Clemente, Francesco
b. Corbett, Young, III
b. Gardenia, Vincent
b. Gesualdo, Carlo
b. Giordano, Luca
b. Heiskell, Andrew
b. Lablache, Luigi
b. Lebrun, Rico
b. Leoncavallo, Ruggiero
b. Marterie, Ralph
b. Merola, Gaetano
b. Mugnone, Leopoldo
b. Muti, Riccardo
b. Nicolini
b. Nobile, Umberto
b. Papi, Genarro
b. Porpora, Niccolo
b. Pucci, Emilio Marchese di Barsento
b. Ricca, Paul
b. Rosa, Salvator
b. Scarlatti, Domenico Girolamo
b. Scotti, Antonio
b. Sodero, Cesare
b. Stignani, Ebe
b. Stradella, Alessandro
b. Urban, VI
b. Vico, Giovanni Battista
b. Victor Emmanuel III

b. Zingarelli, Nicola Antonio
d. Abarbanel, Judah
d. Adam de la Halle
d. Cajetan, St.
d. Caruso, Enrico
d. Charles, IV
d. Cooper, Anthony Ashley, 1st Earl of Shaftesbury
d. Crescentini, Girolamo
d. Crispi, Francesco
d. Croce, Benedetto
d. DeSanctis, Francesco
d. Domenichino, Il
d. Durante, Francesco
d. Fontana, Domenico
d. Galiani, Ferdinando
d. Gentileschi, Artemisia
d. Gesualdo, Carlo
d. Giordano, Luca
d. Jommelli, Niccolo
d. Lablache, Luigi
d. Lardner, Dionysius
d. Leo, Leonardo
d. Leopardi, Giacomo
d. Luciano, Lucky
d. Majorano, Gaetano
d. Mercadante, Saverio
d. Mugnone, Leopoldo
d. Nicolini
d. Nourrit, Adolphe
d. Paisiello, Giovanni
d. Porpora, Niccolo
d. Quasimodo, Salvatore
d. Ribera, Jusepe (Jose) de
d. Scarlatti, Alessandro
d. Scarlatti, Domenico Girolamo
d. Schliemann, Heinrich
d. Scotti, Antonio
d. Shaftesbury, Anthony Ashley Cooper, Earl
d. Vico, Giovanni Battista

Neapolis, Italy
d. Lucilius, Gaius

Nicosia, Sicily, Italy
b. Pecora, Ferdinand

Nola, Italy
b. Bruno, Giordano
d. Augustus

Norcia, Italy
b. Benedict, Saint

Novara, Italy
b. Lombard, Peter
b. Scalfaro, Oscar Luigi

Nvoro, Sardinia, Italy
b. Deledda, Grazia

Oneglia, Italy
b. Amicis, Edmond de
b. Berio, Luciano
b. Doria, Andrea

Orsara, Italy
b. Torrio, Johnny

Ortona, Italy
b. Tosti, Francesco Paolo

Rapallo, Italy
d. Beerbohm, Max
d. Gish, Dorothy

Ravenna, Italy
d. Dante Alighieri
d. Pratella, Francesco Balilla

Reate, Italy
b. Vespasian
d. Vespasian

Recanati, Italy
b. Gigli, Beniamino
b. Leopardi, Giacomo
d. Gregory, XII

Reggio Emilia, Italy
b. Tagliavini, Ferrucio
d. Tagliavini, Ferrucio

Reggio Nell'Emilia, Italy
b. Ariosto, Ludovico
b. Secchi, Pietro Angelo
d. Boiardo, Matteo Maria

Reggio di Calabria, Italy
b. Boccioni, Umberto
b. Versace, Gianni

Ribera, Sicily, Italy
b. Crispi, Francesco

Riese, Italy
b. Pius X

Rimini, Italy
b. Cipriani, Amilcare
b. Fellini, Federico

Riva, Italy
b. Schuschnigg, Kurt von

Rivarola, Italy
b. Cesnola, Luigi Palma di

Rocca d'Arona, Italy
b. Borromeo, Charles, Saint

Roccasecca, Italy
b. Gazzelloni, Severino
b. Thomas Aquinas, Saint
d. Gazzelloni, Severino

Romano, Italy
b. Rubini, Giovanni-Battista
d. Rubini, Giovanni-Battista

Rome, Italy
b. Adrian II
b. Agnes, Saint
b. Allegri, Gregorio
b. Andreotti, Giulio
b. Apollinaire, Guillaume
b. Augustus
b. Baccaloni, Salvatore
b. Bartoli, Cecilia
b. Battistini, Mattia
b. Borgia, Cesare
b. Borgia, Lucrezia
b. Brazza, Pierre Paul Francois
  Camille Savorgnan de
b. Brooks, Romaine

b. Brumidi, Constantino
b. Caccini, Giulio
b. Caesar, Julius
b. Camerini, Mario
b. Cavallini, Pietro
b. Celsus, Aulus Cornelius
b. Cenci, Beatrice
b. Charles Edward Louis Philip
  Casimir Stuart
b. Clement I, Saint
b. Clementi, Muzio
b. Collins, Mike
b. DeLuca, Giuseppe
b. DePaolis, Alessio
b. Fabrizi, Aldo
b. Fermi, Enrico
b. Gerard, Francois
b. Gregory the Great, Saint
b. Gui, Vittorio
b. Hazelton, Nika
b. Jones, R(enato) William
b. Juan Carlos I
b. Julius III, Pope
b. Lauri-Volpi, Giacoma
b. Leone, Sergio
b. Loren, Sophia
b. Mangano, Silvana
b. Marcus Aurelius Antoninus
b. Martinelli, Elsa
b. Metastasio, Pietro
b. Modigliani, Franco
b. Monicelli, Mario
b. Moravia, Alberto
b. Ortese, Anna Maria
b. Ottaviani, Alfredo, Cardinal
b. Pei, Mario Andrew
b. Pella, Giuseppe
b. Peri, Jacopo
b. Persiani, Fanny
b. Petacci, Claretta
b. Petri, Elio
b. Pinza, Ezio
b. Pius XII
b. Pompey the Great
b. Praz, Mario
b. Rienzi, Cola di
b. Romiti, Cesare
b. Rossellini, Isabella
b. Rossellini, Renzo
b. Rossellini, Roberto
b. Salerno-Sonnenberg, Nadja
b. Schiaparelli
b. Simonetta
b. Soria, Dario
b. Stuart, Charles Edward Louis Philip
b. Tamberlik, Enrico
b. Tiberius Julius Caesar Augustus
b. Titus
b. Valla, Lorenzo
b. Valletti, Cesare
b. Vitale, Milly
b. Vitti, Monica
b. Wertmuller, Lina von Eigg
b. Zampa, Luigi
d. Agnes, Saint
d. Alberti, Leon Battista
d. Alfonso XIII
d. Allegri, Gregorio
d. Almirante, Giorgio
d. Amfiteatrof, Daniele
d. Angelico, Fra
d. Animuccia, Giovanni
d. Antonelli, Giacomo
d. Arnold of Brescia
d. Auer, Mischa
d. Balla, Giacomo

d. Balsam, Martin Henry
d. Barzini, Luigi Giorgio, Jr.
d. Bea, Augustinus
d. Bellarmine, Robert, Saint
d. Beltrami, Eugenio
d. Benedict XV
d. Berberian, Cathy
d. Berman, Eugene
d. Bernini, Giovanni Lorenzo
d. Betti, Ugo
d. Biringuccio, Vannoccio
d. Bonaparte, Letizia
d. Bonaparte, Louis
d. Boniface, VIII
d. Borromini, Francesco
d. Bovet, Daniele
d. Bramante, Donata d'Agnolo
d. Brazzi, Rossano
d. Browning, Oscar
d. Bruno, Giordano
d. Buitoni, Giovanni
d. Bulow, Bernhard H M
d. Burdett, Winston M.
d. Bury, John Bagnell
d. Caesar, Julius
d. Cagliostro, Alessandro, Conte di
d. Caligula
d. Caniglia, Maria
d. Cannizzaro, Stanislao
d. Cardano, Geronimo
d. Carissimi, Giacomo
d. Carracci, Annibale
d. Catherine of Siena, Saint
d. Catullus, Gaius Valerius
d. Cecchi, Emilio
d. Cecelia, Saint
d. Celestine V, Saint
d. Cenci, Beatrice
d. Chaliapin, Feodor Ivanovitch, Jr.
d. Charles Edward Louis Philip
  Casimir Stuart
d. Chirico, Giorgio de
d. Christina
d. Christoff, Boris
d. Claudian
d. Claudius I
d. Clement I, Saint
d. Clement VII
d. Clement XIV, Pope
d. Corelli, Arcangelo
d. Cortona, Pietro da
d. Dana, Richard Henry, Jr.
d. Deledda, Grazia
d. Einaudi, Luigi
d. Elsheimer, Adam
d. Escriva de Balaguer, Josemarie
d. Eustachio, Bartolomeo
d. Ezekiel, Moses Jacob
d. Fanfani, Amintore
d. Farouk I
d. Fellini, Federico
d. Firbank, Ronald
d. Flandrin, Hippolyte Jean
d. Frescobaldi, Girolamo
d. Gassman, Vittorio
d. Gaulli, Giovanni Battista
d. Gentile da Fabriano
d. Germi, Pietro
d. Gibson, John
d. Gigli, Beniamino
d. Ginzburg, Natalia
d. Gobbi, Tito
d. Gracchus, Tiberius Sempronius
d. Gramsci, Antonio
d. Grassi, Giovanni Battista
d. Graziani, Rodolfo

Scyllacium, Italy
b. Cassiodorus, Flavius Magnus
Aurelius

Segno, Italy
b. Kino, Eusebio Francisco

Selasca, Italy
d. Riemann, Georg Friedrich

Sella Val Suguna, Italy
d. De Gasperi, Alcide

Senigallia, Italy
b. Pius IX

Sequals, Italy
b. Carnera, Primo
d. Carnera, Primo

Sermoneta, Italy
b. Manutius, Aldus

Sesana, Italy
b. Dolci, Danilo

Settignano, Italy
b. da Settignano, Desiderio
d. Berenson, Bernard

Seveso, Italy
b. Confalonieri, Carlo, Cardinal

Sicily, Italy
d. Dolci, Danilo
d. Sappho

Siena, Italy
b. Bastianini, Ettore
b. Biringuccio, Vannoccio
b. Catherine of Siena, Saint
b. Duccio di Buoninsegna
b. Giorgio, Francesco di
b. Giovanni di Paolo
b. Lorenzetti, Ambrogio
b. Martini, Simone
b. Sassetta
b. Senesino
b. Socinus, Faustus
d. Calvino, Italo
d. Duccio di Buoninsegna
d. Giorgio, Francesco di
d. Giovanni di Paolo
d. Pintuicchio
d. Sassetta
d. Senesino

Siracusa, Italy
b. Vittorini, Elio

Sirmione, Italy
d. Bastianini, Ettore

Sondrio, Italy
b. Nervi, Pier Luigi

Sonnino, Italy
b. Antonelli, Giacomo

Sorrento, Italy
b. Tasso, Torquato
d. Crawford, Francis Marion

Sotto il Monte, Italy
b. John XXIII

Spezia, Italy
b. Giannini, Giancarlo

Stabiae, Italy
d. Pliny the Elder

Stella, Italy
b. Pertini, Sandro

Stilo, Italy
b. Campanella, Tommaso

Subiaco, Italy
b. Lollobrigida, Gina

Sulmona, Italy
b. Ovid

Syracuse, Sicily, Italy
b. Archimedes
b. Damocles
b. Quasimodo, Salvatore
b. Theocritus
d. Archimedes

Taormina, Sicily, Italy
b. Winwar, Frances

Taranto, Italy
b. Paisiello, Giovanni
d. Laclos, Pierre (Ambroise Francois)
Choderlos de

Tarentum, Italy
b. Livius Andronicus

Tempio Pausania, Sardinia, Italy
b. Sironi, Mario

Teni, Italy
d. Savo, Jimmy

Terentino, Italy
b. De Gasperi, Alcide

Termi, Italy
b. Brioni, Gaetano Savini, Marquis

Thurii, Italy
d. Herodotus

Tivoli, Italy
b. Segre, Emilio Gino

Todi, Italy
b. Jacopone da Todi
d. Nicholas of Cusa

Torre Annunziata, Italy
b. DeLaurentiis, Dino

Torre del Greco, Italy
d. Zingarelli, Nicola Antonio

Torremaggiore, Italy
b. Gallo, Fortune
b. Rossi, Luigi

Treviso, Italy
b. Benetton, Luciano
d. Malipiero, Gian Francesco

Trieste, Italy
b. Barbieri, Fedora
b. Cleva, Fausto
b. DeSabata, Victor
b. Henreid, Paul
b. Strehler, Giorgio
b. Svevo, Italo
d. Burton, Richard Francis, Sir
d. Fouche, Joseph
d. Winckelmann, Johann Joachim

Tropea, Italy
b. Anastasia, Albert
b. Vallone, Raf(faele)

Turin, Italy
b. Agnelli, Giovanni
b. Amato, Giuliano
b. Avogadro, Amedeo
b. Balla, Giacomo
b. Bich, Marcel
b. Brosio, Manilo Giovanni
b. Cavour, Camillo Benso, Conte di
b. De Benedetti, Carlo
b. Farina, Giuseppe
b. Giardini, Felice di
b. Huxley, Laura Archera
b. Lagrange, Joseph-Louis
b. Levi, Carlo
b. Levi, Primo
b. Levi-Montalcini, Rita
b. Luria, Salvador Edward
b. Marcoux, Vanni
b. Pasero, Tancredi
b. Ricci, Nina
b. Rocca, Lodovico
b. Rosso, Medardo
b. Saragat, Giuseppe
b. Scalchi, Sofia
b. Soleri, Paolo
b. Tamagno, Francesco
b. Valdengo, Giuseppe
b. Victor Emmanuel II
b. Yon, Pietro Alessandro
d. Agnelli, Giovanni
d. Avogadro, Amedeo
d. Brosio, Manilo Giovanni
d. Cavour, Camillo Benso, Conte di
d. Ferraris, Galileo
d. Gobineau, Joseph Arthur, Comte de
d. Kossuth, Lajos
d. Levi, Primo
d. Lombroso, Cesare
d. Marot, Clement
d. Pavese, Cesare
d. Peano, Giuseppe
d. Pellico, Silvio
d. Sobrero, Ascanio

Tuscany, Italy
b. Collodi, Carlo
b. Fanfani, Amintore
b. Gregory, VII

Tusculum, Italy
b. Cato, Marcus Porcius Censorius

Udine, Italy
b. Gatti-Casazza, Giulio

d. Pickering, William Henry
d. Read, Mary

Blenheim, Jamaica
b. Bustamante, William Alexander
    Clarke, Sir

Clarendon, Jamaica
b. McKay, Festus Claudius

Falmouth, Jamaica
b. Johnson, Ben

Hanover, Jamaica
b. Perry, Lee

Kingston, Jamaica
b. Abercrombie, Josephine
b. Ashley, Maurice
b. Ewing, Patrick Aloysius
b. Fagan, Garth
b. Glasspole, Florizel Augustus
b. Manley, Michael (Norman)
b. Marley, Bob
b. Silvera, Frank
b. Simpson, Louis
b. Sinclair, Madge
d. Bustamante, William Alexander
    Clarke, Sir
d. Coward, Noel Pierce, Sir
d. Manley, Michael (Norman)
d. Parsons, Charles Algernon, Sir
d. Starling, Ernest Henry
d. Tosh, Peter

Lawrencefield, Jamaica
d. Morgan, Henry, Sir

Montego Bay, Jamaica
d. Rose, Billy

Ocho Rios, Jamaica
d. Hench, Philip Showalter

Port Antonio, Jamaica
b. Russwurm, John Brown

Saint Andrew, Jamaica
b. Christie, Linford
b. Patterson, P(ercival Noel) J(ames)

Saint Ann's Bay, Jamaica
b. Garvey, Marcus Moziah

Saint Catherine, Jamaica
b. Cliff, Jimmy

Spanishtown, Jamaica
b. Jones, Grace

Sunny Ville, Jamaica
b. McKay, Claude

Westmoreland, Jamaica
b. Patterson, Orlando
b. Tosh, Peter

JAPAN

b. Aoki, Hiroaki
b. Ashikaga, Takauji

b. Daigo, II
b. Fukuda, Takeo
b. Hasegawa, Kazuo
b. Honda, Ishiro
b. Idei, Nobuyuki
b. Kitaro
b. Korin, Ogata
b. Mabuchi, Kamo
b. Minamoto Yoritomo
b. Nagumo, Chuichi
b. Niwano, Nikkyo
b. Owado, Masako
b. Saionji, Kimmochi
b. Sakamoto, Ryuichi
b. Sasakawa, Ryoichi
b. Shimomura, Tsutomu
b. Shotoku Taishi
b. Suiko
b. Takada, Kenzo
b. Toyoda, Shoichiro
b. Yamashita, Kazuhito
b. Yoshimune, Tokugawa
d. Adams, William
d. Daigo, II
d. Iwakura, Tomomi
d. Mabuchi, Kamo
d. Okubo, Toshimichi
d. Phibun Songkhram, Luang
d. Saionji, Kimmochi
d. Yamagata, Aritomo
d. Yoshimune, Tokugawa

Abiko, Japan
b. Aoki, Isao

Amagasaki, Japan
d. Taoka Kazuo

Anjo City, Japan
b. Iwama, Kazuo

Atami, Japan
d. Tokutomi Soho

Chiba, Japan
b. Hayakawa, Sessue (Kintaro)

Choshu Province, Japan
b. Ito, Hirobumi

Donari, Japan
b. Miki Takeo

Edo, Japan
b. Harunobu, Suzuki
b. Hiroshige, Ando
b. Hokusai, Katsushika
d. Harunobu, Suzuki
d. Hiroshige, Ando
d. Hokusai, Katsushika

Eichizen Province, Japan
b. Chikamatsu, Monzaemon

Fukuoka, Japan
b. Principal, Victoria

Hagi, Japan
b. Yamagata, Aritomo

Hayama, Japan
d. Yoshihito

Hiroshima, Japan
b. Ibuse, Masuji
b. Miyake, Issey
b. Yamamoto, Kenichi

Holdaido, Japan
b. Umeki, Miyoshi

Ichikawa, Japan
d. Nagai, Sokichi

Ichinomiya, Japan
b. Kaifu Toshiki

Ie Shima, Okinawa, Japan
d. Pyle, Ernie

Ikegami, Japan
d. Nichiren

Iwata Gun, Japan
b. Honda, Soichiro

Iwate, Japan
b. Hara, Kei

Kagoshima, Japan
b. Okubo, Toshimichi
b. Saigo, Takamori
b. Togo, Heihachiro

Kamakura, Japan
d. Minamoto Yoritomo
d. Takahama Kyoshi

Kanazawa, Japan
b. Suzuki, Daisetz Teitaro

Kariwa, Japan
b. Tanaka, Kakuei

Kashiwara, Japan
d. Fuchida, Mitsuo

Kinan, Japan
b. Onoda, Hiroo

Kinjo, Japan
b. Toyoda, Eiji

Kobe, Japan
b. Doi, Takako
d. Hadley, Arthur Twining

Kochi, Japan
b. Nagano, Osami
b. Yamashita, Tomoyuki

Kominato, Japan
b. Nichiren

Kyoto, Japan
b. Eitoku, Kano
b. Itami, Juzo
b. Iwakura, Tomomi
b. Mori, Hanae
b. Murasaki, Shikibu, Lady
b. Mutsuhito
b. Oshima, Nagisa
d. Ashikaga, Takauji
d. Fukui, Kenichi
d. Kano, Motonobu

Tsushima-Shi, Japan
b. Sugiura, Kanematsu

Ueno, Iga, Japan
b. Basho

Wakayama-Ken, Japan
b. Nomura, Kichisaburo

Wasa Village, Japan
b. Matsushita, Konosuke

Yamada, Japan
b. Suzuki, Zenko

Yamaguchi Prefecture, Japan
b. Kishi, Nobusuke

Yokohama, Japan
b. Aki, Keiiti
b. Crowe, Colin Tradescant, Sir
b. Kurusu, Saburo
b. Okada, Kenzo
b. Whitney, Phyllis Ayame
d. Watson, Johnny ''Guitar''

Yokosuka, Japan
b. De Grassi, Alex

Yugawara, Japan
d. Tanizaki Jun'ichiro

Zushi, Japan
d. Kawabata, Yasunari

JORDAN

b. Jaabari, Mohammed Ali, Sheik

Amman, Jordan
b. Hussein, I, King
d. Freij, Elias
d. Husein ibn Ali
d. Hussein, I, King
d. Shukairy, Ahmed

Bethlehem, Jordan
b. Freij, Elias

JUDEA

b. John the Baptist
b. Mary, The, Virgin Mother

Anathoth, Judea
b. Jeremiah

Bethlehem, Judea
b. Jesus Christ
d. Jerome, Saint

Jericho, Judea
d. Herod the Great

Jerusalem, Judea
b. Mark, Saint
d. Jesus Christ

Magdala, Judea
b. Mary Magdalene, Saint

KASHMIR

Soura, Kashmir
b. Abdullah, Mohammad, Sheik

Srinagar, Kashmir
d. Abdullah, Mohammad, Sheik

KAZAKHSTAN

b. Nazarbayev, Nursultan (Abishevich)

KEDAH

Alor Star, Kedah
b. Rahman, Abdul, Prince

KENYA

b. Hussein, Ibrahim
b. Kiptanui, Moses
b. Maysa, Ben
d. Adamson, George

Asembo, Kenya
b. Ogot, Grace Emily Akinyi

Bondo, Kenya
b. Odinga, Ajuma Jaramogi

Kambui, Kenya
b. Thuku, Harry

Kilifi, Kenya
b. Ngala, Ronald Gideon

Limuru, Kenya
b. Ngugi, James Thiong'o

Mombasa, Kenya
b. Mazrui, Ali A(l'Amin)
d. Kenyatta, Jomo

Nairobi, Kenya
b. Morris, Edmund
b. Wasow, Omar
d. Leakey, Mary (Douglas)
d. Markham, Beryl
d. Mboya, Tom

Nyeri, Kenya
b. Maathai, Wangari (Muta)

Sacho, Kenya
b. Moi, Daniel arap

Shaba, Kenya
d. Adamson, Joy Friederike Victoria
Gessner

KIRGIZSTAN

Kyzyl-Bairak, Kirgizstan
b. Akayev, Askar Akayevich

KIRIBATI

b. Tabai, Ieremia Tienang

Nonouti, Kiribati
b. Teannaki, Teatao

Tabiteaua North, Kiribati
b. Tito, Teburoro

KOREA

b. Han Yongun
d. Han Yongun

Geoje, Korea
b. Kim Young Sam

Hayi-do, Korea
b. Kim Dae Jung

Hwanghai, Korea
b. Rhee, Syngman

Kwangju Sangsa Ri, Korea
b. Moon, Sung Myung

Mangyongdae, Korea
b. Kim Il Sung

Naechonri, Korea
b. Chun Doo Hwan

Pusan, Korea
b. Pedersen, Charles J

Pyongyang, Korea
b. Park, Tongsun

Seoul, Korea
b. Kahng, Dawon
b. Paik, Nam June

Sosan Gun, Korea
b. Park, Chung Hee

Taegu, Korea
b. Roh Tae Woo

KOREA (NORTH)

Pyongyang, Korea (North)
d. Kim Il Sung

KOREA (SOUTH)

Seoul, Korea (South)
b. Chung, Myung-Whun
d. Cohen, Wilbur Joseph
d. Park, Chung Hee

KUWAIT

b. Bishara, Abdullah Yaccoub
b. Saud (Ibn Abdul Aziz al Saud)

Kuwait City, Kuwait
b. Jaber Al-Sabah, Jaber Al-Ahmad Al-
b. Jabir al-Ahmad al-Jabir Al Sabah, Sheikh

LAOS

b. Sananikone, Phoui
d. Souphanouvong, Prince

Champasak, Laos
b. Khamtay Siphandone

Luang Prabang, Laos
b. Souphanouvong, Prince
b. Souvanna, Phouma

Vientiane, Laos
d. Souvanna, Phouma

LATINUM

Antium, Latinum
b. Nero

Arpinum, Latinum
b. Cicero, Marcus Tullius

Formiae, Latinum
d. Cicero, Marcus Tullius

LATVIA

Libau, Latvia
b. Anders, Edward

Ludza, Latvia
b. Gorbunovs, Anatolijs

Mstislav, Mohilov, Latvia
b. Dubnov, Simon

Riga, Latvia
b. Baryshnikov, Mikhail
b. Hillquit, Morris
b. Kremer, Gidon
b. Moisseiff, Leon Solomon
b. Ulmanis, Guntis
b. von Praunheim, Rosa
d. Dubnov, Simon

LEBANON

b. Gemayel, Pierre, Sheikh
d. Buckley, William F
d. Collett, Alec
d. Douglas, John Leigh
d. Higgins, William R
d. Kilburn, Peter

Al-Muhaydithah, Lebanon
b. Abu Madi, Iliya

Bechari, Lebanon
b. Gibran, Kahlil

Beirut, Lebanon
b. Fairuz
b. Kerr, Malcolm (Hooper)
b. Reeves, Keanu
b. Salam, Saeb
d. Chamoun, Camille N(imer)
d. Gemayel, Bashir
d. Husayni, Al-Hajj Amin al-
d. Husseini, Haj Amin
d. Jumblatt, Kamal Fouad
d. Kerr, Malcolm (Hooper)
d. Kuwatli, Shukri al-
d. Malik, Charles Habib
d. Meloy, Francis Edward, Jr.
d. Philby, Harold St. John Bridger
d. Salam, Saeb

Bikfaya, Lebanon
b. Gemayel, Amin
b. Gemayel, Bashir
d. Gemayel, Pierre, Sheikh

Bterram, Lebanon
b. Malik, Charles Habib

Deir el-Kamar, Lebanon
b. Chamoun, Camille N(imer)

Ghazir, Kisrwan, Lebanon
b. Shihab, Fu'ad

Haret Hreik, Lebanon
b. Aoun, Michel

Jubayl, Lebanon
d. Karami, Rashid Abdul Hamid

Marjayoun, Lebanon
b. Haddad, Saad
d. Haddad, Saad

Mukhtara, Lebanon
b. Jumblatt, Kamal Fouad

Ramallah, Lebanon
b. Mikhail-Ashrawi, Hanan

Shibaniyah, Lebanon
b. Sarkis, Elias

Tripoli, Lebanon
b. Karami, Rashid Abdul Hamid

Zahle, Lebanon
b. Hrawi, Elias

LESOTHO

d. Mofolo, Thomas (Mokopu)

Maseru, Lesotho
d. Moshoeshoe II

Mokhotlong, Lesotho
b. Moshoeshoe II

Teyateyaneng, Lesotho
b. Mokhehle, Ntsu

LIBERIA

b. Taylor, Charles McArthur

Arthington, Liberia
b. Taylor, Charles

Bensonville, Liberia
b. Tolbert, William Richard, Jr.

Grand Cape Mount, Liberia
b. Perry, Ruth (Sando)

Greenville, Liberia
b. Sawyer, Amos

Harper, Liberia
b. Tubman, William Vacanarat Shadrach

Monrovia, Liberia
b. Fuller, Solomon Carter, Jr.
d. Doe, Samuel Kanyon
d. Garnet, Henry Highland
d. Russwurm, John Brown
d. Scripps, Edward Wyllis
d. Tolbert, William Richard, Jr.

Tuzon, Liberia
b. Doe, Samuel Kanyon

Virginia, Liberia
b. Brooks, Angie Elizabeth

LIBYA

b. Romano, Joseph

Jaghbub, Libya
b. Idris I

Sirta, Libya
b. Qadhafi, Muammar al-

Tobruk, Libya
d. Balbo, Italo

Tripoli, Libya
b. Podesta, Rossana

LIECHTENSTEIN

b. Franz Joseph II

Vaduz, Liechtenstein
d. Franz Joseph II

LITHUANIA

b. Bryant, Lane
b. Burton, Montague Maurice, Sir
b. Hoffenstein, Samuel Goodman
b. Parish, Mitchell
b. Slovo, Joe

b. Washkansky, Louis

Austryn, Lithuania
b. Wolfson, Harry Austryn

Druskinikai, Lithuania
b. Lipchitz, Jacques

Eurburg, Lithuania
b. Zorach, William

Janiskis, Lithuania
b. Harvey, Laurence

Kaunas, Lithuania
b. Adamkus, Valdas (V.)
b. Arens, Moshe
b. Beriosova, Svetlana
b. Goldman, Emma
b. Landsbergis, Vytautas
b. Levinas, Emmanuel
b. Shahn, Ben(jamin)

Kovno, Lithuania
b. Ginzberg, Louis
b. Revel, Bernard

Novo-Aleksandrovsk, Lithuania
b. Wrangel, Pietr Nikolayevich

Rokiskis, Lithuania
b. Brazauskas, Algirdas (Mykolas)

Sateiniai, Lithuania
b. Milosz, Czeslaw

Siauliai, Lithuania
b. Schapiro, Meyer

Sirvintos, Lithuania
b. Silver, Abba Hillel

Swenziany, Lithuania
b. Kaplan, Mordecai

Vilnius, Lithuania
b. Berenson, Bernard
b. Elijah Ben Solomon
b. Godowsky, Leopold
b. Heifetz, Jascha
b. Romanoff, Mike

Zagare, Lithuania
b. Hillman, Sidney (Simcha)

LUXEMBOURG

b. Schuman, Robert
b. Steichen, Edward Jean
b. Thorn, Gaston
d. Bech, Joseph
d. Charlotte Aldegonde E M
  Wilhelmine

Chateau de Berg, Luxembourg
b. Charlotte Aldegonde E M
  Wilhelmine

Diekirch, Luxembourg
b. Bech, Joseph

Hallerich, Luxembourg
b. Lippmann, Gabriel Jonas

Luxembourg, Luxembourg
b. Gernsback, Hugo

Redangesur-Attert, Luxembourg
b. Juncker, Jean-Claude

Wasserbillig, Luxembourg
b. Santer, Jacques

MACAO

b. Sun Yat-Sen

MACEDONIA

b. Philip II
b. Ptolemy (Soter), I
b. Seleucus, I
d. Seleucus, I

Kavalla, Macedonia
b. Mohammed Ali

Pella, Macedonia
b. Alexander the Great

Shtip, Macedonia
b. Gligorov, Kiro

MADAGASCAR

Anahidrano, Madagascar
b. Tsiranana, Philibert

Antongil Bay, Madagascar
d. Schouten, William Cornelius

Betsiaka, Antsiranana, Madagascar
b. Zafy, Albert

Tananarive, Madagascar
b. Rabearivelo, Jean Joseph
b. Simon, Claude Eugene Henri
d. Tsiranana, Philibert

Vatomandry, Madagascar
b. Ratsiraka, Didier

MALAWI

Chiwengo, Malawi
b. Banda, Hastings Kamuzu

Machinga, Malawi
b. Muluzi, Bakili

MALAYSIA

Alor Setar, Malaysia
b. Mahathir Bin Mohamad

Kuala Lumpur, Malaysia
d. Rahman, Abdul, Prince

MALI

d. Keita, Modibo
d. Sundiata Keita

Bamako, Mali
b. Cisse, Souleymane
b. Keita, Modibo
b. Sangare, Oumou

Kayes, Mali
b. Konare, Alpha Oumar
b. Traore, Moussa

Mpoti, Mali
b. Toure, Amadou Toumani

Niafenke, Mali
b. Toure, Ali Farka

Timbuktu, Mali
d. Laing, Alexander Gordon

MALTA

b. Brenan, Gerald

Birkirkara, Malta
b. Fenech-Adami, Eddie

Gozo, Malta
b. Buttigieg, Anton
d. Bateman, Henry Mayo

Sliema, Malta
b. Sant, Alfred

Valletta, Malta
d. Reed, Oliver

MARSHALL ISLANDS

Eniwetok Atoll, Marshall Islands
d. Clapper, Raymond Lewis

Enmat, Kwajalein Atoll, Marshall Islands
b. Kabua, Imata

Jaluit Atoll, Marshall Islands
b. Kabua, Amata

MARTINIQUE

b. Fanon, Frantz (Omar)

Basse-Pointe, Martinique
b. Cesaire, Aime Fernand

Fort de France, Martinique
b. Eda-Pierre, Christiane

MASSILIA

b. Pytheas

MAURITANIA

Atar, Mauritania
b. Taya, Maaouya Ould Sid'Ahmed

Boutilimit, Mauritania
b. Daddah, Moktar Ould

MAURITIUS

b. Barbarossa, Dave
b. Jugnauth, Anerood
b. Maunick, Edouard Joseph Marc

Belle River, Mauritius
b. Ramgoolam, Seewoosagur, Sir

Port Louis, Mauritius
d. Ramgoolam, Seewoosagur, Sir

MEDIA

b. Cyrus the Great

MESOPOTAMIA

b. Saladin Yusuf ibn Ayyub

Al Kufa, Mesopotamia
d. Ali

Carrhae, Mesopotamia
d. Caracalla, Marcus Aurelius
Antonius
d. Crassus, Marcus Licinius Dives

MEXICO

b. Corona, Juan
b. Onate, Juan de
d. Alaman, Lucas
d. Bierce, Ambrose Gwinett
d. Coronado, Francisco Vasquez de
d. Cosio Villegas, Daniel
d. Galvez, Bernardo de
d. Ruiz Cortines, Adolfo

Acapulco, Mexico
d. Alvarez, Juan
d. Muncey, Bill
d. Weissmuller, Johnny

Alamos, Mexico
b. Obregon, Alvaro

Anenecuilco, Mexico
b. Zapata, Emiliano

Arizpe, Mexico
d. Anza, Juan Bautista de

Atizapan de Zaragoza, Mexico
b. Lopez Mateos, Adolfo

Autlan, Mexico
b. Santana, Carlos

Campeche, Yucatan, Mexico
b. Sierra, Justo

Cancun, Mexico
d. Marshak, Robert E(ugene)

Casa Alvaredo, Mexico
d. Nuttall, Zelia Maria Magdalena

Cerritos, Mexico
b. Lopez, Josefina Maria

Chiapas, Mexico
d. Gordon, Caroline

Chihuahua, Mexico
b. Allred, Rulon Clark
b. Quinn, Anthony Rudolph Oaxaca
b. Romney, George (Wilcken)
b. Siqueiros, David A
b. Villa, Luz Corral de
d. Hidalgo y Costilla, Miguel
d. Villa, Luz Corral de

Chinameca, Mexico
d. Zapata, Emiliano

Chupederos, Mexico
d. Candy, John (Franklin)

Colima, Mexico
b. Madrid Hurtado, Miguel de la

Colotlan, Mexico
b. Huerta, Victoriano

Concepcion de Atayac, Mexico
b. Alvarez, Juan

Corralejo, Mexico
b. Hidalgo y Costilla, Miguel

Coyoacan, Mexico
b. Kahlo, Frida

Cuatroa Cienegas, Mexico
b. Carranza, Venustiano

Cuernavaca, Mexico
d. Bergen, John Joseph
d. Evans, Gil
d. Mingus, Charles
d. Puig, Manuel
d. Siqueiros, David A

Cuilapan, Mexico
d. Guerrero, Vicente

Culiacan, Mexico
b. Limon, Jose Arcadio

Durango, Mexico
b. DelRio, Dolores
b. Novarro, Ramon

Ensenada, Mexico
b. Bruce, Nigel
b. Ramirez, Raul

Fronteras, Mexico
b. Anza, Juan Bautista de

Guadalajara, Mexico
b. Barragan, Luis
b. Jurado, Katy
b. Lopez-Portillo y Rojas, Jose
d. Close, Upton
d. Janney, Leon
d. Pahlmann, William Carroll
d. Royle, Selena

Guanajuato, Mexico
b. Alaman, Lucas
b. Rivera, Diego
d. Martin, Fletcher
d. Williams, Garth Montgomery

Guaymas, Mexico
b. Calles, Plutarco Elias

Hermosillo, Mexico
b. Barrios, Francisco Javier
d. Barrios, Francisco Javier

Hondo, Mexico
b. Fernandez, Emilio

Itzancanal, Mexico
d. Cuauhtemoc

Jalapa, Mexico
b. Lerdo de Tejada, Sebastian
b. Santa Anna, Antonio Lopez de

Jiquilpan, Mexico
b. Cardenas, Lazaro

Juarez, Mexico
b. Roland, Gilbert
d. McQueen, Steve

Las Mochis, Mexico
b. Higuera, Teddy

Logos de Morena, Mexico
b. Azuela, Mariano

Magdalena de Kino, Mexico
b. Colosio Murrieta, Luis Donaldo

Mexico City, Mexico
b. Ana-Alicia
b. Armendariz, Pedro
b. Cantinflas
b. Cardenas Solorzano, Cuauhtemoc
b. Chavez (y Ramirez), Carlos Antonio de Pauda
b. Cosio Villegas, Daniel
b. Covarrubias, Miguel
b. Echeverria Alvarez, Louis
b. Fernandez de Lizardi, Jose Joaquin
b. Fuentes, Carlos
b. Graham, Robert
b. Lopez Portillo (y Pacheco), Jose
b. Margo
b. Matamoros, Mariano
b. Moats, Alice-Leone
b. Montalban, Ricardo

b. Novi, Carlo
b. Paz, Octavio
b. Salinas de Gortari, Carlos
b. Van Peebles, Mario
b. Zedillo Ponce de Leon, Ernesto
d. Aleman, Miguel
d. Allen, Larry
d. Altamira Y Crevea, Rafael
d. Arbenz Guzman, Jacobo
d. Azuela, Mariano
d. Barragan, Luis
d. Bunuel, Luis
d. Calles, Plutarco Elias
d. Campora, Hector Jose
d. Cantinflas
d. Cardenas, Lazaro
d. Chase, Ilka
d. Chavez (y Ramirez), Carlos Antonio
   de Pauda
d. Covarrubias, Miguel
d. Diaz Ordaz, Gustavo
d. Feldman, Marty
d. Fernandez, Emilio
d. Garcia Robles, Alfonso
d. Garcia Vargas, Joaquin
d. Gurie, Sigrid
d. Juarez, Benito Pablo
d. Kahlo, Frida
d. Krauss, Clemens
d. Kuiper, Gerard Peter
d. Lerdo de Tejada, Miguel
d. Lopez Mateos, Adolfo
d. Lopez-Portillo y Rojas, Jose
d. Madero, Francisco Indalecio
d. Merida, Carlos
d. Motley, Willard Francis
d. Orozco, Jose Clemente
d. Paz, Octavio
d. Reyes, Alfonso
d. Ricketts, Howard T
d. Rivera, Diego
d. Rulfo, Juan
d. Santa Anna, Antonio Lopez de
d. Sontag, Henriette
d. Tamayo, Rufino
d. Toledano, Vicente Lombardo
d. Traven, B.
d. Trotsky, Leon
d. Vasconcelos (Calderon), Jose
d. Wilkinson, James
d. Zumarraga, Juan de

Monterrey, Mexico
b. Kiam, Omar
b. Reyes, Alfonso

Navajoa, Mexico
b. Valenzuela, Fernando

Nochistlan, Mexico
d. Alvarado, Pedro de

Oaxaca, Mexico
b. Diaz, Jose de la Cruz Porfirio
b. Diaz, Porfirio
b. Juarez, Benito Pablo
b. Tamayo, Rufino
b. Vasconcelos (Calderon), Jose

Padillla, Mexico
d. Iturbide, Augustin de

Parral, Mexico
d. Villa, Pancho

Parras, Mexico
b. Madero, Francisco Indalecio

Playa del Carmen, Mexico
d. Barr, Joseph W(alker)

Puebla, Mexico
b. Avila Camacho, Manuel
b. Baez, Albert V.
b. Diaz Ordaz, Gustavo
b. Toledano, Vicente Lombardo

Puerto Vallarta, Mexico
d. Allbritton, Louise
d. Pryor, Roger

Queretaro, Mexico
d. Maximilian
d. Sanchez, Salvador

Rio Grande, Mexico
b. Villa, Pancho

Saltillo, Mexico
b. Brent, Romney

San Angel, Mexico
d. Obregon, Alvaro

San Cristobal, Mexico
d. Morelos y Pavon, Jose Maria

San Luis Potosi, Mexico
b. Velez, Lupe

San Miguel de Allende, Mexico
d. Cassady, Neal

San Miguel de Nepantla, Mexico
b. Juana Ines de la Cruz, Sor

Santiago de Tianquistenco, Mexico
b. Sanchez, Salvador

Sayula, Mexico
b. Aleman, Miguel
b. Rulfo, Juan

Tamaulipas, Mexico
b. Esquivel, Juan
d. Sequoyah

Tampico, Mexico
b. Christian, Linda

Taxco, Mexico
b. Alarcon y Mendoza, Juan Ruiz de

Tenochtitlan, Mexico
b. Cuauhtemoc
b. Montezuma I
b. Montezuma II
d. Montezuma I
d. Montezuma II

Tijuana, Mexico
d. Colosio Murrieta, Luis Donaldo
d. Paulsen, Pat

Tixtla, Mexico
b. Guerrero, Vicente

Tlaxcalantongo, Mexico
d. Carranza, Venustiano

Torreon, Mexico
b. Law, Bernard Francis, Cardinal

Valladolid, Mexico
b. Iturbide, Augustin de
b. Morelos y Pavon, Jose Maria

Veracruz, Mexico
b. Avila, Bobby
b. Lerdo de Tejada, Miguel
b. Ruiz Cortines, Adolfo

Yucatan, Mexico
d. Landa, Diego de

Zamora, Mexico
b. Garcia Robles, Alfonso

Zapotlan, Mexico
b. Orozco, Jose Clemente

MOESIA

Nassius, Moesia
b. Constantine I

MOLDOVA

Kamenetz-Podolsk, Moldova
b. Tracy, Arthur

Radulenii-Vechi, Moldova
b. Lucinschi, Petru

Trifaneshty, Moldova
b. Snegur, Mircea Ion

MONACO

b. Rainier III, Prince
b. Schreker, Franz
d. Darracq, Alexandre
d. Gallico, Paul William

Monaco-Ville, Monaco
b. Stephanie, Princess

Monte Carlo, Monaco
b. Albert, Prince
b. Caroline, Princess
d. Beatty, Alfred Chester, Sir
d. Berry, James Gomer
d. Carol, Martine
d. Casiraghi, Stefano
d. Chaminade, Cecile
d. Darvi, Bella
d. Dongen, Kees van
d. Escoffier, Georges Auguste
d. Kelly, Grace Patricia
d. Langtry, Lillie
d. Loewy, Raymond Fernand
d. Molyneux, Edward H
d. Morgan, Junius Spencer
d. Olcott, Chauncey
d. Paray, Paul
d. Pathe, Charles

d. Rossellini, Renzo
d. Wallmann, Margherita
d. Whitman, Alden
d. Zaharoff, Basil, Sir

MONGOLIA

b. Genghis Khan
d. Lin, Piao (Yu-Yung)

Hovd, Mongolia
b. Elbegdorj, Tsahiagiyn

Kansu, Mongolia
d. Genghis Khan

Ulaanbaatar, Mongolia
b. Enhsaihan, M.

MORAVIA

Brno, Moravia
b. Loos, Adolf

Brunn, Moravia
b. Maretzek, Max

Butschowitz, Moravia
b. Strakosch, Maurice

Chirlitz-Turas, Moravia
b. Mach, Ernst

Dedice, Moravia
b. Gottwald, Klement

Eibenschutz, Moravia
b. Adler, Guido

Freiberg, Moravia
b. Freud, Sigmund

Goding, Moravia
b. Masaryk, Tomas Garrigue

Hodslavice, Moravia
b. Palacky, Frantisek

Horznatin, Moravia
b. Svoboda, Ludvik

Hukvaldy, Moravia
b. Janacek, Leos

Ivancice, Moravia
b. Mucha, Alphonse Marie

Koprivnice, Moravia
b. Zatopek, Emil

Prossnitz, Moravia
b. Husserl, Edmund

Schonberg, Moravia
b. Slezak, Leo

Trest, Moravia
b. Schumpeter, Joseph Alois

Unersky, Moravia
b. Comenius, Johann Amos

Ungarisch Brod, Moravia
b. Jung, Leo

MOROCCO

b. ibn Tumart, Muhammad

Agadir, Morocco
d. Blyden, Larry

Ajdir, Morocco
b. Abd el-Krim el-Khatabi, Mohamed ben

Casablanca, Morocco
b. Portzamparc, Christian de

Ceuta, Morocco
b. Idrisi, Muhammad ibn Muhammad al-
d. Idrisi, Muhammad ibn Muhammad al-

Fez, Morocco
b. Allal al-Fassi, Mohamed
b. Ben Jelloun, Tahar
b. Lahbabi, Mohammed Aziz
b. Mohammed V
d. ibn Battuta, Muhammad
d. Ibn Batutah

Kenitra, Morocco
b. Aouita, Said

Marrakech, Morocco
d. Auchinleck, Claude, Sir
d. Averroes
d. ibn Tufayl, Abu Bakr Muhammad
d. ibn Tumart, Muhammad

Mazagan, Morocco
b. Chraibi, Driss

Oujda, Morocco
b. Bouteflika, Abdelaziz

Rabat, Morocco
b. Hassan II
d. Hassan II
d. Mobutu Sese Seko
d. Mohammed V

Tangiers, Morocco
b. ibn Battuta, Muhammad
b. Ibn Batutah
b. Spotswood, Alexander
b. Tietjen, Heinz
b. Toledano, Ralph de
d. Bowles, Paul (Frederick)
d. Lukas, Paul

MOZAMBIQUE

b. Machel, Graca Simbine
b. Mondlane, Eduardo Chivambo

Chibabava, Sofala Province, Mozambique
b. Dhlakama, Afonso

Chilembene, Mozambique
b. Machel, Samora Moises

Lourenco Marques, Mozambique
b. Honwana, Luis Bernardo

Malehice, Mozambique
b. Chissano, Joaquim Alberto

Maputo, Mozambique
b. Mutola, Maria
d. First, Ruth

MYANMAR

Rangoon, Myanmar
b. Townsend, Peter Wooldridge
d. Nu, U

Yangon, Myanmar
d. Nu Thakin

MYSORE

b. Sabu

Bangalore, Mysore
b. Swinton, Ernest Dunlop, Sir

NAMIBIA

Owambo, Namibia
b. Nujoma, Samuel Shafiihuma

Windhoek, Namibia
b. Mbuende, Kaire (Munionganda)

NAURU

b. Clodumar, Kinza
b. DeRoburt, Hammer, Sir
b. Dowiyogo, Bernard

NEPAL

d. Mahal, Hazrat
d. Mallory, George Leigh

Bharatpur, Nepal
d. Mahendra, Bir Bikram Shah Dev

Kathmandu, Nepal
b. Adhikary, Man Mohan
b. Birendra Bir Bikram, Shah Dev
b. Mahendra, Bir Bikram Shah Dev

Muga, Nepal
b. Thapa, Surya Bahadur

Nieuwegein, Nepal
d. Alfrink, Bernard (Jan), Cardinal

Nijkerk, Nepal
b. Alfrink, Bernard (Jan), Cardinal

Solo Khumbu, Nepal
b. Tenzing Norgay

Tukurkutiya, Nepal
b. Chand, Lokendra Bahadur

NETHERLANDS

b. Agt, Andries Antonius Maria van
b. Clouet, Jean
b. Fabritius, Carel
b. Geertgen tot Sint Jans
b. Hobbema, Meindert
b. Van der Klugt, Cor
b. Van Westerborg, Edward
d. Pavlova, Anna
d. Rembrandt (Harmenszoon van Rijn)
d. Southampton, Henry Wriothesley,
   Earl
d. Tromp, Solco Walle

Acquoi, Netherlands
b. Jansen, Cornelis Otto

Agnietenberg, Netherlands
d. Thomas a Kempis

Amersfoort, Netherlands
b. Mondrian, Piet(er Cornelis)
b. Oldenbarnevelt, Johan van
d. Meinesz, Felix Andries Vening

Amsterdam, Netherlands
b. Appel, Karel Christian
b. Asser, Tobias Michael Carel
b. Berlage, Hendrik Petrus
b. Blankers-Koen, Fanny
b. Cruyff, Johan
b. DeWaart, Edo
b. Drees, Willem
b. Eeckhout, Gerbrand van den
b. Euwe, Max
b. Haitink, Bernard
b. Hooft, Pieter Corneliszoon
b. Keyser, Thomas De
b. Krieghoff, Cornelius
b. Lionni, Leo
b. Matthes, Francois-Emile
b. Pais, Abraham
b. Spier, Peter Edward
b. Spinoza, Baruch (Benedictus de)
b. Swammerdam, Jan
b. Sweelinck, Jan Pieterszoon
b. Ten Boom, Corrie
b. Van Rensselaer, Kiliaen
b. Verwoerd, Hendrik F
b. Zernike, Frits
d. Beinum, Eduard van
d. Clay-Jolles, Tettje Clasina
d. Comenius, Johann Amos
d. Den Uyl, Joop
d. DeVries, Hugo
d. Eeckhout, Gerbrand van den
d. Egorov, Youri
d. Ehrenfest, Paul
d. Euwe, Max
d. Flinck, Govert
d. Hobbema, Meindert
d. Holland, Charles
d. Hooch, Pieter de

d. Kalf, Willem
d. Kapteyn, Jacobus Cornelis
d. Keyser, Thomas De
d. Kondrashin, Kiril Petrovich
d. Locatelli, Pietro Antonio
d. Oistrakh, David Fyodorovich
d. Ruysdael, Jacob van
d. Sweelinck, Jan Pieterszoon
d. Van Rensselaer, Kiliaen
d. Vondel, Joost van den
d. Waals, Johannes Diderik van der
d. Zeeman, Pieter

Anna Paulowna, Netherlands
b. Schenk, Ard

Apeldoorn, Netherlands
b. DeJong, Petrus

Arnhem, Netherlands
b. Beinum, Eduard van
b. Lorentz, Hendrick Antoon
d. Sidney, Philip, Sir

Assen, Netherlands
b. Clay-Jolles, Tettje Clasina

Barneveld, Netherlands
b. Kapteyn, Jacobus Cornelis

Beers, Netherlands
d. DeQuay, Jan E

Bergambacht, Netherlands
b. Kok, Wim

Berkhout, Netherlands
b. Clay, Jacob

Blija, Netherlands
b. DeJong, David Cornel

Breda, Netherlands
b. Bruegel, Pieter, the El
b. Ingenhousz, Jan
b. Parker, Tom, Colonel

Breukelen, Netherlands
b. Hauer, Rutger

Bruges, Netherlands
d. David, Gerard

Bussum, Netherlands
b. Wittop, Freddy
d. Eeden, Fredrik Willem van

Cote-Saint-Andre, Netherlands
d. Jongkind, Johan Barthold

Culemborg, Netherlands
b. Cooper, Wilhelmina Behmenburg
b. Riebeeck, Jan Anthonisz van
b. Van Diemen, Anthony Meuza

De Steeg, Netherlands
d. Couperius, Louis (Marie Anne)
d. Huizinga, Johan

Delfshaven, Netherlands
b. Dongen, Kees van

Delft, Netherlands
b. Grotius, Hugo
b. Leeuwenhoek, Antonie van
b. Vermeer, Jan
d. Fabritius, Carel
d. Vermeer, Jan

Den Helder, Netherlands
b. Bok, Edward William

Deventer, Netherlands
b. Groote, Gerhard
d. Groote, Gerhard
d. Ter Borch, Gerard

Doorn, Netherlands
d. Wilhelm II
d. William, II

Dordrecht, Netherlands
b. Bloembergen, Nicolaas
b. Cuyp, Aelbert Jacobsz(oon)
b. Cuyp, Jacob Gerritsz(oon)
b. Hurkos, Peter
b. Witt, Johan de
d. Cuyp, Aelbert Jacobsz(oon)
d. Cuyp, Jacob Gerritsz(oon)

Dronrijp, Netherlands
b. Alma-Tadema, Lawrence, Sir

Druten, Netherlands
b. Kolvenbach, Peter-Hans

Eijsden, Netherlands
b. Dubois, Eugene

Exeter, Netherlands
b. Ladd, William

Franeker, Netherlands
b. Oort, Jan Hendrik

Goreum, Netherlands
b. Van Paassen, Pierre

Gouda, Netherlands
b. Schilt, Jan

Graveland, Netherlands
b. Koopmans, Tjalling (Charles)

Groningen, Netherlands
b. Bernoulli, Daniel
b. Huizinga, Johan
b. Israels, Josef
b. Kamerlingh Onnes, Heike
b. Vermeij, Geerat J(acobus)

Groot Zundert, Netherlands
b. Van Gogh, Vincent Willem

Haarlem, Netherlands
b. Bouts, Dierick C
b. Coster, Laurens Janszoon
b. DeHartog, Jan
b. DeVries, Hugo
b. Eeden, Fredrik Willem van
b. Meer, Jan van der
b. Ostade, Adriaen van
b. Ruysdael, Jacob van
b. Van Niel, Cornelius B(ernardus)
b. Visser T Hooft, Willem Adolf

d. Hals, Frans
d. Lorentz, Hendrick Antoon
d. Ostade, Adriaen van

Hainaut, Netherlands
b. Ockeghem, Johannes

Harenkarspel, Netherlands
b. Kuiper, Gerard Peter

Hertogenbosch, Netherlands
b. Bosch, Hieronymous
d. Bosch, Hieronymous

Het Loo, Netherlands
d. Wilhelmina

Hilversum, Netherlands
b. Den Uyl, Joop
d. Escher, M(aurits) C(ornelis)

Hoorn, Netherlands
b. Bok, Bart J(an)
b. Coen, Jan Pieterszoon
b. Schouten, William Cornelius

Lattrop, Netherlands
b. Jongkind, Johan Barthold

Leeuwarden, Netherlands
b. Escher, M(aurits) C(ornelis)
b. Mata Hari

Leiden, Netherlands
b. Dou, Gerard
b. Foch, Nina
b. Goyen, Jan Josephszoon van
b. Kolff, Willem Johan
b. Rembrandt (Harmenszoon van Rijn)
b. Steen, Jan
b. Van Leyden, Lucas
b. Velde, Willem van de
b. Waals, Johannes Diderik van der
d. Arminius, Jacobus
d. Boerhaave, Hermann
d. Dou, Gerard
d. Ehrenfest-Afanaseva, Tatiana
d. Einthoven, Willem
d. Elzevir, Louis
d. Kamerlingh Onnes, Heike
d. Sitter, Willem de
d. Steen, Jan
d. Van Leyden, Lucas

Leusden, Netherlands
d. Achterberg, Gerrit
d. Auger, Arleen

Limburg, Netherlands
d. Dubois, Eugene

Lubeck, Netherlands
d. Menno Simonsz(con)

Maastricht, Netherlands
b. Debye, Peter Joseph William

Maeseyck, Netherlands
b. Van Eyck, Jan

Mons, Netherlands
b. Lassus, Orlandus de

Naarden, Netherlands
d. Martin, Frank
d. Zernike, Frits

Neerlangbroek, Netherlands
b. Achterberg, Gerrit

Nijkerk, Netherlands
b. Eijkman, Christiaan

Nijmegen, Netherlands
b. Canisius, Peter
b. Ivens, Joris
b. Van Halen, Alex
b. Van Halen, Eddie

Noordwijk, Netherlands
d. Montessori, Maria

Noordwykerhout, Netherlands
b. Vander Zalm, William

Oegstgeest, Netherlands
d. Keesom, Willem Hendrik

Oudewater, Netherlands
b. Arminius, Jacobus
b. David, Gerard

Portsmouth, Netherlands
d. Ladd, William

Purmerend, Netherlands
b. Oud, Jacobus Johannes Pieter

Roermond, Netherlands
b. Cuypers, Petrus Josephus Hubertus
b. Raemaekers, Louis

Rotterdam, Netherlands
b. Ameling, Elly
b. Brico, Antonia
b. deKooning, Willem
b. Dijkstra, Edsger W(ybe)
b. Erasmus, Desiderius
b. Gibbons, Grinling
b. Hoff, Jacobus Henricus van 't
b. Hooch, Pieter de
b. Kalf, Willem
b. Kindler, Hans
b. Lanting, Frans
b. Lubbers, Ruud
b. Luns, Joseph Marie Antoine Hubert
b. Mandeville, Bernard
b. Monmouth, James Scott, Duke
b. Stove, Betty
b. Van Loon, Hendrik Willem
b. Van Rooy, Anton
b. Van't Hoff, Jacobus Henricus
b. Vlieger, Simon Jacobsz de
d. Bayle, Pierre
d. Colton, Gardner Quincy

S'Hertogenbosch, Netherlands
b. DeQuay, Jan E

Scherpenzeel, Netherlands
b. Stuyvesant, Peter

Scheveninaen, Netherlands
d. Raemaekers, Louis

Scheveningen, Netherlands
b. Meinesz, Felix Andries Vening

Sneek, Netherlands
b. Sitter, Willem de

Soestdijk, Netherlands
b. Beatrix
b. Christina
b. Irene

Sommelsdyk, Netherlands
b. Luyendyk, Arie

Steins, Netherlands
b. Dykstra, John

Terschelling, Netherlands
b. Barents, Willem

Texel, Netherlands
b. Keesom, Willem Hendrik

The Hague, Netherlands
b. Couperius, Louis (Marie Anne)
b. Gallitzin, Demetrius Augustine
b. Goudsmit, Samuel Abraham
b. Huygens, Christian
b. Juliana
b. Meer, Simon van der
b. Thyssen-Bornemisza de Kaszan, Hans Heinrich, Baron
b. Tinbergen, Jan
b. Tinbergen, Nikolaas
b. Van der Meer, Simon
b. Wilhelmina
b. William III
d. Asser, Tobias Michael Carel
d. Berlage, Hendrik Petrus
d. Drees, Willem
d. Fahrenheit, Gabriel Daniel
d. Goyen, Jan Josephszoon van
d. Hooft, Pieter Corneliszoon
d. Huygens, Christian
d. Israels, Josef
d. Maurice of Nassau
d. Oldenbarnevelt, Johan van
d. Spinoza, Baruch (Benedictus de)
d. Stevin, Simon
d. Waldock, Humphrey Meredith, Sir
d. Witt, Johan de

Utrecht, Netherlands
b. Doesburg, Theo van
b. Heem, Jan Davidsz(oon) de
b. Kristel, Sylvia
b. Mengelberg, Willem
b. Rietveld, Gerrit Thomas
b. Van Eekelen, Willem Frederik
d. Eijkman, Christiaan
d. Rietveld, Gerrit Thomas

Voorhout, Netherlands
b. Boerhaave, Hermann

Wassenaar, Netherlands
d. Oud, Jacobus Johannes Pieter

Weesp, Netherlands
d. Vlieger, Simon Jacobsz de

Wierum, Netherlands
b. Dejong, Meindert

Wijk, Netherlands
b. Van Cortlandt, Oloff Stevenszen

Zandvoort, Netherlands
d. Corinth, Lovis

Zeist, Netherlands
b. Blyleven, Bert

Zierikzee, Netherlands
b. Muste, A(braham) J(ohannes)

Zonnemaire, Netherlands
b. Zeeman, Pieter

Zwolle, Netherlands
b. Ter Borch, Gerard

NETHERLANDS ANTILLES

Willemstad, Curacao, Netherlands Antilles
b. Liberia-Peters, Maria Philomena

NEVIS

b. Crosse, Rupert

NEW CALEDONIA

Noumea, New Caledonia
b. Higgins, Colin

NEW ZEALAND

b. Bolitho, Henry Hector
b. Ratana, Taupotiki Wiremu
b. Russell, Franklin Alexander
d. Ngata, Apirana Turupa

Auckland, New Zealand
b. Birley, Oswald Hornby Joseph, Sir
b. Duggan, Maurice Noel
b. Garnett, Gale
b. Hillary, Edmund Percival, Sir
b. Lawless, Lucy
b. Lewis, Chris
b. McLaren, Bruce Leslie
b. Muldoon, Robert David, Sir
b. Walpole, Hugh Seymour, Sir
d. Hobson, William
d. Muldoon, Robert David, Sir

Canterbury, New Zealand
b. Eden, Dorothy

Cartenton, New Zealand
b. Charles, Bob

Christchurch, New Zealand
b. Alda, Frances
b. Denny-Brown, Derek Ernest
b. Marsh, Ngaio, Dame
d. Marsh, Ngaio, Dame

Dannevirke, New Zealand
b. Bjelke-Petersen, Johannes

Dunedin, New Zealand
b. Low, David Alexander Cecil, Sir

Gisborne, New Zealand
b. Partridge, Eric Honeywood
b. Te Kanawa, Kiri, Dame

Gore, New Zealand
b. Shipley, Jenny

Invercargill, New Zealand
b. Todd, Garfield

Kawaka, New Zealand
b. Ngata, Apirana Turupa

Kurow, New Zealand
b. Kerr, Roy Patrick

Levin, New Zealand
b. Silk, George

Motueka, New Zealand
b. Rowling, Wallace Edward

New Plymouth, New Zealand
b. King, Frederic Truby

Ngaruawahia, New Zealand
b. Wilson, Allan C

Opunake, New Zealand
b. Snell, Peter George

Otahuhu, New Zealand
b. Lange, David Russell

Pahiatua, New Zealand
b. Holyoake, Keith Jacka, Sir

Pongaroa, New Zealand
b. Wilkins, Maurice Hugh Frederick

Riverton, New Zealand
b. Arnett, Peter Gregg

Rotorua, New Zealand
b. Batten, Jean Gardner
d. Ironside, Henry Allan

Spring Grove, New Zealand
b. Rutherford, Ernest, Baron

Springfield, New Zealand
b. Alley, Rewi

Stratford, New Zealand
b. Ashton-Warner, Sylvia Constance

Taranaki, New Zealand
b. Bolger, Jim

Tauranga, New Zealand
d. Ashton-Warner, Sylvia Constance

Wanganui, New Zealand
b. Porritt, Arthur Espie, Sir

Wellington, New Zealand
b. Campion, Jane
b. Mansfield, Katherine

b. Revill, Clive Selsby
d. Holyoake, Keith Jacka, Sir
d. Massey, William Ferguson
d. Savage, Michael Joseph
d. Wakefield, Edward Gibbon

NICARAGUA

b. Calero (Portocarrero), Adolfo
b. Fournier, Rafael (Angel) Calderon
b. Robelo, Alfonso

Asuncion, Nicaragua
d. Somoza Debayle, Anastasio

Dario, Nicaragua
b. Pastora (Gomez), Eden

Esteli, Nicaragua
b. Alegria, Claribel

Granada, Nicaragua
b. Cardenal, Ernesto

Jinotepe, Nicaragua
b. Cruz, Arturo

La Libertad, Nicaragua
b. Obando (y Bravo), Miguel
b. Ortega Saavedra, Daniel

Leon, Nicaragua
b. Somoza Debayle, Anastasio
d. Dario, Ruben
d. Pedrarias

Managua, Nicaragua
b. Aleman, Arnoldo
b. Arguello, Alexis
b. Astorga, Nora Gadea
b. Carrera, Barbara
b. Jagger, Bianca Teresa
b. Zelaya, Jose Santos
d. Astorga, Nora Gadea
d. Sandino, Augusto C(esar Calderon)
d. Somoza, Anastasio

Matagalpa, Nicaragua
b. Borge Martinez, Tomas

Metapa, Nicaragua
b. Dario, Ruben

Niquinohomo, Nicaragua
b. Sandino, Augusto C(esar Calderon)

Rivas, Nicaragua
b. Chamorro, Violeta Barrios de

San Marcos, Nicaragua
b. Somoza, Anastasio

NIGER

Dingajibanda, Ouallam, Niger
b. Saibou, Ali

Fandou, Niger
b. Kountche, Seyni

Cappagh, Northern Ireland
b. Hurson, Martin

Cookstown, Northern Ireland
b. Devlin, Bernadette Josephine

County Armagh, Northern Ireland
b. Muldoon, Paul

County Derry, Northern Ireland
b. Connor, William Neil, Sir

County Down, Northern Ireland
b. Garson, Greer
b. Martin, James, Sir

County Fermanagh, Northern Ireland
b. Alanbrooke, Alan Francis Brooke,
  1st Viscount

Dromore, Northern Ireland
b. Ferguson, Harry George

Dungiven, Northern Ireland
b. Lynch, Kevin

Larne, Northern Ireland
b. Hobson, Valerie Babette

Lisburn, Northern Ireland
b. Stewart, Alexander Turney
d. Taylor, Jeremy

Londonderry, Northern Ireland
b. Cary, Joyce
b. Devine, Michael
b. Doherty, Kieran
b. Farquhar, George
b. Hare, William
b. Hume, John
b. Maginnis, Charles Donagh
b. O'Hara, Patrick

Lurgan, Northern Ireland
b. Dill, John Greer, Sir

Mossbawn, Northern Ireland
b. Heaney, Seamus (Justin)

Omagh, Northern Ireland
b. Friel, Brian

Ulster, Northern Ireland
b. Daly, Maureen Patricia

NORWAY

b. Bjorn-Larsen, Knut
b. Eric the Red
b. Olaf, II
b. Rollo
d. Lukeman, Henry A
d. Olaf, II

Asker, Norway
b. Gerhardsen, Einar Henry

Bergen, Norway
b. Bull, Ole Bornemann
b. Giaever, Ivar
b. Grieg, Edvard Hagerup

b. Grieg, Nordahl Brun
b. Ostenso, Martha
b. Parr, A(lbert) E(ide)
b. Rider-Kelsey, Corinne
d. Grieg, Edvard Hagerup
d. Helland-Hansen, Bjorn

Christiania, Norway
b. Aurell, Tage
b. Evinrude, Ole
b. Helland-Hansen, Bjorn
b. Nansen, Fridtjof
d. Ibsen, Henrik Johan

Fetsund, Norway
b. Stenerud, Jan

Findoe, Norway
b. Abel, Niels Henrik

Fredrikshald, Norway
d. Charles XII

Froland, Norway
d. Abel, Niels Henrik

Fryesdal, Norway
b. Quisling, Vidkun Abraham

Geilo, Norway
d. Lie, Trygve Halvdan

Golaa, Norway
d. Evans, Edward Ratcliffe Garth
  Russell

Hamar, Norway
b. Flagstad, Kirsten

Helgeland, Norway
b. Rolvaag, Ole Edvart
b. Sverdrup, Otto

Hokksund in Eiker, Norway
b. Lie, Jonas Laurite Idemil

Horten, Norway
b. Norena, Eide
b. Ronne, Finn

Kongsberg, Norway
b. D'Aulaire, Ingri Mortenson
b. Sinding, Christian

Kristiania, Norway
b. Bjerknes, Vilhelm (Frimann Koren)
b. Hassel, Odd
b. Henie, Sonja

Kvikne, Norway
b. Bjornson, Bjornstjerne Martinius

Larvik, Norway
b. Heyerdahl, Thor

Lilleborg, Norway
d. Gerhardsen, Einar Henry

Lillehammer, Norway
d. Undset, Sigrid

Lom, Norway
b. Hamsun, Knut

Loyten, Norway
b. Munch, Edvard

Lysaker, Norway
d. Nansen, Fridtjof

Lysoe, Norway
d. Bull, Ole Bornemann

Mandal, Norway
b. Vigeland, Gustav

Meraker, Norway
b. Ingstad, Helge Marcus

Molde, Norway
b. Bondevik, Kjell (Magne)

Noerholmen, Norway
d. Hamsun, Knut

Notteroy, Norway
b. Bratteli, Trygve Martin

Orkesdalsoren, Norway
b. Bojer, Johan

Oslo, Norway
b. Andresen, Ivar
b. Brundtland, Gro Harlem
b. Bull, Odd
b. Cammermeyer, Margarethe
b. Frisch, Ragnar Anton Kittil
b. Harald
b. Lie, Trygve Halvdan
b. Onsager, Lars
b. Waitz, Grete
d. Bjerknes, Vilhelm (Frimann Koren)
d. Bojer, Johan
d. Bratteli, Trygve Martin
d. Dobrowen, Issai
d. Flagstad, Kirsten
d. Frisch, Ragnar Anton Kittil
d. Goldschmidt, Victor Moritz
d. Haakon VII
d. Hassel, Odd
d. Lange, Christian Louis
d. Munch, Edvard
d. Olav V
d. Quisling, Vidkun Abraham
d. Sinding, Christian
d. Stormer, Fredrik (Carl Mulertz)
d. Sverdrup, H(arald) U(lrik)
d. Sverdrup, Otto
d. Vigeland, Gustav

Skedsmo, Norway
b. Haavelmo, Trygve Magnus

Skien, Norway
b. Ibsen, Henrik Johan
b. Stormer, Fredrik (Carl Mulertz)

Sogndal, Norway
b. Sverdrup, H(arald) U(lrik)

Spitsbergen, Norway
d. Amundsen, Roald Engelbregt

Rishon Letzion, Palestine
b. Agam, Yaacov

Tel Aviv, Palestine
b. Arison, Ted
b. Bufman, Zev
b. Dinitz, Simcha
b. Geller, Uri
b. Ginott, Haim
b. Perlman, Itzhak
b. Topol, Chaim
b. Weizman, Ezer
d. Ahad Haam
d. Bialik, Chaim Nachman

Tulkarm City, Palestine
b. Abu Salma

al Birwah, Palestine
b. Darwish, Mahmud

PANAMA

b. Arias Madrid, Arnulfo
b. Chiari, Roberto
b. Cobham, Billy
b. Goulet, Leo D
d. Chiari, Roberto
d. Torrijos Herrera, Omar

Acla, Panama
d. Balboa, Vasco Nunez de

Chorillo, Panama
b. Duran, Roberto

Colon, Panama
b. Laguna, Ismael
b. Sanguillen, Manny
d. Anderson, Sherwood

Gatun, Panama
b. Carew, Rod(ney Cline)

La Chorrera, Panama
b. Royo, Aristides

Panama City, Panama
b. Blades, Ruben, Jr.
b. Endara (Galimany), Guillermo
b. Noriega (Moreno), Manuel Antonio
b. Perez Balladares, Ernesto
b. Pincay, Laffit, Jr.
b. Quintero, Jose (Benjamin)
d. Arias, Roberto Emilio
d. Fonteyn, Margot, Dame

Portobelo, Panama
d. Drake, Francis, Sir
d. Laing, David

Santiago de Veraguas, Panama
b. Torrijos Herrera, Omar

PANAMA CANAL ZONE

b. Clark, Kenneth Bancroft
b. McCain, John Sidney, III

PAPAL STATES

b. Gentileschi, Artemisia

Bertinoro, Papal States
b. Bertinoro, Obadiah ben Abraham Yare

Bologna, Papal States
b. Gregory XV
d. Guercino, Il

Cento, Papal States
b. Guercino, Il

Fabriano, Papal States
b. Gentile da Fabriano

Jesi, Papal States
b. Frederick II

Lugo, Papal States
b. Ricci-Curbastro, Gregorio

Macerata, Papal States
b. Ricci, Matteo

Orvieto, Papal States
d. Pisano, Andrea

Rome, Papal States
b. Cecchetti, Enrico
b. Fetti, Domenico
d. Gregory XV
d. Kauffmann, Angelica

PAPUA NEW GUINEA

Ara'ara, Gulf, Papua New Guinea
b. Skate, Bill

Moika, Papua New Guinea
b. Wingti, Paias

Raluana, Kokopo, Papua New Guinea
b. Namaliu, Rabbie Langanai

Tanga, New Ireland, Papua New Guinea
b. Chan, Julius

PARAGUAY

b. Gonzalez Macchi, Luis
d. Lopez, Carlos Antonio
d. Sarmiento, Domingo Faustino

Asuncion, Paraguay
b. Lopez, Carlos Antonio
b. Lopez, Francisco Solano

Borja, Paraguay
b. Rodriguez, Andres

Cerro Cora, Paraguay
d. Lopez, Francisco Solano

Encarnacion, Paraguay
b. Stroessner, Alfredo

Ibiray, Paraguay
d. Artigas, Jose Gervasio

Paraguari, Paraguay
b. Morinigo, Higinio

PEOPLE'S REPUBLIC OF CHINA

Beijing, People's Republic of China
b. Cho, Alfred Y(i)

PERSIA

b. Khosrow, I
b. Mani
b. Shahpur, II
b. Zoroaster
d. Khosrow, I
d. Mani
d. Shahpur, II

Ahwaz, Persia
b. Abu Nuwas

Amol, Tabaristan, Persia
b. Tabari, Muhammad ibn Jarir al-

Ctesiphon, Persia
d. Julian

Hamadan, Persia
d. Avicenna

Hamadan Province, Persia
b. Bani-Sadr, Abolhassan

Isfahan, Persia
b. Beheshti, Mohammad, Ayatollah

Kermanshah, Persia
b. Lessing, Doris May

Kesh, Persia
b. Tamerlane

Khomein, Persia
b. Khomeini, Ruhollah Musavi, Ayatollah

Khurasan, Persia
b. Alp Arslan
b. Nadir Shah

Mazanderan, Persia
d. Abbas I

Nishapur, Persia
b. Omar Khayyam
d. Omar Khayyam

Qishm, Persia
d. Baffin, William

Quazin, Persia
b. Rajai, Mohammed Ali

Ray, Persia
b. Razi

POLAND

b. Basia
b. Biba
b. Bronowski, Jacob
b. Burck, Jacob
b. Charpak, George
b. Lipsig, Harry H(avon)
b. Lowe, Edwin S
b. Mattus, Reuben
b. Mazepa, Ivan Stepanovich
b. Pearlroth, Norbert
b. Radin, Paul
b. Schneiderman, Rose
b. Stulberg, Louis

Akopy, Poland
b. Ba'al Shem Tov, Israel

Auschwitz, Poland
d. Fleischmann, Gisi
d. Hoess, Rudolf Franz
d. Kolbe, Maximilian Maria, Saint
d. Salomon, Charlotte
d. Stein, Edith

Baranovichi, Poland
b. Foxman, Abraham H

Bemberg, Poland
b. Rosenthal, Moriz

Biala, Poland
b. Tworkov, Jack

Bialobrzegi, Poland
b. Gomulka, Wladyslaw

Bialogard, Poland
b. Kwasniewski, Aleksander

Bialystok, Poland
b. Kaufman, Boris
b. Raisa, Rosa
b. Zamenhof, Ludwik Lazar

Blonie, Poland
b. Anders, Wladyslaw

Breslau, Poland
b. Anderssen, Adolf
b. Cohn, Ferdinand Julius
d. Anderssen, Adolf
d. Cohn, Ferdinand Julius
d. Mueller, Otto

Brest-Litovsk, Poland
b. Begin, Menachem (Wolfovitch)
b. Dubinsky, David

Brody, Poland
b. Krochmal, Nachman Kohen

Buczacz, Poland
b. Wiesenthal, Simon

Bukovnia, Poland
b. Appelfeld, Aharon

Bunzlau, Poland
d. Kutuzov, Mikhail Ilarionovich

Chudnov, Poland
b. Masserman, Jules H(oman)

Czernica, Poland
b. Gorecki, Henryk (Mikolaj)

Czestochowa, Poland
b. Huberman, Bronislaw

Danzig, Poland
b. Hevelius, Johannes
d. Hevelius, Johannes

Debica, Poland
b. Penderecki, Krzysztof

Filipowa, Poland
b. Broudy, Harry Samuel

Frauenburg, Poland
d. Copernicus, Nicolaus

Garnek, Poland
d. DeReszke, Edouard

Glinno, Poland
b. Boguslawski, Wojciech

Gradek, Poland
b. Martin, Ross

Grodno, Poland
b. Cohen, Myron
d. Casimir, Saint

Inowroclaw, Poland
b. Glemp, Jozef, Cardinal

Janowa, Poland
b. Negri, Pola

Jarotschin, Poland
b. Schwarzkopf, Elisabeth

Kaminetz-Podolsk, Poland
b. Drachler, Norman

Katowice Voivodship, Poland
b. Babiuch, Edward

Kobiele Wielkie, Poland
b. Reymont, Wladyslaw Stanislaw

Kowalewko, Poland
b. Rakowski, Mieczyslaw Franciszek

Krakow, Poland
b. Casimir, Saint
b. Erteszek, Jan
b. Gray, Gilda
b. Infeld, Leopold
b. Kronold, Selma
b. Malinowski, Bronislaw Kasper
b. Modjeska, Helena
b. Modjeski, Ralph
b. Olga
b. Rosenstock, Joseph
b. Rubinstein, Helena

Kraznashiltz, Poland
b. Warner, Albert
b. Warner, Harry Morris

Kreschov, Poland
b. Schneider, Herman

Kurilovka, Poland
b. Paderewski, Ignace Jan

Kurow, Poland
b. Jaruzelski, Wojciech Witold

Kutno, Poland
b. Asch, Sholem

Kuzinoy, Poland
b. Shamir, Yitzhak

Lemburg, Poland
b. Meinong, Alexius, Ritter von Handschuchsheim

Leszno, Poland
b. Salomon, Haym

Lodz, Poland
b. Factor, Max
b. Ford, Alexander
b. Kosinski, Jerzy (Nikodem)
b. Moczar, Mieczyslaw
b. Morgentaler, Henry
b. Rosten, Leo C(alvin)
b. Rubinstein, Arthur
b. Spychalski, Marian
b. Szyk, Arthur
d. Aldridge, Ira Frederick

Lubaczow, Poland
b. Hertzberg, Arthur

Lublin, Poland
b. Cwiklinska, Mieczyslawa
b. Wieniawski, Henri

Luclawice, Poland
d. Socinus, Faustus

Lvov, Poland
b. Ax, Emanuel
b. Kuron, Jacek
b. Radek, Karl Bernhardovich
b. Rapacki, Adam
b. Skrowaczewski, Stanislaw
b. Sobieski, John, III
b. Taubes, Frederic

Mezshbozsh, Poland
d. Ba'al Shem Tov, Israel

Moloszyee, Poland
b. Gombrowicz, Witold

Nieswicz, Poland
b. Jaroszewicz, Piotr

Niskish, Poland
b. Yeshurun, Avot

Okrzejska, Poland
b. Sienkiewicz, Henryk Adam Aleksander Pius

Ozorkow, Poland
b. Reshevsky, Samuel

Zarnowiec, Poland
d. Barlow, Joel

Zdunska Wola, Poland
b. Kolbe, Maximilian Maria, Saint

Zelazowa Wola, Poland
b. Chopin, Frederic Francois
b. Szeryng, Henryk

Zloczow, Poland
b. Hoffmann, Roald

POMERANIA

Koslin, Pomerania
b. Clausius, Rudolf Julius Emmanuel

PONTUS

Amasia, Pontus
b. Strabo

PORTUGAL

b. Cabrillo, Juan Rodriguez
b. Colon, Diego
b. Covilhao, Pedro de
b. Pinto, Isaac
b. Salazar, Antonio de Oliveira
b. Solis, Juan Diaz de

Alcains, Portugal
b. Eanes, Antonio dos Santos Ramalho

Alcochete, Portugal
b. Manuel I

Alhandra, Portugal
b. Albuquerque, Affonso de

Alverca, Portugal
d. Cousteau, Philippe

Avanca, Portugal
b. Egas Moniz, Antonio C A F

Beira Alta, Portugal
b. Ribeiro, Aquilino Gomez

Boliqueime, Portugal
b. Cavaco Silva, Anibal Antonio

Cascais, Portugal
d. Thomaz, Americo
d. Trifa, Valerian

Coimbra, Portugal
b. Alfonso, III
b. Sa, Mem de
d. Alfonso, I

Estoril, Portugal
d. Carol II
d. Horthy de Nagybanya, Nicholas
d. Lupescu, Magda (Elena)

Guimaraes, Portugal
b. Alfonso, I

Lisbon, Portugal
b. Abarbanel, Isaac Ben Jehudah
b. Abarbanel, Judah
b. Abravanel, Isaac ben Judah
b. Anthony of Padua, Saint
b. Caetano, Marcello
b. Camoes, Luis de
b. da Graca, Carlos Alberto Dias
b. Grey, George
b. Guterres, Antonio Manuel de Oliveira
b. Nesselrode, Karl Robert
b. Pedro I
b. Soares, Mario Alberto Nobre Lopes
b. Thomaz, Americo
b. Vieira, Antonio
b. Vieira Da Silva, Maria Helena
d. Alba, Duke of
d. Alekhine, Alexander
d. Alfonso, III
d. Camoes, Luis de
d. Correia, Natalia
d. Deus, Joao de
d. Egas Moniz, Antonio C A F
d. Fielding, Henry
d. Gulbenkian, Calouste S
d. Lunardi, Vincenzo
d. Manuel I
d. Mendes Pinto, Fernao
d. Pedro I
d. Ribeiro, Aquilino Gomez
d. Salazar, Antonio de Oliveira
d. Sousa, Martim Afonso de
d. Spinola, Antonio (Sebastiao Ribeiro) de
d. Suarez, Francisco
d. Thompson, Dorothy

Madeira, Portugal
d. Mowrer, Edgar Ansel

Marco Canavezes, Portugal
b. Miranda, Carmen

Matosinhos, Portugal
b. Siza, Alvaro (Joaquim Melo)

Montemor-o-Velho, Portugal
b. Mendes Pinto, Fernao

Oporto, Portugal
d. Charles Albert

Porto, Portugal
b. Henry the Navigator

Ribeira de Litem, Portugal
d. Barros, Joao de

Sabrosa, Portugal
b. Magellan, Ferdinand

Sagres, Portugal
d. Henry the Navigator

Sao Bartolemeu, Portugal
b. Deus, Joao de

Sao Miguel, Portugal
b. Correia, Natalia

Setubal, Portugal
d. Campbell, Roy

Sines, Portugal
b. DaGama, Vasco

Soure, Portugal
b. Pombal, Marques de

Vila Vicosa, Portugal
b. Sousa, Martim Afonso de

Viseu, Portugal
b. Barros, Joao de

PORTUGUESE EAST AFRICA

Lourenco Marques, Portuguese East Africa
b. Craveirinha, Jose

PORTUGUESE GUINEA

Bissau, Portuguese Guinea
b. Cabral, Luis de Almeida

PRUSSIA

b. Zweig, Arnold

Aachen, Prussia
b. Blech, Leo
d. Burke, John

Alt-Seidenberg, Prussia
b. Boehme, Jakob

Anklam, Prussia
b. Lilienthal, Otto

Bad Harzburg, Prussia
d. Schmoller, Gustav Friedrich von

Bad Kreuznach, Prussia
b. Driesch, Hans Adolf Eduard

Bad Salzbrunn, Prussia
b. Hauptmann, Gerhart Johann Robert

Barmen, Prussia
b. Engels, Friedrich

Bergen, Prussia
b. Billroth, Theodore

Berlin, Prussia
b. Gutzkow, Karl Ferdinand
d. Busching, Anton Friedrich
d. Grisi, Giulia
d. Seebeck, Thomas Johann

Berlinchen, Prussia
b. Lasker, Emanuel

PUERTO RICO

b. Garcia, Joe
d. Enoch, Kurt

Aguada, Puerto Rico
b. Hernandez, Willie (Guillermo Villaneuva)

Arecibo, Puerto Rico
b. Gonzales, Juan (Alberto)

Barceloneta, Puerto Rico
b. Escobar, Sixto

Barranquitas, Puerto Rico
b. Gonzalez, Jose Ramon
b. Rivera, Luis Munoz

Caguas, Puerto Rico
b. Badillo, Herman

Carolina, Puerto Rico
b. Clemente, Roberto Walker

Fajardo, Puerto Rico
b. Novello, Antonia Coello

Guayama, Puerto Rico
b. Pales Matos, Luis

Gurabo, Puerto Rico
b. Pinero, Miguel

Humacao, Puerto Rico
b. Moreno, Rita

Lajas, Puerto Rico
b. Aponte-Martinez, Luis, Cardinal

Lares, Puerto Rico
b. Feliciano, Jose
b. Velez, Clemente Soto

Mayaguez, Puerto Rico
b. Hostos (y Bonilla), Eugenio Maria de
d. Baez, Buenaventura

Ponce, Puerto Rico
b. Alcala, Jose (Ramon)
b. Cepeda, Orlando Manuel
b. Ferre, Maurice Antonio
b. Hernandez-Colon, Rafael
b. Santiago, Benito

Rincon, Puerto Rico
d. Maxwell, Vera (Huppe)

Rio Piedras, Puerto Rico
b. Rodriguez, Chi-Chi
b. Sierra (Garcia), Ruben Angel
d. Casals, Pablo (Pau Carlos Salvador)

Salinas, Puerto Rico
b. Alomar, Roberto

San Juan, Puerto Rico
b. Diaz, Justino
b. Elvira, Pablo
b. Goodman, Robert O, Jr.
b. Julia, Raul

b. Munoz Marin, Luis
b. Romero Barcelo, Carlos Antonio
b. Schomburg, Arthur Alfonso
d. Adler, Elmer
d. Clemente, Roberto Walker
d. Gautier, Felisa Rincon de
d. Jimenez, Juan Ramon
d. Leopold, Nathan Freudenthal
d. Munoz Marin, Luis
d. Pales Matos, Luis
d. Rivera, Luis Munoz
d. Velez, Clemente Soto
d. Wallenda, Karl

Santurce, Puerto Rico
b. Classen, Willie
b. Cordero, Angel Tomas
b. Ferrer, Jose Vicente

Yabucoa, Puerto Rico
b. Velazquez, Nydia Margarita

QATAR

Doha, Qatar
b. Hamad bin Khalifa al-Thani, Sheikh

Rayyan, Qatar
b. Thani, Shiekh Khalifa Ben Hamad al

REPUBLIC OF KOREA

b. Ch'oe Ch'ung-hn
b. Chong Chung-bu
b. Chongjo
b. Kojong
b. Sejong
b. Yi Hwang
b. Yngjo
d. Ch'oe Ch'ung-hn
d. Chong Chung-bu
d. Chongjo
d. Kojong
d. Sejo
d. Yi Sng-gye

Andong, Republic of Korea
d. Yi Hwang

Seoul, Republic of Korea
b. Hakuta, Ken
b. Yi Sunsin
b. Yun Sondo
d. Min
d. Sejong
d. Yngjo

Yju, Republic of Korea
b. Min

Ynghung, Republic of Korea
b. Yi Sng-gye

RHODESIA

b. Luthuli, Albert John Mvumbi
b. Tekere, Edgar Zivanai

Chinsali, Rhodesia
b. Kaunda, Kenneth D(avid)

Kutama, Rhodesia
b. Mugabe, Robert (Gabriel)

Matabeleland, Rhodesia
b. Nkomo, Joshua (Mqabuko Nyongolo)

Ndola, Rhodesia
d. Hammarskjold, Dag (Hjalmar Agne Carl)

Salisbury, Rhodesia
b. Brutus, Dennis Vincent
b. Welensky, Roy
d. DuPont, Clifford Walter

Seluwke, Rhodesia
b. Smith, Ian Douglas

Umtali, Rhodesia
b. Muzorewa, Abel Tendekai

ROMAN EMPIRE

d. Vercingetorix

Rome, Roman Empire
b. Domitian
d. Domitian
d. Pulcher, Publius Clodius

Sirmium, Roman Empire
b. Gratian

Tyre, Phoenicia, Roman Empire
b. Ulpian, Domitius

ROMANIA

b. Gutfreund, Yosef
b. Leibowitz, Samuel Simon
b. Nechita, Alexandra
b. Schussler Fiorenza, Elisabeth
b. Shorr, Kehat
b. Spitzer, Andre
b. Zuckerman, Ben
d. Allal al-Fassi, Mohamed

Bender, Romania
b. Leonidoff, Leon

Birlad, Romania
b. Gheorghiu-Dej, Gheorghe

Botosani, Romania
b. Covici, Pascal
b. Eminescu, Mihail

Braila, Romania
b. Bercovici, Konrad
b. Xenakis, Iannis

Bucharest, Romania
b. Arghezi, Tudor
b. Ciulei, Liviu
b. Coanda, Henri Marie
b. Comissiona, Sergiu

Bialystok, Russia
b. Litvinov, Maxim
b. Sabin, Albert Bruce
b. Weber, Max

Bolshaya Tes, Russia
b. Chernenko, Konstantin Ustinovich

Borodino, Russia
d. Bagration, Petr Ivanovich

Brest-Litovsk, Russia
b. Auerbach-Levy, William
b. Gingold, Josef

Briansk, Russia
b. Gabo, Naum

Cherepovets, Russia
b. Vereshchagin, Vasily Vasilyevich

Chernigov, Russia
b. Baker, Rachel

Chisinau, Russia
b. Milestone, Lewis

Chitai, Russia
b. Nowicki, Matthew

Chizhovo, Russia
b. Potemkin, Grigori Alexsandrovich

Daugavpils, Russia
b. Rothko, Mark

Denisovka, Russia
b. Lomonosov, Mikhail Vasilyevich

Diyalora, Russia
b. Ilyushin, Sergei Vladimirovich

Dorpat, Russia
d. Baer, Karl Ernst von

Dzhizak, Russia
b. Rashidov, Sharaf Rashidovich

Efremov, Russia
b. Ivanov, Konstantin Konstantinovich

Ekaterinoslav, Russia
b. Blavatsky, Helena Petrovna
b. Esau, Katherine
b. Piatigorsky, Gregor

Elets, Russia
b. Khrennikov, Tikhon Nikolaevich

Elisavetgrad, Russia
b. Petrov, Ossip
b. Trotsky, Leon
b. Zinoviev, Grigori Evseevich

Elisavetpol, Russia
b. Alikhanov, Abram Isaakovich

Elizabethgrad, Russia
b. Podoloff, Maurice

Evpatoria, Russia
b. Vronsky, Vitya

Gatchina, Russia
b. Ippolitov-Ivanov, Mikhail
Mikhailovich

Georgia, Russia
b. Beria, Lavrenti Pavlovich

Glukhov, Russia
b. Shklovsky, Iosif Samvilovitch

Golodaevka, Russia
b. Grechko, Andrei Antonovick

Gori, Russia
b. Stalin, Joseph

Gorki, Russia
b. Lobachevskii, Nikolai Ivanovich
b. Nikon, Nikita Minov

Gorokhovo, Russia
b. Leskov, Nikolai Semyonovich

Gradizhsk, Russia
b. Delaunay-Terk, Sonia

Greshnevo, Russia
b. Nekrasov, Nikolay Alexeyevich

Grodak, Russia
b. Gorin, Igor

Grodna, Russia
b. Lansky, Meyer

Grodno, Russia
b. Weizmann, Chaim

Gurzuf, Russia
d. Petipa, Marius

Irkutsk, Russia
b. Romm, Mikhail

Ivanovka, Russia
b. Metchnikoff, Elie

Ivanovo-Voznessensk, Russia
b. Sarraute, Nathalie

Jamburg, Russia
b. Tammann, Gustav Heinrich Johann
Apollon

Kabany, Russia
b. Kaganovich, Lazar M(oiseevich)

Kaliningrad, Russia
d. Sobchak, Anatoly Aleksandrovich

Kamenskoye, Russia
b. Brezhnev, Leonid Ilyich

Kamyshin, Russia
b. Chernov, Viktor Mikhailovich

Karakol, Russia
d. Przhevalsky, Nikolai Mikhailovich

Karevo, Russia
b. Mussorgsky, Modest Petrovich

Kargopol, Russia
b. Baranov, Aleksandr Andreievich

Karlovka, Russia
b. Lysenko, Trofim Denisovich
b. Podgorny, Nikolai Viktorovich

Kazan, Russia
b. Chaliapin, Feodor Ivanovitch, Jr.
b. Dali, Gala
b. Vishnevsky, Alexandr
Alekandrovich
b. Zabolotskii, Nikolai Alekseevich
d. Lobachevskii, Nikolai Ivanovich

Keatz, Russia
b. Piastro, Michel

Kharkov, Russia
b. Artsybashev, Mikhail Petrovich
b. Artzybasheff, Boris Mikhailovich
b. Cassandre, A(dolphe) M(ouron)
b. Kuznets, Simon Smith
b. Malik, Yakov (Alexandrovich)
b. Schillinger, Joseph
b. Struve, Otto

Kherson, Russia
b. Cooper, Emil
b. Kulish, Mykola
b. Rubinstein, Anton Gregorovitch
b. Sharett, Moshe
b. Vynnychenko, Volodymyr

Kiev, Russia
b. Aronson, Boris
b. Berdyayev, Nikolay Aleksandrovich
b. Brailowsky, Alexander
b. Bulgakov, Mikhail Afanasyevich
b. Cournos, John
b. Deren, Maya
b. Ehrenburg, Ilya Grigoryevich
b. Gliere, Reinhold Moritsevich
b. Gottlieb, Eddie
b. Horowitz, Vladimir
b. Kistiakowsky, George Bogdan
b. Liberman, Alexander
(Semeonovitch)
b. Lifar, Serge
b. Litvak, Anatole
b. Malevich, Kasimir Severinovich
b. Markevitch, Igor
b. Meir, Golda
b. Moiseyev, Igor Alexandrovich
b. Nevelson, Louise Berliawsky
b. Nijinsky, Vaslav
b. Rostovtzeff, Michael Ivanovich
b. Sikorsky, Igor Ivanovich
b. Tarasova, Alla Konstantinovna
b. Tarsis, Valery Yakovlevich
b. Valentina
b. Youskevitch, Igor
b. Zaturenska, Marya
d. Borochov, Dov Ber
d. Mogila, Peter
d. Stolypin, Piotr Arkadevich

Kishinev, Russia
b. Cebotari, Maria
b. Friedman, William Frederick
b. Zemurray, Samuel

Kislovodsk, Russia
b. Adamov, Arthur

Kizlar, Russia
b. Bagration, Petr Ivanovich

Kletsk, Russia
b. Levine, Philip

Kobiankari, Russia
b. Papashvily, George

Kolomenskoye, Russia
b. Ivan IV

Konno, Russia
b. Keyserling, Hermann Alexander
Graf Von

Konstantinovo, Russia
b. Esenin, Sergei Aleksandrovich

Kostroma, Russia
b. Gerasimov, Innokentii Petrovich
b. Vinogradoff, Paul Gavrilovitch

Kovna, Russia
b. Sackheim, Maxwell Byron

Krasnoyarsk, Russia
b. Hvorostovsky, Dmitri
b. Rebikov, Vladimir Ivanovich
d. Rezanov, Nikolay Petrovich

Kronstadt, Russia
b. Gumilev, Nikolai
b. Kapitsa, Pyotr Leonidovich
d. Bellinghausen, Fabian Gottlieb von

Kruzhilin, Russia
b. Sholokhov, Mikhail Aleksandrovich

Kukarka, Russia
b. Molotov, Vyacheslav Mikhaylovich

Kursku, Russia
b. Druzhinin, Nicolai Mikhailovich

Ladeino, Russia
b. Konev, Ivan Stepanovich

Libau, Russia
b. Sterne, Maurice

Livadia, Russia
d. Alexander III

Luban, Russia
b. Epstein, Abraham

Luzhky, Russia
b. Ben-Yehuda, Eliezer

Magadan, Russia
d. Vavilov, Nikolai Ivanovich

Makov, Russia
b. Rickover, Hyman George

Medzhibozh, Russia
b. Berdichevsky, Micah Joseph

Mikhailovka, Russia
b. Karamzin, Nikolai Mikhailovich

Mikilovka, Russia
b. Tschernichowsky, Saul

Minsk, Russia
b. Angoff, Charles
b. Hoffman, Al
b. Hubert, Conrad
b. Lerner, Max
b. Mayer, L(ouis) B(urt)
b. Nabokov, Nicolas
b. Nijinska, Bronislava
b. Rosenthal, Ida Cohen
b. Sarnoff, David
b. Taishoff, Sol Joseph

Mir, Russia
b. Shazar, Zalman

Mitau, Russia
b. Hirshhorn, Joseph Herman

Mitava, Russia
b. Rojankovsky, Feodor Stepanovich

Moltovsk, Russia
b. Oswald, Marina Nikolaevna

Morintsy, Russia
b. Shevchenko, Taras

Moscow, Russia
b. Alekhine, Alexander
b. Alexander II
b. Anna Ivanovna
b. Babin, Victor
b. Baclanova, Olga
b. Bellison, Simeon
b. Bely, Andrey
b. Bukharin, Nikolai Ivanovich
b. Dostoyevsky, Fyodor Mikhailovich
b. Elizabeth Petrovna
b. Godunov, Boris Fedorovich
b. Goldovsky, Boris
b. Gretchaninov, Aleksandr
Tikhonovich
b. Herzen, Aleksandr Ivanovich
b. Ivan III
b. Jakobson, Roman
b. Kandinsky, Wassily
b. Karrar, Paul
b. Khodasevich, Vladislav
b. Kondrashin, Kiril Petrovich
b. Kropotkin, Peter Alekseyevich,
Prince
b. Krylov, Ivan Andreyevich
b. Leonov, Leonid Maximovich
b. Leontovich, Eugenie
b. Lermontov, Mikhail
b. Lhevinne, Josef
b. Lhevinne, Rosina L
b. Lichine, Alexis
b. Massine, Leonide Fedorovich
b. Medtner, Nicholas
b. Melnikov, Konstantin Stepanovich
b. Menchik-Stevenson, Vera Francevna
b. Mikhalkov, Sergei Vladimirovich
b. Miliukov, Pavel Nikolayevich
b. Ostrovsky, Aleksandr Nikolaevich
b. Pasternak, Boris Leonidovich
b. Peter the Great
b. Pfitzner, Hans

b. Pobedonostsev, Konstantin
Petrovich
b. Popova, Liubov Sergeevna
b. Prigogine, Ilya
b. Pushkin, Aleksandr Sergeevich
b. Romanov, Alexis Mikhailovich
b. Scriabin, Alexander Nicholaevich
b. Soloviev, Sergei Mikhailovich
b. Stanislavsky, Konstantin
Sergeyevich
b. Suvorov, Aleksandr V
b. Tikhomirov, Vasily Dmitrievich
b. Troyat, Henri
b. Tsvetaeva, Marina Ivanovna
b. Uspenskii, Petr Dem'yanovich
b. Vassilenko, Sergei
b. Vavilov, Nikolai Ivanovich
b. Yakovlev, Aleksandr Sergeevich
b. Yermolova, Maria Nikolayevna
d. Afinogenov, Aleksandr Nikolaevich
d. Aksakov, Sergei Timofeyevich
d. Beregovoi, Georgi
d. Botvinnik, Mikhail (Moisseyevich)
d. Field, John
d. Frunze, Mikhail Vasilievich
d. Giardini, Felice di
d. Gogol, Nikolai Vasilievich
d. Ivan III
d. Ivan IV
d. Karmal, Babrak
d. Nikon, Nikita Minov
d. Ostrovsky, Aleksandr Nikolaevich
d. Richter, Sviatoslav Theofilovich
d. Rodchenko, Alexander Mikhailovich
d. Romanov, Alexis Mikhailovich
d. Rozanov, Vasili Vasilyevich
d. Scriabin, Alexander Nicholaevich
d. Taneyev, Sergey Ivanovich
d. Tsedenbal, Yumzaghin
d. Ulanova, Galina
d. Vasily III
d. Wieniawski, Henri
d. Yegorov, Boris (Borisovitch)
d. Zetkin, Clara

Mourom, Russia
b. Zworykin, Vladimir K(osma)

Nagaevo, Russia
b. Goncharova, Natalia

Nagutskaia, Russia
b. Andropov, Yuri Vladimirovich

Narovchat, Russia
b. Kuprin, Aleksandr Ivanovich

Nemirov, Russia
b. Dobzhansky, Theodosius
(Grigorievich)

Nikolaevski-Samarskom, Russia
b. Tolstoy, Alexey Nikolaevich

Nikolayev, Russia
b. Schneerson, Menachem M(endel)

Nizhni-Novgorod, Russia
b. Balakirev, Mili Alekseyevich
b. Bulganin, Nikolai Aleksandrovich
b. Diaghilev, Sergei (Pavlovich)
b. Dobrowen, Issai
b. Gorky, Maxim

Nova Kraruka, Russia
b. Granick, Harry

Novaya Chigla, Russia
b. Cherenkov, Pavel Alekseyevich

Novgorod, Russia
d. Rurik

Novospaskoi, Russia
b. Glinka, Mikhail Ivanovich

Odessa, Russia
b. Akhmatova, Anna
b. Babel, Isaac Emmanuelovich
b. Brackman, Robert
b. Brown, Lew
b. Cherkassky, Shura
b. Gamow, George
b. Halpert, Edith Gregor
b. Jabotinsky, Vladimir Evgenevich
b. Kaminska, Ida
b. Katayev, Valentin Petrovich
b. Lapidus, Morris
b. Luboshutz, Pierre
b. Milstein, Nathan
b. Oistrakh, David Fyodorovich
b. Pious, Minerva
b. Reilly, Sidney George
b. Semenenko, Serge
b. Spanel, Abram N
b. Spitalny, Phil
b. Spivakovsky, Tossy

Oesel, Russia
b. Bellinghausen, Fabian Gottlieb von
b. Kahn, Louis I(sadore)

Oneg, Russia
b. Rachmaninoff, Sergei Vasilyevich

Oranienbaum, Russia
b. Stravinsky, Igor Fedorovich

Orel, Russia
b. Andreyev, Leonid Nikolaevich
b. Bakhtin, Mikhail (Mikhailovich)
b. Pevsner, Antoine
b. Turgenev, Ivan Sergeevich

Orenburg, Russia
b. Malenkov, Georgi Maximilianovich

Penza, Russia
b. Meyerhold, Vsevolod Emilievich
b. Pudovkin, Vsevolod

Peredelkino, Russia
d. Stevens, Edmund William

Pereyaslavl, Russia
b. Aleichem, Sholom

Peterhof, Russia
b. Danilova, Alexandra
d. Rubinstein, Anton Gregorovitch

Piep, Russia
b. Baer, Karl Ernst von

Pogar, Russia
b. Hurok, Sol(omon Isaievich)

Polotsk, Russia
b. Antin, Mary

Premukhine, Russia
b. Bakunin, Mikhail Aleksandrovich

Proskurov, Russia
b. Durant, Ariel
b. Mischakoff, Mischa

Pskov, Russia
b. Duke, Vernon
b. Wrangel, Ferdinand Petrovich, Baron

Pustomazovo, Russia
b. Tupolev, Andrei Nikolaevich

Pyatigorsk, Russia
b. Fedorenko, Nikolai Trofimovich
d. Lermontov, Mikhail

Radi, Russia
b. Bialik, Hayyim Nahman

Radomisl, Russia
b. Potofsky, Jacob Samuel

Rady, Russia
b. Bialik, Chaim Nachman

Reval, Russia
b. Kohler, Wolfgang
b. Rosenberg, Alfred

Riga, Russia
b. Berlin, Isaiah, Sir
b. Eisenstein, Sergei Mikhailovich
b. Halsman, Philippe
b. Jadlowker, Hermann
b. Ostwald, Friedrich Wilhelm

Romny, Russia
b. Tairov, Aleksandr Yakovlevich

Rostov-on-Don, Russia
b. Alajalov, Constantin
b. Gordon-Lazareff, Helene
b. Lev, Ray
b. Lichine, David
b. Parry, Albert
b. Zimbalist, Efrem

Rovno, Russia
b. Loeb, Sophia Irene Simon

Rumni, Russia
b. Carr, Alexander

Ryazan, Russia
b. Afinogenov, Aleksandr Nikolaevich
b. Pavlov, Ivan Petrovich

Rybinsk, Russia
b. Schenck, Joseph M
b. Schenck, Nicholas Michael

Saint Petersburg, Russia
b. Abel, Rudolf Ivanovich
b. Alexander I
b. Amfiteatrof, Daniele
b. Andreas-Salome, Lou

b. Andrew, Prince of Russia
b. Auer, Mischa
b. Balanchine, George
b. Berberova, Nina Nikolaevna
b. Berman, Eugene
b. Blok, Aleksandr Aleksandrovich
b. Bolotowsky, Ilya
b. Borodin, Alexander Profirevich
b. Botvinnik, Mikhail (Moisseyevich)
b. Cantor, Georg Ferdinand Ludwig Philipp
b. Chekhov, Michael
b. Chukovsky, Korney Ivanovich
b. Coates, Albert
b. Conway, Tom
b. Doubrovska, Felia
b. Erte
b. Faberge, Peter Carl
b. Fokine, Michel
b. Frank, Ilya Mikaylovich
b. Gabrilowitsch, Ossip Salomonovich
b. Gelfond, Aleksandr Osipovich
b. Gerhardi, William Alexander
b. Geva, Tamara
b. Glazunov, Alexander Constantinovich
b. Guitry, Sacha
b. Hanfmann, George Maxim Anossov
b. Janson, Horst Woldemar
b. Jolson, Al
b. Kabalevsky, Dmitri Borisovich
b. Kantorovich, Leonid Vital'evich
b. Karsavina, Tamara (Platonova)
b. Keyserlingk, Robert Wendelin Henry
b. Kolchak, Aleksandr Vasilievich
b. Kollontai, Alexandra Mikhailovna (Domantovich)
b. Kostelanetz, Andre
b. Kosygin, Aleksei Nikolaevich
b. Krupskaya, Nadezhda Konstantinovna
b. Kurtz, Efrem
b. Kutuzov, Mikhail Ilarionovich
b. Leontief, Wassily W
b. Litvinne, Felia
b. Lopokova, Lydia Vasilievna
b. Merejkowski, Dmitri Sergeyevich
b. Merezhkovsky, Dmitry Sergeyevich
b. Mravinsky, Eugene
b. Nabokov, Vladimir
b. Oldenbourg, Zoe
b. Paul, Prince
b. Pavlova, Anna
b. Rand, Ayn
b. Ratoff, Gregory
b. Rezanov, Nikolay Petrovich
b. Rodchenko, Alexander Mikhailovich
b. Romanov, Anastasia
b. Rudenko, Lyudmila
b. Sanders, George
b. Savitt, Jan
b. Semyonova, Marina
b. Shostakovich, Dmitri Dmitryevich
b. Simonov, Konstantin (Kirill) Mikhailovich
b. Slonimsky, Nicolas
b. Smallens, Alexander
b. Stael, Nicolas de
b. Stravinsky, Vera de Bossett
b. Tcherepnin, Alexander Nikolayevich
b. Tcherepnin, Nicholas
b. Tiomkin, Dimitri
b. Ulanova, Galina
b. Vishniac, Roman
d. Alexander II

d. Balakirev, Mili Alekseyevich
d. Belinsky, Vissarion Grigoryevich
d. Borodin, Alexander Profirevich
d. Burlingame, Anson
d. Catherine the Great
d. Dargomijsky, Alexander
d. Dostoyevsky, Fyodor Mikhailovich
d. Du Chaillu, Paul Belloni
d. Euler, Leonhard
d. Goncharov, Ivan Aleksandrovich
d. Krylov, Ivan Andreyevich
d. Leskov, Nikolai Semyonovich
d. Lomonosov, Mikhail Vasilyevich
d. Martin y Soler, Vicente
d. Mendeleev, Dmitri Ivanovich
d. Mussorgsky, Modest Petrovich
d. Napravnik, Eduard
d. Nekrasov, Nikolay Alexeyevich
d. Nesselrode, Karl Robert
d. Nicholas I
d. Peter the Great
d. Petrov, Ossip
d. Pobedonostsev, Konstantin
Petrovich
d. Popov, Aleksandr Stepanovich
d. Pushkin, Aleksandr Sergeyevich
d. Rasputin, Grigori Efimovich
d. Rimsky-Korsakov, Nikolai
Andreevich
d. Schluter, Andreas
d. Shevchenko, Taras
d. Suvorov, Aleksandr V
d. Tchaikovsky, Peter Ilyich
d. Witte, Sergey Yulyevich

Sakhalin, Russia
b. Brynner, Yul
b. Godunov, Alexander

Samara, Russia
b. Ustinov, Dmitri Fedorovich

Saratov, Russia
b. Chernyshevsky, Nikolai Gavrilovich
b. Fedin, Konstantin Aleksandrovich
b. Mandelstam, Nadezhda Yakovlevna
b. Rykov, Aleksey Ivanovich
b. Semenov, Nikolai Nikolaevich
d. Chernyshevsky, Nikolai Gavrilovich

Sedikov, Russia
b. Schwartz, Maurice

Serebryanye Prudy, Russia
b. Chuikov, Vasili Ivanovitch

Sevastopol, Russia
b. Cassini, Igor Loiewski
b. Papanin, Ivan D
d. Raglan, Fitzroy James Henry
Somerset, Baron

Shakhovskol, Russia
b. Suslov, Mikhail Andreevich

Shirvanta, Russia
b. Shubert, Jacob J
b. Shubert, Lee

Shusha, Russia
b. Takhtadzhian, Armen Leonovich

Siberia, Russia
b. Slobodkina, Esphyr

b. Toumanova, Tamara
d. DeLong, George Washington

Sim, Russia
b. Kurchatov, Igor Vasilyevich

Simbirsk, Russia
b. Goncharov, Ivan Aleksandrovich
b. Kerensky, Alexander Fedorovitch
b. Lenin, Vladimir Ilyich

Skwera, Kiev, Russia
b. Ahad Haam
b. Haam, Ahad

Slednevo, Russia
b. Tukhachevski, Mikhail
Nikolayevich

Slobodka, Russia
b. Stavisky, Serge Alexandre

Smilovich, Russia
b. Soutine, Chaim

Smolensk, Russia
b. Przhevalsky, Nikolai Mikhailovich
b. Zadkine, Ossip

Smorgon, Russia
b. Blume, Peter

Sofilovka, Russia
b. Kuznetzov, Vassili Vasilyevich

Sontsovka, Russia
b. Prokofiev, Sergei Sergeevich

Starchevicvhi, Russia
b. Bleeker, Sonia

Starye Gromyky, Russia
b. Gromyko, Andrei Andreevich

Stelkovka, Russia
b. Zhukov, Georgi Konstantinovich

Sukovoly, Russia
b. Yezierska, Anzia

Sverdlovsk, Russia
b. Gerasimov, Sergei Appolinarievich

Taganrog, Russia
d. Alexander I

Tallinn, Russia
b. Valtman, Edmund Siegfried

Talnoye, Russia
b. Elman, Mischa

Tambov, Russia
b. Chicherin, Georgi Vasilyevich
b. Kolmogorov, Andrey Nikolaevich
b. Plekhanov, Georgi Valentinovich
b. Soyer, Isaac
b. Soyer, Moses
b. Soyer, Raphael

Tarkhovka, Russia
b. Bilibin, Ivan Iakolevich

Tbilisi, Russia
b. Kovalev, Mikhail Aleksandrovich

Teganrog, Russia
b. Chekhov, Anton Pavlovich

Temun, Russia
b. Berlin, Irving

Ternopol, Russia
d. Krochmal, Nachman Kohen

Tiflis, Russia
b. DeSeversky, Alexander Procofieff
b. Galitzine, Irene, Princess
b. Kalatozov, Mikhail
b. Khachaturian, Aram
b. Mamoulian, Rouben (Zachary)
b. Nemirovich-Danchenko, Vladimir I
b. Pressman, David
b. Witte, Sergey Yulyevich

Tikhvin, Russia
b. Rimsky-Korsakov, Nikolai
Andreevich

Timoshovka, Russia
b. Szymanowski, Karol Maciej

Tobolsk, Russia
b. Mendeleev, Dmitri Ivanovich
b. Rasputin, Grigori Efimovich

Tokmak, Russia
b. Grade, Lew, Sir

Torschok, Russia
b. Jawlensky, Alexej von

Troyano, Russia
b. Gordon, Aaron David

Tsarskoe Selo, Russia
b. Nicholas I
b. Nicholas II
b. Obolensky, Serge

Tschuguev, Russia
b. Repin, Ilya Yefimovich

Tula, Russia
b. Dargomijsky, Alexander
b. Ouspenskaya, Maria

Turinskiye Rudniki, Russia
b. Popov, Aleksandr Stepanovich

Turkistan, Russia
b. Kornilov, Lavr Georgyevich

Turya, Russia
b. Sorokin, Pitirim A(lexandrovitch)

Ufa, Russia
b. Aksakov, Sergei Timofeyevich

Uglich, Russia
b. Oparin, Aleksandr Ivanovich

Ukraine, Russia
b. Cooke, Samuel
b. Freeman, Joseph
b. Ukrainka, Lesia

Upper Troitsa, Russia
b. Kalinin, Mikhail (Ivanovich)

Urlow, Russia
d. Lipinski, Carl

Urmanka, Russia
b. Timoshenko, Semen
Konstantinovich

Urzhum, Russia
b. Kirov, Sergei Mironovich

Uslian, Russia
b. Lyons, Eugene

Uzkoe, Russia
d. Soloviev, Vladimir Sergeevich

Verkhneye, Russia
b. Voroshilov, Kliment Efremovich

Vetluga, Russia
b. Rozanov, Vasili Vasilyevich

Viapori, Russia
b. Belinsky, Vissarion Grigoryevich

Vilna, Russia
b. Berkman, Alexander
b. Cahan, Abraham
b. Cui, Cesar Antonovich
b. Dzerzhinsky, Felix Edmundovich
b. Gest, Morris
b. Reisenberg, Nadia
b. Schneider, Alexander
d. Elijah Ben Solomon

Vilnius, Russia
b. Gary, Romain

Vitebsk, Russia
b. Chagall, Marc
b. Chotzinoff, Samuel

Vladimir, Russia
b. Taneyev, Sergey Ivanovich

Vladivostok, Russia
b. Tamm, Igor Evgenevich

Vologda, Russia
b. Shalamov, Varlam Tikhonovich

Volotchok, Russia
b. Sevitzky, Fabien

Voronezh, Russia
b. Bunin, Ivan Alekseevich

Votiwsk, Russia
b. Tchaikovsky, Peter Ilyich

Vyshni Volochek, Russia
b. Furtseva, Ekaterina Alexeyevna
b. Koussevitzky, Serge Alexandrovich

Yalta, Russia
b. Lewton, Val Ivan
b. Nazimova, Alla

Yasnaya Polyana, Russia
b. Tolstoy, Leo Nikolayevich

Yekaterinburg, Russia
b. Alexandrov, Grigori

Zabludora, Russia
b. Lazare, Kaplan

Zhitomir, Russia
b. Kipnis, Alexander
b. Korolenko, Vladimir Galaktionovich
b. Richter, Sviatoslav Theofilovich

Zolotonosha, Ukraine, Russia
b. Borochov, Dov Ber

Zuzela, Russia
b. Wyszynski, Stefan

RWANDA

Kigali, Rwanda
d. Habyarimana, Juvenal

Virunga Mountains, Rwanda
d. Fossey, Dian

SAMOA

Vailima, Samoa
d. Stevenson, Robert Louis (Balfour)

SAN MARINO

b. Gatti, Gabriele

SAO TOME AND PRINCIPE

b. Trovoada, Miguel

Agua Grande, Sao Tome and Principe
b. Pinto da Costa, Manuel

SARDINIA

b. Angeli, Pier
d. Hippolytus, Saint

Cuneo, Sardinia
b. Peano, Giuseppe

Livorno Vercellese, Sardinia
b. Ferraris, Galileo

Mondovi, Sardinia
b. Giolitti, Giovanni

SAUDI ARABIA

d. Ibn Saud
d. Khan, Fazlur Rahman

Mecca, Saudi Arabia
b. Khashoggi, Adnan
b. Yamani, Ahmad Zaki, Sheik

Medina, Saudi Arabia
d. Mohammed

Riyadh, Saudi Arabia
b. Fahd ibn Abdul Aziz, King
b. Faisal ibn Musaed
d. Faisal (Ibn Abdul-Aziz al Saud)
d. Faisal ibn Musaed

Taif, Saudi Arabia
d. Khalid Ibn Abdul Azia Al-Saud

SAXONY

Freiberg, Saxony
b. Charpentier, Johann von

Halle, Saxony
b. Handel, George Frideric

Lutzen, Saxony
d. Gustavus Adophus

Magdeburg, Saxony
b. Guericke, Otto Von

Meissen, Saxony
b. Hahnemann, Samuel

Rocken, Saxony
b. Nietzsche, Friedrich Wilhelm

Wittenberg, Saxony
d. Melanchthon, Philipp

Worbis, Saxony
b. Quaritch, Bernard

Zittau, Saxony
b. Marschner, Heinrich August

SCOTLAND

b. Brackenridge, H(ugh) H(enry)
b. Burnford, Sheila
b. Calder, Frank
b. Darling, Frank Fraser, Sir
b. Dunlop, John Boyd
b. Gray, Nicholas Stuart
b. Hamilton, Andrew
b. Home, Daniel Douglas
b. Macquarrie, John
b. Murchison, Roderick Impey
b. Park, Mungo
b. Robert, II
b. Robert, III
b. Ross, Alex(ander)
b. Ross, Ishbel
b. Thomson, James
b. Walker, David Harry
b. White, Michael Simon

d. Bannen, Ian
d. Bute, 3d Earl of
d. Chalmers, Thomas
d. Inness, George
d. MacTaggart, William, Sir
d. McAdam, John Loudoun
d. Robert, II
d. Robert, III

Abbotsford, Scotland
d. Lockhart, John Gibson
d. Scott, Walter, Sir

Aberdeen, Scotland
b. Bain, Alexander
b. Burton, John Hill, Sir
b. Cruickshank, Andrew John
b. Donald, James
b. Douglas, Norman
b. Dyce, William
b. Ferrier, David, Sir
b. Forbes, Bertie
b. Garden, Mary
b. Keith, William
b. Lennox, Annie
b. MacFarlane, Willie
b. Milne, George Francis, Baron
b. Strachan, John
d. Adler, Alfred
d. Bain, Alexander
d. Barbour, John
d. Garden, Mary
d. MacLeod, John James Rickard

Aberfeldy, Scotland
b. Crisp, Donald

Airdrie, Scotland
b. Bannen, Ian

Allerby, Scotland
d. Brewster, David, Sir

Alloway, Scotland
b. Burns, Robert

Annan, Scotland
b. Clapperton, Hugh
b. Irving, Edward

Anstruther, Scotland
b. Bruce Lockhart, Robert Hamilton, Sir

Arbroth, Scotland
b. Buick, David Dunbar

Arbuthnot, Scotland
b. Arbuthnot, John

Auchterarder, Scotland
b. Maccoll, Ewan

Auchterless, Scotland
b. Gibbon, Lewis Grassic

Aylsbury, Scotland
d. Ross, James Clark, Sir

Ayrshire, Scotland
b. Dent, Alan Holmes
b. McAdam, John Loudoun
b. McCosh, James

d. Kelvin, William Thomson, Baron

Ballater, Scotland
b. Geddes, Patrick, Sir

Ballencrief, Scotland
b. Murray, James

Balsarroch, Scotland
b. Ross, James Clark, Sir

Banchor, Scotland
d. Lang, Andrew

Barrhead, Scotland
b. Davidson, John

Bathgate, Scotland
b. Simpson, James Young, Sir

Bellshill, Scotland
b. Easton, Sheena

Berwickshire, Scotland
d. Douglas-Home, Alexander Frederick, Sir

Bladenock, Scotland
b. McArthur, John

Blairgowrie, Scotland
b. Clyde, Andy

Bonsyde, Scotland
b. Thomson, Charles Wyville, Sir
d. Thomson, Charles Wyville, Sir

Borthwick, Scotland
b. Robertson, William

Braemar, Scotland
b. Waller, Gordon

Brechin, Scotland
b. Watson-Watt, Robert Alexander, Sir
d. Boyd-Orr, John, Baron

Cardross, Scotland
d. Robert I

Carlops, Scotland
d. Wilson, Charles Thomson Rees

Carnoustie, Scotland
b. Smith, Alex

Ceres, Fifeshire, Scotland
b. Gourlay, Robert

Cluny, Scotland
b. MacLeod, John James Rickard

Clydebank, Scotland
b. Reston, James (Barrett)

Coatbridge, Scotland
b. Marshall, Peter

Crieff, Scotland
b. McGregor, Ewan (Gordon)

Crosshouse, Ayrshire, Scotland
b. Fisher, Andrew

Cults, Scotland
b. Wilkie, David, Sir

Dalkeith, Scotland
b. Tait, Peter Guthrie

Dalquhurn, Scotland
b. Smollett, Tobias George

Deanston, Scotland
b. Grierson, John

Deerness, Scotland
b. Muir, Edwin

Dornoch, Scotland
b. Ross, Donald James

Doune, Scotland
b. Neilson, William A(llan)

Dumbarton, Scotland
b. Byrne, David

Dumferline, Scotland
b. MacMillan, Kenneth, Sir

Dumfries, Scotland
b. Richardson, John, Sir
d. Burns, Robert

Dumfriesshire, Scotland
d. Godden, Rumer

Dunbar, Scotland
b. Muir, John

Dunbartonshire, Scotland
b. Stewart, Jackie

Dunbreath, Scotland
d. George Edward Alexander Edmund

Dundee, Scotland
b. Fleming, Williamina Paton Stevens
b. Fyffe, Will
b. Mackenzie, William Lyon
b. Spence, Lewis
b. Wright, Frances
d. Baillie, D(onald) M(acpherson)

Dunfermline, Scotland
b. Anderson, Ian
b. Carnegie, Andrew
b. Charles I
b. Forbes, John
b. James I
b. Shearer, Moira

Dunglass, Scotland
b. Hall, James, Sir

Dunkeld, Scotland
b. Mackenzie, Alexander

Duns, Scotland
b. Duns Scotus, John

Dunure, Scotland
b. Curry, Peggy Simson

Earlsferry Fife, Scotland
b. Braid, James

East Lothian, Scotland
b. Balfour, Arthur James

Ecclefechan, Scotland
b. Carlyle, Thomas

Edinburgh, Scotland
b. Aberdeen, 4th Earl of
b. Adam, James
b. Alison, Archibald
b. Armour, Tommy
b. Aytoun, William Edmonstoune
b. Bannerman, Helen
b. Barnetson, William Denholm
b. Bell, Alexander Graham
b. Bell, Charles
b. Bell, Joseph
b. Blair, James
b. Blair, Tony
b. Boothby, Robert John Graham,
  Lord
b. Boswell, James
b. Burnet, Gilbert
b. Bute, 3d Earl of
b. Charleson, Ian
b. Combe, George
b. Connery, Sean
b. Currie, Finlay
b. Dott, Gerard
b. Dowie, John Alexander
b. Doyle, Arthur Conan, Sir
b. Dyce, Alexander
b. Faulkner, Eric
b. Fergusson, Robert
b. Flint, William Russell, Sir
b. Gardiner, Chuck
b. Ged, William
b. Geikie, Archibald, Sir
b. Grahame, Kenneth
b. Grant, James
b. Haig, Douglas
b. Haldane, John Scott
b. Home, William Douglas
b. Horsbrugh, Florence
b. Hume, David
b. Hurst, George
b. Hutton, James
b. Inescort, Frieda
b. James I
b. James II
b. Jameson, Leander Starr, Sir
b. Jeffrey, Francis Jeffrey, Lord
b. Laing, Alexander Gordon
b. Laing, David
b. Law, John
b. Lehmann-Haupt, Christopher
  Charles Herbert
b. Longmuir, Alan
b. Longmuir, Derek
b. Mackenzie, Alexander Campbell,
  Sir
b. Mackenzie, Henry
b. Maxwell, James Clerk
b. Mitchison, Naomi Margaret
  (Haldane)
b. Musgrave, Thea
b. Napier, John
b. Nasmyth, James
b. Ramsay, Allan

b. Redpath, Jean
b. Sanderson, Ivan Terence
b. Scott, Walter, Sir
b. Shaw, Richard Norman
b. Short, James
b. Sim, Alastair
b. Smibert, John
b. Spark, Muriel Sarah
b. Stevenson, Robert Louis (Balfour)
b. Stewart, Dugald
b. Stewart, J(ohn) I(nnes)
  M(ackintosh)
b. Stopes, Marie Charlotte Carmichael
b. Torrence, Ernest
b. Wheeler, Mortimer
b. Wood, Stuart
d. Alison, Archibald
d. Appleton, Edward Victor, Sir
d. Baillie, John
d. Bannerman, Helen
d. Barkla, Charles Glover
d. Bishop, Isabella Lucy Bird
d. Black, Joseph
d. Bridie, James
d. Buchanan, George
d. Burke, William
d. Burton, John Hill, Sir
d. Calder, Peter Ritchie
d. Darnley, Henry Stuart, Lord
d. DeQuincey, Thomas
d. Fergusson, Robert
d. Gourlay, Robert
d. Grant, James
d. Hall, James, Sir
d. Hamilton, William, Sir
d. Horsbrugh, Florence
d. Hume, David
d. Hutton, James
d. Jeffrey, Francis Jeffrey, Lord
d. Knox, John
d. MacDiarmid, Hugh
d. Mackenzie, Compton
d. Mackenzie, Henry
d. Napier, John
d. Peach, Charles William
d. Raeburn, Henry, Sir
d. Ramsay, Allan
d. Reith, John Charles Walsham
d. Robertson, William
d. Smith, Adam
d. Spence, Lewis
d. Tait, Peter Guthrie
d. Tovey, Donald Francis, Sir

Ednam, Scotland
b. Thomson, James

Edzell, Scotland
d. Orr, John Boyd, 1st Baron of
  Brechin

Elgin, Scotland
b. Young, Andrew
d. Aytoun, William Edmonstoune

Eliock, Scotland
b. Crichton, James

Ettrick, Scotland
b. Hogg, James

Falkirk, Scotland
b. Dollar, Robert
b. Douglas, Thomas Clement

Fearn, Scotland
b. Fraser, Peter

Fetlar, Scotland
d. Cheyne, William Watson, Sir

Fife, Scotland
b. Chalmers, Thomas

Fifeshire, Scotland
b. Wilson, James

Footdeesmire, Scotland
b. Gibbs, James

Forfar, Scotland
b. Calder, Peter Ritchie
b. Neill, A(lexander) S(utherland)

Forres, Scotland
d. Darling, Frank Fraser, Sir

Fyvie, Scotland
b. Lang, William Cosmo Gordon,
  Baron

Gairloch, West Rossshire, Scotland
b. Baillie, D(onald) M(acpherson)
b. Baillie, John

Gifford, Scotland
b. Witherspoon, John

Glamis, Scotland
b. Margaret

Glasgow, Scotland
b. Ballinger, Margaret
b. Bone, Muirhead, Sir
b. Bridie, James
b. Brogan, Denis William, Sir
b. Brown, Arthur Whitten, Sir
b. Bruce, Jack
b. Buchanan, Jack
b. Campbell, Douglas
b. Campbell, Thomas
b. Campbell-Bannerman, Henry, Sir
b. Chesney, Marion
b. Clyde, Colin Campbell, Baron
b. Corri, Adrienne
b. D'Albert, Eugene
b. Dinwiddie, Robert
b. Donegan, Lonnie
b. Donovan
b. Dooley, Rae
b. Forsyth, Bill
b. Fraser, Douglas Andrew
b. Frazer, James George, Sir
b. Gemmell, Alan
b. Graham, Thomas
b. Hamilton, William, Sir
b. Henderson, Arthur
b. Herlie, Eileen
b. Herriot, James
b. Highet, Gilbert (Arthur)
b. Isaacs, Alick
b. Jackson, Gordon Cameron
b. Kelman, James
b. Kennedy, John Stewart
b. Knopfler, Mark
b. Knussen, Oliver
b. Laing, R(onald) D(avid)
b. Lipton, Thomas Johnstone, Sir
b. Lloyd, Frank

b. Loftus, Cissie
b. Logan, Ella
b. Lulu
b. Lynch, Benny
b. MacDonald, John Alexander
b. MacInnes, Helen
b. Macintosh, Charles
b. MacIntyre, Alasdair Chalmers
b. MacKellar, William
b. Mackintosh, Charles Rennie
b. MacLean, Alistair (Stuart)
b. Martyn, John
b. McCallum, David
b. McGill, James
b. Meek, Donald
b. Miller, Frankie
b. Moffatt, James
b. Morgan, Edwin George
b. Motherwell, William
b. Nicoll, (John Ramsay) Allardyce
b. Owen, Robert Dale
b. Pinkerton, Allan
b. Primrose, William
b. Ramsay, William, Sir
b. Reid Dick, William, Sir
b. Stewart, Al
b. Stirling, James
b. Thomson, Bobby
b. Todd, Alexander (Robertus), Sir
b. Ure, Mary
b. Williamson, Robin
b. Wilson, Edward Arthur
b. Young, Angus
b. Young, Malcolm
d. Hardie, James Keir
d. Hutcheson, Francis
d. Irving, Edward
d. Macintosh, Charles
d. Motherwell, William
d. Reid, Thomas
d. Wells, Henry

Glencorse, Scotland
b. Wilson, Charles Thomson Rees

Grangemouth, Scotland
b. Davie, Alan
b. Winton, Alexander

Greenock, Scotland
b. Kidd, William, Captain
b. Watt, James
d. Galt, John

Haddington, Scotland
b. Knox, John

Hamilton, Scotland
b. Williamson, Nicol

Hawick, Scotland
b. Murray, James Augustus Henry, Sir

Hawthornden, Scotland
b. Drummond of Hawthornden, William
d. Drummond of Hawthornden, William

Helensburgh, Scotland
b. Baird, John Logie
b. Kerr, Deborah

Hume-by-Kelso, Scotland
d. Arundel, Honor Morfydd

Huntley, Scotland
b. MacDonald, George

Inner Hebrides, Scotland
b. Macquarie, Lachlan

Inverness, Scotland
b. Mackay, John Alexander
b. Phyfe, Duncan
b. Tey, Josephine
d. Cobb, John Rhodes
d. Watson-Watt, Robert Alexander, Sir

Inverness-Shire, Scotland
d. Baring, Maurice

Iona, Scotland
d. Columba, Saint

Ironside, Scotland
b. Ironside, William Edmund

Irvine, Scotland
b. Galt, John
b. MacMillan, Alexander

Islay, Scotland
b. McDougall, Alexander

Isle of Arran, Scotland
b. MacMillan, Daniel
d. Gemmell, Alan

Isle of Lewis, Scotland
b. Smith, Iain Crichton

Jedburgh, Scotland
b. Brewster, David, Sir

Killearn, Scotland
b. Buchanan, George

Kilmacolm, Scotland
b. Smith, Hedrick Laurence

Kilmany, Scotland
b. Clark, James

Kilmarnock, Scotland
b. Leiper, Robert Thomson
b. Smith, Alexander

Kilmaurs, Scotland
b. Boyd-Orr, John, Baron
b. Orr, John Boyd, 1st Baron of Brechin

Kilmun, Scotland
d. Richardson, Lewis Fry

Kincardine-on-Forth, Scotland
b. Dewar, James, Sir

Kinlochleven, Scotland
b. MacGregor, Ian Kinloch, Sir

Kinnordy, Scotland
b. Lyell, Charles, Sir

Kirkcaldy, Scotland
b. Adam, Robert
b. Fleming, Sandford
b. Smith, Adam
b. Steel, David Martin Scott
b. Wilson, Bertha

Kirkcudbright, Scotland
b. Jones, John Paul

Kirkcudbrightshire, Scotland
b. Selkirk, 5th Earl of

Kirkilston, Scotland
b. Dalzel, Archibald

Kirkintilloch, Dumbartonshire, Scotland
b. Couper, Archibald Scott

Kirkliston, Scotland
d. Murray, John, Sir

Kirkwall, Scotland
b. Baikie, William Balfour
d. Brown, George Mackay

Kirriemuir, Scotland
b. Barrie, James Matthew, Sir
b. Niven, David

Lanarkshire, Scotland
b. Livingstone, David
b. Lockhart, John Gibson
b. Murray, Philip

Langholm, Scotland
b. MacDiarmid, Hugh

Largo, Scotland
b. Selkirk, Alexander

Leadhills, Scotland
b. Ramsay, Allan

Legbrannock, Scotland
b. Hardie, James Keir

Leith, Scotland
d. Ged, William

Lerwick, Scotland
b. Lamont, Norman

Lesmahagow, Scotland
b. Cairncross, Alexander Kirkland, Sir

Lethington, Scotland
b. Maitland, John

Lewis Island, Scotland
b. Mackenzie, Alexander, Sir

Liddesdale, Scotland
b. Oliver, James

Linlithgow, Scotland
b. James V
b. Mary, Queen of Scots

Little Duchrae, Scotland
  b. Crockett, S(amuel) R(utherford)

Loanhead, Scotland
  b. MacTaggart, William, Sir

Lochfield, Scotland
  b. Fleming, Alexander, Sir

Lochgelly, Scotland
  b. Lee, Jennie

Logierat, Perthshire, Scotland
  b. Ferguson, Adam

Long Calderwood, Scotland
  b. Hunter, John
  b. Hunter, William

Lossiemouth, Scotland
  b. MacDonald, James Ramsay
  b. MacDonald, Malcolm John

Lumphanan, Scotland
  d. Macbeth

Melrose, Scotland
  d. Christison, (Alexander Frank) Philip

Midlothian, Scotland
  b. Dalhousie, James Andrew Broun
    Ramsay, Marquess of
  d. Dalhousie, James Andrew Broun
    Ramsay, Marquess of

Moffat, Scotland
  b. Dowding, Hugh Caswell
    Tremenheere, Baron

Montrose, Scotland
  b. Brown, Robert

Morayshire, Scotland
  b. Smith, Donald Alexander

Mull of Kintyre, Scotland
  d. Mitchison, Naomi Margaret
    (Haldane)

Mulnain, Scotland
  d. Mackenzie, Alexander, Sir

Musselburgh, Scotland
  b. Oliphant, Margaret

Nairn, Scotland
  b. Rose, Murray

Newmill, Scotland
  b. Bennett, James Gordon

North Berwick, Scotland
  b. Anderson, Willie
  b. McLeod, Fred(erick)

Northwater Bridge, Scotland
  b. Mill, James

Oldmeldrum, Scotland
  b. Manson, Patrick, Sir

Orkney Islands, Scotland
  d. Grimond, Jo(seph)

Paisley, Scotland
  b. Conti, Tom
  b. Gardner, Alexander
  b. Rafferty, Gerry
  b. Sharp, William
  b. Wilson, Alexander

Peebles, Scotland
  b. Chambers, Robert

Perth, Scotland
  b. Buchan, John, Sir
  b. Soutar, William
  d. James I
  d. Soutar, William

Perthshire, Scotland
  b. Braddock, Edward
  b. Dewar, John

Pitsligo Bay, Scotland
  d. Chancellor, Richard

Portobello, Scotland
  b. Lauder, Harry MacLennan, Sir

Quarry Farm, Scotland
  b. Keith, Arthur

Renfrew, Scotland
  b. Davies, Hunter

Rothiemurchus, Scotland
  b. Grant, Duncan (James Corrowr)

Roxburgh Castle, Scotland
  d. James II

Ruthven, Scotland
  b. Macpherson, James
  d. Macpherson, James

Saint Andrews, Scotland
  b. Aucherlonie, Laurie
  b. Bell, Andrew
  b. Grimond, Jo(seph)
  d. Aucherlonie, Laurie
  d. Chambers, Robert
  d. Fyffe, Will

Sauchieburn, Scotland
  d. James III

Scone, Scotland
  b. Douglas, David

Selkirk, Scotland
  b. Lang, Andrew

Shotts, Scotland
  b. MacBeth, George Mann

Stirling, Scotland
  b. James III
  b. Mathieson, Muir
  b. McLaren, Norman
  b. Tedder, Arthur William Tedder,
    Baron

Stirling Castle, Scotland
  b. James IV

Stirlingshire, Scotland
  b. Bruce, James

Stockbridge, Scotland
  b. Raeburn, Henry, Sir

Stonehaven, Scotland
  b. Reith, John Charles Walsham

Stornoway, Scotland
  b. MacIver, Robert Morrison

Strachan, Scotland
  b. Reid, Thomas

Strathaven, Scotland
  d. Lauder, Harry MacLennan, Sir

Stromness, Scotland
  b. Brown, George Mackay

Tantallon Castle, Scotland
  b. Douglas, Gavin

Taynuilt, Scotland
  d. Smith, Iain Crichton

Thurso, Scotland
  b. Saint Clair, Arthur

Tillypronie, Scotland
  d. Astor, Gavin

Tullibody, Scotland
  b. Abercromby, Ralph, Sir

Turnberry, Scotland
  b. Robert I

Uddingston, Scotland
  b. Black, James Whyte, Sir

Wardie, Scotland
  d. Forbes, Edward
  d. Smith, Alexander

West Calder, Scotland
  b. Kane, John

Wigtown, Scotland
  b. Justice, James Robertson

Yarrow, Scotland
  d. Hogg, James

SENEGAL

  b. Wheatley, Phillis

Dakar, Senegal
  b. Diop, Birago
  b. Mboup, Souleymane
  b. M'Bow, Mahtar-Amadou
  b. Ndour, Youssou
  d. Brazza, Pierre Paul Francois
    Camille Savorgnan de
  d. Diop, Birago

d. Diop, Cheikh Anta
d. Diop, David
d. Gueye, Lamine
d. Laye, Camara

Diourbel, Senegal
b. Diop, Cheikh Anta

Fad Jal, Senegal
b. Faye, Safi

Goree, Senegal
b. Diagne, Blaise

Joal, Senegal
b. Senghor, Leopold Sedar

Louga, Senegal
b. Diouf, Abdou

M'Backe, Senegal
b. Bamba, Amadou

Saint-Louis, Senegal
b. Ly, Abdoulaye

Ziguinchor, Senegal
b. Sembene, Ousmane

SERBIA

Belgrade, Serbia
b. Panic, Milan

Ivanjica, Serbia
b. Mihajlovic, Dragoliub

Sarajevo, Serbia
d. Francis Ferdinand

SEYCHELLES

b. Rene, (France) Albert

SIERRA LEONE

d. Baikie, William Balfour

Allen Town, Sierra Leone
b. Strasser, Valentine (E. M.)

Binkola, Sierra Leone
b. Momoh, Joseph (Saidu)

Freetown, Sierra Leone
b. Berri, Nabih
d. Blyden, Edward Wilmot
d. Stevens, Siaka Probyn

Moyamba, Sierra Leone
b. Stevens, Siaka Probyn

Pendemba, Sierra Leone
b. Kabbah, (Alhaji) Ahmad Tejan

Wilberforce, Sierra Leone
b. Wallace-Johnson, Isaac Theophilus Akunna

SIKKIM

Gangtok, Sikkim
b. Namgyal, Palden Thondup

SILESIA

Breslau, Silesia
d. Clausewitz, Karl (Philipp Gottlieb) von

Heinzendorf, Silesia
b. Mendel, Gregor Johann

Karwin, Silesia
b. Kentner, Louis Philip

Kreisau, Silesia
b. Moltke, Helmuth James, Graf von

Kunern, Silesia
d. Achard, Franz Karl

Neisse, Silesia
b. Grzimek, Bernhard

Ossig, Silesia
b. Schwenckfeld, Kasper von

Parchim, Silesia
b. Moltke, Helmuth Karl Bernhard von

Sargans, Silesia
b. Engler, Adolph Gustav Heinrich

Trebnitz, Silesia
b. Niekisch, Ernest

Troppau, Silesia
b. Adamson, Joy Friederike Victoria Gessner

SINGAPORE

b. Charteris, Leslie
b. Goh Chok Tong
b. Lee Hsien Loong
b. Lee Kuan Yew
b. Marshall, David (Saul)
b. Ong Teng Cheong
b. Sheares, Benjamin Henry
d. Ishak, Yusof bin
d. Marshall, David (Saul)
d. Martinson, Joseph Bertram
d. Parkinson, Norman
d. Sheares, Benjamin Henry

SLOVAKIA

Bratislava, Slovakia
b. Fleischmann, Gisi

Dubravka, Slovakia
b. Husak, Gustav

Zvolen, Slovakia
b. Meciar, Vladimir

SOLOMON ISLANDS

d. Yamamoto, Isoroku

Alite'e Village, Laulasi, Solomon Islands
b. Ulufa'alu, Bart

Koriovuku, Solomon Islands
b. Hilly, Francis Billy

SOMALIA

b. Hassan, Muhammad Abdille

Lugh, Somalia
b. Siad Barre, Mohamed

Mogadishu, Somalia
b. Ali Mahdi Mohamed
d. Micombero, Michel

SOUTH AFRICA

b. Beckett, Wendy
b. Bloom, Harry
b. Cornelius, Henry
b. Lembede, Anton
b. Ndungane, Winston N(jongonkulu)
b. Tshabalala, Headman
d. Dingane
d. Hani, Chris
d. Hertzog, James Barry Munnik
d. Lembede, Anton
d. Muller, Hilgard

Alasht, South Africa
b. Pahlevi, Riza

Alexandra, South Africa
b. Mathabane, Mark

Bandawe, South Africa
b. Kadalie, Clements

Beaufort West, South Africa
b. Barnard, Christiaan Neethling

Benoni, South Africa
b. Nzo, Alfred (Baphethuxolo)

Bloemfontein, South Africa
b. Tolkien, J(ohn) R(onald) R(euel)
d. Swart, Charles Robberts

Bonnievale, South Africa
b. Breytenbach, Breyten

Cape Province, South Africa
b. Mqhayi, S(amuel) E(dward) K(rune Loliwe)
d. Ballinger, Margaret

Cape Town, South Africa
b. Bolitho, William
b. Butlin, William Heygate Edmund,
Sir
b. Cannon, Poppy
b. Chaplin, Sydney Dryden
b. Coetzee, J(ohn) M
b. Cooper, David (Graham)
b. Divine, Arthur Durham
b. Eban, Abba
b. Hunter, Ian
b. Kellaway, Cecil
b. Little, Sally
b. Oliphant, Laurence
b. Seed, Jenny
b. Smuts, Jan Christian
b. Zuckerman, Solly, Lord
d. Blaiberg, Philip
d. Cloete, Stuart
d. Coates, Albert
d. Diederichs, Nicholaas
d. Malan, Daniel Francois
d. Renault, Mary
d. Rhodes, Cecil John
d. Verwoerd, Hendrik F
d. Vorster, Balthazar Johannes
d. Washkansky, Louis

Cofimvaba, South Africa
b. Hani, Chris

Colesberg, South Africa
b. Kruger, Paul

Durban, South Africa
b. Campbell, Roy
b. Curren, Kevin
b. Cusack, Cyril
b. Klug, Aaron, Sir
b. Kunene, Mazisi (Raymond)
b. Langley, Noel
b. Price, Nick
d. Paton, Alan Stewart

Elliotdale, South Africa
b. Woods, Donald

Ermelo, South Africa
b. Dube, Lucky

Germiston, South Africa
b. Brenner, Sydney
b. Locke, Bobby
b. Suzman, Helen

Graaff Reinet, South Africa
b. Pretorius, Andries
b. Pretorius, Marthinus Wessel
b. Sobukwe, Robert Mangaliso

Groutville, South Africa
d. Luthuli, Albert John Mvumbi

Guguletu Township, South Africa
d. Biehl, Amy

Honigfontein, South Africa
b. Botha, Louis

Inanda, Natal, South Africa
b. Dube, John Langalibalele

Irene, South Africa
d. Smuts, Jan Christian

Jamestown, South Africa
b. Vorster, Balthazar Johannes

Johannesburg, South Africa
b. Cormack, Allan MacLeod
b. Dalrymple, Ian (Murray)
b. Daly, John Charles, Jr.
b. De Klerk, F(rederik) W(illem)
b. Duncan, Sheena
b. First, Ruth
b. Gluckman, Max
b. Hayward, Louis
b. Keeton, Kathy
b. Masekela, Barbara
b. Player, Gary Jim
b. Qoboza, Percy
b. Ramaphosa, Cyril
b. Rathbone, Basil
b. Suzman, Janet
d. Banda, Hastings Kamuzu
d. Dart, Raymond Arthur
d. Joseph, Helen
d. Locke, Bobby
d. Oppenheimer, Harry Frederick
d. Pahlevi, Riza
d. Qoboza, Percy
d. Revson, Peter Jeffrey
d. Slovo, Joe
d. Tambo, Oliver

Kakamas, South Africa
b. Boesak, Allan Aubrey

Kalk Bay, South Africa
d. Ardrey, Robert

Khojane, South Africa
b. Mofolo, Thomas (Mokopu)

Kimberley, South Africa
b. Oppenheimer, Harry Frederick
d. Sobukwe, Robert Mangaliso

King William's Town, South Africa
b. Biko, Steven

Klerksdrop, South Africa
b. Tutu, Desmond (Mpilo)

Magaliesberg, South Africa
d. Pretorius, Andries

Mahlabatini, South Africa
b. Buthelezi, Gatsha Mangosuthu

Middleburg, South Africa
b. Fugard, Athol

Mooi River, South Africa
b. Cope, Jack

Muzimi, South Africa
d. Machel, Samora Moises

Natal, South Africa
b. Nkosi, Lewis

Newcastle, South Africa
b. Mabuza, Lindiwe

Orange Free State, South Africa
b. Diederichs, Nicholaas

Paul Roux, South Africa
b. Botha, Pieter Willem

Philioppis, South Africa
b. Van Der Post, Laurens (Jan), Sir

Phiri, South Africa
b. Nkoli, Simon

Pietermaritzburg, South Africa
b. Head, Bessie Emery
b. Paton, Alan Stewart

Pietersburg, South Africa
b. Plomer, William Charles Franklyn

Piketberg, South Africa
b. Treurnicht, Andries Petrus

Pinetown, South Africa
d. Tshabalala, Headman

Ponogola, South Africa
b. Kriek, Johann

Port Elizabeth, South Africa
d. Biko, Steven
d. Blackburn, Molly

Port Natal, South Africa
d. Retief, Pieter

Potchefstroom, South Africa
b. Muller, Hilgard
d. Pretorius, Marthinus Wessel

Pretoria, South Africa
b. Johns, Glynis
b. Mphahlele, Ezekiel
b. Sloane, Dennis
b. Theiler, Max
d. Botha, Louis
d. Jonathan, Leabua, Chief

Prospect Township, South Africa
b. Makeba, Miriam

Queenstown, South Africa
b. Mbeki, Thabo Mvuyelwa

Riebeck, South Africa
b. Malan, Daniel Francois

Rustenburg, South Africa
b. Botha, Roelof Frederik
b. Cranko, John

Siyamu, South Africa
b. Dhlomo, R(olfus) R(eginald)
R(aymond)

Springs, South Africa
b. Gordimer, Nadine

Transkei, South Africa
b. Mandela, Winnie
b. Sisulu, Nontsikelelo Albertina
b. Sisulu, Walter Max Ulyate
b. Tambo, Oliver

Cauca, Spain
b. Thedosius I

Cebreros, Spain
b. Suarez Gonzales, Adolfo

Cifuentes, Spain
b. Landa, Diego de

Comprodon, Spain
b. Albeniz, Isaac Manuel Francisco

Cordoba, Spain
b. Averroes
b. Gongora y Argote, Luis de
b. ibn Hazm, Abu Muhammad Ali
b. Lucan
b. Maimonides, Moses
b. Manolete
b. Quesada, Gonzalo Jimenez de
b. Saavedra, Angel de
b. Seneca, Lucius Annaeus, the
   Younger
d. Abd al-Rahman, I
d. Gongora y Argote, Luis de

Cuellar, Spain
b. Velazquez de Cuellar, Diego

Deya, Majorca, Spain
d. Graves, Robert von Ranke

El Ferrol, Spain
b. Alvarino (de Leira), Angeles
b. Franco, Francisco

Encina, Salamanca, Spain
b. Encina, Juan del

Entralgo, Spain
b. Palacio Valdes, Armando

Figueras, Spain
b. Dali, Salvador
d. Dali, Salvador

Fuendetodos, Spain
b. Goya y Lucientes, Francisco Jose
   de

Fuente Vaqueros, Spain
b. Garcia Lorca, Federico

Fuentes de Cantos, Spain
b. Zurbaran, Francisco

Galicia, Spain
d. Nino, Pedro Alonzo

Gallarta, Spain
b. Ibarruri, Dolores Gomez

Gerona, Spain
b. Nahmanides
d. Dali, Gala

Granada, Spain
b. Eugenie
b. Fortuny
b. Leo Africanus
b. Mendoza, Antonio de
b. Orantes, Manuel

b. Suarez, Francisco
d. Garcia Lorca, Federico

Guadalajara, Spain
b. Buero Vallejo, Antonio
b. DeCreeft, Jose
d. Amalrik, Andrei Alekseyevich
d. Santillana, Inigo Lopez de Mendoza

Guadix, Spain
b. Alarcon, Pedro Antonio de
b. ibn Tufayl, Abu Bakr Muhammad

Guetaria, Spain
b. Balenciaga, Cristobal

Huesca, Spain
b. Saura (Atares), Carlos

Ibiza, Spain
d. Elliott, Denholm Mitchell
d. Sackler, Howard Oliver

Iria Flavia, Spain
b. Cela (Trulock), Camilo Jose

Italica, Spain
b. Hadrian
b. Trajan

Jativa, Spain
b. Ribera, Jusepe (Jose) de

Javea, Spain
d. Balenciaga, Cristobal

Jerez Caballeros, Spain
b. Balboa, Vasco Nunez de

La Coruna, Spain
b. Madariaga (y Rojo), Salvador de
b. Menendez Pidal, Ramon
b. Rey, Fernando

La Serena, Estremadura, Spain
b. Valdivia, Pedro de

Las Palmas, Canary Islands, Spain
b. Kraus, Alfredo
b. Negrin, Juan
b. Perez Galdos, Benito

Leon, Spain
b. Moses de Leon
b. Ponce de Leon, Juan

Lerida, Spain
b. Granados, Enrique

Linares, Spain
b. Raphael
b. Segovia, Andres
d. Manolete

Logrono, Spain
b. Castroviejo, Ramon

Loyola, Spain
b. Ignatius of Loyola, Saint

Luarca, Spain
b. Ochoa, Severo

Macharaviaya, Spain
b. Galvez, Bernardo de

Madrid, Spain
b. Abruzzi, Luigi Amedeo
b. Alfonso XIII
b. Alonso, Damaso
b. Ayala, Francisco J(ose)
b. Aznar, Jose Maria
b. Benavente y Martinez, Jacinto
b. Berganza, Teresa
b. Blanc, Louis
b. Calderon de la Barca, Pedro
b. Calvo Sotelo (y Bustelo), Leopoldo
b. Candela, Felix
b. Castillo, Antonio Canovas del
b. Charles, II
b. Charles, III
b. Churriguera, Jose Benito de
b. Colbran, Isabella
b. DePinies, Jaime
b. Domingo, Placido
b. Dominguin, Luis Miguel
b. Echegaray y Eizaguirre, Jose
b. Ercilla y Zuniga, Alonso de
b. Fernandez-Muro, Jose Antonio
b. Garcia, Manuel Patricio Rodriguez
b. Gris, Juan
b. Halffter, Christobal
b. Hamen y Leon, Juan van der
b. Iglesias, Julio
b. Isabella II
b. Juan Carlos, Count of Barcelona
b. Largo Caballero, Francisco
b. Lope de Vega
b. Lopez Bravo, Gregorio
b. Martinez Sierra, Gregorio
b. Maura, Carmen
b. Montoya, Carlos
b. Ortega y Gasset, Jose
b. Patti, Adelina Juana Maria
b. Philip, III
b. Quevado y Villegas, Francisco
   Gomez de
b. Salinas (y Serrano), Pedro
b. Santayana, George
b. Tamayo y Baus, Manuel
b. Tirso de Molina
b. Torroja (y Miret), Eduardo
d. Alarcon, Pedro Antonio de
d. Alarcon y Mendoza, Juan Ruiz de
d. Aldecoa, Ignacio
d. Aleixandre, Vicente
d. Alonso, Damaso
d. Asturias, Miguel Angel
d. Bacon, Francis
d. Baroja (y Nessi), Pio
d. Becquer, Gustavo Adolfo
   Dominguez
d. Benavente y Martinez, Jacinto
d. Boccherini, Luigi
d. Buero Vallejo, Antonio
d. Calderon de la Barca, Pedro
d. Castroviejo, Ramon
d. Cervantes (Saavedra), Miguel (de)
d. Charriere, Henri
d. Churriguera, Jose Benito de
d. Crosby, Bing
d. Echegaray y Eizaguirre, Jose
d. Ercilla y Zuniga, Alonso de
d. Eugenie
d. Flores, Lola
d. Franco, Francisco
d. Frederika Louise
d. Hamen y Leon, Juan van der
d. Herrera, Juan de

d. Ibarruri, Dolores Gomez
d. Juvara, Filippo
d. Kraus, Alfredo
d. Lope de Vega
d. Machado (y Ruiz), Manuel
d. Mangano, Silvana
d. Martinez Sierra, Gregorio
d. Menendez Pidal, Ramon
d. Ochoa, Severo
d. Ortega y Gasset, Jose
d. Palacio Valdes, Armando
d. Perez Galdos, Benito
d. Power, Tyrone, Jr.
d. Ramon y Cajal, Santiago
d. Rey, Fernando
d. Rojas Zorrilla, Francisco de
d. Ruiz, Jose Martinez
d. Saavedra, Angel de
d. Segovia, Andres
d. Sierra, Justo
d. Starkie, Walter Fitzwilliam
d. Tamayo y Baus, Manuel
d. Tiepolo, Giambattista
d. Torroja (y Miret), Eduardo
d. Velazquez, Diego Rodriguez de
Silva
d. Waln, Nora
d. Yerby, Frank (Garvin)
d. Youlou, Fulbert
d. Zurbaran, Francisco

Madrigal de las Altas Torres, Spain
b. Isabella I

Madrigalejo, Spain
d. Ferdinand V

Majorca, Spain
b. Llull, Ramon
b. Serra, Junipero
d. Batten, Jean Gardner
d. Emerson, Faye Margaret
d. Malcuzynski, Witold

Malaga, Spain
b. Banderas, Antonio
b. Galvez, Jose de
b. Picasso, Pablo Ruiz y
d. Baker, Stanley, Sir
d. Bowles, Jane Sydney
d. Brenan, Gerald
d. Guillen, Jorge

Marbella, Spain
d. Batista y Zaldivar, Fulgencio
d. Carroll, Madeleine

Medellin, Spain
b. Cortez, Hernando

Medina del Campo, Spain
d. Isabella I

Milan, Spain
d. Thedosius I

Mobellan, Spain
b. Herrera, Juan de

Monguer, Spain
b. Jimenez, Juan Ramon
b. Nino, Pedro Alonzo

Monovar, Spain
b. Ruiz, Jose Martinez

Montalban, Spain
d. Colon, Diego

Moraira, Spain
d. Himes, Chester Bomar

Motril, Spain
d. Baudouin, I, King

Murcia, Spain
b. Charo

Nijar, Spain
b. Asencio, Diego Cortes

Oropesa, Spain
b. Toledo, Fernando Alvarez de
b. Toledo, Francisco de

Palma, Spain
b. Lull, Raymond

Palma de Majorca, Spain
d. Fielding, Temple Hornaday
d. Miro, Joan

Palma del Rio, Spain
b. Cordobes, El

Pamplona, Spain
b. Francis Xavier, Saint
b. Sarasate, Pablo de
d. Juan Carlos, Count of Barcelona

Paredes de Navas, Valladolid, Spain
b. Berruguete, Alonso (Gonzalez)

Pedrena, Spain
b. Ballesteros, Seve(riano)

Penuela, Spain
d. John of the Cross, Saint

Petilla de Aragon, Spain
b. Ramon y Cajal, Santiago

Piedrahita, Spain
b. Alba, Duke of

Placiencia, Spain
d. Charles V

Polanco, Spain
b. Pereda, Jose Marie de

Priego, Spain
b. Alcala Zamora, Niceto

Puebla de Caraminal, Spain
b. Valle Inclan, Ramon Maria del

Puerto de Santa Maria, Spain
b. Alberti, Rafael
d. Alberti, Rafael

Puerto del Pico, Spain
d. Verrazano, Giovanni da

Reus, Spain
b. Gaudi y Cornet, Antonio

Salamanca, Spain
b. Coronado, Francisco Vasquez de
d. Stanley, Wendell Meredith
d. Unamuno (y Jugo), Miguel de
d. Vitoria, Francisco de

San Lorenzo del Escorial, Spain
b. Ferdinand, VII

San Sebastian, Spain
b. Baroja (y Nessi), Pio
b. Chillida, Eduard
b. Jorda, Enrique
b. Zabaleta, Nicanor

Sanlucar de Barrameda, Spain
b. Pacheco, Francisco

Santander, Spain
d. Menendez de Aviles, Pedro
d. Pereda, Jose Marie de

Sao Cristovao de la Laguna on, Spain
b. Anchieta, Jose de

Saragossa, Spain
b. Lorengar, Pilar
b. Mendana de Neyra, Alvaro de
b. Molinos, Miguel de

Seville, Spain
b. Aleixandre, Vicente
b. Aleman, Mateo
b. Becquer, Gustavo Adolfo
Dominguez
b. Cueva de Garoza, Juan de la
b. Garcia, Manuel del Popolo Vincente
b. Gonzalez Marquez, Felipe
b. Guerrero, Francisco
b. Las Casas, Bartolome de
b. Machado (y Ruiz), Antonio
b. Machado (y Ruiz), Manuel
b. Mercer, Beryl
b. Murillo, Bartolome Esteban
b. Velazquez, Diego Rodriguez de
Silva
b. Wiseman, Nicholas Patrick Stephen
d. Alfonso, X
d. Bandelier, Adolph Francis Alphonse
d. Caballero, Fernan
d. Guerrero, Francisco
d. Pacheco, Francisco
d. Vespucci, Amerigo

Sos, Spain
b. Ferdinand V

Soto Grande, Spain
d. Dominguin, Luis Miguel

Sotograde, Spain
d. Moore, George Stevens

Talavera, Spain
d. Rojas, Fernando de

Tarazona, Spain
d. Gracian y Morales, Baltasar
Jeronimo

Tenerife, Canary Islands, Spain
d. Saunders, William Laurence

Teruel, Spain
b. Clement VIII

Thomar, Spain
d. Toledo, Fernando Alvarez de

Toledo, Spain
b. Alfonso, X
b. Ayllon, Lucas Vasquez de
b. Caro, Joseph
b. Mariana, Juan de
b. Rojas, Fernando de
b. Rojas Zorrilla, Francisco de
d. Alfonso, VI
d. Castiglione, Baldassare, Conte
d. Greco, El
d. Mariana, Juan de

Torremolinos, Spain
d. Karpis, Alvin

Trujillo, Spain
b. Orellana, Francisco de
b. Pizarro, Francisco

Tudela, Spain
b. Benjamin of Tudela
b. Ha-Levi, Judah
b. Moneo, Jose Rafael

Valencia, Spain
b. Blasco-Ibanez, Vicente
b. Iturbi, Amparo
b. Iturbi, Jose
b. Martin y Soler, Vicente
b. Milan, Luis
d. Cid, El
d. Enrique Tarancon, Vicente, Cardinal
d. Lauri-Volpi, Giacoma
d. Ribalta, Francisco

Valladolid, Spain
b. Guillen, Jorge
b. Narvaez, Panfilo de
d. Matamoros, Mariano

Vendrell, Spain
b. Casals, Pablo (Pau Carlos Salvador)

Verdu, Catalonia, Spain
b. Claver, Peter

Vigo, Spain
d. Norwich, Alfred Duff Cooper, Viscount

Villanueva de Sixena, Spain
b. Servetus, Michael

Villanueva de los Infantes, Spain
d. Quevado y Villegas, Francisco Gomez de

Villava, Spain
b. Indurain, Miguel

Vitoria, Spain
b. Aldecoa, Ignacio
b. Lopez de Ayala, Pero

Xativa, Spain
b. Alexander VI

SPANISH MOROCCO

Melilla, Spanish Morocco
b. Arrabal (Teran), Fernando

SPANISH NETHERLANDS

d. Jansen, Cornelis Otto

Antwerp, Spanish Netherlands
b. Hals, Frans

SRI LANKA

b. Ondaatje, Michael

Colombo, Sri Lanka
b. Premadasa, Ranasinghe
d. Gopallawa, William
d. Jayewardene, J(unius) R(ichard)
d. Senanayake, Dudley Shelton

ST. HELENA

d. Napoleon I

ST. KITTS AND NEVIS

b. Douglas, Denzil
b. Douglas, Robert L
d. Crosse, Rupert

Basseterre, St. Kitts and Nevis
b. Simmonds, Kennedy Alphonse

ST. LUCIA

b. Anthony, Kenny
b. Lewis, Vaughan Allen

Castries, St. Lucia
b. Lewis, Allen Montgomery, Sir
b. Lewis, William Arthur, Sir
b. Walcott, Derek (Alton)

ST. MARTIN

d. Spiegel, Sam
d. Von Wangenheim, Chris

ST. VINCENT AND THE GRENADINES

b. Mitchell, James

Canouan, St. Vincent and the Grenadines
b. Compton, John (George M.)

SUDAN

b. al-Turabi, Hassan
b. Khalil, Sayyid Abdullah
b. Wek, Alek

Dongola, Sudan
b. Mahdi, Mohammed Ahmed

Gogrial, Sudan
b. Bol, Manute

Khartoum, Sudan
b. Naguib, Mohammed
d. Abboud, (El Ferik) Ibrahim
d. Gordon, Charles George
d. Khalil, Sayyid Abdullah

Milo Valley, Sudan
b. Samory Toure

Mohammed-Gol, Sudan
b. Abboud, (El Ferik) Ibrahim

Omdurman, Sudan
b. Azhari, Sayyid Ismail al-
d. Mahdi, Mohammed Ahmed

Wad Nubawi, Sudan
b. Nimeiry, Gaafar Mohammed al

SURINAME

b. Matzeliger, Jan Ernest

Paramaribo, Suriname
b. Sedney, Jules
b. Wijdenbosch, Jules Albert

SWAZILAND

b. Mswati, III

Mbabane, Swaziland
b. Sobhuza II
d. Sobhuza II

SWEDEN

b. Grove, Frederick Philip
b. Nelson, Erik Henning
b. Tenggren, Gustaf Adolf

Algutsboda, Sweden
b. Moberg, Vihelm

Alvik Neder Lulea, Sweden
b. Nordstrom, John

Angelholm, Sweden
d. Widerberg, Bo

Boras, Sweden
b. Carlsson, Ingvar Gosta

Bosjokloster, Sweden
b. Rosenberg, Hilding

b. Engellau, Gunnar Ludwig
b. Faltskog, Agnetha
b. Garbo, Greta
b. Gedda, Nicolai
b. Gentele, Goeran
b. Gustaf Adolf VI
b. Gustavus Adophus
b. Hallstrom, Ivar
b. Hasso, Signe Eleonora Cecilia
b. Hedin, Sven Anders
b. Hoving, Walter
b. Larsson, Carl Olof
b. Lind, Jenny
b. Lindbergh, Charles Augustus
b. Lindbergh, Pelle (Per-Eric)
b. Lindstrom, Pia
b. Lyngstad-Fredriksson, Annifrid
b. Myrdal, Jan
b. Nobel, Alfred Bernhard
b. Nystrom, Bob
b. Oldenburg, Claes Thure
b. Oldenburg, Richard
b. Olin, Lena
b. Onegin, Sigrid
b. Otter, Anne Sofie von
b. Palme, Olof
b. Renvall, Johan Bengt Erik
b. Rosberg, Keke
b. Sjoberg, Alf
b. Soderstrom, Elisabeth Anna
b. Spiegelman, Art
b. Stevens, Inger
b. Strindberg, August
b. Swedenborg, Emanuel
b. Taglioni, Maria
b. Tiselius, Arne Wilhelm Kaurin
b. Toren, Marta
b. Ulvaeus, Bjorn
b. Varnay, Astrid
b. Victoria Ingrid Alice Desiree
b. Von Euler, Ulf
b. Wallenberg, Marcus
b. Wallenberg, Raoul Gustav
d. Alfven, Hannes Olof Gosta
d. Andersson, Johan Gunnar
d. Andresen, Ivar
d. Arnoldson, Klas Pontus
d. Arrhenius, Svante August
d. Asplund, Erik Gunnar
d. Asther, Nils
d. Bernadotte, Jean Baptiste
d. Berzelius, Jons Jacob, Baron
d. Branting, Karl Hjalmar
d. Dalen, Nils Gustaf
d. Descartes, Rene
d. Engellau, Gunnar Ludwig
d. Enskog, David
d. Euler-Chelpin, Hans Karl August Simon von
d. Gullstrand, Allvar
d. Hallstrom, Ivar
d. Hammarskjold, Hjalmar
d. Hedin, Sven Anders
d. Hedtoft (-Hansen), Hans Christian
d. Johnson, Eyvind Olof Verner
d. Karlfeldt, Erik Axel
d. Lagerkvist, Par Fabian
d. Larsen-Todsen, Nanny
d. Lundkvist, Artur Nils
d. Mallory, Molla
d. Martinson, Harry Edmund
d. Milles, Carl Wilhelm Emil
d. Moberg, Vihelm
d. Myrdal, Alva Reimer
d. Myrdal, Karl Gunnar
d. Nilsson, Christine

d. Oland, Warner
d. Oxenstierna, Axel Gustafsson
d. Palme, Olof
d. Ralf, Torsten
d. Sachs, Nelly (Leonie)
d. Siegbahn, Karl Manne Georg
d. Sjoberg, Alf
d. Sjostrom, Victor
d. Stiller, Mauritz
d. Strindberg, August
d. Theorell, (Axel) Hugh Teodor
d. Tiselius, Arne Wilhelm Kaurin
d. Toren, Marta
d. Von Euler, Ulf
d. Wallenberg, Marcus
d. Weiss, Peter Ulrich
d. Wenner-Gren, Axel (Lenard)
d. Wiener, Norbert

Stora Tuna, Sweden
b. Bjoerling, Jussi

Sundsvall, Sweden
b. Ljungberg, Gota

Timra, Sweden
b. Nasland, Mats

Trono, Sweden
b. Soderblom, Nathan

Tuna, Sweden
b. Hammarskjold, Hjalmar

Uddevalla, Sweden
b. Wenner-Gren, Axel (Lenard)

Umea, Sweden
b. Oland, Warner

Uppsala, Sweden
b. Alexanderson, Ernst Frederik Werner
b. Arrhenius, Svante August
b. Bergman, Ingmar (Ernst)
b. Celsius, Anders
b. Lindfors, Viveca
b. Myrdal, Alva Reimer
b. Oxenstierna, Axel Gustafsson
b. Wiesel, Torsten Nils
d. Angstrom, Anders Jonas
d. Barany, Robert
d. Celsius, Anders
d. Cleve, Per Teodor
d. Lindfors, Viveca
d. Linnaeus, Carolus
d. Soderblom, Nathan

Valadalen, Sweden
d. Ohlin, Bertil Gotthard

Valsjobyn, Sweden
b. Ann-Margret

Varmland, Sweden
b. Ericsson, John

Vasteras, Sweden
b. Svanholm, Set
b. Zetterling, Mai (Elisabeth)

Vastervik, Sweden
b. Edberg, Stefan

Vastra Amtervik, Varmland, Sweden
b. Enskog, David

Vaversunda, Sweden
b. Berzelius, Jons Jacob, Baron

Vaxjo, Sweden
b. Lagerkvist, Par Fabian
b. Wilander, Mats

Vimmerby, Sweden
b. Lindgren, Astrid

Vingaker, Sweden
b. Persson, Goran

West Karup, Sweden
b. Nilsson, Birgit

Wexio, Sweden
b. Nilsson, Christine

Ystad, Sweden
b. Nilsson, Anna Q(uerentia)

SWEDISH POMERANIA

Stralsund, Swedish Pomerania
b. Scheele, Karl Wilhelm

SWITZERLAND

b. LeCorbusier
b. Rohrer, Heinrich
b. Sismondi, Jean Charles Leonard Simonde de
d. Bhabha, Homi Jehangir
d. Brunhoff, Jean de
d. Corena, Fernando
d. Necker, Jacques
d. Tata, J(ehangir) R(atanji) D(adbhoy)

Adelboden, Switzerland
b. King, Francis Henry

Aldenbogen, Switzerland
d. Sabatini, Rafael

Ascona, Switzerland
d. Kaiser, Georg
d. Ludwig, Emil

Axenstein, Switzerland
d. Schnabel, Artur

Bad Ragaz, Switzerland
d. Schelling, Friedrich Wilhelm Joseph von

Basel, Switzerland
b. Barth, Karl
b. Bocklin, Arnold
b. Burckhardt, Carl Jacob
b. Euler, Leonhard
b. Haug, Hans
b. His, Wilhelm
b. Jung, Carl Gustav
b. Keller, Marthe
b. Muller, Karl Alex(ander)
b. Oppenheim, Meret

Kreuzlingen, Switzerland
b. Binswanger, Ludwig
d. Binswanger, Ludwig

Kussnacht, Switzerland
b. Frey-Wyssling, Albert F

La Chaux-de-Fonds, Switzerland
b. Chevrolet, Louis Joseph

La Tour de Peilz, Switzerland
d. Courbet, (Jean Desire) Gustave

Lake Constance, Switzerland
d. Flick, Friedrich

Langenthal, Switzerland
b. Holliger, Heinz

Langnau, Switzerland
b. Guggenheim, Meyer

Lausanne, Switzerland
b. Burckhardt, Johann Ludwig
b. Constant de Rebeque, (Henri)
   Benjamin
b. Dutoit, Charles
b. Furstenberg, Egon von
d. Anouilh, Jean Marie Lucien Pierre
d. Capucine
d. Cortot, Alfred-Denis
d. Faberge, Peter Carl
d. Flesch, Karl
d. Haug, Hans
d. Kemble, John Philip
d. Lifar, Serge
d. Mannerheim, Carl Gustav Emil,
   Baron
d. Mason, James Neville
d. May, Edna
d. Norena, Eide
d. Piccard, Auguste
d. Reard, Louis
d. Simenon, Georges
d. Szymanowski, Karol Maciej
d. Viollet le Duc, Eugene Emmanuel

Liestal, Switzerland
b. Spitteler, Karl Friedrich Georg
d. Martinu, Bohuslav

Locarno, Switzerland
d. Hess, Walter Rudolf
d. Highsmith, Patricia
d. Madariaga (y Rojo), Salvador de
d. Remarque, Erich Maria
d. Richter, Hans
d. Willstater, Richard Martin

Locle, Switzerland
b. Tschirky, Oscar

Lucerne, Switzerland
b. Villiger, Kaspar
d. Beernaert, Auguste Marie Francois
d. DeWohl, Louis
d. Kubelik, Rafael (Jeronym)
d. Reynolds, R(ichard) J(oshua), Jr.
d. Ritz, Cesar
d. Scribner, Charles
d. Spitteler, Karl Friedrich Georg
d. Szigeti, Joseph

Lugano, Switzerland
d. Rosbaud, Hans
d. Sirk, Douglas
d. Strehler, Giorgio

Magliasco, Switzerland
d. Onegin, Sigrid

Marbach, Switzerland
d. Reichmann, Theodor

Marengo, Switzerland
b. Delmonico, Lorenzo

Martigny, Switzerland
d. Lefebvre, Marcel Francois

Minusio, Switzerland
d. George, Stefan

Montagnola, Switzerland
d. Hesse, Hermann

Montreux, Switzerland
d. Kokoschka, Oskar
d. Nabokov, Vladimir

Morges, Switzerland
b. Caballero, Fernan

Motier, Switzerland
b. Agassiz, Louis

Mumpf, Switzerland
b. Rachel

Muralto, Switzerland
b. Cotti, Flavio
d. Fromm, Erich
d. Klee, Paul

Muzot, Switzerland
d. Rilke, Rainer Maria

Nant Corsier, Switzerland
d. Huberman, Bronislaw

Neuchatel, Switzerland
b. Agassiz, Alexander Emmanuel
   Rodolphe
b. Bovet, Daniele
b. Breguet, Abraham Louis
b. Marat, Jean Paul
b. Piaget, Jean
d. Durrenmatt, Friedrich
d. Petitpierre, Max

Niederwald, Switzerland
b. Ritz, Cesar

Nyon, Switzerland
b. Cortot, Alfred-Denis
b. De Mestral, Georges
d. Appia, Adolphe

Olsten, Switzerland
b. Muller, Paul Hermann

Oschwand, Switzerland
d. Amiet, Cuno

Passug, Switzerland
d. Bebel, August

Paudex, Switzerland
b. Delamuraz, Jean-Pascal

Porto Ronco, Switzerland
d. Goddard, Paulette

Poschiavo, Switzerland
d. Hildesheimer, Wolfgang

Reconvilier, Switzerland
b. Grock

Riesbach, Switzerland
b. Bodmer, Karl

Rolle, Switzerland
b. Bouquet, Henry

Romont, Switzerland
d. Schumacher, E(rnst) F(riedrich)

Rorschach, Switzerland
b. Jannings, Emil

Saas-Almagell, Switzerland
b. Zurbriggen, Pirmin

Saint Gallen, Switzerland
b. Maag, Peter

Saint Moritz, Switzerland
b. Kreuger, Kurt

Samaden, Switzerland
b. Ikle, Fred Charles
d. Segantini, Giovanni

Schaffhausen, Switzerland
b. Ammann, Othmar Hermann

Schwyz, Switzerland
b. Marty, Martin

Solothurn, Switzerland
b. Amiet, Cuno
d. Kosciuszko, Thaddeus
d. Ratoff, Gregory

St. Gall, Switzerland
b. Notker Balbulus

Stiebschen, Switzerland
b. Wagner, Siegfried (Helferich)

Sursee, Switzerland
b. Kung, Hans

Territet, Switzerland
d. Belin, Edouard

Tolochenaz, Switzerland
d. Hepburn, Audrey (Edda)

Tramelan, Switzerland
b. Gobat, Charles Albert

Triebschen, Switzerland
d. Hauk, Minnie

Ukerewe, Tanzania
b. Mongella, Gertrude

THAILAND

b. Chatichai Choonhavan
b. Kukrit Pramoj, Momrajawong
(M.R.)
d. Buddhadasa Bhikkhu
d. Chulalongkorn

Ayudhya Province, Thailand
b. Pridi Phanomyong

Bangkok, Thailand
b. Banharn Silpa-archa
b. Chulalongkorn
b. Mongkut
b. Osborne, Adam
b. Phibun Songkhram, Luang
b. Sarit Thanarat
d. Kukrit Pramoj, Momrajawong
(M.R.)
d. Merton, Thomas
d. Mongkut
d. Silliphant, Stirling Dale

Meklong, Thailand
b. Chang and Eng

Nguam Phanich, Thailand
b. Buddhadasa Bhikkhu

Nonthaburi, Thailand
b. Chavalit Yongchaiyudh

Phuket, Thailand
d. Jones, Tristan

Songkhla, Thailand
b. Prem Tinsulanonda

Tak, Thailand
b. Kittikachorn, Thanom

Trang, Thailand
b. Chuan Leekpai

THURINGIA

Buttstadt, Thuringia
b. Fischer, Carl

Hainichen, Thuringia
b. Feuerbach, Paul Johann Anselm von

Stolberg, Thuringia
b. Muntzer, Thomas

TIBET

Chhija Nangso, Tibet
b. Dalai Lama, the 14th Incarnate

TOGO

b. Olympio, Sylvanus E.

d. Olympio, Sylvanus E.

Lome, Togo
b. Soglo, Nicephore (Dieudonne)

Pya, Togo
b. Eyadema, Etienne Gnassingbe

TRANSYLVANIA

Koloszvar, Transylvania
b. Matthias Corvinus

Lancram, Transylvania
b. Blaga, Lucien

Sighet, Transylvania
b. Wiesel, Elie(zer)

TRINIDAD

b. Dalgleish, Alice
b. Julian, Hubert Fauntleroy
b. Mallory, Stephen R
b. Primus, Pearl
b. Robinson, A(rthur) N(apoleon)
R(aymond)
b. Williams, Henry Sylvester
d. Williams, Henry Sylvester

Fyzabad, Trinidad
b. Ocean, Billy

Princes Town, Trinidad
b. Panday, Basdeo

San Fernando, Trinidad
b. Manning, Patrick (Augustus
Mervyn)

Tunapuna, Trinidad
b. Klass, Perri Elizabeth

TRINIDAD AND TOBAGO

b. Naipaul, V(idiahar) S(urajprasad)

Diego Martin, Trinidad and Tobago
b. Constantine, Learie Nicholas
Constantine, Baron

Port of Spain, Trinidad and Tobago
b. Carmichael, Stokely
b. Clarke, Ellis Emmanuel Innocent,
Sir
b. Holder, Geoffrey
b. Scott, Hazel Dorothy
b. Williams, Eric Eustace
d. Williams, Eric Eustace

San Fernando, Trinidad and Tobago
b. Guy, Rosa Cuthbert
b. Selvon, Samuel Dickson
d. Beebe, William

TUNIS

d. Louis IX

TUNISIA

Hammamet, Tunisia
d. Craxi, Bettino

Monastir, Tunisia
b. Bourguiba, Habib Ben Ali
d. Bourguiba, Habib Ben Ali

Tunis, Tunisia
b. Alaia, Azzedine
b. Cardinale, Claudia
b. Ibn Khaldun
b. Memmi, Albert
d. Morrice, James Wilson
d. Nicolle, Charles Jules Henri
d. Payne, John Howard

TURKEY

b. Gulbenkian, Calouste S
d. Mazepa, Ivan Stepanovich

Adrianople, Turkey
d. Koprulu, Ahmed

Alasehir, Turkey
b. Evren, Kenan

Ankara, Turkey
d. Ataturk, Kemal
d. Inonu, Ismet
d. Ozal, Turgut

Antioch, Turkey
b. Adams, Walter Sydney

Apana, Turkey
b. Enver Pasha

Bukhara, Turkey
d. Enver Pasha

Constantinople, Turkey
b. Constantine VI
b. Constantine XI Palaeologus
b. Grosvenor, Gilbert Hovey
b. Julian
b. Kazan, Elia
b. Milder-Hauptmann, Pauline Anna
b. Proclus Diadochus
b. Rossi-Lemeni, Nicola
b. Schildkraut, Rudolph
d. Constantine VI
d. Constantine XI Palaeologus
d. Gokalp, Mehmet Ziya

Diyarbakir, Anatolia, Turkey
b. Gokalp, Mehmet Ziya

Farghana, Turkey
b. Babur

Hemite, Turkey
b. Kemal, Yashar

Imvros, Turkey
b. Iakovos, Demetrios A Coucouzis, Archbishop

Islamkoy, Turkey
b. Demirel, Suleyman

Istanbul, Turkey
b. Ciller, Tansu
b. Cornfeld, Bernard
b. Dimitrios I, Patriarch
b. Ecevit, Bulent
b. Ertegun, Ahmet (Munir)
b. Halide Edip Adivar
b. Koruturk, Fahri S
b. Riklis, Meshulam
b. Yilmaz, Mesut
d. Ahmed Hasim
d. Athenagoras I
d. Dimitrios I, Patriarch
d. Halide Edip Adivar
d. Koruturk, Fahri S
d. Sunay, Cevdet

Izmir, Turkey
b. Seferiades, Giorgos Styljanou

Khorkom Vari, Turkey
b. Gorky, Arshile

Malatya, Turkey
b. Agca, Mehmet Ali
b. Ozal, Turgut

Marash, Turkey
b. Bagdikian, Ben Haig

Mugla, Turkey
b. Zaharoff, Basil, Sir

Nicomedia, Turkey
d. Constantine I

Salonika, Turkey
b. Ataturk, Kemal

Sinop, Turkey
b. Erbakan, Necmettin

Smyrna, Turkey
b. Balladur, Edouard
b. Brewer, David Josiah
b. Issigonis, Alec Arnold Constantine, Sir
b. Manoogian, Alex
b. Onassis, Aristotle Socrates
b. Sabbatai Zevi

Trabzon, Turkey
b. Sunay, Cevdet

Trebizona, Turkey
b. Suleiman I

TUVALU

Tawara, Tuvalu
b. Paeniu, Bikenibeu

UBANGI-SHARI

Bouchia, Ubangi-Shari
b. Dacko, David

UGANDA

d. Kiwanuka, Benedicto Kagima Mugumba

Akokoro, Uganda
b. Obote, Milton

Entebbe, Uganda
d. Netanyahu, Yonatan

Kisabwa, Uganda
b. Kiwanuka, Benedicto Kagima Mugumba

Kisule, Uganda
b. Nsubuga, Emmanuel, Cardinal

Koboko, Uganda
b. Amin, Idi

Ntungamo, Uganda
b. Museveni, Yoweri Kaguta

UKRAINE

Chaikine, Ukraine
b. Kuchma, Leonid Danylovich

Crimea, Ukraine
b. Tchernichowski, Saul Gutmanovich

Dnepropetrovsk, Ukraine
b. Baiul, Oksana

Dolina, Ukraine
b. Lubachivsky, Myroslav Ivan, Cardinal

Dub Makarenzi, Ukraine
b. Demjanjuk, John

Kalinovka, Ukraine
b. Khrushchev, Nikita Sergeyevich

Kamenets-Podolsk, Ukraine
b. Gorshkov, Sergei

Kharkov, Ukraine
b. Akimov, Nikolay Pavlovich
b. Tatlin, Vladimir Yevgrapovich

Kiev, Ukraine
b. Archipenko, Alexander Porfirievich
b. Ehrenfest-Afanaseva, Tatiana
b. Shestov, Lev

Kolomea, Ukraine
b. Feuermann, Emanuel

Mariupol, Ukraine
b. Zhdanov, Andrei Alexandrovich

Nikolayev, Ukraine
b. Breit, Gregory

Odessa, Ukraine
b. Gilels, Emil Grigoyevich
b. Malinovsky, Rodion Yakovlevich

Oratova, Ukraine
b. Eshkol, Levi

Pereyaslav, Ukraine
b. Chmielnicki, Bogdan

Priluki, Ukraine
b. Waksman, Selman Abraham

Sorochintsy, Ukraine
b. Gogol, Nikolai Vasilievich

Sosnytsia, Ukraine
b. Dovzhenko, Alexander

Velyky Zhytyn, Ukraine
b. Kravchuk, Leonid Makarovich

UNION OF SOVIET SOCIALIST REPUBLICS

b. Gordeeva, Ekaterina
b. Gutsu, Tatiana
b. Halfin, Eliezer
b. Kozyrev, Andrei Y
b. Kubasov, Valery Nikolaevich
b. Lonsdale, Gordon Arnold
b. Press, Irina Natanovna
b. Press, Tamara
b. Rodnina, Irina
b. Saneyev, Viktor
b. Shukshin, Vasilii Makarovich
b. Slavin, Mark
b. Tretiak, Vladislav
b. Zaitsev, Aleksandr
d. Fedorenko, Fyodor
d. Hvorostovsky, Dmitri
d. Kabalevsky, Dmitri Borisovich
d. Kogan, Leonid Borisovich
d. Kornilov, Lavr Georgyevich
d. Lysenko, Trofim Denisovich
d. Popova, Liubov Sergeevna
d. Vishnevsky, Alexandr Alekandrovich

Aktyubinsk, Union of Soviet Socialist Republics
b. Patsayev, Viktor Ivanovich

Alma-Ata, Union of Soviet Socialist Republics
b. Zhirinovsky, Vladimir

Amavir, Union of Soviet Socialist Republics
b. Avakian, George

Baku, Union of Soviet Socialist Republics
b. Kasparov, Garry Kimovich
b. Rostropovich, Mstislav Leopoldovich

Bar, Union of Soviet Socialist Republics
  b. Timerman, Jacobo

Barnaul, Union of Soviet Socialist Republics
  b. Streich, Rita

Bessarabia, Union of Soviet Socialist Republics
  b. Bertini, Gary

Biysk, Union of Soviet Socialist Republics
  b. Bessmertnykh, Aleksandr Aleksandrovich

Byelozerka, Union of Soviet Socialist Republics
  b. Bondarchuk, Sergei (Fedorovich)

Caucasus, Union of Soviet Socialist Republics
  b. Ilizarov, Gavril A

Chechelnik, Union of Soviet Socialist Republics
  b. Lispector, Clarice

Chita, Union of Soviet Socialist Republics
  b. Sobchak, Anatoly Aleksandrovich

Dmitrov, Union of Soviet Socialist Republics
  d. Kropotkin, Peter Alekseyevich, Prince

Dnepropetrovsk, Union of Soviet Socialist Republics
  b. Kogan, Leonid Borisovich

Dubinkino, Union of Soviet Socialist Republics
  b. Ligachev, Yegor (Kuzmich)

Dubrowna, Union of Soviet Socialist Republics
  b. Zeitlin, Zvi

Ekaterinburg, Union of Soviet Socialist Republics
  d. Alexandra Feodorovna
  d. Nicholas II
  d. Romanov, Anastasia

Engels, Union of Soviet Socialist Republics
  b. Schnittke, Alfred

Estonia, Union of Soviet Socialist Republics
  b. Schmemann, Alexander

Gorki, Union of Soviet Socialist Republics
  b. Ashkenazy, Vladimir Davidovich
  d. Lenin, Vladimir Ilyich
  d. Rakosi, Matyas

Gorlovka, Union of Soviet Socialist Republics
  b. Shevchenko, Arkady N(ikolayevich)

Grodno, Union of Soviet Socialist Republics
  b. Korbut, Olga

Grozny, Union of Soviet Socialist Republics
  b. Turischeva, Ludmila

Gzhatsk, Union of Soviet Socialist Republics
  b. Gagarin, Yuri Alexseyevich

Irkutsk, Union of Soviet Socialist Republics
  b. Nureyev, Rudolf (Hametovich)
  d. Kolchak, Aleksandr Vasilievich

Iskander, Union of Soviet Socialist Republics
  b. Dzhanibekov, Vladimir Alexandrovich

Izhevskoye, Union of Soviet Socialist Republics
  b. Tsiolkovsky, Konstantin Eduardovich

Kalinin District, Union of Soviet Socialist Republics
  b. Ogarkov, Nikolai

Kaluga, Union of Soviet Socialist Republics
  d. Tsiolkovsky, Konstantin Eduardovich

Kazakh, Union of Soviet Socialist Republics
  d. Komarov, Vladimir Mikhaylovich

Kazan, Union of Soviet Socialist Republics
  b. Aksyonov, Vassily Pavlovich
  b. Egorov, Youri

Khabarovsk, Union of Soviet Socialist Republics
  b. Kim Jong Il

Kharkov, Union of Soviet Socialist Republics
  b. Schneider, Alan

Kherson, Union of Soviet Socialist Republics
  b. Latynina, Larisa Semyonovna
  b. Shcherbo, Vitaly

Kiev, Union of Soviet Socialist Republics
  b. Kuznetsov, Anatoli Vasilievich
  d. Podgorny, Nikolai Viktorovich

Kislovodsk, Union of Soviet Socialist Republics
  b. Solzhenitsyn, Aleksandr (Isayevich)

Krasnaya Gorka, Union of Soviet Socialist Republics
  b. Dobrynin, Anatoly Fedorovich

Krasnoarmeyskoye, Union of Soviet Socialist Republics
  b. Chukarin, Viktor Ivanovich

Kreminiecz, Union of Soviet Socialist Republics
  b. Stern, Isaac

Kuntsevo, Union of Soviet Socialist Republics
  d. Andropov, Yuri Vladimirovich

Kurgan, Union of Soviet Socialist Republics
  d. Ilizarov, Gavril A

Leningrad, Union of Soviet Socialist Republics
  b. Berman, Lazar
  b. Brodsky, Joseph (Alexandrovich)
  b. Ginzburg, Aleksandr Ilich
  b. Grebenshikov, Boris
  b. Grigorovich, Yuri Nikolaevich
  b. Krikalev, Sergei
  b. Makarova, Natalia
  b. Obraztsova, Elena
  b. Protopopov, Oleg Alekseevich
  b. Shafran, Daniel
  b. Shostakovich, Maxim
  b. Spassky, Boris Vasilyevich
  b. Szewinska, Irena Kirszenstein
  b. Vishnevskaya, Galina (Pavlovna)
  d. Bilibin, Ivan Iakolevich
  d. Esenin, Sergei Aleksandrovich
  d. Gumilev, Nikolai
  d. Kirov, Sergei Mironovich
  d. Kuprin, Aleksandr Ivanovich
  d. Malevich, Kasimir Severinovich
  d. Mravinsky, Eugene
  d. Pavlov, Ivan Petrovich
  d. Plekhanov, Georgi Valentinovich
  d. Rudenko, Lyudmila

Listvyanka, Union of Soviet Socialist Republics
  b. Leonov, Alexei Arkhipovich

Mamati, Union of Soviet Socialist Republics
  b. Shevardnadze, Eduard Amvrosiyevich

Maslennikovo, Union of Soviet Socialist Republics
  b. Tereshkova-Nikolaeva, Valentina

Melitopol, Union of Soviet Socialist Republics
  b. Chukrai, Grigori

Moscow, Union of Soviet Socialist Republics
  b. Amalrik, Andrei Alekseyevich
  b. Arbatov, Georgi
  b. Bessmertnova, Natalya (Igorevna)
  b. Biryukova, Aleksandra Pavlovna
  b. Bonner, Yelena
  b. Bukovsky, Vladimir

Sheker Village, Union of Soviet Socialist Republics
  b. Aitmatov, Chingiz

Shorshely, Union of Soviet Socialist Republics
  b. Nikolayev, Andriyan Grigoryevich

Siberia, Union of Soviet Socialist Republics
  d. Babel, Isaac Emmanuelovich
  d. Kulish, Mykola

Snovsk, Union of Soviet Socialist Republics
  b. Olitski, Jules

Sverdlovsk, Union of Soviet Socialist Republics
  b. Yeltsin, Boris (Nikolayevich)

Tashkent, Union of Soviet Socialist Republics
  b. Bronfman, Yefim
  d. Shastri, Lal Badahur

Tbilisi, Union of Soviet Socialist Republics
  b. Aganbegyan, Abel Gezevich
  b. Petrosian, Tigran Vartanovich

Tiflis, Union of Soviet Socialist Republics
  b. Medvedev, Zhores Aleksandrovich
  b. Taktakishvili, Otar Vasilevich
  b. Ter-Arutunian, Rouben

Ufa, Union of Soviet Socialist Republics
  b. Spivakov, Valdimir (Teodorovich)

Ukraine, Union of Soviet Socialist Republics
  b. Shcharansky, Anatoly Borisovich

Ulyanousk, Union of Soviet Socialist Republics
  b. Protopopov, Ludmilla Evgenievna Belousova

Usman, Union of Soviet Socialist Republics
  b. Basov, Nikolai Gennadievich

Verkhneye, Union of Soviet Socialist Republics
  b. Titov, Gherman Stepanovich

Veshenskaya, Union of Soviet Socialist Republics
  d. Sholokhov, Mikhail Aleksandrovich

Vilna, Union of Soviet Socialist Republics
  b. Panov, Valery

Vladivostok, Union of Soviet Socialist Republics
  d. Mandelstam, Osip Emilyevich

Voronezh, Union of Soviet Socialist Republics
  b. Feoktistov, Konstantin Petrovich

Voroshilovgrad, Union of Soviet Socialist Republics
  b. Bubka, Sergei (Nazarovich)

Vtoraya Rechka, Union of Soviet Socialist Republics
  d. Mandelstam, Osip Emilyevich

Yalta, Union of Soviet Socialist Republics
  d. Rebikov, Vladimir Ivanovich
  d. Togliatti, Palmiro

Yaroslavl, Union of Soviet Socialist Republics
  b. Lyubimov, Yuri Petrovich

Yelabuga, Union of Soviet Socialist Republics
  d. Tsvetaeva, Marina Ivanovna

Zima, Union of Soviet Socialist Republics
  b. Evtushenko, Evgeniy Alexandrovich
  b. Yevtushenko, Yevgeny

Zlatoust, Union of Soviet Socialist Republics
  b. Karpov, Anatoly Yevgenyevich

UNITED ARAB EMIRATES

Abu Dhabi, United Arab Emirates
  b. Nahayan, Zayed bin al-, Sultan

UNITED STATES

  b. Albert, Marv(in Philip)
  b. Beaver Brown Band
  b. Belew, Adrian
  b. Belle, Regina
  b. Ben & Jerry
  b. Berlin, Ellin (Mackay)
  b. Bible, Alan
  b. Big Foot
  b. Bingham, Barry
  b. Black Elk
  b. Black Kettle
  b. Blues Brothers, The
  b. BoDeans
  b. Brenner, Eleanor P
  b. Burns, James MacGregor
  b. Buttafuoco, Mary Jo
  b. Cameron, Candace
  b. Carter, Stephen L(isle)
  b. Coulier, Dave
  b. Daly, Mary
  b. Danvers, Dennis
  b. Dlugacz, Judy
  b. Freedman, Marcia
  b. Garrow, David J
  b. Gates, Daryl F
  b. Geary, Cynthia
  b. Gebbie, Kristine
  b. Geiger, Ken
  b. George, Clair

  b. Gibbons, Leeza
  b. Gilbert, Sara
  b. Ginsburg, Charles P
  b. Gist, Carole Anne-Marie
  b. Goerlich, John
  b. Goldman, Francisco
  b. Goldmark, Josephine
  b. Goodrich, Bert
  b. Goranson, Lecy
  b. Green, Brian Austin
  b. Greenberg, Stanley B
  b. Grentz, Theresa Shank
  b. Hall, Edd
  b. Hall, Rich
  b. Hardison, Kadeem
  b. Harley, Bill
  b. Harrell, Andre (O'Neal)
  b. Harris, Robert Alton
  b. Hay, John
  b. Healey, Jack
  b. Hensel *Abigail and Brittany*
  b. Henson, Maria
  b. Hervey, Jason
  b. Higgins, William R
  b. Holloway, Wanda
  b. Hooks, Jan
  b. Horovitz, Adam
  b. Horton, Willie
  b. Hudson, Walter
  b. Humphry, Ann Wickett
  b. Hunt, Marsha
  b. Hunter, Madeline Cheek
  b. Ising, Rudolf C
  b. Jacobsen, David P
  b. Jen, Gish
  b. Jones, Star(let Marie)
  b. Jones, Stormie
  b. Karn, Richard
  b. Kelley, Sheila
  b. Kimbrough, Charles
  b. King, Rodney G
  b. Kiplinger, Knight A
  b. Kitaen, Tawny
  b. Koon, Stacey C.
  b. Korda, Michael
  b. Kressy, Edmund
  b. Laettner, Christian
  b. La Haye, Beverly
  b. Lardner, George, Jr.
  b. Laub, Larry
  b. Lauer, Matt
  b. Lauria, Dan
  b. Lavin, Christine
  b. Lawrence, Joey
  b. Lawrence-Lightfoot, Sara
  b. Lazarus, Charles P
  b. Leavitt, Mike
  b. Leavitt, Ron
  b. Lee, Joie
  b. Lennon, Jimmy, Sr.
  b. Leon, Kenny
  b. Levin, Jeremy
  b. Levine, Kathy
  b. Levine, Stuart R
  b. Levy, Allan
  b. Lewis, David
  b. Lewis, Reggie
  b. Liedtke, William C, Jr.
  b. Lipton, Eric
  b. Locklear, Arlinda Faye
  b. Loughlin, Lori
  b. MacDonald, Elizabeth G.
  b. MacKinnon, Catharine A(lice)
  b. Malandro, Kristina
  b. Mallon, Meg
  b. Malone, Dan

Foley, Alabama
b. Stabler, Ken(neth Michael)
d. Coggeshall, L(owell) T(helwell)

Fort Decatur, Alabama
d. Sevier, John

Fort Payne, Alabama
b. Johnson, James Ralph
b. Nelson, Larry Gene
b. Ober, Philip (Nott)

Gadsden, Alabama
b. Cox, Jean
b. Harris, Alice
b. Patrick, Jennie R.
d. Rains, Albert McKinley

Garland, Alabama
b. Shavers, Ernie

Georgiana, Alabama
b. Williams, Hank

Greensboro, Alabama
b. Hobson, Richmond Pearson
b. Sawyer, Eugene, Jr.

Grove Hill, Alabama
b. Mathews, Forrest David

Groveoak, Alabama
b. Rains, Albert McKinley

Guntersville, Alabama
d. Huie, William Bradford

Haleyville, Alabama
b. Hasford, Jerry Gustav

Harlan, Alabama
b. Black, Hugo LaFayette

Hartford, Alabama
b. Wynn, Early

Hartselle, Alabama
b. Huie, William Bradford

Holly Pond, Alabama
b. Hunt, Guy

Hueytown, Alabama
b. Allison, Bobby

Huntsville, Alabama
b. Allen, Viola Emily
b. Bankhead, Tallulah Brockman
b. Lowery, Joseph E
d. Atkinson, Brooks
d. Sparkman, John Jackson

Jackson, Alabama
b. Lynne, Shelby
b. Mathews, Mitford M

Jasper, Alabama
b. Holliday, Polly Dean

Lanett, Alabama
b. Fuller, Millard (Dean)

Leeds, Alabama
b. Barkley, Charles Wade

Lexington, Alabama
b. Louis, Joe

Linden, Alabama
b. Abernathy, Ralph David

Lipscomb, Alabama
b. Hill, Virginia

Marion, Alabama
b. King, Coretta Scott
b. Young, Jean Childs

Mathews, Alabama
b. Rhodes, Dusty

Mobile, Alabama
b. Aaron, Hank
b. Andrews, Mary Raymond Shipman
b. Belmont, Alva Erskine Smith
Vanderbilt
b. Benjamin, Regina (M.)
b. Campbell, William Edward March
b. Cottrell, Comer J(oseph), Jr.
b. Denton, Jeremiah Andrew, Jr.
b. Europe, James Reese
b. Gorgas, William Crawford
b. McCovey, Willie Lee
b. Newman, Joseph Westley
b. Paige, Satchel
b. Reese, Don(ald Francis)
b. Smith, Ozzie
b. Williams, Cootie
d. Semmes, Raphael
d. Sewell, Joe

Monroeville, Alabama
b. Collins, Marva Deloise Nettles
b. Lee, Harper
b. Malone, Vivian
b. Tucker, Cynthia (Anne)

Montgomery, Alabama
b. Butler, Brett
b. Carr, Henry
b. Cater, Douglass
b. Cole, Nat King
b. Fitzgerald, Zelda
b. Franklin, Melvin
b. Hill, Lester
b. Julian, Percy Lavon
b. King, Martin Luther, III
b. King, Yolanda Denise
b. McKinnon, Isaiah
b. Nixon, E(dgar) D(aniel)
b. Starr, Bart
b. Tennille, Toni
b. Thornton, Willie Mae
b. Wilson, Willie James
d. Hill, Lester
d. Nixon, E(dgar) D(aniel)
d. Wallace, George C(orley)
d. Wallace, Lurleen Burns
d. Yancey, William Lowndes

Montgomery County, Alabama
b. Owsley, Frank Lawrence

Morgan County, Alabama
b. Jones, Dean Carroll
b. Sparkman, John Jackson

Moscow, Alabama
b. Bankhead, William Brockman

Mount Meigs, Alabama
b. Dees, Morris S(eligman), Jr.

Mount Willing, Alabama
b. Moorer, Thomas H(inman)

Mugler, Alabama
b. Shuttlesworth, Fred Lee

Nokomis, Alabama
b. Murray, Albert L(ee)

Northport, Alabama
b. Lary, Frank Strong

Phoenix City, Alabama
b. Hawkins, Osie Penman, Jr.

Piper, Alabama
b. Davis, Lorenzo

Portersville, Alabama
b. Keener, Jefferson Ward

Prattville, Alabama
b. Pickett, Wilson

Ragland, Alabama
b. York, Rudy

Red Level, Alabama
b. Terry, Luther Leonidas

Rockville, Alabama
b. Hilliard, David

Samson, Alabama
b. Yates, Bill

Seale, Alabama
b. Smith, Holland McTeire

Selma, Alabama
b. Connor, Bull
b. Gilmore, Eddy Lanier King
d. Liuzzo, Viola

Shelby City, Alabama
b. Walthall, Henry B

Siluria, Alabama
b. O'Donnell, Cathy

Sweet Water, Alabama
b. Logan, Onnie Lee

Sylacauga, Alabama
b. Nabors, Jim

Tallassee, Alabama
b. Judkins, Reba

Titus, Alabama
b. Sewell, Joe

Troy, Alabama
b. Davenport, Willie D
b. Lewis, John Robert

d. McFarland, Ernest William
d. Miranda, Ernesto
d. Moley, Raymond Charles
d. O'Connor, Basil
d. Rausch, James Stevens
d. Russell, Andy
d. Vlasic, Joseph
d. Wright, Frank Lloyd
d. Wrigley, William, Jr.

Prescott, Arizona
b. DeCamp, Rosemary
b. Denny, John Allen
b. Silas, Paul Theron
b. Willis, Mary
d. Kleindienst, Richard Gordon
d. Ortiz, Peter J(ulien)
d. Sommer, Frederick

Sacaton, Arizona
b. Hayes, Ira Hamilton

Saint Johns, Arizona
b. Udall, Morris K(ing)
b. Udall, Stewart Lee

San Luis, Arizona
d. Chavez, Cesar (Estrada)

Sawmill, Arizona
b. Wauneka, Annie Dodge

Scottsdale, Arizona
d. Ameche, Don
d. Astaire, Adele
d. Bayne, Beverly Pearl
d. Conlan, Jocko
d. Crabbe, Buster
d. Crane, Bob
d. Dallis, Nicholas Peter
d. Davis, Loyal
d. Evans, Ronald Ellwin
d. Fiorito, Ted
d. Grimm, Charlie
d. Helmsley, Harry B(rakmann)
d. Hubbell, Carl Owen
d. Hynek, J(oseph) Allen
d. Isbell, Marion William
d. Kelland, Clarence Budington
d. O'Sullivan, Maureen
d. Roosevelt, Elliott
d. Rubicam, Raymond
d. Stoneham, Horace
d. Sunderland, Thomas E(lbert)
d. Swarthout, Glendon (Fred)

Second Mesa, Arizona
b. Loloma, Otellie

Sedona, Arizona
d. Pendleton, Don

Shongopavi, Arizona
b. Kabotie, Fred

Stanfield, Arizona
b. Zepeda, Ofelia

Sun City, Arizona
d. Jacuzzi, Candido

Sun City West, Arizona
d. Ode, Robert C

Tempe, Arizona
b. Finch, Robert H(utchison)
b. Hayden, Carl Trumball
d. Pyle, Howard

Tombstone, Arizona
d. Earp, Morgan
d. Ringo, John(ny)

Tucson, Arizona
b. Alexander, Sue
b. DeConcini, Dennis Webster
b. Eden, Barbara
b. Kay, Ulysses Simpson
b. Ronstadt, Linda
b. Strug, Kerri
d. Abbey, Edward
d. Allen, Rex E., Sr.
d. Ameche, Jim
d. Apache Kid
d. Bennett, Michael
d. Bok, Bart J(an)
d. Bordes, Francois
d. Calkins, Dick
d. Clinton, Larry
d. Donlon, Mary Honor
d. Douglass, Andrew Ellicott
d. Franken, Rose
d. Freyse, William
d. Gorin, Igor
d. Gould, Laurence M(cKinley)
d. Haury, Emil W
d. Hickey, Margaret A.
d. Krutch, Joseph Wood
d. Kuykendall, Ralph Simpson
d. Licavoli, Peter Joseph, Sr.
d. Lowden, Frank O(rren)
d. Marvin, Lee
d. Merrill, James (Ingram)
d. Miller, Olive Beaupre
d. Norstad, Lauris
d. Owens, Jesse
d. Pegler, Westbrook
d. Rockefeller, John D(avison), Jr.
d. Sanger, Margaret
d. Schottland, Charles I(rwin)
d. Sheil, Bernard James, Archbishop
d. Smallens, Alexander
d. Smith, Lowell Herbert
d. Smith, W(illiam) Eugene
d. Speare, Elizabeth George
d. Wood, Evelyn

White Cone, Arizona
b. Begay, Harrison

Wickenberg, Arizona
d. Northrop, John Howard

Wilcox, Arizona
b. Allen, Rex E., Sr.

Winslow, Arizona
b. Kleindienst, Richard Gordon

Yavapai County, Arizona
b. Behn, Harry

Yuma, Arizona
b. Chavez, Cesar (Estrada)

ARKANSAS
b. Clinton, Chelsea Victoria
b. Grisham, John

b. Hobson, Geary
b. Jones, Arthur A

Arkansas City, Arkansas
b. Johnson, John Harold

Black Oak, Arkansas
b. Mangrum, Jim Dandy
b. Reynolds, Ricky

Blytheville, Arkansas
b. Keohane, Nannerl Overholser
b. Walker, Junior

Bodcaw, Arkansas
b. Kelley, Virginia

Brinkley, Arkansas
b. Jordan, Louis

Camden, Arkansas
b. Pryor, David Hampton

Center Point, Arkansas
b. Shaver, Dorothy

Charleston, Arkansas
b. Bumpers, Dale Leon

Clifty, Arkansas
b. Vaughan, Arky

Combs, Arkansas
b. Faubus, Orval E(ugene)

Conway, Arkansas
d. Faubus, Orval E(ugene)

Crossett, Arkansas
b. Oslin, K(ay) T(oinette)
b. Switzer, Barry

De Witt, Arkansas
b. Holt, Ivan Lee

DeQueen, Arkansas
b. Bauer, Helen

Delight, Arkansas
b. Campbell, Glen Travis

Dumas, Arkansas
b. Hines, Jim

El Dorado, Arkansas
b. Brock, Lou(is Clark)
b. Portis, Charles
d. Rowe, Schoolboy

Elmar, Arkansas
b. Sykes, Roosevelt

Eros, Arkansas
b. Tomlin, Pinky

Eureka Springs, Arkansas
d. Castle, Irene Foote
d. Chisum, John Simpson

Fayetteville, Arkansas
b. Stone, Edward Durell

CALIFORNIA
- b. Allen, Elsie
- b. Bergeron, Victor J
- b. Burns, Diane M.
- b. Burum, Stephen H
- b. Castillo, Edward (Daniel)
- b. Childs, Toni
- b. Edmonds, Tracey
- b. Faustino, David
- b. Harper, Ben
- b. Lipkis, Andy
- b. Price, Steve
- b. Rutan, Dick
- b. Toone, Bill
- d. Bancroft, Hubert Howe
- d. Baskin, Burton
- d. Bennett, Harry Herbert
- d. Cubberley, Ellwood Patterson
- d. Fidler, Jimmie
- d. Halop, Billy
- d. Holling, Holling C(lancy)
- d. La Barba, Fidel
- d. Murnau, Friedrich W
- d. Rankin, J(ames) Lee
- d. Reynolds, Quentin James
- d. Ridge, John Rollin
- d. Robinson, Julia (Bowman)
- d. Schmiechen, Richard Kurt
- d. Serra, Junipero
- d. Yarnell, Bruce

Alameda, California
- b. Doolittle, James H(arold)
- b. Erickson, Leif
- b. Heidt, Horace Murray
- b. Knowland, William Fife
- b. Lewis, Wilmarth Sheldon
- b. VonSchmidt, Harold

Alcatraz, California
- d. Barker, Doc

Alhambra, California
- b. Dalrymple, G. Brent
- b. Tiegs, Cheryl
- b. Watkins, James (David)

Allegheny, California
- b. Weber, Lois

Alpha, California
- b. Nevada, Emma

Altadena, California
- b. Nixon, Marni
- b. Rosen, Nathaniel
- d. Akins, Claude
- d. Branzell, Karin
- d. Grey, Zane
- d. Hall, Lloyd Augustus
- d. LaMarr, Barbara

Anaheim, California
- b. Fender, Leo
- b. Huarte, John G
- b. Wilson, Marie (Katherine Elizabeth)
- d. Demara, Ferdinand Waldo, Jr.

Antioch, California
- b. Burke, Johnny
- b. Dragon, Carmen
- b. Marchetti, Gino

Apple Valley, California
- d. Buono, Victor
- d. Mangrum, Lloyd
- d. Rogers, Roy
- d. Sparks, Ned
- d. Thomas, John Charles

Arcadia, California
- b. Worrell, Todd Roland

Arroyo Grande, California
- b. Quimby, Harriet
- d. Saint Johns, Adela Rogers

Atherton, California
- d. Haider, Michael Lawrence

Atwater, California
- b. Hutchins, Will

Auburn, California
- b. Campbell, Ben Nighthorse
- d. Bible, Alan

Aurora, California
- d. Wood, Louise Aletha

Avalon, California
- b. Harrison, Gregory

Azusa, California
- d. Ritchey, George Willis

Bakersfield, California
- b. Deaver, Michael Keith
- b. Engle, Clair
- b. Haggard, Merle Ronald
- b. Madison, Guy
- b. Nofziger, Lyn
- b. Tibbett, Lawrence Mervil
- b. Trevino, Elizabeth Borton de
- b. Williams, Sherley Anne
- d. Shafter, William Rufus

Baldwin Hills, California
- d. Bubbles, John

Barstow, California
- b. Crain, Jeanne

Bay Island, California
- d. Modjeska, Helena

Beaumont, California
- b. Bottel, Helen Alfea

Bel Air, California
- d. Day, Dennis
- d. Hitchcock, Alfred Joseph, Sir
- d. Kelly, Nancy
- d. Kent, Arthur Atwater
- d. Mercer, Johnny
- d. Roach, Hal
- d. Tate, Sharon

Bell Station, California
- b. Hooper, Harry Bartholomew

Belvedere, California
- d. Vance, Vivian

Belvedere Gardens, California
- b. Costigan, James

Benicia, California
- b. Mizner, Addison

Berkeley, California
- b. Anderson, Melissa Sue
- b. Brower, David Ross
- b. Cheney, Sheldon Warren
- b. Clark, Marcia
- b. Culp, Robert
- b. Davies, Rodger Paul
- b. Fogerty, John
- b. Funikawa, Gyo
- b. Goulart, Ron(ald Joseph)
- b. Grassle, Karen Gene
- b. Hafey, Chick
- b. Ivory, James
- b. Keene, Christopher
- b. LeGuin, Ursula K(roeber)
- b. Lesh, Phil
- b. Martin, Billy
- b. Moody, Helen Wills
- b. Paine, Thomas Otten
- b. Profet, Margie
- b. Redman, Joshua
- b. Smith, Roger Guenveur
- b. Wilkes, Jamaal
- b. Zuniga, Daphne
- d. Alvarez, Luis W(alter)
- d. Arnon, Daniel I(srael)
- d. Bishop, Katharine Scott
- d. Calvin, Melvin
- d. Cheney, Sheldon Warren
- d. Compton, Arthur Holly
- d. Coolidge, Dane
- d. Cottrell, Frederick Gardner
- d. Dean, William Frishe
- d. Diebenkorn, Richard C.
- d. Evans, Herbert McLean
- d. Fergusson, Harvey
- d. Giauque, William Francis
- d. Gleason, Ralph Joseph
- d. Harris, Joseph Pratt
- d. Keith, William
- d. Kelsen, Hans
- d. Kroeber, Theodora Kracaw
- d. Li, C(hoh) H(ao)
- d. Lowie, Robert Harry
- d. Matthes, Francois-Emile
- d. Meiklejohn, Alexander
- d. Merriam, Clinton Hart
- d. Miles, Josephine
- d. Powdermaker, Hortense
- d. Scherr, Max
- d. Sproul, Robert Gordon
- d. Stern, Otto
- d. Struve, Otto
- d. Susskind, Walter
- d. Tarski, Alfred
- d. Thomas, W(illiam) I(saac)
- d. Tolman, Edward Chace

Berry Creek, California
- b. Day, Frank

Beverly Hills, California
- b. Barrymore, John Blythe Drew, Jr.
- b. Bergen, Candice
- b. Gilbert, Bruce
- b. Holt, Tim
- b. Rubinstein, John Arthur
- d. Adams, Nick
- d. Angeli, Pier

d. Arthur, Robert
d. Balderston, John Lloyd
d. Barnes, Binnie
d. Baruch, Andre
d. Baxter, Warner
d. Beery, Noah
d. Berman, Pandro Samuel
d. Bern, Paul
d. Bernie, Ben
d. Brackett, Charles
d. Brice, Fanny
d. Broderick, Helen
d. Brooks, Richard
d. Brown, Edmund G.
d. Burns, George
d. Cantor, Eddie
d. Carr, Allan
d. Castle, William
d. Chekhov, Michael
d. Cody, Lew
d. Collier, William, Sr.
d. Connolly, Walter
d. Craven, Frank
d. Dall, John
d. Dantine, Helmut
d. Diamond, I(sidore) A L
d. Duke, Doris
d. Ennis, Skinnay
d. Erwin, Stuart
d. Factor, Max
d. Farrow, John Villiers
d. Fazenda, Louise
d. Field, Rachel Lyman
d. Fields, Joseph
d. Fields, Lew Maurice
d. Finch, Peter
d. Fitzgerald, Ella
d. Foreman, Carl
d. Frank, Bruno
d. Frann, Mary
d. Gershwin, Ira
d. Giesler, Jerry
d. Gordon, Vera
d. Green, Johnny
d. Greenberg, Hank
d. Gruenberg, Louis
d. Hayward, Susan
d. Hearst, William Randolph
d. Hecht, Harold
d. Hersholt, Jean
d. Hitchcock, Raymond
d. Hudson, Rock
d. Huston, Walter
d. Ince, Thomas H(arper)
d. Iturbi, Amparo
d. Jaffe, Herb
d. Jaffe, Sam
d. Janis, Elsie
d. Kahn, Gus
d. Kamen, Milt
d. Kaper, Bronislau
d. Kelly, Gene
d. Kovacs, Ernie
d. Kuchel, Thomas H(enry)
d. LaRocque, Rod
d. Lasky, Jesse L(ouis)
d. Lawrence, Florence
d. Lazar, Irving Paul
d. Leary, Timothy (Francis)
d. Leonard, Sheldon
d. Leroy, Mervyn
d. Levant, Oscar
d. Lyman, Abe
d. Lynde, Paul Edward
d. Malle, Louis
d. Mann, Heinrich Ludwig

d. Marshall, Herbert
d. Martin, Dean
d. Mason, Pamela Helen
d. Maxwell, Marilyn
d. McCoy, Horace
d. McHugh, Jimmy
d. McRae, Carmen
d. Menjou, Adolphe Jean
d. Menzies, William Cameron
d. Minnelli, Vincente
d. Miranda, Carmen
d. Mitchell, Thomas
d. Morgan, Frank
d. Murphy, Jimmy
d. Newton, Robert
d. Norworth, Jack
d. Oldfield, Barney
d. Pal, George
d. Pan, Hermes
d. Pasternak, Joe
d. Pauley, Edwin Wendell
d. Powell, Eleanor
d. Rachmaninoff, Sergei Vasilyevich
d. Reed, Donna
d. Reeves, George
d. Renoir, Jean
d. Robinson, Edward G
d. Robson, May
d. Russell, Rosalind
d. Schafer, Natalie
d. Schenck, Joseph M
d. Seaton, George
d. Seville, David
d. Shore, Dinah
d. Siegel, Bugsy
d. Six, Robert Forman
d. Smith, C Aubrey
d. Stewart, Anita
d. Stewart, James (Maitland)
d. Thomas, Bill
d. Toler, Sidney
d. Tracy, Spencer Bonaventure
d. Velez, Lupe
d. Wald, Jerry
d. Walker, Stuart Armstrong
d. Walter, Bruno
d. Webb, Clifton
d. Webster, Paul Francois
d. Werfel, Franz
d. Whiting, Richard Armstrong
d. Whitty, May, Dame
d. Wyler, William
d. Wynn, Ed

Big Sur, California
d. Flory, Paul John
d. Pauling, Linus C(arl)

Bolinas, California
d. Brautigan, Richard

Borea, California
b. Hosmer, Craig

Boyle Heights, California
b. Olmos, Edward James

Bradbury, California
d. Thompson, Mickey

Brentwood, California
d. Andrews, LaVerne
d. Brown, Joe E(van)
d. Carey, Harry
d. Convy, Bert

d. Friedman, Stephen
d. Gleason, Lucille
d. Hamilton, Joe
d. Nolan, Lloyd
d. Paine, Thomas Otten
d. Schoenberg, Arnold
d. Sloane, Everett
d. Van Dyke, W(oodbridge) S(trong)
d. Wynn, Keenan

Brentwood Heights, California
d. Landis, Carole

Buena Park, California
b. Spenkelink, John Arthur
d. Knott, Walter

Burbank, California
b. Burton, Tim
b. Fisher, Carrie Frances
b. Gold, Andrew
b. Harmon, Mark
b. Howard, Clint
b. Kanaly, Steve(n Francis)
b. Moran, Erin
b. Otto, Whitney
b. Penn, Sean
b. Raitt, Bonnie
b. Ritter, John(athan Southworth)
d. Ackerman, Harry S
d. Arquette, Cliff
d. Avery, Tex
d. Bates, Florence
d. Calhoun, Rory
d. Connelly, Christopher
d. Conreid, Hans
d. Crosby, Gary
d. Disney, Roy O(liver)
d. Dixon, Willie (James)
d. Faylen, Frank
d. Hayes, Gabby
d. Iwerks, Ub(be)
d. Jeffries, James Jackson
d. Johnson, Clarence Leonard
d. Josefsberg, Milt
d. Lantz, Walter
d. Loo, Richard
d. Lupino, Ida
d. Matuszak, John (Daniel)
d. Murray, Ken
d. Nash, Clarence
d. Pyle, Denver
d. Quillan, Eddie
d. Richman, Harry
d. Rose, David
d. Schine, G(erard) David
d. Steele, Bob
d. Waterfield, Bob
d. Weaver, Doodles
d. Wilcoxon, Henry

Burlingame, California
d. Christensen, Lew Farr

Calabasas, California
d. Nelson, Gene

Calistoga, California
b. Vermeil, Dick
d. Hafey, Chick

Camarillo, California
d. Langan, Glenn

Cambria, California
d. Papashvily, George

Canoga Park, California
b. Cameron, Kirk
d. Hood, Darla Jean

Capistrano Beach, California
b. Alter, Hobie

Carmel, California
b. Sargent, Dick
d. Alinsky, Saul David
d. Andrews, Roy Chapman
d. Arthur, Jean
d. Bonestell, Chesley
d. Burgess, Gelett
d. Cone, Fairfax Mastick
d. Farina, Richard
d. Flavin, Martin Archer
d. Greene, Charles Sumner
d. Hatlo, Jimmy
d. Heinlein, Robert Anson
d. Jeffers, (John) Robinson
d. Moody, Helen Wills
d. Rankin, Jeannette
d. Remsen, Ira
d. Steffens, Lincoln
d. Van Niel, Cornelius B(ernardus)
d. Weston, Edward

Castaic, California
d. Morrow, Vic

Castle, California
d. Zambelli, Joseph

Catalina Island, California
d. Wood, Natalie

Cathedral City, California
d. Oakland, Simon

Century City, California
d. Bixby, Bill
d. Lancaster, Burt(on Stephen)

Chatsworth, California
d. Harman, Hugh
d. Henry, William M
d. Sabu
d. Waters, Ethel

Chico, California
b. Hayden, Russell

Claremont, California
b. Davis, Glenn W
b. McGwire, Mark (David)
d. Armour, Richard Willard
d. Bennett, John C(oleman)
d. Mason, Max
d. McFee, Henry Lee
d. Suckow, Ruth

Clear Lake, California
d. Burnette, Johnny

Clinton, California
b. Craft, Ellen

Coalinga, California
b. Stafford, Jo

Coleville, California
b. Dick, Lena Frank

Compton, California
b. Carpenter, Ken(neth)
b. Conner, Nadine
b. Dr. Dre
b. Eazy-E

Concord, California
b. Brubeck, Dave
b. Hanks, Tom

Corona, California
b. Parks, Michael
d. Grapewin, Charley
d. Soule, Olan

Coronado, California
d. Downs, Johnny
d. Haynes, Lloyd
d. Redenbacher, Orville

Corte Madera, California
d. McKernan, Ron

Costa Mesa, California
d. Beneke, Tex
d. Nolan, Bob

Covelo, California
b. Marks, Percy

Covina, California
b. Stafford, Jean

Cressy, California
b. Suzuki, Pat

Culver City, California
b. Carter, Gary Edmund
b. Lennon, Janet
b. Lowrey, Peanuts
b. Richards, Michael
b. Verdon, Gwen
d. Bigard, Albany Barney Leon
d. Chandler, Jeff
d. Conway, Tom
d. Korjus, Miliza
d. Robinson, Sugar Ray
d. Shearer, Douglas

Cypress, California
b. Woods, Tiger

Daly City, California
d. Williams, Tony

Death Valley, California
d. White, Leslie A(lvin)

Del Mar, California
d. Arnaz, Desi

Del Monte, California
b. Gilmore, Virginia

Delano, California
b. Rambo, Dack
b. Valdez, Luis (Miguel)
b. Valente, Benita
d. Rambo, Dack

Denny, California
d. Flanders, Ed

Desert Hot Springs, California
d. Langley, Noel

Diamond Bar, California
d. Martin, Louis E.

Downey, California
d. Brasselle, Keefe
d. Carpenter, Karen (Anne)

Dry Creek Valley, California
d. Burr, Raymond (William Stacy)

Duarte, California
b. Adamek, Donna
d. Dubridge, L(ee) A(lvin)
d. Exner, Judith Campbell

Durango, California
b. Tully, Tom

Eagleville, California
d. Vaughan, Arky

East Oakland, California
b. Pointer, Anita
b. Pointer, Bonnie
b. Pointer, June
b. Pointer, Ruth

Edwards Air Force Base, California
d. Lawrence, Robert (Henry), Jr.

El Centro, California
b. Cher
b. Howard, Ken(neth Joseph, Jr.)
d. West, Nathanael

El Cerrito, California
d. Einstein, Alfred
d. McMillan, Edwin Mattison

El Monte, California
b. McDonald, Country Joe
b. Wiggins, Charles Edward

Encino, California
b. Breathed, Berke
b. Kudrow, Lisa
b. Ovitz, Michael S.
b. Zimbalist, Stephanie
d. Abell, George O(gden)
d. Ball, John Dudley, Jr.
d. Breneman, Tom
d. Burroughs, Edgar Rice
d. Cabot, Susan
d. Carlson, Richard
d. Carson, Jack
d. Cowan, Jerome
d. Dmytryk, Edward
d. Gobel, George Leslie
d. Goren, Charles Henry
d. Hackett, Joan
d. Hartman, Phil
d. Horton, Edward Everett
d. Jordan, Marian Driscoll
d. Marshall, Tully
d. Powers, Francis Gary
d. Talman, William
d. Tuttle, Lurene

b. Yardley, George Harry
b. Zappa, Moon Unit
d. Adler, Buddy
d. Adler, Polly
d. Adrian
d. Albertson, Jack
d. Alexander, Ben
d. Allen, Gracie Ethel Cecil Rosaline
d. Atwill, Lionel
d. Baer, Max
d. Bainter, Fay Okell
d. Barrymore, Ethel Mae Blythe
d. Barrymore, John
d. Baum, L(yman) Frank
d. Baum, Vicki
d. Beavers, Louise
d. Begley, Ed(ward James)
d. Belushi, John
d. Bitzer, George William
d. Blackstone, Harry
d. Bledsoe, Jules
d. Blore, Eric
d. Bondi, Beulah
d. Borg, Veda Ann
d. Borzage, Frank
d. Breen, Joseph Ignatius
d. Brendel, El(mer)
d. Bruce, Lenny
d. Byington, Spring
d. Cambridge, Godfrey
d. Canova, Judy
d. Carmel, Roger C
d. Carroll, Leo G
d. Carter, Boake
d. Castelnuovo-Tedesco, Mario
d. Castle, Peggie
d. Chandler, Dorothy (Buffum)
d. Chase, Charley
d. Clive, Colin
d. Columbo, Russ
d. Conklin, Chester
d. Cooper, Gary
d. Costello, Maurice
d. Crawford, Sam(uel Earl)
d. Curtiz, Michael
d. Dailey, Dan
d. Dalmores, Charles
d. Darin, Bobby
d. Davies, Marion
d. DeForest, Lee
d. Dekker, Albert
d. DeMille, Cecil B(lount)
d. Dolly, Jenny
d. Donnell, Jeff
d. Douglas, Paul
d. Dreiser, Theodore
d. Duel, Peter
d. Eaton, Mary
d. Edeson, Robert
d. Edwards, Cliff
d. Emerson, Hope
d. Fitzgerald, F(rancis) Scott (Key)
d. Flippen, Jay C
d. Flowers, Wayland Parrott, Jr.
d. Foxx, Redd
d. Friml, Rudolf
d. Gable, Clark
d. Garland, Hamlin
d. Gershwin, George
d. Gilbert, Billy
d. Goulding, Edmund
d. Grauman, Sid(ney Patrick)
d. Gray, Gilda
d. Green, Martyn
d. Griffith, D(avid Lewelyn) W(ark)
d. Hackett, Raymond

d. Hale, Alan
d. Hardin, Tim
d. Head, Edith
d. Heflin, Van Emmett Evan
d. Hellinger, Mark
d. Herbert, Hugh
d. Herriman, George
d. Hoffenstein, Samuel Goodman
d. Holmes, Burton
d. Holmes, Taylor
d. Hopper, Hedda
d. Howard, Moe
d. Howard, Shemp
d. Howe, James Wong
d. Irene
d. James, Art
d. James, Will(iam Roderick)
d. Jefferson, Thomas
d. Jones, Isham
d. Joplin, Janis
d. Joyce, Alice
d. Keaton, Buster
d. Kelly, Patsy
d. Kelly, Walt(er Crawford)
d. Kenton, Stan(ley Newcomb)
d. Kilian, Victor
d. Kirby, John
d. Korngold, Erich Wolfgang
d. Laemmle, Carl, Sr.
d. Lesser, Sol
d. Lincoln, Elmo
d. Little, Little Jack
d. Lloyd, Harold
d. Lorre, Peter
d. Marx, Chico
d. Marx, Harpo
d. McDaniel, Hattie
d. McDevitt, Ruth
d. McIntyre, Hal
d. Monroe, Marilyn
d. Mowbray, Alan
d. Nazimova, Alla
d. Nelson, Ozzie
d. Newman, Alfred
d. O'Brien, Willis Harold
d. O'Connell, Hugh
d. Oliver, Edna May
d. Orry-Kelly
d. Patrick, Gail
d. Perkins, Anthony
d. Pitts, Zasu
d. Post, Marjorie Merriweather
d. Powell, Dick
d. Power, Tyrone
d. Pyne, Joe
d. Raft, George
d. Ragland, Rags
d. Rankin, Arthur
d. Redman, Ben Ray
d. Saint Cyr, Lillian
d. Scheuer, Philip K(latz)
d. Schumann-Heink, Ernestine Rossler
d. Selznick, David O(liver)
d. Sheridan, Ann
d. Sherman, Lowell
d. Shields, Larry
d. Skolsky, Sidney
d. Steiner, Max
d. Stevens, Inger
d. Stompanato, Johnny
d. Sullivan, C(harles) Gardner
d. Taylor, Estelle
d. Taylor, William Desmond
d. Tilden, Bill
d. Tobias, George
d. Toland, Gregg

d. Turner, Joe
d. Vallee, Rudy
d. Veidt, Conrad
d. Vincent, Gene
d. VonSternberg, Josef
d. Waldron, Charles D
d. Wallace, Edgar
d. Walter, Eugene
d. Warner, Harry Morris
d. Webster, Ben(jamin)
d. West, Mae
d. Whale, James
d. Wood, Samuel Grosvenor
d. Wright, Cobina
d. Ziegfeld, Flo(renz)
d. Zucco, George

Hollywood Hills, California
d. Fuller, Samuel
d. Inge, William Motter
d. Oates, Warren
d. Scala, Gia
d. Wilson, Marie (Katherine Elizabeth)

Holmby Hills, California
d. Disney, Lillian
d. Lee, Dixie
d. Livingstone, Mary
d. Thornton, Charles Bates

Huntington, California
d. Green, Mitzi

Huntington Beach, California
d. Darro, Frankie
d. Kelly, Jack

Ignacio Valley, California
d. Walker, Joseph Reddeford

Indian Wells, California
d. Lake, Arthur

Indio, California
d. Carey, William F
d. Cochran, Jacqueline
d. Odlum, Floyd Bostwick
d. Van Druten, John William

Inglewood, California
b. Banks, Tyra
b. De Young, Cliff
b. Lawrence, Vicki Ann
b. Sims, Zoot
d. Bell, Ricky Lynn
d. Blocker, Dan
d. Childress, Alvin
d. Condon, Jackie
d. Lowrey, Peanuts
d. O'Brien, Edmond
d. Peckinpah, Sam

Irvine, California
b. Colonius, Lillian
d. Bailey, Raymond

Isleton, California
b. Morita, Pat

Jackson, California
b. Aitkin, Robert Grant

Jonesboro, California
b. Rivers, Thomas Milton

Joshua Tree, California
d. Parsons, Gram

Julian, California
d. Rumann, Sig(fried)

Kingsberg, California
b. Pickens, Slim

La Habre, California
b. Coy, Harold

La Jolla, California
b. Peck, Gregory
b. Robertson, Cliff
d. Baillie, Hugh
d. Brink, Carol Ryrie
d. Bullard, Edward Crisp, Sir
d. Chandler, Raymond Thornton
d. Cole, Kenneth Stewart
d. Daugherty, Carroll Roop
d. Ehricke, Krafft Arnold
d. Foster, Preston
d. Galli-Curci, Amelita
d. Gray, Harold Lincoln
d. McGill, William James
d. Menard, H William
d. Miller, Max (Carlton)
d. Naish, J(oseph) Carrol
d. Parks, Bert
d. Rogers, Carl Ransom
d. Salk, Jonas E(dward)
d. Seuss, Doctor
d. Shawn, Dick
d. Stone, Milburn
d. Szilard, Leo
d. Urey, Harold Clayton
d. Wilder, Robert Ingersoll
d. Wright, Harold Bell

La Mesa, California
b. Walton, Bill
d. Booth, Charles Brandon
d. Wieghorst, Olaf

La Mirada, California
b. Neff, Wallace

La Quinta, California
d. Arzner, Dorothy
d. Capra, Frank

Lafayette, California
d. Seaborg, Glenn T(heodore)
d. Segre, Emilio Gino

Laguna Beach, California
d. Ames, Leon
d. McIntire, John
d. Nelson, Harriet
d. Roman, Ruth
d. Stace, W(alter) T(erence)
d. Summerville, Slim

Laguna Hills, California
d. Mallory, L(ester) D(ewitt)
d. Nelson, Christian
d. Patrick, Lee

Laguna Niguel, California
d. Armstrong, Jack Lawrence
d. Friebus, Florida

Lagunitas, California
d. Kinski, Klaus

Lake Elsinore, California
d. Merrill, Henry Tindall

Lancaster, California
d. Stevens, George (Cooper)

Larkspur, California
d. Gomez, Lefty

Leucadia, California
d. Riggs, Bobby

Lincoln, California
b. Clark, Fred

Linden, California
b. Kuykendall, Ralph Simpson

Livermore, California
b. Davis, Mark William

Lodi, California
b. Cartwright, Bill

Loma Linda, California
b. Modine, Matthew
d. Blackstone, Harry, Jr.

Long Beach, California
b. Anderson, Jack Northman
b. Bartlett, Jennifer Losch
b. Britton, Barbara
b. Cage, Nicolas
b. Costle, Douglas Michael
b. Derek, Bo
b. Forbes, Jack D(ouglas)
b. Garver, Kathy
b. Gortner, Marjoe (Hugh Ross)
b. Irwin, Robert
b. Jaeckel, Richard (Hanley)
b. Jones, Spike
b. Kellerman, Sally Claire
b. King, Billie Jean
b. Okamura, Arthur
b. Phillips, Michelle Gillam
b. Ridgeway, Rick
b. Rigby, Cathy
b. Rippy, Rodney Allen
b. Ryan, Peggy
b. Saint James, Susan
b. Snoop Doggy Dogg
b. Sperling, Godfrey, Jr.
b. Warmerdam, Dutch
b. Zerbe, Anthony
d. Andrus, Ethel Percy
d. Hilton, James
d. Lemon, Bob
d. Lynch, David
d. Merriam, Frank Finley
d. Monroe, Marion
d. Zamboni, Frank J

Los Alamitos, California
d. Andrews, (Carver) Dana

Los Altos, California
d. Lewis, Janet

Los Angeles, California
b. Abdul, Paula (Julie)
b. Abell, George O(gden)
b. Achtenberg, Roberta
b. Ackerman, Forest J
b. Albert, Edward Laurence
b. Alpert, Herb
b. Alvin, Dave
b. Araki, Gregg
b. Archer, Anne
b. Arnaz, Desi(derio Alberto IV), J
b. Ash, Roy Lawrence
b. Ashford, Emmett Littleton
b. Astin, Mackenzie Alexander
b. Auger, Arleen
b. Ayers, Roy
b. Babbitt, Bruce E(dward)
b. Baby Leroy
b. Bainter, Fay Okell
b. Barnes, Billy
b. Barrymore, Drew
b. Baxter, Meredith
b. Beard, Matthew, Jr.
b. Beatty, Roger
b. Beck
b. Begley, Ed, Jr.
b. Benet, Brenda
b. Beradino, John
b. Berkeley, Busby
b. Berry, Jan
b. Billingsley, Barbara
b. Bloomingdale, Betsy
b. Blythe, Betty
b. Bond, Victoria
b. Bonet, Lisa
b. Bonham, Frank
b. Bono, Chastity
b. Bonoff, Karla
b. Boone, Richard
b. Breedlove, Craig
b. Brennan, Eileen Regina
b. Bridges, Beau
b. Bridges, Jeff
b. Brolin, James
b. Brooks, Albert (Lawrence Einstein)
b. Brown, Judie
b. Brown, Ron(ald James)
b. Burden, Carter
b. Burke, Yvonne Watson Brathwaite
b. Burrows, James
b. Busby, Jheryl
b. Buscaglia, Leo
b. Butler, Brett
b. Butler, Robert
b. Cage, John
b. Calhoun, Rory
b. Cannell, Stephen Joseph
b. Carradine, Robert Reed
b. Carrillo, Leo
b. Cassidy, Shaun Paul
b. Castro, George (A.)
b. Chamberlain, Richard
b. Champion, Marge Celeste
b. Chandler, Otis
b. Chaplin, Sydney
b. Clark, Eleanor
b. Cobbs, Price M(ashaw)
b. Cohn, Mindy
b. Cole, Natalie
b. Collett, Wayne
b. Condon, Jackie
b. Constantine, Eddie
b. Cooder, Ry(land Peter)

b. Coogan, Jackie
b. Coolio
b. Coombs, Charles Ira
b. Cooper, Jackie
b. Costello, Chris
b. Crenna, Richard
b. Crosby, Cathy Lee
b. Crosby, David (Van Cortlandt)
b. Crosby, Mary Frances
b. Crosby, Nathaniel
b. Crouch, Andrae Edward
b. Crouch, Stanley
b. Curtis, Jamie Lee
b. Davis, Edward Michael
b. Davis, Eric Keith
b. Davis, Patti
b. Davis, Peter Frank
b. Dee, Frances
b. DeHaven, Gloria
b. De La Hoya, Oscar
b. DeLavallade, Carmen
b. DeLugg, Milton
b. Densmore, John
b. De Patie, David H
b. Disney, Roy E(dward)
b. Doerr, Bobby
b. Dolenz, Mickey
b. Eckstein, George
b. Edelin, Ramona Hoage
b. Einstein, Bob
b. Ellis, Bret Easton
b. Ellis, Dock Phillip, Jr.
b. Farnsworth, Richard
b. Farrow, Mia
b. Fears, Tom
b. Fielder, Cecil Grant
b. Fields, Kim
b. Flake, Floyd H(arold)
b. Fleming, Rhonda
b. Fonda, Bridget
b. Foster, Jodie
b. Fraker, William A
b. Francis, Genie
b. Fratianne, Linda
b. Freeman, Seth
b. French, Victor
b. Gable, John Clark
b. Gardner, John William
b. Garrett, Mike
b. Gautier, Dick
b. Gavin, John Anthony Golenor
b. Getty, Gordon Peter
b. Gilbert, Melissa
b. Gless, Sharon
b. Goldsmith, Jerry
b. Goldwater, Barry M(orris), Jr.
b. Gonzalez, Pancho
b. Goodrich, Gail Charles
b. Gordon, Dexter Keith
b. Gordon, Joe
b. Grahame, Gloria
b. Granz, Norman
b. Graver, Elizabeth
b. Greenwood, Lee
b. Gregory, Cynthia Kathleen
b. Grey, Virginia
b. Gwynn, Tony
b. Haack, Morton R
b. Haines, Randa
b. Haldeman, H(arry) R(obbins)
b. Hale, Alan, Jr.
b. Haley, Jack, Jr.
b. Hamilton, Joe
b. Hannum, Alex(ander Murray)
b. Harrison, Kathryn
b. Harryhausen, Ray

b. Hayward, Brooke
b. Hensley, Pamela Gail
b. Hickman, Darryl
b. Hickman, Dwayne B
b. Hill, Lynn
b. Hillman, Chris
b. Hills, Carla Anderson
b. Hoffman, Dustin (Lee)
b. Hoffs, Susanna
b. Horner, James
b. Horton, Robert
b. Hunt, Helen
b. Huston, Anjelica
b. Hwang, David Henry
b. Ice Cube
b. Ito, Lance
b. Jackson, Sheneska
b. James, Etta
b. Janov, Arthur
b. Johnson, Bill
b. Johnson, Cornelius
b. Jones, Jack
b. Jones, Jerry
b. Jones, Marion (Patrick)
b. Jones, Robert C
b. Joyner, Florence Griffith
b. Judd, Ashley
b. Kassorla, Irene Chamie
b. Katt, William
b. Kavner, Julie Deborah
b. Keaton, Diane
b. Kemp, Jack
b. Kert, Larry
b. Kilmer, Val
b. King, Cammie
b. Kirk, Ruth Kratz
b. Kirkwood, James
b. Klein, Herbert George
b. Knight, Suge
b. Kohner, Susan
b. Krenwinkel, Patricia
b. Krieger, Robby
b. Ladd, Alan Walbridge, Jr.
b. LaDuke, Winona
b. Lahr, John
b. Lamb, Willis Eugene, Jr.
b. Laurel, Alicia Bay
b. Lee, Michele
b. Leigh, Jennifer Jason
b. LeMond, Greg(ory James)
b. Lennon, Dianne
b. Lennon, Peggy
b. Lenz, Kay
b. Leslie, Lisa
b. Lewis, Flora
b. Lewis, Henry (Jay)
b. Lewis, Juliette
b. Lewis, Roger
b. Lindley, Audra
b. Livingston, Barry
b. Livingston, Stanley
b. Lobel, Arnold Stark
b. Locklear, Heather
b. Love, Mike
b. Luft, Lorna
b. Lynn, Diana
b. MacArthur, James
b. Maiman, Theodore Harold
b. Marin, Richard
b. Martin, Quinn
b. Matheson, Tim
b. McCallister, Lon
b. McCarey, Leo
b. McCord, Kent
b. McDonough, Mary Elizabeth
b. McElhenny, Hugh

b. McNichol, Jimmy
b. McNichol, Kristy
b. Meriwether, Lee
b. Miles, Tichi Wilkerson
b. Miller, Barry
b. Miller, Steve
b. Mimieux, Yvette Carmen M
b. Minnelli, Liza
b. Misrach, Richard
b. Mix, Ron(ald J)
b. Molina, Gloria
b. Monroe, Marilyn
b. Montgomery, Elizabeth
b. Moon, Warren (Harold)
b. Moore, Dick(ie)
b. Moore, Terry
b. Morefield, Richard H
b. Morris, Wayne
b. Mosley, Walter
b. Murphy, Jack R
b. Murray, Eddie Clarence
b. Nanula, Richard D.
b. Newman, Randy
b. Newmar, Julie
b. Noguchi, Isamu
b. Nolan, Jeanette
b. North, Sheree
b. O'Brien-Moore, Erin
b. Ochoa, Ellen
b. O'Dell, Scott
b. O'Neal, Ryan
b. O'Neal, Tatum
b. Osmond, Ken
b. Paltrow, Gwyneth
b. Parkening, Christopher William
b. Parker, Brant (Julian)
b. Patterson, Melody
b. Phillips, Chynna
b. Quarry, Jerry
b. Raffin, Deborah
b. Randle, Theresa
b. Reagan, Maureen Elizabeth
b. Reagan, Michael Edward
b. Reagan, Ronald Prescott
b. Reese, Mason
b. Reynolds, William
b. Ride, Sally K
b. Riggs, Bobby
b. Ritenour, Lee
b. Robinson, Rachel
b. Rogers, Darryl D
b. Royal-Allard, Lucille
b. Ruggles, Charles
b. Rushen, Patrice Louise
b. Russell, Andy
b. Saar, Alison
b. Saint James, Synthia
b. Saint John, Jill
b. Saint Johns, Adela Rogers
b. Salt, Jennifer
b. Sand, Paul
b. Sandrich, Jay H
b. Schramm, Tex(as Edward)
b. Schulberg, Stuart
b. Scott, Pippa
b. Sefton, William
b. Shapiro, Arnold
b. Sheen, Charlie
b. Sherman, Harry R
b. Shyer, Charles
b. Sikking, James B
b. Silverman, Jonathan
b. Singleton, John (Daniel)
b. Slatkin, Leonard
b. Slezak, Erika
b. Smiley, Jane (Graves)

d. Factor, Max, Jr.
d. Fain, Sammy
d. Faith, Percy
d. Farnum, William
d. Feldman, Alvin Lindbergh
d. Fenneman, George
d. Feuchtwanger, Lion
d. Feynman, Richard Phillips
d. Fields, Shep
d. Fields, Stanley
d. Fleischer, Max
d. Flood, Curt(is Charles)
d. Flynn, Joe
d. Flynt, Althea Sue
d. Fonda, Henry Jaynes
d. Ford, Mary
d. Forrest, Helen
d. Fowler, Gene
d. Franklin, Melvin
d. Frankovich, Mike J
d. Franz, Eduard
d. Frawley, William
d. Frederick, Pauline
d. Freed, Arthur
d. Freleng, Friz
d. French, Victor
d. Frings, Ketti
d. Fryer, Robert
d. Fuchs, Daniel
d. Fuller, Richard Buckminster
d. Fulton, Maude
d. Furst, Anton
d. Gabor, Eva
d. Garner, Erroll
d. Garrett, Joy
d. Gathers, Hank
d. Gaye, Marvin (Pentz)
d. Geer, Will
d. George, Christopher
d. George, Gladys
d. Gernreich, Rudi
d. Gilbert, John
d. Gillette, King Camp
d. Gillette, Paul
d. Gilliam, Jim
d. Gimpel, Jakob
d. Goldman, Ronald Lyle
d. Goldwyn, Samuel
d. Goodrich, Bert
d. Gordon, C Henry
d. Gordon, Michael
d. Gosden, Freeman Fisher
d. Gottschalk, Robert
d. Goyen, William
d. Graham, Ronny
d. Greenfield, Howard
d. Greenstreet, Sydney Hughes
d. Greenwood, Charlotte
d. Hadley, Reed
d. Hale, Alan, Jr.
d. Haley, Jack
d. Hall, Huntz
d. Hall, Manly Palmer
d. Halop, Florence
d. Halstead, William S
d. Hammer, Armand
d. Hampden, Walter
d. Harburg, E(dgar) Y(ipsel)
d. Harlow, Jean
d. Harmon, Tom
d. Hartley, Fred Lloyd
d. Hartman, Paul
d. Hathaway, Henry
d. Haymes, Dick
d. Healy, Ted
d. Hearst, David W(hitmire)

d. Heggie, O P
d. Heidt, Horace Murray
d. Heifetz, Jascha
d. Heindorf, Ray
d. Henie, Sonja
d. Henning, Doug(las James)
d. Herlihy, James Leo
d. Herman, Woody
d. Herrmann, Bernard
d. Hertz, John Daniel
d. Hexum, Jon-Erik
d. Higgins, Colin
d. Hite, Robert Ernest, Jr.
d. Hofmann, Josef Casimir
d. Holden, Fay
d. Holdren, Judd Clifton
d. Holloway, Sterling Price
d. Holt, Jack
d. Hormel, George Albert
d. Hughes, Rupert
d. Hunter, Ross
d. Hurkos, Peter
d. Hutton, Barbara Woolworth
d. Hutton, Jim
d. Huxley, Aldous (Leonard)
d. Hyde-White, Wilfrid
d. Hyland, Diana
d. Iceberg Slim
d. Ingram, Rex
d. Iturbi, Jose
d. Jarvis, Howard Arnold
d. Jenney, William LeBaron
d. Jessel, George Albert
d. Johnson, Martin Elmer
d. Johnson, Nunnally
d. Jones, Carolyn
d. Jones, Henry
d. Jones, Spike
d. Jordan, Bobby
d. Jordan, Jim
d. Jordan, Louis
d. Jordan, Richard
d. Kalmar, Bert
d. Kalmus, Herbert Thomas
d. Kamp, Irene Kittle
d. Karns, Roscoe
d. Kashdan, Isaac
d. Kath, Terry
d. Kaufman, Andy
d. Kaufman, Louis
d. Kaufman, Murray
d. Kaye, Danny
d. Kellaway, Cecil
d. Kellems, Vivien
d. Kelley, DeForest
d. Kelly, Paul
d. Kennedy, Robert Francis
d. Kilbride, Percy
d. Kirsten, Dorothy
d. Kohler, Fred, Sir
d. Kollsman, Paul
d. Krasna, Norman
d. Kurnitz, Harry
d. Lamas, Fernando
d. Lamour, Dorothy
d. L'Amour, Louis Dearborn
d. Landau, Ely A
d. Lang, Fritz
d. Langdon, Harry
d. Larson, Nicolette
d. Laughton, Charles
d. Lawford, Peter
d. Lea, Homer
d. Lee, Gypsy Rose
d. Legg, W(illiam) Dorr
d. Leginska

d. Lembeck, Harvey
d. Levinson, Richard Leighton
d. Lewis, David
d. Lewis, Robert Q
d. Lewis, Shari
d. Lewis, Tom
d. Libby, Willard Frank
d. Lichine, David
d. Lindley, Audra
d. Lindsay, Margaret
d. Lindsey, Benjamin Barr
d. Livingston, Jerry
d. Long, Richard
d. Love, Nat
d. Lubell, Samuel
d. Lubitsch, Ernst
d. Luckman, Charles
d. Ludden, Allen Ellsworth
d. Lugosi, Bela
d. Lund, John
d. Lundigan, William
d. Lynn, Diana
d. Macready, George
d. Maddow, Ben
d. Main, Marjorie
d. Maltz, Albert
d. Mamoulian, Rouben (Zachary)
d. Mancini, Henry
d. Manne, Shelly
d. Manning, Timothy, Cardinal
d. March, Fredric
d. March, Hal
d. Marion, Frances
d. Marley, John
d. Marx, Groucho
d. Mason, Biddy
d. Massey, Raymond Hart
d. Matlock, Matty
d. Mayer, L(ouis) B(urt)
d. McCarthy, Frank
d. McCulloch, Robert P
d. McDowall, Roddy
d. McIntyre, James Francis Aloysius, Cardinal
d. McMahon, Don(ald John)
d. Meadows, Audrey
d. Meek, Donald
d. Meeker, Ralph
d. Mellinger, Frederick
d. Merivale, Philip
d. Merkel, Una
d. Milestone, Lewis
d. Miller, Olive Thorne
d. Miller, Roger Dean
d. Mills, Donald
d. Mills, Harry
d. Mineo, Sal(vatore)
d. Mitchell, Grant
d. Modjeski, Ralph
d. Monroe, Phil
d. Montana, Bull
d. Montgomery, Elizabeth
d. Moran, Polly
d. Morton, Jelly Roll
d. Moss, Carlton
d. Muir, John
d. Murphy, Franklin D(avid)
d. Murray, Jim
d. Musso, Vido
d. Nathan, Robert
d. Ngor, Haing S
d. Nicholson, Seth Barnes
d. Nick the Greek
d. Nin, Anais
d. Nolan, Jeanette
d. Noone, Jimmie

Malibu Beach, California
d. Janssen, David
d. Woolsey, Robert

Mandena, California
b. Evans, Lee

Manhattan Beach, California
d. MacRae, Meredith
d. Reynolds, Marjorie

Mare Island, California
b. Cochrane, Edward Lull

Marina del Rey, California
b. Gardner, Randy
d. Unruh, Jesse Marvin
d. Wayne, Bernie
d. Wilson, Dennis

Martinez, California
b. DiMaggio, Joe
b. DiMaggio, Vince(nt Paul)
b. McGraw, Tug
d. Ray, Aldo
d. Rodia, Simon

Marysville, California
b. Bacon, Frank

Maywood, California
b. Messina, Jim

Mendocino County, California
d. Hedges, Michael

Menlo Park, California
b. Cowell, Henry Dixon
d. Behrens, Earl Charles
d. Guaraldi, Vince(nt Anthony)
d. Lewis, Clarence Irving
d. Marcus, Luis J
d. Maslow, Abraham Harold
d. Nevins, Allan
d. Poulter, Thomas Charles
d. Sears, Robert Richardson
d. Warne, William E(lmo)

Merced, California
b. Leigh, Janet
b. Ogletree, Charles (J.), Jr.

Mill Valley, California
b. Arden, Eve
b. Fernald, John Bailey
b. Hemingway, Mariel
d. Boyle, Kay
d. Morris, Wright Marion
d. Watts, Alan Wilson

Mission Hills, California
d. Weatherwax, Rudd B

Mission Viejo, California
d. Joyner, Florence Griffith
d. Lee, Pinky

Modesto, California
b. Evans, Herbert McLean
b. Gallo, Ernest
b. Gallo, Julio
b. Lucas, George
b. Meyer, Joseph

b. Presnell, Harve
b. Rudi, Joe
b. Spitz, Mark Andrew
d. Pickens, Slim

Monroe, California
b. Darden, Christine (Mann)

Monrovia, California
b. Baker, Kenny
d. Normand, Mabel
d. Walthall, Henry B

Montecito, California
d. Bayer, Herbert
d. Dresser, Davis
d. McLean, Robert
d. Muni, Paul
d. Rexroth, Kenneth
d. Stone, Dorothy

Monterey, California
b. Dutra, Olin
b. Hagar, Sammy
b. Kennedy, Edgar
b. Panetta, Leon E(dward)
d. Adams, Ansel Easton
d. Berne, Eric Lennard
d. Billings, Josh
d. Cameron, Eleanor Frances
d. Crocker, Charles
d. Davenport, Marcia
d. Dowling, Dan(iel Blair)
d. Freeman, Paul Lamar
d. Mazia, Daniel
d. Shepard, Alan B(artlett), Jr.
d. Stoll, George E

Monterey Bay, California
d. Denver, John

Monterey Park, California
b. Mackie, Bob

Morro Bay, California
d. Rempp, Adolph

Mountain View, California
b. Boitano, Brian
d. Bolet, Jorge

Napa, California
d. West, Jessamyn

National City, California
b. Baldessari, John

Needles, California
d. Kinison, Sam

Nevada City, California
b. Marshall, Tully

Newhall, California
d. Hart, William Surrey
d. Partch, Virgil Franklin, II
d. Williams, Tex

Newman, California
d. Dutra, Olin

Newport, California
b. McGillis, Kelly

Newport Beach, California
b. Aames, Willie
b. Kerwin, Lance
d. Baxter, Les
d. DelRio, Dolores
d. Harris, MacDonald
d. Ising, Rudolf C
d. Martin, Freddy
d. McLaglen, Victor
d. McLaren, Wayne
d. Roosevelt, James
d. Trevor, Claire
d. Tully, Tom
d. Voit, Willard Darby

Nipomo, California
d. Siegel, Don

North Hills, California
d. Scott, Raymond

North Hollywood, California
b. Bernsen, Corbin
b. North, Jay
b. Smithers, Jan
b. Stockwell, Guy
d. Arlen, Richard
d. Barry, Donald
d. Carle, Richard
d. Conrad, William
d. Dell, Gabriel
d. Diegel, Leo
d. DiMaggio, Vince(nt Paul)
d. Felton, Verna
d. Franciscus, James Grover
d. Hardy, Oliver
d. Hauser, Gayelord
d. Morgan, Vicki
d. Price, Roger Taylor
d. Stone, Fred Andrew
d. Yung, Victor Sen

Northridge, California
b. Harrison, Jenilee
d. Coppola, Carmine
d. Davis, Jim

Norwalk, California
b. Tiffany
d. Anderson, Cat

Oakland, California
b. Anderson, Eddie
b. Anderson, Jack Zuinglius
b. Baer, Max, Jr.
b. Bechtel, Stephen Davison, Jr.
b. Bley, Carla
b. Budge, Don
b. Cambra, Jessie G.
b. Cashin, Bonnie
b. Cottrell, Frederick Gardner
b. Crabbe, Buster
b. Curry, Mark
b. Dellums, Ronald Vernie
b. Duncan, Robert Edward
b. Eckersley, Dennis
b. Fields, Debbi
b. Froines, John Radford
b. Gilbreth, Lillian Moller
b. Gorman, Chester
b. Hamill, Mark
b. Hammer
b. Howard, Sidney Coe
b. Hrabosky, Al(an Thomas)
b. Kingman, Dong Moy Shu

b. Evans, Darrell Wayne
b. Field, Sally Margaret
b. Fleming, Victor
b. Freberg, Stan
b. Fussell, Paul
b. Gleason, Lucille
b. Guyer, David Leigh
b. Hamlin, Harry Robinson
b. Harrah, Bill
b. Jewett, Frank Baldwin
b. Lightner, Candy
b. Lilly, Doris
b. Mardian, Robert Charles
b. Matthiessen, Francis Otto
b. Nader, George
b. Quinlan, Kathleen
b. Richardson, Bill
b. Smith, Stan(ley Roger)
b. Sullivan, Kathleen
b. Toomer, Ronald V
b. Vines, Ellsworth
b. Walters, Charles
b. Worrill, Conrad (W.)
d. Adams, Walter Sydney
d. Armstrong, Herbert W
d. Avery, R Stanton
d. Babcock, Harold Delos
d. Barthe, Richmond
d. Biggers, Earl Derr
d. Bronson, Betty
d. Cushman, Austin Thomas
d. Davis, William Morris
d. Delbruck, Max
d. Dreyfuss, Henry
d. Edmunds, George Franklin
d. Fields, W C
d. Finch, Robert H(utchison)
d. Fowler, William A(lfred)
d. Frost, Arthur Burdett
d. Garfield, Lucretia (Rudolph)
d. Greene, Henry Mather
d. Hale, George Ellery
d. Howland, Alfred Cornelius
d. Husing, Ted
d. Krick, Irving P(arkhurst)
d. Leighton, Robert B(enjamin)
d. Maravich, Pete(r Press)
d. Markle, Fletcher
d. Michelson, Albert Abraham
d. Millikan, Clark Blanchard
d. Morgan, Thomas Hunt
d. Neff, Wallace
d. Reed, Robert
d. Richter, Charles Francis
d. Silvera, Frank
d. Sinclair, Harry Ford
d. Sperry, Roger W(olcott)
d. Stans, Maurice H(ubert)
d. Sturtevant, Alfred Henry
d. Tokatyan, Armand
d. Tolman, Richard C(hace)
d. Turner, Frederick Jackson
d. Weyerhaeuser, Frederick
d. Whittingham, Charlie
d. Williams, J(ames) R(obert)
d. Winter, Alice Vivian Ames
d. Zwicky, Fritz

Paso Robles, California
d. Dean, James Byron
d. Moore, Colleen
d. Vidor, King Wallis

Pearblossom, California
d. Voskovec, George

Pebble Beach, California
d. Doolittle, James H(arold)
d. Funt, Allen
d. Little, Lawson
d. McCone, John Alex
d. Spruance, Raymond Ames

Petaluma, California
b. Kael, Pauline

Placentia, California
d. Ten Boom, Corrie

Placerville, California
b. Dunlop, John Thomas

Plumas City, California
b. Marble, Alice

Point Loma, California
d. Spalding, Albert Goodwill

Pomona, California
b. Seagren, Bob
b. Waits, Tom
d. Beadle, George Wells
d. Cleaver, Eldridge

Poway, California
d. Creston, Paul

Prattville, California
b. Adams, Annette Abbott

Ramona, California
d. Martin, Ross

Rancho Chico, California
d. Bidwell, John

Rancho Mirage, California
d. Caray, Harry
d. Carmichael, Hoagy
d. Crawford, Broderick
d. Faye, Alice
d. Field, Virginia (Margaret Cynthia St. John)
d. Foster, Phil
d. Gabor, Jolie
d. Gabor, Magda
d. Harris, Phil
d. Hillings, Patrick J(ohn)
d. Hutson, Don(ald M)
d. Kaye, Stubby
d. Martin, Kiel
d. Martin, Mary
d. Massey, D Curtis
d. Rogers, Buddy
d. Rogers, Ginger
d. Skelton, Red
d. Taurog, Norman
d. Van Heusen, Jimmy
d. Wallis, Hal Brent

Rancho Palos Verdes, California
d. Allen, George Herbert

Rancho Santa Fe, California
d. Applewhite, Marshall Herff
d. Henry, Marguerite
d. Martin, Quinn
d. Mature, Victor (John)
d. Rozelle, Pete

Raymond, California
d. Hill, Thomas

Red Bluff, California
b. Geiberger, Al(len L)
b. Shaw, Robert Lawson

Redding, California
b. Hein, Mel(vin John)

Redlands, California
b. Harris, Harwell Hamilton
d. Holifield, Chet

Redondo Beach, California
b. McMillan, Edwin Mattison
b. Pierpoint, Robert Charles
d. Rosecrans, William Starke

Redwood, California
d. O'Neill, Gerard Kitchen

Redwood City, California
d. Humphries, Rolfe
d. Stevens, Albert William

Reseda, California
b. Feldman, Corey

Richmond, California
b. Darden, Christopher A.
b. Franklin, Carl

Ripon, California
b. Anderson, Roy A(rnold)

Riverside, California
b. Baker, Dusty
b. Bonds, Barry (Lamar)
b. Bonds, Bobby (Lee)
b. Davidson, Jaye
b. Imus, Don
b. Kistler, Darci Anna
b. Miller, Cheryl
b. Miller, Reggie
b. Vera, Billy
d. Kerr, Alexander H
d. LeMay, Curtis Emerson
d. Martin, Dean Paul

Rockport, California
b. Brinegar, Claude Stout

Rodeo, California
b. Armstrong, Billie Joe
b. Gomez, Lefty

Rolling Hills, California
b. Austin, Tracy Ann

Roseville, California
b. Ringwald, Molly

Ross, California
d. Adler, Kurt Herbert

Sacramento, California
b. Anderson, Mary Antoinette
b. Barbeau, Adrienne
b. Benton, Barbie
b. Bowa, Larry
b. Caen, Herb

b. Collins, Ray
b. Colmenares, Margarita (H.)
b. Didion, Joan
b. Eames, Ray
b. Elliott, Sam
b. Everson, William Oliver
b. Forsch, Bob
b. Forsch, Ken(neth Roth)
b. George, Henry, Jr.
b. Goodson, Mark
b. Hathaway, Henry
b. Hayes, James C.
b. Johnson, Hiram Warren
b. Johnson, Kevin
b. Kemble, Edward W(indsor)
b. Kennedy, Anthony McLeod
b. King, Thomas
b. Lescoulie, Jack
b. Matsui, Robert T(akeo)
b. McNamara, John Francis
b. Sanderson, Sybil
b. Schwab, Charles
b. Slenczynska, Ruth
b. Warwick, Robert
d. Adams, Annette Abbott
d. Brand, Neville
d. Gordon, Joe
d. Gorman, Chester
d. Harris, Thomas Anthony
d. Rogers, Don(ald Lavert)
d. Savitt, Jan

Saint Helena, California
d. Strouse, Norman H(ulbert)
d. White, Ellen Gould Harmon

Salinas, California
b. Felton, Verna
b. Steinbeck, John (Ernst)

San Andreas, California
d. Adams, Diana

San Anselmo, California
d. Christensen, Harold

San Bernardino, California
b. Hackman, Gene
b. Head, Edith
b. Karns, Roscoe
b. Kirk, Claude Roy, Jr.
b. Knott, Walter
b. Lemon, Bob
b. McCloskey, Paul Norton, Jr.
b. Stockton, Dave
b. Walker, Wesley Darcel
b. Wayman, Dorothy

San Bruno, California
b. McKernan, Ron
b. Somers, Suzanne
d. Davis, Tommy

San Clemente, California
d. Chaney, Lon, Jr.
d. Hein, Mel(vin John)
d. Jorgensen, Christine

San Diego, California
b. Allen, Marcus
b. Bill, Tony
b. Bishop, Stephen
b. Boone, Bob
b. Buono, Victor

b. Casper, Billy
b. Chadwick, Florence (May)
b. Clampett, Bob
b. Conner, Dennis
b. Connolly, Maureen
b. Danson, Ted
b. Davis, Terrell
b. DeVarona, Donna
b. Duvall, Robert (Selden)
b. Fabray, Nanette
b. Gerstler, Amy
b. Grady, Don
b. Jeakins, Dorothy
b. Jensen, Arthur Robert
b. Kempthorne, Dirk Arthur
b. Lansing, Robert
b. Littler, Gene
b. Louganis, Greg(ory Efthimios)
b. McNeil, Lori
b. Mitchell, Kevin (Darrell)
b. Nettles, Graig
b. O'Brien, Margaret
b. Roberts, Steven K
b. Russell, Theresa
b. Scripps, Robert Paine
b. Simpson, Scott
b. Stadler, Craig Robert
b. Stewart, John
b. Story, Liz
b. Teacher, Brian
b. Tilton, Charlene
b. Van Dyke, W(oodbridge) S(trong)
b. Walford, Roy L(ee, Jr.)
b. Walker, Daniel
b. Whittingham, Charlie
b. Wilcox, Larry Dee
b. Williams, Ted
b. Wilson, Ann
b. Wright, Mickey
d. Allen, Peter Woolnough
d. Armetta, Henry
d. Barnet, Charlie
d. Blitch, Iris F(aircloth)
d. Burdick, Eugene Leonard
d. Chadwick, Florence (May)
d. Cheney, John Vance
d. Coffroth, Jimmy
d. Eigenmann, Rosa Smith
d. Fitzsimmons, Frank Edward
d. Gargan, William
d. Groza, Alex John
d. Heinemann, Edward H
d. Henry, Charlotte
d. Jaffee, Irving
d. Kroc, Ray(mond) Albert
d. Mayer, Maria Goeppert
d. Moore, Archie
d. O'Connell, Helen
d. Parker, Frank
d. Partch, Harry
d. Pendleton, Clarence McLane, Jr.
d. Pendleton, Nat
d. Revelle, Roger Randall
d. Ritz, Harry
d. Rutherford, Joseph Franklin
d. Ryan, T(ubal) Claude
d. Sender, Ramon Jose
d. Smith, Holland McTeire
d. Spock, Benjamin (McLane)
d. Thomason, John William, Jr.
d. Timken, Henry
d. Williams, Sherley Anne

San Fernando, California
b. Crum, Denny
d. Arnold, Edward

d. Burns, Bob

San Francisco, California
b. Adams, Ansel Easton
b. Aitken, Robert
b. Alioto, Joseph L(awrence)
b. Allen, Gracie Ethel Cecil Rosaline
b. Alvarez, Luis W(alter)
b. Alvarez, Walter Clement
b. Andrus, Ethel Percy
b. Anglim, Philip
b. Archer, George
b. Arzner, Dorothy
b. Atherton, Gertrude Franklin
b. Attell, Abe B
b. Bailey, Raymond
b. Beban, Gary Joseph
b. Belasco, David
b. Bixby, Bill
b. Blanc, Mel(vin Jerome)
b. Blinn, Holbrook
b. Bonestell, Chesley
b. Born, Ernest Alexander
b. Bowes, Major
b. Brady, Joan
b. Brady, William Aloysius
b. Breyer, Stephen Gerald
b. Bridges, Todd
b. Brodie, John Riley
b. Brown, Edmund G.
b. Brown, Jerry
b. Camilli, Dolph
b. Casals, Rosemary
b. Catlett, Walter
b. Chamberlain, Owen
b. Chatham, Russell
b. Cho, Margaret
b. Chrystos
b. Church, Sandra
b. Cone, Fairfax Mastick
b. Cook, Elisha, Jr.
b. Cooke, Hope
b. Corbett, James John
b. Crews, Laura Hope
b. Cronin, Joe
b. Curtis, Ann
b. Dahl-Wolfe, Louise
b. De Cuir, John
b. Desmond, Paul Breitenfeld
b. Diller, Barry Charles
b. Dillman, Bradford
b. DiMaggio, Dom(inic Paul)
b. Dorgan, Thomas Aloysius
b. DuBay, William Bryan
b. Dukes, David
b. Duncan, Augustin
b. Duncan, Isadora
b. Dupree, Minnie
b. Eastwood, Clint
b. Egan, Richard
b. Erlanger, Joseph
b. Fassett, Kaffe
b. Fay, Frank
b. Feinstein, Dianne
b. Flavin, Martin Archer
b. Fleisher, Leon
b. Forbes, Kathryn
b. Fossey, Dian
b. Fouts, Dan(iel Francis)
b. Freedman, Russell
b. Frost, Robert Lee
b. Garcia, Jerry
b. Gaxton, William
b. Geertz, Clifford James
b. Glover, Danny
b. Goldberg, Rube

b. Goodwin, Bill	b. Rambeau, Marjorie	d. Claire, Ina
b. Grant, Gordon	b. Rand, Ellen Gertrude Emmet	d. Creel, George Edward
b. Guaraldi, Vince(nt Anthony)	b. Ricci, Ruggiero	d. Crittenton, Charles Nelson
b. Haas, Robert D(ouglas)	b. Roland, Ruth	d. Cunningham, Imogen
b. Haas, Walter A(braham), Sr.	b. Rosburg, Bob	d. Cushman, Pauline
b. Haas, Walter A(braham), Jr.	b. Rubens, Alma	d. Delaplane, Stanton Hill
b. Haid, Charles	b. Ruef, Abraham	d. DeYoung, Michel Harry
b. Hammond, John Hays, Jr.	b. St. Clair, Bob	d. Drew, John
b. Hartman, Grace	b. Salinger, Pierre Emil George	d. Drury, Allen (Stuart)
b. Hartman, Paul	b. Sargeant, Winthrop	d. Duncan, Robert Edward
b. Hawkins, Tramaine	b. Schneider, Rob	d. Elder, Ruth
b. Hayes, Peter Lind	b. Selfridge, Thomas Etholen	d. Feeney, Chub
b. Hearst, Patty	b. Serra, Richard Anthony	d. Feingold, Benjamin Franklin
b. Hearst, William Randolph	b. Sheila E	d. Forbes, Kathryn
b. Heilmann, Harry Edwin	b. Sherman, Lowell	d. Foster, Pops
b. Henry, William M	b. Shields, Alexander	d. Frailberg, Selma
b. Hernandez, Keith	b. Silverstone, Alicia	d. Frankenstein, Alfred Victor
b. Holt, Fritz	b. Simmons, Calvin	d. Freeman, Cynthia
b. Holtz, Lou	b. Simpson, O(renthal) J(ames)	d. Haas, Walter A(braham), Sr.
b. Hulme, Kathryn Cavarly	b. Smith, Robyn Caroline	d. Haas, Walter A(braham), Jr.
b. Irvin, Rea	b. Snyder, Gary Sherman	d. Halston
b. Jackson, Shirley (Hardie)	b. Soss, Wilma Porter	d. Harding, Warren G(amaliel)
b. Jacobs, Al(bert T)	b. Spano, Joe	d. Hawthorne, Julian
b. Jaffe, Sam(uel Anderson)	b. Sproul, Robert Gordon	d. Hayakawa, S(amuel) I(chiye)
b. Janowitz, Tama	b. Steffens, Lincoln	d. Hertz, Alfred
b. Jensen, Jackie	b. Stone, Irving	d. Hoffer, Eric
b. Jones, KC	b. Strong, Austin	d. Hurd, Clement
b. Kagel, Sam	b. Tevis, Walter	d. Jackson, Helen Maria Hunt Fiske
b. Kantner, Paul	b. Toklas, Alice B(abette)	d. Jagel, Frederick
b. Kelly, George Lange	b. Tyrrell, Susan	d. Johnson, Cornelius
b. Kenney, Bill	b. Van Doren, Dorothy Graffe	d. Jolson, Al
b. Kerns, Joanna	b. Varsi, Diane	d. Judson, Egbert Putnam
b. Kilbride, Percy	b. Venturi, Ken(neth)	d. Kaiser, Edgar Fosburgh
b. Kilburn, Peter	b. Venuta, Benay	d. Kalakaua, David
b. Kyne, Peter Bernard	b. Wagner, Robin	d. Kapell, William
b. LaLanne, Jack	b. Wanger, Walter	d. Keeler, James Edward
b. Lamantia, Philip	b. Ward, Jay	d. Kelly, George Lange
b. Lapham, Lewis Henry	b. Warfield, David	d. King, Thomas Starr
b. Lazzeri, Tony	b. Warner, Jack, Jr.	d. Kyne, Peter Bernard
b. Lee, Bruce	b. Weinberger, Caspar Willard	d. Lange, Dorothea Nutzhorn
b. Leroy, Mervyn	b. Weingarten, Violet Brown	d. Larkin, Thomas Oliver
b. Loeb, Gerald Martin	b. Weir, Bob	d. Lawson, John Howard
b. London, Jack	b. Weldon, Joan	d. Lazzeri, Tony
b. Lord, Marjorie	b. Whitman, Stuart	d. Leiber, Fritz (Reuter), Jr.
b. Love, Courtney	b. Williams, Gluyas	d. Loeb, Gerald Martin
b. Luisetti, Hank	b. Wilson, Nancy	d. Logan, John
b. Lyng, Richard E	b. Wolf, Naomi	d. Magnin, Cyril Isaac
b. Mackay, Clarence Hungerford	b. Wong, B D	d. Magnin, Grover Arnold
b. Magnin, Cyril Isaac	b. Woo, Merle	d. Mannes, Marya
b. Magnin, Grover Arnold	b. Wood, Natalie	d. McDowell, Irvin
b. March, Hal	b. Young, John Watts	d. Mendelsohn, Eric
b. Marion, Frances	b. Yung, Victor Sen	d. Merola, Gaetano
b. Martin, Tony	b. Zellerbach, William Joseph	d. Milk, Harvey
b. Mather, Stephen Tyng	b. Zumwalt, Elmo R(ussell), Jr.	d. Miller, Otto Neil
b. Mathis, Johnny	d. Adams, Alice	d. Mooney, Tom
b. McCone, John Alex	d. Alioto, Joseph L(awrence)	d. Morgan, Julia
b. McDougald, Gil(bert James)	d. Alvarez, Walter Clement	d. Moscone, George Richard
b. McGee, Willie Dean	d. Anthony, John J(ason)	d. Murphy, Turk
b. McKuen, Rod Marvin	d. Apostoli, Fred	d. Murray, Philip
b. McNamara, Robert S(trange)	d. Atherton, Gertrude Franklin	d. Nimitz, Chester William
b. Menuhin, Hephzibah	d. Bates, Blanche Lyon	d. Norris, Frank(lin)
b. Miller, Johnny Laurence	d. Bateson, Gregory	d. Norris, Kathleen Thompson
b. Morgan, Julia	d. Bechtel, Stephen Davison	d. Packard, David
b. Moscone, George Richard	d. Belli, Melvin M(ouron)	d. Palmer, Nathaniel Brown
b. Nelson, Barry	d. Black, Winifred Sweet	d. Peers, William Raymond
b. Newell, Allen	d. Bloomfield, Mike	d. Petri, Angelo
b. Nixon, Tricia	d. Bombeck, Erma (Louise)	d. Pleasant, Mary Ellen
b. Nolan, Lloyd	d. Boyd, Louise Arner	d. Pritchard, John Michael, Sir
b. Norris, Kathleen Thompson	d. Bridges, Harry Renton	d. Remenyi, Eduard
b. Nuttall, Zelia Maria Magdalena	d. Brown, Nacio Herb	d. Rudhyar, Dane
b. Obata, Gyo	d. Burton, Phillip	d. Ruef, Abraham
b. O'Brien, George	d. Busch, Niven	d. Russell, Donald Joseph
b. Olds, Sharon	d. Caen, Herb	d. Smith, H(arry) Allen
b. Paris, Jerry	d. Campbell, William Wallace	d. Soong, T V
b. Prichard, Diana Garcia	d. Chaudhuri, Haridas	d. Spreckels, Claus
b. Pringle, Aileen	d. Childs, Marquis William	d. Stephenson, Henry

b. Nelson, Tracy
b. Norton-Taylor, Judy
b. O'Brien, Parry
b. Quisenberry, Dan(iel Raymond)
b. Redford, Robert
b. Scott, Mike
b. Sherman, Bobby
b. Teena Marie
b. Vega, Suzanne
b. Vollmann, William T.
b. Webb, Jack Randolph
b. Williams, Barry
d. Albertson, Frank
d. Allen, Irwin
d. Anderson, Warner
d. Andrews, Edward
d. Armstrong, Robert
d. Bailey, Jack
d. Bancroft, George
d. Bellamy, Ralph
d. Blondell, Joan
d. Bloomingdale, Alfred S
d. Brodie, Fawn McKay
d. Brown, Clarence
d. Browning, Tod
d. Bruce, Nigel
d. Buckley, Tim
d. Burnett, W(illiam) R(iley)
d. Carnap, Rudolf
d. Carrillo, Leo
d. Clark, Dane
d. Clark, Fred
d. Clayton, Lou
d. Cole, Nat King
d. Collins, Ray
d. Coogan, Jackie
d. Cowl, Jane
d. Daniell, Henry
d. Davis, Miles Dewey, III
d. Donaldson, Walter
d. Dozier, William
d. Dragon, Carmen
d. Duke, Vernon
d. Dunn, James Howard
d. Durante, Jimmy
d. Ebert, Carl
d. Egan, Richard
d. Erteszek, Jan
d. Fairbanks, Douglas
d. Fay, Frank
d. Feld, Fritz
d. Fix, Paul
d. Foster, Norman
d. Francis, Sam(uel Lewis)
d. Glaser, Elizabeth
d. Gomez, Thomas
d. Grable, Betty
d. Granger, Stewart
d. Granville, Bonita
d. Greene, Lorne
d. Griffith, Corinne
d. Grofe, Ferde
d. Gross, Robert Ellsworth
d. Haines, William
d. Harris, Roy
d. Heard, Gerald
d. Hemingway, Margaux
d. Henreid, Paul
d. Hilton, Conrad Nicholson
d. Holden, William
d. Humes, Helen
d. Isherwood, Christopher (William)
d. Jagger, Dean
d. Jenkins, Allen
d. Jory, Victor
d. Kaplan, Joseph

d. Kasznar, Kurt
d. Kaye, Nora
d. Knight, James L
d. Lansing, Joi
d. LaRue, Jack
d. Laurel, Stan
d. Lennon, Jimmy, Sr.
d. Lloyd, Frank
d. Lockhart, Gene
d. Lofting, Hugh
d. Loper, Don
d. MacLane, Barton
d. MacMurray, Fred(erick Martin)
d. Mahin, John Lee
d. Maltby, Richard E
d. Matthau, Walter
d. McCarey, Leo
d. McManus, George
d. Melchior, Lauritz
d. Mercer, Beryl
d. Mitchell, Millard
d. Moore, Tom
d. Morton, Arthur
d. Nelson, Ralph
d. Nesbit, Evelyn
d. Norvo, Red
d. Ober, Philip (Nott)
d. O'Brien, Pat
d. O'Keefe, Dennis
d. Olson, Johnny
d. Overman, Lynne
d. Pangborn, Franklin
d. Pankhurst, Christabel Harriette, Dame
d. Parsons, Louella Oettinger
d. Pennel, John (Thomas)
d. Pickford, Mary
d. Pidgeon, Walter
d. Porter, Cole
d. Priest, Ivy (Maude) Baker
d. Righter, Carroll
d. Ring, Blanche
d. Risdon, Elizabeth
d. Ritt, Martin
d. Romero, Cesar
d. Ruggles, Charles
d. Ryan, Irene Noblette
d. Schaffner, Franklin James
d. Segar, Elzie Crisler
d. Seymour, Dan
d. Shaughnessy, Clark Daniel
d. Sheehan, Joseph Green
d. Sheekman, Arthur
d. Stanwyck, Barbara
d. Struss, Karl
d. Taylor, Robert
d. Thalberg, Irving Grant
d. Thomas, Ross (Elmore)
d. Todd, Thelma
d. Toumanova, Tamara
d. Tracy, Lee
d. Traubel, Helen
d. Tufts, Sonny
d. Tynan, Kenneth Peacock
d. Walker, Robert
d. Wayne, David
d. Welk, Lawrence
d. Whorf, Richard
d. Wibberley, Leonard Patrick O'Connor
d. Willson, Meredith
d. Wilson, Richard
d. Wong, Anna May (Lu Tsong)
d. Wood, Robert Dennis
d. Wright, Lloyd

Santa Rosa, California
  b. DeMornay, Rebecca
  b. London, Julie
  b. Perry, Nancy Ling
  b. Ripley, Robert Leroy
  b. Valentine, Karen
  d. Burbank, Luther
  d. Lichty, George
  d. Schulz, Charles M(onroe)

Sausalito, California
  d. Hayden, Sterling Relyea Walter
  d. Oppenheimer, Frank F
  d. Spanier, Muggsy

Sebastopol, California
  d. Edwards, India Moffett

Seeley, California
  b. Steele, Willie

Sepulveda, California
  d. Holmes, John C.
  d. Switzer, Carl

Shasta, California
  b. Behrens, Earl Charles

Sherman Oaks, California
  b. Aniston, Jennifer
  b. Babilonia, Tai (Reina)
  b. Marshack, Megan
  d. Booke, Sorrell
  d. Brian, David
  d. DelRuth, Roy
  d. Dumke, Ralph
  d. Guldahl, Ralph
  d. Harding, Ann
  d. Hayes, Alfred
  d. Little, Cleavon Jake
  d. McAvoy, May
  d. McClure, Doug
  d. Meisner, Sanford
  d. Raines, Ella
  d. Robards, Jason
  d. Rowen, Hobart
  d. Schwartz, Jean
  d. Sheinwold, Alfred
  d. Shulman, Irving
  d. Sullivan, Barry

Sisson, California
  b. Loos, Anita

Solana Beach, California
  d. Brent, George

Solvang, California
  d. Baker, Kenny

Sonoma, California
  d. Arnold, Henry Harley

Sonora, California
  b. Belli, Melvin M(ouron)
  b. Oxnam, G(arfield) Bromley
  b. Pastorini, Dan(te Anthony, Jr.)

South Gate, California
  b. Rozelle, Pete
  b. Smith, Roger
  d. Goodman, Johnny

South Laguna, California
d. Boyd, William

South Lake Tahoe, California
d. Bono, Sonny

South Pasadena, California
b. Harris, MacDonald
b. McCrea, Joel
d. Anderson, Gilbert M
d. De Palma, Ralph
d. Nance, Jack
d. Rosenbloom, Maxie

Squaw Valley, California
b. Erwin, Stuart

Stanford, California
d. Davis, Kingsley
d. Hook, Sidney

Stanton, California
b. Fortensky, Larry

Stockton, California
b. Baxley, Barbara
b. Beck, Dave
b. Etchison, Dennis
b. Goodell, Brian Stuart
b. Isaak, Chris
b. Kingston, Maxine Hong
b. Montana, Bob
b. Six, Robert Forman
b. Walker, Kara
b. Wurster, William
d. Lewis, (Myrtle) Tillie
d. Pollard, Jim
d. Stagg, Amos Alonzo

Stovepipe Wells, California
d. Scott, Walter

Student, California
b. Rutan, Burt

Studio City, California
b. Dragon, Daryl
d. Davis, Brad
d. Miller, Max
d. Parks, Larry
d. Walker, Nancy

Sunland, California
d. DeCordoba, Pedro

Sunnyvale, California
b. Hatcher, Teri
b. Wozniak, Steven
d. Oppen, George

Taft, California
b. Bailey, Martin Jean

Tarzana, California
b. Lovitz, Jon
d. Hodiak, John
d. Stevenson, McLean

Temecula, California
d. Gardner, Erle Stanley

Templeton, California
d. Quarry, Jerry

Terra Bella, California
d. Baker, Dorothy Dodds

Terra Linda, California
d. Bessie, Alvah
d. Gold, Michael

Thousand Oaks, California
d. Kirby, Jack
d. Martin, Strother

Tiburon, California
d. May, Rollo (Reece)

Toluca Lake, California
b. Henning, Linda Kaye
d. King, Henry
d. Pierce, Charles
d. Rorke, Hayden

Torrance, California
b. Carlton, Larry
b. Hite, Robert Ernest, Jr.
b. Lopez, Nancy Marie
b. Rochon, Lela
b. Westphal, Paul Douglas
d. Drake, Tom
d. Lundberg, Daniel
d. Milland, Ray(mond Alton)
d. O'Keefe, Walter
d. Peary, Harold
d. Qualen, John Mandt
d. Wallace, Bobby

Towle, California
b. Towle, Katherine Amelia

Tracy, California
d. Gallo, Julio

Tujunga, California
d. Adoree, Renee

Tulare, California
b. Cromley, Raymond Avolon
b. Farquhar, Marilyn G(ist)
b. Mathias, Bob
b. Zumwalt, Elmo Russell, III

Ukiah, California
b. Near, Holly

Universal City, California
d. Savalas, Telly

Valencia, California
d. Powolny, Frank

Vallejo, California
b. Buckner, Bill
b. Carney, Robert Bostwick
b. Gordon, Jeff
d. Cone, Russell Glenn
d. Graham, Bill

Van Nuys, California
b. Drysdale, Don(ald Scott)
b. Lockwood, Gary
b. Milken, Michael
b. Peters, Jon
b. Saddler, Donald
b. Whitaker, Johnny
b. Williams, Cindy

d. Allison, Fran(ces)
d. Barrymore, Lionel Blythe
d. Conrad, Con
d. Crisp, Donald
d. Hartman, Grace
d. Hunter, Jeffrey
d. Hurrell, George
d. Matzenauer, Margaret
d. Mulhare, Edward
d. Ryan, Tommy
d. Stevens, Onslow
d. Vickers, Martha

Venice, California
d. Feld, Irvin

Ventura, California
b. Vincent, Jan-Michael
d. Carr, Sabin
d. Hutton, Ina Ray
d. Ralston, Esther

Verdugo City, California
d. Burke, Billie

Visalia, California
d. Dederich, Charles (Edwin)
d. Peters, Susan

Vista, California
b. Sasway, Benjamin H
d. Patten, Gilbert

Walnut Creek, California
b. Johnson, Randy
b. Turlington, Christy
d. Baldrige, Malcolm
d. Duffy, Clinton Truman
d. Van Westerborg, Edward
d. Weede, Robert

Weitchpec, California
b. Risling, David

West Covina, California
b. Aikman, Troy (Kenneth)
b. Robbins, Tim(othy Francis)

West Hills, California
d. Moore, Clayton

West Hollywood, California
d. Cassidy, Jack
d. Dandridge, Dorothy
d. Godunov, Alexander
d. Klein, Marty
d. Monette, Paul

West Los Angeles, California
d. Bradley, Tom
d. Louise, Anita

Westlake Village, California
d. Oboler, Arch
d. Scott, George C(ampbell)
d. Young, Robert (George)

Westminister, California
b. Eaton, Mark E

Westwood, California
d. Cousins, Norman
d. Gardiner, Reginald

d. McCarty, Mary

Whittier, California
b. Babashoff, Shirley
b. Jordan, Charles Morrell
b. Kostabi, Mark
b. Moraga, Cherrie
b. Patterson, Lorna
b. Wakoski, Diane
b. Yothers, Tina
d. Luke, Keye

Woodland, California
b. Howard, Eddy

Woodland Hills, California
b. Yount, Robin (R.)
d. Abbott, Bud
d. Alley, Norman William
d. Allgood, Sara
d. Benson, Sally
d. Blythe, Betty
d. Brady, Scott
d. Brown, Johnny Mack
d. Bruce, Virginia
d. Cabot, Bruce
d. Campanella, Roy
d. Catlett, Walter
d. Cavanaugh, Hobart
d. Clarke, Mae
d. Colonna, Jerry
d. Compton, Joyce
d. Cooper, Melville
d. Corby, Ellen
d. Corey, Wendell
d. Dana, Viola
d. Darwell, Jane
d. DeRita, Joe
d. Donlevy, Brian
d. D'Orsay, Fifi
d. Dresser, Louise
d. Dwan, Allan
d. Edelman, Herb
d. Ewell, Tom
d. Fell, Norman
d. Fetchit, Stepin
d. Fine, Larry
d. Ford, Wallace
d. Foy, Eddie, Jr.
d. Frisco, Joe
d. Garner, Peggy Ann
d. Gibson, Hoot
d. Gleason, James
d. Gwenn, Edmund
d. Hagen, Jean
d. Hunnicutt, Arthur
d. Jaeckel, Richard (Hanley)
d. Joslyn, Allyn Morgan
d. Kennedy, Edgar
d. Kennedy, Madge
d. Kennedy, Tom
d. Knowles, Patric
d. Kruger, Otto
d. Lanchester, Elsa
d. Lane, Rosemary
d. LaPlante, Laura
d. Lowe, Edmund Dante
d. Matheson, Murray
d. Maynard, Ken
d. McCrea, Joel
d. Mulhall, Jack
d. Murray, Mae
d. Purviance, Edna
d. Rawlinson, Herbert
d. Robin, Leo
d. Ruby, Harry

d. Sennett, Mack
d. Shearer, Norma
d. Silverheels, Jay
d. Sondergaard, Gale (Edith Holm)
d. Toomey, Regis
d. Tucker, Forrest Meredith
d. Von Zell, Harry
d. Whalen, Michael
d. Young, Clara Kimball

Woodside, California
d. Sterling, John Ewart Wallace

Yorba Linda, California
b. Nixon, Richard M(ilhous)

Yucaipa, California
b. Anton, Susan

Yuma City, California
b. Hohman, Donald

COLORADO
b. Burns, Robin
b. Morgan, Vicki
b. Waters, Frank (Joseph)
d. Barker, Lloyd
d. Reventlow, Lance

Aguilar, Colorado
b. Zamora, Bernice

Alamosa, Colorado
b. Carruthers, Garrey E

Aspen, Colorado
b. Ross, Harold Wallace
d. Sabich, Spider

Atwood, Colorado
b. Shumlin, Herman Elliott

Aurora, Colorado
b. Lowe, Jack (Warren)

Bethune, Colorado
b. Pyle, Denver

Boulder, Colorado
b. Biafra, Jello
b. Burke, Arleigh A(lbert)
b. Carpenter, Scott
b. McDonald, Harl
b. Tatum, Edward Lawrie
d. Boulding, Kenneth E(wart)
d. Condon, Edward Uhler
d. Gamow, George
d. Praeger, Frederick A(mos)
d. Shapley, Harlow T

Brush, Colorado
b. Day, Pat

Buena Vista, Colorado
b. Eaton, Robert James

Canon City, Colorado
d. Clark, Dutch

Central City, Colorado
b. Sabin, Florence Rena

Colorado Springs, Colorado
b. Andrews, Bert
b. Bishop, Kelly
b. Byington, Spring
b. Chaney, Lon
b. Dillon, Mia
b. Dingell, John David, Jr.
b. Gilpin, Laura
b. Gossage, Goose
b. Keys, Ancel Benjamin
b. Morath, Max Edward
b. Parrish, Anne
b. Parsons, Talcott
b. Stringfield, Sherry
b. Taber, Gladys Bagg
d. Blaik, Red
d. Cray, Seymour R.
d. De La Torre(-Bueno), Lillian
d. Etting, Ruth
d. Goodman, Linda
d. James, Daniel, Jr.
d. Lincoln, George A
d. Lucas, Nick
d. Moody, William Vaughn

Conifer, Colorado
b. Parker, Trey

Creede, Colorado
b. Elting, Mary Letha
d. Ford, Bob

Del Norte, Colorado
d. Graves, Alvin Cushman

Denver, Colorado
b. Allen, Tim
b. Amaya, Victor
b. Bailey, Philip
b. Bishop, Julie
b. Bond, Ward
b. Bresler, Jerry
b. Brown, Hank
b. Browning, John
b. Carr, Gerald Paul
b. Carroll, Joe Barry
b. Chapman, John (Arthur)
b. Chase, Mary Coyle
b. Drinkwater, Terry
b. Eisenhower, John Sheldon Doud
b. Fairbanks, Douglas
b. Fodor, Eugene Nicholas
b. Fowler, Gene
b. Gaddis, Thomas (Eugene)
b. Halliday, Richard
b. Handler, Elliot
b. Handler, Ruth
b. Harris, William Bliss
b. Hart, John Richard
b. Hingle, Pat
b. Hogan, Linda
b. Hufstedler, Shirley (Ann) M(ount)
b. Johnson, Robert Willard
b. Kerry, John F(orbes)
b. Kroeber, Theodora Kracaw
b. Lamb, Sydney MacDonald
b. Langan, Glenn
b. Lea, Homer
b. Livingston, Jerry
b. Lustig, Alvin
b. McArthur, Edwin Douglas
b. McDonnell, James Smith
b. McLean, Evalyn Walsh
b. Meselson, Matthew Stanley
b. Morgan, Jaye P

b. Morrison, Trudi Michelle
b. Perry, Antoinette
b. Ramo, Roberta Cooper
b. Reed, Dean
b. Rice, Norm(an Blann)
b. Richter, Curt Paul
b. Rifkin, Jeremy
b. Rush, Barbara
b. Russell, Donald Joseph
b. Stevens, Edmund William
b. Swigert, Jack
b. Walker, Harold Blake
b. Warner, Emily Howell
b. Whiteman, Paul
d. Andrews, Bert
d. Barrett, William Edmund
d. Beckwourth, James Pierson
d. Brico, Antonia
d. Byers, William Newton
d. Carr, William G(eorge)
d. Chase, Mary Coyle
d. Cherrington, Ben Mark
d. Cody, Buffalo Bill
d. Davidson, J Brownlee
d. DeWilde, Brandon
d. Eklund, John M(anly)
d. Evans, John
d. Hoyt, Palmer
d. Packer, Alfred G
d. Raine, William MacLeod
d. Sabin, Florence Rena
d. Tabor, Horace Austin Warner
d. Youmans, Vincent

Dillon, Colorado
b. Markey, Enid

Durango, Colorado
b. Roosa, Stuart Allen

Engelwood, Colorado
b. Van Dyken, Amy

Fort Collins, Colorado
b. White, Byron Raymond

Fort Lyon, Colorado
d. Carson, Kit

Fowler, Colorado
b. Clark, Dutch

Glenwood Springs, Colorado
d. Holliday, Doc
d. Irwin, James Benson

Golden, Colorado
b. Coors, Joseph
b. Coors, William K
b. Hoagland, Dennis Robert

Grand Valley, Colorado
b. Libby, Willard Frank

Greeley, Colorado
b. Baca-Barragan, Polly
b. Gipson, Lawrence Henry
b. Mack, Ted
b. Runnels, Tom

Green Mountain Falls, Colorado
d. Brady, Pat

La Junta, Colorado
b. Kesey, Ken
d. Maxim, Hiram Percy

Lamar, Colorado
b. Curtis, Ken

Las Animas, Colorado
b. Thompson, Llewellyn E, Jr.

Leadville, Colorado
b. Sadler, Barry
d. Tabor, Elizabeth Bonduel McCourt Doe

Littleton, Colorado
b. Grusin, Dave

Longmont, Colorado
b. Brand, Vance DeVoe

Louisville, Colorado
b. Jovanovich, William Iliya

Manassa, Colorado
b. Dempsey, Jack

Manitou Springs, Colorado
d. Goodrich, Benjamin Franklin

Merino, Colorado
b. Edwards, Ralph Livingstone

Middleton, Colorado
b. Wriston, Walter Bigelow

Montrose, Colorado
b. Trumbo, Dalton

Pagosa Springs, Colorado
b. Harman, Hugh

Palisade, Colorado
b. Martin, Fletcher

Pueblo, Colorado
b. Packard, David

Salida, Colorado
b. Blane, Sally
b. Siegel, Morris J
b. White, Leslie A(lvin)

Simla, Colorado
b. Morris, Glenn

Steamboat Springs, Colorado
b. McWilliams, Carey
d. Walker, Doak

Timpas, Colorado
d. Mackaye, James Morrison Steele

Towaoc, Colorado
b. Begay, Fred

Trinidad, Colorado
d. Lane, Ronnie

Vail, Colorado
d. Stevens, S(tanley) S(mith)

Valmont, Colorado
b. Stone, Fred Andrew

CONNECTICUT
b. Brooks, Henry Sands
b. Merrill, Steve
b. Wright, Elizur

Ashford, Connecticut
b. Lyon, Nathaniel

Avon, Connecticut
b. Alsop, Joseph Wright, Jr.
b. Alsop, Stewart Johonnot Oliver

Bantam, Connecticut
b. Bushnell, Horace

Berlin, Connecticut
b. Willard, Emma Hart

Bethany, Connecticut
b. Durand, William F.

Bethel, Connecticut
b. Barnum, P(hineas) T(aylor)
d. Tarbell, Ida Minerva
d. Young, Art(hur Henry)

Black Rock, Connecticut
b. Chauncey, Isaac

Branford, Connecticut
d. Donovan, King
d. Kennedy, Arthur

Bridgeport, Connecticut
b. Belzer, Richard
b. Benzell, Mimi
b. Dennehy, Brian
b. Irving, Isabel
b. Jones, Rosie
b. Judah, Theodore Dehone
b. Kramer, Larry
b. Lowndes, Robert A(ugustine) W(ard)
b. Mitchum, Robert
b. Olsen, Kenneth Harry
b. O'Rourke, Jim
b. Ratzenberger, John Dezso
b. Reynolds, William Bradford
b. Stoddard, Brandon
b. Tom Thumb, General
b. Walley, Deborah
d. Barnum, P(hineas) T(aylor)
d. Bemis, Samuel Flagg
d. Crosby, Fanny
d. Hoyt, Lawrence W
d. Impellitteri, Vincent R(ichard)
d. Lake, Simon
d. Moore, Roy W
d. O'Rourke, Jim
d. Partridge, Bellamy

Bridgewater, Connecticut
d. Brooks, Van Wyck
d. Evergood, Philip (Howard Francis Dixon)

Bristol, Connecticut
b. Burghoff, Gary
b. Humphrey, Gordon John

Brookfield, Connecticut
d. Berrill, Jack

Brooklyn, Connecticut
d. Putnam, Israel

Byram, Connecticut
d. Balaban, Barney

Camden, Connecticut
b. Anderson, Sherwood

Canaan, Connecticut
d. Danielian, Leon

Candlewood Lake, Connecticut
d. Genthe, Arnold

Canterbury, Connecticut
b. Cleaveland, Moses
d. Cleaveland, Moses

Cheshire, Connecticut
b. Hitchcock, Lambert
b. Kensett, John Frederick

Chester, Connecticut
d. Abel, Walter Charles
d. Mendenhall, Dorothy Reed

Clinton, Connecticut
b. Wright, Horatio Gouverneur

Colchester, Connecticut
b. Trumbull, Lyman

Cornwall, Connecticut
d. Hammond, Laurens

Cornwall Hollow, Connecticut
b. Sedgwick, John

Coventry, Connecticut
b. Buel, Jesse
b. Hale, Nathan

Cromwell, Connecticut
b. McIntyre, Hal

Danbury, Connecticut
b. Conniff, Frank
b. Ives, Charles Edward
b. Smith, Kenneth Danforth
d. Addy, Wesley
d. Crothers, Rachel
d. DaCosta, Morton
d. Gianninoto, Frank Anthony
d. Jameson, House
d. Kay, Hershy
d. Kirkus, Virginia
d. Landis, Jessie Royce
d. Lane, Rose Wilder
d. Miller, Merle
d. Nyro, Laura
d. Parrish, Anne
d. Ruml, Beardsley
d. Schell, Orville H, Jr.
d. Stout, Rex Todhunter
d. Wallace, Henry Agard
d. Westermann, H(orace) C(lifford)

Darien, Connecticut
b. Brett, George Platt, Jr.
b. Moby
d. Lopat, Ed(mund Walter)
d. McMaster, John Bach
d. Mulligan, Gerry

Deep River, Connecticut
d. Batchelor, Clarence Daniel

Derby, Connecticut
b. Cobleigh, Ira Underwood
b. Holbrook, Josiah
b. Hull, William

East Guilford, Connecticut
b. Chittenden, Thomas

East Haddam, Connecticut
b. Bulkeley, Morgan G

East Hartford, Connecticut
d. Travers, Jerry

East Windsor, Connecticut
b. Edwards, Jonathan
d. Wolcott, Roger

Easton, Connecticut
d. Carnovsky, Morris
d. Kardiner, Abram
d. Sikorsky, Igor Ivanovich
d. Tandy, Jessica

Enfield, Connecticut
b. Burke, Mike

Essex, Connecticut
d. Bowles, Chester Bliss

Fairfield, Connecticut
b. Boros, Julius (Nicholas)
b. Osborn, Henry Fairfield
b. Ryan, Meg
d. Larsen, Roy Edward
d. Parker, Ely Samuel

Falls Village, Connecticut
d. Neilson, William A(llan)

Farmington, Connecticut
d. Schorr, Friedrich

Georgetown, Connecticut
d. D'Aulaire, Edgar Parin

Glastonbury, Connecticut
b. Disney, Doris Miles
b. Welles, Gideon

Goshen, Connecticut
b. Hall, Asaph

Greenwich, Connecticut
b. Close, Glenn
b. Hack, Shelley
b. Kennedy, Ethel Skakel
b. McWilliams, Alden S
b. Purl, Linda
b. Topping, Dan(iel Reid)
d. Allen, Mel
d. Allyn, Stanley Charles

d. Barrett, Edward Ware
d. Blatch, Harriot Eaton Stanton
d. Burns, John L(awrence)
d. Caldwell, Taylor
d. Collyer, Bud
d. Cooper, Wilhelmina Behmenburg
d. Dole, Charles Minot
d. Donner, Frederic Garrett
d. Dorsey, Tommy
d. Douglass, Lathrop
d. Eberhart, Mignon Good
d. Fox, Fontaine Talbot, Jr.
d. Funston, George Keith
d. Hellmann, Richard
d. Henderson, Ray
d. Henry, George William
d. Laeri, J(ohn) Howard
d. Lasker, Mary (Woodward)
d. Levine, Joseph Edward
d. Linen, James A(lexander), III
d. Mason, Daniel Gregory
d. McHugh, Frank
d. Meek, Samuel Williams
d. Morano, Albert Paul
d. Pace, Frank, Jr.
d. Simpson, Adele (Smithline)
d. Stettinius, Edward R, Jr.
d. Templeton, Alec
d. Tuchman, Barbara Wertheim
d. Tunney, Gene
d. Warburg, James Paul
d. Watson, Thomas J(ohn), Jr.
d. Weiss, George Martin
d. Whitehead, Edwin C(arl)
d. Winterhalter, Hugo
d. Wortman, Sterling

Griswold, Connecticut
b. Stanton, Henry Brewster
b. Tyler, Moses Coit

Groton, Connecticut
b. Deane, Silas
b. Seabury, Samuel
d. Kimmel, Husband Edward

Guilford, Connecticut
b. Halleck, Fritz-Greene
d. Clinchy, Everett Ross
d. Gunn, Moses
d. Halleck, Fritz-Greene
d. Kirkpatrick, Ralph Leonard

Haddam, Connecticut
b. Brainerd, David
b. Field, David Dudley
b. Field, Stephen Johnson

Hadlyme, Connecticut
d. Hamilton, Alice

Hamden, Connecticut
b. Borgnine, Ernest
d. Angell, James Rowland
d. Estes, Eleanor Ruth Rosenfeld
d. Fitzgerald, Robert Stuart
d. Wellek, Rene
d. Wilder, Thornton (Niven)
d. Woodward, C(omer) Vann

Hampton, Connecticut
b. Weld, Theodore Dwight

b. Eikenberry, Jill
b. Elgart, Les
b. Ellsberg, Edward
b. Foote, Andrew Hull
b. Gibbs, J(osiah) Willard
b. Gilbert, Alfred Carlton, Jr.
b. Gilman, Alfred G
b. Goldsmith, Fred Ernest
b. Goodeve, Grant
b. Goodyear, Charles
b. Hadley, Arthur Twining
b. Hall, Donald Andrew
b. Harris, Louis
b. Hemion, Dwight
b. Hendrick, Burton Jesse
b. Ingersoll, Ralph McAllister
b. Jenkins, Newell
b. Kiernan, Walter
b. Lear, Norman Milton
b. Lothrop, Harriet Mulford Stone
b. Mac Cready, Paul Beattie
b. McGuire, Biff
b. McNerney, Walter James
b. Menzies, William Cameron
b. Morrow, Buddy
b. Moses, Robert
b. Motley, Constance Baker
b. Murphy, George Lloyd
b. Newman, Alfred
b. Palillo, Ron
b. Phelps, William Lyon
b. Phillips, Harry Irving
b. Porter, Quincy
b. Powell, Adam Clayton, Jr.
b. Seymour, Charles
b. Sloan, Alfred Pritchard, Jr.
b. Sobol, Louis
b. Sperry, Armstrong W
b. Spivak, Charlie
b. Spock, Benjamin (McLane)
b. Steegmuller, Francis
b. Vare, Glenna Collett
b. Verrill, Alpheus Hyatt
b. Wallant, Edward Lewis
b. Weiss, George Martin
b. Wynn, Stephen A.
d. Albers, Josef
d. Andrews, Charles McLean
d. Ashmun, Jehudi
d. Bacon, Leonard Woolsey
d. Bainton, Roland Herbert
d. Bakeless, John Edwin
d. Balin, Ina
d. Basso, Hamilton
d. Beard, Charles Austin
d. Bentley, Elizabeth Terrill
d. Bloomfield, Leonard
d. Bouchet, Edward Alexander
d. Broderick, James Joseph
d. Brownell, Samuel Miller
d. Chamberlain, John Rensselaer
d. Cochrane, Edward Lull
d. Comstock, Ada Louise
d. Cook, Donald
d. Cross, Wilbur Lucius
d. Cushing, Harvey Williams
d. Dana, James Dwight
d. Dollard, John
d. Druckman, Jacob (Raphael)
d. Durrie, George Henry
d. Dwight, Timothy
d. Eaton, Theophilus
d. Evans, Walker
d. Fischer, John
d. Fischetti, John
d. Fisher, Irving

d. Foote, Andrew Hull
d. Gassner, John Waldhorn
d. Gesell, Arnold
d. Gibbs, J(osiah) Willard
d. Griswold, Alfred Whitney
d. Harrison, Peter
d. Harrison, Ross Granville
d. Hull, Clark Leonard
d. Huntington, Ellsworth
d. Kellogg, Clara Louise
d. Koopmans, Tjalling (Charles)
d. Ladd, George Trumbull
d. Levy, Julien
d. Linton, Ralph
d. Linton, William James
d. Malinowski, Bronislaw Kasper
d. Marsh, Othniel Charles
d. Morse, Jedidiah
d. Nevin, Ethelbert Woodbridge
d. Phelps, William Lyon
d. Podoloff, Maurice
d. Porter, Quincy
d. Rostovtzeff, Michael Ivanovich
d. Rudkin, Margaret Fogarty
d. Sapir, Edward
d. Seymour, Charles
d. Shaw, Robert Lawson
d. Sherman, Roger
d. Silliman, Benjamin
d. Sullavan, Margaret
d. Terry, Alfred Howe
d. Theiler, Max
d. Tunnard, Christopher
d. Webster, Noah
d. Whitney, Eli
d. Whitney, William Dwight
d. Wimsatt, William Kurtz, Jr.
d. Winchester, Oliver Fisher

New London, Connecticut
b. Bolton, Isabel
b. Branch, Anna Hempstead
b. Carter, Jeff
b. Fletcher, Alfonso, Jr.
b. Prentice, George Denison
d. Brackman, Robert
d. Branch, Anna Hempstead
d. Branner, Martin Michael
d. Chidsey, Donald Barr
d. Ferguson, Elsie
d. Hooker, Brian
d. Mansfield, Richard
d. Martin, David Stone
d. O'Neill, James
d. Pastor, Tony
d. Rogers, John
d. Seabury, Samuel
d. Shepard, Odell

New Milford, Connecticut
d. Adams, Leonie Fuller
d. Blume, Peter
d. Cowley, Malcolm
d. Crohn, Burrill Bernard
d. McFee, William
d. Parkhurst, Helen
d. Wunder, George S

Newtown, Connecticut
d. Fosdick, Raymond Blaine
d. Untermeyer, Louis

Norfolk, Connecticut
b. Welch, William Henry
d. Laughlin, James, IV

Norwalk, Connecticut
b. Dolan, Terry
b. McMahon, Brien
b. McMahon, Horace
b. Morton, Bruce Alexander
b. Murphy, Calvin Jerome
b. Silver, Horace Ward Martin Tavares
b. Vaughn, Mo
b. Weitz, Bruce Peter
b. Wilson, Sloan
d. Babcock, Harry
d. Baldwin, Faith
d. Benjamin, Curtis G
d. Blackwell, Betsy Talbot
d. Burnett, Whit
d. Cary, Anne Louise
d. Chatterton, Ruth
d. Christians, Mady
d. DeVries, Peter
d. Drake, Stan(ley Albert)
d. Elliot, Win
d. Flavin, Joseph B(ernard)
d. Johnson, Crockett
d. Lockridge, Frances Louise
d. Maney, Richard
d. Maury, Reuben
d. McMahon, Horace
d. Peyre, Henri Maurice
d. Price, Garrett
d. Rand, Paul
d. Reasoner, Harry
d. Roper, Elmo Burns, Jr.
d. Soby, James Thrall
d. Stuart, Kenneth James
d. Telva, Marion
d. Wallant, Edward Lewis

Norwich, Connecticut
b. Arnold, Benedict
b. Backus, Isaac
b. Coit, Margaret Louise
b. Corning, Erastus
b. Dodd, Thomas Joseph
b. Gilman, Daniel Coit
b. Hazam, Lou(is J)
b. Land, Edwin Herbert
b. Lanman, Charles Rockwell
b. Norwich, William
b. Pratt, Bela Lyon
b. Proulx, E(dna) Annie
b. Roosevelt, Edith Kermit (Carow)
b. Sigourney, Lydia Howard
d. Gilman, Daniel Coit
d. Huntington, Samuel
d. Teale, Edwin Way

Old Greenwich, Connecticut
d. Landis, Walter Savage
d. Seton, Anya Chase

Old Lyme, Connecticut
d. Artzybasheff, Boris Mikhailovich
d. Dodd, Thomas Joseph
d. Ely, Richard Theodore
d. Langer, Suzanne K
d. Peterson, Roger Tory
d. Schlesinger, Frank

Old Saybrook, Connecticut
b. Petry, Ann (Lane)
d. Petry, Ann (Lane)

Plymouth, Connecticut
d. Carlson, Evans Fordyce
d. Thomas, Seth

b. Gallo, Robert Charles
b. Hopkins, Samuel
b. Kainen, Jacob
b. McGivney, Michael Joseph
b. Parker, Daniel Francis
b. Piersall, Jimmy
b. Ralph, Sheryl Lee
b. Russell, Rosalind
b. Sirica, John Joseph
b. Vincent, Fay
b. Walker, Ralph Thomas
d. Connor, Roger
d. Crosby, Sumner McKnight
d. Gabo, Naum
d. Hull, Warren
d. Leighton, Clare Veronica Hope
d. Markert, Russell
d. Parker, Daniel Francis
d. Schacht, Al(exander)

Waterford, Connecticut
d. Enders, John Franklin
d. McDougall, Walt(er)

Watertown, Connecticut
b. Hotchkiss, Benjamin Berkeley
b. Trumbull, John

West Cornwall, Connecticut
d. Skelly, Hal

West Hartford, Connecticut
b. Bush-Brown, Albert
b. Enders, John Franklin
b. Naughton, David
b. Stich-Randall, Teresa
b. Webster, Noah
d. Wilder, Joseph

West Haven, Connecticut
b. Estes, Eleanor Ruth Rosenfeld
b. Ford, Doug
b. Strong, Ken(neth E)

West Redding, Connecticut
d. Steichen, Edward Jean

West Suffield, Connecticut
b. Graham, Sylvester

Westbury, Connecticut
b. Leibovitz, Annie

Weston, Connecticut
d. Bloustein, Edward J.
d. Cadmus, Paul
d. Helburn, Theresa
d. Lawson, Robert
d. Le Gallienne, Eva

Westport, Connecticut
b. Martin, Pamela Sue
d. Adams, James Truslow
d. Chapman, John (Arthur)
d. Dennis, Sandy
d. Egan, Raymond B
d. Fraser, James Earle
d. Glackens, William James
d. Glass, Montague (Marsden)
d. Gramatky, Hardie
d. Keller, Helen Adams
d. Kipnis, Alexander
d. Raymond, Alex(ander Gillespie)
d. Spivakovsky, Tossy

d. VonSchmidt, Harold
d. Wald, Lillian D

Wethersfield, Connecticut
b. Andrews, Charles McLean
d. Beadle, William

Willimantic, Connecticut
b. Dodd, Christopher John
b. Farrell, Eileen

Willington, Connecticut
b. Sparks, Jared

Wilton, Connecticut
d. D'Aulaire, Ingri Mortenson

Windham, Connecticut
b. Huntington, Samuel
b. Wheelock, Eleazar

Windsor, Connecticut
b. Ellsworth, Oliver
b. Fitch, John
b. Ladd-Franklin, Christine
b. Sill, Edward Rowland
b. Wolcott, Oliver, Sr.
b. Wolcott, Roger
d. Ellsworth, Oliver

Windsor Locks, Connecticut
b. Grasso, Ella

Winsted, Connecticut
b. Brinton, Clarence Crane
b. Nader, Ralph

Wolcott, Connecticut
b. Alcott, Amos Bronson
b. Thomas, Seth

Woodbridge, Connecticut
b. Baur, John I(reland) H(owe)
d. Cooper, Louise Field

Woodbury, Connecticut
d. Anderson, Leroy
d. Dalgleish, Alice
d. Tanguy, Yves

Woodstock, Connecticut
b. Arnold, Harold De Forest
b. Morse, Jedidiah

DELAWARE
d. DuPont de Nemours, Pierre Samuel

Christiana, Delaware
b. Copeland, Lammot du Pont

Claymont, Delaware
d. Darley, Felix Octavius Carr

Dagsboro, Delaware
b. Clayton, John Middleton

Delaware County, Delaware
b. Humphreys, Joshua

Dover, Delaware
b. Cannon, Annie Jump
b. Rodney, Caesar

b. Sykes, George
d. Clayton, John Middleton
d. Rodney, Caesar

Frankford, Delaware
b. Williams, John James

Georgetown, Delaware
b. Townsend, George Alfred

Greenville, Delaware
d. McCoy, Charles B(relsford)

Guyencourt, Delaware
b. Chandler, Alfred Du Pont, Jr.

Hosckessin, Delaware
d. Calloway, Cab

Lewes, Delaware
d. Williams, John James

Milton, Delaware
b. Stevenson, Bryan (Allen)

Mount Cuba, Delaware
d. Copeland, Lammot du Pont

New Castle, Delaware
b. Bird, Robert Montgomery
b. Evans, Oliver
b. Ross, George
d. Read, George

New Castle County, Delaware
b. MacDonough, Thomas

Newark, Delaware
d. Crozier, Roger Allan

Newport, Delaware
b. Green, Dallas

Rockland, Delaware
d. DuPont, Pierre Samuel, III

Smyrna, Delaware
b. Cummins, George David
b. Moore, John Bassett

Washington, Delaware
b. Redding, Jay Saunders

Wilmington, Delaware
b. Bayard, Thomas Francis
b. Berry, Bertice
b. Bertinelli, Valerie
b. Canby, Henry Seidel
b. Castle, Michael Newbold
b. Cooke, David Coxe
b. DuPont, Pierre Samuel
b. DuPont, Pierre Samuel, III
b. DuPont, Pierre Samuel, IV
b. Fuller, Edmund
b. Gibson, Michael
b. Heimlich, Henry Jay
b. Kaplan, John
b. Maraldo, Pamela Jean
b. Marquand, John Phillips
b. Nathans, Daniel
b. Pyle, Howard
b. Reinhold, Judge

b. Warner, John William
b. Watterson, Henry
b. Weaver, Robert C(lifton)
b. Weaver, William
b. Wellstone, Paul David
b. West, James Edward
b. Wexler, Nancy Sabin
b. Wheeler, Earle G
b. Wideman, John Edgar
b. Williams, O(swald) S.
b. Wills, Maury
b. Wilson, John Johnston
b. Wimsatt, William Kurtz, Jr.
d. Abrams, Creighton Williams
d. Abu Salma
d. Adams, Charles Francis, Jr.
d. Adams, Henry Brooks
d. Adams, John Quincy
d. Adams, Louisa Catherine
d. Addabbo, Joseph Patrick
d. Agronsky, Martin Zama
d. Allen, Macon B
d. Allen, Robert Sharon
d. Alsop, Joseph Wright, Jr.
d. Alsop, Stewart Johonnot Oliver
d. Altrock, Nick
d. Anderson, George Everett
d. Anderson, Mary
d. Angleton, James J(esus)
d. Aspin, Les
d. Atwater, Lee
d. Auchincloss, Hugh D
d. Bailey, Florence Augusta Merriam
d. Bancroft, George
d. Bauer, Louis Agricola
d. Bazelon, David L(ionel)
d. Becker, Ralph E(lihu)
d. Belknap, William Worth
d. Benjamin, Adam, Jr.
d. Benton, Thomas Hart
d. Berger, Samuel David
d. Berkner, Lloyd Viel
d. Berliner, Emile
d. Berryman, Clifford Kennedy
d. Biddle, Anthony Joseph
d. Bingham, Hiram
d. Biossat, Bruce
d. Blackmun, Harry A(ndrew)
d. Blaine, James Gillespie
d. Bliss, Tasker Howard
d. Bloch, Claude Charles
d. Bohlen, Charles Eustis
d. Bonnin, Gertrude Simmons
d. Bonsal, Philip Wilson
d. Bonsal, Stephen
d. Borah, William Edgar
d. Bowes, Walter
d. Bowie, William
d. Boyce, Westray Battle
d. Bradley, Joseph P
d. Brady, St. Elmo
d. Brandeis, Louis Dembitz
d. Brawley, Benjamin Griffith
d. Brennan, William Joseph, Jr.
d. Brewer, David Josiah
d. Brookings, Robert Somers
d. Brown, George Scratchley
d. Brown, Jacob Jennings
d. Bruce, Blanche Kelso
d. Bruce, David Kirkpatrick Estes
d. Brumidi, Constantino
d. Buford, John
d. Burger, Warren E(arl)
d. Butler, Benjamin Franklin
d. Cabot, John Moors
d. Calhoun, John Caldwell

d. Cantacuzene, Princess
d. Cardozo, Francis Louis
d. Carney, Robert Bostwick
d. Carpenter, Leslie
d. Carroll, Anna Ella
d. Carusi, Ugo
d. Case, Clifford Philip
d. Casey, Dan(iel Maurice)
d. Chace, Marian
d. Chase, Mary Agnes
d. Chauncey, Isaac
d. Chautemps, Camille
d. Cheatham, Adolphus
d. Chretien, Henri
d. Clark, Champ
d. Clay, Henry
d. Clinton, George
d. Cobb, William Montague
d. Cockrell, Ewing
d. Cohen, Benjamin Victor
d. Cole, Sterling W(illiam)
d. Collins, Joseph Lawton, General
d. Connally, Tom
d. Cooke, Jack Kent
d. Cooper, Annie
d. Cooper, John Sherman
d. Cooper, Joseph D
d. Corcoran, Thomas Gardiner
d. Corcoran, William Wilson
d. Corwin, Thomas
d. Cox, Allyn
d. Craig, Malin
d. Crawford, William Hulfish
d. Crockett, George (William), Jr.
d. Crowder, Enoch Herbert
d. Crowder, Henry
d. Curtis, Charles Brent
d. Cushing, William Barker
d. Dahlgren, John Adolphus Bernard
d. Damas, Leon-Gontran
d. Davies, Joseph Edward
d. Davis, Dwight Filley
d. Davis, Elmer Holmes
d. Deming, W(illiam) Edwards
d. Denver, James William
d. DeRegniers, Beatrice Schenk
d. Dewey, Charles Schuveldt
d. Dewey, George
d. Diggs, Charles C(oles), Jr.
d. Dill, John Greer, Sir
d. Dirksen, Everett McKinley
d. Dixon, Jeane (Pinckert)
d. Dolan, Terry
d. Donovan, William Joseph
d. Douglas, Paul Howard
d. Douglas, William Orville
d. Drew, Charles Richard
d. Dulles, Allen Welsh
d. Dulles, Eleanor Lansing
d. Dulles, John Foster
d. Duncan, Todd
d. Eastman, Mary Henderson
d. Eaton, John Henry
d. Eberle, Edward Walter
d. Eisenhower, Dwight D(avid)
d. Eisenhower, Mamie (Geneva) Doud
d. Ellis, John Tracy
d. Elson, Edward L(ee) R(oy)
d. Engle, Clair
d. Fanon, Frantz (Omar)
d. Field, Stephen Johnson
d. Fillmore, Abigail (Powers)
d. Fitzpatrick, Thomas
d. Flanagan, Hallie Mae Ferguson
d. Fleeson, Doris
d. Fletcher, Alice Cunningham

d. Fortas, Abe
d. Fosse, Bob
d. Foster, Vincent
d. Frankfurter, Felix
d. Frazier, Edward Franklin
d. Friedman, William Frederick
d. Friendly, Alfred
d. Fulbright, J(ames) William
d. Gardner, Alexander
d. Gaud, William Steen, Jr.
d. Gerry, Elbridge
d. Ghormley, Robert Lee
d. Gilliss, James Melville
d. Glass, Carter
d. Glasser, Melvin
d. Goddard, Calvin Hooker
d. Goetz, Delia
d. Goldberg, Arthur Joseph
d. Goldberger, Joseph
d. Goldsborough, Louis Malesherbes
d. Goodell, Charles Ellsworth
d. Grant, Julia Dent
d. Gray, Gordon
d. Gray, Horace
d. Greely, Adolphus Washington
d. Greenfield, Meg
d. Griffith, Clark Calvin
d. Grimke, Archibald H(enry)
d. Grimke, Charlotte Lottie Forten
d. Gross, H(arold) R(oyce)
d. Groves, Leslie Richard
d. Grubert, Carl Alfred
d. Gruenther, Alfred Maximillian
d. Guiteau, Charles Julius
d. Halberstam, Michael Joseph
d. Hamilton, Edith
d. Hamilton, Murray
d. Hanna, Mark
d. Hare, Raymond A(rthur)
d. Harlan, John Marshall, I
d. Harlan, John Marshall, II
d. Harlow, Bryce Nathaniel
d. Harris, Patricia Roberts
d. Harrison, Caroline (Lavinia Scott)
d. Harrison, William Henry
d. Hart, Philip Aloysius
d. Hartt, Frederick
d. Haviland, Virginia
d. Hawes, Harriet Ann Boyd
d. Hay, Oliver Perry
d. Hazen, William Babcock
d. Hearst, George
d. Heaton, Leonard
d. Helper, Hinton Rowan
d. Henry, Joseph
d. Henry, Pete
d. Herter, Christian Archibald
d. Hickman, Herman Michael, Jr.
d. Higgins, Marguerite
d. Hirshhorn, Joseph Herman
d. Hitchcock, Gilbert Monell
d. Hoban, James
d. Hodge, John Reed
d. Hokinson, Helen
d. Holland, Leland James
d. Hollerith, Herman
d. Holmes, Oliver Wendell, Jr.
d. Hoover, J(ohn) Edgar
d. Houston, Charles Hamilton
d. Howard, James John
d. Hrdlicka, Ales
d. Huebner, Clarence R
d. Ickes, Harold LeClair
d. Jackson, Robert Houghwout
d. Jagan, Cheddi (Berret)
d. Jefferson, Martha

d. Wurf, Jerry
d. Yost, Charles Woodruff
d. Youngdahl, Luther Wallace
d. Zablocki, Clement John

FLORIDA
b. Kingsley, Gregory
b. Lloyd, John Henry
b. Orange, Walter
d. Ames, Adelbert
d. Deming, Barbara
d. Heade, Martin Johnson
d. Holmes, Hap

Altamonte Springs, Florida
b. Hastings, Alcee L

Apalachicola, Florida
b. Humphries, Frederick (S.)
d. Gorrie, John

Apopka, Florida
b. Anderson, John

Arcadia, Florida
b. Dozier, James Lee

Atlantis, Florida
d. Sullivan, William Hallisey, Jr.

Aventura, Florida
d. Luckman, Sid(ney)

Baker, Florida
b. Henderson, Leon N(esbit)

Bal Harbour, Florida
d. Dewey, Thomas Edmund
d. Stillman, Irwin Maxwell

Bascom, Florida
b. Dunaway, Faye

Belleair Bluffs, Florida
d. Carlson, William S(amuel)

Boca Grande, Florida
d. Lamont, Thomas William

Boca Raton, Florida
d. Bettmann, Otto L(udwig)
d. Curran, Joseph Edwin
d. Gerson, Noel Bertram
d. Hanson, Duane (Elwood)
d. Hughes, Richard J(oseph)
d. Lawrence, Lawrence Shubert, Jr.
d. Wragge, Sidney
d. Zondervan, Peter

Boynton Beach, Florida
d. Farrell, Johnny
d. Lowe, Jack (Warren)
d. Marshall, Catherine
d. McGraw, Donald Cushing
d. Raymond, James C
d. Smith, Mayo

Bradenton, Florida
d. Claytor, W(illiam) Graham, Jr.
d. Doak, Bill
d. Jepson, Helen
d. McKechnie, Bill
d. Roush, Edd J

d. Tebbetts, Birdie

Bunnell, Florida
b. Jones, Bill T.

Cape Canaveral, Florida
d. Chaffee, Roger Bruce
d. Grissom, Virgil Ivan
d. Jarvis, Gregory
d. McAuliffe, Christa
d. McNair, Ronald Ervin
d. Onizuka, Ellison
d. Resnik, Judy
d. Scobee, Dick
d. Smith, Michael John
d. White, Ed(ward Higgins, III)

Cape Coral, Florida
d. Johnston, Johnny

Carrabelle, Florida
b. O'Neil, Buck

Chiefland, Florida
d. Verrill, Alpheus Hyatt

Chipley, Florida
b. Gilmore, Artis

Clearwater, Florida
d. Battles, Cliff(ord Franklin)
d. Burke, Billy
d. Cordiner, Ralph Jarron
d. Fascell, Dante B(runo)
d. Lee, Doris Emrick
d. Merritt, Abraham
d. Zinn, Walter Henry

Cocoa, Florida
d. Debus, Kurt Heinrich
d. Messick, Hank

Coconut Grove, Florida
d. Deering, William
d. Doubleday, Frank Nelson
d. Fairchild, David Grandison
d. Farrell, Wes

Coral Gables, Florida
b. Berliner, Ron
b. Graham, Bob
b. Kurtz, Katherine
d. Auslander, Joseph
d. Ferrer, Jose Vicente
d. Groves, Wallace
d. Onsager, Lars
d. Ryder, James Arthur
d. Slotta, Karl Heinrich

Crescent City, Florida
b. Randolph, Asa Philip

Crystal River, Florida
d. Fleming, Art

Daytona Beach, Florida
b. Hamilton, Lee Herbert
b. Thurman, Howard
d. Bethune, Mary McLeod
d. Hall, Charles Martin
d. Kiernan, Walter
d. Lajoie, Nap(oleon)
d. Maleska, Eugene T.

d. Thompson, Paul W(illiams)

De Land, Florida
d. Stetson, John Batterson

Delray Beach, Florida
d. Bishop, Jim
d. Creavy, Tom
d. Johnson, Arno Hollock
d. Little, Lou(is)
d. Patrick, John
d. Rush, (David) Kenneth
d. Scholz, Jackson Volney
d. Shriner, Herb

Dunedin, Florida
d. MacDonald, Elizabeth G.

Eatonville, Florida
b. Hurston, Zora Neale
b. Jones, Deacon

Eloise, Florida
b. Stafford, Jim

Englewood, Florida
d. Rowan, Dan

Eustis, Florida
b. Lee-Smith, Hughie

Fernandina, Florida
d. Merrill, Frank Dow

Fort Lauderdale, Florida
b. Evert, Chris(tine Marie)
b. Hiassen, Carl
b. Irvin, Michael (Jerome)
b. Richmond, Mitch(ell James)
b. Sudarkasa, Niara
d. Albright, Malvin Marr
d. Boros, Julius (Nicholas)
d. Egan, Eddie
d. Gleason, Jackie
d. Jones, Robert Trent
d. Martin, Joseph William, Jr.
d. McNary, Charles Linza
d. Ortega, Santos
d. Pastorius, Jaco
d. Wesley, Dorothy Porter

Fort Myers, Florida
b. Sanders, Deion (Luwynn)
d. Aardema, Verna Norberg
d. Kirby, Durward
d. Smith, Austin E(dward)
d. Stotz, Charles Morse

Fort Pierce, Florida
d. Bergalis, Kimberly
d. Hurston, Zora Neale

Gainesville, Florida
b. Felder, Don(ald William)
b. Lyons, Henry (J.)
b. Petty, Tom
d. Beck, C(harles) C(larence)
d. Henderson, Leon N(esbit)
d. Maples, William R.
d. Rountree, William M(anning)
d. Sarett, Lew R
d. Wilder, Alec

d. Evans, Billy
d. Fitzsimmons, James E
d. Ford, Arthur A
d. Foxx, Jimmie
d. Furgol, Ed(ward)
d. Gardner, Hy
d. Gordon, John Brown
d. Grosvenor, Melville Bell
d. Hemingway, Leicester
d. Hills, Lee
d. Hoppe, Willie
d. Jacobs, Walter L
d. Kearns, Jack
d. Kenney, George Churchill
d. Klem, Bill
d. Lester, Jerry
d. Lyttle, Hulda Margaret
d. MacPhail, Larry
d. Markey, Lucille (Parker) Wright
d. Marley, Bob
d. Mars, Forrest
d. Mas Canosa, Jorge
d. Papanicolaou, George Nicholas
d. Powell, Adam Clayton, Jr.
d. Read, Albert Cushing
d. Rebozo, Bebe
d. Robbie, Joe
d. Rosenbloom, Carroll D
d. Ross, Alex(ander)
d. Singer, Isaac Bashevis
d. Spitalny, Phil
d. Sullivan, Daniel P
d. Sutherland, Earl Wilbur, Jr.
d. Thurston, Howard
d. Topping, Dan(iel Reid)
d. Walters, Lou
d. Willeford, Charles Ray, II
d. Wood, Gar(field A)
d. Wurdemann, Audrey May
d. Wylie, Philip Gordon
d. Zamora, Pedro

Miami Beach, Florida
b. Baldridge, Letitia Katherine
b. Firestone, Roy
b. Hanks, Nancy
b. Kasdan, Lawrence Edward
b. Spurrier, Steve(n Orr)
d. Abbott, George (Francis)
d. Blaisdell, George G
d. Briggs, Walter Owen
d. Capone, Al(phonse)
d. Carey, Max George
d. Firestone, Harvey Samuel
d. Ghezzi, Vic(tor)
d. Gruelle, Johnny
d. Heatter, Gabriel
d. Heywood, Eddie, Jr.
d. Ingersoll, Ralph McAllister
d. Lansky, Meyer
d. Lewisohn, Ludwig
d. Liberman, Alexander
   (Semeonovitch)
d. Lopez, Vincent
d. MacFarlane, Willie
d. Machado y Morales, Gerardo
d. May, Mortimer
d. Prio Socarras, Carlos
d. Rickard, Tex
d. Schenck, Nicholas Michael
d. Slobodkin, Louis
d. Stover, Russell
d. Thaw, Harry Kendall
d. Troy, Hannah
d. Vanderbilt, Cornelius, Jr.
d. Versace, Gianni

d. Warner, Albert
d. Wilson, William Griffith
d. Zevin, B(enjamin) D(avid)

Naples, Florida
d. Arends, Leslie Cornelius
d. Borch, Fred J.
d. Colbert, Lester L(um)
d. Dial, Morris Grant
d. Henry, David D(odds)
d. Kirby, Robert E(mory)
d. Martin, John C
d. Sarazen, Gene
d. Steelman, John Roy

New Smyrna, Florida
d. Blood, Ernest
d. Paine, Albert Bigelow

Nokomis, Florida
d. Jessup, Richard

North Miami, Florida
d. Lombardo, Carmen

North Miami Beach, Florida
d. Buckley, Emerson

North Palm Beach, Florida
d. Butterfield, Billy
d. Cunningham, Harry Blair
d. Leonidoff, Leon

Ocala, Florida
b. Ashley, Elizabeth
b. O'Neal, Patrick
d. Harbert, Chick

Odessa, Florida
d. Politz, Alfred

Oklawaha, Florida
d. Barker, Fred
d. Barker, Ma

Orlando, Florida
b. Burke, Delta
b. Dawkins, Darryl
b. Garrett, George Palmer, Jr.
b. Johnson, Davey
b. Pihos, Pete(r L)
b. Snipes, Wesley
b. West, Riff
d. Crane, Roy(ston Campbell)
d. Duranty, Walter
d. Gould, Morton
d. Lamarr, Hedy
d. McNeill, Robert Edward, Jr.
d. Mott, John Raleigh
d. Newsom, Bobo
d. Roberts, Elizabeth Madox
d. Shawn, Ted
d. Thompson, Mary
d. Tinker, Joe

Ormond Beach, Florida
d. Boni, Albert
d. Hunt, Jack Reed
d. Kitchell, Iva
d. Mitchell, Howard (Bundy)
d. Rockefeller, John D(avison)

Pahokee, Florida
b. Tillis, Mel(vin)

Palatka, Florida
b. Stilwell, Joseph Warren

Palm Beach, Florida
b. Pulitzer, Lilly
d. Albee, Edward Franklin
d. Bache, Jules Sermon
d. Bishop, Billy
d. Cummings, Nathan
d. Daniels, Frank
d. DeMarco, Tony
d. Dodge, Horace Elgin
d. Donahue, Woolworth
d. Downey, Morton
d. Eyen, Tom
d. Gambling, John Bradley
d. Goodman, Martin
d. Guggenheim, Meyer
d. Jefferson, Joseph
d. Kallen, Horace M(eyer)
d. Keith, Benjamin Franklin
d. Kennedy, David Anthony
d. Mahoney, David Joseph, Jr.
d. McKeen, John Elmer
d. Mizner, Addison
d. Murphy, George Lloyd
d. Sawyer, Charles
d. Sears, Eleonora Randolph
d. Smith, Ethel
d. Uris, Harold David
d. Wood, Craig Ralph

Palm Beach Gardens, Florida
d. Horst, Horst P(aul)

Palm Coast, Florida
d. Long, Dale

Palm Harbor, Florida
d. Klassen, Elmer Theodore

Palm Springs, Florida
d. Custin, Mildred

Pembroke Pines, Florida
d. McHale, Tom

Pensacola, Florida
b. Butterfield, Alexander Porter
b. Byrd, Robert
b. Cherberg, John A(ndrew)
b. Cochran, Jacqueline
b. Dussault, Nancy Elizabeth
b. James, Daniel, Jr.
b. Kurtis, Bill
b. Percy, Charles Harting
b. Smith, Emmitt
d. Bouquet, Henry
d. Erickson, Leif
d. Mallory, Stephen R

Plant City, Florida
b. Tillis, Pam

Plantation Key, Florida
d. Zim, Herbert S(pencer)

Polk City, Florida
d. Van Fleet, James Alward

Pompano Beach, Florida
b. Rolle, Esther
d. Cadieux, Marcel (Joseph David Romeo)
d. Daniel, Dan(iel)
d. Hinton, Walter
d. Ross, Roy G
d. Sanders, Lawrence
d. Sebrell, W(illiam) H(enry), Jr.
d. Walsh, Ed(ward Augustine)

Quincy, Florida
b. Lefall, LaSalle Doheny, Jr.

Riviera Beach, Florida
b. Carter, Anthony Calvin

Saint Augustine, Florida
b. Smith, Edmund Kirby
d. Boone, Richard
d. Caldecott, Randolph
d. Rawlings, Marjorie Kinnan
d. Schofield, John McAllister
d. Young, Owen D

Saint Petersburg, Florida
b. Corinne, Tee A.
b. McNally, Terrence
d. Cable, George Washington
d. Gunnison, Foster
d. Hartmann, Sadakichi
d. Hubbard, Cal
d. Kerouac, Jack
d. Medwick, Joe
d. Pennington, John Selman
d. Seibert, Florence B(arbara)
d. Weinberger, Jaromir
d. Young, Chic

Sanford, Florida
b. Courier, Jim
b. Raines, Tim(othy)

Sanibel Island, Florida
d. Fadiman, Clifton (Paul)
d. Shepherd, Jean Parker

Sarasota, Florida
d. Baldwin, Horace
d. Bartholomew, Freddie
d. Braceland, Francis J(ames)
d. Browne, Dik
d. Chase, Edna Woolman
d. Edwards, Douglas
d. Ferrell, Wes(ley Cheek)
d. Goldenson, Leonard H(arry)
d. Jacobs, Lou
d. Kantor, Mackinlay
d. Kappel, Frederick R(ussell)
d. Kelly, Emmett Lee
d. Kenny, Nick
d. Langer, Walter C
d. Lawrence, David
d. Lowe, Edward
d. Manush, Heinie
d. Mayer, Jean
d. Raushenbush, Stephen
d. Ringling, Charles
d. Roudebush, Richard L(owell)
d. Smith, Thorne
d. Stahl, Ben(jamin Albert)
d. Stern, Philip Van Doren
d. Swayze, John Cameron, Sr.
d. Taubman, (Hyman) Howard
d. Tucker, Tommy

d. Waner, Paul Glee
d. Woltman, Frederick Enos

Satsuma, Florida
d. Barker, Cliff

Sebastian, Florida
d. Jackson, Laura Riding

Sebring, Florida
d. Beach, Rex Ellingwood

Seminole, Florida
d. Hammon, William McDowell

Silver Springs, Florida
d. Remington, Eliphalet

Sommerfield, Florida
b. Hutson, Jean Blackwell

South Miami, Florida
d. Rinehart, Stanley Marshall, Jr.

Spring Hill, Florida
d. Foster, Hal
d. Sutton, Willie

Starke, Florida
d. Bundy, Ted
d. Spenkelink, John Arthur

Stuart, Florida
d. Cozzens, James Gould
d. Dempster, Arthur Jeffrey
d. Monroe, Vaughn
d. Wilson, Lyle Campbell

Tacoma Park, Florida
b. Agee, Philip

Tallahassee, Florida
b. Amos, Wally
b. Davis, Brad
b. Meek, Carrie
b. Perry, Troy D.
b. Thigpen, Bobby
d. Barber, Red
d. Caidin, Martin
d. Chiles, Lawton Mainor, Jr.
d. Dirac, Paul Adrien Maurice
d. Gaither, Jake
d. Griffin, Marvin
d. Jahoda, Gloria (Adelaide Love)
d. Kilenyi, Edward, Sr.

Tamarac, Florida
d. Bernstein, Allan

Tampa, Florida
b. Adderley, Cannonball
b. Brent, Evelyn
b. Garvey, Steve(n Patrick)
b. Gates, Sylvester James, Jr.
b. Gooden, Dwight Eugene
b. LaRussa, Tony
b. Lopez, Al(fonso Ramon)
b. Martinez, Bob
b. McGriff, Fred(erick Stanley)
b. McQueen, Butterfly
b. Piniella, Lou(is Victor)
b. Rebozo, Bebe
b. Sanborn, David

b. Sheffield, Gary (Antonian)
b. Trafficante, Santo, Jr.
d. Paul, Gabe
d. Sissle, Noble
d. Tanny, Vic
d. Vander Meer, Johnny
d. Waugh, Alec
d. Zaharias, George

Tarpon Springs, Florida
b. Higgins, Bertie
d. Lenski, Lois

Tavares, Florida
b. Roberts, Edward Glenn

Titusville, Florida
b. Ford, Arthur A
b. Marshall, Wilbur Buddyhia
d. Fitzgerald, John Dennis
d. Grant, Kirby

Venice, Florida
d. Aherne, Brian de Lacy
d. Farley, Walter Lorimer
d. Haggart, Bob
d. Irish, Ned
d. Moore, Don W
d. Nitschke, Ray(mond E.)
d. Wynn, Early

Vero Beach, Florida
d. Bickmore, Lee Smith

Wabasso, Florida
d. Riding, Laura

Wakulla Springs State Park, Florida
d. Kendall, Henry Way

West Palm Beach, Florida
b. Anderson, O(ttis) J(erome)
b. Canova, Diana
b. Rogers, Adrian Pierce
d. Cooper, Kent
d. Flagler, Henry Morrison
d. Fox, Virgil Keel
d. Graham, Sheilah
d. Herman, Billy
d. Hodges, Gil(bert Raymond)
d. Javits, Jacob Koppel
d. MacArthur, John Donald
d. Miller, Paul
d. Pillsbury, John Sargent
d. Pomerantz, Fred P
d. Ridder, Bernard Herman
d. Ruchlis, Hy(man)
d. Summerfield, Arthur Ellsworth
d. Wicker, Ireene Seaton

Winter Haven, Florida
b. Parsons, Gram
b. Rollins, Wayne Monte
d. Cleaver, William Joseph
d. Skidmore, Louis

Winter Park, Florida
b. Bearse, Amanda
d. Churchill, Winston
d. Feis, Herbert
d. Gaines, Clarence F
d. Gurney, Edward John
d. Homer, Louise
d. Homer, Sidney

d. King, Frank
d. Pattee, Fred Lewis
d. Russell, Annie
d. Stratemeyer, George E, General

Yukon, Florida
b. Smoot, George

GEORGIA
b. Boudinot, Elias
b. Bozeman, John M
b. Daniels, Jeff
b. Hill, Benjamin Harvey
b. Osceola
b. Ridge, John Rollin
b. Soderbergh, Steven
b. Watie, Stand

Albany, Georgia
b. Charles, Ray
b. Coachman, Alice
b. Dawson, William L(evi)
b. James, Harry
b. Jones, Edward Vason
b. Knight, Ray
b. Reagon, Bernice Johnson
b. Riegger, Wallingford
d. Jones, Edward Vason
d. Thomas, Charles Allen

Alma, Georgia
b. Crews, Harry Eugene

Americus, Georgia
b. Bell, Griffin Boyette
d. Carter, Lillian

Andersonville, Georgia
b. Pennington, John Selman

Archery, Georgia
b. Stapleton, Ruth Carter

Ashburn, Georgia
b. Dennison, George

Athens, Georgia
b. Basinger, Kim
b. Derricotte, Juliette Aline
b. Grady, Henry Woodfin
b. Johnson, Hall
b. Kottke, Leo
b. McGarity, Lou
b. Stovall, Luther McKinley
d. Andrews, Raymond
d. Long, Crawford Williamson
d. Michael, Moina Belle
d. Rusk, (David) Dean
d. Sinkwich, Frank
d. Towns, Forrest

Atlanta, Georgia
b. Adams, Brock(man)
b. Allen, Ivan, Jr.
b. Atwater, Lee
b. Blackwell, (Samuel) Earl, Jr.
b. Blomberg, Ron(ald Mark)
b. Boorstin, Daniel J(oseph)
b. Borden, Barry
b. Candler, Charles Howard
b. Cleland, Max
b. Collier, John
b. Conroy, Pat
b. Cook, Barbara

b. Days, Drew S(aunders), III
b. Dickey, James (Lafayette)
b. Dobbs, Mattiwilda
b. Frazier, Walt(er Jr.)
b. Free, World B
b. Fuller, Hoyt William
b. Gaines, Boyd
b. Gordy, Emory, Jr.
b. Hamilton, Grace Towns
b. Harwell, Ernie
b. Heywood, Eddie, Jr.
b. Higginbotham, Jack
b. Hill, Abram
b. Jones, Bobby
b. Jordan, Vernon Eulion, Jr.
b. Joyner, Wally
b. Kelley, DeForest
b. King, Dexter (Scott)
b. King, Martin Luther, Jr.
b. Knight, Gladys Maria
b. Lee, Brenda
b. Lee, Spike
b. Lipshutz, Robert Jerome
b. Lucas, Craig
b. Lundquist, Steve
b. Lyon, Ben
b. Maddox, Lester Garfield
b. Major, Clarence
b. McDaniel, Mildred
b. McDonald, Larry
b. McDougall, Gay J.
b. McKinney, Cynthia A(nn)
b. Metcalfe, Ralph H
b. Miller, James Clifford, III
b. Millis, Walter
b. Mitchell, Margaret
b. Neal, Larry
b. Parks, Bert
b. Pender, Mel(vin)
b. Reed, Jerry
b. Robertson, James D, III
b. Roe, Tommy
b. Russell, Herman J(erome)
b. Russell, Nipsey
b. South, Joe
b. Stone, Doug
b. Sullivan, Louis W(ade)
b. Terry, Bill
b. Torrence, Gwen(dolyn Lenna)
b. Tracy, Lee
b. Tucker, Chris
b. Walker, LeRoy Tashreau
b. Wells, James Lesesne
b. White, Walter Francis
b. Williams, Wayne Bertram
b. Willingham, Calder Baynard, Jr.
b. Wills, Garry
b. Withers, Jane
d. Abernathy, Ralph David
d. Arnall, Ellis (Gibbs)
d. Austin, John Paul
d. Bealer, Alex W(inkler III)
d. Black, Frank J.
d. Boles, Paul Darcy
d. Callahan, Harry (Morey)
d. Candler, Asa Griggs
d. Candler, Charles Howard
d. Casey, Hugh Thomas
d. Cobb, Ty(rus Raymond)
d. Coverdell, Paul
d. Davis, James Curran
d. Ehrlichman, John D(aniel)
d. Felton, Rebecca Ann Latimer
d. Fuller, Hoyt William
d. Goizueta, Roberto C(rispulo)
d. Grady, Henry Woodfin

d. Grizzard, Lewis M., Jr.
d. Hamilton, Grace Towns
d. Harris, Joel Chandler
d. Henderson, Vivian Wilson
d. Hill, Benjamin Harvey
d. Holt, Ivan Lee
d. Hope, John
d. Howell, Clark
d. Jones, Bobby
d. King, Alberta Christine Williams
d. King, Martin Luther, Sr.
d. Kirbo, Charles H(ughes)
d. Mays, Benjamin E(lijah)
d. McConnell, Joseph H(oward)
d. McGill, Ralph Emerson
d. McPherson, James Birdseye
d. Mitchell, Margaret
d. Robinson, Wilbert
d. Robitscher, Jonas Bondi, Jr.
d. Sargent, George
d. Smith, Lillian
d. Stanton, Frank Lebby
d. Stephens, Alexander Hamilton
d. Talmadge, Eugene
d. Woodruff, Robert Winship
d. Young, Jean Childs

Atmore, Georgia
b. Holyfield, Evander

Attapulgis, Georgia
b. Williams, Hosea Lorenzo

Augusta, Georgia
b. Brown, James
b. Fishburne, Laurence
b. Gibbs, Terri
b. Grant, Amy
b. Hogan, Hulk
b. Hope, John
b. Johns, Jasper, (Jr.)
b. McDuffie, George
b. Meigs, Montgomery Cunningham
b. Mize, Larry
b. Norman, Jessye
b. Prince, Faith
b. Tobias, Channing Heggie
b. Wheeler, Joseph
b. Yerby, Frank (Garvin)
d. Billings, John Shaw
d. McLeod, Fred(erick)
d. McQueen, Butterfly
d. Ward, Monte
d. Woodward, William E

Bainbridge, Georgia
b. Griffin, Marvin
b. Hopkins, Miriam
b. Kirbo, Charles H(ughes)
b. Stribling, Young

Barstow, Georgia
b. Coleman, Lonnie William

Bethlehem, Georgia
b. Odum, Howard Washington

Brunswick, Georgia
d. Tower, John Goodwin

Buckhead, Georgia
b. Casey, Hugh Thomas

La Grange, Georgia
b. Austin, John Paul
b. Callaway, Howard Hollis
b. Jarriel, Tom
b. Wright, Louis Tompkins

Lafayette, Georgia
b. Bean, Andy
b. Dodd, Ed(ward) Benton

Lawrenceville, Georgia
b. Charles, Ezzard

Leesburg, Georgia
b. Hamilton, Roy
b. Motley, Marion

Lincoln County, Georgia
b. Curry, Jabez Lamar Monroe

Lithia Springs, Georgia
b. Suggs, Louise

Lumpkin, Georgia
b. Root, John Wellborn

Macon, Georgia
b. Ansa, Tina McElroy
b. Crawford, Randy
b. Douglas, Melvyn
b. Harvard, Beverly
b. Hoving, Jane Pickens
b. Lanier, Sidney
b. Little Richard
b. McDuffie, Robert
b. Moore, Roy W
b. Pate, Jerry
b. Pinchback, P(inckney) B(enton) S(tewart)
b. Stallings, Laurence
d. Allman, Duane
d. Stribling, Young

Marietta, Georgia
b. Clay, Lucius du Bignon
b. McAdoo, William Gibbs
b. Tritt, Travis
b. Walker, Danton MacIntyre
d. Carmichael, James Vinson
d. Haughton, Daniel Jeremiah

Martin, Georgia
b. Landrum, Phil(lip) M(itchell)

McRue, Georgia
b. Folsom, Marion Bayard

Milledgeville, Georgia
b. Vinson, Carl
d. O'Connor, Flannery
d. Vinson, Carl

Monroe, Georgia
d. Van Brocklin, Norm (an Mack)

Monroe County, Georgia
b. George, James Zachariah

Montgomery, Georgia
d. Smith, Frances Scott Fitzgerald Lanahan

Monticello, Georgia
b. Yearwood, Trisha

Moreland, Georgia
b. Caldwell, Erskine Preston

Morgan City, Georgia
b. Andrews, Raymond

Moultrie, Georgia
b. Melton, James

Mount Berry, Georgia
d. Berry, Martha McChesney

Narrows, Georgia
b. Cobb, Ty(rus Raymond)

Nelson, Georgia
b. Akins, Claude

Newnan, Georgia
b. Arnall, Ellis (Gibbs)
b. Jackson, Alan Eugene
b. Upshaw, William David
b. Walton, Jerome O'Terrell

Norcross, Georgia
d. Dean, Man Mountain

Oak Grove, Georgia
b. Johnston, Richard Malcolm

Ocilla, Georgia
b. Prater, Dave

Peach County, Georgia
b. Johnson, Pete

Perry, Georgia
b. Hodges, Courtney
b. Nunn, Sam(uel Augustus, Jr.)

Pike County, Georgia
b. Futrelle, Jacques

Plains, Georgia
b. Carter, Amy Lynn
b. Carter, Billy
b. Carter, Jimmy
b. Carter, Rosalynn
d. Carter, Billy

Poulan, Georgia
b. Heflin, Howell Thomas

Preston, Georgia
b. George, Walter Franklin

Richland, Georgia
b. Dixon, Robert Ellington

Richmond, Georgia
b. Carter, Lillian

Rome, Georgia
b. Berry, Martha McChesney
b. Franklin, Hardy R.
b. Reeves, Dan(iel Edward)
b. Towers, John Henry
d. York, Rudy

Roswell, Georgia
d. Mayfield, Curtis (Lee)

Saint Catherine's Island, Georgia
d. Gwinnett, Button

Saint Simons Island, Georgia
b. Brown, Jim

Sandersville, Georgia
b. Muhammad, Elijah

Savannah, Georgia
b. Adams, Floyd, Jr.
b. Aiken, Conrad Potter
b. Clayton, Eva M.
b. Coburn, Charles Douville
b. Curb, Mike
b. Dent, Bucky
b. Fremont, John Charles
b. Green, Anne
b. Hardee, William Joseph
b. Harmon, Claude
b. Jaffee, Allan
b. Jessup, Richard
b. Kanter, Hal
b. Keach, Stacy, Jr.
b. Low, Juliette Gordon
b. Martin, James Grubbs
b. Matlovich, Leonard P., Jr.
b. McPherson, James Alan
b. Mercer, Johnny
b. Morehouse, Ward
b. O'Connor, Flannery
b. Quinn, Sally
b. Sengstacke, John H(erman Henry)
b. Smith, Merriman
b. Stacy, Hollis
b. Thomas, Clarence
b. Varnedoe, (John) Kirk (Train)
b. Washington, Fredi
b. Wilson, Ellen Axson
b. Young, Trummy
d. Aiken, Conrad Potter
d. Coleman, Lonnie William
d. Greene, Nathanael
d. Low, Juliette Gordon
d. Oliver, Joe
d. Pulaski, Kazimierz
d. Thompson, William Tappan

Sea Island, Georgia
d. Coffin, Howard Earle

Shellman, Georgia
b. Bryant, Boudleaux

Smyrna, Georgia
b. Carmichael, James Vinson
b. Roberts, Julia

Sparta, Georgia
b. Jackson, Hurricane

Stockbridge, Georgia
b. King, Martin Luther, Sr.

Sunbury, Georgia
b. Couper, James Hamilton

Swainsboro, Georgia
b. Guy, Ray

Council, Idaho
b. Craig, Larry Edwin
b. Rainwater, James

Evansville, Idaho
b. Catlett, Big Sid

Gooding, Idaho
b. Cary, Frank Taylor

Hailey, Idaho
b. Pound, Ezra Loomis

Harpster, Idaho
b. Conklin, Gladys Plemon

Henry's Lake, Idaho
d. Winnemucca, Sarah

Hope, Idaho
d. Kienholz, Edward

Idaho Falls, Idaho
b. Kornman, Mary

Jerome, Idaho
d. Fisher, Vardis

Ketchum, Idaho
d. Hemingway, Ernest (Miller)

Lava Hot Springs, Idaho
b. Bell, T(errel) H(oward)

Malad, Idaho
b. Johnson, Sonia

Meridian, Idaho
b. Law, Vern(on Sanders)

Moscow, Idaho
b. Brink, Carol Ryrie

Nampa, Idaho
b. Clark, J.E.
b. Symms, Steven Douglas
b. Young, John Alan

Payette, Idaho
b. Killebrew, Harmon Clayton
b. McClure, James A

Pocatello, Idaho
b. Bucher, Lloyd Mark

Rigby, Idaho
b. Wilson, Larry

Spalding, Idaho
b. Disney, Lillian

Stanley, Idaho
b. Blakeley, Ronee

Twin Falls, Idaho
b. Deiss, Joseph Jay
b. Pike, Gary

Wallace, Idaho
b. Turner, Lana

Whitney, Idaho
b. Benson, Ezra Taft

ILLINOIS
b. Bode, Boyd Henry
b. Courtright, Jim
b. Ernst, Kenneth
b. Goldman, Ronald Lyle
b. McDormand, Frances
b. Ode, Robert C
d. Lundy, Benjamin

Abington, Illinois
b. Stockdale, James

Acton, Illinois
b. Main, Marjorie

Aledo, Illinois
b. Lee, Doris Emrick

Alton, Illinois
b. Aurre, Laura
b. Brodkey, Harold
b. Davis, Miles Dewey, III
b. Ray, James Earl
d. Long, Stephen H
d. Lovejoy, Elijah Parish

Arcola, Illinois
b. Gruelle, Johnny

Argo, Illinois
b. Kluszewski, Ted

Arlington Heights, Illinois
b. Wille, Lois Jean

Auburn, Illinois
b. Leonard, Dutch

Aurora, Illinois
b. Jones, Thom
b. Miller, Olive Beaupre
b. Parrington, Vernon L(ouis)
b. Sereno, Paul C.
d. Mansfield, Arabella
d. White, Deacon

Barrington, Illinois
d. Payton, Walter

Barry, Illinois
b. Dell, Floyd

Batavia, Illinois
b. Anderson, Ken(neth Allan)
b. Issel, Dan(iel Paul)

Beardstown, Illinois
b. Norvo, Red

Belleville, Illinois
b. Dixon, Alan John
b. Ebsen, Buddy
b. Goalby, Bob

Berwyn, Illinois
b. Watt, Richard Martin

Bloomingdale, Illinois
b. Lillie, Gordon William

Bloomington, Illinois
b. Anderson, George Everett
b. Crothers, Rachel
b. Davisson, Clinton Joseph
b. Goudy, Frederic William
b. Hubbard, Elbert Green
b. Mowrer, Edgar Ansel
b. Mowrer, Paul Scott
b. Robinson, James Harvey
b. Rockwell, George Lincoln
b. Smith, (Robert) Sidney
b. Stevenson, McLean
d. Davis, David
d. Radbourn, Old Hoss

Bourbonnais, Illinois
b. Dandurand, Leo

Braidwood, Illinois
b. Mitchell, John

Brocton, Illinois
b. Gard, Wayne

Byron, Illinois
b. Spalding, Albert Goodwill

Cairo, Illinois
b. Hart, George Overbury
b. Ingram, Rex
b. Strode, Hudson
b. Woodruff, Hale (Aspacio)

Camp Point, Illinois
b. Nevins, Allan

Canton, Illinois
b. Duryea, Charles Edgar
b. Mertz, Barbara Louise Gross

Carbondale, Illinois
b. Ayres, Agnes
b. Trumbauer, Frank(ie)
d. Moore, Harry Thornton

Carlinville, Illinois
b. Austin, Mary Hunter
b. Mack, Peter

Carlyle, Illinois
b. Dean, William Frishe
b. Slade, Jack

Carol Stream, Illinois
d. Shoemaker, Vaughn Richard

Carrollton, Illinois
b. Allen, Karen Jane

Carthage, Illinois
d. Smith, Joseph

Cary, Illinois
d. Schnering, Otto

Cedarville, Illinois
b. Addams, Jane

Centralia, Illinois
b. Brady, James Scott
b. Madeira, Jean

b. Friedkin, William
b. Friedman, Jerome
b. Fukuyama, Francis
b. Fuller, Henry Blake
b. Gacy, John Wayne, Jr.
b. Gaedel, Eddie
b. Gardiner, Muriel
b. Gardner, Edward George
b. Gaynor, Mitzi
b. Gelbart, Larry
b. Gelber, Jack
b. Germer, Lester Halbert
b. Gerson, Noel Bertram
b. Geyer, Georgie Anne
b. Giancana, Sam
b. Gibbs, Marla Bradley
b. Gilkey, Langdon Brown
b. Ginsburg, Douglas Howard
b. Giovenco, John Vincent
b. Gobel, George Leslie
b. Godowsky, Leopold, Jr.
b. Goldberg, Arthur Joseph
b. Goldberg, Bertrand
b. Goldman, James
b. Goldman, William
b. Golonka, Arlene
b. Golub, Leon Albert
b. Goodman, Benny
b. Goodman, Steve(n Benjamin)
b. Gorey, Edward St. John
b. Gorton, Slade
b. Gottschalk, Robert
b. Graham, Evarts Ambrose
b. Graham, Virginia
b. Grahn, Judy
b. Gray, Dolores
b. Grebey, Ray
b. Green, Rickey Anthony
b. Greene, Shecky
b. Gross, Michael
b. Groth, John August
b. Grubert, Carl Alfred
b. Gunther, John
b. Hagen, Jean
b. Halas, George Stanley
b. Hale, George Ellery
b. Halper, Albert
b. Hambro, Leonid
b. Hamill, Dorothy Stuart
b. Hampton, Fred
b. Hancock, Herbie
b. Hannah, Daryl
b. Hannah, Marc (Regis)
b. Hansberry, Lorraine
b. Hapgood, Norman
b. Harlan, John Marshall, II
b. Harnick, Sheldon Mayer
b. Harridge, Will(iam)
b. Harris, Robin
b. Harsh, Vivian Gordon
b. Hathaway, Donny
b. Hawkins, La-Van
b. Hefner, Christie
b. Hefner, Hugh Marston
b. Hemphill, Essex
b. Henderson, Rickey (Henley)
b. Henner, Marilu
b. Herblock
b. Hersh, Seymour
b. Heyworth, James
b. Hinton, William Augustus
b. Hoffman, Julius Jennings
b. Hoffman, Paul Gray
b. Hogarth, Burne
b. Holmes, Burton
b. Hovland, Carl I.

b. Howard, Juwan (Antonio)
b. Hunt, Richard (Howard)
b. Hutton, Ina Ray
b. Hyde, Henry J(ohn)
b. Hynek, J(oseph) Allen
b. Iceberg Slim
b. Irsay, Robert
b. Jackson, George
b. Jacobs, Walter L
b. Jacobson, Michael Faraday
b. Jaeger, Andrea
b. Jagan, Janet
b. Jahoda, Gloria (Adelaide Love)
b. Jakes, John (William)
b. Jensen, Mike
b. Johanson, Donald Carl
b. Johnson, Chic
b. Johnson, Lynn-Holly
b. Jones, Jo(nathan)
b. Jones, Quincy Delight
b. Jones, Rickie Lee
b. Jordan, Stanley
b. Kaplan, Henry Seymour
b. Karlin, Frederick James
b. Kath, Terry
b. Keach, Stacy, Sr.
b. Keith, Louis Gerald
b. Kelly, R(obert)
b. Keniston, Kenneth
b. Kennedy, Joseph Patrick, Jr.
b. Kennedy, Madge
b. Keough, Danny
b. Kerner, Otto
b. Kerr, Red
b. Kiley, Richard (Paul)
b. Kilgallen, Dorothy
b. Kirby, George
b. Kline, Otis Adelbert
b. Koenig, Walter
b. Komer, Robert William
b. Kopay, David
b. Korman, Harvey Herschel
b. Kroc, Ray(mond) Albert
b. Krogh, Egil, Jr.
b. Krupa, Gene
b. Krzyzewski, Mike
b. Kunjufu, Jawanza
b. Kupcinet, Irv
b. Kutner, Luis
b. Lafontant-Mankarious, Jewel
   (Stradford)
b. Lahey, Edwin A(loysius)
b. Laine, Frankie
b. Landis, Jessie Royce
b. Landis, John David
b. Lansing, Sherry Lee
b. Lardner, Ring(gold Wilmer), Jr.
b. LaRocque, Rod
b. Larsen, Nella
b. Lattner, Johnny
b. Lawler, Richard Harold
b. Lawrence, Robert (Henry), Jr.
b. Lawson, Donald Elmer
b. Lawson, Victor Fremont
b. Leiber, Fritz (Reuter), Jr.
b. Leonard, Jack E
b. Lester, Jerry
b. Levi, Edward Hirsch
b. Levin, Meyer
b. Lewis, Janet
b. Lewis, Meade Anderson Lux
b. Lewis, Ramsey Emanuel, Jr.
b. Lichty, George
b. Lincoln, Abbey
b. Lindstrom, Freddie
b. Lipman, Clara

b. Loeb, Richard A
b. Lofgren, Nils
b. Long, Richard
b. Loughname, Lee
b. Lubin, Charles W
b. Luboff, Norman
b. Lubovitch, Lar
b. Lundahl, Arthur Charles
b. Lurie, Alison
b. Luzinski, Greg(ory Michael)
b. Lyman, Abe
b. Lynn, Fred(ric Michael)
b. Lynn, Janet
b. MacCameron, Robert L
b. Macy, John Williams, Jr.
b. Mahoney, Jock
b. Mainbocher
b. Malone, Dorothy
b. Maltby, Richard E
b. Mamet, David Alan
b. Manatt, Charles Taylor
b. Manetti, Larry
b. Mann, Michael
b. Mantegna, Joe
b. Manzarek, Ray
b. Margulis, Lynn
b. Mark, Norman (Barry)
b. Markus, Robert
b. Marsala, Joe
b. Marsala, Marty
b. Marshall, William
b. Martin, David Stone
b. Marx, Richard
b. Matalin, Mary (Joe)
b. Matheson, Scott Milne
b. Mayer, Oscar Gottfried
b. Mayer, Oscar Gottfried, II
b. Mayfield, Curtis (Lee)
b. Mazel, Judy
b. McBride, Bryant
b. McCarthy, Jenny
b. McCashin, Constance Broman
b. McCormach, Mark Hume
b. McCormack, Mike
b. McCormick, Cyrus Hall
b. McCormick, Joseph Medill
b. McCormick, Robert Rutherford
b. McDivitt, Jim
b. McGivern, William Peter
b. McGuinn, Roger
b. McLain, Denny
b. McLaughlin, Frederic
b. McNally, Andrew, III
b. McNellis, Maggi
b. McPartland, Jimmy
b. Meland, Bernard Eugene
b. Meyer, Ray(mond Joseph)
b. Mezzrow, Mezz
b. Middleton, Ray
b. Miles, Josephine
b. Miller, Perry Gilbert Eddy
b. Millikan, Clark Blanchard
b. Mills, Donna
b. Minnelli, Vincente
b. Mitchell, Joan
b. Monroe, Harriet
b. Mooney, Tom
b. Moore, Clayton
b. Moore, Stanford
b. Moran, Polly
b. Moseley-Braun, Carol
b. Motley, Willard Francis
b. Mottelson, Benjamin Roy
b. Moutoussamy-Ashe, Jeanne
b. Muczynski, Robert
b. Mull, Martin

Geographic Index

b. Murphy, Jimmy
b. Murray, Elizabeth
b. Nebel, Long John
b. Nelson, Baby Face
b. Ness, Eliot
b. Netsch, Walter Andrew, Jr.
b. Nielsen, Arthur Charles
b. Norris, Bruce A
b. Norris, Frank(lin)
b. Norris, James D
b. Novak, Kim
b. Nussbaum, Karen
b. Oboler, Arch
b. O'Connor, Donald
b. O'Day, Anita
b. O'Donnell, Chris
b. O'Horgan, Tom
b. Olin, Ken
b. O'Neil, Roger
b. Paley, William Samuel
b. Panama, Norman
b. Pankow, James
b. Parazaider, Walter
b. Patinkin, Mandy
b. Patrick, Deval Laurdine
b. Patterson, Alicia
b. Patterson, Eleanor Medill
b. Patterson, Joseph Medill
b. Paxton, Tom
b. Peattie, Donald Culross
b. Pereira, William Leonard
b. Perry, Walt
b. Petrillo, James Caesar
b. Piccard, Jeannette Ridlon
b. Pipp, Wally
b. Pletcher, Stew
b. Pollard, Fritz
b. Poole, Ernest
b. Pritikin, Nathan
b. Pritzker, Abram Nicholas
b. Provensen, Alice Rose Twitchell
b. Provensen, Martin
b. Puckett, Kirby
b. Rader, Doug(las Lee)
b. Radford, Arthur William
b. Randolph, Georgiana Ann
b. Raphael, Frederic Michael
b. Rawls, Lou(is Allen)
b. Rayburn, Gene
b. Redfield, Robert
b. Reed, John S(hepard)
b. Reed, John Shedd
b. Reed, Myrtle
b. Reed, Robert
b. Reiffel, Leonard
b. Reiss, Stuart
b. Reuben, David Robert
b. Rice, Craig
b. Rice, Linda Johnson
b. Richardson, Lee
b. Richman, Charles
b. Riperton, Minnie
b. Robards, Jason, Jr.
b. Robinson, John Alexander
b. Rogers, John W., Jr.
b. Roos, Frank John, Jr.
b. Rose, Helen Bronberg
b. Rostenkowski, Daniel David
b. Roszak, Theodore
b. Rowland, Pleasant
b. Royko, Mike
b. Ruby, Jack
b. Rumsfeld, Donald (Harold)
b. Rusher, William Allen
b. Russell, Gail
b. Ryan, Robert (Bushnell)

b. Saint John, Howard
b. Saint John, Robert
b. Sajak, Pat
b. Salt, Waldo
b. Samuels, Ernest
b. Sands, Tommy
b. Sarett, Lew R
b. Savage, Fred
b. Schaefer, Germany
b. Schnering, Otto
b. Schreiber, Avery
b. Schuyler, James Marcus
b. Seraphine, Danny
b. Seymour, Dan
b. Shandling, Garry
b. Sharpe, Sterling
b. Shaw, Bernard
b. Shawn, William
b. Sheekman, Arthur
b. Sheil, Bernard James, Archbishop
b. Sheldon, Alice Hastings Bradley
b. Sheldon, Sidney
b. Shepherd, Jean Parker
b. Sherman, Allan
b. Shirer, William L(awrence)
b. Shoemaker, Vaughn Richard
b. Shriver, Maria (Owings)
b. Sidaris, Andy
b. Siegel, Don
b. Siegel, Owen R
b. Sills, Milton
b. Silverstein, Shel(by)
b. Simpson, Carole
b. Simpson, George Gaylord
b. Sinise, Gary
b. Sisco, Joseph John
b. Siskel, Gene
b. Skinner, Cornelia Otis
b. Skinner, Sam
b. Skinner, Samuel K(nox)
b. Skowron, Bill
b. Slick, Grace Wing
b. Smith, Patti
b. Snodgrass, Carrie
b. Sobieski, Carol
b. Solomon, Hannah Greenebaum
b. Sosnik, Harry
b. Soul, David
b. Spalding, Albert
b. Spanier, Muggsy
b. Stahl, Ben(jamin Albert)
b. Steele, Claude Mason
b. Steele, Shelby
b. Stein, James R
b. Stettinius, Edward R, Jr.
b. Stevens, John Paul
b. Stevenson, Adlai Ewing, III
b. Stevenson, Janet
b. Stingley, Darryl
b. Stone, W Clement
b. Sturges, Preston
b. Sukman, Harry
b. Swanson, Gloria May Josephine
b. Sweet, Blanche
b. T, Mr.
b. Tabbert, William
b. Targ, William
b. Tate, Larenz
b. Taurog, Norman
b. Tax, Sol
b. Taylor, Henry Junior
b. Taylor, June
b. Taylor, Samuel (Albert)
b. Teichmann, Howard Miles
b. Thinnes, Roy
b. Thomas, Bill

b. Thomas, Isiah
b. Thompson, James Robert
b. Threadgill, Henry
b. Thurstone, Louis Leon
b. Tietjens, Eunice
b. Till, Emmett (Louis)
b. Tillstrom, Burr
b. Torme, Mel(vin Howard)
b. Torrence, Jackie
b. Touhy, Roger
b. Townsend, Robert
b. Tozzi, Giorgio
b. Trafton, George
b. Travis, Dempsey Jerome
b. Tristano, Leonard Joseph
b. Tureck, Rosalyn
b. Turner, Stansfield
b. Turow, Scott
b. Tuthill, Harry J
b. Tyler, Ralph W(infred)
b. Utley, (Clifton) Garrick
b. Valerio, James Robert
b. VanAlstyne, Egbert Anson
b. Van Peebles, Melvin
b. Vedder, Eddie
b. Veeck, Bill
b. Vincent, Marjorie Judith
b. Volner, Jill Wine
b. Vonnegut, Mark
b. Wahl, Ken
b. Wakefield, Dick
b. Walgreen, Charles Rudolph, Jr.
b. Walker, Albertina
b. Wallace, Chris(topher)
b. Wallace, Irving
b. Wallenstein, Alfred Franz
b. Wallis, Hal Brent
b. Wanamaker, Sam
b. Ward, Lynd
b. Warfield, Marsha
b. Warner, Rawleigh, Jr.
b. Washburn, Charles
b. Washington, Harold
b. Washington, Laura S.
b. Watley, Jody
b. Watson, James Dewey
b. Webb, Wellington
b. Weil, Joseph R
b. Weiskopf, Bob
b. Welch, Raquel
b. Welsing, Frances Cress
b. Wendt, George (Robert)
b. Wexler, Haskell
b. Willard, Frank Henry
b. Williams, Robin
b. Williams, Tony
b. Wilson, Phill
b. Wirtz, Arthur Michael
b. Woolley, Catherine
b. Wrigley, Philip Knight
b. Wrigley, William, III
b. Yancey, Jimmy
b. Yates, Sidney R(ichard)
b. Yordan, Philip
b. Young, Chic
b. Young, Clara Kimball
b. Young, Lyman
b. Young, Robert (George)
b. Young, Victor
b. Zabach, Florian
b. Zemeckis, Robert
b. Zevon, Warren
b. Ziegfeld, Flo(renz)
b. Ziff, William Bernard
b. Zmed, Adrian
d. Abbott, Grace

d. Addams, Jane
d. Adler, Dankmar
d. Adler, David
d. Allison, Samuel King
d. Ammons, Albert C
d. Ammons, Jug
d. Anson, Cap
d. Armour, Philip Danforth
d. Armstrong, Charles B
d. Armstrong, Lil(lian Hardin)
d. Arnstein, Bobbie
d. Arvey, Jacob Meyer
d. Avery, Sewell
d. Bacon, Frank
d. Barrow, Keith E
d. Bentley, Charles Edwin
d. Bernardin, Joseph L(ouis), Cardinal
d. Bernstein, Sid(ney Ralph)
d. Bidwell, Charles W
d. Blackburn, Jack
d. Block, Joseph L(eopold)
d. Bloom, Allan David
d. Borglum, John Gutzon de la Mothe
d. Brach, Emil J
d. Brauer, Jerald C(arl)
d. Breckinridge, Sophonisba Preston
d. Broonzy, Big Bill
d. Browning, Alice Crolley
d. Brunis, George
d. Budd, Ralph
d. Burck, Jacob
d. Burr, Henry
d. Cabrini, Frances Xavier, Saint
d. Calderon, Alberto P(edro)
d. Capone, Teresa
d. Carmichael, John P
d. Carpenter, John Alden
d. Cassidy, Claudia
d. Catlett, Big Sid
d. Chalmers, William James
d. Chamberlin, Thomas Chrowder
d. Chandler, Zachariah
d. Chandrasekhar, Subrahmanyan
d. Chanute, Octave
d. Charles, Ezzard
d. Cody, John Patrick
d. Coleman, James S(amuel)
d. Collins, Lee
d. Correll, Charles J
d. Cowles, Henry Chandler
d. Crook, George
d. Crown, Henry
d. Daley, Richard Joseph
d. Darnell, Linda (Monetta Eloyse)
d. Darrow, Clarence Seward
d. Dawson, William L(evi)
d. Dean, Henry Trendley
d. DeKoven, (Henry Louis) Reginald
d. DePriest, Oscar Stanton
d. Dillinger, John Herbert
d. Dodds, Baby
d. Dodds, Johnny
d. Dorsey, Thomas Andrew
d. Douglas, Stephen Arnold
d. Driscoll, Paddy
d. Dye, Babe
d. Eddy, Clarence
d. Eliade, Mircea
d. Engle, Paul (Hamilton)
d. Esposito, Joseph
d. Estes, E(lliott) M(arantette)
d. Estes, Pete
d. Evans, Chick
d. Faber, Red
d. Fairbank, Janet Ayer
d. Farley, Chris

d. Farmer, Moses Gerrish
d. Fermi, Enrico
d. Field, Eugene
d. Field, Marshall, IV
d. Finley, Charles O(scar)
d. Fishbein, Morris
d. Fitzsimmons, Bob
d. Fox, Carol
d. Frost, Edwin Brant
d. Fuller, Henry Blake
d. Gaedel, Eddie
d. Gage, Matilda Joslyn
d. Gale, Zona
d. Ganz, Rudolph
d. Gardner, George
d. Genet, Arthur Samuel
d. Gibbs, Erna Leonhardt
d. Goldberg, Bertrand
d. Halas, George Stanley
d. Hampton, Fred
d. Hansberry, William Leo
d. Harkins, William Draper
d. Harper, William Rainey
d. Harris, Robin
d. Harris, Sydney J(ustin)
d. Hauser, Philip M(orris)
d. Healy, George Peter Alexander
d. Herrick, James Bryan
d. Hess, Sol
d. Hilberseimer, Ludwig Karl
d. Hoffman, Julius Jennings
d. Hornsby, Rogers
d. Howard, Joseph Edgar
d. Howell, Albert S
d. Howlin' Wolf
d. Huggins, Charles B(renton)
d. Irvin, Robert W
d. Jacobson, Leon Orris
d. James, Elmore
d. Janowitz, Morris
d. Jefferson, Blind Lemon
d. Jenco, Lawrence M
d. Kemper, James S(cott)
d. Keppard, Freddie
d. Kerner, Otto
d. Kimball, William Wallace
d. Kitagawa, Joseph Mitsuo
d. Klutznick, Philip M.
d. Knight, Frank Hyneman
d. Kohut, Heinz
d. Kraft, James Lewis
d. Krainik, Ardis
d. Krieghoff, Cornelius
d. Kutner, Luis
d. Lafontant-Mankarious, Jewel
   (Stradford)
d. Landis Kenesaw, Mountain, Judge
d. Lawler, Richard Harold
d. Lawson, Victor Fremont
d. Layden, Elmer Francis
d. Levi, Edward Hirsch
d. Lindstrom, Freddie
d. Lowinsky, Edward Elias
d. Lubin, Charles W
d. Lunt, Alfred
d. Maclean, Norman (Fitzroy)
d. Malone, Annie Minerva Turnbo
   Pope
d. Marsala, Marty
d. Marshal, Alan
d. Masserman, Jules H(oman)
d. Mathews, Mitford M
d. Mayer, Oscar Ferdinand
d. Mayo, Charles Horace
d. McCormick, Cyrus Hall
d. McKay, Claude

d. McLaughlin, Frederic
d. Mead, George Herbert
d. Metcalfe, Ralph H
d. Mies van der Rohe, Ludwig
d. Moholy-Nagy, Laszlo
d. Morgan, Helen Riggins
d. Mowrer, Lilian Thomson
d. Muhammad, Elijah
d. Mundelein, George William
d. Nelson, Battling
d. Nielsen, Arthur Charles
d. Norris, James D
d. Ogilvie, Richard Buell
d. Packard, Elizabeth Parsons Ware
d. Page, Ruth
d. Palmer, Potter
d. Park, Thomas
d. Parker, Francis Wayland
d. Parker, George Safford
d. Parsons, James
d. Peller, Clara
d. Perls, Frederick Salomon
d. Petrillo, James Caesar
d. Phillips, Irna
d. Pinkerton, Allan
d. Price, Florence Beatrice Smith
d. Pritzker, Abram Nicholas
d. Pullman, George Mortimer
d. Quarterman, Lloyd Albert
d. Rainey, Melanie
d. Reed, Myrtle
d. Ricca, Paul
d. Ritchard, Cyril
d. Roebuck, Alvah Curtis
d. Root, John Wellborn
d. Rosenwald, Julius
d. Ross, Barney
d. Royko, Mike
d. Rubloff, Arthur
d. Sampson, Edith Spurlock
d. Saperstein, Abe
d. Schalk, Ray(mond William)
d. Scholl, William M
d. Sengstacke, John H(erman Henry)
d. Shils, Edward Albert
d. Siskel, Gene
d. Slye, Maud
d. Small, Albion W(oodbury)
d. Smith, Clarence
d. Solomon, Hannah Greenebaum
d. Spann, Otis
d. Starrett, Vincent
d. Stevenson, Adlai Ewing
d. Stigler, George Joseph
d. Stock, Frederick A
d. Sullivan, Louis Henri
d. Sunday, Billy
d. Swanson, Carl A
d. Swift, Gustavus Franklin
d. Taft, Lorado
d. Tax, Sol
d. Teschemacher, Frank
d. Thomas, Theodore
d. Thorek, Max
d. Tietjens, Eunice
d. Tillich, Paul Johannes
d. Touhy, Roger
d. Townsend, Willard Saxby
d. Trout, Dizzy
d. Trumbull, Lyman
d. VanAlstyne, Egbert Anson
d. Veeck, Bill
d. Visscher, William Lightfoot
d. Walgreen, Charles Rudolph
d. Washington, Harold
d. Weil, Joseph R

d. Wells, Junior
d. Wells-Barnett, Ida Bell
d. Wirtz, Arthur Michael
d. Wrigley, William, III
d. Yancey, Jimmy

Chicago Heights, Illinois
b. Saberhagen, Bret (William)

Christian County, Illinois
b. Sheean, (James) Vincent

Christopher, Illinois
b. Malkovich, John

Cicero, Illinois
b. Akalaitis, JoAnne
b. Marcinkus, Paul Casimir

Clay City, Illinois
b. Doherty, Robert Ernest

Cullom, Illinois
b. Beckman, Arnold (Orville)

Danville, Illinois
b. Morgan, Helen Riggins
b. Park, Thomas
b. Short, Bobby
b. Van Dyke, Jerry
b. Wainwright, James

De Kalb, Illinois
b. Crawford, Cindy
b. Hale, Barbara
b. Wirtz, William Willard
d. Glidden, Joseph Farwell

Decatur, Illinois
b. Dressen, Chuck
b. Duffy, James Edson
b. Felton, Rebecca Ann Latimer
b. Krauss, Alison (Maria)
b. Reilly, William Kane

Dixon, Illinois
b. Bestor, Arthur Eugene

Donnellson, Illinois
b. Lasswell, Harold Dwight

Downers Grove, Illinois
b. Milnes, Sherrill Eustace
d. Dewar, James A
d. Waters, Muddy

Du Quoin, Illinois
b. East, Edward Murray

Earlville, Illinois
b. Crisler, Fritz

East Saint Louis, Illinois
b. Bauer, Hank
b. Connors, Jimmy
b. Joyner, Al(fred, Jr.)
b. Joyner-Kersee, Jackie
b. Price, Melvin

Edwardsville, Illinois
b. Metcalf, Laurie
b. Musso, George Francis

Effingham, Illinois
d. McNaughton, F(oye) F(isk)

El Paso, Illinois
b. Sheen, Fulton John, Bishop

Elgin, Illinois
b. Boxleitner, Bruce
b. Ernst, Richard
b. Hall, Lloyd Augustus
b. Oldfield, Brian
b. Shales, Tom

Elmhurst, Illinois
b. Sandburg, Helga
d. Debs, Eugene Victor

Elmwood, Illinois
b. Taft, Lorado

Elmwood Park, Illinois
b. Nitschke, Ray(mond E.)

Evanston, Illinois
b. Agase, Alexander A.
b. Christopher, William
b. Cryer, David
b. Cusack, John
b. Dart, Justin Whitlock
b. Downes, Olin
b. Driscoll, Paddy
b. Finley, Karen
b. Gibson, Charles Dewolf
b. Hammond, Laurens
b. Harnwell, Gaylord Probasco
b. Harris, Barbara
b. Hart, Jim
b. Heston, Charlton
b. Johnson, Charles Richard
b. Kerr, Walter F(rancis)
b. Long, Scott
b. Mahin, John Lee
b. Martin, Lynn
b. May, John L.
b. McGovern, Elizabeth
b. Miller, Bob
b. Murray, Bill
b. Naber, John
b. Pearson, Drew
b. Rader, Dotson
b. Wilson, Gahan
b. Zipprodt, Patricia
d. Barrows, Marjorie (Ruth)
d. Britt, Steuart Henderson
d. Dawes, Charles Gates
d. Ed, Carl Frank Ludwig
d. Frank, Clinton Edward
d. Harridge, Will(iam)
d. Hayford, John Fillmore
d. Herskovits, Melville Jean
d. Hillis, Margaret
d. Holabird, William
d. MacDougall, Curtis Daniel
d. Marquis, Albert Nelson
d. May, Robert Lewis
d. McMurtrie, Douglas C
d. McNeill, Don(ald Thomas)
d. Olsen, Harold G
d. Poole, William Frederick
d. Samuels, Ernest
d. Schultz, Theodore W(illiam)
d. Yust, Walter

Evansville, Illinois
b. Hamilton, Bob

b. Ueberroth, Peter Victor

Evergreen Park, Illinois
b. Huizenga, H(arry) Wayne
b. Kaczynski, Theodore (John)
d. Jackson, Mahalia

Fairfield, Illinois
b. Borah, William Edgar

Fillmore, Illinois
b. Short, Walter Campbell

Forrest, Illinois
b. Ross, Roy G

Fort Sheridan, Illinois
b. Shepard, Sam
b. Sheppard, Sam(uel)

Fox River Grove, Illinois
d. Nelson, Baby Face

Freeport, Illinois
b. Bentley, Arthur F.
b. Eckert, William Dole
b. Flockhart, Calista
b. Guiteau, Charles Julius
b. Parsons, Louella Oettinger
b. Thayer, Tiffany Ellsworth

Fullersburg, Illinois
b. Fuller, Loie

Galena, Illinois
b. Gilbertson, Mildred Geiger
b. McNeill, Don(ald Thomas)
b. Rawlins, John A
b. Schwatka, Frederik

Galesburg, Illinois
b. Block, John Rusling
b. Davis, Loyal
b. Ferris, George Washington Gale
b. Huntington, Ellsworth
b. Sandburg, Carl (August)
b. Sundburg, Jim

Galva, Illinois
b. Kirby, Rollin

Geneseo, Illinois
b. Calkins, Earnest Elmo

Geneva, Illinois
b. Champion, Gower
b. Woodward, Bob

Germantown, Illinois
b. Schoendienst, Red

Gillespie, Illinois
b. Keel, Howard

Glencoe, Illinois
b. MacLeish, Archibald

Glenview, Illinois
d. Patterson, William Allan

Golconda, Illinois
b. Alcorn, James Lusk

b. Hodge, John Reed

Grand Ridge, Illinois
b. Finley, John Huston

Granite City, Illinois
b. Butler, Robert Olen
b. Goodpaster, Andrew Jackson
b. Phillip, Andy

Granville, Illinois
b. Ruffing, Red

Great Lakes, Illinois
b. Khan, Chaka

Groveland, Illinois
b. Duniway, Abigail Jane Scott

Hamilton, Illinois
b. Clausen, A(lden) W(inship)

Hartford, Illinois
b. Walker, Clint

Hartsburg, Illinois
b. Fletcher, Grant

Harvard, Illinois
d. Smith, (Robert) Sidney

Harvel, Illinois
b. Schalk, Ray(mond William)

Harvey, Illinois
b. Boudreau, Lou(is)

Highland, Illinois
b. Mosbacher, Georgette
b. Rubin, Barbara Jo

Highland Park, Illinois
b. Carr, Allan
b. Cohen, Joan Lebold
b. Galati, Frank
b. Ray, Shorty
b. Weston, Edward
d. Evans, Bergen Baldwin
d. Martin, John Bartlow
d. Ward, Montgomery

Hinsdale, Illinois
b. Anglund, Joan Walsh

Hope, Illinois
b. Van Doren, Carl Clinton
b. Van Doren, Mark

Hudson, Illinois
b. Stone, Melville Elijah

Humboldt, Illinois
b. Brann, William Cowper

Hume, Illinois
b. Doisy, Edward Adelbert, Sr.

Hunt, Illinois
b. Ives, Burl (Icle Ivanhoe)

Iroquois County, Illinois
b. Chase, Mary Agnes
b. Masterson, Bat

Jacksonville, Illinois
b. Norton, Ken(neth Howard)
b. Powers, James Farl
b. Ray, Charles
b. Rohde, Ruth Bryan Owen
b. Sturtevant, Alfred Henry
b. Udry, Janice May
d. Eddy, Sherwood

Joliet, Illinois
b. Bannon, Ann
b. Barfield, Jesse Lee
b. Bayes, Nora
b. Haley, Margaret A(ngela)
b. Jenco, Lawrence M
b. McCambridge, Mercedes
b. Mikan, George Lawrence, Jr.
b. Novak, Robert
b. Teale, Edwin Way
b. Thigpen Lynne
b. Totter, Audrey
b. Ward, Lester Frank
d. Altgeld, John Peter
d. Gacy, John Wayne, Jr.
d. Speck, Richard Franklin

Kankakee, Illinois
b. Gray, Harold Lincoln
b. MacMurray, Fred(erick Martin)
d. Foster, Rube

Kenilworth, Illinois
b. Andrews, Wayne

Kenwood, Illinois
b. Leopold, Nathan Freudenthal

Kewanee, Illinois
b. Brand, Neville
b. Estes, Richard

Kirkwood, Illinois
b. Speck, Richard Franklin

Knox County, Illinois
b. Walgreen, Charles Rudolph

La Grange, Illinois
b. Lewis, John Aaron
b. Lynd, Helen Merrell

La Harpe, Illinois
b. Martin, Robert Bernard
b. Soule, Olan

La Salle, Illinois
b. Aubrey, James (Thomas), Jr.
b. Keeler, James Edward

Lafayette, Illinois
b. Chandler, Dorothy (Buffum)

Lake Forest, Illinois
b. Proxmire, William
b. Simmons, Adele Smith
b. Wilson, Pete Barton
d. Cochrane, Mickey
d. Douglas, James Henderson, Jr.
d. Frederick, Pauline

d. Ivan, Tommy
d. McCutcheon, John Tinney
d. Morton, Julius Sterling
d. Wood, Robert Elkington

Lake Zurich, Illinois
d. Burnett, Leo

Libertyville, Illinois
d. Harshaw, Margaret

Lincoln, Illinois
b. Madigan, Edward R.
b. Maxwell, William

Lisle, Illinois
d. Morton, Joy

Livingston City, Illinois
b. Townsend, Francis Everett

Lockport, Illinois
b. Lloyd-Jones, Esther McDonald

Macoupin County, Illinois
b. Goodnight, Charles

Mason City, Illinois
b. Buehrig, Gordon

Mattoon, Illinois
b. Chamberlin, Thomas Chrowder
b. Daringer, Helen Fern
b. Harris, Patricia Roberts

Maywood, Illinois
b. Franz, Dennis
b. Griffin, Walter Burley
b. Prine, John

McLeansboro, Illinois
b. Smith, H(arry) Allen

Melrose Park, Illinois
b. Lawrence, Carol

Melvin, Illinois
b. Arends, Leslie Cornelius

Mendota, Illinois
b. Hokinson, Helen

Metropolis, Illinois
b. Malone, Annie Minerva Turnbo Pope
b. Micheaux, Oscar

Milan, Illinois
b. Frisco, Joe

Minooka, Illinois
d. Barry, Leonora Marie Kearney

Moline, Illinois
b. Bendix, Vincent
b. Berry, Ken
b. Ed, Carl Frank Ludwig
d. Deere, John

Monmouth, Illinois
b. Earp, Wyatt Berry Stapp
b. Eigenmann, Rosa Smith

Seneca, Illinois
b. Ellis, John Tracy

Sharpsburg, Illinois
b. Neihardt, John Gneisenau

Shawneetown, Illinois
b. Cassidy, Claudia

Springfield, Illinois
b. Barrow, Ed(ward Grant)
b. Christoff, Steve
b. East, John Porter
b. Eifert, Virginia Snider
b. Hickman, Fred(erick Douglass)
b. Hill, Bonnie Guiton
b. Howard, Jane Temple
b. Lincoln, Robert Todd
b. Lindsay, Vachel
b. Nicholson, Seth Barnes
b. Post, Charles William
b. Post, Marjorie Merriweather
b. Rogell, Billy
b. Rosenwald, Julius
d. Leonard, Dutch
d. Lincoln, Mary Todd
d. Lindsay, Vachel
d. Madigan, Edward R.
d. Smart, Jack Scott

Stateville, Illinois
d. Loeb, Richard A

Sterling, Illinois
b. Flory, Paul John

Streator, Illinois
b. Jamieson, Bob
b. Mulford, Clarence Edward
b. Tombaugh, Clyde W(illiam)

Summun, Illinois
b. Burnette, Smiley

Sumner, Illinois
b. Montgomery, Ruth Shick

Tampico, Illinois
b. Reagan, Ronald (Wilson)

Tiskilwa, Illinois
b. Giles, Warren Crandall

Troy Grove, Illinois
b. Hickok, Wild Bill

Turner Junction, Illinois
b. Gates, John Warne

Union City, Illinois
b. Derringer, Rick

Urbana, Illinois
b. Ebert, Roger (Joseph)
b. Garth, Jennie
b. Holley, Robert W(illiam)
b. Schopf, J(ames) William
d. Caudill, Rebecca
d. Shannon, Fred Albert
d. Steward, Julian Haynes

Vandalia, Illinois
b. Hunt, H(aroldson) L(afayette)

Virden, Illinois
b. Ross, Edward Alsworth

Walnut, Illinois
b. Marquis, Don Robert Perry

Washburn, Illinois
b. Duryea, J(ames) Frank

Watseka, Illinois
b. Bacon, Henry
d. Sumner, Jessie

Waukegan, Illinois
b. Ackerman, Diane
b. Benny, Jack
b. Bradbury, Ray Douglas
b. Graham, Otto Everett, Jr.
d. Julian, Percy Lavon

Wayne, Illinois
b. Anderson, Laurie

Wheaton, Illinois
b. Gary, Elbert Henry
b. Kendrick, Pearl Luella
b. Reber, Grote
d. McCormick, Robert Rutherford

White Oak Township, Illinois
b. Knight, Frank Hyneman

Will County, Illinois
b. Van Horne, William Cornelius, Sir

Wilmette, Illinois
b. King, Mary-Claire

Winnetka, Illinois
b. Hudson, Rock
b. Milford, Penny
b. Porter, Eliot Furness
b. Porter, Fairfield
d. Grant, Bruce

Winstanley Park, Illinois
b. Dean, Henry Trendley

Woodson, Illinois
b. Barber, Jerry

Woodstock, Illinois
d. Gould, Chester

Zion, Illinois
b. Coleman, Gary
b. Nype, Russell
d. Connelly, One-Eyed
d. Dowie, John Alexander

INDIANA
b. Allen, Macon B
b. Baniszewski, Gertrude Wright
b. Coggeshall, L(owell) T(helwell)
b. Dumke, Ralph
b. Lackey, Kenneth
b. Stonesifer, Patty
b. West, Jessamyn

Albany, Indiana
b. Kilgore, Bernard
b. McCormick, Myron

Algiers, Indiana
b. Capehart, Homer Earl

Allen County, Indiana
d. Appleseed, Johnny

Anderson, Indiana
b. Burton, Gary
b. Erskine, Carl Daniel
b. Mattingly, Mack Francis
b. Ryan, Tom Kreusch
d. Harroun, Ray
d. Wilt, Fred(erick Loren)

Angola, Indiana
d. Hershey, Lewis Blaine

Antiock, Indiana
b. Cubberley, Ellwood Patterson

Attica, Indiana
b. Hay, George Dewey

Auburn, Indiana
b. Cuppy, Will(iam Jacob)

Aurora, Indiana
b. Bechtel, Stephen Davison
b. Davis, Elmer Holmes

Bedford, Indiana
b. Coleman, James S(amuel)
b. Guthrie, A(lfred) B(ertram), Jr.
d. Jenner, William Ezra

Bippus, Indiana
b. Schenkel, Chris(topher Eugene)

Bloomington, Indiana
b. Cantrell, Ed
b. Carmichael, Hoagy
b. Helms, Bobby
b. Lockridge, Ross Franklin, Jr.
b. Roth, David Lee
d. Kinsey, Alfred Charles
d. Kirk, Rahsaan Roland
d. McCracken, Branch
d. Rossi-Lemeni, Nicola
d. Rothmuller, Marko A

Boonville, Indiana
b. Denny, Ludwell

Bourbon, Indiana
b. Phillips, Marjorie Acker

Brazil, Indiana
b. Craig, George N(orth)
b. Hoffa, Jimmy
b. Redenbacher, Orville

Brook, Indiana
d. Arthur, Joseph Charles

Brookline, Indiana
b. Van Camp, Gilbert C

Brookville, Indiana
b. Wallace, Lew(is)
d. Ade, George

b. Paige, Robert (John Arthur)
b. Pauley, Edwin Wendell
b. Pauley, Jane
b. Pinckney, Darryl
b. Quayle, Dan
b. Quayle, Marilyn Tucker
b. Randall, James Garfield
b. Reisner, George Andrew
b. Ruckelshaus, William Doyle
b. Russell-McCloud, Patricia (A.)
b. Shirley, George Irving
b. Sissle, Noble
b. Smith, Walter Bedell
b. Spuzich, Sandra Ann
b. Stevens, Ted
b. Tarkington, Booth
b. Vonnegut, Kurt, Jr.
b. Von Tilzer, Albert
b. Von Zell, Harry
b. Wakefield, Dan
b. Webb, Clifton
b. Weber, Dick
b. Young, Marguerite (Vivian)
d. Beveridge, Albert Jeremiah
d. Bobbs, William Conrad
d. Bolton, Sarah Tittle Barrett
d. Capehart, Homer Earl
d. Craig, George N(orth)
d. Duesenberg, August S
d. Fairbanks, Charles Warren
d. Farmer, Frances
d. Harger, Rolla
d. Harrison, Benjamin
d. Hendricks, Thomas Andrews
d. Honeywell, Mark Charles
d. Hubbard, Kin
d. Hulman, Tony, Jr.
d. Irsay, Robert
d. Klein, Chuck
d. Knight, Etheridge
d. Lawson, Yank
d. Lilly, Eli
d. Marcelo, (Edward) Jovy
d. Montgomery, Wes
d. Morton, Oliver Hazard Perry
   Throck
d. Muller, Hermann Joseph
d. Nolan, Jeannette Covert
d. Omlie, Phoebe Jane Fairgrave
d. Riley, James Whitcomb
d. Tarkington, Booth
d. Turner, Roscoe Wilson
d. Van Camp, Gilbert C
d. Welsh, Matthew E(mpson)
d. White, Ryan

Jasper, Indiana
b. Schroeder, William J

Jeffersonville, Indiana
b. Roland, Duane

Johnson County, Indiana
b. Terman, Lewis Madison

Kent, Indiana
b. Wiley, Harvey Washington

Kentland, Indiana
b. Ade, George

Knightstown, Indiana
b. Beard, Charles Austin
b. Elliott, George Paul

Kokomo, Indiana
b. Hillis, Margaret
b. Kroft, Steve
b. Martin, Strother
b. White, Ryan
d. Haynes, Elwood

LaPorte, Indiana
b. Scholl, William M
d. Mennen, Frederick

Lafayette, Indiana
b. DeRegniers, Beatrice Schenk
b. Ewry, Ray C
b. Fazenda, Louise
b. Friend, Bob
b. Hannagan, Steve
b. Lamb, Brian (P.)
b. Roebuck, Alvah Curtis
b. Rogers, Bruce
b. Rose, Axl
d. Halleck, Charles Abraham
d. Lambert, Ward L
d. McIlhenny, Walter S

Lawrenceburg, Indiana
b. Eads, James Buchanan
b. Skidmore, Louis
b. Spooner, John Coit

Lebanon, Indiana
b. Saunders, Allen

Liberty, Indiana
b. Burnside, Ambrose Everett
b. Miller, Joaquin

Linton, Indiana
b. Harris, Phil

Lizton, Indiana
b. Davis, Adelle

Logansport, Indiana
b. Hinkle, Paul
b. Kinnear, Greg
b. Landis, Frederick

Lowell, Indiana
b. Worley, Jo Anne

Lynn, Indiana
b. Jones, Reverend Jim

Macy, Indiana
b. Lane, Lola

Madison, Indiana
b. Philips, David Graham

Marengo, Indiana
b. Jenner, William Ezra

Marion, Indiana
b. Davis, Jim
b. Dean, James Byron
b. Fehr, Donald Martin
b. Jones, Phil(ip Howard)
b. Murphy, Charles
b. Van Devanter, Willis

Martinsville, Indiana
b. Wooden, John Robert

d. Helms, Bobby

Mentone, Indiana
b. Bell, Lawrence Dale

Michigan City, Indiana
b. Baxter, Anne
b. Hatcher, Richard Gordon
b. Just, Ward
b. Larsen, Don(ald James)
d. Judy, Steven

Millville, Indiana
b. Wright, Wilbur

Mishawaka, Indiana
b. Brademas, John
b. Germano, Lisa
b. McKenney, Ruth

Mitchell, Indiana
b. Bass, Sam
b. Grissom, Virgil Ivan

Monrovia, Indiana
b. McCracken, Branch

Montezuma, Indiana
b. Allport, Gordon William

Mooresville, Indiana
b. Rusie, Amos Wilson

Morocco, Indiana
b. Rice, Sam

Mount Pleasant, Indiana
b. Coup, W(illiam) C(ameron)

Mount Vernon, Indiana
b. Monroe, Marion

Mulberry, Indiana
b. Slipher, Vesto Melvin

Muncie, Indiana
b. Cohen, Benjamin Victor
b. Haines, Robert Terrel
b. Kimbrough, Emily
b. Williams, Gregory (Howard)
d. Ball, Edmund B
d. Ball, Frank

Munster, Indiana
d. Lema, Tony

Nappanee, Indiana
b. Neher, Fred

New Albany, Indiana
b. Herman, Billy
b. Lynd, Robert Staughton
b. Zoeller, Fuzzy
d. Minton, Sherman

New Castle, Indiana
b. Indiana, Robert

Noble County, Indiana
b. Butz, Earl Lauer

Algona, Iowa
b. Cowles, Gardner, Jr.
b. Cowles, John, Sr.

Alton, Iowa
b. Schuller, Robert Harold

Ames, Iowa
b. Kirby, Robert E(mory)
b. Paretsky, Sara
b. Schickele, Peter
b. Sunday, Billy
d. Spedding, Frank Harold

Anamosa, Iowa
b. Wood, Grant

Arispe, Iowa
b. Gross, H(arold) R(oyce)

Avoca, Iowa
b. Beymer, Richard

Blockton, Iowa
b. Hickenlooper, Bourke B

Boone, Iowa
b. Eisenhower, Mamie (Geneva) Doud

Burlington, Iowa
b. Carothers, Wallace Hume
b. Duke, Wayne
b. Frawley, William
b. Kent, Jack
b. Mansfield, Arabella
b. Noyce, Robert Norton
b. Orr, Kay Avonne

Burnside, Iowa
b. Mollenhoff, Clark Raymond

Carroll, Iowa
d. Garst, Roswell

Cascade, Iowa
b. Faber, Red

Cedar Falls, Iowa
b. Aldrich, Bess Streeter
b. Cassill, R(onald) V(erlin)
b. Jepsen, Roger William

Cedar Rapids, Iowa
b. Boddicker, Mike
b. Conrad, Paul Francis
b. DeFore, Don
b. Driscoll, Bobby
b. Engle, Paul (Hamilton)
b. Fitch, Bill
b. Hershfield, Harry
b. Ruml, Beardsley
b. Threlkeld, Richard D
b. Van Vechten, Carl
b. Wood, Elijah

Centerville, Iowa
b. Estes, Simon Lamont

Chariton, Iowa
b. Howard, Guy Wesley

Charles City, Iowa
b. Coover, Robert (Lowell)

Charter Oak, Iowa
b. Hansen, James E(dward)

Clarinda, Iowa
b. Maclean, Norman (Fitzroy)
b. Maxwell, Marilyn
b. Miller, Glenn
d. Shambaugh, Jessie Field

Clear Lake, Iowa
d. Big Bopper, The
d. Holly, Buddy
d. Valens, Ritchie

Clinton, Iowa
b. Childs, Marquis William
b. Kraushaar, Otto
b. Russell, Lillian
b. Stewart, Paul Wilbur
d. Stone, George Robert

Colfax, Iowa
b. Hall, James Norman

Columbus Junction, Iowa
b. Wilcox, Francis (Orlando)

Corning, Iowa
b. Carson, Johnny

Council Bluffs, Iowa
b. Beer, Thomas
b. Chandler, Don(ald G)
b. DeForest, Lee
b. Farmer, Art(hur Stewart)
b. Langdon, Harry
b. McCain, John Sidney, Jr.
b. Pusey, Nathan Marsh
d. Bloomer, Amelia Jenks
d. Dodge, Grenville Mellen

Cresco, Iowa
b. Borlaug, Norman Ernest
b. Chamberlain, Samuel
b. Izac, Edouard V(ictor Michel)

Creston, Iowa
b. Cunningham, R Walter

Cumming, Iowa
b. Harkin, Thomas R(ichard)

Dakota City, Iowa
b. Reasoner, Harry

Davenport, Iowa
b. Beiderbecke, Bix
b. Ficke, Arthur Davidson
b. Glaspell, Susan Keating
b. Ketelsen, James Lee
b. Layden, Elmer Francis
b. Margolin, Stuart
b. Pendleton, Nat
b. Russell, Charles Edward
b. Shilts, Randy (Martin)
d. Grant, Cary

Delaware County, Iowa
b. Merriam, Frank Finley

Denison, Iowa
b. Garrison, Jim C.
b. Reed, Donna

Des Moines, Iowa
b. Armstrong, Herbert W
b. Ball, George W(ildman)
b. Bartkowski, Steve(n Joseph)
b. Burton, Michael
b. Collins, Stephen
b. Coverdell, Paul
b. Gartner, Michael Gay
b. Halston
b. Hyman, Libbie Henrietta
b. Jensen, Virginia Allen
b. Kellems, Vivien
b. Leachman, Cloris
b. McCree, Wade Hampton, Jr.
b. Nelson, Harriet
b. Omlie, Phoebe Jane Fairgrave
b. Pierce, John Robinson
b. Prusiner, Stanley (Ben)
b. Ray, Robert D
b. Rense, Paige
b. Schick, Jacob
b. Thompson, Sada Carolyn
d. Alexander, Archie Alphonso
d. Darling, Jay Norwood
d. Marciano, Rocky
d. Waymack, W(illiam) W(esley)
d. Weaver, James Baird

Doon, Iowa
b. Manfred, Frederick Feikema

Dubuque, Iowa
b. Berwanger, J Jay
b. Bissell, Richard Pike
b. Carr, Sabin
b. Keenan, Frank
b. Lindsay, Margaret
b. Rabe, David William
d. Allison, William Boyd
d. Bissell, Richard Pike
d. Mickelson, George Speaker

Emmetsburg, Iowa
b. Bliven, Bruce
b. Gould, Beatrice Blackmar

Fort Dodge, Iowa
b. Arkoff, Samuel Z
b. Heggen, Thomas Orls, Jr.
b. Kent, Corita

Fort Madison, Iowa
b. Boley, Forrest Irving
b. O'Keefe, Dennis

Greenfield, Iowa
b. Sidey, Hugh Swanson

Grinnell, Iowa
b. Schultz, Richard D(ale)

Hampton, Iowa
b. Bailey, Jack
b. Leahy, William Daniel

Harlan, Iowa
b. Miller, Otto Neil

Hawarden, Iowa
b. Emerson, Hope

b. Suckow, Ruth

Hawthorne, Iowa
b. Cessna, Clyde Vernon

Hedrick, Iowa
b. Loveless, Herschel C(ellel)

Humboldt, Iowa
b. Baker, Laura Nelson

Independence, Iowa
b. Yarnell, Harry Ervin

Indianola, Iowa
b. Lane, Priscilla
b. Lane, Rosemary

Iowa City, Iowa
b. Grant, Charity
b. Guthrie, Janet
b. Johnson, Nicholas
b. Leighton, Laura
d. Wood, Grant

Jefferson, Iowa
b. Gallup, George Horace

Jefferson Barracks, Iowa
d. Atkinson, Henry

Keokuk, Iowa
b. Maxwell, Elsa
b. Nagel, Conrad
d. Black Hawk

Keokuk County, Iowa
b. Mott, Frank Luther

Keosauqua, Iowa
b. Strong, Philip Duffield

Knoxville, Iowa
b. Stone, Edward C, Jr.

La Porte City, Iowa
b. Allison, Fran(ces)

Lake Mills, Iowa
b. Stegner, Wallace (Earle)

Lakota, Iowa
b. Griese, Arnold

Lansing, Iowa
b. Krebs, Edwin Gerhard

Le Mars, Iowa
b. Kluckhohn, Clyde
b. Kluckhorn, Clyde Kay Maben
b. Starzl, Thomas Earl

Leland, Iowa
b. Branstad, Terry Edward

Lost Nation, Iowa
b. Stone, George Robert

Luana, Iowa
b. Gould, Charles Bruce

Lucas, Iowa
b. Lewis, John L(lewellyn)

Macksburg, Iowa
b. Martin, Glenn Luther

Manning, Iowa
b. Knudson, Tom

Mapleton, Iowa
b. Wood, Gar(field A)

Marengo, Iowa
b. Whitehill, Clarence Eugene

Marshalltown, Iowa
b. Anson, Cap
b. Hurt, Mary Beth Supinger
b. Seberg, Jean

Mason City, Iowa
b. Arbuthnot, May Hill
b. Willson, Meredith

Maurice, Iowa
b. Keough, Donald Raymond

McGregor, Iowa
b. Ringling, Charles

Montour, Iowa
b. Miller, Merle

Mount Pleasant, Iowa
b. Van Allen, James Alfred

Nashua, Iowa
b. Taylor, Kent

Neola, Iowa
b. Felton, Harold W
b. Lafferty, Raphael Aloysius

Nevada, Iowa
b. Patterson, Neva

New Hartford, Iowa
b. Grassley, Charles Ernest

New Providence, Iowa
b. Clampitt, Amy

Newton, Iowa
b. Maytag, Elmer Henry
b. Murray, Charles Alan

Orient, Iowa
b. Vance, Dazzy

Oskaloosa, Iowa
b. Bell, Steve
b. Conklin, Chester

Ottumwa, Iowa
b. Alexander, Archie Alphonso
b. Arnold, Tom
b. Cone, Russell Glenn
b. Keyhoe, Donald E(dward)
b. Williams, Roy Lee

Paris, Iowa
b. Clark, Richard Clarence

Parkersburg, Iowa
b. Fenton, Carroll Lane

Pella, Iowa
b. Earp, Morgan

Pleasantville, Iowa
b. McKay, Scott

Primghar, Iowa
b. Welch, Joseph Nye

Red Oak, Iowa
b. Hunt, Jack Reed
b. Logan, John

Rock Valley, Iowa
b. Bell, Herbert A

Rockford, Iowa
b. Waller, Robert James

Sac City, Iowa
b. Stouffer, Samuel A.

Scout County, Iowa
b. Cody, Buffalo Bill

Shenandoah, Iowa
b. Haden, Charlie
b. Shambaugh, Jessie Field

Sioux City, Iowa
b. Bancroft, Dave
b. Carey, Macdonald
b. Deming, W(illiam) Edwards
b. Grandy, Fred(erick Lawrence)
b. Herbst, Josephine Frey
b. Hopkins, Harry Lloyd
b. Landers, Ann
b. Mathers, Jerry
b. Means, Marianne Hansen
b. Melcher, John
b. Moore, Constance
b. Van Buren, Abigail
b. Waitt, Tedd

Stanton, Iowa
b. Christine, Virginia

Storm Lake, Iowa
b. Dailey, Janet

Stuart, Iowa
b. Peers, William Raymond

Traer, Iowa
b. Wilson, Margaret

Van Meter, Iowa
b. Feller, Bob

Wall Lake, Iowa
b. Williams, Andy

Waterloo, Iowa
b. Adams, Julie
b. Becker, Carl Lotus
b. Budd, Ralph

b. Funston, George Keith
b. Hoover, Lou Henry
b. Van Duyn, Mona

Webster City, Iowa
b. Eberle, Mary Abastenia St. Leger
b. Kantor, Mackinlay
b. Maclaughlin, Don

West Branch, Iowa
b. Hoover, Herbert C(lark)

Wilton Junction, Iowa
b. Giesler, Jerry

Winterset, Iowa
b. Clarke, Fred Clifford
b. Smith, Courtney Craig
b. Wayne, John

KANSAS
d. Laclede, Pierre

Abilene, Kansas
b. Eisenhower, Milton Stover
b. Engle, Joe Henry

Alamena, Kansas
b. Sebelius, Keith George

Alton, Kansas
b. Stover, Russell

Arkansas City, Kansas
b. Lewis, Delano (Eugene)

Ashland, Kansas
b. Santee, Wes

Atchison, Kansas
b. Earhart, Amelia (Mary)
b. Sanders, Joseph
d. Howe, Edgar Watson

Atlanta, Kansas
b. Cunningham, Glenn Clarence

Baldwin, Kansas
d. Liston, Emil

Baldwin City, Kansas
b. Counts, George S(ylvester)

Baxter Springs, Kansas
b. Harman, Jeanne Perkins

Bazaar, Kansas
d. Rockne, Knute Kenneth

Bucyrus, Kansas
b. Price, Garrett

Bunker Hill, Kansas
d. Bickerdyke, Mary Ann Ball

Burlingame, Kansas
b. Sutherland, Earl Wilbur, Jr.

Burton, Kansas
b. Stone, Milburn

Bushton, Kansas
b. Huebner, Clarence R

Caldwell, Kansas
b. Emerson, Gladys Anderson

Centralia, Kansas
b. Riggins, John

Chanute, Kansas
b. Johnson, Osa Helen Leighty

Chapman, Kansas
b. Poor, Henry Varnum, III

Cherryvale, Kansas
b. Brooks, Louise
b. Vance, Vivian

Claflin, Kansas
b. Hickel, Wally

Coffee City, Kansas
b. Windsor, Claire

Coffeyville, Kansas
d. Dalton, Gratton
d. Dalton, Robert

Colby, Kansas
b. Hayden, Mike
b. Ramey, Samuel Edward

Columbus, Kansas
b. Terris, Norma

Concordia, Kansas
b. Carlson, Frank
d. Carlson, Frank

Council Grove, Kansas
b. Rhodes, John Jacob

Decatur County, Kansas
b. Harger, Rolla

Dodge City, Kansas
b. Hopper, Dennis
b. King, James Ambros

Dunavant, Kansas
b. Curry, John Steuart

El Dorado, Kansas
b. Brodie, Steve
b. Fulton, Maude
b. Walker, Mort

Elk Falls, Kansas
d. Crandall, Prudence

Elwood, Kansas
b. Moran, George

Emporia, Kansas
b. Castle, Wendell Keith
b. Smith, Dean Edwards
b. White, William Allen
b. White, William Lindsay
d. White, William Allen
d. White, William Lindsay

Fairview, Kansas
b. Rogers, Bernard William

Falun, Kansas
b. Johnson, U(ral) Alexis

Fontana, Kansas
b. Hibbs, Ben

Fort Riley, Kansas
b. Beard, Dita Davis

Fort Scott, Kansas
b. Canaday, John (Edwin John)
b. Clifford, Clark M(cAdams)
b. Johnson, Hugh Samuel
b. McCollum, Elmer Verner
b. Parks, Gordon Alexander Buchanan

Franklin County, Kansas
d. Keokuk

Fredonia, Kansas
b. Lamb, Lawrence Edward

Garden City, Kansas
b. Dunn, Katherine (Karen)
b. Romer, Roy R

Garnett, Kansas
b. Capper, Arthur
b. Masters, Edgar Lee

Girard, Kansas
d. Haldeman-Julius, Emanuel

Goessel, Kansas
b. Knight, Shirley

Grenola, Kansas
b. Friganza, Trixie

Halstead, Kansas
b. Rupp, Adolph Frederick

Hillsboro, Kansas
b. Klassen, Elmer Theodore

Humboldt, Kansas
b. Johnson, Walter Perry

Hutchinson, Kansas
b. Stafford, William Edgar

Independence, Kansas
b. Inge, William Motter

Iola, Kansas
b. Adams, John

Junction City, Kansas
b. Chaffee, Adna Romanza
b. Horner, Bob
b. Kitchell, Iva
b. Pennell, Joseph Stanley

Kansas City, Kansas
b. Carr, Harold Noflet
b. Downs, William Randall, Jr.
b. Lomawaima, K(imberly) Tsianina
b. Parker, Charlie
b. Treas, Terri

Bagdad, Kentucky
b. Collins, Martha Layne Hall

Bardstown, Kentucky
d. Fitch, John

Beargrass, Kentucky
b. Johnson, Richard Mentor

Belcher Holler, Kentucky
b. Loveless, Patty

Bluelick, Kentucky
b. Foley, Red

Bourbon County, Kentucky
b. Corwin, Thomas

Bowling Green, Kentucky
b. Hines, Duncan
d. Hines, Duncan

Boyle County, Kentucky
b. Harlan, John Marshall, I

Bracken County, Kentucky
b. Fee, John Gregg

Brooksville, Kentucky
b. Galloway, Don

Brownie, Kentucky
b. Everly, Don(ald)

Bryant Station, Kentucky
b. Rogers, James Gamble

Burgin, Kentucky
b. McDonald, Marie

Burton Fork, Kentucky
b. Kazee, Buell Hilton

Butcher Hollow, Kentucky
b. Lynn, Loretta

Cadiz, Kentucky
b. Mein, John Gordon

Campbellsville, Kentucky
b. Young, Margaret Ann Buckner

Cayce, Kentucky
b. Jones, Casey

Christian County, Kentucky
b. Davis, Jefferson
b. Stevenson, Adlai Ewing

Clay City, Kentucky
b. Jackson, Aunt Molly

Corbin, Kentucky
b. Lake, Arthur

Cordell, Kentucky
b. Skaggs, Ricky

Corydon, Kentucky
b. Chandler, Happy
b. Ramsey, Frank Vernon, Jr.

Covington, Kentucky
b. Burman, Ben Lucien
b. Cauthen, Steve
b. Duveneck, Frank
b. Kirby, Durward
b. Merkel, Una
b. Sperti, George Speri
b. Ziegler, Ron(ald Louis)
d. Peabody, Eddie

Cumberland County, Kentucky
b. Huddleston, Walter Darlington

Cynthiana, Kentucky
b. Hall, Joe Beasman
d. McKinney, Bill

Danville, Kentucky
b. Birney, James Gillespie
b. Duncan, Todd
b. McCormick, Robert K
d. McDowell, Ephraim

Depoy, Kentucky
b. Oates, Warren

Dixon, Kentucky
b. Rice, Cale Young

Dry Ridge, Kentucky
b. Davis, Skeeter

Eddyville, Kentucky
d. Fulks, Joe

Elkton, Kentucky
b. Bristow, Benjamin Helm
b. Reese, Pee Wee
b. Rudolph, Paul Marvin

Flatwoods, Kentucky
b. Cyrus, Billy Ray

Florence, Kentucky
b. Price, Kenny
d. Price, Kenny

Floydsfork, Kentucky
b. Griffith, D(avid Lewelyn) W(ark)

Fort Knox, Kentucky
b. Barker, Len

Frankfort, Kentucky
b. Bledsoe, Albert Taylor
b. Brown, Benjamin Gratz
b. Fall, Albert Bacon
b. Polk, Willis Jefferson
b. Wolfe, George C.
d. Crittenden, John Jordan
d. Johnson, Richard Mentor

Franklin, Kentucky
b. Potts, Annie

Franklin County, Kentucky
b. Blair, Montgomery

Frogtown, Kentucky
b. Atchison, David R

Fulton, Kentucky
b. Rascoe, Burton

Garrard County, Kentucky
b. Nation, Carry A(melia Moore)
b. Smith, Joshua (Isaac)

Geneva, Kentucky
b. Banks, William (Venoid)

Glasgow, Kentucky
b. Goodman, Julian B
b. Krock, Arthur Bernard
b. Sawyer, Diane (K.)

Glensboro, Kentucky
b. Townsend, William H(enry)

Graves County, Kentucky
b. Barkley, Alben William

Grayson County, Kentucky
b. Dargan, Olive Tilford

Guthrie, Kentucky
b. Warren, Robert Penn

Hardinsburg, Kentucky
b. Beard, Ralph Milton

Harlan, Kentucky
b. Cheshire, Maxine
b. Jones, Wallace

Hart County, Kentucky
b. Buckner, Simon Bolivar

Hartford, Kentucky
b. Bland, Richard Parks
b. Curran, Charles Courtney
b. Earp, Virgil W

Hazel, Kentucky
b. DeShannon, Jackie

Henderson, Kentucky
b. Kimmel, Husband Edward
b. Robinson, Francis Arthur

Henry County, Kentucky
b. Berry, Wendell

Hindman, Kentucky
b. Perkins, Carl Dewey

Hodgenville, Kentucky
b. Lincoln, Abraham

Hopkinsville, Kentucky
b. Cayce, Edgar
b. Hooks, Bell

Hyden, Kentucky
d. Breckinridge, Mary

Jenkins, Kentucky
b. Bach, Bert Coates

Kenton County, Kentucky
b. Carlisle, John Griffin

Paintsville, Kentucky
b. Gayle, Crystal

Paris, Kentucky
b. Morgan, Garrett Augustus

Pascagoula, Kentucky
d. Taylor, Margaret (Smith)

Pebworth, Kentucky
b. Combs, Earle Bryan

Perryville, Kentucky
b. Roberts, Elizabeth Madox

Pewee Valley, Kentucky
d. Johnston, Annie Fellows

Pikeville, Kentucky
b. Yoakam, Dwight

Poor Fork, Kentucky
b. Caudill, Rebecca

Prestonsburg, Kentucky
b. Allen, Jack

Providence, Kentucky
b. Benjamin, Curtis G

Pulaski, Kentucky
b. Monroe, Rose Will

Richmond, Kentucky
b. Hunter, Floyd
b. Miller, Samuel Freeman

Rockport, Kentucky
d. Buell, Don Carlos

Rosewood, Kentucky
b. Travis, Merle Robert

Rosine, Kentucky
b. Monroe, Bill

Russellville, Kentucky
b. Crittendon, Thomas Leonidas

Sandy Hook, Kentucky
b. Whitley, Keith

Scott, Kentucky
b. Hatch, William Henry

Scott County, Kentucky
b. Thomas, Charles Allen

Sharpsburg, Kentucky
b. Allen, Henry Tureman

Shelbyville, Kentucky
b. Rice, Alice Caldwell Hegan

Somerset, Kentucky
b. Cooper, John Sherman

Southgate, Kentucky
b. Bunning, Jim

Stoney Pointe, Kentucky
b. Fox, John W, Jr.

Three Springs, Kentucky
b. Altsheler, Joseph Alexander

Trenton, Kentucky
b. Gordon, Caroline

Versailles, Kentucky
b. Berryman, Clifford Kennedy
b. Blackburn, Jack
b. Crittenden, John Jordan
d. Chandler, Happy

Viper, Kentucky
b. Ritchie, Jean

W-Hollow, Kentucky
b. Stuart, Jesse Hilton

Washington, Kentucky
b. Johnston, Albert Sidney

Wayne County, Kentucky
b. Arnow, Harriette Louisa Simpson

Whitehall, Kentucky
d. Clay, Cassius Marcellus

Winchester, Kentucky
b. Tate, Allen (John Orley)
b. Thomas, Helen A.
d. Kazee, Buell Hilton

Woodbury, Kentucky
b. Bloch, Claude Charles

Woodford County, Kentucky
b. Buford, John

LOUISIANA
b. Brown, Dee (Alexander)
b. Ji Jaga, Geronimo
d. Rhett, Robert Barnwell

Abend, Louisiana
b. Oliver, Joe

Alexandria, Louisiana
b. Bontemps, Arna Wendell
b. Riles, Wilson Camanza
b. Woodiwiss, Kathleen (Erin)
d. Granger, Lester
d. Long, Earl Kemp

Algiers, Louisiana
b. Henry, Clarence

Bastrop, Louisiana
b. Dickey, Bill

Baton Rouge, Louisiana
b. Al-Amin, Jamil Abdullah
b. Atkinson, Ti-Grace
b. Brown, H(ubert) Rap
b. Gray, William H, III
b. Hebert, Bobby Joseph
b. Pettit, Bob
b. Spikes, Dolores
b. Taylor, Jim
b. Whitfield, Lynn

d. Kennon, Robert Floyd
d. Long, Huey Pierce
d. Milburn, Rodney, Jr.
d. Myer, Buddy
d. Rathbone, Monroe Jackson
d. Torrance, Jack

Baywood, Louisiana
b. Douglas, Donna

Bogalusa, Louisiana
b. Byrd, Henry
b. Komunyakaa, Yusef
b. Professor Longhair

Bossier City, Louisiana
b. Winchester, Jesse (James Ridout)

Broussard, Louisiana
b. Jacquet, Illinois (Robert Russell)

Brunswick, Louisiana
b. Boggs, Lindy

Bunkie, Louisiana
b. Singleton, Zutty

Burnside, Louisiana
b. Ward, Douglas Turner

Carencro, Louisiana
b. Rockin' Dopsie

Covington, Louisiana
d. Percy, Walker

Creston, Louisiana
b. Hunsaker, Jerome Clarke

Crowley, Louisiana
b. Breaux, John B.
b. Brooks, Jack Bascom

Cut Off, Louisiana
b. Noone, Jimmie

De Ridder, Louisiana
b. Cagle, Red
d. Hamer, Rusty

Delhi, Louisiana
b. Holliman, Earl

Delta, Louisiana
b. Walker, C. J., Madame
b. Walker, Sarah Breedlove
  McWilliams

Elizabeth, Louisiana
b. Emerson, Faye Margaret

Extension, Louisiana
b. Berry, Richard

Ferriday, Louisiana
b. Lewis, Jerry Lee
b. Smith, Howard K(ingsbury)
b. Swaggart, Jimmy Lee
d. DeSoto, Hernando

Forbing, Louisiana
b. Williams, Victoria

Gibsland, Louisiana
d. Barrow, Clyde
d. Parker, Bonnie

Gretna, Louisiana
b. Ott, Mel(vin Thomas)

Gulfport, Louisiana
b. Morton, Jelly Roll

Hall Summit, Louisiana
b. Courtney, Clint(on Dawson)

Hammond, Louisiana
d. Rich, Charlie

Haynesville, Louisiana
b. Beene, Geoffrey

Hico, Louisiana
b. Reed, Willis, Jr.

Jackson, Louisiana
b. Robinson, Eddie

Jamestown, Louisiana
b. Smith, Lee (Arthur)

Jefferson Island, Louisiana
b. Gordy, Robert

La Place, Louisiana
b. Ory, Kid

Lafayette, Louisiana
b. Buckwheat Zydeco
b. Guidry, Ron(ald Ames)
b. Hebert, Jay
b. Hebert, Lionel
b. Richard, Zachary
d. Chenier, Clifton

Lafourche, Louisiana
b. White, Edward Douglass

Lake Charles, Louisiana
b. Boutte, Alvin J
b. DeBakey, Michael Ellis
b. Johnson, Norma L. Holloway
b. Lyons, Ted
b. McLaren, Wayne
b. Perry, Harold R
b. Queen Ida
b. Williams, Lucinda
d. Mitchel, John Purroy

Leesville, Louisiana
b. Connerly, Ward

Lettsworth, Louisiana
b. Guy, Buddy

Mandeville, Louisiana
b. Ladnier, Tommy

Mansfield, Louisiana
b. Blue, Vida Rochelle

Many, Louisiana
b. Joiner, Charlie

Marion, Louisiana
b. Crow, John David

Marksville, Louisiana
b. Cadoria, Sherian Grace
b. Edwards, Edwin Washington
b. Stuart, Ruth McEnery

Marrero, Louisiana
d. Perry, Harold R

Maurice, Louisiana
b. Desormeaux, Kent

McCall, Louisiana
b. Foster, Pops

Metairie, Louisiana
b. DeGeneres, Ellen
b. Gennaro, Peter

Minden, Louisiana
b. Kennon, Robert Floyd

Monroe, Louisiana
b. Fuller, S(amuel) B.
b. McGee, Frank
b. Russell, Bill
d. Delaney, Joe Alton

Montegut, Louisiana
b. Ellender, Allen Joseph

Mooringsport, Louisiana
b. Leadbelly

Natchitoches, Louisiana
b. Hunter, Clementine
b. Johnson, Marques Kevin
d. Croce, Jim
d. Hunter, Clementine

New Iberia, Louisiana
b. Eckart, William Joseph
b. Moore, Audley
d. Johnson, Bunk

New Orleans, Louisiana
b. Allen, Red
b. Armstrong, Anne Legendre
b. Armstrong, Louis
b. Basso, Hamilton
b. Bechet, Sidney
b. Bigard, Albany Barney Leon
b. Bolden, Buddy
b. Borders, James
b. Boswell, Connee
b. Boswell, Martha
b. Boswell, Vet
b. Brunis, George
b. Burke, Paul
b. Cable, George Washington
b. Capote, Truman
b. Carlisle, Kitty
b. Carter, Hodding
b. Clark, Will(iam Nuschler, Jr.)
b. Collins, Janet Faye
b. Collins, Joseph Lawton, General
b. Collins, Lee
b. Connick, Harry, Jr.
b. Cushman, Pauline
b. Dodds, Baby
b. Dodds, Johnny

b. Domino, Fats
b. Dr. John
b. Drexler, Clyde
b. Edeson, Robert
b. Fiske, Minnie Maddern
b. Fountain, Pete(r Dewey)
b. Gottschalk, Louis Moreau
b. Grau, Shirley Ann
b. Gumbel, Bryant (Charles)
b. Gumbel, Greg(ory)
b. Healy, Mary
b. Hebert, F(elix) Edward
b. Hellman, Lillian
b. Herriman, George
b. Hirt, Al(ois Maxwell)
b. Hunter, Jeffrey
b. Jackson, Mahalia
b. Johnson, Bunk
b. Johnson, Dink
b. Johnson, Lonnie
b. Joy, Leatrice
b. Kane, Harnett T(homas)
b. Keppard, Freddie
b. Kiam, Victor Kermit, II
b. King, Grace Elizabeth
b. Labouisse, Henry Richardson
b. Lamour, Dorothy
b. Landrieu, Moon
b. Larroquette, John (Bernard)
b. Lea, Fanny Heaslip
b. Leonard, Elmore John, Jr.
b. Leslie, Miriam Florence Folline
b. Manone, Wingy
b. Marier, Rebecca
b. Marsalis, Branford
b. Marsalis, Wynton
b. Menken, Adah Isaacs
b. Monroe, Bill
b. Morial, Ernest Nathan
b. Morial, Marc (Haydel)
b. Morphy, Paul Charles
b. Nelson, Ed(win Stafford)
b. Neville, Aaron
b. Newman, Joe Dwight
b. Newton, Huey P(ercy)
b. Oswald, Lee Harvey
b. Piazza, Marguerite
b. Plotkin, Mark
b. Plotkin, Mark J.
b. Prima, Louis
b. Rafferty, Max(well Lewis, Jr.)
b. Ransohoff, Martin
b. Reggio, Godfrey
b. Rice, Anne
b. Roberts, Cokie
b. Rosen, Benjamin M(aurice)
b. Rosen, Harold A.
b. RuPaul
b. Shields, Larry
b. Sigmund, Barbara Boggs
b. Simmons, Richard
b. Sothern, Edward Hugh
b. Staub, Rusty
b. Stewart, Ellen
b. Toole, John Kennedy
b. Turpin, Ben
b. Tyler, Parker
b. Verrett, Shirley Carter
b. Walston, Ray
b. Weathers, Carl
b. Wills, Harry
b. Young, Andrew Jackson, Jr.
b. Youngblood, Johnny Ray
d. Agramonte y Simoni, Aristides
d. Ball, Edward

d. Beauregard, Pierre Gustav Toutant de
d. Bilbo, Theodore Gilmore
d. Bolden, Buddy
d. Bradford, Roark Whitney Wickliffe
d. Byrd, Henry
d. Campbell, William Edward March
d. Catledge, Turner
d. Chennault, Claire Lee
d. Clairborne, William Charles Coles
d. Davis, Jefferson
d. Dinwiddie, John Ekin
d. Dix, Dorothy
d. Douvillier, Suzanne Theodore Vaillande
d. Elliott, Robert Brown
d. Garrison, Jim C.
d. Gordy, Robert
d. Hebert, F(elix) Edward
d. Higgins, Andrew J
d. Hirt, Al(ois Maxwell)
d. Hood, John Bell
d. Johnston, Frances Benjamin
d. Kane, Harnett T(homas)
d. Keyes, Frances Parkinson
d. King, Grace Elizabeth
d. Latrobe, Benjamin Henry
d. Mansfield, Jayne
d. Morial, Ernest Nathan
d. Morphy, Paul Charles
d. Neyland, Robert Reese
d. Niblo, Fred
d. Ochsner, Alton
d. Ott, Mel(vin Thomas)
d. Prima, Louis
d. Professor Longhair
d. Reddick, L(awrence) D(unbar)
d. Ritz, Al
d. Sykes, Roosevelt
d. Teagarden, Jack
d. Ubico y Castaneda, Jorge
d. Wallerstein, Lothar
d. Zemurray, Samuel

New Roads, Louisiana
d. Douglas, Emmitt

Newellton, Louisiana
b. Brimmer, Andrew Felton

Norwood, Louisiana
d. Wilson, Charles Erwin

Oak Grove, Louisiana
b. Marshall, Ray

Opelousas, Louisiana
b. Chenier, Clifton
b. Milburn, Rodney, Jr.
b. Prudhomme, Paul
d. Rockin' Dopsie

Oscar, Louisiana
b. Gaines, Ernest J(ames)

Port Allen, Louisiana
b. Fields, Cleo

Rayne, Louisiana
b. Sonnier, Jo-El

Rayville, Louisiana
b. Hayes, Elvin Ernest

Ruston, Louisiana
b. Jones, Bert(ram Hays)

Saint Bernard, Louisiana
b. Beauregard, Pierre Gustav Toutant de

Saint Gabriel, Louisiana
b. Roche, Joyce

Saint James, Louisiana
b. Richardson, Henry Hobson

Saint Rose Parish, Louisiana
b. Burroughs, Margaret Taylor

Scott, Louisiana
b. Doucet, Michael

Sheldon, Louisiana
b. Burdick, Eugene Leonard

Shreveport, Louisiana
b. Ashford, Evelyn
b. Belle, Albert
b. Bookout, John Frank, Jr.
b. Bradshaw, Terry Paxton
b. Burton, James
b. Carroll, Pat(ricia Ann Angela Bridgit)
b. Cliburn, Van
b. Cochran, Johnnie
b. Cramer, Floyd
b. Davis, Tommy
b. Dumars, Joe, III
b. Hawkins, Gus
b. Johnston, J. Bennett, Jr.
b. King, Claude
b. Long, Russell Billiu
b. Morse, Philip McCord
b. Parish, Robert L
b. Roemer, Buddy
b. Simmons, Althea T L
b. Suesse, Dana Nadine
b. Sutton, Hal Evan
b. Williams, Hank, Jr.
b. Young, Faron
d. Garber, Jan
d. Scopes, John Thomas

Simmesport, Louisiana
b. Simon, Joe

Slidell, Louisiana
b. Canzoneri, Tony

Sterlington, Louisiana
b. Perkins, Edward Joseph

Sulphur, Louisiana
d. Lyons, Ted

Summerfield, Louisiana
b. Malone, Karl

Tel Ridge, Louisiana
b. Kershaw, Doug(las James)

Thibodeaux, Louisiana
b. Lawless, Theodore K(enneth)

Trout, Louisiana
b. Jacob, John Edward

Vienna, Louisiana
b. Richard, J(ames) R(odney)

Waterproof, Louisiana
b. Johnson, John Henry

West Baton Rouge, Louisiana
b. DeRivera, Jose Ruiz

West Monroe, Louisiana
b. Pierce, Webb

Winnfield, Louisiana
b. Long, Earl Kemp
b. Long, Huey Pierce
b. Smith, William Jay

Zachary, Louisiana
b. Williams, Doug(las Lee)

MAINE
b. Lewis, Wyndham
d. Eliot, Charles William

Addison, Maine
d. Marin, John

Albion, Maine
b. Lovejoy, Elijah Parish

Auburn, Maine
b. Canham, Erwin Dain
b. Gould, George Milbry
d. Smith, Samantha

Augusta, Maine
b. Cony, Edward Roger
b. Hartford, George Huntington
b. Snowe, Olympia J(ean)
b. Wyman, Willard Gordon
d. Bolte, Charles G(uy)
d. Coxe, Louis Osborne

Bangor, Maine
b. Cahners, Norman Lee
b. Cohen, William S(ebastian)
b. McKernan, John Rettie, Jr.
b. Peirce, Waldo
d. Hamlin, Hannibal

Bar Harbor, Maine
b. Ralston, Esther
b. Rockefeller, Nelson A(ldrich)
d. Farrand, Beatrix Jones
d. Snell, George D(avis)
d. Yourcenar, Marguerite

Bath, Maine
b. Jackson, John Adams
d. Zorach, William

Biddeford, Maine
b. Baker, Carlos Heard
b. Bowie, Norman Ernest

Blue Hill, Maine
b. Chase, Mary Ellen
d. Brace, Gerald Warner
d. Taylor, Samuel (Albert)

Brunswick, Maine
b. Coffin, Robert Peter Tristram

b. Davis, Owen
b. Dow, Neal
b. Gallant, Roy Arthur
b. Gerber, John
b. Gurney, Edward John
b. King, Stephen Edwin
b. Lavin, Linda
b. Nelson, Judd
b. Paine, John Knowles
b. Parton, Sara Payson Willis
b. Pickard, Greenleaf Whittier
b. Reed, Thomas Brackett
b. Rowell, Victoria (Lynn)
b. Sharmat, Marjorie Weinman
b. Thaxter, Phyllis
b. Willis, Nathaniel Parker
b. Wilson, Hazel Hutchins
d. Cooney, Barbara
d. Dow, Neal
d. Fessenden, William Pitt
d. Mulford, Clarence Edward
d. Preston, John
d. Scribner, Fred C(lark), Jr.

Prouts Neck, Maine
d. Homer, Winslow

Rockland, Maine
b. Ames, Adelbert
b. Elliott, Gertrude
b. Elliott, Maxine
b. Millay, Edna St. Vincent
b. Piston, Walter

Rockport, Maine
d. Luboshutz, Pierre
d. Sayao, Bidu

Rumford, Maine
b. Muskie, Edmund S(ixtus)

Rumford Falls, Maine
d. Finck, Henry Theophilus

Saco, Maine
b. Brannan, Samuel
b. Rogers, Edith

Sangerville, Maine
b. Maxim, Hiram Stevens, Sir

Scarboro, Maine
b. King, Rufus

Searsport, Maine
d. Peirce, Waldo

Shirley, Maine
b. Nye, Edgar Wilson

Skowhegan, Maine
b. Dolbier, Maurice (Wyman)
b. Smith, Margaret (Madeline) Chase
d. Smith, Margaret (Madeline) Chase

Somerset County, Maine
b. Coffin, Charles Albert

South Berwick, Maine
b. Jewett, Sarah Orne
d. Jewett, Sarah Orne

South Casco, Maine
d. Gulick, Luther (Halsey)

South China, Maine
b. Jones, Rufus Matthew

South Windham, Maine
b. Donnell, Jeff

Strong, Maine
b. Allen, Elizabeth Ann Chase Akers

Temple, Maine
d. Dennison, George
d. Goodman, Mitchell

Temple Mills, Maine
b. Dryden, John Fairfield

Thomaston, Maine
d. Knox, Henry

Vienna, Maine
b. Bradley, Milton

Waterford, Maine
b. Ward, Artemus

Waterville, Maine
b. Cody, Lew
b. Lovejoy, Clarence Earle
b. Mitchell, George John

Wayne, Maine
b. Cary, Anne Louise

Webster, Maine
b. Simmons, Franklin

West Gardiner, Maine
b. Stevens, John Frank

West Pembroke, Maine
b. Best, Charles Herbert
b. Bridges, Styles

West Southport, Maine
d. Tenggren, Gustaf Adolf

Windham, Maine
b. Andrew, John Albion

Wiscasset, Maine
d. Johnson, James Weldon

Woolwich, Maine
b. Phips, William, Sir

York, Maine
b. Wood, Sarah Sayward Barrell
  Keating
d. Carroll, Gladys Hasty
d. Sarton, May

York Harbor, Maine
d. DeRochemont, Louis

MARYLAND
b. Bowie, Walter
b. Calvert, Charles
b. Clarke, Edith

b. Galloway, Joseph
b. Gist, Christopher
d. Brown, Alexander
d. McCulloch, Hugh
d. Wiley, George A

Aberdeen, Maryland
b. Ripken, Cal(vin Edwin, Sr.)

Abingdon, Maryland
b. Paca, William
d. Paca, William

Anacosta Heights, Maryland
d. Douglass, Frederick

Annapolis, Maryland
b. Cain, James M(allahan)
b. Carroll, Charles
b. Davis, Henry Winter
b. Johnson, Reverdy
b. Kingsolver, Barbara
b. Meyer, Debbie
b. Peale, Raphael
b. Pinkney, William
b. Smith, Thorne
d. Bowie, Walter
d. Byrd, Charlie
d. Cates, Clifton Bledsoe
d. Green, Constance Windsor
  McLaughlin
d. Hall, Asaph
d. Johnson, Reverdy
d. Smith, Cyrus Rowlett
d. Spotswood, Alexander
d. Terrell, Mary Church
d. Thomson, Earl

Anne Arundel, Maryland
b. Hopkins, Johns

Anne Arundel County, Maryland
b. Bowie, William
b. Weems, Mason Locke

Arnold, Maryland
d. Lewis, Elizabeth Foreman

Baltimore, Maryland
b. Adler, Larry
b. Agle, Nan Hayden
b. Agnew, Spiro T(heodore)
b. Alexander, Hattie Elizabeth
b. Angelos, Peter
b. Armstrong, Bess
b. Ashman, Howard
b. Astin, John Allen
b. Atkinson, William Walker
b. Baldwin, Hanson Weightman
b. Bamberger, Louis
b. Bateman, Kate Josephine
b. Beach, Sylvia
b. Blake, Eubie
b. Boehm, Edward M
b. Bogues, Mugsy
b. Bonaparte, Elizabeth Patterson
b. Bonsal, Stephen
b. Breeskin, Adelyn Dohme
b. Bruce, David Kirkpatrick Estes
b. Burns, William John
b. Burt, Maxwell Struthers
b. Bushman, Francis X(avier)
b. Calvert, Catherine
b. Carnegie, Mary Elizabeth Lancaster

d. Clifford, Clark M(cAdams)
d. Cohn, Roy (Marcus)
d. Courlander, Harold
d. Dell, Floyd
d. Dennison, Robert Lee
d. Devers, Jacob Loucks
d. Downs, William Randall, Jr.
d. Ellender, Allen Joseph
d. Forrestal, James Vincent
d. Harris, Bucky
d. Hickerson, John Dewey
d. Hull, Cordell
d. Jaffe, Sam(uel Anderson)
d. Johnson, Hiram Warren
d. Kefauver, Estes
d. Kiplinger, W(illard) M(onroe)
d. Klineberg, Otto
d. Leahy, William Daniel
d. Marshall, George Catlett
d. Marshall, Thurgood
d. Massey, Ilona
d. McCarthy, Joe
d. McGee, Gale William
d. Patman, (John Williams) Wright
d. Ronne, Finn
d. Ruppe, Loret Miller
d. Shear, Murray Jacob
d. Shevchenko, Arkady N(ikolayevich)
d. Solomon, Samuel Joseph
d. Sweet, John Howard
d. Teague, Olin E
d. Tuve, Merle Antony
d. Ullman, Al(bert Conrad)
d. Vandegrift, Alexander Archer
d. Volkov, Leon
d. Walsh, William B(ertalan)
d. White, Stephen
d. Wilson, Hazel Hutchins
d. Wyman, Willard Gordon

Bladensburg, Maryland
d. Decatur, Stephen

Bowie, Maryland
b. Scruggs, Jan

Bryantown, Maryland
b. Mudd, Samuel Alexander

Calvert County, Maryland
b. Taney, Roger Brooke
b. Taylor, Margaret (Smith)
b. Wilkinson, James

Cambridge, Maryland
b. Barth, John (Simmons)

Camp Springs, Maryland
d. Eaker, Ira Clarence

Carroll County, Maryland
b. Key, Francis Scott
d. Chambers, Whittaker

Catonsville, Maryland
b. Crosby, Alexander L

Cecil County, Maryland
b. Brookings, Robert Somers
b. Caswell, Richard
b. Davis, David

Centreville, Maryland
d. Raskob, John J

Charles County, Maryland
b. Hanson, John
b. Henson, Josiah
b. Henson, Matthew Alexander
b. Semmes, Raphael
b. Stone, Thomas

Chestertown, Maryland
b. Peale, James
d. Bode, Carl
d. Cater, Douglass

Cheverly, Maryland
d. Porter, Richard William

Chevy Chase, Maryland
b. King, Gayle
d. Abbe, Cleveland
d. Ball, Joseph H(urst)
d. Daly, John Charles, Jr.
d. Hays, Brooks
d. Larsen, Emmanuel
d. McCloskey, Robert James
d. O'Hara, Mary
d. Trudeau, Arthur G(ilbert)
d. Ward, Paul W
d. Wright, Louis Booker

Clear Springs, Maryland
b. Bobst, Elmer Holmes

College Park, Maryland
d. Bias, Len

Columbia, Maryland
d. Rouse, James W(ilson)
d. Whittle, Frank, Sir

Cumberland, Maryland
b. Ord, Edward Otho Cresap
b. Walsh, James Edward
d. Staggers, Harley O(rrin)

Deer Park, Maryland
d. Garrett, John Work

Derwood, Maryland
d. Turner, Donald F(rank)

Dorchester, Maryland
b. Tubman, Harriet Ross

Easton, Maryland
b. Rouse, James W(ilson)
d. Girdler, Tom Mercer
d. Lawrie, Lee
d. Morton, Rogers Clark Ballard
d. Smith, Gerard C(oad)

Elkton, Maryland
b. Purdie, Bernard

Ellicott City, Maryland
b. Davis, Meyer

Ellicott Mills, Maryland
b. Banneker, Benjamin

Emmitsburg, Maryland
d. Seton, Elizabeth Ann Bayley, Saint

Fallston, Maryland
d. Hartline, Haldan Keffer

Fort Washington, Maryland
d. Cushman, Robert Everton, Jr.

Frederick, Maryland
b. Fritchie, Barbara
b. Mathias, Charles McCurdy, Jr.
b. McCardell, Claire
d. Wheeler, Earle G

Frederick County, Maryland
b. Schley, Winfield Scott
b. Seiss, Joseph Augustus
d. Lee, Thomas Sim

Gaithersburg, Maryland
d. Johnson, Eleanor M
d. Stratton, Samuel S(tuddiford)

Garrett Park, Maryland
d. Leaf, Munro

Georgetown, Maryland
b. Gilliss, James Melville
d. Wallop, Douglass

Glen Burnie, Maryland
d. Eberle, Bob

Glen Echo, Maryland
d. Barton, Clara Harlowe

Glencoe, Maryland
d. Perky, Henry D

Green Hills, Maryland
d. L'Enfant, Pierre Charles

Hagerstown, Maryland
b. Feld, Irvin

Hamilton, Maryland
b. Leaf, Munro

Harford County, Maryland
b. Booth, John Wilkes
b. Rodgers, John

Havre de Grace, Maryland
b. Ripken, Bill
b. Ripken, Cal(vin Edwin, Jr.)
b. Tydings, Millard Evelyn
d. Tydings, Millard Evelyn

Howard County, Maryland
d. Winpisinger, William W(ayne)

Hughesville, Maryland
b. Turner, Thomas Wyatt

Hunt Valley, Maryland
d. Day, J(ames) Edward

Huntsville, Maryland
b. Hunt, George Wylie Paul

Hyattsville, Maryland
b. Bias, Len
d. Barnes-Taeuber, Irene
d. Cain, James M(allahan)

b. Nitze, Paul Henry
b. Symington, Stuart
d. Adams, Herbert Baxter
d. Baker, Ray Stannard
d. Commager, Henry Steele
d. Dickinson, Emily (Elizabeth)
d. Garis, Howard Roger
d. Genung, John Franklin
d. Hitchcock, Edward

Andover, Massachusetts
b. Burns, John Horne
b. Phelps, Elizabeth Stuart Ward
d. Bradstreet, Anne
d. Fitts, Dudley
d. Lane, Priscilla
d. Otis, James
d. Pierce, Jane (Means)

Arlington, Massachusetts
b. Creeley, Robert (White)
b. Hardy, Harriet
b. Whitaker, Rogers E(rnest)
    M(alcolm)
b. Wilson, Samuel
d. Agassiz, Elizabeth Cabot Cary
d. Trowbridge, John Townsend

Ashburnham, Massachusetts
d. Kressy, Edmund

Ashfield, Massachusetts
b. DeMille, Cecil B(lount)
b. Hall, G(ranville) Stanley

Attleboro, Massachusetts
b. Berberian, Cathy
b. Bowen, Roger
b. Conniff, Ray
b. Manchester, William Raymond
b. Rounseville, Robert Field

Auburndale, Massachusetts
b. Clark, Sydney
b. Friebus, Florida
b. Parker, Horatio William

Barnstable, Massachusetts
b. Shaw, Lemuel
b. Warren, Mercy Otis
d. Kittredge, G(eorge) L(yman)

Barre, Massachusetts
d. Riis, Jacob August

Bedford, Massachusetts
b. Haney, Carol

Belchertown, Massachusetts
b. Bartlett, Francis Alonzo

Bellingham, Massachusetts
b. Adams, William Taylor

Belmont, Massachusetts
b. Daily, Thomas V, Bishop
d. Bush, Vannevar
d. Hale, Lucretia Peabody
d. Howard, Cordelia
d. Piston, Walter
d. Walker, Henry Oliver
d. Zacharias, Jerrold R(einarch)

Beverly, Massachusetts
b. Barnet, Will
b. Brown, Frank Arthur, Jr.
b. Carpenter, Bobby
b. Colwell, Rita R(ossi)
b. Larcom, Lucy
b. Whitney, Richard
b. Wylie, Philip Gordon
d. Lodge, Henry Cabot, Jr.
d. Rayburn, Gene

Billerica, Massachusetts
b. Peabody, Elizabeth Palmer

Blackstone, Massachusetts
b. Tappan, Eva March

Boston, Massachusetts
b. Adams, Charles Francis, Sr.
b. Adams, Charles Francis, Jr.
b. Adams, Henry Brooks
b. Adams, Samuel
b. Agassiz, Elizabeth Cabot Cary
b. Akers, John Fellows
b. Albright, Tenley Emma
b. Aldrich, Richard Stoddard
b. Alexander, Jane
b. Allen, Frederick Lewis
b. Ames, Ed(mund Dantes)
b. Anderson, June
b. Bailey, Charles Waldo, II
b. Ballou, Maturin Murray
b. Barber, Bernard
b. Barnes, Joanna
b. Barrasso, Tom
b. Barron, Clarence Walker
b. Barth, Roland Sawyer
b. Bellows, Henry Whitney
b. Benirschke, Rolf Joachim
b. Berle, Adolf Augustus, Jr.
b. Bigelow, Henry Bryant
b. Bitzer, George William
b. Bloomberg, Michael (R.)
b. Bogosian, Eric
b. Bookspan, Martin
b. Borg, Veda Ann
b. Borofsky, Jonathan
b. Borysenko, Joan
b. Boswell, John (Eastburn)
b. Bowdoin, James
b. Bradford, Gamaliel
b. Bradlee, Ben(jamin Crowninshield)
b. Braff, Ruby
b. Braithwaite, William Stanley
    Beaumont
b. Brattle, Thomas
b. Brooks, Phillips
b. Brown, Bobby
b. Brown, William Hill
b. Bulfinch, Charles
b. Bundy, McGeorge
b. Burgess, Gelett
b. Burns, Jack
b. Butcher, Susan
b. Cabot, Susan
b. Carlisle, Mary
b. Carney, Harry Howell
b. Cass, Peggy
b. Chauncy, Charles
b. Ciardi, John Anthony
b. Clapp, Patricia
b. Cole, Maria
b. Coles, Robert
b. Collins, Gary
b. Colonna, Jerry
b. Colson, Chuck

b. Connolly, James B
b. Coolidge, Charles Allerton
b. Cooper, Joseph D
b. Copley, John Singleton
b. Corwin, Norman
b. Costa, Don
b. Cowl, Jane
b. Crafts, James Mason
b. Craven, Frank
b. Crosby, Harry
b. Crosby, Norm(an Lawrence)
b. Curley, James Michael
b. Curtis, Charles Gordon
b. Cushing, Richard James, Cardinal
b. Cushman, Charlotte Saunders
b. Dahlberg, Edward
b. Davis, Margaret B(ryan)
b. Dawes, William
b. Delmar, Kenny
b. DeLue, Donald Harcourt
b. Dewing, Thomas Wilmer
b. Dole, James
b. Donnellan, Nanci
b. Downes, Edward Olin Davenport
b. Duran Ballen, Sixto
b. Durant, William Crapo
b. Eliot, Charles William
b. Elkins, Stanley Maurice
b. Elliott, Bob
b. Elliott, Robert Brown
b. Emerson, Ralph Waldo
b. Eruzione, Mike
b. Evans, Charles
b. Evarts, William Maxwell
b. Faber, Sandra M(oore)
b. Farmer, Fannie Merritt
b. Farnum, William
b. Fellows, Edith
b. Fichandler, Zelda Diamond
b. Fiedler, Arthur
b. Field, Betty
b. Filene, Lincoln
b. Fitts, Dudley
b. Fitzgerald, John Francis
b. Flynn, Ray
b. Flynn, Raymond (Leo)
b. Foley, Martha
b. Forbes, Robert Bennet
b. Francis, Arlene
b. Franklin, Benjamin
b. Frederick, Pauline
b. Giamatti, A(ngelo) Bartlett
b. Gibran, Kahlil George
b. Gilbert, Walter
b. Gomez, Jewelle
b. Goodwin, Nat C
b. Goodwin, Richard N(aradhof)
b. Grandin, Temple
b. Gray, Horace
b. Greenough, Horatio
b. Grew, Joseph Clark
b. Griffis, Stanton
b. Grimke, Angelina Emily Weld
b. Gross, Courtlandt Sherrington
b. Gross, Robert Ellsworth
b. Guber, Peter
b. Guest, C. Z.
b. Guiney, Louise Imogene
b. Guy, Jasmine
b. Hale, Edward Everett
b. Hale, Lucretia Peabody
b. Hale, Nancy
b. Haley, Jack
b. Hall, Anthony Thomas Charles
b. Hartt, Frederick
b. Hassam, Childe

d. Crabtree, Lotta
d. Cram, Ralph Adams
d. Curley, James Michael
d. Cushing, Richard James, Cardinal
d. Cushman, Charlotte Saunders
d. Dallin, Cyrus Edwin
d. Daugherty, James Henry
d. Davenport, John
d. Dawes, William
d. Doriot, Georges Frederic
d. East, Edward Murray
d. Endecott, John
d. Europe, James Reese
d. Everett, Edward
d. Farb, Peter
d. Farmer, Fannie Merritt
d. Fields, James Thomas
d. Fitzgerald, Albert J
d. Fitzgerald, John Francis
d. Fleming, Williamina Paton Stevens
d. Foote, Arthur William
d. Forbes, Robert Bennet
d. Francis, James Bicheno
d. Frazier, Brenda Diana Dudd
d. Frost, Robert Lee
d. Gallen, Hugh J
d. Gardner, Isabella Stewart
d. Garrigue, Jean
d. Geschwind, Norman
d. Gilbert, A(lfred) C(arleton)
d. Griswold, Erwin N(athaniel)
d. Gropius, Walter Adolf
d. Gunn, Hartford Nelson, Jr.
d. Hampton, Henry
d. Harding, Chester
d. Harvard, John
d. Hayes, Roland
d. Herne, Chrystal Katharine
d. Hightower, Florence Josephine Cole
d. Hill, Billy
d. Holmes, Oliver Wendell, Sr.
d. Holt, John Caldwell
d. Howe, Samuel Gridley
d. Hunsaker, Jerome Clarke
d. Jaeger, Werner Wilhelm
d. Jakobson, Roman
d. Jones, Buck
d. Kalmus, Natalie Mabelle Dunfee
d. Kelly, King
d. Kennedy, Patrick Bouvier
d. Kent, Corita
d. Kern, Harold G
d. Kilroy, James, Jr.
d. Koussevitzky, Serge Alexandrovich
d. Lahey, Frank Howard
d. Lanman, Charles Rockwell
d. Larcom, Lucy
d. Lash, Joseph P
d. Lawrence, Abbott
d. Lawson, Thomas William
d. Lincoln, Mary Johnson Bailey
d. Little, Charles Coffin
d. Lodge, Henry Cabot
d. Lowell, Abbott Lawrence
d. Lowell, Francis Cabot
d. MacLeish, Archibald
d. Maginnis, Charles Donagh
d. Mapplethorpe, Robert
d. Mather, Cotton
d. Mather, Increase
d. Mayhew, Jonathan
d. McCarthy, Tommy
d. McCord, David (Thompson Watson)
d. McCullough, Paul
d. Medeiros, Humberto, Cardinal
d. Metalious, Grace de Repentigny

d. Morison, Samuel Eliot
d. Murray, John
d. O'Connor, Edwin Greene
d. O'Donnell, Kenneth P
d. O'Neill, Eugene Gladstone
d. O'Neill, Thomas P(hilip), Jr.
d. Paine, Robert Treat
d. Parker, George Swinnerton
d. Parkman, Francis
d. Perry, Ralph Barton
d. Phillips, Wendell
d. Pincus, Gregory
d. Prescott, William Hickling
d. Quimby, Harriet
d. Remond, Charles Lennox
d. Revere, Paul
d. Rey, Hans Augustus
d. Richardson, Elliot L(ee)
d. Rimmer, William
d. Rodzinski, Artur
d. Rogers, Edith
d. Ross, Art(hur Howie)
d. Ross, Harold Wallace
d. Sacco, Nicola
d. Salinas (y Serrano), Pedro
d. Sauveur, Albert
d. Savage, Henry Wilson
d. Scott, Austin Wakeman
d. Scourby, Alexander
d. Sears, Richard Dudley
d. Sewall, Samuel
d. Shannon, William Vincent
d. Shirer, William L(awrence)
d. Sims, William Sowden
d. Sissman, L(ouis) E(dward)
d. Smith, Samuel Francis
d. Stanley, Freelan O
d. Stone, I(sidor) F(einstein)
d. Stoopnagle, Lemuel Q, Colonel
d. Stratton, Julius A(dams)
d. Stuart, Gilbert Charles
d. Taylor, Phoebe Atwood
d. Taylor, Susie Baker King
d. Thompson, Randall
d. Ticknor, George
d. Trotter, Monroe
d. Tsongas, Paul E(fthemios)
d. Ullman, James Ramsey
d. Updike, Daniel Berkeley
d. Vanzetti, Bartolomeo
d. Walker, David
d. Walsh, Michael Patrick
d. Wang, An
d. Weiland, Cooney
d. West, Dorothy
d. Wheatley, Phillis
d. White, Paul Dudley
d. Williams, Gluyas
d. Winthrop, John
d. Wolff, Mary Evaline
d. Wood, Leonard
d. Woods, Robert Archey
d. Wright, George
d. Yawkey, Thomas Austin

Boxford, Massachusetts
d. Sherrill, Henry Knox

Bradford, Massachusetts
b. Snell, George D(avis)

Braintree, Massachusetts
b. Adams, John
b. Adams, John Quincy
b. Hancock, John
b. Thayer, Sylvanus, General

d. Thayer, Sylvanus, General

Brewster, Massachusetts
b. Lincoln, Joseph C(rosby)

Bridgewater, Massachusetts
b. Ames, Nathaniel
b. Cochrane, Mickey

Brighton, Massachusetts
b. Dysart, Richard (Allan)
b. Hebner, Richie
b. Hoyt, Lawrence W
b. Kennedy, Joseph Patrick, II

Brimfield, Massachusetts
b. Fairbanks, Thaddeus
b. Guthrie, Samuel

Brockton, Massachusetts
b. Davis, Al(len)
b. Dunham, Sonny
b. Higgins, George V.
b. Kaminsky, Max
b. Marciano, Rocky
b. Wind, Herbert Warren

Brookfield, Massachusetts
b. Holmes, Mary Jane Hawes

Brookline, Massachusetts
b. Boutwell, George Sewall
b. Cabot, Richard C
b. Dukakis, Michael Stanley
b. Fowlie, Wallace
b. Kennedy, Edward Moore
b. Kennedy, John F(itzgerald)
b. Kennedy, Robert Francis
b. Lowell, Amy
b. Mason, Daniel Gregory
b. Mirkin, Gabe
b. Monteux, Claude
b. O'Brien, Conan
b. Ouimet, Francis de Sales
b. Pantaleoni, Helenka (Tradeusa
  Adamowski)
b. Shriver, Eunice Mary Kennedy
b. Streeter, Ruth
b. Susskind, David Howard
b. Wallace, Mike
b. Wellman, William Augustus
d. Adams, Hannah
d. Adams, Weston W, Sir
d. Brewster, (Ralph) Owen
d. Coons, Albert Hewett
d. Fiedler, Arthur
d. Fuller, George
d. Katz, Milton
d. Lehr, Lew
d. Liebman, Joshua Loth
d. Lowell, Amy
d. Mather, Stephen Tyng
d. McBurney, Charles
d. Minot, George Richards
d. Olmsted, Frederick Law
d. Rhodes, James Ford
d. Richardson, Henry Hobson
d. Sager, Ruth
d. Soloveitchik, Joseph Baer
d. Williams, Ben Ames

Buckland, Massachusetts
b. Lyon, Mary Mason

d. Emerson, Ralph Waldo
d. Greeley, Dana McLean
d. Kuhn, Irene
d. Morse, Philip McCord
d. Thoreau, Henry David
d. Weeks, Sinclair

Conway, Massachusetts
b. Field, Marshall
b. Harding, Chester
b. Whitney, William Collins
d. Chesbro, Jack

Crookston, Massachusetts
d. Lindbergh, Charles Augustus

Cummington, Massachusetts
b. Bryant, William Cullen
b. Dawes, Henry Laurens

Cutty Hunk, Massachusetts
b. Cuffe, Paul

Danvers, Massachusetts
b. Dodge, Grenville Mellen
b. Kelsey, Alice Geer
b. Sexton, Leo

Dedham, Massachusetts
b. Ames, Fisher
b. D'Amboise, Jacques
b. Nickerson, Albert L(indsay)
d. Ames, Nathaniel
d. Bayard, Thomas Francis
d. McCormack, John William

Deerfield, Massachusetts
b. Fuller, George
b. Hildreth, Richard
b. Hitchcock, Edward

Dorchester, Massachusetts
b. Bolger, Ray(mond Wallace)
b. Channing, Edward Perkins
b. Conant, James Bryant
b. Eliot, Martha May
b. Everett, Edward
b. Herne, Chrystal Katharine
b. Mather, Increase
b. McCarron, Chris
b. Motley, John Lothrop
d. Adams, William Taylor
d. Stone, Lucy

Dover, Massachusetts
d. Saltonstall, Leverett

Dracut, Massachusetts
b. Corey, Wendell

Dunstable, Massachusetts
b. Kendall, Amos
b. Richards, Ellen Henrietta Swallow

Duxbury, Massachusetts
d. Alden, John
d. Alden, Priscilla Mullens
d. Standish, Miles

East Boston, Massachusetts
b. Walker, Hiram

East Brookfield, Massachusetts
b. Mack, Connie
b. Thurber, Charles

East Northfield, Massachusetts
b. Moody, Dwight Lyman

Easthampton, Massachusetts
b. Brubacher, John Seiler

Easton, Massachusetts
b. Ames, Oakes
d. Ames, Oakes

Edgartown, Massachusetts
d. Hough, Henry Beetle

Egypt, Massachusetts
b. McCall, Thomas Lawson

Everett, Massachusetts
b. Bush, Vannevar
b. Sneed, Paula A(nn)

Fairhaven, Massachusetts
b. Bradford, William
b. Jenney, William LeBaron

Fall River, Massachusetts
b. Borden, Lizzie Andrew
b. Clark, Alvin Graham
b. Dean, Morton
b. Lagasse, Emeril
b. Lincoln, Victoria Endicott
b. Raposo, Joseph
b. Stephanopoulos, George (Robert)
d. Borden, Lizzie Andrew
d. Howe, Louis McHenry
d. Porter, William James

Falmouth, Massachusetts
b. Bates, Katharine Lee
b. Dubroff, Jessica
b. Kennedy, Patrick Bouvier
b. Boyd, William Clouser
d. Crawford, Frederick C(oolidge)
d. Harris, William Bliss
d. Langmuir, Irving

Feeding Hills, Massachusetts
b. Sullivan, Anne

Fitchburg, Massachusetts
b. Rugg, Harold

Framingham, Massachusetts
b. Attucks, Crispus
b. Parkhurst, Charles Henry
b. Preston, John
b. Traynor, Pie
d. Nutting, Wallace
d. Wilkins, George Hubert, Sir

Franklin, Massachusetts
b. Mann, Horace

Gardner, Massachusetts
b. Cady, (Walter) Harrison

Gloucester, Massachusetts
b. Lane, Fitz Hugh
b. Poirier, Richard
d. Anthony, Edward

d. Barbour, Walworth
d. Beaux, Cecilia
d. Clark, Bennett Champ
d. Coon, Carleton Stevens
d. Fiske, John
d. Kroll, Leon
d. Twachtman, John Henry
d. Wengenroth, Stow

Grafton, Massachusetts
b. Thomas, Robert B

Granville Centre, Massachusetts
d. Scott, Austin

Great Barrington, Massachusetts
b. Chinn, May (Edward)
b. DuBois, W(illiam) E(dward)
    B(urghardt)
b. Lynes, Joseph Russell, Jr.
d. Cournand, Andre Frederic

Greenfield, Massachusetts
b. Benjamin, Asher
b. Eddy, Clarence
b. Nolan, Thomas Brennan
b. Ripley, George
b. Taylor, Charles Alonzo
d. Niebuhr, Helmut Richard

Groton, Massachusetts
b. Lawrence, Abbott
d. Boutwell, George Sewall
d. Peabody, Endicott

Hadley, Massachusetts
b. Hooker, Joseph
d. Smith, Sophia

Hamilton, Massachusetts
d. Cutler, Manasseh
d. McKay, Donald

Hampden, Massachusetts
d. Burgess, Thornton Waldo

Harwich, Massachusetts
d. Erikson, Erik H(omburger)

Hatfield, Massachusetts
b. Smith, Sophia

Haverhill, Massachusetts
b. Appleton, Daniel
b. Appleton, William Henry
b. Cline, Maggie
b. Crockett, James Underwood
b. Fontaine, Frank
b. Lahey, Frank Howard
b. Whittier, John Greenleaf

Hingham, Massachusetts
b. Brett, Jan Churchill
b. Hall, James
b. Lincoln, Benjamin
b. Stoddard, Richard Henry
d. Dwiggins, William Addison
d. Lincoln, Benjamin

Holbrook, Massachusetts
b. Brightman, Edgar Sheffield

Holyoke, Massachusetts
b. Azinger, Paul
b. Breck, John Henry
b. Cox, Gardner
b. Holmes, John Clellon
b. Moffett, Anthony Toby
b. Sheehan, Neil
b. Wegman, William George
d. Kahn, E(ly) J(acques), Jr.
d. Swados, Harvey
d. Viereck, George Sylvester

Hopkinton, Massachusetts
b. Brown, Walter Augustine
b. Shays, Daniel

Hudson, Massachusetts
b. Coolidge, William David
b. Robinson, Wilbert
b. Wheeler, Burton Kendall
d. Williams, Tommy

Huntington, Massachusetts
b. Rich, Louise Dickinson

Hyannis, Massachusetts
d. Anthony, Joseph
d. Biddle, Francis Beverley
d. Field, Betty
d. Gorey, Edward St. John
d. Jones, Thomas Hudson
d. Knaths, Karl
d. Most, Johnny
d. Taber, Gladys Bagg
d. Waksman, Selman Abraham
d. Walker, Danton MacIntyre
d. Welch, Joseph Nye

Hyannis Port, Massachusetts
d. Kennedy, Joseph Patrick, Sr.
d. Kennedy, Rose (Fitzgerald)
d. Page, Irvine H

Hyde Park, Massachusetts
d. Grimke, Angelina Emily
d. Grimke, Sarah Moore

Ipswich, Massachusetts
b. Choate, Rufus
d. Wise, John

Jamaica Plain, Massachusetts
b. Balch, Emily G
d. Clarke, James Freeman
d. Peabody, Elizabeth Palmer
d. Pratt, Bela Lyon
d. Richards, Ellen Henrietta Swallow

Kingston, Massachusetts
d. Bartlett, Josiah

Lancaster, Massachusetts
b. Burbank, Luther

Lanesboro, Massachusetts
b. Billings, Josh

Lawrence, Massachusetts
b. Antoon, A(lfred) J(oseph)
b. Bernstein, Leonard
b. Demara, Ferdinand Waldo, Jr.
b. Goulet, Robert Gerard
b. Monette, Paul

b. Mungo, Raymond
b. Thayer, Ernest L
b. Todd, Thelma
b. Tree, Marietta Endicott Peabody

Lee, Massachusetts
b. Ayer, Francis Wayland
b. Durant, Thomas Clark
b. Rogers, Shorty

Lenox, Massachusetts
b. Fitzgibbon, Constantine
b. Lathrop, Rose Hawthorne
b. VanDerZee, James
d. Carnegie, Andrew
d. Clampitt, Amy

Leominster, Massachusetts
b. Kirkpatrick, Ralph Leonard
b. Little, Lou(is)

Lexington, Massachusetts
b. Greeley, Dana McLean
b. Parker, Theodore
b. Young, Philip
d. Luria, Salvador Edward
d. Sloane, Dennis

Longmeadow, Massachusetts
b. Brewster, Kingman, Jr.

Lowell, Massachusetts
b. Ames, Blanche
b. Baker, George
b. Chadwick, George Whitefield
b. Davis, Bette
b. Dukakis, Olympia
b. Elias, Rosalind
b. Goulding, Ray(mond Walter)
b. Harmon, Ernest N(ason)
b. Kaplan, Jacob Merrill
b. Kelly, Nancy
b. Kerouac, Jack
b. Metcalf, Willard Leroy
b. Sullivan, William Hallisey, Jr.
b. Tsongas, Paul E(fthemios)
b. Whistler, James Abbott McNeill

Lunenburg, Massachusetts
b. Brown, Earle

Lynn, Massachusetts
b. Andrews, Fannie Fern Phillips
b. Brennan, Walter Andrew
b. Conley, Eugene
b. Estrich, Susan
b. Fitzgerald, Albert J
b. Grimes, Tammy Lee
b. Hamilton, Neil
b. Hegan, Jim
b. Henderson, Lawrence Joseph
b. Lummis, Charles Fletcher
b. Mears, Walter Robert
b. Newhall, Beaumont
b. Newhall, Nancy Wynne
b. Parsons, Estelle
b. Pinkham, Lydia Estes
b. Stahl, Lesley (Rene)
b. Thorndike, Lynn
b. Tozzer, Alfred Marston
d. Matzeliger, Jan Ernest
d. Mitchell, Maria
d. Pinkham, Lydia Estes
d. Van Depoele, Charles Joseph

Magnolia, Massachusetts
d. Cox, Jacob Dolson

Malden, Massachusetts
b. Albertson, Jack
b. Barnard, Chester Irving
b. Gardner, Erle Stanley
b. Greenbaum, Norman
b. Judson, Adoniram
b. Kalem, T(heodore) E(ustace)
b. Melcher, Frederic Gershon
b. Oliver, Edna May
b. Paul, Elliot Harold
b. Reed, Frank H
b. Stella, Frank Philip
b. Traube, Shepard
d. Robinson, Harriet Jane Hanson
d. Wigglesworth, Michael

Manchester, Massachusetts
d. Grew, Joseph Clark

Marblehead, Massachusetts
b. Gerry, Elbridge
b. Story, Joseph
d. Barton, Robert B(rown) M(orison)
d. Chamberlain, Samuel
d. Glover, John
d. Kemelman, Harry

Marion, Massachusetts
b. Ruggles, Carl

Marlborough, Massachusetts
b. Nutting, Wallace
b. Rock, John

Marshfield, Massachusetts
b. Rogers, Isaiah
d. Webster, Daniel

Martha's Vineyard, Massachusetts
b. Mayhew, Jonathan
d. Bacon, Selden D(askam)
d. Eisenstaedt, Alfred
d. Giamatti, A(ngelo) Bartlett
d. Gordon, Ruth
d. Treat, Lawrence

Mattapoisett, Massachusetts
d. Rich, Louise Dickinson

Medfield, Massachusetts
b. Mason, Lowell
d. Loeffler, Charles Martin Tornow

Medford, Massachusetts
b. Adams, Edwin
b. Adams, Hannah
b. Brooks, Maria Gowen
b. Child, Lydia Maria Francis
b. Larkin, Oliver Waterman
b. Marshall, Laurence
b. Ripley, William Zebina
b. Theroux, Paul Edward
d. Pierce, John Davis

Melrose, Massachusetts
b. Atkinson, Brooks
b. Farrar, Geraldine
b. Souter, David Hackett
b. Speare, Elizabeth George
d. Livermore, Mary Ashton Rice

Mendon, Massachusetts
b. Thayer, Eli

Methuen, Massachusetts
b. Bedrosian, Steve
b. Caras, Roger Andrew
b. Corey, Elias James
b. Rogers, Robert

Middleboro, Massachusetts
d. Tom Thumb, General

Middlefield, Massachusetts
b. Emmons, Ebenezer

Milford, Massachusetts
b. Bragg, Mabel Caroline
b. Murray, Joseph

Milton, Massachusetts
b. Bush, George (Herbert Walker)
b. Daniell, Robert F
b. Fuller, Richard Buckminster
d. Higgins, George V.

Monterey, Massachusetts
d. Dyer-Bennet, Richard

Muddy River, Massachusetts
b. Boylston, Zabdiel
d. Boylston, Zabdiel

Nahant, Massachusetts
b. Amory, Cleveland
b. Johnson, Walter
b. Lodge, Henry Cabot, Jr.

Nahunt, Massachusetts
d. Volpe, John A(nthony)

Nantucket, Massachusetts
b. Fowler, Lydia Folger
b. Mitchell, Maria
b. Mott, Lucretia Coffin
d. Baldwin, Billy
d. Dean, Gordon Evans
d. Fawcett, George
d. Irving, Isabel
d. Sarg, Tony
d. Strong, Austin
d. Thayer, Tiffany Ellsworth

Natick, Massachusetts
b. Coolidge, Dane
d. Alger, Horatio
d. Connolly, Tommy

Needham, Massachusetts
b. Wyeth, N(ewell) C(onvers)
d. Coomaraswamy, Ananda Kentish

Needham Heights, Massachusetts
d. Carter, William

New Bedford, Massachusetts
b. Barboza, Anthony
b. Green, Hetty
b. Hough, Henry Beetle
b. Lansky, Aaron
b. Paine, Albert Bigelow
b. Ryder, Albert Pinkham
b. Stone, Ezra (Chaim)
b. Wexler, Norman

Newbury, Massachusetts
d. Parker, Thomas

Newburyport, Massachusetts
b. Andrews, Jane
b. Garrison, William Lloyd
b. Greely, Adolphus Washington
b. Lowell, Francis Cabot
b. Lowell, John
b. Mulliken, Robert Sanderson
b. Perkins, Jacob
b. Wheelwright, William
d. Andrews, Jane
d. Cushing, Caleb
d. Marquand, John Phillips
d. Parton, James
d. Thornton, Matthew
d. Welchman, Gordon
d. Whitefield, George

Newton, Massachusetts
b. Banks, Russell
b. Benchley, Nathaniel Goddard
b. Bulfinch, Thomas
b. Converse, Frederick Shepherd
b. Darrell, R(obert) D(onaldson)
b. Gardner, Isabella
b. Gardner, Mary Sewall
b. Goodman, Ellen Holtz
b. Hull, Josephine
b. Jaffe, Harold W
b. Kimball, Fiske
b. Kirk, Paul G(rattan), Jr.
b. LeBlanc, Matt
b. Morse, Robert Alan
b. Sexton, Anne Harvey
b. Sherman, Roger
d. Hull, William
d. Ouimet, Francis de Sales
d. Pickard, Greenleaf Whittier
d. Spencer, Percy Le Baron
d. Wightman, Hazel Virginia
   Hotchkiss

Newton Centre, Massachusetts
b. Burton, Virginia Lee
b. Daddario, Emilio Quincy
b. Wilkins, Ernest Hatch

Newton Highlands, Massachusetts
b. Preston, Robert
d. Ovington, Mary White

Newton Upper Falls, Massachusetts
b. Switzer, Mary E.

Newtonville, Massachusetts
b. Eltinge, Julian
d. Gray, Elisha
d. Lewin, Kurt

Nonquitt, Massachusetts
d. Sheridan, Philip Henry

North Adams, Massachusetts
b. Chesbro, Jack
b. Durant, Will(iam James)
b. Sibley, Hiram

North Andover, Massachusetts
b. Gagne, Robert Mills
d. Houghton, Henry Oscar

North Attleboro, Massachusetts
b. Martin, Joseph William, Jr.

North Chatham, Massachusetts
d. Booth, Shirley

North Easton, Massachusetts
b. Ames, Winthrop
b. Craig, Jim
d. Ames, Blanche

North Reading, Massachusetts
b. Flint, Timothy
d. Flint, Timothy

North Scituate, Massachusetts
d. Lowes, John Livingston

Northampton, Massachusetts
b. Clark, John Maurice
b. Dwight, Timothy
b. Whitney, Josiah Dwight
b. Whitney, William Dwight
d. Baskin, Leonard
d. Brainerd, David
d. Chase, Mary Ellen
d. Coolidge, Calvin
d. Coolidge, Grace (Anne Goodhue)
d. Foley, Martha
d. Graham, Sylvester
d. Koffka, Kurt
d. Larkin, Oliver Waterman
d. Morrison, Theodore

Northbridge, Massachusetts
b. Thibault, Conrad

Northfield, Massachusetts
d. Moody, Dwight Lyman

Oak Bluffs, Massachusetts
d. Dunnock, Mildred

Onset Bay, Massachusetts
b. Farrell, Charles

Orleans, Massachusetts
d. Mortimer, Charles Greenough

Osterville, Massachusetts
d. Cronin, Joe
d. Hughes, Charles Evans

Otis, Massachusetts
d. Sokolsky, George E

Oxford, Massachusetts
b. Barton, Clara Harlowe

Peabody, Massachusetts
b. Peabody, George
b. Upton, Francis Robbins
b. Welch, John Francis, Jr.

Pelham, Massachusetts
b. Foster, Abigail Kelley
d. Thorp, Willard Long

Petersham, Massachusetts
b. Flint, Austin

Pittsfield, Massachusetts
b. Chappell, Tom
b. Graves, Nancy (Stevenson)
b. Miller, William
b. Piccolo, Brian
b. Thompson, J(ames) Walter
b. Winship, Elizabeth
d. Dawes, Henry Laurens
d. Mercer, Mabel
d. Wheeler, Hugh Callingham

Plainfield, Massachusetts
b. Warner, Charles Dudley

Plymouth, Massachusetts
b. Bartlett, John
b. Gannett, Deborah Sampson
b. Jackson, Charles Thomas
b. Picard, Henry
b. Watson, Elkanah
d. Bradford, William
d. Brewster, William
d. Carver, John
d. Chase, Richard Volney
d. Dunster, Henry
d. Gray, Glen
d. Wakefield, Ruth G

Portland, Massachusetts
b. Longfellow, Henry Wadsworth

Princeton, Massachusetts
b. Savage, Edward
d. Savage, Edward

Provincetown, Massachusetts
b. MacMillan, Donald Baxter
d. Glaspell, Susan Keating
d. Kemp, Harry (Hibbard)
d. MacMillan, Donald Baxter
d. Motherwell, Robert Burns
d. Tworkov, Jack
d. Waugh, Frederick Judd

Quincy, Massachusetts
b. Adams, Brooks
b. Adams, Peter Chardon Brooks
b. Andre, Carl
b. Baker, Elbert Hall, II
b. Cheever, John
b. Dana, Bill
b. Dewson, Mary Williams
b. Priscilla of Boston
b. Remick, Lee
d. Adams, Abigail (Smith)
d. Adams, John
d. Adams, Peter Chardon Brooks
d. Hancock, John

Randolph, Massachusetts
b. Freeman, Mary E Wilkins

Reading, Massachusetts
b. Peabody, Eddie
d. DeMar, Clarence
d. Park, Maud May Wood

Revere, Massachusetts
b. Alger, Horatio
b. Conigliaro, Tony
b. Macy, Bill

Riverdale, Massachusetts
d. Abbot, C(harles) G(reeley)

Rockport, Massachusetts
d. Birnie, William Alfred Hart
d. Kieran, John Francis

Roxbury, Massachusetts
b. Abbott, Lyman
b. Corson, Juliet
b. Currier, Nathaniel
b. Gibson, Charles Dana
b. Heath, William
b. Langley, Samuel Pierpont
b. McBurney, Charles
b. Millner, Wayne E
b. O'Callahan, Joseph Timothy
b. Warren, Joseph
b. White, Paul Dudley
b. Wise, John
d. Dearborn, Henry
d. Dudley, Thomas
d. Eliot, John
d. Hale, Edward Everett
d. Heath, William
d. Lowell, John
d. Shirley, William

Salem, Massachusetts
b. Atwood, Francis Clarke
b. Benson, Frank Weston
b. Bowditch, Henry Ingersoll
b. Bowditch, Nathaniel
b. Bowker, R(ichard) R(ogers)
b. Cabot, George
b. Choate, Joseph Hodges
b. Douglas, Paul Howard
b. Fenollosa, Ernest Francisco
b. Filene, Edward Albert
b. Foote, Arthur William
b. Gifford, Walter Sherman
b. Glover, John
b. Hawthorne, Nathaniel
b. McIntire, Samuel
b. Page, Charles Grafton
b. Parker, George Swinnerton
b. Peabody, Endicott
b. Peirce, Benjamin
b. Pickering, Timothy
b. Poole, William Frederick
b. Poulter, Thomas Charles
b. Prescott, William Hickling
b. Putnam, Israel
b. Remond, Charles Lennox
b. Rogers, John
b. Story, William Wetmore
b. Very, Jones
d. Benson, Frank Weston
d. Bishop, Bridget
d. Conigliaro, Tony
d. Pickering, Timothy
d. Very, Jones

Salisbury, Massachusetts
b. Cushing, Caleb
b. Perdue, Frank

Sandwich, Massachusetts
b. Burgess, Thornton Waldo
b. Swift, Gustavus Franklin

Scituate, Massachusetts
b. Woodworth, Samuel

Sharon, Massachusetts
b. Davis, Arthur Vining
d. Gannett, Deborah Sampson

Sheffield, Massachusetts
b. Barnard, Frederick Augustus Porter

Shelburne Falls, Massachusetts
d. Gregory, Horace Victor
d. Zaturenska, Marya

Shrewsbury, Massachusetts
b. Earle, Ralph

Shutesbury, Massachusetts
b. Adams, Herbert Baxter

Snoquaimie, Massachusetts
b. Raines, Ella

Somerset, Massachusetts
b. Holland, Clifford Milburn

Somerville, Massachusetts
b. Carle, Richard
b. Connolly, Harold
b. Hadley, Henry Kimball
b. Hovhaness, Alan
d. Greenough, Horatio
d. Jackson, Charles Thomas

South Attleboro, Massachusetts
b. Lincoln, Mary Johnson Bailey

South Boston, Massachusetts
b. McCarthy, Tommy

South Duxbury, Massachusetts
d. Davenport, Fanny Lily Gypsy

South Hadley, Massachusetts
b. Mead, George Herbert
d. Lyon, Mary Mason

South Lee, Massachusetts
b. Brown, Henry Billings

South Weymouth, Massachusetts
b. Carsey, Marcy

South Williamston, Massachusetts
d. Vanderbilt, William Henry

Spencer, Massachusetts
b. Howe, Elias

Springfield, Massachusetts
b. Abrams, Creighton Williams
b. Adams, Weston W, Sir
b. Allen, Joel Asaph
b. Appleseed, Johnny
b. Beach, Alfred Ely
b. Birnie, William Alfred Hart
b. Blackmur, Richard Palmer
b. Boland, Edward P(atrick)
b. Bowles, Chester Bliss
b. Bowles, Samuel, II
b. Brown, Rachel Fuller
b. Buoniconti, Nick
b. Cleage, Pearl (Michelle)
b. Ellis, Harry Bearse
b. Gage, Harlow W
b. Gorman, Herbert Sherman
b. Gravel, Mike
b. Greenaway, Emerson
b. Healey, Ed(ward)
b. Irving, George Steven

b. Leary, Timothy (Francis)
b. MacArthur, Arthur
b. Maranville, Rabbit
b. Morello, Joseph A
b. Morgan, Junius Spencer
b. O'Brien, Larry
b. Parker, Robert B(rown)
b. Powell, Eleanor
b. Russell, Kurt (Von Vogel)
b. Sanderson, Julia
b. Seuss, Doctor
b. Wade, Benjamin Franklin
d. Benjamin, Asher
d. Bowles, Samuel, II
d. Bradley, Milton
d. Breck, John Henry
d. Garand, John Cantius
d. Merriam, Charles
d. Sanderson, Julia
d. Shore, Eddie
d. Winterich, John Tracy

Sterling, Massachusetts
b. Butterick, Ebenezer

Stockbridge, Massachusetts
b. Field, Cyrus West
b. Hopkins, Mark
b. Sedgwick, Catherine Maria
d. Bowker, R(ichard) R(ogers)
d. French, Daniel Chester
d. Niebuhr, Reinhold
d. Rockwell, Norman

Stoneham, Massachusetts
b. Kerrigan, Nancy
b. Lewis, Clarence Irving

Sturbridge, Massachusetts
b. Marcy, William Learned

Sutton, Massachusetts
b. Blanchard, Thomas

Swampscott, Massachusetts
b. Stahl, Leslie
d. Hegan, Jim
d. Thomson, Elihu

Taunton, Massachusetts
b. Foster, William Zebulon
b. O'Connor, Basil

Three Rivers, Massachusetts
d. Kelley, Hall Jackson

Truro, Massachusetts
b. Collins, Edward Knight
d. Albert, Stephen Joel

Tyngsboro, Massachusetts
b. Dole, Charles Minot

Tyringham, Massachusetts
d. Clapp, Margaret Antoinette
d. Howard, Sidney Coe

Vineyard Haven, Massachusetts
d. Cornell, Katharine
d. Harding, Chester
d. Haydn, Hiram Collins
d. Hellman, Lillian
d. Mannes, Leopold Damrosch

d. Packard, Vance (Oakley)

Wakefield, Massachusetts
b. Beebe, Lucius Morris
b. Coon, Carleton Stevens
b. Dellinger, David T
b. Galvin, John Rogers
b. Grattan, Clinton Hartley
b. Horovitz, Israel Arthur
b. Little, Royal
b. Volpe, John A(nthony)

Wales, Massachusetts
b. Wales, Salem Howe

Walpole, Massachusetts
d. DeSalvo, Albert

Waltham, Massachusetts
b. Bailey, F(rancis) Lee
b. Howe, Clarence Decatur
b. Keough, William Francis, Jr.
b. Warren, Austin
b. Wilson, Kenneth Geddes
d. Lewis, Reggie

Ware, Massachusetts
b. Cummings, Candy
b. Landes, Bertha Ethel
b. Packard, Elizabeth Parsons Ware

Wareham, Massachusetts
b. Davis, Geena

Watertown, Massachusetts
b. Briggs, Ellis O(rmsbee)
b. Curtis, Benjamin Robbins
b. Hosmer, Harriet Goodhue
b. Pratt, Charles
d. Brown, James
d. Hosmer, Harriet Goodhue
d. Wiesner, Jerome B(ert)
d. Williams, Carroll Milton

Waverly, Massachusetts
d. Copeland, Charles Townsend

Wayland, Massachusetts
d. Child, Lydia Maria Francis

Webster, Massachusetts
b. Warnke, Paul Culliton

Wellesley, Massachusetts
b. Baldwin, Roger Nash
b. Sagansky, Jeff
b. Squier, Billy
d. Bates, Katharine Lee
d. Cattani, Richard J.
d. Kronenberger, Louis
d. Price, Don K.

Wellfleet, Massachusetts
d. Chermayeff, Serge (Ivan)
d. Crowell, Luther Childs

Wenham, Massachusetts
d. Stanley, Francis Edgar

West Barnstable, Massachusetts
b. Otis, James

West Boylston, Massachusetts
b. Bigelow, Erastus Brigham
d. Thomas, Robert B

West Brewster, Massachusetts
b. Sears, Isaac

West Brookfield, Massachusetts
b. Merriam, Charles
b. Stone, Lucy

West Dennis, Massachusetts
b. Crowell, Luther Childs

West Newton, Massachusetts
b. Perkins, Osgood
b. Tolman, Edward Chace
b. Tolman, Richard C(hace)
b. Weeks, Sinclair
d. Jewett, Henry

West Roxbury, Massachusetts
b. Lowell, Josephine Shaw
d. Sedgwick, Catherine Maria

West Somerville, Massachusetts
b. Macdonald, Eleanor Josephine

West Springfield, Massachusetts
b. Bertelli, Angelo B.
b. Day, Benjamin Henry
b. Durocher, Leo Ernest

West Upton, Massachusetts
b. Cloud, Preston (Ercelle)

Westboro, Massachusetts
b. Forbes, Esther
b. Whitney, Eli

Westfield, Massachusetts
b. Andrews, James Frederick
b. Thorpe, Thomas Bangs
d. Taylor, Edward

Westford, Massachusetts
b. Bradley, Pat(ricia Ellen)

Westminster, Massachusetts
b. Miles, Nelson Appleton

Weston, Massachusetts
b. Stoddard, Alexandra
d. Alexander, Leo
d. Ashbrook, Joseph
d. Cabot, Thomas D(udley)
d. Sexton, Anne Harvey

Westport, Massachusetts
d. Cuffe, Paul

Weymouth, Massachusetts
b. Adams, Abigail (Smith)
b. Carver, Jonathan
b. Lewis, Gilbert Newton

Whitman, Massachusetts
b. Spellman, Francis Joseph

Wianno, Massachusetts
d. Kroger, Bernard Henry
d. Underwood, John Thomas

Williamsburg, Massachusetts
b. Thorndike, Edward L(ee)

Williamstown, Massachusetts
b. Bascom, Florence
b. Perry, Bliss
b. Perry, Matthew
d. Bascom, Florence
d. Baxter, James Phinney, III
d. Hopkins, Mark
d. Sprague, R(obert) C(hapman)

Winchendon, Massachusetts
b. Bowker, Albert Hosmer

Winchester, Massachusetts
b. Bellino, Joe
d. Cormack, Allan MacLeod
d. Sorokin, Pitirim A(lexandrovitch)
d. Welch, Robert Henry Winborne, Jr.

Winthrop, Massachusetts
b. Whorf, Richard

Woburn, Massachusetts
b. Rumford, Count

Wollaston, Massachusetts
b. DeWolfe, Billy
b. Gordon, Ruth

Woods Hole, Massachusetts
d. Baird, Spencer Fullerton
d. Sawyer, John E(dward)
d. Szent-Gyorgyi, Albert (von Nagyrapolt)

Worcester, Massachusetts
b. Adams, John Coolidge
b. Allaire, Paul Arthur
b. Bancroft, George
b. Behrman, S(amuel) N(athaniel)
b. Bemis, Samuel Flagg
b. Benchley, Robert Charles
b. Bishop, Elizabeth
b. Dixon, Roland Burrage
b. Earle, Alice Morse
b. Fidrych, Mark Steven
b. Fuller, Samuel
b. Gedman, Rich(ard Leo, Jr.)
b. Gibbs, Georgia
b. Goddard, Robert Hutchings
b. Harrison, Wallace Kirkman
b. Hayes, John Michael
b. Hoffman, Abbie
b. Kennedy, Arthur
b. Kunitz, Stanley Jasspon
b. Leary, Denis
b. Mekka, Eddie
b. O'Donnell, Kenneth P
b. Olson, Charles John
b. Price, Irving L
b. Shannon, William Vincent
b. Smith, Jack
b. Stone, Lewis
b. Thompson, Edward Herbert
b. Wesson, Daniel Baird
b. Workman, Fanny Bullock
d. Burkett, Jesse Cail
d. Chang, M(in) C(heuh), Dr.
d. Forbes, Esther
d. Foster, Abigail Kelley
d. Hall, G(ranville) Stanley
d. Hamilton, Billy

d. Julian, Doggie
d. O'Callahan, Joseph Timothy
d. Tappan, Eva March
d. Thomas, Isaiah
d. Wright, Carroll Davidson

Worthington, Massachusetts
d. Stankiewicz, Richard Peter

MICHIGAN
b. Holland, Robert, Jr.
b. Miller, Howard
b. Sachs, Jeffrey D(avid)

Adrian, Michigan
b. Geddes, Norman Bel

Albion, Michigan
b. Fisher, M(ary) F(rances) K(ennedy)

Allegan, Michigan
d. Curtis, Thomas B(radford)
d. Dejong, Meindert

Ann Arbor, Michigan
b. Baker, Gwendolyn Calvert
b. Bennett, Harry Herbert
b. Cooley, Charles Horton
b. Danto, Arthur C(oleman)
b. Estleman, Loren D
b. Green, Constance Windsor McLaughlin
b. Hewlett, William
b. Hundt, Reed
b. Legg, W(illiam) Dorr
b. Monaghan, Tom
b. Orr, Robert Dunkerson
b. Pop, Iggy
b. Russell, Elizabeth Shull
b. Seger, Bob
b. Sellars, Wilfred
b. Sunderland, Thomas E(lbert)
b. Ting, Samuel Chao Chung
b. Vickers, Martha
b. Weller, Thomas Huckle
d. Angell, James Burrill
d. Angell, Robert Cooley
d. Crisler, Fritz
d. Curtis, Heber Doust
d. Cuyler, Kiki
d. Denikin, Anton Ivanovich
d. Francis, Thomas, Jr.
d. Hayden, Robert Earl
d. Landes, Bertha Ethel
d. McIntyre, Frank J
d. Saarinen, Eero
d. Stowe, Leland
d. Yost, Fielding Harris

Atwood, Michigan
b. Beach, Rex Ellingwood

Battle Creek, Michigan
b. Hutton, Betty
b. Kellogg, Will Keith
b. Martin, Dick
b. Oliver, Sy
b. Sheehan, Joseph Green
d. Barron, Clarence Walker
d. Dett, Robert Nathaniel
d. Holland, Clifford Milburn
d. Kellogg, John Harvey
d. Kellogg, Will Keith
d. Truth, Sojourner

d. Walker, Junior

Bay City, Michigan
b. Billington, Ray Allen
b. Eurich, Alvin C(hristian)
b. Hewitt, Bill
b. Madonna
b. Schneirla, Theodore Christian

Belding, Michigan
b. Ford, Kathleen DuRoss

Benton Harbor, Michigan
b. Johnson, Arte
b. Krone, Julie
b. Moore, Charles Willard
b. Sinbad
b. Walker, Chet

Berkley, Michigan
d. Goldsmith, Fred Ernest

Berlin, Michigan
b. Cole, Edward Nicholas

Birmingham, Michigan
b. Lahti, Christine
b. Sullivan, Pat(rick J)
b. Young, Sheila

Bloomfield Hills, Michigan
b. Mohajer, Dineh
d. Coughlin, Charles Edward, Father
d. Gehringer, Charlie
d. Hoffa, Jimmy
d. Polk, Ralph Lane
d. Romney, George (Wilcken)
d. Saarinen, Eliel

Boyne City, Michigan
b. Tebbel, John William

Breckenridge, Michigan
b. Northrup, Jim

Brooklyn, Michigan
b. Ingels, Marty

Buchanan, Michigan
b. Scholz, Jackson Volney

Calumet, Michigan
b. Smith, Paul Joseph

Capac, Michigan
b. Tucker, Preston Thomas

Cass City, Michigan
b. MacPhail, Larry

Cassopolis, Michigan
b. Lowe, Edward

Central Lake, Michigan
b. Hathaway, Starke R

Charlevoix, Michigan
d. Cash, Norm(an Dalton)

Cheboygan, Michigan
b. Humphrey, George Magoffin
d. Ford, Benson

Chinook, Michigan
b. Maney, Richard

Coldwater, Michigan
b. Crippen, Hawley Harvey
b. McDevitt, Ruth

Colon, Michigan
b. Blackstone, Harry, Jr.

Coopersville, Michigan
b. Shannon, Del

Crystal Falls, Michigan
b. Ott, David Lee

Dearborn, Michigan
b. Ford, Henry
b. James, Art
d. Ford, Henry
d. Washington, Thomas L.

Dearborn Heights, Michigan
b. Sui, Anna

Deer Lodge, Michigan
b. Rice, Gregory

Deerfield, Michigan
b. Thomas, Danny

Detroit, Michigan
b. Algren, Nelson
b. Allen, Byron
b. Altobelli, Joe
b. Angell, Robert Cooley
b. Archer, Dennis W(ayne)
b. Atterbury, Grosvenor
b. Bacon, Leonard Woolsey
b. Bagley, William Chandler
b. Bailey, James Anthony
b. Ballard, Florence
b. Ballard, Hank
b. Barden, Don H.
b. Barr, Alfred Hamilton, Jr.
b. Benson, Renaldo
b. Blaik, Red
b. Blanchard, Jim
b. Bloch, Ivan Sol
b. Boeing, William Edward
b. Boesky, Ivan Frederick
b. Bono, Sonny
b. Brant, Beth
b. Bremen, Barry
b. Brown, Jesse
b. Brundage, Avery
b. Buck, Gene
b. Bunche, Ralph Johnson
b. Burkemo, Walter
b. Burns, Jerry
b. Burstyn, Ellen
b. Byrd, Donald
b. Callahan, Harry (Morey)
b. Canfield, Francis X(avier)
b. Caponi, Donna
b. Carson, Benjamin S.
b. Carter, James
b. Cattani, Richard J.
b. Cavanagh, Jerome Patrick
b. Chapin, Roy Dikeman, Jr.
b. Cicotte, Eddie
b. Cole, Dennis
b. Collins, Barbara-Rose
b. Conyers, John, Jr.

b. Cooper, Alice
b. Coppola, Francis Ford
b. Corman, Gene
b. Corman, Roger William
b. Cox, Wally
b. Crenshaw, Marshall
b. Cunningham, William T(homas)
b. Curtis-Hall, Vondie
b. Czolgosz, Leon F
b. Dawber, Pam
b. DeBusschere, Dave
b. DeLorean, John Zachary
b. Desmond, Johnny
b. Diegel, Leo
b. Diggs, Charles C(oles), Jr.
b. Donahue, Sam Koontz
b. Dyer, Wayne Walter
b. Dyson, Michael Eric
b. Edwards, Helen T(hom)
b. Epps, Jack, Jr.
b. Ewing, Maria Louise
b. Fairbanks, Chuck
b. Fakir, Abdul
b. Fenn, Sherilyn
b. Flanagan, Tommy (Lee)
b. Forche, Carolyn (Louise)
b. Ford, Benson
b. Ford, Bill
b. Ford, Edsel Bryant
b. Ford, Eleanor Clay
b. Ford, Henry, II
b. Ford, William Clay
b. Frailberg, Selma
b. Freehan, Bill
b. Frey, Glenn
b. Freyse, William
b. Gail, Max(well Trowbridge, Jr.)
b. Gervin, George
b. Goines, Donald
b. Gomez-Preston, Cheryl
b. Gordon, Ed
b. Gordy, Berry, Jr.
b. Graves, John Earl
b. Greene, Gael
b. Grier, David Allen
b. Griffin, Bob
b. Guest, Judith Ann
b. Gumbleton, Thomas J
b. Guyton, Tyree
b. Harkless, Necia Desiree
b. Hayden, Robert Earl
b. Henry, Martha
b. Herlihy, James Leo
b. Howard, Bronson Crocker
b. Howe, Mark Steven
b. Hughes, Albert
b. Hughes, Allen
b. Hughes, John
b. Hunter, Kim
b. Ilitch, Mike
b. Inatome, Rick
b. Jackson, Milt(on)
b. Jarvis, Gregory
b. Jenkins, Beverly
b. Jones, Cobi
b. Jones, Ingrid Saunders
b. Kallen, Jackie
b. Karle, Isabella (L.)
b. Kasem, Casey (Kemal Amin)
b. Keith, Damon (Jerome)
b. Kelley, Frank Joseph
b. Kicknosway, Faye
b. Kienzle, William X(avier)
b. Kilpatrick, Carolyn Cheeks
b. Kinsley, Michael (E.)
b. Klugh, Earl

b. Krause, Bernie
b. Kresge, Stanley Sebastian
b. Krickstein, Aaron
b. LaHaye, Tim
b. Lane, Kenneth Jay
b. Lansdale, Edward Geary
b. Laredo, Ruth
b. Laurie, Piper
b. Lee, Helen Elaine
b. LeFlore, Ron(ald)
b. Leslie, Joan
b. Levin, Carl Milton
b. Levine, Philip
b. Liggett, Louis Kroh
b. Lindbergh, Charles A(ugustus)
b. Lipscomb, Eugene
b. Mallett, Conrad (LeRoy), Jr.
b. McCrory, Milton
b. McHale, John Joseph
b. McKee, Lonette
b. McMahon, Ed(ward Lee)
b. Melchers, Gari
b. Milner, Martin Sam
b. Mitchell, Guy
b. Mitchell, John Newton
b. Mitchelson, Marvin M(orris)
b. Moorer, Michael
b. Morgan, Harry
b. Moriarty, Michael
b. Morton, Joy
b. Muhammad, Wallace D
b. Murray, Lenda
b. Nederlander, James Morton
b. Newhouser, Hal
b. Nicholas, Denise
b. Nugent, Ted
b. Pappas, Milt(on Steven)
b. Parker, Ray, Jr.
b. Payne, Freda
b. Payton, Lawrence
b. Peete, Calvin
b. Peppard, George
b. Piercy, Marge
b. Polk, Ralph Lane
b. Quatro, Suzi
b. Quine, Richard
b. Radner, Gilda
b. Reese, Della
b. Reeves, Martha
b. Reulbach, Ed(ward Marvin)
b. Robinson, Smokey
b. Robinson, Sugar Ray
b. Rockwell
b. Roney, William Chapoton, Jr.
b. Ross, Diana
b. Ryder, Mitch
b. Sabo, Chris(topher Andrew)
b. Selleck, Tom
b. Shabazz, Betty
b. Show, Grant
b. Silliphant, Stirling Dale
b. Sillman, Leonard
b. Sissman, L(ouis) E(dward)
b. Skerritt, Tom
b. Slovik, Eddie
b. Smith, Margaret
b. Souther, J(ohn) D(avid)
b. Stein, Herbert
b. Stevens, Roger L(acey)
b. Stritch, Elaine
b. Stroh, Peter W
b. Stubbs, Levi
b. Sturtzel, Jane Levington
b. Tallent, Garry Wayne
b. Talman, William
b. Tanana, Frank Daryl

b. Taylor, Kristin Clark
b. Thomas, Marlo
b. Tomlin, Lily
b. Vanbiesbrouck, John
b. Vance, Courtney B.
b. Vesco, Robert Lee
b. VonTilzer, Harry
b. Wagner, Robert John, Jr.
b. Washington, Thomas L.
b. Webb, Veronica
b. Webber, Chris
b. Welch, Bob
b. Wells, Mary
b. Whiting, Margaret
b. Williams, G(erhard) Mennen
b. Wilson, Jackie
b. Winans, Marvin L.
b. Wine, Sherwin T(heodore)
b. Yawkey, Thomas Austin
b. Yokich, Stephen P.
d. Adams, Jack
d. Ballard, Florence
d. Banks, William (Venoid)
d. Bonstelle, Jessie
d. Booth, George Gough
d. Brownson, Orestes Augustus
d. Buick, David Dunbar
d. Cass, Lewis
d. Chapin, Roy Dikeman
d. Chevrolet, Louis Joseph
d. Cicotte, Eddie
d. Clampett, Bob
d. Cornell, Douglas B
d. Couzens, James Joseph, Jr.
d. Cunningham, William T(homas)
d. Dressen, Chuck
d. Duncanson, Robert Scott
d. Ford, Eleanor Clay
d. Ford, Henry, II
d. Ford, Len
d. Fruehauf, Harvey Charles
d. Gabrilowitsch, Ossip Salomonovich
d. Guest, Edgar A(lbert)
d. Herzog, Arthur, Jr.
d. Houdini, Harry
d. House, Son
d. Hubbard, Orville Liscum
d. Hupp, Louis Gorham
d. Kahn, Albert
d. Knudsen, William Signius
d. Lavigne, Kid
d. Leland, Henry Martyn
d. Lyons, Sophie Levy
d. Manoogian, Alex
d. McCoy, Charles
d. McCree, Wade Hampton, Jr.
d. Moeller, Philip
d. Murphy, Frank
d. Newberry, John Stoughton
d. Reuther, Roy
d. Richard, Gabriel
d. Smith, Horton
d. Thompson, Sam(uel Luther)
d. Trumbull, John
d. Wakefield, Dick
d. Walker, Hiram
d. Wallace, Sippie
d. Washington, Dinah
d. Williams, G(erhard) Mennen
d. Wolfgang, Myra K
d. Yamasaki, Minoru
d. Young, Coleman A(lexander)

East Lansing, Michigan
b. Fairchild, David Grandison
d. Smith, A(rthur) J(ames) M(arshall)

Eaton Rapids, Michigan
b. Curtice, Harlow Herbert

Edmore, Michigan
b. Blough, Glenn Orlando

Eloise, Michigan
d. McCoy, Elijah

Evart, Michigan
b. Voelker, Paul Frederick

Farmington Hills, Michigan
d. Abel, Sid(ney Gerald)
d. Townsend, Lynn Alfred

Flint, Michigan
b. Abbott, Jim
b. Bernhard, Sandra
b. Carter, Betty
b. Harris, E. Lynn
b. Haworth, Leland John
b. MC Breed
b. Moore, Michael
b. Morrow, Ken(neth)
b. Morton, Craig
b. Mott, Stewart Rawlings
b. Riegle, Donald Wayne, Jr.
b. Townsend, Lynn Alfred
d. Curtice, Harlow Herbert
d. Mott, Charles Stewart

Fort Brady, Michigan
b. Drum, Hugh A

Fowlerville, Michigan
b. Gehringer, Charlie

Frankfort, Michigan
d. Catton, Bruce

Fremont, Michigan
b. Gerber, Daniel Frank
d. Gerber, Daniel Frank
d. Goulet, Leo D

Gaylord, Michigan
b. Shannon, Claude Elwood

Grand Rapids, Michigan
b. Calkins, Dick
b. Chaffee, Roger Bruce
b. DeBarge, Bunny
b. DeBarge, El(dra)
b. DeBarge, James
b. DeBarge, Mark
b. DeBarge, Randy
b. DeVos, Richard Marvin
b. Gingrich, Arnold
b. Hannah, John Alfred
b. Jacobsen, Hugh Newell
b. Ketchel, Stanley
b. Kiedis, Anthony
b. Lousma, Jack
b. Luedtke, Kurt (Mamre)
b. Rathbun-Nealy, Melissa
b. Rogers, Lynn L(eroy)
b. Schrader, Paul Joseph
b. Sowerby, Leo
b. Stanley, Mickey
b. Szoka, Edmund Casimir, Cardinal
b. TerHorst, Jerald Franklin
b. VanAllsburg, Chris
b. Van Andel, Jay

b. Vandenberg, Arthur Hendrick
b. Vandenberg, Arthur Hendrick, Jr.
b. White, Stewart Edward
d. Bissell, Melville Reuben
d. Kendrick, Pearl Luella
d. Pipp, Wally
d. Rourke, Constance Mayfield
d. Vandenberg, Arthur Hendrick
d. Vandenberg, Arthur Hendrick, Jr.
d. York, Dick

Grosse Pointe, Michigan
b. Fruehauf, Harvey Charles
b. Lightner, Theodore
b. Ziegler, John Augustus, Jr.
d. Cisler, Walker (Lee)
d. Ferguson, Homer
d. Ford, Edsel Bryant
d. Obolensky, Serge
d. Roney, William Chapoton, Jr.
d. Trendle, George Washington

Grosse Pointe Park, Michigan
b. Eugenides, Jeffrey
b. Harris, Julie

Grosse Pointe Shores, Michigan
d. Roy, Ross

Grosse Pointe Woods, Michigan
b. Allen, George Herbert
d. Buehrig, Gordon

Harbor Beach, Michigan
b. Lincoln, George A
b. Murphy, Frank

Harrisville, Michigan
b. Cuyler, Kiki

Hart, Michigan
b. Winston, George

Highland Park, Michigan
b. Ellmann, Richard David
b. Haley, Bill
b. Irvin, Robert W
d. Goines, Donald

Hillsdale, Michigan
b. Robards, Jason

Holland, Michigan
b. Dinkeloo, John Gerard
b. Walz, Ken
d. DeKruif, Paul Henry
d. Urban, Matt

Holling Corners, Michigan
b. Holling, Holling C(lancy)

Hudson, Michigan
b. Carleton, Will

Idlewild, Michigan
d. Williams, Daniel Hale

Iron Mountain, Michigan
b. Flaherty, Robert Joseph

Ishpeming, Michigan
b. Johnson, Clarence Leonard
b. Pitrone, Jean Maddern

b. Seaborg, Glenn T(heodore)
b. Voelker, John Donaldson
d. Voelker, John Donaldson

Jackson, Michigan
b. Coats, Dan(iel R)
b. Dungy, Tony
b. Porter, Bill
b. Stewart, Potter
b. Worden, Alfred Merrill
d. Gilbert, Grove Karl

Kalamazoo, Michigan
b. Briley, John Richard
b. Ferber, Edna
b. Hupp, Louis Gorham
b. Schippers, Thomas
d. Cole, Edward Nicholas
d. Hannah, John Alfred
d. Tucker, Richard
d. Upjohn, Lawrence Northcote

Kalamazoo County, Michigan
b. Shafter, William Rufus

Kent County, Michigan
b. Moore, Julia A Davis

Lacota, Michigan
b. Gould, Laurence M(cKinley)

Lansing, Michigan
b. Abraham, Spencer
b. Baker, Ray Stannard
b. Busfield, Timothy
b. Canady, Alexa I(rene)
b. Chapin, Roy Dikeman
b. Davis, Rennie
b. Johnson, Earvin, Jr.
b. Little, Robert Langdon
b. Seagal, Steven
d. Little, Robert Langdon
d. Olds, Ranson E(li)

Lapeer, Michigan
b. DeAngeli, Marguerite Lofft

Laurium, Michigan
b. Gipp, George
b. Ross, Percy Nathan

Lowell, Michigan
b. Graham, Ernest Robert

Ludington, Michigan
d. Johnson, Walter
d. Marquette, Jacques, Pere

Mackinac Island, Michigan
d. Day, William Rufus

Manton, Michigan
d. Moore, Julia A Davis

Marquette, Michigan
b. Kidder, Alfred Vincent

Mecosta, Michigan
d. Kirk, Russell (Amos)

Mendon, Michigan
b. Estes, E(lliott) M(arantette)
b. Estes, Pete

Midland, Michigan
b. Hickey, James Aloysius, Cardinal
b. Jarvik, Robert Koffler
b. Studer, Cheryl
d. Gerstacker, Carl A(llan)

Monroe, Michigan
b. Cantrick, Robert
b. Custer, Elizabeth Bacon
b. Sneider, Vernon John
d. Sneider, Vernon John

Mount Clemens, Michigan
b. Cain, Dean
d. Smith, Christopher Columbus

Mount Pleasant, Michigan
b. Engler, John Mathias
b. Pohl, Dan(ny Joe)

Muskegon, Michigan
b. Bakker, Jim
b. Curtis, Heber Doust
b. Morrall, Earl E
b. Nelson, Don(ald Arvid)
b. Stanton, Frank Nicholas

New Era, Michigan
b. Aardema, Verna Norberg

Niles, Michigan
b. Dodge, Horace Elgin
b. Dodge, John Francis
b. Lardner, Ring(gold Wilmer), Sr.

North Dorr, Michigan
b. Bieber, Owen Frederick

Norwood, Michigan
b. Darling, Jay Norwood

Okemos, Michigan
b. Grettenberger, John O

Oscoda, Michigan
b. Abbott, Jack

Overisel, Michigan
b. Birkhoff, George David

Owosso, Michigan
b. Curwood, James Oliver
b. Dewey, Thomas Edmund
b. Hershey, Alfred D(ay)
d. Bentley, Alvin Morell
d. Curwood, James Oliver

Oxford, Michigan
d. Beemer, Brace

Pellston, Michigan
d. Reuther, Walter Philip

Petersburg, Michigan
b. Crosby, Elizabeth Caroline

Petoskey, Michigan
b. Catton, Bruce
d. Mischakoff, Mischa

Pinckney, Michigan
b. Swarthout, Glendon (Fred)

Pinconning, Michigan
b. Summerfield, Arthur Ellsworth

Plymouth, Michigan
b. Corwin, Edward Samuel
b. Kirk, Russell (Amos)

Pontiac, Michigan
b. Allen, Geri
b. Gibson, Kirk Harold
b. Howe, Steve
b. Jones, Elvin
b. Jones, Thad(deus Joseph)
b. Kevorkian, Jack
b. McKechnie, Donna
b. Taubman, A(dolph) Alfred
b. Thomas, Pinklon
d. McCafferty, Don

Port Huron, Michigan
b. Kalmbach, Herbert Warren
b. McMillan, Terry
b. Moore, Colleen
b. Sanborn, Pitts

Portland, Michigan
b. Kelland, Clarence Budington

Redford, Michigan
b. Kiel, Richard

Richmond, Michigan
b. Neddermeyer, Seth H

Riverview, Michigan
b. McCartney, Bill

Rochester, Michigan
d. Kresge, Stanley Sebastian

Romulus, Michigan
b. Lau, Charlie

Royal Oak, Michigan
b. Carter, Ron
b. Dawkins, Pete(r M)
b. George, Christopher
b. Hayden, Tom
b. Hess, Richard
b. Lalas, Alexi
b. L'Esperance Quintuplets
b. Muncey, Bill
d. Breech, Ernest Robert
d. Gordon, John F
d. Heard, J.C.
d. Knudsen, Semon E(mil)
d. Mitchell, William Leroy
d. Thompson, Marshall
d. Tyner, Rob

Saginaw, Michigan
b. Armstrong, Robert
b. Avery, Sewell
b. Begle, Edward G(riffith)
b. Heinemann, Edward H
b. Hughes, Holly
b. Jones, Howard Mumford
b. Lavigne, Kid
b. McCoy, Tim(othy John Fitzgerald)
b. Roethke, Theodore (Huebner)
b. Williams, Serena
b. Wonder, Stevie

Hibbing, Minnesota
b. Bugliosi, Vincent T
b. Maris, Roger (Eugene)
b. McHale, Kevin (Edward)
b. Redig, Patrick

Humboldt, Minnesota
b. Briggs, Austin Eugene

International Falls, Minnesota
b. Messner, Tammy Faye
d. Nagurski, Bronko

Iron, Minnesota
b. Hall, Gus

Keewatin, Minnesota
b. Cappeletti, Gino

Kenyon, Minnesota
b. Volstead, Andrew J

Le Sueur, Minnesota
b. Mayo, William James

Leech Lake, Minnesota
b. Banks, Dennis J.

Litchfield, Minnesota
b. Sondergaard, Gale (Edith Holm)

Little Falls, Minnesota
b. Erdrich, Louise
b. Langer, Jim

Luverne, Minnesota
b. Wiggins, J(ames) R(ussell)

Madison, Minnesota
b. Bly, Robert Elwood

Maine, Minnesota
b. Douglas, William Orville

Mankato, Minnesota
b. Bate, Walter Jackson
b. Wood, Louise Aletha
d. Colfax, Schuyler

Marshall, Minnesota
b. Burchard, John Ely

Melrose, Minnesota
b. Otte, Ruth

Minneapolis, Minnesota
b. Anderson, Richard Dean
b. Andrews, LaVerne
b. Andrews, Maxene
b. Andrews, Patti
b. Arness, James
b. Artist Formerly Known as Prince, The
b. Ayres, Lew
b. Bakke, Allan Paul
b. Baxter, Charles (Morley)
b. Bayne, Beverly Pearl
b. Benton, William
b. Berg, Patty
b. Berrigan, Philip Francis
b. Blegen, Carl William
b. Blumenfeld, Isadore

b. Brinig, Myron
b. Britz, Jerilyn
b. Brousse, Amy Elizabeth Thorpe
b. Bruce, Virginia
b. Carlson, Curtis L.
b. Chorzempa, Daniel Walter
b. Chute, Beatrice Joy
b. Chute, Marchette (Gaylord)
b. Claytor, Helen (Natalie Jackson)
b. Coen, Ethan
b. Coen, Joel
b. Crosby, Sumner McKnight
b. Dahl, Arlene
b. Demento, Dr.
b. Doar, John Michael
b. Douglas, Marjory (Stoneman)
b. Eiseman, Florence
b. Engstrom, Elmer William
b. Flanders, Ed
b. Franken, Al
b. Fraser, Donald Mackay
b. Freeman, Orville Lothrop
b. Friedman, Thomas L(oren)
b. Getty, J(ean) Paul
b. Gilliam, Terry (Vance)
b. Gillman, Sidney
b. Graves, Peter
b. Heffelfinger, Pudge
b. Hill, George Roy
b. Husted, Marjorie Child
b. James, John
b. Johnson, Bob
b. Kelsey, Linda
b. Lamb, Gil
b. Larson, Reed David
b. Laughlin, Tom
b. Leadon, Bernie
b. Lebowsky, Stanley Richard
b. Levin, Harry Tuchman
b. Lord, Mary Pillsbury
b. MacGregor, Clark
b. Meeker, Ralph
b. Morgan, Frank
b. Motley, Arthur Harrison
b. Norstad, Lauris
b. O'Meara, Walter (Andrew)
b. Pegler, Westbrook
b. Pillsbury, John Sargent
b. Pillsbury, Philip Winston
b. Pirsig, Robert M(aynard)
b. Ramsey, Mike
b. Saint Cyr, Lillian
b. Salisbury, Harrison Evans
b. Schulz, Charles M(onroe)
b. Simms, Hilda
b. Slye, Maud
b. Smith, Dora
b. Steger, Will
b. Stoll, George E
b. Sturtzel, Howard Allison
b. Todd, Mike
b. Trenary, Jill
b. Tyler, Anne
b. Vessey, John William, Jr.
b. Vizenor, Gerald
b. Walter, Cyril
b. White, Minor
b. Wilkinson, Bud
b. Youngdahl, Luther Wallace
d. Beach, Joseph Warren
d. Bell, James Ford
d. Berryman, John
d. Brown, Charlie
d. Carlson, Curtis L.
d. Cowles, John, Sr.
d. Donnelly, Ignatius

d. Hathaway, Starke R
d. Humphrey, Muriel Fay Buck
d. Husted, Marjorie Child
d. Lewis, Meade Anderson Lux
d. Masterton, Bill
d. Piccard, Jean Felix
d. Piccard, Jeannette Ridlon
d. Pillsbury, Charles Alfred
d. Pillsbury, John Sargent
d. Pillsbury, Philip Winston
d. Schumann, Walter
d. Simak, Clifford Donald
d. Tiny Tim

Minnesota Lakes, Minnesota
b. Keogan, George

Mohnomen, Minnesota
b. Guyon, Joe

Moorhead, Minnesota
b. Comstock, Ada Louise
b. Hurley, Jack B
b. Magnuson, Warren Grant

Morgan, Minnesota
b. Root, Lynn

Nashwauk, Minnesota
b. Gilruth, Robert Rowe

New Ulm, Minnesota
b. Gag, Wanda
b. Hedren, Tippi
b. Steinbach, Terry Lee
b. Ulric, Lenore

Northfield, Minnesota
b. Chase, Sylvia B
b. Hustvedt, Siri
b. Rolvaag, Karl Fritjof
d. Rolvaag, Karl Fritjof
d. Rolvaag, Ole Edvart

Odin Township, Minnesota
b. Laingen, (Lowell) Bruce

Olivia, Minnesota
b. Winsor, Kathleen

Owatonna, Minnesota
b. Marshall, E(dda) G(unnar)

Pine River, Minnesota
b. Baker, Terry Wayne

Pipestone, Minnesota
b. Petersen, Donald Eugene
b. Steen, Roger

Red Wing, Minnesota
b. Densmore, Frances
d. Anderson, Eugenie M(oore)
d. Densmore, Frances

Rochester, Minnesota
b. Culver, John Chester
b. Mayo, Charles Horace
b. Ryder, Winona
d. Connolly, Mike
d. Dow, Herbert Henry
d. Harrah, Bill
d. Lorant, Stefan

b. Williams, Tennessee

Como, Mississippi
b. Young, Stark

Corinth, Mississippi
b. Knight, Etheridge
b. Meadows, Earle
b. Osborne, John Franklin
b. Turner, Roscoe Wilson

Decatur, Mississippi
b. Evers, James Charles
b. Evers, Medgar Wiley

Doddsville, Mississippi
b. Eastland, James Oliver

Dublin, Mississippi
b. Henry, Aaron

Dumas, Mississippi
b. Wildmon, Donald Ellis

Ellisville, Mississippi
b. Myer, Buddy

Enterprise, Mississippi
b. Harding, Chester

Fayette, Mississippi
b. Truly, Richard H

Friars Point, Mississippi
b. Twitty, Conway

Fulton, Mississippi
b. Lunceford, Jimmy

Gillsburg, Mississippi
d. Van Zant, Ronnie

Glen Allen, Mississippi
b. Taulbert, Clifton Lemoure

Glendora, Mississippi
b. Williamson, Sonny Boy

Gloster, Mississippi
b. Hansberry, William Leo

Goodman, Mississippi
b. Lomax, John Avery

Greenville, Mississippi
b. Foote, Shelby
b. Henson, Jim
b. Scott, George Charles, Jr.
b. Turnbull, Walter (J.)
b. White, Frank, Jr.
b. Wilson, Mary
d. Lomax, John Avery

Greenwood, Mississippi
b. Holland, Endesha Ida Mae
b. Tartt, Donna (Louise)
d. Eastland, James Oliver

Grenada, Mississippi
b. Lott, Trent
b. Winter, William Forrest
d. Hurt, Mississippi John

Gulfport, Mississippi
b. Barney, Lem(uel Jackson)
b. Favre, Brett (Lorenzo)
b. Smiley, Tavis

Hattiesburg, Mississippi
b. Hodges, Eddie
b. Manning, Danny
b. Massey, Walter E(ugene)
b. Parks, Van Dyke

Hazelhurst, Mississippi
b. Ford, Ruth Elizabeth
b. Johnson, Robert

Hermanville, Mississippi
b. Bodenheim, Maxwell

Hickory, Mississippi
b. Johnson, Robert Louis

Holly Springs, Mississippi
b. Crump, Edward Hull
b. McDowell, Katharine Sherwood
   Bonner
b. Wells-Barnett, Ida Bell
d. McDowell, Katharine Sherwood
   Bonner

Hot Coffee, Mississippi
b. Stevens, Stella

Houston, Mississippi
b. Gaines, Lee

Indianola, Mississippi
b. King, Albert
b. Mary Alice
b. Walker, A Maceo, Sr.

Itawamba County, Mississippi
b. Wynette, Tammy

Itta Bena, Mississippi
b. Barry, Marion S(hepilov), Jr.
b. Bevel, James Luther
b. King, B. B.

Iuka, Mississippi
b. Merrill, Henry Tindall

Jackson, Mississippi
b. Barksdale, James L(ove)
b. Colbert, Virgis William
b. Engel, Lehman
b. Ford, Richard
b. Henderson, Jimmy
b. Henley, Beth
b. Hill, Faith
b. Manley, Audrey Forbes
b. Morris, Willie
b. Myricks, Larry
b. Parker, Dave
b. Pittman, Robert W(arren)
b. Rimes, LeAnn
b. Spann, Otis
b. Welty, Eudora
b. Williams, John A(lfred)
b. Wilson, Cassandra
d. Barnett, Ross Robert
d. Evers, Medgar Wiley
d. Meng, John Joseph
d. Morris, Willie

d. Stennis, John C(ornelius)
d. Wickens, Aryness Joy

Kemper County, Mississippi
b. Stennis, John C(ornelius)

Kosciusko, Mississippi
b. Meredith, James Howard
b. Winfrey, Oprah Gail

Laurel, Mississippi
b. Boston, Ralph
b. Calhoun, Lee
b. Ingrassia, Paul
b. Mills, Mary
b. Price, Leontyne

Long Beach, Mississippi
b. Boggs, Hale

Louisville, Mississippi
b. Clark, Thomas Dionysius

Lula, Mississippi
b. Blackwell, Unita

Macon, Mississippi
b. Williams, Ben Ames

Magnolia, Mississippi
b. Diddley, Bo

Marks, Mississippi
b. Smith, Frederick Wallace

McComb, Mississippi
b. Brandy
d. Gaines, Steve

Meridian, Mississippi
b. Bandy, Moe
b. Childress, Alvin
b. Ethridge, Mark Foster
b. Hannah, Barry
b. Ladd, Diane
b. Rodgers, Jimmie
b. Ruffin, David
b. Ruffin, Jimmy

Minter City, Mississippi
b. Stewart, Luisa Harris

Montgomery County, Mississippi
b. Hamer, Fannie Lou Townsend

Mound Bayou, Mississippi
d. Hamer, Fannie Lou Townsend

Natchez, Mississippi
b. Douglas, Ellen
b. Gilley, Mickey Leroy
b. Wright, Richard (Nathaniel)

New Albany, Mississippi
b. Faulkner, William

Okolona, Mississippi
b. Raspberry, William

Olive Branch, Mississippi
b. Perkins, Ray

Oxford, Mississippi
b. Brown, Larry
b. Sims, Naomi
b. Woodward, Ellen S.
d. Faulkner, William

Pascagoula, Mississippi
b. Buffett, Jimmy
b. Miller, William Mosley
d. Miller, William Mosley

Pass Christian, Mississippi
b. Roberts, Robin

Pelahatchie, Mississippi
b. Kinard, Frank M

Philadelphia, Mississippi
b. Cannon, Billy
b. Stuart, Marty

Pontotoc, Mississippi
b. Cochran, Thad
b. Jackson, Cordell

Poplarville, Mississippi
b. Bilbo, Theodore Gilmore

Preston, Mississippi
b. Craig, Roger Timothy

Richland, Mississippi
b. James, Elmore

Richton, Mississippi
b. Cochran, Roy
b. Johnson, George E(llis)

Rolling Fork, Mississippi
b. Waters, Muddy

Scott, Mississippi
b. Broonzy, Big Bill

Shannon, Mississippi
d. Bush, Guy Terrell

Shelby, Mississippi
b. Morgan, Rose Meta

Silver City, Mississippi
b. Haywood, Spencer

Sledge, Mississippi
b. Pride, Charley

Standing Pine, Mississippi
b. Barnett, Ross Robert

Starkville, Mississippi
b. Bell, Cool Papa
b. Jones, Hayes
b. Rice, Jerry (Lee)

Sunflower, Mississippi
b. Claiborne, Craig

Tallahatchie County, Mississippi
d. Till, Emmett (Louis)

Teoc, Mississippi
b. Hurt, Mississippi John

Tippo, Mississippi
b. Allison, Mose

Toomsuba, Mississippi
b. Walker, T. J.

Tupelo, Mississippi
b. Gilliam, Sam, (Jr.)
b. Presley, Elvis Aaron

Vaughan, Mississippi
d. Jones, Casey

Vicksburg, Mississippi
b. Burnett, Charles
b. Dixon, Willie (James)
b. Evers-Williams, Myrlie
b. Freeman, Cliff(ord Lee)
b. Kelly, Patrick
b. Thornell, Jack Randolph
b. Tolliver, William (Mack)
b. Walker, A'lelia

Vienna, Mississippi
b. Brown, Vanessa

Washington, Mississippi
b. Allain, William A

Weathersby, Mississippi
b. Torrance, Jack

West Point, Mississippi
b. Harlan, Louis R
b. Howlin' Wolf
b. Lane, Vincent

Woodville, Mississippi
b. Still, William Grant
b. Young, Lester Willis

Yazoo City, Mississippi
b. Barbour, Haley (Reeves)
b. Brown, Willie
b. Espy, Mike

MISSOURI
b. Brady, Sarah Jane
b. Smedley, Agnes
d. Bothwell, Jean
d. Kelly, Dan
d. Pontiac

Affton, Missouri
b. Goodman, John
d. Busch, August Anheuser, Jr.

Anderson, Missouri
b. Corben, Richard Vance

Atherton, Missouri
b. Cooper, Mort(on Cecil)
b. Cooper, Walker

Aurora, Missouri
b. Barker, Doc
b. Barker, Fred
b. Barker, Herman
b. Barker, Lloyd

b. Phillips, Harvey Gene

Bethel, Missouri
b. Finck, Henry Theophilus

Birch Tree, Missouri
b. Carnahan, Mel Eugene

Bonne Terre, Missouri
b. Williams, Patrick

Boonville, Missouri
b. Hitch, Charles J(ohnston)
d. Ashley, William Henry

Bowling Green, Missouri
b. Clark, Bennett Champ

Butler, Missouri
b. Heinlein, Robert Anson

Butte, Missouri
b. Knievel, Robbie

Cainsville, Missouri
b. Booth, George

Cameron, Missouri
b. Gillis, Don

Canton, Missouri
b. Tate, Eleanora E(laine)

Cape Girardeau, Missouri
b. Hecht, Chic
b. Limbaugh, Rush Hudson, III

Carthage, Missouri
b. Hubbell, Carl Owen
b. Neville, Kris Ottman
b. Perkins, Marlin
b. Starr, Belle

Caruthersville, Missouri
b. Oliver, James A(rthur)

Cass County, Missouri
b. Dalton, Emmett
b. Dalton, Gratton
b. Dalton, Robert
b. Dalton, William

Centerville, Missouri
b. James, Jesse Woodson

Charleston, Missouri
b. Danforth, William H
b. Rollins, Kenny

Chillicothe, Missouri
b. Grant, Harry Johnston

Clark, Missouri
b. Bradley, Omar Nelson

Clay County, Missouri
b. James, Frank
d. James, Frank

Clayton, Missouri
b. Franciscus, James Grover

Clever, Missouri
b. Mandan, Robert

Columbia, Missouri
b. Wiener, Norbert
d. Froman, Jane
d. Lehmann-Haupt, Hellmut Emil
d. Neihardt, John Gneisenau
d. Rickey, Branch

Concordia, Missouri
b. Kuhlman, Kathryn

Crystal City, Missouri
b. Bradley, Bill

Dearborn, Missouri
b. Boyd, William Clouser

Deepwater, Missouri
b. Swarthout, Gladys

Diamond, Missouri
b. Carver, George Washington
b. Miller, Paul

Dundee, Missouri
d. Colter, John

East Saint Louis, Missouri
b. Edwards, Harry, Jr.
b. Hudlin, Reginald
b. Hudlin, Warrington

Easton, Missouri
b. Iba, Hank

Edgerton, Missouri
b. Davis, Jim

Edinburg, Missouri
b. Crowder, Enoch Herbert

Elkton, Missouri
b. Rand, Sally

Eve, Missouri
b. Ghostley, Alice

Excelsior Springs, Missouri
b. Judd, Donald (Clarence)

Farmington, Missouri
b. Asbury, Herbert
b. McBride, Lloyd

Fayette, Missouri
b. Pritchett, Henry S

Flat Creek, Missouri
b. Johnson, Don

Flat River, Missouri
b. Husky, Ferlin

Florida, Missouri
b. Twain, Mark

Franklin, Missouri
b. Hearst, George

Frederick, Missouri
b. Foreman, Chuck

Fulton, Missouri
b. Britt, Steuart Henderson
b. Galbreath, Tony
b. Stephens, Helen

Gallatin, Missouri
b. Burns, Conrad Ray

Garden City, Missouri
b. Kauffman, Ewing Marion

Glasgow, Missouri
b. Vaughan, Harry Hawkins

Gower, Missouri
d. Atchison, David R

Grant City, Missouri
b. Winslow, Ola Elizabeth

Green Ridge, Missouri
b. White, Pearl

Hamilton, Missouri
b. Penney, J(ames) C(ash)
b. Wheat, Zack

Hannibal, Missouri
b. Beckley, Jake
b. Edwards, Cliff
b. Kemp, Barry
b. Lear, William Powell
b. Moore, George Stevens
d. Hatch, William Henry

Hazelton, Missouri
b. Stottlemyre, Mel(vin Leon)

Humansville, Missouri
b. Akins, Zoe
b. Buchanan, Edgar

Illmo, Missouri
b. Jackson, Mannie (L.)

Independence, Missouri
b. DePugh, Robert Bolivar
b. Nash, Clarence
b. Rogers, Ginger
b. Sutcliffe, Rick
b. Truman, Bess
b. Truman, Margaret

Jackson County, Missouri
b. Younger, Cole
d. Younger, Cole

Jamesport, Missouri
b. Allen, Forrest Claire
b. Scott, Martha Ellen

Jefferson City, Missouri
b. Beecher, Janet
b. Himes, Chester Bomar
b. Roehm, Carolyne Jane Smith
d. Dinning, Mark

Joplin, Missouri
b. Allen, Bob

b. Beal, John
b. Cummings, Bob
b. Grant, Jane
b. Hughes, Langston
b. Irwin, Hale S
b. Porter, Darrell Ray
b. Watkins, Perry
b. Weaver, Dennis
b. Wenrich, Percy

Kansas City, Missouri
b. Ace, Goodman
b. Ace, Jane Sherwood
b. Alcott, Amy Strum
b. Altman, Robert B
b. Asner, Ed(ward)
b. Bacharach, Burt
b. Bannon, Jim
b. Beall, Lester Thomas
b. Beery, Noah
b. Beery, Wallace Fitzgerald
b. Bennett, Robert Russell
b. Bloch, Henry W(ollman)
b. Boyle, Harold Vincent
b. Brakhage, Stan
b. Byers, Walter
b. Cheadle, Don
b. Coburn, Julia
b. Connell, Evan Shelby, Jr.
b. Corbett, Scott
b. Cotten, Michael
b. Diemer, Emma Lou
b. Douglass, Lathrop
b. Duncan, David Douglas
b. Eagels, Jeanne
b. Freleng, Friz
b. Glancy, Diane
b. Hall, Donald Joyce
b. Hancock, John D
b. Harlow, Jean
b. Hickey, Margaret A.
b. Hickock, Richard Eugene
b. Horst, Louis
b. Iwerks, Ub(be)
b. Jenkins, Paul
b. Joyce, Alice
b. Kander, John
b. Keller, George Matthew
b. Kelley, Clarence Marion
b. Kennedy, Florynce
b. Kling, Johnny
b. Klutznick, Philip M.
b. Kohler, Fred, Sir
b. Least Heat Moon, William
b. Lockridge, Frances Louise
b. Luckman, Charles
b. MacKenzie, Warren
b. Morris, Robert
b. Moten, Bennie
b. Ogilvie, Richard Buell
b. Opel, John Roberts
b. Parsons, James
b. Peterson, Lorraine Collett
b. Rosen, Moishe Martin
b. Roueche, Berton
b. Ryden, Ernest Edwin
b. Sanders, Ed
b. Saunders, Lori
b. Shawn, Ted
b. Snow, Edgar Parks
b. Stengel, Casey
b. Tate, James
b. Teschemacher, Frank
b. Thomson, Virgil Garnett
b. Trillin, Calvin Marshall
b. Truex, Ernest

b. Burton, Nelson, Jr.
b. Busch, August Adolphus, III
b. Busch, August Anheuser, Jr.
b. Campbell, E Simms
b. Caray, Harry
b. Carlson, Wally
b. Carnovsky, Morris
b. Carter, Don(ald James)
b. Cervantes, Alfonso Juan
b. Chopin, Kate
b. Churchill, Winston
b. Clay, William Lacy
b. Cody, John Patrick
b. Collins, Cardiss (Hortense
   Robertson)
b. Converse, Frank
b. Convy, Bert
b. Conzelman, Jimmy
b. Cornell, Douglas B
b. Danforth, John Claggett
b. Darcy, Tom
b. Davis, Billy, Jr.
b. Davis, Dwight Filley
b. Davis, Phil
b. DeWitt, William Orville, Sr.
b. DeYoung, Michel Harry
b. Dooley, Thomas Anthony, III
b. Dotson, Bob
b. Eagleton, Thomas Francis
b. Eames, Charles
b. Edgell, George Harold
b. Eliot, T(homas) S(tearns)
b. Engelbreit, Mary
b. Evans, Walker
b. Factor, Max, Jr.
b. Falk, Lee Harrison
b. Farmer, Don(ald Edwin)
b. Faylen, Frank
b. Felker, Clay S
b. Fidler, Jimmie
b. Field, Eugene
b. Field, Kate
b. Fishbein, Morris
b. Flavin, Joseph B(ernard)
b. Foxx, Redd
b. Frank, Clinton Edward
b. Frann, Mary
b. Froman, Jane
b. Galvin, Pud
b. Garagiola, Joe
b. Gellhorn, Martha Ellis
b. Gephardt, Richard Andrew
b. Goodman, George Jerome Waldo
b. Grable, Betty
b. Grant, Julia Dent
b. Gray, Louis Patrick
b. Gregory, Dick
b. Grimm, Charlie
b. Guenther, Charles John
b. Guerin, Jules
b. Guillaume, Robert
b. Gunn, Moses
b. Hahn, Emily
b. Hampton, Henry
b. Harkness, Rebekah West
b. Harrington, Michael
b. Hill, Jesse, Jr.
b. Hillenkoetter, Roscoe H(enry)
b. Hirschfeld, Al(bert)
b. Hotchner, Aaron Edward
b. Howard, Elston Gene
b. Ittner, William Butts
b. Jenkins, Ella (Louise)
b. Johnston, Johnny
b. Jones, Joe
b. Kline, Kevin Delaney

b. Kohlmeier, Louis Martin, Jr.
b. Kurland, Bob
b. La Fontaine, Pat
b. Lambert, Gerard Barnes
b. LaPlante, Laura
b. Lemmons, Kasi
b. Lester, Julius
b. Lynch, David
b. Macauley, Ed
b. MacNutt, Francis, Father
b. Mallinckrodt, Edward
b. Marlowe, Marion
b. Martin, William McChesney, Jr.
b. Mason, Marsha
b. May, Morton David
b. Mayo, Virginia
b. McCulloch, Robert P
b. McDonald, Michael
b. McFee, Henry Lee
b. McHenry, Donald Franchot
b. McKenzie, Red
b. McKinley, Chuck
b. McManus, George
b. Merrick, David
b. Moore, Marianne Craig
b. More, Paul Elmer
b. Nader, Michael
b. Nolan, Kathy
b. Perkoff, Stuart Z.
b. Pike, Jim
b. Price, Vincent
b. Pulitzer, Ralph
b. Queeny, Edgar Monsanto
b. Rankin, Judy
b. Redhead, Hugh McCulloch
b. Reid, Wallace Eugene
b. Reiser, Pete
b. Revolta, Johnny
b. Roberts, Doris
b. Robinson, Julia (Bowman)
b. Rombauer, Irma von Starkloff
b. Rosenbloom, Georgia
b. Russell, Charles Marion
b. Russell, Pee Wee
b. Savant, Marilyn vos
b. Schlafly, Phyllis Stewart
b. Schmiechen, Richard Kurt
b. Sims, Billy Ray
b. Smith, Robert Lee
b. Spinks, Leon
b. Spinks, Michael
b. Spofford, Charles M(erville)
b. Stilwell, Richard Dale
b. Stoessel, Albert
b. Stone, Chuck
b. Sutton, Carol
b. Swope, Gerard
b. Swope, Herbert Bayard
b. Taussig, Frank William
b. Teasdale, Sara
b. Telva, Marion
b. Terris, Susan
b. Thomas, Betty
b. Thompson, Kay
b. Thum, Marcella
b. Tjader, Cal(len Radcliffe, Jr.)
b. Traubel, Helen
b. Tucker, Orrin
b. Vaughan, Bill
b. Waddles, Charleszetta, Mother
b. Ward, Fannie
b. Warrick, Ruth
b. Waters, Maxine
b. Wattleton, Faye
b. Weathers, Felicia
b. Weaver, Earl Sidney

b. Weber, Pete(r)
b. Webster, William Hedgcock
b. Westbrook, Peter (J.)
b. White, Jo Jo
b. Wilkins, Roy
b. Williams, Dick
b. Winslow, Kellen Boswell
b. Winters, Shelley
b. Wolfson, Louis Elwood
b. Wyman, Thomas Hunt
d. Aiken, Howard Hathaway
d. Beaumont, William
d. Bell, Cool Papa
d. Blair, Francis Preston, Jr.
d. Bottomley, Jim
d. Boyer, Ken(ton Lloyd)
d. Breitenstein, Ted
d. Cabet, Etienne
d. Cervantes, Alfonso Juan
d. Chopin, Kate
d. Clark, William
d. Conzelman, Jimmy
d. Cori, Gerty Theresa (Radnitz)
d. Danforth, William H
d. Dauss, George August
d. Doisy, Edward Adelbert, Sr.
d. Eames, Charles
d. Elkin, Stanley (Lawrence)
d. Erlanger, Joseph
d. Fitzpatrick, Daniel R
d. Gilmore, Patrick Sarsfield
d. Graham, Evarts Ambrose
d. Ittner, William Butts
d. Johnson, Ban
d. Kearny, Stephen Watts
d. Mallinckrodt, Edward
d. May, John L.
d. May, Morton David
d. McDonnell, James Smith
d. Meriwether, Lee
d. Patrick, Lynn
d. Perkins, Marlin
d. Price, Sterling
d. Pulitzer, Joseph, II
d. Queeny, Edgar Monsanto
d. Randolph, Jennings
d. Rombauer, Irma von Starkloff
d. Scott, Dred
d. Shreve, Henry Miller
d. Smet, Pierre Jean de
d. Stephens, Helen
d. Taussig, Frank William
d. Tuthill, Harry J
d. Wilkinson, Charles (Burnham)

Sedalia, Missouri
  b. Martin, Valerie
  b. Oakie, Jack
  b. Shannon, Fred Albert
  d. Wheat, Zack

Sikeston, Missouri
  b. Adams, John Hanly

Somerset County, Missouri
  b. Chase, Samuel

Speed, Missouri
  b. Corum, Martene Windsor

Springfield, Missouri
  b. Barker, Ma
  b. Hammond, Bray
  b. James, Marquis
  b. Johnson, Virginia E

NEBRASKA
b. Dietz, Angel DeCora
b. LaFlesche Tibbles, Susette
b. Petalesharo
b. Red Cloud, Chief
b. Worth, Irene
d. Snake, Reuben, Jr.

Allande, Nebraska
b. Emanuel, James A

Anselmo, Nebraska
b. Forrester, Jay Wright

Beaver City, Nebraska
b. Pipher, Mary

Blue Springs, Nebraska
b. Chamberlin, B Guy

Burchard, Nebraska
b. Bosley, Harold A
b. Lloyd, Harold

Camp Robinson, Nebraska
d. Crazy Horse

Central City, Nebraska
b. Morris, Wright Marion

Clatonia, Nebraska
b. Burton, Glenn W(illard)

Columbus, Nebraska
b. Higgins, Andrew J

David City, Nebraska
b. Etting, Ruth
b. Hall, Joyce Clyde
b. Hruska, Roman L(ee)

Douglas, Nebraska
b. Davidson, J Brownlee

Elba, Nebraska
b. Alexander, Grover Cleveland

Eustis, Nebraska
b. Yeutter, Clayton Keith

Falls City, Nebraska
b. Erwin, Pee Wee

Filley, Nebraska
b. Taylor, Robert

Fort Lisa, Nebraska
d. Sacagawea

Fremont, Nebraska
b. Armstrong, William L
b. Edgerton, Harold Eugene

Friend, Nebraska
b. Strong, Anna Louise

Gibbon, Nebraska
b. Cavett, Dick
b. Cherrington, Ben Mark

Grand Island, Nebraska
b. Abbott, Edith
b. Abbott, Grace
b. Baird, Bil
b. Fonda, Henry Jaynes
d. Abbott, Edith

Hastings, Nebraska
b. Dennis, Sandy
b. Hefti, Neal Paul
b. Warren, Gerald Lee

Hebron, Nebraska
b. Darby, Ken
b. Roper, Elmo Burns, Jr.

Laurel, Nebraska
b. Calcavecchia, Mark
b. Coburn, James

Lincoln, Nebraska
b. Cheney, Dick
b. Eberhart, Mignon Good
b. Eiseley, Loren Corey
b. Gann, Ernest Kellogg
b. Guthrie, Edwin Ray
b. Kerrey, Bob
b. Lasch, Robert
b. McGee, Gale William
b. Moores, Dick
b. Pound, Louise
b. Pound, Roscoe
b. Ryan, Leo Joseph
b. Sorensen, Ted
b. Starkweather, Charles
b. Sweet, Matthew
b. Turner, Janine
b. Weidman, Charles Edward, Jr.
b. Wilson, Don(ald Harlow)
b. Yorty, Sam(uel William)
d. Aldrich, Bess Streeter
d. MacRae, Gordon
d. Pound, Louise
d. Starkweather, Charles

Loup City, Nebraska
b. Moeller, Michael E

Lyons, Nebraska
b. Mitchell, Howard (Bundy)

McCook, Nebraska
b. Nelson, Ben
d. Norris, George William

Merriman, Nebraska
b. Fitch, Val Logsdon

Naponee, Nebraska
b. Janssen, David

Nebraska City, Nebraska
b. Hayward, Leland

Niobrara, Nebraska
b. Trudell, John

O'Neill, Nebraska
b. Dowling, Dan(iel Blair)
b. Leahy, Frank
b. Owens, Harry

Omaha, Nebraska
b. Addy, Wesley
b. Astaire, Adele
b. Astaire, Fred
b. Baer, Max
b. Baldrige, Malcolm
b. Berlin, Richard E
b. Boggs, Wade (Anthony)
b. Brando, Marlon, Jr.
b. Buffett, Warren Edward
b. Clark, Robert Edward
b. Clift, Montgomery
b. Denenberg, Herbert Sidney
b. Door, Rheta Childe
b. Doyle, David (Fitzgerald)
b. Dozier, William
b. Ford, Gerald R(udolph)
b. Gibson, Bob
b. Goldston, Nathaniel R, III
b. Goodman, Johnny
b. Hitchcock, Gilbert Monell
b. Kalber, Floyd
b. Kinnick, Nile
b. Klein, Lawrence Robert
b. Kurtz, Swoosie
b. Laird, Melvin Robert
b. Malcolm X
b. McGuire, Dorothy Hackett
b. Miles, Buddy
b. Nolte, Nick
b. Olsen, Tillie
b. Olson, Gregg William
b. Peter, Valentine J
b. Rodgers, Johnny
b. Ruscha, Edward
b. Stephenson, Skip
b. Stoltzman, Richard Leslie
b. Sullivan, Mike
b. Swenson, Inga
b. Waybill, Fee
b. Wedemeyer, Albert Coady
b. Williams, Paul Hamilton
b. Williams, Roger
b. Wilson, Julie
b. Zorinsky, Edward
d. Creighton, Edward
d. Hruska, Roman L(ee)
d. Zorinsky, Edward

Omaha Indian Reservation, Nebraska
b. LaFlesche, Francis
d. LaFlesche, Francis
d. LaFlesche Tibbles, Susette

Osceola, Nebraska
b. Hathaway, Stanley Knapp

Papillion, Nebraska
b. Curti, Merle Eugene

Pender, Nebraska
b. Pate, Maurice

Peru, Nebraska
b. Brownell, Herbert, Jr.
b. Brownell, Samuel Miller
b. Conkle, Ellsworth Prouty

Platte Center, Nebraska
b. Gruenther, Alfred Maximillian

Platte County, Nebraska
b. Keogh, James

d. Pierce, Franklin

Cornish, New Hampshire
b. Chase, Philander
b. Chase, Salmon Portland
d. MacKaye, Percy Wallace
d. Saint Gaudens, Augustus

Deerfield, New Hampshire
b. Butler, Benjamin Franklin

Dunbarton, New Hampshire
b. Wright, Carroll Davidson

East Derry, New Hampshire
b. Shepard, Alan B(artlett), Jr.

Enfield, New Hampshire
d. Kohler, Wolfgang

Exeter, New Hampshire
b. Cass, Lewis
b. French, Daniel Chester
b. Hicks, Granville
b. Irving, John
d. Perry, Bliss

Farmington, New Hampshire
b. Wilson, Henry

Fitzwilliam, New Hampshire
d. Drinker, Philip

Francestown, New Hampshire
b. Woodbury, Levi

Franconia, New Hampshire
d. Gilman, Lawrence
d. Poole, Ernest

Franklin, New Hampshire
b. Damon, Ralph Shepard
d. Cannon, Walter Bradford
d. Pierce, George Washington

Gilford, New Hampshire
d. Rolfe, Red

Gilmanton, New Hampshire
b. Mudgett, Herman Webster

Goffstown, New Hampshire
b. Gerould, Gordon Hall

Hampton, New Hampshire
b. Dearborn, Henry
b. Pierce, Jane (Means)

Hampton Falls, New Hampshire
b. Brown, Alice
b. Cram, Ralph Adams
d. Whittier, John Greenleaf

Hanover, New Hampshire
b. Bridgman, Laura Dewey
b. Clarke, James Freeman
b. Young, Charles Augustus
d. Adams, Sherman Llewellyn
d. Brush, George
d. Conant, James Bryant
d. Dwinell, Lane
d. Ford, Corey

d. Logan, Harlan (De Braun)
d. Sloan, John F
d. Sperry, Armstrong W
d. Stefansson, Vihjalmur
d. Stewart, Potter
d. Stibitz, George R.
d. Wheelock, Eleazar
d. Young, Charles Augustus

Henniker, New Hampshire
b. Beach, H H A, Mrs.

Hillsboro, New Hampshire
b. Keith, Benjamin Franklin
b. Pierce, Franklin

Hinsdale, New Hampshire
b. Dana, Charles Anderson

Hopkinton, New Hampshire
b. Long, Stephen H

Jaffrey, New Hampshire
d. Laughlin, James Laurence
d. Von Eckardt, Wolf

Keene, New Hampshire
b. Dutton, E(dward) P(ayson)
b. Ellis, Carleton

Laconia, New Hampshire
b. May, Mortimer
d. Willingham, Calder Baynard, Jr.

Lake Sunapee, New Hampshire
d. Whitney, Josiah Dwight

Lakeport, New Hampshire
b. Chase, Richard Volney

Lebanon, New Hampshire
b. Obomsawin, Alanis
d. Cotton, Norris
d. Kemeny, John G(eorge)

Littleton, New Hampshire
b. Porter, Eleanor H

Londonderry, New Hampshire
b. Stark, John

Lyme, New Hampshire
b. Converse, Marquis M
b. Read, Albert Cushing

Madison, New Hampshire
d. Hocking, William Ernest

Manchester, New Hampshire
b. Blood, Ernest
b. Choquette, Robert Guy
b. Coxe, Louis Osborne
b. Custin, Mildred
b. Flanagan, Mike
b. Freedman, James Oliver
b. Loeb, William
b. Metalious, Grace de Repentigny
b. O'Neil, James F(rancis)
b. Revson, Charles Haskell
d. King, John W(illiam)
d. Lincoln, Robert Todd
d. McDonald, Richard
d. Morris, Ernest Brougham

d. Stark, John

Mason Village, New Hampshire
b. Chickering, Jonas

Meredith, New Hampshire
d. Montana, Bob

Milton, New Hampshire
b. Jones, Robert Edmond
d. Jones, Robert Edmond

Monadnock, New Hampshire
d. Thayer, Abbott Handerson

Nashua, New Hampshire
b. Gorman, Leon Arthur
b. Gregg, Judd
d. Taeuber, Conrad F.
d. Thurber, Charles
d. Welch, Mickey

New Boston, New Hampshire
b. Langdell, Christopher Columbus

New Ipswich, New Hampshire
b. Appleton, Nathan

New London, New Hampshire
d. Greenaway, Emerson

Newbury, New Hampshire
d. Hay, John Milton

Newington, New Hampshire
b. Archibald, Joe

Newport, New Hampshire
b. Hale, Sarah Josepha Buell
d. Edgell, George Harold

North Conway, New Hampshire
b. Shea, John
d. Cummings, E(dward) E(stlin)
d. McNair, Malcolm Perrine

North Hampton, New Hampshire
d. Philbrick, Herbert Arthur

North Stratford, New Hampshire
d. Goodman, Paul

Northwood, New Hampshire
b. Kelley, Hall Jackson

Penacook, New Hampshire
b. Rolfe, Red

Peterborough, New Hampshire
d. Rock, John

Plainfield, New Hampshire
d. Parrish, Maxfield

Plymouth, New Hampshire
d. Hawthorne, Nathaniel

Portsmouth, New Hampshire
b. Aldrich, Thomas Bailey
b. Astor, Brooke Marshall
b. Blalock, Jane

b. Bonerz, Peter
b. Boylston, Helen Dore
b. Coues, Elliott
b. Fields, James Thomas
b. Langdon, John
b. Nicholas, Nicholas John, Jr.
b. Rush, Tom
b. Thaxter, Celia
d. Farragut, David Glasgow
d. King, Ernest Joseph
d. Langdon, John
d. Whipple, William
d. Woodbury, Levi

Randolph, New Hampshire
d. Bridgman, Percy Williams

Rochester, New Hampshire
b. Carroll, Gladys Hasty
b. Hall, Charles Francis
b. Larouche, Lyndon Hermyle, Jr.

Rumney, New Hampshire
b. Clifford, Nathan

Salisbury, New Hampshire
b. Webster, Daniel

Sandwich, New Hampshire
d. Rains, Claude

Somersworth, New Hampshire
b. Chase, Stuart
b. Sullivan, John

Springfield, New Hampshire
d. Downey, Fairfax Davis

Sutton, New Hampshire
b. Pillsbury, John Sargent

Walpole, New Hampshire
b. Howland, Alfred Cornelius

Warner, New Hampshire
b. Pillsbury, Charles Alfred

Wilton, New Hampshire
b. Abbot, C(harles) G(reeley)
b. Smith, William French

Winchester, New Hampshire
b. Wood, Leonard

Wolfeboro, New Hampshire
d. Marriott, John Willard

NEW JERSEY
b. Adams, Cliff
b. Bailey, Radcliffe
b. Block, Rory
b. Giroux, Robert
b. Gorka, John
b. Hegyes, Robert
b. Hill, Lauryn
b. Lipton, Martin
b. Lundy, Benjamin
b. Muses, Charles Arthur
b. Stempel, Robert
b. Sullivan, Kathryn D

Allendale, New Jersey
b. Matheson, Richard Burton

d. Fairfax, Beatrice

Allenhurst, New Jersey
b. Fields, Dorothy

Alliance, New Jersey
b. Seldes, George (Henry)
b. Seldes, Gilbert Vivian

Alpine, New Jersey
b. Lamb, Harold Albert
d. Fokker, Anthony Herman Gerard

Ancochs, New Jersey
b. Woolman, John

Andover, New Jersey
d. Burke, Kenneth

Arlington, New Jersey
b. Scott, Adrian

Asbury Park, New Jersey
b. Abbott, Bud
b. Chase, Edna Woolman
b. Hess, Leon

Atlantic City, New Jersey
b. Banks, Harvey Washington
b. Forrest, Helen
b. Gimbel, Richard
b. Kaprow, Allan
b. Lawrence, Jacob Armstead
b. Smathers, George Armistead
b. Thomas, Dave
b. Throckmorton, Cleon
d. Brady, Diamond Jim
d. Gould, George Milbry
d. Lloyd, John Henry
d. Luden, William H
d. Lurton, Horace Harmon
d. Wanamaker, Lewis Rodman
d. Wright, Harry

Avon, New Jersey
d. Howard, Bronson Crocker

Bayonne, New Jersey
b. Dee, Sandra
b. Donovan, Raymond James
b. Frank, Barney
b. Kahn, Herman
b. Keith, Brian
b. Perle, George
b. Stein, Mark
b. Tully, Grace George
b. Tyson, Laura D'Andrea
b. Wiley, George A

Beach Haven Terrace, New Jersey
d. Bosley, Harold A

Belle Meade, New Jersey
d. Van Dusen, Henry Pitney

Belleville, New Jersey
b. DeVito, Tommy
b. Goodrich, Frances

Belmar, New Jersey
b. Dunn, Alan
b. McMurtrie, Douglas C
d. Held, John, Jr.

d. Moisseiff, Leon Solomon

Belvidere, New Jersey
b. Schelling, Ernest Henry

Bergen County, New Jersey
b. Smith, Allison

Bergen Heights, New Jersey
b. Magonigle, Harold Van Buren

Bergen Point, New Jersey
b. DuPont, Samuel Francis

Bernardsville, New Jersey
d. Fenwick, Millicent Hammond
d. Welles, Sumner

Beverly, New Jersey
b. Merritt, Abraham

Bloomfield, New Jersey
b. Bourne, Randolph Silliman

Boonton, New Jersey
b. Douglas, Helen Mary Gahagan

Bordentown, New Jersey
b. Waugh, Frederick Judd

Bound Brook, New Jersey
b. Bohay, Heidi
b. Talmadge, Thomas de Witt
d. Sinclair, Upton Beall
d. Trefflich, Henry Herbert Frederick

Bridgeton, New Jersey
b. Brown, Lester Russell
d. Goslin, Goose

Brigantine, New Jersey
d. White, Slappy

Browns Mills, New Jersey
d. Patten, Simon Nelson

Bunnvale, New Jersey
b. Decker Slaney, Mary

Burlington, New Jersey
b. Bard, John
b. Cooper, James Fenimore
b. Lawrence, James

Burlington County, New Jersey
b. Shreve, Henry Miller

Caldwell, New Jersey
b. Cleveland, Grover
d. Thornhill, Claude

Camden, New Jersey
b. Camp, Kimberly
b. Cassidy, Joanna
b. Cavanna, Betty
b. Dash, Samuel
b. DeFranco, Buddy
b. Dworkin, Andrea
b. Falana, Lola
b. Huff, Leon
b. Kelleher, Herb(ert David)
b. Pennington, Ann

b. Renaldo, Duncan
b. Rozier, Mike
b. Sterban, Richard
b. Unruh, Howard B
b. Valeriani, Richard Gerard
b. Wilson, Henry Braid
d. Ayer, Francis Wayland
d. Walcott, Joe
d. Whitman, Walt(er)

Cape May, New Jersey
b. O'Hara, Mary
b. Stephens, Uriah
b. Volcker, Paul Adolph

Cape May Court House, New Jersey
d. Shaughnessy, Mickey
d. Voorhees, Donald

Carteret, New Jersey
b. Medwick, Joe

Chatham, New Jersey
b. Day, Chon
b. Strang, Ruth May
b. Ward, Montgomery

Cliffside Park, New Jersey
b. Blair, Betsy
b. Lesnevich, Gus
d. Dunninger, Joseph
d. Lesnevich, Gus

Clifton, New Jersey
d. Bertelli, Angelo B.

Clinton, New Jersey
b. Case, Anna

Collingswood, New Jersey
b. Allen, Richard Vincent

Coytesville, New Jersey
b. Price, George
b. Van Fleet, James Alward

Dover, New Jersey
b. Kennedy, X J

East Orange, New Jersey
b. Blish, James Benjamin
b. Clapp, Margaret Antoinette
b. Cole, Cozy
b. Fletcher, Joseph Francis (III)
b. Heilbrun, Carolyn Gold
b. Hillyer, Robert
b. Houston, Whitney
b. Latifah, Queen
b. MacRae, Gordon
b. Warwick, Dionne
d. Barnes, Jim
d. Brouthers, Dan
d. Dundee, Johnny

Edison, New Jersey
d. Stevens, Robert Ten Broeck

Egg Harbor, New Jersey
b. Morganweck, Frank

Elberon, New Jersey
b. Ferrer, Mel(chor Gaston)
d. Garfield, James Abram

Eldridge Park, New Jersey
d. Gilpin, Charles Sidney

Elizabeth, New Jersey
b. Barry, Rick
b. Blume, Judy Sussman
b. Brown, Hubie
b. Butler, Nicholas Murray
b. Chidsey, Donald Barr
b. Dennis, Jack B(onnell)
b. Halsey, William Frederick, Jr.
b. Johnson, Cletus Merlin
b. Mitchell, Thomas
b. Pena, Elizabeth
b. Solotaroff, Theodore
b. Stratemeyer, Edward L
b. Taylor, Arthur Robert
b. Tregaskis, Richard William
b. Walker, Mickey
d. Blackwell, Antoinette Louisa Brown
d. Dwyer, Florence Price

Elizabethport, New Jersey
b. Gitlow, Benjamin

Elizabethtown, New Jersey
b. Clark, Abraham

Englewood, New Jersey
b. Baldwin, Horace
b. Button, Dick
b. Chapman, Frank Michler
b. Hexum, Jon-Erik
b. Lewis, Richard
b. Lindbergh, Anne Spencer Morrow
b. Parcells, Bill
b. Post, Elizabeth Lindley
b. Sedgwick, Anne Douglas
b. Stewart, Slam
b. Travolta, John
b. Wright, Gary
d. Barrie, Wendy
d. Block, Martin
d. Corio, Ann
d. Elmen, Gustav Waldemar
d. Faye, Joey
d. Franklin, Irene
d. Gillespie, Dizzy
d. Heatherton, Ray(mond Joseph)
d. McCoy, Van
d. Monk, Thelonious Sphere, Jr.
d. Morrow, Dwight Whitney
d. Price, George
d. Scarne, John
d. Schilt, Jan
d. Smith, Joe
d. Sumner, William Graham

Englewood Cliffs, New Jersey
b. Van Devere, Trish
d. Nichols, Anne
d. Sachse, Leopold

Fair Haven, New Jersey
d. Blair, William Richards
d. Cline, Maggie

Fanwood, New Jersey
b. Stevens, Robert Ten Broeck

Far Hills, New Jersey
d. Forbes, Malcolm Stevenson
d. Whitney, Richard

Fieldsboro, New Jersey
b. Crossley, Archibald Maddock

Flemington, New Jersey
b. Federici, Daniel Paul
b. Foran, Dick John Nicholas
d. Bradley, Will
d. De Rochemont, Richard Guertis
d. Limon, Jose Arcadio
d. Teague, Walter Dorwin

Fort Dix, New Jersey
b. Harris, Franco
d. Bennett, Constance Campbell

Franklin County, New Jersey
d. Westley, Helen

Franklin Park, New Jersey
b. Case, Clifford Philip
d. Hicks, Granville

Fredericksville, New Jersey
b. Fauset, Jessie Redmon

Freehold, New Jersey
b. Springsteen, Bruce
d. Walker, Mickey

Garfield, New Jersey
b. Vitale, Dick

Gibbstown, New Jersey
b. Earle, Sylvia Alice

Glen Ridge, New Jersey
b. Muir, Malcolm
b. Sherman, Cindy
b. Stewart, Alison
d. Pei, Mario Andrew
d. Sangster, Margaret Elizabeth

Gloucester, New Jersey
b. Barton, James

Guttenberg, New Jersey
b. Gougelman, Pierre

Hackensack, New Jersey
b. Boone, Debby
b. Carey, Phil(ip)
b. Fratello, Mike
b. Hewitt, Henry Kent
b. Schirra, Wally
d. Fischer, Louis
d. Rice, Gregory
d. Walker, Cyril

Haddonfield, New Jersey
d. Cahill, William T(homas)

Haledon, New Jersey
b. Borgmann, Benny

Hammonton, New Jersey
b. Moore, Victor

Harrington, New Jersey
b. Lydon, James

Harrison, New Jersey
b. Sullivan, A(loysius) M(ichael)

Hightstown, New Jersey
d. Dodds, Harold Willis
d. Engstrom, Elmer William
d. Kelley, Larry
d. Mackay, John Alexander

Hoboken, New Jersey
b. Aiken, Howard Hathaway
b. Bishop, Hazel
b. Chang, Michael
b. Dunlap, Albert J.
b. Kinsey, Alfred Charles
b. Kroeber, Alfred Louis
b. Lange, Dorothea Nutzhorn
b. Shippen, Katherine Binney
b. Sinatra, Frank
b. Stevens, Robert Livingston
b. Stieglitz, Alfred
d. Bethune, Thomas Greene
d. Bissell, Patrick
d. Stevens, John
d. Stevens, Robert Livingston

Hope, New Jersey
d. Krumgold, Joseph (Quincy)

Hopewell, New Jersey
b. Lindbergh, Charles Augustus
d. Gould, Beatrice Blackmar
d. Gould, Charles Bruce
d. Hart, John
d. Lindbergh, Charles Augustus

Idell, New Jersey
d. Wiese, Kurt

Irvington, New Jersey
b. Howard, James John
b. Rudd, Mark
d. Mueller, Christian F

Island Heights, New Jersey
d. Peto, John Frederick

Jefferson, New Jersey
b. Durand, Asher Brown
d. Durand, Asher Brown

Jersey City, New Jersey
b. Allen, Elizabeth
b. Bishop, Jim
b. Brown, George
b. Buttenheim, Edgar Joseph
b. Conte, Richard
b. DiMeola, Al
b. Duffy, Edmund
b. Freeh, Louis J(oseph)
b. Gourdine, Simon (Peter)
b. Hague, Frank
b. Heatherton, Ray(mond Joseph)
b. Heinsohn, Tommy
b. James, Dennis
b. James, Philip
b. Kilian, Victor
b. Kimbro, Dennis (Paul)
b. Krumgold, Joseph (Quincy)
b. Lane, Nathan
b. Maleska, Eugene T.
b. Markert, Russell
b. McCoo, Marilyn
b. McMahon, Jim
b. Mickens, Spike
b. Murphy, Warren B
b. Murray, Kathryn (Hazel)

b. Nelson, Ozzie
b. Newman, Phyllis
b. Nugent, Nelle
b. Okun, Arthur Melvin
b. Rovere, Richard Halworth
b. Secunda, Arthur
b. Sinatra, Frank, Jr.
b. Sinatra, Nancy
b. Smith, Claydes
b. Sonneck, Oscar George Theodore
b. Stoneham, Horace
b. Tagliabue, Paul John
b. Talmadge, Norma
b. Thomas, Dennis
b. Thompson, Vivian Laubach
b. Warner, Malcolm-Jamal
b. Wilson, Flip
d. Anderson, Alexander
d. Catlin, George
d. Hague, Frank
d. Haupt, Herman
d. Macfadden, Bernarr Adolphus
d. Marshall, Frank James
d. Quidor, John
d. Sheed, Frank
d. Washburn, Charles

Juliustown, New Jersey
b. Lippincott, Joshua Ballinger

Kearny, New Jersey
b. Harkes, John
d. Dejongh, Peter

Keyport, New Jersey
d. Hall, Juanita

Kingston, New Jersey
b. Hewes, Joseph

Lake Hopatcong, New Jersey
d. Maxim, Hudson

Lakewood, New Jersey
d. Confrey, Zez

Lamberton, New Jersey
b. Pike, Zebulon Montgomery

Lawnside, New Jersey
b. Bryant, Wayne R(ichard)

Lawrence, New Jersey
b. Stewart, Jon

Leonardo, New Jersey
d. DeLue, Donald Harcourt

Leonia, New Jersey
d. Arnold, Leslie Philip

Lincoln Park, New Jersey
b. Kiick, Jim

Livingston, New Jersey
b. Biondi, Frank J., Jr.
d. Galento, Tony
d. Guarnieri, Johnny
d. Jensen, Alfred Julio
d. Russell, Honey
d. Turnbull, Agnes Sligh

Long Branch, New Jersey
b. Anderson, Richard Norman
b. Barry, Daniel
b. Frank, Waldo
b. Garrison, David
b. Greer, Sonny
b. Hobart, Garret Augustus
b. Love, Susan M(argaret)
b. Mailer, Norman (Kingsley)
d. Howard, Tom
d. Pratt, Fletcher

Lyndhurst, New Jersey
b. Rawl, Lawrence G

Madison, New Jersey
b. McGraw, Donald Cushing
b. Newcombe, Don(ald)

Mahwah, New Jersey
d. Guy-Blache, Alice

Maplewood, New Jersey
b. Mirabella, Grace
d. Hazeltine, (Louis) Alan

Mendham, New Jersey
d. Doubleday, Abner

Merchantville, New Jersey
b. Walcott, Joe

Metuchen, New Jersey
b. Copperfield, David
b. Martin, Luther
d. Ciardi, John Anthony
d. Fisher, Clara
d. Freeman, Mary E Wilkins

Middletown Point, New Jersey
d. Bartlett, John Sherren

Millville, New Jersey
b. Henderson, Leon

Monmouth County, New Jersey
b. Hutchins, Thomas
d. Freneau, Philip Morin

Montclair, New Jersey
b. Aldrin, Edwin E(ugene), Jr.
b. Brown, George Scratchley
b. Cole, Charles Woolsey
b. Durang, Christopher Ferdinand
b. Hamer, Dean H.
b. Hayden, Sterling Relyea Walter
b. Kirsten, Dorothy
b. Kreskin
b. Lederberg, Joshua
b. Liquori, Marty
d. Ball, Thomas
d. Chute, Marchette (Gaylord)
d. Funk, Isaac Kauffman
d. Funk, Wilfred John
d. Gilbreth, Frank Bunker
d. Hartford, George Ludlum
d. Holt, Fritz
d. Keene, Laura
d. Lewis, Isaac Newton
d. Melcher, Frederic Gershon
d. Mennen, William Gerhard
d. Sullivan, A(loysius) M(ichael)
d. Wesson, David

Moorestown, New Jersey
b. Paul, Alice
d. Paul, Alice

Morris County, New Jersey
b. McLean, John

Morris Plains, New Jersey
d. Quinlan, Karen Ann

Morristown, New Jersey
b. Dalrymple, Jean
b. Fillmore, Caroline Carmichael
  McIntosh
b. Forbes, Malcolm Stevenson, Jr.
b. Griswold, Alfred Whitney
b. Harrison, Anna (Tuthill Symmes)
b. Hazeltine, (Louis) Alan
b. Hunt, Linda
b. LaFever Minard
b. Lebowitz, Fran(ces Ann)
b. Lowry, Judith Ives
b. Scott, Tony
b. Vail, Alfred Lewis
d. Duvoisin, Roger Antoine
d. Jones, Joe
d. Streeter, Ruth
d. Vail, Alfred Lewis

Mount Holly, New Jersey
b. Bailey, Gamaliel
b. Parsons, Frank
d. Wilson, Jackie

Mountain Lakes, New Jersey
d. Hinrichs, Gustav

Mountainside, New Jersey
d. Campbell, John W

Neptune, New Jersey
b. Bornstein, Kate
b. DeVito, Danny
b. Lyon, Southside Johnny
b. Nicholson, Jack
b. Schweickart, Russell L
d. Guerin, Jules

New Brunswick, New Jersey
b. Baskin, Leonard
b. Cole, Jack
b. Douglas, Michael Kirk
b. Gilman, Dorothy
b. Guth, Alan Harvey
b. Johnson, James Price
b. Kilmer, Joyce
b. Osterwald, Bibi
b. Pass, Joe
b. Scott, Austin Wakeman
b. Theismann, Joe
b. Vanderbilt, William Henry
b. Veronis, John James
b. Wasserburg, Gerald Joseph
d. Dickson, Earle Ensign
d. Kahng, Dawon

Newark, New Jersey
b. Adams, Harriet Stratemeyer
b. Addonizio, Hugh Joseph
b. Alexander, Jason
b. Amos, John
b. Attles, Al(vin A)
b. Auster, Paul
b. Baraka, Amiri

b. Bellamy, Bill
b. Blacque, Taurean
b. Blaine, Vivian
b. Bouton, Jim
b. Brennan, Robert E
b. Brennan, William Joseph, Jr.
b. Burr, Aaron
b. Campbell, John W
b. Clark, Joe
b. Coleman, Leonard S., Jr.
b. Coles, Joanna
b. Corrigan, Michael Augustine
b. Crane, Stephen
b. Davis, Marvin
b. DePalma, Brian Russell
b. Dickerson, Ernest
b. Ditmars, Raymond Lee
b. Fairchild, John Burr
b. Fiedler, Leslie Aaron
b. Fiorito, Ted
b. Francis, Connie
b. Gaynor, Gloria
b. Ginsberg, Allen
b. Glover, Savion
b. Hagler, Marvelous Marvin
b. Hamilton, Billy
b. Hoest, Bill
b. Holmes, Taylor
b. Houston, Cissy
b. Hughes, Emmet John
b. Ice-T
b. Ismail, Raghib
b. Jeffries, Leonard
b. Kantrowitz, Arnie
b. Kearny, Stephen Watts
b. Kilgore, Al
b. Kruger, Barbara
b. Lasser, Jacob Kay
b. Lawrence, Josephine
b. Lerner, Michael
b. Lewis, Byron E(ugene)
b. Lewis, Jerry
b. Lindsey, Mort
b. Liotta, Ray
b. Lowenstein, Allard Kenneth
b. Lucas, Nick
b. Massi, Nick
b. McDougall, Walt(er)
b. McLaughlin, Ann Dore
b. Meier, Richard Alan
b. Mennen, William Gerhard
b. Moss, Carlton
b. Mott, Charles Stewart
b. Neuwirth, Bebe
b. Northrop, John Knudsen
b. Pangborn, Franklin
b. Payne, Donald M
b. Pearson, Drew
b. Pesci, Joe
b. Pulliam, Keisha Knight
b. Pully, B S
b. Ritz, Al
b. Ritz, Harry
b. Rodino, Peter Wallace, Jr.
b. Roth, Philip (Milton)
b. Saint, Eva Marie
b. Saint Denis, Ruth
b. Schary, Dore
b. Scheuer, Philip K(latz)
b. Shorter, Wayne
b. Simeone, Harry
b. Simon, Paul
b. Stevens, Morton
b. Terhune, Albert Payson
b. Valli, Frankie
b. Vaughan, Sarah Lois

b. Viorst, Judith (Stahl)
b. Warden, Jack
b. Westheimer, Irvin Ferdinand
b. Weston, Edward F
b. Zia, Helen
d. Douglas, Amanda Minnie
d. Dryden, John Fairfield
d. Forsythe, Albert E
d. Healy, Timothy S(tafford)
d. Hepbron, George
d. Holland, John Philip
d. Schultz, Dutch
d. Stratemeyer, Edward L
d. Tough, Dave

Newbold, New Jersey
b. Baxter, Frank Condie

Newport, New Jersey
b. Hall, Juanita

Newton, New Jersey
b. Bradley, Will
b. Garofalo, Janeane
d. Trotta, Maurice S
d. Wright, Henry

North Arlington, New Jersey
b. Eilshemius, Louis Michel

North Bergen, New Jersey
b. Brooks, James L.
b. Leonetti, Tommy
d. Braddock, Jim
d. Castellano, Richard

Nutley, New Jersey
b. Blake, Robert
b. Du Bois, William Pene
b. Goodrich, Lloyd
b. Stewart, Martha
d. Bunner, Henry Cuyler

Oakland, New Jersey
d. Evans, Madge
d. Kingsley, Sidney

Ocean City, New Jersey
b. Andes, Keith
b. Foster, Preston
b. Talese, Gay

Oldwick, New Jersey
d. Hafstad, Lawrence R(andolph)

Oradell, New Jersey
b. Riddle, Nelson

Orange, New Jersey
b. Feeney, Chub
b. Fisher, Gail
b. Galento, Tony
b. Gwaltney, John Langston
b. Harbison, John Harris
b. Hartford, John Augustine
b. Hartke, Stephen Paul
b. Olcott, Henry Steel
b. Pickering, Thomas (Reeve)
b. Richards, Dickinson Woodruff
b. Ringo, Jim
b. Scheider, Roy Richard
b. Smith, Tony
b. Stetson, John Batterson
b. Wiley, W(illiam) Bradford

Rutherford, New Jersey
b. Marin, John
b. Williams, William Carlos
d. LeClear, Thomas
d. Sammartino, Peter
d. Williams, William Carlos

Saddle River, New Jersey
d. Haney, Carol

Salem, New Jersey
b. Goslin, Goose
b. Righter, Carroll
b. Stephens, Alice Barber
d. Pedersen, Charles J

Sayreville, New Jersey
b. Bon Jovi, Jon

Sea Bright, New Jersey
b. Alexander, James Waddell, II
b. Trippe, Juan Terry

Sea Girt, New Jersey
b. D'Alessio, Kitty

Sea Isle City, New Jersey
d. Hergesheimer, Joseph

Shamong, New Jersey
b. Still, William

Shrewsbury, New Jersey
b. Stephens, John Lloyd
d. Graves, William Sidney

Somerdale, New Jersey
d. Lindbergh, Pelle (Per-Eric)

Somerville, New Jersey
b. Morrison, Philip
b. Van Cleef, Lee
b. VonStade, Frederica
b. Wylie, Elinor Hoyt

South Amboy, New Jersey
b. Evigan, Greg(ory Ralph)

South Brunswick, New Jersey
d. Segal, George

South Orange, New Jersey
b. Eisenman, Peter
b. Kraft, Joseph
b. Shue, Andrew
b. Spacey, Kevin
b. Weinberg, Max M
d. Bamberger, Louis

South River, New Jersey
b. Wojciechowicz, Alex(ander)
d. Wojciechowicz, Alex(ander)

South Seaville, New Jersey
b. Daley, Rosie

Spring Lake, New Jersey
b. Boller, Paul Franklin, Jr.
d. Chesebrough, Robert Augustus
d. Hartford, George Huntington

Summit, New Jersey
b. Fleming, Peter
b. Jackson, Charles Reginald
b. Streep, Meryl
d. Arnold, Harold De Forest
d. Jewett, Frank Baldwin
d. Whittredge, Thomas Worthington
d. Wiley, W(illiam) Bradford

Teaneck, New Jersey
b. Christian-Green, Donna M.
b. McBride, Patricia
b. Nelson, Rick
d. Erwin, Pee Wee
d. Hare, James Henry
d. Kay, Ulysses Simpson
d. Messmer, Otto

Tenafly, New Jersey
b. Gore, Lesley
b. Hamer, Rusty
b. Harris, Ed
b. Sorvino, Mira

Toms River, New Jersey
b. Messersmith, Andy

Tranquility, New Jersey
d. Rutherfurd, Lewis Morris

Trenton, New Jersey
b. Antheil, George
b. Bronson, Betty
b. Cristofer, Michael
b. Crooks, Richard Alexander
b. Dinkins, David Norman
b. Donnelly, Ruth
b. Gummere, William Stryker
b. Higginbotham, A(loysius) Leon, Jr.
b. Kovacs, Ernie
b. Lawrence, Margaret
b. Light, Judith Ellen
b. Linowitz, Sol Myron
b. Pitcher, Molly
b. Rodman, Dennis (Keith)
b. Scalia, Antonin
b. Schwarzkopf, H Norman
b. Shange, Ntozake
b. Smith, Robert C
b. Taylor, Peter (Hillsman)
b. Thompson, Frank, Jr.
d. Boehm, Edward M
d. Dix, Dorothea Lynde
d. Hauptmann, Bruno Richard
d. Roebling, Mary G(indhart)
d. Roebling, Washington Augustus

Union City, New Jersey
b. Messmer, Otto

Union Hill, New Jersey
b. Cousins, Norman
b. Lee, Lila
b. Monty, Gloria

Upper Montclair, New Jersey
d. Ives, Herbert Eugene

Vauxhall, New Jersey
b. Kearse, Amalya Lyle

Verona, New Jersey
b. Dana, Margaret Bloxham

Weehawken, New Jersey
b. Bitter, Francis
b. Feigenbaum, Edward A(lbert)
b. Schwarz, Gerard
d. Rogers, Mary Cecilia

West Bend, New Jersey
b. Parker, Dorothy Rothschild

West End, New Jersey
b. Guggenheim, Harry Frank

West Hoboken, New Jersey
b. DiDonato, Pietro

West Long Branch, New Jersey
d. Pryor, Arthur W

West Orange, New Jersey
b. Byrne, Brendan Thomas
b. Caulfield, Joan
b. Chapin, James Ormsbee
b. Stagg, Amos Alonzo
d. Davis, Alexander Jackson
d. Edison, Thomas Alva

Westfield, New Jersey
b. Addams, Charles Samuel
b. Apgar, Virginia
b. McCarthy, Andrew
b. Schifter, Peter Mark
b. Torborg, Jeff(rey Allen)
b. Vagelos, P Roy

Westwood, New Jersey
d. Medina, Harold Raymond

Whippany, New Jersey
d. Dodington, Sven H(enry Marriott)
d. North, Sterling

Whiteboro, New Jersey
b. Graham, Stedman

Wildwood, New Jersey
b. Corle, Edwin

Willingboro, New Jersey
d. Hawkins, Erskine (Ramsey)

Woodbine, New Jersey
b. Pincus, Gregory

Woodbury, New Jersey
b. Browne, Roscoe Lee

Woodstown, New Jersey
b. Shinn, Everett

NEW MEXICO
b. Coloradas, Mangas
b. Martinez, Maria Montoya
b. McKerrow, Amanda

Alamogordo, New Mexico
b. Clayton, Jan(e Byral)
b. Condon, Edward Uhler
d. Lord, Pauline

Albuquerque, New Mexico
b. Bezos, Jeff
b. Chavez, Linda

Akron, New York
  b. Hull, Clark Leonard

Albany, New York
  b. Ackerman, Harry S
  b. Alston, Theodosia Burr
  b. Baker, Kathy
  b. Bradley, Marion Zimmer
  b. Carter, Mandy
  b. Chestnut, Harold
  b. Conkling, Roscoe
  b. Corning, Erastus, III
  b. DeMoss, Arthur S
  b. Devane, William
  b. Florence, William Jermyn
  b. Fort, Charles Hoy
  b. Groves, Leslie Richard
  b. Hand, Learned
  b. Harte, (Francis) Bret
  b. Henry, Joseph
  b. James, Henry, Sr.
  b. Kennedy, William (Joseph)
  b. Lewis, Edmonia
  b. Lipman, Howard W
  b. Livingston, Philip
  b. Loeb, William
  b. Martin, Homer Dodge
  b. Quinn, Martha
  b. Rooney, Andy
  b. Schuyler, Philip John
  b. Sheridan, Philip Henry
  b. Simons, Howard
  b. Slobodkin, Louis
  b. Smith, Theobald
  b. Streibert, Theodore Cuyler
  b. Van Heusen, John
  b. Winter, Alice Vivian Ames
  b. Yunich, David Lawrence
  d. Alexander, William
  d. Clinton, DeWitt
  d. Corning, Erastus
  d. Diamond, Legs
  d. Elliott, Charles Loring
  d. Evers, Johnny
  d. Funk, Casimir
  d. O'Brien, Leo W
  d. Palmer, Erastus Dow
  d. Paterson, William
  d. Pritikin, Nathan
  d. Schuyler, Philip John
  d. Smith, David
  d. Van Buren, Hannah (Hoes)
  d. Van Rensselaer, Stephen
  d. Woolley, Monty

Albany County, New York
  b. Palmer, Potter
  b. Schoolcraft, Henry Rowe

Alexandria Bay, New York
  d. Exley, Frederick (Earl)

Allegheny, New York
  b. Taylor, Paul

Altmar, New York
  b. Avery, Milton Clark

Amagansett, New York
  d. Roueche, Berton

Amenia, New York
  d. Alajalov, Constantin
  d. Mumford, Lewis

Amenia Union, New York
  b. Holabird, William

Amityville, New York
  b. Mayhew, Richard
  b. Munson, Gorham B(ert)
  d. Barrymore, Maurice
  d. Nash, George Frederick
  d. Wood, Robert Williams

Amsterdam, New York
  b. Douglas, Kirk
  b. Waldron, Hicks Benjamin

Angola, New York
  b. Carrier, Willis Haviland

Annandale, New York
  d. Crittendon, Thomas Leonidas

Arden, New York
  d. Harriman, E(dward) Roland (Noel)

Armonk, New York
  b. Barry, Dave
  d. London, George

Astoria, New York
  b. Brooke, Hillary
  b. Gardner, Ed(ward Francis)
  b. Kelly, Jack
  b. Kenny, Nick
  b. Merman, Ethel
  b. Oerter, Al(fred A)
  d. Gallatin, Albert
  d. Montez, Lola

Auburn, New York
  b. Burroughs, William Seward
  b. Hitchcock, Raymond
  b. Holland, Jerome Heartwell
  b. Miller, Olive Thorne
  b. Osborne, Thomas Mott
  d. Seward, William Henry
  d. Tubman, Harriet Ross

Aurora, New York
  b. Morgan, Lewis Henry

Austerlitz, New York
  d. Millay, Edna St. Vincent

Babylon, New York
  b. Dangerfield, Rodney
  d. Kobbe, Gustav

Bainbridge, New York
  b. Smith, Jedediah Strong

Baldwin, New York
  b. Demme, Jonathan

Ballston Spa, New York
  b. Doubleday, Abner
  d. Marcy, William Learned

Batavia, New York
  b. Brisbane, Albert
  b. Gardner, John Champlin, Jr.

Bay Shore, New York
  b. Peck, Dale

  d. Faversham, William Alfred
  d. Kilgour, Joseph
  d. Markey, Enid
  d. Profaci, Joe
  d. Puzo, Mario

Bayonne, New York
  b. Langella, Frank

Beacon, New York
  b. Forrestal, James Vincent
  b. Lavalle, Paul
  b. Montgomery, Robert Henry
  b. Phelps, Digger
  b. Polhill, Robert
  d. Baekeland, Leo Hendrik

Bearsville, New York
  d. Ballantine, Ian (Keith)

Bedford, New York
  b. Lemon, Ted
  d. Adair, Frank E(arl)
  d. Jay, John
  d. Mankiewicz, Joseph (Leo)
  d. Marshall, E(dda) G(unnar)
  d. Oenslager, Donald Mitchell
  d. Root, Oren
  d. Wilder, Clinton

Bedford Hills, New York
  b. Hughes, Barnard
  d. Frankel, Charles

Beekman, New York
  b. Lossing, Benson John

Bennington, New York
  b. Fraser, Simon

Berne, New York
  b. Bradley, Joseph P
  b. Butterfield, John

Binghamton, New York
  b. Baker, Rick
  b. Casey, Dan(iel Maurice)
  b. Garis, Howard Roger
  b. Herbert, Hugh
  b. Hutton, Jim
  b. Luciano, Ron(ald Michael)
  b. Sharkey, Jack
  d. Link, Edwin Albert
  d. Martin, Billy
  d. Stewart, Slam

Bloomingdale, New York
  b. Renwick, James, Jr.

Blue Point, New York
  d. Booth, Ballington

Bolton Landing, New York
  d. Jacobi, Abraham

Boonville, New York
  b. Edmonds, Walter D(umaux)

Brentwood, New York
  d. Gordon, Kitty

Brewster, New York
  b. Branigan, Laura

Charlotte, New York
b. Henry, Charlotte

Chautauqua County, New York
b. Bidwell, John

Chittenango, New York
b. Baum, L(yman) Frank

Churchville, New York
b. Willard, Frances Elizabeth Caroline

Cicero, New York
b. Gage, Matilda Joslyn

Clarkon, New York
b. Selden, George Baldwin

Claverack, New York
b. Lamont, Thomas William

Clayton, New York
b. Bohlen, Charles Eustis

Clermont, New York
d. Livingston, Robert R

Clinton, New York
b. Britton, Jack
b. Root, Elihu
d. Kirkland, Samuel

Clinton Corners, New York
d. Provensen, Martin

Clinton Hollows, New York
d. Cook, Joe

Cohoes, New York
b. Strout, Richard Lee

Cold Spring, New York
b. Maury, Antonia Caetana De Paiva
　Pereira
d. Butterford, Daniel
d. Fish, Hamilton, III

Cold Spring Harbor, New York
d. Abramson, Harold A(lexander)

Colesville, New York
b. Palmer, Alice Elvira Freeman

College Park, New York
b. Nakian, Reuben

Columbia County, New York
b. Livingston, Edward

Commack, New York
b. O'Donnell, Rosie

Conewaugus, New York
b. Cornplanter
b. Handsome Lake

Connery Pond, New York
d. Simmons, Calvin

Cooperstown, New York
d. Beadle, Erastus Flavel

d. Cooper, James Fenimore
d. Potter, Henry Codman

Corning, New York
b. Eddy, Duane
b. Houghton, Amory
b. Sanger, Margaret
b. Tully, Alice
d. Carder, Frederick

Cornwall, New York
b. Blair, Bonnie Kathleen

Cornwall-on-Hudson, New York
b. Barnes, Djuna
d. Allen, Joel Asaph
d. Roe, Edward Payson

Corona, New York
b. Bleyer, Archie

Cortland, New York
b. Carmer, Carl Lamson
b. Dillon, William A
b. Parker, Alton Brooks
b. Silverman, Sime
b. Sperry, Elmer Ambrose
b. Swing, Raymond Gram
d. Fennelly, Parker W

Crestwood, New York
d. Schmemann, Alexander

Croton-on-Hudson, New York
b. Strauss, Peter
d. Biddle, George
d. Blinn, Holbrook
d. Sands, Dorothy

Cutchogue, New York
b. Moore, Douglas Stuart

Decatur, New York
b. Waterman, Lewis Edson

Delaware County, New York
b. Wheeler, Candace Thurber

Delhi, New York
d. Vandercook, John Womack

Depew, New York
b. Clifton, (Thelma) Lucille

Dobbs Ferry, New York
b. Conklin, Peggy
b. Fix, Paul
b. Poe, James
d. Flesch, Rudolf (Franz)
d. Kerr, Walter F(rancis)
d. Maury, Antonia Caetana De Paiva
　Pereira
d. Sheeler, Charles
d. Villard, Helen Francis Garrison
d. Villard, Henry
d. Wilson, Edward Arthur

Douglaston, New York
d. Ewry, Ray C

Dover Plains, New York
d. Lossing, Benson John

Dresden, New York
b. Ingersoll, Robert Green

Dunkirk, New York
b. Adams, Samuel Hopkins

East Aurora, New York
d. Price, Irving L

East Durham, New York
b. Dearie, Blossom

East Hampton, New York
b. Beecher, Catharine (Esther)
d. Bernstein, Felicia Montealegre
d. Bronowski, Jacob
d. deKooning, Willem
d. Dooley, Rae
d. Gaddis, William (Thomas)
d. Hassam, Childe
d. Heller, Joseph
d. Jacobs, Helen (Hull)
d. Lardner, Ring(gold Wilmer), Sr.
d. Pollock, Jackson

East Harlem, New York
b. Fernandez, Joseph

East Islip, New York
d. Kibbee, Guy

East Meadow, New York
b. Morrison, Sterling
b. Viola, Frank John, Jr.

Eaton, New York
b. Judson, Emily Chubbock

Elizabethtown, New York
d. Blakelock, Ralph Albert
d. Fisk, James Brown

Elmhurst, New York
b. Casey, William Joseph
d. Pastor, Tony
d. Ryder, Albert Pinkham

Elmira, New York
b. Collins, Eileen
b. Fitch, (William) Clyde
b. Griffes, Charles Tomlinson
b. Hilfiger, Tommy
b. Holladay, Wilhelmina Cole
b. Lawes, Lewis Edward
b. Pirro, Jeanine (Ferris)
b. Roach, Hal
b. Waterfield, Bob
d. Beecher, Catharine (Esther)
d. Eglevsky, Andre

Elmsford, New York
b. Turnesa, Jim
d. Shrady, Henry M
d. Turnesa, Jim

Endicott, New York
b. Hart, Johnny
b. Paglia, Camille
d. Luciano, Ron(ald Michael)

Euphrates, New York
b. Simmons, Zalmon G

Hartsdale, New York
d. Booth, Evangeline Cory

Hartwick, New York
b. Bissell, Melville Reuben
d. Butterfield, Roger Place

Hastings-on-Hudson, New York
b. Lake, Ricki
d. Draper, John William
d. Hine, Lewis Wickes

Hauppauge, New York
d. Brokenshire, Norman

Haverstraw, New York
b. Heindorf, Ray
b. Hewitt, Abram Stevens

Hawthorne, New York
d. Lathrop, Rose Hawthorne

Hempstead, New York
b. Knight, Hilary
b. Murphy, Eddie
b. Wright, Robert C
d. Earle, Alice Morse
d. Hudson, Walter

Hempstead Township, New York
b. Hicks, Elias

Henderson, New York
b. Burnham, Daniel H(udson)
b. Charles, Glen
b. Crittenton, Charles Nelson
b. Peck, George Wilbur

Henrietta, New York
b. Blackwell, Antoinette Louisa Brown

Herkimer, New York
b. Alpert, Hollis
b. Ambers, Lou
b. Herkimer, Nicholas

Hicksville, New York
b. Joel, Billy

Highland, New York
b. Hunter, Glenn

Highland Falls, New York
b. Dickey, Herbert Spencer
b. Durning, Charles
d. Corbin, Margaret Cochran
d. Warner, Susan Bogert

Hillsdale, New York
d. Jenkins, Newell

Hollis, New York
d. Fiske, Minnie Maddern

Homer, New York
b. Bloomer, Amelia Jenks
b. Carpenter, Francis Bicknell
b. White, Andrew Dickson

Hoosick Falls, New York
b. Carey, William F
b. Eberle, Ray

d. Moses, Grandma

Hopewell, New York
b. Flagler, Henry Morrison
b. Walker, Edyth

Hornell, New York
b. Murphy, Thomas Aquinas

Huddersfield, New York
b. Kitson, Henry Hudson

Hudson, New York
b. Lear, Frances
d. Church, Frederick Edwin
d. Ficke, Arthur Davidson
d. Lewenthal, Raymond
d. Shaver, Dorothy

Hughsonville, New York
d. Gorman, Herbert Sherman

Hunter, New York
d. Jabotinsky, Vladimir Evgenevich

Huntington, New York
b. Grumman, Leroy Randle
b. Heckscher, August
b. McGuire, Dick
d. Coltrane, Trane
d. Davenport, Charles Benedict
d. Dove, Arthur Garfield
d. Plimpton, Francis Taylor Pearson
d. Reed, Stanley Forman
d. Stimson, Henry Lewis
d. Thomas, Norman Mattoon
d. Varipapa, Andy
d. Waller, Fred(erick)

Hurleyville, New York
b. Kamen, Milt

Hyde Park, New York
b. Roosevelt, Anna Eleanor
b. Roosevelt, Franklin D(elano)
b. Roosevelt, John Aspinal
d. Bard, John
d. Roosevelt, Sara Delano

Indian Falls, New York
b. Parker, Ely Samuel

Irvington, New York
b. Morgan, J(ohn) P(ierpont), Jr.

Irvington-on-Hudson, New York
d. Tiffany, Charles Lewis
d. Walker, C. J., Madame

Islip, New York
b. Brace, Gerald Warner

Ithaca, New York
b. Cole, Kenneth Stewart
b. Dean, Arthur H(obson)
b. French, Robert T
b. Fuertes, Louis Agassiz
b. Geller, Margaret J(oan)
b. Haley, Alex (Murray Palmer)
b. Hayes, Alfred
b. Jensen, Oliver Ormerod
b. Kane, Robert Joseph
d. Allen, Arthur Augustus

d. Bailey, Liberty Hyde
d. Becker, Carl Lotus
d. Comstock, John Henry
d. Cornell, Ezra
d. Debye, Peter Joseph William
d. Dillon, William A
d. Jagendorf, Moritz Adolf
d. Kane, Robert Joseph
d. Malott, Deane W(aldo)
d. Morgana, Nina
d. Redding, Jay Saunders
d. Titchener, Edward Bradford
d. White, Andrew Dickson
d. Wilson, Robert R(athbun)

Jackson Heights, New York
b. Casey, Robert P
b. Dobson, Kevin
d. Kane, Helen

Jamaica, New York
b. Beamon, Bob
b. Breslin, Jimmy
b. Egan, Walter Lindsay
b. Shire, Talia Rose Coppola
d. King, Rufus
d. Tristano, Leonard Joseph

Jamestown, New York
b. Arisman, Marshall
b. Ball, Lucille (Desiree)
b. Goodell, Charles Ellsworth
b. Harvey, Hayward Augustus
b. Merchant, Natalie
b. Peterson, Roger Tory
d. Schlamme, Martha

Jericho, New York
d. Chapin, Harry Foster
d. Hicks, Elias

Johnson City, New York
b. Platt, Lewis E

Johnstown, New York
b. Stanton, Elizabeth Cady
d. Johnson, William, Sir

Katonah, New York
d. Delaney, Jack

Keeseville, New York
b. Ferril, Thomas Hornsby
b. Jackson, William Henry

Kew Gardens, New York
b. Van Patten, Dick Vincent

Kinderhook, New York
b. Van Buren, Hannah (Hoes)
b. Van Buren, Martin
d. Van Buren, Martin

Kingston, New York
b. Bogdanovich, Peter
b. Craft, Robert
b. Flemming, Arthur S(herwood)
b. Freer, Charles Lang
b. Hutton, Robert
b. Petersham, Maud
b. Vanderlyn, John
d. Darrell, R(obert) D(onaldson)
d. Gibson, Walter B(rown)
d. Kesselring, Joseph Otto

d. Landi, Elissa
d. Loring, Eugene
d. Vanderlyn, John

Knapps Creek, New York
b. Piper, William Thomas

La Fargeville, New York
b. Lawrenson, Helen Brown

Lackawanna, New York
b. Jaworski, Ron(ald Vincent)

Lake George, New York
b. Irish, Ned
d. Eggleston, Edward
d. Owen, Robert Dale

Lake Placid, New York
b. Wood, Craig Ralph
d. Collins, Ted
d. Grinkov, Sergei

Lancaster, New York
b. Thompson, Dorothy

Lansingburgh, New York
b. Kelly, King

Larchmont, New York
b. Schaefer, Rudolph Jay
d. Armour, Tommy
d. Drew, Louisa Lane
d. Harrington, Michael

Lawrence, New York
b. Auchincloss, Louis
d. Laffan, William Mackay

Le Roy, New York
b. Costanza, Midge

Lew Beach, New York
d. Lazare, Kaplan

Liberty, New York
b. Lasky, Victor
d. Attell, Abe B

Lido Beach, New York
b. Rubin, Rick

Lima, New York
b. Keating, Kenneth B
b. Raymond, Henry Jarvis

Lindenhurst, New York
b. Barry, Jack
b. Hartley, Hal

Little Britain, New York
b. Clinton, DeWitt
b. Clinton, George
b. Clinton, James

Little Falls, New York
b. Gerstenberg, Richard Charles
b. Riccardo, John Joseph
d. Herkimer, Nicholas

Livingston, New York
b. Woolsey, Janette

Livingston Manor, New York
b. Mott, John Raleigh

Lockport, New York
b. Alexis, Kim
b. Hobart, Alice Tisdale Nourse
b. Marsh, Othniel Charles
b. Miller, William E
b. Oates, Joyce Carol
b. Raskob, John J

Locust Grove, New York
b. Bailey, Florence Augusta Merriam

Locust Valley, New York
d. Lovett, Robert A(bercrombie)
d. Revere, Anne

Lomontville, New York
d. Rounds, David

Long Beach, New York
b. Crystal, Billy
d. Atlas, Charles

Long Branch, New York
d. Walker, A'lelia

Long Island, New York
b. Bloom, Eric
b. Bouchard, Joe
b. Capriati, Jennifer
b. Cooke, Donald
b. DeFrank, Vincent
b. Downey, Rick
b. Galvin, Martin
b. Gomez, Thomas
b. Kaufman, Sue
b. Lanier, Allen
b. Longworth, Alice Roosevelt
b. Macchio, Ralph George, Jr.
b. Roeser, Donald
b. Shante
b. Stevens, Eileen
b. Straight, Beatrice Whitney
b. Tartikoff, Brandon
b. Taylor, Cecil Percival
b. Whitfield, Mark
b. York, David
d. Atterbury, Grosvenor
d. Colden, Cadwallader
d. Coolidge, Charles Allerton
d. Goulding, Ray(mond Walter)
d. Hutchinson, Anne
d. Johnson, William Henry
d. Mantle, (Robert) Burns
d. McClintock, Barbara
d. Moore, Victor
d. Muhlenberg, William Augustus
d. Rea, Gardner
d. Somogi, Judith
d. Vought, Chance Milton
d. Whittemore, Arthur Austin
d. Williams, Cootie
d. Wittgenstein, Paul
d. Wodehouse, P(elham) G(renville)
d. Yon, Pietro Alessandro

Lowville, New York
b. Arthur, Joseph Charles

Lucerne, New York
b. Allyson, June

Lynbrook, New York
b. Keeshan, Bob

Lyndonville, New York
b. Butterfield, Lyman Henry
b. Butterfield, Roger Place

Madison Barracks, New York
b. Clark, Mark Wayne

Mahapac, New York
b. Laoretti, Larry

Malba, New York
b. Frankenheimer, John Michael

Malone, New York
b. Mould, Bob
b. Wheeler, William Alrnon
d. Wheeler, William Alrnon

Mamaroneck, New York
b. Sheehy, Gail Henion
b. Wood, James Rushmore
d. Kirstein, George G
d. Skouras, Spyros Panagiotes

Manhasset, New York
b. Grace, J(oseph) Peter, Jr.
d. Adams, Stanley
d. Benzell, Mimi
d. Buck, Gene
d. Cordier, Andrew Wellington
d. Gropper, William
d. Grumman, Leroy Randle
d. Hass, H(enry) B(ohn)
d. Julia, Raul
d. Levitt, William J(aird)
d. Maurer, Emilia Sherman
d. Musial, Joe
d. Siegmeister, Elie
d. Treacher, Arthur
d. Weisgall, Hugo (David)
d. White, Josh(ua Daniel)
d. Whitney, John Hay

Manlius, New York
d. Hillcourt, William

Marbletown, New York
b. Helmsley, Leona Mindy Rosenthal

Marlboro, New York
d. Goudy, Frederic William

Martinsburg, New York
b. Hunt, Walter

Massapequa, New York
b. Baldwin, Alec
b. Baldwin, Stephen
b. Baldwin, William
b. Buttafuoco, Joey
b. Hahn, Jessica
b. Powers, Brian M
b. Snider, Dee
d. Brennan, Peter J(oseph)
d. Gambino, Carlo

Massena, New York
b. Deshaies, Jim

Mechanicville, New York
b. Eberle, Bob

Menands, New York
b. Deukmejian, George

Merrick, New York
b. Gibson, Deborah (Ann)

Middleburg, New York
b. Brayman, Harold

Middletown, New York
d. Kiley, Richard (Paul)
d. Peterson, Edith R.
d. Seredy, Kate

Milbrook, New York
d. Lloyd-Jones, Esther McDonald

Mill Neck, New York
d. DeGraff, Robert F(air)
d. Vanderbilt, Alfred G(wynne)

Millertown, New York
b. Collins, Eddie

Mineola, New York
b. Brannigan, Bill
b. Bruce, Lenny
b. Forman, James Douglas
b. Gerstner, Lou
b. Gerstner, Louis Vincent, Jr.
b. Studds, Gerry E(astman)
d. Barton, James
d. Damon, Ralph Shepard
d. Ford, Paul
d. Sawchuk, Terry
d. Terry, Sonny

Mineville, New York
b. Kelly, Walter C

Minoa, New York
b. Costello, Larry

Montauk Point, New York
d. Greene, Balcomb

Monticello, New York
d. Hayes, Patrick Joseph, Cardinal
d. Lapchick, Joe

Montrose, New York
d. Thorndike, Edward L(ee)

Moreau, New York
d. Winsten, Archer

Morrisania, New York
b. Morris, Gouverneur
b. Morris, Lewis
b. Rutherfurd, Lewis Morris
d. Morris, Gouverneur
d. Morris, Lewis

Mount Kisco, New York
b. Blyth, Ann Marie
b. Eisner, Michael Dammann
b. Halstead, William S
b. Jenner, Bruce
b. MacLeod, Gavin

b. Schneider, John
b. Sulzberger, Arthur O(chs), Jr.
d. Balchen, Bernt
d. Burger, Carl Victor
d. Cerf, Bennett Alfred
d. Crowther, Bosley
d. Davis, Rebecca Blaine Harding
d. Davis, Richard Harding
d. O'Dell, Scott
d. Rinkoff, Barbara Jean
d. Wallace, DeWitt
d. Wallace, Lila Bell Acheson

Mount McGregor, New York
d. Grant, Ulysses Simpson

Mount Morris, New York
b. Powell, John Wesley

Mount Vernon, New York
b. Becker, Stephen David
b. Branca, Ralph Theodore Joseph
b. Buchwald, Art(hur)
b. Carney, Art
b. Clark, Dick
b. Conway, Lynn Ann
b. Harris, Mark
b. Marks, Johnny
b. Moshacher, Robert Adam
b. Schawlow, Arthur L(eonard)
b. Shabazz, Attallah
b. Thomopoulos, Anthony Denis
b. Washington, Denzel, Jr.
b. White, E(lwyn) B(rooks)
b. Williams, Gus
d. Bailey, James Anthony
d. Delany, Annie Elizabeth
d. Hess, Victor Francis
d. Kurtzman, Harvey

Neponsit, New York
d. Levenson, Sam(uel)

New Berlin, New York
b. Burlingame, Anson

New Egypt, New York
b. Dancer, Stanley

New Hyde Park, New York
d. Holzman, Red

New Lebanon, New York
b. Tilden, Samuel Jones

New Milford, New York
d. Fisher, Avery

New Paltz, New York
d. Tschirky, Oscar

New Rochelle, New York
b. Agar, Herbert Sebastian
b. Baldwin, Faith
b. Branley, Franklyn Mansfield
b. Castle, Irene Foote
b. Chew, Peter
b. Denver, Bob
b. Dillon, Kevin
b. Dillon, Matt
b. Faneuil, Peter
b. Foy, Eddie, Jr.
b. Gelb, Leslie Howard
b. Lantz, Walter

b. Leno, Jay
b. McLean, Don
b. Menken, Alan
b. Morrow, Rob
b. Oppen, George
b. Raymond, Alex(ander Gillespie)
b. Roundtree, Richard
b. Sangster, Margaret Elizabeth
b. Schell, Orville H, Jr.
b. Sherwood, Robert Emmet
b. Tower, Joan Peabody
b. Weir, Robert W
d. Bassett, Ben
d. Catt, Carrie Chapman
d. Cook, Frederick Albert
d. Courant, Richard
d. Crean, Robert
d. Crichton, Robert
d. Fry, Franklin Clark
d. Hamilton, Roy
d. Jonas, Hans
d. Leyendecker, Joseph Christian
d. McGraw, John Joseph
d. Opper, Frederick Burr
d. Patterson, Frederick Douglass
d. Primus, Pearl
d. Richardson, Scovel
d. Rothstein, Arthur
d. Shimkin, Leon
d. Wank, Roland A
d. Wertheimer, Max
d. West, James Edward
d. Willis, Paul S
d. Wilson, Malcolm

New Windsor, New York
b. Roe, Edward Payson

New York, New York
b. Abbe, Cleveland
b. Abbott, Gregory
b. Abdul-Jabbar, Kareem
b. Abplanalp, Robert H
b. Abrahams, Doris Cole
b. Abrams, Elliott
b. Abramson, Harold A(lexander)
b. Abzug, Bella (Savitsky)
b. Adams, Brooke
b. Adams, Cindy
b. Adams, Don
b. Adams, James Truslow
b. Adams, Joey
b. Adams, Leonie Fuller
b. Adams, Mason
b. Addabbo, Joseph Patrick
b. Addison, Adele
b. Adler, Buddy
b. Adler, Irving
b. Adler, Luther
b. Adler, Mortimer J(erome)
b. Adler, Richard
b. Adler, Stella
b. Agostini, Peter
b. Aiello, Danny Louis, Jr.
b. Aitken, Hugh
b. Albert, Stephen Joel
b. Alda, Alan
b. Alda, Robert
b. Aldridge, Ira Frederick
b. Alexander, Clifford L, Jr.
b. Alexander, Denise
b. Alexander, Shana
b. Alexander, William
b. Alfred, William
b. Allen, Irwin
b. Allen, Nancy

b. Allen, Steve
b. Allen, Woody
b. Alt, Carol
b. Altman, Benjamin
b. Alvardo, Trini(dad)
b. Alvarez, Julia
b. Alzado, Lyle Martin
b. Amen, Irving
b. Ames, Bruce N(athan)
b. Anderson, Alexander
b. Anderson, Carl David
b. Anderson, Elizabeth Milbank
b. Anderson, Robert Woodruff
b. Anderson, Warner
b. Andrews, Tige
b. Angell, Roger
b. Anhalt, Edward
b. Anson, Jay
b. Anspach, Susan
b. Anthony, Edward
b. Anthony, John J(ason)
b. Aptheker, Herbert
b. Apuzzo, Virginia M.
b. Arbus, Diane
b. Archerd, Army
b. Archibald, Nate
b. Aretsky, Ken
b. Arkin, Alan Wolf
b. Armstrong, Edwin Howard
b. Armstrong, Hamilton Fish
b. Arno, Peter
b. Arnold, Danny
b. Arnold, Edward
b. Arquette, Patricia
b. Arquette, Rosanna
b. Arrow, Kenneth Joseph
b. Arroyo, Martina
b. Arthur, Beatrice
b. Arthur, Robert
b. Assante, Armand
b. Astor, William Vincent
b. Astor, William Waldorf Astor,
    Viscount
b. Auberjonois, Rene Murat
b. Auerbach, Red
b. August, Jan
b. Auletta, Robert
b. Austin, Patti
b. Avakian, Aram A
b. Avallone, Michael Angelo, Jr.
b. Avedon, Richard
b. Avery, Samuel Putnam
b. Axelrod, George
b. Axelrod, Julius
b. Axthelm, Pete(r Macrae)
b. Azenberg, Emanuel
b. Bacall, Lauren
b. Bach, Barbara
b. Bache, Harold Leopold
b. Bache, Jules Sermon
b. Baez, Joan
b. Baillie, Hugh
b. Baio, Scott Vincent
b. Baird, Bill
b. Baird, Cora Eisenberg
b. Baker, Belle
b. Baker, Blanche
b. Baker, Theodore
b. Bald, Kenneth
b. Baldwin, James (Arthur)
b. Balin, Ina
b. Ballantine, Ian (Keith)
b. Balsam, Martin Henry
b. Baltimore, David
b. Balukas, Jean
b. Bambara, Toni Cade

b. Bancroft, Anne
b. Banning, Kendall
b. Barad, Jill E(likann)
b. Barbera, Joseph Roland
b. Barkin, Ellen
b. Barnet, Charlie
b. Barnet, Sylvan M., Jr.
b. Baron, Samuel
b. Barr, William Pelham
b. Barrett, Rona
b. Barrett, William Christopher
b. Barrett, William Edmund
b. Barry, Gene
b. Barrymore, Diana
b. Barthelmess, Richard
b. Basquiat, Jean-Michel
b. Bass, Saul
b. Bassett, Angela
b. Bavier, Frances
b. Beard, Peter Hill
b. Beasley, Allyce
b. Beatty, Alfred Chester, Sir
b. Beatty, Jim
b. Beck, Julian
b. Beckford, Tyson
b. Beckman, Johnny
b. Bedelia, Bonnie
b. Beebe, William
b. Beery, Noah, Jr.
b. Begelman, David
b. Beilenson, Edna Rudolph
b. Belafonte, Harry, Jr.
b. Belafonte, Shari
b. Belinsky, Bo
b. Bell, Arthur (Irving)
b. Bell, Daniel
b. Bellwood, Pamela
b. Belmont, August, Jr.
b. Benaderet, Bea
b. Benarde, Melvin Albert
b. Benatar, Pat
b. Benchley, Peter Bradford
b. Bendick, Jeanne
b. Bendix, William
b. Benedict, Ruth (Fulton)
b. Benjamin, Richard
b. Bennett, Constance Campbell
b. Bennett, James Gordon, Jr.
b. Bennett, Tony
b. Bennett, William John
b. Benzer, Seymour
b. Bereano, Nancy K(irp)
b. Berenson, Marisa
b. Berg, Gertrude
b. Berg, Paul
b. Berger, Arthur
b. Berger, Marilyn
b. Berger, Melvin H
b. Berger, Meyer
b. Berger, Terry
b. Bergh, Henry
b. Bergman, Alan
b. Bergman, Jules Verne
b. Bergman, Marilyn Keith
b. Berkowitz, Bob
b. Berkowitz, David
b. Berkowitz, Joan B.
b. Berle, Milton
b. Berle, Peter A. A.
b. Berlenbach, Paul
b. Berlinger, Warren
b. Berlitz, Charles L Frambach
b. Berman, Emile Zola
b. Bernardi, Hershel
b. Bernbach, William
b. Berndt, Walter

b. Bernhard, Arnold
b. Bernie, Ben
b. Bernstein, Alice Frankau
b. Bernstein, Elmer
b. Bernstein, Robert L(ouis)
b. Bernstein, Theodore Menline
b. Berresford, Susan Vail
b. Berrill, Jack
b. Bessie, Alvah
b. Bester, Alfred
b. Bevilacqua, Anthony Joseph,
    Cardinal
b. Biaggi, Mario
b. Bichler, Joyce
b. Bikoff, James L
b. Biller, Moe
b. Billy the Kid
b. Birch, Stephen
b. Birdseye, Clarence Frank
b. Bishop, Joey
b. Bishop, Katharine Scott
b. Black, David (Jay)
b. Black, Walter J
b. Black, William
b. Blackton, Jay S
b. Blackwell, Betsy Talbot
b. Blackwell, Mr. (Richard)
b. Blaikie, William
b. Blakelock, Ralph Albert
b. Blashfield, Edwin Howland
b. Blatchford, Samuel
b. Blatty, William Peter
b. Bleckner, Jeff
b. Bleeth, Yasmine
b. Bleiberg, Robert Marvin
b. Blige, Mary J(ane)
b. Bloch, Bertram
b. Blondell, Joan
b. Bloom, Harold
b. Bloom, Julius
b. Bloom, Mickey
b. Bloom, Murray Teigh
b. Bloomgarden, Kermit
b. Bloomingdale, Alfred S
b. Bloomingdale, Joseph Bernard
b. Bloomingdale, Samuel
b. Bloustein, Edward J.
b. Blumberg, Baruch Samuel
b. Bochco, Steven Ronald
b. Boehm, Helen
b. Bofill, Angela
b. Bogart, Humphrey de Forest
b. Bogart, Neil
b. Bogert, Tim
b. Bologna, Joseph
b. Boni, Albert
b. Bonilla, Bobby
b. Boosler, Elayne
b. Booth, Charles Brandon
b. Booth, Shirley
b. Borch, Fred J.
b. Boskin, Michael J(ay)
b. Boudin, Kathy
b. Bourgholtzer, Frank
b. Bourke-White, Margaret
b. Bow, Clara Gordon
b. Bowe, Riddick (Lamont)
b. Bowles, Jane Sydney
b. Bowles, Paul (Frederick)
b. Boxer, Barbara Levy
b. Boyd, John W., Jr.
b. Bracken, Eddie
b. Braddock, Jim
b. Brady, Alice
b. Brady, Diamond Jim
b. Brady, James Winston

b. Brady, Nicholas Frederick
b. Brady, Scott
b. Brandon, Barbara
b. Branner, Martin Michael
b. Brasher, Rex
b. Braslau, Sophie
b. Bray, Charles William, III
b. Breese, Edmund
b. Brennan, Peter J(oseph)
b. Brenner, Barbara Johnes
b. Brian, David
b. Brice, Fanny
b. Brigati, Eddie
b. Brisebois, Danielle
b. Bristow, Lonnie
b. Brock, Alice May
b. Brockington, John Stanley
b. Broderick, Matthew
b. Brody, Jane Ellen
b. Bronfman, Edgar Miles, Jr.
b. Bronk, Detlev Wulf
b. Brook, Alexander
b. Brooks, Donald Marc
b. Brooks, Geraldine
b. Brooks, Mel
b. Brooks, Ronald E.
b. Brothers, Joyce Diane Bauer
b. Broun, Heywood Hale
b. Broun, (Matthew) Heywood
    (Campbell)
b. Brown, David
b. Brown, Harold
b. Brown, Kenneth H
b. Brown, Larry
b. Brown, Margaret Wise
b. Brown, Michael Stuart
b. Brown, Tom
b. Browne, Dik
b. Browne, Leslie
b. Brownmiller, Susan
b. Bruner, Jerome Seymour
b. Brustein, Robert Sanford
b. Buchalter, Lepke
b. Buckley, Charles Anthony
b. Buckley, Christopher (Taylor)
b. Buckley, Emerson
b. Buckley, James Lane
b. Buckley, William Frank, Jr.
b. Buechner, Frederick
b. Bunny, John
b. Bunting, Mary Ingraham
b. Burke, Christopher
b. Burns, David
b. Burns, George
b. Burns, Ken(neth Lauren)
b. Burnshaw, Stanley
b. Burrows, Abe
b. Buscemi, Steve
b. Busch, Charles
b. Busch, Niven
b. Bush, Barbara (Pierce)
b. Bushkin, Joe
b. Bushmiller, Ernie
b. Busta Rhymes
b. Butler, Robert N(eil)
b. Buttons, Red
b. Butts, Calvin O(tis), III
b. Buzzell, Eddie
b. Bynner, Harold Witter
b. Byrd, Michelle
b. Byrnes, Edd
b. Caan, James
b. Cadmus, Paul
b. Caesar, Adolph
b. Caesar, Irving
b. Cagney, James

b. Cagney, Jeanne
b. Cahill, Marie
b. Cahn, Sammy
b. Caidin, Martin
b. Calderone, Frank Anthony
b. Calderone, Mary Steichen
b. Calhern, Louis
b. Califano, Joseph Anthony, Jr.
b. Calisher, Hortense
b. Callas, Charlie
b. Callas, Maria
b. Callender, Clive O(rville)
b. Cambridge, Godfrey
b. Cameron, Roderick W
b. Campanella, Joseph Mario
b. Campbell, Joseph
b. Campo, John(ny)
b. Canfield, Cass
b. Cannon, Jimmy
b. Cantor, Eddie
b. Caples, John
b. Capone, Al(phonse)
b. Cara, Irene (Escalera)
b. Carberry, John J(oseph)
b. Carcaterra, Lorenzo
b. Cardozo, Benjamin Nathan
b. Carey, Ernestine Moller Gilbreth
b. Carey, Harry
b. Carey, Hugh Leo
b. Carey, Mariah
b. Carlin, George Dennis
b. Carlino, Lewis John
b. Carlisle, Kevin
b. Carlos, John
b. Carlson, Arne Helge
b. Carmel, Roger C
b. Carnesseca, Lou
b. Caro, Robert A
b. Carr, Caleb
b. Carradine, John
b. Carroll, Diahann
b. Carroll, Jim
b. Carroll, Nancy
b. Carroll, Vinnette
b. Carson, Mindy
b. Carter, Benny
b. Carter, Elliott Cook, Jr.
b. Carter, Jack
b. Cartwright, Alexander Joy, Jr.
b. Caruso, David
b. Casablancas, John(ny)
b. Cassavetes, John
b. Cassidy, David Bruce
b. Cassidy, Jack
b. Castellano, Richard
b. Castle, William
b. Caston, Saul
b. Cates, Gilbert
b. Cates, Joseph
b. Cates, Phoebe
b. Cavallaro, Carmen
b. Celler, Emanuel
b. Cerf, Bennett Alfred
b. Chaikin, Joseph
b. Chaikin, Sol Chick
b. Chamberlin, William Henry
b. Chambers, Robert W
b. Chan, June
b. Chandler, Jeff
b. Channing, Stockard
b. Chapin, F(rancis) Stuart
b. Chapin, Harry Foster
b. Chapin, Schuyler Garrison
b. Chaplin, Saul
b. Chapman, Ceil
b. Charlip, Remy

b. Charnin, Martin
b. Chartoff, Robert
b. Chase, Ilka
b. Chasins, Abram
b. Chast, Roz
b. Chatterton, Ruth
b. Chayefsky, Paddy
b. Chenault, Kenneth I
b. Cherne, Leo
b. Chideya, Farai (Nduu)
b. Chisholm, Shirley Anita St. Hill
b. Chodorov, Edward
b. Chodorov, Jerome
b. Chomsky, Marvin
b. Churchill, Jennie Jerome
b. Chwast, Seymour
b. Cimino, Michael
b. Cisneros, Eleanora
b. Clark, Dane
b. Clark, Mary Higgins
b. Clark, Patrick
b. Clarke, Gilmore David
b. Clarke, Shirley
b. Clay, Andrew Dice
b. Clayburgh, Jill
b. Clayton, Lou
b. Cleland, Thomas Maitland
b. Cleveland, James Harlan
b. Clinchy, Everett Ross
b. Clinton, Larry
b. Clurman, Harold Edgar
b. Cobb, Lee J
b. Cobb, Vicki
b. Coco, James Emil
b. Coffin, Henry Sloane
b. Coffin, William Sloan, Jr.
b. Cohen, Alexander H
b. Cohen, Ben(nett)
b. Cohen, Mickey
b. Cohen, Stanley
b. Cohn, Al
b. Cohn, Edwin Joseph
b. Cohn, Harry
b. Cohn, Roy (Marcus)
b. Cohn, Zanvil (Alexander)
b. Colavito, Rocky
b. Cole, Kenneth Reese
b. Coleman, Cy
b. Colfax, Schuyler
b. Collier, William, Sr.
b. Collins, Ted
b. Collyer, Bud
b. Colombo, Joseph Anthony
b. Colwin, Laurie
b. Combs, Sean
b. Comden, Betty
b. Commoner, Barry
b. Conaway, Jeff
b. Condon, Richard (Thomas)
b. Connors, Chuck
b. Conrad, Con
b. Conrad, Michael
b. Conroy, Frank
b. Conwell, Esther Marly
b. Cook, Blanche Wiesen
b. Cook, Robin
b. Cooke, Terence James
b. Cooney, Barbara
b. Cooney, Gerry
b. Cooper, Leon Neil
b. Cooper, Lester Irving
b. Cooper, Peter
b. Coots, J Fred
b. Copeland, Jo
b. Copland, Aaron
b. Coplon, Judith

b. Coppola, Carmine
b. Corcos, Lucille
b. Corey, Irwin
b. Corey, Jeff
b. Corigliano, John (Paul)
b. Cornell, Don
b. Corsaro, Frank
b. Corso, Gregory Nunzio
b. Cortissoz, Royal
b. Coryell, John Russell
b. Coslow, Sam
b. Costas, Bob
b. Cousy, Bob
b. Cowan, Jerome
b. Cowen, Joshua Lionel
b. Cowings, Patricia S.
b. Cowles, Fleur Fenton
b. Cox, Allyn
b. Cox, Richard Joseph
b. Crabtree, Lotta
b. Crane, Nathalia Clara Ruth
b. Crapsey, Adelaide
b. Crawford, Thomas
b. Creston, Paul
b. Criss, Peter
b. Crist, Judith Klein
b. Crocker, Chester Arthur
b. Crohn, Burrill Bernard
b. Croly, Herbert David
b. Crosby, Floyd Delafield
b. Crosby, John
b. Crosby, Percy L
b. Cross, Milton John
b. Crouse, Lindsay Ann
b. Crummell, Alexander
b. Cukor, George (Dewey)
b. Culkin, Macaulay
b. Cullen, Countee (Porter)
b. Cunningham, Billy
b. Cuomo, Mario Matthew
b. Curran, Joseph Edwin
b. Currie, Barton Wood
b. Curtis, Tony
b. Dailey, Dan
b. Dailey, Irene
b. Dale, Alan
b. Dale, Chester
b. Daley, Arthur (John)
b. Dall, John
b. Dallis, Nicholas Peter
b. Daly, Arnold
b. Daly, Timothy
b. D'Amato, Alfonse Marcello
b. Damon, Stuart
b. Damone, Vic
b. Dana, Viola
b. Danelli, Dino
b. Danes, Claire
b. Danielian, Leon
b. Daniels, William
b. Dannay, Frederic
b. Dante, Nicholas
b. Danton, Ray(mond)
b. Danza, Tony
b. D'Arby, Terence Trent
b. Darin, Bobby
b. Darion, Joseph
b. Darken, Lawrence Stamper
b. Darnton, Robert Choate
b. Darrow, Henry
b. Dash, Julie
b. Davenport, Harry George Bryant
b. Davenport, Marcia
b. David, Hal
b. David, Mack
b. Davidson, Jo

b. Davies, Marion
b. Davis, Alexander Jackson
b. Davis, Clive Jay
b. Davis, Martin S.
b. Davis, Sammy, Jr.
b. Davis, Tommy, Jr.
b. Dawkins, Wayne J(esse)
b. Day, Clarence Shepard, Jr.
b. Day, Dennis
b. Day, Dorothy
b. Day, Joseph Paul
b. Dean, Howard
b. Dean, Man Mountain
b. DeCamp, L(yon) Sprague
b. DeCarava, Roy
b. DeCordoba, Pedro
b. DeCordova, Frederick Timmins
b. Defeo, Ronald
b. DeForest, Calvert
b. Dehner, John Forkum
b. Dehnert, Henry
b. Dekker, Albert
b. DeKooning, Elaine Marie Catherine
   Fried
b. Delacorte, George Thomas, Jr.
b. Delany, Dana
b. Delany, Samuel R.
b. DeLillo, Don
b. DellaFemina, Jerry
b. Dello Joio, Norman Joseph
b. Dell'Olio, Louis
b. Delmar, Vina Croter
b. DeLong, George Washington
b. DeLuise, Dom
b. D'Emilio, John
b. DeMille, Agnes (George)
b. Deming, Barbara
b. DeNiro, Robert
b. Denoff, Sam
b. Densen-Gerber, Judianne
b. DePaul, Gene Vincent
b. DeRose, Peter
b. Dershowitz, Alan M
b. DeSapio, Carmine Gerard
b. DeSylva, Buddy
b. Deutsch, Babette
b. Deutsch, Helen
b. DeValera, Eamon
b. DeVita, Vincent Theodore, Jr.
b. De Vorzon, Barry
b. DeVries, William Castle
b. DeWilde, Brandon
b. Diamond, Neil
b. Dibbs, Eddie
b. Dietz, Howard M
b. Dillon, Leo
b. Dion
b. DiSalle, Michael Vincent
b. Dixon, Dean
b. Dixon, Ivan
b. Dixon, Mort
b. Dobkin, Alix
b. Doctorow, E(dgar) L(aurence)
b. Dodge, Grace Hoadley
b. Dodge, Mary Elizabeth Mapes
b. Dodson, Owen (Vincent)
b. Donahue, Troy
b. Donahue, Woolworth
b. Donaldson, Walter
b. Donleavy, James Patrick
b. Donohue, Jack
b. Donovan, Art(hur, Jr.)
b. Donovan, Arthur
b. Donovan, King
b. Dorfman, Dan
b. Dorne, Albert

b. Doubleday, Frank Nelson
b. Doubleday, Nelson
b. Douglas, Amanda Minnie
b. Douglas, Donald Willis
b. Downey, Robert, Jr.
b. Downs, Johnny
b. Drake, Alfred
b. Drake, Joseph Rodman
b. Drake, Stan(ley Albert)
b. Drake, Tom
b. Draper, Dorothy Tuckerman
b. Draper, Ruth
b. Drescher, Fran
b. Dresselhaus, Mildred S(piewak)
b. Drexler, Millard S
b. Drexler, Rosalyn
b. Dreyfuss, Henry
b. Dreyfuss, Richard (Stephan)
b. Drucker, Daniel Charles
b. Drury, James
b. Dryden, Spencer
b. Dryfoos, Orvil Eugene
b. Duberman, Martin
b. DuBois, Guy Pene
b. Duchin, Peter Oelrichs
b. Duchovny, David
b. Duffy, Ben
b. Duffy, Karen
b. Dugan, Alan
b. Duke, Angier Biddle
b. Duke, Doris
b. Duke, Patty
b. DuMont, Allen Balcom
b. Dumont, Margaret
b. Dunn, James Howard
b. Dunne, Griffin
b. Dunninger, Joseph
b. Durante, Jimmy
b. Duyckinck, Evert Augustus
b. Dvorak, Ann
b. Earl, Ronnie
b. Eastlake, William (Derry)
b. Ebb, Fred
b. Ebbets, Charles Hercules
b. Eberstadt, Ferdinand
b. Economaki, Chris(topher
   Constantine)
b. Edelman, Gerald Maurice
b. Edelman, Herb
b. Ederle, Gertrude Caroline
b. Edwards, Alan
b. Edwards, Joan
b. Edwards, Sherman
b. Edwards, Vince(nt)
b. Eisner, Will(iam E.)
b. Eldredge, Niles
b. Eldridge, Florence
b. Elegant, Robert Sampson
b. Elion, Gertrude B(ell)
b. Eliot, George Fielding
b. Elisofon, Eliot
b. Elizondo, Hector
b. Elkin, Stanley (Lawrence)
b. Elkins, Hillard
b. Ellin, Stanley
b. Ellington, E. David
b. Elliott, Osborn
b. Ellison, Virginia Howell
b. Engel, Lyle Kenyon
b. Ephron, Henry
b. Ephron, Nora
b. Epstein, Alvin
b. Epstein, Edward Jay
b. Epstein, Jacob, Sir
b. Epstein, Julius
b. Epstein, Philip G

b. Erickson, Eric
b. Erskine, John
b. Estevez, Emilio
b. Estrada, Erik
b. Estrin, Thelma (Austern)
b. Ethridge, Mark Foster, Jr.
b. Evans, Bob
b. Evans, Joni
b. Evans, Madge
b. Evergood, Philip (Howard Francis Dixon)
b. Evers, Jason
b. Faderman, Lillian
b. Fadiman, Clifton (Paul)
b. Fahrenkopf, Frank Joseph, Jr.
b. Fain, Sammy
b. Fairbanks, Douglas, Jr.
b. Falco, Louis
b. Falk, Peter
b. Falletta, JoAnn
b. Falls, Joe
b. Faludi, Susan
b. Farb, Peter
b. Farentino, James
b. Farina, Richard
b. Farrakhan, Louis
b. Farrand, Beatrix Jones
b. Farrar, Margaret (Petherbridge)
b. Farrell, Perry
b. Fast, Howard Melvin
b. Fauci, Anthony Stephen
b. Faust, Lotta
b. Faye, Alice
b. Faye, Joey
b. Feelings, Tom
b. Feifel, Herman
b. Feiffer, Jules Ralph
b. Feininger, Lyonel
b. Feis, Herbert
b. Feld, Eliot
b. Feldman, Alvin Lindbergh
b. Feldman, Morton
b. Feldman, Sandra
b. Feldshuh, Tovah
b. Feldstein, Martin Stuart
b. Fenten, D X
b. Fenwick, Millicent Hammond
b. Ferrante, Arthur
b. Ferrigno, Lou
b. Feuer, Cy
b. Feynman, Richard Phillips
b. Field, Marshall, IV
b. Field, Rachel Lyman
b. Field, Ron(ald)
b. Fielding, Lewis J
b. Fielding, Temple Hornaday
b. Fields, Joseph
b. Fields, Lew Maurice
b. Fields, Shep
b. Fierstein, Harvey (Forbes)
b. Fine, Sylvia
b. Fineman, Irving
b. Firbank, Louis
b. Fischetti, John
b. Fischl, Eric
b. Fish, Hamilton
b. Fisher, Amy
b. Fisher, Avery
b. Fisher, Harrison
b. FitzGerald, Frances
b. Fitzsimmons, James E
b. Fixx, James Fuller
b. Flagg, Ernest
b. Flannery, Susan
b. Fleck, Bela
b. Fleischer, Nat(haniel Stanley)

b. Fleischmann, Peter F(rancis)
b. Fleischmann, Sid
b. Fleming, Art
b. Florio, James Joseph
b. Flynn, Edward Joseph
b. Foat, Ginny
b. Folger, Henry Clay
b. Fonda, Jane
b. Fonda, Peter
b. Forbes, Malcolm Stevenson
b. Ford, Constance
b. Ford, Corey
b. Ford, Eileen
b. Ford, Paul Leicester
b. Ford, Whitey
b. Foreman, Richard
b. Forsythe, William
b. Foster, Phil
b. Fox, Charles
b. Foy, Eddie
b. Franciosa, Anthony
b. Frank, Jerome David
b. Frankel, Charles
b. Frankel, Emily
b. Frankel, Gene
b. Frankenthaler, Helen
b. Franklin, Irene
b. Frazetta, Frank
b. Fredericks, Carlton
b. Freed, Bert
b. Freeman, Cynthia
b. Frehley, Ace
b. Freilicher, Jane
b. French, Jay Jay
b. French, Marilyn
b. Freneau, Philip Morin
b. Fried, Gerald
b. Friedman, Bruce Jay
b. Friedman, Herbert
b. Friedman, Max
b. Friedman, Milton
b. Friedman, Stephen
b. Friendly, Ed
b. Friendly, Fred W.
b. Frisch, Frankie
b. Frissell, Toni
b. Frye, David
b. Fuchs, Daniel
b. Fuchs, Joseph (Philip)
b. Fuchs, Michael J(oseph)
b. Fuller, Kathryn S(cott)
b. Funk, Wilfred John
b. Funt, Allen
b. Furman, Rosemary
b. Furness, Betty
b. Futter, Ellen Victoria
b. Gabor, Mark
b. Gaddis, William (Thomas)
b. Gaines, William M(axwell)
b. Gale, Eric
b. Gale, Robert Peter
b. Galella, Ron
b. Gallagher, Helen
b. Gallico, Paul William
b. Gannett, Ruth
b. Gardner, Hy
b. Gardner, Isabella Stewart
b. Garfield, Brian Wynne
b. Garfield, John
b. Gargan, William
b. Garment, Leonard
b. Garraty, John Arthur
b. Garrett, Lila
b. Garrison, Lloyd K(irkham)
b. Gaud, William Steen, Jr.
b. Gaudio, Bob

b. Gavin, James Maurice
b. Gazzara, Ben
b. Geddes, Barbara Bel
b. Geffen, David
b. Gehrig, Lou
b. Gelb, Arthur
b. Gelb, Barbara Stone
b. Gelb, Lawrence
b. Geller, Bruce
b. Gellis, Roberta Leah Jacobs
b. Gell-Mann, Murray
b. Genauer, Emily
b. Genet, Arthur Samuel
b. George, Don
b. George, Grace
b. George, Nelson
b. Gerry, Elbridge Thomas
b. Gershwin, George
b. Gershwin, Ira
b. Gertz, Alison L.
b. Gerulaitis, Vitas
b. Geschwind, Norman
b. Getty, Estelle
b. Giardello, Joey
b. Gibbs, Oliver Wolcott
b. Gibbs, Terry
b. Gibson, Bob
b. Gibson, William
b. Gilder, George
b. Gildersleeve, Virginia Crocheron
b. Gilford, Jack
b. Gillenson, Lewis W
b. Gilligan, Carol
b. Gillmore, Frank
b. Gilpatric, Roswell L(eavitt)
b. Gilroy, Frank Daniel
b. Gimbel, Peter Robin
b. Ginsburg, Ruth Bader
b. Ginzburg, Ralph
b. Giorno, John
b. Giuliani, Rudolph William
b. Givens, Robin
b. Glaser, Elizabeth
b. Glaser, Milton
b. Glashow, Sheldon Lee
b. Glasser, Ira
b. Glazer, Nathan
b. Gleason, Jackie
b. Gleason, James
b. Gleason, John James
b. Gleason, Ralph Joseph
b. Gleason, Thomas W(illiam)
b. Gluck, Louise
b. Godey, Louis Antoine
b. Godfrey, Arthur Michael
b. Goethals, George Washington
b. Goetz, Bernhard
b. Gold, Michael
b. Goldberg, Bernard
b. Goldberg, Gary David
b. Goldberg, Leonard
b. Goldberg, Whoopi
b. Golden, John
b. Golden, Thelma
b. Golden, William
b. Goldfinger, Nathaniel
b. Goldin, Daniel S
b. Goldman, Bo
b. Goldman, Richard Franko
b. Golub, William Weldon
b. Goode, Richard Stephen
b. Gooding, Cuba, Jr.
b. Goodman, Martin
b. Goodman, Mitchell
b. Goodman, Paul
b. Goody, Joan

b. Hugel, Max
b. Hughan, Jessie Wallace
b. Hughes, George
b. Hunter, Evan
b. Hunter, Tab
b. Huntington, Daniel
b. Hurd, Clement
b. Husing, Ted
b. Hutchins, Robert Maynard
b. Hutton, Barbara Woolworth
b. Hutton, Edward F
b. Huxtable, Ada Louise
b. Ian, Janis
b. Ingersoll, Ralph McAllister, II
b. Irving, Clifford Michael
b. Irving, Jules
b. Irving, Larry
b. Irving, Washington
b. Isaacs, Susan
b. Isham, Samuel
b. Istomin, Eugene George
b. Ives, James Merritt
b. Jackson, Freddie
b. Jackson, George
b. Jackson, Mark
b. Jacobs, Joe
b. Jacobs, Joe B
b. Jacobs, Michael S
b. Jacoby, Oswald
b. Jaffe, Herb
b. Jaffe, Rona
b. Jaffe, Sam
b. Jagel, Frederick
b. James, Henry, (Jr.)
b. James, Juanita (T.)
b. James, William
b. Jampolis, Neil Peter
b. Janeway, Eliot
b. Janeway, Elizabeth Hall
b. Janifer, Laurence M(ark)
b. Janis, Conrad
b. Janklow, Morton Lloyd
b. Janssen, Werner
b. Jason, Rick
b. Jastrow, Robert
b. Javits, Jacob Koppel
b. Jay, John
b. Jay, Karla
b. Jay, Ricky
b. Jay, William
b. Jeffreys, Garland
b. Jellinek, Elvin Morton
b. Jenkins, Allen
b. Jenkins, Carol Elizabeth Heiss
b. Jenkins, Sally
b. Jennings, Paul Joseph
b. Jergens, Adele
b. Jessel, George Albert
b. Jessup, Philip Caryl
b. Johnson, Crockett
b. Johnson, Robert T.
b. Jones, Billy
b. Jong, Erica (Mann)
b. Jonsson, John Erik
b. Jordan, June
b. Jordan, Michael (Jeffery)
b. Jordan, Richard
b. Jorgensen, Christine
b. Josefsberg, Milt
b. Joseph, Richard
b. Joseph, Stephen (Carl)
b. Josephson, Matthew
b. Joyce, William
b. Kaempffert, Waldemar (Bernhard)
b. Kahane, Meir David
b. Kahane, Melanie

b. Kahn, Roger
b. Kalb, Bernard
b. Kalb, Marvin Leonard
b. Kalfin, Robert
b. Kalikow, Peter Stephen
b. Kalmanoff, Martin
b. Kalmar, Bert
b. Kamali, Norma
b. Kameny, Frank(lin Edward)
b. Kamp, Irene Kittle
b. Kampelman, Max M
b. Kane, Big Daddy
b. Kane, Helen
b. Kane, Henry
b. Kane, Joseph Nathan
b. Kani, Karl
b. Kanin, Fay
b. Kanokogi, Rusty
b. Kantrowitz, Adrian
b. Kapell, William
b. Kaplan, Gabe
b. Kaplan, Justin
b. Kaplow, Herbert Elias
b. Kapp, Wolfgang
b. Kardiner, Abram
b. Karle, Jerome
b. Karlen, John
b. Karpin, Fred Leon
b. Kashdan, Isaac
b. Kasper, Herbert
b. Katims, Milton
b. Katz, Alex
b. Katz, Jonathan Ned
b. Katzenberg, Jeffrey
b. Kauffmann, Stanley Jules
b. Kaufman, Andy
b. Kaufman, Elaine
b. Kaufman, Irving R(obert)
b. Kaufman, Joseph William
b. Kaufman, Murray
b. Kaye, Danny
b. Kaye, Nora
b. Kaye, Stubby
b. Kazan, Lainie
b. Kazin, Alfred
b. Kean, Thomas Howard
b. Keats, Ezra Jack
b. Keeler, Wee Willie
b. Keene, Donald Lawrence
b. Keene, Thomas Wallace
b. Keitel, Harvey
b. Keith, Minor Cooper
b. Keller, Arthur C
b. Kelly, Patsy
b. Kelly, Paul
b. Kelly, Stephen Eugene
b. Kelman, Charles David
b. Kennedy, Caroline Bouvier
b. Kennedy, George
b. Kennedy, Joan Bennett
b. Kennedy, Tom
b. Keogh, Eugene James
b. Keppel, Francis
b. Kern, Jerome David
b. Kerr, John
b. Kerr, Orpheus C
b. Kesselring, Joseph Otto
b. Kessler, David Aaron
b. Keyes, Alan L(ee)
b. Keyes, Daniel
b. Kheel, Theodore Woodrow
b. Kibbee, Robert Joseph
b. Kidd, Michael
b. Kieran, John Francis
b. King, Alan
b. King, Bernard

b. King, Carole
b. King, Charles
b. King, Evelyn
b. King, Larry
b. King, Thomas Starr
b. King, Warren Thomas
b. Kingsbury-Smith, Joseph
b. Kingsley, Sidney
b. Kirby, Jack
b. Kirkland, Caroline Matilda
  Stansbury
b. Kirshner, Don
b. Kissling, Frances
b. Kleban, Edward Lawrence
b. Klein, Anne
b. Klein, Calvin
b. Klein, Robert
b. Kline, Morris
b. Klopfer, Donald Simon
b. Knopf, Alfred Abraham
b. Knopf, Blanche Wolf
b. Kobbe, Gustav
b. Koch, Ed(ward Irwin)
b. Kohan, Buz
b. Kohl, Herbert R
b. Kolchin, Ellis Robert
b. Kolodin, Irving
b. Komroff, Manuel
b. Kool Moe Dee
b. Koop, C(harles) Everett
b. Kooper, Al
b. Kopell, Bernie
b. Kopit, Arthur Lee
b. Koren, Edward Benjamin
b. Kornberg, Arthur
b. Kotto, Yaphet Frederick
b. Kotzky, Alex Sylvester
b. Koufax, Sandy
b. Kramer, Stanley E
b. Krantz, Judith
b. Krasna, Norman
b. Krasner, Lee
b. Krassner, Paul
b. Kravitz, Lenny
b. Kredel, Fritz
b. Krementz, Jill
b. Krens, Thomas
b. Kreymborg, Alfred
b. Kristol, Irving
b. Kristol, William
b. Kroll, Leon
b. KRS-One
b. Kubrick, Stanley
b. Kuhn, Walt
b. Kunhardt, Dorothy (Meserve)
b. Kunstler, William M(oses)
b. Kunzel, Erich
b. Kurnitz, Harry
b. Kurtzman, Harvey
b. Kurzban, Ira Jay
b. Kurzweil, Raymond C
b. Kushner, Harold S(amuel)
b. Kushner, Tony
b. La Barba, Fidel
b. LaFarge, Christopher
b. LaFarge, John
b. LaFarge, Oliver
b. La Guardia, Fiorello Henry
b. Lahr, Bert
b. Laidler, Harry Wellington
b. Laiken, Deirdre Susan
b. Lake, Anthony
b. Lake, Veronica
b. Lambert, Christopher
b. Lamm, Robert
b. LaMotta, Jake

b. Maywood, Augusta
b. Mazursky, Paul
b. McAdie, Alexander George
b. McAvoy, May
b. McCann, Elizabeth Ireland
b. McCarthy, Carolyn
b. McCarthy, J(oseph) P(riestley)
b. McCartney, Linda
b. McCloskey, John
b. McCord, David (Thompson Watson)
b. McCormack, Patty
b. McCourt, Frank
b. McDermott, Alice
b. McFadden, Mary Josephine
b. McFerrin, Bobby
b. McGill, William James
b. McGinniss, Joe
b. McGiver, John
b. McGoohan, Patrick (Joseph)
b. McGraw, Harold Whittlesey, Jr.
b. McGuire, Al
b. McIntyre, James Francis Aloysius,
   Cardinal
b. McKay, Nellie Yvonne
b. McKean, Michael
b. McKeen, John Elmer
b. MC Lyte
b. McMahon, Don(ald John)
b. McManus, Sean
b. McMaster, John Bach
b. McRae, Carmen
b. Meany, George
b. Meara, Anne
b. Medford, Kay
b. Medina, Harold Raymond
b. Meisner, Sanford
b. Melanie
b. Mellinger, Frederick
b. Melnick, Daniel
b. Melville, George Wallace
b. Melville, Herman
b. Mendl, Lady Elsie de Wolfe
b. Menken, Helen
b. Menuhin, Yehudi
b. Meredith, Scott
b. Meredith, Sidney
b. Merriam, Clinton Hart
b. Merrill, Dina
b. Merrill, James (Ingram)
b. Merrill, Robert
b. Merritt, Wesley
b. Merwin, W(illiam) S(tanley)
b. Messing, Shep
b. Metrano, Art
b. Meyer, Nicholas
b. Meyers, Ari(adne)
b. Michaels, Al
b. Michener, James A(lbert)
b. Milano, Alyssa
b. Milano, Fred
b. Miles, Sylvia
b. Miller, Arthur
b. Miller, Bebe
b. Miller, Gilbert Heron
b. Miller, Henry (Valentine)
b. Miller, Marvin Julian
b. Miller, Max
b. Millo, Aprile
b. Mills, Irving
b. Mills, Stephanie
b. Mineo, Sal(vatore)
b. Minnesota Fats
b. Minsky, Abraham Bennett
b. Minsky, Marvin Lee
b. Minsky, Morton
b. Mintz, Beatrice

b. Mirisch, Walter Mortimer
b. Mitchel, John Purroy
b. Mitchell, Arthur Adam
b. Mitchell, Margaret Julia
b. Mittermeier, Russell A
b. Mizrahi, Isaac
b. Modell, Art(hur B)
b. Moe, Doug(las Edwin)
b. Moeller, Philip
b. Molinari, Susan
b. Monash, Paul
b. Monroe, Elizabeth (Kortright)
b. Monroe, Lucy
b. Montenegro, Hugh
b. Moore, Clement Clarke
b. Moore, Mary Tyler
b. Moore, Melba
b. Moore, William
b. Morales, Esai
b. Morgan, Frank
b. Morgan, Henry
b. Morgan, Ralph
b. Morgenthau, Henry, Jr.
b. Morgenthau, Robert Morris
b. Moriarty, Cathy
b. Morison, Patricia
b. Morris, Chester
b. Morris, Dick
b. Morris, Howard
b. Morris, Newbold
b. Morris, Richard Brandon
b. Morris, William, Jr.
b. Morrow, Vic
b. Mortimer, Charles Greenough
b. Morton, Joe
b. Moses, Robert Parris
b. Moskowitz, J(ay)
b. Moss, Arnold
b. Moss, Geoffrey
b. Moss, Howard
b. Moss, Jerry
b. Most, Donny
b. Mostel, Zero
b. Mott, William Penn, Jr.
b. Mottola, Tommy
b. Muir, Jean
b. Muldaur, Diana Charlton
b. Muldaur, Maria
b. Mullen, Joe
b. Muller, Hermann Joseph
b. Mulligan, Gerry
b. Mulligan, Richard
b. Mundelein, George William
b. Munn, Frank
b. Munshin, Jules
b. Murchison, Kenneth MacKenzie
b. Murphy, Johnny (John Joseph)
b. Murphy, Patrick Vincent
b. Murray, Allen Edward
b. Murray, Arthur
b. Murray, Jan
b. Murray, Ken
b. Myerson, Bess
b. Nagler, Eric
b. Naish, J(oseph) Carrol
b. Naldi, Nita
b. Nast, Conde
b. Nathan, Robert
b. Navasky, Victor Saul
b. Naylor, Gloria
b. Nelson, David
b. Nelson, Jill
b. Nelson, Ralph
b. Nemerov, Howard (Stanley)
b. Nero, Peter
b. Nestle, Joan

b. Neway, Patricia
b. Newhouse, S(amuel) I(rving), Jr.
b. Newhouse, Samuel Irving
b. Newman, Arnold Abner
b. Newman, Barnett
b. Newman, David
b. Newman, Edwin Harold
b. Ney, Richard
b. Nichols, Ruth Rowland
b. Nicolson, Marjorie Hope
b. Nidetch, Jean
b. Nilsson
b. Nirenberg, Marshall Warren
b. Nolte, Henry R, Jr.
b. Noonan, Peggy
b. Norman, Pat
b. Norris, Christopher
b. Norton, Jack
b. Nossiter, Bernard Daniel
b. Notorious B.I.G.
b. Nozick, Robert
b. Nugent, Edward
b. Nyad, Diana
b. Nyro, Laura
b. Oakland, Simon
b. Oates, John William
b. O'Brien, Edmond
b. O'Brien, John J
b. O'Connell, Arthur
b. O'Connell, Hugh
b. O'Connor, Carroll
b. O'Donnell, Emmett, Jr.
b. Ojeda, Eddie
b. Okun, Milton Theodore
b. Olderman, Murray
b. Oliver, Daniel
b. Oliver, Edith
b. O'Malley, Walter Francis
b. Onassis, Christina
b. O'Neill, Eugene Gladstone
b. O'Neill, Gerard Kitchen
b. Opatoshu, David
b. Oppenheimer, Frank F
b. Oppenheimer, J(ulius) Robert
b. Orbach, Jerry
b. Orlando, Tony
b. Ornitz, Samuel
b. Ortega, Santos
b. Osgood, Charles
b. O'Sheel, Shaemas
b. Ostin, Mo
b. O'Sullivan, Timothy H
b. Ovington, Mary White
b. Owens, Rochelle
b. Oxenberg, Catherine
b. Pacino, Al(fredo James)
b. Pakula, Alan J(ay)
b. Palmer, Jim
b. Palmieri, Eddie
b. Palminteri, Chazz
b. Paltrow, Bruce
b. Papp, Joseph
b. Pappas, Ike
b. Park, William Hallock
b. Parnis, Mollie
b. Parsons, Betty Pierson
b. Parsons, Elsie Clews
b. Parsons, Richard Dean
b. Pastor, Tony
b. Paterno, Joe
b. Paterson, Basil Alexander
b. Patrick, Lee
b. Payne, Allen
b. Payne, John Howard
b. Payne, Roger S.
b. Payson, Joan Whitney

b. Ryan, Sylvester James
b. Ryder, Alfred
b. Ryskind, Morrie
b. Saarinen, Aline Bernstein
b. Sachs, Samuel, II
b. Sackler, Howard Oliver
b. Safire, William L
b. Sagan, Carl (Edward)
b. Sager, Carole Bayer
b. Saks, Gene
b. Salant, Richard S
b. Sale, Richard Bernard
b. Salinger, J(erome) D(avid)
b. Salk, Jonas E(dward)
b. Salk, Lee
b. Salmi, Albert
b. Salt
b. Sammartino, Peter
b. Samstag, Nicholas
b. Sanders, Bernard
b. Sanders, Lawrence
b. Sandler, Adam
b. Sands, Diana Patricia
b. Sanford, Isabel Gwendolyn
b. Sann, Paul
b. Sarandon, Susan
b. Sardi, Vincent, Jr.
b. Sarnoff, Robert W(illiam)
b. Sarris, Andrew George
b. Sauter, Eddie
b. Savo, Jimmy
b. Saxon, Charles David
b. Saxon, John
b. Schaap, Dick
b. Schacht, Al(exander)
b. Schaltzberg, Jerry Ned
b. Schank, Roger C(arl)
b. Schayes, Dolph
b. Scheer, Robert
b. Schell, Johnathan Edward
b. Schell, Orville H(ickock), 3rd.
b. Scherman, Thomas Kielty
b. Schiff, Dorothy
b. Schisgal, Murray Joseph
b. Schlein, Miriam
b. Schlesinger, Frank
b. Schlesinger, James Rodney
b. Schlessinger, Laura
b. Schnabel, Julian
b. Schoenbach, Sol Israel
b. Schoenbrun, David
b. Schoenfeld, Gerald
b. Schonberg, Harold C
b. Schorr, Daniel Louis
b. Schulberg, Budd Wilson
b. Schuller, Gunther
b. Schulman, Sarah (Miriam)
b. Schultz, Dutch
b. Schultz, Howard M.
b. Schumacher, Joel
b. Schuman, Patricia Glass
b. Schuman, William Howard
b. Schumann, Walter
b. Schumer, Charles E(llis)
b. Schwartz, Arthur
b. Schwartz, Delmore (David)
b. Schwartz, Felice N(ierenberg)
b. Schwartz, Melvin
b. Schwimmer, David
b. Schwinger, Julian (Seymour)
b. Scorsese, Martin
b. Scott, Norman
b. Scott, Raymond
b. Scourby, Alexander
b. Scribner, Charles
b. Sculley, John

b. Scully, Vin(cent Edward)
b. Sebastian, John
b. Sedaka, Neil
b. Sedran, Barney
b. Seeger, Alan
b. Seeger, Pete(r)
b. Segal, Erich Wolf
b. Segal, George
b. Seinfeld, Jerry
b. Selby, Hubert, Jr.
b. Seldes, Marian
b. Seligman, Edwin Robert Anderson
b. Sellecca, Connie
b. Selznick, Irene Mayer
b. Sendak, Maurice Bernard
b. Serkin, Peter A(dolf)
b. Serpico, Frank
b. Serrano, Andres
b. Sessions, Roger Huntington
b. Seton, Anya Chase
b. Seton, Elizabeth Ann Bayley, Saint
b. Severn, William Irving
b. Seymour, Anne Eckert
b. Seymour, Dan
b. Shagan, Steve
b. Shakur, Assata
b. Shakur, Tupac
b. Shalit, Gene
b. Shanker, Albert
b. Shanley, John Patrick
b. Shapiro, Stanley
b. Sharkey, Ray
b. Sharpton, Al(fred), Jr.
b. Shattuck, Roger Whitney
b. Shaughnessy, Mickey
b. Shaw, Artie
b. Shaw, Irwin
b. Shawn, Wallace
b. Shea, William Alfred
b. Shear, Murray Jacob
b. Sheedy, Ally
b. Sherman, Richard Morton
b. Sherman, Russell
b. Sherrill, Henry Knox
b. Shields, Brooke
b. Shimkin, Leon
b. Shirley, Anne
b. Shrady, Henry M
b. Shulman, Irving
b. Shultz, George Pratt
b. Shutta, Ethel
b. Shuttlesworth, Dorothy Edwards
b. Sickles, Daniel Edgar
b. Sidney, George
b. Sidney, Sylvia
b. Siegel, Bernie S(hepard)
b. Siegel, Bugsy
b. Siegel, Larry
b. Siegmeister, Elie
b. Sills, Beverly
b. Silver, Ron
b. Silverberg, Robert
b. Silverman, Fred
b. Silvers, Phil
b. Silverstein, Alvin
b. Simmons, Russell
b. Simon, Carly
b. Simon, Neil
b. Simon, Norma Feldstein
b. Simon, Richard Leo
b. Simpson, Adele (Smithline)
b. Simpson, Lorna
b. Simpson, Valerie
b. Sinclair, Jo
b. Sinder, Dee
b. Singer, Burns James Hyman

b. Singer, Maxine (Frank)
b. Siskind, Aaron
b. Sister Souljah
b. Skolsky, Sidney
b. Slater, Christian
b. Slesar, Henry
b. Slidell, John
b. Sliwa, Curtis
b. Sloan, Michael
b. Sloane, Eric
b. Sloane, Everett
b. Sloane, John
b. Slotnick, Daniel Leonid
b. Smalls, Charlie
b. Smaltz, Audrey
b. Smith, Alfred Emanuel
b. Smith, Betty
b. Smith, Dennis
b. Smith, Hamilton Othanel
b. Smith, Joe
b. Smith, Kent
b. Smith, Lee
b. Smith, Pete
b. Smits, Jimmy
b. Smothers, Dick
b. Smothers, Tommy
b. Snow, Phoebe Laub
b. Snyder, Mitch
b. Snyder, Richard Elliot
b. Sobell, Morton
b. Soglow, Otto
b. Solarz, Stephen Joshua
b. Solow, Robert Merton
b. Sommers, Ben
b. Somogi, Judith
b. Sondheim, Stephen (Joshua)
b. Sontag, Susan
b. Sorel, Edward
b. Sorvino, Paul
b. Sour, Robert B(andler)
b. Sovern, Michael I(ra)
b. Speck, Frank Gouldsmith
b. Spector, Phil(lip Harvey)
b. Spigelgass, Leonard
b. Spillane, Mickey
b. Spingarn, Arthur Barnett
b. Spingarn, Joel Elias
b. Spivak, Lawrence E(dmund)
b. Sprague, R(obert) C(hapman)
b. Stallone, Sylvester (Enzio)
b. Stander, Lionel (Jay)
b. Stanley, Paul
b. Stanwyck, Barbara
b. Stapleton, Jean
b. Stark, Koo
b. Steel, Danielle Fernande
b. Steel, Dawn
b. Steig, William
b. Stein, Aaron Marc
b. Stein, Joseph
b. Stein, William Howard
b. Steinman, David Barnard
b. Sterling, Jan
b. Stern, Bert
b. Stern, Carl Leonard
b. Stern, David Joel
b. Stern, Howard (Allan)
b. Stern, Leonard B
b. Stern, Leonard Norman
b. Stern, Richard Gustave
b. Stern, Stewart
b. Stevens, Connie
b. Stevens, Emily A
b. Stevens, John
b. Stevens, Rise
b. Stevens, Shane

b. Stewart, Anita
b. Stewart, Michael
b. Stewart, Paul
b. Stiller, Ben
b. Stiller, Jerry
b. Stillman, Irwin Maxwell
b. Stimson, Henry Lewis
b. Stirling, Lord
b. Stockton, Dick
b. Stone, Dick
b. Stone, Dorothy
b. Stone, Grace Zaring
b. Stone, Louis
b. Stone, Oliver
b. Stone, Paula
b. Stone, Robert Anthony
b. Storch, Larry
b. Strand, Paul
b. Strasberg, Susan Elizabeth
b. Strassman, Marcia
b. Straus, Jack Isidor
b. Straus, Roger W(illiams), Jr.
b. Strauss, Robert
b. Streeter, Edward
b. Streisand, Barbra (Joan)
b. Strouse, Charles
b. Struss, Karl
b. Stuart, Lyle
b. Stuart, Mel
b. Sullivan, Barry
b. Sullivan, Ed(ward Vincent)
b. Sullivan, Susan
b. Sullivan, Walter
b. Sulzberger, Arthur Hays
b. Sulzberger, Arthur O(chs)
b. Sulzberger, C(yrus) L(eo)
b. Sutton, Horace (Ashley)
b. Sutton, Willie
b. Sweat, Keith
b. Sweeney, John J(oseph)
b. Swift, Kay
b. Swinburne, Laurence
b. Sylbert, Richard
b. Symington, J Fife, III
b. Syms, Sylvia
b. Taft, Henry Waters, II
b. Taj Mahal
b. Talbot, Nita
b. Talmadge, Constance
b. Tamiris, Helen
b. Tannen, Deborah Frances
b. Tarnower, Herman
b. Tashman, Lilyan
b. Taubman, (Hyman) Howard
b. Tayback, Vic
b. Taylor, (Joseph) Deems
b. Taylor, Laurette
b. Taylor, Susan L.
b. Taylor, Sydney Brenner
b. Terkel, Studs (Louis)
b. Terry, Walter
b. Testaverde, Vinny
b. Thalberg, Irving Grant
b. Thomas, Franklin Augustine
b. Thomas, Piri
b. Thomas, Richard Earl
b. Thompson, Randall
b. Thompson, Tazewell (Alfred)
b. Thon, William
b. Tierney, Gene
b. Tiffany, Louis Comfort
b. Tiny Tim
b. Tisch, Laurence Alan
b. Tobias, Andrew Previn
b. Tobias, George
b. Todman, Bill

b. Toffler, Alvin
b. Tomei, Marisa
b. Torre, Joe
b. Totenberg, Nina
b. Traphagen, Ethel Leigh
b. Traub, Marvin Stuart
b. Travers, Jerry
b. Treat, Lawrence
b. Trevor, Claire
b. Trilling, Diana (Rubin)
b. Trilling, Lionel
b. Tripp, Paul
b. Trotta, Maurice S
b. Troy, Hannah
b. Troyanos, Tatiana
b. Trudeau, Edward Livingston
b. Trudeau, Garry
b. Trump, Donald John
b. Tuchman, Barbara Wertheim
b. Tucker, Richard
b. Tunney, Gene
b. Tunney, John Varick
b. Turkus, Burton B
b. Turturro, John
b. Tweed, Boss
b. Twelvetrees, Helen
b. Tyler, Liv
b. Tyson, Cicely
b. Tyson, Mike
b. Tyson, Neil de Grasse
b. Ubell, Earl
b. Uggams, Leslie (Marian Crayne)
b. Uhnak, Dorothy
b. Ullman, James Ramsey
b. Unger, Irwin
b. Untermeyer, Louis
b. Upson, Ralph Hazlett
b. Uris, Harold David
b. Vaccaro, Brenda
b. Vai, Steve
b. Valachi, Joe
b. Vale, Jerry
b. Valvano, Jim
b. Van Ark, Joan
b. Van Cortlandt, Stephanus
b. Vanderbilt, Cornelius, Jr.
b. Vanderbilt, Gloria Morgan
b. Vanderbilt, William Henry
b. Vanderbilt, William Kissam
b. Van Doren, Charles Lincoln
b. Vandross, Luther
b. Van Nostrand, David
b. Van Patten, Joyce
b. Van Patten, Vince(nt)
b. Van Rensselaer, Stephen
b. Van Zandt, Marie
b. Vanzant, Iyanla (Rhonda)
b. Vaughn, Robert
b. Vedder, Elihu
b. Velez, Eddie
b. Vernon, Jackie
b. Vickrey, Robert (Remsen)
b. Viereck, Peter Robert Edwin
b. Vigoda, Abe
b. Villella, Edward Joseph
b. Viscardi, Henry, Jr.
b. VonHoffman, Nicholas
b. Vought, Chance Milton
b. Wachner, Linda
b. Wagner, Robert Ferdinand, Jr.
b. Wain, Bea
b. Wald, George
b. Wald, Jerry
b. Walden, Robert
b. Waldman, Max
b. Walinsky, Adam

b. Walken, Christopher
b. Walker, Jimmie
b. Walker, Jimmy
b. Wallace, Michele Faith
b. Wallach, Eli
b. Waller, Fats
b. Waller, Fred(erick)
b. Wallerstein, Jusith S.
b. Wallop, Malcolm
b. Walsh, Raoul
b. Walter, Jessica
b. Walters, Vernon Anthony
b. Wang, Vera
b. Wanzer, Bobby
b. Warburg, Frederick Marcus
b. Ward, Benjamin
b. Warner, Susan Bogert
b. Warren, Harry
b. Warren, Leonard
b. Warren, Lesley Ann
b. Wasserstein, Wendy
b. Watt, Douglas Benjamin
b. Wattenberg, Ben J
b. Wayans, Damon
b. Wayans, Keenen Ivory
b. Wayland, Francis
b. Weaver, Sigourney
b. Webb, William Seward
b. Weber, Joseph M
b. Webster, Margaret
b. Webster, Paul Francois
b. Wechsler, James Arthur
b. Weidenbaum, Murray Lew
b. Weidman, Jerome
b. Weill, Claudia
b. Weill, Sanford I.
b. Weinberg, Chester
b. Weinberg, Steven
b. Weinstein, Bob
b. Weinstein, Harvey
b. Weintraub, Jerry
b. Welch, Herbert
b. Welch, Mickey
b. Weld, Tuesday
b. Weller, Michael
b. Welles, Sumner
b. Wengenroth, Stow
b. Wenner, Jann
b. Werblin, Sonny
b. Wesson, David
b. West, Mae
b. West, Nathanael
b. Westlake, Donald E(dwin) Edmund
b. Westley, Helen
b. Wexler, Peter John
b. Wexley, John
b. Whalen, Grover (Michael)
   A(loysius)
b. Wharton, Edith
b. Whitaker, Lou(is Rodman)
b. White, Richard Grant
b. White, Stanford
b. White, William Alanson
b. Whitehead, Edwin C(arl)
b. Whitman, Marina VonNeumann
b. Whitney, C(ornelius) V(anderbilt)
b. Whitney, Gertrude Vanderbilt
b. Whitney, Harry Payne
b. Wiener, Leigh Auston
b. Wilbur, Richard Purdy
b. Wilde, Cornel
b. Wilkens, Lenny
b. Wilkes, Charles
b. Wilkinson, J(ohn) Burke
b. Wille, Frank
b. Williams, Billy Dee

b. Williams, Clarence, III
b. Williams, Garth Montgomery
b. Williams, Gus
b. Williams, Vanessa
b. Willig, George
b. Wilson, Charles Edward
b. Wilson, Malcolm
b. Wilson, Mitchell A
b. Wilson, Theodore Roosevelt
b. Winchell, Paul
b. Winchell, Walter
b. Windom, William
b. Winkler, Henry Franklin
b. Winkler, Irwin
b. Winograd, Arthur
b. Winston, Harry
b. Wise, William H
b. Witcover, Walt
b. Witkin, Joel-Peter
b. Witmark, Isidore
b. Witt, Paul Junger
b. Wolfert, Ira
b. Wolfman Jack
b. Wolheim, Louis
b. Wolper, David Lloyd
b. Wood, Peggy
b. Woolley, Monty
b. Woolrich, Cornell
b. Wouk, Herman
b. Wragge, Sidney
b. Wright, George
b. Wright, Jane Cooke
b. Wright, Steven
b. Wright, Teresa
b. Wunder, George S
b. Wuorinen, Charles (Peter)
b. Wurf, Jerry
b. Wynn, Keenan
b. Yablans, Frank
b. Yalow, Rosalyn Sussman
b. Yarrow, Peter
b. Yetnikoff, Walter
b. Yoba, Malik
b. Youmans, Vincent
b. Young, Burt
b. Zadora, Pia
b. Zaslofsky, Max
b. Zevin, B(enjamin) D(avid)
b. Zim, Herbert S(pencer)
b. Zimbalist, Efrem, Jr.
b. Zindel, Paul
b. Zinn, Howard
b. Zolotow, Maurice
b. Zukofsky, Louis
d. Abbey, Henry Eugene
d. Abbott, Lyman
d. Abrams, Harry Nathan
d. Abu Madi, Iliya
d. Abzug, Bella (Savitsky)
d. Ace, Goodman
d. Ace, Jane Sherwood
d. Acheson, Edward Goodrich
d. Ackerman, Carl William
d. Adams, Franklin P(ierce)
d. Adams, Herbert Samuel
d. Adams, Joey
d. Addams, Charles Samuel
d. Adler, Felix
d. Adler, Jacob Pavlovitch
d. Adler, Julius Ochs
d. Agee, James Rufus
d. Agostini, Peter
d. Agron, Salvador
d. Ailey, Alvin
d. Aitken, Robert
d. Albrand, Martha

d. Alden, Henry M
d. Aldrich, Nelson Wilmarth
d. Aldrich, Winthrop Williams
d. Aleichem, Sholom
d. Allen, Fred
d. Allen, Frederick Lewis
d. Allen, James Lane
d. Allen, Red
d. Allen, Viola Emily
d. Allen, Vivian Beaumont
d. Almendros, Nestor
d. Althouse, Paul Shearer
d. Altman, Benjamin
d. Altsheler, Joseph Alexander
d. Alvary, Lorenzo
d. Amato, Pasquale
d. Amerasinghe, Hamilton Shirley
d. Amory, Cleveland
d. Amsterdam, Birdie
d. Anastasia, Albert
d. Anderson, Dorothy Hansine
d. Anderson, Elizabeth Milbank
d. Anderson, John Murray
d. Angoff, Charles
d. Antheil, George
d. Anthony, Katharine Susan
d. Antoon, A(lfred) J(oseph)
d. Apess, William
d. Apgar, Virginia
d. Appleton, Daniel
d. Appleton, William Henry
d. Aranason, H Harvard
d. Arbus, Diane
d. Archipenko, Alexander Porfirievich
d. Arden, Elizabeth
d. Arenas, Reinaldo
d. Arendt, Hannah
d. Argentinita
d. Arieti, Silvano
d. Arlen, Harold
d. Arlen, Michael
d. Armour, Norman
d. Armstrong, Edwin Howard
d. Armstrong, Hamilton Fish
d. Armstrong, Louis
d. Arthur, Chester A(lan)
d. Arthur, Ellen (Lewis) Herndon
d. Asbury, Herbert
d. Ascoli, Max
d. Ashburn, Richie
d. Ashe, Arthur
d. Ashman, Howard
d. Asimov, Isaac
d. Astor, John Jacob
d. Astor, William Vincent
d. Audubon, John James
d. August, Jan
d. Avakian, Aram A
d. Avery, Milton Clark
d. Avery, Samuel Putnam
d. Ayer, Harriet Hubbard
d. Babbitt, Benjamin Talbot
d. Baccaloni, Salvatore
d. Bacharach, Bert(ram Mark)
d. Bache, Harold Leopold
d. Bacon, Henry
d. Baer, Bugs
d. Bagley, William Chandler
d. Bailey, Mildred
d. Baird, Bil
d. Baird, Cora Eisenberg
d. Baker, Ella
d. Baker, George Fisher
d. Baker, Sara Josephine
d. Baker, Shorty
d. Balanchine, George

d. Ball, George W(ildman)
d. Bandy, Way
d. Bangs, Lester
d. Bankhead, Tallulah Brockman
d. Barber, Samuel
d. Barker, Lex
d. Barnard, Chester Irving
d. Barnard, Frederick Augustus Porter
d. Barnard, George Grey
d. Barnes, Djuna
d. Baron, Samuel
d. Barry, Jack
d. Barry, Philip
d. Barrymore, Diana
d. Bartlett, Robert Abram
d. Bartok, Bela
d. Barton, Bruce
d. Baruch, Bernard Mannes
d. Basquiat, Jean-Michel
d. Baum, Kurt
d. Baur, John I(reland) H(owe)
d. Baxley, Barbara
d. Baxter, Anne
d. Bay, Howard
d. Bayes, Nora
d. Baziotes, William
d. Beach, Alfred Ely
d. Beach, H H A, Mrs.
d. Beard, George Miller
d. Beard, James Andrews
d. Bearden, Romare Howard
d. Beck, Julian
d. Beck, Martin
d. Beckmann, Max
d. Beecher, Henry Ward
d. Beer, Thomas
d. Behn, Noel
d. Behrman, S(amuel) N(athaniel)
d. Beiderbecke, Bix
d. Beilenson, Edna Rudolph
d. Belasco, David
d. Bell, Arthur (Irving)
d. Bell, Herbert A
d. Bellanca, Giuseppe Mario
d. Bellison, Simeon
d. Bellows, George Wesley
d. Belmont, August
d. Belmont, Eleanor Robson
d. Bemelmans, Ludwig
d. Benchley, Robert Charles
d. Bendix, Vincent
d. Benedict, Ruth (Fulton)
d. Benet, Stephen Vincent
d. Benet, William Rose
d. Bennett, James Gordon
d. Bennett, Robert Russell
d. Benton, Brook
d. Benton, Nelson
d. Benton, William
d. Bercovici, Konrad
d. Berg, Gertrude
d. Berger, Meyer
d. Bergh, Henry
d. Bergman, Jules Verne
d. Bergmann, Carl
d. Berigan, Bunny
d. Berle, Adolf Augustus, Jr.
d. Berlin, Ellin (Mackay)
d. Berlin, Irving
d. Berman, Emile Zola
d. Bernbach, William
d. Bernhard, Arnold
d. Bernhard, Lucian
d. Bernstein, Alice Frankau
d. Bernstein, Leonard
d. Bernstein, Theodore Menline

d. Croker, Boss
d. Croly, Jane Cunningham
d. Crosby, Harry
d. Crosby, James Morris
d. Crosby, Percy L
d. Cross, Milton John
d. Crouse, Russel
d. Crowninshield, Francis Welch
d. Cullen, Countee (Porter)
d. Cuppy, Will(iam Jacob)
d. Curran, Charles Courtney
d. Currier, Nathaniel
d. Curtis, Alan (Harold Neberroth)
d. Custer, Elizabeth Bacon
d. Dabney, Virginius
d. Dale, Chester
d. Daley, Arthur (John)
d. Dalrymple, Jean
d. Dalto, Jorge
d. Daly, Arnold
d. Daly, Marcus
d. Damrosch, Frank Heino
d. Damrosch, Leopold
d. Damrosch, Walter Johannes
d. Daniel, Clifton, Jr.
d. Danilova, Alexandra
d. Dante, Nicholas
d. DaPonte, Lorenzo
d. Darvas, Lili
d. Davenport, Homer Calvin
d. Davis, Gary, Reverend
d. Davis, Hal Charles
d. Davis, John Williams
d. Davis, Martin S.
d. Davis, Meyer
d. Davis, Owen
d. Davis, Stuart
d. Davis, Tobe
d. Dawn, Hazel
d. Day, Benjamin Henry
d. Day, Clarence Shepard, Jr.
d. Day, Dorothy
d. Day, Joseph Paul
d. DeBeck, Billy
d. DeCreeft, Jose
d. Dehn, Adolf Arthur
d. Delacorte, George Thomas, Jr.
d. DeLiagre, Alfred
d. del Ray, Lester (Ramon Alvarez)
d. DeLuca, Giuseppe
d. DeMille, Agnes (George)
d. Dempsey, Jack
d. Dennis, Patrick
d. DePaolis, Alessio
d. DeParis, Wilbur
d. Depew, Chauncey Mitchell
d. Deren, Maya
d. DeRivera, Jose Ruiz
d. DeRose, Peter
d. DeSeversky, Alexander Procofieff
d. Desmond, Paul Breitenfeld
d. Deutsch, Babette
d. Deutsch, Helen
d. DeVinne, Theodore Low
d. DeVoto, Bernard Augustine
d. Dewey, John
d. Dewing, Thomas Wilmer
d. Dickerson, Nancy Hanschman
d. Dietz, Angel DeCora
d. Dietz, Howard M
d. Digges, Dudley
d. Dirks, Rudolph
d. DiSant'Angelo, Giorgio
d. Ditmars, Raymond Lee
d. Dix, John Adams
d. Dixon, George

d. Dixon, Jean
d. Dockstader, Lew
d. Dodge, Grace Hoadley
d. Dodge, John Francis
d. Dodson, Owen (Vincent)
d. Doggett, Bill
d. Dohnanyi, Erno von
d. Dolly, Rosie
d. Donghia, Angelo R
d. Donnelly, Ruth
d. Donovan, Arthur
d. Donovan, Hedley Williams
d. Dooley, Thomas Anthony, III
d. Dorne, Albert
d. Dorsey, Jimmy
d. Doubrovska, Felia
d. Douglas, Helen Mary Gahagan
d. Douglas, Melvyn
d. Douglas, Robert L
d. Dow, Charles Henry
d. Downes, Olin
d. Dragonette, Jessica
d. Drake, Alfred
d. Drake, Joseph Rodman
d. Draper, Ruth
d. Drew, Daniel
d. Driscoll, Bobby
d. Dryfoos, Orvil Eugene
d. Dubin, Al
d. Dubinsky, David
d. DuBois, Guy Pene
d. Du Bois, Raoul Pene
d. Dubos, Rene Jules
d. Duchin, Eddy
d. Duff, Mary Ann Dyke
d. Duffy, Edmund
d. Duffy, Francis Patrick
d. Dugdale, Richard Louis
d. Duke, Benjamin Newton
d. Duke, James Buchanan
d. DuMont, Allen Balcom
d. Duncan, Augustin
d. Dunlap, William
d. Dunn, Alan
d. Dunne, Finley Peter
d. Dupree, Minnie
d. Durant, William Crapo
d. Duyckinck, Evert Augustus
d. Eagels, Jeanne
d. Eames, Emma Hayden
d. Easton, Florence Gertrude
d. Ebbets, Charles Hercules
d. Eberle, Mary Abastenia St. Leger
d. Edwards, Joan
d. Edwards, Sherman
d. Eilshemius, Louis Michel
d. Einhorn, David
d. Elisofon, Eliot
d. Ellin, Stanley
d. Ellington, Duke
d. Elliott, George Paul
d. Ellis, Perry Edwin
d. Ellison, Ralph (Waldo)
d. Ellsworth, Lincoln
d. Elman, Mischa
d. Eltinge, Julian
d. Engel, Lehman
d. Englund, Richard
d. Ericsson, John
d. Ernst, Jimmy
d. Erskine, John
d. Eurich, Alvin C(hristian)
d. Eustis, Dorothy Leib Harrison
    Wood
d. Evans, Bill
d. Evans, Oliver

d. Evarts, William Maxwell
d. Evelyn, Judith
d. Everleigh, Minna
d. Fairbanks, Douglas, Jr.
d. Fairchild, Sherman Mills
d. Farago, Ladislas
d. Farley, James A(loysius)
d. Farmer, Art(hur Stewart)
d. Farnham, Eliza Wood Burhans
d. Farnham, Sally James
d. Farnum, Dustin Lancy
d. Farrar, John Chipman
d. Farrar, Margaret (Petherbridge)
d. Farrell, Glenda
d. Farrell, James Thomas
d. Faust, Lotta
d. Fearing, Kenneth Flexner
d. Feininger, Andreas (Bernhard
    Lyonel)
d. Feininger, Lyonel
d. Fellig, Arthur
d. Ferber, Edna
d. Feuermann, Emanuel
d. Field, Cyrus West
d. Field, David Dudley
d. Field, Marshall
d. Field, Marshall, III
d. Field, Ron(ald)
d. Fields, Dorothy
d. Fine, Sylvia
d. Fingesten, Peter
d. Finkelstein, Louis, Dr.
d. Finletter, Thomas Knight
d. Finley, John Huston
d. Fischer, Carl
d. Fish, Hamilton
d. Fishbein, Harry J
d. Fisher, Bud
d. Fisher, Fred
d. Fisher, Ham(mond Edward)
d. Fisher, Harrison
d. Fisher, Rudolph
d. Fisk, Jim
d. Fitch, James Marston
d. Fitzgerald, Ed(ward)
d. Fitzgerald, Pegeen
d. Fizdale, Robert
d. Flagg, Ernest
d. Flagg, James Montgomery
d. Flannagan, John Bernard
d. Flanner, Janet
d. Fleischer, Nat(haniel Stanley)
d. Fleischmann, Peter F(rancis)
d. Fleischmann, Raoul H(erbert)
d. Flint, Austin
d. Flowers, Tiger
d. Fogarty, Anne
d. Folger, Henry Clay
d. Forbes, Bertie
d. Forbes, Ralph
d. Ford, Constance
d. Ford, Paul Leicester
d. Fort, Charles Hoy
d. Foster, Joseph C
d. Foster, Stephen Collins
d. Fox, Kate
d. Fox, Margaret
d. Fox, William
d. France, Harry Clinton
d. Francis, Kay
d. Freeman, Joseph
d. Freer, Charles Lang
d. Fremont, John Charles
d. Frick, Henry Clay
d. Friedman, Max
d. Friendly, Fred W.

d. Frohman, Daniel
d. Fuchs, Joseph (Philip)
d. Fulton, Robert
d. Furness, Betty
d. Gabel, Martin
d. Gag, Wanda
d. Gaines, William M(axwell)
d. Galamian, Ivan
d. Galamison, Milton Arthur
d. Gallatin, Albert Eugene
d. Gallo, Fortune
d. Garbo, Greta
d. Gardner, Isabella
d. Garfield, John
d. Garrison, Lloyd K(irkham)
d. Garrison, William Lloyd
d. Gary, Elbert Henry
d. Gasser, Herbert Spencer
d. Gates, Horatio
d. Gates, Pop
d. Gatling, Richard Jordan
d. Gaxton, William
d. Gayle, Addison, Jr.
d. Geddes, Norman Bel
d. Gehrig, Lou
d. Gelb, Lawrence
d. Gellhorn, Walter
d. Geneen, Harold S(ydney)
d. Genovese, Kitty
d. Gentry, Minnie Lee
d. George, Grace
d. George, Henry, Sr.
d. George, Henry, Jr.
d. Gernsback, Hugo
d. Gerry, Elbridge Thomas
d. Gertz, Alison L.
d. Gervasi, Frank Henry
d. Gest, Morris
d. Geva, Tamara
d. Giannini, Vittorio
d. Gibbs, William Francis
d. Gibran, Kahlil
d. Gibson, Charles Dana
d. Gifford, Walter Sherman
d. Gilford, Jack
d. Gill, Brendan
d. Gillenson, Lewis W
d. Gillmore, Frank
d. Gilpatric, Roswell L(eavitt)
d. Gimbel, Bernard Feustman
d. Gimbel, Peter Robin
d. Gimbel, Sophie Haas
d. Gingold, Hermione Ferdinanda
d. Ginott, Haim
d. Ginsberg, Allen
d. Ginsberg, Mitchell I(rving)
d. Giovannitti, Arturo
d. Gish, Lillian (Diana)
d. Gleason, Thomas W(illiam)
d. Glenn, Carroll
d. Gluck, Alma
d. Godfrey, Arthur Michael
d. Godowsky, Leopold
d. Godowsky, Leopold, Jr.
d. Goethals, George Washington
d. Gogarty, Oliver St. John
d. Gold, Arthur
d. Goldberg, Rube
d. Golden, John
d. Goldman, Edwin Franko
d. Goldman, James
d. Golenpaul, Dan
d. Golschmann, Vladimir
d. Gonzalez, Xavier
d. Goodhue, Bertram G(rosvenor)
d. Goodman, Benny

d. Goodrich, Frances
d. Goodrich, Lloyd
d. Goodrich, Samuel Griswold
d. Goodson, Mark
d. Goody, Sam
d. Goodyear, Charles
d. Gordon, Max
d. Gordon, Steve
d. Gottlieb, Adolph
d. Gould, Jay
d. Grace, J(oseph) Peter, Jr.
d. Grace, William Russell
d. Graham, Martha
d. Graham, Virginia
d. Grahame, Gloria
d. Grant, Gordon
d. Grauer, Ben(jamin Franklin)
d. Graves, Nancy (Stevenson)
d. Gray, Barry
d. Graziano, Rocky
d. Greaza, Walter N
d. Greb, Harry
d. Greeley, Horace
d. Green, Abel
d. Green, Hetty
d. Green, Richard R(eginald)
d. Greene, Belle da Costa
d. Greer, Sonny
d. Gregg, John Robert
d. Gretchaninov, Aleksandr
  Tikhonovich
d. Gribble, Harry Wagstaff Graham
d. Griffes, Charles Tomlinson
d. Griffis, Stanton
d. Griffiths, John Willis
d. Grimke, Angelina Emily Weld
d. Gross, Chaim
d. Groth, John August
d. Gruenberg, Sidonie Matsner
d. Guggenheimer, Minnie
d. Guimard, Hector Germain
d. Gunther, John
d. Gunzberg, Nicolas de, Baron
d. Guthrie, Woody
d. Haas, Ernst
d. Hackett, Albert
d. Hadden, Briton
d. Hadley, Henry Kimball
d. Hahn, Emily
d. Haines, Robert Terrel
d. Haire, Bill Martin
d. Hale, Clara (McBride)
d. Hale, Nathan
d. Halpert, Edith Gregor
d. Halsman, Philippe
d. Hamilton, Alexander
d. Hamilton, Charles
d. Hamilton, Nancy
d. Hammerstein, Oscar
d. Hammett, Dashiell
d. Hammond, E(dward) Cuyler
d. Hammond, John Hays, Jr.
d. Hammond, John Henry, Jr.
d. Hampton, Hope
d. Hand, Learned
d. Handy, W(illiam) C(hristopher)
d. Hanks, Nancy
d. Hansberry, Lorraine
d. Hanson, Howard
d. Harand, Irene
d. Harbach, Otto Abels
d. Hardwicke, Cedric Webster, Sir
d. Haring, Keith
d. Harkness, Anna M Richardson
d. Harkness, Rebekah West
d. Harnett, William Michael

d. Harper, Fletcher
d. Harper, James
d. Harper, John
d. Harper, Joseph Wesley
d. Harper, Ken
d. Harrigan, Edward
d. Harris, Jed
d. Harris, Sam Henry
d. Harrison, G(eorge) Donald
d. Harrison, Mary Scott Lord
  Dimmick
d. Harrison, Rex, Sir
d. Harrison, Wallace Kirkman
d. Hart, Lorenz
d. Hartford, John Augustine
d. Hassenfeld, Stephen David
d. Hathaway, Donny
d. Hauge, Gabriel
d. Hawes, Elizabeth
d. Hawkins, Bean
d. Hawkins, Coleman
d. Hawkins, Erick
d. Hayden, Palmer
d. Hayes, Isaac Israel
d. Haynes, George Edmund
d. Hayworth, Rita
d. Hazelton, Nika
d. Hearst, Millicent Veronica Willson
d. Hearst, William Randolph, Jr.
d. Hechinger, Fred Michael
d. Hecht, Ben
d. Hecht, George Joseph
d. Heckscher, August
d. Heggen, Thomas Orls, Jr.
d. Heiden, Konrad
d. Heiser, Victor George
d. Heisman, John William
d. Hejduk, John
d. Held, Anna
d. Hemingway, Mary Welsh
d. Henderson, Fletcher
d. Hendrick, Burton Jesse
d. Henri, Robert
d. Henry, Edward Lamson
d. Henry, O
d. Henson, Jim
d. Henson, Matthew Alexander
d. Herbert, Victor
d. Herbst, Josephine Frey
d. Herford, Oliver
d. Hershey, Lenore
d. Hershfield, Harry
d. Heschel, Abraham Joshua
d. Hess, Leon
d. Hesse, Eva
d. Hewitt, Alan
d. Higginbotham, Jack
d. Highet, Gilbert (Arthur)
d. Hill, Abram
d. Hill, Chippie
d. Hill, Morton A(nthony)
d. Hill, Patty Smith
d. Hillenkoetter, Roscoe H(enry)
d. Hilliard, Robert Cochran
d. Hillquit, Morris
d. Hirsch, Joseph
d. Hiss, Alger
d. Hobson, Laura Zametkin
d. Hobson, Richmond Pearson
d. Hodges, Johnny
d. Hoest, Bill
d. Hoffman, Al
d. Hoffman, Malvina
d. Hoffman, Paul Gray
d. Hofmann, Hans
d. Hofstadter, Richard

d. Holiday, Billie
d. Holland, Jerome Heartwell
d. Holliday, Judy
d. Holm, Hanya
d. Holman, Bill
d. Holman, Eugene
d. Holman, Nat(han)
d. Holmes, John Haynes
d. Holt, Henry
d. Hoover, Herbert C(lark)
d. Hoover, Lou Henry
d. Hopkins, Arthur
d. Hopkins, Claude
d. Hopkins, Harry Lloyd
d. Hopkins, Miriam
d. Hopper, Edward
d. Horan, James David
d. Horney, Karen Danielson
d. Horowitz, Vladimir
d. Horst, Louis
d. House, Edward Mandell
d. Hovey, Richard
d. Howard, Elston Gene
d. Howard, Eugene
d. Howard, Jane Temple
d. Howard, Roy Wilson
d. Howard, Willie
d. Howe, Elias
d. Howe, Irving
d. Howe, Quincy
d. Howells, William Dean
d. Huggins, Miller James
d. Hughan, Jessie Wallace
d. Hughes, Langston
d. Hull, Josephine
d. Humphrey, Doris
d. Huneker, James Gibbons
d. Hunt, Walter
d. Hunter, Alberta
d. Hunter, Glenn
d. Hunter, Thomas
d. Huntington, Daniel
d. Hurok, Sol(omon Isaievich)
d. Hurst, Fannie
d. Hyman, Libbie Henrietta
d. Hyslop, James Hervey
d. Igoe, Hype
d. Ingersoll, Robert Green
d. Inman, Henry
d. Irwin, May
d. Irwin, Will(iam Henry)
d. Ives, Charles Edward
d. Jackson, Charles Reginald
d. Jackson, Hurricane
d. Jackson, Milt(on)
d. Jackson, William Henry
d. Jacobi, Mary Corinna Putnam
d. Jacobs, Joe B
d. Jacobs, Michael S
d. Janeway, Eliot
d. Janis, Sidney
d. Janney, Russell Dixon
d. Janssen, Herbert
d. Janssen, Werner
d. Jarvis, John Wesley
d. Jobim, Antonio Carlos
d. Joffrey, Robert
d. John, John P(ico)
d. Johnson, Eastman
d. Johnson, Hall
d. Johnson, Howard Deering
d. Johnson, James Price
d. Johnson, Jonathan Eastman
d. Johnson, Osa Helen Leighty
d. Johnson, William
d. Jones, Allan

d. Jones, Billy
d. Jones, Candy
d. Jones, Jo(nathan)
d. Jones, Jonah
d. Joplin, Scott
d. Jordan, Elizabeth Garver
d. Joyce, Peggy Hopkins
d. Juch, Emma
d. Juilliard, Augustus D
d. Jumel, Eliza
d. Jung, Leo
d. Kaempffert, Waldemar (Bernhard)
d. Kahane, Meir David
d. Kahane, Melanie
d. Kahn, Ben
d. Kahn, Louis I(sadore)
d. Kahn, Madeline (Gail)
d. Kahn, Otto Hermann
d. Kalem, T(heodore) E(ustace)
d. Kalish, Max
d. Kaltenborn, H(ans) V(on)
d. Kaminska, Ida
d. Kanin, Garson
d. Kaplan, Jacob Merrill
d. Kaplan, Mordecai
d. Karfiol, Bernard
d. Kauffer, Edward McKnight
d. Kaufman, Boris
d. Kaufman, George S(imon)
d. Kaufman, Irving R(obert)
d. Kaufman, Sue
d. Kazin, Alfred
d. Keating, Kenneth B
d. Keats, Ezra Jack
d. Keeler, Wee Willie
d. Keene, Christopher
d. Keeton, Kathy
d. Keith, Ian
d. Kelley, Edgar Stillman
d. Kelly, Bruce
d. Kelly, Shipwreck
d. Kelly, Stephen Eugene
d. Kempton, (James) Murray
d. Kensett, John Frederick
d. Kent, James
d. Keogh, Eugene James
d. Kerensky, Alexander Fedorovitch
d. Kern, Jerome David
d. Kert, Larry
d. Kertesz, Andre
d. Ketchel, Stanley
d. Kiam, Omar
d. Kibbee, Robert Joseph
d. Kiesler, Frederick John
d. Kilgallen, Dorothy
d. Kilgore, Al
d. Kilpatrick, William H(eard)
d. Kimbrough, Emily
d. King, Alexander
d. King, Dennis
d. King Curtis
d. Kingman, Dong Moy Shu
d. Kipnis, Claude
d. Kirby, Rollin
d. Kirk, Alan Goodrich
d. Kirk, Lisa
d. Kirkland, Caroline Matilda
   Stansbury
d. Kirkwood, James
d. Kirstein, Lincoln (Edward)
d. Kleban, Edward Lawrence
d. Klein, Anne
d. Kline, Franz Joseph
d. Kline, Morris
d. Kline, Nathan Schellenberg
d. Kline, Otis Adelbert

d. Klopfer, Donald Simon
d. Knerr, H(arold) H
d. Knopf, Blanche Wolf
d. Kober, Arthur
d. Koch, John
d. Kohler, Kaufmann
d. Kolchin, Ellis Robert
d. Kollmar, Richard
d. Kolodin, Irving
d. Koo, V(i) K(yuin) Wellington
d. Kosinski, Jerzy (Nikodem)
d. Kotzky, Alex Sylvester
d. Krasner, Lee
d. Kredel, Fritz
d. Kreisler, Fritz
d. Kress, Samuel Henry
d. Kronold, Selma
d. Kuniyoshi, Yasuo
d. Kunstler, William M(oses)
d. Kuralt, Charles (Bishop)
d. Labouisse, Henry Richardson
d. Lachaise, Gaston
d. Ladd-Franklin, Christine
d. Ladnier, Tommy
d. La Guardia, Fiorello Henry
d. Lahr, Bert
d. Laidler, Harry Wellington
d. Laing, Hugh
d. Lancaster, Joseph
d. Landsteiner, Karl
d. Lane, Burton
d. Lang, Daniel
d. Lang, Eddie
d. Langer, Lawrence
d. Larsen, Nella
d. Larson, Jonathan
d. Lasker, Albert D(avis)
d. Lasker, Edward
d. Lasker, Emanuel
d. Lasser, Jacob Kay
d. Lauder, Joseph H
d. Laurie, Joe, Jr.
d. Lawe, John Edward
d. Lawrence, Gertrude
d. Lawrence, Josephine
d. Lawrence, William Beach
d. Lawrenson, Helen Brown
d. Lazarus, Emma
d. Lea, Fanny Heaslip
d. Leadbelly
d. Lear, Frances
d. Lebowsky, Stanley Richard
d. Lee, Canada
d. Lee, Will
d. Leech, Margaret Kernochan
d. Lehman, Herbert Henry
d. Leibowitz, Samuel Simon
d. Leigh, Carolyn
d. Lemoyne, W(illiam) J
d. Lengyel, Emil
d. Lennon, John Winston
d. Lenya, Lotte
d. Leonard, Benny
d. Leonard, Eddie
d. Leonard, Jack E
d. Leontief, Wassily W
d. Leontovich, Eugenie
d. Lerdo de Tejada, Sebastian
d. Lerner, Alan Jay
d. Lerner, Max
d. Lescaze, William
d. Leslie, Edgar
d. Leslie, Frank
d. Lev, Ray
d. Levene, Sam
d. Leventhal, Albert Rice

d. Newell, Edward Theodore
d. Newhouse, Samuel Irving
d. Newman, Barnett
d. Newman, Joe Dwight
d. Nichols, Ruth Rowland
d. Nielsen, Alice
d. Nikolais, Alwin
d. Nixon, Richard M(ilhous)
d. Nizer, Louis
d. Noguchi, Isamu
d. Norell, Norman
d. Nossiter, Bernard Daniel
d. Novotna, Jarmila
d. Nugent, Elliott
d. O'Brien, Larry
d. O'Connor, John Joseph, Cardinal
d. O'Connor, Una
d. O'Dwyer, William
d. O'Hara, Frank
d. Ohrbach, Nathan M
d. Olds, Irving S
d. Oliver, Edith
d. Oliver, James A(rthur)
d. Oliver, Sy
d. Olson, Charles John
d. Olson, James E(lias)
d. Onassis, Jacqueline (Lee Bouvier Kennedy)
d. O'Neal, Frederick
d. O'Neil, James F(rancis)
d. Oppenheim, James
d. Orkin, Ruth
d. Osborn, Paul
d. Osgood, Frances Sargent Locke
d. Oursler, (Charles) Fulton
d. Oursler, Will(iam Charles)
d. Paddleford, Clementine Haskin
d. Paderewski, Ignace Jan
d. Padover, Saul Kussiel
d. Paez, Jose Antonio
d. Page, Geraldine
d. Page, Hot Lips
d. Paine, Thomas
d. Paley, Barbara Cushing
d. Paley, William Samuel
d. Palmer, Frances Flora Bond
d. Pangborn, Clyde Edward
d. Pantaleoni, Helenka (Tradeusa Adamowski)
d. Papi, Genarro
d. Papp, Joseph
d. Parish, Mitchell
d. Parker, Alton Brooks
d. Parker, Charlie
d. Parker, Dorothy Rothschild
d. Parnis, Mollie
d. Parsons, Elsie Clews
d. Parton, Sara Payson Willis
d. Pascal, Gabriel
d. Pate, Maurice
d. Patterson, Alicia
d. Patterson, Joseph Medill
d. Payson, Joan Whitney
d. Pearl, Jack
d. Pearlroth, Norbert
d. Pecora, Ferdinand
d. Peerce, Jan
d. Pelletier, Wilfrid
d. Pemberton, Brock
d. Pennell, Joseph Stanley
d. Penney, J(ames) C(ash)
d. Pennington, Ann
d. Pennock, Herb(ert Jefferis)
d. Perelman, S(idney) J(oseph)
d. Perkins, Frances
d. Perlea, Jonel

d. Perlmutter, Nathan
d. Perrin, Jean Baptiste
d. Perry, Antoinette
d. Perry, Eleanor Bayer
d. Perry, Frank
d. Perry, Matthew Calbraith, Commodore
d. Persinger, Louis
d. Peters, Brandon
d. Pettit, William Thomas
d. Philips, David Graham
d. Phillips, Channing Emery
d. Phyfe, Duncan
d. Piastro, Michel
d. Piccolo, Brian
d. Pierce, Edward Allen
d. Pinchot, Gifford
d. Pinero, Miguel
d. Pinto, Isaac
d. Pious, Minerva
d. Placzek, Adolf K(urt)
d. Platt, Thomas Collier
d. Pogany, Willy
d. Polacco, Giorgio
d. Pollock, Channing
d. Pool, David de Sola
d. Poor, Henry Varnum, III
d. Pope, John Russell
d. Popper, Hans
d. Porter, Edwin
d. Porter, William Trotter
d. Post, Emily (Price)
d. Potofsky, Jacob Samuel
d. Potok, Anna Maximilian Apfelbaum
d. Potthast, Edward Henry
d. Powell, Earl
d. Powell, William Henry
d. Pratt, Charles
d. Preminger, Otto Ludwig
d. Prendergast, Maurice Brazil
d. Price, Sammy
d. Pringle, Aileen
d. Prouty, Jed
d. Puente, Tito
d. Pulitzer, Ralph
d. Pupin, Michael Idvorsky
d. Quill, Mike
d. Quinn, Edmond T
d. Quintero, Jose (Benjamin)
d. Rabi, Isidor Isaac
d. Rabin, Michael
d. Rabin, Yehuda L
d. Rand, Ayn
d. Rand, Ellen Gertrude Emmet
d. Randolph, Asa Philip
d. Rank, Otto
d. Raphaelson, Samson
d. Rascoe, Burton
d. Raskin, A(braham) H(enry)
d. Raskin, Ellen
d. Raskin, Judith
d. Rathbone, Basil
d. Rattner, Abraham
d. Ray, Nicholas
d. Raymond, Henry Jarvis
d. Read, Thomas Buchanan
d. Redman, Don
d. Rehan, Ada
d. Reid, Helen Rogers
d. Reid, Ogden Mills
d. Reik, Theodor
d. Reiner, Fritz
d. Reinhardt, Ad(olph Frederick)
d. Reinhardt, Max
d. Reinhart, Charles S
d. Reisenberg, Nadia

d. Rentner, Maurice
d. Renwick, James, Jr.
d. Resnik, Muriel
d. Resor, Stanley Burnett
d. Revson, Charles Haskell
d. Ribicoff, Abraham A(lexander)
d. Rice, Grantland
d. Rice, Thomas Dartmouth
d. Richards, Stanley
d. Richardson, Lee
d. Richman, Charles
d. Richman, Milton
d. Ridge, Lola
d. Riegger, Wallingford
d. Rifkind, Simon H(irsch)
d. Rigby, Harry
d. Riggs, Lynn
d. Rinehart, Frederick Roberts
d. Rinehart, Mary Roberts
d. Ripley, Elmer Horton
d. Ripley, George
d. Ripley, Robert Leroy
d. Ripley, William Zebina
d. Ritter, Thelma
d. Rivera, Jose Eustasio
d. Rivers, Thomas Milton
d. Roach, John
d. Robbins, Jerome
d. Robeson, Eslanda Cardoza Goode
d. Robinson, Bill
d. Robinson, Claude Everett
d. Robinson, Edward
d. Robinson, Edwin Arlington
d. Robinson, Francis Arthur
d. Robinson, Henry Morton
d. Robinson, James Harvey
d. Robinson, Theodore
d. Rockefeller, Abby Aldrich
d. Rockefeller, Mary French
d. Rockefeller, Nelson A(ldrich)
d. Rockefeller, Rodman C
d. Rodale, Jerome Irving
d. Rodgers, Jimmie
d. Rodgers, Richard
d. Rodriguez, Andres
d. Roebling, John Augustus
d. Rogers, Mary Joseph(ine)
d. Rollins, Howard Ellsworth, Jr.
d. Romano, Umberto
d. Romberg, Sigmund
d. Rome, Harold J(acob)
d. Rooney, Pat
d. Roosevelt, Alice Lee
d. Roosevelt, Anna Eleanor
d. Roosevelt, Eleanor
d. Roosevelt, John Aspinal
d. Root, Elihu
d. Rosenberg, Anna Marie
d. Rosenfeld, Henry J
d. Rosenfeld, Paul
d. Rosenman, Dorothy
d. Rosenstein, Nettie
d. Rosenstock, Joseph
d. Rosenthal, Ida Cohen
d. Rosenthal, Jean E
d. Rosenthal, Moriz
d. Roskolenko, Harry
d. Ross, David
d. Ross, Ishbel
d. Ross, Lanny
d. Rossen, Robert
d. Rosten, Leo C(alvin)
d. Rosten, Norman
d. Roszak, Theodore
d. Roth, Lillian
d. Rothier, Leon

d. Tashman, Lilyan
d. Tatum, Edward Lawrie
d. Taylor, (Joseph) Deems
d. Taylor, Henry Junior
d. Taylor, Laurette
d. Taylor, Sydney Brenner
d. Teasdale, Sara
d. Tebelak, John Michael
d. Teichmann, Howard Miles
d. Teilhard de Chardin, Pierre
d. Ter-Arutunian, Rouben
d. Terhune, Mary Virginia
d. Terry, Paul H
d. Terry, Walter
d. Tesla, Nikola
d. Tevis, Walter
d. Thant, U
d. Thibault, Conrad
d. Thomas, Dylan Marlais
d. Thomas, Edith Matilda
d. Thomas, Lewis
d. Thompson, George Selden
d. Thompson, J(ames) Walter
d. Thompson, Kay
d. Thompson, Oscar
d. Thomson, Virgil Garnett
d. Thorndike, Lynn
d. Thorpe, Thomas Bangs
d. Thurber, James Grover
d. Thurman, Wallace (Henry)
d. Tibbett, Lawrence Mervil
d. Tieri, Frank
d. Tiffany, Louis Comfort
d. Tilberis, Elizabeth
d. Tobias, Channing Heggie
d. Todman, Bill
d. Toffenetti, Dario Louis
d. Toller, Ernst
d. Tomes, Margot
d. Tomlin, Bradley Walker
d. Tone, Franchot
d. Torrence, Ernest
d. Torrence, Ridgely
d. Torrio, Johnny
d. Toscanini, Arturo
d. Tourel, Jennie
d. Towne, Charles Hanson
d. Townsend, George Alfred
d. Tracy, Arthur
d. Train, Arthur Cheney
d. Traphagen, Ethel Leigh
d. Traube, Shepard
d. Tree, Marietta Endicott Peabody
d. Trilling, Diana (Rubin)
d. Trilling, Lionel
d. Trippe, Juan Terry
d. Troyanos, Tatiana
d. Trumbull, John
d. Tucker, Sophie
d. Tudor, Antony
d. Tully, Alice
d. Turkus, Burton B
d. Tweed, Boss
d. Tyler, Parker
d. Typhoid Mary
d. Ullstein, Hermann
d. Untermeyer, Jean Starr
d. Urban, Joseph Maria
d. Urrutia Lleo, Manuel
d. Ussachevsky, Vladimir Alexis
d. Valentina
d. Valentino, Rudolph
d. Vance, Louis Joseph
d. Van Cortlandt, Oloff Stevenszen
d. Van Cortlandt, Stephanus
d. Vanderbilt, Amy

d. Vanderbilt, Cornelius
d. Vanderbilt, William Henry
d. Van Dine, S S
d. Van Fleet, Jo
d. Van Horne, Harriet
d. Van Loon, Hendrik Willem
d. Van Paassen, Pierre
d. Van Slyke, Helen Lenore Vogt
d. Van Vechten, Carl
d. Varese, Edgar
d. Vaux, Calvert
d. Vicious, Sid
d. Victor, Sally Josephs
d. Vila, George Raymond
d. Villard, Oswald (Garrison)
d. Vishniac, Roman
d. VonTilzer, Harry
d. Vreeland, Diana (Dalziel)
d. Vyshinsky, Andrei Yanuarievich
d. Wagner, Robert F(erdinand)
d. Walburn, Raymond
d. Waldman, Max
d. Walker, Edyth
d. Walker, Jimmy
d. Walker, Sarah Breedlove
    McWilliams
d. Wallace, Ed(ward Tatum)
d. Wallack, James William
d. Wallenstein, Alfred Franz
d. Walter, Cyril
d. Wanger, Walter
d. Warburg, Felix Moritz
d. Ward, Fannie
d. Warfield, David
d. Warhol, Andy
d. Warren, Leonard
d. Washington, Buck
d. Washington, Grover, Jr.
d. Wasson, R(obert) Gordon
d. Waterman, Lewis Edson
d. Watson, John Broadus
d. Watson, Thomas J(ohn), Sr.
d. Watts, Richard, Jr.
d. Weaver, Robert C(lifton)
d. Webster, Jean
d. Wechsler, David
d. Wechsler, James Arthur
d. Weed, Thurlow
d. Weidman, Charles Edward, Jr.
d. Weidman, Jerome
d. Weill, Kurt
d. Weinberg, Chester
d. Weingarten, Violet Brown
d. Weir, Julian Alden
d. Weir, Robert W
d. Weiss, Ted
d. Welch, Herbert
d. Wellman, Walter
d. Wells, Carolyn
d. Wells, Horace
d. Weng, Will
d. Wenrich, Percy
d. Werblin, Sonny
d. Westinghouse, George
d. Weston, Jack
d. Whalen, Grover (Michael)
    A(loysius)
d. Wheeler, Bert
d. Wheeler, Candace Thurber
d. Wheeler, Joseph
d. Wheelock, John Hall
d. Whitaker, Rogers E(rnest)
    M(alcolm)
d. White, Miles
d. White, Richard Grant
d. White, Stanford

d. White, Theodore Harold
d. White, Walter Francis
d. Whitehill, Clarence Eugene
d. Whitney, Gertrude Vanderbilt
d. Whitney, Harry Payne
d. Whitney, William Collins
d. Whyte, William H(ollingsworth)
d. Wilkins, Roy
d. Willard, Frances Elizabeth Caroline
d. Williams, Bert
d. Williams, Tennessee
d. Willkie, Wendell Lewis
d. Wills, Harry
d. Wilson, Henry Braid
d. Wilson, Mitchell A
d. Winston, Harry
d. Wise, Stephen Samuel
d. Witherspoon, Herbert
d. Witmark, Isidore
d. Wood, James Rushmore
d. Woodbridge, Frederick James
    Eugene
d. Woodruff, Hale (Aspacio)
d. Woods, Granville T
d. Woodworth, Samuel
d. Woollcott, Alexander Humphreys
d. Woolman, John
d. Woolrich, Cornell
d. Wright, James Arlington
d. Wright, Louis Tompkins
d. Wright, Russel
d. Wrightsman, Charles Bierer
d. Wrightson, Earl
d. Wu, Chien Shiung
d. Wycherley, Margaret
d. Wylie, Elinor Hoyt
d. Yale, Linus
d. Young, Gig
d. Young, Lester Willis
d. Young, Mahonri Mackintosh
d. Young, Roland
d. Young, Stark
d. Youngman, Henny
d. Youskevitch, Igor
d. Yurka, Blanche
d. Zelaya, Jose Santos
d. Zemlinsky, Alexander von
d. Zenatello, Giovanni
d. Zenger, John Peter
d. Ziegler, Edward
d. Ziff, William Bernard
d. Zipprodt, Patricia
d. Zirato, Bruno
d. Zuckerman, Ben

New York Mills, New York
  b. Furgol, Ed(ward)

Newark, New York
  b. O'Neal, Shaquille
  d. Gummere, William Stryker

Newburgh, New York
  b. Belknap, William Worth
  b. Downing, Andrew Jackson
  b. Ferraro, Geraldine Anne
  b. Hart, William Surrey
  b. Inness, George
  b. Kelly, Ellsworth
  b. Leech, Margaret Kernochan
  b. Roosevelt, Sara Delano
  d. Colombo, Joseph Anthony

Newton, New York
  b. Harper, Fletcher

Pittsford, New York
d. Lasch, Christopher

Plainview, New York
d. Pakula, Alan J(ay)

Plandome, New York
d. Burnett, Frances Eliza Hodgson

Plattsburg, New York
b. Arthur, Jean
b. Hagerty, James Campbell
b. Watson, Mark Skinner
d. Kent, Rockwell

Pleasantville, New York
b. King, Morganna
d. Tunnell, Em(len)

Point Lookout, New York
d. Hillman, Sidney (Simcha)

Pompey, New York
b. Fargo, William George
b. Palmer, Erastus Dow

Port Byron, New York
b. Bonelli, Richard

Port Chester, New York
b. Lopez, Barry (Holstun)
d. Arno, Peter
d. Baker, Samm Sinclair
d. Barrow, Ed(ward Grant)
d. Cardozo, Benjamin Nathan
d. Roosa, Robert V(incent)
d. Weinman, Adolph A

Port Jefferson, New York
d. Berndt, Walter
d. Haworth, Leland John
d. Zukofsky, Louis

Port Jervis, New York
b. Harris, Bucky

Port Washington, New York
b. Gunn, Hartford Nelson, Jr.
d. Alexander, Hattie Elizabeth
d. Guggenheim, Daniel

Potsdam, New York
b. Kellogg, Frank Billings

Poughkeepsie, New York
b. Baker, Sara Josephine
b. Butts, Alfred M(osher)
b. Cott, Ted
b. Crew, Rudolph F.
b. Denning, Richard
b. Duke, Bill
b. Holland, Tom
b. Jordy, William H(enry)
b. Rattner, Abraham
b. Thomas, Debi
b. Wood, Edward D., Jr.
d. Cole, Timothy
d. Lipmann, Fritz Albert
d. Morgenthau, Henry, Jr.
d. Morrison, Sterling
d. Roosevelt, Franklin Delano, Jr.
d. Rovere, Richard Halworth
d. Rushmore, Robert (William)

---

d. Vassar, Matthew

Pound Ridge, New York
d. Porter, Sylvia Field

Purchase, New York
d. Knopf, Alfred Abraham
d. Lehman, Adele Lewisohn
d. Tarnower, Herman

Putnam County, New York
b. Crosby, Fanny

Quogue, New York
b. Scribner, Charles, Jr.

Randolph, New York
b. Castlemon, Harry

Raquette Lake, New York
d. Huntington, Collis Potter

Redwood, New York
b. Ryan, Tommy

Remsen, New York
d. Steuben, Friedrich Wilhelm Ludolf
Gerhard Augustin, Baron

Rensselaer, New York
b. Morris, Ernest Brougham
b. Singer, Isaac Merrit

Rensselaerville, New York
b. Farnham, Eliza Wood Burhans

Rhinebeck, New York
b. Bachman, John
d. Butts, Alfred M(osher)
d. Hickok, Lorena A
d. Livingston, Edward
d. Morton, Levi Parsons

Richford, New York
b. Rockefeller, John D(avison)
b. Rockefeller, William

Richmond Hill, New York
b. Gould, Morton
d. Barr, Amelia Edith Huddleston

Richmondville, New York
b. France, Harry Clinton

Ripley, New York
b. Ely, Richard Theodore
b. Goodrich, Benjamin Franklin

Riverdale, New York
d. Joy, Leatrice
d. Willys, John North

Riverhead, New York
b. Pike, Otis Grey
d. Brooks, Geraldine

Rochester, New York
b. Adler, Elmer
b. Alden, Isabella Macdonald
b. Antonelli, John(ny August)
b. Ashbery, John (Lawrence)
b. Baker, Nicholson

---

b. Barry, Philip
b. Bausch, Edward
b. Brown, Marcia
b. Calloway, Cab
b. Curran, Charles E(dward)
b. Diamond, David
b. Duel, Peter
b. Finlay, Virgil
b. Forster, Robert
b. Fullerton, (Charles) Gordon
b. Gannett, Lewis Stiles
b. Gilbert, Grove Karl
b. Gorkin, Jess
b. Hagen, Walter Charles
b. Haviland, Virginia
b. Kanin, Garson
b. Katzen, Mollie
b. Kirstein, Lincoln (Edward)
b. Klem, Bill
b. Lincoln, Elmo
b. Lithgow, John (Arthur)
b. Lund, John
b. Mangione, Chuck
b. McCarthy, Clem
b. Miller, Mitch(ell William)
b. O'Brian, Hugh
b. Paul, Gabe
b. Pringle, Laurence
b. Radbourn, Old Hoss
b. Rauschenbusch, Walter
b. Rico, Don(ato)
b. Rock, Arthur
b. Stein, Clarence S
b. Stern, Bill
b. Terry, Randall A.
b. Wallington, Jimmy
b. Wilder, Alec
b. Williams, Wendy O(rlean)
b. Wilson, Joseph Chamberlain
d. Anthony, Susan B(rownell)
d. Bausch, Edward
d. Bausch, John Jacob
d. Brooks, Louise
d. Courtney, Clint(on Dawson)
d. De Gaetani, Jan
d. Eastman, George
d. Eden, Elizabeth Debbie
d. Ellingson, Mark
d. Folsom, Marion Bayard
d. Gannett, Frank Ernest
d. Lamb, Harold Albert
d. Mawdudi, Abu-I A'la
d. Morgan, Lewis Henry
d. Rauschenbusch, Walter
d. Rochester, Nathaniel
d. Selden, George Baldwin
d. Serling, Rod
d. Sibley, Hiram
d. Wadsworth, James Jeremiah
d. Whipple, George Hoyt

Rockaway Beach, New York
b. Bittan, Roy
b. Rich, John

Rockville Centre, New York
b. DeMott, Benjamin Haile
b. Heatherton, Joey
b. Kearns, Doris H
b. Louie, David Wong
d. Meredith, Sidney
d. O'Brien, John J
d. Rose, Vincent

Rocky Point, New York
d. Leach, Will

Rodman, New York
b. Woolworth, Frank Winfield

Rome, New York
b. Brooks, Walter R(ollin)
b. Fisher, Welthy (Blakesley Honsinger)
b. Riley, Pat(rick James)
b. Wright, Harold Bell

Roosevelt, New York
b. Erving, Julius Winfield

Rosedale, New York
b. Score, Herb(ert Jude)

Roslyn, New York
b. Schwartz, Stephen L(awrence)
d. Black, Walter J
d. Margolius, Sidney Senier

Roslyn Heights, New York
d. Morley, Christopher (Darlington)

Rossville, New York
b. Cropsey, Jasper Francis

Rouses Point, New York
b. Hayford, John Fillmore

Roxbury, New York
b. Burroughs, John
b. Gould, Jay
d. Brooks, Walter R(ollin)

Royalton, New York
b. Lockwood, Belva Ann Bennett

Rushville, New York
b. Whitman, Marcus

Rye, New York
b. Atkins, Christopher
b. Barker, Lex
b. Bateman, Jason
b. Bateman, Justine
b. Bird, Junius Bouton
b. Cort, Bud
b. Ford, Anne McDonnell
b. Nash, Ogden Frederick
d. Ammann, Othmar Hermann
d. Berlin, Richard E
d. Bishop, Hazel
d. Duffy, Ben
d. Goodman, Andrew
d. Ives, James Merritt
d. Marston, William Moulton
d. Stern, Bill

Sackets Harbor, New York
b. Bible, Frances Lillian
d. Guthrie, Samuel

Sag Harbor, New York
b. Sterling, George
d. Algren, Nelson
d. Brook, Alexander

Saint James, New York
d. Frissell, Toni
d. McKim, Charles Follen

Saint Regis Reservation, New York
b. Oakes, Richard

Salamanca, New York
b. Abrams, George H. J.
b. Evans, Ray

Salisbury, New York
b. Yale, Linus

Sands Point, New York
b. Cowles, William Hutchinson, Jr.
d. Guggenheim, Harry Frank
d. Guggenheim, Solomon Robert
d. Leser, Tina
d. Lewyt, Alexander Milton
d. Swope, Herbert Bayard

Sandy Hill, New York
b. Harris, Townsend

Sangerfield, New York
b. Newberry, John Stoughton

Saranac Lake, New York
d. Crapsey, Adelaide
d. Lee, Lila
d. Mathewson, Christy
d. Norton, Jack
d. Quezon (y Molina), Manuel Luis
d. Schaefer, Germany

Saratoga, New York
b. Sullivan, Frank
d. Sullivan, Frank

Saratoga County, New York
b. Scott, Clarence
b. Scott, Edward Irvin

Saratoga Springs, New York
b. Brackett, Charles
b. Bruchac, Joseph, III
b. Humphrey, Elliott S
b. Pierce, David Hyde
b. Valentine, Scott
d. Graham, William Alexander
d. Martin, John
d. Whitney, C(ornelius) V(anderbilt)

Saugerties, New York
b. Fisher, Irving
b. Wortman, Denys

Sauquoit, New York
b. Gray, Asa

Scarsdale, New York
b. Holbrooke, Richard
b. Lucci, Susan
b. Tompkins, Daniel D
d. Folsom, Frank M
d. Harrar, J(acob) George
d. Henle, Guy
d. Van Heusen, John
d. Wilson, Charles Edward

Schenectady, New York
b. Ball, John Dudley, Jr.
b. Blodgett, Katherine Burr
b. Blum, Stella
b. Davis, Ann Bradford
b. Garroway, Dave

b. Mackerras, Charles
b. Ponselle, Carmela
b. Potter, Henry Codman
b. Rourke, Mickey
b. Sayles, John
b. Schaefer, Vincent Joseph
b. Taylor, Graham
b. Tudor, John Thomas
d. Alexanderson, Ernst Frederik Werner
d. Blodgett, Katherine Burr
d. Coolidge, William David
d. Golub, William Weldon
d. Schaefer, Vincent Joseph
d. Steinmetz, Charles Proteus

Schodack, New York
d. Genet, Edmond Charles Edouard

Schroon Lake, New York
b. Knapp, Seaman Asahel

Schuyler Falls, New York
b. Bridges, Calvin Blackman

Scipio, New York
b. Elliott, Charles Loring

Scotia, New York
d. Doherty, Robert Ernest

Seneca Falls, New York
b. Blatch, Harriot Eaton Stanton
b. Dickinson, Edwin W
b. Giusti, Dave

Setauket, New York
b. Mount, William Sidney
d. Mount, William Sidney

Shady, New York
d. Cowell, Henry Dixon

Sharon Springs, New York
d. Delmonico, Lorenzo

Sheepshead Bay, New York
d. McCay, Winsor

Shelter Island, New York
d. Hickenlooper, Bourke B

Sidney, New York
b. Carlson, Evans Fordyce

Silver Creek, New York
b. Ehmke, Howard Jonathan

Sinclairville, New York
b. Tugwell, Rexford Guy

Skaneateles, New York
d. Danforth, William

Smithtown, New York
b. Dean, Laura
b. Weld, William F(loyd)

Sneden's Landing, New York
d. McClintic, Guthrie

Solvay, New York
b. Bacon, Leonard

South Nyack, New York
d. Breger, Dave

South Salem, New York
d. Dewhurst, Colleen

Southampton, New York
b. Cox, Edward Finch
b. Onassis, Jacqueline (Lee Bouvier Kennedy)
b. Thayer, Mary Van Rensselaer
b. Yastrzemski, Carl Michael
d. Barthelmess, Richard
d. DeKooning, Elaine Marie Catherine Fried
d. Duke, Angier Biddle
d. Elson, Robert Truscott
d. Geldzahler, Henry
d. Gerulaitis, Vitas
d. Gwathmey, Robert
d. James, Philip
d. Jones, James
d. Matter, Herbert
d. McIntyre, James
d. Mellon, Andrew William
d. Merrill, Charles Edward
d. Paton, Richard
d. Porter, Fairfield

Southold, New York
d. Parsons, Betty Pierson

Sparta, New York
d. Shays, Daniel

Spring Valley, New York
b. Margulies, Julianna

Springville, New York
b. Warner, Pop
d. Yellen, Jack

Staatsburg, New York
d. Firkusny, Rudolf

Stamford, New York
b. Judson, Edward Zane Carroll
d. Judson, Edward Zane Carroll

Stanfordville, New York
d. Cagney, James

Star Lake, New York
b. Young, Marian

Staten Island, New York
b. Appice, Carmine
b. Bloor, Mother
b. Britton, Nathaniel, Lord
b. Buatta, Mario
b. Dean, Laura
b. Du Bois, Raoul Pene
b. Johansen, David
b. Magruder, Jeb Stuart
b. Miller, Alice Duer
b. Murphy, John Michael
b. Pero, A J
b. Ripley, Elmer Horton
b. Scarpelli, Glenn
b. Scavullo, Francesco

b. Schroder, Rick
b. Sturgeon, Theodore Hamilton
b. Vanderbilt, Amy
b. Vanderbilt, Cornelius
d. Curtis, George William
d. Maretzek, Max
d. O'Sullivan, Timothy H
d. Tompkins, Daniel D

Stephentown, New York
b. Face, Roy

Steuben County, New York
b. Fowler, Orson Squire

Stillwater, New York
b. Fillmore, Abigail (Powers)

Stockbridge, New York
b. Armour, Philip Danforth

Stony Brook, New York
d. DiDonato, Pietro

Stony Pointe, New York
d. Golden, William

Suffern, New York
b. Harper, Valerie
d. Antin, Mary
d. Beard, Dan(iel Carter)
d. Jaegers, Albert
d. Reshevsky, Samuel
d. Shippen, Katherine Binney

Sullivan County, New York
d. Grossinger, Jennie
d. Lease, Mary Elizabeth Clyens

Summerhill, New York
b. Fillmore, Millard

Sylvan Lake, New York
b. Brouthers, Dan

Syosset, New York
d. Hershey, Alfred D(ay)
d. Streibert, Theodore Cuyler

Syracuse, New York
b. Berendt, John
b. Bode, Vaughn
b. Carle, Eric
b. Cruise, Tom
b. Danforth, William
b. Dinneen, Bill
b. Farley, Walter Lorimer
b. Hesburgh, Theodore Martin
b. Judson, Egbert Putnam
b. Kenneth
b. Lundigan, William
b. May, Edna
b. Sage, Margaret Olivia
b. Sears, John Patrick
b. Serling, Rod
b. Tomlin, Bradley Walker
b. Van Heusen, Jimmy
b. Van Horne, Harriet
d. Dinneen, Bill
d. Putch, William Henry
d. Sumner, Edwin V

Talcottville, New York
d. Wilson, Edmund

Tannersville, New York
d. Adams, Maude

Tappan, New York
b. Quidor, John
d. Andre, John

Tarrytown, New York
b. Kent, Rockwell
d. Havell, Robert, Jr.
d. Irving, Washington
d. Lowenfels, Walter
d. Mack, Ted
d. Prince, William
d. Rockefeller, William
d. Willis, Nathaniel Parker

Taughannock, New York
b. Goodwin, Hannibal Williston

Theresa, New York
b. Drummond, Roscoe

Thornwood, New York
d. Gougelman, Pierre

Tilantire Bridge, New York
d. Smith, Kenneth Danforth

Tompkinsville, New York
d. Keene, Thomas Wallace

Townsend, New York
b. Delano, Jane Arminda

Troy, New York
b. Baker, George Fisher
b. Crocker, Charles
b. Evers, Johnny
b. Fitzgerald, Ed(ward)
b. Fuller, Robert
b. Lewis, Tom
b. Peters, Brandon
b. Selzer, Richard (Alan)
b. Stapleton, Maureen
b. Toon, Malcolm
b. Wachter, Ed(ward)
d. Low, George M(ichael)
d. Wachter, Ed(ward)
d. Willard, Emma Hart
d. Wilson, Samuel

Trumansburgh, New York
b. Biggs, Hermann Michael

Truxton, New York
b. McGraw, John Joseph

Tuckahoe, New York
b. Creavy, Tom
d. Allen, Elizabeth Ann Chase Akers

Tuxedo, New York
b. Weiss, Walt(er William, Jr.)

Tuxedo Park, New York
b. Rushmore, Robert (William)

Witherbee, New York
b. Podres, Johnny

Woodhaven, New York
b. Hyland, Brian

Woodmere, New York
b. Chapman, Gilbert Whipple
b. Garth, David
b. Milk, Harvey

Woodside, New York
d. Ault, George Christian
d. Ray, Charlotte E.

Woodstock, New York
b. Chase, Chevy
d. Draper, Paul (Nathaniel Saltonstall)
d. Fischer, Anton Otto
d. Guston, Philip
d. Hague, Raoul (Heukelekian)
d. Komroff, Manuel
d. Rugg, Harold
d. Speicher, Eugene Edward

Yonkers, New York
b. Bunker, Ellsworth
b. Burch, Billy
b. Caesar, Sid
b. Edmiston, Mark Morton
b. Ferlinghetti, Lawrence Monsanto
b. Gajdusek, D(aniel) Carleton
b. Giddings, Paula (Jane)
b. Granville, Joseph E(nsign)
b. Halsey, Margaret (Frances)
b. Lapchick, Joe
b. McMullen, Mary
b. Northrop, John Howard
b. Stratton, Samuel S(tuddiford)
b. Tomes, Margot
b. Tyler, Steven
b. Voight, Jon
b. Yates, Richard
d. Bing, Rudolf (Franz Josef), Sir
d. Coulter, John Merle
d. Fokine, Michel
d. Fredericks, Carlton
d. Jacobs, Joseph
d. Krupa, Gene
d. Otis, Elisha Graves
d. Rainwater, James
d. Tait, Arthur Fitzwilliam
d. Tilden, Samuel Jones
d. Williams, Gus
d. Wilson, Earl
d. Winding, Kai Chresten

Yorktown Heights, New York
d. Harriman, W(illiam) Averell
d. Hayward, Leland
d. Rethberg, Elizabeth

NORTH CAROLINA
b. Atkinson, Henry
b. Parker, Maceo
b. Polk, Leonidas Lafayette
b. Purcell, Lee
b. Williams, Evelyn
d. Jordan, James

Arden, North Carolina
d. Nye, Edgar Wilson

Asheville, North Carolina
b. Anderson, Dorothy Hansine
b. Daugherty, James Henry
b. Dupri, Jermaine
b. Greene, Ward
b. Justice, Choo Choo
b. McKissick, Floyd Bixler
b. Noland, Kenneth Clifton
b. Reynolds, Robert Rice
b. Wolfe, Thomas (Clayton)
d. Burgess, Smoky
d. Chapin, F(rancis) Stuart
d. Curry, Jabez Lamar Monroe
d. Dargan, Olive Tilford
d. Eichelberger, Robert Lawrence
d. Fitzgerald, Zelda
d. Hayne, Robert Young
d. Kraus, Lili
d. Moores, Dick
d. Reynolds, Robert Rice

Ayden, North Carolina
b. Mumford, Lawrence Quincy

Beaufort, North Carolina
b. Smith, Michael John

Bellhaven, North Carolina
b. Little Eva

Belvidere, North Carolina
d. Smith, Robert Weston
d. Wolfman Jack

Black Mountain, North Carolina
b. Flack, Roberta
b. Proctor, Barbara Gardner

Blowing Rock, North Carolina
b. Robbins, Tom

Brevard, North Carolina
b. Mabley, Moms

Brunswick, North Carolina
d. Emmons, Ebenezer

Buncombe County, North Carolina
b. Vance, Zebulon Baird

Burgaw, North Carolina
b. Williams, Samm-Art

Burlington, North Carolina
d. Bennett, Hugh Hammond

Bynum, North Carolina
d. Luboff, Norman

Candor, North Carolina
b. Harris, Joseph Pratt

Canton, North Carolina
b. Chappell, Fred (Davis)

Caroleen, North Carolina
b. Burgess, Smoky

Cary, North Carolina
b. Page, Walter Hines

Chadbourn, North Carolina
b. Lewis, Thomas
b. Towns, Edolphus

Chapel Hill, North Carolina
b. Cotten, Libba
b. Schenkkan, Robert
b. Wainwright, Loudon, III
d. Elion, Gertrude B(ell)
d. Ethridge, Mark Foster, Jr.
d. Green, Paul Eliot
d. Hitchings, George H(erbert)
d. Jarrell, Randall
d. Kyser, Kay (James King Kern)
d. Odum, Howard Washington
d. Reeves, Rosser
d. Stern, Arthur Cecil
d. Thurstone, Louis Leon

Charlotte, North Carolina
b. Bearden, Romare Howard
b. Byars, Betsy
b. Darman, Richard G(ordon)
b. Duke, Charles Moss, Jr.
b. Graham, Billy
b. Gwathmey, Charles
b. Henry, Joe
b. Jordan, Hamilton
b. Lay, Herman Warden
b. Little, Edward Herman
b. McKelway, St. Clair
b. Prince, Prairie
b. Schollander, Don(ald Arthur)
b. Sifford, Charlie
b. Spong, John
b. Trotter, John Scott
d. Bond, George Foote
d. Christopher, Matt(hew F.)
d. Golden, Harry Lewis
d. Hilton, Daisy
d. Hilton, Violet
d. Micheaux, Oscar
d. Roberts, Edward Glenn

Cherryville, North Carolina
b. Tatum, Jack

Chowan County, North Carolina
b. Welch, Robert Henry Winborne, Jr.

Clarkton, North Carolina
b. Owen, Guy, Jr.
b. Spaulding, Charles Clinton

Clayton, North Carolina
b. Dodd, William Edward
b. Horne, Herman Harrell

Columbus, North Carolina
d. Lackey, Kenneth

Concord, North Carolina
d. Cannon, James W

Cross Creek, North Carolina
b. Williams, William T(homas)

Cumberland County, North Carolina
b. Barfield, Velma

Danville, North Carolina
d. Cannon, Joseph Gurney

Montgomery Co., North Carolina
b. Chambers, Julius LeVonne

Mooresville, North Carolina
b. Burke, Selma (Hortense)
b. Washam, Wisner McCamey

Morganton, North Carolina
b. Ervin, Sam(uel James Jr.)

Mount Airy, North Carolina
b. Fargo, Donna
b. Griffith, Andy
d. Chang and Eng

Murfreesboro, North Carolina
d. Brown, William Hill

Nash County, North Carolina
b. Gibbons, Kaye

New Bern, North Carolina
b. Bellamy, Walt(er Jones)
b. Bradham, Caleb D
b. Stallings, George Augustus, Jr.

New Garden, North Carolina
b. Cannon, Joseph Gurney
b. Coffin, Levi

New London, North Carolina
b. Byrd, Donald

Newton, North Carolina
b. Amos, Tori

North Wilkesboro, North Carolina
b. Byrd, Robert C(arlyle)

Ocracoke Island, North Carolina
d. Blackbeard

Orange County, North Carolina
b. Duke, Benjamin Newton

Oxford, North Carolina
b. Chavis, Benjamin Franklin, Jr.

Parmele, North Carolina
b. Greenfield, Eloise

Pembroke, North Carolina
b. Chavers, Dean

Pennert, North Carolina
b. McEachin, James Elton

Pinehurst, North Carolina
d. Page, Walter Hines
d. Ross, Donald James
d. Zorbaugh, Geraldine B(one)

Pineville, North Carolina
b. Davis, Walter Paul

Plymouth, North Carolina
b. Daly, Augustin

Raleigh, North Carolina
b. Campbell, Bill
b. Cooper, Annie

b. Daniels, Jonathan Worth
b. Delany, Annie Elizabeth
b. Howar, Barbara
b. Johnson, Andrew
b. Royster, Vermont C(onnecticut)
d. Barfield, Velma
d. Coffin, Robert Peter Tristram
d. Commons, John Rogers
d. Crittenden, Christopher
d. Daniels, Josephus
d. Dixon, Thomas
d. Harris, Harwell Hamilton
d. Johnson, Jack
d. Johnson, U(ral) Alexis
d. Owen, Guy, Jr.
d. Royster, Vermont C(onnecticut)
d. Sloan, Samuel
d. Smith, Kate

Richmond County, North Carolina
b. Morrison, Cameron

Riverton, North Carolina
b. Johnson, Gerald White

Roanoke Island, North Carolina
b. Dare, Virginia
d. Dare, Virginia

Roanoke Rapids, North Carolina
b. Cheek, James Edward
b. Grizzard, George

Robinsville, North Carolina
b. Milsap, Ronnie

Rockingham, North Carolina
b. Williams, Charles
d. Ford, Russ(ell William)

Rocky Mount, North Carolina
b. Boyce, Westray Battle
b. Ford, Phil Jackson
b. Gurganus, Allan
b. Hyman, Earle
b. Kyser, Kay (James King Kern)
b. Leonard, Buck
b. Monk, Thelonious Sphere, Jr.
b. Williams, Charles Linwood
d. Leonard, Buck

Roxboro, North Carolina
b. Slaughter, Enos Bradsher

Salisbury, North Carolina
b. Blackmer, Sidney Alderman
b. Dole, Elizabeth Hanford
b. Ennis, Skinnay
b. Evans, Mike
b. Koontz, Elizabeth Duncan
d. Koontz, Elizabeth Duncan

Sallsburg, North Carolina
b. Junior, E(ster) J(ames, III)

Sampson County, North Carolina
b. Faircloth, Lauch
b. King, William Rufus de Vane

Seaboard, North Carolina
b. Goode, Wilson

Shelby, North Carolina
b. Bell, Bobby
b. Dixon, Thomas
b. Gibson, Don(ald)
b. Thompson, David O'Neil

Silver City, North Carolina
d. Bavier, Frances

Smithfield, North Carolina
b. Gardner, Ava

Southern Pines, North Carolina
d. Irwin, Wallace (Admah)
d. Stevens, John Frank

Tryon, North Carolina
b. Simone, Nina
d. Banning, Margaret Culkin
d. Heyward, (Edwin) DuBose
d. Lockridge, Richard

Unaka, North Carolina
b. Jenkins, Ray Howard

Waco, North Carolina
b. Patterson, Floyd

Wadesboro, North Carolina
b. Bennett, Hugh Hammond

Wake County, North Carolina
b. Trout, Robert

Wake Forest, North Carolina
b. Billingsley, Ray
b. Crittenden, Christopher
b. Sales, Soupy

Wallace, North Carolina
b. Jordan, James

Warrenton, North Carolina
b. Bragg, Braxton

Washington, North Carolina
b. Little, Joan
b. Wilkins, Dominique

Waynesville, North Carolina
b. Ferguson, Homer Lenoir
d. Miller, Caroline

West Jefferson, North Carolina
b. Bunch, Charlotte

Wilkes County, North Carolina
b. Broyhill, James E

Williamsburg, North Carolina
d. Penn, John

Williamston, North Carolina
b. Perry, Gaylord Jackson
b. Perry, Jim

Wilmington, North Carolina
b. Brinkley, David (McClure)
b. Daniels, Charlie
b. Gabriel, Roman, Jr.
b. Jones, Sam(uel)
b. Jurgenson, Sonny

Bellaire, Ohio
b. Watt, George Willard

Bellefontaine, Ohio
b. Flora, James (Royer)
b. Herskovits, Melville Jean
b. Hubbard, Kin
b. Kiplinger, W(illard) M(onroe)

Berea, Ohio
b. McElroy, Neil Hosler
b. Moley, Raymond Charles

Beverly, Ohio
b. Adair, Frank E(arl)

Birmingham, Ohio
b. Leonard, Dutch

Blaine, Ohio
b. Niekro, Phil(ip Henry)

Boardman, Ohio
b. Hartman, Elizabeth
b. Kosar, Bernie, Jr.

Bowersville, Ohio
b. Peale, Norman Vincent

Bratenahl, Ohio
b. Verdi-Fletcher, Mary (Regina)

Brighton, Ohio
b. Greene, Charles Sumner
b. Greene, Henry Mather

Brown County, Ohio
b. Marquis, Albert Nelson

Cadiz, Ohio
b. Dewey, Charles Schuveldt
b. Gable, Clark

Cambridge, Ohio
b. Boyd, William
b. Eyen, Tom
b. Glenn, John Herschel, Jr.

Campbell, Ohio
b. Allen, Betty (Lou)

Canal Dover, Ohio
b. Quantrill, William Clarke

Canal Winchester, Ohio
b. Speaks, Oley

Canton, Ohio
b. Cordier, Andrew Wellington
b. Craft, Christine
b. Dierdorf, Dan(iel Lee)
b. Garner, Peggy Ann
b. Juilliard, Augustus D
b. Light, Enoch Henry
b. McKinley, Ida Saxton
b. Paar, Jack
b. Page, Alan Cedric
b. Peters, Jean
b. Scali, John (Alfred)
b. Wottle, Dave
d. McKinley, Ida Saxton
d. Munson, Thurman Lee

Carroll County, Ohio
b. Jeffries, James Jackson
b. Vail, Theodore Newton

Cedarville, Ohio
b. Parker, Eleanor

Chagrin Falls, Ohio
b. Kitaj, R(onald) B(rooks)

Chatham, Ohio
b. Thomas, Edith Matilda

Chili, Ohio
b. Crile, George Washington

Chillicothe, Ohio
b. Bennett, John
b. Cook, Greg(ory Lynn)
b. Dun, Robert Graham
b. Finley, Martha
b. Hayes, Lucy Webb
b. Johnston, Neil
b. Trotter, Monroe
b. Wilson, Nancy

Cincinnati, Ohio
b. Altrock, Nick
b. Arcaro, Eddie
b. Balin, Marty
b. Bara, Theda
b. Bauer, Erwin Adam
b. Bauer, Louis Agricola
b. Beard, Dan(iel Carter)
b. Beavers, Louise
b. Bentley, Charles Edwin
b. Berger, Thomas Louis
b. Bishop, Isabel
b. Bowman, Lee
b. Brosnan, Jim
b. Burton, Phillip
b. Carruthers, George Robert, Dr.
b. Cary, Alice
b. Cary, Phoebe
b. Collins, Bootsy
b. Condit, Carl Wilbur
b. Connolly, Walter
b. Crosley, Powel, Jr.
b. Dane, Maxwell
b. Day, Doris
b. Dine, Jim
b. Drew, Elizabeth Brenner
b. Duncanson, Robert Scott
b. Eckstein, Gustav
b. Farrell, Suzanne
b. Finkelstein, Louis, Dr.
b. Fries, Charles W
b. Gamble, James Norris
b. Gilligan, John Joyce
b. Glueck, Nelson
b. Grasselli, Caesar Augustin
b. Grier, Barbara
b. Henize, Karl G(ordon)
b. Henri, Robert
b. Holman, Libby
b. Horchow, S(amuel) Roger
b. Huggins, Miller James
b. Hurrell, George
b. Justice, David
b. Justice, David (Christopher)
b. Keating, Charles H, Jr.
b. Koch, Kenneth Jay
b. Kroger, Bernard Henry
b. Kronenberger, Louis
b. Kuhn, Thomas Samuel

b. Lane, Frank C
b. Larkin, Barry
b. Lelyveld, Joseph Salem
b. Lemon, Ralph
b. Levine, James Lawrence
b. Maddox, Garry Lee
b. Manning, Irene
b. Manson, Charles
b. Matthews, Stanley
b. Matthews, T(homas) S(tanley)
b. Mauchly, John William
b. Morgan, Arthur
b. Ochs, Adolph Simon
b. Pendleton, George Hunt
b. Pettit, William Thomas
b. Phair, Liz
b. Potthast, Edward Henry
b. Power, Tyrone, Jr.
b. Rauh, Joseph Louis, Jr.
b. Resor, Stanley Burnett
b. Reynolds, Jack
b. Rhodes, Hari
b. Richman, Harry
b. Rogers, Roy
b. Rose, Pete(r Edward)
b. Rubin, Jerry
b. Sawyer, Charles
b. Schiess, Betty Bone
b. Schott, Marge
b. Spielberg, Steven
b. Staubach, Roger Thomas
b. Stemrick, Greg(ory Earl, Sr.)
b. Stratemeyer, George E, General
b. Strauss, Joseph Baermann
b. Taft, Helen Herron
b. Taft, Robert A(lphonso)
b. Taft, Robert A(lphonso), Jr.
b. Taft, William (Howard)
b. Tahse, Martin
b. Tekulve, Kent(on Charles)
b. Townsend, Willard Saxby
b. Trabert, Tony
b. Turner, Ted
b. Twachtman, John Henry
b. Vera-Ellen
b. Wald, Lillian D
b. Wesselmann, Tom
b. White, Edmund
b. Zimmer, Don(ald William)
d. Ames, Louise (Bates)
d. Brown, Paul
d. Coffin, Levi
d. Crosley, Powel, Jr.
d. Daubert, Jake
d. DeWitt, William Orville, Sr.
d. Duveneck, Frank
d. Eckstein, Gustav
d. Ewing, Buck
d. Fleischmann, Charles Louis
d. Giles, Warren Crandall
d. Glueck, Nelson
d. Hoyt, Waite Charles
d. Kluszewski, Ted
d. Marcus, Jacon R(ader)
d. McElroy, Neil Hosler
d. Miller, William Ernest
d. Millett, John D(avid)
d. Rixey, Eppa Jephtha
d. Segal, Henry
d. Sperti, George Speri
d. Taft, Charles Phelps
d. Taft, Robert A(lphonso), Jr.
d. Tajo, Italo
d. Westheimer, Irvin Ferdinand
d. Wise, Isaac Mayer
d. Wright, Frances

d. Wurlitzer, Rudolph

Circleville, Ohio
b. Lewis, Ted

Clark County, Ohio
b. Shull, George Harrison

Clayton, Ohio
b. Haines, Jesse Joseph

Cleveland, Ohio
b. Abdul, Raoul
b. Abel, John Jacob
b. Allen, Leslie
b. Anson, Robert Sam
b. Ault, George Christian
b. Backus, Jim
b. Baker, Julius
b. Ball, Ernest
b. Ballard, Kaye
b. Bampton, Rose Elizabeth
b. Bando, Sal(vatore Leonard)
b. Barron, Blue
b. Berry, Halle
b. Beutel, Bill
b. Bolton, Frances Payne
b. Bourjaily, Vance
b. Bravo, Ellen
b. Brooks, William Keith
b. Buckmaster, Henrietta
b. Carey, Drew
b. Carmen, Eric
b. Celeste, Richard F
b. Chapman, Tracy
b. Chesnutt, Charles Waddell
b. Cover, Franklin
b. Craven, Wes
b. Crile, George Washington, Jr.
b. Croft, Arthur C
b. Cushing, Harvey Williams
b. Dandridge, Dorothy
b. DaSilva, Howard
b. Dee, Ruby
b. DeFreeze, Donald David
b. Delahanty, Ed(ward James)
b. Dietz, David
b. Dillard, Harrison
b. Donahue, Phil
b. Donaldson, Stephen Reeder
b. Draper, Sharon M(ills)
b. Dullea, Keir
b. Ellison, Harlan Jay
b. Elson, Robert Truscott
b. Fedoroff, Nina V(sevolod)
b. Fennell, Frederick
b. Fish, Robert Lloyd
b. Frank, Gerold
b. Frazier, Ian
b. Frey, Jim
b. Garwin, Richard Lawrence
b. Gilles, D(onald) B(ruce)
b. Glaser, Donald Arthur
b. Gold, Herbert
b. Gordone, Charles Edward
b. Grey, Joel
b. Gund, Agnes
b. Hall, Arsenio
b. Hamilton, Margaret Brainard
b. Harkness, Edward Stephen
b. Harris, Leslie
b. Hawkins, Screamin' Jay
b. Haworth, Ted
b. Haydn, Hiram Collins
b. Heisman, John William

b. Henkle, Henrietta
b. Hocking, William Ernest
b. Holbrook, Hal
b. Hopkins, Arthur
b. Hopwood, Avery
b. Howard, Desmond
b. Hunter, Ross
b. Hyatt, Joel
b. Johnson, Philip Cortelyou
b. Joyce, Elaine
b. Kane, Carol
b. Kanter, Rosabeth Moss
b. Kenney, Douglas C
b. King, Don(ald)
b. Kovel, Terry Horvitz
b. Krol, John (Joseph), Cardinal
b. Kucinich, Dennis John
b. Lausche, Frank John
b. Lawrence, Jerome
b. Lipscomb, William Nunn
b. Long, Irene D.
b. Lovell, Jim
b. Malcolm, Andrew H(ogarth)
b. Mancini, Henry
b. Marquard, Rube
b. Martin, Freddy
b. Masters, William Howell
b. McCafferty, Don
b. Meng, John Joseph
b. Metzenbaum, Howard M(orton)
b. Michalske, Mike
b. Mitchell, William Leroy
b. Morris, Greg
b. Moses, Gilbert, III
b. Newman, Paul
b. Noll, Chuck
b. Norton, Andre
b. Noyes, Blanche Wilcox
b. O'Leary, Jean
b. Panek, LeRoy Lad
b. Perry, Eleanor Bayer
b. Presser, Jackie
b. Priesand, Sally Jane
b. Rhodes, James Ford
b. Rich, Lee
b. Rockefeller, John D(avison), Jr.
b. Rourke, Constance Mayfield
b. St. James, Lyn
b. Salhany, Lucie
b. Sanders, Marlene
b. Schaefer, Jack Warner
b. Shalala, Donna Edna
b. Shapp, Milton J(errold)
b. Shute, Denny
b. Siebert, Muriel
b. Siegel, Jerry
b. Smith, Barbara
b. Stevens, Mark
b. Stokes, Carl B(urton)
b. Stokes, Louis
b. Stouffer, Vernon B
b. Tidyman, Ernest
b. Uhlenbeck, Karen (Keskulla)
b. Vanik, Charles Albert
b. Vanocur, Sander
b. Vessels, Billy
b. Voinovich, George V(ictor)
b. Votipka, Thelma
b. Walter, Eugene
b. Ward, Robert Eugene
b. Wasserman, Lew(is Robert)
b. Wasserman, Lew R
b. Weston, Jack
b. White, Michael R(eed)
b. Wick, Charles Z
b. Williams, Edward Porter

b. Winger, Debra
b. Winpisinger, William W(ayne)
b. Womack, Bobby
b. Woolsey, Sarah Chauncey
d. Arbuthnot, May Hill
d. Babin, Victor
d. Bee, Clair Francis
d. Brush, Charles Francis
d. Celebrezze, Anthony J(oseph)
d. Chesnutt, Charles Waddell
d. Cline, Genevieve Rose
d. Crile, George Washington
d. Crile, George Washington, Jr.
d. Davis, Ernie
d. Dietz, David
d. Draper, Dorothy Tuckerman
d. Eldjarn, Kristjan
d. Garcia, Mike
d. George, Zelma W(atson)
d. Humphrey, George Magoffin
d. Lausche, Frank John
d. Miller, Don
d. Morgan, Garrett Augustus
d. Motley, Marion
d. Ness, Eliot
d. O'Neill, Steve
d. Ruffing, Red
d. Shera, Jesse Hauk
d. Sill, Edward Rowland
d. Silver, Abba Hillel
d. Stokes, Carl B(urton)
d. Szell, George
d. Toure, Ahmed Sekou
d. Toure, Sekou
d. Walsh, Stella
d. Willard, Archibald MacNeal
d. Winton, Alexander

Cleveland Heights, Ohio
b. Hyland, Diana
d. Cullinan, Thomas P.

Clifton, Ohio
b. Funk, Isaac Kauffman
b. Hayes, Woody

Clinton, Ohio
b. Emmett, Daniel Decatur

Coalton, Ohio
b. Jones, Isham

Columbus, Ohio
b. Baxter, Warner
b. Bellows, George Wesley
b. Buck, Paul Herman
b. Carr, Joe
b. Cassady, Howard
b. Coulter, Ernest Kent
b. Cowans, Adger W.
b. D'Angelo, Beverly
b. Douglas, Buster
b. Eisele, Donn Fulton
b. Feinstein, Michael Jay
b. Firestone, Harvey Samuel
b. Frings, Ketti
b. Goodman, Dody
b. Gowdy, Hank
b. Greene, Bob
b. Griffin, Archie Mason
b. Hammon, William McDowell
b. Heckart, Eileen
b. Howard, Frank Oliver
b. Jackson, Madeline Manning
b. Janis, Elsie

b. Kellor, Frances (Alice)
b. Kirk, Rahsaan Roland
b. LeMay, Curtis Emerson
b. McDowell, Irvin
b. McGovern, Arthur F
b. Mendenhall, Dorothy Reed
b. Mitchell, Grant
b. Nicklaus, Jack William
b. N'Namdi, George R(ichard)
b. Poston, Tom
b. Rickenbacker, Eddie
b. Ryder, James Arthur
b. Schlesinger, Arthur M(eier), Jr.
b. Sheppard, Eugenia Benbow
b. Smith, Roger Bonham
b. Stewart, Donald Ogden
b. Stine, R. L.
b. Thurber, James Grover
b. Thurston, Howard
b. Willis, Bill
b. Woods, Granville T
d. Axis Sally
d. Bricker, John William
d. Bromfield, Louis Brucker
d. Cole, Cozy
d. Curtis, Charlotte Murray
d. Galbreath, John Wilmer
d. Gladden, Washington
d. Gowdy, Hank
d. Janowicz, Vic(tor Felix)
d. Kauff, Benny
d. Licavoli, Thomas
d. McKenney, Ruth
d. Sheppard, Sam(uel)

Columbus Grove, Ohio
b. Jagger, Dean

Conneaut, Ohio
b. Kelley, Larry
d. Berry, Chu

Corsica, Ohio
b. Harding, Warren G(amaliel)

Coshocton, Ohio
b. Brenly, Bob
b. Green, William
d. Green, William

Crestline, Ohio
b. Morgan, Marabel

Cuyahoga County, Ohio
b. Garfield, James Abram

Dalton, Ohio
b. Harkness, Anna M Richardson

Darke County, Ohio
b. Oakley, Annie

Dayton, Ohio
b. Babbitt, Irving
b. Barney, Natalie Clifford
b. Battelle, Phyllis Marie
b. Bombeck, Erma (Louise)
b. Boyer, Ernest L(eroy)
b. Chambers, Anne Cox
b. Clemens, (William) Roger
b. Collinsworth, Cris
b. Cox, James Middleton, Jr.
b. Crook, George
b. Daniels, Frank

b. Dickens, Helen Octavia
b. Dickman, Joseph Theodore
b. Dunbar, Paul Laurence
b. Faust, Gerry
b. Guisewite, Cathy Lee
b. Harbert, Chick
b. Harewood, Dorian
b. Heard, J.C.
b. Hockenberry, John (Charles)
b. Jump, Gordon
b. Knebel, Fletcher
b. Lowe, Chad
b. Madison, Joseph E(dward)
b. Maier, Henry W
b. Marable, Manning
b. Mead, George Houk
b. Moses, Edwin Corley
b. Page, Clarence
b. Sandy, Gary
b. Schmidt, Mike
b. Scofield, John
b. Sheen, Martin
b. Strayhorn, Billy
b. Watson, Thomas J(ohn), Jr.
b. Weaver, James Baird
b. Wexner, Leslie
b. Winters, Jonathan (Harshman, III)
b. Wright, Orville
d. Cox, James Middleton, Sr.
d. Dunbar, Paul Laurence
d. Haines, Jesse Joseph
d. Kettering, Charles Franklin
d. Mead, George Houk
d. Wright, Orville
d. Wright, Wilbur

Deerfield, Ohio
b. Laughlin, James Laurence

Defiance, Ohio
b. Davison, Wild Bill
b. Duerk, Alene B(ertha)
b. Miller, Don

Delaware, Ohio
b. Cooney, Rory
b. Hayes, Rutherford B(irchard)
b. Rodgers, Bob

Delaware County, Ohio
b. Rosecrans, William Starke

Derby, Ohio
b. Galbreath, John Wilmer

Dover, Ohio
b. Nugent, Elliott
b. White, Stan(ley Ray)

Dover Centre, Ohio
b. Miner, Jack

East Liverpool, Ohio
b. Blythe, David Gilmour
d. Blythe, David Gilmour
d. Floyd, Pretty Boy

Elyria, Ohio
b. Janowicz, Vic(tor Felix)
b. Lee, Robert E(dwin)

Euclid, Ohio
b. Adamle, Mike
b. Brush, Charles Francis

b. Tarkanian, Jerry

Fairview Park, Ohio
b. Cousineau, Tom

Findlay, Ohio
b. Bennett, Willard Harrison
b. Crouse, Russel
b. Guyer, Tennyson
b. Miller, Marilyn
b. Ricketts, Howard T

Franklin, Ohio
b. Evans, Bergen Baldwin
b. Mullin, Willard
b. Schenck, Robert Cumming

Fredericktown, Ohio
b. Perry, Luke

Fremont, Ohio
b. Purdy, James
d. Hayes, Lucy Webb
d. Hayes, Rutherford B(irchard)

Gallipolis, Ohio
b. Holzer, Jenny

Galloway, Ohio
d. Power, Donald Clinton

Gambier, Ohio
d. Ransom, John Crowe

Gano, Ohio
b. Howard, Roy Wilson

Garfield Heights, Ohio
b. Wambsganss, Bill

Garrettsville, Ohio
b. Crane, Hart

Geneva, Ohio
b. Olds, Ranson E(li)

Gilmore, Ohio
b. Young, Cy

Glendale, Ohio
b. Procter, William Cooper
d. McCulley, Johnston

Glenville, Ohio
d. Williams, Edward Porter

Grand River, Ohio
b. Shula, Don(ald Francis)

Granville, Ohio
b. Bancroft, Hubert Howe

Green Creek, Ohio
b. McPherson, James Birdseye

Greenfield, Ohio
b. Hull, John Edwin
b. Paycheck, Johnny

Greensburg, Ohio
b. Ball, Edmund B

Minerva, Ohio
b. Wilson, Charles Erwin

Montgomery, Ohio
b. Bobbs, William Conrad

Montpelier, Ohio
b. Siple, Paul Allman

Morgan County, Ohio
b. Christy, Howard Chandler

Mount Healthy, Ohio
b. Hunt, Pee Wee

Mount Holmes, Ohio
b. Perky, Henry D

Mount Vernon, Ohio
b. Lynde, Paul Edward
b. Sockman, Ralph W
d. Emmett, Daniel Decatur

Murray City, Ohio
b. Carlson, Doc

Nelsonville, Ohio
b. Parker, Sarah Jessica

New Carlisle, Ohio
b. Funston, Frederick

New Concord, Ohio
b. Harper, William Rainey

New Knoxville, Ohio
b. Wierwille, Victor Paul

New Lisbon, Ohio
b. Hanna, Mark
b. Vallandigham, Clement Laird

New Matamoras, Ohio
b. Farr, Wanda K.

New Rumley, Ohio
b. Custer, George Armstrong

New York, Ohio
b. Lawton, Henry Ware

Newark, Ohio
d. Ashbrook, John Milan

Niles, Ohio
b. McKinley, William
b. Patchen, Kenneth

North Bend, Ohio
b. Harrison, Benjamin
d. Harrison, Anna (Tuthill Symmes)

Northfield, Ohio
d. Eaton, Cyrus Stephen

Norwalk, Ohio
b. Brown, Paul
b. Johnson, Ban
b. Trendle, George Washington
d. Grove, Lefty

Norwood, Ohio
b. Chakiris, George
b. Rule, Janice

Oberlin, Ohio
b. Hinderas, Natalie Leota Henderson
b. Talbert, Mary Morris Burnett
d. Finney, Charles Grandison

Oldtown, Ohio
b. Tecumseh

Orrville, Ohio
b. Sedelmaier, Joe

Orwell, Ohio
b. Chaffee, Adna Romanza

Ottawa Hills, Ohio
d. Goerlich, John

Oxford, Ohio
b. Harrison, Caroline (Lavinia Scott)
b. Heckert, Richard Edwin
b. Shera, Jesse Hauk
d. Alston, Walter Emmons
d. Ewbank, Weeb
d. Langstroth, Lorenzo Lorraine

Pagetown, Ohio
b. Fillmore, Myrtle Page

Paine Station, Ohio
b. Power, Donald Clinton

Painesville, Ohio
b. Foust, Larry
b. Harrar, J(acob) George
b. Ladd, George Trumbull

Parma, Ohio
d. Boiardi, Hector

Peoli, Ohio
d. Young, Cy

Pigeon Run, Ohio
b. Fairless, Benjamin F

Pioneer, Ohio
b. Schiavo, Mary (Fackler)

Piqua, Ohio
b. Mills, Donald
b. Mills, Harry
b. Mills, Herbert

Plain City, Ohio
b. Barlow, Howard

Point Pleasant, Ohio
b. Grant, Ulysses Simpson

Pomeroy, Ohio
b. Kauff, Benny

Port Clinton, Ohio
d. Sowerby, Leo

Port Washington, Ohio
b. Wyant, Alexander Helwig

Portsmouth, Ohio
b. Battle, Kathleen Deanne
b. Schuler, Mike

Ravenna, Ohio
b. Day, William Rufus
b. Thompson, William Tappan
d. Blum, Stella
d. Petersham, Maud

Ripley, Ohio
b. Smith, Joe

Rittman, Ohio
b. Strawser, Neil Edward

Rockford, Ohio
b. Wilson, Earl

Rocky River, Ohio
b. Steinbrenner, George Michael, III

Sandusky, Ohio
b. Cooke, Jay
b. Frohman, Charles
b. Frohman, Daniel
b. Norris, George William

Sandy Springs, Ohio
b. Wittenmyer, Annie Turner

Sebring, Ohio
b. Woods, Rose Mary

Shaker Heights, Ohio
b. Penske, Roger

Shandon, Ohio
b. Shaw, Albert

Shoshone, Ohio
b. Jennings, Talbot

Springfield, Ohio
b. Abbott, Berenice
b. Burnett, W(illiam) R(iley)
b. Clark, Bobby
b. Embry, Wayne Richard
b. Gish, Lillian (Diana)
b. Lenski, Lois
b. McCullough, Paul
b. Renick, Marion Lewis
b. Whittredge, Thomas Worthington

Steubenville, Ohio
b. Fingers, Rollie
b. Hunter, Dard
b. Martin, Dean
b. Mosel, Tad
b. Perrine, Charles Dillon
b. Scarne, John
b. Snyder, Jimmy the Greek
b. Stanton, Edwin McMasters

Stockdale, Ohio
b. Rickey, Branch

Stonelick Township, Ohio
b. Shively, Charles

Sugar Ridge, Ohio
b. Evans, Bob

b. Hinckley, John Warnock, Jr.

Barnsdall, Oklahoma
b. Bryant, Anita Jane

Bartlesville, Oklahoma
d. Keeler, William Wayne

Beggs, Oklahoma
b. Rowan, Dan

Blaine City, Oklahoma
d. Chisholm, Jesse

Boise City, Oklahoma
b. Miles, Vera

Briartown, Oklahoma
d. Starr, Belle

Broken Arrow, Oklahoma
d. O'Brien, George

Broken Bow, Oklahoma
b. Brecheen, Harry David

Checotah, Oklahoma
b. Lucas, Jim Griffing

Chickasha, Oklahoma
b. Little, Cleavon Jake
b. Moody, Orville

Claremore, Oklahoma
b. Archambault, JoAllyn
b. Riggs, Lynn

Clarence, Oklahoma
b. Page, Patti

Cleo Springs, Oklahoma
b. Owen, Steve

Clinton, Oklahoma
b. Keith, Toby

Comanche, Oklahoma
b. Dark, Alvin Ralph

Doughtery, Oklahoma
b. Starr, Kay

Drury, Oklahoma
b. Dinning, Mark

Duncan, Oklahoma
b. Axton, Hoyt (Wayne)
b. Diffie, Joe
b. Howard, Ron(ald William)
b. Kirkpatrick, Jeane Duane Jordan

Earlsboro, Oklahoma
b. McFarland, Ernest William
b. Stargell, Willie

El Reno, Oklahoma
b. Rhodes, Erik

Elk City, Oklahoma
b. Walters, David
b. Webb, Jim

Enid, Oklahoma
b. Billingsley, Sherman
b. Burch, Dean
b. Farrell, Glenda
b. Garriott, Owen
b. Hedges, Michael
b. Wellman, Paul Iselin

Erick, Oklahoma
b. Wooley, Sheb

Eufaula, Oklahoma
b. Selmon, Lee Roy
b. Watts, J(ulius) C(aesar), (Jr.)

Fairfax, Oklahoma
b. Tallchief, Maria
b. Tallchief, Marjorie

Fairland, Oklahoma
b. New, Lloyd Kiva

Fort Sill, Oklahoma
b. Harris, William
b. Sanapia
d. Geronimo
d. Quanah

Gore, Oklahoma
b. Owens, Steve E

Guthrie, Oklahoma
b. Covey, Cyclone

Guymon, Oklahoma
b. Welch, Larry Dean

Harrah, Oklahoma
b. Waner, Lloyd James
b. Waner, Paul Glee

Haworth, Oklahoma
b. Bolt, Tommy

Healdton, Oklahoma
b. McClanahan, Rue

Hickory, Oklahoma
b. Mosley, Zack Terrell

Hobart, Oklahoma
b. Wayne, Paula

Holdenville, Oklahoma
b. Brown, Zora Kramer
b. Gulager, Clu
b. Pickens, T(homas) Boone, Jr.

Hollis, Oklahoma
b. Royal, Darrell K

Hugo, Oklahoma
b. Cleaver, William Joseph
b. Ling, James J
b. Moyers, Bill

Idabelle, Oklahoma
b. Grant, Earl

Keota, Oklahoma
b. Iness, Sim

Kingfisher, Oklahoma
b. Blanding, Don
b. Walton, Sam Moore

Lawton, Oklahoma
b. Bass, Randy William
b. Momaday, N(avarre) Scott
b. Rhoades, Everett Ronald
b. Russell, Leon

Leedey, Oklahoma
b. Hood, Darla Jean

Lincoln County, Oklahoma
b. Harris, Roy

Madill, Oklahoma
d. Gary, Raymond

Mannford, Oklahoma
b. Hazelwood, Lee

Marshall, Oklahoma
b. Beebe, Burdetta Faye

McAlester, Oklahoma
b. Albert, Carl Bert
b. Berryman, John
b. McEntire, Reba
d. Albert, Carl Bert
d. Martin, Pepper

Miami, Oklahoma
b. Ballard, Louis W.

Mooreland, Oklahoma
b. Ruttman, Troy

Morris, Oklahoma
b. Hill, Anita Faye

Muskogee, Oklahoma
b. Askew, Reubin O'Donovan
b. Clayton, Xernona
b. Jones, James Robert

Nofire Hollow, Oklahoma
b. Studi, Wes

Norman, Oklahoma
b. Cobb, Jerrie
b. Garner, James
b. Gill, Vince(nt Grant)
b. Salle, David

Okemah, Oklahoma
b. Guthrie, Woody
b. Pogue, William R(eid)

Oklahoma City, Oklahoma
b. Allbritton, Louise
b. Avery, R Stanton
b. Bee, Molly
b. Bench, Johnny Lee
b. Bernstein, Jay
b. Boone, Ron(ald Bruce)
b. Brough, Louise Althea
b. Cale, J J
b. Carter, Joe
b. Chaney, Lon, Jr.
b. Cherry, Don
b. Cochran, Eddie
b. Cooper, Kenneth Hardy

b. Lampman, Evelyn Sibley
b. Ray, Johnnie

Eugene, Oregon
b. Ainge, Danny
b. Armstrong, Garner Ted
b. Goldschmidt, Neil Edward
b. Hardin, Tim
b. McCloskey, John Michael
b. Mondale, Joan Adams
b. Simon, Paul M(artin)
b. Wilhelm, Gale
b. Wilkins, Mac
d. Ginsburg, Charles P
d. Owens, Harry
d. Prefontaine, Steve Roland
d. Sturgeon, Theodore Hamilton

Fox Valley, Oregon
b. Graves, Morris Cole

Hood River, Oregon
b. Andrus, Cecil D(ale)
b. Yasui, Minoru

Lake Oswego, Oregon
d. Stafford, William Edgar

Lakeview, Oregon
b. Wright, Cobina

Lebanon, Oregon
b. Hesseman, Howard

Madras, Oregon
b. Phoenix, River

McMinnville, Oregon
b. Cleary, Beverly (Atlee Bunn)
b. Vinton, Will

Medford, Oregon
b. Frohnmayer, John Edward

Merrill, Oregon
b. Barks, Carl

Ontario, Oregon
b. McGinley, Phyllis

Oregon City, Oregon
b. Markham, Edwin
b. Ruttan, Susan
d. McLoughlin, John
d. Ogden, Peter Skene

Pendleton, Oregon
b. Kingman, Dave
b. Lappe, Francis Moore
b. Steele, Bob

Portland, Oregon
b. Bates, Blanche Lyon
b. Beard, James Andrews
b. Braly, Malcolm
b. Brandon, (Thomas) Terrell
b. Cook, Donald
b. Cunningham, Imogen
b. Diebenkorn, Richard C.
b. Dolby, Ray M(ilton)
b. Fosbury, Dick
b. Gallen, Hugh J
b. Ghormley, Robert Lee

b. Groening, Matt
b. Hansen, Julia Butler
b. Hemingway, Margaux
b. Hodel, Donald P(aul)
b. Kaufman, Louis
b. Knight, Phil
b. Knight, Philip H.
b. Lolich, Mickey
b. Lomax, Neil Vincent
b. Mitchell, Chad
b. Munson, Ona
b. Murphy, Dale Bryan
b. Musburger, Brent Woody
b. Packwood, Bob
b. Pauling, Linus C(arl)
b. Poling, Daniel A
b. Popham, William James
b. Powell, Jane
b. Rashad, Ahmad
b. Reed, John Silas
b. Robinson, Claude Everett
b. Schroeder, Patricia Scott
b. Scott, Gordon
b. Simon, Norton Winfred
b. Struthers, Sally Anne
b. Swigert, Ernest Goodnough
b. Yeon, John B
d. Alzado, Lyle Martin
d. Anderson, Marian
d. Barlow, Howard
d. Belluschi, Pietro
d. Bloch, Ernest
d. Coffin, Charles Albert
d. Duniway, Abigail Jane Scott
d. Gaddis, Thomas (Eugene)
d. Griffith, Ernest S(tacey)
d. Hildreth, Horace A(ugusta)
d. Holbrook, Stewart Hall
d. Johnson, Dink
d. Lampman, Evelyn Sibley
d. Leahy, Frank
d. McCall, Dorothy Lawson
d. McCall, Thomas Lawson
d. Morse, Wayne Lyman
d. Schwatka, Frederik
d. Swigert, Ernest Goodnough
d. U'Ren, William Simon

Roseburg, Oregon
b. Kennerly, David Hume

Salem, Oregon
b. Gilbert, A(lfred) C(arleton)
b. Gill, Amory Tingle
b. Mahan, Larry
b. McNary, Charles Linza
d. Breit, Gregory

Seaside, Oregon
d. Lunceford, Jimmy
d. Pennell, Joseph Stanley

Siletz, Oregon
d. Cloud, Henry Roe

Silverton, Oregon
b. Davenport, Homer Calvin

Springfield, Oregon
b. Tomseth, Victor Lloyd

Toledo, Oregon
b. Osborne, Leone Neal

Tualatin, Oregon
d. Green, Edith S(tarrett)

Turner, Oregon
b. Cromwell, Dean Bartlett

Willamette Valley, Oregon
d. Humphry, Ann Wickett

Wilsonville, Oregon
d. Morey, Walt(er Nelson)

Yoncalla, Oregon
b. Davis, Harold Lenoir

PENNSYLVANIA
b. Armstrong, Thomas M
b. Fuisz, Robert E
b. Heiser, Victor George
b. Lease, Mary Elizabeth Clyens
b. Metrinko, Michael John
b. Muhlenberg, William Augustus
b. Ramsay, David
b. Royer, William Blackburn, Jr.
d. Dio, Johnny
d. Noether, (Amalie) Emmy
d. Shippen, Edward
d. Twelvetrees, Helen
d. Zinzendorf, Nikolaus Ludwig von,
Count

Abington, Pennsylvania
d. Balderston, William
d. Walters, Bucky

Aliquippa, Pennsylvania
b. Dorsett, Tony
b. Maravich, Pete(r Press)

Allegheny, Pennsylvania
b. Deland, Margaret Wade
b. Fields, Stanley
b. Jackson, Anne
b. Rinehart, Frederick Roberts
b. Skelly, Hal
b. Stein, Gertrude

Allegheny City, Pennsylvania
b. Cassatt, Mary Stevenson

Allegheny County, Pennsylvania
b. Packer, Alfred G

Allentown, Pennsylvania
b. CasSelle, Malcolm
b. Iacocca, Lee
b. Jarrett, Keith
b. Snelling, Richard
b. Voorhees, Donald

Altoona, Pennsylvania
b. Anslinger, Harry Jacob
b. Blair, Janet
b. Piper, H(enry) Beam
b. Winter, Paul Theodore

Ambler, Pennsylvania
d. Creed, Linda
d. Mauchly, John William

Ardmore, Pennsylvania
d. Pew, J(ohn) Howard

Cochrane's Mill, Pennsylvania
b. Bly, Nellie

Collegeville, Pennsylvania
b. Ashenfelter, Nip

Coloraine, Pennsylvania
b. Latzo, Pete

Connellsville, Pennsylvania
b. Lujack, John(ny)
b. Porter, Edwin
b. Woodruff, John

Conshohocken, Pennsylvania
b. Cairns, John, Jr.

Coplay, Pennsylvania
b. Stofflet, Ty(rone Earl)

Corner Ketch, Pennsylvania
b. Read, Thomas Buchanan

Cornwells Heights, Pennsylvania
d. Drexel, Mary Katherine

Coulterville, Pennsylvania
b. Rooney, Art(hur Joseph)

Cresson, Pennsylvania
b. Peary, Robert Edwin

Cumberland County, Pennsylvania
b. Grier, Robert Cooper

Dallastown, Pennsylvania
b. Mitchell, Cameron

Darby, Pennsylvania
b. Stanford, John (Henry)
d. Scott, Thomas Alexander

Dauphin City, Pennsylvania
b. Hershey, Milton Snavely

Delaware County, Pennsylvania
b. Garrett, Thomas

Derry Township, Pennsylvania
b. Wilson, William Julius

Devon, Pennsylvania
d. Duane, William

Dillsburg, Pennsylvania
b. Quay, Matthew Stanley

Donegal Springs, Pennsylvania
d. Cameron, Simon

Donora, Pennsylvania
b. Griffey, Ken
b. Griffey, Ken, Jr.
b. Musial, Stan(ley Frank)

Dormont, Pennsylvania
b. Goldman, Albert

Doylestown, Pennsylvania
b. Mercer, Henry Chapman
b. Widdemer, Margaret

d. Bester, Alfred
d. Burpee, David
d. Burpee, W(ashington) Atlee
d. Hammerstein, Oscar, II
d. Mercer, Henry Chapman
d. Toomer, Jean
d. Wexley, John
d. Whiteman, Paul

DuBois, Pennsylvania
b. Lyle, Sparky

Dunmore, Pennsylvania
d. Chylak, Nestor

Duquesne, Pennsylvania
b. Hines, Fatha
b. Skurzynski, Gloria

East Liberty, Pennsylvania
b. Conn, Billy

East Norriton, Pennsylvania
d. Hastie, William Henry

East Stroudsburg, Pennsylvania
d. Brannum, Hugh

East Vandergrift, Pennsylvania
b. Maida, Adam (Joseph)

Easton, Pennsylvania
b. Cattell, James McKeen
b. Crater, Joseph Force
b. Deringer, Henry
b. Gross, Samuel Daniel
b. Powers, John Robert
b. Raphael, Sally Jessy
b. Seibert, Florence B(arbara)
d. Taylor, George

Ebensburg, Pennsylvania
b. Hartack, Billy

Economy, Pennsylvania
d. Rapp, George

Edenborn, Pennsylvania
b. Stringer, C. Vivian

Edgeworth, Pennsylvania
b. Nevin, Ethelbert Woodbridge

Ehrenfeld, Pennsylvania
b. Bronson, Charles

Elizabethtown, Pennsylvania
b. Baldwin, Matthias William

Ellwood City, Pennsylvania
b. Wilson, Hack

Ercildoun, Pennsylvania
b. Moore, Charlotte E(mma)

Erie, Pennsylvania
b. Anuszkiewicz, Richard Joseph
b. Berner, Robert A(rbuckle)
b. Biletnikoff, Fred(erick)
b. Boone, Mary
b. Burleigh, Harry Thacker
b. Mennin, Peter

b. Mizener, Arthur Moore
b. Olds, Irving S
b. Spencer, William
d. Wayne, Anthony

Erie County, Pennsylvania
b. Tarbell, Ida Minerva

Everett, Pennsylvania
b. Koontz, Dean R(ay)

Factoryville, Pennsylvania
b. Mathewson, Christy

Forksville, Pennsylvania
b. Grange, Red

Fort Duquesne, Pennsylvania
d. Braddock, Edward

Fort Loudon, Pennsylvania
b. Scott, Thomas Alexander

Fort Pitt, Pennsylvania
b. Fink, Mike

Fox Chapel, Pennsylvania
d. Ridgway, Matthew Bunker

Franklin County, Pennsylvania
b. Corbin, Margaret Cochran
b. Nevin, John Williamson

Gallitzen, Pennsylvania
b. Frederick, Pauline

Germantown, Pennsylvania
b. Alcott, Louisa May
b. Bernier, Rosamond Margaret
b. Coleman, William T, Jr.
b. Gibson, Henry
b. Harrison, Ross Granville
b. Richards, Theodore William
b. Rittenhouse, David
b. Taylor, Frederick Winslow
b. Vandyke, Henry Jackson, Jr.
b. Wister, Owen
d. Kelley, Florence

Gettysburg, Pennsylvania
b. Plank, Eddie
b. Studebaker, John Mohler
d. Plank, Eddie
d. Singmaster, Elsie

Gladwyne, Pennsylvania
b. Arnold, Henry Harley
b. Ferrell, Trevor

Glen Riddle, Pennsylvania
b. Jordan, I(rving) King

Grampian, Pennsylvania
b. Waln, Nora

Granville Summit, Pennsylvania
b. Packard, Vance (Oakley)

Greentree, Pennsylvania
b. Jackson, Chevalier

McKeesport, Pennsylvania
b. Connelly, Marc(us Cook)
b. Janis, Byron
b. MacMahon, Aline Laveen
b. Michals, Duane Steven
b. Parrish, Lance Michael
b. Warhol, Andy
b. Wilson, Richard

Meadville, Pennsylvania
b. Barnaby, Ralph S
b. Haskins, Charles Homer
b. Kirkus, Virginia
b. Stone, Sharon

Mercer, Pennsylvania
b. Reznor, Trent

Mercersburg, Pennsylvania
b. Buchanan, James

Merion, Pennsylvania
d. Currie, Barton Wood
d. Heinz, John

Merion Square, Pennsylvania
b. Neel, Alice Hartley

Meyersdale, Pennsylvania
b. Thomas, John Charles

Milford, Pennsylvania
b. Joslyn, Allyn Morgan
d. Peirce, Charles Sanders

Minooka, Pennsylvania
b. O'Neill, Steve

Mix Run, Pennsylvania
b. Mix, Tom

Monessen, Pennsylvania
b. Anfinsen, Christian Boehmer
b. Thebom, Blanche

Montgomery County, Pennsylvania
b. Hancock, Winfield Scott

Mooresburg, Pennsylvania
b. Sholes, Christopher Latham

Moosehead, Pennsylvania
b. Palmer, Alexander Mitchell

Mornsville, Pennsylvania
d. Clymer, George

Morris Run, Pennsylvania
b. Nearing, Scott

Morristown, Pennsylvania
b. Garber, Jan

Mount Carmel, Pennsylvania
b. Trohan, Walter
d. Carroll, Earl

Mountainhome, Pennsylvania
d. Kresge, Sebastian Spering

Moylan, Pennsylvania
d. Shaw, Anna Howard

Nanticoke, Pennsylvania
b. Adams, Nick
b. Gray, Pete(r)

Neath, Pennsylvania
b. Evans, Alice (Catherine)

New Alexandria, Pennsylvania
b. Turnbull, Agnes Sligh

New Brighton, Pennsylvania
b. Brown, Cecil B
b. Clark, Jack Anthony

New Britain, Pennsylvania
d. Door, Rheta Childe

New Castle, Pennsylvania
b. Sterling, Robert

New Eagle, Pennsylvania
b. Montana, Joe

New Hope, Pennsylvania
d. Burke, Selma (Hortense)
d. Hoffman, Abbie
d. Morris, Chester
d. Savitch, Jessica Beth

New Kensington, Pennsylvania
b. Noble, Elaine

New London, Pennsylvania
b. McKean, Thomas

New Providence, Pennsylvania
d. Muhlenberg, Heinrich Melchior

New Salem, Pennsylvania
b. Davis, Ernie
b. Lewis, Isaac Newton

Newton, Pennsylvania
d. Blanding, Sarah Gibson
d. Burns, Eveline Mabel
d. Kotsching, Walter Maria

Newtown, Pennsylvania
d. Hicks, Edward
d. Hunt, Frazier
d. Jessup, Philip Caryl
d. Quackenbush, Bill

Norristown, Pennsylvania
b. Fisher, Jules Edward
b. Lasorda, Tommy
b. Pastorius, Jaco
b. Piazza, Mike
b. Schweiker, Richard Schultz

Northumberland, Pennsylvania
b. Walker, Robert James
d. Priestley, Joseph

Ogortz, Pennsylvania
d. Cooke, Jay

Oil City, Pennsylvania
b. Smalley, David Bruce

Old Forge, Pennsylvania
b. Jones, Allan

b. Plishka, Paul Peter

Olyphant, Pennsylvania
b. Chylak, Nestor

Osceola Mills, Pennsylvania
b. Liveright, Horace Brisbin

Ottsville, Pennsylvania
d. Darrow, Charles Brace

Pen Argyl, Pennsylvania
b. Ray, Aldo

Penllyn, Pennsylvania
d. Pemberton, John Clifford

Penn Valley, Pennsylvania
d. Hibbs, Ben

Pennsburg, Pennsylvania
b. Buchman, Frank Nathan Daniel

Philadelphia, Pennsylvania
b. Abbey, Edwin Austin
b. Abu-Jamal, Mumia
b. Adderley, Herb(ert Anthony)
b. Agronsky, Martin Zama
b. Alexander, Lloyd Chudley
b. Allen, Ethel D.
b. Allen, Richard
b. Allred, Gloria Rachel
b. Amram, David Werner, III
b. Amsterdam, Jane
b. Arizin, Paul Joseph
b. Ashbrook, Joseph
b. Auslander, Joseph
b. Avalon, Frankie
b. Babbitt, Milton Byron
b. Bacharach, Bert(ram Mark)
b. Bache, Alexander Dallas
b. Backus, John
b. Bacon, Kevin
b. Baer, Bugs
b. Bailey, Pearl Mae
b. Baker, Phil
b. Balderston, John Lloyd
b. Bancroft, George
b. Barris, Chuck
b. Barrymore, Ethel Mae Blythe
b. Barrymore, Georgiana Emma Drew
b. Barrymore, John
b. Barrymore, Lionel Blythe
b. Barthelme, Donald
b. Barton, George
b. Batts, Deborah A.
b. Baugh, Albert Croll
b. Beam, Joseph
b. Beaux, Cecilia
b. Becker, B Jay
b. Bell, Bert
b. Bell, James Ford
b. Bentley, Gladys
b. Bettger, Lyle
b. Biberman, Herbert
b. Biddle, Anthony Joseph
b. Biddle, George
b. Biddle, Nicholas
b. Black, Frank J.
b. Blitzstein, Marc
b. Bluford, Guy
b. Boardman, Eleanor
b. Boland, Mary
b. Bond, James

b. Bonsall, Joe
b. Bose, Amar Gopal
b. Bova, Ben(jamin William)
b. Bowser, Yvette Lee
b. Boyle, Peter
b. Braceland, Francis J(ames)
b. Bradley, Ed(ward R.)
b. Breen, Joseph Ignatius
b. Brendel, El(mer)
b. Brenner, David
b. Breuer, Lee
b. Bricklin, Malcolm N
b. Broderick, Helen
b. Bromberg, David
b. Brooks, Richard
b. Brown, Charles Brockden
b. Brown, Dorothy Lavinia
b. Brown, Elaine
b. Brown, Marie Dutton
b. Bryant, Kobe
b. Bullins, Ed
b. Bullitt, William Christian
b. Bundy, Robert F.
b. Burpee, David
b. Cahill, William T(homas)
b. Calder, Alexander
b. Callan, Michael
b. Campbell, Bebe Moore
b. Cappelletti, John Raymond
b. Carey, Henry Charles
b. Cary, Lorene
b. Chambers, Whittaker
b. Chang, Sarah Yong-chu
b. Charles, Suzette
b. Chase-Riboud, Barbara
b. Chasnoff, Debra
b. Chomsky, Noam Avram
b. Christopher, Dennis
b. Christy, Edwin P.
b. Clark, Joseph Sill
b. Clarke, Mae
b. Clarke, Stanley Marvin
b. Clayton, Constance Elaine
b. Clymer, George
b. Cobb, Will D
b. Coca, Imogene Fernandez y
b. Columbo, Russ
b. Conrad, Charles, Jr.
b. Cope, Edward Drinker
b. Cosby, Bill
b. Covington, Warren
b. Cox, Geraldine V(ang)
b. Coxe, Tench
b. Cramp, Charles Henry
b. Crawford, Broderick
b. Cregar, Laird
b. Creighton, Thomas H(awk)
b. Croce, Jim
b. Crumb, R(obert)
b. Cummings, Sam
b. DaCosta, Morton
b. Dahlgren, John Adolphus Bernard
b. Dallas, George Mifflin
b. Daly, Thomas Augustine
b. Danner, Blythe Katharine
b. Darley, Felix Octavius Carr
b. Darren, James
b. Davis, Richard Harding
b. Davis, Stuart
b. Davis, William Morris
b. Davison, Bruce
b. Deacon, Richard
b. DelRuth, Roy
b. Denslow, W(illiam) W(allace)
b. DePreist, James Anderson
b. DeRita, Joe

b. Diamond, Legs
b. Dicciani, Nance K(atherine)
b. Doggett, Bill
b. Donnelly, Ignatius
b. Douglas, Paul
b. Drew, John
b. Drexel, Anthony Joseph
b. Drexel, Mary Katherine
b. Druckman, Jacob (Raphael)
b. Duane, William
b. Dundee, Angelo Mirena, Jr.
b. Dykes, Jimmy
b. Eakins, Thomas
b. Early, Gerald
b. Eckert, John Presper, Jr.
b. Ehrlich, Paul
b. Elliott, Jumbo
b. Ellsler, Effie
b. Elman, Ziggy
b. Ennis, Del(mer)
b. Erhard, Werner
b. Eubanks, Kevin
b. Eustis, Dorothy Leib Harrison
  Wood
b. Fabian
b. Fallows, James (Mackenzie)
b. Fattah, Chaka
b. Feigenbaum, Mitchell Jay
b. Fell, Norman
b. Fields, W C
b. Fine, Larry
b. Finletter, Thomas Knight
b. Fiorentino, Linda
b. Fischer, Louis
b. Fisher, Eddie
b. Forrest, Edwin
b. Forten, James
b. Frost, Arthur Burdett
b. Fry, William Henry
b. Fuller, Charles
b. Gabel, Martin
b. Galamison, Milton Arthur
b. Galanos, James
b. Gallaudet, Thomas Hopkins
b. Gamble, Kenny
b. Garzarelli, Elaine Marie
b. Gates, Thomas Sovereign, Jr.
b. Gathers, Hank
b. Gaynor, Janet
b. George, Henry, Sr.
b. Gere, Richard
b. Getz, Stan
b. Giannini, Dusolina
b. Giannini, Vittorio
b. Gibbs, William Francis
b. Gibson, Walter B(rown)
b. Glackens, William James
b. Gola, Tom
b. Goldstein, Israel
b. Golson, Benny
b. Goren, Charles Henry
b. Graham, Ronny
b. Grant, Gogi
b. Gratz, Rebecca
b. Greco, Buddy
b. Greenwood, Charlotte
b. Grimke, Charlotte Lottie Forten
b. Guarrera, Frank
b. Guggenheim, Daniel
b. Guggenheim, Solomon Robert
b. Haig, Alexander Meigs, Jr.
b. Haldeman-Julius, Emanuel
b. Hale, Clara (McBride)
b. Hale, Lorraine
b. Hamel, Veronica
b. Hare, Robert

b. Harris, Barbara Clementine
b. Harris, Willard Palmer
b. Harshaw, Margaret
b. Haupt, Herman
b. Head, Howard
b. Hemsley, Sherman
b. Hergesheimer, Joseph
b. Hesselius, John
b. Hill, George Washington
b. Hirsch, Joseph
b. Holm, John Cecil
b. Holmes, John Haynes
b. Hooks, Kevin
b. Hopkinson, Francis
b. Humphries, Rolfe
b. Huneker, James Gibbons
b. Hyman, Phyllis
b. Innaurato, Albert
b. Ives, Herbert Eugene
b. Jaggar, Thomas Augustus
b. Jamison, Judith
b. Jamison, Philip Duane, Jr.
b. Jefferson, Joseph
b. Jett, Joan
b. Jones, Henry
b. Kallen, Kitty
b. Kane, Elisha Kent
b. Katzenbach, Nicholas de Belleville
b. Kay, Hershy
b. Keane, Bil
b. Keen, William Williams
b. Kelley, Florence
b. Kelly, George Edward
b. Kelly, Grace Patricia
b. Kelly, John Brenden
b. Kelly, John Brenden, Jr.
b. Kelly, Thomas
b. Kelly, Walt(er Crawford)
b. Kerr, Alexander H
b. Kirk, Alan Goodrich
b. Kline, Nathan Schellenberg
b. Klugman, Jack
b. Knauer, Virginia Harrington Wright
b. Knight, Arthur
b. Kramm, Joseph
b. Kumin, Maxine Winokur
b. LaBelle, Patti
b. Landers, Audrey
b. Landers, Judy
b. Lang, Eddie
b. Langstroth, Lorenzo Lorraine
b. Lanin, Lester
b. Lanza, Mario
b. Lawrence, David
b. Lawrence, Elliot
b. Lawrence, Lawrence Shubert, Jr.
b. Lea, Henry Charles
b. Lehman, John Francis, Jr.
b. Lehr, Lew
b. Leidy, Joseph
b. Leland, Charles Godfrey
b. Leser, Tina
b. Leslie, Eliza
b. Lester, Richard
b. Levin, Gerald
b. Levinsky, Battling
b. Levinson, Richard Leighton
b. Levy, Uriah Phillips
b. Lewis, Drew
b. Linton, Ralph
b. Lipinski, Tara
b. List, Eugene
b. Lloyd, Lewis Kevin
b. Locke, Alain Leroy
b. Lorne, Marion
b. Loughran, Tommy

b. Loyd, Sam(uel)
b. Lumet, Sidney
b. Lynd, Staughton (Craig)
b. MacDonald, Jeanette
b. Mack, Connie
b. Mann, Abby
b. Mark, Mary Ellen
b. Marlowe, Hugh
b. Marshall, Brenda
b. Martino, Al
b. Martino, Pat
b. May, Elaine
b. McArdle, Andrea
b. McBride, Christian
b. McCarten, John
b. McCarthy, Joe
b. McClellan, George Brinton
b. McCloskey, Robert James
b. McCloy, John Jay
b. McCracken, Joan
b. McDermott, Johnny
b. McIntyre, John Thomas
b. McKay, Jim
b. McLean, Robert
b. Mead, Margaret
b. Medary, Milton B
b. Mellor, Walter
b. Merriam, Eve
b. Merton, Robert King
b. Mitchell, Silas Weir
b. Monaghan, (James) Jay, (IV)
b. Monroe, Earl
b. Morgan, John
b. Morrison, Hobe
b. Mosconi, Willie
b. Mosley, J(ohn) Brooke
b. Mulhern, Matt
b. Nash, George Frederick
b. Nash, N Richard
b. Nipon, Albert
b. Norworth, Jack
b. Nowlan, Phil
b. O'Connor, John Joseph, Cardinal
b. Odets, Clifford
b. Omarr, Sydney
b. Parrish, Maxfield
b. Peale, Titian Ramsay
b. Peete, Holly Robinson
b. Pemberton, John Clifford
b. Pendergrass, Teddy
b. Penn, Arthur Hiller
b. Pennell, Joseph Stanley
b. Penrose, Boies
b. Perret, Gene
b. Persichetti, Vincent
b. Peto, John Frederick
b. Pinkney, Jerry
b. Pitlik, Noam
b. Pitz, Henry Clarence
b. Pleasant, Mary Ellen
b. Powdermaker, Hortense
b. Powell, Mike
b. Prosky, Robert Joseph
b. Quarterman, Lloyd Albert
b. Quillan, Eddie
b. Quindlen, Anna
b. Quinn, Arthur Hobson
b. Quinn, Edmond T
b. Ramsay, Jack
b. Randall, Samuel J
b. Rapp, Danny
b. Ray, Man
b. Reed, Henry Hope
b. Repplier, Agnes
b. Rhone, Sylvia
b. Rice, Joseph Mayer

b. Richards, William Trost
b. Riesman, David
b. Rivlin, Alice Mitchell
b. Rizzo, Frank Lazzaro
b. Roberts, Robin Evan
b. Rodgers, Guy William, Jr.
b. Rodin, Judith
b. Rosenbach, Abraham Simon Wolf
b. Rosenfeld, Alvin Hirsch
b. Ross, Betsy
b. Roth, Ann
b. Rush, Benjamin
b. Rush, William
b. Rydell, Bobby
b. Saget, Bob
b. Sample, Bill
b. Sargent, Alvin
b. Schlessinger, David
b. Segal, Vivienne
b. Seidelman, Susan
b. Sellinger, Frank
b. Sellinger, Joseph A
b. Sembello, Michael
b. Shapey, Ralph
b. Shaplen, Robert Modell
b. Sheeler, Charles
b. Shippen, Margaret
b. Shor, Toots
b. Singleton, Penny
b. Sledge, Debbie
b. Sledge, Joni
b. Sledge, Kathy
b. Sledge, Kim
b. Smith, Jessie Wilcox
b. Smith, Will
b. Smith, Willi Donnell
b. Soren, David
b. Soyer, David
b. Spaeth, Sigmund Gottfried
b. Stankiewicz, Richard Peter
b. Stanky, Eddie
b. Stevenson, Parker
b. Stockton, Frank
b. Stone, I(sidor) F(einstein)
b. Susann, Jacqueline
b. Tassell, Gustave
b. Temin, Howard Martin
b. Terra, Daniel J(ames)
b. Terrell, Tammi
b. Thompson, Ruth Plumly
b. Tilden, Bill
b. Toomey, Bill
b. Tribble, Isreal, Jr.
b. Trumbauer, Horace
b. Tucker, C(ynthia) DeLores
   (Nottage)
b. Tucker, Lorenzo
b. Tyne, George
b. Tyner, McCoy Alfred
b. Van Dusen, Henry Pitney
b. Ventura, Charlie
b. Venturi, Robert
b. Vila, George Raymond
b. von Lipsey, Roderick K.
b. Walcott, Mary Morris Vaux
b. Walker, Nancy
b. Wallace, Horace Binney
b. Walter, Thomas Ustick
b. Walters, Bucky
b. Wanamaker, John
b. Wanamaker, Lewis Rodman
b. Watson, Elizabeth
b. Weil, Andrew (Thomas)
b. Wharton, Joseph
b. Whitaker, Jack
b. Widener, George D

b. Wiggin, Kate Douglas
b. Williams, Walter Edward
b. Williams, Willie Lawrence
b. Willners, Hal
b. Wolfington, Iggie
b. Wood, Fernando
b. Wood, Samuel Grosvenor
b. Woodson, Robert L.
b. Wrigley, William, Jr.
b. Wummer, John
b. Wynn, Ed
b. Yust, Walter
b. Zimmerman, Paul L
d. Adams, Edwin
d. Adler, Cyrus
d. Agnew, David Hayes
d. Allen, Richard
d. Bailey, Pearl Mae
d. Bainbridge, William
d. Baldwin, Matthias William
d. Barry, John
d. Bartram, William
d. Baugh, Albert Croll
d. Bell, Bert
d. Bender, Chief
d. Benezet, Anthony
d. Berberova, Nina Nikolaevna
d. Bergey, David Hendricks
d. Biddle, Nicholas
d. Bird, Robert Montgomery
d. Bond, James
d. Brown, Charles Brockden
d. Burns, David
d. Carey, Henry Charles
d. Carey, Mathew
d. Carothers, Wallace Hume
d. Charleston, Oscar McKinley
d. Childs, George William
d. Churchill, May
d. Clark, Joseph Sill
d. Cleghorn, Sarah Norcliffe
d. Cope, Edward Drinker
d. Coxe, Tench
d. Cramp, Charles Henry
d. Cret, Paul P(hilippe)
d. Dallas, George Mifflin
d. Daly, Thomas Augustine
d. DeAngeli, Marguerite Lofft
d. Divine, Father Major Jealous
d. Drexel, Francis Martin
d. DuPont, Eleuthere Irenee
d. DuPont, Samuel Francis
d. Duryea, Charles Edgar
d. Dykes, Jimmy
d. Eakins, Thomas
d. Ehmke, Howard Jonathan
d. Eiseley, Loren Corey
d. Eklund, Carl Robert
d. Evans, Orrín C
d. Fauset, Jessie Redmon
d. Fels, Joseph
d. Fels, Samuel Simeon
d. Florence, William Jermyn
d. Forbes, John
d. Forrest, Edwin
d. Forten, James
d. Fortune, Timothy Thomas
d. Frank, Gerold
d. Franklin, Benjamin
d. Gardenia, Vincent
d. Gates, Thomas Sovereign, Jr.
d. Girard, Stephen
d. Godey, Louis Antoine
d. Gold, Harry
d. Gordon, Dexter Keith
d. Gottlieb, Eddie

b. Unitas, Johnny
b. Wallace, Bobby
b. Wambaugh, Joseph Aloysius, Jr.
b. Weaver, Fritz William
b. Widdoes, James
b. Wild, Earl
b. Williams, Mary Lou
b. Wilson, August
b. Woods, Robert Archey
b. Wright, Syretta
b. Yablonski, Joseph
b. Yardley, Jonathan
d. Axthelm, Pete(r Macrae)
d. Blumenthal, Monica David
d. Caliguiri, Richard
d. Conn, Billy
d. Cooper, Chuck
d. Duse, Eleanora
d. Eckstine, Billy
d. Ferris, George Washington Gale
d. Foster, Tabatha
d. Galvin, Pud
d. Gibson, Josh(ua)
d. Goode, Mal
d. Guiterman, Arthur
d. Hartman, Elizabeth
d. Heinz, Henry John
d. Holland, William Jacob
d. Hutchins, Thomas
d. Jones, Stormie
d. Kane, John
d. Lipscomb, Eugene
d. Love, George Hutchinson
d. Mellon, Richard King
d. Muller-Munk, Peter
d. Murray, Pauli
d. Newell, Allen
d. Rockwell, Willard F
d. Rooney, Art(hur Joseph)
d. Russell, Lillian
d. Schmitt, Gladys
d. Shiras, George, Jr.
d. Stuhldreher, Harry A
d. Sublette, William L
d. Traynor, Pie

Pittston, Pennsylvania
b. Cefalo, Jimmy
b. Jennings, Hugh(ey Ambrose)
b. MacArthur, John Donald
b. Trippi, Charlie

Plainfield, Pennsylvania
b. Penn, Irving

Plains, Pennsylvania
b. Walsh, Ed(ward Augustine)

Pleasantville, Pennsylvania
b. Palmer, Frederick

Pottsgrove, Pennsylvania
b. Gladden, Washington

Pottstown, Pennsylvania
b. Hall, Daryl
b. Landis, Walter Savage

Pottsville, Pennsylvania
b. Becker, Gary S(tanley)
b. Bergen, John Joseph
b. O'Hara, John Henry
d. Richter, Conrad Michael

Quakertown, Pennsylvania
d. Crosby, Alexander L

Quartzside, Pennsylvania
d. Rapp, Danny

Reading, Pennsylvania
b. Althouse, Paul Shearer
b. Baird, Spencer Fullerton
b. Boone, Daniel
b. Constantine, Michael
b. Dwyer, Florence Price
b. Eichhorn, Lisa
b. Julian, Doggie
b. Kerr, Clark
b. Lampkin, Daisy
b. Moore, Lenny
b. Smith, Martin Cruz
b. Stevens, Wallace
b. Weiss, Theodore (Russell)
d. Sousa, John Philip

Reinerton, Pennsylvania
b. Brown, Les(ter Raymond)

Richboro, Pennsylvania
b. Peale, Rembrandt

Richlandtown, Pennsylvania
d. Bloor, Mother

Ridgeway, Pennsylvania
b. Mayo, Katherine

Ridley Park, Pennsylvania
b. Morton, John
b. Rigby, Bob
d. Morton, John

Riverside, Pennsylvania
b. Blough, Roger Miles

Rose Valley, Pennsylvania
d. Stephens, Alice Barber

Rosemont, Pennsylvania
d. Lattimore, Richmond Alexander

Running Pumps, Pennsylvania
b. Gorgas, Josiah

Russellton, Pennsylvania
b. Tenace, Gene

Saint Davids, Pennsylvania
b. Helms, Richard McGarrah

Saint Mary's, Pennsylvania
b. Daly, Chuck

Saint Thomas, Pennsylvania
b. Fox, Nellie

Saltsburg, Pennsylvania
b. McIlwain, Charles Howard

Sanatoga, Pennsylvania
d. Wittenmyer, Annie Turner

Saxonburg, Pennsylvania
b. Roebling, Washington Augustus

Saylorsburg, Pennsylvania
d. Gibbons, Floyd Phillips

Sayre, Pennsylvania
b. Hennard, George, Jr.

Schuylkill, Pennsylvania
b. Singmaster, Elsie

Scottdale, Pennsylvania
b. Goldenson, Leonard H(arry)

Scranton, Pennsylvania
b. Biden, Joe
b. Carlucci, Frank Charles, III
b. Crowley, Pat
b. Falkenberg, Nanette
b. Keen, Sam
b. Kerr, Jean
b. Levy, David Mordecai
b. MacArthur, Charles
b. Mazia, Daniel
b. McHale, Tom
b. Miller, Jason
b. Morgan, Russ
b. O'Boyle, Patrick Aloysius, Cardinal
b. Quinlan, Karen Ann
b. Reich, Robert B(ernard)
b. Scott, Lizabeth
b. Victor, Sally Josephs
d. Budge, Don
d. Casey, Robert P
d. Crowley, Jim
d. Jennings, Hugh(ey Ambrose)
d. Scranton, George Whitfield

Selinsgrove, Pennsylvania
b. Coxey, Jacob Sechler

Sellersville, Pennsylvania
d. Hewitt, Bill

Sewickley, Pennsylvania
b. Hamilton, Nancy
b. Heinz, Henry John, II
b. Homer, Louise
b. Knox, Chuck
b. Stewart, George Rippey

Shamokin, Pennsylvania
b. Coveleski, Harry Frank
b. Coveleski, Stanley Anthony
b. Daubert, Jake
d. Coveleski, Harry Frank

Sharon, Pennsylvania
b. Butala, Tony
b. MacDonald, John Dann

Shenandoah, Pennsylvania
b. Dorsey, Jimmy
b. Dorsey, Tommy

Shillington, Pennsylvania
b. Updike, John (Hoyer)

Shippensburg, Pennsylvania
b. Bugbee, Emma

Sinking Spring, Pennsylvania
d. Hoopes, Darlington

Wissahickon, Pennsylvania
b. Baker, Hobey

Worcester, Pennsylvania
d. Callender, John Hancock

Wyalusing, Pennsylvania
b. Stern, Philip Van Doren

Wyncote, Pennsylvania
b. Jackson, Reggie
d. Curtis, Cyrus Hermann Kotszchmar

Wynnewood, Pennsylvania
d. Shapp, Milton J(errold)

Yeadon, Pennsylvania
d. McDermott, Johnny

York, Pennsylvania
b. Bishop, J(ohn) Michael
b. Claiborne, Loretta (Lynn)
b. Devers, Jacob Loucks
b. Franklin, William Buel
b. Hunt, Lois
b. Koons, Jeff
b. Lefever, Ernest Warren
b. Woltman, Frederick Enos
d. Hoffman, Robert C
d. Smith, James

Youngstown, Pennsylvania
b. Palmer, Arnold Daniel

Youngwood, Pennsylvania
b. Blanda, George Frederick

RHODE ISLAND
d. Holm, John Cecil

Bristol, Rhode Island
b. Massasoit
d. Burnside, Ambrose Everett
d. Massasoit
d. Mizener, Arthur Moore

Burrillville, Rhode Island
b. Robillard, Duke

Cranston, Rhode Island
b. Aldrich, Robert
b. DiPrete, Edward Daniel
b. Sullivan, William Healy

Foster, Rhode Island
b. Aldrich, Nelson Wilmarth

Hopkinton, Rhode Island
b. Crandall, Prudence

Lime Rock, Rhode Island
d. Lewis, Ida

Middletown, Rhode Island
d. Huston, John

Newport, Rhode Island
b. Anderson, Harry
b. Channing, Walter
b. Channing, William Ellery
b. Ellery, William
b. Ince, Thomas H(arper)

b. Johnson, Van
b. King, Clarence
b. Lewis, Ida
b. Little, Lawson
b. Mills, Ogden Livingston
b. Perry, Matthew Calbraith,
   Commodore
b. Waterhouse, Benjamin
d. Bache, Alexander Dallas
d. Blatchford, Samuel
d. Cary, Phoebe
d. Chadwick, French Ensor
d. Clarke, John
d. Coddington, William
d. Curtis, Benjamin Robbins
d. Eaton, Wyatt
d. Ellery, William
d. Gibbs, Oliver Wolcott
d. Hopkins, Samuel
d. Hoving, Jane Pickens
d. Hoving, Walter
d. Howe, Julia Ward
d. Hunt, Richard Morris
d. Ingersoll, Stuart H
d. Kennedy, John Pendleton
d. Moore, Clement Clarke
d. Richards, William Trost
d. Stephens, Ann Sophia
d. Vanderbilt, Harold Stirling
d. Woolsey, Sarah Chauncey
d. Yarnell, Harry Ervin

North Kingstown, Rhode Island
b. Stuart, Gilbert Charles
d. Pastore, John Orlando
d. Wister, Owen

Pawtucket, Rhode Island
b. Corcoran, Thomas Gardiner
b. Hartman, David Downs
b. Hood, Raymond Matthewson
b. Levine, Irving R(askin)

Peace Dale, Rhode Island
d. Bacon, Leonard
d. Eichenberg, Fritz

Potowomut, Rhode Island
b. Greene, Nathanael

Providence, Rhode Island
b. Aldrich, Winthrop Williams
b. Bartlett, John Russell
b. Brown, John Carter
b. Brown, Moses
b. Carle, Frankie
b. Chace, Marian
b. Chafee, John H(ubbard)
b. Chase, William Curtis
b. Clark, John Bates
b. Cohan, George M(ichael)
b. Cohan, Josephine
b. Colasanto, Nicholas
b. Conti, Bill
b. Curtis, George William
b. Denneny, Michael (Leo)
b. Eddy, Nelson
b. Foster, Joseph C
b. Gorham, Jabez
b. Hackett, Bobby
b. Hassenfeld, Stephen David
b. Hatlo, Jimmy
b. Hedison, David
b. Hopkins, Stephen
b. Howard, Cordelia

b. Hussey, Ruth Carol
b. Kinnell, Galway
b. Lopes, Davey
b. Lovecraft, H(oward) P(hillips)
b. Macready, George
b. McLaughlin, John (Joseph)
b. O'Connor, Edwin Greene
b. Osborne, Jeffrey
b. Pastore, John Orlando
b. Rockefeller, Abby Aldrich
b. Rockwell, Doc
b. Sundlun, Bruce George
b. Updike, Daniel Berkeley
b. Violet, Arlene
b. Ward, David S
b. White, Helen Magill
b. Whitman, Sarah Helen Power
b. Woodcock, Leonard Freel
d. Bannister, Edward Mitchell
d. Bartlett, John Russell
d. Beers, Clifford Whittingham
d. DeJong, David Cornel
d. Dolbier, Maurice (Wyman)
d. Gardner, Mary Sewall
d. Gorham, Jabez
d. Hawkes, John
d. Hopkins, Esek
d. Hopkins, Stephen
d. Jones, Matilda Sissieretta Joyner
d. LaFarge, John
d. Lattimore, Owen
d. Lorillard, Louis Livingston
d. Lovecraft, H(oward) P(hillips)
d. Madeira, Jean
d. Paul, Elliot Harold
d. Roberts, Dennis J(oseph)
d. Ryden, Ernest Edwin
d. Salisbury, Harrison Evans
d. Warren, Austin
d. Wayland, Francis
d. Weir, John F(erguson)
d. Whitman, Sarah Helen Power
d. Williams, Roger

Quonset Point, Rhode Island
b. Myers, Dee Dee

River Point, Rhode Island
b. Duffy, Hugh

Riverside, Rhode Island
d. Jordy, William H(enry)

Scituate, Rhode Island
b. Angell, James Burrill
b. Hopkins, Esek

Smithfield, Rhode Island
d. Dowling, Eddie

South Kingstown, Rhode Island
b. Perry, Oliver Hazard, Admiral

Tiverton, Rhode Island
b. Gray, Robert

Valley Falls, Rhode Island
b. Dearden, John Francis, Cardinal

Warwick, Rhode Island
b. Sheldon, William Herbert
d. Bugbee, Emma
d. Gorton, Samuel

Florence, South Carolina
b. Johnson, William Henry
d. Purvis, Melvin

Fort Moultrie, South Carolina
d. Osceola

Fountain Inn, South Carolina
b. Bates, Peg Leg
d. Bates, Peg Leg

Gaffney, South Carolina
b. MacDowell, Andie

Georgetown, South Carolina
b. Rainey, Joseph Hayne
d. Rainey, Joseph Hayne

Georgetown County, South Carolina
b. Allston, Washington

Goose Creek, South Carolina
d. Middleton, Arthur

Greenville, South Carolina
b. Anderson, Cat
b. Ashmore, Harry Scott
b. Bryson, Peabo
b. Butler, Matthew Calbraith
b. Campbell, Carroll Ashmore, Jr.
b. Gibson, William F(rank)
b. Haynsworth, Clement Furman, Jr.
b. Jackson, Jesse, Jr.
b. Jackson, Jesse Louis
b. Riley, Richard W(ilson)
b. Townes, Charles Hard
b. Watson, John Broadus
b. White, Josh(ua Daniel)
d. Carr, John Dickson
d. Jackson, Joe
d. Jones, Bob
d. Spivak, Charlie

Greenville County, South Carolina
b. Allison, Dorothy E.

Greenwood, South Carolina
b. Buzhardt, J(oseph) Fred, Jr.
b. Hopkins, Bo
b. Wright, Louis Booker

Hartsville, South Carolina
b. Newsom, Bobo
d. Coker, Elizabeth Boatwright

Hilton Head Island, South Carolina
d. Batten, William Milfred
d. Blair, Frank
d. Buzhardt, J(oseph) Fred, Jr.
d. Coxe, George Harmon
d. Daniels, Jonathan Worth
d. Hansell, Haywood Shepherd, Jr.
d. Moore, Garry

Holly Hill, South Carolina
b. Randolph, Willie

Jonesville, South Carolina
b. Dove, Ulysses
b. Littlejohn, Robert McGowan

Kinard, South Carolina
b. Clements, Vassar

Lake City, South Carolina
b. McNair, Ronald Ervin

Lancaster, South Carolina
d. Townsend, William Cameron

Latta, South Carolina
b. Floyd, Carlisle Sessions

Laurens County, South Carolina
b. Davis, Gary, Reverend
b. Peterkin, Julia Mood

Lynchburg, South Carolina
b. Smith, Ellison DuRant
d. Smith, Ellison DuRant

Manning, South Carolina
b. Parish, Peggy
d. Parish, Peggy

Marlboro, South Carolina
b. Roper, Daniel C(alhoun)

Mauldin, South Carolina
b. Garnett, Kevin

Mayesville, South Carolina
b. Bethune, Mary McLeod

Newbury District, South Carolina
b. Hammond, James Henry

North, South Carolina
b. Kitt, Eartha Mae

Orangeburg, South Carolina
b. Nix, Robert N(elson) C(ornelius), Sr.
d. Peterkin, Julia Mood

Parris Island, South Carolina
b. Phillips, John

Pawley's Island, South Carolina
b. Reid, Irvin D.

Pendleton, South Carolina
b. Maverick, Samuel Augustus
d. Earle, Ralph

Pickens District, South Carolina
b. Brown, Joseph Emerson

Red Banks, South Carolina
b. Travis, William Barret

Richburg, South Carolina
b. Marion, Marty

Ridge Spring, South Carolina
b. Woodward, William E

Ridgeland, South Carolina
b. Ike, Reverend

Rock Hill, South Carolina
b. Caddell, Pat(rick Hayward)

Saint Helena's, South Carolina
b. Heyward, Thomas, Jr.

Saint Luke's, South Carolina
d. Heyward, Thomas, Jr.

Saint Matthews, South Carolina
b. Ulmer, James

Seabrook Is., South Carolina
d. Snyder, John Wesley

Seneca, South Carolina
b. Aikens, Willie Mays
b. Hines, John E(lbridge)

Silver, South Carolina
b. Gibson, Althea

Spartanburg, South Carolina
b. Powell, Earl A, III
b. Rawls, Betsy
b. Rosen, Al(bert Leonard)
b. Westmoreland, William Childs

Statesburg, South Carolina
b. Chesnut, Mary Boykin (Miller)
d. Poinsett, Joel Roberts

Sumter, South Carolina
b. Capero, Virginia
b. Goldstein, Joseph Leonard
b. Richardson, Bobby

Sumterville, South Carolina
b. Kellogg, Clara Louise

Timminsville, South Carolina
b. Yarborough, Cale

Timmonsville, South Carolina
b. Purvis, Melvin

Walhalla, South Carolina
b. Portman, John Calvin, Jr.

Waxhaw, South Carolina
b. Jackson, Andrew

Winnsboro, South Carolina
b. Belk, William E

Winyah Bay, South Carolina
d. Ayllon, Lucas Vasquez de

Winyaw, South Carolina
b. Lynch, Thomas, Jr.

Woodruff, South Carolina
b. Harrelson, Ken(neth Smith)

Yemassee, South Carolina
b. Blair, Frank

York, South Carolina
b. Sanders, Dori(nda)

SOUTH DAKOTA
b. Gall
b. Giago, Tim
b. Hart, LeRoy
b. Hump
b. Lame Deer

Athens, Tennessee
b. Culvahouse, Art(hur Boggess, Jr.)

Bakerville, Tennessee
b. Anderson, William Robert
b. Caraway, Hattie Wyatt

Bells, Tennessee
b. Martindale, Wink

Bristol, Tennessee
b. Ford, Tennessee Ernie
b. Henderson, Vivian Wilson
b. Reynolds, Richard S
d. Kulwicki, Alan

Brownsville, Tennessee
b. Chauncey, George
b. Halliburton, Richard
b. Smitherman, Geneva

Camden, Tennessee
d. Cline, Patsy

Campbellsville, Tennessee
b. Davidson, Donald Grady

Carter Station, Tennessee
d. Johnson, Andrew

Carthage, Tennessee
d. Gore, Albert Arnold

Centerville, Tennessee
b. Pearl, Minnie

Chapel Hill, Tennessee
b. Forrest, Nathan Bedford

Charlotte, Tennessee
b. Robertson, Oscar Palmer

Chattanooga, Tennessee
b. Adler, Julius Ochs
b. Barber, Jesse B., Jr.
b. Blanton, Jimmy
b. Brock, Bill
b. Moser, Barry
b. Ochs, Adolph Shelby, II
b. Reed, Ishmael Scott
b. Smith, Bessie
b. White, Reggie
d. Derricotte, Juliette Aline
d. Ochs, Adolph Shelby, II
d. Ochs, Adolph Simon

Clarksville, Tennessee
b. Rudolph, Wilma (Glodean)
b. Scott, Evelyn

Cleveland, Tennessee
d. Smith, Hazel Brannon

Clinton, Tennessee
b. Stribling, Thomas Sigismund

Coal Creek, Tennessee
b. Hightower, John Marmann

Collierville, Tennessee
b. McCray, Nikki
b. Throneberry, Marv(in Eugene)

Covington, Tennessee
b. Hayes, Isaac

Davidson County, Tennessee
b. Love, Nat

Dayton, Tennessee
b. Gaither, Jake
d. Bryan, William Jennings

Del Rio, Tennessee
b. Guffey, Burnett

Dover, Tennessee
d. Bell, John

Etowah, Tennessee
b. Whittle, Christopher

Fayetteville, Tennessee
b. Dempsey, Rick

Giles County, Tennessee
d. Davis, Sam(uel)

Gordonsville, Tennessee
b. Bridges, Tommy

Grand Junction, Tennessee
b. Hearns, Thomas

Grandview, Tennessee
b. Dickson, Earle Ensign

Granville, Tennessee
b. Gore, Albert Arnold

Greene City, Tennessee
b. Crockett, Davy

Greeneville, Tennessee
d. Johnson, Eliza (McCardle)

Halls, Tennessee
b. Middlecoff, Cary

Hardeman County, Tennessee
b. Chisum, John Simpson

Hardin County, Tennessee
b. Blanton, (Leonard) Ray

Harriman, Tennessee
b. Lee, Dixie

Henderson, Tennessee
b. Arnold, Eddy

Hendersonville, Tennessee
d. Orbison, Roy
d. Stewart, Wynn

Huntsville, Tennessee
b. Baker, Howard Henry, Jr.

Iron City, Tennessee
b. Montgomery, Melba

Jackson, Tennessee
b. Dancy, John Albert
b. Jones, Christopher

b. Jones, Too Tall
b. Lindsey, Benjamin Barr
b. Perkins, Carl (Lee)
b. Sheppard, T G
d. Blanton, (Leonard) Ray
d. Perkins, Carl (Lee)

Johnson City, Tennessee
b. Hickman, Herman Michael, Jr.
b. Marshall, Catherine
b. Miller, William Ernest

Knoxville, Tennessee
b. Agee, James Rufus
b. Alexander, Lamar
b. Bergen, Polly
b. Costa, Mary
b. Cullum, John
b. Delaney, Beauford
b. Farragut, David Glasgow
b. Giovanni, Nikki
b. Hastie, William Henry
b. Keith, David Lemuel
b. Krutch, Joseph Wood
b. Richberg, Donald R(andall)
b. Tarantino, Quentin
d. Bryant, Boudleaux
d. Holt, A(ndrew) D(avid, Jr.)
d. Jenkins, Ray Howard
d. Whitehead, Don(ald Ford)

Lauderdale County, Tennessee
b. Bradford, Roark Whitney Wickliffe

Lawrenceberg, Tennessee
b. Jeter, Michael

Leesburg, Tennessee
b. Johnson, Eliza (McCardle)

Lookout Mountain, Tennessee
b. Ross, John
b. Tanner, Roscoe
d. Carter, John Garnet

Luttrell, Tennessee
b. Atkins, Chet

Macon County, Tennessee
b. White, Neva

Madison, Tennessee
d. Snow, Hank

Madisonville, Tennessee
b. Carter, Carlene
b. Kefauver, Estes

Maryville, Tennessee
b. Burger, Carl Victor

Maynardville, Tennessee
b. Acuff, Roy (Claxton)

McLemoresville, Tennessee
b. Carter, Dixie

McMinnville, Tennessee
b. Snow, Dorothea Johnston
b. West, Dottie

Memphis, Tennessee
b. Ace, Johnny

Shelbyville, Tennessee
b. Brush, George
b. Locke, Sondra
b. Martin, Louis E.

Shiloh, Tennessee
d. Johnston, Albert Sidney

Signal Mountain, Tennessee
d. Derthick, L(awrence) G(ridley)

Sneedville, Tennessee
b. Martin, Jimmy

Soddy, Tennessee
b. McGill, Ralph Emerson

Spring City, Tennessee
b. Handy, Thomas Troy

Springfield, Tennessee
d. Monroe, Bill

Stewart's Creek, Tennessee
b. Davis, Sam(uel)

Stony Creek, Tennessee
b. Curtis, Jackie

Summer County, Tennessee
b. Neal, James Foster

Sweetwater, Tennessee
b. Carter, John Garnet
b. O'Steen, Van

Taskigi, Tennessee
b. Sequoyah

Taylorville, Tennessee
b. Purcell, Edward M(ills)

Tiptonville, Tennessee
b. Cates, Clifton Bledsoe

White House, Tennessee
d. Varney, Jim

Whitehaven, Tennessee
b. Isbell, Marion William

Winchester, Tennessee
b. Shore, Dinah

Wolcottville, Tennessee
b. Kercheval, Ken

Woodstock, Tennessee
b. Dix, Dorothy

TEXAS
b. Applewhite, Marshall Herff
b. Church, George W
b. Davis, (Thomas) Cullen
b. Hargrove, Roy
b. Miller, Nolan
b. Murchison, Clint(on Williams, Jr.)
b. Murphey, Michael Martin
b. Schoellkopf, Caroline Rose Hunt
b. Yeager, Jeana
d. Becknell, William
d. Cacers, Ernest

d. Goodnight, Charles
d. La Salle, Rene Robert Cavelier de
d. Smithson, Robert (Irving)

Abbott, Texas
b. Nelson, Willie

Abilene, Texas
b. Crane, Roy(ston Campbell)
b. Olson, Billy Richard
b. Sharman, Bill
b. Williams, Mason

Alba, Texas
b. Payne, Leon

Alvarado, Texas
b. Southern, Terry

Amarillo, Texas
b. Britain, Radie
b. Charisse, Cyd
b. Elfman, Danny
b. Jones, Carolyn
b. Neely, Mark E., Jr.
b. Sargent, Ben

Anson, Texas
b. Riley, Jeannie C

Athens, Texas
b. Justice, William Wayne
b. Richardson, Sid
d. Murchison, Clint(on Williams, Sr.)

Atlanta, Texas
b. Coleman, Bessie

Austin, Texas
b. Baylor, Don(ald Edward)
b. Carpenter, Leslie
b. Coleman, Dabney W
b. Crenshaw, Ben Daniel
b. Faulk, John Henry
b. Griffith, Nanci
b. Hawke, Ethan
b. Ing, Dean
b. Jameson, House
b. Kenty, Hilmer
b. Key, Valdimer Orlando, Jr.
b. Kirk, Ron
b. Kite, Tom
b. Lane, Dick
b. Lomax, Alan
b. Schieffer, Bob
b. Scott, Zachary
b. Wehrwein, Austin Carl
b. Wilson, Teddy
d. Ames, Jessie Daniel
d. Austin, Stephen Fuller
d. Dobie, J(ames) Frank
d. Faulk, John Henry
d. Ferguson, Miriam Amanda
d. Grattan, Clinton Hartley
d. Hines, John E(lbridge)
d. Horton, Johnny
d. Jordan, Barbara C(harline)
d. Lubbock, Francis Richard
d. Mark, Herman Francis
d. Moore, Charles Willard
d. Noyce, Robert Norton
d. Scott, Zachary
d. Watt, George Willard
d. Webb, Walter Prescott

d. Whitman, Charles Joseph
d. Williams, Roger J
d. Wilson, Logan
d. Yarborough, Ralph W(ebster)

Ballinger, Texas
b. Guion, David Wendel Fentress

Bay City, Texas
b. Whitfield, Malvin

Baytown, Texas
b. Griffin, Anthony P.

Beaumont, Texas
b. Crippen, Robert Laurel
b. Davis, Walter
b. Graham, Larry
b. Hofheinz, Roy Mark
b. Parks, Bernard C.
b. Robinson, Frank
b. Vinson, Helen
b. Winter, Edgar Holand
b. Winter, Johnny
b. Zernial, Gus Edward

Bell County, Texas
b. Ferguson, Miriam Amanda

Big Spring, Texas
b. Buckley, Betty Lynn

Birthright, Texas
b. Gregg, Forrest

Blessing, Texas
d. Heffelfinger, Pudge

Bloomington, Texas
b. Storm, Gale

Blossom Prairie, Texas
b. Garner, John Nance

Bonham, Texas
b. Morgan, Joe (Leonard)
d. Rayburn, Sam(uel Taliaferro)

Bonham County, Texas
b. Hardin, John Wesley

Borden, Texas
d. Borden, Gail

Bowie, Texas
b. Blocker, Dan

Brenham, Texas
b. Cooper, Cecil Celester

Brookshire, Texas
b. Gray, Dobie

Brownfield, Texas
b. Swoopes, Sheryl

Brownsville, Texas
b. Kristofferson, Kris
b. Sterling, Bruce
b. Stillman, James
d. Sykes, George

Bryan, Texas
b. Ellerbee, Linda

Caddo Mills, Texas
b. Johnson, Guy Benton

Calvert, Texas
b. Bradley, Tom
b. Foster, Rube
b. McCrary, Tex

Cedar Lake, Texas
b. Parker, Quanah

Celeste, Texas
b. Stratton, Monty Franklin Pierce

Centerville, Texas
b. Hopkins, Lightnin'

Chandler, Texas
b. Yarborough, Ralph W(ebster)

Cherino, Texas
b. Miller, Ann

Cisco, Texas
b. Crofts, Dash

Clarendon, Texas
b. Treybig, James G

Clarksville, Texas
b. Gibbons, Euell
b. Smith, Tommie

Coleman, Texas
b. Birdwell, Russell Juarez

College Station, Texas
d. Barton, Derek H(arold) R(ichard), Sir
d. Gordone, Charles Edward

Colorado, Texas
b. Dies, Martin, Jr.

Commerce, Texas
b. Chennault, Claire Lee

Coppeville, Texas
b. Watson, Charles

Corpus Christi, Texas
b. Berry, Raymond Emmett
b. Bissell, Patrick
b. Browning, Edmond Lee
b. Donath, Helen
b. Farenthold, Frances T(arlton)
b. Fawcett, Farrah Leni
b. Kleberg, Robert Justus, Jr.
b. Leetch, Brian
b. Oldham, Todd
d. Borglum, James Lincoln Delamothe
d. Cottam, Clarence
d. King, Richard
d. Mullin, Willard
d. Selena

Corsicana, Texas
b. Frizzell, Lefty

Couchman, Texas
b. Jefferson, Blind Lemon

Crawford, Texas
b. Hickerson, John Dewey

Crisp, Texas
b. Tubb, Ernest

Crosbyton, Texas
b. Maynard, Don(ald)

Cross Plains, Texas
d. Howard, Robert Ervin

Cuero, Texas
b. Hansen, Fred Morgan

Dallas, Texas
b. Banks, Ernie
b. Baum, William Wakefield, Cardinal
b. Beard, Frank
b. Benson, Robby
b. Bond, Tommy
b. Boykin, Otis Frank
b. Brown, Tim
b. Christian, Charlie
b. Clark, Ramsey
b. Clark, Tom
b. Clements, William Perry, Jr.
b. Corley, Pat
b. Daniels, Bebe
b. Darnell, Linda (Monetta Eloyse)
b. Elder, Lee
b. English, Doug
b. Evans, Clifford
b. Fairchild, Morgan
b. Giuffre, James Peter
b. Gramatky, Hardie
b. Granatelli, Andy
b. Griffin, John Howard
b. Guldahl, Ralph
b. Halaby, Najeeb E(lias)
b. Hall, Bridget
b. Hill, Grant
b. Hilton, William Barron
b. Hunt, Lamar
b. Jackson, Maynard Holbrook, Jr.
b. Jefferson, John Larry
b. Johnson, Michael
b. Lopez, Trini(dad, III)
b. Mangrum, Lloyd
b. Maples, William R.
b. Marcus, Stanley
b. Martin, Harvey Banks
b. Meat Loaf
b. Nance, Jack
b. O'Brien, Davey
b. Ornish, Dean
b. Page, Hot Lips
b. Rote, Kyle, Jr.
b. Scaggs, Boz
b. Seale, Bobby G
b. Spelling, Aaron
b. Stills, Stephen
b. Stone, Sly
b. Tate, Sharon
b. Taylor, Charley
b. Taylor, Regina
b. Trevino, Lee Buck
b. Vaughan, Stevie Ray
b. Walker, Doak
b. Walls, Everson Collins
b. Webb, Spud
b. Wylie, Paul

d. Bond, Ward
d. Condon, Richard (Thomas)
d. Connolly, Maureen
d. Corn, Ira George, Jr.
d. DeBernardi, Forrest S
d. Eckart, William Joseph
d. Elgart, Les
d. Estridge, Philip D
d. Gard, Wayne
d. Garson, Greer
d. Gary, John
d. Guion, David Wendel Fentress
d. Haggar, Joseph M(arion)
d. Hughes, Sarah Tilghman
d. Hunt, H(aroldson) L(afayette)
d. Jacoby, Oswald
d. Jones, Preston St. Vrain
d. Jonsson, John Erik
d. Kennedy, John F(itzgerald)
d. King, Freddy
d. Kusch, P(olycarp)
d. Landry, Tom
d. Lay, Herman Warden
d. Mantle, Mickey (Charles)
d. McKinley, Chuck
d. Murchison, Clint(on Williams, Jr.)
d. O'Shea, Michael
d. Oswald, Lee Harvey
d. Pons, Lily
d. Ruby, Jack
d. Short, Walter Campbell
d. Tabbert, William

Dawson, Texas
b. Comer, Anjanette

Dawson County, Texas
b. Corbin, Barry

De Leon, Texas
b. White, William S(mith)

Dekalb, Texas
d. Nelson, Rick

Denison, Texas
b. Eisenhower, Dwight D(avid)
b. Hillerman, John Benedict

Denton, Texas
b. Eberle, Edward Walter
b. George, Phyllis
b. O'Neill, Cherry Boone
b. Sheridan, Ann
d. Conley, Eugene

Dickinson, Texas
b. Ware, Andre

Dublin, Texas
b. Hogan, Ben

El Paso, Texas
b. Abraham, F(ahrid) Murray
b. Bingaman, Jeff
b. Carr, Vikki
b. Cornell, Lydia
b. Corona, Bert
b. Donaldson, Sam(uel Andrew)
b. Ivey, Judith
b. Kibbee, Guy
b. Lea, Tom
b. Mayer, Norman D
b. Ochs, Phil(ip David)

b. O'Connor, Sandra Day
b. Rechy, John Francisco
b. Reynolds, Debbie (Marie Frances)
b. Richardson, Nolan
b. Roddenberry, Gene
b. Ryan, Irene Noblette
b. Suzy
b. Watson, Jack Hearn, Jr.
d. Fall, Albert Bacon
d. Farah, William F.
d. Hardin, John Wesley
d. Huerta, Victoriano
d. Marshall, S(amuel) L(yman) A(twood)
d. Valachi, Joe

Eldorado, Texas
b. Hunt, Nelson Bunker

Ennis, Texas
b. Banner, Bob

Fabens, Texas
b. Shoemaker, Willie

Fannin County, Texas
b. Boyd, Bill

Farmersviller, Texas
b. Ellis, Herb

Field Creek, Texas
b. Eaker, Ira Clarence

Floresville, Texas
b. Connally, John B.

Floydada, Texas
b. Williams, Don

Fort Hood, Texas
b. Stockman, David Allen

Fort Worth, Texas
b. Bass, Rick
b. Bass, Robert M(use)
b. Beneke, Tex
b. Burke, Jack, Jr.
b. Capshaw, Kate
b. Chapman, Mark David
b. Coleman, Ornette
b. Cruz, Stevie
b. Curry, Donald
b. Franklin, Kirk
b. Garrett, Joy
b. Hagman, Larry
b. Haynie, Sandra
b. Heloise
b. Highsmith, Patricia
b. Hunnicutt, Gayle
b. Hyer, Martha
b. King Curtis
b. Lary, Yale
b. McFarland, Spanky
b. McKinley, Ray
b. McMurtry, James Lawrence
b. Merrifield, R(obert) Bruce
b. Miller, Nicole (Jacqueline)
b. Miller, Roger Dean
b. Moffatt, Katy
b. Morris, Gary
b. Nelson, Byron
b. Parker, Fess
b. Paxton, Bill

b. Reed, Rex
b. Riggs, Marlon
b. Smith, Liz
b. Snow, Clyde Collins
b. Stanton, Robert
b. Thompson, Thomas
b. Whelchel, Lisa
b. Whitman, Charles Joseph
b. Wright, Jim
d. Castle, Vernon
d. Courtright, Jim
d. Griffin, John Howard
d. Hogan, Ben
d. O'Brien, Davey
d. Wills, Bob

Fredericksburg, Texas
b. Nimitz, Chester William

Gainesville, Texas
b. Austin, Gene
b. Buck, Frank
b. Franken, Rose

Galloway, Texas
b. Reeves, Jim

Galveston, Texas
b. Corrigan, Douglas
b. Coryell, Larry
b. Helmond, Katherine
b. Johnson, Jack
b. Perrine, Valerie
b. Phillips, Esther
b. Vidor, King Wallis
b. White, Barry
d. Bragg, Braxton
d. Ewing, William Maurice
d. Zaharias, Babe Didrikson

Gatesville, Texas
b. Weaver, Mike

Gilmer, Texas
b. King, Freddy

Golden Acres, Texas
b. Viguerie, Richard A(rt)

Goose Creek, Texas
b. Busey, Gary

Grand Prairie, Texas
d. Hamilton, Floyd (Garland)

Grand Saline, Texas
b. Post, Wiley

Granger, Texas
b. Danforth, Dave

Grapeland, Texas
b. Simmons, Ruth J(ean)

Greenville, Texas
b. Boles, John
b. Neyland, Robert Reese
d. Stratton, Monty Franklin Pierce

Groesbeck, Texas
b. Baker, Joe Don
b. Roark, Garland

Hallettsville, Texas
b. Willis, Paul S

Harlingen, Texas
b. McLish, Rachel Elizondo
b. Morrow, Bobby
d. Haley, Bill

Haskell, Texas
b. Thornton, Charles Bates

Hearne, Texas
b. George, Zelma W(atson)

Henderson, Texas
b. Delaney, Joe Alton
b. Duncan, Sandy
b. White, Mark Wells, Jr.

Hereford, Texas
b. Ely, Ron
b. Mitchell, Edgar Dean

Hillsboro, Texas
b. Johnson, Rafer Lewis

Honey Grove, Texas
b. Price, Sammy

Hot Wells, Texas
b. Ash, Mary Kay
b. Kay, Mary

Houston, Texas
b. Adair, Red
b. Adams, Yolanda
b. Allen, Debbie
b. Alworth, Lance Dwight
b. Baker, James Addison, III
b. Barry, Donald
b. Bell, Ricky Lynn
b. Bettis, Valerie
b. Black, Clint
b. Blyden, Larry
b. Bradshaw, John Elliot
b. Branch, Cliff(ord)
b. Browles, William Dodson, Jr.
b. Christian, Mary Blount
b. Cobb, Arnett Cleophus
b. Cooley, Denton Arthur
b. Costa, Victor Charles
b. Crosby, Kathryn
b. Crowell, Rodney
b. David
b. Dell, Michael
b. Demaret, Jimmy
b. Drury, Allen (Stuart)
b. Duncan, Charles William, Jr.
b. Duvall, Shelley
b. Edwards, Melvin
b. Flood, Curt(is Charles)
b. Foxworth, Robert
b. Foyt, A(nthony) J(oseph Jr.)
b. Garrison, Zina
b. Gay, John
b. Gimbel, Sophie Haas
b. Gray, John
b. Gruber, Kelly
b. Guerard, Albert Joseph
b. Hampton, Hope
b. Harris, Marcelite Jordan
b. Hartman, Lisa
b. Hayes, Lester
b. Healy, Ted

b. House, Edward Mandell
b. Hughes, Howard Robard
b. Jordan, Barbara C(harline)
b. Knoblauch, Chuck
b. Koresh, David
b. MacRae, Meredith
b. Mandrell, Barbara Ann
b. Manley, Dexter
b. Marr, Dave
b. Martin, Slater
b. Millar, Jeff(rey) Lynn
b. Muhammad, Khallid Abdul
b. Nash, Johnny
b. Nesmith, Mike
b. Parker, Pat
b. Preston, Billy
b. Pruitt, Greg(ory Donald)
b. Quaid, Dennis William
b. Quaid, Randy
b. Rashad, Phylicia
b. Renfro, Mel(vin Lacy)
b. Rogers, Kenny
b. Scott, Gloria Dean Randle
b. Singletary, Mike
b. Smith, Jaclyn
b. Stone, Matt
b. Swayze, Patrick
b. Thomas, B(illy) J(oe)
b. Thomas, Thurman Lee
b. Tower, John Goodwin
b. Valenti, Jack Joseph
b. Vidor, Florence
b. Vinson, Cleanhead
b. Wallace, Sippie
b. Watson, Johnny "Guitar"
b. Whitmire, Kathy
b. Williams, JoBeth
b. Williamson, Marianne
b. Wilson, Robert Woodrow
d. Abercrombie, James Smither
d. Ace, Johnny
d. Ameche, Alan Dante
d. Bankhead, Dan(iel Robert)
d. Barthelme, Donald
d. Bochner, Salomon
d. Bucher, Walter Herman
d. Buck, Frank
d. Chase, William Curtis
d. Cobb, Arnett Cleophus
d. Connally, John B.
d. David
d. Demaret, Jimmy
d. Gerber, John
d. Harmon, Claude
d. Hebert, Jay
d. Hobby, Oveta Culp
d. Hofheinz, Roy Mark
d. Hopkins, Lightnin'
d. Hughes, Howard Robard
d. Jones, Jesse Holman
d. Kleberg, Robert Justus, Jr.
d. Leonetti, Tommy
d. Liedtke, William C, Jr.
d. Lombardo, Guy Albert
d. MacDonald, Jeanette
d. Maris, Roger (Eugene)
d. Marr, Dave
d. Mecom, John Whitfield
d. Sampson, Will, Jr.
d. Tierney, Gene
d. Trafficante, Santo, Jr.

Hubbard City, Texas
b. Speaker, Tris(tram E)

Hughes Springs, Texas
b. Patman, (John Williams) Wright

Humboldt, Texas
b. Atkins, Doug(las L)

Huntsville, Texas
b. Abercrombie, James Smither
b. Forrest, Steve
b. Lovett, Robert A(bercrombie)
b. Thomason, John William, Jr.
b. Wilson, Logan
d. Brooks, Charlie, Jr.
d. Fitzhugh, George
d. Houston, Sam(uel)
d. Satanta

Indian Creek, Texas
b. Porter, Katherine Anne

Irving, Texas
b. Ashton, Susan
b. Bosworth, Brian Keith

Jacksonville, Texas
b. Dexter, Al

Jefferson, Texas
b. Benefield, Barry

Jesus Maria of the Valley, Texas
b. Anzaldua, Gloria

Johnson City, Texas
d. Johnson, Lyndon B(aines)

Justiceburg, Texas
b. Cash, Norm(an Dalton)

Karnack, Texas
b. Johnson, Lady Bird

Kaufman, Texas
d. Parker, Buddy

Kemp, Texas
b. Parker, Buddy

Kerrville, Texas
b. Mahaffey, John

Kilgore, Texas
b. Matson, Randy

Killeen, Texas
b. Hobby, Oveta Culp
d. Hennard, George, Jr.

King Ranch, Texas
b. Cavazos, Lauro F(red, Jr.)

Kingston, Texas
b. Murphy, Audie

Kingsville, Texas
b. Denton, Steve

Kirbyville, Texas
b. Hunter, Ivory Joe

Klein, Texas
b. Lovett, Lyle

La Porte, Texas
d. Edmonds, Emma E

Lackland Air Force Base, Texas
d. Twining, Nathan F(arragut)

Lake Jackson, Texas
b. Selena

Lake Lewisville, Texas
d. Dexter, Al

Lake Whitney, Texas
d. Speaker, Tris(tram E)

Lakeview, Texas
b. Richards, Ann

Lampasas, Texas
b. Walker, Stanley
d. Walker, Stanley

Lanesville, Texas
b. Mosely, Mark DeWayne

Langtry, Texas
d. Bean, Roy

Laredo, Texas
b. Pena, Federico F.

League City, Texas
d. Slayton, Donald Kent

Leesburg, Texas
b. Shelby, Carroll (Hall)

Leona, Texas
b. Collins, Albert

Liberty, Texas
b. Mecom, John Whitfield
d. Daniel, Price

Limestone County, Texas
b. Wills, Bob

Linden, Texas
b. Henley, Don
b. Walker, T-Bone

Littlefield, Texas
b. Jennings, Waylon
b. Jones, Tom

Live Oak County, Texas
b. Dobie, J(ames) Frank

Lockhart, Texas
b. Strauss, Robert Schwarz

Lockney, Texas
b. Ewing, William Maurice
b. Templeton, Garry Lewis

Longview, Texas
b. Whitaker, Forest
d. LeTourneau, Robert Gilmour

Lubbock, Texas
  b. Davis, Mac
  b. Ely, Joe
  b. Holly, Buddy
  b. Leland, Mickey
  b. McClinton, Delbert
  b. Price, Deb(orah Jane)
  b. Richardson, Micheal Ray
  d. Layne, Bobby

Lufkin, Texas
  b. Houston, Ken(neth Ray)
  d. Dies, Martin, Jr.

Mansfield, Texas
  b. Morse, Ella Mae

Marlin, Texas
  b. Humphrey, Bobbi

Marshall, Texas
  b. Farmer, James
  b. Foreman, George
  b. Howard, Susan
  b. Joplin, Scott
  b. Prothrow-Stith, Deborah
  b. Riley, Helen Caldwell Day
  b. Tittle, Y(elberton) A(braham)

Mart, Texas
  b. Thomas, E Donall

Mason County, Texas
  b. Stevenson, Coke Robert

McCarney, Texas
  b. Seals, Dan Wayland

McKinney, Texas
  b. Smith, Owen Guinn

McLennan County, Texas
  b. Connally, Tom

Mercedes, Texas
  b. Hinojosa, Rolando
  b. Spielberg, David

Mesquite, Texas
  b. Hall, Jerry (Faye)

Mexia, Texas
  b. Baxter, Les
  b. Rhodes, Ray

Midland, Texas
  b. Baker, Kathy
  b. Harrelson, Woody
  b. Love, Bessie
  b. Massey, D Curtis
  b. Peters, C(larence) J(ames), (Jr.)

Minden, Texas
  b. Arnold, Oren

Mineola, Texas
  b. Brown, Willie
  b. Hogg, Ima

Minerva, Texas
  b. Smith, Cyrus Rowlett

Mission, Texas
  b. Bentsen, Lloyd Millard, Jr.
  b. Landry, Tom

Monahans, Texas
  b. Clark, Guy
  b. Whitworth, Kathy

Moran, Texas
  b. Barker, Elliott

Mount Calm, Texas
  b. Graves, William Sidney

Mount Vernon, Texas
  b. Meredith, Don

Muleshoe, Texas
  b. Horsley, Lee

Munday, Texas
  b. Cousins, (Sue) Margaret

Murval, Texas
  b. Ritter, Tex

Nacogdoches, Texas
  b. Baker, Charlotte
  d. Roark, Garland

Navasota, Texas
  d. Tex, Joe

Nocona, Texas
  b. Justin, John, Jr.

Normangee, Texas
  d. Roloff, Lester

Oak Cliff, Texas
  b. Brickell, Edie

Oakwood, Texas
  b. Colbert, Lester L(um)

Olney, Texas
  b. Lilly, Bob

Orange, Texas
  b. Baker, Bonnie
  b. Phillips, Bum
  b. Smith, Bubba

Palestine, Texas
  b. Ames, Jessie Daniel

Pampa, Texas
  d. Russell, Charles Taze

Panola County, Texas
  b. Webb, Walter Prescott

Paris, Texas
  b. Johnson, Mordecai Wyatt

Pearsall, Texas
  b. Strait, George

Peaster, Texas
  b. Howard, Robert Ervin

Perryville, Texas
  b. Price, Ray

Petrolia, Texas
  b. Hadley, Reed

Plainview, Texas
  b. Clark, James H.
  b. Dean, Jimmy
  b. January, Don(ald)

Port Arthur, Texas
  b. Johnson, Jimmy
  b. Joplin, Janis
  b. Keyes, Evelyn Louise
  b. Rauschenberg, Robert
  b. Zaharias, Babe Didrikson

Port Lavaca, Texas
  b. Knipling, Edward Fred

Quitman, Texas
  b. Spacek, Sissy

Refugio, Texas
  b. Ryan, Nolan

Rhonesboro, Texas
  b. Inman, Bobby Ray

Richardson, Texas
  d. Lane, Frank C

River Oaks, Texas
  b. Ivins, Molly

Riverside, Texas
  b. Holliday, Jennifer Yvette

Robstown, Texas
  b. Salinas, Luis Omar
  b. Upshaw, Gene

Rockland, Texas
  b. Dorsey, Bob Rawls

Rockport, Texas
  b. Cacers, Ernest
  b. Wood, John Howland, Jr.

Rogers, Texas
  b. Ailey, Alvin
  b. Tex, Joe

Round Rock, Texas
  d. Bass, Sam

Rowena, Texas
  b. Parker, Bonnie

Sabinal, Texas
  b. Rodriguez, Johnny

Sabine Pass, Texas
  b. Big Bopper, The

Salado, Texas
  b. Carpenter, Liz

San Angelo, Texas
  b. Allen, Jay Presson

Wheeler, Texas
b. Bean, Alan L

Wichita Falls, Texas
b. Grant, Bruce
b. Hauptman, William
b. McMurtry, Larry Jeff
b. Quanah
b. Singer, Jane Sherrod
b. Tune, Tommy

Williamson County, Texas
b. Pickett, Bill

Wimberley, Texas
d. Jaworski, Leon

Winters, Texas
b. Hornsby, Rogers

UTAH
b. Manuelito
d. Ouray

American Fork, Utah
d. Westwood, Jean Miles

Beaver, Utah
b. Cassidy, Butch
b. Farnsworth, Philo Taylor

Brigham City, Utah
b. Christensen, Harold
b. Christensen, Lew Farr
b. Christensen, William

Coalville, Utah
b. Geary, Anthony

Duchesne, Utah
b. Mecham, Evan

Eureka, Utah
b. Zamboni, Frank J

Granger, Utah
b. Bangerter, Norman Howard

Holliday, Utah
d. Lund, Art(hur Earl, Jr.)

Huntsville, Utah
b. McKay, David O

Kimberley, Utah
b. Priest, Ivy (Maude) Baker

Logan, Utah
b. Eccles, Marriner Stoddard
b. Gilbert, John
b. Olsen, Merlin Jay
b. Swenson, May

Magna, Utah
b. Jarvis, Howard Arnold

Marriott, Utah
b. Marriott, John Willard

Marysvale, Utah
b. Windsor, Marie

Midway, Utah
b. Watkins, Arthur V(ivian)

Murray, Utah
d. Allred, Rulon Clark

Ogden, Utah
b. Ashby, Hal
b. Borglum, Solon Hannibal
b. Brodie, Fawn McKay
b. Browning, John Moses
b. Bushnell, Nolan Kay
b. Dawn, Hazel
b. DeVoto, Bernard Augustine
b. Janney, Leon
b. Nichols, Red
b. Osmond, Donny
b. Osmond, Marie
b. Richards, Richard
b. Scowcroft, Brent
b. Stevens, S(tanley) S(mith)
b. Wood, Evelyn

Orem, Utah
d. Watkins, Arthur V(ivian)

Paradise, Utah
b. Bickmore, Lee Smith

Point of Mountain, Utah
d. Gilmore, Gary Mark

Price, Utah
b. Westwood, Jean Miles

Provo, Utah
b. Clark, Barney Bailey
b. Sorensen, Virginia
d. Haworth, Ted
d. Primrose, William

Randolph, Utah
b. Kennedy, David M(atthew)

Richfield, Utah
b. Garn, Jake

Roosevelt, Utah
b. Day, Laraine

Saint George, Utah
b. Cannon, Howard Walter
b. Cottam, Clarence
d. McMurrin, Sterling M(oss)

Salt Lake City, Utah
b. Adams, Maude
b. Allen, Florence Ellinwood
b. Barnes, Lee
b. Beesley, H(orace) Brent
b. Borzage, Frank
b. Brimley, Wilford
b. Burnett, Whit
b. Buss, Jerry Hatten
b. Cassady, Neal
b. Covey, Stephen R.
b. Downey, Fairfax Davis
b. Evans, Richard Louis
b. Friendly, Alfred
b. Harbach, Otto Abels
b. Hawkins, Paula Fickes
b. Haywood, William Dudley
b. Held, John, Jr.

b. Johannesen, Grant
b. Kimball, Spencer Woolley
b. Lansing, Joi
b. Lund, Art(hur Earl, Jr.)
b. Moss, Frank Edward
b. Motta, Dick
b. Naisbitt, John
b. Roseanne
b. Russell, Solveig Paulson
b. Smith, Joseph Fielding
b. Squires, James Radcliffe
b. Thurman, Wallace (Henry)
b. Venter, J. Craig
b. Walker, Robert
b. Young, Loretta Gretchen
b. Young, Mahonri Mackintosh
b. Young, Steve
d. Abravanel, Maurice
d. Bell, T(errel) H(oward)
d. Bennett, Wallace F(oster)
d. Benson, Ezra Taft
d. Clark, Barney Bailey
d. Condie, Richard P
d. Eccles, Marriner Stoddard
d. Evans, Richard Louis
d. Farnsworth, Philo Taylor
d. Hill, Joe
d. Kennedy, David M(atthew)
d. Kimball, Spencer Woolley
d. Lander, Toni
d. Lee, J(oseph) Bracken
d. McKay, David O
d. Smith, Joseph Fielding
d. Young, Brigham

Springville, Utah
b. Condie, Richard P

Vernal, Utah
b. Woods, James

Windsor, Utah
b. Douglass, Andrew Ellicott

Woodruff, Utah
b. Pusey, Merlo John

VERMONT
b. Fitzgerald, John Dennis
b. Peck, Robert Newton
b. Straw, Syd
d. Gulick, Luther (Halsey)

Arlington, Vermont
d. Fisher, Dorothy Frances Canfield

Baltimore, Vermont
b. Sherwin, Henry Alden

Barnet, Vermont
b. Flanders, Ralph Edward

Bellows Falls, Vermont
b. Fisk, Carlton Ernest
b. Thompson, Ernest

Bennington, Vermont
b. Fisk, Jim
d. Channing, William Ellery
d. Marsh, Reginald
d. Ruggles, Carl
d. Sloane, John
d. Spargo, John

Brandon, Vermont
b. Douglas, Stephen Arnold

Brattleboro, Vermont
b. Frost, Edwin Brant
b. Hunt, Richard Morris
b. Hunt, William Morris
b. Mead, William Rutherford
b. Noyes, John Humphrey
d. Bunker, Ellsworth
d. Culbertson, Ely
d. Fuller, Ida
d. Phelps, John Wolcott
d. Tyler, Royall

Burlington, Vermont
b. Bean, Orson
b. Bundy, Ted
b. Coolidge, Grace (Anne Goodhue)
b. Dewey, John
b. Farrar, John Chipman
b. Kent, Arthur Atwater
b. Kidd, William
b. Lifshin, Lyn
b. McKenzie, Kevin
b. Muldowney, Shirley
b. Rowen, Hobart
b. Stone, Marvin Lawrence
b. Tebbetts, Birdie
d. Allen, Ethan
d. Austin, Warren R(obinson)
d. Darrow, Whitney, Jr.
d. Howard, Oliver Otis
d. Lake, Veronica

Calais, Vermont
d. LaTouche, John

Cavendish, Vermont
b. Stevens, Nettie Maria

Charlotte, Vermont
d. Grenfell, Wilfred Thomason, Sir

Chester, Vermont
b. Cram, Donald James

Danby, Vermont
d. Buck, Pearl S(ydenstricker)

Danville, Vermont
b. Leland, Henry Martyn
b. Stevens, Thaddeus

Dummerston, Vermont
b. Aiken, George David
d. Flaherty, Robert Joseph

East Dorset, Vermont
b. Wilson, William Griffith

East Dover, Vermont
b. Adams, Sherman Llewellyn

Fairfield, Vermont
b. Arthur, Chester A(lan)

Georgia, Vermont
b. Colton, Gardner Quincy

Guilford, Vermont
b. Phelps, John Wolcott
d. Serkin, Rudolph

Halifax, Vermont
b. Otis, Elisha Graves

Hardwick, Vermont
b. Eaton, Dorman Bridgman
d. Fixx, James Fuller

Hartford, Vermont
b. Lord, Phillips H
b. Wells, Horace

Highgate, Vermont
b. Austin, Warren R(obinson)

Holland, Vermont
b. Tabor, Horace Austin Warner

Irasburg, Vermont
b. Robinson, Theodore

Island Pond, Vermont
b. Vallee, Rudy

Isles of Shoals, Vermont
d. Hunt, William Morris

Ludlow, Vermont
b. Fuller, Ida

Manchester, Vermont
d. Keylor, Arthur W

Middlebury, Vermont
b. Trudeau, Arthur G(ilbert)
d. Hewitt, Henry Kent

Montpelier, Vermont
b. Dewey, George
b. Leahy, Patrick Joseph
d. Aiken, George David

Morrisville, Vermont
d. Trapp, Maria Augusta von

Mount Tabor, Vermont
b. Alden, Henry M

Newburg, Vermont
b. Porter, William Trotter

Newport, Vermont
b. Adams, Charles Francis
b. Holbrook, Stewart Hall

North Bennington, Vermont
d. Jackson, Shirley (Hardie)

North Hartland, Vermont
b. Willard, Daniel

Norwich, Vermont
d. Sample, Paul Starrett

Ogden, Vermont
b. Chambers, Tom

Peacham, Vermont
b. Harvey, George Brinton M

Plymouth, Vermont
b. Coolidge, Calvin

Poultney, Vermont
b. Perry, Ralph Barton

Richmond, Vermont
b. Edmunds, George Franklin
b. LeTourneau, Robert Gilmour

Rock Pointe, Vermont
d. Hopkins, John Henry

Rutland, Vermont
b. Burke, James Edward
b. Deere, John
b. Jeffords, James Merrill
b. Stafford, Robert Theodore

Saint Johnsbury, Vermont
b. Pendleton, Moses Robert Andrew
b. Smith, Robert H
d. Fairbanks, Thaddeus

Salisbury, Vermont
d. Davenport, Thomas

Sharon, Vermont
b. Smith, Joseph

Shelburne, Vermont
d. Walsh, Chad

Shoreham, Vermont
b. Morton, Levi Parsons

Springfield, Vermont
d. Flanders, Ralph Edward

Springville, Vermont
b. Dallin, Cyrus Edwin

Stanstead, Vermont
b. Lee, Jason
d. Lee, Jason

Stockbridge, Vermont
b. Brownson, Orestes Augustus

Strafford, Vermont
b. Morrill, Justin Smith

Stratton, Vermont
d. Warren, Robert Penn

Sutton, Vermont
b. Houghton, Henry Oscar

Thetford, Vermont
b. Wells, Henry
d. Hammond, Bray

Vergennes, Vermont
d. Magonigle, Harold Van Buren

West Concord, Vermont
b. Adams, Herbert Samuel

West Hartford, Vermont
b. Hazen, William Babcock

Weybridge, Vermont
b. James, Edwin

White River Junction, Vermont
d. Harmon, Ernest N(ason)

Whitingham, Vermont
b. Young, Brigham

Wilder, Vermont
d. Parr, A(lbert) E(ide)

Williamstown, Vermont
b. Davenport, Thomas

Williston, Vermont
d. Chittenden, Thomas

Windsor, Vermont
d. Seldes, George (Henry)

Woodstock, Vermont
b. Powers, Hiram
d. Albright, Ivan Le Lorraine

VIRGINIA
b. Beckwourth, James Pierson
b. Byrd, William
b. Cartwright, Peter
b. Foote, Henry Stuart
b. Pendleton, Edmund
b. Pocahontas
b. Randolph, Mary
b. Rochester, Nathaniel
b. Taylor, John
b. Walker, Joseph Reddeford
d. Brent, Margaret
d. Pendleton, Edmund
d. Taylor, John

Abingdon, Virginia
d. Floyd, John Buchanan

Albemarle County, Virginia
b. Jefferson, Martha
b. Jefferson, Mary
b. Jefferson, Thomas
b. Lewis, Meriwether
d. Jefferson, Martha (Wayles Skelton)
d. Jefferson, Mary
d. Jefferson, Thomas

Alexandria, Virginia
b. Fawcett, George
b. Greene, Belle da Costa
b. Phillips, MacKenzie
b. Schultze, Charles Louis
b. Scott, Willard Herman, Jr.
d. Arnold, Thurman Wesley
d. Bane, Frank B
d. Barr, Stringfellow
d. Bledsoe, Albert Taylor
d. Evans, Alice (Catherine)
d. Flemming, Arthur S(herwood)
d. Guyer, Tennyson
d. Hansen, Alvin Harvey
d. Landon, Margaret (Dorothea Mortenson)
d. Mason, James Murray
d. McGarity, Lou
d. Mearns, David Chambers
d. Russell, Pee Wee
d. Schmitt, Bernadotte Everly
d. Smith, Howard Worth
d. Smith, Merriman
d. Stone, Thomas
d. Trist, Nicholas Philip

d. VonBraun, Wernher

Altavista, Virginia
b. Futrell, Mary Alice Franklin Hatwood
b. Worsham, Lew(is Elmer)

Amelia County, Virginia
b. Tabb, John Banister
d. Ruffin, Edmund

Amherst County, Virginia
b. Becknell, William
b. Crawford, William Harris

Annandale, Virginia
b. Hall, Fawn

Appalachia, Virginia
b. Castle, Peggie

Arlington, Virginia
b. Bright, Susie
b. Bullock, Sandra
b. Couric, Katie
b. Elliot, Cass
d. Bean, Louis H(yman)
d. Bolger, William Frederick
d. Hopper, Grace Brewster Murray
d. Lee, Robert E(mmet)
d. Lisagor, Peter Irvin
d. McCarthy, William J.
d. Mulliken, Robert Sanderson
d. Overstreet, Bonaro Wilkinson
d. Rickover, Hyman George
d. Rockwell, George Lincoln
d. Siple, Paul Allman
d. Young, Philip

Arno, Virginia
b. Horton, Willie

Auburn, Virginia
b. Scobee, Dick

Augusta County, Virginia
b. Bingham, George Caleb
b. Breckinridge, John

Austinville, Virginia
b. Austin, Stephen Fuller

Bassett, Virginia
b. Bassett, John D
d. Bassett, John D

Belroi, Virginia
b. Reed, Walter

Berkeley County, Virginia
b. Zane, Ebenezer

Bermuda Hundred, Virginia
d. Rolfe, John

Berryville, Virginia
d. Byrd, Harry Flood

Blackridge, Virginia
b. Person, Waverly

Blacksburg, Virginia
b. Floyd, John Buchanan

Bluefield, Virginia
b. Dudley, Bill

Boyce, Virginia
d. Cooke, John Esten

Brandy Station, Virginia
d. Strauss, Lewis Lichtenstein

Bristol, Virginia
b. Johnson, Charles Spurgeon

Broad Run, Virginia
b. Smith, Howard Worth

Buena Vista, Virginia
b. Jennings, Gary

Buffalo, Virginia
b. Harvey, William Hope

Burlington, Virginia
b. Angell, James Rowland

Campbell County, Virginia
b. Hanks, Nancy

Caroline County, Virginia
b. Clark, William
b. Penn, John

Cawsons, Virginia
b. Randolph, John

Chantilly, Virginia
d. Lee, Richard Henry

Charles City, Virginia
b. Harrison, Benjamin
b. Jefferson, Martha (Wayles Skelton)
b. Tyler, John
d. Harrison, Benjamin

Charles City County, Virginia
b. Harrison, William Henry

Charletown, Virginia
b. Delany, Martin Robinson

Charlotte County, Virginia
d. Henry, Patrick

Charlottesville, Virginia
b. Arlen, Richard
b. Brown, Roosevelt
b. Clark, George Rogers
b. Field, Marshall, V
b. Keyes, Frances Parkinson
b. Lowe, Rob(ert Hepler)
b. MacDonald-Wright, Stanton
b. Trist, Nicholas Philip
b. Vandegrift, Alexander Archer
b. Van Dine, S S
d. Davisson, Clinton Joseph
d. Gilruth, Robert Rowe
d. Hahn, Archie
d. Hale, Nancy
d. Jensen, Jackie
d. Malone, Dumas

Geographic Index

d. Maury, Matthew Fontaine
d. Mollenhoff, Clark Raymond

Loudoun County, Virginia
d. Monroe, Elizabeth (Kortright)

Louisa County, Virginia
b. Langston, John Mercer

Lovingston, Virginia
b. Ryan, Thomas Fortune

Lynch's Station, Virginia
b. Delany, Sarah Louise

Lynchburg, Virginia
b. Christian, Meg
b. Falwell, Jerry L
b. Freeman, Douglas S
b. Glass, Carter
d. Early, Jubal Anderson
d. Holbrook, Josiah

Maces Spring, Virginia
b. Carter, June

Manassas, Virginia
b. Von Bulow, Sunny

Martinsburg, Virginia
b. Boyd, Belle

Mason County, Virginia
b. Owens, Michael Joseph

Mathews County, Virginia
b. Tompkins, Sally Louisa

McLean, Virginia
b. Copeland, Stewart
d. Lansdale, Edward Geary
d. Macy, John Williams, Jr.
d. O'Donnell, Emmett, Jr.
d. Pett, Saul
d. Sheldon, Alice Hastings Bradley

Mecklenburg, Virginia
b. Mitchell, Corinne

Meherrin, Virginia
b. Clark, Roy Linwood

Middlesex County, Virginia
b. Beverley, Robert

Millwood, Virginia
d. Randolph, Edmund Jennings

Morrisonville, Virginia
b. Baker, Russell Wayne

Mount Vernon, Virginia
d. Washington, George
d. Washington, Martha (Dandridge Custis)

Natural Bridge, Virginia
d. Merritt, Wesley

New Canton, Virginia
b. Woodson, Carter Godwin

New Kent County, Virginia
b. Tyler, Letitia Christian
b. Washington, Martha (Dandridge Custis)

New Market, Virginia
b. Sevier, John
d. Keyhoe, Donald E(dward)

Newington, Virginia
b. Braxton, Carter

Newport News, Virginia
b. Christian, Spencer
b. Dobyns, Lloyd Allen, Jr.
b. Fitzgerald, Ella
b. Gayle, Addison, Jr.
b. Granger, Lester
b. O'Leary, Hazel R(eid)
b. Patton, Edward L
b. Rees, Ennis (Samuel, Jr.)
b. Styron, William Clark, Jr.
d. Lewis, Robert Alvin

Nickelsville, Virginia
b. Carter, Mother Maybelle

Norfolk, Virginia
b. Baker, Ella
b. Bowser, Betty Ann
b. Carr, Elizabeth Jordan
b. Cleghorn, Sarah Norcliffe
b. Clemons, Clarence
b. Davis, John Staige
b. Eaton, Mary
b. Gentry, Minnie Lee
b. Groves, Wallace
b. Holland, Charles
b. Jones, Elaine R.
b. Josey, E. J.
b. Joyce, Peggy Hopkins
b. Maynor, Dorothy
b. Newton, Wayne
b. Reid, Tim
b. Smith, Bruce (Bernard)
b. Smith, Keely
b. Strange, Curtis
b. Sullavan, Margaret
b. Vincent, Gene
b. Whitaker, Pernell
b. Zolotow, Charlotte Shapiro
d. Darden, Colgate Whitehead
d. Mitscher, Marc Andrew
d. Pickett, George Edward

Orange County, Virginia
b. Scott, Randolph
b. Taylor, Zachary
d. Madison, Dolly (Payne Todd)
d. Madison, James

Patrick County, Virginia
b. Stuart, Jeb

Pearisburg, Virginia
b. Gearhart, Sally (Miller)

Petersburg, Virginia
b. Cotten, Joseph
b. Cowper, Steve Cambreleng
b. Leach, Will
b. Malone, Moses Eugene
b. Myers, Jerome
b. Scott, Winfield

b. Stern, Arthur Cecil
d. Hill, Ambrose Powell

Phoebus, Virginia
b. Kraft, Chris(topher Columbus, Jr.)

Pittsylvania County, Virginia
b. Hodges, Luther Hartwell
b. Jackson, Rachel (Donelson Robards)

Poquoson, Virginia
d. Worsham, Lew(is Elmer)

Port Conway, Virginia
b. Madison, James

Port Royal, Virginia
d. Booth, John Wilkes

Portsmouth, Virginia
b. Andrews, V(irginia) C(leo)
b. Carter, Jack
b. Garvin, Clifton Canter, Jr.
b. Garwood, Robert Russell
b. Harper, Chandler
b. Jones, Matilda Sissieretta Joyner
b. Lavelle, Rita Marie
b. McCall, Nathan
b. Murray, Mae
b. Parker, Ace
b. Reed, Ralph
b. Sebrell, W(illiam) H(enry), Jr.

Pound, Virginia
b. Powers, Francis Gary

Powhatan County, Virginia
b. Ashley, William Henry

Prince Edward County, Virginia
b. Johnston, Joseph Eggleston
b. Price, Sterling

Prince George County, Virginia
b. Ruffin, Edmund

Prince William County, Virginia
b. Fitzhugh, George

Reedville, Virginia
b. Haynie, Hugh

Reston, Virginia
d. Ford, Tennessee Ernie
d. Ward, Lynd

Richard, Virginia
b. LaMarr, Barbara

Richmond, Virginia
b. Ashe, Arthur
b. Beatty, Warren
b. Bridger, James
b. Brown, Charles Lee
b. Cabell, James Branch
b. Dandridge, Ray(mond)
b. Ezekiel, Moses Jacob
b. Freeman, Charles Eldridge
b. Gabriel
b. Gilpin, Charles Sidney
b. Glasgow, Ellen Anderson Gholson
b. Gosden, Freeman Fisher
b. Gravely, Samuel Lee, Jr.

Aberdeen, Washington
  b. Brown, Trisha
  b. Cobain, Kurt
  b. Motherwell, Robert Burns
  b. Simmons, Pat(rick)

Anacortes, Washington
  d. Ives, Burl (Icle Ivanhoe)

Bainbridge Isle, Washington
  d. Roethke, Theodore (Huebner)

Bellevue, Washington
  b. Horton, Peter William
  d. Bauer, Eddie
  d. Fielding, Gabriel
  d. Patton, Edward L
  d. Wells, Edward

Bellingham, Washington
  b. Wickens, Aryness Joy

Bremerton, Washington
  b. Duff, Howard

Bridgeport, Washington
  b. Pangborn, Clyde Edward

Camas, Washington
  b. Rodgers, Jimmy F

Cashmere, Washington
  b. Uhlman, Wes(ley Carl)

Cathamet, Washington
  d. Hansen, Julia Butler

Centralia, Washington
  b. Bay, Howard
  b. Cunningham, Merce

Clayton, Washington
  b. Carson, Robert

Colfax, Washington
  b. Canutt, Yakima

Colville, Washington
  d. Joseph, Chief

Darrington, Washington
  b. Barker, Bob

Ellensburg, Washington
  b. Bledsoe, Drew

Entiat, Washington
  b. King, Charles Glen

Everett, Washington
  b. Jackson, Henry Martin
  b. Loggins, Kenny
  d. Averill, Earl
  d. Jackson, Henry Martin

Fairfield, Washington
  b. Kienholz, Edward

Fort Walla Walla, Washington
  d. Whitman, Marcus

Fox Island, Washington
  d. Ray, Dixy Lee

Hood River, Washington
  d. Sohappy, David, Sr.

Hoquiam, Washington
  b. Hitchings, George H(erbert)
  b. Morey, Walt(er Nelson)

Kelso, Washington
  b. Close, Upton

Keyser, Washington
  b. Staggers, Harley O(rrin)

Kirkland, Washington
  b. Carner, Joanne Gunderson

Little Falls, Washington
  b. Cantwell, Robert Emmett

Mold, Washington
  b. Edwards, Turk

Nespelem, Washington
  b. Pease-Windy Boy, Jeanine

Olympia, Washington
  b. Strouse, Norman H(ulbert)

Orcas Island, Washington
  b. Bauer, Eddie

Pasco, Washington
  d. Chenoweth, Dean

Port Angeles, Washington
  b. Elway, John (Albert)
  d. Carver, Raymond Clevie, Jr.

Port Ludlow, Washington
  b. Binns, Archie Fred

Renton, Washington
  b. Stigler, George Joseph

Republic, Washington
  b. Conley, Renie

Ritzville, Washington
  b. Adams, James Luther

Saint John, Washington
  b. Lowry, Mike

San Juan Island, Washington
  d. Gann, Ernest Kellogg

Seattle, Washington
  b. Adams, Oleta
  b. Anderson, Daryl
  b. Bailey, Xenobia
  b. Barry, Lynda
  b. Bennett, Ramona
  b. Bernhard, Harvey
  b. Bissett, Josie
  b. Bolcom, William Elden
  b. Brown, Bobby
  b. Carlson, Chester Floyd
  b. Channing, Carol
  b. Collins, Judy

  b. Cornell, Chris
  b. Coryell, Don(ald David)
  b. Couples, Fred
  b. Cummings, Constance
  b. Damon, Cathryn
  b. Dean, Gordon Evans
  b. Devers, Gail
  b. Engle, Eloise Katherine
  b. Englund, Richard
  b. Evans, Daniel Jackson
  b. Farmer, Frances
  b. Faust, Frederick Schiller
  b. Francis, Russ(ell Ross)
  b. Garfinkle, Louis
  b. Gates, William Henry, III
  b. Gordon, Richard Francis, Jr.
  b. Graham, John
  b. Greenfield, Meg
  b. Guterson, David
  b. Hanauer, Chip
  b. Havoc, June
  b. Hendrix, Jimi
  b. Hills, Roderick M
  b. Houbregs, Bob
  b. Joffrey, Robert
  b. Kenny G
  b. Ketcham, Hank
  b. Lee, Gypsy Rose
  b. Livingstone, Mary
  b. McCarthy, Kevin
  b. McCarthy, Mary Therese
  b. McClintic, Guthrie
  b. McNamara, Margaret Craig
  b. Morris, Mark
  b. Murkowski, Frank Hughes
  b. Murray, Patty
  b. Nelson, Gene
  b. Niatum, Duane
  b. Oliver, Stephanie Stokes
  b. Reinking, Ann H
  b. Revelle, Roger Randall
  b. Riney, Hal (Patrick)
  b. Robinson, Earl Hawley
  b. Ross, Lanny
  b. Santo, Ron(ald Edward)
  b. Simpson, Donald C
  b. Smith, Jeff
  b. Stroud, Robert Franklin
  b. Terry, Megan
  b. Utley, Mike
  b. Voit, Willard Darby
  b. Winsten, Archer
  b. Wright, Martha
  b. Wurdemann, Audrey May
  b. Yamasaki, Minoru
  d. Allen, William McPherson
  d. Beck, Dave
  d. Bestor, Arthur (Eugene)
  d. Boeing, William Edward
  d. Brattain, Walter Houser
  d. Carlson, Edward Elmer
  d. Casey, James E
  d. Cherberg, John A(ndrew)
  d. Cobain, Kurt
  d. Edwards, Turk
  d. Foyston, Frank C
  d. Goodman, Steve(n Benjamin)
  d. Graham, John
  d. Guthrie, Edwin Ray
  d. Haley, Alex (Murray Palmer)
  d. Hall, Joe
  d. Heller, Walter Wolfgang
  d. Hovhaness, Alan
  d. Hurley, Jack B
  d. Julesberg, Elizabeth Rider
    Montgomery

Monongalia County, West Virginia
b. Gregg, William

Morgantown, West Virginia
b. Antonini, Joseph
b. Chadwick, French Ensor
b. Knotts, Don
b. Selby, David

Myra, West Virginia
b. Yeager, Chuck

New Martinsville, West Virginia
b. Murtha, John Patrick

Nitro, West Virginia
b. Burdette, Lew

Oak Hill, West Virginia
d. Williams, Hank

Parkersburg, West Virginia
b. Goodman, Linda
b. Heaton, Leonard
b. Neale, Greasy
b. Rathbone, Monroe Jackson
b. Watts, Richard, Jr.
b. Webster, H(arold) T(ucker)

Piedmont, West Virginia
b. Redman, Don

Point Pleasant, West Virginia
b. Jones, Brereton C

Reedy, West Virginia
b. Batten, William Milfred

Salem, West Virginia
b. Randolph, Jennings

Slab Fork, West Virginia
b. Withers, Bill

South Charleston, West Virginia
b. Jakes, Thomas T.D.

Terre Alta, West Virginia
d. Loomis, Mahion

Wellsburg, West Virginia
b. Davis, Glenn

Wheeling, West Virginia
b. Berry, Chu
b. Burkett, Jesse Cail
b. Crosman, Henrietta
b. DeWitt, Joyce
b. Glasscock, Jack
b. Grimes, J William
b. Hamburger, Philip
b. Mazeroski, Bill
b. Morrow, Richard Martin
b. Reuther, Roy
b. Reuther, Walter Philip
b. Sinclair, Harry Ford
b. Steber, Eleanor
d. Glasscock, Jack

Winding Gulf, West Virginia
b. Lewis, Shirley A(nn) R(edd)

Wyoming, West Virginia
b. Warner, Curt

WISCONSIN
b. Bennett, Robert LaFollette
b. Kulwicki, Alan
b. Oshkosh
b. Wellcome, Henry Solomon, Sir

Adell, Wisconsin
b. Hildegarde, Loretta Sell

Algoma, Wisconsin
b. Stakman, Elvin Charles

Alma, Wisconsin
b. Gesell, Arnold

Antigo, Wisconsin
b. Lukas, D. Wayne

Appleton, Wisconsin
b. Bleier, Rocky
b. Christ-Janer, Albert
b. Dafoe, Willem
b. Havighurst, Walter Edwin
b. Reid, Helen Rogers

Ashland, Wisconsin
b. Newquist, Roy

Athens, Wisconsin
b. Winninger, Charles

Augusta, Wisconsin
b. Devine, Dan(iel John)

Baraboo, Wisconsin
b. North, John Ringling
b. Whiteman, Roberta Hill

Batavia, Wisconsin
b. Dietrich, Noah

Bear Creek, Wisconsin
b. Nieman, Lucius William

Beaver Dam, Wisconsin
b. Hatfield, Bobby

Beloit, Wisconsin
b. Andrews, Roy Chapman

Black River Falls, Wisconsin
d. Knowles, Warren Perley
d. Mountain Wolf Woman

Bloomer, Wisconsin
b. Treptow, Martin A

Blue Mounds, Wisconsin
d. Johansen, Gunnar

Brodhead, Wisconsin
b. Livingston, M(ilton) Stanley

Brookfield, Wisconsin
d. Grede, William John

Burlington, Wisconsin
b. Garvey, Ed(ward Robert)

Cambria, Wisconsin
b. Rowlands, Gena (Catherine)

Cashon, Wisconsin
b. King, Frank

Cazenovia, Wisconsin
b. Duren, Ryne

Centerville, Wisconsin
b. Tobey, Mark

Chilton, Wisconsin
b. Black, Winifred Sweet

Chippewa Falls, Wisconsin
b. Cray, Seymour R.

Clear Lake, Wisconsin
b. Grimes, Burleigh Arland
b. Nelson, Gaylord Anton
d. Grimes, Burleigh Arland

Clemansville, Wisconsin
b. Hooton, Earnest Albert

Cumberland, Wisconsin
b. Wolff, Mary Evaline

Delafield, Wisconsin
b. Cushing, William Barker
d. Farber, Edward Rolke

Durand, Wisconsin
b. Parkhurst, Helen

Eagle River, Wisconsin
d. Comiskey, Charlie

East Troy, Wisconsin
b. Hickok, Lorena A
d. Vaughan, Stevie Ray

Eau Claire, Wisconsin
b. Knaths, Karl

Edgerton, Wisconsin
b. Babcock, Harold Delos
b. North, Sterling

Elkhorn, Wisconsin
d. Wrigley, Philip Knight

Elroy, Wisconsin
b. Thompson, Tommy George

Fairchild, Wisconsin
b. Landis, Carole

Fond du Lac, Wisconsin
b. Brauer, Jerald C(arl)
b. Doheny, Edward Lawrence
b. Gillette, King Camp
b. MacDougall, Curtis Daniel
b. Wise, Winifred E

Genesee, Wisconsin
d. Fontanne, Lynn

Grand Chute, Wisconsin
b. McCarthy, Joe

Green Bay, Wisconsin
b. Herber, Arnie
b. Lambeau, Curly
b. Pirner, Dave
b. Simpson, Mona Elizabeth
b. Smith, Red
d. Gronouski, John A(ustin)
d. Herber, Arnie

Green Lake, Wisconsin
b. Anderson, Elda Emma

Hilbert, Wisconsin
b. Berigan, Bunny

Hillsboro, Wisconsin
b. Mitscher, Marc Andrew

Hortonville, Wisconsin
b. Nye, Gerald Prentice

Janesville, Wisconsin
b. Bond, Carrie Jacobs
b. Comstock, John Henry
b. Feingold, Russell D.

Jefferson County, Wisconsin
b. Witte, Edwin Emil

Johnstown, Wisconsin
b. Wilcox, Ella Wheeler

Juneau, Wisconsin
b. Joss, Addie

Kenosha, Wisconsin
b. Ameche, Alan Dante
b. Ameche, Don
b. Ameche, Jim
b. McIntyre, James
b. Molinaro, Al
b. Newell, Edward Theodore
b. Travanti, Daniel J(ohn)
b. Welles, Orson
d. Simmons, Zalmon G

Keshena, Wisconsin
b. Deer, Ada E(lizabeth)
d. Oshkosh

Kewaskum, Wisconsin
b. Wescott, Glenway

Kewaunee, Wisconsin
b. O'Konski, Alvin E(dward)
d. O'Konski, Alvin E(dward)

Kilbourne, Wisconsin
d. Boyd, Belle

La Crosse, Wisconsin
b. Losey, Joseph Walton
b. Lucey, Patrick Joseph
b. Ray, Nicholas
b. Starch, Daniel
b. Sterling, Ford
b. Toland, John Willard
d. Haydon, Julie

Ladysmith, Wisconsin
b. Kovic, Ron

Lake Geneva, Wisconsin
d. Maytag, Elmer Henry

Lancaster, Wisconsin
b. U'Ren, William Simon

Lodi, Wisconsin
b. Wopat, Tom

Madison, Wisconsin
b. Allyn, Stanley Charles
b. Anderson, Carl Thomas
b. Bakken, Jim
b. Bardeen, John
b. Cole, Michael
b. Curtis, Edward Sheriff
b. Daly, Tyne
b. Farley, Chris
b. Fox, Matthew (Timothy James)
b. Heiden, Eric Arthur
b. Hoiby, Lee
b. Johnson, Mark
b. Jones, Jenkin Lloyd
b. LaFollete, Philip Fox
b. Lamm, Richard Douglas
b. Mason, Max
b. Morse, Wayne Lyman
b. Nichols, Kid
b. Prokosch, Frederic
b. Suter, Gary
b. Wilder, Amos Niven
b. Wilder, Thornton (Niven)
d. Anderson, Carl Thomas
d. Babcock, Stephen Moulton
d. Bohrod, Aaron
d. Crowley, Leo Thomas
d. Curry, John Steuart
d. Curti, Merle Eugene
d. Gein, Ed
d. Herbert, Frank (Patrick)
d. Hirschfelder, Joseph Oakland
d. Kerst, Donald W(illiam)
d. LaFollete, Philip Fox
d. Leonard, William Ellery
d. Redding, Otis

Manitowish Waters, Wisconsin
d. Ilg, Frances Lillian

Manitowoc, Wisconsin
b. Bates, Mary Elizabeth
b. Goldsmith, Judith Ann Becker
b. Krainik, Ardis
b. Rankin, K(arl) L(ott)

Marshfield, Wisconsin
d. Joanis, John W
d. Nash, Philleo

Mazomanie, Wisconsin
d. Appleby, John Francis

Medford, Wisconsin
b. Dixon, Jeane (Pinckert)

Menasha, Wisconsin
b. Dollard, John
b. Liberace, George J

Millville, Wisconsin
b. Simak, Clifford Donald

Milton Junction, Wisconsin
b. Crowley, Leo Thomas

Milwaukee, Wisconsin
b. Abrahams, Jim
b. Adler, David
b. Anello, John David
b. Annenberg, Walter Hubert
b. Anthony, Joseph
b. Aspin, Les
b. Ayres, Mitchell
b. Berkner, Lloyd Viel
b. Blatchford, Joseph Hoffer
b. Bode, Carl
b. Bolles, Don F
b. Bremer, Arthur Herman
b. Bryant, Felice
b. Cohen, Wilbur Joseph
b. Crosby, John Campbell
b. Davis, Tobe
b. Dempsey, Tom
b. Deutsch, Harold C(harles)
b. Eagleburger, Lawrence S.
b. Ets, Marie Hall
b. Farber, Edward Rolke
b. Finney, Jack
b. Franz, Eduard
b. Gault, William Campbell
b. Glazer, David
b. Grede, William John
b. Gregory, Horace Victor
b. Grene, Marjorie
b. Groppi, James E
b. Hahn, Archie
b. Hall, Deidre
b. Henry, Marguerite
b. Herman, Woody
b. Hermening, Kevin Jay
b. Jansen, Dan
b. Janzen, Daniel Hunt
b. Jarreau, Al(wyn Lopez)
b. Jens, Salome
b. Jordan, Elizabeth Garver
b. Kaltenborn, H(ans) V(on)
b. Kasten, Robert Walter, Jr.
b. Kennan, George Frost
b. Kohl, Herbert H.
b. Koplovitz, Kay Smith
b. Kovel, Ralph Mallory
b. Kubek, Tony
b. Kuenn, Harvey Edward
b. Lippold, Richard
b. Loring, Eugene
b. Luening, Otto
b. Lunt, Alfred
b. Mikva, Abner Joseph
b. Minow, Newton Norman
b. Murphy, Robert Daniel
b. Neumeier, John
b. O'Brien, Pat
b. Oglesby, Zena, (Jr.)
b. Olson, Nancy
b. Palmer, Peter
b. Parker, Frank
b. Perkins, Milo Randolph
b. Rae, Charlotte
b. Raskin, Ellen
b. Rehnquist, William Hubbs
b. Ruppe, Loret Miller
b. Schickel, Richard
b. Schroeder, Jay Brian
b. Schultz, Michael A.
b. Selig, Bud
b. Simmons, Al(oysius Harry)
b. Simon, Herbert Alexander
b. Snyder, Tom
b. Straub, Peter
b. Stuart, Kenneth James
b. Thorne, Jim

b. Tillman, George, Jr.
b. Tracy, Spencer Bonaventure
b. Uecker, Bob
b. Vandenberg, Hoyt Sanford
b. Wheeler, William Morton
b. Wilder, Gene
b. Yarbrough, Glenn
b. Zablocki, Clement John
d. Anello, John David
d. Berger, Victor Louis
d. Blue, Monte
d. Eiseman, Florence
d. Evinrude, Ole
d. Grant, Harry Johnston
d. Groppi, James E
d. MacArthur, Arthur
d. MacDonald, John Dann
d. Pabst, Frederick
d. Reedy, George E(dward)
d. Sholes, Christopher Latham
d. Simmons, Al(oysius Harry)

Mineral Point, Wisconsin
b. Ludden, Allen Ellsworth

Monroe, Wisconsin
b. Twining, Nathan F(arragut)

Neillsville, Wisconsin
b. Brameld, Theodore

New Glarus, Wisconsin
b. Kubly, Herbert (Oswald)
d. Kubly, Herbert (Oswald)

New Lisbon, Wisconsin
b. Andreessen, Mark

New Richmond, Wisconsin
b. McNally, John Victor

Oak Creek, Wisconsin
b. Matuszak, John (Daniel)

Osceola, Wisconsin
b. Stickley, Gustav

Oshkosh, Wisconsin
b. Hine, Lewis Wickes
b. Owen, Tobias Chant
b. Suits, C(hauncey) G(uy)
b. Tabor, Elizabeth Bonduel McCourt
Doe

Pardeeville, Wisconsin
b. Smith, Gerald Lyman Kenneth

Pepin, Wisconsin
b. Wilder, Laura Elizabeth Ingalls

Plainfield, Wisconsin
b. Gein, Ed

Platteville, Wisconsin
b. Gasser, Herbert Spencer
b. Luce, Charles (Franklin)

Portage, Wisconsin
b. Gale, Zona
b. Turner, Frederick Jackson
d. Dahmer, Jeffrey L

Prairie du Chien, Wisconsin
b. Bowlen, Patrick Dennis
b. Cannon, Walter Bradford

Prentice, Wisconsin
b. Morgan, Dennis

Primrose, Wisconsin
b. LaFollette, Robert Marion

Racine, Wisconsin
b. Corby, Ellen
b. Davis, Marguerite
b. Gillett, George Nield, Jr.
b. Horlick, Alexander James
b. Johnson, Herbert Fisk
b. March, Fredric
b. McNair, Barbara
d. Davis, Marguerite
d. Horlick, Alexander James
d. Horlick, William
d. Johnson, Herbert Fisk

Reedsburgh, Wisconsin
b. Briggs, Clare A

Rhinelander, Wisconsin
b. Wasserman, Dale

Rice Lake, Wisconsin
b. Olsen, Harold G

Richland Center, Wisconsin
b. Thomson, Vernon Wallace
b. Wright, Frank Lloyd

Richmond, Wisconsin
b. Smith, Francis Marion

Ripon, Wisconsin
b. Catt, Carrie Chapman
b. Maltby, Richard Eldridge, Jr.
b. Selfridge, Harry Gordon

River Falls, Wisconsin
b. Knowles, Warren Perley

Sauk City, Wisconsin
b. Derleth, August (William)
b. Schorer, Mark

Sheboygan, Wisconsin
b. Mason, Jackie

Shorewood, Wisconsin
b. Chapelle, Dickey

Shullsburg, Wisconsin
b. Holland, Leland James
b. Parker, George Safford

Sparta, Wisconsin
b. Kelley, Edgar Stillman
b. Nestingen, Ivan Arnold
b. Slayton, Donald Kent

Stoughton, Wisconsin
b. Murphy, William Parry

Sturgeon, Wisconsin
d. Lambeau, Curly

Sun Prairie, Wisconsin
b. O'Keeffe, Georgia

Superior, Wisconsin
b. Bong, Richard Ira
b. Fitzpatrick, Daniel R
b. Grant, Bud
b. Leemans, Tuffy
d. Bancroft, Dave

Thorp, Wisconsin
b. North, Andy

Tomahawk, Wisconsin
b. Eklund, Carl Robert
b. Webster, Mike

Two Rivers, Wisconsin
b. Walsh, Thomas James

Valders, Wisconsin
b. Veblen, Thorstein Bunde

Viola, Wisconsin
b. Nye, Russel Blaine

Viroqua, Wisconsin
b. Lee, Mark
b. Vig, Butch

Washington Island, Wisconsin
d. Blair, Clay, Jr.

Watertown, Wisconsin
b. Davies, Joseph Edward
b. Lasker, Mary (Woodward)

Waukesha, Wisconsin
b. Ben-Shalom, Miriam
b. Bullard, Dexter Means
b. Ford, Mary
b. Paul, Les
d. Sears, Richard Warren

Waupun, Wisconsin
b. Smith, Oliver

Wausau, Wisconsin
b. Hirsch, Crazylegs
b. Otto, Jim
b. Ruder, David Sturtevant

Wauwatosa, Wisconsin
b. Dickerson, Nancy Hanschman

West Allis, Wisconsin
b. Liberace

West Salem, Wisconsin
b. Garland, Hamlin

White Water, Wisconsin
b. Hulce, Thomas

Williams Bay, Wisconsin
d. Barnard, Edward Emerson

Wisconsin Rapids, Wisconsin
b. Daly, James
b. Nash, Philleo

Chulai, Vietnam
d. Chapelle, Dickey

Cuu Long, Vietnam
b. Vo Van Kiet

Da Lat, Vietnam
b. Pisier, Marie-France

Dich Le, Vietnam
b. Le Duc Tho

Dong My, Vietnam
b. Muoi, Do

Hai Hung, Vietnam
b. Linh, Nguyen Van

Haiphong, Vietnam
b. Ardizzone, Edward Jeffrey Irving

Hanoi, Vietnam
b. Thao, Tran Duc
b. Xuan Thuy
d. Capa, Robert
d. Chinh, Truong
d. Garnier, Francis
d. Ho Chi Minh
d. Le Duan
d. Le Duc Tho
d. Thang, Ton Duc

Ho Chi Minh City, Vietnam
d. Linh, Nguyen Van
d. Pham Hung

Hoang Tru, Vietnam
b. Ho Chi Minh

Hue, Vietnam
b. Ngo-Dinh-Diem
d. Fall, Bernard B

Long Xuyen Province, Vietnam
b. Thang, Ton Duc

My Tho, Vietnam
b. Duong Van Minh

Quang Nam, Vietnam
b. Pham van Dong

Quang Tri Province, Vietnam
b. Le Duan

Quangblin, Vietnam
b. Giap, Vo Nguyen

Saigon, Vietnam
b. Dumurcq, Charles
b. Ut, Huynh Cong

Son Tay, Vietnam
b. Ky, Nguyen Cao

Thanh Hoa, Vietnam
b. Phieu, Le Kha

Tri Thuy, Vietnam
b. Nguyen Van Thieu

Vinh Long Province, Vietnam
b. Pham Hung

VIETNAM (NORTH)

Hanoi, Vietnam (North)
d. Xuan Thuy

VIETNAM (SOUTH)

Saigon, Vietnam (South)
d. Ngo-Dinh-Diem

VIRGIN ISLANDS

St. Thomas, Virgin Islands
b. Blyden, Edward Wilmot

VIRGIN ISLANDS OF THE UNITED STATES

b. Griffith, Emile Alphonse

Frederiksted, Saint Croix, Virgin Islands of the United States
d. Irvin, Rea

Saint Croix, Virgin Islands of the United States
b. Innis, Roy Emile Alfredo
d. Lorde, Audre (Geraldine)
d. Raedler, Dorothy (Florence)
d. Spectorsky, Auguste Compte

Saint Thomas, Virgin Islands of the United States
b. Grammer, Kelsey

St. Croix, Virgin Islands of the United States
b. Duncan, Tim(othy Theodore)

WALES

b. Arundel, Honor Morfydd
b. Glendower, Owen
b. Recorde, Robert
d. Glendower, Owen

Abergavenny, Wales
b. Pym, Francis Leslie

Abersychan, Wales
b. Jenkins, Roy Harris

Aberystwyth, Wales
b. Rees, Roger
d. Evans, Geraint Llewellyn, Sir

Anglesey, Wales
b. Griffith, Hugh Emrys

Barry, Wales
b. Illingworth, Leslie Gilbert
b. Livesey, Roger

Beddgelert, Caernarvonshire, Wales
b. Jones, Samuel Milton

Bettws y Coed, Wales
b. Phillips, Sian
d. Flanders, Michael

Blackwood, Wales
b. Jones, Gwynn
b. Price, Margaret Berenice

Bodvel, Wales
b. Piozzi, Hester Lynch Salisbury

Brecknock, Wales
b. Kemble, Charles
d. Patti, Adelina Juana Maria

Brecknockshire, Wales
b. Everest, George, Sir

Brecon, Wales
b. Siddons, Sarah Kemble

Cardiff, Wales
b. Abse, Dannie
b. Bassey, Shirley
b. Cudlipp, Hugh
b. Edmunds, Dave
b. Follett, Ken(neth Martin)
b. Josephson, Brian David
b. Marquand, Richard
b. Novello, Ivor
b. O'Shea, Tessie
b. Ready, William Bernard
b. Sinclair, Iain
b. Templeton, Alec
b. Thomas, Craig D
b. Thomas, Ronald Stuart
d. Lewis, Saunders
d. Thomas, Gwyn
d. Wilde, Jimmy

Carmarthen, Wales
d. Steele, Richard, Sir

Carnarvon, Wales
b. Leonowens, Anna Harriette Crawford

Clydack, Wales
b. Farr, Tommy B

Colwyn Bay, Wales
b. Dalton, Timothy
b. Jones, Terry

Denbigh, Wales
b. Stanley, Henry Morton, Sir

Deri, Wales
b. Cope, Julian

Glamorgan, Wales
b. Baker, Stanley, Sir
b. Gwenn, Edmund
b. Jones, Ernest Alfred

Gyffin, Wales
b. Gibson, John

Kolasin, Yugoslavia
b. Djilas, Milovan

Konjic, Yugoslavia
b. Markovic, Ante

Krasic, Yugoslavia
d. Stepinac, Alojzije

Krizevci, Yugoslavia
b. Kucan, Milan

Kumrovec, Yugoslavia
b. Tito

Ljubljana, Yugoslavia
d. Tito

Maribor, Yugoslavia
b. Jausovec, Mima

Montenegro, Yugoslavia
b. Karadzic, Radovan

Mostar, Yugoslavia
b. Bijedic, Dzemal

Novi Sad, Yugoslavia
b. Seles, Monica

Osijek, Yugoslavia
b. Seper, Franjo

Pancevo, Yugoslavia
b. Mihajlov, Mihajlo

Pisino, Yugoslavia
b. Dallapiccola, Luigi

Pozarevac, Yugoslavia
b. Milosevic, Slobodan

Sarajevo, Yugoslavia
b. Elazar, David
b. Filipovic, Zlata
d. Franz Ferdinand

Skopje, Yugoslavia
b. Teresa, Mother

Slavonski-Brod, Yugoslavia
b. Slavenska, Mia

Sombor, Yugoslavia
b. Maglich, Bogdan C

Split, Yugoslavia
b. Kukoc, Toni
b. Rodzinski, Artur

Subotica, Yugoslavia
b. Simon, John Ivan

Titovo Utice, Yugoslavia
b. Tesich, Steve

Travnik, Yugoslavia
b. Andric, Ivo
b. Jurinac, Sena

Trnjani, Yugoslavia
b. Rothmuller, Marko A

Veskueb, Yugoslavia
b. Wolff, Helen

Vukovar, Yugoslavia
b. Ruzicka, Leopold Stephen

Zagreb, Yugoslavia
b. Milanov, Zinka Kunc
d. Artukovic, Andrija
d. Ternina, Milka

ZAMBIA

Ilala, Zambia
d. Livingstone, David

ZANZIBAR

b. Mercury, Freddie
d. Tippu Tib

ZIMBABWE

Harare, Zimbabwe
d. Nkomo, Joshua (Mqabuko Nyongolo)

Kitwe, Zimbabwe
b. Chiluba, Frederick Jacob Titus

Nyamanandhlovu, Zimbabwe
b. Sithole, Ndabaningi

Occupation Index

AIDS ACTIVIST

Callen, Michael
Fisher, Mary
Gertz, Alison L.
Hemphill, Essex
Jones, Cleve
Kramer, Larry
Wilson, Phill
Zamora, Pedro

ABOLITIONIST

Arkell, Anthony John
Birney, James Gillespie
Blackwell, Antoinette
  Louisa Brown
Brown, John
Burns, Anthony
Chandler, Zachariah
Channing, William Ellery
Clarkson, Thomas
Clay, Cassius Marcellus
Coffin, Levi
Comstock, Elizabeth L
Craft, Ellen
Crandall, Prudence
Cugoano, Ottobah
Equiano, Olaudah
Fee, John Gregg
Foster, Abigail Kelley
Garnet, Henry Highland
Garrett, Thomas
Garrison, William Lloyd
Giddings, Joshua Reed
Grimke, Angelina Emily
Grimke, Sarah Moore
Jay, William
Larcom, Lucy
Lovejoy, Elijah Parish
Nabuco de Araujo,
  Joaquim Aurelio
Phillips, Wendell
Purvis, Robert
Remond, Charles Lennox
Russwurm, John Brown
Stevens, Thaddeus
Still, William
Truth, Sojourner
Tubman, Harriet Ross
Vesey, Denmark
Walker, David
Weld, Theodore Dwight

Wilberforce, William
Wright, Elizur

ACADEMIC ADMINISTRATOR

Andrus, Cecil D(ale)

ACTING TEACHER

Strasberg, Lee

ACTIVIST

Lord, Bette Bao

ACTOR

Aadland, Beverly
Aames, Willie
Abel, Walter Charles
Abington, Fanny
Abraham, F(ahrid) Murray
Ace, Jane Sherwood
Ackerman, Bettye
Ackland, Joss
Adams, Brooke
Adams, Don
Adams, Edie
Adams, Edwin
Adams, Julie
Adams, Mason
Adams, Maud
Adams, Maude
Adams, Nick
Addams, Dawn
Addy, Wesley
Adjani, Isabelle
Adler, Jacob Pavlovitch
Adler, Luther
Adler, Stella
Adoree, Renee
Agar, John
Agutter, Jenny
Aherne, Brian de Lacy
Aiello, Danny Louis, Jr.
Aimee, Anouk
Akins, Claude

Alberghetti, Anna Maria
Albert, Eddie
Albert, Edward Laurence
Albertson, Frank
Albertson, Jack
Albright, Lola Jean
Alda, Alan
Alda, Robert
Aldridge, Ira Frederick
Aldridge, Michael
Alexander, Ben
Alexander, Denise
Alexander, Jane
Alexander, Jason
Alexander, Katherine
Allan, Elizabeth
Allbritton, Louise
Allen, Debbie
Allen, Elizabeth
Allen, Joan
Allen, Karen Jane
Allen, Nancy
Allen, Rex E., Sr.
Allen, Tim
Allen, Viola Emily
Allen, Woody
Alley, Kirstie
Allgood, Sara
Allison, Fran(ces)
Allyson, June
Alvardo, Trini(dad)
Ameche, Don
Ames, Ed(mund Dantes)
Ames, Leon
Amos, John
Amsterdam, Morey
Ana-Alicia
Anders, Merry
Anderson, Daryl
Anderson, Eddie
Anderson, Gilbert M
Anderson, Gillian
Anderson, Harry
Anderson, Herbert
Anderson, Judith, Dame
Anderson, Loni
Anderson, Mary
  Antoinette
Anderson, Melissa Sue
Anderson, Michael, Jr.
Anderson, Richard Dean
Anderson, Richard
  Norman
Anderson, Warner

Andersson, Bibi
Andersson, Harriet
Andes, Keith
Andress, Ursula
Andrews, Anthony Corin
  Gerald
Andrews, (Carver) Dana
Andrews, Edward
Andrews, Harry
Andrews, Julie
Andrews, Tige
Angel, Heather Grace
Angeli, Pier
Angelou, Maya
Anglim, Philip
Anglin, Margaret Mary
Aniston, Jennifer
Ankers, Evelyn
Annabella
Annis, Francesca
Ann-Margret
Anspach, Susan
Anthony, Michael
Anthony, Tony
Antoine, Andre
Anton, Susan
Archer, Anne
Archerd, Army
Arden, Eve
Arkin, Alan Wolf
Arlen, Richard
Arletty
Arliss, George
Armendariz, Pedro
Armetta, Henry
Armstrong, Bess
Armstrong, R G
Armstrong, Robert
Arnaz, Desi
Arnaz, Desi(derio Alberto
  IV), J
Arnaz, Lucie Desiree
Arness, James
Arnold, Edward
Arnold, Tom
Arquette, Cliff
Arquette, Patricia
Arquette, Rosanna
Artaud, Antonin
Arthur, Beatrice
Arthur, Jean
Ashcroft, Peggy, Dame
Ashley, Elizabeth
Asner, Ed(ward)

Assante, Armand
Astaire, Fred
Asther, Nils
Astin, John Allen
Astin, Mackenzie
  Alexander
Astor, Mary
Atherton, William
Atkins, Christopher
Attenborough, Richard
  Samuel, Sir
Atwater, Edith
Atwill, Lionel
Auberjonois, Rene Murat
Audra (Ann), McDonald
Audran, Stephane
Auer, Mischa
Austin, Gene
Autry, Gene
Avalon, Frankie
Avalos, Luis
Avedon, Doe
Avery, James
Aykroyd, Dan(iel Edward)
Ayres, Agnes
Ayres, Lew
Aznavour, Charles
Baby Leroy
Bacall, Lauren
Bach, Barbara
Bach, Catherine
Backus, Jim
Baclanova, Olga
Bacon, Frank
Bacon, Kevin
Baddeley, Angela
Baddeley, Hermione
  Clinton
Baer, Max
Baer, Max, Jr.
Bailey, Pearl Mae
Bailey, Raymond
Bain, Barbara
Bain, Conrad Stafford
Bainter, Fay Okell
Baio, Scott Vincent
Bajor, Gizi
Baker, Belle
Baker, Blanche
Baker, Carroll
Baker, Diane
Baker, Joe Don
Baker, Kathy
Baker, Kenny
Baker, Stanley, Sir
Bakewell, William
Bakula, Scott
Baldwin, Adam
Baldwin, Alec
Baldwin, Stephen
Baldwin, William
Balin, Ina
Ball, Lucille (Desiree)
Ballard, Kaye
Balsam, Martin Henry
Bancroft, Anne
Bancroft, George
Banderas, Antonio
Banerjee, Victor
Bankhead, Tallulah
  Brockman
Banks, Leslie
Banks, Monty
Banks, Tyra
Banky, Vilma
Bannen, Ian

Bannon, Jim
Bara, Theda
Baranski, Christine
Barbeau, Adrienne
Bardot, Brigitte
Bari, Lynn
Barker, Lex
Barker, Ronnie
Barkin, Ellen
Barnes, Binnie
Barnes, Joanna
Barnes, Wade
Barrault, Jean-Louis
Barrie, Barbara
Barrie, Mona
Barrie, Wendy
Barry, Donald
Barry, Gene
Barrymore, Diana
Barrymore, Drew
Barrymore, Elaine Jacobs
Barrymore, Ethel Mae
  Blythe
Barrymore, Georgiana
  Emma Drew
Barrymore, John
Barrymore, John Blythe
  Drew, Jr.
Barrymore, Lionel Blythe
Barrymore, Maurice
Barthelmess, Richard
Bartholomew, Freddie
Bartok, Eva
Barton, James
Basehart, Richard
Basinger, Kim
Bass, Alfie
Bassett, Angela
Bateman, Jason
Bateman, Justine
Bateman, Kate Josephine
Bates, Alan Arthur
Bates, Blanche Lyon
Bates, Florence
Bates, Kathy
Bavier, Frances
Baxley, Barbara
Baxter, Anne
Baxter, Keith
Baxter, Meredith
Baxter, Warner
Bayes, Nora
Bayne, Beverly Pearl
Beacham, Stephanie
Beal, John
Beals, Jennifer
Bean, Orson
Beard, Matthew, Jr.
Bearse, Amanda
Beasley, Allyce
Beaton, Norman
Beatty, Ned
Beatty, Robert
Beatty, Warren
Beaumont, Hugh
Beavers, Louise
Beck, John
Beck, Julian
Beck, Michael
Bedelia, Bonnie
Bedford, Brian
Beecher, Janet
Beemer, Brace
Beery, Noah
Beery, Noah, Jr.
Beery, Wallace Fitzgerald

Begley, Ed, Jr.
Begley, Ed(ward James)
Belafonte, Harry, Jr.
Belafonte, Shari
Bell, Darryl
Bell, Tom
Bellamy, Ralph
Beller, Kathleen
Bellwood, Pamela
Belmondo, Jean-Paul
Belmont, Eleanor Robson
Belushi, Jim
Belushi, John
Belzer, Richard
Benaderet, Bea
Bendix, William
Benedict, Dirk
Benet, Brenda
Bening, Annette
Benjamin, Richard
Bennett, Constance
  Campbell
Bennett, Joan
Bennett, Richard
Benson, Frank Robert, Sir
Benson, Robby
Bentley, John
Benton, Barbie
Benzell, Mimi
Beradino, John
Berenger, Tom
Berenson, Marisa
Beresford, Harry
Berg, Gertrude
Bergen, Candice
Bergen, Polly
Berger, Helmut
Berger, Senta
Bergman, Ingrid
Bergner, Elisabeth
Berle, Milton
Berliner, Ron
Berlinger, Warren
Berman, Shelley
Bernard, Sam
Bernardi, Hershel
Bernhardt, Sarah
Bernsen, Corbin
Bernstein, Felicia
  Montealegre
Berry, Halle
Berry, Ken
Bertinelli, Valerie
Bessell, Ted
Best, Edna
Betterton, Thomas
Bettger, Lyle
Betz, Carl
Bey, Turhan
Beymer, Richard
Bialik, Mayim
Bickford, Charles
  Ambrose
Bikel, Theodore Meir
Bill, Tony
Billingsley, Barbara
Bilon, Michael Patrick
Birney, David Edwin
Bishop, Julie
Bishop, Kelly
Bisset, Jacqueline Fraser
Bissett, Josie
Bixby, Bill
Black, Karen
Black, Shirley Temple
Blackman, Honor

Blackmer, Sidney
  Alderman
Blacque, Taurean
Blaine, Vivian
Blair, Betsy
Blair, Janet
Blair, Linda Denise
Blake, Amanda
Blake, Robert
Blakeley, Ronee
Blakely, Colin (George
  Edward)
Blakely, Susan
Blanc, Mel(vin Jerome)
Blane, Sally
Bledsoe, Jules
Bledsoe, Tempestt Kenieth
Bleeth, Yasmine
Blinn, Holbrook
Blocker, Dan
Blondell, Joan
Bloom, Claire
Blore, Eric
Blue, Monte
Blyden, Larry
Blyth, Ann Marie
Blythe, Betty
Boardman, Eleanor
Bochner, Hart
Bochner, Lloyd
Bogarde, Dirk
Bogart, Humphrey de
  Forest
Bogosian, Eric
Bohannon, Judy
Bohay, Heidi
Boland, Mary
Boles, John
Bolger, Ray(mond
  Wallace)
Bologna, Joseph
Bond, Sudie
Bond, Tommy
Bond, Ward
Bondarchuk, Sergei
  (Fedorovich)
Bondi, Beulah
Bonerz, Peter
Bonet, Lisa
Bonham Carter, Helena
Bonner, Frank
Bono, Sonny
Bonstelle, Jessie
Booke, Sorrell
Boone, Richard
Booth, Edwin Thomas
Booth, Junius Brutus
Booth, Shirley
Boothe, Powers
Bordoni, Irene
Borg, Veda Ann
Borgnine, Ernest
Bosley, Tom
Bosson, Barbara
Bostwick, Barry
Boswell, Connee
Bosworth, Hobart van
  Zandt
Bottoms, Joseph
Bottoms, Sam
Bottoms, Timothy
Boucicault, Dion Lardner
Bow, Clara Gordon
Bowen, Roger
Bowie, David
Bowman, Lee

Boxleitner, Bruce
Boyd, Belle
Boyd, Stephen
Boyd, William
Boyer, Charles
Boyle, Peter
Bracegirdle, Anne
Bracken, Eddie
Brady, Alice
Brady, Pat
Brady, Scott
Brady, William Aloysius
Braga, Sonia
Brambell, Wilfrid
Branagh, Kenneth
  (Charles)
Brand, Neville
Brandauer, Klaus Maria
Brando, Marlon, Jr.
Brandy
Brannigan, Owen
Brasselle, Keefe
Braugher, Andre
Brazzi, Rossano
Breese, Edmund
Brendel, El(mer)
Breneman, Tom
Brennan, Eileen Regina
Brennan, Walter Andrew
Brent, Evelyn
Brent, George
Brent, Romney
Brett, Jeremy
Brewer, Teresa
Brian, David
Brian, Donald
Brice, Fanny
Bridges, Beau
Bridges, Jeff
Bridges, Lloyd
Bridges, Todd
Bridgewater, Dee Dee
Brimley, Wilford
Brisebois, Danielle
Britt, May
Brittany, Morgan
Britton, Barbara
Broadhurst, Kent
Broderick, Helen
Broderick, James Joseph
Broderick, Matthew
Brodie, Steve
Brolin, James
Bromberg, J Edward
Bromfield, John
Bron, Eleanor
Bronson, Betty
Bronson, Charles
Brook, Clive
Brooke, Hillary
Brooks, Albert (Lawrence
  Einstein)
Brooks, Avery
Brooks, Foster Murrell
Brooks, Geraldine
Brooks, James L.
Brooks, Louise
Brosnan, Pierce
Broun, Heywood Hale
Brown, Blair
Brown, Bryan
Brown, Georgia
Brown, Jim
Brown, Joe E(van)
Brown, Johnny Mack
Brown, Kelly

Brown, Oscar, Jr.
Brown, Pamela
Brown, Pamela Beatrice
Brown, Tom
Brown, Vanessa
Browne, Coral Edith
Browne, Leslie
Browne, Roscoe Lee
Bruce, Carol
Bruce, Nigel
Bruce, Virginia
Bryan, Dora
Brynner, Yul
Buchanan, Edgar
Buchanan, Jack
Buchholz, Horst
Buckley, Betty Lynn
Buckstone, John Baldwin
Bujold, Genevieve
Bull, Peter
Bullock, Sandra
Bunny, John
Buono, Victor
Burbage, James
Burbage, Richard
Burghoff, Gary
Burke, Billie
Burke, Christopher
Burke, Delta
Burke, Paul
Burnett, Carol
Burnette, Smiley
Burns, Bob
Burns, David
Burns, George
Burr, Raymond (William
  Stacy)
Burrows, Darren E
Burstyn, Ellen
Burton, Kate
Burton, LeVar(dis Robert
  Martyn Jr.)
Burton, Richard
Buscemi, Steve
Busch, Charles
Busey, Gary
Busfield, Timothy
Bushell, Anthony
Bushman, Francis X(avier)
Butkus, Dick
Butler, Brett
Buttafuoco, Joey
Butterworth, Charles
Buttons, Red
Buttram, Pat
Buzzell, Eddie
Buzzi, Ruth Ann
Byington, Spring
Byrne, Gabriel
Byrnes, Edd
Caan, James
Cabot, Bruce
Cabot, Sebastian
Cabot, Susan
Caesar, Adolph
Caesar, Sid
Cage, Nicolas
Cagney, James
Cagney, Jeanne
Cahill, Marie
Cain, Dean
Caine, Michael
Calder-Marshall, Anna
  Lucia
Caldwell, Zoe
Calhern, Louis

Calhoun, Rory
Callan, Michael
Calvert, Catherine
Calvert, Louis
Calvert, Phyllis
Calvet, Corinne
Cambridge, Godfrey
Cameron, Candace
Cameron, Kirk
Cameron, Rod
Campanella, Joseph Mario
Campbell, Douglas
Campbell, Naomi
Campbell, Neve
Campbell, Patrick, Mrs.
Campbell, Tisha
Canary, David
Candy, John (Franklin)
Cannon, Dyan
Canova, Diana
Canova, Judy
Cantinflas
Cantrell, Lana
Canutt, Yakima
Canzoneri, Tony
Capero, Virginia
Capshaw, Kate
Capucine
Cara, Irene (Escalera)
Cardinal, Tantoo
Cardinale, Claudia
Carey, Clare
Carey, Harry
Carey, Macdonald
Carey, Phil(ip)
Cariou, Len
Carle, Richard
Carlisle, Kitty
Carlisle, Mary
Carlson, Richard
Carmel, Roger C
Carmichael, Ian
Carney, Art
Carney, Don
Carnovsky, Morris
Carol, Martine
Caron, Leslie Clare
  Margaret
Carr, Alexander
Carradine, David
Carradine, John
Carradine, Keith Ian
Carradine, Robert Reed
Carrera, Barbara
Carrere, Tia
Carrey, Jim
Carrillo, Leo
Carroll, Diahann
Carroll, Leo G
Carroll, Madeleine
Carroll, Nancy
Carroll, Pat(ricia Ann
  Angela Bridgit)
Carroll, Vinnette
Carson, Jack
Carson, Mindy
Carter, Caroline Louise
  Dudley
Carter, Dixie
Carter, Leslie, Mrs.
Carter, Lynda Jean
Carter, Nell
Carteris, Gabrielle
Cartwright, Angela
Cartwright, Nancy
Cartwright, Veronica

Caruso, David
Carvey, Dana
Case, Anna
Casella, Max
Cass, Peggy
Cassavetes, John
Cassidy, David Bruce
Cassidy, Jack
Cassidy, Joanna
Cassidy, Shaun Paul
Castellaneta, Dan
Castellano, Richard
Castle, John
Castle, Peggie
Cates, Phoebe
Catlett, Walter
Cattrall, Kim
Caulfield, Joan
Caulfield, Maxwell
Cavanaugh, Hobart
Cazenove, Christopher
Chaikin, Joseph
Chakiris, George
Chamberlain, Richard
Champion, Marge Celeste
Chan, Jackie
Chandler, Jeff
Chandler, Kyle
Chaney, Lon
Chaney, Lon, Jr.
Chaney, Norman
Channing, Carol
Channing, Stockard
Chaplin, Charlie
Chaplin, Geraldine
Chaplin, Sydney Dryden
Chapman, Graham
Charisse, Cyd
Charleson, Ian
Charlip, Remy
Charo
Chase, Chevy
Chase, Ilka
Chatterton, Ruth
Cheadle, Don
Cher
Chevalier, Maurice
  Auguste
Chiang, Ching
Childress, Alvin
Cho, Margaret
Chong, Tommy
Christian, Linda
Christians, Mady
Christie, Audrey
Christie, Julie
Christine, Virginia
Christopher, Dennis
Christopher, Sybil
  Williams Burton
Christopher, William
Church, Sandra
Churchill, Diana Josephine
Churchill, Sarah
Cibber, Colley
Cicciolina
Cilento, Diane
Ciulei, Liviu
Claire, Ina
Clark, Dane
Clark, Fred
Clark, Marguerite
Clark, Susan Nora
  Goulding
Clarke, Mae
Clary, Robert

Clayburgh, Jill
Clayton, Jan(e Byral)
Clayton, Lou
Cleese, John Marwood
Cleghorne, Ellen
Clift, Montgomery
Clive, Colin
Clooney, George
Clooney, Rosemary
Close, Glenn
Clyde, Andy
Cobb, Joe
Cobb, Lee J
Coburn, Charles Douville
Coburn, James
Coca, Imogene Fernandez
    y
Cochran, Steve
Coco, James Emil
Cody, Iron Eyes
Coffield, Kelly
Coghlan, Rose
Cohan, George M(ichael)
Cohen, Alexander H
Cohn, Mindy
Colasanto, Nicholas
Colbert, Claudette
Colby, Anita
Cole, Dennis
Cole, George
Cole, Michael
Cole, Olivia
Coleman, Dabney W
Coleman, Gary
Colicos, John
Collier, Constance
Collier, William, Sr.
Collinge, Patricia
Collins, Joan Henrietta
Collins, Ray
Collins, Stephen
Colman, Ronald
Comer, Anjanette
Compton, Fay
Compton, Joyce
Conaway, Jeff
Condon, Jackie
Conklin, Peggy
Connelly, Christopher
Connery, Sean
Connolly, Walter
Connors, Chuck
Connors, Mike
Conrad, Michael
Conrad, Robert
Conrad, William
Conreid, Hans
Conroy, Frank
Considine, Tim
Constantine, Eddie
Constantine, Michael
Conte, Richard
Conti, Tom
Converse, Frank
Conway, Jack
Conway, Shirl
Conway, Tim
Conway, Tom
Coogan, Jackie
Cook, Barbara
Cook, Donald
Cook, Elisha, Jr.
Cook, Peter
Cooper, Gary
Cooper, Gladys, Dame
Cooper, Jackie

Cooper, Melville
Coote, Robert
Coquelin, Benoit Constant
Corbett, John
Corbin, Barry
Corby, Ellen
Cord, Alex
Corey, Irwin
Corey, Jeff
Corey, Wendell
Corio, Ann
Corley, Pat
Cornell, Katharine
Cornell, Lydia
Corri, Adrienne
Corrigan, Douglas
Corsaro, Frank
Cort, Bud
Cortesa, Valentina
Cortez, Ricardo
Cosby, Bill
Cossart, Ernest
Costello, Chris
Costello, Dolores
Costello, Lou
Costello, Maurice
Costner, Kevin (Michael)
Cotsworth, Staats
Cotten, Joseph
Coulier, Dave
Coulouris, George
Courtenay, Tom
Courtneidge, Cicely, Dame
Cover, Franklin
Cowan, Jerome
Cowl, Jane
Cox, Courteney
Cox, Wally
Crabbe, Buster
Crabtree, Lotta
Craig, May
Craig, Wendy
Crain, Jeanne
Crane, Bob
Craven, Frank
Crawford, Broderick
Crawford, Christina
Crawford, Joan
Crawford, Michael
Cregar, Laird
Crenna, Richard
Crews, Laura Hope
Crisp, Donald
Cristal, Linda
Cronyn, Hume
Crosby, Bing
Crosby, Cathy Lee
Crosby, Gary
Crosby, Kathryn
Crosby, Mary Frances
Crosman, Henrietta
Cross, Ben
Crosse, Rupert
Crothers, Scatman
Crouse, Lindsay Ann
Crowley, Pat
Cruickshank, Andrew John
Cruise, Tom
Cryer, David
Crystal, Billy
Culkin, Macaulay
Cullum, John
Culp, Robert
Cummings, Bob
Cummings, Constance
Cummings, Quinn

Cummins, Peggy
Currie, Finlay
Curry, Mark
Curry, Tim
Curtin, Jane (Therese)
Curtis, Alan (Harold
    Neberroth)
Curtis, Jamie Lee
Curtis, Ken
Curtis, Tony
Curtis-Hall, Vondie
Cusack, Cyril
Cusack, John
Cushing, Peter
Cushman, Charlotte
    Saunders
Cushman, Pauline
Cwiklinska, Mieczyslawa
D'Abo, Maryam
Dafoe, Willem
Dagmar
Dagover, Lil
Dahl, Arlene
Dailey, Dan
Dailey, Irene
Dale, Jim
Dall, John
Dalton, Abby
Dalton, Charles
Dalton, Timothy
Daly, Arnold
Daly, James
Daly, Timothy
Daly, Tyne
Damita, Lily
Damon, Cathryn
Damon, Stuart
Dana, Bill
Dana, Viola
Dandridge, Dorothy
Dandridge, Ruby Jean
Danes, Claire
Danforth, William
D'Angelo, Beverly
Daniell, Henry
Daniels, Bebe
Daniels, Frank
Daniels, Jeff
Daniels, Mickey
Daniels, William
Danner, Blythe Katharine
Danson, Ted
Dantine, Helmut
Danton, Ray(mond)
Danza, Tony
Darby, Kim
Darcel, Denise
Darin, Bobby
Darnell, Linda (Monetta
    Eloyse)
Darren, James
Darrieux, Danielle
Darro, Frankie
Darrow, Henry
Darvas, Lili
Darvi, Bella
Darwell, Jane
DaSilva, Howard
Dauphin, Claude Le Grand
    Maria Eugene
Davenport, Eva
Davenport, Fanny Lily
    Gypsy
Davenport, Harry George
    Bryant
Davenport, Nigel

Davidovich, Lolita
Davidson, Jaye
Davidson, John
Davidson, Tommy
Davies, Marion
Davies, Rupert
Davis, Ann Bradford
Davis, Bette
Davis, Brad
Davis, Clifton
Davis, Geena
Davis, Jim
Davis, Joan
Davis, Judy
Davis, Mac
Davis, Ossie
Davis, Patti
Davis, Sammi
Davis, Sammy, Jr.
Davison, Bruce
Dawber, Pam
Dawn, Hazel
Day, Dennis
Day, Doris
Day, Laraine
Dayan, Assaf
Day-Lewis, Daniel
    Michael Blake
Deacon, Richard
Dean, Basil
Dean, James Byron
Dean, Laura
DeCamp, Rosemary
DeCaprio, Leonardo
DeCarlo, Yvonne
DeCordoba, Pedro
Dee, Frances
Dee, Ruby
Dee, Sandra
DeFore, Don
DeForest, Calvert
DeGeneres, Ellen
DeHaven, Gloria
DeHavilland, Olivia Mary
Dehner, John Forkum
Dekker, Albert
Delany, Dana
Dell, Gabriel
Delmar, Kenny
Delon, Alain
DelRio, Dolores
DeLuise, Dom
DeMarco, Tony
Demarest, William
DeMornay, Rebecca
Dempster, Carol
Dench, Judith Olivia
Deneuve, Catherine
DeNiro, Robert
Dennehy, Brian
Denning, Richard
Dennis, Sandy
Denny, Reginald Leigh
Denver, Bob
Denver, John
Depardieu, Gerard
Depp, Johnny
Derek, Bo
Derek, John
Dern, Bruce MacLeish
Dern, Laura Elizabeth
DeSica, Vittorio
Desmond, Johnny
Desmond, William
Devane, William
Devine, Andy

DeVito, Danny
Dewaere, Patrick
Dewhurst, Colleen
DeWilde, Brandon
DeWitt, Joyce
DeWolfe, Billy
Dey, Susan Hallock
De Young, Cliff
Diamond, Neil
Diamond, Selma
DiCaprio, Leonardo
Dickinson, Angie
Dietrich, Marlene
Digges, Dudley
Dillman, Bradford
Dillon, Kevin
Dillon, Matt
Dillon, Melinda
Dillon, Mia
Divine
Dix, Richard
Dixon, Ivan
Dixon, Jean
Dobson, Kevin
Doggett, Thomas
Doherty, Shannen
Donahue, Elinor
Donahue, Troy
Donald, James
Donald, Peter
Donat, Robert
Donlevy, Brian
Donnell, Jeff
Donnelly, Ruth
Donohue, Jack
Donovan, King
Doohan, James
  Montgomery
Dooley, Rae
Dorleac, Francoise
Dors, Diana
D'Orsay, Fifi
Douglas, Donna
Douglas, Kirk
Douglas, Melvyn
Douglas, Michael Kirk
Douglas, Paul
Dourif, Brad
Dow, Tony
Dowling, Eddie
Down, Lesley-Anne
Downey, Robert, Jr.
Downs, Johnny
Doyle, David (Fitzgerald)
Doyle, Jill
Drake, Alfred
Drake, Betsy
Drake, Tom
Draper, Ruth
Drescher, Fran
Dresser, Louise
Dressler, Marie
Drew, John
Drew, Louisa Lane
Dreyfuss, Richard
  (Stephan)
Driscoll, Bobby
Dru, Joanne
Drury, James
Dryer, Fred
Duchovny, David
Duel, Peter
Duff, Howard
Duff, Mary Ann Dyke
Duffy, Julia
Duffy, Karen

Duffy, Patrick
Duggan, Andrew
Dukakis, Olympia
Duke, Bill
Duke, Patty
Dukes, David
Dullea, Keir
DuMaurier, Gerald Hubert,
  Sir
Dumke, Ralph
Dumont, Margaret
Dunaway, Faye
Duncan, Augustin
Duncan, Sandy
Dunn, James Howard
Dunn, Michael
Dunne, Dominique
Dunne, Griffin
Dunne, Irene Marie
Dunnock, Mildred
Dupree, Minnie
Durang, Christopher
  Ferdinand
Durbin, Deanna
Durning, Charles
Duryea, Dan
Duse, Eleanora
Dussault, Nancy Elizabeth
Dutton, Charles S
Duvall, Robert (Selden)
Duvall, Shelley
Dvorak, Ann
Dysart, Richard (Allan)
Eagels, Jeanne
Eastwood, Clint
Eaton, Mary
Eaton, Shirley
Ebsen, Buddy
Eddy, Nelson
Edelman, Herb
Eden, Barbara
Edeson, Robert
Edwards, Alan
Edwards, Anthony
Edwards, Cliff
Edwards, Vince(nt)
Efron, Marshall
Egan, Richard
Egg, Augustus Leopold
Eggar, Samantha
Eggerth, Marta
Eichhorn, Lisa
Eikenberry, Jill
Ekberg, Anita
Ekhof, Konrad
Ekland, Britt
Elam, Jack
Elder, Ruth
Eldridge, Florence
Elizondo, Hector
Elliott, Denholm Mitchell
Elliott, Gertrude
Elliott, Maxine
Elliott, Sam
Ellis, Robin
Ellsler, Effie
Eltinge, Julian
Elvira
Ely, Ron
Emerson, Faye Margaret
Emerson, Hope
Engel, Georgia Bright
Englund, Robert
Epstein, Alvin
Erickson, Leif
Errol, Leon

Erwin, Stuart
Esmond, Jill
Esposito, Giancarlo
  (Giusseppi)
Essex, David
Estevez, Emilio
Estrada, Erik
Estrada, Joseph (Marcelo
  Ejercito)
Evans, Bob
Evans, Dale
Evans, Edith Mary Booth,
  Dame
Evans, Linda
Evans, Madge
Evans, Maurice
Evans, Mike
Evelyn, Judith
Everett, Chad
Evers, Jason
Evigan, Greg(ory Ralph)
Ewell, Tom
Fabares, Shelley Michelle
  Marie
Fabian
Fabray, Nanette
Fabrizi, Aldo
Fagerbakke, Bill
Fairbanks, Douglas
Fairbanks, Douglas, Jr.
Fairchild, Morgan
Faith, Adam
Faithfull, Marianne
Falconetti, Renee Maria
Falk, Peter
Farentino, James
Farina, Dennis
Farley, Chris
Farmer, Frances
Farmer, Gary Dale
Farnsworth, Richard
Farnum, Dustin Lancy
Farnum, William
Farr, Felicia
Farr, Jamie
Farrell, Charles
Farrell, Glenda
Farrell, Mike
Farrow, Mia
Fassbinder, Rainer Werner
Faulk, John Henry
Faust, Lotta
Faustino, David
Faversham, William
  Alfred
Fawcett, Farrah Leni
Fawcett, George
Fay, Frank
Faye, Alice
Faye, Joey
Faylen, Frank
Fazenda, Louise
Feld, Fritz
Feldman, Corey
Feldman, Marty
Feldon, Barbara
Feldshuh, Tovah
Fell, Norman
Fellows, Edith
Felsenstein, Walter
Felton, Verna
Fenn, Sherilyn
Fenton, Leslie
Ferguson, Elsie
Ferguson, Jay R
Fernandel

Ferrell, Conchata Galen
Ferrer, Jose Vicente
Ferrer, Mel(chor Gaston)
Ferrigno, Lou
Ferris, Barbara Gillian
Fetchit, Stepin
Fickett, Mary
Field, Betty
Field, Kate
Field, Sally Margaret
Field, Virginia (Margaret
  Cynthia St. John)
Fields, Kim
Fields, Stanley
Fiennes, Ralph
Fierstein, Harvey (Forbes)
Finch, Jon
Finch, Peter
Fine, Larry
Finlay, Frank
Finney, Albert
Fiorentino, Linda
Firth, Peter
Fishburne, Laurence
Fisher, Carrie Frances
Fisher, Clara
Fisher, Gail
Fishman, Michael
Fiske, Minnie Maddern
Fitzgerald, Barry
Fitzgerald, Geraldine
Fix, Paul
Flaherty, Joe
Flanders, Ed
Flanders, Michael
Flannery, Susan
Fleming, Erin
Fleming, Ian
Fleming, Rhonda
Fletcher, Bramwell
Fletcher, Louise
Flippen, Jay C
Flockhart, Calista
Florence, William Jermyn
Flynn, Errol
Flynn, Joe
Flynn, Sean
Fo, Dario
Foch, Nina
Fonda, Bridget
Fonda, Henry Jaynes
Fonda, Jane
Fonda, Peter
Fontaine, Joan
Fontanne, Lynn
Foote, Samuel
Foran, Dick John Nicholas
Forbes, Ralph
Forbes-Robertson,
  Johnston, Sir
Ford, Constance
Ford, Glenn
Ford, Harrison
Ford, Paul
Ford, Ruth Elizabeth
Ford, Steven Meigs
Ford, Wallace
Forrest, Edwin
Forrest, Steve
Forster, Robert
Forsyth, Rosemary
Forsythe, Henderson
Forsythe, John
Foster, Jodie
Foster, Julia
Foster, Preston

Foster, Susanna
Fox, Edward
Fox, James
Fox, Michael J.
Fox, Vivica A.
Foxworth, Robert
Foxworthy, Jeff
Foxx, Jamie
Foxx, Redd
Foy, Eddie
Foy, Eddie, Jr.
Franciosa, Anthony
Francis, Anne
Francis, Arlene
Francis, Genie
Francis, Kay
Franciscus, James Grover
Franken, Al
Franklin, Bonnie Gail
Franklin, Irene
Franklin, Pamela
Frann, Mary
Franz, Arthur
Franz, Dennis
Franz, Eduard
Frawley, William
Frederick, Pauline
Freed, Bert
Freeman, Al(bert
   Cornelius), Jr.
Freeman, Morgan
Frelich, Phyllis
French, Victor
Friebus, Florida
Friganza, Trixie
Frisco, Joe
Frobe, Gerd
Froman, Jane
Fugard, Athol
Fuller, Robert
Fulton, Maude
Funicello, Annette
Furness, Betty
Fyffe, Will
Gabel, Martin
Gabin, Jean
Gable, Clark
Gabor, Eva
Gabor, Magda
Gabor, Zsa Zsa
Gail, Max(well
   Trowbridge, Jr.)
Gaines, Boyd
Gallagher, Helen
Gallagher, Richard
Galloway, Don
Gam, Rita Elenore
Garbo, Greta
Garcia, Andy
Garcia Vargas, Joaquin
Gardenia, Vincent
Gardiner, Reginald
Gardner, Ava
Garfield, John
Garfunkel, Art(hur)
Gargan, William
Garland, Beverly
Garland, Judy
Garner, James
Garner, Peggy Ann
Garnett, Gale
Garofalo, Janeane
Garr, Teri Ann
Garrett, Betty
Garrett, Joy
Garrett, Leif

Garrick, David
Garrison, David
Garson, Greer
Garth, Jennie
Garver, Kathy
Gassman, Vittorio
Gates, Larry
Gautier, Dick
Gavin, John Anthony
   Golenor
Gaxton, William
Gaynor, Janet
Gazzara, Ben
Geary, Anthony
Geary, Cynthia
Geddes, Barbara Bel
Geer, Will
Geeson, Judy
Geldof, Bob
Genn, Leo
Gentry, Minnie Lee
George, Christopher
George, Dan, Chief
George, Gladys
George, Grace
George, Lynda Day
George, Susan
Gerard, Gil
Geray, Steven
Gere, Richard
Gersten, Berta
Gerussi, Bruno
Getty, Estelle
Ghostley, Alice
Giannini, Giancarlo
Gibbs, Marla Bradley
Gibson, Henry
Gibson, Hoot
Gibson, Mel
Gielgud, (Arthur) John, Sir
Gift, Roland
Gilbert, Billy
Gilbert, John
Gilbert, Melissa
Gilbert, Sara
Gilford, Jack
Gillette, William Hooker
Gilmore, Virginia
Gilpin, Charles Sidney
Gilstrap, Suzy
Gingold, Hermione
   Ferdinanda
Girardot, Annie
Gish, Dorothy
Gish, Lillian (Diana)
Givens, Robin
Glaser, Paul Michael
Glass, Ron
Gleason, Jackie
Gleason, James
Gleason, Joanna
Gleason, Lucille
Glenn, Scott
Gless, Sharon
Glover, Danny
Glover, Julian
Goddard, Paulette
Godfrey, Arthur Michael
Godunov, Alexander
Goldberg, Whoopi
Goldblum, Jeff
Golonka, Arlene
Gomez, Thomas
Gong Li
Goodeve, Grant
Goodfriend, Lynda

Gooding, Cuba, Jr.
Goodman, Dody
Goodman, John
Goodwin, Bill
Goodwin, Nat C
Goranson, Lecy
Gorcey, Leo
Gordon, C Henry
Gordon, Gale
Gordon, Kitty
Gordon, Ruth
Gordon, Vera
Gorin, Igor
Goring, Marius
Gorman, Cliff
Gorshin, Frank John
Gortner, Marjoe (Hugh
   Ross)
Gossett, Louis, Jr.
Gottschalk, Ferdinand
Gould, Elliott
Goulet, Robert Gerard
Grable, Betty
Grady, Don
Graham, Ronny
Graham, Virginia
Grahame, Gloria
Grahame, Margot
Grammer, Kelsey
Grandy, Fred(erick
   Lawrence)
Granger, Farley
Granger, Stewart
Grant, Cary
Grant, Hugh
Grant, Kirby
Grant, Lee
Grant, Rodney A
Granville, Bonita
Grapewin, Charley
Grassle, Karen Gene
Graves, Peter
Gray, Coleen
Gray, Dolores
Gray, Dulcie
Gray, Gilda
Gray, Linda
Grayson, Kathryn
Greaza, Walter N
Green, Abel
Green, Brian Austin
Green, Martyn
Green, Mitzi
Greene, Graham
Greene, Lorne
Greene, Richard
Greene, Shecky
Greenstreet, Sydney
   Hughes
Greenwood, Charlotte
Greenwood, Joan
Greer, Jane
Gregory, James
Gregson, John
Grenfell, Joyce Irene
Grey, Jennifer
Grey, Joel
Grey, Virginia
Grier, David Allen
Grier, Pam(ela Suzette)
Grier, Rosey
Griffith, Andy
Griffith, Corinne
Griffith, D(avid Lewelyn)
   W(ark)
Griffith, Hugh Emrys

Griffith, Melanie
Grillo, John
Grimes, Tammy Lee
Grizzard, George
Grodin, Charles
Groh, David Lawrence
Gross, Michael
Guardino, Harry
Guillaume, Robert
Guinan, Texas
Guinness, Alec, Sir
Guitry, Sacha
Gulager, Clu
Gunn, Moses
Gurie, Sigrid
Gustafson, Karin
Guttenberg, Steve
Guy, Jasmine
Gwenn, Edmund
Gwilym, Mike
Gwyn, Nell
Gwynne, Fred
Hack, Shelley
Hackett, Joan
Hackett, Raymond
Hackman, Gene
Hadley, Reed
Hagen, Jean
Hagen, Uta Thyra
Haggerty, Dan
Hagman, Larry
Haid, Charles
Haigh, Kenneth
Haines, Robert Terrel
Haines, William
Hale, Alan
Hale, Alan, Jr.
Hale, Barbara
Haley, Jack
Hall, Anthony Thomas
   Charles
Hall, Arsenio
Hall, Deidre
Hall, Huntz
Hall, Juanita
Halop, Billy
Halop, Florence
Hamel, Veronica
Hamer, Rusty
Hamill, Mark
Hamilton, Carrie
Hamilton, George, IV
Hamilton, Linda
Hamilton, Margaret
   Brainard
Hamilton, Murray
Hamilton, Nancy
Hamilton, Neil
Hamilton, Patrick
Hamlin, Harry Robinson
Hampden, Walter
Hampshire, Susan
Hampton, Hope
Hampton, James
Hanks, Tom
Hannah, Daryl
Harding, Ann
Hardison, Kadeem
Hardwicke, Cedric
   Webster, Sir
Hare, John, Sir
Harewood, Dorian
Harlow, Jean
Harmon, Mark
Harper, Tess
Harper, Valerie

Jones, Jennifer	Kempson, Rachel	Ladd, Cheryl	LeBlanc, Matt
Jones, Preston St. Vrain	Kendal, Felicity	Ladd, Diane	Lecouvreur, Adrienne
Jones, Shirley	Kendal, Madge, Dame	Lahr, Bert	Lederer, Francis
Jones, Terry	Kendal, William Hunter	Lahti, Christine	Lee, Bernard
Jones, Tommy Lee	Kendall, Kay	Laine, Cleo	Lee, Brandon
Jordan, Bobby	Kennedy, Arthur	Lake, Arthur	Lee, Bruce
Jordan, Richard	Kennedy, Edgar	Lake, Ricki	Lee, Canada
Jory, Victor	Kennedy, George	Lake, Veronica	Lee, Christopher Frank
Joslyn, Allyn Morgan	Kennedy, Jayne Harrison	LaMarr, Barbara	Carandini
Jourdan, Louis	Kennedy, Madge	Lamarr, Hedy	Lee, Dixie
Jouvet, Louis	Kennedy, Tom	Lamas, Fernando	Lee, Joie
Joy, Leatrice	Kercheval, Ken	Lamas, Lorenzo	Lee, Lila
Joyce, Alice	Kerns, Joanna	Lamb, Gil	Lee, Michele
Joyce, Elaine	Kerr, Deborah	Lambert, Christopher	Lee, Pamela
Joyce, Peggy Hopkins	Kerr, John	Lamour, Dorothy	Lee, Peggy
Judd, Ashley	Kert, Larry	Lampert, Zohra	Lee, Spike
Julia, Raul	Kerwin, Lance	Lancaster, Burt(on	Lee, Will
Jump, Gordon	Keyes, Evelyn Louise	Stephen)	Le Gallienne, Eva
Jurado, Katy	Khambatta, Persis	Landau, Martin	Lehr, Lew
Jurgens, Curt	Kibbee, Guy	Landers, Audrey	Leibman, Ron
Justice, James Robertson	Kidder, Margot	Landers, Harry	Leigh, Janet
Kahn, Madeline (Gail)	Kidman, Nicole	Landers, Judy	Leigh, Jennifer Jason
Kallen, Kitty	Kiel, Richard	Landesberg, Steve	Leigh, Vivien
Kamen, Milt	Kiepura, Jan Wiktor	Landi, Elissa	Leighton, Laura
Kaminska, Ida	Kilbride, Percy	Landis, Carole	Leighton, Margaret
Kanaly, Steve(n Francis)	Kiley, Richard (Paul)	Landis, Jessie Royce	Lembeck, Harvey
Kane, Carol	Kilgour, Joseph	Landon, Michael	Lemmon, Jack
Kane, Helen	Kilian, Victor	Lane, Abbe	Lemmons, Kasi
Kaplan, Gabe	Kilmer, Val	Lane, Diane	Lemoyne, W(illiam) J
Kaprisky, Valerie	Kimbrough, Charles	Lane, Lola	Lenska, Rula
Karlen, John	King, Alan	Lane, Nathan	Lenya, Lotte
Karloff, Boris	King, Cammie	Lane, Priscilla	Lenz, Kay
Karn, Richard	King, Charles	Lane, Rosemary	Leon, Kenny
Karras, Alex(ander G)	King, Dennis	Langan, Glenn	Leonard, Eddie
Kasznar, Kurt	King, Morganna	Langdon, Harry	Leonard, Sheldon
Katt, William	King, Perry	Lange, Hope Elise Ross	Leoni, Tea
Kaufman, Andy	King, Yolanda Denise	Lange, Jessica	Leontovich, Eugenie
Kavner, Julie Deborah	Kingsley, Ben	Lange, Ted	Lepage, Robert
Kay, Dianne	Kinski, Klaus	Langella, Frank	Leslie, Joan
Kaye, Danny	Kinski, Nastassja	Langford, Frances	Lester, Mark
Kaye, Nora	Kirby, Durward	Langtry, Lillie	Levene, Sam
Kaye, Stubby	Kirk, Phyllis	Lansbury, Angela Brigid	Lewis, Emmanuel
Kazan, Lainie	Klein, Robert	Lansing, Joi	Lewis, Joe E
Keach, Stacy, Sr.	Klemperer, Werner	Lansing, Robert	Lewis, Juliette
Keach, Stacy, Jr.	Kline, Kevin Delaney	Lanza, Mario	Lewis, Richard
Kean, Edmund	Klugman, Jack	LaPlante, Laura	Light, Judith Ellen
Keaton, Buster	Knight, Shirley	Lapotaire, Jane	Lincoln, Abbey
Keaton, Diane	Knight, Ted	LaRocque, Rod	Lincoln, Elmo
Keaton, Michael	Knight, Wayne	Larroquette, John	Linden, Hal
Keel, Howard	Knotts, Don	(Bernard)	Lindfors, Viveca
Keeler, Ruby	Knowles, Patric	LaRue, Jack	Lindley, Audra
Keenan, Frank	Knox, Alexander	LaSalle, Eriq	Lindo, Delroy
Keene, Laura	Koenig, Walter	Lasser, Louise	Lindsay, Howard
Keene, Thomas Wallace	Kohler, Fred, Sir	Laughlin, Tom	Lindsay, Margaret
Keitel, Harvey	Kohner, Susan	Laughton, Charles	Linville, Larry Lavon
Keith, Brian	Kollmar, Richard	Lauper, Cyndi	Liotta, Ray
Keith, David Lemuel	Kopell, Bernie	Laurel, Stan	Lipman, Clara
Keith, Ian	Kornman, Mary	Lauria, Dan	Lipton, Peggy
Kellaway, Cecil	Kotto, Yaphet Frederick	Laurie, Piper	Lisi, Virna
Keller, Marthe	Kovacs, Ernie	Lavin, Linda	Liston, Sonny
Kellerman, Annette	Kramm, Joseph	Law, John Phillip	Lithgow, John (Arthur)
Kellerman, Sally Claire	Krauss, Werner	Lawford, Peter	Little, Cleavon Jake
Kelley, DeForest	Kreuger, Kurt	Lawless, Lucy	Livesey, Roger
Kelley, Sheila	Krige, Alice	Lawrence, Carol	Livingston, Barry
Kellin, Mike	Kristel, Sylvia	Lawrence, Florence	Livingston, Stanley
Kelly, Gene	Kristofferson, Kris	Lawrence, Gertrude	Lloyd, Christopher
Kelly, Grace Patricia	Kruger, Hardy	Lawrence, Joey	Lloyd, Harold
Kelly, Jack	Kruger, Otto	Lawrence, Margaret	Locke, Sondra
Kelly, Nancy	Kudrow, Lisa	Lawrence, Martin	Lockhart, Calvin
Kelly, Paul	Kuehl, Sheila James	Lawrence, Steve	Lockhart, Gene
Kelly, Walter C	Kulp, Nancy Jane	Lawrence, Vicki Ann	Lockhart, June
Kelsey, Linda	Kurtz, Swoosie	Lawson, Leigh	Locklear, Heather
Kelton, Pert	Kwan, Nancy Kashen	Leachman, Cloris	Lockwood, Gary
Kemble, Charles	LaBelle, Patti	Learned, Michael	Lockwood, Margaret Mary
Kemble, Fanny	Lackey, Kenneth	Leary, Denis	Loden, Barbara Ann
Kemble, John Philip	Ladd, Alan	Leaud, Jean-Pierre	Loder, John

Milano, Alyssa
Miles, Bernard, Sir
Miles, Elaine
Miles, Sarah
Miles, Vera
Milford, Penny
Milhaud, Darius
Milland, Ray(mond Alton)
Miller, Ann
Miller, Barry
Miller, Henry John
Miller, Jason
Miller, Joe
Miller, Marilyn
Mills, Alley
Mills, Donna
Mills, Hayley
Mills, John, Sir
Mills, Juliet
Mills, Stephanie
Milner, Martin Sam
Mimieux, Yvette Carmen
M
Mineo, Sal(vatore)
Minnelli, Liza
Miranda, Carmen
Mirren, Helen
Mitchell, Cameron
Mitchell, Grant
Mitchell, Margaret Julia
Mitchell, Millard
Mitchell, Thomas
Mitchum, Robert
Mix, Tom
Mobley, Mary Ann
Modine, Matthew
Modjeska, Helena
Moffat, Donald
Moliere
Molinaro, Al
Monroe, Marilyn
Montalban, Ricardo
Montana, Bull
Montand, Yves
Montez, Maria
Montgomery, Belinda
Montgomery, Elizabeth
Montgomery, George
Montgomery, Robert
Henry
Moody, Ron
Moore, Clayton
Moore, Colleen
Moore, Constance
Moore, Demi
Moore, Dick(ie)
Moore, Dudley Stuart
John
Moore, Julianne
Moore, Mary Tyler
Moore, Melba
Moore, Roger George
Moore, Terry
Moore, Tom
Moore, Victor
Moorehead, Agnes
Morales, Esai
Moran, Erin
Moran, George
More, Kenneth Gilbert
Moreau, Jeanne
Moreno, Rita
Morgan, Dennis
Morgan, Frank
Morgan, Harry
Morgan, Helen Riggins

Morgan, Michele
Morgan, Ralph
Morgan, Terence
Moriarty, Cathy
Moriarty, Michael
Morison, Patricia
Morita, Pat
Morley, Robert
Morris, Chester
Morris, Clara
Morris, Greg
Morris, Howard
Morris, Wayne
Morrow, Rob
Morrow, Vic
Morse, Barry
Morse, Robert Alan
Morton, Joe
Moss, Arnold
Most, Donny
Mostel, Zero
Moten, Etta
Mowbray, Alan
Muir, Jean
Muldaur, Diana Charlton
Mulhall, Jack
Mulhare, Edward
Mulhern, Matt
Mull, Martin
Mullavey, Greg
Mulligan, Richard
Muni, Paul
Munshin, Jules
Munson, Ona
Murphy, Audie
Murphy, Ben(jamin
Edward)
Murphy, Eddie
Murphy, George Lloyd
Murphy, Rosemary
Murray, Bill
Murray, Don(ald Patrick)
Murray, Ken
Murray, Mae
Myers, Mike
Nabors, Jim
Nader, George
Nader, Michael
Nagel, Conrad
Naish, J(oseph) Carrol
Naldi, Nita
Nance, Jack
Nash, George Frederick
Natwick, Mildred
Naughton, David
Nazimova, Alla
Neagle, Anna, Dame
Neal, Patricia
Neeson, Liam
Neff, Hildegarde
Negri, Pola
Nelligan, Kate
Nelson, Barry
Nelson, Craig T
Nelson, David
Nelson, Ed(win Stafford)
Nelson, Gene
Nelson, Harriet
Nelson, Judd
Nelson, Ozzie
Nelson, Rick
Nelson, Tracy
Nero, Franco
Nesbit, Evelyn
Nesbitt, Cathleen Mary
Nethersole, Olga

Nettleton, Lois June
Neuwirth, Bebe
Neville, John
Newhart, Bob
Newley, Anthony
(George)
Newman, Barry Foster
Newman, Paul
Newman, Phyllis
Newmar, Julie
Newton, Christopher
Newton, Robert
Newton-John, Olivia
Ney, Richard
Ngor, Haing S
Nicholas, Denise
Nichols, Nichelle
Nicholson, Jack
Nielsen, Leslie
Nielson, Brigitte
Nilsson, Anna Q(uerentia)
Nimoy, Leonard
Niven, David
Nolan, Jeanette
Nolan, Kathy
Nolan, Lloyd
Nolte, Nick
Noone, Kathleen
Norman, Maidie (Ruth)
Normand, Mabel
Norris, Christopher
Norris, Chuck
North, Jay
North, Sheree
Norton, Jack
Norton-Taylor, Judy
Norwich, Diana (Manners)
Cooper, Viscountess
Norworth, Jack
Nouri, Michael
Novak, Kim
Novarro, Ramon
Novello, Ivor
Noyes, Blanche Wilcox
Nugent, Edward
Nuyen, France
Nype, Russell
Oakie, Jack
Oakland, Simon
Oates, Warren
Ober, Philip (Nott)
Oberon, Merle
O'Brian, Hugh
O'Brien, Edmond
O'Brien, George
O'Brien, Margaret
O'Brien, Pat
O'Brien-Moore, Erin
O'Connell, Arthur
O'Connell, Hugh
O'Connor, Carroll
O'Connor, Kevin
O'Connor, Una
O'Day, Dawn
O'Donnell, Cathy
O'Donnell, Chris
O'Donnell, Rosie
O'Driscoll, Martha
Ogilvy, Ian
O'Hara, Jill
O'Hara, Maureen
O'Herlihy, Dan
O'Keefe, Dennis
O'Keefe, Walter
Olaf, Pierre
Oland, Warner

Oldman, Gary
Olin, Ken
Oliver, Edna May
Olivier, Laurence Kerr, Sir
Olmos, Edward James
Olsen, Ashley Fuller
Olsen, Mary Kate
Olsen, Merlin Jay
Olson, Nancy
O'Malley, J Pat
O'Neal, Frederick
O'Neal, Patrick
O'Neal, Ron
O'Neal, Ryan
O'Neal, Tatum
O'Neill, Ed
O'Neill, James
O'Neill, Jennifer
Ontkean, Michael
Opatoshu, David
Orbach, Jerry
Ormond, Julia (Karin)
Ortega, Santos
O'Shea, Michael
O'Shea, Milo
Osmond, Ken
Osterwald, Bibi
O'Sullivan, Maureen
O'Toole, Peter
Ouspenskaya, Maria
Overman, Lynne
Owen, (John) Reginald
Owens, Gary
Oxenberg, Catherine
Pacino, Al(fredo James)
Page, Geraldine
Pagett, Nicola
Paige, Janis
Paige, Robert (John
Arthur)
Palance, Jack
Palillo, Ron
Palin, Michael
Pallette, Eugene
Palmer, Betsy
Palmer, Lilli
Palmer, Peter
Palminteri, Chazz
Paltrow, Gwyneth
Pangborn, Franklin
Papas, Irene
Paris, Jerry
Parker, Cecil
Parker, Eleanor
Parker, Fess
Parker, Jameson
Parker, Jean
Parker, Sarah Jessica
Parkins, Barbara
Parks, Bert
Parks, Larry
Parks, Michael
Parsons, Estelle
Parton, Dolly (Rebecca)
Pastor, Tony
Patinkin, Mandy
Patrick, Gail
Patrick, Lee
Patterson, Lorna
Patterson, Melody
Patterson, Neva
Pavan, Marisa
Pavarotti, Luciano
Paxinou, Katina
Paxton, Bill
Payne, Allen

Payne, John
Payne, John Howard
Payton-Wright, Pamela
Pearce, Alice
Peary, Harold
Peck, Gregory
Peete, Holly Robinson
Peller, Clara
Pena, Elizabeth
Pendleton, Austin
Pendleton, Nat
Penn, Sean
Pennington, Ann
Peppard, George
Perez, Rosie
Perkins, Anthony
Perkins, Millie
Perkins, Osgood
Perlman, Rhea
Perlman, Ron
Perrine, Valerie
Perry, Antoinette
Perry, Luke
Perry, Matthew
Perryman, Jill
Persoff, Nehemiah
Pesci, Joe
Pescow, Donna
Peters, Bernadette
Peters, Brandon
Peters, Brock
Peters, Jean
Peters, Susan
Petersen, Paul
Pettet, Joanna
Pfeiffer, Michelle
Philipe, Gerard
Phillips, Chynna
Phillips, Lou Diamond
Phillips, MacKenzie
Phillips, Michelle Gillam
Phillips, Robin
Phillips, Sian
Phoenix, River
Piazza, Marguerite
Pickens, Slim
Pickett, Cindy
Pickford, Jack
Pickford, Mary
Picon, Molly
Pidgeon, Walter
Pierce, David Hyde
Pinchot, Bronson Alcott
Pinero, Miguel
Pinkett, Jada
Pinsent, Gordon Edward
Pious, Minerva
Pisier, Marie-France
Pitt, Brad
Pitts, Zasu
Place, Mary Kay
Pleasence, Donald
Pleshette, John
Pleshette, Suzanne
Plowright, Joan Anne
Plummer, Amanda
Plummer, (Arthur)
    Christopher
Podesta, Rossana
Poitier, Sidney
Pollard, Michael J
Porizkova, Paulina
Porter, Don
Porter, Eric Richard
Porter, Nyree Dawn
Portman, Eric

Poston, Tom
Potts, Annie
Powell, Dick
Powell, Eleanor
Powell, Jane
Powell, Robert
Powell, William
Power, Tyrone
Power, Tyrone, Jr.
Power, Tyrone William
    Grattan
Powers, Stefanie
Premice, Josephine
Prentiss, Paula
Presle, Micheline
Presley, Elvis Aaron
Presley, Priscilla Ann
    Beaulieu
Presnell, Harve
Pressman, David
Preston, Robert
Price, Dennis
Price, Nancy
Price, Vincent
Priestly, Jason
Prince, Faith
Prince, William
Principal, Victoria
Pringle, Aileen
Printemps, Yvonne
Prinze, Freddie
Prosky, Robert Joseph
Prouty, Jed
Provine, Dorothy Michele
Prowse, Juliet
Pryor, Nicholas
Pryor, Richard (Franklin
    Lennox Thomas)
Pryor, Roger
Pulliam, Keisha Knight
Pully, B S
Purcell, Lee
Purdom, Edmund
Purl, Linda
Purviance, Edna
Pyle, Denver
Quaid, Dennis William
Quaid, Randy
Qualen, John Mandt
Quayle, Anna
Quayle, (John) Anthony,
    Sir
Quillan, Eddie
Quine, Richard
Quinlan, Kathleen
Quinn, Anthony Rudolph
    Oaxaca
Rachel
Rae, Charlotte
Rafferty, Chips
Raffin, Deborah
Raft, George
Ragland, Rags
Raimu
Rainer, Luise
Raines, Cristina
Raines, Ella
Rains, Claude
Ralph, Sheryl Lee
Ralston, Esther
Ralston, Vera
Rambeau, Marjorie
Rambo, Dack
Rampling, Charlotte
Ramsey, Anne
Randall, Tony

Randle, Theresa
Rankin, Arthur
Rashad, Phylicia
Rathbone, Basil
Ratoff, Gregory
Ratzenberger, John Dezso
Rawlinson, Herbert
Ray, Aldo
Ray, Charles
Raymond, Gene
Reardon, John
Redford, Robert
Redgrave, Corin
Redgrave, Lynn
Redgrave, Michael
    Scudamore, Sir
Redgrave, Vanessa
Redman, Joyce
Reed, Alan
Reed, Donna
Reed, Oliver
Reed, Robert
Reems, Harry
Rees, Roger
Reese, Della
Reese, Mason
Reeve, Christopher
Reeves, George
Reeves, Keanu
Reeves, Steve
Rehan, Ada
Reid, Beryl
Reid, Elliott
Reid, Kate
Reid, Tim
Reid, Wallace Eugene
Reiner, Carl
Reiner, Rob(ert)
Reinhold, Judge
Reinking, Ann H
Reiser, Paul
Remick, Lee
Renaldo, Duncan
Renaud, Madeleine
Rennie, Michael
Reuben, Gloria
Reubens, Paul
Revere, Anne
Revill, Clive Selsby
Rey, Alejandro
Rey, Fernando
Reynolds, Burt
Reynolds, Debbie (Marie
    Frances)
Reynolds, Marjorie
Reynolds, William
Rhames, (Ir)ving
Rhodes, Erik
Rhodes, Hari
Ribeiro, Alfonso
Rice, Thomas Dartmouth
Rice-Davies, Mandy
Rich, Adam
Rich, Irene
Richards, Lloyd George
Richards, Michael
Richardson, Lee
Richardson, Miranda
Richardson, Natasha
Richardson, Ralph David,
    Sir
Richardson, Susan
Richman, Charles
Rigg, Diana
Ring, Blanche
Ringwald, Molly

Rippy, Rodney Allen
Risdon, Elizabeth
Ritchard, Cyril
Ritter, John(athan
    Southworth)
Ritter, Tex
Ritter, Thelma
Robards, Jason
Robards, Jason, Jr.
Robbins, Tim(othy
    Francis)
Roberts, Doris
Roberts, Eric
Roberts, Julia
Roberts, Pernell
Roberts, Rachel
Roberts, Tony
Robertson, Cliff
Robertson, Dale
Robeson, Paul Leroy
Robey, George, Sir
Robins, Elizabeth
Robinson, Bill
Robinson, Edward G
Robinson, Jay
Robson, Flora McKenzie,
    Dame
Robson, May
Rochon, Lela
Rock, Chris
Rogers, Buddy
Rogers, Roy
Rogers, Wayne
Rogers, Will, Jr.
Rogers, Will(iam Penn
    Adair)
Roker, Roxie
Roland, Gilbert
Roland, Ruth
Rolle, Esther
Rollins, Howard
    Ellsworth, Jr.
Roman, Ruth
Romero, Cesar
Rooney, Mickey
Rooney, Pat
Rorke, Hayden
Rosay, Francoise
Rose, George Walter
Roseanne
Rosenbloom, Maxie
Ross, Barney
Ross, Katharine
Ross, Marion
Rossellini, Isabella
Roth, Tim
Rounds, David
Roundtree, Richard
Rounseville, Robert Field
Rourke, Mickey
Rowell, Victoria (Lynn)
Rowlands, Gena
    (Catherine)
Royle, Selena
Rubens, Alma
Rubinstein, John Arthur
Rudd, Paul Ryan
Ruehl, Mercedes
Ruggles, Charles
Rule, Janice
Rumann, Sig(fried)
RuPaul
Rush, Barbara
Russell, Annie
Russell, Gail
Russell, Harold

Russell, Jane
Russell, Kurt (Von Vogel)
Russell, Lillian
Russell, Nipsey
Russell, Rosalind
Russell, Theresa
Rutherford, Ann
Rutherford, Margaret
Ruttan, Susan
Ryan, Irene Noblette
Ryan, Meg
Ryan, Peggy
Ryan, Robert (Bushnell)
Ryder, Alfred
Ryder, Winona
Sabu
Sagal, Katey
Saget, Bob
Saint, Eva Marie
Saint Jacques, Raymond
Saint James, Susan
Saint John, Betta
Saint John, Howard
Saint John, Jill
Sakall, S Z
Sale, Charles Partlow
Salmi, Albert
Salt, Jennifer
Samms, Emma
Sampson, Will, Jr.
Sand, Paul
Sanda, Dominique
Sanders, George
Sanders, Richard Kinard
Sanderson, Julia
Sandler, Adam
Sands, Diana Patricia
Sands, Dorothy
Sandy, Gary
Sanford, Isabel Gwendolyn
Sarandon, Chris
Sarandon, Susan
Sargent, Dick
Sarrazin, Michael
Saunders, Lori
Savage, Fred
Savage, John
Savalas, Telly
Savo, Jimmy
Saxon, John
Scala, Gia
Scarpelli, Glenn
Schafer, Natalie
Scheider, Roy Richard
Schell, Maria Margarethe
Schell, Maximilian
Schikaneder, Emanuel
Schildkraut, Joseph
Schildkraut, Rudolph
Schlamme, Martha
Schneider, John
Schneider, Maria
Schneider, Rob
Schneider, Romy
Schreiber, Avery
Schroder, Rick
Schwartz, Maurice
Schwarzenegger, Arnold Alois
Schwimmer, David
Scofield, Paul
Scott, George C(ampbell)
Scott, Gordon
Scott, Lizabeth
Scott, Martha Ellen

Scott, Pippa
Scott, Randolph
Scott, Zachary
Scourby, Alexander
Seagal, Steven
Seal, Elizabeth
Sears, Heather
Seberg, Jean
Sebring, Jay
Secombe, Harry
Seeley, Blossom
Segal, George
Segal, Vivienne
Seinfeld, Jerry
Selby, David
Seldes, Marian
Sellecca, Connie
Selleck, Tom
Sellers, Peter
Serrault, Michel
Seymour, Anne Eckert
Seymour, Dan
Seymour, Jane
Shabazz, Attallah
Shackelford, Ted
Sharif, Omar
Sharkey, Ray
Shatner, William
Shaughnessy, Mickey
Shaver, Helen
Shaw, Mary
Shaw, Robert
Shawn, Dick
Shawn, Wallace
Shea, John
Shean, Al
Shearer, Moira
Shearer, Norma
Sheedy, Ally
Sheen, Charlie
Sheen, Martin
Shelley, Carole Augusta
Shepard, Sam
Shepherd, Cybill (Lynne)
Shepherd, Jean Parker
Sheridan, Ann
Sheridan, Nicollette
Sherman, Bobby
Sherman, Lowell
Shields, Brooke
Shire, Talia Rose Coppola
Shirley, Anne
Shore, Dinah
Short, Martin
Show, Grant
Shue, Andrew
Shue, Elizabeth
Shukshin, Vasilii Makarovich
Shutta, Ethel
Siddons, Sarah Kemble
Sidney, Sylvia
Signoret, Simone Henrietta Charlotte
Sikking, James B
Sillman, Leonard
Sills, Milton
Silver, Ron
Silvera, Frank
Silverheels, Jay
Silverman, Jonathan
Silverstone, Alicia
Simmons, Jean
Simms, Hilda
Simon, Simone

Simpson, O(renthal) J(ames)
Sinatra, Frank
Sinbad
Sinclair, Madge
Sinden, Donald (Alfred)
Singleton, Penny
Sinise, Gary
Skelly, Hal
Skelton, Red
Skerritt, Tom
Skinner, Cornelia Otis
Skinner, Otis
Skipworth, Alison
Skulnik, Menasha
Slater, Christian
Slezak, Erika
Slezak, Walter
Sloane, Everett
Smart, Jack Scott
Smith, Alexis
Smith, Allison
Smith, Anna Deavere
Smith, C Aubrey
Smith, Jaclyn
Smith, Jada Pinkett
Smith, Kent
Smith, Loring
Smith, Maggie Natalie
Smith, Rex
Smith, Roger
Smith, Roger Guenveur
Smith, Samantha
Smith, Will
Smithers, Jan
Smithson, Harriet Constance
Smits, Jimmy
Snipes, Wesley
Snodgress, Carrie
Somers, Brett
Somers, Suzanne
Sommer, Elke
Sondergaard, Gale (Edith Holm)
Soo, Jack
Sorvino, Mira
Sorvino, Paul
Sothern, Ann
Soul, David
Soule, Olan
Spacek, Sissy
Spacey, Kevin
Spader, James
Spano, Joe
Sparks, Ned
Spelling, Tori
Spielberg, David
Springfield, Rick
Stack, Robert Langford
Stacy, James
Staller, Ilona
Stallone, Sylvester (Enzio)
Stamos, John
Stamp, Terence
Stander, Lionel (Jay)
Standing, Guy, Sir
Stang, Arnold
Stanislavsky, Konstantin Sergeyevich
Stanley, Kim
Stanwyck, Barbara
Stapleton, Jean
Stapleton, Maureen
Stark, Koo
Steel, Anthony

Steele, Bob
Steele, Tommy
Steenburgen, Mary
Steiger, Rod
Steinberg, David
Stephens, Robert, Sir
Stephenson, Henry
Sterling, Ford
Sterling, Jan
Sterling, Robert
Stevens, Andrew
Stevens, Connie
Stevens, Emily A
Stevens, Inger
Stevens, K T
Stevens, Mark
Stevens, Onslow
Stevens, Stella
Stevenson, McLean
Stevenson, Parker
Stewart, Anita
Stewart, Donald Ogden
Stewart, James (Maitland)
Stewart, Jon
Stewart, Patrick
Stewart, Paul
Stickney, Dorothy
Stiers, David Ogden
Stiller, Ben
Stiller, Jerry
Stockwell, Dean
Stockwell, Guy
Stone, Dorothy
Stone, Fred Andrew
Stone, Harold J
Stone, Lewis
Stone, Milburn
Stone, Sharon
Stoopnagle, Lemuel Q, Colonel
Storch, Larry
Storm, Gale
Stowe, Madeleine
Straight, Beatrice Whitney
Strasberg, Lee
Strasberg, Susan Elizabeth
Strassman, Marcia
Stratten, Dorothy
Strauss, Peter
Strauss, Robert
Streep, Meryl
Streisand, Barbra (Joan)
Stringfield, Sherry
Stritch, Elaine
Strode, Woody
Strudwick, Shepperd
Struthers, Sally Anne
Studi, Wes
Sullavan, Margaret
Sullivan, Barry
Sullivan, Francis Loftus
Sullivan, Susan
Sullivan, Tom
Susann, Jacqueline
Sutherland, Donald
Sutherland, Keifer
Sutton, John
Suzman, Janet
Suzuki, Pat
Swanson, Gloria May Josephine
Swayze, Patrick
Sweet, Blanche
Swenson, Inga
Swit, Loretta
Switzer, Carl

Syms, Sylvia
T, Mr.
Tabbert, William
Tabori, Kristoffer
Takei, George
Talbot, Lyle
Talma, Francois Joseph
Talmadge, Norma
Talman, William
Tamblyn, Russ
Tamiroff, Akim
Tandy, Jessica
Tanguay, Eva
Tarantino, Quentin
Tarasova, Alla
    Konstantinovna
Tashman, Lilyan
Tate, Larenz
Tate, Sharon
Tauber, Richard
Tayback, Vic
Taylor, Elizabeth
    Rosemond
Taylor, Estelle
Taylor, Kent
Taylor, Laurette
Taylor, Meshach
Taylor, Regina
Taylor, Robert
Taylor, Rod(ney)
Tempest, Marie
Templeton, Fay
Terris, Norma
Terry, Ellen Alicia, Dame
Terry-Thomas
Thaxter, Phyllis
Thayer, Tiffany Ellsworth
Thespis
Thicke, Alan
Thigpen Lynne
Thinnes, Roy
Thomas, Betty
Thomas, Billy
Thomas, Brandon
Thomas, Danny
Thomas, Henry
Thomas, Jonathan Taylor
Thomas, Marlo
Thomas, Philip Michael
Thomas, Richard Earl
Thompson, Emma
Thompson, Marshall
Thompson, Sada Carolyn
Thomson, Gordon
Thorndike, Sybil, Dame
Thornton, Billy Bob
Thulin, Ingrid
Thurman, Uma
Tibbett, Lawrence Mervil
Tiegs, Cheryl
Tierney, Gene
Tiffin, Pamela Kimberley
Tilly, Jennifer
Tilton, Charlene
Tobias, George
Todd, Ann
Todd, Richard
Todd, Thelma
Toler, Sidney
Tomei, Marisa
Tone, Franchot
Toomey, Regis
Topol, Chaim
Toren, Marta
Torn, Rip
Torrence, Ernest

Totter, Audrey
Townsend, Robert
Tozzi, Giorgio
Tracy, Lee
Tracy, Spencer
    Bonaventure
Trask, Diana
Travanti, Daniel J(ohn)
Travers, Bill
Travolta, John
Treacher, Arthur
Treas, Terri
Tree, Herbert Beerbohm
Tremayne, Les
Trevor, Claire
Trintignant, Jean-Louis
    Xavier
Tripp, Paul
Tripplehorn, Jean
Troup, Bobby
Trudell, John
Truex, Ernest
Tryon, Thomas
Tucker, Chris
Tucker, Forrest Meredith
Tucker, Lorenzo
Tucker, Richard
Tufts, Sonny
Tully, Tom
Turner, Janine
Turner, Kathleen
Turner, Lana
Turturro, John
Tushingham, Rita
Tuttle, Lurene
Twelvetrees, Helen
Tyler, Liv
Tyne, George
Tyrrell, Susan
Tyson, Cicely
Tyzack, Margaret Maud
Uecker, Bob
Uggams, Leslie (Marian
    Crayne)
Ullman, Tracey
Ullmann, Liv (Johanne)
Ulric, Lenore
Umeki, Miyoshi
Underwood, Blair
Ure, Mary
Urich, Robert
Ustinov, Peter Alexander
Vaccaro, Brenda
Valentine, Karen
Valentine, Scott
Valentino, Rudolph
Vallee, Rudy
Valli, Alida
Vallone, Raf(faele)
Van Ark, Joan
Vance, Courtney B.
Vance, Vivian
Van Cleef, Lee
Van Damme, Jean-Claude
Van Devere, Trish
Van Doren, Mamie
Van Dyke, Dick
Van Dyke, Jerry
Van Fleet, Jo
Vanity
VanKamp, Merete
Van Patten, Dick Vincent
Van Patten, Joyce
Van Patten, Vince(nt)
Van Peebles, Mario
Van Peebles, Melvin

Van Vooren, Monique
Varney, Jim
Varsi, Diane
Vaughn, Robert
Veidt, Conrad
Velez, Eddie
Velez, Lupe
Venuta, Benay
Vera-Ellen
Verdon, Gwen
Verdugo, Elena
Vernon, John
Veruschka
Vestris, Lucia Elizabeth,
    Madame
Vickers, Martha
Vidor, Florence
Vidov, Oleg
Vigoda, Abe
Villechaize, Herve Jean
    Pierre
Vincent, Jan-Michael
Vinson, Helen
Vitale, Milly
Vitti, Monica
Voight, Jon
VonFurstenberg, Betsy
VonStroheim, Erich
VonSydow, Max Carl
    Adolf
Von Zell, Harry
Voskovec, George
Vysotsky, Vladimir
    Semyonovich
Waggoner, Lyle
Wagner, Jack Peter
Wagner, Lindsay J
Wagner, Robert John, Jr.
Wahl, Ken
Wahlberg, Mark
Wainwright, James
Waite, Ralph
Wakely, Jimmy
Walbrook, Anton
Walburn, Raymond
Walden, Robert
Waldron, Charles D
Walken, Christopher
Walker, Clint
Walker, Jimmie
Walker, Nancy
Walker, Robert
Walker, Zena
Wallach, Eli
Wallack, James William
Walley, Deborah
Wallington, Jimmy
Wallis, Shani
Walmsley, Jon
Walsh, Raoul
Walston, Ray
Walter, Jessica
Walters, Julie
Walthall, Henry B
Wanamaker, Sam
Ward, Burt
Ward, Douglas Turner
Ward, Fannie
Ward, Rachel
Ward, Simon
Warden, Jack
Warfield, David
Warfield, Marsha
Warner, David
Warner, Malcolm-Jamal
Warren, Lesley Ann

Warren, Michael
Warrick, Ruth
Warwick, Robert
Washington, Denzel, Jr.
Washington, Fredi
Waters, Ethel
Waterston, Sam(uel
    Atkinson)
Waxman, Al
Wayans, Damon
Wayne, David
Wayne, John
Wayne, Patrick
Wayne, Paula
Weathers, Carl
Weaver, Dennis
Weaver, Doodles
Weaver, Fritz William
Weaver, Sigourney
Webb, Clifton
Webb, Veronica
Weber, Lois
Webster, Ben(jamin)
Webster, Margaret
Weissmuller, Johnny
Weitz, Bruce Peter
Welch, Joseph Nye
Welch, Raquel
Weld, Tuesday
Weldon, Joan
Weldon, John
Welles, Orson
Wendt, George (Robert)
Werner, Oskar
West, Adam
West, Mae
Westley, Helen
Weston, Jack
Wettig, Patricia
Whalen, Michael
Whelchel, Lisa
Whitaker, Forest
Whitaker, Johnny
White, Betty
White, George
White, Jaleel
White, Jesse
White, Pearl
Whitelaw, Billie
Whitfield, Lynn
Whiting, Leonard
Whitman, Stuart
Whitmore, James Allen
Whitty, May, Dame
Whorf, Richard
Widdoes, James
Widdoes, Kathleen Effie
Widmark, Richard
Wiest, Dianne
Wilcox, Larry Dee
Wilcoxon, Henry
Wild, Jack
Wilde, Cornel
Wilder, Gene
Wilding, Michael
Willard, Jess
William, Warren
Williams, Anson
Williams, Barry
Williams, Bert
Williams, Billy Dee
Williams, Cindy
Williams, Clarence, III
Williams, Darnell
Williams, Emlyn
Williams, Esther

Williams, Gus
Williams, JoBeth
Williams, Robin
Williams, Samm-Art
Williams, Simon
Williams, Tex
Williams, Treat
Williams, Vanessa
Williamson, Nicol
Willig, George
Willis, Bruce
Wills, Chill
Wilson, Demond
Wilson, Dooley
Wilson, Flip
Wilson, Julie
Wilson, Marie (Katherine Elizabeth)
Wilson, Theodore Roosevelt
Winchell, Paul
Windom, William
Windsor, Claire
Windsor, Marie
Winfield, Paul Edward
Winfrey, Oprah Gail
Winger, Debra
Winkler, Henry Franklin
Winninger, Charles
Winters, Jonathan (Harshman, III)
Winters, Shelley
Winwood, Estelle
Wisdom, Norman
Wiseman, Joseph
Witcover, Walt
Withers, Googie
Withers, Jane
Woffington, Margaret
Wolfington, Iggie
Wolfit, Donald, Sir
Wolheim, Louis
Wong, Anna May (Lu Tsong)
Wong, B D
Wood, Elijah
Wood, John
Wood, Natalie
Wood, Peggy
Woodard, Alfre
Woods, Donald
Woods, James
Woodward, Edward
Woodward, Joanne Gignilliat
Wooley, Sheb
Woolley, Monty
Woolsey, Robert
Wopat, Tom
Worley, Jo Anne
Worth, Irene
Wray, Fay
Wright, Martha
Wright, Teresa
Wyatt, Jane
Wycherley, Margaret
Wyle, Noah
Wyler, Gretchen
Wyman, Jane
Wynn, Keenan
Wynter, Dana
Wynyard, Diana
Yarnell, Bruce
Yermolova, Maria Nikolayevna
Yoba, Malik

York, Dick
York, Michael
York, Susannah
Yothers, Tina
Young, Alan (Angus)
Young, Burt
Young, Clara Kimball
Young, Gig
Young, Loretta Gretchen
Young, Robert (George)
Young, Roland
Young, Sean
Young, Stephen
Yung, Victor Sen
Yurka, Blanche
Zadora, Pia
Zal, Roxana
Zappa, Dweezil
Zeami, Kanze
Zerbe, Anthony
Zetterling, Mai (Elisabeth)
Zimbalist, Efrem, Jr.
Zimbalist, Stephanie
Zmed, Adrian
Zorina, Vera
Zucco, George
Zuniga, Daphne

ACTORS

Hallam, Lewis, Sr. an

ADVENTURER

Aguirre, Lope de
Blood, Thomas
Blyth, Chay
Bowles, William Augustus
Canot, Theodore
Casanova (de Seingalt), Giovanni Giacomo
Chang Po-go
Chichester, Francis Charles, Sir
Crichton, James
Garnier, Francis
Horn, Alfred Aloysius
Judson, Edward Zane Carroll
Mendes Pinto, Fernao
Miller, Joaquin
Perkins, Marlin
Ridgeway, Rick
Scott, Walter
Selkirk, Alexander
Slocum, Joshua
Thorne, Jim
Trelawny, Edward John
Varthema, Ludovico di
Walker, William

ADVERTISING EXECUTIVE

Ayer, Francis Wayland
Barton, Bruce
Bates, Ted
Bernbach, William
Burnett, Leo
Burrell, Thomas Jason
Calkins, Earnest Elmo

Caples, John
Cone, Fairfax Mastick
Dane, Maxwell
DellaFemina, Jerry
Duffy, Ben
Freeman, Cliff(ord Lee)
Green, Paula
Harper, Marion, Jr.
Johnson, Arno Hollock
Kroll, Alexander S
Lasker, Albert D(avis)
Lawrence, Mary Wells
Lazarus, Shelly
Lewis, Byron E(ugene)
Maxon, Lou Russell
May, Robert Lewis
Mayer, Edward Newton, Jr.
McElligott, Thomas J
Meek, Samuel Williams
Ogilvy, David Mackenzie
Philbrick, Herbert Arthur
Proctor, Barbara Gardner
Redhead, Hugh McCulloch
Reeves, Rosser
Resor, Stanley Burnett
Riney, Hal (Patrick)
Roy, Ross
Rubicam, Raymond
Saatchi, Charles
Saatchi, Maurice
Sackheim, Maxwell Byron
Samstag, Nicholas
Seymour, Dan
Starch, Daniel
Strouse, Norman H(ulbert)
Thompson, J(ames) Walter

AERONAUTICAL ENGINEER

Cierva, Juan de la
DeSeversky, Alexander Procofieff
Eckener, Hugo
Gilruth, Robert Rowe
Hargrave, Lawrence
Heinkel, Ernst Heinrich
Horikoshi, Jiro
Hunsaker, Jerome Clarke
Johnson, Clarence Leonard
Kollsman, Paul
Martin, James Slattin, Jr.
Shute, Nevil
Sikorsky, Igor Ivanovich
Sopwith, Thomas O M, Sir
Upson, Ralph Hazlett
Von Karman, Theodore
Vought, Chance Milton
Williams, O(swald) S.

AGENT

Bernstein, Jay
Brown, Marie Dutton
Davis, Meyer
Janklow, Morton Lloyd
Klein, Marty
Lazar, Irving Paul
Marx, Gummo
Mengers, Sue

Morris, William, Jr.
Ovitz, Michael S.
Steinberg, Leigh
Weintraub, Jerry

AGRICULTURALIST

Bidwell, John
Buel, Jesse
Couper, James Hamilton
Kelley, Oliver Hudson
Knapp, Seaman Asahel

AGRICULTURIST

Borlaug, Norman Ernest
Brown, Lester Russell
Garst, Roswell
Stakman, Elvin Charles

AIR FORCE OFFICER

Armstrong, Jack Lawrence
Bader, Douglas Robert Steuart, Sir
Cooke, Christopher M
Davis, Benjamin Oliver, Jr.
Dowding, Hugh Caswell Tremenheere, Baron
Gibson, Guy
Harris, Marcelite Jordan
LeMay, Curtis Emerson
Mitchell, Billy
Norstad, Lauris
Twining, Nathan F(arragut)

AIRCRAFT DESIGNER

Beard, Myron Gould
Fokker, Anthony Herman Gerard
Heinemann, Edward H
Hobbs, Leonard Sinclair
Ilyushin, Sergei Vladimirovich
Junkers, Hugo
Messerschmitt, Willy
Mitchell, Reginald Joseph
Rutan, Burt
Yakovlev, Aleksandr Sergeyevich
Zeppelin, Ferdinand Adolf August Heinrich von, Count

AIRCRAFT MANUFACTURER

Allen, William McPherson
Beech, Walter Herschel
Bell, Lawrence Dale
Bellanca, Giuseppe Mario
Boeing, William Edward

Boullioun, E(rnest)
H(erman Jr.)
Breguet, Louis Charles
Cessna, Clyde Vernon
Curtiss, Glenn Hammond
Dassault, Marcel
DeHavilland, Geoffrey, Sir
Dornier, Claude
Douglas, Donald Willis
Gross, Robert Ellsworth
Martin, Glenn Luther
McDonnell, James Smith
McDonnell, John Finney
Northrop, John Knudsen
Page, Frederick Handley,
Sir
Piper, William Thomas
Ryan, T(ubal) Claude

AIRLINE EXECUTIVE

Borman, Frank
Braniff, Thomas Elmer
Branson, Richard
Burr, Donald Calvin
Crandall, Robert Lloyd
Damon, Ralph Shepard
Feldman, Alvin Lindbergh
Gross, Courtlandt
Sherrington
Laker, Freddie, Sir
Patterson, William Allan
Rabin, Yehuda L
Smith, Cyrus Rowlett
Solomon, Samuel Joseph
Trippe, Juan Terry
Wolf, Stephen M

AIRLINE PILOT

Washington, Patrice
Clarke

ANARCHIST

Bakunin, Mikhail
Aleksandrovich
Berkman, Alexander
Goldman, Emma
Proudhon, Pierre Joseph

ANATOMIST

Alcala, Jose (Ramon)
Barr, Murray Llewellyn
Crosby, Elizabeth Caroline
Dubois, Eugene
Luzzi, Mondino de'
Trotter, Mildred
Weidenreich, Franz

ANIMAL DEALER

Buck, Frank
Hagenbeck, Carl

Trefflich, Henry Herbert
Frederick

ANIMAL EXPERT

Adamson, George
Adamson, Joy Friederike
Victoria Gessner
Schneirla, Theodore
Christian
Tuttle, Merlin Devere

ANIMAL TRAINER

Burck, Wade
Gebel-Williams, Gunther
Hagenbeck, Carl
Humphrey, Elliott S
Weatherwax, Rudd B

ANIMATOR

Park, Nick

ANTHROPOLOGIST

Abrams, George H. J.
Archambault, JoAllyn
Barnett, Steve
Bateson, Gregory
Beals, Ralph Leon
Beattie, Owen
Benedict, Ruth (Fulton)
Biebuyck, Daniel Prosper
Bird, Junius Bouton
Black, Davidson
Boas, Franz
Castaneda, Carlos
Coon, Carleton Stevens
Dart, Raymond Arthur
Davis, (William) Allison
Devereux, George
Dixon, Roland Burrage
Douglas, Mary Tew
Dozier, Edward P.
Dubois, Eugene
Du Chaillu, Paul Belloni
Edmonson, Munro Sterling
Eiseley, Loren Corey
Evans-Pritchard, Edward
Evan
Frazer, James George, Sir
Geertz, Clifford James
Gluckman, Max
Goodall, Jane
Gunther, Hans F K
Gwaltney, John Langston
Haury, Emil W
Herdt, Gilbert
Herskovits, Melville Jean
Hewitt, J(ohn) N(apoleon)
B(rinton)
Heyerdahl, Thor
Hodge, Frederick Webb
Hooton, Earnest Albert
Howells, William White
Hrdlicka, Ales
Isaacs, Jorge
Johanson, Donald Carl

Johnson, Guy Benton
Keith, Arthur
Kluckhohn, Clyde
Kluckhorn, Clyde Kay
Maben
Kroeber, Alfred Louis
Kroeber, Theodora Kracaw
LaFarge, Oliver
Leakey, Louis Seymour
Bazett
Leakey, Mary (Douglas)
Levi-Strauss, Claude
Gustave
Levy-Bruhl, Lucien
Lewis, Oscar
Linton, Ralph
Lomawaima, K(imberly)
Tsianina
Lowie, Robert Harry
Maine, Henry James
Sumner
Malinowski, Bronislaw
Kasper
Maples, William R.
Mead, Margaret
Medicine, Beatrice A.
Mercer, Henry Chapman
Montagu, (Montague
Francis) Ashley
Ortiz, Alfonso
Parker, Arthur C(aswell)
Phinney, Archie
Powdermaker, Hortense
Powell, John Wesley
Radcliffe-Brown, A(lfred)
R(eginald)
Radin, Paul
Redfield, Robert
Ripley, William Zebina
Roosevelt, Anna
C(urtenius)
Sapir, Edward
Sauer, Carl Ortwin
Soustelle, Jacques
Speck, Frank Gouldsmith
Steward, Julian Haynes
Tax, Sol
Tozzer, Alfred Marston
Trotter, Mildred
Turnbull, Collin
M(acmillan)
Tylor, Edward Bennett, Sir
Weaver, Thomas
Weidenreich, Franz
Westermarck, Edward
Alexander
White, Leslie A(lvin)
Worl, Rosita

ANTI-FEMINIST

Morgan, Marabel
Schlafly, Phyllis Stewart

ANTIQUARIAN

Dolmetsch, Arnold
Kovel, Ralph Mallory
Kovel, Terry Horvitz
Laing, David
Wood, Anthony

ARCHAEOLOGIST

Albright, William Foxwell
Andersson, Johan Gunnar
Arkell, Anthony John
Bandelier, Adolph Francis
Alphonse
Bell, Gertrude Margaret
Bibby, Thomas Geoffrey
Blegen, Carl William
Bordes, Francois
Breasted, James Henry
Breuil, Henri Abbe
Carter, Howard
Caton-Thompson, Gertrude
Cesnola, Luigi Palma di
Childe, Vere Gordon
ElMallakh, Kamal
Evans, Arthur John, Sir
Evans, Clifford
Fellows, Charles, Sir
Garrod, Dorothy Annie
Elizabeth
Glueck, Nelson
Gorman, Chester
Hanfmann, George Maxim
Anossov
Hawes, Harriet Ann Boyd
Herbert, George Edward
Stanhope Molyneux
Johnson, Guy Benton
Kidder, Alfred Vincent
Layard, Austen Henry, Sir
Love, Iris Cornelia
Mallowan, Max Edgar
Lucien, Sir
Michalowski, Kazimierz
Murray, Margaret Alice
Nuttall, Zelia Maria
Magdalena
Peiresc, Nicholas-Claude
Fabri de
Petrie, (William Matthew)
Flinders, Sir
Reisner, George Andrew
Roosevelt, Anna
C(urtenius)
Schliemann, Heinrich
Soren, David
Sukenik, Eliazer Lipa
Thompson, Edward
Herbert
Tozzer, Alfred Marston
Wheeler, Mortimer
Winckelmann, Johann
Joachim
Woolley, Charles Leonard,
Sir
Yadin, Yigael

ARCHER

Hill, Howard

ARCHITECT

Aalto, Alvar Henrik Hugo
Abramovitz, Max
Adam, James
Adam, Robert
Adler, Dankmar
Adler, David
Alberti, Leon Battista
Aleijadinho, O

Allen of Hurtwood, Lady
Altdorfer, Albrecht
Ando, Tadao
Arnolfo di Cambio
Asplund, Erik Gunnar
Atterbury, Grosvenor
Bacon, Henry
Baltard, Victor
Barnes, Edward Larrabee
Barragan, Luis
Barry, Charles, Sir
Bayer, Herbert
Behrens, Peter
Bellini, Giovanni
Belluschi, Pietro
Benjamin, Asher
Berlage, Hendrik Petrus
Bernini, Giovanni Lorenzo
Bethune, Louise Blanchard
Bill, Max
Blomfield, Reginald
    Theodore, Sir
Boffrand, Gabriel Germain
Bofill, Ricardo
Bogardus, James
Born, Ernest Alexander
Borromini, Francesco
Bramante, Donata
    d'Agnolo
Breuer, Marcel Lajos
Brown, Lancelot
Brunelleschi, Filippo
Bulfinch, Charles
Bunshaft, Gordon
Burlington, Richard Boyle,
    Earl
Burnham, Daniel H(udson)
Butterfield, William
Butts, Alfred M(osher)
Callender, John Hancock
Candela, Felix
Cardinal, Douglas
Casey, Edward Pearce
Catherwood, Frederick
Chalgrin, Francois
Chambers, William, Sir
Chermayeff, Serge (Ivan)
Churriguera, Jose Benito
    de
Clarke, Gilmore David
Coolidge, Charles Allerton
Cooper, Alexander
Cortona, Pietro da
Cosimo, Piero di
Costa, Lucio
Cram, Ralph Adams
Cramp, Charles Henry
Creighton, Thomas
    H(awk)
Cret, Paul P(hilippe)
Cuvillies, Francois
Cuypers, Petrus Josephus
    Hubertus
Davis, Alexander Jackson
Dinkeloo, John Gerard
Dinwiddie, John Ekin
Dolci, Danilo
Douglass, Lathrop
Doxiadis, Constantinos
    Apostolos
Eiermann, Egon
Eisenman, Peter
Erickson, Arthur Charles
Fischer von Erlach,
    Johann Bernhard
Fitch, James Marston

Flagg, Ernest
Fontana, Domenico
Freed, James I(ngo)
Fry, E Maxwell
Fuller, Richard
    Buckminster
Gabriel, Ange-Jacques
Gantt, Harvey Bernard
Gardner, Jean Louis
    Charles
Garnier, Jean Louis
    Charles
Gaudi y Cornet, Antonio
Geddes, Norman Bel
Gehry, Frank Owen
Gibberd, Frederick, Sir
Gibbs, James
Gibbs, William Francis
Gilbert, Cass
Giorgio, Francesco di
Giotto di Bondone
Godwin, Edward William
Goldberg, Bertrand
Goodhue, Bertram
    G(rosvenor)
Goody, Joan
Graham, Ernest Robert
Graham, John
Graves, Michael
Greene, Charles Sumner
Greene, Henry Mather
Griffin, Walter Burley
Griffiths, John Willis
Gropius, Walter Adolf
Gruen, Victor
Guarini, Guarino
Guimard, Hector Germain
Gunnison, Foster
Gwathmey, Charles
Harris, Harwell Hamilton
Harrison, Peter
Harrison, Wallace
    Kirkman
Hastings, Thomas
Hawksmoor, Nicholas
Hejduk, John
Herrera, Juan de
Hilberseimer, Ludwig Karl
Hildebrandt, Johann Lucas
    von
Hoban, James
Hoffmann, Josef
Holabird, William
Hood, Raymond
    Matthewson
Humphreys, Joshua
Hundertwasser,
    Friedensreich
Hunt, Richard Morris
Hussey, Christopher
    Edward Clive
Ictinus
Imhotep
Isozaki, Arata
Ittner, William Butts
Jacobsen, Arne
Jacobsen, Hugh Newell
Jahn, Helmut
Jenney, William LeBaron
Johnson, Philip Cortelyou
Jones, Edward Vason
Jones, Fay
Jones, Inigo
Juvara, Filippo
Kahn, Albert
Kahn, Louis I(sadore)

Kaskey, Ray(mond John)
Kelly, Bruce
Kent, William
Khan, Fazlur Rahman
Kiesler, Frederick John
Kimball, Fiske
Labrouste, Pierre Francois
    Henri
LaFarge, Christopher
LaFever Minard
Lapidus, Morris
Latrobe, Benjamin Henry
LeCorbusier
Ledoux, Claude Nicolas
L'Enfant, Pierre Charles
LeNotre, Andre
Lescaze, William
Lescot, Pierre
Le Vau, Louis
Lin, Maya Ying
Llewelyn-Davies, Richard
Loos, Adolf
l'Orme, Philibert de
Luckman, Charles
Lutyens, Edwin Landseer,
    Sir
Mackintosh, Charles
    Rennie
Maderno, Carlo
Maginnis, Charles Donagh
Magonigle, Harold Van
    Buren
Maher, George
    Washington
Maki, Fumihiko
Mansart, Francois
Mansart, Jules Hardouin
Maybeck, Bernard Ralph
Mayer, Albert
McArthur, John
McIntire, Samuel
McKim, Charles Follen
Mead, William Rutherford
Medary, Milton B
Meier, Richard Alan
Mellor, Walter
Melnikov, Konstantin
    Stepanovich
Mendelsohn, Eric
Michelozzo
Mies van der Rohe,
    Ludwig
Mills, Robert
Mizner, Addison
Moneo, Jose Rafael
Montreuil, Pierre de
Moore, Charles Willard
Morgan, Julia
Mould, Jacob Wrey
Mumford, Lewis
Murchison, Kenneth
    MacKenzie
Nash, John
Neff, Wallace
Nelson, George H
Nervi, Pier Luigi
Netsch, Walter Andrew,
    Jr.
Neumann, Balthasar
Neutra, Richard Joseph
Nichols, Anne
Niemeyer, Oscar
Nowicki, Matthew
Obata, Gyo
Olbrich, Joseph Maria
Orcagna

Orr, Douglas William
Oud, Jacobus Johannes
    Pieter
Owings, Nathaniel
    Alexander
Palladio, Andrea
Paxton, Joseph, Sir
Pedersen, William
Pei, I(eoh) M(ing)
Pelli, Cesar
Pereira, William Leonard
Perrault, Claude
Perret, Auguste
Pevsner, Nikolaus
    Bernhard Leon, Sir
Pisano, Andrea
Pisano, Giovanni
Plater-Zyberk, Elizabeth
Polk, Willis Jefferson
Polshek, James Stewart
Ponti, Gio(vanni)
Pope, John Russell
Porta, Giacomo della
Portman, John Calvin, Jr.
Portzamparc, Christian de
Prandtauer, Jakob
Predock, Antoine Samuel
Primaticcio, Francesco
Pugin, A(ugustus) W(elby)
    N(orthmore)
Raphael
Renwick, James, Jr.
Richardson, Henry Hobson
Rietveld, Gerrit Thomas
Roche, Kevin
Rodia, Simon
Rogers, Isaiah
Rogers, James Gamble
Rogers, Richard
Root, John Wellborn
Ross, Donald James
Rossant, James Stephane
Rossi, Aldo
Rudolph, Paul Marvin
Saarinen, Eero
Saarinen, Eliel
Safdie, Moshe
Sanmicheli, Michele
Scamozzi, Vincenzo
Schinkel, Karl Friedrich
Schluter, Andreas
Scott, George Gilbert, Sir
Sert, Jose Luis
Shaw, Richard Norman
Sherman, Frank Dempster
Sinan, Kodja Mimar
Siza, Alvaro (Joaquim
    Melo)
Skidmore, Louis
Sloan, Samuel
Soane, John, Sir
Soleri, Paolo
Sostratus
Soufflot, Jacques Germain
Speer, Albert
Spence, Basil Urwin, Sir
Spychalski, Marian
Stein, Clarence S
Stirling, James
Stone, Edward Durell
Stotz, Charles Morse
Street, George Edmund
Stuart, James
Sullivan, Louis Henri
Tallmadge, Thomas Eddy
Tange, Kenzo

Torroja (y Miret), Eduardo
Trumbauer, Horace
Tunnard, Christopher
Upjohn, Richard
Urban, Joseph Maria
Utzon, Jorn
Vanbrugh, John, Sir
van de Velde, Henry
Vasari, Giorgio
Vaux, Calvert
Venturi, Robert
Vignola, Giacomo da
Villanueva, Carlos Raul
Viollet le Duc, Eugene
  Emmanuel
Vitruvius
Wagner, Otto
Walker, Ralph Thomas
Walter, Thomas Ustick
Wank, Roland A
White, Stanford
Williams, Paul R(evere)
Wood, John the Elder
Wren, Christopher, Sir
Wright, Frank Lloyd
Wright, Henry
Wright, John Lloyd
Wright, Lloyd
Wurster, William
Yamasaki, Minoru
Yeon, John B
York, Edward Palmer

ARMY OFFICER

Abrams, Creighton
  Williams
Adams Early, Charity
Agrippa, Marcus
  Vipsanius
Aguinaldo, Emilio
Alanbrooke, Alan Francis
  Brooke, 1st Viscount
Alexander, William
Allon, Yigal
Amherst, Jeffrey
Araki Sadao
Arnold, Benedict
Atkinson, Henry
Belisarius
Belknap, William Worth
Ben-Gal, Avigdor
Bonneville, Benjamin
  Louie Eulalie de
Bouquet, Henry
Bradley, Omar Nelson
Bragg, Braxton
Browning, Frederick
  A(rthur) M(ontague),
  Sir
Buell, Don Carlos
Burgoyne, John, Sir
Burnside, Ambrose Everett
Butler, Benjamin Franklin
Cadogan, William, Earl
Cadoria, Sherian Grace
Caesar, Julius
Calles, Plutarco Elias
Calley, William Laws, Jr.
Cardigan, James Thomas
  Brudenell, Earl of
Cassius
Castle, Frederick W
Caswell, Richard
Chaffee, Adna Romanza

Chapman, Leonard F., Jr.
Chase, William Curtis
Chu Te
Clark, Mark Wayne
Clay, Lucius du Bignon
Clinton, James
Clyde, Colin Campbell,
  Baron
Collins, Joseph Lawton,
  General
Conway, Thomas
Cornwallis, Charles,
  Marquis
Costa e Silva, Arthur da
Crassus, Marcus Licinius
  Dives
Crittendon, Thomas
  Leonidas
Cromwell, Oliver
Crook, George
Crowder, Enoch Herbert
Cunningham, Alan
  Gordon, Sir
Cushman, Robert Everton,
  Jr.
Custer, George Armstrong
Davidson, Garrison H(olt)
Davison, Frederic Ellis
Dean, William Frishe
Dempsey, Miles
  Christopher, Sir
Denikin, Anton Ivanovich
Devers, Jacob Loucks
Dodge, Grenville Mellen
Doolittle, James H(arold)
Doubleday, Abner
Dreyfus, Alfred
Duong Van Minh
Eaker, Ira Clarence
Eichelberger, Robert
  Lawrence
Elazar, David
Enver Pasha
Evren, Kenan
Fairfax, Thomas
Forbes, John
Gage, Thomas
Gale, Richard Nelson, Sir
Gallieni, Joseph-Simon
Gamelin, Maurice Gustave
Gates, Horatio
Gavin, James Maurice
Giraud, Henri Honore
Goethals, George
  Washington
Goodpaster, Andrew
  Jackson
Gorbatov, Aleksandr
  Vassil'evich
Gordon, Charles George
Gordon, John Brown
Gowon, Yakubu
Graves, William Sidney
Greene, Nathanael
Groves, Leslie Richard
Haddad, Saad
Haig, Alexander Meigs, Jr.
Hamilton, Ian Standish
  Monteith, Sir
Hampton, Wade
Hancock, Winfield Scott
Handy, Thomas Troy
Hardee, William Joseph
Harding, Chester
Harmon, Ernest N(ason)
Heath, William

Herbert, Anthony B
Hershey, Lewis Blaine
Hindenburg, Paul Ludwig
  Hans Anton von
  Beneckendorff und
Hodge, John Reed
Horrocks, Brian Gwynne,
  Sir
Houston, Sam(uel)
Howard, Oliver Otis
Huebner, Clarence R
Ironside, William Edmund
Iturbide, Augustin de
Jones, David Charles
Josephus, Flavius
Kalb, Johann de
Kearny, Stephen Watts
Kelly, Thomas
Kenney, George Churchill
Kleber, Jean Baptiste
Kuter, Laurence S(herman)
Laclos, Pierre (Ambroise
  Francois) Choderlos de
Lafayette, Marie Joseph
  Paul, Marquis
Lattre de Tassigny, Jean
  de (Marie Gabriel) de
Leclerc, Jacques-Philippe
Lee, Charles
Lee, Fitzhugh
Lee, Robert E(dward)
Longstreet, James
Lucullus, Lucius Licinius
Ludendorff, Erich
  Friedrich Wilhelm
Lyon, Nathaniel
MacArthur, Arthur
MacArthur, Douglas
Marlborough, John
  Churchill, Duke
Marshall, George Catlett
Marshall, S(amuel)
  L(yman) A(ttwood)
McAuliffe, Anthony
  Clement
McDougall, Alexander
McDowell, Irvin
Medina, Ernest L
Meigs, Montgomery
  Cunningham
Merrill, Frank Dow
Montgomery, Richard
Morgan, Daniel
Morgan, Frederick, Sir
Moultrie, William
Napier, Charles James, Sir
Napier, Robert Cornelis
Netanyahu, Yonatan
Nobile, Umberto
Nuri al-Sa'id
Odria Amoretti, Manuel
  Apolinario
Ord, Edward Otho Cresap
Park, Chung Hee
Patton, George Smith, Jr.
Pepperell, William, Sir
Pershing, John J(oseph)
Phelps, John Wolcott
Pike, Zebulon
  Montgomery
Pile, Frederick Alfred
Pilsudski, Jozef
Pompey the Great
Pulaski, Kazimierz
Putnam, Israel
Rawlins, John A

Ridgway, Matthew Bunker
Roberts, Frederick Sleigh
Robertson, William
  Robert, Sir
Rochambeau, Jean
  Baptiste Donatien de
  Vimeur, Comte
Rokossovsky, Konstantin
  Konstantinovich
Rommel, Erwin Johannes
  Eugin
Rosecrans, William Starke
Scipio Africanus, Publius
  Cornelius
Scobie, Ronald Mackenzie
Scott, Winfield
Sedgwick, John
Short, Walter Campbell
Shrapnel, Henry
Simpson, William Hood
Smith, Walter Bedell
Spaatz, Carl Andrew
Stark, John
Stauffenberg, Claus
  (Schenk Graf) Von
Stilwell, Joseph Warren
Stockdale, James
Stratemeyer, George E,
  General
Stuart, Jeb
Sulla, Lucius C
Sumner, Edwin V
Sumter, Thomas
Swinton, Ernest Dunlop,
  Sir
Tarleton, Banastre, Sir
Timoshenko, Semen
  Konstantinovich
Tojo, Hideki
Toledo, Fernando Alvarez
  de
Toure, Amadou Toumani
Tupolev, Andrei
  Nikolaevich
Vandegrift, Alexander
  Archer
Vandenberg, Hoyt Sanford
Van Fleet, James Alward
Van Rensselaer, Stephen
Vaughan, Harry Hawkins
Wainwright, Jonathan
  Mayhew
Waller, William, Sir
Watkins, Perry
Wellington, Arthur
  Wellesley, Duke
Wilkinson, James
Wilson, Louis Hugh
Wingate, Orde Charles
Wood, Leonard
Wrangel, Pietr
  Nikolayevich
Wright, Horatio
  Gouverneur
Yamashita, Tomoyuki
Yeats-Brown, F(rancis
  Charles Claypon)
Zhdanov, Andrei
  Alexandrovich

ART COLLECTOR

Altman, Benjamin
Beatty, Alfred Chester, Sir
Dale, Chester

Duveen, Joseph, Sir
Elgin, Thomas Bruce
Guggenheim, Peggy
Gulbenkian, Calouste S
Halpert, Edith Gregor
Hirshhorn, Joseph Herman
Janis, Sidney
Lehman, Adele Lewisohn
Lipman, Howard W
Maeght, Aime
Molyneux, Edward H
Quinn, John
Soane, John, Sir
Tate, Henry, Sir
Terra, Daniel J(ames)
Thyssen-Bornemisza de
  Kaszan, Hans Heinrich,
  Baron
Wallace, Richard, Sir

ART DEALER

Boone, Mary
Mansion, Gracie
N'Namdi, George
  R(ichard)

ART DIRECTOR

Adam, Ken
Borders, James
De Cuir, John
Levy, Florence
Powell, Earl A, III
Stuart, Kenneth James
Sylbert, Richard
Trauner, Alexander

ART HISTORIAN

Aranason, H Harvard
Barr, Alfred Hamilton, Jr.
Berenson, Bernard
Blunt, Anthony Frederick
Brookner, Anita
Carritt, David Graham
Clark, Kenneth
  MacKenzie, Sir
Crosby, Sumner McKnight
Faure, Elie
Fenollosa, Ernest
  Francisco
Geldzahler, Henry
Hartt, Frederick
Hoving, Thomas Pearsall
  Field
Levy, Julien
Love, Iris Cornelia
Panofsky, Erwin
Pevsner, Nikolaus
  Bernhard Leon, Sir
Rosenberg, Jakob
Varnedoe, (John) Kirk
  (Train)
Waterhouse, Ellis
  Kirkham, Sir

ART PATRON

Burlington, Richard Boyle,
  Earl
Chandler, Dorothy
  (Buffum)
Corsi, Jacopo
Gardner, Isabella Stewart
Hartford, Huntington
Kahn, Otto Hermann
Martinson, Joseph Bertram
Medici, Lorenzo de
Phillips, Marjorie Acker
Rockefeller, Abby Aldrich
Walker, A'lelia
Whitney, Gertrude
  Vanderbilt

ARTIST

Abbey, Edwin Austin
Agam, Yaacov
Alajalov, Constantin
Albers, Josef
Albright, Ivan Le Lorraine
Albright, Malvin Marr
Alechinsky, Pierre
Aleijadinho, O
Allen, Elsie
Allston, Washington
Alma-Tadema, Lawrence,
  Sir
Altdorfer, Albrecht
Amen, Irving
Ames, Blanche
Amorsolo, Fernando
Angelico, Fra
Annigoni, Pietro
Antes, Horst
Antonello da Messina
Anuszkiewicz, Richard
  Joseph
Apelles
Appel, Karel Christian
Archipenko, Alexander
  Porfirievich
Arisman, Marshall
Arman
Artschwager, Richard
  (Ernst)
Auerbach-Levy, William
Ault, George Christian
Avery, Milton Clark
Avery, Samuel Putnam
Aziz, Philip John Andrew
  Ferris
Bacon, Francis
Bacon, Peggy
Bad Heart Bull, Amos
Bailey, Radcliffe
Bailey, Xenobia
Baker, Rick
Baldessari, John
Baldovinetti, Alesso
Baldung(-Grien), Hans
Balla, Giacomo
Balthus
Bannister, Edward
  Mitchell
Barclay, McClelland
Barnaby, Ralph S
Barnes, Eddie, Jr.
Barnet, Will
Bartlett, Jennifer Losch
Bartolommeo, Fra

Basquiat, Jean-Michel
Bassano, Jacopo
Baumeister, Willi
Baziotes, William
Beard, Dan(iel Carter)
Bearden, Romare Howard
Beaux, Cecilia
Beckmann, Max
Begay, Harrison
Behrens, Peter
Behzad
Bell, Vanessa
Bellini, Gentile
Bellini, Giovanni
Bellini, Jacopo
Bellotto, Bernardo
Bellows, George Wesley
Benson, Frank Weston
Benton, Thomas Hart
Berman, Eugene
Bermejo, Bartolome
Bernard, Emile
Bernhard, Lucian
Berruguete, Alonso
  (Gonzalez)
Bertoia, Harry
Beuys, Joseph
Biddle, George
Bierstadt, Albert
Biggers, John (Thomas)
Bill, Max
Bingham, George Caleb
Birley, Oswald Hornby
  Joseph, Sir
Bishop, Isabel
Blake, William
Blakelock, Ralph Albert
Blashfield, Edwin
  Howland
Blume, Peter
Blythe, David Gilmour
Boccioni, Umberto
Bocklin, Arnold
Bodmer, Karl
Bohrod, Aaron
Bok, Hannes Vajn
Bolotowsky, Ilya
Bomberg, Dave
Bone, Muirhead, Sir
Bonheur, Rosa
Bonington, Richard Parkes
Bonnard, Pierre
Borduas, Paul-Emile
Borofsky, Jonathan
Bosch, Hieronymous
Bosin, Blackbear
Botero, Fernando
Botticelli, Sandro
Boucher, Francois
Boudin, Eugene Louis
Bourgeois, Louise
Bouts, Dierick C
Brackman, Robert
Bradford, William
Brandon, Brumsic, Jr.
Brangwyn, Frank, Sir
Braque, Georges
Brasher, Rex
Breton, Jules Adolphe
Breytenbach, Breyten
Bridgman, Frederic Arthur
Briggs, Austin Eugene
Bronzino, Il
Brook, Alexander
Brouwer, Adriaen C
Brown, Donald

Brown, Vanessa
Browne, Phiz
Brownscombe, Jennie
  Augusta
Bruegel, Jan
Bruegel, Pieter, the El
Brumidi, Constantino
Brush, George
Buffet, Bernard
Burchfield, Charles
  Ephraim
Burne-Jones, Edward
  Coley, Sir
Burri, Alberto
Burroughs, Margaret
  Taylor
Busoni, Rafaello
Cadmus, Paul
Caffieri, Jacques
Caldecott, Randolph
Calder, Alexander
Callot, Jacques
Calvert, Edward
Camp, Kimberly
Campin, Robert
Canaletto, Antonio
Canova, Antonio
Caravaggio, Michelangelo
  da
Carle, Eric
Carmichael, Franklin
Carpaccio, Vittore
Carpeaux, Jean Baptiste
Carpenter, Francis
  Bicknell
Carr, Emily
Carra, Carlo
Carracci, Annibale
Carracci, Lodovico
Carriera, Rosalba
  Giovanna
Carriere, Eugene
Carzou, Jean
Cassandre, A(dolphe)
  M(ouron)
Cassatt, Mary Stevenson
Castagno, Andrea del
Castle, Wendell Keith
Catherwood, Frederick
Catlin, George
Cavallini, Pietro
Cezanne, Paul
Chagall, Marc
Chantrey, Francis Legatt,
  Sir
Chao Meng-fu
Chapin, James Ormsbee
Chardin, Jean Baptiste
  Simeon
Charlot, Jean
Chase, William Merritt
Chatham, Russell
Chermayeff, Ivan
Chia, Sandro
Chicago, Judy
Chillida, Eduard
Ch'i Pai-Shih
Chirico, Giorgio de
Christ-Janer, Albert
Christo
Christy, Howard Chandler
Church, Frederick Edwin
Cimabue, Giovanni
Clave, Antoni
Clemente, Francesco
Cleve, Joos van

Hoban, Russell
Hobbema, Meindert
Hockney, David
Hodgkin, Howard
Hodler, Ferdinand
Hofer, Karl
Hofmann, Hans
Hogarth, William
Holbein, Hans, the Elder
Holbein, Hans, the
    Younger
Holzer, Jenny
Homer, Winslow
Hooch, Pieter de
Hopper, Edward
Hoppner, John
Howe, Oscar
Howland, Alfred Cornelius
Hsia Kuei
Hughes, Arthur
Hummel, Berta
Hundertwasser,
    Friedensreich
Hunt, Holman
Hunt, William Morris
Hunter, Clementine
Huntington, Daniel
Hurd, Peter
Indiana, Robert
Ingres, Jean Auguste
    Dominique
Inman, Henry
Inness, George
Ironside, Christopher
Irvin, Rea
Irwin, Robert
Isham, Samuel
Israels, Josef
Ives, James Merritt
Jackson, A(lexander)
    Y(oung)
Jackson, William Henry
Jacob, Max
Jamison, Philip Duane, Jr.
Jarvis, John Wesley
Jenkins, Paul
Jensen, Alfred Julio
John, Augustus Edwin
John, Gwendolyn Mary
Johns, Jasper, (Jr.)
Johnson, Cletus Merlin
Johnson, Eastman
Johnson, Joshua
Johnston, Frank H
Johnston, Joshua
Jones, David
Jones, Joe
Jones, Lois Mailou
Jongkind, Johan Barthold
Jordaens, Jacob
Kabotie, Fred
Kahlo, Frida
Kainen, Jacob
Kalf, Willem
Kandinsky, Wassily
Kane, John
Kane, Paul
Kano, Motonobu
Kaprow, Allan
Karfiol, Bernard
Katz, Alex
Kauffmann, Angelica
Keene, Charles Samuel
Keith, William
Kelly, Ellsworth
Kenojuak

Kensett, John Frederick
Kent, Corita
Kent, Rockwell
Keyser, Thomas De
Kiefer, Anselm Karl
    Albert
Kienholz, Edward
Kingman, Dong Moy Shu
Kirchner, Ernst Ludwig
Kitaj, R(onald) B(rooks)
Klee, Paul
Klimt, Gustav
Kline, Franz Joseph
Klinger, Max
Knaths, Karl
Kneller, Godfrey, Sir
Koch, John
Kokoschka, Oskar
Kollwitz, Kathe Schmidt
Koons, Jeff
Korin, Ogata
Kostabi, Mark
Krasner, Lee
Kredel, Fritz
Krieghoff, Cornelius
Kroll, Leon
Kruger, Barbara
Kuekes, Edward Daniel
Kuhn, Walt
Kuniyoshi, Yasuo
Kupka, Frank
Kurelek, William
Kurtzman, Harvey
LaFarge, John
La Fosse, Charles de
Lancret, Nicolas
Landseer, Charles
Landseer, Edwin Henry,
    Sir
Lane, Fitz Hugh
Larsson, Carl Olof
Lartique, Jacques-Henri
    Charles Auguste
Lasker, Joe
La Tour, Georges
    Dumesnil de
Laurencin, Marie
Lavery, John, Sir
Lawrence, Jacob Armstead
Lawrence, Thomas, Sir
Lawrie, Lee
Le Brun, Charles
Lebrun, Rico
LeClear, Thomas
Lee, Doris Emrick
Lee-Smith, Hughie
Leger, Fernand
Lely, Peter, Sir
Leonardo da Vinci
Leutze, Emanuel
Levi, Julian Edwin
Levine, David
Levine, Jack
Lewis, Wyndham
Lewisohn, Ludwig
LeWitt, Sol
Leyendecker, Joseph
    Christian
L'Hermitte, Leon
    Augustin
Liberman, Alexander
    (Semeonovitch)
Lichtenstein, Roy
Liebermann, Max
Lindner, Richard
Linton, William James

Lionni, Leo
Liotard, Jean-Etienne
Lippi, Filippino
Lippi, Filippo, Fra
Lismer, Arthur
Loloma, Charles
Loloma, Otellie
Lomahaftewa, Linda
Long, Richard
Longo, Robert
Lord, Jack
Lorenzetti, Ambrogio
Lorjou, Bernard Joseph
    Pierre
Lorrain, Claude
Losch, Tilly
Lotto, Lorenzo
Louis, Morris
Lowry, Lawrence Stephen
Lucioni, Luigi
Luini, Bernardino
Luks, George Benjamin
Lurcat, Jean Marie
Luz, Arturo Rogerio
Mabuse, Jan de
MacCameron, Robert L
MacDonald, J(ames)
    E(dward) H(ervey)
MacDonald-Wright,
    Stanton
MacIver, Loren
Macke, August
MacKenzie, Warren
Mackintosh, Charles
    Rennie
Maclise, Daniel
MacTaggart, William, Sir
Magnasco, Alessandro
    Lissandrino
Magritte, Rene Francois
    Ghislain
Maillol, Aristide
Malevich, Kasimir
    Severinovich
Manessier, Alfred
Manet, Edouard
Manso, Leo
Mantegna, Andrea
Marc, Franz
Marca-Relli, Conrad
Marden, Brice
Marin, John
Marquet, Albert
Marsh, Reginald
Martin, Agnes
Martin, Fletcher
Martin, Homer Dodge
Martin, Mungo
Martinez, Maria Montoya
Martini, Simone
Masaccio
Masson, Andre (Aime
    Rene)
Massys, Quentin
Matisse, Henri Emile
    Benoit
Matta, Roberto Sebastian
    Antonio Echaurren
Matteson, Tompkins
    Harrison
Maurer, Alfred Henry
Max, Peter
Mayhew, Richard
McFee, Henry Lee
McGee, Charles
Meer, Jan van der

Meissonier, Jean Louis
    Ernest
Melchers, Gari
Memling, Hans
Mengs, Anton Raphael
Merida, Carlos
Messel, Oliver
Metcalf, Willard Leroy
Metzinger, Jean
Michaux, Henri
Michelangelo (Buonarroti)
Michelozzo
Mi Fei
Millais, John Everett, Sir
Miller, Alfred Jacob
Millet, Jean Francois
Millett, Kate
Milne, David Brown
Miro, Joan
Mitchell, Joan
Modigliani, Amedeo
Moholy-Nagy, Laszlo
Mondrian, Piet(er
    Cornelis)
Monet, Claude-Oscar
Monnoyer, Jean-Baptiste
Moran, Edward
Moran, Thomas
Morandi, Giorgio
Moreau, Gustave
Morisot, Berthe
Morland, George
Moroni, Giovanni Battista
Moronobu, Hishikawa
Morrice, James Wilson
Morrison, Keith (Anthony)
Morrisseau, Norval
Morse, Samuel Finley
    Breese
Moses, Grandma
Motherwell, Robert Burns
Mount, William Sidney
Mucha, Alphonse Marie
Munch, Edvard
Munnings, Alfred James,
    Sir
Murillo, Bartolome
    Esteban
Murray, Elizabeth
Music, Antonio Zoran
Myers, Jerome
Nadelman, Elie
Nakian, Reuben
Namatjira, Albert
Nampeyo
Naranjo-Morse, Nora
Nash, Paul
Nattier, Jean Marc
Nauman, Bruce
Nechita, Alexandra
Neel, Alice Hartley
Neiman, LeRoy
Nevelson, Louise
    Berliawsky
New, Lloyd Kiva
Newman, Barnett
Nicholson, Ben
Noland, Kenneth Clifton
Nolde, Emil
Numan, Eppo
Ochterveldt, Jacob Lucasz
O'Doherty, Brian
Okada, Kenzo
Okamura, Arthur
O'Keeffe, Georgia
Oldenburg, Claes Thure

Olitski, Jules
Ono, Yoko
Oppenheim, Meret
Orcagna
Orley, Bernard van
Orozco, Jose Clemente
Orpen, William Newneham, Sir
Ostade, Adriaen van
Oudry, Jean-Baptiste
Ozenfant, Amedee
Pacheco, Francisco
Pacher, Michael
Paik, Nam June
Palmer, Frances Flora Bond
Pannini, Giovanni Paolo
Parmigano
Parrhasius
Parrish, Maxfield
Parsons, Betty Pierson
Pater, Jean-Baptiste
Peale, Charles Willson
Peale, James
Peale, Raphael
Peale, Rembrandt
Peale, Titian Ramsay
Pears, Charles
Pechstein, Max
Peirce, Waldo
Pennell, Joseph Stanley
Perkoff, Stuart Z.
Perugino
Peto, John Frederick
Pevsner, Antoine
Phillips, Marjorie Acker
Picabia, Francis
Picasso, Pablo Ruiz y
Piero della Francesca
Pierre, Andre
Pintuicchio
Pippin, Horace
Pisano, Antonio
Pisis, Filippo Tibertelli de
Pissaro, Lucien
Pissarro, Camille Jacob
Polke, Sigmar
Pollaiuolo, Antonio
Pollock, Charles
Pollock, Jackson
Polygnotus
Pontormo, Jacopo da
Poons, Lawrence
Poor, Henry Varnum, III
Popova, Liubov Sergeevna
Popovi Da
Porter, Fairfield
Potthast, Edward Henry
Poussin, Nicolas
Powell, William Henry
Pozzi, Lucio
Pratt, Christopher
Prendergast, Maurice Brazil
Prestopino, Gregorio
Primaticcio, Francesco
Prudhon, Pierre-Paul
Puryear, Martin
Puvis de Chavannes, Pierre Cecile
Quidor, John
Raeburn, Henry, Sir
Ramsay, Allan
Rand, Ellen Gertrude Emmet
Raphael

Rattner, Abraham
Rauschenberg, Robert
Ray, Man
Read, Thomas Buchanan
Redon, Odilon
Rees, Lloyd Frederic
Reid, William Ronald
Reinhardt, Ad(olph Frederick)
Reinhart, Charles S
Rembrandt (Harmenszoon van Rijn)
Remington, Frederic
Reni, Guido
Renoir, (Pierre) Auguste
Repin, Ilya Yefimovich
Reynolds, Joshua, Sir
Ribalta, Francisco
Ribera, Jusepe (Jose) de
Richards, William Trost
Richter, Gerhard
Riemenschneider, Tilman
Rigaud, Hyacinthe
Riley, Bridget
Ringgold, Faith
Riopelle, Jean-Paul
Rivera, Diego
Rivers, Larry
Robert, Hubert
Roberti, Ercole
Robinson, Boardman
Rodchenko, Alexander Mikhailovich
Rojankovsky, Feodor Stepanovich
Romano, Umberto
Romney, George
Rosa, Salvator
Rosenberg, Evelyn Edelson
Rosenquist, James Albert
Rossetti, Dante Gabriel
Rothenberg, Susan
Rothenstein, William, Sir
Rothko, Mark
Rothschild, Judith
Rouault, Georges
Rousseau, Henri
Rousseau, Theodore
Rousseau, (Pierre Etienne) Theodore
Rubens, Peter Paul, Sir
Rubin, Reuven
Ruggles, Carl
Ruscha, Edward
Russell, Charles Marion
Russell, Morgan
Ruysdael, Jacob van
Ryder, Albert Pinkham
Saar, Alison
Saint James, Synthia
Saito, Yoshishige
Sakiestewa, Ramona
Salle, David
Salomon, Charlotte
Samaras, Lucas
Sample, Paul Starrett
Sansovino, Andrea
Sansovino, Jacopo
Sargent, John Singer
Sarto, Andrea del
Sassetta
Savage, Edward
Schapiro, Miriam
Schiele, Egon
Schlemmer, Oskar

Schmidt-Rottluf, Karl
Schnabel, Julian
Scholder, Fritz
Schongauer, Martin
Schwitters, Kurt (Hermann Edward Karl Julius)
Scorel, Jan van
Searle, Ronald William Fordham
Secunda, Arthur
Segantini, Giovanni
Serra, Richard Anthony
Serrano, Andres
Serusier, Paul
Sesshu, Toyo
Seurat, Georges Pierre
Severini, Gino
Shahn, Ben(jamin)
Sheeler, Charles
Shepard, Ernest Howard
Sheridan, Clare Consuelo
Sherman, Cindy
Shinn, Everett
Siddal, Elizabeth Eleanor
Signac, Paul
Signorelli, Luca
Simpson, Lorna
Siqueiros, David A
Sironi, Mario
Sisley, Alfred
Sloan, John F
Sloane, Eric
Smith, Juane Quick-to-See
Smithson, Robert (Irving)
Solari, Andrea
Sommer, Frederick
Sorel, Edward
Soutine, Chaim
Soyer, Isaac
Soyer, Moses
Soyer, Raphael
Speicher, Eugene Edward
Spencer, Stanley, Sir
Spier, Peter Edward
Spitzweg, Carl
Spode, Josiah
Spry, Constance
Spyropoulos, Jannis
Stael, Nicolas de
Stahl, Ben(jamin Albert)
Stankiewicz, Richard Peter
Steen, Jan
Steichen, Edward Jean
Steinberg, Saul
Stella, Frank Philip
Stella, Joseph
Stephens, Alice Barber
Sterne, Maurice
Still, Clyfford
Stravinsky, Vera de Bossett
Stuart, Gilbert Charles
Stuart, James
Stubbs, George
Sully, Thomas
Sutherland, Graham Vivian
Szyk, Arthur
Taeuber-Arp, Sophie
Tait, Arthur Fitzwilliam
Tamayo, Rufino
Tanguy, Yves
Tanner, Henry Ossawa
Tao-chi
Tatlin, Vladimir Yevgrapovich

Taubes, Frederic
Tchelitchew, Pavel
Teniers, David, the Younger
Tenniel, John, Sir
Ter Borch, Gerard
Terbrugghen, Hendrick
Thayer, Abbott Handerson
Thiebaud, (Morton) Wayne
Thoma, Hans
Thomson, Tom
Thon, William
Tiepolo, Giambattista
Tiepolo, Giovanni Domenico
Tiffany, Louis Comfort
Tintoretto
Tissot, James Joseph Jacques
Titian
Tobey, Mark
Tolliver, William (Mack)
Tomlin, Bradley Walker
Topolski, Feliks
Toulouse-Lautrec (Monfa), (Henri Marie Raymond de)
Troyon, Constant
Truitt, Anne
Trumbull, John
Tung Ch'i-ch'ang
Tura, Cosme
Turner, Joseph Mallord William
Twachtman, John Henry
Twombly, Cy
Tworkov, Jack
Uccello, Paolo
Ufer, Walter
Utamaro, Kitagawa
Utrillo, Maurice
Valadon, Suzanne
Valdes-Leal, Juan de
Valerio, James Robert
Vanderlyn, John
Van Dyck, Anthony, Sir
Van Eyck, Hubert
Van Eyck, Jan
Van Gogh, Vincent Willem
Van Leyden, Lucas
Vargas, Alberto
Varley, F(rederick) H(orseman)
Vasarely, Victor
Vasari, Giorgio
Vedder, Elihu
Velarde, Pablita
Velazquez, Diego Rodriguez de Silva
Velde, Willem van de
Vereshchagin, Vasily Vasilyevich
Vermeer, Jan
Veronese, Paolo
Verrocchio, Andrea del
Vertes, Marcel
Vickrey, Robert (Remsen)
Vieira Da Silva, Maria Helena
Vigee-Lebrun, Marie-Louise-Elisabeth
Vlaminck, Maurice de
Vlieger, Simon Jacobsz de
Vollbracht, Michaele J

Volpi, Alfredo
Vonnoh, Robert William
Vos, Cornelis de
Vos, Martin de
Vouet, Simon
Vuillard, (Jean) Edouard
Walcott, Mary Morris
  Vaux
Walker, Henry Oliver
Walker, Kara
Walker, Mickey
Wang Wei
Ward, Lynd
Warhol, Andy
Watteau, Jean Antoine
Watts, George Frederic
Waugh, Frederick Judd
Weber, Max
Wedgwood, Josiah
Wegman, William George
Weir, John F(erguson)
Weir, Julian Alden
Weir, Robert W
Wells, James Lesesne
Wesselmann, Tom
West, Benjamin
Weyden, Rogier van der
Whistler, James Abbott
  McNeill
Whittredge, Thomas
  Worthington
Whymper, Edward
Wieghorst, Olaf
Wilkie, David, Sir
Willard, Archibald
  MacNeal
Williams, Kit
Wilson, Edward Arthur
Witz, Konrad
Wood, Grant
Woodruff, Hale (Aspacio)
Woodville, Richard Caton
Wyeth, Andrew
Wyeth, Henriette
  (Zirngiebel)
Wyeth, Jamie
Wyeth, N(ewell)
  C(onvers)
Youngerman, Jack
Zadkine, Ossip
Zao-Wou-Ki
Zorach, William
Zorn, Anders Leonard
Zurbaran, Francisco

ARTISTS

Asam, Cosmas Damian
  and Egid Quirin
Eight, The
Group of Seven
Sangallo Family, The
Zimmermann, Johann
  Baptist and Domenikus

ASSASSIN

Booth, John Wilkes
Corday d'Armount,
  Charlotte
Czolgosz, Leon F
Mercader, Ramon
Oswald, Lee Harvey

Princip, Gavrilo
Ravaillac, Francois
Ray, James Earl
Sirhan, Sirhan Bishara
Zangara, Joseph

ASTROLOGER

Dixon, Jeane (Pinckert)
Dunninger, Joseph
Goodman, Linda
Leek, Sybil
Nostradamus
Omarr, Sydney
Ptolemy, Claudius
Righter, Carroll
Yeh-lu Ch'u-ts'ai

ASTRONAUT

Aldrin, Edwin E(ugene),
  Jr.
Anders, William Alison
Armstrong, Neil Alden
Bean, Alan L
Bluford, Guy
Bolden, Charles F(rank),
  Jr.
Borman, Frank
Brand, Vance DeVoe
Carpenter, Scott
Carr, Gerald Paul
Cernan, Eugene Andrew
Chaffee, Roger Bruce
Collins, Eileen
Collins, Mike
Conrad, Charles, Jr.
Cooper, Gordon
Crippen, Robert Laurel
Cunningham, R Walter
Duke, Charles Moss, Jr.
Eisele, Donn Fulton
Engle, Joe Henry
Evans, Ronald Ellwin
Fullerton, (Charles)
  Gordon
Garneau, Marc
Garriott, Owen
Gibson, Edward George
Glenn, John Herschel, Jr.
Gordon, Richard Francis,
  Jr.
Gregory, Frederick D(rew)
Grissom, Virgil Ivan
Haise, Fred W(allace, Jr.)
Henize, Karl G(ordon)
Irwin, James Benson
Jarvis, Gregory
Jemison, Mae C(arol)
Kerwin, Joseph Peter
Lawrence, Robert (Henry),
  Jr.
Lee, Mark
Lousma, Jack
Lovell, Jim
Lucid, Shannon
McCandless, Bruce, II
McDivitt, Jim
McNair, Ronald Ervin
Mitchell, Edgar Dean
Ochoa, Ellen
Onizuka, Ellison
Pogue, William R(eid)

Resnik, Judy
Ride, Sally K
Roosa, Stuart Allen
Schirra, Wally
Schmitt, Harrison Hagan
Schweickart, Russell L
Scobee, Dick
Scott, David Randolph
Seddon, Rhea
Shepard, Alan B(artlett),
  Jr.
Slayton, Donald Kent
Smith, Michael John
Stafford, Thomas P(atten)
Sullivan, Kathryn D
Swigert, Jack
Truly, Richard H
White, Ed(ward Higgins,
  III)
Worden, Alfred Merrill
Young, John Watts

ASTRONOMER

Abell, George O(gden)
Adams, John Couch
Adams, Walter Sydney
Airy, George Biddell, Sir
Aitkin, Robert Grant
Ambartsumyan, Viktor
  Amazaspovich
Anaximander
Angstrom, Anders Jonas
Argelander, Friedrich
  Wilhelm August
Aristarchus of Samos
Ashbrook, Joseph
Baade, (Wilhelm Heinrich)
  Walter
Babcock, Harold Delos
Babcock, Horace Welcome
Bailly, Jean Sylvain
Baily, Francis
Banks, Harvey
  Washington
Barnard, Edward Emerson
Bell Burnell, Jocelyn
Bessel, Friedrich Wilhelm
Biruni, Abu Rayhan al-
Bitruji, Nur al-Din Abu
  Ishaq al
Bok, Bart J(an)
Bopp, Thomas
Bowditch, Nathaniel
Bradley, James
Brahe, Tycho
Branting, Karl Hjalmar
Burbidge, Margaret
Campbell, William
  Wallace
Cannon, Annie Jump
Celsius, Anders
Clark, Alvin Graham
Copernicus, Nicolaus
Curtis, Heber Doust
Danjon, Andre Louis
Darwin, George Howard,
  Sir
De La Rue, Warren
Delisle, Joseph-Nicolas
Dixon, Jeremiah
Douglass, Andrew Ellicott
Drake, Frank Donald
Dreyer, Johan Ludwig
  Emil

Dunstable, John
Dyson, Frank Watson, Sir
Eddington, Arthur Stanley,
  Sir
Eudoxus of Cnidus
Faber, Sandra M(oore)
Flammarion, Camille
Flamsteed, John
Fleming, Williamina Paton
  Stevens
Frost, Edwin Brant
Galileo
Gilliss, James Melville
Gold, Thomas
Hagen, Johann Georg
Hale, George Ellery
Hall, Asaph
Halley, Edmund
Hamilton, William Rowan,
  Sir
Hansen, Peter Andreas
Henize, Karl G(ordon)
Herschel, John Frederick
  William, Sir
Herschel, William
  Frederick, Sir
Hertzsprung, Ejnar
Hevelius, Johannes
Hill, George William
Hipparchus
Horrocks, Jeremiah
Hoyle, Fred, Sir
Hubble, Edwin Powell
Huggins, William, Sir
Huygens, Christian
Hynek, J(oseph) Allen
Imhotep
Janssen, Pierre Jules Cesar
Jastrow, Robert
Jeans, James Hopwood,
  Sir
Jeffreys, Harold
Kameny, Frank(lin
  Edward)
Kapteyn, Jacobus Cornelis
Keeler, James Edward
Kepler, Johannes
Khwarizmi, Muhammad
  ibn Musa al-
Kohoutek, Lubos
Kopal, Zdenek
Kuiper, Gerard Peter
Lagrange, Joseph-Louis
Lalande, Joseph Jerome
  Lefrancais de
Langley, Samuel Pierpont
Laplace, Pierre Simon,
  Marquis de
Lemaitre, Georges
Lemonnier, Pierre Charles
LeVerrier, Urbain Jean
  Joseph
Levy, David H.
Lockyer, Joseph Norman,
  Sir
Lovell, Bernard, Sir
Lowell, Percival
Lyot, Bernard Ferdinand
Maskelyne, Nevil
Mason, Charles
Maury, Antonia Caetana
  De Paiua Pereira
Mayer, Johann Tobias
Michell, John
Mitchell, Maria
Mobius, August Ferdinand

Newcomb, Simon
Nicholson, Seth Barnes
Olbers, Heinrich Wilhelm
   Matthaus
Omar Khayyam
Oort, Jan Hendrik
Parsons, William
Payne-Gaposchkin, Cecilia
   (Helena)
Peirce, Benjamin
Perrine, Charles Dillon
Picard, Jean
Pickering, Edward Charles
Pickering, William Henry
Pritchett, Henry S
Ptolemy
Ptolemy, Claudius
Quetelet, Lambert Adolphe
   Jacques
Regiomontanus
Richer, Jean
Ritchey, George Willis
Rittenhouse, David
Rosse, William Parsons,
   3rd Earl of
Russell, Henry Norris
Ryle, Martin, Sir
Sagan, Carl (Edward)
Schilt, Jan
Schlesinger, Frank
Schwarzschild, Martin
Secchi, Pietro Angelo
Shapley, Harlow T
Shklovsky, Iosif
   Samvilovitch
Short, James
Slipher, Vesto Melvin
Spitzer, Lyman, Jr.
Stefanik, Milan Rastislav
Stromgren, Bengt Georg
   Daniel
Struve, Friedrich Georg
   Wilhelm von
Struve, Otto
Tombaugh, Clyde
   W(illiam)
Young, Charles Augustus
Zwicky, Fritz

ASTROPHYSICIST

Banks, Harvey
   Washington
Burbidge, Geoffrey
Tyson, Neil de Grasse

ATHEIST

O'Hair, Madalyn Murray

ATHLETE

Blaikie, William
Butcher, Susan
Conacher, Lionel Pretoria
Curren, Tommy
Fay, Michael, Sir
Hill, Lynn
Kanokogi, Rusty
Sears, Eleonora Randolph
Swenson, Rick

ATHLETIC DIRECTOR

Duke, Wayne
Elliott, Jumbo

ATTEMPTED ASSASSIN

Agca, Mehmet Ali
Bremer, Arthur Herman
Collazo, Oscar
Fromme, Lynette Alice
Hinckley, John Warnock,
   Jr.
Moore, Sara Jane
Torresola, Griselio

AUCTIONEER

Christie, James
Sotheby, John
Sotheby, Samuel Leigh

AUTHOR

Aardema, Verna Norberg
Abbas, Khwaja Ahmad
Abbey, Edward
Abbott, Edith
Abbott, Jack
Abdul, Raoul
Abe, Kobo
Abelard, Pierre
Abell, George O(gden)
Abercrombie, Lascelles
About, Edmond-Francois-
   Valentin
Abrahams, Israel
Abrahams, Peter Henry
Abse, Dannie
Abu-L-Ala al-Maarri
Acevedo Diaz, Eduardo
Achebe, Chinua
Ackerman, Forest J
Ackroyd, Peter
Adam, Juliette Lamber
Adam, Paul
Adamic, Louis
Adamov, Arthur
Adams, Alice
Adams, Andy
Adams, Charles Francis,
   Sr.
Adams, Douglas Noel
Adams, Frank Ramsay
Adams, Hannah
Adams, Henry Brooks
Adams, James Truslow
Adams, Joey
Adams, John Hanly
Adams, Leonie Fuller
Adams, Richard
Adams, Samuel Hopkins
Adamson, Joy Friederike
   Victoria Gessner
Ade, George
Adler, Alfred
Adler, Cyrus
Adler, Irving
Adler, Mortimer J(erome)

Adonias (Aguiar) Filho
Aesop
Agar, Herbert Sebastian
Agate, James Evershed
Agee, James Rufus
Agee, Philip
Agnon, S(hmuel) Y(osef)
Agoult, Marie Catherine
   Sophie d'
Agrippa, Heinrich
   Cornelius
Aguilar, Grace
Ahad Haam
Ahlin, Lars
Aiken, Joan Delano
Ailly, Pierre d'
Ainsworth, W(illiam)
   H(arrison)
Aitmatov, Chingiz
Akhmatova, Anna
Aksakov, Sergei
   Timofeyevich
Alain-Fournier
Alarcon, Pedro Antonio de
Albee, Edward
Alberdi, Juan Bautista
Alberti, Leon Battista
Albrand, Martha
Alcott, Louisa May
Aldecoa, Ignacio
Alden, Henry M
Alden, Isabella Macdonald
Aldington, Richard
   (Edward Godfree)
Aldiss, Brian Wilson
Aldrich, Bess Streeter
Aldrich, Richard Stoddard
Aldrich, Thomas Bailey
Alegria, Ciro
Aleichem, Sholom
Aleman, Mateo
Alexander, Lloyd Chudley
Alexander, Shana
Alger, Horatio
Algren, Nelson
Ali, Ahmed
Allal al-Fassi, Mohamed
Allen, Hervey
Allen, Jack
Allen, James Lane
Allen, Jay Presson
Allen, Robert Sharon
Allen, Walter Ernest
Allende, Isabel
Allen of Hurtwood, Lady
Allingham, Margery
Allison, Dorothy E.
Allsop, Kenneth
Almon, John
Almond, Gabriel Abraham
Alsop, Joseph Wright, Jr.
Alsop, Stewart Johonnot
   Oliver
Altea, Rosemary
Aluko, Timothy
   Mofolorunso
Alvarez, Julia
Amado, Jorge
Amalrik, Andrei
   Alekseyevich
Ambler, Eric
Amicis, Edmond de
Amis, Kingsley (William)
Amis, Martin (Louis)
Amory, Cleveland
Anand, Mulk Raj

Andersen, Hans Christian
Anderson, Peggy
Anderson, Sherwood
Anderson, Vernon
   Ellsworth
Andreas-Salome, Lou
Andrews, James Frederick
Andrews, Julie
Andrews, Mary Raymond
   Shipman
Andrews, Michael Alford
Andrews, Raymond
Andrews, V(irginia) C(leo)
Andrews, Wayne
Andreyev, Leonid
   Nikolayevich
Andric, Ivo
Andrzejewski, Jerzy
Angell, Norman
Angell, Roger
Angelou, Maya
Anger, Kenneth
Angoff, Charles
Ansa, Tina McElroy
Anson, Jay
Anthony, Earl
Anthony, Evelyn
Antin, Mary
Apollinaire, Guillaume
Appelfeld, Aharon
Aptheker, Herbert
Apuleius, Lucius
Aqqad, Abbas Mahmud
   al-
Arbuthnot, May Hill
Archer, Jeffrey Howard
Archibald, Joe
Ardizzone, Edward Jeffrey
   Irving
Ardrey, Robert
Arenas, Reinaldo
Arendt, Hannah
Arghezi, Tudor
Arguedas, Alcides
Arguedas, Jose Maria
Aries, Philippe
Arieti, Silvano
Aristotle
Arlen, Michael
Armstrong, Charlotte
Armstrong, Garner Ted
Arnim, Achim von
   (Ludwig Joachim)
Arnold, Edwin
Arnold, Matthew
Arnow, Harriette Louisa
   Simpson
Aron, Raymond Claude
   Ferdinand
Arp, Hans
Artsybashev, Mikhail
   Petrovich
Artzybasheff, Boris
   Mikhailovich
Arundel, Honor Morfydd
Asante, Molefi Kete
Asbury, Herbert
Asch, Sholem
Ascoli, Max
Ashbery, John (Lawrence)
Ashford, Daisy
Ashley, Merrill
Ashmore, Harry Scott
Ashton-Warner, Sylvia
   Constance
Asimov, Isaac

Asquith, Emma Alice
Margot
Asturias, Miguel Angel
Atherton, Gertrude
Franklin
Atwood, Margaret
(Eleanor)
Aubert de Gaspe,
Philippe(-Joseph)
Aubrey, John
Auchincloss, Louis
Auden, W(ystan) H(ugh)
Audiberti, Jacques
Auel, Jean Marie
Aulnoy, Marie-Catherine
Jumel de Berneville
Aumont, Jean-Pierre
Aungervyle, Richard
Aurell, Tage
Auslander, Joseph
Austen, Jane
Auster, Paul
Austin, Mary Hunter
Avallone, Michael Angelo,
Jr.
Awdry, W(ilbert Vere)
Ayer, Alfred Jules, Sir
Ayme, Marcel
Ayres, Ruby Mildred
Aytoun, William
Edmonstoune
Azuela, Mariano
Babb, Howard Selden
Babbitt, Bruce E(dward)
Babbitt, Irving
Babel, Isaac
Emmanuelovich
Babrius
Bacchelli, Riccardo
Bach, Bert Coates
Bach, Richard David
Bacharach, Bert(ram
Mark)
Bacheller, Irving Addison
Bacon, Delia Salter
Baeck, Leo
Bagdikian, Ben Haig
Bagnold, Enid
Bailey, Alice A(nne La
Trobe-Bateman)
Bailey, Charles Waldo, II
Bailey, Florence Augusta
Merriam
Bailey, H(enry)
C(hristopher)
Bailey, Martin Jean
Bainbridge, Beryl
Bakeless, John Edwin
Baker, Carlos Heard
Baker, Charlotte
Baker, Dorothy Dodds
Baker, Laura Nelson
Baker, Nicholson
Baker, Ray Stannard
Baker, Russell Wayne
Baker, Samm Sinclair
Balchin, Nigel Marlin
Baldwin, Faith
Baldwin, James (Arthur)
Ball, John Dudley, Jr.
Ballantrae, Lord
Ballard, J(ames) G(raham)
Ballinger, Margaret
Ballou, Maturin Murray
Balzac, Honore de
Bancroft, George

Bancroft, Hubert Howe
Bandello, Matteo
Bangs, Lester
Banks, Russell
Banning, Kendall
Banning, Margaret Culkin
Bannon, Ann
Banville, John
Barber, Bernard
Bardis, Panos Demetrios
Barea, Arturo
Baring, Maurice
Barker, Clive
Barker, George Granville
Barnaby, Ralph S
Barnes, Clive Alexander
Barnes, Djuna
Barnes, Joanna
Barnes, Julian Patrick
Barnes, Leonard John
Barnes, Margaret Ayer
Barnet, Sylvan M., Jr.
Barney, Natalie Clifford
Baroja (y Nessi), Pio
Barr, Amelia Edith
Huddleston
Barr, Stringfellow
Barraclough, Geoffrey
Barres, (Auguste) Maurice
Barrett, William Edmund
Barrie, James Matthew,
Sir
Barrows, Marjorie (Ruth)
Barth, John (Simmons)
Barth, Roland Sawyer
Barthelme, Donald
Bartlett, Vernon
Barton, Bruce
Barton, George
Barzini, Luigi Giorgio, Jr.
Basso, Hamilton
Bate, Walter Jackson
Bates, Arlo
Bates, H(erbert) E(rnest)
Bauer, Helen
Baugh, Albert Croll
Baum, L(yman) Frank
Baum, Vicki
Bawden, Nina Mary
Mabey
Bax, Arnold Edward
Trevor, Sir
Baxter, Charles (Morley)
Bazin, Andre
Bazin, Rene
Beach, Joseph Warren
Beach, Rex Ellingwood
Beals, Carleton
Beals, Melba Patillo
Beals, Ralph Leon
Beard, James Andrews
Beattie, Ann
Beaumarchais, Pierre
Augustin Caron de
Beauvoir, Simone de
Becker, Stephen David
Beckett, Samuel (Barclay)
Beckford, William
Bedford, Sybille
Beebe, Lucius Morris
Beecher, Catharine
(Esther)
Beer, Thomas
Beerbohm, Max
Beeton, Isabella Mary
Mayson

Begiebing, Robert J.
Behan, Brendan (Francis)
Behn, Aphra
Behn, Noel
Behrman, S(amuel)
N(athaniel)
Bein, Albert
Belbenoit, Rene Lucien
Belinsky, Vissarion
Grigoryevich
Bell, Arthur Donald
Bell, Derrick Albert, Jr.
Bellamy, Edward
Belloc, Hilaire
Bellow, Saul
Bemelmans, Ludwig
Benarde, Melvin Albert
Benary-Isbert, Margot
Benchley, Nathaniel
Goddard
Benchley, Peter Bradford
Benchley, Robert Charles
Benda, Julien
Bendick, Jeanne
Benedictus, David
Benefield, Barry
Benet, Stephen Vincent
Benet, William Rose
Benjamin, Asher
Benjamin of Tudela
Ben Jelloun, Tahar
Benn, Gottfried
Bennett, Arnold
Bennett, James Gordon, Jr.
Bennett, John
Benson, Arthur
Christopher
Benson, Edward Frederic
Benson, Sally
Bentley, Edmund Clerihew
Bentley, Richard
Berberova, Nina
Nikolaevna
Bercovici, Konrad
Berdichevsky, Micah
Joseph
Beresford, Harry
Berger, John
Berger, Melvin H
Berger, Meyer
Berger, Raoul
Berger, Terry
Berger, Thomas Louis
Berkeley, George
Berkow, Ira Harvey
Berlin, Isaiah, Sir
Berlitz, Charles L
Frambach
Bernanos, Georges
Berne, Eric Lennard
Bernstein, Carl
Bernstein, Leonard
Berry, Mary Frances
Berryman, John
Bertinoro, Obadiah ben
Abraham Yare
Berton, Pierre
Besant, Annie Wood
Besant, Walter, Sir
Bester, Alfred
Beverley, Robert
Bhaktivedanta, A(bhay)
C(haranaravinda)
Bialik, Chaim Nachman
Bialik, Hayyim Nahman
Bichler, Joyce

Biddle, George
Biggers, Earl Derr
Billings, Josh
Binchy, Maeve
Binns, Archie Fred
Bioy Casares, Adolfo
Bird, Robert Montgomery
Birmingham, Stephen
Birney, Earle
Birrell, Augustine
Bishop, Isabella Lucy Bird
Bishop, Jim
Biyidi, Alexandre
Blackmore, Richard
Doddridge
Blackstone, William, Sir
Blackwell, (Samuel) Earl,
Jr.
Blackwell, Elizabeth
Blackwood, Algernon
Henry
Blair, Clay, Jr.
Blanc, Louis
Blanding, Don
Blasco-Ibanez, Vicente
Blassingale, Wyatt Rainey
Blatty, William Peter
Bledsoe, Albert Taylor
Blier, Bertrand
Blish, James Benjamin
Blitzstein, Marc
Bliven, Bruce
Blixen, Karen Christentze,
Baroness
Bloch, Robert Albert
Blofeld, John
Blok, Aleksandr
Aleksandrovich
Bloom, Allan David
Bloom, Harry
Bloom, Ursula
Blough, Glenn Orlando
Blount, Charles
Bloy, Leon Marie
Blume, Judy Sussman
Blyth, Chay
Blyton, Carey
Blyton, Enid Mary
Boccaccio, Giovanni
Bodard, Lucien (Albert)
Bode, Carl
Bodenheim, Maxwell
Bodsworth, Charles
Frederick
Boehm, Eric Hartzell
Bogarde, Dirk
Bogart, Leo
Boileau(-Despreaux),
Nicolas
Bojer, Johan
Bok, Edward William
Bok, Hannes Vajn
Boles, Paul Darcy
Boley, Forrest Irving
Bolingbroke, Henry St.
John, Viscount
Bolinger, Dwight
Lemerton
Bolitho, Henry Hector
Bolitho, William
Boll, Heinrich (Theodor)
Boller, Paul Franklin, Jr.
Bolt, Robert (Oxton)
Bolton, Isabel
Bombal, Maria Luisa
Bombeck, Erma (Louise)

Cater, Douglass
Cather, Willa (Sibert)
Catherall, Arthur
Caton-Thompson, Gertrude
Catton, Bruce
Causley, Charles Stanley
Cavendish, William, Duke
   of Newcastle
Cecil, Edgar Algernon
   Robert
Celine, Louis-Ferdinand
Chamberlain, Houston
   Stewart
Chamberlain, Samuel
Chamberlin, William
   Henry
Chambers, Robert
Chambers, Robert W
Champollin-Figeac,
   Jacques-Joseph
Chandler, Jeff
Chandler, Raymond
   Thornton
Chang, Jung
Chaplin, Charlie
Chappell, Fred (Davis)
Charlevoix, Pierre Francis
   Xavier de
Charlip, Remy
Charriere, Henri
Charteris, Leslie
Chartier, Alain
Chase, Stuart
Chateaubriand, Francois
   Rene de
Chatterji, Bankimchandra
Chatwin, Bruce
Chaudhuri, Haridas
Chavez, Linda
Cheever, John
Chekhov, Anton Pavlovich
Chenier, Marie-Andre de
Chennault, Anna Chan
Chermayeff, Serge (Ivan)
Chesney, Marion
Chesnut, Mary Boykin
   (Miller)
Chesnutt, Charles Waddell
Chessman, Caryl Whittier
Chesterfield, Philip
   Dormer, Earl
Chevalier, Jules
Chevallier, Gabriel
Chew, Peter
Cheyney, Peter
Chiang, Yee
Chidsey, Donald Barr
Child, Julia McWilliams
Child, Lydia Maria
   Francis
Childers, Erskine
Childress, Alice
Childs, Marquis William
Chipperfield, Joseph
   Eugene
Chirol, Valentine, Sir
Chisholm, Shirley Anita
   St. Hill
Chodorov, Edward
Chopin, Kate
Chopra, Deepak
Choquette, Robert Guy
Chraibi, Driss
Chretien de Troyes
Christie, Agatha Mary
   Clarissa Miller, Dame

Christine de Pisan
Christ-Janer, Albert
Chuang Tzu
Churchill, Winston
Churchill, Winston
   Leonard Spencer, Sir
Chute, Beatrice Joy
Chute, Marchette
   (Gaylord)
Ciardi, John Anthony
Cibber, Colley
Cisneros, Sandra
Claiborne, Craig
Clancy, Thomas L., Jr.
Clapp, Patricia
Clark, Barrett H
Clark, Eleanor
Clark, Kenneth
   MacKenzie, Sir
Clark, Mary Higgins
Clark, Sydney
Clark, Thomas Dionysius
Clark, Walter van Tilburg
Clarke, Arthur C(harles)
Clarke, John Henrik
Clarke, Marcus (Andrew
   Hislop)
Clarkson, Ewan
Claudel, Paul Louis
   Charles
Clausewitz, Karl (Philipp
   Gottlieb) von
Clavell, James (Edmund
   Du Maresq)
Cleage, Pearl (Michelle)
Cleaver, Eldridge
Cleaver, William Joseph
Cleghorn, Sarah Norcliffe
Cleland, John
Clifton, (Thelma) Lucille
Cloete, Stuart
Close, Upton
Clurman, Harold Edgar
Coates, Robert Myron
Cobb, Irvin Shrewsbury
Cobbett, William
Cobleigh, Ira Underwood
Cocteau, Jean
Codrescu, Andrei
Coetzee, J(ohn) M
Coffin, Robert Peter
   Tristram
Coffin, William Sloan, Jr.
Coghill, Nevill Henry
   Kendall Aylmer
Cohen, Daniel
Cohen, Joan Lebold
Cohen, Morris Raphael
Cohen, Octavus Roy
Cohen, Wilbur Joseph
Coit, Margaret Louise
Coker, Elizabeth
   Boatwright
Colby, Carroll Burleigh
Colden, Cadwallader
Cole, George Douglas
   Howard
Coleman, James S(amuel)
Coleman, Lonnie William
Coleridge, Mary Elizabeth
Coleridge, Samuel Taylor
Coles, Robert
Colette
Collier, Peter
Collins, Jackie
Collins, Larry

Collins, Wilkie
Collodi, Carlo
Colwin, Laurie
Combe, George
Combe, William
Comenius, Johann Amos
Comfort, Alexander
Commager, Steele
Compton-Burnett, Ivy,
   Dame
Comstock, Anthony
Condon, Richard
   (Thomas)
Cone, James H
Connell, Evan Shelby, Jr.
Connolly, James B
Conquest, Robert
Conrad, Joseph
Conrad, Paul Francis
Conroy, Jack
Conroy, Pat
Constant de Rebeque,
   (Henri) Benjamin
Conway, Moncure Daniel
Conze, Edward J D
Cook, Robin
Cooke, John Esten
Cooke, Rose Terry
Coolidge, Dane
Cooper, Douglas
Cooper, J(oan) California
Cooper, James Fenimore
Cooper, Joseph D
Cooper, Kenneth Hardy
Cooper, Louise Field
Coover, Robert (Lowell)
Cope, Jack
Coppard, A(lfred) E(dgar)
Corelli, Marie
Corey, Lewis
Corle, Edwin
Cornwell, Patricia
   (Daniels)
Corson, Juliet
Cortazar, Julio
Cortissoz, Royal
Corvo, Baron
Coryell, John Russell
Cosby, Camille (Olivia
   Hanks)
Costain, Thomas Bertram
Costello, Chris
Cotton, Charles
Cottrell, Alan Howard, Sir
Couperius, Louis (Marie
   Anne)
Coupland, Douglas
Courlander, Harold
Cournos, John
Cousins, Norman
Covey, Cyclone
Covey, Stephen R.
Cowan, Peter Wilkinshaw
Cowles, Fleur Fenton
Cowley, Malcolm
Cox, Palmer
Coxe, George Harmon
Cozzens, James Gould
Craik, Dinah Maria
   Mulock
Crane, Nathalia Clara
   Ruth
Crane, Stephen
Crawford, Christina
Crawford, Francis Marion
Crawford, John Edmund

Creasey, John
Crebillon, Claude Prosper
   Jolyot de
Creeley, Robert (White)
Creighton, Thomas
   H(awk)
Crevecoeur, Michel-
   Guillaume Jean de
Crevecoeur, (Hector) St.
   John de
Crews, Harry Eugene
Crichton, Michael
Crichton, Robert
Crisp, Quentin
Crispin, Edmund
Crockett, S(amuel)
   R(utherford)
Croft-Cooke, Rupert
Crofts, Freeman Willis
Cronin, A(rchibald)
   J(oseph)
Crossman, Richard
   Howard Stafford
Crowley, Aleister (Edward
   Alexander)
Cubberley, Ellwood
   Patterson
Cugoano, Ottobah
Culliford, Peyo
Cummings, E(dward)
   E(stlin)
Cunha, Euclides
   (Rodrigues Pimenta) da
Cunninghame-Graham,
   Robert Bontine
Cuppy, Will(iam Jacob)
Curie, Eve
Curry, Peggy Simson
Curtis, George William
Curwood, James Oliver
Custer, Elizabeth Bacon
Dabney, Virginius
Dabrowska, Maria
   Szumska
Dadie, Bernard Binlin
Dahl, Roald
Dahlberg, Edward
Daiches, David
Dailey, Janet
Daley, Arthur (John)
Daly, Maureen Patricia
Dalzel, Archibald
Dampier, William
Dana, Richard Henry, Jr.
Dane, Clemence
Dangerfield, George Bubb
Daniel, Samuel
Daniels, Jonathan Worth
Dannay, Frederic
D'Annunzio, Gabriele
Danticat, Edwidge
Danvers, Dennis
D'Arcy, Martin Cyril
Dargan, Olive Tilford
Darley, Felix Octavius
   Carr
Darling, Frank Fraser, Sir
Darnton, Robert Choate
Darwin, Charles Robert
Dasgupta, S(urendra)
   N(ath)
Dashwood, Elizabeth
   Monica
Daudet, Leon
Davenport, Marcia
David-Neel, Alexandra

Davie, Donald Alfred
Davies, Hunter
Davies, Leslie Purnell
Davies, (William) Robertson
Davis, Angela (Yvonne)
Davis, Clyde Brion
Davis, Frederick C(lyde)
Davis, Gerry
Davis, Harold Lenoir
Davis, Patti
Davis, Rebecca Blaine Harding
Davis, Richard Harding
Davison, Frank Dalby
Dawkins, Wayne J(esse)
Day, Chon
Day, James Wentworth
Day, Thomas
Day-Lewis, Cecil
DeCamp, L(yon) Sprague
Decoster, Charles Theodore Henri
Dedijer, Vladimir
Deeping, (George) Warwick
Defoe, Daniel
DeHartog, Jan
Deighton, Len
Deiss, Joseph Jay
DeJong, David Cornel
DeKruif, Paul Henry
DeLaMare, Walter
Deland, Margaret Wade
Delano, Isaac O
Delany, Martin Robinson
Delany, Samuel R.
DeLaRoche, Mazo
Delblanc, Sven
Delderfield, Ronald Frederick
Deledda, Grazia
DeLillo, Don
Dell, Floyd
DellaFemina, Jerry
Dellenbaugh, Frederick Samuel
Dellinger, David T
Delmar, Vina Croter
Deloney, Thomas
DeLorean, John Zachary
Deloria, Vine (Victor), Jr.
del Ray, Lester (Ramon Alvarez)
DeMille, Agnes (George)
Deming, Barbara
De Morgan, William Frend
DeMott, Benjamin Haile
Denning, Alfred Thompson
Dennis, Nigel Forbes
Dennis, Patrick
Dennison, George
Denny-Brown, Derek Ernest
Dent, Alan Holmes
DeQuincey, Thomas
Derleth, August (William)
DeSanctis, Francesco
Destouches, Louis-Ferdinand
Deutsch, Babette
Deutsch, Harold C(harles)
DeValois, Ninette, Dame
Devereux, George

DeVoto, Bernard Augustine
DeVries, Hugo
DeVries, Peter
DeWohl, Louis
Dhlomo, R(olfus) R(eginald) R(aymond)
Dibdin, Thomas Frognall
Dick, Philip K(indred)
Dickens, Charles (John Huffam)
Dickens, Monica Enid
Dickson, Gordon Rupert
Didion, Joan
DiDonato, Pietro
Digby, Kenelm, Sir
Dillard, Annie Doak
Dillon, Diane Claire Sorber
Dillon, George
Dillon, Leo
Diop, Birago
Disney, Doris Miles
Disraeli, Benjamin
D'Israeli, Isaac
Ditmars, Raymond Lee
Divine, Arthur Durham
Dix, Dorothy
Dixon, Jeane (Pinckert)
Dixon, Melvin
Dixon, Thomas
Djilas, Milovan
Dobie, J(ames) Frank
Dobozy, Imre
Doctorow, E(dgar) L(aurence)
Dodd, John Bruce, Mrs.
Dolbier, Maurice (Wyman)
Dollard, John
Donaldson, Stephen Reeder
Donleavy, James Patrick
Donnelly, Ignatius
Donoso, Jose
Doolittle, Hilda
Dorfman, Ariel
Dos Passos, John (Roderigo)
Dostoyevsky, Fyodor Mikhailovich
Doughty, Charles Montagu
Douglas, Alfred Bruce, Lord
Douglas, Ellen
Douglas, Emily Taft
Douglas, Lloyd Cassel
Douglas, Mary Tew
Douglas, Norman
Douglas-Home, Charles
Douglass, Frederick
Downes, Edward Olin Davenport
Downes, Olin
Downey, Fairfax Davis
Dowson, Ernest Christopher
Doyle, Arthur Conan, Sir
Doyle, Roddy
Drabble, Margaret
Drachmann, Holger Henrik Herholdt
Draper, Sharon M(ills)
Drayton, Michael
Dreiser, Theodore
Dresser, Davis

Drewry, John Eldridge
Drexler, Rosalyn
Dreyfus, Hubert L(ederer)
Dreyfus, Jack Jonas
Drinkwater, John
Drummond de Andrade, Carlos
Drury, Allen (Stuart)
Dube, John Langalibalele
DuBois, W(illiam) E(dward) B(urghardt)
Dubos, Rene Jules
Ducharme, Rejean
Duggan, Maurice Noel
Duhamel, Georges
Duke, Robin (Anthony Hare)
Dumas, Alexandre Dumas Davy de la Pailleterie
DuMaurier, Daphne
DuMaurier, George Louis P B
Dunbar, Helen Flanders
Dunbar, Paul Laurence
Dunn, Katherine (Karen)
Dunne, Dominick
Dunne, Finley Peter
Dunne, John Gregory
Dunning, William Archibald
Dunsany, Edward J M Plunkett, Baron
Durant, Ariel
Durant, Will(iam James)
Duranty, Walter
Duras, Marguerite
Durrell, Lawrence (George)
Durrenmatt, Friedrich
Dwight, Timothy
Dyer, Wayne Walter
Earle, Alice Morse
Early, Gerald
Eastlake, William (Derry)
Eastman, Mary Henderson
Eastman, Max Forrester
Eaton, Dorman Bridgman
Eberhart, Mignon Good
Eberle, Irmengarde
Ebers, Georg Moritz
Echeverria, Jose Esteban (Antonino)
Eckstein, Gustav
Eco, Umberto
Eddy, Sherwood
Edel, Leon
Edelman, Marian Wright
Eden, Dorothy
Edgell, George Harold
Edmonds, Walter D(umaux)
Edwards, Jonathan
Eeden, Fredrik Willem van
Efron, Marshall
Eggleston, Edward
Ehrenburg, Ilya Grigoryevich
Eichelberger, Robert Lawrence
Eilshemius, Louis Michel
Eisenhower, Julie Nixon
Ekwensi, Cyprian Odiatu Duaka
Elegant, Robert Sampson
Eliot, George

Eliot, George Fielding
Elkin, Stanley (Lawrence)
Ellin, Stanley
Elliott, George Paul
Elliott, Osborn
Ellis, Bret Easton
Ellis, Harry Bearse
Ellison, Harlan Jay
Ellison, Ralph (Waldo)
Ellroy, James
Ellsberg, Daniel
Ellsberg, Edward
Eluard, Paul
Elyot, Thomas, Sir
Emanuel, James A
Emecheta, Buchi
Emery, Anne (McGuigan)
Encina, Juan del
Endo, Shusaku
Engel, Lehman
Engle, Eloise Katherine
Engle, Paul (Hamilton)
Enright, Dennis Joseph
Enright, Elizabeth
Ephron, Nora
Epstein, Edward Jay
Equiano, Olaudah
Erasmus, Desiderius
Erdman, Paul E(mil)
Erdrich, Louise
Ernaux, Annie
Ernst, Jimmy
Ernst, Paul Karl Friedrich
Erskine, John
Ertz, Susan
Espriu, Salvador
Esslin, Martin Julius
Estleman, Loren D
Etchison, Dennis
Eucken, Rudolf Christoph
Eugenides, Jeffrey
Evans, Bergen Baldwin
Evans, Chick
Evans, Clifford
Evans, Harold Matthew
Evans-Pritchard, Edward Evan
Evatt, Herbert Vere
Evelyn, John
Ewen, David
Ewen, Frederic
Ewing, Alfred Cyril
Eysenck, Hans J(urgen)
Faber, Geoffrey Cust, Sir
Fabre, Jean Henri
Fadil al-Jamali, Muhammad
Fadiman, Clifton (Paul)
Fagunwa, D(aniel) O(lorunfemi)
Fairbank, Janet Ayer
Falk, Lee Harrison
Fall, Bernard B
Fallada, Hans
Falls, Joe
Farago, Ladislas
Farb, Peter
Farina, Richard
Farjeon, Eleanor
Farley, Walter Lorimer
Farmer, Philip Jose
Farnol, Jeffery
Farrar, John Chipman
Farrell, James Thomas
Farrere, Claude
Farrow, John Villiers

Fassbinder, Rainer Werner
Fast, Howard Melvin
Faulkner, William
Faure, Edgar Jean
Fauset, Jessie Redmon
Faust, Frederick Schiller
Fearing, Kenneth Flexner
Fedin, Konstantin
  Aleksandrovich
Feigl, Herbert
Feingold, Benjamin
  Franklin
Felton, Harold W
Fenelon, Fania
Fenelon, Francois de
  Salignac
Fenn, George Manville
Fenten, D X
Fenton, Carroll Lane
Ferber, Edna
Fergusson, Francis
Fergusson, Harvey
Ferlinghetti, Lawrence
  Monsanto
Fernandez de Lizardi, Jose
  Joaquin
Ferrer, Gabriel (Francisco
  Victor) Miro
Ferrero, Guglielmo
Feuchtwanger, Lion
Feuillet, Octave
Ficino, Marsilio
Ficke, Arthur Davidson
Field, Kate
Fielding, Gabriel
Fielding, Henry
Fielding, Temple
  Hornaday
Fields, James Thomas
Filipovic, Zlata
Fineman, Irving
Finkelstein, Louis, Dr.
Finley, Martha
Finney, Jack
Firbank, Ronald
First, Ruth
Fischer, John
Fischer, Louis
Fish, Hamilton
Fish, Robert Lloyd
Fishbein, Morris
Fisher, Dorothy Frances
  Canfield
Fisher, Irving
Fisher, James Maxwell
  McConnell
Fisher, John
Fisher, M(ary) F(rances)
  K(ennedy)
Fisher, R(onald) A(ylmer)
Fisher, Rudolph
Fisher, Vardis
Fiske, John
Fitch, James Marston
Fitts, Dudley
Fitzgerald, F(rancis) Scott
  (Key)
FitzGerald, Frances
Fitzgerald, Robert Stuart
Fitzgerald, Zelda
Fitzgibbon, Constantine
Fitzhugh, George
Fixx, James Fuller
Flagg, James Montgomery
Flanders, Michael
Flanner, Janet

Flaubert, Gustave
Flavin, Martin Archer
Fleischer, Nat(haniel
  Stanley)
Fleming, Ian Lancaster
Fleming, Joan Margaret
Flesch, Rudolf (Franz)
Fletcher, John
Fletcher, Joseph Francis
  (III)
Flexner, Abraham
Flint, Timothy
Flora, James (Royer)
Foerster, Friedrich
  Wilhelm
Foerster, Norman
Fogazzaro, Antonio
Follett, Ken(neth Martin)
Fonseca, Rubem
Fontane, Theodor
Foote, Horton
Forbes, Esther
Forbes, Kathryn
Ford, Corey
Ford, Eileen
Ford, Ford Madox
Ford, Paul Leicester
Ford, Richard
Forester, Cecil Scott
Forman, James Douglas
Forster, E(dward)
  M(organ)
Forsyth, Frederick
Fort, Charles Hoy
Fortune, Timothy Thomas
Fosdick, Raymond Blaine
Foucault, Michel
Fowler, Gene
Fowler, Henry Watson
Fowler, Orson Squire
Fowles, John (Robert)
Fowlie, Wallace
Fox, John W, Jr.
Fox, Uffa
Fraenkel, Heinrich
France, Anatole
Francis, Dick
Frank, Bruno
Frank, Gerold
Frank, Waldo
Frankau, Gilbert
Frankau, Pamela
Franken, Rose
Frankl, Viktor E(mil)
Franklin, Benjamin
Franklin, Miles
Franklin, Robert M(ichael)
Frasconi, Antonio
Fraser, Antonia Pakenham,
  Lady
Fraser, George MacDonald
Frayn, Michael
Frazier, Ian
Freberg, Stan
Frederic, Harold
Freedman, Russell
Freeling, Nicolas
Freeman, Cynthia
Freeman, Joseph
Freeman, Mary E Wilkins
Freeman, R(ichard) Austin
Freemantle, Brian Harry
French, Albert
French, Marilyn
Freuchen, Peter

Freyre, Gilberto (de
  Mello)
Freytag, Gustav
Fried, Alfred Hermann
Friedan, Betty (Naomi
  Goldstein)
Friedman, Bruce Jay
Friedman, William
  Frederick
Fries, Jakob Friedrich
Frings, Ketti
Frisch, Max
Froissart, Jean
Fromentin, Eugene
Frost, David
Frum, Barbara
Fry, Charles Burgess
Fuchs, Daniel
Fuentes, Carlos
Fuess, Claude Moore
Fukuyama, Francis
Fulghum, Robert
Fuller, Edmund
Fuller, Henry Blake
Fuller, Loie
Fuller, Richard
  Buckminster
Fuller, Roy Broadbent
Fuller-Maitland, John
  Alexander
Furphy, Joseph
Furstenberg, Diane Halfin
  von
Furstenberg, Egon von
Fuseli, Henry
Futrelle, Jacques
Gabor, Mark
Gadamer, Hans-Georg
Gaddis, Thomas (Eugene)
Gaddis, William (Thomas)
Gage, Matilda Joslyn
Gaines, Ernest J(ames)
Galbraith, John Kenneth
Gale, Zona
Galeano, Eduardo
  (Hughes)
Galen
Galiani, Ferdinando
Gallant, Mavis
Gallatin, Albert Eugene
Gallegos, Romulo
Gallico, Paul William
Galsworthy, John
Galt, John
Gann, Ernest Kellogg
Garcia, Cristina
Garcia-Marquez, Gabriel
  Jose
Garcilaso de la Vega, Inca
Gardiner, Samuel Rawson
Gardner, Erle Stanley
Gardner, John Champlin,
  Jr.
Gardner, Martin
Garfield, Brian Wynne
Garfield, Leon
Garis, Howard Roger
Garland, Hamlin
Garnett, David
Garnett, Richard
Garraty, John Arthur
Garrett, George Palmer, Jr.
Garrod, Heathcote William
Garrow, David J
Gary, Romain

Gaskell, Elizabeth
  Cleghorn
Gass, William Howard
Gassner, John Waldhorn
Gates, Henry Louis, Jr.
Gates, Sylvester James, Jr.
Gault, William Campbell
Gaunt, William
Gautier, Theophile
Gay, John
Gay, Peter Jack
Geertz, Clifford James
Gehlen, Reinhard
Gelb, Arthur
Gelb, Barbara Stone
Gelber, Jack
Gellhorn, Martha Ellis
Gellis, Roberta Leah
  Jacobs
Genauer, Emily
Genet, Jean
Geoffrey of Monmouth
George, Jean Craighead
George, Nelson
Gerhardi, William
  Alexander
Gerould, Gordon Hall
Gerson, Noel Bertram
Geyer, Georgie Anne
Ghose, Sri Chinmoy
  Kumar
Gibberd, Frederick, Sir
Gibbon, Lewis Grassic
Gibbons, Euell
Gibbons, Kaye
Gibbons, Stella (Dorothea)
Gibbs, Anthony
Gibson, Bill
Gibson, Henry
Gibson, Walter B(rown)
Giddings, Franklin Henry
Gide, Andre (Paul
  Guillaume)
Gilbreth, Frank Bunker, Jr.
Gilder, George
Gilkey, Langdon Brown
Gill, Brendan
Gill, Eric
Gillott, Jacky
Gilman, Charlotte Anna
  Perkins
Gilman, Dorothy
Gilman, Lawrence
Gilot, Francoise
Gilpin, Laura
Gingrich, Arnold
Ginott, Haim
Ginzberg, Louis
Ginzburg, Natalia
Giono, Jean
Giovanni, Nikki
Giraudoux, Jean
Gissing, George Robert
Giusti, Giuseppe
Gjellerup, Karl Adolf
Gladstone, William Ewart
Glasgow, Ellen Anderson
  Gholson
Glaspell, Susan Keating
Glass, Montague
  (Marsden)
Glassco, John Stinson
Glazer, Nathan
Glubb, John Bagot, Sir
Glyn, Elinor Sutherland

Heyer, Georgette
Heym, Stefan
Heyse, Paul Johann
  Ludwig von
Heyward, (Edwin) DuBose
Hiassen, Carl
Hibbert, Eleanor Alice
  Burford
Hickok, Lorena A
Hicks, Granville
Hidayat, Sadiq
Higgins, George V.
Higginson, Thomas
  Wentworth Storrow
Highet, Gilbert (Arthur)
Highsmith, Patricia
Hill, George Birkbeck
  Norman
Hill, Grace Livingstone
Hillerman, Tony
Hillyer, Robert
Hilton, James
Himes, Chester Bomar
Himmelfarb, Gertrude
Hinde, Thomas, Sir
Hines, Duncan
Hinojosa, Rolando
Hinton, S(usan) E(loise)
Hirschfeld, Al(bert)
Hite, Shere
Hoagland, Edward Morley
Hoban, Russell
Hobart, Alice Tisdale
  Nourse
Hobbes, Thomas
Hobson, Laura Zametkin
Hochhuth, Rolf
Hoff, Sydney
Hoffer, Eric
Hoffman, Abbie
Hoffman, Al
Hoffmann, E(rnst)
  T(heodor) A(madeus)
Hogg, James
Holbrook, Stewart Hall
Hollander, Xaviera
Holling, Holling C(lancy)
Holloway, Emory
Holme, Constance
Holmes, John Clellon
Holmes, Mary Jane Hawes
Holmes, Oliver Wendell,
  Sr.
Holt, John Caldwell
Holzer, Harold
Homer
Hone, William
Hood, Thomas
Hook, Theodore Edward
Hope-Hawkins, Anthony,
  Sir
Hopkins, John Henry
Horan, James David
Horchow, S(amuel) Roger
Horgan, Paul
Horn, Alfred Aloysius
Hornung, Ernest William
Horowitz, David Joel
Hotchner, Aaron Edward
Household, Geoffrey
  Edward West
Housman, Laurence
Howar, Barbara
Howard, Jane Temple
Howard, Robert Ervin
Howatch, Susan

Howe, Edgar Watson
Howe, Florence Rosenfeld
Howe, Irving
Howe, Joseph
Howe, Julia Ward
Howe, Mark De Wolfe
Howells, William Dean
Howitt, William
Hoyle, Fred, Sir
Hrabal, Bohumil
Hubbard, Elbert Green
Huch, Ricarda (Octavia)
Hudson, William Henry
Hughes, Emmet John
Hughes, Langston
Hughes, Richard Arthur
  Warren
Hughes, Robert Studley
  Forrest
Hughes, Rupert
Hughes, Thomas
Hugo, Victor Marie
Huie, William Bradford
Hulme, Kathryn Cavarly
Humboldt, Wilhelm
  Freiherr von
Humphreys, Christmas
Humphry, Derek John
Huneker, James Gibbons
Hunt, E(verette) Howard
Hunt, Leigh
Hunt, Marsha
Hunter, Dard
Hunter, Evan
Hunter, Floyd
Hurok, Sol(omon
  Isaievich)
Hurst, Fannie
Hurston, Zora Neale
Husayn, Taha
Hustvedt, Siri
Huxley, Aldous (Leonard)
Huxley, Elspeth Josceline
  Grant
Huxley, Julian Sorell, Sir
Huxley, Laura Archera
Huysmans, Joris Karl
Hyams, Joe
Ibn al-Arabi, Muhyi al-
  Din
Ibsen, Henrik Johan
Ibuse, Masuji
Icaza (Coronel), Jorge
Iceberg Slim
Idle, Eric
Ilg, Frances Lillian
Imam, Alhadji Abubakar
  Iman
Indy, Paul (Marie
  Theodore Vincent d')
Infeld, Leopold
Ing, Dean
Inge, William Ralph
Ingelow, Jean
Ingstad, Helge Marcus
Innes, Hammond
Ionesco, Eugene
Irving, Clifford Michael
Irving, John
Irving, Washington
Irwin, James Benson
Irwin, Margaret
Irwin, Wallace (Admah)
Isaacs, Jorge
Isaacs, Susan
Isham, Samuel

Isherwood, Christopher
  (William)
Ishiguro, Kazuo
Jackson, Charles Reginald
Jackson, Helen Maria
  Hunt Fiske
Jackson, Sheneska
Jackson, Shirley (Hardie)
Jacobs, Harriet Ann
Jacobs, Helen (Hull)
Jacobs, Joseph
Jacobs, W(illiam)
  W(ymark)
Jacobsen, Jens Peter
Jacoby, Oswald
Jaeger, Werner Wilhelm
Jaffe, Rona
Jaffee, Allan
Jagendorf, Moritz Adolf
Jahoda, Gloria (Adelaide
  Love)
Jakes, John (William)
Jakes, Thomas T.D.
James, G(eorge) P(ayne)
  R(ainsford)
James, Henry, (Jr.)
James, Marquis
James, Montague Rhodes
James, P(hyllis) D(orothy)
James, Will(iam Roderick)
Jameson, Margaret Storm
Jammes, Francis
Janeway, Eliot
Janeway, Elizabeth Hall
Janifer, Laurence M(ark)
Janney, Russell Dixon
Janson, Horst Woldemar
Japrisot, Sebastien
Jarrell, Randall
Jaspers, Karl
Jastrow, Robert
Jean de Meun
Jeffrey, Francis Jeffrey,
  Lord
Jeffries, Richard
Jen, Gish
Jenkins, Beverly
Jennings, Elizabeth Joan
Jennings, Gary
Jensen, Arthur Robert
Jensen, Johannes Vilhelm
Jensen, Oliver Ormerod
Jensen, Virginia Allen
Jerome, Jerome Klapka
Jessup, Richard
Jesus ben Sira
Jewett, Sarah Orne
Jhabvala, Ruth Prawer
John of Salisbury
Johnson, Arno Hollock
Johnson, Charles Richard
Johnson, Crockett
Johnson, Emily Pauline
Johnson, Eyvind Olof
  Verner
Johnson, Gerald White
Johnson, James Ralph
Johnson, James Weldon
Johnson, Josephine
  Winslow
Johnson, Martin Elmer
Johnson, Pamela Hansford
Johnson, Philip Cortelyou
Johnson, Raynor Carey
Johnston, Basil H.
Johnston, Henry Hamilton

Johnston, Richard
  Malcolm
Joinville, Jean de
Jones, David
Jones, Edward P.
Jones, (Morgan) Glyn
Jones, Gwynn
Jones, Howard Mumford
Jones, James
Jones, Madison Percy, Jr.
Jones, Rufus Matthew
Jones, Thom
Jones, Tristan
Jones, Weyman
Jong, Erica (Mann)
Jordan, Elizabeth Garver
Jordan, June
Joseph, Helen
Josephson, Matthew
Joyce, James Augustus
  Aloysius
Judson, Emily Chubbock
Juenger, Ernst
Julian of Norwich
Just, Ward
Kadare, Ismail
Kael, Pauline
Kaempffert, Waldemar
  (Bernhard)
Kafka, Franz
Kahn, Roger
Kalb, Bernard
Kamp, Irene Kittle
Kane, Harnett T(homas)
Kane, Henry
Kanin, Garson
Kanner, Leo
Kantor, Mackinlay
Kaplan, Mordecai
Karamzin, Nikolai
  Mikhailovich
Kassorla, Irene Chamie
Kastner, Erich
Katayev, Valentin
  Petrovich
Katzen, Mollie
Kaufman, Bel
Kaufman, Sue
Kautilya
Kavan, Anna
Kawabata, Yasunari
Kaye, Mary Margaret
  Mollie
Kaye-Smith, Sheila
Kazan, Elia
Kazantzakis, Nikos
Keane, Mary Nesta
Kearns, Doris H
Keble, John
Kedourie, Elie
Keegan, John
Keeshan, Bob
Keillor, Garrison
Kelland, Clarence
  Budington
Keller, Gottfried
Keller, Helen Adams
Kelley, Kitty
Kelman, James
Kelsey, Alice Geer
Kemal, Yashar
Kemble, Fanny
Kemelman, Harry
Kemp, Harry (Hibbard)
Keneally, Thomas
  (Michael)

Liu Tsung-yuan
Livingston, J(oseph)
  A(rnold)
Llewellyn, Richard
Lobel, Arnold Stark
Locke, Alain Leroy
Locke, William John
Lockridge, Frances Louise
Lockridge, Richard
Lockridge, Ross Franklin,
  Jr.
Lodge, David (John)
Lodge, Thomas
Loeb, Gerald Martin
Lofting, Hugh
Lofts, Norah Robinson
Logan, Daniel
Lomax, Louis
Lomonosov, Mikhail
  Vasilyevich
London, Jack
Long, John Luther
Longinus
Longstreet, James
Longus
Longworth, Alice
  Roosevelt
Loos, Anita
Lopez, Barry (Holstun)
Lopez de Ayala, Pero
Lopez-Portillo y Rojas,
  Jose
Lord, Bette Bao
Lord, Phillips H
Lord, Walter
Lortz, Richard
Lossing, Benson John
Loti, Pierre
Louys, Pierre
Lovecraft, H(oward)
  P(hillips)
Lovejoy, Clarence Earle
Lovelace, Linda
Lovelock, James
Lovesey, Peter Harmer
Lowenfels, Walter
Lowndes, Marie Adelaide
  Belloc
Lowndes, Robert
  A(ugustine) W(ard)
Lowry, Malcolm
Lucan
Luce, Clare Boothe
Lu Chiu-yuan
Lucian
Ludendorff, Erich
  Friedrich Wilhelm
Ludlow, Fitz Hugh
Ludlum, Robert
Ludwig, Emil
Ludwig, Otto
Luhan, Mabel (Ganson)
  Dodge
Lu Hsun
Lukas, J(ay) Anthony
Lummis, Charles Fletcher
Lundkvist, Artur Nils
Lurie, Alison
Lyell, Charles, Sir
Lyly, John
Lynch, Peter
Lynd, Helen Merrell
Lynes, Joseph Russell, Jr.
Lyons, Enid Muriel
Lyons, Eugene
Lytle, Andrew Nelson

Lytton, Edward George
  Earle Lytton Bulwer-
  Lytton, 1st Baron
  Lytton
Maas, Peter
Mabee, Carleton
Mabuchi, Kamo
Mabuza, Lindiwe
Macaulay, (Emilie) Rose,
  Dame
MacDonald, George
MacDonald, John Dann
MacDonald, Ross
Macfadden, Bernarr
  Adolphus
Machado (y Ruiz), Manuel
Machado de Assis,
  Joaquim Maria
Machen, Arthur
Machiavelli, Niccolo
Machlup, Fritz
MacInnes, Helen
Mackenzie, Alexander, Sir
Mackenzie, Compton
Mackenzie, Henry
MacLaine, Shirley
MacLean, Alistair (Stuart)
MacLennan, Hugh
Macpherson, James
Mahfouz, Naguib
Mailer, Norman
  (Kingsley)
Major, Charles
Major, Clarence
Makonnen Endalkacaw
Malamud, Bernard
Malaparte, Curzio
Malcolm, Andrew
  H(ogarth)
Malherbe, Francois de
Mallet-Joris, Francoise
Mallock, William Hurrell
Mallowan, Max Edgar
  Lucien, Sir
Malone, Dumas
Malone, Edmund
Malory, Thomas, Sir
Malouf, David
Malraux, Andre Georges
Maltz, Albert
Manasseh ben Israel
Manchester, William
  Raymond
Mandelstam, Nadezhda
  Yakovlevna
Manfred, Frederick
  Feikema
Mankowitz, Wolf
Mann, Erika
Mann, Heinrich Ludwig
Mann, Klaus
Mann, Thomas
Mannes, Marya
Manning, Irene
Manning, Olivia
Mansfield, Katherine
Manzoni, Alessandro
  (Antonio)
Mao Zedong
Marchetti, Victor L
Marcum, John Arthur
Marcus Aurelius
  Antoninus
Marek, Kurt W
Margolius, Sidney Senier
Marguerite d'Angouleme

Margulis, Lynn
Marie Alexandra Victoria
Marivaux, Pierre Carlet de
Marks, Percy
Marlowe, Derek
Marmol, Jose
Marmontel, Jean Francois
Marquand, John Phillips
Marryat, Frederick
Marsh, Ngaio, Dame
Marshall, Catherine
Marston, John
Martin, Judith
Martin, Robert Bernard
Martin, Valerie
Martin du Gard, Roger
Martineau, Harriet
Marty, Martin Emil
Marvell, Andrew
Masefield, John
Mason, Bobbie Ann
Mason, Daniel Gregory
Mason, F(rancis) van
  Wyck
Massey, Gerald
Masters, John
Masudi, Ali ibn al-Husayn
  al-
Masur, Harold Q
Mathabane, Mark
Mather, Cotton
Mathews, John Joseph
Mathison, Richard
  Randolph
Matisse, Henri Emile
  Benoit
Matthiessen, Francis Otto
Maugham, Robin
Maugham, W(illiam)
  Somerset
Maupassant, Guy de
Mauriac, Claude
Mauriac, Francois
Maurois, Andre
Maxwell, William
May, Karl Friedrich
May, Robert Lewis
Mayer, Edward Newton,
  Jr.
Mayer, Martin Prager
Mayle, Peter
Mayo, Katherine
Mazel, Judy
Mazrui, Ali A(l'Amin)
McAdie, Alexander
  George
McCall, Dorothy Lawson
McCarthy, Justin Huntly
McCarthy, Mary Therese
McClung, Nellie Letitia
  Mooney
McCourt, Frank
McCoy, Horace
McCullers, Carson (Smith)
McCulley, Johnston
McCullough, Colleen
McCullough, David Gaub
McCutcheon, George Barr
McDermott, Alice
McDowell, Katharine
  Sherwood Bonner
McEwan, Ian (Russell)
McFee, William
McGinley, Phyllis
McGinniss, Joe
McGivern, William Peter

McGuane, Thomas Francis
McGuffey, William
  Holmes
McHale, Tom
McInerney, Jay
McIntyre, John Thomas
McKay, Claude
McKay, Festus Claudius
McKay, Nellie Yvonne
McKelway, St. Clair
McKenna, Terence
McKenney, Ruth
McLuhan, (Herbert)
  Marshall
McMillan, Terry
McMullen, Mary
McMurtry, Larry Jeff
McNair, Malcolm Perrine
McNally, T. M.
McNamer, Deirdre
McNeile, Herman Cyril
McNickle, D'Arcy
McPhee, John (Angus)
McPherson, James Alan
McWhirter, A(lan) Ross
McWhirter, Norris Dewar
McWilliams, Carey
Mead, Margaret
Mears, Walter Robert
Mehta, Ved (Parkash)
Meier-Graefe, Julius
Melville, Herman
Memmi, Albert
Menchu, Rigoberta
Mendes, Catulle
Meredith, George
Merejkowski, Dmitri
  Sergeyevich
Merezhkovsky, Dmitry
  Sergeyevich
Merimee, Prosper
Meriwether, Lee
Merriam, Clinton Hart
Merriam, Eve
Merritt, Abraham
Merton, Thomas
Mertz, Barbara Louise
  Gross
Messick, Hank
Messner, Reinhold
Metalious, Grace de
  Repentigny
Michener, James A(lbert)
Mihajlov, Mihajlo
Mikhalkov, Sergei
  Vladimirovich
Miles, Bernard, Sir
Millar, Margaret (Ellis)
Millay, Edna St. Vincent
Miller, Alice Duer
Miller, Caroline
Miller, Henry (Valentine)
Miller, Jonathan (Wolfe)
Miller, Max (Carlton)
Miller, Merle
Miller, Olive Beaupre
Milligan, Spike
Millis, Walter
Milne, A(lan) A(lexander)
Milne, Christopher Robin
Milosz, Czeslaw
Mishima, Yukio
Mistry, Rohinton
Mitchell, Margaret
Mitchell, Silas Weir

Petronius, Gaius
Petry, Ann (Lane)
Peyre, Henri Maurice
Peyrefitte, Roger
Phaedrus
Philbrick, Herbert Arthur
Philby, Harold St. John
  Bridger
Philips, David Graham
Phillips, Caryl
Phillips, Julia
Phillips, Wendell
Phillpotts, Eden
Piercy, Marge
Pike, James Albert, Bishop
Pinckney, Darryl
Piper, H(enry) Beam
Pipher, Mary
Pirandello, Luigi
Pitkin, Walter Boughton
Pitrone, Jean Maddern
Pitt, William, the Younger
Plaatje, Sol(omon)
  T(shekisho)
Plain, Belva
Plath, Sylvia
Plato
Plimpton, George Ames
Plomer, William Charles
  Franklyn
Plotnik, Arthur
Plutarch
Podhoretz, Norman
Poe, Edgar Allan
Pohl, Frederik
Poincare, Raymond
Politi, Leo
Pollock, Channing
Pollock, Jackson
Polo, Marco
Poniatowska, Elena
Pontoppidan, Henrik
Poole, Ernest
Porter, Bernard H
Porter, Eleanor H
Porter, Gene Stratton
Porter, Hal
Porter, Katherine Anne
Porter, Sylvia Field
Portis, Charles
Post, Elizabeth Lindley
Post, Emily (Price)
Potok, Chaim
Potter, Beatrix
Potter, Stephen
Powdermaker, Hortense
Powell, Anthony Dymoke
Powell, Enoch
Powell, Gordon George
Powell, Lawrence Clark
Powers, Anne
Powers, James Farl
Powter, Susan
Powys, John Cowper
Powys, Llewelyn
Powys, Theodore Francis
Praetorius, Michael
Prather, Richard Scott
Pratt, Fletcher
Premchand
Preston, John
Prevost, Marcel
Prevost d'Exiles, Antoine
  Francois, Abbe
Price, Reynolds
Priestley, (J)ohn (B)oynton

Pritchett, V(ictor)
  S(awdon), Sir
Prokosch, Frederic
Proulx, E(dna) Annie
Proust, Marcel
Pudney, John Sleigh
Puig, Manuel
Pulci, Luigi
Puller, Lewis B., Jr.
Purdy, James
Purdy, Susan Gold
Pusey, Edward Bouverie
Pusey, Merlo John
Pushkin, Aleksandr
  Sergeyevich
Puzo, Mario
Pyle, Howard
Pym, Barbara Mary
  Crampton
Pynchon, Thomas
Queen, Ellery
Quiller-Couch, Arthur
  Thomas, Sir
Quindlen, Anna
Quinn, Arthur Hobson
Quiroga, Horacio
Raab, Selwyn
Rabelais, Francois
Radcliffe, Ann
Rader, Dotson
Rafferty, Max(well Lewis,
  Jr.)
Raine, William MacLeod
Rajagopalachari,
  Chakravarti
Rama Rau, Santha
Rand, Ayn
Randall, James Garfield
Randhawa, Mohinder
  Singh
Randisi, Robert Joseph
Randolph, Georgiana Ann
Randolph, Mary
Ransome, Arthur Mitchell
Raphael, Chaim
Raphaelson, Samson
Ratzel, Friedrich
Rawlings, Marjorie
  Kinnan
Rayner, Claire Berenice
Read, Piers Paul
Reade, Charles
Ready, William Bernard
Rebuffat, Gaston Louis
  Simon
Rechy, John Francisco
Redfield, James
Redford, Robert
Redi, Francesco
Reed, Ishmael Scott
Reed, John Silas
Reed, Myrtle
Reed, Peter Hugh
Reik, Theodor
Reiner, Carl
Remarque, Erich Maria
Renard, Jules
Renault, Mary
Rendell, Ruth
Reuben, David Robert
Revel, Jean Francois
Reymont, Wladyslaw
  Stanislaw
Rhodes, Hari
Rhys, Jean
Ribeiro, Aquilino Gomez

Ricardo, David
Ricci, Nino
Rice, Anne
Rice, Cale Young
Rice, Craig
Rich, Louise Dickinson
Richards, Laura Elizabeth
  Howe
Richards, Stanley
Richardson, Dorothy
  Miller
Richardson, Henry Handel
Richardson, Samuel
Richberg, Donald
  R(andall)
Richler, Mordecai
Richter, Conrad Michael
Richter, Jean Paul F
Richter, Johann Paul
  Friedrich
Riesman, David
Rifkin, Jeremy
Riley, Helen Caldwell Day
Rinehart, Mary Roberts
Ringer, Robert J
Ripley, Alexandra
Ritchie, Jean
Rivera, Jose Eustasio
Rives, Amelie Louise
Roa (y Garcia), Raul
Roark, Garland
Robbe-Grillet, Alain
Robbins, Harold
Robbins, Tom
Robert, Paul
Roberts, Charles George
  Douglas, Sir
Roberts, Elizabeth Madox
Roberts, Kenneth Lewis
Robertson, William
Robins, Denise Naomi
Robins, Elizabeth
Robinson, Henry Morton
Robinson, Lennox
Robinson, Rachel
Robitscher, Jonas Bondi,
  Jr.
Roche, John P
Rodale, Jerome Irving
Rodo, Jose Enrique
Roe, Edward Payson
Rogers, Carl Ransom
Rogers, Rosemary
Rogers, Samuel
Rohmer, Sax
Rojas, Fernando de
Rolland, Romain
Rolle of Hampole, Richard
Rollin, Betty
Rolvaag, Ole Edvart
Romains, Jules
Rombauer, Irma von
  Starkloff
Rooney, Andy
Roos, Frank John, Jr.
Roose-Evans, James
Roosevelt, Elliott
Rosebery, Archibald Philip
  Primrose, Earl
Rosenbach, Abraham
  Simon Wolf
Rosenberg, Alfred
Rosenfeld, Alvin Hirsch
Rosenthal, Abraham
  Michael
Roskolenko, Harry

Ross, Edward Alsworth
Ross, Ishbel
Rossegger, Peter
Rossner, Judith
Rosten, Leo C(alvin)
Roszak, Theodore
Roth, Henry
Roth, Philip (Milton)
Rotha, Paul
Roueche, Berton
Rourke, Constance
  Mayfield
Rousseau, Jean Jacques
Rovere, Richard Halworth
Roy, Gabrielle
Royce, Josiah
Royden, Agnes Maude
Rozanov, Vasili
  Vasilyevich
Ruark, Robert Chester
Rubin, Jerry
Rubin, Theodore Isaac
Rubin, Vitalii
Rudhyar, Dane
Ruether, Rosemary
  Radford
Rukeyser, Louis (Richard)
Rulfo, Juan
Runyon, Damon
Rushdie, Salman Ahmed
Rushmore, Robert
  (William)
Ruskin, John
Russell, Bertrand Arthur
  William
Russell, Edward Frederick
  Langley, Baron of
  Liverpool
Russell, Franklin
  Alexander
Russell, Sydney Gordon,
  Sir
Saarinen, Aline Bernstein
Sabatini, Rafael
Sabato, Ernesto
Sacher-Masoch, Leopold
  von
Sackville-West, Edward
  Charles
Sackville-West, Vita
Sade, Marquis (Donatien
  Alphonse Francoise) de
Saerchinger, Cesar Victor
  Charles
Safire, William L
Sagan, Francoise
Saint-Exupery, Antoine
  (Jean Baptiste Marie
  Roger) de
Saint Georges, Jules
Saint John, Robert
Saint Johns, Adela Rogers
Saint-Just, Louis Antoine
  Leon de
Saintsbury, George
  Edward Bateman
Saint-Simon, Duc de
Saki
Sale, Richard Bernard
Salinger, J(erome) D(avid)
Salk, Lee
Samstag, Nicholas
Samuel, Maurice
Samuels, Ernest
Sanborn, Pitts
Sanchez, Sonia (Benita)

Stow, (Julian) Randolph
Stowe, Harriet (Elizabeth) Beecher
Strasberg, Susan Elizabeth
Straub, Peter
Strauss, Lewis Lichtenstein
Streeter, Edward
Stribling, Thomas Sigismund
Strindberg, August
Strode, Hudson
Strong, Austin
Strong, Philip Duffield
Stroup, Thomas Bradley
Struther, Jan
Strutt, Joseph
Stuart, Jesse Hilton
Stuart, Ruth McEnery
Sturgeon, Theodore Hamilton
Styron, William Clark, Jr.
Suckow, Ruth
Sue, Eugene Joseph Marie
Suhl, Yuri
Sullivan, Arthur Seymour, Sir
Sullivan, Mark
Sulzberger, C(yrus) L(eo)
Sunshine, Linda
Surtees, Robert Smith
Susann, Jacqueline
Sutton, Horace (Ashley)
Suzuki, Daisetz Teitaro
Svevo, Italo
Swados, Elizabeth A
Swados, Harvey
Swanberg, William Andrew
Swarthout, Glendon (Fred)
Swift, Graham (Colin)
Swift, Jonathan
Swinnerton, Frank Arthur
Symons, Julian (Gustave)
Synge, John Millington
Tabari, Muhammad ibn Jarir al-
Taber, Gladys Bagg
Taha Hussein
Talese, Gay
Talmadge, Thomas de Witt
Tan, Amy
Tanizaki Jun'ichiro
Tannen, Deborah Frances
Tarbell, Ida Minerva
Tarkington, Booth
Tarnower, Herman
Tarsis, Valery Yakovlevich
Tartt, Donna (Louise)
Tasso, Torquato
Tate, Eleanora E(laine)
Tatum, Edward Lawrie
Taubman, (Hyman) Howard
Taulbert, Clifton Lemoure
Tawney, Richard Henry
Taylor, A(lan) J(ohn) P(ercivale)
Taylor, Bayard
Taylor, Peter (Hillsman)
Taylor, Phoebe Atwood
Teale, Edwin Way
Teasdale, Sara
Tebbel, John William

Tedder, Arthur William Tedder, Baron
Teller, Edward
Ten Boom, Corrie
Tennenbaum, Silvia
Terhune, Albert Payson
Terhune, Mary Virginia
Terkel, Studs (Louis)
Terry, Walter
Tevis, Walter
Tey, Josephine
Thackeray, William Makepeace
Tharaud, Jean
Tharaud, Jerome
Tharoor, Shashi
Tharp, Louise Hall
Thayer, Ernest L
Thayer, Mary Van Rensselaer
Theresa, Saint
Theriault, Yves
Theroux, Paul Edward
Thomas, Caitlin Macnamara
Thomas, Craig D
Thomas, D(onald) M(ichael)
Thomas, Dylan Marlais
Thomas, Edward
Thomas, Gwyn
Thomas, Joyce Carol
Thomas, Lewis
Thomas, Lowell Jackson
Thomas, Lowell Jackson, Jr.
Thomas, Norman Mattoon
Thomas, Piri
Thomas a Kempis
Thompson, Edward Herbert
Thompson, Ernest
Thompson, Kay
Thompson, Oscar
Thompson, Ruth Plumly
Thoreau, Henry David
Thorne, Jim
Thurber, James Grover
Thurman, Wallace (Henry)
Tidyman, Ernest
Tieck, (Johann) Ludwig
Tietjens, Eunice
Timerman, Jacobo
Timmermans, Felix
Tirso de Molina
Tocqueville, Alexis, Comte de
Todd, Mabel Loomis
Toffler, Alvin
Toland, John
Toland, John Willard
Toledano, Ralph de
Tolkien, J(ohn) R(onald) R(euel)
Tolstoy, Alexey Nikolaevich
Tolstoy, Leo Nikolayevich
Tomasi di Lampedusa, Guiseppe
Tomlinson, Henry Major
Toole, John Kennedy
Toomer, Jean
Tourgee, Albion Winegar
Tournier, Michel
Tovey, Donald Francis, Sir
Townsend, George Alfred

Townsend, Peter Wooldridge
Townsend, William H(enry)
Toye, Francis
Toynbee, Philip
Traill, Catharine Parr
Train, Arthur Cheney
Trapp, Maria Augusta von
Traven, B.
Travers, P(amela) L(yndon)
Treat, Lawrence
Treece, Henry
Tregaskis, Richard William
Trevelyan, George Macaulay
Trevor, William
Trifonov, Yuri Valentinovich
Trillin, Calvin Marshall
Trilling, Diana (Rubin)
Trilling, Lionel
Trollope, Anthony
Trollope, Frances
Tromp, Solco Walle
Trotsky, Leon
Trotta, Maurice S
Trowbridge, John Townsend
Troyat, Henri
Trudeau, Margaret Joan Sinclair
Truman, Margaret
Trumbo, Dalton
Tryon, Thomas
Tuchman, Barbara Wertheim
Tuck, Lily
Tugwell, Rexford Guy
Tung Chung-shu
Turgenev, Ivan Sergeevich
Turnbull, Agnes Sligh
Turner, Morrie
Turow, Scott
Tutuola, Amos
Twain, Mark
Tweedale, Violet Chambers
Twitchell, Paul
Tyler, Anne
Tyler, Royall
Tynan, Kenneth Peacock
Tyndall, John
Tyson, Neil de Grasse
Tzara, Tristan
Uhnak, Dorothy
Ullman, James Ramsey
Unamuno (y Jugo), Miguel de
Underhill, Evelyn
Undset, Sigrid
Unsworth, Barry (Foster)
Untermeyer, Jean Starr
Untermeyer, Louis
Unwin, Stanley, Sir
Updike, John (Hoyer)
Upshaw, William David
Uris, Leon Marcus
Urquhart, Jane
Uspenskii, Petr Dem'yanovich
Utley, Freda
Valera y Alcala Galiano, Juan

Valle Inclan, Ramon Maria del
Vance, Louis Joseph
Vanderbilt, Amy
Vandercook, John Womack
Van Der Post, Laurens (Jan), Sir
Van Dine, S S
Van Doren, Dorothy Graffe
Van Doren, Mark
Van Loon, Hendrik Willem
Van Paassen, Pierre
Van Slyke, Helen Lenore Vogt
Van Vechten, Carl
Van Vooren, Monique
Vanzant, Iyanla (Rhonda)
Varese, Edgar
Vargas Llosa, Mario
Varro, Marcus Terentius
Vasari, Giorgio
Vaughan, Bill
Verga, Giovanni
Verissimo, Erico Lopes
Verne, Jules
Verrill, Alpheus Hyatt
Very, Jones
Vidal, Gore
Viereck, George Sylvester
Viertel, Peter
Vigny, Alfred Victor, Comte de
Villiers, Alan John
Vines, Ellsworth
Viorst, Judith (Stahl)
Vittorini, Elio
Vizenor, Gerald
Voelker, John Donaldson
Voelker, Paul Frederick
Vollmann, William T.
Volney, (Constantin) Francois Chasseboeuf, Comte de
Voltaire
VonDaeniken, Erich
VonDoderer, Heimito
Von Eckardt, Wolf
Vonnegut, Kurt, Jr.
Vonnegut, Mark
Vynnychenko, Volodymyr
Wahloo, Per
Wain, John Barrington
Wakefield, Dan
Wakefield, Edward Gibbon
Wakeman, Frederic
Waley, Arthur David
Walford, Roy L(ee, Jr.)
Walker, Adam
Walker, Alice
Walker, David
Walker, David Harry
Walker, Harold Blake
Walker, Margaret (Abigail)
Wallace, Amy
Wallace, Edgar
Wallace, Horace Binney
Wallace, Irving
Wallace, Lew(is)
Wallace, Michele Faith
Wallant, Edward Lewis
Wallechinsky, David

AUTHORS

AUTO EXECUTIVE

AUTO MANUFACTURER

Agnelli, Giovanni
Austin, Herbert
Bentley, Walter Owen
Benz, Karl Friedrich
Bugatti, Ettore Arco
Isidoro
Buick, David Dunbar
Chapman, (Anthony)
Colin (Bruce)
Chrysler, Walter Percy
Citroen, Andre Gustave
Daimler, Gottlieb
(Wilhelm)
Darracq, Alexandre
Dodge, Horace Elgin
Dodge, John Francis
Duesenberg, August S
Duesenberg, Frederick S
Durant, William Crapo
Ford, Henry
Leland, Henry Martyn
Maserati, Ernesto
McLaren, Bruce Leslie
Nuffield, William Richard
Morris
Porsche, Ferdinand
Renault, Louis
Rolls, Charles Stewart
Royce, Frederick Henry,
Sir
Stanley, Francis Edgar
Stanley, Freelan O
Studebaker, John Mohler
Tucker, Preston Thomas
Winton, Alexander

AUTO RACER

Allison, Bobby
Andretti, Mario Gabriel
Arnoux, Rene Alexandre
Ascari, Alberto
Brabham, Jack
Breedlove, Craig
Campbell, Donald
Malcolm
Campbell, Malcolm, Sir
Chevrolet, Louis Joseph
Clark, James
Cobb, John Rhodes
De Palma, Ralph
Fabi, Teo
Fangio, Juan Manuel
Farina, Giuseppe
Fittipaldi, Emerson
Foyt, A(nthony) J(oseph
Jr.)
Gordon, Jeff
Granatelli, Andy
Guerrero, Roberto
Gurney, Dan
Guthrie, Janet
Hailwood, Mike
Harroun, Ray
Hill, Graham
Hill, Phil(ip Toll)
Hunt, James
Jones, Parnelli
Kulwicki, Alan
Laffite, Jacques Henry
Sabin

Lauda, Niki
Luyendyk, Arie
Mansell, Nigel
Marcelo, (Edward) Jovy
Maserati, Ernesto
McLaren, Bruce Leslie
Mears, Rick Ravon
Moss, Stirling Crauford
Muldowney, Shirley
Newman, Paul
Oldfield, Barney
Parsons, Benny
Pearson, David
Penske, Roger
Petty, Richard
Piquet, Nelson
Prost, Alain Marie Pascal
Rahal, Bobby
Reventlow, Lance
Revson, Peter Jeffrey
Ribbs, Willy T
Rindt, Jochen
Roberts, Edward Glenn
Rosberg, Keke
Ruttman, Troy
St. James, Lyn
Segrave, Henry O'Neal de
Hane, Sir
Senna, Ayrton
Shaw, Wilbur
Shelby, Carroll (Hall)
Sneva, Tom
Stewart, Jackie
Sullivan, Danny
Surtees, John
Thompson, Mickey
Unser, Al, Sr.
Unser, Al, Jr.
Unser, Bobby
Villeneuve, Gilles
Villeneuve, Jacques
Waltrip, Darrell Lee
Watson, John
Wendell Oliver, Scott, Sr.
Yarborough, Cale
Yarbrough, Lee Roy
Zanardi, Alex

AUTO RACING EXECUTIVE

Hulman, Tony, Jr.

AUTOMOBILE EXECUTIVE

Goldsberry, Ronald
(Eugene)
Richie, Leroy C.
Roberts, Roy S.

AVIATOR

Abruzzo, Ben(jamine Lou)
Alcock, John William, Sir
Arnold, Leslie Philip
Auriol, Jacqueline Douet
Balchen, Bernt
Batten, Jean Gardner
Bennett, Floyd
Bleriot, Louis

Bong, Richard Ira
Brown, Arthur Whitten,
Sir
Bullard, Eugene
Castle, Frederick W
Castle, Vernon
Chanute, Octave
Chennault, Claire Lee
Cobham, Alan John, Sir
Cochran, Jacqueline
Coleman, Bessie
Corrigan, Douglas
Coste, Dieudonne
Doolittle, James H(arold)
Dubroff, Jessica
Eaker, Ira Clarence
Earhart, Amelia (Mary)
Elder, Ruth
Fonck, Rene
Fuchida, Mitsuo
Galland, Adolf
Grizodubova, Valentina
(Stepanovna)
Harsh, George
Hinton, Walter
Hughes, Howard Robard
Immelmann, Max
Johnson, Amy
Julian, Hubert Fauntleroy
Kingsford-Smith, Charles
Edward, Sir
Kuter, Laurence S(herman)
Lawrence, Robert (Henry),
Jr.
Lindbergh, Charles
A(ugustus)
Link, Edwin Albert
Markham, Beryl
Nelson, Erik Henning
Nichols, Ruth Rowland
Noyes, Blanche Wilcox
Nungesser, Charles
Eugene Jules Marie
Omlie, Phoebe Jane
Fairgrave
Pangborn, Clyde Edward
Post, Wiley
Quimby, Harriet
Read, Albert Cushing
Reitsch, Hanna
Richthofen, Manfred von,
Baron
Rickenbacker, Eddie
Saint-Exupery, Antoine
(Jean Baptiste Marie
Roger) de
Smith, Lowell Herbert
Sopwith, Thomas O M,
Sir
Turner, Roscoe Wilson
Udet, Ernst
Wright, Orville
Wright, Wilbur

BACTERIOLOGIST

Agramonte y Simoni,
Aristides
Bergey, David Hendricks
Biggs, Hermann Michael
Calmette, Albert Leon
Charles
Cheyne, William Watson,
Sir
Cox, Herald Rea

DeKruif, Paul Henry
Evans, Alice (Catherine)
Fleming, Alexander, Sir
Isaacs, Alick
Kitasato Shibasaburo
Klebs, Edwin
Pasteur, Louis
Welch, William Henry
Widal, Fernand Isidore
Wright, Almroth Edward,
Sir

BAKER

Parker, Albert

BALLET PROMOTER

DeCuevas, Marquis
Diaghilev, Sergei
(Pavlovich)
Kirstein, Lincoln (Edward)

BALLOONIST

Abruzzo, Ben(jamine Lou)
Anderson, Max(ie Leroy)
Blanchard, Francois
Glaisher, James
Lunardi, Vincenzo
Montgolfier, Jacques
Etienne
Montgolfier, Joseph
Michel
Nadar
Piccard, Jeannette Ridlon
Santos-Dumont, Alberto
Stevens, Albert William

BANDLEADER

Allen, Red
Alpert, Herb
Anthony, Ray
Armstrong, Louis
August, Jan
Ayres, Mitchell
Barnet, Charlie
Barron, Blue
Basie, Count
Baxter, Les
Bechet, Sidney
Beneke, Tex
Berigan, Bunny
Bernie, Ben
Bley, Carla
Bloch, Raymond A
Bon Jovi, Jon
Bradley, Will
Brown, Les(ter Raymond)
Bushkin, Joe
Busse, Henry
Calloway, Cab
Cavallaro, Carmen
Clinton, Larry
Cole, Nat King
Columbo, Russ
Condon, Eddie
Conniff, Ray

Gordon, Joe
Green, Dallas
Griffith, Clark Calvin
Grimm, Charlie
Harris, Bucky
Herzog, Whitey
Hodges, Gil(bert
  Raymond)
Hornsby, Rogers
Houk, Ralph George
Howser, Dick
Huggins, Miller James
Jennings, Hugh(ey
  Ambrose)
Johnson, Davey
Johnson, Walter Perry
Kelly, Tom
Lanier, Hal
LaRussa, Tony
Lasorda, Tommy
Lemon, Bob
Leyland, Jim
Lopes, Davey
Lopez, Al(fonso Ramon)
Mack, Connie
Martin, Billy
Mauch, Gene William
McCarthy, Joe
McGraw, John Joseph
McKechnie, Bill
McNamara, John Francis
O'Neill, Steve
Piniella, Lou(is Victor)
Rader, Doug(las Lee)
Richards, Paul Rapier
Rickey, Branch
Ripken, Cal(vin Edwin,
  Sr.)
Robinson, Frank
Robinson, Wilbert
Rodgers, Bob
Rolfe, Red
Rose, Pete(r Edward)
Runnels, Tom
Schoendienst, Red
Smith, Mayo
Stanky, Eddie
Stengel, Casey
Tebbetts, Birdie
Terry, Bill
Torborg, Jeff(rey Allen)
Torre, Joe
Weaver, Earl Sidney
Williams, Dick
Williams, Jimy
Wright, Harry
Zimmer, Don(ald William)

**BASEBALL
PIONEER**

Cartwright, Alexander Joy,
  Jr.
Doubleday, Abner

**BASEBALL
PLAYER**

Aaron, Hank
Abbott, Jim
Aikens, Willie Mays
Ainge, Danny

Alexander, Grover
  Cleveland
Allen, Ethan (Nathan)
Allen, Richie
Alomar, Roberto
Alou, Felipe Rojas
Alou, Jesus Maria Rojas
Alou, Matty
Altrock, Nick
Andujar, Joaquin
Anson, Cap
Antonelli, John(ny
  August)
Aparicio, Luis Ernesto
Appling, Luke
Ashburn, Richie
Averill, Earl
Avila, Bobby
Baines, Harold Douglass
Baker, Dusty
Baker, Frank
Bancroft, Dave
Bando, Sal(vatore
  Leonard)
Bankhead, Dan(iel Robert)
Banks, Ernie
Barfield, Jesse Lee
Barker, Len
Barrios, Francisco Javier
Bass, Randy William
Bauer, Hank
Baylor, Don(ald Edward)
Beckley, Jake
Bedrosian, Steve
Belinsky, Bo
Bell, Buddy
Bell, Cool Papa
Bell, George Antonio
Belle, Albert
Bench, Johnny Lee
Bender, Chief
Beradino, John
Berra, Yogi
Blomberg, Ron(ald Mark)
Blue, Vida Rochelle
Blyleven, Bert
Boddicker, Mike
Boggs, Wade (Anthony)
Bonds, Barry (Lamar)
Bonds, Bobby (Lee)
Bonilla, Bobby
Boone, Bob
Bostock, Lyman Wesley
Bottomley, Jim
Boudreau, Lou(is)
Bouton, Jim
Bowa, Larry
Boyer, Ken(ton Lloyd)
Branca, Ralph Theodore
  Joseph
Brecheen, Harry David
Breitenstein, Ted
Brenly, Bob
Bresnaham, Roger Philip
Brett, George (Howard)
Bridges, Tommy
Brissie, Lou
Brock, Lou(is Clark)
Brosnan, Jim
Brouthers, Dan
Brown, Bobby
Brown, Mordecai Peter
  Centennial
Browning, Tom
Buckner, Bill

Bunning, Jim
Burdette, Lew
Burgess, Smoky
Burke, Glenn
Burkett, Jesse Cail
Bush, Guy Terrell
Butler, Brett
Camilli, Dolph
Campanella, Roy
Campaneris, Bert
Campanis, Al
Canseco, Jose
Carew, Rod(ney Cline)
Carey, Max George
Carlton, Steve(n Norman)
Carter, Gary Edmund
Carter, Joe
Carty, Rico
Casey, Dan(iel Maurice)
Casey, Hugh Thomas
Cash, Norm(an Dalton)
Cavarretta, Phil(ip Joseph)
Cepeda, Orlando Manuel
Cey, Ron(ald Charles)
Chance, Dean
Chance, Frank Leroy
Chandler, Spud
Charleston, Oscar
  McKinley
Chesbro, Jack
Cicotte, Eddie
Clark, Jack Anthony
Clark, Will(iam Nuschler,
  Jr.)
Clarke, Fred Clifford
Clarkson, John Gibson
Clemens, (William) Roger
Clemente, Roberto Walker
Cobb, Ty(rus Raymond)
Cochrane, Mickey
Colavito, Rocky
Coleman, Vince(nt
  Maurice)
Collins, Eddie
Collins, Jimmy
Combs, Earle Bryan
Comiskey, Charlie
Conigliaro, Tony
Connor, Roger
Cooper, Cecil Celester
Cooper, Mort(on Cecil)
Cooper, Walker
Courtney, Clint(on
  Dawson)
Coveleski, Harry Frank
Coveleski, Stanley
  Anthony
Cowley, Joe
Craig, Roger Lee
Crandall, Del(mar Wesley)
Crawford, Sam(uel Earl)
Cronin, Joe
Cuellar, Mike
Cummings, Candy
Cuyler, Kiki
Dandridge, Ray(mond)
Danforth, Dave
Dark, Alvin Ralph
Darling, Ron(ald Maurice),
  Jr.
Daubert, Jake
Dauss, George August
Davis, Eric Keith
Davis, Lorenzo
Davis, Mark William

Davis, Tommy, Jr.
Davis, Willie
Dawson, Andre (Nolan)
Dean, Daffy
Dean, Dizzy
Deer, Rob(ert George)
Delahanty, Ed(ward
  James)
Dempsey, Rick
Denny, John Allen
Dent, Bucky
Deshaies, Jim
Dickey, Bill
Dihigo, Martin
DiMaggio, Dom(inic Paul)
DiMaggio, Joe
DiMaggio, Vince(nt Paul)
Dinneen, Bill
Doak, Bill
Doby, Larry
Doerr, Bobby
Drabek, Doug(las Dean)
Dravecky, Dave
Dropo, Walt(er)
Drysdale, Don(ald Scott)
Duffy, Hugh
Duren, Ryne
Durocher, Leo Ernest
Dykes, Jimmy
Dykstra, Lenny
Eckersley, Dennis
Ehmke, Howard Jonathan
Ellis, Dock Phillip, Jr.
Ennis, Del(mer)
Erskine, Carl Daniel
Evans, Darrell Wayne
Evers, Johnny
Ewing, Buck
Faber, Red
Face, Roy
Fain, Ferris Roy
Feller, Bob
Fernandez, Sid
Ferrell, Rick
Ferrell, Wes(ley Cheek)
Fidrych, Mark Steven
Fielder, Cecil Grant
Fingers, Rollie
Fisk, Carlton Ernest
Flanagan, Mike
Flick, Elmer Harrison
Flood, Curt(is Charles)
Ford, Russ(ell William)
Ford, Whitey
Forsch, Bob
Forsch, Ken(neth Roth)
Foster, George Arthur
Foster, Rube
Fox, Nellie
Foxx, Jimmie
Freehan, Bill
Friend, Bob
Frisch, Frankie
Furillo, Carl Anthony
Gaedel, Eddie
Galvin, Pud
Garagiola, Joe
Garcia, Mike
Garcia y Sanchez, Damaso
  Domingo
Garvey, Steve(n Patrick)

Santiago, Benito
Santo, Ron(ald Edward)
Schacht, Al(exander)
Schaefer, Germany
Schalk, Ray(mond
　William)
Schmidt, Mike
Schoendienst, Red
Score, Herb(ert Jude)
Scott, George Charles, Jr.
Scott, Mike
Seaver, Tom
Sewell, Joe
Sheffield, Gary (Antonian)
Sierra (Garcia), Ruben
　Angel
Simmons, Al(oysius
　Harry)
Sisler, George Harold
Skowron, Bill
Slaughter, Enos Bradsher
Smith, Lee (Arthur)
Smith, Ozzie
Smoltz, John
Snider, Duke
Soto, Mario Melvin
Spahn, Warren Edward
Spalding, Albert Goodwill
Speaker, Tris(tram E)
Stanky, Eddie
Stanley, Mickey
Stargell, Willie
Staub, Rusty
Steinbach, Terry Lee
Stengel, Casey
Stewart, Dave
Stieb, Dave
Stone, George Robert
Stone, Toni
Stottlemyre, Mel(vin
　Leon)
Stratton, Monty Franklin
　Pierce
Strawberry, Darryl
　(Eugene)
Sunday, Billy
Sundberg, Jim
Sutcliffe, Rick
Sutter, Bruce
Sutton, Don(ald Howard)
Tanana, Frank Daryl
Tebbetts, Birdie
Tekulve, Kent(on Charles)
Templeton, Garry Lewis
Tenace, Gene
Terry, Bill
Thigpen, Bobby
Thomas, Frank
Thompson, Sam(uel
　Luther)
Thomson, Bobby
Throneberry, Marv(in
　Eugene)
Tiant, Luis Clemente
Tinker, Joe
Torre, Joe
Trammell, Alan Stuart
Traynor, Pie
Trout, Dizzy
Tudor, John Thomas
Uecker, Bob
Valenzuela, Fernando
Vance, Dazzy
Vander Meer, Johnny
Van Slyke, Andy
Vaughan, Arky

Vaughn, Mo
Vernon, Mickey
Versalles, Zoilo Casanova
Viola, Frank John, Jr.
Vuckovich, Pete(r Dennis)
Waddell, Rube
Wagner, Honus
Wakefield, Dick
Walker, Dixie
Wallace, Bobby
Walsh, Ed(ward
　Augustine)
Walters, Bucky
Walton, Jerome O'Terrell
Wambsganss, Bill
Waner, Lloyd James
Waner, Paul Glee
Ward, Monte
Warneke, Lon(nie)
Weiss, Walt(er William,
　Jr.)
Welch, Bob
Welch, Mickey
Wheat, Zack
Whitaker, Lou(is Rodman)
White, Bill
White, Deacon
White, Frank, Jr.
Wilhelm, Hoyt
Williams, Billy Leo
Williams, Dick
Williams, Ted
Wills, Maury
Wilson, Hack
Wilson, Willie James
Winfield, Dave
Witt, Mike
Wood, Joe
Wood, Wilbur Forrester
Worrell, Todd Roland
Wright, George
Wynn, Early
Yastrzemski, Carl Michael
York, Rudy
Young, Cy
Youngs, Ross
　Middlebrook
Yount, Robin (R.)
Zernial, Gus Edward
Zimmer, Don(ald William)

BASEBALL UMPIRE

Ashford, Emmett Littleton
Chylak, Nestor
Conlan, Jocko
Connolly, Tommy
Dinneen, Bill
Evans, Billy
Gregg, Eric
Hubbard, Cal
Klem, Bill
Luciano, Ron(ald Michael)
Passarella, Art
Warneke, Lon(nie)

BASKETBALL
COACH

Allen, Forrest Claire
Attles, Al(vin A)
Auerbach, Red
Bee, Clair Francis

Bird, Larry (Joe)
Blood, Ernest
Brown, Hubie
Brown, Larry
Carlson, Doc
Carnesseca, Lou
Carnevale, Ben
Cervi, Al
Chaney, John
Costello, Larry
Crum, Denny
Cunningham, Billy
Daly, Chuck
Dehnert, Henry
Douglas, Robert L
Fitch, Bill
Fratello, Mike
Gallatin, Harry J
Gill, Amory Tingle
Gottlieb, Eddie
Grentz, Theresa Shank
Guerin, Richard V
Hall, Joe Beasman
Hannum, Alex(ander
　Murray)
Hinkle, Paul
Holman, Nat(han)
Holzman, Red
Iba, Hank
Jackson, Phil(ip D.)
Jones, KC
Julian, Doggie
Keaney, Frank
Keogan, George
Kerr, Red
Knight, Bobby
Krzyzewski, Mike
Kundla, John
Lambert, Piggy
Lambert, Ward L
Lapchick, Joe
Layden, Frank
Liston, Emil
Loeffler, Ken(neth D)
Loughery, Kevin Michael
Lucas, John
McCracken, Branch
McGuire, Al
Meyer, Ray(mond Joseph)
Miller, Cheryl
Moe, Doug(las Edwin)
Motta, Dick
Nelson, Don(ald Arvid)
Newell, Pete
Olsen, Harold G
Phelps, Digger
Ramsay, Jack
Richardson, Nolan
Riley, Pat(rick James)
Ripley, Elmer Horton
Rothstein, Ron
Rupp, Adolph Frederick
Russell, Bill
Russell, Honey
Schayes, Dolph
Schuler, Mike
Sharman, Bill
Shue, Gene
Silas, Paul Theron
Smith, Dean Edwards
Smith, Tubby
Stringer, C. Vivian
Tarkanian, Jerry
Thompson, John
Valvano, Jim
Vitale, Dick

Wilkens, Lenny
Wooden, John Robert
Woolpert, Phil

BASKETBALL
EXECUTIVE

Brown, Walter Augustine
Douglas, Robert L
Embry, Wayne Richard
Gottlieb, Eddie
Irish, Ned
Jackson, Mannie (L.)
Jones, R(enato) William
Kennedy, Walter
Layden, Frank
Morganweck, Frank
O'Brien, John J
O'Brien, Larry
Podoloff, Maurice
Saperstein, Abe
Stern, David Joel
Thomas, Isiah

BASKETBALL
PIONEER

Naismith, James A

BASKETBALL
PLAYER

Abdul-Jabbar, Kareem
Adams, Alvan Leigh
Aguirre, Mark (Anthony)
Ainge, Danny
Archibald, Nate
Arizin, Paul Joseph
Attles, Al(vin A)
Barker, Cliff
Barkley, Charles Wade
Barry, Rick
Baylor, Elgin Gay
Beard, Ralph Milton
Beckman, Johnny
Bellamy, Walt(er Jones)
Bias, Len
Bing, Dave
Bird, Larry (Joe)
Blab, Uwe Konstantine
Bogues, Mugsy
Bol, Manute
Boone, Ron(ald Bruce)
Borgmann, Benny
Bradley, Bill
Brandon, (Thomas) Terrell
Bridges, Bill
Bryant, Kobe
Buse, Don(ald R)
Carroll, Joe Barry
Cartwright, Bill
Cervi, Al
Chamberlain, Wilt(on
　Norman)
Chambers, Tom
Cooper, Chuck
Cooper, Cynthia
Costello, Larry
Cousy, Bob
Cowens, Dave
Cummings, Terry

Cunningham, Billy
Dantley, Adrian (Delano)
Davies, Bob
Davis, Walter Paul
Dawkins, Darryl
DeBernardi, Forrest S
DeBusschere, Dave
Drexler, Clyde
Dumars, Joe, III
Duncan, Tim(othy
  Theodore)
Eaton, Mark E
Edwards, Teresa
Embry, Wayne Richard
Endacott, Paul
English, Alex(ander)
Erving, Julius Winfield
Ewing, Patrick Aloysius
Ford, Phil Jackson
Foust, Larry
Frazier, Walt(er Jr.)
Free, World B
Friedman, Max
Fulks, Joe
Gallatin, Harry J
Garnett, Kevin
Gates, Pop
Gathers, Hank
Gervin, George
Gilmore, Artis
Gola, Tom
Goodrich, Gail Charles
Green, Rickey Anthony
Greer, Hal
Griffith, Darrell Steven
Groza, Alex John
Guerin, Richard V
Hagan, Cliff(ord Oldham)
Hardaway, Anfernee
  (Deon)
Havlicek, John
Hawkins, Connie
Hayes, Elvin Ernest
Haynes, Marques Oreole
Haywood, Spencer
Heinsohn, Tommy
Hill, Grant
Hodges, Craig Anthony
Holman, Nat(han)
Houbregs, Bob
Howard, Juwan (Antonio)
Howell, Bailey E
Hudson, Lou(is C)
Issel, Dan(iel Paul)
Jackson, Mark
Johnson, Dennis Wayne
Johnson, Earvin, Jr.
Johnson, Gus, Jr.
Johnson, Kevin
Johnson, Larry
Johnson, Marques Kevin
Johnson, Steve
Johnston, Neil
Jones, Sam(uel)
Jones, Wallace
Jordan, Michael (Jeffery)
Kemp, Shawn
Kerr, Red
King, Bernard
Kukoc, Toni
Kurland, Bob
Laettner, Christian
Laimbeer, Bill
Lanier, Bob
Lapchick, Joe
Lemon, Meadowlark

Leslie, Lisa
Lewis, Reggie
Lieberman, Nancy
Lloyd, Lewis Kevin
Loughery, Kevin Michael
Lucas, Jerry Ray
Lucas, John
Luisetti, Hank
Macauley, Ed
Macy, Kyle Robert
Majerle, Dan
Malone, Karl
Malone, Moses Eugene
Manigault, Earl
Manning, Danny
Maravich, Pete(r Press)
Martin, Slater
Maxwell, Cedric Bryan
McAdoo, Bob
McCray, Nikki
McDaniel, Xavier Maurice
McGinnis, George
McGuire, Dick
McHale, Kevin (Edward)
McMillen, Thomas
Mikan, George Lawrence,
  Jr.
Mikkelsen, Vern
Miller, Cheryl
Miller, Reggie
Moe, Doug(las Edwin)
Moncrief, Sidney A
Monroe, Earl
Mourning, Alonzo
Mullien, Chris
Murphy, Calvin Jerome
Murphy, Charles
Mutombo, Dikembe
Nelson, Don(ald Arvid)
Olajuwon, Hakeem
O'Neal, Shaquille
Parish, Robert L
Person, Chuck Connors
Pettit, Bob
Phillip, Andy
Pippen, Scottie
Pollard, Jim
Ramsey, Frank Vernon, Jr.
Reed, Willis, Jr.
Richardson, Micheal Ray
Richmond, Mitch(ell
  James)
Ripley, Elmer Horton
Robertson, Alvin
Robertson, Oscar Palmer
Robinson, David
  (Maurice)
Rodgers, Guy William, Jr.
Rodman, Dennis (Keith)
Rollins, Kenny
Rollins, Wayne Monte
Russell, Bill
Russell, Honey
Sampson, Ralph Lee
Schayes, Dolph
Sedran, Barney
Sharman, Bill
Shue, Gene
Silas, Paul Theron
Stewart, Luisa Harris
Stockton, John (Houston)
Swoopes, Sheryl
Thomas, Isiah
Thompson, David O'Neil
Thurmond, Nate

Tisdale, Wayman
  Lawrence
Twyman, Jack
Unseld, Wes(tley Sissel)
Vandeweghe, Kiki
Wachter, Ed(ward)
Walker, Chet
Walton, Bill
Wanzer, Bobby
Webb, Spud
Webber, Chris
West, Jerry
Westphal, Paul Douglas
White, Jo Jo
White, Neva
Wilkens, Lenny
Wilkes, Jamaal
Wilkins, Dominique
Williams, Charles
  Linwood
Williams, Gus
Woodard, Lynette
Worthy, James Ager
Yardley, George Harry
Zaslofsky, Max

BASKETBALL REFEREE

Hepbron, George
O'Brien, John J

BEAUTY CONTEST WINNER

Charles, Suzette
George, Phyllis
Gist, Carole Anne-Marie
Jones, Rosie
McCarty, Kelli
Meriwether, Lee
Mobley, Mary Ann
Myerson, Bess
Sapp, Carolyn
Vincent, Marjorie Judith
Wells, Sharlene
Whitestone, Heather
Williams, Vanessa

BIBLICAL FIGURE

Aaron
Abel
Abraham
Adam
Amos
Andrew, Saint
Barabbas
Bartholomew, Saint
Bathsheba
Cain
Caleb
Daniel
David
Deborah
Delilah
Elijah
Esau
Esther
Eve
Goliath

Herod the Great
Isaac
Jacob
James the Greater, Saint
James the Less, Saint
Job
John the Baptist
Jonah
Joseph
Joseph, Saint
Joseph of Arimathea, Saint
Joshua
Judah
Judas Iscariot
Jude, Saint
Judith
Lazarus
Leah
Lot
Luke, Saint
Mark, Saint
Mary Magdalene, Saint
Matthew, Saint
Methuselah
Michael the Archangel,
  Saint
Miriam
Moses
Nehemiah
Nicodemus
Paul, Saint
Peter, Saint
Philip, Saint
Rachel
Rebecca
Ruth
Salome
Samson
Samuel
Sarah
Shadrach
Simeon
Simon, Saint
Thomas, Saint

BIBLIOGRAPHER

Bartlett, John Russell
Evans, Charles
Greg, Walter Wilson, Sir
McMurtrie, Douglas C
Wise, Thomas J

BILLIARDS PLAYER

Balukas, Jean
Davis, Joe
Hoppe, Willie
Mataya, Ewa
Minnesota Fats
Mosconi, Willie
Pelkey, Edward

BIOCHEMIST

Asimov, Isaac
Bachrach, Howard L.
Beadle, George Wells
Berg, Paul
Bishop, J(ohn) Michael

Boyer, Herbert Wayne
Bressani, Ricardo
Brown, Rachel Fuller
Cech, Thomas Robert
Chain, Ernest Boris, Sir
Chance, Britton
Chargaff, Erwin
Cohen, Stanley
Cohn, Edwin Joseph
Cohn, Mildred
Cordes, Eugene Harold
Cori, Carl Ferdinand
Cori, Gerty Theresa
   (Radnitz)
Dam, (Carl Peter) Henrik
Deisenhofer, Johann
Doisy, Edward Adelbert,
   Sr.
Elion, Gertrude B(ell)
Emerson, Gladys
   Anderson
Farr, Wanda K.
Fischer, Edmond
Funk, Casimir
Henderson, Lawrence
   Joseph
Hitchings, George
   H(erbert)
Hopkins, Frederick
   Gowland, Sir
Huber, Robert
Jordan, Joseph
Kamen, Martin David
Kendall, Edward C(alvin)
King, Charles Glen
Kornberg, Arthur
Krebs, Edwin Gerhard
Krebs, Hans Adolf, Sir
Li, C(hoh) H(ao)
Lipmann, Fritz Albert
Loeb, Jacques
Merrifield, R(obert) Bruce
Monod, Jacques Lucien
Moore, Stanford
Mullis, Kary B(anks)
Neufeld, Elizabeth
   F(ondal)
Northrop, John Howard
Ochoa, Severo
Oparin, Aleksandr
   Ivanovich
Schally, Andrew Victor
Seibert, Florence B(arbara)
Shear, Murray Jacob
Singer, Maxine (Frank)
Slotta, Karl Heinrich
Szent-Gyorgyi, Albert
   (von Nagyrapolt)
Takamine, Jokichi
Tatum, Edward Lawrie
Theorell, (Axel) Hugh
   Teodor
Von Euler, Ulf
Watson, James Dewey
Williams, Roger J
Wilson, Allan C
Zaragosa, Federico Mayor

BIOGRAPHER

Anthony, Katharine Susan
Beer, Thomas
Bonham Carter, Violet
Boswell, James

Cecil, Edward Christian
   David Gascoyne
Chandler, Alfred Du Pont,
   Jr.
Coffin, Robert Peter
   Tristram
Day, Clarence Shepard, Jr.
Drinkwater, John
Forster, John
Hendrick, Burton Jesse
Holroyd, Michael De
   Courcy Fraser
Lockhart, John Gibson
Matthew Paris
Morris, Edmund
Newman, Ernest
Partridge, Bellamy
Ptolemy (Soter), I
Rowse, A(lfred) L(eslie)
Strachey, (Giles) Lytton
Suetonius
Teichmann, Howard Miles
Van Doren, Carl Clinton
Walton, Izaak
Warner, Sylvia Townsend

BIOLOGIST

Abercrombie, Michael
Alvarino (de Leira),
   Angeles
Anderson, W(illiam)
   French
Arber, Werner
Astbury, William
Bachrach, Howard L.
Baer, Karl Ernst von
Bateson, William
Blackburn, Elizabeth
   Helen
Bose, Jagadis Chandra, Sir
Brenner, Sydney
Bronk, Detlev Wulf
Brown, Frank Arthur, Jr.
Burnet, F(rank)
   MacFarlane, Sir
Carrel, Alexis
Carson, Rachel (Louise)
Cech, Thomas Robert
Chan, June
Chang, M(in) C(heuh), Dr.
Cobb, Jewel Plummer
Cohn, Zanvil (Alexander)
Colwell, Rita R(ossi)
Commoner, Barry
Conklin, Edwin Grant
Cottam, Clarence
Cox, Geraldine V(ang)
Crick, Francis Harry
   Compton
Cruz, Oswaldo Goncalves
Dallmeier, Francisco
DiSabato, Giovanni
Dobzhansky, Theodosius
   (Grigorievich)
Dole, Vincent P(aul)
Driesch, Hans Adolf
   Eduard
Ehrlich, Paul
Ehrlich, Paul Ralph
Eisner, Thomas
Farquhar, Marilyn G(ist)
Fedoroff, Nina V(sevolod)
Franklin, Rosalind Elsie
Geddes, Patrick, Sir

Gilbert, Walter
Huxley, Julian Sorell, Sir
Huxley, Thomas Henry
Janzen, Daniel Hunt
Just, Ernest Everett
Kendrick, Pearl Luella
LeVay, Simon
Margulis, Lynn
Matola, Sharon Rose
Mayr, Ernst Walter
Mazia, Daniel
Mboup, Souleymane
McCarty, Maclyn
Medvedev, Zhores
   Aleksandrovich
Meselson, Matthew
   Stanley
Metchnikoff, Elie
Milstein, Cesar
Mintz, Beatrice
Moss, Cynthia Jane
Nathans, Daniel
Palade, George Emil
Payne, Roger S.
Profet, Margie
Rogers, Lynn L(eroy)
Sabin, Albert Bruce
Sagan, Carl (Edward)
Sanger, Frederick
Smith, Hamilton Othanel
Spemann, Hans
Sperry, Roger W(olcott)
Stevens, Nettie Maria
Strasburger, Eduard Adolf
Van Niel, Cornelius
   B(ernardus)
Vermeij, Geerat J(acobus)
Vogelstein, Bert
Wald, George
Weismann, August
   Friedrich Leopold
Wigler, Michael (H.)
Williams, Carroll Milton
Wilson, Edward Osborne
Woodwell, George
   M(asters)

BIOLOGISTS

Owens, Delia and Mark

BIOPHYSICIST

Quimby, Edith H.

BOAT RACER

Campbell, Donald
   Malcolm
Campbell, Malcolm, Sir
Chenoweth, Dean
Cobb, John Rhodes
Hanauer, Chip
Muncey, Bill
Segrave, Henry O'Neal de
   Hane, Sir
Wood, Gar(field A)

BODYBUILDER

Atlas, Charles
LaLanne, Jack
McLish, Rachel Elizondo
Murray, Lenda
Van Damme, Jean-Claude

BOOKSELLER

Dodsley, Robert
Foyle, Christina Agnes
   Lilian
Foyle, Gilbert Samuel
Foyle, William Alfred
Kraus, Hans Peter
Quaritch, Bernard
Rosenbach, Abraham
   Simon Wolf

BOTANIST

Arber, Agnes
Arthur, Joseph Charles
Bailey, Liberty Hyde
Banks, Joseph
Bartram, John
Bartram, William
Bentham, George
Britton, Nathaniel, Lord
Brown, Robert
Camerarius, Rudolf Jakob
Candolle, Augustin
   Pyrame de
Chase, Mary Agnes
Cohn, Ferdinand Julius
Colden, Cadwallader
Coulter, John Merle
Cowles, Henry Chandler
DeBary, Heinrich Anton
DeVries, Hugo
Dioscorides, Pedanius
Douglas, David
Engler, Adolph Gustav
   Heinrich
Esau, Katherine
Fairchild, David
   Grandison
Gerard, John
Gray, Asa
Haberlandt, Gottlieb
Harrar, J(acob) George
Hoagland, Dennis Robert
Hooker, William Jackson,
   Sir
Jussieu, Bernard de
Linnaeus, Carolus
Mendel, Gregor Johann
Plotkin, Mark
Plotkin, Mark J.
Raven, Peter H(amilton)
Ray, John
Schleiden, Matthias Jakob
Shull, George Harrison
Takhtadzhian, Armen
   Leonovich
Vavilov, Nikolai
   Ivanovich

BOWLER

Adamek, Donna
Anthony, Earl Roderick
Burton, Nelson, Jr.
Carter, Don(ald James)
Hardwick, Billy
Laub, Larry
Roth, Mark Stephan
Varipapa, Andy
Weber, Dick
Weber, Pete(r)

BOXER

Akins, Virgil B
Ali, Muhammad
Ambers, Lou
Angott, Sammy
Apostoli, Fred
Arguello, Alexis
Armstrong, Henry
Attell, Abe B
Baer, Max
Basilio, Carmen
Berbick, Trevor
Berlenbach, Paul
Blackburn, Jack
Bonavena, Oscar
Bowe, Riddick (Lamont)
Braddock, Jim
Britton, Jack
Burns, Tommy
Canzoneri, Tony
Carnera, Primo
Carpentier, Georges
Carruthers, John(ny)
Carter, Hurricane
Carter, Jimmy
Cerdan, Marcel B
Charles, Ezzard
Chuvalo, George
Classen, Willie
Conn, Billy
Cooney, Gerry
Cooper, Henry B
Corbett, James John
Corbett, Young, III
Cruz, Stevie
Curry, Donald
De La Hoya, Oscar
Delaney, Jack
Dempsey, Jack
Dixon, George
Douglas, Buster
Dundee, Johnny
Duran, Roberto
Escobar, Sixto
Farr, Tommy B
Firpo, Luis Angel
Fitzsimmons, Bob
Flowers, Tiger
Foreman, George
Frazier, Joe
Galento, Tony
Gans, Joe
Gardner, George
Gavilan, Kid
Genaro, Frankie
Giardello, Joey
Gibbons, Tom
Graziano, Rocky
Greb, Harry
Griffith, Emile Alphonse
Hagler, Marvelous Marvin

Hearns, Thomas
Heenan, John Carmel
Holmes, Larry
Holyfield, Evander
Jackson, Hurricane
Jackson, Peter B
Jeffries, James Jackson
Jofre, Eder
Johansson, Ingemar
Johnson, Harold
Johnson, Jack
Jones, Gorilla
Jordan, Don
Kenty, Hilmer
Ketchel, Stanley
Kid Chocolate
Kim, Duk Koo
La Barba, Fidel
Laguna, Ismael
LaMotta, Jake
Langford, Sam
Latzo, Pete
Lavigne, Kid
Lee, Canada
Leonard, Benny
Leonard, Sugar Ray
Lesnevich, Gus
Levinsky, Battling
Lewis, Ted
Liston, Sonny
Loughran, Tommy
Louis, Joe
Lynch, Benny
Lynch, Joe
Mancini, Ray
Marciano, Rocky
McAuliffe, Jack B
McCoy, Charles
McCrory, Milton
McGovern, Terry
McLarnin, Jimmy
Moore, Archie
Moorer, Michael
Nelson, Battling
Norton, Ken(neth Howard)
O'Grady, Sean
Papp, Laszlo
Patterson, Floyd
Pep, Willie
Quarry, Jerry
Robinson, Sugar Ray
Root, Jack
Rosenbloom, Maxie
Ross, Barney
Ryan, Tommy
Sanchez, Salvador
Schmeling, Max(imilian)
Sharkey, Jack
Shavers, Ernie
Spinks, Leon
Spinks, Michael
Stevenson, Teofilo
Stribling, Young
Sullivan, John L(awrence)
Thomas, Pinklon
Tunney, Gene
Tyson, Mike
Urtain, Jose Manuel Ibar
Villa, Pancho
Walcott, Joe
Walker, Mickey
Weaver, Mike
Whitaker, Pernell
Wilde, Jimmy
Willard, Jess
Wills, Harry

Zale, Tony

BOXING PROMOTER

Abercrombie, Josephine
Carey, William F
Coffroth, Jimmy
Hurley, Jack B
Jacobs, Joe B
Jacobs, Michael S
Kallen, Jackie
Kearns, Jack
King, Don(ald)
Rickard, Tex
Smith, Harold

BOXING REFEREE

Donovan, Arthur

BOXING RING ANNOUNCER

Lennon, Jimmy, Sr.

BOXING TRAINER

Blackburn, Jack
Dundee, Angelo Mirena, Jr.
Steward, Emanuel

BREWER

Busch, Adolphus
Busch, August Adolphus, III
Busch, August Anheuser, Jr.
Coors, Adolph
Coors, Joseph
Coors, William K
Labatt, John Kinder
Miller, Frederic
Molson, John
Pabst, Frederick
Schaefer, Rudolph Jay
Sellinger, Frank
Stroh, Bernard
Stroh, Peter W
Vassar, Matthew

BRIDGE PLAYER

Becker, B Jay
Corn, Ira George, Jr.
Culbertson, Ely
Fishbein, Harry J
Gerber, John
Goren, Charles Henry
Jacoby, Oswald
Lightner, Theodore
Sheinwold, Alfred

BROADCAST JOURNALIST

Abel, Elie
Adamle, Mike
Agronsky, Martin Zama
Amanpour, Christiane
Anderson, Bonnie Marie
Arnett, Peter Gregg
Bazell, Robert Joseph
Bell, Steve
Benton, Nelson
Berger, Marilyn
Bergman, Jules Verne
Berkowitz, Bob
Beutel, Bill
Blair, Frank
Bourgholtzer, Frank
Bowser, Betty Ann
Bradley, Ed(ward R.)
Briggs, Fred
Brinkley, David (McClure)
Brokaw, Tom
Broun, Heywood Hale
Carter, Hodding
Chancellor, John (William)
Chase, Sylvia B
Chung, Connie
Collingwood, Charles Cummings
Compton, Ann (Woodruff)
Cordtz, Dan
Couric, Katie
Craft, Christine
Cronkite, Walter Leland, Jr.
Dancy, John Albert
Dean, Morton
DeManio, Jack
DeVarona, Donna
Dickerson, Nancy Hanschman
Dietz, David
Dobyns, Lloyd Allen, Jr.
Donaldson, Sam(uel Andrew)
Dotson, Bob
Downs, William Randall, Jr.
Economaki, Chris(topher Constantine)
Edwards, Douglas
Ellerbee, Linda
Farmer, Don(ald Edwin)
Frederick, Pauline
Frum, Barbara
Gibson, Charles Dewolf
Goldberg, Bernard
Gordon, Ed
Grauer, Ben(jamin Franklin)
Grimsby, Roger
Gumbel, Bryant (Charles)
Hart, John Richard
Hartz, James Leroy
Harvey, Paul
Herman, George Edward
Hockenberry, John (Charles)
Hume, Brit
Hunter-Gault, Charlayne
Huntley, Chet
Jaffe, Sam(uel Anderson)
Jamieson, Bob
Jarriel, Tom

Jennings, Peter (Charles)
Jensen, Mike
Jones, Phil(ip Howard)
Jones, Star(let Marie)
Kalb, Marvin Leonard
Kalber, Floyd
Kaltenborn, H(ans) V(on)
Kent, Arthur
Kiker, Douglas
Kinsley, Michael (E.)
Koppel, Ted
Kroft, Steve
Kuralt, Charles (Bishop)
Kurtis, Bill
Lamb, Brian (P.)
Lauer, Matt
Lehrer, Jim
Levine, Irving R(askin)
Lewis, Fulton, Jr.
Lloyd, Robin
Lunden, Joan (Elise)
Mackin, Catherine Patricia
MacNeil, Robert
  Breckenridge Ware
Martin, John
McCormick, Robert K
McEwen, Mark
McGee, Frank
Monroe, Bill
Moriarty, Erin
Mudd, Roger Harrison
Murrow, Edward R
Newman, Edwin Harold
Norville, Deborah (Anne)
O'Neil, Roger
Osgood, Charles
Pappas, Ike
Pauley, Jane
Pettit, William Thomas
Pierpoint, Robert Charles
Quint, Bert
Rather, Dan(iel Irvin)
Reasoner, Harry
Reynolds, Frank
Roberts, Cokie
Robinson, Max C
Rollin, Betty
Rudd, Hughes Day
Rukeyser, Louis (Richard)
Safer, Morley
Sanders, Marlene
Savitch, Jessica Beth
Sawyer, Diane (K.)
Sawyer, Forrest
Scherer, Ray(mond Lewis)
Schieffer, Bob
Schorr, Daniel Louis
Sevareid, Eric
Shaw, Bernard
Shriver, Maria (Owings)
Simpson, Carole
Smith, Howard
  K(ingsbury)
Snyder, Tom
Soren, Tabitha
Stahl, Lesley (Rene)
Stern, Carl Leonard
Strawser, Neil Edward
Streithorst, Tom
Sullivan, Kathleen
Suzuki, David T(akayoshi)
Swing, Raymond Gram
Threlkeld, Richard D
Trout, Robert
Ubell, Earl
Valeriani, Richard Gerard

Vandercook, John
  Womack
Vanocur, Sander
Wallace, Chris(topher)
Wallace, Mike
Walters, Barbara
Wertheimer, Linda
  (Cozby)
Whicker, Alan Donald
Woodruff, Judy Carline
Zahn, Paula

BROADCASTER

Bowes, Major
Brown, Cecil B
Conrad, Frank
Cooke, (Alfred) Alistair
Daniels, Faith
Demento, Dr.
Downes, Edward Olin
  Davenport
Drinkwater, Terry
Edwards, Bob
Evans, Richard Louis
Gemmell, Alan
Gerussi, Bruno
Gross, Terry
Harwell, Ernie
Hewitt, Foster
Hibberd, Andrew Stuart
Howe, Quincy
Jay, Peter
Kasem, Casey (Kemal
  Amin)
Liebman, Joshua Loth
Maskell, Dan
McNamee, Graham
Muggeridge, Malcolm
Simpson, Jim
Smiley, Tavis
Stewart, Alison
Taylor, John

BROADCASTING EXECUTIVE

Banks, William (Venoid)
Brunson, Dorothy
Burgess, John Lawrie, Sir
Clayton, Xernona
Cornelius, Don
Dimmock, Peter
Disney, Roy E(dward)
Duffy, James Edson
Gartner, Michael Gay
Goodman, Julian B
Greene, Hugh (Carleton),
  Sir
Grossman, Lawrence
  K(ugelmass)
Haley, William John, Sir
Hewitt, Don S.
Johnson, Robert Louis
Juneau, Pierre
Kluge, John Werner
Koplovitz, Kay Smith
Lawson, Jennifer Karen
Leonard, Bill
McConnell, Joseph
  H(oward)
McManus, Sean
Minow, Newton Norman

Salant, Richard S
Seiler, James, W
Stoddard, Brandon
Valentine, Dean
Zorbaugh, Geraldine
  B(one)

BULLFIGHTER

Cordobes, El
Dominguin, Luis Miguel
Manolete

BUSINESS EXECUTIVE

Abiola, Moshood
Agee, William
  McReynolds
Akers, John Fellows
Albers, Hans
Allaire, Paul Arthur
Allen, Bob
Allen, Paul
Amdahl, Gene M(yron)
Amos, Wally
Anderson, Robert Orville
Anderson, Roy A(rnold)
Andreas, Dwayne Orville
Andrus, Cecil D(ale)
Antonini, Joseph
Appleton, Nathan
Appley, Lawrence A(sa)
Araskog, Rand Vincent
Ash, Roy Lawrence
Ashley, Laura Mountney
Aubrey, James (Thomas),
  Jr.
Austin, John Paul
Axelson, Kenneth Strong
Ayer, Harriet Hubbard
Balderston, William
Ball, Edward
Ballmer, Steve
Barad, Jill E(likann)
Barden, Don H.
Barksdale, James L(ove)
Barnard, Chester Irving
Barnett, Marvin Robert
Bartlett, Francis Alonzo
Barton, Robert B(rown)
  M(orison)
Beals, Vaughn LeRoy, Jr.
Bechtel, Stephen Davison
Bechtel, Stephen Davison,
  Jr.
Beech, Olive Ann (Mellor)
Bell, James Ford
Benn, Anthony
Berge, Pierre (Vital
  Georges)
Berlin, Richard E
Bernstein, Sid(ney Ralph)
Bickmore, Lee Smith
Billingsley, Sherman
Birch, Stephen
Bissell, Anna
Black, Conrad Moffat
Black, William
Block, Joseph L(eopold)
Bloomberg, Michael (R.)
Bloomingdale, Alfred S
Bluhdorn, Charles G

Blumenthal, W Michael
Bobst, Elmer Holmes
Boehm, Helen
Bogart, Neil
Bond, Alan
Bose, Amar Gopal
Bowlen, Patrick Dennis
Bremen, Barry
Brennan, Edward A.
Bricklin, Malcolm N
Briggs, Walter Owen
Bronfman, Edgar Miles,
  Jr.
Brooks, Diana D
Brown, Charles Lee
Brown, William Melvin,
  Jr.
Buffett, Warren Edward
Bugas, John Stephen
Buitoni, Giovanni
Burcham, Lester Arthur
Burke, James Edward
Burns, John L(awrence)
Burns, Robin
Busby, Jheryl
Busch, August Adolphus,
  III
Cabot, Thomas D(udley)
Cain, Herman
Callaway, Howard Hollis
Calloway, (David) Wayne
Candler, Charles Howard
Canfield, Alan B.
Carmichael, James Vinson
Casablancas, John(ny)
Case, Steve
Casey, James E
Chambers, Anne Cox
Chandler, Colby H
Chandler, Norman
Chandler, Otis
Chapman, Gilbert Whipple
Chaudhari, Praveen
Chenault, Kenneth I
Cisler, Walker (Lee)
Clark, Dick
Coffin, Charles Albert
Colbert, Virgis William
Cole, Kenneth Reese
Coleman, Sheldon, Jr.
Connerly, Ward
Cook, Lowdrick M
Cooke, Jack Kent
Cooper, Wilhelmina
  Behmenburg
Cordiner, Ralph Jarron
Cornell, Ezra
Cottrell, Comer J(oseph),
  Jr.
Cowles, John, Sr.
Coxe, Tench
Craig, Cleo F
Crosby, James Morris
Crosley, Powel, Jr.
Cummings, Nathan
Cummings, Sam
Cunningham, Harry Blair
Cunningham, Mary
  Elizabeth
Cunningham, R Walter
Cushman, Austin Thomas
Custin, Mildred
D'Alessio, Kitty
Daly, Marcus
Danforth, William H
Daniell, Robert F

Prada, Miuccia
Preston, Frances Williams
Price, Gwilym Alexander
Price, Hugh B.
Prodi, Romano
Queeny, Edgar Monsanto
Radocy, Robert
Rand, A(ddison) Barry
Rand, James Henry
Rawl, Lawrence G
Redstone, Sumner
(Murray)
Regine
Riklis, Meshulam
Robertson, James D, III
Roche, Joyce
Rock, Arthur
Rockefeller, Laurance
Spelman
Rockefeller, Rodman C
Roderick, David Milton
Rogers, John W., Jr.
Rootes, William Edward
Rootes, Baron
Ross, Percy Nathan
Ross, Steven J
Rothstein, Ruth
Rowland, Pleasant
Rudkin, Margaret Fogarty
Ruml, Beardsley
Ryder, James Arthur
Salhany, Lucie
Saltzman, Charles
E(skridge)
Sarnoff, David
Sarnoff, Robert W(illiam)
Scarne, John
Scherer, Ray(mond Lewis)
Schindler, Oskar
Schott, Marge
Schultz, Howard M.
Schwab, Charles
Schwinn, Edward R, Jr.
Sculley, John
Semenenko, Serge
Shaver, Dorothy
Shelby, Carroll (Hall)
Shrontz, Frank Anderson
Siebert, Muriel
Simon, Norton Winfred
Sims, Naomi
Six, Robert Forman
Sloane, John
Smale, John Gray
Smith, Frederick Wallace
Smith, Joshua (Isaac)
Sneed, Paula A(nn)
Soria, Dario
Soss, Wilma Porter
Spethmann, Dieter
Stern, Leonard Norman
Stern, Max
Stevens, Robert Ten
Broeck
Still, William
Stokely, Alfred Jehu
Stokely, Anna
Strenger, Hermann Josef
Swearingen, John Eldred
Swimmer, Ross
Taft, Henry Waters, II
Tatum, Donn B
Taulbert, Clifton Lemoure
Taylor, Kristin Clark
Thomas, Charles Allen
Thomas, Dave

Thomson, Ken(neth Roy)
Thomson, Roy Herbert
Tisch, Laurence Alan
Tompkins, Susie
Toomer, Ronald V
Traub, Marvin Stuart
Trump, Donald John
Tyson, Don
Van Andel, Jay
Van Camp, Gilbert C
Van der Klugt, Cor
Van Wachem, Lodewijk
Christiaan
Vernon, Lillian
Vila, George Raymond
Villiger, Kaspar
Vlasic, Joseph
Voit, Willard Darby
Wachner, Linda
Walgreen, Charles
Rudolph, III
Walker, Sarah Breedlove
McWilliams
Walters, Lou
Walters, Peter Ingram, Sir
Walton, Sam Moore
Wang, An
Washington, Val J.
Wasserman, Lew R
Watson, Thomas J(ohn),
Sr.
Watson, Thomas J(ohn),
Jr.
Wattleton, Faye
Weill, Sanford I.
Welch, John Francis, Jr.
Werner, Helmut
(Eberhard)
Westbrook, Peter (J.)
Weyerhaeuser, Frederick
Weyerhaeuser, Frederick
Edward
Wheeler, Roger Milton
Whitehead, (Walter)
Edward
Whitehead, Edwin C(arl)
Whitney, Richard
Willis, Paul S
Willkie, Wendell Lewis
Wilson, Charles Edward
Wilson, Charles Erwin
Wilson, Edward Foss
Wilson, Joseph
Chamberlain
Wilson, Peter Cecil
Wolfensohn, James David
Wolper, David Lloyd
Wood, Robert Elkington
Woodruff, Robert Winship
Wrightsman, Charles
Bierer
Wrigley, Philip Knight
Wrigley, William, Jr.
Wrigley, William, III
Young, John Alan
Zanker, Bill

BUSINESS OWNER

Mosbacher, Georgette

BUSINESSMAN

Abercrombie, James
Smither
Aldrin, Edwin E(ugene),
Jr.
Allen, John Polk
Arison, Ted
Armour, Philip Danforth
Armstrong, Thomas M
Ashbrook, John Milan
Avery, R Stanton
Bache, Harold Leopold
Baruch, Bernard Mannes
Baskin, Burton
Bassett, John D
Batten, William Milfred
Bell, Donald J
Benetton, Luciano
Bikoff, James L
Bing, Dave
Black, Eli M
Black, Samuel Duncan
Blaisdell, George G
Bloch, Henry W(ollman)
Blough, Roger Miles
Blount, Winton Malcolm
Bookout, John Frank, Jr.
Borch, Fred J.
Bowes, Walter
Bowles, Chester Bliss
Brassey, Thomas
Breck, John Henry
Brennan, Robert E
Brooks, Henry Sands
Brown, Harold
Brown, John Young, Jr.
Broyhill, James E
Brzezinski, Zbigniew
Kazimierz
Bulova, Joseph
Buss, Jerry Hatten
Butler, Michael
Butlin, William Heygate
Edmund, Sir
Butterfield, John
Calvo Sotelo (y Bustelo),
Leopoldo
Campbell, Joseph
Carlson, Curtis L.
Carlson, Edward Elmer
Carr, Harold Noflet
Carter, John Garnet
Carvel, Thomas A
Cary, Frank Taylor
Cohen, Ben(nett)
Coleman, William
Conover, Harry
Cook, Thomas
Cooke, Samuel
Cooper, Peter
Copeland, Al
Copeland, Lammot du
Pont
Coup, W(illiam)
C(ameron)
Couzens, James Joseph, Jr.
Cowdrey, (Michael) Colin
Creighton, Edward
Crittenton, Charles Nelson
Culligan, Emmett J
Dahl, Gary
Decker, Alonzo G
Dedman, Robert H
Dewar, James A
Dewar, John

Dietrich, Noah
Dole, James
Donner, Frederic Garrett
Douglas, James, Sir
Dryden, John Fairfield
Duke, Angier Biddle
Duke, James Buchanan
Dunton, Davidson
Eisele, Donn Fulton
Ertegun, Ahmet (Munir)
Estridge, Philip D
Famolare, Joseph P
Fargo, William George
Feld, Irvin
Fels, Samuel Simeon
Ferris, George Washington
Gale
Fetzer, John Earl
Feulner, Edwin John, Jr.
Finley, Charles O(scar)
Fitzgerald, John Francis
Folsom, Frank M
Fortune, Michele
Freer, Charles Lang
French, Robert T
Funston, George Keith
Gaines, Clarence F
Gaines, William
M(axwell)
Gary, Elbert Henry
Gaston, Arthur George
Gates, Thomas Sovereign,
Jr.
Geneen, Harold S(ydney)
Getty, Gordon Peter
Golub, William Weldon
Grace, William Russell
Graebner, Clark
Granatelli, Andy
Grede, William John
Greenfield, Jerry
Grosvenor, Gerald
Cavendish
Grunwald, Henry Anatole
Gurney, Dan
Hanna, Mark
Harkness, Edward Stephen
Harmsworth, Harold
Sidney
Harrah, Bill
Harriman, Edward Henry
Hartford, George
Huntington
Hartford, George Ludlum
Hartford, John Augustine
Hay, John
Helmsley, Harry
B(rakmann)
Hewlett, William
Hoffman, Robert C
Hoover, William K
Horchow, S(amuel) Roger
Howell, Albert S
Hubert, Conrad
Hudson, Joseph Lowthian
Hugel, Max
Hyatt, Joel
Ilitch, Mike
Jacobs, Raymond
Jacuzzi, Candido
Johnson, Herbert Fisk
Jones, Arthur A
Jones, Jerry
Kaplan, Jacob Merrill
Katayama, Yutaka
Kauffman, Ewing Marion

BUSINESSWOMAN

CABINETMAKER

CALL GIRL

CANDY MANUFACTURER

CARICATURIST

CARPENTER

CARTOGRAPHER

CARTOONIST

Fox, Fontaine Talbot, Jr.
Fradon, Dana
Frazetta, Frank
Freyse, William
Furniss, Harry
Gerard, Dave
Gillray, James
Goldberg, Rube
Goscinny, Rene
Gould, Chester
Gray, Harold Lincoln
Groening, Matt
Gross, Milt
Gruelle, Johnny
Guisewite, Cathy Lee
Haenigsen, Harry William
Hamilton, William
Hampson, Frank
Hanna, William Denby
Harman, Fred
Harman, Hugh
Harrington, Oliver
  W(endell)
Hart, Johnny
Hatlo, Jimmy
Haynie, Hugh
Held, John, Jr.
Herblock
Herriman, George
Hershfield, Harry
Hess, Sol
Hirschfeld, Al(bert)
Hoest, Bill
Hogarth, Burne
Hokinson, Helen
Holman, Bill
Igoe, Hype
Illingworth, Leslie Gilbert
Ising, Rudolf C
Iwerks, Ub(be)
Jaffee, Allan
Johnson, Crockett
Johnston, Lynn Beverley
Jones, Chuck
Judge, Mike
Justus, Roy Braxton
Kahles, Charles William
Keane, Bil
Kelly, Walt(er Crawford)
Kemble, Edward
  W(indsor)
Kent, Jack
Ketcham, Hank
Key, Ted
Kilgore, Al
King, Frank
King, Warren Thomas
Kirby, Jack
Kirby, Rollin
Knerr, H(arold) H
Koren, Edward Benjamin
Kotzky, Alex Sylvester
Kressy, Edmund
Kuekes, Edward Daniel
Lancaster, Osbert, Sir
Lantz, Walter
Larson, Gary
Lasswell, Fred
Lazarus, Mell
Lee, Stan
Leech, John
Lichty, George
Long, Scott
Low, David Alexander
  Cecil, Sir
Luks, George Benjamin

MacNelly, Jeff(rey
  Kenneth)
Marston, William Moulton
Mauldin, Bill
McCay, Winsor
McCutcheon, John Tinney
McDougall, Walt(er)
McManus, George
McWilliams, Alden S
Meggendorfer, Lothar
Messick, Dale
Messmer, Otto
Mikkelsen, Henning Dahl
Millar, Jeff(rey) Lynn
Monroe, Phil
Montana, Bob
Moore, Don W
Moores, Dick
Mosley, Zack Terrell
Moss, Geoffrey
Mullin, Willard
Murphy, Jimmy
Musial, Joe
Myers, Russell
Nast, Thomas
Neher, Fred
Nowlan, Phil
O'Brien, Willis Harold
Olderman, Murray
Oliphant, Patrick Bruce
Opper, Frederick Burr
Osborn, Robert C(hesley)
Outcault, Richard Felton
Parker, Brant (Julian)
Partch, Virgil Franklin, II
Plumb, Charles
Price, Garrett
Price, George
Raemaekers, Louis
Raymond, Alex(ander
  Gillespie)
Raymond, James C
Rea, Gardner
Ripley, Robert Leroy
Robbins, Frank
Robinson, W Heath
Rockwell, Doc
Rose, Carl
Rowlandson, Thomas
Ryan, Tom Kreusch
Sargent, Ben
Saunders, Allen
Saxon, Charles David
Schultze, Carl Emil
Schulz, Charles M(onroe)
Segar, Elzie Crisler
Shoemaker, Vaughn
  Richard
Shuster, Joe
Siegel, Jerry
Silverstein, Shel(by)
Smith, (Robert) Sidney
Smythe, Reg(inald)
Soglow, Otto
Spiegelman, Art
Spy
Steig, William
Steinberg, Saul
Sterrett, Cliff
Swinnerton, James
  Guilford
Terry, Paul H
Trudeau, Garry
Turner, Morrie
Tuthill, Harry J

Valtman, Edmund
  Siegfried
Walker, Mort
Ward, Jay
Watterson, Bill
Weber, Robert Maxwell
Webster, H(arold)
  T(ucker)
Westover, Russell
  (Channing)
Willard, Frank Henry
Williams, Gluyas
Williams, J(ames) R(obert)
Wilson, Gahan
Wilson, Tom
Wortman, Denys
Wunder, George S
Yates, Bill
Young, Art(hur Henry)
Young, Chic
Young, Lyman

CELEBRITY FRIEND

Marvin, Michelle Triola

CENTENARIAN

Calment, Jean
Delany, Annie Elizabeth
Delany, Sarah Louise
Douglas, Marjory
  (Stoneman)
Parks, Lillian (Adele)
  Rogers
Stickney, Dorothy
Thompson, Mary

CHEF

Appert, Nicolas
Beard, James Andrews
Benoit, Jehane
Bocuse, Paul
Boiardi, Hector
Brillat-Savarin, Jean
  Anthelme
Child, Julia McWilliams
Clark, Patrick
Escoffier, Georges
  Auguste
Farmer, Fannie Merritt
Franey, Pierre
Kerr, Graham
Lagasse, Emeril
Prudhomme, Paul
Puck, Wolfgang
Roy, Mike
Sherrod, Clayton
Smith, Jeff
Thuilier, Raymond

CHEMIST

Abelson, Philip Hauge
Abney, William de
  Wiveleslie, Sir
Achard, Franz Karl
Adler, Kurt

Alder, Kurt
Anders, Edward
Anfinsen, Christian
  Boehmer
Arrhenius, Svante August
Astbury, William
Baekeland, Leo Hendrik
Baeyer, Adolf Johann
  Friedrich Wilhelm, von
Balard, Antoine-Jerome
Baltimore, David
Bartlett, Neil
Barton, Derek H(arold)
  R(ichard), Sir
Beckman, Arnold (Orville)
Bergius, Friedrich Karl
  Rudolph
Berkowitz, Joan B.
Berner, Robert A(rbuckle)
Berthelot, Marcellin
Berthollet, Claude Louis,
  Comte
Berzelius, Jons Jacob,
  Baron
Black, Joseph
Boltwood, Bertram Borden
Bosch, Carl
Bottger, Johann Friedrich
Boussingault, Jean
  Baptiste
Bovet, Daniele
Brady, St. Elmo
Bronsted, Johannes
  Nicolaus
Brooks, Ronald E.
Brown, Herbert Charles
Buchner, Eduard
Bunsen, Robert Wilhelm
  Eberhard
Butenandt, Adolf Fredrick
  Johann
Calvin, Melvin
Cannizzaro, Stanislao
Carothers, Wallace Hume
Carver, George
  Washington
Cassidy, Harold Gomes
Castro, George (A.)
Cavendish, Henry
Chaptal, Jean Antoine,
  Comte de Chanteloup
Chardonnet, Louis Marie
  Hilaire Bernigaud
Chesebrough, Robert
  Augustus
Chevreul, Michel Eugene
Claude, Georges
Cleve, Per Teodor
Corey, Elias James
Cornforth, John Warcup,
  Sir
Cottrell, Frederick Gardner
Couper, Archibald Scott
Courtois, Bernard
Crafts, James Mason
Cram, Donald James
Curie, Marie
Curie, Pierre
Darken, Lawrence Stamper
Davis, Marguerite
Davis, Raymond, Jr.
Debye, Peter Joseph
  William
DeDuve, Christian Rene
  Marie Joseph
Dewar, James, Sir

Diels, Otto Paul Herman
Djerassi, Carl
Dobereiner, Johann
  Wolfgang
Domagk, Gerhard
Dow, Herbert Henry
Duhem, Pierre Maurice
  Marie
Dulong, Pierre-Louis
Dumas, Jean Baptiste
  Andre
DuVigneaud, Vincent
Edelman, Gerald Maurice
Eigen, Manfred
Ellis, Carleton
El-Sayed, Mostafa Amr
Ernst, Richard
Euler-Chelpin, Hans Karl
  August Simon von
Fischer, Emil Herman
Fischer, Hans
Flory, Paul John
Franklin, Rosalind Elsie
Friedel, Charles
Fukui, Kenichi
Gay-Lussac, Joseph-Louis
Gerhardt, Charles Frederic
Giauque, William Francis
Gibbs, Oliver Wolcott
Graham, Thomas
Grignard, Francois
  Auguste Victor
Haber, Fritz
Hahn, Otto
Hall, James, Sir
Hall, Lloyd Augustus
Harden, Arthur, Sir
Hare, Robert
Harkins, William Draper
Harris, James Andrew
Hass, H(enry) B(ohn)
Hassel, Odd
Hawkins, Walter Lincoln
Haworth, Walter Norman,
  Sir
Helmont, Jan Baptista van
Heroult, Paul Louis
  Toussaint
Herschbach, Dudley
  Robert
Herzberg, Gerhard
Hevesy, George Charles
  von
Hinshelwood, Cyril
  Norman, Sir
Hirschfelder, Joseph
  Oakland
Hoff, Jacobus Henricus
  van't
Hoffmann, Roald
Hofmann, August Wilhelm
  von
Ingenhousz, Jan
Ingold, Christopher Kelk,
  Sir
Julian, Percy Lavon
Karle, Isabella (L.)
Karrar, Paul
Kekule, Friedrich August
Kistiakowsky, George
  Bogdan
Kuhn, Richard
Landis, Walter Savage
Langmuir, Irving
Lavoisier, Antoine Laurent
Le Chatelier, Henry-Louis

Lee, Yuan Tseh
Lehn, Jean-Marie
Leloir, Luis Federico
Levi, Primo
Lewis, Gilbert Newton
Libby, Willard Frank
Liebig, Justus von
Lipscomb, William Nunn
Macintosh, Charles
Mark, Herman Francis
Marker, Russell Earl
Martin, Archer John Porter
McCollum, Elmer Verner
McLaughlin, John J
McMillan, Edwin Mattison
Mendeleev, Dmitri
  Ivanovich
Midgeley, Thomas
Mitchell, Peter Dennis
Mitscherlich, Eilhardt
Moissan, Ferdinand
  Frederick Henri
Muller, Paul Hermann
Mulliken, Robert
  Sanderson
Munroe, Charles Edward
Natta, Giulio
Nernst, Walther Hermann
Nirenberg, Marshall
  Warren
Oersted, Hans Christian
Ostwald, Friedrich
  Wilhelm
Paneth, Friedrich Adolf
Pasteur, Louis
Pauling, Linus C(arl)
Payen, Anselme
Pedersen, Charles J
Perkin, William Henry, Sir
Pictet, Raoul-Pierre
Polanyi, John C
Polanyi, Michael
Ponnamperuma, Cyril
  (Andrew)
Porter, Rodney Robert
Pregl, Fritz
Prelog, Vladimir
Priestley, Joseph
Prigogine, Ilya
Proust, Joseph Louis
Quarterman, Lloyd Albert
Reichstein, Tadeus
Remsen, Ira
Richards, Ellen Henrietta
  Swallow
Richards, Theodore
  William
Robinson, Robert, Sir
Ruffin, Edmund
Ruzicka, Leopold Stephen
Sabatier, Paul
Sainte-Clair Deville, Henri
  Etienne
Saussure, Nicolas
  Thoedore de
Scheele, Karl Wilhelm
Schonbein, Christian
  Friedrich
Schopf, J(ames) William
Seaborg, Glenn
  T(heodore)
Semenov, Nikolai
  Nikolaevich
Silliman, Benjamin
Sobrero, Ascanio
Soddy, Frederick

Spedding, Frank Harold
Stahl, Georg Ernst
Stanley, Wendell Meredith
Staudinger, Hermann
Stein, William Howard
Strassmann, Fritz
Sumner, James Batcheller
Svedberg, Theodor H E
Swan, Joseph Wilson, Sir
Synge, Richard Laurence
  Millington
Tammann, Gustav
  Heinrich Johann
  Apollon
Telkes, Maria (de)
Tiselius, Arne Wilhelm
  Kaurin
Todd, Alexander
  (Robertus), Sir
Tolman, Richard C(hace)
Urey, Harold Clayton
Van't Hoff, Jacobus
  Henricus
Virtanen, Artturi Llmari
Wallach, Otto
Watt, George Willard
Welsbach, Carl Auer von,
  Baron
Werner, Alfred
Wesson, David
Wieland, Heinrich Otto
Wiley, Harvey
  Washington
Willstater, Richard Martin
Windaus, Adolf Otto
  Reinhold
Wohler, Friedrich
Zsigmondy, Richard Adolf

CHESS PLAYER

Alekhine, Alexander
Anderssen, Adolf
Ashley, Maurice
Benko, Paul Charles
Botvinnik, Mikhail
  (Moisseyevich)
Bourdonnais, Louis
  Charles de la
Browne, Walter Shawn
Capablanca, Jose Raoul
Euwe, Max
Fischer, Bobby
Karpov, Anatoly
  Yevgenyevich
Kashdan, Isaac
Kasparov, Garry Kimovich
Lasker, Edward
Lasker, Emanuel
Marshall, Frank James
Menchik-Stevenson, Vera
  Francevna
Morphy, Paul Charles
Petrosian, Tigran
  Vartanovich
Philidor, Francois Andre
  Danican
Polgar, Judit
Reshevsky, Samuel
Rudenko, Lyudmila
Smyslov, Vasili
  Vasil'evich
Spassky, Boris
  Vasilyevich
Staunton, Howard

Steinitz, Wilhelm
Tal, Mikhail
  Nekhemyevich

CHIEFTAIN

Lautaro
Maherero, Samuel
Vercingetorix

CHILD ACTORS

Our Gang

CHILD PRODIGY

Lawrence, Ruth

CHILDREN'S AUTHOR

Abbott, Jacob
Adams, Harriet
  Stratemeyer
Adams, William Taylor
Agle, Nan Hayden
Alexander, Sue
A.L.O.E.
Altsheler, Joseph
  Alexander
Anderson, C(larence)
  W(illiam)
Andrews, Jane
Anglund, Joan Walsh
Armstrong, William
  H(oward)
Arnold, Oren
Baker, Rachel
Bannerman, Helen
Bealer, Alex W(inkler III)
Beebe, Burdetta Faye
Behn, Harry
Best, Oswald Herbert
Bianco, Margery Williams
Blake, Quentin
Bleeker, Sonia
Bothwell, Jean
Bragg, Mabel Caroline
Brett, Jan Churchill
Brown, Marcia
Brown, Margaret Wise
Brunhoff, Jean de
Burton, Virginia Lee
Byars, Betsy
Carter, Dorothy Sharp
Carter, Katherine Jones
Castlemon, Harry
Caudill, Rebecca
Cavanna, Betty
Chase, Mary Ellen
Christian, Mary Blount
Christopher, Matt(hew F.)
Chukovsky, Korney
  Ivanovich
Clarke, Rebecca Sophia
Cleary, Beverly (Atlee
  Bunn)
Cleaver, Vera Allen
Coatsworth, Elizabeth Jane
Cobb, Vicki

Coles, Joanna
Colonius, Lillian
Cone, Molly Lamken
Conklin, Gladys Plemon
Cooke, David Coxe
Coombs, Charles Ira
Cooney, Barbara
Corbett, Scott
Cousins, (Sue) Margaret
Coy, Harold
Craig, Helen
Crosby, Alexander L
Dalgleish, Alice
Daringer, Helen Fern
Daugherty, James Henry
D'Aulaire, Edgar Parin
D'Aulaire, Ingri
   Mortenson
Davis, Burke
DeAngeli, Marguerite
   Lofft
Dejong, Meindert
DeLeeuw, Adele Louise
DeRegniers, Beatrice
   Schenk
Dodge, Bertha Sanford
Dodge, Mary Elizabeth
   Mapes
Douglas, Amanda Minnie
Du Bois, William Pene
Duvoisin, Roger Antoine
Eckert, Horst
Edgeworth, Maria
Eifert, Virginia Snider
Elkin, Benjamin
Ellison, Virginia Howell
Elting, Mary Letha
Estes, Eleanor Ruth
   Rosenfeld
Ets, Marie Hall
Ewing, Julianna Horatia
   (Gatty)
Fiedler, Jean(nette
   Feldman)
Field, Rachel Lyman
Fitzgerald, John Dennis
Fleischmann, Sid
Fritz, Jean Guttery
Gag, Wanda
Gallant, Roy Arthur
Garnett, Eve C R
Gerrard, Roy
Gidal, Sonia
Gilbertson, Mildred Geiger
Goffstein, Marilyn
Grahame, Kenneth
Gramatky, Hardie
Gray, Nicholas Stuart
Greenfield, Eloise
Handford, Martin
Henry, Marguerite
Henty, George Alfred
Hightower, Florence
   Josephine Cole
Hoffmann, Heinrich
Houston, James Archibold
Howitt, Mary
Johnston, Annie Fellows
Julesberg, Elizabeth Rider
   Montgomery
Keats, Ezra Jack
Knight, Hilary
Lamb, Mary Ann
Lampman, Evelyn Sibley
Langner, Nola
Lawson, Donald Elmer

Lenski, Lois
Levitin, Sonia
Lewis, Elizabeth Foreman
Lindgren, Astrid
Lionni, Leo
Little, (Flora) Jean
Littledale, Freya Lota
Lively, Penelope
Lothrop, Harriet Mulford
   Stone
MacKellar, William
Maestro, Giulio
Marshall, James Edward
McCloskey, Robert
Miller, Olive Thorne
Morey, Walt(er Nelson)
Nesbit, Edith
Nolan, Jeannette Covert
Norton, Mary
Osborne, Leone Neal
Parish, Peggy
Petersham, Maud
Petersham, Miska
Phelps, Elizabeth Stuart
   Ward
Pilkington, Francis
   Meredyth
Pinkwater, Daniel Manus
Pringle, Laurence
Provensen, Alice Rose
   Twitchell
Provensen, Martin
Pullein-Thompson, Diana
Raskin, Ellen
Rees, Ennis (Samuel, Jr.)
Renick, Marion Lewis
Rey, Margret (Elizabeth)
Rice, Alice Caldwell
   Hegan
Rinkoff, Barbara Jean
Robinson, Joan Mary Gale
   Thomas
Rosen, Sidney
Ruchlis, Hy(man)
Russell, Solveig Paulson
Salten, Felix
Sandburg, Helga
Sanderlin, George William
Sarg, Tony
Sawyer, Ruth
Scarry, Richard (McClure)
Schlein, Miriam
Schneider, Herman
Schneider, Nina
Scholz, Jackson Volney
Seredy, Kate
Serraillier, Ian Lucien
Sharmat, Marjorie
   Weinman
Sherwood, Mary Martha
Shippen, Katherine Binney
Shuttlesworth, Dorothy
   Edwards
Silverstein, Alvin
Simon, Norma Feldstein
Slobodkina, Esphyr
Smith, William Jay
Snow, Dorothea Johnston
Sorensen, Virginia
Speare, Elizabeth George
Sperry, Armstrong W
Steig, William
Stoutenburg, Adrien Pearl
Stratemeyer, Edward L
Sturtzel, Howard Allison
Sturtzel, Jane Levington

Sutton, Margaret Beebe
Swinburne, Laurence
Tappan, Eva March
Taylor, Ann
Taylor, Sydney Brenner
Terris, Susan
Thompson, George Selden
Thompson, Vivian
   Laubach
Thum, Marcella
Tomlinson, Jill
Trevino, Elizabeth Borton
   de
Tripp, Paul
Tunis, Edwin Burdett
Turkle, Brinton Cassaday
Udry, Janice May
Ungerer, Tomi
Unkelbach, Kurt
Uttley, Alice Jane Taylor
VanAllsburg, Chris
Westall, Robert Atkinson
Wiese, Kurt
Wiggin, Kate Douglas
Wildsmith, Brian
Williams, Jay
Williams, Ursula Moray
Wilson, Hazel Hutchins
Wise, Winifred E
Woody, Regina Llewellyn
   Jones
Yates, Elizabeth
Young, Margaret Ann
   Buckner
Zolotow, Charlotte
   Shapiro

CHOREOGRAPHER

Abdul, Paula (Julie)
Ailey, Alvin
Ashton, Frederick
   William, Sir
Balanchine, George
Baryshnikov, Mikhail
Bausch, Pina
Bejart, Maurice
Bennett, Michael
Berkeley, Busby
Bettis, Valerie
Brown, Trisha
Butler, John
Byrd, Donald
Carlisle, Kevin
Champion, Gower
Charmoli, Tony
Christensen, Lew Farr
Christensen, William
Clarke, Hope
Clarke, Martha
Cole, Jack
Collins, Janet Faye
Cranko, John
Cunningham, Merce
Dale, Grover
Danielian, Leon
Danilova, Alexandra
Dean, Laura
DeValois, Ninette, Dame
Dolin, Anton, Sir
Dolly, Jenny
Dolly, Rosie
Dove, Ulysses
Dunham, Katherine
Englund, Richard

Fagan, Garth
Faison, George
Falco, Louis
Feld, Eliot
Fenley, Molissa
Field, Ron(ald)
Flatt, Ernie
Forsythe, William
Fosse, Bob
Franca, Celia
Frankel, Emily
Geiogamah, Hanay
Gennaro, Peter
Geva, Tamara
Glover, Savion
Gordon, David
Graham, Martha
Greco, Jose
Grigorovich, Yuri
   Nikolaevich
Haney, Carol
Hawkins, Erick
Holm, Hanya
Humphrey, Doris
Irwin, Bill
Jamison, Judith
Joffrey, Robert
Johnson, Virginia (Alma
   Fairfax)
Jones, Bill T.
Jooss, Kurt
Kidd, Michael
Kudelka, James
Laban, Rudolf von
Layton, Joe
Lemon, Ralph
Lichine, David
Lifar, Serge
Limon, Jose Arcadio
Loring, Eugene
Lubovitch, Lar
MacMillan, Kenneth, Sir
Markert, Russell
Martins, Peter
Massine, Leonide
   Fedorovich
Maurer, Emilia Sherman
Miller, Bebe
Mitchell, Arthur Adam
Moiseyev, Igor
   Alexandrovich
Monk, Meredith Jane
Morris, Mark
Neumeier, John
Nijinska, Bronislava
Nikolais, Alwin
Pan, Hermes
Parsons, David
Pendleton, Moses Robert
   Andrew
Petipa, Marius
Petit, Roland
Robbins, Jerome
Saddler, Donald
Saint Denis, Ruth
Smuin, Michael
Svetlova, Marina
Takei, Kei
Tamiris, Helen
Taylor, June
Taylor, Paul
Tharp, Twyla
Tomasson, Helgi
Tudor, Antony
Tune, Tommy
Villella, Edward Joseph

Hesburgh, Theodore
Martin
Hidalgo y Costilla, Miguel
Higginson, Thomas
Wentworth Storrow
Hill, Morton A(nthony)
Holland, William Jacob
Holly, James Theodore
Holmes, John Haynes
Holt, Ivan Lee
Honen
Hooker, Thomas
Hooks, Benjamin Lawson
Howard, Guy Wesley
Hsuan Tsang
Hui-yuan
Ignatius of Antioch
Imhotep
Ironside, Henry Allan
Isidore of Seville, St.
Jack, Homer A(lexander)
Jakes, Thomas T.D.
Jasper, John J
Jogues, Isaac
John of Piano Carpini
Jowett, Benjamin
Judson, Adoniram
Keble, John
King, Bernice Albertine
King, Martin Luther, Sr.
King, Martin Luther, Jr.
King, Thomas Starr
Kingsley, Charles
Kukai
Kumarajiva
Lacombe, Albert
Lacordaire, Jean Baptiste
Henri
LaHaye, Tim
Lanfranc
Lang, William Cosmo
Gordon, Baron
Langstroth, Lorenzo
Lorraine
Las Casas, Bartolome de
Laval, Francois Xavier de
Lavigerie, Charles Martel
Allemand
Lowery, Joseph E
Lydgate, John
Lynch, J(ohn) Joseph
Mabillon, Jean
Mackay, John Alexander
MacKillop, Mary
Mahan, Asa
Maida, Adam (Joseph)
Manasseh ben Israel
Mannix, Daniel
Marcus, Jacon R(ader)
Matamoros, Mariano
Mather, Cotton
Mather, Increase
Matthew Paris
Mayhew, Jonathan
McCloskey, John
McGivney, Michael
Joseph
McLaughlin, Leo
(Plowden)
Menno Simonsz(con)
Mogila, Peter
Molinos, Miguel de
Morelos y Pavon, Jose
Maria
Morse, Jedidiah

Muhammad, Khallid
Abdul
Muhlenberg, William
Augustus
Mundelein, George
William
Murray, Cecil (Leonard)
Muste, A(braham)
J(ohannes)
Muzorewa, Abel Tendekai
Ndungane, Winston
N(jongonkulu)
Neri, Philip
Nevin, John Williamson
Newton, John
Nicholas of Oresme
Nikon, Nikita Minov
Nygren, Anders T(heodor)
S(amuel)
Oates, Titus
Oberlin, Johann Friedrich
O'Callahan, Joseph
Timothy
Occom, Samson
Otterbein, Philip William
Paisley, Ian Richard Kyle
Parker, Thomas
Parkhurst, Charles Henry
Pazmany, Peter
Peabody, Endicott
Peale, Norman Vincent
Pelikan, Jaroslav
Phillips, Channing Emery
Pire, Dominique
Powell, Adam Clayton, Jr.
Preus, Jacob A(all)
O(ttesen)
Pusey, Edward Bouverie
Richard, Gabriel
Ripley, George
Roe, Edward Payson
Roloff, Lester
Rosmini-Serbati, Antonio
Royden, Agnes Maude
Rubenstein, Richard
L(owell)
Rugambwa, Laurean
Ruiz, Juan
Ryerson, Adolphus
Egerton
Saicho
Schiess, Betty Bone
Schillebeeckx, Edward
(Cornelis Florentius
Alfons)
Schindler, Solomon
Schmemann, Alexander
Seiss, Joseph Augustus
Sharpton, Al(fred), Jr.
Shinichiro Imaoka
Shinran
Shuttlesworth, Fred Lee
Sin, Jaime L(achica)
Smith, Samuel Francis
Smith, Sydney
Sorin, Edward Frederick
Stoddard, Solomon
Strachan, John
Strong, Josiah
Sullivan, Leon H
Swift, Jonathan
Talmadge, Thomas de
Witt
Taylor, Graham
Teilhard de Chardin,
Pierre

Temple, William
Tennent, Gilbert
Theresa, St.
Toba Sojo
Toplady, Augustus
Montague
Tyrrell, George
Van Dusen, Henry Pitney
Vandyke, Henry Jackson,
Jr.
Van Paassen, Pierre
Vanzant, Iyanla (Rhonda)
Vianney, Jean (Marie)
Baptiste
Vieira, Antonio
Vitry, Philippe de
Waite, Terry
Walker, Harold Blake
Walsh, Chad
Watts, J(ulius) C(aesar),
(Jr.)
Wayland, Francis
Weems, Mason Locke
Weld, Theodore Dwight
Wesley, Charles
Wheelock, Eleazar
Whitechurch, Victor
Lorenzo
Wierwille, Victor Paul
Wigglesworth, Michael
Wilder, Amos Niven
Williams, George
Washington
Williams, Hosea Lorenzo
Williams, Roger
Winans, Marvin L.
Wine, Sherwin T(heodore)
Winebrenner, John
Wise, John
Woodsworth, James
Shaver
Youlou, Fulbert
Youngblood, Johnny Ray
Zinzendorf, Nikolaus
Ludwig von, Count
Zumarraga, Juan de

CLERGYMAN

Gladden, Washington

CLOWN

Eulenspiegel, Till
Grimaldi, Joseph
Grock
Jacobs, Lou
Kelly, Emmett Lee
Popov, Oleg
Konstantinovich

COLONIAL FIGURE

Alden, John
Alden, Priscilla Mullens
Andros, Edmund, Sir
Bacon, Nathaniel
Bowdoin, James
Bradford, William
Brewster, William
Byrd, William
Carver, John

Clarke, John
Coddington, William
Dare, Virginia
Deane, Silas
Dinwiddie, Robert
Dudley, Thomas
Eaton, Theophilus
Eliot, John
Endecott, John
Galvez, Bernardo de
Gorges, Ferdinando, Sir
Hanson, John
Head, Edmund Walker, Sir
Hutchinson, Thomas
Mason, George
Minuit, Peter
Otis, James
Phips, William, Sir
Rolfe, John
Ross, Betsy
Shirley, William
Spotswood, Alexander
Standish, Miles
Stuyvesant, Peter
Taylor, George
Winslow, Edward
Wolcott, Roger
Yale, Elihu
Berkeley, William, Sir

COLONIZER

Austin, Stephen Fuller
Baltimore, George Calvert,
Baron
Bienville, Sieur de
Brazza, Pierre Paul
Francois Camille
Savorgnan de
Cuffe, Paul
Davenport, John
DeVries, David Pietersen
Maclean, George
Maisoneuve, Sieur de
Mason, John
Menendez de Aviles,
Pedro
Oglethorpe, James Edward
Penn, William
Phillip, Arthur
Riebeeck, Jan Anthonisz
van
Selkirk, 5th Earl of
Smith, John
Sousa, Martim Afonso de
Van Rensselaer, Kiliaen

COMEDIAN

Abbott, Bud
Adams, Don
Adams, Joey
Allen, Byron
Allen, Fred
Allen, Gracie Ethel Cecil
Rosaline
Allen, Tim
Amsterdam, Morey
Arbuckle, Fatty
Arnold, Tom
Aykroyd, Dan(iel Edward)
Baddeley, Hermione
Clinton

Baker, Phil
Ball, Lucille (Desiree)
Barker, Ronnie
Bean, Orson
Beaton, Norman
Bellamy, Bill
Belushi, John
Belzer, Richard
Benny, Jack
Berberian, Cathy
Bergen, Edgar John
Berle, Milton
Berman, Shelley
Bernhard, Sandra
Bernie, Ben
Besser, Joe
Bishop, Joey
Blue, Ben
Boosler, Elayne
Borge, Victor
Brendel, El(mer)
Brenner, David
Brooks, Albert (Lawrence
    Einstein)
Brooks, Foster Murrell
Brown, Joe E(van)
Bruce, Lenny
Buchanan, Jack
Burnett, Carol
Burns, George
Burns, Jack
Buttons, Red
Buzzi, Ruth Ann
Caesar, Sid
Callas, Charlie
Cambridge, Godfrey
Candy, John (Franklin)
Canova, Judy
Cantinflas
Cantor, Eddie
Carey, Drew
Carlin, George Dennis
Carne, Judy
Carroll, Pat(ricia Ann
    Angela Bridgit)
Carson, Johnny
Carter, Jack
Carvey, Dana
Chaplin, Sydney Dryden
Chapman, Graham
Chase, Charley
Chase, Chevy
Cho, Margaret
Chong, Tommy
Clark, Bobby
Clay, Andrew Dice
Clyde, Andy
Coca, Imogene Fernandez
    y
Cody, Lew
Cohen, Myron
Colonna, Jerry
Conklin, Chester
Conway, Tim
Corey, Irwin
Correll, Charles J
Cosby, Bill
Costello, Lou
Cox, Wally
Crosby, Norm(an
    Lawrence)
Crystal, Billy
Curry, Mark
Curtin, Jane (Therese)
Dana, Bill
Dangerfield, Rodney

Davis, Joan
DeGeneres, Ellen
DeLuise, Dom
DeRita, Joe
Diller, Phyllis
Dunn, Nora
Efron, Marshall
Elliott, Bob
Erwin, Stuart
Fay, Frank
Faye, Joey
Fields, Gracie
Fields, Lew Maurice
Fields, Totie
Fields, W C
Fine, Larry
Flagg, Fannie
Fontaine, Frank
Foster, Phil
Foxworthy, Jeff
Foxx, Redd
Frye, David
Gardner, Ed(ward Francis)
Garofalo, Janeane
Gleason, Jackie
Gobel, George Leslie
Goldberg, Whoopi
Gorshin, Frank John
Gosden, Freeman Fisher
Goulding, Ray(mond
    Walter)
Greene, Shecky
Gregory, Dick
Hackett, Buddy
Hall, Arsenio
Hall, Rich
Handelman, Stanley
    Myron
Hardy, Oliver
Harris, Phil
Harris, Robin
Hartman, Grace
Harvey, Steve(n Patrick)
Henry, Lenny
Herman, Pee-Wee
Hill, Benny
Hope, Bob
Howard, Curly
Howard, Eugene
Howard, Moe
Howard, Shemp
Howard, Willie
Ingels, Marty
Johnson, Arte
Johnson, Chic
Kabibble, Ish
Kamen, Milt
Kaplan, Gabe
Karns, Roscoe
Kaufman, Andy
Kaye, Danny
Kaye, Stubby
Keaton, Buster
Keaton, Michael
Kelly, Patsy
King, Alan
Kinison, Sam
Kirby, George
Klein, Robert
Knotts, Don
Korman, Harvey Herschel
Lahr, Bert
Lanchester, Elsa
Landesberg, Steve
Laurel, Stan
Laurie, Joe, Jr.

Lee, Pinky
Leno, Jay
Leonard, Jack E
Lester, Jerry
Lewis, Jerry
Lewis, Joe E
Lewis, Richard
Lillie, Beatrice Gladys
Little Tich
Livingstone, Mary
Lloyd, Harold
Lovitz, Jon
Lynde, Paul Edward
Mabley, Moms
Maher, Bill
Mandel, Howie
Marin, Richard
Markham, Pigmeat
Marks, Charles
Martin, Dick
Martin, Steve
Marx, Chico
Marx, Groucho
Marx, Gummo
Marx, Harpo
Marx, Zeppo
Mason, Jackie
Meara, Anne
Miles, Sylvia
Miller, Dennis
Moran, Polly
Morita, Pat
Mull, Martin
Murphy, Eddie
Murray, Bill
Murray, Jan
Myers, Mike
Nealon, Kevin
Newhart, Bob
Novello, Don
O'Brien, Conan
O'Donnell, Rosie
Olsen, Ole
O'Shea, Tessie
Paulsen, Pat
Pearl, Minnie
Penner, Joe
Piscopo, Joe
Poston, Tom
Poundstone, Paula
Prinze, Freddie
Pryor, Richard (Franklin
    Lennox Thomas)
Pully, B S
Radner, Gilda
Raye, Martha
Reilly, Charles Nelson
Reiser, Paul
Reubens, Paul
Rickles, Don
Ritz, Al
Ritz, Harry
Ritz, Jimmy
Rivers, Joan
Robey, George, Sir
Rock, Chris
Roseanne
Rose-Marie
Ross, Joe E
Rowan, Dan
Rubin, Benny
Rudner, Rita
Russell, Anna
Russell, Mark
Russell, Nipsey
Saget, Bob

Sahl, Mort (Lyon)
Samples, Junior
Sandler, Adam
Savo, Jimmy
Schneider, Rob
Schreiber, Avery
Secombe, Harry
Seinfeld, Jerry
Shandling, Garry
Shaughnessy, Mickey
Shawn, Dick
Sherman, Allan
Short, Martin
Shuster, Frank
Silvers, Phil
Sinbad
Skelton, Red
Smirnoff, Yakov
Smith, Joe
Smothers, Dick
Smothers, Tommy
Stang, Arnold
Steinberg, David
Stephenson, Skip
Stewart, Jon
Stiller, Jerry
Storch, Larry
Summerville, Slim
Talbot, Nita
Talmadge, Constance
Tarlton, Richard
Tati, Jacques
Terry-Thomas
Thomas, Danny
Thomas, Dave
Tomlin, Lily
Tucker, Chris
Turpin, Ben
Van Dyke, Dick
Vernon, Jackie
Walker, Jimmie
Warfield, Marsha
Washington, Buck
Wayans, Damon
Wayans, Keenen Ivory
Wayne, Johnny
Weber, Joseph M
Wheeler, Bert
White, Jesse
White, Slappy
Williams, Bert
Williams, Robin
Wilson, Flip
Winters, Jonathan
    (Harshman, III)
Wisdom, Norman
Woolsey, Robert
Worley, Jo Anne
Wright, Steven
Wynn, Ed
Yankovic, Weird Al
Young, Alan (Angus)
Youngman, Henny

COMEDY TEAM

Abbott and Costello
Cheech and Chong
Marx Brothers, The
Monty Python's Flying
    Circus
Ritz Brothers
Three Stooges, The
Wayne and Shuster
Weber and Fields

COMPOSER

Abel, Karl Friedrich
Adam, Adolphe Charles
Adams, John Coolidge
Addinsell, Richard
Addison, John
Adler, Richard
Ager, Milton
Aitken, Hugh
Albeniz, Isaac Manuel
  Francisco
Albert, Stephen Joel
Albinoni, Tommaso
Allegri, Gregorio
Almeida, Laurindo
Amram, David Werner, III
Anderson, Cat
Anderson, Leroy
Animuccia, Giovanni
Antheil, George
Arditi, Luigi
Arne, Thomas Augustine
Arnold, Malcolm, Sir
Auber, Daniel Francois
  Esprit
Auric, Georges
Babbitt, Milton Byron
Bach, Carl Philipp
  Emanuel
Bach, Johann Christian
Bach, Johann Sebastian
Bach, Wilhelm
  Friedmann
Bacharach, Burt
Badalamenti, Angelo
Badings, Henk
Baker, Phil
Balakirev, Mili
  Alekseyevich
Balfe, Michael William
Ball, Ernest
Ballard, Louis W.
Bantock, Granville, Sir
Barber, Samuel
Barnes, Billy
Barry, John
Bart, Lionel
Bartok, Bela
Bax, Arnold Edward
  Trevor, Sir
Beach, H H A, Mrs.
Beethoven, Ludwig van
Bellini, Vincenzo
Ben-Haim, Paul
Benjamin, Arthur
Bennett, Richard Rodney
Bennett, Robert Russell
Bennett, William
  Sterndale, Sir
Berg, Alban
Berger, Arthur
Berio, Luciano
Berlin, Irving
Berlioz, Hector
Bernstein, Elmer
Bernstein, Leonard
Bertini, Gary
Bevel, James Luther
Billings, William
Bizet, Georges (Alexandre
  Cesar Leopold)
Black, Frank J.
Blake, Eubie
Blech, Leo
Bley, Carla

Bliss, Arthur, Sir
Blitzstein, Marc
Bloch, Ernest
Bloom, Mickey
Blow, John
Blyton, Carey
Boccherini, Luigi
Bock, Jerry
Boieldieu, Francois Adrien
Boito, Arrigo
Bolcom, William Elden
Bond, Carrie Jacobs
Bononcini, Giovanni
  Battista
Borodin, Alexander
  Profirevich
Boulanger, Nadia Juliette
Boulez, Pierre
Bowles, Paul (Frederick)
Boyce, William
Brahms, Johannes
Brand, Oscar
Bricusse, Leslie
Bridge, Frank
Britain, Radie
Britten, (Edward)
  Benjamin
Brown, Earle
Brown, Oscar, Jr.
Bruch, Max
Bruckner, Anton
Bruckner, Joseph Anton
Buck, Dudley
Bull, John
Bull, Ole Bornemann
Burnette, Johnny
Bush, Alan (Dudley)
Busoni, Ferruccio
  Benvenuto
Bussotti, Sylvano
Buxtehude, Dietrich
Byrd, Henry
Byrd, William
Byrne, David
Cabezon, Antonio
Caccini, Giulio
Cadman, Charles
  Wakefield
Cage, John
Cambert, Robert
Campion, Thomas
Cantrick, Robert
Carey, Henry
Carissimi, Giacomo
Carle, Frankie
Carmines, Al(vin Allison
  Jr.)
Carpenter, John Alden
Carter, Elliott Cook, Jr.
Casadesus, Robert
Castelnuovo-Tedesco,
  Mario
Catalani, Alfredo
Cavallaro, Carmen
Cavalli, Francesco
Cavalli, Pietro Francesco
Cesti, Pietro
Chabrier, Emmanuel
Chadwick, George
  Whitefield
Chaminade, Cecile
Chaplin, Charlie
Charles, Ray
Charpentier, Gustave
Charpentier, Marc-Antoine
Chasins, Abram

Chausson, Ernest
Chavez (y Ramirez),
  Carlos Antonio de
  Pauda
Cherubini, Luigi Carlo
  Zenobio Salvadore
  Maria
Chopin, Frederic Francois
Chorzempa, Daniel Walter
Cilea, Francesco
Cimarosa, Domenico
Clarke, Jeremiah
Clarke, Stanley Marvin
Clemens non Papa,
  Jacobus
Clementi, Muzio
Clinton, George
Coates, Albert
Cobb, Arnett Cleophus
Cobham, Billy
Cohn, Al
Coleridge-Taylor, Samuel
Confrey, Zez
Conti, Bill
Converse, Frederick
  Shepherd
Cook, Will Marion
Cooney, Rory
Copland, Aaron
Coppola, Carmine
Corigliano, John (Paul)
Cornelius, Peter
Coryell, Larry
Cotten, Libba
Couperin, Francois
Coward, Noel Pierce, Sir
Cowell, Henry Dixon
Cramer, Johann Baptist
Creston, Paul
Crowder, Henry
Crumb, George Henry
Cui, Cesar Antonovich
Czerny, Karl
D'Albert, Eugene
Dallapiccola, Luigi
Damrosch, Walter
  Johannes
Dankworth, John Philip
  William
Darby, Ken
Dargomijsky, Alexander
David, Felicien Cesar
David, Mack
Davies, Henry Walford,
  Sir
Davies, Peter Maxwell
Davis, Anthony
Davis, Chip
Davis, Clifton
Davis, Miles Dewey, III
Dawson, William Levi
Dean, Laura
Debussy, Claude Achille
DeKoven, (Henry Louis)
  Reginald
Delerue, Georges
Delibes, Leo
Delius, Frederick
Dello Joio, Norman
  Joseph
DeLugg, Milton
Deodato
DePaul, Gene Vincent
DeSabata, Victor
DesPres, Josquin
Dessau, Paul

Dett, Robert Nathaniel
Deutsch, Adolph
De Vorzon, Barry
Diamond, David
Diemer, Emma Lou
Ditters, Karl
Dohnanyi, Erno von
Donizetti, Gaetano
Dorati, Antal
Dorsey, Thomas Andrew
Dowland, John
Druckman, Jacob
  (Raphael)
Dufay, Guillaume
Dukas, Paul Abraham
Duke, Vernon
Dunstable, John
DuPre, Marcel
DuPrez, Gilbert
Durante, Francesco
Dury, Ian
Dvorak, Anton
Dykes, John Bacchus
Edwards, Sherman
Egk, Werner
Einem, Gottfried von
Elfman, Danny
Elgar, Edward William,
  Sir
Encina, Juan del
Enesco, Georges
Enya
Erwin, Pee Wee
Evans, Bill
Evans, Gil
Evans, Ray
Falla, Manuel de
Fame, Georgie
Fasch, Johann Friedrich
Faure, Gabriel Urbain
Favart, Charles Simon
Feather, Leonard Geoffrey
Feldman, Morton
Ferguson, Howard
Ferrante, Arthur
Fetis, Francois Joseph
Field, John
Fisher, Fred
Fleck, Bela
Fletcher, Grant
Flotow, Friedrich von,
  Baron
Floyd, Carlisle Sessions
Foerster, Josef Bohuslav
Fogelberg, Dan(iel
  Grayling)
Foote, Arthur William
Foster, Stephen Collins
Fox, Charles
Francaix, Jean
Franck, Cesar Auguste
Fraser, Ian
Freberg, Stan
Frescobaldi, Girolamo
Fried, Gerald
Friml, Rudolf
Froberger, Johann Jakob
Fry, William Henry
Fux, Johann Joseph
Gabrieli, Giovanni
Gade, Niels Vilhelm
Gaines, Lee
Galuppi, Baldassare
Ganz, Rudolph
Garcia, Manuel del Popolo
  Vincente

Montenegro, Hugh
Monteverdi, Claudio
Moore, Douglas Stuart
Morley, Thomas
Morton, Arthur
Moscheles, Ignaz
Moszkowski, Moritz
Mozart, Leopold
Mozart, Wolfgang
  Amadeus
Muczynski, Robert
Mulligan, Gerry
Musgrave, Thea
Mussorgsky, Modest
  Petrovich
Nabokov, Nicolas
Napravnik, Eduard
Nathan, Robert
Nessler, Victor E
Nevin, Ethelbert
  Woodbridge
Newman, Alfred
Nicolai, Carl Otto
  Ehrenfried
Nielsen, Carl August
Nikolais, Alwin
Nin-Culmell, Joaquin
  Maria
Nono, Luigi
North, Alex
Nougues, Jean
Novak, Vitezslav
Obrecht, Jacob
Ockeghem, Johannes
Offenbach, Jacques
Okun, Milton Theodore
Oldfield, Mike
Orff, Carl
Ott, David Lee
Pachelbel, Johann
Pacini, Giovanni
Paer, Ferdinando
Paganini, Niccolo
Paine, John Knowles
Paisiello, Giovanni
Palestrina, Giovanni
Panizza, Ettore
Parker, Horatio William
Parks, Van Dyke
Parry, Charles Hubert
  Hastings, Sir
Part, Arvo
Partch, Harry
Penderecki, Krzysztof
Pennario, Leonard
Pepusch, Johann Christoph
Pergolesi, Giovanni
  Battista
Peri, Jacopo
Perle, George
Perotin
Persichetti, Vincent
Pfitzner, Hans
Philidor, Francois Andre
  Danican
Piazzola, Astor
Piccinni, Nicola
Pierne, Gabriel
Piston, Walter
Pizzetti, Ildebrando
Planquette, Jean(-Robert)
Ponchielli, Amilcare
Porpora, Niccolo
Porter, Cole
Porter, Quincy
Poulenc, Francis

Praetorius, Michael
Pratella, Francesco Balilla
Previn, Andre
Price, Florence Beatrice
  Smith
Prokofiev, Sergei
  Sergeevich
Puccini, Giacomo
Puente, Tito
Purcell, Henry
Rabaud, Henri
Rachmaninoff, Sergei
  Vasilyevich
Rameau, Jean-Philippe
Raposo, Joseph
Ravel, Maurice Joseph
Rebikov, Vladimir
  Ivanovich
Redman, Don
Reger, Max
Reich, Steve
Reichardt, Johann
  Friedrich
Reinhardt, Django (Jean
  Baptiste)
Remenyi, Eduard
Respighi, Ottorino
Reyer, (Louis) Ernest
  (Etienne)
Reznicek, Emil von
Riddle, Nelson
Riegger, Wallingford
Rimsky-Korsakov, Nikolai
  Andreevich
Robertson, Robbie
Robinson, Earl Hawley
Rocca, Lodovico
Rochberg, George
Rodgers, Mary
Rodgers, Richard
Romberg, Bernhard
Romberg, Sigmund
Ronald, Landon, Sir
Rorem, Ned
Rosenberg, Hilding
Rossellini, Renzo
Rossi, Luigi
Rossini, Gioacchino
  Antonio
Roussel, Albert
Rozsa, Miklos
Rudhyar, Dane
Ruggles, Carl
Sablon, Jean Georges
Sacchini, Antonio
Sachs, Hans
Sainte-Marie, Buffy
Saint-Saens, (Charles)
  Camille
Sakamoto, Ryuichi
Salieri, Antonio
Sarasate, Pablo de
Sàrti, Giuseppe
Satie, Erik
Sauguet, Henri
Scarlatti, Alessandro
Scarlatti, Domenico
  Girolamo
Schelling, Ernest Henry
Schickele, Peter
Schifrin, Lalo Claudio
Schillinger, Joseph
Schillings, Max von
Schnittke, Alfred
Schoech, Othmar
Schoenberg, Arnold

Schreker, Franz
Schubert, Franz Peter
Schuller, Gunther
Schuman, William
  Howard
Schumann, Robert
  Alexander
Schumann, Walter
Schutz, Heinrich
Schwartz, Stephen
  L(awrence)
Schwarz, Gerard
Scott, Cyril (Meir)
Scriabin, Alexander
  Nicholaevich
Senfl, Ludwig
Sessions, Roger
  Huntington
Shaffer, Paul
Shankar, Ravi
Shapey, Ralph
Shchedrin, Rodion
  Konstantinovich
Sherman, Richard Morton
Shire, David (Lee)
Shorter, Wayne
Shostakovich, Dmitri
  Dmitryevich
Sibelius, Jean
Siegmeister, Elie
Simeone, Harry
Sinding, Christian
Sinopoli, Giuseppe
Skrowaczewski, Stanislaw
Smalls, Charlie
Smetana, Bedrich
Smith, Paul Joseph
Smyth, Ethel, Dame
Snider, Dee
Sondheim, Stephen
  (Joshua)
Sor, Fernando
Sousa, John Philip
Sowerby, Leo
Spohr, Louis Ludwig
Spontini, Gasparo
Stanford, Charles Villiers,
  Sir
Steffani, Agostino
Steiner, Max
Stevens, Morton
Stewart, Slam
Still, William Grant
Stockhausen, Karlheinz
Stoessel, Albert
Stoll, George E
Stolz, Robert
Story, Liz
Stradella, Alessandro
Straus, Oskar
Strauss, Johann, Sr.
Strauss, Johann, Jr.
Strauss, Richard Georg
Stravinsky, Igor
  Fedorovich
Strouse, Charles
Suesse, Dana Nadine
Suk, Josef
Sukman, Harry
Sullivan, Arthur Seymour,
  Sir
Sullivan, Tom
Sulzer, Salomon
Sun Ra
Suppe, Franz von
Sutermeister, Heinrich

Svetlanov, Evgeni
  Fyodorovich
Swados, Elizabeth A
Swann, Donald (Ibrahim)
Sweelinck, Jan Pieterszoon
Szymanowski, Karol
  Maciej
Tailleferre, Germaine
Taj Mahal
Takemitsu, Toru
Taktakishvili, Otar
  Vasilevich
Tal, Josef
Tallis, Thomas
Taneyev, Sergey
  Ivanovich
Tartini, Giuseppe
Tausig, Karl
Taylor, (Joseph) Deems
Tchaikovsky, Peter Ilyich
Tcherepnin, Alexander
  Nikolayevich
Tcherepnin, Nicholas
Teicher, Louis
Telemann, Georg Philipp
Theodorakis, Mikis
Thomas, (Charles Louis)
  Ambroise
Thompson, Randall
Thomson, Virgil Garnett
Threadgill, Henry
Tiomkin, Dimitri
Tippett, Michael Kemp,
  Sir
Toch, Ernst
Tortelier, Paul
Tosti, Francesco Paolo
Tovey, Donald Francis, Sir
Tower, Joan Peabody
Traetta, Tommaso
Tricky
Tyner, McCoy Alfred
Ussachevsky, Vladimir
  Alexis
Vangelis
Van Peebles, Melvin
Varese, Edgar
Vassilenko, Sergei
Vaughan Williams, Ralph
Verdi, Giuseppe Fortunino
  Francesco
Viardot-Garcia, Pauline
Victoria, Tomas Luis de
Vieuxtemps, Henri
  Francois Joseph
Villa-Lobos, Heitor
Viotti, Giovanni Battista
Vitry, Philippe de
Vivaldi, Antonio (Lucio)
Vogelweide, Walther von
  der
Von Tilzer, Albert
Wagner, Richard
Wagner, Siegfried
  (Helferich)
Wagner-Regeny, Rudolf
Walter, Johann
Walton, William Turner,
  Sir
Ward, Robert Eugene
Watt, Douglas Benjamin
Waxman, Franz
Wayne, Bernie
Webb, Jim
Weber, Carl Maria von

Webern, Anton Friedrich Ernst von
Weill, Kurt
Weinberger, Jaromir
Weingartner, Felix
Weisgall, Hugo (David)
Welch, Ken
Welch, Mitzie
Wellesz, Egon
Wesley, Charles
Whiting, Richard Armstrong
Widor, Charles Marie Jean Albert
Wieniawski, Henri
Wild, Earl
Wilder, Alec
Willaert, Adrian
Williams, John Towner
Williams, Mary Lou
Williams, Mason
Williams, Patrick
Williams, Tony
Willson, Meredith
Wilson, Sandy
Winston, George
Wolf, Hugo
Wolf-Ferrari, Ermanno
Wolpe, Stefan
Wood, Henry Joseph, Sir
Wuorinen, Charles (Peter)
Xenakis, Iannis
Yarrow, Peter
Yon, Pietro Alessandro
Youmans, Vincent
Zandonai, Riccardo
Zarlino, Gioseffo
Zemlinsky, Alexander von
Zimbalist, Efrem
Zimbalist, Efrem, Jr.
Zimmerman, Udo
Zimmermann, Bernd Alois
Zingarelli, Nicola Antonio
Zwilich, Ellen Taaffe

COMPOSERS

Holland-Dozier-Holland
Les Six

COMPUTER ANIMATOR

Lasseter, John

COMPUTER EXECUTIVE

Andreessen, Mark
Bushnell, Nolan Kay
CasSelle, Malcolm
Clark, James H.
Cray, Seymour R.
Dell, Michael
Ellington, E. David
Gates, William Henry, III
Isaacson, Portia
Osborne, Adam
Perlman, Steve
Stonesifer, Patty
Treybig, James G

Waitt, Tedd
Wozniak, Steven

COMPUTER SCIENTIST

Backus, John
Bell, Gordon (Bennett)
Berners-Lee, Tim
Dennis, Jack B(onnell)
Dijkstra, Edsger W(ybe)
Feigenbaum, Edward A(lbert)
Hannah, Marc (Regis)
Hillis, W(illiam) Daniel, (Jr.)
Lanier, Jaron (Zepel)
Raskin, Jef
Shimomura, Tsutomu

CONDUCTOR

Abbado, Claudio
Abravanel, Maurice
Adamowski, Timothee
Adler, Kurt Herbert
Adler, Peter Herman
Alessandro, Victor Nicholas
Allers, Franz
Amfiteatrof, Daniele
Amram, David Werner, III
Ancerl, Karel
Anderson, Leroy
Anello, John David
Ansermet, Ernest Alexandre
Arditi, Luigi
Autori, Franco
Bacharach, Burt
Bantock, Granville, Sir
Barbirolli, John, Sir
Barenboim, Daniel
Barlow, Howard
Baron, Samuel
Barzin, Leon Eugene
Beecham, Thomas, Sir
Beinum, Eduard van
Bell, John Kim
Bergmann, Carl
Berio, Luciano
Bernstein, Elmer
Bernstein, Leonard
Bertini, Gary
Blackton, Jay S
Blech, Leo
Bloch, Raymond A
Bodanzky, Artur
Bohm, Karl
Bond, Victoria
Bonynge, Richard
Boulanger, Nadia Juliette
Boulez, Pierre
Boult, Adrian Cedric, Sir
Brico, Antonia
Bruch, Max
Buckley, Emerson
Buketoff, Igor
Bulow, Hans Guido von
Busch, Fritz
Bush, Alan (Dudley)
Caldwell, Sarah
Carle, Frankie

Caston, Saul
Celibidache, Sergiu
Chailly, Riccardo
Chavez (y Ramirez), Carlos Antonio de Pauda
Christie, William Lincoln
Chung, Myung-Whun
Cleva, Fausto
Cluytens, Andre
Coates, Albert
Colonne, Edouard
Comissiona, Sergiu
Condie, Richard P
Cooper, Emil
Coppola, Carmine
Cortot, Alfred-Denis
Costa, Don
Craft, Robert
Damrosch, Leopold
Damrosch, Walter Johannes
Dankworth, John Philip William
Darby, Ken
Davies, Dennis Russell
Davis, Andrew Frank
Davis, Colin Rex, Sir
Defauw, Desire
DeFrank, Vincent
Delerue, Georges
DeLugg, Milton
DePreist, James Anderson
DeSabata, Victor
DeWaart, Edo
Dixon, Dean
Dobrowen, Issai
Dohnanyi, Christoph von
Dohnanyi, Erno von
Dorati, Antal
Dragon, Carmen
Dutoit, Charles
Ehrling, Sixten
Elgar, Edward William, Sir
Engel, Lehman
Entremont, Phillippe
Eschenbach, Christoph
Faith, Percy
Falletta, JoAnn
Fennell, Frederick
Ferencsik, Janos
Fiedler, Arthur
Fleisher, Leon
Fletcher, Grant
Foss, Lukas
Fox, Charles
Fraser, Ian
Furtwangler, Wilhelm
Fux, Johann Joseph
Gabrilowitsch, Ossip Salomonovich
Ganz, Rudolph
Gardiner, John Eliot
Gellhorn, Peter
Gibbs, Terry
Gibson, Michael
Giulini, Carlo Maria
Godfrey, Isadore
Goldovsky, Boris
Golschmann, Vladimir
Goossens, Eugene, Sir
Gould, Morton
Gui, Vittorio
Haitink, Bernard
Halasz, Laszlo

Halle, Charles, Sir
Hanson, Howard
Harnoncourt, Nikolaus
Hayman, Richard
Hayton, Lennie
Heger, Robert
Heindorf, Ray
Herbert, Victor
Hertz, Alfred
Hillis, Margaret
Hinrichs, Gustav
Hoffman, Irwin
Hogwood, Christopher
Hurst, George
Irving, Robert Augustine
Iturbi, Jose
Ivanov, Konstantin Konstantinovich
Jackson, Isaiah Allen
James, Philip
Janigo, Antonio
Janssen, Werner
Jarvi, Neemi
Jenkins, Gordon
Jenkins, Newell
Jochum, Eugen
Jorda, Enrique
Kalmanoff, Martin
Karajan, Herbert von
Karlin, Frederick James
Katims, Milton
Keene, Christopher
Keilberth, Joseph
Kempe, Rudolf
Kennedy, Nigel Paul
Kertesz, Istvan
Khaikin, Boris
Kindler, Hans
Kleiber, Carlos
Kleiber, Erich
Klemperer, Otto
Klenau, Paul von
Knappertsbusch, Hans
Kondrashin, Kiril Petrovich
Konwitschny, Franz
Kostelanetz, Andre
Koussevitzky, Serge Alexandrovich
Krauss, Clemens
Krips, Josef
Kubelik, Rafael (Jeronym)
Kunzel, Erich
Kurtz, Efrem
Lamoureux, Charles
Lavalle, Paul
Lawrence, Elliot
Lawrence, Robert
Leginska
Legrand, Michel Jean
Leibowitz, Rene
Leinsdorf, Erich
Leitner, Ferdinand
Lemoyne, Jean-Baptiste
Leon, Tania (Justina)
Leppard, Raymond John
Levi, Hermann
Levine, James Lawrence
Lewenthal, Raymond
Lewis, Henry (Jay)
Lindsey, Mort
Lortzing, Gustav Albert
Lualdi, Adriano
Luboff, Norman
Ludwig, Leopold
Maag, Peter

Maazel, Lorin Varencove
Mackerras, Charles
MacMillan, Ernest
  Campbell, Sir
Mahler, Fritz
Mahler, Gustav
Malcolm, George
Maltby, Richard E
Mancinelli, Luigi
Manns, August, Sir
Mantovani, Annunzio
Marinuzzi, Giuseppe
  (Gino)
Markevitch, Igor
Marriner, Neville
Marterie, Ralph
Martinon, Jean
Masur, Kurt
Mathieson, Muir
McArthur, Edwin Douglas
Mehta, Zubin
Mendelssohn, Felix
Mengelberg, Willem
Merola, Gaetano
Messager, Andre Charles
  Prosper
Miller, Mitch(ell William)
Mitchell, Howard (Bundy)
Mitropoulos, Dimitri
Moninari-Pradelli,
  Francesco
Monteux, Claude
Monteux, Pierre
Mottl, Felix
Mravinsky, Eugene
Muck, Karl
Mugnone, Leopoldo
Munch, Charles
Munchinger, Karl
Muti, Riccardo
Napravnik, Eduard
Neel, (Louis) Boyd
Nero, Peter
Neuendorff, Adolf
Newman, Alfred
Nielsen, Carl August
Nikisch, Arthur
Nin-Culmell, Joaquin
  Maria
Norrington, Roger Arthur
  Carver
North, Alex
Ormandy, Eugene
Ozawa, Seiji
Panizza, Ettore
Papi, Genarro
Paray, Paul
Pasdeloup, Jules Etienne
Pelletier, Wilfrid
Perahia, Murray
Perlea, Jonel
Persinger, Louis
Piastro, Michel
Pinnock, Trevor David
Pitt, Percy
Polacco, Giorgio
Pollack, Egon
Previn, Andre
Previtali, Fernando
Pritchard, John Michael,
  Sir
Queler, Eve Rabin
Rabaud, Henri
Rattle, Simon
Reichardt, Johann
  Friedrich

Reiner, Fritz
Richter, Hans
Richter, Karl
Rodzinski, Artur
Ronald, Landon, Sir
Rosbaud, Hans
Rose, David
Rosenberg, Hilding
Rosenstock, Joseph
Rostropovich, Mstislav
  Leopoldovich
Rothwell, Walter Henry
Rozhdestvensky, Gennadi
  Nikolaevich
Rudel, Julius
Rudolf, Max
Sacher, Paul
Saerchinger, Cesar Victor
  Charles
Saidenberg, Daniel
Salieri, Antonio
Sargent, Malcolm, Sir
Sarti, Giuseppe
Schalk, Franz
Schelling, Ernest Henry
Scherchen, Hermann
Scherman, Thomas Kielty
Schifter, Peter Mark
Schillings, Max von
Schippers, Thomas
Schmidt-Isserstedt, Hans
Schoech, Othmar
Schuch, Ernst von
Schuller, Gunther
Schumann, Walter
Secunda, Sholom
Seidl, Anton
Serafin, Tullio
Sevitzky, Fabien
Shapey, Ralph
Shaw, Robert Lawson
Shostakovich, Maxim
Siegmeister, Elie
Simmons, Calvin
Sinopoli, Giuseppe
Skrowaczewski, Stanislaw
Slatkin, Leonard
Smallens, Alexander
Smetana, Bedrich
Sodero, Cesare
Solomon, Izler
Solti, Georg, Sir
Somogi, Judith
Sosnik, Harry
Sousa, John Philip
Spohr, Louis Ludwig
Spontini, Gasparo
Stanford, Charles Villiers,
  Sir
Stein, Horst
Steinberg, William
Steiner, Max
Stevens, Morton
Stiedry, Fritz
Still, William Grant
Stock, Frederick A
Stoessel, Albert
Stokowski, Leopold
  (Anton Stanislaw
  Boleslawawicz)
Strasfogel, Ignace
Strauss, Johann, Sr.
Strauss, Johann, Jr.
Strauss, Richard Georg
Sukman, Harry
Susskind, Walter

Svetlanov, Evgeni
  Fyodorovich
Szell, George
Szenkar, Eugen
Tcherepnin, Nicholas
Tennstedt, Klaus
Thomas, Theodore
Tietjen, Heinz
Tilson Thomas, Michael
Toscanini, Arturo
Varviso, Silvio
Voorhees, Donald
Wagner, Siegfried
  (Helferich)
Wallenstein, Alfred Franz
Walter, Bruno
Ward, Robert Eugene
Waxman, Franz
Weingartner, Felix
Weisgall, Hugo (David)
Williams, John Towner
Winograd, Arthur
Wolff, Albert Louis
Wolff, Hugh
  (MacPherson)
Wood, Henry Joseph, Sir
Woss, Kurt
Young, Victor
Ysaye, Eugene
Zemlinsky, Alexander von

CONJOINED TWINS

Hensel *Abigail and*
  Brittany

CONQUEROR

Almagro, Diego de
Alvarado, Pedro de
Benalcazar, Sebastian de
Castillo, Bernal Diaz del
Cortez, Hernando
Genghis Khan
Guzman, Nuno Beltran de
Lopez de Legaspi, Miguel
Mahmud of Ghazni
Orellana, Francisco de
Pizarro, Francisco
Quesada, Gonzalo Jimenez
  de
Tamerlane
Valdivia, Pedro de
Velazquez de Cuellar,
  Diego

CONSERVATIONIST

Douglas, Marjory
  (Stoneman)
Fuller, Kathryn S(cott)
Payne, Roger S.
Pough, Richard Hooper
Scheffer, Victor
  B(lanchard)

CONSORT

Albert, Prince

Alexandra Caroline Mary
  Charlotte
Alexandra Feodorovna
Anne of Bohemia
Anne of Cleves
Bernhard, Prince
Boleyn, Anne
Catherine de Medici
Catherine of Aragon
Catherine of Valois
Charlotte Sophia
Cooke, Hope
Eleanor of Aquitaine
Elizabeth, Queen Mother
Frederika Louise
Howard, Catherine
Maintenon, Francoise
  d'Aubigne, Marquise de
Margaret of Anjou
Marie Antoinette
Marie de Medicis
Marina
Mary
Nagako, Empress
Noor, Queen
Parr, Catherine
Philip, Prince
Seymour, Jane
Silvia
Theodora
Zita of Bourbon-Parma

CONSPIRATOR

Babington, Anthony

CONSTRUCTION WORKER

King, Rodney G

CONSULTANT

Ailes, Roger Eugene
Atwater, Lee
Carville, James
Covey, Stephen R.
Deming, W(illiam)
  Edwards
Edwards, Harry, Jr.
Foster, Vincent
Henderson, Bruce
Kanter, Rosabeth Moss
Langhart, Janet
Magaziner, Ira C(harles)
Matalin, Mary (Joe)
Morris, Dick
Peters, Tom
Popcorn, Faith
Schlink, Frederick John
Waldron, Hicks Benjamin
Zia, Helen

CONSULTANTS

Hill, Calvin and Janet
  (McDonald)

CONTINENTAL CONGRESSMAN

Bartlett, Josiah
Braxton, Carter
Carroll, Charles
Chase, Samuel
Clark, Abraham
Ellery, William
Floyd, William
Gwinnett, Button
Hall, Lyman
Hancock, John
Harrison, Benjamin
Hart, John
Hewes, Joseph
Heyward, Thomas, Jr.
Hooper, William
Hopkinson, Francis
Huntington, Samuel
Lee, Francis Lightfoot
Lee, Richard Henry
Lewis, Francis
Livingston, Philip
Lowell, John
Lynch, Thomas, Jr.
Middleton, Arthur
Morris, Lewis
Morris, Robert
Morton, John
Nelson, Thomas, Jr.
Paca, William
Penn, John
Randolph, Peyton
Read, George
Rodney, Caesar
Ross, George
Rush, Benjamin
Rutledge, Edward
Sherman, Roger
Smith, James
Stockton, Richard
Stone, Thomas
Taylor, George
Thornton, Matthew
Walton, George
Whipple, William
Wilson, James
Witherspoon, John
Wolcott, Oliver, Sr.
Wythe, George

COOK

Daley, Rosie
Husted, Marjorie Child
Typhoid Mary

COSMETICS EXECUTIVE

Arden, Elizabeth
Ash, Mary Kay
Bergerac, Jacques
Bergerac, Michel C
Bishop, Hazel
Factor, Max
Factor, Max, Jr.
Kay, Mary
Lauder, Estee
Quant, Mary
Revson, Charles Haskell
Rubinstein, Helena

Waldron, Hicks Benjamin
Westmore, Perc(ival)

COSMONAUT

Beregovoi, Georgi
Bykovsky, Valery Fyodorovich
Dobrovolsky, Georgi Timofeyevich
Dzhanibekov, Vladimir Alexandrovich
Feoktistov, Konstantin Petrovich
Gagarin, Yuri Alexseyevich
Khrunov, Evgeny Vasilievich
Komarov, Vladimir Mikhaylovich
Krikalev, Sergei
Kubasov, Valery Nikolaevich
Leonov, Alexei Arkhipovich
Nikolayev, Andriyan Grigoryevich
Patsayev, Viktor Ivanovich
Popovich, Pavel Romanovich
Savitskaya, Svetlana Y
Tereshkova-Nikolaeva, Valentina
Titov, Gherman Stepanovich
Volkov, Vladislav Nikolayevich
Yegorov, Boris (Borisovitch)

COSTUME DESIGNER

Thomas, Bill
White, Miles

COURTESAN

Duplessis, Marie
Lenclos, Ninon de
Phryne

COURTIER

Beaumarchais, Pierre Augustin Caron de
Bellman, Carl Michael
Castiglione, Baldassare, Conte
Damocles
Devereaux, Robert
Lovelace, Richard
Lyndsay, David
Montaigne, Michel Eyquem de
Raleigh, Walter, Sir
Sidney, Philip, Sir
Tyrrell, James, Sir

CRICKET PLAYER

Bradman, Donald George
Constantine, Learie Nicholas Constantine, Baron
Cowdrey, (Michael) Colin
Fry, Charles Burgess

CRIMINAL

Adonis, Joe
Anastasia, Albert
Apache Kid
Barfield, Velma
Barker, Doc
Barker, Fred
Barker, Herman
Barker, Lloyd
Barker, Ma
Biggs, Ronald Arthur
Blumenfeld, Isadore
Bonanno, Joseph
Buchalter, Lepke
Capone, Al(phonse)
Cartouche, Louis Dominique
Chadwick, Cassie L
Chapin, Dwight Lee
Chessman, Caryl Whittier
Churchill, May
Cohen, Mickey
Colombo, Joseph Anthony
Cooper, D B
Costello, Frank
Cutpurse, Moll
Dalton, William
DeSalvo, Albert
Deshayes, Catherine
Diamond, Legs
Dillinger, John Herbert
Dio, Johnny
Diver, Jenny
Escobar Gaviria, Pablo
Esposito, Joseph
Estes, Billie Sol
Fisher, Amy
Floyd, Pretty Boy
Gambino, Carlo
Genovese, Vito
Giacalone, Anthony
Giancana, Sam
Gotti, John
Hamilton, Floyd (Garland)
Harsh, George
Hauptmann, Bruno Richard
Hazelwood, Joe
Hill, Virginia
Holliday, Doc
Holloway, Wanda
Jackson, George
Karpis, Alvin
Kelly, Machine Gun
Kray, Reggie
Kray, Ronnie
Lansky, Meyer
Leopold, Nathan Freudenthal
Lewis, James W
Licavoli, Peter Joseph, Sr.
Licavoli, Thomas
Loeb, Richard A
Lohman, Ann Trow
Lucchese, Thomas

Luciano, Lucky
Lyons, Sophie Levy
Madden, Owen Victor
Mandelbaum, Fredericka
Miranda, Ernesto
Moran, Bugs
Murphy, Jack R
Nelson, Baby Face
Owen, Richard Lee, II
Parker, Bonnie
Profaci, Joe
Ricca, Paul
Rudensky, Morris
Schultz, Dutch
Sheppard, Jack
Shinburn, Mark
Siegel, Bugsy
Stavisky, Serge Alexandre
Stompanato, Johnny
Stroud, Robert Franklin
Surratt, John Harrison
Surratt, Mary Eugenia Jenkins
Sutton, Willie
Taoka Kazuo
Tieri, Frank
Torrio, Johnny
Touhy, Roger
Trafficante, Santo, Jr.
Turpin, Dick
Valachi, Joe
Weil, Joseph R

CRIMINALS

Scottsboro Boys
Yonger Brothers, The

CRIMINOLOGIST

Bertillon, Alphonse
Brown, Lee P(atrick)
Glueck, Sheldon
Goddard, Calvin Hooker
Lawes, Lewis Edward
Lombroso, Cesare
Tarde, Gabriel

CRITIC

Abercrombie, Lascelles
Agate, James Evershed
Aiken, Conrad Potter
Allsop, Kenneth
Alonso, Damaso
Alpert, Hollis
Altamira Y Crevea, Rafael
Alvarez, Alfred
Anderson, Lindsay (Gordon)
Apollinaire, Guillaume
Aqqad, Abbas Mahmud al-
Arnold, Matthew
Atkinson, Brooks
Austin, Alfred
Avakian, George
Babbitt, Irving
Baker, Houston A(lfred), Jr.
Bangs, Lester

Occupation Index

Barnes, Clive Alexander
Barthes, Roland (Gerard)
Bax, Clifford
Bayle, Pierre
Bazin, Andre
Beach, Joseph Warren
Beerbohm, Max
Bell, Clive
Benda, Julien
Bentley, Eric
Bentley, Richard
Berger, Arthur
Binyon, Laurence
Birney, Earle
Blackmur, Richard Palmer
Blackwell, Mr. (Richard)
Bloom, Harold
Blunden, Edmund Charles
Bodmer, Johann Jakob
Bogan, Louise
Boileau(-Despreaux),
  Nicolas
Bookspan, Martin
Bourget, Paul (Charles
  Joseph)
Bowra, Maurice, Sir
Bradley, Andrew Cecil
Braithwaite, William
  Stanley Beaumont
Brandes, Georg Morris
  Cohen
Breen, Joseph Ignatius
Brooks, Cleanth
Brown, John Mason
Burke, Kenneth
Callimachus
Canaday, John (Edwin
  John)
Canby, Henry Seidel
Canby, Vincent
Carducci, Giosue
  Alessandro Guiseppe
Carlyle, Thomas
Cassidy, Claudia
Cassou, Jean
Cecchi, Emilio
Chamberlin, William
  Henry
Chambers, Edmund
  Kerchever, Sir
Chapman, John (Arthur)
Chase, Richard Volney
Cheney, Sheldon Warren
Chernyshevsky, Nikolai
  Gavrilovich
Chesterton, G(ilbert)
  K(eith)
Chotzinoff, Samuel
Coates, Robert Myron
Coleridge, Samuel Taylor
Corey, Lewis
Cowley, Malcolm
Craven, Thomas
Crist, Judith Klein
Crowther, Bosley
Cuppy, Will(iam Jacob)
Darrell, R(obert)
  D(onaldson)
Davenport, Marcia
Davidson, Donald Grady
de Andrade, Mario
DeKooning, Elaine Marie
  Catherine Fried
DeKoven, (Henry Louis)
  Reginald
Denis, Maurice

Dent, Alan Holmes
DeSanctis, Francesco
DeVere, Aubrey Thomas
DeVoto, Bernard
  Augustine
Dickey, James (Lafayette)
Downes, Olin
DuBois, Guy Pene
Dukas, Paul Abraham
Ebert, Roger (Joseph)
Einstein, Alfred
Eliot, T(homas) S(tearns)
Ellmann, Richard David
Elytis, Odysseus
Empson, William, Sir
Ernst, Paul Karl Friedrich
Faure, Elie
Feather, Leonard Geoffrey
Fergusson, Francis
Fiedler, Leslie Aaron
Finck, Henry Theophilus
Fletcher, John Gould
Forster, John
Frankenstein, Alfred
  Victor
Frankfurter, Alfred Moritz
Freytag, Gustav
Fry, Roger Eliot
Fry, William Henry
Frye, (Herman) Northrop
Fuller, Hoyt William
Fuller, Margaret
Fuller-Maitland, John
  Alexander
Gannett, Lewis Stiles
Gates, Henry Louis, Jr.
Gaunt, William
Gautier, Theophile
Gayle, Addison, Jr.
Genauer, Emily
Gibbs, Woolcott
Gide, Andre (Paul
  Guillaume)
Gill, Brendan
Gilliatt, Penelope (Ann
  Douglas Conner)
Gilman, Lawrence
Gissing, George Robert
Glanville-Hicks, Peggy
Gleason, Ralph Joseph
Gordon, Caroline
Gottfried, Martin
Gourmont, Remy (-Marie-
  Charles) de
Granick, Harry
Greenberg, Clement
Gutzkow, Karl Ferdinand
Hanslick, Eduard
Harewood, George Henry
  Hubert Lascelles, Earl
Heine, Heinrich
Hentoff, Nat(han Irving)
Herder, Johann Gottfried
  von
Hewes, Henry
Hobson, Harold
Howe, Irving
Howes, Frank Stewart
Hughes, Robert Studley
  Forrest
Huneker, James Gibbons
Huxley, Aldous (Leonard)
Huxtable, Ada Louise
Johnson, Pamela Hansford
Johnson, Samuel
Kael, Pauline

Kalem, T(heodore)
  E(ustace)
Kauffmann, Stanley Jules
Kazin, Alfred
Keene, Donald Lawrence
Kermode, (John) Frank
Kerr, Walter F(rancis)
Kirkus, Virginia
Knight, Arthur
Kolodin, Irving
Krasna, Norman
Kronenberger, Louis
Krutch, Joseph Wood
Lahr, John
Lambert, J(ack) W(alter)
Lang, Paul Henry
Laski, Marghanita
Laver, James
Lawrence, Robert
Leavis, F(rank)
  R(aymond)
Lehmann-Haupt,
  Christopher Charles
  Herbert
Levin, Bernard
Levin, Harry Tuchman
Lewes, George Henry
Lewis, Saunders
Liu Hsieh
Lowell, Amy
Lubbock, Percy
Lu Chi
Lu Hsun
MacDonald, Dwight
Maltin, Leonard
Mantle, (Robert) Burns
Mayer, Martin Prager
McCarthy, Mary Therese
Meier-Graefe, Julius
Mendes, Catulle
Meres, Francis
Merimee, Prosper
Mi Fei
Millar, Jeff(rey) Lynn
Miller, Perry Gilbert Eddy
Molloy, John T
Montale, Eugenio
Moore, Harry Thornton
Moore, William
More, Paul Elmer
Morehouse, Ward
Morgan, Charles
  Langbridge
Morrison, Hobe
Muir, Edwin
Nathan, George Jean
Newhall, Nancy Wynne
Newman, Ernest
Nicoll, (John Ramsay)
  Allardyce
Nkosi, Lewis
North, Sterling
Norton, Elliot
O'Brian, Jack
Oliver, Edith
Orwell, George
Ozanam, (Antoine)
  Frederic
Pater, Walter (Horatio)
Paz, Octavio
Peterson, Virgilia
Poirier, Richard
Pound, Ezra Loomis
Praz, Mario
Prescott, Orville
Quennell, Peter (Courtney)

Quiller-Couch, Arthur
  Thomas, Sir
Rascoe, Burton
Read, Herbert, Sir
Redman, Ben Ray
Reed, Henry Hope
Reed, Peter Hugh
Reed, Rex
Richards, Ivor Armstrong
Riesman, David
Rodo, Jose Enrique
Rosenfeld, Paul
Rossetti, William Michael
Ruskin, John
Saarinen, Aline Bernstein
Sackville-West, Edward
  Charles
Sainte-Beuve, Charles
  Augustin
Saintsbury, George
  Edward Bateman
Sanborn, Pitts
Sarcey, Francisque
Sargeant, Winthrop
Scheuer, Philip K(latz)
Schickel, Richard
Schlegel, Friedrich von
Schonberg, Harold C
Schwartz, Delmore
  (David)
Seldes, Gilbert Vivian
Shalit, Gene
Shapiro, Karl Jay
Shaw, George Bernard
Shestov, Lev
Simon, John Ivan
Sinyavsky, Andrei
  D(onatovich)
Siskel, Gene
Sitwell, Sacheverell, Sir
Smith, A(rthur) J(ames)
  M(arshall)
Soby, James Thrall
Sontag, Susan
Starrett, Vincent
Stendhal
Stephen, Leslie, Sir
Swinburne, Algernon
  Charles
Swinnerton, Frank Arthur
Symons, Arthur William
Tate, Allen (John Orley)
Taubman, (Hyman)
  Howard
Taylor, (Joseph) Deems
Taylor, John Russell
Terry, Walter
Thompson, Oscar
Thomson, Virgil Garnett
Toynbee, Philip
Trilling, Diana (Rubin)
Trilling, Lionel
Tyler, Parker
Tynan, Kenneth Peacock
Valera y Alcala Galiano,
  Juan
Valery, Paul Ambroise
Valla, Lorenzo
Van Dine, S S
Van Doren, Carl Clinton
Van Doren, Mark
Van Horne, Harriet
Van Vechten, Carl
Vendler, Helen Hennessy
Von Eckardt, Wolf
Wain, John Barrington

Verdi-Fletcher, Mary
  (Regina)
Verdon, Gwen
Verdy, Violette
Villella, Edward Joseph
Warren, Lesley Ann
Watts, Heather
Weidman, Charles
  Edward, Jr.
Wigman, Mary
Youskevitch, Igor
Zorina, Vera

DANDY

Brummell, Beau

DEMOGRAPHER

Carr-Saunders, Alexander
  Morris

DENTIST

Allen, John
Angle, Edward Hartley
Bentley, Charles Edwin
Blaiberg, Philip
Bluitt, Juliann S.
Clark, Barney Bailey
Dean, Henry Trendley
Delany, Annie Elizabeth
Delany, Bessie and Sadie
Holliday, Doc
Loomis, Mahion
Morton, William Thomas
  Green
Sinkford, Jeanne C(raig)
Taylor, Lucy Beaman
  Hobbs
Welch, Thomas B
Wells, Horace

DESIGNER

Adam, Ken
Akimov, Nikolay
  Pavlovich
Aldredge, Theoni
  (Athanasiou)
  V(achliotis)
Alter, Hobie
Appia, Adolphe
Aronson, Boris
Ashley, Laura Mountney
Baker, Rick
Baldwin, Billy
Bandy, Way
Bay, Howard
Beall, Lester Thomas
Beaton, Cecil (Walter
  Hardy), Sir
Benetton, Luciano
Berman, Eugene
Bernstein, Alice Frankau
Bertoia, Harry
Biba
Bogner, Willi
Bosin, Blackbear
Boulle, Andre Charles

Breuer, Marcel Lajos
Brodovitch, Alexey
Buehrig, Gordon
Burne-Jones, Edward
  Coley, Sir
Burtin, Will
Capezio, Salvatore
Carfagno, Edward
Castel, Frederic
Chappell, William
Chwast, Seymour
Cipullo, Aldo Massimo
  Fabrizio
Clark, Peggy
Clodagh
Conley, Renie
Craig, Gordon
Cranach, Lucas
Cuvillies, Francois
Delaunay-Terk, Sonia
DeLotherbourg, Philip
  James
DiCamerino, Roberta
Donati, Danilo
Donghia, Angelo R
Draddy, Vincent de Paul
Dreyfuss, Henry
Du Bois, Raoul Pene
Eames, Charles
Eames, Ray
Eckart, William Joseph
Eigsti, Karl
Eiseman, Florence
Evins, David
Famolare, Joseph P
Fisher, Avery
Fisher, Jules Edward
Ford, Charlotte
Fox, Uffa
Frizon, Maud
Furst, Anton
Galle, Emile
Geddes, Norman Bel
Geddes, Patrick, Sir
Gianninoto, Frank
  Anthony
Gleason, John James
Godwin, Edward William
Goncharova, Natalia
Grumman, Leroy Randle
Haack, Morton R
Harrison, G(eorge) Donald
Hermes, Thierry
Hicks, David (Nightingale)
Ironside, Christopher
Jacobs, Sally
Jaeger, Gustav, Dr.
Jampolis, Neil Peter
Jeakins, Dorothy
John, John P(ico)
Jones, Robert Edmond
Kahane, Melanie
Kahn, Ben
Kepes, Gyorgy
Lane, Kenneth Jay
Lee, Ming Cho
Leiber, Judith
Lelong, Lucien
Lenox, Walter S
Levine, Beth
Levine, Herbert
Lexcen, Ben
Liebes, Dorothy Katherine
  Wright
Lionni, Leo
Loewy, Raymond Fernand

Lubalin, Herbert Frederick
Lustig, Alvin
Mackaye, James Morrison
  Steele
MacLiammoir, Michael
MacNeil, Hermon Atkins
Matter, Herbert
Max, Peter
McCobb, Paul Winthrop
McKay, Donald
Menzies, William
  Cameron
Messel, Oliver
Mielziner, Jo
Mitchell, David
Moholy-Nagy, Laszlo
Mori, Hanae
Morris, William
Morton, Digby
Muller-Munk, Peter
Napier, John
Nash, Paul
Nelson, George H
Noguchi, Isamu
Oenslager, Donald
  Mitchell
O'Hearn, Robert Raymond
Oldham, Todd
Peretti, Elsa
Picasso, Paloma
Ponti, Gio(vanni)
Potok, Anna Maximilian
  Apfelbaum
Pucci, Emilio Marchese di
  Barsento
Pulitzer, Lilly
Rand, Paul
Reiss, Stuart
Revere, Paul
Rhodes, Zandra
Ricci, Nina
Rietveld, Gerrit Thomas
Robbins, Carrie Fishbein
Rodchenko, Alexander
  Mikhailovich
Roebling, John Augustus
Rogers, Bruce
Roller, Alfred
Rosenstein, Nettie
Rosenthal, Jean E
Roth, Ann
Russell, Sydney Gordon,
  Sir
Sanders, Joseph
Schinkel, Karl Friedrich
Schlemmer, Oskar
Scott, Ken
Sharaff, Irene
Sheraton, Thomas
Smith, Oliver
Steinman, David Barnard
Sylbert, Paul
Tassell, Gustave
Tchelitchew, Pavel
Teague, Walter Dorwin
Ter-Arutunian, Rouben
Thompson, Bradbury
  James
Throckmorton, Cleon
Tiffany, Louis Comfort
Toms, Carl
Toomer, Ronald V
Urban, Joseph Maria
Vanderbilt, Gloria Morgan
van de Velde, Henry
Van Heusen, John

Vera
Victor, Sally Josephs
Wagner, Robin
Walton, Tony
Wexler, Peter John
Wheeler, Candace Thurber
Willis, Mary
Wittop, Freddy
Wolsky, Albert
Wragge, Sidney
Wright, Russel
Zipprodt, Patricia

DETECTIVE

Burns, William John
Fabian, Robert Honey
McCloskey, James
Pinkerton, Allan

DIARIST

Frank, Anne
Lister, Anne
Pepys, Samuel
Piozzi, Hester Lynch
  Salisbury
Sevigne, Marie de
  Rabutin-Chantal,
  Marquise de

DICTATOR

Toyotomi Hideyoshi

DIPLOMAT

Aga Khan, Sadruddin,
  Prince
Albright, Madeleine
  K(orbel)
Ali, Ahmed
Alphand, Herve
Amerasinghe, Hamilton
  Shirley
Anderson, Eugenie
  M(oore)
Anderson, George Everett
Angell, James Burrill
Annan, Kofi (Atta)
Annenberg, Walter Hubert
Arciniegas, German
Arens, Moshe
Armour, Norman
Asencio, Diego Cortes
Astorga, Nora Gadea
Asturias, Miguel Angel
Attwood, William
  Hollingsworth
Barbour, Walworth
Barlow, Joel
Bartholomew, Reginald
Bayard, Thomas Francis
Beam, Jacob D(yneley)
Bech, Joseph
Becker, Ralph E(lihu)
Ben-Elissar, Eliahu
Bentley, Alvin Morell
Berger, Samuel David
Berle, Adolf Augustus, Jr.

Williams, G(erhard)
  Mennen
Woodcock, Leonard Freel
Wright, Jerauld
Yost, Charles Woodruff
Young, Owen D
Zafrulla Khan,
  Muhammad, Sir

DIRECTOR

Abbott, George (Francis)
Abrahams, Jim
Achard, Marcel
Ackerman, Robert Allan
Adler, Luther
Akalaitis, JoAnne
Alda, Alan
Aldrich, Robert
Aldridge, Michael
Alexandrov, Grigori
Allegret, Yves
Allen, Debbie
Allen, Irwin
Allen, Woody
Altman, Robert B
Amos, John
Anderson, John Murray
Anderson, Lindsay
  (Gordon)
Anderson, Michael
Anger, Kenneth
Annaud, Jean-Jacques
Anstey, Edgar Harold
  McFarlane
Anthony, Joseph
Antonioni, Michelangelo
Antoon, A(lfred) J(oseph)
Apted, Michael
Arbuckle, Fatty
Arkin, Alan Wolf
Arliss, Leslie
Armstrong, Gillian (May)
Artaud, Antonin
Arzner, Dorothy
Ashby, Hal
Asquith, Anthony
Attenborough, Richard
  Samuel, Sir
Autant-Lara, Claude
Avakian, Aram A
Averback, Hy
Ayckbourn, Alan
Baer, Max, Jr.
Ball, William
Banks, Leslie
Banks, Monty
Banner, Bob
Barrault, Jean-Louis
Baryshnikov, Mikhail
Bass, Saul
Bay, Howard
Beatty, Roger
Beatty, Warren
Becker, Jacques
Benjamin, Richard
Benson, Robby
Benton, Robert Douglass
Bergman, Ingmar (Ernst)
Berkeley, Busby
Bern, Paul
Bernhardt, Melvin
Bertolucci, Bernardo
Biberman, Herbert
Bigelow, Kathryn

Bill, Tony
Bleckner, Jeff
Bloom, Julius
Bogdanovich, Peter
Bogner, Willi
Boguslawski, Wojciech
Bondarchuk, Sergei
  (Fedorovich)
Bonerz, Peter
Bonstelle, Jessie
Boorman, John
Borzage, Frank
Boulting, John
Branagh, Kenneth
  (Charles)
Brent, Romney
Bresson, Robert
Bridges, James
Brook, Peter Stephen Paul
Brooks, James L.
Brooks, Mel
Brooks, Richard
Brosten, Harve
Brown, Clarence
Browne, Roscoe Lee
Browning, Tod
Bunuel, Luis
Burrows, James
Burton, Tim
Butler, Robert
Buzzell, Eddie
Byrd, Robert
Cacoyannis, Michael
Caldwell, Sarah
Camerini, Mario
Cameron, James
Campion, Jane
Camus, Marcel
Capra, Frank
Cariou, Len
Carlisle, Kevin
Carne, Marcel Albert
Carpenter, John Howard
Cassavetes, John
Castle, William
Cates, Joseph
Cavalcanti, Alberto
Cayatte, Andre
Chabrol, Claude
Chaikin, Joseph
Chan, Jackie
Charnin, Martin
Chekhov, Michael
Chereau, Patrice
Chodorov, Edward
Chodorov, Jerome
Chomsky, Marvin
Christian-Jacque
Chukrai, Grigori
Chung, Myung-Whun
Cimino, Michael
Ciulei, Liviu
Clarke, Hope
Clarke, Shirley
Clayton, Jack
Clement, Rene
Clouzot, Henri-George
Clurman, Harold Edgar
Cocteau, Jean
Coe, Frederick H
Collier, William, Sr.
Columbus, Chris
Conway, Jack
Coppola, Francis Ford
Cornelius, Henry
Corsaro, Frank

Corwin, Norman
Costa-Gavras
Crichton, Charles
Crichton, Michael
Croft, Michael
Cromwell, John
Crowe, Cameron
Cukor, George (Dewey)
Curtis, Heber Doust
Curtiz, Michael
DaCosta, Morton
Dale, Grover
Dalrymple, Jean
Danton, Ray(mond)
DaSilva, Howard
Dassin, Jules
Daubeny, Peter
  Lauderdale, Sir
Dean, Basil
Delannoy, Jean
DeLiagre, Alfred
DelRuth, Roy
DeMille, Cecil B(lount)
Demme, Jonathan
Demy, Jacques
DePalma, Brian Russell
DeSantis, Giuseppe
DeSica, Vittorio
Dexter, John
Diamand, Peter
Dickerson, Ernest
Dieterle, William
Dixon, Ivan
Dmytryk, Edward
Donen, Stanley
Donohue, Jack
Dovzhenko, Alexander
Drake, Alfred
Dreyer, Carl Theodore
Duke, Bill
Dunlop, Frank
Duvivier, Julien
Dwan, Allan
Eames, Charles
Eastwood, Clint
Edwards, Blake
Eisenstein, Sergei
  Mikhailovich
Ekhof, Konrad
Epstein, Alvin
Erman, John
Evans, Jerry
Eyen, Tom
Fabri, Zoltan
Faison, George
Farrow, John Villiers
Fassbinder, Rainer Werner
Fellini, Federico
Felsenstein, Walter
Fenton, Leslie
Fernald, John Bailey
Fernandez, Emilio
Feuer, Cy
Feuillade, Louis
Fichandler, Zelda
  Diamond
Field, Ron(ald)
Fields, Joseph
Finney, Albert
Fisher, Terence
Flaherty, Robert Joseph
Fleming, Victor
Forbes, Bryan
Ford, Alexander
Ford, John Sean O'Feeney
Foreman, Carl

Foreman, Richard
Forman, Milos
Forsythe, Henderson
Fosse, Bob
Foster, Jodie
Foster, Norman
Francis, Freddie
Frankel, Gene
Frankenheimer, John
  Michael
Franklin, Carl
Fraser, Brad
Freedman, Gerald
Freleng, Friz
Friedkin, William
Fugard, Athol
Fuller, Samuel
Furie, Sidney J
Furman, Roger
Gabel, Martin
Galati, Frank
Gance, Abel
Garrett, Lila
Gassman, Vittorio
Gentele, Goeran
Gerasimov, Sergei
  Appolinarievich
Germi, Pietro
Gibson, Mel
Gielgud, (Arthur) John, Sir
Godard, Jean Luc
Goldovsky, Boris
Gordon, Michael
Gordon, Steve
Gosho Heinosuke
Goulding, Edmund
Graf, Herbert
Graham, Ronny
Grant, Lee
Gray, F. Gary
Green, Guy
Greenspan, Bud
Gribble, Harry Wagstaff
  Graham
Griffith, D(avid Lewelyn)
  W(ark)
Grodin, Charles
Grosbard, Ulu
Grotowski, Jerzy
Gunn, Moses
Guthrie, Tyrone, Sir
Guy-Blache, Alice
Hackford, Taylor
Haines, Randa
Haley, Jack, Jr.
Hall, Adrian
Hall, Peter Reginald
  Frederick, Sir
Hamer, Robert
Hamilton, Guy
Hancock, John D
Hands, Terry
Harewood, George Henry
  Hubert Lascelles, Earl
Harlan, Veit
Harris, Jed
Harris, Leslie
Hart, Moss
Harvey, Anthony
  (Kesteven)
Hathaway, Henry
Hawke, Ethan
Hawks, Howard
  Winchester
Haworth, Ted
Haydn, Richard

Valdez, Luis (Miguel)
Van Dyke, W(oodbridge)
S(trong)
Varda, Agnes
Verdy, Violette
Vidor, King Wallis
Vidov, Oleg
Vigo, Jean
Visconti, Luchino
VonSternberg, Josef
VonStroheim, Erich
Voskovec, George
Wagner, Jane
Wagner, Wieland Adolf
Gottfried
Wajda, Andrzej
Walker, Stuart Armstrong
Wallerstein, Lothar
Walsh, Raoul
Walston, Ray
Walters, Charles
Wanamaker, Sam
Ward, Douglas Turner
Wayne, John
Webb, Jack Randolph
Weber, Carl
Weber, Lois
Webster, Margaret
Weill, Claudia
Weir, Peter
Welles, Orson
Wellman, William
Augustus
Wenders, Wim
Wertmuller, Lina von Eigg
Wexler, Haskell
Whale, James
Whitaker, Forest
White, George
Whorf, Richard
Widerberg, Bo
Wilde, Cornel
Wilder, Billy (Samuel)
Wilson, Richard
Wise, Robert
Witcover, Walt
Witt, Paul Junger
Wolfe, George C.
Woo, John
Wood, Samuel Grosvenor
Wyler, William
Yates, Peter
Young, Terence
Zampa, Luigi
Zanuck, Lili Fini
Zeffirelli, Franco
Zemeckis, Robert
Zetterling, Mai (Elisabeth)
Zieff, Howard
Zinnemann, Fred

DISTILLER

Beam, James B
Bronfman, Edgar Miles
Bronfman, Edgar Miles,
Jr.
Bronfman, Samuel
Seagram, Joseph Edward
Frowde
Walker, Hiram

DIVER

Desjardins, Pete
King, Micki
Louganis, Greg(ory
Efthimios)
Mingxia, Fu

DRAMATIST

Abbott, George (Francis)
A'Beckett, Gilbert Abbott
Ableman, Paul
Achard, Marcel
Adam de la Halle
Adamov, Arthur
Ade, George
Aeschylus
Akins, Zoe
Alarcon y Mendoza, Juan
Ruiz de
Albee, Edward
Alfred, William
Ambrose, David Edwin
Anderson, Maxwell
Anderson, Robert
Woodruff
Anouilh, Jean Marie
Lucien Pierre
Arden, John
Aretino, Pietro
Aristophanes
Arrabal (Teran), Fernando
Artsybashev, Mikhail
Petrovich
Auletta, Robert
Axelrod, George
Ayckbourn, Alan
Babe, Thomas
Bagnold, Enid
Balderston, John Lloyd
Baraka, Amiri
Barlach, Ernst Heinrich
Barnes, Margaret Ayer
Barnes, Peter
Barry, Philip
Bart, Lionel
Bax, Clifford
Beaumarchais, Pierre
Augustin Caron de
Beaumont, Francis
Beck, Julian
Beckett, Samuel (Barclay)
Behan, Brendan (Francis)
Behn, Aphra
Behrman, S(amuel)
N(athaniel)
Bein, Albert
Belasco, David
Benavente y Martinez,
Jacinto
Bennett, Alan
Betti, Ugo
Bissell, Richard Pike
Bloch, Bertram
Bogosian, Eric
Boguslawski, Wojciech
Bolt, Carol
Bolton, Guy Reginald
Bond, Edward
Bonham, Frank
Bottomley, Gordon
Boucicault, Dion Lardner
Bradford, Roark Whitney
Wickliffe

Brecht, Bertolt (Eugen
Friedrich)
Brent, Romney
Brentano, Clemens Maria
Breuer, Lee
Bridie, James
Brieux, Eugene
Brophy, Brigid Antonia
Brown, Kenneth H
Buchner, Georg
Buckstone, John Baldwin
Buero Vallejo, Antonio
Bulgakov, Mikhail
Afanasyevich
Bullins, Ed
Burgoyne, John, Sir
Burrows, Abe
Busch, Charles
Calderon de la Barca,
Pedro
Carlino, Lewis John
Cary, Elizabeth Tanfield
Cavendish, Margaret
Cervantes (Saavedra),
Miguel (de)
Cesaire, Aime Fernand
Chapman, George
Chase, Mary Coyle
Chayefsky, Paddy
Chekhov, Anton Pavlovich
Chikamatsu, Monzaemon
Childress, Alice
Chodorov, Jerome
Chorell, Walentin
Christie, Agatha Mary
Clarissa Miller, Dame
Churchill, Caryl
Cibber, Colley
Clark, John Pepper
Claus, Hugo
Cleland, John
Coburn, D(onald) L(ee)
Cohan, George M(ichael)
Collier, William, Sr.
Colman, George
Comden, Betty
Congreve, William
Conkle, Ellsworth Prouty
Connelly, Marc(us Cook)
Cook, Michael
Cooper, Giles (Stannus)
Copeau, Jacques
Coppee, Francois Edouard
Joachim
Corneille, Pierre
Coulter, John William
Coward, Noel Pierce, Sir
Cowl, Jane
Cox, Constance
Crean, Robert
Crebillon, Claude Prosper
Jolyot de
Cristofer, Michael
Crommelynck, Fernand
Crothers, Rachel
Crouse, Russel
Cueva de Garoza, Juan de
la
Cumberland, Richard
Curel, Francois de
Curtis, Jackie
Dadie, Bernard Binlin
Daly, Augustin
Dane, Clemence
Dante, Nicholas
Davenant, William, Sir

Davidson, John
Davis, Ossie
Davis, Owen
Day, John
de Acosta, Mercedes
Dekker, Thomas
Delaney, Shelagh
Delavigne, Jean Francois
Casimir
Delderfield, Ronald
Frederick
Dell, Floyd
Dibdin, Charles
Dibdin, Thomas Pitt
Dickens, Charles (John
Huffam)
Dodsley, Robert
Dodson, Owen (Vincent)
Doherty, Brian
Donleavy, James Patrick
Dowling, Eddie
Dryden, John
Ducis, Jean Francois
Dumas, Alexandre
Dumas, Alexandre Dumas
Davy de la Pailleterie
Dunlap, William
Dunsany, Edward J M
Plunkett, Baron
Durang, Christopher
Ferdinand
D'Urfey, Thomas
Eberhart, Richard
(Ghormley)
Echegaray y Eizaguirre,
Jose
Edgar, David
Ephron, Henry
Epstein, Philip G
Ernst, Paul Karl Friedrich
Espriu, Salvador
Etherege, George, Sir
Euripides
Ewald, Johannes
Eyen, Tom
Farquhar, George
Feuillet, Octave
Feydeau, Georges
Fierstein, Harvey (Forbes)
Fitch, (William) Clyde
Fletcher, John
Florence, William Jermyn
Fo, Dario
Foote, Samuel
Ford, John
Foreman, Richard
Foster, Paul
Franken, Rose
Fraser, Brad
Friel, Brian
Frings, Ketti
Fry, Christopher
Fuentes, Carlos
Fugard, Athol
Fuller, Charles
Fulton, Maude
Galsworthy, John
Garcia Lorca, Federico
Gay, John
Geiogamah, Hanay
Gelber, Jack
Genet, Jean
Ghelderode, Michel de
Gibson, Wilfred Wilson
Gibson, William
Gielgud, Val Henry

Gilbert, William S(chwenck), Sir
Gilles, D(onald) B(ruce)
Gillette, William Hooker
Gilroy, Frank Daniel
Giono, Jean
Giraudoux, Jean
Glaspell, Susan Keating
Glass, Montague (Marsden)
Godden, Rumer
Goethe, Johann Wolfgang von
Golden, John
Goldman, James
Goldoni, Carlo
Goldsmith, Oliver
Gordone, Charles Edward
Gorky, Maxim
Granville-Barker, Harley
Gray, Simon James Holliday
Green, Adolf
Green, Paul Eliot
Greene, Robert
Gregory, Isabella Augusta Persse, Lady
Gribble, Harry Wagstaff Graham
Grillo, John
Grillparzer, Franz
Grimke, Angelina Emily Weld
Guare, John
Guitry, Sacha
Gurney, A(lbert) R(amsdell), Jr.
Hamilton, Patrick
Hampton, Christopher James
Hanley, William
Hansberry, Lorraine
Hare, David
Harrigan, Edward
Hart, Moss
Hauptman, William
Havel, Vaclav
Heavysege, Charles
Hebbel, Friedrich
Hecht, Ben
Heggen, Thomas Orls, Jr.
Heller, Joseph
Hellman, Lillian
Henley, Beth
Herbert, John
Hervieu, Paul-Ernest
Heywood, Thomas
Highway, Thomson
Hildesheimer, Wolfgang
Hochhuth, Rolf
Hofmannsthal, Hugo von
Holland, Endesha Ida Mae
Holm, John Cecil
Home, William Douglas
Hooker, Brian
Hopwood, Avery
Horovitz, Israel Arthur
Housman, Laurence
Howard, Bronson Crocker
Howard, Sidney Coe
Howe, Tina
Hughes, Richard Arthur Warren
Hugo, Victor Marie
Hurston, Zora Neale
Hwang, David Henry

Ibsen, Henrik Johan
Inge, William Motter
Innaurato, Albert
Ionesco, Eugene
Isherwood, Christopher (William)
Jarry, Alfred
Jeffers, (John) Robinson
Jellicoe, Ann
Jennings, Talbot
Jones, Preston St. Vrain
Jones, Tom
Jonson, Ben(jamin)
Jouy, Victor (Joseph-Etienne) de
Juana Ines de la Cruz, Sor
Kaiser, Georg
Kalidasa
Kaufman, George S(imon)
Keane, John Brendon
Keefe, Barrie Colin
Kelly, George Edward
Kennedy, Adrienne
Kerr, Jean
Kesselring, Joseph Otto
Kharitonov, Yevgeni
Killigrew, Thomas
Kingsley, Sidney
Kisfaludy, Karoly
Kleist, Heinrich von
Klima, Ivan
Kopit, Arthur Lee
Kramm, Joseph
Krasna, Norman
Kreymborg, Alfred
Kulish, Mykola
Kurnitz, Harry
Kushner, Tony
Kyd, Thomas
Lagerkvist, Par Fabian
Langer, Lawrence
LaPlace, Pierre-Antoine de
Larson, Jonathan
Laurents, Arthur
Lawrence, Jerome
Lawson, John Howard
Laxness, Halldor (Kiljan)
Lea, Fanny Heaslip
Leblanc, Maurice
Lee, Robert E(dwin)
Leonard, Hugh
Leonov, Leonid Maximovich
Lerner, Alan Jay
Lesage, Alain-Rene
Lewis, Saunders
Lewis, Sinclair
Lind, Jakov
Lindsay, Howard
Livius Andronicus
Llewellyn, Richard
Lodge, Thomas
Logan, Josh(ua Lockwood)
Long, John Luther
Loos, Anita
Lope de Vega
Lopez, Josefina Maria
Lortz, Richard
Lowell, Robert Trail Spence, Jr.
Lucas, Craig
Ludlam, Charles
Lupino, Stanley
MacArthur, Charles
MacGrath, Leueen (Emily)

Machado (y Ruiz), Manuel
MacKaye, Percy Wallace
Maeterlinck, Maurice
Mamet, David Alan
Mankowitz, Wolf
Marcel, Gabriel Honore
Marcus, Frank
Margulies, Donald
Marivaux, Pierre Carlet de
Marlowe, Christopher
Marmontel, Jean Francois
Marquis, Don Robert Perry
Marston, John
Martin du Gard, Roger
Martinez Sierra, Gregorio
Masefield, John
Massinger, Philip
Masters, Edgar Lee
Mauriac, Francois
Mayakovsky, Vladimir
McClure, Michael Thomas
McIntyre, John Thomas
McNally, Terrence
Medoff, Mark Howard
Meilhac, Henri
Menander
Mercer, David
Metastasio, Pietro
Middleton, Thomas
Miller, Arthur
Miller, Jason
Moeller, Philip
Moliere
Molnar, Ferenc
Monteleone, Thomas F(rancis)
Moody, William Vaughn
Moore, George Augustus
Morehouse, Ward
Morley, Robert
Mosel, Tad
Mosenthal, Salomon Hermann von
Nash, Thomas
Neal, Larry
Nemirovich-Danchenko, Vladimir I
Nichols, Anne
Nichols, Peter
Norman, Marsha Williams
Nugent, Elliott
Oboler, Arch
O'Casey, Sean
Odets, Clifford
O'Keeffe, John
O'Neill, Eugene Gladstone
Orton, Joe
Osborn, Paul
Osborne, John (James)
Ostrovsky, Aleksandr Nikolaevich
Otway, Thomas
Oursler, (Charles) Fulton
Owens, Rochelle
Pagnol, Marcel Paul
Patrick, John
Payne, John Howard
Peabody, Josephine Preston
Peele, George
Pellico, Silvio
Phillips, Caryl
Pinero, Arthur Wing, Sir
Pinero, Miguel
Pinter, Harold

Pirandello, Luigi
Plautus, Titus Maccius
Plomley, Roy
Pollock, Channing
Porta, Giambattista della
Potter, Dennis (Christopher George)
Prevost, Marcel
Priestley, (J)ohn (B)oynton
Pudney, John Sleigh
Rabe, David William
Racine, Jean Baptiste
Rattigan, Terence Mervyn, Sir
Reade, Charles
Renard, Jules
Rice, Elmer
Richards, Stanley
Richardson, Jack
Riggs, Lynn
Rinehart, Mary Roberts
Robinson, Lennox
Rojas Zorrilla, Francisco de
Rolland, Romain
Root, Lynn
Rostand, Edmond Alexis
Rotimi, Ola
Rowe, Nicholas
Rudnick, Paul
Russell, George William
Ryskind, Morrie
Saavedra, Angel de
Sabatini, Rafael
Sackler, Howard Oliver
Sardou, Victorien
Saroyan, William
Sartre, Jean-Paul
Schenkkan, Robert
Schiller, Friedrich von
Schisgal, Murray Joseph
Schnitzler, Arthur
Schwartz, Stephen L(awrence)
Scribe, (Augustin) Eugene
Segal, Erich Wolf
Seneca, Lucius Annaeus, the Younger
Shadwell, Thomas
Shaffer, Peter Levin
Shakespeare, William
Shange, Ntozake
Shanley, John Patrick
Shaw, George Bernard
Shaw, Irwin
Shaw, Robert
Shawn, Wallace
Shepard, Sam
Sheridan, Richard Brinsley
Sherriff, Robert Cedric
Sherwood, Robert Emmet
Shirley, James
Shulman, Max
Simon, Neil
Slade, Bernard
Smith, Anna Deavere
Smith, Dodie
Sophocles
Spewack, Bella Cohen
Spewack, Samuel
Spigelgass, Leonard
Stallings, Laurence
Stein, Joseph
Stewart, Michael
Storey, David Malcolm
Strindberg, August

Suckling, John
Sudermann, Hermann
Swerling, Jo
Swinburne, Algernon
  Charles
Synge, John Millington
Tamayo y Baus, Manuel
Tarkington, Booth
Taylor, Charles Alonzo
Taylor, Samuel (Albert)
Tebelak, John Michael
Teichmann, Howard Miles
Terence
Terry, Megan
Thespis
Thomas, Brandon
Toller, Ernst
Torrence, Ridgely
Totheroh, Dan
Tourneur, Cyril
Travers, Ben
Treece, Henry
Tremblay, Michel
Trevor, William
Tsegaye, Gabre-Medhin
Tyler, Royall
Udall, Nicholas
Uhry, Alfred
Valle Inclan, Ramon
  Maria del
Vanbrugh, John, Sir
Van Druten, John William
Van Itallie, Jean-Claude
Van Peebles, Melvin
Vicente, Gil
Vidal, Gore
Vigny, Alfred Victor,
  Comte de
Villers, George
Vogel, Paula (Anne)
Vollmer, Lula
Vondel, Joost van den
Voskovec, George
Walter, Eugene
Ward, Douglas Turner
Warren, Mercy Otis
Washburn, Charles
Wasserman, Dale
Wasserstein, Wendy
Webster, John
Wedekind, Frank
Weiss, Peter Ulrich
Weldon, John
Weller, Michael
Wesker, Arnold
Wexley, John
Wilde, Oscar (Fingal
  O'Flahertie Wills)
Wilder, Thornton (Niven)
Williams, Emlyn
Williams, Samm-Art
Williams, Tennessee
Wilson, August
Wilson, Lanford
Wilson, Robert M
Wilson, Sandy
Wolfe, George C.
Wouk, Herman
Wycherley, William
Yeats, William Butler
Zangwill, Israel
Zeami, Kanze
Zindel, Paul
Zuckmayer, Carl
Zweig, Arnold

ECCENTRIC

Connelly, One-Eyed
Kelly, Shipwreck
Ludwig II
Manville, Tommy

ECONOMIST

Aganbegyan, Abel
  Gezevich
Allais, Maurice
Alphand, Herve
Arrow, Kenneth Joseph
Bagehot, Walter
Bean, Louis H(yman)
Becker, Gary S(tanley)
Beveridge, William Henry,
  Lord
Bohm von Bawerk,
  Eugene
Boskin, Michael J(ay)
Boulding, Kenneth E(wart)
Brimmer, Andrew Felton
Buchanan, James McGill
Burns, Arthur Frank
Burns, Eveline Mabel
Cairnes, John Elliott
Campos, Roberto de
  Oliveira
Carazo (Odio), Rodrigo
Carey, Henry Charles
Chase, Stuart
Cherne, Leo
Clapham, John Harold
Clark, Colin Grant
Clark, John Bates
Clark, John Maurice
Cobden, Richard
Cobleigh, Ira Underwood
Commons, John Rogers
Coombs, Herbert Cole
Cournot, Antoine Augustin
Coxe, Tench
Currie, Lauchlin (Bernard)
Daugherty, Carroll Roop
Debreu, Gerard
Delors, Jacques Lucien
  Jean
Douglas, Paul Howard
Duhring, Eugen Karl
Dunlop, John Thomas
DuPont de Nemours,
  Pierre Samuel
Eccles, Marriner Stoddard
Ellsberg, Daniel
Ely, Richard Theodore
Epstein, Abraham
Erdman, Paul E(mil)
Erhard, Ludwig
Fawcett, Henry
Feldstein, Martin Stuart
Fisher, Irving
Friedman, Milton
Frisch, Ragnar Anton
  Kittil
Galbraith, John Kenneth
Galiani, Ferdinando
George, Henry, Sr.
Gilder, George
Gramm, (William) Phil(ip)
Gronouski, John A(ustin)
Haavelmo, Trygve
  Magnus
Hambleton, Hugh George

Hansen, Alvin Harvey
Harris, Abram Lincoln, Jr.
Harvey, William Hope
Hauge, Gabriel
Hawtrey, Ralph George,
  Sir
Hayek, Friedrich August
  von
Heller, Walter Wolfgang
Henderson, Vivian Wilson
Herrera Lane, Felipe
Hicks, John Richard, Sir
Hicks, Ursula Kathleen
  Webb
Hobson, John Atkinson
Hollowood, Albert
  Bernard
Howe, Clarence Decatur
Iglesias, Enrique V.
Innis, Harold Adams
Janeway, Eliot
Jevons, William Stanley
Johnson, Alvin Saunders
Johnson, Arno Hollock
Kahn, Alfred Edward
Kantorovich, Leonid
  Vital'evich
Katona, George
Kaufman, Henry
Keynes, John Maynard,
  Baron
Keyserling, Leon Hirsch
Klein, Lawrence Robert
Knight, Frank Hyneman
Koopmans, Tjalling
  (Charles)
Kuznets, Simon Smith
Laffer, Arthur Betz
Laidler, Harry Wellington
Lalonde, Marc
Laughlin, James Laurence
Law, John
Leontief, Wassily W
Le Play, Guillaume
  Frederic
List, Georg Friedrich
Livingston, J(oseph)
  A(rnold)
Machlup, Fritz
Malthus, Thomas Robert
Marshall, Alfred
McNair, Malcolm Perrine
Meade, James Edward
Mill, John Stuart
Mitchell, Wesley Clair
Modigliani, Franco
Monnet, Jean Omer Marie
  Gabriel
Ohlin, Bertil Gotthard
Okun, Arthur Melvin
Pareto, Vilfredo
Patten, Simon Nelson
Pella, Giuseppe
Penner, Rudolph Gerhard
Petty, William, Sir
Pigou, Arthur Cecil
Prebisch, Raul
Quesnay, Francois
Raphael, Chaim
Ricardo, David
Ripley, William Zebina
Rivlin, Alice Mitchell
Robertson, Dennis Holme
Robinson, Joan Violet
  Maurice
Roosa, Robert V(incent)

Rosovsky, Henry
Rostow, Eugene Victor
Rostow, Walt Whitman
Sachs, Jeffrey D(avid)
Saint-Pierre, Abbe de
Samuelson, Paul Anthony
Say, Jean Baptiste
Schmoller, Gustav
  Friedrich von
Schultze, Charles Louis
Schumacher, E(rnst)
  F(riedrich)
Schuman, Robert
Schumpeter, Joseph Alois
Seligman, Edwin Robert
  Anderson
Shanks, Michael
Simon, Herbert Alexander
Sismondi, Jean Charles
  Leonard Simonde de
Smith, Adam
Solow, Robert Merton
Sowell, Thomas
Sprinkel, Beryl Wayne
Stein, Herbert
Stigler, George Joseph
Stone, John Richard
  Nicholas, Sir
Sumner, William Graham
Taussig, Frank William
Thorp, Willard Long
Thurow, Lester C
Tinbergen, Jan
Tobin, James
Turgot, A(nne) R(obert)
  J(acques), Baron de
  l'Aulne
Tyson, Laura D'Andrea
Veblen, Thorstein Bunde
Vickrey, William
von Mises, Ludwig (Edler)
Wallace, Phyllis A(nn)
Walras, Marie Esprit Leon
Ward, Barbara Mary
Weidenbaum, Murray Lew
Whitman, Marina
  VonNeumann
Wickens, Aryness Joy
Williams, Walter Edward
Witte, Edwin Emil
Wojnilower, Albert Martin
Wootton, Barbara
  (Frances) Adam
Wright, Carroll Davidson

EDITOR

Abbott, Lyman
A'Beckett, Gilbert Abbott
Abercrombie, Michael
Abernethy, Robert Gordon
Ackerman, Forest J
Adams, John Hanly
Ainsworth, W(illiam)
  H(arrison)
Alden, Henry M
Allingham, William
Alpert, Hollis
Amsterdam, Jane
Anderson, Margaret
  (Carolyn)
Andrews, James Frederick
Angell, Roger
Angoff, Charles
Arbatov, Georgi

Rascoe, Burton
Rashidov, Sharaf
　Rashidovich
Raymond, Henry Jarvis
Redman, Ben Ray
Rense, Paige
Rhys, Ernest Percival
Rickword, Edgell
Robinson, M(aurice)
　R(ichard)
Rosenfeld, Alvin Hirsch
Rosenthal, Abraham
　Michael
Ross, Harold Wallace
Rovere, Richard Halworth
Ruder, Melvin
Rukeyser, William Simon
Russell, George William
Ryle, Gilbert
Saerchinger, Cesar Victor
　Charles
Scheuer, Philip K(latz)
Schmitt, Gladys
Schwartz, Delmore
　(David)
Scott, Charles Prestwich
Seaman, Owen, Sir
Seldes, Gilbert Vivian
Seligman, Edwin Robert
　Anderson
Shaw, Albert
Shawn, William
Sherrod, Robert (Lee)
Shirley, Ralph
Shortz, Will(iam Frederic)
Smith, Gerald Lyman
　Kenneth
Sparks, Jared
Spence, Lewis
Steele, Richard, Sir
Stephens, Ann Sophia
Stieglitz, Alfred
Stone, Lucy
Stone, Marvin Lawrence
Sullivan, A(loysius)
　M(ichael)
Sullivan, Andrew
Summers, Anne Fairhurst
Suttner, Bertha Felicie
　Sophie Kinsky von
Sutton, Carol
Swope, Herbert Bayard
Taggard, Genevieve
Taishoff, Sol Joseph
Tarbell, Ida Minerva
Taylor, Susan L.
Thomas, Edith Matilda
Thompson, Hunter
　S(tockton)
Tilberis, Elizabeth
Towne, Charles Hanson
Trotter, Monroe
Untermeyer, Louis
Van Doren, Charles
　Lincoln
Viereck, George Sylvester
Wallace, Henry
Wallace, Lila Bell
　Acheson
Waltari, Mika
Warner, Charles Dudley
Warren, Gerald Lee
Waymack, W(illiam)
　W(esley)
Weiss, Theodore (Russell)
Weld, Theodore Dwight

West, Dorothy
White, William Lindsay
Wilder, Joseph
Winterich, John Tracy
Wintour, Anna
Woodson, Carter Godwin
Yust, Walter

EDUCATOR

Abba Arika
Abbott, Edith
Abbott, Jacob
Abel, Elie
Abel, John Jacob
Abelard, Pierre
Abercrombie, Michael
Abrahams, Israel
Abram, Morris Berthold
Abramson, Lyn
Adams, Herbert Baxter
Adams, James Luther
Adrian, Edgar Douglas,
　Baron
Agassiz, Elizabeth Cabot
　Cary
Agnew, David Hayes
Aiken, Howard Hathaway
Alcott, Amos Bronson
Alexander, Franz Gabriel
Alexander, Leo
Alfred, William
Allen, Betty (Lou)
Allen, Jack
Allred, Gloria Rachel
Almond, Gabriel Abraham
Anderson, Vernon
　Ellsworth
Andrews, Fannie Fern
　Phillips
Andrus, Ethel Percy
Arisman, Marshall
Armstrong, Anne
　Legendre
Armstrong, William
　H(oward)
Arnold, Thomas
Asante, Molefi Kete
Ashton-Warner, Sylvia
　Constance
Asser, Tobias Michael
　Carel
Aytoun, William
　Edmonstoune
Bache, Alexander Dallas
Baeck, Leo
Baer, Karl Ernst von
Baez, Albert V.
Bagley, William Chandler
Baillie, D(onald)
　M(acpherson)
Bainton, Roland Herbert
Baker, Gwendolyn Calvert
Baker, Houston A(lfred),
　Jr.
Bakker, Robert T.
Baldessari, John
Banerjee, Surendranath
Banks, Harvey
　Washington
Barber, Bernard
Barker, Ernest, Sir
Barnard, Edward Emerson
Barnard, Frederick
　Augustus Porter

Barnard, Henry
Barnet, Sylvan M., Jr.
Barnet, Will
Baron, Salo Wittmayer
Barr, Stringfellow
Barraclough, Geoffrey
Barrett, Edward Ware
Barzun, Jacques Martin
Basedow, Johann
　Bernhard
Bate, Walter Jackson
Bates, Katharine Lee
Baugh, Albert Croll
Baur, Ferdinand Christian
Baxter, Frank Condie
Baxter, James Phinney, III
Bayley, Corrine
Beale, Dorothea
Becker, Gary S(tanley)
Beecher, Catharine
　(Esther)
Beecher, Lyman
Begle, Edward G(riffith)
Bell, Andrew
Bell, Arthur Donald
Bell, Daniel
Bell, Derrick Albert, Jr.
Bell, Joseph
Beltrami, Eugenio
Benacerraf, Baruj
Benezet, Anthony
Bentley, Eric
Berlin, Isaiah, Sir
Berry, Martha McChesney
Bestor, Arthur Eugene
Bethune, Mary McLeod
Billington, Ray Allen
Bishop, Katharine Scott
Bitter, Francis
Blackett, Patrick Maynard
　Stuart
Blackmur, Richard Palmer
Blair, James
Blanding, Sarah Gibson
Bledsoe, Albert Taylor
Bloch, Felix
Bloch, Konrad Emil
Bloom, Allan David
Blow, Susan Elizabeth
Blumenthal, Monica David
Blyden, Edward Wilmot
Bode, Boyd Henry
Bode, Carl
Bok, Derek Curtis
Boley, Forrest Irving
Bolinger, Dwight
　Lemerton
Boller, Paul Franklin, Jr.
Bond, Horace Mann
Born, Max
Botstein, Leon
Bouchet, Edward
　Alexander
Boulding, Kenneth E(wart)
Bowker, Albert Hosmer
Bowra, Maurice, Sir
Boyer, Ernest L(eroy)
Brace, Gerald Warner
Brady, St. Elmo
Brameld, Theodore
Branley, Franklyn
　Mansfield
Brauer, Jerald C(arl)
Brawley, Benjamin
　Griffith
Brayman, Harold

Brewer, Ebenezer Cobham
Broudy, Harry Samuel
Brown, Charlotte
　(Eugenia) Hawkins
Brown, Frank Arthur, Jr.
Browning, Alice Crolley
Brubacher, John Seiler
Brustein, Robert Sanford
Brutus, Dennis Vincent
Brzezinski, Zbigniew
　Kazimierz
Bucher, Walter Herman
Buck, Paul Herman
Budenz, Louis Francis
Buisson, Ferdinand
　Edouard
Bullock, Alan Louis
　Charles
Bunch, Charlotte
Bundy, McGeorge
Burns, Arthur Frank
Buscaglia, Leo
Butler, Nicholas Murray
Butler, Paul D.
Caldwell, John Charles
Camerarius, Rudolf Jakob
Canady, Alexa I(rene)
Canby, Henry Seidel
Canfield, Francis X(avier)
Cantrick, Robert
Cardozo, Francis Louis
Carey, William
Carmer, Carl Lamson
Carnap, Rudolf
Carr, William G(eorge)
Carr-Saunders, Alexander
　Morris
Carter, Stephen L(isle)
Carver, George
　Washington
Cash, Jim
Cassidy, Harold Gomes
Castillo, Edward (Daniel)
Cater, Douglass
Catlin, George Edward
　Gordon, Sir
Cavazos, Lauro F(red, Jr.)
Cecil, Edward Christian
　David Gascoyne
Chain, Ernest Boris, Sir
Chamberlain, Owen
Champagne, Duane
　(Willard)
Chase, Mary Ellen
Chase, Richard Volney
Chavers, Dean
Chavis, John
Chayes, Abram J(oseph)
Chermayeff, Serge (Ivan)
Chern, Shiing-shen
Cherrington, Ben Mark
Chiang, Yee
Chiepe, Gaositwe
　Keagakwa Tibe
Chinard, Gilbert
Christ-Janer, Albert
Clapp, Margaret
　Antoinette
Clark, Joe
Clark, Kenneth Bancroft
Clark, Septima
Clayton, Constance Elaine
Cloud, Henry Roe
Cobb, William Montague
Coghill, Nevill Henry
　Kendall Aylmer

Janson, Horst Woldemar
Janzen, Daniel Hunt
Jaques-Dalcroze, Emile
Jaspers, Karl
Jay, Karla
Jeffries, Leonard
Jensen, Johannes Hans
  Daniel
Johanan ben Zakkai
Johnson, Alvin Saunders
Johnson, Charles Spurgeon
Johnson, Marietta Louise
  Pierce
Johnson, Robert Willard
Johnson, Walter
Jojola, Ted
Jones, Gwynn
Jones, Ingrid Saunders
Jones, Lois Mailou
Jordy, William H(enry)
Josephson, Brian David
Jowett, Benjamin
Judd, Charles Hubbard
Justiz, Manuel Jon
Kallen, Horace M(eyer)
Karrar, Paul
Kaufman, Bel
Kearns, Doris H
Keble, John
Kedourie, Elie
Kelsen, Hans
Kemp, Jan
Kendrew, John Cowdery,
  Sir
Keohane, Nannerl
  Overholser
Kepes, Gyorgy
Keppel, Francis
Kerr, Clark
Khorana, Har Gobind
Kilpatrick, William
  H(eard)
Kline, Morris
Kluckhohn, Clyde
Klug, Aaron, Sir
Knapp, Seaman Asahel
Knowles, Malcolm
  Shepherd
Koch, Kenneth Jay
Kohl, Herbert R
Kolchin, Ellis Robert
Koontz, Elizabeth Duncan
Koren, Edward Benjamin
Kozol, Jonathan
Kraushaar, Otto
Krogh, Schack August
  Steenberg
Kusch, P(olycarp)
Laboulaye, Edouard Rose
La Fontaine, Henri Marie
Lamb, Willis Eugene, Jr.
Lancaster, Joseph
Landis, James McCauley
Langdell, Christopher
  Columbus
Langston, J William
Langston, John Mercer
Lanman, Charles Rockwell
Larkin, Oliver Waterman
Laue, Max Theodor Felix
  von
Lavisse, Ernest
Lawrence, Ernest Orlando
Lawrence-Lightfoot, Sara
Lazarsfeld, Paul F(elix)
Leacock, Stephen Butler

Leary, Timothy (Francis)
Lederberg, Joshua
Lee, Sidney, Sir
Lefall, LaSalle Doheny, Jr.
Lefever, Ernest Warren
LeFleming, Christopher
  Kaye
Levi, Edward Hirsch
Levy, Leonard Williams
Lewis, Clarence Irving
Lewis, Elma Ina
Lewis, Shirley A(nn)
  R(edd)
Lewis, Thomas
Lewis, William Arthur, Sir
Liberia-Peters, Maria
  Philomena
Lidz, Theodore
Lieber, Franz
Liebig, Justus von
Lilly, John C
Lin, Yutang
Lincoln, Mary Johnson
  Bailey
Linton, Ralph
Lloyd-Jones, Esther
  McDonald
Locke, Alain Leroy
Logan, John
Lomax, Louis
Lombroso, Cesare
Longfellow, Henry
  Wadsworth
Lorentz, Hendrick Antoon
Lowes, John Livingston
Lowinsky, Edward Elias
Lynch, J(ohn) Joseph
Lynd, Helen Merrell
Lyon, Mary Mason
MacDougall, Curtis Daniel
MacIver, Robert Morrison
Mackinder, Halford John,
  Sir
MacKinnon, Catharine
  A(lice)
Macquarrie, John
Malinowski, Bronislaw
  Kasper
Malott, Deane W(aldo)
Malpighi, Marcello
Mann, Horace
Mannheim, Karl
Marable, Manning
Maraghi, Mustafa al-
Marcus, Jacon R(ader)
Marcus, Rudolph A
Mark, Herman Francis
Martin, Robert Bernard
Mason, Daniel Gregory
Massey, Walter E(ugene)
Mathews, Forrest David
Mattingley, Garrett
Maurice, Frederick
  Denison
Mayr, Ernst Walter
Mays, Benjamin E(lijah)
McAfee, Mildred H(elen)
McCourt, Frank
McDougall, William
McGuffey, William
  Holmes
McIlwain, Charles Howard
McKay, Nellie Yvonne
McLuhan, (Herbert)
  Marshall
McMurrin, Sterling M(oss)

McNair, Malcolm Perrine
McNamara, Margaret
  Craig
Meiklejohn, Alexander
Meinecke, Friedrich
Meng, John Joseph
Mennin, Peter
Merulo, Claudio
Miles, Josephine
Millikan, Clark Blanchard
Milosz, Czeslaw
Minot, George Richards
Minsky, Marvin Lee
Model, Lisette
Moltmann, Juergen
  (Dankwart)
Mondlane, Eduardo
  Chivambo
Montagu, (Montague
  Francis) Ashley
Montessori, Maria
Moody, William Vaughn
Moore, Charles Willard
Moore, John Bassett
Moos, Malcolm Charles
Morgan, Arthur
Morgenthau, Hans
  Joachim
Morrison, Keith (Anthony)
Morrison, Philip
Morton, Nelle Katherine
Moses, Robert Parris
Moss, Carlton
Mott, Frank Luther
Muller, Hermann Joseph
Mundt, Karl Earl
Nagai, Sokichi
Natividad, Irene
Natta, Giulio
Neel, Louis Eugene Felix
Neill, A(lexander)
  S(utherland)
Neurath, Otto
Nicolson, Marjorie Hope
Norman, Maidie (Ruth)
Norrish, Ronald George
  Wreyford
Norton, Charles Eliot
Nye, Russel Blaine
Nygren, Anders T(heodor)
  S(amuel)
Oberlin, Johann Friedrich
O'Callahan, Joseph
  Timothy
Odum, Howard
  Washington
Ogburn, W(illiam)
  F(ielding)
Okamura, Arthur
Old Coyote, Barney
Onsager, Lars
Ortiz, Alfonso
Osler, William, Sir
Owen, Lewis James
Padover, Saul Kussiel
Paine, John Knowles
Palade, George Emil
Palmer, Alice Elvira
  Freeman
Palmer, Austin Norman
Panofsky, Erwin
Parent, Elizabeth Anne
Parker, Francis Wayland
Parker, Horatio William
Parkhurst, Helen
Parrington, Vernon L(ouis)

Parry, Albert
Parsons, Frank
Pattee, Fred Lewis
Patten, Simon Nelson
Patterson, Frederick
  Douglass
Patterson, Orlando
Pauli, Wolfgang Ernst
Peabody, Elizabeth Palmer
Peabody, Endicott
Pease-Windy Boy, Jeanine
Pei, Mario Andrew
Perlea, Jonel
Perry, Bliss
Pestalozzi, Johann
  Heinrich
Petty, William, Sir
Phelps, William Lyon
Pierce, John Davis
Pitkin, Walter Boughton
Pobedonostsev, Konstantin
  Petrovich
Popham, William James
Porter, George, Sir
Pound, Louise
Pound, Roscoe
Poussaint, Alvin F.
Powell, Cecil Frank
Powell, Lawrence Clark
Powell, Maxine
Price, Reynolds
Pritchett, Henry S
Purcell, Edward M(ills)
Pusey, Nathan Marsh
Quiller-Couch, Arthur
  Thomas, Sir
Rafferty, Max(well Lewis,
  Jr.)
Raikes, Robert
Raleigh, Walter
  Alexander, Sir
Rayleigh, John William
  Strutt, Baron
Ready, William Bernard
Reddick, L(awrence)
  D(unbar)
Redding, Jay Saunders
Reed, Henry Hope
Reeve, Tapping
Reisner, George Andrew
Remsen, Ira
Renault, Louis
Revel, Bernard
Revelle, Roger Randall
Rice, Condoleezza
Richard, Gabriel
Richter, Burton
Riles, Wilson Camanza
Risling, David
Robbins, Fredrick
  Chapman
Robertson, Dennis Holme
Robinson, James Harvey
Roche, John P
Rodin, Judith
Rodriguez, Miguel Angel
Rogers, Fred McFeely
Romano, Umberto
Romney, Seymour
  Leonard
Ronan, William John
Rondon, Candido Mariano
  da Silva
Roos, Frank John, Jr.
Rorty, Richard (McKay)
Rose, Leonard

Wang Mang
Wei Hsiao-Wen-ti
Wenceslaus
William, I
William, II
Wu-ti, Han
Yung-lo

EMPRESS

Anna Ivanovna
Elizabeth Petrovna
Irene of Athens
Livia
Suiko
Wu Tse-t'ien
Zoe

EMPRESSES

Julias of Rome, The

ENCYCLOPEDIST

Isidore of Seville, St.

ENDOCRINOLOGIST

Yen, Samuel

ENGINEER

Aadlberg, John O.
Ader, Clement
Adler, Dankmar
Alexander, Archie Alphonso
Alexanderson, Ernst Frederik Werner
Amdahl, Gene M(yron)
Ammann, Othmar Hermann
Armstrong, Edwin Howard
Bailey, Donald Coleman, Sir
Baird, John Logie
Bauersfeld, Walther
Beard, George Miller
Beatty, Alfred Chester, Sir
Bechtel, Stephen Davison
Belin, Edouard
Bell, William Holden
Berkner, Lloyd Viel
Bessemer, Henry, Sir
Biringuccio, Vannoccio
Bleriot, Louis
Boulton, Matthew
Bridgman, Percy Williams
Brill, Yvonne Claeys
Brindley, James
Brunel, Isambard Kingdom
Brunel, Marc Isambard, Sir
Bugatti, Ettore Arco Isidoro
Bunau-Varilla, Philippe Jean

Bundy, Robert F.
Bush, Vannevar
Cambra, Jessie G.
Campbell, Donald Fraser
Candela, Felix
Cayley, George, Sir
Chanute, Octave
Chestnut, Harold
Cho, Alfred Y(i)
Christie, John Walter
Clarke, Edith
Coanda, Henri Marie
Cockerell, Christopher (Sydney), Sir
Coffin, Howard Earle
Colmenares, Margarita (H.)
Condit, Carl Wilbur
Cone, Russell Glenn
Conrad, Frank
Converse, Frederick J
Conway, Lynn Ann
Cooke, William Fothergil, Sir
Crapper, Thomas
Crosthwait, David Nelson, Jr.
Darcy, Henri Philibert Gaspard
Darden, Christine (Mann)
Davidson, J Brownlee
Dejongh, Peter
Dicciani, Nance K(atherine)
Diesel, Rudolf Christian Karl
Dinkeloo, John Gerard
Dodge, Grenville Mellen
Dodington, Sven H(enry Marriott)
Doherty, Robert Ernest
Dornberger, Walter Robert
Draper, Charles Stark
Drew, Richard G
Drinker, Philip
Drucker, Daniel Charles
Dumas, Jean Baptiste Andre
DuMont, Allen Balcom
Durand, William F.
Eads, James Buchanan
Eckert, John Presper, Jr.
Edgerton, Harold Eugene
Ehricke, Krafft Arnold
Eiffel, Alexandre Gustave
Ellsberg, Edward
Elmen, Gustav Waldemar
Estrin, Thelma (Austern)
Feoktistov, Konstantin Petrovich
Fleming, Sandford
Flipper, Henry Ossian
Flores Facusse, Carlos Roberto
Florey, Howard Walter
Forrester, Jay Wright
Francis, James Bicheno
Freyssinet, Eugene
Frontinus, Sextus Julius
Fulton, Robert
Gabor, Dennis
Garand, John Cantius
Geddes, James
Gilbreth, Frank Bunker
Gilbreth, Lillian Moller
Ginsburg, Charles P

Goethals, George Washington
Goetz, Bernhard
Goldmark, Peter Carl
Gramme, Zenobe Theophile
Graydon, James Weir
Grove, George, Sir
Harding, Chester
Hargreaves, James
Harroun, Ray
Haupt, Herman
Hayford, John Fillmore
Hench, Philip Showalter
Hennebique, Francois
Hewlett, William
Hinton, Christopher, Sir
Holland, Clifford Milburn
Hunt, Jack Reed
Ingenhousz, Jan
Issigonis, Alec Arnold Constantine, Sir
Jenner, William, Sir
Jenney, William LeBaron
Jewett, Frank Baldwin
Jones, Casey
Judah, Theodore Dehone
Kettering, Charles Franklin
Kilroy, James, Jr.
Koch, Robert
Kraft, Chris(topher Columbus, Jr.)
Kwoh, Yik San
Labrouste, Pierre Francois Henri
Lake, Simon
Lear, William Powell
L'Enfant, Pierre Charles
Lesseps, Ferdinand Marie de
LeTourneau, Robert Gilmour
Lilienthal, Otto
Long, Crawford Williamson
Macaulay, Herbert
Mac Cready, Paul Beattie
Markle, C(larke) Wilson, Jr.
Martin, James, Sir
Mauchly, John William
McAdam, John Loudoun
Meer, Simon van der
Melville, George Wallace
Mills, Robert
Modjeski, Ralph
Moisseiff, Leon Solomon
Monash, John
Morgan, Arthur
Nasmyth, James
Nervi, Pier Luigi
Norden, Carl Lukas
Ochoa, Ellen
Otto, Nikolaus August
Paine, Thomas Otten
Patrick, Jennie R.
Patton, Edward L
Pickard, Greenleaf Whittier
Pierce, John Robinson
Pincus, Gregory
Porter, Richard William
Ricketts, Howard T
Rillieux, Norbert
Rockwell, Willard F

Roebling, John Augustus
Roebling, Washington Augustus
Rosen, Harold A.
Ross, Mary G.
Rous, Francis Peyton
Rugg, Harold
Russo, Anthony J, Jr.
Sanmicheli, Michele
Saunders, William Laurence
Shearer, Douglas
Shirley-Smith, Hubert
Siemens, William, Sir
Sims, James Marion
Smeaton, John
Sprague, Frank Julian
Steinman, David Barnard
Steinmetz, Charles Proteus
Stephenson, George
Stevens, John Frank
Stevin, Simon
Stout, William Bushnell
Strauss, Joseph Baermann
Stumpf, Richard J
Sutherland, Earl Wilbur, Jr.
Sydenham, Thomas
Taylor, Frederick Winslow
Tesla, Nikola
Theiler, Max
Torroja (y Miret), Eduardo
Tupolev, Andrei Nikolaevich
Vauban, Sebastien LePrestre de
Waksman, Selman Abraham
Wallace, Alfred Russell
Wallis, Barnes Neville, Sir
Wang, An
Wankel, Felix
Warner, Roger Sherman, Jr.
Watson-Watt, Robert Alexander, Sir
Watt, James
Weber, Ernst
Wells, Edward
Wiesner, Jerome B(ert)
Wright, Horatio Gouverneur
Wright, John Lloyd
Zacharias, Jerrold R(einarch)
Zworykin, Vladimir K(osma)

ENGRAVER

Anderson, Alexander
Bewick, Thomas
Cole, Timothy
Cousins, Samuel
Fragonard, Jean-Honore
Gill, Eric
Granjon, Robert
Havell, Robert, Jr.
Hogarth, William
Hokusai, Katsushika
Hollyer, Samuel
Moser, Barry
Piranesi, Giovanni Battista
Sartain, John
Schongauer, Martin

Burckhardt, Johann
　　Ludwig
Burke, Robert O'Hara
Burton, Richard Francis,
　　Sir
Byng, George Torrington,
　　Viscount
Byrd, Richard Evelyn,
　　Admiral
Cabeza de Vaca, Alvar
　　Nunez
Cabot, John
Cabot, Sebastian
Cabral, Pedro Alvarez
Cabrillo, Juan Rodriguez
Cadamosto, Alvise Luigi
　　da
Cadillac, Antoine de la
　　Mothe
Caillie, Rene Auguste
Cameron, Verney Lovett
Cartier, Jacques
Carver, Jonathan
Catlin, George
Champlain, Samuel de
Chancellor, Richard
Charcot, Jean Baptiste
　　Etienne Auguste
Chesney, Francis Rawdon
Clapperton, Hugh
Clark, William
Colter, John
Columbus, Christopher
Conti, Niccolo de'
Cook, Frederick Albert
Cook, James, Captain
Cordoba, Francisco
　　Fernandez
Coronado, Francisco
　　Vasquez de
Corte Real, Gaspar and
　　Miguel
Covilhao, Pedro de
DaGama, Vasco
Dampier, William
David-Neel, Alexandra
Davis, John
DeLong, George
　　Washington
DeSoto, Hernando
Dias de Novais,
　　Bartolomeu
Dickey, Herbert Spencer
Duluth, Daniel
　　(Greysolon)
Eklund, Carl Robert
Ellsworth, Lincoln
Emin Pasha
Ericson, Leif
Estevanico
Eyre, Edward John
Ferraris, Galileo
Fiennes (Twisleton
　　Wykeham), Ranulph
Fitzpatrick, Thomas
Flinders, Matthew
Forrest, John, 1st Baron
　　Forrest of Bunbury
Franklin, John, Sir
Fraser, Simon
Fremont, John Charles
Freuchen, Peter
Fuchs, Vivian (Ernest), Sir
Galton, Francis, Sir
Gilbert, Humphrey, Sir
Giles, Ernest

Gimbel, Peter Robin
Gist, Christopher
Gould, Laurence
　　M(cKinley)
Gray, Robert
Greely, Adolphus
　　Washington
Grey, George
Hall, Charles Francis
Halliburton, Richard
Hayes, Isaac Israel
Hearne, Samuel
Hedin, Sven Anders
Hennepin, Louis
Henson, Matthew
　　Alexander
Heyerdahl, Thor
Hillary, Edmund Percival,
　　Sir
Humboldt, Alexander,
　　Freiherr von
Huntington, Ellsworth
Iberville, Pierre Le
　　Moyne, Sieur d'
James, Edwin
Johnson, Martin Elmer
Johnson, Osa Helen
　　Leighty
Johnston, Henry Hamilton
Jolliet, Louis
Kane, Elisha Kent
Kelsey, Henry
Kino, Eusebio Francisco
Kotzebue, Otto von
Laing, Alexander Gordon
Lander, Richard Lemon
La Salle, Rene Robert
　　Cavelier de
la Verendrye, Sieur de
Lewis, Meriwether
Livingstone, David
Long, Stephen H
Lummis, Charles Fletcher
Mackenzie, Alexander, Sir
MacMillan, Donald Baxter
Magellan, Ferdinand
Maisoneuve, Sieur de
Marchand, Jean-Baptiste
Marquette, Jacques, Pere
Mawson, Douglas, Sir
McClintock, Francis
　　Leopold, Sir
McClure, Robert (John Le
　　Mesurier)
Mendana de Neyra,
　　Alvaro de
Nansen, Fridtjof
Narvaez, Panfilo de
Nicolet, Jean
Nobile, Umberto
Nordenskiold, Nils Adolph
　　Erik, Baron
Nordenskold, Nils Otto
　　Gustaf
Ogden, Peter Skene
Onate, Juan de
Orellana, Francisco de
Palmer, Nathaniel Brown
Papanin, Ivan D
Park, Mungo
Parry, William Edward,
　　Sir
Peary, Robert Edwin
Peters, Carl
Philby, Harold St. John
　　Bridger

Piccard, Jacques Ernest
　　Jean
Pike, Zebulon
　　Montgomery
Ponce de Leon, Juan
Portola, Gaspar de
Poulter, Thomas Charles
Przhevalsky, Nikolai
　　Mikhailovich
Radisson, Pierre Espirit
Rasmussen, Knud Johan
　　Victor
Richardson, John, Sir
Ronne, Finn
Ross, James Clark, Sir
Schiaparelli, Giovanni
Schoolcraft, Henry Rowe
Schouten, William
　　Cornelius
Schwatka, Frederik
Scoresby, William
Scott, Robert Falcon
Shackleton, Ernest Henry,
　　Sir
Siple, Paul Allman
Smith, Jedediah Strong
Solis, Juan Diaz de
Spallanzani, Lazzaro
Speke, John Hanning
Stanley, Henry Morton,
　　Sir
Stefansson, Vihjalmur
Steger, Will
Sturt, Charles
Sublette, William L
Sverdrup, Otto
Tasman, Abel Janszoon
Thompson, David
Thompson, Edward
　　Herbert
Vancouver, George
Verrazano, Giovanni da
Verrill, Alpheus Hyatt
Victor, Paul-Emile
Vincennes, Francois Marie
　　Bissot
Walker, Joseph Reddeford
Weddell, James
Wegener, Alfred Lothar
Whymper, Edward
Wilkes, Charles
Wilkins, George Hubert,
　　Sir
Wilson, Alexander
Workman, Fanny Bullock
Wrangel, Ferdinand
　　Petrovich, Baron
Younghusband, Francis
　　Edward

FARMER

Aiken, George David
Balchin, Nigel Marlin
Bergland, Bob
Boyd, John W., Jr.
Crevecoeur, (Hector) St.
　　John de
Davis, Noel
Morton, John

FASHION
DESIGNER

Adolfo
Adrian
Alaia, Azzedine
Amies, Hardy
Armani, Giorgio
Balenciaga, Cristobal
Balmain, Pierre Alexandre
Banks, Jeffrey (Laurence)
Beene, Geoffrey
Bijan
Blackwell, Mr. (Richard)
Blass, Bill
Blotta, Anthony
Brioni, Gaetano Savini,
　　Marquis
Brooks, Donald Marc
Burberry, Thomas
Cameron, David
Capucci, Roberto
Cardin, Pierre
Carnegie, Hattie
Cashin, Bonnie
Cassini, Oleg Loiewski
Castillo, Antonio Canovas
　　del
Chanel, Coco
Chapman, Ceil
Claiborne, Liz
Connolly, Sybil
Copeland, Jo
Costa, Victor Charles
Courreges, Andre
Dache, Lilly
DeBarentzen, Patrick
DeLaRenta, Oscar
Dell'Olio, Louis
Derby, Jane
De Ribes, Jacqueline
Desses, Jean
Dior, Christian
DiSant'Angelo, Giorgio
Ellis, Perry Edwin
Emanuel, David
Emanuel, Elizabeth
Erte
Estevez (de Galvez), Luis
Fath, Jacques
Ferre, Gianfranco
Fogarty, Anne
Fortuny
Furstenberg, Diane Halfin
　　von
Furstenberg, Egon von
Galanos, James
Galitzine, Irene, Princess
Galliano, John
Garavani, Valentino
Gaultier, Jean-Paul
Gernreich, Rudi
Gigli, Romeo
Gimbel, Sophie Haas
Givenchy, Hubert James
　　Marcel Taffin de
Graham, Nicholas
Greer, Howard
Gres, Alix
Gucci, Rodolfo
Haire, Bill Martin
Halston
Harp, Holly
Hartnell, Norman Bishop,
　　Sir

Hampton, Henry
Hartley, Hal
Howe, James Wong
Hudlin, Reginald
Hudlin, Warrington
Hughes, John
Itami, Juzo
Jarman, Derek
Jarmusch, Jim
Johnson, Martin Elmer
Jordan, Neil
Julien, Isaac
Kaufman, Boris
Kieslowski, Krzysztof
Langman, Claude Berel
Lee, Spike
Leigh, Mike
Lemmons, Kasi
Loach, Ken(neth)
Lorentz, Pare
Lurie, Jane
Lyne, Adrian
Marshall, Garry Kent
McLaren, Norman
Micheaux, Oscar
Mikhalkov, Nikita
Moore, Michael
Mosbacher, Dee
Moss, Carlton
Nair, Mira
Naruse, Mikio
Nuridsany, Claude
Nykvist, Sven Vilhem
Obomsawin, Alanis
Ouedraogo, Idrissa
Parker, Trey
Parkerson, Michelle
Parmar, Pratibha
Pathe, Charles
Perennou, Marie
Phillips, Julia
Plage, Dieter
Priestly, Jack
Reggio, Godfrey
Richter, Hans
Riggs, Marlon
Robbe-Grillet, Alain
Rodriguez, Robert
Roeg, Nicholas (Jack)
Romero, George A
Rotha, Paul
Sayles, John
Schoonmaker, Thelma
Sedelmaier, Joe
Sembene, Ousmane
Singleton, John (Daniel)
Soderbergh, Steven
Spheeris, Penelope
Stark, Ray
Stone, Matt
Strand, Paul
Struss, Karl
Sullivan, C(harles)
  Gardner
Tanaka, Tomoyuki
Tanner, Alain
Taylor, Ronnie
Thornton, Billy Bob
Toland, Gregg
Towne, Robert (Burton)
Townsend, Robert
Trnka, Jiri
Trotta, Margarethe Von
Unsworth, Geoffrey
Vanderbilt, Cornelius, Jr.
Van Sant, Gus

Vinton, Will
von Praunheim, Rosa
Waite, Ric
Waters, John
Wayans, Keenen Ivory
Wexler, Haskell
Williams, Billy
Willis, Gordon
Wiseman, Frederick
Wood, Edward D., Jr.
Zhang Yimou
Zsigmond, Vilmos

FILMMAKERS

Hollywood Ten

FINANCIER

Astor, William Vincent
Astor, William Waldorf
  Astor, Viscount
Bache, Jules Sermon
Baker, George Fisher
Bass, Robert M(use)
Belmont, August
Bergen, John Joseph
Brady, Diamond Jim
Butler, Michael
Camdessus, Michel (Jean)
Catto, Thomas Sivewright,
  Baron
Corcoran, William Wilson
Cornfeld, Bernard
Corning, Erastus
Dow, Charles Henry
Drew, Daniel
Dreyfus, Jack Jonas
Dun, Robert Graham
Durant, Thomas Clark
Eaton, Cyrus Stephen
Estes, Billie Sol
Field, Cyrus West
Fisk, Jim
Fitzgerald, A(rthur) Ernest
Gallatin, Albert
Gates, John Warne
Goldsmith, James
  (Michael), Sir
Gould, Jay
Granville, Joseph E(nsign)
Green, Hetty
Gresham, Thomas, Sir
Groves, Wallace
Guggenheim, Daniel
Gulbenkian, Nubar Sarkis
Halaby, Najeeb E(lias)
Hammer, Armand
Harriman, E(dward)
  Roland (Noel)
Hartford, Huntington
Hirshhorn, Joseph Herman
Hopkins, Johns
Keating, Charles H, Jr.
Kennedy, John Stewart
Kennedy, Joseph Patrick,
  Sr.
Kreuger, Ivar
Laeri, J(ohn) Howard
Lasser, Jacob Kay
Loeb, Gerald Martin
Ludwig, Daniel Keith
Mellon, Andrew William

Morgan, J(ohn) P(ierpont)
Murchison, Clint(on
  Williams, Sr.)
Necker, Jacques
Odlum, Floyd Bostwick
Pierce, Edward Allen
Pritzker, Abram Nicholas
Reed, John S(hepard)
Roney, William Chapoton,
  Jr.
Rothschild, Mayer
  Amschel
Ryan, Thomas Fortune
Sage, Russell
Schacht, Hjalmar Horace
  Greeley
Schultz, Harry D
Semenenko, Serge
Smith, Donald Alexander
Smith, Francis Marion
Soros, George
Vanderbilt, Cornelius
Vanderbilt, William Henry
Vesco, Robert Lee
Zaharoff, Basil, Sir

FIREFIGHTER

Adair, Red
Barker, Elliott

FIRST LADY

Adams, Abigail (Smith)
Adams, Louisa Catherine
Bush, Barbara (Pierce)
Carter, Rosalynn
Cleveland, Frances Folsom
Clinton, Hillary Rodham
Coolidge, Grace (Anne
  Goodhue)
Eisenhower, Mamie
  (Geneva) Doud
Fillmore, Abigail (Powers)
Ford, Betty
Garfield, Lucretia
  (Rudolph)
Grant, Julia Dent
Harding, Florence Kling
  (De Wolfe)
Harrison, Anna (Tuthill
  Symmes)
Harrison, Caroline
  (Lavinia Scott)
Hayes, Lucy Webb
Hoover, Lou Henry
Johnson, Eliza (McCardle)
Johnson, Lady Bird
Lincoln, Mary Todd
Madison, Dolly (Payne
  Todd)
McKinley, Ida Saxton
Monroe, Elizabeth
  (Kortright)
Nixon, Patricia
Onassis, Jacqueline (Lee
  Bouvier Kennedy)
Pierce, Jane (Means)
Polk, Sarah Childress
Reagan, Nancy (Davis)
Roosevelt, Edith Kermit
  (Carow)
Roosevelt, Eleanor

Taft, Helen Herron
Taylor, Margaret (Smith)
Truman, Bess
Tyler, Julia Gardiner
Tyler, Letitia Christian
Washington, Martha
  (Dandridge Custis)
Wilson, Edith Bolling
  (Galt)
Wilson, Ellen Axson

FOLKLORIST

Brown, Sterling (Allen)
Courlander, Harold
Dobie, J(ames) Frank
Grimm, Jakob Ludwig
  Karl
Grimm, Wilhelm Karl
Jacobs, Joseph
Jagendorf, Moritz Adolf
Lomax, Alan
Lomax, John Avery
Smith, Mary Carter
Spence, Lewis
Torrence, Jackie

FOOTBALL COACH

Allen, George Herbert
Berry, Raymond Emmett
Blaik, Red
Blanchard, Doc
Bowden, Bobby
Brown, Paul
Bryant, Bear
Burns, Jerry
Chamberlin, B Guy
Christiansen, Jack L
Clark, Dutch
Clark, Monte Dale
Conzelman, Jimmy
Coryell, Don(ald David)
Crisler, Fritz
Daugherty, Duffy
Devine, Dan(iel John)
Ditka, Mike
Dungy, Tony
Ewbank, Weeb
Fairbanks, Chuck
Faust, Gerry
Flaherty, Ray(mond)
Flores, Tom
Gibbs, Joe Jackson
Gillman, Sidney
Grant, Bud
Green, Dennis
Gregg, Forrest
Halas, George Stanley
Hayes, Woody
Heisman, John William
Hickman, Herman
  Michael, Jr.
Holtz, Lou(is Leo)
Johnson, Jimmy
Kapp, Joe
Knox, Chuck
Lambeau, Curly
Landry, Tom
Leahy, Frank
Little, Lou(is)
Lombardi, Vince(nt
  Thomas)

Lambeau, Curly
Lambert, Jack
Lane, Dick
Langer, Jim
Lanier, Willie E
Largent, Steve M
Lary, Yale
Lattner, Johnny
Lavelli, Dante
Layden, Elmer Francis
Layne, Bobby
Leemans, Tuffy
Lilly, Bob
Lipscomb, Eugene
Lomax, Neil Vincent
Lott, Ronnie
Luckman, Sid(ney)
Lujack, John(ny)
Lundy, Lamar
Lyman, Link
Manley, Dexter
Manning, Archie
Marchetti, Gino
Marinaro, Ed(ward
   Francis)
Marino, Dan
Marshall, Wilbur
   Buddyhia
Martin, Harvey Banks
Matson, Ollie
Matuszak, John (Daniel)
Maynard, Don(ald)
McAfee, George A
McCormack, Mike
McElhenny, Hugh
McMahon, Jim
McNally, John Victor
Meredith, Don
Michalske, Mike
Miller, Don
Millner, Wayne E
Mitchell, Bobby
Mix, Ron(ald J)
Monk, Art
Montana, Joe
Moon, Warren (Harold)
Moore, Lenny
Morrall, Earl E
Morris, Joe
Morris, Mercury
Morton, Craig
Mosely, Mark DeWayne
Motley, Marion
Musso, George Francis
Nagurski, Bronko
Namath, Joe
Neale, Greasy
Nevers, Ernie
Nitschke, Ray(mond E.)
Nomelleni, Leo Joseph
O'Brien, Davey
Okoye, Christian
Olsen, Merlin Jay
Otto, Jim
Owens, Steve E
Page, Alan Cedric
Parker, Ace
Parker, Jim
Pastorini, Dan(te Anthony,
   Jr.)
Payton, Walter
Pearson, Drew
Perry, Joe
Perry, William
Piccolo, Brian
Pihos, Pete(r L)

Plunkett, Jim
Pollard, Fritz
Pruitt, Greg(ory Donald)
Rashad, Ahmad
Reese, Don(ald Francis)
Reeves, Dan(iel Edward)
Renfro, Mel(vin Lacy)
Rentzel, Lance
Reynolds, Jack
Rice, Jerry (Lee)
Riggins, John
Ringo, Jim
Robustelli, Andy
Rodgers, Johnny
Rogers, Don(ald Lavert)
Rogers, George
   Washington, Jr.
Rote, Kyle
Rozier, Mike
Rypien, Mark
St. Clair, Bob
Sanders, Barry
Sanders, Deion (Luwynn)
Sayers, Gale Eugene
Schlicter, Art(hur E)
Schmidt, Joe
Schroeder, Jay Brian
Selmon, Lee Roy
Sharpe, Sterling
Shell, Art
Simms, Phil(ip)
Simpson, O(renthal)
   J(ames)
Sims, Billy Ray
Singletary, Mike
Sinkwich, Frank
Smith, Bruce (Bernard)
Smith, Bruce P
Smith, Bubba
Smith, Emmitt
Smith, Jerry
Spurrier, Steve(n Orr)
Stabler, Ken(neth Michael)
Stallworth, John(ny Lee)
Starr, Bart
Staubach, Roger Thomas
Stautner, Ernie
Stemrick, Greg(ory Earl,
   Sr.)
Stenerud, Jan
Stingley, Darryl
Strong, Ken(neth E)
Stuhldreher, Harry A
Stydahar, Joe
Sullivan, Pat(rick J)
Swann, Lynn Curtis
Tarkenton, Fran(cis
   Asbury)
Tatum, Jack
Taylor, Charley
Taylor, Jim
Taylor, Lawrence Julius
Testaverde, Vinny
Theismann, Joe
Thomas, Thurman Lee
Tittle, Y(elberton)
   A(braham)
Todd, Richard
Trafton, George
Trippi, Charlie
Tunnell, Em(len)
Unitas, Johnny
Upshaw, Gene
Utley, Mike
Van Brocklin, Norm (an
   Mack)

Van Buren, Steve W
Vessels, Billy
Walker, Doak
Walker, Herschel
Walker, Wesley Darcel
Walls, Everson Collins
Ware, Andre
Warfield, Paul Dryden
Warner, Curt
Waterfield, Bob
Watts, J(ulius) C(aesar),
   (Jr.)
Webster, Mike
Weinmesiter, Arnie
White, Charles Raymond
White, Randy Lee
White, Reggie
White, Stan(ley Ray)
Williams, Doug(las Lee)
Willis, Bill
Wilson, Larry
Winslow, Kellen Boswell
Wojciechowicz,
   Alex(ander)
Woodson, Rod(erick
   Kevin)
Yepremian, Garo
Young, Steve
Youngblood, Jack

FOOTBALL PLAYERS

Four Horsemen of Notre
Dame

FOOTBALL COACH

Gaither, Jake

FOUNDATION EXECUTIVE

Berresford, Susan Vail

FUR TRADER

Ashley, William Henry
Astor, John Jacob
Bridger, James
Laclede, Pierre
McGill, James
McLoughlin, John
Smith, Jedediah Strong

FURNITURE DESIGNER

Adam, Robert
Chippendale, Thomas
Hepplewhite, George
Hitchcock, Lambert
McIntire, Samuel
Phyfe, Duncan
Roentgen, David
Sheraton, Thomas
Stickley, Gustav

GAMBLER

Brummell, Beau
Harrah, Bill
Holliday, Doc
Nick the Greek
Rothstein, Arnold

GAS STATION ATTENDANT

Dummar, Melvin

GENETICIST

Ayala, Francisco J(ose)
Barr, Murray Llewellyn
Benzer, Seymour
Brenner, Sydney
Bridges, Calvin Blackman
Brown, Michael Stuart
Burton, Glenn W(illard)
Cohen, Stanley N(orman)
Collins, Francis S(ellers)
Darlington, Cyril Dean
Dukepoo, Frank C.
East, Edward Murray
Hamer, Dean H.
Jacob, Francois
King, Mary-Claire
Krim, Mathilde Galland
Lysenko, Trofim
   Denisovich
McClintock, Barbara
Mendel, Gregor Johann
Nuesslein-Volhard,
   Christiane
Russell, Elizabeth Shull
Sager, Ruth
Singer, Maxine (Frank)
Skolnick, Mark H(enry)
Stahl, Franklin William
Stevens, Nettie Maria
Sturtevant, Alfred Henry
Sutton, Walter
   Stanborough
Swaminathan,
   M(onkombu)
   S(ambisivan)
Tatum, Edward Lawrie
Vavilov, Nikolai
   Ivanovich
Wortman, Sterling

GEOGRAPHER

Anville, Jean Baptiste
   Bourguignon d'
Biruni, Abu Rayhan al-
Bowman, Isaiah
Busching, Anton Friedrich
Christaller, Walter
Davis, William Morris
Everest, George, Sir
Freshfield, Douglas
   William
Gerasimov, Innokentii
   Petrovich
Grosvenor, Gilbert Hovey
Hakluyt, Richard
Haushofer, Karl Ernst

Hedin, Sven Anders
Huntington, Ellsworth
Hutchins, Thomas
Idrisi, Muhammad ibn
  Muhammad al-
Khwarizmi, Muhammad
  ibn Musa al-
Mackinder, Halford John,
  Sir
Morse, Jedidiah
Peel, Ronald Francis
  (Edward Waite)
Przhevalsky, Nikolai
  Mikhailovich
Ptolemy, Claudius
Pytheas
Ratzel, Friedrich
Richthofen, Ferdinand
  Paul Wilhelm
Ritter, Karl
Robinson, Arthur
  H(oward)
Robinson, Edward
Ronne, Finn
Sauer, Carl Ortwin
Siple, Paul Allman
Strabo
Thompson, David
Vidal de la Blache, Paul
Waldseemuller, Martin
Wei Yuan

GEOLOGIST

Andersson, Johan Gunnar
Ballard, Robert Duane
Bascom, Florence
Boule, Marcellin
Bowie, William
Bucher, Walter Herman
Buckland, William
Chamberlin, Thomas
  Chrowder
Cloud, Preston (Ercelle)
Dalrymple, G. Brent
Daly, Reginald Aldworth
Dana, James Dwight
Davis, William Morris
Dawson, George Mercer
Dawson, John William, Sir
Deluc, Jean Andre
Dolomieu, Deodat Guy
  Gratet de
Emmons, Ebenezer
Fuchs, Vivian (Ernest), Sir
Geikie, Archibald, Sir
Gilbert, Grove Karl
Hall, James
Hall, James, Sir
Hitchcock, Edward
Holmes, Arthur
Hutton, James
Jaggar, Thomas Augustus
King, Clarence
Logan, William Edmond
Lyell, Charles, Sir
Masursky, Harold
Matthes, Francois-Emile
Mawson, Douglas, Sir
Menard, H William
Michell, John
Murchison, Roderick
  Impey
Nolan, Thomas Brennan

Nordenskiold, Nils Adolph
  Erik, Baron
Person, Waverly
Powell, John Wesley
Richthofen, Ferdinand
  Paul Wilhelm
Schopf, J(ames) William
Silliman, Benjamin
Smith, William
Tharp, Marie
Tromp, Solco Walle
Tyrrell, Joseph Burr
Wegener, Alfred Lothar
Whitney, Josiah Dwight
Wrather, William Embry

GOLF COURSE ARCHITECT

Jones, Robert Trent

GOLF EXECUTIVE

Beman, Deane Randolph

GOLFER

Aaron, Tommy
Abbott, Margaret I.
Alcott, Amy Strum
Anderson, Willie
Aoki, Isao
Archer, George
Armour, Tommy
Aucherlonie, Laurie
Azinger, Paul
Baker, Kathy
Ballesteros, Seve(riano)
Barber, Jerry
Barnes, Jim
Bean, Andy
Beard, Frank
Beman, Deane Randolph
Berg, Patty
Berning, Susie Maxwell
Blalock, Jane
Bolt, Tommy
Boros, Julius (Nicholas)
Boswell, Charles Albert
Bradley, Pat(ricia Ellen)
Braid, James
Brewer, Gay, Jr.
Britz, Jerilyn
Burke, Billy
Burke, Jack, Jr.
Burkemo, Walter
Calcavecchia, Mark
Caponi, Donna
Carner, Joanne Gunderson
Casper, Billy
Charles, Bob
Chen, T.C.
Coody, Charles
Cotton, Henry, Sir
Couples, Fred
Crampton, Bruce Sidney
Creavy, Tom
Crenshaw, Ben Daniel
Crocker, Fay
Crosby, Nathaniel
Daniel, Beth

Demaret, Jimmy
DeVicenzo, Roberto
Diegel, Leo
Dutra, Olin
Elder, Lee
Evans, Chick
Faldo, Nick
Farrell, Johnny
Ferrier, Jim
Finsterwald, Dow
Floyd, Raymond Loran
Ford, Doug
Furgol, Ed(ward)
Geiberger, Al(len L)
Ghezzi, Vic(tor)
Goalby, Bob
Goodman, Johnny
Graham, David
Graham, Lou
Green, Hubie
Guldahl, Ralph
Hagen, Walter Charles
Hamilton, Bob
Harbert, Chick
Harmon, Claude
Harper, Chandler
Haynie, Sandra
Hebert, Jay
Hebert, Lionel
Hogan, Ben
Irwin, Hale S
Jacklin, Tony
January, Don(ald)
Jones, Bobby
Keiser, Herman
King, Betsy
Kite, Tom
Lacoste, Catherine
Langer, Bernhard
Laoretti, Larry
Lema, Tony
Little, Lawson
Little, Sally
Littler, Gene
Locke, Bobby
Lopez, Nancy Marie
Lyle, Sandy
MacFarlane, Willie
Mahaffey, John
Mallon, Meg
Manero, Tony
Mangrum, Lloyd
Mann, Carol Ann
Marr, Dave
Mayer, Dick
McDermott, Johnny
McLeod, Fred(erick)
McSpaden, Byron
Middlecoff, Cary
Miller, Johnny Laurence
Mills, Mary
Mize, Larry
Moody, Orville
Nagle, Kel(vin David
  George)
Nelson, Byron
Nelson, Larry Gene
Nichols, Bobby
Nicklaus, Jack William
Norman, Greg
North, Andy
O'Meara, Mark
Ouimet, Francis de Sales
Palmer, Arnold Daniel
Parks, Sam(uel
  McLaughlin)

Pate, Jerry
Pavin, Corey
Peete, Calvin
Picard, Henry
Player, Gary Jim
Pohl, Dan(ny Joe)
Post, Sandra
Price, Nick
Rankin, Judy
Rawls, Betsy
Ray, Edward
Revolta, Johnny
Rodriguez, Chi-Chi
Rogers, Bill
Rosburg, Bob
Ross, Alex(ander)
Runyan, Paul Scott
Sarazen, Gene
Sargent, George
Shute, Denny
Sifford, Charlie
Simpson, Scott
Smith, Alex
Smith, Horton
Snead, Sam(uel Jackson)
Spuzich, Sandra Ann
Stacy, Hollis
Stadler, Craig Robert
Stephenson, Jan Lynn
Stockton, Dave
Strange, Curtis
Suggs, Louise
Sutton, Hal Evan
Taylor, J(ohn) H(enry)
Thomson, Peter William
Travers, Jerry
Trevino, Lee Buck
Turnesa, Jim
Tway, Bob
Vardon, Harry
Vare, Glenna Collett
Venturi, Ken(neth)
Wadkins, Lanny
Walker, Cyril
Wall, Art(hur Jonathan),
  Jr.
Watson, Tom
Weiskopf, Tom
Whitworth, Kathy
Wood, Craig Ralph
Woods, Tiger
Worsham, Lew(is Elmer)
Wright, Mickey
Zaharias, Babe Didrikson
Zoeller, Fuzzy

GOVERNESS

Leonowens, Anna
  Harriette Crawford

GOVERNMENT OFFICIAL

Abrams, Elliott
Abravanel, Isaac ben
  Judah
Acheson, Dean
  Gooderham
Adams, Brock(man)
Adams, Eva Bertrand
Adams, Sherman
  Llewellyn

Adelman, Kenneth Lee
Agee, Philip
Albright, Madeleine
  K(orbel)
Alexander, Clifford L, Jr.
Alexander, Donald
  Crichton
Alexander, Lamar
Allen, Richard Vincent
Amerasinghe, Hamilton
  Shirley
Andrus, Cecil D(ale)
Angleton, James J(esus)
Araki Sadao
Arbatov, Georgi
Arens, Moshe
Armstrong, Anne
  Legendre
Artukovic, Andrija
Askew, Reubin
  O'Donovan
Aspin, Les
Atherton, Alfred LeRoy,
  Jr.
Austin, Warren R(obinson)
Aziz, Tariq Mikhayl
Babbitt, Bruce E(dward)
Bailar, Benjamin Franklin
Baker, Bobby
Baker, Howard Henry, Jr.
Baker, James Addison, III
Balbo, Italo
Baldrige, Malcolm
Ball, George W(ildman)
Ballantrae, Lord
Bane, Frank B
Barbie, Klaus
Barnard, Chester Irving
Barr, Joseph W(alker)
Barr, William Pelham
Barre, Raymond
Beard, Dita Davis
Beesley, H(orace) Brent
Bell, T(errel) H(oward)
Bello y Lopez, Andres
Bennett, William John
Benson, Ezra Taft
Bentsen, Lloyd Millard, Jr.
Berchtold, Leopold von
Bergland, Bob
Berri, Nabih
Berry, Mary Frances
Bevin, Ernest
Biddle, Francis Beverley
Bienville, Sieur de
Bigge, John Thomas
Blatchford, Joseph Hoffer
Bloch, Eric
Block, John Rusling
Blount, Winton Malcolm
Blumenthal, W Michael
Blyden, Edward Wilmot
Bolger, William Frederick
Bolz, Lothar
Bondfield, Margaret Grace
Boorstin, Daniel J(oseph)
Borge Martinez, Tomas
Bormann, Martin Ludwig
Boskin, Michael J(ay)
Bowles, Erskine B.
Boyce, Westray Battle
Brady, Nicholas Frederick
Bray, Charles William, III
Brennan, Peter J(oseph)
Bright, John
Brimmer, Andrew Felton

Brinegar, Claude Stout
Briscoe, Robert
Bristow, Benjamin Helm
Broadbent, Ed
Brown, George Alfred
Brown, George Scratchley
Brown, Harold
Brown, Jesse
Brown, Lee P(atrick)
Brown, Ron(ald Harmon)
Brownell, Herbert, Jr.
Brownell, Samuel Miller
Browner, Carol M.
Bruce, Louis R., Jr.
Buchan, John, Sir
Buchanan, Angela Marie
Buisson, Ferdinand
  Edouard
Bundy, William Putnam
Burch, Dean
Burford, Anne McGill
  Gorsuch
Burnley, James H, IV
Butterfield, Alexander
  Porter
Butz, Earl Lauer
Byrnes, James Francis
Callaghan, James
Callaway, Howard Hollis
Cameron, Simon
Campbell, Clifford, Sir
Carleton, Guy
Carlisle, John Griffin
Carlucci, Frank Charles,
  III
Carusi, Ugo
Casey, William Joseph
Cassiodorus, Flavius
  Magnus Aurelius
Cavazos, Lauro F(red, Jr.)
Chang Chih-tung
Chang Chu-cheng
Chao Meng-fu
Chapin, Roy Dikeman
Charnisay, Charles de
  Menou, Seigneur
  d'Aulnay
Chataway, Christopher
  John
Chayes, Abram J(oseph)
Chelmsford, Frederic John
  Napier Thesiger, 1st
  Viscount Chelmsford
Cheney, Dick
Cherberg, John A(ndrew)
Cherwell, Frederick
  Alexander L, Viscount
Chia Ssu-tao
Chicherin, Georgi
  Vasilyevich
Ch'in Kuei
Ch'i-ying
Chou En-Lai
Chretien, Jean (Joseph-
  Jacques)
Christopher, Warren
  M(inor)
Chun Doo Hwan
Chung, Arthur
Ciano (di Cortellazzo),
  Galeazzo
Cisneros, Henry G(abriel)
Civiletti, Benjamin
  Richard
Clark, Georgia Neese
Clark, Ramsey

Clark, William P(atrick
  Jr.)
Clay, Cassius Marcellus
Claybrook, Joan B
Claytor, W(illiam)
  Graham, Jr.
Cleland, Max
Clifford, Clark
  M(cAdams)
Cline, Genevieve Rose
Cochrane, Edward Lull
Cohen, Wilbur Joseph
Cohen, William
  S(ebastian)
Colbert, Jean-Baptiste
Colby, William E(gan)
Coleman, William T, Jr.
Colman, Norman Jay
Conger, Clement Ellis
Constantine, Learie
  Nicholas Constantine,
  Baron
Coombs, Herbert Cole
Cosio Villegas, Daniel
Costa Mendez, Nicanor
Costle, Douglas Michael
Cox, Jacob Dolson
Craig, Malin
Creel, George Edward
Crocker, Chester Arthur
Cromer, 1st Earl of
Crosbie, John (Carnell)
Crowley, Leo Thomas
Cuomo, Andrew M.
Daley, William M.
Dalton, John H.
Dandolo, Enrico
Daniels, Josephus
Darlan, Jean Louis Xavier
  Francois
Darman, Richard G(ordon)
Davis, Dwight Filley
Davis, Edward Michael
Day, J(ames) Edward
Dean, Arthur H(obson)
Dean, Gordon Evans
Dearborn, Henry
Debray, Regis
Debus, Kurt Heinrich
Deer, Ada E(lizabeth)
Demjanjuk, John
Derthick, L(awrence)
  G(ridley)
Derwinski, Edward Joseph
Deutch, John
Dewey, Charles Schuveldt
Dewson, Mary Williams
Dixon, Paul Rand
Dole, Elizabeth Hanford
Dominick, Peter Hoyt
Donovan, Raymond James
Douglas, James
  Henderson, Jr.
Dreyfus, Pierre
Duke, Robin (Anthony
  Hare)
Dulles, John Foster
Dumas, Roland
Duncan, Charles William,
  Jr.
Dupleix, Joseph Francois
Eagleburger, Lawrence S.
Eberstadt, Ferdinand
Eccles, Marriner Stoddard
Eden, Nicholas
Edwards, James Burrows

Eichmann, Adolf
Elders, Joycelyn
Eliot, Martha May
Espy, Mike
Evans, John
Evarts, William Maxwell
Falcone, Giovanni
Fall, Albert Bacon
Fan Chung-yen
Fedorenko, Fyodor
Feng Kuei-fen
Finch, Robert H(utchison)
Fleming, Donald
  M(ethuen)
Flemming, Arthur
  S(herwood)
Fletcher, Arthur Allen
Floyd, John Buchanan
Folsom, Marion Bayard
Forrestal, James Vincent
Fowler, Mark Stapleton
Frank, Anthony Melchior
Frank, Hans
Frankel, Charles
Franklin, William
Franks, Oliver (Shewell),
  Sir
Freeh, Louis J(oseph)
Freeman, Orville Lothrop
Frere, Henry Bartle
  Edward
Frick, Wilhelm
Fritzsche, Hans
Frohnmayer, John Edward
Frontinus, Sextus Julius
Funk, Walther
Furness, Betty
Furtseva, Ekaterina
  Alexeyevna
Gairy, Eric Matthew, Sir
Gao Gang
Gardner, John William
Garrett, Henry Lawrence,
  III
Gates, Robert M(ichael)
Gaud, William Steen, Jr.
Gebbie, Kristine
Gelb, Leslie Howard
George, Clair
George, Walter Franklin
Gergen, David
  (Richmond)
Gero, Erno
Ghotbzadeh, Sadegh
Gilpatric, Roswell
  L(eavitt)
Giuliani, Rudolph William
Glennan, T(homas) Keith
Glickman, Daniel R.
Goebbels, Joseph
Goering, Hermann
  Wilhelm
Goldin, Daniel S
Goldmann, Nahum
Gracchus, Tiberius
  Sempronius
Granger, Lester
Gray, C(layland) Boyden
Gray, Gordon
Gray, Louis Patrick
Grechko, Andrei
  Antonovick
Greenspan, Alan
Grese, Irma
Grolier, Jean
Gronouski, John A(ustin)

Hagerty, James Campbell
Haig, Alexander Meigs, Jr.
Haldeman, H(arry)
  R(obbins)
Han Fei Tzu
Hanks, Nancy
Harriman, Pamela
Harriman, W(illiam)
  Averell
Harris, Patricia Roberts
Hawksmoor, Nicholas
Haykal, Muhammad
  Husain
Healy, Bernadine
Heckler, Margaret Mary
Heller, Walter Wolfgang
Helms, Richard McGarrah
Henderson, Leon
Henry, Edward Richard,
  Sir
Herman, Alexis M.
Herrick, Elinore
  Morehouse
Heruy Walda-Sellase
Heseltine, Michael Ray
  Dibdin
Hess, Rudolf
Heydrich, Reinhard
  Tristan Eugen
Hickerson, John Dewey
Hill, Rowland, Sir
Hills, Carla Anderson
Hills, Roderick M
Himmler, Heinrich
Hiss, Alger
Ho, Ying-Chin
Hobby, Oveta Culp
Hodel, Donald P(aul)
Hodges, Luther Hartwell
Hodgson, James Day
Hoover, J(ohn) Edgar
Houghton, Amory
Howe, Geoffrey Richard
  Edward, Sir
Huang Hua
Hufstedler, Shirley (Ann)
  M(ount)
Hugel, Max
Hundt, Reed
Hurd, Douglas
Ickes, Harold LeClair
Iglesias, Enrique V.
Ikle, Fred Charles
Irving, Larry
Izac, Edouard V(ictor
  Michel)
James, Daniel, Jr.
Jaworski, Leon
Johnson, Hugh Samuel
Johnson, Nicholas
Johnson, William, Sir
Jones, David Charles
Jones, Jesse Holman
Jones, Roger W(arren)
Kalb, Bernard
Kania, Stanislaw
Kantor, Mickey
Kell, Vernon, Sir
Kelley, Clarence Marion
Kelley, Frank Joseph
Kelsen, Hans
Kelsey, Henry
Kennard, William Earl
Kennedy, David
  M(atthew)
Kennedy, Weldon

Keppel, Francis
Kessler, David Aaron
Keyserling, Leon Hirsch
Keyworth, George Albert
Killian, James Rhyne, Jr.
Kim Pusik
Kissinger, Henry Alfred
Klassen, Elmer Theodore
Kleindienst, Richard
  Gordon
Klutznick, Philip M.
Knauer, Virginia
  Harrington Wright
Knox, Frank
Knox, Henry
Koch, Ilse
Komer, Robert William
Koop, C(harles) Everett
Kotsching, Walter Maria
Kozyrev, Andrei Y
Kraft, Chris(topher
  Columbus, Jr.)
Kreps, Juanita Morris
Krishna Menon, V(engalil)
  K(rishnan)
Krogh, Egil, Jr.
Kutschmann, Walter
Labouisse, Henry
  Richardson
LaFollette, Bronson
  Cutting
Lafontant-Mankarious,
  Jewel (Stradford)
Laird, Melvin Robert
Lake, Anthony
Lambsdorff, Otto
Lamont, Norman
Lance, (Thomas)
  Bert(ram)
Landis, James McCauley
Landrieu, Moon
Lansing, Robert
Larson, (Lewis) Arthur
Lavelle, Rita Marie
Lay, James Selden, Jr.
Le Duc Tho
Lee, Robert E(mmet)
Lehman, John Francis, Jr.
Levesque, Rene
Levi, Edward Hirsch
Lewis, Allen Montgomery,
  Sir
Lewis, Drew
Lewis, Stephen Henry
Liddy, G(eorge) Gordon
Li Hung-Chang
Lilienthal, David Eli
Lin, Piao (Yu-Yung)
Lin Tse-hsu
Li Ssu
Logan, James
Lovett, Robert
  A(bercrombie)
Lowery, Robert O
Lucas, Scott Wike
Lu Chiu-yuan
Lugard, Frederick John
  Dealtry
Lujan, Manuel, Jr.
Lundahl, Arthur Charles
Lyautey, Louis Hubert
  Gonzalve
Lyng, Richard E
Lyttleton, Oliver
Mabuza, Lindiwe
MacLeod, Iain Norman

Macy, John Williams, Jr.
Makonnen Endalkacaw
Malenkov, Georgi
  Maximilianovich
Malik, Charles Habib
Malraux, Andre Georges
Mandel, Georges
Marshall, George Catlett
Marshall, Ray
Martin, Lynn
Martin, William
  McChesney, Jr.
Masekela, Barbara
Mather, Stephen Tyng
Mathews, Forrest David
Maverick, Samuel
  Augustus
McCabe, Thomas Bayard
McCloy, John Jay
McCord, James Walter
McCree, Wade Hampton,
  Jr.
McCurry, Michael
  D(emaree)
McElroy, Neil Hosler
McFarlane, Robert Carl
McHenry, Donald
  Franchot
McIntyre, James
  Talmadge, Jr.
McLarty, Thomas F, III
McLaughlin, Ann Dore
McMurrin, Sterling M(oss)
McNamara, Robert
  S(trange)
McNutt, Paul Vories
Meese, Edwin, III
Mellon, Andrew William
Mendoza, Antonio de
Metcalfe, Charles
  Theophilus
Middendorf, John William,
  II
Mielke, Erich
Miller, G(eorge) William
Miller, James Clifford, III
Miller, William Mosley
Mills, Ogden Livingston
Mitchell, John Newton
Moley, Raymond Charles
Moore, Bert C
Morgenthau, Henry, Jr.
Morton, Julius Sterling
Morton, Rogers Clark
  Ballard
Mosbacher, Robert Adam
Moscone, George Richard
Moses, Robert
Moskowitz, J(ay)
Mott, William Penn, Jr.
Muller, Hilgard
Myers, Dee Dee
Myerson, Bess
Nash, Philleo
Ness, Eliot
Nestingen, Ivan Arnold
Niezabitowska, Malgorzata
Norton, Eleanor Holmes
Nott, John William
  Frederic, Sir
Novello, Antonia Coello
Nussbaum, Karen
Nzo, Alfred
  (Baphethuxolo)
O'Brien, Larry
O'Donnell, Kenneth P

Ogata, Sadako (Nakamura)
Oldfield, Maurice, Sir
O'Leary, Hazel R(eid)
Oliver, Daniel
Ortega, Katherine Davalos
Ou-yang Hsiu
Pace, Frank, Jr.
Paine, Robert Treat
Paine, Thomas Otten
Palme, Olof
Palmer, Alexander
  Mitchell
Panetta, Leon E(dward)
Pantaleoni, Helenka
  (Tradeusa Adamowski)
Park, William Hallock
Passy, Frederic
Pate, Maurice
Pena, Federico F.
Pendleton, Clarence
  McLane, Jr.
Perez, Anna
Perkins, Frances
Perkins, Milo Randolph
Perle, Richard Norman
Perry, William J(ames)
Petitpierre, Max
Pierce, Samuel Riley, Jr.
Pindling, Lynden Oscar
Pineau, Christian (Paul
  Francis)
Poinsett, Joel Roberts
Porritt, Arthur Espie, Sir
Price, Byron
Priest, Ivy (Maude) Baker
Profumo, John Dennis
Purvis, Melvin
Pym, Francis Leslie
Quisling, Vidkun Abraham
Raines, Franklin (Delano)
Randall, Samuel J
Rapacki, Adam
Regan, Donald Thomas
Reich, Robert B(ernard)
Reilly, William Kane
Reisman, Simon
Reith, John Charles
  Walsham
Reno, Janet
Resor, Stanley Rogers
Reynolds, William
  Bradford
Rhodes, Cecil John
Richardson, Bill
Richardson, Elliot L(ee)
Riley, Richard W(ilson)
Rivers, L(ucius) Mendel
Rogers, William Pierce
Rolvaag, Karl Fritjof
Ronan, William John
Roosa, Robert V(incent)
Rosenberg, Anna Marie
Rosenfeld, Harry N(athan)
Rothschild, Lionel Nathan
Rothschild, Baron
Roudebush, Richard
  L(owell)
Rountree, William
  M(anning)
Rowe, James Henry, Jr.
Rowley, James Joseph
Rubin, Robert E.
Ruckelshaus, William
  Doyle
Ruder, David Sturtevant

Rumsfeld, Donald
  (Harold)
Ruppe, Loret Miller
Rush, (David) Kenneth
Rusk, (David) Dean
Rykov, Aleksey Ivanovich
Saltzman, Charles
  E(skridge)
Sapir, Pinchas
Satcher, David
Sawyer, Charles
Sayre, Francis Bowes
Schiavo, Mary (Fackler)
Schiller, Karl (August
  Fritz)
Schlesinger, James
  Rodney
Schottland, Charles I(rwin)
Schweiker, Richard
  Schultz
Scribner, Fred C(lark), Jr.
Sessions, William Steele
Seton-Watson, Hugh
Seward, William Henry
Shalala, Donna Edna
Shanks, Michael
Sharett, Moshe
Sharon, Ariel
Shelepin, Aleksandr
  (Nikolaevich)
Shriver, (Robert) Sargent
Shultz, George Pratt
Shushkevich, Stanislav
Sickles, Daniel Edgar
Sierra, Justo
Simcoe, John Graves
Simon, William E(dward)
Singh, (Sardar) Swaran
Sisco, Joseph John
Skinner, Samuel K(nox)
Slater, Rodney E.
Smathers, George
  Armistead
Smith, Gerard C(oad)
Smith, William French
Snepp, Frank Warren, III
Snyder, John Wesley
Soames, Christopher
Sonnenfeldt, Helmut
Sorensen, Ted
Soustelle, Jacques
Sparkman, John Jackson
Speakes, Larry Melvin
Stangl, Franz Paul
Stans, Maurice H(ubert)
Stanton, Robert
Steelman, John Roy
Stephanopoulos, George
  (Robert)
Stettinius, Edward R, Jr.
Stevens, Robert Ten
  Broeck
Stimson, Henry Lewis
Stockman, David Allen
Stone, Michael Patrick
  William
Strauss, Lewis
  Lichtenstein
Streibert, Theodore Cuyler
Sturt, Charles
Sullivan, Daniel P
Sullivan, Louis W(ade)
Summerfield, Arthur
  Ellsworth
Swimmer, Ross
Switzer, Mary E.

Syed Ahmed Khan
Tabor, Horace Austin
  Warner
Talon, Jean
Tekere, Edgar Zivanai
Thang, Ton Duc
Toledo, Francisco de
Tolson, Clyde Anderson
Toure, Amadou Toumani
Train, Russell Errol
Tree, Marietta Endicott
  Peabody
Truly, Richard H
Tryon, William
Tseng Kuo-fan
Tso Tsung-t'ang
Turner, Stansfield
Tutwiler, Margaret
  (DeBardeleben)
Tyson, Laura D'Andrea
Udall, Stewart Lee
Underwood, Oscar Wilder
Ustinov, Dmitri
  Fedorovich
Valenti, Jack Joseph
Vance, Cyrus Roberts
Vandenberg, Arthur
  Hendrick, Jr.
Van Diemen, Anthony
  Meuza
Varmus, Harold E(lliot)
Velasco, Luis de
Velazquez de Cuellar,
  Diego
Verity, C(alvin) William,
  Jr.
Volcker, Paul Adolph
von Lipsey, Roderick K.
Vranitzky, Franz
Wadsworth, James
  Jeremiah
Walker, Robert James
Walsh, Lawrence E
Wang Yang-ming
Ward, Benjamin
Warne, William E(lmo)
Warnke, Paul Culliton
Watkins, James (David)
Watkins, Shirley R.
Watson, Jack Hearn, Jr.
Watt, James Gaius
Weaver, Robert C(lifton)
Webb, James Edwin
Webb, James H(enry), Jr.
Webster, William
  Hedgcock
Weeks, Sinclair
Weidenbaum, Murray Lew
Weinberger, Caspar
  Willard
Wellesley, Richard Colley,
  1st Marquess Wellesley
Wen-hsiang
Wen T'ien-hsiang
West, Togo D., Jr.
Wheeler, Earle G
Whitney, William Collins
Wick, Charles Z
Widnall, Sheila E.
Wilcox, Francis (Orlando)
Wille, Frank
Williams, Maggie
Wilson, Charles Erwin
Wirtz, William Willard
Wo-jen

Woodcock, Amos Walter
  Wright
Woodward, Ellen S.
Woolsey, R James
Wrather, William Embry
Wright, Bruce McMarion
Yamani, Ahmad Zaki,
  Sheik
Yeh-lu Ch'u-ts'ai
Yeutter, Clayton Keith
Young, Philip
Zech, Lando William, Jr.
Ziegler, Ron(ald Louis)
Skinner, Sam

GRAPHIC ARTIST

Baskin, Leonard

GUARD

Wills, Frank

GYMNAST

Caslavska, Vera
Chukarin, Viktor
  Ivanovich
Comaneci, Nadia
Dawes, Dominique
  (Margaux)
Gutsu, Tatiana
Korbut, Olga
Latynina, Larisa
  Semyonovna
Leitzel, Lillian
Miller, Shannon (Lee)
Retton, Mary Lou
Rigby, Cathy
Shcherbo, Vitaly
Strug, Kerri
Thomas, Kurt
Turischeva, Ludmila

GYMNASTICS
COACH

Karolyi, Bela

GYMNASTICS
PIONEER

Jahn, Friedrich Ludwig

HAIRSTYLIST

Alexandre
Kenneth
Leonard
Sassoon, Vidal
Sebring, Jay

HANDWRITING
EXPERT

Hamilton, Charles

HERO

Matamoros, Mariano
Omar al-Mukhtar
Robin Hood

HISTORIAN

Acton, John Emerich
  Edward Dalberg-Acton,
  Baron
Adams, Brooks
Adams, Charles Francis,
  Jr.
Adams, Henry Brooks
Adams, Herbert Baxter
Adams, James Truslow
Adams, Peter Chardon
  Brooks
Alaman, Lucas
Allen, Frederick Lewis
Altamira Y Crevea, Rafael
Amory, Cleveland
Andrews, Charles McLean
Aptheker, Herbert
Arendt, Hannah
Aulard, Francois Victor
  Alphonse
Bancroft, Hubert Howe
Baron, Salo Wittmayer
Barros, Joao de
Bartlett, John Russell
Barzun, Jacques Martin
Beard, Charles Austin
Beard, Mary Ritter
Becker, Carl Lotus
Bembo, Pietro
Bemis, Samuel Flagg
Bestor, Arthur (Eugene)
Bettmann, Otto L(udwig)
Beveridge, Albert
  Jeremiah
Beverley, Robert
Bibaud, Michel
Bickerman, Elias Joseph
Billington, James H(adley)
Billington, Ray Allen
Biruni, Abu Rayhan al-
Bloch, Marc
Boswell, John (Eastburn)
Bowers, Claude Gernade
Boyd, Julian Parks
Brandel, Fernand Paul
Brandes, Georg Morris
  Cohen
Braudel, Fernand (Paul)
Brauer, Jerald C(arl)
Breasted, James Henry
Brinton, Clarence Crane
Brown, Dee (Alexander)
Buckle, Henry Thomas
Burchard, John Ely
Burckhardt, Carl Jacob
Burckhardt, Jacob
  (Christoph)
Burton, John Hill, Sir
Bury, John Bagnell
Butterfield, Lyman Henry

Treitschke, Heinrich
  Gotthard von
Trevelyan, George
  Macaulay
Trevor-Roper, Hugh
  Redwald
Troeltsch, Ernst
Tuchman, Barbara
  Wertheim
Tucker, George
Tung Ch'i-ch'ang
Turner, Frederick Jackson
Tyler, Moses Coit
Unger, Irwin
Van Loon, Hendrik
  Willem
Varnhagen, Francisco
  Adolfo de
Vasconcelos (Calderon),
  Jose
Villani, Giovanni
Villehardouin, Geffroi de
Vinogradoff, Paul
  Gavrilovitch
Voegelin, Eric (Herman
  Wilhelm)
Warren, Mercy Otis
Wedgwood, C(icely)
  V(eronica)
Wei Yuan
Wesley, Charles Harris
William of Malmesbury
William of Tyre
Williams, Eric Eustace
Williams, George
  Washington
Winsor, Justin
Woodward, C(omer) Vann
Wroth, Lawrence
  Counselman
Xenophon
Zinn, Howard

HISTORIANS

Hammond, Lawrence and
  Lucy

HISTORICAL
FIGURE

Bellshazzar
Bishop, Bridget
Corbin, Margaret Cochran
Fritchie, Barbara
Gannett, Deborah
  Sampson
Joan of Arc, Saint
Laurie, Annie
Lewis, Ida
Ludington, Sybil
Pitcher, Molly
Rutledge, Ann
Secord, Laura Ingersoll

HOCKEY COACH

Abel, Sid(ney Gerald)
Adams, Jack
Arbour, Al(ger Joseph)
Berenson, Red

Blake, Toe
Boucher, Frank
Bowman, Scotty
Brooks, Herb(ert Paul)
Burns, Pat
Cherry, Don(ald Stewart)
Demers, Jacques
Gorman, Tommy
Imlach, Punch
Ivan, Tommy
Johnson, Bob
Keenan, Mike
Mathers, Frank
Maxwell, Steamer
Patrick, Lester B
Quinn, Pat
Ross, Art(hur Howie)
Sather, Glen Cameron
Schmidt, Milt(on Conrad)

HOCKEY
EXECUTIVE

Adams, Charles Francis
Adams, Weston W, Sir
Ahearn, Frank
Ballard, Harold
Brown, Walter Augustine
Calder, Frank
Campbell, Clarence
  Sutherland
Clancy, King
Clarke, Bobby
Dandurand, Leo
Dudley, George S
Dutton, Red
Esposito, Phil(ip Anthony)
Esposito, Tony
Ferguson, John Bowie
Francis, Emile Percy
Gorman, Tommy
Imlach, Punch
Ivan, Tommy
Jennings, Bill
Mathers, Frank
McBride, Bryant
McLaughlin, Frederic
Molson, Hartland de
  Montarville
Nanne, Lou(is Vincent)
Norris, Bruce A
Norris, James, Sr.
Norris, James D
Patrick, Frank A
Patrick, Lester B
Patrick, Lynn
Pocklington, Peter H
Pollock, Sam
Sather, Glen Cameron
Schmidt, Milt(on Conrad)
Selke, Frank J, Sr.
Smythe, Conn
Torrey, Bill
Wirtz, Arthur Michael
Ziegler, John Augustus, Jr.

HOCKEY PIONEER

Stanley, Frederick Arthur,
  Earl of Derby

HOCKEY PLAYER

Abel, Sid(ney Gerald)
Abel, Taffy
Adams, Jack
Allan, Montagu, Sir
Anderson, Glenn Chris
Apps, Syl
Arbour, Al(ger Joseph)
Armstrong, George
  Edward
Bailey, Ace
Bain, Dan
Baker, Bill
Baker, Hobey
Barrasso, Tom
Barry, Marty
Bathgate, Andy
Beliveau, Jean (Marc A)
Benedict, Clint(on
  Stephen)
Bentley, Doug(las
  Wagner)
Bentley, Max(well Herbert
  Lloyd)
Berenson, Red
Blake, Toe
Boivin, Leo Joseph
Boon, Dickie
Bossy, Mike
Bouchard, Butch
Boucher, Buck
Boucher, Frank
Bourque, Ray(mond Jean)
Bower, Johnny
Bowie, Russell
Bowman, Scotty
Brimsek, Frankie
Broadbent, Punch
Broda, Turk
Broten, Neal LaMoy
Bucyk, John Paul
Burch, Billy
Cameron, Harry
Carbonneau, Guy
Carlyle, Randy
Carpenter, Bobby
Carson, Jimmy
Cheevers, Gerry
Chelios, Chris
Christian, Dave
Christoff, Steve
Clancy, King
Clapper, Dit
Clark, Wendel
Clarke, Bobby
Cleghorn, Sprague
Coffey, Paul (Douglas)
Colville, Neil McNeil
Conacher, Charlie
Connell, Alex
Cook, Bill
Coulter, Art(hur Edmund)
Courneyor, Yvan Serge
Cowley, Bill
Craig, Jim
Crawford, Rusty
Crozier, Roger Allan
Darragh, Jack
Davidson, Scotty
Day, Hap
Delvecchio, Alex Peter
Denneny, Cy(ril)
Dionne, Marcel Elphege
Drillon, Gordie

Drinkwater, Charles
  Graham
Dryden, Ken(neth Wayne)
Durnan, Bill
Dutton, Red
Dye, Babe
Eagleson, Alan
Eruzione, Mike
Esposito, Phil(ip Anthony)
Esposito, Tony
Federko, Bernie
Fedorov, Sergei
Ferguson, John Bowie
Foyston, Frank C
Francis, Emile Percy
Frederickson, Frank
Froese, Bob
Fuhr, Grant Scott
Gadsby, Bill
Gainey, Bob
Gardiner, Chuck
Gardiner, Herb(ert Martin)
Gardner, Jimmy
Geoffrion, Bernie
Gerard, Eddie
Giacomin, Eddie
Gilbert, Rod(rigue
  Gabriel)
Gillies, Clark
Gilmour, Billy
Gilmour, Doug
Goodfellow, Ebbie
Goring, Butch
Goulet, Michel
Green, Wilf(red Thomas)
Gretzky, Wayne
Hainsworth, George
Hall, Glenn Henry
Hall, Joe
Harvey, Doug(las
  Norman)
Hasek, Dominik
Hawerchuk, Dale
Hay, George W
Hern, Riley
Hextall, Bryan Aldwyn
Hextall, Ron(ald Jeffrey)
Holmes, Hap
Hooper, Tom
Horner, Red
Horton, Tim
Howe, Gordie
Howe, Mark Steven
Howe, Syd(ney Harris)
Howell, Harry
Hull, Bobby
Hull, Brett (A.)
Hutton, Bouse
Hyland, Harry
Irvin, Dick
Jackson, Busher
Jagr, Jaromir
Janaszak, Steve
Jarvis, Doug(las)
Johnson, Ching
Johnson, Mark
Johnson, Moose
Johnson, Tom
Joliat, Aurel
Keats, Duke
Kelly, Red
Kennedy, Ted
Keon, Dave
Kerr, Tim(othy)
Klima, Petr
Konstantinov, Vladimir

HORSE OWNER

HORSE RACING OFFICIAL

HORSE TRAINER

HORTICULTURIST

HOSPITAL ADMINISTRATOR

HOSTAGE

HOTEL EXECUTIVE

Binns, Joseph Patterson
Giovenco, John Vincent
Grossinger, Jennie
Helmsley, Leona Mindy
  Rosenthal
Hilton, Conrad Nicholson
Hilton, William Barron
Isbell, Marion William
Johnson, Wallace Edward
Lewis, Rosa
Ritz, Cesar
Statler, Ellsworth Milton
Tschirky, Oscar
Wilson, Kemmons

HUMORIST

Barry, Dave
Bombeck, Erma (Louise)
Hook, Theodore Edward
Kerr, Orpheus C
Knox, E(dmund) G(eorge)
  V(alpy)
Locke, David Ross
O'Rourke, P J
Richter, Johann Paul
  Friedrich
Rogers, Will(iam Penn
  Adair)
Thompson, William
  Tappan
Thorpe, Thomas Bangs

HUNGER STRIKER

Devine, Michael
Doherty, Kieran
Hughes, Francis
Hurson, Martin
Lynch, Kevin
MacSwiney, Terence
McCreesh, Raymond
McDonnell, Joe
McIlwee, Thomas
O'Hara, Patrick
Sands, Bobby

ILLUSTRATOR

Abbey, Edwin Austin
Alajalov, Constantin
Anderson, Alexander
Anglund, Joan Walsh
Ardizzone, Edward Jeffrey
  Irving
Arisman, Marshall
Artzybasheff, Boris
  Mikhailovich
Barclay, McClelland
Beall, Lester Thomas
Beardsley, Aubrey Vincent
Bendick, Jeanne
Bennett, John
Bewick, Thomas
Bilibin, Ivan Iakolevich
Biro, Val
Blake, Quentin
Blanding, Don

Bonestell, Chesley
Bouche, Rene Robert
Breger, Dave
Brett, Jan Churchill
Briggs, Austin Eugene
Brinkley, Nell
Brooke, L Leslie
Brown, Marcia
Browne, Phiz
Brunhoff, Jean de
Brunhoff, Laurent de
Burger, Carl Victor
Burton, Virginia Lee
Busch, Wilhelm
Cady, (Walter) Harrison
Carle, Eric
Charlot, Jean
Chwast, Seymour
Clarke, Harry
Clave, Antoni
Cleland, Thomas Maitland
Clokey, Art
Cooney, Barbara
Corcos, Lucille
Cowles, Fleur Fenton
Cox, Palmer
Craig, Helen
Crane, Walter
Cruikshank, George
Darley, Felix Octavius
  Carr
Daugherty, James Henry
D'Aulaire, Edgar Parin
D'Aulaire, Ingri
  Mortenson
DeAngeli, Marguerite
  Lofft
Denslow, W(illiam)
  W(allace)
Dillon, Diane Claire
  Sorber
Dillon, Leo
Dohanos, Stevan
Dongen, Kees van
Dorne, Albert
Du Bois, William Pene
Duvoisin, Roger Antoine
Dwiggins, William
  Addison
Eckert, Horst
Eichenberg, Fritz
Engelbreit, Mary
Enright, Elizabeth
Falter, John
Feelings, Tom
Fenton, Carroll Lane
Finlay, Virgil
Fischer, Anton Otto
Fisher, Harrison
Flora, James (Royer)
Folon, Jean-Michel
Fox, Fontaine Talbot, Jr.
Frost, Arthur Burdett
Funikawa, Gyo
Furniss, Harry
Gag, Wanda
Gannett, Ruth
Garnett, Eve C R
Gerard, Jean Ignace
  Isidore
Gerrard, Roy
Gibson, Charles Dana
Gilbert, John, Sir
Gilliam, Terry (Vance)
Glanzman, Louis S
Glaser, Milton

Goffstein, Marilyn
Goodall, John Strickland
Gorey, Edward St. John
Gramatky, Hardie
Grant, Gordon
Greenaway, Kate
Handford, Martin
Helck, Peter
Held, John, Jr.
Herford, Oliver
Hess, Richard
Hoff, Sydney
Hogrogian, Nonny
Houston, James Archibold
Hughes, Arthur
Hughes, George
Hurd, Clement
Hurd, Peter
James, Will(iam Roderick)
Kauffer, Edward
  McKnight
Keats, Ezra Jack
Kemble, Edward
  W(indsor)
Knight, Hilary
Kredel, Fritz
Kurelek, William
Lasker, Joe
Laurel, Alicia Bay
Lawson, Robert
Leaf, Munro
Leech, John
Leighton, Clare Veronica
  Hope
Lenski, Lois
Leslie, Frank
Levine, David
Lindner, Richard
Lobel, Arnold Stark
Lossing, Benson John
Maclise, Daniel
Maestro, Giulio
Marsh, Reginald
Marshall, James Edward
Martin, David Stone
McCloskey, Robert
Meggendorfer, Lothar
Moran, Thomas
Moss, Geoffrey
Nast, Thomas
O'Neill, Rose Cecil
Peake, Mervyn Laurence
Pears, Charles
Peirce, Waldo
Pennell, Joseph Stanley
Petersham, Maud
Petersham, Miska
Pinkney, Jerry
Pinkwater, Daniel Manus
Pitz, Henry Clarence
Pogany, Willy
Politi, Leo
Potter, Beatrix
Price, Garrett
Provensen, Alice Rose
  Twitchell
Provensen, Martin
Purdy, Susan Gold
Pyle, Howard
Rackham, Arthur
Raskin, Ellen
Rey, Hans Augustus
Rico, Don(ato)
Robinson, Boardman
Robinson, W Heath
Rockwell, Norman

Rose, Carl
Scarry, Richard (McClure)
Sendak, Maurice Bernard
Seredy, Kate
Seuss, Doctor
Shepard, Ernest Howard
Slobodkin, Louis
Slobodkina, Esphyr
Smith, Jessie Wilcox
Sperry, Armstrong W
Stahl, Ben(jamin Albert)
Steig, William
Stuart, Kenneth James
Tenggren, Gustaf Adolf
Tenniel, John, Sir
Tomes, Margot
Trnka, Jiri
Ulreich, Nura Woodson
Ungerer, Tomi
Upton, Florence Kate
VanAllsburg, Chris
VonSchmidt, Harold
Whistler, Rex
Wiese, Kurt
Wildsmith, Brian
Williams, Garth
  Montgomery
Wilson, Edward Arthur
Wyeth, N(ewell)
  C(onvers)

IMPOSTER

Demara, Ferdinand Waldo,
  Jr.
Ireland, William Henry
Monmouth, James Scott,
  Duke
Orton, Arthur
Psalmanazar, George
Pugachev, Yemelyan I
Wilson, Sarah

IMPRESARIO

Barbaja, Domenico
Blackwell, (Samuel) Earl,
  Jr.
Chapin, Schuyler Garrison
Cochran, C(harles) B(lake)
Crosby, John
Dent, Edward Joseph
Fox, Carol
Frohman, Charles
Gallo, Fortune
Giardini, Felice di
Granz, Norman
Hammerstein, Oscar
Harris, Augustus, Sir
Hurok, Sol(omon
  Isaievich)
Manners, Charles
Mapleson, James Henry
Maretzek, Max
Morley, Eric Douglas
Rosa, Carl
Russell, Henry
Savage, Henry Wilson
Strakosch, Maurice
Turner, Ted
Whitney, Harry Payne
Wilson, Sunnie

INDUSTRIALIST

Baldwin, Matthias William
Beckman, Arnold (Orville)
Bergen, John Joseph
Berwind, Charles G
Breech, Ernest Robert
Brush, Charles Francis
Butler, Paul
Carnegie, Andrew
Chang Chien
Corey, William Ellis
Cowen, Joshua Lionel
Crawford, Frederick
    C(oolidge)
Crown, Henry
Deere, John
Duke, Benjamin Newton
DuPont, Eleuthere Irenee
Eastman, George
Ferguson, Harry George
Flick, Friedrich
Folger, Henry Clay
Frick, Henry Clay
Goodrich, Benjamin
    Franklin
Gregg, William
Grumman, Leroy Randle
Guggenheim, Meyer
Hewitt, Abram Stevens
Horlick, William
Hughes, Howard Robard
Irving, Kenneth Colin
Kaiser, Edgar Fosburgh
Kaiser, Henry John
Keith, Minor Cooper
Kent, Arthur Atwater
Knudsen, William Signius
Krupp, Alfred
Lowell, Francis Cabot
Matsushita, Konosuke
Michelin, Francois
Morris, William Richard
Mott, Charles Stewart
Oppenheimer, Harry
    Frederick
Patino, Simon Iturri
Pew, J(ohn) Howard
Rathenau, Walter
Rockefeller, William
Sasakawa, Ryoichi
Schwab, Charles Michael
Siemens, (Ernst) Werner
    von
Sloan, Alfred Pritchard, Jr.
Swope, Gerard
Tata, J(ehangir) R(atanji)
    D(adbhoy)
Tata, Jamshedji
    Nusserwanji
Thyssen, Fritz
Wenner-Gren, Axel
    (Lenard)
Willys, John North
Winchester, Oliver Fisher
Wolfson, Louis Elwood

INSURANCE EXECUTIVE

Day, Joseph Paul
DeMoss, Arthur S
Hill, Jesse, Jr.
Joanis, John W

Kemper, James S(cott)
MacArthur, John Donald
Procope, Ernesta Gertrude
    Foster Bowman
Spaulding, Charles Clinton
Walker, A Maceo, Sr.

INTELLECTUAL

Bello y Lopez, Andres
Ram Camul Sen

INTERIOR DECORATOR

Boffrand, Gabriel Germain
Buatta, Mario
Cuvillies, Francois
Draper, Dorothy
    Tuckerman
Hicks, David (Nightingale)
Hoffmann, Josef
Mendl, Lady Elsie de
    Wolfe
Pahlmann, William Carroll
Stoddard, Alexandra

INVENTOR

Abbott, Scott
Abplanalp, Robert H
Acheson, Edward
    Goodrich
Ader, Clement
Alexanderson, Ernst
    Frederik Werner
Allen, John
Appleby, John Francis
Arkwright, Richard, Sir
Armstrong, Edwin Howard
Atwood, Francis Clarke
Babbage, Charles
Babbitt, Benjamin Talbot
Babcock, Harold Delos
Babcock, Horace Welcome
Baekeland, Leo Hendrik
Bailey, Donald Coleman,
    Sir
Banneker, Benjamin
Barnack, Oskar
Bauersfeld, Walther
Bausch, Edward
Bausch, John Jacob
Beach, Alfred Ely
Beach, Moses Yale
Beckman, Arnold (Orville)
Belin, Edouard
Bell, Alexander Graham
Bell, Herbert A
Bendix, Vincent
Berliner, Emile
Bernstein, Allan
Bessemer, Henry, Sir
Bigelow, Erastus Brigham
Birdseye, Clarence Frank
Bissell, Melville Reuben
Bitter, Francis
Bjorn-Larsen, Knut
Blair, William Richards
Blanchard, Thomas
Bogardus, James

Booth, Hubert Cecil
Borden, Gail
Bosch, Robert August
Bowie, Jim
Boykin, Otis Frank
Bradham, Caleb D
Braestrup, Carl Bjorn
Bramah, Joseph
Breguet, Abraham Louis
Browning, John Moses
Brunel, Isambard
    Kingdom
Brunel, Marc Isambard,
    Sir
Brush, Charles Francis
Budding, Edwin
Bunsen, Robert Wilhelm
    Eberhard
Burroughs, William
    Seward
Bushnell, David
Butterick, Ebenezer
Carlson, Chester Floyd
Carrier, Willis Haviland
Cartwright, Edmund
Chardonnet, Louis Marie
    Hilaire Bernigaud
Chretien, Henri
Christie, John Walter
Coanda, Henri Marie
Colt, Samuel
Colton, Gardner Quincy
Coolidge, William David
Coster, Laurens Janszoon
Cowen, Joshua Lionel
Cristofori, Bartolomeo di
    Francesco
Crowell, Luther Childs
Curtis, Charles Gordon
Curtiss, Glenn Hammond
Daguerre, Louis Jacques
    Mande
Dahlgren, John Adolphus
    Bernard
Daimler, Gottlieb
    (Wilhelm)
Daniell, John Frederic
Darrow, Charles Brace
Davenport, Thomas
Davis, Noel
DeForest, Lee
De La Rue, Warren
De Mestral, Georges
Deringer, Henry
Dewar, James A
Dickson, Earle Ensign
Diemer, Walter
Diesel, Rudolf Christian
    Karl
Dines, William Henry
Dolby, Ray M(ilton)
Dunlop, John Boyd
Dunne, John William
Duryea, Charles Edgar
Duryea, J(ames) Frank
Eastman, George
Eckert, John Presper, Jr.
Edgeworth, Richard Lovell
Edison, Thomas Alva
Edwards, Willard Eldridge
Ellis, Carleton
Epperson, Frank W
Essen, Louis
Etscorn, Frank
Evans, Oliver
Evinrude, Ole

Fairbanks, Thaddeus
Fairchild, Sherman Mills
Farber, Edward Rolke
Farmer, Moses Gerrish
Farnsworth, Philo Taylor
Ferris, George Washington
    Gale
Fessenden, Reginald
    Aubrey
Fitch, John
Focke, Heinrich Karl
    Johann
Forrester, Jay Wright
Friese-Greene, William
    Edward
Fry, Art
Garand, John Cantius
Garcia, Joe
Gatling, Richard Jordan
Ged, William
Gerber, Daniel Frank
Gernsback, Hugo
Gillette, King Camp
Glidden, Joseph Farwell
Godowsky, Leopold, Jr.
Goerlich, John
Goldman, Sylvan N
Goldmark, Peter Carl
Goodwin, Hannibal
    Williston
Goodyear, Charles
Gorrie, John
Gougelman, Pierre
Gramme, Zenobe
    Theophile
Gray, Elisha
Graydon, James Weir
Greenwood, Chester
Gregg, John Robert
Hagelstein, Peter
Halstead, William S
Hammond, John Hays, Jr.
Hammond, Laurens
Haney, Chris
Haney, John
Hansom, Joseph Aloysius
Hare, Robert
Hargreaves, James
Hart, LeRoy
Harvey, Hayward
    Augustus
Haynes, Elwood
Hazeltine, (Louis) Alan
Head, Howard
Henry, Joseph
Heron of Alexandria
Hewitt, Peter Cooper
Hoe, Richard March
Holland, John Philip
Hollerith, Herman
Honeywell, Mark Charles
Hotchkiss, Benjamin
    Berkeley
Houdry, Eugene Jules
Howe, Elias
Hubert, Conrad
Hunt, Walter
Ingersoll, Simon
Ives, Frederic Eugene
Ives, Herbert Eugene
Iwatani, Toro
Jacquard, Joseph Marie
Jacuzzi, Candido
Jarvik, Robert Koffler
Jones, Arthur A
Judson, Egbert Putnam

Kahng, Dawon
Kalmus, Herbert Thomas
Kalmus, Natalie Mabelle
  Dunfee
Keller, Arthur C
Kellogg, John Harvey
Kelly, William
Kent, Arthur Atwater
Kloss, Henry E.
Kurzweil, Raymond C
Laennec, Rene Theophile
  Hyacinthe
Lake, Simon
Land, Edwin Herbert
Langley, Samuel Pierpont
Langstroth, Lorenzo
  Lorraine
Lanston, Tolbert
Latimer, Lewis Howard
Lewis, Isaac Newton
Lewyt, Alexander Milton
Libby, Willard Frank
Lilienthal, Otto
Link, Edwin Albert
Loomis, Mahion
Lovelock, James
Loyd, Sam(uel)
Lumiere, Auguste Marie
  Louis
Lumiere, Louis Jean
Lyot, Bernard Ferdinand
Mac Cready, Paul Beattie
MacDonald, Elizabeth G.
Macintosh, Charles
Mackaye, James Morrison
  Steele
Mannes, Leopold
  Damrosch
Mannlicher, Ferdinand
Marconi, Guglielmo
Marcus, Luis J
Mason, John L
Mason, Max
Matzeliger, Jan Ernest
Maxim, Hiram Percy
Maxim, Hiram Stevens,
  Sir
Maxim, Hudson
McCormick, Cyrus Hall
McCoy, Elijah
McMurray, Bette Clair
Mennen, Frederick
Mergenthaler, Ottmar
Midgeley, Thomas
Miller, Carl S
Montgolfier, Jacques
  Etienne
Montgolfier, Joseph
  Michel
Moog, Robert A
Morgan, Garrett Augustus
Morse, Samuel Finley
  Breese
Nelson, Christian
Newcomen, Thomas
Newman, Joseph Westley
Nobel, Alfred Bernhard
Norden, Carl Lukas
Olds, Ranson E(li)
Oliver, James
Otis, Elisha Graves
Oughtred, William
Page, Charles Grafton
Parsons, Charles Algernon,
  Sir
Paul, Les

Perkins, Jacob
Perky, Henry D
Piccard, Jacques Ernest
  Jean
Pierce, George
  Washington
Pitman, Isaac
Pitney, Arthur
Popov, Aleksandr
  Stepanovich
Porsche, Ferdinand
Pullman, George Mortimer
Pupin, Michael Idvorsky
Richter, Charles Francis
Saunders, William
  Laurence
Savery, Thomas
Sax, Adolphe (Antoine-
  Joseph)
Schick, Jacob
Schweppe, Jacob
Seibert, Florence B(arbara)
Selden, George Baldwin
Senefelder, Aloys
Siemens, (Ernst) Werner
  von
Siemens, William, Sir
Singer, Isaac Merrit
Skinner, Halcyon
Smith, Horace
Smith, Robert Lee
Spanel, Abram N
Spencer, Percy Le Baron
Sperry, Elmer Ambrose
Sperti, George Speri
Stanley, Francis Edgar
Stanley, Freelan O
Stephenson, George
Stevens, John
Stevens, Robert Livingston
Stibitz, George R.
Stout, William Bushnell
Suits, C(hauncey) G(uy)
Talbot, William Henry
  Fox
Taylor, Frederick Winslow
Tesla, Nikola
Thomas, Sidney Gilchrist
Thompson, John Taliaferro
Thomson, Elihu
Thurber, Charles
Timken, Henry
Trevithick, Richard
Ts'ai, Lun
Tupper, Earl Silas
Vaaler, Johan
Vail, Alfred Lewis
Van Depoele, Charles
  Joseph
Verrill, Alpheus Hyatt
Walker, Adam
Walker, Joseph
Waller, Fred(erick)
Wallis, Barnes Neville, Sir
Wankel, Felix
Waring, Fred Malcolm
Waterman, Lewis Edson
Watt, James
Welsbach, Carl Auer von,
  Baron
Westinghouse, George
Wheatstone, Charles, Sir
Wheeler, Schuyler Skaats
Whitney, Eli
Whittle, Frank, Sir
Wilson, Jerry

Woods, Granville T
Wright, Orville
Wright, Wilbur
Zamboni, Frank J
Zwicky, Fritz

JAZZ MUSICIAN

Allen, Red
Ammons, Albert C
Armstrong, Lil(lian
  Hardin)
Baker, Shorty
Barnet, Charlie
Basie, Count
Bechet, Sidney
Beiderbecke, Bix
Berigan, Bunny
Berry, Chu
Bigard, Albany Barney
  Leon
Blakey, Art
Blanton, Jimmy
Bolden, Buddy
Bradley, Will
Braff, Ruby
Brubeck, Dave
Brunis, George
Bushkin, Joe
Busse, Henry
Butterfield, Billy
Byrd, Charlie
Byrd, Donald
Cacers, Ernest
Carney, Harry Howell
Carter, Benny
Carter, Ron
Catlett, Big Sid
Christian, Charlie
Clayton, Buck
Cobb, Arnett Cleophus
Cobham, Billy
Cohn, Al
Coleman, Ornette
Collins, Lee
Coltrane, Trane
Condon, Eddie
Connick, Harry, Jr.
Corea, Chick
Crawford, James
  Strickland
Davis, Miles Dewey, III
Davison, Wild Bill
DeFranco, Buddy
DeParis, Wilbur
Desmond, Paul Breitenfeld
Dodds, Baby
Dodds, Johnny
Eldridge, Roy
Erwin, Pee Wee
Farmer, Art(hur Stewart)
Ferguson, Maynard
Firbank, Louis
Foster, Pops
Fountain, Pete(r Dewey)
Freeman, Bud
Garner, Erroll
Getz, Stan
Gillespie, Dizzy
Giuffre, James Peter
Golson, Benny
Gordon, Dexter Keith
Grappelli, Stephane
Guarnieri, Johnny
Hackett, Bobby

Haden, Charlie
Hampton, Lionel Leo
Hancock, Herbie
Hargrove, Roy
Harris, Willard Palmer
Hawkins, Bean
Heard, J.C.
Henderson, Joe
Hill, Chippie
Hines, Fatha
Hirt, Al(ois Maxwell)
Hodges, Johnny
Hubbard, Freddie
Hunt, Pee Wee
Jackson, Milt(on)
Jacquet, Illinois (Robert
  Russell)
Jamal, Ahmad
James, Bob
Johnson, Bunk
Johnson, Dink
Johnson, J J
Jones, Elvin
Jones, Jo(nathan)
Jordan, Louis
Kaminsky, Max
Kenny G
Keppard, Freddie
Kirk, Rahsaan Roland
Konitz, Lee
Ladnier, Tommy
Lang, Eddie
Lawson, Yank
Lewis, Meade Anderson
  Lux
Lunceford, Jimmy
Mangione, Chuck
Mann, Herbie
Manne, Shelly
Manone, Wingy
Marsala, Marty
Marsalis, Branford
Matlock, Matty
May, Billy
Mayall, John Brumwell
McCoy, Clyde
McGarity, Lou
McIntyre, Hal
McPartland, Jimmy
Metheny, Pat(rick Bruce)
Mezzrow, Mezz
Mingus, Charles
Montgomery, Wes
Morello, Joseph A
Morgan, Frank
Morton, Jelly Roll
Mulligan, Gerry
Murphy, Turk
Musso, Vido
Navarro, Fats
Newman, Joe Dwight
Noone, Jimmie
Norvo, Red
Ory, Kid
Page, Hot Lips
Parker, Charlie
Pass, Joe
Pepper, Art(hur Edward)
Peterson, Oscar Emanuel
Pettiford, Oscar
Pletcher, Stew
Powell, Earl
Price, Sammy
Redman, Don
Reinhardt, Django (Jean
  Baptiste)

Rich, Buddy
Roach, Max(well Lemuel)
Rogers, Shorty
Rollini, Adrian
Rollins, Sonny
Rushing, Jimmy
Russell, Pee Wee
Sauter, Eddie
Scott, Hazel Dorothy
Shields, Larry
Silver, Horace Ward
  Martin Tavares
Sims, Zoot
Smith, Clarence
Smith, Joe
Smith, William
Spanier, Muggsy
Stewart, Slam
Stitt, Sonny
Strayhorn, Billy
Tatum, Art(hur)
Taylor, Billy
Teagarden, Charles
Teagarden, Jack
Teschemacher, Frank
Threadgill, Henry
Tjader, Cal(len Radcliffe,
  Jr.)
Tough, Dave
Tristano, Leonard Joseph
Turner, Joe
Ventura, Charlie
Vinson, Cleanhead
Waller, Fats
Washington, Buck
Weatherford, Teddy
Webb, Chick
Whitfield, Mark
Williams, Cootie
Wilson, Teddy
Winding, Kai Chresten
Yancey, Jimmy
Young, Lester Willis
Young, Trummy
Cheatham, Adolphus

JEWELER

Breguet, Abraham Louis
Bulgari, Constantine
Bulgari, Giorgio
Bulova, Joseph
Cartier, Claude
Cartier, Louis J
Cartier, Pierre C
Faberge, Peter Carl
Lalique, Rene
Schlumberger, Jean
Tiffany, Charles Lewis
Winston, Harry

JOCKEY

Adams, John
Arcaro, Eddie
Atkinson, Ted
Cauthen, Steve
Cordero, Angel Tomas
Dancer, Stanley
Day, Pat
Desormeaux, Kent
Hartack, Billy
Haughton, Billy

Krone, Julie
Longden, Johnny
McCarron, Chris
Pincay, Laffit, Jr.
Rubin, Barbara Jo
Sande, Earl
Shoemaker, Willie
Smith, Robyn Caroline
Turcotte, Ron

JOURNALIST

Abbas, Khwaja Ahmad
Abbott, Scott
Abernethy, Robert Gordon
Abu-Jamal, Mumia
Abu Madi, Iliya
Ackerman, Carl William
Adamic, Louis
Adams, Franklin P(ierce)
Adams, Samuel Hopkins
Adelman, Kenneth Lee
Adzhubei, Aleksei
  I(vanovich)
Allen, Frederick Lewis
Allen, Larry
Allen, Robert Sharon
Allsop, Kenneth
Alsop, Joseph Wright, Jr.
Alsop, Stewart Johonnot
  Oliver
Altsheler, Joseph
  Alexander
Anderson, George Everett
Anderson, Jack Northman
Anderson, Terry A
Andrews, Bert
Anson, Robert Sam
Anthony, Edward
Apple, R(aymond)
  W(alter), Jr.
Arcaro, Eddie
Archerd, Army
Armstrong, Hamilton Fish
Arran, Arthur Kattendyke
  Strange David
Archibald Gore, Earl of
Attwood, William
  Hollingsworth
Axthelm, Pete(r Macrae)
Ayer, Harriet Hubbard
Babeuf, Francois-Noel
Bacharach, Bert(ram
  Mark)
Baer, Bugs
Baillie, Hugh
Baker, Russell Wayne
Baldwin, Hanson
  Weightman
Bandeira, Manuel
Bangor, Edward Henry
  Harold Ward, Viscount
Barbanell, Maurice
Barbosa, Ruy
Barlow, Joel
Barnes, Clive Alexander
Barnes, Djuna
Barnetson, William
  Denholm
Barr, Amelia Edith
  Huddleston
Barrett, Rona
Barry, Dave
Bartlett, Charles
  Leffingwell

Bassett, Ben
Bates, Daisy Lee Gatson
Battelle, Phyllis Marie
Baum, L(yman) Frank
Beach, Alfred Ely
Beale, Betty
Beatty, Morgan
Beck, Marilyn (Mohr)
Beebe, Lucius Morris
Bell, Arthur (Irving)
Benchley, Peter Bradford
Benet, William Rose
Bentley, Edmund Clerihew
Berendt, John
Berger, Meyer
Berkow, Ira Harvey
Bernstein, Carl
Bernstein, Theodore
  Menline
Bhattarai, Krishna Prasad
Bierce, Ambrose Gwinett
Bigelow, John
Biossat, Bruce
Birnie, William Alfred
  Hart
Bishop, Jim
Black, Winifred Sweet
Bloom, Murray Teigh
Bly, Nellie
Bodard, Lucien (Albert)
Bolitho, William
Bolles, Don F
Bombeck, Erma (Louise)
Bonsal, Stephen
Bottel, Helen Alfea
Bowell, Mackenzie, Sir
Bowles, Samuel, II
Boyle, Harold Vincent
Bradlee, Ben(jamin
  Crowninshield)
Brann, William Cowper
Brannigan, Bill
Bratteli, Trygve Martin
Brayman, Harold
Breslin, Jimmy
Briand, Rena
Brisbane, Arthur
Broder, David S
Brody, Jane Ellen
Broun, (Matthew)
  Heywood (Campbell)
Brown, Cecil B
Brown, Les(ter Louis)
Brown, Tina
Browne, Walter Shawn
Buchwald, Art(hur)
Buckmaster, Henrietta
Buel, Jesse
Bugbee, Emma
Bunner, Henry Cuyler
Burdett, Winston M.
Burgess, Anthony
Burgess, John Lawrie, Sir
Burgess, Thornton Waldo
Burman, Ben Lucien
Butterfield, Roger Place
Caen, Herb
Calder, Peter Ritchie
Calmer, Ned
Campbell, Donald Guy
Campbell, Roy
Canby, Vincent
Canham, Erwin Dain
Cannon, Jimmy
Cannon, Poppy
Capa, Cornell

Caputo, Philip Joseph
Caras, Roger Andrew
Carbine, Patricia Theresa
Carleton, Will
Carlile, Richard
Carmichael, John P
Carpenter, Leslie
Carpenter, Liz
Carter, Ernestine Marie
Cassini, Igor Loiewski
Catledge, Turner
Cattani, Richard J.
Catton, Bruce
Cerf, Bennett Alfred
Chadwick, Henry
Chamberlain, John
  Rensselaer
Chambers, Whittaker
Chapais, Thomas, Sir
Chennault, Anna Chan
Chernov, Viktor
  Mikhailovich
Chernyshevsky, Nikolai
  Gavrilovich
Cheshire, Maxine
Chew, Peter
Chideya, Farai (Nduu)
Childs, Marquis William
Chirol, Valentine, Sir
Christy, Marian
Clapper, Raymond Lewis
Clark, Robert Edward
Clarke, Marcus (Andrew
  Hislop)
Cobb, Irvin Shrewsbury
Cobbett, William
Cochran, Jacqueline
Cockburn, Claud
Coleridge, Hartley
Collins, Larry
Conniff, Frank
Connolly, Mike
Connor, William Neil, Sir
Connors, Dorsey
Considine, Bob
Constant de Rebeque,
  (Henri) Benjamin
Cony, Edward Roger
Cooke, Janet
Cooper, Kent
Cornell, Douglas B
Cortissoz, Royal
Corum, Martene Windsor
Cose, Ellis
Craig, May
Crankshaw, Edward
Croly, Herbert David
Croly, Jane Cunningham
Cromley, Raymond
  Avolon
Crosby, John Campbell
Crouch, Stanley
Crowley, Diane
Cudlipp, Hugh
Curie, Eve
Currie, Barton Wood
Daley, Arthur (John)
Daly, Thomas Augustine
Dana, Charles Anderson
Daniel, Clifton, Jr.
Daniel, Dan(iel)
Daniels, Jonathan Worth
Daniels, Josephus
Daniloff, Nicholas
Darwin, Bernard Richard
  Meirion

Davis, Clyde Brion
Davis, Elmer Holmes
Davis, Rebecca Blaine Harding
Davis, Richard Harding
Davis, Tobe
Dawkins, Wayne J(esse)
De Bow, James Dunwoody Brownson
Decter, Midge
Deford, Frank
Delaplane, Stanton Hill
Delcasse, Theophile
De Leon, Daniel
Del Pilar, Marcelo Hilario
Denenberg, Herbert Sidney
Denny, Ludwell
Dent, Alan Holmes
Desmoulins, Camille
DeVoto, Bernard Augustine
Dickinson, Brian
Divine, Arthur Durham
Dix, Dorothy
Dolbier, Maurice (Wyman)
Donovan, Hedley Williams
Donovan, Robert John
Door, Rheta Childe
Dorfman, Dan
Dorgan, Thomas Aloysius
Dowd, Maureen (Brigid)
Dreifus, Claudia
Drew, Elizabeth Brenner
Drummond, Roscoe
Dubnov, Simon
Ducommun, Elie
Dunne, Dominick
Dunton, Davidson
Duranty, Walter
Durslag, Melvin
Dwyer, Cynthia
Edel, Leon
Edwards, India Moffett
Edwards, Willard
Elegant, Robert Sampson
Ellis, Harry Bearse
Elson, Robert Truscott
Ethridge, Mark Foster, Jr.
Evans, Heloise Cruse
Evans, Orrin C
Evans, Rowland, Jr.
Evans, Walker
Fairfax, Beatrice
Fallaci, Oriana
Fallows, James (Mackenzie)
Falls, Joe
Fanning, Katherine Woodruff
Farrington, Elizabeth Pruett (Mary)
Faubus, Orval E(ugene)
Faust, Frederick Schiller
Felker, Clay S
Fenten, D X
Fenton, Thomas Trail
Fernandez de Lizardi, Jose Joaquin
Ferrero, Guglielmo
Ferry, Jules Francois Camille
Fidler, Jimmie
Field, Eugene

Fischer, John
FitzGerald, Frances
Flanner, Janet
Fleeson, Doris
Foley, Martha
Foot, Michael
Forbes, Bertie
Fowler, Gene
Fraenkel, Heinrich
France, Harry Clinton
Frankel, Max
Freeman, Douglas S
Freneau, Philip Morin
Freytag, Gustav
Friedman, Milton
Friedman, Thomas L(oren)
Friendly, Alfred
Gage, Nicholas
Gale, Zona
Gallico, Paul William
Garcia, Cristina
Gard, Wayne
Gardner, Hy
Gelb, Arthur
Gelb, Leslie Howard
Gellhorn, Martha Ellis
Genthe, Arnold
Gentz, Friedrich Von
George, Henry, Jr.
Gerold, Karl
Gervasi, Frank Henry
Geyer, Georgie Anne
Gibbons, Floyd Phillips
Gidal, Tim
Gilbreth, Frank Bunker, Jr.
Gillott, Jacky
Gilmore, Eddy Lanier King
Ginzburg, Ralph
Giroud, Francoise
Gleason, Ralph Joseph
Godkin, E(dwin) L(awrence)
Gold, Michael
Gooch, George Peabody
Goode, Mal
Goodman, Ellen Holtz
Gordon-Lazareff, Helene
Goren, Charles Henry
Gorkin, Jess
Gorman, Herbert Sherman
Grady, Henry Woodfin
Graham, Fred P(atterson)
Graham, Sheilah
Grant, Bruce
Grant, Jane
Greene, Bob
Greene, Ward
Greenfield, Meg
Gregory, Bettina Louise
Groth, John August
Grunwald, Henry Anatole
Guerin, Veronica
Guest, Edgar A(lbert)
Guthrie, A(lfred) B(ertram), Jr.
Gutman, Roy
Haber, Joyce
Hagerty, James Campbell
Halberstam, David
Hale, Nancy
Hale, Sarah Josepha Buell
Haley, Alex (Murray Palmer)
Hamill, Pete
Hare, James Henry

Harman, Jeanne Perkins
Harris, Derek
Harris, Frank
Harris, Sydney J(ustin)
Harsch, Joseph Close
Harte, (Francis) Bret
Haskell, Arnold Lionel
Hayford, J(oseph) E(phraim)Casely
Haykal, Muhammad Husain
Hearn, Lafcadio
Heatter, Gabriel
Hebert, Jacques Rene
Heckscher, August
Hellinger, Mark
Helms, Jesse Alexander, Jr.
Heloise
Hemingway, Ernest (Miller)
Hemingway, Mary Welsh
Hendrick, Burton Jesse
Henkle, Henrietta
Henry, O
Henry, William M
Henson, Maria
Hentoff, Nat(han Irving)
Hersey, John (Richard)
Hersh, Seymour
Herzl, Theodor
Hewitt, William Archibald
Hibbs, Ben
Hickok, Lorena A
Higgins, Marguerite
Hightower, John Marmann
Holbrook, Stewart Hall
Hoppe, Arthur Watterson
Hopper, Hedda
Hottelet, Richard C(urt)
Hough, Henry Beetle
Howar, Barbara
Howard, Jane Temple
Howard, Roy Wilson
Howard, Sidney Coe
Howe, Louis McHenry
Howell, Clark
Hubbard, Kin
Hughes, Emmet John
Hughes, Irene Finger
Hughes, Langston
Huie, William Bradford
Hunt, Frazier
Igoe, Hype
Ingersoll, Ralph McAllister
Ingrassia, Paul
Inukai, Tsuyoshi
Irvin, Robert W
Irwin, Wallace (Admah)
Irwin, Will(iam Henry)
Jacoby, Oswald
Johnson, Gerald White
Johnson, Lionel Pigot
Johnson, Paul (Bede)
Joseph, Richard
Kahn, Roger
Kantor, Mackinlay
Kaplow, Herbert Elias
Kapuscinski, Ryszard
Karamzin, Nikolai Mikhailovich
Karpin, Fred Leon
Karsh, Yousuf
Kaufman, George S(imon)
Kempton, (James) Murray

Kendall, Amos
Kenny, Nick
Keogh, James
Keynes, John Maynard, Baron
Khanga, Yelena
Kiernan, Walter
Kilgallen, Dorothy
Kilgore, Bernard
Kilpatrick, James J(ackson), Jr.
Kingsbury-Smith, Joseph
Kiplinger, W(illard) M(onroe)
Kirk, Russell (Amos)
Klein, Abraham Moses
Kleinfield, Sonny
Knebel, Fletcher
Knudson, Tom
Kohlmeier, Louis Martin, Jr.
Kraft, Joseph
Krassner, Paul
Krock, Arthur Bernard
Kuhn, Irene
Kupcinet, Irv
Lahey, Edwin A(loysius)
Lambert, Eleanor
Landers, Ann
Lardner, George, Jr.
Lardner, Ring(gold Wilmer), Sr.
Lasky, Victor
Lawrence, David
Lawson, Thomas William
Lebowitz, Fran(ces Ann)
Lehmann, John Frederick
Lemon, Mark
Lerner, Max
Levin, Bernard
Lewis, Anthony
Lewis, Flora
Lewis, William Arthur, Sir
Liebling, Abbot Joseph
Lilly, Doris
Lincoln, G(eorge) Gould
Lindauer, Lois L
Lindstrom, Pia
Lippmann, Walter
Lipton, Eric
Lisagor, Peter Irvin
Livermore, Mary Ashton Rice
Livingston, J(oseph) A(rnold)
Locke, Richard Adams
Loeb, Sophia Irene Simon
Loeb, William
Lovejoy, Elijah Parish
Lubell, Samuel
Lucas, Jim Griffing
Lyons, Leonard
Macaulay, Herbert
MacCarthy, Desmond Charles Otto, Sir
MacDonald, Dwight
MacDougall, Curtis Daniel
Mackenzie, William Lyon
MacLeish, Archibald
MacLeish, Rod(erick)
Malcolm, Andrew H(ogarth)
Malone, Dan
Maney, Richard
Mankiewicz, Frank Fabian
Mannes, Marya

Occupation Index

Walker, Harold Blake
Walker, Stanley
Wallace, Ed(ward Tatum)
Wallace-Johnson, Isaac
  Theophilus Akunna
Waln, Nora
Ward, Artemus
Ward, Paul W
Warner, Denis Ashton
Washburn, Charles
Washington, Laura S.
Wasson, R(obert) Gordon
Watson, Mark Skinner
Weaver, William
Wechsberg, Joseph
Wechsler, James Arthur
Weed, Thurlow
Wehrwein, Austin Carl
Weingarten, Violet Brown
Weintal, Edward
Wellman, Paul Iselin
Wellman, Walter
Wells, Linton
Wells-Barnett, Ida Bell
Wenner, Jann
Werth, Alexander
Wesley, Valerie Wilson
West, Rebecca, Dame
Whitaker, Rogers E(rnest)
  M(alcolm)
White, William Allen
White, William S(mith)
Whitehead, Don(ald Ford)
Whitman, Alden
Wibberley, Leonard
  Patrick O'Connor
Wicker, Tom
Wiesel, Elie(zer)
Wiggins, J(ames) R(ussell)
Wilder, Robert Ingersoll
Will, George F(rederick)
Wille, Lois Jean
Williams, Ben Ames
Williams, George
  Washington
Willis, Nathaniel Parker
Wills, Garry
Wilson, Earl
Wilson, Lyle Campbell
Winchell, Walter
Wind, Herbert Warren
Wolfert, Ira
Woltman, Frederick Enos
Woods, Donald
Woodward, Bob
Woodworth, Samuel
Worrill, Conrad (W.)
Wright, Cobina
Yardley, Jonathan
Yarmon, Betty
Zaslow, Jeff
Zenger, John Peter
Zhukov, Georgi
  Alexandrovich
Zia, Helen
Zola, Emile (Edouard
  Charles)

JUDGE

Adams, Annette Abbott
Alexander, Joyce London
Allen, Florence Ellinwood
Allen, Macon B
Amsterdam, Birdie

Batts, Deborah A.
Baylor, Robert Emmet
  Bledsoe
Bazelon, David L(ionel)
Bean, Roy
Bigge, John Thomas
Blackstone, William, Sir
Bork, Robert Heron
Bracton, Henry de
Carson, Edward Henry
Cassin, Rene-Samuel
Celebrezze, Anthony
  J(oseph)
Cline, Genevieve Rose
Cockrell, Ewing
Coke, Edward, Sir
Crater, Joseph Force
Davies, Ronald N(orwood)
Denning, Alfred
  Thompson
Diggs-Taylor, Anna
Donlon, Mary Honor
Ellery, William
Evatt, Herbert Vere
Feuerbach, Paul Johann
  Anselm
Garrison, Jim C.
Ginsburg, Douglas
  Howard
Haliburton, Thomas
  Chandler
Hand, Learned
Hastie, William Henry
Haynsworth, Clement
  Furman, Jr.
Higginbotham, A(loysius)
  Leon, Jr.
Hoffman, Julius Jennings
Hopkins, Stephen
Hufstedler, Shirley (Ann)
  M(ount)
Hughes, Richard J(oseph)
Hughes, Sarah Tilghman
Huntington, Samuel
Ito, Lance
Jennings, Robert Yewdall
Johnson, Norma L.
  Holloway
Justice, William Wayne
Kaufman, Irving R(obert)
Kaufman, Joseph William
Kearse, Amalya Lyle
Keith, Damon (Jerome)
Kennon, Robert Floyd
Kent, James
Kerner, Otto
Landis, Frederick
Lausche, Frank John
Lindsey, Benjamin Barr
Lowell, John
Mallett, Conrad (LeRoy),
  Jr.
Mascarenhas Monteiro,
  Antonio
Matthews, Burnita
  S(helton)
McDonald, Gabrielle
  (Anne) Kirk
Medina, Harold Raymond
Meskill, Thomas J
Mikva, Abner Joseph
Miller, William Ernest
Motley, Constance Baker
Murphy, Thomas F(rancis)
O'Dalaigh, Cearbhall

Orlando, Vittorio
  Emanuele
Parker, Alton Brooks
Parsons, James
Pecora, Ferdinand
Posner, Richard Allen
Richardson, Scovel
Rifkind, Simon H(irsch)
Rothwax, Harold
Russell, Edward Frederick
  Langley, Baron of
  Liverpool
Rutledge, John
Ryan, Sylvester James
Sampson, Edith Spurlock
Sears-Collins, Leah J.
Selden, John
Sewall, Samuel
Shaw, Lemuel
Sirica, John Joseph
Stammler, Rudolf
Stout, Juanita Kidd
Thompson, John
  S(parrow) D(avid), Sir
Trumbull, John
Trumbull, Jonathan
Underhill, John
Urrutia Lleo, Manuel
Voelker, John Donaldson
Vyshinsky, Andrei
  Yanurievich
Widgery, John Passmore,
  Baron
Williams, G(erhard)
  Mennen
Williams, William
Wolcott, Oliver, Sr.
Wood, John Howland, Jr.
Wythe, George
Youngdahl, Luther
  Wallace

JURIST

Ahmed, Shahabuddin
Altamira Y Crevea, Rafael
Barton, Edmund
Brown, Henry Billings
Curtis, Benjamin Robbins
Drago, Luis Maria
Elias, Taslim Olawale
Freeman, Charles Eldridge
George, James Zachariah
Gierke, Otto von
Griffith, Samuel Walker
Henderson, Richard
ibn Hazm, Abu
  Muhammad Ali
Iredell, James
Jay, William
McLean, John
Miller, Samuel Freeman
Montesquieu, Charles
  Louis de Secondat,
  Baron
Pobedonostsev, Konstantin
  Petrovich
Pufendorf, Samuel von
Reeve, Tapping
Reuchlin, Johann
Robinson, John Beverley
Sa, Mem de
Savigny, Friedrich Karl
  von
Shippen, Edward

Thomasius
Tourgee, Albion Winegar
Tyler, Royall
Ulpian, Domitius
Whittaker, Charles Evans

KIDNAP VICTIM

Bronfman, Samuel

KING

Affonso, I
Agesilaus, II
Agis, IV
Alaungpaya
Alexander of Yugoslavia
Alfonso, I
Alfonso, III
Alfonso, VI
Alfonso, X
Antigonus, I
Antiochus, III
Antiochus, IV
Baldwin, I
Bernadotte, Jean Baptiste
Bonaparte, Louis
Cetshwayo
Charles, II
Charles, III
Charles, IV
Charles, V
Charles, VI
Charles, VII
Charles Albert
Chongjo
Chulalongkorn
Cleomenes, I
Cleomenes, III
David, I
Dingane
Edward the Elder
Ethelred the Unready
Ezana
Faisal, I
Ferdinand
Ferdinand, II
Ferdinand, VII
Frederick William, III
Frederick William, IV
Fuad, I
Gaiseric
Gustavus, I
Gustavus, III
Harold, I
Harold, III
Harsha
Henry, IV
Jeroboam, I
John, II
Khosrow, I
Kojong
Kwanggaet'o
Kwangjong
Lalibela
Laszlo, I
Leopold, I
Lobengula
Louis, VI
Louis, VII
Louis, XII
Louis, XIII
Louis, XVIII

Occupation Index

Crockett, George (William), Jr.
Culvahouse, Art(hur Boggess, Jr.)
Culver, John Chester
Darden, Christopher A.
Darrow, Clarence Seward
Dash, Samuel
Davies, Joseph Edward
Davis, Clive Jay
Davis, John Williams
Days, Drew S(aunders), III
Dean, Arthur H(obson)
Dean, John Wesley
Dees, Morris S(eligman), Jr.
Denenberg, Herbert Sidney
Dershowitz, Alan M
Diefenbaker, John George
Dies, Martin, Jr.
Doar, John Michael
Doherty, Brian
Dole, Sanford Ballard
Douglas, Cathleen Curran Heffernan
Douglas, James Henderson, Jr.
Dudley, Barbara
Dulles, Allen Welsh
Dulles, John Foster
Dumas, Roland
Eaton, Dorman Bridgman
Echohawk, John E.
Echo-Hawk, Walter R.
Edelman, Marian Wright
Edley, Christopher Fairfield
Edmunds, George Franklin
Edwards, Edwin Washington
Estrada Cabrera, Manuel
Estrich, Susan
Evarts, William Maxwell
Fairstein, Linda
Field, David Dudley
Finletter, Thomas Knight
Foley, Tom
Fong, Hiram Leong
Fosdick, Raymond Blaine
Fouquier-Tinville, Antoine Quentin
Frei, Eduardo
Frohnmayer, John Edward
Frondizi, Arturo
Fuller, Millard (Dean)
Futter, Ellen Victoria
Galloway, Joseph
Galvin, Martin
Gambetta, Leon
Gandhi, Mahatma
Gardner, Erle Stanley
Garment, Leonard
Garrison, Lloyd K(irkham)
Garvey, Ed(ward Robert)
Gary, Willie E.
Gellhorn, Walter
George, James Zachariah
Gerry, Elbridge Thomas
Giesler, Jerry
Glass, Montague (Marsden)
Gobat, Charles Albert
Goodell, Charles Ellsworth
Goodwin, Richard N(aradhof)

Gourdine, Simon (Peter)
Graham, Lawrence Otis
Gray, C(layland) Boyden
Griffin, Anthony P.
Griffin, Bob
Grimke, Archibald H(enry)
Griswold, Erwin N(athaniel)
Guinier, Lani
Gurney, Edward John
Halleck, Charles Abraham
Hamilton, Andrew
Hatch, Carl A
Hawkins, Steven (Wayne)
Hayes, Robert Michael
Hayford, J(oseph) E(phraim)Casely
Hays, Will Harrison
Heyward, Thomas, Jr.
Hickey, William
Higgins, George V.
Hill, Anita Faye
Hills, Roderick M
Hirschorn, Joel
Hiss, Alger
Holder, Eric H., Jr.
Hooper, William
Hopkinson, Francis
Hore-Belisha, Leslie, Baron
Hosmer, Craig
Houston, Charles Hamilton
Hoyle, Edmond
Humes, James Calhoun
Hurley, Patrick Jay
Hutchins, Robert Maynard
Hyatt, Joel
Ingersoll, Robert Green
Innocent, III, Pope
Janklow, Morton Lloyd
Jaworski, Leon
Jenkins, Ray Howard
Johnson, Nicholas
Johnson, Reverdy
Johnson, Robert T.
Jones, Elaine R.
Jordan, Barbara C(harline)
Kagel, Sam
Kalmbach, Herbert Warren
Kampelman, Max M
Katz, Milton
Katzenbach, Nicholas de Belleville
Kaufman, Joseph William
Keating, Kenneth B
Kempner, Robert M(aximilian) W(asilii)
Kennard, William Earl
Kennedy, Florynce
Kennedy, John F(itzgerald), Jr.
Kheel, Theodore Woodrow
Kickingbird, Kirke
King, Bernice Albertine
Kirbo, Charles H(ughes)
Kucan, Milan
Kunstler, William M(oses)
Kurzban, Ira Jay
Kutner, Luis
La Fontaine, Henri Marie
Lafontant-Mankarious, Jewel (Stradford)

La Guardia, Fiorello Henry
Lane, Mark
Langdell, Christopher Columbus
Lansing, Robert
Lawrence, William Beach
Laxalt, Paul
Leibowitz, Samuel Simon
Leonard, Daniel
Lie, Jonas Laurite Idemil
Lie, Trygve Halvdan
Lilienthal, David Eli
Liman, Arthur L(awrence)
Lincoln, Robert Todd
Lindsay, John Vliet
Linowitz, Sol Myron
Lipshutz, Robert Jerome
Lipsig, Harry H(avon)
Lipsky, Eleazar
Lipton, Martin
Locklear, Arlinda Faye
Lockwood, Belva Ann Bennett
Lowden, Frank O(rren)
Lowenstein, Allard Kenneth
Lynd, Staughton (Craig)
MacKinnon, Catharine A(lice)
Maitland, Frederic William
Mansfield, Arabella
Mardian, Robert Charles
Martin, Luther
Martinez, Vilma Socorro
Maverick, Maury
Mays, David John
McCormach, Mark Hume
McCormack, John William
McDougall, Gay J.
McIntyre, James Talmadge, Jr.
McKean, Thomas
McPhail, Sharon
Minow, Newton Norman
Mitchell, George John
Mitchelson, Marvin M(orris)
Mitsotakis, Constantine
Montagu, Ewen
Moore, John Bassett
Morgenthau, Robert Morris
Morrison, Trudi Michelle
Mortimer, John Clifford
Murphy, Thomas F(rancis)
Murray, Pauli
Napolitano, Janet
Neal, James Foster
Nehru, Motilal
Nizer, Louis
Nolte, Henry R, Jr.
Norton, Eleanor Holmes
O'Connor, Basil
O'Dwyer, Paul
Ogletree, Charles (J.), Jr.
O'Hair, Madalyn Murray
Olney, Richard
O'Steen, Van
Patman, (John Williams) Wright
Patrick, Deval Laurdine
Paul, Alice
Penn, John
Phillips, Lena Madesin

Pinchback, P(inckney) B(enton) S(tewart)
Pirro, Jeanine (Ferris)
Plimpton, Francis Taylor Pearson
Power, Donald Clinton
Procter, Bryan Waller
Puccio, Thomas Philip
Quinn, John
Rai, Lala Lajpat
Ramo, Roberta Cooper
Ramphal, Shridath Surendranath
Randolph, Peyton
Rankin, J(ames) Lee
Rauh, Joseph Louis, Jr.
Ray, Charlotte E.
Read, George
Reading, 1st Marquess of
Reynolds, William Bradford
Richberg, Donald R(andall)
Richie, Leroy C.
Rifkind, Simon H(irsch)
Rivera, Jose Eustasio
Roa (y Garcia), Raul
Robb, Charles Spittal
Robinson, Randall
Root, Oren
Roper, Daniel C(alhoun)
Rosenfeld, Harry N(athan)
Ross, George
Rostow, Eugene Victor
Ruder, David Sturtevant
Saavdedra, Lamas Carlos
Saint Clair, James Draper
Sapru, Tej Bahadur
Scherr, Max
Schmidt, Benno C(harles), Jr.
Scribner, Fred C(lark), Jr.
Sears, John Patrick
Segretti, Donald H
Shea, William Alfred
Sheehan, Daniel P
Shriver, (Robert) Sargent
Simmons, Althea T L
Slotnick, Barry Ivan
Slovo, Joe
Smith, James
Soule, Pierre
Spaak, Paul-Henri
Spingarn, Arthur Barnett
Spofford, Charles M(erville)
Starr, Kenneth
Stassen, Harold Edward
Steinberg, Leigh
Stevenson, Adlai Ewing, III
Stevenson, Bryan (Allen)
Stockton, Richard
Stone, Thomas
Story, William Wetmore
Straus, Oscar Solomon
Strauss, Robert Schwarz
Suarez, Xavier Louis
Sunderland, Thomas E(lbert)
Taft, Charles Phelps
Tagliabue, Paul John
Taylor, John
Terry, Alfred Howe
Thomas, Franklin Augustine

Tilden, Samuel Jones
Townsend, William
  H(enry)
Train, Arthur Cheney
Tribe, Laurence Henry
Trist, Nicholas Philip
Trumka, Richard Louis
Tsongas, Paul E(fthemios)
Turkus, Burton B
Turner, Donald F(rank)
Uhlman, Wes(ley Carl)
Vance, Cyrus Roberts
Vanzant, Iyanla (Rhonda)
Vargas, Getulio Dornelles
Violet, Arlene
Volner, Jill Wine
von Mehren, Robert
  Brandt
Vorster, Balthazar
  Johannes
Wagner, Robert Ferdinand,
  Jr.
Walinsky, Adam
Walsh, Lawrence E
Walsh, Thomas James
Walton, George
Warnke, Paul Culliton
Washington, Walter
  Edward
Watkins, Arthur V(ivian)
Watson, Jack Hearn, Jr.
Welch, Joseph Nye
Werner, Pierre
Williams, Edward Bennett
Williams, Evelyn
Williams, Harrison
  Arlington, Jr.
Williams, Henry Sylvester
Williams, Patricia J(oyce)
Wilson, John Johnston
Woodcock, Amos Walter
  Wright
Wythe, George
Yarborough, Ralph
  W(ebster)
Yasui, Minoru
Young, Owen D
Zorbaugh, Geraldine
  B(one)

LECTURER

Ackerman, Forest J
Alexander, Shana
Angell, Norman
Bernier, Rosamond
  Margaret
Blatch, Harriot Eaton
  Stanton
Bolitho, Henry Hector
Bradshaw, John Elliot
Brown, John Mason
Brown, Tony
Carey, Ernestine Moller
  Gilbreth
Carleton, Will
Curtis, George William
Deloria, Vine (Victor), Jr.
Douglass, Frederick
Eliot, George Fielding
Farnham, Eliza Wood
  Burhans
Fletcher, Alice
  Cunningham
Fowler, Orson Squire

France, Harry Clinton
Frost, Edwin Brant
George, Zelma W(atson)
Gilbreth, Frank Bunker
Gilman, Charlotte Anna
  Perkins
Grimke, Sarah Moore
James, Henry, Sr.
Janeway, Eliot
Keen, Sam
Keller, Helen Adams
King, Coretta Scott
Leary, Timothy (Francis)
Lease, Mary Elizabeth
  Clyens
Lindsay, Vachel
Livermore, Mary Ashton
  Rice
Logan, Daniel
Lukas, J(ay) Anthony
Mann, Erika
McKenna, Terence
Norton, Elliot
Rogers, Will, Jr.
Rogers, Will(iam Penn
  Adair)
Ross, Edward Alsworth
Royden, Agnes Maude
Russell-McCloud, Patricia
  (A.)
Smith, Chard Powers
Smith, Gerald Lyman
  Kenneth
Strode, Hudson
Talbert, Mary Morris
  Burnett
Tennenbaum, Silvia
Vanzant, Iyanla (Rhonda)
Ward, Artemus
Westrup, J(ack) A(llan),
  Sir
Williamson, Marianne
Young, Ann Eliza Webb

LEGENDARY
FIGURE

Arthur, King
Helen of Troy
Hiawatha
Manco Capac
Robin Hood
Romulus
Tell, William

LEXICOGRAPHER

Baker, Theodore
Barnhart, Clarence L(ewis)
Bartlett, John
Bradley, Henry
Evans, Bergen Baldwin
Florio, John
Fowler, Henry Watson
Gould, George Milbry
Johnson, Samuel
Larousse, Pierre Athanase
Mathews, Mitford M
Murray, James Augustus
  Henry, Sir
Partridge, Eric
  Honeywood
Robert, Paul

Roget, Peter Mark
Webster, Noah
Worcester, Joseph
  Emerson

LIBRARIAN

Billington, James H(adley)
Carlson, William Hugh
Champollin-Figeac,
  Jacques-Joseph
Dewey, Melvil
Dibdin, Thomas Frognall
Evans, Charles
Franklin, Hardy R.
Greenaway, Emerson
Harsh, Vivian Gordon
Haviland, Virginia
Henderson, Robert W
Hutson, Jean Blackwell
Josey, E. J.
Larkin, Philip Arthur
Mearns, David Chambers
Mumford, Lawrence
  Quincy
Owens, Major (Robert)
Panizzi, Anthony, Sir
Patmore, Coventry Kersey
  Dighton
Placzek, Adolf K(urt)
Poole, William Frederick
Ready, William Bernard
Shera, Jesse Hauk
Sonneck, Oscar George
  Theodore
Teggart, Frederick J.
Tsang, Daniel C.
Wesley, Dorothy Porter
Winsor, Justin
Wroth, Lawrence
  Counselman

LIBRARY
ADMINISTRATOR

Cory, John Mackenzie
Greene, Belle da Costa
Healy, Timothy S(tafford)
Wright, Louis Booker

LIBRETTIST

Barbier, Jules
Boito, Arrigo
DaPonte, Lorenzo
Halevy, Ludovic
Hooker, Brian
Lortzing, Gustav Albert
Marmontel, Jean Francois
Metastasio, Pietro
Mosenthal, Salomon
  Hermann von
Nuitter, Charles Louis
Piave, Francesco Maria
Rice, Tim(othy Miles
  Bindon)
Rinuccini, Ottavio
Romani, Felice
Rossi, Gaetano
Saint Georges, Jules
Schikaneder, Emanuel

Stein, Joseph
Wagner, Richard
Zeno, Apostolo

LINGUIST

Allegro, John Marco
Bloomfield, Leonard
Bolinger, Dwight
  Lemerton
Chomsky, Noam Avram
Gowers, Ernest Arthur, Sir
Jakobson, Roman
Korzybski, Alfred
  Habdank
Kurath, Hans
Lamb, Sydney MacDonald
Menendez Pidal, Ramon
Sequoyah
Tannen, Deborah Frances
Thomas, Michel
Whitney, William Dwight
Zamenhof, Ludwik Lazar
Zepeda, Ofelia

LITHOGRAPHER

Currier, Nathaniel
Gavarni, Paul
Prang, Louis
Wengenroth, Stow

LYRICIST

Adams, Stanley
Ashman, Howard
Barnes, Billy
Bart, Lionel
Bergman, Alan
Bergman, Marilyn Keith
Bricusse, Leslie
Cahn, Sammy
Charnin, Martin
Darion, Joseph
David, Hal
Deutsch, Helen
Dixon, Mort
Dubin, Al
Ebb, Fred
Edwards, Sherman
Fine, Sylvia
Gershwin, Ira
Hammerstein, Oscar, II
Harbach, Otto Abels
Harburg, E(dgar) Y(ipsel)
Harnick, Sheldon Mayer
Hart, Charles
Hart, Lorenz
Jacobs, Al(bert T)
Kalmar, Bert
Kleban, Edward Lawrence
Larson, Jonathan
LaTouche, John
Lawrence, Jack
Lerner, Alan Jay
Marks, Johnny
Moraes, Vinicius de
Parish, Mitchell
Porter, Cole
Previn, Dory Langdon
Razaf, Andy
Robin, Leo

Rose, Billy
Sherman, Richard Morton
Sissle, Noble
Smalls, Charlie
Sondheim, Stephen
(Joshua)
Sour, Robert B(andler)
Swann, Donald (Ibrahim)
Taupin, Bernie
Webster, Paul Francois

MADAM

Adler, Polly
Everleigh, Ada
Everleigh, Minna
Pleasant, Mary Ellen

MAGICIAN

Anderson, Harry
Blackstone, Harry
Blackstone, Harry, Jr.
Cagliostro, Alessandro,
Conte di
Copperfield, David
Crowley, Aleister (Edward
Alexander)
Dee, John
Dunninger, Joseph
Faust, Johann
Goldin, Horace
Henning, Doug(las James)
Houdin, Jean Eugene
Robert
Houdini, Harry
Jay, Ricky
Maskelyne, John Nevil
Randi, James
Scarne, John
Thurston, Howard

MANAGER

Abbey, Henry Eugene
Baylis, Lilian Mary
Beck, Martin
Benson, Frank Robert, Sir
Bing, Rudolf (Franz
Josef), Sir
Boycott, Charles
Cunningham
Chapin, Schuyler Garrison
Coburn, Charles Douville
Dillingham, Charles
Bancroft
Edwardes, George
Epstein, Brian
Evans, Maurice
Forbes-Robertson,
Johnston, Sir
Frohman, Daniel
Gailhard, Pierre
Gatti-Casazza, Giulio
Hammerstein, Oscar
Hare, John, Sir
Hartmann, Rudolph
Juch, Emma
Kellogg, Clara Louise
Liebermann, Rolf
Miller, Henry John
Neumann, Angelo

Parker, Tom, Colonel
Pastor, Tony
Robinson, Francis Arthur
Shubert, Jacob J
Tree, Herbert Beerbohm
Wallack, James William
Ziegler, Edward
Zirato, Bruno

MANAGERS

Hallam, Lewis, Sr. an

MANUFACTURER

Allyn, Stanley Charles
Ames, Oakes
Babbitt, Benjamin Talbot
Ball, Edmund B
Ball, Frank
Bass, Henry
Bendix, Vincent
Bich, Marcel
Bigelow, Erastus Brigham
Boiardi, Hector
Boulton, Matthew
Boussac, Marcel
Bradley, Milton
Brown, Moses
Buitoni, Giovanni
Burnison, Chantal Simone
Cadbury, George Adrian
Hayhurst, Sir
Campagnolo, Gitullio
Campbell, Joseph
Candler, Asa Griggs
Carder, Frederick
Carter, William
Chalmers, William James
Chapin, Roy Dikeman
Chickering, Jonas
Coats, James
Colgate, William
Converse, Marquis M
Coty, Francois Marie
Joseph Spoturno
Danforth, William H
Dassler, Adolf
Deering, William
Dewar, John
Dow, Herbert Henry
Durkee, Eugene R
Duryea, Charles Edgar
Evinrude, Ole
Farah, James
Farah, William F.
Farber, Simon W
Farmer, Moses Gerrish
Fels, Joseph
Fender, Leo
Firestone, Harvey Samuel
Firestone, Harvey Samuel,
Jr.
Fischer, Herman G
Fleischmann, Charles
Louis
Fleischmann, Raoul
H(erbert)
Folger, James A
Fruehauf, Harvey Charles
Fuller, Alfred Carl
Gamble, James Norris
Gilbert, Alfred Carlton, Jr.

Girdler, Tom Mercer
Gucci, Guccio
Haggar, Joseph M(arion)
Hammer, Armand
Handler, Elliot
Handler, Ruth
Hanes, John Wesley
Hanes, Pleasant H
Heinz, Henry John
Hellmann, Richard
Hires, Charles E
Honeywell, Mark Charles
Horlick, Alexander James
Hupp, Louis Gorham
Jantzen, Carl
Jergens, Andrew
Johnson, Samuel C
Jones, Samuel Milton
Kerr, Alexander H
Kimball, William Wallace
Kraft, James Lewis
Lawrence, Abbott
Lear, William Powell
Lee, Henry D
Lenox, Walter S
Lever, William Hesketh
Lilly, Eli
Mack, John M
Mallinckrodt, Edward
Matchabelli, Georges,
Prince
Mattus, Reuben
Maxim, Hiram Percy
Maxim, Hudson
May, Mortimer
Maytag, Elmer Henry
McCormick, Cyrus Hall
Michelin, Andre
Michelin, Edouard
Miller, Howard
Morton, Joy
Mueller, Christian F
Oliver, James
Olivetti, Adriano
Olivetti, Camillo
Otis, Elisha Graves
Owen, Robert
Owens, Michael Joseph
Parker, George Safford
Perky, Henry D
Pfizer, Charles
Phillips, Charles
Pillsbury, Charles Alfred
Pillsbury, John Sargent
Pillsbury, Philip Winston
Pinkham, Lydia Estes
Price, Irving L
Procter, William Cooper
Redenbacher, Orville
Remington, Eliphalet
Rentner, Maurice
Reynolds, Richard S
Richardson, Benjamin
Rockwell, Willard F
Sax, Charles Joseph
Schwinn, Ignaz
Scranton, George
Whitfield
Sherwin, Henry Alden
Short, James
Shorthouse, Joseph Henry
Siegel, Owen R
Simmons, Zalmon G
Smith, Amanda W
Smith, Christopher
Columbus

Smith, Horace
Smucker, Jerome
Sommers, Ben
Spreckels, Claus
Squibb, Edward Robinson
Steinway, Henry
Engelhard
Stetson, John Batterson
Stiegel, Henry William
Strauss, Levi
Studebaker, Clement
Swift, Gustavus Franklin
Swigert, Ernest
Goodnough
Tappan, William J
Tate, Henry, Sir
Thomas, Samuel Bath
Thomas, Seth
Timken, Henry
Underwood, John Thomas
Upjohn, Lawrence
Northcote
Vail, Alfred Lewis
Vickers, Edward
Wakefield, Ruth G
Wellcome, Henry
Solomon, Sir
Wesson, Daniel Baird
Westinghouse, George
Weston, Edward F
Wharton, Joseph
Williams, Edward Porter
Wurlitzer, Rudolph
Yale, Linus
Zeiss, Carl
Zellerbach, William
Joseph
Zuckerman, Ben

MANUFACTURERS

Ben & Jerry
Smith Brothers

MATHEMATICIAN

Abel, Niels Henrik
Aiken, Howard Hathaway
Alembert, Jean le Rond d'
Alexander, James
Waddell, II
Apollonius of Perga
Archimedes
Artin, Emil
Babbage, Charles
Baker, Alan
Banneker, Benjamin
Batchelor, George (Keith)
Begle, Edward G(riffith)
Beltrami, Eugenio
Bernoulli, Daniel
Bernstein, Dorothy Lewis
Bertrand, Joseph Louis
Francois
Birkhoff, George David
Biruni, Abu Rayhan al-
Bochner, Salomon
Bondi, Hermann, Sir
Boole, George
Boscovich, Ruggiero
Giuseppe
Bowditch, Nathaniel
Bronowski, Jacob

MECHANICAL ENGINEER

MERCHANT

Abboud, (El Ferik) Ibrahim
Abercromby, Ralph, Sir
Abruzzi, Luigi Amedeo
Abu Musa
Agesilaus, II
Alba, Duke of
Alcibiades
Alexander of Tunis
Ali, Sunni
Ali Pasha
Allen, Ethan
Allen, Henry Tureman
Allenby, Edmund Henry Hynman
Alp Arslan
Alvarez, Juan
Anders, Wladyslaw
Anderson, Robert
Andrews, Frank M(axwell)
Aoun, Michel
Aratus
Armstrong, Samuel Chapman
Arnold, Henry Harley
Auchinleck, Claude, Sir
Avila Camacho, Manuel
Babur
Baden-Powell, Robert Stephenson Smyth Baden-Powell, Baron
Badoglio, Pietro
Bagramian, Ivan Christofovorich
Bagration, Petr Ivanovich
Barak, Ehud
Barrios, Justo Rufino
Barry, Tom
Batu Khan
Beauregard, Pierre Gustav Toutant de
Beck, Ludwig August Theoder
Belgrano, Manuel
Bishop, Billy
Bliss, Tasker Howard
Bloch, Claude Charles
Blucher, Gebhard Leberecht von
Borgia, Cesare
Botha, Louis
Braddock, Edward
Brauchitsch, Heinrich Alfred
Brown, George Scratchley
Brown, Jacob Jennings
Brunner, Alois
Brutus Albinus, Decimus Junius
Buckingham, 1st Duke of
Buckner, Simon Bolivar
Buckner, Simon Bolivar, Jr.
Buford, John
Bugeaud de la Piconnerie, Thomas Robert
Bullard, Robert Lee
Carleton, Guy
Castilla, Ramon
Cates, Clifton Bledsoe
Caxias, Duque de
Cedras, Raoul
Chang Tso-Lin
Chatichai Choonhavan
Chauncey, Isaac
Cheng Ho

Chen Yi
Chmielnicki, Bogdan
Ch'oe Ch'ung-hn
Chong Chung-bu
Christison, (Alexander Frank) Philip
Chuikov, Vasili Ivanovitch
Clausewitz, Karl (Philipp Gottlieb) von
Clinton, Henry, Sir
Conde, Prince de
Craig, Malin
Crowe, William James, Jr.
Cunningham, Andrew Browne, Viscount
Currie, Arthur William
Cushing, William Barker
Dabrowski, Jan Henryk
Davis, Benjamin Oliver, Sr.
Davout, Louis Nicholas
Diaz, Jose de la Cruz Porfirio
Dickman, Joseph Theodore
Dill, John Greer, Sir
Dixon, Robert Ellington
Douglas, Sholto
Dozier, James Lee
Drum, Hugh A
Du Guesclin, Bertrand
Early, Jubal Anderson
Epaminondas
Ershad, Hussain Mohammad
Eugene of Savoy
Evans, Robley Dunglison
Farragut, David Glasgow
Feng Yu-hsiang
Flamininus, Titus Quinctius
Flores, Juan Jose
Floyd, John Buchanan
Foch, Ferdinand
Forrest, Nathan Bedford
Franklin, William Buel
Freeman, Paul Lamar
Frunze, Mikhail Vasilievich
Funston, Frederick
Galvin, John Rogers
Glubb, John Bagot, Sir
Gneisenau, August Neithardt von
Gomez, Maximo
Graziani, Rodolfo
Grivas, Georgios Theodoros
Grubert, Carl Alfred
Gruenther, Alfred Maximillian
Guderian, Heinz Wilhelm
Guemes, Martin
Guerrero, Vicente
Haig, Douglas
Halleck, Henry Wager
Hamilcar Barca
Hannibal
Hansell, Haywood Shepherd, Jr.
Harris, Arthur Travers, Sir
Harrison, William Kelly, Jr.
Harsha
Haushofer, Karl Ernst
Hazen, William Babcock

Heaton, Leonard
Herkimer, Nicholas
Hill, Ambrose Powell
Hobson, Richmond Pearson
Hodges, Courtney
Hood, John Bell
Hooker, Joseph
Hopper, Grace Brewster Murray
Howe, William, Viscount
Huerta, Victoriano
Hull, Isaac
Hull, John Edwin
Hull, William
Hunyadi, Janos
Hunyadi, John
Ibanez del Campo, Carlos
ibn Tashufin, Yusuf
Ibrahim Pasha
Ieyasu, Tokugawa
Ingersoll, Stuart H
Ismay, Hastings Lionel, Baron
Jackson, Stonewall
Jodl, Alfred
Joffre, Joseph Jacques Cesaire
John Maurice of Nassau
Johnson, John
Johnston, Albert Sidney
Johnston, Joseph Eggleston
Justo, Agustin Pedro
Kamel, Hussein
Keitel, Wilhelm
Kesselring, Albert
Khalil, Sayyid Abdullah
Kirk, Alan Goodrich
Kitchener, Horatio Herbert
Knox, Henry
Kolchak, Aleksandr Vasilievich
Konev, Ivan Stepanovich
Koprulu, Ahmed
Kornilov, Lavr Georgyevich
Kutuzov, Mikhail Ilárionovich
Lansdale, Edward Geary
Lawton, Henry Ware
Lebed, Alexander
Lemnitzer, Lyman Louis
Lewis, Andrew
Lincoln, Benjamin
Lincoln, George A
Littlejohn, Robert McGowan
Lopez, Narciso
Lysander
Maccabeus, Judas
Maceo, Antonio
Macquarie, Lachlan
Malinovsky, Rodion Yakovlevich
Mannerheim, Carl Gustav Emil, Baron
Marion, Francis
Marius, Gaius
Martinez, Maximiliano Hernandez
McClellan, George Brinton
McPherson, James Birdseye
Meade, George Gordon

Mengistu Haile Mariam
Merritt, Wesley
Miles, Nelson Appleton
Milne, George Francis, Baron
Miltiades
Minamoto Yoritomo
Mitscher, Marc Andrew
Mladic, Ratko
Monck, George, 1st Duke of Albemarle
Montcalm, Louis Joseph de
Montgomery of Alamein, Bernard Law Montgomery, Viscount
Morazan, Jose Francisco
Morelos y Pavon, Jose Maria
Murat, Joachim
Murray, James
Ney, Michel de la Moskova, Prince
Nguyen Khanh
O'Donnell, Emmett, Jr.
Ogarkov, Nikolai
Ortiz, Peter J(ulien)
Paez, Jose Antonio
Paige, Emmett, Jr.
Parker, Ely Samuel
Parks, Floyd Lavinius
Patch, Alexander M(c Carrell)
Paulus, Friedrich von
Peers, William Raymond
Pelopidas
Pemberton, John Clifford
Petain, Henri Philippe
Phibun Songkhram, Luang
Pickett, George Edward
Porter, David Dixon
Portola, Gaspar de
Potemkin, Grigori Alexsandrovich
Powell, Colin (Luther)
Power, Thomas S(arsfield)
Prem Tinsulanonda
Prestes, Luiz Carlos
Price, Sterling
Primo de Rivera (y Orbaneja), Miguel
Ptolemy (Soter), I
Raglan, Fitzroy James Henry Somerset, Baron
Raushenbush, Stephen
Reyes, Rafael
Ricimer
Rivera, Fructuoso
Roca, Julio Argentino
Rogers, Bernard William
Rollo
Roosevelt, Elliott
Roosevelt, Theodore, Jr.
Rosas, Juan Manuel de
Rundstedt, Karl Rudolf Gerd von
Saigo, Takamori
Saint Clair, Arthur
Sampson, William T
Samsonov, Aleksandr Vasilievich
Santa Cruz, Andres de
Santana, Pedro
Sarit Thanarat
Saw Maung
Saxe, Maurice

Anastasia, Albert
Anderson, William
Atkins, Susan Denise
Baniszewski, Gertrude
  Wright
Bateman, Mary
Bathory, Elizabeth
Beadle, William
Berkowitz, David
Billington, John
Borden, Lizzie Andrew
Broderick, Elisabeth
  Bisceglia
Brooks, Charlie, Jr.
Brooks, David Owen
Brunner, Alois
Bundy, Ted
Burke, William
Carols
Chapman, Mark David
Charriere, Henri
Chikatilo, Andrei
Christie, John Reginald
  Halliday
Corona, Juan
Crippen, Hawley Harvey
Dahmer, Jeffrey L
Defeo, Ronald
Dillinger, John Herbert
Dumurcq, Charles
Ellis, Ruth
Fish, Albert
Ford, Bob
Franklin, Joseph Paul
Fugate, Caril Ann
Gacy, John Wayne, Jr.
Gein, Ed
Gilmore, Gary Mark
Graham, Barbara
Guiteau, Charles Julius
Hardin, John Wesley
Hare, William
Harris, Jean Witt Struven
Harris, Robert Alton
Hauptmann, Bruno
  Richard
Hennard, George, Jr.
Hickock, Richard Eugene
Horn, Tom
Horton, Willie
Jack the Ripper
Judd, Winnie Ruth
  McKinnell
Judy, Steven
Kray, Reggie
Kray, Ronnie
Krenwinkel, Patricia
Lafarge, Marie
Landru, Henri Desire
Leopold, Nathan
  Freudenthal
Loeb, Richard A
Manning, Maria
Manson, Charles
Mudgett, Herman Webster
Noziere, Violette
Packer, Alfred G
Palmer, William
Ruby, Jack
Slade, Jack
Smith, Madeline Hamilton
Smith, Perry Edward
Snider, Paul
Speck, Richard Franklin
Spenkelink, John Arthur
Starkweather, Charles

Thaw, Harry Kendall
Todd, Sweeney
Unruh, Howard B
Whitman, Charles Joseph
Williams, Wayne Bertram
Zodiac Killer

MUSEUM DIRECTOR

Barr, Alfred Hamilton, Jr.
Baur, John I(reland)
  H(owe)
Blum, Stella
Breeskin, Adelyn Dohme
Brown, John Carter
Camp, Kimberly
Colvin, Sidney, Sir
DeMontebello, Guy-
  Philippe
Edgell, George Harold
Futter, Ellen Victoria
Goodrich, Lloyd
Gund, Agnes
Holladay, Wilhelmina
  Cole
Kimball, Fiske
Krens, Thomas
Oldenburg, Richard
Reagon, Bernice Johnson
Rubin, William Stanley
Sachs, Samuel, II
Smith, Kenneth Danforth
Spargo, John
Waterhouse, Ellis
  Kirkham, Sir
Wolfenden, John
  Frederick, Sir
Woodall, Mary

MUSIC EXECUTIVE

Ackerman, Will
Branson, Richard
Davis, Clive Jay
Gordy, Berry, Jr.
Hammond, John Henry, Jr.
Harrell, Andre (O'Neal)
Kirshner, Don
Moss, Jerry
Phillips, Sam
Rhone, Sylvia
Rubin, Rick
Satherly, Arthur Edward
Simmons, Russell
Witmark, Isidore
Yetnikoff, Walter

MUSIC GROUP

ABBA
ABC
AC-DC
Ace
Adam and the Ants
Aerosmith
Air Supply
Alabama
Allman Brothers Band
Amboy Dukes, The
America

Ames Brothers, The
Andrews Sisters
Animals, The
April Wine
Argent
Ashford and Simpson
Asia
Asleep at the Wheel
Association, The
Atlanta Rhythm Section
Average White Band, The
B-52's
Babys, The
Bachman-Turner
  Overdrive
Bad Company
Badfinger
Bananarama
Band, The
Bangles, The
Barenaked Ladies
Bay City Rollers, The
Beach Boys, The
Beatles, The
Beaver Brown Band
Bee Gees, The
Bellamy Brothers, The
Big Brother and the
  Holding Company
Big Country
Black Crowes, The
Black Oak Arkansas
Black Sabbath
Blind Faith
Blondie
Blood, Sweat and Tears
Blue Oyster Cult
Blues Brothers, The
BoDeans
Boney M.
Bon Jovi
Booker T and the MG's
Boomtown Rats
Boston
Boswell Sisters
Bow Wow Wow
Box Tops, The
Boyz II Men
Bread
Brewer and Shipley
Brickell, Edie
Brothers Johnson, The
Buckinghams, The
Buffalo Springfield
Buzzocks, The
Byrds, The
Canadian Brass, The
Canned Heat
Captain and Tennile, The
Cardigans, The
Carpenters, The
Cars, The
Carter Family, The
Chad and Jeremy
Charlie Daniels Band, The
Cheap Trick
Chic
Chicago
Chieftains, The
Clash, The
Climax Blues Band, The
Club Nouveau
Coasters, The
Commodores, The
Country Gentlemen, The
Country Joe and the Fish

Cowboy Junkies
Cowsills, The
Crazy Horse
Cream
Creedence Clearwater
  Revival
Critters
Crosby, Stills, Nash &
  Young
Crusaders, The
Crystals, The
Culture Club
Cure, The
Damned, The
Danny and the Juniors
Danzig
Dave Clark Five, The
Dazz Band
DeBarge
Deee-Lite
Deep Purple
Def Leppard
Delaney and Bonnie
Depeche Mode
Derek and the Dominoes
Desert Rose Band
Devo
Dion and the Belmonts
Dire Straits
Doobie Brothers, The
Doors, The
Double
Dr. Feelgood
Dr. Hook
Drifters, The
Duran Duran
Eagles, The
Earth, Wind and Fire
Electric Light Orchestra
Emerson, Lake, and
  Palmer
England Dan and John
  Ford Coley
English Beat
En Vogue
E-Street Band
Eurythmics
Everly Brothers
Everything But The Girl
Exile
Expose
Fabulous Thunderbirds,
  The
Faces, The
Fairport Convention
Faith No More
Fifth Dimension
Firefall
Fishbone
Fixx, The
Fleetwood Mac
Flock of Seagulls
Flying Burrito Brothers,
  The
Foghat
Foreigner
Four Freshmen, The
Four Lads, The
Four Seasons, The
Four Tops
Frankie Goes to
  Hollywood
Free
Frijid Pink
Fugs, The
Funkadelic

MUSICIAN

Abel, Karl Friedrich
Ackerman, Will
Adam de la Halle
Adamowski, Timothee
Adams, Bryan Guy
Adams, Cliff
Adderley, Cannonball
Ade, Sunny, King
Adler, Larry
Allen, Duane David
Allen, Rick
Allen, Verden
Allman, Gregg
Almeida, Laurindo
Alpert, Herb
Alvin, Dave
Ammons, Jug
Anderson, Cat
Anderson, Ian
Anderson, John
Anderson, Jon
Anderson, Rich
Andersson, Benny
Anthony, Michael
Argent, Rod(ney Terence)
Armstrong, Louis
Arnold, Eddy
Artist Formerly Known as
  Prince, The
Ashkenazy, Vladimir
  Davidovich
Ashman, Matthew
Atkins, Chet
Auger, Brian
August, Jan
Auldridge, Mike
Ayers, Roy
Bacharach, Burt
Bachman, Randy
Bailey, Philip
Baker, Ginger
Baker, Julius
Ballard, Russ(ell)
Banks, Tony
Barbarossa, Dave
Bar-Ilian, David Jacob
Baron, Samuel
Bebey, Francis
Beck, Jeff
Beefheart, Captain
Belew, Adrian
Bell, Kool
Bell, Ronald
Bellison, Simeon
Bender, Ariel
Bennett, Richard Rodney
Benson, George
Benson, Renaldo
Bentley, John
Berger, Al
Bernstein, Leonard
Berry, John
Best, Peter
Bethune, Thomas Greene
Bishop, Elvin
Bittan, Roy
Black, Clint
Black, Frank J.
Blackmore, Ritchie
Bleyer, Archie
Blind Willie McTell
Block, Rory
Bloom, Eric
Bloom, Mickey

Bloomfield, Mike
Blunstone, Colin
Bogert, Tim
Boggs, Tom
Bolan, Marc
Bonfanti, Jim Alexander
Bonga, Kuenda
Bonham, John Henry
Borden, Barry
Bouchard, Joe
Boult, Adrian Cedric, Sir
Boyd, Liona Maria
Brain, Aubrey
Brain, Dennis
Bream, Julian Alexander
Brock, Tony
Bromberg, David
Broonzy, Big Bill
Brown, George
Bruce, Jack
Brymer, Jack
Bryson, Wally Carter
Buckingham, Lindsey
Buckwheat Zydeco
Bull, Ole Bornemann
Burton, Gary
Burton, James
Busey, Gary
Byrd, Henry
Byrne, David
Caccini, Giulio
Cale, John
Campbell, Glen Travis
Capaldi, Jim
Captain Beefheart
Carlton, Larry
Carmen, Eric
Carpenter, Richard Lynn
Carr, Joe
Carrack, Paul
Carter, James
Casadesus, Gaby (Lhote)
Casadesus, Jean
Casadesus, Robert
Casady, Jack
Casals, Pablo (Pau Carlos
  Salvador)
Casey, H(arry) W(ayne)
Cavaliere, Felix
Cetera, Peter
Chambers, Paul
Charles, Ray
Chenier, Clifton
Cherry, Don
Chorzempa, Daniel Walter
Christie, William Lincoln
Clapton, Eric
Clark, Dave
Clark, Steve
Clarke, Kenny
Clarke, Stanley Marvin
Clayderman, Richard
Clemons, Clarence
Cobain, Kurt
Cocker, Joe
Cole, Cozy
Collins, Albert
Collins, Bootsy
Collins, Phil(ip)
Colonna, Jerry
Contino, Dick
Cooder, Ry(land Peter)
Cook, Will Marion
Cooke, Sam
Corby, Mike
Cornish, Gene

Coryell, Larry
Cotten, Libba
Cotten, Michael
Couperin, Francois
Covington, Warren
Creach, Papa
Crenshaw, Marshall
Criss, Peter
Crosby, David (Van
  Cortlandt)
Crowe, J D
Cummings, Burton
Cunningham, Bill
Dale, Alan
Dallapiccola, Luigi
Damrosch, Frank Heino
Danelli, Dino
Daniels, Charlie
D'Arby, Terence Trent
Darling, Erik
Dart, Thurston
Daugherty, Pat
Davies, Dave
Davies, Ray(mond
  Douglas)
Davis, Chip
Davis, Gary, Reverend
Davis, Spencer
DeBarge, El(dra)
DeBarge, James
DeBarge, Mark
DeBarge, Randy
Debost, Michel H
De Grassi, Alex
De Lucia, Paco
Denner, Johann Christoph
Densmore, John
Deodato
Derringer, Rick
DeVito, Tommy
Dichter, Mischa
Diddley, Bo
Difford, Chris
DiMeola, Al
Ditters, Karl
Dixon, Willie (James)
Doggett, Bill
Dohnanyi, Erno von
Doktor, Paul Karl
Dolby, Thomas
Dolmetsch, Arnold
Donahue, Sam Koontz
Donegan, Lonnie
Dott, Gerard
Dowland, John
Downey, Rick
Dragon, Daryl
Drake, Nick
Dryden, Spencer
Dulfer, Candy
Dunham, Sonny
DuPre, Jacqueline
Earl, Ronnie
Eddy, Duane
Edmunds, Dave
Elgar, Edward William,
  Sir
Ellington, Mercer
Ellis, Herb
Elman, Ziggy
Ely, Joe
Emerson, Keith
Encina, Juan del
Eno, Brian
Entwistle, John Alec
Escovedo, Alejandro

Esquivel, Juan
Etheridge, Melissa
Eubanks, Kevin
Europe, James Reese
Evans, Mark
Everly, Don(ald)
Everly, Phil
Fahey, John
Falco
Fame, Georgie
Faulkner, Eric
Faure, Gabriel Urbain
Federici, Daniel Paul
Feinstein, Michael Jay
Felder, Don(ald William)
Feliciano, Jose
Fenelon, Fania
Ferguson, Howard
Feuermann, Emanuel
Finch, Rick
Firkusny, Rudolf
Fizdale, Robert
Flatt, Lester Raymond
Fleck, Bela
Fleetwood, Mick
Floren, Myron
Ford, Lita
Ford, Mary
Foster, David
Fournier, Pierre
Francaix, Jean
Francescatti, Zino Rene
Franco
Frehley, Ace
French, Jay Jay
Frey, Glenn
Frickie, Janie
Friml, Rudolf
Fripp, Robert
Furay, Richie
Gabrieli, Giovanni
Gaines, Steve
Galamian, Ivan
Gale, Eric
Gallagher, Rory
Galway, James
Ganz, Rudolph
Garcia, Jerry
Gaudio, Bob
Gazda, Ricky
Gazzelloni, Severino
Geldof, Bob
Gendron, Maurice
Giardini, Felice di
Gibb, Andy
Gibbons, Orlando
Gibbs, Terri
Gibbs, Terry
Gibson, Bob
Gieseking, Walter
  Wilhelm
Gilels, Emil Grigoyevich
Gill, Vince(nt Grant)
Gilley, Mickey Leroy
Gilmour, Dave
Gimpel, Jakob
Glazer, David
Godowsky, Leopold
Goodman, Benny
Goossens, Leon Jean
Gordy, Emory, Jr.
Gorka, John
Gorman, Leroy
Gottschalk, Louis Moreau
Goytisolo, Fermin
Graffman, Gary

Reagon, Toshi
Redman, Joshua
Reid, Vernon
Remenyi, Eduard
Respighi, Ottorino
Rey, Alvino
Reynolds, Ricky
Reznor, Trent
Rich, Charlie
Richard, Zachary
Richards, Keith
Richter, Karl
Riddle, Nelson
Ridgeley, Andrew
Ritenour, Lee
Robertson, Robbie
Robillard, Duke
Robinson, Tom
Robison, Paula Judith
Rockin' Dopsie
Rodford, Jim
Rodgers, Nile
Roeser, Donald
Roland, Duane
Romberg, Bernhard
Rose, Leonard
Rosen, Nathaniel
Rostropovich, Mstislav
  Leopoldovich
Roth, David Lee
Rucker, Darius
Rudd, Phil(lip)
Rundgren, Todd
Rush, Billy
Rutherford, Michael
Rydell, Bobby
Saidenberg, Daniel
Saint-Saens, (Charles)
  Camille
Sakamoto, Ryuichi
Sanborn, David
Sanders, Marty
Santana, Carlos
Satriani, Joe
Savage, Rick
Scaggs, Boz
Schickele, Peter
Schillinger, Joseph
Schirmer, Gustave
Schmidt, Tim(othy B)
Schnabel, Karl Ulrich
Schneider, Alexander
Schoenbach, Sol Israel
Scholz, Tom
Schwarz, Gerard
Scofield, John
Scott, Tony
Scriabin, Alexander
  Nicholaevich
Scruggs, Earl Eugene
Seger, Bob
Segovia, Andres
Sembello, Michael
Seraphine, Danny
Severinsen, Doc
Shaffer, Paul
Shafran, Daniel
Shankar, Ravi
Shaw, Artie
Shearing, George Albert
Sheila E
Sheppard, T G
Shorter, Wayne
Simmons, Gene
Singleton, Zutty
Skaggs, Ricky

Slash
Smalley, David Bruce
Smetana, Bedrich
Smith, Claydes
Smith, Jerome
Smith, Ronnie
Snow, Don
Solti, Georg, Sir
Sonnier, Jo-El
Sor, Fernando
South, Joe
Soyer, David
Spivak, Charlie
Spivakovsky, Tossy
Spooner, Bill
Springfield, Rick
Squier, Billy
Squire, Chris
Stanley, Paul
Starker, Janos
Starr, Ringo
Steen, Roger
Stein, Mark
Stevens, Ray
Stewart, David
Stills, Stephen
Sting
Stocker, Wally
Stokowski, Leopold
  (Anton Stanislaw
  Boleslawawicz)
Stoltzman, Richard Leslie
Stone, Sly
Stuart, Marty
Suesse, Dana Nadine
Sullivan, Maxine
Summers, Andy
Sun Ra
Sweet, Matthew
Swift, Kay
Sykes, Roosevelt
Talbot, John Michael
Tallent, Garry Wayne
Talley, Gary
Taylor, Cecil Percival
Taylor, Mick
Terry, Sonny
Tesh, John
Thomas, Dennis
Thompson, Hank
Thompson, Richard
Thomson, Virgil Garnett
Tilbrook, Glenn
Toch, Ernst
Tork, Peter
Tortelier, Paul
Toure, Ali Farka
Townshend, Peter Dennis
  Blandford
Trampler, Walter
Travis, Merle Robert
Tritt, Travis
Trotter, John Scott
Trower, Robin
Trudell, John
Tubb, Ernest
Tuckwell, Barry
  Emmanuel
Turnbull, Walter (J.)
Tyler, Steven
Ulmer, James
Ulvaeus, Bjorn
Vai, Steve
VanAlstyne, Egbert Anson
Vandross, Luther
Van Halen, Alex

Van Halen, Eddie
Van Zant, Ronnie
Vaughan, Stevie Ray
Vieuxtemps, Henri
  Francois Joseph
Vig, Butch
Viotti, Giovanni Battista
Vivaldi, Antonio (Lucio)
Vollenweider, Andreas
Wagner, Roger Frances
Wainwright, Loudon, III
Waits, Tom
Wakeman, Rick
Walker, Junior
Walker, T-Bone
Wallenstein, Alfred Franz
Waller, Gordon
Walsh, Joe
Wariner, Steve
Washington, Grover, Jr.
Waters, Muddy
Watson, Doc
Watson, Johnny "Guitar"
Watts, Andre
Watts, Charlie
Watts, Pete
Wein, George Theodore
Weinberg, Max M
Weir, Bob
Welch, Bob
Wells, Junior
Welnick, Vince(nt)
West, Riff
Westrup, J(ack) A(llan),
  Sir
White, Chris(topher
  Taylor)
Williams, Charles
Williams, Cliff
Williams, Curtis
Williams, Don
Williams, John
Williams, Mary Lou
Williams, Mason
Williams, Milan
Williams, Tex
Williams, Tony
Williamson, Cris
Williamson, Robin
Williamson, Sonny Boy
Wills, Bob
Wilson, Ann
Wilson, Dennis
Wilson, Dooley
Wilson, Nancy
Wilson, Ransom
Winans, Marvin L.
Winter, Edgar Holand
Winter, Johnny
Winter, Paul Theodore
Winwood, Steve
Wonder, Stevie
Wood, Chris
Wood, Ron(ald)
Wood, Stuart
Wooley, Sheb
Wray, Link
Wright, Gary
Wright, Rick
Wummer, John
Wyman, Bill
Wynonna
Yamashita, Kazuhito
Yanni
Yarbrough, Glenn
Young, Angus

Young, Faron
Young, Malcolm
Young, Neil
Zabaleta, Nicanor
Zander, Robin
Zappa, Dweezil
Zappa, Frank
Zeitlin, Zvi
Zingarelli, Nicola Antonio

MUSICIANS

Couperin
Homer and Jethro

MUSICOLOGIST

Adler, Guido
Burney, Charles
Castil-Blaze, Francois-
  Joseph
Chrysander, Karl Franz
  Friedrich
Dart, Thurston
Densmore, Frances
Dent, Edward Joseph
Downes, Edward Olin
  Davenport
Einstein, Alfred
Fetis, Francois Joseph
Haberl, Franz Xaver
Heth, Charlotte
Lang, Paul Henry
Parry, Charles Hubert
  Hastings, Sir
Scholes, Percy Alfred
Slonimsky, Nicolas
Smith, Carleton Sprague
Sonneck, Oscar George
  Theodore
Spaeth, Sigmund Gottfried
Szabolcsi, Bence
Tovey, Donald Francis, Sir
Wellesz, Egon

MYSTIC

Attar, Farid ed-Din
Boehme, Jakob
Eckhart, Johannes
Fox, Kate
Fox, Margaret
Groote, Gerhard
Gurdjieff, George
  Ivanovitch
Hallaj, Al-Husayn ibn
  Mansur al-
Hartmann, Franz
Irving, Edward
Jacopone da Todi
Joachim of Fiore
Juan, Don
Julian of Norwich
Junayd, Abu al-Qasim ibn
  Muhammad al
Luzzato, Moses Hayyim
Ruysbroeck, Jan van
Sabbatai Zevi
Suso, Heinrich
Swedenborg, Emanuel
Wovoka

Occupation Index

Yarnell, Harry Ervin
Zumwalt, Elmo R(ussell),
  Jr.

NAVIGATOR

Adams, William
Baffin, William
Barents, Willem
Bering, Vitus Jonassen
Bermudez, Juan de
Bougainville, Louis-
  Antoine de
Cabot, John
Cartier, Jacques
Cavendish, Thomas
Cook, James, Captain
DaGama, Vasco
Dias, Bartholomew
Dixon, George
Drake, Francis, Sir
Dumont d'Urville, Jules
  Sebastian Cesar
Ericson, Leif
Eric the Red
Frobisher, Martin
Gilbert, Humphrey, Sir
Hudson, Henry
Magellan, Ferdinand
Nino, Pedro Alonzo
Pytheas
Raleigh, Walter, Sir
Verrazano, Giovanni da
Vespucci, Amerigo
Wallis, Samuel

NAVY OFFICER

Garnier, Francis

NEUROLOGIST

Alzheimer, Alois
Berger, Hans
Denny-Brown, Derek
  Ernest
Ferrier, David, Sir
Gibbs, Frederic A
Golgi, Camillo
Jackson, John Hughlings
Levi-Montalcini, Rita
Merritt, Hiram Houston
Mitchell, Silas Weir
Prusiner, Stanley (Ben)
Ramon y Cajal, Santiago
Sacks, Oliver Wolf

NEWSPAPER
EDITOR

Bailey, Charles Waldo, II
Bartlett, John Sherren
Canham, Erwin Dain
Curtis, Charlotte Murray
DeYoung, Michel Harry
Jagan, Janet
Klein, Herbert George
Knight, John Shively, III
Lelyveld, Joseph Salem
Maury, Reuben

Maynard, Robert Clyve
Nelson, William Rockhill
Roberts, Gene
Royster, Vermont
  C(onnecticut)
Simons, Howard
Watterson, Henry
Wilcock, John

NEWSPAPER
EXECUTIVE

Adler, Julius Ochs
Chandler, Dorothy
  (Buffum)
Goodman, Martin Wise
Graham, Donald Edward
Graham, Katharine Meyer
Haley, William John, Sir
Hearst, Randolph
  Apperson
Hearst, William Randolph,
  III
Noyes, Frank B(rett)
Ochs, Adolph Shelby, II
Reid, Helen Rogers
Sulzberger, Arthur O(chs)
Sulzberger, Arthur O(chs),
  Jr.

NEWSPAPER
PUBLISHER

Baker, Elbert Hall, II
Bennett, James Gordon
Bingham, Barry
Brittain, Harry Ernest, Sir
Chandler, Norman
Chandler, Otis
Coty, Francois Marie
  Joseph Spoturno
Curtis, Cyrus Hermann
  Kotszchmar
Dryfoos, Orvil Eugene
Field, Marshall, V
Gannett, Frank Ernest
Grant, Harry Johnston
Harris, Jay T(errence)
Hearst, William Randolph
Hoyt, Palmer
Kern, Harold G
Knight, James L
Knight, John Shivley
Knowland, William Fife
Laffan, William Mackay
Leavell, Dorothy R.
Levy, Joseph Moses
Martin, Harold Eugene
McClure, Samuel Sidney
McCormick, Robert
  Rutherford
McLean, Robert
Newhouse, Samuel Irving
Nieman, Lucius William
Northcliffe, Alfred Charles
  William Harmsworth,
  Viscount
Ochs, Adolph Simon
Reid, Ogden Mills
Ridder, Bernard Herman
Rothermere, Esmond Cecil
  Harmsworth, Viscount
Scripps, Edward Wyllis

Sengstacke, John H(erman
  Henry)
Stone, Melville Elijah
Thomson, Roy Herbert
Walter, John, I

NOBLEMAN

Aberdeen, 4th Earl of
Alba, Duke of
Berchtold, Leopold von
Bothwell, James Hepburn,
  Earl of
Bruce of Melbourne, 1st
  Viscount
Buckingham, 1st Duke of
Calvert, Charles
Chou Kung
Conde, Prince de
Francis Ferdinand
Fujiwara Kamatari
Fujiwara Michinaga
Gloucester, Duke of
Haussmann, Georges
  Eugene
Joinville, Jean de
Leicester, Earl of
Philip the Good
Pulaski, Kazimierz
Queensberry, John Sholto
  Douglas
Schwenckfeld, Kasper von
Sforza, Ludovico
Thibaut, IV
Tupac Amaru
Villers, George
Visconti, Gian Galeazzo,
  Duke of Milan
Warwick and of Salisbury,
  Earl of
William the Silent

NOBLEWOMAN

Accoramboni, Vittoria
Beaufort, Margaret,
  Countess of Richmond
Borgia, Lucrezia
Cenci, Beatrice
Francesca da Rimini
Gioconda, Lisa Gherardini
Matilda of Tuscany

NUCLEAR
TECHNICIAN

Silkwood, Karen

NURSE

Auguste, Rose-Anne
Barrow, Ruth Nita, Dame
Bickerdyke, Mary Ann
  Ball
Breckinridge, Mary
Cammermeyer, Margarethe
Carnegie, Mary Elizabeth
  Lancaster
Carter, Lillian
Cavell, Edith Louisa

Delano, Jane Arminda
Edmonds, Emma E
Gardner, Mary Sewall
Jumper, Betty Mae Tiger
Kelley, Virginia
Kenny, Sister Elizabeth
Lubic, Ruth Watson
Lyttle, Hulda Margaret
Mahoney, Mary Eliza
Mason, Biddy
Nightingale, Florence
Riley, Helen Caldwell Day
Sanger, Margaret

NUTRITIONIST

Boyd-Orr, John, Baron
Davis, Adelle
Emerson, Gladys
  Anderson
Fredericks, Carlton
Hauser, Gayelord
Lappe, Francis Moore
Mayer, Jean
McCollum, Elmer Verner
Pritikin, Nathan
Sebrell, W(illiam) H(enry),
  Jr.

OCEANOGRAPHER

Cousteau, Jacques (Yves)
Cousteau, Jean-Michel
Cousteau, Philippe
Helland-Hansen, Bjorn
Maury, Matthew Fontaine
Murray, John, Sir
Revelle, Roger Randall
Stommel, Henry Melson
Sverdrup, H(arald) U(lrik)

OILMAN

Davis, (Thomas) Cullen
Davis, Marvin
Doheny, Edward
  Lawrence
Dorsey, Bob Rawls
Drake, Edwin Laurentine
Getty, J(ean) Paul
Gulbenkian, Calouste S
Hess, Leon
Holman, Eugene
Hunt, H(aroldson)
  L(afayette)
Kerr, Robert Samuel
McCulloch, Robert P
Mecom, John Whitfield
Pauley, Edwin Wendell
Pratt, Charles
Richardson, Sid
Rockefeller, John
  D(avison)
Sinclair, Harry Ford
Warner, Rawleigh, Jr.

OLYMPIC
ATHLETE

Berger, David

Coroebus
Fiske, Billy
Friedman, Ze'ev
Gutfreund, Yosef
Halfin, Eliezer
Romano, Joseph
Shapira, Amitzur
Shorr, Kehat
Slavin, Mark
Spitzer, Andre
Springer, Ya'acov
Waddell, Tom
Weinberg, Moshe

OLYMPIC
OFFICIAL

Brundage, Avery
Coubertin, Pierre de,
  Baron
Kane, Robert Joseph
Kelly, John Brenden, Jr.
Killanin, Michael Morris,
  Lord
Samaranch, Juan Antonio
Schultz, Richard D(ale)

OPERA SINGER

Abdul, Raoul
Addison, Adele
Albanese, Licia
Alda, Frances
Allen, Betty (Lou)
Althouse, Paul Shearer
Alvary, Lorenzo
Alvary, Max
Amara, Lucine
Amato, Pasquale
Ameling, Elly
Andresen, Ivar
Angeles, Victoria de los
Arroyo, Martina
Auger, Arleen
Austral, Florence Wilson
Baccaloni, Salvatore
Baker, Janet Abbott, Dame
Balfe, Michael William
Bampton, Rose Elizabeth
Barbieri, Fedora
Barrientos, Maria
Bartoli, Cecilia
Bastianini, Ettore
Battistini, Mattia
Baum, Kurt
Bechi, Gino
Behrens, Hildegard
Benzell, Mimi
Berberian, Cathy
Berganza, Teresa
Bergonzi, Carlo
Bernacchi, Antonio Maria
Berry, Walter
Bible, Frances Lillian
Billington, Elizabeth
Bjoerling, Jussi
Blegen, Judith Eyer
Bonci, Alessandro
Bonelli, Richard
Bordoni, Faustina
Borg, Kim
Branzell, Karin
Braslau, Sophie

Brownlee, John
Bumbry, Grace Ann
  Jaeckel
Caballe, Montserrat Folch
Callas, Maria
Calve, Emma
Caniglia, Maria
Carreras, Jose
Carte, Richard d'Oyly
Caruso, Enrico
Cary, Anne Louise
Case, Anna
Castagna, Bruna
Cavalieri, Lina
Cebotari, Maria
Chaliapin, Feodor
  Ivanovitch, Jr.
Christoff, Boris
Cigna, Gina
Cisneros, Eleanora
Colbran, Isabella
Conley, Eugene
Conner, Nadine
Corelli, Franco
Corena, Fernando
Cossotto, Fiorenza
Costa, Mary
Cotrubas, Ileana
Cox, Jean
Crescentini, Girolamo
Crespin, Regine
Crooks, Richard
  Alexander
Cuzzoni, Francesca
Dalis, Irene
Dalla Rizza, Gilda
Dalmores, Charles
DellaCasa, Lisa
Deller, Alfred George
DelMonaco, Mario
DeLuca, Giuseppe
DePaolis, Alessio
DeReszke, Edouard
DeReszke, Jean
Destinn, Emmy
Diaz, Justino
Dimitrova, Ghena
DiStefano, Giuseppe
Dobbs, Mattiwilda
Domingo, Placido
Donath, Helen
Dragonette, Jessica
Dunn, Mignon
DuPrez, Gilbert
Eames, Emma Hayden
Easton, Florence Gertrude
Eda-Pierre, Christiane
Edelmann, Otto
Elias, Rosalind
Elvira, Pablo
Estes, Simon Lamont
Evans, Geraint Llewellyn,
  Sir
Ewing, Maria Louise
Farinelli
Farrar, Geraldine
Farrell, Eileen
Fassbaender, Brigitte
Ferrier, Kathleen
Flagstad, Kirsten
Fleming, Renee
Forrester, Maureen
Freni, Mirella
Frick, Gottlob
Fuchs, Marta
Gadski, Johanna

Gailhard, Pierre
Galli-Curci, Amelita
Galli-Marie, Marie
  Celestine
Garcia, Manuel del Popolo
  Vincente
Garcia, Manuel Patricio
  Rodriguez
Garden, Mary
Gedda, Nicolai
Ghiaurov, Nicolai
Giannini, Dusolina
Gigli, Beniamino
Glossop, Peter
Gluck, Alma
Gobbi, Tito
Gorr, Rita
Grisi, Giulia
Grist, Reri
Guadagni, Gaetano
Guarrera, Frank
Gueden, Hilde
Hadley, Jerry
Hagegard, Hakan
Hampson, Thomas
Harper, Heather Mary
Harshaw, Margaret
Hauk, Minnie
Hawkins, Osie Penman, Jr.
Hayes, Roland
Hempel, Frieda
Hendricks, Barbara
Heppner, Ben
Hidalgo, Elvira de
Hines, Jerome
Holland, Charles
Homer, Louise
Horne, Marilyn Berneice
Hotter, Hans
Howells, Anne Elizabeth
Husch, Gerhard
Hvorostovsky, Dmitri
Ivogun, Maria
Jadlowker, Hermann
Jagel, Frederick
Janssen, Herbert
Jepson, Helen
Jerger, Alfred
Jeritza, Maria
Jerusalem, Siegfried
Jobin, Raoul
Jones, Gwyneth
Journet, Marcel
Juch, Emma
Jurinac, Sena
Kalisch, Paul
Kappel, Gertrude
Kellogg, Clara Louise
Kelly, Michael
Kiepura, Jan Wiktor
King, James Ambros
Kipnis, Alexander
Kirsten, Dorothy
Klafsky, Katharina
Klose, Margarete
Knote, Heinrich
Konetzni, Hilde
Korjus, Miliza
Kraus, Alfredo
Kraus, Felix von
Krauss, Gabrielle
Kronold, Selma
Kunz, Erich
Kurz, Selma
Lablache, Luigi
Lanza, Mario

Larsen-Todsen, Nanny
Lassale, Jean
Laszlo, Magda
Laubenthal, Rudolf
Lauri-Volpi, Giacoma
Lawrence, Marjorie
  Florence
Lazzari, Virgilio
Lear, Evelyn
Lehmann, Lilli
Lehmann, Lotte
Leider, Frida
Lemnitz, Tiana
Levasseur, Nicolas Prosper
Levasseur, Rosalie
Lind, Jenny
List, Emanuel
Litvinne, Felia
Ljungberg, Gota
London, George
Lorengar, Pilar
Lorenz, Max
Lubin, Germaine
Lucca, Pauline
Ludikar, Pavel
Ludwig, Christa
Madeira, Jean
Maison, Rene
Majorano, Gaetano
Malbin, Elaine
Malibran, Maria Felicita
Mallinger, Mathilde
Manners, Charles
Marcoux, Vanni
Mario, Giovanni Matteo
Martinelli, Giovanni
Martini, Nino
Materna, Amalia
Matzenauer, Margaret
Maurel, Victor
Mayr, Richard
McCormack, John
McCracken, James
  (Eugene)
Melba, Nellie, Dame
Melchior, Lauritz
Melton, James
Merrill, Robert
Merriman, Nan
Migenes, Julia
Milanov, Zinka Kunc
Mildenburg, Anna von
Milder-Hauptmann,
  Pauline Anna
Mildmay, Audrey
Millo, Aprile
Milnes, Sherrill Eustace
Modl, Martha
Moffo, Anna
Monk, Allan James
Morris, James Peppler
Moscona, Nicola
Muller, Maria
Muratore, Lucien
Muzio, Claudia
Nachbaur, Franz
Naudin, Emilio
Neumann, Angelo
Nevada, Emma
Neway, Patricia
Nicolini
Nielsen, Alice
Niemann, Albert
Nilsson, Birgit
Nilsson, Christine
Nixon, Marni

Nordica, Lillian
Norena, Eide
Norman, Jessye
Nourrit, Adolphe
Novotna, Jarmila
Obraztsova, Elena
Olczewska, Maria
Olivero, Magda
Onegin, Sigrid
Pacchierotti, Gasparo
Pasero, Tancredi
Pasta, Giuditta Negri
Patti, Adelina Juana Maria
Patzak, Julius
Pavarotti, Luciano
Pears, Peter, Sir
Peerce, Jan
Persiani, Fanny
Peters, Roberta
Petrov, Ossip
Piazza, Marguerite
Pilou, Jeannette
Pinza, Ezio
Plancon, Pol-Henri
Plishka, Paul Peter
Pons, Lily
Ponselle, Carmela
Ponselle, Rosa
Presnell, Harve
Prey, Hermann
Price, Leontyne
Price, Margaret Berenice
Quilico, Louis
Raisa, Rosa
Ralf, Torsten
Ramey, Samuel Edward
Raskin, Judith
Reardon, John
Reichmann, Theodor
Reiss, Albert
Renaud, Maurice
Resnik, Regina
Rethberg, Elizabeth
Robinson, Forbes
Rossi-Lemeni, Nicola
Roswaenge, Helge
Rothier, Leon
Rothmuller, Marko A
Rounseville, Robert Field
Roze, Marie
Rubini, Giovanni-Battista
Ruffo, Titta
Rysanek, Leonie
Sack, Erna
Sammarco, Mario
Sanderson, Sybil
Sayao, Bidu
Scalchi, Sofia
Scheff, Fritzi
Schipa, Tito
Schlusnus, Heinrich
Schmedes, Erik
Schnorr, Ludwig von
  Carolsfeld
Schorr, Friedrich
Schroder-Devrient,
  Wilhelmine
Schumann, Elisabeth
Schumann-Heink,
  Ernestine Rossler
Schutzendorf, Gustav
Schwarzkopf, Elisabeth
Scott, Norman
Scotti, Antonio
Scotto, Renata

Seefried, Irmgard Maria
  Theresia
Sembrich, Marcella
Senesino
Shirley, George Irving
Shirley-Quirk, John
  Stanton
Siepi, Cesare
Sills, Beverly
Simionato, Guilietta
Simoneau, Leopold
Singher, Martial
Slezak, Leo
Soderstrom, Elisabeth
  Anna
Sontag, Henriette
Souzay, Gerard
Stabile, Mariano
Stader, Maria
Steber, Eleanor
Stevens, Rise
Stewart, Thomas
Stich-Randall, Teresa
Stignani, Ebe
Stilwell, Richard Dale
Stoltz, Rosine
Stolz, Teresa
Stracciari, Riccardo
Stratas, Teresa
Streich, Rita
Strepponi, Giuseppina
Studer, Cheryl
Supervia, Conchita
Sutherland, Joan, Dame
Svanholm, Set
Swarthout, Gladys
Taddei, Giuseppe
Tagliabue, Carlo
Tagliavini, Ferrucio
Talvela, Martti Olavi
Tamagno, Francesco
Tamburini, Antonio
Tauber, Richard
Tebaldi, Renata
Te Kanawa, Kiri, Dame
Telva, Marion
Ternina, Milka
Tetrazzini, Luisa
Teyte, Maggie, Dame
Thebom, Blanche
Thill, Georges
Thomas, Jess
Thomas, John Charles
Thorborg, Kerstin
Tibbett, Lawrence Mervil
Tichatschek, Joseph
Tokatyan, Armand
Torrence, Ernest
Tourel, Jennie
Tozzi, Giorgio
Traubel, Helen
Troyanos, Tatiana
Tucker, Richard
Turner, Eva, Dame
Uhde, Hermann
Unger, Caroline
Uppman, Theodor
Ursuleac, Viorica
Valdengo, Giuseppe
Valente, Benita
Valleria, Alwina
Valletti, Cesare
Van Rooy, Anton
Van Zandt, Marie
Varesi, Felice
Varnay, Astrid

Velluti, Giovanni Battista
Verrett, Shirley Carter
Vestris, Lucia Elizabeth,
  Madame
Viardot-Garcia, Pauline
Vickers, Jon
Vinay, Ramon
Vishnevskaya, Galina
  (Pavlovna)
Vogl, Heinrich
VonStade, Frederica
Votipka, Thelma
Vyvyan, Jennifer Brigit
Walker, Edyth
Warren, Leonard
Weathers, Felicia
Welitsch, Ljuba
Whitehill, Clarence
  Eugene
Windgassen, Wolfgang
  Friedrich Hermann
Winkelmann, Hermann
Witherspoon, Herbert
Witte, Erich
Wolff, Fritz
Wunderlich, Fritz
Zanelli, Renato
Zenatello, Giovanni
Zylis-Gara, Teresa

ORATOR

Ames, Fisher
Antiphon of Rhamnus
Apuleius, Lucius
Bevan, Aneurin
Bossuet, Jacques Benigne
Burke, Edmund
Canning, George
Demosthenes
Grady, Henry Woodfin
Grattan, Henry
Hyperides
Ingersoll, Robert Green
Isocrates
Mirabeau, Honore Gabriel
  Riquetti
Phillips, Wendell
Pliny the Younger
Quintilian Marcus Fabius
Sumner, Charles
Tacitus, Cornelius
Webster, Daniel

ORGANIST

Bach, Johann Sebastian
Bach, Wilhelm
  Friedemann
Biggs, Edward George
  Power
Boyce, William
Bruckner, Anton
Buck, Dudley
Bull, John
Burney, Charles
Buxtehude, Dietrich
Byrd, William
Cabezon, Antonio
Courboin, Charles
Davies, Henry Walford,
  Sir
Diemer, Emma Lou

DuPre, Marcel
Eddy, Clarence
Foote, Arthur William
Fox, Virgil Keel
Franck, Cesar Auguste
Frescobaldi, Girolamo
Froberger, Johann Jakob
Gruber, Franz-Xaver
Hofhaimer, Paul
Merulo, Claudio
Morley, Thomas
Pachelbel, Johann
Smith, Ethel
Sowerby, Leo
Sweelinck, Jan Pieterszoon
Tallis, Thomas
Widor, Charles Marie Jean
  Albert
Yon, Pietro Alessandro

ORGANIZATION EXECUTIVE

Dixon, Margaret (A.)
Tucker, C(ynthia) DeLores
  (Nottage)
White, Lois Jean

ORGANIZATION OFFICIAL

Washington, Thomas L.

ORIENTALIST

Binyon, Laurence
Burton, Richard Francis,
  Sir
Lane, Edward William
Selden, John

ORNITHOLOGIST

Ali, Salim A
Allen, Arthur Augustus
Arbib, Robert Simeon, Jr.
Audubon, John James
Bailey, Florence Augusta
  Merriam
Beebe, William
Bond, James
Brasher, Rex
Chapman, Frank Michler
Coues, Elliott
Fuertes, Louis Agassiz
Hosking, Eric J
Miner, Jack
Peterson, Roger Tory
Stroud, Robert Franklin
Toone, Bill

OUTLAW

Allison, Clay
Barrow, Clyde
Bass, Sam
Billy the Kid
Cassidy, Butch

Montefiore, Moses Haim,
  Sir
Montor, Henry
Morgan, J(ohn) P(ierpont),
  Jr.
Morris, William Richard
Mott, Stewart Rawlings
Nobel, Alfred Bernhard
Peabody, George
Pearson, Cyril Arthur, Sir
Perot, H(enry) Ross
Post, Marjorie
  Merriweather
Pratt, Charles
Procter, William Cooper
Reynolds, R(ichard)
  J(oshua), Jr.
Rockefeller, Abby Aldrich
Rockefeller, John
  D(avison), Jr.
Rockefeller, John
  D(avison), III
Rockefeller, Mary French
Rosenstein, Nettie
Ross, Percy Nathan
Rutgers, Henry
Rylands, John
Sage, Margaret Olivia
Sasakawa, Ryoichi
Schiff, Jacob Henry
Sharp, Granville
Simmons, Adele Smith
Sloane, Hans, Sir
Smith, Gerrit
Smith, Sophia
Spanel, Abram N
Stewart, Alexander Turney
Stone, W Clement
Straus, Isidor
Straus, Nathan
Tanner, Marion
Tata, Jamshedji
  Nusserwanji
Tompkins, Sally Louisa
Tulane, Paul
Tully, Alice
Uris, Harold David
Vanderbilt, Cornelius
Vanderbilt, William Henry
Walker, Sarah Breedlove
  McWilliams
Wallace, Richard, Sir
Warburg, Felix Moritz
Warburg, James Paul
Wrightsman, Charles
  Bierer
Yale, Elihu

PHILOLOGIST

Wolf, Friedrich August

PHILOSOPHER

Abarbanel, Judah
Abravanel, Isaac ben
  Judah
Adler, Mortimer J(erome)
Adorno, Theodor
  Wiesengrund
Ahad Haam
Alain
Albert the Great

Alembert, Jean le Rond d'
Alexander, Samuel
Alexander of Hales
Althusser, Louis
Anaxagoras
Anaximander
Anaximenes of Miletus
Antisthenes
Aristotle
Augustine, Saint
Austin, John Langshaw
Averroes
Avicenna
Ayer, Alfred Jules, Sir
Bacon, Francis, Sir
Bacon, Roger
Bain, Alexander
Barrett, William
  Christopher
Bayle, Pierre
Bentham, Jeremy
Berdyayev, Nikolay
  Aleksandrovich
Bergson, Henri Louis
Berkeley, George
Berlin, Isaiah, Sir
Bernard De Chartres
Biddle, John
Blaga, Lucien
Bloch, Ernst
Bode, Boyd Henry
Bodin, Jean
Boethius
Bok, Sissela
Borochov, Dov Ber
Bosanquet, Bernard
Bradley, Francis Herbert
Bradshaw, John Elliot
Brentano, Franz Clemens
Brewster, David, Sir
Brightman, Edgar
  Sheffield
Broad, C(harlie) D(unbar)
Broudy, Harry Samuel
Bruno, Giordano
Buber, Martin
Buddha
Butler, Joseph
Callahan, Daniel John
Campanella, Tommaso
Camus, Albert
Cardano, Geronimo
Carnap, Rudolf
Carneades
Cassirer, Ernst
Cato, Marcus Porcius
  Uticensis
Charron, Pierre
Chrysippus
Chuang Tzu
Chu Hsi
Cicero, Marcus Tullius
Clarke, Samuel
Cohen, Hermann
Cohen, Morris Raphael
Collingwood, Robin
  George
Comte, Auguste
Condillac, Etienne Bonnot
  de
Condorcet, Marie-Jean-
  Antoine
Confucius
Congreve, Richard
Cooper, Anthony Ashley,
  1st Earl of Shaftesbury

Cousin, Victor
Croce, Benedetto
Cudworth, Ralph
Dasgupta, S(urendra)
  N(ath)
Democritus
Derrida, Jacques
Descartes, Rene
Dewey, John
Diderot, Denis
Dilthey, Wilhelm Christian
  Ludwig
Diogenes
Draper, John William
Driesch, Hans Adolf
  Eduard
Duhring, Eugen Karl
Dunne, John William
Eberhard, Johann August
Eckhart, Johannes
Emerson, Ralph Waldo
Empedocles
Epictetus
Epicurus
Erasmus, Desiderius
Erigena, John Scotus
Eucken, Rudolf Christoph
Fanon, Frantz (Omar)
Fechner, Gustav Theodor
Feigl, Herbert
Ferguson, Adam
Feuerbach, Ludwig
  Andreas
Fichte, Johann Gottlieb
Ficino, Marsilio
Fiske, John
Fletcher, Joseph Francis
  (III)
Foucault, Michel
Fourier, Francois Marie
  Charles
Frege, (Friedrich Ludwig)
  Gottlob
Freire, P(aulo)
Fries, Jakob Friedrich
Fukuyama, Francis
Gadamer, Hans-Georg
Garrigou-Lagrange,
  Reginald Marie
Gentile, Giovanni
Ghazali, al
Ghose, Aurobindo
Gilson, Etienne Henry
Gobineau, Joseph Arthur,
  Comte de
Gorgias
Green, Thomas Hill
Grote, George
Guardini, Romano
Guarini, Guarino
Guattari, Felix
Haam, Ahad
Habermas, Juergen
Halevy, Elie
Hamann, Johann Georg
Hamilton, William, Sir
Hanafi, Hassan
Han Fei Tzu
Hartley, David
Hartshorne, Charles
Hegel, Georg Wilhelm
  Friedrich
Heidegger, Martin
Helvetius, Claude Adrien
Heraclides of Pontus
Heraclitus of Ephesus

Herbart, Johann Friedrich
Herbert, Edward, 1st
  Baron Herbert of
  Cherbury
Hesse, Mary B(renda)
Hobbes, Thomas
Hobhouse, Leonard
  Trelawny
Hoffer, Eric
Holbach, Baron d'
Hook, Sidney
Hooke, Robert
Horne, Herman Harrell
Hostos (y Bonilla),
  Eugenio Maria de
Hsiung Shih-Li
Hsun-tzu
Huang Tsung-hsi
Hulme, Thomas Ernest
Hume, David
Husserl, Edmund
Hutcheson, Francis
Hypatia
Hyslop, James Hervey
Ibn al-Arabi, Muhyi al-
  Din
ibn Gabirol, Solomon ben
  Judah
ibn Hazm, Abu
  Muhammad Ali
ibn Tufayl, Abu Bakr
  Muhammad
Iqbal, Mahomed, Sir
Jacobi, Friedrich Heinrich
Jaeger, Werner Wilhelm
James, Henry, Sr.
James, William
Jaspers, Karl
Jeffreys, Harold
Jonas, Hans
Kallen, Horace M(eyer)
Kant, Immanuel
Kaufmann, Ezekiel
Keen, Sam
Keyserling, Hermann
  Alexander Graf Von
Kierkegaard, Soren Aabye
Kindi, Abu-Yusuf Yaqub
  ibn-Ishaq al-
Kolakowski, Leszek
Krishnamurti, Jiddu
Kuhn, Thomas Samuel
LaBruyere, Jean de
Ladd, George Trumbull
Lahbabi, Mohammed Aziz
Lakatos, Imre
La Mettrie, Julien Offray
  de
Langer, Suzanne K
Lao-Tzu
Le Bon, Gustave
Leibniz, Gottfried Wilhelm
  von
Lerner, Michael
Levi ben Gershon
Levinas, Emmanuel
Levy, Bernard-Henri
Levy-Bruhl, Lucien
Lewes, George Henry
Lewis, Clarence Irving
Locke, John
Lotze, Rudolf Hermann
Lovejoy, Arthur Oncken
  (Schauffler)
Lu Chiu-yuan
Lucretius

PHILOSOPHERS

PHOTOGRAPHER

PHOTOJOURNALIST

Alley, Norman William
Bergen, Candice
Bourke-White, Margaret
Chapelle, Dickey
Davidson, Bruce
Duncan, David Douglas
Eisenstaedt, Alfred
Haas, Ernst
Haney, Chris
Mark, Mary Ellen
Rebbot, Olivier
Rosenthal, Joe
Salgado, Sebastiao
Sleet, Moneta, Jr.
Smith, W(illiam) Eugene
Ut, Huynh Cong

PHYSICAL FITNESS EXPERT

Atlas, Charles
LaLanne, Jack
Prudden, Bonnie

PHYSICIAN

Addison, Thomas
Alexander, Franz Gabriel
Alexander, Hattie
  Elizabeth
Allen, Ethel D.
Alvarez, Walter Clement
Anderson, Dorothy
  Hansine
Anderson, Elizabeth
  Garrett
Apgar, Virginia
Appel, James Ziegler
Arbuthnot, John
Avicenna
Baker, Sara Josephine
Baldwin, Horace
Bannister, Roger, Sir
Banting, Frederick Grant,
  Sir
Barany, Robert
Bard, John
Baulieu, Etienne-Emile
Beard, George Miller
Beaumont, William
Benjamin, Regina (M.)
Benn, Gottfried
Berengario da Carpi,
  Jacopo
Bishop, Katharine Scott
Black, Davidson
Black, James Whyte, Sir
Black, Keith Lanier
Blackwell, Elizabeth
Blackwell, Emily
Blumberg, Baruch Samuel
Boerhaave, Hermann
Bond, George Foote
Bowditch, Henry Ingersoll
Bowen, Otis Ray
Boyd, William Clouser
Boylston, Zabdiel
Brazelton, T(homas) Berry
Bretonneau, Pierre Fidele
Breuer, Josef
Bridgman, Percy Williams

Bright, Richard
Bristow, Lonnie
Brown, Bobby
Browne, Thomas
Bruce, David, Sir
Butler, Robert N(eil)
Caius, John
Calderone, Frank Anthony
Calderone, Mary Steichen
Cardozo, W. Warrick
Cardus, David
Channing, Walter
Charcot, Jean Martin
Chinn, May (Edward)
Chopra, Deepak
Christian-Green, Donna
  M.
Cook, Robin
Cooper, Edward S(awyer)
Cooper, Kenneth Hardy
Crohn, Burrill Bernard
Culpeper, Nicholas
Dafoe, Allan Roy
Dale, Henry Hallett
Darwin, Erasmus
Dawson, Bertrand Edward
Destouches, Louis-
  Ferdinand
DeVita, Vincent Theodore,
  Jr.
Dickens, Helen Octavia
Dickey, Herbert Spencer
Dioscorides, Pedanius
Domagk, Gerhard
Dooley, Thomas Anthony,
  III
Doyle, Arthur Conan, Sir
Drake, Daniel
Drummond, William
  Henry
Eastman, Charles
  Alexander
Egas Moniz, Antonio C A
  F
Eijkman, Christiaan
Elders, Joycelyn
Eliot, Martha May
Ellis, Effie O'Neal
Enders, John Franklin
Erasistratus
Eudoxus of Cnidus
Evans, Herbert McLean
Falkner, Frank T(ardrew)
Fauci, Anthony Stephen
Feingold, Benjamin
  Franklin
Fernel, Jean Francois
Finlay, Carlos Juan
Finsen, Niels Ryberg
Fishbein, Morris
Fisher, Rudolph
Flint, Austin
Florey, Howard Walter
Fowler, Lydia Folger
Fracastoro, Gerolamo
Frank, Johann Peter
Fuller, Solomon Carter, Jr.
Gale, Robert Peter
Galen
Gall, Franz Joseph
Galvani, Luigi
Gardiner, Muriel
Garretta, Michel
Geschwind, Norman
Gesell, Arnold
Gilbert, William

Gogarty, Oliver St. John
Goldberger, Joseph
Goldstein, Joseph Leonard
Gorgas, William Crawford
Gorrie, John
Gougelman, Pierre
Gould, George Milbry
Graham, Wallace H(arry)
Gram, Hans Christian
  Joachim
Grau San Martin, Ramon
Grenfell, Wilfred
  Thomason, Sir
Guillotin, Joseph Ignace
Guion, Connie Myers
Gunning, Lucille C
Guthrie, Samuel
Hahnemann, Samuel
Halberstam, Michael
  Joseph
Hamilton, Alice
Hammon, William
  McDowell
Hartmann, Franz
Harvey, William
Hatem, George
Healy, Bernadine
Heaton, Leonard
Heimlich, Henry Jay
Heiser, Victor George
Hench, Philip Showalter
Herrick, James Bryan
Hess, Walter Rudolf
Heymans, Corneille Jean
  Francois
Hingson, Robert A(ndrew)
Hinton, William Augustus
Hippocrates
Hirschfeld, Magnus
Hopkins, Frederick
  Gowland, Sir
Horder, Thomas Jeeves
ibn Tufayl, Abu Bakr
  Muhammad
Ilg, Frances Lillian
Imhotep
Ingenhousz, Jan
Jackson, Charles Thomas
Jacobi, Abraham
Jacobi, Mary Corinna
  Putnam
Jacobs, Joe
Jaffe, Harold W
Jarvik, Robert Koffler
Jaspers, Karl
Jemison, Mae C(arol)
Jenner, Edward
Jenner, William, Sir
Joseph, Stephen (Carl)
Kane, Elisha Kent
Kaplan, Henry Seymour
Keith, Louis Gerald
Kerwin, Joseph Peter
King, Frederic Truby
Klass, Perri Elizabeth
Kocher, Emil Theodor
Kolff, Willem Johan
Kopits, Steven E
Kossel, Karl Martin
  Leonhard Albrecht
Kouchner, Bernard
LaFlesche Picotte, Susan
Lamaze, Fernand
Lamb, Lawrence Edward
La Mettrie, Julien Offray
  de

Landsteiner, Karl
Langston, J William
Laveran, Charles Louis
  Alphonse
Lawless, Theodore
  K(enneth)
Lazear, Jesse William
Leboyer, Frederick
Lee, Rebecca
Levy, Allan
Liebow, Averill
  A(braham)
Lilly, John C
Linacre, Thomas
Loewi, Otto
Lombroso, Cesare
Long, Crawford
  Williamson
Long, Irene D.
Louis, Pierre Charles
  Alexandre
Lovelace, William
  Randolph, II
MacLeod, John James
  Rickard
Malpighi, Marcello
Manley, Audrey Forbes
Manson, Patrick, Sir
Marat, Jean Paul
Margai, Milton Augustus
  Striery
Masters, William Howell
McCrae, John
Mellon, William Larimer,
  Jr.
Mendenhall, Dorothy Reed
Mengele, Josef
Menninger, William C
Meriwether, W(ilhelm)
  Delano
Merrill, John Putnam
Mesmer, Franz Anton
Minot, George Richards
Mirkin, Gabe
Montezuma, Carlos
Morgan, John
Morgan, Russell H(edley)
Morgentaler, Henry
Mudd, Samuel Alexander
Murphy, William Parry
Murray, Joseph
Mutis, Jose Celestino
Negrin, Juan
Nicolle, Charles Jules
  Henri
Niepce, Joseph Nicephore
Nostradamus
Novello, Antonia Coello
Olbers, Heinrich Wilhelm
  Matthaus
Ornish, Dean
Osler, William, Sir
Page, Irvine H
Palmer, Daniel David
Palmer, William
Papanicolaou, George
  Nicholas
Paracelsus, Philippus
  Aureolus
Park, William Hallock
Paton, Richard
Penfield, Wilder Graves
Petty, William, Sir
Pincus, Gregory
Pinel, Philippe
Pitt, David Thomas

Jeffreys, Harold
Jensen, Johannes Hans
  Daniel
Johnson, Raynor Carey
Joliot(-Curie), (Jean)
  Frederic
Joliot-Curie, Irene
Joule, James Prescott
Kahn, Herman
Kahng, Dawon
Kamerlingh Onnes, Heike
Kapitsa, Pyotr
  Leonidovich
Karle, Isabella (L.)
Karle, Jerome
Kastler, Alfred
Kayser, Heinrich Gustav
  Johannes
Keesom, Willem Hendrik
Kelvin, William Thomson,
  Baron
Kendall, Henry Way
Kerst, Donald W(illiam)
Kirchhoff, Gustav Robert
Klitzing, Klaus von
Kurchatov, Igor
  Vasilyevich
Kusch, P(olycarp)
Lamb, Willis Eugene, Jr.
Land, Edwin Herbert
Landau, Lev Davidovich
Laue, Max Theodor Felix
  von
Lawrence, Ernest Orlando
Lederman, Leon Max
Lee, Tsung-Dao
Leighton, Robert
  B(enjamin)
Lippmann, Gabriel Jonas
Livingston, M(ilton)
  Stanley
Lorentz, Hendrick Antoon
Lovins, Amory B(loch)
Mach, Ernst
Maglich, Bogdan C
Maiman, Theodore Harold
Marshak, Robert E(ugene)
Massey, Walter E(ugene)
Mauchly, John William
Maxwell, James Clerk
Mayer, Maria Goeppert
Meitner, Lise
Michelson, Albert
  Abraham
Millikan, Robert Andrews
Moore, Charlotte E(mma)
Morrison, Philip
Morse, Philip McCord
Mossbauer, Rudolf
  Ludwig
Mott, Nevill Francis, Sir
Mottelson, Benjamin Roy
Mueller, Erwin Wilhelm
Muller, Karl Alex(ander)
Neddermeyer, Seth H
Neel, Louis Eugene Felix
Oersted, Hans Christian
Ohm, Georg Simon
O'Neill, Gerard Kitchen
Oppenheimer, Frank F
Oppenheimer, J(ulius)
  Robert
Owen, Tobias Chant
Pais, Abraham
Paul, Wolfgang
Pauli, Wolfgang Ernst

Pauling, Linus C(arl)
Penney, William George
Penrose, Roger
Penzias, Arno Allan
Piccard, Auguste
Planck, Max Karl Ernst
  Ludwig
Plucker, Julius
Powell, Cecil Frank
Poynting, John Henry
Prichard, Diana Garcia
Prokhorov, Alexander
  Mikhailovich
Pupin, Michael Idvorsky
Purcell, Edward M(ills)
Rabi, Isidor Isaac
Rainwater, James
Raman, Chandrasekhara
  Venkata, Sir
Rayleigh, John William
  Strutt, Baron
Richardson, Lewis Fry
Rohrer, Heinrich
Rosendahl, Bruce R
Rowland, Henry Augustus
Rubbia, Carlo
Rumford, Count
Rutherford, Ernest, Baron
Rutherfurd, Lewis Morris
Sakharov, Andrei
  Dmitrievich
Salam, Abdus
Schawlow, Arthur
  L(eonard)
Schlick, Friedrich Albert
  Moritz
Schrieffer, John Robert
Schroedinger, Erwin
Schwartz, Melvin
Schwinger, Julian
  (Seymour)
Seebeck, Thomas Johann
Segre, Emilio Gino
Siegbahn, Kai Manne
  Boerje
Siemens, William, Sir
Smoot, George
Steinberger, Jack
Stern, Otto
Stokes, George Gabriel,
  Sir
Stone, Edward C, Jr.
Stoney, George Johnstone
Stormer, Fredrik (Carl
  Mulertz)
Stromgren, Bengt Georg
  Daniel
Sturgeon, William
Suits, C(hauncey) G(uy)
Swan, Joseph Wilson, Sir
Tait, Peter Guthrie
Tamm, Igor Evgenevich
Taylor, Richard Edward
Teller, Edward
Thomson, George Paget,
  Sir
Tolman, Richard C(hace)
Tomonaga Shinichiro
Townes, Charles Hard
Townsend, John Sealy
  Edward, Sir
Tuve, Merle Antony
Tyndall, John
Upton, Francis Robbins
Van Allen, James Alfred
Van der Meer, Simon

Van Vleck, John
  Hasbrouck
Volta, Alessandro
  Giuseppe Antonio
  Anastasio
Von Klitzing, Klaus
Walton, Ernest Thomas
  Sinton
Weber, Wilhelm Eduard
Weinberg, Steven
Wigner, Eugene P(aul)
Wilson, Kenneth Geddes
Wilson, Robert R(athbun)
Wilson, Robert Woodrow
Witten, Edward
Wood, Robert Williams
Wu, Chien Shiung
Yalow, Rosalyn Sussman
Yang, Chen Ning
Young, Thomas
Yukawa, Hideki
Zacharias, Jerrold
  R(einarch)
Zernike, Frits
Zinn, Walter Henry
Zworykin, Vladimir
  K(osma)

PHYSIOLOGIST

Bayliss, William
  Maddock, Sir
Behring, Emil Adolph von
Bernard, Claude
Best, Charles Herbert
Blumenbach, Johann
  Friedrich
Cannon, Walter Bradford
Cournand, Andre Frederic
Cowings, Patricia S.
Dalton, John Call
Du Bois-Reymond, Emil
Eckstein, Gustav
Edwards, Robert Geoffrey
Einthoven, Willem
Erlanger, Joseph
Gasser, Herbert Spencer
Granit, Ragnar Arthur
Guillemin, Roger Charles
  Louis
Haldane, John Scott
Hales, Stephen
Helmholtz, Hermann
  Ludwig Ferdinand von
Hill, Archibald Vivian
Hodgkin, Alan Lloyd, Sir
Houssay, Bernardo
  Alberto
Howell, William H(enry)
Jellinek, Elvin Morton
Keys, Ancel Benjamin
Ludwig, Karl Friedrich
  Wilhelm
Meyerhof, Otto Fritz
Minkowski, Oskar
Pavlov, Ivan Petrovich
Sanctorius
Schlessinger, Laura
Schwann, Theodor
Starling, Ernest Henry

PIANIST

Albeniz, Isaac Manuel
  Francisco
Allen, Geri
Allison, Mose
Anda, Geza
Arrau, Claudio
Ax, Emanuel
Babin, Victor
Bachauer, Gina
Backhaus, Wilhelm
Badura-Skoda, Paul
Balsam, Artur
Barenboim, Daniel
Bartok, Bela
Bauer, Harold
Benjamin, Arthur
Bennett, William
  Sterndale, Sir
Berman, Lazar
Beroff, Michel
Blake, Eubie
Bley, Carla
Bolcom, William Elden
Bolet, Jorge
Borge, Victor
Brahms, Johannes
Brailowsky, Alexander
Brendel, Alfred
Bronfman, Yefim
Browning, John
Bulow, Hans Guido von
Busoni, Ferruccio
  Benvenuto
Carle, Frankie
Chaminade, Cecile
Chasins, Abram
Cherkassky, Shura
Chopin, Frederic Francois
Chung, Myung-Whun
Clementi, Muzio
Cliburn, Van
Cortot, Alfred-Denis
Cowell, Henry Dixon
Cramer, Floyd
Cramer, Johann Baptist
Crowder, Henry
Curzon, Clifford Michael,
  Sir
Czerny, Karl
D'Albert, Eugene
Dalto, Jorge
Davidovich, Bella
Davies, Dennis Russell
Davis, Anthony
Dearie, Blossom
DeJohnette, Jack
De Larrocha, Alicia
Demus, Joreg
DeRose, Peter
Donegan, Dorothy
Dr. John
Duchin, Eddy
Duchin, Peter Oelrichs
Egorov, Youri
Entremont, Phillippe
Eschenbach, Christoph
Evans, Bill
Fain, Sammy
Feltsman, Vladimir
Ferrante, Arthur
Ferrell, Rachelle
Field, John
Flanagan, Tommy (Lee)
Fleisher, Leon

Gabrilowitsch, Ossip
  Salomonovich
Gold, Arthur
Goldovsky, Boris
Goode, Richard Stephen
Gould, Glenn Herbert
Grainger, Percy Aldridge
Greco, Buddy
Green, Benny
Guaraldi, Vince(nt
  Anthony)
Gulda, Friedrich
Halasz, Laszlo
Halle, Charles, Sir
Hambro, Leonid
Hawkins, Screamin' Jay
Helfgott, David
Henderson, Skitch
Hess, Myra, Dame
Hinderas, Natalie Leota
  Henderson
Hoiby, Lee
Horn, Shirley
Horowitz, Vladimir
Hummel, Johann
  Nepomuk
Iturbi, Amparo
Janis, Byron
Johannesen, Grant
Johansen, Gunnar
Johnson, James Price
Joyce, Eileen
Kapell, William
Kempff, (Wilhelm) Walter
  Friedrich
Kennedy, Joan Bennett
Kissin, Evgeny
Kuerti, Anton
Laredo, Ruth
Lev, Ray
Lewenthal, Raymond
Lhevinne, Josef
Lipatti, Dinu
List, Eugene
Liszt, Franz (Ferencz)
Lowe, Jack (Warren)
Luboshutz, Pierre
Lupu, Radu
Lympany, Moura
MacDowell, Edward
  Alexander
Malcolm, George
Masselos, William
McArthur, Edwin Douglas
McCabe, John
McPartland, Margaret
  Marian
Medtner, Nicholas
Melis, Jose
Memphis Slim
Menuhin, Hephzibah
Moszkowski, Moritz
Nero, Peter
Nin-Culmell, Joaquin
  Maria
Nyiregyhazi, Ervin
Paderewski, Ignace Jan
Palmieri, Eddie
Perahia, Murray
Pogorelich, Ivo
Previn, Andre
Professor Longhair
Reisenberg, Nadia
Richter, Sviatoslav
  Theofilovich

Roberts, Marcus
Rosenstock, Joseph
Rosenthal, Moriz
Rubinstein, Anton
  Gregorovitch
Rubinstein, Arthur
Rushen, Patrice Louise
Samaroff, Olga
Schelling, Ernest Henry
Schnabel, Artur
Schumann, Clara
  Josephine Wieck
Serkin, Peter A(dolf)
Serkin, Rudolph
Sherman, Russell
Short, Bobby
Slenczynska, Ruth
Solal, Martial
Solomon
Spann, Otis
Story, Liz
Sukman, Harry
Tal, Josef
Taneyev, Sergey
  Ivanovich
Tausig, Karl
Tcherepnin, Alexander
  Nikolayevich
Teicher, Louis
Templeton, Alec
Tiomkin, Dimitri
Tureck, Rosalyn
Tyner, McCoy Alfred
Uchida, Mitsuko
Vronsky, Vitya
Walter, Bruno
Walter, Cyril
Weissenberg, Alexis
  Sigismund
Whittemore, Arthur Austin
Wild, Earl
Williams, Roger
Winston, George
Wittgenstein, Paul

PILOT

Beard, Myron Gould
Boyington, Pappy
Brown, A Roy
Cobb, Jerrie
Forsythe, Albert E
Gann, Ernest Kellogg
Guynemer, Georges Marie
Hunt, Jack Reed
Lewis, Robert Alvin
Merrill, Henry Tindall
Numan, Eppo
Powers, Francis Gary
Rutan, Dick
Shreve, Henry Miller
Steger, Will
Tibbets, Paul Warfield
Tiburzi, Bonnie
von Lipsey, Roderick K.
Warner, Emily Howell
Yeager, Chuck
Yeager, Jeana

PIONEER

Applegate, Jesse
Appleseed, Johnny

Beckwourth, James
  Pierson
Boone, Daniel
Bozeman, John M
Bridger, James
Calamity Jane
Carson, Kit
Chisholm, Jesse
Cody, Buffalo Bill
Comstock, Henry
  Tompkins Paige
Crockett, Davy
Daly, Marcus
DuSable, Jean Baptiste
Fink, Mike
Hickok, Wild Bill
Lillie, Gordon William
Love, Nat
Oakley, Annie
Rogers, Robert
Starr, Belle
Sutter, John Augustus
Tabor, Elizabeth Bonduel
  McCourt Doe
Zane, Ebenezer

PIRATE

Blackbeard
Bonny, Anne
Kidd, William, Captain
Laffite, Jean
Morgan, Henry, Sir
Read, Mary

PLAYWRIGHT

Afinogenov, Aleksandr
  Nikolaevich
Moss, Carlton
Smith, Roger Guenveur

POET

Abarbanel, Judah
Abercrombie, Lascelles
Abu-L-Ala al-Maarri
Abu Madi, Iliya
Abu Nuwas
Abu Salma
Achterberg, Gerrit
Adonis
Ady, Endre
Agee, James Rufus
Agustini, Delmira
Ahmed Hasim
Aiken, Conrad Potter
Akhmatova, Anna
Akins, Zoe
Alberti, Rafael
Alegria, Claribel
Aleixandre, Vicente
Alfieri, Vittorio
Allen, Elizabeth Ann
  Chase Akers
Allen, Hervey
Allen, Paula Gunn
Allingham, William
Allston, Washington
Alonso, Damaso
Alvarez, Alfred
Alvarez, Julia

Amrouche, Jean
Anacreon
Andersen, Hans Christian
Anderson, Sherwood
Anhava, Tuomas
Aragon, Louis Marie
  Antoine Alfred
Aretino, Pietro
Ariosto, Ludovico
Armour, Richard Willard
Artaud, Antonin
Attar, Farid ed-Din
Atwood, Margaret
  (Eleanor)
Audiberti, Jacques
Auslander, Joseph
Austin, Alfred
Awoonor, Kofi
Bacchylides
Bacon, Leonard
Bandeira, Manuel
Banks, Russell
Baraka, Amiri
Barbour, John
Barclay, Alexander
Barker, George Granville
Basho
Bates, Katharine Lee
Baudelaire, Charles Pierre
Bax, Clifford
Beaumont, John, Sir
Becquer, Gustavo Adolfo
  Dominguez
Belli, Carlos German
Bellman, Carl Michael
Bely, Andrey
Bembo, Pietro
Benediktsson, Einar
Benet, Stephen Vincent
Ben Jelloun, Tahar
Beranger, Pierre-Jean de
Bernard, Andrew Milroy
Berrigan, Daniel J
Berry, Wendell
Berryman, John
Betjeman, John, Sir
Betti, Ugo
Bialik, Chaim Nachman
Bialik, Hayyim Nahman
Binyon, Laurence
Birney, Earle
Bishop, Elizabeth
Bjornson, Bjornstjerne
  Martinius
Blackmur, Richard Palmer
Blaga, Lucien
Blake, William
Blandiana, Ana
Blok, Aleksandr
  Aleksandrovich
Bloomfield, Robert
Blunden, Edmund Charles
Blunt, Wilfrid Scawen
Bly, Robert Elwood
Bodenheim, Maxwell
Bodmer, Johann Jakob
Bogan, Louise
Boiardo, Matteo Maria
Boileau(-Despreaux),
  Nicolas
Bolton, Sarah Tittle
  Barrett
Borel d'Hauterive, Petrus
Bottomley, Gordon
Bowles, Paul (Frederick)
Bradstreet, Anne

Braithwaite, William Stanley Beaumont
Branch, Anna Hempstead
Brant, Sebastian
Brassens, Georges
Brautigan, Richard
Brecht, Bertolt (Eugen Friedrich)
Brentano, Clemens Maria
Breton, Andre
Breytenbach, Breyten
Bridges, Robert Seymour
Brodsky, Joseph (Alexandrovich)
Bronte, Patrick Branwell
Brooke, Rupert Chawner
Brooks, Gwendolyn Elizabeth
Brooks, Maria Gowen
Broumas, Olga
Brown, Christy
Brown, George Mackay
Browning, Elizabeth Barrett
Browning, Robert
Brutus, Dennis Vincent
Bryant, William Cullen
Bunting, Basil
Burns, Diane M.
Burns, Robert
Burnshaw, Stanley
Busch, Wilhelm
Bush, Barney Furman
Butler, Samuel
Byron, George Gordon, Baron
Cabral de Melo Neto, Joao
Caedmon, Saint
Calderon de la Barca, Pedro
Callimachus
Camoes, Luis de
Campana, Dino
Campanella, Tommaso
Campbell, Thomas
Campion, Thomas
Cardenal, Ernesto
Cardiff, Gladys
Carducci, Giosue Alessandro Guiseppe
Carew, Thomas
Carey, Henry
Carleton, Will
Carman, Bliss
Carroll, Jim
Carruth, Hayden
Cary, Alice
Cary, Phoebe
Castro Alves, Antonio de
Catullus, Gaius Valerius
Cavafy, C(onstantine) P(eter)
Cavalcanti, Guido
Cavendish, Margaret
Cawein, Madison Julius
Celan, Paul
Cervantes (Saavedra), Miguel (de)
Cesaire, Aime Fernand
Chao, Yuen Ren
Chapman, George
Char, Rene (Emile)
Chartier, Alain
Chatterton, Thomas
Chaucer, Geoffrey
Cheney, John Vance

Chenier, Marie-Andre de
Chesterton, G(ilbert) K(eith)
Choquette, Robert Guy
Chretien de Troyes
Christine de Pisan
Churchill, Charles
Ciardi, John Anthony
Cisneros, Sandra
Clampitt, Amy
Clare, John
Clark, Charles Badger
Clarke, Austin
Claudel, Paul Louis Charles
Claudian
Claudius, Matthias
Claus, Hugo
Clemo, Jack
Clough, Arthur Hugh
Coatsworth, Elizabeth Jane
Cocteau, Jean
Coffin, Robert Peter Tristram
Coleridge, Hartley
Coleridge, Mary Elizabeth
Coleridge, Samuel Taylor
Collins, William
Colum, Padraic
Cooke, Rose Terry
Cook-Lynn, Elizabeth
Coppard, A(lfred) E(dgar)
Coppee, Francois Edouard Joachim
Corbiere, Tristan (Edouard Joachim)
Corneille, Pierre
Cornford, Frances Crofts Darwin
Corso, Gregory Nunzio
Cowley, Abraham
Cowper, William
Coxe, Louis Osborne
Crabbe, George
Crane, Hart
Crane, Nathalia Clara Ruth
Crapsey, Adelaide
Crashaw, Richard
Craveirinha, Jose
Creeley, Robert (White)
Cremazie, Octave
Crosby, Harry
Cueva de Garoza, Juan de la
Cullen, Countee (Porter)
Cummings, E(dward) E(stlin)
Cynewulf
Cyrano de Bergerac, Savinien de
Dadie, Bernard Binlin
Daly, Thomas Augustine
Damas, Leon-Gontran
D'Annunzio, Gabriele
Dante Alighieri
DaPonte, Lorenzo
Dargan, Olive Tilford
Dario, Ruben
Darwin, Erasmus
Darwish, Mahmud
Daryush, Elizabeth Bridges
Davenant, William, Sir
Davidson, Donald Grady
Davidson, John

Day-Lewis, Cecil
de Acosta, Mercedes
de Andrade, Mario
Dehmel, Richard
DeLaMare, Walter
Delavigne, Jean Francois Casimir
Deschamps, Eustache
Deus, Joao de
Deutsch, Babette
DeVere, Aubrey Thomas
Dickey, James (Lafayette)
Dickinson, Emily (Elizabeth)
Diop, Birago
Diop, David
Dobell, Sydney Thompson
Dobson, Henry Austin
Dodson, Owen (Vincent)
Donne, John
Doolittle, Hilda
Doughty, Charles Montagu
Douglas, Alfred Bruce, Lord
Douglas, Gavin
Douglas, Keith Castellain
Dove, Rita (Frances)
Dowson, Ernest Christopher
Drake, Joseph Rodman
Drayton, Michael
Drewry, Guy Carleton
Drinkwater, John
Drummond, William Henry
Drummond de Andrade, Carlos
Drummond of Hawthornden, William
Dryden, John
du Bellay, Joachim
Ducis, Jean Francois
Dugan, Alan
Dunbar, Paul Laurence
Dunbar, William
Duncan, Robert Edward
Durcan, Paul
Dyer, Edward, Sir
Eberhart, Richard
Echeverria, Jose Esteban (Antonino)
Eichendorff, Joseph Karl Benedict Freiherr von
Eliot, T(homas) S(tearns)
Elliott, Ebenezer
Elytis, Odysseus
Emerson, Ralph Waldo
Eminescu, Mihail
Empson, William, Sir
Encina, Juan del
Engle, Paul (Hamilton)
Ennius, Quintus
Enright, Dennis Joseph
Ercilla y Zuniga, Alonso de
Esenin, Sergei Aleksandrovich
Espriu, Salvador
Euphorion
Eupolis
Eusden, Laurence
Everson, William Oliver
Evtushenko, Evgeniy Alexandrovich
Ewald, Johannes

Faiz, Faiz Ahmad
Faust, Frederick Schiller
Fergusson, Robert
Ferlinghetti, Lawrence Monsanto
Ferril, Thomas Hornsby
Ficke, Arthur Davidson
Field, Eugene
Finch, Robert Duer Clayton
Firdausi
Fishback, Margaret
FitzGerald, Edward
Fletcher, John Gould
Fogazzaro, Antonio
Forche, Carolyn (Louise)
Ford, Ford Madox
Foscolo, (Niccolo) Ugo
Frechette, Louis-Honore
Freneau, Philip Morin
Froissart, Jean
Frost, Robert Lee
Fuller, Roy Broadbent
Garcia Lorca, Federico
Gardner, Isabella
Garrigue, Jean
Gascoyne, David Emery
Gautier, Theophile
Gay, John
George, Stefan
Gerhardt, Paul(us)
Gershom ben Judah
Gershon, Karen
Gerstler, Amy
Ghose, Aurobindo
Ghose, Sri Chinmoy Kumar
Gibbons, Stella (Dorothea)
Gibran, Kahlil
Gibson, Wilfred Wilson
Gidlow, Elsa
Ginsberg, Allen
Ginzburg, Aleksandr Ilich
Giorno, John
Giovanni, Nikki
Giovannitti, Arturo
Gluck, Louise
Godden, Rumer
Goethe, Johann Wolfgang von
Goldsmith, Oliver
Gongora y Argote, Luis de
Gonzalez Prada, Manuel
Gonzalo de Berceo
Gorbanevskaya, Natalya
Gottfried von Strassburg
Gower, John
Graham, Jorie
Graves, Robert von Ranke
Gray, Thomas
Gregor, Arthur
Gregory, Horace Victor
Grigson, Geoffrey Edward Harvey
Grimke, Angelina Emily Weld
Guest, Edgar A(lbert)
Guillaume de Lorris
Guillen, Jorge
Guillen (y Batista), Nicolas (Cristobal)
Guiney, Louise Imogene
Guinizzelli, Guido
Guiraldes, Ricardo (Guillermo)
Guiterman, Arthur

Gumilev, Nikolai
Gunn, Thom(son William)
Hacker, Marilyn
Hafiz, Shams-al-Din
  Muhammad
Hagedorn, Hermann
Ha-Levi, Judah
Hall, Donald Andrew
Hall, Radclyffe
Halleck, Fritz-Greene
Hammon, Jupiter
Hansen, Joseph
Han Yongun
Han Yu
Hardy, Thomas
Harjo, Joy
Harper, Frances Ellen
  Watkins
Hartmann von Aue
Hassan, Muhammad
  Abdille
Hauptmann, Gerhart
  Johann Robert
Hayden, Robert Earl
Heaney, Seamus (Justin)
Heavysege, Charles
Hecht, Anthony Evan
Heidenstam, Carl Gustaf
  Verner von
Heine, Heinrich
Hemans, Felicia Dorothea
  Browne
Hemphill, Essex
Henley, William Ernest
Herbert, Edward, 1st
  Baron Herbert of
  Cherbury
Herder, Johann Gottfried
  von
Hernandez, Jose
Herrick, Robert
Hesiod
Hill, Geoffrey
Hillyer, Robert
Hinojosa, Rolando
Hoffenstein, Samuel
  Goodman
Hoffman, Charles Fenno
Hofmannsthal, Hugo von
Hogan, Linda
Holderlin, Friedrich
Hollander, John
Holmes, Oliver Wendell,
  Sr.
Hopkins, Gerard Manley
Hopkinson, Francis
Horace
Housman, A(lfred)
  E(dward)
Hovey, Richard
Howe, Susan
Hsieh Ling-yun, Duke of
  K'ang-lo
Huch, Ricarda (Octavia)
Hughes, Langston
Hughes, Ted
Humphries, Rolfe
Hunt, Leigh
Ibn al-Arabi, Muhyi al-
  Din
ibn Gabirol, Solomon ben
  Judah
Ingelow, Jean
Iqbal, Mahomed, Sir
Ivask, Ivar Vidrik
Jackson, Laura Riding

Jacob, Max
Jacopone da Todi
Jami
Jammes, Francis
Jarrell, Randall
Jarry, Alfred
Jeffers, (John) Robinson
Jimenez, Juan Ramon
John of the Cross, Saint
Jong, Erica (Mann)
Jonson, Ben(jamin)
Joyce, James Augustus
  Aloysius
Jozsef, Attila
Juana Ines de la Cruz, Sor
Kafka, Franz
Kalidasa
Karlfeldt, Erik Axel
Kastner, Erich
Kavanagh, Patrick
Keane, John Brendon
Keats, John
Kemp, Harry (Hibbard)
Kenny, Maurice (Francis)
Kerouac, Jack
Kharitonov, Yevgeni
Khodasevich, Vladislav
Kicknosway, Faye
Kilmer, Joyce
Kinnell, Galway
Kipling, Rudyard
Kizer, Carolyn (Ashley)
Klein, Abraham Moses
Kleist, Heinrich von
Klepfisz, Irena
Klopstock, Friedrich
  Gottlieb
Knight, Etheridge
Kogawa, Joy (Nozomi)
Komunyakaa, Yusef
Kops, Bernard
Krea, Henri
Kreymborg, Alfred
Kunene, Mazisi
  (Raymond)
Kunitz, Stanley Jasspon
Laforgue, Jules
Lagerkvist, Par Fabian
Lamartine, Alphonse
  Marie Louis de Prat de
Lampman, Archibald
Landini, Francesco
Landor, Walter Savage
Lang, Andrew
Lanier, Sidney
Lanyer, Aemilia
Larcom, Lucy
Larkin, Philip Arthur
La Tour du Pin, Patrice de
Lautreamont, Comte de
Lawson, Henry (Archibald
  Hertzberg)
Layamon
Lazarus, Emma
Lear, Edward
Leconte de Lisle, Charles
  Marie Rene
Lee-Hamilton, Eugene
  Jacob
LeGallienne, Richard
Leger, Alexis St. Leger
Leland, Charles Godfrey
Leonard, William Ellery
Leopardi, Giacomo
Lermontov, Mikhail
Levertov, Denise

Levine, Philip
Lewis, Janet
Lifshin, Lyn
Liliencron, Detlev von
Lindbergh, Anne Spencer
  Morrow
Lindsay, Vachel
Li Po
Liu Tsung-yuan
Livius Andronicus
Llull, Ramon
Logan, John
Lomonosov, Mikhail
  Vasilyevich
Longfellow, Henry
  Wadsworth
Lope de Vega
Lorde, Audre (Geraldine)
Louys, Pierre
Lovelace, Richard
Lowell, Amy
Lowell, Robert Trail
  Spence, Jr.
Lowenfels, Walter
Lowry, Malcolm
Lu, Yu
Lucan
Lu Chi
Lucilius, Gaius
Lucretius
Lull, Raymond
Luzzato, Moses Hayyim
Lydgate, John
Lyndsay, David
Lytton, Edward George
  Earle Lytton Bulwer-
  Lytton, 1st Baron
  Lytton
Mabuchi, Kamo
MacBeth, George Mann
MacDiarmid, Hugh
MacDonagh, Thomas
MacDonald, George
Machado (y Ruiz),
  Antonio
Machaut, Guillaume de
MacKaye, Percy Wallace
MacLeish, Archibald
MacNeice, Louis
Madhubuti, Haki R.
Maeterlinck, Maurice
Malherbe, Francois de
Mallarme, Stephane
Mandelstam, Osip
  Emilyevich
Manrique, Jorge
Manzoni, Alessandro
  (Antonio)
Marie de France
Marinetti, Filippo
  Tommaso Emilio
Markham, Edwin
Marlowe, Christopher
Marot, Clement
Marquis, Don Robert
  Perry
Marti (y Perez), Jose
  Julian
Martial
Martinson, Harry Edmund
Marvell, Andrew
Marx, Anne Loewenstein
Masaoka, Tsunenori
Masefield, John
Massey, Gerald
Masters, Edgar Lee

Mathieu, Noel Jean
Maunick, Edouard Joseph
  Marc
Mayakovsky, Vladimir
McClure, Michael Thomas
McCord, David
  (Thompson Watson)
McCrae, John
McGinley, Phyllis
McKay, Festus Claudius
McKuen, Rod Marvin
Medici, Lorenzo de
Menken, Adah Isaacs
Meredith, George
Merriam, Eve
Merrill, James (Ingram)
Merton, Thomas
Merwin, W(illiam)
  S(tanley)
Metastasio, Pietro
Mew, Charlotte Mary
Meynell, Alice Christina
  Gertrude
Michelangelo (Buonarroti)
Miles, Josephine
Millay, Edna St. Vincent
Miller, Joaquin
Milton, John
Mistral, Frederic
Mistral, Gabriela
Momaday, N(avarre) Scott
Monroe, Harriet
Montale, Eugenio
Moody, William Vaughn
Moore, Clement Clarke
Moore, George Augustus
Moore, Julia A Davis
Moore, Marianne Craig
Moore, Thomas
Morgan, Edwin George
Morike, Eduard Friedrich
Morin, Paul
Morris, William
Motherwell, William
Moure, Erin
Mowrer, Paul Scott
Mqhayi, S(amuel)
  E(dward) K(rune
  Loliwe)
Muldoon, Paul
Murray, Les(lie) A(llan)
Muske, Carol (Anne)
Naidu, Sarojini
Naranjo-Morse, Nora
Neal, Larry
Nemerov, Howard
  (Stanley)
Nerval, Gerard de
Niatum, Duane
Nietzsche, Friedrich
  Wilhelm
Notker Balbulus
Novalis
Noyes, Alfred
O'Hara, Frank
Okigbo, Christopher
  (Ifenayichukwu)
Olds, Sharon
Olson, Charles John
Omar Khayyam
Oppen, George
Oppenheim, James
Orleans, Charles d'
Ortiz, Simon
Osgood, Frances Sargent
  Locke

Otway, Thomas
Ovid
Owen, Wilfred
Owens, Rochelle
Palamas, Kostes
Pales Matos, Luis
Paludan-Muller, Frederik
Parker, Dorothy
  Rothschild
Parker, Pat
Parra, Nicanor
Pascoli, Giovanni
Patchen, Kenneth
Paterson, A(ndrew)
  B(arton)
Patmore, Coventry Kersey
  Dighton
Paz, Octavio
Peabody, Josephine
  Preston
Peacock, Thomas Love
Pearse, Padraic
Peele, George
Peguy, Charles Pierre
Peret, Benjamin
Perkoff, Stuart Z.
Perrault, Charles
Petrarch, Francesco
Philips, Katherine
Pindar
Plath, Sylvia
Po Chu-i
Poe, Edgar Allan
Poliziano, Angelo
Popa, Vasko
Pope, Alexander
Pound, Ezra Loomis
Pratt, Edwin John
Prior, Matthew
Procter, Bryan Waller
Prokosch, Frederic
Propertius, Sextus
Pushkin, Aleksandr
  Sergeyevich
Pye, Henry
Quasimodo, Salvatore
Quevado y Villegas,
  Francisco Gomez de
Rabearivelo, Jean Joseph
Ramsay, Allan
Randall, Dudley
Ransom, John Crowe
Ransome, Arthur Mitchell
Ratushinskaya, Irina
Read, Herbert, Sir
Read, Thomas Buchanan
Reese, Lizette Woodworth
Revard, Carter
Rexroth, Kenneth
Rice, Cale Young
Rice, Grantland
Rich, Adrienne (Cecile)
Rickword, Edgell
Ridge, Lola
Riley, James Whitcomb
Rilke, Rainer Maria
Rimbaud, (Jean Nicolas)
  Arthur
Rinuccini, Ottavio
Robinson, Edwin
  Arlington
Robinson, Henry Morton
Roethke, Theodore
  (Huebner)
Ronsard, Pierre de
Rosa, Salvator

Rose, Wendy
Rosenberg, Issac
Rossetti, Christina
  Georgina
Rossetti, Dante Gabriel
Rossetti, Gabriele Pasquale
  Giuseppe
Rothenberg, Jerome
Rowe, Nicholas
Ruckert, Friedrich
Ruiz, Juan
Rukeyser, Muriel
Rumi, Jalai ed-Din
Runeberg, Johan Ludwig
Russell, George William
Saavedra, Angel de
Sachs, Hans
Sachs, Nelly (Leonie)
Sackville-West, Vita
Sa'di
Salinas, Luis Omar
Salinas (y Serrano), Pedro
Sandburg, Carl (August)
Santillana, Inigo Lopez de
  Mendoza
Sappho
Sarett, Lew R
Sarton, May
Sassoon, Siegfried
Savage, Richard
Schauffler, Robert Haven
Schuyler, James Marcus
Schwitters, Kurt (Hermann
  Edward Karl Julius)
Scott, Duncan Campbell
Scott, F(rancis) R(eginald)
Scott, Walter, Sir
Seeger, Alan
Seferis, George
Seifert, Jaroslav
Senghor, Leopold Sedar
Service, Robert William
Seward, Anna
Sexton, Anne Harvey
Shaaban Robert
Shadwell, Thomas
Shakespeare, William
Shalamov, Varlam
  Tikhonovich
Shange, Ntozake
Shapiro, Karl Jay
Sharp, William
Shelley, Percy Bysshe
Sherman, Frank Dempster
Shevchenko, Taras
Sidney, Philip, Sir
Sigourney, Lydia Howard
Sikelianos, Angelos
Silkin, Jon
Sill, Edward Rowland
Simic, Charles
Simonov, Konstantin
  (Kirill) Mikhailovich
Simpson, Louis
Sissman, L(ouis) E(dward)
Sisson, Charles Hubert
Sitwell, Edith, Dame
Sjowall, Maj
Skelton, John
Skelton, Robin
Smart, Christopher
Smith, A(rthur) J(ames)
  M(arshall)
Smith, Alexander
Smith, Iain Crichton
Smith, Patti

Smith, Samuel Francis
Smith, Stevie
Smith, William Jay
Snodgrass, W(illiam)
  D(eWitt)
Snyder, Gary Sherman
Solon
Sophocles
Sordello
Soutar, William
Southey, Robert
Spence, Lewis
Spender, Stephen (Harold)
Spenser, Edmund
Spicer, Jack
Spitteler, Karl Friedrich
  Georg
Squires, James Radcliffe
Ssu-ma Hsiang-ju
Stafford, William Edgar
Stanton, Frank Lebby
Stephens, James
Sterling, George
Stevens, Wallace
Stevenson, Robert Louis
  (Balfour)
Stoddard, Richard Henry
Storm, (Hans) Theodor
  (Woldsen)
Strand, Mark
Stuart, Jesse Hilton
Suckling, John
Sully Prudhomme
Su Shih
Swenson, May
Swinburne, Algernon
  Charles
Symonds, John Addington
Symons, Arthur William
Tabb, John Banister
Taggard, Genevieve
Tagore, Rabindranath, Sir
Takahama Kyoshi
TallMountain, Mary
T'ao Ch'ien
Tapahonso, Luci
Tate, Allen (John Orley)
Tate, James
Tate, Nahum
Taylor, Ann
Taylor, Edward
Taylor, Jane
Tchernichowski, Saul
  Gutmanovich
Teasdale, Sara
Tennyson, Alfred, Lord
Terence
Thaxter, Celia
Theocritus
Theodorescu, Ion N
Thespis
Thibaut, IV
Thomas, Edith Matilda
Thomas, Edward
Thomas, Ronald Stuart
Thompson, Francis Joseph
Thomson, James
Thorarensen, Jakob
Tietjens, Eunice
Tiller, Rogers
Timrod, Henry
Toller, Ernst
Toomer, Jean
Torrence, Ridgely
Towne, Charles Hanson
Treece, Henry

Trench, Richard Chenevix
Trumbull, John
Tschernichowsky, Saul
Tsegaye, Gabre-Medhin
Tsvetayeva, Marina
  Ivanovna
Tu, Fu
Tyler, Parker
Tzara, Tristan
Ukrainka, Lesia
Ungaretti, Giuseppe
Valery, Paul Ambroise
Valle Inclan, Ramon
  Maria del
Vallejo, Cesar Abraham
Van Doren, Mark
Van Duyn, Mona
Vandyke, Henry Jackson,
  Jr.
Vaughan, Henry
Velez, Clemente Soto
Vergil
Verlaine, Paul (Marie)
Vicente, Gil
Viereck, Peter Robert
  Edwin
Vigny, Alfred Victor,
  Comte de
Villon, Francois
Viorst, Judith (Stahl)
Visscher, William
  Lightfoot
Vitry, Philippe de
Vogelweide, Walther von
  der
Vondel, Joost van den
Wagner, Richard
Wakoski, Diane
Walcott, Derek (Alton)
Walker, Margaret
  (Abigail)
Wallace, Horace Binney
Waller, Edmund
Wang An-shih
Wang Wei
Warner, Sylvia Townsend
Warren, Robert Penn
Warton, Joseph
Watts-Dunton, Theodore
Weiss, Theodore (Russell)
Wellesley, Dorothy Violet
Wesendonck, Mathilde
  Luckemeyer
Wheatley, Phillis
Wheelock, John Hall
Whitehead, William
Whiteman, Roberta Hill
Whitman, Sarah Helen
  Power
Whitman, Walt(er)
Whittier, John Greenleaf
Widdemer, Margaret
Wieland, Christoph Martin
Wigglesworth, Michael
Wilbur, Richard Purdy
Wilcox, Ella Wheeler
Wilde, Oscar (Fingal
  O'Flahertie Wills)
Wilder, Amos Niven
Williams, William Carlos
Wilson, Alexander
Wolfram von Eschenbach
Woody, Elizabeth
Wordsworth, William
Wright, James Arlington
Wroth, Mary, Lady

Occupation Index — POLITICAL LEADER

Wurdemann, Audrey May
Wyatt, Thomas, Sir
Yeats, William Butler
Yeshurun, Avot
Yevtushenko, Yevgeny
Yi Hwang
Yun Sondo
Zabolotskii, Nikolai
  Alekseevich
Zamora, Bernice
Zaturenska, Marya
Zeno, Apostolo
Zorrilla de San Martin,
  Juan

POLICE CHIEF

Gates, Daryl F
Harvard, Beverly
McKinnon, Isaiah
Murphy, Thomas F(rancis)
Watson, Elizabeth
Williams, Willie Lawrence

POLICE OFFICER

Burke, Robert O'Hara
Cantrell, Ed
Connor, Bull
Delahanty, Thomas K
Egan, Eddie
Glover, Nathaniel, Jr.
Gomez-Preston, Cheryl
Koon, Stacey C.
Lewis, Thomas
Parks, Bernard C.
Sample, Bill
Serpico, Frank
White, Dan(iel James)

POLITICAL ACTIVIST

Abduh ibn Hasan Khayr
  Allah, Muhammad
Abu-Jamal, Mumia
Acevedo Diaz, Eduardo
Agyeman-Rawlings, Nana
  Konadu
Alinsky, Saul David
Alley, Rewi
Anderson, Owanah
Andrews, Fannie Fern
  Phillips
Aquash, Anna Mae Pictou
Arnoldson, Klas Pontus
Ashrawi, Hanan
Baez, Joan
Banerjee, Surendranath
Baum, Herbert (M.)
Berrigan, Daniel J
Berrigan, Elizabeth
  McAlister
Berrigan, Philip Francis
Biko, Steven
Blackburn, Molly
Blackwell, Unita
Bonga, Kuenda
Bourne, Randolph
  Silliman
Boyd, John W., Jr.

Bradlaugh, Charles
Bravo, Ellen
Breytenbach, Breyten
Brown, Elaine
Brown, Zora Kramer
Bukovsky, Vladimir
Cabet, Etienne
Calero (Portocarrero),
  Adolfo
Cesaire, Aime Fernand
Chai Ling
Chomsky, Noam Avram
Claytor, Helen (Natalie
  Jackson)
Cleaver, Eldridge
Cohn-Bendit, Daniel
Corona, Bert
Crow Dog, Mary
Cuong De
de Andrade, Mario
De Leon, Daniel
Dellinger, David T
Deloria, Vine (Victor), Jr.
DePugh, Robert Bolivar
Devlin, Bernadette
  Josephine
Dewson, Mary Williams
Dohrn, Bernadine Rae
Dolan, Terry
Dubnov, Simon
Eaton, Dorman Bridgman
Ellsberg, Daniel
Evans, George Henry
Falkenberg, Nanette
Farenthold, Frances
  T(arlton)
Fela
Ferrell, Trevor
Fleischmann, Gisi
Fonda, Jane
Frank, Billy, Jr.
Froines, John Radford
Furman, Rosemary
Gage, Matilda Joslyn
Galvin, Martin
Gere, Richard
Ghose, Aurobindo
Ginzburg, Aleksandr Ilich
Gitlow, Benjamin
Goerdeler, Karl Friedrich
Grede, William John
Green, Mark J(oseph)
Gregory, Dick
Grieg, Nordahl Brun
Groppi, James E
Hall, Gus
Hampton, Fred
Hani, Chris
Han Yongun
Harand, Irene
Harris, Joseph Pratt
Hayden, Tom
Hoffman, Abbie
Huerta, Dolores
  (Fernandez)
Hughan, Jessie Wallace
Hullinger, Charlotte
Ireland, Patricia
Jemison, Alice Mae
Ji Jaga, Geronimo
Jingsheng, Wei
Jones, Samuel Milton
Joseph, Helen
Katayama, Sen
Kearney, Denis
Kellor, Frances (Alice)

Khan, Abdul Ghaffar
Kielburger, Craig
Kopp, Wendy
Kovic, Ron
Krupskaya, Nadezhda
  Konstantinovna
Kuron, Jacek
Kuti, Fela Anikulapo
LaDuke, Winona
LaFlesche Tibbles, Susette
Lange, Christian Louis
Lee, Arthur
Lembede, Anton
Levinger, Moshe
Lewis, Saunders
Liang Ch'i-ch'ao
Lowenstein, Allard
  Kenneth
Lynd, Staughton (Craig)
Mabuza, Lindiwe
Machel, Graca Simbine
Malcolm X
Mandela, Nelson
  (Rolihlahla)
Mandela, Winnie
Martinez, Vilma Socorro
Masekela, Barbara
Mason, Belinda
Mathews, Dan
Mayer, Norman D
Mbeki, Thabo Mvuyelwa
McGuinness, Martin
Means, Russell
Means, Russell C(harles)
Mendes, Chico
Merritt, Justine
Michelman, Kate
Michnik, Adam
Mihajlov, Mihajlo
Mikhail-Ashrawi, Hanan
Millett, Kate
Moczar, Mieczyslaw
Montezuma, Carlos
Moore, Audley
Muste, A(braham)
  J(ohannes)
Nader, Ralph
Natividad, Irene
Newton, Huey P(ercy)
Niekisch, Ernest
Nzo, Alfred
  (Baphethuxolo)
Oakes, Richard
Ochs, Phil(ip David)
O'Donnell, Peadar
Oglesby, Zena, (Jr.)
Pacciardi, Randolfo
Padmore, George
Paton, Alan Stewart
Peltier, Leonard
Perez Esquivel, Adolfo
Place, Francis
Polk, Leonidas Lafayette
Ram Singh
Rauh, Joseph Louis, Jr.
Reed, Ralph
Rifkin, Jeremy
Robeson, Eslanda Cardoza
  Goode
Robinson, Rachel
Rockwell, George Lincoln
Rosenman, Dorothy
Rubin, Jerry
Sacco, Nicola
Said, Edward W
Sanchez, Sonia (Benita)

Santamaria, Bartholomew
  Augustine
Sasway, Benjamin H
Schiavo, Mary (Fackler)
Schwimmer, Rosika
Scott, F(rancis) R(eginald)
Seale, Bobby G
Sharpton, Al(fred), Jr.
Sieyes, Emmanuel Joseph
Sinclair, Mary
Sisulu, Nontsikelelo
  Albertina
Sisulu, Walter Max Ulyate
Snyder, Mitch
Sobukwe, Robert
  Mangaliso
Soelle, Dorothee
Sohappy, David, Sr.
Stewart, Maria W. Miller
Sung Chiao-jen
Suu Kyi, Aung San
Tambo, Oliver
Thorpe, Grace F.
Trudell, John
Vanzetti, Bartolomeo
Wang T'ao
Welch, Robert Henry
  Winborne, Jr.
Willson, S Brian
Worrill, Conrad (W.)
Wu, Harry
Xiang Jingyu
Yard, Molly
Zetkin, Clara
Zia, Helen

POLITICAL ACTIVISTS

Black Panther Party
Chicago Seven, The

POLITICAL LEADER

Abbas, Ferhat
Abdallah, Ahmed
Abd el-Kadir
Abd el-Krim el-Khatabi,
  Mohamed ben
Abdulkarim, Mohamed
  Taki
Abdullah, Mohammad,
  Sheik
Abe, Isao
Aberdeen, 4th Earl of
Aberhart, William
Abubakar, Abdulsalam
  (Alhaji)
Adamkus, Valdas (V.)
Adams, Gerald
Adams, Tom
Adhikary, Man Mohan
Adler, Victor
Afwerki, Isaias
Aguinaldo, Emilio
Ahern, Bertie
Ahidjo, Ahmadou
Ahmed, Fakhruddin Ali
Ahmed, Shahabuddin
Aho, Esko (Tapani)
Akayev, Askar Akayevich
Albert, Carl Bert

Albuquerque, Affonso de
Alcala Zamora, Niceto
Aleman, Arnoldo
Aleman, Miguel
Alesana, Tofilau Eti
Alessandri, Jorge
Alessandri Palma, Arturo
Alexander of Tunis
Alfaro, Jose Eloy
Alfonsin Foulkes, Raul
  Ricardo
Alia, Ramiz
Ali Mahdi Mohamed
Aliyev, Heydar
al-Khalifa, Sheikh Isa Bin
  Sulman
Allal al-Fassi, Mohamed
Allende Gossens, Salvador
Alp Arslan
Amin, Idi
Andreotti, Giulio
Andropov, Yuri
  Vladimirovich
Antall, Jozsef, Jr.
Anthony, Kenny
Antonescu, Ion
Antony, Marc
Apithy, Sourou Migan
Aptidon, Hassan Gouled
Aquino, Corazon
  (Cojuangco)
Arafat, Yasir
Aramburu, Pedro Eugenio
Arbenz Guzman, Jacobo
Arevalo, Juan Jose
Arias Madrid, Arnulfo
Arias Sanchez, Oscar
Aristide, Jean-Bertrand
Arron, Henck Alphonsus
  Eugene
Arthur, Owen
Arvey, Jacob Meyer
Arzu, Avaro
Asquith, Herbert Henry
Assad, Hafez al-
Assad, Rifaat al-
Astor, Nancy Witcher
  Langhorne
Ataturk, Kemal
Attlee, Clement Richard
  Attlee, Earl
Aung San
Auriol, Vincent
Avila Camacho, Manuel
Awolowo, Obafemi Awo
Aylwin (Azocar), Patricio
Ayub Khan, Mohammad
Azali, Assoumani
Azana y Diaz, Manuel
Azcona Hoyo, Jose Simon
Azhari, Sayyid Ismail al-
Azikiwe, Nnamdi
Aznar, Jose Maria
Babangida, Ibrahim
  Badamasi
Babiuch, Edward
Baez, Buenaventura
Bagaza, Jean-Baptiste
Bakhtiar, Shahpur
Bakr, Ahmad Hasan al
Balaguer, Joaquin
Balewa, Abubakar Tafawa,
  Sir
Ballivian, Jose
Balmaceda Fernandez,
  Jose Manuel

Balopoulos, Michael
Ba Maw
Banda, Hastings Kamuzu
Bandaranaike, S(olomon)
  W(est) R(idgeway)
  D(ias)
Bandaranaike, Sirimavo
  Ratwatte Dias
Banharn Silpa-archa
Bani-Sadr, Abolhassan
Banzer-Suarez, Hugo
Barak, Ehud
Barco Vargas, Virgilio
Barrientos Ortuno, Rene
Barrios, Justo Rufino
Barrow, Errol Walton
Bashir, Omar Hassan
  Ahmed al-
Batista y Zaldivar,
  Fulgencio
Batlle y Ordonez, Jose
Baunsgaard, Hilmar
  Tormod Ingolf
Bebel, August
Beccaria, Cesare
Bedie, Henri Konan
Begin, Menachem
  (Wolfovitch)
Beheshti, Mohammad,
  Ayatollah
Belaunde-Terry, Fernando
Belgrano, Manuel
Bello, (Alhaji Sir)
  Ahmadu
Ben Barka, Mehdi
Ben Bella, Ahmed
Benediktsson, Bjarni
Ben-Gurion, David
Bennett, Richard Bedford
Bennett, W(illiam)
  A(ndrew) C(ecil)
Benton, Thomas Hart
Beregovoy, Pierre
  (Eugene)
Berger, Victor Louis
Beria, Lavrenti Pavlovich
Berisha, Sali
Berlinguer, Enrico
Berlusconi, Silvio
Bernstein, Eduard
Betancur, Belisario
Bethmann Hollweg,
  Theobald von
Bevan, Aneurin
Bhattarai, Krishna Prasad
Bhutto, Benazir
Bhutto, Zulfikar Ali
Bierut, Boleslaw
Bignone, Reynaldo Benito
  Antonio
Bijedic, Dzemal
Bildt, Carl
Bird, Lester
Bird, Vere Cornwall, Sr.
Bishop, Maurice Rupert
Biya, Paul
Bizimungu, Pasteur
Bjornson, Bjornstjerne
  Martinius
Blanc, Louis
Blanco, Antonio Guzman
Bliss, Ray C(harles)
Boeynants, Paul Vanden
Bokassa, Jean-Bedel
Bokassa I
Bolger, Jim

Bonaparte, Francois
  Charles Joseph
Bondevik, Kjell (Magne)
Bongo, Albert-Bernard
  (Omar)
Borden, Robert Laird, Sir
Borja Cevallos, Rodrigo
Botha, Louis
Botha, Pieter Willem
Botha, Roelof Frederik
Boumedienne, Houari
Bourguiba, Habib Ben Ali
Bouteflika, Abdelaziz
Boyer, Jean Pierre
Brandt, Willy
Branting, Karl Hjalmar
Brathwaite, Nicholas
  A(lexander)
Bratteli, Trygve Martin
Braun, Otto
Brazauskas, Algirdas
  (Mykolas)
Brezhnev, Leonid Ilyich
Brooke, James, Sir
Browder, Earl Russell
Brundtland, Gro Harlem
Bruton, John (Gerard)
Bryan, William Jennings
Bucaram, Abdala
Buckard, Alfredo Cristiani
Bukharin, Nikolai
  Ivanovich
Bulatovic, Momir
Bulganin, Nikolai
  Aleksandrovich
Bulow, Bernhard H M
Burnham, Forbes
Burrenchobay,
  Dayendranath
Busia, Kofi A(brefa)
Bustamante, William
  Alexander Clarke, Sir
Bute, 3d Earl of
Buthelezi, Gatsha
  Mangosuthu
Buttigieg, Anton
Buyoya, Pierre
Byng, Julian Hedworth
  George, Viscount
Cabral, Luis de Almeida
Caetano, Marcello
Caillaux, Joseph Marie
  Auguste
Caldera Rodriguez, Rafael
Calderon Sol, Armando
Callejas Romero, Rafael
  Leonardo
Campbell, Kim
Campbell-Bannerman,
  Henry, Sir
Campora, Hector Jose
Canning, Charles John,
  Earl
Cardenas, Lazaro
Cardoso, Fernando
  Henrique
Carias Andino, Tiburcio
Carlsson, Ingvar Gosta
Carranza, Venustiano
Carrera, Jose Rafael
Carstens, Karl Walter
Castello Branco,
  Humberto
Castilla, Ramon
Castro, Raul
Castro (Ruz), Fidel

Cavaco Silva, Anibal
  Antonio
Ceausescu, Nicolae
Cerezo (Arevalo), Vinicio
Chaban-Delmas, Jacques
  Pierre Michel
Chadli, Bendjedid
Chaka
Chamberlain, Neville
Chamorro, Violeta Barrios
  de
Chamoun, Camille
  N(imer)
Chan, Julius
Chand, Lokendra Bahadur
Charles, Mary Eugenia
Chatichai Choonhavan
Chaudhry, Mahendra
Chautemps, Camille
Chavalit Yongchaiyudh
Chernenko, Konstantin
  Ustinovich
Chervenkov, Vulko
Chiang, Ching
Chiang Ching-Kuo
Chiari, Roberto
Chifley, Joseph Benedict
Childers, Erskine
  Hamilton
Chiluba, Frederick Jacob
  Titus
Chinh, Truong
Chissano, Joaquim Alberto
Chuan Leekpai
Ciller, Tansu
Clarke, Ellis Emmanuel
  Innocent, Sir
Cleon
Clerides, Glafcos (John)
Clodumar, Kinza
Cobden, Richard
Collin, Frank
Collor de Mello, Fernando
  Affonso
Colombo, Emilio
Compaore, Blaise
Compton, John (George
  M.)
Constantinescu, Emil
Conte, Lansana
Cosgrave, Liam
Cossiga, Francesco
Costello, John Aloysius
Cotti, Flavio
Couve de Murville,
  (Jacques) Maurice
Cowen, Zelman, Sir
Craxi, Bettino
Crerar, Thomas Alexander
Cresson, Edith Campion
Crispi, Francesco
Cristiani, Alfredo
Cubas, Raul
Curley, James Michael
Curtin, Andrew Gregg
Curtin, John Joseph
Cyrankiewicz, Josef
Cyrus the Great
Dacko, David
Daddah, Moktar Ould
da Graca, Carlos Alberto
  Dias
Daladier, Edouard
Dandolo, Enrico
Danquah, Joseph (Kwame
  Kyeretwi) B(oakye)

Davis, Jefferson
Deakin, Alfred
Debre, Michel (Jean Pierre)
Debs, Eugene Victor
Deby, Idriss
De Gasperi, Alcide
DeGaulle, Charles Andre Joseph Marie
Dehaene, Jean-Luc
DeJong, Petrus
De Klerk, F(rederik) W(illem)
Delamuraz, Jean-Pascal
de Leon Carpio, Ramiro
De Maiziere, Lothar
Demirel, Suleyman
Deng Xiaoping
Denktash, Rauf
DeQuay, Jan E
DeRoburt, Hammer, Sir
Desai, Morarji (Ranchhodji)
Deuba, Sher Bahadur
Dhlakama, Afonso
Diaz, Jose de la Cruz Porfirio
Diaz, Porfirio
Diaz Ordaz, Gustavo
Diederichs, Nicholaas
Diefenbaker, John George
Dimitrov, Georgi Mikhailovich
Dini, Lamberto
Diouf, Abdou
Djohar, Said Mohamed
Doe, Samuel Kanyon
Dollfuss, Engelbert
Dorman, Maurice Henry, Sir
Douglas, Denzil
Douglas, James, Sir
Dowiyogo, Bernard
Drees, Willem
Duarte (Fuentes), Jose Napoleon
Dubcek, Alexander
Duclos, Jacques
Duplessis, Maurice le Noblet
DuPont, Clifford Walter
Duran Ballen, Sixto
Dutra, Eurico Gaspar
Duvalier, Francois
Duvalier, Jean-Claude
Eanes, Antonio dos Santos Ramalho
Ebert, Friedrich
Ecevit, Bulent
Echeverria Alvarez, Louis
Einaudi, Luigi
Eisner, Kurt
Elbegdorj, Tsahiagiyn
Elgin, James Bruce
Endara (Galimany), Guillermo
Engels, Friedrich
Enhsaihan, M.
Enver Pasha
Erbakan, Necmettin
Ershad, Hussain Mohammad
Eshkol, Levi
Esquivel, Manuel
Estrada, Joseph (Marcelo Ejercito)

Estrada Cabrera, Manuel
Estrada Palma, Tomas
Evren, Kenan
Eyadema, Etienne Gnassingbe
Eyskens, Gaston, Viscount
Fabius, Laurent
Fadil al-Jamali, Muhammad
Falldin, Thorbjorn Nils Olof
Fanfani, Amintore
Faulkner, Brian
Faure, Francois Felix
Febres-Cordero, Leon
Feijo, Diogo Antonio
Fenech-Adami, Eddie
Fernandez, Leonel
Figueiredo, Joao Baptista de Oliveira
Figueres Ferrer, Jose
Figueres Olsen, Jose Maria
Finnbogadottir, Vigdis
Fisher, Andrew
FitzGerald, Garret Michael
Flores, Francisco
Flores, Juan Jose
Flores Facusse, Carlos Roberto
Flynn, Elizabeth Gurley
Fonseca, Manuel Deodoro da
Forne Molne, Marc
Foster, William Zebulon
Fournier, Rafael (Angel) Calderon
Franco, Francisco
Franz Ferdinand
Fraser, John Malcolm
Fraser, Peter
Frei, Eduardo
Frei Ruiz-Tagle, Eduardo
Frontenac, Louis de Buade de
Fujimori, Alberto
Fukuda, Takeo
Gaitskell, Hugh (Todd Naylor)
Gajah Mada
Gallegos, Romulo
Galtieri, Leopoldo Fortunato
Gandhi, Indira Priyadarshini Nehru
Gandhi, Rajiv Ratna
Garcia, Carlos Polestico
Garcia Perez, Alan
Garvey, Marcus Moziah
Gatti, Gabriele
Gaviria Trujillo, Cesar Augusto
Gayoom, Maumoon Abdul
Geisel, Ernesto
Gemayel, Amin
Gemayel, Bashir
Gerhardsen, Einar Henry
Gheorghiu-Dej, Gheorghe
Ghiz, Joseph A
Gierek, Edward
Glasspole, Florizel Augustus
Gligorov, Kiro
Goh Chok Tong
Gomez, Juan Vicente

Gomez Castro, Laureano Eleuterio
Gomulka, Wladyslaw
Gonzalez Macchi, Luis
Gonzalez Marquez, Felipe
Gorbachev, Mikhail (Sergeyevich)
Gorbunovs, Anatolijs
Gordon, Pamela (Felicity)
Gorton, John Grey, Sir
Gottwald, Klement
Goulart, Joao
Gowda, H(aradanahalli) D(odde) Deve
Gramsci, Antonio
Grau San Martin, Ramon
Grevy, Francois Paul Jules
Griffith, Arthur
Grosz, Karoly
Guelleh, Ismael Omar
Guerrero, Vicente
Gujral, Inder Kumar
Guterres, Antonio Manuel de Oliveira
Guzman, Antonio
Habash, Georges
Habibie, B(acharuddin) J(usuf)
Habre, Hissene
Habyarimana, Juvenal
Hamad, Sheikh
Hamad bin Khalifa al-Thani, Sheikh
Hammarskjold, Hjalmar
Hans Adam, II
Hara, Kei
Hara Takashi
Hardenberg, Karl August von
Harris, Lagumot
Harun-Al-Rashid
Hasani, Ali Nasir Muhammad
Hashimoto, Ryutaro
Hasina Wajed
Hasluck, Paul Meernaa, Sir
Hatoyama Ichiro
Haughey, Charles James
Havel, Vaclav
Hawke, Bob
Haya de la Torre, Victor Raul
Healy, T(imothy) M(ichael)
Heath, Edward Richard George
Hedtoft (-Hansen), Hans Christian
Heinemann, Gustav Walter
Hermannsson, Steingrimur
Herrera Campins, Luis
Herriot, Edouard
Hertzog, James Barry Munnik
Herzog, Chaim
Herzog, Roman
Hillery, Patrick John
Hillquit, Morris
Hilly, Francis Billy
Hindenburg, Paul Ludwig Hans Anton von Beneckendorff und
Hitler, Adolf
Ho Chi Minh
Holkeri, Harri (Hermanni)

Holt, Harold Edward
Holyoake, Keith Jacka, Sir
Hore-Belisha, Leslie, Baron
Horn, Gyula
Horthy de Nagybanya, Nicholas
Hoveyda, Amir Abbas
Howard, John (Winston)
Hoxha, Enver
Hoyte, Hugh Desmond
Hrawi, Elias
Huerta, Victoriano
Hughes, William Morris
Hunyadi, John
Husain, Zakir
Husak, Gustav
Husein ibn Ali
Hussein, Saddam (Al-Tikriti)
Husseini, Faisal
Husseini, Haj Amin
Hyde, Douglas
Hyndman, Henry Mayers
Ibanez del Campo, Carlos
ibn Tumart, Muhammad
Ibrahim Pasha
Iliescu, Ion
Illia, Arturo Umberto
Ingraham, Hubert
Inukai, Tsuyoshi
Irigoyen, Hipolito
Ishak, Yusof bin
Ismail Pasha
Iwakura, Tomomi
Jabir al-Ahmad al-Jabir Al Sabah, Sheikh
Jablonski, Henryk
Jagan, Janet
Jagland, Thorbjoern
James, Edison
Jameson, Leander Starr, Sir
Jammeh, Yahya A(bdulaziz) J(emus) J.
Jaruzelski, Wojciech Witold
Jaures, Jean Leon
Jawara, Alhaji Dawda Kairaba, Sir
Jawara, Dauda Kairaba
Jayewardene, J(unius) R(ichard)
Jenkins, Roy Harris
Jiang Zemin
Jinnah, Mohammed Ali
Johnson, John
Jonas, Franz
Jonathan, Joseph Leabua
Jonathan, Leabua, Chief
Jorge Blanco, Salvador
Jorgensen, Anker Henrik
Juarez, Benito Pablo
Jugnauth, Anerood
Jumblatt, Kamal Fouad
Jumblatt, Walid
Juncker, Jean-Claude
Justo, Agustin Pedro
Kabbah, (Alhaji) Ahmad Tejan
Kabila, Laurent Desire
Kabua, Amata
Kabua, Imata
Kadar, Janos
Kaganovich, Lazar M(oiseevich)

Kaifu Toshiki
Kalinin, Mikhail
 (Ivanovich)
Kalpokas, Donald
Kamaraj, Kumaraswami
Kang, Sheng
Karadzic, Radovan
Karamanlis, Constantine
Karami, Rashid Abdul
 Hamid
Karim Khan Zand
Karimov, Islam
 Abduganievich
Karmal, Babrak
Kasavubu, Joseph
Kaunda, Kenneth D(avid)
Kawawa, Rashidi Mfaume
Kayibanda, Gregoire
Kaysone Phomvihan
Keating, Paul John
Keita, Modibo
Kekkonen, Urho Kaleva
Kenyatta, Jomo
Kerekou, Mathieu Ahmed
Kerensky, Alexander
 Fedorovitch
Khaleda Zia
Khalil, Mustafa
Khalil, Sayyid Abdullah
Khama, Seretse M., Sir
Khamenei, (Sayed) Ali,
 Hojatolislam
Khamtay Siphandone
Khatami, Mohammad
Khrushchev, Nikita
 Sergeyevich
Kim Il Sung
Kim Jong Il
Kim Young Sam
King, William Lyon
 Mackenzie
Kirchschlager, Rudolf
Kishi, Nobusuke
Kittikachorn, Thanom
Kiwanuka, Benedicto
 Kagima Mugumba
Klaus, Vaclav
Klestil, Thomas
Kocharyan, Robert
Kohl, Helmut (Michael)
Koirala, Girija Prasad
Koivisto, Mauno Henrik
Kok, Wim
Kolingba, Andre-
 Dieudonne
Konare, Alpha Oumar
Konoye, Fumimaro, Prince
Koprulu, Ahmed
Korman, Maxime Carlot
Koroma, Johnny
Koruturk, Fahri S
Kostov, Ivan
Kosygin, Aleksei
 Nikolaevich
Kountche, Seyni
Kovac, Michael
Krag, Jens Otto
Kravchuk, Leonid
 Makarovich
Kreisky, Bruno
Krenz, Egon
Kruger, Paul
Kubitschek (de Oliveira),
 Juscelino
Kuchma, Leonid
 Danylovich

Kukrit Pramoj,
 Momrajawong (M.R.)
Kumaratunga, Chandrika
 Bandaranaike
Kun, Bela
Kuwatli, Shukri al-
Kwasniewski, Aleksander
Ky, Nguyen Cao
Kyprianou, Spyros
 Achilles
Laatasi, Kamuta
Lacalle (Herrera), Luis
 Alberto
Landsbergis, Vytautas
Lange, David Russell
Lanusse, Alejandro
 Agustin
Largo Caballero, Francisco
Lassalle, Ferdinand
Laval, Pierre
Lavalleja, Juan Antonio
Lebrun, Albert
Le Duan
Lee, Teng-Hui
Lee Hsien Loong
Lee Kuan Yew
Lee Teng-hui
Leghari, Sardar Farooq
 Ahmed Khan
Leguia y Salcedo, Augusto
 Bernardino
Lekhanya, Justin Metsing
Lenin, Vladimir Ilyich
Leone, Giovanni
Lerdo de Tejada,
 Sebastian
Lewis, Vaughan Allen
Ley, Robert
Liaquat Ali, Khan
Liebknecht, Karl
Limann, Hilla
Linh, Nguyen Van
Lini, Walter Hadye
Li Peng
Lipponen, Paavo (T.)
Lissouba, Pascal
Liu Shao-Ch'i
Liverpool, 2nd Earl of
Li Xiannian
Lleras Camargo, Alberto
Lleras Restrepo, Carlos
Lopez, Carlos Antonio
Lopez, Francisco Solano
Lopez Mateos, Adolfo
Lopez Portillo (y
 Pacheco), Jose
Losonczi, Pal
Lubbers, Ruud
Lubke, Heinrich
Lucinschi, Petru
Lukanov, Andrei
Lukashenka, Alyaksandr
 Hrihoryevich
Lumumba, Patrice
Lusinchi, Jaime
Luthuli, Albert John
 Mvumbi
Luxemburg, Rosa
Ly, Abdoulaye
Lyons, Joseph Aloysius
Macapagal, Diosdado
 P(angan)
Macarthur, John
Macaulay, Herbert
MacDonald, John
 Alexander

Machado y Morales,
 Gerardo
Machel, Samora Moises
Mackenzie, Alexander
MacMillan, Harold
Madero, Francisco
 Indalecio
Madrid Hurtado, Miguel
 de la
Magana, Alvaro (Alfredo)
Magsaysay, Ramon
Mahathir Bin Mohamad
Mahmud, II
Mainassara, Ibrahim Bare
Malenkov, Georgi
 Maximilianovich
Mamaloni, Solomon
Mandela, Nelson
 (Rolihlahla)
Manley, Michael
 (Norman)
Mannerheim, Carl Gustav
 Emil, Baron
Manning, Ernest (Charles)
Manning, Patrick
 (Augustus Mervyn)
Mansur, (Abu Jafar Ibn
 Muhammad), Al
Mao Zedong
Mara, Ratu Sir Kamisese
Marchais, Georges (Rene
 Louis)
Marcos, Ferdinand Edralin
Margai, Milton Augustus
 Striery
Markovic, Ante
Martens, Wilfried
Martinez, Maximiliano
 Hernandez
Marx, Karl Heinrich
Mascarenhas Monteiro,
 Antonio
Masire, Quett (Ketumile
 Jonny)
Massamba-Debat,
 Alphonse
Massey, William Ferguson
Matteotti, Giacomo
Mauroy, Pierre
Mawdudi, Abu-I A'la
Mazepa, Ivan Stepanovich
Mazowiecki, Tadeusz
Mboya, Tom
McEntee, Peter Donovan
Meciar, Vladimir
Mehmed the Conqueror
Meighen, Arthur
Meir, Golda
Mejia Victores, Oscar
 Humberto
Melbourne, William
 Lamb, Viscount
Meles Zenawi
Mendez, Aparicio
Menem, Carlos Saul
Menguistu Haile Mariam
Menocal, Mario Garcia
Meri, Lennart
Messali Hadj
Metaxas, John
Micombero, Michel
Milosevic, Slobodan
Mitchell, James
Mitchell, Keith
Mitre, Bartolome
Mitsotakis, Constantine

Mitterrand, Francois
 (Maurice Marie)
Miyazawa, Kiichi
Mkapa, Benjamin William
Mobutu Sese Seko
Mogae, Festus Gontebanye
Mohammed, II
Mohammed Ali
Mohieddin, Ahmed Faud
Moi, Daniel arap
Mokhehle, Ntsu
Mollet, Guy
Molotov, Vyacheslav
 Mikhaylovich
Momoh, Joseph (Saidu)
Moneta, Ernesto Teodora
Montfort, Simon de
Montt Torres, Manuel
Morales Bermudez,
 Francisco
Moreno, Gabriel Garcia
Morinigo, Higinio
Mosquera, Tomas
 Cipriano de
Mossadegh, Mohammed
Mswati, III
Muawiya ibn Abu Sufyan
Mubarak, (Mohammed)
 Hosni
Mugabe, Robert (Gabriel)
Muhammad bin Tughluq
Muldoon, Robert David,
 Sir
Mulroney, Brian
Muluzi, Bakili
Muoi, Do
Murayama, Tomiichi
Museveni, Yoweri Kaguta
Mussolini, Benito
 · Amilcare Andrea
Muzorewa, Abel Tendekai
Mwanga
Mwinyi, Ali Hassan
Naguib, Mohammed
Nahayan, Zayed bin al-,
 Sultan
Najib Ahmadzi
Nakamura, Kuniwo
Nakasone, Yasuhiro
Namaliu, Rabbie Langanai
Namphy, Henri
Nano, Fatos
Naoroji, Dadabhai
Nasser, Gamal Abdel
Navon, Yitzhak
Nazarbayev, Nursultan
 (Abishevich)
Ndadaye, Melchior
Nehru, Jawaharlal
Nena, Jacob
Nenni, Pietro Sandro
Netanyahu, Benjamin
Neto, Agostinho
Ne Win, U
Ngo-Dinh-Diem
Nguyen Khanh
Nimeiry, Gaafar
 Mohammed al
Nitti, Francesco Saverio
Niyazov, Saparmurad
 Atayevich
Nkrumah, Kwame
Nol, Lon
Nordli, Odvar
Noriega (Moreno), Manuel
 Antonio

North, Frederick North, Baron
Novotny, Antonin
Ntaryamira, Cyprien
Ntibantunganya, Sylvestre
Nu, U
Nujoma, Samuel Shafiihuma
Nureddin
Nuri al-Sa'id
Nu Thakin
Nyerere, Julius Kambarage
Nyrup Rasmussen, Poul
Nzinga Nkuwu
Obasanjo, Olusegun
Obiang Nguema Mbasogo, Teodoro
Obote, Milton
Ochirbat, Punsalmaagiyn
O'Connell, Daniel
Oddsson, David
Odinga, Ajuma Jaramogi
Odoacer
Odria Amoretti, Manuel Apolinario
Oduber (Quiros), Daniel
Ojukwu, Chukwuemeka Odumegwu
Okubo, Toshimichi
Olter, Bailey
Olympio, Sylvanus E.
Omar ibn Said Tal, Al-Hajj
O'Neill, Terence Marne
Ongania, Juan Carlos
Ong Teng Cheong
Orban, Viktor
Orlando, Vittorio Emanuele
Ortega Saavedra, Daniel
Osman I
Ospina Perez, Mariano
Ousmane, Mahamane
Ovando Candia, Alfredo
Ozal, Turgut
Paasikivi, Juho Kusti
Paasio, Rafael
Paeniu, Bikenibeu
Paez, Jose Antonio
Paisley, Ian Richard Kyle
Panchen Lama
Panday, Basdeo
Panic, Milan
Papadopoulos, George
Papandreou, Andreas (George)
Papandreou, George
Papineau, Louis-Joseph
Parizeau, Jacques
Park, Chung Hee
Parnell, Charles Stewart
Pascal-Trouillot, Ertha
Pastora (Gomez), Eden
Pastrana, Andres
Patasse, Ange (Felix)
Patel, Vallabhbhai
Patten, Chris(topher Francis)
Pauker, Ana
Paz Estenssoro, Victor
Paz Zamora, Jaime
Pearson, Lester B(owles)
Peixoto, Floriano
Pendergast, Thomas Joseph
Pereira, Aristides

Peres, Shimon
Perez, Carlos Andres
Perez Balladares, Ernesto
Peron, Eva Duarte
Peron, Isabel Martinez de
Peron, Juan
Persson, Goran
Pertini, Sandro
Pham Hung
Pham van Dong
Phibun Songkhram, Luang
Phieu, Le Kha
Pieck, Wilhelm
Pilate, Pontius
Pinay, Antoine
Pinochet Ugarte, Augusto
Pinto da Costa, Manuel
Pitt, William, the Younger
Planinc, Milka
Plaza Lasso, Galo
Pollitt, Harry
Pol Pot
Pompidou, Georges Jean Raymond
Premadasa, Ranasinghe
Prem Tinsulanonda
Pretorius, Andries
Preval, Rene
Price, George
Primo de Rivera (y Orbaneja), Miguel
Prio Socarras, Carlos
Prodi, Romano
Ptolemy (Soter), I
Qaboos Bin Al Sai'id
Qadhafi, Muammar al-
Quezon (y Molina), Manuel Luis
Quirino, Elpidio
Rabani, Burhanuddin
Rabin, Yitzhak
Rabuka, Sitiveni (Ligamamada)
Radek, Karl Bernhardovich
Rafsanjani, Hashemi
Rahman, Abdul, Prince
Rahman, Mujibur, Sheik
Rai, Lala Lajpat
Rajagopalachari, Chakravarti
Rajai, Mohammed Ali
Rajaraja, I
Rakhmonov, Imomali
Rakowski, Mieczyslaw Franciszek
Ramgoolam, Navin
Ramgoolam, Seewoosagur, Sir
Ramos, Fidel V(aldez)
Rannaridh, Norodom, Prince
Rao, P V Narasimha
Ratana, Taupotiki Wiremu
Ratsiraka, Didier
Rawlings, Jerry John
Recto, Claro M.
Reddy, N(eelam) Sanjeeva
Reina, Carlos Roberto
Rene, (France) Albert
Renner, Karl
Retief, Pieter
Reyes, Rafael
Reynolds, Albert
Rios Montt, Jose Efrain
Rivadavia, Bernardino

Rivera, Fructuoso
Rivera, Luis Munoz
Robinson, A(rthur) N(apoleon) R(aymond)
Robinson, Mary
Roca, Julio Argentino
Rockingham, 2nd Marquess of
Rodriguez, Andres
Rodriguez, Miguel Angel
Rodriguez Pedotti, Andres
Roh Tae Woo
Rojas Pinilla, Gustavo
Roldos Aguilera, Jamie
Romero, Carlos Humberto
Rosas, Juan Manuel de
Rosebery, Archibald Philip Primrose, Earl
Rosenberg, Alfred
Roxas, Manuel
Ruiz Cortines, Adolfo
Rumor, Mariano
Sadat, Anwar el
Saibou, Ali
Said, Seyyid
St. Laurent, Louis Stephen
Salam, Saeb
Saleh, Ali Abdullah
Salem, Mamdouh
Salih, Ali Abdallah
Salinas de Gortari, Carlos
Samper Pizano, Ernesto
Samrin, Heng
Samudragupta
Sananikone, Phoui
Sanchez de Lozada, Gonzalo
Sandiford, Lloyd Erskine
Sandino, Augusto C(esar Calderon)
Sanguinetti, Julio Maria
Sankara, Thomas
Sant, Alfred
Santa Anna, Antonio Lopez de
Santa Cruz, Andres de
Santana, Pedro
Santer, Jacques
Santos, Jose Eduardo dos
Saragat, Giuseppe
Sarit Thanarat
Sarkis, Elias
Sarmiento, Domingo Faustino
Sarney, Jose
Sassou-Nguesso, Denis
Sato, Eisaku
Sauve, Jeanne Mathilde Benoit
Savage, Michael Joseph
Savimbi, Jonas Malheiro
Saw Maung
Sawyer, Amos
Scalfaro, Oscar Luigi
Scheidemann, Philipp
Schleicher, Kurt von
Schluter, Poul (Holmskov)
Schmidt, Helmut Heinrich Waldemar
Schreyer, Edward Richard
Schuschnigg, Kurt von
Scott, Arleigh Winston, Sir
Scullin, James Henry
Seaga, Edward Phillip George

Seddon, Richard John
Sedney, Jules
Segni, Antonio
Selim, III
Senanayake, Don Stephen
Senghor, Leopold Sedar
Serrano Elias, Jorge Antonio
Shagari, Alhaji Shehu Usman Aliyu
Shamir, Yitzhak
Sharif, Nawaz
Shazar, Zalman
Sheares, Benjamin Henry
Shekhar, Chandra
Shihab, Fu'ad
Shih Le
Shipley, Jenny
Shukairy, Ahmed
Siad Barre, Mohamed
Siles Zuazo, Hernan
Simitis, Costas
Simmonds, Kennedy Alphonse
Singh, Giani Zail
Singh, V(ishwanath) P(ratap)
Skate, Bill
Slovo, Joe
Smallwood, Joey
Smith, Alfred Emanuel
Smith, Ian Douglas
Snegur, Mircea Ion
Soares, Mario Alberto Nobre Lopes
Soeharto
Soglo, Nicephore (Dieudonne)
Somoza, Anastasio
Somoza Debayle, Anastasio
Souphanouvong, Prince
Souvanna, Phouma
Speransky, Mikhail
Spinola, Antonio (Sebastiao Ribeiro) de
Stahlberg, Kaarlo Juho
Stalin, Joseph
Stambuliski, Aleksandr
Stampfli, Jakob
Stanley, Frederick Arthur, Earl of Derby
Stevens, Siaka Probyn
Stolypin, Piotr Arkadevich
Strasser, Valentine (E. M.)
Stroessner, Alfredo
Strougal, Lubomir
Suarez Gonzales, Adolfo
Suharto
Sui, Yang Chien
Sukarno, Achmed
Sulla, Lucius C
Sunay, Gevdet
Sun Yat-Sen
Sun Yat-Sen, Chingling Soong, Madame
Suzuki, Zenko
Svoboda, Ludvik
Swart, Charles Robberts
Tabai, Ieremia Tienang
Taewon'gun, Hungson
Takeshita, Noboru
Tanaka, Kakuei
Taqi Khan Amir-e Kabir, Mirza

Taya, Maaouya Ould
　Sid'Ahmed
Taylor, Charles
Teannaki, Teatao
Tebbit, Norman Beresford
Ter-Petrosyan, Levon
Terra, Gabriel
Thalmann, Ernst
Than Shwe
Thapa, Surya Bahadur
Thatcher, Margaret (Hilda
　Roberts)
Thomas, Norman Mattoon
Thomaz, Americo
Thorpe, Jeremy
Tindemans, Leo(nard)
Tito
Tito, Teburoro
Todd, Garfield
Togliatti, Palmiro
Tojo, Hideki
Tolbert, William Richard,
　Jr.
Tombalbaye, Nagarta
　Francois
Torrijos Herrera, Omar
Tosovsky, Josef
Toure, Ahmed Sekou
Toure, Sekou
Toussaint l'Ouverture,
　Pierre Dominique
Traore, Moussa
Trotsky, Leon
Trovoada, Miguel
Trudeau, Pierre Elliott
Tsankov, Aleksandur
Tsatsos, Constantinos
Tshombe, Moise
Tsiranana, Philibert
Tubman, William
　Vacanarat Shadrach
Tudjman, Franjo
Tung Chee-hwa
Tupou, IV
Tupper, Charles
Turbay Ayala, Julio Cesar
Turner, John Napier
Ubico y Castaneda, Jorge
Ulbricht, Walter
Ulmanis, Guntis
Ulufa'alu, Bart
Urquiza, Justo Jose
Urrutia Lleo, Manuel
Vajpayee, Atal Behari
Vander Zalm, William
Vargas, Getulio Dornelles
Vassiliou, George
　(Vassos)
Vazquez, Horacio
Veil, Simone Annie Jacob
Velasco Alvarado, Juan
Velasco Ibarra, Jose Maria
Venetiaan, Renaldo
Venkataraman,
　Ramaswamy
Verwoerd, Hendrik F
Videla, Jorge Rafael
Videnov, Zhan (Vassilev)
Vieira, Joao (Bernardo)
Villiger, Kaspar
Virchow, Rudolf
Vogel, Julius
Vohor, (Rialuth) Serge
Vo Van Kiet
Walesa, Lech
Wangchuk, Jigme Singye

Wang Hung-Wen
Wang Ming
Wanke, Daouda Malam
Ward, Deighton Harcourt
　Lisle, Sir
Wasmosy, Juan Carlos
Webb, Sidney James
Weizmann, Chaim
Weizsacker, Richard
　Freiherr von
Welensky, Roy
Wijdenbosch, Jules Albert
Wingti, Paias
Witt, Johan de
Yahya Khan, Agha
　Muhammad
Ydigoras Fuentes Miguel
Ye Jianying
Yeltsin, Boris
　(Nikolayevich)
Yilmaz, Mesut
Yoshida, Shigeru
Youlou, Fulbert
Yuan, Shih-Kai
Zafy, Albert
Zaghlul Pasha, Saad
Zayid bin Sultan Al-
　Nahyan, Shaykh
Zedillo Ponce de Leon,
　Ernesto
Zelaya, Jose Santos
Zeroual, Liamine
Zhao Ziyang
Zhdanov, Andrei
　Alexandrovich
Zia(ur) Rahman
Zia-ul-Haq, Mohammad
Zine el Abidine Ben Ali
Zinoviev, Grigori
　Evseevich
Zyuganov, Gennadi
　A(ndreyevich)

POLITICAL
LEADERS

Song Sisters, The

POLITICAL
REFORMER

Friedrich, Carl Joachim
Galvez, Jose de
Halide Edip Adivar
Wang An-shih

POLITICAL
SCIENTIST

Alberdi, Juan Bautista
Barker, Ernest, Sir
Bentley, Arthur F.
Brogan, Denis William,
　Sir
Catlin, George Edward
　Gordon, Sir
Cherne, Leo
Cleveland, James Harlan
Corwin, Edward Samuel
Deutsch, Karl Wolfgang
Dodds, Harold Willis

Filmer, Robert
Griffith, Ernest S(tacey)
Gulick, Luther (Halsey)
Janowitz, Morris
Key, Valdimer Orlando,
　Jr.
Laski, Harold Joseph
Lasswell, Harold Dwight
Lieber, Franz
Lipset, Seymour Martin
Mariana, Juan de
Mazrui, Ali A(l'Amin)
Moley, Raymond Charles
Morgenthau, Hans
　Joachim
Parkinson, C(yril)
　Northcote
Phillips, Kevin (Price)
Price, Don K.
Rice, Condoleezza
Saint-Pierre, Abbe de
Scott, F(rancis) R(eginald)
Shalala, Donna Edna
Tugwell, Rexford Guy
Voegelin, Eric (Herman
　Wilhelm)
Wallas, Graham
Wilcox, Francis (Orlando)

POLITICAL
THEORIST

Harrington, James
Hildreth, Richard

POLITICIAN

Abbott, Diane (Julie)
Abdnor, James S
Abiola, Moshood
Abourezk, James George
Abraham, Spencer
Abzug, Bella (Savitsky)
Achtenberg, Roberta
Adams, Annette Abbott
Adams, Charles Francis,
　Sr.
Adams, Floyd, Jr.
Addabbo, Joseph Patrick
Addison, Christopher,
　Viscount
Addonizio, Hugh Joseph
Adenauer, Konrad
Aflaq, Michel
Agt, Andries Antonius
　Maria van
Agus Salim, Hadji
Aiken, George David
Akaka, Daniel Kahikina
Alaman, Lucas
Alcorn, James Lusk
Alexander, Lamar
Alioto, Joseph L(awrence)
Allain, William A
Allard, Wayne
Allen, Ethel D.
Allen, Ivan, Jr.
Allison, William Boyd
Almirante, Giorgio
Altgeld, John Peter
Amato, Giuliano
Ambedkar, Bhimrao Ramji
Amery, Julian

Ames, Adelbert
Ames, Fisher
Ames, Oakes
Anaya, Toney
Anderson, Clint(on
　Presba)
Anderson, Jack Zuinglius
Anderson, John Bayard
Anderson, Wendell
　Richard
Andrada e Silva, Jose
　Bonifacio de
Andrew, John Albion
Andrews, Mark N
Appleton, Nathan
Aquino, Benigno Simeon,
　Jr.
Aranha, Osvaldo
Aratus
Archer, Dennis W(ayne)
Archer, Jeffrey Howard
Arends, Leslie Cornelius
Armey, Richard K(eith)
Armstrong, William L
Arnall, Ellis (Gibbs)
Arran, Arthur Kattendyke
　Strange David
　Archibald Gore, Earl of
Ashbrook, John Milan
Ashcroft, John David
Ashdown, Paddy
Ashley, Thomas William
　Ludlow
Ashley, William Henry
Ashmun, Jehudi
Askew, Reubin
　O'Donovan
Aspin, Les
Atchison, David R
Babbitt, Bruce E(dward)
Baca-Barragan, Polly
Badillo, Herman
Bahr, Egon
Bailly, Jean Sylvain
Bajer, Fredrik
Baker, Howard Henry, Jr.
Baker, Newton D(iehl)
Baliles, Gerald L
Ball, Joseph H(urst)
Balladur, Edouard
Ballinger, Margaret
Bangerter, Norman
　Howard
Bankhead, William
　Brockman
Barbosa, Ruy
Barnett, Ross Robert
Barr, Joseph W(alker)
Barras, Paul Francois Jean
　Nicolas, Comte de
Barres, (Auguste) Maurice
Barry, Marion S(hepilov),
　Jr.
Bartlett, Vernon
Barton, Edmund
Baucus, Max Sieben
Bayard, Thomas Francis
Bayh, Birch Evans, Jr.
Bayh, Evan
Beame, Abraham David
Beernaert, Auguste Marie
　Francois
Bell, John
Bellmon, Henry Louis
Benjamin, Adam, Jr.
Bennett, Robert F.

Devine, Donald
Dewey, Thomas Edmund
DeWine, Mike
Diagne, Blaise
Dies, Martin, Jr.
Diggs, Charles C(oles), Jr.
Dingell, John David, Jr.
Dinkins, David Norman
DiPrete, Edward Daniel
Dirksen, Everett McKinley
DiSalle, Michael Vincent
Dixon, Alan John
Dixon, Sharon Pratt
Djilas, Milovan
Dodd, Christopher John
Dodd, Thomas Joseph
Doi, Takako
Dole, Robert Joseph
Domenici, Pete V(ichi)
Dominick, Peter Hoyt
Donnelly, Ignatius
Dorgan, Byron Leslie
dos Santos, Marcelino
Douglas, Emily Taft
Douglas, Helen Mary
 Gahagan
Douglas, Paul Howard
Douglas, Stephen Arnold
Douglas, Thomas Clement
Douglas-Home, Alexander
 Frederick, Sir
Dow, Neal
Draco
Drago, Luis Maria
Drapeau, Jean
Drusus, Marcus Livius
Dryden, John Fairfield
Dube, John Langalibalele
Dukakis, Michael Stanley
Dumas, Jean Baptiste
 Andre
Duncan-Sandys, Edwin,
 Lord
Dunmore, 4th Earl of
DuPont, Pierre Samuel, IV
Durbin, Richard J.
Durenberger, David
 Ferdinand
Durham, 1st Earl of
Dwinell, Lane
Dwyer, Florence Price
Dzerzhinsky, Felix
 Edmundovich
Eagleton, Thomas Francis
East, John Porter
Eastland, James Oliver
Eaton, John Henry
Eaton, Theophilus
Eboue, Adolphe Felix
 Sylvestre
Edgar, Jim
Edmunds, George Franklin
Edwards, Edwin
 Washington
Edwards, India Moffett
Eldjarn, Kristjan
Ellender, Allen Joseph
Elliott, Robert Brown
Engle, Clair
Engler, John Mathias
Enzi, Michael B.
Erhard, Ludwig
Erlander, Tage Fritiof
Ervin, Sam(uel James Jr.)
Erzberger, Matthias
Evans, Daniel Jackson

Evatt, Herbert Vere
Exon, (John) James, (Jr.)
Fadlallah, Sayyid
 Muhammad Husayn
Fahrenkopf, Frank Joseph,
 Jr.
Faidherbe, Louis Leon
 Cesar
Faircloth, Lauch
Fairclough, Ellen Louks
Farley, James A(loysius)
Farrington, Elizabeth
 Pruett (Mary)
Fascell, Dante B(runo)
Fattah, Chaka
Faubus, Orval E(ugene)
Fauntroy, Walter E(dward)
Feingold, Russell D.
Feinstein, Dianne
Felton, Rebecca Ann
 Latimer
Fenwick, Millicent
 Hammond
Ferguson, Homer
Ferguson, Miriam Amanda
Ferraro, Geraldine Anne
Ferre, Maurice Antonio
Ferry, Jules Francois
 Camille
Fessenden, William Pitt
Fields, Cleo
Finney, Joan Marie
 McInroy
Fish, Hamilton, III
Fitzgerald, John Francis
Flake, Floyd H(arold)
Flanders, Ralph Edward
Flood, Daniel J(ohn)
Florio, James Joseph
Flynn, Edward Joseph
Flynn, Ray
Flynn, Raymond (Leo)
Foley, Thomas S(tephen)
Foley, Tom
Folsom, James E(lisha)
Fong, Hiram Leong
Foot, Michael
Foote, Henry Stuart
Ford, Harold E(ugene), Jr.
Ford, Wendell Hampton
Fordice, Kirk
Forrest, John, 1st Baron
 Forrest of Bunbury
Foss, Joe
Frahm, Sheila
Frank, Barney
Franks, Gary A
Fraser, Donald Mackay
Freij, Elias
Fremont, John Charles
Frist, Bill
Frondizi, Arturo
Frunze, Mikhail
 Vasilievich
Fulani, Lenora
Fulbright, J(ames) William
Fulton, Richard Harmon
Furcolo, (John) Foster
Gaitan, Jorge Eliecer
Gallen, Hugh J
Galloway, Joseph
Galt, Alexander Tilloch
Galvez, Jose de
Gantt, Harvey Bernard
Gardner, Booth
Garn, Jake

Gary, Raymond
Gasca, Pedro de la
Gautier, Felisa Rincon de
Gemayel, Pierre, Sheikh
George, James Zachariah
George, Walter Franklin
Gephardt, Richard Andrew
Getty, Donald
Gibson, Kenneth Allen
Giddings, Joshua Reed
Gilligan, John Joyce
Gingrich, Newt(on Leroy)
Giroud, Francoise
Giscard d'Estaing, Valery
Giuliani, Rudolph William
Gladstone, James
Glass, Carter
Glenn, John Herschel, Jr.
Gloucester, Duke of
Godoy y Alvarez de Faria,
 Manuel de
Gokhale, Gopal Krishna
Goldschmidt, Neil Edward
Goldwater, Barry M(orris)
Goldwater, Barry M(orris),
 Jr.
Gonzalez, Henry Barbosa
Gooch, George Peabody
Goode, Wilson
Goodell, Charles Ellsworth
Gordon-Walker of Leyton,
 Patrick Chrestien
Gordon-Walker, Baron
Gore, Albert Arnold
Gorton, Slade
Grace, William Russell
Graham, Bob
Graham, William
 Alexander
Gramm, (William) Phil(ip)
Grams, Rod
Grandi, Dino
Grandy, Fred(erick
 Lawrence)
Grassley, Charles Ernest
Grasso, Ella
Grattan, Henry
Gravel, Mike
Green, Edith S(tarrett)
Gregg, Judd
Grey, George
Griffin, Bob
Griffin, Marvin
Griffith, Samuel Walker
Grimond, Jo(seph)
Gronchi, Giovanni
Gross, H(arold) R(oyce)
Grosseteste, Robert
Guericke, Otto Von
Gueye, Lamine
Gurney, Edward John
Guyer, Tennyson
Hagel, Chuck
Hague, Frank
Halleck, Charles Abraham
Hamilcar Barca
Hamilton, Alexander
Hamilton, Grace Towns
Hamilton, Lee Herbert
Hamm-Brucher, Hildegard
Hammond, James Henry
Hanna, Mark
Hansen, Clifford Peter
Hansen, Julia Butler
Hardy, Porter, Jr.
Harkin, Thomas R(ichard)

Harley, Robert, 1st Earl of
 Oxford and Earl
 Mortimer
Harrington, Michael
Harris, Fred Roy
Harris, Joe Frank
Harris, Michael Wesley
Hart, Gary Warren
Hart, Philip Aloysius
Hartke, Vance
Hassan, Muhammad
 Abdille
Hastie, William Henry
Hastings, Alcee L
Hatch, Carl A
Hatch, Orrin G(rant)
Hatch, William Henry
Hatcher, Richard Gordon
Hatfield, Mark Odom
Hatfield, Richard
Hathaway, Stanley Knapp
Hathaway, William Dodd
Hatta, Mohammad
Hawkins, Gus
Hawkins, Paula Fickes
Hayakawa, S(amuel)
 I(chiye)
Hayden, Carl Trumball
Hayden, Mike
Hayden, Tom
Hayes, James C.
Hayford, J(oseph)
 E(phraim)Casely
Hayne, Robert Young
Hays, Brooks
Hays, Wayne Levere
Hearst, George
Hebert, F(elix) Edward
Hecht, Chic
Heflin, Howell Thomas
Heinz, John
Helms, Jesse Alexander,
 Jr.
Hernandez-Colon, Rafael
Hickel, Wally
Hickenlooper, Bourke B
Hicks, Louise Day
Hildreth, Horace
 A(ugusta)
Hill, Benjamin Harvey
Hill, Lester
Hillings, Patrick J(ohn)
Hitchcock, Gilbert Monell
Hobson, William
Hochoy, Solomon, Sir
Holifield, Chet
Hollings, Ernest Frederick
Holtzman, Elizabeth
Honecker, Erich
Hoopes, Darlington
Ho-shen
Hosmer, Craig
Hosokawa, Morihiro
Houphouet-Boigny, Felix
Howard, James John
Howe, Clarence Decatur
Howe, Joseph
Hruska, Roman L(ee)
Hua Guofeng
Hubbard, Orville Liscum
Huddleston, Walter
 Darlington
Hughes, Harold E(verett)
Hughes, Richard J(oseph)
Hume, John
Humphrey, Gordon John

Mikulski, Barbara Ann
Mikva, Abner Joseph
Milk, Harvey
Miller, Bob
Miller, Walter Dale
Miller, William E
Miller, Zell (Bryan)
Milliken, William Grawn
Mills, Wilbur Daigh
Miltiades
Mink, Patsy Takemoto
Mitchel, John Purroy
Mitchell, George John
Moffett, Anthony Toby
Mofford, Rose
Molina, Gloria
Molinari, Susan
Monck, Charles Stanley,
  Sir
Mondlane, Eduardo
  Chivambo
Monroney, Mike (Aimer
  Stillwell)
Montoya, Joseph Manuel
Moore, Arch Alfred, Jr.
Moorhead, William Singer
Morano, Albert Paul
Morgan, Daniel
Morgan, Robert Burren
Morgan, Thomas
  E(llsworth)
Morial, Ernest Nathan
Morial, Marc (Haydel)
Morley, John, Viscount
Moro, Aldo
Morrill, Justin Smith
Morris, Newbold
Morrison, Cameron
Morse, Wayne Lyman
Morton, Oliver Hazard
  Perry Throck
Morton, Thruston Ballard
Moseley-Braun, Carol
Mosley, Oswald Ernald,
  Sir
Moss, Frank Edward
Moultrie, William
Moynihan, Daniel Patrick
Mundt, Karl Earl
Munoz Marin, Luis
Murat, Joachim
Murkowski, Frank Hughes
Murphy, Frank
Murphy, George Lloyd
Murphy, John Michael
Murray, Patty
Murtha, John Patrick
Muskie, Edmund S(ixtus)
Nabuco de Araujo,
  Joaquim Aurelio
Naidu, Sarojini
Narayan, Jayaprakash
Negrin, Juan
Nelson, Ben
Nelson, Gaylord Anton
Ngala, Ronald Gideon
Ngata, Apirana Turupa
Ngo dinh Nhu, Madame
Nguyen Huu Tho
Nguyen thi Binh, Madame
Nicholson, Francis
Nickles, Donald Lee
Nix, Robert N(elson)
  C(ornelius), Sr.
Nixon, Richard M(ilhous)

Nkomo, Joshua (Mqabuko
  Nyongolo)
Noble, Elaine
Norfolk, 3d Duke of
Norris, George William
Northumberland, Duke of
Nunn, Sam(uel Augustus,
  Jr.)
Nye, Gerald Prentice
O'Brien, Leo W
O'Dwyer, Paul
O'Dwyer, William
Ogilvie, Richard Buell
Ogot, Grace Emily Akinyi
O'Konski, Alvin E(dward)
Okuma, Shigenobu
Oldenbarnevelt, Johan van
Olmert, Ehud
Olney, Richard
O'Neill, Thomas P(hilip),
  Jr.
O'Neill, William Atchison
Orr, Kay Avonne
Orr, Robert Dunkerson
Osmena, Sergio, Jr.
Otis, Harrison Gray
Owen, David Anthony
  Llewellyn
Owens, Major (Robert)
Oxenstierna, Axel
  Gustafsson
Packwood, Bob
Palacky, Frantisek
Pandit, Vijaya Lakshmi
  (Nehru)
Papen, Franz von
Parker, Alton Brooks
Parkes, Henry, Sir
Pastore, John Orlando
Pataki, George E(lmer)
Paterson, Basil Alexander
Paterson, William
Patterson, P(ercival Noel)
  J(ames)
Pawley, Howard Russell
Payne, Donald M
Peckford, Brian
Pell, Claiborne DeBorda
Pendleton, Edmund
Pendleton, George Hunt
Penrose, Boies
Pepper, Claude Denson
Percy, Charles Harting
Perez Jimenez, Marcos
Perkins, Carl Dewey
Perpich, Rudy George
Perry, Carrie Saxon
Perry, Ruth (Sando)
Perth, 16th Earl of
Peterson, David Robert
Pickering, Timothy
Pike, Otis Grey
Pillsbury, John Sargent
Pinchback, P(inckney)
  B(enton) S(tewart)
Pinchot, Gifford
Pinckney, Charles
Pitman, James
Pitt, David Thomas
Pitt, William, the Elder
Pitta, Celso
Platt, Thomas Collier
Plimsoll, Samuel
Poage, W(illiam) R(obert)
Pobedonostsev, Konstantin
  Petrovich

Podgorny, Nikolai
  Viktorovich
Pombal, Marques de
Portales, Diego (Jose
  Victor)
Poulson, Norris
Powell, Adam Clayton, Jr.
Powell, Enoch
Pozsgay, Imre
Prasad, Rajendra
Pressler, Larry
Pretorius, Marthinus
  Wessel
Price, Melvin
Pridi Phanomyong
Proxmire, William
Pryor, David Hampton
Pulcher, Publius Clodius
Purtell, William Arthur
Pyle, Howard
Pym, John
Quay, Matthew Stanley
Quayle, Dan
Quiroga, Juan Facundo
Racicot, Marc F
Rae, Bob
Rainey, Joseph Hayne
Rains, Albert McKinley
Rakosi, Matyas
Ram, Jagjivan
Ramphal, Shridath
  Surendranath
Ramsay, David
Randolph, Jennings
Rangel, Charles Bernard
Rankin, Jeannette
Rathbone, Eleanor
Rau, Johannes
Ray, Dixy Lee
Ray, Robert D
Rayburn, Sam(uel
  Taliaferro)
Raymond, Henry Jarvis
Reading, 1st Marquess of
Reagan, Maureen
  Elizabeth
Reed, Jack
Reed, Thomas Brackett
Reid, Harry
Reifel, Ben
Reuter, Ernst
Revels, Hiram Rhodes
Revillagigedo, Conde de
Reynaud, Paul
Reynolds, R(ichard)
  J(oshua), Jr.
Reynolds, Robert Rice
Rhett, Robert Barnwell
Rhodes, James Allen
Rhodes, John Jacob
Ribicoff, Abraham
  A(lexander)
Rice, Norm(an Blann)
Richards, Ann
Richards, Richard
Richardson, Bill
Riegle, Donald Wayne, Jr.
Rienzi, Cola di
Rio Branco, Barao do
Riordan, Richard J
Rizzo, Frank Lazzaro
Robarts, John Parmenter
Robb, Charles Spittal
Robert, II
Roberts, Barbara
Roberts, Dennis J(oseph)

Roberts, Pat
Robinson, John Beverley
Rocard, Michel Louis
  Leon
Rockefeller, John
  D(avison), IV
Rockefeller, Winthrop
Rodino, Peter Wallace, Jr.
Rodney, Caesar
Roemer, Buddy
Rogers, Edith
Rohde, Ruth Bryan Owen
Romer, Roy R
Romero Barcelo, Carlos
  Antonio
Romney, George
  (Wilcken)
Rooney, John (James)
Roosevelt, Franklin
  Delano, Jr.
Roosevelt, James
Root, Oren
Roper, Daniel C(alhoun)
Rosenthal, Benjamin
  Stanley
Ros-Lehtinen, Ileana
Ross, Nellie Taylor
Rostenkowski, Daniel
  David
Roth, William Victor, Jr.
Rothermere, Esmond Cecil
  Harmsworth, Viscount
Rowling, Wallace Edward
Roybal-Allard, Lucille
Royo, Aristides
Rudman, Warren Bruce
Ruef, Abraham
Russell, John, Lord
Russell, Richard Brevard,
  Jr.
Rutledge, John
Ryan, Leo Joseph
Sa, Mem de
Saavedra, Angel de
Sadr, Musa al-
Saigo, Takamori
St. Clair, Arthur
Saint-Just, Louis Antoine
  Leon de
Saionji, Kimmochi
Salinger, Pierre Emil
  George
Sallust
Saltonstall, Leverett
Sanders, Bernard
Sandwich, John Montagu
Sanford, Terry
Santander, Francisco de
  Paula
Santorum, Rick
Sapru, Tej Bahadur
Sarbanes, Paul S(pyros)
Sarpi, Paolo
Sasser, James R(alph)
Savelli, Luca
Sawyer, Eugene, Jr.
Sayles Belton, Sharon
Schaefer, William Donald
Scharping, Rudolf
Schenck, Robert Cumming
Schily, Otto
Schlafly, Phyllis Stewart
Schmitt, Harrison Hagan
Schmoke, Kurt L(idell)
Schonhuber, Franz Xaver
Schroder, Gerhard

Schroeder, Patricia Scott
Schumacher, Kurt
Schumann, Maurice
Schumer, Charles E(llis)
Schurz, Carl
Schwarzhaupt, Elisabeth
Schwinden, Ted
Scott, Hugh (Doggett), Jr.
Scranton, William Warren
Sebelius, Keith George
Servan-Schreiber, Jean-
   Jacques
Sessions, Jeff
Sevier, John
Seymour, Horatio
Seyss-Inquart, Artur von
Shang Yang
Shapp, Milton J(errold)
Shehu, Mehmet
Shelby, Richard C.
Sheridan, Richard Brinsley
Sherman, John
Shields, James
Sidney, Algernon
Sifton, Clifford
Sigmund, Barbara Boggs
Simon, Jules Francois
Simon, Paul M(artin)
Simpson, Alan Kooi
Sinner, George Albert
Sithole, Ndabaningi
Slansky, Rudolf Salzmann
Slidell, John
Smalls, Robert
Smith, Donald Alexander
Smith, Ellison DuRant
Smith, Gordon H.
Smith, Howard Worth
Smith, Margaret
   (Madeline) Chase
Smith, Robert C
Snelling, Richard
Snowe, Olympia J(ean)
Sobchak, Anatoly
   Aleksandrovich
Solarz, Stephen Joshua
Solon
Somerset, Duke of
Soule, Pierre
Spaak, Paul-Henri
Specter, Arlen
Spooner, John Coit
Spychalski, Marian
Ssu-ma kuang
Stafford, Robert Theodore
Staggers, Harley O(rrin)
Staller, Ilona
Stanford, Leland
Stanford, Sally
Stassen, Harold Edward
Steel, David Martin Scott
Stein, Heinrich Friedrich
   Karl vom und zum,
   Baron
Stennis, John C(ornelius)
Stephens, Alexander
   Hamilton
Stevens, Ted
Stevens, Thaddeus
Stevenson, Adlai Ewing, II
Stevenson, Adlai Ewing,
   III
Stevenson, Coke Robert
Stokes, Carl B(urton)
Stokes, Louis
Stone, Dick

Stoneman, George
Strafford, 1st Earl of
Stratton, Samuel
   S(tuddiford)
Strauss, Franz Josef
Streicher, Julius
Strong, James Matthew
Stronge, Norman, Sir
Studds, Gerry E(astman)
Suarez, Xavier Louis
Suazo Cordova, Roberto
Suchocka, Hanna
Sullivan, John
Sullivan, Mike
Sumner, Charles
Sumner, Jessie
Sundlun, Bruce George
Sununu, John Henry
Suslov, Mikhail
   Andreevich
Suzman, Helen
Swigert, Jack
Sydenham, Baron
Symington, J Fife, III
Symington, Stuart
Symms, Steven Douglas
Taft, Robert A(lphonso)
Taft, Robert A(lphonso),
   Jr.
Takahashi, Korekiyo
Talmadge, Eugene
Talmadge, Herman Eugene
Tawley, Howard
Taylor, John
Teague, Olin E
Thayer, Eli
Thomas, Craig
Thomas, Elmer
Thompson, Frank, Jr.
Thompson, Fred
Thompson, James Robert
Thompson, John
   S(parrow) D(avid), Sir
Thompson, Tommy
   George
Thomson, Vernon Wallace
Thorez, Maurice
Thorn, Gaston
Thornburgh, Dick
Thorneycroft, (George
   Edward) Peter
Thuku, Harry
Thurmond, Strom
Tilden, Samuel Jones
Tilley, Samuel Leonard,
   Sir
Tillman, Benjamin Ryan
Timmerman, George Bell,
   Jr.
Tisza, Kalman
Titulescu, Nicolae
Toledano, Vicente
   Lombardo
Torricelli, Robert G.
Tower, John Goodwin
Towns, Edolphus
Traikov, Georgi
Treurnicht, Andries Petrus
Trible, Paul Seward, Jr.
Trimble, (William) David
Trujillo (Molina), Rafael
   Leonidas
Trumbull, Jonathan
Trumbull, Lyman
Tryon, William
Ts'ao Ts'ao

Tsedenbal, Yumzahgin
Tsongas, Paul E(fthemios)
Tunney, John Varick
Tweed, Boss
Tydings, Millard Evelyn
Udall, Morris K(ing)
Uhlman, Wes(ley Carl)
Ullman, Al(bert Conrad)
Unruh, Jesse Marvin
Upshaw, William David
Vallandigham, Clement
   Laird
Vance, Zebulon Baird
Van Cortlandt, Oloff
   Stevenszen
Van Cortlandt, Stephanus
Vandenberg, Arthur
   Hendrick
Vanderbilt, William Henry
Vane, Henry
Van Eekelen, Willem
   Frederik
Vanik, Charles Albert
Van Rensselaer, Stephen
Vaudreuil-Cavagnal,
   Marquis de
Velazquez, Nydia
   Margarita
Vinson, Carl
Vogel, Hans-Jochen
Voinovich, George
   V(ictor)
Volstead, Andrew J
Voroshilov, Kliment
   Efremovich
Vorster, Balthazar
   Johannes
Wade, Benjamin Franklin
Wagner, Robert
   F(erdinand)
Wagner, Robert Ferdinand,
   Jr.
Waihee, John David, III
Walker, Daniel
Walker, Jimmy
Wallace, George C(orley)
Wallace, Lurleen Burns
Wallace-Johnson, Isaac
   Theophilus Akunna
Wallop, Malcolm
Walsh, Thomas James
Walters, David
Walworth, William, Sir
Warner, John William
Washington, Harold
Washington, Val J.
Washington, Walter
   Edward
Waters, Maxine
Watkins, Arthur V(ivian)
Watson, Thomas Edward
Watts, J(ulius) C(aesar),
   (Jr.)
Waxman, Henry Arnold
Weaver, James Baird
Webb, Wellington
Weed, Thurlow
Weicker, Lowell Palmer,
   Jr.
Weiss, Ted
Weizman, Ezer
Weld, William F(loyd)
Welles, Gideon
Wellstone, Paul David
Welsh, Matthew E(mpson)

Wentworth, William
   Charles
Werner, Pierre
Westwood, Jean Miles
Wheat, Alan (Dupree)
Wheeler, Burton Kendall
White, Kevin Hagan
White, Mark Wells, Jr.
White, Michael R(eed)
Whitington, Dick
Whitman, Christine Todd
Whitmire, Kathy
Whittington, Dick
Wigg, George (Edward
   Cecil)
Wiggins, Charles Edward
Wilder, Douglas
Wilkinson, Ellen
Williams, Eric Eustace
Williams, G(erhard)
   Mennen
Williams, George
   Washington
Williams, Harrison
   Arlington, Jr.
Williams, John James
Williams, Shirley
Willkie, Wendell Lewis
Wilmot, David
Wilson, Malcolm
Wilson, Michael
   (Holcombe)
Wilson, Pete Barton
Winter, William Forrest
Winthrop, John
Wirth, Timothy E
Wood, Fernando
Woodbury, Levi
Woodsworth, James
   Shaver
Wright, Jim
Wyatt, Wilson W(atkins)
Wyden, Ron
Xuan Thuy
Xu Guangqi
Yancey, William Lowndes
Yarborough, Ralph
   W(ebster)
Yates, Sidney R(ichard)
Yorty, Sam(uel William)
Young, Andrew Jackson,
   Jr.
Young, Coleman
   A(lexander)
Youngdahl, Luther
   Wallace
Zablocki, Clement John
Zamora, Ruben
Zhirinovsky, Vladimir
Zhivkov, Todor Khristov
Zhukov, Georgi
   Alexandrovich
Zorinsky, Edward

POLLSTER

Caddell, Pat(rick
   Hayward)
Crossley, Archibald
   Maddock
Gallup, George Horace
Greenberg, Stanley B
Harris, Louis
Lubell, Samuel
Robinson, Claude Everett

POLO PLAYER

Hitchcock, Tommy

PRESERVATIONIST

Fitch, James Marston
Placzek, Adolf K(urt)

PRESIDENTIAL AIDE

Baker, James Addison, III
Brady, James Scott
Buchanan, Patrick Joseph
Bundy, McGeorge
Cole, Kenneth Reese
Colson, Chuck
Costanza, Midge
Deaver, Michael Keith
Ehrlichman, John D(aniel)
Fitzwater, Marlin
Harlow, Bryce Nathaniel
Hopkins, Harry Lloyd
Hunt, E(verette) Howard
Jordan, Hamilton
Larue, Frederick Chaney
McLaughlin, John
  (Joseph)
Meese, Edwin, III
Nessen, Ron(ald Harold)
Nofziger, Lyn
North, Oliver Laurence, Jr.
Poindexter, John Marlan
Powell, Jody
Rafshoon, Gerald Monroe
Rowan, Carl Thomas
Scowcroft, Brent
Sloan, Hugh W
Strauss, Robert Schwarz
Sununu, John Henry
Vandenberg, Arthur
  Hendrick, Jr.
Warren, Gerald Lee

PRIEST

Gonzalo de Berceo
Guarini, Guarino

PRIME MINISTER

Maurer, Ion Gheorghe

PRINCE

Albert, Prince
Andrew
Andrew, Prince of Russia
Bohemund, I
Chang Po-go
Charles, Prince of Wales
Charles Edward Louis
  Philip Casimir Stuart
Cuong De
Dracula
Edward
Edward the Black Prince

Faisal ibn Musaed
Frederick Louis
George Edward Alexander
  Edmund
Hardenberg, Karl August
  von
Henry of Wales
Henry the Navigator
Henry William Frederick
  Albert
John of Gaunt
Juan Carlos, Count of
  Barcelona
Llewelyn ap Gruffydd
Maurice of Nassau
Orleans, Charles d'
Rudolf of Hapsburg
Shotoku Taishi
Souvanna, Phouma
Vladimir, I
William of Wales

PRINCESS

Alice
Anne
Beatrice, Princess of York
Caroline, Princess
Christina
Comnena, Anna
Diana, Princess of Wales
Eugenie, Princess of York
Irene
Jezebel
Kelly, Grace Patricia
Margaret
Pocahontas
Romanov, Anastasia
Stephanie, Princess
Victoria Ingrid Alice
  Desiree

PRINTER

Baskerville, John
Beadle, Erastus Flavel
Bradshaw, George
Caxton, William
Cobden-Sanderson,
  Thomas James
Daye, Stephen
DeVinne, Theodore Low
Estienne, Henri
Froben, Johann
Fust, Johann
Gutenberg, Johann
  Gensfleischzur Laden
  Zum
Hunter, Dard
Manutius, Aldus
Plantin, Christophe
Raikes, Robert
Richard, Gabriel
Rollins, Carl Purington
Sholes, Christopher
  Latham
Updike, Daniel Berkeley
Walker, Emery, Sir
Zenger, John Peter

PRINTMAKER

Baldung(-Grien), Hans
Catlett, Elizabeth
Stovall, Luther McKinley

PRISON WARDEN

Duffy, Clinton Truman

PRODUCER

Abrahams, Doris Cole
Ackerman, Harry S
Adams, Tony
Adler, Buddy
Ailes, Roger Eugene
Akimov, Nikolay
  Pavlovich
Aldrich, Richard Stoddard
Aldrich, Robert
Allen, Irwin
Almond, Paul
Altman, Robert B
Ames, Winthrop
Anderson, Gerry
Antoine, Andre
Arkoff, Samuel Z
Arnaz, Desi
Arnold, Danny
Arthur, Robert
Asher, Peter
Attenborough, Richard
  Samuel, Sir
Austin, Dallas
Averback, Hy
Azenberg, Emanuel
Badalamenti, Angelo
Baer, Max, Jr.
Balcon, Michael Elias, Sir
Banner, Bob
Barris, Chuck
Barry, Jack
Bass, Saul
Bayer, Wolfgang
Beatty, Warren
Behn, Noel
Belasco, David
Bellisario, Donald P
Bennett, Harve
Bergman, Ingmar (Ernst)
Berman, Pandro Samuel
Bernhard, Harvey
Biberman, Herbert
Bill, Tony
Blinn, Holbrook
Bloch, Ivan Sol
Bloodworth-Thomason,
  Linda Joyce
Bloomgarden, Kermit
Bochco, Steven Ronald
Bogart, Neil
Bogdanovich, Peter
Bogner, Willi
Bosustow, Stephen
Boulting, Roy
Brackett, Charles
Brady, William Aloysius
Brakhage, Stan
Brasselle, Keefe
Bresler, Jerry
Brisson, Frederick
Brook, Peter Stephen Paul

Brooks, James L.
Brooks, Mel
Brosten, Harve
Brown, David
Bruhn, Erik Belton Evers
Bufman, Zev
Bullins, Ed
Burrows, James
Byrd, Robert
Cannell, Stephen Joseph
Capra, Frank
Carlisle, Kevin
Carr, Allan
Carr, Martin
Carroll, Earl
Carroll, Vinnette
Carsey, Marcy
Castle, William
Cates, Gilbert
Cates, Joseph
Chaplin, Saul
Charles, Glen
Charles, Lee
Charnin, Martin
Chartoff, Robert
Chase, David
Chodorov, Edward
Clark, Dick
Clinton, George
Codron, Michael
Coe, Frederick H
Cohan, George M(ichael)
Cohen, Alexander H
Collins, Bootsy
Combs, Sean
Cooney, Joan Ganz
Corman, Gene
Corman, Roger William
Corwin, Norman
Costello, Robert E
Cousteau, Philippe
Crawford, Cheryl
Crozier, Eric John
DaCosta, Morton
Daley, Robert H
Dalrymple, Jean
Daly, John
DaSilva, Howard
Davis, Peter Frank
DeCordova, Frederick
  Timmins
DeLaurentiis, Dino
DeLaurentiis, Federico
DeLiagre, Alfred
DeMille, Cecil B(lount)
Denoff, Sam
De Passe, Suzanne
De Patie, David H
DeRochemont, Louis
DeSylva, Buddy
Dillingham, Charles
  Bancroft
Disney, Walt(er Elias)
Dixon, Willie (James)
Doherty, Brian
Douglas, Michael Kirk
Dowling, Eddie
Dozier, William
DuMaurier, Gerald Hubert,
  Sir
Duncan, Augustin
Dunne, Griffin
Ebert, Carl
Eckart, William Joseph
Edmunds, Dave
Edwards, Blake

Edwards, Ralph
  Livingstone
Einstein, Bob
Elkins, Hillard
English, Diane
Eno, Brian
Evans, Bob
Fairbanks, Douglas, Jr.
Feld, Irvin
Felsenstein, Walter
Feuer, Cy
Fichandler, Zelda
  Diamond
Fields, Freddie
Fine, Sylvia
Fontana, Tom
Fox, Carol
Frankovich, Mike J
Frederickson, H Gray
Freed, Arthur
Freeman, Seth
Freleng, Friz
Friedman, Stephen
Friendly, Ed
Friendly, Fred W.
Fries, Charles W
Frohman, Charles
Fryer, Robert
Fuisz, Robert E
Funt, Allen
Garrett, Lila
Geffen, David
Gelbart, Larry
Geller, Bruce
Gest, Morris
Gielgud, (Arthur) John, Sir
Gilbert, Bruce
Goldberg, Gary David
Goldberg, Leonard
Golden, John
Goldie, Grace Wyndham
Goldwyn, Samuel
Golenpaul, Dan
Goodson, Mark
Gordon, Max
Gordy, Emory, Jr.
Gottlieb, Morton Edgar
Graham, Bill
Granz, Norman
Greenspan, Bud
Guber, Peter
Hackford, Taylor
Haley, Jack, Jr.
Halliday, Richard
Hamilton, Joe
Harper, Ken
Harris, Jed
Harris, Sam Henry
Hartmann, Rudolph
Hawks, Howard
  Winchester
Hayward, Leland
Hazam, Lou(is J)
Hecht, Harold
Helburn, Theresa
Hemion, Dwight
Holmes, Burton
Holt, Fritz
Hopkins, Arthur
Houseman, John
Hunter, Ross
Hutt, William Ian Dewitt
Ince, Thomas H(arper)
Irving, Jules
Ivory, James
Jaffe, Herb

James, Art
Janney, Russell Dixon
Johnson, Nunnally
Jones, Booker T
Jones, Quincy Delight
Kanin, Fay
Kanter, Hal
Keillor, Garrison
Keitel, Harvey
Kemp, Barry
Kohan, Buz
Kollmar, Richard
Kooper, Al
Korda, Alexander, Sir
Kramer, Stanley E
Krofft, Marty
Krofft, Sid
KRS-One
Landau, Ely A
Lane, Stewart F
Langer, Lawrence
Lanois, Daniel
Lawrence, Bill
Lawrence, Jack
Lear, Norman Milton
Leavitt, Ron
Leonard, Sheldon
Leonidoff, Leon
Leroy, Mervyn
Lesser, Sol
Levine, Joseph Edward
Lewis, David
Lewton, Val Ivan
Liebman, Max
Lindsay, Howard
Liveright, Horace Brisbin
Lloyd Webber, Andrew
Loew, Marcus
Lord, Jack
Lord, Phillips H
Lortel, Lucille
Lowe, Nick
Lucas, Phil
Ludden, Allen Ellsworth
Ludlam, Charles
Ludlum, Robert
Lupino, Stanley
Mackintosh, Cameron
Majors, Lee
Mankiewicz, Joseph (Leo)
Mankowitz, Wolf
Mann, Michael
Mann, Theodore
Manulis, Martin
Mariens, Neal
Marley, Rita
Marsh, Ngaio, Dame
Marshall, Alan Peter
Marshall, Garry Kent
Martin, George
Martin, Quinn
Massey, Raymond Hart
Mayer, L(ouis) B(urt)
McCann, Elizabeth Ireland
McCarthy, Frank
McClintic, Guthrie
Melford, Austin
Melies, Georges
Melnick, Daniel
Merchant, Ismail
Merrick, David
Michaels, Lorne
Miller, Gilbert Heron
Miller, Thomas
Miner, Worthington C
Minsky, Abraham Bennett

Minsky, Harold
Minsky, Morton
Mirisch, Walter Mortimer
Monash, Paul
Monty, Gloria
Moussa, Ibrahim
Moye, Michael
Neagle, Anna, Dame
Nederlander, James
  Morton
Nemirovich-Danchenko,
  Vladimir I
Newman, Paul
Nimoy, Leonard
Nugent, Elliott
Nugent, Nelle
O'Connor, Carroll
O'Connor, Kevin
Olivier, Laurence Kerr, Sir
Pagnol, Marcel Paul
Pal, George
Paltrow, Bruce
Papp, Joseph
Parks, Van Dyke
Pascal, Gabriel
Pasternak, Joe
Patrick, Gail
Pemberton, Brock
Peters, Jon
Ponti, Carlo
Powell, Michael Latham
Power, Jules
Preminger, Otto Ludwig
Price, Nancy
Prince, Hal
Puttnam, David Terence
Raedler, Dorothy
  (Florence)
Ransohoff, Martin
Reinhardt, Max
Reitman, Ivan
Renaldo, Duncan
Rich, John
Richardson, Tony
Rigby, Harry
Roach, Hal
Roddenberry, Gene
Rogell, Albert S
Rooney, Andy
Rose, Billy
Ross, David
Rossen, Robert
Rubin, Rick
Ruddy, Al(bert Stotland)
Rush, Richard
Saint-Subber, Arnold
Schary, Dore
Schenck, Joseph M
Schikaneder, Emanuel
Schmiechen, Richard Kurt
Schneider, Bert
Schulberg, Stuart
Schwartz, Maurice
Schwary, Ronald L
Scott, Adrian
Seidelman, Susan
Selznick, David O(liver)
Selznick, Irene Mayer
Sennett, Mack
Serling, Rod
Shapiro, Arnold
Shapiro, Stanley
Sherman, Harry R
Shubert, Jacob J
Shubert, Lee
Shumlin, Herman Elliott

Sidaris, Andy
Sidney, George
Silliphant, Stirling Dale
Sillman, Leonard
Sim, Alastair
Simpson, Donald C
Siodmark, Curt
Skouras, Spyros
  Panagiotes
Smith, Oliver
Smith, Pete
Spector, Phil(lip Harvey)
Spelling, Aaron
Spiegel, Sam
Spielberg, Steven
Spivak, Lawrence
  E(dmund)
Steel, Dawn
Stern, Leonard B
Stevens, George, Jr.
Stevens, Roger L(acey)
Stewart, Ellen
Stigwood, Robert Colin
Stone, Ezra (Chaim)
Stone, Paula
Stromberg, Hunt
Susskind, David Howard
Tahse, Martin
Tairov, Aleksandr
  Yakovlevich
Tanen, Ned Stone
Taylor, Charles Alonzo
Terry, Paul H
Thalberg, Irving Grant
Thomas, Danny
Thomas, Gerald
Thomas, Lowell Jackson,
  Jr.
Tietjen, Heinz
Tinker, Grant Almerin
Todd, Mike
Todman, Bill
Tors, Ivan
Traube, Shepard
Travers, Bill
Trendle, George
  Washington
Tricky
Tripp, Paul
Van Dyke, W(oodbridge)
  S(trong)
Vig, Butch
Wagner, Wieland Adolf
  Gottfried
Wagner, Wolfgang
Waissman, Kenneth
Wald, Jerry
Walker, Stuart Armstrong
Wallis, Hal Brent
Wallmann, Margherita
Walz, Ken
Wanger, Walter
Wein, George Theodore
Weintraub, Jerry
Weiskopf, Bob
Welles, Orson
Werner, Tom
White, George
White, Michael Simon
Whitehead, Robert
Whitney, C(ornelius)
  V(anderbilt)
Wilcox, Herbert
Wilcoxon, Henry
Wilde, Cornel
Wilder, Billy (Samuel)

Wilder, Clinton
Willners, Hal
Wilson, Richard
Wilson, Robert M
Winkler, Irwin
Wise, Robert
Witt, Paul Junger
Witte, Erich
Wolfe, George C.
Wolper, David Lloyd
Wyler, William
Yablans, Frank
Zaentz, Saul
Zanuck, Darryl Francis
Zanuck, Lili Fini
Zanuck, Richard Darryl
Ziegfeld, Flo(renz)
Zukor, Adolph

PROPHET

Amos
Ezekiel
Hosea
Isaiah
Jeremiah
Micah
Montanus
Zoroaster

PROSPECTOR

Hearst, George

PSYCHIATRIST

Abramson, Harold
    A(lexander)
Alexander, Leo
Berger, Hans
Berne, Eric Lennard
Binswanger, Ludwig
Bleuler, Eugen
Blumenthal, Monica David
Braceland, Francis J(ames)
Brill, Abraham Arden
Bullard, Dexter Means
Butler, Robert N(eil)
Cobbs, Price M(ashaw)
Coles, Robert
Comer, James P(ierpont)
Cooper, David (Graham)
Densen-Gerber, Judianne
Dunbar, Helen Flanders
Fielding, Lewis J
Frank, Jerome David
Frankl, Viktor E(mil)
Henry, George William
Jung, Carl Gustav
Klein, Melanie
Kline, Nathan
    Schellenberg
Krafft-Ebing, Richard von
Kubler-Ross, Elisabeth
Laing, R(onald) D(avid)
Larson, John Augustus
Levy, David Mordecai
Lidz, Theodore
Masserman, Jules
    H(oman)
Menninger, Karl Augustus
Peck, M Scott

Perls, Frederick Salomon
Poussaint, Alvin F.
Radecki, Thomas
Reuben, David Robert
Robitscher, Jonas Bondi,
    Jr.
Rorschach, Hermann
Rubin, Theodore Isaac
Storr, (Charles) Anthony
Sullivan, Harry Stack
Szasz, Thomas Stephen
Welsing, Frances Cress
Westheimer, Ruth
White, William Alanson
Wilder, Joseph

PSYCHIC

Altea, Rosemary
Barbanell, Maurice
Brown, Rosemary
Cayce, Edgar
Garrett, Eileen Jeanette
    Lyttle
Geller, Uri
Home, Daniel Douglas
Hurkos, Peter
Knight, J. Z.
Kreskin
Logan, Daniel
Stokes, Doris

PSYCHOANALYST

Adler, Alfred
Arieti, Silvano
Deutsch, Helene
    R(osenbach)
Erikson, Erik H(omburger)
Fanon, Frantz (Omar)
Frailberg, Selma
Freud, Anna
Freud, Sigmund
Fromm, Erich
Gay, John
Horney, Karen Danielson
Kardiner, Abram
Kohut, Heinz
Lacan, Jacques (Marie
    Emile)
Langer, Walter C
Loulan, JoAnn
May, Rollo (Reece)
Mitscherlich, Alexander
Reich, Wilhelm
Reik, Theodor

PSYCHOLOGIST

Abramson, Lyn
Allport, Gordon William
Ames, Louise (Bates)
Baldwin, James Mark
Bartlett, F(rederic)
    C(harles)
Bateson, Gregory
Bell, Arthur Donald
Bender, Hans
Bettelheim, Bruno
Binet, Alfred
Borysenko, Joan
Britt, Steuart Henderson

Brothers, Joyce Diane
    Bauer
Bruner, Jerome Seymour
Burt, Cyril Lodowic, Sir
Cattell, James McKeen
Clark, Kenneth Bancroft
Cooley, Charles Horton
Coue, Emile
Crawford, John Edmund
Dichter, Ernest
Dollard, John
Ebbinghaus, Hermann
Ellis, Albert (Isaac)
Ellis, Havelock
Feifel, Herman
Fulani, Lenora
Gilligan, Carol
Ginott, Haim
Gordon, Thomas
Guthrie, Edwin Ray
Hall, G(ranville) Stanley
Hathaway, Starke R
Herbart, Johann Friedrich
Heyns, Roger W(illiam)
Hovland, Carl I.
Hull, Clark Leonard
James, William
Janet, Pierre Marie Felix
Janov, Arthur
Jensen, Arthur Robert
Johnson, Virginia E
Jones, Ernest Alfred
Judd, Charles Hubbard
Jung, Carl Gustav
Kanner, Leo
Kassorla, Irene Chamie
Keniston, Kenneth
Koffka, Kurt
Kohler, Wolfgang
Kronhausen, Eberhard
    Wilhelm
Kronhausen, Phyllis
    Carmen
Ladd, George Trumbull
Ladd-Franklin, Christine
Lashley, Karl Spencer
Leach, Penelope
Lewin, Kurt
Marston, William Moulton
Maslow, Abraham Harold
McDougall, William
Mead, George Herbert
Monroe, Marion
Morgan, C(onwy) Lloyd
Myers, Garry Cleveland
Piaget, Jean
Pipher, Mary
Rhine, J(oseph) B(anks)
Rogers, Carl Ransom
Salk, Lee
Salter, Andrew
Sears, Robert Richardson
Sheehan, Joseph Green
Sheldon, William Herbert
Simon, Herbert Alexander
Skinner, B(urrhus)
    F(rederic)
Starch, Daniel
Steele, Claude Mason
Stevens, S(tanley) S(mith)
Terman, Lewis Madison
Thorndike, Edward L(ee)
Thurstone, Louis Leon
Titchener, Edward
    Bradford
Tolman, Edward Chace

Wallerstein, Jusith S.
Watson, John Broadus
Wechsler, David
Wertheimer, Max
Wexler, Nancy Sabin
Wundt, Wilhelm Max
Yerkes, Robert Mearns
Zigler, Edward

PSYCHOTHERAPIST

Rank, Otto
Starhawk

PUBLIC OFFICIAL

Donovan, William Joseph
Lasker, Albert D(avis)
Loeb, William
Longstreet, James
Mackinder, Halford John,
    Sir
McGee, Thomas D'Arcy
Moffett, Ken(neth
    Elwood)

PUBLIC RELATIONS EXECUTIVE

Baldridge, Letitia
    Katherine
Bernays, Edward L.
Birdwell, Russell Juarez
Garth, David
Graham, Stedman
Hannagan, Steve
Kingsley, Pat(ricia)

PUBLICIST

Gokalp, Mehmet Ziya
Hargraves, Edward
    Hammond
Kelley, Hall Jackson
Wallace, Henry

PUBLISHER

Abrams, Harry Nathan
Adler, Elmer
Aitken, Max
Almon, John
Ames, Nathaniel
Annenberg, Walter Hubert
Appleton, Daniel
Appleton, William Henry
Armstrong, Charles B
Astor, Gavin
Attwood, William
    Hollingsworth
Baedeker, Karl
Ballantine, Ian (Keith)
Barron, Clarence Walker
Bartlett, John
Beach, Sylvia
Beadle, Erastus Flavel

Beaverbrook, William
Maxwell Aitken, Baron
Beilenson, Edna Rudolph
Benjamin, Curtis G
Benn, Ernest John
Pickstone, Sir
Bennett, James Gordon, Jr.
Benton, William
Bereano, Nancy K(irp)
Bernhard, Arnold
Bernstein, Robert L(ouis)
Berry, James Gomer
Beuve-Mery, Hubert
Black, Walter J
Blackwell, Basil Henry,
Sir
Blackwell, (Samuel) Earl,
Jr.
Bleiberg, Robert Marvin
Bobbs, William Conrad
Boehm, Eric Hartzell
Boettiger, John
Boni, Albert
Bowker, R(ichard)
R(ogers)
Bracken, Brendan Rendall,
Viscount
Bradley, Milton
Brady, James Winston
Brand, Stewart
Brannan, Samuel
Brett, George Platt, Jr.
Brown, James
Burden, Carter
Bush, Melinda
Buttenheim, Edgar Joseph
Cahners, Norman Lee
Canfield, Cass
Cape, Herbert Jonathan
Capper, Arthur
Carey, Mathew
Cerf, Bennett Alfred
Chambers, Robert
Charney, Nicolas Herman
Childs, George William
Conrad, Con
Covici, Pascal
Cowles, Gardner, Jr.
Cowles, John, Sr.
Cowles, William
Hutchinson, Jr.
Cox, James Middleton, Jr.
Croft, Arthur C
Crosby, Harry
Crowninshield, Francis
Welch
Day, Benjamin Henry
Day, James Wentworth
Debrett, John
DeGraff, Robert F(air)
Delacorte, George
Thomas, Jr.
Dodsley, Robert
Doubleday, Frank Nelson
Doubleday, Nelson
Dow, Charles Henry
Dutton, E(dward) P(ayson)
Economaki, Chris(topher
Constantine)
Elzevir, Louis
Engel, Lyle Kenyon
England, John
Enoch, Kurt
Ethridge, Mark Foster
Evans, Joni
Faber, Geoffrey Cust, Sir

Fairchild, John Burr
Farrar, John Chipman
Field, Marshall, III
Field, Marshall, IV
Fields, James Thomas
Fischer, Carl
Fleischer, Nat(haniel
Stanley)
Fleischmann, Peter
F(rancis)
Fleischmann, Raoul
H(erbert)
Flores Facusse, Carlos
Roberto
Flynt, Althea Sue
Flynt, Larry (Claxton)
Fodor, Eugene
Forbes, Malcolm
Stevenson
Funk, Isaac Kauffman
Funk, Wilfred John
Gaines, William
M(axwell)
Garrett, Eileen Jeanette
Lyttle
Gernsback, Hugo
Giago, Tim
Gillenson, Lewis W
Ginzburg, Ralph
Giroux, Robert
Godey, Louis Antoine
Golden, Harry Lewis
Golenpaul, Dan
Gollancz, Victor, Sir
Goodman, Martin
Goodrich, Samuel
Griswold
Graves, Earl Gilbert
Greeley, Horace
Grier, Barbara
Grosvenor, Melville Bell
Guccione, Bob
Guccione, Bob, Jr.
Guggenheim, Harry Frank
Guptill, Arthur Leighton
Hadden, Briton
Haldeman-Julius, Emanuel
Harper, Fletcher
Harper, James
Harper, John
Harper, Joseph Wesley
Hart-Davis, Rupert
Harvey, George Brinton M
Hearst, David W(hitmire)
Hearst, George
Hearst, William Randolph,
Jr.
Hecht, George Joseph
Hefner, Hugh Marston
Hefti, Neal Paul
Heinemann, William
Heiskell, Andrew
Henson, Lisa
Hillegrass, C(lifton)
K(eith)
Hills, Argentina (Schifano)
Hines, Duncan
Hitchcock, Gilbert Monell
Hobby, Oveta Culp
Hoffman, Rob
Holt, Henry
Houghton, Henry Oscar
Howe, Florence Rosenfeld
Hoyt, Lawrence W
Hubbard, Elbert Green

Ingersoll, Ralph
McAllister
Ingersoll, Ralph
McAllister, II
Johnson, Eleanor M
Johnson, John Harold
Kalikow, Peter Stephen
Keeton, Kathy
Kelly, Stephen Eugene
Keylor, Arthur W
Keyserlingk, Robert
Wendelin Henry
Kiplinger, Austin
Huntington
Kiplinger, Knight A
Kiplinger, W(illard)
M(onroe)
Kirstein, George G
Klopfer, Donald Simon
Knight, Charles
Knopf, Alfred Abraham
Knopf, Blanche Wolf
Korda, Michael
Kristol, William
Kunjufu, Jawanza
Lane, Allen, Sir
Larsen, Roy Edward
Laughlin, James, IV
Lawson, Victor Fremont
Leslie, Frank
Leslie, Miriam Florence
Folline
Leventhal, Albert Rice
Linen, James A(lexander),
III
Lippincott, Joshua
Ballinger
Liss, Alan R
Litolff, Henri Charles
Little, Charles Coffin
Liveright, Horace Brisbin
Loeb, William
Logan, Harlan (De Braun)
Luce, Henry Robinson
Lundy, Benjamin
Macfadden, Bernarr
Adolphus
MacMillan, Alexander
MacMillan, Daniel
Macy, George
Manley, Joan Adele
Daniels
Marquis, Albert Nelson
Maxwell, Robert Ian
Charles
McGraw, Donald Cushing
McGraw, Harold
Whittlesey, Jr.
McNally, Andrew, III
McNaughton, F(oye)
F(isk)
McWhirter, A(lan) Ross
McWhirter, Norris Dewar
Melcher, Frederic Gershon
Merriam, Charles
Mifflin, George Harrison
Miles, Tichi Wilkerson
Moser, Barry
Motley, Arthur Harrison
Muir, Malcolm
Munsey, Frank Andrew
Murdoch, Rupert
Murphy, Arthur Richard,
Jr.
Nast, Conde
Neuharth, Allen Harold

Newbery, John
O'Neil, James F(rancis)
Patterson, Alicia
Patterson, Eleanor Medill
Patterson, Joseph Medill
Pearson, Cyril Arthur, Sir
Pickering, William
Plantin, Christophe
Polk, Ralph Lane
Pope, Generoso
Praeger, Frederick A(mos)
Presser, Theodore
Price, Roger Taylor
Pulitzer, Joseph
Pulitzer, Peter
Pulitzer, Ralph
Qoboza, Percy
Quaritch, Bernard
Ricordi, Giovanni
Rinehart, Frederick
Roberts
Rinehart, Stanley
Marshall, Jr.
Rivera, Luis Munoz
Robinson, M(aurice)
R(ichard)
Rodale, Jerome Irving
Rusher, William Allen
Scherman, Harry
Scherr, Max
Schiff, Dorothy
Schirmer, Gustave
Schocken, Theodore
Schuster, Max Lincoln
Scribner, Charles
Scribner, Charles, Jr.
Seajay, Carol
Sheed, Frank
Shimkin, Leon
Shirley, Ralph
Silverman, Sime
Simon, Richard Leo
Snyder, Richard Elliot
Sonzogno, Edoardo
Springer, Axel Caesar
Stone, Louis
Straus, Roger W(illiams),
Jr.
Stuart, Lyle
Sweet, John Howard
Taishoff, Sol Joseph
Targ, William
Thomas, Isaiah
Thomas, Robert B
Tokutomi Soho
Ullstein, Hermann
Unwin, Stanley, Sir
Updike, Daniel Berkeley
Van Nostrand, David
Van Westerborg, Edward
Veronis, John James
Viguerie, Richard A(rt)
VonTilzer, Harry
Wagnalls, Adam Willis
Wallace, DeWitt
Wallace, Lila Bell
Acheson
Washington, Laura S.
Wenner, Jann
White, William Lindsay
Whitney, John Hay
Whittle, Christopher
Wiley, W(illiam) Bradford
Witmark, Isidore
Wolff, Helen
Woolf, Leonard Sidney

PUBLISHER (continued)

Zenger, John Peter
Zevin, B(enjamin) D(avid)
Ziff, William Bernard
Zuckerman, Mortimer
  Benjamin

PUBLISHERS

Hudson, Wade and Cheryl

PUBLISHING EXECUTIVE

Black, Cathleen Prunty
Bolte, Charles G(uy)
Brownlow, William
  Gannaway
Driver, David E.
Ducksworth, Marilyn
  (Jacoby)
Epstein, Jason
Forbes, Malcolm
  Stevenson, Jr.
Hamilton, Hamish
Hefner, Christie
Hillegass, Clifton Keith
James, Juanita (T.)
Jones, Jenkin Lloyd
Jovanovich, William Iliya
McDonald, Erroll
Mirabella, Grace
Newhouse, S(amuel)
  I(rving), Jr.
Rice, Linda Johnson
Schuman, Patricia Glass
Thompson, Paul
  W(illiams)
Ziff, William B(ernard),
  Jr.
Zondervan, Peter

PUPPETEER

Baird, Bil
Baird, Cora Eisenberg
Dupuy, Diane
Henson, Brian
Henson, Jim
Kevin, Clash
Krofft, Marty
Krofft, Sid
Oz, Frank
Raposo, Joseph
Sarg, Tony
Teschner, Richard
Tillstrom, Burr

PUZZLE MAKER

Farrar, Margaret
  (Petherbridge)
Maleska, Eugene T.
Shortz, Will(iam Frederic)
Weng, Will

QUEEN

Boudicca

Hatshepsut
Margaret of Denmark
Mary, II
Min
Zenobia

QUINTUPLET

Dionne, Emilie
Dionne, Marie

QUINTUPLETS

Dionne Sisters
L'Esperance Quintuplets

RADIO EXECUTIVE

Cott, Ted
Hay, George Dewey
Kintner, Robert Edmonds
Lewis, Delano (Eugene)
Paley, William Samuel

RADIO PERFORMER

Ace, Goodman
Ameche, Don
Ameche, Jim
Anthony, John J(ason)
Barrett, John L
Baruch, Andre
Berle, Milton
Big Bopper, The
Block, Martin
Brokenshire, Norman
Carter, Boake
Close, Upton
Coughlin, Charles Edward,
  Father
Cross, Milton John
Davis, Elmer Holmes
Donnellan, Nanci
Eliot, George Fielding
Elliot, Win
Fadiman, Clifton (Paul)
Faulk, John Henry
Fennelly, Parker W
Fidler, Jimmie
Fitzgerald, Ed(ward)
Fitzgerald, Pegeen
Freed, Alan
Gambling, John Bradley
Gray, Barry
Hamblin, Ken
Hay, George Dewey
Heatter, Gabriel
Imus, Don
Jordan, Jim
Jordan, Marian Driscoll
Joyner, Tom
Kaufman, Murray
King, Larry
Lauck, Chester H
Limbaugh, Rush Hudson,
  III
Lomax, Louis
Madison, Joseph E(dward)
Magliozzi, Ray

Magliozzi, Tom
McBride, Mary Margaret
McCarthy, J(oseph)
  P(riestley)
McNeill, Don(ald Thomas)
Nebel, Long John
Nichols, Red
Pearl, Jack
Plomley, Roy
Quivers, Robin
Reber, Grote
Schlessinger, Laura
Simms, Ginny
Sinclair, Gordon
Stern, Howard (Allan)
Thomas, Lowell Jackson
Tinney, Cal(vin Lawrence)
Wilson, Don(ald Harlow)
Wolfman Jack
Young, Marian

RADIO PERFORMERS

Tex and Jinx

RADIO PERSONALITY

Smith, Robert Weston

RAILROAD EXECUTIVE

Alpert, George
Budd, Ralph
Claytor, W(illiam)
  Graham, Jr.
Crocker, Charles
Durant, Thomas Clark
Hill, James Jerome
Huntington, Collis Potter
Huntington, Henry
  Edwards
Keith, Minor Cooper
Mahone, William
Newberry, John Stoughton
Reed, John Shedd
Scott, Thomas Alexander
Stanford, Leland
Vanderbilt, William Henry
Van Horne, William
  Cornelius, Sir
Webb, William Seward
Willard, Daniel

RANCHER

Abdnor, James S
Adams, Andy
Applegate, Jesse
Chisum, John Simpson
Goodnight, Charles
Kidman, Sidney
King, Richard
Kleberg, Robert Justus, Jr.
Maverick, Samuel
  Augustus
Todd, Garfield

RAP GROUP

Arrested Development
Beastie Boys, The
De La Soul
Digital Underground
DJ Jazzy Jeff and the
  Fresh Prince
Eric B and Rakim
Kid 'n Play
Kriss Kross
N.W.A.
Public Enemy
Run-DMC
Salt n Pepa
Tribe Called Quest, A

RAPPER

Busta Rhymes
Chuck D
Coolio
Dr. Dre
Eazy-E
Gerardo
Hammer
Heavy D
Horovitz, Adam
Ice Cube
Ice-T
Kane, Big Daddy
Kool Moe Dee
KRS-One
Latifah, Queen
LL Cool J
Lover, Ed
MC Lyte
Pepa
Salt
Shakur, Tupac
Shante
Sister Souljah
Smith, Will
Snoop Doggy Dogg
Tone-Loc
Vanilla Ice
Wahlberg, Mark
Young MC

REAL ESTATE EXECUTIVE

Campeau, Robert Joseph
Day, Joseph Paul
Jones, Jesse Holman
Kalikow, Peter Stephen
Keating, Charles H, Jr.
Meyerhoff, Joseph
Rebozo, Bebe
Reichmann, Paul
Rouse, James W(ilson)
Rubloff, Arthur
Travis, Dempsey Jerome
Woods, Donald

REBEL LEADER

An Lu-shan
Huang Ch'ao
Tiradentes

RECORD COMPANY EXECUTIVE

Avant, Clarence
Combs, Sean
Dlugacz, Judy
Dupri, Jermaine
Edmonds, Tracey
Jackson, George
Knight, Suge
Light, Enoch Henry
LiPuma, Tommy
Ostin, Mo
Stein, Jules Caesar

RECORD COMPANY EXECUTIVES

Jimmy Jam and Terry Lewis

RELIGIOUS FIGURE

Agnes, Saint
Albert the Great
Angela Merici, Saint
Anthony of Padua, Saint
Apollinaris Sidonius, Gaius Sollius
Augustine, Saint
Bakhita, Giuseppina
Benedict, Saint
Bernadette of Lourdes, Saint
Bernard De Menthon, Saint
Bernardine of Siena, Saint
Bernard of Cluny
Blaise, Saint
Bonaventure, Saint
Boniface, Saint
Brendan of Clonfert, Saint
Brigid of Kildare
Cabrini, Frances Xavier, Saint
Carpini, Giovanni de Piano
Catherine of Alexandria, Saint
Catherine of Genoa, Saint
Cecelia, Saint
Christopher, Saint
Clare of Assisi, Saint
Columban, Saint
Cyril of Alexandria, Saint
Damian, Saint
David, Saint
Deckers, Jeanine
Dominic, Saint
Elizabeth of Hungary, Saint
Genevieve, Saint
Geoffrey of Monmouth
George, Saint
Gertrude the Great, Saint
Giuliani, Veronica, Saint
Guido d'Arezzo
Hallaj, Al-Husayn ibn Mansur al-

Heloise
Hildegard of Bingen, Saint
Hubert, Saint
Jenco, Lawrence M
Jerome, Saint
John the Apostle, Saint
Juana Ines de la Cruz, Sor
Kolbe, Maximilian Maria, Saint
Koresh, David
Lippi, Filippino
Mary, The, Virgin Mother
Nanak
Neumann, John Nepomucene, Saint
Origen Adamantius
Palamas, Gregory, Saint
Patrick, Saint
Pio da Pietrelcina, Francesco Forgione, Father
Rasputin, Grigori Efimovich
Sabbatai Zevi
Tekakwitha, Kateri, Saint
Theresa, Saint
Therese of Lisieux, Saint
Torquemada, Tomas de
Wolff, Mary Evaline
Wolsey, Thomas, Cardinal

RELIGIOUS FIGURES

Tappan Brothers

RELIGIOUS LEADER

Aaron
Abbott, Lyman
Abd el-Kadir
Abdu'l-Baha
Abdullah ibn Yasin
A'Becket, Thomas, Saint
Abu Bakr
Adler, Cyrus
Adrian II
Aga Khan, I
Aga Khan III
Aga Khan IV
Agus Salim, Hadji
Ahmad, Mirza Ghulam Hazat
Akiba ben Joseph
Alexander VI
Alfrink, Bernard (Jan), Cardinal
Ali
Allen, Richard
Allred, Rulon Clark
al-Turabi, Hassan
Ambrose, Saint
Anan ben David
Anokye, Okomfo
Anselm, Saint
Anthony, Saint
Aponte-Martinez, Luis, Cardinal
Applewhite, Marshall Herff
Arnold of Brescia
Asbury, Francis

Athanasius, Saint
Athenagoras I
Atkinson, William Walker
Augustine of Canterbury, Saint
Ba'al Shem Tov, Israel
Baeck, Leo
Baha'u'llah
Bamba, Amadou
Basil, Saint
Baum, William Wakefield, Cardinal
Bean, Carl
Beissel, Johann Conrad
Ben Badis, Abd al-Hamid
Benedictos I
Benedict XV
Benelli, Giovanni, Cardinal
Ben-Israel, Ben Ami
Benson, Ezra Taft
Bernardin, Joseph L(ouis), Cardinal
Bernard of Clairvaux, Saint
Bevilacqua, Anthony Joseph, Cardinal
Bhaktivedanta, A(bhay) C(haranaravinda)
Bhashani, Maulana Abdul Hamid Khan
Black Elk
Blavatsky, Helena Petrovna
Boehme, Jakob
Boniface, VIII
Booth, William
Borochov, Dov Ber
Borromeo, Charles, Saint
Bourgeoys, Marguerite
Brasch, Rudolph
Brooks, Phillips
Browning, Edmond Lee
Buchman, Frank Nathan Daniel
Buddha
Buddhadasa Bhikkhu
Bukhari, Muhammad ibn Ismail al-
Bushnell, Horace
Cajetan, St.
Callistus II, Pope
Canisius, Peter
Carberry, John J(oseph)
Carey, George Leonard, Archbishop
Carroll, John
Catherine of Siena, Saint
Cauchon, Pierre
Celestine V, Saint
Chang Chueh
Chrysostom, John, Saint
Clement, V
Clement I, Saint
Clement VII
Clement VIII
Clement XIV, Pope
Cody, John Patrick
Coggan, Frederick Donald, Baron
Coligny, Gaspard de Chatillon
Confalonieri, Carlo, Cardinal
Cooke, Terence James
Cotton, John

Cranmer, Thomas
Crowther, Samuel Adjai
Cummins, George David
Cushing, Richard James, Cardinal
Daily, Thomas V, Bishop
Dalai Lama, the 14th Incarnate
Dayananda Saraswati, Swami
Dearden, John Francis, Cardinal
Delaware Prophet
Dharmapala, Anagarika
Dimitrios I, Patriarch
Divine, Father Major Jealous
Donatus
Drexel, Mary Katherine
Eddy, Mary Baker Morse
Eilberg, Amy
Einhorn, David
Eisai
Enrique Tarancon, Vicente, Cardinal
Escriva de Balaguer, Josemarie
Farrakhan, Louis
Fillmore, Myrtle Page
Fleury, Andre Hercule de
Fox, George
Francis of Assisi, Saint
Francis of Sales, St.
Frings, Joseph Richard
Gamaliel the Elder
Gandhi, Mahatma
Gershom ben Judah
Ghose, Aurobindo
Gibbons, James, Cardinal
Glemp, Jozef, Cardinal
Goldstein, Israel
Gordon, Aaron David
Gorton, Samuel
Greeley, Dana McLean
Gregory, VII
Gregory, XII
Gregory the Great, Saint
Gregory XIII
Gregory XV
Guardini, Romano
Gumbleton, Thomas J
Ha-Levi, Judah
Handsome Lake
Harding, Stephen
Harris, Barbara Clementine
Hayes, Patrick Joseph, Cardinal
Heber, Reginald
Heck, Barbara Ruckle
Hertzberg, Arthur
Heschel, Abraham Joshua
Hickey, James Aloysius, Cardinal
Hicks, Elias
Hines, John E(lbridge)
Hippolytus, Saint
Hobart, John Henry
Hocking, Silas
Hoffner, Joseph, Cardinal
Honen
Hopkins, John Henry
Hubbard, L(afayette) Ron(ald)
Huddleston, Trevor
Hui-yuan

Hung Hsiu-ch'uan
Hunter, Howard
Hunthausen, Raymond
  Gerhardt
Hus, Jan
Husayni, Al-Hajj Amin al-
Hutchinson, Anne
Iakovos, Demetrios A
  Coucouzis, Archbishop
ibn Tumart, Muhammad
Ignatius of Loyola, Saint
Ikeda, Daisaku
Inge, William Ralph
Innocent, III, Pope
Innocent XI, Pope
Irving, Edward
Jabotinsky, Vladimir
  Evgenevich
Jackson, Jesse Louis
Jakobovits, Immanuel
Jesus Christ
John, XXIII
John of Leiden
John Paul I
John Paul II
Johnson, Hewlett
John XXIII
Jones, Bob
Jones, Reverend Jim
Jordan, Fred
Julius II, Pope
Julius III, Pope
Jung, Leo
Kahane, Meir David
Kaplan, Mordecai
Karlstadt, Andreas
  Bodenheim von
Kelly, Leontine Turpeau
  Current
Khomeini, Ruhollah
  Musavi, Ayatollah
Kimball, Spencer Woolley
Knorr, Nathan Homer
Knox, John
Knox, Ronald Arbuthnott
Kolvenbach, Peter-Hans
Krol, John (Joseph),
  Cardinal
Kung, Hans
Kushner, Harold S(amuel)
Lamy, Jean Baptist
Landa, Diego de
Langton, Stephen
Latimer, Hugh
Laud, William
Law, Bernard Francis,
  Cardinal
Lee, Ann
Lefebvre, Marcel Francois
Leo, X
Leo, I, St.
Leo, IX, St.
Leo XIII
Levinger, Moshe
Liebman, Joshua Loth
Linus, Saint
Lonergan, Bernard J F
Lubachivsky, Myroslav
  Ivan, Cardinal
Luther, Martin
Lyons, Henry (J.)
MacNutt, Francis, Father
Maharaj Ji, Guru
Mahavira
Mahdi, Mohammed
  Ahmed

Mahesh Yogi, Maharishi
Mahoney, James P(atrick)
Mahony, Roger Michael
Maimonides, Moses
Makarios III, Archbishop
Mani
Manning, Henry Edward
Manning, Timothy,
  Cardinal
Marcellus II, Pope
Marcinkus, Paul Casimir
Marcion
Margaret of Scotland
Marino, Eugene Antonio
Marshall, Peter
Martin, V
May, John L.
Mazarin, Jules, Cardinal
McIntyre, James Francis
  Aloysius, Cardinal
McKay, David O
Medeiros, Humberto,
  Cardinal
Melanchthon, Philipp
Miller, William
Mindszenty, Jozsef,
  Cardinal
Mohammed
Moon, Sung Myung
Mosley, J(ohn) Brooke
Mueller, Reuben Herbert
Muhammad, Elijah
Muhammad, Wallace D
Muhlenberg, Heinrich
  Melchior
Murray, John
Nestorius
Nichiren
Nicholas, Saint
Nicholas of Cusa
Niwano, Nikkyo
Nsubuga, Emmanuel,
  Cardinal
Obando (y Bravo), Miguel
O'Boyle, Patrick Aloysius,
  Cardinal
O'Connor, John Joseph,
  Cardinal
Omar I
Omar ibn Said Tal, Al-
  Hajj
Ottaviani, Alfredo,
  Cardinal
Oxnam, G(arfield)
  Bromley
Panchen Lama
Parker, Theodore
Paul, IV
Paul III
Paul VI
Perry, Harold R
Perry, Troy D.
Peter, Valentine J
Piccard, Jeannette Ridlon
Pike, James Albert, Bishop
Pius, II
Pius, VI
Pius, VII
Pius, IV, Pope
Pius, V, Pope
Pius IX
Pius X
Pius XI
Pius XII
Pontian, Saint
Pool, David de Sola

Potter, Henry Codman
Priesand, Sally Jane
Rajneesh, Bhagwan Shree
Ramakrishna, Sri
Ramsey, Arthur Michael,
  Lord
Ram Singh
Rapp, George
Ratana, Taupotiki Wiremu
Ratzinger, Joseph Alois,
  Cardinal
Rausch, James Stevens
Rogers, Adrian Pierce
Rogers, John
Rogers, Mary Joseph(ine)
Romero y Galdamez,
  Oscar Arnulfo
Rosen, Moishe Martin
Ross, Roy G
Rumi, Jalai ed-Din
Runcie, Robert Alexander
  Kennedy
Russell, Charles Taze
Rutherford, Joseph
  Franklin
Ryden, Ernest Edwin
Sadr, Musa al-
Savonarola, Girolamo
Sayyid Qutb
Schechter, Solomon
Schindler, Alexander
  Moshe
Schneerson, Menachem
  M(endel)
Seabury, Samuel
Seper, Franjo
Seton, Elizabeth Ann
  Bayley, Saint
Shah, Indries
Shariati, Ali
Sharietmadari, Ayatollah
  Seyed
Sheen, Fulton John,
  Bishop
Sheil, Bernard James,
  Archbishop
Sidarouss, Stephanos,
  Cardinal
Silver, Abba Hillel
Simeon Stylites, Saint
Sixtus, V
Smith, Joseph
Smith, Joseph Fielding
Smohalla
Snake, Reuben, Jr.
Sockman, Ralph W
Spellman, Francis Joseph
Spong, John
Spottswood, Stephen Gill
Stallings, George
  Augustus, Jr.
Starhawk
Stepinac, Alojzije
Suenens, Leon Joseph,
  Cardinal
Syed Ahmed Khan
Szoka, Edmund Casimir,
  Cardinal
Taft, Charles Phelps
Tao-an
Tao-hsuan
Taylor, Jeremy
Traglia, Luigi, Cardinal
Trifa, Valerian
Turner, Henry McNeal
Tutu, Desmond (Mpilo)

Urban, VI
Urban II
Ussher, James
Vincent, John Heyl
Vincent de Paul, Saint
Visser T Hooft, Willem
  Adolf
Vivekananda
Waldo, Peter
Walsh, James Edward
Warham, William
Weizmann, Chaim
Welch, Herbert
Wesley, John
White, Ellen Gould
  Harmon
Whitefield, George
Wierwille, Victor Paul
Wildmon, Donald Ellis
William of Tyre
William of Waynflete
Wise, Isaac Mayer
Wise, Stephen Samuel
Wiseman, Nicholas Patrick
  Stephen
Witherspoon, John
Woolman, John
Wovoka
Wright, John Joseph
Wyszynski, Stefan
Young, Brigham
Zoroaster

RELIGIOUS REFORMER

Muhlenberg, William
  Augustus

RESTAURATEUR

Aoki, Hiroaki
Aretsky, Ken
Bergeron, Victor J
Bloch, Ivan Sol
Bocuse, Paul
Bricktop
Brock, Alice May
Church, George W
Delmonico, Lorenzo
Evans, Bob
Goldston, Nathaniel R, III
Harvey, Fred(erick Henry)
Johnson, Howard Brennan
Johnson, Howard Deering
Kaufman, Elaine
Kroc, Ray(mond) Albert
McDonald, Maurice James
McDonald, Richard
Melman, Richard
Puck, Wolfgang
Rempp, Adolph
Rice-Davies, Mandy
Ritz, Cesar
Romanoff, Mike
Sanders, Colonel
Sardi, Vincent, Sr.
Sardi, Vincent, Jr.
Shor, Toots
Smith, Barbara
Stouffer, Vernon B
Thomas, Dave
Toffenetti, Dario Louis

RETAILER

Avery, Sewell
Bean, L(eon) L(eonwood)
Bloomingdale, Samuel
Bryant, Lane
Donahue, Woolworth
Gimbel, Adam
Gimbel, Bernard Feustman
Gimbel, Richard
Lawrence, Abbott
Macy, R(owland) H(ussey)
Magnin, Cyril Isaac
Magnin, Grover Arnold
Marcus, Stanley
Marks, Simon
Reed, Austin Leonard

REVOLUTIONARIES

Gang of Four
Irish Hunger Strikers
S(ymbionese) L(iberation)
  A(rmy)

REVOLUTIONARY

Adams, Samuel
Aguirre, Lope de
Alfaro, Jose Eloy
Anielewicz, Mordecai
Artigas, Jose Gervasio
Astorga, Nora Gadea
Atwood, Angela
Baader, Andreas
Babeuf, Francois-Noel
Bar Kokhba, Simon
Belgrano, Manuel
Ben Bella, Ahmed
Bhave, Acharya Vinoba
Blanqui, Auguste
Bolivar, Simon
Bonifacio, Andres
Borge Martinez, Tomas
Boudin, Kathy
Breshkovsky, Catherine
Cabral, Amilcar Lopes
Carnot, Hippolyte
Carnot, Lazare
Carrera, Jose Miguel
Cavalier, Jean
Cespedes, Carlos Manuel
  de
Chang Chueh
Ch'en Tu-hsiu
Christian, Fletcher
Cinque, Joseph
Cipriani, Amilcare
Collins, Michael
Condorcet, Marie-Jean-
  Antoine
Corday d'Armount,
  Charlotte
Danton, Georges Jacques
Davis, Angela (Yvonne)
Davitt, Michael
Dawes, William
DeFreeze, Donald David
Desmoulins, Camille
Devi, Phoolan
Devine, Michael
Doherty, Kieran
dos Santos, Marcelino

Emmet, Robert
Faisal, I
Fouche, Joseph
Frunze, Mikhail
  Vasilievich
Glendower, Owen
Glover, John
Guerrero, Vicente
Guevara, Che
Hale, Nathan
Hall, Camilla Christine
Harris, Emily Schwartz
Harris, William
Hebert, Jacques Rene
Henry, Patrick
Hereward the Wake
Herzen, Aleksandr
  Ivanovich
Hidalgo y Costilla, Miguel
Ho Chi Minh
Hughes, Francis
Hurson, Martin
Ibarruri, Dolores Gomez
Kamenev, Lev Borisovich
Kirov, Sergei Mironovich
Liebknecht, Karl
Li Ta-chao
Ludd, Ned
Lynch, Kevin
MacSwiney, Terence
Madero, Francisco
  Indalecio
Mahal, Hazrat
Marat, Jean Paul
Markievicz, Constance
  Georgine, Countess
Mazzini, Giuseppe
Mbuende, Kaire
  (Munionganda)
McCreesh, Raymond
McDonnell, Joe
McIlwee, Thomas
Meinhof, Ulrike Marie
Mirabeau, Honore Gabriel
  Riquetti
Miranda, Francisco de
Nguyen Huu Tho
Niekisch, Ernest
O'Hara, Patrick
Percy, Henry, Sir
Perry, Nancy Ling
Primo de Rivera, Jose A
Riel, Louis David, Jr.
Robelo, Alfonso
Robespierre, Maximilien
  Francois de
Roland (de La Platiere),
  Jeanne-Marie
Rudd, Mark
Sands, Bobby
San Martin, Jose de
Santander, Francisco de
  Paula
Soltysik, Patricia Michelle
Sucre, Antonio J de
Tandy, James Napper
Tone, Theobald Wolfe
Tonge, Israel
Tyler, Wat
Villa, Pancho
Wang Ching-wei
Wolfe, Willie
Zapata, Emiliano

RODEO PERFORMER

Ferguson, Tom R
Mahan, Larry
Pickett, Bill
Sampson, Charles

RUGBY PLAYER

Bevan, Brian

RULER

Abbas I
Abd al-Malik
Abd al-Mumin
Abd al-Rahman, I
Abd-Al-Rahman, III
Abdul-Hamid, II
Abdulhamid II
Abdullah al-Salim al-
  Sabah
Abdullah Ibn Hussein
Achab
Agrippina
Akbar
Akihito
Alaric I
Ala-ud-din
Albert, II
Albert I
Albrecht, Duke
Alexander I
Alexander II
Alexander III
Alexander the Great
Alexius Comnenus
Alfonso XIII
Alfred the Great
Amanollah Khan
Amenemhet, I
Amenhotep, III
Anne
Anokye, Okomfo
Antoninus Pius
Artemisia
Ashurbanipal
Asoka the Great
Atahualpa
Attila
Augustus
Augustus II
Aurangzeb
Baudouin, I, King
Beatrix
Bellshazzar
Bhumibol, Adulyadej
Birendra Bir Bikram, Shah
  Dev
Boadicea
Bolkiah, Muda Hassanal,
  Sir
Bonaparte, Jerome
Bonaparte, Joseph
Brian Boru
Caligula
Cambyses, II
Canute
Caracalla, Marcus Aurelius
  Antonius
Carl Gustaf XVI
Carlota

Carol II
Catherine the Great
Charlemagne
Charles I
Charles II
Charles Martel
Charles V
Charles VII
Charles XII
Charlotte Aldegonde E M
  Wilhelmine
Cheops
Ch'ien Lung
Ch'oe Ch'ung-hn
Chong Chung-bu
Christian IV
Christian X
Christina
Christophe, Henri
Claudius I
Cleopatra VII
Clovis I
Constantine I
Constantine V
Constantine VI
Constantine XII
Constantine XI
  Palaeologus
Croesus
Cuauhtemoc
Dalai Lama, the 14th
  Incarnate
Darius I
David
Demetrius I
Dessalines, Jean Jacques
Diocletian
Dionysius the Elder
Duncan I
Edgar
Edmund, Saint
Edward I
Edward II
Edward III
Edward IV
Edward the Confessor
Edward V
Edward VI
Edward VII
Edward VIII
Edwy
Elizabeth I
Elizabeth II
Eric IX
Eugenie
Fahd ibn Abdul Aziz,
  King
Faisal (Ibn Abdul-Aziz al
  Saud)
Faisal II
Farouk I
Ferdinand I
Ferdinand II
Ferdinand V
Francis I
Franz Joseph I
Franz Joseph II
Frederick I
Frederick II
Frederick III
Frederick IX
Frederick the Great
Frederick William
Frederick William I
George I
George II

George III
George IV
George V
George VI
Godfrey of Bouillon
Godunov, Boris
  Fedorovich
Gratian
Grey, Jane, Lady
Gustaf Adolf VI
Gustavus Adophus
Haakon VII
Hadrian
Haidar Ali
Haile Selassie, I
Hammurabi
Harald
Harold II
Hassan II
Hathaway, Sibyl Collings
Heliogabalus
Henry I
Henry II
Henry III
Henry IV
Henry V
Henry VI
Henry VII
Henry VIII
Herod Antipas
Herod the Great
Hirohito
Hitotsubashi
Hugh Capet
Hulagu Khan
Hung-Wu
Hussein, I, King
Ibn Saud
ibn Tashufin, Yusuf
Idris I
Ieyasu, Tokugawa
Ikhnaton, Pharaoh
Isabella I
Isabella II
Iturbide, Augustin de
Ivan III
Ivan IV
Jaber Al-Sabah, Jaber Al-
  Ahmad Al-
Jahangir
James I
James II
James III
James IV
James V
Jean, Prince
John, King of England
Joseph I
Joseph II
Josephine
Juan Carlos I
Julian
Juliana
Justinian I
Kalakaua, David
Kamehameha I
Kamehameha II
Kamehameha III
Kamehameha IV
Kamehameha V
Kanishka
Khalid Ibn Abdul Azia Al-
  Saud
Kropotkin, Peter
  Alekseyevich, Prince
Kublai Khan

Leonidas I
Leopold II
Leopold III
Liliuokalani, Queen
Louis I
Louis IX
Louis Phillippe
Louis XI
Louis XIV
Louis XV
Louis XVI
Ludwig II
Macbeth
Mahendra, Bir Bikram
  Shah Dev
Mahmud of Ghazni
Manuel I
Marcus Aurelius
  Antoninus
Margrethe II
Marguerite d'Angouleme
Maria Theresa
Marie Alexandra Victoria
Mary, Queen of Scots
Mary I
Matthias Corvinus
Mausolus
Maximilian
Maximilian I
Maximilian II
Medici, Cosimo de
Medici, Francesco de
Medici, Lorenzo de
Menelik II
Menes
Michael V
Minamoto Yoritomo
Ming, T'ai-Tsu
Mohammed V
Mohammed Zahir Shah
Mongkut
Montezuma I
Montezuma II
Moshoeshoe II
Mumtaz Mahal
Mutesa I
Mutesa II
Mutsuhito
Nadir Shah
Namgyal, Palden Thondup
Napoleon I
Napoleon III
Nebuchadnezzar I
Nebuchadnezzar II
Nefertiti
Nero
Nicholas I
Nicholas II
Olav V
Orleans, Philippe II d'
Pahlevi, Farah Diba
Pahlevi, Mohammed Riza
Pahlevi, Riza
Paul, Prince
Paul I
Pedrarias
Pedro I
Pedro II
Pepin III
Peter II
Peter the Great
Philip II
Philip V
Philip VI
Pu-Yi, Henry
Quabus bin Saud

Rainier III, Prince
Ramses II
Richard I
Richard II
Richard III
Robert Guiscard
Robert I
Rudolf II
Said bin Taimur
Said ibn Sultan
Saladin Yusuf ibn Ayyub
Samory Toure
Saud (Ibn Abdul Aziz al
  Saud)
Selim I
Sennacherib
Shah Jahan
Sheba
Sigismund
Sihanouk, Norodom
Sobhuza II
Sobieski, John, III
Solomon
Suleiman I
Sundiata Keita
Taharqa
Tai-Tsung
Tewfik Pasha
Tewodros II
Thani, Shiekh Khalifa Ben
  Hamad al
Thedosius I
Tiberius Julius Caesar
  Augustus
Tipu Sultan
Titus
Trajan
Tutankhamen
Tz'u Hsi
Umberto II
Vashti
Vasily III
Vespasian
Victor Emmanuel II
Victor Emmanuel III
Victoria, Queen
Vitellius, Aulus
Wilhelm II
Wilhelmina
William
William II
William III
William the Conqueror
Wu P'ei-fu
Wu wang
Xerxes I
Yakub al-Mansur, Abu
  Yusuf
Yen Hsi-shan
Yi Sng-gye
Yoshihito
Yoshimune, Tokugawa
Zahir Shah, Mohammad
Zayid bin Sultan Al-
  Nahyan, Shaykh
Zhao Kuang-yin
Zog I
Zoser

SAGE

Shammai

SAINT

Justin Martyr
Lalibela
Laszlo, I

SATIRIST

Churchill, Charles
Horace
Juvenal
Mandeville, Bernard
Mencken, H(enry) L(ouis)
Persius
Sanders, Ed
Swift, Jonathan
Waugh, Evelyn Arthur St.
  John

SCHOLAR

Abba Arika
Abrahams, Israel
Aelfric
Ailly, Pierre d'
Alcuin
Allal al-Fassi, Mohamed
Amyot, Jacques
Asante, Molefi Kete
Bainton, Roland Herbert
Bea, Augustinus
Bede the Venerable, Saint
Ben-Yehuda, Eliezer
Biddle, Nicholas
Bodley, Thomas, Sir
Bonaparte, Louis Lucien
Brightman, Edgar
  Sheffield
Bude, Guillaume
Caro, Joseph
Casaubon, Isaac
Chiang K'ang-Hu
Chu Hsi
Chukovsky, Korney
  Ivanovich
Coghill, Nevill Henry
  Kendall Aylmer
Crichton, James
Danquah, Joseph (Kwame
  Kyeretwi) B(oakye)
Diez, Friedrich Christian
Dugdale, William, Sir
Elias, Taslim Olawale
Elijah Ben Solomon
Erasmus, Desiderius
Eratosthenes
Estienne, Henri
Euphorion
Feltre, Vittorino da
Feng Kuei-fen
First, Ruth
Franco of Cologne
Froben, Johann
Fux, Johann Joseph
Gadamer, Hans-Georg
Gamaliel the Elder
Garrod, Heathcote William
Genung, John Franklin
Gershom ben Judah
Ginzberg, Louis
Goldmann, Nahum
Grotius, Hugo
Gumplowicz, Ludwig

Guo Moruo
Halide Edip Adivar
Harnack, Adolf von
Hillel
Himmelfarb, Gertrude
Holbach, Baron d'
Housman, A(lfred)
  E(dward)
Howe, Florence Rosenfeld
Hsuan Tsang
Huang Tsung-hsi
Husayn, Taha
Hu Shih
Hyde, Douglas
Ibn al-Arabi, Muhyi al-
  Din
James, Montague Rhodes
Jowett, Benjamin
Judah, I
K'ang Yu-wei
Kuk, Abraham Isaac
Lee, Sidney, Sir
Legg, W(illiam) Dorr
Lewis, C(live) S(taples)
Lewis, Wilmarth Sheldon
Logan, James
Lomonosov, Mikhail
  Vasilyevich
Lowes, John Livingston
Luria, Isaac ben Solomon
Mabuchi, Kamo
Macquarrie, John
Mandelstam, Nadezhda
  Yakovlevna
Manutius, Aldus
Moore, Clement Clarke
Mphahlele, Ezekiel
Nahmanides
Newell, Edward Theodore
Ngata, Apirana Turupa
Nicolson, Marjorie Hope
Ou-yang Hsiu
Pinto, Isaac
Pliny the Elder
Pound, Louise
Praz, Mario
Rashi
Reuchlin, Johann
Revel, Bernard
Robinson, Edward
Rondon, Candido Mariano
  da Silva
Rossetti, Gabriele Pasquale
  Giuseppe
Rostovtzeff, Michael
  Ivanovich
Rowse, A(lfred) L(eslie)
Rubin, Gayle
Saadia ben Joseph al-
  Fayumi
Scaliger, Joseph Justus
Schechter, Solomon
Schussler Fiorenza,
  Elisabeth
Sequoyah
Shanley, Kathryn W.
Shotoku Taishi
Sol Ch'ong
Tabari, Muhammad ibn
  Jarir al-
Toland, John
Trench, Richard Chenevix
Tseng Kuo-fan
Tyler, Ralph W(infred)
Ulfilas
Valla, Lorenzo

Varro, Marcus Terentius
Wang An-shih
Wilder, Amos Niven
Wilhelm, Hellmut
Wolf, Friedrich August
Wolfson, Harry Austryn
Xu Guangqi
Yen Fu
Yi Hwang
Zunz, Leopold

SCIENTIST

Abbot, C(harles) G(reeley)
Abel, John Jacob
Abu 'Ali al-Hasan ibn al-
  Haytham
Agassiz, Elizabeth Cabot
  Cary
Alfven, Hannes Olof
  Gosta
Altman, Sidney
Ames, Bruce N(athan)
Ampere, Andre Marie
Anderson, Carl David
Andrada e Silva, Jose
  Bonifacio de
Ardrey, Robert
Arnon, Daniel I(srael)
Aston, Francis William
Avery, Oswald T
Axelrod, Julius
Babcock, Stephen Moulton
Bache, Alexander Dallas
Bacon, Roger
Baird, Spencer Fullerton
Barany, Robert
Barkla, Charles Glover
Bauer, Louis Agricola
Baulieu, Etienne-Emile
Beard, George Miller
Bekhterev, Vladimir
  Mikhailovich
Benacerraf, Baruj
Bennett, Hugh Hammond
Bergstrom, Sune
Bhabha, Homi Jehangir
Bichat, Marie Francois
  Xavier
Bishop, Hazel
Bloch, Konrad Emil
Blumberg, Baruch Samuel
Bohr, Aage Niels
Boolootian, Richard
  Andrew
Bordet, Jules Jean Baptiste
  Vincent
Borlaug, Norman Ernest
Boyle, Robert
Braestrup, Carl Bjorn
Brewster, David, Sir
Bridgman, Percy Williams
Cabot, Richard C
Cairns, John, Jr.
Cayley, George, Sir
Cech, Thomas Robert
Chadwick, James, Sir
Charpentier, Johann von
Cherwell, Frederick
  Alexander L, Viscount
Clarke, Alexander Ross
Clarke, Arthur C(harles)
Claude, Albert
Cobb, Vicki

Coggeshall, L(owell)
  T(helwell)
Colton, Gardner Quincy
Compton, Arthur Holly
Comstock, John Henry
Coons, Albert Hewett
Cooper, Thomas
Cormack, Allan MacLeod
Cottrell, Alan Howard, Sir
Cowdry, Edmund Vincent
Crane, Eva
Cutler, Manasseh
Dalton, John
Darling, Frank Fraser, Sir
Dausset, Jean (Baptiste
  Gabriel Joachim)
Davis, Margaret B(ryan)
Davy, Humphrey, Sir
Dehmelt, Hans Georg
Deisenhofer, Johann
Delbruck, Max
Douglass, Andrew Ellicott
Drew, Charles Richard
Dubos, Rene Jules
Dulbecco, Renato
Eads, James Buchanan
Earle, Sylvia Alice
Eccles, John C(arew), Sir
Ehrenberg, Christian
  Gottfried
Eigenmann, Rosa Smith
Elmen, Gustav Waldemar
Elsasser, Walter M, Dr.
Eustachio, Bartolomeo
Ewing, William Maurice
Fabre, Jean Henri
Faraday, Michael
Ferraris, Galileo
Finlay, Carlos Juan
Finsen, Niels Ryberg
Florey, Howard Walter
Fornos, Werner H(orst)
Francis, Thomas, Jr.
Franklin, Benjamin
Frey-Wyssling, Albert F
Gajdusek, D(aniel)
  Carleton
Galdikas, Birute M(arija)
  F(ilomena)
Gallo, Robert Charles
Galton, Francis, Sir
Garriott, Owen
Gayle, Helene Doris
Gerasimov, Innokentii
  Petrovich
Gibbs, Erna Leonhardt
Gibbs, J(osiah) Willard
Gilbert, William
Gilman, Alfred G
Glasser, Melvin
Grandin, Temple
Grew, Nehemiah
Guerin, Camille
Guillaume, Charles
  Edouard
Gullstrand, Allvar
Guyot, Arnold Henry
Haldane, J(ohn) B(urdon)
  S(anderson)
Hall, Charles Martin
Haller, Albrecht von
Hammond, E(dward)
  Cuyler
Hansen, James E(dward)
Harger, Rolla
Hartline, Haldan Keffer

Hench, Philip Showalter
Herelle, Felix d'
Hershey, Alfred D(ay)
Hertz, Gustav Ludwig
Hewish, Antony
Heyrovsky, Jaroslav
His, Wilhelm
Ho, David D.
Holley, Robert W(illiam)
Hooke, Robert
Hounsfield, Godfrey
  Newbold, Sir
Hubel, David Hunter
Humboldt, Alexander,
  Freiherr von
Humboldt, Friedrich
  Heinrich Alexander von
Hunter, William
Huxley, Andrew Fielding,
  Sir
Hyatt, Alpheus
Jabir ibn Hayyan
Jackson, Charles Thomas
Jackson, Chevalier
Jacobson, Leon Orris
Jenner, William, Sir
Jerne, Niels Kaj
Jordan, David Starr
Josephson, Brian David
Kaplan, Henry Seymour
Katz, Bernard, Sir
Kendrew, John Cowdery,
  Sir
Khorana, Har Gobind
Kinsey, Alfred Charles
Knipling, Edward Fred
Koch, Robert
Kocher, Emil Theodor
Koehler, Georges J F
Kossel, Karl Martin
  Leonhard Albrecht
Krogh, Schack August
  Steenberg
Lee, Henry C.
Leidy, Joseph
Leiper, Robert Thomson
Lenard, Philipp Edward
  Anton
Levi ben Gershon
Levine, Philip
Ley, Willy
Lodge, Oliver Joseph, Sir
Loewi, Otto
Lomonosov, Mikhail
  Vasilyevich
Long, Crawford
  Williamson
Lonsdale, Kathleen
  (Yardley)
Lorenz, Konrad Zacharias
Love, Augustus Edward
  Hough
Lovelock, James
Low, George M(ichael)
Lumiere, Auguste Marie
  Louis
Lumiere, Louis Jean
Luria, Salvador Edward
Lwoff, Andre Michel
Lynen, Feodor Felix
  Konrad
Macdonald, Eleanor
  Josephine
Marcus, Rudolph A
Marshall, Barry J(ames)
Martinez, Joseph V

McCarthy, John
Meinesz, Felix Andries
  Vening
Mendenhall, Dorothy Reed
Menninger, William C
Michel, Hartmut
Mikoyan, Artem Ivanovich
Minsky, Marvin Lee
Mittermeier, Russell A
Montagnier, Luc
Morgagni, Giovanni
  Battista
Morgan, Thomas Hunt
Muller, Hermann Joseph
Muller, Johannes Peter
Neher, Erwin
Newell, Allen
Nicholas of Cusa
Nicholas of Oresme
Niepce, Joseph Nicephore
Noyce, Robert Norton
Oberth, Hermann Julius
Orr, John Boyd, 1st Baron
  of Brechin
Patrick, Ruth
Peregrinus, Petrus
Perrin, Jean Baptiste
Perutz, M(ax) F(erdinand)
Peters, C(larence) J(ames),
  (Jr.)
Peterson, Edith R.
Piccard, Jean Felix
Pincus, Gregory
Piret, Edgar L
Porta, Giambattista della
Ramsay, William, Sir
Ramsey, Norman
Regnault, Henri Victor
Reiffel, Leonard
Richardson, Owen
  Williams, Sir
Richet, Charles Robert
Richter, Burton
Richter, Curt Paul
Ricketts, Howard T
Riley, Charles Valentine
Rivers, Thomas Milton
Robbins, Fredrick
  Chapman
Roentgen, Wilhelm
  Konrad
Ross, Ronald, Sir
Rothschild, Miriam Louisa
Rous, Francis Peyton
Roux, Wilhelm
Ruska, Ernst
Sabin, Florence Rena
Salk, Jonas E(dward)
Samuelsson, Bengt
  Ingemar
Saunders, Charles E, Sir
Sauveur, Albert
Schank, Roger C(arl)
Schiaparelli, Giovanni
Schick, Bela
Schultes, Richard Evans
Selye, Hans
Shcharansky, Anatoly
  Borisovich
Shockley, William
  B(radford)
Siegbahn, Karl Manne
  Georg
Simons, Elwyn L(aVerne)
Sims, James Marion
Sloane, Dennis

Slotnick, Daniel Leonid
Smithson, James (Louis
  Macie)
Snell, George D(avis)
Snow, C(harles) P(ercy),
  Sir
Snow, Clyde Collins
Snyder, Solomon H(albert)
Spallanzani, Lazzaro
Sperti, George Speri
Stark, Johannes
Stopes, Marie Charlotte
  Carmichael
Stratton, Julius A(dams)
Struve, Friedrich Georg
  Wilhelm von
Sugiura, Kanematsu
Sutherland, Earl Wilbur,
  Jr.
Swammerdam, Jan
Swedenborg, Emanuel
Sydenham, Thomas
Szilard, Leo
Szmuness, Wolf
Temin, Howard Martin
Theiler, Max
Thomas, Sidney Gilchrist
Thomas, Vivien
Thompson, Starley
Thomson, Elihu
Thomson, Joseph John, Sir
Tinbergen, Nikolaas
Ting, Samuel Chao Chung
Tizard, Henry Thomas, Sir
Tonegawa, Susumu
Torricelli, Evangelista
Tournefort, Joseph Pitton
  de
Tsiolkovsky, Konstantin
  Eduardovich
Unanue, Jose Hipolito
Van Depoele, Charles
  Joseph
Vane, John Robert, Sir
Varmus, Harold E(lliot)
Venter, J. Craig
Vesalius, Andreas
Von Bekesy, Georg
VonBraun, Wernher
Waals, Johannes Diderik
  van der
Wagner-Jaurregg, Julius,
  von
Waksman, Selman
  Abraham
Wallace, Alfred Russell
Warburg, Otto Heinrich
Wasserburg, Gerald
  Joseph
Wasson, R(obert) Gordon
Watson-Watt, Robert
  Alexander, Sir
Wheatstone, Charles, Sir
Wien, Wilhelm Carl
  Werner Otto Fritz Franz
Wiesel, Torsten Nils
Wilkins, Maurice Hugh
  Frederick
Wilmut, Ian
Wilson, Charles Thomson
  Rees
Zeeman, Pieter
Ziegler, Karl
Zuckerman, Solly, Lord

SCREENWRITER

Allen, Jay Presson
Almond, Paul
Ambler, Eric
Ambrose, David Edwin
Anderson, Robert
  Woodruff
Anhalt, Edward
Anthony, Joseph
Audiard, Michel
Behrman, S(amuel)
  N(athaniel)
Benton, Robert Douglass
Bessie, Alvah
Biberman, Herbert
Bloch, Robert Albert
Bridges, James
Briley, John Richard
Brooks, James L.
Brooks, Richard
Busch, Niven
Carriere, Jean-Claude
Cash, Jim
Caspary, Vera
Clarke, Thomas Ernest
  Bennett
Corwin, Norman
Cox, Alex
Curtis, Jackie
Dalrymple, Ian (Murray)
De Passe, Suzanne
Deutsch, Helen
Diamond, I(sidore) A L
Didion, Joan
Eastman, Carol
Ephron, Henry
Ephron, Nora
Epps, Jack, Jr.
Epstein, Philip G
Feiffer, Jules Ralph
Fellini, Federico
Fields, Joseph
Foote, Horton
Forbes, Bryan
Fuller, Samuel
Gance, Abel
Goldman, Bo
Goldman, William
Green, Abel
Green, Paul Eliot
Gruber, Frank
Harris, Leslie
Harrison, Joan (Mary)
Harvey, Frank Laird
Hayes, John Michael
Henry, Buck
Hunter, Evan
Jennings, Talbot
Johnson, Nunnally
Kanter, Hal
Kasdan, Lawrence Edward
Kautner, Helmut
Kenney, Douglas C
Kramer, Larry
Kureishi, Hanif
Kurnitz, Harry
Langley, Noel
Lardner, Ring(gold
  Wilmer), Jr.
Lee, Ang
Leone, Sergio
Levinson, Barry (Michael)
Luedtke, Kurt (Mamre)
Lynch, David K
Maddow, Ben

Mahin, John Lee
Malick, Terence
Maltz, Albert
Mann, Abby
Marion, Frances
Matheson, Richard Burton
Mathison, Melissa
McCoy, Horace
McGuane, Thomas Francis
McKelway, St. Clair
Mercer, David
Meyer, Nicholas
Mucha, Jiri
Murphy, Warren B
Newman, David
Osborn, Paul
Panama, Norman
Perry, Eleanor Bayer
Pierson, Frank R(omer)
Poe, James
Raphael, Frederic Michael
Raphaelson, Samson
Renoir, Jean
Romero, George A
Sale, Richard Bernard
Salt, Waldo
Sargent, Alvin
Saura (Atares), Carlos
Schary, Dore
Schlondorff, Volker
Scorsese, Martin
Scott, Adrian
Seaton, George
Semple, Lorenzo, Jr.
Shagan, Steve
Shapiro, Stanley
Sheekman, Arthur
Shyer, Charles
Silliphant, Stirling Dale
Stallings, Laurence
Stern, Stewart
Stevens, Leslie
Stone, Oliver
Stone, Peter H
Sturges, Preston
Sullivan, C(harles)
  Gardner
Swerling, Jo
Syberberg, Hans Jurgen
Tesich, Steve
Thayer, Tiffany Ellsworth
Thomas, Dave
Tidyman, Ernest
Tillman, George, Jr.
Trumbo, Dalton
Varda, Agnes
Walter, Eugene
Ward, David S
Weber, Lois
Welland, Colin
Weller, Michael
Wells, George
Wexler, Norman
Williamson, David
Yordan, Philip
Young, Burt

SCULPTOR

Adams, Herbert Samuel
Aeschbacher, Hans
Agostini, Peter
Agostino di Duccio
Aitken, Robert
Albright, Malvin Marr

Alcamenes
Andre, Carl
Armitage, Kenneth
Arnolfo di Cambio
Arp, Hans
Ball, Thomas
Barlach, Ernst Heinrich
Barnard, George Grey
Barthe, Richmond
Bartholdi, Auguste
Bartlett, Paul Wayland
Baskin, Leonard
Bernini, Giovanni Lorenzo
Bertoldo di Giovanni
Bitter, Karl Theodore
    Francis
Boehm, Edward M
Bolotowsky, Ilya
Borglum, James Lincoln
    Delamothe
Borglum, John Gutzon de
    la Mothe
Borglum, Solon Hannibal
Bourdelle, Emile-Antoine
Brancusi, Constantin
Brunelleschi, Filippo
Burke, Selma (Hortense)
Caro, Anthony, Sir
Carrier-Belleuse, Albert
    Ernest
Castle, Wendell Keith
Catlett, Elizabeth
Cellini, Benvenuto
Chadwick, Lynn Russell
Chares
Charoux, Siegfried
Chase-Riboud, Barbara
Cherne, Leo
Chihuly, Dale (Patrick)
Churriguera, Jose Benito
    de
Clevenger, Shobal Vail
Clodion
Coysevox, Antoine
Crawford, Thomas
Dallin, Cyrus Edwin
da Settignano, Desiderio
David d'Angers
Davidson, Jo
DeCreeft, Jose
DellaRobbia, Andrea
DellaRobbia, Giovanni
DellaRobbia, Lucia
DeLue, Donald Harcourt
DeRivera, Jose Ruiz
DiSuvero, Mark
Donner, Georg Raphael
Duchamp-Villon,
    Raymond
Edwards, Melvin
Epstein, Jacob, Sir
Ezekiel, Moses Jacob
Falconet, Etienne Maurice
Farnham, Sally James
Fingesten, Peter
Flannagan, John Bernard
Fraser, James Earle
French, Daniel Chester
Gabo, Naum
Giacometti, Alberto
Gibbons, Grinling
Gibran, Kahlil George
Gibson, John
Gilbert, Alfred, Sir
Gill, Eric
Giorgio, Francesco di

Girardon, Francois
Gonzalez, Julio
Gonzalez, Xavier
Goujon, Jean
Greenough, Horatio
Gross, Chaim
Gunther, Ignaz
Haacke, Hans Christoph
Hague, Raoul
    (Heukelekian)
Hanson, Duane (Elwood)
Hare, David
Hepworth, Barbara, Dame
Hesse, Eva
Hoffman, Malvina
Hosmer, Harriet Goodhue
Houdon, Jean Antoine
Houser, Allan
Hunt, Richard (Howard)
Jackson, John Adams
Jaegers, Albert
Jones, Thomas Hudson
Judd, Donald (Clarence)
Kalish, Max
Kaskey, Ray(mond John)
Kiefer, Anselm Karl
    Albert
Kitson, Henry Hudson
Lachaise, Gaston
Laurens, Henri
Lehmbruck, Wilhelm
Lewis, Edmonia
Lin, Maya Ying
Lipchitz, Jacques
Lippold, Richard
Lukeman, Henry A
Lysippus
MacMonnies, Fred W
MacNeil, Hermon Atkins
Manship, Paul
Manzu, Giacomo
Marini, Marino
Marisol (Escobar)
Mestrovic, Ivan
Milles, Carl Wilhelm Emil
Millett, Kate
Moore, Henry Spencer
Morris, Robert
Myron
Noguchi, Isamu
Oldenburg, Claes Thure
Palmer, Erastus Dow
Papashvily, George
Pevsner, Antoine
Phidias
Pilon, Germain
Pisano, Andrea
Pisano, Nicola
Polycletus the Elder
Powers, Hiram
Pratt, Bela Lyon
Praxiteles
Puget, Pierre
Quercia, Jacopo della
Quinn, Edmond T
Raimondi, John
Reid Dick, William, Sir
Remington, Frederic
Riccio, Andrea
Richier, Germaine
Rickey, George Warren
Rimmer, William
Rinehart, William H
Rodin, Auguste
Rogers, John
Rogers, Randolph

Rosso, Medardo
Roszak, Theodore
Rush, William
Saint Gaudens, Augustus
Savage, Augusta Christine
Schadow, Gottfried
Schluter, Andreas
Scopas
Segal, George
Shrady, Henry M
Simmons, Franklin
Slobodkin, Louis
Sluter, Claus
Smith, David
Smith, Tony
Story, William Wetmore
Stoss, Veit
Taft, Lorado
Tatlin, Vladimir
    Yevgrapovich
Thorvaldsen, Albert Bertel
Tinguely, Jean
Truitt, Anne
Vigeland, Gustav
Ward, J(ohn) Q(uincy)
    A(dams)
Watts, George Frederic
Weinman, Adolph A
Westermann, H(orace)
    C(lifford)
Whitney, Gertrude
    Vanderbilt
Young, Mahonri
    Mackintosh
Ziolkowski, Korczak
Zorach, William

SECRETARY

Arnstein, Bobbie
Gies, Miep
Hahn, Jessica
Hall, Fawn
Howe, Louis McHenry
Kopechne, Mary Jo
Lehand, Missy
Marsh, Edward Howard,
    Sir
Marshack, Megan
Pang, May
Ray, Elizabeth
Rutherfurd, Lucy Page
    Mercer
Summersby, Kay
Toklas, Alice B(abette)
Tully, Grace George
Woods, Rose Mary
Zirato, Bruno

SEISMOLOGIST

Aki, Keiiti

SHIPBUILDER

Ericsson, John
McKay, Donald
Roach, John
Stevens, John
Stevens, Robert Livingston

SHIPPING
EXECUTIVE

Collins, Edward Knight
Cramp, Charles Henry
Cunard, Samuel, Sir
Dollar, Robert
Ferguson, Homer Lenoir
Forbes, Robert Bennet
Higgins, Andrew J
Luckenbach, Edgar
    Frederick, Jr.
Niarchos, Stavros (Spyros)
Onassis, Aristotle Socrates
Pao, Y(ue) K(ong), Sir

SIAMESE TWINS

Chang and Eng

SINGER

Aadland, Beverly
Abbott, Gregory
Abdul, Paula (Julie)
Ace, Johnny
Acuff, Roy (Claxton)
Adam Ant
Adams, Bryan Guy
Adams, Edie
Adams, Oleta
Adams, Yolanda
Alberghetti, Anna Maria
Allen, Deborah
Allen, Duane David
Allen, Elizabeth
Allen, Peter Woolnough
Allen, Rex E., Sr.
Allison, Mose
Allman, Duane
Allman, Gregg
Alvin, Dave
Ames, Ed(mund Dantes)
Amos, Tori
Anderson, Bill
Anderson, Ian
Anderson, Ivie
Anderson, John
Anderson, Jon
Anderson, June
Anderson, Lynn
Anderson, Marian
Andersson, Benny
Andrews, Julie
Andrews, LaVerne
Andrews, Maxene
Andrews, Patti
Anka, Paul
Annabella
Anton, Susan
Appice, Carmine
Argent, Rod(ney Terence)
Armatrading, Joan
Armstrong, Billie Joe
Arnaz, Desi
Arnaz, Lucie Desiree
Arnold, Eddy
Artist Formerly Known as
    Prince, The
Asher, Peter
Ashford, Nickolas
Ashton, Susan
Astley, Rick

Audra (Ann), McDonald
Austin, Patti
Autry, Gene
Avalon, Frankie
Axton, Hoyt (Wayne)
Aznavour, Charles
Bachman, Randy
Baez, Joan
Bailey, Mildred
Bailey, Pearl Mae
Bailey, Philip
Baker, Anita
Baker, Bonnie
Baker, Ginger
Baker, Josephine (Carson)
Baker, Kenny
Balin, Marty
Ballard, Florence
Ballard, Hank
Ballard, Russ(ell)
Bandy, Moe
Barrett, Syd
Barrow, Keith E
Basia
Bassey, Shirley
Battle, Kathleen Deanne
Bayes, Nora
Becaud, Gilbert (Francois
    Silly)
Beck
Bedelia, Bonnie
Bee, Molly
Belafonte, Harry, Jr.
Bell, Kool
Belle, Regina
Benatar, Pat
Beneke, Tex
Bennett, Tony
Benson, George
Benson, Renaldo
Bentley, Gladys
Benton, Barbie
Benton, Brook
Berg, Matraca
Berger, Al
Bernardi, Hershel
Berry, Chuck
Berry, Jan
Berry, John
Biafra, Jello
Big Bopper, The
Bikel, Theodore Meir
Billings, William
Bishop, Stephen
Bittan, Roy
Bjork
Black, Clint
Black, David (Jay)
Blades, Ruben, Jr.
Blakeley, Ronee
Bland, Bobby Blue
Bledsoe, Jules
Blige, Mary J(ane)
Blind Willie McTell
Block, Rory
Bloom, Eric
Bloomfield, Mike
Bofill, Angela
Bogert, Tim
Bolton, Michael
Bonds, Gary U S
Bon Jovi, Jon
Bono
Bono, Sonny
Bonoff, Karla
Bonsall, Joe

Boone, Debby
Boone, Pat
Boswell, Connee
Boswell, Martha
Boswell, Vet
Bouchard, Joe
Bowen, Billy
Bowie, David
Boyd, Bill
Boy George
Brady, Pat
Brady, Paul Joseph
Bragg, Billy
Brand, Oscar
Brandy
Branigan, Laura
Brannigan, Owen
Brassens, Georges
Braxton, Toni
Brewer, Teresa
Brian, Donald
Brice, Fanny
Bricktop
Bridgewater, Dee Dee
Brigati, Eddie
Brock, Tony
Bromberg, David
Brooks, Garth
Broonzy, Big Bill
Brown, Bobby
Brown, James
Brown, Jim Ed
Brown, Peter
Browne, Jackson
Bruce, Carol
Bryant, Anita Jane
Bryant, Hugh
Bryson, Peabo
Buckley, Jeff
Buckley, Tim
Buffett, Jimmy
Burdon, Eric
Burleigh, Harry Thacker
Burnette, Johnny
Burr, Henry
Bush, Kate
Butala, Tony
Butterfield, Paul
Caesar, Shirley
Cale, J J
Cale, John
Calloway, Cab
Campbell, Glen Travis
Campbell, Luther
Campbell, Tevin
Campbell, Tisha
Canova, Judy
Cantor, Eddie
Cantrell, Lana
Capaldi, Jim
Captain Beefheart
Cara, Irene (Escalera)
Carey, Mariah
Cariou, Len
Carissimi, Giacomo
Carlisle, Belinda
Carlisle, Kitty
Carmen, Eric
Carnes, Kim
Carpenter, Karen (Anne)
Carpenter, Mary Chapin
Carpenter, Richard Lynn
Carr, Vikki
Carrack, Paul
Carradine, Keith Ian
Carrere, Tia

Carroll, Diahann
Carroll, Jim
Carson, Mindy
Carter, Betty
Carter, Carlene
Carter, June
Carter, Lynda Jean
Carter, Mother Maybelle
Carter, Nell
Carter, Wilf
Casady, Jack
Casey, H(arry) W(ayne)
Cash, Johnny
Cash, Roseanne
Cassidy, David Bruce
Cassidy, Jack
Cassidy, Shaun Paul
Cavaliere, Felix
Cave, Nicholas Edward
Ceasar, Shirley
Cetera, Peter
Chandra, Sheila
Chapin, Harry Foster
Chapman, Tracy
Charlemagne, Manno
Charles, Ray
Charo
Checker, Chubby
Chenier, Clifton
Cher
Cherry, Neneh
Chevalier, Maurice
    Auguste
Childs, Toni
Chilton, Alex
Christian, Meg
Churchill, Sarah
Clark, Dave
Clark, Guy
Clark, Petula
Clark, Roy Linwood
Clarke, Allan
Clegg, Johnny
Clements, Vassar
Clemons, Clarence
Cleveland, James
Cliff, Jimmy
Cline, Maggie
Cline, Patsy
Clinton, George
Clooney, Rosemary
Coates, Edith
Cochran, Eddie
Cocker, Joe
Coe, David Allan
Cohen, Leonard Norman
Cole, Holly
Cole, Lloyd
Cole, Maria
Cole, Nat King
Cole, Natalie
Collins, Bootsy
Collins, Dorothy
Collins, Judy
Collins, Phil(ip)
Colter, Jessie
Columbo, Russ
Como, Perry
Cook, Barbara
Cooke, Sam
Coolidge, Rita
Cooper, Alice
Cope, Julian
Corby, Mike
Corgan, Billy
Cornell, Chris

Cornell, Don
Costello, Elvis
Covington, Warren
Craddock, Crash
Cramer, Floyd
Crawford, Michael
Crawford, Randy
Cray, Robert
Crenshaw, Marshall
Criss, Peter
Croce, Jim
Crofts, Dash
Crosby, Bing
Crosby, Gary
Cross, Christopher
Crothers, Scatman
Crouch, Andrae Edward
Crow, Sheryl
Crowe, J D
Crowell, Rodney
Cruz, Celia
Cummings, Burton
Curry, Tim
Curtin, Phyllis Smith
Cyrus, Billy Ray
Dale, Alan
Dale, Clamma Churita
Dalton, Lacy J
Daltrey, Roger Harry
Damone, Vic
Dandridge, Dorothy
D'Angelo, Beverly
Daniels, Billy
D'Arby, Terence Trent
Darcel, Denise
Darin, Bobby
Darling, Erik
Darren, James
Davidson, John
Davies, Dave
Davies, Ray(mond
    Douglas)
Davis, Billy, Jr.
Davis, Clifton
Davis, Gary, Reverend
Davis, Janette
Davis, Mac
Davis, Sammy, Jr.
Davis, Skeeter
Davis, Spencer
Dawn, Hazel
Day, Dennis
Day, Doris
Dayne, Taylor
Dean, Jimmy
Deane, Sandy
Dearie, Blossom
DeBarge, Bunny
DeBarge, El(dra)
DeBarge, James
DeBarge, Mark
DeBarge, Randy
Deckers, Jeanine
Dee, Kiki
Dee, Sandra
De Gaetani, Jan
Densmore, John
Denver, John
Derringer, Rick
DeShannon, Jackie
Desmond, Johnny
DeVito, Tommy
Dexter, Al
DeYoung, Dennis
Diamond, Neil
Dickens, Little Jimmy

Dietrich, Marlene
Diffie, Joe
Difford, Chris
DiFranco, Ani
Dinning, Mark
Dion
Dion, Celine
Dobkin, Alix
Doggett, Bill
Dolby, Thomas
Dolenz, Mickey
Domino, Fats
Donegan, Lonnie
Donovan
Dott, Gerard
Doucet, Michael
Douglas, Helen Mary
  Gahagan
Douglas, Mike
Downey, Morton
Downey, Rick
Downing, Will
Dr. John
Drake, Alfred
Drake, Nick
Driftwood, Jimmy
Dryden, Spencer
Dube, Lucky
Duncan, Todd
Dunn, Holly
Dury, Ian
Dussault, Nancy Elizabeth
Dyer-Bennet, Richard
Dylan, Bob
Easton, Sheena
Eberle, Bob
Eberle, Ray
Eckstine, Billy
Eddy, Nelson
Edmonds, Kenneth
Edwards, Cliff
Edwards, Dennis
Edwards, Joan
Egan, Walter Lindsay
Eggerth, Marta
Elfman, Danny
Elliman, Yvonne
Elliot, Cass
Elliott, Joe
Ely, Joe
Ennis, Skinnay
Entwistle, John Alec
Enya
Erickson, Leif
Escovedo, Alejandro
Essex, David
Estefan, Gloria
Etheridge, Melissa
Etting, Ruth
Everly, Don(ald)
Everly, Phil
Evora, Cesaria
Fabares, Shelley Michelle
  Marie
Fabian
Fagen, Donald
Fain, Sammy
Fairuz
Faith, Adam
Faithfull, Marianne
Fakir, Abdul
Faltskog, Agnetha
Fame, Georgie
Fargo, Donna
Farina, Richard
Farrell, Perry

Faye, Alice
Federici, Daniel Paul
Fela
Felder, Don(ald William)
Feliciano, Jose
Fellows, Edith
Fender, Freddy
Fenelon, Fania
Ferrell, Rachelle
Ferry, Bryan
Fischer-Dieskau, Dietrich
Fisher, Eddie
Fitzgerald, Ella
Flack, Roberta
Flatt, Lester Raymond
Fleetwood, Mick
Flores, Lola
Flowers, Gennifer
Fogelberg, Dan(iel
  Grayling)
Fogerty, John
Foley, Red
Fontaine, Frank
Ford, Lita
Ford, Mary
Ford, Tennessee Ernie
Forrest, Helen
Foster, Susanna
Fox, Samantha
Frampton, Peter Kenneth
Francis, Connie
Franklin, Aretha
Franklin, Kirk
Franklin, Melvin
Frazier, Dallas June
Frehley, Ace
Frey, Glenn
Frickie, Janie
Friganza, Trixie
Frizzell, Lefty
Froman, Jane
Funicello, Annette
Fury, Billy
Gabriel, Peter
Gaines, Lee
Garcia, Jerry
Garfunkel, Art(hur)
Garland, Judy
Garnett, Gale
Garrett, Leif
Gary, John
Gates, David
Gatlin, Larry Wayne
Gaye, Marvin (Pentz)
Gayle, Crystal
Gaynor, Gloria
Gaynor, Mitzi
Geldof, Bob
Gentry, Bobbie
Gibb, Andy
Gibb, Barry
Gibb, Maurice
Gibb, Robin
Gibbs, Georgia
Gibbs, Terri
Gibson, Bob
Gibson, Deborah (Ann)
Gibson, Don(ald)
Gifford, Kathie Lee
Gift, Roland
Gilder, Nick
Gill, Vince(nt Grant)
Gilmour, Dave
Godfrey, Arthur Michael
Gold, Andrew
Golden, William Lee

Goldsboro, Bobby
Gore, Lesley
Gorin, Igor
Gorka, John
Gorme, Eydie
Goulet, Robert Gerard
Graham, Larry
Grant, Amy
Grant, Eddy
Grant, Gogi
Graves, Denyce
  (Antoinette)
Gray, Dobie
Greco, Buddy
Green, Al(bert Leornes)
Green, Peter
Greenbaum, Norman
Greenwood, Lee
Grey, Joel
Griffith, Nanci
Grundy, Hugh
Guilbert, Yvette
Guthrie, Arlo Davy
Hagar, Sammy
Haggard, Merle Ronald
Haley, Bill
Hall, Daryl
Hall, Juanita
Hall, Tom T
Halliday, Johnny
Hamilton, Roy
Hardin, Tim
Harding, John Wesley
Hare, Ernie
Harper, Ben
Harris, Emmylou
Harrison, George
Harrison, Noel
Harry, Deborah (Ann)
Hart, Mickey
Hartford, John Cowan
Hartman, Dan
Hartman, Lisa
Harvey, Polly Jean
Hatfield, Bobby
Hathaway, Donny
Havens, Richie
Hawkins, Ronnie
Hawkins, Screamin' Jay
Hawkins, Tramaine
Haymes, Dick
Hays, Lee
Hazelwood, Lee
Healey, Jeff
Heatherton, Joey
Heatherton, Ray(mond
  Joseph)
Hedges, Michael
Hellerman, Fred
Helm, Levon
Helms, Bobby
Henderson, Florence
Hendrix, Jimi
Henley, Don
Henry, Clarence
Henry, Joe
Hiatt, John
Hibbler, Al
Higgins, Bertie
Hildegarde, Loretta Sell
Hill, Dan
Hill, Faith
Hill, Lauryn
Hitchcock, Robyn
Hite, Robert Ernest, Jr.
Ho, Don

Hoffs, Susanna
Holiday, Billie
Holliday, Jennifer Yvette
Holly, Buddy
Holman, Libby
Holmes, Rupert
Hooker, John Lee
Hopkin, Mary
Hopkins, Lightnin'
Hopkins, Telma Louise
Horn, Shirley
Horne, Lena Calhoun
Hornsby, Bruce
Horton, Johnny
Houston, Cissy
Houston, Whitney
Hoving, Jane Pickens
Howard, Ken(neth Joseph,
  Jr.)
Howes, Sally Ann
Howlin' Wolf
Hucknall, Mick
Hull, Warren
Humes, Helen
Humperdinck, Engelbert
Hunt, Lois
Hunter, Alberta
Hunter, Ian
Hunter, Ivory Joe
Hurt, Mississippi John
Husky, Ferlin
Hutchence, Michael
Hutton, Betty
Hutton, Ina Ray
Hyland, Brian
Hyman, Phyllis
Hynde, Chrissie
Ian, Janis
Idol, Billy
Iglesias, Julio
Ingram, James
Isaak, Chris
Ives, Burl (Icle Ivanhoe)
Jackson, Alan Eugene
Jackson, Aunt Molly
Jackson, Freddie
Jackson, Jackie
Jackson, Janet Damita
Jackson, Jermaine La
  Jaune
Jackson, Joe
Jackson, La Toya
Jackson, Mahalia
Jackson, Marlon David
Jackson, Michael Joseph
Jackson, Randy
Jackson, Tito
Jagger, Mick
James, Etta
James, Rick
James, Skip
James, Sonny
Jardine, Al(lan)
Jarreau, Al(wyn Lopez)
Jeanmaire, Renee Marcelle
Jefferson, Blind Lemon
Jeffreys, Garland
Jennings, Waylon
Jett, Joan
Joel, Billy
Johansen, David
John, Elton
Johnson, Lonnie
Johnson, Robert
Jolson, Al
Jones, Allan

Jones, Billy
Jones, Bobby
Jones, Brian
Jones, Davy
Jones, George (Glenn)
Jones, Grace
Jones, Howard
Jones, Jack
Jones, Matilda Sissieretta
  Joyner
Jones, Rickie Lee
Jones, Shirley
Jones, Tom
Joplin, Janis
Jordan, Louis
Judd, Naomi (Diana)
Kaas, Patricia
Kallen, Kitty
Kalthoum, Um
Kane, Helen
Kane, Howie
Kantner, Paul
Kath, Terry
Kauokenen, Jorma
Kavanaugh, Kevin
Kazan, Lainie
Kazee, Buell Hilton
Keel, Howard
Keith, Toby
Kelly, R(obert)
Kendricks, Eddie
Khan, Chaka
Kidjo, Anjelique
Kiedis, Anthony
Kiley, Richard (Paul)
King, B. B.
King, Ben E.
King, Carole
King, Claude
King, Evelyn
King, Freddy
King, William
Kirk, Lisa
Kitt, Eartha Mae
Knight, Gladys Maria
Krause, Bernie
Krauss, Alison (Maria)
Kravitz, Lenny
Kristofferson, Kris
LaBelle, Patti
Laine, Cleo
Laine, Frankie
Laird, Rick
Lake, Greg(ory)
Lamm, Robert
Lamour, Dorothy
Lane, Abbe
Lane, Lola
Lane, Priscilla
Lane, Rosemary
Lang, K(atherine) D(awn)
Langford, Frances
Lanier, Allen
Lansbury, Angela Brigid
Lanson, Snooky
Larkin, Patty
LaRosa, Julius
Larson, Nicolette
Lattisaw, Stacy
Lauder, Harry MacLennan,
  Sir
Lauper, Cyndi
Lavin, Christine
Lavin, Linda
Lawrence, Carol
Lawrence, Steve

Leadbelly
Leadon, Bernie
LeBon, Simon
Lee, Brenda
Lee, Geddy
Lee, Johnny
Lee, Peggy
Lennon, Dianne
Lennon, Janet
Lennon, John Winston
Lennon, Julian
Lennon, Kathy
Lennon, Peggy
Lennox, Annie
Lenya, Lotte
Leonetti, Tommy
Lesh, Phil
Lewis, Huey
Lewis, Jerry Lee
Liebling, Estelle
Lightfoot, Gordon
  Meredith
Lincoln, Abbey
Little Eva
Little Richard
Lofgren, Nils
Loggins, Kenny
London, Julie
Long, Avon
Longet, Claudine
  Georgette
Longmuir, Alan
Longmuir, Derek
Lopez, Trini(dad, III)
Lords, Traci
Loring, Gloria Jean
Love, Courtney
Love, Mike
Loveless, Patty
Lovett, Lyle
Lowe, Nick
Luft, Lorna
Lulu
Lydon, John (Joseph)
Lyman, Frankie
Lynch, David
Lyngstad-Fredriksson,
  Annifrid
Lynn, Loretta
Lynne, Shelby
Lynott, Phil(ip)
Lyon, Southside Johnny
Maccoll, Ewan
MacDonald, Jeanette
MacKenzie, Gisele
MacRae, Gordon
MacRae, Sheila
Madonna
Makeba, Miriam
Makem, Tommy
Manchester, Melissa Toni
Mandrell, Barbara Ann
Mangrum, Jim Dandy
Manilow, Barry
Manning, Irene
Manzarek, Ray
Markie, Biz
Marley, Rita
Marley, Ziggy
Marlowe, Marion
Marsden, Gerry
Marshall, Lois
Martin, Dean
Martin, Jimmy
Martin, Mary
Martin, Millicent

Martin, Tony
Martino, Al
Martyn, John
Marx, Richard
Mason, Nick
Massey, D Curtis
Massi, Nick
Mathis, Johnny
Mattea, Kathy
Matthews, Ian
Maxwell
May, Brian
Mayfield, Curtis (Lee)
Maynor, Dorothy
McArdle, Andrea
MC Breed
McCann, Les
McCartney, Paul
McClinton, Delbert
McCoo, Marilyn
McCracken, Joan
McCurdy, Ed
McDonald, Country Joe
McDonald, Michael
McEntire, Reba
McFerrin, Bobby
McGovern, Maureen
  Therese
McGraw, Tim
McKee, Lonette
McKenzie, Red
McKernan, Ron
McKinley, Ray
McKnight, Brian
McKuen, Rod Marvin
McLaughlin, John
McLean, Don
McMurtry, James
  Lawrence
McNair, Barbara
McNichol, Jimmy
McPhatter, Clyde
McRae, Carmen
McVie, Christine Perfect
Medley, Bill
Meisner, Randy
Melanie
Mellencamp, John
Memphis Slim
Mercer, Johnny
Mercer, Mabel
Merchant, Natalie
Mercury, Freddie
Merman, Ethel
Me'Shell Ndegeocello
Messina, Jim
Michael, George
Midler, Bette
Milano, Fred
Miles, Buddy
Miller, Ann
Miller, Frankie
Miller, Roger Dean
Miller, Steve
Mills, Donald
Mills, Harry
Mills, Herbert
Mills, John
Mills, Stephanie
Milsap, Ronnie
Mineo, Sal(vatore)
Minnelli, Liza
Miranda, Carmen
Mitchell, Chad
Mitchell, Guy
Mitchell, Joni

Moffatt, Katy
Monk, Meredith Jane
Monroe, Bill
Monroe, Lucy
Monroe, Vaughn
Montana, Patsy
Montand, Yves
Montgomery, Melba
Moore, Grace
Moore, Melba
Moore, Sam(uel David)
Moreno, Rita
Morgan, Dennis
Morgan, Helen Riggins
Morgan, Jane
Morgan, Jaye P
Morgan, Lorrie
Morgana, Nina
Morissette, Alanis
Morris, Gary
Morrison, Jim
Morrison, Van
Morrissey
Morse, Ella Mae
Moten, Etta
Mould, Bob
Muldaur, Maria
Munn, Frank
Munsel, Patrice Beverly
Murphey, Michael Martin
Murray, Anne
Myles, Alannah
Nabors, Jim
Nascimento, Milton
Nash, Graham
Nash, Johnny
Naughton, David
Near, Holly
Nelson, Harriet
Nelson, Rick
Nelson, Willie
Nesmith, Mike
Neville, Aaron
Newley, Anthony
  (George)
Newman, Phyllis
Newman, Randy
Newton, Juice
Newton, Wayne
Newton-John, Olivia
Nicks, Stevie
Niles, John Jacob
Nilsson
Nolan, Bob
Noone, Peter
Notorious B.I.G.
Nugent, Ted
Numan, Gary
Nyro, Laura
Oates, John William
Ocasek, Ric
Ocean, Billy
Ochs, Phil(ip David)
O'Connell, Helen
O'Connor, Donald
O'Connor, Sinead
O'Day, Anita
Odetta
Olcott, Chauncey
Ongala, Remmy
Orange, Walter
Orbison, Roy
Orlando, Tony
Osborne, Joan
Osbourne, Jeffrey
Osbourne, Ozzy

Oslin, K(ay) T(oinette)
Osmond, Donny
Osmond, Marie
O'Sullivan, Gilbert
Otter, Anne Sofie von
Owens, Buck
Page, Patti
Paige, Janis
Palmer, Peter
Palmer, Robert
Parker, Graham
Parker, Ray, Jr.
Parsons, Gram
Parton, Dolly (Rebecca)
Patti, Carlotta
Patti, Sandi
Paxton, Tom
Paycheck, Johnny
Payne, Freda
Payton, Lawrence
Pendergrass, Teddy
Penn, Michael
Penner, Fred
Perkins, Carl (Lee)
Perry, Lee
Perry, Steve
Peters, Bernadette
Peters, Brock
Petersen, Paul
Petty, Tom
Phair, Liz
Phillips, Chynna
Phillips, Esther
Phillips, John
Phillips, Michelle Gillam
Piaf, Edith
Pickett, Wilson
Pierce, Webb
Pike, Gary
Pike, Jim
Pirner, Dave
Pitney, Gene
Plant, Robert Anthony
Pointer, Anita
Pointer, Bonnie
Pointer, June
Pointer, Ruth
Pop, Iggy
Powell, Jane
Prater, Dave
Premice, Josephine
Presley, Elvis Aaron
Preston, Billy
Previn, Dory Langdon
Price, Alan
Price, Kenny
Price, Ray
Price, Steve
Pride, Charley
Prine, John
Printemps, Yvonne
Purim, Flora
Quatro, Suzi
Queen Ida
Rabbitt, Eddie
Rafferty, Gerry
Raffi
Rainey, Gertrude
Raitt, Bonnie
Raitt, John Emmet
Ralph, Sheryl Lee
Raphael
Rapp, Danny
Rawls, Lou(is Allen)
Ray, Johnnie
Raye, Martha

Redding, Otis
Reddy, Helen
Redpath, Jean
Reed, Dean
Reed, Jerry
Reed, Lou
Reed, Susan
Reese, Della
Reeves, Jim
Reeves, Martha
Regan, Phil
Reno, Mike
Reynolds, Debbie (Marie Frances)
Reznor, Trent
Ribeiro, Alfonso
Rich, Charlie
Richard, Cliff
Richard, Zachary
Richards, Keith
Richie, Lionel (Brockman)
Richman, Harry
Rider-Kelsey, Corinne
Riley, Jeannie C
Rimes, LeAnn
Ring, Blanche
Riperton, Minnie
Ritchie, Jean
Ritter, Tex
Rivera, Chita
Rivers, Johnny
Robbins, Marty
Robeson, Paul Leroy
Robillard, Duke
Robinson, Earl Hawley
Robinson, Smokey
Robinson, Tom
Rockin' Dopsie
Rockwell
Rodgers, Jimmie
Rodgers, Jimmy F
Rodriguez, Johnny
Roe, Tommy
Roeser, Donald
Rogers, Kenny
Rogers, Roy
Ronstadt, Linda
Rose, Axl
Rose, Fred
Ross, Diana
Ross, Lanny
Roth, David Lee
Roth, Lillian
Rucker, Darius
Ruffin, David
Ruffin, Jimmy
Rundgren, Todd
RuPaul
Rush, Tom
Rushen, Patrice Louise
Russell, Andy
Russell, Leon
Russell, Lillian
Rutherford, Michael
Ryder, Mitch
Sablon, Jean Georges
Sade
Sadler, Barry
Sager, Carole Bayer
Sainte-Marie, Buffy
Sanderson, Julia
Sands, Tommy
Sang, Samantha
Sangare, Oumou
Sayer, Leo
Scaggs, Boz

Scarbury, Joey
Schilling, Peter
Schioetz, Aksel
Schlamme, Martha
Schmidt, Tim(othy B)
Schneider, John
Scholz, Tom
Schuur, Diane
Seal
Seals, Dan Wayland
Seals, Jim
Sebastian, John
Secombe, Harry
Sedaka, Neil
Seeger, Pete(r)
Seger, Bob
Selena
Sembello, Michael
Seville, David
Shannon, Del
Sheila E
Sheppard, T G
Sherman, Bobby
Shocked, Michelle
Shore, Dinah
Shorrock, Glenn
Siberry, Jane
Simmons, Gene
Simmons, Pat(rick)
Simms, Ginny
Simon, Carly
Simon, Joe
Simon, Paul
Simone, Nina
Simpson, Valerie
Sinatra, Frank
Sinatra, Frank, Jr.
Sinatra, Nancy
Sinder, Dee
Skaggs, Ricky
Sledge, Debbie
Sledge, Joni
Sledge, Kathy
Sledge, Kim
Slick, Grace Wing
Smith, Bessie
Smith, Cathy Evelyn
Smith, Kate
Smith, Keely
Smith, Michael W
Smith, Patti
Smith, Rex
Smith, Sammi
Smothers, Dick
Smothers, Tommy
Snider, Dee
Snow, Don
Snow, Hank
Snow, Phoebe Laub
Sonnier, Jo-El
Sosa, Mercedes
South, Joe
Souther, J(ohn) D(avid)
Springfield, Dusty
Springfield, Rick
Springsteen, Bruce
Squier, Billy
Squire, Chris
Stafford, Jim
Stafford, Jo
Stanley, Paul
Stanley, Ralph Edmond
Stansfield, Lisa
Starr, Kay
Starr, Ringo
Stein, Mark

Sterban, Richard
Stevens, Cat
Stevens, Connie
Stevens, Ray
Stewart, Al
Stewart, John
Stewart, Rod(erick David)
Stewart, Wynn
Stills, Stephen
Sting
Stipe, Michael
Stocker, Wally
Stone, Doug
Stone, Sly
Stookey, Paul
Strait, George
Straw, Syd
Streisand, Barbra (Joan)
Stritch, Elaine
Stuart, Marty
Stubbs, Levi
Styles, Re
Sullivan, Maxine
Sullivan, Tom
Sumac, Yma
Summer, Donna
Suzuki, Pat
Sweat, Keith
Sweet, Matthew
Sweet, Rachel
Syms, Sylvia
Tabbert, William
Taj Mahal
Talbot, John Michael
Tamberlik, Enrico
Taylor, J T
Taylor, James Vernon
Taylor, KoKo
Taylor, Livingston
Teena Marie
Tennille, Toni
Terrell, Tammi
Terry, Sonny
Tex, Joe
Thibault, Conrad
Thomas, B(illy) J(oe)
Thomas, Rufus
Thompson, Hank
Thompson, Kay
Thompson, Richard
Thornton, Willie Mae
Tiffany
Tikaram, Tanita
Tilbrook, Glenn
Tillis, Mel(vin)
Tillis, Pam
Tork, Peter
Torme, Mel(vin Howard)
Torrence, Dean
Tosh, Peter
Toure, Ali Farka
Tracy, Arthur
Trapp, Maria Augusta von
Trask, Diana
Travers, Mary
Travis, Merle Robert
Travis, Randy
Traynor, John
Trenet, Charles
Tricky
Tritt, Travis
Troup, Bobby
Tshabalala, Headman
Tubb, Ernest
Tucker, Sophie
Tucker, Tanya (Denise)

Tully, Alice
Turner, Ike
Turner, Tina
Twain, Shania
Twitty, Conway
Tyler, Bonnie
Tyler, Steven
Tyner, Rob
Tyson, Ian
Tyson, Sylvia Fricker
Uggams, Leslie (Marian Crayne)
Ulvaeus, Bjorn
Umeki, Miyoshi
Upshaw, Dawn
Vale, Jerry
Valens, Ritchie
Vallee, Rudy
Valli, Frankie
Vance, Kenny
Vandross, Luther
Van Halen, Eddie
Vanity
Vannelli, Gino
Van Shelton, Ricky
Van Zant, Ronnie
Vaughan, Sarah Lois
Vedder, Eddie
Vee, Bobby
Vega, Suzanne
Venuta, Benay
Vera, Billy
Vicious, Sid
Vincent, Gene
Vinson, Cleanhead
Vinton, Bobby
Vogelweide, Walther von der
Vysotsky, Vladimir Semyonovich
Wagner, Jack Peter
Wagoner, Porter
Wahlberg, Donnie
Wain, Bea
Wainwright, Loudon, III
Waite, John
Waits, Tom
Wakely, Jimmy
Walker, Albertina
Walker, Junior
Walker, T-Bone
Wallace, Sippie
Waller, Gordon
Walsh, Joe
Warfield, William Caesar
Wariner, Steve
Warnes, Jennifer
Warwick, Dionne
Washington, Dinah
Waters, Ethel
Waters, Muddy
Watley, Jody
Watts, Charlie
Waybill, Fee
Weede, Robert
Weir, Bob
Wells, Kitty
Wells, Mary
West, Dottie
White, Barry
White, Josh(ua Daniel)
Whiting, Margaret
Whitley, Keith
Wilde, Kim
Williams, Andy
Williams, Anson

Williams, Deniece
Williams, Don
Williams, Hank
Williams, Hank, Jr.
Williams, Joe
Williams, Lucinda
Williams, Milan
Williams, Paul Hamilton
Williams, Vanessa
Williams, Victoria
Williamson, Sonny Boy
Wilson, Ann
Wilson, Brian Douglas
Wilson, Carl (Dean)
Wilson, Cassandra
Wilson, Dennis
Wilson, Jackie
Wilson, Julie
Wilson, Mary
Wilson, Nancy
Winchester, Jesse (James Ridout)
Winter, Edgar Holand
Winter, Johnny
Winwood, Steve
Withers, Bill
Wolf, Peter
Womack, Bobby
Wonder, Stevie
Wood, Stuart
Wooley, Sheb
Worley, Jo Anne
Wray, Link
Wright, Cobina
Wright, Martha
Wright, Rick
Wright, Syretta
Wrightson, Earl
Wynette, Tammy
Wynonna
Yankovic, Weird Al
Yarbrough, Glenn
Yarrow, Peter
Yearwood, Trisha
Yoakam, Dwight
Young, Faron
Young, Paul
Young, Ralph
Zadora, Pia
Zander, Robin
Zappa, Frank
Zappa, Moon Unit
Zevon, Warren

SINGERS

Winans, BeBe and CeCe

SKATER

Albright, Tenley Emma
Babilonia, Tai (Reina)
Baiul, Oksana
Biellmann, Denise
Blair, Bonnie Kathleen
Blumberg, Judy
Boitano, Brian
Bonaly, Surya
Boucher, Gaetan
Button, Dick
Carruthers, Kitty
Carruthers, Peter
Cousins, Robin

Cranston, Toller
Curry, John (Anthony)
Dean, Christopher
Dijkstra, Sjoukje
Enke, Karin
Fleming, Peggy Gale
Fratianne, Linda
Gardner, Randy
Gordeeva, Ekaterina
Grinkov, Sergei
Hamill, Dorothy Stuart
Hamilton, Scott
Heiden, Eric Arthur
Heiss, Carol Elizabeth
Henie, Sonja
Henning, Anne
Hoffmann, Jan
Holum, Dianne
Jaffee, Irving
Jansen, Dan
Jenkins, Carol Elizabeth Heiss
Jenkins, Dave
Jenkins, Hayes Alan
Jewtraw, Charlie
Johnson, Lynn-Holly
Kerrigan, Nancy
Lynn, Janet
McDermott, Terry
Mueller, Peter
Nepela, Ondrej
Niemann, Gunda
Orser, Brian
Paul, Bob
Potzsch, Anett
Protopopov, Ludmilla Evgenievna Belousova
Protopopov, Oleg Alekseevich
Rodnina, Irina
Schenk, Ard
Schuba, Beatrix
Scott, Barbara Ann
Seibert, Michael
Shea, John A
Sumners, Rosalyn
Thomas, Debi
Tickner, Charlie
Torvill, Jayne
Trenary, Jill
Wagner, Barbara
Witt, Katarina
Wood, Tim
Wylie, Paul
Yamaguchi, Kristi Tsuya
Young, Sheila
Zaitsev, Aleksandr
Zayak, Elaine

SKIER

Armstrong, Debbie
Bogatja, Vinto
Chaffee, Suzy
Cochran, Barbara Ann
DiBello, Paul
Duvall, Camille
Fraser, Gretchen Kunigh
Greene, Nancy Catherine
Johnson, Bill
Kidd, William
Killy, Jean-Claude
Kinmont, Jill
Klammer, Franz
Kreiner, Kathy

Kronberger, Petra
Lawrence, Andrea Mead
Lunn, Arnold Henry Moore, Sir
Mahre, Phil(lip)
Mahre, Steve(n Irving)
Mc Kinney, Tamara
Mittermaier, Rosi
Moe, Tommy
Nieminen, Toni
Proell Moser, Annemarie
Sabich, Spider
Schranz, Karl
Stenmark, Ingemar
Tomba, Alberto
Wenzel, Hanni
Zurbriggen, Pirmin

SLAVE

Androcles
Cinque, Joseph
Craft, Ellen
Equiano, Olaudah
Hemings, Sally
Henson, Josiah
Ja Ja of Opobo
Keckley, Elizabeth Hobbs
Scott, Dred
Spartacus
Toussaint l'Ouverture, Pierre Dominique
Turner, Nat
Vesey, Denmark

SLAVE TRADER

Canot, Theodore
Dalzel, Archibald

SOCCER EXECUTIVE

Busby, Matthew, Sir
Ertegun, Ahmet (Munir)
Toye, Clive Roy

SOCCER PLAYER

Akers, Michelle
Best, George
Brand, Jack
Charlton, Bobby
Chinaglia, Giorgio
Cruyff, Johan
Francis, Trevor
Harkes, John
Jones, Cobi
Lalas, Alexi
Maradona, Diego
Matthews, Stanley, Sir
Messing, Shep
Milla, Roger
Pele
Rigby, Bob
Rote, Kyle, Jr.

SOCIAL REFORMER

Abbott, Grace
Adams, Hank
Adler, Felix
Ambedkar, Bhimrao Ramji
Ames, Jessie Daniel
Anthony, Susan B(rownell)
Apuzzo, Virginia M.
Auguste, Rose-Anne
Baden-Powell, Olave St. Claire, Lady
Bailey, Gamaliel
Baird, Bill
Baker, Ella
Baldwin, Roger Nash
Banks, Dennis J.
Barnardo, Thomas John
Barrow, Ruth Nita, Dame
Barton, Clara Harlowe
Bates, Mary Elizabeth
Beecher, Henry Ward
Beers, Clifford Whittingham
Bellamy, Edward
Bellecourt, Clyde
Ben-Shalom, Miriam
Bergalis, Kimberly
Bergh, Henry
Besant, Annie Wood
Bethune, Mary McLeod
Bloomer, Amelia Jenks
Boesak, Allan Aubrey
Bonner, Yelena
Boole, Ella Alexander
Booth, Ballington
Booth, Catherine Mumford
Booth, Charles Brandon
Booth, Evangeline Cory
Booth, William
Brace, Charles Loring
Brady, Sarah Jane
Breckinridge, Sophonisba Preston
Brisbane, Albert
Brower, David Ross
Brown, Judie
Brown, William Wells
Burritt, Elihu
Caldicott, Helen Broinowski
Calvin, John
Carlile, Richard
Chang Chien
Chiang K'ang-Hu
Childers, Erskine
Chisholm, Caroline
Claflin, Tennessee Celeste
Claybrook, Joan B
Coffin, William Sloan, Jr.
Collins, Marva Deloise Nettles
Comstock, Anthony
Cooper, Anthony Ashley, 7th Earl of Shaftesbury
Corrigan-Maguire, Mairead
Coulter, Ernest Kent
Cox, Harvey Gallagher, Jr.
Coxey, Jacob Sechler
Cremer, William Randal, Sir
Davis, Rennie
Deb, Radhakant

Dederich, Charles (Edwin)
Dees, Morris S(eligman), Jr.
Delany, Martin Robinson
Dewson, Mary Williams
Dix, Dorothea Lynde
Dolci, Danilo
Dow, Neal
Drake, Daniel
DuBois, W(illiam) E(dward) B(urghardt)
Duncan, Sheena
Edelman, Marian Wright
Ely, Richard Theodore
Farnham, Eliza Wood Burhans
Fauntroy, Walter E(dward)
Field, David Dudley
Foote, Andrew Hull
Foreman, Dave
Forten, James
Fry, Elizabeth Gurney
Fuller, Ida
Fuller, Margaret
Gabriel
Gage, Matilda Joslyn
Gerry, Elbridge Thomas
Gittings, Barbara
Glaser, Elizabeth
Glasser, Ira
Gmeiner, Hermann
Godiva, Lady
Goldmark, Josephine
Gourlay, Robert
Graham, Sylvester
Groote, Gerhard
Guyer, David Leigh
Hale, Clara (McBride)
Hale, Lorraine
Hamilton, Alice
Harris, LaDonna (Crawford)
Hay, Harry
Hayes, Robert Michael
Healey, Jack
Height, Dorothy Irene
Hill, Morton A(nthony)
Holmes, John Haynes
Howe, Julia Ward
Howe, Samuel Gridley
Hughes, Thomas
Humphry, Ann Wickett
Humphry, Derek John
Huntington, Henry S, Jr.
Jacob, John Edward
Jacobson, Michael Faraday
Jarvis, Anna
Jarvis, Howard Arnold
Joyce, William
Kellor, Frances (Alice)
King, Bernice Albertine
Kissling, Frances
Klarsfeld, Beate
Knox, John
Kollontai, Alexandra Mikhailovna (Domantovich)
Kowalski, Sharon
Kuhn, Maggie
Kutner, Luis
Ladd, William
La Haye, Beverly
Lamont, Corliss
Las Casas, Bartolome de
Leland, Mickey
Lightner, Candy

Lindsey, Benjamin Barr
Livermore, Mary Ashton Rice
Lloyd, Henry Demarest
Lockwood, Belva Ann Bennett
Loeb, Sophia Irene Simon
Lopez-Portillo y Rojas, Jose
Low, Juliette Gordon
Lowell, Josephine Shaw
Luthuli, Albert John Mvumbi
Maguire, Mairead Corrigan
McTaggart, David
Melanchthon, Philipp
Menchu, Rigoberta
Michael, Moina Belle
Miller, Elizabeth Smith
Moltke, Helmuth James, Graf von
Montessori, Maria
Mott, Lucretia Coffin
Muntzer, Thomas
Narayan, Jayaprakash
Nation, Carry A(melia Moore)
Newkirk, Ingrid
Nightingale, Florence
Nkoli, Simon
Norman, Pat
Noyes, John Humphrey
O'Leary, Jean
Osborne, Thomas Mott
Ovington, Mary White
Owen, Robert
Owen, Robert Dale
Packard, Elizabeth Parsons Ware
Parker, Theodore
Patrick, Ted
Pinel, Philippe
Plimsoll, Samuel
Potter, Henry Codman
Rathbone, Eleanor
Rice, Joseph Mayer
Riley, Helen Caldwell Day
Ripley, George
Roddick, Anita Lucia Perella
Rondon, Candido Mariano da Silva
Roosevelt, Eleanor
Roy, Ram Mohun
Russell, Charles Edward
Sanger, Margaret
Sangster, Margaret Elizabeth
Santamaria, Bartholomew Augustine
Schindler, Solomon
Schwartz, Felice N(ierenberg)
Senesh, Hannah
Shaw, Anna Howard
Sheldon, Charles M(onroe)
Shriver, Eunice Mary Kennedy
Silhouette, Etienne de
Sisulu, Nontsikelelo Albertina
Sisulu, Walter Max Ulyate
Sliwa, Curtis
Smith, Robert H

Solomon, Hannah Greenebaum
Stanton, Elizabeth Cady
Stanton, Henry Brewster
Steffens, Lincoln
Stephens, Charlotte Andrews
Stevens, Eileen
Stevens, James (Richard)
Strong, Josiah
Switzer, Mary E.
Szold, Henrietta
Taylor, Lucy Beaman Hobbs
Terrell, Mary Church
Terry, Randall A.
Thayer, Eli
Thompson, Karen
Tobias, Channing Heggie
Townsend, Francis Everett
Velez, Clemente Soto
Villard, Helen Francis Garrison
Wakefield, Edward Gibbon
Wauneka, Annie Dodge
Wildmon, Donald Ellis
Wiley, Harvey Washington
Wilkes, John
Wilkins, Roy
Willard, Frances Elizabeth Caroline
Williams, Betty Smith
Wilson, William Griffith
Wittenmyer, Annie Turner
Wood, Louise Aletha
Woodhull, Victoria Claflin
Wright, Elizur
Wright, Frances
Wyclif, John
Wycliffe, John
Zwingli, Huldreich

SOCIAL REFORMERS

Tappan Brothers
Willmar 8

SOCIAL SCIENTIST

Berelson, Bernard (Reuben)
Booth, Charles
Le Bon, Gustave
Wootton, Barbara (Frances) Adam

SOCIAL WORKER

Addams, Jane
Bates, Daisy Mae
Kelley, Florence
Little, Robert Langdon
Lord, Mary Pillsbury
Wald, Lillian D
West, James Edward
Woods, Robert Archey
York, David

SOCIALITE

Armstrong-Jones, Antony
  Charles Robert
Belmont, Alva Erskine
  Smith Vanderbilt
Blessington, Marguerite
  Gardiner, Countess
Bloomingdale, Betsy
Bonaparte, Elizabeth
  Patterson
Churchill, Jennie Jerome
Cramm, Gottfried von,
  Baron
D'Orsay, Alfred
  Guillaume, Count
Duke, Doris
Ford, Charlotte
Frazier, Brenda Diana
  Dudd
Gardner, Isabella Stewart
Guggenheim, Peggy
Hampton, Hope
Hutton, Barbara
  Woolworth
Jagger, Bianca Teresa
Leverson, Ada
Longworth, Alice
  Roosevelt
Maxwell, Elsa
McLean, Evalyn Walsh
Mosbacher, Georgette
Norwich, Diana (Manners)
  Cooper, Viscountess
Obolensky, Serge
Paley, Barbara Cushing
Recamier, Julie, Madame
Stael-Holstein, Anne
  Louise Germaine
  Necker, Baroness de
Tanner, Marion
Trudeau, Margaret Joan
  Sinclair
Von Bulow, Sunny
Walker, A'lelia

SOCIOLOGIST

Angell, Robert Cooley
Arguedas, Alcides
Bacon, Selden D(askam)
Balch, Emily G
Bardis, Panos Demetrios
Barnes-Taeuber, Irene
Baudrillard, Jean
Bell, Daniel
Bogart, Leo
Bond, Horace Mann
Carey, Henry Charles
Carr-Saunders, Alexander
  Morris
Champagne, Duane
  (Willard)
Chapin, F(rancis) Stuart
Chiang Mei-Ling
Coleman, James S(amuel)
Collier, John
Cooley, Charles Horton
Counts, George S(ylvester)
Davis, Kingsley
Duffey, Joseph Daniel
Dugdale, Richard Louis
Durkheim, Emile
Edwards, Harry, Jr.
Emecheta, Buchi

Etzioni, Amitai Werner
Fitzhugh, George
Frazier, Edward Franklin
Freyre, Gilberto (de
  Mello)
Geddes, Patrick, Sir
Geiger, Theodor Julius
George, Zelma W(atson)
Giddings, Franklin Henry
Glass, David Victor
Gokalp, Mehmet Ziya
Gumplowicz, Ludwig
Habermas, Juergen
Haynes, George Edmund
Hine, Lewis Wickes
Hobhouse, Leonard
  Trelawny
Homans, George Caspar
Hunter, Floyd
Janowitz, Morris
Johnson, Charles Spurgeon
Johnson, Guy Benton
Lazarsfeld, Paul F(elix)
Le Play, Guillaume
  Frederic
Lipset, Seymour Martin
Luhmann, Niklas
Lynd, Helen Merrell
Lynd, Robert Staughton
MacIver, Robert Morrison
Mannheim, Karl
Mayo-Smith, Richmond
Merton, Robert King
Michels, Robert
Mills, C(harles) Wright
Murray, Charles Alan
Myrdal, Alva Reimer
Myrdal, Karl Gunnar
Nearing, Scott
Odum, Howard
  Washington
Ogburn, W(illiam)
  F(ielding)
Park, Robert Ezra
Parsons, Elsie Clews
Parsons, Talcott
Riesman, David
Ross, Edward Alsworth
Shils, Edward Albert
Simmel, Georg
Small, Albion W(oodbury)
Sorokin, Pitirim
  A(lexandrovitch)
Stouffer, Samuel A.
Sumner, William Graham
Taeuber, Conrad F.
Tarde, Gabriel
Taylor, Graham
Teggart, Frederick J.
Thomas, W(illiam) I(saac)
Tonnies, Ferdinand
Touraine, Alain (Louis)
Troeltsch, Ernst
Vasconcelos (Calderon),
  Jose
Wallas, Graham
Ward, Lester Frank
Webb, Beatrice Potter
Weber, Max
Wilson, Logan
Wilson, William Julius
Woodson, Robert L.
Work, Monroe (Nathan)
Yankelovich, Daniel
Znaniecki, Florian

SOFTBALL PLAYER

Stofflet, Ty(rone Earl)

SOLDIER

Antony, Marc
Ashikaga, Takauji
Ataturk, Kemal
Bayard, Pierre du Terrail
Berlichingen, Gotz von
Blair, Francis Preston, Jr.
Boulanger, Georges Ernest
  Jean Marie
Bowie, Jim
Brant, Joseph
Brock, Isaac, Sir
Bunau-Varilla, Philippe
  Jean
Burnaby, Frederick
  Gustavus
Butler, Matthew Calbraith
Butterford, Daniel
Carlson, Evans Fordyce
Castillo, Bernal Diaz del
Chauvin, Nicholas
Chesney, Francis Rawdon
Choiseul, Cesar, Comte
  Du Plessis-Praslin, duc
  de
Cid, El
Clark, George Rogers
Cleaveland, Moses
Clive, Robert
Cordoba, Francisco
  Fernandez
Coriolanus, Gaius
Cui, Cesar Antonovich
Cyrano de Bergerac,
  Savinien de
D'Annunzio, Gabriele
Davis, Sam(uel)
Dayan, Moshe
Delany, Martin Robinson
Denison, George Taylor
Dix, John Adams
Douglas, Keith Castellain
Edmonds, Emma E
Ercilla y Zuniga, Alonso
  de
Farnese, Alessandro
Fastolf, John, Sir
Fawkes, Guy
Fiske, Billy
Flipper, Henry Ossian
Francisco, Peter
Frontinus, Sextus Julius
Garibaldi, Giuseppe
Garwood, Robert Russell
Germain, George Sackville
Godfrey of Bouillon
Gorgas, Josiah
Hayes, Ira Hamilton
Hertzog, James Barry
  Munnik
Hoess, Rudolf Franz
Iberville, Pierre Le
  Moyne, Sieur d'
Johnson, Henry
Juin, Alphonse Pierre
Kosciuszko, Thaddeus
Laing, Alexander Gordon

LaTour D'Auvergne,
  Theophile de
la Verendrye, Sieur de
Lawrence, T(homas)
  E(dward)
Lea, Homer
L'Enfant, Pierre Charles
Li Hung-Chang
Logan, John Alexander
Lubbock, Francis Richard
Maclean, George
Mahone, William
Manrique, Jorge
Marchand, Jean-Baptiste
Matlovich, Leonard P., Jr.
McNaughton, Andrew
Mihajlovic, Dragoliub
Miranda, Francisco de
Moltke, Helmuth Karl
  Bernhard von
Monash, John
Mosby, John Singleton
Munchhausen, Hieronymus
  Karl Friedrich von,
  Baron
Narvaez, Panfilo de
Nelson, Thomas, Jr.
Nevski, Alexander, Saint
Norfolk, 3d Duke of
Northumberland, Duke of
Obregon, Alvaro
O'Higgins, Bernardo
Onoda, Hiroo
Quantrill, William Clarke
Rathbun-Nealy, Melissa
Renault, Gilbert (Leon
  Etienne Theodore)
Richelieu, Louis Francois
  Armand de
Rogers, Robert
Rohm, Ernst
Rutgers, Henry
St. Clair, Arthur
Sampson, Deborah
Sassoon, Siegfried
Selfridge, Thomas Etholen
Shays, Daniel
Sickles, Daniel Edgar
Sidney, Philip, Sir
Slovik, Eddie
Smuts, Jan Christian
Steuben, Friedrich
  Wilhelm Ludolf
  Gerhard Augustin,
  Baron
Stevens, Albert William
Treptow, Martin A
Urban, Matt
Valdivia, Pedro de
Velazquez de Cuellar,
  Diego
Villehardouin, Geffroi de
Voroshilov, Kliment
  Efremovich
Wallace, Lew(is)
Wayne, Anthony
Whipple, William
York, Sergeant
Younghusband, Francis
  Edward
Zeppelin, Ferdinand Adolf
  August Heinrich von,
  Count
Zumwalt, Elmo Russell,
  III

SONGWRITER

Adams, Frank Ramsay
Allen, Deborah
Allen, Peter Woolnough
Allen, Rex E., Sr.
Allen, Steve
Allison, Mose
Alvin, Dave
Amos, Tori
Anderson, Bill
Anka, Paul
Anthony, Ray
Arlen, Harold
Armatrading, Joan
Armstrong, Billie Joe
Artist Formerly Known as
 Prince, The
Ashford, Nickolas
Auger, Brian
Austin, Dallas
Austin, Gene
Axton, Hoyt (Wayne)
Balin, Marty
Barrett, Syd
Barrow, Keith E
Basia
Becaud, Gilbert (Francois
 Silly)
Beck
Beefheart, Captain
Berg, Matraca
Berry, Chuck
Berry, Richard
Bishop, Stephen
Black, Clint
Blades, Ruben, Jr.
Blige, Mary J(ane)
Bofill, Angela
Bonds, Gary U S
Bono
Bonoff, Karla
Bowie, David
Bowling, Roger
Brady, Paul Joseph
Bragg, Billy
Brel, Jacques
Brooks, Garth
Brown, Bobby
Brown, Lew
Brown, Nacio Herb
Brown, Peter
Browne, Jackson
Bryant, Boudleaux
Bryant, Felice
Buck, Gene
Buckley, Tim
Buffett, Jimmy
Burke, Johnny
Burleigh, Harry Thacker
Bush, Kate
Byrd, William
Caesar, Irving
Cale, J J
Callen, Michael
Carey, Mariah
Carmichael, Hoagy
Carnes, Kim
Carpenter, Mary Chapin
Carpenter, Richard Lynn
Carter, Carlene
Carter, Mother Maybelle
Carter, Wilf
Cash, Johnny
Cave, Nicholas Edward
Chapin, Harry Foster

Chaplin, Saul
Chapman, Tracy
Charles, Ray
Christian, Meg
Clark, Guy
Clark, Roy Linwood
Clegg, Johnny
Clements, Vassar
Cliff, Jimmy
Cobb, Will D
Cochran, Eddie
Coe, David Allan
Cohen, Leonard Norman
Cole, Lloyd
Coleman, Cy
Collins, Albert
Connick, Harry, Jr.
Conrad, Con
Cooper, Alice
Coots, J Fred
Cope, Julian
Copeland, Stewart
Corgan, Billy
Cornell, Chris
Coslow, Sam
Costello, Elvis
Cray, Robert
Creed, Linda
Croce, Jim
Crofts, Dash
Crosby, David (Van
 Cortlandt)
Crosby, Fanny
Cross, Christopher
Crouch, Andrae Edward
Crow, Sheryl
Crowell, Rodney
Daniels, Charlie
Davis, Mac
Dayne, Taylor
Dearie, Blossom
Denver, John
DeRose, Peter
DeShannon, Jackie
DeSylva, Buddy
Dexter, Al
Diamond, Neil
Dibdin, Charles
Dibdin, Thomas Pitt
Dickens, Little Jimmy
Diddley, Bo
Dietz, Howard M
Diffie, Joe
DiFranco, Ani
Dillon, William A
DiMeola, Al
Dion
Dixon, Willie (James)
Dobkin, Alix
Doggett, Bill
Donaldson, Walter
Donovan
Dragon, Daryl
Drake, Nick
Driftwood, Jimmy
Dube, Lucky
Dunn, Holly
D'Urfey, Thomas
Dylan, Bob
Edmonds, Kenneth
Edwards, Gus
Edwards, Joan
Egan, Raymond B
Egan, Walter Lindsay
Elfman, Danny
Ellington, Duke

Emmett, Daniel Decatur
Escovedo, Alejandro
Etheridge, Melissa
Fagen, Donald
Fahey, John
Fargo, Donna
Farrell, Wes
Fela
Felder, Don(ald William)
Fender, Freddy
Ferry, Bryan
Fields, Dorothy
Finch, Rick
Fiorito, Ted
Firbank, Louis
Florence, William Jermyn
Foster, David
Frampton, Peter Kenneth
Franklin, Irene
Frazier, Dallas June
Freed, Alan
Freed, Arthur
Frey, Glenn
Gabriel, Peter
Gamble, Kenny
Garner, Erroll
Gates, David
Gatlin, Larry Wayne
Gaudio, Bob
Gentry, Bobbie
George, Don
Gibb, Andy
Gibb, Barry
Gibb, Maurice
Gibb, Robin
Gibson, Deborah (Ann)
Gibson, Don(ald)
Gill, Vince(nt Grant)
Goldsboro, Bobby
Goodman, Steve(n
 Benjamin)
Gordy, Emory, Jr.
Gorka, John
Greco, Buddy
Green, Adolf
Green, Al(bert Leornes)
Green, Johnny
Greenbaum, Norman
Greenfield, Howard
Greenwood, Lee
Griffith, Nanci
Guion, David Wendel
 Fentress
Guthrie, Woody
Haggard, Merle Ronald
Hall, Tom T
Hamilton, Nancy
Handy, W(illiam)
 C(hristopher)
Hardin, Tim
Harding, John Wesley
Harper, Ben
Harris, Emmylou
Harrison, George
Hartford, John Cowan
Hartman, Dan
Harvey, Polly Jean
Hathaway, Donny
Hawkins, Erskine
 (Ramsey)
Hayes, Isaac
Hays, Lee
Hazelwood, Lee
Healey, Jeff
Hedges, Michael
Hellerman, Fred

Henderson, Ray
Henley, Don
Henry, Joe
Herman, Jerry
Herzog, Arthur, Jr.
Hiatt, John
Higgins, Bertie
Hill, Billy
Hill, Joe
Hill, Lauryn
Hitchcock, Robyn
Holly, Buddy
Holmes, Rupert
Hornsby, Bruce
Howard, Eddy
Howard, Joseph Edgar
Howlin' Wolf
Huff, Leon
Hunter, Alberta
Hunter, Ivory Joe
Hynde, Chrissie
Ian, Janis
Iglesias, Julio
Ingram, James
Isaak, Chris
Jackson, Alan Eugene
Jackson, Freddie
Jackson, Michael Joseph
Jagger, Mick
James, Rick
Jarreau, Al(wyn Lopez)
Jeffreys, Garland
Joel, Billy
Johansen, David
John, Elton
Johnson, James Price
Jones, Isham
Jones, Rickie Lee
Jones, Tom
Kahn, Gus
Kane, Big Daddy
Keith, Toby
Kenny, Nick
King, Carole
King, Freddy
Krause, Bernie
Kravitz, Lenny
Kristofferson, Kris
Lane, Ronnie
Lang, K(atherine) D(awn)
Lavin, Christine
Leadbelly
Lehrer, Tom
Leigh, Carolyn
Lennon, John Winston
Leslie, Edgar
Lightfoot, Gordon
 Meredith
Livingston, Jerry
Lofgren, Nils
Loggins, Kenny
Lombardo, Carmen
Love, Courtney
Loveless, Patty
Lovett, Lyle
Lynn, Loretta
Lynne, Shelby
Maccoll, Ewan
Manchester, Melissa Toni
Manilow, Barry
Marks, Johnny
Marley, Rita
Marley, Ziggy
Martin, Jimmy
Massey, D Curtis
Mattea, Kathy

Maxwell
Mayfield, Curtis (Lee)
McCartney, Paul
McCurdy, Ed
McDonald, Country Joe
McDonald, Michael
McHugh, Jimmy
McLean, Don
McMurtry, James
  Lawrence
McPartland, Margaret
  Marian
McVie, Christine Perfect
Melanie
Mellencamp, John
Mercer, Johnny
Merchant, Natalie
Me'Shell Ndegeocello
Messina, Jim
Miller, Roger Dean
Mitchell, Joni
Monk, Thelonious Sphere,
  Jr.
Monroe, Bill
Montgomery, Melba
Morgan, Russ
Morissette, Alanis
Morrison, Jim
Morrison, Sterling
Morrison, Van
Morton, Jelly Roll
Mould, Bob
Murphey, Michael Martin
Myles, Alannah
Nascimento, Milton
Near, Holly
Nelson, Willie
Nesmith, Mike
Newley, Anthony
  (George)
Newman, Randy
Newton, John
Nicks, Stevie
Niles, John Jacob
Nilsson
Nolan, Bob
Norworth, Jack
Novello, Ivor
Nyro, Laura
Oates, John William
Ocasek, Ric
O'Connor, Sinead
Olcott, Chauncey
Osborne, Joan
Parker, Graham
Parks, Van Dyke
Parsons, Gram
Parton, Dolly (Rebecca)
Paxton, Tom
Payne, Leon
Penn, Michael
Penner, Fred
Perkins, Carl (Lee)
Pettiford, Oscar
Petty, Tom
Phair, Liz
Pickett, Wilson
Pirner, Dave
Pitney, Gene
Plant, Robert Anthony
Price, Alan
Prine, John
Rabbitt, Eddie
Rafferty, Gerry
Raffi
Raitt, Bonnie

Redding, Otis
Reddy, Helen
Reed, Jerry
Reed, Lou
Reid, Vernon
Ritenour, Lee
Robertson, Don
Robinson, Smokey
Rodgers, Jimmie
Rome, Harold J(acob)
Rose, David
Rose, Vincent
Rouget de Lisle, Claude
  Joseph
Ruby, Harry
Rucker, Darius
Rush, Tom
Sager, Carole Bayer
Sanders, Marty
Sangare, Oumou
Sauter, Eddie
Schwartz, Arthur
Schwartz, Jean
Scott, Raymond
Scruggs, Earl Eugene
Seal
Seals, Dan Wayland
Seals, Jim
Sedaka, Neil
Seeger, Pete(r)
Shannon, Del
Shocked, Michelle
Siberry, Jane
Simmons, Pat(rick)
Simon, Carly
Simon, Paul
Smith, Bessie
Smith, William
South, Joe
Souther, J(ohn) D(avid)
Speaks, Oley
Springsteen, Bruce
Stafford, Jim
Stanley, Ralph Edmond
Stevens, Cat
Stewart, John
Stewart, Wynn
Stills, Stephen
Sting
Stipe, Michael
Stone, Doug
Stookey, Paul
Straw, Syd
Stuart, Marty
Styne, Jule
Summers, Andy
Sweet, Matthew
Swift, Kay
Taj Mahal
Taylor, James Vernon
Taylor, KoKo
Thomas, Rufus
Thornhill, Claude
Tikaram, Tanita
Tillis, Mel(vin)
Tillis, Pam
Tomlin, Pinky
Torme, Mel(vin Howard)
Trenet, Charles
Tricky
Tritt, Travis
Trotter, John Scott
Troup, Bobby
Trumbauer, Frank(ie)
Tubb, Ernest
Turner, Ike

Twain, Shania
Twitty, Conway
Tyson, Ian
Tyson, Sylvia Fricker
Vai, Steve
VanAlstyne, Egbert Anson
Van Heusen, Jimmy
Vannelli, Gino
Van Shelton, Ricky
Vedder, Eddie
Vega, Suzanne
VonTilzer, Harry
Vysotsky, Vladimir
  Semyonovich
Waite, John
Waits, Tom
Wakely, Jimmy
Walker, Jimmy
Walker, T-Bone
Waller, Fats
Walter, Cyril
Wariner, Steve
Warren, Harry
Welch, Ken
Welch, Mitzie
Wenrich, Percy
Westerman, Floyd
White, Barry
Whitley, Keith
Williams, Hank
Williams, Lucinda
Williams, Paul Hamilton
Williams, Victoria
Wills, Bob
Wilson, Brian Douglas
Winchester, Jesse (James
  Ridout)
Withers, Bill
Womack, Bobby
Wonder, Stevie
Wray, Link
Wright, Syretta
Yearwood, Trisha
Yellen, Jack
Young, Victor
Zevon, Warren

SPECIAL EFFECTS TECHNICIAN

Edlund, Richard
Harryhausen, Ray
Muren, Dennis
O'Brien, Willis Harold
Whitlock, Albert
Zambelli, Joseph

SPECULATOR

Henderson, Richard

SPEECHWRITER

Edmonds, Terry

SPOKESPERSON

Fleming, Sandford

SPORTS EXECUTIVE

Angelos, Peter
Buss, Jerry Hatten
Byers, Walter
Coleman, Leonard S., Jr.
Ilitch, Mike
Jones, Jerry
O'Malley, Susan
Selig, Bud

SPORTS FISHERMAN

Wulff, Lee

SPORTS PROMOTER

McMahon, Vince, Jr.

SPORTSCASTER

Abdul-Jabbar, Kareem
Albert, Marv(in Philip)
Allen, Mel
Barber, Red
Barry, Rick
Bradshaw, Terry Paxton
Brodie, John Riley
Burton, Nelson, Jr.
Caray, Harry
Cauthen, Steve
Cefalo, Jimmy
Cherry, Don(ald Stewart)
Cosell, Howard
Costas, Bob
Dean, Dizzy
Dierdorf, Dan(iel Lee)
Donnellan, Nanci
Drysdale, Don(ald Scott)
Esiason, Boomer
Firestone, Roy
Flemming, Bill
Garagiola, Joe
George, Phyllis
Gifford, Frank
Gowdy, Curt(is)
Gumbel, Greg(ory)
Hickman, Fred(erick
  Douglass)
Hill, Jimmy
Husing, Ted
Jenner, Bruce
Kaline, Al(bert William)
Kell, George (Clyde)
Kelly, Dan
Kiner, Ralph McPherran
Kubek, Tony
Lynn, Fred(ric Michael)
Madden, John
Martyn, Bruce
McCarthy, Clem
McKay, Jim
Meeker, Howie
Meredith, Don
Michaels, Al
Most, Johnny
Musburger, Brent Woody
Namath, Joe

Mazarin, Jules, Cardinal
M'Bow, Mahtar-Amadou
McNary, Charles Linza
Mendes-France, Pierre
Metternich-Winneburg,
  Clemens
Milner, Alfred, Viscount
Mirabeau, Honore Gabriel
  Riquetti
Moltke, Helmuth Karl
  Bernhard von
More, Thomas, Sir
Morgan, Henry, Sir
Morris, Gouverneur
Morrison of Lambeth,
  Herbert Stanley
  Morrison, Baron
Murphy, Robert Daniel
Nagy, Imre
Nansen, Fridtjof
Necker, Jacques
Nguyen Van Thieu
Nicolson, Harold George,
  Sir
Norwich, Alfred Duff
  Cooper, Viscount
Obregon, Alvaro
O'Higgins, Bernardo
Paderewski, Ignace Jan
Palmerston, Henry John
  Temple, Viscount
Paul-Boncour, Joseph
Peel, Robert, Sir
Perez de Cuellar, Javier
Pericles
Petain, Henri Philippe
Petitpierre, Max
Pilsudski, Jozef
Pinay, Antoine
Pinckney, Charles
  Cotesworth
Pleven, Rene Jean
Pliny the Younger
Poincare, Raymond
Pompey the Great
Prado Ugarteche, Manuel
Queensberry, William
  Douglas, Duke
Rabin, Yitzhak
Raffles, Thomas Stamford,
  Sir
Randolph, Edmund
  Jennings
Randolph, John
Rhee, Syngman
Richard, Duke of York
Richelieu, Armand Jean
  du Plessis, Cardinal
Romulo, Carlos Pena
Root, Elihu
Rosebery, Archibald Philip
  Primrose, Earl
Salazar, Antonio de
  Oliveira
Salisbury, Robert Arthur
  Talbot, 3rd Marquess
Sandys, Edwin, Sir
San Martin, Jose de
Schuman, Robert
Schuyler, Philip John
Senanayake, Dudley
  Shelton
Seneca, Lucius Annaeus,
  the Younger
Sforza, Carlo

Shaftesbury, Anthony
  Ashley Cooper, Earl
Shastri, Lal Badahur
Sidney, Philip, Sir
Smuts, Jan Christian
Soong, T V
Southampton, Henry
  Wriothesley, Earl
Spruance, Raymond Ames
Stanton, Edwin McMasters
Stresemann, Gustav
Sully, Maximilien de
  Bethune, Duc
Sykes, Mark, Sir
Talleyrand-Perigord,
  Charles Maurice de
Tanner, Valno Alfred
Thant, U
Thiers, Adolphe
Thou, Jacques Auguste de
Toombs, Robert Augustus
U'Ren, William Simon
Vandervelde, Emile
Venizelos, Eleutherios
  Kyriakos
Waldheim, Kurt
Waldock, Humphrey
  Meredith, Sir
Waller, William, Sir
Walpole, Robert
Walsingham, Francis, Sir
Webster, Daniel
Wellington, Arthur
  Wellesley, Duke
Wilson, (James) Harold,
  Sir
Witte, Sergey Yulyevich
Worner, Manfred
Zaleski, August

STATISTICIAN

Fisher, R(onald) A(ylmer)
Mayo-Smith, Richmond
Ogburn, W(illiam)
  F(ielding)
Quetelet, Lambert Adolphe
  Jacques
Stouffer, Samuel A.
Wright, Carroll Davidson

STOCKBROKER

Fletcher, Alfonso, Jr.

STUDENT

Bakke, Allan Paul
Biehl, Amy
Billings, Grace Bedell
Bridgman, Laura Dewey
Faulkner, Shannon
Grant, Charity
Holdereid, Kristine
Martinez, Andrew
O'Hanlon, Virginia
Smith, Samantha

STUNT
PERFORMER

Barrett, Stan
Canutt, Yakima
Goodrich, Bert
Knievel, Evel
Knievel, Robbie
Needham, Hal
Petit, Philippe
Willig, George

SUFFRAGIST

Addams, Jane
Anthony, Susan
  B(rownell)
Belmont, Alva Erskine
  Smith Vanderbilt
Bugbee, Emma
Duniway, Abigail Jane
  Scott
Miller, Elizabeth Smith
Pankhurst, Christabel
  Harriette, Dame
Pankhurst, Emmeline
  Goulden
Pankhurst, Sylvia
Park, Maud May Wood
Rankin, Jeannette
Robinson, Harriet Jane
  Hanson
Shaw, Anna Howard
Stone, Lucy
Wright, Elizur

SUPREME COURT
JUSTICE

Bartlett, Josiah
Black, Hugo LaFayette
Blackmun, Harry
  A(ndrew)
Blatchford, Samuel
Bradley, Joseph P
Brandeis, Louis Dembitz
Brennan, William Joseph,
  Jr.
Brewer, David Josiah
Breyer, Stephen Gerald
Burger, Warren E(arl)
Cardozo, Benjamin Nathan
Chase, Salmon Portland
Chase, Samuel
Clark, Tom
Clifford, Nathan
Davis, David
Day, William Rufus
Douglas, William Orville
Ellsworth, Oliver
Field, Stephen Johnson
Fortas, Abe
Frankfurter, Felix
Ginsburg, Ruth Bader
Goldberg, Arthur Joseph
Gray, Horace
Grier, Robert Cooper
Harlan, John Marshall, I
Harlan, John Marshall, II
Holmes, Oliver Wendell,
  Jr.
Hughes, Charles Evans

Jackson, Robert
  Houghwout
Jay, John
Johnson, William
Kennedy, Anthony
  McLeod
Lamar, Joseph Rucker
Lamar, Lucius Quintus
  Cincinnatus
Lurton, Horace Harmon
Marshall, John
Marshall, Thurgood
Matthews, Stanley
Minton, Sherman
Murphy, Frank
O'Connor, Sandra Day
Paterson, William
Powell, Lewis F(ranklin),
  Jr.
Reed, Stanley Forman
Rehnquist, William Hubbs
Scalia, Antonin
Shiras, George, Jr.
Souter, David Hackett
Stevens, John Paul
Stewart, Potter
Stone, Harlan Fiske
Story, Joseph
Swayne, Noah Haynes
Taney, Roger Brooke
Thomas, Clarence
Van Devanter, Willis
Vinson, Frederick Moore
Waite, Morrison Remick
Warren, Earl
White, Byron Raymond
White, Edward Douglass
Wilson, Bertha
Wilson, James
Woodbury, Levi

SURGEON

Adair, Frank E(arl)
Agnew, David Hayes
Agpaoa, Tony
Albright, Tenley Emma
Barber, Jesse B., Jr.
Barnard, Christiaan
  Neethling
Bates, Mary Elizabeth
Bell, Charles
Bell, Joseph
Bethune, Norman
Billroth, Theodore
Blalock, Alfred
Brinkley, John Romulus
Brown, Dorothy Lavinia
Callender, Clive O(rville)
Canady, Alexa I(rene)
Carrel, Alexis
Carson, Benjamin S.
Castroviejo, Ramon
Charnley, John, Sir
Cheyne, William Watson,
  Sir
Cooley, Denton Arthur
Cooper, Astley Paston, Sir
Crile, George Washington
Crile, George Washington,
  Jr.
Cushing, Harvey Williams
Davis, John Staige
Davis, Loyal
DeBakey, Michael Ellis

TEACHER

Adler, Guido
Anastas, Robert
Auer, Leopold
Beauchamp, Pierre
Boulanger, Nadia Juliette
Braille, Louis
Brown, Charlie
Burchenal, Elizabeth
Collins, Marva Deloise
  Nettles
Corson, Juliet
Delano, Jane Arminda
Eliot, John
Escalante, Jaime
Fillmore, Abigail (Powers)
Flesch, Karl
Galamian, Ivan
Gallaudet, Thomas
  Hopkins
Garcia, Manuel Patricio
  Rodriguez
Hidalgo, Elvira de
Isocrates
Jagel, Frederick
Kinmont, Jill
Lamperti, Francesco
Lhevinne, Josef
Lhevinne, Rosina L
Liebling, Estelle
Lowenstein, Allard
  Kenneth
Mannes, David
Mason, Lowell
Maurel, Victor
McAuliffe, Christa
Ochsner, Alton
Olcott, Henry Steel
Quinn, Arthur Hobson
Russell, Henry
Schoen-Rene, Anna
Scopes, John Thomas
Shanker, Albert
Sharp, Zerna A
Sullivan, Anne
Thompson, Randall
Walker, Adam

TENNIS PLAYER

Agassi, Andre
Allen, Leslie
Amaya, Victor
Arias, Jimmy
Ashe, Arthur
Austin, Tracy Ann
Barker, Sue
Becker, Boris
Betz, Pauline
Borg, Bjorn Rune
Borotra, Jean Robert
Brough, Louise Althea
Brugnon, Jacques
Budge, Don
Bueno, Maria Ester
  Audion
Capriati, Jennifer
Casals, Rosemary
Cash, Pat(rick)
Chang, Michael
Clerc, Jose-Luis
Cochet, Henri
Connolly, Maureen
Connors, Jimmy

Courier, Jim
Court, Margaret
Cramm, Gottfried von,
  Baron
Curren, Kevin
Dent, Phil
Denton, Steve
Dibbs, Eddie
Durie, Jo
Edberg, Stefan
Emerson, Roy
Evert, Chris(tine Marie)
Fibak, Wojtek
Fleming, Peter
Fromholtz, Dianne
Garrison, Zina
Gerulaitis, Vitas
Gibson, Althea
Gonzalez, Pancho
Goolagong, Evonne
Gottfried, Brian
Graebner, Clark
Graf, Steffi
Hanika, Sylvia
Hoad, Lew(is A.)
Hu Na
Jacobs, Helen (Hull)
Jaeger, Andrea
Jausovec, Mima
Jordan, Kathy
King, Billie Jean
Kramer, Jack
Krickstein, Aaron
Kriek, Johann
Lacoste, Rene
Laver, Rod(ney George)
Lendl, Ivan
Lenglen, Suzanne
Lewis, Chris
Lloyd, John
Lutz, Bob
Mallory, Molla
Mandlikova, Hana
Marble, Alice
Mayer, Gene
Mayer, Sandy
McEnroe, John Patrick, Jr.
McKinley, Chuck
McNeil, Lori
Moody, Helen Wills
Muster, Thomas
Nastase, Ilie
Navratilova, Martina
Newcombe, John
Noah, Yannick Simon
  Camille
Orantes, Manuel
Parker, Frank
Pierce, Mary
Ramirez, Raul
Richards, Rene
Riggs, Bobby
Rinaldi, Kathy
Rosewall, Ken(neth R)
Ruzici, Virginia
Sabatini, Gabriela
Sampras, Pete(r)
Sanchez-Vicario, Arantxa
Sears, Richard Dudley
Sedgman, Frank
Segura, Pancho
Seles, Monica
Shriver, Pam(ela Howard)
Simionescu, Mariana
Smith, Stan(ley Roger)
Solomon, Harold Charles

Stich, Michael
Stockton, Dick
Stove, Betty
Tanner, Roscoe
Teacher, Brian
Tilden, Bill
Trabert, Tony
Turnbull, Wendy
Van Patten, Vince(nt)
Vilas, Guillermo
Vines, Ellsworth
Wade, Virginia
Washington, MaliVai
Wightman, Hazel Virginia
  Hotchkiss
Wilander, Mats
Williams, Serena
Williams, Venus (Ebone
  Starr)

TENNIS PLAYERS

Four Musketeers, The

TERRORIST

Abu Daoud
Agca, Mehmet Ali
Baader, Andreas
Carols
Debus, Sigurd Friedrich
Kaczynski, Theodore
  (John)
Meinhof, Ulrike Marie
Nidal, Abu

TEST TUBE BABY

Brown, Louise Joy
Carr, Elizabeth Jordan

THEATER OWNER

Albee, Edward Franklin
Ames, Winthrop
Grauman, Sid(ney Patrick)
Henslowe, Philip
Hill, Abram
Loew, Marcus
Nederlander, James
  Morton
Schoenfeld, Gerald
Shubert, Lee

THEOLOGIAN

Abarbanel, Isaac Ben
  Jehudah
Abduh ibn Hasan Khayr
  Allah, Muhammad
Abelard, Pierre
Adams, James Luther
Alcuin
Altizer, Thomas
  J(onathan) J(ackson)
Arius
Arminius, Jacobus

Ashari, Abu al-Hasan Ali
  al-
Baillie, D(onald)
  M(acpherson)
Baillie, John
Barth, Karl
Baur, Ferdinand Christian
Baxter, Richard
Bede the Venerable, Saint
Bellarmine, Robert, Saint
Berdyayev, Nikolay
  Aleksandrovich
Berengar of Tours
Bernard of Clairvaux
Boff, Leonardo
Bonhoeffer, Dietrich
Brunner, Emil
Bultmann, Rudolf
Burnet, Gilbert
Butler, Joseph
Calvin, John
Casaubon, Isaac
Chalmers, Thomas
Charron, Pierre
Chauncy, Charles
Clarke, Samuel
Clement of Alexandria
Colet, John
Cone, James H
Cox, Harvey Gallagher, Jr.
Cumberland, Richard
Curran, Charles E(dward)
Daly, Mary
Dodd, Charles Harold
Dollinger, J(ohannes)
  J(osef) I(gnaz) von
Duns Scotus, John
Eck, Johann Maier von
Edwards, Jonathan
Eliade, Mircea
Fenelon, Francois de
  Salignac
Garrigou-Lagrange,
  Reginald Marie
Geiger, Abraham
Gerhardt, Paul(us)
Gilkey, Langdon Brown
Glueck, Nelson
Gutierrez, Gustavo
Harkness, Georgia (Elma)
Harnack, Adolf von
Herberg, Will
Hooker, Richard
Hopkins, Samuel
ibn Hazm, Abu
  Muhammad Ali
Innocent, III, Pope
Jansen, Cornelis Otto
John of Damascus, St.
Justin Martyr
Kitagawa, Joseph Mitsuo
Kohler, Kaufmann
Kung, Hans
Lanfranc
Lavater, Johann Casper
Llull, Ramon
Loisy, Alfred Firmin
Lombard, Peter
Lucaris, Cyril
Lull, Raymond
Malebranche, Nicolas
Manasseh ben Israel
Marcion
Maurice, Frederick
  Denison
Meland, Bernard Eugene

Tschernichowsky, Saul
Tyndale, William
Ulfilas
Weaver, William
Winnemucca, Sarah
Yen Fu

TRANSPLANT PATIENT

Blaiberg, Philip
Clark, Barney Bailey
Foster, Tabatha
Jones, Stormie
Schroeder, William J
Washkansky, Louis

TRANSSEXUAL

Bornstein, Kate
Eden, Elizabeth Debbie
Jorgensen, Christine
Richards, Rene

TRAVELER

Benjamin of Tudela
Bishop, Isabella Lucy Bird
Blunt, Wilfrid Scawen
Burnaby, Frederick
  Gustavus
Burton, Isabel Arundel
Carpini, Giovanni de
  Piano
Charlevoix, Pierre Francis
  Xavier de
Clark, Sydney
Cunninghame-Graham,
  Robert Bontine
Du Chaillu, Paul Belloni
Hickey, William
ibn Battuta, Muhammad
Ibn Batutah
Leo Africanus
Mandeville, John, Sir
Nordhoff, Charles Bernard
Polo, Marco
Royall, Anne Newport
Stephens, John Lloyd
Taylor, Bayard

TREASURE HUNTER

Fisher, Mel

TROUBADOR

Sordello

TYPE DESIGNER

Arrighi, Ludovico degli
Baskerville, John
Bernhard, Lucian
Bodoni, Giambattista

Caslon, William
Cassandre, A(dolphe)
  M(ouron)
Cochin, Charles Nicholas
Dwiggins, William
  Addison
Garamond, Claude
Goudy, Frederic William
Granjon, Robert
McMurtrie, Douglas C
Walker, Emery, Sir
Zapf, Hermann

US PRESIDENT

Adams, John
Adams, John Quincy
Arthur, Chester A(lan)
Buchanan, James
Bush, George (Herbert
  Walker)
Carter, Jimmy
Cleveland, Grover
Clinton, Bill
Coolidge, Calvin
Eisenhower, Dwight
  D(avid)
Fillmore, Millard
Ford, Gerald R(udolph)
Garfield, James Abram
Grant, Ulysses Simpson
Harding, Warren
  G(amaliel)
Harrison, Benjamin
Harrison, William Henry
Hayes, Rutherford
  B(irchard)
Hoover, Herbert C(lark)
Jackson, Andrew
Jefferson, Thomas
Johnson, Andrew
Johnson, Lyndon B(aines)
Kennedy, John
  F(itzgerald)
Lincoln, Abraham
Madison, James
McKinley, William
Monroe, James
Nixon, Richard M(ilhous)
Pierce, Franklin
Polk, James Knox
Reagan, Ronald (Wilson)
Roosevelt, Franklin
  D(elano)
Roosevelt, Theodore
Taft, William (Howard)
Taylor, Zachary
Truman, Harry S
Tyler, John
Van Buren, Martin
Washington, George
Wilson, Woodrow

US VICE PRESIDENT

Agnew, Spiro T(heodore)
Barkley, Alben William
Breckinridge, John Cabell
Burr, Aaron
Calhoun, John Caldwell
Clinton, George
Colfax, Schuyler

Curtis, Charles Brent
Dallas, George Mifflin
Dawes, Charles Gates
Fairbanks, Charles Warren
Garner, John Nance
Gerry, Elbridge
Gore, Albert, Jr.
Hamlin, Hannibal
Hendricks, Thomas
  Andrews
Hobart, Garret Augustus
Humphrey, Hubert
  Horatio, Jr.
Johnson, Richard Mentor
King, William Rufus de
  Vane
Marshall, Thomas Riley
Mondale, Walter
  F(rederick)
Morton, Levi Parsons
Rockefeller, Nelson
  A(ldrich)
Sherman, James
  Schoolcraft
Stevenson, Adlai Ewing
Tompkins, Daniel D
Wallace, Henry Agard
Wheeler, William Alrnon
Wilson, Henry

UNION ORGANIZER

Corona, Bert

UNIVERSITY ADMINISTRATOR

Angell, James Burrill
Angell, James Rowland
Armstrong, Samuel
  Chapman
Bloustein, Edward J.
Bluitt, Juliann S.
Bok, Derek Curtis
Bond, Horace Mann
Bordeaux, Lionel R.
Boren, David (Lyle)
Bowman, Isaiah
Brademas, John
Brattle, Thomas
Brewster, Kingman, Jr.
Bunting, Mary Ingraham
Bush-Brown, Albert
Carlson, William S(amuel)
Casper, Gerhard
Cheek, James Edward
Cobb, Jewel Plummer
Cole, Johnnetta Betsch
Compton, Wilson
  Martindale
Conant, James Bryant
Connerly, Ward
Cook, Samuel DuBois
Cubberley, Ellwood
  Patterson
Currie, Arthur William
Curry, Jabez Lamar
  Monroe
Dew, Thomas Roderick
Dunster, Henry
Eisenhower, Milton Stover
Elliott, Osborn

Freedman, James Oliver
Futter, Ellen Victoria
Giamatti, A(ngelo) Bartlett
Goheen, Robert Francis
Gonzalez, Jose Ramon
Gregorian, Vartan
Hadley, Arthur Twining
Hannah, John Alfred
Healy, Timothy S(tafford)
Henry, David D(odds)
Hesburgh, Theodore
  Martin
Hitch, Charles J(ohnston)
Hitchcock, Edward
Holt, A(ndrew) D(avid,
  Jr.)
Humphries, Frederick (S.)
Jenifer, Franklyn Green
Johnson, Charles Spurgeon
Johnson, Mordecai Wyatt
Jordan, David Starr
Jordan, I(rving) King
Kean, Thomas Howard
Keohane, Nannerl
  Overholser
Kerr, Malcolm (Hooper)
Kibbee, Robert Joseph
Kilpatrick, William
  H(eard)
Kirk, Grayson Louis
Lewis, Shirley A(nn)
  R(edd)
Low, Seth
Lowell, Abbott Lawrence
Lyttle, Hulda Margaret
Mackay, John Alexander
Mahan, Asa
Malloy, Edward Aloysius
Malott, Deane W(aldo)
Manley, Audrey Forbes
Marshak, Robert E(ugene)
Mather, Increase
Mayer, Jean
McCosh, James
McGill, William James
Meiklejohn, Alexander
Millett, John D(avid)
Murphy, Franklin D(avid)
Neilson, William A(llan)
Oppenheimer, Harry
  Frederick
Patterson, Frederick
  Douglass
Reid, Irvin D.
Remsen, Ira
Rodin, Judith
Russell, James Earl
Schmidt, Benno C(harles),
  Jr.
Scott, Gloria Dean Randle
Sellinger, Joseph A
Shalala, Donna Edna
Shapiro, Harold Tafler
Silber, John Robert
Sinkford, Jeanne C(raig)
Severn, Michael I(ra)
Spikes, Dolores
Sterling, John Ewart
  Wallace
Stoodard, George
  Dinsmore
Sudarkasa, Niara
Tedder, Arthur William
Tedder, Baron
Walker, LeRoy Tashreau
Walsh, Michael Patrick

Wharton, Clifton Reginald,
  Jr.
White, Andrew Dickson
Williams, Gregory
  (Howard)

URBAN PLANNER

Cooper, Alexander
Douglass, Lathrop
Howard, Ebenezer, Sir
Levitt, William J(aird)
Llewelyn-Davies, Richard
Mayer, Albert
Pereira, William Leonard
Rouse, James W(ilson)
Stein, Clarence S

VENTRILOQUIST

Bergen, Edgar John
Flowers, Wayland Parrott,
  Jr.
Lewis, Shari
Winchell, Paul

VETERANS'
LEADER

Scruggs, Jan
Willson, S Brian

VETERINARIAN

Herriot, James
Redig, Patrick

VICTIM

Bergalis, Kimberly
Berger, David
Bichler, Joyce
Buttafuoco, Mary Jo
Cruzan, Nancy
Denny, Reginald
Fonyo, Steve
Fox, Terry
Friedman, Ze'ev
Genovese, Kitty
Goldman, Ronald Lyle
Gutfreund, Yosef
Halfin, Eliezer
Hearst, Patty
Iceman
King, Rodney G
Kingsley, Gregory
Little, Joan
Quinlan, Karen Ann
Rogers, Mary Cecilia
Romano, Joseph
Shapira, Amitzur
Shorr, Kehat
Simpson, Nicole Brown
Slavin, Mark
Spitzer, Andre
Springer, Ya'acov
Till, Emmett (Louis)
Von Bulow, Sunny

Weinberg, Moshe
White, Ryan
Zumwalt, Elmo Russell,
  III

VINTNER

Gallo, Ernest
Gallo, Julio
Masson, Paul
Petri, Angelo
Rothschild, Philippe de,
  Baron
Sebastiani, Samuele
Taylor, Walter

VIOLIN MAKER

Amati
Amati, Nicolo
Guarneri, Giuseppe
  Antonio
Stradivari, Antonio

VIOLINIST

Albinoni, Tommaso
Anderson, Laurie
Auer, Leopold
Bauer, Harold
Boccherini, Luigi
Cerovsek, Corey
Chang, Sarah Yong-chu
Clements, Vassar
Corelli, Arcangelo
Doucet, Michael
Elman, Mischa
Enesco, Georges
Flesch, Karl
Fodor, Eugene Nicholas
Fuchs, Joseph (Philip)
Geminiani, Francesco
Germano, Lisa
Gingold, Josef
Glenn, Carroll
Heifetz, Jascha
Hubay, Jeno
Huberman, Bronislaw
Joachim, Joseph
Kaufman, Louis
Kennedy, Nigel Paul
Kreisler, Fritz
Kubelik, Jan
Lamoureux, Charles
Laredo, Jaime
Lipinski, Carl
Locatelli, Pietro Antonio
Loeffler, Charles Martin
  Tornow
Maazel, Lorin Varencove
Mannes, David
Marriner, Neville
McDuffie, Robert
Menuhin, Yehudi
Midori
Milstein, Nathan
Mischakoff, Mischa
Oistrakh, David
  Fyodorovich
Oistrakh, Igor Davidovich
Paganini, Niccolo
Perlman, Itzhak

Piastro, Michel
Ponty, Jean-Luc
Powell, Maud
Primrose, William
Rabin, Michael
Ricci, Ruggiero
Rode, Jacques Pierre
  Joseph
Salerno-Sonnenberg, Nadja
Sarasate, Pablo de
Shaham, Gil
Spalding, Albert
Spivakov, Valdimir
  (Teodorovich)
Spohr, Louis Ludwig
Stern, Isaac
Stoessel, Albert
Strauss, Johann, Jr.
Suk, Josef
Suzuki, Shin'ichi
Szeryng, Henryk
Szigeti, Joseph
Tartini, Giuseppe
Wieniawski, Henri
Ysaye, Eugene
Zabach, Florian
Zimbalist, Efrem
Zukerman, Pinchas

VOLLEYBALL
PLAYER

Kiraly, Karch

VOLUNTEER

Hebard, Caroline

WARRIOR

Little Wolf
Mzilikazi
Nobunaga, Oda

WAX MODELER

Tussaud, Marie Gresholtz,
  Madame

WEIGHTLIFTER

Alekseyev, Vasily
  Ivanovich
Hoffman, Robert C

WRESTLER

Baumgartner, Bruce
Dean, Man Mountain
Hogan, Hulk
Zaharias, George

WRITER

Ackerman, Diane

Adams, Cindy
Adelman, Sybil
Aflaq, Michel
Aga Khan, Sadruddin,
  Prince
Aksyonov, Vassily
  Pavlovich
Akutagawa Ryunosuke
Al-Amin, Jamil Abdullah
Alexie, Sherman
Altman, Dennis
Anderson, Harry
Anzaldua, Gloria
Arciniegas, German
Arnold, Tom
Baker, Houston A(lfred),
  Jr.
Bakhtin, Mikhail
  (Mikhailovich)
Bambara, Toni Cade
Barnes, Wade
Barry, Lynda
Bass, Rick
Bauer, Erwin Adam
Beam, Joseph
Beatts, Anne
Beatty, Roger
Bellisario, Donald P
Benezet, Anthony
Berendt, John
Berlin, Ellin (Mackay)
Beti, Mongo
Blessington, Marguerite
  Gardiner, Countess
Bloodworth-Thomason,
  Linda Joyce
Bochco, Steven Ronald
Bonnin, Gertrude
  Simmons
Boothroyd, John Basil
Bornstein, Kate
Boudjedra, Rachid
Branagh, Kenneth
  (Charles)
Brant, Beth
Braun, Lily von
  Kretschman
Bright, Susie
Brodkey, Harold
Brookner, Anita
Brooks, Albert (Lawrence
  Einstein)
Brosten, Harve
Brown, Sterling (Allen)
Buckley, Christopher
  (Taylor)
Bunch, Charlotte
Butler, Eleanor, Lady
Cabrera Infante, Guillermo
Califia, Pat
Campbell, Maria
Cannell, Stephen Joseph
Carruth, Hayden
Cary, Lorene
Castiglione, Baldassare,
  Conte
Cela (Trulock), Camilo
  Jose
Celsus, Aulus Cornelius
Charles, Glen
Charles, Lee
Chase, David
Chase-Riboud, Barbara
Chotzinoff, Samuel
Chrystos
Chubak, Sadeq-i

Clarke, Thomas Ernest
  Bennett
Cleese, John Marwood
Comer, James P(ierpont)
Connolly, Cyril Vernon
Conroy, Frank
Conway, Jill Kathryn Ker
Cooper, Annie
Cooper, Lester Irving
Correia, Natalia
Costigan, James
Craveirinha, Jose
Cullinan, Thomas P.
Dallis, Nicholas Peter
Dana, Margaret Bloxham
Danto, Arthur C(oleman)
David, Elizabeth
Davis, Peter Frank
De Bow, James
  Dunwoody Brownson
Decter, Midge
Delany, Annie Elizabeth
Delany, Sarah Louise
De La Torre(-Bueno),
  Lillian
Del Pilar, Marcelo Hilario
Denoff, Sam
Dershowitz, Alan M
Dew, Thomas Roderick
Djerassi, Carl
Dobzhansky, Theodosius
  (Grigorievich)
Dorris, Michael (Anthony)
Douglas, Marjory
  (Stoneman)
Drake, Daniel
Drucker, Peter Ferdinand
Duberman, Martin
Dworkin, Andrea
Dyer, Charles (Raymond)
Eames, Charles
Eastman, Charles
  Alexander
Eckstein, George
Ehrenreich, Barbara
Einstein, Bob
Epstein, Julius
Exley, Frederick (Earl)
Faderman, Lillian
Faludi, Susan
Ferguson, Sarah
  (Margaret)
Fisher, Carrie Frances
Flaherty, Joe
Flipper, Henry Ossian
Fontana, Tom
Foote, Shelby
Fox, Matthew (Timothy
  James)
Freeman, Seth
Friedrich, Otto
Frontinus, Sextus Julius
Fuisz, Robert E
Fussell, Paul
Garfinkle, Louis
Garrett, Lila
Garrison, Jim C.
Gillette, Paul
Gilliam, Terry (Vance)
Gilliatt, Penelope (Ann
  Douglas Conner)
Glancy, Diane
Goldberg, Gary David
Goldman, Albert
Gomez, Jewelle
Goodman, Linda

Goscinny, Rene
Grahn, Judy
Granick, Harry
Green, Gerald
Grieg, Nordahl Brun
Grizzard, Lewis M., Jr.
Grodin, Charles
Grosseteste, Robert
Guo Moruo
Gutzkow, Karl Ferdinand
Hamburger, Philip
Hare, Robert
Harman, Jeanne Perkins
Harris, Leonard
Heloise
Helper, Hinton Rowan
Heruy Walda-Sellase
Higgins, Colin
Hildesheimer, Wolfgang
Hillcourt, William
Hirsch, E(ric) D(onald), Jr.
Holland, Tom
Honwana, Luis Bernardo
Hooks, Bell
Hostos (y Bonilla),
  Eugenio Maria de
Huffington, Arianna
Hyde, Douglas
Ikeda, Daisaku
Ingold, Christopher Kelk,
  Sir
Ivins, Molly
James, Henry, Sr.
Janowitz, Tama
Jay, Karla
Jenkins, Sally
Johnson, Nicholas
Jones, Robert C
Jones, Terry
Josefsberg, Milt
Judd, Donald (Clarence)
Kahn, E(ly) J(acques), Jr.
Kane, Paul
Kanin, Fay
Kantrowitz, Arnie
Kaplan, Justin
Karenga, Maulana
Keen, Sam
Keyhoe, Donald E(dward)
Kinsley, Michael (E.)
Kirkwood, James
Klass, Perri Elizabeth
Knight, Etheridge
Kober, Arthur
Kohan, Buz
Kohout, Pavel
Krea, Henri
Kroker, Arthur
Kubly, Herbert (Oswald)
Kurtzman, Harvey
La Follette, Suzanne
Lamennais, Hugues
  Felicite Robert de
Landon, Michael
Lange, Christian Louis
Lapham, Lewis Henry
Lasky, Jesse Louis, Jr.
Lease, Mary Elizabeth
  Clyens
Lee, Laurie
Leonard, Daniel
Lester, Julius
Levi, Primo
Levinson, Richard
  Leighton
Lewis, David Levering

Liebman, Max
Lipsyte, Robert Mitchell
  Michael
Livesay, Dorothy
  (Kathleen)
Lopez de Segura Ruy
Lord, Shirley
Louie, David Wong
Lowell, Josephine Shaw
Lyon, Phyllis Ann
Maclean, Norman
  (Fitzroy)
Mann, Michael
Mariategui, Jose Carlos
Markle, Fletcher
Marshall, Paule
Martin, Del
Maurras, Charles Marie
  Photius
McGrory, Mary
Meehan, Thomas Edward
Michaels, Lorne
Millett, Kate
Min, Anchee
Mitchell, Joseph
Mittermeier, Russell A
Monash, Paul
Monette, Paul
Montalembert, Comte de
Montalvo, Juan Maria
Moraga, Cherrie
Mountain Wolf Woman
Mungo, Raymond
Munro, Alice
Murray, Albert L(ee)
Musset, Alfred de
Nash, N Richard
Nestle, Joan
Nichols, Beverley
Noonan, Peggy
North, Sterling
O'Connor, Carroll
O'Donoghue, Michael
Okamura, Arthur
Owens, Major (Robert)
Palma, Ricardo
Parkerson, Michelle
Perret, Gene
Phillips, Irna
Pinsent, Gordon Edward
Ponsonby, Sarah
Porter, Connie
Posey, Alexander
  Lawrence
Price, Richard
Resnik, Muriel
Rico, Don(ato)
Ridge, John Rollin
Riding, Laura
Ringgold, Faith
Robeson, Eslanda Cardoza
  Goode
Robinson, Harriet Jane
  Hanson
Roddenberry, Gene
Rodman, Selden
Rose, Wendy
Rosten, Norman
Rubenstein, Richard
  L(owell)
Ruiz, Jose Martinez
Rule, Jane
Russell, Charles Edward
Russo, Vito
Ruysbroeck, Jan van
Saint, Assotto

Sanders, Dori(nda)
Sapphire
Sargent, Herb
Saro-Wiwa, Ken
Schrader, Paul Joseph
Schulman, Sarah (Miriam)
Schumacher, E(rnst)
  F(riedrich)
Schumacher, Joel
Shukovsky, Joel
Shuster, Rosie
Siegel, Larry
Sierra, Justo
Silver, Franelle
Simon, Jules Francois
Slesar, Henry
Sloan, Michael
Smith, Barbara
Smith, Frances Scott
  Fitzgerald Lanahan
Sobieski, Carol
Some, Malidoma Patrice
Soto, Gary
Southern, Terry
Speight, Johnny
Spiegelman, Art
Spielhagen, Friedrich von
Stein, James R
Stern, Leonard B
Stern, Sandor
Stevens, Jeremy
Stewart, Maria W. Miller
Strauss, Theodore
Sullivan, Andrew
Summers, Anne Fairhurst
Suttner, Bertha Felicie
  Sophie Kinsky von
Tarantino, Quentin
Tertullian, Quintus
  Septimus Florens
Thomas, Elizabeth
  Marshall
Thomas, Ross (Elmore)
Thomas, Tony
Thomason, Harry
Thompson, William
  Tappan
Tiller, Rogers
Tobias, Andrew Previn
Towne, Robert (Burton)
Treitel, Jonathan
Tsui, Kitty
Ulibarri, Sabine (Reyes)
Ulrichs, Karl Heinrich
Vaid, Urvashi
Valdez, Luis (Miguel)
van de Velde, Henry
Wagner, Jane
Washam, Wisner
  McCamey
Weinberger, Edwin B
Weiskopf, Bob
Welch, Ken
Welch, Mitzie
Welles, Orson
Wentworth, William
  Charles
Wheeler, Hugh
  Callingham
White, Stephen
White, William Alanson
Williams, John A(lfred)
Williams, Matt
Willingham, Calder
  Baynard, Jr.

Wilson, A(ndrew)
  N(orman)
Wincelberg, Shimon
Winter, Alice Vivian
  Ames
Wittig, Monique
Wolfe, Digby
Wolff, Tobias (Jonathan
  Ansell)
Woo, Merle
Wynn, Tracy Keenan

YACHTSMAN

Chichester, Francis
  Charles, Sir

Conner, Dennis
Kelly, John Brenden
Koch, Bill
Lorillard, Pierre

ZOOLOGIST

Agassiz, Alexander
  Emmanuel Rodolphe
Allen, Joel Asaph
Andrews, Roy Chapman
Bigelow, Henry Bryant
Brooks, William Keith
Child, Charles Manning
Christophers, S(amuel)
  Rickard, Sir

Cuvier, Georges, Baron
Davenport, Charles
  Benedict
Durrell, Gerald (Malcolm)
Elton, Charles Sutherland
Frisch, Karl von
Geoffroy Saint-Hilaire,
  Etienne
Grassi, Giovanni Battista
Gray, James, Sir
Grzimek, Bernhard
Haeckel, Ernst Heinrich
  Philipp August
Harrison, Ross Granville
Hyman, Libbie Henrietta
Medawar, Peter Brian, Sir
Morgan, C(onwy) Lloyd

Morgan, Thomas Hunt
Morris, Desmond
Oliver, James A(rthur)
Owen, Richard, Sir
Park, Thomas
Parr, A(lbert) E(ide)
Ray, Dixy Lee
Sanderson, Ivan Terence
Schaudinn, Fritz Richard
Scheffer, Victor
  B(lanchard)
Sedgwick, Adam
Wheeler, William Morton